BUTTERWORTHS

STONE'S JUSTICES' MANUAL 2006

One Hundred and Thirty-Eighth Edition

edited by

A P CARR

District Judge (Magistrates' Courts)

and

A J TURNER

Barrister, Chambers of Adrian Turner, Eastbourne

Human Rights contributor

Keir Starmer QC

Doughty Street Chambers, visiting lecturer at King's College, London

Licensing contributor

Ian Seeley

Principal Solicitor, Ipswich Borough Council

VOLUME 3

Members of the LexisNexis Group worldwide

United Kingdom	LexisNexis Butterworths, a Division of Reed Elsevier (UK) Ltd, Halsbury House, 35 Chancery Lane, London, WC2A 1EL, and RSH, 1–3 Baxter's Place, Leith Walk Edinburgh EH1 3AF
United Kingdom	LexisNexis Butterworths, a Division of Reed Elsevier (UK) Ltd, RSH, 1–3 Baxter's Place, Leith Walk, EDINBURGH EH1 3AF and Halsbury House, 35 Chancery Lane, LONDON WC2A 1EL
Argentina	LexisNexis Argentina, Buenos Aires
Australia	LexisNexis Butterworths, Chatswood, New South Wales
Austria	LexisNexis Verlag ARD Orac GmbH & Co KG, Vienna
Benelux	LexisNexis Benelux, Amsterdam
Canada	LexisNexis Canada, Markham, Ontario
Chile	LexisNexis Chile Ltda, Santiago
China	LexisNexis China, Beijing and Shanghai
France	LexisNexis SA, Paris
Germany	LexisNexis Deutschland GmbH, Munster
Hong Kong	LexisNexis Hong Kong, Hong Kong
India	LexisNexis India, New Delhi
Italy	Giuffrè Editore, Milan
Japan	LexisNexis Japan, Tokyo
Malaysia	Malayan Law Journal Sdn Bhd, Kuala Lumpur
Mexico	LexisNexis Mexico, Mexico
New Zealand	LexisNexis NZ Ltd, Wellington
Poland	Wydawnictwo Prawnicze LexisNexis Sp, Warsaw
Singapore	LexisNexis Singapore, Singapore
South Africa	LexisNexis Butterworths, Durban
USA	LexisNexis, Dayton, Ohio

Published by LexisNexis Butterworths

A CIP Catalogue record for this book is available from the British Library.

ISBN for this volume

ISBN 10: 1405712546
ISBN 13: 9781405712545

ISBN 1-4057-1254-6

9 781405 712545

ISBN for the complete set of volumes

ISBN 10: 1405711000
ISBN 13: 9781405711005

ISBN 1-4057-1100-0

9 781405 711005

Typeset by David Lewis XML Associates Limited
Printed and bound in Great Britain by William Clowes Limited, Beccles, Suffolk

Visit LexisNexis Butterworths at www.lexisnexis.co.uk

CONTENTS

(WITH REFERENCE TO PARAS)

VOLUME 1

VOLUME 2

VOLUME 3

Ready Reference

	Statutory provision		Narrative
Bail	Bail Act 1976	1–1560	1–464
Exceptions to right to bail	Bail Act 1976, Sch 1	1–1570	1–469
Prosecution appeal	Bail (Amend) Act 1993, s 1	1–3447	1–488
Remand	MCA 1980, ss 128–131	1–2211	1–464
Custody time limits	PO (CTL) Regs 1987	1–6220	
Disclosure			
Advance	CrimPR Pt 21	1–7441	1–425
Public interest immunity			1–605
Primary	CPIA 1996, s 3	1–3583	1–602
Code of Practice	CPIA 1996, s 23	1–6539	
A-G Guidelines		1–7750	
Representation order			
Criteria for grant	AJ A 1999, Sch 3 para 5	1–3983	1–884
Application for	CDS (Gen) (No 2) R 2001	1–5691	1–885
Appeal	CDS (Rep Ord App) Regs 2001	1–5681	1–889
Disqualification and Bias			1–119
Abuse of process			1–447
Information			1–386
Time limit	MCA 1980, s 127	1–2210	1–387
Statement of offence	CrimPR Pt 7 r 7.2	1–7427	1–388
Several offences			1–444

	Statutory provision		Narrative
Bad character	CJA 2003, ss 98–112 CrimPR Pt 35	2–1561/ 1575 1–7455	2–494A ff 1–625
Oaths etc	Oaths Act 1978	2–1190	1–645/8
Competence	YJCEA 1999, s 53	2–1553	2–320
Compellability	PACE 1984, s 80	2–1361	2–332
Hostile	Crim Proc Act 1865, s 3	2–851	1–661
Special measures	YJCEA 1999, Pt II	2–1517	2–345A
Protection from cross examination	YJCEA 1999, Pt II, Ch II	2–1534	2–345H
Complainant's sexual history	YJCEA 1999, Pt II, Ch III	2–1541	2–345I
Refreshing memory	CJA 2003, s 139	2–1602	1–663
Accused			
– effect of silence of at trial	CJPOA 1994, s 35	2–1495	2–497
Submission of no case			1–668
Burden and standard of proof			1–685/689
Sentencing			
Purposes	CJA 2003	3–1930	3–10
Available sentences (adults)			3–190
Sentencing guidelines			3–561 and 3080
Fine enforcement	MCA 1980 ss 75–91	1–2125/53	3–208
Imprisonment			3–244/247
– restrictions on	PCC(S)A 2000 s 79	3–1555X	3–218
– consecutive terms	MCA 1980 s 133	1–2217	3–245
– return to	PCC(S)A 2000 s 116	3–1676	
– when custody appropriate			3–219
Sex offenders	SOA 2003 Pt 2	8–28423Z ff	3–528 ff

	Statutory provision		Narrative
Costs	Pros of Offences Act 1985, s 16–19A	1–2910/4	1–800 3–522
Road traffic			
Highway Code		4–2031	
NIPs	RTOA 1988, s 1, Sch 1	4–1642	
Offences			
– careless driving	RTA 1988, s 3	4–1373	
– alcohol (OPL)	RTA 1988, s 5	4–1376	
– fail provide specimen	RTA 1988, s 7	4–1378	
– fail to stop	RTA 1988, s 170	4–1596	
– no insurance	RTA 1988, s 143	4–1560	
Penalties			
– list of maximum penalties and endorseable offences	RTOA 1988, Sch 2	4–1769	
– codes		4–2019	
Disqualification			
– mandatory/special reasons	RTOA 1988, s 34(1)	4–1680	
– discretionary	RTOA 1988, s 34(2)	4–1680	
– penalty points/mitigating circumstances	RTOA 1988, s 35	4–1684	

PART VIII *cont* OFFENCES, MATTERS OF COMPLAINT, ETC

HOUSING, LANDLORD AND TENANT

8–16700 This title contains the following general provisions—

and the following statutes—

DISTRESS

8–16719 Distress for rent. By the Law of Distress Amendment Act 1888, s 4, goods or chattels of the tenant or his family which would be protected from seizure under the County Courts Act 1846, s 96, or any enactment amending or substituted for the same (see the County Courts Act 1984, s 89), are exempt from distress from rent, except (1) where the lease, term, or interest of the tenant has expired; (2) possession of the premises has been demanded; and (3) the distress is made "not earlier than seven days after such demand". Actual entry to seize and impound goods is necessary[1]. The chattels exempted from seizure in execution are "the wearing apparel and[2] bedding of such person or his family, and the tools[3] and implement of his trade to the value of[4] **£50**". An agricultural charge is no protection from distress (Agricultural Credits Act 1928, s 8 (7)). Goods belonging to the Crown which are upon the land of another person are not liable to be distrained for rent due from that person to his landlord (*Secretary of State for War v Wynne* [1905] 2 KB 845). Gas fittings let for hire or lent to a consumer by a public gas supplier and marked or impressed with a sufficient mark or brand indicating the supplier as the owner thereof are not subject to distress (Gas Act 1986, Sch 5, para 19, in title Energy (Gas), ante). So much of 2 Will & M c 5, s 1, as requires appraisement before sale is repealed, except where appraisement is required in writing; and for the purpose of sale the goods and chattels distrained shall, at the request in writing of the tenant or owner, be removed to a public auction room or some other fit and proper place specified in such request, and there[5] sold, but provision has not been made that the goods shall be sold by auction. The costs of appraisement, when required, shall be borne by the tenant; and the costs and expenses attending the removal and any damage to the goods are to be paid by the person requiring the removal (Law of Distress Amendment Act 1888, s 5). The period of five days provided in 2 Will. & M c 5, within which the tenant may reply, is to be extended to not more than fifteen days at tenant's request in writing, and on security being given for additional cost (Law of Distress Amendment Act 1888, s 6).

No person is to act as bailiff to levy any distress for rent unless authorised to act as a bailiff by a certificate in writing under the hand of a county court judge, or by the county court registrar when duly authorised by Rules. The certificate may be cancelled or declared void by the county court judge at any time (Law of Distress Amendment Act 1888, s 7; Law of Distress Amendment Act 1895, s 17). If any person not holding a certificate under s 7 shall levy a distress contrary to the provisions of this Act, the person so levying and the person who authorised him commits a trespass. This applies not only as between landlords and tenants, but also as between landlords and third persons whose goods may be on the demised premises (*Perring & Co v Emerson* [1906] 1 KB 1). If any person not holding a certificate for the time being in force under the Law of Distress Amendment Act 1888, levies a distress contrary to the provisions of that Act, he will without prejudice to any civil liability be liable on summary conviction to a *fine* not exceeding **level 1** on the standard scale (Law of Distress Amendment Act 1895, s 2, as amended by the Criminal Law Act 1977, s 31 and the Criminal Justice Act 1982, s 46). A court of summary jurisdiction, on complaint that goods or chattels exempt under the Law of Distress Amendment Act 1888 from distress for rent have been taken under such distress, may by summary order direct that the goods and chattels so taken, if not sold, be restored; or if they have been sold, that such sum as the court may determine to be the value thereof shall be paid to the complainant by the person who levied the distress or directed it to be levied (Law of Distress Amendment Act 1895, s 4). The order must be enforced under Magistrates' Courts Act 1980, s 63, ante. The Lord Chancellor may make rules for regulating the fees, charges, and expenses incidental to distresses (Law of Distress Amendment Act 1888, s 8). Distress for Rent Rules 1988[6], make provision for the certification of bailiffs, complaints as to fitness to hold certificates, fees, charges and expenses and the procedure for the levy of distress and removal. By r 7, a general certificate shall, unless cancelled, have effect for 2 years from the date of grant. Each county court shall compile a list of bailiffs holding general certificates as at 1st February in every year and the list shall be exhibited in the public area of the court office.

1. *Evans v South Ribble Borough Council* [1999] QB 757, [1992] 2 All ER 695, [1992] 2 WLR 429.

2. A bedstead, as well as the articles of bedding on it, is privileged (*Davis v Harris* [1900] 1 QB 729, 64 JP 136). The expressions "wearing apparel and bedding" and "tools and implements of trade" are not separate classes of articles, so the requirements of the section are satisfied if wearing apparel, or tools, to the prescribed value, see note 3, infra, are left (*Boyd Ltd v Bilham* [1909] 1 KB 14, 72 JP 495).

3. A sewing machine held on a hiring agreement by a dressmaker was a tool of trade (*Masters v Fraser* (1901) 66 JP 100, following *Churchward v Johnson* (1889) 54 JP 326). A cab used by a cabdriver for the purposes of his trade is also within the protection of the section (*Lavell v Richings* [1906] 1 KB 480). So is a pianoforte used for the purpose of giving music lessons to pupils (*Boyd Ltd v Bilham*, supra).

4. The protected value is now £100 in relation to wearing apparel and bedding, and £150 in relation to tools and implements of trade, by reason of the Protection from Execution (Prescribed Value) Order 1980, SI 1980/26 made under the Administration of Justice Act 1956, s 37(2). An implement of trade exceeding the prescribed value is within the exemption, provided it is the only chattel upon the premises (*Lavell v Richings*, supra). A typewriter, carried as a sample by a traveller engaged to sell typewriters, is not a tool or implement of trade within the section (*Addison v Shepherd* [1908] 2 KB 118, 72 JP 239). In an action for unlawful distress the onus of proving that the defendant had not left goods of the prescribed value on the premises lies on the plaintiff (*Gonsky v Durrell* [1918] 2 KB 71).

5. The landlord who distrained the goods cannot himself purchase them (*Moore Nettlefold & Co v Singer Manufacturing Co* [1904] 1 KB 820, 68 JP 369; *King v England* (1864) 4 B & S 782, 28 JP 230, approved and followed). The notice of seizure must not leave it uncertain as to what goods have been seized (*Wakeman v Lindsey* (1850) 14 QB 625; *Kerby v Harding* (1851) 6 Exch 234, 15 JP 294; *Davies v Property and Reversionary Investments Corpn Ltd* [1929] 2 KB 222, 93 JP 167).

6. SI 1988/2050, amended by SI 1993/2072, SI 1999/2360, 2564 and 3186, and SI 2000/1481 and 2737, SI 2001/4026 and SI 2003/1858 and 2141.

8–16720 19 Settlement of disputes as to distress under Agricultural Holdings Act 1986. (1) Where a dispute arises—(*a*) in respect of any distress having been levied on an agricultural holding contrary to the provisions[1] of this Act, (*b*) as to the ownership of any live stock[2] distrained, or as to the price to be paid for the feeding of that stock; or (*c*) as to any other matter or thing relating to a distress on an agricultural holding[3]; the dispute may be determined by the county court or on complaint by a magistrates' court, and the court may make an order for restoration of any live stock or things unlawfully distrained, may declare the price agreed to be paid for feeding, or may make any other order that justice requires.

(2) Any person aggrieved by a decision of a magistrates' court under this section may appeal to the Crown Court.

(3) In this section "livestock" includes any animal capable of being distrained.

[Agricultural Holdings Act 1986, s 19.]

1. Provision is made by s 16 of the Act against distress for more than one year's rent. Live stock at agistment are conditionally exempt from distress. If taken in to be fed at a fair price, such stock is not distrainable when there is other sufficient distress to be found; and when distrainable it should only be for the price agreed to be paid for the feeding or any part thereof which remains unpaid (s 18(2)). Property belonging to a person other than the tenant shall not be distrained for rent if—(*a*) the property is agricultural or other machinery and is on the holding under an agreement for its hire or use in the conduct of the business, or (*b*) the property is livestock and is on the holding solely for breeding purposes (s 18(1)). Where any compensation is due to the tenant, that amount may be set off against the rent and the landlord shall not be entitled to distrain for more than the balance.

2. "Livestock" includes any creature kept for the production of food, wool, skins or fur or for the purpose of its use in the farming of land or the carrying on in relation to land of any agricultural activity (Agricultural Holdings Act 1986, s 96).

3. See *Lord Eldon v Hedley Bros* [1935] 2 KB 1. "Agricultural holding" means the aggregate of the land (whether agricultural land or not) comprised in a contract of tenancy which is a contract for an agricultural tenancy, not being a contract under which the land is let to the tenant during his continuance in any office, appointment or employment held under the landlord (Agricultural Holdings Act 1986, s 1(1)).

8–16721 Costs allowed under Rules. By the Distress for Rent Rules 1988[1], r 10, "No person shall be entitled to charge or recover from the tenant any fees, charges, or expenses for levying a distress, or for doing any act or thing in relation thereto other than those authorised by the table in Appendix I to these Rules." The table is as follows:

1. For levying distress[2]—	
(i) where the sum demanded and due does not exceed £100	
	£12.50
(ii) where the sum demanded and due exceeds £100	12 ½ per cent on the first £100, 4 per cent on the next £400, 2 ½ per cent on the next £1,500, 1 per cent on the next £8,000, and ¼ per cent on any additional sum.

2. For attending to levy distress where the levy is not made, the reasonable costs and charges for attending to levy, not exceeding the fees which would have been due under paragraph 1 if the distress had been levied; the costs and charges are subject to taxation under Rule 11.

3. For taking possession—	
(i) where a man is left in physical possession	£4.50 per day[3]
(ii) where walking possession is taken	45p per day

Note: The charge for walking possession is payable only if a walking possession agreement in Form 8 has been concluded.

A man left in possession must provide his own board in every case.

The possession fee is payable in respect of the day on which the distress is levied, but a fee for physical possession must not be charged where a walking possession agreement is signed at the time when the distress is levied.

4. For appraisement, at the request in writing of the tenant, the reasonable fees, charges and expenses of the broker, subject to taxation under Rule 11[4].

5. For attending to remove, the reasonable costs and charges attending the removal; the costs and charges are subject to taxation under Rule 11[4].

6. For sale—

(i) where the sale is held on the auctioneer's premises, for commission to the auctioneer, an inclusive charge to include all out-of-pocket expenses of 15 per cent on the sum realised, and the reasonable cost of advertising, removal and storage.

(ii) where the sale is held on the debtor's premises, for commission to the auctioneer, in addition to out-of-pocket expenses actually and reasonably incurred, 7½ per cent on the sum realised.

7. Reasonable fees, charges and expenses, where distress is withdrawn or where no sale takes place, and for negotiations between landlord and tenant respecting the distress, subject to taxation under Rule 11.

8. For the purpose of calculating any percentage charges a fraction of £1 is to be reckoned as £1 but any fraction of a penny in the total amount of the fee so calculated is to be disregarded.

9. In addition to any amount authorised by this Table in respect of the supply of goods or services on which value added tax is chargeable there may be added a sum equivalent to value added tax at the appropriate rate on that amount.

1. SI 1988/2050, amended by SI 1993/2072, SI 1999/2360, 2564, 3186 and SI 2000/1481 and 2737.
2. The bailiff (not the landlord) is the person entitled to the fee (*Phillips v Rees* (1889) 24 QBD 17, 54 JP 293; overruling *Coode v Johns* (1886) 17 QBD 714, 51 JP 21).
3. The charge for man in possession must not be made if the man has only been in constructive possession, and not in real possession, of the goods distrained upon, unless, in order to avoid the inconvenience of having a man in real possession, an express agreement has been made to pay that charge (*Lumsden v Burnett* [1898] 2 QB 177). The goods are then in the custody of the law (*Lavell & Co v O'Leary* [1933] 2 KB 200, [1933] All ER Rep 423). As to actions of replevin, see County Courts Act 1984, Sch 1. In possession means in possession of the goods, and is not confined to possession of the goods on the premises on which they are distrained (*Scott v Denton* [1907] 1 KB 456, 71 JP 66).
4. Rule 11 provides for taxation in case of difference by the Registrar of the County Court (now the District Judge: Courts and Legal Services Act 1990, s 74(1), (3)), who may make an order as to costs of taxation.

8–16722 Statutory costs—Penalty. If any person shall in any manner levy, take or receive, or retain, or take from the proceeds of goods sold for the payment of rent any other or[1] greater costs and charges than those allowed by the statute[2], or make any charge for anything mentioned and not really done, the party aggrieved may apply to a justice[3] where the distress was made or in any manner proceeded in, who, if the complaint be found true, shall order such person to pay the party complaining treble the amount unlawfully taken with full costs. (Distress (Costs) Act 1817, s 2), enforceable as a penalty under ss 76 and 79 of Magistrates' Courts Act 1980 (*R v Daly, ex p Newson* (1911) 75 JP 333). But this does not exclude the jurisdiction of the county court to try an action for the recovery of any excess charged (*R v Bridport County Court Judge, ex p Edwards* [1905] 2 KB 108, 69 JP 221). Brokers are in all cases to give notes of their charges to the persons distrained (Distress (Costs) Act 1817, s 6). Where a person had incurred and charged expenses which were not necessary, but acted *bona fide* and in the honest belief that they were necessary, and had not taken other or greater charges than were allowed by the statute, nor charged for what was not really done, he was not liable to be convicted (*Nott v Bound* (1866) LR 1 QB 405).

1. The Divisional Court held that this did not prevent the landlord and bailiff contracting out of the statute and making a special agreement for the latter to receive extra remuneration (*Robson v Biggar* [1907] 1 KB 690, 71 JP 164). This being

a criminal matter within (what is now) s 18(1) (*a*) of the Supreme Court Act 1981, no appeal lay to the Court of Appeal (id [1908] 1 KB 672). In *Day v Davies* [1938] 2 KB 74, [1938] 1 All ER 686; the Court of Appeal held that a bailiff cannot charge for "walking possession" even by agreement. The Distress for Rent Rules 1988, now provide for payment of such fees by agreement.

2. Now by the Rules (*Walker v Retter* [1911] 1 KB 1103).

3. This reference to a justice of the peace shall be construed in relation to any area in England (outside Greater London) or Wales as meaning a justice of the peace for a commission area (as defined in the Justices of the Peace Act 1979, s 1 in PART I: MAGISTRATES' COURTS, PROCEDURE, ante) (Local Government Changes for England Regulations 1996, SI 1996/674 and the Magistrates' Courts (Wales) (Consequences of Local Government Changes) Order 1996, SI 1996/675).

8–16723 Execution of warrant—Insufficient seizure. The entry must not be made before sunrise or after sunset (*Co Litt* 142*a*). The execution of a warrant of distress for rent by forcing the outer door or by entering through a window found closed, but not fastened, is unlawful (*Nash v Lucas* (1867) LR 2 QB 590, 32 JP 23). If, however, a window is at all open a bailiff may raise it higher to enter the house (*Crabtree v Robinson* (1885) 15 QBD 312, 50 JP 70). The ordinary rule of law is that a bailiff may not break open an outer door, but may, if he gets in, break open an inner door. The QB Division refused a *certiorari* to bring up a conviction of a bailiff obtained on complaint of a householder for malicious injuries in breaking open, with excessive force, the door of a lodger to levy an execution, but the writ was refused on the ground that the justices were the persons to decide whether the claim was *bona fide* (*Ex p Smith (In re a conviction by Mr Biron)* (1890) 7 TLR 42). The QB Division held that a bailiff committed a trespass by breaking open the outer door of a warehouse sub-let and abutting on a courtyard to which he had obtained access through another person's property (*American Concentrated Meat Co v Hendry* (1893) 57 JP 788). But climbing over a wall and entering by an open window is not illegal, and the distress is lawful (*Long v Clarke* [1894] 1 QB 119, 58 JP 150). A person cannot distrain twice for the same rent, but the officer may distrain again under the same warrant where there has been some excusable mistake as to the value of the goods seized when they come to be sold, or the first distress has been rendered abortive by the misconduct of the tenant (*Hutchins v Chambers* (1758) 1 Burr 579; *Lee v Cooke* (1858) 3 H & N 203, 22 JP 177; *R v Judge Clements, ex p Ferridge* [1932] 2 KB 535; *Withers & Co v Spicer* [1935] 1 KB 412). But where the first distress is a trespass *ab initio* and void as a distress, the landlord may lawfully distrain under a second warrant for the same rent (*Grunnel v Welch* [1906] 2 KB 555). Goods sent to an auction sale are distrainable for rent (*Lyons v Elliott* (1876) 1 QBD 210, 40 JP 263); but goods distrained for penalties must actually belong to the person distrained upon. Notwithstanding s 141(2) of the Law of Property Act 1925, a *cestui que trust* cannot distrain (*Schalit v Nadler Ltd* [1933] 2 KB 79, [1933] All ER Rep 708). Cf *Allen v IRC* [1914] 1 KB 327; *Baker v Archer-Shee* [1927] AC 844. A landlord may distrain for not more than 6 months' rent accrued due before the commencement of the bankruptcy, subject to s 347 of the Insolvency Act 1986, although he has proved in the bankruptcy, if he has received no dividend; up to that time he has a right of election (*Holmes v Watt* [1935] 2 KB 300, [1935] All ER Rep 496).

8–16724 Fraudulent removal of goods. Goods fraudulently or clandestinely conveyed or carried away from premises to prevent the landlord from distraining for any rent then due, may be seized by the landlord wherever found within thirty days, if not sold *bona fide* before such seizure to some person not privy to the fraud (Distress for Rent Act 1737, ss 1, 2. See *Dibble v Bowater* (1853) 2 E & B 564, 17 JP 792). The statute only applies to cases where a landlord has a right of distress at common law, or under 8 Anne, c 18, s 67, at the time of removal of the goods, and it is a condition of the application of the latter statute that the tenant shall be in actual possession of the demised premises; therefore, when the tenancy has expired, it is too late for the landlord to follow and seize the goods (*Gray v Stait* (1883) 11 QBD 668, 48 JP 86, 290). Goods had been levied upon and the brokers' man had been induced to go out of physical possession temporarily; when he returned the goods had been removed. A metropolitan magistrate has held that as the distraining was over before the man went out of possession, the subsequent removal could not be a fraudulent removal under the statute (*Taylor v Waller* (1900) 64 JP 666).

8–16725 Aid of a justice of the peace. Goods so carried away and put into any house, or other place, locked up, or otherwise secured, so as to prevent them from being taken as a distress, may be seized in the daytime by the landlord or his bailiff, etc (first calling to their assistance the peace-officer of the place, who shall aid therein); and in case of a dwelling-house (oath being first made before a justice having jurisdiction of a reasonable ground to suspect that such goods are therein) they may break open and enter into such house, or other place, and distrain the goods (Distress for Rent Act 1737, s 7). Under this section the landlord apparently has power, after an oath made before a justice, to call to his aid the constable and break open the house without any warrant from a justice. It is, however, usual to issue a warrant, but the right to do so is very questionable (9 JP 819). In *Robinson v Waddington* (1849) 13 QB 753, and *Newnham v Stevenson* (1851) 10 CB 713, it was held that the five days allowed to a landlord for selling a distress for rent must be clear days, ie exclusive both of the day of distress and of sale.

8–16726 Penalty for fraudulent removal. Any tenant[1] so fraudulently carrying off or concealing his goods, or any person wilfully and knowingly aiding the tenant in the fraudulent removal or concealment of goods, to prevent the landlord from distraining for rent then due, to forfeit[2] double the value of the goods so removed or concealed; and when they do not exceed the value of fifty pounds, on information before a justice[3] for the[4] commission area, the offender to be summoned to appear before two or more justices, who, by order under their hands and seals, may and shall adjudge him to pay double the value of the goods, which on non-payment (after notice of the order) may be levied by distress, and for want of distress, imprisonment[5] regulated by scale in Magistrates' Courts Act 1980, Sch 4. (Distress for Rent Act 1737, s 4 amended by the Access to Justice Act 1999, Sch 10). Appeal lies to the Crown Court (Distress for Rent Act 1737, ss 5, 6), upon compliance with Magistrates' Courts Act 1980, s 108, ante) (*R v Shropshire Justices* (1881) 6 QBD 669, 45 JP 196).

---

1. The statute does not apply where the goods have become, by the execution of a bill of sale by the tenant, the property of a bill of sale holder (*Tomlinson v Consolidated Credit and Mortgage Corpn* (1890) 24 QBD 135, 54 JP 644). Nor it would seem, where the article is an implement of trade within the meaning of Law of Distress Amendment Act 1888, 51 & 52 Vict c 21, s 4, though used solely by the tenant's wife. C, a gas stoker, hired a sewing machine for the use of his wife, a seamstress, who used it, and applied her earnings for the maintenance of the household. J, the landlord, having distrained, the Queen's Bench held the machine was privileged from distress (*Churchward v Johnson* (1889) 54 JP 326). This case was followed by the Divisional Court in *Masters v Fraser* (1901) 66 JP 100.

2. The plaintiff is not entitled to administer interrogatories to the defendant in an action for double value under s 3, the action being penal, and the answers tending to criminate (*Hobbs v Hudson* (1890) 54 JP 520).

3. This reference to a justice of the peace shall be construed in relation to any area in England (outside Greater London) or Wales as meaning a justice of the peace for a commission area (as defined in the Justices of the Peace Act 1979, s 1 in PART I: MAGISTRATES' COURTS, PROCEDURE, ante) (Local Government Changes for England Regulations 1996, SI 1996/674 and the Magistrates' Courts (Wales) (Consequences of Local Government Changes) Order 1996, SI 1996/675).

4. The rent must be due when the offence is committed (*Watson v Main* (1799) 3 Esp 15, and *Dibble v Bowater* (1853) 2 E & B 564, 17 JP 792).

5. The proceedings are of a penal nature, and the order should be treated as a conviction. By the Magistrates' Courts Act 1980, s 50, the reference to "information" is substituted for "complaint". The statutory requirement that the complaint shall be in writing and before two or more justices is over-ruled by the Magistrates' Courts Act 1980, s 51. The Magistrates' Courts Rules 1981, ante, in no case require an order to be sealed but the specific provision therefor in this Act has not been repealed. The particular goods need not be specified in the order (*R v Rabbitts* (1825) 6 Dow & Ry KB 341). Costs may be given under Magistrates' Courts Act 1980, s 64, ante.

8–16727 Restoration of under-tenants' or lodgers' goods. Under the[1] Law of Distress Amendment Act 1908, a stipendiary magistrate, or two justices where there is no stipendiary magistrate, may in certain cases order the restoration of the goods of an under-tenant or lodger[2] or any person not being a tenant, and having no beneficial interest in any tenancy of the premises or any part thereof seized for rent by the superior landlord[3].

Such under-tenant, etc, may serve such superior landlord, or the bailiff or other agent employed by him to levy, with a declaration[4] in writing made by such under-tenant, etc, setting forth that the landlord's immediate tenant has no right of property or beneficial interest in the furniture, etc, sought to be distrained, that the same are the[5] property of such under-tenant, etc, and that the same are not goods of live stock to which this Act is expressed[6] not to apply. To the declaration must be annexed a correct inventory[7] of the goods referred to in the declaration subscribed by the under-tenant, etc, and, in the case of an under-tenant or lodger, the declaration must set forth the amount of rent[8] (if any) due from him and the times at which future instalments of rent will become due and the amount thereof, and contain an undertaking to pay to the superior landlord any rent so due or to become due until the arrears of rent to which the distress relates have been paid off (s 1). If, under the foregoing circumstances, the superior landlord, or his agent, proceeds with the distress, he is guilty of an illegal distress[9] and the court may make such order for the recovery of the goods[10] as they may deem just (s 2).

Goods bailed under a hire-purchase agreement[11] or a consumer hire agreement or agreed to be sold under a conditional sale agreement are where the relevant agreement has not been terminated excluded from the application of the 1908 Act except during the period between the service of a default notice under the Consumer Credit Act 1974 in respect of the goods and the date on which the notice expires or is earlier complied with; similar provisions apply to goods comprised in a bill of sale (s 4A added by the Consumer Credit Act 1974, Sch 4 except in relation to consumer hire agreements).

---

1. The Lodgers' Goods Protection Act 1871, wherever and so far as this Act applies, is repealed (s 8). The Act of 1871 (relates to lodgers and not under-tenants) therefore continues to apply to eight classes of goods to which the later Act does not apply. The declaration under the former Act need not contain all the particulars required by the later Act, for instance, if no rent is due from the lodger it need not contain a statement to that effect (*Ex p Harris* (1885) 16 QBD 130, 50 JP 164). As to the exclusion of certain goods and under-tenants under the later Act, see ss 4, 5, and as to payment of rent to superior landlord, see ss 3, 6. The notice under s 6 to under-tenant to pay rent to superior landlord may be served personally as well as by registered post (*Jarvis v Hemmings* [1912] 1 Ch 462, 76 JP Jo 39).

2. "Lodger" is not defined in either Act. The Act of 1871 applies only to lodgers. The question whether a man is a lodger is a question of fact (*Ness v Stephenson* (1882) 9 QBD 245, 47 JP 134) that must be proved by the complainant (*Bensing v Ramsay* (1898) 62 JP 613). He must habitually sleep on the premises (*Heawood v Bone* (1884) 13 QBD 179, 48 JP 710), and, seemingly, he is not a lodger if he occupies the whole house (*Bradley v Baylis* (1881) 8 QBD 195, 45 JP 847). The fact of being an under-tenant does not by itself prevent his also being a lodger under the Act of 1871 (*Phillips v Henson* (1877) 3 CPD 26, 42 JP 137).

3. In the Act of 1908 the words "superior landlord" shall be deemed to include a landlord in cases where the goods

seized are not those of an under-tenant or lodger, and the words "tenant" and "under-tenant" do not include a lodger (s 9). A person who is in ostensible legal possession can unite the relationship of landlord and tenant (*Bensing v Ramsay*, supra). The landlord by himself or his servants must retain some dominion over the house (*Morton v Palmer* (1881) 46 JP 150; *Bradley v Baylis* (1881) 8 QBD 195, 45 JP 847). The lodger may also act as the landlord's caretaker or servant (*Ness v Stephenson, supra*).

4. By the Perjury Act 1911, s 5, it is an offence knowingly to make a false declaration. The declaration need not be a statutory declaration, and, where the goods belong to a partnership, the declaration may be made and subscribed by one partner with the authority of the other members of the firm (*Rogers Eungblut & Co v Martin* [1911] 1 KB 19, 75 JP 10). If made by any one else but the lodger or under-tenant it is a nullity (*ex p Harris*, supra). If the distress be withdrawn and a subsequent levy made under another warrant, a fresh declaration and notice must be served by the lodger (*Thwaites v Wilding* (1883) 12 QBD 4, 48 JP 100).

5. In the absence of evidence, the court will not take judicial notice of the custom of letting pianos on hire-purchase agreement so as to exclude the doctrine of reputed ownership (*Chappell & Co Ltd v Harrison* (1910) 75 JP 20).

6. See s 4. If these words are omitted the declaration is invalid (*Druce & Co Ltd v Beaumont Property Trust Ltd* [1935] 2 KB 257, [1935] All ER Rep 404).

7. Where a declaration was signed but the inventory written on the same paper was unsigned, it was held sufficiently subscribed (*Godlonton v Fulham and Hampstead Property Co* [1905] 1 KB 431).

8. The word "rent" in this section means a sum of money and does not include a contingent profit or advantage agreed to be given by the under-tenant to his immediate landlord (*Parsons v Hambridge* (1916) 33 TLR 346).

9. If the goods be sold before five clear days, and the lodger is deprived of his opportunity of availing himself of the provisions of this statute, the sale is unlawful and wrongful against the lodger, and he is entitled to recover damages by action (*Sharpe v Fowle* (1884) 12 QBD 385, 48 JP 680). An action will lie against the bailiff for levying an illegal distress (*Lowe v Dorling & Son* [1906] 2 KB 772, overruling *Page v Vallis* (1903) 19 TLR 393).

10. But not damages (*Lowe v Dorling & Son* [1905] 2 KB 501).

11. The words "hire-purchase agreement" in sub-s (1) are governed by the words "made by such tenant". (*Shenstone & Co v Freeman* [1910] 2 KB 84.) As to determination of hire-purchase agreement, see *London Furnishing Co Ltd v Solomon* (1912) 106 LT 371, and also *Hackney Furnishing Co v Watts* [1912] 3 KB 225, where the last-mentioned case was not followed. *Hackney Furnishing Co v Watts* was followed in *Jay's Furnishing Co v Brand & Co* [1915] 1 KB 458. When no contractual obligation is subsisting under the agreement when the notice is served (by delivery to the post office, *Drages Ltd v Owen* [1935] All ER Rep 342, 154 LT 12), the goods are not comprised in a hire-purchase agreement (*Smart Bros Ltd v Holt* [1929] 2 KB 303). The word "tenant" includes one of two joint tenants (*A W Gamage Ltd v Payne* [1925] 90 JP 14). A clause that the owner's consent to the hirer's possession shall automatically cease if the landlord threatens or takes any steps to levy a distress does not operate until the service of proper notice (*Times Furnishing Co Ltd v Hutchings* [1938] 1 KB 775, [1938] 1 All ER 422).

JURISDICTION IN EJECTMENT

8–16830 **Deserted premises.** As to deserted premises, see the Distress for Rent Act 1737; the Deserted Tenements Act 1817; and *Edwards v Hodges* (1855) 15 CB 477, 19 JP 102; *Re Emmett* (1850) 14 JP 530; *Ex p Evans* (1908) 72 JP Jo 568. Justices may view premises and give possession if rent not paid and no sufficient distress, Distress for Rent Act 1737, s 16. Proceedings "examinable in a summary way" by next justices of assize, or in London or Middlesex by High Court (ibid, s 17), thereby providing a right of appeal.

8–16831 **Rectories, vicarages, etc.** Agreements for letting by incumbents to be made in writing and to contain a condition for avoiding the same upon a copy of the bishop's order to incumbent to reside therein being served upon the tenant, "otherwise shall be null and void" (ie void not *ab initio*, but upon such order being made (*Rickard v Graham* [1910] 1 Ch 722)). Upon application by incumbent, and verification of bishop's order, a justice is bound to issue a warrant for possession (Pluralities Act 1838, s 59). There are similar provisions in the Lecturers and Parish Clerks Act 1844, s 6. The provisions of the Rent Restrictions Acts relating to the recovery of possession do not apply. (*Gloucester (Bishop) v Cunningham* [1943] KB 101, [1943] 1 All ER 61).

Statement of Rates Act 1919

(9 & 10 Geo 5 c 31)

8–16850 **1. Demands and receipts for rent.** (1) Every document containing a[1] demand for rent or[1] receipt for rent, which includes any sum for rates paid or payable under any statutory enactment by the owner instead of the occupier, shall state either the annual, half-yearly, quarterly, monthly, or weekly amount of such rates paid or payable in accordance with the last demands received by the owner from the rating authorities at the time of making his demand or giving his receipt in respect of the hereditament in question: Provided that, where such a statement as is required by this section has been furnished in connection with a demand for rent or receipt for rent in respect of a particular period, it shall not be necessary to furnish the statement upon any subsequent demand for rent or receipt for rent in respect of that period. (2) This Act shall not apply to weekly lettings at inclusive rentals in any market under or controlled by statute.

[Statement of Rates Act 1919, s 1; Statute Law Revision Act 1927.]

---

1. See s 2 for definition of these expressions.

8–16851 **2. Definitions.** The expressions "demand for rent" and "receipt for rent" shall include[1] a rent-book, rent-card and any document used for the notification or collection of rent due or for the acknowledgment of the receipt of the same.

[Statement of Rates Act 1919, s 2.]

1. As to further information to be given to tenants, see the Landlord and Tenant Act 1985, and the Housing Act 1985, s 332, post.

8–16852 3. Penalty. If any person makes a demand for rent or gives a receipt for rent in contravention of this Act, he shall, in respect of each offence, be liable on summary conviction to a fine not exceeding **level 1** on the standard scale.

[Statement of Rates Act 1919, s 3, as amended by the Criminal Law Act 1977, s 31 and the Criminal Justice Act 1982, s 46.]

Accommodation Agencies Act 1953

(1 & 2 Eliz 2 c 23)

8–16870 1. Illegal commissions and advertisements. (1) Subject to the provisions of this section, any person who—

(*a*) demands or accepts payment of any sum of money in consideration of registering or undertaking to register the name or requirements of any person seeking the tenancy of a house;

(*b*) demands or accepts payment of any sum of money in consideration[1] of supplying, or undertaking to supply, to any person addresses[2] or other particulars of houses to let; or

(*c*) issues any advertisement, list or other document describing any house as being to let without the authority of the owner of the house or his agent,

shall be guilty of an offence.

(2) A person shall not be guilty of an offence under this section by reason of his demanding or accepting payment from the owner of a house of any remuneration payable to him as agent for the said owner.

(3) [Saving for solicitors.]

(4) A person shall not be guilty of an offence under this section by reason of his demanding or accepting any payment in consideration of the display in a shop, or of the publication in a newspaper, of any advertisement or notice, or by reason of the display or publication as aforesaid of an advertisement or notice received for the purpose in the ordinary course of business.

(5) Any person guilty of an offence under this section shall be liable on summary conviction to a fine not exceeding **level 3** on the standard scale or to imprisonment for a term not exceeding **three months**, or to both such fine and imprisonment*.

(6) In this section the following expressions have the meanings hereby assigned to them that is to say:

"house" includes any part of a building which is occupied or intended to be occupied as a dwelling;

"newspaper" includes any periodical or magazine;

"owner", in relation to a house, means the person having power to grant a lease of the house.

[Accommodation Agencies Act 1953, s 1, as amended by the Expiring Laws Continuance Act 1969, Sch and the Criminal Justice Act 1982, ss 38 and 46.]

***Words repealed by the Criminal Justice act 2003, Sch 37 from a date to be appointed.**

1. For instance, a payment described as a commission (*McInnes v Clarke* [1955] 1 All ER 346, 119 JP 208). The section applies whether payment is made before or after the address is provided; nor are agents exempted merely because the money is refundable (*Lawrence v Sinclair-Taylor* (1973) 117 Sol Jo 815).

2. This includes the case where only one address is supplied (*Lawrence v Sinclair-Taylor*, supra). Distinguish payment for the finding of acceptable accommodation (*Saunders v Soper* [1975] AC 239, [1974] 3 All ER 1025).

Rent (Agriculture) Act 1976

(1976 c 80)

8–16880 This Act aims to afford security of tenure for agricultural[1] workers housed by their employers, and creates the status of "protected occupant" (defined by ss 2 and 3). A person ceasing to be a protected occupier can then become a statutory tenant (defined by ss 4 and 5 amended by the New Towns Act 1981, Sch 12, the Local Government Act 1985, Schs 14 and 17, the Housing (Consequential Provisions) Act 1985, Sch 2, and the Housing Act 1988, Schs 4, 17 and 18 and SI 1996/2325). A number of summary offences are created by the Act, as follows: s 20 as amended by the Criminal Justice Act 1982, ss 38 and 46, imposing a prohibited requirement for advance payment or rent, fine not exceeding **level 3** on the standard scale plus order to repay any rent paid thereunder; s 21 as amended by the Criminal Justice Act 1982, ss. 38 and 46, person entering sum in rent book which is irrecoverable under the Act, or landlord refusing or neglecting to cause such entry to be deleted on request within seven days (unless he proves he had a *bona fide* claim), fine not exceeding **level 3** on the standard scale; s 25 as amended by the Criminal Justice Act 1982, ss 39 and 46 and Sch 3, failure or refusal of agent of landlord etc to comply with notice requiring full name and place of abode or place of business of landlord (unless he did not know and could not with reasonable diligence have ascertained the facts), fine not exceeding **level 4** on the standard scale; s 28 as amended by the Criminal Justice Act 1982, ss 38 and 46 and the Housing Act 1988, Sch 17, failure without reasonable cause to notify change of facts in relation to application to housing authority for alternative accommodation, or knowingly or recklessly making false statement to obtain housing, fine not exceeding **level 5** on the standard scale; s 31 as amended by the Criminal Justice Act 1982, ss 38 and 46, failure without reasonable excuse to comply with notice, or knowingly or recklessly furnishing information false in a material particular in compliance with notice from Minister of Agriculture, Fisheries and Food (or the Secretary of State for Wales; SI 1978/272) requiring information as to housing accommodation, fine not exceeding **level 5** on the standard scale.

The Act applies to premises where there is a Crown interest (but the definition of statutory tenant is modified) (s 36). Provision is made for proceedings against a body corporate as well as against a director, manager, secretary or similar officer or person purporting to act in such capacity, or a member managing the affairs of the body corporate. Without prejudice to s 222 of the Local Government Act 1972 (power of local authorities to prosecute or defend legal proceedings) proceedings for an offence under any provision of this Act except s 31(6) may be instituted by the housing authority concerned (s 37).

1. A gamekeeper keeping pheasants for sport was not protected because he was not in employment in "agriculture" as defined by s 1 of the Act (*Lord Glendyne v Rapley* [1978] 2 All ER 110, [1978] 1 WLR 601).

Rent Act 1977

(1977 c 42)

PART III[1]

RENTS UNDER REGULATED TENANCIES

Enforcement provisions

8–16890 57. Recovery from landlord of sums paid in excess of recoverable rent, etc.

(1) Where a tenant has paid on account of rent any amount which, by virtue of this Part of this Act, is irrecoverable by the landlord, the tenant who paid it shall be entitled to recover that amount from the landlord who received it or his personal representatives.

(2) Any amount which a tenant is entitled to recover under subsection (1) above may, without prejudice to any other method of recovery, be deducted by the tenant from any rent payable by him to the landlord.

(3) No amount which a tenant is entitled to recover under subsection (1) above shall be recoverable at any time after the expiry of—

(*a*) one year, in the case of an amount which is irrecoverable by virtue of section 54 of this Act; or
(*b*) two years, in any other case.

(4) Any person who, in any rent book or similar document, makes an entry showing or purporting to show any tenant as being in arrears in respect of any sum on account of rent which is irrecoverable by virtue of this Part of this Act shall be liable to a fine not exceeding **level 3** on the standard scale, unless he proves that, at the time of the making of the entry, the landlord had a bona fide claim that the sum was recoverable.

(5) If, where any such entry has been made by or on behalf of any landlord, the landlord on being requested by or on behalf of the tenant to do so, refuses or neglects to cause the entry to be deleted within 7 days, the landlord shall be liable to a fine not exceeding **level 3** on the standard scale, unless he proves that, at the time of the neglect or refusal to cause the entry to be deleted, he had a bona fide claim that the sum was recoverable.

[Rent Act 1977, s 57, as amended by the Housing Act 1980, s 68 and the Criminal Justice Act 1982, ss 38 and 46.]

1. Part III contains ss 44–61. For meaning of "regulated tenancies", to which Pt III applies, see s 18.

PART V[1]

RENTS UNDER RESTRICTED CONTRACTS

Control of rents

8–16891 77. Reference of contracts to rent tribunals and obtaining by them of information.

(1) Either the lessor or the lessee under a restricted contract[2] may refer the contract to the rent tribunal[3].

(2) Where a restricted contract is referred to a rent tribunal under subsection (1) above they may, by notice in writing served on the lessor, require him to give to them, within such period (not less than 7 days from the date of the service of the notice) as may be specified in the notice, such

information as they may reasonably require regarding such of the prescribed particulars relating to the contract as are specified in the notice.

(3) If, within the period specified in a notice under subsection (2) above, the lessor fails without reasonable cause to comply with the provisions of the notice he shall be liable to a fine not exceeding **level 3** on the standard scale.

(4) Proceedings for an offence under this section shall not be instituted otherwise than by the local authority.

[Rent Act 1977, s 77, as amended by the Housing Act 1980, Sch 26, the Criminal Justice Act 1982, ss 35, 38 and 46 and the Housing Act 1988, Schs 17 and 18.]

---

1. Part V contains ss 76–85.
2. For meaning of "restricted contract", see s 19.
3. For meaning of "rent tribunal", see s 76(1).

8–16892 81. Effect of registration of rent. (1) Where the rent payable for any dwelling is entered in the register[1] under section 79 of this Act, it shall not be lawful to require or receive on account of rent for that dwelling under a restricted contract[2] payment of any amount in excess of the rent so registered—

(*a*) in respect of any period subsequent to the date of the entry, or

(*b*) where a particular period is specified in the register, in respect of that period.

(2) Where subsection (3) of section 79 applies, the amount entered in the register under that section shall be treated for the purposes of this section as increased for any rental period by the amount of the rates for that period, ascertained in accordance with Schedule 5 to this Act.

(3) Where any payment has been made or received in contravention of this section, the amount of the excess[3] shall be recoverable by the person by whom it was paid.

(4) Any person who requires or receives any payment in contravention of this section shall be liable to a fine not exceeding **level 3** on the standard scale or to imprisonment for a term not exceeding **6 months** or both, and, without prejudice to any other method of recovery, the court by which a person is found guilty of an offence under this subsection may order the amount paid in excess to be repaid to the person by whom the payment was made.

(5) Proceedings for an offence under this section shall not be instituted otherwise than by the local authority.

[Rent Act 1977, s 81, as amended by the Criminal Justice Act 1982, ss 38 and 46.]

---

1. This is the register of rents under restricted contracts which a local authority is required to prepare and keep up to date.
2. For meaning of "restricted contract", see s 19.
3. This means the amount paid in excess of the registered rent (*Henry v Taylor* [1954] 1 QB 506, [1954] 1 All ER 721, 118 JP 250). The registered rent remains the rent until the entry is changed or the period for which it was made expires (*De Jean v Fletcher* [1959] 1 All ER 602, 123 JP 244).

PART VI[1]

RENT LIMIT FOR DWELLINGS LET BY HOUSING ASSOCIATIONS, HOUSING TRUSTS AND THE HOUSING CORPN

Conversion to regulated tenancies

8–16893 92. Conversion of housing association tenancies into regulated tenancies. (1) If at any time, by virtue of subsections (1) and (3) of section 15 of this Act, a tenancy[2] ceases to be one to which this Part of this Act applies and becomes a protected tenancy[3], that tenancy shall be a regulated tenancy[3] and the housing association[2] which is the landlord under that tenancy shall give notice in writing to the tenant, informing him that his tenancy is no longer excluded from protection under this Act.

(2) If, without reasonable excuse, a housing association fails to give notice to a tenant under subsection (1) above within the period of 21 days beginning on the day on which his tenancy becomes a protected tenancy, the association shall be liable to a fine not exceeding **level 3** on the standard scale.

(3) Where an offence under subsection (2) above committed by a body corporate is proved to have been committed with the consent or connivance of, or to be attributable to any neglect on the part of, any director, manager or secretary or other similar officer of the body corporate or any person who was purporting to act in any such capacity, he as well as the body corporate shall be guilty of that offence and shall be liable to be proceeded against and punished accordingly.

(4) Schedule 14 to this Act shall have effect for supplementing this section.

(5) In this section—

"housing association" has the same meaning as in the Housing Associations Act 1985.

[Rent Act 1977, s 92, as amended by the Housing Act 1980, Sch 26, the Criminal Justice Act 1982, ss 38 and 46 and the Housing (Consequential Provisions) Act 1985, Sch 2.]

1. Part VI contains ss 86–97.
2. In Pt VI of this Act "tenancy" means a housing association tenancy (s 97(1)). For meaning of "housing association", "housing association tenancy" and "housing trust", see s 86.
3. For meaning of "protected tenancy", see s 1, and for meaning of "regulated tenancy", see s 18.

Miscellaneous

8–16894 **94. Recovery from landlord of sums paid in excess of recoverable rent, etc.** (1) Where a tenant has paid on account of rent any amount which, by virtue of this Part of this Act, is irrecoverable by the landlord, the tenant who paid it shall be entitled to recover that amount from the landlord who received it or his personal representatives.

(2) Any amount which a tenant is entitled to recover under subsection (1) above may, without prejudice to any other method of recovery, be deducted by the tenant from any rent payable by him to the landlord.

(3) No amount which a tenant is entitled to recover under subsection (1) above shall be recoverable at any time after the expiry of 2 years from the date of payment.

(4) Any person who, in any rent book or similar document, makes an entry showing or purporting to show any tenant as being in arrears in respect of any sum on account of rent which is irrecoverable by virtue of this Part of this Act shall be liable to a fine not exceeding **level 3** on the standard scale, unless he proves that, at the time of the making of the entry, the landlord had a *bona fide* claim that the sum was recoverable.

(5) If, where any such entry has been made by or on behalf of any landlord, the landlord on being requested by or on behalf of the tenant to do so, refuses or neglects to cause the entry to be deleted within 7 days, the landlord shall be liable to a fine not exceeding **level 3** on the standard scale, unless he proves that, at the time of the neglect or refusal to cause the entry to be deleted, he had a *bona fide* claim that the sum was recoverable.

[Rent Act 1977, s 94, as amended by the Criminal Justice Act 1982, ss 38 and 46.]

8–16895 **95. Duty of landlord to supply statement of rent under previous tenancy.** (1) Where the rent payable under a tenancy is subject to the rent limit specified in section 88(4)(*b*) of this Act, the landlord shall, on being so requested in writing by the tenant, supply him with a statement in writing of the rent which was payable for the last rental period of the other tenancy referred to in that subsection.

(2) If, without reasonable excuse, a landlord who has received such a request—

(*a*) fails to supply the statement referred to in subsection (1) above within 21 days of receiving the request, or

(*b*) supplies a statement which is false in any material particular,

he shall be liable to a fine not exceeding **level 3** on the standard scale.

(3) Where an offence under this section committed by a body corporate is proved to have been committed with the consent or connivance of, or to be attributable to any neglect on the part of, any director, manager or secretary or other similar officer of the body corporate or any person who was purporting to act in any such capacity, he as well as the body corporate shall be guilty of that offence and shall be liable to be proceeded against and punished accordingly.

[Rent Act 1977, s 95, as amended by the Criminal Justice Act 1982, ss 35, 38 and 46.]

PART IX[1]

PREMIUMS, ETC

8–16896 **119. Prohibition of premiums and loans on grant of protected tenancies.** (1) Any person who, as a condition of the grant, renewal or continuance of a protected tenancy[2] requires, in addition to the rent, the payment of any premium[3] or the making of any loan (whether secured or unsecured) shall be guilty of an offence.

(2) Any person who, in connection with the grant, renewal or continuance of a protected tenancy, receives any premium in addition to the rent shall be guilty of an offence.

(3) A person guilty of an offence under this section shall be liable to a fine not exceeding **level 3** on the standard scale.

(4) The court by which a person is convicted of an offence under this section relating to requiring or receiving any premium may order the amount of the premium to be repaid to the person by whom it was paid.

[Rent Act 1977, s 119, as amended by the Criminal Justice Act 1982, ss 38 and 46.]

1. Part IX contains ss 119–128.
2. For meaning of "protected tenancy", see s 1.
3. "Premium" includes—

(*a*) any fine or other like sum;
(*b*) any other pecuniary consideration in addition to rent; and
(*c*) any sum paid by way of a deposit, other than one which does not exceed one-sixth of the annual rent and is reasonable in relation to the potential liability in respect of which it is paid (s 128(1) as amended by the Housing Act 1980, s 79).

A payment may be a premium although it is required to be made to a third party (*Elmdene Estates Ltd v White* [1960] AC 528, [1960] 1 All ER 306). See (1960) 110 LJ 359. Any attempt to obtain from a prospective tenant excessive prices for furniture is an offence (s 124, post). A master is not liable in respect of an offence under this section committed by a servant outside the general scope of his employment (*Barker v Levinson* [1951] 1 KB 342, [1950] 2 All ER 825, 114 JP 545).

8–16897 **120. Prohibition of premiums and loans on assignment of protected tenancies.** (1) Subject to section 121 of this Act, any person who, as a condition of the assignment of a protected tenancy, requires the payment of any premium or the making of any loan (whether secured or unsecured) shall be guilty of an offence.

(2) Subject to section 121 of this Act, any person who, in connection with the assignment of a protected tenancy, receives any premium shall be guilty of an offence.

(3) Notwithstanding anything in subsections (1) and (2) above, an assignor of a protected tenancy of a dwelling-house may, if apart from this section he would be entitled to do so, require the payment by the assignee or receive from the assignee a payment—

(*a*) of so much of any outgoings discharged by the assignor as is referable to any period after the assignment takes effect;

(*b*) of a sum not exceeding the amount of any expenditure reasonably incurred by the assignor in carrying out any structural alteration of the dwelling-house or in providing or improving fixtures therein, being fixtures which, as against the landlord, he is not entitled to remove;

(*c*) where the assignor became a tenant of the dwelling-house by virtue of an assignment of the protected tenancy, of a sum not exceeding any reasonable amount paid by him to his assignor in respect of expenditure incurred by that assignor, or by any previous assignor of the tenancy, in carrying out any such alteration or in providing or improving any such fixtures as are mentioned in paragraph (*b*) above; or

(*d*) where part of the dwelling-house is used as a shop or office, or for business, trade or professional purposes, of a reasonable amount in respect of any goodwill of the business, trade or profession, being goodwill transferred to the assignee in connection with the assignment or accruing to him in consequence thereof.

(4) Without prejudice to subsection (3) above, the assignor shall not be guilty of an offence under this section by reason only that—

(*a*) any payment of outgoings required or received by him on the assignment was a payment of outgoings referable to a period before the assignment took effect; or

(*b*) any expenditure which he incurred in carrying out structural alterations of the dwelling-house or in providing or improving fixtures therein and in respect of which he required or received the payment of any sum on the assignment was not reasonably incurred; or

(*c*) any amount paid by him as mentioned in subsection (3)(*c*) above was not a reasonable amount; or

(*d*) any amount which he required to be paid, or which he received, on the assignment in respect of goodwill was not a reasonable amount.

(5) Notwithstanding anything in subsections (1) and (2) above, Part I of Schedule 18 to this Act shall have effect in relation to the assignment of protected tenancies which are regulated tenancies in cases where a premium was lawfully required or received at the commencement of the tenancy.

(6) A person guilty of an offence under this section shall be liable to a fine not exceeding **level 3** on the standard scale.

(7) The court by which a person is convicted of an offence under this section relating to requiring or receiving any premium may order the amount of the premium, or so much of it as cannot lawfully be required or received under this section (including any amount which, by virtue of subsection (4) above, does not give rise to an offence), to be repaid to the person by whom it was paid.

[Rent Act 1977, s 120, as amended by the Criminal Justice Act 1982, ss 38 and 46.]

8–16898 **122. Prohibition of premiums on grant or assignment of rights under restricted contracts.** (1) This section applies in relation to any premises if—

(*a*) under Part V of this Act, a rent is registered for those premises in the register kept in pursuance of section 79 of this Act; and

(*b*) in a case where the approval, reduction or increase of the rent by the rent tribunal is limited to rent payable in respect of a particular period, that period has not expired.

(2) Any person who, as a condition of the grant, renewal, continuance or assignment of rights under a restricted contract[1], requires the payment of any premium shall be guilty of an offence.

(3) Nothing in subsection (2) above shall prevent a person from requiring—

(*a*) that there shall be paid so much of any outgoings discharged by a grantor or assignor as is referable to any period after the grant or assignment takes effect; or

(*b*) that there shall be paid a reasonable amount in respect of goodwill of a business, trade, or profession, where the goodwill is transferred to a grantee or assignee in connection with the grant or assignment or accrues to him in consequence thereof.

(4) A person guilty of an offence under this section shall be liable to a fine not exceeding **level 3** on the standard scale.

(5) The court by which a person is convicted of an offence under this section may order the amount of the premium, or so much of it as cannot lawfully be required under this section, to be repaid to the person by whom it was paid.

[Rent Act 1977, s 122, as amended by the Criminal Justice Act 1982, ss 38 and 46.]

1. For meaning of "restricted contract", see s 19.

8–16899 123. Excessive price for furniture to be treated as premium. Where the purchase of any furniture[1] has been required as a condition of the grant, renewal, continuance or assignment—

(*a*) of a protected tenancy[2], or

(*b*) of rights under a restricted contract[3] which relates to premises falling within section 122(1) of this Act,

then, if the price exceeds the reasonable price of the furniture, the excess shall be treated, for the purposes of this Part of this Act, as if it were a premium required to be paid as a condition of the grant, renewal, continuance or assignment of the protected tenancy or, as the case may be, the rights under the restricted contract.

[Rent Act 1977, s 123.]

1. "Furniture" includes fittings and other articles (s 128(1)).
2. For meaning of "protected tenancy", see s 1.
3. For meaning of "restricted contract", see s 19.

8–16900 124. Punishment of attempts to obtain from prospective tenants excessive prices for furniture. (1) Any person who, in connection with the proposed grant, renewal, continuance or assignment, on terms which require the purchase of furniture[1], of a protected tenancy[2]—

(*a*) offers the furniture at a price which he knows or ought to know is unreasonably high, or otherwise seeks to obtain such a price for the furniture, or

(*b*) fails to furnish, to any person seeking to obtain or retain accommodation whom he provides with particulars of the tenancy, a written inventory of the furniture, specifying the price sought for each item,

shall be liable to a fine not exceeding **level 3** on the standard scale.

(2) Where a local authority have reasonable grounds for suspecting that an offence under subsection (1)(*a*) above has been committed with respect to a protected tenancy or proposed protected tenancy of a dwelling-house, they may give notice to the person entitled to possession of the dwelling-house or his agent that, on such date as may be specified in the notice, which shall not be earlier than—

(*a*) 24 hours after the giving of the notice, or

(*b*) if the dwelling-house is unoccupied, the expiry of such period after the giving of the notice as may be reasonable in the circumstances,

facilities will be required for entry to the dwelling-house and inspection of the furniture therein.

(3) A notice under this section may be given by post.

(4) Where a notice is given under this section, any person authorised by the local authority may avail himself of any facilities for such entry and inspection as are referred to in subsection (2) above which are provided on the specified date but shall, if so required, produce some duly authenticated document showing that he is authorised by the local authority.

(5) If it is shown to the satisfaction of a justice of the peace, on sworn information in writing, that a person required to give facilities under this section has failed to give them, the justice may, by warrant under his hand, empower the local authority, by any person authorised by them, to enter the dwelling-house in question, if need be by force, and inspect the furniture therein.

(6) A person empowered by or under the preceding provisions of this section to enter a dwelling-house may take with him such other persons as may be necessary and, if the dwelling-house is unoccupied, shall leave it as effectively secured against trespassers as he found it.

(7) Any person who wilfully obstructs a person acting in pursuance of a warrant issued under subsection (5) above shall be liable to a fine not exceeding **level 3** on the standard scale.

(8) In this section "local authority" means the council of a district (or, in a county of England in which there are no districts having a district council, the council of the county) or the council of a London borough or the Common Council of the City of London or, in Wales, the council of a county or common borough.

[Rent Act 1977, s 124, as amended by the Criminal Justice Act 1982, ss 35, 38 and 46, the Local Government (Wales) Act 1994, Sch 8 and SI 1995/2451.]

1. "Furniture" includes fittings and other articles (s 128(1)).
2. For meaning of "protected tenancy", see s 1.

8–16901 126. Avoidance of requirements for advance payment of rent in certain cases. (1) Where a protected tenancy[1] which is a regulated tenancy[1] is granted, continued or renewed, any requirement that rent shall be payable—

(*a*) before the beginning of the rental period in respect of which it is payable, or
(*b*) earlier than 6 months before the end of the rental period in respect of which it is payable (if that period is more than 6 months),

shall be void, whether the requirement is imposed as a condition of the grant, renewal or continuance of the tenancy or under the terms thereof.

(2) Any requirement avoided by subsection (1) above is, in this section, referred to as a "prohibited requirement".

(3) Rent for any rental period to which a prohibited requirement relates shall be irrecoverable from the tenant.

(4) Any person who purports to impose any prohibited requirement shall be liable to a fine not exceeding **level 3** on the standard scale, and the court by which he is convicted may order any amount of rent paid in compliance with the prohibited requirement to be repaid to the person by whom it was paid.

(5) Where a tenant has paid on account of rent any amount which, by virtue of this section, is irrecoverable the tenant shall be entitled to recover that amount from the landlord who received it or his personal representatives.

(6) Any amount which a tenant is entitled to recover under subsection (5) above may, without prejudice to any other method of recovery, be deducted by the tenant from any rent payable by him to the landlord.

(7) No amount which a tenant is entitled to recover under subsection (5) above shall be recoverable at any time after the expiry of 2 years from the date of payment.

(8) Any person who, in any rent book or similar document, makes an entry showing or purporting to show any tenant as being in arrears in respect of any sum on account of rent which is irrecoverable by virtue of this section shall be liable to a fine not exceeding **level 3** on the standard scale, unless he proves that, at the time of the making of the entry, the landlord had a *bona fide* claim that the sum was recoverable.

(9) If, where any such entry has been made by or on behalf of any landlord, the landlord on being requested by or on behalf of the tenant to do so, refuses or neglects to cause the entry to be deleted within 7 days, the landlord shall be liable to a fine not exceeding **level 3** on the standard scale, unless he proves that, at the time of the neglect or refusal to cause the entry to be deleted, he had a *bona fide* claim that the sum was recoverable.

[Rent Act 1977, s 126, as amended by the Criminal Justice Act 1982, ss 38 and 46.]

1. For meaning of "protected tenancy", see s 1, and for meaning of "regulated tenancy", see s 18.

PART XI[1]
GENERAL

Sublettings

8–16902 139. Obligation to notify sublettings of dwelling-houses let on or subject to protected or statutory tenancies. (1) If the tenant of a dwelling-house let on or subject to a protected or statutory tenancy sublets any part of the dwelling-house on a protected tenancy, then, subject to subsection (2) below, he shall, within 14 days after the subletting, supply the landlord with a statement in writing of the subletting giving particulars of occupancy, including the rent charged.

(2) Subsection (1) above shall not require the supply of a statement in relation to a subletting of any part of a dwelling-house if the particulars which would be required to be included in the statement as to the rent and other conditions of the sub-tenancy would be the same as in the last statement supplied in accordance with that subsection with respect to a previous sub-letting of that part.

(3) A tenant who is required to supply a statement in accordance with subsection (1) above and who, without reasonable excuse—

(*a*) fails to supply a statement, or
(*b*) supplies a statement which is false in any material particular, shall be liable to a fine not exceeding **level 2** on the standard scale.

(4) In this section—

(*a*) "protected tenancy" includes a protected occupancy under the Rent (Agriculture) Act 1976;
(*b*) "statutory tenancy" includes a statutory tenancy under that Act.

[Rent Act 1977, s 139, as amended by the Criminal Justice Act 1982, ss. 38 and 46.]

1. Part XI contains ss 137–156.

8–16903 **150. Prosecution of offences.** (1) Offences under this Act are punishable summarily.

(2) Proceedings for an offence under this Act may be instituted by any local authority to which section 149 of this Act applies.

[Rent Act 1977, s 150, as amended by the Housing Act 1980, Sch 26.]

8–16904 **151. Service of notices on landlord's agents.** (1) Any document required or authorised by this Act to be served by the tenant of a dwelling-house on the landlord thereof shall be deemed to be duly served on him if it is served—

(*a*) on any agent of the landlord named as such in the rent book or other similar document; or
(*b*) on the person who receives the rent of the dwelling-house.

(2) Where a dwelling-house is subject to a regulated tenancy, subsection (1) above shall apply also in relation to any document required or authorised by this Act to be served on the landlord by a person other than the tenant.

(3) If for the purpose of any proceedings (whether civil or criminal) brought or intended to be brought under this Act, any person serves upon any such agent or other person as is referred to in paragraph (*a*) or paragraph (*b*) of subsection (1) above a notice in writing requiring the agent or other person to disclose to him the full name and place of abode or place of business of the landlord, that agent or other person shall forthwith comply with the notice.

(4) If any such agent or other person as is referred to in subsection (3) above fails or refuses forthwith to comply with a notice served on him under that subsection, he shall be liable to a fine not exceeding **level 4** on the standard scale, unless he shows to the satisfaction of the court that he did not know, and could not with reasonable diligence have ascertained, such of the facts required by the notice to be disclosed as were not disclosed by him.

(5) So far as this section relates to Part V or IX or sections 103 to 107 of this Act, references to a landlord and to a tenant shall respectively include references to a lessor and to a lessee as defined by section 85 of this Act.

[Rent Act 1977, s 151, as amended by the Criminal Justice Act 1982, ss 39 and 46, and Sch 3.]

8–16905 **152. Interpretation.** (1) In this Act, except where the context otherwise requires—

"the appropriate day" has the meaning assigned to it by section 25(3) of this Act;

"landlord" includes any person from time to time deriving title under the original landlord and also includes, in relation to any dwelling-house, any person other than the tenant who is, or but for Part VII of this Act would be, entitled to possession of the dwelling-house;

"let" includes "sublet";

"long tenancy" means a tenancy granted for a term of years certain exceeding 21 years, whether or not subsequently extended by act of the parties or by any enactment;

"protected furnished tenancy", "regulated furnished tenancy" and "statutory furnished tenancy" means a protected or, as the case may be, regulated or statutory tenancy—

(*a*) under which the dwelling-house concerned is bona fide let at a rent which includes payments in respect of furniture, and
(*b*) in respect of which the amount of rent which is fairly attributable to the use of furniture, having regard to the value of that use to the tenant, forms a substantial part of the whole rent;

"protected tenant" and "protected tenancy" shall be construed in accordance with section 1 of this Act;

"rates" includes water rates and charges but does not include an owner's drainage rate as defined in section 63(2)(*a*) of the Land Drainage Act 1976;

"rateable value" shall be construed in accordance with section 25 of this Act;

"regulated tenancy" shall be construed in accordance with section 18 of this Act;

"rent tribunal" has the meaning given by section 76(1) of this Act;

"rental period" means a period in respect of which a payment of rent falls to be made;

"restricted contract" shall be construed in accordance with section 19 of this Act;

"statutory tenant" and "statutory tenancy" shall be construed in accordance with section 2 of this Act;

"tenant" includes statutory tenant and also includes a sub-tenant and any person deriving title under the original tenant or sub-tenant;

"tenancy" includes "sub-tenancy";

"tenancy at a low rent" has the meaning assigned to it by section 5 of this Act.

(2) Except in so far as the context otherwise requires, any reference in this Act to any other enactment shall be taken as referring to that enactment as amended by or under any other enactment, including this Act.

[Rent Act 1977, s 152, as amended by the Housing Act 1980, Sch 26.]

Sections 2 and 3

SCHEDULE 1

(Amended by the Housing Act 1980, Sch 26, the Criminal Justice Act 1982, ss 38 and 46 and the Housing Act 1988, Sch 4.)

8–16906

STATUTORY TENANCIES

PART I

8–16907

STATUTORY TENANTS BY SUCCESSION

PART II

8–16908

RELINQUISHING TENANCIES AND CHANGING TENANTS

Payments demanded by statutory tenants as a condition of giving up possession

12. (1) A statutory tenant[1] of a dwelling-house who, as a condition of giving up possession of the dwelling-house, asks for or receives the payment of any sum, or the giving of any other consideration, by any person other than the landlord, shall be guilty of an offence.

(2) Where a statutory tenant of a dwelling-house requires that furniture or other articles shall be purchased as condition of his giving up possession of the dwelling-house, the price demanded shall, at the request of the person on whom the demand is made, be stated in writing, and if the price exceeds the reasonable price[2] of the articles the excess shall be treated, for the purposes of sub-paragraph (1) above, as a sum asked to be paid as a condition of giving up possession.

(3) A person guilty of an offence under this paragraph shall be liable to a fine not exceeding **level 3** on the standard scale.

(4) The court by which a person is convicted of an offence under this paragraph may order the payment—

(*a*) to the person who made any such payment, or gave any such consideration, as is referred to in sub-paragraph (1) above, of the amount of that payment or the value of that consideration, or

(*b*) to the person who paid any such price as is referred to in sub-paragraph (2) above, of the amount by which the price paid exceeds the reasonable price.

13. *Change of statutory tenant by agreement.*

---

1. For meaning of "statutory tenant", see s 2.
2. The market price of the articles is an important, but not the only, consideration determining this figure (*Eales v Dale* [1954] 1 QB 539, [1954] 1 All ER 717, 118 JP 255).

No pecuniary consideration to be required on change of tenant under paragraph 13

8–16909 **14.** (1) Any person who requires the payment of any pecuniary consideration for entering into such an agreement as is referred to in paragraph 13(1) above shall be liable to a fine not exceeding **level 3** on the standard scale.

(2) The court by which a person is convicted of an offence under sub-paragraph (1) above may order the amount of the payment to be repaid by the person to whom it was paid.

(3) Without prejudice to sub-paragraph (2) above, the amount of any such payment as is referred to in sub-paragraph (1) above shall be recoverable by the person by whom it was made either by proceedings for its recovery or, if it was made to the landlord by a person liable to pay rent to the landlord, by deduction from any rent so payable.

(4) Notwithstanding anything in sub-paragraph (1) above, if apart from this paragraph he would be entitled to do so, the outgoing tenant may require the payment by the incoming tenant—

(*a*) of so much of any outgoings discharged by the outgoing tenant as is referable to any period after the transfer date;

(*b*) of a sum not exceeding the amount of any expenditure reasonably incurred by the outgoing tenant in carrying out any structural alteration of the dwelling or in providing or improving fixtures therein, being fixtures which, as against the landlord, the outgoing tenant is not entitled to remove;

(*c*) where the outgoing tenant became a tenant of the dwelling by virtue of an assignment of the previous protected tenancy, of a sum not exceeding any reasonable amount paid by him to his assignor in respect of expenditure incurred by the assignor, or by any previous assignor of the tenancy, in carrying out any such alteration or in providing or improving any such fixtures as are mentioned in paragraph (*b*) above; or

(*d*) where part of the dwelling is used as a shop or office, or for business, trade or professional purposes, of a reasonable amount in respect of any goodwill of the business, trade or profession, being goodwill transferred to the incoming tenant in connection with his becoming a statutory tenant of the dwelling or accruing to him in consequence thereof.

(5) In this paragraph "outgoing tenant", "incoming tenant", "the transfer date" and "the dwelling" have the same meanings as in paragraph 13 above.

SCHEDULE 11

Section 67

APPLICATION FOR REGISTRATION OF RENT

(Amended by SI 1981/1783, the Criminal Justice Act 1982, ss 35, 38 and 46, SI 1993/651 and SI 1999/6.)

PART I

APPLICATION UNSUPPORTED BY CERTIFICATE OF FAIR RENT

8–16921 **1–6.** *Procedure on application to rent officer.*

Determination of fair rent by rent assessment committee

8–16922 **7.** (1) The rent assessment committee to whom a matter is referred under paragraph 6 above—

(*a*) may by notice in the prescribed form served on the landlord or the tenant require him to give to the committee, within such period of not less than 14 days from the service of the notice as may be specified in the notice, such further information, in addition to any given to the rent officer in pursuance of paragraph 1 above, as they may reasonably require; and

(*b*) shall serve on the landlord and on the tenant a notice specifying a period of not less than 7 days from the service of the notice during which either representations in writing or a request to make oral representations may be made by him to the committee.

(2) If any person fails without reasonable cause to comply with any notice served on him under sub-paragraph (1)(*a*) above, he shall be liable to a fine not exceeding **level 3** on the standard scale.

(3) Where an offence under sub-paragraph (2) above committed by a body corporate is proved to have been committed with the consent or connivance of, or to be attributable to any neglect on the part of, any director, manager or secretary or other similar officer of the body corporate or any person who was purporting to act in any such capacity, he as well as the body corporate shall be guilty of that offence and shall be liable to be proceeded against and punished accordingly.

8–9. *Procedure before rent assessment committee.*

Interim registration of rent

9A. In this Schedule references to a fair rent in relation to an application under section 67A of this Act are references to the amount to be registered under section 70A(1)(*b*) of this Act.

Maximum Fair Rent

9B. This Schedule has effect subject to article 2 of the Rent Acts (Maximum Fair Rent) Order 1999 and accordingly—

(*a*) the rent officer, in considering what rent ought to be registered, shall consider whether that article applies; and

(*b*) where a matter is referred to them, the committee shall consider whether that article applies and, where it does apply, they shall not, subject to paragraph (5) of that article, confirm or determine a rent for the dwelling-house that exceeds the maximum fair rent calculated in accordance with that article.

Protection from Eviction Act 1977[1]

(1977 c 43)

PART I
UNLAWFUL EVICTION AND HARASSMENT

8–17030 **1. Unlawful eviction and harassment of occupier.** (1) In this section "residential occupier", in relation to any premises, means a person occupying the premises as a residence, whether under a contract or by virtue of any enactment or rule of law giving him the right to remain in occupation or restricting the right of any other person to recover possession of the premises.

(2) If any person unlawfully[2] deprives[3] the residential occupier of any premises[4] of his occupation of the premises or any part thereof, or attempts to do so, he shall be guilty of an offence unless he proves that he believed, and had reasonable cause to believe, that the residential occupier had ceased to reside in the premises.

(3) If any person with intent[5] to cause the residential occupier of any premises—

(*a*) to give up the occupation of the premises or any part thereof; or

(*b*) to refrain from exercising any right or pursuing any remedy in respect of the premises or part thereof;

does acts[6] likely to interfere with the peace or comfort of the residential occupier or members of his household, or persistently withdraws or withholds services reasonably required for the occupation of the premises as a residence[7], he shall be guilty of an offence.

(3A) Subject to subsection (3B) below, the landlord of a residential occupier or an agent of the landlord shall be guilty of an offence if—

(*a*) he does acts likely to interfere with the peace of comfort of the residential occupier or members of his household, or

(*b*) he persistently withdraws or withholds services reasonably required for the occupation of the premises in question as a residence,

and (in either case) he knows, or has reasonable cause to believe, that that conduct is likely to cause the residential occupier to give up the occupation of the whole or part of the premises or to refrain from exercising any right or pursuing any remedy in respect of the whole or part of the premises.

(3B) A person shall not be guilty of an offence under subsection (3A) above if he proves that he had reasonable grounds for doing the acts or withdrawing or withholding the services in question.

(3C) In subsection (3A) above "landlord", in relation to a residential occupier of any premises, means the person who, but for—

(*a*) the residential occupier's right to remain in occupation of the premises, or
(*b*) a restriction on the person's right to recover possession of the premises,

would be entitled to occupation of the premises and any superior landlord under whom that person derives title.

(4) A person guilty of an offence under this section shall be liable[8]—

(*a*) on summary conviction, to a fine not exceeding the prescribed sum or to imprisonment for a term not exceeding 6 months or to both;
(*b*) on conviction on indictment, to a fine or to imprisonment for a term not exceeding 2 years or to both.

(5) Nothing in this section shall be taken to prejudice any liability or remedy to which a person guilty of an offence thereunder may be subject in civil proceedings.

(6) Where an offence under this section committed by a body corporate is proved to have been committed with the consent or connivance of, or to be attributable to any neglect on the part of, any director, manager or secretary or other similar officer of the body corporate or any person who was purporting to act in any capacity, he as well as the body corporate shall be guilty of that offence and shall be liable to be proceeded against and punished accordingly.

[Protection from Eviction Act 1977, s 1, as amended by the Criminal Law Act 1977, s 28, the Magistrates' Court Act 1980, s 32(2) and the Housing Act 1988, s 29.]

---

1. This Act consolidates, *inter alia*, s 16 of the Rent Act 1957 and Pt III of the Rent Act 1965. The Act applies where a person has been let into possession of a dwelling-house under the terms of a rental purchase agreement (within the meaning of section 88 of the Housing Act 1980) as if—

(*a*) the dwelling-house had been let to him as a dwelling under a tenancy which is not a statutorily protected tenancy (within the meaning of s 3 of the Act); and
(*b*) that tenancy had come to an end on the termination of the agreement or of his right to possession under it (Housing Act 1980, Sch 25, para 61).

"Rental purchase agreement" means an agreement for the purchase of a dwelling-house (whether freehold or leasehold property) under which the whole or part of the purchase price is to be paid in three or more instalments and the completion of the purchase is deferred until the whole or a specified part of the purchase price has been paid (Housing Act 1980, s 88(4)).

2. Contravention of ss 2 or 3, post, would be an unlawful deprivation. The sections do not of themselves create any criminal offence.

3. The unlawful deprivation of occupation complained of has to have the character of an eviction, and while not limited to a permanent deprivation of occupation, has to amount to more than a mere exclusion from premises for more than one day and night (*R v Yuthiwattana* [1984] Crim LR 562; applied in *Costelloe v London Borough of Camden* [1986] Crim LR 249).

4. Such premises may consist of a caravan and the land on which it stands (*Norton v Knowles* [1969] 1 QB 572, [1967] 3 All ER 1061, 132 JP 100).

5. The prosecution must prove *mens rea*; accordingly they must negative any statement of honest belief that the person alleged to have been harassed was not a residential occupier; *R v Phekoo* [1981] 3 All ER 84, [1981] 1 WLR 1117, [1981] Crim LR 399, CA.

6. The words "does acts" do not impose a responsibility to rectify damage which the defendant has already caused by an act when he did not possess either of the intentions necessary to constitute an offence under s 1(3) (*R v Ahmad* (1986) 84 Cr App Rep 64, [1986] Crim LR 739).

7. The act need not amount to a breach of a residential occupier's right of occupation before it is capable of constituting harassment under this section (*R v Yuthiwattana* [1984] Crim LR 562), nor need it be an actionable civil wrong in order to be an offence (*R v Burke* [1991] 1 AC 135, [1990] 2 All ER 385, 154 JP 798, HL).

8. For procedure in respect of this offence triable either way, see the Magistrates' Courts Act 1980, ss 18–21, in PART I, ante. In the absence of unusual mitigation, a sentence of immediate imprisonment is correct in principle where threats or force have been used to evict a tenant (*R v Brennan and Brennan* [1979] Crim LR 603).

8–17031 **2. Restriction on re-entry without due process of law.** Where any premises are let as a dwelling on a lease which is subject to a right of re-entry or forfeiture it shall not be lawful to enforce that right otherwise than by proceedings in the court[1] while any person is lawfully residing in the premises or part of them.

[Protection from Eviction Act 1977, s 2.]

---

1. Ie, the county court or (exceptionally) the High Court (s 9).

8–17032 **3. Prohibition of eviction without due process of law.** (1) Where any premises have been let as a dwelling under a tenancy which is neither a statutorily protected tenancy[1] nor an excluded tenancy and—

(*a*) the tenancy (in this section referred to as the former tenancy) has come to an end, but
(*b*) the occupier continues to reside in the premises or part of them,

it shall not be lawful for the owner[1] to enforce against the occupier, otherwise than by proceedings in the court, his right to recover possession of the premises.

(2) In this section "the occupier", in relation to any premises, means any person lawfully residing in the premises or part of them at the termination of the former tenancy.

(2A) Subsections (1) and (2) above apply in relation to any restricted contract (within the meaning of the Rent Act 1977) which—

(*a*) creates a licence; and
(*b*) is entered into after the commencement of section 69 of the Housing Act 1980;

as they apply in relation to a restricted contract which creates a tenancy.

(2B) Subsections (1) and (2) above apply in relation to any premises occupied as a dwelling under a licence, other than an excluded licence, as they apply in relation to premises let as a dwelling under a tenancy, and in those subsections the expressions "let" and "tenancy" shall be construed accordingly.

(2C) References in the preceding provisions of this section and section 4(2A) below to an excluded tenancy to not apply to—

(*a*) a tenancy entered into before the date[2] on which the Housing Act 1988 came into force, or
(*b*) a tenancy entered into on or after that date but pursuant to a contract made before that date,

but, subject to that, "excluded tenancy" and "excluded licence" shall be construed in accordance with section 3A below.

(3) This section shall, with the necessary modifications, apply where the owner's right to recover possession arises on the death of the tenant under a statutory tenancy within the meaning of the Rent Act 1977 or the Rent (Agriculture) Act 1976.

[Protection from Eviction Act 1977, s 3, as amended by the Housing Act 1980, s 69 and the Housing Act 1988, s 30.]

1. "Statutorily protected tenancy" and "the owner" are defined in s 8, post. The provisions of the Act have no application to a local council providing temporary accommodation for a homeless person pending inquiries under s 63 of the Housing Act 1985. The council who had arranged temporary accommodation in a hotel were not, by the agency of the hotel proprietor, the "owner" of the room nor were they the "licensor" (*Mohamed v Manek and Royal Borough of Kensington and Chelsea* (1995) 27 HLR 439).

2. The commencement date for this purpose was 15 January 1989; see the Housing Act 1988, s 141(3).

8–17033 **3A. Excluded tenancies and licences.** (1) Any reference in this Act to an excluded tenancy or an excluded licence is a reference to a tenancy or licence which is excluded by virtue of any of the following provisions of this section.

(2) A tenancy or licence is excluded if—

(*a*) under its terms the occupier shares any accommodation with the landlord or licensor; and
(*b*) immediately before the tenancy or licence was granted and also at the time it comes to an end, the landlord or licensor occupied as his only or principal home premises of which the whole or part of the shared accommodation formed part.

(3) A tenancy or licence is also excluded if—

(*a*) under its terms the occupier shares any accommodation with a member of the family of the landlord or licensor;
(*b*) immediately before the tenancy or licence was granted and also at the time it comes to an end, the member of the family of the landlord or licensor occupied as his only or principal home premises of which the whole or part of the shared accommodation formed part; and
(*c*) immediately before the tenancy or licence was granted and also at the time it comes to an end, the landlord or licensor occupied as his only or principal home premises in the same building as the shared accommodation and that building is not a purpose-built block of flats.

(4) For the purposes of subsections (2) and (3) above, an occupier shares accommodation with another person if he has the use of it in common with that person (whether or not also in common with others) and any reference in those subsections to shared accommodation shall be construed accordingly, and if, in relation to any tenancy or licence, there is at any time more than one person who is the landlord or licensor, any reference in those subsections to the landlord or licensor shall be construed as a reference to any one of those persons.

(5) In subsection (2) to (4) above—

(*a*) "accommodation" includes neither an area used for storage nor a staircase, passage, corridor or other means of access;
(*b*) "occupier" means, in relation to a tenancy, the tenant and, in relation to a licence, the licensee; and
(*c*) "purpose-built block of flats" has the same meaning as in Part III of Schedule 1 to the Housing Act 1988;

and section 113 of the Housing Act 1985 shall apply to determine whether a person is for the purposes of subsection (3) above a member of another's family as it applies for the purposes of Part IV of that Act.

(6) A tenancy or licence is excluded if it was granted as a temporary expedient to a person who entered the premises in question or any other premises as a trespasser (whether or not, before the beginning of that tenancy or licence, another tenancy or licence to occupy the premises or any other premises had been granted to him).

(7) A tenancy or licence is excluded if—

(*a*) it confers on the tenant or licensee the right to occupy the premises for a holiday only; or (*b*) it is granted otherwise than for money or money's worth.

(7A) A tenancy or licence is excluded if it is granted in order to provide accommodation under Part VI of the Immigration and Asylum Act 1999.*

(7C) A tenancy or licence is excluded if it is granted in order to provide accommodation under the Displaced Persons (Temporary Protection) Regulations 2005.

(8) A licence is excluded if it confers rights of occupation in a hostel, within the meaning of the Housing Act 1985, which is provided by—

(*a*) the council of a county, county borough, district or London Borough, the Common Council of the City of London, the Council of the Isles of Scilly, the Inner London Education Authority, the London Fire and Emergency Planing Authority, a joint authority within the meaning of the Local Government Act 1985 or a residuary body within the meaning of that Act;
(*b*) a development corporation within the meaning of the New Towns Act 1981;
(*c*) the Commission for the New Towns;
(*d*) an urban development corporation established by an order under section 135 of the Local Government, Planning and Land Act 1980;
(*e*) a housing action trust established under Part III of the Housing Act 1988;
(*f*) *Repealed*;
(*g*) the Housing Corporation;
(*ga*) the Secretary of State under section 89 of the Housing Associations Act 1985;
(*h*) a housing trust (within the meaning of the Housing Associations Act 1985) which is a charity or a registered social landlord (within the meaning of the Housing Act 1985); or
(*i*) any other person who is, or whole belongs to a class of person which is, specified in an order[1] made by the Secretary of State.

(9) The power to make an order under subsection (8)(*i*) above shall be exercisable by statutory instrument which shall be subject to annulment in pursuance of a resolution of either House of Parliament.*

[Protection from Eviction Act 1977, s 3A, as inserted by the Housing Act 1988, s 31 and amended by the Local Government (Wales) Act 1994, Sch 8, SI 1996/2325, the Government of Wales Act 1998, Schs 16 and 18, the Immigration and Asylum Act 1999, Sch 14, the Greater London Authority Act 1999, Sch 29 and SI 2005/1379.]

***Sub-section (7B) inserted by the Nationality, Immigration and Asylum Act 2002, s 32 from a date to be appointed.**

1. See the Protection from Eviction (Excluded Licences) Order 1991, SI 1991/1943.

8–17034 **4.** *Special provisions for agricultural employees.*

PART II
NOTICE TO QUIT

8–17035 **5.** *Validity of notices to quit.*

PART III
SUPPLEMENTAL PROVISIONS

8–17036 **6. Prosecution of offences.** Proceedings for an offence under this Act may be instituted by any of the following authorities:

(*a*) councils of districts and London boroughs;
(*aa*) councils of Welsh counties and county boroughs;
(*b*) the Common Council of the City of London;
(*c*) the Council of the Isles of Scilly.

[Protection from Eviction Act 1977, s 6 amended by the Local Government (Wales) Act 1994, Sch 8.]

8–17037 **7. Service of notices.** (1) If for the purpose of any proceedings (whether civil or criminal) brought or intended to be brought under this Act, any person serves upon—

(*a*) any agent of the landlord named as such in the rent book or other similar document, or
(*b*) the person who receives the rent of the dwelling,

a notice in writing requiring the agent or other person to disclose to him the full name and place of abode or place of business of the landlord, that agent or other person shall forthwith comply with the notice.

(2) If any such agent or other person as is referred to in subsection (1) above fails or refuses forthwith to comply with a notice served on him under that subsection, he shall be liable on summary conviction to a fine not exceeding **level 4** on the standard scale, unless he shows to the satisfaction of the court that he did not know, and could not with reasonable diligence have ascertained, such of the facts required by the notice to be disclosed as were not disclosed by him.

(3) In this section "landlord" includes—

(*a*) any person from time to time deriving title under the original landlord,
(*b*) in relation to any dwelling-house, any person other than the tenant who is or, but for Part VII of the Rent Act 1977 would be, entitled to possession of the dwelling-house, and
(*c*) any person who grants to another the right to occupy the dwelling in question as a residence and any person directly or indirectly deriving title from the grantor.

[Protection from Eviction Act 1977, s 7, as amended by the Criminal Justice Act 1982, ss 39 and 46, and Sch 3 and the Housing Act 1988, Schs 17 and 18.]

8–17038 8. Interpretation. (1) In this Act "statutorily protected tenancy" means—

(*a*) a protected tenancy within the meaning of the Rent Act 1977 or a tenancy to which Part I of the Landlord and Tenant Act 1954 applies;
(*b*) a protected occupancy or statutory tenancy as defined in the Rent (Agriculture) Act 1976;
(*c*) a tenancy to which Part II of the Landlord and Tenant Act 1954 applies;
(*d*) a tenancy of an agricultural holding within the meaning of the Agricultural Holdings Act 1986 which is a tenancy in relation to which that Act applies;
(*e*) an assured tenancy or assured agricultural occupancy under Part I of the Housing Act 1988;
(*f*) a tenancy to which Schedule 10 to the Local Government and Housing Act 1989 applies;
(*g*) a farm business tenancy within the meaning of the Agricultural Tenancies Act 1995.

(2) For the purposes of Part I of this Act a person who, under the terms of his employment, had exclusive possession of any premises other than as a tenant shall be deemed to have been a tenant and the expressions "let" and "tenancy" shall be construed accordingly.

(3) In Part I of this Act "the owner", in relation to any premises, means the person who, as against the occupier, is entitled to possession thereof.

(4) In this Act "excluded tenancy" and "excluded licence" have the meaning assigned by section 3A of this Act.

(5)–(6) *Variation of terms of an excluded tenancy or excluded licence.*

[Protection from Eviction Act 1977, s 8, as amended by the Agricultural Holdings Act 1986, Sch 14, the Housing Act 1988, s 33, the Local Government and Housing Act 1989, Sch 11 and the Agricultural Tenancies Act 1995, Sch.]

Housing Act 1985

(1985 c 68)

PART I[1]

INTRODUCTORY PROVISIONS

Local housing authorities

8–17141 1. Local housing authorities. In this Act "local housing authority" means a district council, a London borough council, the Common Council of the City of London, a Welsh county council or county borough council or the Council of the Isles of Scilly.

[Housing Act 1985, s 1, as amended by the Local Government (Wales) Act 1994, Sch 8.]

1. Part I contains ss 1–7.

8–17142 2. The district of a local housing authority. (1) References in this Act to the district of a local housing authority are to the area of the council concerned, that is, to the district, London borough, the City of London, the Welsh county or county borough or the Isles of Scilly, as the case may be.

(2) References in this Act to "the local housing authority", in relation to land, are to the local housing authority in whose district the land is situated.

[Housing Act 1985, s 2, as amended by the Local Government (Wales) Act 1994, Sch 8.]

8–17143 3. Buildings situated in more than one district. (1) Where a building is situated partly in the district of one local housing authority and partly in the district of another, the authorities may agree that—

(*a*) the building, or
(*b*) the building, its site and any yard, garden, outhouses and appurtenances belonging to the building or usually enjoyed with it,

shall be treated for the purposes of the enactments relating to housing as situated in such one of the districts as is specified in the agreement.

(2) Whilst the agreement is in force the enactments relating to housing have effect accordingly.

[Housing Act 1985, s 3.]

Other authorities and bodies

8–17144 4. Other descriptions of authority. In this Act—

(*a*) "housing authority" means a local housing authority or a new town corporation;
(*b*) "new town corporation" means a development corporation or the Commission for the New Towns;
(*c*) "development corporation" means a development corporation established by an order made, or having effect as if made, under the New Towns Act 1981;
(*d*) "urban development corporation" means an urban development corporation established under Part XVI of the Local Government, Planning and Land Act 1980;
(*e*) "local authority" means a county, county borough, district or London borough council, the Common Council of the City of London or the Council of the Isles of Scilly, in sections 43, 44 and 232 includes the Broads Authority, in sections 438, 441, 442, 443 and 458 includes the Broads Authority and a joint authority established by Part IV of the Local Government Act 1985 and the London Fire and Emergency Planning Authority, and in sections 45(2)(*b*), 50(2), 51(6), 80(1), 157(1), 171(2), 573(1), paragraph 2(1) of Schedule 1, grounds 7 and 12 in Schedule 2, ground 5 in Schedule 3, paragraph 7(1) of Schedule 4, paragraph 5(1)(*b*) of Schedule 5 and Schedule 16 includes the Broads Authority, a police authority established under section 3 of the Police Act 1996 a joint authority established by Part IV of the Local Government Act 1985 and the London Fire and Emergency Planning Authority;
(*f*) "housing action trust" means a housing action trust established under Part III of the Housing Act 1988.

[Housing Act 1985, s 4, as amended by the Norfolk and Suffolk Broads Act 1988, Sch 6, the Education Reform Act 1988, Sch 13, the Housing Act 1988, s 62, the Local Government (Wales) Act 1994, Sch 8, the Police and Magistrates' Courts Act 1994, Sch 4, the Police Act 1996, Sch 7, the Police Act 1997, Sch 9, the Government of Wales Act 1998, Sch 15, the Greater London Authority Act 1999, Schs 27 and 29, the Criminal Justice and Police Act 2001, Sch 6 and the Police Reform Act 2002, ss 100 and 107.]

8–17145 5. Housing associations. (1) In this Act "housing association" means a society, body of trustees or company—

(*a*) which is established for the purpose of, or amongst whose objects or powers are included those of, providing, constructing, improving or managing, or facilitating or encouraging the construction or improvement of, housing accommodation, and
(*b*) which does not trade for profit or whose constitution or rules prohibit the issue of capital with interest or dividend exceeding such rate as may be prescribed by the Treasury, whether with or without differentiation as between share and loan capital.

(2) In this Act "fully mutual", in relation to a housing association, means that the rules of the association—

(*a*) restrict membership to persons who are tenants or prospective tenants of the association, and
(*b*) preclude the granting or assignment of tenancies to persons other than members;

and "co-operative housing association" means a fully mutual housing association which is a society registered under the Industrial and Provident Societies Act 1965.

(3) In this Act "self-build society" means a housing association whose object is to provide, for sale to, or occupation by, its members, dwellings built or improved principally with the use of its members' own labour.

(4) In this Act "registered social landlord" means—

(*a*) a housing association registered in the register maintained by the Housing Corporation under section 1 of the Housing Act 1996, or
(*b*) a housing association registered in the register maintained by the Secretary for State under section 1 of the Housing Act 1996,

subject as follows.

(5) References to registered social landlords include, where the context so permits, references to housing associations registered in the register maintained by Scottish Homes under section 3 of the Housing Associations Act 1985 (Scottish registered housing associations).

[Housing Act 1985, s 5, as amended by SI 1996/2325 and the Government of Wales Act 1998, Sch 16.]

8–17146 6. Housing trusts. In this Act "housing trust" means a corporation or body of persons which—

(*a*) is required by the terms of its constituent instrument to use the whole of its funds, including any surplus which may arise from its operations, for the purpose of providing housing accommodation, or
(*b*) is required by the terms of its constituent instrument to devote the whole, or substantially the whole, of its funds for charitable purposes and in fact uses the whole, or substantially the whole, of its funds for the purpose of providing housing accommodation.

[Housing Act 1985, s 6.]

8–17147 **6A.** (1) In this Act "the Relevant Authority" means the Housing Corporation, the Secretary of State or Scottish Homes, subject as follows.

(2) In relation to a housing association which is—

(*a*) a registered charity which has its address for the purposes of registration by the Charity Commissioners in Wales,

(*b*) a society registered under the Industrial and Provident Societies Act 1965 which has its registered office for the purposes of the Act in Wales, or

(*c*) a company registered under the Companies Act 1985 which has its registered office for the purposes of that Act in Wales,

"the Relevant Authority" means the Secretary of State.

(3) In relation to a housing association which is a society registered under the Industrial and Provident Societies Act 1965 which has its registered office for the purposes of that Act in Scotland, "the Relevant Authority" means Scottish Homes.

(4) In relation to any other housing association which is a registered charity, a society registered under the Industrial and Provident Societies Act 1965 or a company registered under the Companies Act 1985, "the Relevant Authority " means the Housing Corporation.

(5) In this section "registered charity" means a charity which is registered under section 3 of the Charities Act 1993 and is not an exempt charity within the meaning of that Act.

[Housing Act 1985, s 6A, as inserted by the Housing Act 1988, Sch 17, substituted by SI 1996/2325 and amended by the Government of Wales Act 1998, Sch 16.]

Supplementary provisions

8–17148 **7. Index of defined expressions: Part I.** The following Table shows provisions defining or otherwise explaining expressions used in this Part (other than provisions defining or explaining an expression used in the same section or paragraph):—

district (of a local housing authority)	section 2(1)
local housing authority	section 1, 2(2)
tenancy and tenant	section 621

[Housing Act 1985, s 7.]

PART II[1]
PROVISION OF HOUSING ACCOMMODATION

Restriction on service charges payable after disposal of house

8–17149 **45. Disposals in relation to which ss 46 to 51 apply.** (1) The following provisions of this Part down to section 51 (restrictions on, and provision of information about, service charges) apply where—

(*a*) the freehold of a house has been conveyed by a public sector authority; and

(*b*) the conveyance enabled the vendor to recover from the purchaser a service charge.

(2) In subsection (1)(*a*)—

"public sector authority" means—

a local authority,
a National Park authority,
a new town corporation,
an urban development corporation,
a housing action trust,
the Housing Corporation or Scottish Homes, or
a registered social landlord.

(2A) In subsection (1)(*a*) "public sector authority" also includes the Secretary of State if the freehold has been conveyed by him (or Housing for Wales) under section 90 of the Housing Association Act 1985.

(3) The following provisions—

section 170 (power of Secretary of State to give assistance in connection with legal proceedings), and
section 181 (jurisdiction of county court),

apply to proceedings and questions arising under this section and sections 46 to 51 as they apply to proceedings and questions arising under Part V (the right to buy).

[Housing Act 1985, s 45, as amended by the Landlord, Tenant Act 1987, Schs 4 and 5, the Housing Act 1988, s 79 and Sch 17, the Environment Act 1995, Sch 10, SI 1996/2325 and the Government of Wales Act 1998, Schs 16 and 18.]

---

1. Part II contains ss 8–57.

8–17150 47. Limitation of service charges. (1) Relevant costs shall be taken into account in determining the amount of a service charge payable for a period—

(*a*) only to the extent that they are reasonably incurred, and

(*b*) where they are incurred on the provision of services or the carrying out of works, only if the services or works are of a reasonable standard;

and the amount payable shall be limited accordingly.

(2) Where the service charge is payable before the relevant costs are incurred, no greater amount than is reasonable is so payable and after the relevant costs have been incurred any necessary adjustment shall be made by repayment, reduction of subsequent charges or otherwise.

(3) An agreement by the payer (other than an arbitration agreement within the meaning of Part 1 of the Arbitration Act 1996) is void in so far as it purports to provide for a determination in a particular manner or on particular evidence of any question—

(*a*) whether an amount payable before costs for services, repairs, maintenance, insurance or management are incurred is reasonable,

(*b*) whether such costs were reasonably incurred, or

(*c*) whether services or works for which costs were incurred are of a reasonable standard.

(4) Where relevant costs are incurred or to be incurred on the carrying out of works in respect of which a grant has been or is to be paid under section 523 of the Housing Act 1985 (assistance for provision of separate service pipe for water supply) or any provision of Part I of the Housing Grants, Construction and Regeneration Act 1996 (grants, &c. for renewal of private sector housing) or any corresponding earlier enactment, the amount of the grant shall be deducted from the costs and the amount of the service charge payable shall be reduced accordingly.

[Housing Act 1985, s 47, as amended by the Housing and Planning Act 1986, Sch 5, the Local Government and Housing Act 1989, Sch 11, the Arbitration Act 1996, Sch 3 and the Housing Grants, Construction and Regeneration Act 1996, Sch 1.]

8–17151 48. Information as to relevant costs. (1) The payer may require the payee in writing to supply him with a written summary of the costs incurred—

(*a*) if the relevant accounts are made up for periods of twelve months, in the last such period ending not later than the date of the request, or

(*b*) if the accounts are not so made up, in the period of twelve months ending with the date of the request,

and which are relevant to the service charges payable or demanded as payable in that or any other period.

(2) The payee shall comply with the request within one month of the request or within six months of the end of the period referred to in subsection (1)(*a*) or (*b*), whichever is the later.

(3) The summary shall set out those costs in a way showing how they are or will be reflected in demands for service charges and must be certified by a qualified accountant as in his opinion a fair summary complying with this requirement and as being sufficiently supported by accounts, receipts and other documents which have been produced to him.

(3A) The summary shall also state whether any of the costs relate to works in respect of which a grant has been or is to be paid under section 523 of the Housing Act 1985 (assistance for provision of separate service pipe for water supply) or any provision of Chapter I of Part I of the Housing Grants, Construction and Regeneration Act 1996 (grants for renewal of private sector housing) or any corresponding earlier enactment.

(4) Where the payer has obtained such a summary as is referred to in subsection (1) (whether in pursuance of this section or otherwise), he may within six months of obtaining it require the payee in writing to afford him reasonable facilities—

(*a*) for inspecting the accounts, receipts and other documents supporting the summary, and

(*b*) for taking copies or extracts from them,

and the payee shall then make such facilities available to the payer for a period of two months beginning not later than one month after the request is made.

(5) A request under this section shall be deemed to be served on the payee if it is served on a person who receives the service charge on behalf of the payee; and a person on whom a request is so served shall forward it as soon as possible to the payee.

(6) A disposal of the house by the payer does not affect the validity of a request made under this section before the disposal; but a person is not obliged to provide a summary or make the facilities available more than once for the same house and for the same period.

[Housing Act 1985, s 48, as amended by the Housing and Planning Act 1986, Sch, the Local Government and Housing Act 1989, Sch 11 and the Housing Grants, Construction and Regeneration Act 1996, Sch 1.]

8–17152 50. Offences. (1) If a person fails without reasonable excuse to perform a duty imposed on him by section 48 (provision of information, etc), he commits a summary offence and is liable on conviction to a fine not exceeding **level 4** on the standard scale.

(2) Subsection (1) does not apply where the payee is—

a local authority, or
a new town corporation.

[Housing Act 1985, s 50, as amended by the Landlord and Tenant Act 1987, Schs 4 and 5, and the Government of Wales Act 1998, Schs 15 and 18.]

8–17153 **51. Meaning of "qualified accountant".** (1) The reference to a "qualified accountant" in section 48(3) (certification of summary of information about relevant costs) is to a person who, in accordance with the following provisions, has the necessary qualification and is not disqualified from acting.

(2) A person has the necessary qualification only if he is eligible for appointment as a company auditor under section 25 of the Companies act 1989.

(3) (*Repealed*).

(4) The following are disqualified from acting—

(*a*) where the payee is a company, the payee or any associated company of the payee;

(*b*) an officer or employee of the payee or, where the payee is a company, of an associated company;

(*c*) a person who is a partner or employee of any such officer or employee.

(5) For the purposes of subsection (4)(*a*) and (*b*) a company is associated with the payee company if it is (within the meaning of section 736 of the Companies Act 1985) the payee's holding company or subsidiary or is a subsidiary of the payee's holding company.

(6) Where the payee is a local authority or a new town corporation—

(*a*) the persons who have the necessary qualification include members of the Chartered Institute of Public Finance and Accountancy, and

(*b*) subsection (4)(*b*) (disqualification of officers and employees) does not apply.

[Housing Act 1985, s 51, as amended by SI 1991/1997 and the Government of Wales Act 1998, Sch 15.]

Supplementary provisions

8–17154 **54. Powers of entry.** (1) A person authorised by a local housing authority or the Secretary of State may, at any reasonable time, on giving 24 hours' notice of his intention to the occupier, and to the owner if the owner is known, enter premises for the purpose of survey and examination—

(*a*) where it appears to the authority or Secretary of State that survey or examination is necessary in order to determine whether any powers under this Part should be exercised in respect of the premises, or

(*b*) in the case of premises which the authority are authorised by this Part to purchase compulsorily.

(2) An authorisation for the purposes of this section shall be in writing stating the particular purpose[1] or purposes for which the entry is authorised and shall, if so required, be produced for inspection by the occupier or anyone acting on his behalf.

[Housing Act 1985, s 54, as amended by the Local Government and Housing Act 1989, Sch 11.]

1. This is a general power, not depending upon reasonable ground to suspect the existence of any state of things (*Bedingfield v Jones* (1959) 124 JP 11).

8–17155 **55. Penalty for obstruction.** (1) It is a summary offence intentionally to obstruct an officer of the local housing authority, or of the Secretary of State, or any person authorised to enter premises in pursuance of this Part, in the performance of anything which he is by this Part required or authorised to do.

(2) A person who commits such an offence is liable on conviction to a fine not exceeding **level 3** on the standard scale.

[Housing Act 1985, s 55, as amended by the Local Government and Housing Act 1989, Sch 11.]

8–17156 **56. Minor definitions.** In this Part—

"house" includes any yard, garden, outhouses and appurtenances belonging to the house or usually enjoyed with it;

"housing accommodation" includes flats, lodging-houses and hotels, and "house" shall be similarly construed;

"introductory tenancy" has the same meaning as in Chapter I of Part V of the Housing Act 1996;

"lodging-houses" means houses not occupied as separate dwellings;

"member of family", in relation to a person, has the same meaning as in Part V (the right to buy);

"owner", in relation to premises—

(*a*) means a person (other than a mortgagee not in possession) who is for the time being entitled to dispose of the fee simple in the premises, whether in possession or in reversion, and

(*b*) includes also a person holding or entitled to the rents and profits of the premises under a lease of which the unexpired term exceeds three years.

[Housing Act 1985, s 56, as amended by SI 1997/74.]

8–17157 57. Index of defined expressions: Part II. The following Table shows provisions defining or otherwise explaining expressions used in this Part (other than provisions defining or explaining an expression used in the same section or paragraph):—

Bank	section 622
building society	section 622
compulsory disposal	section 40
development corporation	section 4(*c*)
district (of a local housing authority)	section 2(1)
exempted disposal	section 39
family (member of)	sections 56 and 186
friendly society	section 622
Hostel	section 622
House	section 56
housing accommodation	section 56
housing association	section 5(1)
Housing Revenue Account	section 417
insurance company	section 622
introductory tenancy	section 56
Lease	section 621
local authority	section 4(*e*)
local housing authority	sections 1, 2(2)
local housing authority's houses	section 20
lodging-houses	section 56
new town corporation	section 4(*b*)
Owner	section 56
payee and payer (in relation to a service charge)	section 621A
qualified accountant (for the purposes of section 48(3))	section 51
registered social landlord	section 5(4) and (5)
relevant costs (in relation to a service charge)	section 621A
relevant disposal	section 38 (and see section 452(3))
secure tenancy	section 79
service charge	section 621A
shared ownership lease	section 622
standard scale (in reference to the maximum fine on summary conviction)	section 622
Street	section 622
tenancy and tenant	section 621
trustee savings bank	section 622
urban development corporation	section 4(*d*)

[Housing Act 1985, s 57, as amended by the Housing and Planning Act 1986, Sch, the Housing Act 1988, Sch 17, SI 1996/2325, SI 1997/74 and the Government of Wales Act 1998, Schs 16 and 18.]

8–17168

PART IV[1]
SECURE TENANCIES AND RIGHTS OF SECURE TENANTS

1. Part IV contains ss 79–117. This Part is not printed in this work.

8–17169

PART V[1]
THE RIGHT TO BUY

1. Part V contains ss 118–188. This Part is not printed in this work.

PART VI[1]
REPAIR NOTICES

Repair Notices

8–17174 189. Repair notice in respect of unfit house. (1) Subject to subsection (1A), where the local housing authority are satisfied that a dwelling-house or house in multiple occupation is unfit for human habitation, they shall serve a repair notice on the person having control[3] of the dwelling-house, or house in multiple occupation, if they are satisfied, in accordance with section 604A that serving a notice under this subsection is the most satisfactory course of action.

(1A) Where the local housing authority are satisfied that either a dwelling-house which is a flat or a flat in multiple occupation is unfit for human habitation by virtue of section 604(2), they shall serve a repair notice on the person having control of the part of the building in question if they are satisfied, in accordance with section 604A, that serving a notice under this subsection is the most satisfactory course of action.

(1B) In the case of a house in multiple occupation, a repair notice may be served on the person instead of on the person having control; and where a notice is so served, then, subject to section 191, the person managing the house shall be regarded as the person having control of it for the purposes of the provisions of this Part following that section.

(2) A repair notice under this section shall—

(*a*) require the person on whom it is served to execute the works specified in the notice (which may be works of repair or improvement or both) and to begin those works not later than such reasonable date, being not earlier than the twenty-eighth day after the notice is served, as is specified in the notice and to complete those works within such reasonable time as is so specified, and

(*b*) state that in the opinion of the authority the works specified in the notice will render the dwelling-house or, as the case may be, house in multiple occupation fit for human habitation.

(3) The authority, in addition to serving the notice—

(*a*) on the person having control of the dwelling-house or part of the building concerned, or

(*b*) on the person having control of or, as the case may, on the person managing the house in multiple occupation which is concerned,

shall serve a copy of the notice on any other person having an interest in the dwelling-house, part of the building or house concerned, whether as freeholder, mortgagee, or lessee.

(4) The notice becomes operative, if no appeal is brought, on the expiration of 21 days from the date of the service of the notice and is final and conclusive as to matters which could have been raised on an appeal.

(5) A repair notice under this section which has become operative is a local land charge.

(6) This section has effect subject to the provisions of section 190A.

[Housing Act 1985, s 189, as amended by the Housing Act 1988, Sch 15 and the Local Government and Housing Act 1989, s 165 and Sch 9, Part I.]

---

1. Part VI contains ss 189–208.
2. This section deals with dwelling-houses or houses in multiple occupation which are unfit for human habitation; s 190, post, deals with the permissive power to serve a repair notice in respect of such houses in a state of disrepair but not unfit.
3. "Person having control" is defined in s 207, post.

8–17175 **190. Power notice in respect of house in state of disrepair but not unfit.** (1) Subject to subsection (1B) where the local housing authority—

(*a*) are satisfied that a dwelling-house or house in multiple occupation is in such a state of disrepair that, although not unfit for human habitation, substantial repairs are necessary to bring it up to a reasonable standard, having regard to its age, character and locality, or

(*b*) are satisfied whether on a representation made by an occupying tenant or otherwise that a dwelling-house or house in multiple occupation is in such a state of disrepair that, although not unfit for human habitation, its condition is such as to interfere materially with the personal comfort of the occupying tenant, or, in the case of a house in multiple occupation, the persons occupying it (whether as tenants or licensees), they may serve a repair notice on the person having control of the dwelling-house or house in multiple occupation.

(1A) Subject to subsection (1B). Where the local housing authority—

(*a*) are satisfied that a building containing a flat including a flat in multiple occupation is in such a state of disrepair that, although the flat is not unfit for human habitation, substantial repairs are necessary to a part of the building outside the flat to bring the flat up to a reasonable standard, having regard to its age, character and locality, or

(*b*) are satisfied, whether on a representation made by an occupying tenant or otherwise, that a building containing a flat is in such a state of disrepair that, although the flat is not unfit for human habitation, the condition of a part of the building outside the flat is such as to interfere materially with the personal comfort of the occupying tenant, or, in the case of a flat in multiple occupation, the persons occupying it (whether as tenants or licensees),

they may serve a repair notice on the persons having control of the part of the building concerned.

(1B) The authority may not serve a notice under subsection (1) or subsection (1A) unless—

(*a*) there is an occupying tenant of the dwelling-house or flat concerned, or

(*b*) the dwelling-house or building concerned falls within a renewal area within the meaning of Part VII of the Local Government and Housing Act 1989.

(1C) In the case of a house in multiple occupation, a notice under subsection (1) or subsection (1A) may be served on the person managing the house instead of on the person having control of it; and where a notice is so served, then, subject to section 191, the person managing the house shall be regarded as the person having control of it for the purposes of the provisions of this part following that section.

(2) A repair notice under this section shall require the person on whom it is served, to execute the works specified in the notice, not being works of internal decorative repair, and—

(*a*) to begin those works not later than such reasonable date, being not earlier than the twenty-eighth day after the notice is served, as is specified in the notice; and

(*b*) to complete those works within such reasonable time as is so specified

(3) The authority, in addition to serving the notice—

(*a*) on the person having control of the dwelling-house or part of the building concerned, or

(*b*) on the person having control of or, as the case may be, on the person managing the house in multiple occupation which is concerned,

shall serve a copy of the notice on any other person having an interest in the dwelling-house, part of the building or house concerned, whether as a freeholder, mortgagee or lessee.

(4) The notice becomes operative, if no appeal is brought, on the expiry of 21 days from the date of service of the notice and is final and conclusive as to matters which could have been raised on an appeal.

(5) A repair notice under this section which has become operative is a local land charge.

[Housing Act 1985, s 190, as amended by the Housing Act 1988, s 130 and Sch 15, and the Local Government and Housing Act 1989, s 165 and Sch 9, Part I.]

8–17176 190A. Effect on section 189 of proposal to include premises in group repair scheme. (1) A local housing authority shall not be under a duty to serve a repair notice under subsection (1) or, as the case may be, subsection (1A) of section 189 if, at the same time as they satisfy themselves as mentioned in the subsection in question, they determine—

(*a*) that the premises concerned form part of a building which would be a qualifying building in relation to a group repair scheme; and

(*b*) that, within the period of twelve months beginning at that time, they expect to prepare a group repair scheme in respect of the qualifying building (in this section referred to as a "relevant scheme");

but where, having so determined, the authority do serve such a notice, they may do so with respect only to those works which, in their opinion, will not be carried out to the premises concerned in pursuance of the relevant scheme.

(2) Subject to subsection (3), subsection (1) shall apply in relation to the premises concerned from the time referred to in subsection (1) until the date on which the works specified in a relevant scheme are completed to the authority's satisfaction (as certified under section 66(1) of the Housing Grants, Construction and Regeneration Act 1996).

(2) Subsection (1) shall cease to have effect in relation to the premises concerned on the day when the first of the following events occurs, that is to say,—

(*a*) the local housing authority determine not to submit a relevant scheme to the Secretary of State for approval; or

(*b*) the expiry of the period referred to in subsection (1)(*b*) without either the approval of a relevant scheme within that period or the submission of a relevant scheme to the Secretary of State within that period; or

(*c*) the Secretary of State notifies the authority that he does not approve a relevant scheme; or

(*d*) the authority ascertain that a relevant scheme, as submitted or approved, will not, for whatever reason, involve the carrying out of any works to the premises concerned.

(4) In any case where, in accordance with subsection (1), the authority serve a repair notice under subsection (1) or, as the case may be, subsection (1A) of section 189 with respect only to certain of the works which would otherwise be specified in the notice, subsection (2)(*b*) of that section shall have effect with respect to the notice as if after the word "notice" there were inserted the words "when taken together with works proposed to be carried out under a group repair scheme".

(5) In this section and section 189 "group repair scheme" and "qualifying building" have the same meaning as in Chapter II of Part I of the Housing Grants, Construction and Regeneration Act 1996 (group repair schemes).

[Housing Act 1985, s 190A, as inserted by the Local Government and Housing Act 1989, s 165 and Sch 9, Part I and amended by the Housing Grants, Construction and Regeneration Act 1996, Sch 1.]

8–17177 191. Appeals against repair notices. A person aggrieved by a repair notice may within 21 days after the date of service of the notice, appeal to the county court.

[Housing Act 1985, s 191—summarised.]

8–17178 191A. Execution of works by local housing authority by agreement. (1) The local housing authority may by agreement with the person having control of any premises execute at his expense any works which he is required to execute in respect of the premises in pursuance of a repair notice served under section 189 or section 190.

(2) For that purpose the authority shall have all such rights as that person would have against any occupying tenant of, and any other person having an interest in, the premises (or any part of the premises).
[Housing Act 1985, s 191A, as inserted by the Local Government and Housing Act 1989, s 165 and Sch 9, Part I.]

Enforcement

8-17179 **193. Power of local housing authority to execute works.** (1) If a repair notice is not complied with the local housing authority may themselves do the work required to be done by the notice.

(2) For this purpose of this Part compliance with the notice means beginning and completing the works specified in the notice,—

(*a*) if no appeal is brought against the notice, not later than such date and within such period as is specified in the notice;
(*b*) if an appeal is brought against the notice and is not withdrawn, not later than such date and within such period as may be fixed by the court determining the appeal; and
(*c*) if an appeal brought against the notice is withdrawn, not later than the twenty-first day after the date on which the notice becomes operative and within such period (beginning on that twenty-first day) as is specified in the notice.

(2A) If, before the expiry of the period which under subsection (2) is appropriate for completion of the works specified in the notice, it appears to the local housing authority that reasonable progress is not being made towards compliance with the notice, the authority may themselves do the work required to be done by the notice.

(3) The provisions of Schedule 10[1] apply with respect to the recovery by the local housing authority of expenses incurred by them under this section.

(4) If, after the local housing authority have given notice under section 194 of their intention to enter and do any works, the works are in fact carried out by the person having control of the dwelling-house, house in multiple occupation or part of the building in question, any administrative and other expenses incurred by the authority with a view to doing the works themselves shall be treated for the purposes of Schedule 10 as expenses incurred by them under this section in carrying out works in a case where the repair notice has not been complied with.
[Housing Act 1985, s 193, as amended by the Housing Act 1988, Sch 15 and the Local Government and Housing Act 1989, Sch 9.]

1. Schedule 10 is not printed in this work.

8-17180 **194. Notice of authority's intention to execute works.** (1) Where the local housing authority are about to enter upon any premises under the provisions of section 193 for the purpose of doing any work, they shall give notice in writing of their intention to do so to the person having control of the premises and, if they think fit, to any owner of the premises.

(2) If at any time after the expiration of seven days from the service of the notice on him and whilst any workman or contractor employed by the local housing authority is carrying out works in the premises—

(*a*) the person on whom the notice was served is in the premises for the purpose of carrying out any works, or
(*b*) any workman employed by him or by any contractor employed by him is in the premises for such purpose,

the person on whom the notice was served shall be deemed for the purpose of section 198 (penalty for obstruction) to be obstructing the authority in the execution of this Part unless he shows that there was urgent necessity to carry out the works in order to obviate danger to occupants of the premises.
[Housing Act 1985, s 194, as amended by the Housing Act 1988, Sch 15.]

8-17181 **195. Power of court to order occupier or owner to permit things to be done.** (1) If a person, after receiving notice of the intended action—

(*a*) being the occupier of premises, prevents the owner or person having control of the premises, or his officers, servants or agents, from carrying into effect with respect to the premises any of the provisions of this Part, or
(*b*) being the occupier, owner or person having control of premises, prevents an officer, servant or agent of the local housing authority from so doing,

a magistrates' court may order him to permit to be done on the premises all things requisite for carrying into effect those provisions.

(2) A person who fails to comply with an order of the court under this section commits a summary

offence and is liable on conviction to a fine not exceeding **£20** in respect of each day during which the failure continues.
[Housing Act 1985, s 195.]

8–17182 **196. Power of court to authorise owner to execute works on default of another owner.** (1) If it appears to a magistrates' court, on the application of an owner of premises in respect of which a repair notice has been served, that owing to the default of another owner of the premises in executing works required to be executed, the interests of the applicant will be prejudiced, the court may make an order empowering the applicant forthwith to enter on the premises and execute the works within a period fixed by the order.

(2) Where the court makes such an order, the court may, where it seems to the court just to do so, make a like order in favour of any other owner.

(3) Before an order is made under this section, notice of the application shall be given to the local housing authority.
[Housing Act 1985, s 196.]

8–17183 **197. Powers of entry.** (1) A person authorised by the local housing authority or the Secretary of State may at any reasonable time, on giving seven days' notice of his intention to the occupier, and to the owner if the owner is known, enter premises for the purpose of survey and examination—

(*a*) where it appears to the authority that survey or examination is necessary in order to determine whether any powers under this Part should be exercised in respect of the premises, or

(*b*) where a repair notice has been served in respect of the premises, or

(2) An authorisation for the purposes of this section shall be in writing stating the particular purpose[1] or purposes for which the entry is authorised and shall, if so required, be produced for inspection by the occupier or anyone acting on his behalf.
[Housing Act 1985, s 197, as amended by the Local Government and Housing Act 1989, Schs 9 and 12.]

1. This is a general power, not depending upon reasonable ground to suspect the existence of any state of things (*Bedingfield v Jones* (1959) 124 JP 11).

8–17184 **198. Penalty for obstruction.** (1) It is a summary offence intentionally to obstruct an officer of the local housing authority or of the Secretary of State, or a person authorised in pursuance of this Part to enter premises, in the performance of anything which that officer, authority or person is required or authorised by this Part to do.

(2) A person who commits such an offence is liable on conviction to a fine not exceeding **level 3** on the standard scale.
[Housing Act 1985, s 198, as amended by the Housing Act 1988, Sch 15 and the Local Government and Housing Act 1989, Sch 9.]

8–17185 **198A. Penalty for failure to execute works.** (1) A person having control of premises to which a repair notice relates who intentionally fails to comply with the notice commits a summary offence and is liable on conviction to a fine not exceeding **level 4** on the standard scale.

(2) The obligation to execute the works specified in the notice continues notwithstanding that the period for completion of the works has expired.

(3) Section 193(2) shall have effect to determine whether a person has failed to comply with a notice and what is the period for completion of any works.

(4) The provisions of this section are without prejudice to the exercise by the local housing authority of the powers conferred by the preceding provisions of this Part.
[Housing Act 1985, s 198A, as inserted by the Housing Act 1988, Sch 15.]

Supplementary provisions

8–17186 **207. Minor definitions.** (1) In this Part—

"dwelling-house" and "flat" shall be construed in accordance with subsection (2) and "the building", in relation to a flat, means the building containing the flat;

"occupying tenant", in relation to a dwelling-house, means a person (other than an owner-occupier) who—

(*a*) occupies or is entitled to occupy the dwelling-house as a lessee; or
(*b*) is a statutory tenant of the dwelling-house; or
(*c*) occupies the dwelling-house as a residence under a restricted contract; or
(*d*) is a protected occupier, within the meaning of the Rent (Agriculture) Act 1976; or
(*e*) is a licensee under an assured agricultural occupancy;

"owner" in relation to premises—

(*a*) means a person (other than a mortgagee not in possession) who is for the time being entitled to dispose of the fee simple in the premises, whether in possession or reversion, and (*b*) includes also a person holding or entitled to the rents and profits of the premises under a lease of which the unexpired term exceeds three years;

"owner-occupier", in relation to a dwelling-house, means the person who, as owner or lessee under a long tenancy, within the meaning of Part I of the Leasehold Reform Act 1967, occupies or is entitled to occupy the dwelling-house;

"person managing" has the same meaning as in Part XI

"person having control", subject to sections 189(1B), 190(1C) and 191

(*a*) in relation to a dwelling-house or house in multiple occupation, means the person who receives the rack-rent of the premises (that is to say, a rent which is not less than 2/3rds of the full net annual value of the premises), whether on his own account or as agent or trustee[1] for another person, or who would so receive it if the premises were let at such a rack-rent and

(*b*) in relation to a part of a building to which relates a repair notice served under subsection (1A) of section 189 or section 190, means a person who is an owner in relation to that part of the building (or the building as a whole) and who, in the opinion of the authority by whom the notice is served, ought to execute the works specified in the notice

"Premises" includes a dwelling-house, house in multiple occupation or part of a building and, in relation to any premises, any reference to a person having control shall be construed accordingly.

(2) For the purposes of this Part a "dwelling-house or house in multiple occupation" includes any yard garden, outhouses and appurtenances belonging to it or usually enjoyed with it and section 183 shall have effect to determine whether a dwelling-house is a flat.

[Housing Act 1985, s 207, as amended by the Housing and Planning Act 1986, Sch 5, the Housing Act 1988, Sch 15 and the Local Government and Housing Act 1989, Sch 9.]

1. For cases in which a collector of rent was not an "agent or trustee", see *Bottomley v Harrison* [1952] 1 All ER 368, 116 JP 113; *Midland Bank Ltd v Conway Borough Council* [1965] 2 All ER 972, [1965] 1 WLR 1165, 129 JP 466.

8–17187 **208. Index of defined expressions: Part VI.** The following Table shows provisions defining or otherwise explaining expressions used in this Part (other than provisions defining or explaining an expression used in the same section or paragraph):—

district (of a local housing authority)	section 2(1)
dwelling-house	sections 205 and 207
fit for human habitation	section 604
Flat	section 207
house in multiple occupation (and flat in multiple occupation)	section 345
lease, lessee and lessor	section 261
local housing authority	sections 1, 2(2)
occupying tenant	section 207
Owner	section 207
owner-occupier	section 207
person having control	section 207
person managing	section 398
Premises	section 207
repair notice	sections 189 and 190
restricted contract	section 622
standard scale (in reference to the maximum fine on summary conviction)	section 622
statutory tenant	section 622
unfit for human habitation	section 604

[Housing Act 1985, s 208 amended by the Local Government and Housing Act 1989, Schs 9 and 12.]

8–17188

PART VIII[1]
AREA IMPROVEMENT

Housing action areas

1. The provisions of Part VII of the Local Government and Housing Act 1989, on renewal areas, have effect now in place of Part VIII of the 1985 Act.

PART IX[1]
SLUM CLEARANCE

Demolition or closing of unfit premises beyond repair at reasonable cost

8–17215 **Sections 264–269** contain the power to make a closing order or a demolition order, with administrative provisions including a right of appeal to the county court.

Demolition orders

8–17231 270. Demolition orders: recovery of possession of premises to be demolished. (1) Where a demolition order has become operative with respect to any premises, the local housing authority shall[1] serve on any occupier of the premises or any part of the premises a notice—

(*a*) stating the effect of the order,
(*b*) specifying the date by which the order requires the premises to be vacated, and
(*c*) requiring him to quit the premises before that date or before the expiration of 28 days from the service of the notice, whichever may be the later.

(2) If any person is in occupation of the premises, or any part of them at any time after the date on which the notice requires the premises to be vacated, the local housing authority or an owner of the premises may apply to the county court which shall thereupon order vacant possession of the premises or part to be given to the applicant within such period, of not less than two or more than four weeks, as the court may determine.

(3) Nothing in the Rent Acts or Part I of the Housing Act 1988 affects the provisions of this section relating to the obtaining possession of any premises.

(4) Expenses incurred by the local housing authority under this section in obtaining possession of any premises, or part of any premises, may be recovered by them by action from the owner, or from any of the owners, of the premises.

(5) A person who, knowing that a demolition order has become operative and applies to any premises—

(*a*) enters into occupation of the premises, or a part of them, after the date by which the order requires them to be vacated, or
(*b*) permits another person to enter into such occupation after that date,

commits a summary offence and is liable on conviction to a fine not exceeding **level 5** on the standard scale and to a further fine not exceeding **£5** for every day or part of a day on which the occupation continues after conviction.

[Housing Act 1985, s 270, as amended by the Housing Act 1988, Sch 17 and the Local Government and Housing Act 1989, Sch 9.]

1. Service of this notice by the local authority is mandatory: see *R v Epsom and Ewell Corpn, ex p R B Property Investments (Eastern) Ltd* [1964] 2 All ER 832, [1964] 1 WLR 1060, 128 JP 478.

8–17232 271. Demolition orders: execution of order. When a demolition order has become operative, the owner of the premises to which it applies shall demolish the premises within the time limited by the order, and if the premises are not demolished within that time the local housing authority shall enter and demolish them and sell the materials.

[Housing Act 1985, s 271—summarised.]

Closing orders

8–17233 276. Closing orders: recovery of possession of house. Nothing in the Rent Acts or Part I of the Housing Act 1988 prevents possession being obtained by the owner of premises in respect of which a closing order is in force.

[Housing Act 1985, s 276, as amended by the Housing Act 1988, Sch 17.]

8–17234 277. Closing orders: enforcement. If a person, knowing that a closing order has become operative[1] and applies to premises, uses the premises in contravention of the order, or permits them to be so used, he commits a summary offence and is liable on conviction to a fine not exceeding **level 5** on the standard scale and to a further fine not exceeding **£20** for every day or part of a day on which he so uses them or permits them to be so used after conviction.

[Housing Act 1985, s 277.]

1. Despite s 198 of the Law of Property Act 1925 registration of the closing order will not mean a defendant will be deemed to have notice of the order for the purpose of proceedings under this section; actual knowledge must be proved beyond reasonable doubt (*Wrekin District Council v Shah* (1985) 150 JP 22).

Miscellaneous

8–17235 315. Power of court to order occupier or owner to permit things to be done. (1) If a person, after receiving notice of the intended action—

(*a*) being the occupier of premises, prevents the owner of the premises, or his officers, servants or agents, from carrying into effect with respect to the premises any of the provisions of this Part, or
(*b*) being the occupier or owner of premises, prevents an officer, servant or agent of the local housing authority from so doing,

a magistrates' court may order him to permit to be done on the premises all things requisite for carrying into effect those provisions.

(2) A person who fails to comply with an order of the court under this section commits a summary offence and is liable on conviction to a fine not exceeding **£20** in respect of each day during which the failure continues.
[Housing Act 1985, s 315, as amended by the Local Government and Housing Act 1989, Schs 9 and 12.]

8–17236 **316. Power of court to authorise owner to demolish premises on default of another owner.** (1) If it appears to a magistrates' court on the application of an owner of premises in respect of which a demolition order, or obstructive building order has been made, that owing to the default of another owner of the premises in demolishing the premises, the interests of the applicant will be prejudiced, the court may make an order empowering the applicant forthwith to enter on the premises, and, within a period fixed by the order, demolish them.

(2) Where the court makes an order under subsection (1), the court may, where it seems to the court just to do so, make a like order in favour of any other owner.

(3) Before an order is made under this section, notice of the application shall be given to the local housing authority.
[Housing Act 1985, s 316.]

Supplementary provisions

8–17237 **319. Powers of entry.** (1) A person authorised by the local housing authority or the Secretary of State may at any reasonable time, on giving seven days' notice of his intention to the occupier, and to the owner if the owner is known, enter premises—

(*a*) for the purpose of survey and examination where it appears to the authority or the Secretary of State that survey or examination is necessary in order to determine whether any powers under this Part should be exercised in respect of the premises; or

(*b*) for the purpose of survey and examination where a demolition or closing order, or an obstructive building order, has been made in respect of the premises; or

(*c*) for the purpose of survey or valuation where the authority are authorised by this Part to purchase the premises compulsorily.

(2) An authorisation for the purposes of this section shall be in writing stating the particular purpose[1] or purposes for which the entry is authorised and shall, if so required, be produced for inspection by the occupier or anyone acting on his behalf.
[Housing Act 1985, s 319, as amended by the Local Government and Housing Act 1989, Sch 9.]

---

1. This is a general power, not depending upon reasonable ground to suspect the existence of any state of things (*Bedingfield v Jones* (1959) 124 JP 11).

8–17238 **320. Penalty for obstruction.** (1) It is a summary offence intentionally to obstruct an officer of the local housing authority or of the Secretary of State, or any person authorised to enter premises in pursuance of this Part, in the performance of anything which he is by this Part required or authorised to do.

(2) A person committing such an offence is liable on conviction to a fine not exceeding **level 3** on the standard scale.
[Housing Act 1985, s 319, as amended by the Local Government and Housing Act 1989, Sch 9.]

8–17239 **322. Minor definitions.** In this Part—

"dwelling-house" and "flat", except in the expression "flat in multiple occupation", shall be construed in accordance with subsection (2) and "the building", in relation to a flat, means the building containing the flat;

"house in multiple occupation" and "flat in multiple occupation" have the same meaning as in Part XI

"owner", in relation to premises—

(*a*) means a person (other than a mortgagee not in possession) who is for the time being entitled to dispose of the fee simple in the premises, whether in possession or in reversion, and

(*b*) includes also a person holding or entitled to the rents and profits of the premises under a lease of which the unexpired term exceeds three years;

"premises", in relation to a demolition or closing order, means the dwelling-house, house in multiple occupation, building or part of a building in respect of which the closing order, as the case may be, demolition order is made.

(2) For the purposes of this Part, "dwelling-house" includes any yard, garden, outhouses and appurtenances belonging to it or usually enjoyed with it and section 183 shall have effect to determine whether a dwelling-house is a flat.

(3) Except where the context otherwise requires, any reference in this Part (other than this section) to a flat is a reference to a dwelling-house which is a flat or to a flat in multiple occupation.
[Housing Act 1985, s 322, as amended by the Housing and Planning Act 1986, Sch 5 and the Local Government and Housing Act 1989, Schs 9 and 12.]

8–17240 323. Index of defined expressions: Part IX. The following Table shows provisions defining or otherwise explaining expressions used in this Part (other than provisions defining or explaining an expression used in the same section or paragraph)—

assured agricultural occupancy	section 622
assured tenancy	section 622
clearance area	section 289(1)
closing order	section 267(2)
demolition order	section 267(1)
district (of a local housing authority)	section 2(1)
dwelling-house	sections 266 and 322
fit (or unfit) for human habitation	section 604
flat	section 322
house in multiple occupation	section 322
lease, lessee and lessor	section 621
listed building	section 303
local housing authority	section 1, 2(2)
obstructive building	section 283
obstructive building order	section 284
owner (of premises)	section 322
premises	section 322
prescribed	section 614
reasonable expense	section 321
rehabilitation order	Schedule 11
the Rent Acts	section 622
standard scale (in reference to the maximum fine on summary conviction)	section 622
underground room	section 280
unfit (or fit) for human habitation	section 604

[Housing Act 1985, s 323, as amended by the Housing Act 1988, Sch 17 and the Local Government and Housing Act 1989, Schs 9 and 12.]

PART X[1]
OVERCROWDING

Definition of overcrowding

8–17241 324. Definition of overcrowding. A dwelling is overcrowded for the purposes of this Part when the number of persons sleeping in the dwelling is such as to contravene—

(*a*) the standard specified in section 325 (the room standard), or
(*b*) the standard specified in section 326 (the space standard).

[Housing Act 1985, s 324.]

1. Part X contains ss 324–344.

8–17242 325. The room standard. (1) The room standard is contravened when the number of person sleeping in a dwelling and the number of rooms available as sleeping accommodation is such that two persons of opposite sexes who are not living together as husband and wife must sleep in the same room.

(2) For this purpose—

(*a*) children under the age of ten shall be left out of account, and
(*b*) a room is available as sleeping accommodation if it is of a type normally used in the locality either as a bedroom or as a living room.

[Housing Act 1985, s 325.]

8–17243 326. The space standard. (1) The space standard is contravened when the number of persons sleeping in a dwelling is in excess of the permitted number, having regard to the number and floor area of the rooms of the dwelling available as sleeping accommodation.

(2) For this purpose—

(*a*) no account shall be taken of a child under the age of one and a child aged one or over but under ten shall be reckoned as one-half of a unit, and
(*b*) a room is available as sleeping accommodation if it is of a type normally used in the locality either as a living room or as a bedroom.

(3) The permitted number of persons in relation to a dwelling is whichever is the less of—

(*a*) the number specified in Table I in relation to the number of rooms in the dwelling available as sleeping accommodation, and (*b*) the aggregate for all such rooms in the dwelling of the numbers specified in column 2 of Table II in relation to each room of the floor area specified in column 1.

No account shall be taken for the purposes of either Table of a room having a floor area of less than 50 square feet.

TABLE I

Number of rooms	*Number of persons*
1	2
2	3
3	5
4	7 1/2
5 or more	2 for each room

TABLE II

Floor area of room	*Number of persons*
110 sq ft or more	2
90 sq ft or more but less than 110 sq ft	1 1/2
70 sq ft or more but less than 90 sq ft	1
50 sq ft or more but less than 70 sq ft	1/2

(4)–(5) *Power of the Secretary of State by regulations to prescribe the manner in which the floor area of a room is to be ascertained for the purposes of this section.*

(6) A certificate of the local housing authority stating the number and floor areas of the rooms in a dwelling, and that the floor areas have been ascertained in the prescribed manner, is prima facie evidence for the purposes of legal proceedings of the facts stated in it.

[Housing Act 1985, s 326.]

Responsibility of occupier

8–17244 **327. Penalty for occupier causing or permitting overcrowding.** (1) The occupier of a dwelling who causes or permits it to be overcrowded commits a summary offence, subject to subsection (2).

(2) The occupier is not guilty of an offence—

(*a*) if the overcrowding is within the exceptions specified in sections 328 or 329 (children attaining age of 10 or visiting relatives), or

(*b*) by reason of anything done under the authority of, and in accordance with any conditions specified in, a licence granted by the local housing authority under section 330.

(3) A person committing an offence under this section is liable on conviction to a fine not exceeding **level 2** on the standard scale and to a further fine not exceeding one-tenth of the amount corresponding to that level in respect of every day subsequent to the date on which he is convicted on which the offence continues.

[Housing Act 1985, s 327, as amended by the Local Government and Housing Act 1989, Sch 11.]

8–17245 **328. Exception: children attaining age of 1 or 10.** (1) Where a dwelling which would not otherwise be overcrowded becomes overcrowded by reason of a child attaining the age of one or ten, then if the occupier—

(*a*) applies to the local housing authority for suitable alternative accommodation, or

(*b*) has so applied before the date when the child attained the age in question,

he does not commit an offence under section 327 (occupier causing or permitting overcrowding), so long as the condition in subsection (2) is met and the occupier does not fail to take action in the circumstances specified in subsection (3).

(2) The condition is that all the persons sleeping in the dwelling are persons who were living there when the child attained that age and thereafter continuously live there, or children born after that date of any of those persons.

(3) The exception provided by this section ceases to apply if—

(*a*) suitable alternative accommodation is offered to the occupier on or after the date on which the child attains that age, or, if he has applied before that date, is offered at any time after the application, and he fails to accept it, or

(*b*) the removal from the dwelling of some person not a member of the occupier's family is on that date or thereafter becomes reasonably practicable having regard to all the circumstances (including the availability of suitable alternative accommodation for that person), and the occupier fails to require his removal.

[Housing Act 1985, s 328.]

8–17246 **329. Exception; visiting member of family.** Where the persons sleeping in an overcrowded dwelling include a member of the occupier's family who does not live there but is

sleeping there temporarily, the occupier is not guilty of an offence under section 327 (occupier causing or permitting overcrowding) unless the circumstances are such that he would be so guilty if that member of his family were not sleeping there.
[Housing Act 1985, s 329.]

8–17247 **330. Licence of local housing authority.** The occupier or intending occupier of a dwelling may apply to the local housing authority for a licence authorising him to permit a number of persons in excess of the permitted number to sleep in the dwelling. The authority may grant such a licence if it appears to them that there are exceptional circumstances and that it is expedient to do so; and they shall specify in the licence the number of persons authorised in excess of the permitted number. The licence shall be in the prescribed form and may be granted either unconditionally or subject to conditions specified in it.
[Housing Act 1985, s 330—summarised.]

Responsibilities of landlord

8–17248 **331. Penalty for landlord causing or permitting overcrowding.** (1) The landlord of a dwelling commits a summary offence if he causes or permits it to be overcrowded.

(2) He shall be deemed to cause or permit it to be overcrowded in the following circumstances, and not otherwise—

(*a*) if he or a person effecting the letting on his behalf had reasonable cause to believe that the dwelling would become overcrowded in circumstances rendering the occupier guilty of an offence;

(*b*) if he or a person effecting the letting on his behalf failed to make inquiries of the proposed occupier as to the number, age and sex of the persons who would be allowed to sleep in the dwelling;

(*c*) if notice is served on him or his agent by the local housing authority that the dwelling is overcrowded in such circumstances as to render the occupier guilty of an offence and he fails to take such steps as are reasonably open to him for securing the abatement of the overcrowding, including if necessary legal proceedings for possession of the dwelling.

(3) A person committing an offence under this section is liable on conviction to a fine not exceeding **level 2** on the standard scale and to a further fine not exceeding **one tenth of the amount corresponding to that level** in respect of every day subsequent to the day on which he is convicted on which the offence continues.
[Housing Act 1985, s 331, as amended by the Local Government and Housing Act 1989, Sch 11.]

8–17249 **332. Information to be contained in rent book.** (1) Every rent book or similar document used in relation to a dwelling by or on behalf of the landlord shall contain—

(*a*) a summary in the prescribed form of the preceding provisions of this Part, and
(*b*) a statement of the permitted number of persons in relation to the dwelling.

(2) If a rent book or similar document not containing such a summary and statement is used by or on behalf or the landlord, the landlord is guilty of a summary offence and liable on conviction to a fine not exceeding **level 1** on the standard scale.

(3) The local housing authority shall on the application of the landlord or the occupier of a dwelling inform him in writing of the permitted number of persons in relation to the dwelling; and a statement inserted in a rent book or similar document which agrees with information so given shall be deemed to be a sufficient and correct statement.
[Housing Act 1985, s 332.]

8–17260 **333. Duty to inform local housing authority of overcrowding.** (1) Where it comes to the knowledge of the landlord of a dwelling, or of his agent, that the dwelling is overcrowded, then, except in the cases mentioned in subsection (2), the landlord or, as the case may be, the agent shall give notice of the fact of overcrowding to the local housing authority within seven days after that fact first comes to his knowledge.

(2) The obligation to notify does not arise in the case of overcrowding which—

(*a*) has already been notified to the local housing authority,
(*b*) has been notified to the landlord or his agent by the local housing authority, or
(*c*) is constituted by the use of the dwelling for sleeping by such number of persons as the occupier is authorised to permit to sleep there by a licence in force under section 330 (licence of local housing authority).

(3) A landlord or agent who fails to give notice in accordance with this section commits a summary offence and is liable on conviction to a fine not exceeding **level 1** on the standard scale.
[Housing Act 1985, s 333.]

Powers and duties of local housing authority

8–17261 **334.** *Duty to inspect, report and prepare proposals.*

8–17262 **335. Power to require information about persons sleeping in dwelling.** (1) The local housing authority may, for the purpose of enabling them to discharge their duties under this Part, serve notice on the occupier of a dwelling requiring him to give them within 14 days a written statement of the number, ages and sexes of the persons sleeping in the dwelling.

(2) The occupier commits a summary offence if—

(*a*) he makes default in complying with the requirement, or

(*b*) he gives a statement which to his knowledge is false in a material particular,

and is liable on conviction to a fine not exceeding **level 1** on the standard scale.
[Housing Act 1985, s 335.]

8–17263 **336. Power to require production of rent book.** (1) A duly authorised officer of the local housing authority may require an occupier of a dwelling to produce for inspection any rent book or similar document which is being used in relation to the dwelling and is in his custody or under his control.

(2) On being so required, or within seven days thereafter, the occupier shall produce any such book or document to the officer or at the offices of the authority.

(3) An occupier who fails to do so commits a summary offence and is liable on conviction to a fine not exceeding **level 1** on the standard scale.
[Housing Act 1985, s 336.]

8–17264 **337. Power of entry to determine permitted number of persons.** (1) A person authorised by the local housing authority may at any reasonable time, on giving 24 hours' notice of his intention to the occupier, and to the owner if the owner is known, enter premises for the purpose of measuring the rooms of a dwelling in order to ascertain for the purposes of this Part the number of persons permitted to use the dwelling for sleeping.

(2) An authorisation for the purposes of this section shall be in writing stating the particular purpose for which the entry is authorised.
[Housing Act 1985, s 337.]

8–17265 **338. Notice to abate overcrowding.** Where a dwelling is overcrowded in circumstances such as to render the occupier guilty of an offence, the local housing authority may serve on the occupier notice in writing requiring him to abate the overcrowding within 14 days from the date of service of the notice; if within three months from the end of that period the dwelling is in the occupation of the same person and is overcrowded, the local housing authority may apply to the county court which shall order vacant possession of the dwelling.
[Housing Act 1985, s 338—summarised.]

Supplementary provisions

8–17266 **339. Enforcement of this Part.** (1) The local housing authority shall enforce the provisions of this Part.

(2) A prosecution for an offence against those provisions may be brought only—

(*a*) by the local housing authority, or

(*b*) in the case of a prosecution against the authority themselves, with the consent[1] of the Attorney General.

[Housing Act 1985, s 339.]

1. See PART I: MAGISTRATES' COURTS, PROCEDURE, para **1–380 Criminal prosecutions**, ante.

8–17267 **340. Powers of entry.** (1) A person authorised by the local housing authority may at all reasonable times, on giving 24 hours' notice to the occupier, and to the owner if the owner is known, enter any premises for the purpose of survey and examination where it appears to the authority that survey or examination is necessary in order to determine whether any powers under this Part should be exercised.

(2) An authorisation for the purposes of this section shall be in writing stating the particular purpose[1] for which it is given and shall, if so required, be produced for inspection by the occupier or anyone acting on his behalf.
[Housing Act 1985, s 340, as amended by the Local Government and Housing Act 1989, Sch 11.]

1. This is a general power, not depending upon reasonable ground to suspect the existence of any state of things (*Bedingfield v Jones* (1959) 124 JP 11).

8–17268 **341. Penalty for obstruction.** (1) It is a summary offence intentionally to obstruct an officer of the local housing authority, or any person authorised to enter premises in pursuance of this Part, in the performance of anything which he is by this Part required or authorised to do.

(2) A person committing such an offence is liable on conviction to a fine not exceeding **level 3** on the standard scale.
[Housing Act 1985, s 341, as amended by the Local Government and Housing Act 1989, Sch 11.]

8–17269 342. Meaning of "suitable alternative accommodation". (1) In this Part "suitable alternative accommodation", in relation to the occupier of a dwelling, means a dwelling as to which the following conditions are satisfied—

(*a*) he and his family can live in it without causing it to be overcrowded;

(*b*) it is certified by the local housing authority to be suitable to his needs and those of his family as respects security of tenure, proximity to place of work and otherwise, and to be suitable in relation to his means;

(*c*) where the dwelling belongs to the local housing authority, it is certified by them to be suitable to his needs and those of his family as respects accommodation.

(2) For the purpose of subsection (1)(*c*) a dwelling containing two bedrooms shall be treated as providing accommodation for four persons, a dwelling containing three bedrooms shall be treated as providing accommodation for five persons and a dwelling containing four bedrooms shall be treated as providing accommodation for seven persons.

[Housing Act 1985, s 342.]

8–17270 343. Minor definitions. In this Part—

"agent", in relation to the landlord of a dwelling—

(*a*) means a person who collects rent in respect of the dwelling on behalf of the landlord, or is authorised by him to do so, and

(*b*) in the case of a dwelling occupied under a contract of employment under which the provision of the dwelling for his occupation forms part of the occupier's remuneration, includes a person who pays remuneration on behalf of the employer, or is authorised by him to do so;

"dwelling" means premises used or suitable for use as a separate dwelling;

"landlord", in relation to a dwelling—

(*a*) means the immediate landlord of an occupier of the dwelling, and

(*b*) in the case of a dwelling occupied under a contract of employment under which the provision of the dwelling for his occupation forms part of the occupier's remuneration, includes the occupier's employer;

"owner", in relation to premises—

(*a*) means a person (other than a mortgagee not in possession) who is for the time being entitled to dispose of the fee simple, whether in possession or in reversion, and

(*b*) includes also a person holding or entitled to the rents and profits of the premises under a lease of which the unexpired term exceeds three years.

[Housing Act 1985, s 343.]

8–17271 344. Index of defined expressions: Part X. The following Table shows provisions defining or otherwise explaining expressions used in this Part (other than provisions defining or explaining an expression used in the same section or paragraph):—

agent (in relation to the landlord of a dwelling)	sections 343
district (of a local housing authority)	section 2(1)
Dwelling	section 343
Landlord	sections 343 and 621
local housing authority	section 1, 2(2)
overcrowding (and related expressions)	section 324
Owner	section 343
permitted number (of persons sleeping in a dwelling)	section 326
Prescribed	section 614
standard scale (in reference to the maximum fine on summary conviction)	section 622
suitable alternative accommodation	section 342

[Housing Act 1985, s 344.]

PART XI[1]
HOUSES IN MULTIPLE OCCUPATION

Introductory

8–17272 345. Meaning of "multiple occupation". (1) In this Part "house in multiple occupation"[2] means a house which is occupied by persons who do not form a single household.

(2) For the purposes of this section "house", in the expression "house in multiple occupation", includes any part of a building which—

(*a*) apart from this subsection would not be regarded as a house; and (*b*) was originally constructed or subsequently adapted for occupation by a single household;

and any reference to this Part to a flat in multiple occupation is a reference to a part of a building which, whether by virtue of this subsection or without regard to it, constitutes a house in multiple occupation.

[Housing Act 1985, s 345, as amended by the Local Government and Housing Act 1989, Sch 9.]

1. Part XI contains ss 345–400.

2. Where rooms in a house were let under individual oral agreements for unspecified periods to up to 9 single adults, each having his or her own bedroom and entitled to share the living room, kitchen and bathrooms, it was held that this was a house in multiple occupation (*Rogers v Islington London Borough Council* [1999] 37 EG 178, CA; distinguished from *Barnes v Sheffield City Council* (1995) 27 HLR 719, CA which related to shared student accommodation.

Registration schemes

8–17273 346. Registration schemes[1]**.** (1) A local housing authority may make a registration scheme authorising the authority to compile and maintain a register for their district of houses in multiple occupation.

(2) A registration scheme need not be for the whole of the authority's district and need not apply to every description of house in multiple occupation.

(3) A registration scheme may vary or revoke a previous registration scheme; and the local housing authority may at any time by order revoke a registration scheme.

[Housing Act 1985, s 346, as substituted by the Housing Act 1996, s 65.]

1. The amendments made by ss 65–69 of the Housing Act 1996 to Pt XI of the Housing Act 1985 do not apply to registration schemes in force immediately before the coming into force of ss 65 to 69 of the 1996 Act. The unamended provisions of Pt XI of the Housing Act 1985 continue to apply to such schemes, subject as follows:—

(i) any such scheme may be revoked—

(*a*) by a new scheme complying with the provisions of that Part as amended, or

(*b*) by order of the local housing authority;

(ii) if not so revoked any such scheme shall cease to have effect at the end of the period of two years beginning with the date on which the amendments come into force.

[Housing Act 1996, s 70.]

8–17274 346A. Contents of registration scheme. (1) A registration scheme shall make it the duty of such person as may be specified by the scheme to register a house to which the scheme applies and to renew the registration as and when required by the scheme.

(2) A registration scheme shall provide that registration under the scheme—

(*a*) shall be for a period of five years from the date of first registration, and

(*b*) may on application be renewed, subject to such conditions as are specified in the scheme, for further periods of five years at a time.

(3) A registration scheme may—

(*a*) specify the particulars to be inserted in the register,

(*b*) make it the duty of such persons as may be specified by the scheme to give the authority as regards a house all or any of the particulars specified in the scheme.

(*c*) make it the duty of such persons as may be specified by the scheme to notify the authority of any change which makes it necessary to alter the particulars inserted in the register as regards a house.

(4) A registration scheme shall, subject to subsection (5)—

(*a*) require the payment on first registration of a reasonable fee of an amount determined by the local housing authority, and

(*b*) require the payment on any renewal of registration of half the fee which would then have been payable on a first registration of the house.

(5) The Secretary of State may by order make provision as to the fee payable on registration—

(*a*) specifying the maximum permissible fee (whether by specifying an amount or a method for calculating an amount), and

(*b*) specifying cases in which no fee is payable.

(6) An order under subsection (5)—

(*a*) may make different provision with respect to different cases or descriptions of case (including different provision for different areas), and

(*b*) shall be made by statutory instrument which shall be subject to annulment in pursuance of a resolution of either House of Parliament.

[Housing Act 1985, s 346A, as inserted by the Housing Act 1996, s 65.]

8–17275 346B. Model schemes and confirmation of schemes. (1) The Secretary of State may prepare model registration schemes.

(2) Model registration schemes may be prepared with or without control provisions (see section

347) or special control provisions (see section 348B); and different model schemes may be prepared for different descriptions of authorities and for different areas.

(3) A registration scheme which conforms to a model scheme—

(*a*) does not require confirmation by the Secretary of State, and

(*b*) comes into force on such date (at least one month after the making of the scheme) as may be specified in the scheme.

(4) Any other registration scheme does not come into force unless and until confirmed by the Secretary of State.

(5) The Secretary of State may if he thinks fit confirm such a scheme with or without modifications.

(6) A scheme requiring confirmation shall not come into force before it has been confirmed but, subject to that, comes into force on such date as may be specified in the scheme or, if no date is specified, one month after it is confirmed.

[Housing Act 1985, s 346B, as inserted by the Housing Act 1996, s 65.]

8–17276 **347. Control provisions.** (1) A registration scheme may contain control provisions, that is to say, provisions for preventing multiple occupation of a house unless—

(*a*) the house is registered, and

(*b*) the number of households or persons occupying it does not exceed the number registered for it.

(2) Control provisions may prohibit persons from permitting others to take up residence in a house or part of a house but shall not prohibit a person from taking up or remaining in residence in the house.

(3) Control provisions shall not prevent the occupation of a house by a greater number of households or persons than the number registered for it if all of those households or persons have been in occupation of the house without interruption since before the number was first registered.

[Housing Act 1985, s 347, as substituted by the Housing Act 1996, s 66.]

8–17277 **348. Control provisions: decisions on applications and appeals.** (1) Control provisions may enable the local housing authority, on an application for first registration of a house or a renewal or variation of registration—

(*a*) to refuse the application on the ground that the house is unsuitable and incapable of being made suitable for such occupation as would be permitted if the application were granted;

(*b*) to refuse the application on the ground that the person having control of the house or the person intended to be the person managing the house is not a fit and proper person;

(*c*) to require as a condition of granting the application that such works as will make the house suitable for such occupation as would be permitted if the application were granted are executed within such time as the authority may determine;

(*d*) to impose such conditions relating to the management of the house during the period of registration as the authority may determine.

(2) Control provisions shall provide that the local housing authority shall give an applicant a written statement of their reasons where they—

(*a*) refuse to grant his application for first registration or for a renewal or variation of registration,

(*b*) require the execution of works as a condition of granting such an application, or

(*c*) impose conditions relating to the management of the house.

(3) Where the local housing authority—

(*a*) notify an applicant that they refuse to grant his application for first registration or for the renewal or variation of a registration,

(*b*) notify an applicant that they require the execution of works as a condition of granting such an application,

(*c*) notify an applicant that they intend to impose conditions relating to the management of the house, or

(*d*) do not within five weeks of receiving the application, or such longer period as may be agreed in writing between the authority and the applicant, register the house or vary or renew the registration in accordance with the application,

the applicant may, within 21 days of being so notified or of the end of the period mentioned in paragraph (*d*), or such longer period as the authority may in writing allow, appeal to the county court.

(4) On appeal the court may confirm, reverse or vary the decision of the authority.

(5) Where the decision of the authority was a refusal—

(*a*) to grant an application for first registration of a house, or

(*b*) for the renewal or variation of the registration,

the court may direct the authority to grant the application as made or as varied in such manner as the court may direct.

(6) For the purposes of subsections (4) and (5) an appeal under subsection (3)(*d*) shall be treated as an appeal against a decision of the authority to refuse the application.

(7) Where the decision of the authority was to impose conditions relating to the management of the house, the court may direct the authority to grant the application without imposing the conditions or to impose the conditions as varied in such manner as the court may direct.
[Housing Act 1985, s 348, as substituted by the Housing Act 1996, s 66.]

8–17278 **348A. Control provisions: other decisions and appeals.** (1) Control provisions may enable the local housing authority at any time during a period of registration (whether or not an application has been made)—

(*a*) to alter the number of households or persons for which a house is registered or revoke the registration on the ground that the house is unsuitable and incapable of being made suitable for such occupation as is permitted by virtue of the registration; or

(*b*) to alter the number of households or persons for which a house is registered or revoke the registration unless such works are executed within a specified time as will make the house in question suitable for such occupation as is permitted by virtue of the registration.

(2) Control provisions which confer on a local housing authority any such power as is mentioned in subsection (1) shall provide that the authority shall, in deciding whether to exercise the power, apply the same standards in relation to the circumstances existing at the time of the decision as were applied at the beginning of the period of registration.

(3) Control provisions may enable the local housing authority to revoke a registration if they consider that—

(*a*) the person having control of the house or the person managing it is not a fit and proper person, or

(*b*) there has been a breach of conditions relating to the management of the house.

(4) Control provisions shall also provide that the local housing authority shall—

(*a*) notify the person having control of a house and the person managing it of any decision by the authority to exercise a power mentioned in subsection (1) or (3) in relation to the house, and

(*b*) at the same time give them a written statement of the authority's reasons.

(5) A person who has been so notified may within 21 days of being so notified, or such longer period as the authority may in writing allow, appeal to the county court.

(6) On appeal the court may confirm, reverse or vary the decision of the authority.
[Housing Act 1985, s 348A, as inserted by the Housing Act 1996, s 66.]

8–17279 **348B. Special control provisions.** (1) A registration scheme which contains control provisions may also contain special control provisions, that is, provisions for preventing houses in multiple occupation, by reason of their existence or the behaviour of their residents, from adversely affecting the amenity or character of the area in which they are situated.

(2) Special control provisions may provide for the refusal or revocation of registration, for reducing the number of households or persons for which a house is registered and for imposing conditions of registration.

(3) The conditions of registration may include conditions relating to the management of the house or the behaviour of its occupants.

(4) Special control provisions may authorise the revocation of registration in the case of—

(*a*) occupation of the house by more households or persons than the registration permits, or

(*b*) a breach of any condition imposed in pursuance of the special control provisions,

which is due to a relevant management failure.

(5) Special control provisions shall not authorise the refusal of—

(*a*) an application for first registration of a house which has been in operation as a house in multiple occupation since before the introduction by the local housing authority of a registration scheme with special control provisions, or

(*b*) any application for renewal of registration of a house previously registered under such a scheme,

unless there has been a relevant management failure.

(6) Special control provisions may provide that in any other case where an application is made for first registration of a house the local housing authority may take into account the number of houses in multiple occupation in the vicinity in deciding whether to permit or refuse registration.
[Housing Act 1985, s 348B, as inserted by the Housing Act 1996, s 67.]

8–17280 **348C. Special control provisions: general provisions as to decisions and appeals.** (1) Special control provisions shall provide that the local housing authority shall give a written statement of their reasons to the applicant where they refuse to grant his application for first registration, or for a renewal or variation of a registration, or impose conditions of registration on such an application.

(2) Special control provisions shall provide that the authority shall give written notice to the person having control of the house and the person managing it of any decision by the authority—

(*a*) to vary the conditions of registration (otherwise than on an application to which subsection (1) applies), or

(*b*) to revoke the registration of the house,

and at the same time give them a written statement of the authority's reasons.

(3) Where in accordance with special control provisions the local housing authority—

(*a*) notify an applicant that they refuse to grant his application for first registration or for the renewal or variation of a registration,

(*b*) notify such an applicant of the imposition of conditions of registration, or

(*c*) give notice to the person having control or the person managing the house of any such decision as is mentioned in subsection (2),

that person may, within 21 days of being so notified, or such longer period as the authority may in writing allow, appeal to the county court.

(4) If on appeal it appears to the court—

(*a*) that there has been any informality, defect or error in, or in connection with, the authority's decision, or

(*b*) that the authority acted unreasonably,

the court may reverse or vary the decision of the authority.

(5) In so far as an appeal is based on the ground mentioned in subsection (4)(*a*), the court shall dismiss the appeal if it is satisfied that the informality, defect or error was not a material one.

(6) Where the decision of the authority was a refusal—

(*a*) to grant an application for first registration of a house, or

(*b*) for the renewal or variation of the registration,

the court may direct the authority to grant the application as made or as varied in such manner as the court may direct.

(7) Where the decision of the authority was to impose conditions of registration, the court may direct the authority to grant the application without imposing the conditions or to impose the conditions as varied in such manner as the court may direct.

[Housing Act 1985, s 348C, as inserted by the Housing Act 1996, s 67.]

8–17281 348D. Special control provisions: occupancy directions:—(1) Special control provisions may provide that where the local housing authority decide that the registration of a house should be revoked the authority may direct that the level of occupation of the house be reduced, within such period of not less than 28 days as they may direct, to a level such that the registration scheme does not apply.

Such a direction is referred to in this Part as an "occupancy direction".

(2) Special control provisions shall provide that the authority shall only make an occupancy direction if it appears to the authority that there has been a relevant management failure resulting in a serious adverse effect on the amenity or character of the area in which the house is situated.

(3) In considering whether to make an occupancy direction the authority shall take into account the interests of the occupants of the house and the person having control of the house as well as the interests of local residents and businesses.

(4) Special control provisions may require the person having control of the house, and the person managing it, to take all reasonably practicable steps to comply with an occupancy direction.

(5) Nothing in Part I of the Housing Act 1988 prevents possession being obtained by any person in order to comply with an occupancy direction.

(6) Nothing in this section affects any liability in respect of any other contravention or failure to comply with control provisions or special control provisions.

[Housing Act 1985, s 348D, as inserted by the Housing Act 1996, s 67.]

8–17282 348E. Special control provisions: decisions and appeals relating to occupancy directions. (1) Special control provisions shall provide that where the local housing authority make an occupancy direction in respect of a house they shall give written notice of the direction to the person having control of the house and the person managing it and at the same time give them a written statement of the authority's reasons.

(2) A person aggrieved by an occupancy direction may, within 21 days after the date of the service of notice as mentioned in subsection (1), appeal to the county court.

(3) If on appeal it appears to the court—

(*a*) that there has been any informality, defect or error in, or in connection with, the authority's decision, or

(*b*) that the authority acted unreasonably,

the court may make such order either confirming, quashing or varying the notice as it thinks fit.

(4) In so far as an appeal is based on the ground mentioned in subsection (3)(*a*), the court shall dismiss the appeal if it is satisfied that the informality, defect or error was not a material one.

(5) If an appeal is brought the direction does not become operative until—

(*a*) a decision on the appeal confirming the direction (with or without variation) is given and the period within which an appeal to the Court of Appeal may be brought expires without any such appeal having been brought, or

(*b*) if a further appeal to the Court of Appeal is brought, a decision on that appeal is given confirming the direction (with or without variation).

(6) For this purpose the withdrawal of an appeal has the same effect as a decision confirming the direction or decision appealed against.

[Housing Act 1985, s 348E, as inserted by the Housing Act 1996, s 67.]

8–17283 **348F. Special control provisions: "relevant management failure".** A "relevant management failure" for the purposes of sections 348B to 348E (special control provisions) means a failure on the part of the person having control of, or the person managing, a house in multiple occupation to take such steps as are reasonably practicable to prevent the existence of the house or the behaviour of its residents from adversely affecting the amenity or character of the area in which the house is situated, or to reduce any such adverse effect.

[Housing Act 1985, s 348F, as inserted by the Housing Act 1996, s 67.]

8–17284 **348G. Offences in connection with registration schemes.** (1) A person who contravenes or fails to comply with a provision of a registration scheme commits an offence.

(2) A person who commits an offence under this section consisting of a contravention of so much of control provisions as relates—

(*a*) to occupation to a greater extent than permitted under those provisions of a house which is not registered, or

(*b*) to occupation of a house which is registered by more households or persons that the registration permits,

is liable on summary conviction to a fine not exceeding **level 5** on the standard scale.

(3) A person who commits an offence under this section consisting of a contravention of so much of special control provisions as requires all reasonably practicable steps to be taken to comply with an occupancy direction is liable on summary conviction to a fine not exceeding **level 5** on the standard scale.

(4) A person who commits any other offence under this section is liable on summary conviction to a fine not exceeding **level 4** on the standard scale.

[Housing Act 1985, s 348G, as inserted by the Housing Act 1996, s 68.]

8–17285 **349. Steps required to inform public about schemes.** (1) Where a local housing authority intend to make a registration scheme which does not require confirmation by the Secretary of State, they shall publish notice of their intention at least one month before the scheme is made.

As soon as the scheme is made, the local housing authority shall publish a notice stating—

(*a*) that a registration scheme which does not require confirmation has been made, and

(*b*) the date on which the scheme is to come into force.

(2) Where a local housing authority intend to submit to the Secretary of State a registration scheme which requires his confirmation, they shall publish notice of their intention at least one month before the scheme is submitted.

As soon as the scheme is confirmed, the local housing authority shall publish a notice stating—

(*a*) that a registration scheme has been confirmed, and

(*b*) the date on which the scheme is to come into force.

(3) A notice under subsection (1) or (2) of the authority's intention to make a scheme or submit a scheme for confirmation shall—

(*a*) describe any steps which will have to be taken under the scheme by those concerned with registrable houses (other than steps which have only to be taken after a notice from the authority), and

(*b*) name a place where a copy of the scheme may be seen at all reasonable hours.

(4) After publication of notice under subsection (1) or (2) that a registration scheme has been made or confirmed, and for as long as the scheme is in force, the local housing authority—

(*a*) shall keep a copy of the scheme, and of the register, available for public inspection at the offices of the authority free of charge at all reasonable hours, and

(*b*) on request, and on payment of such reasonable fee as the authority may require, shall supply a copy of the scheme or the register, or of any entry in the register, to any person.

(5) If the local housing authority revoke a registration scheme by order they shall publish notice of the order.

(6) In this section "publish" means publish in one or more newspapers circulating in the district of the local housing authority concerned.

[Housing Act 1985, s 349, as substituted by the Housing Act 1996, s 69.]

8–17286 **350. Power to require information for purposes of scheme.** (1) The local housing authority may—

(*a*) for the purpose of ascertaining whether a house is registrable, and

(*b*) for the purpose of ascertaining the particulars to be entered in the register as regards a house,

require the person having control of the house or the person managing the house or any person who has an estate or interest in, or who lives in, the house to state in writing any information in his possession which the authority may reasonably require for that purpose.

(2) A person who, having been required in pursuance of this section to give information to a local housing authority, fails to give the information, or knowingly makes a mis-statement in respect of it, commits a summary offence and is liable on conviction to a fine not exceeding (*a*) **level 3** on the standard scale in the case of such a failure; or (*b*) **level 5** on the standard scale in the case of such a mis-statement.

[Housing Act 1985, s 350, as amended by the Local Government and Housing Act 1989, Schs 9 and 12 and the Housing Act 1996, ss 69 and 78.]

8–17287 **351. Proof of scheme and contents of register.** (1) If there is produced a printed copy of a registration scheme purporting to be made by a local housing authority, upon which there is endorsed a certificate purporting to be signed by the proper officer of the authority stating—

(*a*) that the scheme was made by the authority,

(*b*) that the copy is a true copy of the scheme, and

(*c*) that the scheme did not require confirmation by the Secretary of State or that on a specified date the scheme was confirmed by the Secretary of State,

the certificate is prima facie evidence of the facts so stated without proof of the handwriting or official position of the person by whom it purports to be signed.

(2) A document purporting to be a copy of an entry in a register kept under a registration scheme and to be certified as a true copy by the proper officer of the authority is prima facie evidence of the entry without proof of the handwriting or official position of the person by whom it purports to be signed.

[Housing Act 1985, s 351, as amended by the Housing Act 1996, s 65.]

Fitness for the number of occupants

8–17288 **352. Power to require execution of works to render premises fit for number of occupants.** (1) Subject to section 365 the local housing authority may serve a notice under this section where in the opinion of the authority, a house in multiple occupation fails to meet one or more of the requirements in paragraphs (*a*) to (*e*) of subsection (1A) and, having regard to the number of individuals or households or both for the time being accommodated on the premises, by reason of that failure the premises are not reasonably suitable for occupation by those individuals or households.

(1A) The requirements in respect of a house in multiple occupation referred to in subsection (1) are the following, that is to say,—

(*a*) there are satisfactory facilities for the storage, preparation and cooking of food including an adequate number of sinks with a satisfactory supply of hot and cold water;

(*b*) it has an adequate number of suitably located water-closets for the exclusive use of the occupants;

(*c*) it has, for the exclusive use of the occupants, an adequate number of suitably located fixed baths or showers and wash-hand basins each of which is provided with a satisfactory supply of hot and cold water;

(*d*) subject to section 365, there are adequate means of escape from fire; and

(*e*) there are adequate other fire precautions.

(2) Subject to subsection (2A) the notice shall specify the works which in the opinion of the authority are required for rendering the house reasonably suitable—

(*a*) for occupation by the individuals and households for the time being accommodated there, or

(*b*) for a smaller number of individuals or households and the number of individuals or households, or both, which, in the opinion of the authority, the house could reasonably accommodate if the works were carried out

but the notice shall not specify any works to any premises outside the house.

(2A) Where the authority have exercised or propose to exercise their powers under section 368 to secure that part of the house is not used for human habitation, they may specify in the notice such work only as in their opinion is required to meet such of the requirements in subsection (1A) as may be applicable if that part is not so used.

(3) The notice may be served—

(*a*) on the person having control of the house, or
(*b*) on the person managing the house;

and the authority shall inform any other person who is to their knowledge an owner, lessee, occupier or mortgagee of the house of the fact that the notice has been served.

(4) The notice shall require the person on whom it is served to execute the works specified in the notice as follows, namely,—

(*a*) to begin those works not later than such reasonable date, being not earlier than the twenty-first day after the date of service of the notice, as is specified in the notice; and
(*b*) to complete those works within such reasonable period as is so specified.

(5) If the authority are satisfied that—

(*a*) after the service of a notice under this section the number of individuals living on the premises has been reduced to a level which will make the works specified in the notice unnecessary, and
(*b*) that number will be maintained at or below that level, whether in consequence of the exercise of the authority's powers under section 354 (power to limit number of occupants of house) or otherwise,

they may withdraw the notice by notifying that fact in writing to the person on whom the notice was served, but without prejudice to the issue of a further notice.

(5A) A notice served under this section is a local land charge.

(5B) Each local housing authority shall—

(*a*) maintain a register of notices served by the authority under subsection (1) after the coming into force of this subsection;
(*b*) ensure the register is open to inspection by the public free of charge at all reasonable hours; and
(*c*) on request, and on payment of any such reasonable fee as the authority may require, supply copies of entries in the register to any person.

(6) (*Repealed*).

(7) Where a local housing authority serve a notice under this section in respect of any of the requirements specified in subsection (1A), and the works specified in the notice are carried out, whether by the person on whom the notice was served or by the local housing authority under section 375, the authority shall not, within the period of five years from the service of the notice, serve another notice under this section in respect of the same requirement unless they consider that there has been a change of circumstances in relation to the premises.

(8) Such a change may, in particular, relate to the condition of the premises or the availability or use of the facilities mentioned in subsection (1A).

[Housing Act 1985, s 352, as amended by the Local Government and Housing Act 1989, Schs 9 and 12 and the Housing Act 1996, s 71.]

8–17289 352A. Recovery of expenses of notice under s 352[1]. (1) A local housing authority may, as a means of recovering certain administrative and other expenses incurred by them in serving a notice under section 352, make such reasonable charge as they consider appropriate.

[Housing Act 1985, s 352A, as inserted by the Housing Act 1996, s 72—summarised.]

---

1. Schedule 10 to the Act, which is not printed in this Manual, provides for the recovery by the authority of a charge under s 352A. The expenses recoverable by virtue of this section, together with the interest accrued due, are until recovered, a charge on the premises to which the notice under s 352 related (Housing Act 1985, Sch 10, para 7). The amount of the charge made by a local housing authority under s 352A shall not exceed £300 (Housing (Recovery of Expenses for Section 352 Notices) Order 1997, SI 1997/228.

8–17290 353. Appeal against notice under s 352.—(1) A person on whom a notice is served under section 352 (notice requiring works to render premises fit for number of occupants), or any other person who is an owner, lessee or mortgagee of the premises to which the notice relates, may, within 21 days from the service of the notice, or such longer period as the local housing authority may in writing allow, appeal to the county court.

[Housing Act 1985, s 353(1).]

8–17291 353A. Duty to keep premises fit for number of occupants. (1) It is the duty of the person having control of a house in multiple occupation, and of the person managing it, to take such steps as are reasonably practicable to prevent the occurrence of a state of affairs calling for the service of a notice or further notice under section 352 (notice requiring execution of works to render house fit for number of occupants).

(2) A breach of that duty is actionable in damages at the suit of any tenant or other occupant of the premises, or any other person who suffers loss, damage or personal injury in consequence of the breach.

(3) A person who fails to comply with the duty imposed on him by subsection (1) commits a summary offence and is liable on conviction to a fine not exceeding **level 5** on the standard scale.

[Housing Act 1985, s 353A, as inserted by the Housing Act 1996, s 73.]

8–17292 354. Power to limit number of occupants of house. (1) The local housing authority may, for the purpose of preventing the occurrence of, or remedying, a state of affairs calling for the service of a notice or further notice under section 352 (notice requiring execution of works to render house fit for number of occupants)—

(*a*) fix as a limit for the house what is in their opinion the highest number of individuals or households, or both, who should, having regard to the requirements set out in subsection (1A) of that section, occupy the house in its existing condition, and
(*b*) give a direction applying that limit to the house.

(2) The authority may also exercise the powers conferred by subsection (1) in relation to a part of a house; and the authority shall have regard to the desirability of applying separate limits where different parts of a house are, or are likely to be, occupied by different persons.

(3) Not less than seven days before giving a direction under this section, the authority shall—

(*a*) serve on an owner of the house, and on every person who is to their knowledge a lessee of the house, notice of their intention to give the direction, and
(*b*) post such a notice in some position in the house where it is accessible to those living in the house,

and shall afford to any person on whom a notice is so served an opportunity of making representations regarding their proposal to give the direction.

(4) The authority shall within seven days from the giving of the direction—

(*a*) serve a copy of the direction on an owner of the house and on every person who is to their knowledge a lessee of the house, and
(*b*) post a copy of the direction in some position in the house where it is accessible to those living in the house.

(5) A direction may be given notwithstanding the existence of a previous direction laying down a higher maximum for the same house or part of a house.

(6) Where the local housing authority have in pursuance of section 352 served a notice specifying the number of individuals or households, or both, which in the opinion of the authority the house could reasonably accommodate if the works specified in the notice were carried out, the authority may adopt that number in fixing a limit under subsection (1) as respects the house.

(7) The powers conferred by this section—

(*a*) are exercisable whether or not a notice has been given under section 352, and
(*b*) are without prejudice to the powers conferred by section 358 (overcrowding notices).

(8) A direction under this section is a local land charge.

[Housing Act 1985, s 354, as amended by the Local Government and Housing Act 1989, Sch 9 and the Housing Act 1996, s 74.]

8–17293 355. Effect of direction under s 354. (1) Where a direction under section 354 is given (direction limiting number of occupants), it is the duty of—

(*a*) the occupier for the time being of the house, or part of a house, to which the direction relates, and
(*b*) any other person who is for the time being entitled or authorised to permit individuals to take up residence in that house or part,

not to permit any individual to take up residence in that house or part unless the number of individuals or households[1] then occupying the house or part would not exceed the limit specified in the direction.

(2) A person who knowingly[2] fails to comply with the requirements imposed on him by subsection (1) commits a summary offence and is liable on conviction to a fine not exceeding **level 5** on the standard scale.

[Housing Act 1985, s 355, as amended by the Housing Act 1996, ss 78 and 79.]

---

1. In *Simmons v Pizzey* [1979] AC 37, [1977] 2 All ER 432, 141 JP 414, HL concerning a house used as a refuge for battered women, the House of Lords held it was irrelevant whether the occupants formed a single household.

2. A person may act "knowingly" if, intending what is happening, he deliberately looks the other way (*Ross v Moss* [1965] 2 QB 396, [1965] 3 All ER 145, 129 JP 537).

8–17294 356. Power to require information about occupation of house. (1) The local housing authority may from time to time serve on the occupier of a house or part of a house in respect of which there is in force a direction under section 354 (direction limiting number of occupants) a notice requiring him to furnish them within seven days with a statement in writing giving all or any of the following particulars—

(*a*) the number of individuals who are, on a date specified in the notice, living in the house or part of the house, as the case may be;
(*b*) the number of families or households to which those individuals belong;
(*c*) the names of those individuals and of the heads of each of those families or households;
(*d*) the rooms used by those individuals and families or households respectively.

(2) An occupier who makes default in complying with the requirements of a notice under this section, or furnishes a statement which to his knowledge is false in a material particular, commits a summary offence and is liable on conviction to a fine not exceeding **level 3** on the standard scale.
[Housing Act 1985, s 356, as amended by the Housing Act 1996, s 78.]

8–17295 **357. Revocation or variation of direction under s 354.** Power of local housing authority on the application of a person having an estate or interest in a house in respect of which a direction is in force to revoke or vary the direction; right of appeal to the county court against refusal of such application.
[Housing Act 1985, s 357—summarised.]

Overcrowding

8–17296 **358. Service of overcrowding notice.** (1) Where it appears to the local housing authority in the case of a house in multiple occupation—

(*a*) that an excessive number of persons is being accommodated on the premises, having regard to the rooms available, or
(*b*) that it is likely that an excessive number of persons will be accommodated on the premises, having regard to the rooms available,

they may serve an overcrowding notice on the occupier of the premises or on the person managing the premises, or on both.

(2) At least seven days before serving an overcrowding notice, the local housing authority shall—

(*a*) inform the occupier of the premises and any person appearing to them to be managing the premises, in writing, of their intention to do so, and
(*b*) ensure that, so far as is reasonably possible, every person living in the premises is informed of that intention;

and they shall afford those persons an opportunity of making representations regarding their proposal to serve the notice.

(3) If no appeal is brought under section 362, the overcrowding notice becomes operative at the end of the period of 21 days from the date of service, and is final and conclusive as to matters which could have been raised on such an appeal.

(4) A person who contravenes an overcrowding notice commits a summary offence and is liable on conviction to a fine not exceeding **level 4** on the standard scale.
[Housing Act 1985, s 358.]

8–17297 **359. Contents of overcrowding notice.** (1) An overcrowding notice shall state in relation to every room on the premises—

(*a*) what in the opinion of the local housing authority is the maximum number of persons by whom the room is suitable to be occupied as sleeping accommodation at any one time, or
(*b*) that the room is in their opinion unsuitable to be occupied as sleeping accommodation;

and the notice may specify special maxima applicable where some or all of the persons occupying the room are under such age as may be specified in the notice.

(2) An overcrowding notice shall contain either—

(*a*) the requirement set out in section 360 (not to permit excessive number of persons to sleep on premises), or
(*b*) the requirement set out in section 361 (not to admit new residents if number of persons is excessive);

and where the local housing authority have served on a person an overcrowding notice containing the latter requirement, they may at any time withdraw the notice and serve on him in its place an overcrowding notice containing the former requirement.
[Housing Act 1985, s 359.]

8–17298 **360. Requirement as to overcrowding generally.** (1) The first requirement referred to in section 359(2) is that the person on whom the notice is served must refrain from knowingly—

(*a*) permitting a room to be occupied as sleeping accommodation otherwise than in accordance with the notice, or
(*b*) permitting persons to occupy the premises as sleeping accommodation in such numbers that it is not possible to avoid persons of opposite sexes who are not living together as husband and wife sleeping in the same room.

(2) For the purposes of subsection (1)(*b*)—

(*a*) children under the age of 12 shall be left out of account, and
(*b*) it shall be assumed that the persons occupying the premises as sleeping accommodation sleep only in rooms for which a maximum is set by the notice and that the maximum set for each room is not exceeded.

[Housing Act 1985, s 360.]

8–17299 361. Requirement as to new residents. (1) The second requirement referred to in section 359(2) is that the person on whom the notice is served must refrain from knowingly—

(*a*) permitting a room to be occupied by a new resident as sleeping accommodation otherwise than in accordance with the notice, or

(*b*) permitting a new resident to occupy any part of the premises as sleeping accommodation if that is not possible without persons of opposite sexes who are not living together as husband and wife sleeping in the same room;

and for this purpose "new resident" means a person who was not living in the premises immediately before the notice was served.

(2) For the purposes of subsection (1)(*b*)—

(*a*) children under the age of 12 shall be left out of account, and

(*b*) it shall be assumed that the persons occupying any part of the premises as sleeping accommodation sleep only in rooms for which a maximum is set by the notice and that the maximum set for each room is not exceeded.

[Housing Act 1985, s 361.]

8–17300 362. Appeal against overcrowding notice. *Appeal to the county court.*

8–17301 363. Revocation and variation of notice. Power of local housing authority on application to revoke or vary an overcrowding notice; right of appeal to the county court against refusal of application.

[Housing Act 1985, s 363—summarised.]

8–17302 364. Power to require information where notice in force. (1) The local housing authority may from time to time serve on the occupier of premises in respect of which an overcrowding notice is in force a notice requiring him to furnish them within seven days with a statement in writing giving any of the following particulars—

(*a*) the number of individuals who are, on a date specified in the notice, occupying any part of the premises as sleeping accommodation;

(*b*) the number of families or households to which those individuals belong;

(*c*) the names of those individuals and of the heads of each of those families or households;

(*d*) the rooms used by those individuals and families or households respectively.

(2) A person who—

(*a*) knowingly fails to comply with the requirements of such a notice, or

(*b*) furnishes a statement which he knows to be false in a material particular,

commits a summary offence and is liable on conviction to a fine not exceeding, in the case of such failure, **level 3** on the standard scale and, in the case of furnishing such a statement, **level 5** on the standard scale.

[Housing Act 1985, s 364, as amended by the Housing Act 1996, s 78.]

Means of escape from fire

8–17303 365. Means of escape from fire: general provisions as to exercise of powers. Where local housing authority could serve a notice under s 352(1) it can accept undertaking or make a closing order under s 368; Secretary of State may specify exercise of powers by Order[1].

[Housing Act 1985, s 365, as amended by the Local Government and Housing Act 1989, Sch 9, the Housing Act 1996, s 75 and Sch 19 and the Fire and Rescue Services Act 2004, Sch 1—summarised.]

1. See the Housing (Fire Safety in Houses in Multiple Occupation) Order 1997, SI 1997/230 amended by SI 2005/1541.

8–17304 368. Means of escape from fire: power to secure that part of house not used for human habitation. (1) Subject to section 365, if it appears to the local housing authority that the means of escape from fire would be adequate if part of the house were not used for human habitation, they may secure that that part is not so used.

(2) For that purpose, the authority may, if after consultation with any owner or mortgagee they think fit to do so, accept an undertaking from him that that part will not be used for human habitation without the permission of the authority.

(3) A person who, knowing that such an undertaking has been accepted—

(*a*) uses the part of the house to which the undertaking relates in contravention of the undertaking, or

(*b*) permits that part of the house to be so used,

commits a summary offence and is liable on conviction to a fine not exceeding **level 5** on the standard scale.

(4) If the local housing authority do not accept an undertaking under subsection (2) with respect to a part of a house, or where they have accepted such an undertaking and that part of the house is at

any time used in contravention of the undertaking, the authority may make a closing order with respect to that part of the house.

(5) *Application of the provisions of Part IX with modifications to a closing order under sub-s (4).*

(6) Nothing in the Rent Acts or Part I of the Housing Act 1988 prevents possession being obtained of a part of a house which in accordance with an undertaking in pursuance of this section cannot for the time being be used for human habitation.

[Housing Act 1985, s 368, as amended by the Housing Act 1988, Sch 17 the Local Government and Housing Act 1989, Sch 9 and the Housing Act 1996, s 78 and Sch 19.]

Standards of management

8–17305 **369. The management code.** (1) The Secretary of State may, with a view to providing a code for the management of houses in multiple occupation, by regulations[1] make provision for ensuring that the person managing a house in multiple occupation observes proper standards of management.

(2)–(4) *Further provisions as to regulations.*

(5) A person who knowingly[2] contravenes or[3] without reasonable excuse[4] fails to comply with a regulation under this section commits a summary offence and is liable on conviction to a fine not exceeding **level 5** on the standard scale.

(6) Regulations under this section shall be made by statutory instrument which shall be subject to annulment in pursuance of a resolution of either House of Parliament.

[Housing Act 1985, s 369, as amended by the Local Government and Housing Act 1989, Schs 9 and 12 and the Housing Act 1996, s 78.]

---

1. See the Housing (Management of Houses in Multiple Occupation) Regulations 1990, SI 1990/380.

2. A person may act "knowingly" if, intending what is happening, he deliberately looks the other way *Ross v Moss* [1965] 2 QB 396, [1965] 3 All ER 145, 129 JP 537).

3. The word "or" is used disjunctively, and therefore the subsection creates two separate offences (*Wandsworth London Borough Council v Sparling* (1987) 152 JP 315).

4. This subsection is divided into two limbs; the first of which "knowingly contravenes" requires knowledge of the defects complained of; but the second "without reasonable excuse fails to comply with any regulations" does not (*Neville v Mavroghenis* [1984] Crim LR 42).

8–17306 **372. Power to require execution of works to remedy neglect of management.** (1) If in the opinion of the local housing authority the condition of a house is defective in consequence of—

(*a*) neglect to comply with the requirements imposed by regulations under section 369 (regulations prescribing management code), or

(*b*) (*Repealed*),

the authority may serve on the person managing the house a notice specifying the works which, in the opinion of the authority, are required to make good the neglect.

(2) If it is not practicable after reasonable inquiry to ascertain the name or address of the person managing the house, the notice may be served by addressing it to him by the description of "manager of the house" (naming the house to which it relates) and delivering it to some person on the premises.

(3) The notice shall require the person on whom it is served to execute the works specified in the notice as follows, namely,—

(*a*) to begin those works not later than such reasonable date, being not earlier than the twenty-first day after the date of service of the notice, as is specified in the notice; and

(*b*) to complete those works within such reasonable period as is so specified.

(4) Where the authority serve a notice under this section on the person managing a house, they shall inform any other person who is to their knowledge an owner, lessee or mortgagee of the house of the fact that the notice has been served.

(5) References in this section to the person managing a house have the same meaning as in section 369 (and accordingly are subject to amendment by regulations under that section).

[Housing Act 1985, s 372, as amended by the Local Government and Housing Act 1989, Sch 9.]

8–17307 **373.** *Appeal against notice under s 372.*

Supplementary provisions as to works notices

8–17320 **375. Carrying out of works by local housing authority.** (1) If a notice under section 352 or 372 (notices requiring the execution of works) is not complied with, the local housing authority may themselves do the work required to be done by the notice.

(2) Compliance with a notice means beginning and completing the works specified in the notice—

(*a*) if no appeal is brought against the notice, not later than such date and within such period as is specified in the notice;

(*b*) if an appeal is brought against the notice and is not withdrawn, not later than such date and within such period as may be fixed by the court determining the appeal; and (*c*) if an appeal brought against the notice is withdrawn, not later than the twenty-first day after the date of withdrawal of the appeal and within such period (beginning on that twenty-first day) as is specified in the notice.

(3) If, before the expiry of the period which under subsection (2) is appropriate for completion of the works specified in the notice, it appears to the local housing authority that reasonable progress is not being made towards compliance with the notice, the authority may themselves do the work required to be done by the notice.

(3A) Not less than seven days before a local housing authority enter any house for the purpose of doing any works by virtue of subsection (1) or subsection (3), they shall serve notice of their intention to do so on the person on whom the notice referred to in subsection (1) was served and, if they think fit, also on any other owner of the house.

(3B) If, after a local housing authority have served notice under subsection (3A), the works are in fact carried out (otherwise than by the authority), any administrative and other expenses incurred by the authority with a view to doing the work themselves in accordance with subsection (1) or subsection (3) shall be treated for the purposes of subsection (4) (and Schedule 10) as expenses incurred by them under this section in carrying out the works in a case where the notice referred to in subsection (1) has not been complied with.

(4) The provisions of Schedule 10 apply with respect to the recovery by the local housing authority of expenses incurred by them under this section.

[Housing Act 1985, s 375, as amended by the Local Government and Housing Act 1989, Schs 9 and 12]

8–17321 **376. Penalty for failure to execute works.** (1) A person on whom a notice has been served under section 352 or 372 (notices requiring the execution of works) who wilfully fails to comply with the notice commits a summary offence[1] and is liable on conviction to a fine not exceeding **level 5** on the standard scale.

(2) The obligation to execute the works specified in the notice continues notwithstanding the expiry of the period which under section 375(2) is appropriate for completion of the works in question; and a person who wilfully fails to comply with that obligation, after being convicted of an offence in relation to the notice under subsection (1) or this subsection, commits a further summary offence and is liable on conviction to a fine not exceeding **level 5** on the standard scale.

(3) References in this section to compliance with a notice shall be construed in accordance with section 375(2).

(4) (*Repealed*).

(5) The provisions of this section are without prejudice to the exercise by the local housing authority of their power under section 375 to carry out the works themselves.

[Housing Act 1985, s 376 amended by the Local Government and Housing Act 1989, Schs 9 and 12 and the Housing Act 1996, s 78.]

---

1. A notice served under s 352 comprises three requirements namely to do the works; to begin the works within time and to complete them within the time specified. Breach of the second and third requirements occurs when the time for compliance expires. The obligation to execute the works however is made a continuing obligation by s 376(2).

As the offence may take place over the whole period from when it should have been done until when it is finally done, the time limit in s 127 of the Magistrates' Courts Act 1980 does not run from the date specified for the completion of the works (*Camden London Borough Council v Marshall* [1996] 1 WLR 1345).

8–17322 **377. Powers of court to facilitate execution of works, etc.** (1) Where—

(*a*) a person is required by a notice under section 352 or 372 to execute works and

(*b*) another person having an estate or interest in the premises unreasonably refuses to give a consent required to enable the works to be executed,

the person required to execute the works may apply to the county court and the court may give the necessary consent in place of that other person.

(2) If a person, after receiving notice of the intended action—

(*a*) being the occupier of premises, prevents the owner or his officers, agents, servants or workmen, from carrying into effect with respect to the premises any of the preceding provisions of this Part, or

(*b*) being the owner or occupier of premises, prevents an officer, agent, servant or workman of the local housing authority from so doing,

a magistrates' court may order him to permit to be done on the premises all things requisite for carrying into effect those provisions.

(3) A person who fails to comply with an order of the court under subsection (2) commits a summary offence and is liable on conviction to a fine not exceeding **level 5** on the standard scale; and if the failure continues, he commits a further summary offence and is liable on conviction to a fine not exceeding one-tenth of the amount corresponding to that level for every day or part of a day during which the failure continues.

[Housing Act 1985, s 377, as amended by the Local Government and Housing Act 1989, Schs 9 and 12 and the Housing Act 1996, s 78.]

8–17323 **377A. Works notices: improvement of enforcement procedures.** (1) The Secretary of State may by order[1] provide that a local housing authority shall act as specified in the order before serving a works notice.

In this section a "works notice" means a notice under section 352 or 372 (notices requiring the execution of works).

(2) An order under this section may provide that the authority—

(*a*) shall as soon as practicable give to the person on whom the works notice is to be served a written notice which satisfies the requirements of subsection (3); and

(*b*) shall not serve the works notice until after the end of such period beginning with the giving of a notice which satisfies the requirements of subsection (3) as may be determined by or under the order.

(3) A notice satisfies the requirements of this subsection if it—

(*a*) states the works which in the authority's opinion should be undertaken, and explains why and within what period;

(*b*) explains the grounds on which it appears to the authority that the works notice might be served;

(*c*) states the type of works notice which is to be served, the consequences of serving it and whether there is a right to make representations before, or a right of appeal against, the serving of it.

(4) An order[1] under this section may also provide that, before the authority serves the works notice on any person, they—

(*a*) shall give to that person a written notice stating—

(i) that they are considering serving the works notice and the reasons why they are considering serving the notice; and

(ii) that the person may, within a period specified in the written notice, make written representations to them or, if the person so requests, make oral representations to them in the presence of a person determined by or under the order; and

(*b*) shall consider any representations which are duly made and not withdrawn.

(5) An order[1] under this section may in particular—

(*a*) make provision as to the consequences of any failure to comply with a provision made by the order;

(*b*) contain such consequential, incidental, supplementary or transitional provisions and savings as the Secretary of State considers appropriate (including provisions modifying enactments relating to the periods within which proceedings must be brought).

(6) An order[1] under this section—

(*a*) may make different provision with respect to different cases or descriptions of case (including different provision for different areas), and

(*b*) shall be made by statutory instrument which shall be subject to annulment in pursuance of a resolution of either House of Parliament.

(7) Nothing in any order under this section shall—

(*a*) preclude a local housing authority from serving a works notice on any person, or from requiring any person to take immediate remedial action to avoid a works notice being served on him, in any case where it appears to them to be necessary to serve such a notice or impose such a requirement; or

(*b*) require such an authority to disclose any information the disclosure of which would be contrary to the public interest.

[Housing Act 1985, s 377A, as inserted by the Housing Act 1996, s 76.]

---

1. The Housing (Enforcement Procedures for Houses in Multiple Occupation) Order 1997, SI 1997/227, art 2 provides—

"2. Except in a case where it appears to the local housing authority necessary to take such action immediately, before a local housing authority serve a works notice on any person they—

(1) shall give to that person a written notice stating:

(*a*) that they are considering serving the works notice;

(*b*) the reasons why they are considering serving the works notice and the works which should be undertaken to remedy the relevant defect;

(*c*) that the person may, within a period specified in the notice (not being less than 14 days) make either written representations to the authority or, if the person so requests, make oral representations to the authority in the presence of an officer appointed by the authority (such a request being made not later than the expiry of 7 days beginning with the day on which that notice is given); and

(2) shall consider any representations which are duly made and not withdrawn."

Where a works notice is served and the authority have failed to comply with Article 2 above, that failure shall be a ground for appeal additional to those specified in s 353(2) and 373(2) of the Housing Act 1985 (ibid, Article 3)."

8–17324 **378.** *Provisions for protection of owners.*

Control orders

8–17325 379–381. *Local authority powers to make a control order in respect of a house in multiple occupation.*

8–17326 387. Right of entry for inspection and carrying out of works. (1) The local housing authority, and any person authorised in writing by the authority, have, as against a person having an estate or interest in a house which is subject to a control order, the right at all reasonable times to enter any part of the house for the purpose of survey and examination or of carrying out works.

(2) The right conferred by subsection (1) is without prejudice to the rights conferred on the authority by section 381 (general effect of control order).

(3) Where part of a house is excluded from the provisions of a control order under section 380 (modification of order where dispossessed proprietor resides in part of the house), the right conferred by subsection (1) is exercisable as respects that part so far as is reasonably required for the purpose of survey and examination of, or carrying out works in, the part of the house which is subject to the control order.

(4) If the occupier of part of a house subject to a control order, after receiving notice of the intended action, prevents any officers, agents, servants, or workmen of the local housing authority from carrying out work in the house a magistrates' court may order him to permit to be done on the premises anything which the authority consider necessary.

(5) A person who fails to comply with an order of the court under subsection (4) commits a summary offence and is liable to a fine not exceeding **level 5** on the standard scale.

[Housing Act 1985, s 387, as amended by the Local Government and Housing Act 1989, Sch 9 and the Housing Act 1996, s 78.]

General supplementary provisions

8–17327 395. Powers of entry. (1) Where it appears to the local housing authority that survey or examination of any premises is necessary in order to determine whether any powers under this Part should be exercised in respect of the premises, a person authorised by the authority may at any reasonable time, on giving 24 hours' notice of his intention to the occupier, and to the owner if the owner is known, enter the premises for the purpose of such a survey and examination.

(2) A person authorised by the local housing authority may at any reasonable time, without any such prior notice as is mentioned in subsection (1), enter any premises for the purpose of ascertaining whether an offence has been committed under any of the following provisions of this Part—

section 348G (contravention of or failure to comply with provision of registration scheme),
section 353A (failure to keep premises fit for number of occupants),
section 355(2) (failure to comply with requirements of direction limiting number of occupants of house),
section 358(4) (contravention of overcrowding notice),
section 368(3) (use or permitting use of part of house with inadequate means of escape from fire in contravention of undertaking),
section 369(5) (contravention of or failure to comply with regulations prescribing management code),
section 376(1) or (2) (failure to comply with notice requiring execution of works).

(3) An authorisation for the purposes of this section shall be in writing stating the particular purpose[1] or purposes for which the entry is authorised and shall, if so required, be produced for inspection by the occupier or anyone acting on his behalf.

[Housing Act 1985, s 395, as amended by the Local Government and Housing Act 1989, Sch 9 and the Housing Act 1996, ss 68 and 73.]

---

1. This is a general power, not depending upon reasonable ground to suspect the existence of any state of things (*Bedingfield v Jones* (1959) 124 JP 11).

8–17328 395A. Codes of practice. (1) The Secretary of State may by order—

(*a*) approve any code of practice (whether prepared by him or another person) which, in his opinion, gives suitable guidance to any person in relation to any matter arising under this Part;
(*b*) approve any modification of such a code; or
(*c*) withdraw such a code or modification.

(2) The Secretary of State shall only approve a code of practice or a modification of a code if he is satisfied that—

(*a*) the code or modification has been published (whether by him or by another person) in such manner as he considers appropriate for the purpose of bringing the code or modification to the notice of those likely to be affected by it; or
(*b*) arrangements have been made for the code or modification to be so published.

(3) The Secretary of State may approve—

(*a*) more than one code of practice in relation to the same matter;

(*b*) a code of practice which makes different provision with respect to different cases or descriptions of case (including different provision for different areas).

(4) A failure to comply with a code of practice for the time being approved under this section shall not of itself render a person liable to any civil or criminal proceedings; but in any civil or criminal proceedings—

(*a*) any code of practice approved under this section shall be admissible in evidence, and
(*b*) any provision of any such code which appears to the court to be relevant to any question arising in the proceedings shall be taken into account in determining that question.

(5) An order under this section shall be made by statutory instrument which shall be subject to annulment in pursuance of a resolution of either House of Parliament.

(6) In this section references to a code of practice include references to a part of a code of practice.
[Housing Act 1985, s 395A, as inserted by the Housing Act 1996, s 77.]

8–17329 396. Penalty for obstruction. (1) It is a summary offence intentionally to obstruct an officer of the local housing authority, or any person authorised to enter premises in pursuance of this Part, in the performance of anything which he is by this Part required or authorised to do.

(2) A person committing such an offence is liable on conviction to a fine not exceeding **level 4** on the standard scale.
[Housing Act 1985, s 396, as amended by the Local Government and Housing Act 1989, Sch 9 and the Housing Act 1996, s 78.]

8–17330 397. Warrant to authorise entry. (1) Where it is shown to the satisfaction of a justice of the peace, on sworn information in writing, that admission to premises specified in the information is reasonably required by a person employed by, or acting on the instructions of, the local housing authority—

(*a*) for the purpose of survey and examination to determine whether any powers under this Part should be exercised in respect of the premises, or
(*b*) for the purpose of ascertaining whether an offence has been committed under any of the provisions of this Part listed in section 395(2),

the justice may by warrant under his hand authorise that person to enter on the premises for those purposes or for such of those purposes as may be specified in the warrant.

(2) The justice shall not grant the warrant unless he is satisfied—

(*a*) that admission to the premises has been refused and, except where the purpose specified in the information is that mentioned in subsection (1)(*b*), that admission was sought after not less than 24 hours' notice of the intended entry had been given to the occupier, or
(*b*) that application for admission would defeat the purpose of the entry.

(3) The power of entry conferred by the warrant includes power to enter by force, if need be, and may be exercised by the person on whom it is conferred either alone or together with other persons.

(4) If the premises are unoccupied or the occupier is temporarily absent, a person entering under the authority of the warrant shall leave the premises as effectively secured against trespassers as he found them.

(5) The warrant continues in force until the purpose for which the entry is required is satisfied.
[Housing Act 1985, s 397.]

8–17331 398. Meaning of "lessee", "owner", "person having control" and similar expressions. (1) In this Part the expressions "lessee", "owner", "person having an estate or interest", "person having control", and "person managing" shall be construed as follows.

(2) "Lessee" includes a statutory tenant of the premises, and references to a lease or to a person to whom premises are let shall be construed accordingly.

(3) "Owner"—

(*a*) means a person (other than a mortgagee not in possession) who is for the time being entitled to dispose of the fee simple of the premises whether in possession or in reversion, and
(*b*) includes also a person holding or entitled to the rents and profits of the premises under a lease having an unexpired term exceeding three years.

(4) "Person having an estate or interest" includes a statutory tenant of the premises.

(5) "Person having control" means the person who receives the rack-rent of the premises, whether on his own account or as agent or trustee of another person, or who would so receive it if the premises were let at a rack-rent (and for this purpose a "rack-rent" means a rent which is not less than 2/3rds of the full net annual value of the premises).

(6) "Person managing"—

(*a*) means the person who, being an owner or lessee of the premises—

(i) receives, directly or through an agent or trustee, rents or other payments from persons who are tenants of parts of the premises, or who are lodgers, or

(ii) would so receive those rents or other payments but for having entered into an arrangement (whether in pursuance of a court order or otherwise) with another person who is not an owner or lessee of the premises by virtue of which that other person receives the rents or other payments, and

(*b*) includes, where those rents or other payments are received through another person as agent or trustee, that other person.

[Housing Act 1985, s 398, as amended by the Housing Act 1996, s 79.]

8–17332 **399. Minor definitions.** In this Part—

"dispossessed proprietor", in relation to a house subject to a control order, means the person by whom the rent or other periodical payments to which the local housing authority become entitled on the coming into force of the order would have been receivable but for the making of the order, and the successors in title of that person;

"final determination", in relation to an appeal, includes the withdrawal of the appeal, which has the same effect for the purposes of this Part as a decision dismissing the appeal;

"house" includes any yard, garden, outhouses and appurtenances belonging to the house or usually enjoyed with it.

[Housing Act 1985, s 399.]

8–17333 **400. Index of defined expressions: Part XI.** The following Table shows provisions defining or otherwise explaining expressions used in this Part (other than provisions defining or explaining an expression used in the same section or paragraph):—

appropriate multiplier	Schedule 13, paragraph 13
assured tenancy	section 622
assured agricultural occupancy	section 622
control order	section 379(1)
control provisions	section 347(1)
dispossessed proprietor	section 399
district (of a local housing authority)	section 2(1)
district valuer	section 622
expenditure incurred (in respect of a house subject to a control order)	section 385(3) and Schedule 13, paragraph 2(3)
final determination (in relation to an appeal)	section 399
flat in multiple occupation	section 345
gross value	Schedule 13, paragraphs 8 to 12
house	section 399
house in multiple occupation	section 345
lessee (and "lease" and "let")	sections 398 and 621
local housing authority	section 1, 2(2)
management code	section 369
management scheme	section 386
occupancy direction (in connection with special control provisions)	section 348D
overcrowding notice	section 358(1)
owner	section 398(3)
person having control	section 398(5)
person having an estate or interest	section 398(4)
person managing	sections 369(4), 372(5) and 398(6)
registration scheme	section 346
relevant management failure (for purposes of sections 348B to 348E)	section 348F
the Rent Acts	section 622
rents or other payments	Schedule 13, paragraph 2(2)
special control provisions	section 348B
standard scale (in reference to the maximum fine on summary conviction)	section 622
statutory tenant	section 622
surpluses on revenue account as settled by the scheme (in Schedule 13)	Schedule 13, paragraph 2(1)
tenant	section 621

[Housing Act 1985, s 400, as amended by the Housing Act 1988, Sch 1, the Local Government and Housing Act 1989, Sch 9 and the Housing Act 1996, s 67.]

PART XVII[1]

COMPULSORY PURCHASE AND LAND COMPENSATION

Supplementary provisions

8–17358 **600. Powers of entry.** (1) A person authorised by the local housing authority or the Secretary of State may at any reasonable time, on giving seven days' notice of his intention to the occupier, and to the owner if the owner is known, enter premises for the purpose of survey and examination where it appears to the authority or the Secretary of State that survey or examination is necessary in order to determine whether any powers under this Part should be exercised in respect of the premises.

(2) An authorisation for the purposes of this section shall be in writing stating the particular purpose[2] or purposes for which the entry is authorised and shall, if so required, be produced for inspection by the occupier or anyone acting on his behalf.

[Housing Act 1985, s 600 amended by the Local Government and Housing Act 1989, Sch 9.]

1. Part XVII contains ss 578–603.

2. This is a general power, not depending upon reasonable ground to suspect the existence of any state of things (*Bedingfield v Jones* (1959) 124 JP 11).

8–17359 **601. Penalty for obstruction.** (1) It is a summary offence intentionally to obstruct an officer of the local housing authority or of the Secretary of State, or any person authorised to enter premises in pursuance of this Part, in the performance of anything which he is by this Part required or authorised to do.

(2) A person committing such an offence is liable on conviction to a fine not exceeding **level 3** on the standard scale.

[Housing Act 1985, s 601, as amended by the Local Government and Housing Act 1989, Sch 9.]

8–17360 **602. Minor definitions.** In this Part—

"owner", in relation to premises—

(*a*) means a person (other than a mortgagee not in possession) who is for the time being entitled to dispose of the fee simple in the premises, whether in possession or in reversion, and

(*b*) includes also a person holding or entitled to the rents and profits of the premises or part of the premises under a lease of which the unexpired term exceeds three years.

[Housing Act 1985, s 602, as amended by the Local Government and Housing Act 1989, Sch 9.]

PART XVIII[1]

MISCELLANEOUS AND GENERAL PROVISIONS

General provisions relating to housing conditions

8–17361 **604. Fitness for human habitation.** (1) Subject to subsection (2) below, a dwelling-house is fit for human habitation for the purposes of this Act unless, in the opinion of the local housing authority, it fails to meet one or more of the requirements in paragraphs (*a*) to (i) below and, by reason of that failure, is not reasonably suitable for occupation,—

(*a*) it is structurally stable;

(*b*) it is free from serious disrepair;

(*c*) it is free from dampness prejudicial to the health of the occupants (if any);

(*d*) it has adequate provision for lighting, heating and ventilation;

(*e*) it has an adequate piped supply of wholesome water;

(*f*) there are satisfactory facilities in the dwelling-house for the preparation and cooking of food, including a sink with a satisfactory supply of hot and cold water;

(*g*) it has a suitably located water-closet for the exclusive use of the occupants (if any);

(*h*) it has, for the exclusive use of the occupants (if any), a suitably located fixed bath or shower and wash-hand basin each of which is provided with a satisfactory supply of hot and cold water; and

(*i*) it has an effective system for the draining of foul, waste and surface water;

and any reference to a dwelling-house being unfit for human habitation shall be construed accordingly.

(2) Whether or not a dwelling-house which is a flat satisfies the requirements in subsection (1), it is unfit for human habitation for the purposes of this Act if, in the opinion of the local housing authority, the building or a part of the building outside the flat fails to meet one or more of the requirements in paragraphs (*a*) to (*e*) below and, by reason of that failure, the flat is not reasonably suitable for occupation,—

(*a*) the building or part is structurally stable;

(*b*) it is free from serious disrepair;

(*c*) it is free from dampness;

(*d*) it has adequate provision for ventilation; and

(*e*) it has an effective system or the draining of foul, waste and surface water.

(3) Subsection (1) applies in relation to a house in multiple occupation with the substitution of a reference to the house for any reference to a dwelling-house.

(4) Subsection (2) applies in relation to a flat in multiple occupation with the substitution for any reference to a dwelling-house which is a flat of a reference to the flat in multiple occupation.

(5) *Secretary of State may amend sub-ss (1) and (2) by Order.*

[Housing Act 1985, s 604 as substituted by the Local Government and Housing Act 1989 Sch 9.]

1. Part XVIII contains ss 604–625.

8–17361A 604A. *Authority to consider guidance given by Secretary of State in deciding whether to take action under ss 189, 264, 265 or 289.*

8–17362 606. Reports on particular houses or areas. (1) The proper officer of the local housing authority shall make a report in writing to the authority whenever he is of the opinion—

(*a*) that a dwelling-house or house in multiple occupation in their district is unfit for human habitation, or

(*b*) that an area in their district should be dealt with as a clearance area;

and the authority shall take into consideration as soon as may be any such report made to them.

(2) If a complaint in writing that a dwelling-house or house in multiple occupation is unfit for human habitation, or that an area should be dealt with as a clearance area, is made to the proper officer of the local housing authority by—

(*a*) a justice of the peace having jurisdiction in any part of their district, or

(*b*) a parish or community council for a parish or community within their district,

the officer shall forthwith inspect the dwelling-house or house in multiple occupation or area and make a report to the authority stating the facts of the case and whether in his opinion the dwelling-house or house in multiple occupation is unfit for human habitation or the area should be dealt with as a clearance area.

(3) The absence of a complaint under subsection (2) does not excuse the proper officer of the authority from inspecting a dwelling-house or house in multiple occupation or area or making a report on it under subsection (1).

[Housing Act 1985, s 606, as amended by the Local Government and Housing Act 1989, Sch 9.]

General provisions

8–17363 612. Exclusion of Rent Act protection. Nothing in the Rent Acts or Part I of the Housing Act 1988 prevents possession being obtained of a dwelling-house of which possession is required for the purpose of enabling a local housing authority to exercise their powers under any enactment relating to housing[1].

[Housing Act 1985, s 612, as amended by the Housing Act 1988, Sch 17 and the Local Government and Housing Act 1989, Sch 9.]

1. The requiring of possession of premises for the purposes of re-letting, whatever the reason, is an exercise of the power of management under s 21(1) of this Act (*R v Snell, ex p Marylebone Borough Council* [1942] 2 KB 137, [1942] 1 All ER 612, 106 JP 160, followed, but criticised in *LCC v Shelley, Harcourt v LCC*, infra). See Art 106 JP Jo 472.

8–17364 613. Liability of directors, etc in case of offence by body corporate. (1) Where an offence under this Act committed by a body corporate is proved to have been committed with the consent or connivance of, or to be attributable to any neglect on the part of, a director, manager, secretary or other similar officer of the body corporate, or a person purporting to act in any such capacity, he, as well as the body corporate, is guilty of an offence and liable to be proceeded against and punished accordingly.

(2) Where the affairs of a body corporate are managed by its members, subsection (1) applies in relation to the acts and defaults of a member in connection with his functions of management as if he were a director of the body corporate.

[Housing Act 1985, s 613.]

8–17365 617. Service of notices. (1) Where under any provision of this Act it is the duty of a local housing authority to serve a document on a person who is to the knowledge of the authority—

(*a*) a person having control of premises, however defined, or

(*b*) a person managing premises, however defined, or

(*c*) a person having an estate or interest in premises, whether or not restricted to persons who are owners or lessees or mortgagees or to any other class of those having an estate or interest in premises,

the authority shall take reasonable steps to identify the person or persons coming within the description in that provision.

(2) A person having an estate or interest in premises may for the purposes of any provision to which subsection (1) applies give notice to the local housing authority of his interest in the premises and they shall enter the notice in their records.

(3) A document required or authorised by this Act to be served on a person as being a person having control of premises (however defined) may, if it is not practicable after reasonable enquiry to ascertain the name or address of that person, be served by—

(*a*) addressing it to him by the description of "person having control of" the premises (naming them) to which it relates, and

(*b*) delivering it to some person on the premises or, if there is no person on the premises to whom it can be delivered, by affixing it, or a copy of it, to some conspicuous part of the premises.

(4) Where under any provision of this Act a document is to be served on—

(*a*) the person having control of premises, however defined, or

(*b*) the person managing premises, however defined, or

(*c*) the owner of premises, however defined,

and more than one person comes within the description in the enactment, the document may be served on more than one of those persons.

[Housing Act 1985, s 617.]

8–17366 **618.** *The Common Council of the City of London; the Inner and Middle Temples.*

8–17367 **620. The Isles of Scilly.** (1) This Act applies to the Isles of Scilly subject to such exceptions, adaptations and modifications as the Secretary of State may by order direct.

(2) An order shall be made by statutory instrument which shall be subject to annulment in pursuance of a resolution of either House of Parliament.

[Housing Act 1985, s 620.]

8–17368 **621. Meaning of "lease" and "tenancy" and related expressions.** (1) In this Act "lease" and "tenancy" have the same meaning.

(2) Both expressions include—

(*a*) a sub-lease or sub-tenancy, and

(*b*) an agreement for a lease or tenancy (or sub-lease or sub-tenancy).

(3) The expressions "lessor" and "lessee" and "landlord" and "tenant", and references to letting, to the grant of a lease or to covenants or terms, shall be construed accordingly.

[Housing Act 1985, s 621.]

8–17369 **621A. Meaning of "service charge" and related expressions.** (1) In this Act "service charge" means an amount payable by a purchaser or lessee of premises—

(*a*) which is payable, directly or indirectly, for services, repairs, maintenance or insurance or the vendor's or lessor's costs of management, and

(*b*) the whole or part of which varies or may vary according to the relevant costs.

(2) The relevant costs are the costs or estimated costs incurred or to be incurred by or on behalf of the payee, or (in the case of a lease) a superior landlord, in connection with the matters for which the service charge is payable.

(3) For this purpose—

(*a*) "costs" includes overheads, and

(*b*) costs are relevant costs in relation to a service charge whether they are incurred, or to be incurred, in the period for which the service charge is payable or in an earlier or later period.

(4) In relation to a service charge—

(*a*) the "payee" means the person entitled to enforce payment of the charge, and

(*b*) the "payer" means the person liable to pay it.

(5) But this section does not apply in relation to Part 14.

[Housing Act 1985, s 621A, as inserted by the Housing and Planning Act 1986, Sch 5 and amended by the Commonhold and Leasehold Reform Act 2002, s 150.]

8–17380 **622. Minor definitions: general.** (1) In this Act—

"assured tenancy" has the same meaning as in Part I of the Housing Act 1988;

"assured agricultural occupancy" has the same meaning as in Part I of the Housing Act 1988;

"authorised deposit taker" means—

(*a*) a person who has permission under Part 4 of the Financial Services and Markets Act 2000 to accept deposits, or

(*b*) an EEA firm of the kind mentioned in paragraph 5(*b*) of Schedule 3 to that Act who has permission under paragraph 15 of that Schedule (as a result of qualifying for authorisation under paragraph 12(1) of that Schedule) to accept deposits;

"authorised insurer" means—

(*a*) a person who has permission under Part 4 of the Financial Services and Markets Act 2000 to effect or carry out contracts of insurance, or

(*b*) an EEA firm of the kind mentioned in paragraph 5(*b*) of Schedule 3 to that Act who has permission under paragraph 15 of that Schedule (as a result of qualifying for authorisation under paragraph 12(1) of that Schedule) to effect or carry out contracts of insurance;

"building regulations" means—

(*a*) building regulations made under Part I of the Building Act 1984,

(*b*) (*Repealed*), or

(*c*) any provision of a local Act, or of a byelaw made under a local Act, dealing with the construction and drainage of new buildings and the laying out and construction of new streets;

"cemetery" has the same meaning as in section 214 of the Local Government Act 1972;

"charity" has the same meaning as in the Charities Act 1993;

"district valuer" means an officer of the Commissioners of Inland Revenue appointed to be, in relation to the valuation list for the area in which the land in question is situated, the valuation or deputy valuation officer or one of the valuation officers or deputy valuation officers;

"friendly society" means a friendly society, or a branch of a friendly society, registered under the Friendly Societies Act 1974 or earlier legislation;

"general rate fund" means—

(*a*) in relation to the Council of the Isles of Scilly, the general fund of that council;

(*b*) in relation to the Common Council of the City of London, that council's general rate;

"hostel" means a building in which is provided, for persons generally or for a class or classes of persons—

(*a*) residential accommodation otherwise than in separate and self-contained sets of premises, and

(*b*) either board or facilities for the preparation of food adequate to the needs of those persons, or both;

"protected occupancy" and "protected occupier" have the same meaning as in the Rent (Agriculture) Act 1976;

"protected tenancy" has the same meaning as in the Rent Act 1977;

"regular armed forces of the Crown" means the Royal Navy, the regular forces as defined by section 225 of the Army Act 1955, or the regular air force as defined by section 223 of the Air Force Act 1955;

"the Rent Acts" means the Rent Act 1977 and the Rent (Agriculture) Act 1976;

"restricted contract" has the same meaning as in the Rent Act 1977;

"shared ownership lease" means a lease—

(*a*) granted on payment of a premium calculated by reference to a percentage of the value of the dwelling or of the cost of providing it, or

(*b*) under which the tenant (or his personal representatives) will or may be entitled to a sum calculated by reference, directly or indirectly, to the value of the dwelling;

"statutory tenancy" and "statutory tenant" mean a statutory tenancy or statutory tenant within the meaning of the Rent Act 1977 or the Rent (Agriculture) Act 1976;

"street" includes any court, alley, passage, square or row of houses, whether a thoroughfare or not;

"subsidiary" has the meaning given by section 736 of the Companies Act 1985.

[Housing Act 1985, s 622, as amended by the Building Societies Act 1986, Sch 18, the Banking Act 1987, Sch 6, the Housing Act 1988, Sch 17, the Companies Act 1989, Sch 18, the Planning and Compensation Act 1991, Sch 19, the Charities Act 1993, Sch 6, the Statute Law (Repeals) Act 1993, Sch 1, the Armed Forces Act 2001, Sch 6 and SI 2001/3649.]

8–17381 623. Minor definitions: Part XVIII. (1) In this Part—

"dwelling-house" and "flat", except in the expression "flat in multiple occupation", shall be construed in accordance with subsection (2);

"house in multiple occupation" and "flat in multiple occupation" have the same meaning as in Part XI;

"owner", in relation to premises—

(*a*) means a person (other than a mortgagee not in possession) who is for the time being entitled to dispose of the fee simple absolute in the premises, whether in possession or in reversion, and

(*b*) includes also a person holding or entitled to the rents and profits of the premises under a lease of which the unexpired term exceeds three years.

(2) For the purposes of this Part, "dwelling-house" includes any yard, garden, outhouses and

appurtenances belonging to it or usually enjoyed with it and section 183 shall have effect to determine whether a dwelling-house is a flat.
[Housing Act 1985, s 623, as amended by the Local Government and Housing Act 1989, Sch 9.]

8–17382 **624. Index of defined expressions: Part XVIII.** The following Table shows provisions defining or otherwise explaining expressions used in this Part (other than provisions defining or explaining an expression used in the same section)—

clearance area	section 289
district (of a local housing authority)	section 2(1)
dwelling-house	section 623
flat	section 623
flat in multiple occupation	section 623
house in multiple occupation	section 623
lease and let	section 621
local housing authority	section 1, 2(2)
owner	section 623
Rent Acts	section 622
standard scale (in reference to the maximum fine on summary conviction)	section 622
street	section 622
unfit for human habitation	section 604

[Housing Act 1985, s 624, as amended by the Local Government and Housing Act 1989, Sch 9.]

Landlord and Tenant Act 1985[1]

(1985 c 70)

Information to be given to tenant

8–17490 **1. Disclosure of landlord's identity.** (1) If the tenant of premises occupied as a dwelling makes a written request for the landlord's name and address to—

(*a*) any person who demands, or the last person who received, rent payable under the tenancy, or
(*b*) any other person for the time being acting as agent for the landlord, in relation to the tenancy,

that person shall supply the tenant with a written statement of the landlord's name and address within the period of 21 days beginning with the day on which he receives the request.

(2) A person who, without reasonable excuse, fails to comply with subsection (1) commits a summary offence and is liable on conviction to a fine not exceeding **level 4** on the standard scale.

(3) In this section and section 2—

(*a*) "tenant" includes a statutory tenant; and
(*b*) "landlord" means the immediate landlord.

[Landlord and Tenant Act 1985, s 1.]

1. This Act consolidates certain provisions of the law of landlord and tenant formerly found in the Housing Acts, together with the Landlord and Tenant Act 1962, with amendments to give effect to recommendations of the Law Commission.

8–17491 **2. Disclosure of directors, etc of corporate landlord.** (1) Where a tenant is supplied under section 1 with the name and address of his landlord and the landlord is a body corporate, he may make a further written request to the landlord for the name and address of every director and of the secretary of the landlord.

(2) The landlord shall supply the tenant with a written statement of the information requested within the period of 21 days beginning with the day on which he receives the request.

(3) A request under this section is duly made to the landlord if it is made to—

(*a*) an agent of the landlord, or
(*b*) a person who demands the rent of the premises concerned;

and any such agent or person to whom such a request is made shall forward it to the landlord as soon as may be.

(4) A landlord who, without reasonable excuse, fails to comply with a request under this section, and a person who, without reasonable excuse, fails to comply with a requirement imposed on him by subsection (3), commits a summary offence and is liable on conviction to a fine not exceeding **level 4** on the standard scale.

[Landlord and Tenant Act 1985, s 2.]

8–17492 **3. Duty to inform tenant of assignment of landlord's interest.** (1) If the interest of the landlord under a tenancy of premises which consist of or include a dwelling is assigned, the new landlord shall give notice in writing of the assignment, and of his name and address, to the tenant not later than the next day on which rent is payable under the tenancy or, if that is within two months of the assignment, the end of that period of two months.

(2) If trustees constitute the new landlord, a collective description of the trustees as the trustees of the trust in question may be given as the name of the landlord, and where such a collective description is given—

(*a*) the address of the new landlord may be given as the address from which the affairs of the trust are conducted, and

(*b*) a change in the persons who are for the time being the trustees of the trust shall not be treated as an assignment of the interest of the landlord.

(3) A person who is the new landlord under a tenancy falling within subsection (1) and who fails, without reasonable excuse, to give the notice required by that subsection, commits a summary offence and is liable on conviction to a fine not exceeding **level 4** on the standard scale.

(3A) The person who was the landlord under the tenancy immediately before the assignment ("the old landlord") shall be liable to the tenant in respect of any breach of any covenant, condition or agreement under the tenancy occurring before the end of the relevant period in like manner as if the interest assigned were still vested in him; and where the new landlord is also liable to the tenant in respect of any such breach occurring within that period, he and the old landlord shall be jointly and severally liable in respect of it.

(3B) In subsection (3A) "the relevant period" means the period beginning with the date of the assignment and ending with the date when—

(*a*) notice in writing of the assignment, and of the new landlord's name and address, is given to the tenant by the new landlord (whether in accordance with subsection (1) or not), or

(*b*) notice in writing of the assignment, and of the new landlord's name and last-known address, is given to the tenant by the old landlord,

which happens first.

(4) In this section—

(*a*) "tenancy" includes a statutory tenancy, and

(*b*) references to the assignment of the landlord's interest include any conveyance other than a mortgage or charge.

[Landlord and Tenant Act 1985, s 3, as amended by the Landlord and Tenant Act 1987, s 50.]

8–17493 **3A. Duty to inform tenant of possible right to acquire landlord's interest.** (1) Where a new landlord is required by section 3(1) to give notice to a tenant of an assignment to him, then if—

(*a*) the tenant is a qualifying tenant within the meaning of Part I of the Landlord and Tenant Act 1987 (tenants' rights of first refusal), and

(*b*) the assignment was a relevant disposal within the meaning of that Part affecting premises to which at the time of the disposal that Part applied,

the landlord shall give also notice in writing to the tenant to the following effect.

(2) The notice shall state—

(*a*) that the disposal to the landlord was one to which Part I of the Landlord and Tenant Act 1987 applied;

(*b*) that the tenant (together with other qualifying tenants) may have the right under that Part—

(i) to obtain information about the disposal, and

(ii) to acquire the landlord's interest in the whole or part of the premises in which the tenant's flat is situated; and

(*c*) the time within which any such right must be exercised, and the fact that the time would run from the date of receipt of notice under this section by the requisite majority of qualifying tenants (within the meaning of that Part).

(3) A person who is required to give notice under this section and who fails, without reasonable excuse, to do so within the time allowed for giving notice under section 3(1) commits a summary offence and is liable on conviction to a fine not exceeding **level 4** on the standard scale.

[Landlord and Tenant Act 1985, s 3A, as inserted by the Housing Act 1996, s 93.]

Provision of rent books

8–17494 **4. Provision of rent books.** (1) Where a tenant has a right to occupy premises as a residence in consideration of a rent payable weekly, the landlord shall provide a rent book or other similar document for use in respect of the premises.

(2) Subsection (1) does not apply to premises if the rent includes a payment in respect of board and the value of that board to the tenant forms a substantial proportion of the whole rent.

(3) In this section and sections 5 to 7—

(*a*) "tenant" includes a statutory tenant and a person having a contractual right to occupy the premises; and (*b*) "landlord", in relation to a person having such a contractual right, means the person who granted the right or any successor in title of his, as the case may require.

[Landlord and Tenant Act 1985, s 4.]

8–17495 5. Information to be contained in rent books. (1) A rent book or other similar document provided in pursuance of section 4 shall contain notice of the name and address of the landlord of the premises and—

(*a*) if the premises are occupied by virtue of a restricted contract, particulars of the rent and of the other terms and conditions of the contract and notice of such other matters as may be prescribed;

(*b*) if the premises are let on or subject to a protected or statutory tenancy or let on an assured tenancy within the meaning of Part I of the Housing Act 1988, notice of such matters as may be prescribed.

(2) If the premises are occupied by virtue of a restricted contract or let on or subject to a protected or statutory tenancy or let on an assured tenancy within the meaning of Part I of the Housing Act 1988, the notice and particulars required by this section shall be in the prescribed form.

(3) *In this section "prescribed" means prescribed by regulations[1] made by the Secretary of State.*

[Landlord and Tenant Act 1985, s 5, as amended by the Housing Act 1988, Sch 17.]

1. See the Rent Book (Forms of Notice) Regulations 1982, SI 1982/1474, amended by SI 1988/2198, SI 1990/1067 and SI 1993/656.

8–17496 6. Information to be supplied by companies. (1) Where the landlord of premises to which section 4(1) applies (premises occupied as a residence at a weekly rent) is a company, and the tenant serves on the landlord a request in writing to that effect, the landlord shall give the tenant in writing particulars of the name and address of every director and of the secretary of the company.

(2) A request under this section is duly served on the landlord if it is served—

(*a*) on an agent of the landlord named as such in the rent book or other similar document, or

(*b*) on the person who receives the rent of the premises;

and a person on whom a request is so served shall forward it to the landlord as soon as may be.

[Landlord and Tenant Act 1985, s 6.]

8–17497 7. Offences. (1) If the landlord of premises to which section 4(1) applies (premises occupied as a residence at a weekly rent) fails to comply with any relevant requirement of—

section 4 (provision of rent book),
section 5 (information to be contained in rent book), or
section 6 (information to be supplied by companies),

he commits a summary offence and is liable on conviction to a fine not exceeding **level 4** on the standard scale.

(2) If a person demands or receives rent on behalf of the landlord of such premises while any relevant requirement of—

section 4 (provision of rent book), or
section 5 (information to be contained in rent book),

is not complied with, then, unless he shows that he neither knew nor had reasonable cause to suspect that any such requirement had not been complied with, he commits a summary offence and is liable to a fine not exceeding **level 4** on the standard scale.

(3) If a person fails to comply with a requirement imposed on him by section 6(2) (duty to forward request to landlord), he commits a summary offence and is liable on conviction to a fine not exceeding level 4 on the standard scale.

(4) If a default in respect of which—

(*a*) a landlord is convicted of an offence under subsection (1), or

(*b*) another person is convicted of an offence under subsection (3),

continues for more than 14 days after the conviction, the landlord or other person commits a further offence under that subsection in respect of the default.

[Landlord and Tenant Act 1985, s 7.]

Service charges

8–17498 18. Meaning of "service charge" and "relevant costs". (1) In the following provisions of this Act "service charge" means an amount payable by a tenant of a dwelling as part of or in addition to the rent—

(*a*) which is payable, directly or indirectly, for services, repairs, maintenance, improvements or insurance or the landlord's costs of management, and

(*b*) the whole or part of which varies or may vary according to the relevant costs.

(2) The relevant costs are the costs or estimated costs incurred or to be incurred by or on behalf

of the landlord, or a superior landlord, in connection with the matters for which the service charge is payable.

(3) For this purpose—

(*a*) "costs" includes overheads, and

(*b*) costs are relevant costs in relation to a service charge whether they are incurred, or to be incurred, in the period for which the service charge is payable or in an earlier or later period.

[Landlord and Tenant Act 1985, s 18, as amended by the Landlord and Tenant Act 1987, Sch 2 and the Commonhold and Leasehold Reform Act 2002, s 150.]

8–17499 19. Limitation of service charges: reasonableness. (1) Relevant costs shall be taken into account in determining the amount of a service charge payable for a period—

(*a*) only to the extent that they are reasonably incurred, and

(*b*) where they are incurred on the provision of services or the carrying out of works, only if the services or works are of a reasonable standard;

and the amount payable shall be limited accordingly.

[Landlord and Tenant Act 1985, s 19 amended by the Landlord and Tenant Act 1987, Sch 2, the Courts and Legal Services Act 1990, Sch 20 and the Housing Act 1996, s 83 and Sch 19—summarised.]

8–17500 20, 20A, 20B, 20C. *Limitation of service charges: estimates and consultation.*

8–17501 21. Request for summary of relevant costs. (1) A tenant may require the landlord in writing to supply him with a written summary of the costs incurred—

(*a*) if the relevant accounts are made up for periods of twelve months, in the last such period ending not later than the date of the request, or

(*b*) if the accounts are not so made up, in the period of twelve months ending with the date of the request,

and which are relevant costs in relation to the service charges payable or demanded as payable in that or any other period.

(2) If the tenant is represented by a recognised tenants' association and he consents, the request may be made by the secretary of the association instead of by the tenant and may then be for the supply of the summary to the secretary.

(3) A request is duly served on the landlord if it is served on—

(*a*) an agent of the landlord named as such in the rent book or similar document, or

(*b*) the person who receives the rent on behalf of the landlord;

and a person on whom a request is so served shall forward it as soon as may be to the landlord.

(4) The landlord shall comply with the request within one month of the request or within six months of the end of the period referred to in subsection (1)(*a*) or (*b*) whichever is the later.

(5) The summary shall state whether any of the costs relate to works in respect of which a grant has been or is to be paid under section 523 of the Housing Act 1985 (assistance for provision of separate service pipe for water supply) or any provision of Part I of the Housing Grants, Construction and Regeneration Act 1996 (grants, &c. for renewal of private sector housing) or any corresponding earlier enactment and set out the costs in a way showing how they have been or will be reflected in demands for services charges, and, in addition, shall summarise each of the following items, namely—

(*a*) any of the costs in respect of which no demand for payment was received by the landlord within the period referred to in subsection (1)(*a*) or (*b*),

(*b*) any of the costs in respect of which—

(i) a demand for payment was so received, but

(ii) no payment was made by the landlord within that period, and

(*c*) any of the costs in respect of which—

(i) a demand for payment was so received, and

(ii) payment was made by the landlord within that period,

and specify the aggregate of any amounts received by the landlord down to the end of that period on account of service charges in respect of relevant dwellings and still standing to the credit of the tenants of whose dwellings at the end of that period.

(5A) In subsection (5) "relevant dwelling" means a dwelling whose tenant is either—

(*a*) the person by or with the consent of whom the request was made, or

(*b*) a person whose obligations under the terms of his lease as regards contributing to relevant costs relate to the same costs as the corresponding obligations of the person mentioned in paragraph (*a*) above relate to.

(5B) The summary shall state whether any of the costs relate to works which are included in the external works specified in a group repair scheme, within the meaning of Chapter II of Part I of the Housing Grants, Construction and Regeneration Act 1996 or any corresponding earlier enactment in which the landlord participated or is participating as an assisted participant.

(6) If the service charges in relation to which the costs are relevant costs as mentioned in subsection (1) are payable by the tenants of more than four dwellings, the summary shall be certified by a qualified accountant as—

(*a*) in this opinion a fair summary complying with the requirements of subsection (5), and
(*b*) being sufficiently supported by accounts, receipts and other documents which have been produced to him.*

[Landlord and Tenant Act 1985, s 21, as amended by the Housing and Planning Act 1986, Sch 5, the Landlord and Tenant Act 1987, Sch 2, the Local Government and Housing Act 1989, Sch 11 and the Housing Grants, Construction and Regeneration Act 1996, Sch 1.]

***Section substituted by new ss 21 and 21A by the Commonhold and Leasehold Reform Act 2002, s 152 from a date to be appointed. New s 21B inserted by the Commonhold and Leasehold Reform Act 2002, s 153 from a date to be appointed.**

8–17502 **22. Request to inspect supporting accounts, etc.** (1) This section applies where a tenant, or the secretary of a recognised tenants' association, has obtained such a summary as is referred to in section 21(1) (summary of relevant costs), whether in pursuance of that section or otherwise.

(2) The tenant, or the secretary with the consent of the tenant, may within six months of obtaining the summary require the landlord in writing to afford him reasonable facilities—

(*a*) for inspecting the accounts, receipts and other documents supporting the summary, and
(*b*) for taking copies or extracts from them.

(3) A request under this section is duly served on the landlord if it is served on—

(*a*) an agent of the landlord named as such in the rent book or similar document, or
(*b*) the person who receives the rent on behalf of the landlord;

and a person on whom a request is so served shall forward it as soon as may be to the landlord.

(4) The landlord shall make such facilities available to the tenant or secretary for a period of two months beginning not later than one month after the request is made.

(5) The landlord shall—

(*a*) where such facilities are for the inspection of any documents, make them so available free of charge;
(*b*) where such facilities are for the taking of copies or extracts, be entitled to make them so available on payment of such reasonable charge as he may determine.

(6) The requirement imposed on the landlord by subsection (5)(*a*) to make any facilities available to a person free of charge shall not be construed as precluding the landlord from treating as part of his costs of management any costs incurred by him in connection with making those facilities so available.*

[Landlord and Tenant Act 1985, s 22, as amended by the Landlord and Tenant Act 1987, Sch 2.]

***Section substituted by the Commonhold and Leasehold Reform Act 2002, s 154 from a date to be appointed.**

8–17503 **23. Information held by superior landlord.** (1) If a statement of account which the landlord is required to supply under section 21 relates to matters concerning a superior landlord and the landlord is not in possession of the relevant information—

(*a*) he may by notice in writing require the person who is his landlord to give him the relevant information (and so on, if that person is not himself the superior landlord), and
(*b*) the superior landlord must comply with the requirement within a reasonable time.

(2) If a notice under section 22 imposes a requirement in relation to documents held by a superior landlord—

(*a*) the landlord shall immediately inform the tenant or secretary of that fact and of the name and address of the superior landlord, and
(*b*) section 22 then applies in relation to the superior landlord (as in relation to the landlord).*

[Landlord and Tenant Act 1985, s 23, as substituted by the Commonhold and Leasehold Reform Act 2002, s 157.]

***Section in force in England 30 September 2003, date in force in Wales to be appointed.**

8–17503A **23A. Effect of change of landlord.** (1) This section applies where, at a time when a duty imposed on the landlord or a superior landlord by or by virtue of any of sections 21 to 23 remains to be discharged by him, he disposes of the whole or part of his interest as landlord or superior landlord to another person.

(2) If the landlord or superior landlord is, despite the disposal, still in a position to discharge the duty to any extent, he remains responsible for discharging it to that extent.

(3) If the other person is in a position to discharge the duty to any extent, he is responsible for discharging it to that extent.

(4) Where the other person is responsible for discharging the duty to any extent (whether or not the landlord or superior landlord is also responsible for discharging it to that or any other extent)—

(*a*) references to the landlord or superior landlord in sections 21 to 23 are to, or include, the other person so far as is appropriate to reflect his responsibility for discharging the duty to that extent, but

(*b*) in connection with its discharge by the other person, section 22(6) applies as if the reference to the day on which the landlord receives the notice were to the date of the disposal referred to in subsection (1).*

[Landlord and Tenant Act 1985, s 23A, as inserted by the Commonhold and Leasehold Reform Act 2002, s 157.]

***Section in force in England 30 September 2003, date in force in Wales to be appointed.**

8–17504 **24. Effect of assignment.** The assignment of a tenancy does not affect any duty imposed by or by virtue of any of sections 21 to 23A; but a person is not required to comply with more than a reasonable number of requirements imposed by any one person.*

[Landlord and Tenant Act 1985, s 24, as amended by the Landlord and Tenant Act 1987, Sch 2 and substituted by the Commonhold and Leasehold Reform Act 2002, s 157.]

***In force in England and Wales for certain purposes.**

8–17505 **25. Failure to comply with s 21, 22, or 23 an offence.** (1) It is summary offence for a person to fail, without reasonable excuse, to perform a duty imposed on him by or by virtue of any of sections 21 to 23A*.

(2) A person committing such an offence is liable on conviction to a fine not exceeding **level 4** on the standard scale.

[Landlord and Tenant Act 1985, s 25, as amended by the Commonhold and Leasehold Reform Act 2002, s 157.]

***Reproduced as amended, in force in England and Wales for certain purposes.**

8–17506 **26. Exception: tenants of certain public authorities.** (1) Sections 18 to 25 (limitation on service charges and requests for information about costs)* do not apply to a service charge payable by a tenant of—

a local authority,
a National Park authority, or
a new town corporation,

unless the tenancy is a long tenancy, in which case sections 18 to 24 apply but section 25 (offence of failure to comply) does not.

(2) The following are long tenancies for the purposes of subsection (1), subject to subsection (3)—

(*a*) a tenancy granted for a term certain exceeding 21 years, whether or not it is (or may become) terminable before the end of that term by notice given by the tenant or by re-entry or forfeiture;

(*b*) a tenancy for a term fixed by law under a grant with a covenant or obligation for perpetual renewal, other than a tenancy by sub-demise from one which is not a long tenancy;

(*c*) any tenancy granted in pursuance of Part V of the Housing Act 1985 (the right to buy, including any tenancy granted in pursuance of that Part as it has effect by virtue of section 17 of the Housing Act 1996 (the right to acquire).

(3) A tenancy granted so as to become terminable by notice after a death is not a long tenancy for the purposes of subsection (1), unless—

(*a*) it is granted by a housing association which at the time of the grant is a registered social landlord,

(*b*) it is granted at a premium calculated by reference to a percentage of the value of the dwelling-house or the cost of providing it, and

(*c*) at the time it is granted it complied with the requirements of the regulations then in force under section 140(4)(*b*) of the Housing Act 1980 or paragraph 4(2)(*b*) of Schedule 4A to the Leasehold Reform Act 1967 (conditions for exclusion of shared ownership leases from Part I of Leasehold Reform Act 1967) or, in the case of a tenancy granted before any such regulations were brought into force, with the first such regulations to be in force.

[Landlord and Tenant Act 1985, s 26, as amended by the Housing Act 1988, Sch 17, the Environment Act 1995, Sch 10, SI 1996/2325, SI 1997/627, the Government of Wales Act 1998, Schs 15 and 18 and the Commonhold and Leasehold Reform Act 2002, s 157.]

***Reproduced as amended, in force in England and Wales for certain purposes.**

8–17507 **27. Exception: rent registered and not entered as variable.** Sections 18 to 25 (limitation on service charges, statements of account and inspection etc of documents) do not apply

to a service charge payable by the tenant of a dwelling the rent of which is registered under Part IV of the Rent Act 1977, unless the amount registered is, in pursuance of section 71(4) of that Act, entered as a variable amount.
[Landlord and Tenant Act 1985, s 27, as amended by the Landlord and Tenant Act 1987, Sch 2 and the Commonhold and Leasehold Reform Act 2002, s 157.]

***Reproduced as amended, in force in England and Wales for certain purposes.**

8–17507A **27A. Liability to pay service charges: jurisdiction.** (1) An application may be made to a leasehold valuation tribunal for a determination whether a service charge is payable and, if it is, as to—

(*a*) the person by whom it is payable,
(*b*) the person to whom it is payable,
(*c*) the amount which is payable,
(*d*) the date at or by which it is payable, and
(*e*) the manner in which it is payable.

(2) Subsection (1) applies whether or not any payment has been made.

(3) An application may also be made to a leasehold valuation tribunal for a determination whether, if costs were incurred for services, repairs, maintenance, improvements, insurance or management of any specified description, a service charge would be payable for the costs and, if it would, as to—

(*a*) the person by whom it would be payable,
(*b*) the person to whom it would be payable,
(*c*) the amount which would be payable,
(*d*) the date at or by which it would be payable, and
(*e*) the manner in which it would be payable.

(4) No application under subsection (1) or (3) may be made in respect of a matter which—

(*a*) has been agreed or admitted by the tenant,
(*b*) has been, or is to be, referred to arbitration pursuant to a post-dispute arbitration agreement to which the tenant is a party,
(*c*) has been the subject of determination by a court, or
(*d*) has been the subject of determination by an arbitral tribunal pursuant to a post-dispute arbitration agreement.

(5) But the tenant is not to be taken to have agreed or admitted any matter by reason only of having made any payment.

(6) An agreement by the tenant of a dwelling (other than a post-dispute arbitration agreement) is void in so far as it purports to provide for a determination—

(*a*) in a particular manner, or
(*b*) on particular evidence,

of any question which may be the subject of an application under subsection (1) or (3).

(7) The jurisdiction conferred on a leasehold valuation tribunal in respect of any matter by virtue of this section is in addition to any jurisdiction of a court in respect of the matter.*
[Landlord and Tenant Act 1985, s 27A, as inserted by the Commonhold and Leasehold Reform Act 2002, s 157.]

***Reproduced as amended, in force in England and Wales for certain purposes.**

8–17508 **28. Meaning of "qualified accountant".** (1) The reference to a "qualified accountant" in section 21(3)(*a*) (certification of statements of account) is to a person who, in accordance with the following provisions, has the necessary qualification and is not disqualified from acting.

(2) A person has the necessary qualification if he is eligible for appointment as a company auditor under section 25 of the Companies Act 1989.

(3) *Repealed.*

(4) The following are disqualified from acting—

(*a*) *Repealed*;
(*b*) an officer, employee or partner of the landlord or, where the landlord is a company, of an associated company;
(*c*) a person who is a partner or employee of any such officer or employee.
(*d*) an agent of the landlord who is a managing agent for any premises to which the statement of account in question relates;
(*e*) an employee or partner of any such agent.

(5) For the purposes of subsection (4)(*b*) a company is associated with a landlord company if it is (within the meaning of section 736 of the Companies Act 1985) the landlord's holding company, a subsidiary of the landlord or another subsidiary of the landlord's holding company.

(5A) For the purposes of subsection (4)(*d*) a person is a managing agent for any premises to which a statement of account relates if he has been appointed to discharge any of the landlord's obligations relating to the management by him of the premises and owed to the tenants who may be required under the terms of their leases to contribute to costs covered by the statement of account by the payment of service charges.

(6) Where the landlord is an emanation of the Crown a local authority, a National Park authority or a new town corporation—

(*a*) the persons who have the necessary qualification include members of the Chartered Institute of Public Finance and Accountancy, and

(*b*) subsection (4)(*b*) (disqualification of officers and employees of landlord) does not apply.*

[Landlord and Tenant Act 1985, s 28, as amended by the Landlord and Tenant Act 1987, Sch 2, SI 1991/1997, the Environment Act 1995, Sch 10, the Government of Wales Act 1998, Sch 15 and.]

***Reproduced as amended by the Commonhold and Leasehold Reform Act 2002, s 157, in force in England and Wales for certain purposes.**

8–17509 **29. Meaning of "recognised tenants' association".** (1) A recognised tenants' association is an association of qualifying tenants (whether with or without other tenants) which is recognised for the purposes of the provisions of this Act relating to service charges either—

(*a*) by notice in writing given by the landlord to the secretary of the association, or

(*b*) by a certificate of a member of the local rent assessment committee panel.

(2) A notice given under subsection (1)(*a*) may be withdrawn by the landlord by notice in writing given to the secretary of the association not less than six months before the date on which it is to be withdrawn.

(3) A certificate given under subsection (1)(*b*) may be cancelled by any member of the local rent assessment committee panel.

(4) In this section the "local rent assessment committee panel" means the persons appointed by the Lord Chancellor under the Rent Act 1977 to the panel of persons to act as members of a rent assessment committee for the registration area in which the dwellings let to the qualifying tenants are situated, and for the purposes of this section a number of tenants are qualifying tenants if each of them may be required under the terms of his lease to contribute to the same costs by the payment of a service charge.

(5)—(6) *Power of the Secretary of State may by regulations to specify the matters to which regard is to be had in giving or cancelling a certificate under subsection (1)(b).*

[Landlord and Tenant Act 1985, s 29, as amended by the Landlord and Tenant Act 1987, Sch 2.]

8–17510 **30. Meaning of "landlord" and "tenant".** In the provisions of this Act relating to service charges—

"landlord" includes any person who has a right to enforce payment of a service charge;
"tenant" includes—

(*a*) a statutory tenant, and

(*b*) where the dwelling or part of it is sub-let, the sub-tenant.

[Landlord and Tenant Act 1985, s 30, as amended by the Landlord and Tenant Act 1987, Schs 2 and 5.]

Insurance

8–17520 **30A. Rights of tenants with respect to insurance.** The Schedule[1] to this Act (which confers on tenants certain rights with respect to the insurance of their dwellings) shall have effect.

[Landlord and Tenant Act 1985, s 30A, as inserted by the Landlord and Tenant Act 1987, s 43.]

1. The Schedule is printed, in this PART, post.

Managing agents

8–17521 **30B.** *Recognised tenants' associations to be consulted about managing agents.*

Supplementary provisions

8–17522 **32. Provisions not applying to tenancies within Part II of the Landlord and Tenant Act 1954.** (1) The following provisions do not apply to a tenancy to which Part II of the Landlord and Tenant Act 1954 (business tenancies) applies—

sections 1 to 3A (information to be given to tenant),
section 17 (specific performance of landlord's repairing obligations).

(2)–(3) *Section 11 and 31 not to apply to such tenancies.*

[Landlord and Tenant Act 1985, s 32, as amended by the Housing Act 1996, s 93.]

8–17523 **33. Liability of directors, etc for offences by body corporate.** (1) Where an offence under this Act which has been committed by a body corporate is proved—

(*a*) to have been committed with the consent or connivance of a director, manager, secretary or other similar officer of the body corporate, or a person purporting to act in any such capacity, or

(*b*) to be attributable to any neglect on the part of such an officer or person,

he, as well as the body corporate, is guilty of an offence and liable to be proceeded against and punished accordingly.

(2) Where the affairs of a body corporate are managed by its members, subsection (1) applies in relation to the acts and defaults of a member in connection with his functions of management as if he were a director of the body corporate.

[Landlord and Tenant Act 1985, s 33.]

8–17524 **34. Power of local housing authority to prosecute.** Proceedings for an offence under any provision of this Act may be brought by a local housing authority.

[Landlord and Tenant Act 1985, s 34.]

8–17525 **35. Application to Isles of Scilly.** (1) This Act applies to the Isles of Scilly subject to such exceptions, adaptations and modifications as the Secretary of State may by order direct.

(2) An order shall be made by statutory instrument which shall be subject to annulment in pursuance of a resolution of either House of Parliament.

[Landlord and Tenant Act 1985, s 35.]

8–17526 **36. Meaning of "lease" and "tenancy" and related expressions.** (1) In this Act "lease" and "tenancy" have the same meaning.

(2) Both expressions include—

(*a*) a sub-lease or sub-tenancy, and

(*b*) an agreement for a lease or tenancy (or sub-lease or sub-tenancy).

(3) The expressions "lessor" and "lessee" and "landlord" and "tenant", and references to letting, to the grant of a lease or to covenants or terms, shall be construed accordingly.

[Landlord and Tenant Act 1985, s 36.]

8–17527 **37. Meaning of "statutory tenant" and related expressions.** In this Act—

(*a*) "statutory tenancy" and "statutory tenant" mean a statutory tenancy or statutory tenant within the meaning of the Rent Act 1977 or the Rent (Agriculture) Act 1976; and

(*b*) "landlord", in relation to a statutory tenant, means the person who, apart from the statutory tenancy, would be entitled to possession of the premises.

[Landlord and Tenant Act 1985, s 37.]

8–17528 **38. Minor definitions.** In this Act—

"address" means a person's place of abode or place of business or, in the case of a company, its registered office;

"arbitration agreement", "arbitration proceedings" and "arbitral tribunal" have the same meaning as in Part I of the Arbitration Act 1996 and post-dispute arbitration agreement, in relation to any matter, means an arbitration agreement made after a dispute about the matter has arisen;*

"co-operative housing association" has the same meaning as in the Housing Associations Act 1985;

"dwelling" means a building or part of a building occupied or intended to be occupied as a separate dwelling, together with any yard, garden, outhouses and appurtenances belonging to it or usually enjoyed with it;

"housing association" has the same meaning as in the Housing Associations Act 1985;

"local authority" means a district, county, county borough or London borough council, the Common Council of the City of London or the Council of the Isles of Scilly and in sections 14(4), 26(1) and 28(6) includes the Broads Authority, a police authority established under section 3 of the Police Act 1996, the Metropolitan Police Authority, a joint authority established by Part IV of the Local Government Act 1985 and the London Fire and Emergency Planning Authority;

"local housing authority" has the meaning given by section 1 of the Housing Act 1985;

"new town corporation" means—

(*a*) a development corporation established by an order made, or treated as made, under the New Towns Act 1981, or

(*b*) the Commission for the New Towns;

"protected tenancy" has the same meaning as in the Rent Act 1977;

"registered social landlord" has the same meaning as in the Housing Act 1985 (see section 5(4) and (5) of that Act);

"restricted contract" has the same meaning as in the Rent Act 1977;

"urban development corporation" has the same meaning as in Part XVI of the Local Government, Planning and Land Act 1980.

[Landlord and Tenant Act 1985, s 38, as amended by the Norfolk and Suffolk Broads Act 1988, Sch 6, the Education Reform Act 1988, Sch 13, the Local Government (Wales) Act 1994, Sch 8, the Police and Magistrates' Courts Act 1994, Sch 4, the Police Act 1996, Sch 7, SI 1996/2325, the Housing Act 1996 s 83, the Police Act 1997 Sch 9, the Greater London Authority Act 1999, Schs 27, 29 and 34, the Criminal Justice and Police Act 2001, Sch 6 and the Commonhold and Leasehold Reform Act 2002, s 155(2).]

***These definitions as amended by the Commonhold and Leasehold Reform Act 2002, s 157 in force in England and Wales (except in relation to applications made to or proceedings transferred to a LVT before that date).**

8–17529 **39. Index of defined expressions.** The following Table shows provisions defining or otherwise explaining expressions used in this Act (other than provisions defining or explaining an expression in the same section):

Address	section 38
arbitration agreement, arbitration proceedings, arbitral tribunal and post-dispute arbitration agreement*	section 38
co-operative housing association	section 38
Dwelling	section 38
dwelling-house (in the provisions relating to repairing obligations)	section 16
fit for human habitation	section 10
housing association	section 38
landlord—	
(generally)	section 36(3)
(in sections 1 and 2)	section 1(3)
(in the provisions relating to rent books)	section 4(3)
(in the provisions relating to service charges)	section 30
(in relation to a statutory tenancy)	section 37(*b*)
lease, lessee and lessor—	
(generally)	section 36
(in the provisions relating to repairing obligations)	section 16
local authority	section 38
local housing authority	section 38
new town corporation	section 38
protected tenancy	section 38
qualified accountant (for the purposes of section 21(3)(*a*))*	section 28
registered social landlord	section 38
recognised tenants' association	section 29
relevant costs (in relation to a service charge)	section 18(2)
restricted contract	section 38
service charge	section 18(1)
statutory tenant	section 37(*a*)
tenancy and tenant—	
(generally)	section 36
(in sections 1 and 2)	section 1(3)
(in the provisions relating to rent books)	section 4(3)
(in the provisions relating to service charges)	section 30
urban development corporation	section 38

[Landlord and Tenant Act 1985, s 39, as amended by the Housing Act 1996, s 83, SI 1996/2325 and the Commonhold and Leasehold Reform Act 2002, ss 155(3) and 180.]

***Reproduced as amended by the Commonhold and Leasehold Reform Act 2002; in force in England and Wales (except in relation to applications made to or proceedings transferred to a LVT before that date).**

Final provisions

8–17530 **40. Short title, commencement and extent.** (1) This Act may be cited as the Landlord and Tenant Act 1985.

(2) This Act comes into force on 1st April 1986.

(3) This Act extends to England and Wales.

[Landlord and Tenant Act 1985, s 40.]

SCHEDULE
RIGHTS OF TENANTS WITH RESPECT TO INSURANCE

(As inserted by the Landlord and Tenant Act 1987, s 43 and Sch 3 and amended by the Environment Act 1995, Sch 10, the Government of Wales Act 1998, Schs 15 and 18. the Commonhold and Leasehold Reform Act 2002, s 157 and the Commonhold and Leasehold Reform Act 2002, s 165.)

Construction

8–17531 **1.** In this Schedule—

"landlord", in relation to a tenant by whom a service charge is payable which includes an amount payable directly or indirectly for insurance, includes any person who has a right to enforce payment of that service charge;

"relevant policy, in relation to a dwelling, means any policy of insurance under which the dwelling is insured (being, in the case of a flat, a policy covering the building containing it); and

"tenant" includes a statutory tenant.

Summary of insurance cover

2. (1) Where a service charge is payable by the tenant of a dwelling which consists of or includes an amount payable directly or indirectly for insurance, the tenant may by notice in writing require the landlord to supply him with a written summary of the insurance for the time being effected in relation to the dwelling.

(2) If the tenant is represented by a recognised tenants' association and he consents, the notice may be served by the secretary of the association instead of by the tenant and may then be for the supply of the summary to the secretary.

(3) A notice under this paragraph is duly served on the landlord if it is served on—

(*a*) an agent of the landlord named as such in the rent book or similar document, or

(*b*) the person who receives the rent on behalf of the landlord;

and a person on whom such a notice under this paragraph is duly served shall forward it as soon as may be to the landlord.

(4) The landlord shall, within the period of twenty-one days beginning with the day on which he receives the notice, comply with it by supplying to the tenant or the secretary of the recognised tenants' association (as the case may require) such a summary as is mentioned in sub-paragraph (1), which shall include—

(*a*) the insured amount or amounts under any relevant policy, and

(*b*) the name of the insurer under any such policy, and

(*c*) the risks in respect of which the dwelling or (as the case may be) the building containing it is insured under any such policy.

(5) In sub-paragraph (4)(*a*) "the insured amount or amounts", in relation to a relevant policy, means—

(*a*) in the case of a dwelling other than a flat, the amount for which the dwelling is insured under the policy; and

(*b*) in the case of a flat, the amount for which the building containing it is insured under the policy and, if specified in the policy, the amount for which the flat is insured under it.

(6) The landlord shall be taken to have complied with the notice if, within the period mentioned in sub-paragraph (4), he instead supplies to the tenant or the secretary (as the case may require) a copy of every relevant policy.

(7) In a case where two or more buildings are insured under any relevant policy, the summary or copy supplied under sub-paragraph (4) or (6) so far as relating to that policy need only be of such parts of the policy as relate—

(*a*) to the dwelling, and

(*b*) if the dwelling is a flat, to the building containing it.

Inspection of insurance policy etc

3. (1) Where a service charge is payable by the tenant of a dwelling which consists of or includes an amount payable directly or indirectly for insurance, the tenant may by notice in writing require the landlord—

(*a*) to afford him reasonable facilities for inspecting any relevant policy or associated documents and for taking copies of or extracts from them, or

(*b*) to take copies of or extracts from any such policy or documents and either send them to him or afford him reasonable facilities for collecting them (as he specifies).

(2) If the tenant is represented by a recognised tenants' association and he consents, the notice may be served by the secretary of the association instead of by the tenant (and in that case any requirement imposed by it is to afford reasonable facilities, or to send copies or extracts, to the secretary).

(3) A notice under this paragraph is duly served on the landlord if it is served on—

(*a*) an agent of the landlord named as such in the rent book or similar document, or

(*b*) the person who receives the rent on behalf of the landlord;

and a person on whom such a notice is so served shall forward it as soon as may be to the landlord.

(4) The landlord shall comply with a requirement imposed by a notice under this paragraph within the period of twenty-one days beginning with the day on which he receives the notice.

(5) To the extent that a notice under this paragraph requires the landlord to afford facilities for inspecting documents—

(*a*) he shall do so free of charge, but
(*b*) he may treat as part of his costs of management any costs incurred by him in doing so.

(6) The landlord may make a reasonable charge for doing anything else in compliance with a requirement imposed by a notice under this paragraph.

(7) In this paragraph—

"relevant policy" includes a policy of insurance under which the dwelling was insured for the period of insurance immediately preceding that current when the notice is served (being, in the case of a flat, a policy covering the building containing it), and

"associated documents" means accounts, receipts or other documents which provide evidence of payment of any premiums due under a relevant policy in respect of the period of insurance which is current when the notice is served or the period of insurance immediately preceding that period.

Insurance effected by superior landlord

4. (1) If a notice is served under paragraph 2 in a case where a superior landlord has effected, in whole or in part, the insurance of the dwelling in question and the landlord on whom the notice is served is not in possession of the relevant information—

(*a*) he shall in turn by notice in writing require the person who is his landlord to give him the relevant information (and so on, if that person is not himself the superior landlord),
(*b*) the superior landlord shall comply with the notice within a reasonable time, and
(*c*) the immediate landlord shall then comply with the tenant's or secretary's notice in the manner provided by sub-paragraphs (4) to (7) of paragraph 2 within the time allowed by that paragraph or such further time, if any, as is reasonable in the circumstances.

(2) If, in a case where a superior landlord has effected, in whole or in part, the insurance of the dwelling in question, a notice under paragraph 3 imposes a requirement relating to any policy of insurance effected by the superior landlord—

(*a*) the landlord on whom the notice is served shall forthwith inform the tenant or secretary of that fact and of the name and address of the superior landlord, and
(*b*) that paragraph shall then apply to the superior landlord in relation to that policy as it applies to the immediate landlord.

Effect of change of landlord

4A. (1) This paragraph applies where, at a time when a duty imposed on the landlord or a superior landlord by virtue of any of paragraphs 2 to 4 remains to be discharged by him, he disposes of the whole or part of his interest as landlord or superior landlord).

(2) If the landlord or superior landlord is, despite the disposal, still in a position to discharge the duty to any extent, he remains responsible for discharging it to that extent.

(3) If the other person is in a position to discharge the duty to any extent, he is responsible for discharging it to that extent.

(4) Where the other person is responsible for discharging the duty to any extent (whether or not the landlord or superior landlord is also responsible for discharging it to that or any other extent)—

(*a*) references to the landlord or superior landlord in paragraphs 2 to 4 are to, or include, the other person so far as is appropriate to reflect his responsibility for discharging the duty to that extent, but
(*b*) in connection with its discharge by that person, paragraphs 2(4) and 3(4) apply as if the reference to the day on which the landlord receives the notice were to the date of the disposal referred to in sub-paragraph (1).

Effect of assignment

5. The assignment of a tenancy does not affect any duty imposed by virtue of any of paragraphs 2 to 4A; but a person is not required to comply with more than a reasonable number of requirements imposed by any one person.

Offence of failure to comply

6. (1) It is a summary offence for a person to fail, without reasonable excuse, to perform a duty imposed on him by or by virtue of any of paragraphs 2 to 4A.

(2) A person committing such an offence is liable on conviction to a fine not exceeding **level 4** on the standard scale.

7. *Tenant's right to notify insurers of possible claim.*

8. *Right to challenge landlord's choice of insurers.*

Exception for tenants of certain public authorities

9. (1) Paragraphs 2 to 8 do not apply to a tenant of—

a local authority,
a National Park authority, or
a new town corporation,

unless the tenancy is a long tenancy, in which case paragraphs 2 to 5 and 7 and 8 apply but paragraph 6 does not.

(2) Subsections (2) and (3) of section 26 shall apply for the purposes of subparagraph (1) as they apply for the purposes of subsection (1) of that section.

Landlord and Tenant Act 1987

(1987 c 31)

PART I[1]

TENANTS' RIGHTS OF FIRST REFUSAL

Preliminary

8–17532 **1. Qualifying tenants to have rights of first refusal on disposals by landlord.** (1) A landlord shall not make a relevant disposal affecting any premises to which at the time of the disposal this Part applies unless—

(*a*) he has in accordance with section 5 previously served a notice under that section with respect to the disposal on the qualifying tenants of the flats contained in those premises (being a notice by virtue of which rights of first refusal are conferred on those tenants); and

(*b*) the disposal is made in accordance with the requirements of sections 6 to 10.

(2) Subject to subsections (3) and (4), this Part applies to premises if—

(*a*) they consist of the whole or part of a building; and

(*b*) they contain two or more flats held by qualifying tenants; and

(*c*) the number of flats held by such tenants exceeds 50 per cent of the total number of flats contained in the premises.

(3) This Part does not apply to premises falling within subsection (2) if—

(*a*) any part or parts of the premises is or are occupied or intended to be occupied otherwise than for residential purposes; and

(*b*) the internal floor area of that part or those parts (taken together) exceeds 50 per cent of the internal floor area of the premises (taken as a whole);

and for the purposes of this subsection the internal floor area of any common parts shall be disregarded.

(4) This Part also does not apply to any such premises at a time when the interest of the landlord in the premises is held by an exempt landlord or a resident landlord.

(5) The Secretary of State may by order substitute for the percentage for the time being specified in subsection (3)(*b*) such other percentage as is specified in the order.

[Landlord and Tenant Act 1987, s 1.]

1. Part I contains ss 1–20.

8–17533 **2. Landlords for the purposes of Part I.** (1) Subject to subsection (2) and section 4(1A), a person is for the purposes of this Part the landlord in relation to any premises consisting of the whole or part of a building if he is—

(*a*) the immediate landlord of the qualifying tenants of the flats contained in those premises, or

(*b*) where any of those tenants is a statutory tenant, the person who, apart from the statutory tenancy, would be entitled to possession of the flat in question.

(2) Where the person who is, in accordance with subsection (1), the landlord in relation to any such premises for the purposes of this Part ("the immediate landlord" is himself a tenant of those premises under a tenancy which is either—

(*a*) a tenancy for a term of less than seven years, or

(*b*) a tenancy for a longer term but terminable within the first seven years at the option of the person who is the landlord under that tenancy ("the superior landlord"),

the superior landlord shall also be regarded as the landlord in relation to those premises for the purposes of this Part and, if the superior landlord is himself a tenant of those premises under a tenancy falling within paragraph (*a*) or (*b*) above, the person who is the landlord under that tenancy shall also be so regarded (and so on).

[Landlord and Tenant Act 1987, s 2, as amended by the Housing Act 1988, s 119 and Sch 13.]

8–17534 **3. Qualifying tenants.** (1) Subject to the following provisions of this section, a person is for the purposes of this Part a qualifying tenant of a flat if he is the tenant of the flat under a tenancy other than—

(*a*) a protected shorthold tenancy as defined in section 52 of the Housing Act 1980;

(*b*) a tenancy to which Part II of the Landlord and Tenant Act 1954 (business tenancies) applies;

(*c*) a tenancy terminable on the cessation of his employment or

(*d*) an assured tenancy or assured agricultural occupancy within the meaning of Part I of the Housing Act 1988.

(2) A person is not to be regarded as being a qualifying tenant of any flat contained in any particular premises consisting of the whole or part of a building if by virtue of one or more tenancies

none of which falls within paragraphs (*a*) to (*d*) of subsection (1), he is the tenant not only of the flat in question but also of at least two other flats contained in those premises.

(3) For the purposes of subsection (2) any tenant of a flat contained in the premises in question who is a body corporate shall be treated as the tenant of any other flat so contained and let to an associated company.

(4) A tenant of a flat whose landlord is a qualifying tenant of that flat is not to be regarded as being a qualifying tenant of that flat.

[Landlord and Tenant Act 1987, s 3, as amended by the Housing Act 1988, s 119, 140 and Sch 13.]

8–17535 **4. Relevant disposals.** (1) In this Part references to a relevant disposal affecting any premises to which this Part applies are references to the disposal by the landlord of any estate or interest (whether legal or equitable) in any such premises, including the disposal of any such estate or interest in any common parts of any such premises but excluding—

(*a*) the grant of any tenancy under which the demised premises consist of a single flat (whether with or without any appurtenant premises); and

(*b*) any of the disposals falling within subsection (2).

(1A) Where an estate or interest of the landlord has been mortgaged, the reference in subsection (1) above to the disposal of an estate or interest by the landlord includes a reference to its disposal by the mortgagee in exercise of a power of sale or leasing, whether or not the disposal is made in the name of the landlord; and, in relation to such a proposed disposal by the mortgagee, any reference in the following provisions of this Part to the landlord shall be construed as a reference to the mortgagee.

(2) The disposals referred to in subsection (1)(*b*) are—

(*a*) a disposal of—

(i) any interest of a beneficiary in settled land within the meaning of the Settled Land Act 1925, or

(ii) *Repealed*;

(iii) any incorporeal hereditament;

(*aa*) a disposal by way of security for a loan

(*b*) a disposal to a trustee in bankruptcy or to the liquidator of a company;

(*c*) a disposal in pursuance of an order made under—

(i) section 24* of the Matrimonial Causes Act 1973 (property adjustment orders in connection with matrimonial proceedings),

(ii) section 24A of the Matrimonial Causes Act 1973 (orders for the sale of property in connection with matrimonial proceedings) where the order includes provision requiring the property concerned to be offered for sale to a person or class of persons specified in the order,

(iii) section 2 of the Inheritance (Provision for Family and Dependants) Act 1975 (orders as to financial provision to be made from estate),

(iv) section 17(1) of the Matrimonial and Family Proceedings Act 1984 (property adjustment orders after overseas divorce, &c.),

(v) section 17(2) of the Matrimonial and Family Proceedings Act 1984 (orders for the sale of property after overseas divorce, &c.) where the order includes provision requiring the property concerned to be offered for sale to a person or class of persons specified in the order,

(vi) paragraph 1 of Schedule 1 to the Children Act 1989 (orders for financial relief against parents);

(vii) Part 2 of Schedule 5, or paragraph 9(2) or (3) of Schedule 7, to the Civil Partnership Act 2004 (property adjustment orders in connection with civil partnership proceedings or after overseas dissolution of a civil partnership, etc), or

(viii) Part 3 of Schedule 5, or paragraph 9(4) of Schedule 7, to the Civil Partnership Act 2004 (orders for the sale of property in connection with civil partnership proceedings or after overseas dissolution of a civil partnership, etc) where the order includes provision requiring the property concerned to be offered for sale to a person or class of persons specified in the order;

(*d*) a disposal in pursuance of a compulsory purchase order or in pursuance of an agreement entered into in circumstances where, but for the agreement, such an order would have been made or (as the case may be) carried into effect;

(*da*) a disposal of any freehold or leasehold interest in pursuance of Chapter I of Part I of the Leasehold Reform, Housing and Urban Development Act 1993;

(*e*) a disposal by way of gift to a member of the landlord's family or to a charity;

(*f*) a disposal by one charity to another of an estate or interest in land which prior to the disposal is functional land of the first-mentioned charity and which is intended to be functional land of the other charity once the disposal is made;

(*g*) a disposal consisting of the transfer of an estate or interest held on trust for any person where the disposal is made in connection with the appointment of a new trustee or in connection with the discharge of any trustee;

(*h*) a disposal consisting of a transfer by two or more persons who are members of the same family either—
 (i) to fewer of their number or,
 (ii) to a different combination of members of the family (but one that includes at least one of the transferors);

(*i*) a disposal in pursuance of a contract, option or right of pre-emption binding on the landlord (except as provided by section 8D (application of sections 11 to 17 to disposal in pursuance of option or right of pre-emption));

(*j*) a disposal consisting of the surrender of a tenancy in pursuance of any covenant, condition or agreement contained in it;

(*k*) a disposal to the Crown; and

(*l*) a disposal by a body corporate to a company which has been an associated company of that body for at least two years.

(3) In this Part "disposal" means a disposal whether by the creation or the transfer of an estate or interest and—

(*a*) includes the surrender of a tenancy and the grant of an option or right of pre-emption, but
(*b*) excludes a disposal under the terms of a will or under the law relating to intestacy;

and references in this Part to the transferee in connection with a disposal shall be construed accordingly.

(4) In this section "appurtenant premises", in relation to any flat, means any yard, garden, outhouse or appurtenance (not being a common part of the building containing the flat) which belongs to, or is usually enjoyed with, the flat.

(5) A person is a member of another's family for the purposes of this section if—

(*a*) that person is the spouse or civil partner of that other person, or the two of them live together as husband and wife or as if they were civil partners, or
(*b*) that person is that other person's parent, grandparent, child, grandchild, brother, sister, uncle, aunt, nephew or niece.

(6) For the purposes of subsection (5) (*b*)—

(*a*) a relationship by marriage or civil partnership shall be treated as a relationship by blood,
(*b*) a relationship of the half-blood shall be treated as a relationship of the whole blood,
(*c*) the stepchild of a person shall be treated as his child, and
(*d*) the illegitimate child shall be treated as the legitimate child of his mother and reputed father.

[Landlord and Tenant Act 1987, s 4, as amended by the Housing Act 1988, ss 119, 140 and Schs 13 and 18, the Leasehold Reform, Housing and Urban Development Act 1993, s 187 and Sch 21, the Housing Act 1996, ss 89 and 90, Schs 18 and 19 and the Civil Partnership Act 2004, Schs 8 and 30.]

8–17536 4A. Application of provisions to contracts. (1) The provisions of this Part apply to a contract to create or transfer an estate or interest in land, whether conditional or unconditional and whether or not enforceable by specific performance, as they apply in relation to a disposal consisting of the creation or transfer of such an estate or interest.

As they so apply—

(*a*) references to a disposal of any description shall be construed as references to a contract to make such a disposal;
(*b*) references to making a disposal of any description shall be construed as references to entering into a contract to make such a disposal; and
(*c*) references to the transferee under the disposal shall be construed as references to the other party to the contract and include a reference to any other person to whom an estate or interest is to be granted or transferred in pursuance of the contract.

(2) The provisions of this Part apply to an assignment of rights under such a contract as is mentioned in subsection (1) as they apply in relation to a disposal consisting of the transfer of an estate or interest in land.

As they so apply—

(*a*) references to a disposal of any description shall be construed as references to an assignment of rights under a contract to make such a disposal;
(*b*) references to making a disposal of any description shall be construed as references to making an assignment of rights under a contract to make such a disposal;
(*c*) references to the landlord shall be construed as references to the assignor; and
(*d*) references to the transferee under the disposal shall be construed as references to the assignee of such rights.

(3) The provisions of this Part apply to a contract to make such an assignment as is mentioned in subsection (2) as they apply (in accordance with subsection (1)) to a contract to create or transfer an estate or interest in land.

(4) Nothing in this section affects the operation of the provisions of this Part relating to options or rights of pre-emption.
[Landlord and Tenant Act 1987, s 4A, as inserted by the Housing Act 1996 s 89.]

Rights of first refusal

8–17537 **5. Landlord required to serve offer notice on tenants.** (1) Where the landlord proposes to make a relevant disposal affecting premises to which this Part applies, he shall serve a notice under this section (an "offer notice") on the qualifying tenants of the flats contained in the premises (the "constituent flats").

(2) An offer notice must comply with the requirements of whichever is applicable of the following sections—

section 5A (requirements in case of contract to be completed by conveyance, &c.),
section 5B (requirements in case of sale at auction),
section 5C (requirements in case of grant of option or right of pre-emption),
section 5D (requirements in case of conveyance not preceded by contract, &c.);

and in the case of a disposal to which section 5E applies (disposal for non-monetary consideration) shall also comply with the requirements of that section.

(3) Where a landlord proposes to effect a transaction involving the disposal of an estate or interest in more than one building (whether or not involving the same estate or interest), he shall, for the purpose of complying with this section, sever the transaction so as to deal with each building separately.

(4) If, as a result of the offer notice being served on different tenants on different dates, the period specified in the notice as the period for accepting the offer would end on different dates, the notice shall have effect in relation to all the qualifying tenants on whom it is served as if it provided for that period to end with the latest of those dates.

(5) A landlord who has not served an offer notice on all of the qualifying tenants on whom it was required to be served shall nevertheless be treated as having complied with this section—

(*a*) if he has served an offer notice on not less than 90% of the qualifying tenants on whom such a notice was required to be served, or
(*b*) where the qualifying tenants on whom it was required to be served number less than ten, if he has served such a notice on all but one of them.

[Landlord and Tenant Act 1987, s 5, as substituted by the Housing Act 1996, Sch 6.]

8–17538 **5A. Offer notice: requirements in case of contract to be completed by conveyance, &c.** (1) The following requirements must be met in relation to an offer notice where the disposal consists of entering into a contract to create or transfer an estate or interest in land.

(2) The notice must contain particulars of the principal terms of the disposal proposed by the landlord, including in particular—

(*a*) the property, and the estate or interest in that property, to which the contract relates.
(*b*) the principal terms of the contract (including the deposit and consideration required).

(3) The notice must state that the notice constitutes an offer by the landlord to enter into a contract on those terms which may be accepted by the requisite majority of qualifying tenants of the constituent flats.

(4) The notice must specify a period within which that offer may be so accepted, being a period of not less than two months which is to begin with the date of service of the notice.

(5) The notice must specify a further period of not less than two months within which a person or persons may be nominated by the tenants under section 6.

(6) This section does not apply to the grant of an option or right of pre-emption (see section 5C).
[Landlord and Tenant Act 1987, s 5A, as inserted by the Housing Act 1996, Sch 6.]

8–17539 **5B. Offer notice: requirements in case of sale by auction.** (1) The following requirements must be met in relation to an offer notice where the landlord proposes to make the disposal by means of a sale at a public auction held in England and Wales.

(2) The notice must contain particulars of the principal terms of the disposal proposed by the landlord, including in particular the property to which it relates and the estate or interest in that property proposed to be disposed of.

(3) The notice must state that the disposal is proposed to be made by means of a sale at a public auction.

(4) The notice must state that the notice constitutes an offer by the landlord, which may be accepted by the requisite majority of qualifying tenants of the constituent flats, for the contract (if any) entered into by the landlord at the auction to have effect as if a person or persons nominated by them, and not the purchaser, had entered into it.

(5) The notice must specify a period within which that offer may be so accepted, being a period of not less than two months beginning with the date of service of the notice.

(6) The notice must specify a further period of not less than 28 days within which a person or persons may be nominated by the tenants under section 6.

(7) The notice must be served not less than four months or more than six months before the date of the auction; and—

(*a*) the period specified in the notice as the period within which the offer may be accepted must end not less than two months before the date of the auction, and

(*b*) the period specified in the notice as the period within which a person may be nominated under section 6 must end not less than 28 days before the date of the auction.

(8) Unless the time and place of the auction and the name of the auctioneers are stated in the notice, the landlord shall, not less than 28 days before the date of the auction, serve on the requisite majority of qualifying tenants of the constituent flats a further notice stating those particulars.

[Landlord and Tenant Act 1987, s 5B, as inserted by the Housing Act 1996, Sch 6.]

8–17540 5C. Offer notice: requirements in case of grant or option or right of pre-emption. (1) The following requirements must be met in relation to an offer notice where the disposal consists of the grant of an option or right of pre-emption.

(2) The notice must contain particulars of the principal terms of the disposal proposed by the landlord, including in particular—

(*a*) the property, and the estate or interest in that property, to which the option or right of pre-emption relates,

(*b*) the consideration required by the landlord for granting the option or right of pre-emption, and

(*c*) the principal terms on which the option or right of pre-emption would be exercisable, including the consideration payable on its exercise.

(3) The notice must state that the notice constitutes an offer by the landlord to grant an option or right of pre-emption on those terms which may be accepted by the requisite majority of qualifying tenants of the constituent flats.

(4) The notice must specify a period within which that offer may be so accepted, being a period of not less than two months which is to begin with the date of service of the notice.

(5) The notice must specify a further period of not less than two months within which a person or persons may be nominated by the tenants under section 6.

[Landlord and Tenant Act 1987, s 5C, as inserted by the Housing Act 1996, Sch 6.]

8–17541 5D. Offer notice: requirements in case of conveyance not preceded by contract, &c. (1) The following requirements must be met in relation to an offer notice where the disposal is not made in pursuance of a contract, option or right of pre-emption binding on the landlord.

(2) The notice must contain particulars of the principal terms of the disposal proposed by the landlord, including in particular—

(*a*) the property to which it relates and the estate or interest in that property proposed to be disposed of, and

(*b*) the consideration required by the landlord for making the disposal.

(3) The notice must state that the notice constitutes an offer by the landlord to dispose of the property on those terms which may be accepted by the requisite majority of qualifying tenants of the constituent flats.

(4) The notice must specify a period within which that offer may be so accepted, being a period of not less than two months which is to begin with the date of service of the notice.

(5) The notice must specify a further period of not less than two months within which a person or persons may be nominated by the tenants under section 6.

[Landlord and Tenant Act 1987, s 5D, as inserted by the Housing Act 1996, Sch 6.]

8–17542 5E. Offer notice: disposal for non-monetary consideration. (1) This section applies where, in any case to which section 5 applies, the consideration required by the landlord for making the disposal does not consist, or does not wholly consist, of money.

(2) The offer notice, in addition to complying with whichever is applicable of sections 5A to 5D, must state—

(*a*) that an election may [be]* made under section 8C (explaining its effect), and

(*b*) that, accordingly, the notice also constitutes an offer by the landlord, which may be accepted by the requisite majority of qualifying tenants of the constituent flats, for a person or persons nominated by them to acquire the property in pursuance of sections 11 to 17.

(3) The notice must specify a period within which that offer may be so accepted, being a period of not less than two months which is to begin with the date of service of the notice.

[Landlord and Tenant Act 1987, s 5E, as inserted by the Housing Act 1996, Sch 6.]

***This word appears to have been omitted from the text of the Act in the Queen's Printer's copy.**

8–17543 6. Acceptance of landlord's offer: general provisions. (1) Where a landlord has served an offer notice, he shall not during—

(*a*) the period specified in the notice as the period during which the offer may be accepted, or
(*b*) such longer period as may be agreed between him and the requisite majority of the qualifying tenants of the constituent flats,

dispose of the protected interest except to a person or persons nominated by the tenants under this section.

(2) Where an acceptance notice is duly served on him, he shall not during the protected period (see subsection (4) below) dispose of the protected interest except to a person duly nominated for the purposes of this section by the requisite majority of qualifying tenants of the constituent flats (a "nominated person").

(3) An "acceptance notice" means a notice served on the landlord by the requisite majority of qualifying tenants of the constituent flats informing him that the persons by whom it is served accept the offer contained in his notice.

An acceptance notice is "duly served" if it is served within—

(*a*) the period specified in the offer notice as the period within which the offer may be accepted, or
(*b*) such longer period as may be agreed between the landlord and the requisite majority of qualifying tenants of the constituent flats.

(4) The "protected period" is the period beginning with the date of service of the acceptance notice and ending with—

(*a*) the end of the period specified in the offer notice as the period for nominating a person under this section, or
(*b*) such later date as may be agreed between the landlord and the requisite majority of qualifying tenants of constituent flats.

(5) A person is "duly nominated" for the purposes of this section if he is nominated at the same time as the acceptance notice is served or at any time after that notice is served and before the end of—

(*a*) the period specified in the offer notice as the period for nomination, or
(*b*) such longer period as may be agreed between the landlord and the requisite majority of qualifying tenants of the constituent flats.

(6) A person nominated for the purposes of this section by the requisite majority of qualifying tenants of the constituent flats may be replaced by another person so nominated if, and only if, he has (for any reason) ceased to be able to act as a nominated person.

(7) Where two or more persons have been nominated and any of them ceases to act without being replaced, the remaining person or persons so nominated may continue to act.

[Landlord and Tenant Act 1987, s 6, as substituted by the Housing Act 1996, Sch 6.]

8–17544 7. Failure to accept landlord's offer or to make nomination. (1) Where a landlord has served an offer notice on the qualifying tenants of the constituent flats and—

(*a*) no acceptance notice is duly served on the landlord, or
(*b*) no person is nominated for the purposes of section 6 during the protected period,

the landlord may, during the period of 12 months beginning with the end of that period, dispose of the protected interest to such person as he thinks fit, but subject to the following restrictions.

(2) Where the offer notice was one to which section 5B applied (sale by auction) the restrictions are—

(*a*) that the disposal is made by means of a sale at a public auction, and
(*b*) that the other terms correspond to those specified in the offer notice.

(3) In any other case the restrictions are—

(*a*) that the deposit and consideration required are not less than those specified in the offer notice, and
(*b*) that the other terms correspond to those specified in the offer notice.

(4) The entitlement of a landlord, by virtue of this section or any other corresponding provision of this Part, to dispose of the protected interest during a specified period of 12 months extends only to a disposal of that interest, and accordingly the requirements of section 1 (1) must be satisfied with respect to any other disposal by him during that period of 12 months (unless the disposal is not a relevant disposal affecting any premises to which at the time of the disposal this Part applies).

[Landlord and Tenant Act 1987, s 7, as substituted by the Housing Act 1996, Sch 6.]

8–17545 8. Landlord's obligations in case of acceptance and nomination. (1) This section applies where a landlord serves an offer notice on the qualifying tenants of the constituent flat and—

(*a*) an acceptance notice is duly served on him, and
(*b*) a person is duly nominated for the purposes of section 6,

by the requisite majority of qualifying tenants of the constituent flats.

(2) Subject to the following provisions of this Part, the landlord shall not dispose of the protected interest except to the nominated person.

(3) The landlord shall, within the period of one month beginning with the date of service of notice of nomination, either—

(*a*) serve notice on the nominated person indicating an intention no longer to proceed with the disposal of the protected interest, or

(*b*) be obliged to proceed in accordance with the following provisions of this Part.

(4) A notice under subsection (3)(*a*) is a notice of withdrawal for the purposes of section 9B(2) to (4) (consequences of notice of withdrawal by landlord).

(5) Nothing in this section shall be taken as prejudicing the application of the provisions of this Part to any further offer notice served by the landlord on the qualifying tenants of the constituent flats.

[Landlord and Tenant Act 1987, s 8, as substituted by the Housing Act 1996, Sch 6.]

8–17546 8A. Landlord's obligation: general provisions. (1) This section applies where the landlord is obliged to proceed and the offer notice was not one to which section 5B applied (sale by auction).

(2) The landlord shall, within the period of one month beginning with the date of service of the notice of nomination, send to the nominated person a form of contract for the acquisition of the protected interest on the terms specified in the landlord's offer notice.

(3) If he fails to do so, the following provisions of this Part apply as if he had given notice under section 9B (notice of withdrawal by landlord) at the end of that period.

(4) If the landlord complies with subsection (2), the nominated person shall, within the period of two months beginning with the date on which it is sent or such longer period beginning with that date as may be agreed between the landlord and that person, either—

(*a*) serve notice on the landlord indicating an intention no longer to proceed with the acquisition of the protected interest, or

(*b*) offer an exchange of contracts, that is to say, sign the contract and send it to the landlord, together with the requisite deposit.

In this subsection "the requisite deposit" means a deposit of an amount determined by or under the contract or an amount equal to 10 per cent of the consideration, whichever is the less.

(5) If the nominated person—

(*a*) serves notice in pursuance of paragraph (*a*) of subsection (4), or

(*b*) fails to offer an exchange of contracts within the period specified in that subsection,

the following provisions of this Part apply as if he had given notice under section 9A (withdrawal by nominated person) at the same time as that notice or, as the case may be, at the end of that period.

(6) If the nominated person offers an exchange of contracts within the period specified in subsection (4), but the landlord fails to complete the exchange within the period of seven days beginning with the day on which he received that person's contract, the following provisions of this Part apply as if the landlord had given notice under section 9B (withdrawal by landlord) at the end of that period.

[Landlord and Tenant Act 1987, s 8A, as inserted by the Housing Act 1996, Sch 6.]

8–17547 8B. Landlord's obligation: election in case of sale at auction—(1) This section applies where the landlord is obliged to proceed and the offer notice was one to which section 5B applied (sale by auction).

(2) The nominated person may, by notice served on the landlord not less than 28 days before the date of the auction, elect that the provisions of this section shall apply.

(3) If a contract for the disposal is entered into at the auction, the landlord shall, within the period of seven days beginning with the date of the auction, send a copy of the contract to the nominated person.

(4) If, within the period of 28 days beginning with the date on which such a copy is so sent, the nominated person—

(*a*) serves notice on the landlord accepting the terms of the contract, and

(*b*) fulfils any conditions falling to be fulfilled by the purchaser on entering into the contract,

the contract shall have effect as if the nominated person, and not the purchaser, had entered into the contract.

(5) Unless otherwise agreed, any time limit in the contract as it has effect by virtue of subsection (4) shall start to run again on the service of notice under that subsection; and nothing in the contract as it has effect by virtue of a notice under this section shall require the nominated person to complete the purchase before the end of the period of 28 days beginning with the day on which he is deemed to have entered into the contract.

(6) If the nominated person—

(*a*) does not serve notice on the landlord under subsection (2) by the time mentioned in that subsection, or

(*b*) does not satisfy the requirements of subsection (4) within the period mentioned in that subsection,

the following provisions of this Part apply as if he had given notice under section 9A (withdrawal by nominated person) at the end of that period.
[Landlord and Tenant Act 1987, s 8B, as inserted by the Housing Act 1996, Sch 6.]

8–17548 8C. Election in case of disposal for non-monetary consideration. (1) This section applies where an acceptance notice is duly served on the landlord indicating an intention to accept the offer referred to in section 5E (offer notice: disposal for non-monetary consideration).

(2) The requisite majority of qualifying tenants of the constituent flats may, by notice served on the landlord within—

(*a*) the period specified in the offer notice for nominating a person or persons for the purposes of section 6, or

(*b*) such longer period as may be agreed between the landlord and the requisite majority of qualifying tenants of the constituent flats,

elect that the following provisions shall apply.

(3) Where such an election is made and the landlord disposes of the protected interest on terms corresponding to those specified in his offer notice in accordance with section 5A, 5B, 5C or 5D, sections 11 to 17 shall have effect as if—

(*a*) no notice under section 5 had been served;

(*b*) in section 11A(3)(period for serving notice requiring information, &c.), the reference to four months were a reference to 28 days; and

(*c*) in section 12A(2) and 12B(3) (period for exercise of tenants' rights against purchaser) each reference to six months were a reference to two months.

(4) For the purposes of sections 11 to 17 as they have effect by virtue of subsection (3) so much of the consideration for the original disposal as did not consist of money shall be treated as such amount in money as was equivalent to its value in the hands of the landlord.

The landlord or the nominated person may apply to have that amount determined by a leasehold valuation tribunal.
[Landlord and Tenant Act 1987, s 8C, as inserted by the Housing Act 1996, Sch 6.]

8–17549 8D. Disposal in pursuance of option or right of pre-emption. (1) Where—

(*a*) the original disposal was the grant of an option or right of pre-emption, and

(*b*) in pursuance of the option or right, the landlord makes another disposal affecting the premises ("the later disposal") before the end of the period specified in subsection (2),

sections 11 to 17 shall have effect as if the later disposal, and not the original disposal, were the relevant disposal.

(2) The period referred to in subsection (1)(*b*) is the period of four months beginning with the date by which—

(*a*) notices under section 3A of the Landlord and Tenant Act 1985 (duty of new landlord to inform tenants of rights) relating to the original disposal, or

(*b*) where that section does not apply, documents of any other description—

(i) indicating that the original disposal has taken place, and

(ii) alerting the tenants to the existence of their rights under this Part and the time within which any such rights must be exercised,

have been served on the requisite majority of qualifying tenants of the constituent flats.
[Landlord and Tenant Act 1987, s 8D, as inserted by the Housing Act 1996, Sch 6.]

8–17550 8E. Covenant, &c. affecting landlord's power to dispose.—(1) Where the landlord is obliged to proceed but is precluded by a covenant, condition or other obligation from disposing of the protected interest to the nominated person unless the consent of some other person is obtained—

(*a*) he shall use his best endeavours to secure that the consent of that person to that disposal is given, and

(*b*) if it appears to him that that person is obliged not to withhold his consent unreasonably but has nevertheless so withheld it, he shall institute proceedings for a declaration to that effect.

(2) Subsection (1) ceases to apply if a notice of withdrawal is served under section 9A or 9B, (withdrawal of either party from transaction) or if notice is served under section 10 (lapse of landlord's offer: premises ceasing to be premises to which this Part applies).

(3) Where the landlord has discharged any duty imposed on him by subsection (1) but any such consent as is there mentioned has been withheld, and no such declaration as is there mentioned has been made, the landlord may serve a notice on the nominated person stating that to be the case.

When such a notice has been served, the landlord may, during the period of 12 months beginning with the date of service of the notice, dispose of the protected interest to such person as he thinks fit, but subject to the following restrictions.

(4) Where the offer notice was one to which section 5B applied (sale by auction), the restrictions are—

(*a*) that the disposal is made by means of a sale at a public auction, and
(*b*) that the other terms correspond to those specified in the offer notice.

(5) In any other case the restrictions are—

(*a*) that the deposit and consideration required are not less than those specified in the offer notice or, if higher, those agreed between the landlord and the nominated person (subject to contract), and
(*b*) that the other terms correspond to those specified in the offer notice.

(6) Where notice is given under subsection (3), the landlord may recover from the nominated party and the qualifying tenants who served the acceptance notice any costs reasonably incurred by him in connection with the disposal between the end of the first four weeks of the nomination period and the time when that notice is served by him.

Any such liability of the nominated person and those tenants is a joint and several liability.

[Landlord and Tenant Act 1987, s 8E, as inserted by the Housing Act 1996, Sch 6.]

8–17551 9A. Notice of withdrawal by nominated person. (1) Where the landlord is obliged to proceed, the nominated person may serve notice on the landlord (a "notice of withdrawal") indicating his intention no longer to proceed with the acquisition of the protected interest.

(2) If at any time the nominated person becomes aware that the number of the qualifying tenants of the constituent flats desiring to proceed with the acquisition of the protected interest is less than the requisite majority of qualifying tenants of those flats, he shall forthwith serve a notice of withdrawal.

(3) Where notice of withdrawal is given by the nominated person under this section, the landlord may, during the period of 12 months beginning with the date of service of the notice, dispose of the protected interest to such person as he thinks fit, but subject to the following restrictions.

(4) Where the offer notice was one to which section 5B applied (sale by auction), the restrictions are—

(*a*) that the disposal is made by means of a sale at a public auction, and
(*b*) that the other terms correspond to those specified in the offer notice.

(5) In any other case the restrictions are—

(*a*) that the deposit and consideration required are not less than those specified in the offer notice or, if higher, those agreed between the landlord and the nominated person (subject to contract), and
(*b*) that the other terms correspond to those specified in the offer notice.

(6) If notice of withdrawal is served under this section before the end of the first four weeks of the nomination period specified in the offer notice, the nominated person and the qualifying tenants who served the acceptance notice are not liable for any costs incurred by the landlord in connection with the disposal.

(7) If notice of withdrawal is served under this section after the end of those four weeks, the landlord may recover from the nominated person and the qualifying tenants who served the acceptance notice any costs reasonably incurred by him in connection with the disposal between the end of those four weeks and the time when the notice of withdrawal was served on him.

Any such liability of the nominated person and those tenants is a joint and several liability.

(8) This section does not apply after a binding contract for the disposal of the protected interest—

(*a*) has been entered into by the landlord and the nominated person, or
(*b*) has otherwise come into existence between the landlord and the nominated person by virtue of any provision of this Part.

[Landlord and Tenant Act 1987, s 9A, as inserted by the Housing Act 1996, Sch 6.]

8–17552 9B. Notice of withdrawal by landlord. (1) Where the landlord is obliged to proceed, he may serve notice on the nominated person (a "notice of withdrawal") indicating his intention no longer to proceed with the disposal of the protected interest.

(2) Where a notice of withdrawal is given by the landlord, he is not entitled to dispose of the protected interest during the period of 12 months beginning with the date of service of the notice.

(3) If a notice of withdrawal is served before the end of the first four weeks of the nomination period specified in the offer notice, the landlord is not liable for any costs incurred in connection with the disposal by the nominated person and the qualifying tenants who served the acceptance notice.

(4) If a notice of withdrawal is served after the end of those four weeks, the nominated person and the qualifying tenants who served the acceptance notice may recover from the landlord any costs reasonably incurred by them in connection with the disposal between the end of those four weeks and the time when the notice of withdrawal was served.

(5) This section does not apply after a binding contract for the disposal of the protected interest—

(*a*) has been entered into by the landlord and the nominated person, or

(*b*) has otherwise come into existence between the landlord and the nominated person by virtue of any provision of this Part.

[Landlord and Tenant Act 1987, s 9B, as inserted by the Housing Act 1996, Sch 6.]

8–17553 **10. Lapse of landlord's offer.** (1) If after a landlord has served an offer notice the premises concerned cease to be premises to which this Part applies, the landlord may serve a notice on the qualifying tenants of the constituent flats stating—

(*a*) that the premises have ceased to be premises to which this Part applies, and

(*b*) that the offer notice, and anything done in pursuance of it, is to be treated as not having been served or done;

and on the service of such a notice the provisions of this Part cease to have effect in relation to that disposal.

(2) A landlord who has not served such a notice on all of the qualifying tenants of the constituent flats shall nevertheless be treated as having duly served a notice under subsection (1)—

(*a*) if he has served such a notice on not less than 90% of those tenants, or

(*b*) where those qualifying tenants number less than ten, if he has served such a notice on all but one of them.

(3) Where the landlord is entitled to serve a notice under subsection (1) but does not do so, this Part shall continue to have effect in relation to the disposal in question as if the premises in question were still premises to which this Part applies.

(4) The above provisions of this section do not apply after a binding contract for the disposal of the protected interest—

(*a*) has been entered into by the landlord and the nominated person, or

(*b*) has otherwise come into existence between the landlord and the nominated person by virtue of any provision of this Part.

(5) Where a binding contract for the disposal of the protected interest has been entered into between the landlord and the nominated person but it has been lawfully rescinded by the landlord, the landlord may, during the period of 12 months beginning with the date of the rescission of the contract, dispose of that interest to such person (and on such terms) as he thinks fit.

[Landlord and Tenant Act 1987, s 10, as substituted by the Housing Act 1996, Sch 6.]

8–17554 **10A. Offence of failure to comply with requirements of Part I.** (1) A landlord commits an offence if, without reasonable excuse, he makes a relevant disposal affecting premises to which this Part applies—

(*a*) without having first compiled with the requirements of section 5 as regards the service of notices on the qualifying tenants of flats contained in the premises, or

(*b*) in contravention of any prohibition or restriction imposed by sections 6 to 10.

(2) A person guilty of an offence under this section is liable on summary conviction to a fine not exceeding **level 5** on the standard scale.

(3) Where an offence under this section committed by a body corporate is proved—

(*a*) to have been committed with the consent or connivance of a director, manager, secretary or other similar officer of the body corporate, or a person purporting to act in such a capacity, or

(*b*) to be due to any neglect on the part of such an officer or person,

he, as well as the body corporate, is guilty of the offence and liable to be proceeded against and punished accordingly.

Where the affairs of a body corporate are managed by its members, the above provision applies in relation to the acts and defaults of a member in connection with his functions of management as if he were a director of the body corporate.

(4) Proceedings for an offence under this section may be brought by a local housing authority (within the meaning of section 1 of the Housing Act 1985).

(5) Nothing in this section affects the validity of the disposal.

[Landlord and Tenant Act 1987, s 10A, as inserted by the Housing Act 1996, s 91.]

Supplementary

8–17555 **19.** *Enforcement of obligations under Part I*

8–17556 **20. Construction of Part I and power of Secretary of State to prescribe modifications.** (1) In this Part—

"acceptance notice" has the meaning given by section 6(3);

"associated company", in relation to a body corporate, means another body corporate which is (within the meaning of section 736 of the Companies Act 1985) that body's holding company, a subsidiary of that body or another subsidiary of that body's holding company;

"constituent flat" shall be construed in accordance with section 5(1) or 11(2), as the case may require;

"disposal" shall be construed in accordance with section 4(3) and section 4A (application of provisions to contracts), and references to the acquisition of an estate or interest shall be construed accordingly;

"landlord", in relation to any premises, shall be construed in accordance with section 2;

"the nominated person" means the person or persons for the time being nominated by the requisite majority of the qualifying tenants of the constituent flats for the purposes of section 6, 12A, 12B or 12C, as the case may require;

"offer notice" means a notice served by a landlord under section 5;

"the original disposal" means the relevant disposal referred to in section 11(1);

"the protected interest" means the estate, interest or other subject-matter of an offer notice;

"the protected period" has the meaning given by section 6(4);

"purchase notice" has the meaning given by section 12B(2);

"purchaser" has the meaning given by section 11(3);

"qualifying tenant", in relation to a flat, shall be construed in accordance with section 3;

"relevant disposal" shall be construed in accordance with section 4;

"the requisite majority", in relation to qualifying tenants, shall be construed in accordance with section 18A;

"transferee", in relation to a disposal, shall be construed in accordance with section 4(3).

(2) In this Part—

(*a*) any reference to an offer is a reference to an offer made subject to contract, and

(*b*) any reference to the acceptance of an offer is a reference to its acceptance subject to contract.

(3) Any reference in this Part to a tenant of a particular description shall be construed, in relation to any time when the interest under his tenancy has ceased to be vested in him, as a reference to the person who is for the time being the successor in title to that interest.

(4) The Secretary of State may by regulations make such modifications of any of the provisions of sections 5 to 18 as he considers appropriate, and any such regulations may contain such incidental, supplemental or transitional provisions as he considers appropriate in connection with the regulations.

(5) In subsection (4) "modifications" includes additions, omissions and alterations.

[Landlord and Tenant Act 1987, s 20, as amended by the Housing Act 1996, s 89 and Schs 6 and 19.]

PART VII[1]
GENERAL

8–17557 53. *Regulations and orders.*

8–17558 54. Notices. (1) Any notice required or authorised to be served under this Act—

(*a*) shall be in writing; and

(*b*) may be sent by post.

(2) Any notice purporting to be a notice served under any provision of Part I or III by the requisite majority of any qualifying tenants (as defined for the purposes of that provision) shall specify the names of all of the persons by whom it is served and the addresses of the flats of which they are qualifying tenants.

(3) The Secretary of State may by regulations prescribe—

(*a*) the form of any notices required or authorised to be served under or in pursuance of any provision of Parts I to III, and

(*b*) the particulars which any such notices must contain (whether in addition to, or in substitution for, any particulars required by virtue of the provision in question).

(4) Subsection (3)(*b*) shall not be construed as authorising the Secretary of State to make regulations under subsection (3) varying any of the periods specified in section 5A(4) or (5), 5B(5) or (6), 5C(4) or (5), 5D(4) or (5) or 5E(3) (which accordingly can only be varied by regulations under section 20(4)).

[Landlord and Tenant Act 1987, s 54, as amended by the Housing Act 1966, Sch 6.]

1. Part VII contains ss 52–62.

8–17559 55. *Application to Isles of Scilly.*

8–17560 56. Crown Land. (1) Parts 1 and 3 and sections 42 to 42B (and so much of this Part as relates to those provisions)* shall apply to a tenancy from the Crown if there has ceased to be a Crown interest in the land subject to it.

(2) (*Repealed*).*

(3) Where there exists a Crown interest in any land subject to a tenancy from the Crown and the person holding that tenancy is himself the landlord under any other tenancy whose subject-matter comprises the whole or part of that land, the provisions mentioned in subsection (1)* shall apply to that other tenancy, and to any derivative sub-tenancy, notwithstanding the existence of that interest.

(4) For the purposes of this section "tenancy from the Crown" means a tenancy of land in which there is, or has during the subsistence of the tenancy been, a Crown interest superior to the tenancy, and "Crown interest" means—

(*a*) an interest comprised in the Crown Estate;
(*b*) an interest belonging to Her Majesty in right of the Duchy of Lancaster;
(*c*) an interest belonging to the Duchy of Cornwall;
(*d*) any other interest belonging to a government department or held on behalf of Her Majesty for the purposes of a government department.

[Landlord and Tenant Act 1987, s 56.]

***Reproduced as amended by the Commonhold and Leasehold Reform Act 2002, ss 172(6) and 180, in force in England from 30 September 2003, and in Wales from a date to be appointed.**

8–17561 **58. Exempt landlords and resident landlords.** (1) In this Act "exempt landlord" means a landlord who is one of the following bodies, namely—

(*a*) a district, county, county borough or London borough council, the Common Council of the City of London, the London Fire and Emergency Planning Authority, the Council of the Isles of Scilly, a police authority established under section 3 of the Police Act 1996 or a joint authority established by Part IV of the Local Government Act 1985;
(*b*) the Commission for the New Towns or a development corporation established by an order made (or having effect as if made) under the New Towns Act 1981;
(*c*) an urban development corporation within the meaning of Part XVI of the Local Government, Planning and Land Act 1980;
(*ca*) a housing action trust established under Part III of the Housing Act 1988;
(*d*) (*Repealed*);
(*dd*) the Broads Authority;
(*de*) a National Park authority;
(*e*) the Housing Corporation;
(*ea*) (*Repealed*);
(*f*) a housing trust (as defined in section 6 of the Housing Act 1985) which is a charity;
(*g*) a registered social landlord, or a fully mutual housing association which is not a registered social landlord; or
(*h*) an authority established under section 10 of the Local Government Act 1985 (joint arrangements for waste disposal functions).

(1A) In subsection (1)(*g*)—

"fully mutual housing association" has the same meaning as in the Housing Associations Act 1985 (see section 1(1) and (2) of that Act); and

"registered social landlord" has the same meaning as in the Housing Act 1985 (see section 5(4) and (5) of that Act).

(2) For the purposes of this Act the landlord of any premises consisting of the whole or part of a building is a resident landlord of those premises at any time if—

(*a*) the premises are not, and do not form part of, a purpose-built block of flats; and
(*b*) at that time the landlord occupies a flat contained in the premises as his only or principal residence; and
(*c*) he has so occupied such a flat throughout a period of not less than 12 months ending with that time.

(3) In subsection (2) "purpose-built block of flats" means a building which contained as constructed, and contains, two or more flats.

[Landlord and Tenant Act 1987, s 58, as amended by the Housing Act 1988, ss 119, 140, and Schs 13 and 17, the Norfolk and Suffolk Broads Act 1988, s 21 and Sch 6, the Education Reform Act 1989, s 237 and Sch 13, the Local Government (Wales) Act 1994, Sch 8, the Police and Magistrates' Courts Act 1994, Sch 4, the Environment Act 1995, Sch 10, the Police Act 1996, Sch 7, SI 1996/2325, the Police Act 1997, Sch 9, the Government of Wales Act 1998, Sch 18, the Greater London Authority Act 1999, Sch 29 and the Criminal Justice and Police Act 2001, Sch 7.]

8–17562 **59. Meaning of "lease", "long lease" and related expressions.** (1) In this Act "lease" and "tenancy" have the same meaning; and both expressions include—

(*a*) a sub-lease or sub-tenancy, and
(*b*) an agreement for a lease or tenancy (or for a sub-lease or sub-tenancy).

(2) The expressions "landlord" and "tenant", and references to letting, to the grant of a lease or to covenants or the terms of a lease shall be construed accordingly.

(3) In this Act "long lease" means—

(*a*) a lease granted for a term certain exceeding 21 years, whether or not it is (or may become) terminable before the end of that term by notice given by the tenant or by re-entry or forfeiture;

(*b*) a lease for a term fixed by law under a grant with a covenant or obligation for perpetual renewal, other than a lease by sub-demise from one which is not a long lease; or

(*c*) a lease granted in pursuance of Part V of the Housing Act 1985 (the right to buy), including a lease granted in pursuance of that Part as it has effect by virtue of section 17 of the Housing Act 1996 (the right to acquire).

[Landlord and Tenant Act 1987, s 59, as amended by SI 1997/627.]

8–17563 60. General interpretation. (1) In this Act—

"the 1985 Act" means the Landlord and Tenant Act 1985;

"charity" means a charity within the meaning of the Charities Act 1993, and "charitable purposes", in relation to a charity, means charitable purposes whether of that charity or of that charity and other charities;

"common parts", in relation to any building or part of a building, includes the structure and exterior of that building or part and any common facilities within it;

"the court" means the High Court or a county court;

"dwelling" means a building or part of a building occupied or intended to be occupied as a separate dwelling, together with any yard, garden, outhouses and appurtenances belonging to it or usually enjoyed with it;

"exempt landlord" has the meaning given by section 58(1);

"flat" means a separate set of premises, whether or not on the same floor, which—

(*a*) forms part of a building, and

(*b*) is divided horizontally from some other part of that building, and

(*c*) is constructed or adapted for use for the purposes of a dwelling;

"functional land," in relation to a charity, means land occupied by the charity, or by trustees for it, and wholly or mainly used for charitable purposes;

"landlord" (except for the purposes of Part I) means the immediate landlord or, in relation to a statutory tenant, the person who, apart from the statutory tenancy, would be entitled to possession of the premises subject to the tenancy;

"lease" and related expressions shall be construed in accordance with section 59(1) and (2);

"long lease" has the meaning given by section 59(3);

"mortgage" includes any charge or lien, and references to a mortgagee shall be construed accordingly;

"notices in proceedings" means notices or other documents served in, or in connection with, any legal proceedings;

"resident landlord" shall be construed in accordance with section 58(2);

"statutory tenancy" and "statutory tenant" mean a statutory tenancy or statutory tenant within the meaning of the Rent Act 1977 or the Rent (Agriculture) Act 1976;

"tenancy" includes a statutory tenancy.

(2) (*Repealed*).

[Landlord and Tenant Act 1987, s 60, as amended by the Housing Act 1988, s 140 and Sch 18, the Charities Act 1993, Sch 6 and the Housing Act 1996, Sch 19.]

8–17564 62. *Short title, commencement and extent.*

Local Government and Housing Act 1989

(1989 c 42)

PART VII
RENEWAL AREAS

8–17565 97. Powers of entry and penalty for obstruction. (1) A person authorised by the local housing authority or the Secretary of State may at any reasonable time, on giving not less than seven days' notice of his intention to the occupier, and to the owner if the owner is known, enter premises—

(*a*) for the purpose of survey and examination where it appears to the authority or the Secretary of State that survey or examination is necessary in order to determine whether any powers under this Part should be exercised; or

(*b*) for the purpose of survey or valuation where the authority are authorised by this Part to acquire the premises compulsorily.

(2) An authorisation for the purposes of this section—

(*a*) shall be in writing stating the particular purpose or purposes for which the entry is authorised; and

(*b*) shall, if so required, be produced for inspection by the occupier or anyone acting on his behalf.

(3) It is a summary offence intentionally to obstruct an officer of the local housing authority or of the Secretary of State, or a person authorised to enter premises under subsection (1) above, in the performance of anything which that officer, authority or person is by this Part required or authorised to do.

(4) A person who commits an offence under subsection (3) above is liable on conviction to a fine not exceeding **level 3** on the standard scale.

(5) In this section "owner", in relation to premises,—

(*a*) means a person (other than a mortgagee not in possession) who is for the time being entitled to dispose of the fee simple in the premises, whether in possession or reversion, and

(*b*) includes also a person holding or entitled to the rents and profits of the premises under a lease of which the unexpired term exceeds three years.

[Local Government and Housing Act 1989, s 97.]

Leasehold Reform, Housing and Urban Development Act 1993

(1993 c 28)

Part III[1]

Development of Urban and Other Areas

The Urban Regeneration Agency

8–17570 **163. Power to enter and survey land.** (1) Any person who is duly authorised in writing by the Agency[2] may at any reasonable time enter any land for the purpose of surveying it, or estimating its value, in connection with—

(*a*) any proposal to acquire that land or any other land; or

(*b*) any claim for compensation in respect of any such acquisition.

(2) The power to survey land shall be construed as including power to search and bore for the purpose of ascertaining the nature of the subsoil or the presence of minerals in it.

(3) A person authorised under this section to enter any land—

(*a*) shall, if so required, produce evidence of his authority before entry, and

(*b*) shall not demand admission as of right to any land which is occupied unless 28 days' notice of the intended entry has been given to the occupier by the Agency.

(4) Any person who wilfully obstructs a person acting in exercise of his powers under this section shall be guilty of an offence and liable on summary conviction to a fine not exceeding **level 2** on the standard scale.

(5) If any person who, in compliance with the provisions of this section, is admitted into a factory, workshop or workplace discloses to any person any information obtained by him in it as to any manufacturing process or trade secret, he shall be guilty of an offence.

(6) Subsection (5) does not apply if the disclosure is made by a person in the course of performing his duty in connection with the purpose for which he was authorised to enter the premises.

(7) A person who is guilty of an offence under subsection (5) shall be liable[3] on summary conviction to a fine not exceeding the **statutory maximum** or on conviction on indictment to imprisonment for a term not exceeding **two years** or a **fine** or both.

(8) Where any land is damaged—

(*a*) in the exercise of a right of entry under this section, or

(*b*) in the making of any survey under this section,

compensation in respect of that damage may be recovered by any person interested in the land from the Agency.

(9) The provisions of section 118 of the Town and Country Planning Act 1990 (determination of claims for compensation) shall apply in relation to compensation under subsection (8) as they apply in relation to compensation under Part IV of that Act.

(10) No person shall carry out under this section any works authorised by virtue of subsection (2) unless notice of his intention to do so was included in the notice required by subsection (3).

(11) The authority of the appropriate Minister shall be required for the carrying out of any such works if—

(*a*) the land in question is held by statutory undertakers; and

(*b*) they object to the proposed works on the ground that the execution of the works would be seriously detrimental to the carrying on of their undertaking;

and expressions used in this subsection have the same meanings as they have in section 325(9) of the Town and Country Planning Act 1990 (supplementary provisions as to rights of entry).

[Leasehold Reform, Housing and Urban Development Act 1993, s 163.]

1. Part III contains ss 158–185.
2. "The Agency" means the Urban Regeneration Agency (s 185).
3. For procedure in respect of this offence which is triable either way, see the Magistrates' Courts Act 1980, ss 17A–21, in PART I: MAGISTRATES' COURTS, PROCEDURE, ante.

Housing Act 1996

(1996 c 52)

PART I[1]
SOCIAL RENTED SECTOR

CHAPTER I
REGISTERED SOCIAL LANDLORDS

Registration

8–17580 **1. The register of social landlords.** (1) The Relevant Authority shall maintain a register of social landlords which shall be open to inspection at all reasonable times.

(1A) In this Part "the Relevant Authority" means the Housing Corporation or the Secretary of State, as provided by section 56.

(1B) The register maintained by the Housing Corporation shall be maintained at its head office.

(2) (*Repealed*).

[Housing Act 1996, s 1, as amended by the Government of Wales Act 1998, Schs 16 and 18.]

1. This Act makes provision about housing, including provision about the social rented sector, houses in multiple occupation, landlord and tenant matters, and homelessness. The Act contains a number of penal provisions and it is not practicable to include all of them in this Manual. However, we have included in this title those provisions of the Act which are most likely to be relevant to proceedings in magistrates' courts.

The Housing Act 1996 is to be brought into force in accordance with the provisions of s 232, post. Of the provisions printed in this Manual, the following had not been brought into force at the date of going to press:

Part I s 35;
Part II ss 65–75, 78, 79, 80(1), (2);
Part VII ss 175, 214. Sections 175 and 214 were to be brought into force on 20 January 1997 by virtue of SI 1996/2959).

2. Part I contains ss 1–64.

8–17580A **7.** *Regulation of registered social landlords.*

CHAPTER IV[1]
GENERAL POWERS OF THE CORPORATION

Information

8–17581 **30. General power to obtain information.** (1) The Relevant Authority may for any purpose connected with the discharge of any of its functions in relation to registered social landlords serve a notice on a person requiring him—

(*a*) to give to the Relevant Authority, at a time and place and in the form and manner specified in the notice, such information relating to the affairs of a registered social landlord as may be specified or described in the notice, or
(*b*) to produce to the Relevant Authority or a person authorised by the Relevant Authority, at a time and place specified in the notice, any documents relating to the affairs of the registered social landlord which are specified or described in the notice and are in his custody or under his control.

(2) A notice under this section may be served on—

(*a*) a registered social landlord,
(*b*) any person who is, or has been, an officer, member, employee or agent of a registered social landlord,
(*c*) a subsidiary or associate of a registered social landlord,
(*d*) any person who is, or has been, an officer, member, employee or agent of a subsidiary or associate of a registered social landlord, or
(*e*) any other person whom the Relevant Authority has reason to believe is or may be in possession of relevant information.

In this section "agent" includes banker, solicitor and auditor.

(3) No notice shall be served on a person within paragraphs (*b*) to (*e*) of subsection (2) unless—

(*a*) a notice has been served on the registered social landlord and has not been complied with, or
(*b*) the Relevant Authority believes that the information or documents in question are not in the possession of the landlord.

(4) Nothing in this section authorises the Relevant Authority to require—

(*a*) the disclosure of anything which a person would be entitled to refuse to disclose on grounds of legal professional privilege in proceedings in the High Court, or

(*b*) the disclosure by a banker of anything in breach of any duty of confidentiality owed by him to a person other than a registered social landlord or a subsidiary or associate of a registered social landlord.

(5) A notice under this section—

(*a*) if given by the Housing Corporation, shall be given under its seal, and

(*b*) if given by the Secretary of State, shall be given in writing.

(6) References in this section to a document are to anything in which information of any description is recorded; and in relation to a document in which information is recorded otherwise than in legible form, references to producing it are to producing it in legible form.

(7) Where by virtue of this section documents are produced to any person, he may take copies of or make extracts from them.

[Housing Act 1996, s 30, as amended by the Government of Wales Act 1998, Sch 16.]

1. Chapter IV contains ss 30–50.

8–17582 31. Enforcement of notice to provide information, &c. (1) A person who without reasonable excuse fails to do anything required of him by a notice under section 30 commits an offence and is liable on summary conviction to a fine not exceeding level 5 on the standard scale.

(2) A person who intentionally alters, suppresses or destroys a document which he has been required by a notice under section 30 to produce commits an offence and is liable[1]—

(*a*) on summary conviction, to a fine not exceeding **the statutory maximum**,

(*b*) on conviction on indictment, to **imprisonment** for a term not exceeding two years or to a **fine**, or both.

(3) Proceedings for an offence under subsection (1) or (2) may be brought only by or with the consent of the Relevant Authority or the Director of Public Prosecutions.

(4) If a person makes default in complying with a notice under section 30, the High Court may, on the application of the Relevant Authority, make such order as the court thinks fit for requiring the default to be made good.

Any such order may provide that all the costs or expenses of and incidental to the application shall be borne by the person in default or by any officers of a body who are responsible for its default.

[Housing Act 1996, s 31, as amended by the Government of Wales Act 1998, Sch 16 and the Housing Act 2004, Sch 11.]

1. For procedure in respect of this offence which is triable either way, see the Magistrates' Courts Act 1980, ss 17A–21, in PART I: MAGISTRATES' COURTS, PROCEDURE, ante.

8–17583 32. Disclosure of information to the Relevant Authority. (1) A body or person to whom this section applies may, subject to the following provisions, disclose to the Relevant Authority, for the purpose of enabling the Relevant Authority to discharge any of its functions relating to registered social landlords, any information received by that body or person under or for the purposes of any enactment.

(2) This section applies to the following bodies and persons—

(*a*) any government department (including a Northern Ireland department);

(*b*) any local authority;

(*c*) any constable; and

(*d*) any other body or person discharging functions of a public nature (including a body or person discharging regulatory functions in relation to any description of activities).

(3) This section has effect subject to any express restriction on disclosure imposed by or under any other enactment.

(4) Nothing in this section shall be construed as affecting any power of disclosure exercisable apart from this section.

[Housing Act 1996, s 32, as amended by the Government of Wales Act 1998, Sch 16.]

8–17584 33. Disclosure of information by the Relevant Authority. (1) The Relevant Authority may disclose to a body or person to whom this section applies any information received by it relating to a registered social landlord—

(*a*) for any purpose connected with the discharge of the functions of the Relevant Authority in relation to such landlords, or

(*b*) for the purpose of enabling or assisting that body or person to discharge any of its or his functions.

(2) This section applies to the following bodies and persons—

(*a*) any government department (including a Northern Ireland department);
(*b*) any local authority;
(*c*) any constable; and
(*d*) any other body or person discharging functions of a public nature (including a body or person discharging regulatory functions in relation to any description of activities).

Paragraph (*d*) extends to any such body or person in a country or territory outside the United Kingdom.

(3) Where any information disclosed to the Relevant Authority under section 32 is so disclosed subject to any express restriction on the further disclosure of the information, the Relevant Authority's power of disclosure under this section is exercisable subject to that restriction.

A person who discloses information in contravention of any such restriction commits an offence and is liable on summary conviction to a fine not exceeding **level 3** on the standard scale.

(4) Any information disclosed by the Relevant Authority under this section may be subject by the Relevant Authority to any express restriction on the further disclosure of the information.

(5) A person who discloses information in contravention of any such restriction commits an offence and is liable on summary conviction to a fine not exceeding **level 3** on the standard scale.

Proceedings for such an offence may be brought only by or with the consent of the Relevant Authority or the Director of Public Prosecutions.

(6) Nothing in this section shall be construed as affecting any power of disclosure exercisable apart from this section.

[Housing Act 1996, s 33, as amended by the Government of Wales Act 1998, Sch 16.]

Standards of performance

8–17585 34. *Standards of performance.*

8–17586 35. Information as to levels of performance. (1) The Relevant Authority shall from time to time collect information as to the levels of performance achieved by registered social landlords in connection with the provision of housing.

(2) On or before such date in each year as may be specified in a direction given by the Relevant Authority, each registered social landlord shall provide the Relevant Authority, as respects each standard determined under section 34, with such information as to the level of performance achieved by him as may be so specified.

(3) A registered social landlord who without reasonable excuse fails to do anything required of him by a direction under subsection (2) commits an offence and is liable on summary conviction to a fine not exceeding **level 5** on the standard scale.

Proceedings for such an offence may be brought only by or with the consent of the Relevant Authority or the Director of Public Prosecutions.

(4) The Relevant Authority shall at least once in every year arrange for the publication, in such form and in such manner as it considers appropriate, of such of the information collected by or provided to it under this section as appears to it expedient to give to tenants or potential tenants of registered social landlords.

(5) In arranging for the publication of any such information the Relevant Authority shall have regard to the need for excluding, so far as that is practicable—

(*a*) any matter which relates to the affairs of an individual, where publication of that matter would or might, in the opinion of the Relevant Authority, seriously and prejudicially affect the interests of that individual; and
(*b*) any matter which relates specifically to the affairs of a particular body or persons, whether corporate or unincorporate, where publication of that matter would or might, in the opinion of the Relevant Authority, seriously and prejudicially affect the interests of that body.

[Housing Act 1996, s 35, as amended by the Government of Wales Act 1998, Sch 16.]

Housing management

8–17587 36. Issue of guidance by the Relevant Authority. (1) The Relevant Authority may issue guidance with respect to the management of housing accommodation by registered social landlords.

[Housing Act 1996, s 36(1), as amended by the Government of Wales Act 1998, Sch 16.]

8–17588 37. Powers of entry. (1) This section applies where it appears to the Relevant Authority that a registered social landlord may be failing to maintain or repair any premises in accordance with guidance issued under section 36.

(2) A person authorised by the Relevant Authority may at any reasonable time, on giving not less than 28 days' notice of his intention to the landlord concerned, enter any such premises for the purpose of survey and examination.

(3) Where such notice is given to the landlord, the landlord shall give the occupier or occupiers of the premises not less than seven days' notice of the proposed survey and examination.

A landlord who fails to do so commits an offence and is liable on summary conviction to a fine not exceeding **level 3** on the standard scale.

(4) Proceedings for an offence under subsection (3) may be brought only by or with the consent of the Relevant Authority or the Director of Public Prosecutions.

(5) An authorisation for the purposes of this section shall be in writing stating the particular purpose or purposes for which the entry is authorised and shall, if so required, be produced for inspection by the occupier or anyone acting on his behalf.

(6) The Relevant Authority shall give a copy of any survey carried out in exercise of the powers conferred by this section to the landlord concerned.

(7) The Relevant Authority may require the landlord concerned to pay to it such amount as the Relevant Authority may determine towards the costs of carrying out any survey under this section.
[Housing Act 1996, s 37, as amended by the Government of Wales Act 1998, Sch 16.]

8–17589 **38. Penalty for obstruction of person exercising power of entry.** (1) It is an offence for a registered social landlord or any of its officers or employees to obstruct a person authorised under section 37 (powers of entry) to enter premises in the performance of anything which he is authorised by that section to do.

(2) A person who commits such an offence is liable on summary conviction to a fine not exceeding **level 3** on the standard scale.

(3) Proceedings for such an offence may be brought only by or with the consent of the Relevant Authority or the Director of Public Prosecutions.
[Housing Act 1996, s 38, as amended by the Government of Wales Act 1998, Sch 16.]

CHAPTER V[1]
MISCELLANEOUS AND GENERAL PROVISIONS

Interpretation

8–17590 **56. Meaning of "the Relevant Authority".** (1) In this Part "the Relevant Authority" means the Housing Corporation or the Secretary of State, as follows.

(2) In relation to a registered social landlord, or a body applying for such registration, which is—

(*a*) a registered charity which has its address for the purposes of registration by the Charity Commissioners in Wales,

(*b*) an industrial and provident society which has its registered office for the purposes of the Industrial and Provident Societies Act 1965 in Wales, or

(*c*) a company registered under the Companies Act 1985 which has its registered office for the purposes of that Act in Wales,

"the Relevant Authority" means the Secretary of State.

(3) In relation to any other registered social landlord or a body applying for such registration, "the Relevant Authority" means the Housing Corporation.

(4) Nothing in this Part shall be construed as requiring the Housing Corporation and the Secretary of State to establish the same criteria for registration as a social landlord, or otherwise to act on the same principles in respect of any matter in relation to which they have functions under this Part.
[Housing Act 1996, s 56, as amended by the Government of Wales Act 1998, Sch 16.]

1. Chapter V contains ss 51–64.

8–17591 **57.** *Definitions relating to industrial and provident societies.*

8–17592 **58.** *Definitions relating to charities.*

8–17593 **59. Meaning of "officer" of registered social landlord.** (1) References in this Part to an officer of a registered social landlord are—

(*a*) in the case of a registered charity which is not a company registered under the Companies Act 1985, to any trustee, secretary or treasurer of the charity;

(*b*) in the case of an industrial and provident society, to any officer of the society as defined in section 74 of the Industrial and Provident Societies Act 1965; and

(*c*) in the case of a company registered under the Companies Act 1985 (including such a company which is also a registered charity), to any director or other officer of the company within the meaning of that Act.

(2) Any such reference includes, in the case of an industrial and provident society, a co-opted member of the committee of the society.
[Housing Act 1996, s 59.]

8–17594 **60. Meaning of "subsidiary".** (1) In this Part "subsidiary", in relation to a registered social landlord, means a company with respect to which one of the following conditions is fulfilled—

(*a*) the landlord is a member of the company and controls the composition of the board of directors;
(*b*) the landlord holds more than half in nominal value of the company's equity share capital; or
(*c*) the company is a subsidiary, within the meaning of the Companies Act 1985 or the Friendly and Industrial and Provident Societies Act 1968, of another company which, by virtue of paragraph (*a*) or paragraph (*b*), is itself a subsidiary of the landlord.

(2) For the purposes of subsection (1)(*a*), the composition of a company's board of directors shall be deemed to be controlled by a registered social landlord if, but only if, the landlord, by the exercise of some power exercisable by him without the consent or concurrence of any other person, can appoint or remove the holders of all or a majority of the directorships.

(3) In relation to a company which is an industrial and provident society—

(*a*) any reference in this section to the board of directors is a reference to the committee of management of the society; and
(*b*) the reference in subsection (2) to the holders of all or a majority of the directorships is a reference—
  (i) to all or a majority of the members of the committee, or
  (ii) if the landlord is himself a member of the committee, such number as together with him would constitute a majority.

(4) In the case of a registered social landlord which is a body of trustees, references in this section to the landlord are to the trustees acting as such.
[Housing Act 1996, s 60.]

8–17595 **61. Meaning of "associate".** (1) In this Part "associate", in relation to a registered social landlord, means—

(*a*) any body of which the landlord is a subsidiary, and
(*b*) any other subsidiary of such a body.

(2) In this section "subsidiary" has the same meaning as in the Companies Act 1985 or the Friendly and Industrial and Provident Societies Act 1968 or, in the case of a body which is itself a registered social landlord, has the meaning given by section 60.
[Housing Act 1996, s 61.]

8–17596 **62.** *Members of a person's family: Part I.*

8–17597 **63. Minor definitions: Part I.** (1) In this Part—

"dwelling" means a building or part of a building occupied or intended to be occupied as a separate dwelling, together with any yard, garden, outhouses and appurtenances belonging to it or usually enjoyed with it;
"fully mutual", in relation to a housing association, and "co-operative housing association" have the same meaning as in the Housing Associations Act 1985 (see section 1(2) of that Act);
"hostel" means a building in which is provided for persons generally or for a class or classes of persons—
  (*a*) residential accommodation otherwise than in separate and self-contained premises, and
  (*b*) either board or facilities for the preparation of food adequate to the needs of those persons, or both;
"house" includes—
  (*a*) any part of a building occupied or intended to be occupied as a separate dwelling, and
  (*b*) any yard, garden, outhouses and appurtenances belonging to it or usually enjoyed with it;
"housing accommodation" includes flats, lodging-houses and hostels;
"housing activities" means, in relation to a registered social landlord, all its activities in pursuance of the purposes, objects and powers mentioned in or specified under section 2;
"information" includes accounts, estimates and returns;
"local authority" has the same meaning as in the Housing Associations Act 1985;
"long tenancy" has the same meaning as in Part V of the Housing Act 1985;
"modifications" includes additions, alterations and omissions and cognate expressions shall be construed accordingly;
"notice" means notice in writing;
"public sector landlord" means any of the authorities or bodies within section 80(1) of the Housing Act 1985 (the landlord condition for secure tenancies);
"registrar of companies" has the same meaning as in the Companies Act 1985;
"statutory tenancy" has the same meaning as in the Housing Act 1985.

(2) References in this Part to the provision of a dwelling or house include the provision of a dwelling or house—

(*a*) by erecting the dwelling or house, or converting a building into dwellings or a house, or (*b*) by altering, enlarging, repairing or improving an existing dwelling or house;

and references to a dwelling or house provided by means of a grant or other financial assistance are to its being so provided directly or indirectly.
[Housing Act 1996, s 63.]

8–17598 **64. Index of defined expressions: Part I.** The following Table shows provisions defining or otherwise explaining expressions used in this Part (others than provisions defining or explaining an expression used in the same section)—

Appointed person (in relation to inquiry into affairs of registered social landlord)	paragraph 20 of Schedule 1
Associate (in relation to a registered social landlord)	section 61(1)
assured tenancy	section 230
assured agricultural occupancy	section 230
assured shorthold tenancy	section 230
charity	section 58(1)(*a*)
committee member (in relation to an industrial and provident society)	section 57(2)
company registered under the Companies Act 1985	section 58(2)
co-operative housing association	section 63
co-opted member (of committee of industrial and provident society)	section 57(1)
disposal proceeds fund	section 24
dwelling	section 63
enactment	section 230
fully mutual housing association	section 63
hostel	section 63
house	section 63
housing accommodation	section 63
housing activities	section 63
housing association	section 230
industrial and provident society	section 2(1)(*b*)
information	section 63
lease	section 229
local authority	section 63
long tenancy	section 63
member of family	section 62
modifications	section 63
notice	section 63
officer of registered social landlord	section 59
provision (in relation to dwelling or house)	section 63(2)
public sector landlord	section 63
register, registered and registration (in relation to social landlords)	section 1
registered charity	section 58(1)(*b*)
registrar of companies	section 63
the Relevant Authority	section 56
relevant disposal which is not an exempted disposal (in sections 11 to 14)	section 15
secure tenancy	section 230
social housing grant	section 18(1)
statutory tenancy	section 63
subsidiary (in relation to a registered social landlord)	section 60(1)
trustee and trusts (in relation to a charity)	section 58(1)(*a*)

[Housing Act 1996, s 64, as amended by the Government of Wales Act 1998, Schs 16 and 18 and SI 2001/3649.]

PART II[1]
HOUSES IN MULTIPLE OCCUPATION

1. Part II contains ss 65–80. Part II of the Housing Act 1996 makes various amendments to Part XI of the Housing Act 1985 (para **8–17272** et seq, ante).

PART VII[1]
HOMELESSNESS

Homelessness and threatened homelessness

8–17613 **175. Homelessness and threatened homelessness.** (1) A person is homeless if he has no accommodation available for his occupation, in the United Kingdom or elsewhere, which he—

(*a*) is entitled to occupy by virtue of an interest in it or by virtue of an order of a court,
(*b*) has an express or implied licence to occupy, or
(*c*) occupies as a residence by virtue of any enactment or rule of law giving him the right to remain in occupation or restricting the right of another person to recover possession.

(2) A person is also homeless if he has accommodation but—
(*a*) he cannot secure entry to it, or
(*b*) it consists of a moveable structure, vehicle or vessel designed or adapted for human habitation and there is no place where he is entitled or permitted both to place it and to reside in it.

(3) A person shall not be treated as having accommodation unless it is accommodation which it would be reasonable for him to continue to occupy.

(4) A person is threatened with homelessness if it is likely that he will become homeless within 28 days.
[Housing Act 1996, s 175.]

1. Part VII contains ss 175–218.

General provisions

8–17614 **214. False statements, withholding information and failure to disclose change of circumstances.** (1) It is an offence for a person, with intent to induce a local housing authority to believe in connection with the exercise of their functions under this Part that he or another person is entitled to accommodation or assistance in accordance with the provisions of this Part, or is entitled to accommodation or assistance of a particular description—
(*a*) knowingly or recklessly to make a statement which is false in a material particular, or
(*b*) knowingly to withhold information which the authority have reasonably required him to give in connection with the exercise of those functions.

(2) If before an applicant receives notification of the local housing authority's decision on his application there is any change of facts material to his case, he shall notify the authority as soon as possible.

The authority shall explain to every applicant, in ordinary language, the duty imposed on him by this subsection and the effect of subsection (3).

(3) A person who fails to comply with subsection (2) commits an offence unless he shows that he was not given the explanation required by that subsection or that he had some other reasonable excuse for non-compliance.

(4) A person guilty of an offence under this section is liable on summary conviction to a fine not exceeding level 5 on the standard scale.
[Housing Act 1996, s 214.]

PART VIII[1]
MISCELLANEOUS AND GENERAL PROVISIONS

General

8–17615 **223. Offences by body corporate.** (1) Where an offence under this Act committed by a body corporate is proved to have been committed with the consent or connivance of a director, manager, secretary or other similar officer of the body corporate, or a person purporting to act in such a capacity, he as well as the body corporate is guilty of an offence and liable to be proceeded against and punished accordingly.

(2) Where the affairs of a body corporate are managed by its members, subsection (1) applies in relation to the acts and defaults of a member in connection with his functions of management as if he were a director of the body corporate.
[Housing Act 1996, s 223.]

1. Part VIII contains ss 219–233.

8–17616 **232. Commencement.** (1) The following provisions of this Act come into force on Royal Assent—

section 110 (new leases: valuation principles),
section 120 (payment of housing benefit to third parties), and
sections 223 to 226 and 228 to 233 (general provisions).

(2) The following provisions of this Act come into force at the end of the period of two months beginning with the date on which this Act is passed—

sections 81 and 82 (restriction on termination of tenancy for failure to pay service charge),
section 85 (appointment of manager by the court),
section 94 (provision of general legal advice about residential tenancies),
section 95 (jurisdiction of county courts),

section 221 (exercise of compulsory purchase powers in relation to Crown land),
paragraph 24 (powers of local housing authorities to acquire land for housing purposes), paragraph 26 (preserved right to buy) and paragraphs 27 to 29 of Schedule 18 (local authority assistance in connection with mortgages), and
sections 222 and 227, and Schedule 19 (consequential repeals), in so far as they relate to those paragraphs.

(3) The other provisions of this Act come into force on a day appointed by order[1] of the Secretary of State, and different days may be appointed for different areas and different purposes.

(4) An order under subsection (3) shall be made by statutory instrument and may contain such transitional provisions and savings as appear to the Secretary of State to be appropriate.
[Housing Act 1996, s 232.]

1. At the date of going to press, the following commencement orders had been made: Commencement No 1 Order, SI 1996/2048; Commencement No. 2 and Savings Order, SI 1996/2212, and Commencement No 3 and Transitional Provisions Order, SI 1996/2402, Commencement No 4 Order, SI 1996/2658, and Commencement No 5 and Transitional Provisions Order 1996, SI 1996/2959.

8–17617 **233. Short title.** This Act may be cited as the Housing Act 1996.
[Housing Act 1996, s 233.]

SCHEDULES

Section 7

SCHEDULE 1
REGISTERED SOCIAL LANDLORDS: REGULATION

(As amended by the Government of Wales Act, Schs 16 and 18.)

PART III
ACCOUNTS AND AUDIT

General requirements as to accounts and audit

8–17618 **16.** (1) The Relevant Authority may from time to time determine accounting requirements for registered social landlords with a view to ensuring that the accounts of every registered social landlord—

(*a*) are prepared in a proper form, and
(*b*) give a true and fair view of—

(i) the state of affairs of the landlord, so far as its housing activities are concerned, and
(ii) the disposition of funds and assets which are, or at any time have been, in its hands in connection with those activities.

(2) The Relevant Authority by a determination under sub-paragraph (1) may lay down a method by which a registered charity is to distinguish in its accounts between its housing activities and other activities.

(3) The accounts of every registered social landlords shall comply with the requirements laid down under this paragraph.

(4) The auditor's report shall state, in addition to any other matters which it is required to state, whether in the auditor's opinion the accounts do so comply.

(5) Every registered social landlord shall furnish to the Relevant Authority a copy of its accounts and auditor's report within six months of the end of the period to which they relate.

8–17619 **17.** Appointment of auditors by industrial and provident societies.

Accounting and audit requirements for charities

8–17620 **18.** (1) A registered social landlord which is a registered charity shall, in respect of its housing activities (and separately from its other activities, if any), be subject to the following provisions (which impose accounting and audit requirements corresponding to those imposed by the Friendly and Industrial and Provident Societies Act 1968).

This does not affect any obligation of the charity under sections 41 to 45 of the Charities Act 1993 (charity accounts).

(2) The charity shall in respect of its housing activities—

(*a*) cause to be kept properly books of account showing its transactions and its assets and liabilities, and
(*b*) establish and maintain a satisfactory system of control of its books of accounts, its cash holdings and all its receipts and remittances.

The books of account must be such as to enable a true and fair view to be given of the state of affairs of the charity in respect of its housing activities, and to explain its transactions in the course of those activities.

(3) The charity shall for each period of account prepare—

(*a*) a revenue account giving a true and fair view of the charity's income and expenditure in the period, so far as arising in connection with its housing activities, and
(*b*) a balance sheet giving a true and fair view as at the end of the period of the state of the charity's affairs.

The revenue account and balance sheet must be signed by at least two directors or trustees of the charity.

(4) The charity shall in each period of account appoint a qualified auditor to audit the accounts prepared in accordance with sub-paragraph (3).

A qualified auditor means a person who is eligible for appointment as auditor of the charity under Part II of the

Companies Act 1989 or who would be so eligible if the charity were a company registered under the Companies Act 1985.

(5) The auditor shall make a report to the charity on the accounts audited by him, stating whether in his opinion—

(*a*) the revenue account gives a true and fair view of the state of income and expenditure of the charity in respect of its housing activities and of any other matters to which it relates, and

(*b*) the balance sheet gives a true and fair view of the state of affairs of the charity as at the end of the period of account.

(6) The auditor in preparing his report shall carry out such investigations as will enable him to form an opinion as to the following matters—

(*a*) whether the association has kept, in respect of its housing activities, proper books of account in accordance with the requirements of this paragraph,

(*b*) whether the charity has maintained a satisfactory system of control over its transactions in accordance with those requirements, and

(*c*) whether the accounts are in agreement with the charity's books;

and if he is of opinion that the charity has failed in any respect to comply with this paragraph, or if the accounts are not in agreement with the books, he shall state that fact in his report.

(7) The auditor—

(*a*) has a right of access at all times to the books, deeds and accounts of the charity, so far as relating to its housing activities, and to all other documents relating to those activities, and

(*b*) is entitled to require from officers of the charity such information and explanations as he thinks necessary for the performance of his duties;

and if he fails to obtain all the information and explanations which, to the best of his knowledge and belief, are necessary for the purposes of his audit, he shall state that fact in his report.

(8) A period of account for the purposes of this paragraph is twelve months or such other period not less than six months or more than 18 months as the charity may, with the consent of the Relevant Authority, determine.

Responsibility for securing compliance with accounting requirements

8–17621 **19.** (1) Every responsible person, that is to say, every person who—

(*a*) is directly concerned with the conduct and management of the affairs of a registered social landlord, and

(*b*) is in that capacity responsible for the preparation and audit of accounts,

shall ensure that paragraph 16 (general requirements as to accounts and audit) and, where applicable, paragraph 18 (accounting and audit requirements for charities) are complied with by the registered social landlord.

(2) If—

(*a*) paragraph 16(5) (furnishing of accounts and auditor's report) is not complied with,

(*b*) the accounts furnished to the Relevant Authority under that provision do not comply with the accounting requirements laid down under paragraph 16(1),

(*c*) paragraph 18 (accounting and audit requirements for charities), where applicable, is not complied with,

(*d*) section 55(9) of the Housing Act 1988 (surplus rental income: power to require information) is not complied with, or

(*e*) any notice under section 26 (information relating to disposal proceeds fund) is not complied with,

every responsible person, and the registered social landlord itself, commits a summary offence and is liable on conviction to a fine not exceeding **level 3** on the standard scale.

(3) In proceedings for an offence under this paragraph it is a defence—

(*a*) for a responsible person to prove that he did everything that could reasonably have been expected of him by way of discharging the relevant duty;

(*b*) for a registered social landlord to prove that every responsible person did everything that could reasonably have been expected of him by way of discharging the relevant duty in relation to the registered social landlord.

(4) Proceedings for an offence under this paragraph may be brought only by or with the consent of the Relevant Authority or the Director of Public Prosecutions.

PART IV
INQUIRY INTO AFFAIRS OF REGISTERED SOCIAL LANDLORDS
Inquiry

8–17622 **20.** (1) The Relevant Authority may direct an inquiry into the affairs of a registered social landlord if it appears to the Relevant Authority that there may have been misconduct or mismanagement.

For this purpose "misconduct" includes any failure to comply with the requirements of this Part of this Act.

(2) Any such inquiry shall be conducted by one or more persons appointed by the Relevant Authority.

(3) If one person is appointed by the Housing Corporation to conduct an inquiry he must be a person who is not a member or an employee of the Housing Corporation and has not been such a member or employee within the previous five years; and if more than one person is so appointed at least one of them must be such a person.

(4) If the Relevant Authority so directs, or if during the course of the inquiry the person or persons conducting the inquiry consider it necessary, the inquiry shall extend to the affairs of any other body which at any material time is or was a subsidiary or associate of the registered social landlord.

(5) The person or persons conducting the inquiry may, if they think fit during the course of the inquiry, make one or more interim reports on such matters as appear to them to be appropriate.

(6) On completion of the inquiry the person or persons conducting the inquiry shall make a final report on such matters as the Relevant Authority may specify.

(7) An interim or final report shall be in such form as the Relevant Authority may specify.

Power of appointed person to obtain information

8–17623 **21.** (1) A person appointed by the Relevant Authority under paragraph 20 to conduct an inquiry (or, if more than one person is so appointed, each of those persons) has, for the purposes of the inquiry, the same powers as are conferred on the Relevant Authority by section 30 (general power to obtain information).

(2) Where by virtue of a notice under that section given by an appointed person any documents are produced to any person, the person to whom they are produced may take copies of or make extracts from them.

(3) Section 31 (enforcement of notice to provide information, &c.) applies in relation to a notice given under this paragraph by an appointed person as it applies in relation to a notice given under section 30 by the Relevant Authority.

Extraordinary audit for purposes of inquiry

8–17624 **22.** (1) For the purposes of an inquiry under paragraph 20 the Relevant Authority may require the accounts and balance sheet of the registered social landlord concerned, or such of them as the Relevant Authority may specify, to be audited by a qualified auditor appointed by the Relevant Authority.

(2) A person is a qualified auditor for this purpose if he would be eligible for appointment as auditor of the ordinary accounts of the registered social landlord.

(3) On completion of the audit the appointed auditor shall make a report to the Relevant Authority on such matters and in such form as the Relevant Authority may specify.

(4) The expenses of the audit, including the remuneration of the auditor, shall be paid by the Relevant Authority.

(5) An audit under this paragraph is additional to, and does not affect, any audit made or to be made under any other enactment.

Powers exercisable on interim basis

8–17625 **23.** (1) The Relevant Authority may make an order under this paragraph—

(*a*) where an inquiry has been directed under paragraph 20 and the Relevant Authority has reasonable grounds to believe—

(i) that there has been misconduct or mismanagement in the affairs of the registered social landlord, and

(ii) that immediate action is needed to protect the interests of the tenants of the registered social landlord or to protect the assets of the landlord; or

(*b*) where an interim report has been made under paragraph 20(5) as a result of which the Relevant Authority is satisfied that there has been misconduct or mismanagement in the affairs of a registered social landlord.

(2) The orders that may be made under this paragraph are—

(*a*) an order suspending any officer, employee or agent of the registered social landlord who appears to the Relevant Authority to have been responsible for or privy to the misconduct or mismanagement or by his conduct to have contributed to or facilitated it;

(*b*) an order directing any bank or other person who holds money or securities on behalf of the registered social landlord not to part with the money or securities without the approval of the Relevant Authority;

(*c*) an order restricting the transactions which may be entered into, or the nature or amount of the payments which may be made, by the registered social landlord without the approval of the Relevant Authority.

(3) An order under this paragraph, if not previously revoked by the Relevant Authority, shall cease to have effect six months after the making of the final report under paragraph 20(6) unless the Relevant Authority renews it, which it may do for a further period of up to six months.

(4) A person suspended by an order under sub-paragraph 2(*a*) may appeal against the order to the High Court.

(5) Where a person is suspended by such an order, the Relevant Authority may give directions with respect to the performance of his functions and otherwise as to matters arising from his suspension.

The Relevant Authority may, in particular, appoint a named person to perform his functions.

(6) A person who contravenes an order under sub-paragraph (2)(*b*) commits an offence and is liable on summary conviction to a fine not exceeding **level 5** on the standard scale or imprisonment for a term not exceeding **three months**, or both.

Proceedings for such an offence may be brought only by or with the consent of the Relevant Authority or the Director of Public Prosecutions.

Powers exercisable as a result of final report or audit

8–17626 **24.** (1) Where the Relevant Authority is satisfied, as the result of an inquiry under paragraph 20 or an audit under paragraph 22, that there has been misconduct or mismanagement in the affairs of a registered social landlord, it may make an order under this paragraph.

(2) The orders that may be made under this paragraph are—

(*a*) an order removing any officer, employee or agent of the registered social landlord who appears to the Relevant Authority to have been responsible for or privy to the misconduct or mismanagement or by his conduct to have contributed to or facilitated it;

(*b*) an order suspending any such person for up to six months, pending determination whether he should be removed;

(*c*) an order directing any bank or other person who holds money or securities on behalf of the registered social landlord not to part with the money or securities without the approval of the Relevant Authority;

(*d*) an order restricting the transactions which may be entered into, or the nature or amount of the payments which may be made, by the registered social landlord without the approval of the Relevant Authority.

(3) Before making an order under sub-paragraph (2)(*a*) the Relevant Authority shall give at least 14 days' notice of its intention to do so—

(*a*) to the person it intends to remove, and
(*b*) to the registered social landlord concerned.

Notice under this sub-paragraph may be given by post, and if so given to the person whom the Relevant Authority intends to remove may be addressed to his last known address in the United Kingdom.

(4) A person who is ordered to be removed under sub-paragraph (2)(*a*) or suspended under sub-paragraph (2)(*b*) may appeal against the order to the High Court.

(5) Where a person is suspended under sub-paragraph (2)(*b*), the Relevant Authority may give directions with respect to the performance of his functions and otherwise as to matters arising from the suspension.

The Relevant Authority may, in particular, appoint a named person to perform his functions.

(6) A person who contravenes an order under sub-paragraph (2)(*c*) commits an offence and is liable on summary conviction to a fine not exceeding **level 5** on the standard scale or imprisonment for a term not exceeding **three months**, or both.

Proceedings for such an offence may be brought only by or with the consent of the Relevant Authority or the Director of Public Prosecutions.

Disqualification as officer of registered social landlord

8–17627 **25.** (1) A person is disqualified from being an officer of a registered social landlord if the Relevant Authority has made an order against him under—

(*a*) paragraph 24(2)(*a*) (removal for misconduct or mismanagement), or
(*b*) section 30(1)(*a*) of the Housing Associations Act 1985 or section 20(1)(*a*) of the Housing Act 1974 (corresponding earlier provisions).

(2) The Relevant Authority may, on the application of any such person, waive his disqualification either generally or in relation to a particular registered social landlord or particular class of registered social landlord.

(3) Any waiver shall be notified in writing to the person concerned.

(4) For the purposes of this paragraph the Relevant Authority shall keep, in such manner as it thinks fit, a register of all persons who have been removed from office by the Relevant Authority under the provisions mentioned in sub-paragraph (1).

(5) The register shall be available for public inspection at all reasonable times.

Persons acting as officer while disqualified

8–17628 **26.** (1) A person who acts as an officer of a registered social landlord while he is disqualified under paragraph 25(1) commits an offence.

A person guilty of such an offence is liable[1]—

(*a*) on summary conviction, to imprisonment for a term not exceeding **six months** or to a fine not exceeding **the statutory maximum**, or both;
(*b*) on conviction on indictment, to imprisonment for a term not exceeding **two years** or to a **fine**, or both.

(2) Proceedings for an offence under sub-paragraph (1) may be brought only by or with the consent of the Relevant Authority or the Director of Public Prosecutions.

(3) Acts done as an officer of a registered social landlord by a person who is disqualified under paragraph 25(1) are not invalid by reason only of that disqualification.

(4) Where the Relevant Authority is satisfied—

(*a*) that a person has acted as an officer of a registered social landlord while disqualified under paragraph 25(1), and
(*b*) that while so acting he has received from the registered social landlord any payments or benefits in connection with his so acting,

it may by order direct him to repay to the registered social landlord the whole or part of any such sums or, as the case may be, to pay to it the whole or part of the monetary value (as determined by it) of any such benefit.

---

1. For procedure in respect of an offence which is triable either way, see the Magistrates' Courts Act 1980, ss 18–21, in PART I: MAGISTRATES' COURTS, PROCEDURE, ante.

Housing Act 2004[1]

(2004 c 34)

PART 1[2]

Housing Conditions

CHAPTER 1[3]

Enforcement of Housing Standards: General

New system for assessing housing conditions

8–17628A **1. New system for assessing housing conditions and enforcing housing standards.**

(1) This Part provides—

(*a*) for a new system of assessing the condition of residential premises, and
(*b*) for that system to be used in the enforcement of housing standards in relation to such premises.

(2) The new system—

(*a*) operates by reference to the existence of category 1 or category 2 hazards on residential premises (see section 2), and

(*b*) replaces the existing system based on the test of fitness for human habitation contained in section 604 of the Housing Act 1985 (c 68).

(3) The kinds of enforcement action which are to involve the use of the new system are—

(*a*) the new kinds of enforcement action contained in Chapter 2 (improvement notices, prohibition orders and hazard awareness notices),

(*b*) the new emergency measures contained in Chapter 3 (emergency remedial action and emergency prohibition orders), and

(*c*) the existing kinds of enforcement action dealt with in Chapter 4 (demolition orders and slum clearance declarations).

(4) In this Part "residential premises" means—

(*a*) a dwelling;

(*b*) an HMO;

(*c*) unoccupied HMO accommodation;

(*d*) any common parts of a building containing one or more flats.

(5) In this Part—

"building containing one or more flats" does not include an HMO;

"common parts", in relation to a building containing one or more flats, includes—

(*a*) the structure and exterior of the building, and

(*b*) common facilities provided (whether or not in the building) for persons who include the occupiers of one or more of the flats;

"dwelling" means a building or part of a building occupied or intended to be occupied as a separate dwelling;

"external common parts", in relation to a building containing one or more flats, means common parts of the building which are outside it;

"flat" means a separate set of premises (whether or not on the same floor)—

(*a*) which forms part of a building,

(*b*) which is constructed or adapted for use for the purposes of a dwelling, and

(*c*) either the whole or a material part of which lies above or below some other part of the building;

"HMO" means a house in multiple occupation as defined by sections 254 to 259, as they have effect for the purposes of this Part (that is, without the exclusions contained in Schedule 14);

"unoccupied HMO accommodation" means a building or part of a building constructed or adapted for use as a house in multiple occupation but for the time being either unoccupied or only occupied by persons who form a single household.

(6) In this Part any reference to a dwelling, an HMO or a building containing one or more flats includes (where the context permits) any yard, garden, outhouses and appurtenances belonging to, or usually enjoyed with, the dwelling, HMO or building (or any part of it).

(7) The following indicates how this Part applies to flats—

(*a*) references to a dwelling or an HMO include a dwelling or HMO which is a flat (as defined by subsection (5)); and

(*b*) subsection (6) applies in relation to such a dwelling or HMO as it applies in relation to other dwellings or HMOs (but it is not to be taken as referring to any common parts of the building containing the flat).

(8) This Part applies to unoccupied HMO accommodation as it applies to an HMO, and references to an HMO in subsections (6) and (7) and in the following provisions of this Part are to be read accordingly.

[Housing Act 2004, s 1.]

---

1. This Act replaces the existing housing fitness standard with the Housing Health and Safety System. It introduces two new licensing regimes for private rented properties: the first for licensing houses in multiple occupation; the second for selective licensing of other residential accommodation. It also introduces a new makes a new requirement for sellers or estate agents to produce a home information pack before marketing any residential property for sale, together with an ombudsman scheme for estate agents. The Act also makes various others provisions about housing. These include enabling local authorities to secure occupation of long-term empty private sector homes, and establishing tenancy deposit protection schemes to safeguard deposits paid in connection with assured shorthold tenancies. Finally, the Act requires housing authorities to assess the accommodation needs of Gypsies and travellers in their area and to produce a strategy on how those needs can be met.

The Act is in 7 parts and has 16 Schedules.

Part 1 is concerned with the replacement of the existing housing fitness standards contained in the Housing Act 1985 with the Housing Health and Safety Rating System. It also adapts and extends the enforcement powers currently available to local housing authorities (LHAs) to tackle poor housing conditions, with the intention of helping LHAs to prioritise their intervention on the basis of the severity of the health and safety hazards in the home. The new framework is largely free-standing, though some provisions of the 1985 Act remain with appropriate amendments.

Part 2 is concerned with the licensing of houses in multiple occupation (HMOs). It introduces a mandatory scheme to licence HMOs of a description contained in regulations. It is intended initially only to apply to the larger risk HMOs, though LHAs are given power to extend licensing in their districts to other categories of HMOs subject to local consultation and with the approval of the appropriate national authority.

Part 3 introduces a new power for LHAs to bring in selective licensing to deal with particular problems in an area. This will focus on areas of low house-purchase demand and other areas suffering from anti-social behaviour. LHAs are given the discretionary power, subject to consultation and with the approval of the appropriate national authority, to license all landlords in a designated area to ensure minimum standards of management. The appropriate national authority is also provided with powers to prescribe by regulation other circumstances in which discretionary schemes may be made.

Part 4 contains additional control provisions in relation to residential accommodation.

Part 5 is concerned with home information packs. It imposes new legal duties on those marketing residential properties in England and Wales. Part 5 aims to bring forward the availability of documents and information the seller has to provide to the start of the process rather than waiting until after agreement 'subject to contract' has been reached. The vendor's pack will also include a report on the condition of the property.

Part 6 makes other provision about housing.

Part 7 contains supplementary and final provisions.

Most of the Act's provisions will be brought into force in accordance with commencement orders made under s 270. At the date of going to press, the following commencement orders had been made: Housing Act 2004 (Commencement No 1) (England) Order 2005, SI 2005/326; Housing Act 2004 (Commencement No 2) (England) Order 2005, SI 2005/1120; Housing Act 2004 (Commencement No 3) (England) Order 2005, SI 2005/1451; Housing Act 2004 (Commencement No 4 and Transitional Provisions) (England) Order 2005, SI 2005/1729; Housing Act 2004 (Commencement No 1) (Wales) Order 2005, SI 2005/1814; and Housing Act 2004 (Commencement No 2) (Wales) Order 2005, SI 2005/3237. This work reproduces only the provisions that are relevant to magistrates' courts. Readers should refer to the notes to the titles of each Part for commencement information.

2. Part 1 contains ss 1–54. Section 2 and 9 came into force on the day on which the Act was passed (see s 270). Section 4 is in force in relation to Wales only (see Housing Act 2004 (Commencement No 2) (Wales) Order 2005, SI 2005/3237). Otherwise, at the date of going to press Part 1 was not in force save for the provisions that confer any powers to make orders or regulations which are exercisable by the Secretary of State or the National Assembly of Wales (see s 270(2)(*b*)).

3. Chapter 1 contains ss 1-10.

8–17628A 2. Meaning of "category 1 hazard" and "category 2 hazard". (1) In this Act—

"category 1 hazard" means a hazard of a prescribed description which falls within a prescribed band as a result of achieving, under a prescribed method for calculating the seriousness of hazards of that description, a numerical score of or above a prescribed amount;

"category 2 hazard" means a hazard of a prescribed description which falls within a prescribed band as a result of achieving, under a prescribed method for calculating the seriousness of hazards of that description, a numerical score below the minimum amount prescribed for a category 1 hazard of that description; and

"hazard" means any risk of harm to the health or safety of an actual or potential occupier of a dwelling or HMO which arises from a deficiency in the dwelling or HMO or in any building or land in the vicinity (whether the deficiency arises as a result of the construction of any building, an absence of maintenance or repair, or otherwise).

(2) In subsection (1)—

"prescribed" means prescribed by regulations made by the appropriate national authority (see section 261(1)); and

"prescribed band" means a band so prescribed for a category 1 hazard or a category 2 hazard, as the case may be.

(3) Regulations under this section may, in particular, prescribe a method for calculating the seriousness of hazards which takes into account both the likelihood of the harm occurring and the severity of the harm if it were to occur.

(4) In this section—

"building" includes part of a building;

"harm" includes temporary harm.

(5) In this Act "health" includes mental health.

[Housing Act 2004, s 2.]

Procedure for assessing housing conditions

8–17628B 3. Local housing authorities to review housing conditions in their districts. (1) A local housing authority must keep the housing conditions in their area under review with a view to identifying any action that may need to be taken by them under any of the provisions mentioned in subsection (2).

(2) The provisions are—

(*a*) the following provisions of this Act—

(i) this Part,

(ii) Part 2 (licensing of HMOs),

(iii) Part 3 (selective licensing of other houses), and

(iv) Chapters 1 and 2 of Part 4 (management orders);

(*b*) Part 9 of the Housing Act 1985 (c 68) (demolition orders and slum clearance);
(*c*) Part 7 of the Local Government and Housing Act 1989 (c 42) (renewal areas); and
(*d*) article 3 of the Regulatory Reform (Housing Assistance) (England and Wales) Order 2002 (SI 2002/1860).

(3) For the purpose of carrying out their duty under subsection (1) a local housing authority and their officers must—

(*a*) comply with any directions that may be given by the appropriate national authority, and
(*b*) keep such records, and supply the appropriate national authority with such information, as that authority may specify.

[Housing Act 2004, s 3.]

8–17628C 4. Inspections by local housing authorities to see whether category 1 or 2 hazards exist. (1) If a local housing authority consider—

(*a*) as a result of any matters of which they have become aware in carrying out their duty under section 3, or
(*b*) for any other reason,

that it would be appropriate for any residential premises in their district to be inspected with a view to determining whether any category 1 or 2 hazard exists on those premises, the authority must arrange for such an inspection to be carried out.

(2) If an official complaint about the condition of any residential premises in the district of a local housing authority is made to the proper officer of the authority, and the circumstances complained of indicate—

(*a*) that any category 1 or category 2 hazard may exist on those premises, or
(*b*) that an area in the district should be dealt with as a clearance area,

the proper officer must inspect the premises or area.

(3) In this section "an official complaint" means a complaint in writing made by—

(*a*) a justice of the peace having jurisdiction in any part of the district, or
(*b*) the parish or community council for a parish or community within the district.

(4) An inspection of any premises under subsection (1) or (2)—

(*a*) is to be carried out in accordance with regulations made by the appropriate national authority; and
(*b*) is to extend to so much of the premises as the local housing authority or proper officer (as the case may be) consider appropriate in the circumstances having regard to any applicable provisions of the regulations.

(5) Regulations under subsection (4) may in particular make provision about—

(*a*) the manner in which, and the extent to which, premises are to be inspected under subsection (1) or (2), and
(*b*) the manner in which the assessment of hazards is to be carried out.

(6) Where an inspection under subsection (2) has been carried out and the proper officer of a local housing authority is of the opinion—

(*a*) that a category 1 or 2 hazard exists on any residential premises in the authority's district, or
(*b*) that an area in their district should be dealt with as a clearance area,

the officer must, without delay, make a report in writing to the authority which sets out his opinion together with the facts of the case.

(7) The authority must consider any report made to them under subsection (6) as soon as possible.

[Housing Act 2004, s 4.]

Enforcement of housing standards

8–17628D 5. Category 1 hazards: general duty to take enforcement action. (1) If a local housing authority consider that a category 1 hazard exists on any residential premises, they must take the appropriate enforcement action in relation to the hazard.

(2) In subsection (1) "the appropriate enforcement action" means whichever of the following courses of action is indicated by subsection (3) or (4)—

(*a*) serving an improvement notice under section 11;
(*b*) making a prohibition order under section 20;
(*c*) serving a hazard awareness notice under section 28;
(*d*) taking emergency remedial action under section 40;
(*e*) making an emergency prohibition order under section 43;
(*f*) making a demolition order under subsection (1) or (2) of section 265 of the Housing Act 1985 (c 68);

(*g*) declaring the area in which the premises concerned are situated to be a clearance area by virtue of section 289(2) of that Act.

(3) If only one course of action within subsection (2) is available to the authority in relation to the hazard, they must take that course of action.

(4) If two or more courses of action within subsection (2) are available to the authority in relation to the hazard, they must take the course of action which they consider to be the most appropriate of those available to them.

(5) The taking by the authority of a course of action within subsection (2) does not prevent subsection (1) from requiring them to take in relation to the same hazard—

(*a*) either the same course of action again or another such course of action, if they consider that the action taken by them so far has not proved satisfactory, or

(*b*) another such course of action, where the first course of action is that mentioned in subsection (2)(*g*) and their eventual decision under section 289(2F) of the Housing Act 1985 means that the premises concerned are not to be included in a clearance area.

(6) To determine whether a course of action mentioned in any of paragraphs (*a*) to (*g*) of subsection (2) is "available" to the authority in relation to the hazard, see the provision mentioned in that paragraph.

(7) Section 6 applies for the purposes of this section.

[Housing Act 2004, s 5.]

8–17628E 6. Category 1 hazards: how duty under section 5 operates in certain cases. (1) This section explains the effect of provisions contained in subsection (2) of section 5.

(2) In the case of paragraph (*b*) or (*f*) of that subsection, the reference to making an order such as is mentioned in that paragraph is to be read as a reference to making instead a determination under section 300(1) or (2) of the Housing Act 1985 (c 68) (power to purchase for temporary housing use) in a case where the authority consider the latter course of action to be the better alternative in the circumstances.

(3) In the case of paragraph (*d*) of that subsection, the authority may regard the taking of emergency remedial action under section 40 followed by the service of an improvement notice under section 11 as a single course of action.

(4) In the case of paragraph (*e*) of that subsection, the authority may regard the making of an emergency prohibition order under section 43 followed by the service of a prohibition order under section 20 as a single course of action.

(5) In the case of paragraph (*g*) of that subsection—

(*a*) any duty to take the course of action mentioned in that paragraph is subject to the operation of subsections (2B) to (4) and (5B) of section 289 of the Housing Act 1985 (procedural and other restrictions relating to slum clearance declarations); and

(*b*) that paragraph does not apply in a case where the authority have already declared the area in which the premises concerned are situated to be a clearance area in accordance with section 289, but the premises have been excluded by virtue of section 289(2F)(*b*).

[Housing Act 2004, s 6.]

8–17628F 7. Category 2 hazards: powers to take enforcement action. (1) The provisions mentioned in subsection (2) confer power on a local housing authority to take particular kinds of enforcement action in cases where they consider that a category 2 hazard exists on residential premises.

(2) The provisions are—

(*a*) section 12 (power to serve an improvement notice),

(*b*) section 21 (power to make a prohibition order),

(*c*) section 29 (power to serve a hazard awareness notice),

(*d*) section 265(3) and (4) of the Housing Act 1985 (power to make a demolition order), and

(*e*) section 289(2ZB) of that Act (power to make a slum clearance declaration).

(3) The taking by the authority of one of those kinds of enforcement action in relation to a particular category 2 hazard does not prevent them from taking either—

(*a*) the same kind of action again, or

(*b*) a different kind of enforcement action,

in relation to the hazard, where they consider that the action taken by them so far has not proved satisfactory.

[Housing Act 2004, s 7.]

8–17628G 8. Reasons for decision to take enforcement action. (1) This section applies where a local housing authority decide to take one of the kinds of enforcement action mentioned in section 5(2) or 7(2) ("the relevant action").

(2) The authority must prepare a statement of the reasons for their decision to take the relevant action.

(3) Those reasons must include the reasons why the authority decided to take the relevant action rather than any other kind (or kinds) of enforcement action available to them under the provisions mentioned in section 5(2) or 7(2).

(4) A copy of the statement prepared under subsection (2) must accompany every notice, copy of a notice, or copy of an order which is served in accordance with—

(*a*) Part 1 of Schedule 1 to this Act (service of improvement notices etc),
(*b*) Part 1 of Schedule 2 to this Act (service of copies of prohibition orders etc), or
(*c*) section 268 of the Housing Act 1985 (service of copies of demolition orders),

in or in connection with the taking of the relevant action.

(5) In subsection (4)—

(*a*) the reference to Part 1 of Schedule 1 to this Act includes a reference to that Part as applied by section 28(7) or 29(7) (hazard awareness notices) or to section 40(7) (emergency remedial action); and
(*b*) the reference to Part 1 of Schedule 2 to this Act includes a reference to that Part as applied by section 43(4) (emergency prohibition orders).

(6) If the relevant action consists of declaring an area to be a clearance area, the statement prepared under subsection (2) must be published—

(*a*) as soon as possible after the relevant resolution is passed under section 289 of the Housing Act 1985, and
(*b*) in such manner as the authority consider appropriate.

9. Guidance about inspections and enforcement action

10. Consultation with fire and rescue authorities in certain cases

CHAPTER 2[1]
Improvement Notices, Prohibition Orders and Hazard Awareness Notices

Improvement notices

8–17628H 11. Improvement notices relating to category 1 hazards: duty of authority to serve notice. (1) If—

(*a*) the local housing authority are satisfied that a category 1 hazard exists on any residential premises, and
(*b*) no management order is in force in relation to the premises under Chapter 1 or 2 of Part 4,

serving an improvement notice under this section in respect of the hazard is a course of action available to the authority in relation to the hazard for the purposes of section 5 (category 1 hazards: general duty to take enforcement action).

(2) An improvement notice under this section is a notice requiring the person on whom it is served to take such remedial action in respect of the hazard concerned as is specified in the notice in accordance with subsections (3) to (5) and section 13.

(3) The notice may require remedial action to be taken in relation to the following premises—

(*a*) if the residential premises on which the hazard exists are a dwelling or HMO which is not a flat, it may require such action to be taken in relation to the dwelling or HMO;
(*b*) if those premises are one or more flats, it may require such action to be taken in relation to the building containing the flat or flats (or any part of the building) or any external common parts;
(*c*) if those premises are the common parts of a building containing one or more flats, it may require such action to be taken in relation to the building (or any part of the building) or any external common parts.

Paragraphs (*b*) and (*c*) are subject to subsection (4).

(4) The notice may not, by virtue of subsection (3)(*b*) or (*c*), require any remedial action to be taken in relation to any part of the building or its external common parts that is not included in any residential premises on which the hazard exists, unless the authority are satisfied—

(*a*) that the deficiency from which the hazard arises is situated there, and
(*b*) that it is necessary for the action to be so taken in order to protect the health or safety of any actual or potential occupiers of one or more of the flats.

(5) The remedial action required to be taken by the notice—

(*a*) must, as a minimum, be such as to ensure that the hazard ceases to be a category 1 hazard; but
(*b*) may extend beyond such action.

(6) An improvement notice under this section may relate to more than one category 1 hazard on the same premises or in the same building containing one or more flats.

(7) The operation of an improvement notice under this section may be suspended in accordance with section 14.

(8) In this Part "remedial action", in relation to a hazard, means action (whether in the form of carrying out works or otherwise) which, in the opinion of the local housing authority, will remove or reduce the hazard.

[Housing Act 2004, s 11.]

---

1. Chapter 1 contains ss 11–39.

8–17628I 12. Improvement notices relating to category 2 hazards: power of authority to serve notice. (1) If—

(*a*) the local housing authority are satisfied that a category 2 hazard exists on any residential premises, and

(*b*) no management order is in force in relation to the premises under Chapter 1 or 2 of Part 4,

the authority may serve an improvement notice under this section in respect of the hazard.

(2) An improvement notice under this section is a notice requiring the person on whom it is served to take such remedial action in respect of the hazard concerned as is specified in the notice in accordance with subsection (3) and section 13.

(3) Subsections (3) and (4) of section 11 apply to an improvement notice under this section as they apply to one under that section.

(4) An improvement notice under this section may relate to more than one category 2 hazard on the same premises or in the same building containing one or more flats.

(5) An improvement notice under this section may be combined in one document with a notice under section 11 where they require remedial action to be taken in relation to the same premises.

(6) The operation of an improvement notice under this section may be suspended in accordance with section 14.

[Housing Act 2004, s 12.]

8–17628J 13. Contents of improvement notices. (1) An improvement notice under section 11 or 12 must comply with the following provisions of this section.

(2) The notice must specify, in relation to the hazard (or each of the hazards) to which it relates—

(*a*) whether the notice is served under section 11 or 12,

(*b*) the nature of the hazard and the residential premises on which it exists,

(*c*) the deficiency giving rise to the hazard,

(*d*) the premises in relation to which remedial action is to be taken in respect of the hazard and the nature of that remedial action,

(*e*) the date when the remedial action is to be started (see subsection (3)), and

(*f*) the period within which the remedial action is to be completed or the periods within which each part of it is to be completed.

(3) The notice may not require any remedial action to be started earlier than the 28th day after that on which the notice is served.

(4) The notice must contain information about—

(*a*) the right of appeal against the decision under Part 3 of Schedule 1, and

(*b*) the period within which an appeal may be made.

(5) In this Part of this Act "specified premises", in relation to an improvement notice, means premises specified in the notice, in accordance with subsection (2)(*d*), as premises in relation to which remedial action is to be taken in respect of the hazard.

[Housing Act 2004, s 13.]

8–17628K 14. Suspension of improvement notices. (1) An improvement notice may provide for the operation of the notice to be suspended until a time, or the occurrence of an event, specified in the notice.

(2) The time so specified may, in particular, be the time when a person of a particular description begins, or ceases, to occupy any premises.

(3) The event so specified may, in particular, be a notified breach of an undertaking accepted by the local housing authority for the purposes of this section from the person on whom the notice is served.

(4) In subsection (3) a "notified breach", in relation to such an undertaking, means an act or omission by the person on whom the notice is served—

(*a*) which the local housing authority consider to be a breach of the undertaking, and

(*b*) which is notified to that person in accordance with the terms of the undertaking.

(5) If an improvement notice does provide for the operation of the notice to be suspended under this section—

(*a*) any periods specified in the notice under section 13 are to be fixed by reference to the day when the suspension ends, and

(*b*) in subsection (3) of that section the reference to the 28th day after that on which the notice is served is to be read as referring to the 21st day after that on which the suspension ends.

[Housing Act 2004, s 14.]

8–17628L 15. Operation of improvement notices. (1) This section deals with the time when an improvement notice becomes operative.

(2) The general rule is that an improvement notice becomes operative at the end of the period of 21 days beginning with the day on which it is served under Part 1 of Schedule 1 (which is the period for appealing against the notice under Part 3 of that Schedule).

(3) The general rule is subject to subsection (4) (suspended notices) and subsection (5) (appeals).

(4) If the notice is suspended under section 14, the notice becomes operative at the time when the suspension ends.

This is subject to subsection (5).

(5) If an appeal against the notice is made under Part 3 of Schedule 1, the notice does not become operative until such time (if any) as is the operative time for the purposes of this subsection under paragraph 19 of that Schedule (time when notice is confirmed on appeal, period for further appeal expires or suspension ends).

(6) If no appeal against an improvement notice is made under that Part of that Schedule within the period for appealing against it, the notice is final and conclusive as to matters which could have been raised on an appeal.

[Housing Act 2004, s 15.]

8–17628M 16. Revocation and variation of improvement notices. (1) The local housing authority must revoke an improvement notice if they are satisfied that the requirements of the notice have been complied with.

(2) The local housing authority may revoke an improvement notice if—

(*a*) in the case of a notice served under section 11, they consider that there are any special circumstances making it appropriate to revoke the notice; or

(*b*) in the case of a notice served under section 12, they consider that it is appropriate to revoke the notice.

(3) Where an improvement notice relates to a number of hazards—

(*a*) subsection (1) is to be read as applying separately in relation to each of those hazards, and

(*b*) if, as a result, the authority are required to revoke only part of the notice, they may vary the remainder as they consider appropriate.

(4) The local housing authority may vary an improvement notice—

(*a*) with the agreement of the person on whom the notice was served, or

(*b*) in the case of a notice whose operation is suspended, so as to alter the time or events by reference to which the suspension is to come to an end.

(5) A revocation under this section comes into force at the time when it is made.

(6) If it is made with the agreement of the person on whom the improvement notice was served, a variation under this section comes into force at the time when it is made.

(7) Otherwise a variation under this section does not come into force until such time (if any) as is the operative time for the purposes of this subsection under paragraph 20 of Schedule 1 (time when period for appealing expires without an appeal being made or when decision to vary is confirmed on appeal).

(8) The power to revoke or vary an improvement notice under this section is exercisable by the authority either—

(*a*) on an application made by the person on whom the improvement notice was served, or

(*b*) on the authority's own initiative.

[Housing Act 2004, s 16.]

8–17628N 17. Review of suspended improvement notices. (1) The local housing authority may at any time review an improvement notice whose operation is suspended.

(2) The local housing authority must review an improvement notice whose operation is suspended not later than one year after the date of service of the notice and at subsequent intervals of not more than one year.

(3) Copies of the authority's decision on a review under this section must be served—

(*a*) on the person on whom the improvement notice was served, and

(*b*) on every other person on whom a copy of the notice was required to be served.

[Housing Act 2004, s 17.]

8–17628O 18. Service of improvement notices etc and related appeals. Schedule 1 (which deals with the service of improvement notices, and notices relating to their revocation or variation, and with related appeals) has effect.

[Housing Act 2004, s 18.]

8–17628P 19. Change in person liable to comply with improvement notice. (1) This section applies where—

(*a*) an improvement notice has been served on any person ("the original recipient") in respect of any premises, and

(*b*) at a later date ("the changeover date") that person ceases to be a person of the relevant category in respect of the premises.

(2) In subsection (1) the reference to a person ceasing to be a "person of the relevant category" is a reference to his ceasing to fall within the description of person (such as, for example, the holder of a licence under Part 2 or 3 or the person managing a dwelling) by reference to which the improvement notice was served on him.

(3) As from the changeover date, the liable person in respect of the premises is to be in the same position as if—

(*a*) the improvement notice had originally been served on him, and

(*b*) he had taken all steps relevant for the purposes of this Part which the original recipient had taken.

(4) The effect of subsection (3) is that, in particular, any period for compliance with the notice or for bringing any appeal is unaffected.

(5) But where the original recipient has become subject to any liability arising by virtue of this Part before the changeover date, subsection (3) does not have the effect of—

(*a*) relieving him of the liability, or

(*b*) making the new liable person subject to it.

(6) Subsection (3) applies with any necessary modifications where a person to whom it applies (by virtue of any provision of this section) ceases to be the liable person in respect of the premises.

(7) Unless subsection (8) or (9) applies, the person who is at any time the "liable person" in respect of any premises is the person having control of the premises.

(8) If—

(*a*) the original recipient was served as the person managing the premises, and

(*b*) there is a new person managing the premises as from the changeover date,

that new person is the "liable person".

(9) If the original recipient was served as an owner of the premises, the "liable person" is the owner's successor in title on the changeover date.

[Housing Act 2004, s 19.]

Prohibition orders

8–17628Q 20. Prohibition orders relating to category 1 hazards: duty of authority to make order. (1) If—

(*a*) the local housing authority are satisfied that a category 1 hazard exists on any residential premises, and

(*b*) no management order is in force in relation to the premises under Chapter 1 or 2 of Part 4,

making a prohibition order under this section in respect of the hazard is a course of action available to the authority in relation to the hazard for the purposes of section 5 (category 1 hazards: general duty to take enforcement action).

(2) A prohibition order under this section is an order imposing such prohibition or prohibitions on the use of any premises as is or are specified in the order in accordance with subsections (3) and (4) and section 22.

(3) The order may prohibit use of the following premises—

(*a*) if the residential premises on which the hazard exists are a dwelling or HMO which is not a flat, it may prohibit use of the dwelling or HMO;

(*b*) if those premises are one or more flats, it may prohibit use of the building containing the flat or flats (or any part of the building) or any external common parts;

(*c*) if those premises are the common parts of a building containing one or more flats, it may prohibit use of the building (or any part of the building) or any external common parts.

Paragraphs (*b*) and (*c*) are subject to subsection (4).

(4) The notice may not, by virtue of subsection (3)(*b*) or (*c*), prohibit use of any part of the building or its external common parts that is not included in any residential premises on which the hazard exists, unless the authority are satisfied—

(*a*) that the deficiency from which the hazard arises is situated there, and

(*b*) that it is necessary for such use to be prohibited in order to protect the health or safety of any actual or potential occupiers of one or more of the flats.

(5) A prohibition order under this section may relate to more than one category 1 hazard on the same premises or in the same building containing one or more flats.

(6) The operation of a prohibition order under this section may be suspended in accordance with section 23.
[Housing Act 2004, s 20.]

8–17628R 21. Prohibition orders relating to category 2 hazards: power of authority to make order. (1) If—

(*a*) the local housing authority are satisfied that a category 2 hazard exists on any residential premises, and
(*b*) no management order is in force in relation to the premises under Chapter 1 or 2 of Part 4,

the authority may make a prohibition order under this section in respect of the hazard.

(2) A prohibition order under this section is an order imposing such prohibition or prohibitions on the use of any premises as is or are specified in the order in accordance with subsection (3) and section 22.

(3) Subsections (3) and (4) of section 20 apply to a prohibition order under this section as they apply to one under that section.

(4) A prohibition order under this section may relate to more than one category 2 hazard on the same premises or in the same building containing one or more flats.

(5) A prohibition order under this section may be combined in one document with an order under section 20 where they impose prohibitions on the use of the same premises or on the use of premises in the same building containing one or more flats.

(6) The operation of a prohibition order under this section may be suspended in accordance with section 23.
[Housing Act 2004, s 21.]

8–17628S 22. Contents of prohibition orders. (1) A prohibition order under section 20 or 21 must comply with the following provisions of this section.

(2) The order must specify, in relation to the hazard (or each of the hazards) to which it relates—

(*a*) whether the order is made under section 20 or 21,
(*b*) the nature of the hazard concerned and the residential premises on which it exists,
(*c*) the deficiency giving rise to the hazard,
(*d*) the premises in relation to which prohibitions are imposed by the order (see subsections (3) and (4)), and
(*e*) any remedial action which the authority consider would, if taken in relation to the hazard, result in their revoking the order under section 25.

(3) The order may impose such prohibition or prohibitions on the use of any premises as—

(*a*) comply with section 20(3) and (4), and
(*b*) the local housing authority consider appropriate in view of the hazard or hazards in respect of which the order is made.

(4) Any such prohibition may prohibit use of any specified premises, or of any part of those premises, either—

(*a*) for all purposes, or
(*b*) for any particular purpose,

except (in either case) to the extent to which any use of the premises or part is approved by the authority.

(5) A prohibition imposed by virtue of subsection (4)(*b*) may, in particular, relate to—

(*a*) occupation of the premises or part by more than a particular number of households or persons; or
(*b*) occupation of the premises or part by particular descriptions of persons.

(6) The order must also contain information about—

(*a*) the right under Part 3 of Schedule 2 to appeal against the order, and
(*b*) the period within which an appeal may be made,

and specify the date on which the order is made.

(7) Any approval of the authority for the purposes of subsection (4) must not be unreasonably withheld.

(8) If the authority do refuse to give any such approval, they must notify the person applying for the approval of—

(*a*) their decision,
(*b*) the reasons for it and the date on which it was made,
(*c*) the right to appeal against the decision under subsection (9), and
(*d*) the period within which an appeal may be made,

within the period of seven days beginning with the day on which the decision was made.

(9) The person applying for the approval may appeal to a residential property tribunal against the

decision within the period of 28 days beginning with the date specified in the notice as the date on which it was made.

(10) In this Part of this Act "specified premises", in relation to a prohibition order, means premises specified in the order, in accordance with subsection (2)(*d*), as premises in relation to which prohibitions are imposed by the order.
[Housing Act 2004, s 22.]

8–17628T 23. Suspension of prohibition orders. (1) A prohibition order may provide for the operation of the order to be suspended until a time, or the occurrence of an event, specified in the order.

(2) The time so specified may, in particular, be the time when a person of a particular description begins, or ceases, to occupy any premises.

(3) The event so specified may, in particular, be a notified breach of an undertaking accepted by the local housing authority for the purposes of this section from a person on whom a copy of the order is served.

(4) In subsection (3) a "notified breach", in relation to such an undertaking, means an act or omission by such a person—

(*a*) which the local housing authority consider to be a breach of the undertaking, and
(*b*) which is notified to that person in accordance with the terms of the undertaking.

[Housing Act 2004, s 23.]

8–17628U 24. Operation of prohibition orders. (1) This section deals with the time when a prohibition order becomes operative.

(2) The general rule is that a prohibition order becomes operative at the end of the period of 28 days beginning with the date specified in the notice as the date on which it is made.

(3) The general rule is subject to subsection (4) (suspended orders) and subsection (5) (appeals).

(4) If the order is suspended under section 23, the order becomes operative at the time when the suspension ends.

This is subject to subsection (5).

(5) If an appeal is brought against the order under Part 3 of Schedule 2, the order does not become operative until such time (if any) as is the operative time for the purposes of this subsection under paragraph 14 of that Schedule (time when order is confirmed on appeal, period for further appeal expires or suspension ends).

(6) If no appeal against a prohibition order is made under that Part of that Schedule within the period for appealing against it, the order is final and conclusive as to matters which could have been raised on an appeal.

(7) Sections 584A and 584B of the Housing Act 1985 (c 68) provide for the payment of compensation where certain prohibition orders become operative, and for the repayment of such compensation in certain circumstances.
[Housing Act 2004, s 24.]

8–17628V 25. Revocation and variation of prohibition orders. (1) The local housing authority must revoke a prohibition order if at any time they are satisfied that the hazard in respect of which the order was made does not then exist on the residential premises specified in the order in accordance with section 22(2)(*b*).

(2) The local housing authority may revoke a prohibition order if—

(*a*) in the case of an order made under section 20, they consider that there are any special circumstances making it appropriate to revoke the order; or
(*b*) in the case of an order made under section 21, they consider that it is appropriate to do so.

(3) Where a prohibition order relates to a number of hazards—

(*a*) subsection (1) is to be read as applying separately in relation to each of those hazards, and
(*b*) if, as a result, the authority are required to revoke only part of the order, they may vary the remainder as they consider appropriate.

(4) The local housing authority may vary a prohibition order—

(*a*) with the agreement of every person on whom copies of the notice were required to be served under Part 1 of Schedule 2, or
(*b*) in the case of an order whose operation is suspended, so as to alter the time or events by reference to which the suspension is to come to an end.

(5) A revocation under this section comes into force at the time when it is made.

(6) If it is made with the agreement of every person within subsection (4)(*a*), a variation under this section comes into force at the time when it is made.

(7) Otherwise a variation under this section does not come into force until such time (if any) as is the operative time for the purposes of this subsection under paragraph 15 of Schedule 2 (time when period for appealing expires without an appeal being made or when decision to revoke or vary is confirmed on appeal).

(8) The power to revoke or vary a prohibition order under this section is exercisable by the authority either—

(*a*) on an application made by a person on whom a copy of the order was required to be served under Part 1 of Schedule 2, or

(*b*) on the authority's own initiative.

[Housing Act 2004, s 25.]

8–17628W 26. Review of suspended prohibition orders. (1) The local housing authority may at any time review a prohibition order whose operation is suspended.

(2) The local housing authority must review a prohibition order whose operation is suspended not later than one year after the date on which the order was made and at subsequent intervals of not more than one year.

(3) Copies of the authority's decision on a review under this section must be served on every person on whom a copy of the order was required to be served under Part 1 of Schedule 2.

[Housing Act 2004, s 26.]

8–17628X 27. Service of copies of prohibition orders etc and related appeals. Schedule 2 (which deals with the service of copies of prohibition orders, and notices relating to their revocation or variation, and with related appeals) has effect.

[Housing Act 2004, s 27.]

Hazard awareness notices

8–17628Y 28. Hazard awareness notices relating to category 1 hazards: duty of authority to serve notice. (1) If—

(*a*) the local housing authority are satisfied that a category 1 hazard exists on any residential premises, and

(*b*) no management order is in force in relation to the premises under Chapter 1 or 2 of Part 4,

serving a hazard awareness notice under this section in respect of the hazard is a course of action available to the authority in relation to the hazard for the purposes of section 5 (category 1 hazards: general duty to take enforcement action).

(2) A hazard awareness notice under this section is a notice advising the person on whom it is served of the existence of a category 1 hazard on the residential premises concerned which arises as a result of a deficiency on the premises in respect of which the notice is served.

(3) The notice may be served in respect of the following premises—

(*a*) if the residential premises on which the hazard exists are a dwelling or HMO which is not a flat, it may be served in respect of the dwelling or HMO;

(*b*) if those premises are one or more flats, it may be served in respect of the building containing the flat or flats (or any part of the building) or any external common parts;

(*c*) if those premises are the common parts of a building containing one or more flats, it may be served in respect of the building (or any part of the building) or any external common parts.

Paragraphs (*b*) and (*c*) are subject to subsection (4).

(4) The notice may not, by virtue of subsection (3)(*b*) or (*c*), be served in respect of any part of the building or its external common parts that is not included in any residential premises on which the hazard exists, unless the authority are satisfied—

(*a*) that the deficiency from which the hazard arises is situated there, and

(*b*) that it is desirable for the notice to be so served in the interests of the health or safety of any actual or potential occupiers of one or more of the flats.

(5) A notice under this section may relate to more than one category 1 hazard on the same premises or in the same building containing one or more flats.

(6) A notice under this section must specify, in relation to the hazard (or each of the hazards) to which it relates—

(*a*) the nature of the hazard and the residential premises on which it exists,

(*b*) the deficiency giving rise to the hazard,

(*c*) the premises on which the deficiency exists,

(*d*) the authority's reasons for deciding to serve the notice, including their reasons for deciding that serving the notice is the most appropriate course of action, and

(*e*) details of the remedial action (if any) which the authority consider that it would be practicable and appropriate to take in relation to the hazard.

(7) Part 1 of Schedule 1 (which relates to the service of improvement notices and copies of such notices) applies to a notice under this section as if it were an improvement notice.

(8) For that purpose, any reference in that Part of that Schedule to "the specified premises" is, in relation to a hazard awareness notice under this section, a reference to the premises specified under subsection (6)(*c*).

[Housing Act 2004, s 28.]

8–17628Z 29. Hazard awareness notices relating to category 2 hazards: power of authority to serve notice. (1) If—

(*a*) the local housing authority are satisfied that a category 2 hazard exists on any residential premises, and

(*b*) no management order is in force in relation to the premises under Chapter 1 or 2 of Part 4,

the authority may serve a hazard awareness notice under this section in respect of the hazard.

(2) A hazard awareness notice under this section is a notice advising the person on whom it is served of the existence of a category 2 hazard on the residential premises concerned which arises as a result of a deficiency on the premises in respect of which the notice is served.

(3) Subsections (3) and (4) of section 28 apply to a hazard awareness notice under this section as they apply to one under that section.

(4) A notice under this section may relate to more than one category 2 hazard on the same premises or in the same building containing one or more flats.

(5) A notice under this section must specify, in relation to the hazard (or each of the hazards) to which it relates—

(*a*) the nature of the hazard and the residential premises on which it exists,

(*b*) the deficiency giving rise to the hazard,

(*c*) the premises on which the deficiency exists,

(*d*) the authority's reasons for deciding to serve the notice, including their reasons for deciding that serving the notice is the most appropriate course of action, and

(*e*) details of the remedial action (if any) which the authority consider that it would be practicable and appropriate to take in relation to the hazard.

(6) A notice under this section may be combined in one document with a notice under section 28 where they are served in respect of the same premises.

(7) Part 1 of Schedule 1 (which relates to the service of improvement notices and copies of such notices) applies to a notice under this section as if it were an improvement notice.

(8) For that purpose, any reference in that Part of that Schedule to "the specified premises" is, in relation to a hazard awareness notice under this section, a reference to the premises specified under subsection (5)(*c*).

[Housing Act 2004, s 29.]

Enforcement: improvement notices

8–17628ZA 30. Offence of failing to comply with improvement notice. (1) Where an improvement notice has become operative, the person on whom the notice was served commits an offence if he fails to comply with it.

(2) For the purposes of this Chapter compliance with an improvement notice means, in relation to each hazard, beginning and completing any remedial action specified in the notice—

(*a*) (if no appeal is brought against the notice) not later than the date specified under section 13(2)(*e*) and within the period specified under section 13(2)(*f*);

(*b*) (if an appeal is brought against the notice and is not withdrawn) not later than such date and within such period as may be fixed by the tribunal determining the appeal; and

(*c*) (if an appeal brought against the notice is withdrawn) not later than the 21st day after the date on which the notice becomes operative and within the period (beginning on that 21st day) specified in the notice under section 13(2)(*f*).

(3) A person who commits an offence under subsection (1) is liable on summary conviction to a fine not exceeding level 5 on the standard scale.

(4) In proceedings against a person for an offence under subsection (1) it is a defence that he had a reasonable excuse for failing to comply with the notice.

(5) The obligation to take any remedial action specified in the notice in relation to a hazard continues despite the fact that the period for completion of the action has expired.

(6) In this section any reference to any remedial action specified in a notice includes a reference to any part of any remedial action which is required to be completed within a particular period specified in the notice.

[Housing Act 2004, s 30.]

8–17628ZB 31. Enforcement action by local housing authorities. Schedule 3 (which enables enforcement action in respect of an improvement notice to be taken by local housing authorities either with or without agreement and which provides for the recovery of related expenses) has effect.

[Housing Act 2004, s 31.]

Enforcement: prohibition orders

8–17628ZC 32. Offence of failing to comply with prohibition order etc. (1) A person commits an offence if, knowing that a prohibition order has become operative in relation to any specified premises, he—

(*a*) uses the premises in contravention of the order, or
(*b*) permits the premises to be so used.

(2) A person who commits an offence under subsection (1) is liable on summary conviction—

(*a*) to a fine not exceeding level 5 on the standard scale, and
(*b*) to a further fine not exceeding £20 for every day or part of a day on which he so uses the premises, or permits them to be so used, after conviction.

(3) In proceedings against a person for an offence under subsection (1) it is a defence that he had a reasonable excuse for using the premises, or (as the case may be) permitting them to be used, in contravention of the order.
[Housing Act 2004, s 32.]

8–17628ZD 33. Recovery of possession of premises in order to comply with order. Nothing in—

(*a*) the Rent Act 1977 (c 42) or the Rent (Agriculture) Act 1976 (c 80), or
(*b*) Part 1 of the Housing Act 1988 (c 50),

prevents possession being obtained by the owner of any specified premises in relation to which a prohibition order is operative if possession of the premises is necessary for the purpose of complying with the order.
[Housing Act 2004, s 33.]

34. Power of tribunal to determine or vary lease

Enforcement: improvement notices and prohibition orders

8–17628ZE 35. Power of court to order occupier or owner to allow action to be taken on premises. (1) This section applies where an improvement notice or prohibition order has become operative.

(2) If the occupier of any specified premises—

(*a*) has received reasonable notice of any intended action in relation to the premises, but
(*b*) is preventing a relevant person, or any representative of a relevant person or of the local housing authority, from taking that action in relation to the premises,

a magistrates' court may order the occupier to permit to be done on the premises anything which the court considers is necessary or expedient for the purpose of enabling the intended action to be taken.

(3) If a relevant person—

(*a*) has received reasonable notice of any intended action in relation to any specified premises, but
(*b*) is preventing a representative of the local housing authority from taking that action in relation to the premises,

a magistrates' court may order the relevant person to permit to be done on the premises anything which the court considers is necessary or expedient for the purpose of enabling the intended action to be taken.

(4) A person who fails to comply with an order of the court under this section commits an offence.

(5) In proceedings for an offence under subsection (4) it is a defence that the person had a reasonable excuse for failing to comply with the order.

(6) A person who commits an offence under subsection (4) is liable on summary conviction to a fine not exceeding £20 in respect of each day or part of a day during which the failure continues.

(7) In this section "intended action", in relation to any specified premises, means—

(*a*) where an improvement notice has become operative, any action which the person on whom that notice has been served is required by the notice to take in relation to the premises and which—
   (*a*) (in the context of subsection (2)) is proposed to be taken by or on behalf of that person or on behalf of the local housing authority in pursuance of Schedule 3, or
   (*b*) (in the context of subsection (3)) is proposed to be taken on behalf of the local housing authority in pursuance of Schedule 3;
(*b*) where a prohibition order has become operative, any action which is proposed to be taken and which either is necessary for the purpose of giving effect to the order or is remedial action specified in the order in accordance with section 22(2)(*e*).

(8) In this section—

"relevant person", in relation to any premises, means a person who is an owner of the premises, a person having control of or managing the premises, or the holder of any licence under Part 2 or 3 in respect of the premises;

"representative" in relation to a relevant person or a local housing authority, means any officer, employee, agent or contractor of that person or authority.
[Housing Act 2004, s 35.]

8–17628ZF 36. Power of court to authorise action by one owner on behalf of another. (1) Where an improvement notice or prohibition order has become operative, an owner of any specified premises may apply to a magistrates' court for an order under subsection (2).

(2) A magistrates' court may, on an application under subsection (1), make an order enabling the applicant—

(*a*) immediately to enter on the premises, and
(*b*) to take any required action within a period fixed by the order.

(3) In this section "required action" means—

(*a*) in the case of an improvement notice, any remedial action which is required to be taken by the notice;
(*b*) in the case of a prohibition order, any action necessary for the purpose of complying with the order or any remedial action specified in the order in accordance with section 22(2)(*e*).

(4) No order may be made under subsection (2) unless the court is satisfied that the interests of the applicant will be prejudiced as a result of a failure by another person to take any required action.

(5) No order may be made under subsection (2) unless notice of the application has been given to the local housing authority.

(6) If it considers that it is appropriate to do so, the court may make an order in favour of any other owner of the premises which is similar to the order that it is making in relation to the premises under subsection (2).
[Housing Act 2004, s 36.]

Supplementary provisions

37. Effect of improvement notices and prohibition orders as local land charges

38. Savings for rights arising from breach of covenant etc

39. Effect of Part 4 enforcement action and redevelopment proposals

CHAPTER 3[1]

Emergency Measures

Emergency remedial action

8–17628ZG 40. Emergency remedial action. (1) If—

(*a*) the local housing authority are satisfied that a category 1 hazard exists on any residential premises, and
(*b*) they are further satisfied that the hazard involves an imminent risk of serious harm to the health or safety of any of the occupiers of those or any other residential premises, and
(*c*) no management order is in force under Chapter 1 or 2 of Part 4 in relation to the premises mentioned in paragraph (*a*),

the taking by the authority of emergency remedial action under this section in respect of the hazard is a course of action available to the authority in relation to the hazard for the purposes of section 5 (category 1 hazards: general duty to take enforcement action).

(2) "Emergency remedial action" means such remedial action in respect of the hazard concerned as the authority consider immediately necessary in order to remove the imminent risk of serious harm within subsection (1)(*b*).

(3) Emergency remedial action under this section may be taken by the authority in relation to any premises in relation to which remedial action could be required to be taken by an improvement notice under section 11 (see subsections (3) and (4) of that section).

(4) Emergency remedial action under this section may be taken by the authority in respect of more than one category 1 hazard on the same premises or in the same building containing one or more flats.

(5) Paragraphs 3 to 5 of Schedule 3 (improvement notices: enforcement action by local authorities) apply in connection with the taking of emergency remedial action under this section as they apply in connection with the taking of the remedial action required by an improvement notice which has become operative but has not been complied with.

But those paragraphs so apply with the modifications set out in subsection (6).

(6) The modifications are as follows—

(*a*) the right of entry conferred by paragraph 3(4) may be exercised at any time; and
(*b*) the notice required by paragraph 4 (notice before entering premises) must (instead of being served in accordance with that paragraph) be served on every person, who to the authority's knowledge—

(i) is an occupier of the premises in relation to which the authority propose to take emergency remedial action, or

(ii) if those premises are common parts of a building containing one or more flats, is an occupier of any part of the building; but

(*c*) that notice is to be regarded as so served if a copy of it is fixed to some conspicuous part of the premises or building.

(7) Within the period of seven days beginning with the date when the authority start taking emergency remedial action, the authority must serve—

(*a*) a notice under section 41, and
(*b*) copies of such a notice,

on the persons on whom the authority would be required under Part 1 of Schedule 1 to serve an improvement notice and copies of it.

(8) Section 240 (warrant to authorise entry) applies for the purpose of enabling a local housing authority to enter any premises to take emergency remedial action under this section in relation to the premises, as if—

(*a*) that purpose were mentioned in subsection (2) of that section, and
(*b*) the circumstances as to which the justice of the peace must be satisfied under subsection (4) were that there are reasonable grounds for believing that the authority will not be able to gain admission to the premises without a warrant.

(9) For the purposes of the operation of any provision relating to improvement notices as it applies by virtue of this section in connection with emergency remedial action or a notice under section 41, any reference in that provision to the specified premises is to be read as a reference to the premises specified, in accordance with section 41(2)(*c*), as those in relation to which emergency remedial action has been (or is to be) taken.
[Housing Act 2004, s 40.]

---

1. Chapter 3 contains ss 40–45.

8–17628ZH 41. Notice of emergency remedial action. (1) The notice required by section 40(7) is a notice which complies with the following requirements of this section.

(2) The notice must specify, in relation to the hazard (or each of the hazards) to which it relates—

(*a*) the nature of the hazard and the residential premises on which it exists,
(*b*) the deficiency giving rise to the hazard,
(*c*) the premises in relation to which emergency remedial action has been (or is to be) taken by the authority under section 40 and the nature of that remedial action,
(*d*) the power under which that remedial action has been (or is to be) taken by the authority, and
(*e*) the date when that remedial action was (or is to be) started.

(3) The notice must contain information about—

(*a*) the right to appeal under section 45 against the decision of the authority to make the order, and
(*b*) the period within which an appeal may be made.
[Housing Act 2004, s 41.

42. Recovery of expenses of taking emergency remedial action

Emergency prohibition orders

8–17628ZI 43. Emergency prohibition orders. (1) If—

(*a*) the local housing authority are satisfied that a category 1 hazard exists on any residential premises, and
(*b*) they are further satisfied that the hazard involves an imminent risk of serious harm to the health or safety of any of the occupiers of those or any other residential premises, and
(*c*) no management order is in force under Chapter 1 or 2 of Part 4 in relation to the premises mentioned in paragraph (*a*),

making an emergency prohibition order under this section in respect of the hazard is a course of action available to the authority in relation to the hazard for the purposes of section 5 (category 1 hazards: general duty to take enforcement action).

(2) An emergency prohibition order under this section is an order imposing, with immediate effect, such prohibition or prohibitions on the use of any premises as are specified in the order in accordance with subsection (3) and section 44.

(3) As regards the imposition of any such prohibition or prohibitions, the following provisions apply to an emergency prohibition order as they apply to a prohibition order under section 20—

(*a*) subsections (3) to (5) of that section, and
(*b*) subsections (3) to (5) and (7) to (9) of section 22.

(4) Part 1 of Schedule 2 (service of copies of prohibition orders) applies in relation to an emergency prohibition order as it applies to a prohibition order, but any requirement to serve copies within a specified period of seven days is to be read as a reference to serve them on the day on which the emergency prohibition order is made (or, if that is not possible, as soon after that day as is possible).

(5) The following provisions also apply to an emergency prohibition order as they apply to a prohibition order (or to a prohibition order which has become operative, as the case may be)—

(*a*) section 25 (revocation and variation);
(*b*) sections 32 to 36 (enforcement);
(*c*) sections 37 to 39 (supplementary provisions); and
(*d*) Part 2 of Schedule 2 (notices relating to revocation or variation);
(*e*) Part 3 of that Schedule (appeals) so far as it relates to any decision to vary, or to refuse to revoke or vary, a prohibition order; and
(*f*) sections 584A and 584B of the Housing Act 1985 (c 68) (payment, and repayment, of compensation).

(6) For the purposes of the operation of any provision relating to prohibition orders as it applies in connection with emergency prohibition orders by virtue of this section or section 45, any reference in that provision to the specified premises is to be read as a reference to the premises specified, in accordance with section 44(2)(*c*), as the premises in relation to which prohibitions are imposed by the order.
[Housing Act 2004, s 43.]

8–17628ZJ 44. Contents of emergency prohibition orders. (1) An emergency prohibition order under section 43 must comply with the following requirements of this section.

(2) The order must specify, in relation to the hazard (or each of the hazards) to which it relates—

(*a*) the nature of the hazard concerned and the residential premises on which it exists,
(*b*) the deficiency giving rise to the hazard,
(*c*) the premises in relation to which prohibitions are imposed by the order (see subsections (3) and (4) of section 22 as applied by section 43(3)), and
(*d*) any remedial action which the authority consider would, if taken in relation to the hazard, result in their revoking the order under section 25 (as applied by section 43(5)).

(3) The order must contain information about—

(*a*) the right to appeal under section 45 against the order, and
(*b*) the period within which an appeal may be made,

and specify the date on which the order is made.
[Housing Act 2004, s 44.]

Appeals

8–17628ZK 45. Appeals relating to emergency measures

CHAPTER 4[1]

Demolition Orders and Slum Clearance Declarations

1. Chapter 4 contains ss 46–48. This chapter is concerned with demolition orders, slum clearance declarations and appeals. It amends various provisions of the Housing Act 1985.

CHAPTER 5[1]

General and Miscellaneous Provisions Relating to Enforcement Action

1. Chapter 5 contains ss 49–54. Sections 49–53 provide for the recovery of expenses relating to enforcement action and for certain repeals.

Index

8–17628ZL 54. Index of defined expressions: Part 1. The following table shows where expressions used in this Part are defined or otherwise explained.

Expression	*Provision of this Act*
Appropriate national authority	Section 261(1)
Building containing one or more flats	Section 1(5)
Category 1 hazard	Section 2(1)
Category 2 hazard	Section 2(1)
Common parts	Section 1(5)
Compliance with improvement notice	Section 30(2)

Expression	*Provision of this Act*
District of local housing authority	Section 261(6)
Dwelling	Section 1(5), (6)
External common parts	Section 1(5)
Flat	Section 1(5) to (7)
Hazard	Section 2(1)
Hazard awareness notice	Section 28(2) or 29(2)
Health	Section 2(5)
HMO	Section 1(5), (6) (and see also section 1(8))
Improvement notice	Section 11(2) or 12(2)
Lease, lessee etc	Section 262(1) to (4)
Local housing authority	Section 261(2) to (5)
Occupier (and related expressions)	Section 262(6)
Owner	Section 262(7)
Person having control	Section 263(1) and (2)
Person managing	Section 263(3) and (4)
Prohibition order	Section 20(2) or 21(2)
Remedial action	Section 11(8)
Residential premises	Section 1(4)
Residential property tribunal	Section 229
Specified premises, in relation to an improvement notice	Section 13(5)
Specified premises, in relation to a prohibition order	Section 22(10)
Tenancy, tenant	Section 262(1) to (5)
Unoccupied HMO accommodation	Section 1(5) (and see also section 1(8)).

PART 2[1]
LICENSING OF HOUSES IN MULTIPLE OCCUPATION

Introductory

8–17628ZM 55. Licensing of HMOs to which this Part applies. (1) This Part provides for HMOs to be licensed by local housing authorities where—

(*a*) they are HMOs to which this Part applies (see subsection (2)), and

(*b*) they are required to be licensed under this Part (see section 61(1)).

(2) This Part applies to the following HMOs in the case of each local housing authority—

(*a*) any HMO in the authority's district which falls within any prescribed description of HMO, and

(*b*) if an area is for the time being designated by the authority under section 56 as subject to additional licensing, any HMO in that area which falls within any description of HMO specified in the designation.

(3) The appropriate national authority may by order prescribe descriptions of HMOs for the purposes of subsection (2)(*a*).

(4) The power conferred by subsection (3) may be exercised in such a way that this Part applies to all HMOs in the district of a local housing authority.

(5) Every local housing authority have the following general duties—

(*a*) to make such arrangements as are necessary to secure the effective implementation in their district of the licensing regime provided for by this Part;

(*b*) to ensure that all applications for licences and other issues falling to be determined by them under this Part are determined within a reasonable time; and

(*c*) to satisfy themselves, as soon as is reasonably practicable, that there are no Part 1 functions that ought to be exercised by them in relation to the premises in respect of which such applications are made.

(6) For the purposes of subsection (5)(*c*)—

(*a*) "Part 1 function" means any duty under section 5 to take any course of action to which that section applies or any power to take any course of action to which section 7 applies; and

(*b*) the authority may take such steps as they consider appropriate (whether or not involving an inspection) to comply with their duty under subsection (5)(*c*) in relation to each of the premises in question, but they must in any event comply with it within the period of 5 years beginning with the date of the application for a licence.

[Housing Act 2004, s 55.]

1. Part 2 contains ss 55–78. Section 55 (1), (2) and (5)(*a*) and (*b*), and ss 56 and 57 came into force in relation to England and Wales on 15 June 2005 (see Housing Act 2004 (Commencement No 3) (England) Order 2005, SI 2005/1451;

and Housing Act 2004 (Commencement No 2) (Wales) Order 2005, SI 2005/3237). Otherwise, at the date of going to press Part 2 was not in force save for the provisions that confer any powers to make orders or regulations which are exercisable by the Secretary of State or the National Assembly of Wales (see s 270(2)(*b*)).

Designation of additional licensing areas

8–17628ZN 56. Designation of areas subject to additional licensing. (1) A local housing authority may designate either—

(*a*) the area of their district, or
(*b*) an area in their district,

as subject to additional licensing in relation to a description of HMOs specified in the designation, if the requirements of this section are met.

(2) The authority must consider that a significant proportion of the HMOs of that description in the area are being managed sufficiently ineffectively as to give rise, or to be likely to give rise, to one or more particular problems either for those occupying the HMOs or for members of the public.

(3) Before making a designation the authority must—

(*a*) take reasonable steps to consult persons who are likely to be affected by the designation; and
(*b*) consider any representations made in accordance with the consultation and not withdrawn.

(4) The power to make a designation under this section may be exercised in such a way that this Part applies to all HMOs in the area in question.

(5) In forming an opinion as to the matter mentioned in subsection (2), the authority must have regard to any information regarding the extent to which any codes of practice approved under section 233 have been complied with by persons managing HMOs in the area in question.

(6) Section 57 applies for the purposes of this section.

[Housing Act 2004, s 56.]

8–17628ZO 57. Designations under section 56: further considerations. (1) This section applies to the power of a local housing authority to make designations under section 56.

(2) The authority must ensure that any exercise of the power is consistent with the authority's overall housing strategy.

(3) The authority must also seek to adopt a co-ordinated approach in connection with dealing with homelessness, empty properties and anti-social behaviour affecting the private rented sector, both—

(*a*) as regards combining licensing under this Part with other courses of action available to them, and
(*b*) as regards combining such licensing with measures taken by other persons.

(4) The authority must not make a particular designation under section 56 unless—

(*a*) they have considered whether there are any other courses of action available to them (of whatever nature) that might provide an effective method of dealing with the problem or problems in question, and
(*b*) they consider that making the designation will significantly assist them to deal with the problem or problems (whether or not they take any other course of action as well).

(5) In this Act "anti-social behaviour" means conduct on the part of occupiers of, or visitors to, residential premises—

(*a*) which causes or is likely to cause a nuisance or annoyance to persons residing, visiting or otherwise engaged in lawful activities in the vicinity of such premises, or
(*b*) which involves or is likely to involve the use of such premises for illegal purposes.

[Housing Act 2004, s 57.]

8–17628ZP 58. Designation needs confirmation or general approval to be effective. (1) A designation of an area as subject to additional licensing cannot come into force unless—

(*a*) it has been confirmed by the appropriate national authority; or
(*b*) it falls within a description of designations in relation to which that authority has given a general approval in accordance with subsection (6).

(2) The appropriate national authority may either confirm, or refuse to confirm, a designation as it considers appropriate.

(3) If the appropriate national authority confirms a designation, the designation comes into force on the date specified for this purpose by that authority.

(4) That date must be no earlier than three months after the date on which the designation is confirmed.

(5) A general approval may be given in relation to a description of designations framed by reference to any matters or circumstances.

(6) Accordingly a general approval may (in particular) be given in relation to—

(*a*) designations made by a specified local housing authority;

(*b*) designations made by a local housing authority falling within a specified description of such authorities;

(*c*) designations relating to HMOs of a specified description.

"Specified" means specified by the appropriate national authority in the approval.

(7) If, by virtue of a general approval, a designation does not need to be confirmed before it comes into force, the designation comes into force on the date specified for this purpose in the designation.

(8) That date must be no earlier than three months after the date on which the designation is made.

[Housing Act 2004, s 58.]

8–17628ZQ 59. Notification requirements relating to designations. (1) This section applies to a designation—

(*a*) when it is confirmed under section 58, or

(*b*) (if it is not required to be so confirmed) when it is made by the local housing authority.

(2) As soon as the designation is confirmed or made, the authority must publish in the prescribed manner a notice stating—

(*a*) that the designation has been made,

(*b*) whether or not the designation was required to be confirmed and either that it has been confirmed or that a general approval under section 58 applied to it (giving details of the approval in question),

(*c*) the date on which the designation is to come into force, and

(*d*) any other information which may be prescribed.

(3) After publication of a notice under subsection (2), and for as long as the designation is in force, the local housing authority must make available to the public in accordance with any prescribed requirements—

(*a*) copies of the designation, and

(*b*) such information relating to the designation as is prescribed.

(4) In this section "prescribed" means prescribed by regulations made by the appropriate national authority.

[Housing Act 2004, s 59.]

8–17628ZR 60. Duration, review and revocation of designations. (1) Unless previously revoked under subsection (4), a designation ceases to have effect at the time that is specified for this purpose in the designation.

(2) That time must be no later than five years after the date on which the designation comes into force.

(3) A local housing authority must from time to time review the operation of any designation made by them.

(4) If following a review they consider it appropriate to do so, the authority may revoke the designation.

(5) If they do revoke the designation, the designation ceases to have effect at the time that is specified by the authority for this purpose.

(6) On revoking a designation the authority must publish notice of the revocation in such manner as is prescribed by regulations made by the appropriate national authority.

[Housing Act 2004, s 60.]

HMOs required to be licensed

8–17628ZS 61. Requirement for HMOs to be licensed. (1) Every HMO to which this Part applies must be licensed under this Part unless—

(*a*) a temporary exemption notice is in force in relation to it under section 62, or

(*b*) an interim or final management order is in force in relation to it under Chapter 1 of Part 4.

(2) A licence under this Part is a licence authorising occupation of the house concerned by not more than a maximum number of households or persons specified in the licence.

(3) Sections 63 to 67 deal with applications for licences, the granting or refusal of licences and the imposition of licence conditions.

(4) The local housing authority must take all reasonable steps to secure that applications for licences are made to them in respect of HMOs in their area which are required to be licensed under this Part but are not.

(5) The appropriate national authority may by regulations provide for—

(*a*) any provision of this Part, or

(*b*) section 263 (in its operation for the purposes of any such provision),

to have effect in relation to a section 257 HMO with such modifications as are prescribed by the regulations.

A "section 257 HMO" is an HMO which is a converted block of flats to which section 257 applies.

(6) In this Part (unless the context otherwise requires)—

(*a*) references to a licence are to a licence under this Part,

(*b*) references to a licence holder are to be read accordingly, and

(*c*) references to an HMO being (or not being) licensed under this Part are to its being (or not being) an HMO in respect of which a licence is in force under this Part.

[Housing Act 2004, s 61.]

62. Temporary exemption from licensing requirement

Grant or refusal of licences

63. Applications for licences

64. Grant or refusal of licence

65. Tests as to suitability for multiple occupation

66. Tests for fitness etc and satisfactory management arrangements

8–17628ZT **67. Licence conditions.** (1) A licence may include such conditions as the local housing authority consider appropriate for regulating all or any of the following—

(*a*) the management, use and occupation of the house concerned, and

(*b*) its condition and contents.

(2) Those conditions may, in particular, include (so far as appropriate in the circumstances)—

(*a*) conditions imposing restrictions or prohibitions on the use or occupation of particular parts of the house by persons occupying it;

(*b*) conditions requiring the taking of reasonable and practicable steps to prevent or reduce anti-social behaviour by persons occupying or visiting the house;

(*c*) conditions requiring facilities and equipment to be made available in the house for the purpose of meeting standards prescribed under section 65;

(*d*) conditions requiring such facilities and equipment to be kept in repair and proper working order;

(*e*) conditions requiring, in the case of any works needed in order for any such facilities or equipment to be made available or to meet any such standards, that the works are carried out within such period or periods as may be specified in, or determined under, the licence;

(*f*) conditions requiring the licence holder or the manager of the house to attend training courses in relation to any applicable code of practice approved under section 233.

(3) A licence must include the conditions required by Schedule 4.

(4) As regards the relationship between the authority's power to impose conditions under this section and functions exercisable by them under or for the purposes of Part 1 ("Part 1 functions")—

(*a*) the authority must proceed on the basis that, in general, they should seek to identify, remove or reduce category 1 or category 2 hazards in the house by the exercise of Part 1 functions and not by means of licence conditions;

(*b*) this does not, however, prevent the authority from imposing licence conditions relating to the installation or maintenance of facilities or equipment within subsection (2)(*c*) above, even if the same result could be achieved by the exercise of Part 1 functions;

(*c*) the fact that licence conditions are imposed for a particular purpose that could be achieved by the exercise of Part 1 functions does not affect the way in which Part 1 functions can be subsequently exercised by the authority.

(5) A licence may not include conditions imposing restrictions or obligations on a particular person other than the licence holder unless that person has consented to the imposition of the restrictions or obligations.

(6) A licence may not include conditions requiring (or intended to secure) any alteration in the terms of any tenancy or licence under which any person occupies the house.

[Housing Act 2004, s 67.]

8–17628ZU **68. Licences: general requirements and duration.** (1) A licence may not relate to more than one HMO.

(2) A licence may be granted before the time when it is required by virtue of this Part but, if so, the licence cannot come into force until that time.

(3) A licence—

(*a*) comes into force at the time that is specified in or determined under the licence for this purpose, and

(*b*) unless previously terminated by subsection (7) or revoked under section 70, continues in force for the period that is so specified or determined.

(4) That period must not end more than 5 years after—

(*a*) the date on which the licence was granted, or

(*b*) if the licence was granted as mentioned in subsection (2), the date when the licence comes into force.

(5) Subsection (3)(*b*) applies even if, at any time during that period, the HMO concerned subsequently ceases to be one to which this Part applies.

(6) A licence may not be transferred to another person.

(7) If the holder of the licence dies while the licence is in force, the licence ceases to be in force on his death.

(8) However, during the period of 3 months beginning with the date of the licence holder's death, the house is to be treated for the purposes of this Part and Part 3 as if on that date a temporary exemption notice had been served in respect of the house under section 62.

(9) If, at any time during that period ("the initial period"), the personal representatives of the licence holder request the local housing authority to do so, the authority may serve on them a notice which, during the period of 3 months after the date on which the initial period ends, has the same effect as a temporary exemption notice under section 62.

(10) Subsections (6) to (8) of section 62 apply (with any necessary modifications) in relation to a decision by the authority not to serve such a notice as they apply in relation to a decision not to serve a temporary exemption notice.

[Housing Act 2004, s 68.]

Variation and revocation of licences

69. Variation of licences

70. Revocation of licences

Procedure and appeals

71. Procedural requirements and appeals against licence decisions

Enforcement

8–17628ZV **72. Offences in relation to licensing of HMOs.** (1) A person commits an offence if he is a person having control of or managing an HMO which is required to be licensed under this Part (see section 61(1)) but is not so licensed.

(2) A person commits an offence if—

(*a*) he is a person having control of or managing an HMO which is licensed under this Part,

(*b*) he knowingly permits another person to occupy the house, and

(*c*) the other person's occupation results in the house being occupied by more households or persons than is authorised by the licence.

(3) A person commits an offence if—

(*a*) he is a licence holder or a person on whom restrictions or obligations under a licence are imposed in accordance with section 67(5), and

(*b*) he fails to comply with any condition of the licence.

(4) In proceedings against a person for an offence under subsection (1) it is a defence that, at the material time—

(*a*) a notification had been duly given in respect of the house under section 62(1), or

(*b*) an application for a licence had been duly made in respect of the house under section 63,

and that notification or application was still effective (see subsection (8)).

(5) In proceedings against a person for an offence under subsection (1), (2) or (3) it is a defence that he had a reasonable excuse—

(*a*) for having control of or managing the house in the circumstances mentioned in subsection (1), or

(*b*) for permitting the person to occupy the house, or

(*c*) for failing to comply with the condition,

as the case may be.

(6) A person who commits an offence under subsection (1) or (2) is liable on summary conviction to a fine not exceeding £20,000.

(7) A person who commits an offence under subsection (3) is liable on summary conviction to a fine not exceeding level 5 on the standard scale.

(8) For the purposes of subsection (4) a notification or application is "effective" at a particular time if at that time it has not been withdrawn, and either—

(*a*) the authority have not decided whether to serve a temporary exemption notice, or (as the case may be) grant a licence, in pursuance of the notification or application, or (*b*) if they have decided not to do so, one of the conditions set out in subsection (9) is met.

(9) The conditions are—

(*a*) that the period for appealing against the decision of the authority not to serve or grant such a notice or licence (or against any relevant decision of a residential property tribunal) has not expired, or

(*b*) that an appeal has been brought against the authority's decision (or against any relevant decision of such a tribunal) and the appeal has not been determined or withdrawn.

(10) In subsection (9) "relevant decision" means a decision which is given on an appeal to the tribunal and confirms the authority's decision (with or without variation).

[Housing Act 2004, s 72.]

73. Other consequences of operating unlicensed HMOs: rent repayment orders

74. Further provisions about rent repayment orders

75. Other consequences of operating unlicensed HMOs: restriction on terminating tenancies

Supplementary provisions

8–17628ZW **76. Transitional arrangements relating to introduction and termination of licensing.** (1) Subsection (2) applies where—

(*a*) an order under section 55(3) which prescribes a particular description of HMOs comes into force; or

(*b*) a designation under section 56 comes into force in relation to HMOs of a particular description.

(2) This Part applies in relation to the occupation by persons or households of such HMOs on or after the coming into force of the order or designation even if their occupation began before, or in pursuance of a contract made before, it came into force.

This is subject to subsections (3) to (5).

(3) Subsection (4) applies where—

(*a*) an HMO which is licensed under this Part, or a part of such an HMO, is occupied by more households or persons than the number permitted by the licence; and

(*b*) the occupation of all or any of those households or persons began before, or in pursuance of a contract made before, the licence came into force.

(4) In proceedings against a person for an offence under section 72(2) it is a defence that at the material time he was taking all reasonable steps to try to reduce the number of households or persons occupying the house to the number permitted by the licence.

(5) Subsection (4) does not apply if the licence came into force immediately after a previous licence in respect of the same HMO unless the occupation in question began before, or in pursuance of a contract made before, the coming into force of the original licence.

(6) An order under section 270 may make provision as regards the licensing under this Part of HMOs—

(*a*) which are registered immediately before the appointed day under a scheme to which section 347 (schemes containing control provisions) or 348B (schemes containing special control provisions) of the Housing Act 1985 (c 68) applies, or

(*b*) in respect of which applications for registration under such a scheme are then pending.

(7) In subsection (6) "the appointed day" means the day appointed for the coming into force of section 61.

[Housing Act 2004, s 76.]

8–17628ZX **77. Meaning of "HMO".** In this Part—

(*a*) "HMO" means a house in multiple occupation as defined by sections 254 to 259, and

(*b*) references to an HMO include (where the context permits) any yard, garden, outhouses and appurtenances belonging to, or usually enjoyed with, it (or any part of it).

[Housing Act 2004, s 77.]

8–17628ZY **78. Index of defined expressions: Part 2.** The following table shows where expressions used in this Part are defined or otherwise explained.

Expression	*Provision of this Act*
Anti-social behaviour	Section 57(5)
Appropriate national authority	Section 261(1)

Expression	*Provision of this Act*
Category 1 hazard	Section 2(1)
Category 2 hazard	Section 2(1)
District of local housing authority	Section 261(6)
HMO	Section 77
HMO to which this Part applies	Section 55(2)
Licence and licence holder	Section 61(6)
Licence (to occupy premises)	Section 262(9)
Local housing authority	Section 261(2) to (5)
Modifications	Section 250(7)
Occupier (and related expressions)	Section 262(6)
Person having control	Section 263(1) and (2) (and see also section 66(7))
Person having estate or interest	Section 262(8)
Person managing	Section 263(3)
Person involved in management	Section 263(5)
Residential property tribunal	Section 229
Tenant	Section 262(1) to (5).

[Housing Act 2004, s 78.]

PART 3[1]
SELECTIVE LICENSING OF OTHER RESIDENTIAL ACCOMMODATION

Introductory

8–17628ZZ 79. Licensing of houses to which this Part applies. (1) This Part provides for houses to be licensed by local housing authorities where—

(*a*) they are houses to which this Part applies (see subsection (2)), and
(*b*) they are required to be licensed under this Part (see section 85(1)).

(2) This Part applies to a house if—

(*a*) it is in an area that is for the time being designated under section 80 as subject to selective licensing, and
(*b*) the whole of it is occupied either—
  (i) under a single tenancy or licence that is not an exempt tenancy or licence under subsection (3) or (4), or
  (ii) under two or more tenancies or licences in respect of different dwellings contained in it, none of which is an exempt tenancy or licence under subsection (3) or (4).

(3) A tenancy or licence is an exempt tenancy or licence if it is granted by a body which is registered as a social landlord under Part 1 of the Housing Act 1996 (c 52).

(4) In addition, the appropriate national authority may by order provide for a tenancy or licence to be an exempt tenancy or licence—

(*a*) if it falls within any description of tenancy or licence specified in the order; or
(*b*) in any other circumstances so specified.

(5) Every local housing authority have the following general duties—

(*a*) to make such arrangements as are necessary to secure the effective implementation in their district of the licensing regime provided for by this Part; and
(*b*) to ensure that all applications for licences and other issues falling to be determined by them under this Part are determined within a reasonable time.

[Housing Act 2004, s 79.]

---

1. Part 3 contains ss 79–100. Sections 79, 80 and 81 came in to force in relation to England and Wales on 25 November 2005 (see Housing Act 2004 (Commencement No 3) (England) Order 2005, SI 2005/1451; and Housing Act 2004 (Commencement No 2) (Wales) Order 2005, SI 2005/3237). Otherwise, at the date of going to press Part 3 was not in

force save for the provisions that confer any powers to make orders or regulations which are exercisable by the Secretary of State or the National Assembly of Wales (see s 270(2)(*b*)).

Designation of selective licensing areas

8–17629 **80. Designation of selective licensing areas.** (1) A local housing authority may designate either—

(*a*) the area of their district, or
(*b*) an area in their district,

as subject to selective licensing, if the requirements of subsections (2) and (9) are met.

(2) The authority must consider that—

(*a*) the first or second set of general conditions mentioned in subsection (3) or (6), or
(*b*) any conditions specified in an order under subsection (7) as an additional set of conditions,

are satisfied in relation to the area.

(3) The first set of general conditions are—

(*a*) that the area is, or is likely to become, an area of low housing demand; and
(*b*) that making a designation will, when combined with other measures taken in the area by the local housing authority, or by other persons together with the local housing authority, contribute to the improvement of the social or economic conditions in the area.

(4) In deciding whether an area is, or is likely to become, an area of low housing demand a local housing authority must take into account (among other matters)—

(*a*) the value of residential premises in the area, in comparison to the value of similar premises in other areas which the authority consider to be comparable (whether in terms of types of housing, local amenities, availability of transport or otherwise);
(*b*) the turnover of occupiers of residential premises;
(*c*) the number of residential premises which are available to buy or rent and the length of time for which they remain unoccupied.

(5) The appropriate national authority may by order amend subsection (4) by adding new matters to those for the time being mentioned in that subsection.

(6) The second set of general conditions are—

(*a*) that the area is experiencing a significant and persistent problem caused by anti-social behaviour;
(*b*) that some or all of the private sector landlords who have let premises in the area (whether under leases or licences) are failing to take action to combat the problem that it would be appropriate for them to take; and
(*c*) that making a designation will, when combined with other measures taken in the area by the local housing authority, or by other persons together with the local housing authority, lead to a reduction in, or the elimination of, the problem.

"Private sector landlord" does not include a registered social landlord within the meaning of Part 1 of the Housing Act 1996 (c 52).

(7) The appropriate national authority may by order provide for any conditions specified in the order to apply as an additional set of conditions for the purposes of subsection (2).

(8) The conditions that may be specified include, in particular, conditions intended to permit a local housing authority to make a designation for the purpose of dealing with one or more specified problems affecting persons occupying Part 3 houses in the area.

"Specified" means specified in an order under subsection (7).

(9) Before making a designation the local housing authority must—

(*a*) take reasonable steps to consult persons who are likely to be affected by the designation; and
(*b*) consider any representations made in accordance with the consultation and not withdrawn.

(10) Section 81 applies for the purposes of this section.

[Housing Act 2004, s 80.]

81. Designations under section 80: further considerations

82. Designation needs confirmation or general approval to be effective

83. Notification requirements relating to designations

84. Duration, review and revocation of designations

Houses required to be licensed

8–17629A **85. Requirement for Part 3 houses to be licensed.** (1) Every Part 3 house must be licensed under this Part unless—

(*a*) it is an HMO to which Part 2 applies (see section 55(2)), or
(*b*) a temporary exemption notice is in force in relation to it under section 86, or
(*c*) a management order is in force in relation to it under Chapter 1 or 2 of Part 4.

(2) A licence under this Part is a licence authorising occupation of the house concerned under one or more tenancies or licences within section 79(2)(*b*).

(3) Sections 87 to 90 deal with applications for licences, the granting or refusal of licences and the imposition of licence conditions.

(4) The local housing authority must take all reasonable steps to secure that applications for licences are made to them in respect of houses in their area which are required to be licensed under this Part but are not so licensed.

(5) In this Part, unless the context otherwise requires—

(*a*) references to a Part 3 house are to a house to which this Part applies (see section 79(2)),
(*b*) references to a licence are to a licence under this Part,
(*c*) references to a licence holder are to be read accordingly, and
(*d*) references to a house being (or not being) licensed under this Part are to its being (or not being) a house in respect of which a licence is in force under this Part.

[Housing Act 2004, s 85.]

86. Temporary exemption from licensing requirement

Grant or refusal of licences

87. Applications for licences

88. Grant or refusal of licence

89. Tests for fitness etc and satisfactory management arrangements

8–17629B 90. Licence conditions. (1) A licence may include such conditions as the local housing authority consider appropriate for regulating the management, use or occupation of the house concerned.

(2) Those conditions may, in particular, include (so far as appropriate in the circumstances)—

(*a*) conditions imposing restrictions or prohibitions on the use or occupation of particular parts of the house by persons occupying it;
(*b*) conditions requiring the taking of reasonable and practicable steps to prevent or reduce anti-social behaviour by persons occupying or visiting the house.

(3) A licence may also include—

(*a*) conditions requiring facilities and equipment to be made available in the house for the purpose of meeting standards prescribed for the purposes of this section by regulations made by the appropriate national authority;
(*b*) conditions requiring such facilities and equipment to be kept in repair and proper working order;
(*c*) conditions requiring, in the case of any works needed in order for any such facilities or equipment to be made available or to meet any such standards, that the works are carried out within such period or periods as may be specified in, or determined under, the licence.

(4) A licence must include the conditions required by Schedule 4.

(5) As regards the relationship between the authority's power to impose conditions under this section and functions exercisable by them under or for the purposes of Part 1 ("Part 1 functions")—

(*a*) the authority must proceed on the basis that, in general, they should seek to identify, remove or reduce category 1 or category 2 hazards in the house by the exercise of Part 1 functions and not by means of licence conditions;
(*b*) this does not, however, prevent the authority from imposing (in accordance with subsection (3)) licence conditions relating to the installation or maintenance of facilities or equipment within subsection (3)(*a*) above, even if the same result could be achieved by the exercise of Part 1 functions;
(*c*) the fact that licence conditions are imposed for a particular purpose that could be achieved by the exercise of Part 1 functions does not affect the way in which Part 1 functions can be subsequently exercised by the authority.

(6) A licence may not include conditions imposing restrictions or obligations on a particular person other than the licence holder unless that person has consented to the imposition of the restrictions or obligations.

(7) A licence may not include conditions requiring (or intended to secure) any alteration in the terms of any tenancy or licence under which any person occupies the house.

[Housing Act 2004, s 90.]

8–17629C 91. Licences: general requirements and duration. (1) A licence may not relate to more than one Part 3 house.

(2) A licence may be granted before the time when it is required by virtue of this Part but, if so, the licence cannot come into force until that time.

(3) A licence—

(*a*) comes into force at the time that is specified in or determined under the licence for this purpose, and

(*b*) unless previously terminated by subsection (7) or revoked under section 93, continues in force for the period that is so specified or determined.

(4) That period must not end more than 5 years after—

(*a*) the date on which the licence was granted, or

(*b*) if the licence was granted as mentioned in subsection (2), the date when the licence comes into force.

(5) Subsection (3)(*b*) applies even if, at any time during that period, the house concerned subsequently ceases to be a Part 3 house or becomes an HMO to which Part 2 applies (see section 55(2)).

(6) A licence may not be transferred to another person.

(7) If the holder of the licence dies while the licence is in force, the licence ceases to be in force on his death.

(8) However, during the period of 3 months beginning with the date of the licence holder's death, the house is to be treated for the purposes of this Part as if on that date a temporary exemption notice had been served in respect of the house under section 86.

(9) If, at any time during that period ("the initial period"), the personal representatives of the licence holder request the local housing authority to do so, the authority may serve on them a notice which, during the period of 3 months after the date on which the initial period ends, has the same effect as a temporary exemption notice under section 86.

(10) Subsections (6) to (8) of section 86 apply (with any necessary modifications) in relation to a decision by the authority not to serve such a notice as they apply in relation to a decision not to serve a temporary exemption notice.

[Housing Act 2004, s 91.]

Variation and revocation of licences

92. Variation of licences

93. Revocation of licences

Procedure and appeals

94. Procedural requirements and appeals against licence decisions

Enforcement

8–17629D 95. Offences in relation to licensing of houses under this Part. (1) A person commits an offence if he is a person having control of or managing a house which is required to be licensed under this Part (see section 85(1)) but is not so licensed.

(2) A person commits an offence if—

(*a*) he is a licence holder or a person on whom restrictions or obligations under a licence are imposed in accordance with section 90(6), and

(*b*) he fails to comply with any condition of the licence.

(3) In proceedings against a person for an offence under subsection (1) it is a defence that, at the material time—

(*a*) a notification had been duly given in respect of the house under section 62(1) or 86(1), or

(*b*) an application for a licence had been duly made in respect of the house under section 87,

and that notification or application was still effective (see subsection (7)).

(4) In proceedings against a person for an offence under subsection (1) or (2) it is a defence that he had a reasonable excuse—

(*a*) for having control of or managing the house in the circumstances mentioned in subsection (1), or

(*b*) for failing to comply with the condition,

as the case may be.

(5) A person who commits an offence under subsection (1) is liable on summary conviction to a fine not exceeding £20,000.

(6) A person who commits an offence under subsection (2) is liable on summary conviction to a fine not exceeding level 5 on the standard scale.

(7) For the purposes of subsection (3) a notification or application is "effective" at a particular time if at that time it has not been withdrawn, and either—

(*a*) the authority have not decided whether to serve a temporary exemption notice, or (as the case may be) grant a licence, in pursuance of the notification or application, or

(*b*) if they have decided not to do so, one of the conditions set out in subsection (8) is met.

(8) The conditions are—

(*a*) that the period for appealing against the decision of the authority not to serve or grant such a notice or licence (or against any relevant decision of a residential property tribunal) has not expired, or

(*b*) that an appeal has been brought against the authority's decision (or against any relevant decision of such a tribunal) and the appeal has not been determined or withdrawn.

(9) In subsection (8) "relevant decision" means a decision which is given on an appeal to the tribunal and confirms the authority's decision (with or without variation).

[Housing Act 2004, s 95.]

96. Other consequences of operating unlicensed houses: rent repayment orders

97. Further provisions about rent repayment orders

98. Other consequences of operating unlicensed houses: restriction on terminating tenancies

Supplementary provisions

8–17629E 99. Meaning of "house" etc. In this Part—

"dwelling" means a building or part of a building occupied or intended to be occupied as a separate dwelling;

"house" means a building or part of a building consisting of one or more dwellings;

and references to a house include (where the context permits) any yard, garden, outhouses and appurtenances belonging to, or usually enjoyed with, it (or any part of it).

[Housing Act 2004, s 99.]

8–17629F 100. Index of defined expressions: Part 3. The following table shows where expressions used in this Part are defined or otherwise explained.

Expression	*Provision of this Act*
Anti-social behaviour	Section 57(5)
Appropriate national authority	Section 261(1)
Category 1 hazard	Section 2(1)
Category 2 hazard	Section 2(1)
District of local housing authority	Section 261(6)
Dwelling	Section 99
House	Section 99
Licence and licence holder	Section 85(5)
Licence (to occupy premises)	Section 262(9)
Local housing authority	Section 261(2) to (5)
Occupier (and related expressions)	Section 262(6)
Part 3 house	Section 85(5), together with section 79(2)
Person having control	Section 263(1) and (2) (and see also section 89(7))
Person having estate or interest	Section 262(8)
Person managing	Section 263(3)
Person involved in management	Section 263(5)
Residential property tribunal	Section 229
Tenant	Section 262(1) to (5)

PART 4[1]

ADDITIONAL CONTROL PROVISIONS IN RELATION TO RESIDENTIAL ACCOMMODATION

CHAPTER 1[2]

Interim and Final Management Orders

Introductory

8–17629G 101. Interim and final management orders: introductory. (1) This Chapter deals with the making by a local housing authority of—

(*a*) an interim management order (see section 102), or
(*b*) a final management order (see section 113),

in respect of an HMO or a Part 3 house.

(2) Section 103 deals with the making of an interim management order in respect of a house to which that section applies.

(3) An interim management order is an order (expiring not more than 12 months after it is made) which is made for the purpose of securing that the following steps are taken in relation to the house—

(*a*) any immediate steps which the authority consider necessary to protect the health, safety or welfare of persons occupying the house, or persons occupying or having an estate or interest in any premises in the vicinity, and
(*b*) any other steps which the authority think appropriate with a view to the proper management of the house pending the grant of a licence under Part 2 or 3 in respect of the house or the making of a final management order in respect of it (or, if appropriate, the revocation of the interim management order).

(4) A final management order is an order (expiring not more than 5 years after it is made) which is made for the purpose of securing the proper management of the house on a long-term basis in accordance with a management scheme contained in the order.

(5) In this Chapter any reference to "the house", in relation to an interim or final management order (other than an order under section 102(7)), is a reference to the HMO or Part 3 house to which the order relates.

(6) Subsection (5) has effect subject to sections 102(8) and 113(7) (exclusion of part occupied by resident landlord).

(7) In this Chapter "third party", in relation to a house, means any person who has an estate or interest in the house (other than an immediate landlord and any person who is a tenant under a lease granted under section 107(3)(*c*) or 116(3)(*c*)).

[Housing Act 2004, s 101.]

---

1. Part 4 contains ss 101–147. At the date of going to press these provisions were not in force save for the provisions that confer any powers to make orders or regulations which are exercisable by the Secretary of State or the National Assembly of Wales (see s 270(2)(*b*)).
2. Chapter 1 contains ss 101–131.

Interim management orders: making and operation of orders

8–17629H 102. Making of interim management orders. (1) A local housing authority—

(*a*) are under a duty to make an interim management order in respect of a house in a case within subsection (2) or (3), and
(*b*) have power to make an interim management order in respect of a house in a case within subsection (4) or (7).

(2) The authority must make an interim management order in respect of a house if—

(*a*) it is an HMO or a Part 3 house which is required to be licensed under Part 2 or Part 3 (see section 61(1) or 85(1)) but is not so licensed, and
(*b*) they consider either—
  (i) that there is no reasonable prospect of its being so licensed in the near future, or
  (ii) that the health and safety condition is satisfied (see section 104).

(3) The authority must make an interim management order in respect of a house if—

(*a*) it is an HMO or a Part 3 house which is required to be licensed under Part 2 or Part 3 and is so licensed,
(*b*) they have revoked the licence concerned but the revocation is not yet in force, and
(*c*) they consider either—
  (i) that, on the revocation coming into force, there will be no reasonable prospect of the house being so licensed in the near future, or
  (ii) that, on the revocation coming into force, the health and safety condition will be satisfied (see section 104).

(4) The authority may make an interim management order in respect of a house if—

(*a*) it is an HMO other than one that is required to be licensed under Part 2, and
(*b*) on an application by the authority to a residential property tribunal, the tribunal by order authorises them to make such an order, either in the terms of a draft order submitted by them or in those terms as varied by the tribunal;

and the authority may make such an order despite any pending appeal against the order of the tribunal (but this is without prejudice to any order that may be made on the disposal of any such appeal).

(5) The tribunal may only authorise the authority to make an interim management order under subsection (4) if it considers that the health and safety condition is satisfied (see section 104).

(6) In determining whether to authorise the authority to make an interim management order in respect of an HMO under subsection (4), the tribunal must have regard to the extent to which any applicable code of practice approved under section 233 has been complied with in respect of the HMO in the past.

(7) The authority may make an interim management order in respect of a house if—

(*a*) it is a house to which section 103 (special interim management orders) applies, and

(*b*) on an application by the authority to a residential property tribunal, the tribunal by order authorises them to make such an order, either in the terms of a draft order submitted by them or in those terms as varied by the tribunal;

and the authority may make such an order despite any pending appeal against the order of the tribunal (but this is without prejudice to any order that may be made on the disposal of any such appeal).

Subsections (2) to (6) of section 103 apply in relation to the power of a residential property tribunal to authorise the making of an interim management order under this subsection.

(8) The authority may make an interim management order which is expressed not to apply to a part of the house that is occupied by a person who has an estate or interest in the whole of the house.

In relation to such an order, a reference in this Chapter to "the house" does not include the part so excluded (unless the context requires otherwise, such as where the reference is to the house as an HMO or a Part 3 house).

(9) Nothing in this section requires or authorises the making of an interim management order in respect of a house if—

(*a*) an interim management order has been previously made in respect of it, and

(*b*) the authority have not exercised any relevant function in respect of the house at any time after the making of the interim management order.

(10) In subsection (9) "relevant function" means the function of—

(*a*) granting a licence under Part 2 or 3,

(*b*) serving a temporary exemption notice under section 62 or section 86, or

(*c*) making a final management order under section 113.

[Housing Act 2004, s 102.]

8–17629I 103. Special interim management orders. (1) This section applies to a house if the whole of it is occupied either—

(*a*) under a single tenancy or licence that is not an exempt tenancy or licence under section 79(3) or (4), or

(*b*) under two or more tenancies or licences in respect of different dwellings contained in it, none of which is an exempt tenancy or licence under section 79(3) or (4).

(2) A residential property tribunal may only authorise the authority to make an interim management order in respect of such a house under section 102(7) if it considers that both of the following conditions are satisfied.

(3) The first condition is that the circumstances relating to the house fall within any category of circumstances prescribed for the purposes of this subsection by an order under subsection (5).

(4) The second condition is that the making of the order is necessary for the purpose of protecting the health, safety or welfare of persons occupying, visiting or otherwise engaging in lawful activities in the vicinity of the house.

(5) The appropriate national authority may by order—

(*a*) prescribe categories of circumstances for the purposes of subsection (3),

(*b*) provide for any of the provisions of this Act to apply in relation to houses to which this section applies, or interim or final management orders made in respect of them, with any modifications specified in the order.

(6) The categories prescribed by an order under subsection (5) are to reflect one or more of the following—

(*a*) the first or second set of general conditions mentioned in subsection (3) or (6) of section 80, or

(*b*) any additional set of conditions specified under subsection (7) of that section,

but (in each case) with such modifications as the appropriate national authority considers appropriate to adapt them to the circumstances of a single house.

(7) In this section "house" has the same meaning as in Part 3 (see section 99).

(8) In this Chapter—

(*a*) any reference to "the house", in relation to an interim management order under section 102(7), is a reference to the house to which the order relates, and

(*b*) any such reference includes (where the context permits) a reference to any yard, garden, outhouses and appurtenances belonging to, or usually enjoyed with, it (or any part of it).

[Housing Act 2004, s 103.]

8–17629J 104. The health and safety condition. (1) This section explains what "the health and safety condition" is for the purposes of section 102.

(2) The health and safety condition is that the making of an interim management order is necessary for the purpose of protecting the health, safety or welfare of persons occupying the house, or persons occupying or having an estate or interest in any premises in the vicinity.

(3) A threat to evict persons occupying a house in order to avoid the house being required to be licensed under Part 2 may constitute a threat to the welfare of those persons for the purposes of subsection (2).

This does not affect the generality of that subsection.

(4) The health and safety condition is not to be regarded as satisfied for the purposes of section 102(2)(*b*)(ii) or (3)(*c*)(ii) where both of the conditions in subsections (5) and (6) are satisfied.

(5) The first condition is that the local housing authority either—

(*a*) (in a case within section 102(2)(*b*)(ii)) are required by section 5 (general duty to take enforcement action in respect of category 1 hazards) to take a course of action within subsection (2) of that section in relation to the house, or

(*b*) (in a case within section 102(3)(*c*)(ii)) consider that on the revocation coming into force they will be required to take such a course of action.

(6) The second condition is that the local housing authority consider that the health, safety or welfare of the persons in question would be adequately protected by taking that course of action.

[Housing Act 2004, s 104.]

8–17629K 105. Operation of interim management orders. (1) This section deals with the time when an interim management order comes into force or ceases to have effect.

(2) The order comes into force when it is made, unless it is made under section 102(3).

(3) If the order is made under section 102(3), it comes into force when the revocation of the licence comes into force.

(4) The order ceases to have effect at the end of the period of 12 months beginning with the date on which it is made, unless it ceases to have effect at some other time as mentioned below.

(5) If the order provides that it is to cease to have effect on a date falling before the end of that period, it accordingly ceases to have effect on that date.

(6) If the order is made under section 102(3)—

(*a*) it must include a provision for determining the date on which it will cease to have effect, and

(*b*) it accordingly ceases to have effect on the date so determined.

(7) That date must be no later than 12 months after the date on which the order comes into force.

(8) Subsections (9) and (10) apply where—

(*a*) a final management order ("the FMO") has been made under section 113 so as to replace the order ("the IMO"), but

(*b*) the FMO has not come into force because of an appeal to a residential property tribunal under paragraph 24 of Schedule 6 against the making of the FMO.

(9) If—

(*a*) the house would (but for the IMO being in force) be required to be licensed under Part 2 or 3 of this Act (see section 61(1) or 85(1)), and

(*b*) the date on which—

(i) the FMO,

(ii) any licence under Part 2 or 3, or

(iii) another interim management order,

comes into force in relation to the house (or part of it) following the disposal of the appeal is later than the date on which the IMO would cease to have effect apart from this subsection,

the IMO continues in force until that later date.

(10) If, on the application of the authority, the tribunal makes an order providing for the IMO to continue in force, pending the disposal of the appeal, until a date later than that on which the IMO would cease to have effect apart from this subsection, the IMO accordingly continues in force until that later date.

(11) This section has effect subject to sections 111 and 112 (variation or revocation of orders by authority) and to the power of revocation exercisable by a residential property tribunal on an appeal made under paragraph 24 or 28 of Schedule 6.

[Housing Act 2004, s 105.]

106. Local housing authority's duties once interim management order in force

107. General effect of interim management orders

108. General effect of interim management orders: leases and licences granted by authority

109. General effect of interim management orders: immediate landlords, mortgagees etc

110. Financial arrangements while order is in force

Interim management orders: variation and revocation

111. Variation of interim management orders

112. Revocation of interim management orders

Final management orders: making and operation of orders

8–17629L 113. Making of final management orders. (1) A local housing authority who have made an interim management order in respect of a house under section 102 ("the IMO")—

(*a*) have a duty to make a final management order in respect of the house in a case within subsection (2), and
(*b*) have power to make such an order in a case within subsection (3).

(2) The authority must make a final management order so as to replace the IMO as from its expiry date if—

(*a*) on that date the house would be required to be licensed under Part 2 or 3 of this Act (see section 61(1) or 85(1)), and
(*b*) the authority consider that they are unable to grant a licence under Part 2 or 3 in respect of the house that would replace the IMO as from that date.

(3) The authority may make a final management order so as to replace the IMO as from its expiry date if—

(*a*) on that date the house will not be one that would be required to be licensed as mentioned in subsection (2)(*a*), and
(*b*) the authority consider that making the final management order is necessary for the purpose of protecting, on a long-term basis, the health, safety or welfare of persons occupying the house, or persons occupying or having an estate or interest in any premises in the vicinity.

(4) A local housing authority who have made a final management order in respect of a house under this section ("the existing order")—

(*a*) have a duty to make a final management order in respect of the house in a case within subsection (5), and
(*b*) have power to make such an order in a case within subsection (6).

(5) The authority must make a new final management order so as to replace the existing order as from its expiry date if—

(*a*) on that date the condition in subsection (2)(*a*) will be satisfied in relation to the house, and
(*b*) the authority consider that they are unable to grant a licence under Part 2 or 3 in respect of the house that would replace the existing order as from that date.

(6) The authority may make a new final management order so as to replace the existing order as from its expiry date if—

(*a*) on that date the condition in subsection (3)(*a*) will be satisfied in relation to the house, and
(*b*) the authority consider that making the new order is necessary for the purpose of protecting, on a long-term basis, the health, safety or welfare of persons within subsection (3)(*b*).

(7) The authority may make a final management order which is expressed not to apply to a part of the house that is occupied by a person who has an estate or interest in the whole of the house.

In relation to such an order, a reference in this Chapter to "the house" does not include the part so excluded (unless the context requires otherwise, such as where the reference is to the house as an HMO or a Part 3 house).

(8) In this section "expiry date", in relation to an interim or final management order, means—

(*a*) where the order is revoked, the date as from which it is revoked, and
(*b*) otherwise the date on which the order ceases to have effect under section 105 or 114;

and nothing in this section applies in relation to an interim or final management order which has been revoked on an appeal under Part 3 of Schedule 6.
[Housing Act 2004, s 113.]

8–17629M 114. Operation of final management orders. (1) This section deals with the time when a final management order comes into force or ceases to have effect.

(2) The order does not come into force until such time (if any) as is the operative time for the purposes of this subsection under paragraph 27 of Schedule 6 (time when period for appealing expires without an appeal being made or when order is confirmed on appeal).

(3) The order ceases to have effect at the end of the period of 5 years beginning with the date on which it comes into force, unless it ceases to have effect at some other time as mentioned below.

(4) If the order provides that it is to cease to have effect on a date falling before the end of that period, it accordingly ceases to have effect on that date.

(5) Subsections (6) and (7) apply where—

(*a*) a new final management order ("the new order") has been made so as to replace the order ("the existing order"), but

(*b*) the new order has not come into force because of an appeal to a residential property tribunal under paragraph 24 of Schedule 6 against the making of that order.

(6) If—

(*a*) the house would (but for the existing order being in force) be required to be licensed under Part 2 or 3 of this Act (see section 61(1) or 85(1)), and

(*b*) the date on which—

(i) the new order, or

(ii) any licence under Part 2 or 3, or

(iii) a temporary exemption notice under section 62 or 86,

comes into force in relation to the house (or part of it) following the disposal of the appeal is later than the date on which the existing order would cease to have effect apart from this subsection,

the existing order continues in force until that later date.

(7) If, on the application of the authority, the tribunal makes an order providing for the existing order to continue in force, pending the disposal of the appeal, until a date later than that on which it would cease to have effect apart from this subsection, the existing order accordingly continues in force until that later date.

(8) This section has effect subject to sections 121 and 122 (variation or revocation of orders) and to the power of revocation exercisable by a residential property tribunal on an appeal made under paragraph 24 or 28 of Schedule 6.

[Housing Act 2004, s 114.

115. Local housing authority's duties once final management order in force

116. General effect of final management orders

117. General effect of final management orders: leases and licences granted by authority

118. General effect of final management orders: immediate landlords, mortgagees etc

119. Management schemes and accounts

120. Enforcement of management scheme by relevant landlord

Final management orders: variation and revocation

121. Variation of final management orders

122. Revocation of final management orders

Interim and final management orders: procedure and appeals

123. Procedural requirements and appeals

Interim and final management orders: other general provisions

124. Effect of management orders: occupiers

125. Effect of management orders: agreements and legal proceedings

126. Effect of management orders: furniture

127. Management orders: power to supply furniture

128. Compensation payable to third parties

129. Termination of management orders: financial arrangements

130. Termination of management orders: leases, agreements and proceedings

8–17629N **131. Management orders: power of entry to carry out work.** (1) The right mentioned in subsection (2) is exercisable by the local housing authority, or any person authorised in writing by them, at any time when an interim or final management order is in force.

(2) That right is the right at all reasonable times to enter any part of the house for the purpose of carrying out works, and is exercisable as against any person having an estate or interest in the house.

(3) Where part of a house is excluded from the provisions of an interim or final management order under section 102(8) or 113(7), the right conferred by subsection (1) is exercisable as respects that part so far as is reasonably required for the purpose of carrying out works in the part of the house which is subject to the order.

(4) If, after receiving reasonable notice of the intended action, any occupier of the whole or part of the house prevents any officer, employee, agent or contractor of the local housing authority from carrying out work in the house, a magistrates' court may order him to permit to be done on the premises anything which the authority consider to be necessary.

(5) A person who fails to comply with an order of the court under subsection (4) commits an offence.

(6) A person who commits an offence under subsection (5) is liable on summary conviction to a fine not exceeding level 5 on the standard scale.

[Housing Act 2004, s 131.]

CHAPTER 2[1]
Interim and Final Empty Dwelling Management Orders
Introductory

---

1. Chapter 2 contains ss 132–138. These provisions are concerned with empty dwelling management orders.

CHAPTER 3[1]
Overcrowding Notices

8–17629O 139. Service of overcrowding notices. (1) This Chapter applies to any HMO—

(*a*) in relation to which no interim or final management order is in force; and

(*b*) which is not required to be licensed under Part 2.

(2) The local housing authority may serve an overcrowding notice on one or more relevant persons if, having regard to the rooms available, it considers that an excessive number of persons is being, or is likely to be, accommodated in the HMO concerned.

(3) The authority must, at least 7 days before serving an overcrowding notice—

(*a*) inform in writing every relevant person (whether or not the person on whom the authority is to serve the notice) of their intention to serve the notice; and

(*b*) ensure that, so far as is reasonably possible, every occupier of the HMO concerned is informed of the authority's intention.

(4) The authority must also give the persons informed under subsection (3) an opportunity of making representations about the proposal to serve an overcrowding notice.

(5) An overcrowding notice becomes operative, if no appeal is brought under section 143, at the end of the period of 21 days from the date of service of the notice.

(6) If no appeal is brought under section 143, an overcrowding notice is final and conclusive as to matters which could have been raised on such an appeal.

(7) A person who contravenes an overcrowding notice commits an offence and is liable on summary conviction to a fine not exceeding level 4 on the standard scale.

(8) In proceedings for an offence under subsection (7) it is a defence that the person had a reasonable excuse for contravening the notice.

(9) In this section "relevant person" means a person who is, to the knowledge of the local housing authority—

(*a*) a person having an estate or interest in the HMO concerned, or

(*b*) a person managing or having control of it.

[Housing Act 2004, s 139.]

---

1. Chapter 3 contains ss 139–147.

8–17629P 140. Contents of overcrowding notices. (1) An overcrowding notice must state in relation to each room in the HMO concerned—

(*a*) what the local housing authority consider to be the maximum number of persons by whom the room is suitable to be occupied as sleeping accommodation at any one time; or

(*b*) that the local housing authority consider that the room is unsuitable to be occupied as sleeping accommodation.

(2) An overcrowding notice may specify special maxima applicable where some or all of the persons occupying a room are under such age as may be specified in the notice.

(3) An overcrowding notice must contain—

(*a*) the requirement prescribed by section 141 (not to permit excessive number of persons to sleep in the house in multiple occupation); or (*b*) the requirement prescribed by section 142 (not to admit new residents if number of persons is excessive).

(4) The local housing authority may at any time—

(*a*) withdraw an overcrowding notice which has been served on any person and which contains the requirement prescribed by section 142, and

(*b*) serve on him instead an overcrowding notice containing the requirement prescribed by section 141.

[Housing Act 2004, s 140.]

141. Requirement as to overcrowding generally

142. Requirement as to new residents

143. Appeals against overcrowding notices

144. Revocation and variation of overcrowding notices

CHAPTER 4

SUPPLEMENTARY PROVISIONS

145. Supplementary provisions

8–17629Q 146. Interpretation and modification of this Part. (1) In this Part—

"HMO" means a house in multiple occupation as defined by sections 254 to 259,

"Part 3 house" means a house to which Part 3 of this Act applies (see section 79(2)),

and any reference to an HMO or Part 3 house includes (where the context permits) a reference to any yard, garden, outhouses and appurtenances belonging to, or usually enjoyed with, it (or any part of it).

(2) For the purposes of this Part "mortgage" includes a charge or lien, and "mortgagee" is to be read accordingly.

(3) The appropriate national authority may by regulations provide for—

(*a*) any provision of this Part, or

(*b*) section 263 (in its operation for the purposes of any such provision),

to have effect in relation to a section 257 HMO with such modifications as are prescribed by the regulations.

(4) A "section 257 HMO" is an HMO which is a converted block of flats to which section 257 applies.

[Housing Act 2004, s 146.]

8–17629R 147. Index of defined expressions: Part 4. The following table shows where expressions used in this Part are defined or otherwise explained.

Expression	*Provision of this Act*
Appropriate national authority	Section 261(1)
Dwelling	Section 132(4)(*a*) and (*b*)
Final EDMO	Section 132(1)(*b*)
Final management order	Section 101(4)
Health	Section 2(5)
HMO	Section 146(1)
The house	Section 101(5) or 103(8)
Immediate landlord	Section 109(6) or 118(6)
Interim EDMO	Section 132(1)(*a*)
Interim management order	Section 101(3)
Landlord	Section 262(3)
Lease, lessee, etc	Section 262(1) to (4)
Licence (to occupy premises)	Section 262(9)
Local housing authority	Section 261(2) to (5)
Modifications	Section 250(7)
Mortgage, mortgagee	Section 146(2)
Occupier (and related expressions)	Section 262(6)
Owner	Section 262(7)
Part 3 house	Section 146(1)
Person having control	Section 263(1) and (2)
Person having estate or interest	Section 262(8)
Person managing	Section 263(3)
Relevant proprietor	Section 132(4)(*c*) and (5)

Expression	*Provision of this Act*
Rent or other payments (in Chapter 2)	Section 132(4)(*e*)
Residential property tribunal	Section 229
Tenancy, tenant, etc	Section 262(1) to (5)
Third party (in Chapter 1)	Section 101(7)
Third party (in Chapter 2)	Section 132(4)(*d*).

[Housing Act 2004, s 147.]

PART 5[1]
HOME INFORMATION PACKS
Preliminary

8–17629S 148. Meaning of "residential property" and "home information pack". (1) In this Part—

"residential property" means premises in England and Wales consisting of a single dwelling-house, including any ancillary land; and

"dwelling-house" means a building or part of a building occupied or intended to be occupied as a separate dwelling (and includes one that is being or is to be constructed).

(2) References in this Part to a home information pack, in relation to a residential property, are to a collection of documents relating to the property or the terms on which it is or may become available for sale.

[Housing Act 2004, s 148.]

1. Part 5 contains ss 148–178. Sections 161-164 and 176 came into force on the day on which the Act was passed (see s 270(2)). Otherwise, at the date of going to press Part 5 was not in force save for the provisions that confer any powers to make orders or regulations which are exercisable by the Secretary of State or the National Assembly of Wales (see s 270(2)(*b*)).

8–17629T 149. Meaning of "on the market" and related expressions. (1) In this Part references to "the market" are to the residential property market in England and Wales.

(2) A residential property is put on the market when the fact that it is or may become available for sale is, with the intention of marketing the property, first made public in England and Wales by or on behalf of the seller.

(3) A residential property which has been put on the market is to be regarded as remaining on the market until it is taken off the market or sold.

(4) A fact is made public when it is advertised or otherwise communicated (in whatever form and by whatever means) to the public or to a section of the public.

[Housing Act 2004, s 149.]

8–17629U 150. Acting as estate agent. (1) A person acts as estate agent for the seller of a residential property if he does anything, in the course of a business in England and Wales, in pursuance of marketing instructions from the seller.

(2) For this purpose—

"business in England and Wales" means a business carried on (in whole or in part) from a place in England and Wales; and

"marketing instructions" means instructions to carry out any activities with a view to—

(*a*) effecting the introduction to the seller of a person wishing to buy the property; or

(*b*) selling the property by auction or tender.

(3) It is immaterial for the purposes of this section whether or not a person describes himself as an estate agent.

[Housing Act 2004, s 150.]

Responsibility for marketing residential properties

8–17629V 151. Responsibility for marketing: general. (1) References in this Part to a responsible person, in relation to a residential property, are to any person who is for the time being responsible for marketing the property.

(2) Sections 152 and 153 identify for the purposes of this Part—

(*a*) the person or persons who are responsible for marketing a residential property which is on the market ("the property"); and

(*b*) when the responsibility of any such person arises and ceases.

(3) Only the seller or a person acting as estate agent for the seller may be responsible for marketing the property.

(4) A person may be responsible for marketing the property on more than one occasion.

[Housing Act 2004, s 151.]

8–17629W 152. Responsibility of person acting as estate agent. (1) A person acting as estate agent becomes responsible for marketing the property when action taken by him or on his behalf—

(*a*) puts the property on the market; or
(*b*) makes public the fact that the property is on the market.

(2) That responsibility ceases when the following conditions are satisfied, namely—

(*a*) his contract with the seller is terminated (whether by the withdrawal of his instructions or otherwise);
(*b*) he has ceased to take any action which makes public the fact that the property is on the market; and
(*c*) any such action being taken on his behalf has ceased.

(3) Any responsibility arising under this section also ceases when the property is taken off the market or sold.

[Housing Act 2004, s 152.]

8–17629X 153. Responsibility of the seller. (1) The seller becomes responsible for marketing the property when action taken by him or on his behalf—

(*a*) puts the property on the market; or
(*b*) makes public the fact that the property is on the market.

(2) That responsibility ceases when the following conditions are satisfied, namely—

(*a*) there is at least one person acting as his estate agent who is responsible for marketing the property;
(*b*) the seller has ceased to take any action which makes public the fact that the property is on the market; and
(*c*) any such action being taken on the seller's behalf has ceased.

(3) In this section the references to action taken on behalf of the seller exclude action taken by or on behalf of a person acting as his estate agent.

(4) Any responsibility arising under this section also ceases when the property is taken off the market or sold.

[Housing Act 2004, s 153.]

Duties of a responsible person where a property is on the market

8–17629Y 154. Application of sections 155 to 158. (1) Where a residential property is on the market, a person responsible for marketing the property is subject to the duties relating to home information packs that are imposed by sections 155 to 158 until his responsibility ceases.

(2) Each of those duties is subject to any exception relating to that duty which is provided for in those sections.

(3) The duty under section 156(1) is also subject to any condition imposed under section 157.

[Housing Act 2004, s 154.]

8–17629Z 155. Duty to have a home information pack. (1) It is the duty of a responsible person to have in his possession or under his control a home information pack for the property which complies with the requirements of any regulations under section 163.

(2) That duty does not apply where the responsible person is the seller at any time when—

(*a*) there is another person who is responsible for marketing the property under section 152; and
(*b*) the seller believes on reasonable grounds that the other responsible person has a home information pack for the property in his possession or under his control which complies with the requirements of any regulations under section 163.

[Housing Act 2004, s 155.]

8–17629ZA 156. Duty to provide copy of home information pack on request. (1) Where a potential buyer makes a request to a responsible person for a copy of the home information pack, or of a document (or part of a document) which is or ought to be included in that pack, it is the duty of the responsible person to comply with that request within the permitted period.

(2) The responsible person does not comply with that duty unless—

(*a*) he provides the potential buyer with a document which is—
 (i) a copy of the home information pack for the property as it stands at the time when the document is provided, or
 (ii) a copy of a document (or part of a document) which is included in that pack,

as the case may be; and

(*b*) that pack or document complies with the requirements of any regulations under section 163 at that time.

(3) In subsection (2) "the home information pack" means the home information pack intended by the responsible person to be the one required by section 155.

(4) That duty does not apply if, before the end of the permitted period, the responsible person believes on reasonable grounds that the person making the request—

(*a*) is unlikely to have sufficient means to buy the property in question;

(*b*) is not genuinely interested in buying a property of a general description which applies to the property; or

(*c*) is not a person to whom the seller is likely to be prepared to sell the property.

Nothing in this subsection authorises the doing of anything which constitutes an unlawful act of discrimination.

(5) Subsection (4) does not apply if the responsible person knows or suspects that the person making the request is an officer of an enforcement authority.

(6) That duty does not apply where the responsible person is the seller if, when the request is made, the duty under section 155 does not (by virtue of subsection (2) of that section) apply to him.

(7) But where the duty under this section is excluded by subsection (6), it is the duty of the seller to take reasonable steps to inform the potential buyer that the request should be made to the other person.

(8) The responsible person may charge a sum not exceeding the reasonable cost of making and, if requested, sending a paper copy of the pack or document.

(9) The permitted period for the purposes of this section is (subject to section 157(5)) the period of 14 days beginning with the day on which the request is made.

(10) If the responsible person ceases to be responsible for marketing the property before the end of the permitted period (whether because the property has been taken off the market or sold or for any other reason), he ceases to be under any duty to comply with the request.

(11) A person does not comply with the duty under this section by providing a copy in electronic form unless the potential buyer consents to receiving it in that form.

[Housing Act 2004, s 156.]

8–17629ZB 157. Section 156 (1) duty: imposition of conditions. (1) A potential buyer who has made a request to which section 156(1) applies may be required to comply with either or both of the following conditions before any copy is provided.

(2) The potential buyer may be required to pay a charge authorised by section 156(8).

(3) The potential buyer may be required to accept any terms specified in writing which—

(*a*) are proposed by the seller or in pursuance of his instructions; and

(*b*) relate to the use or disclosure of the copy (or any information contained in or derived from it).

(4) A condition is only effective if it is notified to the potential buyer before the end of the period of 14 days beginning with the day on which the request is made.

(5) Where the potential buyer has been so notified of either or both of the conditions authorised by this section, the permitted period for the purposes of section 156 is the period of 14 days beginning with—

(*a*) where one condition is involved, the day on which the potential buyer complies with it by—

(i) making the payment demanded, or

(ii) accepting the terms proposed (or such other terms as may be agreed between the seller and the potential buyer in substitution for those proposed),

as the case may be; or

(*b*) where both conditions are involved, the day (or the later of the days) on which the potential buyer complies with them by taking the action mentioned in paragraph (*a*)(i) and (ii).

[Housing Act 2004, s 157.]

8–17629ZC 158. Duty to ensure authenticity of documents in other situations. (1) Where a responsible person provides a potential buyer with, or allows a potential buyer to inspect, any document purporting to be—

(*a*) a copy of the home information pack for the property, or

(*b*) a copy of a document (or part of a document) included in that pack,

the responsible person is under a duty to ensure that the document is authentic.

(2) A document is not authentic for the purposes of subsection (1) unless, at the time when it is provided or inspected—

(*a*) it is a copy of the home information pack for the property or a document (or part of a document) included in that pack, as the case may be; and

(*b*) that pack or document complies with the requirements of any regulations under section 163.

(3) In subsection (2) "the home information pack" means the pack intended by the responsible person to be the one required by section 155.

(4) The duty under this section does not apply to anything provided in pursuance of the duty under section 156.

[Housing Act 2004, s 158.]

Other duties of person acting as estate agent

8–17629ZD 159. Other duties of person acting as estate agent. (1) This section applies to a person acting as estate agent for the seller of a residential property where—

(*a*) the property is not on the market; or

(*b*) the property is on the market but the person so acting is not a person responsible for marketing the property.

(2) It is the duty of a person to whom this section applies to have in his possession or under his control, when any qualifying action is taken by him or on his behalf, a home information pack for the property which complies with the requirements of any regulations under section 163.

(3) In subsection (2) "qualifying action" means action taken with the intention of marketing the property which—

(*a*) communicates to any person in England and Wales the fact that the property is or may become available for sale; but

(*b*) does not put the property on the market or make public the fact that the property is on the market.

(4) Where a person to whom this section applies provides a potential buyer with, or allows a potential buyer to inspect, any document purporting to be—

(*a*) a copy of the home information pack for the property; or

(*b*) a copy of a document (or part of a document) included in that pack;

it is his duty to ensure that it is an authentic copy.

(5) A document is not authentic for the purposes of subsection (4) unless, at the time when it is provided or inspected—

(*a*) it is a copy of the home information pack for the property or a document (or part of a document) included in that pack, as the case may be; and

(*b*) that pack or document complies with the requirements of any regulations under section 163.

(6) In subsection (5) "the home information pack" means the home information pack intended by the person to whom this section applies to be the one required by subsection (2).
[Housing Act 2004, s 159.]

Exceptions from the duties

8–17629ZE 160. Residential properties not available with vacant possession. (1) The duties under sections 155 to 159 do not apply in relation to a residential property at any time when it is not available for sale with vacant possession.

(2) But for the purposes of this Part a residential property shall be presumed to be available with vacant possession, at any time when any of those duties would apply in relation to the property if it is so available, unless the contrary appears from the manner in which the property is being marketed at that time.
[Housing Act 2004, s 160.]

8–17629ZF 161. Power to provide for further exceptions. The Secretary of State may by regulations provide for other exceptions from any duty under sections 155 to 159 in such cases and circumstances, and to such extent, as may be specified in the regulations.
[Housing Act 2004, s 161.]

8–17629ZG 162. Suspension of duties under sections 155 to 159. (1) The Secretary of State may make an order suspending (or later reviving) the operation of any duty imposed by sections 155 to 159.

(2) An order under this section may provide for the suspension of a duty to take effect only for a period specified in the order.

(3) A duty which is (or is to any extent) revived after being suspended under this section is liable to be suspended again.
[Housing Act 2004, s 162.]

Contents of home information packs

8–17629ZH 163. Contents of home information packs. (1) The Secretary of State may make regulations prescribing—

(*a*) the documents which are required or authorised to be included in the home information pack for a residential property; and

(*b*) particular information which is required or authorised to be included in, or which is to be excluded from, any such document.

(2) A document prescribed under subsection (1) must be one that the Secretary of State considers would disclose relevant information.

(3) Any particular information required or authorised to be included in a prescribed document must be information that the Secretary of State considers to be relevant information.

(4) In this section "relevant information" means information about any matter connected with the property (or the sale of the property) that would be of interest to potential buyers.

(5) Without prejudice to the generality of subsection (4), the information which the Secretary of State may consider to be relevant information includes any information about—

(*a*) the interest which is for sale and the terms on which it is proposed to sell it;
(*b*) the title to the property;
(*c*) anything relating to or affecting the property that is contained in—

(i) a register required to be kept by or under any enactment (whenever passed); or
(ii) records kept by a person who can reasonably be expected to give information derived from those records to the seller at his request (on payment, if required, of a reasonable charge);

(*d*) the physical condition of the property (including any particular characteristics or features of the property);
(*e*) the energy efficiency of the property;
(*f*) any warranties or guarantees subsisting in relation to the property;
(*g*) any taxes, service charges or other charges payable in relation to the property.

(6) The regulations may require or authorise the home information pack to include—

(*a*) replies the seller proposes to give to prescribed pre-contract enquiries; and
(*b*) documents or particular information indexing or otherwise explaining the contents of the pack.

(7) The regulations may require a prescribed document—

(*a*) to be in such form as may be prescribed; and
(*b*) to be prepared by a person of a prescribed description on such terms (if any) as may be prescribed.

(8) The terms mentioned in subsection (7)(*b*) may include terms which enable provisions of the contract under which the document is to be prepared to be enforced by—

(*a*) a potential or actual buyer;
(*b*) a mortgage lender; or
(*c*) any other person involved in the sale of the property who is not a party to that contract.

(9) The regulations may—

(*a*) provide for the time at which any document is to be included in or removed from the home information pack; and
(*b*) make different provision for different areas, for different descriptions of properties or for other different circumstances (including the manner in which a residential property is marketed).

(10) In this section "prescribed" means prescribed by regulations under this section.
[Housing Act 2004, s 163.]

8–17629ZI 164. Home condition reports. (1) Regulations under section 163 may make the provision mentioned in this section in relation to any description of document dealing with matters mentioned in section 163(5)(*d*) or (*e*) (reports on physical condition or energy efficiency) which is to be included in the home information pack.

(2) In this section "home condition report" means a document of that description.

(3) The regulations may require a home condition report to be made by an individual who is a member of an approved certification scheme following an inspection carried out by him in accordance with the provisions of the scheme.

(4) The regulations shall, if the provision mentioned in subsection (3) is made, make provision for the approval by the Secretary of State of one or more suitable certification schemes (and for the withdrawal by him of any such approval).

(5) The regulations shall require the Secretary of State to be satisfied, before approving a certification scheme, that the scheme contains appropriate provision—

(*a*) for ensuring that members of the scheme are fit and proper persons who are qualified (by their education, training and experience) to produce home condition reports;
(*b*) for ensuring that members of the scheme have in force suitable indemnity insurance;
(*c*) for facilitating the resolution of complaints against members of the scheme;
(*d*) for requiring home condition reports made by members of the scheme to be entered on the register mentioned in section 165;
(*e*) for the keeping of a public register of the members of the scheme; and
(*f*) for such other purposes as may be specified in the regulations.

(6) Subsection (5)(*d*) only applies where provision for a register of home condition reports is made under section 165.

(7) The regulations may require or authorise an approved certification scheme to contain provision about any matter relating to the home condition reports with which the scheme is concerned (including the terms on which members of the scheme may undertake to produce a home condition report).

(8) Nothing in this section limits the power under section 163 to make provision about home condition reports in the regulations.

[Housing Act 2004, s 164.]

Register of home condition reports

165. Register of home condition reports

Enforcement

8–17629ZJ 166. Enforcement authorities. (1) Every local weights and measures authority is an enforcement authority for the purposes of this Part.

(2) It is the duty of each enforcement authority to enforce—

(*a*) the duties under sections 155 to 159 and 167(4), and

(*b*) any duty imposed under section 172(1),

in their area.

[Housing Act 2004, s 166.]

8–17629ZK 167. Power to require production of home information packs. (1) An authorised officer of an enforcement authority may require a person who appears to him to be or to have been subject to the duty under section 155 or 159(2), in relation to a residential property, to produce for inspection a copy of, or of any document included in, the home information pack for that property.

(2) The power conferred by subsection (1) includes power—

(*a*) to require the production in a visible and legible documentary form of any document included in the home information pack in question which is held in electronic form; and

(*b*) to take copies of any document produced for inspection.

(3) A requirement under this section may not be imposed more than six months after the last day on which the person concerned was subject to the duty under section 155 or 159(2) in relation to the property (as the case may be).

(4) Subject to subsection (5), it is the duty of a person subject to such a requirement to comply with it within the period of 7 days beginning with the day after that on which it is imposed.

(5) A person is not required to comply with such a requirement if he has a reasonable excuse for not complying with the requirement.

(6) In this section "the home information pack" means—

(*a*) where a requirement under this section is imposed on a person at a time when he is subject to the duty under section 155 or 159(2), the home information pack intended by him to be the one he is required to have at that time; or

(*b*) in any other case, the home information pack intended by the person concerned, when he was last subject to the duty under section 155 or 159(2), to be the one he was required to have at that time.

[Housing Act 2004, s 167.]

168. Penalty charge notices

8–17629ZL 169. Offences relating to enforcement officers. (1) A person who obstructs an officer of an enforcement authority acting in pursuance of section 167 is guilty of an offence.

(2) A person who, not being an authorised officer of an enforcement authority, purports to act as such in pursuance of section 167 or 168 is guilty of an offence.

(3) A person guilty of an offence under this section is liable on summary conviction to a fine not exceeding level 5 on the standard scale.

[Housing Act 2004, s 169.]

170. Right of private action

Supplementary

8–17629ZM 171. Application of Part to sub-divided buildings. (1) This section applies where—

(*a*) two or more dwelling-houses in a sub-divided building are marketed for sale (with any ancillary land) as a single property; and

(*b*) any one or more of those dwelling-houses—

(i) is not available for sale (with any ancillary land) as a separate residential property; but

(ii) is available with vacant possession.

(2) This Part applies to the dwelling-houses mentioned in subsection (1)(*a*) (with any ancillary land) as if—

(*a*) they were a residential property, and
(*b*) section 160 were omitted.

(3) Subsection (2) does not affect the application of this Part to any of those dwelling-houses which is available for sale (with any ancillary land) as a separate residential property.

(4) In this section "sub-divided building" means a building or part of a building originally constructed or adapted for use as a single dwelling which has been divided (on one or more occasions) into separate dwelling-houses.
[Housing Act 2004, s 171.]

172. Power to require estate agents to belong to a redress scheme

173. Approval of redress schemes

174. Withdrawal of approval of redress schemes

175. Office of Fair Trading

176. Grants

8–17629ZN 177. Interpretation of Part 5. (1) In this Part—

"ancillary land", in relation to a dwelling-house or a sub-divided building, means any land intended to be occupied and enjoyed together with that dwelling-house or building;

"long lease" means—

(*a*) a lease granted for a term certain exceeding 21 years, whether or not it is (or may become) terminable before the end of that term by notice given by the tenant or by re-entry or forfeiture; or
(*b*) a lease for a term fixed by law under a grant with a covenant or obligation for perpetual renewal, other than a lease by sub-demise from one which is not a long lease;

and for this purpose "lease" does not include a mortgage term;

"potential buyer" means a person who claims that he is or may become interested in buying a residential property;

"sale", in relation to a residential property, means a disposal, or agreement to dispose, by way of sale of—

(*a*) the freehold interest;
(*b*) the interest under a long lease;
(*c*) an option to acquire the freehold interest or the interest under a long lease;

and "seller" means a person contemplating disposing of such an interest (and related expressions shall be construed accordingly).

(2) Any reference in the definition of "sale" to the disposal of an interest of a kind mentioned in that definition includes a reference to the creation of such an interest.

(3) A document which is not in electronic form is only to be regarded for the purposes of this Part as being under the control of a person while it is in the possession of another if he has the right to take immediate possession of the document on demand (and without payment).

(4) A document held in electronic form is only to be regarded for the purposes of this Part as being in a person's possession or under his control if he is readily able (using equipment available to him)—

(*a*) to view the document in a form that is visible and legible; and
(*b*) to produce copies of it in a visible and legible documentary form.

[Housing Act 2004, s 177.]

8–17629ZO 178. Index of defined expressions: Part 5. In this Part, the expressions listed in the left-hand column have the meaning given by, or are to be interpreted in accordance with, the provisions inserted in the right-hand column.

Expression	*Provision of this Act*
Acting as estate agent for the seller	Section 150
Ancillary land	Section 177(1)
Control of documents	Section 177(3) and (4)
Dwelling-house	Section 148(1)

Expression	*Provision of this Act*
Enforcement authority	Section 166
Home information pack	Section 148(2)
Long lease	Section 177(1)
Make public	Section 149(4)
Possession of electronic documents	Section 177(4)
Potential buyer	Section 177(1)
Putting on the market	Section 149(2)
Remaining on the market	Section 149(3)
Residential property	Section 148(1)
Responsible person	Section 151(1)
Sale (and related expressions)	Section 177(1)
Seller (and related expressions)	Section 177(1)
The market	Section 149(1).

PART 6[1]
OTHER PROVISIONS ABOUT HOUSING

1. Part 7 contains ss 179–228. See Part 6 makes other provision about housing, including: secure tenancies; right to buy; other disposals attracting discounts; mobile homes; tenancy deposit schemes; overcrowding; energy efficiency; social landlords and housing; disabled facilities grants; accommodation needs of gypsies and travellers; annual reports by local housing authorities; and the establishment of a social housing ombudsman for Wales.

PART 7[1]
SUPPLEMENTARY AND FINAL PROVISIONS

1. Part 7 contains ss 229–270. See s 270(2) for the provisions that came into effect on the day on which the Act was passed. See s 270(3) for the provisions that came into effect two months after the aforementioned date. See s 270(5) for the provisions to be brought into effect by commencement orders. As to the latter, s 237 came into effect on 6 June, 2005 in relation to England and 25 November, 2005 in relation to Wales (see, respectively, Housing Act 2004 (Commencement No 3) (England) Order 2005, SI 2005/1451, and Housing Act 2004 (Commencement No 2) (Wales) Order 2005, SI 2005/3237); s 229 and Sch 13 came into force in relation to England on 4 July, 2005 (see Housing Act 2004 (Commencement No 4 and Transitional Provisions) (England) Order 2005, SI 2005/1729); and s 265(1), Sch 12 and various paras of Sch 15 cam into force in relation to Wales on 5 July, 2005 (see Housing Act 2004 (Commencement No 1) (Wales) Order 2005, SI 2005/1814).

229–231. *These provisions are concerned with residential property tribunals.*

Register of licences and management orders

8–17629ZP 232. Register of licences and management orders. (1) Every local housing authority must establish and maintain a register of—

(*a*) all licences granted by them under Part 2 or 3 which are in force;
(*b*) all temporary exemption notices served by them under section 62 or section 86 which are in force; and
(*c*) all management orders made by them under Chapter 1 or 2 of Part 4 which are in force.

(2) The register may, subject to any requirements that may be prescribed, be in such form as the authority consider appropriate.

(3) Each entry in the register is to contain such particulars as may be prescribed.

(4) The authority must ensure that the contents of the register are available at the authority's head office for inspection by members of the public at all reasonable times.

(5) If requested by a person to do so and subject to payment of such reasonable fee (if any) as the authority may determine, a local housing authority must supply the person with a copy (certified to be true) of the register or of an extract from it.

(6) A copy so certified is prima facie evidence of the matters mentioned in it.

(7) In this section "prescribed" means prescribed by regulations made by the appropriate national authority.

[Housing Act 2004, s 232.]

Codes of practice and management regulations relating to HMOs etc

233. Approval of codes of practice with regard to the management of HMOs etc

234. Management regulations in respect of HMOs

Information provisions

8–17629ZQ 235. Power to require documents to be produced. (1) A person authorised in writing by a local housing authority may exercise the power conferred by subsection (2) in relation to documents reasonably required by the authority—

(*a*) for any purpose connected with the exercise of any of the authority's functions under any of Parts 1 to 4 in relation to any premises, or

(*b*) for the purpose of investigating whether any offence has been committed under any of those Parts in relation to any premises.

(2) A person so authorised may give a notice to a relevant person requiring him—

(*a*) to produce any documents which—

(i) are specified or described in the notice, or fall within a category of document which is specified or described in the notice, and

(ii) are in his custody or under his control, and

(*b*) to produce them at a time and place so specified and to a person so specified.

(3) The notice must include information about the possible consequences of not complying with the notice.

(4) The person to whom any document is produced in accordance with the notice may copy the document.

(5) No person may be required under this section to produce any document which he would be entitled to refuse to provide in proceedings in the High Court on grounds of legal professional privilege.

(6) In this section "document" includes information recorded otherwise than in legible form, and in relation to information so recorded, any reference to the production of a document is a reference to the production of a copy of the information in legible form.

(7) In this section "relevant person" means, in relation to any premises, a person within any of the following paragraphs—

(*a*) a person who is, or is proposed to be, the holder of a licence under Part 2 or 3 in respect of the premises, or a person on whom any obligation or restriction under such a licence is, or is proposed to be, imposed,

(*b*) a person who has an estate or interest in the premises,

(*c*) a person who is, or is proposing to be, managing or having control of the premises,

(*d*) a person who is, or is proposing to be, otherwise involved in the management of the premises,

(*e*) a person who occupies the premises.

[Housing Act 2004, s 235.]

8–17629ZR 236. Enforcement of powers to obtain information. (1) A person commits an offence if he fails to do anything required of him by a notice under section 235.

(2) In proceedings against a person for an offence under subsection (1) it is a defence that he had a reasonable excuse for failing to comply with the notice.

(3) A person who commits an offence under subsection (1) is liable on summary conviction to a fine not exceeding level 5 on the standard scale.

(4) A person commits an offence if he intentionally alters, suppresses or destroys any document which he has been required to produce by a notice under section 235.

(5) A person who commits an offence under subsection (4) is liable—

(*a*) on summary conviction, to a fine not exceeding the statutory maximum;

(*b*) on conviction on indictment, to a fine.

(6) In this section "document" includes information recorded otherwise than in legible form, and in relation to information so recorded—

(*a*) the reference to the production of a document is a reference to the production of a copy of the information in legible form, and

(*b*) the reference to suppressing a document includes a reference to destroying the means of reproducing the information.

[Housing Act 2004, s 236.]

237. Use of information obtained for certain other statutory purposes

8–17629ZS 238. False or misleading information. (1) A person commits an offence if—

(*a*) he supplies any information to a local housing authority in connection with any of their functions under any of Parts 1 to 4 or this Part,

(*b*) the information is false or misleading, and

(*c*) he knows that it is false or misleading or is reckless as to whether it is false or misleading.

(2) A person commits an offence if—

(*a*) he supplies any information to another person which is false or misleading,

(*b*) he knows that it is false or misleading or is reckless as to whether it is false or misleading, and

(*c*) he knows that the information is to be used for the purpose of supplying information to a local housing authority in connection with any of their functions under any of Parts 1 to 4 or this Part.

(3) A person who commits an offence under subsection (1) or (2) is liable on summary conviction to a fine not exceeding level 5 on the standard scale.

(4) In this section "false or misleading" means false or misleading in any material respect.

[Housing Act 2004, s 238.]

Enforcement

8–17629ZT 239. Powers of entry. (1) Subsection (3) applies where the local housing authority consider that a survey or examination of any premises is necessary and any of the following conditions is met—

(*a*) the authority consider that the survey or examination is necessary in order to carry out an inspection under section 4(1) or otherwise to determine whether any functions under any of Parts 1 to 4 or this Part should be exercised in relation to the premises;

(*b*) the premises are (within the meaning of Part 1) specified premises in relation to an improvement notice or prohibition order;

(*c*) a management order is in force under Chapter 1 or 2 of Part 4 in respect of the premises.

(2) Subsection (3) also applies where the proper officer of the local housing authority considers that a survey or examination of any premises is necessary in order to carry out an inspection under section 4(2).

(3) Where this subsection applies—

(*a*) a person authorised by the local housing authority (in a case within subsection (1)), or

(*b*) the proper officer (in a case within subsection (2)),

may enter the premises in question at any reasonable time for the purpose of carrying out a survey or examination of the premises.

(4) If—

(*a*) an interim or final management order is in force under Chapter 1 of Part 4 in respect of any premises consisting of part of a house ("the relevant premises"), and

(*b*) another part of the house is excluded from the order by virtue of section 102(8) or 113(7),

the power of entry conferred by subsection (3) is exercisable in relation to any premises comprised in that other part so far as is necessary for the purpose of carrying out a survey or examination of the relevant premises.

(5) Before entering any premises in exercise of the power conferred by subsection (3), the authorised person or proper officer must have given at least 24 hours' notice of his intention to do so—

(*a*) to the owner of the premises (if known), and

(*b*) to the occupier (if any).

(6) Subsection (7) applies where the local housing authority consider that any premises need to be entered for the purpose of ascertaining whether an offence has been committed under section 72, 95 or 234(3).

(7) A person authorised by the local housing authority may enter the premises for that purpose—

(*a*) at any reasonable time, but

(*b*) without giving any prior notice as mentioned in subsection (5).

(8) A person exercising the power of entry conferred by subsection (3) or (7) may do such of the following as he thinks necessary for the purpose for which the power is being exercised—

(*a*) take other persons with him;

(*b*) take equipment or materials with him;

(*c*) take measurements or photographs or make recordings;

(*d*) leave recording equipment on the premises for later collection;

(*e*) take samples of any articles or substances found on the premises.

(9) An authorisation for the purposes of this section—

(*a*) must be in writing; and

(*b*) must state the particular purpose or purposes for which the entry is authorised.

(10) A person authorised for the purposes of this section must, if required to do so, produce his

authorisation for inspection by the owner or any occupier of the premises or anyone acting on his behalf.

(11) If the premises are unoccupied or the occupier is temporarily absent, a person exercising the power of entry conferred by subsection (3) or (7) must leave the premises as effectively secured against trespassers as he found them.

(12) In this section "occupier", in relation to premises, means a person who occupies the premises, whether for residential or other purposes.

[Housing Act 2004, s 239.]

8–17629ZU 240. Warrant to authorise entry. (1) This section applies where a justice of the peace is satisfied, on a sworn information in writing, that admission to premises specified in the information is reasonably required for any of the purposes mentioned in subsection (2) by a person—

(*a*) employed by, or

(*b*) acting on the instructions of,

the local housing authority.

(2) The purposes are—

(*a*) surveying or examining premises in order to carry out an inspection under section 4(1) or (2) or otherwise to determine whether any functions under any of Parts 1 to 4 or this Part should be exercised in relation to the premises;

(*b*) surveying or examining premises—

(i) which are (within the meaning of Part 1) specified premises in relation to an improvement notice or prohibition order, or

(ii) in respect of which a management order is in force under Chapter 1 or 2 of Part 4;

(*c*) ascertaining whether an offence has been committed under section 72, 95 or 234(3).

(3) The justice may by warrant under his hand authorise the person mentioned in subsection (1) to enter on the premises for such of those purposes as may be specified in the warrant.

(4) But the justice must not grant the warrant unless he is satisfied—

(*a*) that admission to the premises has been sought in accordance with section 239(5) or (7) but has been refused;

(*b*) that the premises are unoccupied or that the occupier is temporarily absent and it might defeat the purpose of the entry to await his return; or

(*c*) that application for admission would defeat the purpose of the entry.

(5) The power of entry conferred by a warrant under this section includes power to enter by force (if necessary).

(6) Subsection (8) of section 239 applies to the person on whom that power is conferred as it applies to a person exercising the power of entry conferred by subsection (3) or (7) of that section.

(7) A warrant under this section must, if so required, be produced for inspection by the owner or any occupier of the premises or anyone acting on his behalf.

(8) If the premises are unoccupied or the occupier is temporarily absent, a person entering under the authority of a warrant under this section must leave the premises as effectively secured against trespassers as he found them.

(9) A warrant under this section continues in force until the purpose for which the entry is required is satisfied.

(10) In a case within section 239(4)(*a*) and (*b*), the powers conferred by this section are exercisable in relation to premises comprised in the excluded part of the house as well as in relation to the relevant premises.

(11) In this section "occupier", in relation to premises, means a person who occupies the premises, whether for residential or other purposes.

[Housing Act 2004, s 240.]

8–17629ZV 241. Penalty for obstruction. (1) A person who obstructs a relevant person in the performance of anything which, by virtue of any of Parts 1 to 4 or this Part, that person is required or authorised to do commits an offence.

(2) In proceedings against a person for an offence under subsection (1) it is a defence that he had a reasonable excuse for obstructing the relevant person.

(3) A person who commits an offence under subsection (1) is liable on summary conviction to a fine not exceeding level 4 on the standard scale.

(4) In this section "relevant person" means an officer of a local housing authority or any person authorised to enter premises by virtue of any of Parts 1 to 4 or section 239 or 240.

[Housing Act 2004, s 241.]

8–17629ZW 242. Additional notice requirements for protection of owners. (1) This section applies where an owner of premises gives a notice to the local housing authority for the purposes of this section informing them of his interest in the premises.

(2) The authority must give him notice of any action taken by them under any of Parts 1 to 4 or this Part in relation to the premises.
[Housing Act 2004, s 242.]

Authorisations

8–17629ZX **243. Authorisations for enforcement purposes etc.** (1) This section applies to any authorisation given for the purposes of any of the following provisions—

(*a*) section 131 (management orders: power of entry to carry out work),
(*b*) section 235 (power to require documents to be produced),
(*c*) section 239 (powers of entry),
(*d*) paragraph 3(4) of Schedule 3 (improvement notices: power to enter to carry out work), and
(*e*) paragraph 25 of Schedule 7 (EDMOs: power of entry to carry out work).

(2) Any such authorisation must be given by the appropriate officer of the local housing authority.

(3) For the purposes of this section a person is an "appropriate officer" of a local housing authority, in relation to an authorisation given by the authority, if either—

(*a*) he is a deputy chief officer of the authority (within the meaning of section 2 of the Local Government and Housing Act 1989 (c 42)), and
(*b*) the duties of his post consist of or include duties relating to the exercise of the functions of the authority in connection with which the authorisation is given,

or he is an officer of the authority to whom such a deputy chief officer reports directly, or is directly accountable, as respects duties so relating.
[Housing Act 2004, s 243.]

Documents

244. Power to prescribe forms

245. Power to dispense with notices

8–17629ZY **246. Service of documents.** (1) Subsection (2) applies where the local housing authority is, by virtue of any provision of Parts 1 to 4 or this Part, under a duty to serve a document on a person who, to the knowledge of the authority, is—

(*a*) a person having control of premises,
(*b*) a person managing premises, or
(*c*) a person having an estate or interest in premises,

or a person who (but for an interim or final management order under Chapter 1 of Part 4) would fall within paragraph (*a*) or (*b*).

(2) The local housing authority must take reasonable steps to identify the person or persons falling within the description in that provision.

(3) A person having an estate or interest in premises may for the purposes of any provision to which subsections (1) and (2) apply give notice to the local housing authority of his interest in the premises.

(4) The local housing authority must enter a notice under subsection (3) in its records.

(5) A document required or authorised by any of Parts 1 to 4 or this Part to be served on a person as—

(*a*) a person having control of premises,
(*b*) a person managing premises,
(*c*) a person having an estate or interest in premises, or
(*d*) a person who (but for an interim or final management order under Chapter 1 of Part 4) would fall within paragraph (*a*) or (*b*),

may, if it is not practicable after reasonable enquiry to ascertain the name or address of that person, be served in accordance with subsection (6).

(6) A person having such a connection with any premises as is mentioned in subsection (5)(*a*) to (*d*) is served in accordance with this subsection if—

(*a*) the document is addressed to him by describing his connection with the premises (naming them), and
(*b*) delivering the document to some person on the premises or, if there is no person on the premises to whom it can be delivered, by fixing it, or a copy of it, to some conspicuous part of the premises.

(7) Subsection (1)(*c*) or (5)(*c*) applies whether the provision requiring or authorising service of the document refers in terms to a person having an estate or interest in premises or instead refers to a class of person having such an estate or interest (such as owners, lessees or mortgagees).

(8) Where under any provision of Parts 1 to 4 or this Part a document is to be served on—

(*a*) the person having control of premises,

(*b*) the person managing premises, or
(*c*) the owner of premises,

and more than one person comes within the description in the provision, the document may be served on more than one of those persons.

(9) Section 233 of the Local Government Act 1972 (c 70) (service of notices by local authorities) applies in relation to the service of documents for any purposes of this Act by the authorities mentioned in section 261(2)(*d*) and (*e*) of this Act as if they were local authorities within the meaning of section 233.

(10) In this section—

(*a*) references to a person managing premises include references to a person authorised to permit persons to occupy premises; and
(*b*) references to serving include references to similar expressions (such as giving or sending).

(11) In this section—

"document" includes anything in writing;
"premises" means premises however defined.

[Housing Act 2004, s 246.]

8–17629ZZ 247. Licences and other documents in electronic form. (1) A local housing authority may, subject to subsection (3), issue a licence to a person under Part 2 or 3 by transmitting the text of the licence to him by electronic means, provided the text—

(*a*) is received by him in legible form, and
(*b*) is capable of being used for subsequent reference.

(2) A local housing authority may, subject to subsection (3), serve a relevant document on a person by transmitting the text of the document to him in the way mentioned in subsection (1).

(3) The recipient, or the person on whose behalf the recipient receives the document, must have indicated to the local housing authority the recipient's willingness to receive documents transmitted in the form and manner used.

(4) An indication for the purposes of subsection (3)—

(*a*) must be given to the local housing authority in such manner as they may require;
(*b*) may be a general indication or one that is limited to documents of a particular description;
(*c*) must state the address to be used and must be accompanied by such other information as the local housing authority require for the making of the transmission; and
(*d*) may be modified or withdrawn at any time by a notice given to the local housing authority in such manner as they may require.

(5) In this section any reference to serving includes a reference to similar expressions (such as giving or sending).

(6) In this section—

"document" includes anything in writing; and
"relevant document" means any document which a local housing authority are, by virtue of any provision of Parts 1 to 4 or this Part, under a duty to serve on any person.

[Housing Act 2004, s 247.]

8–17629ZZA 248. Timing and location of things done electronically. (1) The Secretary of State may by regulations make provision specifying, for the purposes of any of Parts 1 to 4 or this Part, the manner of determining—

(*a*) the times at which things done under any of Parts 1 to 4 or this Part by means of electronic communications networks are done;
(*b*) the places at which things done under any of Parts 1 to 4 or this Part by means of such networks are done; and
(*c*) the places at which things transmitted by means of such networks are received.

(2) The Secretary of State may by regulations make provision about the manner of proving in any legal proceedings—

(*a*) that something done by means of an electronic communications network satisfies any requirements of any of Parts 1 to 4 or this Part for the doing of that thing; and
(*b*) the matters mentioned in subsection (1)(*a*) to (*c*).

(3) Regulations under this section may provide for such presumptions to apply (whether conclusive or not) as the Secretary of State considers appropriate.

(4) In this section "electronic communications network" has the meaning given by section 32 of the Communications Act 2003 (c 21).

[Housing Act 2004, s 248.]

249. Proof of designations

250. Orders and regulations

8–17629ZZB 251. Offences by bodies corporate. (1) Where an offence under this Act committed by a body corporate is proved to have been committed with the consent or connivance of, or to be attributable to any neglect on the part of—

(*a*) a director, manager, secretary or other similar officer of the body corporate, or
(*b*) a person purporting to act in such a capacity,

he as well as the body corporate commits the offence and is liable to be proceeded against and punished accordingly.

(2) Where the affairs of a body corporate are managed by its members, subsection (1) applies in relation to the acts and defaults of a member in connection with his functions of management as if he were a director of the body corporate.
[Housing Act 2004, s 251.]

252. Power to up-rate level of fines for certain offences

253. Local inquiries

Meaning of "house in multiple occupation"

8–17629ZZC 254. Meaning of "house in multiple occupation". (1) For the purposes of this Act a building or a part of a building is a "house in multiple occupation" if—

(*a*) it meets the conditions in subsection (2) ("the standard test");
(*b*) it meets the conditions in subsection (3) ("the self-contained flat test");
(*c*) it meets the conditions in subsection (4) ("the converted building test");
(*d*) an HMO declaration is in force in respect of it under section 255; or
(*e*) it is a converted block of flats to which section 257 applies.

(2) A building or a part of a building meets the standard test if—

(*a*) it consists of one or more units of living accommodation not consisting of a self-contained flat or flats;
(*b*) the living accommodation is occupied by persons who do not form a single household (see section 258);
(*c*) the living accommodation is occupied by those persons as their only or main residence or they are to be treated as so occupying it (see section 259);
(*d*) their occupation of the living accommodation constitutes the only use of that accommodation;
(*e*) rents are payable or other consideration is to be provided in respect of at least one of those persons' occupation of the living accommodation; and
(*f*) two or more of the households who occupy the living accommodation share one or more basic amenities or the living accommodation is lacking in one or more basic amenities.

(3) A part of a building meets the self-contained flat test if—

(*a*) it consists of a self-contained flat; and
(*b*) paragraphs (*b*) to (*f*) of subsection (2) apply (reading references to the living accommodation concerned as references to the flat).

(4) A building or a part of a building meets the converted building test if—

(*a*) it is a converted building;
(*b*) it contains one or more units of living accommodation that do not consist of a self-contained flat or flats (whether or not it also contains any such flat or flats);
(*c*) the living accommodation is occupied by persons who do not form a single household (see section 258);
(*d*) the living accommodation is occupied by those persons as their only or main residence or they are to be treated as so occupying it (see section 259);
(*e*) their occupation of the living accommodation constitutes the only use of that accommodation; and
(*f*) rents are payable or other consideration is to be provided in respect of at least one of those persons' occupation of the living accommodation.

(5) But for any purposes of this Act (other than those of Part 1) a building or part of a building within subsection (1) is not a house in multiple occupation if it is listed in Schedule 14.

(6) The appropriate national authority may by regulations—

(*a*) make such amendments of this section and sections 255 to 259 as the authority considers appropriate with a view to securing that any building or part of a building of a description specified in the regulations is or is not to be a house in multiple occupation for any specified purposes of this Act;
(*b*) provide for such amendments to have effect also for the purposes of definitions in other enactments that operate by reference to this Act;
(*c*) make such consequential amendments of any provision of this Act, or any other enactment, as the authority considers appropriate.

(7) Regulations under subsection (6) may frame any description by reference to any matters or circumstances whatever.

(8) In this section—

"basic amenities" means—

(*a*) a toilet,
(*b*) personal washing facilities, or
(*c*) cooking facilities;

"converted building" means a building or part of a building consisting of living accommodation in which one or more units of such accommodation have been created since the building or part was constructed;

"enactment" includes an enactment comprised in subordinate legislation (within the meaning of the Interpretation Act 1978 (c 30);

"self-contained flat" means a separate set of premises (whether or not on the same floor)—

(*a*) which forms part of a building;
(*b*) either the whole or a material part of which lies above or below some other part of the building; and
(*c*) in which all three basic amenities are available for the exclusive use of its occupants.

[Housing Act 2004, s 254.]

8–17629ZZD 255. HMO declarations. (1) If a local housing authority are satisfied that subsection (2) applies to a building or part of a building in their area, they may serve a notice under this section (an "HMO declaration") declaring the building or part to be a house in multiple occupation.

(2) This subsection applies to a building or part of a building if the building or part meets any of the following tests (as it applies without the sole use condition)—

(*a*) the standard test (see section 254(2)),
(*b*) the self-contained flat test (see section 254(3)), or
(*c*) the converted building test (see section 254(4)),

and the occupation, by persons who do not form a single household, of the living accommodation or flat referred to in the test in question constitutes a significant use of that accommodation or flat.

(3) In subsection (2) "the sole use condition" means the condition contained in—

(*a*) section 254(2)(*d*) (as it applies for the purposes of the standard test or the self-contained flat test), or
(*b*) section 254(4)(*e*),

as the case may be.

(4) The notice must—

(*a*) state the date of the authority's decision to serve the notice,
(*b*) be served on each relevant person within the period of seven days beginning with the date of that decision,
(*c*) state the day on which it will come into force if no appeal is made under subsection (9) against the authority's decision, and
(*d*) set out the right to appeal against the decision under subsection (9) and the period within which an appeal may be made.

(5) The day stated in the notice under subsection (4)(*c*) must be not less than 28 days after the date of the authority's decision to serve the notice.

(6) If no appeal is made under subsection (9) before the end of that period of 28 days, the notice comes into force on the day stated in the notice.

(7) If such an appeal is made before the end of that period of 28 days, the notice does not come into force unless and until a decision is given on the appeal which confirms the notice and either—

(*a*) the period within which an appeal to the Lands Tribunal may be brought expires without such an appeal having been brought, or
(*b*) if an appeal to the Lands Tribunal is brought, a decision is given on the appeal which confirms the notice.

(8) For the purposes of subsection (7), the withdrawal of an appeal has the same effect as a decision which confirms the notice appealed against.

(9) Any relevant person may appeal to a residential property tribunal against a decision of the local housing authority to serve an HMO declaration.

The appeal must be made within the period of 28 days beginning with the date of the authority's decision.

(10) Such an appeal—

(*a*) is to be by way of a re-hearing, but
(*b*) may be determined having regard to matters of which the authority were unaware.

(11) The tribunal may—

(*a*) confirm or reverse the decision of the authority, and
(*b*) if it reverses the decision, revoke the HMO declaration.

(12) In this section and section 256 "relevant person", in relation to an HMO declaration, means any person who, to the knowledge of the local housing authority, is—

(*a*) a person having an estate or interest in the building or part of the building concerned (but is not a tenant under a lease with an unexpired term of 3 years of less), or
(*b*) a person managing or having control of that building or part (and not falling within paragraph (*a*)).

[Housing Act 2004, s 255.]

8–17629ZZE 256. Revocation of HMO declarations. (1) A local housing authority may revoke an HMO declaration served under section 255 at any time if they consider that subsection (2) of that section no longer applies to the building or part of the building in respect of which the declaration was served.

(2) The power to revoke an HMO declaration is exercisable by the authority either—

(*a*) on an application made by a relevant person, or
(*b*) on the authority's own initiative.

(3) If, on an application by such a person, the authority decide not to revoke the HMO declaration, they must without delay serve on him a notice informing him of—

(*a*) the decision,
(*b*) the reasons for it and the date on which it was made,
(*c*) the right to appeal against it under subsection (4), and
(*d*) the period within which an appeal may be made under that subsection.

(4) A person who applies to a local housing authority for the revocation of an HMO declaration under subsection (1) may appeal to a residential property tribunal against a decision of the authority to refuse to revoke the notice.

The appeal must be made within the period of 28 days beginning with the date specified under subsection (3) as the date on which the decision was made.

(5) Such an appeal—

(*a*) is to be by way of a re-hearing, but
(*b*) may be determined having regard to matters of which the authority were unaware.

(6) The tribunal may—

(*a*) confirm or reverse the decision of the authority, and
(*b*) if it reverses the decision, revoke the HMO declaration.

[Housing Act 2004, s 256.]

8–17629ZZF 257. HMOs: certain converted blocks of flats. (1) For the purposes of this section a "converted block of flats" means a building or part of a building which—

(*a*) has been converted into, and
(*b*) consists of,

self-contained flats.

(2) This section applies to a converted block of flats if—

(*a*) building work undertaken in connection with the conversion did not comply with the appropriate building standards and still does not comply with them; and
(*b*) less than two-thirds of the self-contained flats are owner-occupied.

(3) In subsection (2) "appropriate building standards" means—

(*a*) in the case of a converted block of flats—
  (i) on which building work was completed before 1st June 1992 or which is dealt with by regulation 20 of the Building Regulations 1991 (SI 1991/2768), and
  (ii) which would not have been exempt under those Regulations,

  building standards equivalent to those imposed, in relation to a building or part of a building to which those Regulations applied, by those Regulations as they had effect on 1st June 1992; and
(*b*) in the case of any other converted block of flats, the requirements imposed at the time in relation to it by regulations under section 1 of the Building Act 1984 (c 55).

(4) For the purposes of subsection (2) a flat is "owner-occupied" if it is occupied—

(*a*) by a person who has a lease of the flat which has been granted for a term of more than 21 years,
(*b*) by a person who has the freehold estate in the converted block of flats, or
(*c*) by a member of the household of a person within paragraph (*a*) or (*b*).

(5) The fact that this section applies to a converted block of flats (with the result that it is a house

in multiple occupation under section 254(1)(*e*)), does not affect the status of any flat in the block as a house in multiple occupation.

(6) In this section "self-contained flat" has the same meaning as in section 254.

[Housing Act 2004, s 257.]

8–17629ZZH 258. HMOs: persons not forming a single household. (1) This section sets out when persons are to be regarded as not forming a single household for the purposes of section 254.

(2) Persons are to be regarded as not forming a single household unless—

(*a*) they are all members of the same family, or

(*b*) their circumstances are circumstances of a description specified for the purposes of this section in regulations made by the appropriate national authority.

(3) For the purposes of subsection (2)(*a*) a person is a member of the same family as another person if—

(*a*) those persons are married to each other or live together as husband and wife (or in an equivalent relationship in the case of persons of the same sex);

(*b*) one of them is a relative of the other; or

(*c*) one of them is, or is a relative of, one member of a couple and the other is a relative of the other member of the couple.

(4) For those purposes—

(*a*) a "couple" means two persons who are married to each other or otherwise fall within subsection (3)(*a*);

(*b*) "relative" means parent, grandparent, child, grandchild, brother, sister, uncle, aunt, nephew, niece or cousin;

(*c*) a relationship of the half-blood shall be treated as a relationship of the whole blood; and

(*d*) the stepchild of a person shall be treated as his child.

(5) Regulations under subsection (2)(*b*) may, in particular, secure that a group of persons are to be regarded as forming a single household only where (as the regulations may require) each member of the group has a prescribed relationship, or at least one of a number of prescribed relationships, to any one or more of the others.

(6) In subsection (5) "prescribed relationship" means any relationship of a description specified in the regulations.

[Housing Act 2004, s 258.]

8–17629ZZI 259. HMOs: persons treated as occupying premises as only or main residence. (1) This section sets out when persons are to be treated for the purposes of section 254 as occupying a building or part of a building as their only or main residence.

(2) A person is to be treated as so occupying a building or part of a building if it is occupied by the person—

(*a*) as the person's residence for the purpose of undertaking a full-time course of further or higher education;

(*b*) as a refuge, or

(*c*) in any other circumstances which are circumstances of a description specified for the purposes of this section in regulations made by the appropriate national authority.

(3) In subsection (2)(*b*) "refuge" means a building or part of a building managed by a voluntary organisation and used wholly or mainly for the temporary accommodation of persons who have left their homes as a result of—

(*a*) physical violence or mental abuse, or

(*b*) threats of such violence or abuse,

from persons to whom they are or were married or with whom they are or were co-habiting.

[Housing Act 2004, s 259.]

8–17629ZZJ 260. HMOs: presumption that sole use condition or significant use condition is met. (1) Where a question arises in any proceedings as to whether either of the following is met in respect of a building or part of a building—

(*a*) the sole use condition, or

(*b*) the significant use condition,

it shall be presumed, for the purposes of the proceedings, that the condition is met unless the contrary is shown.

(2) In this section—

(*a*) "the sole use condition" means the condition contained in—

(i) section 254(2)(*d*) (as it applies for the purposes of the standard test or the self-contained flat test), or

(ii) section 254(4)(*e*),

as the case may be; and

(*b*) "the significant use condition" means the condition contained in section 255(2) that the occupation of the living accommodation or flat referred to in that provision by persons who do not form a single household constitutes a significant use of that accommodation or flat.

[Housing Act 2004, s 260.]

Other general interpretation provisions

8–17629ZZK 261. Meaning of "appropriate national authority", "local housing authority" etc. (1) In this Act "the appropriate national authority" means—

(*a*) in relation to England, the Secretary of State; and

(*b*) in relation to Wales, the National Assembly for Wales.

(2) In this Act "local housing authority" means, in relation to England—

(*a*) a unitary authority;

(*b*) a district council so far as it is not a unitary authority;

(*c*) a London borough council;

(*d*) the Common Council of the City of London (in its capacity as a local authority);

(*e*) the Sub-Treasurer of the Inner Temple or the Under-Treasurer of the Middle Temple (in his capacity as a local authority); and

(*f*) the Council of the Isles of Scilly.

(3) In subsection (2) "unitary authority" means—

(*a*) the council of a county so far as it is the council for an area for which there are no district councils;

(*b*) the council of any district comprised in an area for which there is no county council.

(4) In this Act "local housing authority" means, in relation to Wales, a county council or a county borough council.

(5) References in this Act to "the local housing authority", in relation to land, are to the local housing authority in whose district the land is situated.

(6) References in this Act to the district of a local housing authority are to the area of the council concerned, that is to say—

(*a*) in the case of a unitary authority, the area or district;

(*b*) in the case of a district council so far as it is not a unitary authority, the district;

(*c*) in the case of an authority within subsection (2)(*c*) to (*f*), the London borough, the City of London, the Inner or Middle Temple or the Isles of Scilly (as the case may be); and

(*d*) in the case of a Welsh county council or a county borough council, the Welsh county or county borough.

(7) Section 618 of the Housing Act 1985 (c 68) (committees and members of Common Council of City of London) applies in relation to this Act as it applies in relation to that Act.

[Housing Act 2004, s 261.]

8–17629ZZL 262. Meaning of "lease", "tenancy", "occupier" and "owner" etc. (1) In this Act "lease" and "tenancy" have the same meaning.

(2) Both expressions include—

(*a*) a sub-lease or sub-tenancy; and

(*b*) an agreement for a lease or tenancy (or sub-lease or sub-tenancy).

And see sections 108 and 117 and paragraphs 3 and 11 of Schedule 7 (which also extend the meaning of references to leases).

(3) The expressions "lessor" and "lessee" and "landlord" and "tenant" and references to letting, to the grant of a lease or to covenants or terms, are to be construed accordingly.

(4) In this Act "lessee" includes a statutory tenant of the premises; and references to a lease or to a person to whom premises are let are to be construed accordingly.

(5) In this Act any reference to a person who is a tenant under a lease with an unexpired term of 3 years or less includes a statutory tenant as well as a tenant under a yearly or other periodic tenancy.

(6) In this Act "occupier", in relation to premises, means a person who—

(*a*) occupies the premises as a residence, and

(*b*) (subject to the context) so occupies them whether as a tenant or other person having an estate or interest in the premises or as a licensee;

and related expressions are to be construed accordingly.

This subsection does not apply for the purposes of Part 5 and has effect subject to any other provision defining "occupier" for any purposes of this Act.

(7) In this Act "owner", in relation to premises—

(*a*) means a person (other than a mortgagee not in possession) who is for the time being entitled to dispose of the fee simple of the premises whether in possession or in reversion; and (*b*) includes also a person holding or entitled to the rents and profits of the premises under a lease of which the unexpired term exceeds 3 years.

(8) In this Act "person having an estate or interest", in relation to premises, includes a statutory tenant of the premises.

(9) In this Act "licence", in the context of a licence to occupy premises—

(*a*) includes a licence which is not granted for a consideration, but
(*b*) excludes a licence granted as a temporary expedient to a person who entered the premises as a trespasser (whether or not, before the grant of the licence, another licence to occupy those or other premises had been granted to him);

and related expressions are to be construed accordingly.

And see sections 108 and 117 and paragraphs 3 and 11 of Schedule 7 (which also extend the meaning of references to licences).

[Housing Act 2004, s 262.]

8–17629ZZM 263. Meaning of "person having control" and "person managing" etc. (1) In this Act "person having control", in relation to premises, means (unless the context otherwise requires) the person who receives the rack-rent of the premises (whether on his own account or as agent or trustee of another person), or who would so receive it if the premises were let at a rack-rent.

(2) In subsection (1) "rack-rent" means a rent which is not less than two-thirds of the full net annual value of the premises.

(3) In this Act "person managing" means, in relation to premises, the person who, being an owner or lessee of the premises—

(*a*) receives (whether directly or through an agent or trustee) rents or other payments from—
  (i) in the case of a house in multiple occupation, persons who are in occupation as tenants or licensees of parts of the premises; and
  (ii) in the case of a house to which Part 3 applies (see section 79(2)), persons who are in occupation as tenants or licensees of parts of the premises, or of the whole of the premises; or
(*b*) would so receive those rents or other payments but for having entered into an arrangement (whether in pursuance of a court order or otherwise) with another person who is not an owner or lessee of the premises by virtue of which that other person receives the rents or other payments;

and includes, where those rents or other payments are received through another person as agent or trustee, that other person.

(4) In its application to Part 1, subsection (3) has effect with the omission of paragraph (*a*)(ii).

(5) References in this Act to any person involved in the management of a house in multiple occupation or a house to which Part 3 applies (see section 79(2)) include references to the person managing it.

[Housing Act 2004, s 263.]

8–17629ZZN 264. Calculation of numbers of persons. (1) The appropriate national authority may prescribe rules with respect to the calculation of numbers of persons for the purposes of—

(*a*) any provision made by or under this Act which is specified in the rules, or
(*b*) any order or licence made or granted under this Act of any description which is so specified.

(2) The rules may provide—

(*a*) for persons under a particular age to be disregarded for the purposes of any such calculation;
(*b*) for persons under a particular age to be treated as constituting a fraction of a person for the purposes of any such calculation.

(3) The rules may be prescribed by order or regulations.

[Housing Act 2004, s 264.]

8–17629ZZO 265. Minor and consequential amendments. (1) Schedule 15 (which contains minor and consequential amendments) has effect.

(2) The Secretary of State may by order make such supplementary, incidental or consequential provision as he considers appropriate—

(*a*) for the general purposes, or any particular purpose, of this Act; or
(*b*) in consequence of any provision made by or under this Act or for giving full effect to it.

(3) An order under subsection (2) may modify any enactment (including this Act).

"Enactment" includes an enactment comprised in subordinate legislation (within the meaning of the Interpretation Act 1978 (c 30)).

(4) The power conferred by subsection (2) is also exercisable by the National Assembly for Wales in relation to provision dealing with matters with respect to which functions are exercisable by the Assembly.

(5) Nothing in this Act affects the generality of the power conferred by this section.
[Housing Act 2004, s 265.]

8-17629ZZP 266. Repeals. Schedule 16 (which contains repeals) has effect.
[Housing Act 2004, s 266.]

8-17629ZZQ 267. Devolution: Wales. In Schedule 1 to the National Assembly for Wales (Transfer of Functions) Order 1999 (SI 1999/672) references to the following Acts are to be treated as references to those Acts as amended by virtue of this Act—

(*a*) the Housing Act 1985 (c 68);
(*b*) the Housing Act 1988 (c 50);
(*c*) the Housing Act 1996 (c 52).
[Housing Act 2004, s 267.]

8-17629ZZR 268. The Isles of Scilly. (1) This Secretary of State may by order provide that, in its application to the Isles of Scilly, this Act is have effect with such modifications as are specified in the order.

(2) Where a similar power is exercisable under another Act in relation to provisions of that Act which are amended by this Act, the power is exercisable in relation to those provisions as so amended.
[Housing Act 2004, s 268.]

8-17629ZZS 269. Expenses. There shall be paid out of money provided by Parliament—

(*a*) any expenditure incurred by the Secretary of State by virtue of this Act;
(*b*) any increase attributable to this Act in the sums payable out of money so provided under any other enactment.
[Housing Act 2004, s 269.]

8-17629ZZT 270. Short title, commencement and extent. (1) This Act may be cited as the Housing Act 2004.

(2) The following provisions come into force on the day on which this Act is passed—

(*a*) sections 2, 9, 161 to 164, 176, 190, 208, 216, 233, 234, 244, 248, 250, 252, 264, 265(2) to (5), 267 to 269 and this section, and
(*b*) any other provision of this Act so far as it confers any power to make an order or regulations which is exercisable by the Secretary of State or the National Assembly for Wales.

Subsections (3) to (7) have effect subject to paragraph (*b*).

(3) The following provisions come into force at the end of the period of two months beginning with the day on which this Act is passed—

(*a*) sections 180, 182 to 189, 195 to 207, 209 to 211, 217, 218, 219, 222, 224, 245 to 247, 249, 251 and 253 to 263,
(*b*) Schedule 9,
(*c*) Schedule 11, except paragraphs 15 and 16, and
(*d*) Schedule 14.

(4) The provisions listed in subsection (5) come into force—

(*a*) where they are to come into force in relation only to Wales, on such day as the National Assembly for Wales may by order appoint, and
(*b*) otherwise, on such day as the Secretary of State may by order appoint.

(5) The provisions referred to in subsection (4) are—

(*a*) Part 1 (other than sections 2 and 9),
(*b*) Parts 2 to 4,
(*c*) sections 179, 181, 191 to 194, 212 to 215, 220, 221, 223, 225, 226, 227, 229 to 232, 235 to 243, 265(1) and 266,
(*d*) Schedule 10,
(*e*) paragraphs 15 and 16 of Schedule 11, and
(*f*) Schedules 13, 15 and 16.

(6) Part 5 (other than sections 161 to 164 and 176) comes into force on such day as the Secretary of State may by order appoint.

(7) Section 228 and Schedule 12 come into force on such day as the National Assembly for Wales may by order appoint.

(8) Different days may be appointed for different purposes or different areas under subsection (4), (6) or (7).

(9) The Secretary of State may by order make such provision as he considers necessary or expedient for transitory, transitional or saving purposes in connection with the coming into force of any provision of this Act.

(10) The power conferred by subsection (9) is also exercisable by the National Assembly for

Wales in relation to provision dealing with matters with respect to which functions are exercisable by the Assembly

(11) Subject to subsections (12) and (13), this Act extends to England and Wales only.

(12) Any amendment or repeal made by this Act has the same extent as the enactment to which it relates, except that any amendment or repeal in—

the Mobile Homes Act 1983 (c 34), or
the Crime and Disorder Act 1998 (c 37),

extends to England and Wales only.

(13) This section extends to the whole of the United Kingdom.
[Housing Act 2004, s 270.]

---

1. For details of commencement orders, see the note to the title of the Act.

8–17629ZZU

Section 18

SCHEDULE 1
Procedure and Appeals Relating to Improvement Notices

Part 1
Service of Improvement Notices

Service of improvement notices: premises licensed under Part 2 or 3

1. (1) This paragraph applies where the specified premises in the case of an improvement notice are—

(*a*) a dwelling which is licensed under Part 3 of this Act, or
(*b*) an HMO which is licensed under Part 2 or 3 of this Act.

(2) The local housing authority must serve the notice on the holder of the licence under that Part.

Service of improvement notices: premises which are neither licensed under Part 2 or 3 nor flats

2. (1) This paragraph applies where the specified premises in the case of an improvement notice are—

(*a*) a dwelling which is not licensed under Part 3 of this Act, or
(*b*) an HMO which is not licensed under Part 2 or 3 of this Act,

and which (in either case) is not a flat.

(2) The local housing authority must serve the notice—

(*a*) (in the case of a dwelling) on the person having control of the dwelling;
(*b*) (in the case of an HMO) either on the person having control of the HMO or on the person managing it.

Service of improvement notices: flats which are not licensed under Part 2 or 3

3. (1) This paragraph applies where any specified premises in the case of an improvement notice are—

(*a*) a dwelling which is not licensed under Part 3 of this Act, or
(*b*) an HMO which is not licensed under Part 2 or 3 of this Act,

and which (in either case) is a flat.

(2) In the case of dwelling which is a flat, the local housing authority must serve the notice on a person who—

(*a*) is an owner of the flat, and
(*b*) in the authority's opinion ought to take the action specified in the notice.

(3) In the case of an HMO which is a flat, the local housing authority must serve the notice either on a person who—

(*a*) is an owner of the flat, and
(*b*) in the authority's opinion ought to take the action specified in the notice,

or on the person managing the flat.

Service of improvement notices: common parts

4. (1) This paragraph applies where any specified premises in the case of an improvement notice are—

(*a*) common parts of a building containing one or more flats; or
(*b*) any part of such a building which does not consist of residential premises.

(2) The local housing authority must serve the notice on a person who—

(*a*) is an owner of the specified premises concerned, and
(*b*) in the authority's opinion ought to take the action specified in the notice.

(3) For the purposes of this paragraph a person is an owner of any common parts of a building if he is an owner of the building or part of the building concerned, or (in the case of external common parts) of the particular premises in which the common parts are comprised.

Service of copies of improvement notices

5. (1) In addition to serving an improvement notice in accordance with any of paragraphs 1 to 4, the local housing authority must serve a copy of the notice on every other person who, to their knowledge—

(*a*) has a relevant interest in any specified premises, or
(*b*) is an occupier of any such premises.

(2) A "relevant interest" means an interest as freeholder, mortgagee or lessee.
(3) For the purposes of this paragraph a person has a relevant interest in any common parts of a building if he has a relevant interest in the building or part of the building concerned, or (in the case of external common parts) in the particular premises in which the common parts are comprised.
(4) The copies required to be served under sub-paragraph (1) must be served within the period of seven days beginning with the day on which the notice is served.

PART 2
SERVICE OF NOTICES RELATING TO REVOCATION OR VARIATION OF IMPROVEMENT NOTICES

PART 3
APPEALS RELATING TO IMPROVEMENT NOTICES

"The operative time" for the purposes of section 15(5)

19. (1) This paragraph defines "the operative time" for the purposes of section 15(5) (operation of improvement notices).
(2) If an appeal is made under paragraph 10 against an improvement notice which is not suspended, and a decision on the appeal is given which confirms the notice, "the operative time" is as follows—

(*a*) if the period within which an appeal to the Lands Tribunal may be brought expires without such an appeal having been brought, "the operative time" is the end of that period;
(*b*) if an appeal to the Lands Tribunal is brought, "the operative time" is the time when a decision is given on the appeal which confirms the notice.

(3) If an appeal is made under paragraph 10 against an improvement notice which is suspended, and a decision is given on the appeal which confirms the notice, "the operative time" is as follows—

(*a*) the time that would be the operative time under sub-paragraph (2) if the notice were not suspended, or
(*b*) if later, the time when the suspension ends.

(4) For the purposes of sub-paragraph (2) or (3)—

(*a*) the withdrawal of an appeal has the same effect as a decision which confirms the notice, and
(*b*) references to a decision which confirms the notice are to a decision which confirms it with or without variation.

"The operative time" for the purposes of section 16(7)

20. (1) This paragraph defines "the operative time" for the purposes of section 16(7) (postponement of time when a variation of an improvement notice comes into force).
(2) If no appeal is made under paragraph 13 before the end of the period of 28 days mentioned in paragraph 14(2), "the operative time" is the end of that period.
(3) If an appeal is made under paragraph 13 before the end of that period and a decision is given on the appeal which confirms the variation, "the operative time" is as follows—

(*a*) if the period within which an appeal to the Lands Tribunal may be brought expires without such an appeal having been brought, "the operative time" is the end of that period;
(*b*) if an appeal to the Lands Tribunal is brought, "the operative time" is the time when a decision is given on the appeal which confirms the variation.

(4) For the purposes of sub-paragraph (3)—

(*a*) the withdrawal of an appeal has the same effect as a decision which confirms the variation, and
(*b*) references to a decision which confirms the variation are to a decision which confirms it with or without variation.

8–17629ZZV

Section 27

SCHEDULE 2
PROCEDURE AND APPEALS RELATING TO PROHIBITION ORDERS

PART 1
SERVICE OF COPIES OF PROHIBITION ORDERS

Service on owners and occupiers of dwelling or HMO which is not a flat

1. (1) This paragraph applies to a prohibition order where the specified premises are a dwelling or HMO which is not a flat.
(2) The authority must serve copies of the order on every person who, to their knowledge, is—

(*a*) an owner or occupier of the whole or part of the specified premises;
(*b*) authorised to permit persons to occupy the whole or part of those premises; or
(*c*) a mortgagee of the whole or part of those premises.

(3) The copies required to be served under sub-paragraph (2) must be served within the period of seven days beginning with the day on which the order is made.
(4) A copy of the order is to be regarded as having been served on every occupier in accordance with sub-paragraphs (2)(*a*) and (3) if a copy of the order is fixed to some conspicuous part of the specified premises within the period of seven days mentioned in sub-paragraph (3).

Service on owners and occupiers of building containing flats etc

2. (1) This paragraph applies to a prohibition order where the specified premises consist of or include the whole or any part of a building containing one or more flats or any common parts of such a building.

(2) The authority must serve copies of the order on every person who, to their knowledge, is—

(*a*) an owner or occupier of the whole or part of the building;
(*b*) authorised to permit persons to occupy the whole or part of the building; or
(*c*) a mortgagee of the whole or part of the building.

(3) Where the specified premises consist of or include any external common parts of such a building, the authority must, in addition to complying with sub-paragraph (2), serve copies of the order on every person who, to their knowledge, is an owner or mortgagee of the premises in which the common parts are comprised.

(4) The copies required to be served under sub-paragraph (2) or (3) must be served within the period of seven days beginning with the day on which the order is made.

(5) A copy of the order is to be regarded as having been served on every occupier in accordance with sub-paragraphs (2)(*a*) and (4) if a copy of the order is fixed to some conspicuous part of the building within the period of seven days mentioned in sub-paragraph (4).

PART 2
SERVICE OF NOTICES RELATING TO REVOCATION OR VARIATION OF PROHIBITION ORDERS

PART 3
APPEALS RELATING TO PROHIBITION ORDERS

"The operative time" for the purposes of section 24(5)

14. (1) This paragraph defines "the operative time" for the purposes of section 24(5) (operation of prohibition orders).

(2) If an appeal is made under paragraph 7 against a prohibition order which is not suspended, and a decision on the appeal is given which confirms the order, "the operative time" is as follows—

(*a*) if the period within which an appeal to the Lands Tribunal may be brought expires without such an appeal having been brought, "the operative time" is the end of that period;
(*b*) if an appeal to the Lands Tribunal is brought, "the operative time" is the time when a decision is given on the appeal which confirms the order.

(3) If an appeal is made under paragraph 7 against a prohibition order which is suspended, and a decision is given on the appeal which confirms the order, "the operative time" is as follows—

(*a*) the time that would be the operative time under sub-paragraph (2) if the order were not suspended, or
(*b*) if later, the time when the suspension ends.

(4) For the purposes of sub-paragraph (2) or (3)—

(*a*) the withdrawal of an appeal has the same effect as a decision which confirms the notice, and
(*b*) references to a decision which confirms the order are to a decision which confirms it with or without variation.

"The operative time" for the purposes of section 25(7)

15. (1) This paragraph defines "the operative time" for the purposes of section 25(7) (revocation or variation of prohibition orders).

(2) If no appeal is made under paragraph 9 before the end of the period of 28 days mentioned in paragraph 10(2), "the operative time" is the end of that period.

(3) If an appeal is made under paragraph 10 within that period and a decision is given on the appeal which confirms the variation, "the operative time" is as follows—

(*a*) if the period within which an appeal to the Lands Tribunal may be brought expires without such an appeal having been brought, "the operative time" is the end of that period;
(*b*) if an appeal to the Lands Tribunal is brought, "the operative time" is the time when a decision is given on the appeal which confirms the variation.

(4) For the purposes of sub-paragraph (3)—

(*a*) the withdrawal of an appeal has the same effect as a decision which confirms the variation, and
(*b*) references to a decision which confirms the variation are to a decision which confirms it with or without variation.

8–17629ZZW

Section 31

SCHEDULE 3
IMPROVEMENT NOTICES: ENFORCEMENT ACTION BY LOCAL HOUSING AUTHORITIES

PART 1
ACTION TAKEN BY AGREEMENT

Power to take action by agreement

1. (1) The local housing authority may, by agreement with the person on whom an improvement notice has been served, take any action which that person is required to take in relation to any premises in pursuance of the notice.

(2) For that purpose the authority have all the rights which that person would have against any occupying tenant of, and any other person having an interest in, the premises (or any part of the premises).

(3) In this paragraph—

"improvement notice" means an improvement notice which has become operative under Chapter 2 of Part 1 of this Act;

"occupying tenant", in relation to any premises, means a person (other than an owner-occupier) who—

(*a*) occupies or is entitled to occupy the premises as a lessee;
(*b*) is a statutory tenant of the premises;
(*c*) occupies the premises under a restricted contract;
(*d*) is a protected occupier within the meaning of the Rent (Agriculture) Act 1976 (c 80); or
(*e*) is a licensee under an assured agricultural occupancy;

"owner-occupier", in relation to any premises, means the person who occupies or is entitled to occupy the premises as owner or lessee under a long tenancy (within the meaning of Part 1 of the Leasehold Reform Act 1967 (c 88)).

Expenses of taking action by agreement

2. Any action taken by the local housing authority under paragraph 1 is to be taken at the expense of the person on whom the notice is served.

PART 2
POWER TO TAKE ACTION WITHOUT AGREEMENT

Power to take action without agreement

3. (1) The local housing authority may themselves take the action required to be taken in relation to a hazard by an improvement notice if sub-paragraph (2) or (3) applies.

(2) This sub-paragraph applies if the notice is not complied with in relation to that hazard.

(3) This sub-paragraph applies if, before the end of the period which under section 30(2) is appropriate for completion of the action specified in the notice in relation to the hazard, they consider that reasonable progress is not being made towards compliance with the notice in relation to the hazard.

(4) Any person authorised in writing by the authority may enter any part of the specified premises for the purposes of the taking of any action which the authority are authorised to take under this paragraph.

(5) The right of entry conferred by sub-paragraph (4) may be exercised at any reasonable time.

(6) Any reference in this Part of this Schedule (of whatever nature) to a local housing authority entering any premises under this paragraph is a reference to their doing so in accordance with sub-paragraph (4).

(7) In this paragraph "improvement notice" means an improvement notice which has become operative under Chapter 2 of Part 1 of this Act.

Notice requirements in relation to taking action without agreement

4. (1) The local housing authority must serve a notice under this paragraph before they enter any premises under paragraph 3 for the purpose of taking action in relation to a hazard.

(2) The notice must identify the improvement notice to which it relates and state—

(*a*) the premises and hazard concerned;
(*b*) that the authority intend to enter the premises;
(*c*) the action which the authority intend to take on the premises; and
(*d*) the power under which the authority intend to enter the premises and take the action.

(3) The notice must be served on the person on whom the improvement notice was served, and a copy of the notice must be served on any other person who is an occupier of the premises.

(4) The notice and any such copy must be served sufficiently in advance of the time when the authority intend to enter the premises as to give the recipients reasonable notice of the intended entry.

(5) A copy of the notice may also be served on any owner of the premises.

Obstruction of action taken without agreement

5. (1) If, at any relevant time—

(*a*) the person on whom the notice under paragraph 4 was served is on the premises for the purpose of carrying out any works, or
(*b*) any workman employed by that person, or by any contractor employed by that person, is on the premises for such a purpose,

that person is to be taken to have committed an offence under section 241(1).

(2) In proceedings for such an offence it is a defence that there was an urgent necessity to carry out the works in order to prevent danger to persons occupying the premises.

(3) In sub-paragraph (1) "relevant time" means any time—

(*a*) after the end of the period of 7 days beginning with the date of service of the notice under paragraph 4, and
(*b*) when any workman or contractor employed by the local housing authority is taking action on the premises which has been mentioned in the notice in accordance with paragraph 4(2)(*c*).

Expenses in relation to taking action without agreement

6. (1) Part 3 of this Schedule applies with respect to the recovery by the local housing authority of expenses incurred by them in taking action under paragraph 3.

(2) Sub-paragraph (3) applies where, after a local housing authority have given notice under paragraph 4 of their intention to enter premises and take action, the action is in fact taken by the person on whom the improvement notice is served.

(3) Any administrative and other expenses incurred by the authority with a view to themselves taking the action

are to be treated for the purposes of Part 3 of this Schedule as expenses incurred by them in taking action under paragraph 3.

PART 3
RECOVERY OF CERTAIN EXPENSES

8–17629ZZX

Sections 67 and 90

SCHEDULE 4
LICENCES UNDER PARTS 2 AND 3: MANDATORY CONDITIONS

Conditions to be included in licences under Part 2 or 3

1. (1) A licence under Part 2 or 3 must include the following conditions.

(2) Conditions requiring the licence holder, if gas is supplied to the house, to produce to the local housing authority annually for their inspection a gas safety certificate obtained in respect of the house within the last 12 months.

(3) Conditions requiring the licence holder—

(*a*) to keep electrical appliances and furniture made available by him in the house in a safe condition;
(*b*) to supply the authority, on demand, with a declaration by him as to the safety of such appliances and furniture.

(4) Conditions requiring the licence holder—

(*a*) to ensure that smoke alarms are installed in the house and to keep them in proper working order;
(*b*) to supply the authority, on demand, with a declaration by him as to the condition and positioning of such alarms.

(5) Conditions requiring the licence holder to supply to the occupiers of the house a written statement of the terms on which they occupy it.

Additional conditions to be included in licences under Part 3

2. A licence under Part 3 must include conditions requiring the licence holder to demand references from persons who wish to occupy the house.

Power to prescribe conditions

3. The appropriate national authority may by regulations amend this Schedule so as to alter (by the addition or removal of conditions) the conditions which must be included—

(*a*) in a licence under Part 2 or 3, or
(*b*) only in a licence under one of those Parts.

Interpretation

4. In this Schedule "the house" means the HMO or Part 3 house in respect of which the licence is granted.

SCHEDULE 5
LICENCES UNDER PARTS 2 AND 3: PROCEDURE AND APPEALS

8–17629ZZY

SCHEDULE 6
MANAGEMENT ORDERS: PROCEDURE AND APPEALS

"The operative time" for the purposes of section 114(2)

27. (1) This paragraph defines "the operative time" for the purposes of section 114(2).

(2) If no appeal is made under paragraph 24 before the end of the period of 28 days mentioned in paragraph 25(2), "the operative time" is the end of that period.

(3) If an appeal is made under paragraph 24 before the end of that period, and a decision is given on the appeal which confirms the order, "the operative time" is as follows—

(*a*) if the period within which an appeal to the Lands Tribunal may be brought expires without such an appeal having been brought, "the operative time" is the end of that period;
(*b*) if an appeal to the Lands Tribunal is brought, "the operative time" is the time when a decision is given on the appeal which confirms the order.

(4) For the purposes of sub-paragraph (3)—

(*a*) the withdrawal of an appeal has the same effect as a decision which confirms the order, and
(*b*) references to a decision which confirms the order are to a decision which confirms it with or without variation.

SCHEDULE 7
FURTHER PROVISIONS REGARDING EMPTY DWELLING MANAGEMENT ORDERS

SCHEDULE 8
PENALTY CHARGE NOTICES UNDER SECTION 168

SCHEDULE 9
NEW SCHEDULE 5A TO THE HOUSING ACT 1985: INITIAL DEMOLITION NOTICES

SCHEDULE 10
PROVISIONS RELATING TO TENANCY DEPOSIT SCHEMES

SCHEDULE 11

REGISTERED SOCIAL LANDLORDS

SCHEDULE 12

NEW SCHEDULE 2A TO THE HOUSING ACT 1996

SCHEDULE 13

RESIDENTIAL PROPERTY TRIBUNALS: PROCEDURE

8–17629ZZZ

Section 254

SCHEDULE 14

BUILDINGS WHICH ARE NOT HMOS FOR PURPOSES OF THIS ACT (EXCLUDING PART 1)

Introduction: buildings (or parts) which are not HMOs for purposes of this Act (excluding Part 1)

1. (1) The following paragraphs list buildings which are not houses in multiple occupation for any purposes of this Act other than those of Part 1.

(2) In this Schedule "building" includes a part of a building.

Buildings controlled or managed by public sector bodies etc

2. (1) A building where the person managing or having control of it is—

(*a*) a local housing authority,
(*b*) a body which is registered as a social landlord under Part 1 of the Housing Act 1996 (c 52),
(*c*) a police authority established under section 3 of the Police Act 1996 (c 16),
(*d*) the Metropolitan Police Authority established under section 5B of that Act,
(*e*) a fire and rescue authority, or
(*f*) a health service body within the meaning of section 4 of the National Health Service and Community Care Act 1990 (c 19).

(2) In sub-paragraph (1)(*e*) "fire and rescue authority" means a fire and rescue authority under the Fire and Rescue Services Act 2004 (c 21).

Buildings regulated otherwise than under this Act

3. Any building whose occupation is regulated otherwise than by or under this Act and which is of a description specified for the purposes of this paragraph in regulations made by the appropriate national authority.

Buildings occupied by students

4. (1) Any building—

(*a*) which is occupied solely or principally by persons who occupy it for the purpose of undertaking a full-time course of further or higher education at a specified educational establishment or at an educational establishment of a specified description, and
(*b*) where the person managing or having control of it is the educational establishment in question or a specified person or a person of a specified description.

(2) In sub-paragraph (1) "specified" means specified for the purposes of this paragraph in regulations made by the appropriate national authority.

(3) Sub-paragraph (4) applies in connection with any decision by the appropriate national authority as to whether to make, or revoke, any regulations specifying—

(*a*) a particular educational establishment, or
(*b*) a particular description of educational establishments.

(4) The appropriate national authority may have regard to the extent to which, in its opinion—

(*a*) the management by or on behalf of the establishment in question of any building or buildings occupied for connected educational purposes is in conformity with any code of practice for the time being approved under section 233 which appears to the authority to be relevant, or
(*b*) the management of such buildings by or on behalf of establishments of the description in question is in general in conformity with any such code of practice,

as the case may be.

(5) In sub-paragraph (4) "occupied for connected educational purposes", in relation to a building managed by or on behalf of an educational establishment, means occupied solely or principally by persons who occupy it for the purpose of undertaking a full-time course of further or higher education at the establishment.

Buildings occupied by religious communities

5. (1) Any building which is occupied principally for the purposes of a religious community whose principal occupation is prayer, contemplation, education or the relief of suffering.

(2) This paragraph does not apply in the case of a converted block of flats to which section 257 applies.

Buildings occupied by owners

6. (1) Any building which is occupied only by persons within the following paragraphs—

(*a*) one or more persons who have, whether in the whole or any part of it, either the freehold estate or a leasehold interest granted for a term of more than 21 years;
(*b*) any member of the household of such a person or persons;
(*c*) no more than such number of other persons as is specified for the purposes of this paragraph in regulations made by the appropriate national authority.

(2) This paragraph does not apply in the case of a converted block of flats to which section 257 applies, except for the purpose of determining the status of any flat in the block.

Buildings occupied by two persons

7. Any building which is occupied only by two persons who form two households.

SCHEDULE 15
MINOR AND CONSEQUENTIAL AMENDMENTS

SCHEDULE 16
REPEALS

HUMAN RIGHTS

8–17630 This title contains the following statute—

8–17631 HUMAN RIGHTS ACT 1998

Human Rights Act 1998[1]

(1998 c 42 as amended by SI 2004/1574)

Introduction

8–17631 1. The Convention Rights. (1) In this Act "the Convention rights" means the rights and fundamental freedoms set out in—

(*a*) Articles 2 to 12 and 14 of the Convention,
(*b*) Articles 1 to 3 of the First Protocol, and
(*c*) Article 1 of the Thirteenth Protocol,

as read with Articles 16 to 18 of the Convention[2].

(2) Those Articles are to have effect for the purposes of this Act subject to any designated derogation or reservation (as to which see sections 14 and 15)[3].

(3) The Articles are set out in Schedule 1.

(4) The Secretary of State may by order make such amendments to this Act as he considers appropriate to reflect the effect, in relation to the United Kingdom, of a protocol[4].

(5) In subsection (4) "protocol" means a protocol to the Convention—

(*a*) which the United Kingdom has ratified; or
(*b*) which the United Kingdom has signed with a view to ratification[5].

(6) No amendment may be made by an order under subsection (4) so as to come into force before the protocol concerned is in force in relation to the United Kingdom.
[Human Rights Act 1998, s 1, as amended by SI 2001/3500, SI 2003/1887 and SI 2004/1574.]

---

1. This Act incorporates into domestic law the rights (and fundamental freedoms) of individuals arising under certain provisions of the Convention for the Protection of Human Rights and Fundamental Freedoms, agreed by the Council of Europe at Rome on 4 November 1950. The provisions covered by the Act are those in arts 2-12 and 14 of the Convention, arts 1–3 of the First Protocol and art 1 of the Thirteenth Protocol as read with arts 16–18 of the Convention. These are set out in Schedule 1 to the Act: see para **8–17631W**, post.

Articles 1 and 13 of the Convention are not included in schedule 1 to the Human Rights Act 1998. Article 1 obliges contracting states to 'secure' Convention rights to 'everyone within their jurisdiction'. Article 13 provides that anyone whose Convention rights are violated shall have an 'effective remedy' before a national authority. According to the Lord Chancellor, the Act gives effect to art 1 by securing to people in the UK the rights and freedoms of the Convention and gives effect to art 13 by establishing a scheme under which Convention rights can be raised and remedies before UK courts: HL Debs (committee stage) col 475, 18 November 1997. Therefore courts can have regard to Article 13 when considering the provisions of s 8(1) (remedies) of the Act: HL Debs (committee stage) col 477, 18 November 1997.

Sections 18, 20, 21(5) and 22 came into force when the Act was passed (9 November 1998). The remaining provisions came into force on 2 October 2000. For the effect of s 22(4) between the passing of the Act and its entry into force see *R v DPP, ex p Kebilene* [1999] 4 All ER 801, HL. Where a person appeals subsequent to the implementation of the 1998 Act against a conviction prior to the implementation of the Act, he cannot rely on an alleged breach of his convention rights by the trial court (*R v Lambert* [2001] UKHL 37, [2002] 2 AC 545, [2001] 3 All ER 577, [2001] 3 WLR 206. See also, *R v Kansal (No2)* [2001] UKHL 62, [2002] 2 AC 69, [2002] 1 All ER 257, [2001] 3 WLR 1562, [2002] 1 Cr App Rep 36 where a differently constituted panel of the House of Lords considered, by a majority, that on the issue of retrospectivity, *Lambert* was wrongly decided but, in view of its transitional nature should nevertheless be followed). See also *Wilson v First County Trust Ltd (No 2)* [2003] UKHL 40, [2004] 1 AC 816,[2003] 4 All ER 97, [2003] 3 WLR 568 Where the European Court has adjudged a defendant's Convention rights to have been violated by provisions in force in domestic statute law at the time, the United Kingdom's treaty obligations, particularly under Article 46, do not require the relevant domestic conviction to be quashed or re-opened. Even if the failure to re-open a conviction were a violation of Article 46, the defendant would be tried according to the law in force at the date of the trial as the Human Rights Act 1998 is not retrospective in effect and the court must apply the law as then enacted by Parliament (*R v Lyons* [2001] EWCA Crim 2860, [2002] 2 Cr App Rep 210; affd [2002] UKHL 44, [2003] 1 AC 976, [2002] 4 All ER 1028, [2003] 1 Cr App Rep 24, [2003] Crim LR 623).

The Convention itself is divided into three sections. Section I describes and defines the rights and freedoms guaranteed under the Convention. Section II of the Convention establishes the European Court of Human Rights and provides for its operation. Section III deals with miscellaneous provisions such as territorial application (art 56), reservations (art 57, denunciations (art 58), signature and ratification (art 59).

Since it was first drafted, the Convention has been amplified by a number of Protocols. One of the most important is Protocol 11, which came into force on 11 November 1998 and which abolished the European Commission of Human Rights. As a result, the Convention is now administered by two bodies: the European Court of Human Rights and the Committee of Ministers of the Council of Europe.

At the international level, any individual, non-governmental organisation or group of individuals can petition the European Court of Human Rights in Strasbourg alleging a violation of Convention rights. Three judges of the Court sitting in Committee determine whether a petition is 'admissible'. If so, seven judges of the Court sitting as a Chamber determine the merits of the petition. Cases involving a serious question affecting the interpretation of the Convention are dealt with by a Grand Chamber of eleven judges (art 30).

2. See footnote (1) above.

3. See para **8–17631M**, post.

4. This enables Convention rights to be updated in line with obligations assumed by the UK by the ratification of further Protocols.

5. The UK has signed but not ratified the Fourth Protocol which covers the right not to be deprived of liberty on the ground of inability to fulfil a contractual obligation; the right to liberty of movement for those lawfully in a country, and the right of a person to leave any country, including his own; the right to enter the territory of a country of which one is a national and the right not to be expelled from such territory; and the prohibition on the collective expulsion of aliens.

8–17631A 2. Interpretation of Convention rights. (1) A court or tribunal determining a question which has arisen in connection with a Convention right must take into account any—

(*a*) judgment, decision, declaration or advisory opinion of the European Court of Human Rights,
(*b*) opinion of the Commission[1] given in a report adopted under Article 31 of the Convention[2],
(*c*) decision of the Commission in connection with Article 26[3] or 27(2)[4] of the Convention, or
(*d*) decision of the Committee of Ministers taken under Article 46 of the Convention,

whenever made or given[5], so far as, in the opinion of the court or tribunal, it is relevant to the proceedings in which that question has arisen.

(2) Evidence of any judgment, decision, declaration or opinion of which account may have to be taken under this section is to be given in proceedings before any court or tribunal in such manner as may be provided by rules.

(3) In this section "rules" means rules of court or, in the case of proceedings before a tribunal, rules made for the purposes of this section—

(*a*) by the Lord Chancellor or the Secretary of State, in relation to any proceedings outside Scotland;
(*b*) by the Secretary of State, in relation to proceedings in Scotland; or
(*c*) by a Northern Ireland department, in relation to proceedings before a tribunal in Northern Ireland—
   (i) which deals with transferred matters; and
   (ii) for which no rules made under paragraph (*a*) are in force.

[Human Rights Act 1998, s 2, as amended by SI 2003/1887 and SI 2005/3429.]

1. The Commission was abolished by Protocol 11, which came into force on 11 November 1998.

2. Opinions of the Commission on the merits of an application.

3. Opinions of the Commission on the exhaustion of domestic remedies in an application.

4. Opinions of the Commission on the admissibility of any application.

5. This includes future jurisprudence. It also includes all judgments, decisions and opinions regardless of the identity of the respondent state: see Lord Chancellor, HL Debs (committee) stage, col 513, 18 November 1997.

Legislation

8–17631B 3. Interpretation of legislation. (1) So far as it is possible to do so, primary legislation and subordinate legislation must be read and given effect in a way which is compatible with the Convention rights[1].

(2) This section—

(*a*) applies to primary legislation and subordinate legislation whenever enacted;
(*b*) does not affect the validity, continuing operation or enforcement of any incompatible primary legislation[2]; and
(*c*) does not affect the validity, continuing operation or enforcement of any incompatible subordinate legislation if (disregarding any possibility of revocation) primary legislation prevents removal of the incompatibility[3].

[Human Rights Act 1998, s 3.]

1. This means is that UK courts and tribunals must strive to find a construction consistent with the intentions of Parliament and the wording of legislation which is nearest to the Convention rights: Lord Chancellor. 18 November, House of Lords Committee Stage. Hansard, col 535. Courts should proceed on the basis that Parliament is deemed to have intended its statutes to be compatible with the Convention to which the UK is bound: the only basis for courts concluding that Parliament has failed to carry that intention into effect is where it is impossible to construe a statute so as to be compatible with the Convention: Lord Chancellor. 18 November. House of Lords Committee Stage. Hansard, col.535.

The intention underlying s 3(1) was expressed by the Lord Chancellor as follows-

"We want the courts to strive to find an interpretation of the legislation which is consistent with Convention rights as far as the language of the legislation allows and only in the last resort to conclude that the legislation is simply incompatible with them." (Hansard, HL, 18 November 1997, col 535; see also the Home Secretary, Hansard, HC, 3 June 1998, cols 421–422).

Courts should not "contort the meaning of words to produce implausible or incredible meanings" (Home Secretary, Hansard, HC, 3 June 1998, cols. 422), but it is significant that the Government rejected an attempt to amend s 3 so as to impose an obligation to interpret statutory provisions in accordance with the Convention only where it is "reasonable" to do so: Hansard, HL, 18 November 1997, cols 533–536.

This new rule of statutory construction was described in the White Paper: Rights Brought Home (Cm 3782, 1997) as going-

"... far beyond the present rule which enables the courts to take the Convention into account in resolving any ambiguity in a legislative provision. The courts will be required to interpret legislation so as to uphold the Convention rights unless legislation itself is so clearly incompatible with the Convention that it is impossible to do so." (para 2.7).

The proper approach to the way in which s 3 should be used was considered by the House of Lords in *R v A (No 2)* [2001] UKHL 25, [2001] 3 All ER, [2001] 1 WLR 1546 and *R v Lambert* [2001] UKHL 37, [2002] 2 AC 545, [2001] 3 All ER 577, [2001] 3 WLR 206. The approach adopted by Lord Hope in the former case (and reiterated by his lordship in *Lambert*) was: "The rule of construction which s 3 lays down is quite unlike any previous rule of statutory interpretation. There is no need to identify an ambiguity or absurdity. Compatibility with Convention rights is the sole guiding principle . . . But the rule is only a rule of interpretation. It does not entitle the judges to act as legislators . . . The compatibility is to be achieved only so far as this is possible. Plainly this will not be possible if the legislation contains provisions which expressly contradict the meaning which the enactment would have to be given to make it compatible. It seems to be the same result must follow if they do so by necessary implication, as this too is a means of identifying the plain intention of Parliament ... (cf the rather broader view of the scope of s 3 taken by Lord Steyn in *R v A*).

Section 3(1) applies to past as well as to future legislation (see s 3(2)(*a*)). To the extent that it affects the meaning of a legislative provision, the courts will not be bound by previous interpretations. They will be able to build a new body of case law, taking into account the Convention rights: White Paper: Rights Brought Home (Cm 3782, 1997), para 2.8.

2. This is intended to maintain the sovereignty of Parliament. It primary legislation is held incompatible with the Convention, then it is for Parliament to remedy that after a declaration of incompatibility under s 4: HL Debs, col 583, 18 November 1997.

3. This too is intended to maintain the sovereignty of Parliament. Its purpose was explained by the (then) Parliamentary Secretary at the Lord Chancellor's Department in debate-

" ... it is perfectly reasonable to require that subordinate legislation be consistent both with the terms of its parent statute and with the Human Rights Act. That is what the Bill provides. It is inherent in the public authority provisions in [section 6] that Ministers will be acting unlawfully if they make subordinate legislation that is incompatible with a Convention right, unless the parent statute requires the subordinate legislation to take that form ... If it is the will of Parliament that something should be done that is incompatible with a Convention right, Parliament must be prepared to say so in primary legislation ... The nature of primary legislation under which an order is made may be such that any subordinate legislation will necessarily be held in conflict with Convention rights. If the courts were to have the power to strike down such subordinate legislation, it would, at least indirectly, amount to a challenge to the primary legislation itself. That would place the courts at odds with Parliament." (HC Debs, col 433, 3 June 1998).

If subordinate legislation is incompatible with Convention rights, and the incompatibility is not required by primary legislation, the then Human Rights Act 1998 will affect the validity, continued operation and enforcement of that subordinate legislation. Either the court would interpret the subordinate legislation compatibly with Convention rights under s 3(1), or the court would set aside the subordinate legislation under s 6(1).

8–17631C 4. Declaration of incompatibility. (1) Subsection (2) applies in any proceedings in which a court determines whether a provision of primary legislation is compatible with a Convention right.

(2) If the court is satisfied that the provision is incompatible with a Convention right, it may make a declaration of that incompatibility[1].

(3) Subsection (4) applies in any proceedings in which a court determines whether a provision of subordinate legislation, made in the exercise of a power conferred by primary legislation, is compatible with a Convention right.

(4) If the court is satisfied—

(*a*) that the provision is incompatible with a Convention right, and
(*b*) that (disregarding any possibility of revocation) the primary legislation concerned prevents removal of the incompatibility,

it may make a declaration of that incompatibility.

(5) In this section "court" means—

(*a*) the House of Lords;*
(*b*) the Judicial Committee of the Privy Council;
(*c*) the Courts-Martial Appeal Court;
(*d*) in Scotland, the High Court of Justiciary sitting otherwise than as a trial court or the Court of Session;
(*e*) in England and Wales or Northern Ireland, the High Court or the Court of Appeal.*

(6) A declaration under this section ("a declaration of incompatibility")—

(*a*) does not affect the validity, continuing operation or enforcement of the provision in respect of which it is given; and
(*b*) is not binding on the parties to the proceedings in which it is made.

[Human Rights Act 1998, s 4.]

***Paragraph (5)(*a*) substituted and para (5)(*f*) inserted by the Constitutional Reform Act 2005, Sch 9 from a date to be appointed.**

1. It is a fundamental principle of the Human Rights Act 1998 that the courts cannot strike down incompatible primary legislation or incompatible subordinate legislation if primary legislation prevent the removal of the incompatibility. This reflects the priority afforded to Parliamentary Sovereignty by the government.

A declaration of incompatibility does not affect the validity, continuing operation or enforcement of any incompatible primary legislation, but the declaration is "very likely" to prompt the Government and Parliament to respond: Lord Chancellor, HL Debs, col 1231, 3 November 1997.

In any proceedings the court's power under s 4 to make a declaration of incompatibility in respect of primary legislation does not arise unless the court has first construed the legislation in accordance with section 3(1) and concluded that it is not possible to read and give effect to it in a way which is compatible with the Convention rights: *Wilson v First County Trust Ltd (No 2)* [2003] UKHL 40, [2004] 1 AC 816,[2003] 3 WLR 568.

When the court is considering the compatibility of primary legislation with Convention rights, it must identify the policy objective of the legislation and assess whether the means employed to achieve that objective were proportionate to any adverse effects of the legislation; in doing so the court is entitled, if necessary, to have regard to relevant background material, including ministerial statements and explanatory departmental notes when the Bill was proceeding through Parliament, but parliamentary debates are not a proper matter for investigation or consideration by the courts in deciding issues of compatibility, and the court should be careful not to treat ministerial statements as indicative of the objective intention of Parliament or to give them determinative weight; the cardinal constitutional principle remains that the will of Parliament is expressed in the language used in the enactments, and that the proportionality of the legislation is to be judged on that basis: *Wilson v First County Trust (No 2),* supra.

There is no power to make a declaration of incompatibility "in cases where the problem is an absence of legislation, because there is nothing to stop the courts providing a remedy in those cases": Lord Chancellor, HL Debs, col 815 (24 November 1997).

8–17631D 5. Right of Crown to intervene. (1) Where a court is considering whether to make a declaration of incompatibility, the Crown is entitled to notice in accordance with rules of court.

(2) In any case to which subsection (1) applies—

(*a*) a Minister of the Crown[1] (or a person nominated by him),
(*b*) a member of the Scottish Executive,
(*c*) a Northern Ireland Minister,
(*d*) a Northern Ireland department,

is entitled, on giving notice in accordance with rules of court, to be joined as a party to the proceedings.

(3) Notice under subsection (2) may be given at any time during the proceedings.

(4) A person who has been made a party to criminal proceedings (other than in Scotland) as the result of a notice under subsection (2) may, with leave, appeal to the House of Lords* against any declaration of incompatibility made in the proceedings[2].

(5) In subsection (4)—

"criminal proceedings" includes all proceedings before the Courts-Martial Appeal Court; and
"leave" means leave granted by the court making the declaration of incompatibility or by the House of Lords*.

[Human Rights Act 1998, s 5.]

***Words in paras (4) and (5) substituted by the Constitutional Reform Act 2005, Sch 9 from a date to be appointed.**

1. Where a court is considering whether to make a declaration of incompatibility in respect of:

(*a*) subordinate legislation made by the National Assembly for Wales; and
(*b*) subordinate legislation made, in relation to Wales, by a Minister of the Crown in exercise of a function which is exercisable by the National Assembly, the power under this provision to be joined as a party shall be exercisable by the National Assembly concurrently with any Minister of the Crown by whom it is exercisable (National Assembly for Wales (Transfer of Functions) (No 2) Order 2000, SI 2000/1830).

2. Only criminal proceedings are mentioned because in civil proceedings any person joined as a party is able to exercise the rights of appeal open to any party.

Public authorities

8–17631E 6. Acts of public authorities. (1) It is unlawful for a public authority to act in a way which is incompatible with a Convention right.

(2) Subsection (1) does not apply to an act if—

(*a*) as the result of one or more provisions of primary legislation, the authority could not have acted differently; or
(*b*) in the case of one or more provisions of, or made under, primary legislation which cannot be read or given effect in a way which is compatible with the Convention rights, the authority was acting so as to give effect to or enforce those provisions.

(3) In this section "public authority" includes—

(*a*) a court or tribunal, and
(*b*) any person certain of whose functions are functions of a public nature[1],

but does not include either House of Parliament or a person exercising functions in connection with proceedings in Parliament.

(4) In subsection (3) "Parliament" does not include the House of Lords in its judicial capacity.*

(5) In relation to a particular act, a person is not a public authority by virtue only of subsection (3)(*b*) if the nature of the act is private.

(6) "An act" includes a failure to act but does not include a failure to—

(*a*) introduce in, or lay before, Parliament a proposal for legislation; or

(*b*) make any primary legislation or remedial order.

[Human Rights Act 1998, s 6.]

***Paragraph (4) repealed by the Constitutional Reform Act 2005, Sch 9 from a date to be appointed.**

1. The inclusion of "any person certain of whose functions are functions of a public nature" is intended to expand, rather than restrict, the meaning of "public authority". In debate the Lord Chancellor stated that "We think that it is far better to have a principle rather than a list which would be regarded as exhaustive": HL Debs, col 796, 24 November 1997. He also commented that the principle is deliberately broad "because we want to provide as much protection as possible for the rights of individuals against the misuse of power by the state". The White Paper *Rights Brought Home* (Cm 3782, 1997), para 2.2, stated that the concept of a 'public authority' is intended to be broad. It includes central government (including executive agencies); local government; the police; immigration officers; prisons, courts and tribunals themselves; and, to the extent that they are exercising public functions, companies responsible for areas of activity which were previously within the public sector, such as the privatised utilities. For the meaning of "public authority", which can include hybrid organisations (see s 6(5)), see *Polar Housing and Regeneration Community Association Ltd v Donahue* [2001] 3 WLR 183; *R (on the application of Heather) v Leonard Cheshire Foundation* [2002] EWCA Civ 366, [2002] 2 All ER 936; and *R (on the application of A) v Partnerships in Care Ltd* [2002] EWHC 529 (Admin), [2002] All ER (D) 23 (Apr), [2002] 1 WLR 2610.

8–17631F 7. Proceedings. (1) A person who claims that a public authority has acted (or proposes to act) in a way which is made unlawful[1] by section 6(1) may—

(*a*) bring proceedings against the authority under this Act in the appropriate court or tribunal, or

(*b*) rely on the Convention right or rights concerned in any legal proceedings,

but only if he is (or would be) a victim[2] of the unlawful act.

(2) In subsection (1)(*a*) "appropriate court or tribunal" means such court or tribunal as may be determined in accordance with rules; and proceedings against an authority include a counterclaim or similar proceeding.

(3) If the proceedings are brought on an application for judicial review, the applicant is to be taken to have a sufficient interest in relation to the unlawful act only if he is, or would be, a victim of that act.

(4) If the proceedings are made by way of a petition for judicial review in Scotland, the applicant shall be taken to have title and interest to sue in relation to the unlawful act only if he is, or would be, a victim of that act.

(5) Proceedings under subsection (1)(*a*) must be brought before the end of—

(*a*) the period of one year beginning with the date on which the act complained of took place; or

(*b*) such longer period as the court or tribunal considers equitable having regard to all the circumstances,

but that is subject to any rule imposing a stricter time limit in relation to the procedure in question.

(6) In subsection (1)(*b*) "legal proceedings" includes—

(*a*) proceedings brought by or at the instigation of a public authority; and

(*b*) an appeal against the decision of a court or tribunal.

(7) For the purposes of this section, a person is a victim of an unlawful act only if he would be a victim for the purposes of Article 34 of the Convention if proceedings were brought in the European Court of Human Rights in respect of that act.

(8) Nothing in this Act creates a criminal offence.

(9) In this section "rules"[3] means—

(*a*) in relation to proceedings before a court or tribunal outside Scotland, rules made by the Lord Chancellor or the Secretary of State for the purposes of this section or rules of court,

(*b*) in relation to proceedings before a court or tribunal in Scotland, rules made by the Secretary of State for those purposes,

(*c*) in relation to proceedings before a tribunal in Northern Ireland—

(i) which deals with transferred matters; and

(ii) for which no rules made under paragraph (*a*) are in force,

rules made by a Northern Ireland department for those purposes,

and includes provision made by order under section 1 of the Courts and Legal Services Act 1990.

(10) In making rules, regard must be had to section 9.

(11) The Minister who has power to make rules in relation to a particular tribunal may, to the extent he considers it necessary to ensure that the tribunal can provide an appropriate remedy in relation to an act (or proposed act) of a public authority which is (or would be) unlawful as a result of section 6(1), by order add to—

(*a*) the relief or remedies which the tribunal may grant; or

(*b*) the grounds on which it may grant any of them.

(12) An order made under subsection (11) may contain such incidental, supplemental, consequential or transitional provision as the Minister making it considers appropriate.

(13) "The Minister" includes the Northern Ireland department concerned.

[Human Rights Act 1998, s 7, as amended by SI 2003/1887 and SI 2005/3429.]

---

1. Where a party to proceedings had incurred additional costs resulting from a rehearing on account of apparent bias on the part of the original tribunal, the appeal court had remedied the defect so there was no violation of Article 6(1) and the Lord Chancellor was not liable for the costs: *Director General of Fair Trading v Proprietary Association of Great Britain* [2001] EWCA Civ 1217, [2002] 1 All ER 853, [2002] 1 WLR 269.

2. A person is a victim of an unlawful act only if he would be a victim for the purposes of Article 34 of the Convention if proceedings were brought in the European Court of Human Rights in relation to that act. As a general rule, only those "directly affected" by an act or omission can claim to be victims under the Convention. Representative actions are not permitted: *Lindsay v United Kingdom* (1997) 24 EHRR CD 199. However, the following principles apply—

1 There is no requirement that a victim show detriment in the sense of prejudice: *Johnston v Ireland* (1986) 9 EHRR 203; *Eckle v Germany* (1982) 5 EHRR 1.

2. Those "at risk" of being affected by an act or omission qualify as victims, including those at risk of prosecution (but not actually prosecuted): *Norris v Ireland* (1988) 13 EHRR 186; *Sutherland v United Kingdom* (1998) EHRLR 117.

3. The procedural provisions are part of the Convention designed "to protect the individual" and so they must be applied in a manner which serves to make the system of individual applications efficacious: *Klass v Germany* (1978) 2 EHRR 214.

3. The Prescribed Organizations Appeal Commission (Human Rights Act Proceedings) Rules 2001, SI 2001/127 have been made.

8–17631G 8. Judicial remedies. (1) In relation to any act (or proposed act) of a public authority which the court finds is (or would be) unlawful, it may grant such relief or remedy, or make such order, within its powers as it considers just and appropriate.

(2) But damages may be awarded only by a court which has power to award damages, or to order the payment of compensation, in civil proceedings[1].

(3) No award of damages is to be made unless, taking account of all the circumstances of the case, including—

(*a*) any other relief or remedy granted, or order made, in relation to the act in question (by that or any other court), and

(*b*) the consequences of any decision (of that or any other court) in respect of that act,

the court is satisfied that the award is necessary to afford just satisfaction to the person in whose favour it is made.

(4) In determining—

(*a*) whether to award damages, or

(*b*) the amount of an award,

the court must take into account the principles applied by the European Court of Human Rights in relation to the award of compensation under Article 41 of the Convention[2].

(5) A public authority against which damages are awarded is to be treated—

(*a*) in Scotland, for the purposes of section 3 of the Law Reform (Miscellaneous Provisions) (Scotland) Act 1940 as if the award were made in an action of damages in which the authority has been found liable in respect of loss or damage to the person to whom the award is made;

(*b*) for the purposes of the Civil Liability (Contribution) Act 1978 as liable in respect of damage suffered by the person to whom the award is made.

(6) In this section—

"court" includes a tribunal;

"damages" means damages for an unlawful act of a public authority; and

"unlawful" means unlawful under section 6(1).

[Human Rights Act 1998, s 8.]

---

1. As the Lord Chancellor explained in the committee stage of the Bill, "it is not the Bill's aim that, for example, the Crown Court should be able to make an award of damages where it finds, during the course of a trial, that a violation of a person's Convention rights has occurred. We believe that it is appropriate for an individual who considers that his rights have been infringed in such a case to pursue any matter of damages through civil courts where this type of issue is normally dealt with": HL Debs, col 855, 24 November 1997. Where the High Court determines an appeal by way of case stated, or by way of judicial review, it probably does have the power to award damages under s 8(2) because it, generally, does have the "power to award damages ... in civil proceedings". The same applies where the Court of Appeal allows an appeal against conviction because of a breach of Convention rights.

2. The principles upon which the European Court of Human Rights operates are not clear. Most cases are decided on an "equitable" basis. The most useful starting point is the European Court's recognition that the purpose of an award under Article 41 is to put the victim as far as possible in the position he would have been in had the violation of the Convention not taken place: *Piersack v Belgium (Article 50)* (1984) 7 EHRR 251. Although a domestic court should take into account the scale of damages awarded by the Strasbourg Court, the domestic court would be free to depart from this scale in order to award adequate compensation in United Kingdom terms: *R (KB) v Mental Health Review Tribunal* [2003] EWHC 193 (Admin), [2003] 2 All ER 209.

8–17631H 9. Judicial acts. (1) Proceedings under section 7(1)(*a*) in respect of a judicial act may be brought only—

(*a*) by exercising a right of appeal;
(*b*) on an application (in Scotland a petition) for judicial review; or
(*c*) in such other forum as may be prescribed by rules.

(2) That does not affect any rule of law which prevents a court from being the subject of judicial review.

(3) In proceedings under this Act in respect of a judicial act done in good faith, damages may not be awarded otherwise than to compensate a person to the extent required by Article 5(5) of the Convention[1].

(4) An award of damages permitted by subsection (3) is to be made against the Crown; but no award may be made unless the appropriate person, if not a party to the proceedings, is joined.

(5) In this section—

"appropriate person" means the Minister responsible for the court concerned, or a person or government department nominated by him;

"court" includes a tribunal;

"judge" includes a member of a tribunal, a justice of the peace* and a clerk or other officer entitled to exercise the jurisdiction of a court;

"judicial act" means a judicial act of a court and includes an act done on the instructions, or on behalf, of a judge; and

"rules" has the same meaning as in section 7(9).

[Human Rights Act 1998, s 9.]

***Sub-section (5) amended by the Justice (Northern Ireland) Act 2002, Sch 4, from a date to be appointed.**

1. As to the personal liability of magistrates, see the Justices of the Peace Act 1997, ss 51–52: s 51 gives immunity to a justice of the peace for acts done in the execution of his duty, provided they are done wihtin his jurisdiction; s 52 provides that an action may be brought against a justice for an act which is done in the purported execution of his duty but which is beyond his jurisdiction, but only if he acts in bad faith.

Remedial action

8–17631I **10. Power to take remedial action[1].** (1) This section applies if—

(*a*) a provision of legislation has been declared under section 4 to be incompatible with a Convention right and, if an appeal lies—

(i) all persons who may appeal have stated in writing that they do not intend to do so;
(ii) the time for bringing an appeal has expired and no appeal has been brought within that time; or
(iii) an appeal brought within that time has been determined or abandoned; or

(*b*) it appears to a Minister of the Crown or Her Majesty in Council that, having regard to a finding of the European Court of Human Rights made after the coming into force of this section in proceedings against the United Kingdom, a provision of legislation is incompatible with an obligation of the United Kingdom arising from the Convention.

(2) If a Minister of the Crown considers that there are compelling reasons for proceeding under this section, he may by order make such amendments to the legislation as he considers necessary to remove the incompatibility.

(3) If, in the case of subordinate legislation, a Minister of the Crown considers—

(*a*) that it is necessary to amend the primary legislation under which the subordinate legislation in question was made, in order to enable the incompatibility to be removed, and
(*b*) that there are compelling reasons for proceeding under this section,

he may by order make such amendments to the primary legislation as he considers necessary.

(4) This section also applies where the provision in question is in subordinate legislation and has been quashed, or declared invalid, by reason of incompatibility with a Convention right and the Minister proposes to proceed under paragraph 2(b) of Schedule 2.

(5) If the legislation is an Order in Council, the power conferred by subsection (2) or (3) is exercisable by Her Majesty in Council.

(6) In this section "legislation" does not include a Measure of the Church Assembly or of the General Synod of the Church of England.

(7) Schedule 2 makes further provision about remedial orders.

[Human Rights Act 1998, s 10.]

---

1. The purpose of s 10 is to enable provisions of legislation declared to be incompatible with a Convention right to be amended speedily. Remedial orders are statutory instruments. They are to be used "to protect human rights, not to infringe the"': Lord Chancellor, HL Debs col 1231, 3 November 1987.

Other rights and proceedings

8–17631J **11. Safeguard for existing human rights[1].** A person's reliance on a Convention right does not restrict—

(*a*) any other right or freedom conferred on him by or under any law having effect in any part of the United Kingdom; or

(*b*) his right to make any claim or bring any proceedings which he could make or bring apart from sections 7 to 9.

[Human Rights Act 1998, s 11.]

1. The purpose of s 11 was explained in debate by the Lord Chancellor as follows—

"Convention rights are, as it were, a floor of rights; and if there are different or superior rights or freedoms conferred by or under any law having effect in the United Kingdom, this is a Bill which only gives and does not take away."

(HL Debs, col 510, 18 November 1997).

8–17631K 12. Freedom of expression. (1) This section applies if a court is considering whether to grant any relief which, if granted, might affect the exercise of the Convention right to freedom of expression.

(2) If the person against whom the application for relief is made ("the respondent") is neither present nor represented, no such relief is to be granted unless the court is satisfied—

(*a*) that the applicant has taken all practicable steps to notify the respondent; or

(*b*) that there are compelling reasons why the respondent should not be notified.

(3) No such relief is to be granted so as to restrain publication before trial unless the court is satisfied that the applicant is likely[1] to establish that publication should not be allowed.

(4) The court must have particular regard to the importance of the Convention right to freedom of expression and, where the proceedings relate to material which the respondent claims, or which appears to the court, to be journalistic, literary or artistic material (or to conduct connected with such material), to—

(*a*) the extent to which—

(i) the material has, or is about to, become available to the public; or

(ii) it is, or would be, in the public interest for the material to be published;

(*b*) any relevant privacy code.

(5) In this section—

"court" includes a tribunal; and

"relief" includes any remedy or order (other than in criminal proceedings).

[Human Rights Act 1998, s 12.]

1. For guidance as to the meaning of "likely" in s 12(3), and the new parameters provided by arts 8 and 10 within which the court is to decide, in an action for breach of confidence, whether a person is entitled to have his privacy protected by a court or whether the restriction of freedom of expression which such protection involves cannot be justified, see *A v B plc* [2002] EWCA Civ 337, [2003] QB 195, [2002] 2 FCR 158, [2002] 1 FLR 1021 and the authorities considered therein.

8–17631L 13. Freedom of thought, conscience and religion. (1) If a court's determination of any question arising under this Act might affect the exercise by a religious organisation (itself or its members collectively) of the Convention right to freedom of thought, conscience and religion, it must have particular regard to the importance of that right.

(2) In this section "court" includes a tribunal.

[Human Rights Act 1998, s 13.]

Derogations and reservations

8–17631M 14. Derogations. (1) In this Act "designated derogation" means—

(*a*) *repealed*

(*b*) any derogation by the United Kingdom from an Article of the Convention, or of any protocol to the Convention, which is designated for the purposes of this Act in an order made by the Secretary of State.

(2) *Repealed.*

(3) If a designated derogation is amended or replaced it ceases to be a designated derogation.

(4) But subsection (3) does not prevent the Secretary of State from exercising his power under subsection (1) to make a fresh designation order in respect of the Article concerned.

(5) The Secretary of State must by order make such amendments to Schedule 3 as he considers appropriate to reflect—

(*a*) any designation order; or

(*b*) the effect of subsection (3).

(6) A designation order may be made in anticipation of the making by the United Kingdom of a proposed derogation.

[Human Rights Act 1998, s 14, as amended by SI 2001/1216, 3500 and SI 2003/1887.]

8–17631N 15. Reservations. (1) In this Act "designated reservation" means—

(*a*) the United Kingdom's reservation to Article 2 of the First Protocol to the Convention; and
(*b*) any other reservation by the United Kingdom to an Article of the Convention, or of any protocol to the Convention, which is designated for the purposes of this Act in an order made by the Secretary of State.

(2) The text of the reservation referred to in subsection (1)(*a*) is set out in Part II of Schedule 3.

(3) If a designated reservation is withdrawn wholly or in part it ceases to be a designated reservation.

(4) But subsection (3) does not prevent the Secretary of State from exercising his power under subsection (1)(*b*) to make a fresh designation order in respect of the Article concerned.

(5) The Secretary of State must by order make such amendments to this Act as he considers appropriate to reflect—

(*a*) any designation order; or
(*b*) the effect of subsection (3).

[Human Rights Act 1998, s 15, as amended by SI 2001/3500 and SI 2003/1887.]

8–17631P 16. Period for which designated derogations have effect. (1) If it has not already been withdrawn by the United Kingdom, a designated derogation ceases to have effect for the purposes of this Act—

(*a*) *repealed*
(*b*) in the case of any other derogation, at the end of the period of five years beginning with the date on which the order designating it was made.

(2) At any time before the period—

(*a*) fixed by subsection (1), or
(*b*) extended by an order under this subsection,

comes to an end, the Secretary of State may by order extend it by a further period of five years.

(3) An order under section 14(1) ceases to have effect at the end of the period for consideration, unless a resolution has been passed by each House approving the order.

(4) Subsection (3) does not affect—

(*a*) anything done in reliance on the order; or
(*b*) the power to make a fresh order under section 14(1).

(5) In subsection (3) "period for consideration" means the period of forty days beginning with the day on which the order was made.

(6) In calculating the period for consideration, no account is to be taken of any time during which—

(*a*) Parliament is dissolved or prorogued; or
(*b*) both Houses are adjourned for more than four days.

(7) If a designated derogation is withdrawn by the United Kingdom, the Secretary of State must by order make such amendments to this Act as he considers are required to reflect that withdrawal.

[Human Rights Act 1998, s 16, as amended by SI 2001/1216, 3500 and SI 2003/1887.]

8–17631Q 17. Periodic review of designated reservations. (1) The appropriate Minister must review the designated reservation referred to in section 15(1)(*a*)—

(*a*) before the end of the period of five years beginning with the date on which section 1(2) came into force; and
(*b*) if that designation is still in force, before the end of the period of five years beginning with the date on which the last report relating to it was laid under subsection (3).

(2) The appropriate Minister must review each of the other designated reservations (if any)—

(*a*) before the end of the period of five years beginning with the date on which the order designating the reservation first came into force; and
(*b*) if the designation is still in force, before the end of the period of five years beginning with the date on which the last report relating to it was laid under subsection (3).

(3) The Minister conducting a review under this section must prepare a report on the result of the review and lay a copy of it before each House of Parliament.

[Human Rights Act 1998, s 17.]

Judges of the European Court of Human Rights

8–17631R 18. Appointment to European Court of Human Rights. (1) In this section "judicial office" means the office of—

(*a*) Lord Justice of Appeal, Justice of the High Court or Circuit judge, in England and Wales;
(*b*) judge of the Court of Session or sheriff, in Scotland;
(*c*) Lord Justice of Appeal, judge of the High Court or county court judge, in Northern Ireland.

(2) The holder of a judicial office may become a judge of the European Court of Human Rights ("the Court") without being required to relinquish his office.

(3) But he is not required to perform the duties of his judicial office while he is a judge of the Court.

(4) In respect of any period during which he is a judge of the Court—

(*a*) a Lord Justice of Appeal or Justice of the High Court is not to count as a judge of the relevant court for the purposes of section 2(1) or 4(1) of the Supreme Court Act 1981 (maximum number of judges) nor as a judge of the Supreme Court for the purposes of section 12(1) to (6) of that Act (salaries etc);

(*b*) a judge of the Court of Session is not to count as a judge of that court for the purposes of section 1(1) of the Court of Session Act 1988 (maximum number of judges) or of section 9(1)(*c*) of the Administration of Justice Act 1973 ("the 1973 Act") (salaries etc);

(*c*) a Lord Justice of Appeal or judge of the High Court in Northern Ireland is not to count as a judge of the relevant court for the purposes of section 2(1) or 3(1) of the Judicature (Northern Ireland) Act 1978 (maximum number of judges) nor as a judge of the Supreme Court of Northern Ireland for the purposes of section 9(1)(*d*) of the 1973 Act (salaries etc);

(*d*) a Circuit judge is not to count as such for the purposes of section 18 of the Courts Act 1971 (salaries etc);

(*e*) a sheriff is not to count as such for the purposes of section 14 of the Sheriff Courts (Scotland) Act 1907 (salaries etc);

(*f*) a county court judge of Northern Ireland is not to count as such for the purposes of section 106 of the County Courts Act (Northern Ireland) 1959 (salaries etc).

(5) If a sheriff principal is appointed a judge of the Court, section 11(1) of the Sheriff Courts (Scotland) Act 1971 (temporary appointment of sheriff principal) applies, while he holds that appointment, as if his office is vacant.

(6) Schedule 4 makes provision about judicial pensions in relation to the holder of a judicial office who serves as a judge of the Court.

(7) The Lord Chancellor or the Secretary of State may by order make such transitional provision (including, in particular, provision for a temporary increase in the maximum number of judges) as he considers appropriate in relation to any holder of a judicial office who has completed his service as a judge of the Court.

[Human Rights Act 1998, s 18.]

Parliamentary procedure

8–17631S 19. Statements of compatibility. (1) A Minister of the Crown in charge of a Bill in either House of Parliament must, before Second Reading of the Bill—

(*a*) make a statement to the effect that in his view the provisions of the Bill are compatible with the Convention rights ("a statement of compatibility"); or

(*b*) make a statement to the effect that although he is unable to make a statement of compatibility the government nevertheless wishes the House to proceed with the Bill.

(2) The statement must be in writing and be published in such manner as the Minister making it considers appropriate.

[Human Rights Act 1998, s 19.]

Supplemental

8–17631T 20. Orders etc under this Act. (1) Any power of a Minister of the Crown to make an order under this Act is exercisable by statutory instrument.

(2) The power of the Lord Chancellor or the Secretary of State to make rules (other than rules of court) under section 2(3) or 7(9) is exercisable by statutory instrument.

(3) Any statutory instrument made under section 14, 15 or 16(7) must be laid before Parliament.

(4) No order may be made by the Lord Chancellor or the Secretary of State under section 1(4), 7(11) or 16(2) unless a draft of the order has been laid before, and approved by, each House of Parliament.

(5) Any statutory instrument made under section 18(7) or Schedule 4, or to which subsection (2) applies, shall be subject to annulment in pursuance of a resolution of either House of Parliament.

(6) The power of a Northern Ireland department to make—

(*a*) rules under section 2(3)(*c*) or 7(9)(*c*), or

(*b*) an order under section 7(11),

is exercisable by statutory rule for the purposes of the Statutory Rules (Northern Ireland) Order 1979.

(7) Any rules made under section 2(3)(*c*) or 7(9)(*c*) shall be subject to negative resolution; and section 41(6) of the Interpretation Act (Northern Ireland) 1954 (meaning of "subject to negative resolution") shall apply as if the power to make the rules were conferred by an Act of the Northern Ireland Assembly.

(8) No order may be made by a Northern Ireland department under section 7(11) unless a draft of the order has been laid before, and approved by, the Northern Ireland Assembly.

[Human Rights Act 1998, s 20, as amended by SI 2003/1887 and SI 2005/3429.]

8–17631U 21. Interpretation, etc. (1) In this Act—

"amend" includes repeal and apply (with or without modifications);

"the appropriate Minister" means the Minister of the Crown having charge of the appropriate authorised government department (within the meaning of the Crown Proceedings Act 1947);

"the Commission" means the European Commission of Human Rights;

"the Convention" means the Convention for the Protection of Human Rights and Fundamental Freedoms, agreed by the Council of Europe at Rome on 4th November 1950 as it has effect for the time being in relation to the United Kingdom;

"declaration of incompatibility" means a declaration under section 4;

"Minister of the Crown" has the same meaning as in the Ministers of the Crown Act 1975;

"Northern Ireland Minister" includes the First Minister and the deputy First Minister in Northern Ireland;

"primary legislation" means any—

(*a*) public general Act;

(*b*) local and personal Act;

(*c*) private Act;

(*d*) Measure of the Church Assembly;

(*e*) Measure of the General Synod of the Church of England;

(*f*) Order in Council—

(i) made in exercise of Her Majesty's Royal Prerogative;

(ii) made under section 38(1)(*a*) of the Northern Ireland Constitution Act 1973 or the corresponding provision of the Northern Ireland Act 1998; or

(iii) amending an Act of a kind mentioned in paragraph (*a*), (*b*) or (*c*);

and includes an order or other instrument made under primary legislation (otherwise than by the National Assembly for Wales, a member of the Scottish Executive, a Northern Ireland Minister or a Northern Ireland department) to the extent to which it operates to bring one or more provisions of that legislation into force or amends any primary legislation;

"the First Protocol" means the protocol to the Convention agreed at Paris on 20th March 1952;

"the Eleventh Protocol" means the protocol to the Convention (restructuring the control machinery established by the Convention) agreed at Strasbourg on 11th May 1994;

"the Thirteenth Protocol" means the protocol to the Convention (concerning the abolition of the death penalty in all circumstances) agreed at Vilnius on 3rd May 2002;

"remedial order" means an order under section 10;

"subordinate legislation" means any—

(*a*) Order in Council other than one—

(i) made in exercise of Her Majesty's Royal Prerogative;

(ii) made under section 38(1)(*a*) of the Northern Ireland Constitution Act 1973 or the corresponding provision of the Northern Ireland Act 1998; or

(iii) amending an Act of a kind mentioned in the definition of primary legislation;

(*b*) Act of the Scottish Parliament;

(*c*) Act of the Parliament of Northern Ireland;

(*d*) Measure of the Assembly established under section 1 of the Northern Ireland Assembly Act 1973;

(*e*) Act of the Northern Ireland Assembly;

(*f*) order, rules, regulations, scheme, warrant, byelaw or other instrument made under primary legislation (except to the extent to which it operates to bring one or more provisions of that legislation into force or amends any primary legislation);

(*g*) order, rules, regulations, scheme, warrant, byelaw or other instrument made under legislation mentioned in paragraph (*b*), (*c*), (*d*) or (*e*) or made under an Order in Council applying only to Northern Ireland;

(*h*) order, rules, regulations, scheme, warrant, byelaw or other instrument made by a member of the Scottish Executive, a Northern Ireland Minister or a Northern Ireland department in exercise of prerogative or other executive functions of Her Majesty which are exercisable by such a person on behalf of Her Majesty;

"transferred matters" has the same meaning as in the Northern Ireland Act 1998; and

"tribunal" means any tribunal in which legal proceedings may be brought.

(2) The references in paragraphs (*b*) and (*c*) of section 2(1) to Articles are to Articles of the Convention as they had effect immediately before the coming into force of the Eleventh Protocol.

(3) The reference in paragraph (*d*) of section 2(1) to Article 46 includes a reference to Articles 32

and 54 of the Convention as they had effect immediately before the coming into force of the Eleventh Protocol.

(4) The references in section 2(1) to a report or decision of the Commission or a decision of the Committee of Ministers include references to a report or decision made as provided by paragraphs 3, 4 and 6 of Article 5 of the Eleventh Protocol (transitional provisions).

(5) Any liability under the Army Act 1955, the Air Force Act 1955 or the Naval Discipline Act 1957 to suffer death for an offence is replaced by a liability to imprisonment for life or any less punishment authorised by those Acts; and those Acts shall accordingly have effect with the necessary modifications.

[Human Rights Act 1998, s 21, as amended by SI 2004/1574.]

8–17631V 22. Short title, commencement, application and extent. (1) This Act may be cited as the Human Rights Act 1998.

(2) Sections 18, 20 and 21(5) and this section come into force on the passing of this Act.

(3) The other provisions of this Act come into force on such day as the Secretary of State may by order[1] appoint; and different days may be appointed for different purposes.

(4) Paragraph (*b*) of subsection (1) of section 7 applies to proceedings brought by or at the instigation of a public authority[2] whenever the act in question took place; but otherwise that subsection does not apply to an act taking place before the coming into force of that section[3].

(5) This Act binds the Crown.

(6) This Act extends to Northern Ireland.

(7) Section 21(5), so far as it relates to any provision contained in the Army Act 1955, the Air Force Act 1955 or the Naval Discipline Act 1957, extends to any place to which that provision extends.

[Human Rights Act 1998, s 22.]

---

1. At the date of going to press, the following orders had been made: Human Rights Act 1998 (Commencement) Order 1998, SI 1998/2882. and the Human Rights Act 1998 (Commencement No 2) Order 2000, SI 2000/1851. All provisions of the Act that were not already in force were brought into force on 2 October 2000.

2. Judicial review proceedings are not brought by or at the instigation of the Crown; the involvement of the Crown in such proceedings is only nominal: *R (Ben-Abdelaziz) v Haringey London Borough Council* [2001] EWCA Civ 803, [2001] 1 WLR 1485.

3. For the effect of s 22(4) between the passing of the Act and its entry into force see *R v DPP, ex p Kebilene* [1999] 4 All ER 801, HL.

Section 1(3)

SCHEDULE 1
THE ARTICLES[1]

(Amended by SI 2004/1574.)

PART I
THE CONVENTION

RIGHTS AND FREEDOMS

---

1. The rights protected in Schedule 1 of the Human Rights Act 1998 can be divided into three categories-

1. *Absolute rights*: ie those which cannot be restricted in any circumstances (even in times of war or other public emergency) and which are not to be balanced with any general public interest. These are arts 2, 3, 4(1) and 7.
2. *Limited rights*: ie those in relation to which the Government can enter a derogation, but which otherwise are not to be balanced with any general public interest. These are arts 4(2) and (3), 5 and 6. The only limitations on these rights are those found in the text of the arts themselves.
3. *Qualified rights*: ie those which although set out in positive form are subject to limitation or restriction clauses which enable the general public interest to be taken into account. These are arts 8, 9, 10, 11, 12, 14 and arts 1, 2 and 3 of the First Protocol.

The operation of the limitation or accommodation clauses in relation to *qualified rights* is crucial to the proper approach to the protection of Convention rights. According to the constant case law of the European Court and Commission of Human Rights, a limitation or restriction on these rights can only be justified if the person or body imposing the limitation or restriction can show-

1. That the limitation or restriction in question is "prescribed by law". This does not simply mean permitted under domestic law. Two of the further requirements that flow from the expression "prescribed by law" are-
   a. that the law must be accessible, ie individuals must be able to have an indication that is adequate in the circumstances of the legal rules applicable to a given case; and
   b. that a norm cannot be regarded as "law" unless formulated with sufficient precision to enable individuals to regulate their conduct (*Sunday Times v United Kingdom* (1979) 2 EHRR 245). This test does not demand absolute certainty but individuals must be able to foresee, if necessary with appropriate advice, what activity would infringe the law.
2. That the limitation or restriction pursues a "legitimate aim". Legitimate aims include the protection of national security, territorial integrity or public safety, the prevention of disorder or crime and the protection of health, morals or the rights of others. They are to be interpreted narrowly (*Klass v Germany* (1978) 2 EHRR 214).
3. That the limitation or restriction is "necessary in a democratic society". To satisfy this test, the person or body imposing the limitation or restriction on qualified rights must show that the limitation or restriction in question is necessary and proportionate. The word "necessary" in this context, although not synonymous with 'indispensable', is not as flexible as 'reasonable' or 'desirable'. In some cases, it will be obvious that a measure is disproportionate. In others, a more sophisticated approach is needed, taking into account the following factors (not all of which will be relevant in all cases)-

a. whether "relevant and sufficient" reasons have been advanced in support of it
b. whether there is a less restrictive alternative
c. whether there has been a measure of procedural fairness in the decision-making process
d. whether safeguards exists to protect the individual from arbitrary or excessive restrictions
e. whether effect of the restriction in question is to extinguish the "very essence" of the Convention right in issue.

4. That the limitation or restriction is not discriminatory. In issue here are differences in treatment that have "no objective and reasonable justification" (*Belgian Linguistic Case* (1967) 1 EHRR 241). Discrimination on grounds of sex or race is always very closely scrutinised (*Abdulaziz, Cabales & Balkindali v United Kingdom* (1985) 7 EHRR 471). See also *Saunders v United Kingdom* (1997) 23 EHRR 313, and to the contrary, *Funke v France* (1993) 16 EHRR 297 and *Heaney and McGuinness v Ireland* [2001] Crim LR 481. Similarly as regards use of transcripts of interviews obtained under the compulsory questioning powers of DTI inspectors under s 435 of the Companies Act 1985 (*IJL, GMR and AKP v United Kingdom* [2001] Crim LR 133, ECtHR).

8–17631W

Article 2
Right to life

1. Everyone's right to life shall be protected by law. No one shall be deprived of his life[2] intentionally save in the execution of a sentence of a court following his conviction of a crime for which this penalty is provided by law.

2. Deprivation of life shall not be regarded as inflicted in contravention of this Article when it results from the use of force which is no more than absolutely necessary:

(*a*) in defence of any person from unlawful violence;
(*b*) in order to effect a lawful arrest or to prevent the escape of a person lawfully detained;
(*c*) in action lawfully taken for the purpose of quelling a riot or insurrection.

---

2. This imports a deliberate act and an omission, for example to provide treatment, is only incompatible with article 2 where the circumstances are such as to impose a positive obligation on the state to take steps to prolong life (*NHS Trust A v M* [2001] 1 All ER 801, [2001] 1 FCR 406, FD).

Article 2 enunciates the principle of the sanctity of life and prevents the deliberate taking of life save in very narrowly defined circumstances; it cannot be interpreted as conferring a right to die or to enlist the aid of another in bringing out one's own death (*R (on the application of Pretty) v DPP* [2001] UKHL 61, [2002] 1 AC 800, [2002] 1 All ER 1, [2002] 1 FCR 1).

Article 3
Prohibition of torture

No one shall be subjected to torture or to inhuman or degrading treatment[3] or punishment.

---

3. "Treatment" should not be given an unrestricted or extravagant meaning; thus, where a terminally ill person sought an assurance from the DPP that he would not prosecute her husband if he assisted her to commit suicide, it could not plausibly be suggested that the DPP was inflicting the proscribed treatment since her suffering arose from her disease (*R (on the application of Pretty) v DPP* [2001] UKHL 61, [2002] 1 AC 800, [2002] 1 All ER 1, [2002] 1 FCR 1).

The concept that no person shall be subjected to inhuman or degrading treatment is singularly inapt to convey the idea that the state must guarantee to individuals a right to die with the deliberate assistance of third parties (*R (on the application of Pretty) v DPP*, supra).

An order disqualifying an offender from working with children does not begin to approach the level of severity required to breach art 3 (*R v G* [2005] EWCA Crim 1300, [2006] 1 Cr App R (S) 30.

Article 4
Prohibition of slavery and forced labour

1. No one shall be held in slavery or servitude.

2. No one shall be required to perform forced or compulsory labour.

3. For the purpose of this Article the term "forced or compulsory labour" shall not include:

(*a*) any work required to be done in the ordinary course of detention imposed according to the provisions of Article 5 of this Convention or during conditional release from such detention;
(*b*) any service of a military character or, in case of conscientious objectors in countries where they are recognised, service exacted instead of compulsory military service;
(*c*) any service exacted in case of an emergency or calamity threatening the life or well-being of the community;
(*d*) any work or service which forms part of normal civic obligations.

Article 5
Right to liberty and security

1. Everyone has the right to liberty and security of person. No one shall be deprived of his liberty save in the following cases and in accordance with a procedure prescribed by law:

(*a*) the lawful detention of a person after conviction by a competent court;
(*b*) the lawful arrest or detention of a person for non-compliance with the lawful order of a court or in order to secure the fulfilment of any obligation prescribed by law;
(*c*) the lawful arrest or detention of a person effected for the purpose of bringing him before the competent legal authority on reasonable suspicion of having committed an offence or when it is reasonably considered necessary to prevent his committing an offence or fleeing after having done so;

(*d*) the detention of a minor by lawful order for the purpose of educational supervision or his lawful detention for the purpose of bringing him before the competent legal authority;

(*e*) the lawful detention of persons for the prevention of the spreading of infectious diseases, of persons of unsound mind, alcoholics or drug addicts or vagrants;

(*f*) the lawful arrest or detention of a person to prevent his effecting an unauthorised entry into the country or of a person against whom action is being taken with a view to deportation or extradition[4].

2. Everyone who is arrested shall be informed promptly, in a language which he understands, of the reasons for his arrest and of any charge against him.

3. Everyone arrested or detained in accordance with the provisions of paragraph 1 (c) of this Article shall be brought promptly before a judge or other officer authorised by law to exercise judicial power and shall be entitled to trial within a reasonable time or to release pending trial. Release may be conditioned by guarantees to appear for trial.

4. Everyone who is deprived of his liberty by arrest or detention shall be entitled to take proceedings by which the lawfulness of his detention shall be decided speedily by a court and his release ordered if the detention is not lawful[5].

5. Everyone who has been the victim of arrest or detention in contravention of the provisions of this Article shall have an enforceable right to compensation.

---

4. The Human Rights Act 1998 (Designated Derogation) Order 2001, SI 2001/3644 has been made which designates the proposed derogation from art 5(1)(*f*) in the light of the Anti-terrorism, Crime and Security Act 2001.

5. In extradition proceedings it is clear that a court and not the Secretary of State is the appropriate forum to decide the lawfulness of a fugitive's detention, and to comply with art 5(4) requirement of a speedy decision the magistrates' court dealing with the committal proceedings had jurisdiction to determine the lawfulness of the fugitive's detention *(R (Kashamu) v Governor of Brixton Prison, R (Kashamu) v Bow Street Magistrates' Court, R (Makhlulif) v Bow Street Magistrates' Court* [2001] EWHC Admin 980, [2002] QB 887).

Article 6

Right to a fair trial

1. In the determination of his civil rights and obligations[6] or of any criminal[7] charge against him, everyone is entitled to a fair[8] and public hearing within a reasonable time[9] by an independent and impartial tribunal established by law[10]. Judgment shall be pronounced publicly but the press and public may be excluded from all or part of the trial in the interest of morals, public order or national security in a democratic society, where the interests of juveniles or the protection of the private life of the parties so require, or to the extent strictly necessary[11] in the opinion of the court in special circumstances where publicity would prejudice the interests of justice.

2. Everyone charged with a criminal offence shall be presumed innocent until proved guilty according to law[12].

3. Everyone charged with a criminal offence has the following minimum rights:

(*a*) to be informed promptly, in a language which he understands[13] and in detail, of the nature and cause of the accusation against him;

(*b*) to have adequate time and facilities for the preparation of his defence;

(*c*) to defend himself in person or through legal assistance of his own choosing or, if he has not sufficient means to pay for legal assistance, to be given it free when the interests of justice so require;

(*d*) to examine or have examined witnesses against him and to obtain the attendance and examination of witnesses on his behalf under the same conditions as witnesses against him[14];

(*e*) to have the free assistance of an interpreter if he cannot understand or speak the language used in court.

---

6. Article 6 of the Convention does not create substantive civil rights but only guarantees the procedural right to have a claim in respect of existing civil rights and obligations adjudicated by an independent tribunal: *Wilson v First County Trust Ltd (No 2)* [2003] UKHL 40, [2004] 1 AC 816,[2003] 4 All ER 97, [2003] 3 WLR 568.

7. Disciplinary fines imposed in tax evasion proceedings are essentially punitive and deterrent in nature so that the fines are "penal" in character and that the determination of the tax proceedings are characterised as criminal in nature (*JB v Switzerland* [2001] Crim LR 748, ECtHR; see also *Benham v United Kingdom* (1996) 22 EHRR 293 (Community charge proceedings). The imposition of penalty pursuant to s 60(1) of the Value Added tax 1994 gave rise to a criminal charge within the meaning of art 6(1) of the Convention; accordingly, a person made subject to such a penalty was entitled to the minimum rights provided by art 6(3): *Han v Customs and Excise Comrs, Martins v Customs and Excise Comrs, Morris v Customs and Excise Comrs* [2001] EWCA Civ 1040, [2001] 4 All ER 687, [2001] 1 WLR 2253. Proceedings for an anti-social behaviour order under s 1(1) of the Crime and Disorder Act 1998 are civil, not criminal, both as a matter of domestic law and for the purposes of art 6, their true purpose being preventative, accordingly, hearsay evidence is admissible; magistrates must, however, apply, in relation to s 1(1)(a), the criminal standard of proof, though the inquiry under s 1(1)(b) does not involve a standard of proof but is an exercise of judgment or evaluation (*R (on the application of McCann) v Crown Court at Manchester, Clingham v Kensington and Chelsea Royal London Borough Council* [2002] UKHL 39, [2003] 1 AC 787, [2002] 4 All ER 593, [2002] 3 WLR 1313). The same principles apply to an application for an anti-social behaviour order under s 1C of the Crime and Disorder Act 1998 (ie after conviction) (*R (on the application of W) v Acton Youth Court* [2005] EWHC Admin 954, [2006] 170 JP 31).

Similarly, proceedings under s 2 of the Crime and Disorder Act 1998 (sex offender orders) are civil rather than criminal in character (though a bare balance of probability is not to be applied): *B v Chief Constable of the Avon and Somerset Constabulary* [2001] 1 All ER 562, DC; as are condemnation proceedings under s 139 of, and Sch 3 to, the Customs and Excise Management Act 1979: *Goldsmith v Customs and Excise Comrs* [2001] 1 WLR 1673). Followed in *R (Mudie) v Dover Magistrates' Court* [2003] EWCA Civ 237, [2003] QB 1238, [2003] 2 WLR 1344, [2003] RTR 25 and held in *Gora v Customs and Excise Comrs, Dannatt v Customs and Excise Comrs* [2003] EWCA Civ 525, [2004] QB 93, [2003] 3 WLR 160 to apply to proceedings for restoration in the VAT and duties tribunal. Proceedings for a closure order under s 2 of the Ant-social Behaviour Act 2003 are also civil in nature: *Metropolitan Police Comr v Hooper* [2005] EWHC 199 (Admin), [2005] 4 All ER 1095, [2005] 1 WLR 1995, (2005) 169 JP 409. The criminal charge provisions of Article 6 do not apply to procedures for determining whether a mentally ill defendant 'did the act' as these proceedings cannot result in a conviction: *R v M* [2001] EWCA Crim 2024, [2002] 1 Cr App Rep 25; and neither the warning nor the decision to warn under the final warning scheme contained in ss 65 & 66 of the Crime and Disorder Act 1998 involves the determination of a criminal charge against a young person such as to engage the right fair trial under art 6: *R (on the application of R) v Durham Constabulary* [2005] UKHL 21, [2005] 2 All ER 369, [2005] 1 WLR 1184.

Parenting orders under s 8 of the Crime and Disorder Act 1998 do not breach art 6; there is no specified standard of proof and the exercise whether or not to make a parenting order is one of judgment or evaluation, which requires justices to act on all relevant evidence before them, including information about family circumstances, and to reach a judgment that was rational: *R (on the application of M) v Inner London Crown Court* [2003] EWHC 301 (Admin), [2004] 1 FCR 178.

A confiscation order, either under the Criminal Justice Act 1988 or under the Drug Trafficking Act 1994, is a financial penalty (with a custodial term in default of payment), but it is a penalty imposed for an offence of which the defendant has already been convicted; no accusation of any other offence is involved and art 6(2) (presumption of innocence) is not, therefore, engaged. The defendant still has the full protection of art 6(1), but the Acts pursue important objectives, their measures are rationally connected with the furtherance of those objective and the devised procedures are a fair and proportionate response to the need to protect the public interest. The critical point is that the judge must be astute to avoid injustice, and if there is or might be a serious risk of injustice he must not make a confiscation order (*R v Revzi* [2002] UKHL 1, [2002] 1 All ER 801, [2002] 2 WLR 235, [2002] 2 Cr App Rep 54; *R v Benjafield* [2002] UKHL 2, [2002] 1 AC 1099, [2002] 1 All ER 815, [2002] 2 WLR 235, [2002] 2 Cr App Rep 72).

Section 20(1) of the Taxes Management Act 1970 and the Hansard Procedure (which provides a mechanism for settling tax liabilities without recourse to criminal or civil proceedings) provide legitimate means of furthering the core function of the revenue to collect taxes in a prompt, fair and complete manner and they underpin the revenue's selective prosecution policy; both the s 20(1) notice and the Hansard Procedure are civil in nature, they do not constitute "criminal" proceedings for the purpose of the Convention and they belong to an investigative process to which art 6 does not apply; moreover, the notice under s 20(1) cannot constitute a violation of the right against self-incrimination (*R v Dimsey* [2001] UKHL 46, [2002] 1 AC 509, [2001] 4 All ER 786).

8. This includes the right not to incriminate oneself but this right is primarily concerned with respecting the will of the accused person to remain silent and does not extend to the use in criminal proceedings of materials which might be obtained from the accused through the use of compulsory powers and which have an existence independent of the will of the accused such as the compulsory production of an adverse expert's report especially where the expert did not question or interview the applicant and thereby pass on in his report any confidences from her (*L v United Kingdom* [2000] 2 FCR 145, [2000] 2 FLR 322, ECtHR). See also *Saunders v United Kingdom* (1997) 23 EHRR 313, and to the contrary, *Funke v France* (1993) 16 EHRR 297 and *Heaney and McGuinness v Ireland* [2001] Crim LR 481. See also *A-G's Reference (No 7 of 2000)* [2001] EWCA Crim 888, [2001] 2 Cr App Rep 286 (documents compulsorily delivered up by the defendant to the Official Receiver, but which did not contain statements by the defendant under compulsion, were admissible in a criminal trial and their use did not violate art 6).

Limited qualification of the rights against self-incrimination is acceptable if it is reasonably directed towards a clear and proper objective and represents no greater qualification than the situation requires. There is a clear public interest in enforcing road traffic legislation and s 172 of the Road Traffic Act 1988 (duty to give information as to identity of driver etc in certain circumstances), properly applied, does not represent a disproportionate response to the high incidence of vehicle related death and injury on the roads. Section 172 provides for the putting of a single, simple question and the answer cannot in itself incriminate the suspect since it is not without more an offence to drive a car; the section does not sanction prolonged questioning about facts alleged to give rise to criminal offences and the penalty for declining to answer is moderate. Accordingly, it does not infringe a defendant's rights under art 6 for the prosecution to lead evidence of an admission obtained under s 172(2)(*a*): *Brown v Stott (Procurator Fiscal, Dumfermline)* [2003] 1 AC 681, [2001] 2 All ER 97, [2001] 2 WLR 817, [2001] RTR 121, PC. (See, however, *Heaney and McGuinnes v Ireland* [2001] Crim LR 481, ECtHR, where it was held that the requirement under s 52 of the Offences Against the State Act 1939 to give a full account to the police of, inter alia, movements and actions within a specified period upon pain of a penalty of up to 6 months' imprisonment violated art 6(1) and art 6(2)).

The use of a "police stooge" to carry out the equivalent of an interrogation after the defendant had exercised his right of silence breached art 6, and the admission in evidence of the incriminating statements which were thereby elicited rendered the trial unfair: *R v Allan* [2004] EWCA Crim 2236, [2005] Crim LR 716.

The minimum requirements for a fair hearing at a criminal trial are: (i) the defendant has to understand what he is said to have done wrong; (ii) the court has to be satisfied that the defendant, when he has done wrong by act or omission, has the means of knowing that was wrong; (iii) the defendant has to understand what defences, if any, were available to him; (iv) the defendant has to have a reasonable opportunity to make relevant representations if he wishes; and (v) the defendant has to have the opportunity to consider what representations he wishes to make once he has understood the issues involved. The defendant therefore has to be able to give proper instructions and to participate by way of providing answers to questions and suggesting questions to his lawyers in the circumstances of the trial as they arisen (*R (on the application of Wotton) v Central Devon Magistrates' Court* [2003] EWHC 146 (Admin), [2003] All ER (D) 114 (Feb), 167 JPN 102 (where a stroke had rendered the defendant unfit to stand trial)).

A judge conducting a trial, whether a lay justice or a district judge, has final responsibility for ensuring justice at the trial, and where there has been an ex parte application to withhold material on the ground of public interest immunity justice can best be achieved by the same tribunal conducting the trial: *R (DPP) v Acton Youth Court* [2001] EWHC Admin 402, [2001] 1 WLR 1828.

9. It was held in *A-G's Ref (No 2 of 2001)* UKHL 68, [2004] 2 WLR 1 that, if through the action or inaction of a public authority, a criminal charge was not determined within a reasonable time there was necessarily a breach of the defendant's rights under article 6(1) of the Convention, and for such a breach there had to be afforded such remedy as was just and appropriate pursuant to s 8(1) of the Human Rights Act 1998.

The appropriate remedy would depend on the nature of the breach and all the circumstances, including particularly the stage of the proceedings at which the breach was established. (However, special reasons for expunging or reducing a term of disqualification below the minimum period cannot be widened so as to include and permit the granting of just satisfaction where that was required in response to an art 6 breach: *Myles v DPP* [2004] EWHC 594 (Admin), [2004] 2 All ER 902. [Cf the position in relation to points' disqualification, where an excessive delay that breaches the defendant's rights under art 6 can be taken into account in deciding whether in all the circumstances there are grounds for mitigating the normal consequences of the defendant's conviction: *Miller v DPP* [2004] EWHC 595, [2005] RTR 3]).I It would be appropriate to stay or dismiss the proceedings only if either a fair hearing was no longer possible or it would be, for any compelling reason, unfair to try the defendant. The public interest in the final determination of criminal charges required that such a charge should not be stayed or dismissed if any lesser remedy would be just and proportionate in all the circumstances.

In the absence of such unfairness the prosecutor and the court would not act incompatibly with the defendant's Convention right in prosecuting or entertaining proceedings after a breach had been established as the breach consisted in the delay which had accrued and not in the prospective hearing. If the breach were established retrospectively it would not be appropriate to quash any conviction unless the hearing was unfair or it had been unfair to try the defendant at all.

The category of cases in which it might be unfair to try a defendant included cases of bad faith, unlawfulness and executive manipulation but was not confined to such cases. However, such cases would be exceptional, and a stay would never be an appropriate remedy if any lesser remedy would adequately vindicate the defendant's Convention right.

Their lordships also confirmed that, as a general rule, time would begin to run for the purposes of art 6(1) from the earliest time at which a person was officially alerted to the likelihood of criminal proceedings being brought against him; and that such period would ordinarily begin when a defendant was formally charged or served with a summons rather than when he was arrested or interviewed under caution.

The reasonable time guarantee afforded by art 6(1) applies to enforcement proceedings, by the issue of a warrant of commitment to prison, against a defendant who has failed to pay a confiscation order; the fact that the defaulter is in breach of his continuing duty to satisfy the order is irrelevant (*R (on the application of Lloyd) v Bow Street Magistrates' Court* [2003] EWHC 2294 (Admin), (2003) 168 JP 51).

10. Where by an oversight the required authorisation is not given for a judge to sit in certain proceedings, the judge will be a de facto judge and the tribunal in which he sat will be a "tribunal established by law" if the judge was believed to be a judge in the court in which he sat and he did not know, and had not shut his eyes to the obvious fact, that he lacked authority: *Coppard v Customs and Excise Comrs* [2003] EWCA Civ 511, [2003] QB 1428, [2003] 3 All ER 351, [2003] 2 WLR 1618.

11. Where a witness refused to testify because she felt "uncomfortable" doing so in front of the public and she would not testify until the gallery was cleared, it was "strictly necessary" to do so in order to secure that justice was done. The court's ruling did not therefore, breach art 6 of the ECHR (*R v Richards* (1998) 163 JP 246, CA).

12. There have been various cases concerning statutory defences that must be "proved" by the defendant and whether, having regard to Art 6(2), they should now be regarded as imposing only an evidential or a persuasive burden. This is a matter of proper approach and context. In *R v Johnstone* [2003] UKHL 28, [2003] 3 All ER 884, [2003] 1 WLR 1736, 167 JP 281 Lord Nicholls, with whom the remainder of the House agreed, stated:

"[48] . . . The European Court of Human Rights has recognised that the convention does not, in principle, prohibit presumptions of fact or law. What art 6(2) requires is that they must be confined within reasonable limits which take into account the importance of what is at stake and maintain the rights of the defence (see *Salabiaku v France* (1988) 13 EHRR 379 at 388 (para 28)). Thus, as elsewhere in the convention, a reasonable balance has to be held between the public interest and the interests of the individual. In each case it is for the state to show that the balance held in the legislation is reasonable. The derogation from the presumption of innocence requires justification.

[49] Identifying the requirements of a reasonable balance is not as easy as it might seem. One is seeking to balance incommensurables. At the heart of the difficulty is the paradox noted by Sachs J in *State v Coetzee* [1997] 2 LRC 593 at 677 (para 220): the more serious the crime and the greater the public interest in securing convictions of the guilty, the more important the constitutional protection of the accused becomes. In the face of this paradox all that can be said is that for a reverse burden of proof to be acceptable there must be a compelling reason why it is fair and reasonable to deny the accused person the protection normally guaranteed to everyone by the presumption of innocence.

[50] The relevant factors to be take into account when considering whether such a reason exists have been considered in several recent authorities, in particular the decisions of the House in *R v DPP, ex p Kebeline, R v DPP, ex p Rechachi* [2000] 2 AC 326, [1999] 4 All ER 801, and *R v Lambert* [2001] UKHL 37, [2002] 2 AC 545, [2001] 3 All ER 577. And there is now a lengthening list of decisions of the Court of Appeal and other courts in respect of particular statutory provisions. A sound starting point is to remember that if an accused is required to prove a fact on the balance of probability to avoid conviction, this permits a conviction in spite of the fact-finding tribunal having a reasonable doubt as to the guilt of the accused (see Dickson CJC in *R v Whyte* (1988) 51 DLR (4th) 481 at 493). This consequence of a reverse burden of proof should colour one's approach when evaluating the reasons why it is said that, in the absence of a persuasive burden on the accused, the public interest will be prejudiced to an extent which justifies placing a persuasive burden on the accused. The more serious the punishment which may flow from conviction, the more compelling must be the reasons. The extent and nature of the factual matters required to be proved by the accused, and their importance relative to the matters required to be proved by the prosecution, have to be taken into account. So also does the extent to which the burden on the accused relates to facts which, if they exist, are readily provable by him as matters within his own knowledge or to which he has ready access.

[51] In evaluating these factors the court's role is one of review. Parliament, not the court, is charged with the primary responsibility for deciding, as a matter of policy, what should be the constituent elements of a criminal offence. I echo the words of Lord Woolf in *A-G of Hong Kong v Lee Kwong-kut, A-G of Hong Kong v Lo Chak-man* [1993] AC 951 at 975, [1993] 3 All ER 939 at 955:

'In order to maintain the balance between the individual and the society as a whole, rigid and inflexible standards should not be imposed on the legislature's attempts to resolve the difficult and intransigent problems with which society is faced when seeking to deal with serious crime.'

The court will reach a different conclusion from the legislature only when it is apparent the legislature has attached insufficient importance to the fundamental right of an individual to be presumed innocent until proved guilty."

Where an offence is clearly intended by the relevant enactment to be an offence of strict liability, this does not engage art 6(2) of the Convention; art 6(2) provides a criterion against which the court could scrutinise procedural and evidential matters but not the substantive elements of an offence (*Barnfather v Islington Education Authority* [2003] EWHC 418 (Admin), [2003] 1 WLR 2318. See also *R (on the application of Grundy & Co Excavations Ltd) v Halton Division Magistrates' Court* [2003] EWHC Admin 272, (2003) 167 JP 387).

13. The ECHR has held that where, following a guilty plea, a judge has granted a request for an interpreter to attend the sentencing hearing, the latter hearing should not be allowed to proceed without a satisfactory interpreter even though defence counsel is prepared to proceed on a "make do and mend" basis (*Cuscani v United Kingdom* [2003] Crim LR 50).

14. Since Parliament has decided that the normal practice will be for children under 17 years to give evidence by live link, there will have to be special reasons for departing from that practice; there is nothing inconsistent in the special measures provisions with art 6 of the ECHR, since the accused has every opportunity to challenge and question the prosecutions witnesses at the trial itself and the only thing missing is a face-to-face confrontation which the ECHR does not guarantee: *R v Camberwell Green Youth Court ex p D (a minor), R (on the application of the DPP) v Camberwell Green Youth Court, ex p G* [2005] UKHL 4, [2005] 1 All ER 999, [2005] 1 WLR 393, (2005) 169 JP 105.

In *Luca v Italy* [2001] Crim LR 747, ECtHR the court found a violation of art 6(1) and (3)(d) where the principal evidence against the applicant came from a witness and the applicant, because he had decided to exercise his right of silence, was unable to obtain that witness' presence at the trial or to cross examine him.

Art 6(3)(*d*) is designed to secure equality of arms. As the hearsay provisions of the Criminal Justice Act 2003 apply equally to prosecution and defence, there is no inherent inequality of arms arising out of those provisions. It does not give a defendant an absolute right to examine every witness whose testimony is adduced against him. The touchstone is whether fairness of the trial so requires. Thus, in a case where almost all the hearsay evidence derived directly or indirectly from the complainant and she was available for examination there was no breach of art 6(3)(*d*): *R v Xhabri* [2005] EWCA Crim 3135, [2006] 1 All ER 776.

Article 7
No punishment without law

1. No one shall be held guilty of any criminal[15] offence on account of any act or omission which did not constitute a criminal offence under national or international law at the time when it was committed. Nor shall a heavier penalty[16] be imposed than the one that was applicable at the time the criminal offence was committed.

2. This Article shall not prejudice the trial and punishment of any person for any act or omission which, at the time when it was committed, was criminal according to the general principles of law recognised by civilised nations.

---

15. The scope of the offence of perverting the course of justice is sufficiently clear so as not to be incompatible with art 7; the article permits the gradual clarification of the rules of criminal liability from case to case through judicial interpretation provided that that development was consistent with the essence of the offence and could have been foreseen (*R v Cotter, Clair and Wynn* [2002] EWCA Crim 1033, [2003] QB 951, [2003] 2 WLR 115, [2002] 2 Cr App Rep 405, [2002] Crim LR 824). Article 7 is not a bar to a prosecution for "marital rape" that occurred before the decision in *R v R* [1992] 1 AC 599 that a husband could be convicted of raping his wife: *R v C* [2004] EWCA Crim 292, [2004] 1 WLR 2098, [2004] 2 Cr App R 253.

16. Whether a measure amounts to a "penalty" depends on a number of factors including whether it followed a criminal conviction, its nature and purpose, its characterisation in national law, the procedurses involved in its implementation and its severity (*Welch v United Kingdom* (1995) 20 EHRR 247, ECtHR). An order for registration under the Sex Offenders Act 1997 is preventative rather than punitive in nature and purpose and does not amount to a "penalty" within the terms of art 7 (*Ibbotson v United Kingdom* [1999] Crim LR 153, ECtHR). In *Gough v Chief Constable of Derbyshire* [2002] EWCA Civ 351, [2002] QB 1213, [2002] 2 All ER 351, [2002] 3 WLR 289 the Court of Appeal held as follows in relation to the legislative regime on football banning orders. The objective of these provisions was sufficiently important to justify their limits on the right of freedom of movement and they did not, therefore, contravene EC law. However, those that have to apply them are under a duty to interpret them in a manner that is compatible with EC law and the ECHR. While banning orders are not "penalties", and proceedings under s 14B below are not "criminal", banning orders fall into the same category as anti-social behaviour orders and sex offender orders. Therefore, magistrates should apply an exacting standard of proof that will, in practice, be hard to distinguish from the criminal standard. An increase in the conventional level of sentencing for a particular offence or class of offence, as opposed to an increase in the maximum sentence, does not violate art 7: *R v Alden and Wright* [2001] EWCA Crim 296, [2001] Crim LR 414. Where a conspiracy straddles an increase in the maximum penalty for the offence, the court is bound by the former maximum penalty: *R v Hobbs* [2002] EWCA Crim 387, [2002] 2 Cr App Rep 324, [2002] Crim LR 414.

A disqualification order pursuant to s 28 is not a "penalty" for the purposes of art 7 of the Convention; therefore, a disqualification order can be made in respect of offences committed before s 28 came into force (*R v Field* [2002] EWCA Crim 2913, [2003] 3 All ER 769, [2003] 1 WLR 882, [2003] 2 Cr App Rep 38; followed in (*R v G* [2005] EWCA Crim 1300, [2006] 1 Cr App R (S) 30.

Article 8
Right to respect for private and family life[17]

1. Everyone has the right to respect for his private and family life[18], his home[19] and his correspondence.

2. There shall be no interference by a public authority with the exercise of this right except such as is in accordance with the law[20] and is necessary in a democratic society in the interests of national security, public safety or the economic well-being of the country, for the prevention of disorder or crime[21], for the protection of health[22] or morals, or for the protection of the rights and freedoms of others.

---

17. The guarantee under art 8 prohibits interference with the way an individual leads his life and does not relate to the manner in which in which he wishes to die (*R (on the application of Pretty) v DPP* [2001] UKHL 61, [2002] 1 AC 800, [2002] 1 All ER 1, [2002] 1 FCR 1).

There was, however, no existing tort of invasion of privacy at the time of the enactment of the Human Rights Act 1998, and there would be definitional and conceptual problems were the courts to attempt to develop such a tort: *Wainwright v Home Office* [2001] EWCA Civ 2081, [2003] 3 All ER 943. As to cases involving alleged infringement of rights to confidence, see *Douglas v Hello! Ltd* [2001] QB 967, [2001] 2 All ER 289; *Douglas v Hello! Ltd (No 3)* [2005] EWCA Civ 595, [2005] 4 All ER 128, [2005] 3 WLR 881.

18. Where a covert surveillance video was made in breach of a defendant's right to a private life, the court did not breach art 8 by admitting the video in evidence in a criminal trial; the latter decision had to be taken in accordance with art 6, but the breach of art 8 had already occurred: *R v Button* [2005] EWCA Crim 516, [2005] Crim LR 571. See further *Attorney-General's Reference (No 2) of 2001)* [2003] UKHL 68, [2004] 2 A.C. 72; *Schenk v Switzerland* (1998) 13 EHRR 242; *Khan (Sultan)* [1997] AC 558; *P* [2002] 1 AC 146; *Loveridge* [2001] EWCA Crim 973, [2001] 2 Cr App R 29; and *Mason* [2002] EWCA Crim 385, [2002] 2 Cr.App.R. 38.

Articles 8 and 10 provide new parameters within which the court is to decide, in an action for breach of confidence, whether a person is entitled to have his privacy protected by a court or whether the restriction of freedom of expression which such protection involves cannot be justified, see *A v B plc* [2002] EWCA Civ 337, [2003] QB 195, [2002] 2 FCR 158, [2002] 1 FLR 1021 and the authorities considered therein.

19. When purporting to exercise a power of entry preserved by s 17(6) of the Police and Criminal Evidence Act 1984 to enter premises to prevent a breach of the peace, the police must adopt a proportionate response, *McLeod v United Kingdom* [1999] 1 FCR 193, [1999] Crim LR 155, ECtHR (police accompanying husband seeking to recover property from house where wife lived failed to check whether husband had a court order to verify whether he was

entitled to enter and remove property, further, as the wife was absent there was little or no risk of disorder or crime occurring)).

20. Article 8 does not require magistrates generally to make a note of an application for a search warrant, provided the safeguards in the relevant legislation are complied with, where they accept an information as containing all the material upon which they rely. If a particular matter is elicited in the courts of questioning the deponent, it is desirable to make a note of that matter for the benefit a person who wishes to challenge the legality of the warrant and for the protection of the magistrates and the police (*R (Cronin) v Sheffield Magistrates' Court* [2002] EWHC 2568 (Admin), 166 JP 777).

21. An offender naming scheme, operated by the police to prevent crime, infringes the art 8 rights of those named and their families; whether or not such a scheme would be found to be justified under art 8(2) would depend on a number of factors (*R (Ellis) v Chief Constable of Essex Police* [2003] EWHC 1321 (Admin), [2003] 2 FLR 566). Parenting orders under s 8 of the Crime and Disorder Act 1998 do not breach art 8; such orders are necessary in a democratic society: *R (on the application of M) v Inner London Crown Court* [2003] EWHC 301 (Admin), [2004] 1 FCR 178.

22. For principles regarding disclosure by local authorities arising from their child protection responsibilities, see eg *R v Local Authority and Police Authority in the Midlands, ex p LM* [2000] 1 FLR 612; *R (J and P) v West Sussex County Council* [2002] EWHC 1143 (Admin), [2002] 2 FLR 1192.

Article 9
Freedom of thought, conscience and religion[23]

1. Everyone has the right to freedom of thought, conscience and religion; this right includes freedom to change his religion or belief and freedom, either alone or in community with others and in public or private, to manifest his religion or belief, in worship, teaching, practice and observance.

2. Freedom to manifest one's religion or beliefs shall be subject only to such limitations as are prescribed by law and are necessary in a democratic society in the interests of public safety, for the protection of public order, health or morals, or for the protection of the rights and freedoms of others[24].

---

23. Article 9 does not give individuals the right to perform any act in pursuance of whatever beliefs they may hold (*R (on the application of Pretty) v DPP* [2001] UKHL 61, [2002] 1 AC 800, [2002] 1 All ER 1, [2002] 1 FCR 1).

24. In the light of inter alia the Single Convention on Narcotic Drugs 1961 to which the United Kingdom is a contracting party, the limitations on the possession and supply of drugs in the Misuse of Drugs Act 1971 are part of the United Kingdom's policy to combat the dangers of narcotic drugs to public health and do not amount to an interference with Article 8 or 9 rights: *R v Taylor (Paul)* [2001] EWCA Crim 2263, [2002] 1 Cr App Rep 519, [2002] Crim LR 314.

Article 10
Freedom of expression

1. Everyone has the right to freedom of expression[25]. This right shall include freedom to hold opinions and to receive and impart information and ideas without interference by public authority and regardless of frontiers. This Article shall not prevent States from requiring the licensing of broadcasting, television or cinema enterprises.

2. The exercise of these freedoms, since it carries with it duties and responsibilities, may be subject to such formalities, conditions, restrictions or penalties as are prescribed by law and are necessary in a democratic society, in the interests of national security, territorial integrity or public safety, for the prevention of disorder or crime, for the protection of health or morals, for the protection of the reputation or rights of others, for preventing the disclosure of information received in confidence, or for maintaining the authority and impartiality of the judiciary.

---

25. In a case involving the defacement of the American flag (the defendant's own property) near the gate of an RAF base, in the course of a protest against the use of weapons of mass destruction and American military policy including the national missile defence system, it was held that the court had to presume that the defendant's conduct was protected by art 10 unless and until is was established that a restriction on her freedom was strictly necessary. While the district judge had been entitled to find that there was a pressing social need in a multicultural society to prevent the denigration of objects veneration and symbolic importance for one social group, the next stage was to assess whether or not interference, by means of prosecution, with the defendant's right to free expression by using her own property to convey a lawful message, was a proportionate response to that aim, and the fact that the defendant could have demonstrated in other ways was only one factor to be taken into account when determining the overall reasonableness of the defendant's behaviour and the state's response to it: *Percy v DPP* [2001] EWHC Admin 1125, (2001) 166 JP 93, [2002] Crim LR 835. See also *Norwood v DPP* [2002] EWHC 1564 (Admin), [2002] Crim LR 888; *Hammond v DPP* [2004] EWHC 69 (Admin), (2004) 168 JP 601, [2004] Crim LR 851; and *Dehal v CPS* [2005] EWHC Admin 2154, (2005) 169 JP 581.

Article 11
Freedom of assembly and association

1. Everyone has the right to freedom of peaceful assembly and to freedom of association with others, including the right to form and to join trade unions for the protection of his interests.

2. No restrictions shall be placed on the exercise of these rights other than such as are prescribed by law and are necessary in a democratic society in the interests of national security or public safety, for the prevention of disorder or crime, for the protection of health or morals or for the protection of the rights and freedoms of others. This Article shall not prevent the imposition of lawful restrictions on the exercise of these rights by members of the armed forces, of the police or of the administration of the State.

Article 12
Right to marry

Men and women of marriageable age have the right to marry and to found a family, according to the national laws governing the exercise of this right.

Article 14
Prohibition of discrimination

The enjoyment of the rights and freedoms set forth in this Convention shall be secured without discrimination on any ground such as sex, race, colour, language, religion, political or other opinion, national or social origin, association with a national minority, property, birth or other status.

Article 16
Restrictions on political activity of aliens

Nothing in Articles 10, 11 and 14 shall be regarded as preventing the High Contracting Parties from imposing restrictions on the political activity of aliens.

Article 17
Prohibition of abuse of rights

Nothing in this Convention may be interpreted as implying for any State, group or person any right to engage in any activity or perform any act aimed at the destruction of any of the rights and freedoms set forth herein or at their limitation to a greater extent than is provided for in the Convention.

Article 18
Limitation on use of restrictions on rights

The restrictions permitted under this Convention to the said rights and freedoms shall not be applied for any purpose other than those for which they have been prescribed.

PART II
THE FIRST PROTOCOL

Article 1
Protection of property

Every natural or legal person is entitled to the peaceful enjoyment of his possessions[1]. No one shall be deprived of his possessions except in the public interest and subject to the conditions provided for by law and by the general principles of international law.

The preceding provisions shall not, however, in any way impair the right of a State to enforce such laws as it deems necessary to control the use of property in accordance with the general interest or to secure the payment of taxes or other contributions or penalties.

Article 2
Right to education

No person shall be denied the right to education. In the exercise of any functions which it assumes in relation to education and to teaching, the State shall respect the right of parents to ensure such education and teaching in conformity with their own religious and philosophical convictions.

Article 3
Right to free elections

The High Contracting Parties undertake to hold free elections at reasonable intervals by secret ballot, under conditions which will ensure the free expression of the opinion of the people in the choice of the legislature.

---

[1] In *Wilson v First County Trust Ltd (No 2)* [2003] UKHL 40, [2004] 1 AC 816, [2003] 4 All ER 97, [2003] 3 WLR 568 it was stated, per Lord Nicholls, Lord Hope, Lord Hobhouse and Lord Scott, that "possessions" within the meaning of article 1 of the First Protocol included contractual rights.

Any system of law will regulate in many respects the use of private possessions, for example, preventing cars from using bus lanes; while Art.1 extends beyond cases of mere expropriation and that material interference with business interests may be incompatible with peaceful enjoyment of possessions, a regulation that merely prevents certain uses of vehicles in defined and limited areas, does not really involve a material interference with the enjoyment of the vehicle, or with the business conducted by means of the vehicle, at all (*Phillips v DPP* [2002] EWHC 2093 (Admin), [2003] RTR 132, [2003] Crim LR 481).

A goods vehicle operator's licence is a "possession" for the purposes of art 1 (*Crompton v Department of Transport* [2003] EWCA Civ 64, [2003] RTR 517).

PART III
THE THIRTEENTH PROTOCOL

Article 1
Abolition of the death penalty

The death penalty shall be abolished. No one shall be condemned to such penalty or executed.

Article 2
Death penalty in time of war

A State may make provision in its law for the death penalty in respect of acts committed in time of war or of imminent threat of war; such penalty shall be applied only in the instances laid down in the law and in accordance with its provisions. The State shall communicate to the Secretary General of the Council of Europe the relevant provisions of that law.

Section 10

SCHEDULE 2
REMEDIAL ORDERS

(*Amended by the Scotland Act (Consequential Modifications) Order 2000, SI 2000/2040, Sch*)

Orders

8–17631X **1.** (1) A remedial order may—

(*a*) contain such incidental, supplemental, consequential or transitional provision as the person making it considers appropriate;
(*b*) be made so as to have effect from a date earlier than that on which it is made;
(*c*) make provision for the delegation of specific functions;
(*d*) make different provision for different cases.

(2) The power conferred by sub-paragraph (1)(a) includes—

(*a*) power to amend primary legislation (including primary legislation other than that which contains the incompatible provision); and
(*b*) power to amend or revoke subordinate legislation (including subordinate legislation other than that which contains the incompatible provision).

(3) A remedial order may be made so as to have the same extent as the legislation which it affects.
(4) No person is to be guilty of an offence solely as a result of the retrospective effect of a remedial order.

Procedure

2. No remedial order may be made unless—

(*a*) a draft of the order has been approved by a resolution of each House of Parliament made after the end of the period of 60 days beginning with the day on which the draft was laid; or
(*b*) it is declared in the order that it appears to the person making it that, because of the urgency of the matter, it is necessary to make the order without a draft being so approved.

Orders laid in draft

3. (1) No draft may be laid under paragraph 2(*a*) unless—

(*a*) the person proposing to make the order has laid before Parliament a document which contains a draft of the proposed order and the required information; and
(*b*) the period of 60 days, beginning with the day on which the document required by this sub-paragraph was laid, has ended.

(2) If representations have been made during that period, the draft laid under paragraph 2(*a*) must be accompanied by a statement containing—

(*a*) a summary of the representations; and
(*b*) if, as a result of the representations, the proposed order has been changed, details of the changes.

Urgent cases

4. (1) If a remedial order ("the original order") is made without being approved in draft, the person making it must lay it before Parliament, accompanied by the required information, after it is made.

(2) If representations have been made during the period of 60 days beginning with the day on which the original order was made, the person making it must (after the end of that period) lay before Parliament a statement containing—

(*a*) a summary of the representations; and
(*b*) if, as a result of the representations, he considers it appropriate to make changes to the original order, details of the changes.

(3) If sub-paragraph (2)(*b*) applies, the person making the statement must—

(*a*) make a further remedial order replacing the original order; and
(*b*) lay the replacement order before Parliament.

(4) If, at the end of the period of 120 days beginning with the day on which the original order was made, a resolution has not been passed by each House approving the original or replacement order, the order ceases to have effect (but without that affecting anything previously done under either order or the power to make a fresh remedial order).

Definitions

5. In this Schedule—

"representations" means representations about a remedial order (or proposed remedial order) made to the person making (or proposing to make) it and includes any relevant Parliamentary report or resolution; and
"required information" means—

(*a*) an explanation of the incompatibility which the order (or proposed order) seeks to remove, including particulars of the relevant declaration, finding or order; and
(*b*) a statement of the reasons for proceeding under section 10 and for making an order in those terms.

Calculating periods

6. In calculating any period for the purposes of this Schedule, no account is to be taken of any time during which—

(*a*) Parliament is dissolved or prorogued; or
(*b*) both Houses are adjourned for more than four days.

7. (1) This paragraph applies in relation to—

(a) any remedial order made, and any draft of such an order proposed to be made,—
  (i) by the Scottish Ministers; or
  (ii) within devolved competence (within the meaning of the Scotland Act 1998) by Her Majesty in Council; and
(b) any document or statement to be laid in connection with such an order (or proposed order).

(2) This Schedule has effect in relation to any such order (or proposed order), document or statement subject to the following modifications.

(3) Any reference to Parliament, each House of Parliament or both Houses of Parliament shall be construed as a reference to the Scottish Parliament.

(4) Paragraph 6 does not apply and instead, in calculating any period for the purposes of this Schedule, no account is to be taken of any time during which the Scottish Parliament is dissolved or is in recess for more than four days.

SCHEDULE 3
Derogation and Reservation

(Amended by SI 2001/4032 and SI 2005/1071.)

Sections 14 and 15

Part I
Derogation[1]

8–17631Y *Repealed.*

---

1. Part I of this Schedule was repealed by the Human Rights Act 1998 (Amendment) Order 2005, SI 2005/1071.

Part II
Reservation

At the time of signing the present (First) Protocol, I declare that, in view of certain provisions of the Education Acts in the United Kingdom, the principle affirmed in the second sentence of Article 2 is accepted by the United Kingdom only so far as it is compatible with the provision of efficient instruction and training, and the avoidance of unreasonable public expenditure.

Dated 20 March 1952. Made by the United Kingdom Permanent Representative to the Council of Europe.

Section 18(6)

SCHEDULE 4
Judicial Pensions

Duty to make orders about pensions

8–17631Z **1.** (1) The appropriate Minister must by order make provision with respect to pensions payable to or in respect of any holder of a judicial office who serves as an ECHR judge.

(2) A pensions order must include such provision as the Minister making it considers is necessary to secure that—

(*a*) an ECHR judge who was, immediately before his appointment as an ECHR judge, a member of a judicial pension scheme is entitled to remain as a member of that scheme;
(*b*) the terms on which he remains a member of the scheme are those which would have been applicable had he not been appointed as an ECHR judge; and
(*c*) entitlement to benefits payable in accordance with the scheme continues to be determined as if, while serving as an ECHR judge, his salary was that which would (but for section 18(4)) have been payable to him in respect of his continuing service as the holder of his judicial office.

Contributions

2. A pensions order may, in particular, make provision—

(*a*) for any contributions which are payable by a person who remains a member of a scheme as a result of the order, and which would otherwise be payable by deduction from his salary, to be made otherwise than by deduction from his salary as an ECHR judge; and
(*b*) for such contributions to be collected in such manner as may be determined by the administrators of the scheme.

Amendments of other enactments

3. A pensions order may amend any provision of, or made under, a pensions Act in such manner and to such extent as the Minister making the order considers necessary or expedient to ensure the proper administration of any scheme to which it relates.

Definitions

4. In this Schedule—

"appropriate Minister" means—

(*a*) in relation to any judicial office whose jurisdiction is exercisable exclusively in relation to Scotland, the Secretary of State; and

(*b*) otherwise, the Lord Chancellor;

"ECHR judge" means the holder of a judicial office who is serving as a judge of the Court;

"judicial pension scheme" means a scheme established by and in accordance with a pensions Act;

"pensions Act" means—

(*a*) the County Courts Act (Northern Ireland) 1959;

(*b*) the Sheriffs' Pensions (Scotland) Act 1961;

(*c*) the Judicial Pensions Act 1981; or

(*d*) the Judicial Pensions and Retirement Act 1993; and

"pensions order" means an order made under paragraph 1.

HYPNOTISM

Hypnotism Act 1952

(15 & 16 Geo 6 & 1 Eliz 2 c 46)

8–17640 **1. Control of demonstrations of hypnotism at places licensed for public entertainment.** (1) Where under any enactment an authority in any area in Scotland have power to grant licences for the regulation of theatres or other places of public amusement or public entertainment[1], any power conferred by any enactment to attach conditions to any such licence shall include power to attach conditions[2] regulating or prohibiting the giving of an exhibition, demonstration or performance of hypnotism[3] on any person at the place to which the licence relates.

(2) *Repealed.*

[Hypnotism Act 1952, s 1 as amended by the Licensing Act 2003, Sch 6.]

1. See title LOCAL GOVERNMENT, post.
2. Guidance regarding appropriate conditions is contained in Home Office Circular No 28/1953, dated 10 February, 1953.
3. Except where the context otherwise requires, "hypnotism" includes hypnotism, mesmerism and any similar act or process which produces or is intended to produce in any person any form of induced sleep or trance in which the susceptibility of the mind of that person to suggestion or direction is increased or intended to be increased, but does not include hypnotism, mesmerism or any such similar act or process which is self-induced (s 6).

8–17641 **2. Control of demonstrations of hypnotism at other places.** (1) No person shall give an exhibition, demonstration or performance of hypnotism[1] on any living person at or in connection with an entertainment to which the public are admitted, whether on payment or otherwise, at any place, unless—

(*a*) the controlling authority have authorised that exhibition, demonstration or performance under this section, or

(*b*) the place is in Scotland and a licence mentioned in section 1 of this Act is in force in relation to it..

(1A) The foregoing subsection shall not apply to an exhibition, demonstration or performance of hypnotism that takes place in the course of a performance of a play (within the meaning of the Theatres Act 1968) given at premises in Scotland in respect of which a licence under that Act is in force.

(2) Any authorisation under this section may be made subject to any conditions[2].

(3A) A function conferred by this section on a licensing authority is, for the purposes of section 7 of the Licensing Act 2003 (exercise and delegation by licensing authority of licensing functions), to be treated as a licensing function within the meaning of that Act.

(4) In this section—

"controlling authority" means—

(*a*) in relation to a place in England and Wales, the licensing authority in whose area the place, or the greater or greatest part of it, is situated, and

(*b*) in relation to a place in Scotland, the authority having power to grant licences of the kind mentioned in section 1 in that area, and

"licensing authority" has the meaning given by the Licensing Act 2003.

[Hypnotism Act 1952, s 2, as amended by the Theatres Act 1968, Sch 2, the Local Government (Miscellaneous Provisions) Act 1982, Sch 2 and the Criminal Justice Act 1982, ss 38 and 46 and the Licensing Act 2003, Sch 6.]

1. See note 3 at para **8–17640**.
2. Guidance regarding appropriate conditions is contained in Home Office Circular No 28/1953, dated 10 February, 1953.

8–17641A 2A. Fee[1]**.** The person making an application to a controlling authority, being the council of a London borough, for an authorisation under section 2 of this Act shall on making the application pay to the council such reasonable fee as the council may determine.
[Hypnotism Act 1952, s 2A, as inserted by the London Local Authorities Act 1994, s 7.]

1. If any regulations are made under s 150 of the Local Government and Housing Act 1989 whereby a borough council may impose a charge in connection with the granting of an authorisation under s 2 of the Hypnotism Act 1952, then upon the coming into force of those regulations this section shall cease to have effect (London Local Authorities Act 1994, s 7(2)).

8–17642 3. Prohibition on hypnotising persons under eighteen. A person who gives an exhibition, demonstration or performance of hypnotism[1] on a person who had not attained the age of eighteen years at or in connection with an entertainment to which the public are admitted, whether on payment or otherwise, shall, unless he had reasonable cause to believe that that person had attained that age, be liable on summary conviction to a fine not exceeding **level 3** on the standard scale.
[Hypnotism Act 1952, s 3, as amended by the Family Law Reform Act 1969 and the Criminal Justice Act 1982, ss 38 and 46.]

1. See note 3 at para **8–17640**.

8–17643 4. Entry of premises. Any police constable may enter any premises where any entertainment is held if he has reasonable cause to believe that any act is being or may be done in contravention of this Act.
[Hypnotism Act 1952, s 4.]

8–17644 5. Saving for scientific purposes. Nothing in this Act shall prevent the exhibition, demonstration or performance of hypnotism (otherwise than at or in connection with an entertainment) for scientific or research purposes or for the treatment of mental or physical disease.
[Hypnotism Act 1952, s 5.]

IMMIGRATION[1]

8–17669 This title contains references to the following statutes—

8–17670 Aliens Restriction (Amendment) Act 1919
8–17690 Immigration Act 1971
8–17860 British Nationality Act 1981
8–17880 Immigration Act 1988
8–17886 Asylum and Immigration Act 1996
8–17888 Immigration and Asylum Act 1999
8–18029A Nationality, Immigration and Asylum Act 2002
8–18029Q Asylum and Immigration (Treatment of Claimants, etc) Act 2004

The following statutory instrument is also included—

8–18030 Immigration (Restrictions on Employment) Order 2004

1. The European Convention does not guarantee any right to enter, reside or remain in a particular country: *Vilvarajah v United Kingdom* (1991) 14 EHRR 248; *Chahal v United Kingdom* (1996) 23 EHRR 413. Moreover Article 16 permits certain restrictions on the political activity of aliens. Nonetheless, decisions about admission to or expulsion from a state party to the Convention must be carried out within the framework of Convention rights. Such decisions will be vulnerable to challenge where they expose individuals to risk of conduct prohibited under Article 3 (the prohibition on torture and degrading treatment) or unduly interfere with family rights under Article 8. Where life is at stake, Article 2 may also be relevant.

8–17669A European Communities Act 1972: regulations. Within the scope of the title Immigration would logically fall the subject matter of a number of regulations made under the very wide enabling power provided in s 2(2) of the European Communities Act 1972. Where such regulations create offences they are noted below in chronological order: Accession (Immigration and Worker Registration) Regulations 2004, SI 2004/1219 amended by SI 2005/2400.

Aliens Restriction (Amendment) Act 1919[1]

(9 & 10 Geo 5 c 92)

8–17670 3. Incitement to sedition, etc. (1) If any alien attempts or does any act calculated or likely to cause sedition or disaffection amongst any of Her Majesty's forces or the forces of Her Majesty's allies, or amongst the civilian population, he shall be liable[2] on conviction on indictment to imprisonment for a term not exceeding **ten years**, or on summary conviction to imprisonment for a term not exceeding **three months**.

(2) If any alien promotes or attempts to promote industrial unrest in any industry in which he has not been *bona fide* engaged for at least two years immediately preceding in the United Kingdom, he shall be liable on summary conviction to imprisonment for a term not exceeding **three months**.
[Aliens Restriction (Amendment) Act 1919, s 3.]

1. The European Convention does not guarantee any right to enter, reside or remain in a particular country: *Vilvarajah v United Kingdom* (1991) 14 EHRR 248; *Chahal v United Kingdom* (1996) 23 EHRR 413. Moreover art 16 permits certain restrictions on the political activity of aliens. Nonetheless, decisions about admission to or expulsion from a state party to the Convention must be carried out within the framework of Convention rights. Such decisions will be vulnerable to challenge where they expose individuals to risk of conduct prohibited under art 3 (the prohibition on torture and degrading treatment) or unduly interfere with family rights under art 8. Where life is at stake, art 2 may also be relevant.

2. For procedure in respect of this offence which is triable either way, see Magistrates' Courts Act 1980, ss 17A–21, in PART I: MAGISTRATES' COURTS, PROCEDURE, ante. The maximum fine which may be imposed on summary conviction is **the statutory maximum** (Magistrates' Courts Act 1980, ss 32 and 34(3)).

8–17672 6. Appointment of aliens to the Civil Service. After the[1] passing of this Act no alien shall be appointed to any office or place in the Civil Service of the State.
[Aliens Restriction (Amendment) Act 1919, s 6.]

1. 23 December 1919.

8–17673 13. Offences and penalties. (1) If any person acts in contravention of or fails to comply with the provisions of this Act, he shall be guilty of an[1] offence against this Act.

(2) If any person aids or abets any person in any contravention of this Act or knowingly harbours any person whom he knows or has reasonable ground for believing to have acted in contravention of this Act, he shall be guilty of an[1] offence against this Act.

(4) A person who is guilty of an offence against this Act shall be liable on summary conviction to a fine not exceeding **level 3** on the standard scale or to imprisonment for a term not exceeding **six months**[2], or to both such fine and imprisonment.
[Aliens Restriction (Amendment) Act 1919, s 13, as amended by the Statute Law (Repeals) Act 1975, Sch, Part XIII and the Criminal Justice Act 1982, ss 35, 38 and 46.]

1. See sub-s (4).

2. Six months has been substituted for 12 months in view of the fact that the maximum period of imprisonment which may now be imposed by a magistrates' court for any one offence is six months (Magistrates' Courts Act 1980, s 31).

Immigration Act 1971

(1971 c 77)

PART I

REGULATION OF ENTRY INTO AND STAY IN UNITED KINGDOM

8–17690 1. General principles. (1) All those who are in this Act expressed to have the right of abode in the United Kingdom shall be free to live in, and to come and go into and from, the United Kingdom without let or hindrance except such as may be required under and in accordance with this Act to enable their right to be established or as may be otherwise lawfully imposed on any person.

(2) Those not having that right may live, work and settle in the United Kingdom by permission and subject to such regulation and control of their entry into, stay in and departure from the United Kingdom as is imposed by this Act; and indefinite leave to enter or remain in the United Kingdom shall, by virtue of this provision, be treated as having been given under this Act to those in the United Kingdom at its coming into force, if they are then settled[1] there (and not exempt under this Act from the provisions relating to leave to enter or remain).

(3) Arrival in and departure from the United Kingdom on a local journey[2] from or to any of the Islands (that is to say, the Channel Islands and Isle of Man) or the Republic of Ireland shall not be subject to control under this Act, nor shall a person require leave to enter the United Kingdom on so arriving, except in so far as any of those places is for any purpose excluded from this subsection under the powers conferred by this Act; and in this Act the United Kingdom and those places, or such of them as are not so excluded, are collectively referred to as "the common travel area".

(4) The rules laid down by the Secretary of State as to the practice to be followed in the administration of this Act for regulating the entry into and stay in the United Kingdom of persons not having the right of abode shall include provision for admitting (in such cases and subject to such restrictions as may be provided by the rules, and subject or not to conditions as to length of stay or otherwise) persons coming for the purpose of taking employment, or for purposes of study, or as visitors, or as dependants of persons lawfully in or entering the United Kingdom.

(5) *Repealed.*
[Immigration Act 1971, s 1, as amended by the Immigration Act 1988, s 1.]

1. Persons in breach of the immigration laws (see s 33) are not settled here for this purpose (*Azam v Secretary of State for the Home Department* [1974] AC 18, [1973] 2 All ER 765, 137 JP 626).
2. See s 11(4), post, for definition of "local journey".

8–17691 2. Statement of right of abode in United Kingdom[1]**.** (1) A person is under this Act to have the right of abode in the United Kingdom if—

(*a*) he is a British citizen; or
(*b*) he is a Commonwealth citizen who—
(i) immediately before the commencement of the British Nationality Act 1981 was a Commonwealth citizen having the right of abode in the United Kingdom by virtue of section 2(1)(*d*) or section 2 (2) of this Act as then in force; and
(ii) has not ceased to be a Commonwealth citizen in the meanwhile.

(2) In relation to Commonwealth citizens who have the right of abode in the United Kingdom by virtue of subsection (1)(*b*) above; this Act, except this section and section 5(2), shall apply as if they were British citizens; and in this Act (except as aforesaid) "British citizen" shall be construed accordingly.

[Immigration Act 1971, s 2, as substituted by the British Nationality Act 1981, s 39 and amended by the Immigration Act 1988, s 3.]

1. For restriction on the exercise of the right of abode in the UK in cases of polygamy, see the Immigration Act 1988, s 2, post.

8–17692 3. General provisions for regulation and control. (1) Except as otherwise provided by or under this Act, where a person is not a British citizen—

(*a*) he shall not enter[1] the United Kingdom unless given leave to do so in accordance with the provisions of, or made under, this Act;
(*b*) he may be given leave to enter the United Kingdom (or, when already there, leave to remain in the United Kingdom) either for a limited or for an indefinite period;
(*c*) if he is given limited leave to enter or remain in the United Kingdom, it may be given subject to all or any of the following conditions, namely—
(i) a condition restricting his employment or occupation in the United Kingdom;
(ii) a condition requiring him to maintain and accommodate himself, and any dependants of his, without recourse to public funds; and
(iii) a condition requiring him to register with the police.

(2) *Secretary of State to lay before Parliament rules laid down by him as to the practice to be followed for regulating entry and stay in UK.*

(3) In the case of a limited leave to enter or remain in the United Kingdom—

(*a*) a person's leave may be varied, whether by restricting, enlarging or removing the limit on its duration[2] or by adding, varying, or revoking conditions, but if the limit on its duration is removed, any conditions attached to the leave shall cease to apply; and
(*b*) the limitation on and any conditions attached to a person's leave (whether imposed originally or on a variation) shall, if not superseded, apply also to any subsequent leave he may obtain after an absence from the United Kingdom within the period limited for the duration of the earlier leave.

(4) A person's leave to enter or remain in the United Kingdom shall lapse on his going to a country or territory outside the common travel area[3] (whether or not he lands there), unless within the period for which he had the leave he returns to the United Kingdom in circumstances in which he is not required to obtain leave to enter; but, if he does so return, his previous leave (and any limitation on it or conditions attached to it) shall continue to apply.

(5) A person who is not a British citizen is liable to deportation from the United Kingdom if—

(*a*) the Secretary of State deems his deportation to be conducive to the public good; or
(*b*) another person to whose family he belongs is or has been ordered to be deported.

(6) Without prejudice to the operation of subsection (5) above, a person who is not a British citizen[4] shall also be liable to deportation from the United Kingdom if, after he has attained the age of seventeen[5], he is convicted of an offence for which he is punishable with imprisonment[5] and on his conviction is recommended[6] for deportation by a court empowered by this Act[7] to do so.

(7) Where it appears to Her Majesty proper to do so by reason of restrictions or conditions imposed on British citizens, British overseas territories citizens or British Overseas citizens when leaving or seeking to leave any country or the territory subject to the government of any country, Her Majesty may by Order in Council make provision for prohibiting persons who are nationals or citizens of that country and are not British citizens from embarking in the United Kingdom, or from doing so elsewhere than at a port of exit, or for imposing restrictions or conditions on them when embarking or about to embark in the United Kingdom; and Her Majesty may also make provisions by Order in Council to enable those who are not British citizens, to be, in such cases as may be

prescribed by the Order, prohibited in the interests of safety from so embarking on a ship or aircraft specified or indicated in the prohibition.

Any Order in Council under this subsection shall be subject to annulment in pursuance of a resolution of either House of Parliament.

(8) When any question arises under this Act whether or not a person is a British citizen, or is entitled to any exemption under this Act, it shall lie on the person asserting it to prove that he is.

(9) A person seeking to enter the United Kingdom and claiming to have the right of abode there shall prove that he has that right by means of either—

(*a*) a United Kingdom passport[8] describing him as a British citizen or as a citizen of the United Kingdom and Colonies having the right of abode in the United Kingdom; or

(*b*) a certificate of entitlement.

[Immigration Act 1971, s 3, as amended by the British Nationality Act 1981, s 39 and Sch 4, the Immigration Act 1988, s 3 and Sch, the Asylum and Immigration Act 1996, Sch 2, the Immigration and Asylum Act 1999, Sch 14, the British Overseas Territories Act 2002, s 2(3) and the Nationality, Immigration and Asylum Act 2002, Sch 9.]

---

1. See s 8, post, for exceptions for seamen, aircrews and other special cases and for construction of "enter": see s 11, post.
2. See the Immigration (Variation of Leave) Order 1976, SI 1976/1572, amended by SI 1989/1005, SI 1993/1657 and SI 2000/2445.
3. "The common travel area" is defined in s 1(3), ante.
4. A person liable to deportation should have legal aid; see *R v Edgehill* [1963] 1 QB 593, [1963] 1 All ER 181.
5. See s 6(3), post, as to determination of age and whether offence punishable by imprisonment.
6. Before making a recommendation for deportation in respect of a national of a member state of the European Economic Community, the court shall have regard to Community law, particularly art 48 of the EEC Treaty, in this PART, title EUROPEAN COMMUNITIES, ante.

Note also Directive No 64/221, art 3: "(1) Measures taken on grounds of public policy or of public security shall be based exclusively on the personal conduct of the individual concerned. (2) Previous criminal convictions shall not in themselves constitute grounds for the taking of such measures. . . ."

In *R v Bouchereau* [1978] QB 732, [1981] 2 All ER 924, the European Court of Justice ruled: (*a*) that any action affecting the right of persons covered by Article 48 of the EEC Treaty to enter and reside freely in a member state under the same conditions as nationals of that state constituted a "measure" for the purposes of art 3(1) and (2) of Directive No 64/221; and that a recommendation by a court of a member state, pursuant to national law, for the deportation of a national of another member state was such an action; (*b*) thataArt 3(2) of Directive No 64/221 must be interpreted to mean that previous criminal convictions are relevant only in so far as the circumstances which gave rise to them are evidence of personal conduct constituting a present threat to the requirements of public policy; (*c*) that the justification of restrictions on the free movement of persons subject to Community law on the ground of public policy, as provided for by art 48 of the EEC Treaty, presupposed the existence of a genuine and sufficiently serious threat affecting one of the fundamental interests of society additional to the disturbance of order which any infringement of the law involved. See also *R v Kraus* [1982] Crim LR 468; affd 4 Cr App Rep (S) 113, CA.

7. See s 6, post.
8. This means a current passport and not an expired one, see s 33(1) post and *Akewushola v Secretary of State for the Home Department* [2000] 2 All ER 148, CA.

8–17692A 3A. Further provision as to leave to enter. (1) The Secretary of State may by order[1] make further provision with respect to the giving, refusing or varying of leave to enter the United Kingdom.

(2) An order[1] under subsection (1) may, in particular, provide for—

(*a*) leave to be given or refused before the person concerned arrives in the United Kingdom;

(*b*) the form or manner in which leave may be given, refused or varied;

(*c*) the imposition of conditions;

(*d*) a person's leave to enter not to lapse on his leaving the common travel area.

(3) The Secretary of State may by order[1] provide that, in such circumstances as may be prescribed—

(*a*) an entry visa, or

(*b*) such other form of entry clearance as may be prescribed,

is to have effect as leave to enter the United Kingdom.

(4) An order[1] under subsection (3) may, in particular—

(*a*) provide for a clearance to have effect as leave to enter—

(i) on a prescribed number of occasions during the period for which the clearance has effect;

(ii) on an unlimited number of occasions during that period;

(iii) subject to prescribed conditions; and

(*b*) provide for a clearance which has the effect referred to in paragraph (*a*)(i) or (ii) to be varied by the Secretary of State or an immigration officer so that it ceases to have that effect.

(5) Only conditions of a kind that could be imposed on leave to enter given under section 3 may be prescribed.

(6) In subsections (3), (4) and (5) "prescribed" means prescribed in an order[1] made under subsection (3).

(7) The Secretary of State may, in such circumstances as may be prescribed in an order made by him, give or refuse leave to enter the United Kingdom.

(8) An order under subsection (7) may provide that, in such circumstances as may be prescribed

by the order, paragraphs 2, 4, 6, 7, 8, 9 and 21 of Part I of Schedule 2 to this Act are to be read, in relation to the exercise by the Secretary of State of functions which he has as a result of the order, as if references to an immigration officer included references to the Secretary of State.

(9) Subsection (8) is not to be read as affecting any power conferred by subsection (10).

(10) An order[1] under this section may—

(*a*) contain such incidental, supplemental, consequential and transitional provision as the Secretary of State considers appropriate; and

(*b*) make different provision for different cases.

(11) This Act and any provision made under it has effect subject to any order made under this section.

(12) An order under this section must be made by statutory instrument.

(13) But no such order is to be made unless a draft of the order has been laid before Parliament and approved by a resolution of each House.

[Immigration Act 1971, s 3A, as inserted by the Immigration and Asylum Act 1999, s 1.]

1. The Immigration (Leave to Enter and Remain) Order 2000, SI 2000/1161 amended by SI 2004/475 and SI 2005/1159, and the Immigration (Leave to Enter) Order 2001, SI 2000/2590 have been made.

8–17692B 3B. Further provision as to leave to remain. (1) The Secretary of State may by order make provision as to further provision with respect to the giving, refusing or varying of leave to remain in the United Kingdom.

(2) An order[1] under subsection (1) may, in particular, provide for—

(*a*) the form or manner in which leave may be given, refused or varied;

(*b*) the imposition of conditions;

(*c*) a person's leave to remain in the United Kingdom not to lapse on his leaving the common travel area.

(3) An order[1] under this section may—

(*a*) contain such incidental, supplemental, consequential and transitional provision as the Secretary of State considers appropriate; and

(*b*) make different provision for different cases.

(4) This Act and any provision made under it has effect subject to any order made under this section.

(5) An order under this section must be made by statutory instrument.

(6) But no such order is to be made unless a draft of the order has been laid before Parliament and approved by a resolution of each House.

[Immigration Act 1971, s 3B, as inserted by the Immigration and Asylum Act 1999, s 2.]

1. The Immigration (Leave to Enter and Remain) Order 2000, SI 2000/1161 amended by SI 2004/475 and SI 2005/1159, has been made.

8–17692C 3C. Continuation of leave pending variation decision. (1) This section applies if—

(*a*) a person who has limited leave to enter or remain in the United Kingdom applies to the Secretary of State for variation of the leave,

(*b*) the application for variation is made before the leave expires, and

(*c*) the leave expires without the application for variation having been decided.

(2) The leave is extended by virtue of this section during any period when—

(*a*) the application for variation is neither decided nor withdrawn,

(*b*) an appeal under section 82(1) of the Nationality, Asylum and Immigration Act 2002 could be brought against the decision on the application for variation (ignoring any possibility of an appeal out of time with permission), or

(*c*) an appeal under that section against that decision is pending (within the meaning of section 104 of that Act).

(3) Leave extended by virtue of this section shall lapse if the applicant leaves the United Kingdom.

(4) A person may not make an application for variation of his leave to enter or remain in the United Kingdom while that leave is extended by virtue of this section.

(5) But subsection (4) does not prevent the variation of the application mentioned in subsection (1)(a).

(6) In this section a reference to an application being decided is a reference to notice of the decision being given in accordance with regulations under section 105 of that Act (notice of immigration decision).

[Immigration Act 1971, s 3C, as inserted by the Immigration and Asylum Act 1999, s 3, and as amended by the Nationality, Immigration and Asylum Act 2002, s 118.]

8–17693 4. Administration of control. (1) The power under this Act to give or refuse leave to enter the United Kingdom shall be exercised by immigration officers, and the power to give leave to remain in the United Kingdom, or to vary any leave under section 3(3)(*a*) (whether as regards duration or conditions), shall be exercised by the Secretary of State and, unless otherwise allowed by or under this Act, those powers shall be exercisable by notice in writing[1] given to the person affected, except that the powers under section 3(3)(*a*) may be exercised generally in respect of any class of persons by order made by statutory instrument[2].

(2) The provisions of Schedule 2 to this Act shall have effect with respect to—

(*a*) the appointment and powers of immigration officers and medical inspectors for purposes of this Act;

(*b*) the examination of persons arriving in or leaving the United Kingdom by ship or aircraft, and the special powers exercisable in the case of those who arrive as, or with a view to becoming, members of the crews of ships and aircraft or through the tunnel system; and

(*c*) the exercise by immigration officers of their powers in relation to entry into the United Kingdom, and the removal from the United Kingdom of persons refused leave to enter or entering or remaining unlawfully; and

(*d*) the detention of persons pending examination or pending removal from the United Kingdom;

and for other purposes supplementary to the foregoing provisions of this Act.

(3) The Secretary of State may by regulations[3] made by statutory instrument, which shall be subject to annulment in pursuance of a resolution of either House of Parliament, make provision as to the effect of a condition under this Act requiring a person to register with the police; and the regulations may include provision—

(*a*) as to officers of police by whom registers are to be maintained, and as to the form and content of the registers;

(*b*) as to the place and manner in which anyone is to register and as to the documents and information to be furnished by him, whether on registration or on any change of circumstances;

(*c*) as to the issue of certificates of registration and as to the payment of fees for certificates of registration;

and the regulations may require anyone who is for the time being subject to such a condition to produce a certificate of registration to such persons and in such circumstances as may be prescribed by the regulations.

(4) The Secretary of State may by order made by statutory instrument[4], which shall be subject to annulment in pursuance of a resolution of either House of Parliament, make such provision as appears to him to be expedient in connection with this Act for records to be made and kept of persons staying at hotels and other premises where lodging or sleeping accommodation is provided, and for persons (whether British citizens or not) who stay at any such premises to supply the necessary information.

[Immigration Act 1971, s 4, as amended by the British Nationality Act 1981, Sch 4, SI 1990/2227, SI 1993/1813 and the Immigration and Asylum Act 1999, Sch 14.]

---

1. In *Lamptey v Owen* [1982] Crim LR 42, a defective stamp on a passport was held not sufficient to satisfy the requirement for notice in writing.

2. The Immigration (Variation of Leave) Order 1976, SI 1976/1572, amended by SI 1989/1005, SI 1993/1657 and SI 2000/2445, has been made.

3. The Immigration (Registration with Police) Regulations 1972, SI 1972/1758 amended by SI 1982/502 and 1024, SI 1990/400, SI 1991/965, SI 1992/1503 and SI 1995/2928 have been made.

4. See the Immigration (Hotel Records) Order 1972, SI 1972/1689, as amended by SI 1982/1025.

8-17694 **5. Procedure for, and further provisions as to, deportation.** (1) Where a person is under section 3(5) or (6) above liable to deportation, then subject to the following provisions of this Act the Secretary of State may make a deportation order against him, that is to say an order requiring him to leave and prohibiting him from entering the United Kingdom; and a deportation order against a person shall invalidate any leave to enter or remain in the United Kingdom given him before the order is made or while it is in force.

(2) A deportation order against a person may at any time be revoked by a further order of the Secretary of State, and shall cease to have effect if he becomes a British citizen.

(3) A deportation order shall not be made against a person as belonging to the family of another person if more than eight weeks have lapsed since the other person left the United Kingdom after the making of the deportation order against him; and a deportation order made against a person on that ground shall cease to have effect if he ceases to belong to the family of the other person, or if the deportation order made against the other person ceases to have effect.

(4) For purposes of deportation the following shall be those who are regarded as belonging to another person's family—

(*a*) where that other person is a man, his wife or civil partner, and his or her children under the age of eighteen; and

(*b*) where that other person is a woman, her husband or civil partner, and her or his children under the age of eighteen;

and for purposes of this subsection an adopted child, whether legally adopted or not, may be treated as the child of the adopter and, if legally adopted[1], shall be regarded as the child only of the adopter;

an illegitimate child (subject to the foregoing rule as to adoptions) shall be regarded as the child of the mother; and "wife" includes each of two or more wives.

(5) The provisions of Schedule 3 to this Act shall have effect with respect to the removal from the United Kingdom of persons against whom deportation orders are in force and with respect to the detention or control of persons in connection with deportation.

(6) Where a person is liable to deportation under section 3(5) or (6) above but, without a deportation order being made against him, leaves the United Kingdom to live permanently abroad, the Secretary of State may make payments of such amounts as he may determine to meet that person's expenses in so leaving the United Kingdom, including travelling expenses for members of his family or household.

[Immigration Act 1971, s 5, as amended by the British Nationality Act 1981, Sch 4, the Immigration Act 1988, Sch and the Asylum and Immigration Act 1996, Sch 2 and the Civil Partnership Act 2004, Sch 27.]

1. "Legally adopted" is defined in s 33(1), post.

8–17695 6. Recommendations by court for deportation. (1) Where under section 3(6) above a person[1] convicted of an offence is liable to deportation on the recommendation of a court, he may be recommended for deportation[2] by any court having power to sentence him for the offence unless the court commits him to be sentenced or further dealt with for that offence by another court:

(Proviso applicable to Scotland.)

(2) A court shall not recommend a person for deportation unless he has been given not less than seven days'[3] notice in writing stating that a person is not liable to deportation if he is a British citizen, describing the persons who are British citizens and stating (so far as material) the effect of section 3(8) above and section 7 below; but the powers of adjournment conferred by section 10(3) of the Magistrates' Courts Act 1980, section 179 or 380 of the Criminal Procedure (Scotland) Act 1975 or any corresponding enactment for the time being in force in Northern Ireland shall include power to adjourn, after convicting an offender, for the purpose of enabling a notice to be given to him under this subsection or, if a notice was so given to him less than seven days previously, for the purpose of enabling the necessary seven days to elapse.

(3) For purposes of section 3(6) above—

(*a*) a person shall be deemed to have attained the age of seventeen at the time of his conviction if, on consideration of any available evidence, he appears to have done so to the court making or considering a recommendation for deportation; and

(*b*) the question whether an offence is one for which a person is punishable with imprisonment shall be determined without regard to any enactment restricting the imprisonment of young offenders or persons who have not previously been sentenced to imprisonment;

and for purposes of deportation a person who on being charged with an offence is found to have committed it shall, notwithstanding any enactment to the contrary and notwithstanding that the court does not proceed to conviction, be regarded as a person convicted of the offence, and references to conviction shall be construed accordingly.

(4) Notwithstanding any rule of practice restricting the matters which ought to be taken into account in dealing with an offender who is sentenced to imprisonment, a recommendation for deportation may be made in respect of an offender who is sentenced to imprisonment for life.

(5) Where a court recommends or purports to recommend a person for deportation, the validity of the recommendation shall not be called in question except on an appeal against the recommendation or against the conviction on which it is made; but the recommendation shall be treated as a sentence for the purpose of any enactment providing an appeal against sentence.

(6) A deportation order shall not be made on the recommendation of a court so long as an appeal or further appeal is pending against the recommendation or against the conviction on which it was made; and for this purpose an appeal or further appeal shall be treated as pending (where one is competent but has not been brought) until the expiration of the time for bringing that appeal or, in Scotland, until the expiration of twenty-eight days from the date of the recommendation.

(7) *Scotland.*

[Immigration Act 1971, s 6, as amended by the Criminal Justice Act 1972, Sch 5, the Criminal Procedure (Scotland) Act 1975, Sch 9, the Magistrates' Courts Act 1980, Sch 7, the Criminal Justice (Scotland) Act 1980, Sch 8, the British Nationality Act 1981, Sch 4 and the Criminal Justice Act 1982, Sch 16.]

1. A person liable to deportation should have legal aid: see *R v Edgehill* [1963] 1 QB 593, [1963] 1 All ER 181.

2. For consideration of the general principles governing the power to recommend offenders for deportation, see *R v Nazari* [1980] 3 All ER 880, [1980] 1 WLR 1336, and *R v Escauriaza* (1987) 9 Cr App Rep (S) 542, (EEC citizen), and see also *R v Spura* [1989] Crim LR 165; the potential detriment to the country must justify the recommendation, there must be a full enquiry and reasons must be given. The first matter which the court must consider is whether there is a real threat that the defendant will commit further crimes (*R v Cravioto* (1990) 12 Cr App Rep (S) 71). The defendant should first have an opportunity of making submissions to the court; but his fear of persecution if returned to his own country is a matter for the Minister and not the court (*R v Antypas* (1972) 57 Cr App Rep 207; but see *R v Walters* [1978] Crim LR 175, where the court did consider circumstances in the country of origin which were peculiar to the offender and not of an economic or political nature. Also in *R v Thoseby and Krawczyk* (1979) 1 Cr App Rep (S) 280 that nature and seriousness of the offence, the convicted person's previous convictions and the consequences of deportation where these were indeed serious were all taken into consideration. The court may also take into account the effect of deportation on the offender's

family (*R v Cravioto*, supra); See also *R v Odendaal* (1991) 13 Cr App Rep (S) 341. In *R v Sandhu* [1978] Crim LR 103, it was held inappropriate to recommend deportation where the defendant had lived in this country for 12 years but had spent a few months in India four years previously. The fact that an offender has been living on social security in this country is not a factor which should be taken into account in deciding whether to make a recommendation for deportation (*R v Serry* (1980) 2 Cr App Rep (S) 336) nor the fact that the offender was unlawfully present in the country (*R v Nunu* [1991] Crim LR 653). The fact that an accused possessed refugee status does not affect the courts considerations (*R v Valli and Valli* (1993) 14 Cr App Rep (S) 34). The recommendation should be made in open court and reasons should be given (*R v Rodney* (1996) 2 Cr App Rep (S) 230, [1996] Crim LR 357). However, a failure to do so is not fatal to the recommendation (*R v Bozat* [1997] 1 Cr App Rep (S) 270, [1996] Crim LR 840). Where such a recommendation is made a certificate in form set out in Home Office Circular No 215/1972, should be sent as soon as possible to: The Court Collator, Group 3R, Home Office, Lunar House, 40, Wellesley Road, Croydon, CR9 2BY. With this certificate there should be sent a copy of any probation officer's report considered by the court.

Where the court makes a recommendation and the offender is not sentenced to imprisonment or liable to be detained for any other reason, he is liable to be detained under para 2 of Schedule 3 to the Act (ie until a deportation order is made and until his removal from the United Kingdom). Where the court makes a recommendation for deportation of an offender not otherwise liable to be detained and does not direct that he shall not be detained in custody, a copy, certified by the clerk, of the court's certificate of recommendation should be given to the officer whose duty it is to take the offender to prison (or other place of detention), as an authority for his conveyance and detention there. Where a commitment is issued for non-payment of a fine (after time has been allowed) it should be noted thereon that the offender is also subject to a recommendation for deportation. Although the Bail Act 1976 does not apply, it is suggested that courts consider, when deciding whether or not to order the release of a person recommended for deportation, the principal grounds for withholding bail in criminal proceedings. A person who is recommended for deportation may be released subject to such restrictions as to residence and as to reporting to the police as the court may direct; see Sch 3, para 4, post. If the court directs that the offender should not be detained pending consideration of the recommendation, the Secretary of State asks that his attention shall be called to this fact in a separate covering letter when the certificate of recommendation is forwarded. Where an offender who has been recommended for deportation appeals against the recommendation or the related conviction or against sentence, notification should be sent to the Home Office (at the address quoted above) of the appeal.

For general guidance as to the appropriate practice when a recommendation for deportation is made, see Home Office Circulars No 215/1972, 113/1978 and 37/1988. The application of the appropriate EEC Council Directive can be seen in *R v Secretary of State for the Home Department, ex p Santillo* [1981] QB 778, [1981] 2 All ER 897. In particular it should be noted that all the material on which the executive may base its decision to deport must be placed before the court and the person concerned must have the opportunity to make representations, and that an oral statement by the presiding magistrate of the court's reasons for recommending deportation should be given; it is important to comply with art 9 of the Council Directive 64/221/EEC which requires reasons (*R v Secretary of State for the Home Department, ex p Dannenberg* [1984] QB 766, [1984] 2 All ER 481, 148 JP 321. That case envisages written reasons being given, which will indicate the extent to which current and previous criminal convictions of the defendant have been taken into account and the light they throw on likely future conduct; of particular importance is the court's assessment of gravity of the defendant's conduct and the likelihood of his re-offending. A copy of the statement should go to the Home Secretary and to the offender and should indicate that that has happened.

3. This means seven clear days, ie eight days.

8–17696 **7. Exemption from deportation for certain existing residents.** (1) Notwithstanding anything in section 3(5) or (6) above but subject to the provisions of this section, a Commonwealth citizen or citizen of the Republic of Ireland who was such a citizen at the coming into force of this Act and was then ordinarily resident in the United Kingdom—

(*a*) *repealed*;
(*b*) shall not be liable to deportation under section 3(5) if at the time of the Secretary of State's decision he had for the last five years been ordinarily resident in the United Kingdom and Islands; and
(*c*) shall not on conviction of an offence be recommended for deportation under section 3(6) if at the time of the conviction he had for the last five years been ordinarily resident in the United Kingdom and Islands.

(2) A person who has at any time become ordinarily resident in the United Kingdom or in any of the Islands shall not be treated for the purposes of this section as having ceased to be so by reason only of his having remained there in breach of the immigration laws.

(3) The "last five years" before the material time under subsection (1)(*b*) or (*c*) above is to be taken as a period amounting in total to five years exclusive of any time during which the person claiming exemption under this section was undergoing imprisonment or detention by virtue of a sentence passed for an offence on a conviction in the United Kingdom and Islands, and the period for which he was imprisoned or detained by virtue of the sentence amounted to six months or more.

(4) For purposes of subsection (3) above—

(*a*) "sentence" includes any order made on conviction of an offence; and
(*b*) two or more sentences for consecutive (or partly consecutive) terms shall be treated as a single sentence; and
(*c*) a person shall be deemed to be detained by virtue of a sentence—
   (i) at any time when he is liable to imprisonment or detention by virtue of the sentence, but is unlawfully at large; and
   (ii) (unless the sentence is passed after the material time) during any period of custody by which under any relevant enactment the term to be served under the sentence is reduced.

In paragraph (*c*)(ii) above "relevant enactment" means section 240 of the Criminal Justice Act 2003 (or, before that section operated, section 17(2) of the Criminal Justice Administration Act

1962) and any similar enactment which is for the time being or has (before or after the passing of this Act) been in force in any part of the United Kingdom and Islands.

(5) Nothing in this section shall be taken to exclude the operation of section 3(8) above in relation to an exemption under this section.

[Immigration Act 1971, s 7, as amended by the Immigration and Asylum Act 1999, Sch 14 and the Nationality, Immigration and Asylum Act 2002, s 75 and the Criminal Justice Act 2003, Sch 32.]

8–17697 8. Exceptions for seamen, aircrews and other special cases. (1) Where a person arrives at a place in the United Kingdom as a member of the crew of a ship or aircraft under an engagement requiring him to leave on that ship as a member of the crew, or to leave within seven days on that or another aircraft as a member of its crew, then unless either—

(*a*) there is in force a deportation order made against him; or

(*b*) he has at any time been refused leave to enter the United Kingdom and has not since then been given leave to enter or remain in the United Kingdom; or

(*c*) an immigration officer requires him to submit to examination in accordance with Schedule 2 to this Act;

he may without leave enter the United Kingdom at that place and remain until the departure of the ship or aircraft on which he is required by his engagement to leave.

(2) The Secretary of State may by order exempt[1] any person or class of persons, either unconditionally or subject to such conditions as may be imposed by or under the order, from all or any of the provisions of this Act relating to those who are not British citizens.

An order under this subsection, if made with respect to a class of persons, shall be made by statutory instrument, which shall be subject to annulment in pursuance of a resolution of either House of Parliament.

(3) Subject to subsection (3A) below, the provisions of this Act relating to those who are not British citizens shall not apply to any person so long as he is a member of a mission (within the meaning of the Diplomatic Privileges Act 1964), a person who is a member of the family and forms part of the household of such a member, or a person otherwise entitled to the like immunity from jurisdiction as is conferred by that Act on a diplomatic agent.

(3A) For the purposes of subsection (3), a member of a mission other than a diplomatic agent (as defined by the 1964 Act) is not to count as a member of a mission unless—

(*a*) he was resident outside the United Kingdom, and was not in the United Kingdom, when he was offered a post as such a member; and

(*b*) he has not ceased to be such a member after having taken up the post.

(4) The provisions of this Act relating to those who are not British citizens, other than the provisions relating to deportation, shall also not apply to any person so long as either—

(*a*) he is subject, as a member of the home forces, to service law; or

(*b*) being a member of a Commonwealth force or of a force raised under the law of any colony, protectorate or protected state, is undergoing or about to undergo training in the United Kingdom with any body, contingent or detachment of the home forces; or

(*c*) he is serving or posted for service in the United Kingdom as a member of a visiting force or of any force raised as aforesaid or as a member of an international headquarters or defence organisation designated for the time being by an Order in Council under section 1 of the International Headquarters and Defence Organisations Act 1964.

(5) Where a person having a limited leave to enter or remain in the United Kingdom becomes entitled to an exemption under this section, that leave shall continue to apply after he ceases to be entitled to the exemption, unless it has by then expired; and a person is not to be regarded for purposes of this Act as having been settled in the United Kingdom at any time when he was entitled under the former immigration laws to any exemption corresponding to any of those afforded by subsection (3) or (4)(*b*) or (*c*) above or by any order under subsection (2) above.

(5A) An order under subsection (2) above may, as regards any person or class of persons to whom it applies, provide for that person or class to be in specified circumstances regarded (notwithstanding the order) as settled in the United Kingdom for the purposes of section 1(1) of the British Nationality Act 1981.

(6) In this section "the home forces" means any of Her Majesty's forces other than a Commonwealth force or a force raised under the law of any associated state, colony protectorate or protected state; "Commonwealth force" means a force of any country to which provisions of the Visiting Forces Act 1952, apply without an Order in Council under section 1 of the Act; and "visiting force" means a body, contingent or detachment of the forces of a country to which any of those provisions apply, being a body, contingent or detachment for the time being present in the United Kingdom on the invitation of Her Majesty's Government in the United Kingdom.

[Immigration Act 1971, s 8, as amended by the British Nationality Act 1981, s 39 and Sch 1, the Immigration Act 1988, s 4, the Statute Law (Repeals) Act 1995 and the Immigration and Asylum Act 1999, s 6.]

---

1. By the Immigration (Exemption from Control) Order 1972, SI 1972/1613 amended by SI 1975/617, SI 1977/693, SI 1982/1649, SI 1985/1809, SI 1997/1402 and 2207 and SI 2004/3171, specified consular officers, etc, members of

foreign and Commonwealth governments, etc, and, in specified circumstances, Commonwealth citizens, also certain persons engaged on or with respect to the business of the International Criminal Court are exempted.

8–17697A 8A. Persons ceasing to be exempt. (1) A person is exempt for the purposes of this section if he is exempt from provisions of this Act as a result of section 8(2) or (3).

(2) If a person who is exempt—

(*a*) ceases to be exempt, and
(*b*) requires leave to enter or remain in the United Kingdom as a result,

he is to be treated as if he had been given leave to remain in the United Kingdom for a period of 90 days beginning on the day on which he ceased to be exempt.

(3) If—

(*a*) a person who is exempt ceases to be exempt, and
(*b*) there is in force in respect of him leave for him to enter or remain in the United Kingdom which expires before the end of the period mentioned in subsection (2),

his leave is to be treated as expiring at the end of that period.

[Immigration Act 1971, s 8A, as inserted by the Immigration and Asylum Act 1999, s 7.]

8–17697B 8B. Persons excluded from the United Kingdom under international obligations. (1) An excluded person must be refused—

(*a*) leave to enter the United Kingdom;
(*b*) leave to remain in the United Kingdom.

(2) A person's leave to enter or remain in the United Kingdom is cancelled on his becoming an excluded person.

(3) A person's exemption from the provisions of this Act as a result of section 8(1),(2) or (3) ceases on his becoming an excluded person.

(4) "Excluded person" means a person—

(*a*) named by or under, or
(*b*) of a description specified in

a designated instrument.

(5) The Secretary of State may by order[1] designate an instrument if it is a resolution of the Security Council of the United Nations or an instrument made by the Council of the European Union and it—

(*a*) requires that a person is not to be admitted to the United Kingdom (however that requirement is expressed); or
(*b*) recommends that a person should not be admitted to the United Kingdom (however that recommendation is expressed).

(6) Subsections (1) to (3) are subject to such exceptions (if any) as may specified in the order[1] designating the instrument in question.

(7) An order under this section must be made by statutory instrument.

(8) Such a statutory instrument shall be laid before Parliament without delay.

[Immigration Act 1971, s 8B, as inserted by the Immigration and Asylum Act 1999, s 8.]

---

1. The Immigration (Designation of Travel Bans) Order 2000, SI 2000/2724 amended by SI 2001/2377, SI 2002/192 and 3018, SI 2003/236 and 3285, SI 2004/3316 and SI 2005/3310, has been made.

8–17698 9. Further provisions as to common travel area. (1) Subject to subsection (5) below the provisions of Schedule 4 to this Act shall have effect for the purpose of taking account in the United Kingdom of the operation in any of the Islands of the immigration laws there.

(2) Persons who lawfully enter the United Kingdom on a local journey from a place in the common travel area[1] after having either—

(*a*) entered any of the Islands[2] or the Republic of Ireland on coming from a place outside the common travel area; or
(*b*) left the United Kingdom while having a limited leave to enter or remain which has since expired;

if they are not British citizens (and are not to be regarded under Schedule 4 to this Act as having leave to enter the United Kingdom), shall be subject in the United Kingdom to such restrictions on the period for which they may remain, and such conditions restricting their employment or occupation or requiring them to register with the police or both, as may be imposed by an order of the Secretary of State and may be applicable to them.

(3) Any provision of this Act applying to a limited leave or to conditions attached to a limited leave shall, unless otherwise provided, have effect in relation to a person subject to any restriction or condition by virtue of an order under subsection (2) above as if the provisions of the order applicable to him were terms on which he had been given leave under this Act to enter the United Kingdom.

(4) Section 1(3) above shall not be taken to affect the operation of a deportation order; and, subject to Schedule 4 to this Act, a person who is not a British citizen may not by virtue of section

1(3) enter the United Kingdom without leave on a local journey from a place in the common travel area[1] if either—

(*a*) he is on arrival in the United Kingdom given written notice by an immigration officer stating that, the Secretary of State having issued directions for him not to be given entry to the United Kingdom on the ground that his exclusion is conducive to the public good as being in the interests of national security, he is accordingly refused leave to enter the United Kingdom; or

(*b*) he has at any time been refused leave to enter the United Kingdom and has not since then been given leave to enter or remain in the United Kingdom.

(5) If it appears to the Secretary of State necessary so to do by reason of differences between the immigration laws of the United Kingdom and any of the Islands, he may by order exclude that island from section 1(3) above for such purposes as may be specified in the order, and references in this Act to the Islands shall apply to an island so excluded so far only as may be provided by order of the Secretary of State.

(6) The Secretary of State shall also have power by order[3] to exclude the Republic of Ireland from section 1(3) for such purposes as may be specified in the order.

(7) An order of the Secretary of State under this section shall be made by statutory instrument, which shall be subject to annulment in pursuance of a resolution of either House of Parliament.

[Immigration Act 1971, s 9, as amended by the British Nationality Act 1981, Schs 4 and 9.]

1. "The common travel area" is defined in s 1(3), ante; see also s 11(4), post.
2. "The Islands" means the Channel Islands and the Isle of Man: s 33(1), post.
3. See the Immigration (Control of Entry through Republic of Ireland) Order 1972, SI 1972/1610, amended by SI 1979/730, SI 1980/1859, SI 1982/1028, SI 1985/1854, SI 1987/2092 and SI 2000/1776.

8–17699 **10.** *Power to Order[1] that the provisions of this Act apply to entry otherwise than by ship or aircraft.*

1. The Immigration (Entry Otherwise than by Sea or Air) Order 2002, SI 2002/1832 has been made.

Other provisions as to export of horses

8–17700 **11. Construction of references to entry, and other phrases relating to travel.** (1) A person arriving in the United Kingdom by ship or aircraft shall for purposes of this Act be deemed not to enter the United Kingdom unless and until he disembarks, and on disembarkation at a port shall further be deemed not to enter the United Kingdom so long as he remains in such area (if any) at the port as may be approved for this purpose by an immigration officer; and a person who has not otherwise entered the United Kingdom shall be deemed not to do so as long as he is detained, or temporarily admitted or released while liable to detention, under the powers conferred by Schedule 2 to this Act or section 62 of the Nationality, Immigration and Asylum Act 2002 or by section 68 of the Nationality, Immigration and Asylum Act 2002.*

(1A) (*Repealed*).

(2) In this Act "disembark" means disembark from a ship or aircraft, and "embark" means embark in a ship or aircraft; and, except in subsection (1) above,—

(*a*) references to disembarking in the United Kingdom do not apply to disembarking after a local journey from a place in the United Kingdom or elsewhere in the common travel area; and

(*b*) references to embarking in the United Kingdom do not apply to embarking for a local journey to a place in the United Kingdom or elsewhere in the common travel area.

(3) Except in so far as the context otherwise requires, references in this Act to arriving in the United Kingdom by ship shall extend to arrival by any floating structure, and "disembark" shall be construed accordingly; but the provisions of this Act specially relating to members of the crew of a ship shall not by virtue of this provision apply in relation to any floating structure not being a ship.

(4) For purposes of this Act "common travel area" has the meaning given by section 1(3), and a journey is in relation to the common travel area, a local journey if but only if it begins and ends in the common travel area and is not made by a ship or aircraft which—

(*a*) in the case of a journey to a place in the United Kingdom, began its voyage from, or has during its voyage called at, a place not in the common travel area; or

(*b*) in the case of a journey from a place in the United Kingdom, is due to end its voyage in, or call in the course of its voyage at, a place not in the common travel area.

(5) A person who enters the United Kingdom lawfully by virtue of section 8(1) above, and seeks to remain beyond the time limited by section 8(1), shall be treated for purposes of this Act as seeking to enter the United Kingdom.

[Immigration Act 1971, s 11 amended by SI 1990/2227, SI 1993/1813, the Nationality, Immigration and Asylum Act 2002, s 62 and S! 2003/1016.]

***Section 11 amended by Immigration and Asylum Act 1999, s 170, as from a day to be appointed.**

PART III
CRIMINAL PROCEEDINGS

8–17702 **24. Illegal entry and similar offences.** (1) A person who is not a British citizen shall be guilty of an offence punishable on summary conviction with a fine of not more than **level 5** on the standard scale or with imprisonment for not more than **six months** or with both, in any of the following cases:

(*a*) if contrary to this Act he knowingly enters the United Kingdom in breach of a deportation order or without leave[1];

(*b*) if, having only a limited leave to enter or remain in the United Kingdom, he knowingly either—

(i) remains beyond the time limited by the leave[1]; or

(ii) fails to observe a condition of the leave[3];

(*c*) if, having lawfully entered the United Kingdom without leave by virtue of section 8(1) above, he remains without leave beyond the time allowed by section 8(1)[1];

(*d*) if, without reasonable excuse, he fails to comply with any requirement imposed on him under Schedule 2 to this Act to report to a medical officer of health, or to attend, or submit to a test or examination, as required by such an officer;

(*e*) if, without reasonable excuse, he fails to observe any restriction imposed on him under Schedule 2 or 3 to this Act as to residence, as to his employment or occupation or as to reporting to the police, to an immigration officer or to the Secretary of State;

(*f*) if he disembarks in the United Kingdom from a ship or aircraft after being placed on board under Schedule 2 or 3 to this Act with a view to his removal from the United Kingdom;

(*g*) if he embarks in contravention of a restriction imposed by or under an Order in Council under section 3(7) of this Act.

(1A) A person commits an offence under subsection (1)(*b*)(i) above on the day when he first knows that the time limited by his leave has expired and continues to commit it throughout any period during which he is in the United Kingdom thereafter; but a person shall not be prosecuted under that provision more than once in respect of the same limited leave.

(2) (*Repealed*).

(3) The extended time limit for prosecutions which is provided for by section 28 below shall apply to offences under subsection (1)(*a*) and (*c*) above.

(4) In proceedings for an offence against subsection (1)(*a*) above of entering the United Kingdom without leave—

(*a*) any stamp purporting to have been imprinted on a passport or other travel document by an immigration officer on a particular date for the purpose of giving leave shall be presumed to have been duly so imprinted, unless the contrary is proved;

(*b*) proof that a person had leave to enter the United Kingdom shall lie on the defence if, but only if, he is shown to have entered within six months before the date when the proceedings were commenced.

[Immigration Act 1971, s 24, as amended by the British Nationality Act 1981, Sch 4, the Criminal Justice Act 1982, ss 38 and 46, the Immigration Act 1988, s 6 and Sch, the Asylum and Immigration Act 1996, ss 4 and 6, the Immigration and Asylum Act 1999, Schs 14 and 16, and the Nationality, Immigration and Asylum Act 2002, 62.]

---

1. See sub-s (3), infra, as to extended time limit for prosecutions under sub-s (1)(*a*) and (*c*). The offence under sub-s (1)(*b*)(i) is a continuing offence; see sub-s (1A), infra. Where an appeal is lodged the period of leave is extended by virtue of s 14(1), and an offence under s 24(1)(*b*)(i) is not committed until either the appeal has been determined or withdrawn (*Horne v Gaygusuz* [1979] Crim LR 594). In Case 157/79 *R v Pieck* [1981] QB 571, [1981] 3 All ER 46, a Netherlands national overstayed the period of leave to enter the United Kingdom stamped on his passport. In a reference, the European Court of Justice considering art 3(2) of the Council Directive 68/360/EEC said that member States might not require a person enjoying the protection of Community law to have a residence permit such as was required for aliens in general. Failure to obtain the special residence permit provided for by art 4 might not be punished by a recommendation for deportation or imprisonment.

2. For power of arrest and power to issue search warrants with respect to offences under paras (*a*), (*aa*) and (*b*) of s 24(1) of this Act, see the Asylum and Immigration Act 1996, s 7, post.

3. In order to found a conviction under s 24(1)(*b*) a notice in writing under s 4 of the Act must be proved (*Lamptey v Owen* [1982] Crim LR 42). The offence under sub-s (1)(*b*)(ii) is a continuing offence which may be prosecuted at any time whilst the limited leave and condition remain (*Manickavasagar v Metropolitan Police Comr* [1987] Crim LR 50).

4. This power of arrest is preserved by the Police and Criminal Evidence Act 1984, s 26 and Sch 2.

8–17702A **24A. Deception.** (1) A person who is not a British citizen is guilty of an offence if, by means which include deception by him—

(*a*) he obtains or seeks to obtain leave to enter or remain in the United Kingdom; or

(*b*) he secures or seeks to secure the avoidance, postponement or revocation of enforcement action against him.

(2) "Enforcement action", in relation to a person, means—

(*a*) the giving of directions for his removal from the United Kingdom ("directions") under Schedule 2 to this Act or section 10 of the Immigration and Asylum Act 1999;

(*b*) the making of a deportation order against him under section 5 of this Act; or
(*c*) his removal from the United Kingdom in consequence of directions or a deportation order.

(3) A person guilty of an offence[1] under this section is liable[2]—

(*a*) on summary conviction, to imprisonment for a term not exceeding **six months** or to a fine not exceeding **the statutory maximum**, or to *both*; or
(*b*) on conviction on indictment, to imprisonment for a term not exceeding **two years** or to a **fine**, or to **both**.

(4) (*Repealed*).

[Immigration Act 1971, s 24A, as inserted by the Immigration and Asylum Act 1999, s 28, and amended by the Nationality, Immigration and Asylum Act 2002, Sch 9.]

---

1. For defence based on art 31(1) of the Refugee Convention, see the Immigration and Asylum Act 1999, s 31, in this title, post.
2. For procedure in respect of this offence which is triable either way, see the Magistrates' Courts Act 1980, ss 18–21, in PART I: MAGISTRATES' COURTS, PROCEDURE, ante. See sub-s (4), infra, as to extended time liit for prosecutions under this section.

8–17703 25. Assisting unlawful immigration to member State. (1) A person commits an offence if he—

(*a*) does an act which facilitates[1] the commission of a breach of immigration law by an individual who is not a citizen of the European Union,
(*b*) knows or has reasonable cause for believing that the act facilitates the commission of a breach of immigration law by the individual, and
(*c*) knows or has reasonable cause for believing that the individual is not a citizen of the European Union.

(2) In subsection (1) "immigration law" means a law which has effect in a member State and which controls, in respect of some or all persons who are not nationals of the State, entitlement to—

(*a*) enter the State,
(*b*) transit across the State, or
(*c*) be in the State.

(3) A document issued by the government of a member State certifying a matter of law in that State—

(*a*) shall be admissible in proceedings for an offence under this section, and
(*b*) shall be conclusive as to the matter certified.

(4) Subsection (1) applies to anything done—

(*a*) in the United Kingdom,
(*b*) outside the United Kingdom by an individual to whom subsection (5) applies, or
(*c*) outside the United Kingdom by a body incorporated under the law of a part of the United Kingdom.

(5) This subsection applies to—

(*a*) a British citizen,
(*b*) a British overseas territories citizen,
(*c*) a British National (Overseas),
(*d*) a British Overseas citizen,
(*e*) a person who is a British subject under the British Nationality Act 1981 (c 61), and
(*f*) a British protected person within the meaning of that Act.

(6) A person guilty of an offence under this section shall be liable—

(*a*) on conviction on indictment, to imprisonment for a term not exceeding 14 years, to a fine or to both, or
(*b*) on summary conviction, to imprisonment for a term not exceeding six months, to a fine not exceeding the statutory maximum or to both.[2]

(7) In this section—

(*a*) a reference to a member State includes a reference to a State on a list prescribed for the purposes of this section by order[3] of the Secretary of State (to be known as the "Section 25 List of Schengen Acquis States"), and
(*b*) a reference to a citizen of the European Union includes a reference to a person who is a national of a State on that list.

(8) An order under subsection (7)(*a*)—

(*a*) may be made only if the Secretary of State thinks it necessary for the purpose of complying with the United Kingdom's obligations under the Community Treaties,
(*b*) may include transitional, consequential or incidental provision,
(*c*) shall be made by statutory instrument, and
(*d*) shall be subject to annulment in pursuance of a resolution of either House of Parliament.

[Immigration Act 1971, s 25, as substituted by the Nationality, Immigration and Asylum Act 2002, s 143 and the Asylum and Immigration (Treatment of Claimants, etc) Act 2004, s 1.]

1. Help to get a person into the country may be continued without any break after the illegal entry has been effected; there may be no dividing line between helping to effect an entry and helping by way of harbouring; thus a person may be guilty of an offence under sub-s (1) after a person has entered the country illegally (*R v Amar Jit Singh* [1973] 1 All ER 122, 137 JP 112). An offence under s 24(1)(*b*) is not a continuing offence; it is committed when the leave to remain expires; a condition not to enter into employment, attached to the limited leave, expires with the leave itself (*Singh (Gurdev) v R* [1974] 1 All ER 26, 138 JP 85). The conduct of a person charged with a s 25(1) offence must inevitably precede or be contemporaneous with any entry by those he is assisting. The material times for the knowledge or belief required by s 25(1) are the times at which the defendant makes or carries out the arrangements. Therefore, an offence under s 25(1)(*a*) may relate to a person who sought or intended to become an illegal entrant as well as to someone who had become an illegal entrant by reason of passing or attempting to pass through immigration control by concealment or deception. Similarly, an offence under s 25(1)(*b*) may relate to an intending asylum claimant (*R v Eyck* [2000] 3 All ER 569, [2000] 1 WLR 1389, [2000] Crim LR 299, CA).

2. For procedure in respect of this offence triable either way, see Magistrates' Courts Act 1980, ss 18–21, in PART I, ante. See sub-s (4), infra, as to extended time limit for prosecutions under this section.

3. The Immigration (Assisting Unlawful Immigration) (Section 25 List of Schengen Acquis States) Order 2004, SI 2004/2877 has been made which prescribes Norway and Iceland.

8–17703A 25A. Helping asylum-seeker to enter United Kingdom. (1) A person commits an offence if—

(*a*) he knowingly and for gain facilitates the arrival in the United Kingdom of an individual, and
(*b*) he knows or has reasonable cause to believe that the individual is an asylum-seeker.

(2) In this section "asylum-seeker" means a person who intends to claim that to remove him from or require him to leave the United Kingdom would be contrary to the United Kingdom's obligations under—

(*a*) the Refugee Convention (within the meaning given by section 167(1) of the Immigration and Asylum Act 1999 (c 33) (interpretation)), or
(*b*) the Human Rights Convention (within the meaning given by that section).

(3) Subsection (1) does not apply to anything done by a person acting on behalf of an organisation which—

(*a*) aims to assist asylum-seekers, and
(*b*) does not charge for its services.

(4) Subsections (4) to (6) of section 25 apply for the purpose of the offence in subsection (1) of this section as they apply for the purpose of the offence in subsection (1) of that section.
[Immigration Act 1971, s 25A, as substituted by the Nationality, Immigration and Asylum Act 2002, s 143.]

8–17703B 25B. Assisting entry to United Kingdom in breach of deportation or exclusion order]. (1) A person commits an offence if he—

(*a*) does an act which facilitates a breach of a deportation order in force against an individual who is a citizen of the European Union, and
(*b*) knows or has reasonable cause for believing that the act facilitates a breach of the deportation order.

(2) Subsection (3) applies where the Secretary of State personally directs that the exclusion from the United Kingdom of an individual who is a citizen of the European Union is conducive to the public good.

(3) A person commits an offence if he—

(*a*) does an act which assists the individual to arrive in, enter or remain in the United Kingdom,
(*b*) knows or has reasonable cause for believing that the act assists the individual to arrive in, enter or remain in the United Kingdom, and
(*c*) knows or has reasonable cause for believing that the Secretary of State has personally directed that the individual's exclusion from the United Kingdom is conducive to the public good.

(4) Subsections (4) to (6) of section 25 apply for the purpose of an offence under this section as they apply for the purpose of an offence under that section.
[Immigration Act 1971, s 25B, as inserted by the Nationality, Immigration and Asylum Act 2002, s 143.]

8–17703C 25C. Forfeiture of vehicle, ship or aircraft. (1) This section applies where a person is convicted on indictment of an offence under section 25, 25A or 25B.

(2) The court may order the forfeiture of a vehicle used or intended to be used in connection with the offence if the convicted person—

(*a*) owned the vehicle at the time the offence was committed,
(*b*) was at that time a director, secretary or manager of a company which owned the vehicle,
(*c*) was at that time in possession of the vehicle under a hire-purchase agreement,
(*d*) was at that time a director, secretary or manager of a company which was in possession of the vehicle under a hire-purchase agreement, or
(*e*) was driving the vehicle in the course of the commission of the offence.

(3) The court may order the forfeiture of a ship or aircraft used or intended to be used in connection with the offence if the convicted person—

(*a*) owned the ship or aircraft at the time the offence was committed,
(*b*) was at that time a director, secretary or manager of a company which owned the ship or aircraft,
(*c*) was at that time in possession of the ship or aircraft under a hire-purchase agreement,
(*d*) was at that time a director, secretary or manager of a company which was in possession of the ship or aircraft under a hire-purchase agreement,
(*e*) was at that time a charterer of the ship or aircraft, or
(*f*) committed the offence while acting as captain of the ship or aircraft.

(4) But in a case to which subsection (3)(*a*) or (*b*) does not apply, forfeiture may be ordered only—

(*a*) in the case of a ship, if subsection (5) or (6) applies;
(*b*) in the case of an aircraft, if subsection (5) or (7) applies.

(5) This subsection applies where—

(*a*) in the course of the commission of the offence, the ship or aircraft carried more than 20 illegal entrants, and
(*b*) a person who, at the time the offence was committed, owned the ship or aircraft or was a director, secretary or manager of a company which owned it, knew or ought to have known of the intention to use it in the course of the commission of an offence under section 25, 25A or 25B.

(6) This subsection applies where a ship's gross tonnage is less than 500 tons.

(7) This subsection applies where the maximum weight at which an aircraft (which is not a hovercraft) may take off in accordance with its certificate of airworthiness is less than 5,700 kilogrammes.

(8) Where a person who claims to have an interest in a vehicle, ship or aircraft applies to a court to make representations on the question of forfeiture, the court may not make an order under this section in respect of the ship, aircraft or vehicle unless the person has been given an opportunity to make representations.

(9) In the case of an offence under section 25, the reference in subsection (5)(*a*) to an illegal entrant shall be taken to include a reference to—

(*a*) an individual who seeks to enter a member State in breach of immigration law (for which purpose "member State" and "immigration law" have the meanings given by section 25(2) and (7)), and
(*b*) an individual who is a passenger for the purpose of section 145 of the Nationality, Immigration and Asylum Act 2002 (traffic in prostitution) or section 4 of the Asylum and Immigration (Treatment of Claimants, etc) Act 2004 (trafficking people for exploitation).

(10) In the case of an offence under section 25A, the reference in subsection (5)(*a*) to an illegal entrant shall be taken to include a reference to—

(*a*) an asylum-seeker (within the meaning of that section), and
(*b*) an individual who is a passenger for the purpose of section 145(1) of the Nationality, Immigration and Asylum Act 2002 or section 4 of the Asylum and Immigration (Treatment of Claimants, etc) Act 2004 (trafficking people for exploitation).

(11) In the case of an offence under section 25B, the reference in subsection (5)(*a*) to an illegal entrant shall be taken to include a reference to an individual who is a passenger for the purpose of section 145(1) of the Nationality, Immigration and Asylum Act 2002 or section 4 of the Asylum and Immigration (Treatment of Claimants, etc) Act 2004 (trafficking people for exploitation).

[Immigration Act 1971, s 25C, as inserted by the Nationality, Immigration and Asylum Act 2002, s 143 and amended by the Nationality, Immigration and Asylum Act 2002, s 1 and 5.]

8–17703D 25D. Detention of ship, aircraft or vehicle. (1) If a person has been arrested for an offence under [section 25, 25A or 25B], a senior officer or a constable may detain a relevant ship, aircraft or vehicle—

(*a*) until a decision is taken as to whether or not to charge the arrested person with that offence; or
(*b*) if the arrested person has been charged—
    (i) until he is acquitted, the charge against him is dismissed or the proceedings are discontinued; or
    (ii) if he has been convicted, until the court decides whether or not to order forfeiture of the ship, aircraft or vehicle.

(2) A ship, aircraft or vehicle is a relevant ship, aircraft or vehicle, in relation to an arrested person, if it is one which the officer or constable concerned has reasonable grounds for believing could, on conviction of the arrested person for the offence for which he was arrested, be the subject of an order for forfeiture made under section 25C.

(3) A person (other than the arrested person) may apply to the court for the release of a ship, aircraft or vehicle on the grounds that—

(*a*) he owns the ship, aircraft or vehicle,
(*b*) he was, immediately before the detention of the ship, aircraft or vehicle, in possession of it under a hire-purchase agreement, or
(*c*) he is a charterer of the ship or aircraft.

(4) The court to which an application is made under subsection (3) may, on such security or surety being tendered as it considers satisfactory, release the ship, aircraft or vehicle on condition that it is made available to the court if—

(*a*) the arrested person is convicted; and
(*b*) an order for its forfeiture is made under section 25C.

(5) In the application to Scotland of subsection (1), for paragraphs (*a*) and (*b*) substitute—

"(*a*) until a decision is taken as to whether or not to institute criminal proceedings against the arrested person for that offence; or
(*b*) if criminal proceedings have been instituted against the arrested person—
(i) until he is acquitted or, under section 65 or 147 of the Criminal Procedure (Scotland) Act 1995, discharged or liberated or the trial diet is deserted simpliciter;
(ii) if he has been convicted, until the court decides whether or not to order forfeiture of the ship, aircraft or vehicle,

and for the purposes of this subsection, criminal proceedings are instituted against a person at whichever is the earliest of his first appearance before the sheriff on petition, or the service on him of an indictment or complaint."

(6) "Court" means—

(*a*) in England and Wales—
(ia) if the arrested person has not been charged, or he has been charged but proceedings for the offence have not begun to be heard, a magistrates' court;
(iii) if he has been charged and proceedings for the offence are being heard, the court hearing the proceedings;
(*b*) in Scotland, the sheriff; and
(*c*) in Northern Ireland—
(i) if the arrested person has not been charged, the magistrates' court for the county court division in which he was arrested;
(ii) if he has been charged but proceedings for the offence have not begun to be heard, the magistrates' court for the county court division in which he was charged;
(iii) if he has been charged and proceedings for the offence are being heard, the court hearing the proceedings.

(7) *Repealed.*

(8) "Senior officer" means an immigration officer not below the rank of chief immigration officer.

[Immigration Act 1971, s 25D, as inserted by the Nationality, Immigration and Asylum Act 2002, s 143 and amended by the Nationality, Immigration and Asylum Act 2002, s 144, the Asylum and Immigration (Treatment of Claimants, etc) Act 2004, ss 38 and 144 and the Courts Act 2003, s 109(1), Sch 8.]

8–17704 **26. General offences in connection with administration of Act.** (1) A person shall be guilty of an offence[1] punishable on summary conviction with a fine of not more than **level 5** on the standard scale or with imprisonment for not more than **six months**, or with **both**, in any of the following cases—

(*a*) if, without reasonable excuse, he refuses or fails to submit to examination under Schedule 2 to this Act;
(*b*) if, without reasonable excuse, he refuses or fails to furnish or produce any information in his possession, or any documents in his possession or control, which he is on an examination under that Schedule required to furnish or produce;
(*c*) if on any such examination or otherwise he makes or causes to be made to an immigration officer or other person[2] lawfully acting in the execution of a relevant enactment a return, statement or representation which he knows to be false or does not believe to be true[3];
(*d*) if, without lawful authority, he alters any certificate of entitlement, entry clearance, work permit or other document issued or made under or for the purposes of this Act, or uses for the purposes of this Act, or has in his possession for such use, any passport[4], certificate of entitlement, entry clearance, work permit or other document which he knows or has reasonable cause to believe to be false[3];
(*e*) if, without reasonable excuse, he fails to complete and produce a landing or embarkation card in accordance with any order under Schedule 2 to this Act;
(*f*) if, without reasonable excuse, he fails to comply with any requirement of regulations under section 4(3) or of an order under section 4(4) above;

(*g*) if, without reasonable excuse, he obstructs an immigration officer or other person lawfully acting in the execution of this Act.

(2) The extended time limit for prosecutions which is provided for by section 28 below shall apply to offences under subsection (1)(*c*) and (*d*) above.

(3) "Relevant enactment" means—

(*a*) this Act;
(*b*) the Immigration Act 1988;
(*c*) the Asylum and Immigration Appeals Act 1993 (apart from section 4 or 5);
(*d*) the Immigration and Asylum Act 1999 (apart from Part VI); or
(*e*) the Nationality, Immigration and Asylum Act 2002 (apart from Part 5).

[Immigration Act 1971, s 26, as amended by the British Nationality Act 1981, Sch 4, the Criminal Justice Act 1982, ss 38 and 46, the Asylum and Immigration Act 1996, s 6 and the Immigration and Asylum Act 1999, s 30, and the Nationality, Immigration and Asylum Act 2002, s 151.]

---

1. For defence based on art 31(1) of the Refugee Convention, see the Immigration and Asylum Act 1999, s 31, in this title, post.
2. "Other person" does not include a constable investigating a suspected illegal entry under s 24, ante (*R v Gill* [1976] 2 All ER 893, 63 Cr App Rep 83; approved by the House of Lords in *R v Clarke* [1985] AC 1037, [1985] 2 All ER 777).
3. See sub-s (2), infra, as to extended time limit for prosecutions under paras (*c*) and (*d*) of this subsection.
4. See *R v Zaman* [1975] Crim LR 710.

8–17704A 26A. Registration card. (1) In this section "registration card" means a document which—

(*a*) carries information about a person (whether or not wholly or partly electronically), and
(*b*) is issued by the Secretary of State to the person wholly or partly in connection with a claim for asylum (whether or not made by that person).

(2) In subsection (1) "claim for asylum" has the meaning given by section 18 of the Nationality, Immigration and Asylum Act 2002.

(3) A person commits an offence if he—

(*a*) makes a false registration card,
(*b*) alters a registration card with intent to deceive or to enable another to deceive,
(*c*) has a false or altered registration card in his possession without reasonable excuse,
(*d*) uses or attempts to use a false registration card for a purpose for which a registration card is issued,
(*e*) uses or attempts to use an altered registration card with intent to deceive,
(*f*) makes an article designed to be used in making a false registration card,
(*g*) makes an article designed to be used in altering a registration card with intent to deceive or to enable another to deceive, or
(*h*) has an article within paragraph (f) or (g) in his possession without reasonable excuse.

(4) In subsection (3) "false registration card" means a document which is designed to appear to be a registration card.

(5) A person who is guilty of an offence under subsection (3)(a), (b), (d), (e), (f) or (g) shall be liable—

(*a*) on conviction on indictment, to imprisonment for a term not exceeding ten years, to a fine or to both, or
(*b*) on summary conviction, to imprisonment for a term not exceeding six months, to a fine not exceeding the statutory maximum or to both.

(6) A person who is guilty of an offence under subsection (3)(c) or (h) shall be liable—

(*a*) on conviction on indictment, to imprisonment for a term not exceeding two years, to a fine or to both, or
(*b*) on summary conviction, to imprisonment for a term not exceeding six months, to a fine not exceeding the statutory maximum or to both.

(7) The Secretary of State may by order—

(*a*) amend the definition of "registration card" in subsection (1);
(*b*) make consequential amendment of this section.

(8) An order under subsection (7)—

(*a*) must be made by statutory instrument, and
(*b*) may not be made unless a draft has been laid before and approved by resolution of each House of Parliament.

[Immigration Act 1971, s 26A, as inserted by the Nationality, Immigration and Asylum Act 2002, s 148.]

8–17704B 26B. Possession of immigration stamp. (1) A person commits an offence if he has an immigration stamp in his possession without reasonable excuse.

(2) A person commits an offence if he has a replica immigration stamp in his possession without reasonable excuse.

(3) In this section—

(*a*) "immigration stamp" means a device which is designed for the purpose of stamping documents in the exercise of an immigration function,

(*b*) "replica immigration stamp" means a device which is designed for the purpose of stamping a document so that it appears to have been stamped in the exercise of an immigration function, and

(*c*) "immigration function" means a function of an immigration officer or the Secretary of State under the Immigration Acts.

(4) A person who is guilty of an offence under this section shall be liable—

(*a*) on conviction on indictment, to imprisonment for a term not exceeding two years, to a fine or to both, or

(*b*) on summary conviction, to imprisonment for a term not exceeding six months, to a fine not exceeding the statutory maximum or to both.

[Immigration Act 1971, s 26B, as inserted by the Nationality, Immigration and Asylum Act 2002, s 149.]

8–17705 **27. Offences by persons connected with ships or aircraft or with ports.** A person shall be guilty of an offence punishable on summary conviction with a fine of not more than **level 5** on the standard scale or with imprisonment for not more than **six months**, or with **both**, in any of the following cases—

(*a*) if, being the captain of a ship or aircraft,—

(i) he knowingly permits a person to disembark in the United Kingdom when required under Schedule 2 or 3 to this Act to prevent it, or fails without reasonable excuse to take any steps he is required by or under Schedule 2 to take in connection with the disembarkation or examination of passengers or for furnishing a passenger list or particulars of members of the crew; or

(ii) he fails, without reasonable excuse, to comply with any directions given him under Schedule 2 or 3 or under the Immigration and Asylum Act 1999 with respect to the removal of a person from the United Kingdom;

(*b*) if, as owner or agent of a ship or aircraft,—

(i) he arranges, or is knowingly concerned in any arrangements, for the ship or aircraft to call at a port other than a port of entry contrary to any provision of Schedule 2 to this Act; or

(ii) he fails, without reasonable excuse, to take any steps required by an order under Schedule 2 for the supply to passengers of landing or embarkation cards; or

(iii) he fails, without reasonable excuse, to make arrangements for or in connection with the removal of a person from the United Kingdom when required to do so by directions given under Schedule 2 or 3 to this Act or under the Immigration and Asylum Act 1999; or

(iv) he fails, without reasonable excuse, to comply with the requirements of paragraph 27B or 27C of Schedule 2;

(*c*) if, as owner or agent of a ship or aircraft or as a person concerned in the management of a port, he fails, without reasonable excuse, to take any steps required by Schedule 2 in relation to the embarkation or disembarkation of passengers where a control area is designated;

(*d*) *Repealed.*

[Immigration Act 1971, s 27, as amended by the Criminal Justice Act 1982, ss 38 and 46, SI 1990/2227, SI 1993/1813, the Asylum and Immigration Act 1996, s 6 and the Immigration and Asylum Act 1999, Sch 14.]

8–17706 **28. Proceedings.** (1) Where the offence is one to which, under section 24 or 26 above, an extended time limit for prosecutions is to apply, then—

(*a*) an information relating to the offence may in England and Wales be tried[1] by a magistrates' court if it is laid within six months after the commission of the offence, or if it is laid within three years after the commission of the offence and not more than two months after the date certified by an officer of police above the rank of chief superintendent to be the date on which evidence[2] sufficient to justify proceedings came to the notice of an officer of the police force to which he belongs; and

(*b*) *Scotland*;

(*c*) *Northern Ireland.*

(2) *Scotland.*

(3) For the purposes of the trial of a person for an offence under this Part of this Act, the offence shall be deemed to have been committed either at the place at which it actually was committed or at any place at which he may be.

(4) Any powers exercisable under this Act in the case of any person may be exercised notwithstanding that proceedings for an offence under this Part of this Act have been taken against him.

[Immigration Act 1971, s 28, as amended by the Immigration Act 1988, Schedule the Immigration and Asylum Act 1999, Sch 14 and the Nationality, Immigration and Asylum Act 2002, Sch 9.]

1. The stage at which the conditions in this paragraph must be shown to be complied with is the stage at which the matter comes before the magistrates' court for trial. For this purpose, the entering of a plea of not guilty does not mark the commencement of the trial, but merely the need for a trial, and the trial itself begins with the hearing of the information (*Quazi v DPP* (1988) 152 JP 385).

2. "Evidence" means something more than mere information given to a police officer over the telephone (*Enaas v Dovey* (1986) Times, 25 November).

8–17706A 28A. Arrest without warrant. (1) An immigration officer may arrest without warrant a person—

(*a*) who has committed or attempted to commit an offence under section 24 or 24A; or
(*b*) whom he has reasonable grounds for suspecting has committed or attempted to commit such an offence.

(2) But subsection (1) does not apply in relation to an offence under section 24(1)(*d*).
(3) An immigration officer may arrest without warrant a person—

(*a*) who has committed an offence under section 25, 25A or 25B; or
(*b*) whom he has reasonable grounds for suspecting has committed that offence.

(4) *Repealed.*
(5) An immigration officer may arrest without warrant a person ("the suspect") who, or whom he has reasonable grounds for suspecting—

(*a*) has committed or attempted to commit an offence under section 26(1)(*g*); or
(*b*) is committing or attempting to commit that offence.

(6) The power conferred by subsection (5) is exercisable only if either the first or the second condition is satisfied.
(7) The first condition is that it appears to the officer that service of a summons (or, in Scotland, a copy complaint) is impracticable or inappropriate because—

(*a*) he does not know, and cannot readily discover, the suspect's name;
(*b*) he has reasonable grounds for doubting whether a name given by the suspect as his name is his real name;
(*c*) the suspect has failed to give him a satisfactory address for service; or
(*d*) he has reasonable grounds for doubting whether an address given by the suspect is a satisfactory address for service.

(8) The second condition is that the officer has reasonable grounds for believing that arrest is necessary to prevent the suspect—

(*a*) causing physical injury to himself or another person;
(*b*) suffering physical injury; or
(*c*) causing loss of or damage to property.

(9) For the purposes of subsection (7), an address is a satisfactory address for service if it appears to the officer—

(*a*) that the suspect will be at that address for a sufficiently long period for it to be possible to serve him with a summons (or copy complaint); or
(*b*) that some other person specified by the suspect will accept service of a summons (or copy complaint) for the suspect at that address.

(9A) An immigration officer may arrest without warrant a person—

(*a*) who has committed an offence under section 26A or 26B; or
(*b*) whom he has reasonable grounds for suspecting has committed an offence under section 26A or 26B.

(10) In relation to the exercise of the powers conferred by subsections (3)(*b*) and (5), it is immaterial that no offence has been committed.

(11) In Scotland the powers conferred by subsections (3) and (5) may also be exercised by a constable.
[Immigration Act 1971, s 28A, as inserted by the Immigration and Asylum Act 1999, s 128, the Nationality, Immigration and Asylum Act 2002, Sch 9 and the Serious Organised Crime and Police Act 2005, Sch 7.]

8–17706AA 28AA. Arrest with warrant. (1) This section applies if on an application by an immigration officer a justice of the peace is satisfied that there are reasonable grounds for suspecting that a person has committed an offence under—

(*a*) section 24(1)(*d*), or
(*b*) section 8 of the Asylum and Immigration Act 1996 (c 49) (employment: offence).

(2) The justice of the peace may grant a warrant authorising any immigration officer to arrest the person.
(3) In the application of this section to Scotland a reference to a justice of the peace shall be treated as a reference to the sheriff or a justice of the peace.
Immigration Act 1971, s 28AA is inserted by the Nationality, Immigration and Asylum Act 2002, s 152.

8–17706B 28B. Search and arrest by warrant. (1) Subsection (2) applies if a justice of the peace is, by written information on oath, satisfied that there are reasonable grounds for suspecting that a person ("the suspect") who is liable to be arrested for a relevant offence is to be found on any premises.

(2) The justice may grant a warrant authorising any immigration officer or constable to enter, if need be by force, the premises named in the warrant for the purpose of searching for and arresting the suspect.

(3) Subsection (4) applies if in Scotland the sheriff or a justice of the peace is by evidence on oath satisfied as mentioned in subsection (1).

(4) The sheriff or justice may grant a warrant authorising any immigration officer or constable to enter, if need be by force, the premises named in the warrant for the purpose of searching for and arresting the suspect.

(5) "Relevant offence" means an offence under section 24(1)(*a*), (*b*), (*c*), (*d*), (*e*) or (*f*), 24A, 24A, 26A or 26B.

[Immigration Act 1971, s 28B, as inserted by the Immigration and Asylum Act 1999, s 129 and amended by the Nationality, Immigration and Asylum Act 2002, ss 144 and 150.]

8–17706C 28C. Search and arrest without warrant. (1) An immigration officer may enter and search any premises for the purpose of arresting a person for an offence under section25, 25A or 25B.

(2) The power may be exercised—

(*a*) only to the extent that it is reasonably required for that purpose; and
(*b*) only if the officer has reasonable grounds for believing that the person whom he is seeking is on the premises.

(3) In relation to premises consisting of two or more separate dwellings, the power is limited to entering and searching—

(*a*) any parts of the premises which the occupiers of any dwelling comprised in the premises use in common with the occupiers of any such other dwelling; and
(*b*) any such dwelling in which the officer has reasonable grounds for believing that the person whom he is seeking may be.

(4) The power may be exercised only if the officer produces identification showing that he is an immigration officer (whether or not he is asked to do so).

[Immigration Act 1971, s 28C, as inserted by the Immigration and Asylum Act 1999, s 130, and amended by the Nationality, Immigration and Asylum Act 2002, s 144.]

8–17706CA 28CA. Business premises: entry to arrest. (1) A constable or immigration officer may enter and search any business premises for the purpose of arresting a person—

(*a*) for an offence under section 24,
(*b*) for an offence under section 24A, or
(*c*) under paragraph 17 of Schedule 2.

(2) The power under subsection (1) may be exercised only—

(*a*) to the extent that it is reasonably required for a purpose specified in subsection (1),
(*b*) if the constable or immigration officer has reasonable grounds for believing that the person whom he is seeking is on the premises,
(*c*) with the authority of the Secretary of State (in the case of an immigration officer) or a Chief Superintendent (in the case of a constable), and
(*d*) if the constable or immigration officer produces identification showing his status.

(3) Authority for the purposes of subsection (2)(c)—

(*a*) may be given on behalf of the Secretary of State only by a civil servant of the rank of at least Assistant Director, and
(*b*) shall expire at the end of the period of seven days beginning with the day on which it is given.

(4) Subsection (2)(d) applies—

(*a*) whether or not a constable or immigration officer is asked to produce identification, but
(*b*) only where premises are occupied.

(5) Subsection (6) applies where a constable or immigration officer—

(*a*) enters premises in reliance on this section, and
(*b*) detains a person on the premises.

(6) A detainee custody officer may enter the premises for the purpose of carrying out a search.

(7) In subsection (6)—

"detainee custody officer" means a person in respect of whom a certificate of authorisation is in force under section 154 of the Immigration and Asylum Act 1999 (c 33) (detained persons: escort and custody), and "search" means a search under paragraph 2(1)(a) of Schedule 13 to that Act (escort arrangements: power to search detained person).

[Immigration Act 1971, s 28CA, as inserted by the Nationality, Immigration and Asylum Act 2002, s 153.]

8–17706D 28D. Entry and search of premises. (1) If, on an application made by an immigration officer, a justice of the peace is satisfied that there are reasonable grounds for believing that—

(*a*) a relevant offence has been committed,

(*b*) there is material on premises specified in the application which is likely to be of substantial value (whether by itself or together with other material) to the investigation of the offence,

(*c*) the material is likely to be relevant evidence,

(*d*) the material does not consist of or include items subject to legal privilege, excluded material or special procedure material, and

(*e*) any of the conditions specified in subsection (2) applies,

he may issue a warrant authorising an immigration officer to enter and search the premises.

(2) The conditions are that—

(*a*) it is not practicable to communicate with any person entitled to grant entry to the premises;

(*b*) it is practicable to communicate with a person entitled to grant entry to the premises but it is not practicable to communicate with any person entitled to grant access to the evidence;

(*c*) entry to the premises will not be granted unless a warrant is produced;

(*d*) the purpose of a search may be frustrated or seriously prejudiced unless an immigration officer arriving at the premises can secure immediate entry to them.

(3) An immigration officer may seize and retain anything for which a search has been authorised under subsection (1).

(4) "Relevant offence" means an offence under section 24(1)(*a*), (*b*), (*c*), (*d*), (*e*) or (*f*), section 24A, 25, 25A, 25B, 26A or 26B.

(5) In relation to England and Wales, expressions which are given a meaning by the Police and Criminal Evidence Act 1984 have the same meaning when used in this section.

(6) In relation to Northern Ireland, expressions which are given a meaning by the Police and Criminal Evidence (Northern Ireland) Order 1989 have the same meaning when used in this section

(7) In the application of subsection (1) to Scotland—

(*a*) read the reference to a justice of the peace as a reference to the sheriff or a justice of the peace; and

(*b*) in paragraph (*b*), omit the reference to excluded material and special procedure material.

[Immigration Act 1971, s 28D, as inserted by the Immigration and Asylum Act 1999, s 131, and amended by the Nationality, Immigration and Asylum Act 2002, ss 144 and 150.]

8–17706E 28E. Entry and search of premises following arrest. (1) This section applies if a person is arrested for an offence under this Part at a place other than a police station.

(2) An immigration officer may enter and search any premises—

(*a*) in which the person was when arrested, or

(*b*) in which he was immediately before he was arrested,

for evidence relating to the offence for which the arrest was made ("relevant evidence").

(3) The power may be exercised—

(*a*) only if the officer has reasonable grounds for believing that there is relevant evidence on the premises; and

(*b*) only to the extent that it is reasonably required for the purpose of discovering relevant evidence.

(4) In relation to premises consisting of two or more separate dwellings, the power is limited to entering and searching—

(*a*) any dwelling in which the arrest took place or in which the arrested person was immediately before his arrest; and

(*b*) any parts of the premises which the occupier of any such dwelling uses in common with the occupiers of any other dwellings comprised in the premises.

(5) An officer searching premises under subsection (2) may seize and retain anything he finds which he has reasonable grounds for believing is relevant evidence.

(6) Subsection (5) does not apply to items which the officer has reasonable grounds for believing are items subject to legal privilege.

[Immigration Act 1971, s 28E, as inserted by the Immigration and Asylum Act 1999, s 132(1).]

8–17706F 28F. Entry and search of premises following arrest under section 25(1)*. (1) An immigration officer may enter and search any premises occupied or controlled by a person arrested for an offence under section 25, 25A, 25B.

(2) The power may be exercised—

(*a*) only if the officer has reasonable grounds for suspecting that there is relevant evidence on the premises;

(*b*) only to the extent that it is reasonably required for the purpose of discovering relevant evidence; and

(*c*) subject to subsection (3), only if a senior officer has authorised it in writing.

(3) The power may be exercised—

(*a*) before taking the arrested person to a place where he is to be detained; and

(*b*) without obtaining an authorisation under subsection (2)(*c*),

if the presence of that person at a place other than one where he is to be detained is necessary for the effective investigation of the offence.

(4) An officer who has relied on subsection (3) must inform a senior officer as soon as is practicable.

(5) The officer authorising a search, or who is informed of one under subsection (4), must make a record in writing of—

(*a*) the grounds for the search; and

(*b*) the nature of the evidence that was sought.

(6) An officer searching premises under this section may seize and retain anything he finds which he has reasonable grounds for suspecting is relevant evidence.

(7) "Relevant evidence" means evidence, other than items subject to legal privilege, that relates to the offence in question.

(8) "Senior officer" means an immigration officer not below the rank of chief immigration officer.

[Immigration Act 1971, s 28F, as inserted by the Immigration and Asylum Act 1999, s 133, and amended by the Nationality, Immigration and Asylum Act 2002, s 144.]

***Section heading substituted by the Nationality, Immigration and Asylum Act 2002, s 144 from a date to be appointed.**

8–17706FA 28FA. Search for personnel records: warrant unnecessary. (1) This section applies where—

(*a*) a person has been arrested for an offence under section 24(1) or 24A(1),

(*b*) a person has been arrested under paragraph 17 of Schedule 2,

(*c*) a constable or immigration officer reasonably believes that a person is liable to arrest for an offence under section 24(1) or 24A(1), or

(*d*) a constable or immigration officer reasonably believes that a person is liable to arrest under paragraph 17 of Schedule 2.

(2) A constable or immigration officer may search business premises where the arrest was made or where the person liable to arrest is if the constable or immigration officer reasonably believes—

(*a*) that a person has committed an immigration employment offence in relation to the person arrested or liable to arrest, and

(*b*) that employee records, other than items subject to legal privilege, will be found on the premises and will be of substantial value (whether on their own or together with other material) in the investigation of the immigration employment offence.

(3) A constable or officer searching premises under subsection (2) may seize and retain employee records, other than items subject to legal privilege, which he reasonably suspects will be of substantial value (whether on their own or together with other material) in the investigation of—

(*a*) an immigration employment offence, or

(*b*) an offence under section 105 or 106 of the Immigration and Asylum Act 1999 (c 33) (support for asylum-seeker: fraud).

(4) The power under subsection (2) may be exercised only—

(*a*) to the extent that it is reasonably required for the purpose of discovering employee records other than items subject to legal privilege,

(*b*) if the constable or immigration officer produces identification showing his status, and

(*c*) if the constable or immigration officer reasonably believes that at least one of the conditions in subsection (5) applies.

(5) Those conditions are—

(*a*) that it is not practicable to communicate with a person entitled to grant access to the records,

(*b*) that permission to search has been refused,

(*c*) that permission to search would be refused if requested, and

(*d*) that the purpose of a search may be frustrated or seriously prejudiced if it is not carried out in reliance on subsection (2).

(6) Subsection (4)(b) applies—

(*a*) whether or not a constable or immigration officer is asked to produce identification, but (*b*) only where premises are occupied.

(7) In this section "immigration employment offence" means an offence under section 8 of the Asylum and Immigration Act 1996 (c 49) (employment).

[Immigration Act 1971, s 28FA, as inserted by the Nationality, Immigration and Asylum Act 2002, s 154.]

8–17706G 28G. Searching arrested persons. (1) This section applies if a person is arrested for an offence under this Part at a place other than a police station.

(2) An immigration officer may search the arrested person if he has reasonable grounds for believing that the arrested person may present a danger to himself or others.

(3) The officer may search the arrested person for—

(*a*) anything which he might use to assist his escape from lawful custody; or
(*b*) anything which might be evidence relating to the offence for which he has been arrested.

(4) The power conferred by subsection (3) may be exercised—

(*a*) only if the officer has reasonable grounds for believing that the arrested person may have concealed on him anything of a kind mentioned in that subsection; and
(*b*) only to the extent that it is reasonably required for the purpose of discovering any such thing.

(5) A power conferred by this section to search a person is not to be read as authorising an officer to require a person to remove any of his clothing in public other than an outer coat, jacket or glove; but it does authorise the search of a person's mouth.

(6) An officer searching a person under subsection (2) may seize and retain anything he finds, if he has reasonable grounds for believing that that person might use it to cause physical injury to himself or to another person.

(7) An officer searching a person under subsection (3) may seize and retain anything he finds, if he has reasonable grounds for believing—

(*a*) that that person might use it to assist his escape from lawful custody; or
(*b*) that it is evidence which relates to the offence in question.

(8) Subsection (7)(*b*) does not apply to an item subject to legal privilege.

[Immigration Act 1971, s 28G, as inserted by the Immigration and Asylum Act 1999, s 134(1).]

8–17706H 28H. Searching persons in police custody. (1) This section applies if a person—

(*a*) has been arrested for an offence under this Part; and
(*b*) is in custody at a police station or in police detention at a place other than a police station.

(2) An immigration officer may, at any time, search the arrested person in order to see whether he has with him anything—

(*a*) which he might use to—

(i) cause physical injury to himself or others;
(ii) damage property;
(iii) interfere with evidence; or
(iv) assist his escape; or

(*b*) which the officer has reasonable grounds for believing is evidence relating to the offence in question.

(3) The power may be exercised only to the extent that the custody officer concerned considers it to be necessary for the purpose of discovering anything of a kind mentioned in subsection (2).

(4) An officer searching a person under this section may seize anything he finds, if he has reasonable grounds for believing that—

(*a*) that person might use it for one or more of the purposes mentioned in subsection (2)(*a*); or
(*b*) it is evidence relating to the offence in question.

(5) Anything seized under subsection (4)(*a*) may be retained by the police.

(6) Anything seized under subsection (4)(*b*) may be retained by an immigration officer.

(7) The person from whom something is seized must be told the reason for the seizure unless he is—

(*a*) violent or appears likely to become violent; or
(*b*) incapable of understanding what is said to him.

(8) An intimate search may not be conducted under this section.

(9) The person carrying out a search under this section must be of the same sex as the person searched.

(10) "Custody officer"—

(*a*) in relation to England and Wales, has the same meaning as in the Police and Criminal Evidence Act 1984;
(*b*) in relation to Scotland, means the officer in charge of a police station; and

(*c*) in relation to Northern Ireland, has the same meaning as in the Police and Criminal Evidence (Northern Ireland) Order 1989.

(11) "Intimate search"—

(*a*) in relation to England and Wales, has the meaning given by section 65 of the Act of 1984;

(*b*) in relation to Scotland, means a search which consists of the physical examination of a person's body orifices other than the mouth; and

(*c*) in relation to Northern Ireland, has the same meaning as in the 1989 Order.

(12) "Police detention"—

(*a*) in relation to England and Wales, has the meaning given by section 118(2) of the 1984 Act; and

(*b*) in relation to Northern Ireland, has the meaning given by Article 2 of the 1989 Order.

(13) In relation to Scotland, a person is in police detention if—

(*a*) he has been taken to a police station after being arrested for an offence; or

(*b*) he is arrested at a police station after attending voluntarily at the station, accompanying a constable to it or being detained under section 14 of the Criminal Procedure (Scotland) Act 1995,

and is detained there or is detained elsewhere in the charge of a constable, but is not in police detention if he is in court after being charged.

[Immigration Act 1971, s 28H, as inserted by the Immigration and Asylum Act 1999, s 135(1).]

8–17706I 28I. Seized material: access and copying. (1) If a person showing himself—

(*a*) to be the occupier of the premises on which seized material was seized, or

(*b*) to have had custody or control of the material immediately before it was seized,

asks the immigration officer who seized the material for a record of what he seized, the officer must provide the record to that person within a reasonable time.

(2) If a relevant person asks an immigration officer for permission to be granted access to seized material, the officer must arrange for him to have access to the material under the supervision—

(*a*) in the case of seized material within subsection (8)(*a*), of an immigration officer;

(*b*) in the case of seized material within subsection (8)(*b*), of a constable.

(3) An immigration officer may photograph or copy, or have photographed or copied, seized material.

(4) If a relevant person asks an immigration officer for a photograph or copy of seized material, the officer must arrange for—

(*a*) that person to have access to the material for the purpose of photographing or copying it under the supervision—

(i) in the case of seized material within subsection (8)(*a*), of an immigration officer;

(ii) in the case of seized material within subsection (8)(*b*), of a constable; or

(*b*) the material to be photographed or copied.

(5) A photograph or copy made under subsection (4)(*b*) must be supplied within a reasonable time.

(6) There is no duty under this section to arrange for access to, or the supply of a photograph or copy of, any material if there are reasonable grounds for believing that to do so would prejudice—

(*a*) the exercise of any functions in connection with which the material was seized; or

(*b*) an investigation which is being conducted under this Act, or any criminal proceedings which may be brought as a result.

(7) "Relevant person" means—

(*a*) a person who had custody or control of seized material immediately before it was seized, or

(*b*) someone acting on behalf of such a person.

(8) "Seized material" means anything—

(*a*) seized and retained by an immigration officer, or

(*b*) seized by an immigration officer and retained by the police,

under this Part.

[Immigration Act 1971, s 28I, as inserted by the Immigration and Asylum Act 1999, s 136(1).]

8–17706J 28J. Search warrants: safeguards. (1) The entry or search of premises under a warrant is unlawful unless it complies with this section and section 28K.

(2) If an immigration officer applies for a warrant, he must—

(*a*) state the ground on which he makes the application and the provision of this Act under which the warrant would be issued;

(*b*) specify the premises which it is desired to enter and search; and (*c*) identify, so far as is practicable, the persons or articles to be sought.

(3) In Northern Ireland, an application for a warrant is to be supported by a complaint in writing and substantiated on oath.

(4) Otherwise, an application for a warrant is to be made ex parte and supported by an information in writing or, in Scotland, evidence on oath.

(5) The officer must answer on oath any question that the justice of the peace or sheriff hearing the application asks him.

(6) A warrant shall authorise an entry on one occasion only.

(7) A warrant must specify—

(*a*) the name of the person applying for it;
(*b*) the date on which it is issued;
(*c*) the premises to be searched; and
(*d*) the provision of this Act under which it is issued.

(8) A warrant must identify, so far as is practicable, the persons or articles to be sought.

(9) Two copies of a warrant must be made.

(10) The copies must be clearly certified as copies.

(11) "Warrant" means a warrant to enter and search premises issued to an immigration officer under this Part or under paragraph 17(2) of Schedule 2.

[Immigration Act 1971, s 28J, as inserted by the Immigration and Asylum Act 1999, s 137.]

8–17706K 28K. Execution of warrants. (1) A warrant may be executed by any immigration officer.

(2) A warrant may authorise persons to accompany the officer executing it.

(3) Entry and search under a warrant must be—

(*a*) within one month from the date of its issue; and
(*b*) at a reasonable hour, unless it appears to the officer executing it that the purpose of a search might be frustrated.

(4) If the occupier of premises which are to be entered and searched is present at the time when an immigration officer seeks to execute a warrant, the officer must—

(*a*) identify himself to the occupier and produce identification showing that he is an immigration officer;
(*b*) show the occupier the warrant; and
(*c*) supply him with a copy of it.

(5) If—

(*a*) the occupier is not present, but
(*b*) some other person who appears to the officer to be in charge of the premises is present,

subsection (4) has effect as if each reference to the occupier were a reference to that other person.

(6) If there is no person present who appears to the officer to be in charge of the premises, the officer must leave a copy of the warrant in a prominent place on the premises.

(7) A search under a warrant may only be a search to the extent required for the purpose for which the warrant was issued.

(8) An officer executing a warrant must make an endorsement on it stating—

(*a*) whether the persons or articles sought were found; and
(*b*) whether any articles, other than articles which were sought, were seized.

(9) A warrant which has been executed, or has not been executed within the time authorised for its execution, must be returned—

(*a*) if issued by a justice of the peace in England and Wales, to the justices' chief executive appointed by the magistrates' court committee whose area includes the petty sessions area for which the justice acts;
(*b*) if issued by a justice of the peace in Northern Ireland, to the clerk of petty sessions for the petty sessions district in which the premises are situated;
(*c*) if issued by a justice of the peace in Scotland, to the clerk of the district court for the commission area for which the justice of the peace was appointed;
(*d*) if issued by the sheriff, to the sheriff clerk.

(10) A warrant returned under subsection (9)(*a*) must be retained for 12 months by the justices' chief executive.

(11) A warrant issued under subsection (9)(*b*) or (*c*) must be retained for 12 months by the clerk.

(12) A warrant returned under subsection (9)(*d*) must be retained for 12 months by the sheriff clerk.

(13) If during that 12 month period the occupier of the premises to which it relates asks to inspect it, he must be allowed to do so.

(14) "Warrant" means a warrant to enter and search premises issued to an immigration officer under this Part or under paragraph 17(2) of Schedule 2.
[Immigration Act 1971, s 28K, as inserted by the Immigration and Asylum Act 1999, s 138.]

8–17706L 28L. Interpretation of Part III. (1) In this Part, "premises" and "items subject to legal privilege" have the same meaning—

(*a*) in relation to England and Wales, as in the Police and Criminal Evidence Act 1984;
(*b*) in relation to Northern Ireland, as in the Police and Criminal Evidence (Northern Ireland) Order 1989"; and
(*c*) in relation to Scotland, as in section 412 of the Proceeds of Crime Act 2002.

(2) In this Part "business premises" means premises (or any part of premises) not used as a dwelling.

(3) In this Part "employee records" means records which show an employee's—

(*a*) name,
(*b*) date of birth,
(*c*) address,
(*d*) length of service,
(*e*) rate of pay, or
(*f*) nationality or citizenship.

(4) The Secretary of State may by order amend section 28CA(3)(a) to reflect a change in nomenclature.

(5) An order under subsection (4)—

(*a*) must be made by statutory instrument, and
(*b*) shall be subject to annulment in pursuance of a resolution of either House of Parliament.

[Immigration Act 1971, s 28L, as inserted by the Immigration and Asylum Act 1999, s 139(1), and amended by the Nationality, Immigration and Asylum Act, s 155, and the Proceeds of Crime Act 2002, s 456.]

PART IV
SUPPLEMENTARY

8–17706M 31A. *Procedural Requirements as to applications*

8–17707 32. General provisions as to Orders in Council, etc[1]. (1) Any power conferred by Part I of this Act to make an Order in Council or order (other than a deportation order) or to give any directions includes power to revoke or vary the Order in Council, order or directions.

(2) Any document purporting to be an order, notice or direction made or given by the Secretary of State for the purposes of the Immigration Acts and to be signed by him or on his behalf, and any document purporting to be a certificate of the Secretary of State so given and to be signed by him or on his behalf, shall be received in evidence, and shall, until the contrary is proved, be deemed to be made or issued by him.

(3) Prima facie evidence of any such order, notice, direction or certificate as aforesaid may, in any legal proceedings or other proceedings under the Immigration Acts, be given by the production of a document bearing a certificate purporting to be signed by or on behalf of the Secretary of State and stating that the document is a true copy of the order, notice, direction or certificate.

(4) Where an order under section 8(2) above applies to persons specified in a schedule to the order, or any direction of the Secretary of State given for the purposes of the Immigration Acts apply to persons specified in a schedule to the directions, prima facie evidence of the provisions of the order or directions other than the schedule and of any entry contained in the schedule may, in any legal proceedings or other proceedings under the Immigration Acts, be given by the production of a document purporting to be signed by or on behalf of the Secretary of State and stating that the document is a true copy of the said provisions and of the relevant entry.

(5) In subsection (4) "the Immigration Acts" has the meaning given by section 44 of the Asylum and Immigration (Treatment of Claimants, etc) Act 2004.

[Immigration Act 1971, s 32, as amended by the Immigration and Asylum Act 1999, Sch 14, and amended by the Nationality, Immigration and Asylum Act, s 158 and the Asylum and Immigration (Treatment of Claimants, etc) Act 2004, s 44.]

---

1. The amendments made to s 32 by sub-paras (2)(*a*) and (5) of Sch 14 to the Immigration and Asylum Act 1999, apply whenever the document in question was made or issued (Immigration and Asylum Act 1999, Sch 14, para 6).

8–17708 33. Interpretation. (1) For purposes of this Act, except in so far as the context otherwise requires—

"aircraft" includes hovercraft, "airport" includes hoverport and "port" includes airport;
"captain" means master (of a ship) or commander (of an aircraft);
"certificate of entitlement" means such a certificate as is referred to in section 3(9) above;*

"Convention adoption" has the same meaning as in the Adoption Act 1976 and the Adoption (Scotland) Act 1978 or in the Adoption and Children Act 2002;

"crew", in relation to a ship or aircraft, means all persons actually employed in the working or service of the ship or aircraft, including the captain, and "member of the crew" shall be construed accordingly;

"entrant" means a person entering or seeking to enter the United Kingdom and "illegal entrant" means a person—

(*a*) unlawfully entering or seeking to enter in breach of a deportation order or of the immigration laws, or

(*b*) entering or seeking to enter by means which include deception by another person,

and includes also a person who has entered as mentioned in paragraph (*a*) or (*b*) above;

"entry clearance" means a visa, entry certificate or other document which, in accordance with the immigration rules, is to be taken as evidence or the requisite evidence of a person's eligibility, though not a British citizen, for entry into the United Kingdom (but does not include a work permit);

"immigration laws" means this Act and any law for purposes similar to this Act which is for the time being or has before or after the passing of this Act) been in force in any part of the United Kingdom and Islands;

"immigration rules" means the rules for the time being laid down as mentioned in section 3(2) above;

"the Islands" means the Channel Islands and the Isle of Man, and "the United Kingdom and Islands" means the United Kingdom and the Islands taken together;

"legally adopted" means adopted in pursuance of an order made by any court in the United Kingdom and Islands, under a Convention adoption or by any adoption specified as an overseas adoption by order of the Secretary of State under section 87 of the Adoption and Children Act 2002;

"limited leave" and "indefinite leave" mean respectively leave under this Act to enter or remain in the United Kingdom which is, and one which is not, limited as to duration;

"settled" shall be construed in accordance with subsection (2A) below;

"ship" includes every description of vessel used in navigation;

"United Kingdom passport" means a current passport issued by the Government of the United Kingdom, or by the Lieutenant-Governor of any of the Islands, or by the Government of any territory which is for the time being a British overseas territory within the meaning of the British Nationality Act 1981;

"work permit" means a permit indicating, in accordance with the immigration rules, that a person named in it is eligible, though not a British citizen, for entry into the United Kingdom for the purpose of taking employment.

(1A) A reference to being an owner of a vehicle, ship or aircraft includes a reference to being any of a number of persons who jointly own it.

(2) It is hereby declared that, except as otherwise provided in this Act, a person is not to be treated for the purposes of any provision of this Act as ordinarily resident in the United Kingdom or in any of the Islands at a time when he is there in breach of the immigration laws[2].

(2A) Subject to section 8(5) above, references to a person being settled in the United Kingdom are references to his being ordinarily resident there without being subject under the immigration laws to any restriction on the period for which he may remain.

(3) The ports of entry for purposes of this Act, and the ports of exit for purposes of any Order in Council under section 3(7) above, shall be such ports as may from time to time be designated for the purpose by order of the Secretary of State made by statutory instrument[3].

(4) For the purposes of this Act, the question of whether an appeal is pending shall be determined in accordance with section 104 of the Nationality, Immigration and Asylum Act 2002 (pending appeals)—

(*a*) in relation to an appeal to the Special Immigration Appeals Commission, in accordance with section 7A of the Special Immigration Appeals Commission Act 1997;

(*b*) in any other case, in accordance with section 58(5) to (10) of the Immigration and Asylum Act 1999.

(5) This Act shall not be taken to supersede or impair any power exercisable by Her Majesty in relation to aliens by virtue of Her prerogative[4].

[Immigration Act 1971, s 33, as amended by the Adoption Act 1976, Sch 3, the British Nationality Act 1981, Sch 4, the Immigration Act 1988, Sch, SI 1990/2227, SI 1993/1813, the Asylum and Immigration Act 1996, Sch 2, the Immigration and Asylum Act 1999, Sch 14, the British Overseas Territories Act 2002, s 1(2), and the Nationality, Immigration and Asylum Act 2002, Sch 7 and the Adoption and Children Act 2002, Sch 3.]

1. The term "illegal entrant" is not confined to a person who enters the United Kingdom by clandestine means, thereby avoiding immigration controls, but includes a person who obtains leave to enter by the use of deception or fraud. Silence as to a material fact coupled with conduct can amount to deception or fraud, but the 1971 Act does not impose a positive

duty of candour on an applicant seeking leave to enter, so non-disclosure of relevant facts does not in itself constitute fraud or deception (*Khawaja v Secretary of State for the Home Department* [1984] AC 74, [1983] 1 All ER 765, HL).

2. A person who had illegally entered the country but who could no longer be prosecuted because a limitation period had expired, was still "in breach of the immigration laws"; (*Azam v Secretary of State for the Home Department* [1974] AC 18, [1973] 2 All ER 765, 137 JP 626). A person who has overstayed leave to enter is not lawfully resident and thus not ordinarily resident (*R v Secretary of State for the Home Department, ex p Marguerritte* [1983] QB 180, [1982] 3 All ER 909).

3. See the Immigration (Ports of Entry) Order 1987, SI 1987/177.

4. The Crown is entitled, by virtue of this prerogative, to intern an alien enemy as a prisoner of war (*R v Vine Street Police Station Superintendent, ex p Liebmann* [1916] 1 KB 268, 80 JP 49; *Ex p Weber* [1916] 1 AC 421, 80 JP 249 followed; *R v Knockaloe Camp Commandant, ex p Forman* (1917) 82 JP 41).

8–17709 36. *Power to extend to the Channel Islands and the Isle of Man*[1].

---

1. The Immigration (Isle of Man) Order, SI 1991/2630 amended by SI 1997/275, the Immigration (Jersey) Order, SI 1993/1797 amended by SI 2003/1252, and the Immigration (Guernsey) Order, SI 1993/1796, have been made.

8–17720

Section 4

SCHEDULE 2

ADMINISTRATIVE PROVISIONS AS TO CONTROL ON ENTRY ETC

(*Amended by the Criminal Justice Act 1972, Sch 6, the British Nationality Act 1981, Sch 4, the Immigration Act 1988, Sch, SI 1990/2227, SI 1993/1813, the Asylum and Immigration Act 1996, Schs 2 and 4, the Justices of the Peace Act 1997, Sch 5, the Immigration and Asylum Act 1999, ss 18, 19, 132(2), 134(2), 135(2), 136(2), 139(2), 140 and Schs 14 and 16, the Nationality, Immigration and Asylum Act 2002, ss 63, 64, 73 and 119 and Sch 7, the Courts Act 2003, Sch 8 and the Asylum and Immigration (Treatment of Claimants etc) Act 2004, ss 11, 16 and 18 and Sch 2.*)

PART I
GENERAL PROVISIONS

Immigration officers and medical inspectors

8–17721 1. (1) Immigration officers for the purposes of this Act shall be appointed by the Secretary of State, and he may arrange with the Commissioners of Customs and Excise for the employment of officers of customs and excise as immigration officers under this Act.

(2) Medical inspectors for the purposes of this Act may be appointed by the Secretary of State or, in Northern Ireland, by the Minister of Health and Social Services or other appropriate Minister of the Government of Northern Ireland in pursuance of arrangement made between that Minister and the Secretary of State, and shall be fully qualified medical practitioners.

(2A) The Secretary of State may direct that his function of appointing medical inspectors under sub-paragraph (2) is also to be exercisable by such persons specified in the direction who exercise functions relating to health in England or Wales.

(3) In the exercise of their functions under this Act immigration officers shall act in accordance with such instructions (not inconsistent with the immigration rules) as may be given them by the Secretary of State, and medical inspectors shall act in accordance with such instructions as may be given them by the Secretary of State or, in Northern Ireland, as may be given in pursuance of the arrangements mentioned in sub-paragraph (2) above by the Minister making appointments of medical inspectors in Northern Ireland.

(4) An immigration officer or medical inspector may board any ship or aircraft for the purpose of exercising his functions under this Act.

(5) An immigration officer, for the purpose of satisfying himself whether there are persons he may wish to examine under paragraph 2 below, may search any ship or aircraft and anything on board it, or any vehicle taken off a ship or aircraft on which it has been brought to the United Kingdom.

Examination by immigration officers, and medical examination

8–17722 2. (1) An immigration officer may examine[1] any persons who have arrived in the United Kingdom by ship, or aircraft (including transit passengers, members of the crew and others not seeking to enter the United Kingdom) for the purpose of determining—

(*a*) whether any of them is or is not a British citizen; and
(*b*) whether, if he is not, he may or may not enter the United Kingdom without leave; and
(*c*) whether, if he may not—
  (i) he has been given leave which is still in force,
  (ii) he should be given leave and for what period or on what conditions (if any), or
  (iii) he should be refused leave.

(2) Any such person, if he is seeking to enter the United Kingdom, may be examined also by a medical inspector or by any qualified person carrying out a test or examination required by a medical inspector.

(3) A person, on being examined under this paragraph by an immigration officer or medical inspector, may be required in writing by him to submit to further examination; but a requirement under this sub-paragraph shall not prevent a person who arrives as a transit passenger, or as a member of the crew of a ship or aircraft, or for the purpose of joining a ship or aircraft as a member of the crew, from leaving by his intended ship or aircraft.

Examination of persons who arrive with continuing leave

2A. (1) This paragraph applies to a person who has arrived in the United Kingdom with leave to enter which is in force but which was given to him before his arrival.

(2) He may be examined by an immigration officer for the purpose of establishing—

(*a*) whether there has been such a change in the circumstances of his case, since that leave was given, that it should be cancelled;

(*b*) whether that leave was obtained as a result of false information given by him or his failure to disclose material facts; or

(*c*) whether there are medical grounds on which that leave should be cancelled.

(2A) Where the person's leave to enter derives, by virtue of section 3A(3), from an entry clearance, he may also be examined by an immigration officer for the purpose of establishing whether the leave should be cancelled on the grounds that the person's purpose in arriving in the United Kingdom is different from the purpose specified in the entry clearance.

(3) He may also be examined by an immigration officer for the purpose of determining whether it would be conducive to the public good for that leave to be cancelled.

(4) He may also be examined by a medical inspector or by any qualified person carrying out a test or examination required by a medical inspector.

(5) A person examined under this paragraph may be required by the officer or inspector to submit to further examination.

(6) A requirement under sub-paragraph (5) does not prevent a person who arrives—

(*a*) as a transit passenger,

(*b*) as a member of the crew of a ship or aircraft, or

(*c*) for the purpose of joining a ship or aircraft as a member of the crew,

from leaving by his intended ship or aircraft.

(7) An immigration officer examining a person under this paragraph may by notice suspend his leave to enter until the examination is completed.

(8) An immigration officer may, on the completion of any examination of a person under this paragraph, cancel his leave to enter.

(9) Cancellation of a person's leave under sub-paragraph (8) is to be treated for the purposes of this Act and Part 5 of the Nationality, Immigration and Asylum Act 2002 (immigration and asylum appeals) as if he had been refused leave to enter at a time when he had a current entry clearance.

(10) A requirement imposed under sub-paragraph (5) and a notice given under sub-paragraph (7) must be in writing.

3. (1) An immigration officer may examine any person who is embarking or seeking to embark in the United Kingdom for the purpose of determining whether he is a British citizen and, if he is not, for the purpose of establishing his identity.

(2) So long as any Order in Council is in force under section 3(7) of this Act, an immigration officer may examine any person who is embarking or seeking to embark in the United Kingdom for the purpose of determining—

(*a*) whether any of the provisions of the Order apply to him; and

(*b*) whether, if so, any power conferred by the Order should be exercised in relation to him and in what way.

---

1. This is not limited to an examination at the port or airport of entry; see *Singh v Hammond* [1987] 1 All ER 829, [1987] 1 WLR 283.

Information and documents

8–17723 **4.** (1) It shall be the duty of any person examined under paragraph 2, 2A or 3 above to furnish to the person carrying out the examination all such information in his possession as that person may require for the purpose of his functions under that paragraph.

(2) A person on his examination under paragraph 2, 2A or 3 above by an immigration officer, if so required by the immigration officer—

(*a*) produce either a valid passport with photograph or some other document satisfactorily establishing his identity and nationality or citizenship; and

(*b*) declare whether or not he is carrying or conveying, or has carried or conveyed, documents of any relevant description specified by the immigration officer, and produce any documents of that description which he is carrying or conveying.

In paragraph (*b*), "relevant description" means any description appearing to the immigration officer to be relevant for the purposes of the examination.

(2A) An immigration officer may detain any passport or other document produced pursuant to sub-paragraph (2)(*a*) above until the person concerned is given leave to enter the United Kingdom or is about to depart or be removed following refusal of leave.

(3) Where under sub-paragraph (2)(*b*) above a person has been required to declare whether or not he is carrying or conveying, or has carried or conveyed, documents of any description,

(*a*) he and any baggage or vehicle belonging to him or under his control; and

(*b*) any ship, aircraft or vehicle in which he arrived in the United Kingdom,

may be searched with a view to ascertaining whether he is doing or, as the case may be, has done so by the immigration officer or a person acting under the directions of the officer:

Provided that no woman or girl shall be searched except by a woman.

(4) An immigration officer may examine any documents produced pursuant to sub-paragraph (2)(*b*) above or found on a search under sub-paragraph (3), and may for that purpose detain them for any period not exceeding seven days; and if on examination of any document so produced or found the immigration officer is of the opinion that it may be needed in connection with proceedings on an appeal under the Nationality, Immigration and Asylum Act 2002 or for an offence, he may detain it until he is satisfied that it will not be so needed.

5. The Secretary of State may by order made by statutory instrument[1] make provision requiring passengers disembarking or embarking in the United Kingdom, or any class of such passengers, to produce to an immigration officer, if so required, landing or embarkation cards in such form as the Secretary of State may direct, and for requiring the owners or agents of ships and aircraft to supply such cards to those passengers.

---

1. See the Immigration (Landing and Embarkation Cards) Order 1975, SI 1975/65, amended by SI 1993/1813.

Notice of leave to enter or of refusal of leave

8–17724 **6.** (1) Subject to sub-paragraph (3) below, where a person examined by an immigration officer under paragraph 2 above is to be given a limited leave to enter the United Kingdom or is to be refused leave, the notice giving or refusing leave shall be given not later than twenty-four hours after the conclusion of his examination (including any further examination) in pursuance of that paragraph; and if notice giving or refusing leave is not given him before the end of those twenty-four hours, he shall (if not a British citizen) be deemed to have been given leave to enter the United Kingdom for a period of six months subject to a condition prohibiting his taking employment and the immigration officer shall as soon as may be give him written notice of that leave.

(2) Where on a person's examination under paragraph 2 above he is given notice of leave to enter the United Kingdom, then at any time before the end of twenty-four hours from the conclusion of the examination he may be given a further notice in writing by an immigration officer cancelling the earlier notice and refusing him leave to enter.

(3) Where in accordance with this paragraph a person is given notice refusing him leave to enter the United Kingdom, that notice may at any time be cancelled by notice in writing given him by an immigration officer; and where a person is given a notice of cancellation under this sub-paragraph, and the immigration officer does not at the same time give him indefinite or limited leave to enter or require him to submit to further examination, he shall be deemed to have been given leave to enter for a period of six months subject to a condition prohibiting his taking employment and the immigration officer shall as soon as may be give him written notice of that leave.

(4) Where an entrant is a member of a party in charge of a person appearing to the immigration officer to be a responsible person, any notice to be given in relation to that entrant in accordance with this paragraph shall be duly given if delivered to the person in charge of the party.

Power to require medical examination after entry

8–17725 **7.** (1) This paragraph applies if an immigration officer examining a person under paragraph 2 decides—

(*a*) that he may be given leave to enter the United Kingdom; but
(*b*) that a further medical test or examination may be required in the interests of public health.

(2) This paragraph also applies if an immigration officer examining a person under paragraph 2A decides—

(*a*) that his leave to enter the United Kingdom should not be cancelled; but
(*b*) that a further medical test or examination may be required in the interests of public health.

(3) The immigration officer may give the person concerned notice in writing requiring him—

(*a*) to report his arrival to such medical officer of health as may be specified in the notice; and
(*b*) to attend at such place and time and submit to such test or examination (if any), as that medical officer of health may require.

(4) In reaching a decision under paragraph (*b*) of sub-paragraph (1) or (2), the immigration officer must act on the advice of—

(*a*) a medical inspector; or
(*b*) if no medical inspector is available, a fully qualified medical practitioner.

Removal of persons refused leave to enter and illegal entrants

8–17726 **8.** (1) Where a person arriving in the United Kingdom is refused leave to enter, an immigration officer may, subject to sub-paragraph (2) below—

(*a*) give the captain of the ship or aircraft in which he arrives directions requiring the captain to remove him from the United Kingdom in that ship or aircraft; or
(*b*) give the owners or agents of that ship or aircraft directions requiring them to remove him from the United Kingdom in any ship or aircraft specified or indicated in the directions, being a ship or aircraft of which they are the owners or agents; or
(*c*) give those owners or agents, or, where the person has arrived through the tunnel system, the Concessionaires, directions requiring them to make arrangements for his removal from the United Kingdom in any ship or aircraft specified or indicated in the directions to a county or territory so specified, being either—

(i) a country of which he is a national or citizen; of
(ii) a country or territory in which he has obtained a passport or other document of identity; or
(iii) a country or territory in which he embarked for the United Kingdom; or
(iv) a country or territory to which there is reason to believe that he will be admitted.

(2) No directions shall be given under this paragraph in respect of anyone after the expiration of two months beginning with the date on which he was refused leave to enter the United Kingdom (ignoring any period during which an appeal by him under the Immigration Acts is pending) except that directions may be given under sub-paragraph (1)(*b*) or (*c*) after the end of that period if the immigration officer has within that period given written notice to the owners or agents in question of his intention to give directions to them in respect of that person.

9. (1) Where an illegal entrant[1] is not given leave to enter or remain in the United Kingdom, an immigration officer may give any such directions in respect of him as in a case within paragraph 8 above are authorised by paragraph 8(1).

(2) Any leave to enter the United Kingdom which is obtained by deception shall be disregarded for the purposes of this paragraph.

10. (1) Where it appears to the Secretary of State either—

(*a*) that directions might be given in respect of a person under paragraph 8 or 9 above, but that it is not practicable for them to be given or that, if given, they would be ineffective; or
(*b*) that directions might have been given in respect of a person under paragraph 8 above but that the requirements of paragraph 8(2) have not been complied with;

then the Secretary of State may give to the owners or agents of any ship or aircraft any such directions in respect of that person as are authorised by paragraph 8(1)(*c*).

(2) Where the Secretary of state may give directions for a person's removal in accordance with sub-paragraph (1) above, he may instead give directions for his removal in accordance with arrangements to be made by the Secretary of State to any country or territory to which he could be removed under sub-paragraph (1).

(3) The costs of complying with any directions given under this paragraph shall be defrayed by the Secretary of State.

10A. Where directions are given in respect of a person under any of paragraphs 8 to 10 above, directions to the same effect may be given under that paragraph in respect of a member of the person's family.

11. A person in respect of whom directions are given under any of paragraphs 8 to 10 above may be placed, under the authority of an immigration officer, on board any ship or aircraft in which he is to be removed in accordance with the directions.

---

1. This applies to persons who had entered illegally before this Act came into force; see s 33(1), and *Azam v Secretary of State for the Home Department* [1974] AC 18, [1973] 2 All ER 765, 137 JP 626. Leave to enter given at a time when it was not known that an entry was illegal is to be treated as irrelevant for the purposes of para 9 (*R v Secretary of State for the Home Department, ex p Lapinid* [1984] 3 All ER 257, [1984] 1 WLR 1269, CA.

Seamen and aircrews

8–17727 **12.** (1) If, on a person's examination by an immigration officer under paragraph 2 above, the immigration officer is satisfied that he has come to the United Kingdom for the purpose of joining a ship or aircraft as a member of the crew then the immigration officer may limit the duration of any leave he gives that person to enter the United Kingdom by requiring him to leave the United Kingdom in a ship or aircraft specified or indicated by the notice giving leave.

(2) Where a person (not being a British citizen) arrives in the United Kingdom for the purpose of joining a ship or aircraft as a member of the crew and, having been given leave to enter as mentioned in sub-paragraph (1) above, remains beyond the time limited by that leave, or is reasonably suspected by an immigration officer of intending to do so, an immigration officer may—

(*a*) give the captain of that ship or aircraft directions requiring the captain to remove him from the United Kingdom in that ship or aircraft; or

(*b*) give the owners or agents of that ship or aircraft directions requiring them to remove him from the United Kingdom in any ship or aircraft specified or indicated in the directions, being a ship or aircraft of which they are the owners or agents; or

(*c*) give those owners or agents directions requiring them to make arrangements for his removal from the United Kingdom in any ship or aircraft specified or indicated in the directions to a country or territory so specified, being either—

(i) a country in which he is a national or citizen; or

(ii) a country or territory in which he has obtained a passport or other document of identity; or

(iii) a country or territory in which he embarked for the United Kingdom; or

(iv) a country or territory where he was engaged as a member of the crew of the ship or aircraft which he arrived in the United Kingdom to join; or

(v) a country or territory to which there is reason to believe that he will be admitted.

13. (1) Where a person being a member of the crew of a ship or aircraft is examined by an immigration officer under paragraph 2 above, the immigration officer may limit the duration of any leave he gives that person to enter the United Kingdom—

(*a*) in the manner authorised by paragraph 12(1) above; or

(*b*) if that person is to be allowed to enter the United Kingdom in order to receive hospital treatment, by requiring him, on completion of that treatment, to leave the United Kingdom in accordance with arrangements to be made for his repatriation; or

(*c*) by requiring him to leave the United Kingdom within a specified period in accordance with arrangements to be made for his repatriation.

(2) Where a person (not being a British citizen) arrives in the United Kingdom as a member of the crew of a ship or aircraft, and either—

(A) having lawfully entered the United Kingdom without leave by virtue of section 8(1) of this Act, he remains without leave beyond the time allowed by section 8(1), or is reasonably suspected by an immigration officer of intending to do so; or

(B) having been given leave limited as mentioned in sub-paragraph (1) above, he remains beyond the time limited by that leave, or is reasonably suspected by an immigration officer of intending to do so;

an immigration officer may—

(*a*) give the captain of the ship or aircraft in which he arrived directions requiring the captain to remove him from the United Kingdom in that ship or aircraft; or

(*b*) give the owners or agents of that ship or aircraft directions requiring them to remove him from the United Kingdom in any ship or aircraft or indicated in the directions, being a ship or aircraft of which they are the owners or agents; or

(*c*) give those owners or agents directions requiring them to make arrangements for his removal from the United Kingdom in any ship or aircraft specified or indicated in the directions to a country or territory so specified, being either—

(i) a country of which he is a national or citizen; or

(ii) a country or territory in which he has obtained a passport or other document of identity; or;

(iii) a country in which he embarked for the United Kingdom; or

(iv) a country or territory in which he was engaged as a member of the crew of the ship or aircraft in which he arrived in the United Kingdom; or

(v) a country or territory to which there is reason to believe that he will be admitted.

14. (1) Where it appears to the Secretary of State that directions might be given in respect of a person under paragraph 12 or 13 above, but that it is not practicable for them to be given or that, if given they would be ineffective, then the Secretary of State may give to the owners or agents of any ship or aircraft any such directions in respect of that person as are authorised by paragraph 12(2)(*c*) or 13(2)(*c*).

(2) Where the Secretary of State may give directions for a person's removal in accordance with sub-paragraph (1) above, he may instead give directions for his removal in accordance with arrangements to be made by the Secretary of State to any country or territory to which he could be removed under sub-paragraph (1).

(3) The costs of complying with any directions given under this paragraph shall be defrayed by the Secretary of State.

15. A person in respect of whom directions are given under any of paragraphs 12 to 14 above may be placed, under the authority of an immigration officer, on board any ship or aircraft in which he is to be removed in accordance with the directions.

Detention of persons liable to examination or removal

8–17728 **16.** (1) A person who may be required to submit to examination under paragraph 2 above may be detained under the authority of an immigration officer pending his examination and pending a decision to give or refuse him leave to enter[1].

(1A) A person whose leave to enter has been suspended under paragraph 2A may be detained under the authority of an immigration officer pending—

(*a*) completion of his examination under that paragraph; and
(*b*) a decision on whether to cancel his leave to enter.

(2) If there are reasonable grounds for suspecting that a person is someone in respect of whom directions may be given under any of paragraphs 8 to 10A or 12 to 14, that person may be detained under the authority of an immigration officer pending—

(*a*) a decision whether or not to give such directions;
(*b*) his removal in pursuance of any directions given.

(3) A person on board a ship or aircraft may, under the authority of an immigration officer, be removed from the ship or aircraft for detention under this paragraph; but if an immigration officer so requires the captain of a ship or aircraft shall prevent from disembarking in the United Kingdom any person who has arrived in the United Kingdom in the ship or aircraft and been refused leave to enter, and the captain may for that purpose detain him in custody on board the ship or aircraft.

(4) The captain of a ship or aircraft, if so required by an immigration officer, shall prevent from disembarking in the United Kingdom or before the directions for his removal have been fulfilled any person placed on board the ship or aircraft under paragraph 11 or 15 above, and the captain may for that purpose detain him in custody on board the ship or aircraft.

(4A) *Repealed.*

17. (1) A person liable to be detained under paragraph 16 above may be arrested[2] without warrant by a constable or by an immigration officer.

(2) If—

(*a*) a justice of the peace is by written information on oath satisfied that there is reasonable ground for suspecting that a person liable to be arrested under this paragraph is to be found on any premises; or
(*b*) in Scotland, a sheriff or a justice of the peace, having jurisdiction in the place where the premises are situated is by evidence on oath so satisfied;

he may grant a warrant[3] authorising any immigration officer or constable to enter, if need be by reasonable force, the premises named in the warrant for the purposes of searching for and arresting that person.

(3) Sub-paragraph (4) applies where an immigration officer or constable—

(*a*) enters premises in reliance on a warrant under sub-paragraph (2), and
(*b*) detains a person on the premises.

(4) A detainee custody officer may enter the premises, if need be by reasonable force, for the purpose of carrying out a search.

(5) In sub-paragraph (4)—

"detainee custody officer" means a person in respect of whom a certificate of authorisation is in force under section 154 of the Immigration and Asylum Act 1999 (c 33) (detained persons: escort and custody), and

"search" means a search under paragraph 2(1)(a) of Schedule 13 to that Act (escort arrangements: power to search detained person).

18. (1) Persons may be detained under paragraph 16 above in such places as the Secretary of State may direct (when not detained in accordance with paragraph 16 on board a ship or aircraft).

(2) Where a person is detained under paragraph 16, any immigration officer, constable or prison officer, or any other person authorised by the Secretary of State, may take all such steps as may be reasonably necessary for photographing, measuring or otherwise identifying him.

(2A) The power conferred by sub-paragraph (2) includes the power to take fingerprints.

(3) Any person detained under paragraph 16 may be taken in the custody of a constable, or of any person acting under the authority of an immigration officer, to and from any place where his attendance is required for the purpose of ascertaining his citizenship or nationality or of making arrangements for his admission to a country or territory other than the United Kingdom, or where he is required to be for any other purpose connected with the operation of this Act.

(4) A person shall be deemed to be in legal custody at any time when he is detained under paragraph 16 or is being removed in pursuance of sub-paragraphs (3) above.

19. (1) Where a person is refused leave to enter the United Kingdom and directions are given in respect of him under paragraph 8 or 10 above, then subject to the provisions of this paragraph the owners or agents of the ship or aircraft in which he arrived shall be liable to pay the Secretary of State on demand any expenses incurred by the latter in respect of the custody, accommodation or maintenance of that person for any period (not exceeding 14 days) after his arrival while he was detained or liable to be detained under paragraph 16 above.

(2) Sub-paragraph (1) above shall not apply to expenses in respect of a person who, when he arrived in the United Kingdom, held a certificate of entitlement or a current entry clearance or was the person named in a current work permit; and for this purpose a document purporting to be a certificate of entitlement, entry clearance or work permit is to be regarded as being one unless its falsity is reasonably apparent.

(3) If, before the directions for a person's removal under paragraph 8 or 10 above have been carried out, he is given leave to enter the United Kingdom, or if he is afterwards given that leave in consequence of the determination in his favour of an appeal under this Act (being an appeal against a refusal of leave to enter by virtue of which the directions were given), or it is determined on an appeal under this Act that he does not require leave to enter (being an appeal against a refusal of leave to enter by virtue of which the directions were given), or it is determined on an appeal under this Act that he does not require leave to enter (being an appeal occasioned by such a refusal), no sum shall be demanded under sub-paragraph (1) above for expenses incurred in respect of that person and any sum already demanded and paid shall be refunded.

(4) Sub-paragraph (1) above shall not have effect in relation to directions which in consequence of an appeal under this Act, have ceased to have effect or are for the time being of no effect; and the expenses to which that sub-paragraph applies include expenses in conveying the person in question to and from the place where he is detained or accommodated unless the journey is made for the purpose of attending an appeal by him under this Act.

20. (1) Subject to the provisions of this paragraph, in either of the following cases, that is to say—

(*a*) where directions are given in respect of an illegal entrant under paragraph 9 or 10 above; and

(*b*) where a person has lawfully entered the United Kingdom without leave by virtue of section 8(1) of this Act, but directions are given in respect of him under paragraph 13(2)(A) above or, in a case within paragraph 13(2)(A), under paragraph 14;

the owners or agents of the ship or aircraft in which he arrived in the United Kingdom shall be liable to pay the Secretary of State on demand any expenses incurred by the latter in respect of the custody, accommodation or maintenance of that person for any period (not exceeding 14 days) after his arrival while he was detained or liable to be detained under paragraph 16 above.

(1A) Sub-paragraph (1) above shall not apply to expenses in respect of an illegal entrant if he obtained leave to enter by deception and the leave has not been cancelled under paragraph 6(2) above.

(2) If, before the directions for a person's removal from the United Kingdom have been carried out, he is given leave to remain in the United Kingdom, no sum shall be demanded under sub-paragraph (1) above for expenses incurred in respect of that person and any sum already demanded and paid shall be refunded.

(3) Sub-paragraph (1) above shall not have effect in relation to direction which, in consequence of an appeal under this Act, are for the time being of no effect; and the expenses to which that sub-paragraph applies includes expenses in conveying the person in question to and from the place where he is detained or accommodated unless the journey is made for the purposes of attending an appeal by him under this Act.

---

1. The Secretary of State's policy providing for short term detention in reception centres was lawful in domestic law and does not breach art 5(1) of the European Convention on Human Rights (*R (on the application of Saadi) v Secretary of State for the Home Department* [2001] EWCA Civ 1512, [2001] 4 All ER 961.

2. This power of arrest is preserved by the Police and Criminal Evidence Act 1984, s 26 and Sch 2.

3. See also the Police and Criminal Evidence Act 1984, ss 15 and 16 (applications for, and execution of warrants) and ss 24 and 25 (arrest), in PART I: MAGISTRATES' COURTS, PROCEDURE, ante.

Temporary admission or release of persons liable to detention

8–17729 **21.** (1) A person liable to detention or detained under paragraph 16 above may, under the written authority of an immigration officer, be temporarily admitted to the United Kingdom without being detained or be released from detention; but this shall not prejudice a later exercise of the power to detain him.

(2) So long as a person is at large in the United Kingdom by virtue of this paragraph, he shall be subject to such restrictions as to residence, as to his employment or occupation and as to reporting to the police or an immigration officer as may from time to time be notified to him in writing by an immigration officer.

(2A) The provisions that may be included in restrictions as to residence imposed under sub-paragraph (2) include provisions of such a description as may be prescribed by regulations made by the Secretary of State.

(2B) The regulations may, among other things, provide for the inclusion of provisions—

(*a*) prohibiting residence in one or more particular areas;

(*b*) requiring the person concerned to reside in accommodation provided under section 4 of the Immigration and Asylum Act 1999 and prohibiting him from being absent from that accommodation except in accordance with the restrictions imposed on him.

(2C) The regulations may provide that a particular description of provision may be imposed only for prescribed purposes.

(2D) The power to make regulations conferred by this paragraph is exercisable by statutory instrument and includes a power to make different provision for different cases.

(2E) But no regulations under this paragraph are to be made unless a draft of the regulations has been laid before Parliament and approved by a resolution of each House.

(3) Sub-paragraph (4) below applies where a person who is at large in the United Kingdom by virtue of this paragraph is subject to a restriction as to reporting to an immigration officer with a view to the conclusion of his examination under paragraph 2 or 2A above.

(4) If the person fails at any time to comply with that restriction—

(*a*) an immigration officer may direct that the person's examination shall be treated as concluded at that time; but (*b*) nothing in paragraph 6 above shall require the notice giving or refusing him leave to enter the United Kingdom to be given within twenty-four hours after that time.

22. (1) The following, namely—

(*a*) a person detained under paragraph 16(1) above pending examination;

(*aa*) a person detained under paragraph 16(1A) above pending completion of his examination or a decision on whether to cancel his leave to enter; and

(*b*) a person detained under paragraph 16(2) above pending the giving of directions,

may be released on bail in accordance with this paragraph.

(1A) An immigration officer not below the rank of chief immigration officer or the Asylum and Immigration Tribunal may release a person so detained on his entering into a recognizance or, in Scotland, bail bond conditioned for his appearance before an immigration officer at a time and placed named in the recognizance or bail bond or at such other time and place as may in the meantime be notified to him in writing by an immigration officer.

(1B) Sub-paragraph (1)(*a*) above shall not apply unless seven days have elapsed since the date of the person's arrival in the United Kingdom.

(2) The conditions of a recognizance or bail bond taken under this paragraph may include conditions appearing to the immigration officer or the Asylum and Immigration Tribunal to be likely to result in the appearance of the person bailed at the required time and place; and any recognizance shall be with or without sureties as the officer or the Asylum and Immigration Tribunal may determine.

(3) In any case in which an immigration officer or the Asylum and Immigration Tribunal has power under this paragraph to release a person on bail, the officer or the Asylum and Immigration Tribunal may, instead of taking the bail, fix the amount and conditions of the bail (including the amount in which any sureties are to be bound) with a view to its being taken subsequently by any such person as may be specified by the officer or the Asylum and Immigration Tribunal; and on the recognizance or bail bond being so taken the person to be bailed shall be released.

23. (1) Where a recognizance entered into under paragraph 22 above appears to the Asylum and Immigration Tribunal to be forfeited, the Asylum and Immigration Tribunal may by order declare it to be forfeited and adjudge the persons bound thereby, whether as principal or sureties or any of them, to pay the sum in which they are respectively bound or such part of it, if any, as the Asylum and Immigration Tribunal thinks fit; and an order under this sub-paragraph shall specify a magistrates' court or, in Northern Ireland, court of summary jurisdiction, and—

(*a*) the recognizance shall be treated for the purposes of collection, enforcement and remission of the sum forfeited as having been forfeited by the court so specified; and

(*b*) the Asylum and Immigration Tribunal shall, as soon as practicable, give particulars of the recognizance to the proper officer of that court.*

(1A) In sub-paragraph (1) "proper officer" means—

(*a*) in relation to a magistrates' court in England and Wales, the designated officer for the court; and

(*b*) in relation to a court of summary jurisdiction in Northern Ireland, the clerk of the court.

(2) Where a person released on bail under paragraph 22 above as it applies in Scotland fails to comply with the terms of his bail bond, the Asylum and Immigration Tribunal may declare the bail to be forfeited, and any bail so forfeited shall be transmitted by the Asylum and Immigration Tribunal * to the sheriff court having jurisdiction in the area where the proceedings took place, and shall be treated as having been forfeited by that court.

(3) Any sum the payment of which is enforceable by a magistrates' court in England or Wales by virtue of this paragraph shall be treated for the purposes of section 38 of the Courts Act 2003 (aplication of receipts of deisnated officers) due under a recognizance forfeited by such a court.

(4) Any sum the payment of which is enforceable by virtue of this paragraph by a court of summary jurisdiction in Northern Ireland shall, for the purposes of section 20(5) of the Administration of Justice Act (Northern Ireland) 1954, be treated as a forfeited recognizance.

24. (1) An immigration officer or constable may arrest[1] without warrant a person who has been released by virtue of paragraph 22 above—

(*a*) if he has reasonable grounds for believing that that person is likely to break the condition of his recognizance or bail bond that he will appear at the time and place required or to break any other condition of it, or has reasonable ground to suspect that that person is breaking or has broken any such other condition; or

(*b*) if, a recognizance with sureties having been taken, he is notified in writing by any surety if the surety's belief that that person is likely to break the first-mentioned condition, and of the surety's wish for that reason to be relieved of his obligations as a surety;

and paragraph 17(2) above shall apply for the arrest of a person under this paragraph as it applies for the arrest of a person under paragraph 17.

(2) A person arrested under this paragraph—

(*a*) if not required by a condition on which he was released to appear before an immigration officer within twenty-four hours after the time of his arrest, shall as soon as practicable be brought before the Asylum and Immigration Tribunal or, if that is not practicable within those twenty-four hours, before in Engalnd and Wales, a justice of the peace, in Northern Ireland, a justice of the peace acting for the petty sessions area in which he is arrested or, in Scotland, the sheriff; and

(*b*) if required by such a condition to appear within those twenty-four hours before an immigration officer, shall be brought before that officer.

(3) Where a person is brought before the Asylum and Immigration Tribunal, a justice of the peace or the sheriff by virtue of sub-paragraph (2)(*a*), the Tribunal, justice of the peace or sheriff—

(*a*) if of the opinion that that person has broken or is likely to break any condition on which he was released, may either—

(i) direct that he be detained under the authority of the person by whom he was arrested; or

(ii) release him, on his original recognizance or on a new recognizance, with or without sureties, or, in Scotland, on his original bail or on new bail; and

(*b*) if not of that opinion, shall release him on his original recognizance or bail.

25. The power to make rules[2] of procedure conferred by section 106 of the Nationality, Immigration and Asylum Act 2002 (appeals) shall include power to make rules with respect to application to the Asylum and Immigration Tribunal under paragraphs 22 to 24 above and matters arising out of such applications.

---

1. This power of arrest is preserved by the Police and Criminal Evidence Act 1984, s 26 and Sch 2.
2. The Immigration Appeals (Procedure) Rules 1984, SI 1984/2041, amended by SI 1991/1545 and SI 1993/1662, and the Asylum Appeals (Procedure) Rules 1993, SI 1993/1661, have been made.

Entry and search of premises

8–17729A 25A. (1) This paragraph applies if—

(*a*) a person is arrested under this Schedule; or

(*b*) a person who was arrested by a constable (other than under this Schedule) is detained by an immigration officer under this Schedule.

(2) An immigration officer may enter and search any premises—

(*a*) occupied or controlled by the arrested person, or

(*b*) in which that person was when he was arrested, or immediately before he was arrested,

for relevant documents.

(3) The power may be exercised—

(*a*) only if the officer has reasonable grounds for believing that there are relevant documents on the premises;

(*b*) only to the extent that it is reasonably required for the purpose of discovering relevant documents; and

(*c*) subject to sub-paragraph (4), only if a senior officer has authorised its exercise in writing.

(4) An immigration officer may conduct a search under sub-paragraph (2)—

(*a*) before taking the arrested person to a place where he is to be detained; and

(*b*) without obtaining an authorisation under sub-paragraph (3)(*c*),

if the presence of that person at a place other than one where he is to be detained is necessary to make an effective search for any relevant documents.

(5) An officer who has conducted a search under sub-paragraph (4) must inform a senior officer as soon as is practicable.

(6) The officer authorising a search, or who is informed of one under sub-paragraph (5), must make a record in writing of—

(*a*) the grounds for the search; and

(*b*) the nature of the documents that were sought.

(7) An officer searching premises under sub-paragraph (2)—

(*a*) may seize and retain any documents he finds which he has reasonable grounds for believing are relevant documents; but

(*b*) may not retain any such document for longer than is necessary in view of the purpose for which the person was arrested.

(8) But sub-paragraph (7)(*a*) does not apply to documents which the officer has reasonable grounds for believing are items subject to legal privilege.

(9) "Relevant documents" means any documents which might—

(*a*) establish the arrested person's identity, nationality or citizenship; or

(*b*) indicate the place from which he has travelled to the United Kingdom or to which he is proposing to go.

(10) "Senior officer" means an immigration officer not below the rank of chief immigration officer.

Searching persons arrested by immigration officers

8–17729B 25B. (1) This paragraph applies if a person is arrested under this Schedule.

(2) An immigration officer may search the arrested person if he has reasonable grounds for believing that the arrested person may present a danger to himself or others.

(3) The officer may search the arrested person for—

(*a*) anything which he might use to assist his escape from lawful custody; or

(*b*) any document which might—

(i) establish his identity, nationality or citizenship; or

(ii) indicate the place from which he has travelled to the United Kingdom or to which he is proposing to go.

(4) The power conferred by sub-paragraph (3) may be exercised—

(*a*) only if the officer has reasonable grounds for believing that the arrested person may have concealed on him anything of a kind mentioned in that sub-paragraph; and

(*b*) only to the extent that it is reasonably required for the purpose of discovering any such thing.

(5) A power conferred by this paragraph to search a person is not to be read as authorising an officer to require a person to remove any of his clothing in public other than an outer coat, jacket or glove; but it does authorise the search of a person's mouth.

(6) An officer searching a person under sub-paragraph (2) may seize and retain anything he finds, if he has

reasonable grounds for believing that the person searched might use it to cause physical injury to himself or to another person.

(7) An officer searching a person under sub-paragraph (3)(*a*) may seize and retain anything he finds, if he has reasonable grounds for believing that he might use it to assist his escape from lawful custody.

(8) An officer searching a person under sub-paragraph (3)(*b*) may seize and retain anything he finds, other than an item subject to legal privilege, if he has reasonable grounds for believing that it might be a document falling within that sub-paragraph.

(9) Nothing seized under sub-paragraph (6) or (7) may be retained when the person from whom it was seized—

(*a*) is no longer in custody, or
(*b*) is in the custody of a court but has been released on bail.

Searching persons in police custody

8–17729C 25C. (1) This paragraph applies if a person—

(*a*) has been arrested under this Schedule; and
(*b*) is in custody at a police station.

(2) An immigration officer may, at any time, search the arrested person in order to ascertain whether he has with him—

(*a*) anything which he might use to—

(i) cause physical injury to himself or others;
(ii) damage property;
(iii) interfere with evidence; or
(iv) assist his escape; or

(*b*) any document which might—

(i) establish his identity, nationality or citizenship; or
(ii) indicate the place from which he has travelled to the United Kingdom or to which he is proposing to go.

(3) The power may be exercised only to the extent that the officer considers it to be necessary for the purpose of discovering anything of a kind mentioned in sub-paragraph (2).

(4) An officer searching a person under this paragraph may seize and retain anything he finds, if he has reasonable grounds for believing that—

(*a*) that person might use it for one or more of the purposes mentioned in sub-paragraph (2)(*a*); or
(*b*) it might be a document falling within sub-paragraph (2)(*b*).

(5) But the officer may not retain anything seized under sub-paragraph (2)(*a*)—

(*a*) for longer than is necessary in view of the purpose for which the search was carried out; or
(*b*) when the person from whom it was seized is no longer in custody or is in the custody of a court but has been released on bail.

(6) The person from whom something is seized must be told the reason for the seizure unless he is—

(*a*) violent or appears likely to become violent; or
(*b*) incapable of understanding what is said to him.

(7) An intimate search may not be conducted under this paragraph.
(8) The person carrying out a search under this paragraph must be of the same sex as the person searched.
(9) "Intimate search" has the same meaning as in section 28H(11).

Access and copying

8–17729D 25D. (1) If a person showing himself—

(*a*) to be the occupier of the premises on which seized material was seized, or
(*b*) to have had custody or control of the material immediately before it was seized,

asks the immigration officer who seized the material for a record of what he seized, the officer must provide the record to that person within a reasonable time.

(2) If a relevant person asks an immigration officer for permission to be granted access to seized material, the officer must arrange for that person to have access to the material under the supervision of an immigration officer.

(3) An immigration officer may photograph or copy, or have photographed or copied, seized material.

(4) If a relevant person asks an immigration officer for a photograph or copy of seized material, the officer must arrange for—

(*a*) that person to have access to the material under the supervision of an immigration officer for the purpose of photographing or copying it; or
(*b*) the material to be photographed or copied.

(5) A photograph or copy made under sub-paragraph (4)(*b*) must be supplied within a reasonable time.

(6) There is no duty under this paragraph to arrange for access to, or the supply of a photograph or copy of, any material if there are reasonable grounds for believing that to do so would prejudice—

(*a*) the exercise of any functions in connection with which the material was seized; or
(*b*) an investigation which is being conducted under this Act, or any criminal proceedings which may be brought as a result.

(7) "Relevant person" means—

(*a*) a person who had custody or control of seized material immediately before it was seized, or
(*b*) someone acting on behalf of such a person.

(8) "Seized material" means anything which has been seized and retained under this Schedule.

8–17729E 25E. Section 28L applies for the purposes of this Schedule as it applies for the purposes of Part III.

Supplementary duties of those connected with ships or aircraft or with ports

8–17730 26. (1) The owners or agents of a ship or aircraft employed to carry passengers for reward shall not, without the approval of the Secretary of State, arrange for the ship or aircraft to call at a port in the United Kingdom other than a port of entry for the purpose of disembarking passengers, if any of the passengers on board may not enter the United Kingdom without leave, or for the purpose of embarking passengers unless the owners or agents have reasonable cause to believe all of them to be British citizens.

(1A) Sub-paragraph (1) does not apply in such circumstances, if any, as the Secretary of State may by order prescribe.

(2) The Secretary of State may from time to time give written notice to the owners or agents of any ships or aircraft designating control areas for the embarkation or disembarkation of passengers in any port in the United Kingdom, and specifying the conditions and restrictions (if any) to be observed in any control area; and where by notice given to any owners or agents a control area is for the time being designated for the embarkation or disembarkation of passengers at any port, the owners or agents shall take all reasonable steps to secure that, in the case of their ships or aircraft, passengers do not embark or disembark, as the case may be, at the port outside the control area and that any conditions or restrictions notified to them are observed.

(3) The Secretary of State may also from time to time give to any persons concerned with the management of a port in the United Kingdom written notice designating control areas in the port and specifying conditions or restrictions to be observed in any control area; and any such person shall take all reasonable steps to secure that any conditions or restrictions as notified to him are observed.

(3A) The power conferred by sub-paragraph (1A) is exercisable by statutory instrument; and any such instrument shall be subject to annulment by a resolution of either House of Parliament.

27. (1) The captain of a ship or aircraft arriving in the United Kingdom—

(*a*) shall take such steps as may be necessary to secure that persons on board do not disembark there unless either they have been examined by an immigration officer, or they disembark in accordance with arrangements approved by an immigration officer, or they are members of the crew who may lawfully enter the United Kingdom without leave by virtue of section 8(1) of this Act; and
(*b*) where the examination of persons on board is to be carried out on the ship or aircraft, shall take such steps as may be necessary to secure that those to be examined are presented for the purpose in an orderly manner.

(2) The Secretary of State may by order made by statutory instrument[1] make provision for requiring captains of ships or aircraft arriving in the United Kingdom, or of such of them as arrive from or by way of countries or places specified in the order, to furnish to immigration officers—

(*a*) a passenger list showing the names and nationality or citizenship of passengers arriving on board the ship or aircraft;
(*b*) particulars of members of the crew of the ship or aircraft;

and for enabling an immigration officer to dispense with the furnishing of any such list or particulars.

---

1. See the Immigration (Particulars of Passengers and Crew) Order 1972, SI 1972/1667, amended by SI 1975/980 and SI 1993/1813.

Supplementary duties of the Concessionaires

8–17731 27A. *Repealed.*

Passenger information

8–17731A 27B. (1) This paragraph applies to ships or aircraft—

(*a*) which have arrived, or are expected to arrive, in the United Kingdom; or
(*b*) which have left, or are expected to leave, the United Kingdom.

(2) If an immigration officer asks the owner or agent ("the carrier") of a ship or aircraft for passenger information, the carrier must provide that information to the officer.

(3) The officer may ask for passenger information relating to—

(*a*) a particular ship or particular aircraft of the carrier;
(*b*) particular ships or aircraft (however described) of the carrier; or
(*c*) all of the carrier's ships or aircraft.

(4) The officer may ask for—

(*a*) all passenger information in relation to the ship or aircraft concerned; or
(*b*) particular passenger information in relation to that ship or aircraft.*

(5) A request under sub-paragraph (2)—

(*a*) must be in writing;
(*b*) must state the date on which it ceases to have effect; and
(*c*) continues in force until that date, unless withdrawn earlier by written notice by an immigration officer.

(6) The date may not be later than six months after the request is made.

(7) The fact that a request under sub-paragraph (2) has ceased to have effect as a result of sub-paragraph (5) does not prevent the request from being renewed.

(8) The information must be provided—

(*a*) in such form and manner as the Secretary of State may direct; and
(*b*) at such time as may be stated in the request.

(9) "Passenger information" means such information relating to the passengers carried, or expected to be carried, by the ship or aircraft as may be specified[1].

(10) "Specified"[1] means specified in an order made by statutory instrument by the Secretary of State.

(11) Such an instrument shall be subject to annulment in pursuance of a resolution of either House of Parliament.

***New sub-para (4A) inserted by the Asylum and Immigration (Treatment of Claimants etc) Act 2004, s 16 from a date to be appointed.**

1. The Immigration (Passenger Information) Order 2000, SI 2000/912 has been made.

Notification of non-EEA arrivals

8–17731B **27C.** (1) If a senior officer, or an immigration officer authorised by a senior officer, gives written notice to the owner or agent ("the carrier") of a ship or aircraft, the carrier must inform a relevant officer of the expected arrival in the United Kingdom of any ship or aircraft—

(*a*) of which he is the owner or agent; and
(*b*) which he expects to carry a person who is not an EEA national.

(2) The notice may relate to—

(*a*) a particular ship or particular aircraft of the carrier;
(*b*) particular ships or aircraft (however described) of the carrier; or
(*c*) all of the carrier's ships or aircraft.

(3) The notice—

(*a*) must state the date on which it ceases to have effect; and
(*b*) continues in force until that date, unless withdrawn earlier by written notice given by a senior officer.

(4) The date may not be later than six months after the notice is given.

(5) The fact that a notice under sub-paragraph (1) has ceased to have effect as a result of sub-paragraph (3) does not prevent the notice from being renewed.

(6) The information must be provided—

(*a*) in such form and manner as the notice may require; and
(*b*) before the ship or aircraft concerned departs for the United Kingdom.

(7) If a ship or aircraft travelling to the United Kingdom stops at one or more places before arriving in the United Kingdom, it is to be treated as departing for the United Kingdom when it leaves the last of those places.

(8) "Senior officer" means an immigration officer not below the rank of chief immigration officer.

(9) "Relevant officer" means—

(*a*) the officer who gave the notice under sub-paragraph (1); or
(*b*) any immigration officer at the port at which the ship or aircraft concerned is expected to arrive.

(10) "EEA national" means a national of a State which is a Contracting Party to the Agreement on the European Economic Area signed at Oporto on 2nd May 1992 as it has effect for the time being.

PART II
EFFECT OF APPEALS

8–17732 **28.** *Repealed.*

Grant of bail pending appeal

8–17733 **29.** (1) Where a person (in the following provisions of this Schedule referred to as "an appellant") has an appeal pending under Part 5 of the Nationality, Immigration and Asylum Act 2002 and is for the time being detained under Part I of this Schedule, he may be released on bail in accordance with this paragraph.

(2) An immigration officer not below the rank of chief immigration officer or a police officer not below the rank of inspector may release an appellant on his entering into a recognizance or, in Scotland, bail bond conditioned for his appearance before the Asylum and Immigration Tribunal or the Immigration Appeal Tribunal at a time and place named in the recognizance or bail bond.

(3) the Asylum and Immigration Tribunal may release an appellant on his entering into a recognizance or, in Scotland, bail bond conditioned for his appearance before the Tribunal or the Immigration Appeal Tribunal at a time and place named in the recognizance or bail bond.

(4) *Repealed.*

(5) The conditions of a recognizance or bail bond taken under this paragraph may include conditions appearing to the person fixing the bail to be likely to result in the appearance of the appellant at the time and place named; and any recognizance shall be with or without sureties as that person may determine.

(6) In any case in which the Tribunal has power or is required by this paragraph to release an appellant on bail, the Tribunal may, instead of taking the bail, fix the amount and conditions of the bail (including the amount in which any sureties are to be bound) with a view to its being taken subsequently by any such person as may be specified by the Tribunal; and on the recognizance or bail bond being so taken the appellant shall be released.

Restrictions on grant of bail

8–17734 **30.** (1) An appellant shall not be released under paragraph 29 above without the consent of the Secretary of State if directions for the removal of the appellant from the United Kingdom are for the time being in force, or the power to give such directions is for the time being exercisable.

(2) Notwithstanding paragraph 29(3) or (4) above, the Tribunal shall not be obliged to release an appellant

unless the appellant enters into a proper recognizance, with sufficient and satisfactory sureties if required, or in Scotland sufficient and satisfactory bail is found if so required; and the Tribunal shall not be obliged to release an appellant if it appears to the Tribunal —

(*a*) that the appellant, having on any previous occasion been released on bail (whether under paragraph 24 or under any other provision), has failed to comply with the conditions of any recognizance or bail bond entered into by him on that occasion;
(*b*) that the appellant is likely to commit an offence unless he is retained in detention;
(*c*) that the release of the appellant is likely to cause danger to public health;
(*d*) that the appellant is suffering from mental disorder and that his continued detention is necessary in his own interests or for the protection of any other person; or
(*e*) that the appellant is under the age of seventeen, that arrangements ought to be made for his care in the event of his release and that no satisfactory arrangements for that purpose have been made.

Forfeiture of recognizances

8–17735 **31.** (1) Where under paragraph 29 above (as it applies in England and Wales or in Northern Ireland) a recognizance is entered into conditioned for the appearance of an appellant before the Tribunal, and it appears to the Tribunal, to be forfeited, the Tribunal may by order declare it to be forfeited and adjudge the persons bound thereby, whether as principal or sureties, or any of them, to pay the sum in which they are respectively bound or such part of it, if any, as the Tribunal thinks fit.

(2) An order under this paragraph shall, for the purposes of this sub-paragraph, specify a magistrates' court or, in Northern Ireland, court of summary jurisdiction; and the recognizance shall be treated for the purposes of collection, enforcement and remission of the sum forfeited as having been forfeited by the court so specified.

(3) Where the Tribunal makes an order under this paragraph the Tribunal shall, as soon as practicable, give particulars of the recognizance to the proper officer of the court specified in the order in pursuance of sub-paragraph (2) above.

(3A) In sub-paragraph (3) "proper officer" means—

(*a*) in relation to a magistrates' court in England and Wales, the designated officer for the court; and
(*b*) in relation to a court of summary jurisdiction in Northern Ireland, the clerk of the court.

(4) Any sum the payment of which is enforceable by a magistrates' court in England or Wales by virtue of this paragraph shall be treated for the purposes of section 38 of the Courts Act 2003 (application of receipts of designated officers) as being due under a recognizance forfeited by such a court.

(5) Any sum the payment of which is enforceable by virtue of this paragraph by a court of summary jurisdiction in Northern Ireland shall, for the purposes of section 20(5) of the Administration of Justice Act (Northern Ireland) 1954, be treated as a forfeited recognizance.

32. Where under paragraph 29 above (as it applies in Scotland) a person released on bail fails to comply with the terms of a bail bond conditioned for his appearance before the Tribunal, the Tribunal may declare the bail to be forfeited, and any bail so forfeited shall be transmitted by the Tribunal to the sheriff court having jurisdiction in the area where the proceedings took place, and shall be treated as having been forfeited by that court.

Arrest of appellants released on bail

8–17736 **33.** (1) An immigration officer or constable may arrest[1] without warrant a person who has been released by virtue of this Part of this Schedule—

(*a*) if he has reasonable grounds for believing that that person is likely to break the condition of his recognizance or bail bond that he will appear at the time and place required or to break any other condition of it, or has reasonable ground to suspect that that person is breaking or has broken any such other condition; or
(*b*) if, a recognizance with sureties having been taken, he is notified in writing by any surety of the surety's belief that that person is likely to break the first-mentioned condition, and of the surety's wish for that reason to be relieved of his obligations as a surety;

and paragraph 17(2) above shall apply for the arrest of a person under this paragraph as it applies for the arrest of a person under paragraph 17.

(2) A person arrested under this paragraph—

(*a*) if not required by a condition on which he was released to appear before the Tribunal within twenty-four hours after the time of his arrest, shall as soon as practicable be brought before the Tribunal or, if that is not practicable within those twenty-four hours, before in England and Wales, a justice of the peace, in Northern Ireland, a justice of the peace acting for the petty sessions area in which he is arrested or, in Scotland, the sheriff; and
(*b*) if required by such a condition to appear within those twenty-four hours before the Tribunal, shall be brought before it.

(3) Where a person is brought before the Asylum and Immigration Tribunal, a justice of the peace or the sheriff by virtue of sub-paragraph (2)(*a*), the Tribunal, justice of the peace or sheriff—

(*a*) if of the opinion that that person has broken or is likely to break any condition on which he was released, may either—
   (i) direct that he be detained under the authority of the person by whom he was arrested; or
   (ii) release him on his original recognizance or on a new recognizance, with or without sureties, or, in Scotland, on his original bail or on new bail; and
(*b*) if not of that opinion, shall release him on his original recognizance or bail.

1. This power of arrest is preserved by the Police and Criminal Evidence Act 1984, s 26 and Sch 2.

Grant of bail pending removal

8–17737 **34.** (1) Paragraph 22 above shall apply in relation to a person—

(*a*) directions for whose removal from the United Kingdom are for the time being in force; and
(*b*) who is for the time being detained under Part I of this Schedule,

as it applies in relation to a person detained under paragraph 16(1) above pending examination, detained under paragraph 16(1A) above pending completion of his examination or a decision on whether to cancel his leave to enter or detained under paragraph 16(2) above pending the giving of directions.

(2) Paragraphs 23 to 25 above shall apply as if any reference to paragraph 22 above included a reference to that paragraph as it applies by virtue of this paragraph.

8–17738

Section 5 SCHEDULE 3

SUPPLEMENTARY PROVISIONS AS TO DEPORTATION

(*As amended by the Criminal Justice Act 1982, Sch 10, the Immigration Act 1988, Sch, the Asylum and Immigration Act 1996, Sch 2, the Immigration and Asylum Act 1999, Schs 14 and 16, the Nationality, Immigration and Asylum Act 2002,s 54 and Sch 7 and the Asylum and Immigration (Treatment of Claimants etc) Act 2004, s 34.*)

Removal of persons liable to deportation

8–17739 **1.** (1) Where a deportation order is in force against any person, the Secretary of State may give directions for his removal to a country or territory specified in the directions being either—

(*a*) a country of which he is a national or citizen; or
(*b*) a country or territory to which there is reason to believe that he will be admitted.

(2) The directions under sub-paragraph (1) above may be either—

(*a*) directions given to the captain of a ship or aircraft about to leave the United Kingdom requiring him to remove the person in question in that ship or aircraft; or
(*b*) directions given to the owners or agents of any ship or aircraft requiring them to make arrangements for his removal in a ship or aircraft specified or indicated in the directions; or
(*c*) directions for his removal in accordance with arrangements to be made by the Secretary of State.

(3) In relation to directions given under this paragraph, paragraphs 11 and 16(4) of Schedule 2 to this Act shall apply, with the substitution of references to the Secretary of State for references to an immigration officer, as they apply in relation to directions for removal given under paragraph (8) of that Schedule.

(4) The Secretary of State, if he thinks fit, may apply in or towards payment of the expenses of or incidental to the voyage from the United Kingdom of a person against whom a deportation order is in force, or the maintenance until departure of such a person and his dependants, if any, any money belonging to that person; and except so far as they are paid as aforesaid, those expenses shall be defrayed by the Secretary of State.

Detention or control pending deportation

8–17740 **2.** (1) Where a recommendation for deportation made by a court is in force in respect of any person, and that person is not detained in pursuance of the sentence or order of any court, he shall, unless the court by which the recommendation is made otherwise directs[2], or a direction is given under sub-paragraph (1A) below, be detained pending the making of a deportation order in pursuance of the recommendation, unless the Secretary of State directs him to be released pending further consideration of his case or he is released on bail.

(1A) Where—

(*a*) a recommendation for deportation made by a court on conviction of a person is in force in respect of him; and
(*b*) he appeals against his conviction or against that recommendation,

the powers that the court determining the appeal may exercise include power to direct him to be released without setting aside the recommendation.

(2) Where notice has been given to a person in accordance with regulations under section 105 of the Nationality, Immigration and Asylum Act 2002 (notice of decision) of a decision to make a deportation order against him, and he is not detained in pursuance of the sentence or order of a court, he may be detained under the authority of the Secretary of State pending the making of the deportation order.

(3) Where a deportation order is in force against any person, he may be detained under the authority of the Secretary of State pending his removal or departure from the United Kingdom (and if already detained by virtue of sub-paragraph (1) or (2) above when the order is made, shall continue to be detained unless he is released on bail or the Secretary of State directs otherwise).

(4) In relation to detention under sub-paragraph (2) or (3) above, paragraphs 17, 18 and 25A to 25E of Schedule 2 to this Act shall apply as they apply in relation to detention under paragraph 16 of that Schedule.

(4A) Paragraphs 22 to 25 of Schedule 2 to this Act apply in relation to a person detained under sub-paragraph (1), (2) or (3) as they apply in relation to a person detained under paragraph 16 of that Schedule.

(5) A person to whom this sub-paragraph applies shall be subject to such restrictions as to residence, as to his employment or occupation and as to reporting to the police or an immigration officer as may from time to time be notified to him in writing by the Secretary of State.

(6) The persons to whom sub-paragraph (5) above applies are—

(*a*) a person liable to be detained under sub-paragraph (1) above, while by virtue of a direction of the Secretary of State he is not so detained; and
(*b*) a person liable to be detained under sub-paragraph (2) or (3) above, while he is not so detained.

---

1. So where the original recommendation was made by a circuit judge, only he will have the power subsequently to release on bail, and not the court to which an appeal is unsuccessfully taken (*R v Zaman* (1975) 119 Sol Jo 657). But in *R*

v Governor of Holloway Prison, ex p Giambi [1982] 1 All ER 434, [1982] 1 WLR 535, it was held that the words "released on bail by any court having power so to release him" related to a court which was seized of the question of deportation, whether it be the recommending court, a Crown Court on appeal or a judge of the High Court exercising its inherent jurisdiction. Moreover, in the case of an appeal from justices the Crown Court has power under s 48(2)(c) of the Supreme Court Act 1981 to make any order which the justices could have made; accordingly, applying the provisions of para 2(1) of this Schedule the Crown Court has power to release a person pending the Home Secretary's decision (*R v Inner London Crown Court, ex p Obajuwana* (1979) 69 Cr App Rep 125).

2. See note 2 to s 6(1), ante.

Effect of appeals

8–17741 **3.** So far as they relate to an appeal under section 82(1) of the Nationality, Immigration and Asylum Act 2002 against a decision of the kind referred to in section 82(2)(j) or (k) of that Act (decision to make deportation order and refusal to revoke deportation order), paragraphs 29 to 33 of Schedule 2 to this Act shall apply for the purposes of this Schedule as if the reference in paragraph 29(1) to Part I of that Schedule were a reference to this Schedule.

Powers of courts pending deportation

8–17750 **4.** Where the release of a person recommended for deportation is directed by a court, he shall be subject to such restrictions as to residence and as to reporting to the police as the court may direct.

5. (1) On an application made—

(*a*) by or on behalf of a person recommended for deportation whose release was so directed; or
(*b*) by a constable; or
(*c*) by an immigration officer,

the appropriate court shall have the powers specified in sub-paragraph (2) below.

(2) The powers mentioned in sub-paragraph (1) above are—

(*a*) if the person to whom the application relates is not subject to any such restrictions imposed by a court as are mentioned in paragraph 4 above, to order that he shall be subject to any such restrictions as the court may direct; and
(*b*) if he is subject to such restrictions imposed by a court by virtue of that paragraph or this paragraph—
 (i) to direct that any of them shall be varied or shall cease to have effect; or
 (ii) to give further directions as to his residence and reporting.

6. (1) In this Schedule "the appropriate court" means, except in a case to which sub-paragraph (2) below applies, the court which directed release.

(2) This sub-paragraph applies where the court which directed release was—

(*a*) the Crown Court;
(*b*) the Court of Appeal;
(*c*) the High Court of Justiciary;
(*d*) the Crown Court in Northern Ireland; or
(*e*) the Court of Appeal in Northern Ireland.*

(3) Where the Crown Court* or the Crown Court in Northern Ireland directed release, the appropriate court is—

(*a*) the court that directed release; or
(*b*) a magistrates' court acting for the commission area* or county court division where the person to whom the application relates resides.

(4) Where the Court of Appeal or the Court of Appeal in Northern Ireland gave the direction, the appropriate court is the Crown Court or the Crown Court in Northern Ireland, as the case may be.

(5) Where the High Court of Justiciary directed release, the appropriate court is—

(*a*) that court; or
(*b*) in a case where release was directed by that court on appeal, the court from which the appeal was made.

7. (1) A constable or immigration officer may arrest without warrant any person who is subject to restrictions imposed by a court under this Schedule and who at the time of the arrest is in the relevant part of the United Kingdom—

(*a*) if he has reasonable grounds to suspect that that person is contravening or has contravened any of those restrictions; or
(*b*) if he has reasonable grounds for believing that that person is likely to contravene any of them.

(2) In sub-paragraph (1) above "the relevant part of the United Kingdom" means—

(*a*) England and Wales, in a case where a court with jurisdiction in England or Wales imposed the restrictions;
(*b*) Scotland, in a case where a court with jurisdiction in Scotland imposed them; and
(*c*) Northern Ireland, in a case where a court in Northern Ireland imposed them.

8. (1) A person arrested in England or Wales or* Northern Ireland in pursuance of paragraph 7 above shall be brought as soon as practicable and in any event within 24 hours after his arrest before a justice of the peace for the petty sessions area or district in which he was arrested.

(2) In reckoning for the purposes of this paragraph any period of 24 hours, no account shall be taken of Christmas Day, Good Friday or any Sunday.

9. *Scotland.*

10. Any justice of the peace or court before whom a person is brought by virtue of paragraph 8 or 9 above—

(*a*) if of the opinion that that person is contravening, has contravened or is likely to contravene any restriction imposed on him by a court under this Schedule, may direct—

(i) that he be detained; or

(ii) that he be released subject to such restrictions as to his residence and reporting to the police as the court may direct; and

(*b*) if not of that opinion, shall release him without altering the restrictions as to his residence and his reporting to the police.

***Words substituted and sub-para (2A) inserted by the Courts Act 2003, Sch 8 from a date to be appointed.**

Section 9

SCHEDULE 4

INTEGRATION WITH UNITED KINGDOM LAW OF IMMIGRATION LAW OF ISLANDS

(*As amended by the British Nationality Act 1981, Sch 4 and the Immigration and Asylum Act 1999, Sch 14.*)

Leave to enter

8–17752 **1.** (1) Where under the immigration laws of any of the Islands a person is or has been given leave to enter or remain in the island, or is or has been refused leave, this Act shall have effect in relation to him, if he is not a British citizen, as if the leave were leave (of like duration) given under this Act to enter or remain in the United Kingdom, or, as the case may be, as if he had under this Act been refused leave to enter the United Kingdom.

(2) Where under the immigration laws of any of the Islands a person has a limited leave to enter or remain in the island subject to any such conditions as are authorised in the United Kingdom by section 3(1) of this Act (being conditions imposed by notice given to him, whether the notice of leave or a subsequent notice), then on his coming to the United Kingdom this Act shall apply, if he is not a British citizen, as if those conditions related to his stay in the United Kingdom and had been imposed by notice under this Act.

(3) Without prejudice to the generality of sub-paragraphs (1) and (2) above, anything having effect in the United Kingdom by virtue of either of those sub-paragraphs may in relation to the United Kingdom be varied or revoked under this Act in like manner, and subject to the like appeal (if any), as if it had originated under this Act as mentioned in that sub-paragraph.

(4) Where anything having effect in the United Kingdom by virtue of sub-paragraph (1) or (2) above ceases to have effect or is altered in effect as mentioned in sub-paragraph (3) or otherwise by anything done under this Act, sub-paragraph (1) or (2) shall not thereafter apply to it or, as the case may be, shall apply to it as so altered in effect.

(5) Nothing in this paragraph shall be taken as conferring on a person a right of appeal under this Act against any decision or action taken in any of the Islands.

2. Notwithstanding section 3(4) of this Act, leave given to a person under this Act to enter or remain in the United Kingdom shall not continue to apply on his return to the United Kingdom after an absence if he has during that absence entered any of the Islands in circumstances in which he is required under the immigration laws of that island to obtain leave to enter.

Deportation

8–17753 **3.** (1) This Act has effect in relation to a person who is subject to an Islands deportation order as if the order were a deportation order made against him under this Act.

(2) Sub-paragraph (1) does not apply if the person concerned is—

(*a*) a British citizen;

(*b*) an EEA national;

(*c*) a member of the family of an EEA national; or

(*d*) a member of the family of a British citizen who is neither such a citizen nor an EEA national.

(3) The Secretary of State does not, as a result of sub-paragraph (1), have power to revoke an Islands deportation order.

(4) In any particular case, the Secretary of State may direct that paragraph (*b*), (*c*) or (*d*) of sub-paragraph (2) is not to apply in relation to the Islands deportation order.

(5) Nothing in this paragraph makes it unlawful for a person in respect of whom an Islands deportation order is in force in any of the Islands to enter the United Kingdom on his way from that island to a place outside the United Kingdom.

(6) "Islands deportation order" means an order made under the immigration laws of any of the Islands under which a person is, or has been, ordered to leave the island and forbidden to return.

(7) Subsections (10) and (12) to (14) of section 80 of the Immigration and Asylum Act 1999 apply for the purposes of this section as they apply for the purposes of that section.

Illegal entrants

8–17754 **4.** Notwithstanding anything in section (1)(3) of this Act, it shall not be lawful for a person who is not a British citizen to enter the United Kingdom from any of the Islands where his presence was unlawful under the immigration laws of that island, unless he is given leave to enter.

British Nationality Act 1981[1]

(1981 c 61)

PART I[2]

BRITISH CITIZENSHIP

8–17860 The Act makes provision for the acquisition of British citizenship by those born in the United Kingdom to a parent who is a British citizen or who is settled in the United Kingdom; by foundlings;

by persons born in the United Kingdom one of whose parents subsequently becomes settled here or a British citizen; and by children adopted by an order of a court in the United Kingdom (s 1). British citizenship may also be acquired by descent (s 2); by registration by the Secretary of State of a minor (s 3); by registration of a person who is a British Dependent Territories[3] citizen, a British Overseas citizen, a British subject under the Act or a British protected person (s 4); by registration of a British Dependent Territories citizen who falls to be treated as a national of the United Kingdom for the purposes of the Community Treaties (s 5) and by naturalisation[4] (s 6). Other special cases for acquiring British citizenship after commencement by virtue of residence in the United Kingdom or relevant employment, marriage, father's citizenship etc, or following renunciation of citizenship of the United Kingdom and Colonies are provided for by the Act (ss 8–10). Subject to certain qualifications, a person who immediately before commencement of the Act[5] (a) was a citizen of the United Kingdom and Colonies; and (b) had the right of abode in the United Kingdom under the Immigration Act 1971 at commencement became a British citizen (s 11). Provision is made for renunciation and resumption of British citizenship (ss 12 and 13), and the meaning of British citizen "by descent" is defined (s 14).

1. This Act makes fresh provision about citizenship and nationality, and amends the Immigration Act 1971 as regards the right of abode in the United Kingdom. Only those provisions of the Act which are relevant to magistrates' courts, are printed in full in this work.

The British Nationality (Falkland Islands) Act 1983 makes further provision for the acquisition of British citizenship by persons having connections with the Falkland Islands.

The British Nationality (Hong Kong) Act 1990 provides for the acquisition of British citizenship by selected Hong Kong residents, their spouses and minor children.

2. Part I contains ss 1–14.

3. "Dependent territory" means a territory mentioned in Sch 6 (amended by SI 2001/3497) (s 50); namely—Anguilla, Bermuda, British Antarctic Territory, British Indian Ocean Territory, Cayman Islands, Falkland Islands, Gibraltar, Hong Kong, Montserrat, Pitcairn, Henderson, Ducie and Oeno Islands, St. Christopher and Nevis, St. Helena and Dependencies, South Georgia and the South Sandwich Islands, The Sovereign Base Areas of Akrotiri and Dhekelia (that is to say the areas mentioned in s 2(1) of the Cyprus Act 1960), Turks and Caicos Islands and Virgin Islands.

4. Schedule 1 contains requirements for naturalisation.

5. This was 1 January 1983.

PART II[1]

BRITISH DEPENDENT TERRITORIES CITIZENSHIP

8–17861 The provisions relating to citizenship of the British Dependent territories[14] are analogous to those set out above for British citizenship, with references to dependencies being substituted for those to the United Kingdom (ss 15–25).

1. Part II contains ss 15–25.

PART III[1]

BRITISH OVERSEAS CITIZENSHIP

8–17862 A citizen of the United Kingdom and Colonies, who did not at the commencement of the Act become a British Citizen or a citizen of the British Dependent Territories, became a British Overseas citizen (s 26). The Secretary of State may, if he thinks fit, register a minor as a British Overseas citizen (s 27). A woman whose husband has become a British Overseas citizen may in certain circumstances apply for registration as a British Overseas citizen (s 28). British Overseas citizenship may be the subject of a declaration of renunciation in accordance with s 12 (s 29).

1. Part III contains ss 26–29.

PART IV[1]

BRITISH SUBJECTS

8–17863 British subjects without citizenship under the British Nationality Act 1948, and women who were registered as British subjects under the British Nationality Act 1965 continue to be British subjects (s 30). The Act makes further provision with respect to registration as a British subject and the renunciation and loss of the status of British subject (ss 31–35).

1. Part IV contains ss 30–35.

PART V[1]

MISCELLANEOUS AND SUPPLEMENTARY

8–17864 The provisions of Schedule 2 shall have effect for the purpose of reducing statelessness (s 36). Every person who—(a) under this Act is a British citizen, a British Dependent Territories citizen, a British Overseas citizen or a British subject; or (b) under any enactment for the time being in force in any country mentioned in Schedule 3[2] is a citizen of that country, shall have the status of a Commonwealth citizen (s 37). Her Majesty may by Order[3] in Council made in relation to any territory which was at any time before the commencement of this Act (a) a protectorate or protected state; or (b) a United Kingdom trust territory, declare to be British protected persons for the purposes of this Act any class of persons who are connected with that territory and are not citizens of any country mentioned in Schedule 3[2] which consists of or includes that territory (s 38).

1. Part V contains ss 36–53.
2. The countries mentioned in Sch 3, as amended, are as follows—Antigua and Barbuda, Australia, The Bahamas, Bangladesh, Barbados, Belize, Botswana, Cameroon, Canada, Republic of Cyprus, Dominica, Fiji, The Gambia, Ghana, Grenada, Guyana, India, Jamaica, Kenya, Kiribati, Lesotho, Malawi, Malaysia, Maldives, Malta, Mauritius, Mozambique, Namibia, Nauru, New Zealand, Nigeria, Papua New Guinea, Pakistan, Saint Lucia, Saint Vincent and the Grenadines, Seychelles, Sierra Leone, Singapore, Solomon Islands, South Africa, Sri Lanka, Swaziland, Tanzania, Tonga, Trinidad and Tobago, Tuvalu, Uganda, Vanuatu, Western Samoa, Zambia and Zimbabwe.
3. See the British Protectorates, Protected States and Protected Persons Order 1982, SI 1982/1070.

8–17865 40. Deprivation of citizenship[1]. (1) In this section a reference to a person's "citizenship status" is a reference to his status as—

(*a*) a British citizen,
(*b*) a British overseas territories citizen,
(*c*) a British Overseas citizen,
(*d*) a British National (Overseas),
(*e*) a British protected person, or
(*f*) a British subject.

(2) The Secretary of State may by order deprive a person of a citizenship status if the Secretary of State is satisfied that the person has done anything seriously prejudicial to the vital interests of—

(*a*) the United Kingdom, or
(b) a British overseas territory.

(3) The Secretary of State may by order deprive a person of a citizenship status which results from his registration or naturalisation if the Secretary of State is satisfied that the registration or naturalisation was obtained by means of—

(*a*) fraud,
(*b*) false representation, or
(*c*) concealment of a material fact.

(4) The Secretary of State may not make an order under subsection (2) if he is satisfied that the order would make a person stateless.

(5) Before making an order under this section in respect of a person the Secretary of State must give the person written notice specifying—

(*a*) that the Secretary of State has decided to make an order,
(*b*) the reasons for the order, and
(*c*) the person's right of appeal under section 40A(1) or under section 2B of the Special Immigration Appeals Commission Act 1997 (c 68).

(6) Where a person acquired a citizenship status by the operation of a law which applied to him because of his registration or naturalisation under an enactment having effect before commencement, the Secretary of State may by order deprive the person of the citizenship status if the Secretary of State is satisfied that the registration or naturalisation was obtained by means of—

(*a*) fraud,
(*b*) false representation, or
(*c*) concealment of a material fact.

[British Nationality Act 1981, s 40 as substituted by the Nationality, Immigration and Asylum Act 2002, s 4(1).]

1. See also the British Citizenship (Deprivation) Rules 1982, SI 1982/988, the British Dependent Territories Citizenship (Deprivation) Order 1982, SI 1982/989 and the Status of British Nationals (Overseas) (Deprivation) Rules 1986, SI 1986/2176.

8–17865A 40A. Deprivation of citizenship: appeal. (1) A person who is given notice under section 40(5) of a decision to make an order in respect of him under section 40 may appeal against the decision to the Asylum and Immigration Tribunal.

(2) Subsection (1) shall not apply to a decision if the Secretary of State certifies that it was taken wholly or partly in reliance on information which in his opinion should not be made public—

(*a*) in the interests of national security,
(*b*) in the interests of the relationship between the United Kingdom and another country, or
(*c*) otherwise in the public interest.

(3) The following provisions of the Nationality, Immigration and Asylum Act 2002 (c 41) shall apply in relation to an appeal under this section as they apply in relation to an appeal under section 82 or 83 of that Act—

(*a*) section 87 (successful appeal: direction) (for which purpose a direction may, in particular, provide for an order under section 40 above to be treated as having had no effect),
(*b*) sections 103A to 103E (review and appeal),
(*c*) section 106 (rules), and
(*d*) section 107 (practice directions).

(6)–(8) *Repealed.*

[British Nationality Act 1981, s 40A, as inserted by the Nationality, Immigration and Asylum Act 2002, s 4 and Sch 2.]

8–17866 41. *Regulations*[1] *and Orders in Council.*

---

1. The British Nationality (Dependent Territories) Regulations 1982, SI 1982/987 amended by SI 2003/539 and 3159 and SI 2005/2114, the Registration of Overseas Births, and Deaths Regulations 1982, SI 1982/1123, the British Nationality (Falkland Islands) Regulations 1983, SI 1983/479, the British Nationality (Hong Kong) Order 1986, SI 1986/2175 amended by SI 2003/540, the British Nationality (Hong Kong) (Registration of Citizens) Regulations 1990, SI 1990/2211, the British Nationality (General) Regulations 2003, SI 2003/548 amended by SI 2005/2114 and 2785and the British Nationality (Fees) Regulations 2003, SI 2003/3157 amended by SI 2005/2114, have been made.

8–17867 42. Registration and naturalisation: citizenship ceremony, oath and pledge. (1) A person of full age shall not be registered under this Act as a British citizen unless he has made the relevant citizenship oath and pledge specified in Schedule 5 at a citizenship ceremony.

(2) A certificate of naturalisation as a British citizen shall not be granted under this Act to a person of full age unless he has made the relevant citizenship oath and pledge specified in Schedule 5 at a citizenship ceremony.

(3) A person of full age shall not be registered under this Act as a British overseas territories citizen unless he has made the relevant citizenship oath and pledge specified in Schedule 5.

(4) A certificate of naturalisation as a British overseas territories citizen shall not be granted under this Act to a person of full age unless he has made the relevant citizenship oath and pledge specified in Schedule 5.

(5) A person of full age shall not be registered under this Act as a British Overseas citizen or a British subject unless he has made the relevant citizenship oath specified in Schedule 5.

(6) Where the Secretary of State thinks it appropriate because of the special circumstances of a case he may—

(*a*) disapply any of subsections (1) to (5), or
(*b*) modify the effect of any of those subsections.

(7) Sections 5 and 6 of the Oaths Act 1978 (c 19) (affirmation) apply to a citizenship oath; and a reference in this Act to a citizenship oath includes a reference to a citizenship affirmation.

[British Nationality Act 1981, s 42, as substituted by the Nationality, Immigration and Asylum Act 2002, Sch 1.]

8–17867A 42A. Registration and naturalisation: fee. (1) A person shall not be registered under a provision of this Act as a citizen of any description or as a British subject unless any fee payable by virtue of this Act in connection with the registration has been paid.

(2) A certificate of naturalisation shall not be granted to a person under a provision of this Act unless any fee payable by virtue of this Act in connection with the grant of the certificate has been paid.

[British Nationality Act 1981, s 42A, as inserted by the Nationality, Immigration and Asylum Act 2002, Sch 1.]

8–17867B 42B. Registration and naturalisation: timing. (1) A person who is registered under this Act as a citizen of any description or as a British subject shall be treated as having become a citizen or subject—

(*a*) immediately on making the required citizenship oath and pledge in accordance with section 42, or
(*b*) where the requirement for an oath and pledge is disapplied, immediately on registration.

(2) A person granted a certificate of naturalisation under this Act as a citizen of any description shall be treated as having become a citizen—

(*a*) immediately on making the required citizenship oath and pledge in accordance with section 42, or
(*b*) where the requirement for an oath and pledge is disapplied, immediately on the grant of the certificate.

(3) In the application of subsection (1) to registration as a British Overseas citizen or as a British subject the reference to the citizenship oath and pledge shall be taken as a reference to the citizenship oath.

[British Nationality Act 1981, s 42B, as inserted by the Nationality, Immigration and Asylum Act 2002, Sch 1.]

8–17868 45. Evidence. (1) Every document purporting to be a notice, certificate, order or declaration, or an entry in a register, or a subscription of an oath of allegiance, given, granted or made under this Act or any of the former nationality Acts shall be received in evidence and shall, unless the contrary is proved, be deemed to have been given, granted or made by or on behalf of the person by whom or on whose behalf it purports to have been given, granted or made.

(2) Prima facie evidence of any such document may be given by the production of a document purporting to be certified as a true copy of it by such person and in such manner as may be prescribed.

(3) Any entry in a register made under this Act or any of the former nationality Acts shall be received as evidence (and in Scotland as sufficient evidence) of the matters stated in the entry.

(4) A certificate given by or on behalf of the Secretary of State that a person was at any time in Crown service under the government of the United Kingdom or that a person's recruitment for such service took place in the United Kingdom shall, for the purposes of this Act, be conclusive evidence of that fact.

[British Nationality Act 1981, s 45.]

8–17869 46. Offences and proceedings. (1) Any person who for the purpose of procuring anything to be done or not to be done under this Act—

(*a*) makes any statement which he knows to be false in a material particular; or

(*b*) recklessly makes any statement which is false in a material particular,

shall be liable on summary conviction in the United Kingdom to imprisonment for a term not exceeding **three months*** or to a fine not exceeding **level 5** on the standard scale, or both.

(2) Any person who without reasonable excuse fails to comply with any requirement imposed on him by regulations made under this Act with respect to the delivering up of certificates of naturalisation shall be liable on summary conviction in the United Kingdom to a fine not exceeding **level 4** on the standard scale.

(3) In the case of an offence under subsection (1)—

(*a*) any information relating to the offence may in England and Wales be tried by a magistrates' court if it is laid within six months after the commission of the offence, or if it is laid within three years after the commission of the offence and not more than two months after the date certified by a chief officer of police to be the date on which evidence sufficient to justify proceedings came to the notice of an officer of his police force; and

(*b*)–(*c*) *Scotland and Northern Ireland.*

(4) *Scotland.*

(5) For the purposes of the trial of a person for an offence under subsection (1) or (2), the offence shall be deemed to have been committed either at the place at which it actually was committed or at any place at which he may be.

(6) In their application to the Bailiwick of Jersey subsections (1) and (2) shall have effect with the omission of the words "on summary conviction".

[British Nationality Act 1981, s 46, as amended by the Criminal Justice Act 1982, s 46.]

***"51 weeks" substituted by the Criminal Justice Act 2003, Sch 26, from a date to be appointed.**

Section 42(1)

SCHEDULE 5
CITIZENSHIP OATH AND PLEDGE

(*As substituted by the Nationality, Immigration and Asylum Act 2002, Sch 1.*)

8–17870 1. The form of citizenship oath and pledge is as follows for registration of or naturalisation as a British citizen—

Oath

"I, *[name]*, swear by Almighty God that, on becoming a British citizen, I will be faithful and bear true allegiance to Her Majesty Queen Elizabeth the Second, Her Heirs and Successors according to law."

Pledge

"I will give my loyalty to the United Kingdom and respect its rights and freedoms. I will uphold its democratic values. I will observe its laws faithfully and fulfil my duties and obligations as a British citizen."

2. The form of citizenship oath and pledge is as follows for registration of or naturalisation as a British overseas territories citizen—

Oath

"I, *[name]*, swear by Almighty God that, on becoming a British overseas territories citizen, I will be faithful and bear true allegiance to Her Majesty Queen Elizabeth the Second, Her Heirs and Successors according to law."

Pledge

"I will give my loyalty to *[name of territory]* and respect its rights and freedoms. I will uphold its democratic values. I will observe its laws faithfully and fulfil my duties and obligations as a British overseas territories citizen."

3. The form of citizenship oath is as follows for registration of a British Overseas citizen—

I, *[name]*, swear by Almighty God that, on becoming a British Overseas citizen, I will be faithful and bear true allegiance to Her Majesty Queen Elizabeth the Second, Her Heirs and Successors according to law."

4. The form of citizenship oath is as follows for registration of a British subject—

"I, *[name]*, swear by Almighty God that, on becoming a British subject, I will be faithful and bear true allegiance to Her Majesty Queen Elizabeth the Second, Her Heirs and Successors according to law.

Immigration Act 1988[1]

(1988 c 14)

8–17880 **1. Termination of saving in respect of Commonwealth citizens settled before 1973.** Section 1(5) of the Immigration Act 1971 (in this Act referred to as "the principal Act") is hereby repealed.
[Immigration Act 1988, s 1.]

1. This Act makes further provision for the regulation of immigation into the United Kingdom and the necessary amendments have been made to the Immigration Act 1971, this title, ante.

8–17881 **2. Restriction on exercise of right of abode in cases of polygamy.** (1) This section applies to any woman who—

(*a*) has the right of abode in the United Kingdom under section 2(1)(*b*) of the principal Act as, or as having been, the wife of a man ("the husband")—

(i) to whom she is or was polygamously married; and

(ii) who is or was such a citizen of the United Kingdom and Colonies, Commonwealth citizen or British subject as is mentioned in section 2(2)(*a*) or (*b*) of that Act as in force immediately before the commencement of the British Nationality Act 1981; and

(*b*) has not before the coming into force of this section and since her marriage to the husband been in the United Kingdom.

(2) A woman to whom this section applies shall not be entitled to enter the United Kingdom in the exercise of the right of abode mentioned in subsection (1)(*a*) above or to be granted a certificate of entitlement in respect of that right if there is another woman living (whether or not one to whom this section applies) who is the wife or widow of the husband and who—

(*a*) is, or at any time since her marriage to the husband has been, in the United Kingdom; or

(*b*) has been granted a certificate of entitlement in respect of the right of abode mentioned in subsection (1)(*a*) above or an entry clearance to enter the United Kingdom as the wife of the husband.

(3) So long as a woman is precluded by subsection (2) above from entering the United Kingdom in the exercise of her right of abode or being granted a certificate of entitlement in respect of that right the principal Act shall apply to her as it applies to a person not having a right of abode.

(4) Subsection (2) above shall not preclude a woman from re-entering the United Kingdom if since her marriage to the husband she has at any time previously been in the United Kingdom and there was at that time no such other woman living as is mentioned in that subsection.

(5) Where a woman claims that this section does not apply to her because she had been in the United Kingdom before the coming into force of this section and since her marriage to the husband it shall be for her to prove that fact.

(6) For the purposes of this section a marriage may be polygamous although at its inception neither party has any spouse additional to the other.

(7) For the purposes of subsections (1)(*b*), (2)(*a*), (4) and (5) above there shall be disregarded presence in the United Kingdom as a visitor or an illegal entrant and presence in circumstances in which a person is deemed by section 11(1) of the principal Act not to have entered the United Kingdom.

(8) In subsection (2)(*b*) above the reference to a certificate of entitlement includes a reference to a certificate treated as such a certificate by virtue of section 39(8) of the British Nationality Act 1981.

(9) No application by a woman for a certificate of entitlement in respect of such a right of abode as is mentioned in subsection (1)(*a*) above or for an entry clearance shall be granted if another application for such a certificate or clearance is pending and that application is made by a woman as the wife or widow of the same husband.

(10) For the purposes of subsection (9) above an application shall be regarded as pending so long as it and any appeal proceedings relating to it have not been finally determined.
[Immigration Act 1988, s 2.]

8–17882 **7. Persons exercising Community rights and nationals of member States.** (1) A person shall not under the principal Act require leave to enter or remain in the United Kingdom in any case in which he is entitled to do so by virtue of an enforceable Community right or of any provision made under section 2(2) of the European Communities Act 1972.

(2) The Secretary of State may by order made by statutory instrument give leave to enter the United Kingdom for a limited period to any class of persons who are nationals of member States but who are not entitled to enter the United Kingdom as mentioned in subsection (1) above; and any such order may give leave subject to such conditions as may be imposed by the order.

(3) References in the principal Act to limited leave shall include references to leave given by an order under subsection (2) above and a person having leave by virtue of such an order shall be treated

as having been given that leave by a notice given to him by an immigration officer within the period specified in paragraph 6(1) of Schedule 2 to that Act.
[Immigration Act 1988, s 7.]

8–17883 **8. Examination of passengers prior to arrival.** (1) This section applies to a person who arrives in the United Kingdom with a passport or other travel document bearing a stamp which—

(*a*) has been placed there by an immigration officer before that person's departure on his journey to the United Kingdom or in the course of that journey; and

(*b*) states that the person may enter the United Kingdom either for an indefinite or a limited period and, if for a limited period, subject to specified conditions.

(2) A person to whom this section applies shall for the purposes of the principal Act be deemed to have been given on arrival in the United Kingdom indefinite or, as the case may be, limited leave in terms corresponding to those of the stamp.

(3) A person who is deemed to have leave by virtue of this section shall be treated as having been given it by a notice given to him by an immigration officer within the period specified in paragraph 6(1) of Schedule 2 to the principal Act.

(4) A person deemed to have leave by virtue of this section shall not on his arrival in the United Kingdom be subject to examination under paragraph 2 of Schedule 2 to the principal Act but may be examined by an immigration officer for the purpose of establishing that he is such a person.

(5) The leave which a person is deemed to have by virtue of this section may, at any time before the end of the period of twenty-four hours from his arrival at the port at which he seeks to enter the United Kingdom or, if he has been examined under subsection (4) above, from the conclusion of that examination, be cancelled by an immigration officer by giving him a notice in writing refusing him leave to enter.

(6) Sub-paragraphs (3) and (4) of paragraph 6 of Schedule 2 to the principal Act shall have effect as if any notice under subsection (5) above were a notice under that paragraph.

(7) References in this section to a person's arrival in the United Kingdom are to the first occasion on which he arrives after the time when the stamp in question was placed in his passport or travel document, being an occasion not later than seven days after that time.

(8) *Repealed.*
[Immigration Act 1988, s 8 as amended by SI 1993/1813.]

***Prospectively repealed by the Immigration and Asylum Act 1999, s 169(1), (3), Sch 14, paras 83, 85, Sch 16.**

8–17884 **12. Short title, interpretation, commencement and extent.** (1) This Act may be cited as the Immigration Act 1988.

(2) In this Act "the principal Act" means the Immigration Act 1971 and any expression which is also used in that Act has the same meaning as in that Act.

(3) Except as provided in subsection (4) below this Act shall come into force at the end of the period of two months beginning with the day on which it is passed.

(4) Sections 1, 2, 3, 4, 5 and 7(1) and paragraph 1 of the Schedule shall come into force on such day as may be appointed by the Secretary of State by an order made by statutory instrument; and such an order may appoint different days for different provisions and contain such transitional provisions and savings as the Secretary of State thinks necessary or expedient in connection with any provision brought into force.

(5) This Act extends to Northern Ireland and section 36 of the principal Act (power to extend any of its provisions to the Channel Islands or the Isle of Man) shall apply also to the provisions of this Act.
[Immigration Act 1988, s 12.]

Asylum and Immigration Act 1996[1]

(1996 c 49)

Immigration offences

Persons subject to immigration control

8–17886 **8 Restrictions on employment.** Restrictions on employment—(1) Subject to subsection (2) below, if any person ("the employer") employs a person subject to immigration control ("the employee") who has attained the age of 16, the employer shall be guilty of an offence if—

(*a*) the employee has not been granted leave to enter or remain in the United Kingdom; or

(*b*) the employee's leave is not valid and subsisting, or is subject to a condition precluding him from taking up the employment, and (in either case) the employee does not satisfy such conditions as may be specified in an order[2] made by the Secretary of State.

(2) It is a defence for a person charged with an offence under this section to prove that before the employment began any relevant requirement of an order of the Secretary of State under subsection (2A) was complied with.

(2A) An order under this subsection may—

(*a*) require the production to an employer of a document of a specified description;
(*b*) require the production to an employer of one document of each of a number of specified descriptions;
(*c*) require an employer to take specified steps to retain, copy or record the content of a document produced to him in accordance with the order;
(*d*) make provision which applies generally or only in specified circumstances;
(*e*) make different provision for different circumstances.

(3) The defence afforded by subsection (2) above shall not be available in any case where the employer knew that his employment of the employee would constitute an offence under this section.

(4) A person guilty of an offence under this section shall be liable—

(*a*) on conviction on indictment, to a fine, or
(*b*) on summary conviction, to a fine not exceeding the **statutory maximum**..

(5) Where an offence under this section committed by a body corporate is proved to have been committed with the consent or connivance of, or to be attributable to any neglect on the part of—

(*a*) any director, manager, secretary or other similar officer of the body corporate; or
(*b*) any person who was purporting to act in any such capacity,

he as well as the body corporate shall be guilty of the offence and shall be liable to be proceeded against and punished accordingly.

(6) Where the affairs of a body corporate are managed by its members, subsection (5) above shall apply in relation to the acts and defaults of a member in connection with his functions of management as if he were a director of the body corporate.

(6A) Where an offence under this section is committed by a partnership (other than a limited partnership) each partner shall be guilty of the offence and shall be liable to be proceeded against and punished accordingly.

(6B) Subsection (5) shall have effect in relation to a limited partnership as if—

(*a*) a reference to a body corporate were a reference to a limited partnership, and
(*b*) a reference to an officer of the body were a reference to a partner.

(7) An order under this section shall be made by statutory instrument which shall be subject to annulment in pursuance of a resolution of either House of Parliament.

(8) In this section—

"contract of employment" means a contract of service or apprenticeship, whether express or implied, and (if it is express) whether it is oral or in writing;

"employ" means employ under a contract of employment and "employment" shall be construed accordingly.

(9) *Repealed.*

(10) An offence under this section shall be treated as—

(a) a relevant offence for the purpose of sections 28B and 28D of that Act (search, entry and arrest), and
(b) an offence under Part III of that Act (criminal proceedings) for the purposes of sections 28E, 28G and 28H (search after arrest).

[Asylum and Immigration Act 1996, s 8, as amended by the Nationality, Immigration and Asylum Act 2002, s 147 and the Asylum and Immigration (Treatment of Claimants, etc) Act 2004, s 6.]

1. This Act amends and supplements the Immigration Act 1971 and the Asylum and Immigration Appeals Act 1993.
2. See the Immigration (Restrictions on Employment) Order 2004, in this TITLE, post.

8–17886A 8A Code of practice. (1) The Secretary of State must issue a code of practice as to the measures which an employer is to be expected to take, or not to take, with a view to securing that, while avoiding the commission of an offence under section 8, he also avoids unlawful discrimination.

(2) "Unlawful discrimination" means—

(*a*) discrimination in contravention of section 4(1) of the Race Relations Act 1976 ("the 1976 Act"); or
(*b*) in relation to Northern Ireland, discrimination in contravention of Article 6(1) of the Race Relations (Northern Ireland) Order 1997 ("the 1997 Order").

(3) Before issuing the code, the Secretary of State must—

(*a*) prepare and publish a draft of the proposed code; and
(*b*) consider any representations about it which are made to him.

(4) In preparing the draft, the Secretary of State must consult—

(*a*) the Commission for Racial Equality;
(*b*) the Equality Commission for Northern Ireland; and
(*c*) such organisations and bodies (including organisations or associations of organisations representative of employers or of workers) as he considers appropriate.

(5) If the Secretary of State decides to proceed with the code, he must lay a draft of the code before both Houses of Parliament.

(6) The draft code may contain modifications to the original proposals made in the light of representations to the Secretary of State.

(7) After laying the draft code before Parliament, the Secretary of State may bring the code into operation by an order made by statutory instrument.

(8) An order under subsection (7)—

(*a*) shall be subject to annulment in pursuance of a resolution of either House of Parliament;
(*b*) may contain such transitional provisions or savings as appear to the Secretary of State to be necessary or expedient in connection with the code.

(9) A failure on the part of any person to observe a provision of the code does not of itself make him liable to any proceedings.

(10) But the code is admissible in evidence—

(*a*) in proceedings under the 1976 Act before an employment tribunal;
(*b*) in proceedings under the 1997 Order before an industrial tribunal.

(11) If any provision of the code appears to the tribunal to be relevant to any question arising in such proceedings, that provision is to be taken into account in determining the question.

(12) The Secretary of State may from time to time revise the whole or any part of the code and issue the code as revised.

(13) The provisions of this section also apply (with appropriate modifications) to any revision, or proposed revision, of the code.

[Asylum and Immigration Act 1996, s 8A as inserted by the Immigration Act 1999,s 22.]

Miscellaneous and supplemental

8–17887 **13 Short title, interpretation, commencement and extent.** (1) This Act may be cited as the Asylum and Immigration Act.

(2) In this Act—

"the 1971 Act" means the Immigration Act 1971;
"the 1993 Act" means the Asylum and Immigration Appeals Act 1993;
"person subject to immigration control" means a person who under the 1971 Act requires leave to enter or remain in the United Kingdom (whether or not such leave has been given).

(3) This Act, except section 11 and Schedule 1, shall come into force on such day as the Secretary of State may by order[1] made by statutory instrument appoint, and different days may be appointed for different purposes.

(4) An order under subsection (3) above may make such transitional and supplemental provision as the Secretary of State thinks necessary or expedient.

(5) Her Majesty may by Order[2] in Council direct that any of the provisions of this Act shall extend, with such modifications as appear to Her Majesty to be appropriate, to any of the Channel Islands or the Isle of Man.

(6) This Act extends to Northern Ireland.

[Asylum and Immigration Act 1996, s 13.]

---

1. At the date of going to press, the following orders had been made: Asylum and Immigration Act 1996 (Commencement No 1) Order 1996, SI 1996/2053 and Asylum and Immigration Act 1996 (Commencement No 2) Order 1996, SI 1996/2127.

2. The Asylum and Immigration Act 1996 (Jersey) Order 1998, SI 1998/1070 and the Ayslum and Immigration Act 1996 (Guernsey) Order 1996, SI 1996/1264 have been made.

Immigration and Asylum Act 1999[1]

(1999 c 33)

PART I[2]

IMMIGRATION: GENERAL

Leave to enter, or remain in, the United Kingdom

8–17888 **1–3.** *Inserts new ss 3A–3C in the Immigration Act 1971.*

8–17891 4. Accommodation for those temporarily admitted or released from detention. (1) The Secretary of State may provide, or arrange for the provision of, facilities for the accommodation of persons—

(*a*) temporarily admitted to the United Kingdom under paragraph 21 of Schedule 2 to the 1971 Act;
(*b*) released from detention under that paragraph; or
(*c*) released on bail from detention under any provision of the Immigration Acts.

(2) The Secretary of State may provide, or arrange for the provision of, facilities for the accommodation of a person if—

(*a*) he was (but is no longer) an asylum-seeker, and
(*b*) his claim for asylum was rejected.

(3) The Secretary of State may provide, or arrange for the provision of, facilities for the accommodation of a dependant of a person for whom facilities may be provided under subsection (2).

(4) The following expressions have the same meaning in this section as in Part VI of this Act (as defined in section 94)—

(*a*) asylum-seeker,
(*b*) claim for asylum, and
(*c*) dependant.

(5) The Secretary of State may make regulations[1] specifying criteria to be used in determining—

(*a*) whether or not to provide accommodation, or arrange for the provision of accommodation, for a person under this section;
(*b*) whether or not to continue to provide accommodation, or arrange for the provision of accommodation, for a person under this section.

(6) The regulations may, in particular—

(*a*) provide for the continuation of the provision of accommodation for a person to be conditional upon his performance of or participation in community activities in accordance with arrangements made by the Secretary of State;
(*b*) provide for the continuation of the provision of accommodation to be subject to other conditions;
(*c*) provide for the provision of accommodation (or the continuation of the provision of accommodation) to be a matter for the Secretary of State's discretion to a specified extent or in a specified class of case.

(7) For the purposes of subsection (6)(*a*)—

(*a*) "community activities" means activities that appear to the Secretary of State to be beneficial to the public or a section of the public, and
(*b*) the Secretary of State may, in particular—
   (i) appoint one person to supervise or manage the performance of or participation in activities by another person;
   (ii) enter into a contract (with a local authority or any other person) for the provision of services by way of making arrangements for community activities in accordance with this section;
   (iii) pay, or arrange for the payment of, allowances to a person performing or participating in community activities in accordance with arrangements under this section.

(8) Regulations by virtue of subsection (6)(*a*) may, in particular, provide for a condition requiring the performance of or participation in community activities to apply to a person only if the Secretary of State has made arrangements for community activities in an area that includes the place where accommodation is provided for the person.

(9) A local authority or other person may undertake to manage or participate in arrangements for community activities in accordance with this section.
[Immigration and Asylum Act 1999, s 4, as amended by the the Nationality, Immigration and Asylum Act 2002, s 49 and the Asylum and Immigration (Treatment of Claimants, etc) Act 2004, s 10.]

---

1. The Immigration and Asylum (Provision of Accommodation to Failed Asylum-Seekers) Regulations 2005, SI 2005/930 have been made.

8–17892 5. Charges. (1) The Secretary of State may, with the approval of the Treasury, make regulations prescribing fees to be paid in connection with applications for—

(*a*) leave to remain in the United Kingdom;
(*b*) the variation of leave to enter, or remain in, the United Kingdom;
(*c*) the fixing of a limited leave stamp or indefinite leave stamp on a passport or other document issued to the applicant where the stamp was previously fixed on another passport or document issued to the applicant.

(2) If a fee prescribed in connection with an application of a particular kind is payable, no such application is to be entertained by the Secretary of State unless the fee has been paid in accordance with the regulations.

(3) But—

(*a*) a fee prescribed in connection with such an application is not payable if the basis on which the application is made is that the applicant is—

(i) a person making a claim for asylum which claim either has not been determined or has been granted; or

(ii) a dependant of such a person; and

(*b*) the regulations may provide for no fee to be payable in prescribed circumstances.

(4) If no fee is payable in respect of some part of the application, the Secretary of State must entertain that part of the application.

(5) In this section—

(*a*) "limited leave stamp" means a stamp, sticker or other attachment which indicates that a person has been granted limited leave to enter or remain in the United Kingdom, and

(*b*) "indefinite leave stamp" means a stamp, sticker or other attachment which indicates that a person has been granted indefinite leave to enter or remain in the United Kingdom.

(6) "Claim for asylum" has the meaning given in subsection (1) of section 94; and subsection (3) of that section applies for the purposes of this section as it applies for the purposes of Part VI.

(7) "Dependant" has such meaning as may be prescribed.

[Immigration and Asylum Act 1999, s 5, as amended by the Asylum and Immigration (Treatment of Claimants, etc) Act 2004, s 43.]

Exemption from immigration control

8–17893 6. Members of missions other than diplomatic agents. *Inserts sub-s (3A) into s 8 of the Immigration Act 1971.*

8–17894 7–8. *Inserts ss 8A and 8B into s 8 of the Immigration Act 1971.*

8–17895 8. Persons excluded from the United Kingdom under international obligations. *Inserts new s 8B in the Immigration Act 1971.*

Removal from the United Kingdom

8–17896 9. Treatment of certain overstayers. (1) During the regularisation period overstayers may apply, in the prescribed[1] manner, for leave to remain in the United Kingdom.

(2) The regularisation period begins on the day prescribed[1] for the purposes of this subsection and is not to be less than three months.

(3) The regularisation period ends—

(*a*) on the day prescribed[1] for the purposes of this subsection; or

(*b*) if later, on the day before that on which section 65 comes into force.

(4) Section 10 and paragraph 12 of Schedule 15 come into force on the day after that on which the regularisation period ends.

(5) The Secretary of State must publicise the effect of this section in the way appearing to him to be best calculated to bring it to the attention of those affected.

(6) "Overstayer" means a person who, having only limited leave to enter or remain in the United Kingdom, remains beyond the time limited by the leave.

[Immigration and Asylum Act 1999, s 9.]

1. See the Immigration (Regularisation Period for Overstayers) Regulations 2000, SI 2000/265.

8–17897 10. Removal of certain persons unlawfully in the United Kingdom. (1) A person who is not a British citizen may be removed from the United Kingdom, in accordance with directions[1] given by an immigration officer, if—

(*a*) having only a limited leave to enter or remain, he does not observe a condition attached to the leave or remains beyond the time limited by the leave;

(*b*) he uses deception in seeking (whether successfully or not) leave to remain; or

(*ba*) his indefinite leave to enter or remain has been revoked under section 76(3) of the Nationality, Immigration and Asylum Act 2002 (person ceasing to be refugee);

(*c*) directions have been given for the removal, under this section, of a person to whose family he belongs.

(2) Directions may not be given under subsection (1)(*a*) if the person concerned has made an application for leave to remain in accordance with regulations made under section 9.

(3) Directions for the removal of a person may not be given under subsection (1)(*c*) unless the Secretary of State has given the person written notice of the intention to remove him.

(4) A notice under subsection (3) may not be given if—

(*a*) the person whose removal under subsection (1)(*a*) or (*b*) is the cause of the proposed directions under subsection (1)(*c*) has left the United Kingdom, and

(*b*) more than eight weeks have elapsed since that person's departure.

(5) If a notice under subsection (3) is sent by first class post to a person's last known address, that subsection shall be taken to be satisfied at the end of the second day after the day of posting.

(5A) Directions for the removal of a person under subsection (1)(*c*) cease to have effect if he ceases to belong to the family of the person whose removal under subsection (1)(*a*) or (*b*) is the cause of the directions under subsection (1)(*c*).

(6) Directions under this section—

(*a*) may be given only to persons falling within a prescribed class;

(*b*) may impose any requirements of a prescribed kind.

(7) In relation to any such directions, paragraphs 10, 11, 16 to 18, 21 and 22 to 24 of Schedule 2 to the 1971 Act (administrative provisions as to control of entry), apply as they apply in relation to directions given under paragraph 8 of that Schedule.

(8) Directions for the removal of a person given under this section invalidate any leave to enter or remain in the United Kingdom given to him before the directions are given or while they are in force.

(9) The costs of complying with a direction given under this section (so far as reasonably incurred) must be met by the Secretary of State.

(10) A person shall not be liable to removal from the United Kingdom under this section at a time when section 7(1)(b) of the Immigration Act 1971 (Commonwealth and Irish citizens ordinarily resident in United Kingdom) would prevent a decision to deport him.

[Immigration and Asylum Act 1999, s 10, as amended by the Nationality, Immigration and Asylum Act 2002, ss 73–76.]

1. See the Immigration (Removal Directions) Regulations 2000, SI 2000/2243.

8–17898 11. Removal of asylum claimant under standing arrangement with member States. *Repealed.**

***. Repealed by the Asylum and Immigration (Treatment of Claimants, etc) Act 2004, Sch 4 as from 1 October 2004 except in relation to a person subject to a certificate under ss 11 or 12 issued by the Secretary of State before that date.**

8–17899 12. Removal of asylum claimants in other circumstances. *Repealed.**

***. Repealed by the Asylum and Immigration (Treatment of Claimants, etc) Act 2004, Sch 4 as from 1 October 2004 except in relation to a person subject to a certificate under ss 11 or 12 issued by the Secretary of State before that date.**

8–17900 13. Proof of identity of persons to be removed or deported. (1) This section applies if a person—

(*a*) is to be removed from the United Kingdom to a country of which he is a national or citizen; but

(*b*) does not have a valid passport or other document establishing his identity and nationality or citizenship and permitting him to travel.

(2) If the country to which the person is to be removed indicates that he will not be admitted to it unless identification data relating to him are provided by the Secretary of State, he may provide them with such data.

(3) In providing identification data, the Secretary of State must not disclose whether the person concerned has made a claim for asylum.

(4) For the purposes of paragraph 4(1) of Schedule 4 to the Data Protection Act 1998, the provision under this section of identification data is a transfer of personal data which is necessary for reasons of substantial public interest.

(5) "Identification data" means—

(*a*) fingerprints taken under section 141; or

(*b*) data collected in accordance with regulations made under section 144.

(6) "Removed" means removed as a result of directions given under section 10 or under Schedule 2 or 3 to the 1971 Act.

[Immigration and Asylum Act 1999, s 13.]

8–17901 14. Escorts for persons removed from the United Kingdom under directions. (1) Directions for, or requiring arrangements to be made for, the removal of a person from the

United Kingdom may include or be amended to include provision for the person who is to be removed to be accompanied by an escort consisting of one or more persons specified in the directions.

(2) The Secretary of State may by regulations make further provision supplementing subsection (1).

(3) The regulations may, in particular, include provision—

(*a*) requiring the person to whom the directions are given to provide for the return of the escort to the United Kingdom;

(*b*) requiring him to bear such costs in connection with the escort (including, in particular, remuneration) as may be prescribed;

(*c*) as to the cases in which the Secretary of State is to bear those costs;

(*d*) prescribing the kinds of expenditure which are to count in calculating the costs incurred in connection with escorts.

[Immigration and Asylum Act 1999, s 14.]

8–17902 **15.** *Repealed.*

Provision of financial security

8–17903 **16. Security on grant of entry clearance.** (1) In such circumstances as may be specified, the Secretary of State may require security to be given, with respect to a person applying for entry clearance, before clearance is given.

(2) In such circumstances as may be specified—

(*a*) the Secretary of State may accept security with respect to a person who is applying for entry clearance but for whom security is not required; and

(*b*) in determining whether to give clearance, account may be taken of any security so provided.

(3) "Security" means—

(*a*) the deposit of a sum of money by the applicant, his agent or any other person, or

(*b*) the provision by the applicant, his agent or any other person of a financial guarantee of a specified kind,

with a view to securing that the applicant will, if given leave to enter the United Kingdom for a limited period, leave the United Kingdom at the end of that period.

(4) Immigration rules must make provision as to the circumstances in which a security provided under this section—

(*a*) is to be repaid, released or otherwise cancelled; or

(*b*) is to be forfeited or otherwise realised by the Secretary of State.

(5) No security provided under this section may be forfeited or otherwise realised unless the person providing it has been given an opportunity, in accordance with immigration rules, to make representations to the Secretary of State.

(6) Immigration rules may, in particular—

(*a*) fix the maximum amount that may be required, or accepted, by way of security provided under this section;

(*b*) specify the form and manner in which such a security is to be given or may be accepted;

(*c*) make provision, where such a security has been forfeited or otherwise realised, for the person providing it to be reimbursed in such circumstances as may be specified;

(*d*) make different provision for different cases or descriptions of case.

(7) "Specified" means specified by immigration rules.

(8) Any security forfeited or otherwise realised by the Secretary of State under this section must be paid into the Consolidated Fund.

[Immigration and Asylum Act 1999, s 16.]

8–17904 **17. Provision of further security on extension of leave.** (1) This section applies if security has been provided under section 16(1) or (2) with respect to a person who, having entered the United Kingdom (with leave to do so), applies—

(*a*) to extend his leave to enter the United Kingdom; or

(*b*) for leave to remain in the United Kingdom for a limited period.

(2) The Secretary of State may refuse the application if security of such kind as the Secretary of State considers appropriate is not provided, or continued, with respect to the applicant.

(3) Immigration rules must make provision as to the circumstances in which a security provided under this section—

(*a*) is to be repaid, released or otherwise cancelled; or

(*b*) is to be forfeited or otherwise realised by the Secretary of State.

(4) No security provided under this section may be forfeited or otherwise realised unless the person providing it has been given an opportunity, in accordance with immigration rules, to make representations to the Secretary of State.

(5) Subsection (7) of section 16 applies in relation to this section as it applies in relation to that section.

(6) Any security forfeited or otherwise realised by the Secretary of State under this section must be paid into the Consolidated Fund.
[Immigration and Asylum Act 1999, s 17.]

Information

8–17905 18. Passenger information. *Inserts para 27B into Sch 7 to the Immigration Act 1971.*

8–17906 19. Notification of non-EEA arrivals. *Inserts para 27C into Sch 7 to the Immigration Act 1971.*

8–17907 20. Supply of information to Secretary of State. (1) This section applies to information held by—

(*a*) a chief officer of police;
(*b*) the Director General of the National Criminal Intelligence Service;
(*c*) the Director General of the National Crime Squad;*
(*d*) the Commissioners of Customs and Excise, or a person providing services to them in connection with the provision of those services;
(*e*) a person with whom the Secretary of State has made a contract or other arrangements under section 95 or 98 or a sub-contractor of such a person; or
(*f*) any specified person, for purposes specified in relation to that person.

(1A) This section also applies to a document or article which—

(*a*) comes into the possession of a person listed in subsection (1) or someone acting on his behalf, or
(*b*) is discovered by a person listed in subsection (1) or someone acting on his behalf.

(2) The information, document or article may be supplied to the Secretary of State for use for immigration purposes.

(2A) The Secretary of State may—

(*a*) retain for immigration purposes a document or article supplied to him under subsection (2), and
(*b*) dispose of a document or article supplied to him under subsection (2) in such manner as he thinks appropriate (and the reference to use in subsection (2) includes a reference to disposal).

(3) "Immigration purposes" means any of the following—

(*a*) the administration of immigration control under the Immigration Acts;
(*b*) the prevention, detection, investigation or prosecution of criminal offences under those Acts;
(*c*) the imposition of penalties or charges under Part II;
(*d*) the provision of support for asylum-seekers and their dependants under Part VI;
(*e*) such other purposes as may be specified.

(4) "Chief officer of police" means—

(*a*) the chief officer of police for a police area in England and Wales;
(*b*) the chief constable of a police force maintained under the Police (Scotland) Act 1967;
(*c*) the Chief Constable of the Royal Ulster Constabulary.

(5) "Specified" means specified in an order made by the Secretary of State.

(6) This section does not limit the circumstances in which information, documents or articles may be supplied apart from this section.
[Immigration and Asylum Act 1999, s 20, as amended by the the Nationality, Immigration and Asylum Act 2002, s132.]

***Substituted by the Serious Organised Crime and Police Act 2005, Sch 4 from a date to be appointed.**

8–17908 21. Supply of information by Secretary of State. (1) This section applies to information held by the Secretary of State in connection with the exercise of functions under any of the Immigration Acts.

(2) The information may be supplied to—

(*a*) a chief officer of police, for use for police purposes;
(*b*) the Director General of the National Criminal Intelligence Service, for use for NCIS purposes;
(*c*) the Director General of the National Crime Squad, for use for NCS purposes;*
(*d*) the Commissioners of Customs and Excise, or a person providing services to them, for use for customs purposes; or
(*e*) any specified person, for use for purposes specified in relation to that person.

(3) "Police purposes" means any of the following—

(*a*) the prevention, detection, investigation or prosecution of criminal offences;

(*b*) safeguarding national security;
(*c*) such other purposes as may be specified.

(4) "NCIS purposes" means any of the functions of the National Criminal Intelligence Service mentioned in section 2 of the Police Act 1997.*

(5) "NCS purposes" means any of the functions of the National Crime Squad mentioned in section 48 of that Act.*

(6) "Customs purposes" means any of the Commissioners' functions in relation to—

(*a*) the prevention, detection, investigation or prosecution of criminal offences;
(*b*) the prevention, detection or investigation of conduct in respect of which penalties which are not criminal penalties are provided for by or under any enactment;
(*c*) the assessment or determination of penalties which are not criminal penalties;
(*d*) checking the accuracy of information relating to, or provided for purposes connected with, any matter under the care and management of the Commissioners or any assigned matter (as defined by section 1(1) of the Customs and Excise Management Act 1979);
(*e*) amending or supplementing any such information (where appropriate);
(*f*) legal or other proceedings relating to anything mentioned in paragraphs (*a*) to (*e*);
(*g*) safeguarding national security; and
(*h*) such other purposes as may be specified.

(7) "Chief officer of police" and "specified" have the same meaning as in section 20.

(8) This section does not limit the circumstances in which information may be supplied apart from this section.
[Immigration and Asylum Act 1999, s 21.]

***Substituted by the Serious Organised Crime and Police Act 2005, Sch 4 from a date to be appointed.**

Employment: code of practice

8–17909 22. Restrictions on employment: code of practice. *Inserts s 8A in the Asylum and Immigration Act 1996.*

Monitoring entry clearance

8–17910 23. Monitoring refusals of entry clearance. (1) The Secretary of State must appoint a person to monitor, in such a manner as the Secretary of State may determine, refusals of entry clearance in cases where there is, as a result of section 90 or 91 of the Nationality, Immigration and Asylum Act 2002, no right of appeal.

(2) But the Secretary of State may not appoint a member of his staff.

(3) The monitor must make an annual report on the discharge of his functions to the Secretary of State.

(4) The Secretary of State must lay a copy of any report made to him under subsection (3) before each House of Parliament.

(5) The Secretary of State may pay to the monitor such fees and allowances as he may determine.
[Immigration and Asylum Act 1999, s 23, as amended by the Nationality, Immigration and Asylum Act 2002, s 114.]

Reporting suspicious marriages

8–17911 24. Duty to report suspicious marriages. (1) Subsection (3) applies if—

(*a*) a superintendent registrar to whom a notice of marriage has been given under section 27 of the Marriage Act 1949,
(*b*) any other person who, under section 28(2) of that Act, has attested a declaration accompanying such a notice,
(*c*) a district registrar to whom a marriage notice or an approved certificate has been submitted under section 3 of the Marriage (Scotland) Act 1977, or
(*d*) a registrar or deputy registrar to whom notice has been given under section 13 of the Marriages (Ireland) Act 1844 or section 4 of the Marriage Law (Ireland) Amendment Act 1863,

has reasonable grounds for suspecting that the marriage will be a sham marriage.

(2) Subsection (3) also applies if—

(*a*) a marriage is solemnized in the presence of a registrar of marriages or, in relation to Scotland, an authorised registrar (within the meaning of the Act of 1977); and
(*b*) before, during or immediately after solemnization of the marriage, the registrar has reasonable grounds for suspecting that the marriage will be, or is, a sham marriage.

(3) The person concerned must report his suspicion to the Secretary of State without delay and in such form and manner as may be prescribed by regulations.

(4) The regulations are to be made—

(*a*) in relation to England and Wales, by the Registrar General for England and Wales with the approval of the Chancellor of the Exchequer;
(*b*) in relation to Scotland, by the Secretary of State after consulting the Registrar General of Births, Deaths and Marriages for Scotland;
(*c*) in relation to Northern Ireland, by the Secretary of State after consulting the Registrar General in Northern Ireland.

(5) "Sham marriage" means a marriage (whether or not void)—

(*a*) entered into between a person ("A") who is neither a British citizen nor a national of an EEA State other than the United Kingdom and another person (whether or not such a citizen or such a national); and
(*b*) entered into by A for the purpose of avoiding the effect of one or more provisions of United Kingdom immigration law or the immigration rules.*

[Immigration and Asylum Act 1999, s 24.]

8–17911A 24A. Duty to report suspicious civil partnerships. (1) Subsection (3) applies if—

(*a*) a registration authority to whom a notice of proposed civil partnership has been given under section 8 of the Civil Partnership Act 2004,
(*b*) any person who, under section 8 of the 2004 Act, has attested a declaration accompanying such a notice,
(*c*) a district registrar to whom a notice of proposed civil partnership has been given under section 88 of the 2004 Act, or
(*d*) a registrar to whom a civil partnership notice has been given under section 139 of the 2004 Act,

has reasonable grounds for suspecting that the civil partnership will be a sham civil partnership.

(2) Subsection (3) also applies if—

(*a*) two people register as civil partners of each other under Part 2, 3 or 4 of the 2004 Act in the presence of the registrar, and
(*b*) before, during or immediately after they do so, the registrar has reasonable grounds for suspecting that the civil partnership will be, or is, a sham civil partnership.

(3) The person concerned must report his suspicion to the Secretary of State without delay and in such form and manner as may be prescribed by regulations[1].

(4) The regulations are to be made—

(*a*) in relation to England and Wales, by the Registrar General for England and Wales with the approval of the Chancellor of the Exchequer;
(*b*) in relation to Scotland, by the Secretary of State after consulting the Registrar General of Births, Deaths and Marriages for Scotland;
(*c*) in relation to Northern Ireland, by the Secretary of State after consulting the Registrar General in Northern Ireland.

(5) "Sham civil partnership" means a civil partnership (whether or not void)—

(*a*) formed between a person ("A") who is neither a British citizen nor a national of an EEA State other than the United Kingdom and another person (whether or not such a citizen or such a national), and
(*b*) formed by A for the purpose of avoiding the effect of one or more provisions of United Kingdom immigration law or the immigration rules.

(6) "The registrar" means—

(*a*) in relation to England and Wales, the civil partnership registrar acting under Part 2 of the 2004 Act;
(*b*) in relation to Scotland, the authorised registrar acting under Part 3 of the 2004 Act;
(*c*) in relation to Northern Ireland, the registrar acting under Part 4 of the 2004 Act.

[Immigration and Asylum Act 1999, s 24A as inserted by the Civil Partnership Act 2004, Sch 27.]

1. The Reporting of Suspicious Civil Partnership Regulations 2005, SI 2005/3174 have been made.

Immigration control: facilities and charges

8–17912 25. Provision of facilities for immigration control at ports. (1) The person responsible for the management of a control port ("the manager") must provide the Secretary of State free of charge with such facilities at the port as the Secretary of State may direct as being reasonably necessary for, or in connection with, the operation of immigration control there.

(2) Before giving such a direction, the Secretary of State must consult such persons likely to be affected by it as he considers appropriate.

(3) If the Secretary of State gives such a direction, he must send a copy of it to the person appearing to him to be the manager.

(4) If the manager persistently fails to comply with the direction (or part of it), the Secretary of State may—

(*a*) in the case of a control port which is not a port of entry, revoke any approval in relation to the port given under paragraph 26(1) of Schedule 2 to the 1971 Act;
(*b*) in the case of a control port which is a port of entry, by order revoke its designation as a port of entry.

(5) A direction under this section is enforceable, on the application of the Secretary of State—

(*a*) by injunction granted by a county court; or
(*b*) in Scotland, by an order under section 45 of the Court of Session Act 1988.

(6) "Control port" means a port in which a control area is designated under paragraph 26(3) of Schedule 2 to the 1971 Act.

(7) "Facilities" means accommodation, facilities, equipment and services of a class or description specified in an order[1] made by the Secretary of State.
[Immigration and Asylum Act 1999, s 25.]

1. The Immigration Control (Provision of Facilities at Ports) Order 2003, SI 2003/612 has been made.

8–17913 26. *Charges: immigration control*

Charges: travel documents

8–17914 27. Charges: travel documents. (1) The Secretary of State may, with the approval of the Treasury, make regulations[1] prescribing fees to be paid in connection with applications to him for travel documents.

(2) If a fee is prescribed in connection with an application of a particular kind, no such application is to be entertained by the Secretary of State unless the fee has been paid in accordance with the regulations.

(3) In respect of any period before the coming into force of this section, the Secretary of State is to be deemed always to have had power to impose charges in connection with—

(*a*) applications to him for travel documents; or
(*b*) the issue by him of travel documents.

(4) "Travel document" does not include a passport.
[Immigration and Asylum Act 1999, s 27.]

1. The Travel Documents (Fees) Regulations 1999, SI 1999/339 have been made.

Offences

8–17915 28. Deception. *Inserts s 24 into the Immigration Act 1971.*

8–17916 29. Facilitation of entry. *Amends s 25 of the Immigration Act 1971.*

8–17917 30. False statements etc. *Amends s 26 of the Immigration Act 1971.*

8–17918 31. Defences based on Article 31(1) of the Refugee Convention[1]. (1) It is a defence for a refugee charged with an offence to which this section applies to show that, having come to the United Kingdom directly from a country where his life or freedom was threatened (within the meaning of the Refugee Convention), he—

(*a*) presented himself to the authorities in the United Kingdom without delay;
(*b*) showed good cause for his illegal entry or presence; and
(*c*) made a claim for asylum as soon as was reasonably practicable after his arrival in the United Kingdom.

(2) If, in coming from the country where his life or freedom was threatened, the refugee[2] stopped in another country outside the United Kingdom, subsection (1) applies only if he shows that he could not reasonably have expected to be given protection under the Refugee Convention in that other country.

(3) In England and Wales and Northern Ireland the offences to which this section applies are any offence, and any attempt to commit an offence, under—

(*a*) Part I of the Forgery and Counterfeiting Act 1981 (forgery and connected offences);
(*b*) section 24A of the 1971 Act (deception); or
(*c*) section 26(1)(*d*) of the 1971 Act (falsification of documents).

(4) In Scotland, the offences to which this section applies are those—

(*a*) of fraud,
(*b*) of uttering a forged document,
(*c*) under section 24A of the 1971 Act (deception), or

(*d*) under section 26(1)(*d*) of the 1971 Act (falsification of documents),

and any attempt to commit any of those offences.

(5) A refugee who has made a claim for asylum is not entitled to the defence provided by subsection (1) in relation to any offence committed by him after making that claim.

(6) "Refugee"[3] has the same meaning as it has for the purposes of the Refugee Convention.

(7) If the Secretary of State has refused to grant a claim for asylum made by a person who claims that he has a defence under subsection (1), that person is to be taken not to be a refugee unless he shows that he is.

(8) A person who—

(*a*) was convicted in England and Wales or Northern Ireland of an offence to which this section applies before the commencement of this section, but

(*b*) at no time during the proceedings for that offence argued that he had a defence based on Article 31(1),

may apply to the Criminal Cases Review Commission with a view to his case being referred to the Court of Appeal by the Commission on the ground that he would have had a defence under this section had it been in force at the material time.

(9) A person who—

(*a*) was convicted in Scotland of an offence to which this section applies before the commencement of this section, but

(*b*) at no time during the proceedings for that offence argued that he had a defence based on Article 31(1),

may apply to the Scottish Criminal Cases Review Commission with a view to his case being referred to the High Court of Justiciary by the Commission on the ground that he would have had a defence under this section had it been in force at the material time.

(10) The Secretary of State may by order amend—

(*a*) subsection (3), or
(*b*) subsection (4),

by adding offences to those for the time being listed there.

(11) Before making an order under subsection (10)(*b*), the Secretary of State must consult the Scottish Ministers.

[Immigration and Asylum Act 1999, s 31.]

---

1. This section gives legislative effect to art 31 of the United Nations Convention relating to the Status of Refugees (Geneva, 28 July 1951; TS 39 (1954); Cmd 9171). Article 31(1) provides:

> 'The Contracting States shall not impose penalties, on account of their illegal entry or presence, on refugees who, coming directly from a territory where their life or freedom was threatened in the sense of article 1, enter or are present in their territory without authorisation, provided they present themselves without delay to the authorities and show good cause for their illegal entry or presence.'

Article 31(2) provides for the validity of administrative detention while refugee status is regularised or entry is obtained to another country. Section 31 is Parliament's interpetation of the requirements of art 31 and supersedes the interpretation of art 31 in *R v Uxbridge Magistrates' Court, ex p Adimi* [2001] QB 667, [1999] 4 All ER 520, [2000] 3 WLR 434, DC. Furthermore, the United Kingdom's obligations under article 31 of the Convention are set out authoritatively in s 31 of the 1999 Act so that the focus is on the law set out in that section and not in art 31 of the Convention as interpreted in *ex p Adimi (R (Hussain) v Secretary of State for the Home Department* [2001] EWHC Admin 555). Accordingly, there can be no legitimate expectation that the CPS will have regard to art 31 as, in instituting a prosecution, the CPS is required to apply the domestic law (*R (Pepushi) v Crown Prosecution Service* [2004] EWHC 798 (Admin), [2004] TLR 279).

2. Defined in sub-s (6), infra. "A person is a refugee with the meaning of the 1951 Convention as soon as he fulfils the criteria contained in the definition. This would necessarily occur prior to the time at which his refugee status is formally determined. Recognition of his refugee status does not therefore make him a refugee but declares him to be one. He does not become a refugee because of recognition, but is recognized because he is a refugee." (UNHCR Handbook on Procedures and Criteria for Determining Refugee Status para 28). We would submit it includes: those who have been granted asylum; those who have been refused asylum but are able to persuade the criminal court hearing the case that the decision was wrong; those who have not received a decision on their claim for asylum. Where an application for asylum has not been finally determined (eg an application has not yet been processed or an appeal is outstanding), Home Office (Immigration and Nationality Directorate) advice is that prosecutions should not be instituted unless the person falls outside the defence in s 31 for some reason other than that relating to his refugee status.

3. In Article 1.A(2) of the 1951 Convention "refugee" is defined as apply to any person who: "owing to well-founded fear of being persecuted for reasons of race, religion, nationality, membership of a particular social group or political opinion, is outside the country of his nationality and is unable or, owing to such fear, is unwilling to avail himself of the protection of that country; or who, not having a nationality and being outside the country of his former habitual resdence ... is unable or, owing to such fear, is unwilling to return to it ..." (cited by Thomas LJ in *R (Pepushi) v Crown Prosecution Service* [2004] EWHC 798 (Admin))

PART II[1]
CARRIERS' LIABILITY

8–17919 32–43. *Clandestine entrants and passengers without proper documents*

---

1. Part II comprises ss 32–43.

PART III[1]
BAIL

Routine bail hearings

8–17924 44–52. *Repealed.*

1. Part III comprises ss 44 to 55.

Bail hearings under other enactments

8–17933 53. Applications for bail in immigration cases. (1) The Secretary of State may by regulations make new provision in relation to applications for bail by persons detained under the 1971 Act or under section 62 of the Nationality, Immigration and Asylum Act 2002.

(2) The regulations may confer a right to be released on bail in prescribed circumstances.

(3) The regulations may, in particular, make provision—

(*a*) creating or transferring jurisdiction to hear an application for bail by a person detained under the 1971 Act or under section 62 of the Nationality, Immigration and Asylum Act 2002;

(*b*) as to the places in which such an application may be held;

(*c*) as to the procedure to be followed on, or in connection with, such an application;

(*d*) as to circumstances in which, and conditions (including financial conditions) on which, an applicant may be released on bail;

(*e*) amending or repealing any enactment so far as it relates to such an application.

(4) The regulations must include provision for securing that an application for bail made by a person who has brought an appeal under any provision of the Nationality, Immigration and Asylum Act 2002 or the Special Immigration Appeals Commission Act 1997 is heard by the appellate authority hearing that appeal.

(5) *Repealed.*

(6) Regulations under this section require the approval of the Lord Chancellor.

(7) In so far as regulations under this section relate to the sheriff or the Court of Session, the Lord Chancellor must obtain the consent of the Scottish Ministers before giving his approval.

[Immigration and Asylum Act 1999, s 53, as amended by the Nationality, Immigration and Asylum Act 2002, s 62, Schs 7 and 9.]

Grants

8–17935 55. *Repealed.*

PART IV[1]
APPEALS

8–17936 56–81. *Appeals against decisions of the Secretary of State and immigration officers to an adjudicator or the Immigration Appeal Tribunal.* *Repealed*).

1. Part IV comprises ss 56 to 81, now repealed except in relation to events which took place before 1 April 2003.

PART V[1]
IMMIGRATION ADVISERS AND IMMIGRATION SERVICE PROVIDERS

Interpretation

8–17937 82. Interpretation of Part V. (1) In this Part—

"claim for asylum" means a claim that it would be contrary to the United Kingdom's obligations under—

(*a*) the Refugee Convention, or

(*b*) Article 3 of the Human Rights Convention,

for the claimant to be removed from, or required to leave, the United Kingdom;

"the Commissioner" means the Immigration Services Commissioner;

"the complaints scheme" means the scheme established under paragraph 5(1) of Schedule 5;

"designated judge" has the same meaning as in section 119(1) of the Courts and Legal Services Act 1990;

"designated professional body" has the meaning given by section 86;

"immigration advice" means advice which—

(*a*) relates to a particular individual;

(*b*) is given in connection with one or more relevant matters;

(*c*) is given by a person who knows that he is giving it in relation to a particular individual and in connection with one or more relevant matters; and

(*d*) is not given in connection with representing an individual before a court in criminal proceedings or matters ancillary to criminal proceedings;

"immigration services" means the making of representations on behalf of a particular individual—

(*a*) in civil proceedings before a court, tribunal or adjudicator in the United Kingdom, or
(*b*) in correspondence with a Minister of the Crown or government department,

in connection with one or more relevant matters;

"Minister of the Crown" has the same meaning as in the Ministers of the Crown Act 1975;
"qualified person" means a person who is qualified for the purposes of section 84;
"registered person" means a person who is registered with the Commissioner under section 85;
"relevant matters" means any of the following—

(*a*) a claim for asylum;
(*b*) an application for, or for the variation of, entry clearance or leave to enter or remain in the United Kingdom;
(*ba*) an application for an immigration employment document;
(*c*) unlawful entry into the United Kingdom;
(*d*) nationality and citizenship under the law of the United Kingdom;
(*e*) citizenship of the European Union;
(*f*) admission to Member States under Community law;
(*g*) residence in a Member State in accordance with rights conferred by or under Community law;
(*h*) removal or deportation from the United Kingdom;
(*i*) an application for bail under the Immigration Acts or under the Special Immigration Appeals Commission Act 1997;
(*j*) an appeal against, or an application for judicial review in relation to, any decision taken in connection with a matter referred to in paragraphs (*a*) to (*i*); and

"the Tribunal" means the Immigration Services Tribunal.

(2) In this Part, references to the provision of immigration advice or immigration services are to the provision of such advice or services by a person—

(*a*) in the United Kingdom (regardless of whether the persons to whom they are provided are in the United Kingdom or elsewhere); and
(*b*) in the course of a business carried on (whether or not for profit) by him or by another person.

(3) In the definition of "relevant matters" in subsection (1) "immigration employment document" means—

(a) a work permit (within the meaning of section 33(1) of the Immigration Act 1971 (interpretation)), and
(b) any other document which relates to employment and is issued for a purpose of immigration rules or in connection with leave to enter or remain in the United Kingdom.

[Immigration and Asylum Act 1999, s 82 as amended by the Nationality, Immigration and Asylum Act 2002, s 123.]

1. Part V comprises ss 82 to 93.

The Immigration Services Commissioner

8–17938 **83. The Commissioner.** (1) There is to be an Immigration Services Commissioner (referred to in this Part as "the Commissioner").

(2) The Commissioner is to be appointed by the Secretary of State after consulting the Lord Chancellor and the Scottish Ministers.

(3) It is to be the general duty of the Commissioner to promote good practice by those who provide immigration advice or immigration services.

(4) In addition to any other functions conferred on him by this Part, the Commissioner is to have the regulatory functions set out in Part I of Schedule 5.

(5) The Commissioner must exercise his functions so as to secure, so far as is reasonably practicable, that those who provide immigration advice or immigration services—

(*a*) are fit and competent to do so;
(*b*) act in the best interests of their clients;
(*c*) do not knowingly mislead any court, tribunal or adjudicator in the United Kingdom;
(*d*) do not seek to abuse any procedure operating in the United Kingdom in connection with immigration or asylum (including any appellate or other judicial procedure);
(*e*) do not advise any person to do something which would amount to such an abuse.

(6) The Commissioner—

(*a*) must arrange for the publication, in such form and manner and to such extent as he considers appropriate, of information about his functions and about matters falling within the scope of his functions; and
(*b*) may give advice about his functions and about such matters.

(7) Part II of Schedule 5 makes further provision with respect to the Commissioner.
[Immigration and Asylum Act 1999, s 83.]

The general prohibition

8–17939 **84. Provision of immigration services.** (1) No person may provide immigration advice or immigration services unless he is a qualified person.

(2) A person is a qualified person if he is—

(*a*) a registered person,

(*b*) authorised by a designated professional body to practise as a member of the profession whose members the body regulates,

(*c*) the equivalent in an EEA State of—

(i) a registered person, or

(ii) a person within paragraph (b),

(*d*) a person permitted, by virtue of exemption from a prohibition, to provide in an EEA State advice or services equivalent to immigration advice or services, or

(*e*) acting on behalf of, and under the supervision of, a person within any of paragraphs (*a*) to (*d*) (whether or not under a contract of employment).

(3) Subsection (2)(*a*) and (*e*) are subject to any limitation on the effect of a person's registration imposed under paragraph 2(2) of Schedule 6.

(4) Subsection (1) does not apply to a person who—

(*a*) is certified by the Commissioner as exempt ("an exempt person");

(*b*) is employed by an exempt person;

(*c*) works under the supervision of an exempt person or an employee of an exempt person; or

(*d*) who falls within a category of person specified in an order[1] made by the Secretary of State for the purposes of this subsection.

(5) A certificate under subsection (4)(*a*) may relate only to a specified description of immigration advice or immigration services.

(6) Subsection (1) does not apply to a person—

(*a*) holding an office under the Crown, when acting in that capacity;

(*b*) employed by, or for the purposes of, a government department, when acting in that capacity;

(*c*) acting under the control of a government department; or

(*d*) otherwise exercising functions on behalf of the Crown.

(7) An exemption given under subsection (4) may be withdrawn by the Commissioner.
[Immigration and Asylum Act 1999, s 84, as amended by the Asylum and Immigration (Treatment of Claimants, etc) Act 2004, s 37.]

1. The Immigration and Asylum Act 1999 (Part V Exemption: Eligible Voluntary Bodies and Relevant Employers) Order 2001, SI 2001/1393, the Immigration and Asylum Act 1999 (Part V Exemption: Institutions and Health Sector Bodies) Order 2001, SI 2001/1403, the Immigration and Asylum Act 1999 (Part V Exemption: Relevant Employers) Order 2001, SI 2002/9, the Immigration and Asylum Act 1999 (Part V Exemption: Relevant Employers) Order 2002, SI 2002/3025 and the Immigration and Asylum Act 1999 (Part V Exemption: Relevant Employers) Order 2003, SI 2003/3214 have been made.

8–17940 **85. Registration exemption by the Commissioner.** (1) The Commissioner must prepare and maintain a register for and the purposes of section 84(2)(*a*).

(2) The Commissioner must keep a record of the persons to whom he has issued a certificate of exemption under section 84(4)(*a*).

(3) Schedule 6 makes further provision with respect to registration.
[Immigration and Asylum Act 1999, s 85, as amended by the Asylum and Immigration (Treatment of Claimants, etc) Act 2004, Sch 4.]

8–17941 **86. Designated professional bodies.** (1) "Designated professional body" means—

(*a*) The Law Society;

(*b*) The Law Society of Scotland;

(*c*) The Law Society of Northern Ireland;

(*d*) The Institute of Legal Executives;

(*e*) The General Council of the Bar;

(*f*) The Faculty of Advocates; or

(*g*) The General Council of the Bar of Northern Ireland.

(2) The Secretary of State may by order remove a body from the list in subsection (1) if he considers that the body—

(*a*) has failed to provide effective regulation of its members in their provision of immigration advice or immigration services, or (*b*) has failed to comply with a request of the Commissioner for the provision of information (whether general or in relation to a particular case or matter).

(3) If a designated professional body asks the Secretary of State to amend subsection (1) so as to remove its name, the Secretary of State may by order do so.

(4) If the Secretary of State is proposing to act under subsection (2) he must, before doing so—

(*a*) consult the Commissioner;

(*b*) consult the Legal Services Ombudsman, if the proposed order would affect a designated professional body in England and Wales;

(*c*) consult the Scottish Legal Services Ombudsman, if the proposed order would affect a designated professional body in Scotland;

(*d*) consult the lay observers appointed under Article 42 of the Solicitors (Northern Ireland) Order 1976, if the proposed order would affect a designated professional body in Northern Ireland;

(*e*) notify the body concerned of his proposal and give it a reasonable period within which to make representations; and

(*f*) consider any representations so made.

(5) An order under subsection (2) requires the approval of—

(*a*) the Lord Chancellor, if it affects a designated professional body in England and Wales or Northern Ireland;

(*b*) the Scottish Ministers, if it affects a designated professional body in Scotland.

(6) Before deciding whether or not to give his approval under subsection (5)(*a*), the Lord Chancellor must consult—

(*a*) the designated judges, if the order affects a designated professional body in England and Wales;

(*b*) the Lord Chief Justice of Northern Ireland, if it affects a designated professional body in Northern Ireland.

(7) Before deciding whether or not to give their approval under subsection (5)(*b*), the Scottish Ministers must consult the Lord President of the Court of Session.

(8) If the Secretary of State considers that a body which—

(*a*) is concerned (whether wholly or in part) with regulating the legal profession, or a branch of it, in an EEA State,

(*b*) is not a designated professional body, and

(*c*) is capable of providing effective regulation of its members in their provision of immigration advice or immigration services,

ought to be designated, he may by order amend subsection (1) to include the name of that body.

(9) The Commissioner must—

(*a*) keep under review the list of designated professional bodies set out in subsection (1); and

(*b*) report to the Secretary of State if the Commissioner considers that a designated professional body—

(i) is failing to provide effective regulation of its members in their provision of immigration advice or immigration services, or

(ii) has failed to comply with a request of the Commissioner for the provision of information (whether general or in relation to a particular case or matter).

(9A) A designated professional body shall comply with a request of the Commissioner for the provision of information (whether general or in relation to a specified case or matter).

(10) For the purpose of meeting the costs incurred by the Commissioner in discharging his functions under this Part, each designated professional body must pay to the Commissioner, in each year and on such date as may be specified, such fee as may be specified.

(11) Any unpaid fee for which a designated professional body is liable under subsection (10) may be recovered from that body as a debt due to the Commissioner.

(12) "Specified" means specified by an order[1] made by the Secretary of State.

[Immigration and Asylum Act 1999, s 86, as amended by the Asylum and Immigration (Treatment of Claimants, etc) Act 2004, s 41.]

1. The Immigration Services Commissioner (Designated Professional Body) (Fees) Order 2005, SI 2005/348 has been made.

The Immigration Services Tribunal

8–17942 **87. The Tribunal.** (1) There is to be a tribunal known as the Immigration Services Tribunal (referred to in this Part as "the Tribunal").

(2) Any person aggrieved by a relevant decision of the Commissioner may appeal to the Tribunal against the decision.

(3) "Relevant decision" means a decision—

(*a*) to refuse an application for registration made under paragraph 1 of Schedule 6;
(*b*) to withdraw an exemption given under section 84(4)(*a*);
(*c*) under paragraph 2(2) of that Schedule to register with limited effect;
(*d*) to refuse an application for continued registration made under paragraph 3 of that Schedule;
(*e*) to vary a registration on an application under paragraph 3 of that Schedule; or
(*ea*) to vary a registration under paragraph 3A of that Schedule; or
(*f*) *repealed.*

(4) The Tribunal is also to have the function of hearing disciplinary charges laid by the Commissioner under paragraph 9(1)(*e*) of Schedule 5.

(5) Schedule 7 makes further provision with respect to the Tribunal and its constitution and functions.

[Immigration and Asylum Act 1999, s 87, as amended by the Nationality, Immigration and Asylum Act 2002, s 140 and the Asylum and Immigration (Treatment of Claimants, etc) Act 2004, Sch 4.]

8–17943 88. Appeal upheld by the Tribunal. (1) This section applies if the Tribunal allows an appeal under section 87.

(2) If the Tribunal considers it appropriate, it may direct the Commissioner—

(*a*) to register the applicant or to continue the applicant's registration;
(*b*) to make or vary the applicant's registration so as to have limited effect in any of the ways mentioned in paragraph 2(2) of Schedule 6;
(*c*) to restore an exemption granted under section 84(4)(*a*); or
(*d*) to quash a decision recorded under paragraph 9(1)(*a*) of Schedule 5 and the record of that decision.

[Immigration and Asylum Act 1999, s 88.]

8–17944 89. Disciplinary charge upheld by the Tribunal. (1) This section applies if the Tribunal upholds a disciplinary charge laid by the Commissioner under paragraph 9(1)(*e*) of Schedule 5 against a person ("the person charged").

(2) If the person charged is a registered person or acts on behalf of a registered person, the Tribunal may—

(*a*) direct the Commissioner to record the charge and the Tribunal's decision for consideration in connection with the registered person's next application for continued registration;
(*b*) direct the registered person to apply for continued registration as soon as is reasonably practicable.

(4) If the person charged is certified by the Commissioner as exempt under section 84(4)(*a*), the Tribunal may direct the Commissioner to consider whether to withdraw his exemption.

(5) If the person charged is found to have charged unreasonable fees for immigration advice or immigration services, the Tribunal may direct him to repay to the clients concerned such portion of those fees as it may determine.

(6) The Tribunal may direct the person charged to pay a penalty to the Commissioner of such sum as it considers appropriate.

(7) A direction given by the Tribunal under subsection (5) (or under subsection (6)) may be enforced by the clients concerned (or by the Commissioner)—

(*a*) as if it were an order of a county court; or
(*b*) in Scotland, as if it were an extract registered decree arbitral bearing a warrant for execution issued by the sheriff court of any sheriffdom in Scotland.

(8) The Tribunal may direct that the person charged or any person acting on his behalf or working under his supervision is to be—

(*a*) subject to such restrictions on the provision of immigration advice or immigration services as the Tribunal considers appropriate;
(*b*) suspended from providing immigration advice or immigration services for such period as the Tribunal may determine; or
(*c*) prohibited from providing immigration advice or immigration services indefinitely.

(9) The Commissioner must keep a record of the persons against whom there is in force a direction given by the Tribunal under subsection (8).

[Immigration and Asylum Act 1999, s 89, as amended by the Asylum and Immigration (Treatment of Claimants, etc) Act 2004, s 37.]

8–17945 90. Orders by disciplinary bodies. (1) A disciplinary body may make an order directing that a person subject to its jurisdiction is to be—

(*a*) subject to such restrictions on the provision of immigration advice or immigration services as the body considers appropriate;
(*b*) suspended from providing immigration advice or immigration services for such period as the body may determine; or
(*c*) prohibited from providing immigration advice or immigration services indefinitely.

(2) "Disciplinary body" means any body—

(*a*) appearing to the Secretary of State to be established for the purpose of hearing disciplinary charges against members of a designated professional body; and

(*b*) specified in an order made by the Secretary of State.

(3) The Secretary of State must consult the designated professional body concerned before making an order under subsection (2)(*b*).

(4) For the purposes of this section, a person is subject to the jurisdiction of a disciplinary body if he is an authorised person or is acting on behalf of an authorised person.

(5) "Authorised person" means a person who is authorised by the designated professional body concerned to practise as a member of the profession whose members are regulated by that body.

[Immigration and Asylum Act 1999, s 90, as amended by the Asylum and Immigration (Treatment of Claimants, etc) Act 2004, s 37.]

Enforcement

8–17946 91. Offences. (1) A person who provides immigration advice or immigration services in contravention of section 84 or of a restraining order is guilty of an offence and liable—

(*a*) on summary conviction, to imprisonment for a term not exceeding **six months** or to a **fine** not exceeding **the statutory maximum**, or to **both**; or

(*b*) on conviction on indictment, to imprisonment for a term not exceeding **two years** or to a **fine**, or to **both**.

(2) "Restraining order" means—

(*a*) a direction given by the Tribunal under section 89(8) or paragraph 9(3) of Schedule 5; or

(*b*) an order made by a disciplinary body under section 90(1).

(3) If an offence under this section committed by a body corporate is proved—

(*a*) to have been committed with the consent or connivance of an officer, or

(*b*) to be attributable to neglect on his part,

the officer as well as the body corporate is guilty of the offence and liable to be proceeded against and punished accordingly.

(4) "Officer", in relation to a body corporate, means a director, manager, secretary or other similar officer of the body, or a person purporting to act in such a capacity.

(5) If the affairs of a body corporate are managed by its members, subsection (3) applies in relation to the acts and defaults of a member in connection with his functions of management as if he were a director of the body corporate.

(6) If an offence under this section committed by a partnership in Scotland is proved—

(*a*) to have been committed with the consent or connivance of a partner, or

(*b*) to be attributable to neglect on his part,

the partner as well as the partnership is guilty of the offence and liable to be proceeded against and punished accordingly.

(7) "Partner" includes a person purporting to act as a partner.

[Immigration and Asylum Act 1999, s 91.]

8–17947 92. Enforcement. (1) If it appears to the Commissioner that a person—

(*a*) is providing immigration advice or immigration services in contravention of section 84 or of a restraining order, and

(*b*) is likely to continue to do so unless restrained,

the Commissioner may apply to a county court for an injunction, or to the sheriff for an interdict, restraining him from doing so.

(2) If the court is satisfied that the application is well-founded, it may grant the injunction or interdict in the terms applied for or in more limited terms.

(3) "Restraining order" has the meaning given by section 91.

[Immigration and Asylum Act 1999, s 92.]

8–17947A 92A. Investigation of offence: power of entry. (1) On an application made by the Commissioner a justice of the peace may issue a warrant authorising the Commissioner to enter and search premises.

(2) A justice of the peace may issue a warrant in respect of premises only if satisfied that there are reasonable grounds for believing that—

(*a*) an offence under section 91 has been committed,

(*b*) there is material on the premises which is likely to be of substantial value (whether by itself or together with other material) to the investigation of the offence, and

(*c*) any of the conditions specified in subsection (3) is satisfied.

(3) Those conditions are—

(*a*) that it is not practicable to communicate with a person entitled to grant entry to the premises,
(*b*) that it is not practicable to communicate with a person entitled to grant access to the evidence,
(*c*) that entry to the premises will be prevented unless a warrant is produced, and
(*d*) that the purpose of a search may be frustrated or seriously prejudiced unless the Commissioner can secure immediate entry on arrival at the premises.

(4) The Commissioner may seize and retain anything for which a search is authorised under this section.

(5) A person commits an offence if without reasonable excuse he obstructs the Commissioner in the exercise of a power by virtue of this section.

(6) A person guilty of an offence under subsection (5) shall be liable on summary conviction to—

(*a*) imprisonment for a term not exceeding six months,
(*b*) a fine not exceeding level 5 on the standard scale, or
(*c*) both.

(7) In this section—

(*a*) a reference to the Commissioner includes a reference to a member of his staff authorised in writing by him,
(*b*) a reference to premises includes a reference to premises used wholly or partly as a dwelling, and
(*c*) a reference to material—
  (i) includes material subject to legal privilege within the meaning of the Police and Criminal Evidence Act 1984 (c 60),
  (ii) does not include excluded material or special procedure material within the meaning of that Act, and
  (iii) includes material whether or not it would be admissible in evidence at a trial.

(8) *Scotland.*

(9) *Northern Ireland.*

[Immigration and Asylum Act 1999, s 92A, as inserted by the Asylum and Immigration (Treatment of Claimants, etc) Act 2004, s 38.]

8–17947B 92B. Advertising. (1) A person commits an offence if—

(*a*) he offers to provide immigration advice or immigration services, and
(*b*) provision by him of the advice or services would constitute an offence under section 91.

(2) For the purpose of subsection (1) a person offers to provide advice or services if he—

(*a*) makes an offer to a particular person or class of person,
(*b*) makes arrangements for an advertisement in which he offers to provide advice or services, or
(*c*) makes arrangements for an advertisement in which he is described or presented as competent to provide advice or services.

(3) A person guilty of an offence under this section shall be liable on summary conviction to a fine not exceeding level 4 on the standard scale.

(4) Subsections (3) to (7) of section 91 shall have effect for the purposes of this section as they have effect for the purposes of that section.

(5) An information relating to an offence under this section may in England and Wales be tried by a magistrates' court if—

(*a*) it is laid within the period of six months beginning with the date (or first date) on which the offence is alleged to have been committed, or
(*b*) it is laid—
  (i) within the period of two years beginning with that date, and
  (ii) within the period of six months beginning with a date certified by the Immigration Services Commissioner as the date on which the commission of the offence came to his notice.

(6) *Scotland.*

(7) *Scotland.*

(8) *Northern Ireland.*

[Immigration and Asylum Act 1999, s 92B, as inserted by the Asylum and Immigration (Treatment of Claimants, etc) Act 2004, s 38.]

Miscellaneous

8–17948 93. Information. (1) No enactment or rule of law prohibiting or restricting the disclosure of information prevents a person from—

(*a*) giving the Commissioner information which is necessary for the discharge of his functions; or
(*b*) giving the Tribunal information which is necessary for the discharge of its functions.

(2) No relevant person may at any time disclose information which—

(*a*) has been obtained by, or given to, the Commissioner under or for purposes of this Act,
(*b*) relates to an identified or identifiable individual or business, and
(*c*) is not at that time, and has not previously been, available to the public from other sources,

unless the disclosure is made with lawful authority.

(3) For the purposes of subsection (2), a disclosure is made with lawful authority only if, and to the extent that—

(*a*) it is made with the consent of the individual or of the person for the time being carrying on the business;
(*b*) it is made for the purposes of, and is necessary for, the discharge of any of the Commissioner's functions under this Act or any Community obligation of the Commissioner;
(*c*) it is made for the purposes of any civil or criminal proceedings arising under or by virtue of this Part, or otherwise; or
(*d*) having regard to the rights and freedoms or legitimate interests of any person, the disclosure is necessary in the public interest.

(4) A person who knowingly or recklessly discloses information in contravention of subsection (2) is guilty of an offence and liable—

(*a*) on summary conviction, to a **fine** not exceeding **the statutory maximum**; or
(*b*) on conviction on indictment, to a **fine**.

(5) "Relevant person" means a person who is or has been—

(*a*) the Commissioner;
(*b*) a member of the Commissioner's staff; or
(*c*) an agent of the Commissioner.

[Immigration and Asylum Act 1999, s 93.]

PART VI[1]
SUPPORT FOR ASYLUM-SEEKERS

Interpretation

8–17949 **94. Interpretation of Part VI.** (1) In this Part—

"adjudicator" has the meaning given in section 102(2);

"asylum-seeker" means a person who is not under 18 and has made a claim for asylum which has been recorded by the Secretary of State but which has not been determined;*

"claim for asylum" means a claim that it would be contrary to the United Kingdom's obligations under the Refugee Convention, or under Article 3 of the Human Rights Convention, for the claimant to be removed from, or required to leave, the United Kingdom;

"the Department" means the Department of Health and Social Services for Northern Ireland;

"dependant", in relation to an asylum-seeker or a supported person, means a person in the United Kingdom who—

(*a*) is his spouse;
(*b*) is a child of his, or of his spouse, who is under 18 and dependent on him; or
(*c*) falls within such additional category, if any, as may be prescribed;*

"the Executive" means the Northern Ireland Housing Executive;

"housing accommodation" includes flats, lodging houses and hostels;

"local authority" means—

(*a*) in England and Wales, a county council, a county borough council, a district council, a London borough council, the Common Council of the City of London or the Council of the Isles of Scilly;
(*b*) in Scotland, a council constituted under section 2 of the Local Government etc (Scotland) Act 1994;

"Northern Ireland authority" has the meaning given by section 110(9);

"supported person" means—

(*a*) an asylum-seeker, or
(*b*) a dependant of an asylum-seeker,

who has applied for support and for whom support is provided under section 95.

(2) References in this Part to support provided under section 95 include references to support which is provided under arrangements made by the Secretary of State under that section.

(3) For the purposes of this Part, a claim for asylum is determined at the end of such period beginning—

(*a*) on the day on which the Secretary of State notifies the claimant of his decision on the claim, or
(*b*) if the claimant has appealed against the Secretary of State's decision, on the day on which the appeal is disposed of,

as may be prescribed.

(4) An appeal is disposed of when it is no longer pending for the purposes of the Immigration Acts or the Special Immigration Appeals Commission Act 1997.

(5) If an asylum-seeker's household includes a child who is under 18 and a dependant of his, he is to be treated (for the purposes of this Part) as continuing to be an asylum-seeker while—

(*a*) the child is under 18; and
(*b*) he and the child remain in the United Kingdom.**

(6) Subsection (5) does not apply if, on or after the determination of his claim for asylum, the asylum-seeker is granted leave to enter or remain in the United Kingdom (whether or not as a result of that claim).***

(7) For the purposes of this Part, the Secretary of State may inquire into, and decide, the age of any person.

(8) A notice under subsection (3) must be given in writing.

(9) If such a notice is sent by the Secretary of State by first class post, addressed—

(*a*) to the asylum-seeker's representative, or
(*b*) to the asylum-seeker's last known address,

it is to be taken to have been received by the asylum-seeker on the second day after the day on which it was posted.

[Immigration and Asylum Act 1999, s 93, as amended by the Nationality, Immigration and Asylum Act 2002, s 60.]

***Definitions and sub-section (3) substituted by the Nationality, Immigration and Asylum Act 2002, s 44, from a date to be appointed.**

****Sub-sections (5) and (6) repealed by the Nationality, Immigration and Asylum Act 2002, Sch 9, from a date to be appointed.**

1. Part VI comprises ss 94–127.

Provision of support

8–17950 **95. Persons for whom support may be provided.** (1) The Secretary of State may provide, or arrange for the provision of, support for—

(*a*) asylum-seekers, or
(*b*) dependants of asylum-seekers,

who appear to the Secretary of State to be destitute or to be likely to become destitute within such period as may be prescribed.

(2) In prescribed circumstances, a person who would otherwise fall within subsection (1) is excluded.

(3) For the purposes of this section, a person is destitute if—

(*a*) he does not have adequate accommodation or any means of obtaining it (whether or not his other essential living needs are met); or
(*b*) he has adequate accommodation or the means of obtaining it, but cannot meet his other essential living needs.

(4) If a person has dependants, subsection (3) is to be read as if the references to him were references to him and his dependants taken together.

(5) In determining, for the purposes of this section, whether a person's accommodation is adequate, the Secretary of State—

(*a*) must have regard to such matters as may be prescribed[1] for the purposes of this paragraph; but
(*b*) may not have regard to such matters as may be prescribed for the purposes of this paragraph or to any of the matters mentioned in subsection (6).

(6) Those matters are—

(*a*) the fact that the person concerned has no enforceable right to occupy the accommodation;
(*b*) the fact that he shares the accommodation, or any part of the accommodation, with one or more other persons;
(*c*) the fact that the accommodation is temporary;
(*d*) the location of the accommodation.

(7) In determining, for the purposes of this section, whether a person's other essential living needs are met, the Secretary of State—

(*a*) must have regard to such matters as may be prescribed[1] for the purposes of this paragraph; but
(*b*) may not have regard to such matters as may be prescribed for the purposes of this paragraph.

(8) The Secretary of State may by regulations[1] provide that items or expenses of such a description as may be prescribed[1] are, or are not, to be treated as being an essential living need of a person for the purposes of this Part.

(9) Support may be provided subject to conditions.

(10) The conditions must be set out in writing.

(11) A copy of the conditions must be given to the supported person.

(12) Schedule 8 gives the Secretary of State power to make regulations supplementing this section.

(13) Schedule 9 makes temporary provision for support in the period before the coming into force of this section.

[Immigration and Asylum Act 1999, s 95.]

---

1. See the Asylum Support Regulations 2000, SI 2000/704 amended by SI 2000/472 and 3053, SI 20032/3110, SI 2004/763 and 1313 and SI 2005/11, 738, 2078 and 2114.

8–17951 **96. Ways in which support may be provided.** (1) Support may be provided under section 95—

(*a*) by providing accommodation appearing to the Secretary of State to be adequate for the needs of the supported person and his dependants (if any);

(*b*) by providing what appear to the Secretary of State to be essential living needs of the supported person and his dependants (if any);

(*c*) to enable the supported person (if he is the asylum-seeker) to meet what appear to the Secretary of State to be expenses (other than legal expenses or other expenses of a prescribed description) incurred in connection with his claim for asylum;

(*d*) to enable the asylum-seeker and his dependants to attend bail proceedings in connection with his detention under any provision of the Immigration Acts; or

(*e*) to enable the asylum-seeker and his dependants to attend bail proceedings in connection with the detention of a dependant of his under any such provision.

(2) If the Secretary of State considers that the circumstances of a particular case are exceptional, he may provide support under section 95 in such other ways as he considers necessary to enable the supported person and his dependants (if any) to be supported.

(3) *Repealed.*

(4) But the Secretary of State may by order provide for subsection (3) not to apply—

(*a*) in all cases, for such period as may be specified;

(*b*) in such circumstances as may be specified;

(*c*) in relation to specified categories of person; or

(*d*) in relation to persons whose accommodation is in a specified locality.

(5) The Secretary of State may by order repeal subsection (3).

(6) "Specified" means specified in an order made under subsection (4).

[Immigration and Asylum Act 1999, s 96, as amended by SI 2002/782.]

8–17952 **97. Supplemental.** (1) When exercising his power under section 95 to provide accommodation, the Secretary of State must have regard to—

(*a*) the fact that the accommodation is to be temporary pending determination of the asylum-seeker's claim;

(*b*) the desirability, in general, of providing accommodation in areas in which there is a ready supply of accommodation; and

(*c*) such other matters (if any) as may be prescribed.

(2) But he may not have regard to—

(*a*) any preference that the supported person or his dependants (if any) may have as to the locality in which the accommodation is to be provided; or

(*b*) such other matters (if any) as may be prescribed.

(3) The Secretary of State may by order repeal all or any of the following—

(*a*) subsection (1)(*a*);

(*b*) subsection (1)(*b*);

(*c*) subsection (2)(*a*).

(4) When exercising his power under section 95 to provide essential living needs, the Secretary of State—

(*a*) must have regard to such matters as may be prescribed for the purposes of this paragraph; but

(*b*) may not have regard to such other matters as may be prescribed for the purposes of this paragraph.

(5) In addition, when exercising his power under section 95 to provide essential living needs, the Secretary of State may limit the overall amount of the expenditure which he incurs in connection with a particular supported person—

(*a*) to such portion of the income support applicable amount provided under section 124 of the Social Security Contributions and Benefits Act 1992, or (*b*) to such portion of any components of that amount,

as he considers appropriate having regard to the temporary nature of the support that he is providing.

(6) For the purposes of subsection (5), any support of a kind falling within section 96(1)(*c*) is to be treated as if it were the provision of essential living needs.

(7) In determining how to provide, or arrange for the provision of, support under section 95, the Secretary of State may disregard any preference which the supported person or his dependants (if any) may have as to the way in which the support is to be given.
[Immigration and Asylum Act 1999, s 97.]

8–17953 **98. Temporary support.** (1) The Secretary of State may provide, or arrange for the provision of, support for—

(*a*) asylum-seekers, or
(*b*) dependants of asylum-seekers,

who it appears to the Secretary of State may be destitute.

(2) Support may be provided under this section only until the Secretary of State is able to determine whether support may be provided under section 95.

(3) Subsections (2) to (11) of section 95 apply for the purposes of this section as they apply for the purposes of that section.
[Immigration and Asylum Act 1999, s 98.]

Support and assistance by local authorities etc

8–17954 **99. Provision of support by local authorities.** (1) A local authority may provide support for asylum-seekers and their dependants (if any) in accordance with arrangements made by the Secretary of State under section 95.

(2) Such support may be provided by the local authority—

(*a*) in one or more of the ways mentioned in section 96(1) and (2);
(*b*) whether the arrangements in question are made with the authority or with another person.

(3) The Executive may provide support by way of accommodation for asylum-seekers and their dependants (if any) in accordance with arrangements made by the Secretary of State under section 95, whether the arrangements in question are made with the Executive or with another person.

(4) A local authority may incur reasonable expenditure in connection with the preparation of proposals for entering into arrangements under section 95.

(5) The powers conferred on a local authority by this section include power to—

(*a*) provide services outside their area;
(*b*) provide services jointly with one or more bodies who are not local authorities;
(*c*) form a company for the purpose of providing services;
(*d*) tender for contracts (whether alone or with any other person).

[Immigration and Asylum Act 1999, s 99.]

8–17955 **100. Local authority and other assistance for Secretary of State.** (1) This section applies if the Secretary of State asks—

(*a*) a local authority,
(*b*) a registered social landlord,
(*c*) a registered housing association in Scotland or Northern Ireland, or
(*d*) the Executive,

to assist him to exercise his power under section 95 to provide accommodation.

(2) The person to whom the request is made must co-operate in giving the Secretary of State such assistance in the exercise of that power as is reasonable in the circumstances.

(3) Subsection (2) does not require a registered social landlord to act beyond its powers.

(4) A local authority must supply to the Secretary of State such information about their housing accommodation (whether or not occupied) as he may from time to time request.

(5) The information must be provided in such form and manner as the Secretary of State may direct.

(6) "Registered social landlord" has the same meaning as in Part I of the Housing Act 1996.

(7) "Registered housing association" has the same meaning—

(*a*) in relation to Scotland, as in the Housing Associations Act 1985; and
(*b*) in relation to Northern Ireland, as in Part II of the Housing (Northern Ireland) Order 1992.

[Immigration and Asylum Act 1999, s 100.]

8–17956 **101. Reception zones.** (1) The Secretary of State may by order designate as reception zones—

(*a*) areas in England and Wales consisting of the areas of one or more local authorities;
(*b*) areas in Scotland consisting of the areas of one or more local authorities;
(*c*) Northern Ireland.

(2) Subsection (3) applies if the Secretary of State considers that—

(*a*) a local authority whose area is within a reception zone has suitable housing accommodation within that zone; or

(*b*) the Executive has suitable housing accommodation.

(3) The Secretary of State may direct the local authority or the Executive to make available such of the accommodation as may be specified in the direction for a period so specified—

(*a*) to him for the purpose of providing support under section 95; or

(*b*) to a person with whom the Secretary of State has made arrangements under section 95.

(4) A period specified in a direction under subsection (3)—

(*a*) begins on a date so specified; and

(*b*) must not exceed five years.

(5) A direction under subsection (3) is enforceable, on an application made on behalf of the Secretary of State, by injunction or in Scotland an order under section 45(*b*) of the Court of Session Act 1988.

(6) The Secretary of State's power to give a direction under subsection (3) in respect of a particular reception zone must be exercised by reference to criteria specified for the purposes of this subsection in the order designating that zone.

(7) The Secretary of State may not give a direction under subsection (3) in respect of a local authority in Scotland unless the Scottish Ministers have confirmed to him that the criteria specified in the designation order concerned are in their opinion met in relation to that authority.

(8) Housing accommodation is suitable for the purposes of subsection (2) if it—

(*a*) is unoccupied;

(*b*) would be likely to remain unoccupied for the foreseeable future if not made available; and

(*c*) is appropriate for the accommodation of persons supported under this Part or capable of being made so with minor work.

(9) If housing accommodation for which a direction under this section is, for the time being, in force—

(*a*) is not appropriate for the accommodation of persons supported under this Part, but

(*b*) is capable of being made so with minor work,

the direction may require the body to whom it is given to secure that that work is done without delay.

(10) The Secretary of State must make regulations with respect to the general management of any housing accommodation for which a direction under subsection (3) is, for the time being, in force.

(11) Regulations under subsection (10) must include provision—

(*a*) as to the method to be used in determining the amount of rent or other charges to be payable in relation to the accommodation;

(*b*) as to the times at which payments of rent or other charges are to be made;

(*c*) as to the responsibility for maintenance of, and repairs to, the accommodation;

(*d*) enabling the accommodation to be inspected, in such circumstances as may be prescribed, by the body to which the direction was given;

(*e*) with respect to the condition in which the accommodation is to be returned when the direction ceases to have effect.

(12) Regulations under subsection (10) may, in particular, include provision—

(*a*) for the cost, or part of the cost, of minor work required by a direction under this section to be met by the Secretary of State in prescribed circumstances;

(*b*) as to the maximum amount of expenditure which a body may be required to incur as a result of a direction under this section.

(13) The Secretary of State must by regulations make provision ("the dispute resolution procedure") for resolving disputes arising in connection with the operation of any regulations made under subsection (10).

(14) Regulations under subsection (13) must include provision—

(*a*) requiring a dispute to be resolved in accordance with the dispute resolution procedure;

(*b*) requiring the parties to a dispute to comply with obligations imposed on them by the procedure; and

(*c*) for the decision of the person resolving a dispute in accordance with the procedure to be final and binding on the parties.

(15) Before—

(*a*) designating a reception zone in Great Britain,

(*b*) determining the criteria to be included in the order designating the zone, or

(*c*) making regulations under subsection (13),

the Secretary of State must consult such local authorities, local authority associations and other persons as he thinks appropriate.

(16) Before—

(*a*) designating Northern Ireland as a reception zone, or
(*b*) determining the criteria to be included in the order designating Northern Ireland,

the Secretary of State must consult the Executive and such other persons as he thinks appropriate.

(17) Before making regulations under subsection (10) which extend only to Northern Ireland, the Secretary of State must consult the Executive and such other persons as he thinks appropriate.

(18) Before making any other regulations under subsection (10), the Secretary of State must consult—

(*a*) such local authorities, local authority associations and other persons as he thinks appropriate; and
(*b*) if the regulations extend to Northern Ireland, the Executive.

[Immigration and Asylum Act 1999, s 100.]

8–17957 102–104. *Appeals*

Offences

8–17958 105. False representations. (1) A person is guilty of an offence if, with a view to obtaining support for himself or any other person under any provision made by or under this Part, he—

(*a*) makes a statement or representation which he knows is false in a material particular;
(*b*) produces or gives to a person exercising functions under this Part, or knowingly causes or allows to be produced or given to such a person, any document or information which he knows is false in a material particular;
(*c*) fails, without reasonable excuse, to notify a change of circumstances when required to do so in accordance with any provision made by or under this Part; or
(*d*) without reasonable excuse, knowingly causes another person to fail to notify a change of circumstances which that other person was required to notify in accordance with any provision made by or under this Part.

(2) A person guilty of an offence under this section is liable on summary conviction to imprisonment for a term not exceeding three months* or to a fine not exceeding **level 5** on the standard scale, or to both.

[Immigration and Asylum Act 1999, s 105.]

***"51 weeks" substituted by the Criminal Justice Act 2003, Sch 26, from a date to be appointed,**

8–17959 106. Dishonest representations. (1) A person is guilty of an offence if, with a view to obtaining any benefit or other payment or advantage under this Part for himself or any other person, he dishonestly—

(*a*) makes a statement or representation which is false in a material particular;
(*b*) produces or gives to a person exercising functions under this Part, or causes or allows to be produced or given to such a person, any document or information which is false in a material particular;
(*c*) fails to notify a change of circumstances when required to do so in accordance with any provision made by or under this Part; or
(*d*) causes another person to fail to notify a change of circumstances which that other person was required to notify in accordance with any provision made by or under this Part.

(2) A person guilty of an offence under this section is liable—

(*a*) on summary conviction, to imprisonment for a term not exceeding **six months** or to a **fine** not exceeding **the statutory maximum**, or to both; or
(*b*) on conviction on indictment, to imprisonment for a term not exceeding **seven years** or to a fine, or to **both**.

(3) In the application of this section to Scotland, in subsection (1) for "dishonestly" substitute "knowingly".

[Immigration and Asylum Act 1999, s 106.]

8–17960 107. Delay or obstruction. (1) A person is guilty of an offence if, without reasonable excuse, he—

(*a*) intentionally delays or obstructs a person exercising functions conferred by or under this Part; or
(*b*) refuses or neglects to answer a question, give any information or produce a document when required to do so in accordance with any provision made by or under this Part.

(2) A person guilty of an offence under subsection (1) is liable on summary conviction to a fine not exceeding **level 3** on the standard scale.
[Immigration and Asylum Act 1999, s 107.]

8–17961 **108. Failure of sponsor to maintain.** (1) A person is guilty of an offence if, during any period in respect of which he has given a written undertaking in pursuance of the immigration rules to be responsible for the maintenance and accommodation of another person—

(*a*) he persistently refuses or neglects, without reasonable excuse, to maintain that person in accordance with the undertaking; and
(*b*) in consequence of his refusal or neglect, support under any provision made by or under this Part is provided for or in respect of that person.

(2) A person guilty of an offence under this section is liable on summary conviction to imprisonment for a term not exceeding **3 months*** or to a fine not exceeding **level 4** on the standard scale, or to **both**.

(3) For the purposes of this section, a person is not to be taken to have refused or neglected to maintain another person by reason only of anything done or omitted in furtherance of a trade dispute.
[Immigration and Asylum Act 1999, s 108.]

***"51 weeks" substituted by the Criminal Justice Act 2003, Sch 26, from a date to be appointed,**

8–17962 **109. Supplemental.** (1) If an offence under section 105, 106, 107 or 108 committed by a body corporate is proved—

(*a*) to have been committed with the consent or connivance of an officer, or
(*b*) to be attributable to neglect on his part,

the officer as well as the body corporate is guilty of the offence and liable to be proceeded against and punished accordingly.

(2) "Officer", in relation to a body corporate, means a director, manager, secretary or other similar officer of the body, or a person purporting to act in such a capacity.

(3) If the affairs of a body corporate are managed by its members, subsection (1) applies in relation to the acts and defaults of a member in connection with his functions of management as if he were a director of the body corporate.

(4) If an offence under section 105, 106, 107 or 108 committed by a partnership in Scotland is proved—

(*a*) to have been committed with the consent or connivance of a partner, or
(*b*) to be attributable to neglect on his part,

the partner as well as the partnership is guilty of the offence and liable to be proceeded against and punished accordingly.

(5) "Partner" includes a person purporting to act as a partner.
[Immigration and Asylum Act 1999, s 109.]

Expenditure

8–17963 **110. Payments to local authorities. Secretary of State may from time to time pay to any local authority such sums as he considers appropriate in respect of expenditure incurred, or to be incurred, by the authority in connection with—**

(*a*) persons who are, or have been, asylum-seekers; and
(*b*) their dependants.

[Immigration and Asylum Act 1999, s 110—summarised.]

8–17964 **111.** *Grants to voluntary organisations*

8–17965 **112. Recovery of expenditure on support: misrepresentation etc.** Application may be made by the Secretary of State to the county court for recovery of expenditure on support in cases of misrepresentation.
[Immigration and Asylum Act 1999, s 112—summarised.]

8–17966 **113. Recovery of expenditure on support from sponsor.** (1) This section applies if—

(*a*) a person ("the sponsor") has given a written undertaking in pursuance of the immigration rules to be responsible for the maintenance and accommodation of another person; and
(*b*) during any period in relation to which the undertaking applies, support under section 95 is provided to or in respect of that other person.

(2) The Secretary of State may make a complaint against the sponsor to a magistrates' court for an order under this section.

(3) The court—

(*a*) must have regard to all the circumstances (and in particular to the sponsor's income); and (*b*) may order him to pay to the Secretary of State such sum (weekly or otherwise) as it considers appropriate.

(4) But such a sum is not to include any amount attributable otherwise than to support provided under section 95.

(5) In determining—

(*a*) whether to order any payments to be made in respect of support provided under section 95 for any period before the complaint was made, or

(*b*) the amount of any such payments,

the court must disregard any amount by which the sponsor's current income exceeds his income during that period.

(6) An order under this section is enforceable as a magistrates' court maintenance order within the meaning of section 150(1) of the Magistrates' Courts Act 1980.

(7) In the application of this section to Scotland—

(*a*) omit subsection (6);

(*b*) for references to a complaint substitute references to an application; and

(*c*) for references to a magistrates' court substitute references to the sheriff.

[Immigration and Asylum Act 1999, s 113.]

8–17967 **114. Overpayments.** (1) Subsection (2) applies if, as a result of an error on the part of the Secretary of State, support has been provided to a person under section 95 or 98.

(2) The Secretary of State may recover from a person who is, or has been, a supported person an amount representing the monetary value of support provided to him as a result of the error.

(3) An amount recoverable under subsection (2) may be recovered as if it were a debt due to the Secretary of State.

(4) The Secretary of State may by regulations[1] make provision for other methods of recovery, including deductions from support provided under section 95.

[Immigration and Asylum Act 1999, s 114.]

1. See the Asylum Support Regulations 2000, SI 2000/704 amended by SI 2000/472 and 3053, SI 2002/3110, SI 2004/763 and 1313 and SI 2005/11, 738, 2078 and 2114.

Exclusions

8–17968 **115. Exclusion from benefits.** (1) No person is entitled to income-based jobseeker's allowance under the Jobseekers Act 1995 or to state pension credit under the State Pension Credit Act 2002 or to—

(*a*) attendance allowance,

(*b*) severe disablement allowance,

(*c*) carer's allowance,*

(*d*) disability living allowance,

(*e*) income support,

(*f*) *repealed*

(*g*) *repealed*

(*h*) a social fund payment,

(*i*) child benefit,

(*j*) housing benefit, or

(*k*) council tax benefit,

under the Social Security Contributions and Benefits Act 1992 while he is a person to whom this section applies.

(2) No person in Northern Ireland is entitled to—

(*a*) income-based jobseeker's allowance under the Jobseekers (Northern Ireland) Order 1995, or

(*b*) any of the benefits mentioned in paragraphs (*a*) to (*j*) of subsection (1),

under the Social Security Contributions and Benefits (Northern Ireland) Act 1992 while he is a person to whom this section applies.

(3) This section applies to a person subject to immigration control unless he falls within such category or description, or satisfies such conditions, as may be prescribed.

(4) Regulations under subsection (3) may provide for a person to be treated for prescribed purposes only as not being a person to whom this section applies.

(5) In relation to child benefit, "prescribed" means prescribed by regulations made by the Treasury.

(6) In relation to the matters mentioned in subsection (2) (except so far as it relates to child benefit), "prescribed" means prescribed by regulations made by the Department.

(7) Section 175(3) to (5) of the Social Security Contributions and Benefits Act 1992 (supplemental powers in relation to regulations) applies to regulations made by the Secretary of State or the Treasury under subsection (3) as it applies to regulations made under that Act.

(8) Sections 133(2), 171(2) and 172(4) of the Social Security Contributions and Benefits (Northern Ireland) Act 1992 apply to regulations made by the Department under subsection (3) as they apply to regulations made by the Department under that Act.

(9) "A person subject to immigration control" means a person who is not a national of an EEA State and who—

(*a*) requires leave to enter or remain in the United Kingdom but does not have it;
(*b*) has leave to enter or remain in the United Kingdom which is subject to a condition that he does not have recourse to public funds;
(*c*) has leave to enter or remain in the United Kingdom given as a result of a maintenance undertaking; or
(*d*) has leave to enter or remain in the United Kingdom only as a result of paragraph 17 of Schedule 4.

(10) "Maintenance undertaking", in relation to any person, means a written undertaking given by another person in pursuance of the immigration rules to be responsible for that person's maintenance and accommodation.

[Immigration and Asylum Act 1999, s 115, as amended by the Tax Credits Act 2002, s 60 and the State Pension Credit Act 2002, s 4.]

***Please note, for some purposes, this text still reads " invalid care allowance". See SI 2002/1457.**

8–17970 **122. Support for children.** (1) In this section "eligible person" means a person who appears to the Secretary of State to be a person for whom support may be provided under section 95.

(2) Subsections (3) and (4) apply if an application for support under section 95 has been made by an eligible person whose household includes a dependant under the age of 18 ("the child").

(3) If it appears to the Secretary of State that adequate accommodation is not being provided for the child, he must exercise his powers under section 95 by offering, and if his offer is accepted by providing or arranging for the provision of, adequate accommodation for the child as part of the eligible person's household.

(4) If it appears to the Secretary of State that essential living needs of the child are not being met, he must exercise his powers under section 95 by offering, and if his offer is accepted by providing or arranging for the provision of, essential living needs for the child as part of the eligible person's household.

(5) No local authority may provide assistance under any of the child welfare provisions in respect of a dependant under the age of 18, or any member of his family, at any time when—

(*a*) the Secretary of State is complying with this section in relation to him; or
(*b*) there are reasonable grounds for believing that—

(i) the person concerned is a person for whom support may be provided under section 95; and
(ii) the Secretary of State would be required to comply with this section if that person had made an application under section 95.

(6) "Assistance" means the provision of accommodation or of any essential living needs.

(7) "The child welfare provisions" means—

(*a*) section 17 of the Children Act 1989 (local authority support for children and their families);
(*b*) section 22 of the Children (Scotland) Act 1995 (equivalent provision for Scotland); and
(*c*) Article 18 of the Children (Northern Ireland) Order 1995 (equivalent provision for Northern Ireland).

(8) Subsection (9) applies if accommodation provided in the discharge of the duty imposed by subsection (3) has been withdrawn.

(9) Only the relevant authority may provide assistance under any of the child welfare provisions in respect of the child concerned.

(10) "Relevant authority" means—

(*a*) in relation to Northern Ireland, the authority within whose area the withdrawn accommodation was provided;
(*b*) in any other case, the local authority within whose area the withdrawn accommodation was provided.

(11) In such circumstances as may be prescribed, subsection (5) does not apply.

[Immigration and Asylum Act 1999, s 122.]

8–17971 **123. Back-dating of benefits where person recorded as refugee.** (1) This section applies if—

(*a*) a person is recorded by the Secretary of State as a refugee within the meaning of the Refugee Convention; and (*b*) before the refugee was so recorded, he or his dependant was a person to whom section 115 applied.

(2) Regulations may provide that a person mentioned in subsection (1)(*b*) may, within a prescribed period, claim the whole, or any prescribed proportion, of any benefit to which he would have been entitled had the refugee been so recorded when he made his claim for asylum.

(3) Subsections (5) and (6) apply if the refugee has resided in the areas of two or more local authorities and he or his dependant makes a claim under the regulations in relation to housing benefit.

(4) Subsections (5) and (6) also apply if the refugee has resided in the areas of two or more local authorities in Great Britain and he or his dependant makes a claim under the regulations in relation to council tax benefit.

(5) The claim must be investigated and determined, and any benefit awarded must be paid or allowed, by such one of those authorities as may be prescribed by the regulations ("the prescribed authority").

(6) The regulations may make provision requiring a local authority who are not the prescribed authority to supply that authority with such information as they may reasonably require in connection with the exercise of their functions under the regulations.

(7) The regulations may make provision in relation to a person who has received support under this Part or who is a dependant of such a person*—

(*a*) for the determination, or for criteria for the calculation, of the value of that support; and

(*b*) for the sum which he would be entitled to claim under the regulations to be reduced by the whole, or any prescribed proportion, of that valuation.

(8) The reductions permitted by subsection (7) must not exceed the amount of the valuation.

(9) "Regulations" means—

(*a*) in relation to jobseeker's allowance under the Jobseekers Act 1995, regulations made by the Secretary of State under that Act or the Social Security Administration Act 1992;

(*b*) in relation to jobseeker's allowance under the Jobseekers (Northern Ireland) Order 1995, regulations made by the Department under that Order or the Social Security Administration (Northern Ireland) Act 1992;

(*ba*) in relation to child benefit (and guardian's allowance), regulations made by the Treasury;

(*c*) in relation to a benefit (apart from child benefit and guardian's allowance) under the Social Security Contributions and Benefits Act 1992 or state pension credit, regulations made by the Secretary of State under that Act or the Social Security Administration Act 1992;

(*d*) in relation to a benefit (apart from child benefit and guardian's allowance) under the Social Security Contributions and Benefits (Northern Ireland) Act 1992, regulations made by the Department under that Act or the Social Security Administration (Northern Ireland) Act 1992.

[Immigration and Asylum Act 1999, s 123, as amended by the Tax Credits Act 2002, s 51 and the State Pension Credit Act 2002, s 14.]

Miscellaneous

8–17972 **124. Secretary of State to be corporation sole for purposes Part VI.** (1) For the purpose of exercising his functions under this Part, the Secretary of State is a corporation sole.

(2) Any instrument in connection with the acquisition, management or of disposal of property, real or personal, heritable or moveable, by the Secretary of State under this Part may be executed on his behalf by a person authorised by him for that purpose.

(3) Any instrument purporting to have been so executed on behalf of the Secretary of State is to be treated, until the contrary is proved, to have been so executed on his behalf.

[Immigration and Asylum Act 1999, s 124.]

8–17973 **125. Entry of premises.** (1) This section applies in relation to premises in which accommodation has been provided under section 95 or 98 for a supported person.

(2) If, on an application made by a person authorised in writing by the Secretary of State, a justice of the peace is satisfied that there is reason to believe that—

(*a*) the supported person or any dependants of his for whom the accommodation is provided is not resident in it,

(*b*) the accommodation is being used for any purpose other than the accommodation of the asylum-seeker or any dependant of his, or

(*c*) any person other than the supported person and his dependants (if any) is residing in the accommodation,

he may grant a warrant to enter the premises to the person making the application.

(3) A warrant granted under subsection (2) may be executed—

(*a*) at any reasonable time;

(*b*) using reasonable force.

(4) In the application of subsection (2) to Scotland, read the reference to a justice of the peace as a reference to the sheriff or a justice of the peace.

[Immigration and Asylum Act 1999, s 125.]

8–17974 **126. Information from property owners.** (1) The power conferred by this section is to be exercised with a view to obtaining information about premises in which accommodation is or has been provided for supported persons.

(2) The Secretary of State may require any person appearing to him—

(*a*) to have any interest in, or

(*b*) to be involved in any way in the management or control of,

such premises, or any building which includes such premises, to provide him with such information with respect to the premises and the persons occupying them as he may specify.

(3) A person who is required to provide information under this section must do so in accordance with such requirements as may be prescribed.

(4) Information provided to the Secretary of State under this section may be used by him only in the exercise of his functions under this Part.

[Immigration and Asylum Act 1999, s 126.]

8–17975 **127. Requirement to supply information about redirection of post.** (1) The Secretary of State may require any person conveying postal packets to supply redirection information to the Secretary of State—

(*a*) for use in the prevention, detection, investigation or prosecution of criminal offences under this Part;

(*b*) for use in checking the accuracy of information relating to support provided under this Part; or

(*c*) for any other purpose relating to the provision of support to asylum-seekers.

(2) The information must be supplied in such manner and form, and in accordance with such requirements, as may be prescribed.

(3) The Secretary of State must make payments of such amount as he considers reasonable in respect of the supply of information under this section.

(4) "Postal packet" has the same meaning as in the Postal Services Act 2000.

(5) "Redirection information" means information relating to arrangements made with any person conveying postal packets for the delivery of postal packets to addresses other than those indicated by senders on the packets.

[Immigration and Asylum Act 1999, s 127, as amended by SI 2001/1149.]

PART VII[1]

POWER TO ARREST, SEARCH AND FINGERPRINT

Power to arrest

8–17576 **128–140.** *Powers of arrest, search and entry*

1. Part VII comprises ss 128–146.

Fingerprinting

8–17989 **141. Fingerprinting.** (1) Fingerprints may be taken by an authorised person from a person to whom this section applies.

(2) Fingerprints may be taken under this section only during the relevant period.

(3) Fingerprints may not be taken under this section from a person under the age of sixteen ("the child") except in the presence of a person of full age who is—

(*a*) the child's parent or guardian; or

(*b*) a person who for the time being takes responsibility for the child.

(4) The person mentioned in subsection (3)(*b*) may not be—

(*a*) an officer of the Secretary of State who is not an authorised person;

(*b*) an authorised person.

(5) "Authorised person" means—

(*a*) a constable;

(*b*) an immigration officer;

(*c*) a prison officer;

(*d*) an officer of the Secretary of State authorised for the purpose; or

(*e*) a person who is employed by a contractor in connection with the discharge of the contractor's duties under a removal centre contract.

(6) In subsection (5)(*e*) "contractor" and "removal centre contract" have the same meaning as in Part VIII.

(7) This section applies to—

(*a*) any person ("A") who, on being required to do so by an immigration officer on his arrival in the United Kingdom, fails to produce a valid passport with photograph or some other document satisfactorily establishing his identity and nationality or citizenship;

(*b*) any person ("B") who has been refused leave to enter the United Kingdom but has been temporarily admitted under paragraph 21 of Schedule 2 to the 1971 Act if an immigration officer reasonably suspects that B might break any condition imposed on him relating to residence or as to reporting to the police or an immigration officer;

(*c*) any person ("C") in respect of whom a relevant immigration decision has been made;

(*d*) any person ("D") who has been arrested under paragraph 17 of Schedule 2 to the 1971 Act;

(*e*) any person ("E") who has made a claim for asylum;

(*f*) any person ("F") who is a dependant of any of those persons.

(8) "The relevant period" begins—

(*a*) for A, on his failure to produce the passport or other document;

(*b*) for B, on the decision to admit him temporarily;

(*c*) for C, on the service on him of notice of the relevant immigration decision by virtue of section 105 of the Nationality, Immigration and Asylum Act 2002 (c 41);

(*d*) for D, on his arrest;

(*e*) for E, on the making of his claim for asylum; and

(*f*) for F, at the same time as for the person whose dependant he is.

(9) "The relevant period" ends on the earliest of the following—

(*a*) the grant of leave to enter or remain in the United Kingdom;

(*b*) for A, B, C or D, his removal or deportation from the United Kingdom;

(*c*) for C—

(i) the time when the relevant immigration decision ceases to have effect, whether as a result of an appeal or otherwise, or

(ii) if a deportation order has been made against him, its revocation or its otherwise ceasing to have effect;

(*d*) for D, his release if he is no longer liable to be detained under paragraph 16 of Schedule 2 to the 1971 Act;

(*e*) for E, the final determination or abandonment of his claim for asylum; and

(*f*) for F, at the same time as for the person whose dependant he is.

(10) No fingerprints may be taken from A if the immigration officer considers that A has a reasonable excuse for the failure concerned.

(11) No fingerprints may be taken from B unless the decision to take them has been confirmed by a chief immigration officer.

(12) An authorised person may not take fingerprints from a person under the age of sixteen unless his decision to take them has been confirmed—

(*a*) if he is a constable, by a person designated for the purpose by the chief constable of his police force;

(*b*) if he is a person mentioned in subsection (5)(*b*) or (*e*), by a chief immigration officer;

(*c*) if he is a prison officer, by a person designated for the purpose by the governor of the prison;

(*d*) if he is an officer of the Secretary of State, by a person designated for the purpose by the Secretary of State.

(13) Neither subsection (3) nor subsection (12) prevents an authorised person from taking fingerprints if he reasonably believes that the person from whom they are to be taken is aged sixteen or over.

(14) For the purposes of subsection (7)(*f*), a person is a dependant of another person if—

(*a*) he is that person's spouse or child under the age of eighteen; and

(*b*) he does not have a right of abode in the United Kingdom or indefinite leave to enter or remain in the United Kingdom.

(15) "Claim for asylum" has the same meaning as in Part VI.

(16) "Relevant immigration decision" means a decision of the kind mentioned in section 82(2)(*g*), (*h*), (*i*), (*j*) or (*k*) of the Nationality, Immigration and Asylum Act 2002 (c 41).

[Immigration and Asylum Act 1999, s 141, as amended by the Nationality, Immigration and Asylum Act 2002, s 66 and the Asylum and Immigration (Treatment of Claimants, etc) Act 2004, s 15.]

8–17990 142. Attendance for fingerprinting. (1) The Secretary of State may, by notice in writing, require a person to whom section 141 applies to attend at a specified place for fingerprinting.

(2) The notice—

(*a*) must give the person concerned a period of at least seven days within which to attend, beginning not earlier than seven days after the date of the notice; and

(*b*) may require him to attend at a specified time of day or during specified hours.

(3) A constable or immigration officer may arrest without warrant a person who has failed to

comply with a requirement imposed on him under this section (unless the requirement has ceased to have effect).

(4) Before a person arrested under subsection (3) is released—

(*a*) he may be removed to a place where his fingerprints may conveniently be taken; and
(*b*) his fingerprints may be taken (whether or not he is so removed).

(5) A requirement imposed under subsection (1) ceases to have effect at the end of the relevant period (as defined by section 141).

[Immigration and Asylum Act 1999, s 142.]

8–17991 **143. Destruction of fingerprints.** (1) If they have not already been destroyed, fingerprints must be destroyed before the end of the specified period beginning with the day on which they were taken.

(2) If a person from whom fingerprints were taken proves that he is—

(*a*) a British citizen, or
(*b*) a Commonwealth citizen who has a right of abode in the United Kingdom as a result of section 2(1)(*b*) of the 1971 Act,

the fingerprints must be destroyed as soon as reasonably practicable.

(3)–(8) (*Repealed*).

(9) Fingerprints taken from F (within the meaning of section 141(7)) must be destroyed when fingerprints taken from the person whose dependant he is have to be destroyed.

(10) The obligation to destroy fingerprints under this section applies also to copies of fingerprints.

(11) The Secretary of State must take all reasonably practicable steps to secure—

(*a*) that data which are held in electronic form and which relate to fingerprints which have to be destroyed as a result of this section are destroyed or erased; or
(*b*) that access to such data is blocked.

(12) The person to whom the data relate is entitled, on request, to a certificate issued by the Secretary of State to the effect that he has taken the steps required by subsection (11).

(13) A certificate under subsection (12) must be issued within three months of the date of the request for it.

(14) (*Repealed*).

(15) "Specified period" means—

(*a*) such period as the Secretary of State may specify by order;
(*b*) if no period is so specified, ten years.

[Immigration and Asylum Act 1999, s 143, as amended by the Anti-terrorism, Crime and Security Act 2001, s 36.]

8–17992 **144. Other methods of collecting data about physical characteristics.** (1) The Secretary of State may make regulations containing provisions equivalent to sections 141, 142 and 143 in relation to such other methods of collecting data about external physical characteristics as may be prescribed.

(2) In subsection (1) "external physical characteristics" includes, in particular, features of the iris or any other part of the eye.

[Immigration and Asylum Act 1999, s 144, as amended by the Nationality, Immigration and Asylum Act 2002, s 128.]

Codes of practice

8–17993 **145. Codes of practice.** (1) An immigration officer exercising any specified power to—

(*a*) arrest, question, search or take fingerprints from a person,
(*b*) enter and search premises, or
(*c*) seize property found on persons or premises,

must have regard to such provisions of a code as may be specified.

(2) Subsection (1) also applies to an authorised person exercising the power to take fingerprints conferred by section 141.

(2A) A person exercising a power under regulations made by virtue of section 144 must have regard to such provisions of a code as may be specified.

(3) Any specified provision of a code may have effect for the purposes of this section subject to such modifications as may be specified.

(4) "Specified" means specified in a direction given by the Secretary of State.

(5) "Authorised person" has the same meaning as in section 141.

(6) "Code" means—

(*a*) in relation to England and Wales, any code of practice for the time being in force under the Police and Criminal Evidence Act 1984;
(*b*) in relation to Northern Ireland, any code of practice for the time being in force under the Police and Criminal Evidence (Northern Ireland) Order 1989.

(7) This section does not apply to any person exercising powers in Scotland.
[Immigration and Asylum Act 1999, s 145, as amended by the Nationality, Immigration and Asylum Act 2002, s 128.]

Use of force

8–17994 **146. Use of force.** (1) An immigration officer exercising any power conferred on him by the 1971 Act or this Act may, if necessary, use reasonable force.

(2) A person exercising a power under any of the following may if necessary use reasonable force—

(*a*) section 28CA, 28FA or 28FB of the 1971 Act (business premises: entry to arrest or search),
(*b*) section 141 or 142 of this Act, and
(*c*) regulations under section 144 of this Act.

[Immigration and Asylum Act 1999, s 146, as amended by the Nationality, Immigration and Asylum Act 2002, s 153.]

PART VIII[1]
REMOVAL CENTRES AND DETAINED PERSONS

Interpretation

8–17995 **147. Interpretation of Part VIII.** In this Part—

"certificate of authorisation" means a certificate issued by the Secretary of State under section 154;

"certified prisoner custody officer" means a prisoner custody officer certified under section 89 of the Criminal Justice Act 1991, or section 114 of the Criminal Justice and Public Order Act 1994, to perform custodial duties;

"contract monitor" means a person appointed by the Secretary of State under section 149(4);

"contracted out removal centre" means a removal centre in relation to which a removal centre contract is in force;

"contractor", in relation to a removal centre which is being run in accordance with a removal centre contract, means the person who has contracted to run it;

"custodial functions" means custodial functions at a removal centre;

"detained persons" means persons detained or required to be detained under the 1971 Act or under section 62 of the Nationality, Immigration and Asylum Act 2002 (detention by Secretary of State);

"detainee custody officer" means a person in respect of whom a certificate of authorisation is in force;

"removal centre contract" means a contract entered into by the Secretary of State under section 149;

"removal centre rules" means rules made by the Secretary of State under section 153;

"directly managed removal centre" means a removal centre which is not a contracted out removal centre;

"escort arrangements" means arrangements made by the Secretary of State under section 156;

"escort functions" means functions under escort arrangements;

"escort monitor" means a person appointed under paragraph 1 of Schedule 13;

"prisoner custody officer"—

(*a*) in relation to England and Wales, has the same meaning as in the Criminal Justice Act 1991;
(*b*) in relation to Scotland, has the meaning given in section 114(1) of the Criminal Justice and Public Order Act 1994;
(*c*) in relation to Northern Ireland, has the meaning given in section 122(1) of that Act of 1994;

"removal centre" means a place which is used solely for the detention of detained persons but which is not a short-term holding facility, a prison or part of a prison;

"short-term holding facility" means a place used solely for the detention of detained persons for a period of not more than seven days or for such other period as may be prescribed.

[Immigration and Asylum Act 1999, s 147, as amended by the Nationality, Immigration and Asylum Act 2002, ss 62 and 66.]

1. Part VIII comprises ss 147–159.

Removal centres

8–17996 **148. Management of removal centres.** (1) A manager must be appointed for every removal centre.

(2) In the case of a contracted out removal centre, the person appointed as manager must be a detainee custody officer whose appointment is approved by the Secretary of State.

(3) The manager of a removal centre is to have such functions as are conferred on him by removal centre rules.

(4) The manager of a contracted out removal centre may not—

(*a*) enquire into a disciplinary charge laid against a detained person;
(*b*) conduct the hearing of such a charge; or
(*c*) make, remit or mitigate an award in respect of such a charge.

(5) The manager of a contracted out removal centre may not, except in cases of urgency, order—

(*a*) the removal of a detained person from association with other detained persons;
(*b*) the temporary confinement of a detained person in special accommodation; or
(*c*) the application to a detained person of any other special control or restraint (other than handcuffs).

[Immigration and Asylum Act 1999, s 148, as amended by the Nationality, Immigration and Asylum Act 2002, s 66.]

8–17997 149. Contracting out of certain removal centres. (1) The Secretary of State may enter into a contract with another person for the provision or running (or the provision and running) by him, or (if the contract so provides) for the running by sub-contractors of his, of any removal centre or part of a removal centre.

(2) While a removal centre contract for the running of a removal centre or part of a removal centre is in force—

(*a*) the removal centre or part is to be run subject to and in accordance with the provisions of or made under this Part; and
(*b*) in the case of a part, that part and the remaining part are to be treated for the purposes of those provisions as if they were separate removal centres.

(3) If the Secretary of State grants a lease or tenancy of land for the purposes of a removal centre contract, none of the following enactments applies to the lease or tenancy—

(*a*) Part II of the Landlord and Tenant Act 1954 (security of tenure);
(*b*) section 146 of the Law of Property Act 1925 (restrictions on and relief against forfeiture);
(*c*) section 19(1), (2) and (3) of the Landlord and Tenant Act 1927 and the Landlord and Tenant Act 1988 (covenants not to assign etc);
(*d*) the Agricultural Holdings Act 1986;
(*e*) sections 4 to 7 of the Law Reform (Miscellaneous Provisions) (Scotland) Act 1985 (irritancy clauses);
(*f*) the Agricultural Holdings (Scotland) Act 1991 and the Agricultural Holdings (Scotland) Act 2003 (asp 11);
(*g*) section 14 of the Conveyancing Act 1881;
(*h*) the Conveyancing and Law of Property Act 1892;
(*i*) the Business Tenancies (Northern Ireland) Order 1996.

(4) The Secretary of State must appoint a contract monitor for every contracted out removal centre.

(5) A person may be appointed as the contract monitor for more than one removal centre.

(6) The contract monitor is to have—

(*a*) such functions as may be conferred on him by removal centre rules;
(*b*) the status of a Crown servant.

(7) The contract monitor must—

(*a*) keep under review, and report to the Secretary of State on, the running of a removal centre for which he is appointed; and
(*b*) investigate, and report to the Secretary of State on, any allegations made against any person performing custodial functions at that centre.

(8) The contractor, and any sub-contractor of his, must do all that he reasonably can (whether by giving directions to the officers of the removal centre or otherwise) to facilitate the exercise by the contract monitor of his functions.

(9) "Lease or tenancy" includes an underlease, sublease or sub-tenancy.

(10) In relation to a removal centre contract entered into by the Secretary of State before the commencement of this section, this section is to be treated as having been in force at that time.

[Immigration and Asylum Act 1999, s 149, as amended by the Nationality, Immigration and Asylum Act 2002, s 66 and the Agricultural Holdings (Scotland) Act 2003, s 94.]

8–17998 150. Contracted out functions at directly managed removal centres. (1) The Secretary of State may enter into a contract with another person—

(*a*) for functions at, or connected with, a directly managed removal centre to be performed by detainee custody officers provided by that person; or
(*b*) for such functions to be performed by certified prisoner custody officers who are provided by that person.

(2) For the purposes of this section "removal centre" includes a short-term holding facility.

[Immigration and Asylum Act 1999, s 150, as amended by the Nationality, Immigration and Asylum Act 2002, s 66.]

8–17999 **151. Intervention by Secretary of State.** (1) The Secretary of State may exercise the powers conferred by this section if it appears to him that—

(*a*) the manager of a contracted out removal centre has lost, or is likely to lose, effective control of the centre or of any part of it; or
(*b*) it is necessary to do so in the interests of preserving the safety of any person, or of preventing serious damage to any property.

(2) The Secretary of State may appoint a person (to be known as the Controller) to act as manager of the removal centre for the period—

(*a*) beginning with the time specified in the appointment; and
(*b*) ending with the time specified in the notice of termination under subsection (5).

(3) During that period—

(*a*) all the functions which would otherwise be exercisable by the manager or the contract monitor are to be exercisable by the Controller;
(*b*) the contractor and any sub-contractor of his must do all that he reasonably can to facilitate the exercise by the Controller of his functions; and
(*c*) the staff of the removal centre must comply with any directions given by the Controller in the exercise of his functions.

(4) The Controller is to have the status of a Crown servant.

(5) If the Secretary of State is satisfied that a Controller is no longer needed for a particular removal centre, he must (by giving notice to the Controller) terminate his appointment at a time specified in the notice.

(6) As soon as practicable after making an appointment under this section, the Secretary of State must give notice of the appointment to those entitled to notice.

(7) As soon as practicable after terminating an appointment under this section, the Secretary of State must give a copy of the notice of termination to those entitled to notice.

(8) Those entitled to notice are the contractor, the manager, the contract monitor and the Controller.

[Immigration and Asylum Act 1999, s 152, as amended by the Nationality, Immigration and Asylum Act 2002, s 66.]

8–18000 **152. Visiting Committees and inspections.** (1) The Secretary of State must appoint a committee (to be known as the Visiting Committee) for each removal centre.

(2) The functions of the Visiting Committee for a removal centre are to be such as may be prescribed by the removal centre rules.

(3) Those rules must include provision—

(*a*) as to the making of visits to the centre by members of the Visiting Committee;
(*b*) for the hearing of complaints made by persons detained in the centre;
(*c*) requiring the making of reports by the Visiting Committee to the Secretary of State.

(4) Every member of the Visiting Committee for a removal centre may at any time enter the centre and have free access to every part of it and to every person detained there.

(5) In section 5A of the Prison Act 1952 (which deals with the appointment and functions of Her Majesty's Chief Inspector of Prisons), after subsection (5), insert—

"(5A) Subsections (2) to (5) apply to removal centres (as defined by section 147 of the Immigration and Asylum Act 1999 and including any in Scotland) and persons detained in such removal centres as they apply to prisons and prisoners."

[Immigration and Asylum Act 1999, s 152, as amended by the Nationality, Immigration and Asylum Act 2002, s 66.]

8–18001 **153. Removal centre rules.** (1) The Secretary of State must make rules[1] for the regulation and management of removal centres.

(2) Removal centre rules may, among other things, make provision with respect to the safety, care, activities, discipline and control of detained persons.

[Immigration and Asylum Act 1999, s 153, as amended by the Nationality, Immigration and Asylum Act 2002, s 66.]

1. The Detention Centre Rules 2001, SI 2001/238 amended by SI 2005/673 have been made.

Custody and movement of detained persons

8–18002 **154. Detainee custody officers.** (1) On an application made to him under this section, the Secretary of State may certify that the applicant—

(*a*) is authorised to perform escort functions; or
(*b*) is authorised to perform both escort functions and custodial functions.

(2) The Secretary of State may not issue a certificate of authorisation unless he is satisfied that the applicant—

(*a*) is a fit and proper person to perform the functions to be authorised; and

(*b*) has received training to such standard as the Secretary of State considers appropriate for the performance of those functions.

(3) A certificate of authorisation continues in force until such date, or the occurrence of such event, as may be specified in the certificate but may be suspended or revoked under paragraph 7 of Schedule 11.

(4) A certificate which authorises the performance of both escort functions and custodial functions may specify one date or event for one of those functions and a different date or event for the other.

(5) If the Secretary of State may confer functions of detainee custody officers on prsion officers or prisoner custody officers.

(6) A prison officer acting under arrangements made under subsection (5) has all the powers, authority, protection and privileges of a constable.

(7) Schedule 11 makes further provision about detainee custody officers.

[Immigration and Asylum Act 1999, s 154, as amended by the Nationality, Immigration and Asylum Act 2002, s 65.]

8–18003 **155. Custodial functions and discipline etc at removal centres.** (1) Custodial functions may be discharged at a removal centre only by—

(*a*) a detainee custody officer authorised, in accordance with section 154(1), to perform such functions; or

(*b*) a prison officer, or a certified prisoner custody officer, exercising functions in relation to the removal centre—

(i) in accordance with arrangements made under section 154(5); or

(ii) as a result of a contract entered into under section 150(1)(*b*).

(2) Schedule 12 makes provision with respect to discipline and other matters at removal centres and short-term holding facilities.

[Immigration and Asylum Act 1999, s 155, as amended by the Nationality, Immigration and Asylum Act 2002, s 66.]

8–18004 **156. Arrangements for the provision of escorts and custody.** (1) The Secretary of State may make arrangements for—

(*a*) the delivery of detained persons to premises in which they may lawfully be detained;

(*b*) the delivery of persons from any such premises for the purposes of their removal from the United Kingdom in accordance with directions given under the 1971 Act or this Act;

(*c*) the custody of detained persons who are temporarily outside such premises;

(*d*) the custody of detained persons held on the premises of any court.

(2) Escort arrangements may provide for functions under the arrangements to be performed, in such cases as may be determined by or under the arrangements, by detainee custody officers.

(3) "Court" includes—

(*a*) the Asylum and Immigration Tribunal;

(*c*) the Commission.

(4) Escort arrangements may include entering into contracts with other persons for the provision by them of—

(*a*) detainee custody officers; or

(*b*) prisoner custody officers who are certified under section 89 of the Criminal Justice Act 1991, or section 114 or 122 of the Criminal Justice and Public Order Act 1994, to perform escort functions.

(5) Schedule 13 makes further provision about escort arrangements.

(6) A person responsible for performing a function of a kind mentioned in subsection (1), in accordance with a transfer direction, complies with the direction if he does all that he reasonably can to secure that the function is performed by a person acting in accordance with escort arrangements.

(7) "Transfer direction" means

(*a*) a transfer direction given under—

(i) section 48 of the Mental Health Act 1983 (removal to hospital of, among others, persons detained under the 1971 Act); or

(ii) *Northern Ireland*

(*b*) *Scotland*

[Immigration and Asylum Act 1999, s 156 as amended by the Asylum and Immigration (Treatment of Claimants, etc) Act 2004, Sch 2 and SI 2005/2078.]

8–18005 **157. Short-term holding facilities.** (1) The Secretary of State may by regulations[1] extend any provision made by or under this Part in relation to removal centres (other than one mentioned in subsection (2)) to short-term holding facilities.

(2) Subsection (1) does not apply to section 150.

(3) The Secretary of State may make rules for the regulation and management of short-term holding facilities.
[Immigration and Asylum Act 1999, s 157.]

1. The Immigration (Short-term Holding Facilities) Regulations 2002, SI 2002/2538 have been made.

Miscellaneous

8–18006 **158. Wrongful disclosure of information.** (1) A person who is or has been employed (whether as a detainee custody officer, prisoner custody officer or otherwise)—

(*a*) in accordance with escort arrangements,
(*b*) at a contracted out removal centre, or
(*c*) to perform contracted out functions at a directly managed removal centre,

is guilty of an offence if he discloses, otherwise than in the course of his duty or as authorised by the Secretary of State, any information which he acquired in the course of his employment and which relates to a particular detained person.

(2) A person guilty of such an offence is liable—

(*a*) on conviction on indictment, to imprisonment for a term not exceeding **two years** or to a fine or to **both**;
(*b*) on summary conviction, to imprisonment for a term not exceeding **six months** or to a fine not exceeding the **statutory maximum** or to **both**.

(3) "Contracted out functions" means functions which, as the result of a contract entered into under section 150, fall to be performed by detainee custody officers or certified prisoner custody officers.
[Immigration and Asylum Act 1999, s 158, as amended by the Nationality, Immigration and Asylum Act 2002, s 66.]

8–18007 **159. Power of constable to act outside his jurisdiction.** (1) For the purpose of taking a person to or from a removal centre under the order of any authority competent to give the order, a constable may act outside the area of his jurisdiction.

(2) When acting under this section, the constable concerned retains all the powers, authority, protection and privileges of his office.
[Immigration and Asylum Act 1999, s 159, as amended by the Nationality, Immigration and Asylum Act 2002, s 66.]

8–18008

PART IX[1]

REGISTRAR'S CERTIFICATES: PROCEDURE

1. Part IX comprises ss 160–163.

PART X[1]

MISCELLANEOUS AND SUPPLEMENTAL

8–18010 **166. Regulations and orders.** (1) Any power to make rules, regulations or orders conferred by this Act is exercisable by statutory instrument.

(2) But subsection (1) does not apply in relation to orders made under section 90(1), rules made under paragraph 1 of Schedule 5 or immigration rules.

(3) Any statutory instrument made as a result of subsection (1) may—

(*a*) contain such incidental, supplemental, consequential and transitional provision as the person making it considers appropriate;
(*b*) make different provision for different cases or descriptions of case; and
(*c*) make different provision for different areas.

(4) No order is to be made under—

(*a*) section 20,
(*b*) section 21,
(*c*) section 31(10),
(*d*) section 86(2),
(*e*) *repealed*
(*f*) section 97(3),
(*g*) section 143(15), or
(*h*) paragraph 4 of Schedule 5,

unless a draft of the order has been laid before Parliament and approved by a resolution of each House.

(5) No regulations are to be made under—

(*za*) section 4(5),

(*a*) section 9,
(*b*) section 46(8),
(*c*) section 53, or
(*d*) section 144,

unless a draft of the regulations has been laid before Parliament and approved by a resolution of each House.

(6) Any statutory instrument made under this Act, apart from one made—

(*a*) under any of the provisions mentioned in subsection (4) or (5), or
(*b*) under section 24(3), 24A(3) or 170(4) or (7),

shall be subject to annulment by a resolution of either House of Parliament.
[Immigration and Asylum Act 1999, s 166, as amended by the Asylum and Immigration (Treatment of Claimants, etc) Act 2004, s 41 and the Civil Partnership Act 2004, Sch 27.]

---

1. Part X comprises ss 164–170.

8–18011 167. Interpretation. (1) In this Act—

"the 1971 Act" means the Immigration Act 1971;
"adjudicator" (except in Part VI) means an adjudicator appointed under section 57;
"Chief Adjudicator" means the person appointed as Chief Adjudicator under section 57(2);
"claim for asylum" (except in Parts V and VI and section 141) means a claim that it would be contrary to the United Kingdom's obligations under the Refugee Convention for the claimant to be removed from, or required to leave, the United Kingdom;
"the Commission" means the Special Immigration Appeals Commission;
"country" includes any territory;
"EEA State" means a State which is a Contracting Party to the Agreement on the European Economic Area signed at Oporto on 2nd May 1992 as it has effect for the time being;
"the Human Rights Convention" means the Convention for the Protection of Human Rights and Fundamental Freedoms, agreed by the Council of Europe at Rome on 4th November 1950 as it has effect for the time being in relation to the United Kingdom;
"the Immigration Acts" has the meaning given by section 44 of the Asylum and Immigration (Treatment of Claimants, etc) Act 2004

(*c*) the Asylum and Immigration Appeals Act 1993;
(*d*) the Asylum and Immigration Act 1996; and
(*e*) this Act;

"prescribed" means prescribed by regulations made by the Secretary of State;
"the Refugee Convention" means the Convention relating to the Status of Refugees done at Geneva on 28 July 1951 and the Protocol to the Convention;
"voluntary organisations" means bodies (other than public or local authorities) whose activities are not carried on for profit.

(2) The following expressions have the same meaning as in the 1971 Act—

"certificate of entitlement";
"entry clearance";
"illegal entrant";
"immigration officer";
"immigration rules";
"port";
"United Kingdom passport";
"work permit".

[Immigration and Asylum Act 1999, s 167, as amended by the Nationality, Immigration and Asylum Act 2002, s 66 and the Asylum and Immigration (Treatment of Claimants, etc) Act 2004, s 44.]

8–18012 168. *Expenditure and receipts*

8–18013 169. Minor and consequential amendments, transitional provisions and repeals. (1) Schedule 14 makes minor and consequential amendments.

(2) Schedule 15 contains transitional provisions and savings.

(3) The enactments set out in Schedule 16 are repealed.
[Immigration and Asylum Act 1999, s 169.]

8–18014 170. Short title, commencement and extent. (1) This Act may be cited as the Immigration and Asylum Act 1999.

(2) Subsections (1) and (2) of section 115 come into force on the day on which the first regulations made under Schedule 8 come into force.

(3) The following provisions come into force on the passing of this Act—

(*a*) section 4;

(*b*) section 9;
(*c*) section 15;
(*d*) section 27;
(*e*) section 31;
(*f*) section 94;
(*g*) section 95(13);
(*h*) section 99(4) and (5);
(*i*) sections 105 to 109;
(*j*) section 110(1), (2) and (8) (so far as relating to subsections (1) and (2));
(*k*) section 111;
(*l*) section 124;
(*m*) section 140;
(*n*) section 145;
(*o*) section 146(1);
(*p*) sections 166 to 168;
(*q*) this section;
(*r*) Schedule 9;
(*s*) paragraphs 62(2), 73, 78, 79, 81, 82, 87, 88 and 102 of Schedule 14;
(*t*) paragraphs 2 and 13 of Schedule 15.

(4) The other provisions of this Act, except section 10 and paragraph 12 of Schedule 15 (which come into force in accordance with section 9), come into force on such day as the Secretary of State may by order[1] appoint.

(5) Different days may be appointed for different purposes.

(6) This Act extends to Northern Ireland.

(7) Her Majesty may by Order in Council[2] direct that any of the provisions of this Act are to extend, with such modifications (if any) as appear to Her Majesty to be appropriate, to any of the Channel Islands or the Isle of Man.

[Immigration and Asylum Act 1999, s 170.]

1. At the date of going to press, the following commencement orders had been made:

Immigration and Asylum Act 1999 (Commencement No 1) Order 1999, SI 1999/3190;
Immigration and Asylum Act 1999 (Commencement No 2 and Transitional Provisions) Order 2000, SI 2000/168;
Immigration and Asylum Act 1999 (Commencement No 3) Order 2000, SI 2000/464;
Immigration and Asylum Act 1999 (Commencement No 4) Order 2000, SI 2000/1282;
Immigration and Asylum Act 1999 (Commencement No 5 and Transitional Provisions) Order 2000, SI 2000/1985;
Immigration and Asylum Act 1999, (Commencement No 6, Transitional and Consequential Provisions) Order 2000, SI 2000/2444;
Immigration and Asylum Act 1999 (Commencement No 7) Order 2000, SI 2000/ 2698;
Immigration and Asylum Act 1999 (Commencement No 8 and Transitional Provisions) Order 2000, SI 2000/3099.

2. The Immigration and Asylum Act 1999 (Jersey) Order 2003, SI 2003/1252 and the Immigration and Asylum Act 1999 (Guernsey) Order 2003, SI 2003/2900 have been made.

8–18015

Sections 37(6) and 42(8)

SCHEDULE 1
SALE OF TRANSPORTERS

8–18016

Section 56(2)

SCHEDULE 2
THE IMMIGRATION APPEAL TRIBUNAL

8–18017

Section 57(3)

SCHEDULE 3
ADJUDICATORS

8–18018

Section 58(2) to (4)

SCHEDULE 4
APPEALS

Section 83

SCHEDULE 5
THE IMMIGRATION SERVICES COMMISSIONER

(*Amended by the Nationality, Immigration and Asylum Act 2002, s 140 and the Asylum and Immigration (Treatment of Claimants, etc) Act 2004, ss 37 and 38.*)

PART I
REGULATORY FUNCTIONS

The Commissioner's rules

8–18019 **1.** (1) The Commissioner may make rules regulating any aspect of the professional practice, conduct or discipline of—

(*a*) registered persons, and
(*b*) those acting on behalf of registered persons,

in connection with the provision of immigration advice or immigration services.

(2) Before making or altering any rules, the Commissioner must consult such persons appearing to him to represent the views of persons engaged in the provision of immigration advice or immigration services as he considers appropriate.

(3) In determining whether a registered person is competent or otherwise fit to provide immigration advice or immigration services, the Commissioner may take into account any breach of the rules by—

(*a*) that person; and
(*b*) any person acting on behalf of that person.

(4) The rules may, among other things, make provision requiring the keeping of accounts or the obtaining of indemnity insurance.

2. (1) The Commissioner's rules must be made or altered by an instrument in writing.

(2) Such an instrument must specify that it is made under this Schedule.

(3) Immediately after such an instrument is made, it must be printed and made available to the public.

(4) The Commissioner may charge a reasonable fee for providing a person with a copy of the instrument.

(5) A person is not to be taken to have contravened a rule made by the Commissioner if he shows that at the time of the alleged contravention the instrument containing the rule had not been made available in accordance with this paragraph.

(6) The production of a printed copy of an instrument purporting to be made by the Commissioner on which is endorsed a certificate signed by an officer of the Commissioner authorised by him for that purpose and stating—

(*a*) that the instrument was made by the Commissioner,
(*b*) that the copy is a true copy of the instrument, and
(*c*) that on a specified date the instrument was made available to the public in accordance with this paragraph,

is evidence (or in Scotland sufficient evidence) of the facts stated in the certificate.

(7) A certificate purporting to be signed as mentioned in sub-paragraph (6) is to be treated as having been properly signed unless the contrary is shown.

(8) A person who wishes in any legal proceedings to rely on an instrument containing the Commissioner's rules may require him to endorse a copy of the instrument with a certificate of the kind mentioned in sub-paragraph (6).

Code of Standards

3. (1) The Commissioner must prepare and issue a code setting standards of conduct which those to whom the code applies are expected to meet.

(2) The code is to be known as the Code of Standards but is referred to in this Schedule as "the Code".

(3) The Code is to apply to any person providing immigration advice or immigration services other than—

(*a*) a person who is authorised by a designated professional body to practise as a member of the profession whose members are regulated by that body;
(*b*) a person who is acting on behalf of a person who is within paragraph (*a*); or
(*c*) a person mentioned in section 84(6).

(4) It is the duty of any person to whom the Code applies to comply with its provisions in providing immigration advice or immigration services.

(5) If the Commissioner alters the Code, he must re-issue it.

(6) Before issuing the Code or altering it, the Commissioner must consult—

(*a*) each of the designated professional bodies;
(*b*) the designated judges;
(*c*) the Lord President of the Court of Session;
(*d*) the Lord Chief Justice of Northern Ireland; and
(*e*) such other persons appearing to him to represent the views of persons engaged in the provision of immigration advice or immigration services as he considers appropriate.

(7) The Commissioner must publish the Code in such form and manner as the Secretary of State may direct.

Extension of scope of the Code

4. (1) The Secretary of State may by order provide for the provisions of the Code, or such provisions of the Code as may be specified by the order, to apply to—

(*a*) persons authorised by any designated professional body to practise as a member of the profession whose members are regulated by that body; and
(*b*) persons acting on behalf of persons who are within paragraph (*a*);

(2) If the Secretary of State is proposing to act under sub-paragraph (1) he must, before doing so, consult—

(*a*) the Commissioner;
(*b*) the Legal Services Ombudsman, if the proposed order would affect a designated professional body in England and Wales;
(*c*) the Scottish Legal Services Ombudsman, if the proposed order would affect a designated professional body in Scotland;
(*d*) the lay observers appointed under Article 42 of the Solicitors (Northern Ireland) Order 1976, if the proposed order would affect a designated professional body in Northern Ireland.

(3) An order under sub-paragraph (1) requires the approval of—

(*a*) the Lord Chancellor, if it affects a designated professional body in England and Wales or Northern Ireland;
(*b*) the Scottish Ministers, if it affects a designated professional body in Scotland.

(4) Before deciding whether or not to give his approval under sub-paragraph (3)(*a*), the Lord Chancellor must consult—

(*a*) the designated judges, if the order affects a designated professional body in England and Wales;
(*b*) the Lord Chief Justice of Northern Ireland, if it affects a designated professional body in Northern Ireland.

(5) Before deciding whether or not to give their approval under sub-paragraph (3)(*b*), the Scottish Ministers must consult the Lord President of the Court of Session.

Investigation of complaints

5. (1) The Commissioner must establish a scheme ("the complaints scheme") for the investigation by him of relevant complaints made to him in accordance with the provisions of the scheme.

(2) Before establishing the scheme or altering it, the Commissioner must consult—

(*a*) each of the designated professional bodies; and
(*b*) such other persons appearing to him to represent the views of persons engaged in the provision of immigration advice or immigration services as he considers appropriate.

(3) A complaint is a relevant complaint if it relates to—

(*a*) the competence or fitness of a person acting on behalf ofa person providing immigration advice or Immigration services,
(*b*) the competence or fitness of a person employed by, or working under the supervision of, a person providing immigration advice or immigration services,
(*c*) an alleged breach of the Code,
(*d*) an alleged breach of one or more of the Commissioner's rules by a person to whom they apply, or
(*e*) an alleged breach of a rule of a relevant regulatory body,

but not if it relates to a person who is excluded from the application of subsection (1) of section 84 by subsection (6) of that section.

(4) The Commissioner may, on his own initiative, investigate any matter which he would have power to investigate on a complaint made under the complaints scheme.

(5) In investigating any such matter on his own initiative, the Commissioner must proceed as if his investigation were being conducted in response to a complaint made under the scheme.

6. (1) The complaints scheme must provide for a person who is the subject of an investigation under the scheme to be given a reasonable opportunity to make representations to the Commissioner.

(2) Any person who is the subject of an investigation under the scheme must—

(*a*) take such steps as are reasonably required to assist the Commissioner in his investigation; and
(*b*) comply with any reasonable requirement imposed on him by the Commissioner.

(3) If a person fails to comply with sub-paragraph (2)(*a*) or with a requirement imposed under sub-paragraph (2)(*b*) the Commissioner may—

(*a*) in the case of a registered person, cancel his registration;
(*b*) in the case of a person certified by the Commissioner as exempt under section 84(4)(*a*), withdraw his exemption; or
(*c*) in any other case, refer the matter to any relevant regulatory body.

Power to enter premises

7. (1) This paragraph applies if—

(*a*) the Commissioner is investigating a complaint under the complaints scheme;
(*b*) the complaint falls within paragraph 5(3)(*a*), (*b*), (*c*) or (*d*); and
(*c*) there are reasonable grounds for believing that particular premises are being used in connection with the provision of immigration advice or immigration services by a registered or exempt person.

(1A) This paragraph also applies if the Commissioner is investigating a matter under paragraph 5(5) and—

(*a*) the matter is of a kind described in paragraph 5(3)(*a*), (*b*), (*c*) or (*d*) (for which purpose a reference to an allegation shall be treated as a reference to a suspicion of the Commissioner), and
(*b*) there are reasonable grounds for believing that particular premises are being used in connection with the provision of immigration advice or immigration services by a registered or exempt person.

(2) The Commissioner, or a member of his staff authorised in writing by him, may enter the premises at reasonable hours.

(3) Sub-paragraph (2) does not apply to premises to the extent to which they constitute a private residence.

(4) A person exercising the power given by sub-paragraph (2) ("the investigating officer") may—

(*a*) take with him such equipment as appears to him to be necessary;
(*b*) require any person on the premises—

(i) to produce any document which he considers relates to any matter relevant to the investigation; and
(ii) if the document is produced, to provide an explanation of it;

(*c*) require any person to state, to the best of his knowledge and belief, where any such document is to be found;
(*d*) take copies of, or extracts from, any document which is produced;
(*e*) require any information which is held in a computer and is accessible from the premises and which the investigating officer considers relates to any matter relevant to the investigation, to be produced in a form—

(i) in which it can be taken away; and
(ii) in which it is visible and legible.

(5) Instead of exercising the power under sub-paragraph (2), the Commissioner may require such person as he may determine ("his agent") to make a report on the provision of immigration advice or immigration services from the premises.

(6) If the Commissioner so determines, his agent may exercise the power conferred by sub-paragraph (2) as if he were a member of the Commissioner's staff appropriately authorised.

(7) If a registered person fails without reasonable excuse to allow access under sub-paragraph (2) or (6) to any premises under his occupation or control, the Commissioner may cancel his registration.

(8) The Commissioner may also cancel the registration of a registered person who—

(*a*) without reasonable excuse fails to comply with a requirement imposed on him under sub-paragraph (4);
(*b*) intentionally delays or obstructs any person exercising functions under this paragraph; or
(*c*) fails to take reasonable steps to prevent an employee of his from obstructing any person exercising such functions.

(9) Sub-paragraphs (7) and (8) shall apply to an exempt person as they apply to a registered person, but with a reference to cancellation of registration being treated as reference to withdarwal of exemption.

(10) In this paragraph "exempt person" means a person certified by the Commissioner as exempt under section 84(4)(*a*)

Determination of complaints

8. (1) On determining a complaint under the complaints scheme, the Commissioner must give his decision in a written statement.

(2) The statement must include the Commissioner's reasons for his decision.

(3) A copy of the statement must be given by the Commissioner to—

(*a*) the person who made the complaint; and
(*b*) the person who is the subject of the complaint.

9. (1) On determining a complaint under the complaints scheme, the Commissioner may—

(*a*) if the person to whom the complaint relates is a registered person or is acting on behalf of a registered person, record the complaint and the decision on it for consideration when that registered person next applies for his registration to be continued;
(*b*) if the person to whom the complaint relates is a registered person or is acting on behalf of a registered person and the Commissioner considers the matter sufficiently serious to require immediate action, require that registered person to apply for continued registration without delay;
(*c*) refer the complaint and his decision on it to a relevant regulatory body;
(*d*) if the person to whom the complaint relates is certified by the Commissioner as exempt under section 84(4)(*a*) or is employed by, or working under the supervision of, such a person, consider whether to withdraw that person's exemption;
(*e*) lay before the Tribunal a disciplinary charge against a relevant person.

(2) Sub-paragraph (3) applies if—

(*a*) the Tribunal is considering a disciplinary charge against a relevant person; and
(*b*) the Commissioner asks it to exercise its powers under that sub-paragraph.

(3) The Tribunal may give directions (which are to have effect while it is dealing with the charge)—

(*a*) imposing restrictions on the provision of immigration advice or immigration services by the relevant person or by a person acting on his behalf or under his supervision;
(*b*) prohibiting the provision of immigration advice or immigration services by the relevant person or a person acting on his behalf or under his supervision.

(4) "Relevant person" means a person providing immigration advice or immigration services who is—

(*a*) a registered person;
(*b*) a person acting on behalf of a registered person;
(*c*) a member or employee of a body which is a registered person;
(*d*) a person working under the supervision of a member or employee of such a body;
(*e*) a person certified by the Commissioner as exempt under section 84(4)(*a*);
(*f*) a person to whom section 84(4)(*d*) applies; or
(*g*) a person employed by, or working under the supervision of, a person to whom paragraph (*e*) or (*f*) applies.

Complaints referred to designated professional bodies

10. (1) This paragraph applies if the Commissioner refers a complaint to a designated professional body under paragraph 9(1)(*c*).

(2) The Commissioner may give directions setting a timetable to be followed by the designated professional body—

(*a*) in considering the complaint; and
(*b*) if appropriate, in taking disciplinary proceedings in connection with the complaint.

(3) In making his annual report to the Secretary of State under paragraph 21, the Commissioner must take into account any failure of a designated professional body to comply (whether wholly or in part) with directions given to it under this paragraph.

(4) Sub-paragraph (5) applies if the Commissioner or the Secretary of State considers that a designated professional body has persistently failed to comply with directions given to it under this paragraph.

(5) The Commissioner must take the failure into account in determining whether to make a report under section 86(9)(*b*) and the Secretary of State must take it into account in determining whether to make an order under section 86(2).

PART II

COMMISSIONER'S STATUS, REMUNERATION AND STAFF ETC

11–25. *Not reproduced in this work.*

Section 85(3)

SCHEDULE 6
REGISTRATION

(Amended by the Nationality, Immigration and Asylum Act 2002, s 140 and the Asylum and Immigration (Treatment of Claimants, etc) Act 2004, ss 37 and 38.)

Applications for registration

8–18020 **1.** (1) An application for registration under section 84(2)(*a*) must—

(*a*) be made to the Commissioner in such form and manner, and
(*b*) be accompanied by such information and supporting evidence,

as the Commissioner may from time to time determine.

(2) When considering an application for registration, the Commissioner may require the applicant to provide him with such further information or supporting evidence as the Commissioner may reasonably require.

Registration

2. (1) If the Commissioner considers that an applicant for registration is competent and otherwise fit to provide immigration advice and immigration services, he must register the applicant.

(2) Registration may be made so as to have effect—

(*a*) only in relation to a specified field of advice or services;
(*b*) only in relation to the provision of advice or services to a specified category of person;
(*c*) only in relation to the provision of advice or services to a member of a specified category of person; or
(*d*) only in specified circumstances.

Review of qualifications

3. (1) At such intervals as the Commissioner may determine, each registered person must submit an application for his registration to be continued.

(2) Different intervals may be fixed by the Commissioner in relation to different registered persons or descriptions of registered person.

(3) An application for continued registration must—

(*a*) be made to the Commissioner in such form and manner, and
(*b*) be accompanied by such information and supporting evidence,

as the Commissioner may from time to time determine.

(4) When considering an application for continued registration, the Commissioner may require the applicant to provide him with such further information or supporting evidence as the Commissioner may reasonably require.

(5) If the Commissioner considers that an applicant for continued registration is no longer competent or is otherwise unfit to provide immigration advice or immigration services, he must cancel the applicant's registration.

(6) Otherwise, the Commissioner must continue the applicant's registration but may, in doing so, vary the registration—

(*a*) so as to make it have limited effect in any of the ways mentioned in paragraph 2(2); or
(*b*) so as to make it have full effect.

(7) If a registered person fails, without reasonable excuse—

(*a*) to make an application for continued registration as required by sub-paragraph (1) or by a direction given by the Tribunal under section 89(2)(*b*), or
(*b*) to provide further information or evidence under sub-paragraph (4),

the Commissioner may cancel the person's registration as from such date as he may determine.

Variation of registration

3A. The Commissioner may vary a person's registration—

(*a*) so as to make it have limited effect in any of the ways mentioned in paragraph 2(2); or
(*b*) so as to make it have full effect.

Disqualification of certain persons

4. A person convicted of an offence under section 25 or 26(1)(*d*) or (*g*) of the 1971 Act is disqualified for registration under paragraph 2 or for continued registration under paragraph 3.

Fees

5. (1) The Secretary of State may by order[1] specify fees for the registration or continued registration of persons on the register.

(2) No application under paragraph 1 or 3 is to be entertained by the Commissioner unless it is accompanied by the specified fee.

Open registers

6. (1) The register must be made available for inspection by members of the public in a legible form at reasonable hours.

(2) A copy of the register or of any entry in the register must be provided—

(*a*) on payment of a reasonable fee;[1]
(*b*) in written or electronic form; and
(*c*) in a legible form.

(3) Sub-paragraphs (1) and (2) also apply to—

(*a*) the record kept by the Commissioner of the persons to whom he has issued a certificate of exemption under section 84(4)(*a*); and
(*b*) the record kept by the Commissioner of the persons against whom there is in force a direction given by the Tribunal under section 89(8).

1. The Immigration Services Commissioner (Registration Fee) Order 2000, SI 2000/2735 has been made.

8–18021

Section 87(5)

SCHEDULE 7
THE IMMIGRATION SERVICES TRIBUNAL

Section 95(12)

SCHEDULE 8
PROVISION OF SUPPORT: REGULATIONS

General regulation-making power

8–18022 **1.** The Secretary of State may by regulations[1] make such further provision with respect to the powers conferred on him by section 95 as he considers appropriate.

1. See the Asylum Support Regulations 2000, SI 2000/704, amended by SI 2000/472 amended by SI 2000/472 and 3053, SI 2002/3110, SI 2004/763 and 1313 and SI 2005/11, 738, 2078 and 2114.

Determining whether a person is destitute

2. (1) The regulations[2] may provide, in connection with determining whether a person is destitute, for the Secretary of State to take into account, except in such circumstances (if any) as may be prescribed—

(*a*) income which the person concerned, or any dependant of his, has or might reasonably be expected to have, and
(*b*) support which is, or assets of a prescribed kind which are, or might reasonably be expected to be, available to him or to any dependant of his,

otherwise than by way of support provided under section 95.

(2) The regulations may provide that in such circumstances (if any) as may be prescribed, a person is not to be treated as destitute for the purposes of section 95.

2. See the Asylum Support Regulations 2000, SI 2000/704, as amended, note 1 supra.

Prescribed levels of support

3. The regulations[3] may make provision—

(*a*) as to the circumstances in which the Secretary of State may, as a general rule, be expected to provide support in accordance with prescribed levels or of a prescribed kind;
(*b*) as to the circumstances in which the Secretary of State may, as a general rule, be expected to provide support otherwise than in accordance with the prescribed levels.

3. See the Asylum Support Regulations 2000, SI 2000/704, as amended, note 1 supra.

Provision of items and services

4. The regulations may make provision for prescribed items or services to be provided or made available to persons receiving support under section 95 for such purposes and in such circumstances as may be prescribed.

Support and assets to be taken into account

5. The regulations may make provision requiring the Secretary of State, except in such circumstances (if any) as may be prescribed, to take into account, when deciding the level or kind of support to be provided—

(*a*) income which the person concerned, or any dependant of his, has or might reasonably be expected to have, and
(*b*) support which is, or assets of a prescribed kind which are, or might reasonably be expected to be, available to him or to any dependant of his,

otherwise than by way of support provided under section 95.

Valuation of assets

6. The regulations may make provision as to the valuation of assets.

Breach of conditions

7. The regulations may make provision for the Secretary of State to take into account, when deciding—

(*a*) whether to provide, or to continue to provide, support under section 95, or
(*b*) the level or kind of support to be provided,

the extent to which any condition on which support is being, or has previously been, provided has been complied with.

Suspension or discontinuation of support

8. (1) The regulations may make provision for the suspension or discontinuance of support under section 95 in prescribed circumstances (including circumstances in which the Secretary of State would otherwise be under a duty to provide support).

(2) The circumstances which may be prescribed include the cessation of residence—

(*a*) in accommodation provided under section 95; or
(*b*) at an address notified to the Secretary of State in accordance with the regulations.

Notice to quit

9. (1) The regulations may provide that if—

(*a*) as a result of support provided under section 95, a person has a tenancy or a licence to occupy accommodation,
(*b*) one or more of the conditions mentioned in sub-paragraph (2) are satisfied, and
(*c*) he is given such notice to quit as may be prescribed by the regulations,

his tenancy or licence is to be treated as ending with the period specified in that notice, regardless of when it could otherwise be brought to an end.

(2) The conditions are that—

(*a*) the support provided under section 95 is suspended or discontinued as a result of any provision of a kind mentioned in paragraph 8;
(*b*) the relevant claim for asylum has been determined;
(*c*) the supported person has ceased to be destitute;
(*d*) he is to be moved to other accommodation.

Contributions to support

10. The regulations may make provision requiring a supported person to make payments to the Secretary of State, in prescribed circumstances, by way of contributions to the cost of the provision of that support.

Recovery of sums by Secretary of State

11. (1) The regulations may provide for the recovery by the Secretary of State of sums representing the whole or part of the monetary value of support provided to a person under section 95 where it appears to the Secretary of State—

(*a*) that that person had, at the time when he applied for support, assets of any kind in the United Kingdom or elsewhere which were not capable of being realised; but
(*b*) that those assets have subsequently become, and remain, capable of being realised.

(2) An amount recoverable under regulations made by virtue of sub-paragraph (1) may be recovered—

(*a*) as if it were a debt due to the Secretary of State; or
(*b*) by such other method of recovery, including by deduction from support provided under section 95 as may be prescribed.

Procedure

12. The regulations may make provision with respect to procedural requirements including, in particular, provision as to—

(*a*) the procedure to be followed in making an application for support;
(*b*) the information which must be provided by the applicant;
(*c*) the circumstances in which an application may not be entertained;
(*d*) the making of further enquiries by the Secretary of State;
(*e*) the circumstances in which, and person by whom, a change of circumstances of a prescribed description must be notified to the Secretary of State.

Section 95(13)

SCHEDULE 9
ASYLUM SUPPORT: INTERIM PROVISIONS

8–18023 **1.** (1) The Secretary of State may by regulations make provision requiring prescribed local authorities or local authorities falling within a prescribed description of authority to provide support, during the interim period, to eligible persons.

(2) "Eligible persons" means—

(*a*) asylum-seekers, or
(*b*) their dependants,

who appear to be destitute or to be likely to become destitute within such period as may be prescribed.

(3) For the purposes of sub-paragraph (1), in Northern Ireland, a Health and Social Services Board established under Article 16 of the Health and Personal Social Services (Northern Ireland) Order 1972 is to be treated as a local authority.

2. (1) The regulations must provide for the question whether a person is an eligible person to be determined by the local authority concerned.

(2) The regulations may make provision for support to be provided, before the determination of that question, to a person making a claim for support under the regulations by the Secretary of State or such local authority as may be prescribed.

(3) "The local authority concerned" has such meaning as may be prescribed.

3. Subsections (3) to (8) of section 95 apply for the purposes of the regulations as they apply for the purposes of that section, but for the references in subsections (5) and (7) to the Secretary of State substitute references to the local authority concerned.

4. The regulations may prescribe circumstances in which support for an eligible person—

(*a*) must be provided;
(*b*) must or may be refused; or
(*c*) must or may be suspended or discontinued.

5. The regulations[1] may provide that support—

(*a*) is to be provided in prescribed ways;
(*b*) is not to be provided in prescribed ways.

---

1. See the Asylum Support (Interim Provisions) Regulations 1999, SI 1999/3056 amended by SI 2002/471 amended by SI 2005/595 and 2114.

6. The regulations[2] may include provision—

(*a*) as to the level of support that is to be provided;
(*b*) for support to be provided subject to conditions;
(*c*) requiring any such conditions to be set out in writing;
(*d*) requiring a copy of any such conditions to be given to such person as may be prescribed.

7. The regulations may make provision that, in providing support, a local authority—

(*a*) are to have regard to such matters as may be prescribed;
(*b*) are not to have regard to such matters as may be prescribed.

8. The regulations may include provision—

(*a*) prescribing particular areas, or descriptions of area, (which may include a locality within their own area) in which a local authority may not place asylum-seekers while providing support for them;
(*b*) prescribing circumstances in which a particular area, or description of area, (which may include a locality within their own area) is to be one in which a local authority may not place asylum-seekers while providing support for them;
(*c*) as to the circumstances (if any) in which any such provision is not to apply.

9. (1) The regulations may make provision for the referral by one local authority to another of a claim for support made under the regulations if the local authority to whom the claim is made consider that it is not manifestly unfounded but—

(*a*) they are providing support for a number of asylum-seekers equal to, or greater than, the maximum number of asylum-seekers applicable to them; or
(*b*) they are providing support for a number of eligible persons equal to, or greater than, the maximum number of eligible persons applicable to them.

(2) For the purposes of any provision made as a result of sub-paragraph (1), the regulations may make provision for the determination by the Secretary of State of—

(*a*) the applicable maximum number of asylum-seekers;
(*b*) the applicable maximum number of eligible persons.

(3) The regulations may make provision for any such determination to be made—

(*a*) for local authorities generally;
(*b*) for prescribed descriptions of local authority; or
(*c*) for particular local authorities.

(4) The regulations may provide that a referral may not be made—

(*a*) to a prescribed local authority;
(*b*) to local authorities of a prescribed description; or
(*c*) in prescribed circumstances.

(5) The regulations may make provision for the payment by a local authority of any reasonable travel or subsistence expenses incurred as a result of a referral made by them.

(6) The regulations may make provision for the transfer of a claim for support, or responsibility for providing support, under the regulations from one local authority to another on such terms as may be agreed between them.

(7) In exercising any power under the regulations to refer or transfer, a local authority must have regard to such guidance as may be issued by the Secretary of State with respect to the exercise of the power.

10. (1) The regulations may make provision for the referral of claims for support made to the Secretary of State to prescribed local authorities or local authorities of a prescribed description.

(2) The regulations may make provision for the payment by the Secretary of State of any reasonable travel or subsistence expenses incurred as a result of a referral made by him as a result of provision made by virtue of sub-paragraph (1).

11. The regulations may make provision requiring prescribed local authorities or other prescribed bodies to give reasonable assistance to local authorities providing support under the regulations.

12. The regulations may make provision for the procedure for making and determining claims for support.

13. The regulations may make provision for an asylum-seeker or a dependant of an asylum-seeker who has received, or is receiving, any prescribed description of support from a local authority to be taken to have been accepted for support under the regulations by a prescribed local authority.

14. A person entitled to support under the regulations is not entitled to any prescribed description of support, except to such extent (if any) as may be prescribed.

15. "The interim period" means the period—

(*a*) beginning on such day as may be prescribed for the purposes of this paragraph; and
(*b*) ending on such day as may be so prescribed.

8–18024

Section 102(3)

SCHEDULE 10
ASYLUM SUPPORT ADJUDICATORS

Section 154(7)

SCHEDULE 11
DETAINEE CUSTODY OFFICERS

(*Amended by the Nationality, Immigration and Asylum Act 2002, ss 65 and 66.*)

Obtaining certificates of authorisation by false pretences

8–18025 **1.** A person who, for the purpose of obtaining a certificate of authorisation for himself or for any other person—

(*a*) makes a statement which he knows to be false in a material particular, or
(*b*) recklessly makes a statement which is false in a material particular,

is guilty of an offence and liable on summary conviction to a fine not exceeding **level** 4 on the standard scale.

Powers and duties of detainee custody officers

2. (1) A detainee custody officer exercising custodial functions has power—

(*a*) to search (in accordance with rules made by the Secretary of State) any detained person in relation to whom the officer is exercising custodial functions; and
(*b*) to search any other person who is in, or is seeking to enter, any place where any such detained person is or is to be held, and any article in the possession of such a person.

(2) The power conferred by sub-paragraph (1)(*b*) does not authorise requiring a person to remove any of his clothing other than an outer coat, jacket or glove.

(3) As respects a detained person in relation to whom he is exercising custodial functions, it is the duty of a detainee custody officer—

(*a*) to prevent that person's escape from lawful custody;
(*b*) to prevent, or detect and report on, the commission or attempted commission by him of other unlawful acts;
(*c*) to ensure good order and discipline on his part; and
(*d*) to attend to his wellbeing.

(4) The powers conferred by sub-paragraph (1), and the powers arising by virtue of sub-paragraph (3), include power to use reasonable force where necessary.

Short-term holding facilities

3. (1) A detainee custody officer may perform functions of a custodial nature at a short-term holding facility (whether or not he is authorised to perform custodial functions at a removal centre).

(2) When doing so, he is to have the same powers and duties in relation to the facility and persons detained there as he would have if the facility were a removal centre.

Assaulting a detainee custody officer

4. A person who assaults a detainee custody officer who is—

(*a*) acting in accordance with escort arrangements,
(*b*) performing custodial functions, or
(*c*) performing functions of a custodial nature at a short-term holding facility,

is guilty of an offence and liable on summary conviction to a fine not exceeding **level 5** on the standard scale or to imprisonment for a term not exceeding **six months** or to **both**.

Obstructing detainee custody officers

5. A person who resists or wilfully obstructs a detainee custody officer who is—

(*a*) acting in accordance with escort arrangements,
(*b*) performing custodial functions, or
(*c*) performing functions of a custodial nature at a short-term holding facility,

is guilty of an offence and liable on summary conviction to a fine not exceeding **level 3** on the standard scale.

Uniforms and badges

6. For the purposes of paragraphs 4 and 5, a detainee custody officer is not to be regarded as acting in accordance with escort arrangements at any time when he is not readily identifiable as such an officer (whether by means of a uniform or badge which he is wearing or otherwise).

Suspension and revocation of certificates of authorisation

7. (1) If it appears to the Secretary of State that a detainee custody officer is not a fit and proper person to perform escort functions or custodial functions, he may revoke that officer's certificate so far as it authorises the performance of those functions.

(2) If it appears to the escort monitor that a detainee custody officer is not a fit and proper person to perform escort functions, he may—

(*a*) refer the matter to the Secretary of State; or

(*b*) in such circumstances as may be prescribed, suspend the officer's certificate pending a decision by the Secretary of State as to whether to revoke it.

(3) If it appears to the contract monitor for the removal centre concerned that a detainee custody officer is not a fit and proper person to perform custodial functions, he may—

(*a*) refer the matter to the Secretary of State; or

(*b*) in such circumstances as may be prescribed, suspend the officer's certificate pending a decision by the Secretary of State as to whether to revoke it.

Prison officers and prisoner custody officers

8. A reference in this Schedule to a detainee custody officer includes a reference to a prison officer or prisoner custody officer exercising custodial functions.

Section 155(2)

SCHEDULE 12

DISCIPLINE ETC AT DETENTION CENTRES

(*Amended by the Nationality, Immigration and Asylum Act 2002, ss 65 and 66.*)

Measuring and photographing detained persons

8–18026 **1.** (1) Removal centre rules may (among other things) provide for detained persons to be measured and photographed.

(2) The rules may, in particular, prescribe—

(*a*) the time or times at which detained persons are to be measured and photographed;

(*b*) the manner and dress in which they are to be measured and photographed; and

(*c*) the numbers of copies of measurements or photographs that are to be made and the persons to whom they are to be sent.

Testing for drugs or alcohol

2. (1) If an authorisation is in force, a detainee custody officer may, at the centre to which the authorisation applies and in accordance with removal centre rules, require a detained person who is confined in the centre to provide a sample for the purpose of ascertaining—

(*a*) whether he has a drug in his body; or

(*b*) whether he has alcohol in his body.

(2) The sample required may be one or more of the following—

(*a*) a sample of urine;

(*b*) a sample of breath;

(*c*) a sample of a specified description.

(3) Sub-paragraph (2)(*c*)—

(*a*) applies only if the authorisation so provides; and

(*b*) does not authorise the taking of an intimate sample.

(4) "Authorisation" means an authorisation given by the Secretary of State for the purposes of this paragraph in respect of a particular removal centre.

(5) "Drug" means a drug which is a controlled drug for the purposes of the Misuse of Drugs Act 1971.

(6) "Specified" means specified in the authorisation.

(7) "Intimate sample"—

(*a*) in relation to England and Wales, has the same meaning as in Part V of the Police and Criminal Evidence Act 1984;

(*b*) in relation to Scotland, means—

(i) a sample of blood, semen or any other tissue fluid, urine or pubic hair;

(ii) a dental impression;

(iii) a swab taken from a person's body orifice other than the mouth; and

(*c*) in relation to Northern Ireland, has the same meaning as in Part VI of the Police and Criminal Evidence (Northern Ireland) Order 1989.

Medical examinations

3. (1) This paragraph applies if—

(*a*) an authorisation is in force for a removal centre; and

(*b*) there are reasonable grounds for believing that a person detained in the centre is suffering from a disease which is specified in an order in force under sub-paragraph (7).

(2) A detainee custody officer may require the detained person to submit to a medical examination at the centre.

(3) The medical examination must be conducted in accordance with removal centre rules.

(4) A detained person who fails, without reasonable excuse, to submit to a medical examination required under this paragraph is guilty of an offence.

(5) A person guilty of an offence under sub-paragraph (4) is liable on summary conviction to imprisonment for a term not exceeding six months or to a fine not exceeding **level 5** on the standard scale.

(6) "Authorisation" means an authorisation given by the manager of the removal centre for the purpose of this paragraph.

(7) The Secretary of State may by order specify any disease which he considers might, if a person detained in a removal centre were to suffer from it, endanger the health of others there.

Assisting detained persons to escape

4. (1) A person who aids any detained person in escaping or attempting to escape from a removal centre or short-term holding facility is guilty of an offence.

(2) A person who, with intent to facilitate the escape of any detained person from a removal centre or short-term holding facility—

(*a*) conveys any thing into the centre or facility or to a detained person,
(*b*) sends any thing (by post or otherwise) into the centre or facility or to a person detained there,
(*c*) places any thing anywhere outside the centre or facility with a view to its coming into the possession of a person detained there,

is guilty of an offence.

(3) A person guilty of an offence under this section is liable—

(*a*) on summary conviction, to imprisonment for a term not exceeding **six months** or to a fine not exceeding **the statutory maximum** or to **both**; or
(*b*) on conviction on indictment, to imprisonment for a term not exceeding **two years** or to a fine or to **both**.

Alcohol

5. (1) A person who, contrary to removal centre rules, brings or attempts to bring any alcohol into a removal centre, or to a detained person, is guilty of an offence.

(2) A person who places alcohol anywhere outside a removal centre, intending that it should come into the possession of a detained person there, is guilty of an offence.

(3) A detainee custody officer or any other person on the staff of a removal centre who, contrary to removal centre rules, allows alcohol to be sold or used in the centre is guilty of an offence.

(4) A person guilty of an offence under this paragraph is liable on summary conviction to imprisonment for a term not exceeding **six months** or to a fine not exceeding **level 3** on the standard scale or to both.

(5) "Alcohol" means any spirituous or fermented liquor.

Introduction of other articles

6. (1) A person who—

(*a*) conveys or attempts to convey any thing into or out of a removal centre or to a detained person, contrary to removal centre rules, and
(*b*) is not as a result guilty of an offence under paragraph 4 or 5,

is guilty of an offence under this paragraph.

(2) A person who—

(*a*) places any thing anywhere outside a removal centre, intending it to come into the possession of a detained person, and
(*b*) is not as a result guilty of an offence under paragraph 4 or 5,

is guilty of an offence under this paragraph.

(3) A person guilty of an offence under this paragraph is liable on summary conviction to a fine not exceeding **level 3** on the standard scale.

Notice of penalties

7. (1) In the case of a contracted out removal centre, the contractor must cause a notice setting out the penalty to which a person committing an offence under paragraph 4, 5 or 6 is liable to be fixed outside the centre in a conspicuous place.

(2) In the case of any other removal centre, the Secretary of State must cause such a notice to be fixed outside the centre in a conspicuous place.

8. (1) In the case of a contracted out short-term holding facility, the contractor must cause a notice setting out the penalty to which a person committing an offence under paragraph 4 is liable to be fixed outside the facility in a conspicuous place.

(2) In the case of any other short-term holding facility, the Secretary of State must cause such a notice to be fixed outside the facility in a conspicuous place.

Prison officers and prisoner custody officers

8. A reference in this Schedule to a detainee custody officer includes a reference to a prison officer or prisoner custody officer exercising custodial functions.

Section 156(5)

SCHEDULE 13
ESCORT ARRANGEMENTS

(*Amended by the Nationality, Immigration and Asylum Act 2002, ss 66.*)

Monitoring of escort arrangements

8–18027 **1.** (1) Escort arrangements must include provision for the appointment of a Crown servant as escort monitor.

(2) The escort monitor must—

(*a*) keep the escort arrangements under review and report on them to the Secretary of State as required in accordance with the arrangements;

(*b*) from time to time inspect the conditions in which detained persons are transported or held in accordance with the escort arrangements;

(*c*) make recommendations to the Secretary of State, with a view to improving those conditions, whenever he considers it appropriate to do so;

(*d*) investigate, and report to the Secretary of State on, any allegation made against a detainee custody officer or prisoner custody officer in respect of any act done, or failure to act, when carrying out functions under the arrangements;

(3) Paragraph (*d*) of sub-paragraph (2) does not apply in relation to—

(*a*) detainee custody officers employed as part of the Secretary of State's staff; or

(*b*) an act or omission of a prisoner custody officer so far as it falls to be investigated by a prisoner escort monitor under section 81 of the Criminal Justice Act 1991 or under section 103 or 119 of the Criminal Justice and Public Order Act 1994.

Powers and duties of detainee custody officers

2. (1) A detainee custody officer acting in accordance with escort arrangements has power—

(*a*) to search (in accordance with rules made by the Secretary of State) any detained person for whose delivery or custody the officer is responsible in accordance with the arrangements; and

(*b*) to search any other person who is in, or is seeking to enter, any place where any such detained person is or is to be held, and any article in the possession of such a person.

(2) The power conferred by sub-paragraph (1)(*b*) does not authorise requiring a person to remove any of his clothing other than an outer coat, jacket or glove.

(3) As respects a detained person for whose delivery or custody he is responsible in accordance with escort arrangements, it is the duty of a detainee custody officer—

(*a*) to prevent that person's escape from lawful custody;

(*b*) to prevent, or detect and report on, the commission or attempted commission by him of other unlawful acts;

(*c*) to ensure good order and discipline on his part; and

(*d*) to attend to his wellbeing.

(4) The Secretary of State may make rules with respect to the performance by detainee custody officers of their duty under sub-paragraph (3)(*d*).

(5) The powers conferred by sub-paragraph (1), and the powers arising by virtue of sub-paragraph (3), include power to use reasonable force where necessary.

Breaches of discipline

3. (1) Sub-paragraph (2) applies if a detained person for whose delivery or custody a person ("A") has been responsible in accordance with escort arrangements is delivered to a removal centre.

(2) The detained person is to be treated, for the purposes of such removal centre rules as relate to disciplinary offences, as if he had been in the custody of the director of the removal centre at all times while A was so responsible.

(3) Sub-paragraph (4) applies if a detained person for whose delivery or custody a person ("B") has been responsible in accordance with escort arrangements is delivered to a prison.

(4) The detained person is to be treated, for the purposes of such prison rules as relate to disciplinary offences, as if he had been in the custody of the governor or controller of the prison at all times while B was so responsible.

(5) "Director" means—

(*a*) in the case of a contracted out removal centre, the person appointed by the Secretary of State in relation to the centre under section 149 or such other person as the Secretary of State may appoint for the purposes of this paragraph;

(*b*) in the case of any other removal centre, the manager of the removal centre.

(6) This paragraph does not authorise the punishment of a detained person under removal centre rules or prison rules in respect of any act or omission of his for which he has already been punished by a court.

(7) "Prison rules" means—

(*a*) rules made under section 47 of the Prison Act 1952;

(*b*) rules made under section 19 of the Prisons (Scotland) Act 1989;

(*c*) rules made under section 13 of the Prison Act (Northern Ireland) 1953.

8–18027A
Section 169(1)

SCHEDULE 14
CONSEQUENTIAL AMENDMENTS

Section 169(2)

SCHEDULE 15
TRANSITIONAL PROVISIONS AND SAVINGS

(*Amended by the Mental Health (Care and Treatment) (Scotland) Act 2003, Sch 6.*)

Leave to enter or remain

8–18028 **1.** (1) An order made under section 3A of the 1971 Act may make provision with respect to leave given before the commencement of section 1.

(2) An order made under section 3B of the 1971 Act may make provision with respect to leave given before the commencement of section 2.

Section 2 of the Asylum and Immigration Act 1996

2. (1) This paragraph applies in relation to any time before the commencement of the repeal by this Act of section 2 of the Asylum and Immigration Act 1996.

(2) That section has effect, and is to be deemed always to have had effect, as if the reference to section 6 of the Asylum and Immigration Appeals Act 1993 were a reference to section 15, and any certificate issued under that section is to be read accordingly.

Adjudicators and the Tribunal

3. (1) Each existing member of the Tribunal is to continue as a member of the Tribunal as if he had been duly appointed by the Lord Chancellor under Schedule 2.

(2) Each existing adjudicator is to continue as an adjudicator as if he had been duly appointed by the Lord Chancellor under Schedule 3.

(3) The terms and conditions for a person to whom sub-paragraph (1) or (2) applies remain those on which he held office immediately before the appropriate date.

(4) The provisions of Schedule 7 to the Judicial Pensions and Retirement Act 1993 (transitional provisions for retirement dates), so far as applicable in relation to an existing member or adjudicator immediately before the appropriate date, continue to have effect.

(5) The repeal by this Act of Schedule 5 to the 1971 Act (provisions with respect to adjudicators and the Tribunal) does not affect any entitlement which an existing member or adjudicator had immediately before the appropriate date as a result of a determination made under paragraph 3(1)(*b*) or 9(1)(*b*) of that Schedule.

(6) "The appropriate date" means—

(*a*) in relation to existing members of the Tribunal, the date on which section 56 comes into force; and
(*b*) in relation to existing adjudicators, the date on which section 57 comes into force.

(7) "Existing member" means a person who is a member of the Tribunal immediately before the appropriate date.

(8) "Existing adjudicator" means a person who is an adjudicator immediately before the appropriate date.

References to justices' chief executive

4. At any time before the coming into force of section 90 of the Access to Justice Act 1999—

(*a*) the reference in section 48(3)(*b*) to the justices' chief executive appointed by the magistrates' court committee whose area includes the petty sessions area for which the specified court acts is to be read as a reference to the clerk of that court; and
(*b*) the reference in section 28K(9)(*a*) and (10) of the 1971 Act (inserted by section 138) to the justices' chief executive appointed by the magistrates' court committee whose area includes the petty sessions area for which the justice acts is to be read as a reference to the clerk to the justices for the petty sessions area for which the justice acts.

Duties under National Assistance Act 1948

5. Section 116 has effect, in relation to any time before section 115 is brought into force, as if section 115 came into force on the passing of this Act.

Duties under Health Services and Public Health Act 1968

6. Section 117(1) has effect, in relation to any time before section 115 is brought into force, as if section 115 came into force on the passing of this Act.

Duties under Social Work (Scotland) Act 1968

7. Subsections (1) to (3) of section 120 have effect, in relation to any time before section 115 is brought into force, as if section 115 came into force on the passing of this Act.

Duties under Health and Personal Social Services (Northern Ireland) Order 1972

8. Subsections (1) and (2) of section 121 have effect, in relation to any time before section 115 is brought into force, as if section 115 came into force on the passing of this Act.

Duties under National Health Service Act 1977

9. Section 117(2) has effect, in relation to any time before section 115 is brought into force, as if section 115 came into force on the passing of this Act.

Duties under Mental Health (Scotland) Act 1984

10. *Repealed.*

Appeals relating to deportation orders

11. Section 15 of the 1971 Act, section 5 of the Immigration Act 1988 and the Immigration (Restricted Right of Appeal against Deportation) (Exemption) Order 1993 are to continue to have effect in relation to any person on whom the Secretary of State has, before the commencement of the repeal of those sections, served a notice of his decision to make a deportation order.

12. (1) Sub-paragraph (2) applies if, on the coming into force of section 10, sections 15 of the 1971 Act and 5 of the Immigration Act 1988 have been repealed by this Act.

(2) Those sections are to continue to have effect in relation to any person—

(*a*) who applied during the regularisation period fixed by section 9, in accordance with the regulations made under that section, for leave to remain in the United Kingdom, and

(*b*) on whom the Secretary of State has since served a notice of his decision to make a deportation order.

Assistance under Part VII of the Housing Act 1996

13. (1) The Secretary of State may by order provide for any provision of Part VII of the Housing Act 1996 (homelessness) to have effect in relation to section 185(2) persons, during the interim period, with such modifications as may be specified in the order.

(2) An order under this paragraph may, in particular, include provision—

(*a*) for the referral of section 185(2) persons by one local housing authority to another by agreement between the authorities;

(*b*) as to the suitability of accommodation for such persons;

(*c*) as to out-of-area placements of such persons.

(3) "Interim period" means the period beginning with the passing of this Act and ending on the coming into force of the repeal of section 186 of the Act of 1996 (asylum-seekers and their dependants) by this Act (as to which see section 117(5)).

(4) "Local housing authority" has the same meaning as in the Act of 1996.

(5) "Section 185(2) person" means a person who—

(*a*) is eligible for housing assistance under Part VII of the Act of 1996 as a result of regulations made under section 185(2) of that Act; and

(*b*) is not made ineligible by section 186 (or any other provision) of that Act.

(6) The fact that an order may be made under this paragraph only in respect of the interim period does not prevent it from containing provisions of a kind authorised under section 166(3)(*a*) which are to have continuing effect after the end of that period.

Provision of support

14. (1) The Secretary of State may, by directions given to a local authority to whom Schedule 9 applies, require the authority to treat the interim period fixed for the purposes of that Schedule as coming to an end—

(*a*) for specified purposes,

(*b*) in relation to a specified area or locality, or

(*c*) in relation to persons of a specified description,

on such earlier day as may be specified.

(2) The Secretary of State may, by directions given to an authority to whom an amended provision applies, provide for specified descriptions of person to be treated—

(*a*) for specified purposes, or

(*b*) in relation to a specified area or locality,

as being persons to whom section 115 applies during such period as may be specified.

(3) Directions given under this paragraph may—

(*a*) make such consequential, supplemental or transitional provision as the Secretary of State considers appropriate; and

(*b*) make different provision for different cases or descriptions of case.

(4) "Specified" means specified in the directions.

(5) "Amended provision" means any provision amended by—

(*a*) section 116;

(*b*) section 117(1) or (2);

(*c*) section 120; or

(*d*) section 121.

8–18029 Section 169(3)

SCHEDULE 16

REPEALS

Nationality, Immigration and Asylum Act 2002[1]

(2002 c 41)

PART 1

NATIONALITY[2]

8–18029A 10. Right of abode: certificate of entitlement. *(Power of Secretary of State by regulations to make provision for the issue to a person of a certificate that he has the right of abode on the United Kingdom).*

1. This Act is to be brought into force in accordance with s 162, post and orders made thereunder.
2. Part 1 comprises ss 1–15 and Schs 1 and 2.

8–18029B 11. Unlawful presence in United Kingdom. (1) This section applies for the construction of a reference to being in the United Kingdom "in breach of the immigration laws" in section 4(2) or (4) or 50(5) of, or Schedule 1 to, the British Nationality Act 1981 (c 61).

(2) A person is in the United Kingdom in breach of the immigration laws if (and only if) he—

(a) is in the United Kingdom,

(b) does not have the right of abode in the United Kingdom within the meaning of section 2 of the Immigration Act 1971,

(c) does not have leave to enter or remain in the United Kingdom (whether or not he previously had leave),

(d) is not a qualified person within the meaning of the Immigration (European Economic Area) Regulations 2000 (SI 2000/2326) (person entitled to reside in United Kingdom without leave) (whether or not he was previously a qualified person),

(e) is not a family member of a qualified person within the meaning of those regulations (whether or not he was previously a family member of a qualified person),

(f) is not entitled to enter and remain in the United Kingdom by virtue of section 8(1) of the Immigration Act 1971 (crew) (whether or not he was previously entitled), and

(g) does not have the benefit of an exemption under section 8(2) to (4) of that Act (diplomats, soldiers and other special cases) (whether or not he previously had the benefit of an exemption).

(3) Section 11(1) of the Immigration Act 1971 (person deemed not to be in United Kingdom before disembarkation, while in controlled area or while under immigration control) shall apply for the purposes of this section as it applies for the purposes of that Act.

(4) This section shall be treated as always having had effect except in relation to a person who on the commencement of this section is, or has been at any time since he last entered the United Kingdom—

(a) a qualified person within the meaning of the regulations referred to in subsection (2)(d), or

(b) a family member of a qualified person within the meaning of those regulations.

(5) This section is without prejudice to the generality of—

(a) a reference to being in a place outside the United Kingdom in breach of immigration laws, and

(b) a reference in a provision other than one specified in subsection (1) to being in the United Kingdom in breach of immigration laws.

[Nationality, Immigration and Asylum Act 2002, s 11.]

PART 2
ACCOMMODATION CENTRES[1]

General

8–18029C 35. Ancillary provisions. (1) The following provisions of the Immigration and Asylum Act 1999 (c 33) shall apply for the purposes of this Part as they apply for the purposes of Part VI of that Act (support for asylum-seeker)—

(a) section 105 (false representation),
(b) section 106 (dishonest representation),
(c) section 107 (delay or obstruction),
(d) section 108 (failure of sponsor to maintain),
(e) section 109 (offence committed by body),
(f) section 112 (recovery of expenditure),
(g) section 113 (recovery of expenditure from sponsor),
(h) section 124 (corporation sole), and
(i) section 127 (redirection of post).

(2) In the application of section 112 a reference to something done under section 95 or 98 of that Act shall be treated as a reference to something done under section 17 or 24 of this Act.

(3) In the application of section 113 a reference to section 95 of that Act shall be treated as a reference to section 17 of this Act.

[Nationality, Immigration and Asylum Act 2002, s 35.]

1. Part 2 comprises ss 16–42.

PART 4
DETENTION AND REMOVAL[1]

Removal

8–18029D 72. Serious criminal. (1) This section applies for the purpose of the construction and application of Article 33(2) of the Refugee Convention (exclusion from protection).

(2) A person shall be presumed to have been convicted by a final judgment of a particularly serious crime and to constitute a danger to the community of the United Kingdom if he is—

(a) convicted in the United Kingdom of an offence, and

(b) sentenced to a period of imprisonment of at least two years.

(3) A person shall be presumed to have been convicted by a final judgment of a particularly serious crime and to constitute a danger to the community of the United Kingdom if—

(a) he is convicted outside the United Kingdom of an offence,

(b) he is sentenced to a period of imprisonment of at least two years, and

(c) he could have been sentenced to a period of imprisonment of at least two years had his conviction been a conviction in the United Kingdom of a similar offence.

(4) A person shall be presumed to have been convicted by a final judgment of a particularly serious crime and to constitute a danger to the community of the United Kingdom if—

(a) he is convicted of an offence specified by order[2] of the Secretary of State, or

(b) he is convicted outside the United Kingdom of an offence and the Secretary of State certifies that in his opinion the offence is similar to an offence specified by order under paragraph (a).

(5) An order under subsection (4)—

(a) must be made by statutory instrument, and

(b) shall be subject to annulment in pursuance of a resolution of either House of Parliament.

(6) A presumption under subsection (2), (3) or (4) that a person constitutes a danger to the community is rebuttable by that person.

(7) A presumption under subsection (2), (3) or (4) does not apply while an appeal against conviction or sentence—

(a) is pending, or

(b) could be brought (disregarding the possibility of appeal out of time with leave).

(8) Section 34(1) of the Anti-terrorism, Crime and Security Act 2001 (c 24) (no need to consider gravity of fear or threat of persecution) applies for the purpose of considering whether a presumption mentioned in subsection (6) has been rebutted as it applies for the purpose of considering whether Article 33(2) of the Refugee Convention applies.

(9) Subsection (10) applies where—

(a) a person appeals under section 82, 83 or 101 of this Act or under section 2 of the Special Immigration Appeals Commission Act 1997 (c 68) wholly or partly on the ground that to remove him from or to require him to leave the United Kingdom would breach the United Kingdom's obligations under the Refugee Convention, and

(b) the Secretary of State issues a certificate that presumptions under subsection (2), (3) or (4) apply to the person (subject to rebuttal).

(10) The Tribunal or Commission hearing the appeal—

(a) must begin substantive deliberation on the appeal by considering the certificate, and

(b) if in agreement that presumptions under subsection (2), (3) or (4) apply (having given the appellant an opportunity for rebuttal) must dismiss the appeal in so far as it relies on the ground specified in subsection (9)(a).

(11) For the purposes of this section—

(a) "the Refugee Convention" means the Convention relating to the Status of Refugees done at Geneva on 28th July 1951 and its Protocol, and

(b) a reference to a person who is sentenced to a period of imprisonment of at least two years—

(i) does not include a reference to a person who receives a suspended sentence (unless at least two years of the sentence are not suspended),

(ii) includes a reference to a person who is sentenced to detention, or ordered or directed to be detained, in an institution other than a prison (including, in particular, a hospital or an institution for young offenders), and

(iii) includes a reference to a person who is sentenced to imprisonment or detention, or ordered or directed to be detained, for an indeterminate period (provided that it may last for two years).

[Nationality, Immigration and Asylum Act 2002, s 72 as amended by the Asylum and Immigration (Treatment of Claimants, etc) Act 2004, Sch 2 .]

1. Part 4 comprises ss 62–80.

2. See the Nationality, Immigration and Asylum Act 2002 (Specification of Particularly Serious Crimes) Order 2004, SI 2004/1910.

PART 6
IMMIGRATION PROCEDURE[1]

Disclosure of information by public authority

8–18029E 129. Local authority. (1) The Secretary of State may require a local authority to supply information for the purpose of establishing where a person is if the Secretary of State reasonably suspects that—

(a) the person has committed an offence under section 24(1)(a), (b), (c), (e) or (f), 24A(1) or 26(1)(c) or (d) of the Immigration Act 1971 (c 77) (illegal entry, deception, &c), and

(b) the person is or has been resident in the local authority's area.

(2) A local authority shall comply with a requirement under this section.

(3) In the application of this section to England and Wales "local authority" means—

(a) a county council,

(b) a county borough council,

(c) a district council,

(d) a London borough council,

(e) the Common Council of the City of London, and

(f) the Council of the Isles of Scilly.

(4) In the application of this section to Scotland "local authority" means a council constituted under section 2 of the Local Government etc (Scotland) Act 1994 (c 39).

(5) In the application of this section to Northern Ireland—

(a) a reference to a local authority shall be taken as a reference to the Northern Ireland Housing Executive, and

(b) the reference to a local authority's area shall be taken as a reference to Northern Ireland.

[Nationality, Immigration and Asylum Act 2002, s 129.]

1. Part 6 comprises ss 118–142 and Sch 8.

Disclosure of information by private person

8–18029F 134. Employer. (1) The Secretary of State may require an employer to supply information about an employee whom the Secretary of State reasonably suspects of having committed an offence under—

(a) section 24(1)(a), (b), (c), (e) or (f), 24A(1) or 26(1)(c) or (d) of the Immigration Act 1971 (c 77) (illegal entry, deception, &c),

(b) section 105(1)(a), (b) or (c) of the Immigration and Asylum Act 1999 (c 33) (support for asylum-seeker: fraud), or

(c) section 106(1)(a), (b) or (c) of that Act (support for asylum-seeker: fraud).

(2) The power under subsection (1) may be exercised to require information about an employee only if the information—

(a) is required for the purpose of establishing where the employee is, or

(b) relates to the employee's earnings or to the history of his employment.

(3) In this section a reference to an employer or employee—

(a) includes a reference to a former employer or employee, and

(b) shall be construed in accordance with section 8(8) of the Asylum and Immigration Act 1996 (c 49) (restrictions on employment).

(4) Where—

(a) a business (the "employment agency") arranges for one person (the "worker") to provide services to another (the "client"), and

(b) the worker is not employed by the employment agency or the client,

this section shall apply as if the employment agency were the worker's employer while he provides services to the client.

[Nationality, Immigration and Asylum Act 2002, s 134.]

8–18029G 135. Financial institution. (1) The Secretary of State may require a financial institution to supply information about a person if the Secretary of State reasonably suspects that—

(a) the person has committed an offence under section 105(1)(a), (b) or (c) or 106(1)(a), (b) or (c) of the Immigration and Asylum Act 1999 (c 33) (support for asylum-seeker: fraud),

(b) the information is relevant to the offence, and

(c) the institution has the information.

(2) In this section "financial institution" means—

(a) a person who has permission under Part 4 of the Financial Services and Markets Act 2000 (c 8) to accept deposits, and

(b) a building society (within the meaning given by the Building Societies Act 1986 (c 53)).

[Nationality, Immigration and Asylum Act 2002, s 135.]

8–18029H 136. Notice. (1) A requirement to provide information under section 134 or 135 must be imposed by notice in writing specifying—

(a) the information,

(b) the manner in which it is to be provided, and

(c) the period of time within which it is to be provided.

(2) A period of time specified in a notice under subsection (1)(c)—

(a) must begin with the date of receipt of the notice, and
(b) must not be less than ten working days.

(3) A person on whom a notice is served under subsection (1) must provide the Secretary of State with the information specified in the notice.

(4) Information provided under subsection (3) must be provided—

(a) in the manner specified under subsection (1)(b), and
(b) within the time specified under subsection (1)(c).

(5) In this section "working day" means a day which is not—

(a) Saturday,
(b) Sunday,
(c) Christmas Day,
(d) Good Friday, or
(e) a day which is a bank holiday under the Banking and Financial Dealings Act 1971 (c 80) in any part of the United Kingdom.

[Nationality, Immigration and Asylum Act 2002, s 136.]

8–18029I 137. Disclosure of information: offences. (1) A person commits an offence if without reasonable excuse he fails to comply with section 136(3).

(2) A person who is guilty of an offence under subsection (1) shall be liable on summary conviction to—

(a) imprisonment for a term not exceeding three months*,
(b) a fine not exceeding level 5 on the standard scale, or
(c) both.

[Nationality, Immigration and Asylum Act 2002, s 137.]

***"51 weeks" substituted by the Criminal Justice Act 2003, Sch 26, from a date to be appointed.**

8–18029J 138. Offence by body. (1) Subsection (2) applies where an offence under section 137 is committed by a body corporate and it is proved that the offence—

(a) was committed with the consent or connivance of an officer of the body, or
(b) was attributable to neglect on the part of an officer of the body.

(2) The officer, as well as the body, shall be guilty of the offence.

(3) In this section a reference to an officer of a body corporate includes a reference to—

(a) a director, manager or secretary,
(b) a person purporting to act as a director, manager or secretary, and
(c) if the affairs of the body are managed by its members, a member.

(4) Where an offence under section 137 is committed by a partnership (other than a limited partnership), each partner shall be guilty of the offence.

(5) Subsection (1) shall have effect in relation to a limited partnership as if—

(a) a reference to a body corporate were a reference to a limited partnership, and
(b) a reference to an officer of the body were a reference to a partner.

[Nationality, Immigration and Asylum Act 2002, s 138.]

8–18029K 139. Privilege against self-incrimination. (1) Information provided by a person pursuant to a requirement under section 134 or 135 shall not be admissible in evidence in criminal proceedings against that person.

(2) This section shall not apply to proceedings for an offence under section 137.

[Nationality, Immigration and Asylum Act 2002, s 139.]

PART 7
OFFENCES[1]
Substance

8–18029L 145. Traffic in prostitution. *Repealed.*

---

1. Part 7 comprises ss 143–156.

8–18029M 146. Section 145: supplementary. (1) Subsections (1) to (3) of section 145 apply to anything done—

(a) in the United Kingdom,
(b) outside the United Kingdom by an individual to whom subsection (2) applies, or

(c) outside the United Kingdom by a body incorporated under the law of a part of the United Kingdom.

(2) This subsection applies to—

(a) a British citizen,
(b) a British overseas territories citizen,
(c) a British National (Overseas),
(d) a British Overseas citizen,
(e) a person who is a British subject under the British Nationality Act 1981 (c 61), and
(f) a British protected person within the meaning of that Act.

(3) Sections 25C and 25D of the Immigration Act 1971 (c 77) (forfeiture or detention of vehicle, &c) shall apply in relation to an offence under section 145 of this Act as they apply in relation to an offence under section 25 of that Act.

(4) The following shall be inserted after paragraph 2(m) of Schedule 4 to the Criminal Justice and Court Services Act 2000 (c 43) (offence against child)—

"(n) an offence under section 145 of the Nationality, Immigration and Asylum Act 2002 (traffic in prostitution)."

[Nationality, Immigration and Asylum Act 2002, s 146.]

PART 8
GENERAL[1]

8–18029N 162. Commencement. (1) Subject to subsections (2) to (5), the preceding provisions of this Act shall come into force in accordance with provision made by the Secretary of State by order[2].

(2) The following provisions shall come into force on the passing of this Act—

(a) section 6,
(b) section 7,
(c) section 10(1) to (4) and (6),
(d) section 11,
(e) section 15 (and Schedule 2),
(f) section 16,
(g) section 35(1)(h),
(h) section 38,
(i) section 40(1),
(j) section 41(1),
(k) section 42,
(l) section 43,
(m) section 48,
(n) section 49,
(o) section 50,
(p) section 56,
(q) section 58,
(r) section 59,
(s) section 61,
(t) section 67,
(u) section 69,
(v) section 70,
(w) section 115 and paragraph 29 of Schedule 7 (and the relevant entry in Schedule 9),
(x) section 157, and
(y) section 160.

(3) Section 5 shall have effect in relation to—

(a) an application made after the passing of this Act, and
(b) an application made, but not determined, before the passing of this Act.

(4) Section 8 shall have effect in relation to—

(a) an application made on or after a date appointed by the Secretary of State by order, and
(b) an application made, but not determined, before that date.

(5) Section 9 shall have effect in relation to a child born on or after a date appointed by the Secretary of State by order.

(6) An order under subsection (1) may—

(a) make provision generally or for a specified purpose only (which may include the purpose of the application of a provision to or in relation to a particular place or area);
(b) make different provision for different purposes;
(c) include transitional provision;
(d) include savings;

(e) include consequential provision;
(f) include incidental provision.

(7) An order under this section must be made by statutory instrument.
[Nationality, Immigration and Asylum Act 2002, s 162.]

1. Part 8 comprises ss 157–164 and Sch 9.
2. At the date of going to press the following commencement orders had been made: (No 1) SI 2002/2811; (No 2) SI 2003/1; (No 3) SI 2003/249; (No 4) SI 2003/754 amended by SI 2003/1040, 1339 and 2993; (No 5) SI 2003/1040; (No 6) SI 2003/3156; (No 7) SI 2004/1201; (No 8) SI 2004/1707; (No 9) SI 2004/2998; (No 10) 2005/2782. At the date of going to press, the provisions reproduced above with the exception of ss 10(5) and 35(1)(a)–(g) and (i), (2)–(3), were in force.

8–18029O **163.** *Extent*

8–18029P **164.** *Short title*

Asylum and Immigration (Treatment of Claimants, etc) Act 2004[1]

(2004 c 19)

1. This Act is arranged under 9 headings: Offences; Treatment of claimants; Enforcement powers; Procedure for marriage; Appeals; Removal and detention; Immigration services; Fees and General.

In summary, the Act contains provisions that: unify the immigration and asylum appeals system into a single tier of appeal with limited onward review or appeal; deal with undocumented arrivals and those who fail to comply with steps to co-operate with the re-documentation process; provide additional powers to the OISC; provide for failed asylum seekers to participate in community activities; create a system of integration loans for refugees and tackle sham marriages.

Nearly all of the Act's provisions are to be brought into force in accordance with Commencement Orders made under s 48. At the time of going to press the following commencement orders had been made: Asylum and Immigration (Treatment of Claimants, etc) Act 2004 (Commencement No 1) Order 2004, SI 2004/2523; Asylum and Immigration (Treatment of Claimants etc) Act 2004 (Commencement) (Scotland) Order 2004, SSI 2004/494; Asylum and Immigration (Treatment of Claimants, etc) Act 2004 (Commencement No 2) Order 2004, SI 2004/2999; Asylum and Immigration (Treatment of Claimants, etc) Act 2004 (Commencement No 3) Order 2004, SI 2004/3398 and SI 2005/565. Most of the Act's provisions are now in force.

Offences

8–18029Q **1. Assisting unlawful immigration.** (1) At the end of section 25 of the Immigration Act 1971 (c 77) (offence of assisting unlawful immigration to member State) add—

"(7) In this section—

(*a*) a reference to a member State includes a reference to a State on a list prescribed for the purposes of this section by order of the Secretary of State (to be known as the "Section 25 List of Schengen Acquis States"), and
(*b*) a reference to a citizen of the European Union includes a reference to a person who is a national of a State on that list.

(8) An order under subsection (7)(*a*)—

(*a*) may be made only if the Secretary of State thinks it necessary for the purpose of complying with the United Kingdom's obligations under the Community Treaties,
(*b*) may include transitional, consequential or incidental provision,
(*c*) shall be made by statutory instrument, and
(*d*) shall be subject to annulment in pursuance of a resolution of either House of Parliament."

(2) In section 25C(9)(*a*) of that Act (forfeiture of vehicle, ship or aircraft) for "(within the meaning of section 25)" substitute "(for which purpose "member State" and "immigration law" have the meanings given by section 25(2) and (7))".
[Asylum and Immigration (Treatment of Claimants, etc) Act 2004, s 1.]

8–18029R **2. Entering United Kingdom without passport, &c.** (1) A person commits an offence if at a leave or asylum interview he does not have with him an immigration document which—

(*a*) is in force, and
(*b*) satisfactorily establishes his identity and nationality or citizenship.

(2) A person commits an offence[1] if at a leave or asylum interview he does not have with him, in respect of any dependent child with whom he claims to be travelling or living, an immigration document which—

(*a*) is in force, and
(*b*) satisfactorily establishes the child's identity and nationality or citizenship.

(3) But a person does not commit an offence under subsection (1) or (2) if—

(*a*) the interview referred to in that subsection takes place after the person has entered the United Kingdom, and

(*b*) within the period of three days beginning with the date of the interview the person provides to an immigration officer or to the Secretary of State a document of the kind referred to in that subsection.

(4) It is a defence[2] for a person charged with an offence under subsection (1)—

(*a*) to prove that he is an EEA national,

(*b*) to prove that he is a member of the family of an EEA national and that he is exercising a right under the Community Treaties in respect of entry to or residence in the United Kingdom,

(*c*) to prove that he has a reasonable excuse[3] for not being in possession of a document of the kind specified in subsection (1),

(*d*) to produce a false immigration document and to prove that he used that document as an immigration document for all purposes in connection with his journey to the United Kingdom, or

(*e*) to prove that he travelled to the United Kingdom without, at any stage since he set out on the journey, having possession of an immigration document.

(5) It is a defence for a person charged with an offence under subsection (2) in respect of a child—

(*a*) to prove that the child is an EEA national,

(*b*) to prove that the child is a member of the family of an EEA national and that the child is exercising a right under the Community Treaties in respect of entry to or residence in the United Kingdom,

(c) to prove that the person has a reasonable excuse[3] for not being in possession of a document of the kind specified in subsection (2),

(*d*) to produce a false immigration document and to prove that it was used as an immigration document for all purposes in connection with the child's journey to the United Kingdom, or

(*e*) to prove that he travelled to the United Kingdom with the child without, at any stage since he set out on the journey, having possession of an immigration document in respect of the child.

(6) Where the charge for an offence under subsection (1) or (2) relates to an interview which takes place after the defendant has entered the United Kingdom—

(*a*) subsections (4)(*c*) and (5)(*c*) shall not apply, but

(*b*) it is a defence for the defendant to prove that he has a reasonable excuse[3] for not providing a document in accordance with subsection (3).

(7) For the purposes of subsections (4) to (6)—

(*a*) the fact that a document was deliberately destroyed or disposed of is not a reasonable excuse for not being in possession of it or for not providing it in accordance with subsection (3), unless it is shown that the destruction or disposal was—

(i) for a reasonable cause, or

(ii) beyond the control of the person charged with the offence, and

(*b*) in paragraph (a)(i) "reasonable cause" does not include the purpose of—

(i) delaying the handling or resolution of a claim or application or the taking of a decision,

(ii) increasing the chances of success of a claim or application, or

(iii) complying with instructions or advice given by a person who offers advice about, or facilitates, immigration into the United Kingdom, unless in the circumstances of the case it is unreasonable to expect non-compliance with the instructions or advice.

(8) A person shall be presumed for the purposes of this section not to have a document with him if he fails to produce it to an immigration officer or official of the Secretary of State on request.

(9) A person guilty of an offence under this section shall be liable—

(*a*) on conviction on indictment, to imprisonment for a term not exceeding two years, to a fine or to both, or

(*b*) on summary conviction, to imprisonment for a term not exceeding twelve months, to a fine not exceeding the statutory maximum or to both[4].

(10) If an immigration officer reasonably suspects that a person has committed an offence under this section he may arrest the person without warrant.

(11) An offence under this section shall be treated as—

(*a*) a relevant offence for the purposes of sections 28B and 28D of the Immigration Act 1971 (c 77) (search, entry and arrest), and

(*b*) an offence under Part III of that Act (criminal proceedings) for the purposes of sections 28(4), 28E, 28G and 28H (search after arrest, &c) of that Act.

(12) In this section—

"EEA national" means a national of a State which is a contracting party to the Agreement on the European Economic Area signed at Oporto on 2nd May 1992 (as it has effect from time to time), "immigration document" means—

(*a*) a passport, and

(*b*) a document which relates to a national of a State other than the United Kingdom and which is designed to serve the same purpose as a passport, and

"leave or asylum interview" means an interview with an immigration officer or an official of the Secretary of State at which a person—

(*a*) seeks leave to enter or remain in the United Kingdom, or

(*b*) claims that to remove him from or require him to leave the United Kingdom would breach the United Kingdom's obligations under the Refugee Convention or would be unlawful under section 6 of the Human Rights Act 1998 (c 42) as being incompatible with his Convention rights.

(13) For the purposes of this section—

(*a*) a document which purports to be, or is designed to look like, an immigration document, is a false immigration document, and

(*b*) an immigration document is a false immigration document if and in so far as it is used—

(i) outside the period for which it is expressed to be valid,

(ii) contrary to provision for its use made by the person issuing it, or

(iii) by or in respect of a person other than the person to or for whom it was issued.

(14) Section 11 of the Immigration Act 1971 (c 77) shall have effect for the purpose of the construction of a reference in this section to entering the United Kingdom.

(15) In so far as this section extends to England and Wales, subsection (9)(*b*) shall, until the commencement of section 154 of the Criminal Justice Act 2003 (c 44) (increased limit on magistrates' power of imprisonment), have effect as if the reference to twelve months were a reference to six months.

(16) In so far as this section extends to Scotland, subsection (9)(*b*) shall have effect as if the reference to twelve months were a reference to six months.

(17) In so far as this section extends to Northern Ireland, subsection (9)(*b*) shall have effect as if the reference to twelve months were a reference to six months.

[Asylum and Immigration (Treatment of Claimants, etc) Act 2004, s 2 as amended by the Serious Organised Crime and Police Act 2005, Sch 7.]

---

1. The legislation does not require that an application for asylum be determined before a trial for an alleged breach of the requirements of this section (*R v Navabi* [2005] EWCA Crim 2865, (2005) Times, 5 December).

2. Parliament has decided that this section should reflect in domestic law the obligations of article 31 of the European Convention on Human Rights even though those obligations are not fully reflected in the legislation. Therefore, the court is only concerned with the statutory defences in s 2 and not with the terms of article 31. The burden of proof is on the defendant on the balance of probabilities which is compliant with the requirements of the European Convention on Human Rights (*R v Navabi* [2005] EWCA Crim 2865, (2005) Times, 5 December).

3. For this, see sub-s (7), post.

4. For procedure in respect of offences triable either way see the Magistrates' Courts Act 1980, ss 17A–21 in PART I: MAGISTRATES' COURTS' PROCEDURE, ante.

8–18029S 3. Immigration documents: forgery. (1) Section 5 of the Forgery and Counterfeiting Act 1981 (c 45) (offences relating to various documents) shall be amended as follows.

(2) After subsection (5)(f) (passports) insert—

"*(fa)* immigration documents;".

(3) After subsection (8) add—

"(9) In subsection (5)(*fa*) "immigration document" means a card, adhesive label or other instrument which satisfies subsection (10) or (11).

(10) A card, adhesive label or other instrument satisfies this subsection if it—

(*a*) is designed to be given, in the exercise of a function under the Immigration Acts (within the meaning of section 44 of the Asylum and Immigration (Treatment of Claimants, etc) Act 2004), to a person who has been granted leave to enter or remain in the United Kingdom, and

(*b*) carries information (whether or not wholly or partly electronically) about the leave granted.

(11) A card, adhesive label or other instrument satisfies this subsection if it is given to a person to confirm a right of his under the Community Treaties in respect of entry to or residence in the United Kingdom."

[Asylum and Immigration (Treatment of Claimants, etc) Act 2004, s 3.]

8–18029T 4. Trafficking people for exploitation. (1) A person commits an offence if he arranges or facilitates the arrival in the United Kingdom of an individual (the "passenger") and—

(*a*) he intends to exploit the passenger in the United Kingdom or elsewhere, or (*b*) he believes that another person is likely to exploit the passenger in the United Kingdom or elsewhere.

(2) A person commits an offence if he arranges or facilitates travel within the United Kingdom by an individual (the "passenger") in respect of whom he believes that an offence under subsection (1) may have been committed and—

(*a*) he intends to exploit the passenger in the United Kingdom or elsewhere, or

(*b*) he believes that another person is likely to exploit the passenger in the United Kingdom or elsewhere.

(3) A person commits an offence if he arranges or facilitates the departure from the United Kingdom of an individual (the "passenger") and—

(*a*) he intends to exploit the passenger outside the United Kingdom, or

(*b*) he believes that another person is likely to exploit the passenger outside the United Kingdom.

(4) For the purposes of this section a person is exploited if (and only if)—

(*a*) he is the victim of behaviour that contravenes Article 4 of the Human Rights Convention (slavery and forced labour),

(*b*) he is encouraged, required or expected to do anything as a result of which he or another person would commit an offence under the Human Organ Transplants Act 1989 (c 31) or under section 32 or 33 of the Human Tissue Act 2004,

(*c*) he is subjected to force, threats or deception designed to induce him—

(i) to provide services of any kind,

(ii) to provide another person with benefits of any kind, or

(iii) to enable another person to acquire benefits of any kind, or

(*d*) he is requested or induced to undertake any activity, having been chosen as the subject of the request or inducement on the grounds that—

(i) he is mentally or physically ill or disabled, he is young or he has a family relationship with a person, and

(ii) a person without the illness, disability, youth or family relationship would be likely to refuse the request or resist the inducement.

(5) A person guilty of an offence under this section shall be liable—

(*a*) on conviction on indictment, to imprisonment for a term not exceeding 14 years, to a fine or to both, or

(*b*) on summary conviction, to imprisonment for a term not exceeding twelve months, to a fine not exceeding the statutory maximum or to both[1].

[Asylum and Immigration (Treatment of Claimants, etc) Act 2004, s 4 as amended by the Human Tissue Act 2004, Sch 6.]

1. For procedure in respect of offences triable either way see the Magistrates' Courts Act 1980, ss 17A–21 in PART I: MAGISTRATES' COURTS' PROCEDURE, ante.

8–18029U 5. Section 4: supplemental. (1) Subsections (1) to (3) of section 4 apply to anything done—

(*a*) in the United Kingdom,

(*b*) outside the United Kingdom by an individual to whom subsection (2) below applies, or

(*c*) outside the United Kingdom by a body incorporated under the law of a part of the United Kingdom.

(2) This subsection applies to—

(*a*) a British citizen,

(*b*) a British overseas territories citizen,

(*c*) a British National (Overseas),

(*d*) a British Overseas citizen,

(*e*) a person who is a British subject under the British Nationality Act 1981 (c 61), and

(*f*) a British protected person within the meaning of that Act.

(3) In section 4(4)(*a*) "the Human Rights Convention" means the Convention for the Protection of Human Rights and Fundamental Freedoms agreed by the Council of Europe at Rome on 4th November 1950.

(4) Sections 25C and 25D of the Immigration Act 1971 (c 77) (forfeiture or detention of vehicle, &c) shall apply in relation to an offence under section 4 of this Act as they apply in relation to an offence under section 25 of that Act.

(5) At the end of section 25C(9)(*b*), (10)(*b*) and (11) of that Act add "or section 4 of the Asylum and Immigration (Treatment of Claimants, etc) Act 2004 (trafficking people for exploitation)."

(6) After paragraph 2(*n*) of Schedule 4 to the Criminal Justice and Court Services Act 2000 (c 43) (offence against child) insert—

"(*o*) an offence under section 4 of the Asylum and Immigration (Treatment of Claimants, etc) Act 2004 (trafficking people for exploitation).".

(7) At the end of paragraph 4 of Schedule 2 to the Proceeds of Crime Act 2002 (c 29) (lifestyle offences: England and Wales: people trafficking) add—

"(3) An offence under section 4 of the Asylum and Immigration (Treatment of Claimants, etc) Act 2004 (exploitation).".

(8) At the end of paragraph 4 of Schedule 4 to the Proceeds of Crime Act 2002 (lifestyle offences: Scotland: people trafficking) add "or under section 4 of the Asylum and Immigration (Treatment of Claimants, etc) Act 2004 (exploitation)".

(9) At the end of paragraph 4 of Schedule 5 to the Proceeds of Crime Act 2002 (lifestyle offences: Northern Ireland: people trafficking) add—

"(3) An offence under section 4 of the Asylum and Immigration (Treatment of Claimants, etc) Act 2004 (exploitation).".

(10) After paragraph 2(l) of the Schedule to the Protection of Children and Vulnerable Adults (Northern Ireland) Order 2003 (SI 2003/417 (NI 4)) (offence against child) insert—

"(*m*)an offence under section 4 of the Asylum and Immigration (Treatment of Claimants, etc) Act 2004 (trafficking people for exploitation).".

(11) In so far as section 4 extends to England and Wales, subsection (5)(*b*) shall, until the commencement of section 154 of the Criminal Justice Act 2003 (c 44) (increased limit on magistrates' power of imprisonment), have effect as if the reference to twelve months were a reference to six months.

(12) In so far as section 4 extends to Scotland, subsection (5)(*b*) shall have effect as if the reference to twelve months were a reference to six months.

(13) In so far as section 4 extends to Northern Ireland, subsection (5)(*b*) shall have effect as if the reference to twelve months were a reference to six months.

[Asylum and Immigration (Treatment of Claimants, etc) Act 2004, s 5.]

8–18029V 6. Employment. (1) For section 8(4) of the Asylum and Immigration Act 1996 (c 49) (employment: penalty) substitute—

"(4) A person guilty of an offence under this section shall be liable—

(*a*) on conviction on indictment, to a fine, or

(*b*) on summary conviction, to a fine not exceeding the statutory maximum.".

(2) Section 8(9) of that Act (extension of time limit for prosecution) shall cease to have effect.

[Asylum and Immigration (Treatment of Claimants, etc) Act 2004, s 6.]

8–18029W 7. Advice of Director of Public Prosecutions. In section 3(2) of the Prosecution of Offences Act 1985 (c 23) (functions of Director of Public Prosecutions) after paragraph (eb) insert—

"(*ec*)to give, to such extent as he considers appropriate, advice to immigration officers on matters relating to criminal offences;".

[Asylum and Immigration (Treatment of Claimants, etc) Act 2004, s 7.]

8–18029X 8. Claimant's credibility

8–18029Y 9. Failed asylum seekers: withdrawal of support

8–18029Z 10. Failed asylum seekers: accommodation

8–18029ZA 11. Accommodation for asylum seekers: local connection

8–18029ZB 12. Refugee: back-dating of benefits

8–18029ZC 13. Integration loan for refugees

Enforcement powers

8–18029ZD 14. Immigration officer: power of arrest. (1) Where an immigration officer in the course of exercising a function under the Immigration Acts forms a reasonable suspicion that a person has committed or attempted to commit an offence listed in subsection (2), he may arrest the person without warrant.

(2) Those offences are—

(*a*) the offence of conspiracy at common law (in relation to conspiracy to defraud),

(*b*) at common law in Scotland, any of the following offences—

(i) fraud,

(ii) conspiracy to defraud,

(iii) uttering and fraud,
(iv) bigamy,
(v) theft, and
(vi) reset,

(*c*) an offence under section 57 of the Offences against the Person Act 1861 (c 100) (bigamy),
(*d*) an offence under section 3 or 4 of the Perjury Act 1911 (c 6) (false statements),
(*e*) an offence under section 7 of that Act (aiding, abetting &c.) if it relates to an offence under section 3 or 4 of that Act,
(*f*) an offence under section 53 of the Registration of Births, Deaths and Marriages (Scotland) Act 1965 (c 49) (knowingly giving false information to district registrar, &c),
(*g*) an offence under any of the following provisions of the Theft Act 1968 (c 60)—

(i) section 1 (theft),
(ii) section 15 (obtaining property by deception),
(iii) section 16 (obtaining pecuniary advantage by deception),
(iv) section 17 (false accounting), and
(v) section 22 (handling stolen goods),

(*h*) an offence under section 1, 15, 16, 17 or 21 of the Theft Act (Northern Ireland) 1969 (c 16) (NI),
(*i*) an offence under section 1 or 2 of the Theft Act 1978 (c 31) (obtaining services, or evading liability, by deception),
(*j*) an offence under Article 3 or 4 of the Theft (Northern Ireland) Order 1978 (SI 1978/1407 (NI 23)),
(*k*) an offence under Article 8 or 9 of the Perjury (Northern Ireland) Order 1979 (SI 1979/1714 (NI 19)),
(*l*) an offence under Article 12 of that Order if it relates to an offence under Article 8 or 9 of that Order,
(*m*) an offence under any of the following provisions of the Forgery and Counterfeiting Act 1981 (c 45)—

(i) section 1 (forgery),
(ii) section 2 (copying false instrument),
(iii) section 3 (using false instrument),
(iv) section 4 (using copy of false instrument), and
(v) section 5(1) and (3) (false documents),

(*n*) an offence under any of sections 57 to 59 of the Sexual Offences Act 2003 (c 42) (trafficking for sexual exploitation),
(*o*) an offence under section 22 of the Criminal Justice (Scotland) Act 2003 (asp 7) (trafficking in prostitution), and
(*p*) an offence under section 4 of this Act.

(3) The following provisions of the Immigration Act 1971 (c 77) shall have effect for the purpose of making, or in connection with, an arrest under this section as they have effect for the purpose of making, or in connection with, arrests for offences under that Act—

(*a*) section 28C (entry and search before arrest),
(*b*) sections 28E and 28F (entry and search after arrest),
(*c*) sections 28G and 28H (search of arrested person), and
(*d*) section 28I (seized material).

(4) In section 19D(5)(a) of the Race Relations Act 1976 (c 74) (permitted discrimination)—

(*a*) for "(within the meaning of section 158 of the Nationality, Immigration and Asylum Act 2002)" substitute "(within the meaning of section 44 of the Asylum and Immigration (Treatment of Claimants, etc) Act 2004)", and
(*b*) at the end add "and excluding section 14 of the Asylum and Immigration (Treatment of Claimants, etc) Act 2004".

[Asylum and Immigration (Treatment of Claimants, etc) Act 2004, s 14.]

8–18029ZE 15. Fingerprinting. (1) Section 141 of the Immigration and Asylum Act 1999 (c 33) (fingerprinting) shall be amended as follows.

(2) In subsection (7) for paragraph (c) substitute—

"(*c*) any person ("C") in respect of whom a relevant immigration decision has been made;".

(3) In subsection (8) for paragraph (c) substitute—

"(*c*) for C, on the service on him of notice of the relevant immigration decision by virtue of section 105 of the Nationality, Immigration and Asylum Act 2002 (c 41);".

(4) In subsection (9) for paragraph (c) substitute—

"(*c*) for C—

(i) the time when the relevant immigration decision ceases to have effect, whether as a result of an appeal or otherwise, or

(ii) if a deportation order has been made against him, its revocation or its otherwise ceasing to have effect;".

(5) After subsection (15) add—

"(16) "Relevant immigration decision" means a decision of the kind mentioned in section 82(2)(*g*), (*h*), (*i*), (*j*) or (*k*) of the Nationality, Immigration and Asylum Act 2002 (c 41).".

[Asylum and Immigration (Treatment of Claimants, etc) Act 2004, s 15.]

8–18029ZF 16. Information about passengers

8–18029ZG 17. Retention of documents

8–18029ZH 18. Control of entry

Procedure for marriage

8–18029ZI 19. England and Wales. (1) This section applies to a marriage—

(*a*) which is to be solemnised on the authority of certificates issued by a superintendent registrar under Part III of the Marriage Act 1949 (c 76), and

(*b*) a party to which is subject to immigration control.

(2) In relation to a marriage to which this section applies, the notices under section 27 of the Marriage Act 1949—

(*a*) shall be given to the superintendent registrar of a registration district specified for the purpose of this paragraph by regulations made by the Secretary of State,

(*b*) shall be delivered to the superintendent registrar in person by the two parties to the marriage,

(*c*) may be given only if each party to the marriage has been resident in a registration district for the period of seven days immediately before the giving of his or her notice (but the district need not be that in which the notice is given and the parties need not have resided in the same district), and

(*d*) shall state, in relation to each party, the registration district by reference to which paragraph (*c*) is satisfied.

(3) The superintendent registrar shall not enter in the marriage notice book notice of a marriage to which this section applies unless satisfied, by the provision of specified evidence, that the party subject to immigration control—

(*a*) has an entry clearance granted expressly for the purpose of enabling him to marry in the United Kingdom,

(*b*) has the written permission of the Secretary of State to marry in the United Kingdom, or

(*c*) falls within a class specified for the purpose of this paragraph by regulations made by the Secretary of State.

(4) For the purposes of this section—

(*a*) a person is subject to immigration control if—

(i) he is not an EEA national, and

(ii) under the Immigration Act 1971 (c 77) he requires leave to enter or remain in the United Kingdom (whether or not leave has been given),

(*b*) "EEA national" means a national of a State which is a contracting party to the Agreement on the European Economic Area signed at Oporto on 2nd May 1992 (as it has effect from time to time),

(*c*) "entry clearance" has the meaning given by section 33(1) of the Immigration Act 1971, and

(*d*) "specified evidence" means such evidence as may be specified in guidance issued by the Registrar General.

[Asylum and Immigration (Treatment of Claimants, etc) Act 2004, s 19.]

8–18029ZJ 20. England and Wales: supplemental. (1) The Marriage Act 1949 (c 76) shall have effect in relation to a marriage to which section 19 applies—

(*a*) subject to that section, and

(*b*) with any necessary consequential modification.

(2) In particular—

(*a*) section 28(1)(*b*) of that Act (declaration: residence) shall have effect as if it required a declaration that—

(i) the notice of marriage is given in compliance with section 19(2) above, and

(ii) the party subject to immigration control satisfies section 19(3)(a), (b) or (c), and (*b*) section 48 of that Act (proof of certain matters not essential to validity of marriage) shall have effect as if the list of matters in section 48(1)(*a*) to (*e*) included compliance with section 19 above.

(3) Regulations of the Secretary of State under section 19(2)(*a*) or (3)(*c*)—

(*a*) may make transitional provision,
(*b*) shall be made by statutory instrument, and
(*c*) shall be subject to annulment in pursuance of a resolution of either House of Parliament.

(4) Before making regulations under section 19(2)(*a*) the Secretary of State shall consult the Registrar General.

(5) An expression used in section 19 or this section and in Part III of the Marriage Act 1949 (c 76) has the same meaning in section 19 or this section as in that Part.

(6) An order under the Regulatory Reform Act 2001 (c 6) may include provision—

(*a*) amending section 19, this section or section 25 in consequence of other provision of the order, or
(*b*) repealing section 19, this section and section 25 and re-enacting them with modifications consequential upon other provision of the order.

[Asylum and Immigration (Treatment of Claimants, etc) Act 2004, s 20.]

8–18029ZK 21. Scotland

8–18029ZL 22. Scotland: supplemental

8–18029ZM 23. Northern Ireland

8–18029ZN 24. Northern Ireland: supplemental

8–18029ZO 25. Application for permission under section 19(3)(b), 21(3)(b) or 23(3)(b)

8–18029ZP 26–32. *Appeals*

8–18029ZQ 33–36. *Deportation and removal*

Immigration services

8–18029ZR 37. Provision of immigration services. (1) For section 84(2) and (3) of the Immigration and Asylum Act 1999 (c 33) (person qualified to provide immigration services) substitute—

"(2) A person is a qualified person if he is—

(*a*) a registered person,
(*b*) authorised by a designated professional body to practise as a member of the profession whose members the body regulates,
(*c*) the equivalent in an EEA State of—

(i) a registered person, or
(ii) a person within paragraph (b),

(*d*) a person permitted, by virtue of exemption from a prohibition, to provide in an EEA State advice or services equivalent to immigration advice or services, or
(*e*) acting on behalf of, and under the supervision of, a person within any of paragraphs (*a*) to (*d*) (whether or not under a contract of employment).

(3) Subsection (2)(*a*) and (*e*) are subject to any limitation on the effect of a person's registration imposed under paragraph 2(2) of Schedule 6.".

(2) In section 85(1) of that Act (registration by the Commissioner) omit "and (*b*)".

(3) In section 89 of that Act (disciplinary charge upheld by Immigration Services Tribunal)—

(*a*) for subsections (2) and (3) substitute—

"(2) If the person charged is a registered person or acts on behalf of a registered person, the Tribunal may—

(*a*) direct the Commissioner to record the charge and the Tribunal's decision for consideration in connection with the registered person's next application for continued registration;
(*b*) direct the registered person to apply for continued registration as soon as is reasonably practicable.", and

(*b*) in subsection (8) for "employed by him or working" substitute "acting on his behalf or".

(4) In section 90(4) of that Act (orders by disciplinary bodies) for "works under the supervision of" substitute "is acting on behalf of".

(5) In Schedule 5 to that Act (Immigration Services Commissioner)—

(*a*) for paragraph 1(1)(*b*) substitute—

"(*b*) those acting on behalf of registered persons,",

(*b*) for paragraph 1(3)(*b*) substitute—

"(*b*) any person acting on behalf of that person.",

(*c*) for paragraph 3(3)(*b*) substitute—

"(*b*) a person who is acting on behalf of a person who is within paragraph (*a*);",

(*d*) for paragraph 4(1)(*b*) substitute—

"(*b*) persons acting on behalf of persons who are within paragraph (a).",

(*e*) in paragraph 5(3)(*b*) for "employed by, or working under the supervision of," substitute "acting on behalf of",

(*f*) for paragraph 5(3)(*e*) substitute—

"(*e*) an alleged breach of a rule of a relevant regulatory body,",

(*g*) for paragraph 6(3)(c) substitute—

"(*c*) in any other case, refer the matter to any relevant regulatory body.",

(*h*) in paragraphs 9(1)(*a*) and (*b*) for "or a person employed by, or working under the supervision of," substitute "or is acting on behalf of",

(*i*) for paragraph 9(1)(*c*) substitute—

"(*c*) refer the complaint and his decision on it to a relevant regulatory body;",

(*j*) for paragraphs 9(3)(a) and (b) substitute—

"(*a*) imposing restrictions on the provision of immigration advice or immigration services by the relevant person or by a person acting on his behalf or under his supervision;

(*b*) prohibiting the provision of immigration advice or immigration services by the relevant person or a person acting on his behalf or under his supervision.", and

(*k*) for paragraphs 9(4)(*b*) to (*d*) substitute—

"(*b*) a person acting on behalf of a registered person;".

(6) In Schedule 6 to that Act (registration)—

(*a*) in paragraph 1(1) omit "or (*b*)", and

(*b*) in paragraph 3(7)(*a*) for "section 89(3)(*b*)" substitute "section 89(2)(*b*)".

[Asylum and Immigration (Treatment of Claimants, etc) Act 2004, s 37.]

8–18029ZS 38. Immigration Services Commissioner: power of entry. (1) After section 92 of the Immigration and Asylum Act 1999 (c 33) (offences: enforcement) insert—

"**92A. Investigation of offence: power of entry.** (1) On an application made by the Commissioner a justice of the peace may issue a warrant authorising the Commissioner to enter and search premises.

(2) A justice of the peace may issue a warrant in respect of premises only if satisfied that there are reasonable grounds for believing that—

(*a*) an offence under section 91 has been committed,

(*b*) there is material on the premises which is likely to be of substantial value (whether by itself or together with other material) to the investigation of the offence, and

(*c*) any of the conditions specified in subsection (3) is satisfied.

(3) Those conditions are—

(*a*) that it is not practicable to communicate with a person entitled to grant entry to the premises,

(*b*) that it is not practicable to communicate with a person entitled to grant access to the evidence,

(*c*) that entry to the premises will be prevented unless a warrant is produced, and

(*d*) that the purpose of a search may be frustrated or seriously prejudiced unless the Commissioner can secure immediate entry on arrival at the premises.

(4) The Commissioner may seize and retain anything for which a search is authorised under this section.

(5) A person commits an offence if without reasonable excuse he obstructs the Commissioner in the exercise of a power by virtue of this section.

(6) A person guilty of an offence under subsection (5) shall be liable on summary conviction to—

(*a*) imprisonment for a term not exceeding six months,

(*b*) a fine not exceeding level 5 on the standard scale, or

(*c*) both.

(7) In this section—

(*a*) a reference to the Commissioner includes a reference to a member of his staff authorised in writing by him,

(*b*) a reference to premises includes a reference to premises used wholly or partly as a dwelling, and

(*c*) a reference to material—

(i) includes material subject to legal privilege within the meaning of the Police and Criminal Evidence Act 1984 (c 60),

(ii) does not include excluded material or special procedure material within the meaning of that Act, and

(iii) includes material whether or not it would be admissible in evidence at a trial.

(8) *Scotland.*

(9) *Northern Ireland.*

[Asylum and Immigration (Treatment of Claimants, etc) Act 2004, s 38.]

8–18029ZT 39. Offence of advertising services. After section 92A of the Immigration and Asylum Act 1999 (c 33) (inserted by section 38 above) insert—

"**92B. Advertising.** (1) A person commits an offence if—

(*a*) he offers to provide immigration advice or immigration services, and

(*b*) provision by him of the advice or services would constitute an offence under section 91.

(2) For the purpose of subsection (1) a person offers to provide advice or services if he—

(*a*) makes an offer to a particular person or class of person,

(*b*) makes arrangements for an advertisement in which he offers to provide advice or services, or

(*c*) makes arrangements for an advertisement in which he is described or presented as competent to provide advice or services.

(3) A person guilty of an offence under this section shall be liable on summary conviction to a fine not exceeding level 4 on the standard scale.

(4) Subsections (3) to (7) of section 91 shall have effect for the purposes of this section as they have effect for the purposes of that section.

(5) An information relating to an offence under this section may in England and Wales be tried by a magistrates' court if—

(*a*) it is laid within the period of six months beginning with the date (or first date) on which the offence is alleged to have been committed, or

(*b*) it is laid—

(i) within the period of two years beginning with that date, and

(ii) within the period of six months beginning with a date certified by the Immigration Services Commissioner as the date on which the commission of the offence came to his notice.

(6) *Scotland.*

[Asylum and Immigration (Treatment of Claimants, etc) Act 2004, s 39.]

8–18029ZU 40. Appeal to Immigration Services Tribunal. Section 87(3)(*f*) of the Immigration and Asylum Act 1999 (c 33) (appeal to Tribunal against deferral of decision) shall cease to have effect.

[Asylum and Immigration (Treatment of Claimants, etc) Act 2004, s 40.]

8–18029ZV 41. Professional bodies. (1) Section 86 of the Immigration and Asylum Act 1999 (designated professional bodies) shall be amended as follows.

(2) For subsection (2) substitute—

"(2) The Secretary of State may by order remove a body from the list in subsection (1) if he considers that the body—

(*a*) has failed to provide effective regulation of its members in their provision of immigration advice or immigration services, or

(*b*) has failed to comply with a request of the Commissioner for the provision of information (whether general or in relation to a particular case or matter).".

(3) For subsection (9)(b) substitute—

"(*b*) report to the Secretary of State if the Commissioner considers that a designated professional body—

(i) is failing to provide effective regulation of its members in their provision of immigration advice or immigration services, or

(ii) has failed to comply with a request of the Commissioner for the provision of information (whether general or in relation to a particular case or matter).".

(4) After subsection (9) insert—

"(9A) A designated professional body shall comply with a request of the Commissioner for the provision of information (whether general or in relation to a specified case or matter).".

(5) In section 166(2) of the Immigration and Asylum Act 1999 (c 33) (regulations and orders) after "in relation to" insert "orders made under section 90(1),".

(6) For paragraph 21(2) of Schedule 5 to the Immigration and Asylum Act 1999 (Commissioner: annual report) substitute—

"(2) The report must, in particular, set out the Commissioner's opinion as to the extent to which each designated professional body has—

(*a*) provided effective regulation of its members in their provision of immigration advice or immigration services, and

(*b*) complied with requests of the Commissioner for the provision of information.".

[Asylum and Immigration (Treatment of Claimants, etc) Act 2004, s 41.]

Fees

8–18029ZW 42. Amount of fees

8–18029ZX 43. Transfer of leave stamps

General

8–18029ZY 44. Interpretation: "the Immigration Acts". (1) A reference to "the Immigration Acts" is to—

(*a*) the Immigration Act 1971 (c 77),
(*b*) the Immigration Act 1988 (c 14),
(*c*) the Asylum and Immigration Appeals Act 1993 (c 23),
(*d*) the Asylum and Immigration Act 1996 (c 49),
(*e*) the Immigration and Asylum Act 1999,
(*f*) the Nationality, Immigration and Asylum Act 2002 (c 41), and
(*g*) this Act.

(2) This section has effect in relation to a reference in this Act or any other enactment (including an enactment passed or made before this Act).

(3) For section 158(1) and (2) of the Nationality, Immigration and Asylum Act 2002 (c 41) substitute—

"(1) A reference to "the Immigration Acts" shall be construed in accordance with section 44 of the Asylum and Immigration (Treatment of Claimants, etc) Act 2004.".

(4) In the following provisions for "section 158 of the Nationality, Immigration and Asylum Act 2002" substitute "section 44 of the Asylum and Immigration (Treatment of Claimants, etc) Act 2004"—

(*a*) section 32(5) of the Immigration Act 1971 (c 77), and
(*b*) section 167(1) of the Immigration and Asylum Act 1999 (c 33).

[Asylum and Immigration (Treatment of Claimants, etc) Act 2004, s 44.]

8–18029ZZ 45. Interpretation: immigration officer. In this Act "immigration officer" means a person appointed by the Secretary of State as an immigration officer under paragraph 1 of Schedule 2 to the Immigration Act 1971.

[Asylum and Immigration (Treatment of Claimants, etc) Act 2004, s 45.]

8–18029ZZA 46. Money

8–18029ZZB 47. Repeals. The enactments listed in Schedule 4 are hereby repealed to the extent specified.

[Asylum and Immigration (Treatment of Claimants, etc) Act 2004, s 47.]

8–18029ZZC 48. Commencement. (1) Sections 2, 32(2) and 35 shall come into force at the end of the period of two months beginning with the date on which this Act is passed.

(2) Section 32(1) shall have effect in relation to determinations of the Special Immigration Appeals Commission made after the end of the period of two months beginning with the date on which this Act is passed.

(3) The other preceding provisions of this Act shall come into force in accordance with provision made—

(*a*) in the case of section 26 or Schedule 1 or 2, by order of the Lord Chancellor, (*b*) in the case of sections 4 and 5 in so far as they extend to Scotland, by order of the Scottish Ministers, and

(*c*) in any other case, by order of the Secretary of State[1].

(4) An order under subsection (3)—

(*a*) may make transitional or incidental provision,

(*b*) may make different provision for different purposes, and

(*c*) shall be made by statutory instrument.

(5) Transitional provision under subsection (4)(*a*) in relation to the commencement of section 26 may, in particular, make provision in relation to proceedings which, immediately before commencement—

(*a*) are awaiting determination by an adjudicator appointed, or treated as if appointed, under section 81 of the Nationality, Immigration and Asylum Act 2002 (c 41),

(*b*) are awaiting determination by the Immigration Appeal Tribunal,

(c) having been determined by an adjudicator could be brought before the Immigration Appeal Tribunal,

(*d*) are awaiting the determination of a further appeal brought in accordance with section 103 of that Act,

(*e*) having been determined by the Immigration Appeal Tribunal could be brought before another court by way of further appeal under that section,

(*f*) are or could be made the subject of an application under section 101 of that Act (review of decision on permission to appeal to Tribunal), or

(*g*) are or could be made the subject of another kind of application to the High Court or the Court of Session.

(6) Provision made under subsection (5) may, in particular—

(*a*) provide for the institution or continuance of an appeal of a kind not generally available after the commencement of section 26,

(*b*) provide for the termination of proceedings, or

(*c*) make any other provision that the Lord Chancellor thinks appropriate.

[Asylum and Immigration (Treatment of Claimants, etc) Act 2004, s 48.]

---

1. At the time of going to press the following commencement orders had been made: Asylum and Immigration (Treatment of Claimants, etc) Act 2004 (Commencement No 1) Order 2004, SI 2004/2523; Asylum and Immigration (Treatment of Claimants etc) Act 2004 (Commencement) (Scotland) Order 2004, SSI 2004/494; Asylum and Immigration (Treatment of Claimants, etc) Act 2004 (Commencement No 2) Order 2004, SI 2004/2999; and Asylum and Immigration (Treatment of Claimants, etc) Act 2004 (Commencement No 3) Order 2004, SI 2004/3398. Most of the Act's provisions are now in force.

8–18029ZZD **49. Extent.** (1) This Act extends (subject to subsection (2)) to—

(*a*) England and Wales,

(*b*) Scotland, and

(*c*) Northern Ireland.

(2) An amendment effected by this Act has the same extent as the enactment, or as the relevant part of the enactment, amended (ignoring extent by virtue of an Order in Council).

(3) Her Majesty may by Order in Council direct that a provision of this Act is to extend, with or without modification or adaptation, to—

(*a*) any of the Channel Islands;

(*b*) the Isle of Man.

[Asylum and Immigration (Treatment of Claimants, etc) Act 2004, s 49.]

8–18029ZZE **50. Short title.** This Act may be cited as the Asylum and Immigration (Treatment of Claimants, etc) Act 2004.

[Asylum and Immigration (Treatment of Claimants, etc) Act 2004, s 50.]

8–18029ZZF

SCHEDULE 1

NEW SCHEDULE 4 TO THE NATIONALITY, IMMIGRATION AND ASYLUM ACT 2002

8–18029ZZG

SCHEDULE 2

ASYLUM AND IMMIGRATION TRIBUNAL: CONSEQUENTIAL AMENDMENTS AND TRANSITIONAL PROVISION

PART 1

CONSEQUENTIAL AMENDMENTS[1]

---

1. Where these relate to provisions reproduced in this work the amendments will be incorporated when they take effect.

PART 2
TRANSITIONAL PROVISION

8–18029ZZH SCHEDULE 3
REMOVAL OF ASYLUM SEEKER TO SAFE COUNTRY

8–18029ZZI SCHEDULE 4
REPEALS[1]

1. Where these relate to provisions reproduced in this work the repeals will be shown when they take effect.

Immigration (Restrictions on Employment) Order 2004

(SI 2004/755)

8–18030 1. Citation and commencement. This Order may be cited as the Immigration (Restrictions on Employment) Order 2004 and shall come into force on 1st May 2004[1].

1. Made by the Secretary of State, in exercise of the powers conferred upon him by s 8(1) and (2A) of the Asylum and Immigration Act 1996.

8–18031 2. Interpretation. In this Order—

"the 1996 Act" means the Asylum and Immigration Act 1996;

"the Immigration Rules" has the meaning given in section 33(1) of the Immigration Act 1971;

"Immigration Status Document" means a document issued by the Home Office containing an endorsement, which confirms that the holder has been granted indefinite or limited leave to enter or remain in the United Kingdom; and

"registration card" has the meaning given in section 26A(1) of the Immigration Act 1971.

8–18032 3. Conditions specified under section 8(1) of the 1996 Act. (1) The set of conditions in paragraph (2) and the condition in paragraph (3) are specified for the purposes of section 8(1) of the 1996 Act (no offence committed in employing a person who satisfies such conditions).

(2) The set of conditions are that—

(*a*) the employee had limited leave to enter or remain in the United Kingdom which did not preclude his taking the employment in question;

(*b*) the employee applied to the Secretary of State for variation of that leave; and

(*c*) the employee is within the period during which an appeal could be brought or has a pending appeal under Part 5 of the Nationality, Immigration and Asylum Act 2002, against refusal of that application.

(3) The employee is permitted to work under the Immigration Rules.

8–18033 4. Requirements for the purposes of section 8(2) of the 1996 Act. (1) The requirements set out in paragraphs (2) to (5) are requirements for the purposes of section 8(2) of the 1996 Act (defence for a person charged with an offence under section 8 to prove that before the employment began any such requirement was complied with).

(2) There must have been produced to the employer either—

(*a*) a document of a description specified in Part 1 of the Schedule, or

(*b*) one document of a description specified in—

(i) each of sub-paragraphs (*a*) and (*b*) of paragraph 1 of Part 2 of the Schedule; or

(ii) each of sub-paragraphs (*a*) and (*b*) of paragraph 2 of that Part.

(3) The employer must have taken the steps specified in Part 3 of the Schedule to copy or record the content of any document produced to him in accordance with paragraph (2).

(4) The employer must have satisfied himself that each document produced in accordance with paragraph (2), appears to relate to the employee in question; in particular—

(*a*) if a document contains a photograph, the employer must have satisfied himself that the person photographed is the employee in question, and

(*b*) if a document contains a date of birth, the employer must have satisfied himself that the date of birth is consistent with the appearance of the employee.

(5) If either—

(*a*) the name on a document produced under paragraph 1(*a*) of Part 2 of the Schedule differs from the name on a document produced under paragraph 1(*b*) of that Part; or

(*b*) the name on a document produced under paragraph 2(*a*) of Part 2 of the Schedule differs from the name on a document produced under paragraph 2(*b*) of that Part,

a document must have been produced to the employer explaining the difference.

8–18034 5. Revocation. The Immigration (Restrictions on Employment) Order 1996 is hereby revoked.

8–18035 SCHEDULE

PART 1

DESCRIPTIONS OF DOCUMENTS FOR THE PURPOSES OF ARTICLE 4(2)(*a*)

Article 4(2)(*a*)

1. A United Kingdom passport describing the holder as a British citizen or as a citizen of the United Kingdom and Colonies having the right of abode in the United Kingdom.

2. A passport containing a certificate of entitlement issued by or on behalf of the Government of the United Kingdom, certifying that the holder has the right of abode in the United Kingdom.

3. A passport or national identity card, issued by a State which is a party to the European Economic Area Agreement or any other agreement forming part of the Communities Treaties which confers rights of entry to or residence in the United Kingdom, which describes the holder as a national of a State which is a party to that Agreement.

4. A United Kingdom residence permit issued to a national of a State which is a party to the European Economic Area Agreement or any other agreement forming part of the Communities Treaties which confirms that the holder has rights of entry to, or residence in, the United Kingdom.

5. A passport or other travel document or a residence document issued by the Home Office which is endorsed to show that the holder has a current right of residence in the United Kingdom as the family member of a named national of a State which is a party to the European Economic Area Agreement or any other agreement forming part of the Communities Treaties which confers rights of entry to, or residence in, the United Kingdom, and who is resident in the United Kingdom.

6. A passport or other travel document endorsed to show that the holder is exempt from immigration control, has indefinite leave to enter, or remain in, the United Kingdom or has no time limit on his stay.

7. A passport or other travel document endorsed to show that the holder has current leave to enter, or remain in, the United Kingdom and is permitted to take the employment in question, provided that it does not require the issue of a work permit.

8. A registration card which indicates that the holder is entitled to take employment in the United Kingdom.

PART 2

DESCRIPTIONS OF DOCUMENTS FOR THE PURPOSES OF ARTICLE 4(2)(*b*)

Article 4(2)(*b*)

1. (*a*) A document issued by a previous employer, Inland Revenue, the Department for Work and Pensions' Jobcentre Plus, the Employment Service, the Training and Employment Agency (Northern Ireland) or the Northern Ireland Social Security Agency, which contains the National Insurance number of the person named in the document; and

(*b*) either:—

(i) a birth certificate issued in the United Kingdom, which specifies the names of the holder's parents; or

(ii) a birth certificate issued in the Channel Islands, the Isle of Man or Ireland; or

(iii) a certificate of registration or naturalisation as a British citizen; or

(iv) a letter issued by the Home Office, to the holder, which indicates that the person named in it has been granted indefinite leave to enter, or remain in, the United Kingdom; or

(v) an Immigration Status Document issued by the Home Office, to the holder, endorsed with a United Kingdom Residence Permit, which indicates that the holder has been granted indefinite leave to enter, or remain in, the United Kingdom; or

(vi) a letter issued by the Home Office, to the holder, which indicates that the person named in it has subsisting leave to enter, or remain in, the United Kingdom and is entitled to take the employment in question in the United Kingdom; or

(vii) an Immigration Status Document issued by the Home Office, to the holder, endorsed with a United Kingdom Residence Permit, which indicates that the holder has been granted limited leave to enter, or remain in, the United Kingdom and is entitled to take the employment in question in the United Kingdom.

2. (*a*) A work permit or other approval to take employment issued by Work Permits UK; and

(*b*) either:—

(i) a passport or other travel document endorsed to show that the holder has current leave to enter, or remain in, the United Kingdom and is permitted to take the work permit employment in question, or

(ii) a letter issued by the Home Office to the holder, confirming the same.

PART 3

STEPS WHICH MUST BE TAKEN TO COPY OR RECORD THE CONTENT OF A DOCUMENT PRODUCED TO AN EMPLOYER

Article 4(3)

1. In the case of a passport or other travel document, the following parts must be photocopied or scanned into a database, using the technology known as "Write Once Read Many"—

(*a*) the front cover; and

(*b*) any page containing;

(i) the holder's personal details including nationality;

(ii) the holder's photograph and/or signature;

(iii) the date of expiry; and

(iv) the information referrred to in paragraphs 1 (other than citizenship) and 2 of Part 1 and the endorsements referred to in paragraphs 5, 6 and 7 of Part 1 and paragraph 2(b)(i) of Part 2.

2. All other documents must be photocopied or scanned in their entirety into a database, using the technology known as "Write Once Read Many".

INDUSTRY AND COMMERCE

8–18050 This title contains the following statutes—

The following statutes which are relevant to this title are not reproduced in this Manual—

The following statutory instrument is also included—

8–18051 European Communities Act 1972: regulations. Within the scope of the title Industry would logically fall the subject matter of a number of regulations made under the very wide enabling power provided in section 2(2) of the European Communities Act 1972. Where such regulations create offences they are noted below in chronological order:

Construction Products Regulations 1991, SI 1991/1620;
Export of Dangerous Chemicals Regulations 1992, SI 1992/2415;
Telecommunications Terminal Equipment Regulations 1992, SI 1992/2423;
Public Offers of Securities Regulations 1995, SI 1995/1537 amended by SI 2005/1433;
Money Laundering Regulations 2003, in this title, post;
Financial Services (Distance Marketing) Regulations 2004, SI 2004/2095.

8–18052

Statistics of Trade Act 1947

(10 & 11 Geo 6 c 39)

(Not reproduced in this Manual)

Emergency Laws (Re-enactments and Repeals) Act 1964

(1964 c 60)

8–18053 This Act repeals defence Regulations relating to trade, industry and finance.

By certain re-enactments, Government control is maintained over hire purchase agreements and the movement of gold and various Ministers are empowered to make Orders for purposes of defence and in respect of welfare foods.

If any person contravenes or fails to comply with Part I of the Act, or any Order made thereunder he is guilty of an offence and liable[1] on summary conviction to imprisonment for not exceeding **three months** or fine not exceeding **the statutory maximum or both**, or, on conviction on indictment, to imprisonment for not exceeding **two years** or fine or both. A corporate body convicted on indictment may be fined such larger amount as the court thinks just.

Proceedings for an offence against such Orders or directions may be instituted only by or with the consent of the Director of Public Prosecutions, or the Board of Trade or the Minister of Transport or the Treasury.

Proceedings may be taken before the appropriate court in the United Kingdom having jurisdiction in the place where the defendant is for the time being.

An officer of a Minister of the Crown is empowered to require the production of documents from any person carrying on a relevant undertaking or employed in connection therewith.

Failure to comply with such requirement is an offence punishable on summary conviction by imprisonment for not exceeding **three months** or fine not exceeding **level 3** on the standard scale **or both**.

A justice of the peace, on information on oath, may grant a search warrant in respect of such documents. Any person who obstructs the execution of such warrant is guilty of an offence punishable on summary conviction by imprisonment for not exceeding **three months** or fine not exceeding **level 3** on the standard scale **or both**.

[Emergency laws (Re-enactments and Repeals) Act 1964, as amended by the Criminal Law Act 1977, ss 28 and 32 and the Criminal Justice Act 1982, ss 38 and 46—summarised.]

---

1. For procedure in respect of this offence which is triable either way, see the Magistrates' Courts Act 1980, ss 17A–21 in PART I: MAGISTRATES' COURTS, PROCEDURE, ante.

Scrap Metal Dealers Act 1964

(1964 c 69)

8–18054 **1. Registration of scrap metal dealers.** (1) Every local authority[1] shall maintain a register of persons carrying on business in their area as scrap metal dealers[2]; and, after the expiration of three months beginning with the commencement of this Act[3] no person shall carry on business as a scrap metal dealer in the area of a local authority unless the appropriate particulars relating to him are for the time being entered in the register maintained by the authority under this section.

(2) For the purposes of this section a person carrying on business as a scrap metal dealer shall be treated as carrying on that business in the area of a local authority if, but only if—

(*a*) a place[4] in that area is occupied by him as a scrap metal store[5] or

(*b*) no place is occupied by him as a scrap metal store, whether in that area or elsewhere, but he has his usual place of residence in that area, or

(*c*) no place is occupied by him as a scrap metal store, whether in that area or elsewhere, but a place in that area is occupied by him wholly or partly for the purposes of that business.

(3) Any person at the commencement of this Act[3] carrying on, or thereafter proposing to carry on, business as a scrap metal dealer in the area of a local authority may apply to the authority, on furnishing the authority in writing with the appropriate particulars relating to him, or, as the case may be, with what would be the appropriate particulars relating to him if he were then carrying on the business, to enter those particulars in the register maintained by the authority under this section; and where such an application is made, the local authority shall thereupon enter those particulars relating to the applicant in the register.

(4) For the purposes of this section the appropriate particulars relating to a scrap metal dealer, in relation to the area of a local authority are—

(*a*) the full name of the dealer[6];

(*b*) the address—

(i) if the dealer is an individual, of his usual place of residence;

(ii) if the dealer is a body corporate, of its registered or principal office;

(*c*) the address of each place in the area (if any) which is occupied by the dealer as a scrap metal store;

(*d*) if the business is carried on in the circumstances mentioned in subsection (2)(*b*) of this section, the fact that the business is so carried on;

(*e*) if the business is carried on in the circumstances mentioned in subsection (2)(*c*) of this section, the fact that the business is so carried on, and the address of the place which is occupied by the dealer as mentioned in that paragraph.

(5) Where the appropriate particulars relating to a scrap metal dealer are for the time being entered in the register maintained by a local authority under this section—

(*a*) if any event occurs which involves an alteration of those particulars, the dealer shall give notice of the alteration to the local authority and the authority shall thereupon amend the register accordingly[7];

(*b*) if the dealer ceases to carry on business as a scrap metal dealer in the area of the local authority, he shall give notice of that fact to the authority and the authority shall thereupon cancel the entry relating to him in the register[8];

and any notice required to be given to a local authority under this subsection shall be given within the period of twenty-eight days beginning with the day on which the event in question occurs.

(6) The entry of the appropriate particulars relating to a scrap metal dealer in the register maintained by a local authority under this section shall include a note of the day on which the entry is made; and—

(*a*) any such entry shall be cancelled by the authority at the end of the period of three years beginning with the said day, unless before the end of that period the dealer applies to the authority for the registration to be continued for a further period of three years, and

(*b*) where such an application has been made, the preceding paragraph shall apply, with respect to each successive period of three years, as if the reference in the paragraph to the said day were a reference to the day as from which the registration was last continued under that paragraph.

(7) Any person who carries on business as a scrap metal dealer in contravention of subsection (1) of this section[9], or who fails to comply with the requirements of subsection (5) of this section as to the notice specified in paragraph (*a*) thereof, shall be guilty of an offence, and liable on summary conviction to a fine not exceeding **level 3** on the standard scale.

(8) Any person who fails to comply with the requirements of subsection (5) of this section as to the notice specified in paragraph (*b*) thereof shall be guilty of an offence and liable on summary conviction to a fine not exceeding **level 1** on the standard scale.

(9) It shall be the duty of every local authority to enforce the preceding provisions of this section with respect to persons carrying on business as scrap metal dealers in their area.

(10) In relation to the carrying on of business as a scrap metal dealer by a local authority in their area, this section shall apply with the modifications that the following provisions, that is to say, subsection (3), subsection (6)(*a*) and (*b*), and subsection (8) shall be omitted, and for subsection (5) there shall be substituted the following subsection—

"(5) Where the appropriate particulars relating to a local authority who are carrying on business as a scrap metal dealer are for the time being entered in the register maintained by that local authority under this section—

(*a*) If any event occurs which involves the alteration of those particulars, the authority shall thereupon amend the register;

(*b*) if the local authority cease to carry on business as a scrap metal dealer in their area, they shall thereupon cancel the entry relating to them in the register."

[Scrap Metal Dealers Act 1964, s 1, as amended by the Criminal Justice Act 1982, ss 38 and 46.]

---

1. "Local authority" means the council of a county borough or county district, the Common Council of the City of London or the council of a London borough (s 9(2)).

2. For the purposes of this Act a person carries on business as a scrap metal dealer if he carries on a business which consists wholly or partly of buying and selling scrap metal, whether the scrap metal sold is in the form in which it was bought or otherwise, other than a business in the course of which scrap metal is not bought except as materials for the manufacture of other articles and is not sold except as a by-product of such manufacture or as surplus materials bought but not required for such manufacture; and "scrap metal dealer" (where that expression is used in this Act otherwise than in a reference to carrying on business as a scrap metal dealer) means a person who (in accordance with the preceding provisions of this subsection) carries on business as a scrap metal dealer.

"Scrap metal" includes any old metal, and any broken, worn out, defaced or partly manufactured articles made wholly or partly of metal, and any metallic wastes, and also includes old, broken, worn out or defaced tooltips or dies made of any of the materials commonly known as hard metals or of cemented or sintered metallic carbides;

"Article" includes any part of an article.

Any reference in the preceding provisions of this Act to metal, except in the phrases "hard metal" and "metallic carbides" shall be taken as a reference to magnesium, nickel, tin and zinc, or, subject to the next following subsection, to brass, bronze, gunmetal, steel, white metal or any other alloy of any of the said metals.

For the purposes of this Act, a substance being an alloy referred to in the last preceding subsection shall not be treated as being such an alloy if, of its weight, two per cent or more is attributable to gold or silver or any one or more of the following metals, that is to say, platinum, iridium, osmium, palladium, rhodium and ruthenium.

Any reference in this Act to a person registered under this Act as a scrap metal dealer is a reference to a person in respect of whom the particulars required by s 1 of this Act are for the time being entered in a register maintained by a local authority under that section (s 9(1)–(5)).

In *Such v Gibbons* [1981] RTR 126, on the facts of that case, it was held that a dealer in scrap motor vehicles was not a "scrap metal dealer".

3. Ie 1 April, 1965. This Act repealed and replaced earlier enactments relating to scrap metal dealers, including relevant provisions contained in many local Acts.

4. "Place" includes any land whether consisting of enclosed premises or not (s 9(2)).

5. "Scrap metal store" means a place where scrap metal is received or kept in the course of the business of a scrap metal dealer (s 9(2)).

6. Provisions relating to partnerships are contained in s 7, post.

7. Contravention of this paragraph is punishable in accordance with sub-s (7), post.

8. Contravention of this paragraph is punishable in accordance with sub-s (8), post.

9. On conviction of a contravention of s 1(1) of the Act, restrictive requirements may be imposed relating to future trading: see s 4, post.

8–18055 2. Records of dealings. (1) Subject to the provisions of this and the next following section, every scrap metal dealer[1] shall, at each place[1] occupied by him as a scrap metal store[1] keep a book for the purposes of this section, and shall enter in the book the particulars required by this section with respect to—

(*a*) all scrap metal[1] received at that place, and

(*b*) all scrap metal either processed[2] at, or despatched from, that place:

Provided that at any such place a scrap metal dealer may at his option keep two books for the purposes of this section, one for recording the said particulars with respect to scrap metal falling within paragraph (*a*) of this subsection and the other for recording that said particulars, with respect to scrap metal falling within paragraph (*b*) thereof, but shall not at any one place and at any one time have in use, for the purposes of this section, more than one book for recording the said particulars with respect to scrap metal falling within each of those paragraphs.

(2) The said particulars, in the case of scrap metal falling within paragraph (*a*) of the preceding subsection, are—

(*a*) the description[3] and weight of the scrap metal;
(*b*) the date and time of the receipt of the scrap metal;
(*c*) if the scrap metal is received from another person, the full name and address of that person;
(*d*) the price, if any, payable in respect of the receipt of the scrap metal, if that price has been ascertained at the time when the entry in the book relating to that scrap metal is to be made;
(*e*) where the last preceding paragraph does not apply, the value of the scrap metal at the time when the entry is to be made as estimated by the dealer;
(*f*) in the case of scrap metal delivered at the place in question by means of a mechanically propelled vehicle bearing a registration mark (whether the vehicle belongs to the dealer or not) the registration mark borne by the vehicle[4].

(3) The said particulars, in the case of scrap metal falling within subsection (1)(*b*) of this section, are—

(*a*) the description and weight of the scrap metal;
(*b*) the date of processing or, as the case may be, despatch of the scrap metal, and, if processed, the process applied;
(*c*) in the case of scrap metal despatched on sale or exchange, the full name and address of the person to whom the scrap metal is sold or with whom it is exchanged, and the consideration for which it is sold or exchanged;
(*d*) in the case of scrap metal processed or despatched otherwise than on sale or exchange, the value of the scrap metal immediately before its processing or despatch as estimated by the dealer.

(4) Any particulars required to be entered in a book by virtue of the preceding provisions of this section, in respect of scrap metal falling within subsection (1)(*a*) of this section, shall be so entered immediately after the receipt of the scrap metal at the place in question; and any particulars so requested to be entered, in respect of scrap metal falling within subsection (1)(*b*) of this section, shall be so entered immediately after the processing or despatch.

(5) Any book kept by a person in pursuance of subsection (1) of this section shall be a bound book kept exclusively for the purposes of this section and shall be retained by him until the end of the period of two years beginning with the day on which the last entry was made in the book.

(6) Any person who fails to comply with any of the requirements imposed on him by this section shall be guilty of an offence and liable on summary conviction to a fine not exceeding **level 3** on the standard scale[5].

(7) In this section "processing", in relation to scrap metal, includes melting down and any other process whereby the material ceases to be scrap metal, but does not include dismantling or breaking up, and "processed" shall be construed accordingly.
[Scrap Metal Dealers Act 1964, s 2, as amended by the Criminal Justice Act 1982, s 38 and 46.]

---

1. See notes 2, 4 and 5 in para **8–18054**, ante. Provisions relating to partnership records are contained in s 7, post.
2. See sub-s (7), post.
3. The entry must give a fair, though not necessarily detailed, description: see *Jenkins v A Cohen & Co Ltd* [1971] 2 All ER 1384, [1971] 1 WLR 1280.
4. Any reference in this Act to a registration mark borne by a vehicle is a reference to any mark which is displayed on the vehicle and is of a kind usually displayed on mechanically propelled vehicles for the purpose of complying with the provisions of the Vehicles (Excise) Act 1971, as to registration marks (s 9(6)).
5. On conviction, restrictive requirements relating to future trading may be imposed in accordance with s 4, post.

8–18056 3. Special provisions as to records in certain cases. (1) Where a person, who is registered by a local authority under this Act as a scrap metal dealer, satisfies the authority that he carries on, or proposes to carry on, the business of a scrap metal dealer as part of the business of an itinerant collector[1], and not otherwise, the authority may make an order directing that, while the order remains in force, he shall be exempt from the requirements of the last preceding section, but instead shall be subject to the following requirements, that is to say—

(*a*) that, on the sale by him of any scrap metal, he shall obtain from the purchase a receipt showing the weight of the scrap metal comprised in the sale and the aggregate price at which it is sold; and
(*b*) that he shall keep every such receipt as he is required to obtain under the preceding paragraph, until the end of the period of two years beginning with the day on which the receipt is obtained, in such a way as to be able to produce it on demand to any person authorised, in accordance with the following provisions of this Act, to require its production.

(2) A local authority shall not make an order under the preceding subsection except after consultation with the chief officer of police for the police area (or, if more than one, for every police area) in which the area of the local authority, or any part of their area, is comprised.

(3) An order under subsection (1) of this section may be revoked at any time by the local authority by whom it was made.

(4) Any person who fails to comply with any of the requirements imposed on him by virtue of the foregoing provisions of this section shall be guilty of an offence and liable on summary conviction to a fine not exceeding **level 3** on the standard scale.

(5) Where a scrap metal dealer does not occupy any place as a scrap metal store, but for the time being no order under subsection (1) of this section is in force exempting him from the requirements of the last preceding section, the provisions of that section shall apply to him subject to the following modifications, that is to say—

(*a*) any reference to keeping a book at each place occupied by the dealer as a scrap metal store shall be construed as a reference to keeping a book either at his usual place of residence or at any other place occupied by him wholly or partly for the purposes of his business as a scrap metal dealer;

(*b*) any reference to the receipt of scrap metal at a place shall be construed as a reference to the receipt of scrap metal for the purposes of that business;

(*c*) any reference to the processing of scrap metal at a place, or to the despatch of scrap metal from a place, shall be construed as a reference to the disposal of scrap metal in the course of that business;

(*d*) subsection (4) of that section shall be omitted, and any particulars required to be entered in a book by virtue of this subsection shall be so entered as soon as is practicable.

(6) Where a scrap metal dealer occupies a place as a scrap metal store, but for the time being no order under subsection (1) of this section is in force exempting him from the requirements of the last preceding section, and any scrap metal is, for the purposes of his business as a scrap metal dealer, received otherwise than at a place so occupied by him and is disposed of in the course of that business without its being received at such a place, then—

(*a*) the obligation imposed by subsection (1) of the last preceding section to enter particulars in a book or books shall extend to the entry, as soon as is practicable, of the like particulars with respect to that scrap metal as would be required by subsections (2) and (3) of the last preceding section if they were modified so that—

(i) any reference therein to the receipt of scrap metal at a place were construed as a reference to the receipt of scrap metal for the purposes of that business; and

(ii) any reference therein to the processing of scrap metal at a place or to the despatch of scrap metal from a place, were construed as a reference to the disposal of scrap metal in the course of that business;

(*b*) if the dealer occupies more than one place as a scrap metal store, the particulars required by virtue of the preceding paragraph shall be entered in the book or books kept by him under the last preceding section at such of the places so occupied by him as is the nearer, or, as the case may be, the nearest, to the place at which the scrap metal is received for the purposes aforesaid; and

(*c*) subsection (4) of the last preceding section shall not have effect in relation to the particulars so required.

[Scrap Metal Dealers Act 1964, s 3, as amended by the Criminal Justice Act 1982, ss 38 and 46.]

1. "Itinerant collector" means a person regularly engaged in collecting waste materials, and old, broken, worn out or defaced articles, by means of visits from house to house (s 9(2)).

8–18057 4. Power of court to impose additional requirements on convicted dealers. (1) Where a person—

(*a*) is convicted of the offence of carrying on business as a scrap metal dealer in contravention of section 1(1) of this Act[1], or

(*b*) being a person for the time being registered under this Act as a scrap metal dealer, is convicted of an offence under s 2 of this Act[2], or is convicted of any offence which, in the opinion of the court convicting him, is an offence involving dishonesty[3],

the court by which he is convicted may, if it thinks fit, make an order directing that, while the order is in force, he shall be subject to the requirements specified in the next following subsection, in addition to the requirements which apply to him under the preceding provisions of this Act.

(2) The said requirements are that, at any place occupied by him as a scrap metal store—

(*a*) no scrap metal shall be received between the hours of six o'clock in the evening and eight o'clock in the morning;

(*b*) all scrap metal received at that place shall be kept, in the form in which it is received there, for a period of not less than seventy-two hours beginning with the time when it is so received.

(3) An order under subsection (1) of this section shall specify a period, not exceeding two years, for which the order (if not revoked) is to remain in force; and any such order may at any time, on the application of the person to whom the order relates, be revoked by the court by which the order was made.

(4) If any requirement of an order under subsection (1) of this section is contravened, the person

to whom the order relates shall be guilty of an offence and liable on summary conviction to a fine not exceeding **level 3** on the standard scale and the court by which he is convicted may, if it thinks fit, make in relation to him a further order under that subsection.
[Scrap Metal Dealers Act 1964, s 4, as amended by the Criminal Justice Act 1982, ss 38 and 46.]

1. Carrying on business as a scrap metal dealer without having been registered, ante.
2. Failing to keep prescribed records, ante.
3. This conviction could, for example, be for theft or handling stolen goods.

8–18057A 4A. Notification of destruction of motor vehicles. (1)–(3) *Regulations may provide for notification of destruction of vehicles.*

(4) A person who contravenes any provision to which this subsection applies shall be guilty of an offence and liable on summary conviction to a fine not exceeding level 3 on the standard scale.

(5)–(6) *Further provisions about regulations.*

(7) In this section—

"contravene", in relation to any provision of regulations, includes fail to comply with it;

"motor vehicle" means any vehicle whose function is or was to be used on roads as a mechanically propelled vehicle; and

"road" means any highway and any other road to which the public has access.*

[Scrap Metal Dealers Act 1964, s 4A, as inserted by the Vehicles (Crime) Act 2001, s 35.]

***Section inserted by the Vehicles (Crime) Act 2001, s 35, from a date to be appointed.**

8–18058 5. Other offences relating to scrap metal. (1) If a scrap metal dealer acquires any scrap metal from a person apparently under the age of sixteen years, whether the scrap metal is offered by that person on his own behalf or on behalf of another person, he shall be guilty of an offence and liable on summary conviction to a fine not exceeding **level 1** on the standard scale:

Provided that, where a person is charged with an offence under this subsection, it shall be a defence to prove that the person from whom he acquired the scrap metal was in fact of or over the age of sixteen years.

(2) Any person who, on selling scrap metal to a scrap metal dealer, gives the dealer a false name or false address shall be guilty of an offence and liable on summary conviction to a fine not exceeding **level 1** on the standard scale.
[Scrap Metal Dealers Act 1964, s 5, as amended by the Criminal Justice Act 1982, ss 38 and 46.]

8–18059 6. Rights of entry and inspection. (1) Subject to the provisions of this section, any constable shall have a right at all reasonable times—

(*a*) to enter and inspect any place for the time being entered in a register under section 1 of this Act as a place which is occupied by a scrap metal dealer as a scrap metal store[1], or as a place which is occupied by a scrap metal dealer wholly or partly for the purposes of his business;

(*b*) to require production of, and to inspect, any scrap metal kept at that place and any book or record which the dealer is required by virtue of this Act to keep at that place, or, as the case may be, any receipt which the dealer is required to keep as mentioned in section 3(1)(*b*) of this Act, and to take copies of or extracts from any such book, record or receipt.*

(2) Subject to the provisions of this section, if any officer of a local authority[2] duly authorised in writing by the authority in that behalf has reasonable grounds for believing that a place in the area of the authority is being used as a scrap metal store[1], and that place is not for the time being entered in the register kept by the authority under section 1 of this Act as a place which is occupied as a scrap metal store, the officer shall have a right at any reasonable time, on producing (if required to do so) evidence of this authority, to enter that place for the purpose of ascertaining whether it is being used as a scrap metal store.

(3) If a justice of the peace is satisfied by information on oath that admission to a place specified in the information is reasonably required in order to secure compliance with the provisions of, or made under, this Act, or to ascertain whether those provisions are being complied with, he may by warrant under his hand authorise a person having a right of entry to that place in accordance with the preceding provisions of this section to enter that place at any time within one month from the date of the warrant, if need be by force.*

(4) Except under the authority of a warrant granted under the last preceding subsection, no person shall be entitled by virtue of this section to enter any place by force.

(5) Any person who obstructs the exercise of any right of entry or inspection conferred by this section, or who fails to produce any book, record or other document which a person has a right to inspect thereunder, shall be guilty of an offence and liable on summary conviction to a fine not exceeding **level 1** on the standard scale.*
[Scrap Metal Dealers Act 1964, s 6, as amended by the Criminal Justice Act 1982, ss 38 and 46.]

***Amended by the Vehicles (Crime) Act 2001, s 43, from a date to be appointed.**

1. See note 5 to s 1, ante.
2. For definition of "local authority", see note 1 to s 1, ante.

8–18060 **7. Partnerships.** (1) In relation to any person who carries on, or proposes to carry on, the business of a scrap metal dealer in partnership with any other person—

(*a*) this Act shall have effect as if any reference to the occupation of a place by a person as a scrap metal store were a reference to the occupation of that place for the purposes of the partnership by that person, alone or jointly with a member of the partnership or by another member of the partnership alone; and

(*b*) the particulars which that person is required by section 1(3) of this Act to furnish shall include, in addition to those specified in section 1(4) of this Act, the name under which the partnership is carried on, the name and place of residence of each other member of the partnership who is an individual and the name and registered or principal office of each other member of the partnership who is a body corporate.

(2) Where a place is occupied as a scrap metal store for the purposes of a business carried on in partnership, there shall not be kept at that place in compliance with section 2(1) of this Act more than one book, or, in accordance with the proviso to the said section 2(1), two books, and the requirements imposed on a person by that section in respect of that place shall if complied with by a partner, be taken to be complied with by that person.
[Scrap Metal Dealers Act 1964, s 7.]

8–18080

Restrictive Trade Practices Act 1976

(1976 c 34)

(NOT REPRODUCED IN THIS MANUAL)

8–18100

Development of Rural Wales Act 1976

(1976 c 75)

(NOT REPRODUCED IN THIS MANUAL)

Estate Agents Act 1979[1]

(1979 c 38)

Application of Act

8–18140 **1. Estate agency work.** (1) This Act applies, subject to subsections (2) to (4) below to things done by any person in the course of a business (including a business in which he is employed) pursuant to instructions received from another person (in this section referred to as "the client") who wishes to dispose of or acquire an interest in land—

(*a*) for the purpose of, or with a view to, effecting the introduction to the client of a third person who wishes to acquire or, as the case may be, dispose of such an interest; and

(*b*) after such an introduction has been effected in the course of that business, for the purpose of securing the disposal or, as the case may be, the acquisition of that interest;

and in this Act the expression "estate agency work" refers to things done as mentioned above to which this Act applies.

(2) This Act does not apply to things done—

(*a*) in the course of his profession by a practising solicitor or a person employed by him or by an incorporated practice (within the meaning of the Solicitors (Scotland) Act 1980) or a person employed by it; or

(*b*) in the course of credit brokerage, within the meaning of the Consumer Credit Act 1974; or

(*c*) *repealed*

(*d*) in the course of carrying out any survey or valuation pursuant to a contract which is distinct from that under which other things falling within subsection (1) above are done; or

(*e*) in connection with applications and other matters arising under the Town and Country Planning Act 1990, the Planning (Listed Buildings and Conservation Areas) Act 1990, the Planning (Hazardous Substances) Act 1990, or the Town and Country Planning (Scotland) Act 1972 or the Planning (Northern Ireland) Order 1972.

(3) This Act does not apply to things done by any person—

(*a*) pursuant to instructions received by him in the course of his employment in relation to an interest in land if his employer is the person who, on his own behalf, wishes to dispose of or acquire that interest; or

(*b*) in relation to any interest in any property if the property is subject to a mortgage and he is the receiver of the income of it; or

(*c*) in relation to a present, prospective or former employee of his or of any person by whom he also is employed if the things are done by reason of the employment (whether past, present or future).

(4) This Act does not apply to the publication of advertisements or the dissemination of information by a person who does no other acts which fall within subsection (1) above.

(5) In this section—

(*a*) "practising solicitor" means, except in Scotland, a solicitor who is qualified to act as such under section 1 of the Solicitors Act 1974 or Article 4 of the Solicitors (Northern Ireland) Order 1976, and in Scotland includes a firm of practising solicitors;

(*b*) "mortgage" includes a debenture and any other charge on property for securing money or money's worth; and

(*c*) any reference to employment is a reference to employment under a contract of employment.

[Estate Agents Act 1979, s 1, as amended by the Law Reform (Miscellaneous Provisions) (Scotland) Act 1985, Sch 1, the Planning (Consequential Provisions) Act 1990, Sch 2 and SI 2001/1283.]

---

1. Of the provisions printed in this work, only ss 16, 17 and 22 were not brought into force by SI 1981/1517.

8–18141 **2. Interests in land.** (1) Subject to subsection (3) below, any reference in this Act to disposing of an interest in land is a reference to—

(*a*) transferring a legal estate in fee simple absolute in possession; or

(*b*) transferring or creating, elsewhere than in Scotland, a lease which, by reason of the level of the rent, the length of the term or both, has a capital value which may be lawfully realised on the open market; or

(*c*) *Scotland*;

and any reference to acquiring an interest in land shall be construed accordingly.

(2) In subsection (1)(*b*) above the expression "lease" includes the rights and obligations arising under an agreement to grant a lease.

(3) Notwithstanding anything in subsections (1) and (2), references in this Act to disposing of an interest in land do not extend to disposing of—

(*a*) the interest of a creditor whose debt is secured by way of a mortgage or charge of any kind over land or an agreement for any such mortgage or charge; or

(*b*) *Scotland*.

[Estate Agents Act 1979, s 2.]

Orders by Director General of Fair Trading

8–18142 **3. Orders prohibiting unfit persons from doing estate agency work.** (1) The power of the Director General of Fair Trading (in this Act referred to as "the Director") to make an order under this section with respect to any person shall not be exercisable unless the Director is satisfied that that person—

(*a*) has been convicted[1] of—

(i) an offence involving fraud or other dishonesty or violence, or

(ii) an offence under any provision of this Act, other than section 10(6), section 22(3) or section 23(4), or

(iii) any other offence which, at the time it was committed, was specified for the purposes of this section by an order[2] made by the Secretary of State; or

(*b*) has committed discrimination in the course of estate agency work; or

(*c*) has failed to comply with any obligation imposed on him under any of sections 15 and 18 to 21 below; or

(*d*) has engaged in a practice which, in relation to estate agency work[3], has been declared undesirable by an order made by the Secretary of State;

and the provisions of Schedule 1 to the Act shall have effect for supplementing paragraphs (*a*) and (*b*) above.

(2) Subject to subsection (1) above, if the Director is satisfied that any person is unfit to carry on estate agency work[3] generally or of a particular description he may make an order prohibiting that person—

(*a*) from doing any estate agency work[3] at all; or

(*b*) from doing estate agency work of a description specified in the order;

and in determining whether a person is so unfit the Director may, in addition to taking account of any matters falling within subsection (1) above, also take account of whether, in the course of estate agency work or any other business activity, that person has engaged in any practice which involves breaches of a duty owed by virtue of any enactment, contract or rule of law and which is material to his fitness to carry on estate agency work.

(3) For the purposes of paragraphs (*c*) and (*d*) of subsection (1) above,—

(*a*) anything done by a person in the course of his employment shall be treated as done by his employer as well as by him, whether or not it was done with the employer's knowledge or approval, unless the employer shows that he took such steps as were reasonably practicable to prevent the employee from doing that act, or from doing in the course of his employment acts of that description; and

(*b*) anything done by a person as agent for another person with authority (whether express or implied, and whether precedent or subsequent) of that person shall be treated as done by that other person as well as by him; and

(*c*) anything done by a business associate[4] of a person shall be treated as done by that person as well, unless he can show that the act was done without his connivance or consent.

(4) In an order under this section the Director shall specify as the grounds for the order those matters falling within paragraphs (*a*) to (*d*) of subsection (1) above as to which he is satisfied and on which, accordingly, he relies to give him power to make the order.

(5) If the Director considers it appropriate, he may in an order under this section limit the scope of the prohibition imposed by the order to a particular part of or area within the United Kingdom.

(6) An order under paragraph (*a*)(iii) or paragraph (*d*) of subsection (1) above—

(*a*) shall be made by statutory instrument;

(*b*) shall be laid before Parliament after being made; and

(*c*) shall cease to have effect (without prejudice to anything previously done in reliance on the order) after the expiry of the period of twenty-eight days beginning with the date on which it was made unless within that period it has been approved by a resolution of each House of Parliament.

(7) In reckoning for the purposes of subsection (6)(*c*) above any period of twenty-eight days, no account shall be taken of any period during which Parliament is dissolved or prorogued or during which both Houses are adjourned for more than four days.

(8) A person who fails without reasonable excuse to comply with an order of the Director under this section shall be liable[5] on conviction on indictment or on summary conviction to a fine which on summary conviction shall not exceed **the statutory maximum**[6].

[Estate Agents Act 1979, s 3.]

1. Including a conviction for an offence committed abroad before this Act came into force (*Antonelli v Secretary of State for Trade and Industry* [1998] 1 All ER 997, [1998] 2 WLR 826, CA).
2. See the Estate Agents (Specified Offences) (No 2) Order 1991, SI 1991/1091 amended by SI 1992/2833 and SI 2001/2966.
3. For meaning of "estate agency work", see s 1(1), ante.
4. For meaning of "business associate", see s 31, post.
5. For procedure in respect of this offence which is triable either way, see ss 17A–21 of the Magistrates' Courts Act 1980 in PART I: MAGISTRATES' COURTS, PROCEDURE, ante.
6. For meaning of "the statutory maximum", see s 33, post.

8–18143 **4.** *Warning orders.*

8–18144 **5. Supplementary provisions as to orders under sections 3 and 4.** (1) The provisions of Part I of Schedule 2 to this Act shall have effect—

(*a*) with respect to the procedure to be followed before an order is made by the Director under section 3 or section 4 above; and

(*b*) in connection with the making and coming into operation of any such order.

(2) Where an order is made by the Director under section 3 or section 4 above against a partnership, it may, if the Director thinks it appropriate, have effect also as an order against some or all of the partners individually, and in such a case the order shall so provide and shall specify the names of the partners affected by the order.

(3) Nothing in section 62 of the Sex Discrimination Act 1975, section 53 of the Race Relations Act 1976 or Article 62 of the Sex Discrimination (Northern Ireland) Order 1976 (restriction of sanctions for breaches of those Acts and that Order) shall be construed as applying to the making of an order by the Director under section 3 above.

(4) In any case where—

(*a*) an order of the Director under section 3 above specifies a conviction as a ground for the order, and

(*b*) the conviction becomes spent for the purposes of the Rehabilitation of Offenders Act 1974 or any corresponding enactment for the time being in force in Northern Ireland, then, unless the order also specifies other grounds which remain valid, the order shall cease to have effect on the day on which the conviction becomes so spent.

(5) In any case where—

(*a*) an order of the Director under section 3 above specifies as grounds for the order the fact that the person concerned committed discrimination by reason of the existence of any such finding or notice as is referred to in paragraph 2 of Schedule 1 to this Act, and

(*b*) the period expires at the end of which, by virtue of paragraph 3 of that Schedule, the person concerned would no longer be treated for the purposes of section 3(1)(*b*) above as having committed discrimination by reason only of that finding or notice,

then, unless the order also specifies other grounds which remain valid, the order shall cease to have effect at the end of that period.

[Estate Agents Act 1979, s 5.]

8–18145 **6–8** *Revocation and variation of orders under sections 3 and 4; appeals*[1]*; register of orders etc.*

1. The Estate Agents (Appeals) Regulations 1981, SI 1981/1518 amended by SI 2003/1400, have been made.

Information, entry and inspection

8–18146 **9. Information for the Director.** (1) The Director[1] may, for the purpose of assisting him—

(*a*) to determine whether to make an order under section 3 or section 4 above, and

(*b*) in the exercise of any of his functions under sections 5, 6 and 8 above and 13 and 17 below,

by notice require any person to furnish to him such information as may be specified or described in the notice or to produce to him any documents so specified or described.

(2) A notice under this section—

(*a*) may specify the way in which and the time within which it is to be complied with and, in the case of a notice requiring the production of documents, the facilities to be afforded for making extracts, or taking copies of, the documents; and

(*b*) may be varied or revoked by a subsequent notice.

(3) Nothing in this section shall be taken to require a person who has acted as counsel or solicitor for any person to disclose any privileged communication made by or to him in that capacity.

(4) A person who—

(*a*) refuses or wilfully neglects to comply with a notice under this section, or

(*b*) in furnishing any information in compliance with such a notice, makes any statement which he knows to be false in a material particular or recklessly makes any statement which is false in a material particular, or

(*c*) with intent to deceive, produces in compliance with such a notice a document which is false in a material particular,

shall be liable[2] on conviction on indictment or on summary conviction to a fine which, on summary conviction, shall not exceed **the statutory maximum**[3].

(5) *Repealed.*

(6) It shall be the duty of—

(*a*) the Equal Opportunities Commission,

(*b*) the Equal Opportunities Commission for Northern Ireland, and

(*c*) the Commission for Racial Equality,

to furnish to the Director such information relating to any finding, notice, injunction or order falling within paragraph 2 of Schedule 1 to this Act as is in their possession and appears to them to be relevant to the functions of the Director under this Act.

[Estate Agents Act 1979, s 9, as amended by the Enterprise Act 2002, Schedule.]

1. For meaning of "Director", see s 33, post.
2. For procedure in respect of this offence which is triable either way, see the Magistrates' Courts Act 1980, ss 17A–21 in PART I: MAGISTRATES' COURTS, PROCEDURE, ante.
3. For meaning of "statutory maximum", see s 33, post.

8–18147 **10. Restriction on disclosure of information.** (*Repealed*).

8–18148 **11. Powers of entry and inspection.** (1) A duly authorised officer of an enforcement authority, at all reasonable hours and on production, if required, of his credentials may—

(*a*) if he has reasonable cause to suspect that an offence has been committed under this Act, in order to ascertain whether it has been committed, enter any premises (other than premises used only as a dwelling);

(*b*) if he has reasonable cause to suspect that an offence has been committed under this Act, in order to ascertain whether it has been committed, require any person—

(i) carrying on, or employed in connection with, a business to produce any books or documents relating to it, or

(ii) having control of any information relating to a business recorded otherwise than in a legible form, to provide a document containing a legible reproduction of the whole or any part of the information;

and take copies of, or of any entry in, the books or documents;

(*c*) seize and detain any books or documents which he has reason to believe may be required as evidence in proceedings for an offence under this Act;

(*d*) for the purpose of exercising his powers under this subsection to seize books and documents, but only if and to the extent that it is reasonably necessary for securing that the provisions of this Act are duly observed, require any person having authority to do so to break open any container and, if that person does not comply, break it open himself.

(2) An officer seizing books or documents in exercise of his powers under this section shall not do so without informing the person from whom he seizes them.

(3) If and so long as any books or documents which have been seized under this section are not required as evidence in connection with proceedings which have been begun for an offence under this Act, the enforcement authority[1] by whose officer they were seized shall afford to the person to whom the books or documents belong and to any person authorised by him in writing reasonable facilities to inspect them and to take copies of or make extracts from them.

(4) If a justice of the peace, on sworn information in writing, or, in Scotland, a sheriff or a justice of the peace, on evidence on oath,—

(*a*) is satisfied that there is reasonable ground to believe either—

(i) that any books or documents which a duly authorised officer has power to inspect under this section are on any premises and their inspection is likely to disclose evidence of the commission of an offence under this Act, or

(ii) that an offence under this Act has been, or is being or is about to be, committed on any premises; and

(*b*) is also satisfied either—

(i) that admission to the premises has been or is likely to be refused and that notice of intention to apply for a warrant under this subsection has been given to the occupier, or

(ii) that an application for admission, or the giving of such a notice, would defeat the object of the entry or that the premises are unoccupied or that the occupier is temporarily absent and it might defeat the object of the entry to wait for his return,

the justice or, as the case may be, the sheriff may by warrant under his hand, which shall continue in force for a period of one month, authorise an officer of an enforcement authority to enter the premises, by force if need be.

(5) An officer entering premises by virtue of this section may take such other persons and equipment with him as he thinks necessary, and on leaving premises entered by virtue of a warrant under subsection (4) above shall, if the premises are unoccupied or the occupier is temporarily absent, leave them as effectively secured against trespassers as he found them.

(6) The Secretary of State may by regulations provide that, in cases specified in the regulations[2], an officer of a local weights and measures authority is not to be taken to be duly authorised for the purposes of this section unless he is authorised by the Director[3].

(7) The power to make regulations under subsection (6) above shall be exercisable by statutory instrument which shall be subject to annulment in pursuance of a resolution of either House of Parliament.

(8) Nothing in this section shall be taken to require a person who has acted as counsel or solicitor[4] for any person to produce a document containing a privileged communication made by or to him in that capacity or authorises the seizing of any such document in his possession.

[Estate Agents Act 1979, s 11.]

---

1. For meaning of "enforcement authority", see s 26(1), post.
2. See the Estate Agents (Entry and Inspection) Regulations 1981, SI 1981/1519.
3. For meaning of "Director", see s 33, post.
4. This reference to a solicitor shall be construed as including a reference to a licensed conveyancer or to a recognised body (Administration of Justice Act 1985, s 34).

Clients' money and accounts

8–18149 12. Meaning of "clients' money" etc. (1) In this Act "clients' money", in relation to a person engaged in estate agency work[1], means any money received by him in the course of that work which is a contract or pre-contract deposit—

(*a*) in respect of the acquisition of an interest in land[2] in the United Kingdom, or

(*b*) in respect of a connected contract,

whether that money is held or received by him as agent, bailee, stakeholder or in any other capacity.

(2) In this Act "contract deposit" means any sum paid by a purchaser—

(*a*) which in whole or in part is, or is intended to form part of, the consideration for acquiring such an interest as is referred to in subsection (1)(*a*) above or for a connected contract; and

(*b*) which is paid by him at or after the time at which he acquires the interest or enters into an enforceable contract to acquire it.

(3) In this Act "pre-contract deposit" means any sum paid by any person—

(*a*) in whole or in part as an earnest of his intention to acquire such an interest as is referred to in subsection (1)(*a*) above, or

(*b*) in whole or in part towards meeting any liability of his in respect of the consideration for the acquisition of such an interest which will arise if he acquires or enters into an enforceable contract to acquire the interest, or

(*c*) in respect of a connected contract,

and which is paid by him at a time before he either acquires the interest or enters into an enforceable contract to acquire it.

(4) In this Act "connected contract", in relation to the acquisition of an interest in land, means a contract which is conditional upon such an acquisition or upon entering into an enforceable contract for such an acquisition (whether or not it is also conditional on other matters).
[Estate Agents Act 1979, s 12.]

1. For meaning of "estate agency work", see s 1(1), ante.
2. For interpretation of the expression "acquisition of an interest in land", see s 2, ante.

8–18150 13. Clients' money held on trust or as agent. (1) It is hereby declared that clients' money received by any person in the course of estate agency work[1] in England, Wales or Northern Ireland—

(*a*) is held by him on trust for the person who is entitled to call for it to be paid over to him or to be paid on his direction or to have it otherwise credited to him, or

(*b*) if it is received by him as stakeholder, is held by him on trust for the person who may become so entitled on the occurrence of the event against which the money is held.

(2) *Scotland.*

(3) The provisions of sections 14 and 15 below as to the investment of clients' money, the keeping of accounts and records and accounting for interest shall have effect in place of the corresponding duties which would be owed by a person holding clients' money as trustee, or in Scotland as agent, under the general law.

(4) Where an order of the Director[2] under section 3 above has the effect of prohibiting a person from holding clients' money the order may contain provision—

(*a*) appointing another person as trustee, or in Scotland as agent, in place of the person to whom the order relates to hold and deal with clients' money held by that person when the order comes into effect; and

(*b*) requiring the expenses and such reasonable remuneration of the new trustee or agent as may be specified in the order to be paid by the person to whom the order relates or, if the order so provides, out of the clients' money;

but nothing in this subsection shall affect the power conferred by section 41 of the Trustee Act 1925 or section 40 of the Trustee Act (Northern Ireland) 1958 to appoint a new trustee to hold clients' money.

(5) For the avoidance of doubt it is hereby declared that the fact that any person has or may have a lien on clients' money held by him does not affect the operation of this section and also that nothing in this section shall prevent such a lien from being given effect.
[Estate Agents Act 1979, s 13.]

1. For meaning of "estate agency work", see s 1(1), ante.
2. For meaning of "Director", see s 33, post.

8–18151 14. Keeping of client accounts. (1) Subject to such provision as may be made by accounts regulations[1], every person who receives clients' money in the course of estate work[2] shall, without delay, pay the money into a client account maintained by him or by a person in whose employment he is.

(2) In this Act a "client account" means a current or deposit account which—

(*a*) is with an institution authorised for the purposes of this section, and

(*b*) is in the name of a person who is or has been engaged in estate agency work; and

(*c*) contains in its title the word "client".

(3) The Secretary of State may make provision by regulations[1] (in this section referred to as "accounts regulations") as to the opening and keeping of client accounts, the keeping of accounts and records relating to clients' money and the auditing of those accounts; and such regulations shall

be made by statutory instrument which shall be subject to annulment in pursuance of a resolution of either House of Parliament.

(4) As to the opening and keeping of client accounts, accounts regulations may in particular specify—

(*a*) the institutions which are authorised for the purposes of this section;

(*b*) any persons or classes of persons to whom, or any circumstances in which, the obligation imposed by subsection (1) above does not apply;

(*c*) any circumstances in which money other than clients' money may be paid into a client account; and

(*d*) the occasions on which, and the persons to whom, money held in a client account may be paid out.

(5) As to the auditing of accounts relating to clients' money accounts regulations may in particular make provision—

(*a*) requiring such accounts to be drawn up in respect of specified accounting periods and to be audited by a qualified auditor within a specified time after the end of each such period;

(*b*) requiring the auditor to report whether in his opinion the requirements of this Act and of the accounts regulations have been complied with or have been substantially complied with;

(*c*) as to the matters to which such a report is to relate and the circumstances in which a report of substantial compliance may be given; and

(*d*) requiring a person who maintains a client account to produce on demand to a duly authorised officer of an enforcement authority[3] the latest auditor's report.

(6) Subject to subsection (7) below, "qualified auditor" in subsection (5)(*a*) above means a person who is—

(*a*) eligible for appointment as a company auditor under section 25 of the Companies Act 1989; or

(*b*) in Northern Ireland, is eligible for appointment as a company auditor under Article 28 of the Companies (Northern Ireland) Order 1990.

(7) A person is not a qualified auditor for the purposes of subsection (5)(*a*) above if, in the case of a client account maintained by a company, he is ineligible for appointment as auditor to the company by virtue of Part II of the Companies Act 1989 or Part III of the Companies (Northern Ireland) Order 1990.

(8) A person who—

(*a*) contravenes any provision of this Act or of accounts regulations[1] as to the manner in which clients' money is to be dealt with or accounts and records relating to such money are to be kept, or

(*b*) fails to produce an auditor's report when required to do so by accounts regulations,

shall be liable on summary conviction to a fine not exceeding **level 4** on the standard scale.

[Estate Agents Act 1979, s 14, as amended by the Criminal Justice Act 1982, s 46, the Companies Consolidation (Consequential Provisions) Act 1985, Sch 2, SI 1991/1997 and the Companies (1990 Order) (Eligibility for Appointment as Company Auditor) (Consequential Amendments) Regulations (Northern Ireland) Order 1993.]

1. See the Estate Agents (Accounts) Regulations 1981, SI 1981/1520 amended by SI 1993/3218.
2. For meaning of "estate agency work", see s 1(1), ante.
3. For meaning of "enforcement authority", see s 26(1), post.

8–18152 **15.** *Interest on clients' money.*

8–18153 **16. Insurance cover for clients' money.** (1) Subject to the provisions of this section, a person may not accept clients' money in the course of estate agency work unless there are in force authorised arrangements under which, in the event of his failing to account for such money to the person entitled to it, his liability will be made good by another.

(2) *Power of Secretary of State to make regulations.*

(3) Every guarantee entered into by a person (in this subsection referred to as "the insurer") who provides authorised arrangements covering another person (in this subsection referred to as "the agent") carrying on estate agency work shall enure for the benefit of every person from whom the agent has received clients' money as if—

(*a*) the guarantee were contained in a contract made by the insurer with every such person; and

(*b*) except in Scotland, that contract were under seal; and

(*c*) where the guarantee is given by two or more insurers, they had bound themselves jointly and severally.

(4) No person who carries on estate agency work may describe himself as an "estate agent" or so use any name or in any way hold himself out as to indicate or reasonably be understood to indicate that he is carrying on a business in the course of which he is prepared to act as a broker in the acquisition or disposal of interests in land unless, in such manner as may be prescribed,—

(*a*) there is displayed at his place of business, and
(*b*) there is included in any relevant document issued or displayed in connection with his business,

any prescribed information relating to arrangements authorised for the purposes of this section.

(5) For the purposes of subsection (4) above,—

(*a*) any business premises at which a person carries on estate agency work[1] and to which the public has access is a place of business of his; and
(*b*) "relevant document" means any advertisement, notice or other written material which might reasonably induce any person to use the services of another in connection with the acquisition or disposal of an interest in land.

(6) A person who fails to comply with any provision of subsection (1) or subsection (4) above or of regulations under subsection (2) above which is binding on him shall be liable[2] on conviction on indictment or on summary conviction to a fine which, on summary conviction, shall not exceed **the statutory maximum**[3].
[Estate Agents Act 1979, s 16.]

1. For meaning of "estate agency work", see s 1(1), ante.
2. For procedure in respect of this offence which is triable either way, see the Magistrates' Courts Act 1980, ss 17A–21 in PART I: MAGISTRATES' COURTS, PROCEDURE, ante.
3. For meaning of "statutory maximum", see s 33, post.

8–18154 **17. Exemptions from section 16.** (1) If, on an application made to him in that behalf, the Director considers that a person engaged in estate agency work[1] may, without loss of adequate protection to consumers, be exempted from all or any of the provisions of subsection (1) of section 16 above or of regulations under subsection (2) of that section, he may issue to that person a certificate of exemption under this section.

(2) An application under subsection (1) above—

(*a*) shall state the reasons why the applicant considers that he should be granted a certificate of exemption; and
(*b*) shall be accompanied by the prescribed fee.

(3) A certificate of exemption under this section—

(*a*) may impose conditions of exemption on the person to whom it is issued;
(*b*) may be issued to have effect for a period specified in the certificate or without limit of time.

(4) If and so long as—

(*a*) a certificate of exemption has effect, and
(*b*) the person to whom it is issued complies with any conditions of exemption specified in the certificate,

that person shall be exempt, to the extent so specified, from the provisions of subsection (1) of section 16 above and of any regulations made under subsection (2) of that section.

(5) If the Director decides to refuse an application under subsection (1) above he shall give the applicant notice of his decision and of the reasons for it, including any facts which in his opinion justify the decision.

(6) If a person who made an application under subsection (1) above is aggrieved by a decision of the Director—

(*a*) to refuse his application, or
(*b*) to grant him a certificate of exemption subject to conditions,

he may appeal against the decision to the Secretary of State; and subsections (2) to (6) of section 7 above shall apply to such an appeal as they apply to an appeal under that section.

(7) A person who fails to comply with any condition of exemption specified in a current certificate of exemption issued to him shall be liable[2] on conviction on indictment or on summary conviction to a fine which, on summary conviction, shall not exceed **the statutory maximum**[3].
[Estate Agents Act 1979, s 17.]

1. For meaning of "estate agency work", see s 1(1), ante.
2. For procedure in respect of this offence which is triable either way, see the Magistrates' Courts Act 1980, ss 17A–21 in PART I: MAGISTRATES' COURTS, PROCEDURE, ante.
3. For meaning of "the statutory maximum", see s 33, post.

Regulation of other aspects of estate agency work

8–18155 **22. Standards of competence.** (1) The Secretary of State may by regulations made by statutory instrument make provision for ensuring that persons engaged in estate agency work[1] satisfy minimum standards of competence.

(2) If the Secretary of State exercises his power to make regulations under subsection (1) above, he shall in the regulations prescribe a degree of practical experience which is to be taken as evidence

of competence and, without prejudice to the generality of subsection (1) above, the regulations may, in addition,—

(*a*) prescribe professional or academic qualifications which shall also be taken to be evidence of competence;

(*b*) designate any body of persons as a body which may itself specify professional qualifications the holding of which is to be taken as evidence of competence;

(*c*) make provision for and in connection with the establishment of a body having power to examine and inquire into the competence of persons engaged or professing to engage in estate agency work; and

(*d*) delegate to a body established as mentioned in paragraph (*c*) above powers of the Secretary of State with respect to the matters referred to in paragraph (*a*) above;

and any reference in the following provisions of this section to a person is a reference to a person who has that degree of practical experience which, in accordance with the regulations, is to be taken as evidence of competence or, where the regulations so provide, holds such qualifications or otherwise fulfils such conditions as, in accordance with the regulations, are to be taken to be evidence of competence.

(3) After the day appointed for the coming into force of this subsection,—

(*a*) no individual may engage in estate agency work on his own account unless he has attained the required standard of competence;

(*b*) no member of a partnership may engage in estate agency work on the partnership's behalf unless such number of the partners as may be prescribed have attained the required standard of competence; and

(*c*) no body corporate or unincorporated association may engage in estate agency work unless such numbers and descriptions of the officers, members or employees as may be prescribed have attained the required standard of competence;

and any person who contravenes this subsection shall be liable[2] on conviction on indictment or on summary conviction to a fine which on summary conviction, shall not exceed **the statutory maximum**[3].

(4) In subsection (3) above "prescribed" means prescribed by the Secretary of State by order made by statutory instrument, which shall be subject to annulment in pursuance of a resolution of either House of Parliament.

(5) No regulations shall be made under this section unless a draft of them has been laid before Parliament and approved by a resolution of each House.

[Estate Agents Act 1979, s 22.]

---

1. For meaning of "estate agency work", see s 1(1), ante.
2. For procedure in respect of this offence which is triable either way, see the Magistrates' Courts Act 1980, ss 17A–21, in PART I: MAGISTRATES' COURTS, PROCEDURE, ante.
3. For meaning of "statutory maximum", see s 33, post.

8–18156 23. Bankrupts not to engage in estate agency work. (1) An individual who is adjudged bankrupt after the day appointed for the coming into force of this section or, in Scotland, whose estate is sequestrated after that day shall not engage in estate agency work of any description except as an employee of another person.

(2) The prohibition imposed on an individual by subsection (1) above shall cease to have effect if and when—

(*a*) the adjudication of bankruptcy against him is annulled, or, in Scotland, the sequestration of his estate is recalled or reduced; or

(*b*) he is discharged from bankruptcy.

(3) The reference in subsection (1) above to employment of an individual by another person does not include employment of him by a body corporate of which he is a director or controller.

(4) If a person engages in estate agency work in contravention of subsection (1) above he shall be liable[1] on conviction on indictment or on summary conviction to a fine which on summary conviction shall not exceed **the statutory maximum**[2].

[Estate Agents Act 1979, s 23, as amended by the Bankruptcy (Scotland) Act 1985, Sch 7 and the Insolvency Act 1985, Sch 8.]

---

1. For procedure in respect of this offence which is triable either way, see the Magistrates' Courts Act 1980, ss 17A–21, in PART I: MAGISTRATES' COURTS, PROCEDURE, ante.
2. For meaning of "the statutory maximum", see s 33, post.

Supervision, enforcement, publicity etc

8–18157 25. *General duties of Director.*

8–18158 26. Enforcement authorities. (1) Without prejudice to section 25(1) above, the following authorities (in this Act referred to as "enforcement authorities") have a duty to enforce this Act—

(*a*) the Director,
(*b*) in Great Britain, a local weights and measures authority, and
(*c*) in Northern Ireland, the Department of Commerce for Northern Ireland.

(2) Where a local weights and measures authority in England and Wales propose to institute proceedings for an offence under this Act it shall, as between the authority and the Director, be the duty of the authority to give the Director notice of the intended proceedings, together with a summary of the facts on which the charges are to be founded, and postpone the institution of the proceedings until either—

(*a*) twenty-eight days have expired since that notice was given, or
(*b*) the Director has notified them of receipt of the notice and summary.

(3) *Scotland.*

(4) Every local weights and measures authority shall, whenever the Director requires, report to him in such form and with such particulars as he requires on the exercise of their functions under this Act.

(5)–(8) (*Repealed*).

[Estate Agents Act 1979, s 26, as amended by the Local Government, Planning and Land Act 1980, Schs 4 and 34.]

8–18159 27. Obstruction and personation of authorised officers. (1) Any person who—

(*a*) wilfully obstructs an authorised officer, or
(*b*) wilfully fails to comply with any requirement properly made to him under section 11 above by an authorised officer, or
(*c*) without reasonable cause fails to give an authorised officer other assistance or information he may reasonably require in performing his functions under this Act, or
(*d*) in giving information to an authorised officer, makes any statement which he knows to be false,

shall be liable on summary conviction to a fine not exceeding **level 4** on the standard scale.

(2) A person who is not an authorised officer but purports to act as such shall be liable on summary conviction to a fine not exceeding **level 5** on the standard scale.

(3) In this section "authorised officer" means a duly authorised officer of an enforcement authority who is acting in pursuance of this Act.

(4) Nothing in subsection (1) above requires a person to answer any question or give any information if to do so might incriminate that person or that person's spouse or civil partner.

[Estate Agents Act 1979, s 27, as amended by the Criminal Justice Act 1982, s 46 and the Civil Partnership Act 2004, Sch 27.]

Supplementary

8–18170 28. General provisions as to offences. (1) In any proceedings for an offence under this Act it shall be a defence for the person charged to prove that he took all reasonable precautions and exercised all due diligence to avoid the commission of an offence by himself or any person under his control.

(2) Where an offence under this Act committed by a body corporate is proved to have been committed with the consent or connivance of, or to be attributable to any neglect on the part of, any director, manager, secretary or other similar officer of the body corporate, or any person who was purporting to act in any such capacity, he as well as the body corporate shall be guilty of that offence and shall be liable to be proceeded against and punished accordingly.

[Estate Agents Act 1979, s 28.]

8–18171 29. Service of notices etc. (1) Any notice which under this Act is to be given to any person by the Director shall be so given—

(*a*) by delivering it to him, or
(*b*) by leaving it at his proper address, or
(*c*) by sending it by post to him at that address.

(2) Any such notice may—

(*a*) in the case of a body corporate or incorporated association, be given to the secretary or clerk of that body or association; and
(*b*) in the case of a partnership, be given to a partner or a person having the control or management of the partnership business.

(3) Any application or other document which under this Act may be made or given to the Director may be so made or given by sending it by post to the Director at such address as may be specified for the purposes of this Act by a general notice.

(4) For the purposes of subsections (1) and (2) above and section 7 of the Interpretation Act 1978 (service of documents by post) in its application to those subsections, the proper address of any person to whom a notice is to be given shall be his last-known address, except that—

(*a*) in the case of a body corporate or their secretary or clerk, it shall be the address of the registered or principal office of that body;

(*b*) in the case of an unincorporated association or their secretary or clerk, it shall be that of the principal office of that association;

(*c*) in the case of a partnership or a person having the control or management of the partnership business, it shall be that of the principal office of the partnership;

and for the purposes of this subsection the principal office of a company registered outside the United Kingdom or of an unincorporated association or partnership carrying on business outside the United Kingdom shall be their principal office within the United Kingdom.

(5) If the person to be given any notice mentioned in subsection (1) above has specified an address within the United Kingdom other than his proper address, within the meaning of subsection (4) above, as the one at which he or someone on his behalf will accept notices under this Act, that address shall also be treated for the purposes mentioned in subsection (4) above as his proper address.
[Estate Agents Act 1979, s 29.]

8–18172 **30.** *Orders and regulations.*

8–18173 **31. Meaning of "business associate" and "controller".** (1) The provisions of this section shall have effect for determining the meaning of "business associate" and "controller" for the purposes of this Act.

(2) As respects acts done in the course of a business carried on by a body corporate, every director and controller of that body is a business associate of it.

(3) As respects acts done in the course of a business carried on by a partnership, each partner is a business associate of every other member of the partnership and also of the partnership itself and, in the case of a partner which is a body corporate, every person who, by virtue of subsection (2) above, is a business associate of that body is also a business associate of every other member of the partnership.

(4) As respects acts done in the course of a business carried on by an unincorporated association, every officer of the association and any other person who has the management or control of its activities is a business associate of that association.

(5) In relation to a body corporate "controller" means a person—

(*a*) in accordance with whose directions or instructions the directors of the body corporate or of any other body corporate which is its controller (or any of them) are accustomed to act; or

(*b*) who, either alone or with any associate or associates, is entitled to exercise, or control the exercise of, one third or more of the voting power at any general meeting of the body corporate or of another body corporate which is its controller.

[Estate Agents Act 1979, s 31.]

8–18174 **32. Meaning of "associate".** (1) In this Act "associate" includes a business associate and otherwise has the meaning given by the following provisions of this section.

(2) A person is an associate of another if he is the spouse or civil partner or a relative of that other or of a business associate of that other.

(3) In subsection (2) above "relative" means brother, sister, uncle, aunt, nephew, niece, lineal ancestor or linear descendent, and references to a spouse include a former spouse and a reputed spouse, and references to a civil partner include a former civil partner and a reputed civil partner; and for the purposes of this subsection a relationship shall be established as if an illegitimate child or step-child of a person were the legitimate child of the relationship in question.

(4) A body corporate is an associate of another body corporate—

(*a*) if the same person is a controller of both, or a person is a controller of one and persons who are his associates, or he and persons who are his associates, are controllers of the other; or

(*b*) if a group of two or more persons is a controller of each company, and the groups either consist of the same persons or could be regarded as consisting of the same persons by treating (in one or more cases) a member of either group as replaced by a person of whom he is an associate.

(5) An unincorporated association is an associate of another unincorporated association if any person—

(*a*) is an officer of both associations;

(*b*) has the management or control of the activities of both associations; or

(*c*) is an officer of one association and has the management or control of the activities of the other association.

(6) A partnership is an associate of another partnership if—

(*a*) any person is a member of both partnerships; or

(*b*) a person who is a member of one partnership is an associate of a member of the other partnership; or (*c*) a member of one partnership has an associate who is also an associate of a member of the other partnership.

[Estate Agents Act 1979, s 32 as amended by the Civil Partnership Act 2004, Sch 27.]

8–18175 **33. General interpretation provisions.** (1) In this Act, unless the context otherwise requires—

"associate" has the meaning assigned to it by section 32 above and "business associate" has the meaning assigned to it by section 31 above;

"client account" has the meaning assigned to it by section 14(2) above;

"clients' money" has the meaning assigned to it by section 12(1) above;

"connected contract", in relation to the acquisition of an interest in land, has the meaning assigned to it by section 12(4) above;

"contract deposit" has the meaning assigned to it by section 12(2) above;

"controller", in relation to a body corporate, has the meaning assigned to it by section 31(5) above;

"Director" means the Director General of Fair Trading;

"enforcement authority" has the meaning assigned to it by section 26(1) above;

"estate agency work" has the meaning assigned to it by section 1(1) above;

"general notice" means a notice published by the Director at a time and in a manner appearing to him suitable for securing that the notice is seen within a reasonable time by persons likely to be affected by it;

"pre-contract deposit" has the meaning assigned to it by section 12(3) above;

"prescribed fee" means such fee as may be prescribed by regulations made by the Secretary of State;

"unincorporated association" does not include a partnership.

(2) The power to make regulations under subsection (1) above prescribing fees shall be exercisable by statutory instrument which shall be subject to annulment in pursuance of a resolution of either House of Parliament.

[Estate Agents Act 1979, s 33 amended by the Magistrates' Courts Act 1980, Sch 7 and the Statute Law (Repeals) Act 1993, Sch 1.]

SCHEDULE 1

Provisions supplementary to section 3(1)

SCHEDULE 2

Procedure, etc

8–18280

Competition Act 1980

(1980 c 21)

(NOT REPRODUCED IN THIS MANUAL)

8–18281

Protection of Trading Interests Act 1980

(1980 c 11)

(NOT REPRODUCED IN THIS MANUAL)

8–18282

Industrial Development Act 1982

(1982 c 52)

(NOT REPRODUCED IN THIS MANUAL)

Motor Cycle Noise Act 1987[1]

(1987 c 34)

8–18285 **1. Prohibition of supply of exhaust systems etc not complying with prescribed requirements.** (1) Subject to subsections (3) and (4) below, no person shall, in the course of carrying on a business, supply or offer or agree to supply[2] or expose or have in his possession for the purpose of supplying—

(*a*) an exhaust system for a motor cycle[3]; or

(*b*) a silencer, or any component other than a silencer or fixing, for such a system,

unless the system, silencer or component complies with such requirements as may be prescribed by regulations[4] made by the Secretary of State and, as respects such a system or silencer, the requirements of the regulations as to packaging, labelling and the provision of accompanying instructions are complied with.

(2) The regulations made by the Secretary of State for the purposes of this section shall be such as he considers necessary for preventing the supply of exhaust systems, silencers and components which are likely to result in motor cycles to which they are fitted emitting excessive noise; and those regulations may—

(*a*) prescribe requirements by reference to any British Standard Specification, any regulations made or having effect as if made under section 41 of the Road Traffic Act 1988, any Community instrument or any other instrument issued by an international authority; and

(*b*) make different provision for different cases.

(3) Exemptions from this section or any requirements imposed under it may be conferred by regulations made by the Secretary of State or, in the case of an exemption applying to a particular person, by a notice in writing given by him to that person.

(4) Subsection (1) above does not apply in any case in which the person in question reasonably believes that the exhaust system, silencer or component will not be used in the United Kingdom.

(5) Before making any regulations under this section the Secretary of State shall consult such representative organisations as he thinks fit.

(6) The power to make regulations under this section shall be exercisable by statutory instrument subject to annulment in pursuance of a resolution of either House of Parliament.

(7) The Schedule to this Act shall have effect with respect to contraventions of this section and the enforcement of its provisions.

[Motor Cycle Noise Act 1987, s 1 amended by the Road Traffic (Consequential Provisions) Act 1988, Sch 3.]

---

1. As to commencement of this Act, see s 2, post.
2. References to "supply" include references to gratuitous supply, see s 2(2), post.
3. References to "motor cycle" includes references to a moped and a motor scooter, see s 2(2), post.
4. The Motor Cycle Silencer and Exhaust Systems Regulations 1995, SI 1995/2370 have been made. These prescribe requirements to be met by motorcycle silencers and exhaust systems supplied in the course of carrying on a business. For offences and enforcement, see the Schedule to the Act, post.

8–18286 **2.** Short title, interpretation, commencement and extent.—(1) This Act may be cited as the Motor Cycle Noise Act 1987.

(2) In this Act references to a motor cycle include references to a moped and a motor scooter and references to supply include references to gratuitous supply.

(3) This Act shall come into force on such day as may be appointed by the Secretary of State by an order[1] made by statutory instrument; and different days may be appointed for different provisions or different purposes.

(4) This Act does not extend to Northern Ireland.

[Motor Cycle Noise Act 1987, s 2.]

---

1. The Act was brought into force on 1 August 1996 by the Motor Cycle Noise Act 1987 (Commencement) Order 1995, SI 1995/2367.

Section 1(7)

SCHEDULE

OFFENCES AND ENFORCEMENT

(*As amended by the Consumer Protection Act 1987, Sch 4.*)

Offences

8–18287 **1.** (1) Any person who contravenes section 1 of this Act shall be guilty of an offence and liable on summary conviction to imprisonment for a term not exceeding **three months** or to a fine not exceeding the **fifth level** on the standard scale.

(2) Where the commission by any person of such an offence is due to the act or default of some other person the other person shall be guilty of the offence and may be charged with and convicted of the offence whether or not proceedings are taken against the first-mentioned person.

(3) It shall be a defence to a charge of committing an offence under this paragraph that the accused took all reasonable steps and exercised all due diligence to avoid committing the offence.

2. (1) Where an offence under paragraph 1 above which has been committed by a body corporate is proved to have been committed with the consent or connivance of, or to be attributable to any neglect on the part of, a director, manager, secretary or other similar officer of the body corporate or any person who was purporting to act in any such capacity, he as well as the body corporate shall be guilty of that offence and shall be liable to be proceeded against and punished accordingly.

(2) Where the affairs of a body corporate are managed by its members sub-paragraph (1) above shall apply in relation to the acts and defaults of a member in connection with his functions of management as if he were a director of the body corporate.

Enforcement

3. Part IV of the Consumer Protection Act 1987 (enforcement), except section 31 (power of customs officers to detain goods), shall have effect as if the provisions of this Act were safety provisions within the meaning of that Act; and in Part V of that Act (miscellaneous and supplemental), except in section 49 (Northern Ireland), references to provisions of the said Part IV shall include references to those provisions as applied by this paragraph.

8–18288

Regional Development Agencies Act 1998

(1998 c 45)

(NOT REPRODUCED IN THIS MANUAL)

8–18289

Competition Act 1998

(1998 c 41)

(NOT REPRODUCED IN THIS MANUAL)

Financial Services and Markets Act 2000[1]

(2000 c 8)

PART I[2]
THE REGULATOR

8–18290 1. The Financial Services Authority. (1) The body corporate known as the Financial Services Authority ("the Authority") is to have the functions conferred on it by or under this Act.

(2) The Authority must comply with the requirements as to its constitution set out in Schedule 1[3].

(3) Schedule 1 also makes provision about the status of the Authority and the exercise of certain of its functions.

[Financial Services and Markets Act 2000, s 1.]

1. The Financial Services and Markets Act 2000 makes provision about the regulation of financial services and markets; and provides for the transfer of certain statutory functions relating to building societies, friendly societies, industrial and provident societies and certain other mutual societies.

The Act contains many offences and it is not practicable in a Manual of this nature to set out fully all the penal provisions of the Act. Nevertheless, we have included in this title those provisions of the Act which are most likely to be of relevance to the work of magistrates' courts.

The Act is to be brought into force in accordance with s 431 below. At the date of going to press, no commencement orders had been made.

2. Part I comprises ss 1 to 18.
3. Schedule 1 is not reproduced in this work.

PART II[1]
REGULATED AND PROHIBITED ACTIVITIES

The general prohibition

8–18290A 19. The general prohibition. (1) No person may carry on a regulated activity in the United Kingdom, or purport to do so, unless he is—

(*a*) an authorised person[2]; or
(*b*) an exempt person.

(2) The prohibition is referred to in this Act as the general prohibition.

[Financial Services and Markets Act 2000, s 19.]

1. Part II comprises ss 19 to 30.
2. "Authorised person" has the meaning given in s 31(2), below (s 417, post).

Requirement for permission

8–18290B 20. Authorised persons acting without permission. (1) If an authorised person carries on a regulated activity in the United Kingdom, or purports to do so, otherwise than in accordance with permission—

(*a*) given to him by the Authority under Part IV, or
(*b*) resulting from any other provision of this Act,

he is to be taken to have contravened a requirement imposed on him by the Authority under this Act.

(2) The contravention does not—

(*a*) make a person guilty of an offence;
(*b*) make any transaction void or unenforceable; or
(*c*) (subject to subsection (3)) give rise to any right of action for breach of statutory duty.

(3) In prescribed cases the contravention is actionable at the suit of a person who suffers loss as a result of the contravention, subject to the defences and other incidents applying to actions for breach of statutory duty.

[Financial Services and Markets Act 2000, s 20.]

Financial promotion

8–18290C 21. Restrictions on financial promotion. (1) A person ("A") must not, in the course of business, communicate an invitation or inducement to engage in investment activity.

(2) But subsection (1) does not apply if—

(*a*) A is an authorised person; or
(*b*) the content of the communication is approved for the purposes of this section by an authorised person.

(3) In the case of a communication originating outside the United Kingdom, subsection (1) applies only if the communication is capable of having an effect in the United Kingdom.

(4) The Treasury may by order specify circumstances in which a person is to be regarded for the purposes of subsection (1) as—

(*a*) acting in the course of business;
(*b*) not acting in the course of business.

(5) The Treasury may by order[1] specify circumstances (which may include compliance with financial promotion rules) in which subsection (1) does not apply.

(6) An order under subsection (5) may, in particular, provide that subsection (1) does not apply in relation to communications—

(*a*) of a specified description;
(*b*) originating in a specified country or territory outside the United Kingdom;
(*c*) originating in a country or territory which falls within a specified description of country or territory outside the United Kingdom; or
(*d*) originating outside the United Kingdom.

(7) The Treasury may by order repeal subsection (3).

(8) "Engaging in investment activity" means—

(*a*) entering or offering to enter into an agreement the making or performance of which by either party constitutes a controlled activity; or
(*b*) exercising any rights conferred by a controlled investment to acquire, dispose of, underwrite or convert a controlled investment.

(9) An activity is a controlled activity if—

(*a*) it is an activity of a specified kind or one which falls within a specified class of activity; and
(*b*) it relates to an investment of a specified kind, or to one which falls within a specified class of investment.

(10) An investment is a controlled investment if it is an investment of a specified kind or one which falls within a specified class of investment.

(11) Schedule 2 (except paragraph 26) applies for the purposes of subsections (9) and (10) with references to section 22 being read as references to each of those subsections.

(12) Nothing in Schedule 2, as applied by subsection (11), limits the powers conferred by subsection (9) or (10).

(13) "Communicate" includes causing a communication to be made.

(14) "Investment" includes any asset, right or interest.

(15) "Specified" means specified in an order made by the Treasury.

[Financial Services and Markets Act 2000, s 21.]

1. The Financial Services and Markets Act 2000 (Financial Promotion) Order 2005, SI 2005/1529 amended by SI 2005/3392 has been made. See also The Financial Services and Markets Act 2000, (Miscellaneous Provisions) Order 2001, SI 2001/3650 amended by SI 2002/1777 and SI 2005/1529.

Regulated Activities

8–18290D 22. The classes of activity and categories of investment. (1) An activity is a regulated activity for the purposes of this Act if it is an activity of a specified kind which is carried on by way of business and—

(*a*) relates to an investment of a specified kind; or

(*b*) in the case of an activity of a kind which is also specified for the purposes of this paragraph, is carried on in relation to property of any kind.

(2) Schedule 2 makes provision supplementing this section.

(3) Nothing in Schedule 2 limits the powers conferred by subsection (1).

(4) "Investment" includes any asset, right or interest.

(5) "Specified" means specified in an order[1] made by the Treasury.

[Financial Services and Markets Act 2000, s 22.]

1. The Financial Services and Markets Act 2000 (Regulated Activities) Order 2001, SI 2001/544 amended by SI 2001/3544, SI 2002/682 and 1776, SI 2003/1475, 1476 and 2822, SI 2004/1610, 2737 and 3379 and SI 2005/593, 1518 and 2114 has been made.

Offences

8–18290E 23. Contravention of the general prohibition. (1) A person who contravenes the general prohibition is guilty of an offence and liable[1]—

(*a*) on summary conviction, to imprisonment for a term not exceeding six months or a fine not exceeding the statutory maximum, or both;

(*b*) on conviction on indictment, to imprisonment for a term not exceeding two years or a fine, or both.

(2) In this Act "an authorisation offence" means an offence under this section.

(3) In proceedings for an authorisation offence it is a defence for the accused to show that he took all reasonable precautions and exercised all due diligence to avoid committing the offence.

[Financial Services and Markets Act 2000, s 23.]

1. For procedure in respect of this offence which is triable either way, see the Magistrates' Courts Act 1980, ss 17A–21, in PART I: MAGISTRATES' COURTS, PROCEDURE, ante.

8–18290F 24. False claims to be authorised or exempt. (1) A person who is neither an authorised person nor, in relation to the regulated activity in question, an exempt person is guilty of an offence if he—

(*a*) describes himself (in whatever terms) as an authorised person;

(*b*) describes himself (in whatever terms) as an exempt person in relation to the regulated activity; or

(*c*) behaves, or otherwise holds himself out, in a manner which indicates (or which is reasonably likely to be understood as indicating) that he is—

(i) an authorised person; or

(ii) an exempt person in relation to the regulated activity.

(2) In proceedings for an offence under this section it is a defence for the accused to show that he took all reasonable precautions and exercised all due diligence to avoid committing the offence.

(3) A person guilty of an offence under this section is liable on summary conviction to imprisonment for a term not exceeding six months or a fine not exceeding level 5 on the standard scale, or both.

(4) But where the conduct constituting the offence involved or included the public display of any material, the maximum fine for the offence is level 5 on the standard scale multiplied by the number of days for which the display continued.

[Financial Services and Markets Act 2000, s 24.]

8–18290G 25. Contravention of section 21. (1) A person who contravenes section 21(1) is guilty of an offence and liable[1]—

(*a*) on summary conviction, to imprisonment for a term not exceeding six months or a fine not exceeding the statutory maximum, or both;

(*b*) on conviction on indictment, to imprisonment for a term not exceeding two years or a fine, or both.

(2) In proceedings for an offence under this section it is a defence for the accused to show—

(*a*) that he believed on reasonable grounds that the content of the communication was prepared, or approved for the purposes of section 21, by an authorised person; or

(*b*) that he took all reasonable precautions and exercised all due diligence to avoid committing the offence.

[Financial Services and Markets Act 2000, s 25.]

1. For procedure in respect of this offence which is triable either way, see the Magistrates' Courts Act 1980, ss 17A–21, in PART I: MAGISTRATES' COURTS, PROCEDURE, ante.

PART V[1]
PERFORMANCE AND REGULATED ACTIVITIES

Prohibition orders

8–18290H 56. Prohibition orders. (1) Subsection (2) applies if it appears to the Authority that an individual is not a fit and proper person to perform functions in relation to a regulated activity carried on by an authorised person.

(2) The Authority may make an order ("a prohibition order") prohibiting the individual from performing a specified function, any function falling within a specified description or any function.

(3) A prohibition order may relate to—

(*a*) a specified regulated activity, any regulated activity falling within a specified description or all regulated activities;

(*b*) authorised persons generally or any person within a specified class of authorised person.

(4) An individual who performs or agrees to perform a function in breach of a prohibition order is guilty of an offence and liable on summary conviction to a fine not exceeding level 5 on the standard scale.

(5) In proceedings for an offence under subsection (4) it is a defence for the accused to show that he took all reasonable precautions and exercised all due diligence to avoid committing the offence.

(6) An authorised person must take reasonable care to ensure that no function of his, in relation to the carrying on of a regulated activity, is performed by a person who is prohibited from performing that function by a prohibition order.

(7) The Authority may, on the application of the individual named in a prohibition order, vary or revoke it.

(8) This section applies to the performance of functions in relation to a regulated activity carried on by—

(*a*) a person who is an exempt person in relation to that activity, and

(*b*) a person to whom, as a result of Part XX, the general prohibition does not apply in relation to that activity,

as it applies to the performance of functions in relation to a regulated activity carried on by an authorised person.

(9) "Specified" means specified in the prohibition order.

1. Part V comprises ss 56 to 71.

[Financial Services and Markets Act 2000, s 56.]

8–18290I 57. Prohibition orders: procedure and right to refer to Tribunal. (1) If the Authority proposes to make a prohibition order it must give the individual concerned a warning notice.

(2) The warning notice must set out the terms of the prohibition.

(3) If the Authority decides to make a prohibition order it must give the individual concerned a decision notice.

(4) The decision notice must—

(*a*) name the individual to whom the prohibition order applies;

(*b*) set out the terms of the order; and

(*c*) be given to the individual named in the order.

(5) A person against whom a decision to make a prohibition order is made may refer the matter to the Tribunal.

[Financial Services and Markets Act 2000, s 57.]

8–18290J 58. Applications relating to prohibitions: procedure and right to refer to Tribunal. (1) This section applies to an application for the variation or revocation of a prohibition order.

(2) If the Authority decides to grant the application, it must give the applicant written notice of its decision.

(3) If the Authority proposes to refuse the application, it must give the applicant a warning notice.

(4) If the Authority decides to refuse the application, it must give the applicant a decision notice.

(5) If the Authority gives the applicant a decision notice, he may refer the matter to the Tribunal.

[Financial Services and Markets Act 2000, s 58.]

PART VI[1]
OFFICIAL LISTING

The competent authority

8–18290K 72. The competent authority. (1) On the coming into force of this section, the functions conferred on the competent authority by this Part are to be exercised by the Authority.

(2) Schedule 7 modifies this Act in its application to the Authority when it acts as the competent authority.

(3) But provision is made by Schedule 8 allowing some or all of those functions to be transferred by the Treasury so as to be exercisable by another person.

[Financial Services and Markets Act 2000, s 72.]

---

1. Part VI comprises ss 72–103.

8–18290L 73. General duty of the competent authority. (1) In discharging its general functions the competent authority must have regard to—

(*a*) the need to use its resources in the most efficient and economic way;

(*b*) the principle that a burden or restriction which is imposed on a person should be proportionate to the benefits, considered in general terms, which are expected to arise from the imposition of that burden or restriction;

(*c*) the desirability of facilitating innovation in respect of listed securities and in respect of financial instruments which have otherwise been admitted to trading on a regulated market or for which a request for admission to trading on such a market has been made;

(*d*) the international character of capital markets and the desirability of maintaining the competitive position of the United Kingdom;

(*e*) the need to minimise the adverse effects on competition of anything done in the discharge of those functions;

(*f*) the desirability of facilitating competition in relation to listed securities and in relation to financial instruments which have otherwise been admitted to trading on a regulated market or for which a request for admission to trading on such a market has been made.

(2) The competent authority's general functions are—

(*a*) its function of making rules under this Part (considered as a whole);

(*b*) its functions in relation to the giving of general guidance in relation to this Part (considered as a whole);

(*c*) its function of determining the general policy and principles by reference to which it performs particular functions under this Part.

[Financial Services and Markets Act 2000, s 73 as amended by SI 2005/381.]

8–18290LA 73A. Part 6 Rules. (1) The competent authority may make rules ("Part 6 rules") for the purposes of this Part.

(2) Provisions of Part 6 rules expressed to relate to the official list are referred to in this Part as "listing rules".

(3) Provisions of Part 6 rules expressed to relate to disclosure of information in respect of financial instruments which have been admitted to trading on a regulated market or for which a request for admission to trading on such a market has been made, are referred to in this Part as "disclosure rules".

(4) Provisions of Part 6 rules expressed to relate to transferable securities are referred to in this Part as "prospectus rules".

(5) In relation to prospectus rules, the purposes of this Part include the purposes of the prospectus directive.

[Financial Services and Markets Act 2000, s 73A as inserted by SI 2005/381 and amended by SI 2005/1433.]

The official list

8–18290M 74. The official list. (1) The competent authority must maintain the official list.

(2) The competent authority may admit to the official list such securities and other things as it considers appropriate.

(3) But—

(*a*) nothing may be admitted to the official list except in accordance with this Part; and

(*b*) the Treasury may by order provide that anything which falls within a description or category specified in the order may not be admitted to the official list.

(4) *Repealed.*

(5) In the following provisions of this Part—

"listing" means being included in the official list in accordance with this Part.

[Financial Services and Markets Act 2000, s 74 as amended by SI 2005/381 and SI 2005/1433.]

Listing particulars

8–18290N 79. Listing particulars and other documents. (1) Listing rules may provide that securities of a kind specified in the rules may not be admitted to the official list unless—

(*a*) listing particulars have been submitted to, and approved by, the competent authority and published; or (*b*) in such cases as may be specified by listing rules, such document (other than listing particulars or a prospectus of a kind required by listing rules) as may be so specified has been published.

(2) "Listing particulars" means a document in such form and containing such information as may be specified in listing rules.

(3) For the purposes of this Part, the persons responsible for listing particulars are to be determined in accordance with regulations[1] made by the Treasury.

(3A) Listing rules made under subsection (1) may not specify securities of a kind for which an approved prospectus is required as a result of section 85.

(4) Nothing in this section affects the competent authority's general power to make listing rules.

[Financial Services and Markets Act 2000, s 79 as amended by SI 2005/1433.]

1. The Financial Services and Markets Act 2000 (Official Listing of Securities) Regulations 2001, SI 2001/2956 amended by SI 2005/1433 have been made.

8–18290O 80. General duty of disclosure in listing particulars. (1) Listing particulars submitted to the competent authority under section 79 must contain all such information as investors and their professional advisers would reasonably require, and reasonably expect to find there, for the purpose of making an informed assessment of—

(*a*) the assets and liabilities, financial position, profits and losses, and prospects of the issuer of the securities; and

(*b*) the rights attaching to the securities.

(2) That information is required in addition to any information required by—

(*a*) listing rules, or

(*b*) the competent authority,

as a condition of the admission of the securities to the official list.

(3) Subsection (1) applies only to information—

(*a*) within the knowledge of any person responsible for the listing particulars; or

(*b*) which it would be reasonable for him to obtain by making enquiries.

(4) In determining what information subsection (1) requires to be included in listing particulars, regard must be had (in particular) to—

(*a*) the nature of the securities and their issuer;

(*b*) the nature of the persons likely to consider acquiring them;

(*c*) the fact that certain matters may reasonably be expected to be within the knowledge of professional advisers of a kind which persons likely to acquire the securities may reasonably be expected to consult; and

(*d*) any information available to investors or their professional advisers as a result of requirements imposed on the issuer of the securities by a recognised investment exchange, by listing rules or by or under any other enactment.

[Financial Services and Markets Act 2000, s 80.]

8–18290P 81. Supplementary listing particulars. (1) If at any time after the preparation of listing particulars which have been submitted to the competent authority under section 79 and before the commencement of dealings in the securities concerned following their admission to the official list—

(*a*) there is a significant change affecting any matter contained in those particulars the inclusion of which was required by—

(i) section 80,

(ii) listing rules, or

(iii) the competent authority, or

(*b*) a significant new matter arises, the inclusion of information in respect of which would have been so required if it had arisen when the particulars were prepared,

the issuer must, in accordance with listing rules, submit supplementary listing particulars of the change or new matter to the competent authority, for its approval and, if they are approved, publish them.

(2) "Significant" means significant for the purpose of making an informed assessment of the kind mentioned in section 80(1).

(3) If the issuer of the securities is not aware of the change or new matter in question, he is not under a duty to comply with subsection (1) unless he is notified of the change or new matter by a person responsible for the listing particulars.

(4) But it is the duty of any person responsible for those particulars who is aware of such a change or new matter to give notice of it to the issuer.

(5) Subsection (1) applies also as respects matters contained in any supplementary listing particulars previously published under this section in respect of the securities in question.

[Financial Services and Markets Act 2000, s 81.]

8–18290Q 82. Exemptions from disclosure. (1) The competent authority may authorise the omission from listing particulars of any information, the inclusion of which would otherwise be required by section 80 or 81, on the ground—

(*a*) that its disclosure would be contrary to the public interest;
(*b*) that its disclosure would be seriously detrimental to the issuer; or
(*c*) in the case of securities of a kind specified in listing rules, that its disclosure is unnecessary for persons of the kind who may be expected normally to buy or deal in securities of that kind.

(2) But—

(*a*) no authority may be granted under subsection (1)(*b*) in respect of essential information; and
(*b*) no authority granted under subsection (1)(*b*) extends to any such information.

(3) The Secretary of State or the Treasury may issue a certificate to the effect that the disclosure of any information (including information that would otherwise have to be included in listing particulars for which they are themselves responsible) would be contrary to the public interest.

(4) The competent authority is entitled to act on any such certificate in exercising its powers under subsection (1)(*a*).

(5) This section does not affect any powers of the competent authority under listing rules made as a result of section 101(2).

(6) "Essential information" means information which a person considering acquiring securities of the kind in question would be likely to need in order not to be misled about any facts which it is essential for him to know in order to make an informed assessment.

(7) "Listing particulars" includes supplementary listing particulars.

[Financial Services and Markets Act 2000, s 82.]

8–18290R 83. Registration of listing particulars. *Repealed.*

Prospectuses

8–18290S 84. Matters which may be dealt with by prospectus rules. (1) Prospectus rules may make provision as to—

(*a*) the required form and content of a prospectus (including a summary);
(*b*) the cases in which a summary need not be included in a prospectus;
(*c*) the languages which may be used in a prospectus (including a summary);
(*d*) the determination of the persons responsible for a prospectus;
(*e*) the manner in which applications to the competent authority for the approval of a prospectus are to be made.

(2) Prospectus rules may also make provision as to—

(*a*) the period of validity of a prospectus;
(*b*) the disclosure of the maximum price or of the criteria or conditions according to which the final offer price is to be determined, if that information is not contained in a prospectus;
(*c*) the disclosure of the amount of the transferable securities which are to be offered to the public or of the criteria or conditions according to which that amount is to be determined, if that information is not contained in a prospectus;
(*d*) the required form and content of other summary documents (including the languages which may be used in such a document);
(*e*) the ways in which a prospectus that has been approved by the competent authority may be made available to the public;
(*f*) the disclosure, publication or other communication of such information as the competent authority may reasonably stipulate;
(*g*) the principles to be observed in relation to advertisements in connection with an offer of transferable securities to the public or admission of transferable securities to trading on a regulated market and the enforcement of those principles;
(*h*) the suspension of trading in transferable securities where continued trading would be detrimental to the interests of investors;
(*i*) elections under section 87 or under Article 2.1(m)(iii) of the prospectus directive as applied for the purposes of this Part by section 102C

(3) Prospectus rules may also make provision as to—

(*a*) access to the register of investors maintained under section 87R; and
(*b*) the supply of information from that register.

(4) Prospectus rules may make provision for the purpose of dealing with matters arising out of or related to any provision of the prospectus directive.

(5) In relation to cases where the home State in relation to an issuer of transferable securities is an EEA State other than the United Kingdom, prospectus rules may make provision for the recognition of elections made in relation to such securities under the law of that State in accordance with Article 1.3 or 2.1(m)(iii) of the prospectus directive.

(6) In relation to a document relating to transferable securities issued by an issuer incorporated in

a non-EEA State and drawn up in accordance with the law of that State, prospectus rules may make provision as to the approval of that document as a prospectus.

(7) Nothing in this section affects the competent authority's general power to make prospectus rules.

[Financial Services and Markets Act 2000, s 84 as substituted by SI 2005/1433.]

8–18290T 85. Prohibition of dealing etc in transferable securities without approved prospectus. (1) It is unlawful for transferable securities to which this subsection applies to be offered to the public in the United Kingdom unless an approved prospectus has been made available to the public before the offer is made.

(2) It is unlawful to request the admission of transferable securities to which this subsection applies to trading on a regulated market situated or operating in the United Kingdom unless an approved prospectus has been made available to the public before the request is made.

(3) A person who contravenes subsection (1) or (2) is guilty of an offence and liable—

(*a*) on summary conviction, to imprisonment for a term not exceeding 3 months or a fine not exceeding the statutory maximum or both;

(*b*) on conviction on indictment, to imprisonment for a term not exceeding 2 years or a fine or both.

(4) A contravention of subsection (1) or (2) is actionable, at the suit of a person who suffers loss as a result of the contravention, subject to the defences and other incidents applying to actions for breach of statutory duty.

(5) Subsection (1) applies to all transferable securities other than—

(*a*) those listed in Schedule 11A;

(*b*) such other transferable securities as may be specified in prospectus rules.

(6) Subsection (2) applies to all transferable securities other than—

(*a*) those listed in Part 1 of Schedule 11A;

(*b*) such other transferable securities as may be specified in prospectus rules.

(7) "Approved prospectus" means, in relation to transferable securities to which this section applies, a prospectus approved by the competent authority of the home State in relation to the issuer of the securities.

[Financial Services and Markets Act 2000, s 85 as substituted by SI 2005/1433.]

---

1. For procedure in respect of this offence which is triable either way, see the Magistrates' Courts Act 1980, ss 17A–21, in PART I: MAGISTRATES' COURTS, PROCEDURE, ante.

8–18290U 86. Exempt offers to the public. (1) A person does not contravene section 85(1) if—

(*a*) the offer is made to or directed at qualified investors only;

(*b*) the offer is made to or directed at fewer than 100 persons, other than qualified investors, per EEA State;

(*c*) the minimum consideration which may be paid by any person for transferable securities acquired by him pursuant to the offer is at least 50,000 euros (or an equivalent amount);

(*d*) the transferable securities being offered are denominated in amounts of at least 50,000 euros (or equivalent amounts); or

(*e*) the total consideration for the transferable securities being offered cannot exceed 100,000 euros (or an equivalent amount).

(2) Where—

(*a*) a person who is not a qualified investor ("the client") has engaged a qualified investor falling within Article 2.1(*e*)(i) of the prospectus directive to act as his agent, and

(*b*) the terms on which the qualified investor is engaged enable him to make decisions concerning the acceptance of offers of transferable securities on the client's behalf without reference to the client,

an offer made to or directed at the qualified investor is not to be regarded for the purposes of subsection (1) as also having been made to or directed at the client.

(3) For the purposes of subsection (1)(b), the making of an offer of transferable securities to—

(*a*) trustees of a trust,

(*b*) members of a partnership in their capacity as such, or

(*c*) two or more persons jointly,

is to be treated as the making of an offer to a single person.

(4) In determining whether subsection (1)(e) is satisfied in relation to an offer ("offer A"), offer A is to be taken together with any other offer of transferable securities of the same class made by the same person which—

(*a*) was open at any time within the period of 12 months ending with the date on which offer A is first made; and (*b*) had previously satisfied subsection (1)(*e*).

(5) For the purposes of this section, an amount (in relation to an amount denominated in euros) is an "equivalent amount" if it is an amount of equal value denominated wholly or partly in another currency or unit of account.

(6) The equivalent is to be calculated at the latest practicable date before (but in any event not more than 3 working days before) the date on which the offer is first made.

(7) "Qualified investor" means—

(*a*) an entity falling within Article 2.1(*e*)(i), (ii) or (iii) of the prospectus directive;
(*b*) an investor registered on the register maintained by the competent authority under section 87R;
(*c*) an investor authorised by an EEA State other than the United Kingdom to be considered as a qualified investor for the purposes of the prospectus directive.

[Financial Services and Markets Act 2000, s 86 as substituted by SI 2005/1433.]

8–18290V 87. Election to have prospectus. (1) A person who proposes—

(*a*) to issue transferable securities to which this section applies,
(*b*) to offer to the public transferable securities to which this section applies, or
(*c*) to request the admission to a regulated market of transferable securities to which this section applies,

may elect, in accordance with prospectus rules, to have a prospectus in relation to the securities.

(2) If a person makes such an election, the provisions of this Part and of prospectus rules apply in relation to those transferable securities as if, in relation to an offer of the securities to the public or the admission of the securities to trading on a regulated market, they were transferable securities for which an approved prospectus would be required as a result of section 85.

(3) Listing rules made under section 79 do not apply to securities which are the subject of an election.

(4) The transferable securities to which this section applies are those which fall within any of the following paragraphs of Schedule 11A—

(*a*) paragraph 2,
(*b*) paragraph 4,
(*c*) paragraph 8, or
(*d*) paragraph 9,

where the United Kingdom is the home State in relation to the issuer of the securities.

[Financial Services and Markets Act 2000, s 87 as substituted by SI 2005/1433.]

---

1. See the Financial Services and Markets Act 2000 (Offers of Securities) Order 2001, SI 2001/2958 amended by SI 2005/1433.

87A–87R. *Prospectuses, admissions to market and list of investors*

8–18290W 98. Advertisements etc in connection with listing applications. *Repealed.*

8–18290X 103. Interpretation of this Part. (1) In this Part, save where the context otherwise requires—

"disclosure rules" has the meaning given in section 73A;
"inside information" has the meaning given in section 118C;
"listed securities" means anything which has been admitted to the official list;
"listing" has the meaning given in section 74(5);
"listing particulars" has the meaning given in section 79(2);
"listing rules" has the meaning given in section 73A;
"market operator" means a person who manages or operates the business of a regulated market;
"offer of transferable securities to the public" has the meaning given in section 102B;
"the official list" means the list maintained by the competent authority as that list has effect for the time being;
"Part 6 rules" has the meaning given in section 73A;
"the prospectus directive" means Directive 2003/71/EC of the European Parliament and of the Council of 4 November 2003 on the prospectus to be published when securities are offered to the public or admitted to trading;
"prospectus rules" has the meaning given in section 73A;
"regulated market" has the meaning given in Article 1.13 of the investment services directive;
"supplementary prospectus" has the meaning given in section 87G;
"working day" means any day other that a Saturday, a Sunday, Christmas Day, Good Friday or a day which is a bank holiday under the Banking and Financial Dealings Act 1971 (c 80) in any part of the United Kingdom.

(2) In relation to any function conferred on the competent authority by this Part, any reference in this Part to the competent authority is to be read as a reference to the person by whom that function is for the time being exercisable.

(3) If, as a result of an order under Schedule 8, different functions conferred on the competent authority by this Part are exercisable by different persons, the powers conferred by section 91 are exercisable by such person as may be determined in accordance with the provisions of the order.
[Financial Services and Markets Act 2000, s 103 as substituted by SI 2005/1433.]

PART XI[1]
INFORMATION GATHERING AND INVESTIGATIONS
Powers to gather investigation

8–18290Z 165. Authority's power to require information. (1) The Authority may, by notice in writing given to an authorised person, require him—

(*a*) to provide specified information or information of a specified description; or
(*b*) to produce specified documents or documents of a specified description.

(2) The information or documents must be provided or produced—

(*a*) before the end of such reasonable period as may be specified; and
(*b*) at such place as may be specified.

(3) An officer who has written authorisation from the Authority to do so may require an authorised person without delay—

(*a*) to provide the officer with specified information or information of a specified description; or
(*b*) to produce to him specified documents or documents of a specified description.

(4) This section applies only to information and documents reasonably required in connection with the exercise by the Authority of functions conferred on it by or under this Act.

(5) The Authority may require any information provided under this section to be provided in such form as it may reasonably require.

(6) The Authority may require—

(*a*) any information provided, whether in a document or otherwise, to be verified in such manner, or
(*b*) any document produced to be authenticated in such manner,

as it may reasonably require.

(7) The powers conferred by subsections (1) and (3) may also be exercised to impose requirements on—

(*a*) a person who is connected with an authorised person;
(*b*) an operator, trustee or depositary of a scheme recognised under section 270 or 272 who is not an authorised person;
(*c*) a recognised investment exchange or recognised clearing house.

(8) "Authorised person" includes a person who was at any time an authorised person but who has ceased to be an authorised person.

(9) "Officer" means an officer of the Authority and includes a member of the Authority's staff or an agent of the Authority.

(10) "Specified" means—

(*a*) in subsections (1) and (2), specified in the notice; and
(*b*) in subsection (3), specified in the authorisation.

(11) For the purposes of this section, a person is connected with an authorised person ("A") if he is or has at any relevant time been—

(*a*) a member of A's group;
(*b*) a controller of A;
(*c*) any other member of a partnership of which A is a member; or
(*d*) in relation to A, a person mentioned in Part I of Schedule 15.

[Financial Services and Markets Act 2000, s 165.]

---

1. Part XI comprises ss 165–177.

8–18291 166. Reports by skilled persons. (1) The Authority may, by notice in writing given to a person to whom subsection (2) applies, require him to provide the Authority with a report on any matter about which the Authority has required or could require the provision of information or production of documents under section 165.

(2) This subsection applies to—

(*a*) an authorised person ("A"),
(*b*) any other member of A's group,
(*c*) a partnership of which A is a member, or
(*d*) a person who has at any relevant time been a person falling within paragraph (*a*), (*b*) or (*c*),

who is, or was at the relevant time, carrying on a business.

(3) The Authority may require the report to be in such form as may be specified in the notice.

(4) The person appointed to make a report required by subsection (1) must be a person—

(*a*) nominated or approved by the Authority; and

(*b*) appearing to the Authority to have the skills necessary to make a report on the matter concerned.

(5) It is the duty of any person who is providing (or who at any time has provided) services to a person to whom subsection (2) applies in relation to a matter on which a report is required under subsection (1) to give a person appointed to provide such a report all such assistance as the appointed person may reasonably require.

(6) The obligation imposed by subsection (5) is enforceable, on the application of the Authority, by an injunction or, in Scotland, by an order for specific performance under section 45 of the Court of Session Act 1988.

[Financial Services and Markets Act 2000, s 166.]

Appointment of investigators

8–18291A 167. Appointment of persons to carry out general investigations. (1) If it appears to the Authority or the Secretary of State ("the investigating authority") that there is good reason for doing so, the investigating authority may appoint one or more competent persons to conduct an investigation on its behalf into—

(*a*) the nature, conduct or state of the business of an authorised person or of an appointed representative;

(*b*) a particular aspect of that business; or

(*c*) the ownership or control of an authorised person.

(2) If a person appointed under subsection (1) thinks it necessary for the purposes of his investigation, he may also investigate the business of a person who is or has at any relevant time been—

(*a*) a member of the group of which the person under investigation ("A") is part; or

(*b*) a partnership of which A is a member.

(3) If a person appointed under subsection (1) decides to investigate the business of any person under subsection (2) he must give that person written notice of his decision.

(4) The power conferred by this section may be exercised in relation to a former authorised person (or appointed representative) but only in relation to—

(*a*) business carried on at any time when he was an authorised person (or appointed representative); or

(*b*) the ownership or control of a former authorised person at any time when he was an authorised person.

(5) "Business" includes any part of a business even if it does not consist of carrying on regulated activities.

[Financial Services and Markets Act 2000, s 167.]

8–18291B 168. Appointment of persons to carry out investigations in particular cases. (1) Subsection (3) applies if it appears to an investigating authority that there are circumstances suggesting that—

(*a*) a person may have contravened any regulation made under section 142; or

(*b*) a person may be guilty of an offence under section 177, 191, 346 or 398(1) or under Schedule 4.

(2) Subsection (3) also applies if it appears to an investigating authority that there are circumstances suggesting that—

(*a*) an offence under section 24(1) or 397 or under Part V of the Criminal Justice Act 1993 may have been committed;

(*b*) there may have been a breach of the general prohibition;

(*c*) there may have been a contravention of section 21 or 238; or

(*d*) market abuse may have taken place.

(3) The investigating authority may appoint one or more competent persons to conduct an investigation on its behalf.

(4) Subsection (5) applies if it appears to the Authority that there are circumstances suggesting that—

(*a*) a person may have contravened section 20;

(*b*) a person may be guilty of an offence under prescribed[1] regulations relating to money laundering;

(*c*) an authorised person may have contravened a rule made by the Authority;

(*d*) an individual may not be a fit and proper person to perform functions in relation to a regulated activity carried on by an authorised or exempt person;

(*e*) an individual may have performed or agreed to perform a function in breach of a prohibition order;
(*f*) an authorised or exempt person may have failed to comply with section 56(6);
(*g*) an authorised person may have failed to comply with section 59(1) or (2);
(*h*) a person in relation to whom the Authority has given its approval under section 59 may not be a fit and proper person to perform the function to which that approval relates; or
(*i*) a person may be guilty of misconduct for the purposes of section 66.

(5) The Authority may appoint one or more competent persons to conduct an investigation on its behalf.

(6) "Investigating authority" means the Authority or the Secretary of State.

[Financial Services and Markets Act 2000, s 168.]

---

1. See the Money Laundering Regulations 2003, in this title, post.

Assistance to overseas regulators

8–18291C 169. Investigations etc in support of overseas regulator. (1) At the request of an overseas regulator, the Authority may—

(*a*) exercise the power conferred by section 165; or
(*b*) appoint one or more competent persons to investigate any matter.

(2) An investigator has the same powers as an investigator appointed under section 168(3) (as a result of subsection (1) of that section).

(3) If the request has been made by a competent authority in pursuance of any Community obligation the Authority must, in deciding whether or not to exercise its investigative power, consider whether its exercise is necessary to comply with any such obligation.

(4) In deciding whether or not to exercise its investigative power, the Authority may take into account in particular—

(*a*) whether in the country or territory of the overseas regulator concerned, corresponding assistance would be given to a United Kingdom regulatory authority;
(*b*) whether the case concerns the breach of a law, or other requirement, which has no close parallel in the United Kingdom or involves the assertion of a jurisdiction not recognised by the United Kingdom;
(*c*) the seriousness of the case and its importance to persons in the United Kingdom;
(*d*) whether it is otherwise appropriate in the public interest to give the assistance sought.

(5) The Authority may decide that it will not exercise its investigative power unless the overseas regulator undertakes to make such contribution towards the cost of its exercise as the Authority considers appropriate.

(6) Subsections (4) and (5) do not apply if the Authority considers that the exercise of its investigative power is necessary to comply with a Community obligation.

(7) If the Authority has appointed an investigator in response to a request from an overseas regulator, it may direct the investigator to permit a representative of that regulator to attend, and take part in, any interview conducted for the purposes of the investigation.

(8) A direction under subsection (7) is not to be given unless the Authority is satisfied that any information obtained by an overseas regulator as a result of the interview will be subject to safeguards equivalent to those contained in Part XXIII.

(9) The Authority must prepare a statement of its policy with respect to the conduct of interviews in relation to which a direction under subsection (7) has been given.

(10) The statement requires the approval of the Treasury.

(11) If the Treasury approve the statement, the Authority must publish it.

(12) No direction may be given under subsection (7) before the statement has been published.

(13) "Overseas regulator" has the same meaning as in section 195.

(14) "Investigative power" means one of the powers mentioned in subsection (1).

(15) "Investigator" means a person appointed under subsection (1)(*b*).

[Financial Services and Markets Act 2000, s 169.]

Conduct of investigations

8–18291D 170. Investigations: general. (1) This section applies if an investigating authority appoints one or more competent persons ("investigators") under section 167 or 168(3) or (5) to conduct an investigation on its behalf.

(2) The investigating authority must give written notice of the appointment of an investigator to the person who is the subject of the investigation ("the person under investigation").

(3) Subsections (2) and (9) do not apply if—

(*a*) the investigator is appointed as a result of section 168(1) or (4) and the investigating authority believes that the notice required by subsection (2) or (9) would be likely to result in the investigation being frustrated; or (*b*) the investigator is appointed as a result of subsection (2) of section 168.

(4) A notice under subsection (2) must—

(*a*) specify the provisions under which, and as a result of which, the investigator was appointed; and

(*b*) state the reason for his appointment.

(5) Nothing prevents the investigating authority from appointing a person who is a member of its staff as an investigator.

(6) An investigator must make a report of his investigation to the investigating authority.

(7) The investigating authority may, by a direction to an investigator, control—

(*a*) the scope of the investigation;

(*b*) the period during which the investigation is to be conducted;

(*c*) the conduct of the investigation; and

(*d*) the reporting of the investigation.

(8) A direction may, in particular—

(*a*) confine the investigation to particular matters;

(*b*) extend the investigation to additional matters;

(*c*) require the investigator to discontinue the investigation or to take only such steps as are specified in the direction;

(*d*) require the investigator to make such interim reports as are so specified.

(9) If there is a change in the scope or conduct of the investigation and, in the opinion of the investigating authority, the person subject to investigation is likely to be significantly prejudiced by not being made aware of it, that person must be given written notice of the change.

(10) "Investigating authority", in relation to an investigator, means—

(*a*) the Authority, if the Authority appointed him;

(*b*) the Secretary of State, if the Secretary of State appointed him.

[Financial Services and Markets Act 2000, s 170.]

8–18291E 171. Powers of persons appointed under section 167. (1) An investigator may require the person who is the subject of the investigation ("the person under investigation") or any person connected with the person under investigation—

(*a*) to attend before the investigator at a specified time and place and answer questions; or

(*b*) otherwise to provide such information as the investigator may require.

(2) An investigator may also require any person to produce at a specified time and place any specified documents or documents of a specified description.

(3) A requirement under subsection (1) or (2) may be imposed only so far as the investigator concerned reasonably considers the question, provision of information or production of the document to be relevant to the purposes of the investigation.

(4) For the purposes of this section and section 172, a person is connected with the person under investigation ("A") if he is or has at any relevant time been—

(*a*) a member of A's group;

(*b*) a controller of A;

(*c*) a partnership of which A is a member; or

(*d*) in relation to A, a person mentioned in Part I or II of Schedule 15.

(5) "Investigator" means a person conducting an investigation under section 167.

(6) "Specified" means specified in a notice in writing.

[Financial Services and Markets Act 2000, s 171.]

8–18291F 172. Additional power of persons appointed as a result of section 168(1) or (4). (1) An investigator has the powers conferred by section 171.

(2) An investigator may also require a person who is neither the subject of the investigation ("the person under investigation") nor a person connected with the person under investigation—

(*a*) to attend before the investigator at a specified time and place and answer questions; or

(*b*) otherwise to provide such information as the investigator may require for the purposes of the investigation.

(3) A requirement may only be imposed under subsection (2) if the investigator is satisfied that the requirement is necessary or expedient for the purposes of the investigation.

(4) "Investigator" means a person appointed as a result of subsection (1) or (4) of section 168.

(5) "Specified" means specified in a notice in writing.

[Financial Services and Markets Act 2000, s 172.]

8–18291G 173. Powers of persons appointed as a result of section 168(2). (1) Subsections (2) to (4) apply if an investigator considers that any person ("A") is or may be able to give information which is or may be relevant to the investigation.

(2) The investigator may require A—

(*a*) to attend before him at a specified time and place and answer questions; or

(*b*) otherwise to provide such information as he may require for the purposes of the investigation.

(3) The investigator may also require A to produce at a specified time and place any specified documents or documents of a specified description which appear to the investigator to relate to any matter relevant to the investigation.

(4) The investigator may also otherwise require A to give him all assistance in connection with the investigation which A is reasonably able to give.

(5) "Investigator" means a person appointed under subsection (3) of section 168 (as a result of subsection (2) of that section).

[Financial Services and Markets Act 2000, s 173.]

8–18291H 174. Admissibility of statements made to investigators. (1) A statement made to an investigator by a person in compliance with an information requirement is admissible in evidence in any proceedings, so long as it also complies with any requirements governing the admissibility of evidence in the circumstances in question.

(2) But in criminal proceedings in which that person is charged with an offence to which this subsection applies or in proceedings in relation to action to be taken against that person under section 123—

(*a*) no evidence relating to the statement may be adduced, and

(*b*) no question relating to it may be asked,

by or on behalf of the prosecution or (as the case may be) the Authority, unless evidence relating to it is adduced, or a question relating to it is asked, in the proceedings by or on behalf of that person.

(3) Subsection (2) applies to any offence other than one—

(*a*) under section 177(4) or 398;

(*b*) under section 5 of the Perjury Act 1911 (false statements made otherwise than on oath);

(*c*) under section 44(2) of the Criminal Law (Consolidation)(Scotland) Act 1995 (false statements made otherwise than on oath); or

(*d*) under Article 10 of the Perjury (Northern Ireland) Order 1979.

(4) "Investigator" means a person appointed under section 167 or 168(3) or (5).

(5) "Information requirement" means a requirement imposed by an investigator under section 171, 172, 173 or 175.

[Financial Services and Markets Act 2000, s 174.]

8–18291I 175. Information and documents: supplemental provisions. (1) If the Authority or an investigator has power under this Part to require a person to produce a document but it appears that the document is in the possession of a third person, that power may be exercised in relation to the third person.

(2) If a document is produced in response to a requirement imposed under this Part, the person to whom it is produced may—

(*a*) take copies or extracts from the document; or

(*b*) require the person producing the document, or any relevant person, to provide an explanation of the document.

(3) If a person who is required under this Part to produce a document fails to do so, the Authority or an investigator may require him to state, to the best of his knowledge and belief, where the document is.

(4) A lawyer may be required under this Part to furnish the name and address of his client.

(5) No person may be required under this Part to disclose information or produce a document in respect of which he owes an obligation of confidence by virtue of carrying on the business of banking unless—

(*a*) he is the person under investigation or a member of that person's group;

(*b*) the person to whom the obligation of confidence is owed is the person under investigation or a member of that person's group;

(*c*) the person to whom the obligation of confidence is owed consents to the disclosure or production; or

(*d*) the imposing on him of a requirement with respect to such information or document has been specifically authorised by the investigating authority.

(6) If a person claims a lien on a document, its production under this Part does not affect the lien.

(7) "Relevant person", in relation to a person who is required to produce a document, means a person who—

(*a*) has been or is or is proposed to be a director or controller of that person;

(*b*) has been or is an auditor of that person;

(*c*) has been or is an actuary, accountant or lawyer appointed or instructed by that person; or

(*d*) has been or is an employee of that person.

(8) "Investigator" means a person appointed under section 167 or 168(3) or (5).
[Financial Services and Markets Act 2000, s 175.]

8–18291J 176. Entry of premises under warrant. (1) A justice of the peace may issue a warrant under this section if satisfied on information on oath given by or on behalf of the Secretary of State, the Authority or an investigator that there are reasonable grounds for believing that the first, second or third set of conditions is satisfied.

(2) The first set of conditions is—

(*a*) that a person on whom an information requirement has been imposed has failed (wholly or in part) to comply with it; and

(*b*) that on the premises specified in the warrant—

(i) there are documents which have been required; or

(ii) there is information which has been required.

(3) The second set of conditions is—

(*a*) that the premises specified in the warrant are premises of an authorised person or an appointed representative;

(*b*) that there are on the premises documents or information in relation to which an information requirement could be imposed; and

(*c*) that if such a requirement were to be imposed—

(i) it would not be complied with; or

(ii) the documents or information to which it related would be removed, tampered with or destroyed.

(4) The third set of conditions is—

(*a*) that an offence mentioned in section 168 for which the maximum sentence on conviction on indictment is two years or more has been (or is being) committed by any person;

(*b*) that there are on the premises specified in the warrant documents or information relevant to whether that offence has been (or is being) committed;

(*c*) that an information requirement could be imposed in relation to those documents or information; and

(*d*) that if such a requirement were to be imposed—

(i) it would not be complied with; or

(ii) the documents or information to which it related would be removed, tampered with or destroyed.

(5) A warrant under this section shall authorise a constable—

(*a*) to enter the premises specified in the warrant;

(*b*) to search the premises and take possession of any documents or information appearing to be documents or information of a kind in respect of which a warrant under this section was issued ("the relevant kind") or to take, in relation to any such documents or information, any other steps which may appear to be necessary for preserving them or preventing interference with them;

(*c*) to take copies of, or extracts from, any documents or information appearing to be of the relevant kind;

(*d*) to require any person on the premises to provide an explanation of any document or information appearing to be of the relevant kind or to state where it may be found; and

(*e*) to use such force as may be reasonably necessary.

(6) In England and Wales, sections 15(5) to (8) and section 16 of the Police and Criminal Evidence Act 1984 (execution of search warrants and safeguards) apply to warrants issued under this section.

(7) In Northern Ireland, Articles 17(5) to (8) and 18 of the Police and Criminal Evidence (Northern Ireland) Order 1989 apply to warrants issued under this section.

(8) Any document of which possession is taken under this section may be retained—

(*a*) for a period of three months; or

(*b*) if within that period proceedings to which the document is relevant are commenced against any person for any criminal offence, until the conclusion of those proceedings[1].

(9) In the application of this section to Scotland—

(*a*) for the references to a justice of the peace substitute references to a justice of the peace or a sheriff; and

(*b*) for the references to information on oath substitute references to evidence on oath.

(10) "Investigator" means a person appointed under section 167 or 168(3) or (5).

(11) "Information requirement" means a requirement imposed—

(*a*) by the Authority under section 87C, 87J, 165 or 175; or

(*b*) by an investigator under section 171, 172, 173 or 175.
[Financial Services and Markets Act 2000, s 176 as amended by SI 2005/1433.]

---

1. See the Criminal Justice and Police Act 2001, Part 2 (PART I, ante). These provisions confer, by ss 50 and 51, additional powers of seizure of property in relation to searches carried out under existing powers. However, s 57 (retention of seized items) does not authorise the retention of any property which could not be retained under the provisions listed in s 57(1), which include s 176(8) of the Financial Services and Markets Act 2000, if the property was seized under the new powers (ie those conferred by ss 50 and 51) in reliance on one of those powers (ie those conferred by the provisions listed in s 57(1)). Section 57(4) further provides that nothing in any of the provisions listed in s 57(1) authorises the retention of anything after an obligation to return it has arisen under Part 2.

Offences

8–18291K 177. Offences. (1) If a person other than the investigator ("the defaulter") fails to comply with a requirement imposed on him under this Part the person imposing the requirement may certify that fact in writing to the court.

(2) If the court is satisfied that the defaulter failed without reasonable excuse to comply with the requirement, it may deal with the defaulter (and in the case of a body corporate, any director or officer) as if he were in contempt; and "officer", in relation to a limited liability partnership, means a member of the limited liability partnership.

(3) A person who knows or suspects that an investigation is being or is likely to be conducted under this Part is guilty of an offence if—

(*a*) he falsifies, conceals, destroys or otherwise disposes of a document which he knows or suspects is or would be relevant to such an investigation, or

(*b*) he causes or permits the falsification, concealment, destruction or disposal of such a document,

unless he shows that he had no intention of concealing facts disclosed by the documents from the investigator.

(4) A person who, in purported compliance with a requirement imposed on him under this Part—

(*a*) provides information which he knows to be false or misleading in a material particular, or

(*b*) recklessly provides information which is false or misleading in a material particular,

is guilty of an offence.

(5) A person guilty of an offence under subsection (3) or (4) is liable[1]—

(*a*) on summary conviction, to imprisonment for a term not exceeding six months or a fine not exceeding the statutory maximum, or both;

(*b*) on conviction on indictment, to imprisonment for a term not exceeding two years or a fine, or both.

(6) Any person who intentionally obstructs the exercise of any rights conferred by a warrant under section 176 is guilty of an offence and liable on summary conviction to imprisonment for a term not exceeding three months* or a fine not exceeding level 5 on the standard scale, or both.

(7) "Court" means—

(*a*) the High Court;

(*b*) in Scotland, the Court of Session.

[Financial Services and Markets Act 2000, s 177, as amended by SI 2001/1090.]

***"51 weeks" substituted by the Criminal Justice Act 2993, Sch 26, from a date to be appointed.**

1. For procedure in respect of this offence which is triable either way, see the Magistrates' Courts Act 1980, ss 17A–21, in Part I: Magistrates' Courts, Procedure, ante.

PART XII[1]
CONTROL OVER AUTHORISED PERSONS

Notice of control

8–18291L 178. Obligation to notify the Authority. (1) If a step which a person proposes to take would result in his acquiring—

(*a*) control over a UK authorised person,

(*b*) an additional kind of control over a UK authorised person, or

(*c*) an increase in a relevant kind of control which he already has over a UK authorised person,

he must notify the Authority of his proposal.

(2) A person who, without himself taking any such step, acquires any such control or additional or increased control must notify the Authority before the end of the period of 14 days beginning with the day on which he first becomes aware that he has acquired it.

(3) A person who is under the duty to notify the Authority imposed by subsection (1) must also give notice to the Authority on acquiring, or increasing, the control in question.

(4) In this Part "UK authorised person" means an authorised person who—

(*a*) is a body incorporated in, or an unincorporated association formed under the law of, any part of the United Kingdom; and (*b*) is not a person authorised as a result of paragraph 1 of Schedule 5.

(5) A notice under subsection (1) or (2) is referred to in this Part as "a notice of control".
[Financial Services and Markets Act 2000, s 178.]

1. Part XII comprises ss 178–192.

8–18291M 190. Notification. (1) If a step which a controller of a UK authorised person proposes to take would result in his—

(*a*) ceasing to have control of a relevant kind over the authorised person, or
(*b*) reducing a relevant kind of control over that person,

he must notify the Authority of his proposal.

(2) A controller of a UK authorised person who, without himself taking any such step, ceases to have that control or reduces that control must notify the Authority before the end of the period of 14 days beginning with the day on which he first becomes aware that—

(*a*) he has ceased to have the control in question; or
(*b*) he has reduced that control.

(3) A person who is under the duty to notify the Authority imposed by subsection (1) must also give a notice to the Authority—

(*a*) on ceasing to have the control in question; or
(*b*) on reducing that control.

(4) A notice under this section must—

(*a*) be given to the Authority in writing; and
(*b*) include details of the extent of the control (if any) which the person concerned will retain (or still retains) over the authorised person concerned.

[Financial Services and Markets Act 2000, s 190.]

Offences

8–18291N 191. Offences under this Part. (1) A person who fails to comply with the duty to notify the Authority imposed on him by section 178(1) or 190(1) is guilty of an offence.

(2) A person who fails to comply with the duty to notify the Authority imposed on him by section 178(2) or 190(2) is guilty of an offence.

(3) If a person who has given a notice of control to the Authority carries out the proposal to which the notice relates, he is guilty of an offence if—

(*a*) the period of three months beginning with the date on which the Authority received the notice is still running; and
(*b*) the Authority has not responded to the notice by either giving its approval or giving him a warning notice under section 183(3) or 185(3).

(4) A person to whom the Authority has given a warning notice under section 183(3) is guilty of an offence if he carries out the proposal to which the notice relates before the Authority has decided whether to give him a notice of objection.

(5) A person to whom a notice of objection has been given is guilty of an offence if he acquires the control to which the notice applies at a time when the notice is still in force.

(6) A person guilty of an offence under subsection (1), (2), (3) or (4) is liable on summary conviction to a fine not exceeding level 5 on the standard scale.

(7) A person guilty of an offence under subsection (5) is liable[1]—

(*a*) on summary conviction, to a fine not exceeding the statutory maximum; and
(*b*) on conviction on indictment, to imprisonment for a term not exceeding two years or a fine, or both.

(8) A person guilty of an offence under subsection (5) is also liable on summary conviction to a fine not exceeding one tenth of the statutory maximum for each day on which the offence has continued.

(9) It is a defence for a person charged with an offence under subsection (1) to show that he had, at the time of the alleged offence, no knowledge of the act or circumstances by virtue of which the duty to notify the Authority arose.

(10) If a person—

(*a*) was under the duty to notify the Authority imposed by section 178(1) or 190(1) but had no knowledge of the act or circumstances by virtue of which that duty arose, but
(*b*) subsequently becomes aware of that act or those circumstances,

he must notify the Authority before the end of the period of 14 days beginning with the day on which he first became so aware.

(11) A person who fails to comply with the duty to notify the Authority imposed by subsection

(10) is guilty of an offence and liable, on summary conviction, to a fine not exceeding level 5 on the standard scale.
[Financial Services and Markets Act 2000, s 191.]

1. For procedure in respect of this offence which is triable either way, see the Magistrates' Courts Act 1980, ss 17A–21, in PART I: MAGISTRATES' COURTS, PROCEDURE, ante.

PART XIII[1]
INCOMING FIRMS: INTERVENTION BY AUTHORITY

Interpretation

8–18291O 193. Interpretation of this Part. (1) In this Part—

"additional procedure" means the procedure described in section 199;

"incoming firm" means—

(*a*) an EEA firm which is exercising, or has exercised, its right to carry on a regulated activity in the United Kingdom in accordance with Schedule 3; or

(*b*) a Treaty firm which is exercising, or has exercised, its right to carry on a regulated activity in the United Kingdom in accordance with Schedule 4; and

"power of intervention" means the power conferred on the Authority by section 196.

(2) In relation to an incoming firm which is an EEA firm, expressions used in this Part and in Schedule 3 have the same meaning in this Part as they have in that Schedule.
[Financial Services and Markets Act 2000, s 193.]

1. Part XIII comprises ss 193–204.

8–18291P 194. General grounds on which power of intervention is exercisable. (1) The Authority may exercise its power of intervention in respect of an incoming firm if it appears to it that—

(*a*) the firm has contravened, or is likely to contravene, a requirement which is imposed on it by or under this Act (in a case where the Authority is responsible for enforcing compliance in the United Kingdom);

(*b*) the firm has, in purported compliance with any requirement imposed by or under this Act, knowingly or recklessly given the Authority information which is false or misleading in a material particular; or

(*c*) it is desirable to exercise the power in order to protect the interests of actual or potential customers.

(2) Subsection (3) applies to an incoming EEA firm falling within sub-paragraph (*a*) or (*b*) of paragraph 5 of Schedule 3 which is exercising an EEA right to carry on any Consumer Credit Act business in the United Kingdom.

(3) The Authority may exercise its power of intervention in respect of the firm if the Director General of Fair Trading has informed the Authority that—

(*a*) the firm,

(*b*) any of the firm's employees, agents or associates (whether past or present), or

(*c*) if the firm is a body corporate, a controller of the firm or an associate of such a controller,

has done any of the things specified in paragraphs (*a*) to (*d*) of section 25(2) of the Consumer Credit Act 1974.

(4) "Associate", "Consumer Credit Act business" and "controller" have the same meaning as in section 203.
[Financial Services and Markets Act 2000, s 194.]

Powers of Director General of Fair Trading

8–18291Q 203. Power to prohibit the carrying on of Consumer Credit Act business. (1) If it appears to the Director General of Fair Trading ("the Director") that subsection (4) has been, or is likely to be, contravened as respects a consumer credit EEA firm, he may by written notice given to the firm impose on the firm a consumer credit prohibition.

(2) If it appears to the Director that a restriction imposed under section 204 on an EEA consumer credit firm has not been complied with, he may by written notice given to the firm impose a consumer credit prohibition.

(3) "Consumer credit prohibition" means a prohibition on carrying on, or purporting to carry on, in the United Kingdom any Consumer Credit Act business which consists of or includes carrying on one or more listed activities.

(4) This subsection is contravened as respects a firm if—

(*a*) the firm or any of its employees, agents or associates (whether past or present), or

(*b*) if the firm is a body corporate, any controller of the firm or an associate of any such controller, does any of the things specified in paragraphs (*a*) to (*d*) of section 25(2) of the Consumer Credit Act 1974.

(5) A consumer credit prohibition may be absolute or may be imposed—

(*a*) for such period,
(*b*) until the occurrence of such event, or
(*c*) until such conditions are complied with,

as may be specified in the notice given under subsection (1) or (2).

(6) Any period, event or condition so specified may be varied by the Director on the application of the firm concerned.

(7) A consumer credit prohibition may be withdrawn by written notice served by the Director on the firm concerned, and any such notice takes effect on such date as is specified in the notice.

(8) Schedule 16 has effect as respects consumer credit prohibitions and restrictions under section 204.

(9) A firm contravening a prohibition under this section is guilty of an offence and liable—

(*a*) on summary conviction, to a fine not exceeding the statutory maximum;
(*b*) on conviction on indictment, to a fine.

(10) In this section and section 204—

"a consumer credit EEA firm" means an EEA firm falling within any of paragraphs (*a*) to (*c*) of paragraph 5 of Schedule 3 whose EEA authorisation covers any Consumer Credit Act business;

"Consumer Credit Act business" means consumer credit business, consumer hire business or ancillary credit business;

"consumer credit business", "consumer hire business" and "ancillary credit business" have the same meaning as in the Consumer Credit Act 1974;

"listed activity" means an activity listed in [Annex 1 to the banking consolidation directive] or the Annex to the investment services directive;

"associate" has the same meaning as in section 25(2) of the Consumer Credit Act 1974;

"controller" has the meaning given by section 189(1) of that Act.

[Financial Services and Markets Act 2000, s 203.]

8–18291R 204. Power to restrict the carrying on of Consumer Credit Act business. (1) In this section "restriction" means a direction that a consumer credit EEA firm may not carry on in the United Kingdom, otherwise than in accordance with such condition or conditions as may be specified in the direction, any Consumer Credit Act business which—

(*a*) consists of or includes carrying on any listed activity; and
(*b*) is specified in the direction.

(2) If it appears to the Director that the situation as respects a consumer credit EEA firm is such that the powers conferred by section 203(1) are exercisable, the Director may, instead of imposing a prohibition, impose such restriction as appears to him desirable.

(3) A restriction—

(*a*) may be withdrawn, or
(*b*) may be varied with the agreement of the firm concerned,

by written notice served by the Director on the firm, and any such notice takes effect on such date as is specified in the notice.

(4) A firm contravening a restriction is guilty of an offence and liable[1]—

(*a*) on summary conviction, to a fine not exceeding the statutory maximum;
(*b*) on conviction on indictment, to a fine.

[Financial Services and Markets Act 2000, s 204.]

---

1. For procedure in respect of this offence which is triable either way, see the Magistrates' Courts Act 1980, ss 17A–21, in PART I: MAGISTRATES' COURTS, PROCEDURE, ante.

PART XXII[1]
AUDITORS AND ACTUARIES

Offence

8–18291S 346. Provision of false or misleading information to auditor or actuary. (1) An authorised person who knowingly or recklessly gives an appointed auditor or actuary information which is false or misleading in a material particular is guilty of an offence and liable[2]—

(*a*) on summary conviction, to imprisonment for a term not exceeding six months or a fine not exceeding the statutory maximum, or both;
(*b*) on conviction on indictment, to imprisonment for a term not exceeding two years or a fine, or both.

(2) Subsection (1) applies equally to an officer, controller or manager of an authorised person.

(3) "Appointed" means appointed under or as a result of this Act.
[Financial Services and Markets Act 2000, s 346.]

---

1. Part XXII comprises ss 340–346.
2. For procedure in respect of this offence which is triable either way, see the Magistrates' Courts Act 1980, ss 17A–21, in PART I: MAGISTRATES' COURTS, PROCEDURE, ante.

PART XXIII[1]

PUBLIC RECORD, DISCLOSURE OF INFORMATION AND CO-OPERATION

The public record

8–18291T 347. The record of authorised persons etc. (1) The Authority must maintain a record of every—

(*a*) person who appears to the Authority to be an authorised person;
(*b*) authorised unit trust scheme;
(*c*) authorised open-ended investment company;
(*d*) recognised scheme;
(*e*) recognised investment exchange;
(*f*) recognised clearing house;
(*g*) individual to whom a prohibition order relates;
(*h*) approved person; and
(*i*) person falling within such other class (if any) as the Authority may determine.

(2) The record must include such information as the Authority considers appropriate and at least the following information—

(*a*) in the case of a person appearing to the Authority to be an authorised person—
 (i) information as to the services which he holds himself out as able to provide; and
 (ii) any address of which the Authority is aware at which a notice or other document may be served on him;
(*b*) in the case of an authorised unit trust scheme, the name and address of the manager and trustee of the scheme;
(*c*) in the case of an authorised open-ended investment company, the name and address of—
 (i) the company;
 (ii) if it has only one director, the director; and
 (iii) its depositary (if any);
(*d*) in the case of a recognised scheme, the name and address of—
 (i) the operator of the scheme; and
 (ii) any representative of the operator in the United Kingdom;
(*e*) in the case of a recognised investment exchange or recognised clearing house, the name and address of the exchange or clearing house;
(*f*) in the case of an individual to whom a prohibition order relates—
 (i) his name; and
 (ii) details of the effect of the order;
(*g*) in the case of a person who is an approved person—
 (i) his name;
 (ii) the name of the relevant authorised person;
 (iii) if the approved person is performing a controlled function under an arrangement with a contractor of the relevant authorised person, the name of the contractor.

(3) If it appears to the Authority that a person in respect of whom there is an entry in the record as a result of one of the paragraphs of subsection (1) has ceased to be a person to whom that paragraph applies, the Authority may remove the entry from the record.

(4) But if the Authority decides not to remove the entry, it must—

(*a*) make a note to that effect in the record; and
(*b*) state why it considers that the person has ceased to be a person to whom that paragraph applies.

(5) The Authority must—

(*a*) make the record available for inspection by members of the public in a legible form at such times and in such place or places as the Authority may determine; and
(*b*) provide a certified copy of the record, or any part of it, to any person who asks for it—
 (i) on payment of the fee (if any) fixed by the Authority; and
 (ii) in a form (either written or electronic) in which it is legible to the person asking for it.

(6) The Authority may—

(*a*) publish the record, or any part of it;
(*b*) exploit commercially the information contained in the record, or any part of that information.

(7) "Authorised unit trust scheme", "authorised open-ended investment company" and "recognised scheme" have the same meaning as in Part XVII, and associated expressions are to be read accordingly.

(8) "Approved person" means a person in relation to whom the Authority has given its approval under section 59 and "controlled function" and "arrangement" have the same meaning as in that section.

(9) "Relevant authorised person" has the meaning given in section 66.
[Financial Services and Markets Act 2000, s 347.]

1. Part XXIII comprises ss 347–354.

Disclosure of information

8–18291U 348. Restrictions on disclosure of confidential information by Authority etc. (1) Confidential information must not be disclosed by a primary recipient, or by any person obtaining the information directly or indirectly from a primary recipient, without the consent of—

(*a*) the person from whom the primary recipient obtained the information; and
(*b*) if different, the person to whom it relates.

(2) In this Part "confidential information" means information which—

(*a*) relates to the business or other affairs of any person;
(*b*) was received by the primary recipient for the purposes of, or in the discharge of, any functions of the Authority, the competent authority for the purposes of Part VI or the Secretary of State under any provision made by or under this Act; and
(*c*) is not prevented from being confidential information by subsection (4).

(3) It is immaterial for the purposes of subsection (2) whether or not the information was received—

(*a*) by virtue of a requirement to provide it imposed by or under this Act;
(*b*) for other purposes as well as purposes mentioned in that subsection.

(4) Information is not confidential information if—

(*a*) it has been made available to the public by virtue of being disclosed in any circumstances in which, or for any purposes for which, disclosure is not precluded by this section; or
(*b*) it is in the form of a summary or collection of information so framed that it is not possible to ascertain from it information relating to any particular person.

(5) Each of the following is a primary recipient for the purposes of this Part—

(*a*) the Authority;
(*b*) any person exercising functions conferred by Part VI on the competent authority;
(*c*) the Secretary of State;
(*d*) a person appointed to make a report under section 166;
(*e*) any person who is or has been employed by a person mentioned in paragraphs (*a*) to (*c*);
(*f*) any auditor or expert instructed by a person mentioned in those paragraphs.

(6) In subsection (5)(*f*) "expert" includes—

(*a*) a competent person appointed by the competent authority under section 97;
(*b*) a competent person appointed by the Authority or the Secretary of State to conduct an investigation under Part XI;
(*c*) any body or person appointed under paragraph 6 of Schedule 1 to perform a function on behalf of the Authority.

[Financial Services and Markets Act 2000, s 348.]

8–18291V 349. Exceptions from section 348. (1) Section 348 does not prevent a disclosure of confidential information which is—

(*a*) made for the purpose of facilitating the carrying out of a public function; and
(*b*) permitted by regulations[1] made by the Treasury under this section.

(2) The regulations[1] may, in particular, make provision permitting the disclosure of confidential information or of confidential information of a prescribed kind—

(*a*) by prescribed recipients, or recipients of a prescribed description, to any person for the purpose of enabling or assisting the recipient to discharge prescribed public functions;
(*b*) by prescribed recipients, or recipients of a prescribed description, to prescribed persons, or persons of prescribed descriptions, for the purpose of enabling or assisting those persons to discharge prescribed public functions;
(*c*) by the Authority to the Treasury or the Secretary of State for any purpose;
(*d*) by any recipient if the disclosure is with a view to or in connection with prescribed proceedings.

(3) The regulations[1] may also include provision—

(*a*) making any permission to disclose confidential information subject to conditions (which may relate to the obtaining of consents or any other matter);

(*b*) restricting the uses to which confidential information disclosed under the regulations may be put.

(4) In relation to confidential information, each of the following is a "recipient"—

(*a*) a primary recipient;

(*b*) a person obtaining the information directly or indirectly from a primary recipient.

(5) "Public functions" includes—

(*a*) functions conferred by or in accordance with any provision contained in any enactment or subordinate legislation;

(*b*) functions conferred by or in accordance with any provision contained in the Community Treaties or any Community instrument;

(*c*) similar functions conferred on persons by or under provisions having effect as part of the law of a country or territory outside the United Kingdom;

(*d*) functions exercisable in relation to prescribed disciplinary proceedings.

(6) "Enactment" includes—

(*a*) an Act of the Scottish Parliament;

(*b*) Northern Ireland legislation.

(7) "Subordinate legislation" has the meaning given in the Interpretation Act 1978 and also includes an instrument made under an Act of the Scottish Parliament or under Northern Ireland legislation.

[Financial Services and Markets Act 2000, s 349.]

1. The Financial Services and Markets Act 2000 (Disclosure of Confidential Information) Regulations 2001, SI 2001/2188 amended by Enterprise Act 2002 (c 40), section 2, SI 2001/3437, 3624 and 3648, SI 2002/1775, SI 2003/693, 1092, 1473, 2174 and 2817, SI 2004/3379 and SI 2005/3071 have been made.

8–18291W 350. Disclosure of information by the Inland Revenue. (1) No obligation as to secrecy imposed by statute or otherwise prevents the disclosure of Revenue information to—

(*a*) the Authority, or

(*b*) the Secretary of State,

if the disclosure is made for the purpose of assisting in the investigation of a matter under section 168 or with a view to the appointment of an investigator under that section.

(2) A disclosure may only be made under subsection (1) by or under the authority of the Commissioners of Inland Revenue.

(3) Section 348 does not apply to Revenue information.

(4) Information obtained as a result of subsection (1) may not be used except—

(*a*) for the purpose of deciding whether to appoint an investigator under section 168;

(*b*) in the conduct of an investigation under section 168;

(*c*) in criminal proceedings brought against a person under this Act or the Criminal Justice Act 1993 as a result of an investigation under section 168;

(*d*) for the purpose of taking action under this Act against a person as a result of an investigation under section 168;

(*e*) in proceedings before the Tribunal as a result of action taken as mentioned in paragraph (*d*).

(5) Information obtained as a result of subsection (1) may not be disclosed except—

(*a*) by or under the authority of the Commissioners of Inland Revenue;

(*b*) in proceedings mentioned in subsection (4)(*c*) or (*e*) or with a view to their institution.

(6) Subsection (5) does not prevent the disclosure of information obtained as a result of subsection (1) to a person to whom it could have been disclosed under subsection (1).

(7) "Revenue information" means information held by a person which it would be an offence under section 182 of the Finance Act 1989 for him to disclose.

[Financial Services and Markets Act 2000, s 350.]

8–18291X 351. Competition information. (1) *Repealed.*

(2) *Repealed.*

(3) *Repealed.*

(4) Section 348 does not apply to competition information.

(5) "Competition information" means information which—

(*a*) relates to the affairs of a particular individual or body;

(*b*) is not otherwise in the public domain; and

(*c*) was obtained under or by virtue of a competition provision.

(6) "Competition provision" means any provision of—

(*a*) an order made under section 95;

(*b*) Chapter III of Part X; or

(*c*) Chapter II of Part XVIII.

(7) *Repealed.*

[Financial Services and Markets Act 2000, s 351, as amended by the Enterprise Act 2002, Sch 26.]

---

1. For procedure in respect of this offence which is triable either way, see the Magistrates' Courts Act 1980, ss 17A–21, in PART I: MAGISTRATES' COURTS, PROCEDURE, ante.

8–18291Y 352. Offences. (1) A person who discloses information in contravention of section 348 or 350(5) is guilty of an offence.

(2) A person guilty of an offence under subsection (1) is liable[1]—

(*a*) on summary conviction, to imprisonment for a term not exceeding three months or a fine not exceeding the statutory maximum, or both;

(*b*) on conviction on indictment, to imprisonment for a term not exceeding two years or a fine, or both.

(3) A person is guilty of an offence if, in contravention of any provision of regulations made under section 349, he uses information which has been disclosed to him in accordance with the regulations.

(4) A person is guilty of an offence if, in contravention of subsection (4) of section 350, he uses information which has been disclosed to him in accordance with that section.

(5) A person guilty of an offence under subsection (3) or (4) is liable on summary conviction to imprisonment for a term not exceeding three months* or a fine not exceeding level 5 on the standard scale, or both.

(6) In proceedings for an offence under this section it is a defence for the accused to prove—

(*a*) that he did not know and had no reason to suspect that the information was confidential information or that it had been disclosed in accordance with section 350;

(*b*) that he took all reasonable precautions and exercised all due diligence to avoid committing the offence.

[Financial Services and Markets Act 2000, s 352.]

***"51 weeks" substituted by the Criminal Justice Act 2993, Sch 26, from a date to be appointed.**

1. For procedure in respect of this offence which is triable either way, see the Magistrates' Courts Act 1980, ss 17A–21, in PART I: MAGISTRATES' COURTS, PROCEDURE, ante.

8–18291Z 353. Removal of other restrictions on disclosure. (1) The Treasury may make regulations[1] permitting the disclosure of any information, or of information of a prescribed kind—

(*a*) by prescribed persons for the purpose of assisting or enabling them to discharge prescribed functions under this Act or any rules or regulations made under it;

(*b*) by prescribed persons, or persons of a prescribed description, to the Authority for the purpose of assisting or enabling the Authority to discharge prescribed functions.

(2) Regulations under this section may not make any provision in relation to the disclosure of confidential information by primary recipients or by any person obtaining confidential information directly or indirectly from a primary recipient.

(3) If a person discloses any information as permitted by regulations under this section the disclosure is not to be taken as a contravention of any duty to which he is subject.

[Financial Services and Markets Act 2000, s 353.]

---

1. The Financial Services and Markets Act 2000 (Disclosure of Information by Prescribed Persons) Regulations 2001, SI 2001/1857 amended by SI 2005/272 have been made.

PART XXVII[1]
OFFENCES

Miscellaneous offences

8–18292 397. Misleading statements and practices. (1) This subsection applies to a person who—

(*a*) makes a statement, promise or forecast which he knows to be misleading, false or deceptive in a material particular;

(*b*) dishonestly conceals any material facts whether in connection with a statement, promise or forecast made by him or otherwise; or

(*c*) recklessly makes (dishonestly or otherwise) a statement, promise or forecast which is misleading, false or deceptive in a material particular.

(2) A person to whom subsection (1) applies is guilty of an offence if he makes the statement, promise or forecast or conceals the facts for the purpose of inducing, or is reckless as to whether it

may induce, another person (whether or not the person to whom the statement, promise or forecast is made)—

(*a*) to enter or offer to enter into, or to refrain from entering or offering to enter into, a relevant agreement; or

(*b*) to exercise, or refrain from exercising, any rights conferred by a relevant investment.

(3) Any person who does any act or engages in any course of conduct which creates a false or misleading impression as to the market in or the price or value of any relevant investments is guilty of an offence if he does so for the purpose of creating that impression and of thereby inducing another person to acquire, dispose of, subscribe for or underwrite those investments or to refrain from doing so or to exercise, or refrain from exercising, any rights conferred by those investments.

(4) In proceedings for an offence under subsection (2) brought against a person to whom subsection (1) applies as a result of paragraph (*a*) of that subsection, it is a defence for him to show that the statement, promise or forecast was made in conformity with—

(*a*) price stabilising rules;

(*b*) control of information rules;

(*c*) the relevant provisions of Commission Regulation (EC) No 2273/2003 of 22 December 2003 implementing Directive 2003/6/EC of the European Parliament and of the Council as regards exemptions for buy-back programmes and stabilisation of financial instruments.

(5) In proceedings brought against any person for an offence under subsection (3) it is a defence for him to show—

(*a*) that he reasonably believed that his act or conduct would not create an impression that was false or misleading as to the matters mentioned in that subsection;

(*b*) that he acted or engaged in the conduct—

(i) for the purpose of stabilising the price of investments; and

(ii) in conformity with price stabilising rules;

(*c*) that he acted or engaged in the conduct in conformity with control of information rules; or

(*d*) that he acted or engaged in the conduct in conformity with the relevant provisions of Commission Regulation (EC) No 2273/2003 of 22 December 2003 implementing Directive 2003/6/EC of the European Parliament and of the Council as regards exemptions for buy-back programmes and stabilisation of financial instruments.

(6) Subsections (1) and (2) do not apply unless—

(*a*) the statement, promise or forecast is made in or from, or the facts are concealed in or from, the United Kingdom or arrangements are made in or from the United Kingdom for the statement, promise or forecast to be made or the facts to be concealed;

(*b*) the person on whom the inducement is intended to or may have effect is in the United Kingdom; or

(*c*) the agreement is or would be entered into or the rights are or would be exercised in the United Kingdom.

(7) Subsection (3) does not apply unless—

(*a*) the act is done, or the course of conduct is engaged in, in the United Kingdom; or

(*b*) the false or misleading impression is created there.

(8) A person guilty of an offence under this section is liable[2]—

(*a*) on summary conviction, to imprisonment for a term not exceeding six months or a fine not exceeding the statutory maximum, or both;

(*b*) on conviction on indictment, to imprisonment for a term not exceeding seven years or a fine, or both.

(9) "Relevant agreement" means an agreement—

(*a*) the entering into or performance of which by either party constitutes an activity of a specified kind or one which falls within a specified class of activity; and

(*b*) which relates to a relevant investment.

(10) "Relevant investment" means an investment of a specified kind or one which falls within a prescribed class of investment.

(11) Schedule 2 (except paragraphs 25 and 26) applies for the purposes of subsections (9) and (10) with references to section 22 being read as references to each of those subsections.

(12) Nothing in Schedule 2, as applied by subsection (11), limits the power conferred by subsection (9) or (10).

(13) "Investment" includes any asset, right or interest.

(14) "Specified" means specified in an order[3] made by the Treasury.

[Financial Services and Markets Act 2000, s 397 as amended by SI 2005/381.]

---

1. Part XXVII comprises ss 397–403.

2. For procedure in respect of this offence which is triable either way, see the Magistrates' Courts Act 1980, ss 17A–21, in PART I: MAGISTRATES' COURTS, PROCEDURE, ante.

3. The Financial Services and Markets Act 2000 (Misleading Statements and Practices) Order 2001, SI 2001/3544 amended by SI 2001/3624, SI 2002/1777 and SI 2003/1474 has been made.

8–18292A 398. Misleading the Authority: residual cases. (1) A person who, in purported compliance with any requirement imposed by or under this Act, knowingly or recklessly gives the Authority information which is false or misleading in a material particular is guilty of an offence.

(2) Subsection (1) applies only to a requirement in relation to which no other provision of this Act creates an offence in connection with the giving of information.

(3) A person guilty of an offence under this section is liable[1]—

(*a*) on summary conviction, to a fine not exceeding the statutory maximum;
(*b*) on conviction on indictment, to a fine.

[Financial Services and Markets Act 2000, s 398.]

1. For procedure in respect of this offence which is triable either way, see the Magistrates' Courts Act 1980, ss 17A–21, in PART I: MAGISTRATES' COURTS, PROCEDURE, ante.

8–18292B 399. Misleading the Director General of Fair Trading. Section 44 of the Competition Act 1998 (offences connected with the provision of false or misleading information) applies in relation to any function of the Director General of Fair Trading under this Act as if it were a function under Part I of that Act.
[Financial Services and Markets Act 2000, s 399.]

Bodies corporate and partnerships

8–18292C 400. Offences by bodies corporate etc. (1) If an offence under this Act committed by a body corporate is shown—

(*a*) to have been committed with the consent or connivance of an officer, or
(*b*) to be attributable to any neglect on his part,

the officer as well as the body corporate is guilty of the offence and liable to be proceeded against and punished accordingly.

(2) If the affairs of a body corporate are managed by its members, subsection (1) applies in relation to the acts and defaults of a member in connection with his functions of management as if he were a director of the body.

(3) If an offence under this Act committed by a partnership is shown—

(*a*) to have been committed with the consent or connivance of a partner, or
(*b*) to be attributable to any neglect on his part,

the partner as well as the partnership is guilty of the offence and liable to be proceeded against and punished accordingly.

(4) In subsection (3) "partner" includes a person purporting to act as a partner.

(5) "Officer", in relation to a body corporate, means—

(*a*) a director, member of the committee of management, chief executive, manager, secretary or other similar officer of the body, or a person purporting to act in any such capacity; and
(*b*) an individual who is a controller of the body.

(6) If an offence under this Act committed by an unincorporated association (other than a partnership) is shown—

(*a*) to have been committed with the consent or connivance of an officer of the association or a member of its governing body, or
(*b*) to be attributable to any neglect on the part of such an officer or member,

that officer or member as well as the association is guilty of the offence and liable to be proceeded against and punished accordingly.

(7) Regulations may provide for the application of any provision of this section, with such modifications as the Treasury consider appropriate, to a body corporate or unincorporated association formed or recognised under the law of a territory outside the United Kingdom.
[Financial Services and Markets Act 2000, s 400.]

Institution of proceedings

8–18292D 401. Proceedings for offences. (1) In this section "offence" means an offence under this Act or subordinate legislation made under this Act.

(2) Proceedings for an offence may be instituted in England and Wales only—

(*a*) by the Authority or the Secretary of State; or
(*b*) by or with the consent of the Director of Public Prosecutions.

(3) Proceedings for an offence may be instituted in Northern Ireland only—

(*a*) by the Authority or the Secretary of State; or
(*b*) by or with the consent of the Director of Public Prosecutions for Northern Ireland.

(4) Except in Scotland, proceedings for an offence under section 203 may also be instituted by the Director General of Fair Trading.

(5) In exercising its power to institute proceedings for an offence, the Authority must comply with any conditions or restrictions imposed in writing by the Treasury.

(6) Conditions or restrictions may be imposed under subsection (5) in relation to—

(*a*) proceedings generally; or

(*b*) such proceedings, or categories of proceedings, as the Treasury may direct.

[Financial Services and Markets Act 2000, s 401.]

8–18292E 402. Power of the Authority to institute proceedings for certain other offences. (1) Except in Scotland, the Authority may institute proceedings for an offence under—

(*a*) Part V of the Criminal Justice Act 1993 (insider dealing); or

(*b*) prescribed regulations[1] relating to money laundering.

(2) In exercising its power to institute proceedings for any such offence, the Authority must comply with any conditions or restrictions imposed in writing by the Treasury.

(3) Conditions or restrictions may be imposed under subsection (2) in relation to—

(*a*) proceedings generally; or

(*b*) such proceedings, or categories of proceedings, as the Treasury may direct.

[Financial Services and Markets Act 2000, s 402.]

1. See the Money Laundering Regulations 2003, in this title, post.

8–18292F 403. Jurisdiction and procedure in respect of offences. (1) A fine imposed on an unincorporated association on its conviction of an offence is to be paid out of the funds of the association.

(2) Proceedings for an offence alleged to have been committed by an unincorporated association must be brought in the name of the association (and not in that of any of its members).

(3) Rules of court relating to the service of documents are to have effect as if the association were a body corporate.

(4) In proceedings for an offence brought against an unincorporated association—

(*a*) section 33 of the Criminal Justice Act 1925 and Schedule 3 to the Magistrates' Courts Act 1980 (procedure) apply as they do in relation to a body corporate;

(*b*) section 70 of the Criminal Procedure (Scotland) Act 1995 (procedure) applies as if the association were a body corporate;

(*c*) section 18 of the Criminal Justice (Northern Ireland) Act 1945 and Schedule 4 to the Magistrates' Courts (Northern Ireland) Order 1981 (procedure) apply as they do in relation to a body corporate.

(5) Summary proceedings for an offence may be taken—

(*a*) against a body corporate or unincorporated association at any place at which it has a place of business;

(*b*) against an individual at any place where he is for the time being.

(6) Subsection (5) does not affect any jurisdiction exercisable apart from this section.

(7) "Offence" means an offence under this Act.

[Financial Services and Markets Act 2000, s 403.]

Part XXIX[1]
Interpretation

8–18292G 417. Definitions. (1) In this Act—

"appointed representative" has the meaning given in section 39(2);

"auditors and actuaries rules" means rules made under section 340;

"authorisation offence" has the meaning given in section 23(2);

"authorised open-ended investment company" has the meaning given in section 237(3);

"authorised person" has the meaning given in section 31(2);

"the Authority" means the Financial Services Authority;

"body corporate" includes a body corporate constituted under the law of a country or territory outside the United Kingdom;

"chief executive"—

(*a*) in relation to a body corporate whose principal place of business is within the United Kingdom, means an employee of that body who, alone or jointly with one or more others, is responsible under the immediate authority of the directors, for the conduct of the whole of the business of that body; and

(*b*) in relation to a body corporate whose principal place of business is outside the United Kingdom, means the person who, alone or jointly with one or more others, is responsible for the conduct of its business within the United Kingdom;

"collective investment scheme" has the meaning given in section 235;
"the Commission" means the European Commission (except in provisions relating to the Competition Commission);
"the compensation scheme" has the meaning given in section 213(2);
"control of information rules" has the meaning given in section 147(1);
"director", in relation to a body corporate, includes—

(*a*) a person occupying in relation to it the position of a director (by whatever name called); and

(*b*) a person in accordance with whose directions or instructions (not being advice given in a professional capacity) the directors of that body are accustomed to act;

"documents" includes information recorded in any form and, in relation to information recorded otherwise than in legible form, references to its production include references to producing a copy of the information in legible form, or in a form from which it can be readily produced in visible and legible form;
"electronic commerce directive" means Directive 2000/31/EC of the European Parliament and the Council of 8 June 2000 on certain legal aspects of information society services, in particular electronic commerce, in the Internal Market (Directive on electronic commerce);
"exempt person", in relation to a regulated activity, means a person who is exempt from the general prohibition in relation to that activity as a result of an exemption order made under section 38(1) or as a result of section 39(1) or 285(2) or (3);
"financial promotion rules" means rules made under section 145;
"friendly society" means an incorporated or registered friendly society;
"general prohibition" has the meaning given in section 19(2);
"general rules" has the meaning given in section 138(2);
"incorporated friendly society" means a society incorporated under the Friendly Societies Act 1992;
"industrial and provident society" means a society registered or deemed to be registered under the Industrial and Provident Societies Act 1965 or the Industrial and Provident Societies Act (Northern Ireland) 1969;
"information society service" means an information society service within the meaning of Article 2(*a*) of the electronic commerce directive;
"market abuse" has the meaning given in section 118;
"Minister of the Crown" has the same meaning as in the Ministers of the Crown Act 1975;
"money laundering rules" means rules made under section 146;
"notice of control" has the meaning given in section 178(5);
"the ombudsman scheme" has the meaning given in section 225(3);
"open-ended investment company" has the meaning given in section 236;
"Part IV permission" has the meaning given in section 40(4);
"partnership" includes a partnership constituted under the law of a country or territory outside the United Kingdom;
"prescribed" (where not otherwise defined) means prescribed in regulations made by the Treasury;
"price stabilising rules" means rules made under section 144;
"private company" has the meaning given in section 1(3) of the Companies Act 1985 or in Article 12(3) of the Companies (Northern Ireland) Order 1986;
"prohibition order" has the meaning given in section 56(2);
"recognised clearing house" and "recognised investment exchange" have the meaning given in section 285;
"registered friendly society" means a society which is—

(*a*) a friendly society within the meaning of section 7(1)(*a*) of the Friendly Societies Act 1974; and

(*b*) registered within the meaning of that Act;

"regulated activity" has the meaning given in section 22;
"regulating provisions" has the meaning given in section 159(1);
"regulatory objectives" means the objectives mentioned in section 2;
"regulatory provisions" has the meaning given in section 302;
"rule" means a rule made by the Authority under this Act;
"rule-making instrument" has the meaning given in section 153;
"the scheme manager" has the meaning given in section 212(1);
"the scheme operator" has the meaning given in section 225(2);
"scheme particulars rules" has the meaning given in section 248(1);
"Seventh Company Law Directive" means the European Council Seventh Company Law Directive of 13 June 1983 on consolidated accounts (No 83/349/EEC);
"threshold conditions", in relation to a regulated activity, has the meaning given in section 41;
"the Treaty" means the treaty establishing the European Community;
"trust scheme rules" has the meaning given in section 247(1);
"UK authorised person" has the meaning given in section 178(4); and

"unit trust scheme" has the meaning given in section 237.

(2) In the application of this Act to Scotland, references to a matter being actionable at the suit of a person are to be read as references to the matter being actionable at the instance of that person.

(3) For the purposes of any provision of this Act (other than a provision of Part 6) authorising or requiring a person to do anything within a specified number of days no account is to be taken of any day which is a public holiday in any part of the United Kingdom.

(4) For the purposes of this Act—

(*a*) an information society service is provided from an EEA State if it is provided from an establishment in that State;

(*b*) an establishment, in connection with an information society service, is the place at which the provider of the service (being a national of an EEA State or an company or firm as mentioned in Article 48 of the Treaty) effectively pursues an economic activity for an indefinite period;

(*c*) the presence or use in a particular place of equipment or other technical means of providing an information society service does not, of itself, constitute that place as an establishment of the kind mentioned in paragraph (*b*);

(*d*) where it cannot be determined from which of a number of establishments a given information society service is provided, that service is to be regarded as provided from the establishment where the provider has the centre of his activities relating to the service.

[Financial Services and Markets Act 2000, s 417 as amended by SI 2002/1775, the Criminal Justice and Police Act 2001, Sch 2 and SI 2005/1433.]

1. Part XXIX comprises ss 417 to 425.

8–18292H 418. Carrying on regulated activities in the United Kingdom. (1) In the five cases described in this section, a person who—

(*a*) is carrying on a regulated activity, but

(*b*) would not otherwise be regarded as carrying it on in the United Kingdom,

is, for the purposes of this Act, to be regarded as carrying it on in the United Kingdom.

(2) The first case is where—

(*a*) his registered office (or if he does not have a registered office his head office) is in the United Kingdom;

(*b*) he is entitled to exercise rights under a single market directive as a UK firm; and

(*c*) he is carrying on in another EEA State a regulated activity to which that directive applies.

(3) The second case is where—

(*a*) his registered office (or if he does not have a registered office his head office) is in the United Kingdom;

(*b*) he is the manager of a scheme which is entitled to enjoy the rights conferred by an instrument which is a relevant Community instrument for the purposes of section 264; and

(*c*) persons in another EEA State are invited to become participants in the scheme.

(4) The third case is where—

(*a*) his registered office (or if he does not have a registered office his head office) is in the United Kingdom;

(*b*) the day-to-day management of the carrying on of the regulated activity is the responsibility of—

(i) his registered office (or head office); or

(ii) another establishment maintained by him in the United Kingdom.

(5) The fourth case is where—

(*a*) his head office is not in the United Kingdom; but

(*b*) the activity is carried on from an establishment maintained by him in the United Kingdom.

(5A) The fifth case is any other case where the activity—

(*a*) consists of the provision of an information society service to a person or persons in one or more EEA States; and

(*b*) is carried on from an establishment in the United Kingdom.

(6) For the purposes of subsections (2) to (5A) it is irrelevant where the person with whom the activity is carried on is situated.

[Financial Services and Markets Act 2000, s 418 as amended by SI 2002/1775.]

8–18292I 419. Carrying on regulated activities by way of business. (1) The Treasury may by order[1] make provision—

(*a*) as to the circumstances in which a person who would otherwise not be regarded as carrying on a regulated activity by way of business is to be regarded as doing so;

(*b*) as to the circumstances in which a person who would otherwise be regarded as carrying on a regulated activity by way of business is to be regarded as not doing so.

(2) An order under subsection (1) may be made so as to apply—

(*a*) generally in relation to all regulated activities;
(*b*) in relation to a specified category of regulated activity; or
(*c*) in relation to a particular regulated activity.

(3) An order under subsection (1) may be made so as to apply—

(*a*) for the purposes of all provisions;
(*b*) for a specified group of provisions; or
(*c*) for a specified provision.

(4) "Provision" means a provision of, or made under, this Act.
(5) Nothing in this section is to be read as affecting the provisions of section 428(3).
[Financial Services and Markets Act 2000, s 419.]

1. The Financial Services and Markets Act 2000 (Carrying on Regulated Activities by Way of Business) Order 2001, SI 2001/1177 amended by SI 2005/922 has been made.

8–18292J 420. Parent and subsidiary undertaking. (1) In this Act, except in relation to an incorporated friendly society, "parent undertaking" and "subsidiary undertaking" have the same meaning as in Part VII of the Companies Act 1985 (or Part VIII of the Companies (Northern Ireland) Order 1986).

(2) But—

(*a*) "parent undertaking" also includes an individual who would be a parent undertaking for the purposes of those provisions if he were taken to be an undertaking (and "subsidiary undertaking" is to be read accordingly);
(*b*) "subsidiary undertaking" also includes, in relation to a body incorporated in or formed under the law of an EEA State other than the United Kingdom, an undertaking which is a subsidiary undertaking within the meaning of any rule of law in force in that State for purposes connected with implementation of the Seventh Company Law Directive (and "parent undertaking" is to be read accordingly).

(3) In this Act "subsidiary undertaking", in relation to an incorporated friendly society, means a body corporate of which the society has control within the meaning of section 13(9)(*a*) or (*aa*) of the Friendly Societies Act 1992 (and "parent undertaking" is to be read accordingly).
[Financial Services and Markets Act 2000, s 420.]

8–18292K 421. Group. (1) In this Act "group", in relation to a person ("A"), means A and any person who is—

(*a*) a parent undertaking of A;
(*b*) a subsidiary undertaking of A;
(*c*) a subsidiary undertaking of a parent undertaking of A;
(*d*) a parent undertaking of a subsidiary undertaking of A;
(*e*) an undertaking in which A or an undertaking mentioned in paragraph (*a*), (*b*), (*c*) or (*d*) has a participating interest;
(*f*) if A or an undertaking mentioned in paragraph (*a*) or (*d*) is a building society, an associated undertaking of the society; or
(*g*) if A or an undertaking mentioned in paragraph (*a*) or (*d*) is an incorporated friendly society, a body corporate of which the society has joint control (within the meaning of section 13(9)(*c*) or (*cc*) of the Friendly Societies Act 1992).

(2) "Participating interest" has the same meaning as in Part VII of the Companies Act 1985 or Part VIII of the Companies (Northern Ireland) Order 1986; but also includes an interest held by an individual which would be a participating interest for the purposes of those provisions if he were taken to be an undertaking.

(3) "Associated undertaking" has the meaning given in section 119(1) of the Building Societies Act 1986.
[Financial Services and Markets Act 2000, s 421.]

8–18292L 422. Controller. (1) In this Act "controller", in relation to an undertaking ("A"), means a person who falls within any of the cases in subsection (2).

(2) The cases are where the person—

(*a*) holds 10% or more of the shares in A;
(*b*) is able to exercise significant influence over the management of A by virtue of his shareholding in A;
(*c*) holds 10% or more of the shares in a parent undertaking ("P") of A;
(*d*) is able to exercise significant influence over the management of P by virtue of his shareholding in P;
(*e*) is entitled to exercise, or control the exercise of, 10% or more of the voting power in A;

(*f*) is able to exercise significant influence over the management of A by virtue of his voting power in A;
(*g*) is entitled to exercise, or control the exercise of, 10% or more of the voting power in P; or
(*h*) is able to exercise significant influence over the management of P by virtue of his voting power in P.

(3) In subsection (2) "the person" means—

(*a*) the person;
(*b*) any of the person's associates; or
(*c*) the person and any of his associates.

(4) "Associate", in relation to a person ("H") holding shares in an undertaking ("C") or entitled to exercise or control the exercise of voting power in relation to another undertaking ("D"), means—

(*a*) the spouse or civil partner of H;
(*b*) a child or stepchild of H (if under 18);
(*c*) the trustee of any settlement under which H has a life interest in possession (or in Scotland a life interest);
(*d*) an undertaking of which H is a director;
(*e*) a person who is an employee or partner of H;
(*f*) if H is an undertaking—

(i) a director of H;
(ii) a subsidiary undertaking of H;
(iii) a director or employee of such a subsidiary undertaking; and

(*g*) if H has with any other person an agreement or arrangement with respect to the acquisition, holding or disposal of shares or other interests in C or D or under which they undertake to act together in exercising their voting power in relation to C or D, that other person.

(5) "Settlement", in subsection (4)(*c*), includes any disposition or arrangement under which property is held on trust (or subject to a comparable obligation).

(6) "Shares"—

(*a*) in relation to an undertaking with a share capital, means allotted shares;
(*b*) in relation to an undertaking with capital but no share capital, means rights to share in the capital of the undertaking;
(*c*) in relation to an undertaking without capital, means interests—

(i) conferring any right to share in the profits, or liability to contribute to the losses, of the undertaking; or
(ii) giving rise to an obligation to contribute to the debts or expenses of the undertaking in the event of a winding up.

(7) "Voting power", in relation to an undertaking which does not have general meetings at which matters are decided by the exercise of voting rights, means the right under the constitution of the undertaking to direct the overall policy of the undertaking or alter the terms of its constitution.
[Financial Services and Markets Act 2000, s 422.]

***Words "civil partner" inserted by the Civil Partnership Act 2004, Sch 27 from a date to be appointed.**

8–18292M 423. Manager. (1) In this Act, except in relation to a unit trust scheme or a registered friendly society, "manager" means an employee who—

(*a*) under the immediate authority of his employer is responsible, either alone or jointly with one or more other persons, for the conduct of his employer's business; or
(*b*) under the immediate authority of his employer or of a person who is a manager by virtue of paragraph (*a*) exercises managerial functions or is responsible for maintaining accounts or other records of his employer.

(2) If the employer is not an individual, references in subsection (1) to the authority of the employer are references to the authority—

(*a*) in the case of a body corporate, of the directors;
(*b*) in the case of a partnership, of the partners; and
(*c*) in the case of an unincorporated association, of its officers or the members of its governing body.

(3) "Manager", in relation to a body corporate, means a person (other than an employee of the body) who is appointed by the body to manage any part of its business and includes an employee of the body corporate (other than the chief executive) who, under the immediate authority of a director or chief executive of the body corporate, exercises managerial functions or is responsible for maintaining accounts or other records of the body corporate.
[Financial Services and Markets Act 2000, s 423.]

8–18292N 424. Insurance. (1) In this Act, references to—

(*a*) contracts of insurance,
(*b*) reinsurance,
(*c*) contracts of long-term insurance,
(*d*) contracts of general insurance,

are to be read with section 22 and Schedule 2.

(2) In this Act "policy" and "policyholder", in relation to a contract of insurance, have such meaning as the Treasury may by order[1] specify.

(3) The law applicable to a contract of insurance, the effecting of which constitutes the carrying on of a regulated activity, is to be determined, if it is of a prescribed description, in accordance with regulations[2] made by the Treasury.
[Financial Services and Markets Act 2000, s 424.]

1. The Financial Services and Markets Act 2000 (Meaning of 'Policy' and 'Policyholder') Order 2001, SI 2001/2361 has been made.
2. The Financial Services and Markets Act 2000 (Law Applicable to Contracts of Insurance) Regulations 2001, SI 2001/2635 amended by SI 2001/3542 have been made.

8–18292O 425. Expressions relating to authorisation elsewhere in the single market. (1) In this Act—

(*a*) "banking consolidation directive", "life assurance consolidation dirctive", "EEA authorisation", "EEA firm", "EEA right", "EEA State", "first non-life insurance directive", "insurance directives", "insurance mediation directive", "investment services directive", "single market directives" and "UCITS directive" have the meaning given in Schedule 3; and
(*b*) "home state regulator", in relation to an EEA firm, has the meaning given in Schedule 3.

(2) In this Act—

(*a*) "home state authorisation" has the meaning given in Schedule 4;
(*b*) "Treaty firm" has the meaning given in Schedule 4; and
(*c*) "home state regulator", in relation to a Treaty firm, has the meaning given in Schedule 4.

[Financial Services and Markets Act 2000, s 425, as amended by SI 2003/2066 and SI 2004/3379.]

PART XXX[1]
SUPPLEMENTAL

8–18292P 431. Commencement. (1) The following provisions come into force on the passing of this Act—

(*a*) this section;
(*b*) sections 428, 430 and 433;
(*c*) paragraphs 1 and 2 of Schedule 21.

(2) The other provisions of this Act come into force on such day as the Treasury may by order[2] appoint; and different days may be appointed for different purposes.
[Financial Services and Markets Act 2000, s 431.]

1. Part XXX comprises ss 426–433.
2. At the date of going to press, no order had been made.

8–18292Q 432. Minor and consequential amendments, transitional provisions and repeals. (1) Schedule 20 makes minor and consequential amendments.

(2) Schedule 21 makes transitional provisions.

(3) The enactments set out in Schedule 22 are repealed.
[Financial Services and Markets Act 2000, s 432.]

8–18292R 433. Short title. This Act may be cited as the Financial Services and Markets Act 2000.
[Financial Services and Markets Act 2000, s 433.]

Vehicles (Crime) Act 2001[1]

(2001 c 3)

PART 1
REGULATION OF MOTOR SALVAGE OPERATORS

Registration

8–18293 1. Requirement of registration for motor salvage operators. (1) Any person who carries on business as a motor salvage operator in the area of a local authority without being registered for that area by the authority shall be guilty of an offence and liable on summary conviction to a fine not exceeding level 5 on the standard scale.

(2) For the purposes of this Part a person carries on business as a motor salvage operator if he carries on a business which consists—

(*a*) wholly or partly in the recovery for re-use or sale of salvageable parts from motor vehicles and the subsequent sale or other disposal for scrap of the remainder of the vehicles concerned;

(*b*) wholly or mainly in the purchase of written-off vehicles and their subsequent repair and re-sale;

(*c*) wholly or mainly in the sale or purchase of motor vehicles which are to be the subject (whether immediately or on a subsequent re-sale) of any of the activities mentioned in paragraphs (*a*) and (*b*); or

(*d*) wholly or mainly in activities falling within paragraphs (*b*) and (*c*).

(3) In this Part "registered" means registered in accordance with the provisions of this Part in a register established and maintained by a local authority under section 2; and cognate expressions shall be construed accordingly.

[Vehicles (Crime) Act 2001, s 1.]

---

1. Sections 39–42, 44–46 came into force on 10 April 2001. The remaining provisions of the Act are to be brought into force in accordance with commencement orders made under s 44. At the date of going to press the following have been made: Commencement (No 1) Order 2001, SI 2001/3215 which brought into force s 37 as from 1 October 2001.

Vehicles (Crime) Act 2001 ((No 2) Order 2001, SI 2001/4059;
Vehicles (Crime) Act 2001 ((No 3) Order 2002, SI 2002/1914;
Vehicles (Crime) Act 2001 ((No 4) Order 2002, SI 2002/2377;
Vehicles (Crime) Act 2001 ((No 5) Order 2002, SI 2002/2957.

All the provisions reproduced in this work, except s 36, are in force.

8–18294 2–5. *Registers of motor salvage operators*[1]; *applications for, renewals and cancellations of registration and the right to make representations.Registers of motor salvage operators.*

---

1. Applications must be made in accordance with requirements prescribed in the Motor Salvage Operators Regulations 2002, SI 2002/1916.

The local authority must satisfy itself that the applicant is a fit and proper person to carry on business as a motor salvage operator. In deciding whether it is so satisfied the local authority must have particular regard to whether the applicant has been convicted of any offences of a description specified by the Secretary of State, see the Motor Salvage Operators (Specified Offences) Order 2002, SI 2002/1917.

8–18295 6. Appeals. (1) An appeal against—

(*a*) a refusal by a local authority to register in the register for their area a person who has made an application under section 3(1);

(*b*) a refusal by a local authority to renew the registration in the register for their area of a person who has made an application under section 3(1); or

(*c*) the cancellation by a local authority of a person's registration in the register for their area;

may be brought to a magistrates' court.

(2) An appeal under this section shall be brought within the period of 21 days beginning with the day on which the person concerned is served with a notice under section 5(7).

(3) The procedure on an appeal under this section shall be by way of complaint for an order and in accordance with the Magistrates' Courts Act 1980 (c 43)[1].

(4) For the purposes of the time limit for bringing an appeal under this section the making of the complaint shall be treated as the bringing of the appeal.

(5) On an appeal under this section, the magistrates' court concerned may confirm, vary or reverse the local authority's decision and generally give such directions as it considers appropriate having regard to the provisions of this Part.

(6) It shall be the duty of the local authority to comply with any directions given by a magistrates' court under subsection (5); but the authority need not comply with any directions given by the court—

(*a*) until the time for making an application under section 111 of the Magistrates' Courts Act 1980 (application by way of case stated) has passed; or

(*b*) if such an application is made, until the final determination or withdrawal of the application.

[Vehicles (Crime) Act 2001, s 6.]

---

1. In PART I: MAGISTRATES' COURTS, PROCEDURE, ante. See also the Magistrates' Courts Rules 1981, r 34 and notes thereto in PART I: MAGISTRATES' COURTS, PROCEDURE, ante.

Keeping of records etc

8–18296 7. Keeping of records. (1) The Secretary of State may by regulations[1] provide for the keeping of records by registered persons.

(2) In subsection (1) "registered" includes formerly registered.

(3) Regulations under this section may specify provisions of the regulations as provisions to which subsection (4) applies.

(4) A person who contravenes any provision to which this subsection applies shall be guilty of an offence and liable on summary conviction to a fine not exceeding level 4 on the standard scale.
[Vehicles (Crime) Act 2001, s 7.]

1. The Motor Salvage Operators Regulations 2002, SI 2002/1916 have been made.

8–18297 **8. Notification of destruction of motor vehicles.** (1) The Secretary of State may by regulations provide for the notification by registered persons of the destruction of motor vehicles.

(2) Regulations under this section may specify provisions of the regulations as provisions to which subsection (3) applies.

(3) A person who contravenes any provision to which this subsection applies shall be guilty of an offence and liable on summary conviction to a fine not exceeding level 3 on the standard scale.
[Vehicles (Crime) Act 2001, s 8.]

Supplementary provisions and offences

8–18298 **9. Rights to enter and inspect premises.** (1) A constable may at any reasonable time enter and inspect premises for the time being entered in the register of a local authority as premises which are—

(*a*) occupied as a motor salvage yard by a person carrying on business as a motor salvage operator; or

(*b*) occupied by a person carrying on business as a motor salvage operator wholly or partly for the purposes of his business so far as it consists of any of the activities mentioned in section 1(2).

(2) A constable may at any reasonable time—

(*a*) require production of, and inspect, any motor vehicles or salvageable parts kept at premises falling within subsection (1); and

(*b*) require production of, inspect and take copies of or extracts from any records which the person carrying on business as a motor salvage operator is required to keep at such premises by virtue of this Part.

(3) Subsection (4) applies where, on an application made by a constable, a justice of the peace is satisfied that admission to premises specified in the application is reasonably required in order to secure compliance with the provisions of this Part, or to ascertain whether those provisions are being complied with.

(4) The justice may issue a warrant authorising a constable to enter and inspect the premises concerned.

(5) A constable—

(*a*) shall not be entitled to use force to enter premises in the exercise of his powers under subsection (1); but

(*b*) may if necessary use reasonable force in the exercise of his powers under a warrant issued under subsection (4).

(6) A constable, in seeking to enter any premises in the exercise of his powers under subsection (1), shall, if required by or on behalf of the owner or occupier or person in charge of the premises, produce evidence of his identity, and of his authority for entering, before doing so.
[Vehicles (Crime) Act 2001, s 9.]

8–18299 **10. Offence of making false statements.** (1) A person who, in making an application to be registered in the register of a local authority or to renew his registration in such a register—

(*a*) makes a statement which he knows to be false in a material particular; or

(*b*) recklessly makes a statement which is false in a material particular;

shall be guilty of an offence and, subject to subsection (2), liable on summary conviction to a fine not exceeding level 3 on the standard scale.

(2) A person who is guilty of an offence under subsection (1) shall be liable on summary conviction to a fine not exceeding level 5 on the standard scale if—

(*a*) any previous application of his to the local authority concerned for registration or renewal of registration was refused under section 3(3); or

(*b*) any previous registration of his in the register of the local authority concerned was cancelled under section 4(1).

[Vehicles (Crime) Act 2001, s 10.]

8–18300 **11. Notification requirements.** (1) A person applying to be registered in the register of a local authority or to renew his registration in such a register shall give notice to the local authority of any changes affecting in a material particular the accuracy of the information which he has provided in connection with his application.

(2) A person who is registered in the register of a local authority shall give notice to the local authority of any changes affecting his entry in the register within 28 days of the changes occurring; and the local authority shall amend the register accordingly.

(3) A person who is registered in the register of a local authority and is not carrying on business as a motor salvage operator in the area of the local authority shall give notice to the local authority concerned of that fact within 28 days of the beginning of the period in which he is not carrying on business in that area while registered.

(4) A person who fails to give notice to a local authority in accordance with subsection (1), (2) or (3) shall be guilty of an offence and liable on summary conviction to a fine not exceeding level 3 on the standard scale.

(5) In proceedings for an offence under subsection (4) it shall be a defence for the accused to show that he took all reasonable steps and exercised all due diligence to avoid committing the offence.
[Vehicles (Crime) Act 2001, s 11.]

8–18301 12. Offence of giving false particulars on sale for salvage. Any person who, on selling a motor vehicle to a person who is in the course of carrying on business as a motor salvage operator so far as it consists of any of the activities mentioned in section 1(2), gives that person a false name or address shall be guilty of an offence and liable on summary conviction to a fine not exceeding level 3 on the standard scale.
[Vehicles (Crime) Act 2001, s 12.]

General

8–18301A 13. *Application of "fit and proper" test to companies etc*

8–18302 14. Proceedings for offences under Part 1. Proceedings for an offence under this Part shall not be instituted except—

(*a*) by a local authority or a constable; or

(*b*) in any other case, with the consent of the Attorney General.

[Vehicles (Crime) Act 2001, s 14.]

8–18303 15. *Power to amend or repeal private or local Acts*

8–18304 16. Interpretation of Part 1. (1) In this Part, unless the context otherwise requires—

"carrying on business as a motor salvage operator" has the meaning given by section 1(2);

"contravene", in relation to any provision of regulations, includes fail to comply with it;

"motor salvage yard" means any premises where any motor vehicles are received or kept in the course of the carrying on of business as a motor salvage operator so far as the business consists of any of the activities mentioned in section 1(2) (excluding any premises where only salvageable parts of motor vehicles are so received or kept);

"motor vehicle" means any vehicle whose function is or was to be used on roads as a mechanically propelled vehicle;

"notice" means notice in writing;

"premises" includes any land or other place (whether or not enclosed);

"prescribed" means prescribed by regulations made by the Secretary of State;

"a register" means a register established and maintained under section 2;

"registered" (and cognate expressions) have the meaning given by section 1(3);

"road" means any highway and any other road to which the public has access; and

"written-off motor vehicle" means a motor vehicle which is in need of substantial repair but in relation to which a decision has been made not to carry out the repairs.

(2) The reference in section 5(5) to representations being made in writing includes a reference to representations being made in a text which—

(*a*) is transmitted by means of an electronic communications network or by other means but while in an electronic form;

(*b*) is received in legible form; and

(*c*) is capable of being used for subsequent reference.

(3) In this Part "local authority" means—

(*a*) in relation to England—

(i) a unitary authority;

(ii) a district council so far as they are not a unitary authority;

(*b*) in relation to Wales, a county council or a county borough council.

(4) In subsection (3) "unitary authority" means—

(*a*) the council of a county so far as they are the council for an area for which there are no district councils;
(*b*) the council of any district comprised in an area for which there is no county council;
(*c*) a London borough council;
(*d*) the Common Council of the City of London in its capacity as a local authority;
(*e*) the Council of the Isles of Scilly.

(5) For the purposes of this Part a person carrying on business as a motor salvage operator shall be treated as carrying on that business in the area of a local authority if, but only if—

(*a*) premises in that area are occupied by him as a motor salvage yard;
(*b*) no premises are occupied by him as a motor salvage yard (whether in that area or elsewhere) but he has his usual place of residence in that area; or
(*c*) no premises are occupied by him as a motor salvage yard (whether in that area or elsewhere) but premises in that area are occupied by him wholly or partly for the purposes of that business so far as it consists of any of the activities mentioned in section 1(2).

(6) Subsection (5) shall have effect, in relation to any person who carries on business as a motor salvage operator in partnership with another person, as if any reference to the occupation of a place (whether as a motor salvage yard or otherwise) by a person were a reference to the occupation of that place for the purposes of the partnership by that person, alone or jointly with a member of the partnership, or by another member of the partnership alone.

(7) References in this Part to offences under this Part include references to anything which is an offence by virtue of section 7(3) and (4) or 8(2) and (3).

(8) References in this Part to an appeal under section 6 being finally determined or withdrawn include references to the final determination or withdrawal of proceedings by way of case stated which relate to a decision by a magistrates' court on an appeal under that section.
[Vehicles (Crime) Act 2001, s 16 as amended by the Communications Act 2003, Sch 17.]

PART 2
REGULATION OF REGISTRATION PLATE SUPPLIERS

Registration

8–18305 17. Requirement of registration for registration plate suppliers. (1) Any person who carries on business as a registration plate supplier in England or Wales without being registered by the Secretary of State shall be guilty of an offence and liable on summary conviction to a fine not exceeding level 5 on the standard scale.

(2) For the purposes of this Part a person carries on business as a registration plate supplier if he—

(*a*) carries on a business which consists wholly or partly in selling registration plates; and
(*b*) is not an exempt person.

(3) The Secretary of State may by regulations[1] provide for—

(*a*) activities of a prescribed description to be treated for the purposes of this Part as not being activities which consist in selling registration plates;
(*b*) persons of a prescribed description to be exempt persons for the purposes of this Part.

(4) In this Part "registered" means registered in accordance with the provisions of this Part in a register established and maintained by the Secretary of State under section 18; and cognate expressions shall be construed accordingly.
[Vehicles (Crime) Act 2001, s 17.]

1. The Vehicles Crime (Registration Plate Suppliers) (England and Wales) Regulations 2002, SI 2002/2977 amended by SI 2005/2981 have been made.

8–18306 18. *Registration of registration plate suppliers*

8–18307 19. Applications for registration. (1)–(2) *Form of application and fees.*

(3) A person who, in making an application for registration—

(*a*) makes a statement which he knows to be false in a material particular; or
(*b*) recklessly makes a statement which is false in a material particular;

shall be guilty of an offence and liable on summary conviction to a fine not exceeding level 3 on the standard scale.

(4) Where an order under section 20(1)(*b*) has effect in relation to a person who has been convicted of an offence under subsection (3), no application for registration shall be made by that person under subsection (1) in contravention of the order.

(5) No application for registration shall be made under subsection (1) by a person while his registration is suspended by an order of a court under section 20(2).

(6) A person who makes an application in contravention of subsection (4) or (5) shall be guilty of an offence and liable on summary conviction to a fine not exceeding level 5 on the standard scale.

(7) The Secretary of State shall, on receiving an application under subsection (1), register the applicant.
[Vehicles (Crime) Act 2001, s 19.]

8–18308 20. Removal or suspension of registration by a court. (1) Where a person is convicted of an offence under section 19(3) the court before which he is convicted may, instead of or in addition to imposing a fine, by order do either or both of the following—

(*a*) provide for the removal of any entry relating to him in the register;
(*b*) prohibit him from making an application for registration under section 19(1) within such period not exceeding five years as may be specified in, or determined under, the order.

(2) Where a registered person is convicted of an offence under this Part (other than an offence under section 19(3)) the court before which he is convicted may, instead of or in addition to imposing a fine, by order suspend his registration for any period of up to five years.

(3) No order under subsection (1) or (2) shall have effect—

(*a*) if no appeal is brought, before the end of the period for bringing an appeal has passed;
(*b*) if an appeal is brought, before the final determination or withdrawal of the appeal.

(4) A court shall give notice to the Secretary of State of the contents of any order which has been made by it under subsection (1) or (2) and which has effect.

(5) The Secretary of State shall amend the register—

(*a*) to give effect to any order of a court under subsection (1)(*a*); or
(*b*) to reflect any suspension effected by an order of a court under subsection (2);

but may not do so until the order concerned has effect.

(6) In this section "appeal" includes an application under section 111 of the Magistrates' Courts Act 1980 (c 43) (application by way of case stated).
[Vehicles (Crime) Act 2001, s 20.]

8–18309 21. Cancellation of registration by the Secretary of State. (1) The Secretary of State may cancel a person's registration if he is satisfied that the person concerned is not carrying on business as a registration plate supplier and has not, while registered, been doing so for at least 28 days.

(2) A cancellation under subsection (1) shall not have effect—

(*a*) if no appeal is brought under section 23, before the end of the period of 21 days mentioned in subsection (2) of that section;
(*b*) if an appeal is brought under that section, before the final determination or withdrawal of the appeal.

(3) This section is subject to section 22.
[Vehicles (Crime) Act 2001, s 21.]

8–18310 22. *Right to make representations: Part 2*

8–18311 23. Appeals: Part 2. (1) An appeal against the cancellation by the Secretary of State under section 21 of a person's registration may be brought to a magistrates' court.

(2) An appeal under this section shall be brought within the period of 21 days beginning with the day on which the person concerned is served with a notice under section 22(7).

(3) The procedure on an appeal under this section shall be by way of complaint for an order and in accordance with the Magistrates' Courts Act 1980 (c 43)[1].

(4) For the purposes of the time limit for bringing an appeal under this section the making of the complaint shall be treated as the bringing of the appeal.

(5) On an appeal under this section, the magistrates' court concerned may confirm, vary or reverse the Secretary of State's decision and generally give such directions as it considers appropriate having regard to the provisions of this Part.

(6) It shall be the duty of the Secretary of State to comply with any directions given by a magistrates' court under subsection (5); but the Secretary of State need not comply with any directions given by the court—

(*a*) until the time for making an application under section 111 of the Magistrates' Courts Act 1980 (c 43) (application by way of case stated) has passed; or
(*b*) if such an application is made, until the final determination or withdrawal of the application.

[Vehicles (Crime) Act 2001, s 23.]

1. In PART I: MAGISTRATES' COURTS, PROCEDURE, ante. See also the Magistrates' Courts Rules 1981, r 34 and notes thereto in PART I: MAGISTRATES' COURTS, PROCEDURE, ante.

Keeping of records etc

8–18312 24–25. *Regulations may provide for the keeping of records and provision of information on sale of registration plates. Contravention of regulations to which s 24(4) or 25(3) applies to be an offence penalty* *fine not exceeding **level 3** subject to a defence that the accused shows that he took all reasonable steps and exercised all due diligence to avoid committing the offence.*

Supplementary provisions and offences

8–18313 26. Rights to enter and inspect premises: Part 2. (1) A constable or an authorised person may at any reasonable time enter and inspect premises for the time being entered in the register as premises which are occupied by a person carrying on business as a registration plate supplier wholly or partly for the purposes of his business so far as it consists in selling registration plates.

(2) A constable or an authorised person may at any reasonable time—

(*a*) require production of, and inspect, any registration plates kept at premises falling within subsection (1); and

(*b*) require production of, inspect and take copies of or extracts from any records which the person carrying on business as a registration plate supplier is required to keep at such premises by virtue of this Part.

(3) Subsection (4) applies where, on an application made by a constable or an authorised person, a justice of the peace is satisfied that admission to premises specified in the application is reasonably required in order to secure compliance with the provisions of this Part, or to ascertain whether those provisions are being complied with.

(4) The justice may issue a warrant authorising a constable or (as the case may be) an authorised person to enter and inspect the premises concerned.

(5) A constable or an authorised person—

(*a*) shall not be entitled to use force to enter premises in the exercise of his powers under subsection (1); but

(*b*) may, if necessary, use reasonable force in the exercise of his powers under a warrant issued under subsection (4).

(6) A constable or an authorised person in seeking to enter any premises in the exercise of his powers under subsection (1), and an authorised person in seeking to enter any premises in the exercise of his powers under a warrant issued under subsection (4), shall, if required by or on behalf of the owner or occupier or person in charge of the premises, produce evidence of his identity, and of his authority for entering, before doing so.

(7) Any person who obstructs an authorised person in the exercise of his powers under subsection (1) or (2) or under a warrant issued under subsection (4) shall be guilty of an offence and liable on summary conviction to a fine not exceeding level 2 on the standard scale.

(8) In this section "an authorised person" means a person authorised for the purposes of this section by a local authority in respect of premises situated in the area of the local authority.
[Vehicles (Crime) Act 2001, s 26.]

8–18314 27. Notification requirements: Part 2. (1) A person applying to be registered in the register shall give notice to the Secretary of State of any changes affecting in a material particular the accuracy of the information which he has provided in connection with his application.

(2) A registered person shall give notice to the Secretary of State of any changes affecting his entry in the register within 28 days of the changes occurring; and the Secretary of State shall amend the register accordingly.

(3) A registered person who is not carrying on business as a registration plate supplier shall give notice to the Secretary of State of that fact within 28 days of the beginning of the period in which he is not carrying on business while registered.

(4) A person who fails to give notice to the Secretary of State in accordance with subsection (1), (2) or (3) shall be guilty of an offence and liable on summary conviction to a fine not exceeding level 3 on the standard scale.

(5) In proceedings for an offence under subsection (4) it shall be a defence for the accused to show that he took all reasonable steps and exercised all due diligence to avoid committing the offence.
[Vehicles (Crime) Act 2001, s 27.]

8–18315 28. Offences relating to counterfeit registration plates. (1) A person who sells a plate or other device which is not a registration plate as a registration plate knowing that it is not a registration plate or being reckless as to whether it is a registration plate shall be guilty of an offence.

(2) A person who—

(*a*) supplies a plate, device or other object to a person who is carrying on a business which consists wholly or partly in activities which are unlawful by virtue of subsection (1); and

(*b*) knows or reasonably suspects that the plate, device or other object will be used for the purposes of that other person's unlawful activities;

shall be guilty of an offence.

(3) A person guilty of an offence under subsection (1) or (2) shall be liable on summary conviction to a fine not exceeding level 4 on the standard scale.
[Vehicles (Crime) Act 2001, s 28.]

8–18316 **29. Offence of supplying plates etc to unregistered persons.** (1) A person who—

(*a*) supplies a plate, device or other object to an unregistered person (other than an exempt person) who is carrying on a business which consists wholly or partly in selling registration plates; and

(*b*) knows or reasonably suspects that the plate, device or other object will be used for the purposes of that other person's business (or part of his business) as a registration plate or as part of a registration plate;

shall be guilty of an offence.

(2) A person guilty of an offence under subsection (1) shall be liable on summary conviction to a fine not exceeding level 5 on the standard scale.
[Vehicles (Crime) Act 2001, s 29.]

General

8–18317 **30. Proceedings for offences under Part 2.** Proceedings for an offence under this Part shall not be instituted except—

(*a*) by a local authority or a constable; or

(*b*) in any other case, with the consent of the Attorney General.

[Vehicles (Crime) Act 2001, s 30.]

8–18318 **31. Interpretation of Part 2.** (1) In this Part, unless the context otherwise requires—

"the 1994 Act" means the Vehicle Excise and Registration Act 1994 (c 22);

"carrying on business as a registration plate supplier" has the meaning given by section 17(2);

"contravene", in relation to any provision of regulations, includes fail to comply with it;

"exempt person" means any person who is an exempt person by virtue of regulations made under section 17(3)(*b*);

"local authority" has the same meaning as in Part 1; "notice" means notice in writing;

"premises" includes any land or other place (whether or not enclosed);

"prescribed" means prescribed by regulations made by the Secretary of State;

"a register" means a register established and maintained under section 18;

"registered" (and cognate expressions) have the meaning given by section 17(4);

"registration mark" has the meaning given by section 23(1) of the 1994 Act; and includes a mark indicating the registered number of a vehicle or trailer and assigned to that vehicle or trailer by virtue of regulations under section 22(2) of that Act;

"registration plate" means a plate or other device which—

(*a*) displays (whether alone or in conjunction with other information) a registration mark;

(*b*) complies with requirements imposed by regulations made under section 27A(1)(*a*) of the 1994 Act; and

(*c*) is designed to be fixed to a vehicle or trailer in accordance with regulations made under section 22(2) or 23(3) of that Act; and

"selling registration plates" is to be construed in accordance with any regulations made under section 17(3)(*a*).

(2) The reference in section 22(5) to representations being made in writing includes a reference to representations being made in a text which—

(*a*) is transmitted by means of an electronic communications network or by other means but while in an electronic form;

(*b*) is received in legible form; and

(*c*) is capable of being used for subsequent reference.

(3) References in this Part to offences under this Part include references to anything which is an offence by virtue of section 24(3) and (4) or 25(2) and (3).

(4) References in this Part to an appeal under section 23 being finally determined or withdrawn include references to the final determination or withdrawal of proceedings by way of case stated which relate to a decision by a magistrates' court on an appeal under that section.
[Vehicles (Crime) Act 2001, s 31 as amended by the Communications Act 2003, Sch 17.]

PART 3

OTHER PROVISIONS RELATING TO VEHICLE CRIME

Information requirements

8–18319 **36. Access to certain motor insurance information.** (1) The Secretary of State may by regulations provide for relevant information which is required to be kept by regulation 10 of the

Motor Vehicles (Third Party Risks) Regulations 1972 (SI 1972/1217) or by any subsequent regulation made under any corresponding power in the Road Traffic Act 1988 (c 52) to be made available to the Police Information Technology Organisation for use by constables.

(2) Regulations under subsection (1) may, in particular—

(*a*) require all such information or such information of a particular description to be made available to the Organisation;

(*b*) determine the purposes for which constables may be given access to the information;

(*c*) determine the circumstances in which any of the information to which they have been given access may be further disclosed by them.

(3) In this section—

"constables" includes—

(*a*) persons employed by a police authority under section 15(1) of the Police Act 1996 who are under the direction and control of the chief officer of police of the police force maintained by that authority,

(*b*) persons employed by a police authority under section 9(1) of the Police (Scotland) Act 1967 who are under the direction and control of the chief constable of the police force maintained for the authority's area, and

(*c*) persons employed by the British Transport Police Authority under section 27(1) of the Railways and Transport Safety Act 2003 who are under the direction and control of the Chief Constable of the British Transport Police Force;

"information" means information held in any form; and

"relevant information" means—

(*a*) information relating to policies of insurance, or securities, in relation to the use of motor vehicles, or information relating to any certificates issued in connection with such policies or securities; or

(*b*) information relating to motor vehicles to which section 143 of the Act of 1988 does not apply or to any certificates or other documents issued in connection with such vehicles.

[Vehicles (Crime) Act 2001, s 36 as amended by the Serious Organised Crime and Police Act 2005, s 123.]

Miscellaneous

8–18320 38. Unified power for Secretary of State to fund speed cameras etc. (1) The Secretary of State may make payments in respect of the whole or any part of the expenditure of a public authority in relation to—

(*a*) the prevention or detection of offences to which subsection (2) applies; or

(*b*) any enforcement action or proceedings in respect of such offences or any alleged such offences.

(2) This subsection applies to offences under—

(*a*) section 16 of the Road Traffic Regulation Act 1984 (c 27) which consist in contraventions of restrictions on the speed of vehicles imposed under section 14 of that Act;

(*b*) subsection (4) of section 17 of that Act which consist in contraventions of restrictions on the speed of vehicles imposed under that section;

(*c*) section 88(7) of that Act (temporary minimum speed limits);

(*d*) section 89(1) of that Act (speeding offences generally);

(*e*) section 36(1) of the Road Traffic Act 1988 (c 52) which consist in the failure to comply with an indication given by a light signal that vehicular traffic is not to proceed.

(3) Payments under this section shall be made to—

(*a*) the public authority in respect of whose expenditure the payments are being made; or

(*b*) any other public authority for payment, in accordance with arrangements agreed with the Secretary of State, to, or on behalf of, the public authority in respect of whose expenditure the payments are being made.

(4) Payments under this section shall be paid at such times, in such manner and subject to such conditions as the Secretary of State may determine.

(5) In this section "public authority" means—

(*a*) any highway authority (within the meaning of the Highways Act 1980 (c 66));

(*b*) any police authority established under section 3 of the Police Act 1996 (c 16), the Metropolitan Police Authority or the Common Council of the City of London in its capacity as a police authority;

(*c*) any responsible authority (within the meaning of section 55 of the Justices of the Peace Act 1997 (c 25)) or the Greater London Magistrates' Courts Authority; and

(*d*) any body or other person not falling within paragraphs (*a*) to (*c*) and so far as exercising functions of a public nature.

[Vehicles (Crime) Act 2001, s 38.]

PART 4
SUPPLEMENTARY

General

8–18321 **39. Offences by bodies corporate.** (1) Where an offence under this Act committed by a body corporate is proved to have been committed with the consent or connivance of, or to be attributable to any neglect on the part of, a director, manager, secretary or other similar officer of the body corporate, he as well as the body corporate commits the offence and shall be liable to be proceeded against and punished accordingly.

(2) Where the affairs of a body corporate are managed by its members, subsection (1) applies in relation to the acts and defaults of a member in connection with his functions of management as if he were a director of the body corporate.

[Vehicles (Crime) Act 2001, s 39.]

8–18322 **40. Service of notices.** (1) Any document required or authorised by virtue of this Act to be served on any person may be served—

(*a*) by delivering it to him or by leaving it at his proper address or by sending it by post to him at that address;

(*b*) if the person is a body corporate other than a limited liability partnership, by serving it in accordance with paragraph (*a*) on the secretary of the body;

(*c*) if the person is a limited liability partnership, by serving it in accordance with paragraph (*a*) on a member of the partnership; or

(*d*) if the person is a partnership, by serving it in accordance with paragraph (*a*) on a partner or a person having the control or management of the partnership business.

(2) For the purposes of this section and section 7 of the Interpretation Act 1978 (c 30) (service of documents by post) in its application to this section, the proper address of any person on whom a document is to be served shall be his last known address, except that—

(*a*) in the case of service on a body corporate (other than a limited liability partnership) or its secretary, it shall be the address of the registered or principal office of the body;

(*b*) in the case of service on a limited liability partnership or a member of the partnership, it shall be the address of the registered or principal office of the partnership;

(*c*) in the case of service on a partnership or a partner or a person having the control or management of a partnership business, it shall be the address of the principal office of the partnership.

(3) For the purposes of subsection (2) the principal office of a company constituted under the law of a country or territory outside the United Kingdom or of a partnership carrying on business outside the United Kingdom is its principal office within the United Kingdom.

(4) Subsection (5) applies if a person to be served under this Act with any document by another has specified to that other an address within the United Kingdom other than his proper address (as determined under subsection (2)) as the one at which he or someone on his behalf will accept documents of the same description as that document.

(5) In relation to that document, that address shall be treated as his proper address for the purposes of this section and section 7 of the Interpretation Act 1978 in its application to this section, instead of that determined under subsection (2).

(6) Any notice in writing or other document required or authorised by virtue of this Act to be served on any person may be served on that person by transmitting the text of the notice or other document to him by means of an electronic communications network or by other means but while in an electronic form provided the text is received by that person in legible form and is capable of being used for subsequent reference.

(7) This section does not apply to any document if rules of court make provision about its service.

(8) In this section references to serving include references to similar expressions (such as giving or sending).

[Vehicles (Crime) Act 2001, s 40 as amended by the Communications Act 2003, Sch 17.]

8–18323 **41.** *Orders and regulations under this Act*

8–18324 **42.** *General financial provision*

8–18325 **43.** *Consequential amendments*

Final

8–18326 **44. Commencement.** Parts 1 to 3 and section 43 and the Schedule shall come into force on such day as the Secretary of State may by order[1] appoint; and different days may be appointed for different purposes or different areas.

[Vehicles (Crime) Act 2001, s 44.]

1. For commencement of this Act see note to the title to this Act, ante.

8–18327 **45.** *Extent*

8–18328 **46.** *Short title*

Private Security Industry Act 2001[1]

(2001 c 12)

The Security Industry Authority

8–18329 **1. The Security Industry Authority.** (1) There shall be a body corporate to be known as the Security Industry Authority (in this Act referred to as "the Authority").

(2) The functions of the Authority shall be—

(*a*) to carry out the functions relating to licensing and approvals that are conferred on it by this Act;

(*b*) to keep under review generally the provision of security industry services and other services involving the activities of security operatives;

(*c*) for the purpose of protecting the public, to monitor the activities and effectiveness of persons carrying on businesses providing any such services as are mentioned in paragraph (*b*);

(*d*) to ensure the carrying out of such inspections as it considers necessary of the activities and businesses of—

(i) persons engaged in licensable conduct; and

(ii) persons registered under section 14 as approved providers of security industry services;

(*e*) to set or approve standards of conduct, training and levels of supervision for adoption by—

(i) those who carry on businesses providing security industry services or other services involving the activities of security operatives; and

(ii) those who are employed for the purposes of such businesses;

(*f*) to make recommendations and proposals for the maintenance and improvement of standards in the provision of security industry services and other services involving the activities of security operatives;

(*g*) to keep under review the operation of this Act.

(3) The Authority may do anything that it considers is calculated to facilitate, or is incidental or conducive to, the carrying out of any of its functions.

(4) Without prejudice to subsection (3), the Authority may, for any purpose connected with the carrying out of its functions—

(*a*) make proposals to the Secretary of State for the modification of any provision contained in or made under this Act; and

(*b*) undertake, or arrange for or support (whether financially or otherwise), the carrying out of research relating to the provision of security industry services and of other services involving the activities of security operatives.

(5) The Authority shall not be regarded—

(*a*) as the servant or agent of the Crown; or

(*b*) as enjoying any status, immunity or privilege of the Crown;

and the property of the Authority shall not be regarded as property of, or property held on behalf of, the Crown.

(6) Schedule 1 (which makes provision about the Authority) shall have effect.

[Private Security Industry Act 2001, s 1.]

1. The Private Security Industry Act 2001 makes provision for the regulation of the private security industry. With the exception of s 26 which came into force on the 11 May 2001, the provisions of this Act are to be brought into force in accordance with orders made under s 26(2). At the date of going to press the following order had been made: (No 1) Order 2002, SI 2002/3125; (No 2) SI 2003/2710; (No 3) SI 2004/1431 (s 3 (2)(a) to (i) in force on 24 May 2004 in the police area of Hampshire; s 3(2)(a) to (i) in force on 1 June 2004 in the police areas of Avon and Somerset; Devon and Cornwall; Dorset; Gloucestershire; Wiltshire; s 3(1) in force on 4 June 2004 in the police area of Hampshire); (No 4) SI 2004/2191 (s 3(1) in force on 13 September 2004 in the police areas of Avon and Somerset; Devon and Cornwall; Dorset; Gloucestershire; Wiltshire; s 3(1) and (2)(a) to (i) in force on 27 September 2004 in the police areas of Dyfed Powys; Gwent; North Wales; South Wales); (No 5) SI 2004/2591 (s 3(1) and (2)(a) to (i) in force on 18 October 2004 in the police areas of Leicestershire; Northamptonshire; Staffordshire; Warwickshire; West Mercia; West Midlands; in force on 15 November 2004 in the police areas of Cheshire; Cumbria; Greater Manchester; Lancashire; Merseyside; (No 6) (s 5 into force on 1 December 2004 in the police areas of Avon and Somerset; Cheshire; Cumbria; Devon and Cornwall; Dorset; Dyfed Powys; Gloucestershire; Greater Manchester; Gwent; Hampshire; Lancashire; Leicestershire; Merseyside; North Wales; South Wales; Staffordshire; Warwickshire; West Mercia; West Midlands; and Wiltshire) (on 13 December 2004 – s 3(1) and (2)(*a*) to (*i*) and s 5 in the police areas of Cleveland; Durham; Humberside; Northumbria; North Yorkshire; South Yorkshire; and West Yorkshire) (on 3 January 2005 s 3(1) and (2)(*a*) to (*i*) and s 5 in the police areas of

Cambridgeshire; Derbyshire; Lincolnshire; Norfolk; Nottinghamshire; and Suffolk); (No 7) SI 2004/3230 (s 5 in force on on 13 December 2004 in the Northamptonshire police area); (No 8) SI 2005/243 amended by SI 2005/362 (28 February 2005, s 3(1) to the extent not already in force; s 3(2)(j); s 3(2)(a) to (i) s 5 in the police areas of Bedfordshire; Essex; Hertfordshire; Kent; Surrey; Sussex; and Thames Valley; 11 April 2005 s 3(2)(a) to (i) and s 5 to the extent not already in force); (No 9) SI 2005/1104 s 6 in force on 3 May 2005). All the provisions reproduced here are in force except ss 15 (part), 17(2)–(4), 18 and 21.

8–18329A 2. *Directions etc by the Secretary of State*

3. *Scotland*

Licence requirement

8–18329B 3. Conduct prohibited without a licence. (1) Subject to the following provisions of this Act, it shall be an offence for a person to engage in any licensable conduct except under and in accordance with a licence.

(2) For the purposes of this Act a person engages in licensable conduct if—

(*a*) he carries out any designated activities for the purposes of, or in connection with, any contract for the supply of services under which—

(i) he,
(ii) a body corporate of which he is a director, or
(iii) a firm of which he is a partner,

is or may be required to secure that any such activities are carried out;

(*b*) in the course of any employment of his by any person he carries out any designated activities for the purposes of, or in connection with, any contract for the supply of services under which his employer is or may be so required;

(*c*) he carries out any designated activities in accordance with directions given to him by or on behalf of a person to whom his services are supplied (whether or not for the carrying out of any such activities) by—

(i) a body corporate of which he is a director,
(ii) a firm of which he is a partner,
(iii) a person by whom he is employed, or
(iv) a person to whom he supplies his services under a contract for the purposes of which, or in connection with which, he is or may be required to work in accordance with the directions of another;

(*d*) he acts—

(i) in the course of any employment of his by any person, or
(ii) in accordance with any directions given as mentioned in paragraph (*c*),

as the manager or supervisor of one or more individuals required in the course of their employment to engage in licensable conduct falling within paragraph (*b*);

(*e*) he acts—

(i) in the course of any employment of his by any person, or
(ii) in accordance with any directions given as mentioned in paragraph (*c*),

as the manager or supervisor of individuals who are required in accordance with any such directions to engage in conduct which would be licensable conduct falling within paragraph (*b*) if they were required to engage in that conduct as the employees of the person to whom their services are supplied;

(*f*) he is the director of any body corporate or the partner of any firm at a time when another of the directors or partners of the body or firm, or any employee of the body or firm, engages in licensable conduct falling within any of paragraphs (*a*) to (*e*);

(*g*) he is the employer of an individual who in the course of any employment of his with that employer carries out any designated activities subject to additional controls;

(*h*) in the course of any employment of his, or for purposes connected with his being a director or partner of a body corporate or firm, he carries out designated activities subject to additional controls;

(*i*) in the course of any employment of his by any person he acts as the manager or supervisor of one or more individuals the duties of whose employment involve the carrying out of any designated activities subject to additional controls; or

(*j*) in circumstances in which it is proposed to impose a charge for the release of immobilised vehicles, he carries out on his own behalf or on behalf of another person any designated activities consisting in activities to which paragraph 3 of Schedule 2 (immobilisation of vehicles) applies.

(3) In this Act "designated activities" means such of the activities of a security operative as are for the time being designated for the purposes of this section by an order[1] made by the Secretary of State;

and an order under this subsection may designate different activities for the purposes of different paragraphs of subsection (2).*

(4) For the purposes of this section a person shall not be treated as acting as the manager or supervisor of an individual by reason only of his giving directions to that individual in a case in which—

(*a*) the directions are given on behalf of a person to whom the individual's services are provided under a contract for services, and

(*b*) the person who under the contract provides the individual's services or another person acting on his behalf, acts as the manager or supervisor of that individual in relation to the activities carried out by him in accordance with those directions.

(5) Schedule 2 (which defines the activities that are to be treated as the activities of a security operative for the purposes of this Act and those which, so far as they are designated, are subject to additional controls) shall have effect.

(6) A person guilty of an offence under this section shall be liable, on summary conviction, to imprisonment for a term not exceeding six months or to a fine not exceeding level 5 on the standard scale, or to both.

[Private Security Industry Act 2001, s 3.]

***New sub-s (3A) inserted in relation to Scotland by the Serious Organised Crime and Police Act 2005, Sch 15 from a date to be appointed.**

1. The Private Security Industry Act 2001 (Designated Activities) (No 3) Order 2005, SI 2005/2251 (revoking previous orders) has been made which designates the activities of door supervisors of licensed premises in those police areas in respect of which s 3(1) has been brought into force; security operatives engaged in the immobilisation of vehicles which covers the wheel clamping of vehicles, also the restriction and removal of vehicles. The No 2 Order 2005, SI 2005/234 which designated the activities of security operatives who engage in the immobilisation, restriction and removal of vehicles was revoked before it came into effect by the Revocation Order 2005, SI 2005/361 in order to permit more time for training and certification.

8–18329C **4. Exemptions from licensing requirement.** (1) If—

(*a*) it appears to the Secretary of State that there are circumstances in which licensable conduct is engaged in only by persons to whom suitable alternative arrangements will apply, and

(*b*) the Secretary of State is satisfied that, as a consequence, it is unnecessary for persons engaging in any such conduct in those circumstances to be required to be licensed under this Act,

then he may by regulations prescribing those circumstances provide that a person shall not be guilty of an offence under section 3 in respect of any conduct engaged in by him in those circumstances.

(2) The provision that may be made by regulations under subsection (1) includes provision that a person is not to be guilty of an offence in respect of any conduct which is engaged in by him in the course of his employment by, or otherwise under the direction of, a person who is certified by the Authority in accordance with the regulations to be a person who the Authority is satisfied will secure that suitable alternative arrangements apply.

(3) In subsections (1) and (2) references to suitable alternative arrangements are references to arrangements that the Secretary of State or, as the case may be, the Authority is satisfied are equivalent, for all practical purposes so far as the protection of the public is concerned, to those applying to persons applying for and granted licences.

(4) A person shall not be guilty of an offence under section 3 in respect of any activities of his as a security operative if—

(*a*) he carries out those activities in his capacity as the director of a body corporate, the partner of any firm or the employee of any person;

(*b*) he has applied to the Authority for the grant of a licence and that application is pending;

(*c*) the licence applied for would authorise him to carry out those activities and is not one he has previously been refused;

(*d*) the body, firm or, as the case may be, the employer is a person who is for the time being registered under section 14 as an approved provider of security industry services; and

(*e*) the Authority has given notice to the body, firm or employer that it has authorised that body, firm or employer to use directors, partners or employees whose applications are pending to carry out activities that consist in or include those activities.

(5) Subsection (4) shall apply in the case of a person who carries out activities under directions given by or on behalf of another person in pursuance of a contract for the supply of the services of the first person as if the first person were an employee of the other one.

[Private Security Industry Act 2001, s 4.]

8–18329D **5. Offence of using unlicensed security operative.** (1) A person is guilty of an offence if—

(*a*) he provides any security industry services to another;

(*b*) those services are provided wholly or partly by means of the activities of an individual as a security operative; and (*c*) that individual's activities in connection with the provision of those services involve his engaging in licensable conduct in respect of which he is not the holder of a licence.

(2) In proceedings against any person for an offence under this section it shall be a defence for that person to show either—

(*a*) that he did not know, and had no reasonable grounds for suspecting, at the time when the activities were carried out, that the individual in question was not the holder of a licence in respect of those activities; or

(*b*) that he took all reasonable steps, in relation to the services in question, for securing that that individual would not engage in any licensable conduct in respect of which he was not the holder of a licence.

(3) A person shall not be guilty of an offence under this section in respect of any services in so far as those services are provided by means of conduct in which a person who is not the holder of a licence is entitled to engage by virtue of section 4.

(4) A person guilty of an offence under this section shall be liable[1]—

(*a*) on summary conviction, to imprisonment for a term not exceeding six months or to a fine not exceeding the statutory maximum, or to both;

(*b*) on conviction on indictment, to imprisonment for a term not exceeding five years or to a fine, or to both.

[Private Security Industry Act 2001, s 5.]

1. For procedure in respect of this offence which is triable either way, see the Magistrates' Courts Act 1980, ss 17A–21, in PART I: MAGISTRATES' COURTS, PROCEDURE, ante.

8–18329E 6. Offence of using unlicensed wheel-clampers. (1) A person who is an occupier of any premises is guilty of an offence if—

(*a*) any individual carries out, in relation to vehicles on those premises, any designated activities consisting in activities to which paragraph 3 of Schedule 2 (immobilisation of vehicles) applies;

(*b*) the carrying out of those activities involves that individual's engaging in licensable conduct in respect of which he is not the holder of a licence; and

(*c*) those activities are carried out with the permission of that occupier or for the purposes of, or in connection with, any contract for the supply of services to him.

(2) In proceedings against any person for an offence under this section it shall be a defence for that person to show either—

(*a*) that he did not know, and had no reasonable grounds for suspecting, at the time when the activities were carried out, that the individual in question was not the holder of a licence in respect of those activities; or

(*b*) that he took all reasonable steps, in relation to the carrying out of those activities, for securing that that individual would not engage in any licensable conduct in respect of which he was not the holder of a licence.

(3) A person shall not be guilty of an offence under this section in respect of the carrying out of activities which are comprised in any conduct of an individual in which he is entitled to engage by virtue of section 4.

(4) A person guilty of an offence under this section shall be liable[1]—

(*a*) on summary conviction, to imprisonment for a term not exceeding six months or to a fine not exceeding the statutory maximum, or to both;

(*b*) on conviction on indictment, to imprisonment for a term not exceeding five years or to a fine, or to both.

[Private Security Industry Act 2001, s 6.]

1. For procedure in respect of this offence which is triable either way, see the Magistrates' Courts Act 1980, ss 17A–21, in PART I: MAGISTRATES' COURTS, PROCEDURE, ante.

Licensing functions of the Authority

8–18329F 7. Licensing criteria. (*Duty of Security Industry Authority to prepare and publish document setting out criteria for granting, revoking or modifying a licence.*)

8–18329G 8. *Licences to engage in licensable conduct*

8–18329H 9. Licence conditions. (1) The power of the Secretary of State to prescribe the conditions on which a licence must be granted and the power of the Authority to impose additional conditions for such a licence shall include power to prescribe[1] or impose—

(*a*) conditions containing requirements as to the training, registration and insurances which the licensee is to undergo, or to maintain, while the licence remains in force;

(*b*) conditions as to the manner in which the licensee is to carry out specified activities of a security operative that he is licensed to carry out;
(*c*) conditions imposing obligations as to the production and display of the licence;
(*d*) conditions imposing obligations as to the information to be provided from time to time by the licensee to the Authority; and
(*e*) such other conditions (whether or not relating to the criteria that would be applied by the Authority in determining whether to grant the licence) as the Secretary of State or the Authority thinks fit.

(2) The conditions that may be prescribed or imposed in relation to any description of licence may include conditions imposing obligations on a licensee by reference to requirements made or directions given by the Authority.

(3) In relation to a licence authorising licensable conduct falling within subsection (2)(*g*) of section 3, the references in subsection (1) of this section to the licensee include references to any of his employees who carry out any designated activities subject to additional controls.

(4) Any person who contravenes the conditions of any licence granted to him shall be guilty of an offence and liable, on summary conviction, to a term of imprisonment not exceeding six months or to a fine not exceeding level 5 on the standard scale, or to both.

(5) In proceedings against any person for an offence under subsection (4) it shall be a defence for that person to show that he exercised all due diligence to avoid a contravention of the conditions of the licence.

[Private Security Industry Act 2001, s 9.]

1. See the Private Security Industry (Licences) Regulations 2004, SI 2004/255 amended by SI 2005/237 and 2118.

8–18329I **10.** *Revocation and modification of licences*

8–18329J **11. Appeals in licensing matters.** (1) Where—

(*a*) an application for a licence is refused,
(*b*) a licence is granted subject to conditions imposed under section 8(6), or
(*c*) a licence is modified or revoked,

the applicant or, as the case may be, the holder of the licence may appeal[1] to the appropriate magistrates' court against the Authority's decision to refuse to grant the licence, to impose those conditions or, as the case may be, to modify or to revoke the licence.*

(2) An appeal under subsection (1) must be brought before the end of the period of twenty-one days beginning with the day on which the decision appealed against was first notified to the appellant by the Authority.

(3) For the purposes of subsection (1) the appropriate magistrates' court is the magistrates' court for the petty sessions area in which is situated, as the case may be—

(*a*) the address for the appellant that has been supplied for the purpose of being recorded (if a licence is granted) in the register maintained under section 12; or
(*b*) the address for the appellant that is for the time being recorded in that register.

(4) Where a magistrates' court makes a decision on an appeal under subsection (1), an appeal to the Crown Court may be brought against that decision either by the Authority or by the person on whose appeal that decision was made.*

(5) A court to which an appeal is brought under this section shall determine the appeal in accordance with the criteria for the time being applicable under section 7.

(6) Where an application for the grant of a licence by way of a renewal is refused or a licence is revoked, the licence to which the application or revocation relates shall be deemed to remain in force—

(*a*) for the period during which an appeal may be brought under subsection (1);
(*b*) for the period from the bringing of any such appeal until it is determined or abandoned;
(*c*) for the period from any determination on appeal that a licence should be granted until effect is given to that determination, or it is overturned on a further appeal;
(*d*) during any such period as the appropriate magistrates' court or the Crown Court may direct, pending an appeal from a determination made on an appeal to that magistrates' court.*

[Private Security Industry Act 2001, s 11.]

***Amended in relation to Scotland by the Serious Organised Crime and Police Act 2005, Sch 15 from a date to be appointed.**

1. For procedure, see the Magistrates' Courts Rules 1981, r 34 (appeal to be by complaint) and ss 51–57 (proceedings on complaint) in PART I: MAGISTRATES' COURTS, PROCEDURE, ante.

8–18329K **12.** *Register of licences*

8–18329L **13. Licensing at local authority level.** (1) The Secretary of State may by order make provision for local authorities to carry out some or all of the Authority's relevant licensing functions in relation to such cases and such areas, and for such purposes, as may be specified or described in the order.

(2) References in this section to the Authority's relevant licensing functions are references to such of its functions under this Act (other than section 7) as relate to the grant, revocation or modification of licences to engage in any such licensable conduct as will or may involve, or relate to, the carrying out of activities to which paragraph 8 of Schedule 2 (door supervisors etc for public houses and clubs and comparable venues) applies.

(3) An order under this section may—

(*a*) impose such conditions and requirements in respect of the carrying out of any of the Authority's relevant licensing functions by a local authority as the Secretary of State thinks fit;

(*b*) provide for any of those conditions or requirements to be framed by reference to directions given by the Secretary of State in accordance with the order;

(*c*) provide for any of the powers exercisable by a local authority by virtue of such an order to be exercisable concurrently in relation to the same case by the Authority and that local authority; and

(*d*) authorise a local authority to retain any fee paid to them by virtue of section 8(7).

(4) Section 11 shall apply in relation to a decision made by a local authority in accordance with an order under subsection (1) as it applies in relation to a decision of the Authority; and where it so applies it shall have effect as if the references in subsections (2) and (4) of that section to the Authority were a reference to the local authority that made the decision in question.

(5) The Secretary of State may by order[1] make such provision repealing or modifying the provisions of any local enactment as he considers appropriate in consequence of the coming into force of any of the provisions of this Act or of an order under subsection (1).

(6) The Secretary of State shall consult the Authority before making an order under this section.

(7) In this section "local authority" means—

(*a*) the council for any county or district in England other than a metropolitan county the districts comprised in which are districts for which there are councils;

(*b*) the council for any London borough;

(*c*) the Common Council of the City of London;

(*d*) the Council of the Isles of Scilly;

(*e*) the council for any county or county borough in Wales.*

[Private Security Industry Act 2001, s 13.]

***New sub-s (8) inserted by the Serious Organised Crime and Police Act 2005, Sch 15 from a date to be appointed.**

1. Various orders have been made which repeal those provisions in local acts relating to activities now regulated by the 2001 Act.

Approved contractors

8–18329M **14.** *Register of approved contractors*

8–18329N **15.** *Arrangements for the grant of approvals*

8–18329O **16. Right to use approved status.** (1) The Authority may approve the terms in which a person who is for the time being registered under section 14 as an approved provider of security industry services may hold himself out as so registered.

(2) A person is guilty of an offence if—

(*a*) he holds himself out as registered under section 14 as an approved provider of any security industry services when he is not so registered; or

(*b*) he is so registered but holds himself out as so registered in terms that have not been approved by the Authority in relation to his case.

(3) A person guilty of an offence under this section shall be liable[1]—

(*a*) on summary conviction, to a fine not exceeding the statutory maximum;

(*b*) on conviction on indictment, to a fine.

(4) For the purposes of this section references in this section to a person's holding himself out as registered as an approved provider of any services include references to his holding himself out to be a person who is for the time being approved in respect of those services in accordance with arrangements under section 15.

[Private Security Industry Act 2001, s 16.]

---

1. For procedure in respect of this offence which is triable either way, see the Magistrates' Courts Act 1980, ss 17A–21, in PART I: MAGISTRATES' COURTS, PROCEDURE, ante.

8–18329P **17. Imposition of requirements for approval.** (1) The Secretary of State may by regulations provide that persons of prescribed descriptions are to be prohibited from providing prescribed security industry services unless they are for the time being approved in respect of those services in accordance with arrangements under section 15.

(2) A person is guilty of an offence if he contravenes any prohibition imposed on him by regulations under subsection (1).

(3) A person who—

(*a*) is approved in respect of any security industry services in accordance with arrangements under section 15, and

(*b*) would be prohibited by regulations under subsection (1) from providing those services except while for the time being so approved,

is guilty of an offence if he contravenes any of the conditions of his approval in respect of those services.

(4) A person guilty of an offence under this section is liable[1]—

(*a*) on summary conviction, to a fine not exceeding the statutory maximum;

(*b*) on conviction on indictment, to a fine.

(5) The Secretary of State may by regulations make provision in relation to cases in which a person is required by regulations under subsection (1) to be approved in respect of any services in accordance with arrangements under section 15—

(*a*) for the conditions that are to be contained in his approval in relation to the handling of complaints made about the provision of those services; and

(*b*) generally in relation to the arrangements under that section that are to be made for such cases.

[Private Security Industry Act 2001, s 17.]

---

1. For procedure in respect of this offence which is triable either way, see the Magistrates' Courts Act 1980, ss 17A–21, in PART I: MAGISTRATES' COURTS, PROCEDURE, ante.

8–18329Q 18. Appeals relating to approvals. (1) Where—

(*a*) an application for an approval for the purposes of section 15 is refused,

(*b*) conditions are included as conditions of such an approval, or

(*c*) such an approval is modified or withdrawn,

the applicant or, as the case may be, the approved person may appeal[1] to the appropriate magistrates' court against the Authority's decision to refuse to grant the approval, to include those conditions or, as the case may be, to modify or to withdraw the approval.*

(2) An appeal under subsection (1) must be brought before the end of the period of twenty-one days beginning with the day on which the decision appealed against was first notified to the appellant by the Authority.

(3) For the purposes of subsection (1) the appropriate magistrates' court is the magistrates' court for the petty sessions area in which is situated, as the case may be—

(*a*) the address for the appellant that has been supplied for the purpose of being recorded (if an approval is granted) in the register maintained under section 14; or

(*b*) the address for the appellant that is for the time being recorded in that register.

(4) Where a magistrates' court makes a decision on an appeal under subsection (1), an appeal to the Crown Court may be brought against that decision either by the Authority or by the person on whose appeal that decision was made.*

(5) Where an application for the grant of an approval by way of a renewal is refused or an approval is withdrawn, the approval to which the application or withdrawal relates shall be deemed to remain in force—

(*a*) for the period during which an appeal may be brought under subsection (1);

(*b*) for the period from the bringing of any such appeal until it is determined or abandoned;

(*c*) for the period from any determination on appeal that an approval should be granted until effect is given to that determination, or it is overturned on a further appeal;

(*d*) during any such period as the appropriate magistrates' court or the Crown Court may direct, pending an appeal from a determination made on an appeal to that magistrates' court.*

[Private Security Industry Act 2001, s 18.]

***Amended in relation to Scotland by the Serious Organised Crime and Police Act 2005, Sch 15 from a date to be appointed.**

1. For procedure, see the Magistrates' Courts Rules 1981, r 34 (appeal to be by complaint) and ss 51–57 (proceedings on complaint) in PART I: MAGISTRATES' COURTS, PROCEDURE, ante

Entry, inspection and information

8–18329R 19. Powers of entry and inspection. (1) Subject to subsections (3) and (4), a person authorised in writing for the purpose by the Authority may enter any premises owned or occupied by any person appearing to him to be a regulated person other than premises occupied exclusively for residential purposes as a private dwelling.

(2) A person authorised in writing for the purpose by the Authority may require any person appearing to him to be a regulated person to produce to him any documents or other information relating to any matter connected with—

(*a*) any licensable conduct which has been or may be engaged in by the person so appearing;
(*b*) the provision by the person so appearing of any security industry services;
(*c*) any matters in respect of which conditions are imposed on the person so appearing by virtue of a licence or of an approval granted in accordance with arrangements under section 15.

(3) A person exercising the power conferred by subsection (1) shall do so only at a reasonable hour.

(4) A person exercising such a power shall—

(*a*) comply with any reasonable request made (whether before or after entry is gained to the premises) by any person present on the premises to do any one or more of the following—
  (i) state the purpose for which the power is being exercised;
  (ii) show the authorisation by the Authority for his exercise of the power;
  (iii) produce evidence of his identity;
(*b*) make a record of the date and time of his entry, the period for which he remained there and his conduct while there; and
(*c*) if requested to do so by any person present on the premises at the time of the entry, provide that person with a copy of that record.

(5) A person is guilty of an offence if—

(*a*) he intentionally obstructs any person in the exercise of any power conferred by subsection (1);
(*b*) he fails, without reasonable excuse, to comply with any requirement imposed by subsection (2); or
(*c*) he makes an unauthorised disclosure of any information obtained by him in the exercise of any power conferred by this section, or as a consequence of the exercise of any such power by another.

(6) For the purposes of this section a disclosure of information obtained by any person as mentioned in subsection (5)(*c*) is authorised if, and only if, it is made—

(*a*) for the purposes of the carrying out by the Authority of any of its functions under this Act; or
(*b*) for the purposes of any criminal proceedings.

(7) A person guilty of an offence under this section shall be liable, on summary conviction, to a term of imprisonment not exceeding six months or to a fine not exceeding level 5 on the standard scale, or to both.

(8) In this section "regulated person" means—

(*a*) the holder of any licence granted under this Act;
(*b*) any person who engages in licensable conduct without being the holder of a licence under this Act;
(*c*) any person who is for the time being approved in accordance with arrangements under section 15 in respect of any services which regulations under section 17 prohibit him from providing unless so approved; or
(*d*) any person who is not so approved but provides security industry services which he is prohibited by any such regulations from providing.

[Private Security Industry Act 2001, s 19.]

8–18329S 20. Guidance as to exercise of power of entry. (1) It shall be the duty of the Authority to prepare and publish a document containing its guidance as to the manner in which persons authorised to enter premises under subsection (1) of section 19 should—

(*a*) exercise the power conferred by that subsection; and
(*b*) conduct themselves after entering premises in exercise of that power.

(2) The Authority may from time to time revise the guidance published under this section; and, if it does so, it shall publish the revised guidance.

(3) A requirement under this section for the Authority to publish guidance or revised guidance shall be a requirement to publish it in such manner as appears to the Authority appropriate for bringing it to the attention of persons likely to be affected by it.

[Private Security Industry Act 2001, s 20.]

8–18329T 21. Access to enhanced criminal records certificates. (*Amends Police Act 1997, s 115*(*5*)).

8–18329U 22. False information. (1) A person is guilty of an offence if for any purposes connected with the carrying out by the Authority of any of its functions under this Act—

(*a*) he makes any statement to the Authority which he knows to be false in a material particular; or

(*b*) he recklessly makes any statement to the Authority which is false in a material particular.

(2) A person guilty of an offence under this section shall be liable, on summary conviction, to imprisonment for a term not exceeding six months or to a fine not exceeding level 5 on the standard scale, or to both.

[Private Security Industry Act 2001, s 22.]

Supplemental

8–18329V 23. Criminal liability of directors etc. Where an offence under any provision of this Act is committed by a body corporate and is proved to have been committed with the consent or connivance of, or to be attributable to any neglect on the part of—

(*a*) a director, manager, secretary or other similar officer of the body corporate, or

(*b*) any person who was purporting to act in any such capacity,

he (as well as the body corporate) shall be guilty of that offence and liable to be proceeded against and punished accordingly.*

[Private Security Industry Act 2001, s 23.]

***Amended in relation to Scotland by the Serious Organised Crime and Police Act 2005, Sch 15 from a date to be appointed.**

8–18329W 24. *Orders and regulations*

8–18329X 25. Interpretation. (1) In this Act—

"activities of a security operative" shall be construed in accordance with Part 1 of Schedule 2;

"activities subject to additional controls" shall be construed in accordance with Part 2 of that Schedule;

"the Authority" means the Security Industry Authority;

"contravention" includes a failure to comply, and cognate expressions shall be construed accordingly;

"designated activities" has the meaning given by section 3(3);

"director"—

(*a*) in relation to a company (within the meaning of the Companies Act 1985 (c 6)), includes a shadow director;

(*b*) in relation to any such company that is a subsidiary of another, includes any director or shadow director of the other company; and

(*c*) in relation to a body corporate whose affairs are managed by its members, means a member of that body corporate;

"information" includes reports, references and other documents, photographs and data of any description;

"licence" means a licence from the Authority under this Act;

"licensable conduct" shall be construed in accordance with section 3(2);

"local statutory provision" means—

(*a*) a provision of any local Act;

(*b*) a provision of any instrument in the nature of a local enactment;

(*c*) a provision of any instrument made under a local statutory provision;

"modification" includes amendments, additions and omissions, and cognate expressions shall be construed accordingly;

"motor vehicle" means a mechanically propelled vehicle or a vehicle designed or adapted for towing by a mechanically propelled vehicle;

"premises" includes any vehicle or moveable structure and any other place whatever, whether or not occupied as land;

"relevant accountancy body" means any of the following—

(*a*) the Institute of Chartered Accountants in England and Wales;

(*b*) the Institute of Chartered Accountants of Scotland;

(*c*) the Institute of Chartered Accountants in Ireland;

(*d*) the Association of Chartered Certified Accountants;

(*e*) the Chartered Institute of Management Accountants;

(*f*) the Chartered Institute of Public Finance and Accountancy;

"security industry services" means services which are provided under a contract for services and in the course of which the person providing the services secures—

(*a*) that the activities of a security operative are carried out; or (*b*) that a person is made available to carry out, under directions given by or on behalf of another person, any activities which will or are likely to consist of or include the activities of a security operative;

"surveillance" includes covertly listening to or recording conversations or other sounds and any method of covertly obtaining information;

"shadow director" means a shadow director as defined in section 741(2) of the Companies Act 1985;

"subsidiary" means a subsidiary as defined in section 736 of the Companies Act 1985 (c 6);

"vehicle" includes any vessel, aircraft or hovercraft.

(2) In this Act references, in relation to a firm, to a member of the firm include references to any person who, in relation to that firm, is liable as a partner under section 14 of the Partnership Act 1890 (c 39) (persons liable by "holding out").

[Private Security Industry Act 2001, s 25.]

8–18329Y **26.** *Short title, commencement and extent*

8–18329Z

Section 3

SCHEDULE 2
ACTIVITIES LIABLE TO CONTROL UNDER THE ACT

(Amended by SI 2005/224.)

PART 1
ACTIVITIES OF SECURITY OPERATIVES

General

1. (1) Subject to sub-paragraph (2), the activities which are referred to in this Act as the activities of a security operative are those to which any one or more of the following paragraphs of this Part of this Schedule applies.

(2) The Secretary of State may by order amend this Part of this Schedule for the purpose of adding or excluding any such activities as he thinks fit to or from those that fall to be regarded for the purposes of this Act as the activities of a security operative.

(3) The Secretary of State shall not make an order containing (with or without any other provision) any provision authorised by sub-paragraph (2) unless a draft of the order has been laid before Parliament and approved by a resolution of each House.

Manned guarding

2. (1) This paragraph applies (subject to the following provisions of this paragraph) to any of the following activities—

(*a*) guarding premises against unauthorised access or occupation, against outbreaks of disorder or against damage;

(*b*) guarding property against destruction or damage, against being stolen or against being otherwise dishonestly taken or obtained;

(*c*) guarding one or more individuals against assault or against injuries that might be suffered in consequence of the unlawful conduct of others.

(2) In this paragraph references to guarding premises against unauthorised access include references to being wholly or partly responsible for determining the suitability for admission to the premises of persons applying for admission.

(3) In this paragraph references to guarding against something happening include references to so providing a physical presence, or carrying out any form of patrol or surveillance, as—

(*a*) to deter or otherwise discourage it from happening; or

(*b*) to provide information, if it happens, about what has happened.

(4) This paragraph does not apply to the activities of an individual who exercises control over the persons allowed access to any premises to the extent only of securing, or checking, that persons allowed access—

(*a*) have paid for admission; or

(*b*) have invitations or passes allowing admission.

(5) This paragraph does not apply to the activities of a person who, incidentally to the carrying out of any activities in relation to a group of individuals which (disregarding this sub-paragraph) are neither—

(*a*) the activities of a security operative, nor

(*b*) activities comprising the exercise of any such control as is mentioned in sub-paragraph (4),

maintains order or discipline amongst those individuals.

(6) This paragraph does not apply to the activities of a person who, incidentally to the carrying out of activities which (disregarding this sub-paragraph) are not wholly or mainly the activities of a security operative, responds to a sudden or unexpected occurrence.

Immobilisation of vehicles

3. (1) This paragraph applies (subject to the following provisions of this paragraph) to the immobilisation of a motor vehicle by the attachment to the vehicle, or to a part of it, of an immobilising device.

(2) This paragraph applies only to activities carried out for the purpose of preventing or inhibiting the removal of a vehicle by a person otherwise entitled to remove it.

(2A) This paragraph applies only in circumstances in which it is proposed to impose a charge for the release of the vehicle.

(3) This paragraph does not apply to any activities carried out in relation to a vehicle while it is on a road within the meaning of the Road Traffic Act 1988 (c 52).*

Restriction and removal of vehicles

3A. (1) This paragraph applies (subject to the following provisions of this paragraph) to—

(*a*) the moving of a vehicle by any means; and
(*b*) the restriction of the movement of a vehicle by any means.

(2) This paragraph applies only to activities carried out for the purpose of preventing or inhibiting the removal of a vehicle by a person otherwise entitled to remove it.

(3) This paragraph applies only in circumstances in which it is proposed to impose a charge for the release of the vehicle.

(4) This paragraph does not apply to any activities carried out in relation to a vehicle while it is on a road within the meaning of the Road Traffic Act 1988.

(5) This paragraph does not apply to restricting the movement of a vehicle by a fixed barrier which was present when that vehicle was parked and which is reasonably understood to be for the purpose of ensuring payment which has been accepted as a condition of parking.

Private investigations

4. (1) This paragraph applies (subject to the following provisions of this paragraph) to any surveillance, inquiries or investigations that are carried out for the purpose of—

(*a*) obtaining information about a particular person or about the activities or whereabouts of a particular person; or
(*b*) obtaining information about the circumstances in which or means by which property has been lost or damaged.

(2) This paragraph does not apply to activities carried out exclusively for the purposes of market research.

(3) This paragraph does not apply to activities carried out exclusively for the purpose of determining whether a particular person is credit-worthy.

(4) This paragraph does not apply to any activities of a person with a general qualification within the meaning of section 71 of the Courts and Legal Services Act 1990 (c 41) which are carried out by him for the purposes of any legal practice carried on—

(*a*) by him;
(*b*) by any firm of which he is a partner or by which he is employed;
(*c*) by any body corporate of which he is a director or member or by which he is employed.*

(5) This paragraph does not apply to any activities of a member of a relevant accountancy body which are carried out by him as such and for the purposes of any accountancy practice carried on—

(*a*) by him;
(*b*) by any firm of which he is a partner or by which he is employed;
(*c*) by any body corporate of which he is a director or member or by which he is employed.

(6) This paragraph does not apply to activities carried out for the purpose of obtaining information exclusively with a view to its use, or the use of information to which it relates, for the purposes of or in connection with the publication to the public or to a section of the public of any journalistic, literary or artistic material or of any work of reference.

(7) This paragraph does not apply to activities carried out exclusively by means of references to one or more of the following—

(*a*) registers or other records that are open (whether or not on the payment of a fee) to public inspection;
(*b*) registers or other records which are kept by the person by whom or on whose behalf the activities are carried out or to which that person has a right of access;
(*c*) published works.

(8) This paragraph does not apply to activities carried out with the knowledge or consent of—

(*a*) the person about whom, or about whose activities or whereabouts, information is sought; or
(*b*) every person whose interest in any property has been affected by the loss or damage about which information is sought.

(9) This paragraph does not apply to the activities of any person who carries out any inquiries or investigation merely incidentally to the carrying out of any activities which (disregarding this sub-paragraph) are not the activities of a security operative.

(10) In this paragraph "market research" includes—

(*a*) discovering whether a person is a potential customer for any goods or services or the extent of his satisfaction with goods or services supplied to him; and
(*b*) obtaining information from any person for the purpose of analysing public opinion on any matter (whether or not relating to the market for any goods or services).*

Security consultants

5. (1) This paragraph applies (subject to the following provisions of this paragraph) to the giving of advice about—

(*a*) the taking of security precautions in relation to any risk to property or to the person; or
(*b*) the acquisition of any services involving the activities of a security operative.

(2) This paragraph does not apply to the giving of legal or financial advice or to the giving of any advice about the conduct of any business involving the provision of any such services as are mentioned in sub-paragraph (1)(*b*).

(3) This paragraph does not apply to any activities of a member of a relevant accountancy body which are carried out by him as such and for the purposes of any accountancy practice carried on—

(*a*) by him;
(*b*) by any firm of which he is a partner or by which he is employed;
(*c*) by any body corporate of which he is a director or member or by which he is employed.

(4) This paragraph does not apply to the provision of training to persons for the purpose of giving them qualifications, knowledge or skill for use in the carrying out of the activities of a security operative for others.

Keyholders

6. (1) This paragraph applies (subject to the following provisions of this paragraph) to keeping custody of, or controlling access to, any key or similar device for operating (whether mechanically, electronically or otherwise) any lock.

(2) This paragraph does not apply to activities carried out merely incidentally to the provision of any services in connection with a proposal for the sale of any premises or other property to which the key or similar device gives access.

(3) This paragraph does not apply to the activities of a person who holds a key or other device for obtaining access to any premises for purposes incidental to the provision in relation to those premises, or in relation to an individual present on those premises, of any services that do not consist in or include the carrying out of any of the activities of a security operative.

(4) In this paragraph "lock" means a lock or similar device (whether operated mechanically, electronically or otherwise) that is designed or adapted—

(*a*) for protecting any premises against unauthorised entry; or
(*b*) for securing any safe or other container specifically designed or adapted to hold valuables.

***Amended and para 4A inserted in relation to Scotland by the Serious Organised Crime and Police Act 2005, Sch 15 from a date to be appointed.**

PART 2
ACTIVITIES SUBJECT TO ADDITIONAL CONTROLS
General

7. (1) Subject to sub-paragraph (2), the activities which are referred to in this Act as activities subject to additional controls are any activities which, so far as they are designated activities, are activities to which any one or more of the following paragraphs of this Part of this Schedule applies.

(2) The Secretary of State may by order amend this Part of this Schedule for the purpose of adding or excluding any such activities as he thinks fit to or from those that fall to be regarded for the purposes of this Act as activities subject to additional controls.

(3) The Secretary of State shall not make an order containing (with or without any other provision) any provision authorised by sub-paragraph (2) unless a draft of the order has been laid before Parliament and approved by a resolution of each House.

Door supervisors etc for public houses, clubs and comparable venues

8. (1) This paragraph applies to any activities which are activities of a security operative by virtue of paragraph 2 of this Schedule and are carried out—

(*a*) in relation to licensed premises; and
(*b*) at or in relation to times when those premises are open to the public.

(2) In this paragraph "licensed premises" means (subject to sub-paragraph (3))—

(*a*) any premises in respect of which a premises licence or temporary event notice has effect under the Licensing Act 2003 to authorise the supply of alcohol (within the meaning of section 14 of that Act) for consumption on the premises;
(*b*) any premises in respect of which a premises licence or temporary event notice has effect under that Act to authorise the provision of regulated entertainment;
(*e*) any premises in respect of which a licence of a prescribed description under any prescribed local statutory provision is for the time being in force.* **

(3) For the purposes of this paragraph, premises are not licensed premises—

(*a*) if there is in force in respect of the premises a premises licence which authorises regulated entertainment within paragraph 2(1)(a) or (b) of Schedule 1 to the Licensing Act 2003 (plays and films);
(*b*) in relation to any occasion on which the premises are being used—

(i) exclusively for the purposes of a club which holds a club premises certificate in respect of the premises, or
(ii) for regulated entertainment of the kind mentioned in paragraph (a), in circumstances where that use is a permitted temporary activity by virtue of Part 5 of that Act;

(*c*) in relation to any occasion on which a licence is in force in respect of the premises under the Gaming Act 1968 (c 65) and the premises are being used wholly or mainly for the purposes of gaming to which Part 2 of that Act applies; or

(*d*) in relation to any such other occasion as may be prescribed for the purposes of this sub-paragraph.

(4) For the purposes of this paragraph the times when premises are open to the public shall be taken to include any time when they are open to a section of the public comprising the individuals who qualify for admission to the premises as the members of a particular club, association or group or otherwise as being persons to whom a particular description applies or in relation to whom particular conditions are satisfied.

(5) References in this paragraph to the occasion on which any premises are being used for a particular purpose include references to any time on that occasion when the premises are about to be used for that purpose, or have just been used for that purpose.

(6) Sub-paragraphs (2)(*a*) and (*b*) and (3)(*a*) and (*b*) are to be construed in accordance with the Licensing Act 2003.

Immobilisation of vehicles

9. This paragraph applies to any activities which are activities of a security operative by virtue of paragraph 3 of this Schedule.

Restriction and removal of vehicles

9A. This paragraph applies to any activities which are activities of a security operative by virtue of paragraph 3A of this Schedule.**

***Sub-paragraph 8(2)(*e*) substituted by the Gambling Act 2005, Sch 16 from a date to be appointed.**
****New sub-paras 8(2)(*f*)–(*l*) and para 10 inserted in relation to Scotland by the Serious Organised Crime and Police Act 2005, Sch 15 from a date to be appointed.**

Money Laundering Regulations 2003[1]

(2003/3075 amended SI 2006/308)

PART I
GENERAL

8–18329ZA 1. Citation, commencement etc. (1) These Regulations may be cited as the Money Laundering Regulations 2003.

(2) These Regulations come into force—

(a) for the purposes of regulation 10 in so far as it relates to a person who acts as a high value dealer, on 1st April 2004;
(b) for the purposes of regulation 2(3)(h), on 31st October 2004;
(c) for the purposes of regulation 2(3)(i), on 14th January 2005;
(d) for all other purposes, on 1st March 2004.

(3) These Regulations are prescribed for the purposes of sections 168(4)(b) and 402(1)(b) of the 2000 Act.

(4) The following Regulations are revoked—

(a) the Money Laundering Regulations 1993;
(b) the Financial Services and Markets Act 2000 (Regulations Relating to Money Laundering) Regulations 2001;
(c) the Money Laundering Regulations 2001.

1. Made by the Treasury, in exercise of the powers conferred on them by s 2(2) of the European Communities Act 1972, and ss 168(4)(b), 402(1)(b), 417(1) and 428(3) of the Financial Services and Markets Act 2000.

8–18329ZB 2. Interpretation. (1) In these Regulations—

"the 2000 Act" means the Financial Services and Markets Act 2000;

"applicant for business" means a person seeking to form a business relationship, or carry out a one-off transaction, with another person acting in the course of relevant business carried on by that other person in the United Kingdom;

"applicant for registration" means an applicant for registration as a money service operator, or as a high value dealer;

"the appropriate judicial authority" means—

(a) in England and Wales, a magistrates' court,
(b) in Scotland, the sheriff,
(c) in Northern Ireland, a court of summary jurisdiction;

"authorised person" has the meaning given by section 31(2) of the 2000 Act;

"the Authority" means the Financial Services Authority;

"the Banking Consolidation Directive" means Directive 2000/12/EC of the European Parliament and of the Council of 20th March 2000 relating to the taking up and pursuit of the business of credit institutions as last amended by Directive 2002/87/EC of the European Parliament and of the Council of 16th December 2002;

"business relationship" means any arrangement the purpose of which is to facilitate the carrying out of transactions on a frequent, habitual or regular basis where the total amount of any payments to be made by any person to any other in the course of the arrangement is not known or capable of being ascertained at the outset;

"cash" means notes, coins or travellers' cheques in any currency;

"the Commissioners" means the Commissioners of Customs and Excise;

"constable" includes a person commissioned by the Commissioners and a person authorised for the purposes of these Regulations by the Director General of the National Criminal Intelligence Service;

"EEA State" means a State which is a contracting party to the agreement on the European Economic Area signed at Oporto on 2nd May 1992 as it has effect for the time being;

"estate agency work" has the meaning given by section 1 of the Estate Agents Act 1979 save for the omission of the words " (including a business in which he is employed)" in subsection (1) and includes a case where, in relation to a disposal or acquisition, the person acts as principal;

"high value dealer" means a person who carries on the activity mentioned in paragraph (2)(n);

"the Life Assurance Consolidation Directive" means Directive 2002/83/EC of the European Parliament and of the Council of 5th November 2002 concerning life assurance;

"justice" means a justice of the peace or, in relation to Scotland, a justice within the meaning of section 307 of the Criminal Procedure (Scotland) Act 1995;

"money laundering" means an act which falls within section 340(11) of the Proceeds of Crime Act 2002 or an offence under section 18 of the Terrorism Act 2000;

"the Money Laundering Directive" means Council Directive 91/308/EEC of 10th June 1991 on prevention of the use of the financial system for the purpose of money laundering as amended by Directive 2001/97/EC of the European Parliament and of the Council of 4th December 2001;

"money service business" means any of the activities mentioned in paragraph (2)(d) (so far as not excluded by paragraph (3)) when carried on by way of business;

"money service operator" means a person who carries on money service business other than a person who carries on relevant business falling within any of sub-paragraphs (a) to (c) of paragraph (2);

"nominated officer" has the meaning given by regulation 7;

"officer" (except in regulations 7, 10 and 27) has the meaning given by section 1(1) of the Customs and Excise Management Act 1979;

"officer in overall charge of the investigation" means the person whose name and address are endorsed on the order concerned as being the officer so in charge;

"one-off transaction" means any transaction other than one carried out in the course of an existing business relationship;

"operator" means a money service operator;

"recorded information" includes information recorded in any form and any document of any nature whatsoever;

"registered number" has the meaning given by regulation 9(2);

"relevant business" has the meaning given by paragraph (2);

"the review procedure" means the procedure under regulation 21;

"satisfactory evidence of identity" has the meaning given by paragraphs (5) and (6);

"supervisory authority" has the meaning given by paragraphs (7) and (8);

"tribunal" means a VAT and duties tribunal.

(2) For the purposes of these Regulations, "relevant business" means—

(a) the regulated activity of—

(i) accepting deposits;
(ii) effecting or carrying out contracts of long-term insurance when carried on by a person who has received official authorisation pursuant to Article 4 or 51 of the Life Assurance Consolidation Directive;
(iii) dealing in investments as principal or as agent;
(iv) arranging deals in investments;
(v) managing investments;
(vi) safeguarding and administering investments;
(vii) sending dematerialised instructions;
(viii) establishing (and taking other steps in relation to) collective investment schemes;
(ix) advising on investments; or
(x) issuing electronic money;

(b) the activities of the National Savings Bank;

(c) any activity carried on for the purpose of raising money authorised to be raised under the National Loans Act 1968 under the auspices of the Director of Savings;

(d) the business of operating a bureau de change, transmitting money (or any representation of monetary value) by any means or cashing cheques which are made payable to customers;

(e) any of the activities in points 1 to 12 or 14 of Annex 1 to the Banking Consolidation Directive (which activities are, for convenience, set out in Schedule 1 to these Regulations) when carried on by way of business, ignoring an activity falling within any of sub-paragraphs (a) to (d);
(f) estate agency work;
(g) operating a casino by way of business;
(h) the activities of a person appointed to act as an insolvency practitioner within the meaning of section 388 of the Insolvency Act 1986 or Article 3 of the Insolvency (Northern Ireland) Order 1989;
(i) the provision by way of business of advice about the tax affairs of another person by a body corporate or unincorporate or, in the case of a sole practitioner, by an individual;
(j) the provision by way of business of accountancy services by a body corporate or unincorporate or, in the case of a sole practitioner, by an individual;
(k) the provision by way of business of audit services by a person who is eligible for appointment as a company auditor under section 25 of the Companies Act 1989 or Article 28 of the Companies (Northern Ireland) Order 1990;
(l) the provision by way of business of legal services by a body corporate or unincorporate or, in the case of a sole practitioner, by an individual and which involves participation in a financial or real property transaction (whether by assisting in the planning or execution of any such transaction or otherwise by acting for, or on behalf of, a client in any such transaction);
(m) the provision by way of business of services in relation to the formation, operation or management of a company or a trust; or
(n) the activity of dealing in goods of any description by way of business (including dealing as an auctioneer) whenever a transaction involves accepting a total cash payment of 15,000 euro or more.

(3) Paragraph (2) does not apply to—

(a) the issue of withdrawable share capital within the limit set by section 6 of the Industrial and Provident Societies Act 1965 by a society registered under that Act;
(b) the acceptance of deposits from the public within the limit set by section 7(3) of that Act by such a society;
(c) the issue of withdrawable share capital within the limit set by section 6 of the Industrial and Provident Societies Act (Northern Ireland) 1969 by a society registered under that Act;
(d) the acceptance of deposits from the public within the limit set by section 7(3) of that Act by such a society;
(e) activities carried on by the Bank of England;
(f) any activity in respect of which an exemption order under section 38 of the 2000 Act has effect if it is carried on by a person who is for the time being specified in the order or falls within a class of persons so specified;
(g) any activity (other than one falling within sub-paragraph (f)) in respect of which a person was an exempted person for the purposes of section 45 of the Financial Services Act 1986 immediately before its repeal;
(h) the regulated activities of arranging deals in investments or advising on investments, in so far as the investment consists of rights under a regulated mortgage contract;
(i) the regulated activities of dealing in investments as agent, arranging deals in investments, managing investments or advising on investments, in so far as the investment consists of rights under, or any right to or interest in, a contract of insurance which is not a qualifying contract of insurance; or
(j) the Official Solicitor to the Supreme Court when acting as trustee in his official capacity.

(4) The following must be read with section 22 of the 2000 Act, any relevant order under that section and Schedule 2 to that Act—

(a) paragraphs (2)(a) and (3)(h) and (i);
(b) regulation 25 (authorised persons operating a bureau de change);
(c) references in these Regulations to a contract of long-term insurance.

(5) For the purposes of these Regulations, and subject to paragraph (6), "satisfactory evidence of identity" is evidence which is reasonably capable of establishing (and does in fact establish to the satisfaction of the person who obtains it) that the applicant for business is the person he claims to be.

(6) Where the person who obtains the evidence mentioned in paragraph (5) knows or has reasonable grounds for believing that the applicant for business is a money service operator, satisfactory evidence of identity must also include the applicant's registered number (if any).

(7) For the purposes of these Regulations, each of the following is a supervisory authority—

(a) the Bank of England;
(b) the Authority;
(c) the Council of Lloyd's;
(d) the Office of Fair Trading;
(e) the Occupational Pensions Regulatory Authority;
(f) a body which is a designated professional body for the purposes of Part 20 of the 2000 Act;
(g) the Gaming Board for Great Britain.

(8) The Secretary of State and the Treasury are each a supervisory authority in the exercise, in relation to a person carrying on relevant business, of their respective functions under the enactments relating to companies or insolvency or under the 2000 Act.

(9) In these Regulations, references to amounts in euro include references to equivalent amounts in another currency.

(10) For the purpose of the application of these Regulations to Scotland, "real property" means "heritable property".

PART II
OBLIGATIONS ON PERSONS WHO CARRY ON RELEVANT BUSINESS

8–18329ZC **3. Systems and training etc to prevent money laundering.** (1) Every person must in the course of relevant business carried on by him in the United Kingdom—

(a) comply with the requirements of regulations 4 (identification procedures), 6 (record-keeping procedures) and 7 (internal reporting procedures);

(b) establish such other procedures of internal control and communication as may be appropriate for the purposes of forestalling and preventing money laundering; and

(c) take appropriate measures so that relevant employees are—

(i) made aware of the provisions of these Regulations, Part 7 of the Proceeds of Crime Act 2002 (money laundering) and sections 18 and 21A of the Terrorism Act 2000; and

(ii) given training in how to recognise and deal with transactions which may be related to money laundering.

(2) A person who contravenes this regulation is guilty of an offence and liable[1]—

(a) on conviction on indictment, to imprisonment for a term not exceeding 2 years, to a fine or to both;

(b) on summary conviction, to a fine not exceeding the statutory maximum.

(3) In deciding whether a person has committed an offence under this regulation, the court must consider whether he followed any relevant guidance which was at the time concerned—

(a) issued by a supervisory authority or any other appropriate body;

(b) approved by the Treasury; and

(c) published in a manner approved by the Treasury as appropriate in their opinion to bring the guidance to the attention of persons likely to be affected by it.

(4) An appropriate body is any body which regulates or is representative of any trade, profession, business or employment carried on by the alleged offender.

(5) In proceedings against any person for an offence under this regulation, it is a defence for that person to show that he took all reasonable steps and exercised all due diligence to avoid committing the offence.

(6) Where a person is convicted of an offence under this regulation, he shall not also be liable to a penalty under regulation 20 (power to impose penalties).

---

1. For procedure in respect of this offence which is triable either way, see the Magistrates' Courts Act 1980, ss 17A–21, in PART I: MAGISTRATES' COURTS, PROCEDURE, ante.

8–18329ZD **4. Identification procedures.** (1) In this regulation and in regulations 5 to 7—

(a) "A" means a person who carries on relevant business in the United Kingdom; and

(b) "B" means an applicant for business.

(2) This regulation applies if—

(a) A and B form, or agree to form, a business relationship;

(b) in respect of any one-off transaction—

(i) A knows or suspects that the transaction involves money laundering; or

(ii) payment of 15,000 euro or more is to be made by or to B; or

(c) in respect of two or more one-off transactions, it appears to A (whether at the outset or subsequently) that the transactions are linked and involve, in total, the payment of 15,000 euro or more by or to B.

(3) A must maintain identification procedures which—

(a) require that as soon as is reasonably practicable after contact is first made between A and B—

(i) B must produce satisfactory evidence of his identity; or

(ii) such measures specified in the procedures must be taken in order to produce satisfactory evidence of B's identity;

(b) take into account the greater potential for money laundering which arises when B is not physically present when being identified;

(c) require that where satisfactory evidence of identity is not obtained, the business relationship or one-off transaction must not proceed any further; and

(d) require that where B acts or appears to act for another person, reasonable measures must be taken for the purpose of establishing the identity of that person.

8–18329ZE 5. Exceptions. (1) Except in circumstances falling within regulation 4(2)(b)(i), identification procedures under regulation 4 do not require A to take steps to obtain evidence of any person's identity in any of the following circumstances.

(2) Where A has reasonable grounds for believing that B—

(a) carries on in the United Kingdom relevant business falling within any of sub-paragraphs (a) to (e) of regulation 2(2), is not a money service operator and, if carrying on an activity falling within regulation 2(2)(a), is an authorised person with permission under the 2000 Act to carry on that activity;
(b) does not carry on relevant business in the United Kingdom but does carry on comparable activities to those falling within sub-paragraph (a) and is covered by the Money Laundering Directive; or
(c) is regulated by an overseas regulatory authority (within the meaning given by section 82 of the Companies Act 1989) and is based or incorporated in a country (other than an EEA State) whose law contains comparable provisions to those contained in the Money Laundering Directive.

(3) Where—

(a) A carries out a one-off transaction with or for a third party pursuant to an introduction effected by a person who has provided a written assurance that evidence of the identity of all third parties introduced by him will have been obtained and recorded under procedures maintained by him;
(b) that person identifies the third party; and
(c) A has reasonable grounds for believing that that person falls within any of sub-paragraphs (a) to (c) of paragraph (2).

(4) In relation to a contract of long-term insurance—

(a) in connection with a pension scheme taken out by virtue of a person's contract of employment or occupation where the contract of long-term insurance—
  (i) contains no surrender clause; and
  (ii) may not be used as collateral for a loan; or
(b) in respect of which a premium is payable—
  (i) in one instalment of an amount not exceeding 2,500 euro; or
  (ii) periodically and where the total payable in respect of any calendar year does not exceed 1,000 euro.

(5) Where the proceeds of a one-off transaction are payable to B but are instead directly reinvested on his behalf in another transaction—

(a) of which a record is kept; and
(b) which can result only in another reinvestment made on B's behalf or in a payment made directly to B.

8–18329ZF 6. Record-keeping procedures. (1) A must maintain procedures which require the retention of the records prescribed in paragraph (2) for the period prescribed in paragraph (3).

(2) The records are—

(a) where evidence of identity has been obtained under the procedures stipulated by regulation 4 (identification procedures) or pursuant to regulation 8 (casinos)—
  (i) a copy of that evidence;
  (ii) information as to where a copy of that evidence may be obtained; or
  (iii) information enabling the evidence of identity to be re-obtained, but only where it is not reasonably practicable for A to comply with paragraph (i) or (ii); and
(b) a record containing details relating to all transactions carried out by A in the course of relevant business.

(3) In relation to the records mentioned in paragraph (2)(a), the period is—

(a) where A and B have formed a business relationship, at least five years commencing with the date on which the relationship ends; or
(b) in the case of a one-off transaction (or a series of such transactions), at least five years commencing with the date of the completion of all activities taking place in the course of that transaction (or, as the case may be, the last of the transactions).

(4) In relation to the records mentioned in paragraph (2)(b), the period is at least five years commencing with the date on which all activities taking place in the course of the transaction in question were completed.

(5) Where A is an appointed representative, his principal must ensure that A complies with this regulation in respect of any relevant business carried out by A for which the principal has accepted responsibility pursuant to section 39(1) of the 2000 Act.

(6) Where the principal fails to do so, he is to be treated as having contravened regulation 3 and he, as well as A, is guilty of an offence.

(7) "Appointed representative" has the meaning given by section 39(2) of the 2000 Act and "principal" has the meaning given by section 39(1) of that Act.

8–18329ZG 7. Internal reporting procedures. (1) A must maintain internal reporting procedures which require that—

(a) a person in A's organisation is nominated to receive disclosures under this regulation ("the nominated officer");

(b) anyone in A's organisation to whom information or other matter comes in the course of relevant business as a result of which he knows or suspects or has reasonable grounds for knowing or suspecting that a person is engaged in money laundering must, as soon as is practicable after the information or other matter comes to him, disclose it to the nominated officer or a person authorised for the purposes of these Regulations by the Director General of the National Criminal Intelligence Service;

(c) where a disclosure is made to the nominated officer, he must consider it in the light of any relevant information which is available to A and determine whether it gives rise to such knowledge or suspicion or such reasonable grounds for knowledge or suspicion; and

(d) where the nominated officer does so determine, the information or other matter must be disclosed to a person authorised for the purposes of these Regulations by the Director General of the National Criminal Intelligence Service.

(2) Paragraph (1) does not apply where A is an individual who neither employs nor acts in association with any other person.

(3) Paragraph (1)(b) does not apply in relation to a professional legal adviser where the information or other matter comes to him in privileged circumstances.

(4) Information or other matter comes to a professional legal adviser in privileged circumstances if it is communicated or given to him—

(a) by (or by a representative of) a client of his in connection with the giving by the adviser of legal advice to the client;

(b) by (or by a representative of) a person seeking legal advice from the adviser; or

(c) by a person in connection with legal proceedings or contemplated legal proceedings.

(5) But paragraph (4) does not apply to information or other matter which is communicated or given with the intention of furthering a criminal purpose.

(6) "Professional legal adviser" includes any person in whose hands information or other matter may come in privileged circumstances.

8–18329ZH 8. Casinos. (1) A person who operates a casino by way of business in the United Kingdom must obtain satisfactory evidence of identity of any person before allowing that person to use the casino's gaming facilities.

(2) A person who fails to do so is to be treated as having contravened regulation 3.

PART III
MONEY SERVICE OPERATORS AND HIGH VALUE DEALERS

Registration

8–18329ZI 9. Registers of money service operators and high value dealers. (1) The Commissioners must maintain a register of operators.

(2) The Commissioners must allocate to every registered operator a number, which is to be known as his registered number.

(3) The Commissioners must maintain a register of high value dealers.

(4) The Commissioners may keep the registers in any form they think fit.

8–18329ZJ 10. Requirement to be registered. (1) A person who acts as an operator or as a high value dealer must first be registered by the Commissioners.

(2) An applicant for registration must—

(a) make an application to be registered in such manner as the Commissioners may direct; and

(b) furnish the following information to the Commissioners—

(i) his name and (if different) the name of the business;

(ii) his VAT registration number or, if he is not registered for VAT, any other reference number issued to him by the Commissioners;

(iii) the nature of the business;

(iv) the address of each of the premises at which he proposes to carry on the business;

(v) any agency or franchise agreement relating to the business, and the names and addresses of all relevant principals, agents, franchisors or franchisees;

(vi) the name of the nominated officer (if any); and

(vii) whether any person concerned (or proposed to be concerned) in the management, control or operation of the business has been convicted of money laundering or an offence under these Regulations.

(3) At any time after receiving an application for registration and before determining it, the Commissioners may require the applicant for registration to furnish them, within 21 days beginning with the date of being requested to do so, with such further information as they reasonably consider necessary to enable them to determine the application.

(4) Any information to be furnished to the Commissioners under this regulation must be in such form or verified in such manner as they may specify.

(5) In this regulation, "the business" means money service business (or, in the case of a high value dealer, the business of dealing in goods) which the applicant for registration carries on or proposes to carry on.

(6) In paragraph (2)(b)(vii), the reference to "money laundering or an offence under these Regulations" includes an offence referred to in regulation 2(3) of the Money Laundering Regulations 1993 or an offence under regulation 5 of those Regulations.

8–18329ZK 11. Supplementary information. (1) If at any time after a person has furnished the Commissioners with any information under regulation 10—

(a) there is a change affecting any matter contained in that information; or
(b) it becomes apparent to that person that the information contains an inaccuracy;

he must supply the Commissioners with details of the change or, as the case may be, a correction of the inaccuracy (hereafter "supplementary information") within 30 days beginning with the date of the occurrence of the change (or the discovery of the inaccuracy) or within such later time as may be agreed with the Commissioners.

(2) The supplementary information must be supplied in such manner as the Commissioners may direct.

(3) The obligation in paragraph (1) applies also to changes affecting any matter contained in any supplementary information supplied pursuant to this regulation.

8–18329ZL 12. Determination of application to register. (1) The Commissioners may refuse to register an applicant for registration if, and only if—

(a) any requirement of—

(i) paragraphs (2) to (4) of regulation 10 (requirement to be registered);
(ii) regulation 11 (supplementary information); or
(iii) regulation 14 (fees);

has not been complied with; or

(b) it appears to them that any information furnished pursuant to regulation 10 or 11 is false or misleading in a material particular.

(2) The Commissioners must, by the end of the period of 45 days beginning with the date on which they receive the application or, where applicable, the date on which they receive any further information required under regulation 10(3), give notice in writing to the applicant for registration of—

(a) their decision to register him and, in the case of an applicant for registration as an operator, his registered number; or
(b) the following matters—

(i) their decision not to register him;
(ii) the reasons for their decision;
(iii) the review procedure; and
(iv) the right to appeal to a tribunal.

8–18329ZM 13. Cancellation of registration. (1) The Commissioners may cancel the registration of an operator or high value dealer if, at any time after registration, it appears to them that they would have had grounds to refuse registration under paragraph (1) of regulation 12 (determination of application to register).

(2) Where the Commissioners decide to cancel the registration of an operator or high value dealer, they must forthwith inform him, in writing, of—

(a) their decision and the date from which the cancellation takes effect;
(b) the reasons for their decision;
(c) the review procedure; and
(d) the right to appeal to a tribunal.

8–18329ZN 14. Fees

Powers of the Commissioners

8–18329ZO 15. Entry, inspection etc. (1) Where an officer has reasonable cause to believe that any premises are used in connection with money service business or relevant business falling within regulation 2(2)(n), he may at any reasonable time enter and inspect the premises and inspect any recorded information or currency found on the premises.

(2) An operator or high value dealer must—

(a) furnish to an officer, within such time and in such form as the officer may reasonably require, such information relating to the business as the officer may reasonably specify; and

(b) upon demand made by the officer, produce or cause to be produced for inspection by the officer at such place, and at such time, as the officer may reasonably require, any recorded information relating to the business.

(3) An officer may take copies of, or make extracts from, any recorded information produced under paragraph (2).

8–18329ZP **16. Order for access to recorded information.** (1) Where, on an application by an officer, a justice is satisfied that there are reasonable grounds for believing—

(a) that an offence under these Regulations is being, has been or is about to be committed by an operator or high value dealer; and
(b) that any recorded information which may be required as evidence for the purpose of any proceedings in respect of such an offence is in the possession of any person;

he may make an order under this regulation.

(2) An order under this regulation is an order that the person who appears to the justice to be in possession of the recorded information to which the application relates must—

(a) give an officer access to it;
(b) permit an officer to take copies of, or make extracts from, any information produced; or
(c) permit an officer to remove and take away any of it which he reasonably considers necessary;

not later than the end of the period of 7 days beginning with the date of the order or the end of such longer period as the order may specify.

(3) Where the recorded information consists of information stored in any electronic form, an order under this regulation has effect as an order to produce the information in a form in which it is visible and legible, or from which it can readily be produced in a visible and legible form, and, if the officer wishes to remove it, in a form in which it can be removed.

8–18329ZQ **17. Procedure where recorded information is removed.** (1) An officer who removes any recorded information in the exercise of a power conferred by regulation 16 must, if so requested by a person showing himself—

(a) to be the occupier of premises from which the information was removed; or
(b) to have had custody or control of the information immediately before the removal;

provide that person with a record of what he has removed.

(2) The officer must provide the record within a reasonable time from the making of the request for it.

(3) Subject to paragraph (7), if a request for permission to be granted access to anything which—

(a) has been removed by an officer; and
(b) is retained by the Commissioners for the purposes of investigating an offence;

is made to the officer in overall charge of the investigation by a person who had custody or control of the thing immediately before it was so removed or by someone acting on behalf of such a person, that officer must allow the person who made the request access to it under the supervision of an officer.

(4) Subject to paragraph (7), if a request for a photograph or copy of any such thing is made to the officer in overall charge of the investigation by a person who had custody or control of the thing immediately before it was so removed, or by someone acting on behalf of such a person, that officer must—

(a) allow the person who made the request access to it under the supervision of an officer for the purpose of photographing it or copying it; or
(b) photograph or copy it, or cause it to be photographed or copied.

(5) Where anything is photographed or copied under paragraph (4)(b), the photograph or copy must be supplied to the person who made the request.

(6) The photograph or copy must be supplied within a reasonable time from the making of the request.

(7) There is no duty under this regulation to grant access to, or supply a photograph or a copy of, anything if the officer in overall charge of the investigation for the purposes of which it was removed has reasonable grounds for believing that to do so would prejudice—

(a) that investigation;
(b) the investigation of an offence other than the offence for the purposes of the investigation of which the recorded information was removed; or
(c) any criminal proceedings which may be brought as a result of—
    (i) the investigation of which he is in charge; or
    (ii) any such investigation as is mentioned in sub-paragraph (b).

8–18329ZR **18. Failure to comply with requirements under regulation 17.** (1) Where, on an application made as mentioned in paragraph (2), the appropriate judicial authority is satisfied that a person has failed to comply with a requirement imposed by regulation 17, the authority may order that person to comply with the requirement within such time and in such manner as may be specified in the order.

(2) An application under paragraph (1) may only be made—

(a) in the case of a failure to comply with any of the requirements imposed by regulation 17(1) and (2), by the occupier of the premises from which the thing in question was removed or by the person who had custody or control of it immediately before it was so removed;

(b) in any other case, by the person who had such custody or control.

(3) In England and Wales and Northern Ireland, an application for an order under this regulation is to be made by complaint; and sections 21 and 42(2) of the Interpretation Act (Northern Ireland) 1954 apply as if any reference in those provisions to any enactment included a reference to this regulation.

8–18329ZS 19. Entry, search etc. (1) Where a justice is satisfied on information on oath that there is reasonable ground for suspecting that an offence under these Regulations is being, has been or is about to be committed by an operator or high value dealer on any premises or that evidence of the commission of such an offence is to be found there, he may issue a warrant in writing authorising any officer to enter those premises, if necessary by force, at any time within one month from the time of the issue of the warrant and search them.

(2) A person who enters the premises under the authority of the warrant may—

(a) take with him such other persons as appear to him to be necessary;

(b) seize and remove any documents or other things whatsoever found on the premises which he has reasonable cause to believe may be required as evidence for the purpose of proceedings in respect of an offence under these Regulations; and

(c) search or cause to be searched any person found on the premises whom he has reasonable cause to believe to be in possession of any such documents or other things; but no woman or girl may be searched except by a woman.

(3) The powers conferred by a warrant under this regulation may not be exercised—

(a) outside such times of day as may be specified in the warrant; or

(b) if the warrant so provides, otherwise than in the presence of a constable in uniform.

(4) An officer seeking to exercise the powers conferred by a warrant under this regulation or, if there is more than one such officer, that one of them who is in charge of the search must provide a copy of the warrant endorsed with his name as follows—

(a) if the occupier of the premises concerned is present at the time the search is to begin, the copy must be supplied to the occupier;

(b) if at that time the occupier is not present but a person who appears to the officer to be in charge of the premises is present, the copy must be supplied to that person;

(c) if neither sub-paragraph (a) nor (b) applies, the copy must be left in a prominent place on the premises.

Penalties, Review and Appeals

8–18329ZT 20. Power to impose penalties. (1) The Commissioners may impose a penalty of such amount as they consider appropriate, not exceeding £5,000, on a person to whom regulation 10 (requirement to be registered) applies, where that person fails to comply with any requirement in regulation 3 (systems and training etc to prevent money laundering), 10, 11 (supplementary information), 14 (fees) or 15 (entry, inspection etc).

(2) The Commissioners must not impose a penalty on a person where there are reasonable grounds for them to be satisfied that the person took all reasonable steps for securing that the requirement would be complied with.

(3) Where the Commissioners decide to impose a penalty under this regulation, they must forthwith inform the person, in writing, of—

(a) their decision to impose the penalty and its amount;

(b) their reasons for imposing the penalty;

(c) the review procedure; and

(d) the right to appeal to a tribunal.

(4) Where a person is liable to a penalty under this regulation, the Commissioners may reduce the penalty to such amount (including nil) as they think proper.

8–18329ZU 21. Review procedure. (1) This regulation applies to the following decisions of the Commissioners—

(a) a decision under regulation 12 to refuse to register an applicant;

(b) a decision under regulation 13 to cancel the registration of an operator or high value dealer;

(c) a decision under regulation 20 to impose a penalty.

(2) Any person who is the subject of a decision as mentioned in paragraph (1) may by notice in writing to the Commissioners require them to review that decision.

(3) The Commissioners need not review any decision unless the notice requiring the review is given before the end of the period of 45 days beginning with the date on which written notification of the decision was first given to the person requiring the review.

(4) A person may give a notice under this regulation to require a decision to be reviewed for a second or subsequent time only if—

(a) the grounds on which he requires the further review are that the Commissioners did not, on any previous review, have the opportunity to consider certain facts or other matters; and

(b) he does not, on the further review, require the Commissioners to consider any facts or matters which were considered on a previous review except in so far as they are relevant to any issue to which the facts or matters not previously considered relate.

(5) Where the Commissioners are required under this regulation to review any decision they must either—

(a) confirm the decision; or

(b) withdraw or vary the decision and take such further steps (if any) in consequence of the withdrawal or variation as they consider appropriate.

(6) Where the Commissioners do not, within 45 days beginning with the date on which the review was required by a person, give notice to that person of their determination of the review, they are to be assumed for the purposes of these Regulations to have confirmed the decision.

8–18329ZV 22. Appeals to a VAT and duties tribunal. On an appeal from any decision by the Commissioners on a review under regulation 21, the tribunal have the power to—

(a) quash or vary any decision of the Commissioners, including the power to reduce any penalty to such amount (including nil) as they think proper; and

(b) substitute their own decision for any decision quashed on appeal.

Miscellaneous

8–18329ZW 23. Prosecution of offences by the Commissioners. (1) Proceedings for an offence under these Regulations may be instituted by order of the Commissioners.

(2) Such proceedings may be instituted only against an operator or high value dealer or, where such a person is a body corporate, a partnership or an unincorporated association, against any person who is liable to be proceeded against under regulation 27 (offences by bodies corporate etc).

(3) Any such proceedings which are so instituted must be commenced in the name of an officer.

(4) In the case of the death, removal, discharge or absence of the officer in whose name any such proceedings were commenced, those proceedings may be continued by another officer.

(5) Where the Commissioners investigate, or propose to investigate, any matter with a view to determining—

(a) whether there are grounds for believing that an offence under these Regulations has been committed by any person mentioned in paragraph (2); or

(b) whether such a person should be prosecuted for such an offence;

that matter is to be treated as an assigned matter within the meaning of the Customs and Excise Management Act 1979.

(6) In exercising their power to institute proceedings for an offence under these Regulations, the Commissioners must comply with any conditions or restrictions imposed in writing by the Treasury.

(7) Conditions or restrictions may be imposed under paragraph (6) in relation to—

(a) proceedings generally; or

(b) such proceedings, or categories of proceedings, as the Treasury may direct.

8–18329ZX 24. Recovery of fees and penalties through the court. Where any fee is charged, or any penalty is imposed, by virtue of these Regulations—

(a) if the person from whom it is recoverable resides in England and Wales or Northern Ireland, it is recoverable as a civil debt; and

(b) if that person resides in Scotland, it may be enforced in the same manner as an extract registered decree arbitral bearing a warrant for execution issued by the sheriff court of any sheriffdom in Scotland.

8–18329ZY 25. Authorised persons operating a bureau de change. (1) No authorised person may, as from 1st April 2004, carry on the business of operating a bureau de change unless he has first informed the Authority that he proposes to do so.

(2) Where an authorised person ceases to carry on that business, he must inform the Authority forthwith.

(3) Any information to be supplied to the Authority under this regulation must be in such form or verified in such manner as the Authority may specify.

(4) Any requirement imposed by this regulation is to be treated as if it were a requirement imposed by or under the 2000 Act.

(5) Any function of the Authority under this regulation is to be treated as if it were a function of the Authority under the 2000 Act.

PART IV
MISCELLANEOUS

8–18329ZZ 26. Supervisory authorities etc to report evidence of money laundering. (1) Where a supervisory authority, in the light of any information obtained by it, knows or suspects, or has reasonable grounds for knowing or suspecting, that someone has or may have been engaged in money laundering, the supervisory authority must disclose the information to a constable as soon as is reasonably practicable.

(2) Where a supervisory authority passes the information to any other person who has such knowledge or suspicion or such reasonable grounds for knowledge or suspicion as is mentioned in paragraph (1), he may disclose the information to a constable.

(3) Where any person within paragraph (6), in the light of any information obtained by him, knows or suspects or has reasonable grounds for knowing or suspecting that someone has or may have been engaged in money laundering, he must, as soon as is reasonably practicable, disclose that information either to a constable or to the supervisory authority by whom he was appointed or authorised.

(4) Where information has been disclosed to a constable under this regulation, he (or any person obtaining the information from him) may disclose it in connection with the investigation of any criminal offence or for the purpose of any criminal proceedings, but not otherwise.

(5) A disclosure made under this regulation is not to be taken to breach any restriction on the disclosure of information (however imposed).

(6) Persons within this paragraph are—

(a) a person or inspector appointed under section 65 or 66 of the Friendly Societies Act 1992;
(b) an inspector appointed under section 49 of the Industrial and Provident Societies Act 1965 or section 18 of the Credit Unions Act 1979;
(c) an inspector appointed under section 431, 432, 442 or 446 of the Companies Act 1985 or under Article 424, 425, 435 or 439 of the Companies (Northern Ireland) Order 1986;
(d) a person or inspector appointed under section 55 or 56 of the Building Societies Act 1986;
(e) a person appointed under section 167, 168(3) or (5), 169(1)(b) or 284 of the 2000 Act, or under regulations made as a result of section 262(2)(k) of that Act, to conduct an investigation; and
(f) a person authorised to require the production of documents under section 447 of the Companies Act 1985, Article 440 of the Companies (Northern Ireland) Order 1986 or section 84 of the Companies Act 1989.

8–18329ZZA 27. Offences by bodies corporate etc. (1) If an offence under regulation 3 committed by a body corporate is shown—

(a) to have been committed with the consent or the connivance of an officer; or
(b) to be attributable to any neglect on his part;

the officer as well as the body corporate is guilty of an offence and liable to be proceeded against and punished accordingly.

(2) If an offence under regulation 3 committed by a partnership is shown—

(a) to have been committed with the consent or the connivance of a partner; or
(b) to be attributable to any neglect on his part;

the partner as well as the partnership is guilty of an offence and liable to be proceeded against and punished accordingly.

(3) If an offence under regulation 3 committed by an unincorporated association (other than a partnership) is shown—

(a) to have been committed with the consent or the connivance of an officer of the association or a member of its governing body; or
(b) to be attributable to any neglect on the part of such an officer or member;

that officer or member as well as the association is guilty of an offence and liable to be proceeded against and punished accordingly.

(4) If the affairs of a body corporate are managed by its members, paragraph (1) applies in relation to the acts and defaults of a member in connection with his functions of management as if he were a director of the body.

(5) In this regulation—

(a) "partner" includes a person purporting to act as a partner; and
(b) "officer", in relation to a body corporate, means a director, manager, secretary, chief executive, member of the committee of management, or a person purporting to act in such a capacity.

8–18329ZZB 28. Prohibitions in relation to certain countries. (1) The Treasury may direct any person who carries on relevant business—

(a) not to enter a business relationship;
(b) not to carry out any one-off transaction; or
(c) not to proceed any further with a business relationship or one-off transaction;

in relation to a person who is based or incorporated in a country (other than an EEA State) to which the Financial Action Task Force has decided to apply counter-measures.

(2) A person who fails to comply with a Treasury direction is to be treated as having contravened regulation 3.

8–18329ZZC 29. Minor and consequential amendments

8–18329ZZD 30. Transitional provisions. (1) Nothing in these Regulations obliges any person who carries on relevant business falling within any of sub-paragraphs (a) to (e) of regulation 2(2) to maintain identification procedures which require evidence to be obtained in respect of any business relationship formed by him before 1st April 1994.

(2) Nothing in these Regulations obliges any person who carries on relevant business falling within any of sub-paragraphs (f) to (n) of regulation 2(2)—

(a) to maintain identification procedures which require evidence to be obtained in respect of any business relationship formed by him before 1st March 2004; or

(b) to maintain internal reporting procedures which require any action to be taken in respect of any knowledge, suspicion or reasonable grounds for knowledge or suspicion which came to that person before 1st March 2004.

8–18329ZZE

Regulation 2(2)(e)

SCHEDULE 1

ACTIVITIES LISTED IN ANNEX 1 TO THE BANKING CONSOLIDATION DIRECTIVE

1. Acceptance of deposits and other repayable funds.
2. Lending.
3. Financial leasing.
4. Money transmission services.
5. Issuing and administering means of payment (eg credit cards, travellers' cheques and bankers' drafts).
6. Guarantees and commitments.
7. Trading for own account or for account of customers in—

(a) money market instruments (cheques, bills, certificates of deposit, etc);
(b) foreign exchange;
(c) financial futures and options;
(d) exchange and interest-rate instruments;
(e) transferable securities.

8. Participation in securities issues and the provision of services related to such issues.
9. Advice to undertakings on capital structure, industrial strategy and related questions and advice as well as services relating to mergers and the purchase of undertakings.
10. Money broking.
11. Portfolio management and advice.
12. Safekeeping and administration of securities.
13. Credit reference services.
14. Safe custody services.

SCHEDULE 2

MINOR AND CONSEQUENTIAL AMENDMENTS

INSOLVENCY

8–18330 This title contains the following statutes—

Debtors Act 1869

(32 & 33 Vict c 62)

Preliminary

8–18339 1–2. *Short title; extent.*

8–18340 3. Construction. Words and expressions defined or explained in the Bankruptcy Act 1869[1] shall have the same meaning in this Act.

[Debtors Act 1869, s 3, amended by the Statute Law Revision (No 2) Act 1893.]

1. The Bankruptcy Act 1869 was repealed by the Bankruptcy Act 1883 which was itself almost entirely repealed by the Bankruptcy Act 1914. The Act of 1914 was repealed by the Insolvency Act 1985, now repealed and consolidated with other enactments by the Insolvency Act 1986, post.

PART II

PUNISHMENT OF FRAUDULENT DEBTORS

8–18341 **13. Penalty on fraudulently obtaining credit, etc.** Any person shall in each of the cases following be deemed guilty[1] of a misdemeanour, and on conviction thereof shall be liable to be imprisoned for any time not exceeding one year; that is to say,

(1) (*Repealed*);

(2) If he has with intent to defraud[2] his creditors, or any of them, made or caused to be made any gift, delivery, or transfer of or any charge on his property;

(3) If he has, with intent to defraud his creditors, concealed or removed[3] any part of his property since or within two months before the date of any unsatisfied judgment or order for payment of money obtained against him.

[Debtors Act 1869, s 13, as amended by the Criminal Justice Act 1948, s 1, and the Theft Act 1968, ss 33 and 35, and Sch 3.]

1. Offences under this section are triable either way (Magistrates' Courts Act 1980, Sch 1, in PART I: MAGISTRATES' COURTS, PROCEDURE, ante). For procedure, see ibid, ss 17A–21 ante.

2. The Queen's Bench Division held that a deed, executed before judgment was signed in an action for breach of promise of marriage, was not executed with intent to defraud a creditor (*R v Hopkins* [1896] 1 QB 652).

3. A judgment debtor moved his goods to defeat an execution creditor. The conviction was quashed on the ground that intent to defeat one creditor did not amount to intent to defraud all the creditors (*R v Rowlands* (1882) 8 QBD 530, 46 JP 437). Intent to defraud one creditor may be evidence from which a jury may infer intent to defraud all within the meaning of this section (ibid).

Deeds of Arrangement Act 1914

(4 & 5 Geo 5 c 47)

PART I

APPLICATION OF ACT

8–18360 **1. Deeds of arrangement to which Act applies.** (1) A deed of arrangement to which this Act applies shall include any instrument of the classes hereinafter mentioned whether under seal or not—

(*a*) made by, for or in respect of the affairs of a debtor for the benefit of his creditors generally;

(*b*) made by, for or in respect of the affairs of a debtor who was insolvent at the date of the execution of the instrument for the benefit of any three or more of his creditors:

otherwise than in pursuance of the law for the time being in force relating to bankruptcy.

(2) The classes of instrument hereinbefore referred to are—

(*a*) an assignment of property;

(*b*) a deed of or agreement for a composition;

and in cases where creditors of the debtor obtain any control over his property or business—

(*c*) a deed of inspectorship entered into for the purpose of carrying on or winding up a business;

(*d*) a letter of licence authorising the debtor or any other person to manage, carry on, realise or dispose of a business with a view to the payment of debts; and

(*e*) any agreement or instrument entered into for the purpose of carrying on or winding up the debtor's business, or authorising the debtor or any other person to manage, carry on, realise or dispose of the debtor's business with a view to the payment of his debts.

[Deeds of Arrangement Act 1914, s 1.]

PART IV

PROVISIONS AS TO TRUSTEES

8–18361 **12. Penalty on trustee acting when deed of arrangement void.** If a trustee acts under a deed of arrangement—

(*a*) after it has to his knowledge become void by reason of non-compliance with any of the requirements of this Act or any enactment repealed by this Act; or

(*b*) after he has failed to give security within the time and in the manner provided for by this Act or any enactment repealed by this Act,

he shall be liable on summary conviction to a fine not exceeding **£5** for every day between the date on which the deed became void or the expiration of the time within which security should have been given, as the case may be, and the last day on which he is proved to have acted as trustee, unless he satisfies the court before which he is accused that his contravention of the law was due to inadvertence, or that his action has been confined to taking such steps as were necessary for the protection of the estate.

[Deeds of Arrangement Act 1914, s 12.]

8–18362 **13. Transmission of accounts to Board of Trade.** (1) Every trustee under a deed of arrangement shall, at such times as may be prescribed, transmit to the Board of Trade, or as they direct, an account of his receipts and payments as trustee, in the prescribed form and verified in the prescribed manner.

(2) If any trustee fails to transmit such account, he shall be liable on summary conviction to a fine not exceeding **£5** for each day during which the default continues, and, in addition, shall be guilty of contempt of court and liable to be punished accordingly.

(3) The accounts transmitted to the Board of Trade in pursuance of this section shall be open to inspection by the debtor or any creditor or other person interested on payment of the prescribed fee, and copies of or extracts from the accounts shall, on payment of the prescribed fee, be furnished to the debtor, the creditors, or any other persons interested.

(4) In this section the expression "trustee" shall include any person appointed to distribute a composition or to act in any fiduciary capacity under any deed of arrangement.

[Deeds of Arrangement Act 1914, s 13 as amended by the Administration of Justice Act 1925, s 29 and the Insolvency Act 1985, Sch 8.]

8–18363 **17. Preferential payment to creditor an offence.** If a trustee under a deed of arrangement pays to any creditor out of the debtor's[1] property a sum larger in proportion to the creditor's claim than that paid to other creditors entitled to the benefit of the deed, then, unless the deed authorises him to do so, or unless such payments are either made to a creditor entitled to enforce his claim by distress or are such as would be lawful in a bankruptcy, he shall be guilty of a[2] misdemeanour.

[Deeds of Arrangement Act 1914, s 17.]

1. "Property" has the same meaning as in the Insolvency Act 1986 (s 30, post), see Insolvency Act 1986, s 436.
2. This offence is triable either way (Magistrates' Courts Act 1980, Sch 1). For procedure, see Magistrates' Courts Act 1980, ss 17A–21, ante.

8–18364 **20. Notice to creditors of avoidance of deed.** When a deed of arrangement is void by virtue of this Act for any reason other than that, being for the benefit of creditors generally, it has not been registered within the time allowed for the purpose by this Act, the trustee shall, as soon as practicable after he has become aware that the deed is void, give notice in writing thereof to each creditor whose name and address he knows, and file a copy of the notice with the Registrar of Bills of Sale, and, if he fails to do so, he shall be liable on summary conviction to a fine not exceeding **level 2** on the standard scale.

[Deeds of Arrangement Act 1914, s 20, as amended by the Criminal Law Act 1977, s 31 and the Criminal Justice Act 1982, s 46.]

8–18365 **22. Application of Part IV.** The provisions of this Part of this Act, except such of those provisions—

(*a*) as relate to the transmission of accounts to the Board of Trade;
(*b*) as provide for the protection of trustees under void deeds;
(*c*) as require a notice to be given to creditors of avoidance of deeds;
(*d*) as provide for the payment of expenses incurred by trustees;

shall not apply to a deed of arrangement made for the benefit of any three or more of the debtor's creditors unless it is in fact for the benefit of the debtor's creditors generally.

[Deeds of Arrangement Act 1914, s 22.]

Part V
General

8–18366 **30. Interpretation of terms.** (1) In this Act, unless the context otherwise requires,—

"Creditors generally" includes all creditors who may assent to, or take the benefit of, a deed of arrangement;
"Property" has the meaning given by section 436 of the Insolvency Act 1986;
"Rules" includes forms.

(2) For the purpose of determining the number of creditors for whose benefit a deed is made, any two or more joint creditors shall be treated as a single creditor.

[Deeds of Arrangement Act 1914, s 30, as amended by the Administration of Justice Act 1925, s 29 and Sch 5, the Insolvency Act 1985, Sch 8, and the Insolvency Act 1986, Sch 14.]

Insolvency Act 1986[1]

(1986 c 45)

THE FIRST GROUP OF PARTS

COMPANY INSOLVENCY; COMPANIES WINDING UP

PART I[2]

8–18380 **6A. False representations, etc.** (1) If, for the purpose of obtaining the approval of the members or creditors of a company to a proposal for a voluntary arrangement, a person who is an officer of the company—

(*a*) makes any false representation, or

(*b*) fraudulently does, or omits to do, anything,

he commits an offence.

(2) Subsection (1) applies even if the proposal is not approved.

(3) For purposes of this section "officer" includes a shadow director.

(4) A person guilty of an offence under this section is liable to imprisonment or a fine, or both.

[Insolvency Act 1986, s 6A, as inserted by the Insolvency Act 2000, Sch 2.]

---

1. This Act consolidates the enactments relating to company insolvency and winding up (including the winding up of companies that are not solvent, and of unregistered companies); and enactments relating to the insolvency and bankruptcy of individuals. The Act contains many offences and it is not practicable in a Manual of this nature to set out fully all the penal provisions of the Act. However, we have included in this title sections of the Act which are most likely to be the subject of prosecutions, together with procedural and evidential provisions relevant to criminal trials and the work of magistrates' courts.

The punishment of offences under the Insolvency Act 1986 is provided for by Schedule 10 which is printed in an abridged form so as to correspond to the substantive provisions of the Act contained in the Manual.

The Insolvency Rules 1986, SI 1986/1925, amended by SI 1987/1919, SI 1989/397, SI 1991/495, SI 1993/602, SI 1995/586, SI 1998/1129, SI 1999/359 and 1022, SI 2001/763, 3634 and 3649, SI 2002/1307 and 2712, SI 2003/1730, SI 2004/584 and 1070 and SI 2005/527 and 2114 set out the detailed procedure for the conduct of all company and individual insolvency proceedings in England and Wales under the Insolvency Act 1986. The Rules also create further offences, punishment of which is provided for under the Rules.

The Insolvent Partnerships Order 1994, SI 1994/2421 amended by SI 2001/767 and 3649, SI 2002/1308 and 1555 and SI 2005/1516 and 2114 applies parts of this legislation, with appropriate modifications to insolvent partnerships. Only those modifications which affect the treatment of offences are printed in this work.

The Financial Markets and Insolvency (Settlement Finality) Regulations 1999, SI 1999/2979 amended by SI 2006/50 made under s 2(2) of the European Communities Act 1972 implement Directive 98/26/EC and modify the law of insolvency in so far as it applies to transfer orders effected through and security provided in connection with participation in a payment and securities settlement system designated by the Financial Services Authority or the Bank of England.

Part 10 of the Enterprise Act 2002 changed insolvency law by providing for a new regime for company administration and restricting the future use of administrative receivership; abolishing Crown Preference; establishing a new regime for the insolvency of individuals; and making changes to the operation of the Insolvency Services Account.

2. Part 1 contains ss 1–7B. It is not reproduced in this work, save for s 6A above.

PART II[1]

ADMINISTRATION

8–18380A **8. Administration.** Schedule B1 to this Act (which makes provision about the administration of companies) shall have effect.

[Insolvency Act 1986, s 8, as substituted by the Enterprise Act 2002, s 248.]

---

1. Part II was substituted by Part 10 of the Insolvency Act 1986. Para 1 of Sch 17 to the Enterprise Act 2002 (not reproduced) makes saving provisions in relation to instruments made before the commencement of the new Part II of, and Sch B1 to, the Insolvency Act 1986 and Sch 17.

The Banks (Administration Proceedings) Order 1989, SI 1989/1276, as amended, applies provisions in Pt II of the Insolvency Act 1986 with modifications to companies with are authorised institutions or former authorised institutions under the Banking Act 1987. The Order enables administration orders to be made in relation to such bodies, and makes special provision to permit the Bank of England to petition for such orders and for the involvement of the Bank of England and the Deposit Protection Board in the conduct of administration proceedings.

8–18390

PART IV[1]

WINDING UP OF COMPANIES REGISTERED UNDER THE COMPANIES ACTS

---

1. Part IV contains Chapters I—X, ss 73–219.

CHAPTER VI[1]

WINDING UP BY THE COURT

Jurisdiction (England and Wales)

8–18391 **117. High Court and county court jurisdiction.** (1) The High Court has jurisdiction to wind up any company registered in England and Wales.

(2) Where the amount of a company's share capital paid up or credited as paid up does not exceed £120,000, then (subject to this section) the county court of the district in which the company's registered office is situated has concurrent jurisdiction with the High Court to wind up the company.

(3) The money sum for the time being specified in subsection (2) is subject to increase or reduction by order under section 416 in Part XV.

(4) The Lord Chancellor may by order in a statutory instrument exclude a county court from having winding-up jurisdiction, and for the purposes of that jurisdiction may attach its district, or any part thereof, to any other county court, and may by statutory instrument revoke or vary any such order.

In exercising the powers of this section, the Lord Chancellor shall provide that a county court is not to have winding-up jurisdiction unless it has for the time being jurisdiction for the purposes of Parts VIII to XI of this Act (individual insolvency).

(5) Every court in England and Wales having winding-up jurisdiction has for the purposes of that jurisdiction all the powers of the High Court; and every prescribed officer of the court shall perform any duties which an officer of the High Court may discharge by order of a judge of that court or otherwise in relation to winding up.

(6) For the purposes of this section, a company's "registered office" is the place which has longest been its registered office during the 6 months immediately preceding the presentation of the petition for winding up.

(7) This section is subject to Article 3 of the EC Regulation (jurisdiction under EC Regulation).
[Insolvency Act 1986, s 117, as amended by SI 2002/1240.]

---

1. Chapter VI contains ss 117–160.

8–18392 **118. Proceedings taken in wrong court.** (1) Nothing in section 117 invalidates a proceeding by reason of its being taken in the wrong court.

(2) The winding up of a company by the court in England and Wales, or any proceedings in the winding up, may be retained in the court in which the proceedings were commenced, although it may not be the court in which they ought to have been commenced.
[Insolvency Act 1986, s 118.]

8–18393 **119. Proceedings in county court; case stated for High Court.** (1) If any question arises in any winding-up proceedings in a county court which all the parties to the proceedings, or which one of them and the judge of the court, desire to have determined in the first instance in the High Court, the judge shall state the facts in the form of a special case for the opinion of the High Court.

(2) Thereupon the special case and the proceedings (or such of them as may be required) shall be transmitted to the High Court for the purposes of the determination.
[Insolvency Act 1986, s 119.]

Grounds and effect of winding-up petition

8–18394 **122.** Circumstances in which company may be wound up by the court[1].—(1) A company may be wound up by the court if—

(*a*) the company has by special resolution resolved that the company be wound up by the court,
(*b*) being a public company which was registered as such on its original incorporation, the company has not been issued with a certificate under section 117 of the Companies Act (public company share capital requirements) and more than a year has expired since it was so registered,
(*c*) it is an old public company, within the meaning of the Consequential Provisions Act,
(*d*) the company does not commence its business within a year from its incorporation or suspends its business for whole year,
(*e*) the number of members is reduced below 2,
(*f*) the company is unable to pay its debts,
(*fa*) at the time at which a moratorium for the company under section 1A comes to an end, no voluntary arrangement approved under Part I has effect in relation to the company,
(*g*) the court is of the opinion that it is just and equitable that the company should be wound up.

(2) (*Applies only to companies registered in Scotland.*)
[Insolvency Act 1986, s 122 as amended by SI 1992/1699 and the Insolvency Act 2000, s 1.]

---

1. As to rules applicable to the winding up of a company by the court, see the Insolvency Rules 1986, SI 1986/1925, amended by SI 1987/1919, SI 1989/397, SI 1991/495, SI 1993/602, SI 1995/586, SI 1998/1129, SI 1999/359 and 1022, SI 2001/763, 3634 and 3649, SI 2002/1307 and 2712, SI 2003/1730, SI 2004/584 and 1070 and SI 2005/527 and 2114.

8–18395 **123. Definition of inability to pay debts.** (1) A company is deemed unable to pay its debts—

(*a*) if a creditor (by assignment or otherwise) to whom the company is indebted in a sum exceeding £750 then due has served on the company, by leaving it at the company's registered office, a written demand (in the prescribed form) requiring the company to pay the sum so due and the company has for 3 weeks thereafter neglected to pay the sum or to secure or compound for it to the reasonable satisfaction of the creditor, or

(*b*) if, in England and Wales, execution or other process issued on a judgment, decree or order of any court in favour of a creditor of the company is returned unsatisfied in whole or in part, or

(*c*) (*applies in Scotland only*), or

(*d*) if, in Northern Ireland, a certificate of unenforceability has been granted in respect of a judgment against the company, or

(*e*) if it is proved to the satisfaction of the court that the company is unable to pay its debts as they fall due.

(2) A company is also deemed unable to pay its debts if it is proved to the satisfaction of the court that the value of the company's assets is less than the amount of its liabilities, taking into account its contingent and prospective liabilities.

(3) The money sum for the time being specified in subsection (1)(*a*) is subject to increase or reduction by order under section 416 in Part XV.

[Insolvency Act 1986, s 123.]

8–18396 **124. Application for winding up.** (1) Subject to the provisions of this section, an application to the court for the winding up of a company shall be by petition presented either by the company, or the directors, or by any creditor or creditors (including any contingent or prospective creditor or creditors), contributory or contributories, or by a liquidator (within the meaning of Article 2(*b*) of the EC Regulation) appointed in proceedings by virtue of Article 3(1) of the EC Regulation or a temporary administrator (within the meaning of Article 38 of the EC Regulation) or by the designated officer for a magistrates' court in the exercise of the power conferred by section 87A of the Magistrates' Courts Act 1980 (enforcement of fines imposed on companies), or by all or any of those parties, together or separately.

(2) Except as mentioned below, a contributory is not entitled to present a winding-up petition unless either—

(*a*) the number of members is reduced below 2, or

(*b*) the shares in respect of which he is a contributory, or some of them, either were originally allotted to him, or have been held by him, and registered in his name, for at least 6 months during the 18 months before the commencement of the winding up, or have devolved on him through the death of a former holder.

(3) A person who is liable under section 76 to contribute to a company's assets in the event of its being wound up may petition on either of the grounds set out in section 122(1)(*f*) and (*g*), and subsection (2) above does not then apply; but unless the person is a contributory otherwise than under section 76, he may not in his character as contributory petition on any other ground.

This subsection is deemed included in Chapter VII of Part V of the Companies Act (redeemable shares; purchase by a company of its own shares) for the purposes of the Secretary of State's power to make regulations under section 179 of that Act.

(3A) A winding-up petition on the ground set out in section 122(1)(*fa*) may only be presented by one or more creditors.

(4) A winding-up petition may be presented by the Secretary of State—

(*a*) if the ground of the petition is that in section 122(1)(*b*) or (*c*), or

(*b*) in a case falling within section 124A or 124B below.

(4A) A winding-up petition may be presented by the Regulator of Community Interest Companies in a case falling within section 50 of the Companies (Audit, Investigations and Community Enterprise Act 2004.

(5) Where a company is being wound up voluntarily in England and Wales, a winding-up petition may be presented by the official receiver attached to the court as well as by any other person authorised in that behalf under the other provisions of this section; but the court shall not make a winding-up order on the petition unless it is satisfied that the voluntary winding up cannot be continued with due regard to the interests of the creditors or contributories.

[Insolvency Act 1986, s 124, as amended by the Criminal Justice Act 1988, s 62, the Companies Act 1989, s 60, the Access to Justice Act 1999, Sch 13, the Insolvency Act 2000, s 1, SI 2002/1240, SI 2004/2326 and the Companies (Audit, Investigations and Community Enterprise Act 2004, s 50.]

1. An application to the court for the winding up of a company shall be made in accordance with the Insolvency Rules 1986, SI 1986/1925, as amended by SI 1987/1919, SI 1989/397, SI 1991/495, SI 1993/602, SI 1995/586, SI 1998/1129, SI 1999/359 and 1022, SI 2001/763, 3634 and 3649, SI 2002/1307, 2712 and SI 2003/1730, SI 2004/584 and 1070 and SI 2005/527.

8–18397 **124A. Petition for winding up on grounds of public interest.** (1) Where it appears to the Secretary of State from—

(*a*) any report made or information obtained under Part XIV (except section 448A) of the Companies Act 1985 (company investigations, etc),
(*b*) any report made under section 94 or 177 of the Financial Services Act 1986 or any information obtained under section 105 of that Act,
(*c*) any information obtained under section 2 of the Criminal Justice Act 1987 or section 52 of the Criminal Justice (Scotland) Act 1987 (fraud investigations), or
(*d*) any information obtained under section 83 of the Companies Act 1989 (powers exercisable for purpose of assisting overseas regulatory authorities),

that it is expedient in the public interest that a company should be wound up, he may present a petition for it to be wound up if the court thinks it just and equitable for it to be so.

(2) This section does not apply if the company is already being wound up by the court.
[Insolvency Act 1986, s 124A, as inserted by the Companies Act 1989, s 60 and amended by the Companies (Audit, Investigations and Community Enterprise Act 2004, Sch 2.]

8–18397A **124B. Petition for winding up of SE.** (1) Where—

(*a*) an SE whose registered office is in Great Britain is not in compliance with Article 7 of Council Regulation (EC) No 2157/2001 on the Statute for a European company (the "EC Regulation") (location of head office and registered office), and
(*b*) it appears to the Secretary of State that the SE should be wound up, he may present a petition for it to be wound up if the court thinks it is just and equitable for it to be so.

(2) This section does not apply if the SE is already being wound up by the court.
(3) In this section "SE" has the same meaning as in the EC Regulation.
[Insolvency Act 1986, s 124B, as inserted by SI 2004/2326.]

8–18398 **125. Powers of court on hearing of petition.** (1) On hearing a winding-up petition the court may dismiss it, or adjourn the hearing conditionally or unconditionally, or make an interim order, or any other order that it thinks fit; but the court shall not refuse to make a winding-up order on the ground only that the company's assets have been mortgaged to an amount equal to or in excess of those assets, or that the company has no assets.

(2) If the petition is presented by members of the company as contributories on the ground that it is just and equitable that the company should be wound up, the court, if it is of opinion—

(*a*) that the petitioners are entitled to relief either by winding up the company or by some other means, and
(*b*) that in he absence of any other remedy it would be just and equitable that the company should be wound up,

shall make a winding-up order; but this does not apply if the court is also of the opinion both that some other remedy is available to the petitioners and that they are acting unreasonably in seeking to have the company wound up instead of pursuing that other remedy.
[Insolvency Act 1986, s 125.]

8–18399 **126. Power to stay or restrain proceedings against company.** (1) At any time after the presentation of a winding-up petition, and before a winding-up order has been made, the company, or any creditor or contributory, may—

(*a*) where any action or proceeding against the company is pending in the High Court or Court of Appeal in England and Wales or Northern Ireland, apply to the court in which the action or proceeding is pending for a stay of proceedings therein, and
(*b*) where any other action or proceeding is pending against the company, apply to the court having jurisdiction to wind up the company to restrain further proceedings in the action or proceeding;

and the court to which application is so made may (as the case may be) stay, sist or restrain the proceedings accordingly on such terms as it thinks fit.

(2) In the case of a company registered under section 680 of the Companies Act (pre-1862 companies; companies formed under legislation other than the Companies Acts) or the previous corresponding legislation, where the application to stay, sist or restrain is by a creditor, this section extends to actions and proceedings against any contributory of the company.
[Insolvency Act 1986, s 126.]

8–18400 **127. Avoidance of property dispositions, etc.** (1) In a winding up by the court, any disposition[1] of the company's property, and any transfer of shares, or alteration in the status of the company's members, made after the commencement of the winding up is, unless the court otherwise orders, void.

(2) This section has no effect in respect of anything done by an administrator of a company while a winding-up petition is suspended under paragraph 40 of Schedule B1.
[Insolvency Act 1986, s 127, as amended by the Enterprise Act 2002, Sch 17.]

1. It is only the disposition by a company which is invalidated by this provision not a loan made to the company to enable it to make that disposition so that a bank which honoured cheques drawn by the company in favour of third parties after a petition was advertised, could enforce a guarantee given to secure the company's overdraft: *Coutts & Co v Stock* [2000] 2 All ER 56, Ch D.

8–18401 **128. Avoidance of attachments, etc.** (1) Where a company registered in England and Wales is being wound up by the court, any attachment, sequestration, distress or execution put in force against the estate or effects of the company after the commencement of the winding up is void.

(2) This section, so far as relates to any estate or effects of the company situated in England and Wales, applies in the case of a company registered in Scotland as it applies in the case of a company registered in England and Wales.
[Insolvency Act 1986, s 128.]

Commencement of winding up

8–18402 **129. Commencement of winding up by the court.** (1) If, before the presentation of a petition for the winding up of a company by the court, a resolution has been passed by the company for voluntary winding up, the winding up of the company is deemed to have commenced at the time of the passing of the resolution; and unless the court, on proof of fraud or mistake, directs otherwise, all proceedings taken in the voluntary winding up are deemed to have been validly taken.

(1A) Where the court makes a winding-up order by virtue of paragraph 13(1)(e) of Schedule B1, the winding up is deemed to commence on the making of the order.

(2) In any other case, the winding up of a company by the court is deemed to commence at the time of the presentation of the petition for winding up.
[Insolvency Act 1986, s 129, as amended by the Enterprise Act 2002, Sch 17.]

8–18403 **130. Consequences of winding-up order.** (1) On the making of a winding-up order, a copy of the order must forthwith be forwarded by the company (or otherwise as may be prescribed) to the registrar of companies, who shall enter it in his records relating to the company.

(2) When a winding-up order has been made or a provisional liquidator has been appointed, no action or proceeding[1] shall be proceeded with or commenced against the company or its property, except by leave of the court and subject to such terms as the court may impose.

(3) When an order has been made for winding up a company registered under section 680 of the Companies Act, no action or proceeding shall be commenced or proceeded with against the company or its property or any contributory of the company, in respect of any debt of the company, except by leave of the court, and subject to such terms as the court may impose.

(4) An order for winding up a company operates in favour of all the creditors and of all contributories of the company as if made on the joint petition of a creditor and of a contributory.
[Insolvency Act 1986, s 130.]

1. This includes criminal proceedings (*R v Dickson* and *R v Wright* (1991) 94 Cr App Rep 7, CA).

8–18404 **131–134.** *Investigation procedures.*

8–18405 **135–146.** *Appointment of liquidator; liquidation committees; the liquidator's functions.*

8–18406 **147–160.** *General powers of court.*

CHAPTER X[1]

MALPRACTICE BEFORE AND DURING LIQUIDATION; PENALISATION OF COMPANIES AND COMPANY OFFICERS; INVESTIGATIONS AND PROSECUTIONS

Offences of fraud, deception, etc

8–18415 **206. Fraud, etc in anticipation of winding up.** (1) When a company is ordered to be wound up by the court, or passes a resolution for voluntary winding up, any person, being a past or present officer of the company, is deemed to have committed an offence if, within the 12 months immediately preceding the commencement of the winding up, he has—

(*a*) concealed any part of the company's property to the value of £120 or more, or concealed any debt due to or from the company, or
(*b*) fraudulently removed any part of the company's property to the value of £120 or more, or
(*c*) concealed, destroyed, mutilated or falsified any book or paper affecting or relating to the company's property or affairs, or
(*d*) made any false entry in any book or paper affecting or relating to the company's property or affairs, or

(*e*) fraudulently parted with, altered or made any omission in any document affecting or relating to the company's property or affairs, or

(*f*) pawned, pledged or disposed of any property of the company which has been obtained on credit and has not been paid for (unless the pawning, pledging or disposal was in the ordinary way of the company's business).

(2) Such a person is deemed to have committed an offence if within the period above mentioned he has been privy to the doing by others of any of the things mentioned in paragraphs (*c*), (*d*) and (*e*) of subsection (1); and he commits an offence if, at any time after the commencement of the winding up, he does any of the things mentioned in paragraphs (*a*) to (*f*) of that subsection, or is privy to the doing by others of any of the things mentioned in paragraphs (*c*) to (*e*) of it.

(3) For purposes of this section, "officer" includes a shadow director.

(4) It is a defence—

(*a*) for a person charged under paragraph (*a*) or (*f*) of subsection (1) (or under subsection (2) in respect of the things mentioned in either of those two paragraphs) to prove[2] that he had no intent to defraud, and

(*b*) for a person charged under paragraph (*c*) or (*d*) of subsection (1) (or under subsection (2) in respect of the things mentioned in either of those two paragraphs) to prove that he had no intent to conceal the state of affairs of the company or to defeat the law.

(5) Where a person pawns, pledges or disposes of any property in circumstances which amount to an offence under subsection (1)(*f*), every person who takes in pawn or pledge, or otherwise receives, the property knowing it to be pawned, pledged or disposed of in such circumstances, is guilty of an offence.

(6) A person guilty of an offence under this section is liable to imprisonment or a fine, or both.

(7) The money sums specified in paragraphs (*a*) and (*b*) of subsection (1) are subject to increase or reduction by order under section 416 in Part XV.

[Insolvency Act 1986, s 206.]

1. Chapter X contains ss 206–219.

2. A defendant who raises the defence of no intent to defraud bears only an evidential burden, not a legal burden, and it is appropriate to read the word "prove" in sub-s (4) as "adduce sufficient evidence": *R v Carass* [2001] EWCA Crim 2845, [2002] 1 WLR 1714, [2002] 2 Cr App Rep 72. It was held, however, in *A- G's Reference (No 1 of 2004), R v Edwards* [2004] EWCA Crim 1025, [2004] 1 WLR 2111 that *Carass* had been impliedly overruled by the House of Lords decision in *R v Johnstone* [2003] UKHL 28, [2003] 3 All ER 884, [2003] 1 WLR 1736, and a different view of the defence in s 206 may be taken in the future.

8–18416 **207. Transactions in fraud of creditors.** (1) When a company is ordered to be wound up by the court or passes a resolution for voluntary winding up, a person is deemed to have committed an offence if he, being at the time an officer of the company—

(*a*) has made or caused to be made any gift or transfer of, or charge on, or has caused or connived at the levying of any execution against, the company's property, or

(*b*) has concealed or removed any part of the company's property since, or within 2 months before, the date of any unsatisfied judgment or order for the payment of money obtained against the company.

(2) A person is not guilty of an offence under this section—

(*a*) by reason of conduct constituting an offence under subsection (1)(*a*) which occurred more than 5 years before the commencement of the winding up, or

(*b*) if he proves that, at the time of the conduct constituting the offence, he had no intent to defraud the company's creditors.

(3) A person guilty of an offence under this section is liable to imprisonment or a fine, or both.

[Insolvency Act 1986, s 207.]

8–18417 **208. Misconduct in course of winding up.** (1) When a company is being wound up, whether by the court or voluntarily, any person, being a past or present officer of the company, commits an offence if he—

(*a*) does not to the best of his knowledge and belief fully and truly discover to the liquidator all the company's property, and how and to whom and for what consideration and when the company disposed of any part of that property (except such part as has been disposed of in the ordinary way of the company's business), or

(*b*) does not deliver up to the liquidator (or as he directs) all such part of the company's property as is in his custody or under his control, and which he is required by law to deliver up, or

(*c*) does not deliver up to the liquidator (or as he directs) all books and papers in his custody or under his control belonging to the company and which he is required by law to deliver up, or

(*d*) knowing or believing that a false debt has been proved by any person in the winding up, fails to inform the liquidator as soon as practicable, or

(*e*) after the commencement of the winding up, prevents the production of any book or paper affecting or relating to the company's property or affairs.

(2) Such a person commits an offence if after the commencement of the winding up he attempts to account for any part of the company's property by fictitious losses or expenses; and he is deemed to have committed that offence if he has so attempted at any meeting of the company's creditors within the 12 months immediately preceding the commencement of the winding up.

(3) For purposes of this section, "officer" includes a shadow director.

(4) It is a defence—

(*a*) for a person charged under paragraph (*a*), (*b*) or (*c*) of subsection (1) to prove that he had no intent to defraud, and

(*b*) for a person charged under paragraph (*e*) of that subsection to prove that he had no intent to conceal the state of affairs of the company or to defeat the law.

(5) A person guilty of an offence under this section is liable to imprisonment or a fine, or both.

[Insolvency Act 1986, s 208.]

8–18418 209. Falsification of company's books. (1) When a company is being wound up, an officer or contributory of the company commits an offence if he destroys, mutilates, alters or falsifies any books, papers or securities, or makes or is privy to the making of any false or fraudulent entry in any register, book of account or document belonging to the company with intent to defraud or deceive any person.

(2) A person guilty of an offence under this section is liable to imprisonment or a fine, or both.

[Insolvency Act 1986, s 209.]

8–18419 210. Material omissions from statement relating to company's affairs. (1) When a company is being wound up, whether by the court or voluntarily, any person, being a past or present officer of the company, commits an offence if he makes any material omission in any statement relating to the company's affairs.

(2) When a company has been ordered to be wound up by the court, or has passed a resolution for voluntary winding up, any such person is deemed to have committed that offence if, prior to the winding up, he has made any material omission in any such statement.

(3) For purposes of this section, "officer" includes a shadow director.

(4) It is a defence for a person charged under this section to prove that he had no intent to defraud.

(5) A person guilty of an offence under this section is liable to imprisonment or a fine, or both.

[Insolvency Act 1986, s 210.]

8–18420 211. False representations to creditors[1]. (1) When a company is being wound up, whether by the court or voluntarily, any person, being a past or present officer of the company—

(*a*) commits an offence if he makes any false representation or commits any other fraud for the purpose of obtaining the consent of the company's creditors or any of them to an agreement with reference to the company's affairs or to the winding up, and

(*b*) is deemed to have committed that offence if, prior to the winding up, he has made any false representation, or committed any other fraud, for that purpose.

(2) For purposes of this section, "officer" includes a shadow director.

(3) A person guilty of an offence under this section is liable to imprisonment or a fine, or both.

[Insolvency Act 1986, s 211.]

1. This section and s 356(2)(*d*) are modified in their application to insolvent partnerships by the Insolvent Partnerships Order 1994, SI 1994/2421 as amended. The modified section is as noted below. Please note that the application of other parts of this legislation to insolvent partnerships which may impact on this section, albeit indirectly, are not printed in this work.

211.—(1) This section applies where insolvency orders are made against an insolvent partnership and any insolvent member or members of it by virtue of article 8 of the Insolvent Partnerships Order 1994.

(2) Any person, being a past or present officer of the partnership or a past or present officer (which for these purposes includes a shadow director) of a corporate member against which an insolvency order has been made—

(a) commits an offence if he makes any false representation or commits any other fraud for the purpose of obtaining the consent of the creditors of the partnership (or any of them) or of the creditors of any of its members (or any of such creditors) to an agreement with reference to the affairs of the partnership or of any of its members or to the winding up of the partnership or of a corporate member, or the bankruptcy of an individual member, and

(b) is deemed to have committed that offence if, prior to the winding up or bankruptcy (as the case may be), he has made any false representation, or committed any other fraud, for that purpose.

(3) A person guilty of an offence under this section is liable to imprisonment or a fine, or both.

Penalisation of directors and officers

8–18421 216. Restriction on re-use of company names. (1) This section applies to a person where a company ("the liquidating company") has gone into insolvent liquidation on or after the appointed day and he was a director or shadow director of the company at any time in the period of 12 months ending with the day before it went into liquidation.

(2) For the purposes of this section, a name is a prohibited name in relation to such a person if—

(*a*) it is a name by which the liquidating company was known at any time in that period of 12 months, or

(*b*) it is a name which is so similar to a name falling within paragraph (*a*) as to suggest an association with that company.

(3) Except with leave of the court or in such circumstances as may be prescribed, a person to whom this section applies shall not at any time in the period of 5 years beginning with the day on which the liquidating company went into liquidation—

(*a*) be a director of any other company that is known by a prohibited name, or

(*b*) in any way, whether directly or indirectly, be concerned or take part in the promotion, formation or management of any such company, or

(*c*) in any way, whether directly or indirectly, be concerned or take part in the carrying on of a business carried on (otherwise than by a company) under a prohibited name.

(4) If a person acts in contravention of this section, he is liable to imprisonment or a fine, or both.

(5) In subsection (3) "the court" means any court having jurisdiction to wind up companies; and on an application for leave under that subsection, the Secretary of State or the official receiver may appear and call the attention of the court to any matters which seem to him to be relevant.

(6) References in this section, in relation to any time, to a name by which a company is known are to the name of the company at that time or to any name under which the company carries on business at that time.

(7) For the purposes of this section a company goes into insolvent liquidation if it goes into liquidation at a time when its assets are insufficient for the payment of its debts and other liabilities and the expenses of the winding up.

(8) In this section "company" includes a company which may be wound up under Part V of this Act.

[Insolvency Act 1986, s 216.]

8–18422 **217. Personal liability for debts, following contravention of s 216.** (1) A person is personally responsible for all the relevant debts of a company if at any time—

(*a*) in contravention of section 216, he is involved in the management of the company, or

(*b*) as a person who is involved in the management of the company, he acts or is willing to act on instructions given (without the leave of the court) by a person whom he knows at that time to be in contravention in relation to the company of section 216.

(2) Where a person is personally responsible under this section for the relevant debts of a company, he is jointly and severally liable in respect of those debts with the company and any other person who, whether under this section or otherwise, is so liable.

(3) For the purposes of this section the relevant debts of a company are—

(*a*) in relation to a person who is personally responsible under paragraph (*a*) of subsection (1), such debts and other liabilities of the company as are incurred at a time when that person was involved in the management of the company, and

(*b*) in relation to a person who is personally responsible under paragraph (*b*) of that subsection, such debts and other liabilities of the company as are incurred at a time when that person was acting or was willing to act on instructions given as mentioned in that paragraph.

(4) For the purposes of this section, a person is involved in the management of a company if he is a director of the company or if he is concerned, whether directly or indirectly, or takes part, in the management of the company.

(5) For the purposes of this section a person who, as a person involved in the management of a company, has at any time acted on instructions given (without the leave of the court) by a person whom he knew at that time to be in contravention in relation to the company of section 216 is presumed, unless the contrary is shown, to have been willing at any time thereafter to act on any instructions given by that person.

(6) In this section "company" includes a company which may be wound up under Part V.

[Insolvency Act 1986, s 217.]

Investigation and prosecution of malpractice

8–18423 **218. Prosecution of delinquent officers and members of company.** (1) If it appears to the court in the course of a winding up by the court that any past or present officer, or any member, of the company has been guilty of any offence in relation to the company for which he is criminally liable, the court may (either on the application of a person interested in the winding up or of its own motion) direct the liquidator to refer the matter

(*a*) in the case of a winding up in England and Wales, to the Secretary of State, and

(*b*) in the case of a winding up in Scotland, to the Lord Advocate.

(2) (*Repealed*)

(3) If in the case of a winding up by the court in England and Wales it appears to the liquidator, not being the official receiver, that any past or present officer of the company, or any member of it,

has been guilty of an offence in relation to the company for which he is criminally liable, the liquidator shall report the matter to the official receiver.

(4) If it appears to the liquidator in the course of a voluntary winding up that any past or present officer of the company, or any member of it, has been guilty of an offence in relation to the company for which he is criminally liable, he shall forthwith report the matter—

(*a*) in the case of a winding up in England and Wales, to the Secretary of State, and
(*b*) in the case of a winding up in Scotland, to the Lord Advocate,

and shall furnish to the Secretary of State or (as the case may be) the Lord Advocate such information and give to him such access to and facilities for inspecting and taking copies of documents (being information or documents in the possession or under the control of the liquidator and relating to the matter in question) as the Secretary of State or (as the case may be) the Lord Advocate requires.

(5) Where a report is made to the Secretary of State under subsection (4) he may, for the purpose of investigating the matter reported to him and such other matters relating to the affairs of the company as appear to him to require investigation, exercise any of the powers which are exercisable by inspectors appointed under section 431 or 432 of the Companies Act to investigate a company's affairs.

(6) If it appears to the court in the course of a voluntary winding up that—

(*a*) any past or present officer of the company, or any member of it, has been guilty as above-mentioned, and
(*b*) no report with respect to the matter has been made by the liquidator under subsection (4),

the court may (on the application of any person interested in the winding up or of its own motion) direct the liquidator to make such a report.

On a report being made accordingly, this section has effect as though the report had been made in pursuance of subsection (4).

[Insolvency Act 1986, s 218 as amended by the Companies Act 1989, s 78 and the Insolvency Act 2000, s 16 and Sch 5.]

8–18424 **219. Obligations arising under s 218.** (1) For the purpose of an investigation by the Secretary of State in consequence of a report made to him under section 218(4), any obligation imposed on a person by any provision of the Companies Act to produce documents or give information to, or otherwise to assist, inspectors appointed as mentioned in section 218(5) is to be regarded as an obligation similarly to assist the Secretary of State in his investigation.

(2) An answer given by a person to a question put to him in exercise of the powers conferred by section 218(5) may be used in evidence against him.

(2A) However, in criminal proceedings in which that person is charged with an offence to which this subsection applies—

(*a*) no evidence relating to the answer may be adduced, and
(*b*) no question relating to it may be asked,

by or on behalf of the prosecution, unless evidence relating to it is adduced, or a question relating to it is asked, in the proceedings by or on behalf of that person.

(2B) Subsection (2A) applies to any offence other than—

(*a*) an offence under section 2 or 5 of the Perjury Act 1911 (false statements made on oath otherwise than in judicial proceedings or made otherwise than on oath), or
(*b*) an offence under section 44(1) or (2) of the Criminal Law (Consolidation) (Scotland) Act 1995 (false statements made on oath or otherwise than on oath).

(3) Where criminal proceedings are instituted by the Director of Public Prosecutions, the Lord Advocate or the Secretary of State following any report or reference under section 218, it is the duty of the liquidator and every officer and agent of the company past and present (other than the defendant or defender) to give to the Director of Public Prosecutions, the Lord Advocate or the Secretary of State (as the case may be) all assistance in connection with the prosecution which he is reasonably able to give.

For this purpose "agent" includes any banker or solicitor of the company and any person employed by the company as auditor, whether that person is or is not an officer of the company.

(4) If a person fails or neglects to give assistance in the manner required by subsection (3), the court may, on the application of the Director of Public Prosecutions, the Lord Advocate or the Secretary of State (as the case may be) direct the person to comply with that subsection; and if the application is made with respect to a liquidator, the court may (unless it appears that the failure or neglect to comply was due to the liquidator not having in his hands sufficient assets of the company to enable him to do so) direct that the costs shall be borne by the liquidator personally.

[Insolvency Act 1986, s 219, as amended by the Insolvency Act 2000, ss 10 and 11.]

PART VIII[1]

INDIVIDUAL VOLUNTARY ARRANGEMENTS

Moratorium for insolvent debtor

8–18424A 252. Interim order of court. (1) In the circumstances specified below, the court may in the case of a debtor (being an individual) make an interim order under this section.

(2) An interim order has the effect that, during the period for which it is in force—

(*a*) no bankruptcy petition relating to the debtor may be presented or proceeded with,

(*aa*) no landlord or other person to whom rent is payable may exercise any right of forfeiture by peaceable re-entry in relation to premises let to the debtor in respect of a failure by the debtor to comply with any term or condition of his tenancy of such premises, except with the leave of the court and

(*b*) no other proceedings, and no execution or other legal process, may be commenced or continued and no distress may be levied against the debtor or his property except with the leave of the court.

[Insolvency Act 1986, s 252 as amended by the Insolvency Act 2000, s 3.]

---

1. Part VIII comprises ss 252 to 263.

8–18424B 253. Application for interim order. (1) Application to the court for an interim order may be made where the debtor intends to make a proposal under this Part, that is, a proposal to his creditors for a composition in satisfaction of his debts or a scheme of arrangement of his affairs (from here on referred to, in either case, as a "voluntary arrangement").

(2) The proposal must provide for some person ("the nominee") to act in relation to the voluntary arrangement either as trustee or otherwise for the purpose of supervising its implementation and the nominee must be a person who is qualified to act as an insolvency practitioner, or authorised to act as nominee, in relation to the voluntary arrangement.

(3) Subject as follows, the application may be made—

(*a*) if the debtor is an undischarged bankrupt, by the debtor, the trustee of his estate, or the official receiver, and

(*b*) in any other case, by the debtor.

(4) An application shall not be made under subsection (3)(*a*) unless the debtor has given notice of the proposal to the official receiver and, if there is one, the trustee of his estate.

(5) An application shall not be made while a bankruptcy petition presented by the debtor is pending, if the court has, under section 273 below, appointed an insolvency practitioner to inquire into the debtor's affairs and report.

[Insolvency Act 1986, s 253 as amended by the Insolvency Act 2000, s 3.]

8–18424C 254. Effect of application. (1) At any time when an application under section 253 for an interim order is pending,

(a) no landlord or other person to whom rent is payable may exercise any right of forfeiture by peaceable re-entry in relation to premises let to the debtor in respect of a failure by the debtor to comply with any term or condition of his tenancy of such premises, except with the leave of the court, and

(*b*) the court may forbid the levying of any distress on the debtor's property or its subsequent sale, or both, and stay any action, execution or other legal process against the property or person of the debtor.

(2) Any court in which proceedings are pending against an individual may, on proof that an application under that section has been made in respect of that individual, either stay the proceedings or allow them to continue on such terms as it thinks fit.

[Insolvency Act 1986, s 254 as amended by the Insolvency Act 2000, s 3.]

8–18424D 255. Cases in which interim order can be made. (1) The court shall not make an interim order on an application under section 253 unless it is satisfied—

(*a*) that the debtor intends to make a proposal under this Part;

(*b*) that on the day of the making of the application the debtor was an undischarged bankrupt or was able to petition for his own bankruptcy;

(*c*) that no previous application has been made by the debtor for an interim order in the period of 12 months ending with that day; and

(*d*) that the nominee under the debtor's proposal is willing to act in relation to the proposal.

(2) The court may make an order if it thinks that it would be appropriate to do so for the purpose of facilitating the consideration and implementation of the debtor's proposal.

(3) Where the debtor is an undischarged bankrupt, the interim order may contain provision as to the conduct of the bankruptcy, and the administration of the bankrupt's estate, during the period for which the order is in force.

(4) Subject as follows, the provision contained in an interim order by virtue of subsection (3) may include provision staying proceedings in the bankruptcy or modifying any provision in this Group of Parts, and any provision of the rules in their application to the debtor's bankruptcy.

(5) An interim order shall not, in relation to a bankrupt, make provision relaxing or removing any of the requirements of provisions in this Group of Parts, or of the rules, unless the court is satisfied that that provision is unlikely to result in any significant diminution in, or in the value of, the debtor's estate for the purposes of the bankruptcy.

(6) Subject to the following provisions of this Part, and interim order made on an application under section 253 ceases to have effect at the end of the period of 14 days beginning with the day after the making of the order.

[Insolvency Act 1986, s 255 as amended by the Insolvency Act 2000, s 3.]

8–18424E 256. Nominee's report on debtor's proposal. (1) Where an interim order has been made on an application under section 253, the nominee shall, before the order ceases to have effect, submit a report to the court stating—

(*a*) whether, in his opinion, the voluntary arrangement which the debtor is proposing has a reasonable prospect of being approved and implemented,

(*aa*) whether, in his opinion, a meeting of the debtor's creditors should be summoned to consider the debtor's proposal, and

(*b*) if in his opinion such a meeting should be summoned, the date on which, and time and place at which, he proposes the meeting should be held.

(2) For the purpose of enabling the nominee to prepare his report the debtor shall submit to the nominee—

(*a*) a document setting out the terms of the voluntary arrangement which the debtor is proposing, and

(*b*) a statement of his affairs containing—

(i) such particulars of his creditors and of his debts and other liabilities and of his assets as may be prescribed, and

(ii) such other information as may be prescribed.

(3) The court may—

(*a*) on an application made by the debtor in a case where the nominee has failed to submit the report required by this section or has died, or

(*b*) on an application made by the debtor or the nominee in a case where it is impracticable or inappropriate for the nominee to continue to act as such,

direct that the nominee shall be replaced as such by another person qualified to act as an insolvency practitioner, or authorised to act as nominee, in relation to the voluntary arrangement.

(3A) The court may, on an application made by the debtor in a case where the nominee has failed to submit the report required by this section, direct that the interim order shall continue, or (if it has ceased to have effect) be renewed, for such further period as the court may specify in the direction.

(4) The court may, on the application of the nominee, extend the period for which the interim order has effect so as to enable the nominee to have more time to prepare his report.

(5) If the court is satisfied on receiving the nominee's report that a meeting of the debtor's creditors should be summoned to consider the debtor's proposal, the court shall direct that the period for which the interim order has effect shall be extended, for such further period as it may specify in the direction, for the purpose of enabling the debtor's proposal to be considered by his creditors in accordance with the following provisions of this Part.

(6) The court may discharge the interim order if it is satisfied, on the application of the nominee—

(*a*) that the debtor has failed to comply with his obligations under subsection (2), or

(*b*) that for any other reason it would be inappropriate for a meeting of the debtor's creditors to be summoned to consider the debtor's proposal.

[Insolvency Act 1986, s 256 as amended by the Insolvency Act 2000, s 3.]

Procedure where no interim order made

8–18424F 256A. Debtor's proposal and nominee's report. (1) This section applies where a debtor (being an individual)—

(*a*) intends to make a proposal under this Part (but an interim order has not been made in relation to the proposal and no application for such an order is pending), and

(*b*) if he is an undischarged bankrupt, has given notice of the proposal to the official receiver and, if there is one, the trustee of his estate,

unless a bankruptcy petition presented by the debtor is pending and the court has, under section 273, appointed an insolvency practitioner to inquire into the debtor's affairs and report.

(2) For the purpose of enabling the nominee to prepare a report to the court, the debtor shall submit to the nominee—

(*a*) a document setting out the terms of the voluntary arrangement which the debtor is proposing, and

(*b*) a statement of his affairs containing—

(i) such particulars of his creditors and of his debts and other liabilities and of his assets as may be prescribed, and

(ii) such other information as may be prescribed.

(3) If the nominee is of the opinion that the debtor is an undischarged bankrupt, or is able to petition for his own bankruptcy, the nominee shall, within 14 days (or such longer period as the court may allow) after receiving the document and statement mentioned in subsection (2), submit a report to the court stating—

(*a*) whether, in his opinion, the voluntary arrangement which the debtor is proposing has a reasonable prospect of being approved and implemented,

(*b*) whether, in his opinion, a meeting of the debtor's creditors should be summoned to consider the debtor's proposal, and

(*c*) if in his opinion such a meeting should be summoned, the date on which, and time and place at which, he proposes the meeting should be held.

(4) The court may—

(*a*) on an application made by the debtor in a case where the nominee has failed to submit the report required by this section or has died, or

(*b*) on an application made by the debtor or the nominee in a case where it is impracticable or inappropriate for the nominee to continue to act as such,

direct that the nominee shall be replaced as such by another person qualified to act as an insolvency practitioner, or authorised to act as nominee, in relation to the voluntary arrangement.

(5) The court may, on an application made by the nominee, extend the period within which the nominee is to submit his report.

[Insolvency Act 1986, s 256A, as inserted by the Insolvency Act 2000, s 3.]

Creditors' meeting

8–18424G 257. Summoning of creditors' meeting. (1) Where it has been reported to the court under section 256 or 256A that a meeting of the debtor's creditors should be summoned, the nominee (or his replacement under section 256(3) or 256A(4)) shall, unless the court otherwise directs, summon that meeting for the time, date and place proposed in his report.

(2) The persons to be summoned to the meeting are every creditor of the debtor of whose claim and address the person summoning the meeting is aware.

(3) For this purpose the creditors of a debtor who is an undischarged bankrupt include—

(*a*) every person who is a creditor of the bankrupt in respect of a bankruptcy debt, and

(*b*) every person who would be such a creditor if the bankruptcy had commenced on the day on which notice of the meeting is given.

[Insolvency Act 1986, s 257 as amended by the Insolvency Act 2000, s 3.]

Consideration and implementation of debtor's proposal

8–18424H 258. Decisions of creditors' meeting. (1) A creditors' meeting summoned under section 257 shall decide whether to approve the proposed voluntary arrangement.

(2) The meeting may approve the proposed voluntary arrangement with modifications, but shall not do so unless the debtor consents to each modification.

(3) The modifications subject to which the proposed voluntary arrangement may be approved may include one conferring the functions proposed to be conferred on the nominee on another person qualified to act as an insolvency practitioner or authorised to act as nominee, in relation to the voluntary arrangement.

But they shall not include any modification by virtue of which the proposal ceases to be a proposal under this Part.

(4) The meeting shall not approve any proposal or modification which affects the right of a secured creditor of the debtor to enforce his security, except with the concurrence of the creditor concerned.

(5) Subject as follows, the meeting shall not approve any proposal or modification under which—

(a) any preferential debt of the debtor is to be paid otherwise than in priority to such of his debts as are not preferential debts, or

(b) a preferential creditor of the debtor is to be paid an amount in respect of a preferential debt that bears to that debt a smaller proportion than is borne to another preferential debt by the amount that is to be paid in respect of that other debt.

However, the meeting may approve such a proposal or modification with the concurrence of the preferential creditor concerned.

(6) Subject as above, the meeting shall be conducted in accordance with the rules.

(7) In this section "preferential debt" has the meaning given by section 386 in Part XII; and "preferential creditor" is to be construed accordingly.
[Insolvency Act 1986, s 258 as amended by the Insolvency Act 2000, s 3.]

8–18424I 259. Report of decisions to court. (1) After the conclusion in accordance with the rules of the meeting summoned under section 257, the chairman of the meeting shall report the result of it to the court and, immediately after so reporting, shall give notice of the result of the meeting to such persons as may be prescribed.

(2) If the report is that the meeting has declined (with or without modifications) to approve the debtor's proposal, the court may discharge any interim order which is in force in relation to the debtor.
[Insolvency Act 1986, s 259.]

8–18424J 260. Effect of approval. (1) This section has effect where the meeting summoned under section 257 approves the proposed voluntary arrangement (with or without modifications).

(2) The approved arrangement—

(*a*) takes effect as if made by the debtor at the meeting, and

(*b*) binds every person who in accordance with the rules—

(i) was entitled to vote at the meeting (whether or not he was present or represented at it), or

(ii) would have been so entitled if he had had notice of it,

as if he were a party to the arrangement.

(2A) If—

(*a*) when the arrangement ceases to have effect any amount payable under the arrangement to a person bound by virtue of subsection (2)(*b*)(ii) has not been paid, and

(*b*) the arrangement did not come to an end prematurely,

the debtor shall at that time become liable to pay to that person the amount payable under the arrangement.

(3) The Deeds of Arrangement Act 1914 does not apply to the approved voluntary arrangement.

(4) Any interim order in force in relation to the debtor immediately before the end of the period of 28 days beginning with the day on which the report with respect to the creditors' meeting was made to the court under section 259 ceases to have effect at the end of that period.

This subsection applies except to such extent as the court may direct for the purposes of any application under section 262 below.

(5) Where proceedings on a bankruptcy petition have been stayed by an interim order which ceases to have effect under subsection (4), the petition is deemed, unless the court otherwise orders, to have been dismissed.
[Insolvency Act 1986, s 260 as amended by the Insolvency Act 2000, s 3.]

8–18424K 261. Additional effect on undischarged bankrupt. (1) This section applies where—

(*a*) the creditors' meeting summoned under section 257 approves the proposed voluntary arrangement (with or without modifications), and

(*b*) the debtor is an undischarged bankrupt.

(2) Where this section applies the court shall annul the bankruptcy order on an application made—

(*a*) by the bankrupt, or

(*b*) where the bankrupt has not made an application within the prescribed period, by the official receiver.

(3) An application under subsection (2) may not be made—

(*a*) during the period specified in section 262(3)(a) during which the decision of the creditors' meeting can be challenged by application under section 262,

(*b*) while an application under that section is pending, or

(*c*) while an appeal in respect of an application under that section is pending or may be brought.

(4) Where this section applies the court may give such directions about the conduct of the bankruptcy and the administration of the bankrupt's estate as it thinks appropriate for facilitating the implementation of the approved voluntary arrangement.
[Insolvency Act 1986, s 262, as substituted by the Enterprise Act 2003, Sch 22.]

8–18424L 262. Challenge of meeting's decision. (1) Subject to this section, an application to the court may be made, by any of the persons specified below, on one or both of the following grounds, namely—

(*a*) that a voluntary arrangement approved by a creditors' meeting summoned under section 257 unfairly prejudices the interests of a creditor of the debtor;

(*b*) that there has been some material irregularity at or in relation to such a meeting.

(2) The persons who may apply under this section are—

(*a*) the debtor;
(*b*) a person who—
  (i) was entitled, in accordance with the rules, to vote at the creditors' meeting, or
  (ii) would have been so entitled if he had had notice of it;
(*c*) the nominee (or his replacement under section 256(3), 256A(4) or 258(3)); and
(*d*) if the debtor is an undischarged bankrupt, the trustee of his estate or the official receiver.

(3) An application under this section shall not be made

(*a*) after the end of the period of 28 days beginning with the day on which the report of the creditors' meeting was made to the court under section 259, or
(*b*) in the case of a person who was not given notice of the creditors' meeting, after the end of the period of 28 days beginning with the day on which he became aware that the meeting had taken place,

but (subject to that) an application made by a person within subsection (2)(*b*)(ii) on the ground that the arrangement prejudices his interests may be made after the arrangement has ceased to have effect, unless it has come to an end prematurely.

(4) Where on an application under this section the court is satisfied as to either of the grounds mentioned in subsection (1), it may do one or both of the following, namely—

(*a*) revoke or suspend any approval given by the meeting;
(*b*) give a direction to any person for the summoning of a further meeting of the debtor's creditors to consider any revised proposal he may make or, in a case falling within subsection (1)(*b*), to reconsider his original proposal.

(5) Where at any time after giving a direction under subsection (4)(*b*) for the summoning of a meeting to consider a revised proposal the court is satisfied that the debtor does not intend to submit such a proposal, the court shall revoke the direction and revoke or suspend any approval given at the previous meeting.

(6) Where the court gives a direction under subsection (4)(*b*), it may also give a direction continuing or, as the case may require, renewing, for such period as may be specified in the direction, the effect in relation to the debtor of any interim order.

(7) In any case where the court, on an application made under this section with respect to a creditors' meeting, gives a direction under subsection (4)(*b*) or revokes or suspends an approval under subsection (4)(*a*) or (5), the court may give such supplemental directions as it thinks fit and, in particular, directions with respect to—

(*a*) things done since the meeting under any voluntary arrangement approved by the meeting, and
(*b*) such things done since the meeting as could not have been done if an interim order had been in force in relation to the debtor when they were done.

(8) Except in pursuance of the preceding provisions of this section, an approval given at a creditors' meeting summoned under section 257 is not invalidated by any irregularity at or in relation to the meeting.

[Insolvency Act 1986, s 262 as amended by the Insolvency Act 2000, s 3.]

8–18424M 262A. False representations etc. (1) If for the purpose of obtaining the approval of his creditors to a proposal for a voluntary arrangement, the debtor—

(*a*) makes any false representation, or
(*b*) fraudulently does, or omits to do, anything,

he commits an offence.

(2) Subsection (1) applies even if the proposal is not approved.

(3) A person guilty of an offence under this section is liable to imprisonment or a fine, or both.

[Insolvency Act 1986, s 262A, as inserted by the Insolvency Act 2000, s 3.]

8–18424N 262B. Prosecution of delinquent debtors. (1) This section applies where a voluntary arrangement approved by a creditors' meeting summoned under section 257 has taken effect.

(2) If it appears to the nominee or supervisor that the debtor has been guilty of any offence in connection with the arrangement for which he is criminally liable, he shall forthwith—

(*a*) report the matter to the Secretary of State, and
(*b*) provide the Secretary of State with such information and give the Secretary of State such access to and facilities for inspecting and taking copies of documents (being information or documents in his possession or under his control and relating to the matter in question) as the Secretary of State requires.

(3) Where a prosecuting authority institutes criminal proceedings following any report under subsection (2), the nominee or, as the case may be, supervisor shall give the authority all assistance in connection with the prosecution which he is reasonably able to give.

For this purpose, "prosecuting authority" means the Director of Public Prosecutions or the Secretary of State.

(4) The court may, on the application of the prosecuting authority, direct a nominee or supervisor to comply with subsection (3) if he has failed to do so.
[Insolvency Act 1986, s 262B, as inserted by the Insolvency Act 2000, s 3.]

8–18424O 262C. Arrangements coming to an end prematurely. For the purposes of this Part, a voluntary arrangement approved by a creditors' meeting summoned under section 257 comes to an end prematurely if, when it ceases to have effect, it has not been fully implemented in respect of all persons bound by the arrangement by virtue of section 260(2)(*b*)(i).
[Insolvency Act 1986, s 262C, as inserted by the Insolvency Act 2000, s 3.]

8–18424P 263. Implementation and supervision of approved voluntary arrangement. (1) This section applies where a voluntary arrangement approved by a creditors' meeting summoned under section 257 has taken effect.

(2) The person who is for the time being carrying out, in relation to the voluntary arrangement, the functions conferred by virtue of the approval on the nominee (or his replacement under section 256(3), 256A(4) or 258(3)) shall be known as the supervisor of the voluntary arrangement.

(3) If the debtor, any of his creditors or any other person is dissatisfied by any act, omission or decision of the supervisor, he may apply to the court; and on such an application the court may—

(*a*) confirm, reverse or modify any act or decision of the supervisor,
(*b*) give him directions, or
(*c*) make such other order as it thinks fit.

(4) The supervisor may apply to the court for directions in relation to any particular matter arising under the voluntary arrangement.

(5) The court may, whenever—

(*a*) it is expedient to appoint a person to carry out the functions of the supervisor, and
(*b*) it is inexpedient, difficult or impracticable for an appointment to be made without the assistance of the court,

make an order appointing a person who is qualified to act as an insolvency practitioner or authorised to act as supervisor, in relation to the voluntary arrangement, either in substitution for the existing supervisor or to fill a vacancy.

This is without prejudice to section 41(2) of the Trustee Act 1925 (power of court to appoint trustees of deeds of arrangement).

(6) The power conferred by subsection (5) is exercisable so as to increase the number of persons exercising the functions of the supervisor or, where there is more than one person exercising those functions, so as to replace one or more of those persons.
[Insolvency Act 1986, s 263 as amended by the Insolvency Act 2000, s 3.]

8–18424PA 263A. Availability. Section 263B applies where an individual debtor intends to make a proposal to his creditors for a voluntary arrangement and—

(*a*) the debtor is an undischarged bankrupt,
(*b*) the official receiver is specified in the proposal as the nominee in relation to the voluntary arrangement, and
(*c*) no interim order is applied for under section 253.

[Insolvency Act 1986, s 263A, as inserted by the Enterprise Act 2003, Sch 22.]

8–18424PB 263B. Decision. (1) The debtor may submit to the official receiver—

(*a*) a document setting out the terms of the voluntary arrangement which the debtor is proposing, and
(*b*) a statement of his affairs containing such particulars as may be prescribed of his creditors, debts, other liabilities and assets and such other information as may be prescribed.

(2) If the official receiver thinks that the voluntary arrangement proposed has a reasonable prospect of being approved and implemented, he may make arrangements for inviting creditors to decide whether to approve it.

(3) For the purposes of subsection (2) a person is a "creditor" only if—

(*a*) he is a creditor of the debtor in respect of a bankruptcy debt, and
(*b*) the official receiver is aware of his claim and his address.

(4) Arrangements made under subsection (2)—

(*a*) must include the provision to each creditor of a copy of the proposed voluntary arrangement,
(*b*) must include the provision to each creditor of information about the criteria by reference to which the official receiver will determine whether the creditors approve or reject the proposed voluntary arrangement, and

(*c*) may not include an opportunity for modifications to the proposed voluntary arrangement to be suggested or made.

(5) Where a debtor submits documents to the official receiver under subsection (1) no application under section 253 for an interim order may be made in respect of the debtor until the official receiver has—

(*a*) made arrangements as described in subsection (2), or
(*b*) informed the debtor that he does not intend to make arrangements (whether because he does not think the voluntary arrangement has a reasonable prospect of being approved and implemented or because he declines to act).

[Insolvency Act 1986, s 263B, as inserted by the Enterprise Act 2003, Sch 22.]

8–18424PC 263C. Result. As soon as is reasonably practicable after the implementation of arrangements under section 263B(2) the official receiver shall report to the court whether the proposed voluntary arrangement has been approved or rejected.
[Insolvency Act 1986, s 263C, as inserted by the Enterprise Act 2003, Sch 22.]

8–18424PD 263D. Approval of voluntary arrangement. (1) This section applies where the official receiver reports to the court under section 263C that a proposed voluntary arrangement has been approved.

(2) The voluntary arrangement—

(*a*) takes effect,
(*b*) binds the debtor, and
(*c*) binds every person who was entitled to participate in the arrangements made under section 263B(2).

(3) The court shall annul the bankruptcy order in respect of the debtor on an application made by the official receiver.

(4) An application under subsection (3) may not be made—

(*a*) during the period specified in section 263F(3) during which the voluntary arrangement can be challenged by application under section 263F(2),
(*b*) while an application under that section is pending, or
(*c*) while an appeal in respect of an application under that section is pending or may be brought.

(5) The court may give such directions about the conduct of the bankruptcy and the administration of the bankrupt's estate as it thinks appropriate for facilitating the implementation of the approved voluntary arrangement.

(6) The Deeds of Arrangement Act 1914 (c 47) does not apply to the voluntary arrangement.

(7) A reference in this Act or another enactment to a voluntary arrangement approved under this Part includes a reference to a voluntary arrangement which has effect by virtue of this section.
[Insolvency Act 1986, s 263D, as inserted by the Enterprise Act 2003, Sch 22.]

8–18424PE 263E. Implementation. Section 263 shall apply to a voluntary arrangement which has effect by virtue of section 263D(2) as it applies to a voluntary arrangement approved by a creditors' meeting.
[Insolvency Act 1986, s 263E, as inserted by the Enterprise Act 2003, Sch 22.]

8–18424PF 263F. Revocation. (1) The court may make an order revoking a voluntary arrangement which has effect by virtue of section 263D(2) on the ground—

(*a*) that it unfairly prejudices the interests of a creditor of the debtor, or
(*b*) that a material irregularity occurred in relation to the arrangements made under section 263B(2).

(2) An order under subsection (1) may be made only on the application of—

(*a*) the debtor,
(*b*) a person who was entitled to participate in the arrangements made under section 263B(2),
(*c*) the trustee of the bankrupt's estate, or
(*d*) the official receiver.

(3) An application under subsection (2) may not be made after the end of the period of 28 days beginning with the date on which the official receiver makes his report to the court under section 263C.

(4) But a creditor who was not made aware of the arrangements under section 263B(2) at the time when they were made may make an application under subsection (2) during the period of 28 days beginning with the date on which he becomes aware of the voluntary arrangement.
[Insolvency Act 1986, s 263E, as inserted by the Enterprise Act 2003, Sch 22.]

8–18424PG 263G. Offences. (1) Section 262A shall have effect in relation to obtaining approval to a proposal for a voluntary arrangement under section 263D.

(2) Section 262B shall have effect in relation to a voluntary arrangement which has effect by virtue of section 263D(2) (for which purposes the words "by a creditors' meeting summoned under section 257" shall be disregarded).
[Insolvency Act 1986, s 263G, as inserted by the Enterprise Act 2003, Sch 22.]

PART IX[1]
BANKRUPTCY

CHAPTER I[2]
BANKRUPTCY PETITIONS: BANKRUPTCY ORDERS

Commencement and duration of bankruptcy; discharge

8–18425 **278. Commencement and continuance.** The bankruptcy of an individual against whom a bankruptcy order has been made—

(*a*) commences with the day on which the order is made, and
(*b*) continues until the individual is discharged under the following provisions of this Chapter.

[Insolvency Act 1986, s 278.]

1. Part IX contains Chapters I–VII, (ss 264–371).
2. Chapter I contains ss 264–282.

8–18426 **279. Duration.** (1) A bankrupt is discharged from bankruptcy at the end of the period of one year beginning with the date on which the bankruptcy commences.

(2) If before the end of that period the official receiver files with the court a notice stating that investigation of the conduct and affairs of the bankrupt under section 289 is unnecessary or concluded, the bankrupt is discharged when the notice is filed.

(3) On the application of the official receiver or the trustee of a bankrupt's estate, the court may order that the period specified in subsection (1) shall cease to run until—

(*a*) the end of a specified period, or
(*b*) the fulfilment of a specified condition.

(4) The court may make an order under subsection (3) only if satisfied that the bankrupt has failed or is failing to comply with an obligation under this Part.

(5) In subsection (3)(*b*) "condition" includes a condition requiring that the court be satisfied of something.

(6) In the case of an individual who is adjudged bankrupt on a petition under section 264(1)(d)—

(*a*) subsections (1) to (5) shall not apply, and
(*b*) the bankrupt is discharged from bankruptcy by an order of the court under section 280.

(7) This section is without prejudice to any power of the court to annul a bankruptcy order.
[Insolvency Act 1986, s 279, as substituted by the Enterprise Act 2002, s 256.]

8–18427 **280. Discharge by order of the court.** (1) An application for an order of the court discharging an individual from bankruptcy in a case falling within section 279(6) may be made by the bankrupt at any time after the end of the period of 5 years beginning with the date on which the bankruptcy commences.

(2) On an application under this section the court may—

(*a*) refuse to discharge the bankrupt from bankruptcy,
(*b*) make an order discharging him absolutely, or
(*c*) make an order discharging him subject to such conditions with respect to any income which may subsequently become due to him, or with respect to property devolving upon him, or acquired by him, after his discharge, as may be specified in the order.

(3) The court may provide for an order falling within subsection (2)(*b*) or (*c*) to have immediate effect or to have its effect suspended for such period, or until the fulfilment of such conditions (including a condition requiring the court to be satisfied as to any matter), as may be specified in the order.
[Insolvency Act 1986, s 280, as amended by the Enterprise Act, Sch 23.]

8–18428 **281. Effect of discharge.** (1) Subject as follows, where a bankrupt is discharged, the discharge releases him from all the bankruptcy debts, but has no effect—

(*a*) on the functions (so far as they remain to be carried out) of the trustee of his estate, or
(*b*) on the operation, for the purposes of the carrying out of those functions, of the provisions of this Part;

and, in particular, discharge does not affect the right of any creditor of the bankrupt to prove in the bankruptcy for any debt from which the bankrupt is released.

(2) Discharge does not affect the right of any secured creditor of the bankrupt to enforce his security for the payment of a debt from which the bankrupt is released.

(3) Discharge does not release the bankrupt from any bankruptcy debt which he incurred in respect of, or forbearance in respect of which was secured by means of, any fraud or fraudulent breach of trust[1] to which he was a party.

(4) Discharge does not release the bankrupt from any liability in respect of a fine imposed for an offence or from any liability under a recognisance except, in the case of a penalty imposed for an offence under an enactment relating to the public revenue or of a recognisance, with the consent of the Treasury.

(4A) In subsection (4) the reference to a fine includes a reference to a confiscation order under Part 2, 3 or 4 of the Proceeds of Crime Act 2002.

(5) Discharge does not, except to such extent and on such conditions as the court may direct, release the bankrupt from any bankruptcy debt which—

(*a*) consists in a liability to pay damages for negligence, nuisance or breach of a statutory, contractual or other duty, or to pay damages by virtue of Part I of the Consumer Protection Act 1987, being in either case damages in respect of personal injuries to any person, or

(*b*) arises under any order made in family proceedings or under a maintenance calculation made under the Child Support Act 1991.*

(6) Discharge does not release the bankrupt from such other bankruptcy debts, not being debts provable in his bankruptcy, as are prescribed.

(7) Discharge does not release any person other than the bankrupt from any liability (whether as partner or co-trustee of the bankrupt or otherwise) from which the bankrupt is released by the discharge, or from any liability as surety for the bankrupt or as a person in the nature of such a surety.

(8) In this section—

"family proceedings" means—

(*a*) family proceedings within the meaning of the Magistrates' Courts Act 1980 and any proceedings which would be such proceedings but for section 65(1)(ii) of that Act (proceedings for variation of order for periodical payments); and

(*b*) family proceedings within the meaning of Part V of the Matrimonial and Family Proceedings Act 1984.

"fine" means the same as in the Magistrates' Courts Act 1980; and

"personal injuries" includes death and any disease or other impairment of a person's physical or mental condition.

[Insolvency Act 1986, s 281 as amended by the Consumer Protection Act 1987, Sch 4, the Children Act 1989, Schs 11 and 15, the Child Support Act 1991, Sch 5, the Proceeds of Crime Act 2002, s 456 and the Child Support, Pensions and Social Security Act 2000, Sch 3.]

***Reproduced as amended by the Child Support, Pensions and Social Security Act 2000, Sch 3, in force for certain purposes.**

1. Dishonesty is an essential ingredient of "fraudulent breach of trust", and a finding by the Pensions Ombudsman of "wilful default" in relation to the administration by a trustee of a pension fund was not precisely the same as a finding of "fraudulent breach trust" such as to establish unequivocally conduct of the requisite character (*Woodland-Ferrari v UCL Group Retirement Benefits Scheme* [2002] EWHC 1354, [2002] 3 All ER 670, [2002] 3 WLR 1154.

8–18428A 281A. Post-discharge restrictions. Schedule 4A to this Act (bankruptcy restrictions order and bankruptcy restrictions undertaking) shall have effect.

[Insolvency Act 1986, s 281A, as inserted by the Enterprise Act 2002, s 257.]

8–18429 282. Court's power to annul bankruptcy order. (1) The court may annul a bankruptcy order if it at any time appears to the court—

(*a*) that, on the grounds existing at the time the order was made, the order ought not to have been made, or

(*b*) that, to the extent required by the rules, the bankruptcy debts and the expenses of the bankruptcy have all, since the making of the order, been either paid or secured for to the satisfaction of the court.

(2) The court may annul a bankruptcy order made against an individual on a petition under paragraph (*a*), (*b*) or (*c*) of section 264(1) if it at any time appears to the court, on an application by the Official Petitioner—

(*a*) that the petition was pending at a time when a criminal bankruptcy order was made against the individual or was presented after such an order was so made, and

(*b*) no appeal is pending (within the meaning of section 277) against the individual's conviction of any offence by virtue of which the criminal bankruptcy order was made;

and the court shall annul a bankruptcy order made on a petition under section 264(1)(*d*) if it at any time appears to the court that the criminal bankruptcy order on which the petition was based has been rescinded in consequence of an appeal.*

(3) The court may annul a bankruptcy order whether or not the bankrupt has been discharged from the bankruptcy.

(4) Where the court annuls a bankruptcy order (whether under this section or under section 261 or 263D in Part VIII)—

(*a*) any sale or other disposition of property, payment made or other thing duly done, under any provision in this Group of Parts, by or under the authority of the official receiver or a trustee of the bankrupt's estate or by the court is valid, but

(*b*) if any of the bankrupt's estate is then vested, under any such provision, in such a trustee, it shall vest in such person as the court may appoint or, in default of any such appointment, revert to the bankrupt on such terms (if any) as the court may direct;

and the court may include in its order such supplemental provisions as may be authorised by the rules.

(5) *Repealed.*

[Insolvency Act 1986, s 282, as amended by the Enterprise Act 2002, Sch 23.]

***Repealed by the Criminal Justice Act 1988, Sch 16, when in force.**

CHAPTER II[1]

PROTECTION OF BANKRUPT'S ESTATE AND INVESTIGATION OF HIS AFFAIRS

8–18440 **283. Definition of bankrupt's estate.** (1) Subject as follows, a bankrupt's estate for the purposes of any of this Group of Parts comprises—

(*a*) all property belonging to or vested in the bankrupt at the commencement of the bankruptcy, and

(*b*) any property which by virtue of any of the following provisions of this Part is comprised in that estate or is treated as falling within the preceding paragraph.

(2) Subsection (1) does not apply to—

(*a*) such tools, books, vehicles and other items of equipment as are necessary to the bankrupt for use personally by him in his employment, business or vocation;

(*b*) such clothing, bedding, furniture, household equipment and provisions are as necessary for satisfying the basic domestic needs of the bankrupt and his family.

This subsection is subject to section 308 in Chapter IV (certain excluded property reclaimable by trustee).

(3) Subsection (1) does not apply to—

(*a*) property held by the bankrupt on trust for any other person, or

(*b*) the right of nomination to a vacant ecclesiastical benefice.

(3A) Subject to section 308A in Chapter IV, subsection (1) does not apply to—

(*a*) a tenancy which is an assured tenancy or an assured agricultural occupancy, within the meaning of Part I of the Housing Act 1988, and the terms of which inhibit an assignment as mentioned in section 127(5) of the Rent Act 1977, or

(*b*) a protected tenancy, within the meaning of the Rent Act 1977, in respect of which, by virtue of any provision of Part IX of that Act, no premium can lawfully be required as a condition of assignment, or

(*c*) as tenancy of a dwelling-house by virtue of which the bankrupt is, within the meaning of the Rent (Agriculture) Act 1976, a protected occupier of the dwelling-house, and the terms of which inhibit an assignment as mentioned in section 127(5) of the Rent Act 1977, or

(*d*) a secure tenancy, within the meaning of Part IV of the Housing Act 1985, which is not capable of being assigned, except in the cases mentioned in section 91(3) of that Act.

(4) References in any of this Group of Parts to property, in relation to a bankrupt, include references to any power exercisable by him over or in respect of property except in so far as the power is exercisable over or in respect of property not for the time being comprised in the bankrupt's estate and—

(*a*) is so exercisable at a time after either the official receiver has had his release in respect of that estate under section 299(2) in Chapter III or a meeting summoned by the trustee of that estate under section 331 in Chapter IV has been held, or

(*b*) cannot be so exercised for the benefit of the bankrupt;

and a power exercisable over or in respect of property is deemed for the purposes of any of this Group of Parts to vest in the person entitled to exercise it at the time of the transaction or event by virtue of which it is exercisable by that person (whether or not it becomes so exercisable at that time).

(5) For the purposes of any such provision in this Group of Parts, property comprised in a bankrupt's estate is so comprised subject to the rights of any person other than the bankrupt (whether as a secured creditor of the bankrupt or otherwise) in relation thereto, but disregarding—

(*a*) any rights in relation to which a statement such as is required by section 269(1)(*a*) was made in the petition on which the bankrupt was adjudged bankrupt, and

(*b*) any rights which have been otherwise given up in accordance with the rules.

(6) This section has effect subject to the provisions of any enactment not contained in this Act under which any property is to be excluded from a bankrupt's estate.
[Insolvency Act 1986, s 283 as amended by the Housing Act 1988, s 117.]

1. Chapter II contains ss 283–291.

8–18440A **283A. Bankrupt's home ceasing to form part of estate.** (1) This section applies where property comprised in the bankrupt's estate consists of an interest in a dwelling-house which at the date of the bankruptcy was the sole or principal residence of—

(*a*) the bankrupt,
(*b*) the bankrupt's spouse*, or
(*c*) a former spouse* of the bankrupt.

(2) At the end of the period of three years beginning with the date of the bankruptcy the interest mentioned in subsection (1) shall—

(*a*) cease to be comprised in the bankrupt's estate, and
(*b*) vest in the bankrupt (without conveyance, assignment or transfer).

(3) Subsection (2) shall not apply if during the period mentioned in that subsection—

(*a*) the trustee realises the interest mentioned in subsection (1),
(*b*) the trustee applies for an order for sale in respect of the dwelling-house,
(*c*) the trustee applies for an order for possession of the dwelling-house,
(*d*) the trustee applies for an order under section 313 in Chapter IV in respect of that interest, or
(*e*) the trustee and the bankrupt agree that the bankrupt shall incur a specified liability to his estate (with or without the addition of interest from the date of the agreement) in consideration of which the interest mentioned in subsection (1) shall cease to form part of the estate.

(4) Where an application of a kind described in subsection (3)(b) to (d) is made during the period mentioned in subsection (2) and is dismissed, unless the court orders otherwise the interest to which the application relates shall on the dismissal of the application—

(*a*) cease to be comprised in the bankrupt's estate, and
(*b*) vest in the bankrupt (without conveyance, assignment or transfer).

(5) If the bankrupt does not inform the trustee or the official receiver of his interest in a property before the end of the period of three months beginning with the date of the bankruptcy, the period of three years mentioned in subsection (2)—

(*a*) shall not begin with the date of the bankruptcy, but
(*b*) shall begin with the date on which the trustee or official receiver becomes aware of the bankrupt's interest.

(6) The court may substitute for the period of three years mentioned in subsection (2) a longer period—

(*a*) in prescribed circumstances, and
(*b*) in such other circumstances as the court thinks appropriate.

(7) The rules may make provision for this section to have effect with the substitution of a shorter period for the period of three years mentioned in subsection (2) in specified circumstances (which may be described by reference to action to be taken by a trustee in bankruptcy).

(8) The rules may also, in particular, make provision—

(*a*) requiring or enabling the trustee of a bankrupt's estate to give notice that this section applies or does not apply;
(*b*) about the effect of a notice under paragraph (a);
(*c*) requiring the trustee of a bankrupt's estate to make an application to the Chief Land Registrar.

(9) Rules under subsection (8)(b) may, in particular—

(*a*) disapply this section;
(*b*) enable a court to disapply this section;
(*c*) make provision in consequence of a disapplication of this section;
(*d*) enable a court to make provision in consequence of a disapplication of this section;
(*e*) make provision (which may include provision conferring jurisdiction on a court or tribunal) about compensation.

[Insolvency Act 1986, s 283A, as inserted by the Enterprise Act 2002, s 261.]

***Words inserted by the Civil Partnership Act 2004, Sch 27 from a date to be appointed.**

8–18441 **284. Restrictions on dispositions of property.** (1) Where a person is adjudged bankrupt, any disposition of property made by that person in the period to which this section applies is void except to the extent that it is or was made with the consent of the court, or is or was subsequently ratified by the court.

(2) Subsection (1) applies to a payment (whether in cash or otherwise) as it applies to a disposition of property and, accordingly, where any payment is void by virtue of that subsection, the person paid shall hold the sum paid for the bankrupt as part of his estate.

(3) This section applies to the period beginning with the day of the presentation of the petition for the bankruptcy order and ending with the vesting, under Chapter IV of this Part, of the bankrupt's estate in a trustee.

(4) The preceding provisions of this section do not give a remedy against any person—

(*a*) in respect of any property or payment which he received before the commencement of the bankruptcy in good faith, for value and without notice that the petition had been presented, or

(*b*) in respect of any interest in property which derives from an interest in respect of which there is, by virtue of this subsection, no remedy.

(5) Where after the commencement of his bankruptcy the bankrupt has incurred a debt to a banker or other person by reason of the making of a payment which is void under this section, that debt is deemed for the purposes of any of this Group of Parts to have been incurred before the commencement of the bankruptcy unless—

(*a*) that banker or person had notice of the bankruptcy before the debt was incurred, or

(*b*) it is not reasonably practicable for the amount of the payment to be recovered from the person to whom it was made.

(6) A disposition of property is void under this section notwithstanding that the property is not or, as the case may be, would not be comprised in the bankrupt's estate; but nothing in this section affects any disposition made by a person of property held by him on trust for any other person.
[Insolvency Act 1986, s 284.]

8–18442 **285. Restriction on proceedings and remedies.** (1) At any time when proceedings on a bankruptcy petition are pending or an individual has been adjudged bankrupt the court may stay any action, execution or other legal process[1] against the property or person of the debtor or, as the case may be, of the bankrupt.

(2) Any court in which proceedings are pending against any individual may, on proof that a bankruptcy petition has been presented in respect of that individual or that he is an undischarged bankrupt, either stay the proceedings or allow them to continue on such terms as it thinks fit.

(3) After the making of a bankruptcy order no person who is a creditor of the bankrupt in respect of a debt provable[2] in the bankruptcy shall—

(*a*) have any remedy against the property[3] or person of the bankrupt in respect of that debt, or

(*b*) before the discharge of the bankrupt, commence any action or other legal proceedings against the bankrupt except with the leave of the court and on such terms as the court may impose.

This is subject to sections 346 (enforcement procedures) and 347 (limited right to distress).

(4) Subject as follows, subsection (3) does not affect the right of a secured creditor of the bankrupt to enforce his security.

(5) Where any goods of an undischarged bankrupt are held by any person by way of pledge, pawn or other security, the official receiver may, after giving notice in writing of his intention to do so, inspect the goods.

Where such a notice has been given to any person, that person is not entitled, without leave of the court, to realise his security unless he has given the trustee of the bankrupt's estate a reasonable opportunity of inspecting the goods and of exercising the bankrupt's right of redemption.

(6) References in this section to the property or goods of the bankrupt are to any of his property or goods, whether or not comprised in his estate.
[Insolvency Act 1986, s 285.]

1. It has been held that the words "or other legal process" cover proceedings in the magistrates' court for the issue of a committal warrant for non-payment of rates, and that, accordingly, the bankruptcy court had jurisdiction to stay those proceedings (*Smith v Braintree District Council* [1990] 2 AC 215, [1989] 3 All ER 897, HL).

2. Rule 12.3 of the Insolvency Rules 1986 provides that an obligation arising under an order made in family proceedings (defined for this purpose in s 281(8) ante), is not provable in bankruptcy and, therefore, is capable of being enforced as against the bankrupt, or against income or property acquired by the bankrupt after the making of the bankruptcy order (*Re G (Children Act 1989, Sch 1)* [1996] 2 FLR 171).

3. The Secretary of State for Social Security is not precluded from exercising his power to recover money by making deductions from prescribed benefits when the intended recipient of those benefits has become bankrupt since the recipient is only entitled to the net amount of those benefits (*R v Secretary of State for Social Security, ex p Taylor* (1996) Times, 5 February, DC).

CHAPTER VI[1]

BANKRUPTCY OFFENCES

Preliminary

8–18443 **350. Scheme of this Chapter.** (1) Subject to section 360(3) below, this Chapter applies where the court has made a bankruptcy order on a bankruptcy petition.

(2) This Chapter applies whether or not the bankruptcy order is annulled, but proceedings for an offence under this Chapter shall not be instituted after the annulment.

(3) Without prejudice to his liability in respect of a subsequent bankruptcy, the bankrupt is not guilty of an offence under this Chapter in respect of anything done after his discharge; but nothing in this Group of Parts prevents the institution of proceedings against a discharged bankrupt for an offence committed before his discharge.

(3A) Subsection (3) is without prejudice to any provision of this Chapter which applies to a person in respect of whom a bankruptcy restrictions order is in force.

(4) It is not a defence in proceedings for an offence under this Chapter that anything relied on, in whole or in part, as constituting that offence was done outside England and Wales.

(5) Proceedings for an offence under this Chapter or under the rules shall not be instituted except by the Secretary of State or by or with the consent of the Director of Public Prosecutions.

(6) A person guilty of any offence under this Chapter is liable to imprisonment or a fine, or both.

[Insolvency Act 1986, s 350, as inserted by the Enterprise Act 2002, Sch 21.]

1. Chapter VI contains ss 350–362.

8–18444 351. Definitions. In the following provisions of this Chapter—

(*a*) references to property comprised in the bankrupt's estate or to property possession of which is required to be delivered up to the official receiver or the trustee of the bankrupt's estate include any property which would be such property if a notice in respect of it were given under section 307 (after-acquired property), section 308 (personal property and effects of bankrupt having more than replacement value) or section 308A (vesting in trustee of certain tenancies);

(*b*) "the initial period" means the period between the presentation of the bankruptcy petition and the commencement of the bankruptcy; and

(*c*) a reference to a number of months or years before petition is to that period ending with the presentation of the bankruptcy petition.

[Insolvency Act 1986, s 351 as amended by the Housing Act 1988, Sch 17.]

8–18445 352. Defence of innocent intention. Where in the case of an offence under any provision of this Chapter it is stated that this section applies, a person is not guilty of the offence if he proves[1] that, at the time of the conduct constituting the offence, he had no intent to defraud or to conceal the state of his affairs.

[Insolvency Act 1986, s 352.]

1. It was stated in *R v Daniel* [2002] EWCA Crim 959, [2003] 1 Cr App Rep 99 (following the Court of Appeal's decision in *R v Carass* [2001] EWCA Crim 2845, [2002] 2 Cr App Rep 77, see para **8–18415**, above) that s 352 should be read as merely creating an evidential burden; the issue of a defendant's intent to defraud or conceal the state of his affairs, though not spelled out in the charge, is what it is all about. *Carass* was not, however, followed in *A-G's Reference (No 1 of 2004), R v Edwards* [2004] EWCA Crim 1025, [2004] 1 WLR 2111, in which it was held that it would be a normal inference from a failure to inform the official receiver of an unusual disposal that a bankrupt intended to defeat the claims of creditors or to conceal the state of his affairs, and there was nothing unreasonable for a bankrupt against whom those facts had been proved beyond reasonable doubt to have to establish on a balance of probabilities that when he failed to inform the official receiver of the disposal he did not intend to defraud or to conceal the state of his affairs, since his intention would be peculiarly within his knowledge, and he would know what his motive was; therefore, s 353(1)(*b*) post, read together with s 352, was compatible with article 6(2). However, the ambit of s 357 post was very wide and to require the bankrupt, against whom it was proved only that he had made a gift or other disposal or created a charge within five years before his bankruptcy, to prove that he had no intent to defraud was not justified and infringed art 6(2). Therefore, in relation to s 357(1), s 352 had to be read down as imposing no more than an evidential burden of proof.

Wrongdoing by the bankrupt before and after bankruptcy

8–18446 353. Non-disclosure. (1) The bankrupt is guilty of an offence if—

(*a*) he does not to the best of his knowledge and belief disclose all the property comprised in his estate to the official receiver or the trustee, or

(*b*) he does not inform the official receiver or the trustee of any disposal of any property which but for the disposal would be so comprised, stating how, when, to whom and for what consideration the property was disposed of.

(2) Subsection (1)(*b*) does not apply to any disposal in the ordinary course of a business carried on by the bankrupt or to any payment of the ordinary expenses of the bankrupt or his family.

(3) Section 352 applies to this offence.

[Insolvency Act 1986, s 353.]

8–18447 354. Concealment of property. (1) The bankrupt is guilty of an offence if—

(*a*) he does not deliver up possession to the official receiver or trustee, or as the official receiver or trustee may direct, of such part of the property comprised in his estate as is in his possession or under his control and possession of which he is required by law so to deliver up, (*b*) he conceals any debt due to or from him or conceals any property the value of which is not less than the prescribed amount[1] and possession of which he is required to deliver up to the official receiver or trustee, or

(*c*) in the 12 months before petition, or in the initial period, he did anything which would have been an offence under paragraph (*b*) above if the bankruptcy order had been made immediately before he did it.

Section 352 applies to this offence.

(2) The bankrupt is guilty of an offence if he removes, or in the initial period removed, any property the value of which was not less than the prescribed amount[1] and possession of which he has or would have been required to deliver up to the official receiver or the trustee.

Section 352 applies to this offence.

(3) The bankrupt is guilty of an offence if he without reasonable excuse fails, on being required to do so by the official receiver, the trustee or the court[2]—

(*a*) to account for the loss of any substantial part of his property incurred in the 12 months before petition or in the initial period, or

(*b*) to give a satisfactory explanation of the manner in which such a loss was incurred.

[Insolvency Act 1986, s 354, as inserted by the Enterprise Act 2002, Sch 23.]

---

1. The "prescribed sum" for the purposes of s 354(1) and (2) is £1000; s 384(2) and the Insolvency Proceedings (Monetary Limits) Order 1986, SI 1986/1996 amended by SI 2004/547.

2. This provision does not infringe the defendant's right to a fair trial under art 6(1) of the European Convention on Human Rights by being contrary to his right to remain silent nor does it violate the presumption of innocence in art 6(2). The purpose of this section is to provide a necessary sanction for the regulatory regime for the administration of bankrupt estates. The demand for information to be supplied to the Official Receiver is part of the extra-judicial procedure and its purpose is not to provide a case against the accused. Section 354 is a proportionate legislative response to the problem of administering and investigating bankrupt estates (*R v Kearns* [2002] EWCA Crim 748, [2002] 1 WLR 2815, [2003] 1 Cr App R 111, [2002] Crim LR 653).

8–18448 **355. Concealment of books and papers; falsification.** (1) The bankrupt is guilty of an offence if he does not deliver up possession to the official receiver or the trustee, or as the official receiver or trustee may direct, of all books, papers and other records of which he has possession or control and which relate to his estate or his affairs.

Section 352 applies to this offence.

(2) The bankrupt is guilty of an offence if—

(*a*) he prevents, or in the initial period prevented, the production of any books, papers or records relating to his estate or affairs;

(*b*) he conceals, destroys, mutilates or falsifies, or causes or permits the concealment, destruction, mutilation or falsification of, any books, papers or other records relating to his estate or affairs;

(*c*) he makes, or causes or permits the making of, any false entries in any book, document or record relating to his estate or affairs; or

(*d*) in the 12 months before petition, or in the initial period, he did anything which would have been an offence under paragraph (*b*) or (*c*) above if the bankruptcy order had been made before he did it.

Section 352 applies to this offence.

(3) The bankrupt is guilty of an offence if—

(*a*) he disposes of, or alters or makes any omission in, or causes or permits the disposal, altering or making of any omission in, any book, document or record relating to his estate or affairs, or

(*b*) in the 12 months before petition, or in the initial period he did anything which would have been an offence under paragraph (*a*) if the bankruptcy order had been made before he did it.

Section 352 applies to this offence.

(4) In their application to a trading record subsections (2)(*d*) and (3)(*b*) shall have effect as if the reference to 12 months were a reference to two years.

(5) In subsection (4) "trading record" means a bool, doument or record which shows or explains the transactions or financial position of a preson's business, including—

(*a*) a periodic record of cash paid and received,

(*b*) a statement of periodic stock-taking, and

(*c*) except in the case of goods sold by way of retail trade, a record of goods sold and purchased which identifies the buyer and seller or enables them to be identified.

[Insolvency Act 1986, s 355, as amended by the Enterprise Act 2002, Sch 23.]

8–18449 **356. False statements[1].** (1) The bankrupt is guilty of an offence if he makes or has made any material omission in any statement made under any provision in this Group of Parts and relating to his affairs.

Section 352 applies to this offence.

(2) The bankrupt is guilty of an offence if—

(*a*) knowing or believing that a false debt has been proved by any person under the bankruptcy, he fails to inform the trustee as soon as practicable; or

(*b*) he attempts to account for any part of his property by fictitious losses or expenses; or

(*c*) at any meeting of his creditors in the 12 months before petition or (whether or not at such a meeting) at any time in the initial period, he did anything which would have been an offence under paragraph (*b*) if the bankruptcy order had been made before he did it; or

(*d*) he is, or at any time has been, guilty of any false representation or other fraud for the purpose of obtaining the consent of his creditors, or any of them, to an agreement with reference to his affairs or to his bankruptcy.

[Insolvency Act 1986, s 356.]

---

1. This section has been applied, with modifications, to insolvent partnerships by the Insolvent Partnerships Order 1994, SI 1994/2421 amended by SI 2001/767 and 3649,SI 2002/1308 and 1555 and SI 2005/1516 and 2114. (See note 1 to s 211, ante.)

8–18450 **357. Fraudulent disposal of property.** (1) The bankrupt is guilty of an offence if he makes or causes to be made, or has in the period of 5 years ending with the commencement of the bankruptcy made or caused to be made, any gift or transfer of, or any charge on, his property.

Section 352 applies to this offence.

(2) The reference to making a transfer of or charge on any property includes causing or conniving at the levying of any execution against that property.

(3) The bankrupt is guilty of an offence[1] if he conceals or removes, or has at any time before the commencement of the bankruptcy concealed or removed, any part of his property after, or within 2 months before, the date on which a judgment or order for the payment of money has been obtained against him, being a judgment or order which was not satisfied before the commencement of the bankruptcy.

Section 352 applies to this offence.

[Insolvency Act 1986, s 357.]

---

1. A person who has concealed assets and used them to pay personal debts, can expect to receive a custodial sentence, even if of previous exemplary character (*R v Mungroo* (1997) 25 LS Gaz R 33, CA).

8–18451 **358. Absconding.** The bankrupt is guilty of an offence if—

(*a*) he leaves, or attempts or makes preparations to leave, England and Wales with any property the value of which is not less than the prescribed amount[1] and possession of which he is required to deliver up to the official receiver or the trustee, or

(*b*) in the 6 months before petition, or in the initial period, he did anything which would have been an offence under paragraph (*a*) if the bankruptcy order had been made immediately before he did it.

Section 352 applies to this offence.

[Insolvency Act 1986, s 358.]

---

1. The "prescribed sum" for the purposes of s 358 is £1000; s 384(2) and the Insolvency Proceedings (Monetary Limits) Order 1986, SI 1986/1996 amended by SI 2004/547.

8–18452 **359. Fraudulent dealing with property obtained on credit.** (1) The bankrupt is guilty of an offence if, in the 12 months before petition, or in the initial period, he disposed of any property which he had obtained on credit and, at the time he disposed of it, had not paid for.

Section 352 applies to this offence.

(2) A person is guilty of an offence if, in the 12 months before petition or in the initial period, he acquired or received property from the bankrupt knowing or believing—

(*a*) that the bankrupt owed money in respect of the property, and

(*b*) that the bankrupt did not intend, or was unlikely to be able, to pay the money he so owed.

(3) A person is not guilty of an offence under subsection (1) or (2) if the disposal, acquisition or receipt of the property was in the ordinary course of a business carried on by the bankrupt at the time of the disposal, acquisition or receipt.

(4) In determining for the purposes of this section whether any property is disposed of, acquired or received in the ordinary course of a business carried on by the bankrupt, regard may be had, in particular, to the price paid for the property.

(5) In this section references to disposing of property include pawning or pledging it; and references to acquiring or receiving property shall be read accordingly.

[Insolvency Act 1986, s 359.]

8–18453 **360. Obtaining credit; engaging in business.** (1) The bankrupt is guilty of an offence if—

(*a*) either alone or jointly with any other person, he obtains credit[1] to the extent of the prescribed amount[2] or more without giving the person from whom he obtains it the relevant information about his status; or

(*b*) he engages (whether directly or indirectly) in any business under a name other than that in which he was adjudged bankrupt without disclosing to all persons with whom he enters into any business transaction the name in which he was so adjudged.

(2) The reference to the bankrupt obtaining credit includes the following cases—

(*a*) where goods are bailed to him under a hire-purchase agreement, or agreed to be sold to him under a conditional sale agreement, and

(*b*) where he is paid in advance (whether in money or otherwise) for the supply of goods or services.

(3) A person whose estate has been sequestrated in Scotland, or who has been adjudged bankrupt in Northern Ireland, is guilty of an offence if, before his discharge, he does anything in England and Wales which would be an offence under subsection (1) if he were an undischarged bankrupt and the sequestration of his estate or the adjudication in Northern Ireland were an adjudication under this Part.

(4) For the purposes of subsection (1)(*a*), the relevant information about the status of the person in question is the information that he is an undischarged bankrupt or, as the case may be, that his estate has been sequestrated in Scotland and that he has not been discharged.

(5) This section applies to the bankrupt after discharge while a bankruptcy restrictions order is in force in respect of him.

(6) For the purposes of subsection (1)(*a*) as it applies by virtue of subsection (5), the relevant information about the status of the person in question is the information that a bankruptcy restrictions order is in force in respect of him.

[Insolvency Act 1986, s 360, as amended by the Enterprise Act 2002, Sch 21.]

1. The offence under s 360(1) is absolute and does not depend on proof of dishonesty. The giving of credit involves an agreement to postpone payment of what in the absence of such agreement would be immediately due. It is the nature of the agreement which determines whether or not credit has been obtained: *R v Ramzan* [1998] 2 Cr App Rep 328, CA (where, had the defendant fraudulently obtained an advance of money for the purpose of a capital injection into a proposed joint business, the defendant's fraudulent intent would not convert that into a loan or giving of credit; it gave the person who advanced the money an immediate right of action to avoid the agreement and recover his monies).

2. The "prescribed sum" for the purposes of s 360(1) is £500; s 384(2) and the Insolvency Proceedings (Monetary Limits) Order 1986, SI 1986/1996 amended by SI 2004/547.

8–18454 **361. Failure to keep proper accounts of business.** *Repealed.*

8–18455 **362. Gambling.** *Repealed.*

PART XI[1]
INTERPRETATION FOR SECOND GROUP OF PARTS

8–18456 **380. Introductory.** The next five sections have effect for the interpretation of the provisions of this Act which are comprised in this Group of Parts; and where a definition is provided for a particular expression, it applies except so far as the context otherwise requires.

[Insolvency Act 1986, s 380.]

1. Part XI contains ss 380–385.

8–18457 **381. "Bankrupt" and associated terminology.** (1) "Bankrupt" means an individual who has been adjudged bankrupt and, in relation to a bankruptcy order, it means the individual adjudged bankrupt by that order.

(2) "Bankruptcy order" means an order adjudging an individual bankrupt.

(3) "Bankruptcy petition" means a petition to the court for a bankruptcy order.

[Insolvency Act 1986, s 381.]

8–18458 **382. "Bankruptcy debt", etc.** (1) "Bankruptcy debt", in relation to a bankrupt, means (subject to the next subsection) any of the following—

(*a*) any debt or liability to which he is subject at the commencement of the bankruptcy,

(*b*) any debt or liability to which he may become subject after the commencement of the bankruptcy (including after his discharge from bankruptcy) by reason of any obligation incurred before the commencement of the bankruptcy,

(*c*) any amount specified in pursuance of section 39(3)(*c*) of the Powers of Criminal Courts Act 1973 in any criminal bankruptcy order made against him before the commencement of the bankruptcy, and* (*d*) any interest provable as mentioned in section 322(2) in Chapter IV of Part IX.

(2) In determining for the purposes of any provision in this Group of Parts whether any liability in tort is a bankruptcy debt, the bankrupt is deemed to become subject to that liability by reason of an obligation incurred at the time when the cause of action accrued.

(3) For the purposes of references in this Group of Parts to a debt or liability, it is immaterial whether the debt or liability is present or future, whether it is certain or contingent or whether its amount is fixed or liquidated, or is capable of being ascertained by fixed rules or as a matter of opinion; and references in this Group of Parts to owing a debt are to be read accordingly.

(4) In this Group of Parts, except in so far as the context otherwise requires, "liability" means (subject to subsection (3) above) a liability to pay money or money's worth, including any liability under an enactment, any liability for breach of trust, any liability in contract, tort or bailment and any liability arising out of an obligation to make restitution.
[Insolvency Act 1986, s 382.]

***Repealed by the Criminal Justice Act 1988, Sch 16, when in force**.

8–18459 383. "Creditor", "security", etc. (1) "Creditor"—

(*a*) in relation to a bankrupt, means a person to whom any of the bankruptcy debts is owed (being, in the case of an amount falling within paragraph (*c*) of the definition in section 382(1) of "bankruptcy debt", the person in respect of whom that amount is specified in the criminal bankruptcy order in question), and*

(*b*) in relation to an individual to whom a bankruptcy petition relates, means a person who would be a creditor in the bankruptcy if a bankruptcy order were made on that petition.

(2) Subject to the next two subsections and any provision of the rules requiring a creditor to give up his security for the purposes of proving a debt, a debt is secured for the purposes of this Group of Parts to the extent that the person to whom the debt is owed holds any security for the debt (whether a mortgage, charge, lien or other security) over any property of the person by whom the debt is owed.

(3) Where a statement such as is mentioned in section 269(1)(*a*) in Chapter I of Part IX has been made by a secured creditor for the purposes of any bankruptcy petition and a bankruptcy order is subsequently made on that petition, the creditor is deemed for the purposes of the Parts in this Group to have given up the security specified in the statement.

(4) In subsection (2) the reference to a security does not include a lien on books, papers or other records, except to the extent that they consist of documents which give a title to property and are held as such.
[Insolvency Act 1986, s 383.]

***Amended by the Criminal Justice Act 1988, Sch 16, when in force**.

8–18470 384. "Prescribed" and "the rules". (1) Subject to the next subsection and sections 342C(7) and 342F(9) in Chapter V of Part IX, "prescribed" means prescribed by the rules; and "the rules" means[1] made under section 412 in Part XV.

(2) References in this Group of Parts to the amount prescribed[2] for the purposes of any of the following provisions.

section 273;
section 313A;
section 346(3);
section 354(1) and (2);
section 358;
section 360(1);
section 361(2); and
section 364(2)(*d*),

and references in those provisions to the prescribed amount are to be read in accordance with section 418 in Part XV and orders made under that section.
[Insolvency Act 1986, s 384, as amended by the Welfare Reform and Pensions Act 1999, s 84(1) and amended by the Enterprise Act 2002, s 261.]

---

1. See the Insolvency Rules 1986, SI 1986/1925, amended by SI 1987/1919, SI 1989/397, SI 1991/495, SI 1993/602, SI 1995/586, SI 1998/1129, SI 1999/359 and 1022, SI 2001/763, 3634 and 3649, SI 2002/1307 and 2712, SI 2003/1730, SI 2004/584 and 1070 and SI 2005/527 and 2114.

2. By virtue of s 418 of this Act the Secretary of State may by order prescribe amounts for the purposes of the provisions specified in s 384(2) and references to the "amount prescribed" for the purposes of these provisions and references in these provisions to the "prescribed amount" are to be construed accordingly. For the amount prescribed by order, see the Insolvency Proceedings (Monetary Limits) Order 1986, SI 1986/1996 amended by SI 2004/547.

8–18471 385. Miscellaneous definitions. (1) The following definitions have effect—

"the court", in relation to any matter, means the court to which, in accordance with section 373 in Part X and the rules, proceedings with respect to that matter are allocated or transferred;

"creditor's petition" means a bankruptcy petition under section 264(1)(*a*);

"criminal bankruptcy order" means an order under section 39(1) of the Powers of Criminal Courts Act 1973;*

"debt" is to be construed in accordance with section 382(3);

"the debtor"—

(*a*) in relation to a proposal for the purposes of Part VIII, means the individual making or intending to make that proposal, and

(*b*) in relation to a bankruptcy petition, means the individual to whom the petition relates;

"debtor's petition" means a bankruptcy petition presented by the debtor himself under section 264(1)(*b*);

"dwelling house" includes any building or part of a building which is occupied as a dwelling and any yard, garden, garage or outhouse belonging to the dwelling house and occupied with it;

"estate", in relation to a bankrupt is to be construed in accordance with section 283 in Chapter II of Part IX;

"family", in relation to a bankrupt, means the persons (if any) who are living with him and are dependent on him;

"secured" and related expressions are to be construed in accordance with section 383; and

"the trustee", in relation to a bankruptcy and the bankrupt, means the trustee of the bankrupt's estate.

(2) References in this Group of Parts to a person's affairs include his business, if any.

[Insolvency Act 1986, 385.]

***This definition is repealed by the Criminal Justice Act 1988, Sch 16, when in force.**

THE THIRD GROUP OF PARTS
MISCELLANEOUS MATTERS BEARING ON BOTH COMPANY AND INDIVIDUAL INSOLVENCY; GENERAL INTERPRETATION; FINAL PROVISIONS

PART XII[1]

PREFERENTIAL DEBTS IN COMPANY AND INDIVIDUAL INSOLVENCY

8–18472 386. Categories of preferential debts. (1) A reference in this Act to the preferential debts of a company or an individual is to the debts listed in Schedule 6[2] to this Act (contributions to occupational pension schemes; remineration, &c of employees; levies on coal and steel production); and references to preferential creditors are to be read accordingly.

(2) In that Schedule "the debtor" means the company or the individual concerned.

(3) Schedule 6 is to be read with Schedule 4 to the Pension Schemes Act 1993 (occupational pension scheme contributions).

[Insolvency Act 1986, s 386, as amended by SI 1987/2093, the Finance Act 1991, Sch 2, the Finance (No 2) Act 1992, s 9, the Finance Act 1993, s 36, the Pension Schemes Act 1993, Sch 8, the Finance Act 1994, Sch 7, the Finance Act 1995, s 17, the Finance Act 1996, Sch 5, the Finance Act 2000, Sch 7, the Finance Act 2001, Sch 5 and by the Enterprise Act 2002, s 251.]

1. Part XII contains ss 386, 387.
2. Schedule 6 is not printed in this work.

8–18473 387. "The relevant date". (1) This section explains references in Schedule 6 to the relevant date (being the date which determines the existence and amount of a preferential debt).

(2) For the purposes of section 4 in Part I (meetings to consider company voluntary arrangement), and the relevant date in relation to a company which is not being wound up is—

(*a*) if the company is in administration, the date on which it entered administration, and

(*b*) if the company is not in administration, the date on which the voluntary arrangement takes effect.

(2A) For the purposes of paragraph 31 of Schedule A1 (meetings to consider company voluntary arrangement where a moratorium under section 1A is in force), the relevant date in relation to a company is the date of filing.

(3) In relation to a company which is being wound up, the following applies—

(*a*) if the winding up is by the court, and the winding-up order was made immediately upon the discharge of an administration order, the relevant date is the date on which the company entered administration;

(*aa*) if the winding up is by the court and the winding-up order was made following conversion of administration into winding up by virtue of Article 37 of the EC Regulation, the relevant date is the date on which the company entered administration;

(*ab*) if the company is deemed to have passed a resolution for voluntary winding up by virtue of an order following conversion of administration into winding up under Article 37 of the EC Regulation, the relevant date is the date on which the company entered administration;

(*b*) if the case does not fall within paragraph (*a*), (*aa*) or (*ab*) and the company—

(i) is being wound up by the court, and

(ii) had not commenced to be wound up voluntarily before the date of the making of the winding-up order,

the relevant date is the date of the appointment (or first appointment) of a provisional liquidator or, if no such appointment has been made, the date of the winding-up order;*

(*ba*) if the case does not fall within paragraph (a), (aa), (ab) or (b) and the company is being wound up following administration pursuant to paragraph 83 of Schedule B1, the relevant date is the date on which the company entered administration;

(*c*) if the case does not fall within either paragraph (*a*), (*aa*), (*ab*), (*b*) or (*ba*), the relevant date is the date of the passing of the resolution for the winding up of the company.

(3A) In relation to a company which is in administration (and to which no other provision of this section applies) the relevant date is the date on which the company enters administration.

(4) In relation to a company in receivership (where section 40 or, as the case may be, section 59 applies), the relevant date is—

(*a*) in England and Wales, the date of the appointment of the receiver by debenture-holders, and

(*b*) *Scotland.*

(5) For the purposes of section 258 in Part VIII (individual voluntary arrangements), the relevant date is, in relation to a debtor who is not an undischarged bankrupt, the date of the interim order made under section 252 with respect to his proposal.

(*a*) where an interim order has been made under section 252 with respect to his proposal, the date of that order,and

(*b*) in any other case, the date on which the voluntary arrangement takes effect.

(6) In relation to a bankrupt, the following applies—

(*a*) where at the time the bankruptcy order was made there was an interim receiver appointed under section 286, the relevant date is the date on which the interim receiver was first appointed after the presentation of the bankruptcy petition;

(*b*) otherwise, the relevant date is the date of the making of the bankruptcy order.

[Insolvency Act 1986, s 387, as amended by the Insolvency Act 2000, ss 1, 2 and SI 2002/1240 and the Enterprise Act 2002, s 248.]

PART XIII[1]

INSOLVENCY PRACTITIONERS AND THEIR QUALIFICATION

Restrictions on unqualified persons acting as liquidator, trustee in bankruptcy, etc

8–18474 388. Meaning of "act as insolvency practitioner". (1) A person acts as an insolvency practitioner in relation to a company by acting—

(*a*) as its liquidator, provisional liquidator, administrator or administrative receiver, or

(*b*) where a voluntary arrangement in relation to the company is proposed or approved under Part I, as nominee or supervisor.

(2) A person acts as an insolvency practitioner in relation to an individual by acting—

(*a*) as his trustee in bankruptcy or interim receiver of his property or as permanent or interim trustee in the sequestration of his estate; or

(*b*) as trustee under a deed which is a deed of arrangement made for the benefit of his creditors or, in Scotland, a trust deed for his creditors; or

(*c*) where a voluntary arrangement in relation to the individual is proposed or approved under Part VIII, as nominee or supervisor

(*d*) in the case of a deceased individual to the administration of whose estate this section applies by virtue of an order under section 421 (application of provisions of this Act to insolvent estates of deceased persons), as administrator of that estate.

(2A) A person acts as an insolvency practitioner in relation to an insolvent partnership by acting—

(*a*) as its liquidator, provisional liquidator or administrator, or

(*b*) as trustee of the partnership under article 11 of the Insolvent Partnerships Order 1994, or

(*c*) where a voluntary arrangement in relation to the insolvent partnership is proposed or approved under Part I of this Act, as nominee or supervisor.

(2B) In relation to a voluntary arrangement proposed under Part I or VIII, a person acts as nominee if he performs any of the functions conferred on nominees under the Part in question.

(3) References in this section to an individual include, except in so far as the context otherwise requires, references to any debtor within the meaning of the Bankruptcy (Scotland) Act 1985.

(4) In this section—

"administrative receiver" has the meaning given by section 251 in Part VII;

"company" means a company within the meaning given by section 735(1) of the Companies Act or a company which may be wound up under Part V of this Act (unregistered companies); and

"interim trustee" and "permanent trustee" mean the same as in the Bankruptcy (Scotland) Act 1985.

(5) Nothing in this section applies to anything done by—

(*a*) the official receiver; or

(*b*) the Accountant in Bankruptcy (within the meaning of the Bankruptcy (Scotland) Act 1985).

(6) Nothing in this section applies to anything done (whether in the United Kingdom or elsewhere) in relation to insolvency proceedings under the EC Regulation in a member State other than the United Kingdom.

[Insolvency Act 1986, s 388 as amended by the Bankruptcy (Scotland) Act 1993, s 11, SI 1994/2421 and SI 2002/1240 and 2708, and the Insolvency Act 2000, s 4.]

---

1. Part XIII contains ss 388–398.

8–18475 **389. Acting without qualification an offence.** (1) A person who acts as an insolvency practitioner in relation to a company or an individual at a time when he is not qualified to do so is liable to imprisonment or a fine, or to both.

(1A) This section is subject to section 389A.

(2) This section does not apply to the official receiver or the Accountant in Bankruptcy (within the meaning of the Bankruptcy (Scotland) Act 1985).

[Insolvency Act 1986, s 389 as amended by the Bankruptcy (Scotland) Act 1993, s 11 and the Insolvency Act 2000, s 4.]

8–18475A **389A Authorisation of nominees and supervisors.** (1) Section 389 does not apply to a person acting, in relation to a voluntary arrangement proposed or approved under Part I or Part VIII, as nominee or supervisor if he is authorised so to act.

(2) For the purposes of subsection (1) and those Parts, an individual to whom subsection (3) does not apply is authorised to act as nominee or supervisor in relation to such an arrangement if—

(*a*) he is a member of a body recognised for the purpose by the Secretary of State, and

(*b*) there is in force security (in Scotland, caution) for the proper performance of his functions and that security or caution meets the prescribed requirements with respect to his so acting in relation to the arrangement.

(3) This subsection applies to a person if—

(*a*) he has been adjudged bankrupt or sequestration of his estate has been awarded and (in either case) he has not been discharged,

(*b*) he is subject to a disqualification order made or a disqualification undertaking accepted under the Company Directors Disqualification Act 1986 or to a disqualification order made under Part II of the Companies (Northern Ireland) Order 1989 or a disqualification undertaking accepted under the Company Directors Disqualification (Northern Ireland) Order 2002, or

(*c*) he is a patient within the meaning of Part VII of the Mental Health Act 1983 or section 125(1) of the Mental Health (Scotland) Act 1984.

(4) The Secretary of State may by order declare a body which appears to him to fall within subsection (5) to be a recognised body for the purposes of subsection (2)(*a*).

(5) A body may be recognised if it maintains and enforces rules for securing that its members—

(*a*) are fit and proper persons to act as nominees or supervisors, and

(*b*) meet acceptable requirements as to education and practical training and experience.

(6) For the purposes of this section, a person is a member of a body only if he is subject to its rules when acting as nominee or supervisor (whether or not he is in fact a member of the body).

(7) An order made under subsection (4) in relation to a body may be revoked by a further order if it appears to the Secretary of State that the body no longer falls within subsection (5).

(8) An order of the Secretary of State under this section has effect from such date as is specified in the order; and any such order revoking a previous order may make provision for members of the body in question to continue to be treated as members of a recognised body for a specified period after the revocation takes effect.

[Insolvency Act 1986, s 389A as inserted by the Insolvency Act 2000, s 4 and SI 2004/1941.]

8–18475B **389B. Official receiver as nominee or supervisor.** (1) The official receiver is authorised to act as nominee or supervisor in relation to a voluntary arrangement approved under Part VIII provided that the debtor is an undischarged bankrupt when the arrangement is proposed.

(2) The Secretary of State may by order repeal the proviso in subsection (1).

(3) An order under subsection (2)—

(*a*) must be made by statutory instrument, and
(*b*) shall be subject to annulment in pursuance of a resolution of either House of Parliament.
[Insolvency Act 1986, s 389B, as inserted by the Enterprise Act 2002, s 264(1), Sch 22.]

The requisite qualification, and the means of obtaining it

8–18476 390. Persons not qualified to act as insolvency practitioners. (1) A person who is not an individual is not qualified to act as an insolvency practitioner.

(2) A person is not qualified to act as an insolvency practitioner at any time unless at that time—

(*a*) he is authorised so to act by virtue of membership of a professional body recognised under section 391 below, being permitted so to act by or under the rules of that body, or
(*b*) he holds an authorisation granted by a competent authority under section 393.

(3) A person is not qualified to act as an insolvency practitioner in relation to another person at any time unless—

(*a*) there is in force at that time security or, in Scotland, caution for the proper performance of his functions, and
(*b*) that security or caution meets the prescribed[1] requirements with respect to his so acting in relation to that other person.

(4) A person is not qualified to act as an insolvency practitioner at any time if at that time—

(*a*) he has been adjudged bankrupt or sequestration of his estate has been awarded and (in either case) he has not been discharged,
(*b*) he is subject to a disqualification order made or a disqualification undertaking accepted under the Company Directors Disqualification Act 1986 or to a disqualification order made under Part II of the Companies (Northern Ireland) Order 1989 or a disqualification undertaking accepted under the Company Directors Disqualification (Northern Ireland) Order 2002, or
(*c*) he is a patient within the meaning of Part VII of the Mental Health Act 1983 or section 125(1) of the Mental Health (Scotland) Act 1984 or has had a guardian appointed to him under the Adults with Incapacity (Scotland) Act 2000 (asp 4)[2].

(5) A person is not qualified to act as an insolvency practitioner while a bankruptcy restrictions order is in force in respect of him.
[Insolvency Act 1986, s 390, as amended by the Insolvency Act 2000, Sch 4 and the Adults with Incapacity (Scotland) Act 2000, s 88(2), the Enterprise Act 2002, Sch 21 and SI 2004/1941.]

---

1. See the Insolvency Practitioners Regulations 1990, SI 1990/439 amended by SI 1993/221, SI 2002/2710 and 2748 and SI 2005/524.
2. Adults with Incapacity (Scotland) Act 2000, Sch 5.

8–18477 391. Recognised professional bodies. (1) The Secretary of State may by order declare a body which appears to him to fall within subsection (2) below to be a recognised professional body for the purposes of this section.

(2) A body may be recognised if it regulates the practice of a profession and maintains and enforces rules for securing that such of its members as are permitted by or under the rules to act as insolvency practitioners—

(*a*) are fit and proper persons so to act, and
(*b*) meet acceptable requirements as to education and practical training and experience.

(3) References to members of a recognised professional body are to persons who, whether members of that body or not, are subject to its rules in the practice of the profession in question.

The reference in section 390(2) above to membership of a professional body recognised under this section is to be read accordingly.

(4)–(5) *Further provisions as to orders.*
[Insolvency Act 1986, s 391.]

8–18478 392–393. *Authorisation by competent authority; grant, refusal and withdrawal of authorisation.*

8–18479 394. Notices. (1) Where a competent authority grants an authorisation under section 393, it shall give written notice of that fact to the applicant, specifying the date on which the authorisation takes effect.

(2) Where the authority proposes to refuse an application, or to withdraw an authorisation under section 393(4), it shall give the applicant or holder of the authorisation written notice of its intention to do so, setting out particulars of the grounds on which it proposes to act.

(3) In the case of a proposed withdrawal the notice shall state the date on which it is proposed that the withdrawal should take effect.

(4) A notice under subsection (2) shall give particulars of the rights exercisable under the next two sections by a person on whom the notice is served.
[Insolvency Act 1986, s 394.]

8-18480 **396. Reference to Tribunal.** *The Insolvency Practitioners Tribunal ("the Tribunal") continues in being; and the provisions of Schedule 7 apply to it.*

PART XVII[1]
MISCELLANEOUS AND GENERAL

8-18481 **426. Co-operation between courts exercising jurisdiction in relation to insolvency.** (1) An order made by a court in any part of the United Kingdom in the exercise of jurisdiction in relation to insolvency law shall be enforced in any other part of the United Kingdom as if it were made by a court exercising the corresponding jurisdiction in that other part.

(2) However, without prejudice to the following provisions of this section, nothing in subsection (1) requires a court in any part of the United Kingdom to enforce, in relation to property situated in that part, any order made by a court in any other part of the United Kingdom.

(3) The Secretary of State, with the concurrence in relation to property situated in England and Wales of the Lord Chancellor, may by order make provision for securing that a trustee or assignee under the insolvency law of any part of the United Kingdom has, with such modifications as may be specified in the order, the same rights in relation to any property situated in another part of the United Kingdom as he would have in the corresponding circumstances if he were a trustee or assignee under the insolvency law of that other part.

(4) The courts having jurisdiction in relation to insolvency law in any part of the United Kingdom shall assist the courts having the corresponding jurisdiction in any other part of the United Kingdom or any relevant country or territory.

(5) For the purposes of subsection (4) a request made to a court in any part of the United Kingdom by a court in any other part of the United Kingdom or in a relevant country or territory is authority for the court to which the request is made to apply, in relation to any matters specified in the request, the insolvency law which is applicable by either court in relation to comparable matters falling within its jurisdiction.

In exercising its discretion under this subsection, a court shall have regard in particular to the rules of private international law.

(6) Where a person who is a trustee or assignee under the insolvency law of any part of the United Kingdom claims property situated in any other part of the United Kingdom (whether by virtue of an order under subsection (3) or otherwise), the submission of that claim to the court exercising jurisdiction in relation to insolvency law in that other part shall be treated in the same manner as a request made by a court for the purpose of subsection (4).

(7) Section 38 of the Criminal Law Act 1977 (execution of warrant of arrest throughout the United Kingdom) applies to a warrant which, in exercise of any jurisdiction in relation to insolvency law, is issued in any part of the United Kingdom for the arrest of a person as it applies to a warrant issued in that part of the United Kingdom for the arrest of a person charged with an offence.

(8) Without prejudice to any power to make rules of court, any power to make provision by subordinate legislation for the purpose of giving effect in relation to companies or individuals to the insolvency law of any part of the United Kingdom includes power to make provision for the purpose of giving effect in that part to any provision made by or under the preceding provisions of this section.

(9) An order under subsection (3) shall be made by statutory instrument subject to annulment in pursuance of a resolution of either House of Parliament.

(10) In this section "insolvency law" means—

(*a*) in relation to England and Wales, provision extending to England and Wales and made by or under this Act or sections 1A, 6 to 10, 12 to 15, 19(c) and 20 (with Schedule 1) of the Company Directors Disqualification Act 1986 and sections 1 to 17 of that Act as they apply for the purposes of those provisions of that Act;
(*b*) *Scotland*;
(*c*) *Northern Ireland*;
(*d*) in relation to any relevant country or territory, so much of the law of that country or territory as corresponds to provisions falling within any of the foregoing paragraphs;

and references in this subsection to any enactment include, in relation to any time before the coming into force of that enactment the corresponding enactment in force at that time.

(11) In this section "relevant country or territory" means—

(*a*) any of the Channel Islands or the Isle of Man, or
(*b*) any country or territory designated for the purposes of this section by the Secretary of State by order[2] made by statutory instrument.

[Insolvency Act 1986, s 426, as amended by the Insolvency Act 2000, Sch 4.]

---

1. Part XVII contains ss 426–434.
2. Orders have been made in respect of: Anguilla, Australia, The Bahamas, Bermuda, Botswana, Canada, Cayman Islands, Falkland Islands, Gibraltar, Hong Kong, Republic of Ireland, Montserrat, New Zealand, St Helena, Turks and Caicos Islands, Tuvalu and Virgin Islands (SI 1986/2123); Malaysia and the Republic of South Africa (SI 1996/253); Brunei Darussalam (SI 1998/2766). The courts of these countries may request assistance in insolvency matters from courts with jurisdiction in insolvency law in the United Kingdom.

8–18481A 426A. Disqualification from Parliament (England and Wales). (1) A person in respect of whom a bankruptcy restrictions order has effect shall be disqualified—

(*a*) from membership of the House of Commons,

(*b*) from sitting or voting in the House of Lords, and

(*c*) from sitting or voting in a committee of the House of Lords or a joint committee of both Houses.

(2) If a member of the House of Commons becomes disqualified under this section, his seat shall be vacated.

(3) If a person who is disqualified under this section is returned as a member of the House of Commons, his return shall be void.

(4) No writ of summons shall be issued to a member of the House of Lords who is disqualified under this section.

(5) If a court makes a bankruptcy restrictions order or interim order in respect of a member of the House of Commons or the House of Lords the court shall notify the Speaker of that House.

(6) If the Secretary of State accepts a bankruptcy restrictions undertaking made by a member of the House of Commons or the House of Lords, the Secretary of State shall notify the Speaker of that House.

[Insolvency Act 1986, s 426A, as inserted by the Enterprise Act 2002, s 266.]

8–18481B 426B. Devolution. (1) If a court makes a bankruptcy restrictions order or interim order in respect of a member of the Scottish Parliament, the Northern Ireland Assembly or the National Assembly for Wales, the court shall notify the presiding officer of that body.

(2) If the Secretary of State accepts a bankruptcy restrictions undertaking made by a member of the Scottish Parliament, the Northern Ireland Assembly or the National Assembly for Wales, the Secretary of State shall notify the presiding officer of that body.

[Insolvency Act 1986, s 426B, as inserted by the Enterprise Act 2002, s 266.]

8–18481C 426C. Irrelevance of privilege. (1) An enactment about insolvency applies in relation to a member of the House of Commons or the House of Lords irrespective of any Parliamentary privilege.

(2) In this section "enactment" includes a provision made by or under—

(*a*) an Act of the Scottish Parliament, or

(*b*) Northern Ireland legislation.

[Insolvency Act 1986, s 426C, as inserted by the Enterprise Act 2002, s 266.]

8–18482 430. Provision introducing Schedule of punishments. (1) Schedule 10 to this Act has effect with respect to the way in which offences under this Act are punishable on conviction.

(2) In relation to an offence under a provision of this Act specified in the first column of the Schedule (the general nature of the offence being described in the second column), the third column shows whether the offence is punishable on conviction on indictment, or on summary conviction, or either in the one way or the other.

(3) The fourth column of the Schedule shows, in relation to an offence, the maximum punishment by way of fine or imprisonment under this Act which may be imposed on a person convicted of the offence in the way specified in relation to it in the third column (that is to say, on indictment or summarily), a reference to a period of years or months being to a term of imprisonment of that duration.

(4) The fifth column shows (in relation to an offence for which there is an entry in that column) that a person convicted of the offence after continued contravention is liable to a daily default fine; that is to say, he is liable on a second or subsequent conviction of the offence to the fine specified in that column for each day on which the contravention is continued (instead of the penalty specified for the offence in the fourth column of the Schedule).

(5) For the purpose of any enactment in this Act whereby an officer of a company who is in default is liable to a fine or penalty, the expression "officer who is in default" means any officer of the company who knowingly and wilfully authorises or permits the default, refusal or contravention mentioned in the enactment.

[Insolvency Act 1986, s 430.]

8–18483 431. Summary proceedings. (1) Summary proceedings for any offence under any of Parts I to VII of this Act may (without prejudice to any jurisdiction exercisable apart from this subsection) be taken against a body corporate at any place at which the body has a place of business, and against any other person at any place at which he is for the time being.

(2) Notwithstanding anything in section 127(1) of the Magistrates' Courts Act 1980, an information relating to such an offence which is triable by a magistrates' court in England and Wales may be so tried if it is laid at any time within 3 years after the commission of the offence and within 12 months after the date on which evidence sufficient in the opinion of the Director of Public Prosecutions or the Secretary of State (as the case may be) to justify the proceedings comes to his knowledge.

(3) Summary proceedings in Scotland for such an offence shall not be commenced after the expiration of 3 years from the commission of the offence.

Subject to this (and notwithstanding anything in section 136 of the Criminal Procedure (Scotland) Act 1995), such proceedings may (in Scotland) be commenced at any time within 12 months after the date on which evidence sufficient in the Lord Advocate's opinion to justify the proceedings came to his knowledge or, where such evidence was reported to him by the Secretary of State, within 12 months after the date on which it came to the knowledge of the latter; and subsection (3) of that section applies for the purpose of this subsection as it applies for the purpose of that section.

(4) For purposes of this section, a certificate of the Director of Public Prosecutions, the Lord Advocate or the Secretary of State (as the case may be) as to the date on which such evidence as is referred to above came to his knowledge is conclusive evidence.

[Insolvency Act 1986, s 431 as amended by the Criminal Procedure (Consequential Provisions) (Scotland) Act 1995, Sch 4.]

8–18484 **432. Offences by bodies corporate.** (1) This section applies to offences under this Act other than those excepted by subsection (4).

(2) Where a body corporate is guilty of an offence to which this section applies and the offence is proved to have been committed with the consent or connivance of, or to be attributable to any neglect on the part of, any director, manager, secretary or other similar officer of the body corporate or any person who was purporting to act in any such capacity he, as well as the body corporate, is guilty of the offence and liable to be proceeded against and punished accordingly.

(3) Where the affairs of a body corporate are managed by its members, subsection (2) applies in relation to the acts and defaults of a member in connection with his functions of management as if he were a director of the body corporate.

(4) The offences excepted from this section are those under sections 30, 39, 51, 53, 54, 62, 64, 66, 85, 89, 164, 188, 201, 206, 207, 208, 209, 210 and 211 and those under paragraphs 16(2), 17(3)(*a*), 18(3)(*a*), 19(3)(*a*), 22(1) and 23(1)(*a*) of Schedule A1.

[Insolvency Act 1986, s 432 as amended by the Insolvency Act 2000, s 1.]

8–18485 **433. Admissibility in evidence of statements of affairs, etc.** (1) In any proceedings (whether or not under this Act)—

(*a*) a statement of affairs prepared for the purposes of any provision of this Act which is derived from the Insolvency Act 1985, and

(*b*) any other statement made in pursuance of a requirement imposed by or under any such provision or by or under rules made under this Act,

may be used in evidence against any person making or concurring in making the statement.

(2) However, in criminal proceedings in which any such person is charged with an offence to which this subsection applies—

(*a*) no evidence relating to the statement may be adduced, and

(*b*) no question relating to it may be asked,

by or on behalf of the prosecution, unless evidence relating to it is adduced, or a question relating to it is asked, in the proceedings by or on behalf of that person.

(3) Subsection (2) applies to any offence other than—

(*a*) an offence under section 22(6), 47(6), 48(8), 66(6), 67(8), 95(8), 98(6), 99(3)(*a*), 131(7), 192(2), 208(1)(*a*) or (*d*) or (2), 210, 235(5), 353(1), 354(1)(*b*) or (3) or 356(1) or (2)(*a*) or (*b*) or paragraph 4(3)(*a*) of Schedule 7;

(*b*) an offence which is—

(i) created by rules made under this Act, and

(ii) designated for the purposes of this subsection by such rules or by regulations made by the Secretary of State;

(*c*) an offence which is—

(i) created by regulations made under any such rules, and

(ii) designated for the purposes of this subsection by such regulations;

(*d*) an offence under section 1, 2 or 5 of the Perjury Act 1911 (false statements made on oath or made otherwise than on oath); or

(*e*) an offence under section 44(1) or (2) of the Criminal Law (Consolidation) (Scotland) Act 1995 (false statements made on oath or otherwise than on oath).

(4) Regulations under subsection (3)(b)(ii) shall be made by statutory instrument and, after being made, shall be laid before each House of Parliament.

[Insolvency Act 1986, s 433, as amended by the Youth Justice and Criminal Evidence Act 1999, Sch 3.]

8–18486 **434. Crown application.** For the avoidance of doubt it is hereby declared that provisions of this Act which derive from the Insolvency Act 1985 bind the Crown so far as affecting or relating to the following matters, namely—

(*a*) remedies against, or against the property of, companies or individuals;
(*b*) priorities of debts;
(*c*) transactions at an undervalue or preferences;
(*d*) voluntary arrangements approved under Part I or Part VIII, and
(*e*) discharge from bankruptcy.

[Insolvency Act 1986, s 434.]

PART XVIII[1]
INTERPRETATION

8–18487 **435. Meaning of "associate".** (1) For the purposes of this Act any question whether a person is an associate of another person is to be determined in accordance with the following provisions of this section (any provision that a person is an associate of another person being taken to mean that they are associates of each other).

(2) A person is an associate of an individual if that person is—

(*a*) the individual's husband or wife or civil partner,
(*b*) a relative of—
  (i) the individual, or
  (ii) the individual's husband or wife or civil partner, or
(*c*) the husband or wife or civil partner of a relative of—
  (i) the individual, or
  (ii) the individual's husband or wife or civil partner.

(3) A person is an associate of any person with whom he is in partnership, and of the husband or wife or civil partner or a relative of any individual with whom he is in partnership; and a Scottish firm is an associate of any person who is a member of the firm.

(4) A person is an associate of any person whom he employs or by whom he is employed.

(5) A person in his capacity as trustee of a trust other than—

(*a*) a trust arising under any of the second Group of Parts or the Bankruptcy (Scotland) Act 1985, or
(*b*) a pension scheme or an employees' share scheme (within the meaning of the Companies Act),

is an associate of another person if the beneficiaries of the trust include, or the terms of the trust confer a power that may be exercised for the benefit of, that other person or an associate of that other person.

(6) A company is an associate of another company—

(*a*) if the same person has control of both, or a person has control of one and persons who are his associates, or he and persons who are his associates, have control of the other, or
(*b*) if a group of two or more persons has control of each company, and the groups either consist of the same persons or could be regarded as consisting of the same persons by treating (in one or more cases) a member of either group as replaced by a person of whom he is an associate.

(7) A company is an associate of another person if that person has control of it or if that person and persons who are his associates together have control of it.

(8) For the purposes of this section a person is a relative of an individual if he is that individual's brother, sister, uncle, aunt, nephew, niece, lineal ancestor or lineal descendant, treating—

(*a*) any relationship of the half blood as a relationship of the whole blood and the stepchild or adopted child of any person as his child, and
(*b*) an illegitimate child as the legitimate child of his mother and reputed father;

and references in this section to a husband or wife include a former husband or wife and a reputed husband or wife and references to a civil partner include a former civil partner and a reputed civil partner.

(9) For the purposes of this section any director or other officer of a company is to be treated as employed by that company.

(10) For the purposes of this section a person is to be taken as having control of a company if—

(*a*) the directors of the company or of another company which has control of it (or any of them) are accustomed to act in accordance with his directions or instructions, or
(*b*) he is entitled to exercise, or control the exercise of, one third or more of the voting power at any general meeting of the company or of another company which has control of it;

and where two or more persons together satisfy either of the above conditions, they are to be taken as having control of the company.

(11) In this section "company" includes any body corporate (whether incorporated in Great Britain or elsewhere); and references to directors and other officers of a company and to voting power at any general meeting of a company have effect with any necessary modifications.

[Insolvency Act 1986, s 435 as amended by the Civil Partnership Act 2004, Sch 27.]

---

1. Part XVIII contains ss 435–436.

8–18488 436. Expressions used generally. In this Act, except in so far as the context otherwise requires (and subject to Parts VII and XI)—

"the appointed day" means the day on which this Act comes into force under section 443;
"associate" has the meaning given by section 435;
"business" includes a trade or profession;
"the Companies Act" means the Companies Act 1985;
"conditional sale agreement" and "hire-purchase agreement" have the same meanings as in the Consumer Credit Act 1974;
"the EC Regulation" means Council Regulation (EC) No 1346/2000;
"modifications" includes additions, alterations and omissions and cognate expressions shall be construed accordingly;
"property" includes money, goods, things in action, land and every description of property wherever situated and also obligations and every description of interest, whether present or future or vested or contingent, arising out of, or incidental to, property;
"records" includes computer records and other non-documentary records;
"subordinate legislation" has the same meaning as in the Interpretation Act 1978; and
"transaction" includes a gift, agreement or arrangement, and references to entering into a transaction shall be construed accordingly.

[Insolvency Act 1986, s 436, as amended by SI 2002/1037.]

8–18488A 436A. Proceedings under EC Regulation: modified definition of property. In the application of this Act to proceedings by virtue of Article 3 of the EC Regulation, a reference to property is a reference to property which may be dealt with in the proceedings.

[Insolvency Act 1986, s 436A, as inserted by SI 2002/1240.]

PART XIX[1]

FINAL PROVISIONS

8–18489 437. Transitional provisions, and savings. The transitional provisions and savings set out in Schedule 11 to this Act shall have effect, the Schedule comprising the following Parts—

Part I: company insolvency and winding up (matters arising before appointed day, and continuance of proceedings in certain cases as before that day);

Part II: individual insolvency (matters so arising, and continuance of bankruptcy proceedings in certain cases as before that day);

Part III: transactions entered into before the appointed day and capable of being affected by orders of the court under Part XVI of this Act;

Part IV: insolvency practitioners acting as such before the appointed day; and

Part V: general transitional provisions and savings required consequentially on, and in connection with, the repeal and replacement by this Act and the Company Directors Disqualification Act 1986 of provisions of the Companies Act, the greater part of the Insolvency Act 1985 and other enactments.

[Insolvency Act 1986, s 437.]

1. Part XIX contains ss 437–444.

8–18500 438. *Repeals.*

8–18501 439. Amendment of enactments. (1) The Companies Act is amended as shown in Parts I and II of Schedule 13 to this Act, being amendments consequential on this Act and the Company Directors Disqualification Act 1986.

(2) The enactments specified in the first column of Schedule 14 to this Act (being enactments which refer, or otherwise relate, to those which are repealed and replaced by this Act or the Company Directors Disqualification Act 1986) are amended as shown in the second column of that Schedule.

(3) The Lord Chancellor may by order make such consequential modifications of any provision contained in any subordinate legislation made before the appointed day and such transitional provisions in connection with those modifications as appear to him necessary or expedient in respect of—

(*a*) any reference in that subordinate legislation to the Bankruptcy Act 1914;
(*b*) any reference in that subordinate legislation to any enactment repealed by Part III or IV of Schedule 10 to the Insolvency Act 1985; or
(*c*) any reference in that subordinate legislation to any matter provided for under the Act of 1914 or under any enactment so repealed.

(4) An order under this section shall be made by statutory instrument subject to annulment in pursuance of a resolution of either House of Parliament.

[Insolvency Act 1986, s 439.]

8–18502 440–442. *Extent (Scotland, Northern Ireland, Other territories).*

8–18503 443. *Commencement.*

8–18504 444. Citation. This Act may be cited as the Insolvency Act 1986.
[Insolvency Act 1986, s 444.]

8–18504A

Section 8

SCHEDULE B1
ADMINISTRATION

(*Inserted by the Enterprise Act 2002, Sch 16, amended by SI 2003/2096*).

NATURE OF ADMINISTRATION

Administration

1. (1) For the purposes of this Act "administrator" of a company means a person appointed under this Schedule to manage the company's affairs, business and property.

(2) For the purposes of this Act—

(*a*) a company is "in administration" while the appointment of an administrator of the company has effect,
(*b*) a company "enters administration" when the appointment of an administrator takes effect,
(*c*) a company ceases to be in administration when the appointment of an administrator of the company ceases to have effect in accordance with this Schedule, and
(*d*) a company does not cease to be in administration merely because an administrator vacates office (by reason of resignation, death or otherwise) or is removed from office.

2. A person may be appointed as administrator of a company—

(*a*) by administration order of the court under paragraph 10,
(*b*) by the holder of a floating charge under paragraph 14, or
(*c*) by the company or its directors under paragraph 22.

Purpose of administration

3. (1) The administrator of a company must perform his functions with the objective of—

(*a*) rescuing the company as a going concern, or
(*b*) achieving a better result for the company's creditors as a whole than would be likely if the company were wound up (without first being in administration), or
(*c*) realising property in order to make a distribution to one or more secured or preferential creditors.

(2) Subject to sub-paragraph (4), the administrator of a company must perform his functions in the interests of the company's creditors as a whole.

(3) The administrator must perform his functions with the objective specified in sub-paragraph (1)(a) unless he thinks either—

(*a*) that it is not reasonably practicable to achieve that objective, or
(*b*) that the objective specified in sub-paragraph (1)(*b*) would achieve a better result for the company's creditors as a whole.

(4) The administrator may perform his functions with the objective specified in sub-paragraph (1)(*c*) only if—

(*a*) he thinks that it is not reasonably practicable to achieve either of the objectives specified in sub-paragraph (1)(*a*) and (*b*), and
(*b*) he does not unnecessarily harm the interests of the creditors of the company as a whole.

4. The administrator of a company must perform his functions as quickly and efficiently as is reasonably practicable.

Status of administrator

5. An administrator is an officer of the court (whether or not he is appointed by the court).

General restrictions

6. A person may be appointed as administrator of a company only if he is qualified to act as an insolvency practitioner in relation to the company.

7. A person may not be appointed as administrator of a company which is in administration (subject to the provisions of paragraphs 90 to 97 and 100 to 103 about replacement and additional administrators).

8. (1) A person may not be appointed as administrator of a company which is in liquidation by virtue of—

(*a*) a resolution for voluntary winding up, or
(*b*) a winding-up order.

(2) Sub-paragraph (1)(*a*) is subject to paragraph 38.

(3) Sub-paragraph (1)(*b*) is subject to paragraphs 37 and 38.

9. (1) A person may not be appointed as administrator of a company which—

(*a*) has a liability in respect of a deposit which it accepted in accordance with the Banking Act 1979 (c 37) or 1987 (c 22), but
(*b*) is not an authorised deposit taker.

(2) A person may not be appointed as administrator of a company which effects or carries out contracts of insurance.

(3) But sub-paragraph (2) does not apply to a company which—

(*a*) is exempt from the general prohibition in relation to effecting or carrying out contracts of insurance, or
(*b*) is an authorised deposit taker effecting or carrying out contracts of insurance in the course of a banking business.

(4) In this paragraph—

"authorised deposit taker" means a person with permission under Part IV of the Financial Services and Markets Act 2000 (c 8) to accept deposits, and
"the general prohibition" has the meaning given by section 19 of that Act.

(5) This paragraph shall be construed in accordance with—

(*a*) section 22 of the Financial Services and Markets Act 2000 (classes of regulated activity and categories of investment),
(*b*) any relevant order under that section, and
(*c*) Schedule 2 to that Act (regulated activities).

APPOINTMENT OF ADMINISTRATOR BY COURT

Administration order

10. An administration order is an order appointing a person as the administrator of a company.

Conditions for making order

11. The court may make an administration order in relation to a company only if satisfied—

(*a*) that the company is or is likely to become unable to pay its debts, and
(*b*) that the administration order is reasonably likely to achieve the purpose of administration.

Administration application

12. (1) An application to the court for an administration order in respect of a company (an "administration application") may be made only by—

(*a*) the company,
(*b*) the directors of the company,
(*c*) one or more creditors of the company,
(*d*) the justices' chief executive for a magistrates' court in the exercise of the power conferred by section 87A of the Magistrates' Courts Act 1980 (c 43) (fine imposed on company), or
(*e*) a combination of persons listed in paragraphs (a) to (d).

(2) As soon as is reasonably practicable after the making of an administration application the applicant shall notify—

(*a*) any person who has appointed an administrative receiver of the company,
(*b*) any person who is or may be entitled to appoint an administrative receiver of the company,
(*c*) any person who is or may be entitled to appoint an administrator of the company under paragraph 14, and
(*d*) such other persons as may be prescribed.

(3) An administration application may not be withdrawn without the permission of the court.
(4) In sub-paragraph (1) "creditor" includes a contingent creditor and a prospective creditor.
(5) Sub-paragraph (1) is without prejudice to section 7(4)(*b*).

Powers of court

13. (1) On hearing an administration application the court may—

(*a*) make the administration order sought;
(*b*) dismiss the application;
(*c*) adjourn the hearing conditionally or unconditionally;
(*d*) make an interim order;
(*e*) treat the application as a winding-up petition and make any order which the court could make under section 125;
(*f*) make any other order which the court thinks appropriate.

(2) An appointment of an administrator by administration order takes effect—

(*a*) at a time appointed by the order, or
(*b*) where no time is appointed by the order, when the order is made.

(3) An interim order under sub-paragraph (1)(*d*) may, in particular—

(*a*) restrict the exercise of a power of the directors or the company;
(*b*) make provision conferring a discretion on the court or on a person qualified to act as an insolvency practitioner in relation to the company.

(4) This paragraph is subject to paragraph 39.

APPOINTMENT OF ADMINISTRATOR BY HOLDER OF FLOATING CHARGE

Power to appoint

14. (1) The holder of a qualifying floating charge in respect of a company's property may appoint an administrator of the company.
(2) For the purposes of sub-paragraph (1) a floating charge qualifies if created by an instrument which—

(*a*) states that this paragraph applies to the floating charge,
(*b*) purports to empower the holder of the floating charge to appoint an administrator of the company,
(*c*) purports to empower the holder of the floating charge to make an appointment which would be the appointment of an administrative receiver within the meaning given by section 29(2), or
(*d*) purports to empower the holder of a floating charge in Scotland to appoint a receiver who on appointment would be an administrative receiver.

(3) For the purposes of sub-paragraph (1) a person is the holder of a qualifying floating charge in respect of a company's property if he holds one or more debentures of the company secured—

(*a*) by a qualifying floating charge which relates to the whole or substantially the whole of the company's property,
(*b*) by a number of qualifying floating charges which together relate to the whole or substantially the whole of the company's property, or
(*c*) by charges and other forms of security which together relate to the whole or substantially the whole of the company's property and at least one of which is a qualifying floating charge.

Notice of appointment

18. (1) A person who appoints an administrator of a company under paragraph 14 shall file with the court—

(*a*) a notice of appointment, and
(*b*) such other documents as may be prescribed.

(2) The notice of appointment must include a statutory declaration by or on behalf of the person who makes the appointment—

(*a*) that the person is the holder of a qualifying floating charge in respect of the company's property,
(*b*) that each floating charge relied on in making the appointment is (or was) enforceable on the date of the appointment, and
(*c*) that the appointment is in accordance with this Schedule.

(3) The notice of appointment must identify the administrator and must be accompanied by a statement by the administrator—

(*a*) that he consents to the appointment,
(*b*) that in his opinion the purpose of administration is reasonably likely to be achieved, and
(*c*) giving such other information and opinions as may be prescribed.

(4) For the purpose of a statement under sub-paragraph (3) an administrator may rely on information supplied by directors of the company (unless he has reason to doubt its accuracy).

(5) The notice of appointment and any document accompanying it must be in the prescribed form.

(6) A statutory declaration under sub-paragraph (2) must be made during the prescribed period.

(7) A person commits an offence if in a statutory declaration under sub-paragraph (2) he makes a statement—

(*a*) which is false, and
(*b*) which he does not reasonably believe to be true.

20. A person who appoints an administrator under paragraph 14—

(*a*) shall notify the administrator and such other persons as may be prescribed as soon as is reasonably practicable after the requirements of paragraph 18 are satisfied, and
(*b*) commits an offence if he fails without reasonable excuse to comply with paragraph (*a*).

APPOINTMENT OF ADMINISTRATOR BY COMPANY OR DIRECTORS

Power to appoint

22. (1) A company may appoint an administrator.

(2) The directors of a company may appoint an administrator.

Notice of intention to appoint

26. (1) A person who proposes to make an appointment under paragraph 22 shall give at least five business days' written notice to—

(*a*) any person who is or may be entitled to appoint an administrative receiver of the company, and
(*b*) any person who is or may be entitled to appoint an administrator of the company under paragraph 14.

(2) A person who proposes to make an appointment under paragraph 22 shall also give such notice as may be prescribed to such other persons as may be prescribed.

(3) A notice under this paragraph must—

(*a*) identify the proposed administrator, and
(*b*) be in the prescribed form.

27. (1) A person who gives notice of intention to appoint under paragraph 26 shall file with the court as soon as is reasonably practicable a copy of—

(*a*) the notice, and
(*b*) any document accompanying it.

(2) The copy filed under sub-paragraph (1) must be accompanied by a statutory declaration made by or on behalf of the person who proposes to make the appointment—

(*a*) that the company is or is likely to become unable to pay its debts,
(*b*) that the company is not in liquidation, and
(*c*) that, so far as the person making the statement is able to ascertain, the appointment is not prevented by paragraphs 23 to 25, and
(*d*) to such additional effect, and giving such information, as may be prescribed.

(3) A statutory declaration under sub-paragraph (2) must—

(*a*) be in the prescribed form, and
(*b*) be made during the prescribed period.

(4) A person commits an offence if in a statutory declaration under sub-paragraph (2) he makes a statement—

(*a*) which is false, and
(*b*) which he does not reasonably believe to be true.

Notice of appointment

29. (1) A person who appoints an administrator of a company under paragraph 22 shall file with the court—

(*a*) a notice of appointment, and
(*b*) such other documents as may be prescribed.

(2) The notice of appointment must include a statutory declaration by or on behalf of the person who makes the appointment—

(*a*) that the person is entitled to make an appointment under paragraph 22,
(*b*) that the appointment is in accordance with this Schedule, and
(*c*) that, so far as the person making the statement is able to ascertain, the statements made and information given in the statutory declaration filed with the notice of intention to appoint remain accurate.

(3) The notice of appointment must identify the administrator and must be accompanied by a statement by the administrator—

(*a*) that he consents to the appointment,
(*b*) that in his opinion the purpose of administration is reasonably likely to be achieved, and
(*c*) giving such other information and opinions as may be prescribed.

(4) For the purpose of a statement under sub-paragraph (3) an administrator may rely on information supplied by directors of the company (unless he has reason to doubt its accuracy).

(5) The notice of appointment and any document accompanying it must be in the prescribed form.

(6) A statutory declaration under sub-paragraph (2) must be made during the prescribed period.

(7) A person commits an offence if in a statutory declaration under sub-paragraph (2) he makes a statement—

(*a*) which is false, and
(*b*) which he does not reasonably believe to be true.

EFFECT OF ADMINISTRATION

Moratorium on other legal process

43. (1) This paragraph applies to a company in administration.

(2) No step may be taken to enforce security over the company's property except—

(*a*) with the consent of the administrator, or
(*b*) with the permission of the court.

(3) No step may be taken to repossess goods in the company's possession under a hire-purchase agreement except—

(*a*) with the consent of the administrator, or
(*b*) with the permission of the court.

(4) A landlord may not exercise a right of forfeiture by peaceable re-entry in relation to premises let to the company except—

(*a*) with the consent of the administrator, or
(*b*) with the permission of the court.

(5) In Scotland, a landlord may not exercise a right of irritancy in relation to premises let to the company except—

(*a*) with the consent of the administrator, or
(*b*) with the permission of the court.

(6) No legal process (including legal proceedings[1], execution, distress and diligence) may be instituted or continued against the company or property of the company except—

(*a*) with the consent of the administrator, or
(*b*) with the permission of the court.

(6A) An administrative receiver of the company may not be appointed.

(7) Where the court gives permission for a transaction under this paragraph it may impose a condition on or a requirement in connection with the transaction.

(8) In this paragraph "landlord" includes a person to whom rent is payable.

---

1. It was held, it relation to the predecessor of this provision, namely s 11(3)(d) of the Insolvency Act 1986, that "other proceedings", the phrase then used, included a criminal prosecution, which could not be instituted without the leave of the court: *In re Rhondda Waste Disposal Co Ltd (in administration)* [2001] Ch 57, [2000] 3 WLR 1304, CA.

PROCESS OF ADMINISTRATION

Announcement of administrator's appointment

46. (1) This paragraph applies where a person becomes the administrator of a company.

(2) As soon as is reasonably practicable the administrator shall—

(*a*) send a notice of his appointment to the company, and

(*b*) publish a notice of his appointment in the prescribed manner.

(3) As soon as is reasonably practicable the administrator shall—

(*a*) obtain a list of the company's creditors, and

(*b*) send a notice of his appointment to each creditor of whose claim and address he is aware.

(4) The administrator shall send a notice of his appointment to the registrar of companies before the end of the period of 7 days beginning with the date specified in sub-paragraph (6).

(5) The administrator shall send a notice of his appointment to such persons as may be prescribed before the end of the prescribed period beginning with the date specified in sub-paragraph (6).

(6) The date for the purpose of sub-paragraphs (4) and (5) is—

(*a*) in the case of an administrator appointed by administration order, the date of the order,

(*b*) in the case of an administrator appointed under paragraph 14, the date on which he receives notice under paragraph 20, and

(*c*) in the case of an administrator appointed under paragraph 22, the date on which he receives notice under paragraph 32.

(7) The court may direct that sub-paragraph (3)(b) or (5)—

(*a*) shall not apply, or

(*b*) shall apply with the substitution of a different period.

(8) A notice under this paragraph must—

(*a*) contain the prescribed information, and

(*b*) be in the prescribed form.

(9) An administrator commits an offence if he fails without reasonable excuse to comply with a requirement of this paragraph.

Statement of company's affairs

47. (1) As soon as is reasonably practicable after appointment the administrator of a company shall by notice in the prescribed form require one or more relevant persons to provide the administrator with a statement of the affairs of the company.

(2) The statement must—

(*a*) be verified by a statement of truth in accordance with Civil Procedure Rules,

(*b*) be in the prescribed form,

(*c*) give particulars of the company's property, debts and liabilities,

(*d*) give the names and addresses of the company's creditors,

(*e*) specify the security held by each creditor,

(*f*) give the date on which each security was granted, and

(*g*) contain such other information as may be prescribed.

(3) In sub-paragraph (1) "relevant person" means—

(*a*) a person who is or has been an officer of the company,

(*b*) a person who took part in the formation of the company during the period of one year ending with the date on which the company enters administration,

(*c*) a person employed by the company during that period, and

(*d*) a person who is or has been during that period an officer or employee of a company which is or has been during that year an officer of the company.

(4) For the purpose of sub-paragraph (3) a reference to employment is a reference to employment through a contract of employment or a contract for services.

(5) In Scotland, a statement of affairs under sub-paragraph (1) must be a statutory declaration made in accordance with the Statutory Declarations Act 1835 (c 62) (and sub-paragraph (2)(a) shall not apply).

48. (1) A person required to submit a statement of affairs must do so before the end of the period of 11 days beginning with the day on which he receives notice of the requirement.

(2) The administrator may—

(*a*) revoke a requirement under paragraph 47(1), or

(*b*) extend the period specified in sub-paragraph (1) (whether before or after expiry).

(3) If the administrator refuses a request to act under sub-paragraph (2)—

(*a*) the person whose request is refused may apply to the court, and

(*b*) the court may take action of a kind specified in sub-paragraph (2).

(4) A person commits an offence if he fails without reasonable excuse to comply with a requirement under paragraph 47(1).

Administrator's proposals

49. (1) The administrator of a company shall make a statement setting out proposals for achieving the purpose of administration.

(2) A statement under sub-paragraph (1) must, in particular—

(*a*) deal with such matters as may be prescribed, and
(*b*) where applicable, explain why the administrator thinks that the objective mentioned in paragraph 3(1)(*a*) or (*b*) cannot be achieved.

(3) Proposals under this paragraph may include—

(*a*) a proposal for a voluntary arrangement under Part I of this Act (although this paragraph is without prejudice to section 4(3));
(*b*) a proposal for a compromise or arrangement to be sanctioned under section 425 of the Companies Act (compromise with creditors or members).

(4) The administrator shall send a copy of the statement of his proposals—

(*a*) to the registrar of companies,
(*b*) to every creditor of the company of whose claim and address he is aware, and
(*c*) to every member of the company of whose address he is aware.

(5) The administrator shall comply with sub-paragraph (4)—

(*a*) as soon as is reasonably practicable after the company enters administration, and
(*b*) in any event, before the end of the period of eight weeks beginning with the day on which the company enters administration.

(6) The administrator shall be taken to comply with sub-paragraph (4)(*c*) if he publishes in the prescribed manner a notice undertaking to provide a copy of the statement of proposals free of charge to any member of the company who applies in writing to a specified address.

(7) An administrator commits an offence if he fails without reasonable excuse to comply with sub-paragraph (5).

(8) A period specified in this paragraph may be varied in accordance with paragraph 107.

Requirement for initial creditors' meeting

51. (1) Each copy of an administrator's statement of proposals sent to a creditor under paragraph 49(4)(*b*) must be accompanied by an invitation to a creditors' meeting (an "initial creditors' meeting").

(2) The date set for an initial creditors' meeting must be—

(*a*) as soon as is reasonably practicable after the company enters administration, and
(*b*) in any event, within the period of ten weeks beginning with the date on which the company enters administration.

(3) An administrator shall present a copy of his statement of proposals to an initial creditors' meeting.

(4) A period specified in this paragraph may be varied in accordance with paragraph 107.

(5) An administrator commits an offence if he fails without reasonable excuse to comply with a requirement of this paragraph.

52. (1) Paragraph 51(1) shall not apply where the statement of proposals states that the administrator thinks—

(*a*) that the company has sufficient property to enable each creditor of the company to be paid in full,
(*b*) that the company has insufficient property to enable a distribution to be made to unsecured creditors other than by virtue of section 176A(2)(*a*), or
(*c*) that neither of the objectives specified in paragraph 3(1)(*a*) and (*b*) can be achieved.

(2) But the administrator shall summon an initial creditors' meeting if it is requested—

(a) by creditors of the company whose debts amount to at least 10% of the total debts of the company,
(b) in the prescribed manner, and
(c) in the prescribed period.

(3) A meeting requested under sub-paragraph (2) must be summoned for a date in the prescribed period.

(4) The period prescribed under sub-paragraph (3) may be varied in accordance with paragraph 107.

Business and result of initial creditors' meeting

53. (1) An initial creditors' meeting to which an administrator's proposals are presented shall consider them and may—

(*a*) approve them without modification, or
(*b*) approve them with modification to which the administrator consents.

(2) After the conclusion of an initial creditors' meeting the administrator shall as soon as is reasonably practicable report any decision taken to—

(*a*) the court,
(*b*) the registrar of companies, and
(*c*) such other persons as may be prescribed.

(3) An administrator commits an offence if he fails without reasonable excuse to comply with sub-paragraph (2).

Revision of administrator's proposals

54. (1) This paragraph applies where—

(*a*) an administrator's proposals have been approved (with or without modification) at an initial creditors' meeting,
(*b*) the administrator proposes a revision to the proposals, and
(*c*) the administrator thinks that the proposed revision is substantial.

(2) The administrator shall—

(*a*) summon a creditors' meeting,
(*b*) send a statement in the prescribed form of the proposed revision with the notice of the meeting sent to each creditor,
(*c*) send a copy of the statement, within the prescribed period, to each member of the company of whose address he is aware, and
(*d*) present a copy of the statement to the meeting.

(3) The administrator shall be taken to have complied with sub-paragraph (2)(*c*) if he publishes a notice undertaking to provide a copy of the statement free of charge to any member of the company who applies in writing to a specified address.

(4) A notice under sub-paragraph (3) must be published—

(*a*) in the prescribed manner, and
(*b*) within the prescribed period.

(5) A creditors' meeting to which a proposed revision is presented shall consider it and may—

(*a*) approve it without modification, or
(*b*) approve it with modification to which the administrator consents.

(6) After the conclusion of a creditors' meeting the administrator shall as soon as is reasonably practicable report any decision taken to—

(*a*) the court,
(*b*) the registrar of companies, and
(*c*) such other persons as may be prescribed.

(7) An administrator commits an offence if he fails without reasonable excuse to comply with sub-paragraph (6).

Further creditors' meetings

56. (1) The administrator of a company shall summon a creditors' meeting if—

(*a*) it is requested in the prescribed manner by creditors of the company whose debts amount to at least 10% of the total debts of the company, or
(*b*) he is directed by the court to summon a creditors' meeting.

(2) An administrator commits an offence if he fails without reasonable excuse to summon a creditors' meeting as required by this paragraph.

FUNCTIONS OF ADMINISTRATOR

Charged property: non-floating charge

71. (1) The court may by order enable the administrator of a company to dispose of property which is subject to a security (other than a floating charge) as if it were not subject to the security.

(2) An order under sub-paragraph (1) may be made only—

(*a*) on the application of the administrator, and
(*b*) where the court thinks that disposal of the property would be likely to promote the purpose of administration in respect of the company.

(3) An order under this paragraph is subject to the condition that there be applied towards discharging the sums secured by the security—

(*a*) the net proceeds of disposal of the property, and
(*b*) any additional money required to be added to the net proceeds so as to produce the amount determined by the court as the net amount which would be realised on a sale of the property at market value.

(4) If an order under this paragraph relates to more than one security, application of money under sub-paragraph (3) shall be in the order of the priorities of the securities.

(5) An administrator who makes a successful application for an order under this paragraph shall send a copy of the order to the registrar of companies before the end of the period of 14 days starting with the date of the order.

(6) An administrator commits an offence if he fails to comply with sub-paragraph (5) without reasonable excuse.

Hire-purchase property

72. (1) The court may by order enable the administrator of a company to dispose of goods which are in the possession of the company under a hire-purchase agreement as if all the rights of the owner under the agreement were vested in the company.

(2) An order under sub-paragraph (1) may be made only—

(*a*) on the application of the administrator, and
(*b*) where the court thinks that disposal of the goods would be likely to promote the purpose of administration in respect of the company.

(3) An order under this paragraph is subject to the condition that there be applied towards discharging the sums payable under the hire-purchase agreement—

(*a*) the net proceeds of disposal of the goods, and
(*b*) any additional money required to be added to the net proceeds so as to produce the amount determined by the court as the net amount which would be realised on a sale of the goods at market value.

(4) An administrator who makes a successful application for an order under this paragraph shall send a copy of the order to the registrar of companies before the end of the period of 14 days starting with the date of the order.

(5) An administrator commits an offence if he fails without reasonable excuse to comply with sub-paragraph (4).

ENDING ADMINISTRATION

Automatic end of administration

76. (1) The appointment of an administrator shall cease to have effect at the end of the period of one year beginning with the date on which it takes effect.

(2) But—

(*a*) on the application of an administrator the court may by order extend his term of office for a specified period, and

(*b*) an administrator's term of office may be extended for a specified period not exceeding six months by consent.

78. (1) In paragraph 76(2)(*b*) "consent" means consent of—

(*a*) each secured creditor of the company, and

(*b*) if the company has unsecured debts, creditors whose debts amount to more than 50% of the company's unsecured debts, disregarding debts of any creditor who does not respond to an invitation to give or withhold consent.

(2) But where the administrator has made a statement under paragraph 52(1)(*b*) "consent" means—

(*a*) consent of each secured creditor of the company, or

(*b*) if the administrator thinks that a distribution may be made to preferential creditors, consent of—

(i) each secured creditor of the company, and

(ii) preferential creditors whose debts amount to more than 50% of the preferential debts of the company, disregarding debts of any creditor who does not respond to an invitation to give or withhold consent.

(3) Consent for the purposes of paragraph 76(2)(*b*) may be—

(*a*) written, or

(*b*) signified at a creditors' meeting.

(4) An administrator's term of office—

(*a*) may be extended by consent only once,

(*b*) may not be extended by consent after extension by order of the court, and

(*c*) may not be extended by consent after expiry.

(5) Where an administrator's term of office is extended by consent he shall as soon as is reasonably practicable—

(*a*) file notice of the extension with the court, and

(*b*) notify the registrar of companies.

(6) An administrator who fails without reasonable excuse to comply with sub-paragraph (5) commits an offence.

Moving from administration to dissolution

84. (1) If the administrator of a company thinks that the company has no property which might permit a distribution to its creditors, he shall send a notice to that effect to the registrar of companies.

(2) The court may on the application of the administrator of a company disapply sub-paragraph (1) in respect of the company.

(3) On receipt of a notice under sub-paragraph (1) the registrar shall register it.

(4) On the registration of a notice in respect of a company under sub-paragraph (1) the appointment of an administrator of the company shall cease to have effect.

(5) If an administrator sends a notice under sub-paragraph (1) he shall as soon as is reasonably practicable—

(*a*) file a copy of the notice with the court, and

(*b*) send a copy of the notice to each creditor of whose claim and address he is aware.

(6) At the end of the period of three months beginning with the date of registration of a notice in respect of a company under sub-paragraph (1) the company is deemed to be dissolved.

(7) On an application in respect of a company by the administrator or another interested person the court may—

(*a*) extend the period specified in sub-paragraph (6),

(*b*) suspend that period, or

(*c*) disapply sub-paragraph (6).

(8) Where an order is made under sub-paragraph (7) in respect of a company the administrator shall as soon as is reasonably practicable notify the registrar of companies.

(9) An administrator commits an offence if he fails without reasonable excuse to comply with sub-paragraph (5).

Discharge of administration order where administration ends

85. (1) This paragraph applies where—

(*a*) the court makes an order under this Schedule providing for the appointment of an administrator of a company to cease to have effect, and

(*b*) the administrator was appointed by administration order.

(2) The court shall discharge the administration order.

Notice to Companies Registrar where administration ends

86. (1) This paragraph applies where the court makes an order under this Schedule providing for the appointment of an administrator to cease to have effect.

(2) The administrator shall send a copy of the order to the registrar of companies within the period of 14 days beginning with the date of the order.

(3) An administrator who fails without reasonable excuse to comply with sub-paragraph (2) commits an offence.

Replacing Administrator

Administrator ceasing to be qualified

89. (1) The administrator of a company shall vacate office if he ceases to be qualified to act as an insolvency practitioner in relation to the company.

(2) Where an administrator vacates office by virtue of sub-paragraph (1) he shall give notice in writing—

(*a*) in the case of an administrator appointed by administration order, to the court,

(*b*) in the case of an administrator appointed under paragraph 14, to the holder of the floating charge by virtue of which the appointment was made,

(*c*) in the case of an administrator appointed under paragraph 22(1), to the company, or

(*d*) in the case of an administrator appointed under paragraph 22(2), to the directors of the company.

(3) An administrator who fails without reasonable excuse to comply with sub-paragraph (2) commits an offence.

General

Joint and concurrent administrators

100. (1) In this Schedule—

(*a*) a reference to the appointment of an administrator of a company includes a reference to the appointment of a number of persons to act jointly or concurrently as the administrator of a company, and

(*b*) a reference to the appointment of a person as administrator of a company includes a reference to the appointment of a person as one of a number of persons to act jointly or concurrently as the administrator of a company.

(2) The appointment of a number of persons to act as administrator of a company must specify—

(*a*) which functions (if any) are to be exercised by the persons appointed acting jointly, and

(*b*) which functions (if any) are to be exercised by any or all of the persons appointed.

101. (1) This paragraph applies where two or more persons are appointed to act jointly as the administrator of a company.

(2) A reference to the administrator of the company is a reference to those persons acting jointly.

(3) But a reference to the administrator of a company in paragraphs 87 to 99 of this Schedule is a reference to any or all of the persons appointed to act jointly.

(4) Where an offence of omission is committed by the administrator, each of the persons appointed to act jointly—

(*a*) commits the offence, and

(*b*) may be proceeded against and punished individually.

(5) The reference in paragraph 45(1)(*a*) to the name of the administrator is a reference to the name of each of the persons appointed to act jointly.

(6) Where persons are appointed to act jointly in respect of only some of the functions of the administrator of a company, this paragraph applies only in relation to those functions.

Penalties

106. (1) A person who is guilty of an offence under this Schedule is liable to a fine (in accordance with section 430 and Schedule 10).

(2) A person who is guilty of an offence under any of the following paragraphs of this Schedule is liable to a daily default fine (in accordance with section 430 and Schedule 10)—

(*a*) paragraph 20,
(*b*) paragraph 32,
(*c*) paragraph 46,
(*d*) paragraph 48,
(*e*) paragraph 49,
(*f*) paragraph 51,
(*g*) paragraph 53,
(*h*) paragraph 54,
(*i*) paragraph 56,
(*j*) paragraph 71,
(*k*) paragraph 72,
(*l*) paragraph 77,
(*m*) paragraph 78,
(*n*) paragraph 80,
(*o*) paragraph 84,
(*p*) paragraph 86, and
(*q*) paragraph 89.

Interpretation

111. (1) In this Schedule—

"administrative receiver" has the meaning given by section 251,

"administrator" has the meaning given by paragraph 1 and, where the context requires, includes a reference to a former administrator,

"company" includes a company which may enter administration by virtue of Article 3 of the EC Regulation,

"correspondence" includes correspondence by telephonic or other electronic means,

"creditors' meeting" has the meaning given by paragraph 50,

"enters administration" has the meaning given by paragraph 1,

"floating charge" means a charge which is a floating charge on its creation,

"in administration" has the meaning given by paragraph 1,

"hire-purchase agreement" includes a conditional sale agreement, a chattel leasing agreement and a retention of title agreement,

"holder of a qualifying floating charge" in respect of a company's property has the meaning given by paragraph 14,

"market value" means the amount which would be realised on a sale of property in the open market by a willing vendor,

"the purpose of administration" means an objective specified in paragraph 3, and

"unable to pay its debts" has the meaning given by section 123.

(2) A reference in this Schedule to a thing in writing includes a reference to a thing in electronic form.

(3) In this Schedule a reference to action includes a reference to inaction.

Section 396

SCHEDULE 7
INSOLVENCY PRACTITIONERS TRIBUNALS

(*Amended by the Courts and Legal Services Act 1990, Sch 10.*)

Procedure of Tribunal

8–18505 **4.** (1) Any investigation by the Tribunal shall be so conducted as to afford a reasonable opportunity for representations to be made to the Tribunal by or on behalf of the person whose case is the subject of the investigation.

(2) For the purposes of any such investigation, the Tribunal—

(*a*) may by summons require any person to attend, at such time and place as is specified in the summons, to give evidence or to produce any books, papers and other records in his possession or under his control which the Tribunal consider it necessary for the purposes of the investigation to examine, and

(*b*) may take evidence on oath, and for the purpose administer oaths, or may, instead of administering an oath, require the person examined to make and subscribe a declaration of the truth of the matter respecting which he is examined;

but no person shall be required, in obedience to such a summons, to go more than ten miles from his place of residence, unless the necessary expenses of his attendance are paid or tendered to him.

(3) Every person who—

(*a*) without reasonable excuse fails to attend in obedience to a summons issued under this paragraph, or refuses to give evidence, or

(*b*) intentionally alters, suppresses, conceals or destroys or refuses to produce any document which he may be required to produce for the purpose of an investigation by the Tribunal,

is liable to a fine.

(4) Subject to the provisions of this paragraph, the Secretary of State may make rules for regulating the procedure on any investigation by the Tribunal.

(5) *Scotland.*

SCHEDULE 10[1]

PUNISHMENT OF OFFENCES UNDER THIS ACT

(abridged and amended by the Statute Law (Repeals) Act 1993, Sch 1, the Insolvency Act 2000, Sch 3 and the Enterprise Act 2002, Schs 17 and 26)

[1] Schedule 10 is printed in an abridged form and contains references only to those offences in respect of which the substantive provisions creating the offences are printed in this manual.

Section (Section of Act creating offence)	General nature of offence	Mode of prosecution[2]	Punishment	Daily default fine (where applicable)
6A(1)	False presentation or fraud for purpose of obtaining members' or creditors' approval of proposed voluntary arrangement.	1. On indictment. 2. Summary.	7 years or a fine, or both. 6 months or the statutory maximum, or both.	
12(2)	*Repealed.*	*Repealed.*	*Repealed.*	
15(8)	*Repealed.*	*Repealed.*	*Repealed.*	*Repealed.*
18(5)	*Repealed.*	*Repealed.*	*Repealed.*	*Repealed.*
21(3)	*Repealed.*	*Repealed.*	*Repealed.*	*Repealed.*
22(6)	*Repealed.*	*Repealed.*	*Repealed.*	*Repealed.*
	Repealed.	Repealed.	Repealed.	Repealed.
23(3)	*Repealed.*	*Repealed.*	*Repealed.*	*Repealed.*
24(7)	*Repealed.*	*Repealed.*	*Repealed.*	*Repealed.*
27(6)	*Repealed.*	*Repealed.*	*Repealed.*	*Repealed.*
30	Body corporate acting as receiver.	1. On indictment. 2. Summary.	A fine. The statutory maximum.	
31	Bankrupt acting as receiver or manager.	1. On indictment. 2. Summary.	2 years or a fine, or both. 6 months or the statutory maximum, or both.	
38(5)	Receiver failing to deliver accounts to registrar.	Summary.	One-fifth of the statutory maximum.	One-fiftieth of the statutory maximum.
39(2)	Company and others failing to state in correspondence that receiver appointed.	Summary.	One-fifth of the statutory maximum.	
43(6)	Administrative receiver failing to file office copy of order permitting disposal of charged property.	Summary.	One-fifth of the statutory maximum.	One-fiftieth of the statutory maximum.
45(5)	Administrative receiver failing to file notice of vacation of office.	Summary.	One-fifth of the statutory maximum.	One-fiftieth of the statutory maximum.*
46(4)	Administrative receiver failing to give notice of his appointment.	Summary.	One-fifth of the statutory maximum.	One-fiftieth of the statutory maximum.
47(6)	Failure to comply with provisions relating to statement of affairs, where administrative receiver appointed.	1. On indictment. 2. Summary.	A fine. The statutory maximum.	One-tenth of the statutory maximum.
48(8)	Administrative receiver failing to comply with requirements as to his report.	Summary.	One-fifth of the statutory maximum.	One-fiftieth of the statutory maximum.

Section (Section of Act creating offence)	General nature of offence	Mode of prosecution[2]	Punishment	Daily default fine (where applicable)
51(4)	Body corporate or Scottish firm acting as receiver.	1. On indictment. 2. Summary.	A fine. The statutory maximum.	
51(5)	Undischarged bankrupt acting as receiver (Scotland).	1. On indictment. 2. Summary.	2 years or a fine, or both. 6 months or the statutory maximum, or both.	
53(2)	Failing to deliver to registrar copy of instrument of appointment of receiver.	Summary.	One-fifth of the statutory maximum.	One-fiftieth of the statutory maximum.*
54(3)	Failing to deliver to registrar the court's interlocutor appointing receiver.	Summary.	One-fifth of the statutory maximum.	One-fiftieth of the statutory maximum.*
61(7)	Receiver failing to send to registrar certified copy of court order authorising disposal of charged property.	Summary.	One-fifth of the statutory maximum.	One-fiftieth of the statutory maximum.
62(5)	Failing to give notice to registrar of cessation or removal of receiver.	Summary.	One-fifth of the statutory maximum.	One-fiftieth of the statutory maximum.*
64(2)	Company and others failing to state on correspondence etc that receiver appointed.	Summary.	One-fifth of the statutory maximum.	
65(4)	Receiver failing to send or publish notice of his appointment.	Summary.	One-fifth of the statutory maximum.	One-fiftieth of the statutory maximum.
66(6)	Failing to comply with provisions concerning statement of affairs, where receiver appointed.	1. On indictment. 2. Summary.	A fine. The statutory maximum.	One-tenth of the statutory maximum.
67(8)	Receiver failing to comply with requirements as to his report.	Summary.	One-fifth of the statutory maximum.	One-fiftieth of the statutory maximum.
85(2)	Company failing to give notice in Gazette of resolution for voluntary winding up.	Summary.	One-fifth of the statutory maximum.	One-fiftieth of the statutory maximum.
89(4)	Director making statutory declaration of company's solvency without reasonable grounds for his opinion.	1. On indictment. 2. Summary.	2 years or a fine, or both. 6 months or the statutory maximum, or both.	
89(6)	Declaration under section 89 not delivered to registrar within prescribed time.	Summary.	One-fifth of the statutory maximum.	One-fiftieth of the statutory maximum.
93(3)	Liquidator failing to summon general meeting of company at each year's end.	Summary.	One-fifth of the statutory maximum.	
94(4)	Liquidator failing to send to registrar a copy of account of winding up and return of final meeting.	Summary.	One-fifth of the statutory maximum.	One-fiftieth of the statutory maximum.
94(6)	Liquidator failing to call final meeting.	Summary.	One-fifth of the statutory maximum.	
95(8)	Liquidator failing to comply with s 95, where company insolvent.	Summary.	The statutory maximum.	

Section (Section of Act creating offence)	General nature of offence	Mode of prosecution[2]	Punishment	Daily default fine (where applicable)
98(6)	Company failing to comply with s. 98 in respect of summoning and giving notice of creditors' meeting.	1. On indictment. 2. Summary.	A fine. The statutory maximum.	
99(3)	Directors failing to attend and lay statement in prescribed form before creditors' meeting.	1. On indictment. 2. Summary.	A fine. The statutory maximum.	
105(3)	Liquidator failing to summon company general meeting and creditors' meeting at each year's end.	Summary.	One-fifth of the statutory maximum.	
106(4)	Liquidator failing to send to registrar account of winding up and return of final meetings.	Summary.	One-fifth of the statutory maximum.	One-fiftieth of the statutory maximum.
106(6)	Liquidator failing to call final meeting of company or creditors.	Summary.	One-fifth of the statutory maximum.	
109(2)	Liquidator failing to publish notice of his appointment.	Summary.	One-fifth of the statutory maximum.	One-fiftieth of the statutory maximum.
114(4)	Directors exercising powers in breach of s 114, where no liquidator.	Summary.	The statutory maximum.	
131(7)	Failing to comply with requirements as to statement of affairs, where liquidator appointed.	1. On indictment. 2. Summary.	A fine. The statutory maximum.	One-tenth of the statutory maximum.
164	Giving, offering etc. corrupt inducement affecting appointment of liquidator.	1. On indictment. 2. Summary.	A fine. The statutory maximum.	
166(7)	Liquidator failing to comply with requirements of s 166 in creditors' voluntary winding up.	Summary.	The statutory maximum.	
188(2)	Default in compliance with s 188 as to notification that company being wound up.	Summary.	One-fifth of the statutory maximum.	
192(2)	Liquidator failing to notify registrar as to progress of winding up.	Summary.	One-fifth of the statutory maximum.	One-fiftieth of the statutory maximum.
201(4)	Failing to deliver to registrar office copy of court order deferring dissolution.	Summary.	One-fifth of the statutory maximum.	One-fiftieth of the statutory maximum.
203(6)	Failing to deliver to registrar copy of directions or result of appeal under s 203.	Summary.	One-fifth of the statutory maximum.	One-fiftieth of the statutory maximum.
204(7)	Liquidator failing to deliver to registrar copy of court order for early dissolution.	Summary.	One-fifth of the statutory maximum.	One-fiftieth of the statutory maximum.
204(8)	Failing to deliver to registrar copy of court order deferring early dissolution.	Summary.	One-fifth of the statutory maximum.	One-fiftieth of the statutory maximum.
205(7)	Failing to deliver to registrar copy of Secretary of State's directions or court order deferring dissolution.	Summary.	One-fifth of the statutory maximum.	One-fiftieth of the statutory maximum.

Section (Section of Act creating offence)	General nature of offence	Mode of prosecution[2]	Punishment	Daily default fine (where applicable)
206(1)	Fraud etc. in anticipation of winding up.	1. On indictment. 2. Summary.	7 years or a fine, or both. 6 months or the statutory maximum, or both.	
206(2)	Privity to fraud in anticipation of winding up; fraud, or privity to fraud, after commencement of winding up.	1. On indictment. 2. Summary.	7 years or a fine, or both. 6 months or the statutory maximum, or both.	
206(5)	Knowingly taking in pawn or pledge, or otherwise receiving, company property.	1. On indictment. 2. Summary.	7 years or a fine, or both. 6 months or the statutory maximum, or both.	
207	Officer of company entering into transaction in fraud of company's creditors.	1. On indictment. 2. Summary.	2 years or a fine, or both. 6 months or the statutory maximum, or both.	
208	Officer of company misconducting himself in course of winding up.	1. On indictment. 2. Summary.	7 years or a fine, or both. 6 months or the statutory maximum, or both.	
209	Officer or contributory destroying, falsifying, etc company's books.	1. On indictment. 2. Summary.	7 years or a fine, or both. 6 months or the statutory maximum, or both.	
210	Officer of company making material omission from statement relating to company's affairs.	1. On indictment. 2. Summary.	7 years or a fine, or both. 6 months or the statutory maximum, or both.	
211	False representation or fraud for purpose of obtaining creditors' consent to an agreement in connection with winding up.	1. On indictment. 2. Summary.	7 years or a fine, or both. 6 months or the statutory maximum, or both.	
216(4)	Contravening restrictions on re-use of name of company in insolvent liquidation.	1. On indictment. 2. Summary.	2 years or a fine, or both. 6 months or the statutory maximum, or both.	
235(5)	Failing to co-operate with office-holder.	1. On indictment. 2. Summary.	A fine. The statutory maximum.	One-tenth of the statutory maximum.
262A(1)	False representation or fraud for purpose of obtaining creditors' approval of proposed voluntary arrangement	1. On indictment 2. Summary.	7 years or a fine, or both. 6 months or the statutory maximum, or both	
353(1)	Bankrupt failing to disclose property or disposals to official receiver or trustee.	1. On indictment. 2. Summary.	7 years or a fine, or both. 6 months or the statutory maximum, or both.	

Section (Section of Act creating offence)	General nature of offence	Mode of prosecution[2]	Punishment	Daily default fine (where applicable)
354(1)	Bankrupt failing to deliver property to, or concealing property from, official receiver or trustee.	1. On indictment 2. Summary.	7 years or a fine, or both. 6 months or the statutory maximum, or both.	
354(2)	Bankrupt removing property which he is required to deliver to official receiver or trustee.	1. On indictment. 2. Summary.	7 years or a fine, or both. 6 months or the statutory maximum, or both.	
354(3)	Bankrupt failing to account for loss of substantial part of property.	1 On indictment. 2. Summary.	2 years or a fine, or both. 6 months or the statutory maximum, or both.	
355(1)	Bankrupt failing to deliver books, papers and records to official receiver or trustee.	1. On indictment. 2. Summary.	7 years or a fine, or both. 6 months or the statutory maximum, or both.	
355(2)	Bankrupt concealing, destroying etc books, papers or records, or making false entries in them.	1. On indictment. 2. Summary.	7 years or a fine, or both. 6 months or the statutory maximum, or both.	
355(3)	Bankrupt disposing of, or altering, books, papers or records relating to his estate or affairs.	1. On indictment. 2. Summary.	7 years or a fine, or both. 6 months or the statutory maximum, or both.	
356(1)	Bankrupt making material omission in statement relating to his affairs.	1. On indictment. 2. Summary.	7 years or a fine, or both. 6 months or the statutory maximum, or both.	
356(2)	Bankrupt making false statement, or failing to inform trustee, where false debt proved.	1. On indictment. 2. Summary.	7 years or a fine, or both. 6 months or the statutory maximum, or both.	
357	Bankrupt fraudulently disposing of property.	1. On indictment 2. Summary.	2 years or a fine, or both. 6 months or the statutory maximum, or both.	
358	Bankrupt absconding with property he is required to deliver to official receiver or trustee.	1. On indictment. 2. Summary.	2 years or a fine, or both. 6 months or the statutory maximum, or both.	
359(1)	Bankrupt disposing of property obtained on credit and not paid for.	1. On indictment. 2. Summary.	7 years or a fine, or both. 6 months or the statutory maximum, or both.	

Section (Section of Act creating offence)	General nature of offence	Mode of prosecution[2]	Punishment	Daily default fine (where applicable)
359(2)	Obtaining property in respect of which money is owed by a bankrupt.	1. On indictment. 2. Summary.	7 years or a fine, or both. 6 months or the statutory maximum, or both.	
360(1)	Bankrupt obtaining credit or engaging in business without disclosing his status or name in which he was made bankrupt.	1. On indictment. 2. Summary.	2 years or a fine, or both. 6 months or the statutory maximum, or both.	
360(3)	Person made bankrupt in Scotland or Northern Ireland obtaining credit, etc in England and Wales.	1. On indictment. 2. Summary.	2 years or a fine, or both. 6 months or the statutory maximum, or both.	
361(1)	*Repealed.*	*Repealed.* Repealed.	*Repealed.* Repealed.	
362	*Repealed.*	*Repealed.* Repealed.	*Repealed.* Repealed.	
389	Acting as insolvency practitioner when not qualified.	1. On indictment. 2. Summary.	2 years or a fine, or both. 6 months or the statutory maximum or both.	
429(5)	Contravening s 429 in respect of disabilities imposed by county court on revocation of administration order.	1. On indictment. 2. Summary.	2 years or a fine, or both. 6 months or the statutory maximum, or both.	
Sch A1, para 9(2)	Directors failing to notify nominee of beginning of moratorium.	1 On indictment 2 Summary	2 years or a fine, or both. 6 months or the statutory maximum, or both.	
Sch A1, para 10(3)	Nominee failing to advertise or notify beginning of moratorium.	Summary	One-fifth of the statutory maximum.	
Sch A1, para 11(2)	Nominee failing to advertise or notify end of moratorium.	Summary	One-fifth of the statutory maximum.	
Sch A1, para 16(2)	Company and officers failing to state in correspondence etc that moratorium in force.	Summary	One-fifth of the statutory maximum.	
Sch A1, para 17(3)(*a*)	Company obtaining credit without disclosing existence of moratorium.	1 On indictment 2 Summary	A fine. The statutory maximum.	
Sch A1, para 17(3)(*b*)	Obtaining credit for company without disclosing existence of moratorium.	1 On indictment 2 Summary	2 years or a fine, or both. 6 months or the statutory maximum, or both.	

Section (Section of Act creating offence)	General nature of offence	Mode of prosecution[2]	Punishment	Daily default fine (where applicable)
Sch A1, para 18(3)(*a*)	Company disposing of property otherwise than in ordinary way of business.	1 On indictment 2 Summary	A fine. The statutory maximum.	
Sch A1, para 18(3)(*b*)	Authorising or permitting disposal of company property.	1 On indictment 2 Summary	2 years or a fine, or both. 6 months or the statutory maximum, or both.	
Sch A1, para 19(3)(*a*)	Company making payments in respect of liabilities existing before beginning of moratorium.	1 On indictment 2 Summary	A fine. The statutory maximum.	
Sch A1, para 19(3)(*b*)	Authorising or permitting such a payment.	1 On indictment 2 Summary	2 years or a fine, or both. 6 months or the statutory maximum, or both.	
Sch A1, para. 20(9)	Directors failing to send to registrar office copy of court order permitting disposal of charged property.	Summary	One-fifth of the statutory maximum.	
Sch A1, para 22(1)	Company disposing of charged property.	1 On indictment 2 Summary	A fine. The statutory maximum.	
Sch A1, para 22(2)	Authorising or permitting such a disposal.	1 On indictment 2 Summary	2 years or a fine, or both. 6 months or the statutory maximum, or both.	
Sch A1, para 23(1)(*a*)	Company entering into market contract, etc.	1 On indictment 2 Summary	A fine. The statutory maximum.	
Sch A1, para 23(1)(*b*)	Authorising or permitting company to do so.	1 On indictment 2 Summary	2 years or a fine, or both. 6 months or the statutory maximum, or both.	
Sch A1, para 25(6)	Nominee failing to give notice of withdrawal of consent to act.	Summary	One-fifth of the statutory maximum.	
Sch A1, para 34(3)	Nominee failing to give notice of extension of moratorium.	Summary	One-fifth of the statutory maximum.	
Sch A1, para 41(2)	Fraud or privity to fraud in anticipation of moratorium.	1 On indictment 2 Summary	7 years or a fine, or both. 6 months or the statutory maximum, or both.	
Sch A1, para 41(3)	Fraud or privity to fraud during moratorium.	1 On indictment 2 Summary	7 years or a fine, or both. 6 months or the statutory maximum, or both.	
Sch A1, para 41(7)	Knowingly taking in pawn or pledge, or otherwise receiving, company property.	1 On indictment 2 Summary	7 years or a fine, or both. 6 months or the statutory maximum, or both.	

Section (Section of Act creating offence)	General nature of offence	Mode of prosecution[2]	Punishment	Daily default fine (where applicable)
Sch A1, para 42(1)	False representation or fraud for purpose of obtaining or extending moratorium.	1 On indictment 2 Summary	7 years or a fine, or both. 6 months or the statutory maximum, or both.	
Sch B1, para 18(7)	Making false statement in statutory declaration where administrator appointed by holder of floating charge.	1 On indictment 2 Summary	2 years, or a fine or both. 6 months, or the statutory maximum or both.	
Sch B1, para 20	Holder of floating charge failing to notify administrator or others of commencement of appointment.	1 On indictment 2 Summary	2 years, or a fine or both. 6 months, or the statutory maximum or both.	One-tenth of the statutory maximum.
Sch B1, para 27(4)	Making false statement in statutory declaration where appointment of administrator proposed by company or directors.	1 On indictment 2 Summary	2 years, or a fine or both. 6 months, or the statutory maximum or both.	
Sch B1, para 29(7)	Making false statement in statutory declaration where administrator appointed by company or directors.	1 On indictment 2 Summary	2 years, or a fine or both. 6 months, or the statutory maximum or both.	
Sch B1, para 32	Company or directors failing to notify administrator or others of commencement of appointment.	1 On indictment 2 Summary	2 years, or a fine or both.	One-tenth of the statutory maximum. 6 months, or the statutory maximum or both.
Sch B1, para 45(2)	Administrator, company or officer failing to state in business document that administrator appointed.	Summary	One-fifth of the statutory maximum.	
Sch B1, para 46(9)	Administrator failing to give notice of his appointment.	Summary	One-fifth of the statutory maximum.	One-fiftieth of the statutory maximum.
Sch B1, para 48(4)	Failing to comply with provisions about statement of affairs where administrator appointed.	1 On indictment 2 Summary	A fine. The statutory maximum.	One-tenth of the statutory maximum.
Sch B1, para 49(7)	Administrator failing to send out statement of his proposals.	Summary	One-fifth of the statutory maximum.	One-fiftieth of the statutory maximum.
Sch B1, para 51(5)	Administrator failing to arrange initial creditors' meeting.	Summary	One-fifth of the statutory maximum.	One-fiftieth of the statutory maximum.
Sch B1, para 53(3)	Administrator failing to report decision taken at initial creditors' meeting.	Summary	One-fifth of the statutory maximum.	One-fiftieth of the statutory maximum.
Sch B1, para 54(7)	Administrator failing to report decision taken at creditors' meeting summoned to consider revised proposal.	Summary	One-fifth of the statutory maximum.	One-fiftieth of the statutory maximum.
Sch B1, para 56(2)	Administrator failing to summon creditors' meeting.	Summary	One-fifth of the statutory maximum.	One-fiftieth of the statutory maximum.

Section (Section of Act creating offence)	General nature of offence	Mode of prosecution[2]	Punishment	Daily default fine (where applicable)
Sch B1, para 71(6)	Administrator failing to file court order enabling disposal of charged property.	Summary	One-fifth of the statutory maximum.	One-fiftieth of the statutory maximum.
Sch B1, para 72(5)	Administrator failing to file court order enabling disposal of hire-purchase property.	Summary	One-fifth of the statutory maximum.	One-fiftieth of the statutory maximum.
Sch B1, para 77(3)	Administrator failing to notify Registrar of Companies of automatic end of administration.	Summary	One-fifth of the statutory maximum.	One-fiftieth of the statutory maximum.
Sch B1, para 78(6)	Administrator failing to give notice of extension by consent of term of office.	Summary	One-fifth of the statutory maximum.	One-fiftieth of the statutory maximum.
Sch B1, para 80(6)	Administrator failing to give notice of termination of administration where objective achieved.	Summary	One-fifth of the statutory maximum.	One-fiftieth of the statutory maximum.
Sch B1, para 84(9)	Administrator failing to comply with provisions where company moves to dissolution.	Summary	One-fifth of the statutory maximum.	One-fiftieth of the statutory maximum.
Sch B1, para 86(3)	Administrator failing to notify Registrar of Companies where court terminates administration.	Summary	One-fifth of the statutory maximum.	One-fiftieth of the statutory maximum.
Sch B1, para 89(3)	Administrator failing to give notice on ceasing to be qualified.	Summary	One-fifth of the statutory maximum.	One-fiftieth of the statutory maximum.
Sch 7, para 4(3)	Failure to attend and give evidence to Insolvency Practitioners Tribunal; suppressing, concealing, etc relevant documents.	Summary.	Level 3 on the standard scale within the meaning given by section 75 of the Criminal Justice Act 1982.	

***Repealed by the Companies Act 1989, s 212, from a date to be appointed.**

2. For procedure in respect of an offence which is triable either way, see the Magistrates' Courts Act 1980, ss 17A–21, in PART I: MAGISTRATES' COURTS, PROCEDURE, ante.

JURIES

Juries Act 1974

(1974 c 23)

8–18610 20. Offences. (1) Subject to the provisions of subsections (2) to (4) below—

(*a*) if a person duly summoned under this Act fails to attend (on the first or any subsequent day on which he is required to attend by the summons or by the appropriate officer) in compliance with the summons, or

(*b*) if a person, after attending in pursuance of a summons, is not available when called on to serve as a juror, or is unfit for service by reason of drink or drugs,

he shall be liable to a fine not exceeding **level 3** on the standard scale.

(2) An offence under subsection (1) above shall be punishable either on summary conviction or as if it were criminal contempt of court committed in the face of the court.

(3) Subsection (1)(*a*) above shall not apply to a person summoned, otherwise than under s 6 of this Act[1], unless the summons was duly served on him on a date not later than fourteen days before the date fixed by the summons for his first attendance.

(4) A person shall not be liable to be punished under the preceding provisions of this section if he can show some reasonable cause for his failure to comply with the summons, or for not being available when called on to serve, and those provisions have effect subject to the provisions of this Act about the withdrawal or alteration of a summons and about the granting of any excusal or deferral.

(5) If any person—

(*a*) having been summoned under this Act makes, or causes or permits to be made on his behalf, any false representation to the appropriate officer with the intention of evading jury service; or

(*b*) makes or causes to be made on behalf of another person who has been so summoned any false representation to that officer with the intention of enabling the other to evade jury service; or

(*c*) when any question is put to him in pursuance of section 2(5) of this Act, refuses without reasonable excuse to answer, or gives an answer he knows to be false in a material particular, or recklessly gives an answer which is false in a material particular; or

(*d*) knowing that he is not qualified for jury service by reason of section 40 of the Criminal Justice and Public Order Act 1994,, serves on a jury, or

(*e*) knowing that he is not qualified for jury service by reason of section 40 of the Criminal Justice and Public Order Act 1994, serves on a jury,

he shall be liable on summary conviction to a fine of not more than **level 5** on the standard scale in the case of an offence of serving on a jury when disqualified and, in any other case, a fine of not more than **level 3** on the standard scale.

[Juries Act 1974, s 20, as amended by the Criminal Justice Act 1982, ss 38 and 46, the Criminal Justice Act 1988, Sch 15, the Criminal Justice and Public Order Act 1994, Sch 10 and the Criminal Justice Act 2003, Sch 33.]

---

1. Section 6 contains a power to summon a person in exceptional circumstances without any written notice.

LIBEL

8–18619 This title contains the following statutes—

8–18620 Defined. A libel consists of slanders expressed either in printing, writing, signs or pictures, tending to blacken the memory of one that is dead, or the reputation of one who is alive, and to expose him to disgrace, ridicule, or contempt (3 *Burn's Justice*, 30th ed, p 331)[1]. It would seem from Lord Kenyon's ruling in 1791 (*R v Topham* (1791) 4 Term Rep 126), that the publication must be with a view to injure living persons, or to induce them to commit a breach of the peace. Mr. Justice Stephen laid down, at Cardiff Assizes, February 10th, 1887, on grounds which he had put into writing, that to make a libel on a dead person a crime there must be a vilifying of the dead with a view to injure his posterity (*R v Ensor* (1887) 3 TLR 366). It has been contended that *R v Labouchere* (1884) 15 QBD 320, 48 JP 165, is an authority that an indictment will not lie for a libel on a deceased person, but a motion in the QB Division to quash such an indictment was refused (*R v Carr* (1886)

82 LT Jo 100). Words spoken can in no case be a libel, although they may convey defamatory matter. Lord Coleridge CJ, directed the grand jury at Berkshire Assizes, Reading, February 1889, that there ought to be some public interest concerned, something affecting the Crown or in guardians of the public peace, to justify the recourse by a private person to a criminal remedy by way of indictment. If either by reason of the continued repetition or infamous character of the libel a breach of the peace was likely to ensue, then the libeller should be indicted; but in the absence of any such conditions, a personal squabble between two private individuals ought not to be permitted by grand juries, as indeed it was not permitted by sound law, to be the subject of a criminal indictment, and he invited them to throw out the bill, which, in accordance with his suggestion, was done (33 Sol Jo 250). The essentials of a criminal libel were explained in *R v Wicks* [1936] 1 All ER 384. It is, however, not every libel that warrants a criminal prosecution. To warrant prosecution the libel must be sufficiently serious to require the intervention of the Crown in the public interest", per Lord Scarman in *Gleaves v Deakin* [1979] 2 WLR 665, HL, applied in *Gleaves v Insall* [1999] 2 Cr App Rep 466. Leave was given to commence proceedings where the integrity of someone associated with the Bank of England was impugned (*Goldsmith v Pressdram Ltd* [1977] 2 All ER 557).

1. By Defamation Act 1952, s 1, broadcast statements may be a medium for libel. For the purposes of the law of libel and slander (including the law of criminal libel so far as it relates to the publication of defamatory matter) the publication of words in the course of any programme included in a programme service shall be treated as publication in permanent form (Broadcasting Act 1990, s 166, title TELECOMMUNICATIONS AND BROADCASTING post).

8–18630 The following are indictable misdemeanours:

(1) Maliciously publishing any defamatory libel knowing it to be false.—Pun. imprisonment not exceeding two years and fine (Libel Act 1843, s 4).

(2) Maliciously[1] publishing any defamatory[2] libel (s 5).—Pun. fine or imprisonment or both, but imprisonment[3] not to exceed one year.

1. Omission of "maliciously" and use of "unlawfully" did not invalidate an indictment. The CCR held the indictment was good for a common law offence but so framed as to bring it within the statute. If the averment was imperfect it was cured by verdict (*R v Munslow* [1895] 1 QB 758).

2. B was indicted under s 4, though only committed for trial under s 5:—*Held*, the conviction was no bar to an action for malicious prosecution under s 4 (*Boaler v Holder* (1887) 51 JP 277; but see *Boaler v R* (1888) 21 QBD 284, 52 JP 791, which was before the CCR later). Where a defendant had been committed under s 5, and the indictment contained one count only, and that was framed in accordance with s 4, Hawkins J, refused to quash the indictment, but quashed the words "well knowing the same defamatory libel to be false" (*R v Felbermann and Wilkinson* (1887) 51 JP 168). But application must be made before pleading.

3. Accused may also be ordered, at expiration of imprisonment, to find sureties for a specified period, and, in default, to be further imprisoned for such period (*R v Trueman* [1913] 3 KB 164, 77 JP 428).

8–18631 Plea of justification.—At the time of trial by indictment for a defamatory libel, the truth of the matters charged in the alleged libel may be inquired into upon the defendant pleading justification in the special form specified in the Libel Act 1843, s 6, but will not amount to a defence unless it was for the public benefit that such matter should be published (see Form of Plea in Appendix to Crown Office Rules 1906). If justification is pleaded to an indictment for a defamatory libel, which libel makes several distinct imputations, and the plea alleges the truth of all, but the evidence fails on any one of them, a verdict will be entered generally against the defendant. The only function allotted to the jury is to say whether the whole plea is proved or not. If they find that it is the defendant is acquitted. If they think that it is not they are to declare that the defendant wrongly published the libel without the cause alleged and he is convicted (*R v Lady Scott*) (1897) Times, 8 January, p 9, following *R v Newman* (1853) 1 E & B 558). The court in pronouncing sentence may consider whether the guilt of defendant is aggravated or mitigated by the plea and by the evidence given to prove or disprove it. The statute contains special provisions as to evidence to rebut *prima facie* case of publication by an agent (Libel Act 1843, s 7). With the assent of the defendant a libel in a newspaper may be dealt with summarily. See Newspaper Libel and Registration Act 1881, post.

The fact that the truth of the matters charged is not a defence almost certainly breaches Article 10 of the European Convention on Human Rights (freedom of expression). Even before the Human Rights Act 1998 entered into force, the House of Lords had expressed the view that the criminal offence of defamatory libel was difficult to reconcile with the international obligations of the United Kingdom. See *Gleaves v Deakin* [1979] 2 All ER 497.

8–18632 Observations.—The fact that the allegations in the libel are true is an answer to civil proceedings, but is not in itself a defence to criminal proceedings[1]. In the latter case the defendant must show that he was not actuated by malice, and that publication was for the public benefit. The proceedings must not be postponed by justices until a pending action between the parties as to a different libel arising out of the same facts has been decided (*R v Evans* (1890) 54 JP 471. And see *Ex p Edgar* (1913) 77 JP 283). When it is intended to proceed by *indictment*, the proceedings will be the same as in the case of any other misdemeanour; but the truth of a defamatory libel (Libel Act 1843, s 5, ante) (except a libel published in a newspaper, see 1881 Act, post) is no defence in proceedings before justices, and it is not within their province to determine whether the libel may be justified, or to receive evidence by cross-examination or direct testimony to establish its truth. The justices' duty is: First, to see whether the written matter charged is libellous in point of law on the face of the libel; next, whether the publication is brought so far home to the defendant that he ought to be put on his trial. Any inquiry into the *truth* of the libellous matter is wholly irrelevant. That defence can only be raised by plea upon the trial of an indictment (*R v Carden* (1879) 5 QBD 1, 44 JP 137; *R v Flowers* (1879) 44 JP 377). Moreover, at committal proceedings evidence of the general bad reputation of the prosecutor is not relevant to the proceedings and is not admissible (*Gleaves v Deakin* [1979] 2 All ER 497). But where the charge is for publishing a defamatory libel, knowing it to be false (s 4, ante), the justices are bound to take such evidence, as it goes to the very gist of the accusation (*R v Lord Mayor of London, ex p Ellison* November 1878, unreported), Queen's Bench Division quoted on the argument of the above case).

A newspaper is published when and where it is offered to the public and may be published at more than one place at the same time (*McFarlane v Hulton* [1899] 1 Ch 884). A criminal information was granted against a newspaper proprietor for charging justices with "arbitrary" and cruel conduct (*R v Steel* (1875) 39 JP Jo 357); also against a solicitor for saying, "What a shame," to the gentleman opposed to him after a conviction by a bench of magistrates, and repeating the observation, and adding, "You are not fit to sit on the bench", to one of the magistrates who overheard him, and asked what he had said (*R v Watson* (1878) 23 Sol Jo 86). The publisher and printer of the *Kent Messenger and Dartford Telegraph* were found guilty on a criminal information for a libel which described justices as "devoid of every sentiment of mercy", and their conduct such as to excite "disgust". The article stated there was a doubt whether the offence of larceny referred to in the libel was committed, but if it was, a lighter punishment than 21 days would have met the circumstances of the case. "It is such cases as this which disclose the incompetency of an unpaid magistracy." The court had no power to inflict costs as under the Libel Act, but the defendants were fined £150, and ordered to be imprisoned until the fine was paid (*R v Masters* (1889) 6 TLR 44). A rule *nisi* was granted against a newspaper proprietor on the application of a clerk to magistrates. One passage in the article was: "As to the conduct of the sitting magistrates and their clerk, it is enough to say that if they had acted with the set purpose of throwing contempt on the administration of the law, they could not have better gained their ends" (*Re Clerk to The Magistrates at Great Grimsby* (8 May 1879, unreported), Queen's Bench Division). But where magistrates had been held up to ridicule, for ordering goods (the subject of a charge of larceny which had been dismissed) to be delivered to the prosecutors, the court discharged a rule *nisi* upon condition that the defendant paid all the costs (*Re Justices Aberystwith and Cambrian News* (27 November 1879, unreported), Queen's Bench Division). Damages (£400) were recovered against the proprietors of the *Derby Express* for libels, which in effect said that the appointment of plaintiff as a magistrate would be a direct insult to the borough bench. Defendants pleaded that the alleged libels related to matters of public interest, and were true in substance and in fact, and witnesses were called to bear out this defence (*Johnstone v Midland Counties Newspaper Co* (1887) 23 L Jo 401). Where a magistrate has been libelled in the discharge of his duties as a magistrate and has demanded an apology and threatened an action for damages he cannot afterwards apply for a criminal information for libel (*Ex p Pollard* (1901) 17 TLR 773). It is a good defence to a criminal information against a newspaper proprietor to show that the libel was published without his authority, consent, or knowledge, and from no want of due care or caution on his part (*R v Holbrook* (1878) 4 QBD 42, 43 JP 38; *R v Judd* (1888) 37 WR 143; *R v Allison* (1888) 59 LT 933).

The House of Lords held that a *bona fide* publication of an accurate report of a delivered judgment was privileged, but a doubt was raised whether it would have been so held if it had been contended that the judge's conclusions were not an accurate representation of the facts (*McDougall v Knight* (1889) 14 App Cas 194, 53 JP 691). The question of whether the report is fair is for the jury (*Milissich v Lloyds* (1877) 46 LJQB 404). A fair and impartial report of proceedings in an open justices' court was held to be privileged before the Law of Libel Amendment Act 1888, although the statements were highly defamatory, and made upon an *Ex p* application, which was dismissed because the magistrate had not jurisdiction; but per LOPES J, it may be doubtful whether this rule applies to a matter in the nature of a preliminary inquiry if the ultimate judicial determination is to remain in abeyance until further investigation (*Usill v Hales*, overruling older cases (1878) 3 CPD 319, 42 JP 113). The Court of Appeal has since held that a fair report of what takes place at such proceedings is privileged, although no evidence is given on oath, and although such proceedings do not result in a final decision and lead to further inquiry, but the burden of making out the report was fair is on the defendant (*Kimber v Press Association* [1893] 1 QB 65, 57 JP 247). A report which represented as proved facts statements opened by the solicitor for the prosecution, but contradicted by the evidence, was not a fair report (*Ashmore v Borthwick* (1885) 49 JP 792). A justice of the peace enjoys the same absolute privilege as a judge of the superior courts; but if he acts without jurisdiction and speaks maliciously and without reasonable and probable ground, his liability is identical with that of an ordinary individual (*Seaman v Netherclift* (1876) 2 CPD 53, 41 JP 389). This privilege is strictly confined to the magistrate; no officer of the court has a corresponding right to privilege (*Delegall v Highley* (1837) 4 Bing NC 114). A printed report issued by the chief constable of Liverpool in accordance with an order of the justices, to facilitate their business at sessions, was sent to the justices, and sold at 10*s* 6*d* a copy to professional men, upon their signing a declaration that they required it for the purposes of their business at the sessions. The Court of Appeal held that the occasion of the publication of the report was privileged (*Andrews v Nott-Bower* [1895] 1 QB 888, 59 JP 420). B was indicted at Central Criminal Court, 11 March, 1897, for maliciously publishing a libel, in dictating a statement to a police inspector at a police station, which he afterwards signed, to the effect that the prosecutor had conspired with other persons to set fire to certain premises. Mr. Commissioner Kerr directed the jury that if they were of opinion that when B made the statement he believed it to be true he was entitled to be acquitted; if he did not believe it to be true he ought to be convicted (*R v Fitch* (1897) 61 JP 233). A communication transmitted by post-card is not privileged (*Robinson v Jones* (1879) 4 LR Ir 391).

Although in civil cases publication of a libel to the party libelled is not sufficient to support an action, yet in criminal cases such publication will support an indictment or information. But the document must reasonably or probably tend to provoke a breach of the peace (*R v Adams* (1888) 22 QBD 66, 53 JP 377, 58 LJMC 1; *R v Brooke* (1856) 7 Cox CC 251). Publication is the making known defamatory matter to some person other than the person of whom it is written. Sending a libel straight to the person of whom it is written, without showing it to any other person, is not a publication for which an action will lie; but there is publication, when defamatory matter is communicated to a servant of the plaintiff, the defendant or a third person, unless it is communicated accidentally and the defendant has no means of knowledge that the communication is likely, in the ordinary course of events, to occur (*Pullman v Hill & Co* [1891] 1 QB 524; *Gomersall v Davies* (1898) 14 TLR 430; *Huth v Huth* [1915] 3 KB 32). Although there may be publication, it may be privileged. If a business communication is privileged, as being made on a privileged occasion, the privilege covers incidents of the transmission and treatment of that communication which are in accordance with the reasonable and usual course of business (*Boxsius v Goblet Freres* [1894] 1 QB 842, 58 JP 670; *Edmondson v Birch & Co Ltd* [1907] 1 KB 371; *Osborn v Thomas Boulter & Son* [1930] 2 KB 226, [1930] All ER Rep 154). After reading an anonymous letter the receiver read it aloud to other persons: *Held*, he was liable for publication of a libel (*Forrester v Tyrrell* (1893) 57 JP 532).

A wife cannot prosecute her husband for a personal libel upon herself (*R v Lord Mayor of London* (1886) 16 QBD 772, 50 JP 614). An action will not lie for charging a corporation, as distinguished from its individual members or officials, with corruption, for only individual members can be guilty of such an offence (*Manchester Corpn v Williams* [1891] 1 QB 94, 54 JP 712). As to mitigation of punishment on criminal information for a reckless publication, see *R v Tanfield* (1878) 42 JP 423. As to evidence of bad character and of rumours of the offence imputed to the person libelled, see *Scott v Sampson* (1882) 8 QBD 491, 46 JP 408; and *Hobbs v Tinling* [1929] 2 KB 1. As to an action by a limited company see *D and L Caterers Ltd and Jackson v D'Ajou* [1945] KB 364, [1945] 1 All ER 563; and as to a trade union, see *National Union of General and Municipal Workers v Gillian* [1946] KB 81, [1945] 2 All ER 593. B wrote to E in reply to her advertisement for a situation, and proposed to pay her a sum of money if she would allow him to have immoral intercourse with her. The CCR sustained a conviction upon a court for writing a defamatory libel of E likely to lead to a breach of the peace (*R v Adams* (1888) 22 QBD 66, 58 LJMC 1, 53 JP 377). Counts in an indictment for offences committed on separate days and withdrawn before the committing magistrate were quashed (*R v Bradlaugh* (1882) 47 JP 71).

When defamatory words are written of a class of persons, and where the plaintiff is not named, the test is whether the words are such as would reasonably lead persons acquainted with the plaintiff to believe that he was the person referred to. If the words used in reference to a limited class may be reasonably understood to refer to every member of the class, every member may have a cause of action (*Knupffer v London Express Newspaper Ltd* [1944] AC 116, [1944] 1 All ER 495).

1. As to the compatibility of the rule in criminal proceedings with the European Convention on Human Rights see para **8–18631**, ante.

Law of Libel Amendment Act 1888

(51 & 52 Vict c 64)

8–18650 8. Order of judge for newspaper prosecution. No criminal prosecution shall be commenced[1] against any proprietor, publisher, editor, or any person responsible for the publication[2] of a newspaper for any libel published therein, without the order of a judge[3] at chambers being first had and obtained.

Such application shall be made on notice to the person accused, who shall have an opportunity of being heard against such application.
[Law of Libel Amendment Act 1888, s 8.]

1. It is the publishers and proprietors who are the subject-matter of s 8, and the words "person responsible for the publication of a newspaper" are to be construed *ejusdem generis* with the preceding words "any proprietor, publisher, editor". Accordingly, leave does not have to be sought from a High Court judge before commencing a prosecution against a journalist (*Gleaves v Insall* [1999] 2 Cr App Rep 466).

2. A newsvendor is not liable for selling in the ordinary course of his business a newspaper which he had no reason to suppose contained a libel (*Emmens v Pottle* (1885) 16 QBD 354, 50 JP 228). The word "printers" does not occur in this section, but it is found in s 9 of the Newspaper Libel and Registration Act 1881, post.

3. The order having been made in a criminal matter cannot be appealed against (*Ex p Pulbrook* [1892] 1 QB 86, 56 JP 293). The judge is bound to look at all the circumstances, not merely the applicant's evidence, before coming to a conclusion whether there is a clear *prima facie* case and whether the public interest requires the institution of proceedings (*Desmond v Thorne* [1982] 3 All ER 268, [1983] 1 WLR 163).

Newspaper Libel and Registration Act 1881

(44 & 45 Vict c 60)

8–18670 1. Interpretation. The word "registrar" shall mean the registrar of joint stock companies, or such persons as the Board of Trade may authorise in that behalf. "Registry office" shall mean the principal office of the registrar. "Newspaper" shall mean any paper containing public news, intelligence, or occurrences, or any remarks or observations therein printed for sale, and published in England or Ireland periodically, or in parts or numbers at intervals not exceeding twenty-six days between the publication of any two such papers, parts, or numbers. Also any paper printed in order to be dispersed, and made public weekly or oftener, or at intervals not exceeding twenty-six days, containing only or principally advertisements. "Occupation" when applied to any person shall mean his trade or following, and if none, then his rank or usual title, as esquire, gentleman. "Place of residence" shall include the street, square, or place where the person to whom it refers shall reside, and the number (if any) or other designation of the house in which he shall so reside. "Proprietor" shall mean and include as well the sole proprietor of any newspaper, as also in the case of a divided proprietorship the persons who, as partners or otherwise, represent and are responsible for any share or interest in the newspaper as between themselves and the person in like manner representing or responsible for the other shares or interest therein, and no other person.
[Newspaper Libel and Registration Act 1881, s 1.]

8–18670A 4. Hearing—Evidence. A court of summary jurisdiction, upon the hearing of a charge against a proprietor, publisher, or editor or any person responsible for the publication of a newspaper, for a libel published therein may receive evidence as to the publication being for the public benefit[1], and as to the matters charged in the libel being true, and as to the report being fair and accurate and published without malice, and as to any matter which under this or any other Act, or otherwise, might be given in[2] evidence by way of defence by the person charged on his trial on indictment, and the court, if of opinion after hearing such evidence that there is a strong or probable presumption (see Treat 47 JP 323) that the jury on the trial would acquit the person charged, may dismiss the case.
[Newspaper Libel and Registration Act 1881, s 4.]

1. The statute does not apply to seditious libels (*Ex p O'Brien* (1883) 12 LR Ir 29).
2. This supersedes, as to libels in newspapers, the law as laid down in *R v Carden* (1879) 5 QBD 1, 44 JP 119, 137 and *R v Flowers* (1879) 44 JP 377.

8–18671 7, 8 & 9. Register of newspaper proprietors.— A register of the proprietors of newspapers as[1] defined by this Act shall be established under the superintendence of the registrar. [Newspaper Libel and Registration Act 1881, s 8.] Board of Trade may authorise the registration of names of only a portion of the proprietors. [Newspaper Libel and Registration Act 1881, s 7.] It shall be the duty of the printers and publishers for the time being of every newspaper to make or cause to be made to the registry office annually in the month of July in every year, a[2] return in the form prescribed by the schedule of—(1) The title of a newspaper; (2) The names of all the proprietors of such newspaper, together with their respective occupations, places of business (if any), and places of residence.
[Newspaper Libel and Registration Act 1881, s 9.]

1. The provisions as to registration are not to apply to a newspaper belonging to a joint stock company (s 18).
2. Any party to a transfer or dealing with a share may at any time make a return in the form prescribed by the schedule (s 11).

8–18672 10. Omission to make annual returns. If within the further period of one month after the time hereinbefore appointed for the making of any return as to any newspaper such return be not made, then each printer and publisher of such newspaper shall, on conviction thereof, be liable to a penalty not exceeding **level 2** on the standard scale, and also to be directed by a summary order to make a return within a specified time.
[Newspaper Libel and Registration Act 1881, s 10, as amended by the Criminal Law Act 1977, s 31 and the Criminal Justice Act 1982, s 46.]

8–18673 12. Wilful misrepresentation in or omission from return. If any person shall knowingly and wilfully make or cause to be made any return by this Act required or permitted to be made in which shall be inserted or set forth the name of any person as a proprietor of a newspaper who shall not be a proprietor thereof, or in which there shall be any misrepresentation, or from which there shall be any omission in respect of any of the particulars by this Act required to be contained therein whereby such return shall be misleading, or if any proprietor of a newspaper shall knowingly and wilfully permit any such return to be made which shall be misleading as to any of the particulars with reference to his own name, occupation, place of business (if any), or place of residence, then and in every such case every such offender being convicted thereof shall be liable to a penalty not exceeding **level 3** on the standard scale.

[Newspaper Libel and Registration Act 1881, s 12, as amended by the Criminal Justice Act 1982, ss 38 and 46.]

8–18674 15. Extracts from register to be evidence. Every copy of[1] entry in or extract from the register of newspaper proprietors, purporting to be certified by the registrar or his deputy for the time being, or under the official seal of the registrar, shall be received as conclusive evidence of the contents of the said register of newspaper proprietors, so far as the same appear in such copy or extract without proof of the signature thereto or of the seal of office affixed thereto, and every such certified copy or extract shall in all proceedings, civil or criminal, be accepted as sufficient *prima facie* evidence of all the matters and things thereby appearing, unless and until the contrary thereof be shown.

[Newspaper Libel and Registration Act 1881, s 15.]

---

1. Any person may inspect the register and require a copy or extract to be certified (s 13) on payment of fee to be fixed by the Board of Trade (s 14).

8–18675 16. Procedure. All penalties under this Act may be recovered before a court of summary jurisdiction in manner provided by the Summary Jurisdiction Acts[1].

[Newspaper Libel and Registration Act 1881, s 16, as amended by the Courts Act 1971, Sch 11.]

---

1. Repealed and consolidated in the Magistrates' Courts Act 1952, now the Magistrates' Courts Act 1980.

Judicial Proceedings (Regulation of Reports) Act 1926

(16 & 17 Geo 5 c 61)

8–18690 1. Reports of judicial proceedings. (1) It shall not be lawful to print or publish, or cause or procure to be printed or published—

(*a*) in relation to any judicial proceedings[1] any indecent matter or indecent medical, surgical or physiological details, being matter or details the publication of which would be calculated to injure public morals;

(*b*) in relation to any judicial proceedings for dissolution of marriage, for nullity of marriage, or for judicial separation[2], or for the dissolution or annulment of a civil partnership or for the separation of civil partners, any particulars other than the following, that is to say:

(i) the names, addresses and occupations of the parties and witnesses;

(ii) a concise statement of the charges, defences and countercharges in support of which evidence has been given;

(iii) submissions on any point of law arising in the course of the proceedings and the decision of the court thereon;

(iv) the summing up of the judge and the finding of the jury (if any) and the judgment of the court and observations made by the judge in giving judgment:

Provided that nothing in this part of this subsection shall be held to permit the publication of anything contrary to the provisions of paragraph (*a*) of this subsection.*

(2) If any person acts in contravention of the provisions of this Act, he shall in respect of each offence be liable, on summary conviction, to imprisonment for a term not exceeding **four months**** or to a fine not exceeding **level 5** on the standard scale, or to both such imprisonment and fine: Provided that no person, other than a proprietor, editor, master printer or publisher, shall be liable to be convicted under this Act.

(3) No prosecution to be commenced without the Attorney-General's sanction.

(4) Nothing in this section shall apply to the printing of any pleading, transcript of evidence or other document for use in connection with any judicial proceedings or the communication thereof to persons concerned in the proceedings, or to the printing or publishing of any notice or report in pursuance of the directions of the court; or to the printing or publishing of any matter in any separate volume or part of any bona fide series of law reports which does not form part of any other publication and consists solely of reports of proceedings in courts of law, or in any publication of a technical character bona fide intended for circulation among members of the legal or medical professions.

(5) *Repealed.*

[Judicial Proceedings (Regulation of Reports) Act 1926, s 1 as amended by the Criminal Justice Act 1982, ss 38 and 46 and the Civil Partnership Act 2004, Sch 27.]

***Amended by the Family Law Act 1996, Sch 8, in PART IV, ANTE, WHEN IN FORCE.**

****"51 weeks" substituted by the Criminal Justice Act 2003, Sch 26, from a date to be appointed.**

1. Not defined by this Act. Cf Perjury Act 1911, s 1(2), post.

2. For newspaper reports of domestic proceedings, see Magistrates' Courts Act 1980, s 71 in PART I: MAGISTRATES' COURTS, PROCEDURE, ante.

8–18691 **Minors and Youth Courts.** Prohibition against publication of certain matter in newspapers. See Children and Young Persons Act 1933, ss 39, 49 in PART V: YOUTH COURTS.

8–18692 **Committal proceedings before examining justices.** See Magistrates' Courts Act 1980, ss 6(5) and (8) in **PART I: MAGISTRATES' COURTS, PROCEDURE**.

Defamation Act 1996[1]

(1996 c 31)

Statutory privilege

8–18710 **14. Reports of court proceedings absolutely privileged.** (1) A fair and accurate report of proceedings in public before a court to which this section applies, if published contemporaneously with the proceedings, is absolutely privileged.

(2) A report of proceedings which by an order of the court, or as a consequence of any statutory provision, is required to be postponed shall be treated as published contemporaneously if it is published as soon as practicable after publication is permitted.

(3) This section applies to—

(*a*) any court in the United Kingdom,

(*b*) the European Court of Justice or any court attached to that court,

(*c*) the European Court of Human Rights, and

(*d*) any international criminal tribunal established by the Security Council of the United Nations or by an international agreement to which the United Kingdom is a party.

In paragraph 1 "court" includes any tribunal or body exercising the judicial power of the State.

(4) In section 8(6) of the Rehabilitation of Offenders Act 1974 and in Article 9(6) of the Rehabilitation of Offenders (Northern Ireland) Order 1978 (defamation actions: reports of court proceedings), for "section 3 of the Law of Libel Amendment Act 1888" substitute "section 14 of the Defamation Act 1996".

[Defamation Act 1996, s 14.]

1. The Defamation Act 1996 amends the law of defamation and amends the law of limitation with respect to actions for defamation or malicious falsehood.Only those provisions of the Act which are relevant to the work of magistrates' courts are included in this manual.

8–18711 **15.** Reports, &c. protected by qualified privilege.—(1) The publication of any report or other statement mentioned in Schedule 1 to this Act is privileged unless the publication is shown to be made with malice, subject as follows.

(2) In defamation proceedings in respect of the publication of a report or other statement mentioned in Part II of that Schedule, there is no defence under this section if the plaintiff shows that the defendant—

(*a*) was requested by him to publish in a suitable manner a reasonable letter or statement by way of explanation or contradiction, and

(*b*) refused or neglected to do so.

For this purpose "in a suitable manner" means in the same manner as the publication complained of or in a manner that is adequate and reasonable in the circumstances.

(3) This section does not apply to the publication to the public, or a section of the public, of matter which is not of public concern and the publication of which is not for the public benefit.

(4) Nothing in this section shall be construed—

(*a*) as protecting the publication of matter the publication of which is prohibited by law, or

(*b*) as limiting or abridging any privilege subsisting apart from this section.

[Defamation Act 1996, s 15.]

Supplementary provisions

8–18712 **17. Interpretation.** (1) In this Act—

"publication" and "publish", in relation to a statement, have the meaning they have for the purposes of the law of defamation generally, but "publisher" is specially defined for the purposes of section 1;

"statement" means words, pictures, visual images, gestures or any other method of signifying meaning; and

"statutory provision" means—

(*a*) a provision contained in an Act or in subordinate legislation within the meaning of the Interpretation Act 1978, or

(*aa*) a provision contained in an Act of the Scottish Parliament or in an instrument made under such an Act, or (*b*) a statutory provision within the meaning given by section 1 (*f*) of the Interpretation Act (Northern Ireland) 1954.

(2) In this Act as it applies to proceedings in Scotland—
"costs" means expenses; and
"plaintiff" and "defendant" mean pursuer and defender.
[Defamation Act 1996, s 17, as amended by the Scotland Act 1998, Sch 8.]

General provisions

8–18713 **18.** *Extent.*

8–18714 **19. Commencement.** (1) Sections 18 to 20 (extent, commencement and other general provisions) come into force on Royal Assent.

(2) The following provisions of this Act come into force at the end of the period of two months beginning with the day on which this Act is passed—

section 1 (responsibility for publication),
sections 5 and 6 (time limit for actions for defamation or malicious falsehood),
section 12 (evidence of convictions),
section 13 (evidence concerning proceedings in Parliament),
section 16 and the repeals in Schedule 2, so far as consequential on the above provisions, and
section 17 (interpretation), so far as relating to the above provisions.

(3) The provisions of this Act otherwise come into force on such day as may be appointed—

(*a*) for England and Wales or Northern Ireland, by order[1] of the Lord Chancellor, or
(*b*) for Scotland, by order of the Secretary of State,

and different days may be appointed for different purposes.

(4) Any such order shall be made by statutory instrument and may contain such transitional provisions as appear to the Lord Chancellor or Secretary of State to be appropriate.
[Defamation Act 1996, s 19.]

1. The Defamation Act 1996 (Commencement No 1) Order 1999, SI 1999/817, brought into force on 1 April 1999 ss 14, 15 and 17, so far as it applies to those provisions, of and Sch 1 to the Defamation Act 1996, as well as consequential repeals; the Defamation Act 1996 (Commencement No 2) Order 2000, SI 2000/222.

8–18715 **20. Short title and saving.** (1) This Act may be cited as the Defamation Act 1996.

(2) Nothing in this Act affects the law relating to criminal libel.
[Defamation Act 1996, s 20.]

SCHEDULES

Section 15

SCHEDULE 1
Qualified Privilege

Part I
Statements Having Qualified Privilege Without Explanation or Contradiction

8–18716 **1.** A fair and accurate report of proceedings in public of a legislature anywhere in the world.

2. A fair and accurate report of proceedings in public before a court anywhere in the world.

3. A fair and accurate report of proceedings in public of a person appointed to hold a public inquiry by a government or legislature anywhere in the world.

4. A fair and accurate report of proceedings in public anywhere in the world of an international organisation or an international conference.

5. A fair and accurate copy of or extract from any register or other document required by law to be open to public inspection.

6. A notice or advertisement published by or on the authority of a court, or of a judge or officer of a court, anywhere in the world.

7. A fair and accurate copy of or extract from matter published by or on the authority of a government or legislature anywhere in the world.

8. A fair and accurate copy of or extract from matter published anywhere in the world by an international organisation or an international conference.

Part II
Statements Privileged Subject to Explanation or Contradiction

(*Amended by the Scotland Act 1998, Sch 8 and SI 2001/2237 and SI 2002/808 and 1057.*)

8–18717 **9.** (1) A fair and accurate copy of or extract from a notice or other matter issued for the information of the public by or on behalf of—

(*a*) a legislature in any member State or the European Parliament;
(*b*) the government of any member State, or any authority performing governmental functions in any member State or part of a member State, or the European Commission;

(*c*) an international organisation or international conference.

(2) In this paragraph "governmental functions" includes police functions.

10. A fair and accurate copy of or extract from a document made available by a court in any member State or the European Court of Justice (or any court attached to that court) or by a judge or officer of any such court.

11. (1) A fair and accurate report of proceedings at any public meeting or sitting in the United Kingdom of—

(*a*) a local authority or local authority committee;

(*aa*) in the case of a local authority which are operating executive arrangements, the executive of that authority or a committee of that executive;

(*b*) a justice or justices of the peace acting otherwise than as a court exercising judicial authority;

(*c*) a commission, tribunal, committee or person appointed for the purposes of any inquiry by any statutory provision, by Her Majesty or by a Minister of the Crown a member of the Scottish Executive or a Northern Ireland Department;

(*d*) a person appointed by a local authority to hold a local inquiry in pursuance of any statutory provision;

(*e*) any other tribunal, board, committee or body constituted by or under, and exercising functions under, any statutory provision.

(1A) In the case of a local authority which are operating executive arrangements, a fair and accurate record of any decision made by any member of the executive where that record is required to be made and available for public inspection by virtue of section 22 of the Local Government Act 2000 or of any provision in regulations made under that section.

(2) In sub-paragraphs (1)(*a*), (1)(*aa*) and (1A)—

"local authority" means—

(*a*) in relation to England and Wales, a principal council within the meaning of the Local Government Act 1972, any body falling within any paragraph of section 100J(1) of that Act or an authority or body to which the Public Bodies (Admission to Meetings) Act 1960 applies,

(*b*) in relation to Scotland, a council constituted under section 2 of the Local Government etc. (Scotland) Act 1994 or an authority or body to which the Public Bodies (Admission to Meetings) Act 1960 applies,

(*c*) in relation to Northern Ireland, any authority or body to which sections 23 to 27 of the Local Government Act (Northern Ireland) 1972 apply; and

"local authority committee" means any committee of a local authority or of local authorities, and includes—

(*a*) any committee or sub-committee in relation to which sections 100A to 100D of the Local Government Act 1972 apply by virtue of section 100E of that Act (whether or not also by virtue of section 100J of that Act), and

(*b*) any committee or sub-committee in relation to which sections 50A to 50D of the Local Government (Scotland) Act 1973 apply by virtue of section 50E of that Act.

(2A) In sub-paragraphs (1) and (1A)—

"executive" and "executive arrangements" have the same meaning as in Part II of the Local Government Act 2000.

(3) A fair and accurate report of any corresponding proceedings in any of the Channel Islands or the Isle of Man or in another member State.

12. (1) A fair and accurate report of proceedings at any public meeting held in a member State.

(2) In this paragraph a "public meeting" means a meeting bona fide and lawfully held for a lawful purpose and for the furtherance or discussion of a matter of public concern, whether admission to the meeting is general or restricted.

13. (1) A fair and accurate report of proceedings at a general meeting of a UK public company.

(2) A fair and accurate copy of or extract from any document circulated to members of a UK public company—

(*a*) by or with the authority of the board of directors of the company,

(*b*) by the auditors of the company, or

(*c*) by any member of the company in pursuance of a right conferred by any statutory provision.

(3) A fair and accurate copy of or extract from any document circulated to members of a UK public company which relates to the appointment, resignation, retirement or dismissal of directors of the company.

(4) In this paragraph "UK public company" means—

(*a*) a public company within the meaning of section 1(3) of the Companies Act 1985 or Article 12(3) of the Companies (Northern Ireland) Order 1986, or

(*b*) a body corporate incorporated by or registered under any other statutory provision, or by Royal Charter, or formed in pursuance of letters patent.

(5) A fair and accurate report of proceedings at any corresponding meeting of, or copy of or extract from any corresponding document circulated to members of, a public company formed under the law of any of the Channel Islands or the Isle of Man or of another member State.

14. A fair and accurate report of any finding or decision of any of the following descriptions of association, formed in the United Kingdom or another member State, or of any committee or governing body of such an association—

(*a*) an association formed for the purpose of promoting or encouraging the exercise of or interest in any art, science, religion or learning, and empowered by its constitution to exercise control over or adjudicate on matters of interest or concern to the association, or the actions or conduct of any person subject to such control or adjudication;

(*b*) an association formed for the purpose of promoting or safeguarding the interests of any trade, business, industry or profession, or of the persons carrying on or engaged in any trade, business, industry or profession, and empowered by its constitution to exercise control over or adjudicate upon matters connected with that trade, business, industry or profession, or the actions or conduct of those persons;

(*c*) an association formed for the purpose of promoting or safeguarding the interests of a game, sport or pastime to the playing or exercise of which members of the public are invited or admitted, and empowered by its constitution to exercise control over or adjudicate upon persons connected with or taking part in the game, sport or pastime;

(*d*) an association formed for the purpose of promoting charitable objects or other objects beneficial to the community and empowered by its constitution to exercise control over or to adjudicate on matters of interest or concern to the association, or the actions or conduct of any person subject to such control or adjudication.

15. (1) A fair and accurate report of, or copy of or extract from, any adjudication, report, statement or notice issued by a body, officer or other person designated for the purposes of this paragraph—

(*a*) for England and Wales or Northern Ireland, by order of the Lord Chancellor, and
(*b*) for Scotland, by order of the Secretary of State.

(2) An order under this paragraph shall be made by statutory instrument which shall be subject to annulment in pursuance of a resolution of either House of Parliament.

PART III
SUPPLEMENTARY PROVISIONS

8–18718 **16.** (1) In this Schedule—

"court" includes any tribunal or body exercising the judicial power of the State;
"international conference" means a conference attended by representatives of two or more governments;
"international organisation" means an organisation of which two or more governments are members, and includes any committee or other subordinate body of such an organisation; and
"legislature" includes a local legislature.

(2) References in this Schedule to a member State include any European dependent territory of a member State.

(3) In paragraphs 2 and 6 "court" includes—

(*a*) the European Court of Justice (or any court attached to that court) and the Court of Auditors of the European Communities,
(*b*) the European Court of Human Rights,
(*c*) any international criminal tribunal established by the Security Council of the United Nations or by an international agreement to which the United Kingdom is a party, and
(*d*) the International Court of Justice and any other judicial or arbitral tribunal deciding matters in dispute between States.

(4) In paragraphs 1, 3 and 7 "legislature" includes the European Parliament.

17. (1) Provision may be made by order identifying—

(*a*) for the purposes of paragraph 11, the corresponding proceedings referred to in sub-paragraph (3);
(*b*) for the purposes of paragraph 13, the corresponding meetings and documents referred to in sub-paragraph (5).

(2) An order under this paragraph may be made—

(*a*) for England and Wales or Northern Ireland, by the Lord Chancellor, and
(*b*) for Scotland, by the Secretary of State.

(3) An order under this paragraph shall be made by statutory instrument which shall be subject to annulment in pursuance of a resolution of either House of Parliament.

LOCAL GOVERNMENT

8–18770 This title contains the following statutes—

The following statutory instruments are also printed—

Local Government Act 1972

(1972 c 70 as amended by SI 2006/88)

PART I

LOCAL GOVERNMENT AREAS AND AUTHORITIES IN ENGLAND

8–18800 1. Local government areas in England. With the exception of Greater London[1] and the Isles of Scilly, England is divided into local government areas to be known as counties and in those counties there shall be local government areas known as districts[2]. The counties are either metropolitan counties or non-metropolitan counties.

[Local Government Act 1972, s 1—summarised.]

---

1. There shall be a council for every London borough (Sch 2).
2. The districts in metropolitan counties are to be known as "metropolitan districts" (Sch 2). Districts in non-metropolitan countries are to be established under Sch 3; and "non-metropolitan district" means any district other than a metropolitan district (s 270(2)).

8–18801 2. Councils. There shall be a council for each non-metropolitan county and district: the "County Council" and "District Council" respectively.

[Local Government Act 1972, s 2, amended by the Local Government Act 1985, Sch 16 and the Local Government Act 2000, Sch 3—summarised.]

PART II

LOCAL GOVERNMENT AREAS AND AUTHORITIES IN WALES

8–18802 20. Local Government areas in Wales. With effect from 1st April 1996 Wales is divided into local government areas to be known as counties and county boroughs ("principal areas") and communities[1].

[Local Government Act 1972, s 20 amended by the Local Government (Wales) Act 1994, s 1—summarised.]

---

1. References in pre-existing legislation to councils or areas of a county or district are to be construed as references to the principal areas (Local Government (Wales) Act 1994, s 17. Other transitional provisions are made by Pt VI of the Act.)

8–18803 21. Councils in Wales. There shall be a council for every county and county borough.

[Local Government Act 1972, s 21 amended by the Local Government (Wales) Act 1994, s 2 and the Local Government Act 2000, Sch 3—summarised.]

8–18803A 27–35. *Community Councils.*

PART V

8–18804 92. Proceedings for disqualification. (1) Proceedings against any person on the ground that he acted or claims to be entitled to act as a member of a local authority while disqualified[1] for so acting within the meaning of this section may be instituted by, and only by, any local government elector for the area concerned—

(*a*) in the High Court or a magistrates' court if that person so acted;
(*b*) in the High Court if that person claims to be entitled so to act;

but proceedings under paragraph (*a*) above shall not be instituted against any person after the expiration of more than six months from the date on which he so acted.

(2) Where in proceedings instituted under this section it is proved that the defendant has acted as a member of a local authority while disqualified for so acting, then—

(*a*) if the proceedings are in the High Court, the High Court may—
  (i) make a declaration to that effect and declare that the office in which the defendant has acted is vacant;
  (ii) grant an injunction restraining the defendant from so acting;
  (iii) order that the defendant shall forfeit to Her Majesty such sum as the court think fit, not exceeding **£50** for each occasion on which he so acted while disqualified;

(*b*) if the proceedings are in a magistrates' court, the magistrates' court may, subject to the provisions of this section, convict the defendant and impose on him a fine not exceeding **level 3** on the standard scale for each occasion on which he so acted while disqualified.

(3) Where proceedings under this section are instituted in a magistrates' court, then—

(*a*) if the court is satisfied that the matter would be more properly dealt with in the High Court, it shall by order discontinue the proceedings;
(*b*) if the High Court, on application made to it by the defendant within fourteen days after service of the summons, is satisfied that the matter would be more properly dealt with in the

High Court, it may make an order, which shall not be subject to any appeal, requiring the magistrates' court by order to discontinue the proceedings.

(4) Where in proceedings instituted under this section in the High Court it is proved that the defendant claims to act as a member of a local authority and is disqualified for so acting, the court may make a declaration to that effect and declare that the office in which the defendant claims to be entitled to act is vacant and grant an injunction restraining him from so acting.

(5) No proceedings shall be instituted against a person otherwise than under this section on the ground that he has, while disqualified for acting as a member of a local authority, so acted or claimed to be entitled so to act.

(6) For the purposes of this section a person shall be deemed to be disqualified for acting as a member of a local authority—

(*a*) if he is not qualified to be, or is disqualified for being, a member of the authority; or

(*b*) if by reason of failure to make and deliver the declaration of acceptance of office within the period required, or by reason of resignation or failure to attend meetings of the local authority, he has ceased to be a member of the authority.

(7) In this section "local authority" includes a joint authority; and in relation to a joint authority the reference in subsection (1) above to a local government elector for the area concerned shall be construed as a reference to a local government elector for any local government area in the area for which the authority is established.

(8) In relation to the Broads Authority, the reference in subsection (1) above to a local government elector for the area concerned shall be construed as a reference to a local government elector for the area of any of the local authorities mentioned in section 1(3)(*a*) of the Norfolk and Suffolk Broads Act 1988.

[Local Government Act 1972, s 92, as amended by the Criminal Justice Act 1982, ss 38 and 46, the Local Government Act 1985, Sch 14, the Norfolk and Suffolk Broads Act 1988, Sch 6 and the Education Reform Act 1988, Sch 13.]

---

1. See ss 79 and 80 for provisions as to qualification and disqualification; and see *Bishop v Deakin* [1936] Ch 409, [1936] 1 All ER 255, 100 JP 201, as to time within which proceedings must be commenced.

8–18805 **94.** Disability of members of authorities for voting on account of interest in contracts, etc—(1) Subject to the provisions of section 97[1] below, if a member of a local authority has any pecuniary interest[2], direct or indirect, in any contract, proposed contract or other matter, and is present at a meeting of the local authority at which the contract or other matter is the subject of consideration, he shall at the meeting and as soon as practicable after its commencement disclose[3] the fact and shall not take part in the consideration or discussion of the contract or other matter or vote on any question with respect to it.

(2) If any person fails to comply with the provisions of subsection (1) above he shall for each offence be liable on summary conviction to a fine not exceeding **level 4** on the standard scale unless he proves that he did not know that the contract, proposed contract or other matter in which he had a pecuniary interest was the subject of consideration at that meeting.

(3) A prosecution for an offence under this section shall not be instituted except by or on behalf of the Director of Public Prosecutions.

(4) A local authority may by standing orders provide for the exclusion of a member of the authority from a meeting of the authority while any contract, proposed contract or other matter in which he has a pecuniary interest, direct or indirect, is under consideration.

(5) The following, that is to say—

(*a*) the receipt by the chairman, vice-chairman or deputy chairman of a principal council of an allowance to meet the expenses of his office or his right to receive, or the possibility of his receiving, such an allowance;

(*b*) the receipt by a member of a local authority of an allowance or other payment under any provision of sections 173 to 176 below or under any scheme made by virtue of section 18 of the Local Government and Housing Act 1989 or paragraph 25 of Schedule 2 to the Police Act or his right to receive, or the possibility of his receiving, any such payment;

shall not be treated as a pecuniary interest for the purposes of this section.*

[Local Government Act 1972, s 94, as amended by the Criminal Justice Act 1982, ss 38 and 46, the Local Government and Housing Act 1989, Sch 11, the Police and Magistrates' Courts Act 1994, Sch 4, the Police Act 1996, Sch 7, the Police Act 1997, Sch 6 and the Criminal Justice and Police Act 2001, Sch 7.]

***Prospectively repealed by the Local Government Act 2000, Schs 5 and 6.**

1. Section 97, which is not quoted in this work, contains provisions for the removal or exclusion of a disability.

2. See s 95, not quoted in this work, for provisions as to pecuniary interests. See also s 94(5): specified allowances not to be treated as a pecuniary interest. Where a pecuniary interest exists, the disability extends to a vote which is disadvantageous to that interest (*Brown v DPP* [1956] 2 QB 369, [1956] 2 All ER 189, 120 JP 303; *Rands v Oldroyd* [1959] 1 QB 204, [1958] 3 All ER 344, 123 JP 1). For the precise application of exemptions see *Readman v Payne* (1991) 155 JP 884, DC.

3. See s 96, not quoted in this work, containing provisions as to general notice of disclosure.

PART VA[1]

ACCESS TO MEETINGS AND DOCUMENTS OF CERTAIN AUTHORITIES, COMMITTEES AND SUB-COMMITTEES

8–18806 **100A. Admission to meetings of principal councils.** (1) A meeting of a principal council[2] shall be open to the public except to the extent that they are excluded (whether during the whole or part of the proceedings) under subsection (2) below or by resolution under subsection (4) below.

(2) Public shall be excluded from a meeting of a principal council during an item of business whenever it is likely confidential information would be disclosed in breach of the obligation of confidence; and nothing in this Part shall be taken to authorise or require the disclosure of confidential information in breach of the obligation of confidence (*summarised*).

(3)–(8) *Supplementary provisions as to admission of the public.*

[Local Government Act 1972, s 100A, as inserted by the Local Government (Access to Information) Act 1985, s 1 and amended by SI 2002/715.]

1. Part VA contains ss 100A–100K, and was inserted by the Local Government (Access to Information) Act 1985, s 1. Sections 100A to 100D, 100H, 100I of and Sch 12A to this Act are applied, with modifications, to a "joint committee", being a joint consultative committee appointed pursuant to an order under s 22 of the National Health Service Act 1977, or a sub-committee of such a committee, or a joint sub-committee of 2 or more such committees (Health Service Joint Consultative Committees (Access to Information) Act 1986, ss 1 and 2). Sections 100A to 100D are also applied, with modifications, to a Community Health Council, established under s 20 of the National Health Service Act 1977, and the Committees of those Councils (Community Health Councils (Access to Information) Act 1988, ss 1 and 2).

2. For meaning of "principal council", see ss 100J and 270(1), post.

8–18807 **100B. Access to agenda and connected reports.** (1) Copies of the agenda for a meeting of a principal council[1] and, subject to subsection (2) below, copies of any report for the meeting shall be open to inspection by members of the public at the offices of the council in accordance with subsection (3) below.

(2) If the proper officer thinks fit, there may be excluded from the copies of reports provided in pursuance of subsection (1) above the whole of any report which, or any part which, relates only to items during which, in his opinion, the meeting is likely not to be open to the public.

(3) Any document which is required by subsection (1) above to be open to inspection shall be so open at least five clear days before the meeting, except that—

(*a*) where the meeting is convened at shorter notice, the copies of the agenda and reports shall be open to inspection from the time the meeting is convened, and

(*b*) where an item is added to an agenda copies of which are open to inspection by the public, copies of the item (or of the revised agenda), and the copies of any report for the meeting relating to the item, shall be open to inspection from the time the item is added to the agenda;

but nothing in this subsection requires copies of any agenda, item or report to be open to inspection by the public until copies are available to members of the council.

(4) An item of business may not be considered at a meeting of a principal council unless either—

(*a*) a copy of the agenda including the item (or a copy of the item) is open to inspection by members of the public in pursuance of subsection (1) above for at least five clear days before the meeting or, where the meeting is convened at shorter notice, from the time the meeting is convened; or

(*b*) by reason of special circumstances, which shall be specified in the minutes, the chairman of the meeting is of the opinion that the item should be considered at the meeting as a matter of urgency.

(5) Where by virtue of subsection (2) above the whole or any part of a report for a meeting is not open to inspection by the public under subsection (1) above—

(*a*) every copy of the report or of the part shall be marked "Not for publication"; and

(*b*) there shall be stated on every copy of the whole or any part of the report the description, in terms of Schedule 12A to this Act, of the exempt information by virtue of which the council are likely to exclude the public during the item to which the report relates.

(6) Where a meeting of a principal council is required by section 100A above to be open to the public during the proceedings or any part of them, there shall be made available for the use of members of the public present at the meeting a reasonable number of copies of the agenda and, subject to subsection (8) below, of the reports for the meeting.

(7) There shall, on request and on payment of postage or other necessary charge for transmission, be supplied for the benefit of any newspaper—

(*a*) a copy of the agenda for a meeting of a principal council and, subject to subsection (8) below, a copy of each of the reports for the meeting;

(*b*) such further statements or particulars, if any, as are necessary to indicate the nature of the items included in the agenda; and

(*c*) if the proper officer thinks fit in the case of any item, copies of any other documents supplied to members of the council in connection with the item.

(8) Subsection (2) above applies in relation to copies of reports provided in pursuance of subsection (6) or (7) above as it applies in relation to copies of reports provided in pursuance of subsection (1) above.

[Local Government Act 1972, s 100B, as inserted by the Local Government (Access to Information) Act 1985, s 1 and amended by SI 2002/715.]

1. For meaning of "principal council", see ss 100J and 270(1), post.

8–18808 100C. Inspection of minutes and other documents after meetings. (1) After a meeting of a principal council[1] the following documents shall be open to inspection by members of the public at the offices of the council until the expiration of the period of six years beginning with the date of the meeting, namely—

(*a*) the minutes, or a copy of the minutes, of the meeting, excluding so much of the minutes of proceedings during which the meeting was not open to the public as discloses exempt information;
(*b*) where applicable, a summary under subsection (2) below;
(*c*) a copy of the agenda for the meeting; and
(*d*) a copy of so much of any report for the meeting as relates to any item during which the meeting was open to the public.

(2) Where, in consequence of the exclusion of parts of the minutes which disclose exempt information, the document open to inspection under subsection (1)(*a*) above does not provide members of the public with a reasonably fair and coherent record of the whole or part of the proceedings, the proper officer shall make a written summary of the proceedings or the part, as the case may be, which provides such a record without disclosing the exempt information.

[Local Government Act 1972, s 100C, as inserted by the Local Government (Access to Information) Act 1985, s 1.]

1. For meaning of "principal council", see ss 100J and 270(1), post.

8–18809 100D. Inspection of background papers. (1) Subject, in the case of section 100C(1), to subsection (2) below, if and so long as copies of the whole or part of a report for a meeting of a principal council are required by section 100B(1) or 100C(1) above to be open to inspection by members of the public—

(*a*) those copies shall each include a copy of a list, compiled by the proper officer, of the background papers for the report or the part of the report, and
(*b*) at least one copy of each of the documents included in that list shall also be open to inspection at the offices of the council.

(2) Subsection (1) above does not require a copy of any document included in the list, to be open to inspection after the expiration of the period of four years beginning with the date of the meeting.

(3) Where a copy of any of the background papers for a report is required by subsection (1) above to be open to inspection by members of the public, the copy shall be taken for the purposes of this Part to be so open if arrangements exist for its production to members of the public as soon as is reasonably practicable after the making of a request to inspect the copy.

(4) Nothing in this section—

(*a*) requires any document which discloses exempt information to be included in the list referred to in subsection (1) above; or
(*b*) without prejudice to the generality of subsection (2) of section 100A above, requires or authorises the inclusion in the list of any document which, if open to inspection by the public, would disclose confidential information in breach of the obligation of confidence, within the meaning of that subsection.

(5) For the purposes of this section the background papers for a report are those documents relating to the subject matter of the report which—

(*a*) disclose any facts or matters on which, in the opinion of the proper officer, the report or an important part of the report is based, and
(*b*) have, in his opinion, been relied on to a material extent in preparing the report,

but do not include any published works.

[Local Government Act 1972, s 100D, as inserted by the Local Government (Access to Information) Act 1985, s 1 and amended by the Local Government Act 2000, s 97 and Sch 6.]

8–18810 100E. Application to committees and sub-committees. (1) Sections 100A to 100D above shall apply in relation to a committee or sub-committee of a principal council as they apply in relation to a principal council.

(2) In the application by virtue of this section of sections 100A to 100D above in relation to a committee or sub-committee—

(*a*) section 100A(6)(*a*) shall be taken to have been complied with if the notice is given by posting it at the time there mentioned at the offices of every constituent principal council and, if the meeting of the committee or sub-committee to which that section so applies is to be held at premises other than the offices of such a council, at those premises;

(*b*) for the purposes of section 100A(6)(*c*), premises belonging to a constituent principal council shall be treated as belonging to the committee or sub-committee; and

(*c*) for the purposes of sections 100B(1), 100C(1) and 100D(1), offices of any constituent principal council shall be treated as offices of the committee or sub-committee.

(3) Any reference in this Part to a committee or sub-committee of a principal council is a reference to—

(*a*) a committee which is constituted under an enactment specified in section 101(9) below or which is appointed by one or more principal councils under section 102 below; or

(*b*) a joint committee not falling within paragraph (*a*) above which is appointed or established under any enactment by two or more principal councils and is not a body corporate; or

(*bb*) the Navigation Committee of the Broads Authority; or

(*c*) a sub-committee appointed or established under any enactment by one or more committees falling within paragraphs (*a*) to (*bb*) above.

(4) Any reference in this Part to a constituent principal council, in relation to a committee or sub-committee, is a reference—

(*a*) in the case of a committee, to the principal council, or any of the principal councils, of which it is a committee; and

(*b*) in the case of a sub-committee, to any principal council which, by virtue of paragraph (*a*) above, is a constituent principal council in relation to the committee, or any of the committees, which established or appointed the sub-committee.

[Local Government Act 1972, s 100E, as inserted by the Local Government (Access to Information) Act 1985, s 1 and amended by the Norfolk and Suffolk Broads Act 1988, Sch 6.]

8–18811 100F–100G. *Additional rights*[1] *of access to documents for members of principal councils; principal councils to publish additional information.*

1. See also the Local Government (Inspection of Documents) (Summary of Rights) Order 1986, SI 1986/854, which specifies for these purposes additional enactments which confer rights to attend meetings and to inspect, copy and be furnished with documents.

8–18812 100H. Supplemental provisions and offences. (1) A document directed by any provision of this Part to be open to inspection shall be so open at all reasonable hours and—

(*a*) in the case of a document open to inspection by virtue of section 100D(1) above, upon payment of such reasonable fee as may be required for the facility; and

(*b*) in any other case, without payment.

(2) Where a document is open to inspection by a person under any provision of this Part, the person may, subject to subsection (3) below—

(*a*) make copies of or extracts from the document, or

(*b*) require the person having custody of the document to supply to him a photographic copy of or of extracts from the document,

upon payment of such reasonable fee as may be required for the facility.

(3) Subsection (2) above does not require or authorise the doing of any act which infringes the copyright in any work except that, where the owner of the copyright is a principal council, nothing done in pursuance of that subsection shall constitute an infringement of the copyright.

(4) If, without reasonable excuse, a person having the custody of a document which is required by section 100B(1) or 100C(1) above to be open to inspection by the public—

(*a*) intentionally obstructs any person exercising a right conferred by this Part to inspect, or to make a copy of or extracts from the document, or

(*b*) refuses to furnish copies to any person entitled to obtain them under any provision of this Part,

he shall be liable on summary conviction to a fine not exceeding **level 1** on the standard scale.

(5) Where any accessible document for a meeting to which this subsection applies—

(*a*) is supplied to, or open to inspection by, a member of the public, or

(*b*) is supplied for the benefit of any newspaper, in pursuance of section 100B(7) above,

the publication thereby of any defamatory matter contained in the document shall be privileged unless the publication is proved to be made with malice.

(6) Subsection (5) above applies to any meeting of a principal council and any meeting of a committee or sub-committee of a principal council; and, for the purposes of that subsection, the "accessible documents" for a meeting are the following—

(*a*) any copy of the agenda or of any item included in the agenda for the meeting;
(*b*) any such further statements or particulars for the purpose of indicating the nature of any item included in the agenda as are mentioned in section 100B(7)(*b*) above;
(*c*) any copy of a document relating to such an item which is supplied for the benefit of a newspaper in pursuance of section 100B(7)(*c*) above;
(*d*) any copy of the whole or part of a report for the meeting;
(*e*) any copy of the whole or part of any background papers for a report for the meeting, within the meaning of section 100D above.

(7) The rights conferred by this Part to inspect, copy and be furnished with documents are in addition, and without prejudice, to any such rights conferred by or under any other enactment.
[Local Government Act 1972, s 100H, as inserted by the Local Government (Access to Information) Act 1985, s 1.]

8–18813 100I. Exempt information and power to vary Schedule 12A. (1) In relation to principal councils in England, the descriptions of information which are, for the purposes of this Part, exempt information are those for the time being specified in Part I of Schedule 12A to this Act, but subject to any qualifications contained in Part II of that Schedule; and Part III has effect for the interpretation of Parts 1 to 3 of that Schedule.

(1A) In relation to principal councils in Wales, the descriptions of information which are, for the purposes of this Part, exempt information are those for the time being specified in Part 4 of Schedule 12A to this Act, but subject to any qualifications contained in Part 5 of that Schedule; and Part 6 has effect for the interpretation of Parts 4 to 6 of that Schedule.

(2) The appropriate person may by order vary Schedule 12A to this Act by adding to it any description or other provision or by deleting from it or varying any description or other provision for the time being specified or contained in it.

(3) The appropriate person may exercise the power conferred by subsection (2) above by amending any Part of Schedule 12A to this Act, with or without amendment of any other Part.

(3A) In this section "the appropriate person" means—

(*a*) in relation to England, the Secretary of State;
(*b*) in relation to Wales, the National Assembly for Wales.

(4) Any statutory instrument containing an order under this section made by the Secretary of State shall be subject to annulment in pursuance of a resolution of either House of Parliament.
[Local Government Act 1972, s 100I, as inserted by the Local Government (Access to Information) Act 1985, s 1 and amended by SI 2006/88.]

1. See, post.

8–18814 100J. Application to new authorities, Common Council, etc. (1) Except in this section, any reference in this Part to a principal council1 includes a reference to—

(*a*) *repealed*;
(*b*) a joint authority;
(*bb*) the London Fire and Emergency Planning Authority;
(*c*) the Common Council;
(*cc*) the Broads Authority;
(*cd*) a National Park authority;
(*d*) a joint board or joint committee falling within subsection (2) below;
(*e*) a police authority established under section 3 of the Police Act 1996;
(*eza*)the Metropolitan Police Authority
(*ea*) *repealed*
(*f*) a fire and rescue authority constituted by a scheme under section 2 of the Fire and Rescue Services Act 2004 or scheme to which section 4 of that Act applies.

(2) A joint board or joint committee falls within this subsection if—

(*a*) it is constituted under any enactment as a body corporate; and
(*b*) it discharges functions of two or more principal councils;

and for the purposes of this subsection any body falling within paragraph (*a*), (*b*), (*bb*) or (*c*) of subsection (1) above shall be treated as a principal council.

(3) In its application by virtue of subsection (1) above in relation to a body falling within paragraph (*b*), (*bb*), (*cc*), (*cd*), (*d*), (*e*), (*eza*)or (*f*) of that subsection, section 100A(6)(*a*) above shall have effect with the insertion after the word "council" of the words "(and, if the meeting is to be held at premises other than those offices, at those premises)".

(3A) *Repealed.*

(4) In its application by virtue of subsection (1) above, section 100G(1)(*a*) above shall have effect—

(*a*) in relation to a joint authority or a police authority established under section 3 of the Police Act 1996 or the Metropolitan Police Authority, with the substitution for the words from "ward" onwards of the words "name or description of the body or other person that appointed him"; and

(*aa*) in relation to the Broads Authority or its Navigation Committee or any National Park authority, with the substitution for the words from "ward" onwards of the words "name of the person who appointed him"; and

(*b*) in relation to a joint board or joint committee falling within subsection (2) above, with the omission of the words from "and the ward" onwards; and

(*c*) in relation to a fire and rescue authority falling withn subsection (1)(*f*) above, with the substitution for the words "ward or division" of the words "constituent area".

(4A) In its application by virtue of subsection (1)(*bb*) above in relation to the London Fire and Emergency Authority, section 100G(1)(*a*) shall have effect with the substitution for the words "the ward or division which he represents" of the words "whether he is an Assembly representative of a borough representative and—

(i) if he is an Assembly representative, whether he is a London member or a constituency member and, if a constituency member, the Assembly constituency for which he is a member; or

(ii) if he is a borough representative, the council of which he is a member (whether a London borough council or the Common Council).

(5) In this section "combined fire authority" means a fire authority constituted by a combination scheme under the Fire Services Act 1947.

[Local Government Act 1972, s 100J, as inserted by the Local Government (Access to Information) Act 1985, s 1 and amended by the Norfolk and Suffolk Broads Act 1988, Sch 6, the Education Reform Act 1988, Sch 13, the Police and Magistrates' Courts Act 1994, Sch 4, the Environment Act 1995, Sch 7, the Police Act 1996, Sch 7, the Police Act 1997, Sch 6, the Greater London Authority Act 1999, ss 313 and 331, the Criminal Justice and Police Act 2001, Schs 6 and 7 and the Fire and Rescue Services Act 2004, Sch 1.]

1. For meaning of "principal council", see also s 270(1), post.

8–18815 100K. Interpretation and application of Part VA. (1) In this Part—

"committee or sub-committee of a principal council" shall be construed in accordance with section 100E(3) above;

"constituent principal council" shall be construed in accordance with section 100E(4) above;

"copy", in relation to any document, includes a copy made from a copy;

"exempt information" has the meaning given by section 100I above;

"information" includes an expression of opinion, any recommendations and any decision taken;

"newspaper" includes—

(*a*) a news agency which systematically carries on the business of selling and supplying reports or information to newspapers; and

(*b*) any organisation which is systematically engaged in collecting news—

(i) for sound or television broadcasts; or

(ii) for inclusion in programmes to be included in any programme service (within the meaning of the Broadcasting Act 1990) other than a sound or television broadcasting service;

"principal council" shall be construed in accordance with section 100J above.

(2) Any reference in this Part to a meeting is a reference to a meeting held after 1st April 1986.

(3) The Secretary of State may by order amend sections 100A(6)(*a*) and 100B(3) and (4)(*a*) above so as to substitute for each reference to three clear days such greater number of days as may be specified in the order.

(4) Any statutory instrument containing an order under subsection (3) above shall be subject to annulment in pursuance of a resolution of either House of Parliament.

[Local Government Act 1972, s 100K, as inserted by the Local Government (Access to Information) Act 1985, s 1 and amended by the Broadcasting Act 1990, Sch 20 and the Local Government Act 2000, s 98(1).]

PART VII
MISCELLANEOUS POWERS OF LOCAL AUTHORITIES

8–18816 117. Disclosure by officers of interest in contracts. (1) If it comes to the knowledge of an officer employed, whether under this Act or any other enactment, by a local authority that a contract in which he has any pecuniary interest, whether direct or indirect (not being a contract to which he is himself a party), has been, or is proposed to be, entered into by the authority or any committee thereof, he shall as soon as practicable give notice in writing to the authority of the fact that he is interested therein.

For the purposes of this section an officer shall be treated as having indirectly a pecuniary interest in a contract or proposed contract if he would have been so treated by virtue of section 95[1] above had he been a member of the authority.

(2) An officer of a local authority shall not, under colour of his office or employment, accept any fee or reward whatsoever other than his proper remuneration.

(3) Any person who contravenes the provisions of subsection (1) or (2) above shall be liable on summary conviction to a fine not exceeding **level 4** on the standard scale.

(4) References in this section to a local authority shall include references to a joint committee appointed under Part VI of this Act or any other enactment.

[Local Government Act 1972, s 117, as amended by the Criminal Justice Act 1982, ss 38 and 46.]

1. Section 95 is not reproduced in this work.

PART X
JUDICIAL AND RELATED MATTERS

[See Part I: The Justices and the Clerk, ante.]

PART XI
GENERAL PROVISIONS AS TO LOCAL AUTHORITIES

Legal proceedings

8–18817 222. Power of local authorities to prosecute or defend legal proceedings. (1) Where a local authority consider[1] it expedient for the promotion or protection of the interests of the inhabitants of their area—

(*a*) they may prosecute or defend or appear in any legal proceedings and, in the case of civil proceedings, may institute[2] them in their own name, and

(*b*) they may, in their own name, make representations in the interests of the inhabitants at any public inquiry held by or on behalf of any Minister or public body under any enactment.

(2) In this section "local authority" includes the Common Council and the London Fire and Emergency Planning Authority.

[Local Government Act 1972, s 222, as amended by the Greater London Authority Act 1999, Sch 29.]

1. In certain circumstances a local authority may institute proceedings in its own name seeking an injunction in the civil courts as a means of preventing a breach of the criminal law (*Stoke-on-Trent City Council v B & Q (Retail) Ltd* [1984] AC 754, [1984] 2 All ER 332, HL). A local authority can bring proceedings in public nuisance without having to show it has a special responsibility for enforcement of the criminal law eg against a person arrested for dealing in drugs for an injunction restraining him from entering a housing estate (*Nottingham City Council v Zain (a minor)* [2001] EWCA Civ 1248, [2002] 1 WLR 607). It is the duty of a local planning authority to protect the amenities of its area through a proper observance of planning control, and in order to perform that duty the authority is entitled in appropriate circumstances to seek a civil remedy under this section without first exhausting the processes of the criminal law (*Runnymede Borough Council v Ball* [1986] 1 All ER 629, [1986] 1 WLR 353). Where the conditions in sub-s (1) are met, a local authority is not precluded by s 4 of the Road Traffic Offenders Act 1988 from prosecuting an offence of using a motor vehicle without insurance contrary to s 143 of the Road Traffic Act 1988, (*Middlesborough Borough Council v Safeer* [2001] EWHC Admin 525, [2001] 4 All ER 630, [2002] 1 Cr App Rep 23, [2001] Crim LR 922, DC).

2. In determining whether a local authority has considered whether it is expedient to prosecute, the maxim omnia praesumuntur rite esse acta applies. The burden of displacing this presumption is on the defendant by showing that the local authority made their decision on the basis of facts they should not have taken into account, or failed to take into account matters they should have taken into account (*R v Richards* [1999] Crim LR 598).

8–18818 223. Appearance of local authorities in legal proceedings. (1) Any member or officer of a local authority who is authorised by that authority to prosecute or defend on their behalf, or to appear on their behalf in, proceedings before a magistrates' court shall be entitled to prosecute or defend or to appear in any such proceedings, and, notwithstanding anything contained in the Solicitors Act 1974, to conduct any such proceedings although he is not a solicitor holding a current practising certificate.

(2) In this section "local authority" includes the Common Council, a joint authority, the Greater London Authority, a police authority established under section 3 of the Police Act 1996 and the Metropolitan Police Authority

[Local Government Act 1972, s 223, as amended by the Local Government Act 1985, Sch 14, the Education Reform Act 1988, Sch 13, the Water Act 1989, Sch 25, the Police and Magistrates' Courts Act 1994, Sch 4, the Environment Act 1995, Sch 22, the Police Act 1996, Sch 7, the Police Act 1997, Sch 6, the Greater London Authority Act 1999, Sch 27, SI 2001/3719 and the Criminal Justice and Police Act 2001, Sch 6.]

Documents and Notices, etc

8–18819 225. Deposit of documents with proper officer of authority, etc. (1) In any case in which a document of any description is deposited[1] with the proper officer[2] of a local authority[3], or with the chairman of a parish or community council or with the chairman of a parish meeting, pursuant to the standing orders of either House of Parliament or to any enactment or instrument, the proper officer or chairman, as the case may be, shall receive and retain the document in the manner and for the purposes directed by the standing orders or enactment or instrument, and shall make such notes or endorsements on, and give such acknowledgments and receipts in respect of, the document as may be so directed.

(2) All documents required by any enactment or instrument to be deposited with the proper officer[1] of a parish or community shall, in the case of a parish or community not having a separate

parish or community council, be deposited in England with the chairman of the parish meeting or in Wales with the proper officer of the principal council.

(3) In this section "local authority" includes a joint authority.

[Local Government Act 1972, s 225, as amended by the Local Government Act 1985, Sch 14, the Education Reform Act 1988, Sch 13 and the Local Government (Wales) Act 1994, Sch 15.]

---

1. Claim forms submitted to a local authority pursuant to the Local Government (Allowances) Regulations 1974 are not documents deposited with a proper officer within the meaning of s 225(1) of this Act (*Brookman v Green* (1983) 147 JP 555).

2. Any reference in this Act to a proper officer shall, in relation to any purpose and any local authority or other body or any area, be construed as a reference to an officer appointed for that purpose by that body or for that area, as the case may be (s 270(3)).

3. "Local authority" means a county council, a district council, a London borough council or a parish and in relation to Wales, a county council, county borough or community council (s 270(1)).

8–18830 228. Inspection of documents. (1) The minutes of proceedings of a parish or community council shall be open to the inspection of any local government elector[1] for the area of the council and any such local government elector may make a copy of or extract from the minutes.

(2) A local government elector[1] for the area of a local authority[2] may inspect and make a copy of or extract from an order for the payment of money made by the local authority.

(3) The accounts of a local authority and of any proper officer of a local authority shall be open to the inspection of any member of the authority, and any such member may make a copy of or extract from the accounts.

(4) *Repealed.*

(5) Subject to any provisions to the contrary in any other enactment or instrument, a person interested in any document deposited as mentioned in section 225 above may, at all reasonable hours, inspect and make copies thereof or extracts therefrom on payment to the person having custody thereof of the sum of 10p for every such inspection, and of the further sum of 10p for every hour during which such inspection continues after the first hour.

(6) A document directed by this section to be open to inspection shall be so open at all reasonable hours and, except where otherwise expressly provided, without payment.

(7) If a person having the custody of any such document[3]—

(*a*) obstructs any person entitled to inspect the document or to make a copy thereof or extract therefrom in inspecting the document or making a copy or extract,

(*b*) refuses to give copies or extracts to any person entitled to obtain copies or extracts,[4]

he shall be liable on summary conviction to a fine not exceeding **level 1** on the standard scale.

(7A) This section shall apply to the minutes of proceedings and the accounts of a joint authority or a police authority established under section 3 of the Police Act 1996 or the Metropolitan Police Authority as if that authority were a local authority and as if, references to a local government elector for the area of the authority were a reference to a local government elector for any local government area in the area for which the authority is established.

(8) This section shall apply to the minutes of proceedings and to the accounts of a parish meeting as if that meeting were a parish council.

(9) In relation to the Broads Authority, the references in this section to a local government elector for the area of the authority shall be construed as references to a local government elector for the area of any of the local authorities mentioned in section 1(3)(*a*) of the Norfolk and Suffolk Broads Act 1988.

[Local Government Act 1972, s 228, as amended by the Criminal Justice Act 1982, ss 38 and 46, the Local Government Finance Act 1982, Sch 6, the Local Government (Access to Information) Act 1985, Sch 2, the Local Government Act 1985, Sch 14, the Norfolk and Suffolk Broads Act 1988, Sch 6, the Education Reform Act 1988, Sch 13, the Police and Magistrates' Courts Act 1994, Sch 4, the Police Act 1996, Sch 7, the Police Act 1997, Sch 6, the Greater London Authority Act 1999, Sch 27 and the Criminal Justice and Police Act 2001, Sch 6.]

---

1. "Local government elector" means a person registered as a local government elector in the register of electors in accordance with the provisions of the Representation of the People Acts (s 270(1)).

2. For meaning of "local authority", see note 3 at para **8–18819**, ante.

3. Claim forms submitted to a local authority pursuant to the Local Government (Allowances) Regulations 1974 are not documents deposited with a proper officer within the meaning of s 225(1) of this Act (*Brookman v Green* (1983) 147 JP 555).

4. There is no longer any obligation to give copies or extracts to any person entitled, since paragraph (*b*) related only to the circumstances in sub-s (4) which has now been repealed; see *Russell-Walker v Gimblett* (1985) 149 JP 448.

8–18831 229. Photographic copies of documents. (1) Subject to subsections (3) and (7) below, any requirement imposed by any enactment that a local authority or parish meeting shall keep a document of any description shall be satisfied by their keeping a photographic copy of the document.

(2) Subject to subsection (7) below, any requirement imposed by any enactment that a document of any description in the custody or under the control of a local authority or parish meeting shall be made available for inspection shall be satisfied by their making available for inspection a photographic copy of the document.

(3) Subsection (1) above shall not apply to any document deposited with a local authority under the Public Records Act 1958.

(4) In legal proceedings a photographic copy of a document in the custody of a local authority or parish meeting, or of a document which has been destroyed while in the custody of a local authority or parish meeting, or of any part of any such document, shall, subject to subsection (6) below, be admissible in evidence to the like extent as the original.

(5) A certificate purporting to be signed by the proper officer of the local authority, or the chairman of the parish meeting, concerned that a document is such a photographic copy as is mentioned in subsection (4) above, shall, subject to subsection (7) below, be evidence to that effect.

(6) The court before which a photographic copy is tendered in evidence in pursuance of subsection (4) above may, if the original is in existence, require its production and thereupon that subsection shall not apply to the copy.

(7) A photographic copy of a document in colour where the colours are relevant to the interpretation of the document shall not suffice for the purposes of this section unless it so distinguishes between the colours as to enable the document to be interpreted.

(8) In this section "court" and "legal proceedings" have the same meanings as in the Civil Evidence Act 1968 and "local authority" includes a joint authority or a police authority established under section 3 of the Police Act 1996 and the Metropolitan Police Authority.

[Local Government Act 1972, s 229, as amended by the Local Government Act 1985, Sch 14, the Education Reform Act 1988, Sch 13, the Police and Magistrates' Courts Act 1994, Sch 4, the Police Act 1996, Sch 7, the Police Act 1997, Sch 6, the Greater London Authority Act 1999, Sch 27 and the Criminal Justice and Police Act 2001, Sch 6.]

8–18832 **231. Service of notices on local authorities, etc.** (1) Subject to sub-section (3) below, any notice, order or other document required or authorised by any enactment or any instrument made under an enactment to be given to or served on a local authority or the chairman or an officer of a local authority shall be given or served by addressing it to the local authority and leaving it at, or sending it by post to, the principal office of the authority or any other office of the authority specified by them as one at which they will accept documents of the same description as that document.

(2) Any notice, order or other document so required or authorised to be given to or served on a parish meeting, or the chairman of the parish meeting, shall be given or served by addressing it to the chairman of the parish meeting and by delivering it to him, or by leaving it at his last known address, or by sending it by post to him at that address.

(3) The foregoing provisions of this section do not apply to a document which is to be given or served in any proceedings in court, but except as aforesaid the method of giving or serving documents provided for by those provisions are in substitution for the methods provided for by any other enactment or any instrument made under an enactment so far as it relates to the giving or service of documents to or on a local authority, the chairman or an officer of a local authority or a parish meeting or the chairman of a parish meeting.

(4) In this section "local authority" includes a joint authority or a police authority established under section 3 of the Police Act 1996 and the Metropolitan Police Authority.

[Local Government Act 1972, s 231, as amended by the Local Government Act 1985, Sch 14, the Education Reform Act 1988, Sch 13, the Police and Magistrates' Courts Act 1994, Sch 4, the Police Act 1996, Sch 7, the Police Act 1997, Sch 6, the Greater London Authority Act 1999, Sch 27 and the Criminal Justice and Police Act 2001, Sch 7.]

8–18833 **233. Service of notices by local authorities.** (1) Subject to subsection (8) below, subsections (2) to (5) below shall have effect in relation to any notice, order or other document required or authorised by or under any enactment to be given to or served on any person by or on behalf of a local authority or by an officer of a local authority.

(2) Any such document may be given to or served on the person in question either by delivering it to him, or by leaving it at his proper address, or by sending it by post to him at that address.

(3) Any such document may—

(*a*) in the case of a body corporate, be given to or served on the secretary or clerk of that body;

(*b*) in the case of a partnership, be given to or served on a partner or a person having the control or management of the partnership business.

(4) For the purposes of this section and of section 26 of the Interpretation Act 1889 (service of documents by post) in its application to this section, the proper address of any person to or on whom a document is to be given or served shall be his last known address, except that—

(*a*) in the case of a body corporate or their secretary or clerk, it shall be the address of the registered or principal office of that body;

(*b*) in the case of a partnership or a person having the control or management of the partnership business, it shall be that of the principal office of the partnership;

and for the purposes of this subsection the principal office of a company registered outside the United Kingdom or of a partnership carrying on business outside the United Kingdom shall be their principal office within the United Kingdom.

(5) If the person to be given or served with any document mentioned in subsection (1) above has

specified an address within the United Kingdom other than his proper address within the meaning of subsection (4) above as the one at which he or someone on his behalf will accept documents of the same description as that document, that address shall also be treated for the purposes of this section and section 26 of the Interpretation Act 1889 as his proper address.

(6) *Repealed.*

(7) If the name or address of any owner, lessee or occupier of land to or on whom any document mentioned in subsection (1) above is to be given or served cannot after reasonable inquiry be ascertained, the document may be given or served either by leaving it in the hands of a person who is or appears to be resident or employed on the land or by leaving it conspicuously affixed to some building or object on the land.

(8) This section shall apply to a document required or authorised by or under any enactment to be given to or served on any person by or on behalf of the chairman of a parish meeting as it applies to a document so required or authorised to be given to or served on any person by or on behalf of a local authority.

(9) The foregoing provisions of this section do not apply to a document which is to be given or served in any proceedings[1] in court.

(10) Except as aforesaid and subject to any provision of any enactment or instrument excluding the foregoing provisions of this section, the methods of giving or serving documents which are available under those provisions are in addition to the methods which are available under any other enactment or any instrument made under any enactment.

(11) In this section "local authority" includes a joint authority or a police authority established under section 3 of the Police Act 1996 and the Metropolitan Police Authority.

[Local Government Act 1972, s 233, as amended by the Local Government (Miscellaneous Provisions) Act 1976, Sch 2, the Local Government Act 1985, Sch 14, the Education Reform Act 1988, Sch 13, the Police and Magistrates' Courts Act 1994, Sch 4, the Police Act 1996, Sch 7, the Police Act 1997, Sch 6, the Greater London Authority Act 1999, Sch 27 and the Criminal Justice and Police Act 2001, Sch 6.]

1. However, it would seem that these provisions may enable proof of the service of documents which took place before proceedings commenced or were in contemplation, otherwise they would have no purpose.

8–18834 **234. Authentication of documents.** (1) Any notice, order or other document which a local authority are authorised or required by or under any enactment (including any enactment in this Act) to give, make or issue may be signed[1] on behalf of the authority by the proper officer of the authority.

(2) Any document purporting to bear the signature of the proper officer of the authority shall be deemed, until the contrary is proved, to have been duly given, made or issued by the authority of the local authority.

In this subsection the word "signature" includes a facsimile of a signature by whatever process reproduced.

(3) Where any enactment or instrument made under an enactment makes, in relation to any document or class of documents, provision with respect to the matters dealt with by one of the two foregoing sub-sections, that subsection shall not apply in relation to that document or class of documents.

(4) In this section "local authority" includes a joint authority or a police authority established under section 3 of the Police Act 1996 and the Metropolitan Police Authority.

[Local Government Act 1972, s 234, as amended by the Local Government Act 1985, Sch 14, the Education Reform Act 1988, Sch 13, the Police and Magistrates' Courts Act 1994, Sch 4, the Police Act 1996, Sch 7, the Police Act 1997, Sch 6, the Greater London Authority Act 1999, Sch 27 and the Criminal Justice and Police Act 2001, Sch 6.]

1. The requirement of a signature may be satisfied by a facsimile: see *Plymouth City Corpn v Hurrell* [1968] 1 QB 455, [1967] 3 All ER 354, 131 JP 479.

Bye-laws

8–18835 **235. Power of councils to make bye-laws for good rule and government and suppression of nuisances.** (1) The council of a district, the council of a principal area in Wales and the council of a London borough may make bye-laws[1] for the good rule and government of the whole or any part of the district, principal area or borough, as the case may be, and for the prevention and suppression of nuisances therein[2].

(2) The confirming authority in relation to bye-laws made under this section shall be the Secretary of State.

(3) Bye-laws shall not be made under this section for any purpose as respects any area if provision for that purpose as respects that area is made by, or is or may be made under, any other enactment.

[Local Government Act 1972, s 235 amended by the Local Government (Wales) Act 1994, Sch 15.]

1. Justices are bound to decide on any objection to the validity of a bye-law, although it may have been regularly made and confirmed; and they will exceed their jurisdiction if they convict on the mere proof of facts bringing the case within the bye-law without also deciding the bye-law is good (*R v Rose* (1855) 19 JP 676). It was decided in that case that a power

to make bye-laws for removal of dust, filth, etc, from streets by occupiers did not authorise the making a bye-law for removal of pure snow. Applied in *R v Crown Court at Reading, ex p Hutchinson* [1988] QB 384, [1988] 1 All ER 333, 152 JP 47, where it was held that it is neither necessary nor appropriate for proceedings before magistrates to be adjourned so that the validity of the byelaw can be determined in the High Court by way of judicial review. If byelaws are to be upheld as good in part notwithstanding that they are bad in part, they must be substantially severable. If textual severance is possible, the test of substantial severability will be satisfied when the valid text is unaffected by, and independent of, the invalid. But when the court must modify the text in order to achieve severance, the test of substantial severability will be satisfied only if the substance of what remains is essentially unchanged in its legislative purpose, operation and effect; see *DPP v Hutchinson* [1990] 2 AC 783, [1990] 2 All ER 836, 155 JP 71, HL. Where a properly constituted criminal court has ruled that byelaws on which a prosecution has been based are invalid, the authority responsible for promulgating those byelaws must have regard to that decision in its dealings with others who were not parties to those proceedings and if it fails to do so it may be acting *Wednesbury* unreasonably even if it is not bound by judicial precedent such as where the decision declaring the byelaw invalid is that of a magistrates' court or the Crown Court. If however there are serious doubts about the correctness of the Criminal court's decision as to the validity of the byelaws, and there are serious reasons of public safety or security which require the retention of the byelaws pending an appeal, a case might be made for retaining them, provided an appeal is pursued with expedition, or other means found urgently to establish their validity in a court. See the remarks of Carnwath J in *Secretary of State for Defence v Percy* [1999] 1 All ER 732, Ch D (a case concerning byelaws made under s 14 of the Military Lands Act 1892).

As to a nuisance caused by a failure to remove snow, see *Slater v Worthington's Cash Stores (1930) Ltd* [1941] 1 KB 488, [1941] 3 All ER 28. As to infraction of bye-laws against collecting a crowd by shouting, etc, see *Phillips v Canham* (1872) 36 JP 310. A bye-law made by the Worcester County Council under the repealed s 16 of the Local Government Act 1888, against using obscene language in a street or public place or on land adjacent thereto without words importing that the language must be used to cause annoyance was held to be invalid, and repugnant to the general law because it was not limited to the use of such language to the annoyance of the public or by any limitation to the like effect (*Strickland v Hayes* [1896] 1 QB 290, 60 JP 164). This case was commented on in a later case, and it was held that a bye-law, made under s 16 of the Local Government Act 1888, which provided that "No person shall in any house, building, garden, land, or other place abutting on or near to a street or public place, make use of any violent, abusive, profane, indecent, or obscene language, gesture, or conduct, to the annoyance of any person in such street or public place", was a valid bye-law, and justified a conviction for using such language in a private house abutting on a street to the annoyance of the persons in the street (*Mantle v Jordan* [1897] 1 QB 248, 61 JP 119). *Strickland v Hayes* seems to conflict with *Kruse v Johnson*, infra, as to reasonableness, and it may be doubted whether it is now good law. Further doubt was thrown in this case in *Gentel v Rapps* [1902] 1 KB 160, 66 JP 117, where it was held that a tramway bye-law was not invalid because it omitted the words "to the annoyance of the passengers". See also *Brabham v Wookey* (1901) 18 TLR 99. A publican using indecent language in a public house to two constables who had entered the house on business does not infringe a bye-law prohibiting the use of indecent language in a "public place to the annoyance of passengers" (*Russon v Dutton* (*No* 2) (1911) 75 JP 207).

A bye-law relating to betting in a public place which did not make available to a person charged defences for which the public Acts provided, was held to be repugnant to the general law and invalid (*Powell v May* [1946] KB 330, [1946] 1 All ER 444, 110 JP 157). A bye-law against selling any paper devoted wholly or mainly to giving information as to the probable result of races, steeplechases, or other competitions was held by the Divisional Court (ALVERSTONE LCJ and KENNEDY J, PHILLIMORE J, diss) to be invalid on the ground of its being uncertain and unreasonable (*Scott v Pilliner* [1904] 2 KB 855, 68 JP 518). RUSSELL LCJ, laid down a general rule with regard to the construction that should be put upon bye-laws, and said in his opinion the courts were bound to support as far as possible bye-laws issued by local authorities unless it could be shown the bye-law was made without jurisdiction or was obviously unreasonable. He said the court ought not willingly to "pick holes" in rules that dealt with local matters and local requirements, which the local authorities were often better able to judge than the courts (*Walker v Stretton* (1896) 60 JP 313). Great regard will be paid to findings of local justices upon a bye-law made by a body with knowledge of local conditions (*Everton v Walker* (1927) 91 JP 125). See also *Friend v Brehout* (1914) 79 JP 25.

A local bye-law at Cambridge rendered liable to a penalty any person making a violent noise or outcry in the street "to the annoyance of the inhabitants". A newsboy cried his papers outside the house of one of the inhabitants for some minutes to the annoyance of that inhabitant. The Queen's Bench Division held the bye-law was reasonable and the defendant was not the less liable to conviction because one particular inhabitant only was annoyed (*Innes v Newman* [1894] 2 QB 292, 58 JP 543; followed in *Raymond v Cook* [1958] 3 All ER 407, 123 JP 35). A bye-law provided that "every person who shall sound or play upon any musical instrument, or sing, or make any noise whatsoever in any street, or near any house within the borough, after having been required by any householder resident in such street or by any police constable to desist from making such sound or noise either on account of the illness of any inmate or from any other reasonable cause", shall be liable, etc. The defendant, a "Captain" in the Salvation Army, played on a concertina on a Sunday morning surrounded by a crowd in a square in Truro, and refused to desist at the request of the superintendent of police, who told him he had reasonable cause for the request by reason of the complaints of the inhabitants. The Queen's Bench Division held there was nothing unreasonable or void in such a bye-law, and it was for the justices to decide whether there was a reasonable cause for requiring the appellant to desist (*R v Powell, etc, Truro Justices* (1884) 48 JP 740). A bye-law at St Albans made liable to a penalty any person blowing a horn "or any other noisy instrument", to the annoyance of any of the inhabitants. The justices found that a concertina was a noisy instrument, and a conviction was upheld. The Queen'sBench Division held it was sufficient to prove the instrument was a nuisance or annoyance to some of the inhabitants (*Booth v Howell* (1889) 53 JP 678); if, indeed, it is found as a fact that the noise in question was calculated to be an annoyance, evidence that inhabitants were annoyed is unnecessary (*Raymond v Cook* [1958] 3 All ER 407, 123 JP 35). Similarly, in relation to the use of obscene language in a street, justices are entitled to infer annoyance in the absence of positive evidence that any person was annoyed (*Nicholson v Glasspool* (1959) 123 JP 229).

A bye-law made by the county council of Kent provided that "No person shall sound or play upon any musical or noisy instrument, or sing in any public place or highway within fifty yards of any dwelling-house, after being required by any constable, or by an inmate of such house personally, or by his or her servant to desist". Defendant was conducting an open-air religious service on a public highway, and persisted in singing within fifty yards of a dwelling-house, after having been requested by a police constable to desist. The case was considered of such great importance that it was heard by a specially constituted court of seven judges and the conviction was upheld. RUSSELL LCJ, made some important observations as to the principles to be applied by the court in deciding as to the validity of bye-laws and held that bye-laws made by local authorities ought to be benevolently interpreted, and credit ought to be given to those who have to administer them that they will be benevolently administered. This case must be looked upon as a leading case (*Kruse v Johnson* [1898] 2 QB 91, 62 JP 469. See also *Brownscombe v Johnson* (1898) 62 JP 326, which led to the case of *Kruse v Johnson*). A bye-law made by the Town Council of Southend under a local Act provided that "No organ or other musical instrument worked by steam or other mechanical means shall be used within the borough provided that this bye-law shall not apply to any locomotive or steam engine in use on any railway within the borough"; (other steam whistles, etc, then permitted by statute were also excluded). A travelling showman erected in a field within the borough a roundabout worked by steam, to which an organ was attached, also worked by steam. The organ was in the centre of a field 116 yards from a public road, and played from 7 a.m. until 9.30 p.m. The Queen's Bench Division held the bye-law was valid (*Southend Corpn v Davis* (1900) 16 TLR 167). A bye-law made by the Town Council of Croydon provided that "No person not being a member of Her Majesty's Army or Auxiliary Forces, under the orders of his commanding officer, shall sound or play upon any musical instrument in any of the streets in the borough on Sunday". The appellant, one of the Salvation Army, played a musical instrument on a Sunday and was fined. The Queen's Bench Division held that as the bye-law stated no qualification or exception in any circumstances, it was unreasonable and void (*Johnson v Croydon Corpn* (1886) 16 QBD 708, 50 JP 487, Treat 163). So also was a bye-law that every person who shall play a noisy instrument or sing or preach in any street without a previously written licence from the mayor shall be fined, etc, as it would enable a mayor to legalise a nuisance or prohibit a lawful act which was not a nuisance (*Munro v Watson* (1887) 51 JP 660). But a bye-law which prohibited the exposure for sale of any commodity, etc, or for hire of any chair, etc, on the sea beach, esplanade, etc, except by direction of the sanitary authority, or in such parts as they might by notice appoint, made under a local Act, which authorised bye-laws to be made for regulation of the esplanade, was upheld (*Gray v Sylvester* (1897) 61 JP 807). The court distinguished a bye-law for the good government of a town from bye-laws for the regulation of an esplanade. See also *Slee v Meadows* (1911) 75 JP 246. A bye-law that no person shall wilfully annoy passengers in the public streets was held to be invalid for uncertainty (*Nash v Finlay* (1901) 66 JP 183). So was a bye-law preventing any person hawking on beach or foreshore except in pursuance of agreement with corporation (*Parker v Bournemouth Corpn* (1902) 66 JP 440). This was followed in *Moorman v Tordoff* (1908) 72 JP 142. But see *Williams v Weston-super-Mare UDC (No 1)* (1907) 72 JP 54, where *Parker v Bournemouth Corpn, supra*, was distinguished; *Williams v Weston-super-Mare UDC (No 2)* (1910) 74 JP 370 and *Cassell v Jones* (1913) 77 JP 197. A bye-law made under s 69 (repealed by the Statute Law (Repeals) Act 1975) of the Town Police Clauses Act 1847, as to bathing, and providing that the prescribed charges should include charges for the use of towels and bathing costume, thus purporting to prohibit any extra charge being made therefore, was declared *ultra vires* (*Parker v Clegg* (1903) 2 LGR 608).

A bye-law at Luton provided that "no person shall to the annoyance or disturbance of residents or passengers keep or manage a shooting gallery, swing boat, roundabout, or other like thing in any street or public place or on land adjoining or near to such street or public place, provided that the bye-law shall not apply to any fair lawfully held". It was contended by the appellant that the bye-law was *ultra vires* on the ground that the town council had no authority to make a bye-law affecting private property, and because it created a new criminal offence. The Queen's Bench Division upheld the bye-law (*Teale v Harris* (1896) 60 JP 744). Where a bye-law prohibited touting for hackney carriages in any public thoroughfare, it was held that the respondent committed an offence though he stood at the time on a piece of land adjoining the street and belonging to private persons (*Dereham v Strickland* (1911) 75 JP 300; *McQuade v Barnes* [1949] 1 All ER 154, 113 JP 89).

A licence proposed to be granted by the Edinburgh magistrates under the provisions of an Act regulating the selling of ice-cream, and professing to limit the days and hours when premises should be kept open, was held by the House of Lords to be *ultra vires* (*Rossi v Edinburgh Corpn* [1905] AC 21). Football had been played many years on open ground crossed by footpaths. Appellants set up that the paths were not streets within the meaning of a bye-law, and claimed a right as sons of freemen to play on the open space. The Queen's Bench Division held that justices properly overruled the claim, as such a right could not possibly exist (*Pearson v Whitfield* (1888) 52 JP Jo 708). As to bye-laws regulating games on a public common, see *Harris v Harrison* (1914) 78 JP 398. A local authority has no power to sanction building plans not in accordance with bye-laws; they have no dispensing power, any purported approval of plans contravening bye-laws is inoperative (*Yabbicom v King* [1899] 1 QB 444, 63 JP 149).

2. As to offences against bye-laws, and penalties, see s 237 and notes thereto, post.

8–18836 **236. Procedure etc, for bye-laws.** (1) Subject to subsection (2) below, the following provisions of this section shall apply to bye-laws[1] to be made by a local authority under this Act and to byelaws made by a local authority, the Greater London Authority, Transport for London or a metropolitan county passenger transport authority under any other enactment and conferring on the authority, a power to make bye-laws and for which specific provision is not otherwise made.

(2) This section shall not apply to bye-laws made by the Civil Aviation Authority under section 29 of the Civil Aviation Act 1982 and the Local Government Act 1985, Sch 14.

(3)–(11) *Procedure for making and confirming bye-laws.*

[Local Government Act 1972, s 236, as amended by the Civil Aviation Act 1982, Sch 15, the Local Government Act 1985, Sch 14, the Education Reform Act 1988, Sch 12, the Water Act 1989, Sch 27, the Local Government (Wales) Act 1994, Sch 15, the Greater London Authority Act 1999, ss 76 and 166 and SI 2001/3719.]

---

1. Section 236 is modified by SI 1986/143 in relation to byelaws for marine nature reserves made under ss 36 and 37 of the Wildlife and Countryside Act 1981.

8–18837 **237. Offences against bye-laws[1].** Bye-laws to which section 236 above applies may provide that persons contravening the bye-laws shall be liable on summary conviction to a fine not exceeding such sum as may be fixed by the enactment conferring the power to make the bye-laws, or, if no sum is so fixed, the sum of **level 2** on the standard scale[1], and in the case of a continuing offence a further fine not exceeding such sum as may be fixed as aforesaid, or, if no sum is so fixed, the sum of **£5**[2] for each day during which the offence continues after conviction thereof.

[Local Government Act 1972, s 237, as amended by the Criminal Law Act 1977, s 31(3) and the Criminal Justice Act 1982, s 46.]

---

1. Notwithstanding its repeal, byelaws made under the Local Government Act 1933, are by virtue of s 272(2) of the Local Government Act 1972, preserved and remain in force (*DPP v Jackson* (1990) 154 JP 967).

2. Justices always have jurisdiction to inquire into the validity of a byelaw (*R v Crown Court at Reading, ex p Hutchinson* [1988] QB 384, [1988] 1 All ER 333, 152 JP 47).

A bye-law made by virtue of the Public Health Act 1875, s 183 or the Local Government Act 1933, s 251, or the Local Government Act 1972, s 237, which was in force on 17 July 1978 and specified £20 as the maximum fine (including a bye-law which specified £5 and was increased to £20 by virtue of the Criminal Justice Act 1967 s 92(3) and Sch 3 Part II), had effect as if the bye-law specified a fine of £50 (Criminal Law Act 1977, s 31(2) and (3)). By virtue of s 46 of the Criminal Justice Act 1982 the reference to a maximum of £50 was converted to a reference to level 2 on the standard scale. However, if on 17 July 1978 such bye-law specified an amount less than £20 it remains unchanged (Criminal Law Act

1977, s 31(2) and (3)). In the case of a bye-law made by virtue of an enactment or instrument after 30th April 1984 and before the commencement of s 52 of the Criminal Justice Act 1988, the maximum fine on conviction of a summary offence specified in the bye-law shall be construed as the level in the first column of the standard scale corresponding to that amount (Criminal Justice Act 1988, s 52, when in force).

Byelaws of local authorities made under this section dealing with the burning of straw, stubble or other crop residues on agricultural land have been repealed by the Burning of Crop Residues (Repeal of Byelaws) Order 1992, SI 1992/693. Section 152 of the Environmental Protection Act 1990, title **Public Health**, post, enables regulations to be made prohibiting or restricting the burning of crop residue on agricultural land. Where the byelaws were made under ss 36 or 37 of the Wildlife and Countryside Act 1981 for marine nature reserves, the penalty prescribed here by SI 1986/143 is £1,000.

8–18838 238. Evidence of bye-laws. The production of a printed copy of a bye-law purporting to be made by a local authority, the Greater London Authority or metropolitan county passenger transport authority upon which is endorsed a certificate purporting to be signed by the proper officer of the authority stating—

(*a*) that the bye-law was made by the authority;

(*b*) that the copy is a true copy of the bye-law;

(*c*) that on a specified date the bye-law was confirmed by the authority named in the certificate or, as the case may require, was sent to the Secretary of State and has not been disallowed[1];

(*d*) the date, if any, fixed by the confirming authority for the coming into operation of the bye-law[1];

shall be prima facie evidence of the facts stated in the certificate and without proof of the handwriting or official position of any person purporting to sign the certificate.

[Local Government Act 1972, s 238, as amended by the Local Government Act 1985, Sch 14, the Education Reform Act 1988, Sch 12 and SI 2001/3719.]

---

1. Where the byelaws were made under s 37 of the Wildlife and Countryside Act 1981 for marine nature reserves, paras (*c*) and (*d*) are omitted by the operation of SI 1986/143.

8–18839 265–265A. *Application of Act to Isles of Scilly; application in relation to the Broads Authority.*

8–18840 270. General provisions as to interpretation. (1) In the Act, except where the context otherwise requires, the following expressions have the following meanings respectively, that is to say—

"alternative arrangements" has the same meaning as in Part II of the Local Government Act 2000;

"the Broads" has the same meaning as in the Norfolk and Suffolk Broads Act 1988;

"joint authority" means an authority established by Part IV of the Local Government Act 1985;

"local authority" means a county council, a district council, a London borough council or a parish council, but in relation to Wales, means a county council, county borough or community council;

"principal area" means a county, Greater London, a district or a London borough;

"principal council" means a council elected for a principal area.

(2) In this Act and in any other enactment, whether passed before, at the same time as, or after this Act, the expression "non-metropolitan county" means any county other than a metropolitan county, and the expression "non-metropolitan district" means any district other than a metropolitan district.

(3) Any reference in this Act to a proper officer and any reference which by virtue of this Act is to be construed as such a reference shall, in relation to any purpose and any local authority or other body or any area, be construed as a reference to an officer appointed for that purpose by that body or for that area, as the case may be.

(4) In any provision of this Act which applies to a London borough, except Schedule 2 to this Act,—

(*a*) any reference to the chairman of the council or of any class of councils comprising the council or to a member of a local authority shall be construed as or, as the case may be, as including a reference to the mayor of the borough;

(*b*) any reference to the vice-chairman of the council or any such class of councils shall be construed as a reference to the deputy mayor of the borough; and

(*c*) any reference to the proper officer of the council or any such class of councils shall be construed as a reference to the proper officer of the borough.

(4A) Where a London borough council are operating executive arrangements which involve a mayor and cabinet executive or a mayor and council manager executive, subsection (4) above shall have effect with the omission of paragraphs (*a*) and (*b*).

(5) In this Act, except where the context otherwise requires, references to any enactment shall be construed as references to that enactment as amended, extended or applied by or under any other enactment, including any enactment contained in this Act.

[Local Government Act 1972, s 270, as amended by the Local Government Act 1985, Schs 14 and 17, the Norfolk and Suffolk Broads Act 1988, Sch 6, the Local Government (Wales) Act 1994, s 1(5), the Local Government Act 2000, s 46 and SI 2001/2237.]

SCHEDULE 12A

ACCESS TO INFORMATION: EXEMPT INFORMATION

(*As substituted by SI 2006/88.*)

PART 1
DESCRIPTIONS OF EXEMPT INFORMATION

8–18841 **1.** Information relating to any individual.

2. Information which is likely to reveal the identity of an individual.

3. Information relating to the financial or business affairs of any particular person (including the authority holding that information).

4. Information relating to any consultations or negotiations, or contemplated consultations or negotiations, in connection with any labour relations matter arising between the authority or a Minister of the Crown and employees of, or office holders under, the authority.

5. Information in respect of which a claim to legal professional privilege could be maintained in legal proceedings.

6. Information which reveals that the authority proposes—

(*a*) to give under any enactment a notice under or by virtue of which requirements are imposed on a person; or

(*b*) to make an order or direction under any enactment.

7. Information relating to any action taken or to be taken in connection with the prevention, investigation or prosecution of crime.

8–18842

PART 2
QUALIFICATIONS: ENGLAND

8. Information falling within paragraph 3 above is not exempt information by virtue of that paragraph if it is required to be registered under—

(*a*) the Companies Act 1985;
(*b*) the Friendly Societies Act 1974;
(*c*) the Friendly Societies Act 1992;
(*d*) the Industrial and Provident Societies Acts 1965 to 1978;
(*e*) the Building Societies Act 1986; or
(*f*) the Charities Act 1993.

9. Information is not exempt information if it relates to proposed development for which the local planning authority may grant itself planning permission pursuant to regulation 3 of the Town and Country Planning General Regulations 1992.

10. Information which—

(*a*) falls within any of paragraphs 1 to 7 above; and
(*b*) is not prevented from being exempt by virtue of paragraph 8 or 9 above,

is exempt information if and so long, as in all the circumstances of the case, the public interest in maintaining the exemption outweighs the public interest in disclosing the information.

8–18843

PART III
INTERPRETATION: ENGLAND

11. (1) In Parts 1 and 2 and this Part of this Schedule—

"employee" means a person employed under a contract of service;

"financial or business affairs" includes contemplated, as well as past or current, activities;

"labour relations matter" means—

(*a*) any of the matters specified in paragraphs (a) to (g) of section 218(1) of the Trade Union and Labour Relations (Consolidation) Act 1992 (matters which may be the subject of a trade dispute, within the meaning of that Act); or

(*b*) any dispute about a matter falling within paragraph (a) above;

and for the purposes of this definition the enactments mentioned in paragraph (a) above, with the necessary modifications, shall apply in relation to office-holders under the authority as they apply in relation to employees of the authority;

"office-holder", in relation to the authority, means the holder of any paid office appointments to which are or may be made or confirmed by the authority or by any joint board on which the authority is represented or by any person who holds any such office or is an employee of the authority;

"registered" in relation to information required to be registered under the Building Societies Act 1986, means recorded in the public file of any building society (within the meaning of that Act).

(2) Any reference in Parts 1 and 2 and this Part of this Schedule to "the authority" is a reference to the principal council or, as the case may be, the committee or sub-committee in relation to whose proceedings or documents the question whether information is exempt or not falls to be determined and includes a reference—

(*a*) in the case of a principal council, to any committee or sub-committee of the council; and

(*b*) in the case of a committee, to—

(i) any constituent principal council;

(ii) any other principal council by which appointments are made to the committee or whose functions the committee discharges; and

(iii) any other committee or sub-committee of a principal council falling within sub-paragraph (i) or (ii) above; and

(*c*) in the case of a sub-committee, to—

(i) the committee, or any of the committees, of which it is a sub-committee; and

(ii) any principal council which falls within paragraph (b) above in relation to that committee.

8–18844

PART 4
DESCRIPTIONS OF EXEMPT INFORMATION: WALES

12. Information relating to a particular employee, former employee or applicant to become an employee of, or a particular office-holder, former office-holder or applicant to become an office-holder under, the authority.

13. Information relating to a particular employee, former employee or applicant to become an employee of, or a particular officer, former officer or applicant to become an officer appointed by—

(*a*) a magistrates' court committee;

(*b*) a probation committee within the meaning of the Probation Service Act 1993;

(*c*) a local probation board within the meaning of the Criminal Justice and Court Services Act 2000.

14. Information relating to a particular chief officer, former chief officer or applicant to become a chief officer of a local probation board within the meaning of the Criminal Justice and Court Services Act 2000.

15. Information relating to any particular occupier or former occupier of, or applicant for, accommodation provided by or at the expense of the authority.

16. Information relating to any particular applicant for, or recipient or former recipient of, any service provided by the authority.

17. Information relating to any particular applicant for, or recipient or former recipient of, any financial assistance provided by the authority.

18. Information relating to the adoption, care, fostering or education of any particular child.

19. Information relating to the financial or business affairs of any particular person (other than the authority).

20. The amount of any expenditure proposed to be incurred by the authority under any particular contract for the acquisition of property or the supply of goods or services.

21. Any terms proposed or to be proposed by or to the authority in the course of negotiations for a contract for the acquisition or disposal of property or the supply of goods or services.

22. The identity of the authority (as well as of any other person, by virtue of paragraph 19 above) as the person offering any particular tender for a contract for the supply of goods or services.

23. Information relating to any consultations or negotiations, or contemplated consultations or negotiations, in connection with any labour relations matter arising between the authority or a Minister of the Crown and employees of, or office-holders under, the authority.

24. Any instructions to counsel and any opinion of counsel (whether or not in connection with any proceedings) and any advice received, information obtained or action to be taken in connection with—

(*a*) any legal proceedings by or against the authority, or

(*b*) the determination of any matter affecting the authority,

(whether, in either case, proceedings have been commenced or are in contemplation).

25. Information which, if disclosed to the public, would reveal that the authority proposes—

(*a*) to give under any enactment a notice under or by virtue of which requirements are imposed on a person; or

(*b*) to make an order or direction under any enactment.

26. Any action taken or to be taken in connection with the prevention, investigation or prosecution of crime.

27. The identity of a protected informant.

8–18845

PART 5
QUALIFICATIONS: WALES

28. Information relating to a person of a description specified in any of paragraphs 12 to 17 above is not exempt information by virtue of that paragraph unless it relates to an individual of that description in the capacity indicated by the description.

29. Information falling within paragraph 19 above is not exempt information by virtue of that paragraph if it is required to be registered under—

(*a*) the Companies Act 1985;

(*b*) the Friendly Societies Act 1974;

(*c*) the Industrial and Provident Societies Acts 1965 to 1978;

(*d*) the Building Societies Act 1986; or

(*e*) the Charities Act 1960.

30. Information falling within paragraph 20 above is exempt information if and so long as disclosure to the public of the amount there referred to would be likely to give an advantage to a person entering into, or seeking to enter into, a contract with the authority in respect of the property, goods or services, whether the advantage would arise as against the authority or as against other such persons.

31. Information falling within paragraph 21 above is exempt information if and so long as disclosure to the public of the terms would prejudice the authority in those or any other negotiations concerning the property or goods or services.

32. Information falling within paragraph 23 above is exempt information if and so long as disclosure to the public of the information would prejudice the authority in those or any other consultations or negotiations in connection with a labour relations matter arising as mentioned in that paragraph.

33. Information falling within paragraph 25 above is exempt information if and so long as disclosure to the public might afford an opportunity to a person affected by the notice, order or direction to defeat the purpose or one of the purposes for which the notice, order or direction is to be given or made.

34. Information falling within any paragraph of Part 4 above is not exempt information by virtue of that paragraph if it relates to proposed development for which the local planning authority can grant itself planning permission pursuant to regulation 3 of the Town and Country Planning General Regulations 1992 (SI 1992/1492).

8–18846

PART 6
INTERPRETATION: WALES

35. (1) In Parts 4 and 5 and this Part of this Schedule—

"child" means a person under the age of eighteen years and any person who has attained that age and—

(*a*) is registered as a pupil at a school; or
(*b*) is the subject of a care order, within the meaning of section 31 of the Children Act 1989;

"disposal", in relation to property, includes the granting of an interest in or right over it;
"employee" means a person employed under a contract of service;
"financial or business affairs" includes contemplated, as well as past or current, activities;
"labour relations matter" means—

(*a*) any of the matters specified in paragraphs (a) to (g) of section 29(1) of the Trade Union and Labour Relations Act 1974 (matters which may be the subject of a trade dispute, within the meaning of that Act); or
(*b*) any dispute about a matter falling within paragraph (a) above;

and for the purposes of this definition the enactments mentioned in paragraph (a) above, with the necessary modifications, shall apply in relation to office-holders under the authority as they apply in relation to employees of the authority;

"office-holder", in relation to the authority, means the holder of any paid office appointments to which are or may be made or confirmed by the authority or by any joint board on which the authority is represented or by any person who holds any such office or is an employee of the authority;

"protected informant" means a person giving the authority information which tends to show that—

(*a*) a criminal offence,
(*b*) a breach of statutory duty,
(*c*) a breach of planning control, as defined in section 171A of the Town and Country Planning Act 1990, or
(*d*) a nuisance,

has been, or is being or is about to be committed;

"registered", in relation to information required to be registered under the Building Societies Act 1986, means recorded in the public file of any building society (within the meaning of that Act);

"tender for a contract" includes a written statement prepared by the authority in pursuance of section 9(2) of the Local Government, Planning and Land Act 1980 (estimated cost of carrying out functional work by direct labour).

(2) Any reference in Parts 4 and 5 and this Part of this Schedule to "the authority" is a reference to the principal council or, as the case may be, the committee or sub-committee in relation to whose proceedings or documents the question whether information is exempt or not falls to be determined and includes a reference—

(*a*) in the case of a principal council, to any committee or sub-committee of the council; and
(*b*) in the case of a committee, to—

(i) any constituent principal council;
(ii) any other principal council by which appointments are made to the committee or whose functions the committee discharges; and
(iii) any other committee or sub-committee of a principal council falling within sub-paragraph (i) or (ii) above; and

(*c*) in the case of a sub-committee, to—

(i) the committee, or any of the committees, of which it is a sub-committee; and
(ii) any principal council which falls within paragraph (b) above in relation to that committee."

Local Government (Miscellaneous Provisions) Act 1976

(1976 c 57)

PART I
GENERAL

Highways

8–18950 **7. Control of road-side sales.** (1) If a highway authority considers that, for the purpose of avoiding danger on or facilitating the passage of traffic over a highway for which it is the highway authority, it is appropriate to make an order under this subsection in respect of the highway, the authority may make an order (hereafter in this section referred to as a "control order") specifying the highway and providing that, subject to subsection (5) of this section—

(*a*) no person shall sell anything on the highway or offer or expose anything for sale on the highway; and

(*b*) no person shall, for the purpose of selling anything or offering or exposing anything for sale on the highway or of attracting from users of the highway offers to buy anything, put, keep or use on the highway or on land within fifteen metres from any part of the highway any stall or similar structure or any container or vehicle.

(2) The highway authority for a highway in respect of which a control order is in force may vary or revoke the order by a subsequent order.

(3) Paragraphs 20 to 23, paragraph 24 (except so much of it as relates to appeals by district councils) and paragraph 25 of Schedule 9 to the Road Traffic Regulation Act 1984 (which relates to the procedure for making orders under the provisions of that Act mentioned in paragraphs 20(1) and 24(*a*) and (*b*) of that Schedule) shall have effect as if subsections (1) and (2) of this section were included among those provisions[1].

(4) If a person contravenes a control order which is in force for a highway, the highway authority for the highway may by a notice served on him require him not to contravene the order after a date specified in the notice (which must not be before the expiration of the period of 7 days beginning with the date of service of the notice); and—

(*a*) if a person on whom a notice relating to a contravention of a control order is served in pursuance of this subsection contravenes the order after the expiration of that period, or causes, permits or procures another person to contravene it after the expiration of that period, he shall be guilty of an offence and liable on summary conviction to a fine not exceeding **level 3** on the standard scale;

(*b*) if a contravention in respect of which a person is convicted of an offence in pursuance of the preceding paragraph is continued by him after the expiration of the period of 7 days beginning with the date of the conviction he shall, as respects each day on which the contravention is so continued, be guilty of a further offence and liable on summary conviction to a fine not exceeding **£10**.

(5) A control order does not apply—

(*a*) to anything done at premises used as a shop or petrol filling station either—

(i) in pursuance of planning permission granted or deemed to be granted under the Town and Country Planning Act 1990, or

(ii) in a case where the premises are, without such permission, lawfully used as a shop or petrol filling station;

(*b*) to anything done at a market in respect of which tolls, stallages or rents are payable;

(*c*) to the sale, offer or exposure for sale of things from or on a vehicle which is used only for the purposes of itinerant trading with the occupiers of premises or which is used only for that purpose and for purposes other than trading;

(*d*) to such a vehicle as is mentioned in the preceding paragraph or to containers on the vehicle;

(*e*) to, or to containers used in connection with, the sale, offer or exposure for sale, by or on behalf of the occupier of land used for agriculture and on that land, of agricultural produce produced on that land;

(*f*) to the provision, in a lay-by situated on a highway, of facilities for the purchase of refreshments by persons travelling on the highway or on another highway near to the highway;

(*g*) to anything as respects which the control order provides that the order is not to apply to it.

In paragraph (*e*) of this subsection "agriculture" and "agricultural" have the same meanings as in the Agriculture Act 1947.

(6) References in the preceding provisions of this section to a control order are, in the case of a control order which has been varied in pursuance of subsection (2) of this section, references to the order as so varied.

[Local Government (Miscellaneous Provisions) Act 1976, s 7, as amended by the Criminal Justice Act 1982, ss 38 and 46, the Road Traffic Regulation Act 1984, Sch 13, the Planning (Consequential Provisions) Act 1990, Sch 2 and the Planning and Compensation Act 1991, Sch 7.]

---

1. The Control of Road-side Sales Orders (Procedure) Regulations 1978, SI 1978/932, have been made.

Heating etc

8–18951 **11.** *Production and supply of heat etc by local authorities.*

8–18952 **12. Provisions supplementary to section 11.** (1) A local authority which supplies or proposes to supply heat, hot air, hot water or steam in pursuance of the preceding section may make byelaws—

(*a*) with respect to the works and apparatus to be provided or used by persons other than the authority in connection with the supply;

(*b*) for preventing waste and unauthorised use of the supply and unauthorised interference with works and apparatus used by the authority or any other person in connection with the supply;

(*c*) providing for any specified contravention of the byelaws to be an offence punishable on summary conviction with a fine of such an amount, not exceeding **level 3** on the standard scale, as is specified in the byelaws.

[Local Government (Miscellaneous Provisions) Act 1976, s 12, as amended by the Criminal Justice Act 1982, ss 40 and 46 and the Building Act 1984, Sch 6.]

Land

8–18953 **15. Power of local authorities to survey land which they propose to acquire compulsorily.** (1) A person authorised in writing in that behalf by a local authority may at any reasonable time—

(*a*) survey any land in connection with a proposal by the authority to acquire compulsorily an interest in the land or a right over the land which is not such an interest; and

(*b*) for the purpose of surveying any land in pursuance of the preceding paragraph, enter on the land and other land.

(2) The power to survey land conferred by the preceding subsection includes power to search and bore on and in the land for the purpose of ascertaining the nature of the subsoil or whether minerals are present in the subsoil, and the power to enter on land conferred by that subsection includes power to place and leave, on or in the land, apparatus for use in connection with the survey in question and power to remove the apparatus; and it is hereby declared that references to surveying in this section include surveying from the air.

(3)[1] A person authorised by a local authority to enter on land in pursuance of subsection (1) of this section—

(*a*) shall, if so required before or after entering on the land, produce evidence of his authority to enter;

(*b*) may take with him on to the land such other persons and such equipment as are necessary for the survey in question;

(*c*) shall not if the land is occupied demand admission to the land as of right unless notice of the intended entry has been served by the local authority on the occupier not less than fourteen days before the demand;

(*d*) shall, if the land is unoccupied when he enters or the occupier is then temporarily absent, leave the land as effectually secured against trespassers as he found it;

(*e*) shall not place or leave apparatus on or in the land or remove apparatus from the land—

(i) unless notice of his intention to do so has been served by the local authority on an owner of the land, and if the land is occupied on the occupier, not less than fourteen days before he does so, and

(ii) if the land is held by relevant undertakers who within that period serve on the local authority a notice stating that they object to the placing or leaving or removal of the apparatus on the ground that to do so would be seriously detrimental to the carrying on of their undertaking, unless the Secretary of State authorises him in writing to do so;

(*f*) shall not search or bore on or in the land which is the subject of the survey in question if the land is held by relevant undertakers—

(i) unless notice of his intention to do so has been served by the local authority on the undertakers not less than fourteen days before he does so, and

(ii) if within that period the undertakers serve on the local authority a notice stating that they object to the searching or boring on the ground that to do so would be seriously detrimental to the carrying on of their undertaking, unless the Secretary of State authorises him in writing to do so;

and in paragraphs (*e*) and (*f*) of this subsection "relevant undertakers" means any statutory undertakers, any person authorised to carry on a light railway undertaking, a ferry undertaking or an undertaking for supplying district heating, the Civil Aviation Authority and a person who holds a licence under Chapter I of Part I of the Transport Act 2000 (air traffic services).

(3A) For the purposes of subsection (3) of this section—

(*a*) a person who holds a licence under Chapter I of Part I of the Transport Act 2000 shall not be considered to be a relevant undertaker unless the person is carrying out activities authorised by the licence;

(*b*) the person's undertaking shall not be considered to be that of a relevant undertaker except to the extent that it is the person's undertaking as licence holder.

(4)–(6) *Survey in a street or controlled land within the meaning of the New Roads and Street Works Act* 1991; *compensation for damage arising from a survey.*

(7) If a person—

(*a*) wilfully obstructs another person in the exercise of a power conferred on the other person by subsection (1) or (3)(*b*) of this section; or (*b*) while another person is on any land in pursuance of the said subsection (3)(*b*), wilfully obstructs him in doing things connected with the survey in question; or

(*c*) removes or otherwise interferes with apparatus left on or in land in pursuance of this section,

he shall be guilty of an offence and liable on summary conviction to a fine not exceeding **level 3** on the standard scale.

(8) If a person who has entered on any land in pursuance of this section discloses to another person information obtained by him there about a manufacturing process or trade secret, then, unless the disclosure is made in the course of performing his duty in connection with the purposes for which he was authorised to enter on the land, he shall be guilty of an offence and liable[2], on summary conviction, to a fine not exceeding **the statutory maximum** or, on conviction on indictment, to imprisonment for a term not exceeding **two years** or a fine or both.

(9) A local authority which has power by virtue of section 289(1) of the Highways Act 1980, section 324(6) of the Town and Country Planning Act 1990, section 88(5) of the Planning (Listed Buildings and Conservation Areas) Act 1990, or paragraph 20(1) of Schedule 4 to the Community Land Act 1975 to authorise a person to survey or enter on any land as mentioned in subsection (1) of this section shall not be entitled by virtue of that subsection to authorise a person to survey or enter on the land.

[Local Government (Miscellaneous Provisions) Act 1976, s 15, as amended by the Criminal Law Act 1977, s 28, the Highways Act 1980, Sch 24, the Criminal Justice Act 1982, ss 38 and 46, the Airports Act 1986, Sch 6, the Coal Industry Act 1987, Sch 1, the Planning (Consequential Provisions) Act 1990, Sch 2, the New Roads and Street Works Act 1991, Sch 8, the Coal Industry Act 1994, Sch 9 and SI 2001/4050.]

---

1. For the purposes of s 15(3) of this Act, the holder of a licence under s 6(1) of the Electricity Act 1989 shall be deemed to be a statutory undertaker and his undertaking a statutory undertaking (Electricity Act 1989, Sch 16, para 1).
2. For procedure in respect of this offence which is triable either way, see the Magistrates' Courts Act 1980, ss 17A–21, in PART I: MAGISTRATES' COURTS, PROCEDURE, ante.

8–18954 16. Power[1] of local authorities to obtain particulars of persons interested in land. (1) Where, with a view to performing a function conferred on a local authority by any enactment, the authority considers that it ought to have information connected with any land, the authority may serve on one or more of the following persons, namely—

(*a*) the occupier of the land; and

(*b*) any person who has an interest in the land either as freeholder, mortgagee or lessee or who directly or indirectly receives rent for the land; and

(*c*) any person who, in pursuance of an agreement between himself and a person interested in the land, is authorised to manage the land or to arrange for the letting of it,

a notice specifying the land and the function and the enactment which confers the function and requiring the recipient of the notice to furnish to the authority, within a period specified in the notice (which shall not be less than fourteen days beginning with the day on which the notice is served) the nature of his interest in the land and the name and address of each person whom the recipient of the notice believes is the occupier of the land and of each person whom he believes is, as respects the land, such a person as is mentioned in the provisions of paragraphs (*b*) and (*c*) of this subsection.

(2) A person who—

(*a*) fails to comply with the requirements of a notice served on him in pursuance of the preceding subsection; or

(*b*) in furnishing any information in compliance with such a notice makes a statement which he knows to be false in a material particular or recklessly makes a statement which is false in a material particular,

shall be guilty of an offence and liable[2] on summary conviction to a fine not exceeding **level 5** on the standard scale.

[Local Government (Miscellaneous Provisions) Act 1976, s 16, as amended by the Criminal Justice Act 1982, ss 38 and 46.]

---

1. This power shall not be exercisable with a view to performing any function under Pt I of the Local Government Finance Act 1992 (council tax): Local Government Finance Act 1992, Sch 13.
2. For liability of director, etc, where offence is committed by a body corporate, see s 44(3), post.

Bathing and boating

8–18955 17. Byelaws about bathing and boating. The power of a local authority to make byelaws under section 231 of the Public Health Act 1936 and section 76 of the Public Health Act 1961 may be exercised as respects any area of sea which is outside the area of the authority and within 1,000 metres to seaward of any place where the low water mark is within or on the boundary of the area of the authority; an offence against a byelaw made under the above provision may be dealt with as if committed within the area of the authority.

[Local Government (Miscellaneous Provisions) Act 1976, s 17—summarised.]

Places of entertainment

8–18956 19. *Recreational facilities.*

8–18957 20. Provision of sanitary appliances at places of entertainment. (1) A local authority (other than a county council and the Greater London Council[1]) may, by a notice served on an owner or occupier of a relevant place[2] in the area of the authority, require him—

(*a*) to provide, before the expiration of a period specified in the notice and in such positions at the place as are so specified, sanitary appliances[2] of such kinds and numbers as are so specified;
(*b*) to maintain and keep clean the appliances to the reasonable satisfaction of the authority;
(*c*) to provide and maintain a proper supply of such things for use in connection with the appliances as are so specified (which may be or include cold water or hot water or both); and
(*d*) to make the appliances and things available for use by members of the public resorting to the place and, if the notice so requires, to make them so available free of charge.

(2) A notice in pursuance of this section may require the provision of sanitary appliances on such occasions as are specified in the notice but if it does so it shall not also require the provision of sanitary appliances as respects which occasions are not so specified.

(3) A notice in pursuance of this section—

(*a*) shall not require the provision, in connection with any building for which fixed sanitary appliances could be required by virtue of building regulations in force when the notice is served if the building were to be newly constructed then, of fixed sanitary appliances which are of a different kind from, or which as respects a particular kind are more numerous than, those which could be required as aforesaid;
(*b*) shall not require the provision of movable sanitary appliances at a betting office[2];
(*c*) shall, unless it is an occasional notice[2], specify as the period before the expiration of which sanitary appliances are to be provided in pursuance of the notice a period equal to or longer than that during which the recipient of the notice may appeal against it in pursuance of the following section.

(4) It is hereby declared that a notice in pursuance of this section in respect of a relevant place may—

(*a*) be served on an owner or occupier of the place notwithstanding that he is for the time being required to comply with a previous notice served on him in pursuance of this section in respect of the place;
(*b*) require the provision at the place of appliances already provided there.

(5) A person authorised in writing in that behalf by a local authority (other than a county council and the Greater London Council) may at any reasonable time, upon producing if so required evidence that he is so authorised, enter any relevant place for the purpose of determining whether the authority should serve a notice in pursuance of this section in respect of the place or of ascertaining whether the requirements of such a notice served on a person who is an owner or occupier of the place are being complied with; and a person who wilfully obstructs another person acting in the exercise of powers conferred on the other person by this subsection shall be guilty of an offence and liable on summary conviction to a fine not exceeding **level 3** on the standard scale.

(6) Subject to subsections (7) and (8) of this section, a person who without reasonable excuse fails to comply with a notice in respect of a relevant place which was served on him in pursuance of this section when he was an owner or occupier of the place shall be guilty of an offence and liable[3] on summary conviction to a fine not exceeding **the statutory maximum** or, on conviction on indictment, to a fine; and if after the conviction of a person of such an offence the failure in question continues he shall, as respects each day on which it continues, be guilty of a further offence and liable on summary conviction to a fine not exceeding **£50** or, on conviction on indictment, to a fine.

(7) In proceedings for an offence under the preceding subsection of failing to comply with a notice it shall be a defence to prove that at the time of the failure the person on whom the notice was served was neither an owner nor an occupier of the relevant place in question and that he did not cease to be an owner or occupier of it by reason of anything done or omitted by him or any other person with a view to avoiding compliance with the notice.

(8) In proceedings for an offence under subsection (6) of this section which is alleged to have been committed on a particular day it shall be a defence to prove that on that day the relevant place in question was closed to members of the public or was used neither as a betting office nor for any of the purposes mentioned in paragraph (*a*) of the definition of relevant place in the following subsection; and in proceedings for an offence under subsection (6) of this section of failing to comply with an occasional notice it shall be a defence to prove—

(*a*) that the alleged offence is in respect of a requirement of the notice which is unreasonable; or
(*b*) that it would have been fairer to serve the notice on a person, other than the defendant—

(i) who was an owner or occupier of the relevant place in question when the notice was served on the defendant, and

(ii) whose name and address were furnished by the defendant, to the local authority which served the notice, before the expiration of the period specified in the notice in pursuance of subsection (1)(*a*) of this section.

(9) In this section and the following section—

"betting office" means a place for which a betting office licence within the meaning of the Betting, Gaming and Lotteries Act 1963 is in force;*

"occasional notice" means a notice in pursuance of this section requiring the provision of sanitary appliances on occasions specified in the notice;

"sanitary appliances" means water closets, other closets, urinals and wash basins;

"relevant place" means any of the following places—

(*a*) a place which is normally used or is proposed to be normally used for any of the following purposes, namely—

(i) the holding of any entertainment, exhibition or sporting event to which members of the public are admitted either as spectators or otherwise,

(ii) the sale of food or drink to members of the public for consumption at the place;

(*b*) a place which is used on some occasion or occasions or is proposed to be used on some occasion or occasions for any of the purposes aforesaid; and

(*c*) a betting office.

(10) *Consequential amendment.*

(11) A notice under this section shall draw the attention of the person on whom it is served—

(*a*) to sections 6(1) and 7 of the Chronically Sick and Disabled Persons Act 1970; and

(*b*) to the Code of Practice for Access for the Disabled to Buildings.

(12) In subsection (11) of this section "the Code of Practice for Access for the Disabled to Buildings" means, subject to subsection (13) of this section, the British Standards Institution code of practice referred to as BS 5810: 1979.

(13) Section 28 of the Chronically Sick and Disabled Persons Act 1970 (power to define certain expressions for the purposes of provisions of that Act) shall have effect as if any reference in it to a provision of that Act included a reference to this section.

[Local Government (Miscellaneous Provisions) Act 1976, s 20, as amended by the Criminal Law Act 1977, s 28, the Disabled Persons Act 1981, s 4 and the Criminal Justice Act 1982, ss 38 and 46.]

***Definition substituted by the Gambling Act 2005, Sch 16 from a date to be appointed.**

1. The Greater London Council was abolished by the Local Government Act 1985, s 1.
2. Defined in sub-s (9), post.
3. For procedure in respect of this offence which is triable either way, see the Magistrates' Courts Act 1980, ss 17A–21, in PART I: MAGISTRATES' COURTS, PROCEDURE, ante. For liability of director, etc, where offence is committed by a body corporate, see s 44(3), post.

8–18958 **21.** *Appeal to county court against certain notices under s 20.*

Dangerous trees and excavations

8–18959 **23.** *Power of local authorities to deal with dangerous trees.*

8–18960 **24. Provisions supplementary to section 23.** (1) A person authorised in writing in that behalf by such a council as is mentioned in subsection (1)[1] of the preceding section may enter on any land for the purpose of—

(*a*) determining whether the council should take steps in pursuance of subsection (2) or (7)[2] or serve a notice in pursuance of subsection (3)[2] of that section in respect of a tree on the land; or

(*b*) exercising on behalf of the council a power conferred on the council by subsection (2) or (7)[2] of that section in respect of a tree on the land.

(2) A person authorised to enter on any land in pursuance of the preceding subsection—

(*a*) shall, if so required before or after entering on the land, produce evidence of his authority to enter;

(*b*) may take with him on to the land such other persons and such equipment as are necessary for achieving the purpose for which he was authorised to enter on the land;

(*c*) shall, if the land is unoccupied when he enters or the occupier is then temporarily absent, leave the land as effectually secured against trespassers as he found it.

(3) If a person—

(*a*) wilfully obstructs another person in the exercise of a power conferred on the other person by subsection (1) or (2)(*b*) of this section; or (*b*) while another person is on land in pursuance of the said subsection (1) or (2)(*b*), wilfully obstructs the other person in doing things connected with the purpose for which the other person is authorised to be on the land,

he shall be guilty of an offence and liable on summary conviction to a fine not exceeding **level 3** on the standard scale.

(4) If a person interested in any land suffers damage by reason of—

(*a*) the exercise of the power to enter on the land which is conferred by virtue of subsection (1)(*a*) of this section; or

(*b*) the exercise on the land, in connection with the exercise of the power mentioned in the preceding paragraph, of the power conferred by subsection (2)(*b*) of this section; or

(*c*) a failure to perform the duty imposed by subsection (2)(*c*) of this section in respect of the land,

he shall be entitled to recover compensation for the damage from the local authority which authorised the entry in question.

(5)–(6) *Compensation for damage; council to recover expenses with interest.*

[Local Government (Miscellaneous Provisions) Act 1976, s 24 amended by the Local Government, Planning and Land Act 1980, Sch 6 and the Criminal Justice Act 1982, ss 38 and 46.]

---

1. This means a district council, a London borough council or the Common Council (s 23(1)).
2. Where a council receives from an owner or occupier of land a notice requesting that it makes safe a tree on other land which is not owned or occupied by that person, and the council considers that the tree is likely to cause damage, and does not know the name and address of the owner or occupier of the other land, it may take steps on the land, by felling or otherwise, to make the tree safe (s 23(2)—SUMMARISED). Where a council receives such a request to make a tree safe, and considers the tree is likely to cause damage, and knows the name and address of the owner or occupier of the land, the council may serve on such person a notice requiring him within a specified time to make the tree safe (s 23(3)—SUMMARISED). If a person fails to comply with a notice under s 23(3), the council may take the steps specified in the notice and recover from that person the expenses reasonably incurred (s 23(7)—SUMMARISED).

8–18961 **25.** *Power of certain councils with respect to dangerous excavations.*

8–18962 **26.** Provisions supplementary to s 25[1].—(1) A person authorised in writing in that behalf by such a council as is mentioned in subsection (1)[2] of the preceding section may enter on any land in the area of the council for the purpose of—

(*a*) ascertaining whether the land is suitable as the site of works which the council may carry out or for which the council may serve a notice in pursuance of that section[3]; or

(*b*) carrying out, maintaining, repairing or removing in pursuance of that section[3] any works on behalf of the council; or

(*c*) ascertaining whether any works carried out by the council in pursuance of that section[3] should be or have been maintained, repaired or removed.

(2) A person authorised by a council to enter on land in pursuance of the preceding subsection—

(*a*) shall, if so required before or after entering on the land, produce evidence of his authority to enter;

(*b*) may take with him on to the land such other persons and such equipment as are necessary for achieving the purpose for which he was authorised to enter on the land;

(*c*) shall, if the land is unoccupied when he enters or the occupier is then temporarily absent, leave the land as effectually secured against trespassers as he found it.

(3)–(4) *Compensation for damage.*

(5) If a person—

(*a*) wilfully obstructs another person in the exercise of a power conferred on the other person by subsection (1) or (2)(*b*) of this section; or

(*b*) while another person is on land in pursuance of the said subsection (2)(*b*) wilfully obstructs him in doing things connected with the works in question; or

(*c*) without the agreement of the council by which works have been carried out in pursuance of the preceding section, removes or otherwise interferes with the works,

he shall be guilty of an offence and liable on summary conviction to a fine not exceeding **level 3** on the standard scale.

(6) Nothing in the preceding section or the preceding provisions of this section applies to an excavation—

(*a*) on operational land of statutory undertakers; or

(*b*) on land of the Coal Authority of such a description as the Secretary of State may specify by regulations made by statutory instrument;

and the definition of "operational land" in section 263 of the Town and Country Planning Act 1990 shall apply for the purposes of paragraph (*a*) of this subsection as if in that section "statutory undertakers" had the same meaning as in that paragraph and "undertaking" had a corresponding meaning.

[Local Government (Miscellaneous Provisions) Act 1976, s 26, as amended by the Criminal Justice Act 1982, ss 38 and 46, the Coal Industry Act 1987, Sch 1, the Planning (Consequential Provisions) Act 1990, Sch 2 and the Coal Industry Act 1994, Sch 9.]

1. For the purposes of s 26 of this Act, the holder of a licence under s 6(1) of the Electricity Act 1989 shall be deemed to be a statutory undertaker and his undertaking a statutory undertaking (Electricity Act 1989, Sch 16, para 1).
2. This means a district council, a London borough council or the Common Council (s 25(1)).
3. Where a council considers that an excavation on land is accessible to the public from a highway or a place of public resort and, by reason of its being unenclosed or inadequately enclosed, is a danger to the public, and the council does not know the name and address of the owner or occupier of the land on which works to remove the danger should be carried out, the council may carry out on that land works for the purpose of removing the danger (s 25(1)—SUMMARISED). Where a council considers that an excavation is as mentioned in s 25(1), and knows the name and address of the owner or occupier of the land on which works to remove the danger should be carried out, the council may serve on the owner or occupier of the land a notice specifying the excavation and stating that the council proposes to carry out works specified in the notice (s 25(2)—SUMMARISED).

Miscellaneous

8–18963 **35. Removal of obstructions from private sewers.** (1) If a private sewer is obstructed at a point within the area of a local authority (other than a county council, the authority may serve on each of the persons who is an owner or occupier of premises served by the sewer, or on each of such of those persons as the authority thinks fit, a notice requiring the recipients of notices in pursuance of this subsection in respect of the obstruction to remove it before a time specified in the notice; and that time shall not be earlier than forty-eight hours after the service of the notice or, if different notices in respect of the same obstruction are served in pursuance of this subsection at different times, shall not be earlier than forty-eight hours after the latest of those times.

(2) If an obstruction in respect of which notices have been served by an authority in pursuance of the preceding subsection is not removed within the period specified in the notices, the authority may remove it.

(3)–(6) *Recovery of expenses incurred in pursuance of subsection* (2).

(7) Expressions used in this section and in Part II of the Public Health Act 1936 have the same meanings in this section as in that Part; and sections 287 and 288 of that Act[1] (which confer power to enter premises and penalise obstruction) shall have effect as if references to that Act included references to this section.

[Local Government (Miscellaneous Provisions) Act 1976, s 35, as amended by the Local Government Act 1985, Sch 17.]

1. See title PUBLIC HEALTH, post.

8–18964 **36.** *Power of local authorities to appoint times and charges for markets.*

8–18965 **41.** Evidence[1] of resolutions and minutes of proceedings etc.—(1) A document which—

(*a*) purports to be a copy of—

(i) a resolution, order or report of a local authority or a precursor of a local authority, or

(ii) the minutes of the proceedings at a meeting of a local authority or a precursor of a local authority; and

(*b*) bears a certificate purporting to be signed by the proper officer of the authority or a person authorised in that behalf by him or the authority and stating that the resolution was passed or the order or report was made by the authority or precursor on a date specified in the certificate or, as the case may be, that the minutes were signed in accordance with paragraph 41 of Schedule 12 to the Local Government Act 1972 or the corresponding provision specified in the certificate of the enactments relating to local government which were in force when the minutes were signed,

shall be evidence in any proceedings of the matters stated in the certificate and of the terms of the resolution, order, report or minutes in question.

(2) In the preceding subsection references to a local authority, except the first and second references in paragraph (*b*), include references to a committee of a local authority and a sub-committee of such a committee and references to a precursor of a local authority include references to a committee of such a precursor and a sub-committee of such a committee.

(2A) In the case of a local authority which are operating executive arrangements, a document which—

(a) purports to be a copy of a record of any decision made by the executive of that authority, or any person acting on behalf of that executive, where that record is required to be kept or produced by section 22 of the Local Government Act 2000 or any regulations made under that section; and

(b) bears a certificate purporting to be signed by the proper officer of the authority or by a person authorised in that behalf by him or any other person who, by virtue of regulations made under section 22 of the Local Government Act 2000, is authorised or required to produce such a record, stating that the decision was made on the date specified in the certificate by that executive, or as the case may be, by the person acting on behalf of that executive,

shall be evidence in any proceedings of the matters stated in the certificate and of the terms of the decision in question.

(3) A document which—

(*a*) purports to be a copy of an instrument by which the proper officer of a local authority appointed a person to be an officer of the authority or authorised a person to perform functions specified in the instrument; and

(*b*) bears a certificate purporting to be signed as mentioned in subsection (1)(*b*) of this section and stating that the document is a copy of the instrument in question,

shall be evidence in any proceedings of the fact that the instrument was made by the said proper officer and of the terms of the instrument.

(4) In the preceding provisions of this section "precursor", in relation to a local authority, means any authority which has ceased to exist but which when it existed was constituted, in pursuance of the enactments relating to local government which were then in force, for an area any part of which is included in the area of the local authority.

[Local Government (Miscellaneous Provisions) Act 1976, s 41, as amended by SI 2001/2237.]

1. Note the requirement for strict compliance with s 41(1) when prosecuting an alleged breach of the system of licensing sex establishments (*Smakowski v Westminster City Council* (1989) 154 JP 345).

Supplemental

8–18966 **44. Interpretation etc of Part I.** (1) In this Part of this Act, except where the contrary intention appears—

"apparatus" includes any structure constructed in order that apparatus may be lodged in it;

"the Common Council" means the Common Council of the City of London;

"executive" and "executive arrangements" have the same meaning as in Part II of the Local Government Act 2000;

"functions" includes powers and duties;

"highway" has the same meaning as in the Highways Act 1980[1];

"local Act" includes a provisional order confirmed by an Act;

"local authority" means a county council, a county borough council, a district council, a London borough council, the Common Council, the Council of the Isles of Scilly and—

(*a*) in sections 13 to 16, 29, 30, 38, 39 and 41 of this Act, a police authority established under section 3 of the Police Act 1996, the Metropolitan Police Authority, a joint authority established by Part IV of the Local Government Act 1985 and the London Fire and Emergency Planning Authority;

(*b*) in sections 1, 16, 19, 30, 36, 39 and 41 of this Act, a parish council and a community council;

(*c*) in section 40 of this Act, a joint authority established by Part IV of the Local Government Act 1985, an authority established under section 10 of that Act (waste regulation and disposal authorities), the London Fire and Emergency Planning Authority and the South Yorkshire Pensions Authority;

"notice" means notice in writing;

"owner", in relation to any land, place or premises, means a person who, either on his own account or as agent or trustee for another person, is receiving the rackrent of the land, place or premises or would be entitled to receive it if the land, place or premises were let at a rackrent, and "owned" shall be construed accordingly;

"statutory undertakers" means any of the following bodies, namely, any statutory undertakers within the meaning of [the Highways Act 1980; and, a universal service provider in connection with the provision of a universal postal service; and

"traffic sign" has the same meaning as in the Road Traffic Regulation Act 1984;

"universal service provider" has the same meaning as in the Postal Services Act 2000; and references to the provision of a universal postal service shall be construed in accordance with that Act.

(1ZA) The undertaking of a universal service provider so far as relating to the provision of a universal postal service shall be taken to be his statutory undertaking for the purposes of this Part; and references in this Part to his undertaking shall be construed accordingly.

(1A) Sections 13, 15, 16, 29, 30, 32, 38, 39 and 41 of this Act shall have effect as if the Broads Authority were a local authority and the Broads (as defined in the Norfolk and Suffolk Broads Act 1988) were its local government area.

(1B) Section 16 of this Act shall have effect as if the Environment Agency were a local authority.

(2) Section 322 of the Highways Act 1980 (which relates to the service of documents) shall apply to the service of any document by or on the Secretary of State in pursuance of section 7 of this Act as if that section were a provision of that Act.

(3) When an offence under this Part of this Act (including an offence under byelaws made by virtue of section 12 of this Act) which has been committed by a body corporate is proved to have been committed with the consent or connivance of, or to be attributable to any neglect on the part of, any director, manager, secretary or other similar officer of the body corporate or any person who was purporting to act in any such capacity, he as well as the body corporate shall be guilty of that offence and be liable to be proceeded against and punished accordingly.

Where the affairs of a body corporate are managed by its members the preceding provisions of this subsection shall apply in relation to the acts and defaults of a member in connection with his functions of management as if he were a director of the body corporate.

(4) Except so far as this Part of this Act expressly provides otherwise and subject to the provisions of section 33 of the Interpretation Act 1889[3] (which relates to offences under two or more laws), nothing in this Part of this Act—

(*a*) confers a right of action in any civil proceedings (other than proceedings for the recovery of a fine) in respect of any contravention of this Part of this Act or an instrument made in pursuance of this Part of this Act;

(*b*) affects any restriction imposed by or under any other enactment, whether public, local or private; or

(*c*) derogates from any right of action or other remedy (whether civil or criminal) in proceedings instituted otherwise than under this Part of this Act.

(5) Nothing in paragraph (*a*) of the preceding subsection applies to the failure of a person to perform a duty imposed on him by section 1(4), 2(5), 25(6) or (7)(*b*) of this Act or section 61(2)(*c*) of the Road Traffic Regulation Act 1984.

(6) References in this Part of this Act to any enactment are references to it as amended by or under any other enactment.

[Local Government (Miscellaneous Provisions) Act 1976, s 44, as amended by the Highways Act 1980, Schs 24 and 25, the British Telecommunications Act 1981, Sch 3, the Road Traffic Regulation Act 1984, Sch 13, the Local Government Act 1985, Schs 14 and 17, the Telecommunications Act 1984, Sch 7, the Norfolk and Suffolk Broads Act 1988, Sch 6, the Education Reform Act 1988, Sch 13, the Water Act 1989, Sch 27, SI 1990/1765, the Police and Magistrates' Courts Act 1994, Sch 4, the Environment Act 1995, Sch 22, the Police Act 1996, Sch 7, the Police Act 1997, Sch 6, the Greater London Authority Act 1999, Schs 27, 29 and 34, SI 2001/1149, the Criminal Justice and Police Act 2001, Sch 6 and SI 2002/808.]

1. See s 328 of the Highways Act 1980, PART VII: TRANSPORT, title HIGHWAYS.
2. The National Rivers Authority, every water undertaker and every sewerage undertaker is deemed to be a statutory undertaker for the purposes of this Act (Water Act 1989, Sch 25, para 1).
3. Now s 18 of the Interpretation Act 1978.

PART II[1]
HACKNEY CARRIAGES AND PRIVATE HIRE VEHICLES

8–18967 **45. Application of Part II.** (1) The provisions of this Part of this Act, except this section, shall come into force in accordance with the following provisions of this section.

(2) If the Act of 1847[2] is in force in the area of a district council, the council may resolve that the provisions of this Part of this Act, other than this section, are to apply to the relevant area; and if the council do so resolve those provisions shall come into force in the relevant area on the day specified in that behalf in the resolution (which must not be before the expiration of the period of one month beginning with the day on which the resolution is passed).

In this subsection "the relevant area", in relation to a council, means—

(*a*) if the Act of 1847 is in force throughout the area of the council, that area; and

(*b*) if the Act of 1847 is in force for part only of the area of the council, that part of that area.

(3) A council shall not pass a resolution in pursuance of the foregoing subsection unless they have—

(*a*) published in two consecutive weeks, in a local newspaper circulating in their area, notice of their intention to pass the resolution; and

(*b*) served a copy of the notice, not later than the date on which it is first published in pursuance of the foregoing paragraph, on the council of each parish or community which would be affected by the resolution or, in the case of such a parish which has no parish council, on the chairman of the parish meeting.

(4) If after a council has passed a resolution in pursuance of subsection (2) of this section the Act of 1847 comes into force for any part of the area of the council for which it was not in force when the council passed the resolution, the council may pass a resolution in accordance with the foregoing provisions of this section in respect of that part as if that part were included in the relevant area for the purposes of subsection (2) of this section.

[Local Government (Miscellaneous Provisions) Act 1976, s 45.]

1. Part II of this Act amended and extended the controls over hackney carriages under the Town Police Clauses Act 1847, and introduced new powers to control private hire vehicles and their drivers, proprietors and operators. Part II does

not apply to London. Sections 1, 2, and 42 of the Public Passenger Vehicles Act 1981, post, provide certain exemptions from the PSV licensing system; it shall however continue to be treated as such for the purposes of a local Act or Pt II of this Act (Public Passenger Vehicles Act 1981, s 79, post).

Part II of this Act, to the extent to which it is part of the taxi code, subject to modifications and exceptions, shall apply to a licensed taxi which is being used to provide a local service under a special licence under s 12 of the Transport Act 1985 (Local Services (Operation by Taxis) Regulations 1986, SI 1986/567).

Sections 47, 65(5), 66 and 67 of the Act are modified or disapplied in relation to the hiring of taxis at separate fares under ss 10 and 11 of the Transport Act 1985 (Licensed Taxis (Hiring at Separate Fares) Order 1986, SI 1986/1386).

2. "The Act of 1847" means the provisions of the Town Police Clauses Act 1847 with respect to hackney carriages (s 80(1), post). For that Act, see title TOWNS IMPROVEMENTS: TOWN POLICE, post.

8-18968 **46. Vehicle, drivers' and operators' licences.** (1) Except as authorised by this Part of this Act—

(*a*) no person being the proprietor[1] of any vehicle, not being a hackney carriage[1] or London cab in respect of which a vehicle licence[1] is in force, shall use or permit the same to be used in a controlled district[1] as a private hire vehicle[1] without having for such a vehicle a current licence under section 48 of this Act[2];

(*b*) no person shall in a controlled district act as driver[3] of any private hire vehicle without having a current licence under section 51 of this Act[4];

(*c*) no person being the proprietor of a private hire vehicle licensed under this Part of this Act shall employ as the driver[3] thereof for the purpose of any hiring any person who does not have a current licence under the said section 51;

(*d*) no person shall in a controlled district operate[1] any vehicle as a private hire vehicle without having a current licence under section 55 of this Act[5];

(*e*) no person licensed under the said section 55 shall in a controlled district operate[1] any vehicle as a private hire vehicle—

(i) if for the vehicle a current licence under the said section 48 is not in force; or

(ii) if the driver does not have a current licence under the said section 51[6].

(2) If any person knowingly contravenes the provisions of this section, he shall be guilty of an offence[7].

[Local Government (Miscellaneous Provisions) Act 1976, s 46, as amended by the Transport Act 1985, Sch 7.]

---

1. For meaning of "proprietor", "hackney carriage", "vehicle licence", "controlled district", "operate" and "private hire vehicle", see s 80(1), post. The fact that a vehicle is licensed as a hackney carriage by one local authority does not preclude its being a private hire vehicle in the area of another local authority (*Kingston upon Hull City Council v Wilson* (1995) Times, 25 July). For the purposes of s 46(1)(*d*) and (*e*), the meaning of "operate" is that provided in s 80(1), post (*Adur District Council v Fry* [1997] RTR 257).

The word "operate" in s 46(1)(*d*) has the technical meaning set out in s 80(1), post, and the definitions in the latter provision of "operate", "operator's licence" and "private hire vehicle" make clear that "hackney carriages" are excluded from s 46(1)(*d*); therefore, when such a vehicle is being used as a private hire vehicle by a licensed hackney carriage driver there is no need for the person accepting the bookings to be licensed under s 55, post: *Brentwood Borough Council v Gladen* [2004] EWHC (Admin) 2500, [2005] RTR 12.

2. Where a hackney carriage, in respect of which a vehicle licence was in force, was used to collect a passenger in a controlled district outside the area of the local authority that had issued the vehicle licence, it was held no offence had been committed (*Britain v ABC Cabs (Camberley) Ltd* [1981] RTR 395).

3. A short-staffed licensed operator whose wife drove pre-arranged bookings for no cost was "operating" for the purposes of this section and s 80(1) post and thus liable as his wife was not a licensed driver: (*St Albans District Council v Taylor* [1991] RTR 400, DC).

4. Section 46(1)(*b*) applies to all driving in a controlled district of a vehicle characterised under s 80(1), post, as a private hire vehicle, whatever the specific activity in connection with which the vehicle is in fact being driven. Accordingly, it is no defence in a prosecution under s 46(1)(*b*) that the vehicle was not actually being used for private hire (*Benson v Boyce* [1997] RTR 226). Section 46(2) requires the prosecution, if it is to establish guilt in relation to s 46(1)(*b*), to prove that the defendant knew that: (i) he was driving in a controlled district; (ii) the vehicle he was driving was a private hire vehicle; and (iii) at the time, he was not the holder of a driver's licence to drive such a vehicle. Providing knowledge of those three factors is proved, it matters not that the defendant did not appreciate that he was committing an offence (*Reading Borough Council v Ahmad* (1998) 163 JP 451).

5. The collection of a passenger within a controlled district in pursuance of a contract for hire made outside the controlled district is not "operating" for the purposes of s 46(1)(*d*) (*Britain v ABC Cabs (Camberley) Ltd* [1981] RTR 395).

6. Section 46(1)(*e*) must be read subject to the provisions of s 80(2), post, so as to require private hire operators licensed under s 55, post, to make use only of vehicles and drivers licensed by the council of the district by which the operators are licensed when operating in that controlled district (*Dittah v Birmingham City Council* (1993) 157 JP 1110, [1993] RTR 356, [1993] Crim LR 610).

7. For penalty, see s 76, post, and note possible defences under s 75, post.

8-18969 **47. Licensing of hackney carriages.** (1) A district council may attach to the grant of a licence of a hackney carriage under the Act of 1847[1] such conditions[2] as the district council may consider reasonably necessary.

(2) Without prejudice to the generality of the foregoing subsection, a district council may require any hackney carriage licensed by them under the Act of 1847 to be of such design or appearance or bear such distinguishing marks as shall clearly identify it as a hackney carriage.

(3) Any person aggrieved by any conditions attached to such a licence may appeal[3] to a magistrates' court.

[Local Government (Miscellaneous Provisions) Act 1976, s 47.]

1. See note 2 to para **8–18967**, supra.

2. A condition requiring adaptation of vehicles and applying only to new licences is valid (*R v Manchester City Justices, ex p McHugh* [1989] RTR 285—disabled facilities). Conditions cannot be imposed to restrict new licences to certain parts of the District Council's area; such an approach would create a two-tier system that flew in the face of the legislative approach to remove restraints and to allow market forces to take effect (*R (on the application of Maud) v Castle Point Borough Council* [2002] EWCA Civ 1526, [2002] JPN 782, [2003] RTR 122).

3. The procedure shall be in accordance with ss 300–302 of the Public Health Act 1936, title PUBLIC HEALTH, post (s 77, post). See also Magistrates' Court's Rules 1981, r 34, in PART I: MAGISTRATES' COURTS PROCEDURE, ante.

8–18970 48. Licensing of private hire vehicles. (1) Subject to the provisions of this Part of this Act, a district council may on the receipt of an application from the proprietor[1] of any vehicle for the grant in respect of such vehicle of a licence to use the vehicle as a private hire vehicle[1], grant in respect thereof a vehicle licence:

Provided that a district council shall not grant such a licence unless they are satisfied—

(*a*) that the vehicle is—

(i) suitable[1A] in type, size and design for use as a private hire vehicle;

(ii) not of such design and appearance as to lead any person to believe that the vehicle is a hackney carriage;

(iii) in a suitable mechanical condition;

(iv) safe; and

(v) comfortable;

(*b*) that there is in force in relation to the use of the vehicle a policy of insurance or such security as complies with the requirements of Part VI of the Road Traffic Act 1988,

and shall not refuse such a licence for the purpose of limiting the number of vehicles in respect of which such licences are granted by the council.

(2) A district council may attach to the grant of a licence under this section such conditions as they may consider reasonably necessary[2] including, without prejudice to the generality of the foregoing provisions of this subsection, conditions requiring or prohibiting the display of signs on or from the vehicle to which the licence relates.

(3) In every vehicle licence granted under this section there shall be specified—

(*a*) The name and address of—

(i) the applicant; and

(ii) every other person who is a proprietor of the private hire vehicle in respect of which the licence is granted, or who is concerned, either solely or in partnership with any other person, in the keeping, employing or letting on hire of the private hire vehicle;

(*b*) the number of the licence which shall correspond with the number to be painted or marked on the plate or disc to be exhibited on the private hire vehicle in accordance with subsection (6) of this section;

(*c*) the conditions attached to the grant of the licence; and

(*d*) such other particulars as the district council consider reasonably necessary.

(4) Every licence granted under this section shall—

(*a*) be signed by an authorised officer[3] of the council which granted it;

(*b*) relate to not more than one private hire vehicle; and

(*c*) remain in force for such period not being longer than one year as the district council may specify in the licence.

(5) Where a district council grant under this section a vehicle licence in respect of a private hire vehicle they shall issue a plate or disc identifying that vehicle as a private hire vehicle in respect of which a vehicle licence has been granted.

(6)

(*a*) Subject to the provisions of this Part of this Act, no person shall use or permit to be used in a controlled district as a private hire vehicle a vehicle in respect of which a licence has been granted under this section unless the plate or disc issued in accordance with subsection (5) of this section is exhibited on the vehicle in such manner as the district council shall prescribe by condition attached to the grant of the licence.

(*b*) If any person without reasonable excuse contravenes the provisions of this subsection he shall be guilty of an offence[4].

(7) Any person aggrieved[5] by the refusal of a district council to grant a vehicle licence under this section, or by any conditions specified in such a licence, may appeal[6] to a magistrates' court.

[Local Government (Miscellaneous Provisions) Act 1976, s 48, as amended by the Road Traffic (Consequential Provisions) Act 1988, Sch 3.]

1. See note 1 to para **8–18968**, supra.

1A. Safety of the vehicle for use as a private hire vehicle is part of the suitability for such proposed use. "Safe" in para (iv) might refer to whether the vehicle, suitable in other respects, is safe in the sense, for example, that its components are not defective (*Chauffeur Bikes v Leeds City Council* [2005] EWHC 2369 (Admin), 170 JP 24).

2. A condition which prohibited a private hire vehicle to stand in any public place other than in connection with a pre-arranged booking was held to be beyond the purpose envisaged by the statute and to be unenforceable, or alternatively, not "reasonably necessary" (*R v Blackpool Borough Council, ex p Red Cab Taxis Ltd* (1994) 158 JP 1069).

3. For meaning of "authorised officer", see s 80(1), post.

4. For penalty, see s 76, post.

5. A hackney carriage licence holder may be a 'person aggrieved' by a condition imposed on private hire vehicles (*R v Swansea City and County, ex p Davies* [2001] RTR 54, (2000) Times 7 July, DC).

6. The procedure shall be in accordance with ss 300–302 of the Public Health Act 1936, title PUBLIC HEALTH, post (s 77, post). See also Magistrates' Courts Rules 1981, r 34, in PART I: MAGISTRATES' COURTS PROCEDURE, ante. The size and design of a licence disc or plate cannot be the subject of an appeal, the only exemptions from display are contained in s 75, post, the nature of the appellant's business is irrelevant to the appeal (*Solihull Metropolitan Borough Council v Silverline Cars* (1988) 153 JP 209, [1989] RTR 142 DC).

8–18971 **49. Transfer of hackney carriages and private hire vehicles.** (1) If the proprietor[1] of a hackney carriage[1] or of a private hire vehicle[1] in respect of which a vehicle licence has been granted by a district council transfers his interest in the hackney carriage or private hire vehicle to a person other than the proprietor whose name is specified in the licence, he shall within fourteen days after such transfer give notice in writing thereof to the district council specifying the name and address of the person to whom the hackney carriage or private hire vehicle has been transferred.

(2) If a proprietor without reasonable excuse fails to give notice to a district council as provided by subsection (1) of this section he shall be guilty of an offence[2].

[Local Government (Miscellaneous Provisions) Act 1976, s 49.]

1. For meaning of "proprietor", "hackney carriage" and "private hire vehicle", see s 80(1), post.

2. For penalty, see s 76 post.

8–18972 **50. Provisions as to proprietors.** (1) Without prejudice to the provisions of section 68 of this Act, the proprietor[1] of any hackney carriage[1] or of any private hire vehicle[1] licensed by a district council shall present such hackney carriage or private hire vehicle for inspection and testing by or on behalf of the council within such period and at such place within the area of the council as they may by notice reasonably require:

Provided that a district council shall not under the provisions of this subsection require a proprietor to present the same hackney carriage or private hire vehicle for inspection and testing on more than three separate occasions during any one period of twelve months.

(2) The proprietor of any hackney carriage or private hire vehicle—

(*a*) licensed by a district council under the Act of 1847[2] or under this Part of this Act; or

(*b*) in respect of which an application for a licence has been made to a district council under the Act of 1847 or under this Part of this Act;

shall, within such period as the district council may by notice reasonably require, state in writing the address of every place where such hackney carriage or private hire vehicle is kept when not in use, and shall if the district council so require afford to them such facilities as may be reasonably necessary to enable them to cause such hackney carriage or private hire vehicle to be inspected and tested there.

(3) Without prejudice to the provisions of section 170 of the Road Traffic Act 1988, the proprietor of a hackney carriage or of a private hire vehicle licensed by a district council shall report to them as soon as reasonably practicable, and in any case within seventy-two hours of the occurrence thereof, any accident to such hackney carriage or private hire vehicle causing damage materially affecting the safety, performance or appearance of the hackney carriage or private hire vehicle or the comfort or convenience of persons carried therein.

(4) The proprietor of any hackney carriage or of any private hire vehicle licensed by a district council shall at the request of any authorised officer[4] of the council produce for inspection the vehicle, licence for such hackney carriage or private hire vehicle and the certificate of the policy of insurance or security required by Part VI of the Road Traffic Act 1988 in respect of such hackney carriage or private hire vehicle.

(5) If any person without reasonable excuse contravenes the provisions of this section, he shall be guilty of an offence[5].

[Local Government (Miscellaneous Provisions) Act 1976, s 50 amended by the Road Traffic (Consequential Provisions) Act 1988, Sch 3.]

1. For meaning of "proprietor", "hackney carriage" and "private hire vehicle", see s 80(1), post.

2. "The Act of 1847" means the provisions of the Town Police Clauses Act 1847 with respect to hackney carriages (s 80(1), post). For that Act, see title TOWNS IMPROVEMENTS: TOWN POLICE, post.

4. For meaning of "authorised officer", see s 80(1), post.

5. See note 4 to para **8–18970**, supra.

8–18973 **51. Licensing of drivers of private hire vehicles.** (1) Subject to the provisions of this Part of this Act, a district council shall, on the receipt of an application from any person for the grant to that person of a licence to drive private hire vehicles, grant to that person a driver's licence: Provided that a district council shall not grant a licence—

(*a*) unless they are satisfied that the applicant is a fit and proper person to hold a driver's licence; or (*b*) to any person who has not for at least twelve months[1] been authorised to drive a motor car, or is not at the date of the application for a driver's licence so authorised.

(1) For the purposes of subsection (1) of this section a person is authorised to drive a motor car if—

(*a*) he holds a licence granted under Part III of the Road Traffic Act 1988 (not being a provisional licence) authorising him to drive a motor car, or

(*b*) he is authorised by virtue of section 99A(1) or section 109(1) of that Act to drive in Great Britain a motor car.*

(2) A district council may attach to the grant of a licence under this section such conditions as they may consider reasonably necessary[2].

(3) It shall be the duty of a council by which licences are granted in pursuance of this section to enter, in a register maintained by the council for the purpose, the following particulars of each such licence, namely—

(*a*) the name of the person to whom it is granted;

(*b*) the date on which and the period for which it is granted; and

(*c*) if the licence has a serial number, that number,

and to keep the register available at its principal offices for inspection by members of the public during office hours free of charge.

[Local Government (Miscellaneous Provisions) Act 1976, s 51 amended by the Road Traffic (Consequential Provisions) Act 1988, Sch 3, the Road Traffic Act 1991, s 47, SI 1996/1974, the Police Act 1997, Sch 9 and SI 1998/1946.]

***It would appear that this sub-section has been numbered incorrectly by the amending SI 1996/1974.**

1. A person who has held a licence for 12 months in the past, and does in fact hold a licence at the date of the application, is entitled to qualify, notwithstanding that there is no continuity between the two periods (*Crawley Borough Council v Crabb* [1996] RTR 201).

2. See note 2 to s 48(2) in para **8–18970**.

8–18974 **52. Appeals in respect of drivers' licences.** Any person aggrieved[1] by—

(1) the refusal of the district council to grant a driver's licence under section 51 of this Act; or

(2) any conditions attached to the grant of a driver's licence;

may appeal[2] to a magistrates' court.

[Local Government (Miscellaneous Provisions) Act 1976, s 52.]

---

1. A person is not a "person aggrieved" and cannot bring an appeal under this section unless he has applied for a licence and his application has been refused or granted with conditions and he is aggrieved by that refusal or with those conditions: *Peddubriwny v Cambridge City Council* [2001] EWHC Admin 200, [2001] RTR 461.

2. See note 5 to para **8–18970**, ante. Where the holder of a driver's licence in this application for renewal of the licence failed to give details of his conviction, it was held, on an appeal against the refusal of the district council to renew the licence, that the justices in determining whether the appellant was a fit and proper person had to consider whether the false statement was made knowingly or recklessly, in such circumstances, it was not permissible for the justices to review the question of whether or not the convictions recorded in earlier criminal proceedings were incorrectly arrived at (*Nottingham City Council v Farooq* (1998) Times, 28 October). In determining whether a person is "fit and proper" justices are entitled to rely on any evidential material which might reasonably and properly influence the making of a responsible judgment in good faith. Some evidence such as gossip, speculation and hearsay, might by its source, nature and inherent probability carry a greater degree of credibility. The civil standard of proof applies and in seeking to rebut the applicant's contention that he is a fit and proper person the onus on the local authority is to do this on the civil standard of proof even if the substance of what they seek to prove amounts to a criminal offence. (*McCool v Rushcliffe Borough Council* (1998) 163 JP 46, DC).

8–18975 **53. Drivers' licences for hackney carriages and private hire vehicles.** (1)

(*a*) Every licence granted by a district council under the provisions of this Part of this Act to any person to drive a private hire vehicle[1] shall remain in force for three years from the date of such licence or for such lesser period as the district council may specify in such licence.

(*b*) Notwithstanding the provisions of the Public Health Act 1875 and the Town Police Clauses Act 1889, every licence granted by a district council under the provisions of the Act of 1847[2] to any person to drive a hackney carriage[1] shall remain in force for three years from the date of such licence or for such lesser period as they may specify in such licence.

(2) Notwithstanding the provisions of the Act of 1847, a district council may demand and recover for the grant to any person of a licence to drive a hackney carriage, or a private hire vehicle, as the case may be, such a fee as they consider reasonable with a view to recovering the costs of issue and administration and may remit the whole or part of the fee in respect of a private hire vehicle in any case in which they think it appropriate to do so.

(3) The driver of any hackney carriage or of any private hire vehicle licensed by a district council shall at the request of any authorised officer[1] of the council or of any constable produce for inspection his driver's licence either forthwith or—

(*a*) in the case of a request by an authorised officer, at the principal offices of the council before the expiration of the period of five days beginning with the day following that on which the request is made;

(*b*) in the case of a request by a constable, before the expiration of the period aforesaid at any police station which is within the area of the council and is nominated by the driver when the request is made.

(4) If any person without reasonable excuse contravenes the provisions of this section, he shall be guilty of an offence[3].

[Local Government (Miscellaneous Provisions) Act, 1976, s 53.]

1. For meaning of "private hire vehicle", "hackney carriage", and "authorised officer", see s 80(1), post.
2. See note 2 to para **8–18972**, ante.
3. For penalty, see s 76, post.

8–18976 54. Issue of drivers' badges. (1) When granting a driver's licence under section 51 of this Act a district council shall issue a driver's badge in such a form as may from time to time be prescribed by them.

(2)

(*a*) A driver shall at all times when acting in accordance with the driver's licence granted to him wear such badge in such position and manner as to be plainly and distinctly visible.

(*b*) If any person without reasonable excuse contravenes the provisions of this subsection, he shall be guilty of an offence[1].

[Local Government (Miscellaneous Provisions) Act 1976, s 54.]

1. For penalty, see s 76, post.

8–18977 55. Licensing of operators of private hire vehicles. (1) Subject to the provisions of this Part of this Act, a district council shall, on receipt of an application from any person for the grant to that person of a licence to operate private hire vehicles grant to that person an operator's licence:

Provided that a district council shall not grant a licence unless they are satisfied that the applicant is a fit and proper person to hold an operator's licence.

(2) Every licence granted under this section shall remain in force for such period, not being longer than five years, as a district council may specify in the licence.

(3) A district council may attach to the grant of a licence under this section such conditions as they may consider reasonably necessary[1].

(4) Any applicant aggrieved by the refusal of a district council to grant an operator's licence under this section, or by any conditions attached to the grant of such a licence, may appeal[2] to a magistrates' court.

[Local Government (Miscellaneous Provisions) Act 1976, s 55.]

1. See note 2 to s 48(2) at para **8–18970**, ante.
2. See note 5 to para **8–18970**, ante.

8–18978 56. Operators of private hire vehicles. (1) For the purposes of this Part of this Act every contract for the hire of a private hire vehicle licensed under this Part of this Act shall be deemed to be made with the operator who accepted the booking for that vehicle whether or not he himself provided the vehicle.

(2) Every person to whom a licence in force under section 55 of this Act has been granted by a district council shall keep a record in such form as the council may, by condition attached to the grant of the licence, prescribe and shall enter therein, before the commencement of each journey, such particulars of every booking of a private hire vehicle invited or accepted by him, whether by accepting the same from the hirer or by undertaking it at the request of another operator, as the district council may by condition prescribe and shall produce such record on request to any authorised officer[1] of the council or to any constable for inspection.

(3) Every person to whom a licence in force under section 55 of this Act has been granted by a district council shall keep such records as the council may, by conditions attached to the grant of the licence, prescribe of the particulars of any private hire vehicle operated by him and shall produce the same on request to any authorised officer of the council or to any constable for inspection.

(4) A person to whom a licence in force under section 55 of this Act has been granted by a district council shall produce the licence on request to any authorised officer of the council or any constable for inspection.

(5) If any person without reasonable excuse contravenes the provisions of this section, he shall be guilty of an offence[2].

[Local Government (Miscellaneous Provisions) Act 1976, s 56.]

1. For meaning of "authorised officer", see s 80(1), post.
2. For penalty, see s 76, post.

8–18979 57. Power to require applicants to submit information. (1) A district council may require any applicant for a licence under the Act of 1847[1] or under this Part of this Act to submit to them such information as they may reasonably consider necessary to enable them to determine whether the licence should be granted and whether conditions should be attached to any such licence.

(2) Without prejudice to the generality of the foregoing subsection—

(*a*) a district council may require an applicant for a driver's licence[2] in respect of a hackney carriage[2] or a private hire vehicle[2]—

(i) to produce a certificate signed by a registered medical practitioner to the effect that he is physically fit to be the driver of a hackney carriage or a private hire vehicle; and

(ii) whether or not such a certificate has been produced, to submit to examination by a registered medical practitioner selected by the district council as to his physical fitness to be the driver of a hackney carriage or a private hire vehicle;

(*b*) a district council may require an applicant for an operator's licence to submit to them such information as to—

(i) the name and address of the applicant;

(ii) the address or addresses whether within the area of the council or not from which he intends to carry on business in connection with private hire vehicles licensed under this Part of this Act;

(iii) any trade or business activities he has carried on before making the application;

(iv) any previous application he has made for an operator's licence;

(v) the revocation or suspension of any operator's licence previously held by him;

(vi) any convictions recorded against the applicant;

as they may reasonably consider necessary to enable them to determine whether to grant such licence;

(*c*) in addition to the information specified in paragraph (*b*) of this subsection, a district council may require an applicant for an operator's licence[3] to submit to them—

(i) if the applicant is or has been a director or secretary of a company, information as to any convictions recorded against that company at any relevant time; any trade or business activities carried on by that company; any previous application made by that company for an operator's licence; and any revocation or suspension of an operator's licence previously held by that company;

(ii) if the applicant is a company, information as to any convictions recorded against a director or secretary of that company; any trade or business activities carried on by any such director or secretary; any previous application made by any such director or secretary for an operator's licence; and any revocation or suspension of an operator's licence previously held by such director or secretary;

(iii) if the applicant proposes to operate the vehicle in partnership with any other person, information as to any convictions recorded against that person; any trade or business activities carried on by that person; any previous application made by that person for an operator's licence; and any revocation or suspension of an operator's licence previously held by him.

(3) If any person knowingly or recklessly makes a false statement or omits any material particular in giving information under this section, he shall be guilty of an offence[4].

[Local Government (Miscellaneous Provisions) Act 1976, s 57.]

1. "The Act of 1847" means the provisions of the Town Police Clauses Act 1847 with respect to hackney carriages (s 80(1), post). For that Act, see title TOWNS IMPROVEMENTS: TOWN POLICE, post.
2. For meaning of "driver's licence", "hackney carriage" and "private hire vehicle", see s 80(1), post.
3. "Operator's licence" means a licence under section 55 of this Act (s 80(1), post).
4. For penalty, see s 76, post.

8–18980 58. Return of identification plate or disc on revocation or expiry of licence etc. (1) On—

(*a*) the revocation or expiry of a vehicle licence[1] in relation to a hackney carriage[1] or private hire vehicle[1]; or

(*b*) the suspension of a licence under section 68 of this Act;

a district council may by notice require the proprietor of that hackney carriage or private hire vehicle licensed by them to return to them within seven days after the service on him of the notice the plate or disc which—

(*a*) in the case of a hackney carriage, is required to be affixed to the carriage as mentioned in section 38 of the Act of 1847; and

(*b*) in the case of a private hire vehicle, was issued for the vehicle under section 48(5) of this Act.

(2) If any proprietor[1] fails without reasonable excuse to comply with the terms of a notice under subsection (1) of this section—

(*a*) he shall be guilty of an offence and liable on summary conviction to a fine not exceeding **level 3** on the standard scale and to a daily fine[1] not exceeding **£10**; and (*b*) any authorised officer[1] of the council or constable shall be entitled to remove and retain the said plate or disc from the said hackney carriage or private hire vehicle.

[Local Government (Miscellaneous Provisions) Act 1976, s 58, as amended by the Criminal Justice Act 1982, ss 38 and 46.]

1. For meaning of "vehicle licence", "hackney carriage", "private hire vehicle", "proprietor", "daily fine" and "authorised officer", see s 80(1), post.

8–18981 59. Qualifications for drivers of hackney carriages. (1) Notwithstanding anything in the Act of 1847[1], a district council shall not grant a licence to drive a hackney carriage—

(*a*) unless they are satisfied that the applicant is a fit and proper person[2] to hold a driver's licence; or

(*b*) to any person who has not for at least twelve months been authorised to drive a motor car, or is not at the date of the application for a driver's licence so authorised.

(1A) For the purposes of subsection (1) of this section a person is authorised to drive a motor car if—

(*a*) he holds a licence granted under Part III of the Road Traffic Act 1988 (not being a provisional licence) authorising him to drive a motor car, or

(*b*) he is authorised by virtue of section 99A(1) or section 109(1) of that Act to drive in Great Britain a motor car.

(2) Any applicant aggrieved by the refusal of a district council to grant a driver's licence on the ground that he is not a fit and proper person to hold such licence may appeal[3] to a magistrates' court.

[Local Government (Miscellaneous Provisions) Act 1976, s 59 amended by the Road Traffic (Consequential Provisions) Act 1988, Sch 3, the Road Traffic Act 1991, s 47, SI 1996/1974, the Police Act 1997, Sch 9 and SI 1998/1946.]

1. See note 1 to para **8–18979**, ante.

2. A local authority is entitled in considering whether a person is a fit and proper person to hold a licence to have regard to that person's standard of driving, and to adopt, following proper consultation, a policy to apply in the generality of cases that it will not to regard as fit and proper somebody who has not passed the Driving Standards Agency taxi driver test: *Darlington Borough Council v Kaye* [2004] EWHC (Admin) 2836, [2005] RTR 14.

When deciding, exceptionally, to admit spent convictions under s 7(3) of the Rehabilitation of Offenders Act 1974 (in PART III: SENTENCING, ante) the local authority or justices hearing an appeal should first identify the issue before them to which those convictions must relate. The party furnishing the spent convictions should consider objectively whether any are relevant to that issue, and give a broad indication of the nature, age and seriousness of the offence. The justices will then consider whether to admit some or all of the convictions in the light of the issue before them. Once some or all of the convictions have been admitted, the applicant is entitled to be heard and make representations to persuade the local authority or the justices of the irrelevancy of those convictions to the issue before them (*Adamson v Waveney District Council* [1997] 2 All ER 898, 161 JP 787, DC).

3. The procedure shall be in accordance with ss 300–302 of the Public Health Act 1936, title PUBLIC HEALTH, post (s 77, post). See also Magistrates' Courts Rules 1981, r 34, in PART I, ante. The appeal is by way of a complete rehearing (*Darlington Borough Council v Wakefield* (1989) 153 JP 481).

8–18982 60. Suspension and revocation of vehicle licences. (1) Notwithstanding anything in the Act of 1847[1] or in this Part of this Act, a district council may suspend or revoke, or (on application therefor under section 40 of the Act of 1847 or section 48 of this Act, as the case may be) refuse to renew a vehicle licence[2] on any of the following grounds—

(*a*) that the hackney carriage[2] or private hire vehicle[2] is unfit for use as a hackney carriage or private hire vehicle;

(*b*) any offence under, or non-compliance with, the provisions of the Act of 1847 or of this Part of this Act by the operator or driver; or

(*c*) any other reasonable cause[3].

(2) Where a district council suspend, revoke or refuse to renew any licence under this section they shall give to the proprietor of the vehicle notice of the grounds on which the licence has been suspended or revoked or on which they have refused to renew the licence within fourteen days of such suspension, revocation or refusal.

(3) Any proprietor aggrieved by a decision of a district council under this section may appeal[4] to a magistrates' court.

[Local Government (Miscellaneous Provisions) Act 1976, s 60.]

1. See note 1 to para **8–18979**, ante.

2. For meaning of "vehicle licence", "hackney carriage", "private hire vehicle", and see s 80(1), post.

3. "Any other reasonable cause" confers a wide discretion on a council; where there is a pending prosecution there is no need for a conclusion to be reached as to the chance of the licence holder being convicted, there is no requirement before deciding to suspend the licence to hear evidence from witnesses to the alleged offence and hearsay evidence is admissible (*Leeds City Council v Hussain* [2002] EWHC 1145 (Admin), [2003] RTR 199). The impact of a suspension on the driver and the absence of compensation if he is ultimately acquitted of the offence are not relevant considerations; personal circumstances are irrelevant save perhaps in very rare cases to explain or to excuse the conduct of the driver (*Leeds City Council v Hussain*, supra).

4. The procedure shall be in accordance with ss 300–302 of the Public Health Act 1936, title PUBLIC HEALTH, post (s 77, post). See also Magistrates' Courts Rules 1981, r 34, in PART I: MAGISTRATES' COURTS, PROCEDURE, ante.

8–18983 61. Suspension and revocation of drivers' licences. (1) Notwithstanding any thing in the Act of 1847[1] or in this Part of this Act, a district council may suspend or revoke or (on application therefor under section 46 of the Act of 1847 or section 51 of this Act, as the case may be) refuse to renew the licence of a driver of a hackney carriage or a private hire vehicle on any of the following grounds—

(*a*) that he has since the grant of the licence—

(i) been convicted of an offence involving dishonesty, indecency or violence; or

(ii) been convicted of an offence under or has failed to comply with the provisions of the Act of 1847 or of this Part of this Act; or

(*b*) any other reasonable cause[2].

(2)

(*a*) Where a district council suspend, revoke or refuse to renew any licence under this section they shall give to the driver notice of the grounds on which the licence has been suspended or revoked or on which they have refused to renew such licence within fourteen days of such suspension, revocation or refusal and the driver shall on demand return to the district council the driver's badge issued to him in accordance with section 54 of this Act.

(*b*) If any person without reasonable excuse contravenes the provisions of this section he shall be guilty of an offence and liable on summary conviction to a fine not exceeding **level 1** on the standard scale.

(3) Any driver aggrieved by a decision of a district council under this section may appeal[3] to a magistrates' court.

[Local Government (Miscellaneous Provisions) Act 1976, s 61, as amended by the Criminal Justice Act 1982, ss 38 and 46.]

1. See note 1 to para **8–18979**, ante.
2. See note to s 60(1)(*c*), supra.
3. See note 2 to para **8–18981**, ante. On the hearing of an appeal under this section justices should make findings of fact and record reasons for their decision and the appellant is entitled to be so informed (*R v Burton-upon-Trent Justices, ex p Hussain* (1996) 160 JP 808).

8–18984 62. Suspension and revocation of operators' licences. (1) Notwithstanding anything in this Part of this Act a district council may suspend or revoke, or (on application therefor under section 55 of this Act) refuse to renew an operator's licence[1] on any of the following grounds—

(*a*) any offence under, or non-compliance with, the provisions of this Part of this Act;

(*b*) any conduct on the part of the operator which appears to the district council to render him unfit to hold an operator's licence;

(*c*) any material change since the licence was granted in any of the circumstances of the operator on the basis of which the licence was granted; or

(*d*) any other reasonable cause.

(2) Where a district council suspend, revoke or refuse to renew any licence under this section they shall give to the operator notice of the grounds on which the licence has been suspended or revoked or on which they have refused to renew such licence within fourteen days of such suspension, revocation or refusal.

(3) Any operator aggrieved by a decision of a district council under this section may appeal[2] to a magistrates' court.

[Local Government (Miscellaneous Provisions) Act 1976, s 62.]

1. "Operator's licence" means a licence under s 55 of this Act (s 80(1), post).
2. See note 2 to para **8–18981**, ante. On the hearing of an appeal under this section justices should make findings of fact and record reasons for their decision and the appellant is entitled to be so informed (*R v Burton-upon-Trent Justices, ex p Hussain* (1996) 160 JP 808).

8–18985 63. Stands for hackney carriages. (1) For the purposes of their functions under the Act of 1847[1], a district council may from time to time appoint stands for hackney carriages[2] for the whole or any part of a day in any highway in the district which is maintainable at the public expense and, with the consent of the owner, on any land in the district which does not form part of a highway so maintainable and may from time to time vary the number of hackney carriages permitted to be at each stand.

(2) Before appointing any stand for hackney carriages or varying the number of hackney carriages to be at each stand in exercise of the powers of this section, a district council shall give notice to the chief officer of police for the police area in which the stand is situated and shall also give public notice of the proposal by advertisement in at least one local newspaper circulating in the district and shall

take into consideration any objections or representations in respect of such proposal which may be made to them in writing within twenty-eight days of the first publication of such notice.

(3) Nothing in this section shall empower a district council to appoint any such stand—

(*a*) so as unreasonably to prevent access to any premises;

(*b*) so as to impede the use of any points authorised to be used in connection with a road service licence or PSV operator's licence granted under the Public Passenger Vehicles Act 1981, as points for the taking up or setting down of passengers, or in such a position as to interfere unreasonably with access to any station or depot of any passenger road transport operators, except with the consent of those operators;

(*c*) on any highway except with the consent of the highway authority;

and in deciding the position of stands a district council shall have regard to the position of any bus stops for the time being in use.

(4) Any hackney carriage byelaws[3] for fixing stands for hackney carriages which were made by a district council before the date when this section comes into force in the area of the council and are in force immediately before that date shall cease to have effect, but any stands fixed by such byelaws shall be deemed to have been appointed under this section.

(5) The power to appoint stands for hackney carriages under subsection (1) of this section shall include power to revoke such appointment and to alter any stand so appointed and the expressions "appointing" and "appoint" in subsections (2) and (3) of this section shall be construed accordingly.

[Local Government (Miscellaneous Provisions) Act 1976, s 63, as amended by the Transport Act 1980, Sch 5, Part II and the Public Passenger Vehicles Act 1981, Sch 7.]

1. "The Act of 1847" means the provisions of the Town Police Clauses Act 1847 with respect to hackney carriages (s 80(1), post). For that Act, see title TOWNS IMPROVEMENTS: TOWN POLICE, post.
2. For meaning of "hackney carriage", see s 80(1), post.
3. For meaning of "hackney carriage byelaws", see s 80(1), post.

8–18986 64. Prohibition of other vehicles on hackney carriage stands. (1) No person shall cause or permit any vehicle other than a hackney carriage to wait on any stand for hackney carriages during any period for which that stand has been appointed, or is deemed to have been appointed, by a district council under the provisions of section 63 of this Act.

(2) Notice of the prohibition in this section shall be indicated by such traffic signs as may be prescribed or authorised for the purpose by the Secretary of State in pursuance of his powers under section 64 of the Road Traffic Regulation Act 1984[1].

(3) If any person without reasonable excuse contravenes the provisions of this section, he shall be guilty of an offence[2].

(4) In any proceedings under this section against the driver of a public service vehicle it shall be a defence to show that, by reason of obstruction to traffic or for other compelling reason, he caused his vehicle to wait on a stand or part thereof and that he caused or permitted his vehicle so to wait only for so long as was reasonably necessary for the taking up or setting down of passengers.

[Local Government (Miscellaneous Provisions) Act 1976, s 64, as amended by the Road Traffic Regulation Act 1984, Sch 13.]

1. See PART VII: TRANSPORT, title ROAD TRAFFIC.
2. For penalty, see s 76, post.

8–18987 65. *Fixing of fares for hackney carriages.*

8–18988 66. Fares for long journeys. (1) No person, being the driver of a hackney carriage[1] licensed by a district council, and undertaking for any hirer a journey ending outside the district[1] and in respect of which no fare and no rate of fare was agreed before the hiring was effected, shall require for such journey a fare greater than that indicated on the taximeter[1] with which the hackney carriage is equipped or, if it is not equipped with a taximeter, greater than that which, if the current byelaws fixing rates or fares and in force in the district in pursuance of section 68 of the Act of 1847[2] or, as the case may be, the current table of fares in force within the district in pursuance of section 65 of this Act had applied to the journey, would have been authorised for the journey by the byelaws or table.

(2) If any person knowingly contravenes the provisions of this section, he shall be guilty of an offence[3].

[Local Government (Miscellaneous Provisions) Act 1976, s 66.]

1. For meaning of "hackney carriage", "district" and "taximeter", see s 80(1), post.
2. See note 1 to para **8–18985**, ante.
3. For penalty, see s 76, post.

8–18989 67. Hackney carriages used for private hire. (1) No hackney carriage[1] shall be used in the district[1] under a contract or purported contract for private hire except at a rate of fares or charges not greater than that fixed by the byelaws or table mentioned in section 66 of this Act, and, when any such hackney carriage is so used, the fare or charge shall be calculated from the point in the district at which the hirer commences his journey.

(2) Any person who knowingly contravenes this section shall be guilty of an offence[2].

(3) In subsection (1) of this section "contract" means—

(*a*) a contract made otherwise than while the relevant hackney carriage is plying for hire in the district or waiting at a place in the district which, when the contract is made, is a stand for hackney carriages appointed by the district council under section 63 of this Act; and

(*b*) a contract made, otherwise than with or through the driver of the relevant hackney carriage, while it is so plying or waiting.

[Local Government (Miscellaneous Provisions) Act 1976, s 67.]

1. For meaning of "hackney carriage", and "district" see s 80(1), post.
2. For penalty, see s 76, post.

8–18990 68. Fitness of hackney carriages and private hire vehicles. Any authorised officer[1] of the council in question or any constable shall have power at all reasonable times to inspect and test, for the purpose of ascertaining its fitness, any hackney carriage[1] or private hire vehicle[1] licensed by a district council, or any taximeter[1] affixed to such a vehicle, and if he is not satisfied as to the fitness of the hackney carriage or private hire vehicle or as to the accuracy of its taximeter he may by notice in writing require the proprietor[1] of the hackney carriage or private hire vehicle to make it or its taximeter available for further inspection and testing at such reasonable time and place as may be specified in the notice and suspend the vehicle licence[1] until such time as such authorised officer or constable is so satisfied:

Provided that, if the authorised officer or constable is not so satisfied before the expiration of a period of two months, the said licence shall, by virtue of this section, be deemed to have been revoked and subsections (2) and (3) of section 60[2] of this Act shall apply with any necessary modifications.

[Local Government (Miscellaneous Provisions) Act 1976, s 68.]

1. For meaning of "authorised officer", "hackney carriage", "private hire vehicle", "proprietor", "taximeter", and "vehicle licence", see s 80(1), post.
2. Ante.

8–18991 69. Prolongation of journeys. (1) No person being the driver of a hackney carriage[1] or of a private hire vehicle[1] licensed by a district council shall without reasonable cause unnecessarily prolong, in distance or in time, the journey for which the hackney carriage or private hire vehicle has been hired.

(2) If any person contravenes the provisions of this section, he shall be guilty of an offence[2].

[Local Government (Miscellaneous Provisions) Act 1976, s 69.]

1. For meaning of "hackney carriage", and "private hire vehicle", see s 80(1), post.
2. For penalty, see s 76, post.

8–18992 70. *Fees*[1] *for vehicle and operators' licences.*

1. A local authority is entitled to charge fees for inspections at the time they are carried out and whether or not the vehicle passed the inspection. Furthermore it is lawful for there to be a graduated scale of fees where further tests were required and an additional fee on grant of the licence (*Kelly v Liverpool City Council* [2003] EWCA Civ 197, [2003] 2 All ER 772, [2003] RTR 236).

8–18993 71. Taximeters. (1) Nothing in this Act shall require any private hire vehicle[1] to be equipped with any form of taximeter[1] but no private hire vehicle so equipped shall be used for hire in a controlled district[1] unless such taximeter has been tested and approved by or on behalf of the district council for the district or any other district council by which a vehicle licence[1] in force for the vehicle was issued.

(2) Any person who—

(*a*) tampers with any seal on any taximeter without lawful excuse; or

(*b*) alters any taximeter with intent to mislead; or

(*c*) knowingly causes or permits a vehicle of which he is the proprietor to be used in contravention of subsection (1) of this section,

shall be guilty of an offence[2].

[Local Government (Miscellaneous Provisions) Act 1976, s 71.]

1. For meaning of "controlled district", "private hire vehicle", "taximeter", and "vehicle licence", see s 80(1), post.
2. For penalty, see s 76, post.

8–18994 72. Offences due to fault of other person etc. (1) Where an offence by any person under this Part of this Act is due to the act or default of another person, then, whether proceedings are taken against the first-mentioned person or not, that other person may be charged with and convicted of that offence, and shall be liable on conviction to the same punishment as might have been imposed on the first-mentioned person if he had been convicted of the offence.

(2) Section 44(3)[1] of this Act shall apply to an offence under this Part of the Act as it applies to an offence under Part I of this Act.

[Local Government (Miscellaneous Provisions) Act 1976, s 72.]

1. Ante.

8–18995 **73. Obstruction of authorised officer.** (1) Any person who—

(*a*) wilfully obstructs an authorised officer[1] or constable acting in pursuance of this Part of this Act or the Act of 1847[2]; or

(*b*) without reasonable excuse fails to comply with any requirement properly made to him by such officer or constable under this Part of this Act; or

(*c*) without reasonable cause fails to give such an officer or constable so acting any other assistance or information which he may reasonably require of such person for the purpose of the performance of his functions under this Part of this Act or the Act of 1847;

shall be guilty of an offence[3].

(2) If any person, in giving any such information as is mentioned in the preceding subsection, makes any statement which he knows to be false, he shall be guilty of an offence[3].

[Local Government (Miscellaneous Provisions) Act 1976, s 73.]

1. For meaning of "authorised officer", see s 80(1), post.
2. "The Act of 1847" means the provisions of the Town Police Clauses Act 1847 with respect to hackney carriages (s 80(1), post). For that Act, see title TOWNS IMPROVEMENTS: TOWN POLICE, post.
3. For penalty, see s 76, post.

8–18996 **74.** *Saving for certain businesses.*

8–18997 **75. Saving for certain vehicles etc.** (1) Nothing in this Part of this Act shall—

(*a*) apply to a vehicle used for bringing passengers or goods within a controlled district[1] in pursuance of a contract for the hire of the vehicle made outside the district if the vehicle is not made available for hire within the district;

(*b*) apply to a vehicle used only for carrying passengers for hire or reward under a contract[2] for the hire of the vehicle for a period of not less than seven days;

(*c*) apply to a vehicle while it is being used in connection with a funeral or a vehicle used wholly or mainly, by a person carrying on the business of a funeral director, for the purpose of funerals;

(*cc*) apply to a vehicle while it is being used in connection with a wedding;

(*d*) require the display of any plate, disc or notice in or on any private hire vehicle licensed by a council under this Part of this Act during such period that such vehicle is used for carrying passengers for hire or reward—

(i) *Repealed*;

(ii) under a contract for the hire of the vehicle for a period of not less than 24 hours.

(2) Paragraphs (*a*), (*b*) and (*c*) of section 46(1) of this Act shall not apply to the use or driving of a vehicle or to the employment of a driver of a vehicle while the vehicle is used as a private hire vehicle in a controlled district if a licence issued under section 48 of this Act by the council whose area consists of or includes another controlled district is then in force for the vehicle and a driver's licence issued by such a council is then in force for the driver of the vehicle.

(2A) Where a vehicle is being used as a taxi or private hire car, paragraphs (*a*), (*b*) and (*c*) of section 46(1) of this Act shall not apply to the use or driving of the vehicle or the employment of a person to drive it if—

(*a*) a licence issued under section 10 of the Civic Government (Scotland) Act 1982 for its use as a taxi or, as the case may be, private hire car is then in force, and

(*b*) the driver holds a licence issued under section 13 of that Act for the driving of taxis or, as the case may be, private hire cars.

In this subsection "private hire car" and "taxi" have the same meaning as in sections 10 to 22 of the Civic Government (Scotland) Act 1982.

(2B) Paragraphs (*a*), (*b*) and (*c*) of section 46(1) of this Act shall not apply to the use or driving of a vehicle, or to the employment of a driver of a vehicle, if—

(*a*) a London PHV licence issued under section 7 of the Private Hire Vehicles (London) Act 1998 is in force in relation to that vehicle; and

(*b*) the driver of the vehicle holds a London PHV driver's licence issued under section 13 of that Act.]

(3) Where a licence under section 48 of this Act is in force for a vehicle, the council which issued the licence may, by a notice in writing given to the proprietor of the vehicle, provide that paragraph

(*a*) of subsection (6) of that section shall not apply to the vehicle on any occasion specified in the notice or shall not so apply while the notice is carried in the vehicle; and on any occasion on which by virtue of this subsection that paragraph does not apply to a vehicle section 54(2)(*a*) of this Act shall not apply to the driver of the vehicle.

[Local Government (Miscellaneous Provisions) Act 1976, s 75, as amended by the Civic Government (Scotland) Act 1982, s 16, the Transport Act 1985, Sch 7 and the Private Hire Vehicles (London) Act 1998, Sch 1.]

1. For meaning of "controlled district", see s 80(1), post. Section 75(1)(*a*) is concerned with the vehicle which brings passengers into a controlled district; it is not concerned with a vehicle which makes an initial journey within the controlled district; see *Braintree District Council v Howard* [1993] RTR 193.

2. The burden of establishing this exception by reason of a contract for hire within the terms of this paragraph is on the defendant on the balance of probabilities; see *Leeds City Council v Azam and Fazi* (1988) 153 JP 157, [1989] RTR 66. The contract must relate to a particular vehicle, but that vehicle may return to the proprietor's premises when not in use, and there is no need for there to be a fixed fee (*Pitts v Lewis* (1988) 153 JP 220, [1989] RTR 71n). In *Crawley Borough Council v Ovenden* (1991) 156 JP 877 there was not a written contract but an implied contract for a self-employed driver paid by monthly invoice; in the absence of an agreed minimum notice period the exemption did not apply.

8–18998 76. Penalties. Any person who commits an offence against any of the provisions of this Part of this Act in respect of which no penalty is expressly provided shall be liable on summary conviction to a fine not exceeding **level 3** on the standard scale.

[Local Government (Miscellaneous Provisions) Act 1976, s 76, as amended by the Criminal Justice Act 1982, ss 38 and 46.]

8–18999 77. Appeals. (1) Sections 300 to 302 of the Act of 1936[1], which relate to appeals, shall have effect as if this Part of this Act were part of that Act.

(2) If any requirement, refusal or other decision of a district council against which a right of appeal is conferred by this Act—

(*a*) involves the execution of any work or the taking of any action; or

(*b*) makes it unlawful for any person to carry on a business which he was lawfully carrying on up to the time of the requirement, refusal or decision;

then, until the time for appealing has expired, or, when an appeal is lodged, until the appeal is disposed of or withdrawn or fails for want of prosecution—

(i) no proceedings shall be taken in respect of any failure to execute the work, or take the action; and

(ii) that person may carry on that business.

[Local Government (Miscellaneous Provisions) Act 1976, s 77.]

1. See title PUBLIC HEALTH, post.

8–19000 78. Application of provisions of Act of 1936. Subsection (1) of section 283[1] and section 304[2] of the Act of 1936 shall have effect as if references therein to that Act included a reference to this Part of this Act.

[Local Government (Miscellaneous Provisions) Act 1976, s 78.]

1. Section 283(1) of the Public Health Act 1936 provides that all notices, etc shall be in writing.

2. Section 304 of the Public Health Act 1936 provides that judges and justices shall not be disqualified by liability to pay rates.

8–19001 79. Authentication of licences. Notwithstanding anything in section 43 of the Act of 1847, any vehicle licence or driver's licence granted by a district council under that Act, or any licence granted by a district council under this Part of this Act, shall not be required to be under the common seal of the district council, but if not so sealed shall be signed by an authorised officer of the council.

[Local Government (Miscellaneous Provisions) Act 1976, s 79.]

8–19002 80. Interpretation of Part II. (1) In this Part of this Act, unless the subject or context otherwise requires—

"the Act of 1847" means the provisions of the Town Police Clauses Act 1847 with respect to hackney carriages;

"the Act of 1936" means the Public Health Act 1936;

"authorised officer" means any officer of a district council authorised in writing by the council for the purposes of this Part of this Act;

"contravene" includes fail to comply;

"controlled district" means any area for which this Part of this Act is in force by virtue of—

(*a*) a resolution passed by a district council under section 45 of this Act; or

(*b*) section 255(4) of the Greater London Authority Act 1999;

"daily fine" means a fine for each day during which an offence continues after conviction thereof;

"the district", in relation to a district council in whose area the provisions of this Part of this Act are in force, means—

(*a*) if those provisions are in force throughout the area of the council, that area; and

(*b*) if those provisions are in force for part only of the area of the council, that part of that area;

"driver's badge" means, in relation to the driver of a hackney carriage, any badge issued by a district council under byelaws made under section 68 of the Act of 1847 and, in relation to the driver of a private hire vehicle, any badge issued by a district council under section 54 of this Act;

"driver's licence" means, in relation to the driver of a hackney carriage, a licence under section 46 of the Act of 1847 and, in relation to the driver of a private hire vehicle, a licence under section 51 of this Act;

"hackney carriage" has the same meaning as in the Act of 1847;

"hackney carriage byelaws" means the byelaws for the time being in force in the controlled district in question relating to hackney carriages;

"London cab" means a vehicle which is a hackney carriage within the meaning of the Metropolitan Public Carriage Act 1869;

"operate" means in the course of business to make provision for the invitation[1] or acceptance of bookings for a private hire vehicle[2];

"operator's licence" means a licence under section 55 of this Act;

"private hire vehicle" means a motor vehicle constructed or adapted to seat fewer than nine passengers, other than a hackney carriage or public service vehicle or a London cab or tramcar, which is provided for hire[3] with the services of a driver for the purpose of carrying passengers;

"proprietor" includes a part-proprietor and, in relation to a vehicle which is the subject of a hiring agreement or hire-purchase agreement, means the person in possession of the vehicle under that agreement;

"public service vehicle" has the same meaning as in the Public Passenger Vehicles Act 1981;

"taximeter" means any device for calculating the fare to be charged in respect of any journey in a hackney carriage or private hire vehicle by reference to the distance travelled or time elapsed since the start of the journey, or a combination of both; and

"vehicle licence" means in relation to a hackney carriage a licence under sections 37 to 45 of the Act of 1847 in relation to a London cab in a licence under section 6 of the Metropolitan Public Carriage Act 1869 and in relation to a private hire vehicle means a licence under section 48 of this Act.

(2) In this Part of this Act references to a licence, in connection with a controlled district, are references to a licence issued by the council whose area consists of or includes that district, and "licensed" shall be construed accordingly.

(3) Except where the context otherwise requires, any reference in this Part of this Act to any enactment shall be construed as a reference to that enactment as applied, extended, amended or varied by, or by virtue of, any subsequent enactment including this Act.

(4) In this Part of this Act, except where the context otherwise requires, references to a district council shall, in relation to Wales, be construed as references to a county council or county borough council.

[Local Government (Miscellaneous Provisions) Act 1976, s 80, as amended by the Transport Act 1980, Sch 5, Part II, the Public Passenger Vehicles Act 1981, Sch 7, the Transport Act 1985, Sch 7, the Road Traffic (Consequential Provisions) Act 1988, Sch 1, the Transport and Works Act 1992, s 62, SI 1996/3071 and SI 2000/412.]

---

1. The determining factor is not whether any individual booking was accepted, let alone where it was accepted, but whether the defendant had in the area in question made provision for the invitation or acceptance of bookings in general (*Windsor and Maidenhead Royal Borough Council v Khan)* [1994] RTR 87).

2. It would seem that activity taking place outside an operator's premises may come within the definition of "operate"; see *Adur District Council v Fry* [1997] RTR 257.

3. The words "provided for hire" relate to the nature of the vehicle rather than to the nature of the activity (*Benson v Boyce* [1997] RTR 226).

Local Government, Planning and Land Act 1980

(1980 c 65)

PART XVI[1]
URBAN DEVELOPMENT

Highways

8–19110 **157B. Traffic regulation orders for private streets.** (1) Where—

(*a*) an urban development corporation[2] submits to the Secretary of State that an order under this section should be made in relation to any road in the urban development area[2] which is a private street; and (*b*) it appears to the Secretary of State that the traffic authority do not intend to make an order under section 1 or, as the case may be, section 6 of the Road Traffic Regulation Act 1984 (orders concerning traffic regulation) in relation to the road,

the Secretary of State may by order under this section make in relation to the road any such provision as he might have made by order under that section if he had been the traffic authority.

(2) The Road Traffic Regulation Act 1984 applies to an order under this section as it applies to an order made by the Secretary of State under section 1 or, as the case may be, section 6 of that Act in relation to a road for which he is the traffic authority.

(3) In this section—

"private street" has the same meaning as in Part XI of the Highways Act 1980;

"road" and "traffic authority" have the same meanings as in the Road Traffic Regulation Act 1984.

(4) This section does not extend to Scotland.

[Local Government, Planning and Land Act 1980, s 157B inserted by the Leasehold Reform, Housing and Urban Development Act 1993, s 178.]

---

1. Part XVI contains ss 134–172. For the purposes of Pt XVI of this Act, the holder of a licence under s 6(1) of the Electricity Act 1989 shall be deemed to be a statutory undertaker and his undertaking a statutory undertaking (Electricity Act 1989, Sch 16, para 1).

2. For the meaning of "urban development area" and "urban development corporation", see ss 134 and 135 respectively.

Miscellaneous

8–19111 **167. Power to survey land etc.** (1) A person to whom this subsection applies may at any reasonable time—

(*a*) survey any land, or estimate its value, in connection with a proposal by an urban development corporation[1] to acquire the land compulsorily;

(*b*) for the purpose of surveying, or estimating the value of, any land in pursuance of paragraph (*a*) above, enter on the land and other land.

(2) Subsection (1) above applies—

(*a*) to a person authorised in writing by the urban development corporation; and

(*b*) to an officer of the Valuation Office.

(3) The power to survey land conferred by subsection (1) above includes power for a person to whom that subsection applies by virtue of subsection (2)(*a*) above to search and bore on and in the land for the purpose of ascertaining the nature of the subsoil or whether minerals are present in the subsoil, and the power to enter on land conferred by that subsection includes power for such a person to place and leave, on or in the land, apparatus for use in connection with the survey in question and to remove the apparatus.

(4) A person authorised by an urban development corporation to enter on land in pursuance of subsection (1) above—

(*a*) shall, if so required before or after entering on the land, produce evidence of his authority to enter;

(*b*) may take with him on to the land such other persons and such equipment as are necessary for the survey in question;

(*c*) shall not (if the land is occupied) demand admission to the land as of right unless notice of the intended entry has been served by the corporation on the occupier not less than 28 days before the demand;

(*d*) shall (if the land is unoccupied when he enters or the occupier is then temporarily absent) leave the land as effectually secured against trespassers as he found it;

(*e*) shall not place or leave apparatus on or in the land or remove apparatus from the land—

(i) unless notice of his intention to do so has been served by the corporation on an owner of the land, and if the land is occupied on the occupier, not less than 28 days before he does so, and

(ii) if the land is held by a local authority or statutory undertakers[2] who within that period serve on the corporation a notice stating that they object to the placing or leaving or removal of the apparatus on the ground that to do so would be seriously detrimental to the performance of any of their functions or, as the case may be, the carrying on of their undertakings unless he has a written Ministerial authorisation to do so;

(*f*) shall not search or bore on or in the land which is the subject of the survey in question if the land is held by a local authority or statutory undertakers—

(i) unless notice of his intention to do so has been served by the corporation on the authority or undertakers not less than 28 days before he does so, and

(ii) if within that period the authority or undertakers serve on the corporation a notice stating that they object to the searching or boring on the ground that to do so would be seriously detrimental to the performance of any of their functions or, as the case may be, the carrying on of their undertaking, unless he has a written Ministerial authorisation to do so.

(5) In subsection (4) above "Ministerial authorisation" means—

(*a*) in relation to land held by a local authority, the authorisation of the Secretary of State; and

(*b*) in relation to land held by statutory undertakers, the authorisation of the Secretary of State and the appropriate Minister.

(6) In exercising the powers of this section to survey land held by a local authority or statutory undertakers a person to whom subsection (1) above applies shall comply with all reasonable conditions imposed by the authority or undertakers with regard to the entry on, surveying of, searching or boring on or in the land, or placing or leaving on, or removal of apparatus from the land.

(7) Where it is proposed to search or bore in pursuance of this section in a street within the meaning of Part III of the New Roads and Street Works Act 1991 or, in Scotland, a road within the meaning of Part IV of that Act—

(*a*) section 55 or 114 of that Act (notice of starting date of works), so far as it requires notice to be given to a person having apparatus in the street or road which is likely to be affected by the works,

(*b*) section 69 or 128 of that Act (requirements to be complied with where works likely to affect another person's apparatus in the street or road), and

(*c*) section 82 or 141 of that Act (liability for damage or loss caused),

have effect in relation to the searching or boring as if they were street works within the meaning of the said Part III or (*Scotland*).

(8) If, in connection with such a proposal of a corporation as is mentioned in subsection (1)(*a*) above, a person interested in any land suffers damage in consequence of the exercise of a power conferred by subsection (1) or (4)(*b*) above or a failure to perform the duty imposed by subsection (4)(*d*) above in respect of the land, he shall be entitled to recover compensation for the damage from the corporation.

(9) Any dispute as to a person's entitlement to compensation in pursuance of subsection (8) above or as to the amount of the compensation shall be determined by the Lands Tribunal, and sections 2(2) to (5) and 4 of the Land Compensation Act 1961 (which relate to the conduct of certain proceedings before the Tribunal and costs) shall with the necessary modifications apply in relation to the determination by the Tribunal of such a dispute.

(10) If a person—

(*a*) wilfully obstructs another person in the exercise of a power conferred on the other person by subsection (1) or (4)(*b*) above; or

(*b*) while another person is on any land in pursuance of the said subsection (4)(*b*), wilfully obstructs him in doing things connected with the survey in question; or

(*c*) removes or otherwise interferes with apparatus left on or in land in pursuance of this section,

he shall be guilty of an offence and liable on summary conviction to a fine not exceeding **level 3** on the standard scale.

(11) If a person who has entered on any land in pursuance of this section discloses to another person information obtained by him there about a manufacturing process or trade secret, then, unless the disclosure is made in the course of performing his duty in connection with the purposes for which he was authorised to enter on the land, he shall be guilty of an offence and liable[3], on summary conviction, to a **fine** not exceeding the statutory maximum or, on conviction on indictment, to imprisonment for a term not exceeding **2 years** or a **fine** or both.

(12) It is hereby declared that references to surveying in this section include references to surveying from the air.

(13) *Scotland.*

(14) In this section—

"the Valuation Office" means the Valuation Office of the Inland Revenue Department.

(15) *Repealed.*

[Local Government, Planning and Land Act 1980, s 167, as amended by the Criminal Justice Act 1982, s 46, the New Roads and Street Works Act 1991, Sch 8 and the Statute Law (Repeals) Act 1993, Sch 1.]

1. For meaning of "urban development corporation", see s 135.
2. For meaning of "statutory undertakers", see s 170, post.
3. For procedure in respect of this offence which is triable either way, see the Magistrates' Courts Act 1980, ss 17A–21, in PART I: MAGISTRATES' COURTS, PROCEDURE, ante.

8–19112 **168. Service of notices.** (1) This section has effect in relation to any notice required or authorised by this Part of this Act to be served on any person by an urban development corporation.

(2) Any such notice may be served on the person in question either by delivering it to him, or by leaving it at his proper address, or by sending it by post to him at that address.

(3) Any such notice may—

(*a*) in the case of a body corporate, be given to or served on the secretary or clerk of that body;

(*b*) in the case of a partnership, be given to or served on a partner or a person having the control or management of the partnership business.

(4) For the purposes of this section and of section 7 of the Interpretation Act 1978 (service of documents by post) in its application to this section, the proper address of any person to or on whom a notice is to be given or served shall be his last known address, except that—

(*a*) in the case of a body corporate or its secretary or clerk, it shall be the address of the registered or principal office of that body;

(*b*) in the case of a partnership or a person having the control or management of the partnership business, it shall be that of the principal office of the partnership;

and for the purposes of this subsection the principal office of a company registered outside the United Kingdom or of a partnership carrying on business outside the United Kingdom shall be its principal office within the United Kingdom.

(5) If the person to be given or served with any notice mentioned in subsection (1) above has specified an address within the United Kingdom other than his proper address within the meaning of subsection (4) above as the one at which he or someone on his behalf will accept documents of the same description as that notice, that address shall also be treated for the purposes of this section and section 7 of the Interpretation Act 1978 as his proper address.

(6) If the name or address of any owner, lessee or occupier of land to or on whom any notice mentioned in subsection (1) above is to be served cannot after reasonable inquiry be ascertained, the document may be served either by leaving it in the hands of a person who is or appears to be resident or employed on the land or by leaving it conspicuously affixed to some building or object on the land.

[Local Government, Planning and Land Act 1980, s 168.]

8–19113 170. Interpretation; statutory undertakers etc. (1) In this Part of this Act, unless the context otherwise requires, "statutory undertakers"[1] means—

(*a*) persons authorised by any enactment to carry on any railway, light railway, tramway, road transport, water transport, canal, inland navigation, dock, harbour, pier or lighthouse undertaking, or any undertaking for the supply of hydraulic power,

(*b*) the Civil Aviation Authority, a universal service provider in connection with the provision of a universal postal service and any other authority, body or undertakers which by virtue of any enactment are to be treated as statutory undertakers for any of the purposes of the 1990 Act or of the 1972 Act,

(*c*) any other authority, body or undertakers specified in an order made by the Secretary of State under this paragraph, and

(*d*) any wholly-owned subsidiary as defined by section 736 of the Companies Act 1985) of any person, authority, body or undertakers mentioned in paragraphs (*a*) and (*b*) above or specified in an order made under paragraph (*c*) above,

and "statutory undertaking" shall be construed accordingly.

(2) In section 141 above "statutory undertakers" also includes British Shipbuilders, and any wholly-owned subsidiary as defined by section 736 of the Companies Act 1985) of any of them.

(2A) The undertaking of a universal service provider so far as relating to the provision of a universal postal service shall be taken to be his statutory undertaking for the purposes of this Part of this Act; and references in this Part of this Act to his undertaking shall be construed accordingly.

(2B) In subsection (1) and (2A) above "universal service provider" has the same meaning as in the Postal Services Act 2000; and references to the provision of a universal postal service shall be construed in accordance with that Act.

(3) In this Part of this Act the expression "the appropriate Minister", and any reference to the Secretary of State and the appropriate Minister—

(*a*) in relation to any statutory undertakers who are also statutory undertakers for the purposes of any provision of Part XI of the 1990 Act or Part XI of the 1972 Act, shall have the same meanings as in the said Part XI, and

(*b*) in relation to any other statutory undertakers, shall have the meanings given by an order made by the Secretary of State under this subsection.

(4) If, in relation to anything required or authorised to be done under this Part of this Act, any question arises as to which Minister is the appropriate Minister in relation to any statutory undertakers; that question shall be determined by the Treasury.

(5) An order made under this section shall be made by statutory instrument subject to annulment in pursuance of a resolution of either House of Parliament.

[Local Government, Planning and Land Act 1980, s 170, as amended by the Companies Consolidation (Consequential Provisions) Act 1985, Sch 2, the Airports Act 1986, Sch 6, the Gas Act 1986 Sch 9, the Coal Industry Act 1987, Sch 1, the British Steel Act 1988, Sch 2, the Water Act 1989, Sch 25, the Companies Act 1989, Sch 18, the Electricity Act 1989, Sch 18, the Planning (Consequential Provisions) Act 1990, Sch 2, the British Technology Group Act 1991, Sch 2, the Coal Industry Act 1994, Schs 9 and 11 and SI 2001/1149.]

---

1. The Environment Agency, every water undertaker and every sewerage undertaker is deemed to be a statutory undertaker for the purposes of Part XVI of this Act (Water Act 1989, Sch 25, para 1).

8–19114 **171. Interpretation: general.** In this Part of this Act, except in so far as the context otherwise requires—

"ecclesiastical property" means land belonging to an ecclesiastical benefice, or being or forming part of a church subject to the jurisdiction of a bishop, of any diocese or the site of such a church, or being or forming part of a burial ground subject to such jurisdiction;

"the 1981 Act" means the Acquisition of Land Act 1981;

"the 1947 Act" means the Acquisition of Land (Authorisation Procedure) (Scotland) Act 1947;

"the 1990 Act" means the Town and Country Planning Act 1990;

"the 1972 Act" means the Town and Country Planning (Scotland) Act 1972;

"urban development area" means so much of an area designated by an order under subsection (1) of section 134 above as is not excluded from it by an order under subsection (3A) of that section;

"urban development corporation" means a corporation established by an order under section 135 above.

[Local Government, Planning and Land Act 1980, s 171, as amended by the Acquisition of Land Act 1981, Sch 4, the Planning (Consequential Provisions) Act 1990, Sch 2 and the Leasehold Reform, Housing and Urban Development Act 1993, s 179(5).]

PART XIX[1]

MISCELLANEOUS AND SUPPLEMENTARY

Pleasure Boats

8–19115 **185. Pleasure boats bye laws.** (1) Subject to the provisions of this section, any of the following authorities, namely—

(i) a district council;
(ii) a London borough council;
(iii) the Common Council of the City of London;
(iv) the council of a Welsh county or county borough,

may make byelaws—

(*a*) for regulating the numbering and naming of pleasure boats and vessels which are let for hire to the public and the mooring places for such boats and vessels; and
(*b*) for fixing the qualifications of the boatmen or other persons in charge of such boats or vessels; and
(*c*) for securing their good and orderly conduct while in charge.

(2) No authority mentioned in subsection (1) above shall have power to make byelaws under that subsection in relation to pleasure boats or vessels operating—

(*a*) on any water owned or managed by the British Waterways Board;
(*b*) on any inland waters (within the meaning of the Water Resources Act 1991) in respect of which the National Rivers Authority may make byelaws by virtue of paragraph 1 of Schedule 25 to that Act;
(*c*) subject to subsection (3) below, on any canal or other inland navigation which a navigation authority, as defined in section 135(1) of the Water Resources Act 1963[2], are required or empowered to manage or maintain under any enactment; or
(*d*) on any harbour maintained or managed by a harbour authority, as defined in section 57(1) of the Harbours Act 1964.

(3) Subsection 2(*c*) above does not preclude a local authority making byelaws under subsection (1) above in relation to pleasure boats or vessels operating on any canal or inland navigation which they themselves are required or empowered to manage or maintain.

[Local Government, Planning and Land Act 1980, s 185, as amended by the Water Act 1989, Sch 25, the Water Consolidation (Consequential Provisions) Act 1991, Sch 1, and the Local Government (Wales) 1994 Act, Sch 16.]

1. Part XIX contains ss 180–197.
2. This reference continues to have effect despite the repeal and re-enactment of those provisions: see the Water Consolidation (Consequential Provisions) Act 1991, Sch 1, para 35.

Local Government (Miscellaneous Provisions) Act 1982

(1982 c 30)

PART I[1]

LICENSING OF PUBLIC ENTERTAINMENTS

8–19220 **1. Licensing of public entertainments.** *Repealed.*

1. Part I contains s 1.

PART II[1]
CONTROL OF SEX ESTABLISHMENTS

8–19221 **2. Control of sex establishments.** (1) A local authority may resolve that Schedule 3 to this Act is to apply to their area; and if a local authority do so resolve, that Schedule shall come into force in their area on the day specified in that behalf in the resolution (which must not be before the expiration of the period of one month beginning with the day on which the resolution is passed).

(2) A local authority shall publish notice that they have passed a resolution under this section in two consecutive weeks in a local newspaper circulating in their area.

(3) The first publication shall not be later than 28 days before the day specified in the resolution for the coming into force of Schedule 3 to this Act in the local authority's area.

(4) The notice shall state the general effect of that Schedule.

(5) In this Part of this Act "local authority" means—

(*a*) the council of a district;

(*b*) the council of a London borough; and

(*c*) the Common Council of the City of London.

[Local Government (Miscellaneous Provisions) Act 1982, s 2.]

1. Part II contains s 2.

PART III[1]
STREET TRADING

8–19222 **3. Power of district council to adopt Schedule 4.** A district council may resolve that Schedule 4 to this Act shall apply to their district and, if a council so resolve, that Schedule shall come into force in their district on such day as may be specified in the resolution.

[Local Government (Miscellaneous Provisions) Act 1982, s 3.]

1. Part III contains s 3.

PART IV[1]
CONTROL OF REFRESHMENT PREMISES
Take-away food shops

8–19223 **4. Closing hours for take-away food shops.** *Repealed.*

1. Part IV contains ss 4–7.
2. Section 7(1) and (2) came into force on 13 October 1982 (s 7(3)).

8–19224 **5. Closing orders etc—procedure and appeals.** *Repealed.*

8–19225 **6. Contraventions of closing orders.** *Repealed.*

PART V[1]
FIRE PRECAUTIONS
Fireman's switches

8–19226 **9. Application of section 10.** *Repealed.*

1. Part V contains ss 8–10.

8–19227 **10. Firemen's switches for luminous tube signs.** *Repealed.*

PART VI[1]
ABOLITION OF REGISTRATION OF THEATRICAL EMPLOYERS

PART VII[2]
BYELAWS

8–19228 **12. General provisions relating to byelaws.** (1) Notwithstanding anything in section 298 of the Public Health Act 1936 or section 253 of the Public Health Act 1875 or any other enactment, a constable may take proceedings in respect of an offence against a byelaw made by a relevant local authority under any enactment without the consent of the Attorney General.

(2) In subsection (1) above "relevant local authority" means—

(*a*) a local authority, as defined in section 270 of the Local Government Act 1972; and

(*b*) any body that was the predecessor of a local authority as so defined.

(3) It is immaterial for the purposes of this section that a byelaw was made after the passing of this Act.

[Local Government (Miscellaneous Provisions) Act 1982, s 12.]

1. Part VI contains s 11.
2. Part VII contains s 12.

PART VIII[1]

ACUPUNCTURE, TATTOOING, EAR-PIERCING AND ELECTROLYSIS

8–19229 **13.** Application of Part VIII—(1) The provisions of this Part of this Act, except this section, shall come into force in accordance with the following provisions of this section.

(2) A local authority may resolve that the provisions of this Part of this Act which are mentioned in paragraph (*a*), (*b*) or (*c*) of subsection (3) below are to apply to their area; and if a local authority do so resolve, the provisions specified in the resolution shall come into force in their area on the day specified in that behalf in the resolution (which must not be before the expiration of the period of one month beginning with the day on which the resolution is passed).

(3) The provisions that may be specified in a resolution under subsection (2) above are—

(*a*) sections 14, 16 and 17 below; or
(*b*) sections 15 to 17 below; or
(*c*) sections 14 to 17 below.

(4) A resolution which provides that section 15 below is to apply to the area of a local authority need not provide that it shall apply to all the descriptions of persons specified in subsection (1) of that section; and if such a resolution does not provide that section 15 below is to apply to persons of all of those descriptions, the reference in subsection (2) above to the coming into force of provisions specified in the resolution shall be construed, in its application to section 15 below, and to section 16 below so far as it has effect for the purposes of section 15 below, as a reference to the coming into force of those sections only in relation to persons of the description or descriptions specified in the resolution.

(5) If a resolution provides for the coming into force of section 15 below in relation to persons of more than one of the descriptions specified in subsection (1) of that section, it may provide that that section, and section 16 below so far as it has effect for the purposes of that section, shall come into force on different days in relation to persons of each of the descriptions specified in the resolution.

(6) A local authority shall publish notice that they have passed a resolution under this section in two consecutive weeks in a local newspaper circulating in their area.

(7) The first publication shall not be later than 28 days before the day specified in the resolution for the coming into force of the provisions specified in it in the local authority's area.

(8) The notice shall state which provisions are to come into force in that area.

(9) The notice shall also—

(*a*) if the resolution provides for the coming into force of section 14 below, explain that that section applies to persons carrying on the practice of acupuncture; and
(*b*) if it provides for the coming into force of section 15 below, specify the descriptions of persons in relation to whom that section is to come into force.

(10) Any such notice shall state the general effect, in relation to persons to whom the provisions specified in the resolution will apply, of the coming into force of those provisions.

(11) In this Part of the Act "local authority" means—

(*a*) the council of a district;
(*b*) the council of a London borough; and
(*c*) the Common Council of the City of London.

[Local Government (Miscellaneous Provisions) Act 1982, s 13.]

1. Part VIII contains ss 13–17.

8–19230 **14. Acupuncture.** (1) A person shall not in any area in which this section is in force carry on the practice of acupuncture unless he is registered by the local authority for the area under this section.

(2) A person shall only carry on the practice of acupuncture in any area in which this section is in force in premises registered by the local authority for the area under this section; but a person who is registered under this section does not contravene this subsection merely because he sometimes visits people to give them treatment at their request.

(3) Subject to section 16(8)(*b*) below, on application for registration under this section a local authority shall register the applicant and the premises where he desires to practise and shall issue to the applicant a certificate of registration.

(4) An application for registration under this section shall be accompanied by such particulars as the local authority may reasonably require.

(5) The particulars that the local authority may require include, without prejudice to the generality of subsection (4) above,—

(*a*) particulars as to the premises where the applicant desires to practise; and
(*b*) particulars of any conviction of the applicant under section 16 below,

but do not include information about individual people to whom the applicant has given treatment.

(6) A local authority may charge such reasonable fees as they may determine for registration under this section.

(7) A local authority may make byelaws for the purpose of securing—

(*a*) the cleanliness of premises registered under this section and fittings in such premises;
(*b*) the cleanliness of persons so registered and persons assisting persons so registered in their practice;
(*c*) the cleansing and, so far as is appropriate, the sterilisation of instruments, materials and equipment used in connection with the practice of acupuncture.

(8) Nothing in this section shall extend to the practice of acupuncture by or under the supervision of a person who is registered as a medical practitioner or a dentist or to premises on which the practice of acupuncture is carried on by or under the supervision of such a person.
[Local Government (Miscellaneous Provisions) Act 1982, s 14.]

8–19231 15. Tattooing, ear-piercing and electrolysis. (1) A person shall not in any area in which this section is in force carry on the business—

(*a*) of tattooing;
(*b*) of ear-piercing; or
(*c*) of electrolysis,

unless he is registered by the local authority for the area under this section.

(2) A person shall only carry on a business mentioned in subsection (1) above in any area in which this section is in force in premises registered under this section for the carrying on of that business; but a person who carries on the business of tattooing, ear-piercing or electrolysis and is registered under this section as carrying on that business does not contravene this subsection merely because he sometimes visits people at their request to tattoo them or, as the case may be, to pierce their ears or give them electrolysis.

(3) Subject to section 16(8)(*b*) below, on application for registration under this section a local authority shall register the applicant and the premises where he desires to carry on his business and shall issue to the applicant a certificate of registration.

(4) An application for registration under this section shall be accompanied by such particulars as the local authority may reasonably require.

(5) The particulars that the local authority may require include, without prejudice to the generality of subsection (4) above,—

(*a*) particulars as to the premises where the applicant desires to carry on his business; and
(*b*) particulars of any conviction of the applicant under section 16 below,

but do not include information about individual people whom the applicant has tattooed or given electrolysis or whose ears he has pierced.

(6) A local authority may charge such reasonable fees as they may determine for registration under this section.

(7) A local authority may make byelaws for the purposes of securing—

(*a*) the cleanliness of premises registered under this section and fittings in such premises;
(*b*) the cleanliness of persons so registered and persons assisting persons so registered in the business in respect of which they are registered;
(*c*) the cleansing and, so far as is appropriate, the sterilisation of instruments, materials and equipment used in connection with a business in respect of which a person is registered under this section.

(8) Nothing in this section shall extend to the carrying on of a business such as is mentioned in subsection (1) above by or under the supervision of a person who is registered as a medical practitioner or to premises on which any such business is carried on by or under the supervision of such a person.
[Local Government (Miscellaneous Provisions) Act 1982, s 15.]

8–19232 16. Provisions supplementary to ss 14 and 15. (1) Any person who contravenes—

(*a*) section 14(1) or (2) above; or
(*b*) section 15(1) or (2) above,

shall be guilty of an offence and liable on summary conviction to a fine not exceeding **level 3** on the standard scale.

(2) Any person who contravenes a byelaw made—

(*a*) under section 14(7) above; or

(*b*) under section 15(7) above,

shall be guilty of an offence and liable on summary conviction to a fine not exceeding **level 3** on the standard scale.

(3) If a person registered under section 14 above is found guilty of an offence under subsection (2)(*a*) above, the court, instead of or in addition to imposing a fine under subsection (2) above, may order the suspension or cancellation of his registration.

(4) If a person registered under section 15 above is found guilty of an offence under subsection (2)(*b*) above, the court, instead of or in addition to imposing a fine under subsection (2) above, may order the suspension or cancellation of his registration.

(5) A court which orders the suspension or cancellation of a registration by virtue of subsection (3) or (4) above may also order the suspension or cancellation of any registration under section 14 or, as the case may be, 15 above of the premises in which the offence was committed, if they are occupied by the person found guilty of the offence.

(6) Subject to subsection (7) below, a court ordering the suspension or cancellation of registration by virtue of subsection (3) or (4) above may suspend the operation of the order until the expiration of the period prescribed by Crown Court Rules for giving notice of appeal to the Crown Court.

(7) If notice of appeal is given within the period so prescribed, an order under subsection (3) or (4) above shall be suspended until the appeal is finally determined or abandoned.

(8) Where the registration of any person under section 14 or 15 above is cancelled by order of the court under this section—

(*a*) he shall within 7 days deliver up to the local authority the cancelled certificate of registration, and, if he fails to do so, he shall be guilty of an offence and liable on summary conviction to a fine not exceeding **level 2** on the standard scale and thereafter to a daily fine not exceeding **£5**; and

(*b*) he shall not again be registered by the local authority under section 14 or, as the case may be, 15 above except with the consent of the magistrates' court which convicted him.

(9) A person registered under this Part of this Act shall keep a copy—

(*a*) of any certificate of registration issued to him under this Part of this Act; and

(*b*) of any byelaws under this Part of this Act relating to the practice or business in respect of which he is so registered,

prominently displayed at the place where he carries on that practice or business.

(10) A person who contravenes subsection (9) above shall be guilty of an offence and liable on summary conviction to a fine not exceeding **level 2** on the standard scale.

(11) It shall be a defence for a person charged with an offence under subsection (1), (2), (8) or (10) above to prove that he took all reasonable precautions and exercised all due diligence to avoid commission of the offence.

(12) Nothing in this Part of this Act applies to anything done to an animal.

[Local Government (Miscellaneous Provisions) Act 1982, s 16, as amended by the Criminal Justice Act 1982, s 46.]

8–19233 **17. Power to enter premises (acupuncture etc).** (1) Subject to subsection (2) below, an authorised officer of a local authority may enter any premises in the authority's area if he has reason to suspect that an offence under section 16 above is being committed there.

(2) The power conferred by this section may be exercised by an authorised officer of a local authority only if he has been granted a warrant by a justice of the peace.

(3) A justice may grant a warrant under this section only if he is satisfied—

(*a*) that admission to any premises has been refused, or that refusal is apprehended, or that the case is one of urgency, or that an application for admission would defeat the object of the entry; and

(*b*) that there is reasonable ground for entry under this section.

(4) A warrant shall not be granted unless the justice is satisfied either that notice of the intention to apply for a warrant has been given to the occupier, or that the case is one of urgency, or that the giving of such notice would defeat the object of the entry.

(5) A warrant shall continue in force—

(*a*) for seven days; or

(*b*) until the power conferred by this section has been exercised in accordance with the warrant,

whichever period is the shorter.

(6) Where an authorised officer of a local authority exercises the power conferred by this section, he shall produce his authority if required to do so by the occupier of the premises.

(7) Any person who without reasonable excuse refuses to permit an authorised officer of a local authority to exercise the power conferred by this section shall be guilty of an offence and shall for every such refusal be liable on summary conviction to a fine not exceeding **level 3** on the standard scale.

[Local Government (Miscellaneous Provisions) Act 1982, s 17, as amended by the Criminal Justice Act 1982, s 46.]

PART IX[1]
SALE OF FOOD BY HAWKERS

PART X[2]
HIGHWAYS

PART XI[3]
PUBLIC HEALTH, ETC

PART XII[4]
MISCELLANEOUS

8–19234 33. Enforceability by local authorities of certain covenants relating to land. (1) The provisions of this section shall apply if a principal council (in the exercise of their powers under section 111 of the Local Government Act 1972 or otherwise) and any other person are parties to an instrument under seal which—

(*a*) is executed for the purpose of securing the carrying out of works on land in the council's area in which the other person has an interest; or

(*b*) is executed for the purpose of regulating the use of or otherwise connected with land in or outside the council's area in which the other person has an interest,

and which is neither executed for the purpose of facilitating nor connected with the development of the land in question.

(2) If, in a case where this section applies,—

(*a*) the instrument contains a covenant on the part of any person having an interest in land, being a covenant to carry out any works or do any other thing on or in relation to that land, and

(*b*) the instrument defines the land to which the covenant relates, being land in which that person has an interest at the time the instrument is executed, and

(*c*) the covenant is expressed to be one to which this section or section 126 of the Housing Act 1974 (which is superseded by this section) applies,

the covenant shall be enforceable (without any limit of time) against any person deriving title from the original covenantor in respect of his interest in any of the land defined as mentioned in paragraph (*b*) above and any person deriving title under him in respect of any lesser interest in that land as if that person had also been an original covenanting party in respect of the interest for the time being held by him.

(3) Without prejudice to any other method of enforcement of a covenant falling within subsection (2) above, if there is a breach of the covenant in relation to any of the land to which the covenant relates, then, subject to subsection (4) below, the principal council who are a party to the instrument in which the covenant is contained may—

(*a*) enter on the land concerned and carry out the works or do anything which the covenant requires to be carried out or done or remedy anything which has been done and which the covenant required not to be done; and

(*b*) recover from any person against whom the covenant is enforceable (whether by virtue of subsection (2) above or otherwise) any expenses incurred by the council in exercise of their powers under this subsection.

(4) Before a principal council exercise their powers under subsection (3)(*a*) above they shall give not less than 21 days notice of their intention to do so to any person—

(*a*) who has for the time being an interest in the land on or in relation to which the works are to be carried out or other thing is to be done; and

(*b*) against whom the covenant is enforceable (whether by virtue of subsection (2) above or otherwise).

(5) If a person against whom a covenant is enforceable by virtue of subsection (2) above requests the principal council to supply him with a copy of the covenant, it shall be their duty to do so free of charge.

(6) The Public Health Act 1936 shall have effect as if any reference to that Act in—

(*a*) section 283[5] of that Act (notices to be in writing; forms of notices, etc),

(*b*) section 288[5] of that Act (penalty for obstructing execution of Act), and

(*c*) section 291 of that Act (certain expenses recoverable from owners to be a charge on the premises; power to order payment by instalments),

included a reference to subsections (1) to (4) above and as if any reference in those sections of that Act—

(i) to a local authority were a reference to a principal council; and

(ii) to the owner of the premises were a reference to the holder of an interest in land.

(7) Section 16[6] of the Local Government (Miscellaneous Provisions) Act 1976 shall have effect as

if references to a local authority and to functions conferred on a local authority by any enactment included respectively references to such a board as is mentioned in subsection (9) below and to functions of such a board under this section.

(8) In its application to a notice or other document authorised to be given or served under subsection (4) above or by virtue of any provision of the Public Health Act 1936 specified in subsection (6) above, section 233 of the Local Government Act 1972 (service of notices by local authorities) shall have effect as if any reference in that section to a local authority included a reference to the Common Council of the City of London and such a board as is mentioned in the following subsection.

(9) In this section—

(*a*) "principal council" means the council of a county, district or London borough, the Broads Authority, a board constituted in pursuance of section 2 of the Town and Country Planning Act 1990, the Common Council of the City of London, the London Residuary Body, the London Fire and Emergency Planning Authority, a police authority established under section 3 of the Police Act 1996, the Metropolitan Police Authority, the Residuary Body for Wales (Corff Gweddilliol Cymru) or a joint authority established by Part IV of the Local Government Act 1985; and

(*b*) "area" in relation to such a board means the district for which the board is constituted in relation to the London Residuary Body means Greater London, in relation to the Residuary Body for Wales (Corff Gweddilliol Cymru) means Wales and in relation to such a joint authority means the area for which the authority was established.

(10) Section 126 of the Housing Act 1974 (which is superseded by this section) shall cease to have effect; but in relation to a covenant falling within subsection (2) of that section, section 1(1)(*d*) of the Local Land Charges Act 1975 shall continue to have effect as if the reference to the commencement of that Act had been a reference to the coming into operation of the said section 126. [Local Government (Miscellaneous Provisions) Act 1982, s 33, as amended by the Local Government Act 1985, Schs 14 and 17, the Education Reform Act 1988, Sch 13, the Norfolk and Suffolk Broads Act 1988, Sch 6, the Planning (Consequential Provisions) Act 1990, Sch 2, the Planning and Compensation Act 1991, Sch 7, the Police and Magistrates' Courts Act 1994, Sch 4, the Environment Act 1995, Sch 24, the Police Act 1996, Sch 7, the Police Act 1997, Sch 6, the Greater London Authority Act 1999, Schs 27 and 29 and the Criminal Justice and Police Act 2001, Sch 6.]

1. Part IX, which contained ss 18, 19, has been repealed by the Food Act 1984, Sch 11.
2. Part X contains ss 20–23.
3. Part XI contains ss 24–32.
4. Part XII contains ss 33–46.
5. See title, PUBLIC HEALTH, post.
6. Ante.

8–19235 **37. Temporary markets.** (1) The council of a district or a London borough may resolve that the following provisions of this section shall apply to their district or borough; and if a council so resolve and within 14 days of the passing of the resolution give notice of the resolution by advertising in a local newspaper circulating in their area, those provisions shall come into force in their district or borough on the day specified in the resolution.

(2) Subject to subsection (3) below, any person intending to hold a temporary market in a district or London borough where the provisions of this section have come into force, and any occupier of land in such a district or borough who intends to permit the land to be used as the site of a temporary market or for purposes of that market, shall give the council of the district or the borough not less than one month before the date on which it is proposed to hold the market notice of his intention to hold it or to permit the land to be so used, as the case may be.

(3) No notice is required under subsection (2) above if the proceeds of the temporary market are to be applied solely or principally for charitable, social, sporting or political purposes.

(4) Any notice given under subsection (2) above shall state—

(*a*) the full name and address of the person intending to hold the market;
(*b*) the day or days on which it is proposed that the market shall be held and its proposed opening and closing times;
(*c*) the site on which it is proposed that it shall be held;
(*d*) the full name and address of the occupier of that site, if he is not the person intending to hold the market.

(5) A person who without giving the notice required by subsection (2) above holds a temporary market or permits land occupied by him to be used as the site of a temporary market shall be guilty of an offence and liable on summary conviction to a fine not exceeding **level 4** on the standard scale.

(6) In this section "temporary market" means a concourse of buyers and sellers of articles held otherwise than in a building or on a highway, and comprising not less than five stalls, stands, vehicles (whether movable or not) or pitches from which articles are sold, but does not include—

(*a*) a market or fair the right to hold which was acquired by virtue of a grant (including a presumed grant) or acquired or established by virtue of an enactment or order; or (*b*) a sale by auction of farm livestock or deadstock.

(7) A person holds a temporary market for the purposes of this section if—

(*a*) he is entitled to payment for any space or pitch hired or let on the site of the market to persons wishing to trade in the market; or

(*b*) he is entitled, as a person promoting the market, or as the agent, licensee or assignee of a person promoting the market, to payment for goods sold or services rendered to persons attending the market.

(8) This section does not apply to a market held on any land in accordance with planning permission granted on an application made under Part III of the Town and Country Planning Act 1990.

[Local Government (Miscellaneous Provisions) Act 1982, s 37, as amended by the Criminal Justice Act 1982, s 46 and the Planning (Consequential Provisions) Act 1990, Sch 2.]

8–19236 **40. Nuisance and disturbance on educational premises**[1]**.** (1) Any person who without lawful authority is present on premises to which this section applies and causes or permits nuisance[2] or disturbance to the annoyance of persons who lawfully use those premises (whether or not any such persons are present at the time) shall be guilty of an offence and shall be liable on summary conviction to a fine not exceeding **level 2** on the standard scale.

(2) This section applies to premises, including playing fields and other premises for outdoor recreation, of an institution (other than a school) which—

(*a*) is maintained by a local education authority; and;

(*b*) provides further education or higher education (or both)

(3) If—

(*a*) a police constable; or

(*b*) a person whom a local education authority have authorised to exercise the power conferred by this subsection,

has reasonable cause to suspect that any person is committing or has committed an offence under this section, he may remove him from the premises in question.

(4) No proceedings under this section shall be brought by any person other than—

(*a*) a police constable; or

(*b*) a local education authority.

(5) Expressions used in this section and in the Education Act 1996 have the same meaning as in that Act.

[Local Government (Miscellaneous Provisions) Act 1982, s 40, as amended by the Criminal Justice Act 1982, s 46 and the Education Act 1996, Sch 37.]

1. This offence relates to premises in the further and higher eduation sectors. For offences in relation to premises in the primary and secondary education sectors, see title EDUCATION, this PART, ante.
2. In *Sykes v Holmes and Maw* [1985] Crim LR 791, it was held that the act of inhaling solvents in a school playground after school hours when the staff and pupils were not present could constitute a nuisance for the purposes of this section.

PART XIII[1]
SUPPLEMENTARY

8–19237 **48. Consequential repeal or amendment of local statutory provisions.** (1) The Secretary of State may by order—

(*a*) repeal any provision of a local Act passed before or in the same Session as this Act or of an order or other instrument made under or confirmed by any Act so passed if it appears to him that the provision is inconsistent with or has become unnecessary in consequence of any provision of this Act; and

(*b*) amend any provision of such a local Act, order or instrument if it appears to him that the provision requires amendment in consequence of any provision contained in this Act or any repeal made by virtue of paragraph (*a*) above.

(2) An order under subsection (1) above may contain such incidental or transitional provisions as the Secretary of State considers appropriate in connection with the order.

(3) It shall be the duty of the Secretary of State, before he makes an order under subsection (1) above repealing or amending any provision of a local Act, to consult each local authority which he considers would be affected by the repeal or amendment of that provision.

(4) A statutory instrument containing an order under subsection (1) above shall be subject to annulment in pursuance of a resolution of either House of Parliament.

[Local Government (Miscellaneous Provisions) Act 1982, s 48.]

1. Part XIII contains ss 47–49.

8–19238 49. Citation and extent. (1) This Act may be cited as the Local Government (Miscellaneous Provisions) Act 1982.

(2) Subject to sections 11(2), 38(3) and 47(4) above, and to paragraph 8(2) of Schedule 6 to this Act, this Act extends to England and Wales only.

[Local Government (Miscellaneous Provisions) Act 1982, s 49.]

SCHEDULES

Section 1

SCHEDULE 1
LICENSING OF PUBLIC ENTERTAINMENTS

8–19239 *Repealed by the Licensing Act 2003, Sch 6.*

Section 2

SCHEDULE 3
CONTROL OF SEX ESTABLISHMENTS

(As amended by the Criminal Justice Act 1982, s 46, SI 1984 No 447, the Cinemas Act 1985, Sch 2, the London Local Authorities Act 1990, s 18, SI 2005/886, the Licensing Act 2005, Sch 6, SI 2005/1541 and the Serious Organised Crime and Police Act 2005, Sch 7.)

Saving for existing law

8–19260 1. Nothing in this Schedule—

(*a*) shall afford a defence to a charge in respect of any offence at common law or under an enactment other than this Schedule; or

(*b*) shall be taken into account in any way—

(i) at a trial for such an offence; or

(ii) in proceedings for forfeiture under section 3 of the Obscene Publications Act 1959 or section 5 of the Protection of Children Act 1978; or

(iii) in proceedings for condemnation under Schedule 3 to the Customs and Excise Management Act 1979 of goods which section 42 of the Customs Consolidation Act 1876 prohibits to be imported or brought into the United Kingdom as being indecent or obscene; or

(*c*) shall in any way limit the other powers exercisable under any of those Acts.

Meaning of "sex establishment"

8–19261 2. In this Schedule "sex establishment" means a sex cinema or a sex shop.

Meaning of "sex cinema"

8–19262 3. (1) In this Schedule, "sex cinema" means any premises, vehicle, vessel or stall used to a significant degree for the exhibition of moving pictures, by whatever means produced, which—

(*a*) are concerned primarily with the portrayal of, or primarily deal with or relate to, or are intended to stimulate or encourage—

(i) sexual activity; or

(ii) acts of force or restraint which are associated with sexual activity; or

(*b*) are concerned primarily with the portrayal of, or primarily deal with or relate to, genital organs or urinary or excretory functions,

but does not include a dwelling-house to which the public is not admitted.

(2) No premises shall be treated as a sex cinema by reason only—

(*a*) if they may be used for an exhibition of a film (within the meaning of paragraph 15 of Schedule 1 to the Licensing Act 2003) by virtue of an authorisation (within the meaning of section 136 of that Act), of their use in accordance with that authorisation; or

(*b*) of their use for an exhibition to which section 6 of that Act (certain non-commercial exhibitions) applies given by an exempted organisation within the meaning of section 6(6) of the Cinemas Act 1985.

8–19262A 3A. In this schedule "sex encounter establishment" means—

(*a*) premises at which performances which are not unlawful are given by one or more persons present and performing, which wholly or mainly comprise the sexual stimulation of persons admitted to the premises (whether by verbal or any other means); or

(*b*) premises at which any services which are not unlawful and which do not constitute sexual activity are provided by one or more persons who are without clothes or who expose their breasts or genital, urinary or excretory organs at any time while they are providing the service; or

(*c*) premises at which entertainments which are not unlawful[1] are provided by one or more persons who are without clothes or who expose their breasts or genital, urinary or excretory organs during the entertainment; or

(*d*) premises (not being a sex cinema) at which pictures are exhibited by whatever means (and whether or not to the accompaniment of music) in such circumstances that it is reasonable for the appropriate authority to decide that the principle purpose of the exhibition, other than the purpose of generating income, is to stimulate or encourage sexual activity or acts of force or restraint associated with sexual activity,

Provided that no premises which are—

(i) for the time being, being used for the provision of regulated entertainment (within the meaning of the Licensing Act 2003), in circumstances where that use is authorised under that Act; or

(ii) for the time being, being used for the purposes of late night refreshment (within the meaning of that Act), in circumstances where that use is so authorised; or

(iii) a private dwelling-house to which the public are not admitted; shall be regarded as a "sex encounter establishment"[3].

1. In *McMonagle v Westminster City Council* [1990] 2 AC 716, [1990] 1 All ER 993, 154 JP 854, HL, the appellant was not successful in a defence on the basis that he was committing offences of outraging public decency and keeping a disorderly house: it would be manifestly absurd if legislation were to apply only to inoffensive establishments.

2. Lewd sexual displays which include gyrating to loud music are not "music or dancing or a like public entertainment" and therefore are not exempted from the provisions of Sch 3 where the premises has been granted a music and dancing licence under Sch 12 of the London Government Act 1963: *Willowcell Ltd v Westminster City Council* (1995) 160 JP101, 139 Sol Jo LB 129, CA.

3. Section 12 of the Greater London Council (General Powers) Act 1986 enables London Borough Councils to apply Sch 3 to their areas: they may also resolve that numerous amendments to Sch 3 apply. Only the added para 3A is printed here but the effect is to apply Sch 3 to sex encounter establishments.

Meaning of "sex shop" and "sex article"

8–19263 **4.** (1) In this Schedule "sex shop" means any premises, vehicle, vessel or stall used for a business which consists to a significant[2] degree of selling, hiring, exchanging, lending, displaying or demonstrating—

(*a*) sex articles; or

(*b*) other things intended for use in connection with, or for the purpose of stimulating or encouraging—

(i) sexual activity; or

(ii) acts of force or restraint which are associated with sexual activity.

(2) No premises shall be treated as a sex shop by reason only of their use for the exhibition of moving pictures by whatever means produced.

(3) In this Schedule "sex article" means—

(*a*) anything made for use in connection with, or for the purpose of stimulating or encouraging—

(i) sexual activity; or

(ii) acts of force or restraint which are associated with sexual activity; and

(*b*) anything to which sub-paragraph (4) below applies.

(4) This sub-paragraph applies—

(*a*) to any article containing or embodying matter to be read or looked at or anything intended to be used, either alone or as one of a set, for the reproduction or manufacture of any such article; and

(*b*) to any recording of vision or sound, which—

(i) is concerned primarily with the portrayal of, or primarily deals with or relates to, or is intended to stimulate or encourage, sexual activity or acts of force or restraint which are associated with sexual activity; or

(ii) is concerned primarily with the portrayal of, or primarily deals with or relates to, genital organs, or urinary or excretory functions.

1. This Schedule is additionally amended by the Greater London Council (General Powers) Act 1986, s 12 where a borough council so resolves. This is to enable there to be regulation of sex encounter establishments. See also *McMonagle v Westminster City Council* [1990] 2 AC 716, [1990] 1 All ER 993, 154 JP 854, HL.

2. "Significant" means more than "more than trifling"; in deciding whether an establishment is a "sex shop", the ratio between the sexual and other aspects of the business will always be material, so also will be the absolute quantity of sales, and the character of the remainder of the business. The court must decide which considerations are material to the individual case and what weight is to be attached to them (*Lambeth London Borough Council v Grewal* (1985) 150 JP 138, [1986] Crim LR 260).

Miscellaneous definitions

8–19264 **5.** (1) In this Schedule—

"the appropriate authority" means, in relation to any area for which a resolution has been passed under section 2 above, the local authority who passed it;

"the chief officer of police", in relation to any locality, means the chief officer of police for the police area in which the locality is situated; and

"vessel" includes any ship, boat, raft or other apparatus constructed or adapted for floating on water.

(2) This Schedule applies to hovercraft as it applies to vessels.

Requirement for licences for sex establishments

8–19265 **6.** (1) Subject to the provisions of this Schedule, no person shall in any area in which this Schedule is in force use any premises, vehicle, vessel or stall as a sex establishment except under and in accordance with the terms of a licence granted under this Schedule by the appropriate authority.

(2) Sub-paragraph (1) above does not apply to the sale, supply or demonstration of articles which—

(*a*) are manufactured for use primarily for the purposes of birth control; or

(*b*) primarily relate to birth control.

7. (1) Any person who—

(*a*) uses any premises, vehicle, vessel or stall as a sex establishment; or
(*b*) proposes to do so,

may apply to the appropriate authority for them to waive the requirement of a licence.

(2) An application under this paragraph may be made either as part of an application for a licence under this Schedule or without any such application.

(3) An application under this paragraph shall be made in writing and shall contain the particulars specified in paragraph 10(2) to (5) below and such particulars as the appropriate authority may reasonably require in addition.

(4) The appropriate authority may waive the requirement of a licence in any case where they consider that to require a licence would be unreasonable or inappropriate.

(5) A waiver may be for such period as the appropriate authority think fit.

(6) Where the appropriate authority grant an application for a waiver, they shall give the applicant for the waiver notice that they have granted his application.

(7) The appropriate authority may at any time give a person who would acquire a licence but for a waiver notice that the waiver is to terminate on such date not less than 28 days from the date on which they give the notice as may be specified in the notice.

Grant, renewal and transfer of licences for sex establishments

8–19266 **8.** (1) Subject to sub-paragraph (2) and paragraph 12(1) below, the appropriate authority may grant to any applicant, and from time to time renew, a licence under this Schedule for the use of any premises, vehicle, vessel or stall specified in it for a sex establishment on such terms and conditions and subject to such restrictions as may be so specified.

(2) No term, condition or restriction may be specified under sub-paragraph (1) above in so far as it relates to any matter in relation to which requirements or prohibitions are or could be imposed by or under the Regulatory Reform (Fire Safety) Order 2005 in respect of the premises, vehicle, vessel or stall.

9. (1) Subject to paragraphs 11 and 27 below, any licence under this Schedule shall, unless previously cancelled under paragraph 16 or revoked under paragraph 17(1) below, remain in force for one year or for such shorter period specified in the licence as the appropriate authority may think fit.

(2) Where a licence under this Schedule has been granted to any person, the appropriate authority may, if they think fit, transfer that licence to any other person on the application of that other person.

10. (1) An application for the grant, renewal or transfer of a licence under this Schedule shall be made in writing to the appropriate authority.

(2) An application made otherwise than by or on behalf of a body corporate or an unincorporated body shall state—

(*a*) the full name of the applicant;
(*b*) his permanent address; and
(*c*) his age.

(3) An application made by a body corporate or an unincorporated body shall state—

(*a*) the full name of the body;
(*b*) the address of its registered or principal office; and
(*c*) the full names and private addresses of the directors or other persons responsible for its management.

(4) An application relating to premises shall state the full address of the premises.

(5) An application relating to a vehicle, vessel or stall shall state where it is to be used as a sex establishment.

(6) Every application shall contain such particulars as the appropriate authority may reasonably require in addition to any particulars required under sub-paragraphs (2) to (5) above.

(7) An applicant for the grant, renewal or transfer of a licence under this Schedule shall give public notice of the application.

(8) Notice shall in all cases be given by publishing an advertisement in a local newspaper circulating in the appropriate authority's area.

(9) The publication shall not be later than 7 days after the date of the application.

(10) Where the application is in respect of premises, notice of it shall in addition be displayed for 21 days beginning with the date of the application on or near the premises and in a place where the notice can conveniently be read by the public.

(11) Every notice under this paragraph which relates to premises shall identify the premises.

(12) Every such notice which relates to a vehicle, vessel or stall shall specify where it is to be used as a sex establishment.

(13) Subject to sub-paragraphs (11) and (12) above, a notice under this paragraph shall be in such form as the appropriate authority may prescribe.

(14) An applicant for the grant, renewal or transfer of a licence under this Schedule shall, not later than 7 days after the date of the application, send a copy of the application to the chief officer of police.

(15) Any person objecting to an application for the grant, renewal or transfer of a licence under this Schedule shall give notice in writing of his objection to the appropriate authority, stating in general terms the grounds of the objection, not later than 28 days after the date of the application.

(16) Where the appropriate authority receive notice of any objection under sub-paragraph (15) above, the authority shall, before considering the application, give notice in writing of the general terms of the objection to the applicant.

(17) The appropriate authority shall not without the consent of the person making the objection reveal his name or address to the applicant.

(18) In considering any application for the grant, renewal or transfer of a licence the appropriate authority shall have regard to any observations submitted to them by the chief officer of police and any objections of which notice has been sent to them under subparagraph (15) above.

(19) The appropriate authority shall give an opportunity of appearing before and of being heard by a committee or sub-committee of the authority—

(*a*) before refusing to grant a licence, to the applicant;
(*b*) before refusing to renew a licence, to the holder; and
(*c*) before refusing to transfer a licence, to the holder and the person to whom he desires that it shall be transferred.

(20) Where the appropriate authority refuse to grant, renew or transfer a licence, they shall, if required to do so by the applicant or holder of the licence, give him a statement in writing of the reasons for their decision within 7 days of his requiring them to do so.

11. (1) Where, before the date of expiry of a licence, an application has been made for its renewal, it shall be deemed to remain in force notwithstanding that the date has passed until the withdrawal of the application or its determination by the appropriate authority.

(2) Where, before the date of expiry of a licence, an application has been made for its transfer, it shall be deemed to remain in force with any necessary modifications until the withdrawal of the application or its determination, notwithstanding that the date has passed or that the person to whom the licence is to be transferred if the application is granted is carrying on the business of the sex establishment.

Refusal of licences

8–19267 **12.** (1) A licence under this Schedule shall not be granted—

(*a*) to a person under the age of 18; or
(*b*) to a person who is for the time being disqualified under paragraph 17(3) below; or
(*c*) to a person, other than a body corporate, who is not resident in the United Kingdom or was not so resident throughout the period of six months immediately preceding the date when the application was made; or
(*d*) to a body corporate which is not incorporated in the United Kingdom; or
(*e*) to a person who has, within a period of 12 months immediately preceding the date when the application was made, been refused the grant or renewal of a licence for the premises, vehicle, vessel or stall in respect of which the application is made, unless the refusal has been reversed on appeal.

(2) Subject to paragraph 27 below, the appropriate authority may refuse—

(*a*) an application for the grant or renewal of a licence on one or more of the grounds specified in sub-paragraph (3) below;
(*b*) an application for the transfer of a licence on either or both of the grounds specified in paragraphs (*a*) and (*b*) of that sub-paragraph.

(3) The grounds mentioned in sub-paragraph (2) above are—

(*a*) that the applicant is unsuitable to hold the licence by reason of having been convicted of an offence or for any other reason;
(*b*) that if the licence were to be granted, renewed or transferred the business to which it relates would be managed by or carried on for the benefit of a person, other than the applicant, who would be refused the grant, renewal or transfer of such a licence if he made the application himself;
(*c*) that the number of sex establishments in the relevant locality at the time the application is made is equal to or exceeds the number which the authority consider is appropriate for that locality;
(*d*) that the grant or renewal[1] of the licence would be inappropriate, having regard—

(i) to the character of the relevant locality; or
(ii) to the use to which any premises in the vicinity are put; or
(iii) to the layout, character or condition of the premises, vehicle, vessel or stall in respect of which the application is made.

(4) Nil may be an appropriate number for the purposes of sub-paragraph (3)(*c*) above.

(5) In this paragraph "the relevant locality" means—

(*a*) in relation to premises, the locality where they are situated; and
(*b*) in relation to a vehicle, vessel or stall, any locality where it is desired to use it as a sex establishment.

---

1. The licensing authority is entitled to refuse to renew an existing licence on the grounds specified in para 12(3)(d), despite the fact that there has not been any change of circumstances, provided it gives due weight to the fact that the licence has previously been granted and gives rational reasons for its refusal (*R v Birmingham City Council, ex p Sheptonhurst Ltd* [1990] 1 All ER 1026, 87 LGR 830, CA).

Power to prescribe standard conditions

8–19268 **13.** (1) Subject to the provisions of this Schedule, the appropriate authority may make regulations prescribing standard conditions applicable to licences for sex establishments, that is to say, terms, conditions and restrictions on or subject to which licences under this Schedule are in general to be granted, renewed or transferred by them.*

(1A) No standard condition may be prescribed by regulation under sub-paragraph (1) above in so far as it relates to any matter in relation to which requirements or prohibitions are or could be imposed by or under the Regulatory Reform (Fire Safety) Order 2005.

(2) Regulations under sub-paragraph (1) above may make different provision—

(*a*) for sex cinemas and sex shops; and
(*b*) for different kinds of sex cinemas and sex shops.*

(3) Without prejudice to the generality of sub-paragraphs (1) and (2) above, regulations under this paragraph may prescribe conditions regulating—

(*a*) the hours of opening and closing of sex establishments;
(*b*) displays or advertisements on or in such establishments;
(*c*) the visibility of the interior of sex establishments to passers-by; and
(*d*) any change of a sex cinema to a sex shop or a sex shop to a sex cinema.*

(4) Where the appropriate authority have made regulations under sub-paragraph (1) above, every such licence

granted, renewed or transferred by them shall be presumed to have been so granted, renewed or transferred subject to any standard conditions applicable to it unless they have been expressly excluded or varied.

(5) Where the appropriate authority have made regulations under sub-paragraph (1) above, they shall, if so requested by any person, supply him with a copy of the regulations on payment of such reasonable fee as the authority may determine.

(6) In any legal proceedings the production of a copy of any regulations made by the appropriate authority under sub-paragraph (1) above purporting to be certified as a true copy by an officer of the authority authorised to give a certificate for the purposes of this paragraph shall be prima facie evidence of such regulations, and no proof shall be required of the handwriting or official position or authority of any person giving such certificate.

***Sub-paragraph (2) amended and sub-para (3)(*d*) substituted , in relation to certain London Boroughs by the Greater London Council (General Powers) Act 1986, s 12, from a date to be determined.**

Copies of licences and standard conditions

8–19269 **14.** (1) The holder of a licence under this Schedule shall keep exhibited in a suitable place to be specified in the licence a copy of the licence and any regulations made under paragraph 13(1) above which prescribe standard conditions subject to which the licence is held.

(2) The appropriate authority shall send a copy of any licence granted under this Schedule to the chief officer of police for the area where the sex establishment is situated.

Transmission and cancellation of licences

8–19280 **15.** In the event of the death of the holder of a licence granted under this Schedule, that licence shall be deemed to have been granted to his personal representatives and shall, unless previously revoked, remain in force until the end of the period of 3 months beginning with the death and shall then expire; but the appropriate authority may from time to time, on the application of those representatives, extend or further extend the period of three months if the authority are satisfied that the extension is necessary for the purpose of winding up the deceased's estate and that no other circumstances make it undesirable.

16. The appropriate authority may, at the written request of the holder of a licence, cancel the licence.

Revocation of licences

8–19281 **17.** (1) The appropriate authority may, after giving the holder of a licence under this Schedule an opportunity of appearing before and being heard by them, at any time revoke the licence—

(*a*) on any ground specified in sub-paragraph (1) of paragraph 12 above; or
(*b*) on either of the grounds specified in sub-paragraph (3)(*a*) and (*b*) of that paragraph.

(2) Where a licence is revoked, the appropriate authority shall, if required to do so by the person who held it, give him a statement in writing of the reasons for their decision within 7 days of his requiring them to do so.

(3) Where a licence is revoked, its holder shall be disqualified from holding or obtaining a licence in the area of the appropriate authority for a period of 12 months beginning with the date of revocation.

Variation of licences

8–19282 **18.** (1) The holder of a licence under this Schedule may at any time apply to the appropriate authority for any such variation of the terms, conditions or restrictions on or subject to which the licence is held as may be specified in the application.

(2) Subject to sub-paragraph (4) below, the appropriate authority—

(*a*) may make the variation specified in the application; or
(*b*) may make such variations as they think fit; or
(*c*) may refuse the application.*

(3) The variations that an authority may make by virtue of sub-paragraph (2)(*b*) above include, without prejudice to the generality of that sub-paragraph, variations involving the imposition of terms, conditions or restrictions other than those specified in the application.

(4) No variation is to be made under this paragraph in so far as it relates to any matter in relation to which requirements or prohibitions are or could be imposed by or under the Regulatory Reform (Fire Safety) Order 2005.

Fees

8–19283 **19.** An applicant for the grant, renewal or transfer of a licence under this Schedule shall pay a reasonable fee determined by the appropriate authority.

Enforcement

8–19284 **20.** (1) A person who—

(*a*) knowingly[1] uses, or knowingly causes or permits the use of, any premises, vehicle, vessel or stall contrary to paragraph 6 above[2]; or
(*b*) being the holder of a licence for a sex establishment, employs in the business of the establishment any person known to him to be disqualified from holding such a licence; or
(*c*) being the holder of a licence under this Schedule, without reasonable excuse knowingly contravenes, or without reasonable excuse knowingly permits the contravention of, a term, condition or restriction specified in the licence; or
(*d*) being the servant or agent of the holder of a licence under this Schedule, without reasonable excuse knowingly contravenes, or without reasonable excuse knowingly permits the contravention of, a term, condition or restriction specified in the licence,

shall be guilty of an offence.

21. Any person who, in connection with an application for the grant, renewal or transfer of a licence under this Schedule, makes a false statement which he knows to be false in any material respect or which he does not believe to be true, shall be guilty of an offence.

22. (1) A person guilty of an offence under paragraph 20 or 21 above shall be liable on summary conviction to a fine not exceeding **£20,000**.

(2) A person who, being the holder of a licence under this Schedule, fails without reasonable excuse to comply with paragraph 14(1) above shall be guilty of an offence and liable on summary conviction to a fine not exceeding **level 3** on the standard scale.

1. The prosecution must establish not only that the person knew that the premises were used as a sex establishment but also that he knew that they were being so used without a licence. Such knowledge may be proved either by proving actual knowledge or by showing that the defendant had deliberately shut his eyes to the obvious or refrained from inquiry because he suspected the truth but did not want to have his suspicions confirmed (*Westminster City Council v Croyalgrange Ltd* [1986] 2 All ER 353, [1986] 1 WLR 674, HL).

2. On such a prosecution, the court cannot investigate and determine the validity of a licensing authority's refusal to grant a licence (*Quietlynn Ltd v Plymouth City Council* [1988] QB 114, [1987] 2 All ER 1040, 151 JP 810, DC).

Offences relating to persons under 18

8–19285 **23.** (1) A person who, being the holder of a licence for a sex establishment—

(*a*) without reasonable excuse knowingly permits a person under 18 years of age to enter the establishment; or

(*b*) employs a person known to him to be under 18 years of age in the business of the establishment,

shall be guilty of an offence.

(2) A person guilty of an offence under this paragraph shall be liable on summary conviction to a fine not exceeding **£20,000**.

Powers of constables and local authority officers

8–19286 **24.** *Repealed.*

25. (1) A constable may, at any reasonable time, enter and inspect any sex establishment in respect of which a licence under this Schedule is for the time being in force, with a view to seeing—

(i) whether the terms, conditions or restrictions on or subject to which the licence is held are complied with;

(ii) whether any person employed in the business of the establishment is disqualified from holding a licence under this Schedule;

(iii) whether any person under 18 years of age is in the establishment; and

(iv) whether any person under that age is employed in the business of the establishment.

(2) Subject to sub-paragraph (4) below, a constable may enter and inspect a sex establishment if he has reason to suspect that an offence under paragraph 20, 21 or 23 above has been, is being, or is about to be committed in relation to it.

(3) An authorised officer of a local authority may exercise the powers conferred by sub-paragraphs (1) and (2) above in relation to a sex establishment in the local authority's area.

(4) No power conferred by sub-paragraph (2) above may be exercised by a constable or an authorised officer of a local authority unless he has been authorised to exercise it by a warrant granted by a justice of the peace.

(5) Where an authorised officer of a local authority exercises any such power, he shall produce his authority if required to do so by the occupier of the premises or the person in charge of the vehicle, vessel or stall in relation to which the power is exercised.

(6) Any person who without reasonable excuse refuses to permit a constable or an authorised officer of a local authority to exercise any such power shall be guilty of an offence and shall for every such refusal be liable on summary conviction to a fine not exceeding **level 5** on the standard scale.

Offences by bodies corporate

8–19287 **26.** (1) Where an offence under this Schedule committed by a body corporate is proved to have been committed with the consent or connivance of, or to be attributable to any neglect on the part of, any director, manager, secretary or other similar officer of the body corporate, or any person who was purporting to act in any such capacity, he, as well as the body corporate, shall be guilty of the offence.

(2) Where the affairs of a body corporate are managed by its members sub-paragraph (1) above shall apply to the acts and defaults of a member in connection with his function of management as if he were a director of the body corporate.

Appeals

8–19288 **27.** (1) Subject to sub-paragraphs (2) and (3) below, any of the following persons, that is to say—

(*a*) an applicant for the grant, renewal or transfer of a licence under this Schedule whose application is refused;

(*b*) an applicant for the variation of the terms, conditions or restrictions on or subject to which any such licence is held whose application is refused;

(*c*) a holder of any such licence who is aggrieved by any term, condition or restriction on or subject to which the licence is held; or

(*d*) a holder of any such licence whose licence is revoked,

may at any time before the expiration of the period of 21 days beginning with the relevant date appeal to amagistrates' court

(2) An applicant whose application for the grant or renewal of a licence is refused, or whose licence is revoked, on any ground specified in paragraph 12(1) above shall not have a right to appeal under this paragraph unless the applicant seeks to show that the ground did not apply to him.

(3) An applicant whose application for the grant or renewal of a licence is refused on either ground specified in paragraph 12(3)(*c*) or (*d*) above shall not have the right to appeal under this paragraph.

(4) In this paragraph—

"the relevant date" means the date on which the person in question is notified of the refusal of his application, the imposition of the term, condition or restriction by which he is aggrieved or the revocation of his licence, as the case may be.

(5) An appeal against the decision of a magistrates' court under this paragraph may be brought to the Crown Court.

(6) Where an appeal is brought to the Crown Court under sub-paragraph (5) above, the decision of the Crown Court shall be final

(7) On an appeal to the magistrates' court or the Crown Court under this paragraph the court may make such order as it thinks fit.

(8) Subject to sub-paragraphs (9) to (12) below, it shall be the duty of the appropriate authority to give effect to an order of the magistrates' court or the Crown Court.

(9) The appropriate authority need not give effect to the order of the magistrates' court until the time for bringing an appeal under sub-paragraph (5) above has expired and, if such an appeal is duly brought, until the determination or abandonment of the appeal.

(10) Where a licence is revoked or an application for the renewal of a licence is refused, the licence shall be deemed to remain in force—

(*a*) until the time for bringing an appeal under this paragraph has expired and, if such an appeal is duly brought, until the determination or abandonment of the appeal; and

(*b*) where an appeal relating to the refusal of an application for such a renewal is successful and no further appeal is available, until the licence is renewed by the appropriate authority.

(11) Where—

(*a*) the holder of a licence makes an application under paragraph 18 above; and

(*b*) the appropriate authority impose any term, condition or restriction other than one specified in the application,

the licence shall be deemed to be free of it until the time for bringing an appeal under this paragraph has expired.

(12) Where an appeal is brought under this paragraph against the imposition of any such term, condition or restriction, the licence shall be deemed to be free of it until the determination or abandonment of the appeal.

Provisions relating to existing premises

8–19289 **28.** (1) Without prejudice to any other enactment it shall be lawful for any person who—

(*a*) was using any premises, vehicle, vessel or stall as a sex establishment immediately before the date of the first publication under subsection (2) of section 2 above of a notice of the passing of a resolution under that section by the local authority for the area; and

(*b*) had before the appointed day duly applied to the appropriate authority for a licence for the establishment,

to continue to use the premises, vehicle, vessel or stall as a sex establishment until the determination of his application.

(2) In this paragraph and paragraph 29 below "the appointed day", in relation to any area, means the day specified in the resolution passed under section 2 above as the date upon which this Schedule is to come into force in that area.

29. (1) This paragraph applies to an application for the grant of a licence under this Schedule made before the appointed day.

(2) A local authority shall not consider any application to which this paragraph applies before the appointed day.

(3) A local authority shall not grant any application to which this paragraph applies until they have considered all such applications.

(4) In considering which of several applications to which this paragraph applies should be granted a local authority shall give preference over other applicants to any applicant who satisfies them—

(*a*) that he is using the premises, vehicle, vessel or stall to which the application relates as a sex establishment; and

(*b*) that some person was using the premises, vehicle, vessel or stall as a sex establishment on 22nd December 1981; and

(*c*) that—

(i) he is that person; or

(ii) he is a successor of that person in the business or activity which was being carried on there on that date.

Commencement of Schedule

8–19290 **30.** (1) So far as it relates to sex cinemas, this Schedule shall come into force on such day as the Secretary of State may by order[1] may by statutory instrument appoint.

(2) Subject to sub-paragraph (1) above, this Schedule shall come into force on the day on which this Act is passed.

(3) Where, in relation to any area, the day appointed under sub-paragraph (1) above falls after the day specified in a resolution passed under section 2 above as the day upon which this Schedule is to come into force in that area, the day so appointed shall, for the purposes of paragraphs 28 and 29 above, be the appointed day in relation to sex cinemas in the area.

---

1. The Local Government (Miscellaneous Provisions) Act 1982 (Commencement No 1) Order 1982, SI 1982/1119, brought into force on 13 October 1982, Sch 3 so far as it relates to sex cinemas.

Section 3

SCHEDULE 4
STREET TRADING

(*As amended by the Criminal Justice Act 1982, s 46, the Food Act 1984, Sch 10 and the Government of Wales Act 1998, Sch 15 and Sch 18.*)

Interpretation

8–19291 **1.** (1) In this Schedule—

"consent street" means a street in which street trading is prohibited without the consent of the district council;

"licence street" means a street in which street trading is prohibited without a licence granted by the district council;

"principal terms", in relation to a street trading licence, has the meaning assigned to it by paragraph 4(3) below;

"prohibited street" means a street in which street trading is prohibited;

"street" includes—

(*a*) any road, footway, beach or other area to which the public have access without payment; and

(*b*) a service area as defined in section 329 of the Highways Act 1980,

and also includes any part of a street;

"street trading" means, subject to sub-paragraph (2) below, the selling or exposing or offering for sale of any article (including a living thing) in a street; and

"subsidiary terms", in relation to a street trading licence, has the meaning assigned to it by paragraph 4(4) below.

(2) The following are not street trading for the purposes of this Schedule—

(*a*) trading by a person acting as a pedlar[1] under the authority of a pedlar's certificate granted under the Pedlars Act 1871;

(*b*) anything done in a market[2] or fair the right to hold which was acquired by virtue of a grant (including a presumed grant) or acquired or established by virtue of an enactment or order.

(*c*) trading in a trunk road picnic area provided by the Secretary of State under section 112 of the Highways Act 1980;

(*d*) trading as a news vendor;

(*e*) trading which—

(i) is carried on at premises used as a petrol filling station; or

(ii) is carried on at premises used as a shop or in a street adjoining premises so used and as part of the business of the shop;

(*f*) selling things, or offering or exposing them for sale, as a roundsman[3];

(*g*) the use for trading under Part VIIA of the Highways Act 1980 of an object or structure placed on, in or over a highway;

(*h*) the operation of facilities for recreation or refreshment under Part VIIA of the Highways Act 1980;

(*j*) the doing of anything authorised by regulations made under section 5 of the Police, Factories, etc (Miscellaneous Provisions) Act 1916.*

(3) The reference to trading as a news vendor in sub-paragraph (2)(*d*) is a reference to trading where—

(*a*) the only articles sold or exposed or offered for sale are newspapers or periodicals; and

(*b*) they are sold or exposed or offered for sale without a stall or receptacle for them or with a stall or receptacle for them which does not—

(i) exceed one metre in length or width or two metres in height;

(ii) occupy a ground area exceeding 0·25 square metres; or

(iii) stand on the carriageway of a street.

***Amended by the Charities Act 1992, Sch 6, when in force.**

1. See the definition of "pedlar" in s 3 of the 1871 Act in this PART, post.

2. In the first instance, it is for the defendant to prove that the place where he was trading was a market. The holder of a market right may, however, restrict the holding of the market to an area smaller than that over which his right subsists; see *Jones v Lewis* (1989) Times, 14 June, DC.

3. "Roundsman" means "one who goes the round of his customers for orders and the delivery of goods" and "denotes a person who follows a set route to attend on specific/identifiable customers for the purpose of either taking orders or for the delivery of goods"; the Act clearly envisages that "intermediate sales" may be made, but that is ancillary to the "round": *Kempin (t/a British Bulldog) v Brighton and Hove Council* [2001] EWHC Admin 140, [2001] All ER (D) 125 (Feb)).

Designation of streets

8–19292 **2.** (1) A district council may by resolution designate any street in their district as—

(*a*) a prohibited street;

(*b*) a licence street; or

(*c*) a consent street.

(2) If a district council pass such a resolution as is mentioned in sub-paragraph (1) above, the designation of the street shall take effect on the day specified in that behalf in the resolution (which must not be before the expiration of the period of one month beginning with the day on which the resolution is passed).

(3) A council shall not pass such a resolution unless—

(*a*) they have published notice of their intention to pass such a resolution in a local newspaper circulating in their area;

(*b*) they have served a copy of the notice—

(i) on the chief officer of police for the area in which the street to be designated by the resolution is situated; and

(ii) on any highway authority responsible for that street; and

(*c*) where sub-paragraph (4) below applies, they have obtained the necessary consent.

(4) This sub-paragraph applies—

(*a*) where the resolution relates to a street which is owned or maintainable by a relevant corporation; and

(*b*) where the resolution designates as a licence street any street maintained by a highway authority;

and in sub-paragraph (3) above "necessary consent" means—

(i) in the case mentioned in paragraph (*a*) above, the consent of the relevant corporation; and

(ii) in the case mentioned in paragraph (*b*) above, the consent of the highway authority.

(5) The following are relevant corporations for the purposes of this paragraph—

(*a*) the British Railways Board;

(*b*) the Commission for the New Towns;

(*c*) a development corporation for a new town; and

(*d*) an urban development corporation established under the Local Government, Planning and Land Act 1980.

(*e*) *Repealed.*

(6) The notice referred to in sub-paragraph (3) above—

(*a*) shall contain a draft of the resolution; and

(*b*) shall state that representations relating to it may be made in writing to the council within such period, not less than 28 days after publication of the notice, as may be specified in the notice.

(7) As soon as practicable after the expiry of the period specified under sub-paragraph (6) above, the council shall consider any representations relating to the proposed resolution which they have received before the expiry of that period.

(8) After the council have considered those representations, they may, if they think fit, pass such a resolution relating to the street as is mentioned in sub-paragraph (1) above.

(9) The council shall publish notice that they have passed such a resolution in two consecutive weeks in a local newspaper circulating in their area.

(10) The first publication shall not be later than 28 days before the day specified in the resolution for the coming into force of the designation.

(11) Where a street is designated as a licence street, the council may resolve—

(*a*) in the resolution which so designates the street; or

(*b*) subject to sub-paragraph (12) below, by a separate resolution at any time,

that a street trading licence is not to be granted to any person who proposes to trade in the street for a number of days in every week less than a number specified in the resolution.

(12) Sub-paragraphs (3)(*a*) and (6) to (10) above shall apply in relation to a resolution under sub-paragraph (11)(*b*) above as they apply in relation to a resolution under sub-paragraph (1) above.

(13) Any resolution passed under this paragraph may be varied or rescinded by a subsequent resolution so passed.

Street trading licences

8–19293 **3.** (1) An application for a street trading licence or the renewal of such a licence shall be made in writing to the district council.

(2) The applicant shall state—

(*a*) his full name and address;

(*b*) the street in which, days on which and times between which he desires to trade;

(*c*) the description of articles in which he desires to trade and the description of any stall or container which he desires to use in connection with his trade in those articles; and

(*d*) such other particulars as the council may reasonably require.

(3) If the council so require, the applicant shall submit two photographs of himself with his application.

(4) A street trading licence shall not be granted—

(*a*) to a person under the age of 17 years; or

(*b*) for any trading in a highway in relation to which a control order under section 7 of the Local Government (Miscellaneous Provisions) Act 1976 (road-side sales) is in force, other than trading to which the control order does not apply.

(5) Subject to sub-paragraph (4) above, it shall be the duty of the council to grant an application for a street trading licence or the renewal of such a licence unless they consider that the application ought to be refused on one or more of the grounds specified in sub-paragraph (6) below.

(6) Subject to sub-paragraph (8) below, the council may refuse an application on any of the following grounds—

(*a*) that there is not enough space in the street for the applicant to engage in the trading in which he desires to engage without causing undue interference or inconvenience to persons using the street;

(*b*) that there are already enough traders trading in the street from shops or otherwise in the goods in which the applicant desires to trade;

(*c*) that the applicant desires to trade on fewer days than the minimum number specified in a resolution under paragraph 2(11) above;

(*d*) that the applicant is unsuitable to hold the licence by reason of having been convicted of an offence or for any other reason;

(*e*) that the applicant has at any time been granted a street trading licence by the council and has persistently refused or neglected to pay fees due to them for it or charges due to them under paragraph 9(6) below for services rendered by them to him in his capacity as licence-holder;
(*f*) that the applicant has at any time been granted a street trading consent by the council and has persistently refused or neglected to pay fees due to them for it;
(*g*) that the applicant has without reasonable excuse failed to avail himself to a reasonable extent of a previous street trading licence.

(7) If the council consider that grounds for refusal exist under sub-paragraph (6)(*a*), (*b*) or (*g*) above, they may grant the applicant a licence which permits him—

(*a*) to trade on fewer days or during a shorter period in each day than specified in the application; or
(*b*) to trade only in one or more of the descriptions of goods specified in the application.

(8) If—

(*a*) a person is licensed or otherwise authorised to trade in a street under the provisions of any local Act; and
(*b*) the street becomes a licence street; and
(*c*) he was trading from a fixed position in the street immediately before it became a licence street; and
(*d*) he applied for a street trading licence to trade in the street, his application shall not be refused on any of the grounds mentioned in sub-paragraph (6)(*a*) to (*c*) above.

4. (1) A street trading licence shall specify—

(*a*) the street in which, days on which and times between which the licence-holder is permitted to trade; and
(*b*) the description of articles in which he is permitted to trade.

(2) If the district council determine that a licence-holder is to confine his trading to a particular place in the street, his street trading licence shall specify that place.

(3) Matters that fall to be specified in a street trading licence by virtue of sub-paragraph (1) or (2) above are referred to in this Schedule as the "principal terms" of the licence.

(4) When granting or renewing a street trading licence, the council may attach such further conditions (in this Schedule referred to as the "subsidiary terms" of the licence) as appear to them to be reasonable.

(5) Without prejudice to the generality of sub-paragraph (4) above, the subsidiary terms of a licence may include conditions—

(*a*) specifying the size and type of any stall or container which the licence-holder may use for trading;
(*b*) requiring that any stall or container so used shall carry the name of the licence-holder or the number of his licence or both; and
(*c*) prohibiting the leaving of refuse by the licence-holder or restricting the amount of refuse which he may leave or the places in which he may leave it.

(6) A street trading licence shall, unless previously revoked or surrendered, remain valid for a period of 12 months from the date on which it is granted or, if a shorter period is specified in the licence, for that period.

(7) If a district council resolve that the whole or part of a licence street shall be designated a prohibited street, then, on the designation taking effect, any street trading licence issued for trading in that street shall cease to be valid so far as it relates to the prohibited street.

5. (1) A district council may at any time revoke a street trading licence if they consider—

(*a*) that, owing to circumstances which have arisen since the grant or renewal of the licence, there is not enough space in the street for the licence-holder to engage in the trading permitted by the licence without causing undue interference or inconvenience to persons using the street;
(*b*) that the licence-holder is unsuitable to hold the licence by reason of having been convicted of an offence or for any other reason;
(*c*) that, since the grant or renewal of the licence, the licence-holder has persistently refused or neglected to pay fees due to the council for it or charges due to them under paragraph 9(6) below for services rendered by them to him in his capacity as licence-holder; or
(*d*) that, since the grant or renewal of the licence, the licence-holder has without reasonable excuse failed to avail himself of the licence to a reasonable extent.

(2) If the council consider that they have ground for revoking a licence by virtue of sub-paragraph (1)(*a*) or (*d*) above, they may, instead of revoking it, vary its principal terms—

(*a*) by reducing the number of days or the period in any one day during which the licence-holder is permitted to trade; or
(*b*) by restricting the descriptions of goods in which he is permitted to trade.

(3) A licence-holder may at any time surrender his licence to the council and it shall then cease to be valid.

6. (1) When a district council receive an application for the grant or renewal of a street trading licence, they shall within a reasonable time—

(*a*) grant a licence in the terms applied for; or
(*b*) serve notice on the applicant under sub-paragraph (2) below.

(2) If the council propose—

(*a*) to refuse an application for the grant or renewal of a licence; or
(*b*) to grant a licence on principal terms different from those specified in the application; or
(*c*) to grant a licence confining the applicant's trading to a particular place in a street; or
(*d*) to vary the principal terms of a licence; or
(*e*) to revoke a licence,

they shall first serve a notice on the applicant or, as the case may be, the licence-holder—

(i) specifying the ground or grounds on which their decision would be based; and
(ii) stating that within 7 days of receiving the notice he may in writing require them to give him an opportunity to make representations to them concerning it.

(3) Where a notice has been served under sub-paragraph (2) above, the council shall not determine the matter until either—

(*a*) the person on whom it was served has made representations to them concerning their decision; or
(*b*) the period during which he could have required them to give him an opportunity to make representations has elapsed without his requiring them to give him such an opportunity; or
(*c*) the conditions specified in sub-paragraph (4) below are satisfied.

(4) The conditions mentioned in sub-paragraph (3)(*c*) above are—

(*a*) that the person on whom the notice under sub-paragraph (2) above was served has required the council to give him an opportunity to make representations to them concerning it, as provided by sub-paragraph (2)(ii) above;
(*b*) that the council have allowed him a reasonable period for making his representations; and
(*c*) that he has failed to make them within that period.

(5) A person aggrieved—

(*a*) by the refusal of a council to grant or renew a licence, where—
  (i) they specified in their notice under sub-paragraph (2) above one of the grounds mentioned in paragraph 3(6)(*d*) to (*g*) above as the only ground on which their decision would be based; or
  (ii) they specified more than one ground in that notice but all the specified grounds were grounds mentioned in those paragraphs; or
(*b*) by a decision of a council to grant him a licence with principal terms different from those of a licence which he previously held, where they specified in their notice under sub-paragraph (2) above the ground mentioned in paragraph 3(6)(*g*) above as the only ground on which their decision would be based; or
(*c*) by a decision of a council—
  (i) to vary the principal terms of a licence; or
  (ii) to revoke a licence,

  in a case where they specified in their notice under sub-paragraph (2) above one of the grounds mentioned in paragraph 5(1)(*b*) to (*d*) above as the only ground on which their decision would be based or they specified more than one ground in that notice but all the specified grounds were grounds mentioned in those paragraphs,

may, at any time before the expiration of the period of 21 days beginning with the date upon which he is notified of the refusal or decision, appeal to the magistrates' court acting for the petty sessions area in which the street is situated.

(6) An appeal[1] against the decision of a magistrates' court under this paragraph may be brought to the Crown Court.

(7) On an appeal to the magistrates' court or the Crown Court under this paragraph the court may make such order as it thinks fit.

(8) Subject to sub-paragraphs (9) to (11) below, it shall be the duty of the council to give effect to an order of the magistrates' court or the Crown Court.

(9) The council need not give effect to the order of the magistrates' court until the time for bringing an appeal under sub-paragraph (6) above has expired and, if such an appeal is duly brought, until the determination or abandonment of the appeal.

(10) If a licence-holder applies for renewal of his licence before the date of its expiry, it shall remain valid—

(*a*) until the grant by the council of a new licence with the same principal terms; or
(*b*) if—
  (i) the council refuse renewal of the licence or decide to grant a licence with principal terms different from those of the existing licence, and
  (ii) he has a right of appeal under this paragraph,

  until the time for bringing an appeal has expired or, where an appeal is duly brought, until the determination or abandonment of the appeal; or
(*c*) if he has no right of appeal under this paragraph, until the council either grant him a new licence with principal terms different from those of the existing licence or notify him of their decision to refuse his application.

(11) Where—

(*a*) a council decide—
  (i) to vary the principal terms of a licence; or
  (ii) to revoke a licence; and
(*b*) a right of appeal is available to the licence-holder under this paragraph,

the variation or revocation shall not take effect until the time for bringing an appeal has expired or, where an appeal is duly brought, until the determination or abandonment of the appeal.

1. The position in London is governed by the London County Council (General Powers) Act 1947 and is somewhat different: see *R v Crown Court at Southwark, ex p Watts* (1989) 153 JP 666, 88 LGR 86, DC.

Street trading consents

8–19294 7. (1) An application for a street trading consent or the renewal of such a consent shall be made in writing to the district council.

(2) Subject to sub-paragraph (3) below, the council may grant a consent if they think fit.

(3) A street trading consent shall not be granted—

(*a*) to a person under the age of 17 years; or
(*b*) for any trading in a highway to which a control order under section 7 of the Local Government (Miscellaneous Provisions) Act 1976 is in force, other than trading to which the control order does not apply.

(4) When granting or renewing a street trading consent the council may attach such conditions to it as they consider reasonably necessary.

(5) Without prejudice to the generality of sub-paragraph (4) above, the conditions that may be attached to a street trading consent by virtue of that sub-paragraph include conditions to prevent—

(*a*) obstruction of the street or danger to persons using it; or
(*b*) nuisance or annoyance (whether to persons using the street or otherwise).

(6) The council may at any time vary the conditions of a street trading consent.

(7) Subject to sub-paragraph (8) below, the holder of a street trading consent shall not trade in a consent street from a van or other vehicle or from a stall, barrow or cart.

(8) The council may include in a street trading consent permission for its holder to trade in a consent street—

(*a*) from a stationary van, cart, barrow or other vehicle; or
(*b*) from a portable stall.

(9) If they include such a permission, they may make the consent subject to conditions—

(*a*) as to where the holder of the street trading consent may trade by virtue of the permission; and
(*b*) as to the times between which or periods for which he may so trade.

(10) A street trading consent may be granted for any period not exceeding 12 months but may be revoked at any time.

(11) The holder of a street trading consent may at anytime surrender his consent to the council and it shall then cease to be valid.

General

8–19295 **8.** The holder of a street trading licence or a street trading consent may employ any other person to assist him in his trading without a further licence or consent being required.

9. (1) A district council may charge such fees as they consider reasonable for the grant or renewal of a street trading licence or a street trading consent.

(2) A council may determine different fees for different types of licence or consent and, in particular, but without prejudice to the generality of this sub-paragraph, may determine fees differing according—

(*a*) to the duration of the licence or consent;
(*b*) to the street in which it authorises trading; and
(*c*) to the descriptions of articles in which the holder is authorised to trade.

(3) A council may require that applications for the grant or renewal of licences or consents shall be accompanied by so much of the fee as the council may require, by way of a deposit to be repaid by the council to the applicant if the application is refused.

(4) A council may determine that fees may be paid by instalments.

(5) Where a consent is surrendered or revoked, the council shall remit or refund, as they consider appropriate, the whole or a part of any fee paid for the grant or renewal of the consent.

(6) A council may recover from a licence-holder such reasonable charges as they may determine for the collection of refuse, the cleansing of streets and other services rendered by them to him in his capacity as licence-holder.

(7) Where a licence—

(*a*) is surrendered or revoked; or
(*b*) ceases to be valid by virtue of paragraph 4(7) above,

the council may remit or refund, as they consider appropriate, the whole or a part—

(i) of any fee paid for the grant or renewal of the licence; or
(ii) of any charges recoverable under sub-paragraph (6) above.

(8) The council may determine—

(*a*) that charges under sub-paragraph (6) above shall be included in a fee payable under sub-paragraph (1) above; or
(*b*) that they shall be separately recoverable.

(9) Before determining charges to be made under sub-paragraph (6) above or varying the amount of such charges the council—

(*a*) shall give notice of the proposed charges to licence-holders; and
(*b*) shall publish notice of the proposed charges in a local newspaper circulating in their area.

(10) A notice under sub-paragraph (9) above shall specify a reasonable period within which representations concerning the proposed charges may be made to the council.

(11) It shall be the duty of a council to consider any such representations which are made to them within the period specified in the notice.

Offences

8–19296 **10.** (1) A person who—

(*a*) engages in street trading in a prohibited street; or
(*b*) engages in street trading in a licence street or a consent street without being authorised to do so under this Schedule; or

(*c*) contravenes any of the principal terms of a street trading licence; or
(*d*) being authorised by a street trading consent to trade in a consent street, trades in that street—
(i) from a stationary van, cart, barrow or other vehicle; or
(ii) from a portable stall,

without first having been granted permission to do so under paragraph 7(8) above; or

(*e*) contravenes a condition imposed under paragraph 7(9) above,

shall be guilty of an offence[1].

(2) It shall be a defence for a person charged with an offence under sub-paragraph (1) above to prove that he took all reasonable precautions and exercised all due diligence to avoid commission of the offence.

(3) Any person who, in connection with an application for a street trading licence or for a street trading consent, makes a false statement which he knows to be false in any material respect, or which he does not believe to be true, shall be guilty of an offence.

(4) A person guilty of an offence under this paragraph shall be liable on summary conviction to a fine not exceeding **level 3** on the standard scale.

---

1. In *Caradon District Council v Cheeseman* [2000] Crim LR 190, it was held that a trader had common law rights, including the right to be treated fairly and that justices rightly held that a public law challenge was available as a defence to a criminal charge for an offence under this Schedule.

Savings

8–19297 **11.** Nothing in this Schedule shall affect—

(*a*) section 13 of the Markets and Fairs Clauses Act 1847 (prohibition of sales elsewhere than in market or in shops etc) as applied by any other Act;
(*b*) section 56 of the Food Act 1984 (prohibition of certain sales during market hours).

Local Government Act 1986

(1986 c 10)

PART II[1]
LOCAL AUTHORITY PUBLICITY

8–19630 **2. Prohibition of political publicity.** (1) A local authority shall not publish any material which, in whole or in part, appears to be designed to affect public support for a political party.

(2) In determining whether material falls within the prohibition regard shall be had to content and style of the material, the time and other circumstances of publication and the likely effect on those to whom it is directed and, in particular, to the following matters—

(*a*) whether material refers to a political party or to persons identified with a political party or promotes or opposes a point of view on a question of political controversy which is identifiable as the view of one political party and not of another;
(*b*) where the material is part of a campaign, the effect which the campaign appears to be designed to achieve.

(3) A local authority shall not give financial or other assistance to a person for the publication of material which the authority are prohibited by this section from publishing themselves.
[Local Government Act 1986, s 2, as amended by the Local Government Act 1988, s 27.]

---

1. Part II contains ss 2–6.

8–19631 **4. Codes of recommended practice as regards publicity.** *Secretary of State may issue codes of recommended practice as regards the content, style, distribution and cost of local authority publicity.*

8–19632 **5. Separate account of expenditure on publicity.** (1) A local authority shall keep a separate account of their expenditure on publicity.

(2) Any person interested may at any reasonable time and without payment inspect the account and make copies of it or any part of it.

(3) A person having custody of the account who intentionally obstructs a person in the exercise of the rights conferred by subsection (2) commits an offence and is liable on summary conviction to a fine not exceeding **level 3** on the standard scale.

(4) The regulation making power conferred by section 27(1)(*e*) of the Audit Commission Act 1998[1], section 39(1)(*e*) of the Public Audit (Wales) Act 2004 or section 105(1)(*d*) of the Local Government (Scotland) Act 1973 (power to make provision as to exercise of right of inspection and as to informing persons of those rights) applies to the right of inspection conferred by subsection (2).

(5) The Secretary of State may by order[2] provide that subsection (1) does not apply to publicity or expenditure of a prescribed description.

(6) Before making an order the Secretary of State shall consult such associations of local authorities as appear to him to be concerned and any local authority with whom consultation appears to him to be desirable.

(7) An order shall be made by statutory instrument which shall be subject to annulment in pursuance of a resolution of either House of Parliament.

[Local Government Act 1986, s 5, as amended by the Audit Commission Act 1998, Sch 3 and the Public Audit (Wales) Act 2004, Sch 2.]

---

1. See this title, post.
2. The Local Authorities (Publicity Account) (Exemption) Order 1987, SI 1987/2004 has been made.

8–19633 6. Interpretation and application of Part II. (1) References in this Part to local authorities and to publicity, and related expressions, shall be construed in accordance with the following provisions.

(2) "Local authority" means—

(*a*) in England and Wales—

a county, district or London borough council,
the Common Council of the City of London,
the Broads Authority (except in section 3),
a police authority established under section 3 of the Police Act 1996,
the Metroplitan Police Authority,
a joint authority established by Part IV of the Local Government Act 1985,
the London Fire and Emergency Planning Authority
the Council of the Isles of Scilly, or
a parish or community council;

(*b*) (*Scotland*);

and includes any authority, board or committee which discharges functions which would otherwise fall to be discharged by two or more such authorities.

(3) This Part applies to the Common Council of the City of London as local authority, police authority or port health authority.

(4) "Publicity", "publish" and "publication" refer to any communication, in whatever form, addressed to the public at large or to a section of the public.

(5) This Part applies to any such publicity expressly or impliedly authorised by any statutory provision, including—

section 111 of the Local Government Act 1972 or section 69 of the Local Government (Scotland) Act 1973 (general subsidiary powers of local authorities),
section 141 of the Local Government Act 1972 or section 87 of the Local Government (Scotland) Act 1973 (research and collection of information), and
section 145(1)(*a*) of the Local Government Act 1972 or section 16(1)(*a*) of the Local Government and Planning (Scotland) Act 1982 (provision of entertainments, etc).

(6) Nothing in this Part shall be construed as applying to anything done by a local authority in the discharge of their duties under Part VA of the Local Government Act 1972 or Part IIIA of the Local Government (Scotland) Act 1973 (duty to afford public access to meetings and certain documents).

(7) Nothing in this Part shall be construed as applying to anything done by a person in the discharge of any duties under regulations made under section 22 of the Local Government Act 2000 (access to information etc).

[Local Government Act 1986, s 6, as amended by the Norfolk and Suffolk Broads Act 1988, Sch 6, the Education Reform Act 1988, Sch 13, the Police and Magistrates' Courts Act 1994, Sch 4, the Police Act 1996, Sch 7, the Police Act 1997, Sch 6, the Greater London Authority Act 1999, Sch 27, SI 2001/2237 and the Criminal Justice and Police Act 2001, Sch 7.]

Local Government Finance Act 1988

(1988 c 41)

Introduction

8–19650 Non-domestic rate. Part III of the 1988 Act and Regulations make provision for the payment of rates for non-domestic hereditaments; see in particular the Non-Domestic Rating (Collection and Enforcement) (Local Lists) Regulations 1989 ("the Regulations"), post. Under reg 12(5) of the Regulations a magistrates' court to whom a charging authority has applied shall make a liability order if satisfied that the sum has become payable and has not been paid, to include costs.

Section 43 deals with liability for occupied hereditaments and s 45 for unoccupied hereditaments. Exemptions are covered by Sch 5, valuation by Sch 6 and administration by Sch 9.

At the liability order hearing, the magistrates' court will need satisfying on the following matters:

1. The local authority officer conducting proceedings is duly authorised under s 233 of the Local Government Act 1972 (ante).

2. An entry appears in the local rating list and the sums have been calculated, demanded or notified in accordance with statutory provision.

3. Full payment has not been made by the due date.

4. A second notice or remainder has been issued, and the sum not having been paid within 7 days of the service thereof thus making the full sum due.

5. A summons has been served for the remaining year's rates and the full sum claimed has not been paid.

The following defences may be raised:

1. The property in respect of which the amount is claimed did not appear for the relevant period in the local rating list.

2. The amount due has not been demanded or notified in accordance with statutory provisions.

3. The amount has not been paid.

4. The amount has not been calculated correctly.

5. Joint and several liability has been alleged and the defendant's relationship with the defaulting ratepayer was not such at the time the debt was incurred.

6. The defendant is not in occupation of the hereditament.

Once the liability order has been made, enforcement is under the Regulations alone; reg 14 provides for distress (with appeal to a magistrates' courts by a person aggrieved, under reg 15); thereafter imprisonment (see comments on this above in relation to community charge). The authority may consider insolvency (reg 18).

PART II
CHARGES AND MULTIPLIERS

Repealed.

PART III[1]
NON-DOMESTIC RATING
Local rating

8–19667 **41.** *Local rating lists.*

1. Part III contains ss 41–67. Part III is extensively amended by the Local Government and Housing Act 1989, Sch 5. Provision for the exchange of information between rating officials is made by the Non-Domestic Rating (Information) Act 1996.

8–19667A **41A.** *Local non-domestic rating lists for Welsh billing authorities.*

8–19668 **42.** *Contents of local lists*[1].

1. Section 42 is supplemented by SI 1989/1060 amended by SI 1993/616.

8–19668A **42A–B.** *Rural settlement list.*

8–19669 **43. Occupied hereditaments: liability.** (1) A person (the ratepayer) shall as regards a hereditament be subject to a non-domestic rate in respect of a chargeable financial year if the following conditions are fulfilled in respect of any day in the year—

(*a*) on the day the ratepayer is in occupation[1] of all or part of the hereditament, and
(*b*) the hereditament is shown for the day in a local non-domestic rating list in force for the year.

(2) In such a case the ratepayer shall be liable to pay an amount calculated by—

(*a*) finding the chargeable amount for each chargeable day, and
(*b*) aggregating the amounts found under paragraph (*a*) above.

(3) A chargeable day is one which falls within the financial year and in respect of which the conditions mentioned in subsection (1) above are fulfilled.

(4) Subject to subsections (4A), (5) and (6A) below, the chargeable amount for a chargeable day shall be calculated in accordance with the formula—

$$\frac{A \times B}{C}$$

(4A) Where subsection (4B) below applies, the chargeable amount for a chargeable day shall be calculated—

(*a*) in relation to England, in accordance with the formula—

$$\frac{A \times D}{C \times E}$$

(*b*) in relation to Wales, in accordance with the formula—

$$\frac{A \times B}{C \times E}$$

(4B) This subsection applies—

(*a*) in relation to England, where—

(i) the rateable value of the hereditament shown in the local non-domestic rating list for the first day of the chargeable financial year is not more than any amount prescribed by the Secretary of State by order[2],

(ii) on the day concerned any conditions prescribed by the Secretary of State by order[2] are satisfied, and

(iii) the ratepayer has made an application for the purposes of this subsection to the billing authority concerned by such date as may be prescribed by the Secretary of State by order[2],

(*b*) in relation to Wales, where—

(i) the rateable value of the hereditament shown in the local non-domestic rating list for the first day of the chargeable financial year is not more than any amount prescribed by the National Assembly for Wales by order, and

(ii) on the day concerned any conditions prescribed by the National Assembly for Wales by order are satisfied.

(4C) An application under subsection (4B)(*a*)(iii) above shall be made in such form, and contain such information, as may be prescribed by the Secretary of State by order[2].

(4D) If the ratepayer—

(*a*) makes a statement in an application under subsection (4B)(*a*)(iii) above which he knows to be false in a material particular, or

(*b*) recklessly makes a statement in such an application which is false in a material particular,

he shall be liable on summary conviction to imprisonment for a term not exceeding 3 months or to a fine not exceeding level 3 on the standard scale or to both.

(5) Where subsection (6) below applies the chargeable amount for a chargeable day shall be calculated in accordance with the formula—

$$\frac{A \times B}{C \times 5}$$

(6) This subsection applies where on the day concerned the ratepayer is a charity or trustees for a charity and the hereditament is wholly or mainly used for charitable purposes (whether of that charity or of that and other charities).

(6A) Where subsection (6B) below applies, or, subject to subsection (6I) below, subsection (6F) below applies, the chargeable amount for a chargeable day shall be calculated in accordance with the formula—

$$\frac{A \times B}{C \times 2}$$

(6B) This subsection applies where—*

(*a*) on the day concerned the hereditament is within a settlement identified in the billing authority's rural settlement list for the chargeable financial year,

(*b*) the rateable value of the hereditament shown in the local non-domestic rating list at the beginning of that year is not more than any amount prescribed by the Secretary of State by order[3], and

(*c*) on the day concerned—

(i) the whole or part of the hereditament is used as a qualifying general store, a qualifying food store or qualifying post office, or

(ii) any conditions prescribed by the Secretary of State by order[4] are satisfied;

and subsections (6C) to (6E) below apply for the purposes of this subsection.

(6C) A hereditament, or part of a hereditament, is used as a qualifying general store on any day in a chargeable financial year if—

(*a*) a trade or business consisting wholly or mainly of the sale by retail of both food for human consumption (excluding confectionery) and general household goods is carried on there, and

(*b*) such a trade or business is not carried on in any other hereditament, or part of a hereditament, in the settlement concerned.

(6CA) A hereditament, or part of a hereditament, is used as a qualifying food store on any day in a chargeable financial year if a trade or business consisting wholly or mainly of the sale by retail of food for human consumption (excluding confectionery and excluding the supply of food in the course of catering) is carried on there.

(6CB) In subsection (6CA) above the supply of food in the course of catering includes—

(*a*) any supply of food for consumption on the premises on which it is supplied; and

(*b*) any supply of hot food for consumption off those premises;

and for the purposes of paragraph (*b*) above "hot food" means food which, or any part of which—

(i) has been heated for the purposes of enabling it to be consumed at a temperature above the ambient air temperature; and

(ii) is at the time of supply above that temperature.

(6D) A hereditament, or part of a hereditament, is used as a qualifying post office on any day in a chargeable financial year if—

(*a*) it is used for the purposes of a universal service provider (within the meaning of the Postal Services Act 2000) and in connection with the provision of a universal postal service (within the meaning of that Act), and

(*b*) no other hereditament, or part of a hereditament, in the settlement concerned is so used.

(6E) Where a hereditament or part is used as a qualifying general store or qualifying post office on any day in a chargeable financial year, it is not to be treated as ceasing to be so used on any subsequent day in that year merely because the condition in subsection (6C)(*b*) or (6D)(*b*) above ceases to be satisfied.

(6F) This subsection applies where—

(*a*) on the day concerned the condition mentioned in subsection (6G) below is fulfilled in respect of the hereditament; and

(*b*) the rateable value of the hereditament shown in the local non-domestic rating list at the beginning of the chargeable financial year is not more than any amount prescribed by the Secretary of State by order[5].

(6G) The condition is that the hereditament—

(*a*) consists wholly or mainly of land or buildings which were, on at least 183 days during the period of one year ending immediately before this subsection comes into effect, agricultural land or agricultural buildings for the purposes of the exemption under paragraph 1 of Schedule 5 to this Act; and

(*b*) includes land or a building which is not agricultural for the purposes of that exemption but was agricultural for those purposes on at least 183 days during the period mentioned in paragraph (*a*) above.

(6H) For the purposes of subsection (6G) above—

(*a*) in relation to any hereditament which includes property which is domestic within the meaning of section 66 below, paragraph (a) has effect as if that part of the hereditament which does not consist of such property were the entire hereditament; and

(*b*) a building which has replaced a building which was an agricultural building for the purposes of the exemption mentioned in that subsection ("the original building") is to be treated as if it were the original building.

(6I) Subsection (6A) above shall not have effect, in relation to a hereditament to which subsection (6F) above applies, on a chargeable day on which paragraph 2A of Schedule 6 to this Act applies in relation to the hereditament.

(6J) Subject to subsection (6K) below, subsections (6F) to (6I) above shall cease to have effect at the end of the period of five years beginning with the day on which those subsections come into effect.

(6K) The Secretary of State may by order extend or further extend the period mentioned in subsection (6J).

(6L) If the period is so extended or further extended—

(*a*) subsection (6F) above cannot apply to a hereditament after the end of the period of five years beginning with the day on which it first applies; and

(*b*) where a hereditament to which subsection (6F) above applies ("the original hereditament") includes land or a building which is subsequently included in a different hereditament, that subsection cannot apply to the different hereditament after the end of the period of five years beginning with the day on which it first applies to the original hereditament.

(7) The amount the ratepayer is liable to pay under this section shall be paid to the billing authority in whose local non-domestic rating list the hereditament is shown.

(8) The liability to pay any such amount shall be discharged by making a payment or payments in accordance with regulations under Schedule 9 below.

(8A) In relation to any hereditament in respect of which both subsections (4A) and (6A) above (but not subsection (5) above) have effect on the day concerned, the chargeable amount—

(*a*) in relation to England, shall be calculated in accordance with subsection (6A) above,
(*b*) in relation to Wales, shall be calculated in accordance with whichever of subsections (4A) and (6A) above produces the smaller amount.

(8B) In relation to any hereditament in respect of which—

(*a*) subsections (4A), (5) and (6A) above each have effect on the day concerned,
(*b*) subsections (4A) and (5) above both have effect on that day, or
(*c*) subsections (5) and (6A) above both have effect on that day,

the chargeable amount shall be calculated in accordance with subsection (5) above.
[Local Government Finance Act 1988, s 43, as amended by the Local Government Finance Act 1992, Sch 13, the Local Government and Finance Act 1997, Sch 1, the Rating (Former Agricultural Premises and Rural Shops) Act 2001, ss 1(1), 3(1) and the Local Government Act 2003, s 61.]

***New para (*aa*) inserted by the Local Government Act 2003, s 63 from a date to be appointed.**

1. The actions of a receiver and manager in running a company's business do not, without more, amount to rateable occupation of the company's premises by him, since his occupation amounts to occupation by the company; if the company subsequently goes into liquidation (which terminates the receiver's agency by virtue of s 44(1)(a) of the Insolvency Act 1986), but the receiver continues to run the company as before, the company remains in rateable occupation and the receiver does not become liable for the rates (*Rees v Boston Borough Council* [2001] EWCA Civ 1934, [2002] 1 WLR 1304).
2. The Non-domestic Rating (Small Business Rate Relief) (England) Order 2004, SI 2004/3315 has been made.
3. See the Non-Domestic Rating (Rural Settlements) (England) Order 1997, SI 1997/2792 amended by SI 2000/521, SI 2001/1346 and SI 2004/3153, the Non-Domestic Rating (Rural Settlements) (Wales) Order 1998, SI 1998/2963 amended by SI 2002/331 and the Non-domestic Rating (Rural Rate Relief) (Wales) Order 2002, SI 2002/331.
4. The Non-domestic Rating Contributions (Public Houses and Petrol Filling Stations) (England) Order 2001, SI 2001/1345 has been made.
5. The Non-domestic Rating (Former Agricultural Premises) (England) Order 2004, SI 2004/3152 has been made.

8–19670 44. Occupied hereditaments: supplementary. (1) This section applies for the purposes of section 43 above.

(2) A is the rateable value shown for the day under section 42(4) above as regards the hereditament.

(3) *Repealed.*

(4) Subject to subsection (5) below, B is the non-domestic rating multiplier for the financial year.

(5) Where the billing authority is a special authority, B is the authority's non-domestic rating multiplier for the financial year.

(6) C is the number of days in the financial year.

(7) Subject to subsection (8) below, D is the small business non-domestic rating multiplier for the financial year.

(8) Where the billing authority is a special authority, D is the authority's small business non-domestic rating multiplier for the financial year.

(9) E is such amount as may be prescribed—

(*a*) in relation to England, by the Secretary of State by order[1],
(*b*) in relation to Wales, by the National Assembly for Wales by order.

[Local Government Finance Act 1988, s 44, as amended by the Local Government and Housing Act 1989, Schs 5 and 12, the Local Government Finance Act 1992, Sch 13 and the Local Government Act 2003, s 61.]

---

1. The Non-domestic Rating (Small Business Rate Relief) (England) Order 2004, SI 2004/3315 has been made.

8–19670A 44A. Partly occupied hereditaments. (1) Where a hereditament is shown in a billing authority's local non-domestic rating list and it appears to the authority that part of the hereditament is unoccupied but will remain so for a short time only the authority may require the valuation officer for the authority to apportion the rateable value of the hereditament between the occupied and unoccupied parts of the hereditament and to certify the apportionment to the authority.

(2) The reference in subsection (1) above to the rateable value of the hereditament is a reference to the rateable value shown under section 42(4) above as regards the hereditament for the day on which the authority makes its requirement.

(3) For the purposes of this section an apportionment under subsection (1) above shall be treated as applicable for any day which—

(*a*) falls within the operative period in relation to the apportionment, and
(*b*) is a day for which the rateable value shown under section 42(4) above as regards the hereditament to which the apportionment relates is the same as that so shown for the day on which the authority requires the apportionment.

(4) References in this section to the operative period in relation to an apportionment are references to the period beginning—

(*a*) where requiring the apportionment does not have the effect of bringing to an end the operative period in relation to a previous apportionment under subsection (1) above, with the day on which the hereditament to which the apportionment relates became partly unoccupied, and (*b*) where requiring the apportionment does have the effect of bringing to an end the operative period in relation to a previous apportionment under subsection (1) above, with the day immediately following the end of that period,

and ending with the first day on which one or more of the events listed below occurs.

(5) The events are—

(*a*) the occupation of any of the unoccupied part of the hereditament to which the apportionment relates;

(*b*) the ending of the rate period in which the authority requires the apportionment;

(*c*) the requiring of a further apportionment under subsection (1) above in relation to the hereditament to which the apportionment relates;

(*d*) the hereditament to which the apportionment relates becoming completely unoccupied.

(6) Subsection (7) below applies where—

(*a*) a billing authority requires an apportionment under subsection (1) above, and

(*b*) the hereditament to which the apportionment relates does not fall within the class prescribed under section 45(1)(*d*) below.

(7) In relation to any day for which the apportionment is applicable, section 43 above shall have effect as regards the hereditament as if the following subsections were substituted for section 44(2)—

"(2) A is such part of the rateable value shown for the day under section 42(4) above as regards the hereditament as is assigned by the relevant apportionments to the occupied part of the hereditament.

(2A) In subsection (2) above "the relevant apportionment" means the apportionment under section 44A(1) below which relates to the hereditament and is treated for the purposes of section 44A below as applicable for the day."

(8) Subsection (9) below applies where—

(*a*) a billing authority requires an apportionment under subsection (1) above, and

(*b*) the hereditament to which the apportionment relates falls within a class prescribed under section 45(1)(*d*) below.

(9) In relation to any day for which the apportionment is applicable, section 43 above shall have effect as regards the hereditament as if the following subsections were substituted for section 44(2)—

"(2) A is the sum of—

(*a*) such part of the rateable value shown for the day under section 42(4) above as regards the hereditament as is assigned by the relevant apportionment to the occupied part of the hereditament, and

(*b*) one half of such part of that rateable value as is assigned by the relevant apportionment to the unoccupied part of the hereditament.

(2A) In subsection (2) above "the relevant apportionment" means the apportionment under section 44A(1) below which relates to the hereditament and is treated for the purposes of section 44A below as applicable for the day.".

(10) References in subsections (1) to (5) above to the hereditament, in relation to a hereditament which is partly domestic property or partly exempt from local non-domestic rating, shall, except where the reference is to the rateable value of the hereditament, be construed as references to such part of the hereditament as is neither domestic property nor exempt from local non-domestic rating.

[Local Government Finance Act 1988, s 44A, as inserted with retrospective effect by the Local Government and Housing Act 1989, s 139, Sch 5, paras 22, 79(3). by the Local Government and Housing Act 1989, Schs 5 and 12 and the Local Government Finance Act 1992, Sch 13.]

8–19671 45. Unoccupied hereditaments: liability. (1) A person (the ratepayer) shall as regards a hereditament be subject to a non-domestic rate in respect of a chargeable financial year if the following conditions are fulfilled in respect of any day in the year—

(*a*) on the day none of the hereditament is occupied,

(*b*) on the day the ratepayer is the owner[1] of the whole of the hereditament,

(*c*) the hereditament is shown for the day in a local non-domestic rating list in force for the year, and

(*d*) on the day the hereditament falls within a class prescribed by the Secretary of State by regulations[2].

(2) In such a case the ratepayer shall be liable to pay an amount calculated by—

(*a*) finding the chargeable amount for each chargeable day, and

(*b*) aggregating the amounts found under paragraph (*a*) above.

(3) A chargeable day is one which falls within the financial year and in respect of which the conditions mentioned in subsection (1) above are fulfilled.

(4) Subject to subsection (5) below, the chargeable amount for a chargeable day shall be calculated in accordance with the formula—

$$\frac{A \times B}{C \times 2}$$

(5) Where subsection (6) below applies the chargeable amount for a chargeable day shall be calculated in accordance with the formula—

$$\frac{A \times B}{C \times 10}$$

(6) This subsection applies where on the day concerned the ratepayer is a charity or trustees for a charity and it appears that when next in use the hereditament will be wholly or mainly used for charitable purposes (whether of that charity or of that and other charities).

(7) The amount the ratepayer is liable to pay under this section shall be paid to the billing authority in whose local non-domestic rating list the hereditament is shown.

(8) The liability to pay any such amount shall be discharged by making a payment or payments in accordance with regulations under Schedule 9 below.

(9) For the purposes of subsection (1)(*d*) above a class may be prescribed by reference to such factors as the Secretary of State sees fit.

(10) Without prejudice to the generality of subsection (9) above a class may be prescribed by reference to one or more of the following factors—

(*a*) the physical characteristics of the hereditaments;

(*b*) the fact that hereditaments have been unoccupied at any time preceding the day mentioned in subsection (1) above;

(*c*) the fact that the owners of hereditaments fall within prescribed descriptions.

[Local Government Finance Act 1988, s 45, as amended by the Local Government and Housing Act 1989, Sch 5 and the Local Government Finance Act 1992, Sch 13.]

---

1. Where a landlord brings a claim for forfeiture of a lease and the tenant accepts that repudiation of the lease and vacates the premises, it is the landlord who is responsible for the non-domestic rate in respect of the unoccupied premises (*Royal Borough of Kingston upon Thames v Marlow* (1995) 160 JP 502, DC).
2. The Non-Domestic Rating (Unoccupied Property) Regulations 1989, post, have been made.

8–19672 46. Unoccupied hereditaments: supplementary. (1) This section applies for the purposes of section 45 above.

(2) A is the rateable value shown for the day under section 42(4) above as regards the hereditament.

(3) Subject to subsection (4) below, B is the non-domestic rating multiplier for the financial year.

(4) Where the billing authority is a special authority, B is the authority's non-domestic rating multiplier for the financial year.

(5) C is the number of days in the financial year.

[Local Government Finance Act 1988, s 46, as amended by the Local Government and Housing Act 1989, Sch 5 and the Local Government Finance Act 1992, Sch 13.]

8–19672A 46A. Unnoccupied hereditaments: new buildings. (1) Schedule 4A below (which makes provision with respect to the determination of a day as the completion day in relation to a new building) shall have effect.

(2) Where—

(*a*) a completion notice is served under Schedule 4A below, and

(*b*) the building to which the notice relates is not completed on or before the relevant day,

then for the purposes of section 42 above and Schedule 6 below the building shall be deemed to be completed on that day.

(3) For the purposes of subsection (2) above the relevant day in relation to a completion notice is—

(*a*) where an appeal against the notice is brought under paragraph 4 of Schedule 4A below, the day stated in the notice, and

(*b*) where no appeal against the notice is brought under that paragraph, the day determined under that Schedule as the completion day in relation to the building to which the notice relates.

(4) Where—

(*a*) a day is determined under Schedule 4A below as the completion day in relation to a new building, and

(*b*) the building is not occupied on that day,

it shall be deemed for the purposes of section 45 above to become unoccupied on that day.

(5) Where—

(*a*) a day is determined under Schedule 4A below as the completion day in relation to a new building, and (*b*) the building is one produced by the structural alteration of an existing building,

the hereditament which comprised the existing building shall be deemed for the purposes of section 45 above to have ceased to exist, and to have been omitted from the list, on that day.

(6) In this section—

(*a*) "building" includes part of a building, and

(*b*) references to a new building include references to a building produced by the structural alteration of an existing building where the existing building is comprised in a hereditament which, by virtue of the alteration, becomes, or becomes part of, a different hereditament or different hereditaments.

[Local Government Finance Act 1988, s 46A inserted with retrospective effect by the Local Government and Housing Act 1989, s 139, Sch 5, paras 25, 79(3)., as amended by the Local Government and Housing Act 1989, Sch 5 and the Local Government Finance Act 1992, Sch 13.]

8–19673 47. Discretionary relief. (1) Where the first and second conditions mentioned in subsections (2) and (3) below or the rural settlement condition and the second condition mentioned in subsection (3) below, or the condition relating to relief for former agricultural premises mentioned in subsection (3C) below and the second condition mentioned in subsection (3) below, are fulfilled for a day which is a chargeable day within the meaning of section 43 or 45 above (as the case may be)—

(*a*) the chargeable amount for the day shall be such as is determined by, or found in accordance with rules determined by, the billing authority concerned, and

(*b*) sections 43(4) to (6B) and 44 above, sections 45(4) to (6) and 46 above, regulations under section 57A or 58 below or any provision of or made under Schedule 7A below (as the case may be) shall not apply as regards the day.

(2) The first condition is that one or more of the following applies on the chargeable day—

(*a*) the ratepayer is a charity or trustees for a charity, and the hereditament is wholly or mainly used for charitable purposes (whether of that charity or of that and other charities);

(*b*) the hereditament is not an excepted hereditament, and all or part of it is occupied for the purposes of one or more institutions or other organisations none of which is established or conducted for profit and each of whose main objects are charitable or are otherwise philanthropic or religious or concerned with education, social welfare, science, literature or the fine arts;

(*c*) the hereditament is not an excepted hereditament, it is wholly or mainly used for purposes of recreation, and all or part of it is occupied for the purposes of a club, society or other organisation not established or conducted for profit.

(3) The second condition is that, during a period which consists of or includes the chargeable day, a decision of the billing authority concerned operates to the effect that this section applies as regards the hereditament concerned.

(3A) The rural settlement condition is—*

(*a*) that on the chargeable day the hereditament is within a settlement identified in the billing authority's rural settlement list for the chargeable financial year in which that day falls, and

(*b*) that the rateable value of the hereditament shown in the local non-domestic rating list at the beginning of the chargeable financial year is not more than any amount prescribed by the Secretary of State by order[1].

(3B) Where section 43(6B)(*c*) above does not apply, the billing authority shall not, by virtue of subsection (3A) above, make such a decision as is referred to in subsection (3) above unless it is satisfied that—

(*a*) the hereditament is used for purposes which are of benefit to the local community, and

(*b*) it would be reasonable for the billing authority to make such a decision, having regard to the interests of persons liable to pay council tax set by it.

(3C) The condition relating to relief for former agricultural premises is that on the chargeable day section 43(6F) above applies to the hereditament.

(4) A determination under subsection (1)(*a*) above—

(*a*) must be such that the chargeable amount for the day is less than the amount it would be apart from this section;

(*b*) may be such that the chargeable amount for the day is 0;

(*c*) may be varied by a further determination of the authority under subsection (1)(*a*) above.

(5) In deciding what the chargeable amount for the day would be apart from this section the effect of any regulations under section 57A or 58 below or any provision of or made under Schedule 7A below shall be taken into account but anything which has been done or could be done under section 49 below shall be ignored.

(6) A decision under subsection (3) above may be revoked by a further decision of the authority.

(7) A decision under subsection (3) above is invalid as regards a day if made more than six months after the end of the financial year in which the day falls.

(8) *Regulations.*[2]

(9) A hereditament is an excepted hereditament if all or part of it is occupied (otherwise than as trustee) by—

(*a*) a billing authority; or

(*b*) a precepting authority, other than the Receiver for the Metropolitan Police District or** charter trustees; or

(*c*) a functional body, within the meaning of the Greater London Authority Act 1999, s 138.

[Local Government Finance Act 1988, s 47, as amended by the Local Government and Housing Act 1989, Sch 5, the Local Government Finance Act 1992, Sch 13, the Local Government and Rating Act 1997, Schs 1 and 3, the Greater London Authority Act 1999, s 138, the Rating (Former Agricultural Premises and Rural Shops) Act 2001, s 2(1) and the Local Government Act 2003, Sch 7.]

***New para (*aa*) inserted by the Local Government Act 2003, s 63 from a date to be appointed.**

****Repealed by the Greater London Authority Act 1999, Sch 34, as from a day to be appointed.**

1. See the Non-Domestic Rating (Rural Settlements) (England) Order 1997, SI 1997/2792 amended by SI 2000/521; and the Non-Domestic Rating (Rural Settlements) (Wales) Order 1998, SI 1998/2963.

2. The Non-Domestic Rating (Discretionary Relief) Regulations 1989, SI 1989/1059 amended by SI 1993/616 have been made. See also the Non Domestic Rating Contributions (England) Regulations 1992, SI 1992/3082 amended by SI 1992/3259, SI 1993/1496 and 3082, SI 1994/421, 1431 and 3139, SI 1995/3181, SI 1996/561 and 3245, SI 1997/3031, SI 1998/3038 and SI 2005/3333; and the Non-Domestic Rating Contributions (Wales) Regulations 1992, SI 1992/3238 amended by SI 1993/1505 and 3077, SI 1994/547, 1742 and 3125, SI 1995/3235, SI 1996/3018, SI 1997/3003, SI 1998/2962 and SI 2005/3345.

8–19674 48. Discretionary relief: supplementary. (1) This section applies for the purposes of section 47 above (but subsection (5) below does not apply for the purposes of subsection (3B)(*a*) of that section).

(2) A hereditament not in use shall be treated as wholly or mainly used for charitable purposes if it appears that when next in use it will be wholly or mainly used for charitable purposes.

(3) A hereditament not in use shall be treated as wholly or mainly used for purposes of recreation if it appears that when next in use it will be wholly or mainly used for purposes of recreation.

(4) A hereditament which is wholly unoccupied shall be treated as an excepted hereditament if it appears that when any of it is next occupied the hereditament will be an excepted hereditament.

(5) If a hereditament is wholly unoccupied but it appears that it or any part of it when next occupied will be occupied for particular purposes, the hereditament or part concerned (as the case may be) shall be treated as occupied for those purposes.

[Local Government Finance Act 1988, s 48, as amended by the Local Government and Rating Act 1997, Sch 1.]

8–19675 49. Reduction or remission of liability. (1) A billing authority may—

(*a*) reduce any amount a person is liable to pay to it under section 43 or 45 above, or

(*b*) remit payment of the whole of any amount a person would otherwise be liable to pay to it under section 43 or 45 above.

(2) But an authority may not act under this section unless it is satisfied that—

(*a*) the ratepayer would sustain hardship if the authority did not do so, and

(*b*) it is reasonable for the authority to do so, having regard to the interests of persons liable to pay council tax set by it.

(3) The amount as regards which a reduction or remittance may be made under subsection (1) above is the amount the person would be liable to pay (apart from this section) taking account of anything done under section 47 above, the effect of any regulations under section 57A or 58 below, and the effect of any provision of or made under Schedule 7A below.

(4) Where an authority acts under this section, section 43 or 45 above shall be construed accordingly as regards the case concerned.

[Local Government Finance Act 1988, s 49, as amended by the Local Government and Housing Act 1989, Sch 5, the Local Government Finance Act 1992, Sch 13 and the Local Government Act 2003, Sch 7.]

8–19676 50. Joint owners or occupiers. (1) The Secretary of State may make such regulations[1] as he sees fit to deal with any case where (apart from the regulations) there would be more than one owner or occupier of a hereditament or part or of land at a particular time.

(2) Nothing in the following provisions of this section shall prejudice the generality of subsection (1) above.

(3) The regulations may provide for the owner or occupier at the time concerned to be taken to be such one of the owners or occupiers as is identified in accordance with prescribed rules.

(4) The regulations may provide that—

(*a*) as regards any time when there is only one owner or occupier, section 43 or 45 above (as the case may be) shall apply;

(*b*) as regards any time when there is more than one owner or occupier, the owners or occupiers shall be jointly and severally liable to pay a prescribed amount by way of non-domestic rate.

(5) The regulations may include provision that prescribed provisions shall apply instead of

prescribed provisions of this Part, or that prescribed provisions of this Part shall not apply or shall apply subject to prescribed amendments or adaptations.
[Local Government Finance Act 1988, s 50.]

1. See Part II of the Non-Domestic Rating (Collection and Enforcement) (Miscellaneous Provisions) Regulations 1990, SI 1990/145 amended by SI 1993/616, 774 and 894. The occupier of part of a hereditament is not liable under these Regulations to a liability order being made against him for the whole of the hereditament since it is not the intention of the Regulations themselves to impose such a liability (*Ford v Burnley Borough Council* (1995) 160 JP 541, [1995] RA 205).

8–19677 **51. Exemption.** Schedule 5 below shall have effect to determine the extent (if any) to which a hereditament is for the purposes of this Part exempt from local non-domestic rating.
[Local Government Finance Act 1988, s 51.]

Central rating

8–19678 **52. Central rating lists.** (1) In accordance with this Part the central valuation officer shall compile, and then maintain, lists (to be called central non-domestic rating lists).

(2) A list must be compiled on 1 April 1990 and on 1 April in every fifth year afterwards.

(3) A list shall come into force on the day on which it is compiled and shall remain in force until the next one is compiled five years later.

(4) Before a list is compiled the central valuation officer must take such steps as are reasonably practicable to ensure that it is accurately compiled on 1 April concerned.

(5) Not later than 31 December preceding a day on which a list is to be compiled the central valuation officer shall send to the Secretary of State a copy of the list he proposes (on the information then before him) to compile.

(6) As soon as is reasonably practicable after receiving the copy the Secretary of State shall deposit it at his principal office.

(6A) As soon as is reasonably practicable after compiling a list the central valuation officer shall send a copy of it to the Secretary of State.

(6B) As soon as is reasonably practicable after receiving the copy the Secretary of State shall deposit it at his principal office.

(7) A list must be maintained for so long as is necessary for the purposes of this Part, so that the expiry of the five year period for which it is in force does not detract from the duty to maintain it.
[Local Government Finance Act 1988, s 52, as amended by the Local Government and Housing Act 1989, Sch 5.]

8–19679 **53. Contents of central lists.** (1) With a view to securing the central rating en bloc of certain hereditaments, the Secretary of State may by regulations[1] designate a person and prescribe in relation to him one or more descriptions of relevant non-domestic hereditament.

(2) Where the regulations so require, a central non-domestic rating list must show, for each day in each chargeable financial year for which it is in force, the name of the designated person and, against it, each hereditament (wherever situated) which on the day concerned—

(*a*) is occupied or (if unoccupied) owned by him, and
(*b*) falls within any description prescribed in relation to him.

(3) For each such day the list must also show against the name of the designated person the rateable value (as a whole) of the hereditaments so shown.

(4) Where regulations are for the time being in force under this section prescribing a description of non-domestic hereditament in relation to a person designated in the regulations ("the previously designated person"), amending regulations altering the designated person in relation to whom that description of hereditament is prescribed may have effect from a date earlier than that on which the amending regulations are made.

(4A) Where, by virtue of subsection (4) above, the designated person in relation to any description of non-domestic hereditament is changed from a date earlier than the making of the regulation,—

(*a*) any necessary alteration shall be made with effect from that date to a central non-domestic rating list on which any hereditament concerned is shown; and
(*b*) an order making the provision referred to in paragraph 3(2) of Schedule 6 below and specifying a description of hereditament by reference to the previously designated person shall be treated, with effect from that date, as referring to the person designated by the amending regulations.

(5) A central non-domestic rating list must also contain such information about hereditaments shown in it as may be prescribed by the Secretary of State by regulations.
[Local Government Finance Act 1988, s 53, as amended by the Local Government and Housing Act 1989, Sch 5.]

1. The Non Domestic Rating (Collection and Enforcement) (Central Lists) Regulations 1989, SI 1989/2260 amended by SI 1991/142, SI 1992/1513 and SI 1993/1494, the Central Rating Lists (England) Regulations 2000, SI 2000/525 amended by SI 2001/737 and SI 2005/551and the Central Rating Lists (Wales) Regulations 2005, SI 2005/422 have been made.

8–19680 54. Central rating: liability. (1) A person (the ratepayer) shall be subject to a non-domestic rate in respect of a chargeable financial year if for any day in the year his name is shown in a central non-domestic rating list in force for the year.

(2) In such a case the ratepayer shall be liable to pay an amount calculated by—

(*a*) finding the chargeable amount for each chargeable day, and
(*b*) aggregating the amounts found under paragraph (*a*) above.

(3) A chargeable day is one which falls within the financial year and for which the ratepayer's name is shown in the list.

(4) The chargeable amount for a chargeable day shall be calculated in accordance with the formula—

$$\frac{A \times B}{C}$$

(5) A is the rateable value shown for the day in the list against the ratepayer's name.

(6) B is the non-domestic rating multiplier for the financial year.

(7) C is the number of days in the financial year.

(8) The amount the ratepayer is liable to pay under this section shall be paid to the Secretary of State.

(9) The liability to pay any such amount shall be discharged by making a payment or payments in accordance with regulations under Schedule 9 below.

[Local Government Finance Act 1988, s 54.]

General

8–19681 55. *Alteration of lists.*

8–19682 62. Administration. Schedule 9 below (which contains provisions about administration, including collection and recovery) shall have effect.

[Local Government Finance Act 1988, s 62.]

8–19683 63. *Death.*

Interpretation

8–19689 64. Hereditaments. (1) A hereditament is anything which, by virtue of the definition of hereditament in section 115(1) of the 1967 Act, would have been a hereditament for the purposes of that Act had this Act not been passed.

(2) In addition, a right is a hereditament if it is a right to use any land for the purpose of exhibiting advertisements and—

(*a*) the right is let out or reserved to any person other than the occupier[1] of the land, or
(*b*) where the land is not occupied for any other purpose, the right is let out or reserved to any person other than the owner of the land.

(2A) In addition, a right is a hereditament if—

(*a*) it is a right to use any land for the purpose of operating a meter to measure a supply of gas or electricity or such other service as—
  (i) the Secretary of State in relation to England, or
  (ii) the National Assembly for Wales in relation to Wales,

may by order specify, and

(*b*) the meter is owned by a person other than the consumer of the service.

(3) The Secretary of State may make regulations[2] providing that in prescribed cases—

(*a*) anything which would (apart from the regulations) be one hereditament shall be treated as more than one hereditament;
(*b*) anything which would (apart from the regulations) be more than one hereditament shall be treated as one hereditament[3].

(3A) The Secretary of State may make regulations providing that where on any land there are two or more moorings which—

(*a*) are owned by the same person,
(*b*) are not domestic property, and
(*c*) are separately occupied, or available for separate occupation, by persons other than that person,

a valuation officer may determine that, for the purposes of the compilation or alteration of a local non-domestic rating list, all or any of the moorings, or all or any of them together with any adjacent moorings or land owned and occupied by that person, shall be treated as one hereditament.

(3B) Regulations under subsection (3A) above may provide that—

(*a*) where a valuation officer makes a determination as mentioned in that subsection, he shall, if prescribed conditions are fulfilled, supply prescribed persons with prescribed information;

(*b*) while such a determination is in force—

(i) the person who on any day is the owner of the moorings (or the moorings and land) which constitute the hereditament shall be treated for the purposes of sections 43, 44A and 45 above as being in occupation of all of the hereditament on that day; and

(ii) no other person shall be treated for those purposes as being in occupation of all or any part of the hereditament on that day.

(4) A hereditament is a relevant hereditament if it consists of property of any of the following descriptions—

(*a*) lands;

(*b*) coal mines;

(*c*) mines of any other description, other than a mine of which the royalty or dues are for the time being wholly reserved in kind;

(*d*) *Repealed;*

(*e*) any right which is a hereditament by virtue of subsection (2) or (2A) above.

(5)–(7D) *Repealed.*

(8) A hereditament is non-domestic if either—

(*a*) it consists entirely of property which is not domestic, or

(*b*) it is a composite hereditament.

(9) A hereditament is composite if part only of it consists of domestic property.

(10) A hereditament shall be treated as wholly or mainly used for charitable purposes at any time if at the time it is wholly or mainly used for the sale of goods donated to a charity and the proceeds of sale of the goods (after any deduction of expenses) are applied for the purposes of a charity.

(11) In subsection (2) above "land" includes a wall or other part of a building and a sign, hoarding, frame, post or other structure erected or to be erected on land.

(11A) The Secretary of State in relation to England, and the National Assembly in relation to Wales, may by regulations make provision as to what is to be regarded as being a meter for the purposes of subsection (2A) above.

(11B) In subsection (2A) above "land" includes a wall or other part of a building.

(12) In subsections (3A) and (3B) above "owner", in relation to a mooring, means the person who (if the mooring is let) is entitled to receive rent, whether on his own account or as agent or trustee for any other person, or (if the mooring is not let) would be so entitled if the mooring were let, and "owned" shall be construed accordingly.

[Local Government Finance Act 1988, s 64, as amended by the Local Government and Housing Act 1989, Sch 5, the Local Government Finance Act 1992, Sch 10, the Local Government and Rating Act 1997, s 2 and Sch 3 and the Local Government Act 2003, s 66.]

---

1. Where a person has been granted the right to use a flank wall of a building for advertising and place structures thereon, it is the wall on which a fixture is placed that is the "land" and not the fixture so that a hereditament in the advertising structure is created within the terms of s 64(2)(*a*) as the beneficiary of the right is a person other than the occupier of the land (*O'Brien v Secker* [1996] RA 409, CA).

2. See the Non-Domestic Rating (Miscellaneous Provisions) Regulations 1989, SI 1989/1060 amended by SI 1993/616, the Non-Domestic Rating (Caravan Sites) Regulations 1990, SI 1990/673 amended by SI 1991/471, the Non-Domestic Rating (Electricity Generators) Regulations 1991, SI 1991/475, the Non-Domestic Rating (Police Authorities) Order 1995, SI 1995/1679 and the Non-Domestic Rating (Communications and Light Railways) (England) Regulations 2005, SI 2005/549.

3. Cross-boundary property is dealt with by SI 1989/1060 amended by SI 1993/616.

8–19690 **65. Owners and occupiers.** (1) The owner of a hereditament or land is the person entitled to possession of it[1].

(2) Whether a hereditament or land is occupied, and who is the occupier, shall be determined by reference to the rules which would have applied for the purposes of the 1967 Act had this Act not been passed (ignoring any express statutory rules such as those in sections 24 and 46A of that Act).

(3) Subsections (1) and (2) above shall have effect subject to the following provisions of this section.

(4) Regulations under section 64(3) above may include rules for ascertaining—

(*a*) whether the different hereditaments or the one hereditament (as the case may be) shall be treated as occupied or unoccupied;

(*b*) who shall be treated as the owner or occupier of the different hereditaments or the one hereditament (as the case may be).

(5) A hereditament which is not in use shall be treated as unoccupied if (apart from this subsection) it would be treated as occupied by reason only of there being kept in or on the hereditament plant, machinery or equipment—

(*a*) which was used in or on the hereditament when it was last in use, or

(*b*) which is intended for use in or on the hereditament.

(6) A hereditament shall be treated as unoccupied if (apart from this subsection) it would be treated as occupied by reason only of—

(*a*) the use of it for the holding of public meetings in furtherance of a person's candidature at a parliamentary or local government election, or

(*b*) if it is a house, the use of a room in it by a returning officer for the purpose of taking the poll in a parliamentary or local government election.

(7) In subsection (6) above "returning officer" shall be construed in accordance with section 24 or 35 of the Representation of the People Act 1983 (as the case may be).

(8) A right which is a hereditament by virtue of section 64(2) above shall be treated as occupied by the person for the time being entitled to the right.

(8A) In a case where—

(*a*) land consisting of a hereditament is used (permanently or temporarily) for the exhibition of advertisements or for the erection of a structure used for the exhibition of advertisements,

(*b*) section 64(2) above does not apply, and

(*c*) apart from this subsection, the hereditament is not occupied,

the hereditament shall be treated as occupied by the person permitting it to be so used or, if that person cannot be ascertained, its owner.

(9) *Repealed.*

[Local Government Finance Act 1988, s 65, as amended by the Local Government and Housing Act 1989, Sch 5 and the Local Government and Rating Act 1997, s 2.]

1. If a landlord claims forfeiture of a lease, it is open to the tenant to accept it and thereby terminate all future rights and liabilities under the lease including his right to possession as well as his liability for rent (*Royal Borough of Kingston upon Thames v Marlow* (1995) 160 JP 502, DC). Receivers who were appointed as agents under the terms of the debentures to take possession of the charged properties were held not to be entitled, by reason only of that appointment, to possession of the premises and thus were not "owners" for the purposes of s 65(1) of the Act; accordingly, the receivers were not personally liable for the non-domestic unoccupied property rates (*Brown v City of London Corpn* [1996] 1 WLR 1070).

8–19690A 65A. Crown Property. (1) This Part applies to the Crown as it applies to other persons.

(2) Accordingly, liability to a non-domestic rate in respect of a hereditament is not affected by the fact that—

(*a*) the hereditament is occupied by the Crown or by a person acting on behalf of the Crown or is used for Crown purposes, or

(*b*) the Crown or a person acting on behalf of the Crown is the owner of the hereditament.

(3) If (apart from this subsection) any property would consist of two or more Crown hereditaments, the property is to be treated for the purposes of this Part as if it were a single hereditament occupied by such one of the occupiers as appears to the billing authority to occupy the largest part of the property.

(4) In this section, "Crown hereditament" means a hereditament which—

(*a*) is occupied by a Minister of the Crown or Government department or by any officer or body exercising functions on behalf of the Crown, but

(*b*) is not provided or maintained by a local authority or by a police authority established under section 3 of the Police Act 1996.

(5) In this section—

(*a*) references to this Part include any subordinate legislation (within the meaning of the Interpretation Act 1978) made under it, and

(*b*) "local authority" has the same meaning as in the Local Government Act 1972, and includes the Common Council of the City of London.

(6) The Secretary of State may by order amend subsection (4)(*b*) above so as to alter the persons for the time being referred to there.

(7) Subsection (3) above does not affect the power conferred by section 64(3) above.

[Local Government Finance Act 1988, s 65A as inserted by the Local Government and Rating Act 1997, s 3 and amended by the Police Act 1997, Sch 9 and the Criminal Justice and Police Act 2001, Sch 6.]

8–19691 66. Domestic property. (1) Subject to subsections (2), (2B) and (2E) below, property is domestic if—

(*a*) it is used wholly for the purposes of living accommodation,

(*b*) it is a yard, garden, outhouse or other appurtenance belonging to or enjoyed with property falling within paragraph (*a*) above,

(*c*) it is a private garage which either has a floor area of 25 square metres or less or is used wholly or mainly for the accommodation of a private motor vehicle, or

(*d*) it is private storage premises used wholly or mainly for the storage of articles of domestic use.

(2) Property is not domestic property if it is wholly or mainly used in the course of a business for the provision of short-stay accommodation, that is to say accommodation—

(*a*) Which is provided for short periods to individuals whose sole or main residence is elsewhere, and

(*b*) which is not self-contained self-catering accommodation provided commercially.

(2A) Subsection (2) above does not apply if—

(*a*) it is intended that within the year beginning with the end of the day in relation to which the question is being considered, short-stay accommodation will not be provided within the hereditament for more than six persons simultaneously; and

(*b*) the person intending to provide such accommodation intends to have his sole or main residence within that hereditament throughout any period when such accommodation is to be provided, and that any use of living accommodation within the hereditament which would, apart from this subsection, cause any part of it to be treated as non-domestic, will be subsidiary to the use of the hereditament for, or in connection with, his sole or main residence.

(2B) A building or self-contained part of a building is not domestic property if—

(*a*) the relevant person intends that, in the year beginning with the end of the day in relation to which the question is being considered, the whole of the building or self-contained part will be available for letting commercially, as self-catering accommodation, for short periods totalling 140 days or more, and

(*b*) on that day his interest in the building or part is such as to enable him to let it for such periods.

(2C) For the purposes of subsection (2B) the relevant person is—

(*a*) where the property in question is a building and is not subject as a whole to a relevant leasehold interest, the person having the freehold interest in the whole of the building; and

(*b*) in any other case, any person having a relevant leasehold interest in the building or self-contained part which is not subject (as a whole) to a single relevant leasehold interest inferior to his interest.

(2D) Subsection (2B) above does not apply where the building or self-contained part is used as the sole or main residence of any person.

(2E) Property is not domestic property if it is timeshare accommodation within the meaning of the Timeshare Act 1992.

(3) Subsection (1) above does not apply in the case of a pitch occupied by a caravan, but if in such a case the caravan is the sole or main residence of an individual, the pitch and the caravan, together with any garden, yard, outhouse or other appurtenance belonging to or enjoyed with them, are domestic property[1].

(4) Subsection (1) above does not apply in the case of a mooring occupied by a boat, but if in such a case the boat is the sole or main residence of an individual, the mooring and the boat, together with any garden, yard, outhouse or other appurtenance belonging to or enjoyed with them, are domestic property.

(4A) Subsection (3) or (4) above does not have effect in the case of a pitch occupied by a caravan, or a mooring occupied by a boat, which is an appurtenance enjoyed with other property to which subsection (1)(*a*) above applies[1].

(5) Property not in use is domestic if it appears that when next in use it will be domestic.

(6) *Repealed.*

(7) Whether anything is a caravan shall be construed in accordance with Part I of the Caravan Sites and Control of Development Act 1960.

(8) *Repealed.*

(8A) In this section—

"business" includes—

(*a*) any activity carried on by a body of persons, whether corporate or unincorporate, and

(*b*) any activity carried on by a charity;

"commercially" means on a commercial basis, and with a view to the realisation of profits; and

"relevant leasehold interest" means an interest under a lease or underlease which was granted for a term of 6 months or more and conferred the right to exclusive possession throughout the term.

(9) The Secretary of State may by order amend, or substitute another definition for, any definition of domestic property for the time being effective for the purposes of this Part.

[Local Government Finance Act 1988, s 66 amended by SI 1990/162, the Caravans (Standard Community Charge and Rating) Act 1991, s 1, SI 1991/474, the Local Government Finance Act 1992, Sch 13, SI 1993/542 and the Rating (Caravan and Boats) Act 1996, s 1(2) and (3).]

---

1. The Rating (Caravan and Boats) Act 1996, s 1(4) and (5) provides that sub-ss (3) and (4) of the 1988 Act as substituted by the 1996 Act are to be treated as having had effect on and after 1 April 1990 and any additional sums payable thereby in respect of non-domestic rates may accordingly be recovered. Exception is made in respect of a hereditament where—

(*a*) a proposal for the alteration of a local non-domestic rating list in respect of the hereditament has been made, and not withdrawn, before 30 January 1995 in accordance with regulations under s 55 of the Local Government Finance Act 1988.

(*b*) the ground for the proposal was that the list was inaccurate because the hereditament ought not to be shown in the list or, in the case of a composite hereditament, the rateable value shown in the list was too high, and

(*c*) the reason or one of the reasons given in the proposal, or on an appeal (in accordance with those regulations) to a tribunal against a refusal to make the proposed alteration, for the list being inaccurate was that any pitch occupied by a caravan or (as the case may be) mooring occupied by a boat was domestic property by virtue of s 66(1)(*a*) or (*b*) of that Act.

It is further provided by sub-section (6) that—

> Local non-domestic rating lists compiled on 1 April 1990, 1 April 1995 or 1 April 1996 must be altered so far as required in consequence of this section: and the alterations are to be treated as having had effect from 1 April 1990 or, in the case of lists compiled on 1 April 1995 or 1 April 1996, from 1 April 1995 or from such other date as may be applicable in accordance with regulations under s 2.

8–19692 67. Interpretation: other provisions. (1) Unless the context otherwise requires, references to lists are to local and central non-domestic rating lists.

(2) Unless the context otherwise requires, references to valuation officers are to valuation officers for billing authorities and the central valuation officer.

(3) A right or other property is a hereditament on a particular day if (and only if) it is a hereditament immediately before the day ends.

(4) A hereditament is relevant, non-domestic, composite, unoccupied or wholly or partly occupied on a particular day if (and only if) it is relevant, non-domestic, composite, unoccupied or wholly or partly occupied (as the case may be) immediately before the day ends.

(5) For the purpose of deciding the extent (if any) to which a hereditament consists of domestic property on a particular day, or is exempt from local non-domestic rating on a particular day, the state of affairs existing immediately before the day ends shall be treated as having existed throughout the day.

(5A) In subsection (5) above "Crown hereditament" has the same meaning as in section 65A above.

(6) A person is the owner, or in occupation of all or part, of a hereditament on a particular day if (and only if) he is its owner or in such occupation (as the case may be) immediately before the day ends.

(7) A relevant provision applies on a particular day if (and only if) it applies immediately before the day ends; and for this purpose relevant provisions are sections 43(6), 45(6) and 47(2) above.

(8) For the purpose of deciding what is shown in a list for a particular day the state of the list as it has effect immediately before the day ends shall be treated as having been its state throughout the day; and "effect" here includes any effect which is retrospective by virtue of an alteration of the list.

(9) A hereditament shall be treated as shown in a central non-domestic rating list for a day if on the day it falls within a class of hereditament shown for the day in the list; and for this purpose a hereditament falls within a class on a particular day if (and only if) it falls within the class immediately before the day ends.

(9A) In subsection (9) above "class" means a class expressed by reference to whether hereditaments—

(a) are occupied or owned by a person designated under section 53(1) above, and

(b) fall within any description prescribed in relation to him under section 53(1).

(10) A charity is an institution or other organisation established for charitable purposes only or any persons administering a trust established for charitable purposes only.

(11) The 1967 Act is the General Rate Act 1967.

(12) Nothing in a private or local Act passed before this Act shall have the effect that a hereditament is exempt as regards non-domestic rating, or prevent a person being subject to a non-domestic rate, or prevent a person being designated or a description of hereditament being prescribed under section 53 above.

(13) This section and sections 64 to 66 above apply for the purposes of this Part.

[Local Government Finance Act 1988, s 67, as amended by the Local Government Finance Act 1992, Sch 13 and the Local Government and Rating Act 1997, Sch 3.]

8–19693

PART IV[1]
PRECEPTS AND LEVIES

1. Part IV contains ss 68–75.

PART IX[1]
EXISTING RATES, PRECEPTS AND GRANTS

8–19694 118. *Rates: power to abolish or modify.*

1. Part IX contains ss 117–127. The Local Government and Housing Act 1989, s 149 replaces s 119 by giving the Secretary of State powers to make regulations to provide for references to be made to some other factor than rating or amending such a factor.

8–19695 **119.** *Statutory references to rating.*

PART XI[1]
MISCELLANEOUS AND GENERAL

General

8–19696 **138. Judicial review.** (1) The matters mentioned in subsection (2) below shall not be questioned except by an application for judicial review.

(2) The matters are—

(*a*)–(*d*) *Repealed,*
(*e*) a levy issued under regulations under section 74 above,
(*f*) a special levy issued under regulations under section 75 above,
(*g*) *Repealed,*
(*h*) the specification of a non-domestic rating multiplier under paragraph 2 of Schedule 7 below,
(*i*) the specification of a non-domestic rating multiplier under paragraph 7 of Schedule 7 below, and
(*j*) the setting by a special authority of a non-domestic rating multiplier or small business non-domestic rating multiplier under Schedule 7 below, whether originally or by way of substitute.

(3) If on an application for judicial review the court decides to grant relief in respect of the matters mentioned in subsection (2)(*e*) or (*f*) or (*h*) to (*j*) above, it shall quash the levy, special levy, specification or setting (as the case may be).

[Local Government Finance Act 1988, s 138, as amended by the Local Government Finance Act 1992, Sch 13 and the Local Government Act 2003, Sch 7.]

1. Part XI contains ss 130–152.

SCHEDULES

8–19722 SCHEDULE 4A
NON-DOMESTIC RATING: NEW BUILDINGS (COMPLETION DAYS)

(*Inserted by the Local Government and Housing Act 1989, Sch 5 and amended by the Local Government Finance Act 1992, Sch 13.*)

Section 51 SCHEDULE 5
NON-DOMESTIC RATING: EXEMPTION

(*As amended by the Water Act 1989, Sch 25, the Local Government and Housing Act 1989, Sch 5, the Water Consolidation (Consequential Provisions) Act 1991, Sch 1, the Local Government Finance Act 1992, Sch 10, the Merchant Shipping Act 1995 Sch 13, the Local Government and Rating Act 1997, ss 2 and 4 and Sch 3 and the Transport Act 2000, s 200.*)

Agricultural premises

8–19722 **1.** A hereditament is exempt to the extent that it consists of any of the following—

(*a*) agricultural land;
(*b*) agricultural buildings.

2. (1) Agricultural land is—

(*a*) land used as arable, meadow or pasture ground only,
(*b*) land used for a plantation or a wood or for the growth of saleable underwood.
(*c*) land exceeding 0.10 hectare and used for the purposes of poultry farming,
(*d*) anything which consists of a market garden, nursery ground, orchard or allotment (which here includes an allotment garden within the meaning of the Allotments Act 1922), or
(*e*) land occupied with, and used solely in connection with the use of, a building which (or buildings each of which) is an agricultural building by virtue of paragraph 4, 5, 6 or 7 below.

(2) But agricultural land does not include—

(*a*) land occupied together with a house as a park,
(*b*) gardens (other than market gardens),
(*c*) pleasure grounds,
(*d*) land used mainly or exclusively for purposes of sport or recreation, or
(*e*) land used as a racecourse.

3. A building is an agricultural building if it is not a dwelling and—

(*a*) it is occupied together with agricultural land and is used solely in connection with agricultural operations on the land, or
(*b*) it is or forms part of a market garden and is used solely in connection with agricultural operations at the market garden.

4. (1) A building is an agricultural building if it is used solely in connection with agricultural operations carried on on agricultural land and sub-paragraph (2) or (3) below applies.

(2) This sub-paragraph applies if the building is occupied by the occupiers of all the land concerned.

(3) This sub-paragraph applies if the building is occupied by individuals each of whom is appointed by the occupiers of the land concerned to manage the use of the building and is—

(*a*) an occupier of some of the land concerned, or
(*b*) a member of the board of directors or other governing body of a person who is both a body corporate and an occupier of the land concerned.

(4) This paragraph does not apply unless the number of occupiers of the land concerned is less than 25.

5. (1) A building is an agricultural building if—

(*a*) it is used for the keeping or breeding of livestock, or
(*b*) it is not a dwelling, it is occupied together with a building or buildings falling within paragraph (*a*) above, and it is used in connection with the operations carried on in that building or those buildings.

(2) Sub-paragraph (1)(*a*) above does not apply unless—

(*a*) the building is solely used as there mentioned, or
(*b*) the building is occupied together with agricultural land and used also in connection with agricultural operations on that land, and that other use together with the use mentioned in sub-paragraph (1)(*a*) is its sole use.

(3) Sub-paragraph (1)(*b*) above does not apply unless—

(*a*) the building is solely used as there mentioned, or
(*b*) the building is occupied also together with agricultural land and used also in connection with agricultural operations on that land, and that other use together with the use mentioned in sub-paragraph (1)(*b*) is its sole use.

(4) A building (the building in question) is not an agricultural building by virtue of this paragraph unless it is surrounded by or contiguous to an area of agricultural land which amounts to not less than 2 hectares.

(5) In deciding for the purposes of sub-paragraph (4) above whether an area is agricultural land and what is its size, the following shall be disregarded—

(*a*) any road, watercourse or railway (which here includes the former site of a railway from which railway lines have been removed);
(*b*) any agricultural building other than the building in question;
(*c*) any building occupied together with the building in question.

6. (1) A building is an agricultural building if it is not a dwelling, is occupied by a person keeping bees, and is used solely in connection with the keeping of those bees.

(2) Sub-paragraphs (4) and (5) of paragraph 5 above apply for the purposes of this paragraph as for those of that.

7. (1) A building is an agricultural building if it is not a dwelling and—

(*a*) it is used in connection with agricultural operations carried on on agricultural land, and
(*b*) it is occupied by a body corporate any of whose members are or are together with the body the occupiers of the land.

(2) A building is also an agricultural building if it is not a dwelling and—

(*a*) it is used in connection with the operations carried on in a building which, or buildings each of which, is used for the keeping or breeding of livestock and is an agricultural building by virtue of paragraph 5 above, and
(*b*) sub-paragraph (3), (4) or (5) below applies as regards the building first mentioned in this sub-paragraph (the building in question).

(3) This sub-paragraph applies if the building in question is occupied by a body corporate any of whose members are or are together with the body the occupiers of the building or buildings mentioned in sub-paragraph (2)(*a*) above.

(4) This sub-paragraph applies if the building in question, and the building or buildings mentioned in sub-paragraph (2)(*a*) above, are occupied by the same persons.

(5) This sub-paragraph applies if the building in question is occupied by individuals each of whom is appointed by the occupiers of the building or buildings mentioned in sub-paragraph (2)(*a*) above to manage the use of the building in question and is—

(*a*) an occupier of part of the building, or of part of one of the buildings, mentioned in sub-paragraph (2)(*a*) above, or
(*b*) a member of the board of directors or other governing body of a person who is both a body corporate and an occupier of the building or buildings mentioned in sub-paragraph (2)(*a*) above.

(6) Sub-paragraph (1) above does not apply unless the use there mentioned, or that use together with the use mentioned in sub-paragraph (2) above, is its sole use.

(7) Sub-paragraph (2) above does not apply unless the use there mentioned, or that use together with the use mentioned in sub-paragraph (1) above, is its sole use.

(8) Sub-paragraph (4) or (5) above does not apply unless the number of occupiers of the building or buildings mentioned in sub-paragraph (2)(*a*) above is less than 25.

8. (1) In paragraphs 1 and 3 to 7 above "agricultural land" shall be construed in accordance with paragraph 2 above.

(2) In paragraphs 1 and 5(5)(*b*) above "agricultural building" shall be construed in accordance with paragraphs 3 to 7 above.

(3) In determining for the purposes of paragraphs 3 to 7 above whether a building used in any way is solely so used, no account shall be taken of any time during which it is used in any other way, if that time does not amount to a substantial part of the time during which the building is used.

(4) In paragraphs 2 to 7 above and sub-paragraph (2) above "building" includes a separate part of a building.

(5) In paragraphs 5 and 7 above "livestock" includes any mammal or bird kept for the production of food or wool or for the purpose of its use in the farming of land.

Fish farms

8–19723 **9.** (1) A hereditament is exempt to the extent that it consists of any of the following—

(*a*) land used solely for or in connection with fish farming;
(*b*) buildings (other than dwellings) so used.

(2) In determining whether land or a building used for or in connection with fish farming is solely so used, no account shall be taken of any time during which it is used in any other way, if that time does not amount to a substantial part of the time during which the land or building is used.

(3) "Building" includes a separate part of a building.

(4) "Fish farming" means the breeding or rearing of fish, or the cultivation of shellfish, for the purpose of (or for purposes which include) transferring them to other waters or producing food for human consumption.

(4A) But an activity does not constitute fish farming if the fish or shellfish are or include fish or shellfish which—

(*a*) are purely ornamental, or
(*b*) are bred, reared or cultivated for exhibition.

(5) "Shellfish" includes crustaceans and molluscs of any description.

Fishing

8–19724 **10.** *Repealed.*

Places of religious worship etc

8–19725 **11.** (1) A hereditament is exempt to the extent that it consists of any of the following—

(*a*) a place of public religious worship which belongs to the Church of England or the Church in Wales (within the meaning of the Welsh Church Act 1914) or is for the time being certified as required by law as a place of religious worship;
(*b*) a church hall, chapel hall or similar building used in connection with a place falling within paragraph (*a*) above for the purposes of the organisation responsible for the conduct of public religious worship in that place.

(2) A hereditament is exempt to the extent that it is occupied by an organisation responsible for the conduct of public religious worship in a place falling within sub-paragraph (1)(*a*) above, and—

(*a*) is used for carrying out administrative or other activities relating to the organisation of the conduct of public religious worship in such a place;
(*b*) is used as an office or for office purposes, or for purposes ancillary to its use as an office or for office purposes.

(3) In this paragraph "office purposes" include administration, clerical work and handling money; and "clerical work" includes writing, book-keeping, sorting papers or information, filing, typing, duplicating, calculating (by whatever means), drawing and the editorial preparation of matter for publication.

Certain property of Trinity House

8–19726 **12.** (1) A hereditament is exempt to the extent that it belongs to or is occupied by the Trinity House and consists of any of the following—

(*a*) a lighthouse;
(*b*) a buoy;
(*c*) a beacon;
(*d*) property within the same curtilage as, and occupied for the purposes of, a lighthouse.

(2) No other hereditament (or part of a hereditament) belonging to or occupied by the Trinity House is exempt, notwithstanding anything in section 221 (1) of the Merchant Shipping Act 1995.

Sewers

8–19727 **13.** (1) A hereditament is exempt to the extent that it consists of any of the following—

(*a*) a sewer;
(*b*) an accessory belonging to a sewer.

(2) "Sewer" has the meaning given by section 343 of the Public Health Act 1936.

(3) "Accessory" means a manhole, ventilating shaft, pumping station, pump or other accessory.

(4) The Secretary of State may by order repeal sub-paragraphs (1) to (3) above.

Property of drainage authorities

8–19728 **14.** (1) A hereditament is exempt to the extent that it consists of any of the following—

(*a*) land which is occupied by a drainage authority and which forms part of a main river or of a watercourse maintained by the authority;
(*b*) a structure maintained by a drainage authority for the purpose of controlling or regulating the flow of water in, into or out of a watercourse which forms part of a main river or is maintained by the authority;
(*c*) an appliance so maintained for that purpose.

(2) "Drainage authority", means the National Rivers Authority[1] or any internal drainage board and "main river" and "watercourse" have the same meanings, respectively as they have in the Water Resources Act 1991 and the Land Drainage Act 1991.

(3) *Repealed.*

1. To be construed as the Environment Agency (Environment Act 1995 (Consequential Amendments) Regulations 1996, SI 1996/593).

Parks

8–19729 **15.** (1) A hereditament is exempt to the extent that it consists of a park which—

(*a*) has been provided by, or is under the management of, a relevant authority or two or more relevant authorities acting in combination, and
(*b*) is available for free and unrestricted use by members of the public.

(2) The reference to a park includes a reference to a recreation or pleasure ground, a public walk, an open space within the meaning of the Open Spaces Act 1906, and a playing field provided under the Physical Training and Recreation Act 1937.

(3) Each of the following is a relevant authority—

(aa) a Minister of the Crown or Government department or any officer or body exercising functions on behalf of the Crown,
(a) a county council,
(aa) a county borough council;
(b) a district council,
(c) a London borough council,
(d) the Common Council,
(e) the Council of the Isles of Scilly,
(f) a parish or community council, and
(g) the chairman of a parish meeting.

(4) In construing sub-paragraph (1)(*b*) above any temporary close (at night or otherwise) shall be ignored.

Property used for the disabled

8–19740 **16.** (1) A hereditament is exempt to the extent that it consists of property used wholly for any of the following purposes—

(*a*) the provision of facilities for training, or keeping suitably occupied, persons who are disabled or who are or have been suffering from illness;
(*b*) the provision of welfare services for disabled persons;
(*c*) the provision of facilities under section 15 of the Disabled Persons (Employment) Act 1944;
(*d*) the provision of a workshop or of other facilities under section 3(1) of the Disabled Persons (Employment) Act 1958.

(2) A person is disabled if he is blind, deaf or dumb or suffers from mental disorder of any description or is substantially and permanently handicapped by illness, injury, congenital deformity or any other disability for the time being prescribed for the purposes of section 29(1) of the National Assistance Act 1948.

(3) "Illness" has the meaning given by section 128(1) of the National Health Service Act 1977.

(4) "Welfare services for disabled persons" means services or facilities (by whomsoever provided) of a kind which a local authority has power to provide under section 29 of the National Assistance Act 1948.

Air-raid protection works

8–19741 **17.** A hereditament is exempt to the extent that it consists of property which—

(*a*) is intended to be occupied or used solely for the purpose of affording protection in the event of hostile attack from the air, and
(*b*) is not occupied or used for any other purpose.

Swinging moorings

8–19742 **18.** A hereditament is exempt to the extent that it consists of a mooring which is used or intended to be used by a boat or ship and which is equipped only with a buoy attached to an anchor, weight or other device—

(*a*) which rests on or in the bed of the sea or any river or other waters when in use, and
(*b*) which is designed to be raised from that bed from time to time.

Road crossings over watercourses etc

8–19743 **18A.** (1) A hereditament which is occupied (as mentioned in section 65 of this Act) is exempt to the extent that it consists of, or of any of the appurtenances of, a fixed road crossing over an estuary, river or other watercourse.

(2) For the purposes of this paragraph, a fixed road crossing means a bridge, viaduct, tunnel or other construction providing a means for road vehicles or pedestrians or both to cross the estuary, river or other watercourse concerned.

(3) For the purposes of sub-paragraph (2) above—

(*a*) a bridge may be a fixed road crossing notwithstanding that it is designed so that part of it can be swung, raised or otherwise moved in order to facilitate passage across, above or below it; but
(*b*) the expression "bridge" does not include a floating bridge, that is to say, a ferry operating between fixed chains.

(4) The reference in sub-paragraph (1) above to the appurtenances of a fixed road crossing is a reference to—

(*a*) the carriageway and any footway thereof;
(*b*) any building, other than office buildings, used in connection with the crossing; and
(*c*) any machinery, apparatus or works used in connection with the crossing or with any of the items mentioned in paragraphs (*a*) and (*b*) above.

Property used for road user charging schemes

18B. (1) A hereditament which is occupied (as mentioned in section 65 of this Act) is exempt to the extent that—

(a) it consists of a road in respect of which charges are imposed by a charging scheme under Schedule 23 to the Greater London Authority Act 1999 or Part III of the Transport Act 2000, or
(b) it is used solely for or in connection with the operation of such a scheme.

(2) But office buildings are not exempt under sub-paragraph (1)(b) above.

Property in enterprise zones

8–19744 **19.** (1) A hereditament is exempt to the extent that it is situated in an enterprise zone.

(2) An enterprise zone is an area for the time being designated as an enterprise zone under Schedule 32 to the Local Government, Planning and Land Act 1980.

Visiting Forces etc.

8–19744A **19A.** (1) A hereditament is exempt to the extent that it consists of property which is occupied for the purposes of a visiting force, or a headquarters, in pursuance of arrangements made in that behalf with any Government department.

(2) In this paragraph—

"headquarters" means an international headquarters or defence organisation designated by an Order in Council under section 1 of the International Headquarters and Defence Organisations Act 1964; and

"visiting force" means any such body, contingent or detachment of the forces of any country as is a visiting force for the purposes of any provision of the Visiting Forces Act 1952.

Power to confer exemption

8–19745 **20.** (1) The Secretary of State may make regulations providing that prescribed hereditaments or hereditaments falling within any prescribed description are exempt to such extent (whether as to the whole or some lesser extent) as may be prescribed.

(2) But the power under sub-paragraph (1) above may not be exercised so as to confer exemption which in his opinion goes beyond such exemption or privilege (if any) as fulfils the first and second conditions.

(3) The first condition is that the exemption or privilege operated or was enjoyed in practice, immediately before the passing of this Act, in respect of a general rate in its application to the hereditaments prescribed or falling within the prescribed description.

(4) The second condition is that the exemption or privilege—

(*a*) was conferred by a local Act or order passed or made on or after 22 December 1925, or
(*b*) was conferred by a local Act or order passed or made before 22 December 1925 and was saved by section 117(5)(b) of the 1967 Act.

(5) Regulations under sub-paragraph (1) above in their application to a particular financial year (including regulations amending or revoking others) shall not be effective unless they come into force before 1 January in the preceding financial year.

Interpretation

8–19746 **21.** (1) This paragraph applies for the purposes of this Schedule.

(2) "Exempt" means exempt from local non-domestic rating.

(3) Any land, building or property not in use shall be treated as used in a particular way if it appears that when next in use it will be used in that way.

(4) Any land or building which is not occupied shall be treated as occupied in a particular way if it appears that when next occupied it will be used in that way.

(5) A person shall be treated as an occupier of any land or building which is not occupied if it appears that when it is next occupied he will be an occupier of it.

8–19746A

Section 56

SCHEDULE 6

NON-DOMESTIC RATING: VALUATION[1]

(*Amended by the Local Government and Housing Act 1989, Schs 5 and 12, the Local Government Finance Act 1992, Sch 10, SI 1993/544, the Local Government and Rating Act 1997, s 2 and the Rating (Valuation) Act 1999, s 1.*)

1. See the Non-Domestic Rating (Miscellaneous Provisions) Regulations 1989, SI 1989/1060 amended by SI 1989/2303, SI 1993/616, SI 1994/3122 and SI 1996/619, the Non-Domestic Rating (Miscellaneous Provisions) (No 2) Regulations 1989, SI 1989/2303 amended by SI 1991/2906, SI 1993/544 and 616, SI 1994/3122, SI 2000/532 (England) and 908 (Wales) and SI 2004/1000 (W) and 1494 (E); Non-Domestic Rating (Material Day for List Alterations) Regulations 2005, SI 1992/556 amended by SI 2005/658 (E); the Water Undertakers (Rateable Values) (Wales) Order 2000, SI 2000/299 amended by SI 2003/944, the BG plc (Rateable Value) (Wales) Order 2000, amended by SI 2003/944, the Railtrack plc (Rateable Value) (Wales) Order 2000, SI 2003/555 amended by SI 2003/944, the Valuation for Rating (Plant and Machinery) (England) Regulations 2000, SI 2000/540 amended by SI 2001/846, the Valuation for Rating (Plant and Machinery) (Wales) Regulations 2000, SI 2000/1097 amended by SI 2001/2357 (Wales), the Rating Lists (Valuation

Date) (Wales) Order 2002, SI 2002/3186, the Rating Lists (Valuation Date) (England) Order 2003, SI 2003/329; Non-domestic Rating (Stud Farms) (England) Order 2004, SI 2004/3151.

8–19746B

SCHEDULE 7A
NON-DOMESTIC RATING: 1990–95[1]

(*Inserted by the Local Government and Housing Act 1989, Sch 5 and amended by the Local Government Finance Act 1992, Sch 13, the Non-Domestic Rating Act 1992, ss 1, 2, the Non-Domestic Rating Act 1993 and the Non-Domestic Rating Act 1994, s 1.*)

1. This Schedule makes provision for the transitional period, and enables the making of regulations.

Section 62

SCHEDULE 9
NON-DOMESTIC RATING: ADMINISTRATION

(*As amended by the Local Government and Housing Act 1989, Sch 5 and 12, the Local Government Finance Act 1992, Sch 13 and the Local Government (Wales) Act 1994, Sch 16.*)

Collection and recovery

8–19747 **1.** The Secretary of State may make regulations containing such provision as he sees fit in relation to the collection and recovery of amounts persons are liable to pay under sections 43, 45 and 54 above.

2–4A. *Regulations*[1].

1. See the Non-Domestic Rating (Collection and Enforcement) (Local Lists) Regulations 1989, post, the Non-Domestic Rating (Collection and Enforcement) (Central Lists) Regulations 1989, SI 1989/2260, amended by SI 1991/142, SI 1992/1513 and SI 1993/1494, the Environment Act 1995, Sch 22, para 233(1), SI 1996/1880 and SI 2002/180, and the Community Charge and Non Domestic Rating (Demand Notices) (Wales) Regulations 1993, SI 1993/252 amended by SI 1993/1506, SI 1994/415, SI 1995/284, SI 1997/356, SI 1998/155, SI 2000/793, SI 2003/414 and SI 2005/256; the Council Tax and Non-domestic Rating (Demand Notices) (England) Regulations 2003, SI 2003/2613 amended by SI 2003/3081 and SI 2004/3389 and SI 2006/217 have been made.

Information

8–19748 **5.** (1) A valuation officer may serve a notice on a person who is an owner or occupier of a hereditament requesting him to supply to the officer information—

(*a*) which is specified in the notice, and

(*b*) which the officer reasonably believes will assist him in carrying out functions conferred or imposed on him by or under this Part.

(1A) A notice under this paragraph must state that the officer believes the information requested will assist him in carrying out functions conferred or imposed on him by or under this Part.

(2) A person on whom a notice is served under this paragraph shall supply the information requested if it is in his possession or control, and he shall do so in such form and manner as is specified in the notice and within the period of 21 days beginning with the day on which the notice is served.

(3) If a person on whom a notice is served under this paragraph fails without reasonable excuse to comply with sub-paragraph (2) above, he shall be liable on summary conviction to a fine not exceeding **level 2** on the standard scale.

(4) If a notice has been served on a person under this paragraph, and in supplying information in purported compliance with sub-paragraph (2) above he makes a statement which he knows to be false in a material particular or recklessly makes a statement which is false in a material particular, he shall be liable on summary conviction to imprisonment for a term not exceeding **3 months** or to a fine not exceeding **level 3** on the standard scale or to both.

6. (1) If in the course of the exercise of its functions any information comes to the notice of a billing authority which leads it to suppose that a list requires alteration it shall be the authority's duty to inform the valuation officer who has the duty to maintain the list.

(1A) *Regulations.*

8–19749 **6A.** *Regulations may require information to be supplied to the billing authority.*

Power of entry

8–19750 **7.** (1) If a valuation officer needs to value a hereditament for the purpose of carrying out functions conferred or imposed on him by or under this Part, he and any person authorised by him in writing may enter on, survey and value the hereditament if sub-paragraph (2) below is fulfilled and (where it applies) sub-paragraph (3) below is fulfilled.

(2) At least 24 hours' notice in writing of the proposed exercise of the power must be given.

(3) In a case where a person authorised by the valuation officer proposes to exercise the power, the person must if required produce his authority.

(4) If a person wilfully delays or obstructs a person in the exercise of a power under this paragraph, he shall be liable on summary conviction to a fine not exceeding **level 1** on the standard scale.

Inspection

8–19751 **8.** (1) A person may require a valuation officer to give him access to such information as will enable him to establish what is the state of a list, or has been its state at any time since it came into force, if—

(*a*) the officer is maintaining the list, and
(*b*) the list is in force or has been in force at any time in the preceding 5 years.

(2) A person may require a billing authority to give him access to such information as will enable him to establish what is the state of a copy of a list, or has been its state at any time since it was deposited, if—

(*a*) the authority has deposited the copy under section 41(6B) or 41A(10) above, and
(*b*) the list is in force or has been in force at any time in the preceding 5 years.

(3) A person may require the Secretary of State to give him access to such information as will enable him to establish what is the state of a copy of a list, or has been its state at any time since it was deposited, if—

(*a*) the Secretary of State has deposited the copy under section 52(6B) above, and
(*b*) the list is in force or has been in force at any time in the preceding 5 years.

(4) A person may require a billing authority to give him access to such information as will enable him to establish what is the state of a copy of a proposed list if—

(*a*) the authority has deposited the copy under section 41(6) above, and
(*b*) the list itself is not yet in force.

(5) A person may require the Secretary of State to give him access to such information as will enable him to establish what is the state of a copy of a proposed list if—

(*a*) the Secretary of State has deposited the copy under section 52(6) above, and
(*b*) the list itself is not yet in force.

(6) A requirement under any of the preceding provisions of this paragraph must be complied with at a reasonable time and place and without payment being sought; but the information may be in documentary or other form, as the person or authority of whom the requirement is made thinks fit.

(7) Where access is given under this paragraph to information in documentary form the person to whom access is given may—

(*a*) make copies of (or of extracts from) the document;
(*b*) require a person having custody of the document to supply to him a photographic copy of (or of extracts from) the document.

(8) Where access is given under this paragraph to information in a form which is not documentary the person to whom access is given may—

(*a*) make transcripts of (or of extracts from) the information;
(*b*) require a person having control of access to the information to supply to him a copy in documentary form of (or of extracts from) the information.

(9) If a reasonable charge is required for a facility under sub-paragraph (7) or (8) above, the sub-paragraph concerned shall not apply unless the person seeking to avail himself of the facility pays the charge.

(10) If without reasonable excuse a person having custody of a document containing, or having control of access to, information access to which is sought under this paragraph—

(*a*) intentionally obstructs a person in exercising a right under sub-paragraph (1), (2), (3), (4), (5), (7)(*a*) or (8)(*a*) above, or
(*b*) refuses to comply with a requirement under sub-paragraph (7)(*b*) or 8(*b*) above,

he shall be liable on summary conviction to a fine not exceeding **level 1** on the standard scale.

9. (1) A person may, at a reasonable time and without making payment, inspect any proposal made or notice of appeal given under regulations made under section 55 above, if made or given as regards a list which is in force when inspection is sought or has been in force at any time in the preceding years.

(2) A person may—

(*a*) make copies of (or of extracts from) a document mentioned in sub-paragraph (1) above, or
(*b*) require a person having custody of such a document to supply him a photographic copy of (or of extracts from) the document.

(3) If a reasonable charge is required for a facility under sub-paragraph (2) above, the sub-paragraph shall not apply unless the person seeking to avail himself of the facility pays the charge.

(4) If without reasonable excuse a person having custody of a document mentioned in sub-paragraph (1) above—

(*a*) intentionally obstructs a person in exercising a right under sub-paragraph (1) or (2)(*a*) above, or
(*b*) refuses to supply a copy to a person entitled to it under sub-paragraph (2)(*b*) above,

he shall be liable on summary conviction to a fine not exceeding **level 1** on the standard scale.

Local Government Finance Act 1992

(1992 c 14)

INTRODUCTION

8–19765 Council tax. The Local Government Finance Act 1992 ("the Act") and regulations made thereunder establish a system of council tax replacing the community charge ("poll tax") and thus reverting to a property-based liability.

Part I (ss 1–69) is divided into six Chapters. Chapter I gives the main provisions of the council tax, Chapter II sets out provisions relating to valuation lists; intentional delay or obstruction exercising a power of entry following three clear days' notice (excluding Saturday, Sunday, Christmas Day, Good Friday, bank holidays) is punishable by a level 2 fine (s 26); failing to comply with notice requiring information about property is punishable by a level 2 fine (s **27(4)** and knowingly or recklessly making a statement false in a material particular is punishable by 3 months' imprisonment and/or a level 3 fine (s **27(5)**). Chapter III is concerned with the setting of the council tax and Chapter IV with precepts. Limitation of council tax and precepts by the Secretary of State is dealt with in Chapter V and Chapter VI (ss 65–69) covers miscellaneous and supplemental matters including Part I interpretation. Part III (ss 100–102) provides for transition from community charges.

PART I
COUNCIL TAX: ENGLAND AND WALES

CHAPTER I
MAIN PROVISIONS

Preliminary

8–19766 1. Council tax in respect of dwellings. (1) As regards the financial year beginning in 1993 and subsequent financial years, each billing authority shall, in accordance with this Part, levy and collect a tax, to be called council tax, which shall be payable in respect of dwellings situated in its area.

(2) In this Part "billing authority" means—

(*a*) in relation to England, a district council or London borough council, the Common Council or the Council of the Isles of Scilly, and

(*b*) in relation to Wales, a county council or county borough council.

(3) For the purposes of this Part the Secretary of State may make regulations[1] containing rules for treating a dwelling as situated in a billing authority's area if part only of the dwelling falls within the area.

[Local Government Finance Act 1992, s 1, as amended by the Local Government (Wales) Act 1994, s 35(5).]

1. See Pt II of the Council Tax (Situation and Valuation of Dwellings) Regulations 1992, SI 1992/550 amended by SI 1994/1747.

8–19767 2. Liability to tax determined on a daily basis. (1) Liability to pay council tax shall be determined on a daily basis.

(2) For the purposes of determining for any day—

(*a*) whether any property is a chargeable dwelling;

(*b*) which valuation band is shown in the billing authority's valuation list as applicable to any chargeable dwelling;

(*c*) the person liable to pay council tax in respect of any such dwelling; or

(*d*) whether any amount of council tax is subject to a discount and (if so) the amount of the discount,

it shall be assumed that any state of affairs subsisting at the end of the day had subsisted throughout the day.

[Local Government Finance Act 1992, s 2.]

Chargeable dwellings

8–19768 3. Meaning of "dwelling". (1) This section has effect for determining what is a dwelling for the purposes of this Part.

(2) Subject to the following provisions of this section, a dwelling is any property which—

(*a*) by virtue of the definition of hereditament in section 115(1) of the General Rate Act 1967, would have been a hereditament for the purposes of that Act if that Act remained in force; and

(*b*) is not for the time being shown or required to be shown in a local or a central non-domestic rating list in force at that time; and

(*c*) is not for the time being exempt from local non-domestic rating for the purposes of Part III of the Local Government Finance Act 1988 ("the 1988 Act");

and in applying paragraphs (*b*) and (*c*) above no account shall be taken of any rules as to Crown exemption.

(3) A hereditament which—

(*a*) is a composite hereditament for the purposes of Part III of the 1988 Act; and

(*b*) would still be such a hereditament if paragraphs (b) to (d) of section 66(1) of that Act (domestic property) were omitted,

is also, subject to subsection (6) below, a dwelling for the purposes of this Part.

(4) Subject to subsection (6) below, none of the following property, namely—

(*a*) a yard, garden, outhouse or other appurtenance belonging to or enjoyed with property used wholly for the purposes of living accommodation; or

(*b*) a private garage which either has a floor area of not more than 25 square metres or is used wholly or mainly for the accommodation of a private motor vehicle; or

(*c*) private storage premises used wholly or mainly for the storage of articles of domestic use,

is a dwelling except in so far as it forms part of a larger property which is itself a dwelling by virtue of subsection (2) above.

(5) The Secretary of State may by order[1] provide that in such cases as may be prescribed by or determined under the order—

(*a*) anything which would (apart from the order) be one dwelling shall be treated as two or more dwellings; and

(*b*) anything which would (apart from the order) be two or more dwellings shall be treated as one dwelling.

(6) The Secretary of State may by order amend any definition of "dwelling" which is for the time being effective for the purposes of this Part.

[Local Government Finance Act 1992, s 3.]

---

1. The Council Tax (Chargeable Dwellings) Order 1992, SI 1992/549 amended by SI 1997/656, SI 2003/3121 and SI 2004/2921 (W) has been made.

8–19769 **4. Dwellings chargeable to council tax.** (1) Council tax shall be payable in respect of any dwelling which is not an exempt dwelling.

(2) In this Chapter—

"chargeable dwelling" means any dwelling in respect of which council tax is payable;

"exempt dwelling" means any dwelling of a class prescribed[1] by an order made by the Secretary of State.

(3) For the purposes of subsection (2) above, a class of dwellings may be prescribed by reference to such factors as the Secretary of State sees fit.

(4) Without prejudice to the generality of subsection (3) above, a class of dwellings may be prescribed by reference to one or more of the following factors—

(*a*) the physical characteristics of dwellings;

(*b*) the fact that dwellings are unoccupied or are occupied for prescribed purposes or are occupied or owned by persons of prescribed descriptions.

[Local Government Finance Act 1992, s 4.]

---

1. The Council Tax (Exempt Dwellings) Order 1992, SI 1992/558 amended by SI 1992/2941, SI 1993/150, SI 1994/539, SI 1997/74, SI 1998/291, SI 1996/536,SI 2000/424 and 1025 (Wales), SI 2003/3121, SI 2004/2921 (W) and SI 2005/2865 (E) and 3302 (W).

8–19770 **5. Different amounts for dwellings in different valuation bands.** (1) The amounts of council tax payable in respect of dwellings situated in the same billing authority's area (or the same part of such an area) and listed in different valuation bands shall be in the proportion—

6: 7: 8: 9: 11: 13: 15: 18

where 6 is for dwellings listed in valuation band A, 7 is for dwellings listed in valuation band B, and so on.

(1A) For the purposes of the application of subsection (1) to dwellings situated in Wales, for the purposes of financial years beginning on or after 1st April 2005, for the proportion specified in that subsection there is substituted the following proportion:

6: 7: 8: 9: 11: 13: 15: 18: 21

(2) The valuation bands for dwellings in England are set out in the following Table—

Range of values	**Valuation band**
Values not exceeding £40,000	A
Values exceeding £40,000 but not exceeding £52,000	B
Values exceeding £52,000 but not exceeding £68,000	C
Values exceeding £68,000 but not exceeding £88,000	D
Values exceeding £88,000 but not exceeding £120,000	E
Values exceeding £120,000 but not exceeding £160,000	F
Values exceeding £160,000 but not exceeding £320,000	G
Values exceeding £320,000	H

(3) The valuation bands for dwellings in Wales are set out in the following Table—

Range of values	**Valuation band**
Values not exceeding £44,000	A
Values exceeding £44,000 but not exceeding £65,000	B
Values exceeding £65,000 but not exceeding £91,000	C
Values exceeding £91,000 but not exceeding £123,000	D
Values exceeding £123,000 but not exceeding £162,000	E
Values exceeding £162,000 but not exceeding £223,000	F
Values exceeding £223,000 but not exceeding £324,000	G
Values exceeding £324,000 but not exceeding £424,000	H
Values exceeding £424,000	I

(4) The Secretary of State may by order[1], as regards financial years beginning on or after such date as is specified in the order—

(*a*) substitute another proportion for that which is for the time being effective for the purposes of subsection (1) above;

(*b*) substitute other valuation bands for those which are for the time being effective for the purposes of subsection (2) or (3) above.

(4A) The power under subsection (4)(*b*) above includes powere to make provision for a different number of valuation bands from those which are for the time being effective for the purposes of subsection (2) or (3) above.

(5) No order under subsection (4) above shall be made unless a draft of the order has been laid before and approved by resolution of the House of Commons.

(6) Any reference in this Part to dwellings listed in a particular valuation band shall be construed as a reference to dwellings to which that valuation band is shown as applicable in the billing authority's valuation list.

[Local Government Finance Act 1992, s 5, amended by SI 2003/3046 and the Local Governement Act 2003, s 78.]

---

1. The Council Tax (Valuation Bands) (Wales) Order 2003, SI 2003/3046 has been made.

Liability to tax

8–19771 **6. Persons liable to pay council tax.** (1) The person who is liable to pay council tax in respect of any chargeable dwelling and any day is the person who falls within the first paragraph of subsection (2) below to apply, taking paragraph (*a*) of that subsection first, paragraph (*b*) next, and so on.

(2) A person falls within this subsection in relation to any chargeable dwelling and any day if, on that day—

(*a*) he is a resident of the dwelling and has a freehold interest in the whole or any part of it;

(*b*) he is such a resident and has a leasehold interest in the whole or any part of the dwelling which is not inferior to another such interest held by another such resident;

(*c*) he is both such a resident and a statutory, secure or introductory tenant of the whole or any part of the dwelling;

(*d*) he is such a resident and has a contractual licence to occupy the whole or any part of the dwelling;

(*e*) he is such a resident; or

(*f*) he is the owner of the dwelling.

(3) Where, in relation to any chargeable dwelling and any day, two or more persons fall within the first paragraph of subsection (2) above to apply, they shall each be jointly and severally liable to pay the council tax in respect of the dwelling and that day.

(4) Subsection (3) above shall not apply as respects any day on which one or more of the persons there mentioned fall to be disregarded for the purposes of discount by virtue of paragraph 2 of Schedule 1 to this Act (the severely mentally impaired) and one or more of them do not; and liability to pay the council tax in respect of the dwelling and that day shall be determined as follows—

(*a*) if only one of those persons does not fall to be so disregarded, he shall be solely liable;

(*b*) if two or more of those persons do not fall to be so disregarded, they shall each be jointly and severally liable.

(5) In this Part, unless the context otherwise requires—

"owner", in relation to any dwelling, means the person as regards whom the following conditions are fulfilled—

(*a*) he has a material interest in the whole or any part of the dwelling; and

(*b*) at least part of the dwelling or, as the case may be, of the part concerned is not subject to a material interest inferior to his interest;

"resident", in relation to any dwelling, means an individual who has attained the age of 18 years and has his sole or main residence[1] in the dwelling.

(6) In this section—

"introductory tenant" means a tenant under an introductory tenancy within the meaning of Chapter I of Part V of the Housing Act 1996;

"material interest" means a freehold interest or a leasehold interest which was granted for a term of six months or more;

"secure tenant" means a tenant under a secure tenancy within the meaning of Part IV of the Housing Act 1985;

"statutory tenant" means a statutory tenant within the meaning of the Rent Act 1977 or the Rent (Agriculture) Act 1976.

[Local Government Finance Act 1992, s 6, as amended by SI 1997/74.]

---

1. The words "sole or main residence" in s 6(5) of the 1992 Act refer to premises in which a taxpayer actually resided, and the qualification "sole or main" addresses the fact that a person could reside in more than one place: *Williams v Horsham District Council* [2004] EWCA Civ 39, [2004] 3 All ER 30.

8–19772 7. Liability in respect of caravans and boats. (1) Subsections (2) to (4) below shall have effect in substitution for section 6 above in relation to any chargeable dwelling which consists of a pitch occupied by a caravan, or a mooring occupied by a boat.

(2) Where on any day the owner of the caravan or boat is not, but some other person is, a resident of the dwelling, that other person shall be liable to pay the council tax in respect of the dwelling and that day.

(3) Where on any day subsection (2) above does not apply, the owner of the caravan or boat shall be liable to pay the council tax in respect of the dwelling and that day.

(4) Where on any day two or more persons fall within subsection (2) or (3) above, they shall each be jointly and severally liable to pay the council tax in respect of the dwelling and that day.

(5) Subsection (4) of section 6 above shall apply for the purposes of subsection (4) above as it applies for the purposes of subsection (3) of that section.

(6) In this section "caravan" shall be construed in accordance with Part I of the Caravan Sites and Control of Development Act 1960.

(7) Any reference in this section to the owner of a caravan or boat shall be construed—

(*a*) in relation to a caravan or boat which is subject to an agreement for hire-purchase or conditional sale, as a reference to the person in possession under the agreement;

(*b*) in relation to a caravan or boat which is subject to a bill of sale or mortgage, as a reference to the person entitled to the property in it apart from the bill or mortgage.

[Local Government Finance Act 1992, s 7.]

8–19773 8. Liability in prescribed cases. (1) Subsections (3) and (4) below shall have effect in substitution for section 6 or (as the case may be) section 7 above in relation to any chargeable dwelling of a class prescribed[1] for the purposes of this subsection.

(2) Subsections (3) and (4) below shall have effect in substitution for section 6 or (as the case may be) section 7 above in relation to any chargeable dwelling of a class prescribed for the purposes of this subsection, if the billing authority so determines in relation to all dwellings of that class which are situated in its area.

(3) Where on any day this subsection has effect in relation to a dwelling, the owner of the dwelling shall be liable to pay the council tax in respect of the dwelling and that day.

(4) Where on any day two or more persons fall within subsection (3) above, they shall each be jointly and severally liable to pay the council tax in respect of the dwelling and that day.

(5) Subsection (4) of section 6 above shall apply for the purposes of subsection (4) above as it applies for the purposes of subsection (3) of that section.

(6) Regulations prescribing a class of chargeable dwellings for the purposes of subsection (1) or (2) above may provide that, in relation to any dwelling of that class, subsection (3) above shall have effect as if for the reference to the owner of the dwelling there were substituted a reference to the person falling within such description as may be prescribed[1].

(7) Subsections (3) and (4) of section 4 above shall apply for the purposes of subsections (1) and (2) above as they apply for the purposes of subsection (2) of that section.

[Local Government Finance Act 1992, s 8.]

---

1. The Council Tax (Liability for Owners) Regulations 1992, SI 1992/551 amended by SI 1993/151, SI 1997/74, SI 2000/537 (England) and 1024 (Wales), SI 2003/3125 and SI 2004/2920 (W) have been made.

8–19774 9. Liability of spouses. (1) Where—

(*a*) a person who is liable to pay council tax in respect of any chargeable dwelling of which he is a resident and any day is married, or is the civil partner of, to another person; and*

(*b*) that other person is also a resident of the dwelling on that day but would not, apart from this section, be so liable, those persons shall each be jointly and severally liable to pay the council tax in respect of the dwelling and that day.

(2) Subsection (1) above shall not apply as respects any day on which the other person there mentioned falls to be disregarded for the purposes of discount by virtue of paragraph 2 of Schedule 1 to this Act (the severely mentally impaired).

(3) For the purposes of this section two persons are married to each other if they are a man and a woman—

(*a*) who are married to each other; or

(*b*) who are not married to each other but are living together as husband and wife.

(4) For the purposes of this section two persons are civil partners of each other if they are of the same sex and either—

(*a*) they are civil partners of each other; or

(*b*) They are not civil partners of each other but are living together as if they were civil partners.

[Local Government Finance Act 1992, s 9 as amended by the Civil Partnership Act 2004, Sch 27.]

Amounts of tax payable

8–19775 **10. Basic amounts payable.** (1) Subject to sections 11 to 13 below, a person who is liable to pay council tax in respect of any chargeable dwelling and any day shall, as respects the dwelling and the day, pay to the billing authority for the area in which the dwelling is situated an amount calculated in accordance with the formula—

$$\frac{A}{D}$$

where—

A is the amount which, for the financial year in which the day falls and for dwellings in the valuation band listed for the dwelling, has been set by the authority for its area or (as the case may be) the part of its area in which the dwelling is situated;

D is the number of days in the financial year.

(2) For the purposes of this Part the Secretary of State may make regulations containing rules for ascertaining in what part of a billing authority's area a dwelling is situated (whether situated in the area in fact or by virtue of regulations[1] made under section 1(3) above).

[Local Government Finance Act 1992, s 10.]

---

1. See Pt III of the Council Tax (Situation and Valuation of Dwellings) Regulations 1992, SI 1992/550.

8–19776 **11. Discounts.** (1) The amount of council tax payable in respect of any chargeable dwelling and any day shall be subject to a discount equal to the appropriate percentage of that amount if on that day—

(*a*) there is only one resident of the dwelling and he does not fall to be disregarded for the purposes of discount; or

(*b*) there are two or more residents of the dwelling and each of them except one falls to be disregarded for those purposes.

(2) Subject to section 12 below, the amount of council tax payable in respect of any chargeable dwelling and any day shall be subject to a discount equal to twice the appropriate percentage of that amount if on that day—

(*a*) there is no resident of the dwelling; or

(*b*) there are one or more residents of the dwelling and each of them falls to be disregarded for the purposes of discount.

(3) In this section and section 12 below "the appropriate percentage" means 25 per cent or, if the Secretary of State by order so provides in relation to the financial year in which the day falls, such other percentage as is specified in the order.

(4) No order under subsection (3) above shall be made unless a draft of the order has been laid before and approved by resolution of the House of Commons.

(5) Schedule 1 to this Act shall have effect for determining who shall be disregarded for the purposes of discount.

[Local Government Finance Act 1992, s 11.]

8–19776A **11A. Discounts: special provision for England.** (1) The Secretary of State may for any financial year by regulations[1] prescribe one or more classes of dwelling in England for the purposes of subsection (3) or (4) below.

(2) A class of dwellings may be prescribed under subsection (1) above by reference to such factors as the Secretary of State sees fit and may, in particular, be prescribed by reference to—

(*a*) the physical characteristics of dwellings, or

(*b*) the fact that dwellings are unoccupied.

(3) For any financial year for which a class of dwellings is prescribed for the purposes of this subsection, a billing authority in England may by determination provide in relation to all dwellings of that class in its area, or in such part of its area as it may specify in the determination, that the discount under section 11(2)(a) shall be such lesser percentage of at least 10 as it may so specify.

(4) For any financial year for which a class of dwellings is prescribed for the purposes of this subsection, a billing authority in England may by determination provide in relation to all dwellings of that class in its area, or in such part of its area as it may specify in the determination—

(*a*) that the discount under section 11(2)(a) above shall not apply, or

(*b*) that the discount under that provision shall be such lesser percentage as it may so specify.

(5) A billing authority may make a determination varying or revoking a determination under subsection (3) or (4) for a financial year, but only before the beginning of the year.

(6) A billing authority which makes a determination under this section shall publish a notice of it in at least one newspaper circulating in its area and do so before the end of the period of 21 days beginning with the date of the determination.

(7) Failure to comply with subsection (6) above shall not affect the validity of a determination.

[Local Government Finance Act 1992, s 11A, as inserted by the Local Government Act 2003, s 75(1).]

1. The Council Tax (Prescribed Classes of Dwellings) (England) Regulations 2003, SI 2003/3011 amended by SI 2004/926 and SI 2005/416 and 2866 have been made.

8–19777 **12. Discounts: special provision for Wales.** (1) Where any class of dwellings in Wales is prescribed[1] for the purposes of this section for any financial year, a Welsh billing authority may determine that for the year subsection (2) or (3) below shall have effect in substitution for section 11(2)(a) above in relation to all dwellings of that class which are situated in its area.

(2) Where this subsection has effect for any year in relation to any class of dwellings, the amount of council tax payable in respect of—

(*a*) any chargeable dwelling of that class; and

(*b*) any day in the year on which there is no resident of the dwelling,

shall be subject to a discount equal to the appropriate percentage of that amount.

(3) Where this subsection has effect for any year in relation to any class of dwellings, the amount of council tax payable in respect of—

(*a*) any chargeable dwelling of that class; and

(*b*) any day in the year on which there is no resident of the dwelling,

shall not be subject to a discount.

(4) A determination under subsection (1) above for a financial year may be varied or revoked at any time before the year begins.

(5) Subsections (3) and (4) of section 4 above shall apply for the purposes of subsection (1) above as they apply for the purposes of subsection (2) of that section.

(6) A billing authority which has made a determination under subsection (1) above shall, before the end of the period of 21 days beginning with the day of doing so, publish a notice of the determination in at least one newspaper circulating in the authority's area.

(7) Failure to comply with subsection (6) above does not make the making of the determination invalid.

[Local Government Finance Act 1992, s 12.]

1. The Council Tax (Prescribed Class of Dwellings) (Wales) Regulations 1992, SI 1992/3023 amended by SI 1998/105, SI 2004/452 and SI 2005/3302 have been made.

8–19778 **13. Reduced amounts.** (1) The Secretary of State may make regulations[1] as regards any case where—

(*a*) a person is liable to pay an amount to a billing authority in respect of council tax for any financial year which is prescribed; and

(*b*) prescribed conditions are fulfilled.

(2) The regulations may provide that the amount he is liable to pay shall be an amount which—

(*a*) is less than the amount it would be apart from the regulations; and

(*b*) is determined in accordance with prescribed rules.

(3) This section applies whether the amount mentioned in subsection (1) above is determined under section 10 above or under that section read with section 11 or 12 above.

(4) The conditions mentioned in subsection (1) above may be prescribed by reference to such factors as the Secretary of State thinks fit; and in particular such factors may include the making of an application by the person concerned and all or any of—

(*a*) the factors mentioned in subsection (5) below; or

(*b*) the factors mentioned in subsection (6) below.

(5) The factors referred to in subsection (4)(*a*) above are—

(*a*) community charges for a period before 1st April 1993;

(*b*) the circumstances of, or other matters relating to, the person concerned;

(*c*) an amount relating to the authority concerned and specified, or to be specified, for the purposes of the regulations in a report laid, or to be laid, before the House of Commons;

(*d*) such other amounts as may be prescribed or arrived at in a prescribed manner.

(6) The factors referred to in subsection (4)(*b*) above are—

(*a*) a disabled person having his sole or main residence in the dwelling concerned;

(*b*) the circumstances of or other matters relating to, that person;

(*c*) the physical characteristics of, or other matters relating to, that dwelling.

(7) The rules mentioned in subsection (2) above may be prescribed by reference to such factors as the Secretary of State thinks fit; and in particular such factors may include all or any of the factors mentioned in subsection (5) or subsection (6)(*b*) or (*c*) above.

(8) Without prejudice to the generality of section 113(2) below, regulations under this section may include—

(*a*) provision requiring the Secretary of State to specify in a report, for the purposes of the regulations, an amount in relation to each billing authority;

(*b*) provision requiring him to lay the report before the House of Commons;

(*c*) provision for the review of any prescribed decision of a billing authority relating to the application or operation of the regulations;

(*d*) provision that no appeal may be made to a valuation tribunal in respect of such a decision, notwithstanding section 16(1) below.

(9) To the extent that he would not have power to do so apart from this subsection, the Secretary of State may—

(*a*) include in regulations under this section such amendments of any social security instrument as he thinks expedient in consequence of the regulations under this section;

(*b*) include in any social security instrument such provision as he thinks expedient in consequence of regulations under this section.

(10) In subsection (9) above "social security instrument" means an order or regulations made, or falling to be made, by the Secretary of State under the Social Security Acts, that is to say, the Social Security Contributions and Benefits Act 1992 and the Social Security Administration Act 1992.
[Local Government Finance Act 1992, s 13.]

1. The Council Tax (Reductions for Disabilities) Regulations 1992, SI 1992/554 amended by SI 1993/195, SI 1999/1004 and SI 2005/702 (W), the Local Government Reorganisation (Wales) (Council Tax Reduction Scheme) Regulations 1996, SI 1996/309, the Local Government Reorganisation (Wales) (Council Tax Reduction Scheme) Regulations 1997, SI 1997/261 and the Council Tax Reduction Scheme (Wales) Regulations 1998, SI 1998/266, the Council Tax Reduction Scheme (Wales) Regulations 1999, SI 1999/347 and the Council Tax (Reduction Scheme) and (Demand Notices Transitional Provisions) (Wales) Regulations 2000, SI 2000/501 have been made. Transitional relief for the year 1993/4 is afforded by the Council Tax (Transitional Reduction Scheme) (England) Regulations 1993, SI 1993/175 amended by SI 1993/253 and 401 for the year 1995/6 by SI 1995/209 and for the year 1996/7 by SI 1996/176 (the 1996 Regulations) amended by SI 1996/333 and SI 1997/215.

The 1996 Regulations are modified by the Local Government Changes for England (Council Tax) (Transitional Reduction) Regulations 1997, SI 1997/215 and 1998, SI 1998/214 and are revoked with savings by the Local Government Changes for England (Council Tax) (Transitional Reduction) Regulations 1999, SI 1999/259 which have effect for the financial year 1999/2000.

8–19778A 13A. Billing authority's power to reduce amount of tax payable. (1) Where a person is liable to pay council tax in respect of any chargeable dwelling and any day, the billing authority for the area in which the dwelling is situated may reduce the amount which he is liable to pay as respects the dwelling and the day to such extent as it thinks fit.

(2) The power under subsection (1) above includes power to reduce an amount to nil.

(3) The power under subsection (1) may be exercised in relation to particular cases or by determining a class of case in which liability is to be reduced to an extent provided by the determination.
[Local Government Finance Act 1992, s 13A, inserted by the Local Government Act 2003, s 76.]

8–19778B 13B. *Transitional arrangements*[1]

1. The Council Tax (Transitional Arrangements) (Wales) Regulations 2004, SI 2004/3142 amended by SI 2005/702 have been made which make transitional arrangements for the period from 1 April 2005 (which is the date on which new s 22B lists came into force in Wales) to 31 March 2008.

Administration and appeals

8–19779 14. Administration, penalties and enforcement. (1) Schedule 2 to this Act (which contains provisions about administration, including collection) shall have effect.

(2) Schedule 3 to this Act (which contains provisions about civil penalties) shall have effect.

(3) Schedule 4 to this Act (which contains provisions about the recovery of sums due, including sums due as penalties) shall have effect.

[Local Government Finance Act 1992, s 14.]

8–19780 **15. Valuation tribunals.** (1) Valuation and community charge tribunals established under Schedule 11 to the 1988 Act shall be known as valuation tribunals.

(2) Such tribunals shall exercise, in addition to the jurisdiction conferred on them by or under the 1988 Act, the jurisdiction conferred on them by—

(*a*) section 16 below;
(*b*) regulations made under section 24 below; and
(*c*) paragraph 3 of Schedule 3 to this Act.

[Local Government Finance Act 1992, s 15.]

8–19781 **16. Appeals: general.** (1) A person may appeal to a valuation tribunal if he is aggrieved by—

(*a*) any decision of a billing authority that a dwelling is a chargeable dwelling, or that he is liable to pay council tax in respect of such a dwelling; or
(*b*) any calculation made by such an authority of an amount which he is liable to pay to the authority in respect of council tax.

(2) In subsection (1) above the reference to any calculation of an amount includes a reference to any estimate of the amount.

(3) Subsection (1) above shall not apply where the grounds on which the person concerned is aggrieved fall within such category or categories as may be prescribed[1].

(4) No appeal may be made under subsection (1) above unless—

(*a*) the aggrieved person serves a written notice under this subsection; and
(*b*) one of the conditions mentioned in subsection (7) below is fulfilled.

(5) A notice under subsection (4) above must be served on the billing authority concerned.

(6) A notice under subsection (4) above must state the matter by which and the grounds on which the person is aggrieved.

(7) The conditions are that—

(*a*) the aggrieved person is notified in writing, by the authority on which he served the notice, that the authority believes the grievance is not well founded, but the person is still aggrieved;
(*b*) the aggrieved person is notified in writing, by the authority on which he served the notice, that steps have been taken to deal with the grievance, but the person is still aggrieved;
(*c*) the period of two months, beginning with the date of service of the aggrieved person's notice, has ended without his being notified under paragraph (*a*) or (*b*) above.

(8) Where a notice under subsection (4) above is served on an authority, the authority shall—

(*a*) consider the matter to which the notice relates;
(*b*) include in any notification under subsection (7)(*a*) above the reasons for the belief concerned;
(*c*) include in any notification under subsection (7)(*b*) above a statement of the steps taken.

[Local Government Finance Act 1992, s 16.]

1. See reg 30 of the Council Tax (Administration and Enforcement) Regulations 1992, in this PART, post.

Miscellaneous

8–19782 **17. Completion of new dwellings.** (1) Subject to the provisions of this section, Schedule 4A to the 1988 Act (which makes provision with respect to the determination of a day as the completion day in relation to a new building) shall, with the exception of paragraph 6, apply for the purposes of this Part as it applies for the purposes of Part III of that Act.

(2) Any reference in this section to the Schedule is a reference to Schedule 4A to the 1988 Act as it applies for the purposes of this Part.

(3) Where—

(*a*) a completion notice is served under the Schedule; and
(*b*) the building to which the notice relates is not completed on or before the relevant day,

any dwelling in which the building or any part of it will be comprised shall be deemed for the purposes of this Part to have come into existence on that day.

(4) For the purposes of subsection (3) above the relevant day in relation to a completion notice is—

(*a*) where an appeal against the notice is brought under paragraph 4 of the Schedule, the day stated in the notice; and
(*b*) where no appeal against the notice is brought under that paragraph, the day determined under the Schedule as the completion day in relation to the building to which the notice relates.

(5) Where—

(*a*) a day is determined under the Schedule as the completion day in relation to a new building; and

(*b*) the building is one produced by the structural alteration of a building which is comprised in one or more existing dwellings,

the existing dwelling or dwellings shall be deemed for the purposes of this Part to have ceased to exist on that day.

(6) Any reference in this section or the Schedule to a new building includes a reference to a building produced by the structural alteration of an existing building where—

(*a*) the existing building or any part of it is comprised in a dwelling which, by virtue of the alteration, becomes, or becomes part of a different dwelling or different dwellings; or

(*b*) neither the existing building nor any part of it is, except by virtue of the alteration, comprised in any dwelling.

(7) Any reference in this section to a building includes a reference to a part of a building; and any reference in the Schedule to the valuation officer shall be construed as a reference to the listing officer.
[Local Government Finance Act 1992, s 17.]

8–19783 18. Death of persons liable. *Secretary of State may make regulations*[1]
[Local Government Finance Act 1992, s 18—summarised.]

1. See reg 58 of the Council Tax (Administration and Enforcement) Regulations in this PART post.

8–19784 19. *Exclusion of Crown exemption in certain cases.*

SCHEDULES

Sections 11(5) and 79(5)

SCHEDULE 1

PERSONS DISREGARDED FOR PURPOSES OF DISCOUNT

(*As amended by the Powers of Criminal Courts (Sentencing) Act 2000, Sch 9, the Care Standards Act 2000, Schs 3 and 4 and SSI 2005/465.*)

Persons in detention

8–19785 1. (1) A person shall be disregarded for the purposes of discount on a particular day if on the day—

(*a*) he is detained in a prison, a hospital or any other place by virtue of an order of a court to which sub-paragraph (2) below applies;

(*b*) he is detained under paragraph 2 of Schedule 3 to the Immigration Act 1971 (deportation);

(*c*) he is detained under Part II or section 46, 47, 48 or 136 of the Mental Health Act 1983; or

(*d*) he is detained under Parts 5, 6 and 7 or sections 136 or 297 of the Mental Health (Care and Treatment) (Scotland) Act 2003 or sections 52D or 52M or the Criminal Procedure (Scotland) Act 1995;

(2) This sub-paragraph applies to the following courts—

(*a*) a court in the United Kingdom; and

(*b*) a Standing Civilian Court established under the Armed Forces Act 1976.

(3) If a person—

(*a*) is temporarily discharged under section 28 of the Prison Act 1952, or temporarily released under rules under section 47(5) of that Act; or

(*b*) is temporarily discharged under section 27 of the Prisons (Scotland) Act 1989, or temporarily released under rules under section 39(6) of that Act,

for the purposes of sub-paragraph (1) above he shall be treated as detained.

(4) Sub-paragraph (1) above does not apply where the person—

(*a*) is detained under regulations made under paragraph 8 of Schedule 4 to this Act;

(*b*) is detained under section 76 of the Magistrates' Courts Act 1980, or section 108 of the Powers of Criminal Courts (Sentencing) Act 2000,* for default in payment of a fine; or

(*c*) is detained only under section 407 of the Criminal Procedure (Scotland) Act 1975.

(5) In sub-paragraph (1) above "order" includes a sentence, direction, warrant or other means of giving effect to the decision of the court concerned.

(6) The Secretary of State may by order[1] provide that a person shall be disregarded for the purposes of discount on a particular day if—

(*a*) on the day he is imprisoned, detained or in custody under the Army Act 1955, the Air Force Act 1955 or the Naval Discipline Act 1957; and

(*b*) such conditions as may be prescribed by the order are fulfilled.

***Repealed by the Criminal Justice and Court Services Act 2000, Sch 8 from a date to be appointed.**

1. The Council Tax (Disregards) Order 1992, SI 1992/548 amended by SI 1994/543, SI 1995/619, SI 1996/636 and 3143, SI 1997/656, SI 1998/291, SI 2003/673 (W) and SI 2004/2921 (W) has been made.

The severely mentally impaired

8–19786 **2.** (1) A person shall be disregarded for the purposes of discount on a particular day if—

(*a*) on the day he is severely mentally impaired;
(*b*) as regards any period which includes the day he is stated in a certificate of a registered medical practitioner to have been or to be likely to be severely mentally impaired; and
(*c*) as regards the day he fulfils such conditions as may be prescribed by order[1] made by the Secretary of State.

(2) For the purposes of this paragraph a person is severely mentally impaired if he has a severe impairment of intelligence and social functioning (however caused) which appears to be permanent.

(3) The Secretary of State may by order substitute another definition for the definition in sub-paragraph (2) above as for the time being effective for the purposes of this paragraph.

---

1. The Council Tax (Disregards) Order 1992, SI 1992/548 amended by SI 1994/543, SI 1995/619, SI 1996/636 and 3143, SI 1997/656, SI 1998/291, SI 2003/673 (W) and SI 2004/2921 (W) has been made.

Persons in respect of whom child benefit is payable

8–19787 **3.** (1) A person shall be disregarded for the purposes of discount on a particular day if on the day he—

(*a*) has attained the age of 18 years; but
(*b*) is a person in respect of whom another person is entitled to child benefit, or would be so entitled but for paragraph 1(*c*) of Schedule 9 to the Social Security Contributions and Benefits Act 1992.

(2) The Secretary of State may by order substitute another provision for sub-paragraph (1)(*b*) above as for the time being effective for the purposes of this paragraph.

Students etc

8–19788 **4.** (1) A person shall be disregarded for the purposes of discount on a particular day if—

(*a*) on the day he is a student, student nurse, apprentice or youth training trainee; and
(*b*) such conditions as may be prescribed by order[1] made by the Secretary of State are fulfilled.

(2) In this paragraph "apprentice", "student", "student nurse" and "youth training trainee" have the meanings for the time being assigned to them by order[1] made by the Secretary of State.

---

1. The Council Tax (Disregards) Order 1992, SI 1992/548 amended by SI 1994/543, SI 1995/619, SI 1996/636 and 3143, SI 1997/656, SI 1998/291, SI 2003/673 (W) and SI 2004/2921 (W) has been made.

8–19789 **5.** (1) An institution shall, on request, supply a certificate under this paragraph to any person who is following or, subject to sub-paragraph (3) below, has followed a course of education at that institution as a student or student nurse.

(2) A certificate under this paragraph shall contain such information about the person to whom it refers as may be prescribed by order[1] made by the Secretary of State.

(3) An institution may refuse to comply with a request made more than one year after the person making it has ceased to follow a course of education at that institution.

(4) In this paragraph—

"institution" means any such educational establishment or other body as may be prescribed by order[1] made by the Secretary of State; and

"student" and "student nurse" have the same meanings as in paragraph 4 above.

---

1. The Council Tax (Disregards) Order 1992, SI 1992/548 amended by SI 1994/543, SI 1995/619, SI 1996/636 and 3143, SI 1997/656, SI 1998/291, SI 2003/673 (W) and SI 2004/2921 (W) has been made.

Hospital patients

8–19790 **6.** (1) A person shall be disregarded for the purposes of discount on a particular day if on the day he is a patient who has his sole or main residence in a hospital.

(2) In this paragraph "hospital" means—

(*a*) a health service hospital within the meaning of the National Health Service Act 1977 or section 108(1) (interpretation) of the National Health Service (Scotland) Act 1978; and
(*b*) a military, air-force or naval unit or establishment at or in which medical or surgical treatment is provided for persons subject to military law, air-force law or the Naval Discipline Act 1957.

(3) The Secretary of State may by order substitute another definition for the definition in sub-paragraph (2) above as for the time being effective for the purposes of this paragraph.

Patients in homes in England and Wales

8–19791 **7.** (1) A person shall be disregarded for the purposes of discount on a particular day if on the day—

(*a*) he has his sole or main residence in a care home, independent hospital or hostel in England and Wales; and
(*b*) he is receiving care or treatment (or both) in the home, hospital or hostel.

(2) In this paragraph—

"care home" means—

(*a*) a care home within the meaning of the Care Standards Act 2000; or
(*b*) a building or part of a building in which residential accommodation is provided under section 21 of the National Assistance Act 1948;

"hostel" means anything which falls within any definition of hostel for the time being prescribed by order made by the Secretary of State under this sub-paragraph;

"independent hospital" has the same meaning as in the Care Standards Act 2000.

(3) The Secretary of State may by order[1] substitute another definition for any definition of "care home" or "independent hospital" for the time being effective for the purposes of this paragraph.

---

1. The Council Tax (Disregards) Order 1992, SI 1992/548 amended by SI 1994/543, SI 1995/619, SI 1996/636 and 3143, SI 1997/656, SI 1998/291, SI 2003/673 (W) and SI 2004/2921 (W) has been made.

Patients in homes in Scotland

8–19792 **8.** (1) A person shall be disregarded for the purposes of discount on a particular day if on the day—

(*a*) either—

(i) he has as his sole or main residence a private hospital in Scotland; or

(ii) a care home service provides, in Scotland, accommodation which is his sole or main residence; and

(*b*) he is receiving care or treatment (or both) in the hospital or in the accommodation so provided.

(2) In this paragraph—

"care home service" has the same meaning as in the Regulation of Care (Scotland) Act 2001 (asp 8); and

"private hospital" means an independent health care service as defined in section 329(1) of the Mental Health (Care and Treatment)(Scotland) Act 2003;

(3) *Repealed.*

(4) The Secretary of State may by order substitute another definition for any definition of, "private hospital" or "care home service" for the time being effective for the purposes of this paragraph.

Care workers

8–19793 **9.** (1) A person shall be disregarded for the purposes of discount on a particular day if—

(*a*) on the day he is engaged in providing care or support (or both) to another person or other persons; and

(*b*) such conditions as may be prescribed[1] are fulfilled.

(2) Without prejudice to the generality of sub-paragraph (1)(*b*) above the conditions may—

(*a*) require the care or support (or both) to be provided on behalf of a charity or a person fulfilling some other description;

(*b*) relate to the period for which the person is engaged in providing care or support (or both);

(*c*) require his income for a prescribed period (which contains the day concerned) not to exceed a prescribed amount;

(*d*) require his capital not to exceed a prescribed amount;

(*e*) require him to be resident in prescribed premises;

(*f*) require him not to exceed a prescribed age;

(*g*) require the other person or persons to fulfil a prescribed description (whether relating to age, disablement or otherwise).

---

1. The Council Tax (Additional Provision for Discount Disregards) Regulations 1992, SI 1992/552, amended by SI 1992/2942, SI 1993/149 and 540, SI 1994/540, SI 1996/637, SI 1997/657, SI 1998/294 and SI 2005/2866 (E) and 3302 (W) have been made.

Residents of certain dwellings

8–19794 **10.** (1) A person shall be disregarded for the purposes of discount on a particular day if on the day he has his sole or main residence in a dwelling to which sub-paragraph (2) below applies.

(2) This sub-paragraph applies to any dwelling if—

(*a*) it is for the time being providing residential accommodation, whether as a hostel or night shelter or otherwise; and

(*b*) the accommodation is predominantly provided—

(i) otherwise than in separate and self-contained sets of premises;

(ii) for persons of no fixed abode and no settled way of life; and

(iii) under licences to occupy which do not constitute tenancies.

Persons of other descriptions

8–19795 **11.** A person shall be disregarded for the purposes of discount on a particular day if—

(*a*) on the day he falls within such description as may be prescribed[1]; and

(*b*) such conditions as may be prescribed[1] are fulfilled.

---

1. The Council Tax (Additional Provisions for Discount Disregards) Regulations 1992, SI 1992/552 amended by SI 1992/2942, SI 1993/149 and 540, SI 1994/540, SI 1996/637, SI 1997/657, SI 1998/294 and SI 2005/2866 (E) and 3302 (W) have been made.

8–19796

Sections 14(1) and 97(3)

SCHEDULE 2

ADMINISTRATION[1]

---

1. This Schedule empowers the Secretary of State to make regulations covering specific matters such as collection, discounts, reduction for lump sum payments, exempt dwellings, supply of information and its use. See Pts I to IV of the Council Tax (Administration and Enforcement) Regulations 1992.

8–19797
Sections 14(2) and 97(4)

SCHEDULE 3
PENALTIES[1]

1. This Schedule enables a billing authority or levying authority to impose penalties for failure to supply information. Appeal lies to a valuation tribunal. The same conduct shall not lead both to a conviction and a penalty. As to the collection of penalties see reg 29 of the Council Tax (Administration and Enforcement) Regulations 1992 in this PART post.

8–19798
Section 14(3)

SCHEDULE 4
ENFORCEMENT: ENGLAND AND WALES[1]
(*Amended by Local Government Act 2003, s 76.*)

Quashing of liability orders

12A. Regulations under paragraph 1(1) above may provide—

(*a*) that, where on an application by the authority concerned a magistrates' court is satisfied that a liability order should not have been made, it shall quash the order;

(*b*) that, where on an application to a magistrates' court for the quashing of a liability order, the court is satisfied that, had the original application been for a liability order in respect of a lesser sum payable, such an order could properly have been made, it shall substitute a liability order in respect of the aggregate of—

(i) that lesser sum, and

(ii) any sum included in the quashed order in respect of the costs incurred in obtaining it.

1. This Schedule empowers the Secretary of State to make regulations covering specific matters such as liability orders, attachment of earnings, deductions from income support, distress, commitment to prison, bankruptcy, winding up, charging orders, admissibility of evidence, costs. See Pt V of the Council Tax (Administration and Enforcement) Regulations 1992 in this PART post.

Audit Commission Act 1998[1]

(1998 c 18)

PART I[2]
THE AUDIT COMMISSION

8–19800 **1. The Audit Commission.** (1) There shall continue to be a body known as the Audit Commission for Local Authorities and the National Health Service in England and Wales.

(2)–(5) *Constitution and Appointment of the Commission.*

[Audit Commission Act 1998, s 1.]

1. This Act consolidates part III of the Local Government Finance Act 1982 and other enactments relating to the Audit Commission for Local Authorities and the National Health Service in England and Wales.
2. Part I contains s 1.

PART II[1]
ACCOUNTS AND AUDIT OF PUBLIC BODIES

Audit of accounts

8–19801 **2. Required audit of accounts.** (1) The accounts to which this section applies—

(*a*) shall be made up each year to 31st March or such other date as the Secretary of State may generally or in any special case direct, and

(*b*) shall be audited in accordance with this Act by an auditor or auditors appointed by the Commission.

(2) This section applies to the accounts mentioned in Schedule 2[2].

[Audit Commission Act 1998, s 2.]

1. Part II contains ss 2–32.
2. See, post.

8–19802 **3.** *Appointment of Auditors*

8–19803 **4.** *Code of audit practice*

8–19804 **5. General duties of auditors.** (1) In auditing accounts required to be audited in accordance with this Act, an auditor shall by examination of the accounts and otherwise satisfy himself—

(*a*) if they are accounts of a health service body, that they are prepared in accordance with directions under subsection (2) or (2B) of section 98 of the National Health Service Act 1977;

(*b*) in any other case, that they are prepared in accordance with regulations under section 27;
(*c*) that they comply with the requirements of all other statutory provisions applicable to the accounts;
(*d*) that proper practices have been observed in the compilation of the accounts;
(*e*) that the body whose accounts are being audited has made proper arrangements for securing economy, efficiency and effectiveness in its use of resources; and
(*f*) that that body if required to publish information in pursuance of a direction under section 44 (performance information), has made such arrangements for collecting and recording the information and for publishing it as are required for the performance of its duties under that section.

(2) The auditor shall comply with the code of audit practice applicable to the accounts being audited as that code is for the time being in force.
[Audit Commission Act 1998, s 5, as amended by the Health Act 1999, Sch 4.]

8–19805 **6. Auditors' right to documents and information.** (1) An auditor has a right of access at all reasonable times to every document relating to a body subject to audit which appears to him necessary for the purposes of his functions under this Act.

(2) An auditor may—

(*a*) require a person holding or accountable for any such document to give him such information and explanation as he thinks necessary for the purposes of his functions under this Act; and
(*b*) if he thinks it necessary, require the person to attend before him in person to give the information or explanation or to produce the document.

(3) *Repealed.*

(4) Without prejudice to subsection (2), the auditor may—

(*a*) require any officer or member of a body subject to audit to give him such information or explanation as he thinks necessary for the purposes of his functions under this Act; and
(*b*) if he thinks it necessary, require the officer or member to attend before him in person to give the information or explanation.

(5) Without prejudice to subsections (1) to (4), every body subject to audit shall provide the auditor with every facility and all information which he may reasonably require for the purposes of his functions under this Act.

(6) A person who without reasonable excuse fails to comply with any requirement of an auditor under subsection (1), (2) or (4) is guilty of an offence and liable on summary conviction—

(*a*) to a fine not exceeding **level 3** on the standard scale, and
(*b*) to an additional fine not exceeding **£20** for each day on which the offence continues after conviction for that offence.

(7) Any expenses incurred by an auditor in connection with proceedings for an offence under subsection (6) alleged to have been committed in relation to the audit of the accounts of any body, so far as not recovered from any other source, are recoverable from that body.
[Audit Commission Act 1998, s 6, as amended by the Health Act 1999, Sch 5.]

Auditors' reports and recommendations

8–19806 **8. Immediate and other reports in public interest.** In auditing accounts required to be audited in accordance with this Act, the auditor shall consider—

(*a*) whether, in the public interest, he should make a report on any matter coming to his notice in the course of the audit, in order for it to be considered by the body concerned or brought to the attention of the public, and
(*b*) whether the public interest requires any such matter to be made the subject of an immediate report rather than of a report to be made at the conclusion of the audit.

[Audit Commission Act 1998, s 8.]

8–19807 **9. General report.** (1) When an auditor has concluded his audit of the accounts of any body under this Act he shall, subject to subsection (2), enter on the relevant statement of accounts prepared pursuant to regulations under section 27 (or, where no such statement is required to be prepared, on the accounts)—

(*a*) a certificate that he has completed the audit in accordance with this Act, and
(*b*) his opinion on the statement (or, as the case may be, on the accounts).

(2) Where an auditor makes a report to the body concerned under section 8 at the conclusion of the audit, he may include the certificate and opinion referred to in subsection (1) in that report instead of making an entry on the statement or accounts.
[Audit Commission Act 1998, s 9.]

8–19808 **10. Transmission and consideration of section 8 reports.** (1) Any report under section 8 shall be sent by the auditor to the body concerned or (if it is a parish meeting) to its chairman—

(*a*) forthwith if it is an immediate report;
(*b*) otherwise not later than 14 days after conclusion of the audit.

(2) A copy of the report shall be sent by the auditor to the Commission and (in the case of a health service body) to the Secretary of State and (in the case of a functional body or the London Pensions Fund Authority) to the Mayor of London—

(*a*) forthwith if it is an immediate report;
(*b*) otherwise not later than 14 days after conclusion of the audit.

(3) The body concerned (and, in the case of the Greater London Authority, the London Assembly) shall take the report into consideration—

(*a*) in accordance with sections 11, 11A and 12, or
(*b*) if section 11 does not apply to the body, as soon as practicable after receiving it.

(4) The agenda supplied to the members for the meeting of the body at which the report is considered shall be accompanied by the report.

(4A) In the case of a report relating to the Greater London Authority, subsection (4) shall apply in relation to the meeting of the London Assembly under section 11A(3) (taking the reference to the body as a reference to that Assembly).

(5) The report shall not be excluded—

(*a*) from the matter supplied under section 1(4)(*b*) of the Public Bodies (Admission to Meetings) Act 1960 or section 100B(7) of the 1972 Act (supply of agenda etc to newspapers); or
(*b*) from the documents open to inspection under section 100B(1) of the 1972 Act (public access to agenda and reports before meetings).

(6) Part VA of the 1972 Act has effect in relation to the report as if section 100C(1)(*d*) of that Act (public access to copies of reports for six years after meeting) were not limited to so much of the report as relates to an item during which the meeting was open to the public.
[Audit Commission Act 1998, s 10, as amended by the Greater London Authority Act 1999, Sch 8.]

8–19809 **11. Consideration of reports or recommendations.** (1) A body to which this section applies shall consider in accordance with this section and section 12 (and, in the case of a report or recommendations sent to the Greater London Authority, section 11A)—

(*a*) any report under section 8, and
(*b*) any written recommendation within subsection (3),

sent to the body or (if a parish meeting) its chairman in connection with the audit of its accounts.

(2) This section applies to every body subject to audit except—

(*a*) charter trustees constituted under section 246 of the 1972 Act;
(*b*) health service bodies;
(*c*) port health authorities;
(*d*) licensing planning committees;
(*e*) internal drainage boards;
(*f*) local probation noards established under section 4 of the Criminal Justice and Court Services Act 2000;
(*g*) Passenger Transport Executives.

(2A) Where a written recommendation within subsection (3) is sent to a functional body or the London Pensions Fund Authority, a copy shall be sent at the same time to the Mayor of London.

(3) A written recommendation is within this subsection if it is made to the body concerned (and, in the case of the Greater London Authority, the London Assembly) by an auditor and is stated in the document containing it to be one which in the auditor's opinion should be considered under this section.

(3A) In relation to the Greater London Authority, subsections (4) to (7) shall not apply (but section 11A has effect in place of them).

(4) The body concerned shall consider the report or recommendation at a meeting held before the end of one month beginning with the day on which the report or recommendation was sent to the body or its chairman (as the case may be).

(5) At that meeting the body shall decide—

(*a*) whether the report requires the body to take any action or whether the recommendation is to be accepted; and
(*b*) what, if any, action to take in response to the report or recommendation.

(6) If an auditor is satisfied that it is reasonable to allow more time for the body to comply with its duties under subsections (4) and (5) in relation to a report or recommendation, the auditor may, in relation to that report or recommendation, extend the period of four months* mentioned in subsection (4).

(7) A period may be extended under subsection (6) whether or not it has already been extended under that subsection once or more than once.

(7A) In the case of each of the following bodies, namely—

(*a*) Transport for London,
(*b*) the London Development Agency,
(*c*) the London Pensions Fund Authority,

Part VA of the 1972 Act (access to meetings etc) shall have effect in relation to the meeting as if that body were a principal council, but subject to the provisions of sections 10(5) and (6) and 12(3).

(8) Nothing in section 101 of the 1972 Act (delegation of functions) applies to a duty imposed on a body by this section.

(8A) In the case of the London Development Agency or Transport for London, neither—

(*a*) paragraph 7 of Schedule 2 to the Regional Development Agencies Act 1998 (delegation by London Development Agency etc), nor
(*b*) paragraph 7 of Schedule 10 to the Greater London Authority Act 1999 (delegation by Transport for London),

shall apply to a duty imposed on either of those bodies by this section.

(9) This section is without prejudice to any duties (so far as they relate to the subject-matter of a report or recommendation sent to a body to which this section applies) which are imposed by or under this Act, sections 114 to 116 of the Local Government Finance Act 1988 (functions and reports of finance officers), section 5 of the Local Government and Housing Act 1989 (functions of monitoring officers) or any other enactment.

[Audit Commission Act 1998, s 11, as amended by the Greater London Authority Act 1999, Sch 8, the Criminal Justice and Court Services Act 2000, Sch 1 and the Local Government Act 2003, s 107.]

8–19809A 11A. Greater London Authority: consideration of reports and recommendations.
(1) This section applies where—

(a) a report under section 8, or
(b) any written recommendation within subsection (3) of section 11,

is sent to the Greater London Authority in connection with the audit of its accounts.

(2) The Mayor shall consider the report or recommendation preparatory to making the decisions under subsection (6).

(3) The Assembly shall consider the report or recommendation at a meeting.

(4) At that meeting the Assembly shall decide what recommendations to make to the Mayor as to the decisions to be made under subsection (6).

(5) The Mayor must attend the meeting.

(6) After the meeting, the Mayor shall decide—

(a) whether the report requires the Authority to take any action or whether the recommendation is to be accepted; and
(b) what (if any) action to take in response to the report or recommendation.

(7) In making any decision under subsection (6), the Mayor shall take account of any recommendations made by the Assembly pursuant to subsection (4).

(8) The duties imposed on the Mayor and Assembly by subsections (2) to (6) must be performed before the end of the period of one month beginning with the day on which the report or recommendation was sent to the Authority.

(9) If an auditor is satisfied that it is reasonable to allow more time for the performance of those duties in relation to a report or recommendation, he may, in relation to that report or recommendation, extend the period of one month mentioned in subsection (8).

(10) A period may be extended under subsection (9) whether or not it has already been extended under that subsection once or more than once.

(11) Any functions of the Mayor under this section must be exercised by the Mayor personally.

(12) Section 54 of the Greater London Authority Act 1999 (discharge of Assembly functions by committees etc) shall not apply in relation to any function of the Assembly under this section.

(13) Subsection (9) of section 11 applies in relation to this section as it applies in relation to that section.

(14) In this section—

"the Assembly" means the London Assembly;
"the Authority" means the Greater London Authority;
"the Mayor" means the Mayor of London.

[Audit Commission Act 1998, s 11A, as inserted by the Greater London Authority Act 1999, Sch 8 and amended by the Local Government Act 2003, s 107.]

8–19810 12. Publicity for meetings under section 11. (1) A meeting shall not be held for the purposes of section 11 or 11A unless, at least seven clear days before the meeting, there has been published, in a newspaper circulating in the area of the body concerned, a notice which—

(*a*) states the time and place of the meeting,
(*b*) indicates that the meeting is to be held to consider an auditor's report or recommendation (as the case may be), and

(*c*) describes the subject-matter of the report or recommendation.

(2) The body concerned shall ensure that, as soon as practicable after the meeting (or, in the case of the Greater London Authority, the making of the decisions under section 11A(6))—

(*a*) the auditor of its accounts is notified of the decisions made in pursuance of section 11(5) or 11A(6); and

(*b*) a notice containing a summary of those decisions which has been approved by the auditor is published in a newspaper circulating in that body's area.

(3) The notice required by subsection (2)(b) in relation to a meeting—

(*a*) need not summarise any decision made while the public were excluded from the meeting—

(i) under section 100A(2) of the 1972 Act (confidential matters);

(ii) in pursuance of a resolution under section 100A(4) of that Act (exempt information); or

(iii) in pursuance of a resolution under section 1(2) of the Public Bodies (Admission to Meetings) Act 1960 (protection of public interest);

but

(*b*) if sections 100C and 100D of the 1972 Act (availability for inspection after meetings of minutes, background papers and other documents) apply in relation to the meeting, shall indicate the documents in relation to the meeting which are open for inspection in accordance with those sections.

(4) This section is without prejudice to, and in addition to, any provision made in relation to meetings of the body in question by section 10(4) to (6) or by or under the 1972 Act, the Public Bodies (Admission to Meetings) Act 1960 or any other enactment.

[Audit Commission Act 1998, s 12, as amended by the Greater London Authority Act 1999, Sch 8.]

8–19811 **13. Additional publicity for immediate reports.** (1) This section applies where under section 10(1) an auditor has sent an immediate report to a body or its chairman, except where the body is a health service body.

(2) From the time when the report is received by virtue of section 10(1), any member of the public may—

(*a*) inspect the report at all reasonable times without payment,

(*b*) make a copy of it, or of any part of it, and

(*c*) require the body or chairman to supply him with a copy of it, or of any part of it, on payment of a reasonable sum.

(3) On receiving the report by virtue of section 10(1), the body or (if a parish meeting) its chairman shall forthwith publish in one or more local newspapers circulating in the area of the body a notice which—

(*a*) identifies the subject-matter of the report, and

(*b*) states that any member of the public may inspect the report and make a copy of it or any part of it between such times and at such place or places as are specified in the notice;

and the body, if not a parish meeting, shall in addition forthwith supply a copy of the report to every member of the body.

(4) The auditor may—

(*a*) notify any person he thinks fit of the fact that he has made the report, and

(*b*) supply a copy of it or of any part of it to any person he thinks fit.

(5) A person who has the custody of an immediate report and—

(*a*) obstructs a person in the exercise of a right conferred by subsection (2)(*a*) or (b), or

(*b*) refuses to supply a copy of the report or of part of it (as the case may be) to a person entitled to the copy by virtue of subsection (2)(*c*),

is guilty of an offence and liable on summary conviction to a fine not exceeding **level 3** on the standard scale.

(6) A person who fails to comply with a requirement of subsection (3) is guilty of an offence and liable on summary conviction to a fine not exceeding **level 3** on the standard scale.

(7) Nothing in this section affects the operation of section 10(4) to (6).*

[Audit Commission Act 1998, s 13.]

8–19811A **13A. Additional publicity for non-immediate reports.** (1) This section applies where under section 10(1) an auditor has sent a report that is not an immediate report to a body or its chairman, except where the body is a health service body.

(2) The auditor may—

(*a*) notify any person he thinks fit of the fact that he has made the report,

(*b*) publish the report in any way he thinks fit, and

(*c*) supply a copy of the report, or of any part of it, to any person he thinks fit.

(3) From the time when the report is sent under section 10(1), but subject to subsection (4)—

(*a*) the auditor shall ensure that any member of the public may—

(i) inspect the report at all reasonable times without payment, and

(ii) make a copy of the report or of any part of it;

(*b*) any member of the public may require the auditor to supply him with a copy of the report, or of any part of it, on payment of a reasonable sum.

(4) From the end of the period of one year beginning with the day when the report is sent under section 10(1), the obligations of the auditor under subsection (3)—

(*a*) cease to be his obligations, but

(*b*) become obligations of the Commission instead.

[Audit Commission Act 1998, s 13A as inserted by the Local Government Act 2003, s 108.]

8–19812

Public inspection etc and action by the auditor

14. Inspection of statements of accounts and auditors' reports. (1) A local government elector for the area of a body subject to audit, other than a health service body, may—

(*a*) inspect and make copies of any statement of accounts prepared by the body pursuant to regulations under section 27;

(*b*) inspect and make copies of any report, other than an immediate report, made to the body by an auditor; and

(*c*) require copies of any such statement or report to be delivered to him on payment of a reasonable sum for each copy.

(2) A document which a person is entitled to inspect under this section may be inspected by him at all reasonable times and without payment.

(3) A person who has the custody of any such document and—

(*a*) obstructs a person in the exercise of a right under this section to inspect or make copies of the document, or

(*b*) refuses to give copies of the document to a person entitled under this section to obtain them,

is guilty of an offence and liable on summary conviction to a fine not exceeding level 3 on the standard scale.

(4) References in this section to copies of a document include references to copies of any part of it.

[Audit Commission Act 1998, s 14.]

8–19813 **15. Inspection of documents and questions at audit.** (1) At each audit under this Act, other than an audit of accounts of a health service body, any persons interested may—

(*a*) inspect the accounts[1] to be audited and all books, deeds, contracts, bills, vouchers and receipts relating to them, and

(*b*) make copies of all or any part of the accounts and those other documents.

(2) At the request of a local government elector for any area to which the accounts relate, the auditor shall give the elector, or any representative of his, an opportunity to question the auditor about the accounts.

(3) Nothing in this section entitles a person—

(*a*) to inspect so much of any accounts or other document as contains personal information about a member of the staff of the body whose accounts are being audited; or

(*b*) to require any such information to be disclosed in answer to any question.

(4) For the purposes of subsection (3), information is to be regarded as personal information about a member of a body's staff if it relates specifically to a particular individual and is available to the body for reasons connected with the fact—

(*a*) that that individual holds or has held an office or employment under that body; or

(*b*) that payments or other benefits in respect of an office or employment under any other person are or have been made or provided to that individual by that body.

(5) For the purposes of subsection (4)(*b*), payments made or benefits provided to an individual in respect of an office or employment include any payment made or benefit provided to him in respect of his ceasing to hold the office or employment.

[Audit Commission Act 1998, s 15.]

1. A wages book or its computerised equivalent relating to an authority's employees is a book of account within the meaning of this subsection and, therefore, open to inspection; confidentiality of such a document is irrelevant (Oliver v Northampton Borough Council (1986) 151 JP 44). The exercise of such right of inspection is provided for by s 27(1)(*e*), post, and the Accounts and Audit Regulations 1983, SI 1983/1761.

Miscellaneous

8–19814 **25. Extraordinary audit.** (1) The Commission may direct an auditor or auditors appointed by it to hold an extraordinary audit of the accounts of a body subject to audit—

(*a*) if it appears to the Commission to be desirable to do so in consequence of a report made under this Act by an auditor or for any other reason; or

(*b*) where the accounts are not those of a health service body, if an application for such an audit is made by a local government elector for the area of the body in question.

(2) If it appears to the Secretary of State that it is desirable in the public interest that there should be an extraordinary audit of the accounts of a body subject to audit he may require the Commission to direct such an audit by an auditor or auditors appointed by it.

(3) The following provisions apply to an extraordinary audit under this section as they apply to an ordinary audit under this Act—

(*a*) in relation to the accounts of a body other than a health service body, sections 3, 5, 6, 8 to 13 and 16 to 18; and

(*b*) in relation to the accounts of a health service body, sections 3, 5, 6 and 8 to 10.

(4) An extraordinary audit under this section may be held after three clear days' notice in writing to be given to the body whose accounts are to be audited or (if it is a parish meeting) to be given to its chairman.

(5) The expenditure incurred in holding an extraordinary audit of the accounts of any body—

(*a*) shall be defrayed in the first instance by the Commission, but

(*b*) may be recovered by the Commission, if it thinks fit, in whole or part from the body concerned.

[Audit Commission Act 1998, s 25.]

8–19815 **26. Audit of accounts of officers.** (1) Where an officer of a body subject to audit receives money or other property—

(*a*) on behalf of that body, or

(*b*) for which he ought to account to that body,

the accounts of the officer shall be audited by the auditor of the accounts of that body, and the provisions mentioned in subsection (2) apply with the necessary modifications to the accounts and audit.

(2) Those provisions are—

(*a*) in the case of an officer of a health service body, sections 2(1), 5 to 10 and 25;

(*b*) in any other case, sections 2(1), 5 to 10, 13 to 18, 25 and 27.

[Audit Commission Act 1998, s 26.]

8–19816 **27. Accounts and audit regulations.** (1) The Secretary of State may by regulations[1] applying to bodies subject to audit other than health service bodies make provision with respect to—

(*a*) the keeping of accounts;

(*b*) the form, preparation and certification of accounts and of statements of accounts;

(*c*) the deposit of the accounts of any body at the offices of the body or at any other place;

(*d*) the publication of information relating to accounts and the publication of statements of accounts;

(*e*) the exercise of any rights of objection or inspection conferred by section 14, 15 or 16 and the steps to be taken by any body for informing local government electors for the area of that body of those rights.

(2) Regulations under this section may make different provision in relation to bodies of different descriptions.

(3) Before making any regulations under this section the Secretary of State shall consult—

(*a*) the Commission,

(*b*) such associations of local authorities as appear to him to be concerned, and

(*c*) such bodies of accountants as appear to him to be appropriate.

(4) If a person without reasonable excuse contravenes a provision of regulations under this section and the regulations declare that contravention of the provision is an offence, that person is liable on summary conviction to a fine not exceeding level 3 on the standard scale.

(5) Any expenses incurred by an auditor in connection with proceedings in respect of an offence under subsection (4) alleged to have been committed in relation to the accounts of any body, so far as not recovered from any other source, are recoverable from that body.

[Audit Commission Act 1998, s 27.]

1. See the Accounts and Audit Regulations 1996, SI 1996/590, and theAccounts and Audit (Passenger Transport Executives and London Transport Executive) Regulations 1983 SI 1983/1849.

Performance standards of local authorities etc

8–19817 44. Publication of information as to standards of performance. (1) The Commission shall give such directions as it thinks fit for requiring relevant bodies to publish such information relating to their activities in any financial year as will, in the Commission's opinion, facilitate the making of appropriate comparisons (by reference to the criteria of cost, economy, efficiency and effectiveness) between—

(*a*) the standards of performance achieved by different relevant bodies in that financial year; and
(*b*) the standards of performance achieved by such bodies in different financial years.

(2) Where a relevant body is required by a direction under this section to publish information in relation to any financial year, it shall—

(*a*) make such arrangements for collecting and recording the information as secure that the information is available for publication and, so far as practicable, that everything published in pursuance of the direction is accurate and complete;
(*b*) within the period of nine months or, in the case of a relevant body in England, seven months beginning with the end of that financial year, publish the information in accordance with the direction and by one of the methods permitted by section 45; and
(*c*) keep a document containing any information published in pursuance of the direction available for inspection by local government electors for its area.

(3) The Secretary of State may by order vary the period for the time being specified in paragraph (*b*) of subsection (2) so as to fix the latest time for the publication of information in accordance with that paragraph at any such time, within the period of nine months after the end of the financial year in question, as may be specified in the order.

(4) A local government elector for the area of a relevant body may—

(*a*) at all reasonable times and without payment, inspect and make copies of the whole or any part of a document kept available for inspection under subsection (2)(*c*) by the body; and
(*b*) require copies of the whole or part of any such document to be delivered to him on payment of a reasonable sum for each copy.

(5) A person who has custody of a document kept available for inspection under subsection (2)(*c*) and—

(*a*) obstructs a person in the exercise of his rights under subsection (4), or
(*b*) refuses to comply with a requirement under subsection (4)(*b*),

is guilty of an offence and liable, on summary conviction, to a fine not exceeding **level 3** on the standard scale.

(6) In this section and sections 45 and 46 "relevant body" means any body subject to audit other than one within subsection (7).

(7) Subject to section 47, the following are not relevant bodies for the purposes of this section and sections 45 and 46—

(*a*) parish and community councils and any parish meeting of a parish not having a separate parish council;
(*b*) charter trustees constituted under section 246 of the 1972 Act;
(*c*) health service bodies;
(*d*) port health authorities;
(*e*) licensing planning committees;
(*f*) internal drainage boards;
(*g*) probation committees; and
(*h*) Passenger Transport Executives.

[Audit Commission Act 1998, s 44, as amended by SI 2000/2253.]

1. Part III contains ss 33–47.

8–19818 45. Permitted methods of publishing information under section 44. (1) The permitted methods of publication referred to in section 44(2)(b) are as follows.

(2) The relevant body may publish the information in a newspaper printed for sale and circulating in its area.

(3) If the relevant body ensures that the distribution condition is satisfied with respect to the information, it may publish the information in a newspaper or periodical publication which is produced and distributed by another person (other than a local authority company) and which is free of charge to the recipient.

(4) For the purposes of subsection (3), a relevant body ensures that the distribution condition is satisfied with respect to information if—

(*a*) the body takes all reasonable steps to secure that a copy of a publication containing the information is distributed to each dwelling in its area; and (*b*) in a case where the body considers that the information is of concern to persons carrying on business in its area, the body takes such steps as it considers reasonable and practicable to secure that a copy of a publication containing the information is distributed to business premises in its area.

(5) For the purposes of subsection (3) a local authority company is any company under the control of a local authority; and section 68(1) of the Local Government and Housing Act 1989 (company under control of local authority) has effect for the purposes of this subsection as it has effect for the purposes of Part V of that Act.
[Audit Commission Act 1998, s 45.]

8–19819 **46. Directions under section 44.** (1) A direction under section 44 requiring the publication of information shall—

(*a*) identify the financial year or years in relation to which the information is to be published;
(*b*) specify or describe the activities to which the information is to relate; and
(*c*) make provision as to the matters to be contained in the information and as to the form in which it is to be published.

(2) A direction under section 44—

(*a*) may be given so as to apply either to all relevant bodies or to all such bodies as are of a description specified in the direction; and
(*b*) may be varied or revoked by any subsequent direction under that section.

(3) Before giving a direction under section 44 which imposes a new requirement on a relevant body as to the publication of any information the Commission shall consult such associations of relevant bodies and such other persons as it thinks fit.

(4) A direction under section 44 imposing a new requirement on a relevant body as to the publication of any information shall not be given any later than the 31st December in the financial year which precedes that in relation to which the information is to be published.

(5) Where the Commission gives a direction under section 44, it shall—

(*a*) publish the direction in such manner as it considers appropriate for bringing it to the attention of members of the public; and
(*b*) send a copy of the direction to every relevant body on whom duties are imposed by virtue of the direction.

(6) References in this section to the imposition of a new requirement on a relevant body as to the publication of information are references to—

(*a*) the imposition of any requirement by the first direction under section 44 to apply to that body; or
(*b*) any subsequent extension of, or addition to, either—
 (i) the matters to be contained in the information which that body is required to publish in relation to any financial year in pursuance of directions under section 44; or
 (ii) the activities to which any such information is to relate.

[Audit Commission Act 1998, s 46.]

8–19820 **47. Application to parish councils and charter trustees.** (1) The Secretary of State may by order provide for sections 44 to 46 to have effect as if—

(*a*) parish and community councils in England and Wales, and
(*b*) charter trustees constituted under section 246 of the 1972 Act,

were relevant bodies for the purposes of those sections.

(2) The power to make an order under this section includes power—

(*a*) to make such incidental, consequential, transitional or supplementary provision as the Secretary of State thinks necessary or expedient; and
(*b*) to make different provision for different cases, including different provision for different localities and for different bodies.

[Audit Commission Act 1998, s 47 as amended by the Public Audit (Wales) Act 2004, Sch 2.]

PART IV
GENERAL

Information etc

8–19821 **48. Provision of information and documents to Commission.** (1) Without prejudice to any other provision of this Act, the Commission may require—

(*a*) any body subject to audit, and
(*b*) any officer or member of such a body,

to provide the Commission or a person authorised by it with all such information as the Commission or that person may reasonably require for the discharge of the functions under this Act of the Commission or of that person, including the carrying out of any study under section 33 or 34.

(2) Subsection (1) does not apply to functions under section 36.

(3) For the purpose of assisting the Commission to maintain proper standards in the auditing of the accounts of a body subject to audit the Commission may require that body to make available for inspection by or on behalf of the Commission—

(*a*) the accounts concerned; and

(*b*) such other documents relating to the body as might reasonably be required by an auditor for the purposes of the audit.

(4) A person who without reasonable excuse fails to comply with a requirement of the Commission under subsection (1)(*b*) is guilty of an offence and liable on summary conviction—

(*a*) to a fine not exceeding **level 3** on the standard scale, and

(*b*) to an additional fine not exceeding **£20** for each day on which the offence continues after conviction for that offence.

(5) Any expenses incurred by the Commission in connection with proceedings for an offence under subsection (4) alleged to have been committed by an officer or member of a body, so far as not recovered from any other source, are recoverable from that body.
[Audit Commission Act 1998, s 48.]

1. Part IV contains ss 48–55.

8–19822 **49. Restriction on disclosure of information.** (1) No information relating to a particular body or other person and obtained by the Commission or an auditor, or by a person acting on behalf of the Commission or an auditor, pursuant to any provision of this Act or of Part I of the Local Government Act 1999 or in the course of any audit or study under any such provision shall be disclosed except—

(*a*) with the consent of the body or person to whom the information relates;

(*b*) for the purposes of any functions of the Commission or an auditor under this Act or under Part I of the 1999 Act;

(*ba*) to the Commission for Social Care Inspection for the purposes of its functions under Chapter 5 of Part 2 of the Health and Social Care (Community Health and Standards) Act 2003;

(*bb*) to the National Assembly for Wales for the purposes of its functions under Chapter 4 of that Part of that Act;

(*c*) in the case of a health service body, for those purposes or for the purposes of the functions of the Secretary of State and the Comptroller and Auditor General under the National Health Service Act 1977 or for the purposes of the functions of the Commission for Healthcare Audit and Inspection under Chapter 3 of Part 2 of the Health and Social Care (Community Health and Standards) Act 2003;

(*d*) for the purposes of the functions of the Secretary of State relating to social security;

(*da*) for the purposes of the functions of the Auditor General for Wales under the Public Audit (Wales) Act 2004 or (in relation to a health service body) under the Government of Wales Act 1998;

(*dd*) to the Mayor of London, where the information relates to the Greater London Authority or a functional body;

(*de*) for the purposes of the functions of an ethical standards officer or the Public Services Ombudsman for Wales under Part 3 of the Local Government Act 2000;

(*e*) *repealed*

(*f*) for the purposes of any criminal proceedings.

(1A) Subsection (1) does not apply in relation to disclosure by a person who is, or acts on behalf of a person who is, a public authority for the purposes of the Freedom of Information 2000.

(2) References in subsection (1) to studies and to functions of the Commission do not include studies or functions under section 36.

(3) A person who discloses information in contravention of subsection (1) is guilty of an offence and liable[1]—

(*a*) on summary conviction, to imprisonment for a term not exceeding **six months** or to a **fine** not exceeding the **statutory maximum** or to both; or

(*b*) on conviction on indictment, to imprisonment for a term not exceeding **two years** or to a fine or to both.

[Audit Commission Act 1998, s 49, as amended by the Local Government Act 1999, s 22, the Greater London Authority Act 1999, Sch 8, the Local Government Act 2000, Sch 5, the Health and Social Care (Community Health and Standards) Act 2003, Sch 9, SI 2004/3363, the Public Audit (Wales) Act 2004, Sch 2 and the Public Services Ombudsman (Wales) Act 2005, Sch 6.]

1. For procedure in respect of this offence which is triable either way, see the Magistrates' Courts Act 1980 ss 17A–21, in PART I: MAGISTRATES' COURTS PROCEDURE, ante.

8–19822A 49A. Disclosure of information by or on behalf of public authorities. (1) This section applies if information relating to a particular body or other person is obtained by the Commission or an auditor, or a person acting on behalf of the Commission or an auditor—

(*a*) pursuant to a provision of this Act or of Part 1 of the Local Government Act 1999, or
(*b*) in the course of an audit of study under this Act or under Part 1 of the Local Government Act 1999.

(2) A person who is, or acts on behalf of a person who is, a public authority for the purposes of the Freedom of Information Act 2000, may disclose any such information—

(*a*) in the circumstances in which he would (but for section 49A(1)) be authorised to do so under section 49(1);
(*b*) in accordance with section 41(4); or
(*c*) in any other circumstances, except where such a disclosure would, or would be likely to, prejudice the effective performance by such a person of a function imposed or conferred on the person by or under an enactment.

(3) A person mentioned in subsection (2) who discloses any such information otherwise than as authorised by subsection (2) is guilty of an offence and liable on summary conviction to a fine not exceeding the statutory maximum.
[Audit Commission Act 1998, s 49A, as inserted by SI 2004/3363.]

8–19823 50. Supply of benefit information to Commission. The Secretary of State may supply to the Commission any information held by him which relates to housing benefit or council tax benefit and which appears to him to be relevant to the exercise of any function of the Commission.
[Audit Commission Act 1998, s 50.]

8–19824 51. Publication of information by the Commission. (1) Subject to subsections (2) to (4), the Commission may publish such information as it thinks fit with respect to any of the following—

(*a*) a contravention by a body subject to audit of any obligation imposed on that body by virtue of section 44(2);
(*b*) the making by an auditor of a report under section 8 to any such body, the subject-matter of any such report and the decision made and other action taken by any such body in response to the receipt of any such report or to anything contained in it;
(*c*) a contravention by any such body of regulations made under section 27.

(2) The information that may be published by virtue of subsection (1)(*b*) does not include—

(*a*) information with respect to a report made to a health service body or to any decision or other action by such a body; or
(*b*) information excluded under subsection (3)(*a*) of section 12 from any notice published for the purposes of subsection (2)(*b*) of that section.

(3) Before publishing information under this section relating to—

(*a*) the conduct or decisions of a body subject to audit, or
(*b*) a report made to such a body,

the Commission shall notify the body of its proposal to publish the information.

(4) Information published under this section shall be published in such manner as the Commission considers appropriate for bringing the information to the attention of those members of the public who may be interested.*
[Audit Commission Act 1998, s 51.]

8–19824A 51A. Co-operation with the Auditor General for Wales. [The Commission must co-operate with the Auditor General for Wales where it seems to it appropriate to do so for the efficient and effective discharge of—

(*a*) its functions under sections 33 and 34, or
(*b*) its functions in relation to bodies mentioned in paragraph 1(g) of Schedule 2.

[Audit Commission Act 1998, s 51A as inserted by the Public Audit (Wales) Act 2004, Sch 2.]

8–19824B 51B. Provision of information to Auditor General for Wales. The Commission must, on request, provide the Auditor General for Wales with any information he may reasonably require for the purpose of making comparisons, in the discharge of his functions under sections 41 and 42 of the Public Audit (Wales) Act 2004, between local government bodies in Wales and other local government bodies.
[Audit Commission Act 1998, s 51B as inserted by the Public Audit (Wales) Act 2004, Sch 2.]

Supplementary

8–19825 **52. Orders and regulations.** (1) Any power conferred on the Secretary of State by this Act to make orders or regulations is exercisable by statutory instrument.

(2) No order shall be made under paragraph 9(2) of Schedule 1 unless a draft of the order has been approved by a resolution of the House of Commons.

(3) In any other case, an order or regulations contained in a statutory instrument made by the Secretary of State under this Act shall be subject to annulment in pursuance of a resolution of either House of Parliament.

[Audit Commission Act 1998, s 52 as amended by the Local Government Act 2003, s 109 and the Public Audit (Wales) Act 2004, s 73.]

8–19826 **53. Interpretation.** (1) In this Act—

"the 1972 Act" means the Local Government Act 1972;

"auditor", in relation to the accounts of any body, means (except in section 31(1)) the person or any of the persons appointed by the Commission to act as auditor in relation to those accounts and, to the extent provided by section 3(11), includes a person assisting an auditor under arrangements approved under section 3(9);

"best value authority" means a best value authority for the purposes of Part I of the Local Government Act 1999;

"body subject to audit" means a body whose accounts are required to be audited in accordance with this Act;

"the Commission" means the Audit Commission for Local Authorities and the National Health Service in England and Wales;

"functional body" means a functional body within the meaning of the Greater London Authority Act 1999 (see section 424(1) of that Act);

"the health service" has the same meaning as in the National Health Service Act 1977;

"health service body" means—

(*a*) a body specified in section 98(1) of the National Health Service Act 1977,

(*b*) *Repealed*;

"local government body" means a body mentioned in paragraph 1 of Schedule 2, other than one mentioned in paragraph (*g*) of that paragraph;

"local government body in Wales" has the meaning given in section 12(1) of the Public Audit (Wales) Act 2004;

"statutory provision" means any provision contained in or having effect under any enactment;

"Welsh NHS body" has the meaning given in section 60 of the Public Audit (Wales) Act 2004

(2) Subject to paragraph 11(5) of Schedule 1, section 270 of the 1972 Act (general interpretation) applies for the interpretation of this Act.

(3) A reference in this Act to the accounts of a body—

(*a*) in relation to the Common Council is a reference to the accounts mentioned in paragraph 2(*a*) and (*b*) of Schedule 2;

(*b*) *Repealed.*

(4) A reference in this Act to a local government elector for any area—

(*a*) in relation to the Broads Authority, is a reference to a local government elector for the area of any participating authority (as defined by section 25 of the Norfolk and Suffolk Broads Act 1988); and

(*b*) in relation to a National Park authority which is the local planning authority for a National Park, is a reference to a local government elector for any area the whole or any part of which is comprised in that Park.

(5) Any functions conferred or imposed on the Greater London Authority under or by virtue of this Act shall be functions which are exercisable by the Mayor of London acting on behalf of the Authority.

(6) Subsection (5) does not apply in relation to any function expressly conferred on the London Assembly.

[Audit Commission Act 1998, s 53, as amended by the Local Government Act 1999, s 22, the Health Act 1999, Sch 5 and the Greater London Authority Act 1999, Sch 8 and the Public Audit (Wales) Act 2004, Sch 2.]

8–19827 **54.** *Consequential amendments, transitionals and repeals*

8–19828 **55.** *Short title, commencement and extent*

Section 2

SCHEDULE 2
ACCOUNTS SUBJECT TO AUDIT

(*As amended by the Heath Act 1999, Sch 5, the Greater London Authority Act 1999, s 133, the Countryside and Rights of Way Act 2000, Sch 13, the Criminal Justice and Court Services Act 2000, Sch 7, the Criminal Justice and Police Act 2001, Sch 7, SI 2003/1324, Si 2004/1714, the Fire and Rescue Services Act 2004, Sch 1 and the Public Audit (Wales) Act 2004, s 66.*)

8–19829 **1.** Section 2 applies to all accounts of—

(*a*) a local authority;
(*b*) a joint authority;
(*bb*) the Greater London Authority;
(*bc*) a functional body
(*bd*) the London Pensions Fund Authority
(*c*) a parish meeting of a parish not having a separate parish council;
(*d*) a committee of a local authority, including a joint committee of two or more such authorities;
(*e*) the Council of the Isles of Scilly;
(*f*) any charter trustees constituted under section 246 of the 1972 Act;
(*g*) a body specified in section 98(1) of the National Health Service Act 1977, other than a Welsh NHS body;
(*h*) a port health authority;
(*i*) the Broads Authority;
(*j*) a National Park authority;
(*jj*) a conservation board established under section 86 of the Countryside and Rights of Way Act 2000;
(*k*) a police authority established under section 3 of the Police Act 1996;
(*l*) *repealed*;
(*m*) A fire and rescue authority constituted by a scheme under section 2 of the Fire and Rescue Services Act 2004 or a scheme to which section 4 of that Act applies;
(*n*) a licensing planning committee;
(*o*) an internal drainage board; and
(*p*) a local probation board established under section 4 of the Criminal Justice and Court Services Act 2000.

1A. But section 2 does not apply to accounts of—

(*a*) a Special Health Authority established as at 1st April 2003, in respect of a financial year ending on or after 31st March 2004,
(*b*) the Dental Practice Board, in respect of a financial year ending on or after 31st March 2004,
(*c*) NHSU and NHS Professionals Special Health Authority, in respect of a financial year ending on or after 31st March 2004,
(*d*) NHS Direct and NHS Pensions Agency, in respect of a financial year ending on or after 31st March 2005.

1B. Section 2 does not apply to the accounts of a local government body in Wales.

2. Section 2 also applies to—

(*a*) the accounts of the collection fund of the Common Council and the accounts of the City fund; and
(*b*) the accounts relating to the superannuation fund maintained and administered by the Common Council under the Local Government Pension Scheme Regulations 1995.

3. *Repealed.*

4. Subject to section 30, section 2 also applies to the accounts of a Passenger Transport Executive.

Annex Licensing Act 2003

INTRODUCTION

8–19829A The Licensing Act 2003 has introduced a new regime for the licensing of alcohol (both in premises open to the general public and to qualifying clubs), and has amalgamated it with the licensing of regulated entertainment (previously called "public entertainment" under the provisions of the Local Government (Miscellaneous Provisions) Act 1982, or licensed separately under legislation dealing with theatres and cinemas), and, for the first time, "late night refreshment".

8–19829B **Transfer of responsibilities.** The Act removes the responsibility for licensing such activities from the licensing justices (who were previously responsible for the licensing of alcohol) and hands the responsibilities to "licensing authorities". These are defined in LA 2003, s 3, and include district councils, unitary authorities and London boroughs. The role of magistrates' courts is to act as an appellate court against the myriad of decisions that can be appealed; to deal with the raft of criminal offences under the Act; and to consider closure orders made by the Police under Part 8 of the Act. Because primary responsibility for such matters has been removed from licensing justices, what follows is a short commentary by way of an overview of the Licensing Act 2003, and a more detailed commentary on those parts of the Act that magistrates' courts retain jurisdiction over.

LICENSABLE ACTIVITIES AND QUALIFYING CLUB ACTIVITIES

8–19829C These are defined as the sale by retail[1] of alcohol[2]; the supply of alcohol by or on behalf of a club to, or to the order of, a member of the club; the provision of regulated entertainment; and the provision of late night refreshment[3]. Regulated entertainment is defined fully in Sch 1, and includes both entertainment and entertainment facilities that are provided for the public or a section of the public, and to entertainment provided exclusively for members of a qualifying club. The previous public entertainment regime did not require entertainment provided for club members to be licensed because it was not "public". Entertainment includes those activities listed in Sch 1, para 2. Certain activities listed in Sch 1, Part 2 are exempt from the definition. The provision of late night refreshment is defined in Sch 2. It involves the provision of hot food or hot drink to members of the public between 11pm and 5am on or from any premises, whether for consumption on or off the premises[4]. Certain supplies, such as to residents in hotels, are exempt[5]. If a licensable activity is taking place, it must be licensed either by virtue of a premises licence issued under Part 3 of the Act or by virtue of it being a "permitted temporary activity" under Part 5[6]. A qualifying club activity can only take place by virtue of a club premises certificate issued under Part 4[7].

1. Defined in LA 2003, s 192.
2. Defined in LA 2003, s 191.
3. Licensing Act 2003, s 1(1). Qualifying club activities are further defined in ss 1(2) and (3). Activities that are carried on in certain locations are not licensable activities: Licensing Act 2003, s 173. However, licensable activities or qualifying club activities that take place on vessels, vehicles or other moveable structures do require a premises licence: Licensing Act 2003, s 189. Premises licences that purport to licence roadside service areas or premises used primarily as a garage for the sale or supply of alcohol are invalid: Licensing Act 2003, s 176.
4. Licensing Act 2003, Sch 2, para 1(1).
5. For a full list, see LA 2003, Sch 2, paras 3, 4 and 5.
6. Licensing Act 2003, s 2(1).
7. Licensing Act 2003, s 2(2).

Functions of Licensing Authorities and Licensing Objectives

8–19829D A licensing authority must carry out its functions under the Act with a view to promoting the four licensing objectives of prevention of crime and disorder; public safety; prevention of public nuisance; and the protection of children from harm[1]. In addition, those licensing authorities that are local authorities within the meaning of s 270(1) of the Local Government Act 1972, must have regard to the need to do all that they reasonably can to prevent crime and disorder in their areas[2]. Magistrates' courts dealing with appeals must also have regard to the need to promote the licensing objectives and, because they stand in the feet of licensing authorities when carrying out their appellate functions, it is submitted that they must also have regard to the duty imposed on licensing authorities by the Crime and Disorder Act 1998. Licensing authorities (and magistrates' courts dealing with appeals) must also have regard to the Statement of Licensing Policy issued under s 5 of the Act; and the Secretary of State's guidance issued under s 182 of the Act[3]. A licensing authority must establish a licensing committee of between 10 and 15 members of the authority[4], and most matters are delegated to that committee[5] (or sub-committees consisting of three members[6]) to deal with. Matters can be further delegated to local government officers to determine if they are uncontested[7]. A licensing authority is required to keep a register containing prescribed information[8].

1. Licensing Act 2003, s 4.
2. Crime and Disorder Act 1998, s 17(1).
3. See the Guidance issued under s 182 of the Licensing Act 2003 issued by the DCMS in July 2004.
4. Licensing Act 2003, s 6(1).
5. Licensing Act 2003, s 7.
6. Licensing Act 2003, s 9.
7. Licensing Act 2003, s 10.
8. Licensing Act 2003, s 8 and Sch 3.

Premises Licences

8–19829E A person listed in s 16 of the Act may apply to a licensing authority for a premises licence which authorises premises to be used for one or more licensable activities[1]. The application must be in the prescribed manner and must be properly advertised[2]. The application must be accompanied by an "operating schedule", which must be in the prescribed form and must summarise, amongst other things, the licensable activities (and the times during which they will take place); details about the "premises supervisor" (if one of the licensable activities is the supply of alcohol); and the steps that the applicant intends to take to promote the licensing objectives[3]. A licensing authority receiving a valid application must grant the licence (subject only to such conditions as are consistent with the operating schedule submitted and any mandatory conditions[4]) unless "relevant representations"[5] have been received. Relevant representations can only be made by an "interested party"[6] or a "responsible authority"[7]. If relevant representations are received, the authority must hold a hearing to consider them (unless all parties to the application agree that a hearing is unnecessary)[8] and, having regard to the representations, must take such of the prescribed steps[9] (if any) as it considers necessary for the promotion of the licensing objectives[10]. Once granted, a premises licence has effect until it is revoked, unless the licence has been granted for a limited period or it has been suspended[11]. Application can be made to vary a premises licence[12], and an interested party or responsible authority may make relevant representations about such an application. An application can also be made to transfer a premises licence into the name of any person who could, by virtue of s 16, apply for a licence in his own right. An applicant can apply for such an application to have interim effect[13], and only the chief officer of police can object to a transfer application[14].

1. Licensing Act 2003, s 11. Applications can also be made for provisional statements under s 29 in respect of premises that are being, or are about to be constructed, extended or otherwise altered. There are only limited powers to make relevant representations in respect of an application for a premises licence where the premises already enjoys the benefit of a provisional statement: Licensing Act 2003, s 32.
2. Licensing Act 2003, s 17(2) and the Licensing Act 2003 (Premises licences and club premises certificates) Regulations 2005, SI 2004/42.
3. Licensing Act 2003, s 17(4).
4. Licensing Act 2003, s 18(2). Mandatory conditions are those listed in LA 2003, ss 19–21.
5. Defined in s 18(6) as those which are about the likely effect of the grant of the premises licence on the promotion of the licensing objectives, and which are, in all other requirements, valid.
6. Defined in LA 2003, s 13(3).
7. Defined in LA 2003, s 13(4).
8. Licensing Act 2003, s 18(3)(*a*).
9. The prescribed steps are listed in LA 2003, s 18(4). The licensing authority has a wide discretion, including modifying or adding to proposed conditions, excluding certain licensable activities, refusing to specify a person as the premises supervisor, and rejecting the application outright.
10. Licensing Act 2003, s 18(3)(*b*).
11. Licensing Act 2003, s 26. A premises licence will also lapse in any of the circumstances listed in s 27, and it can be surrendered under s 28. If it has lapsed, s 47 provides for a person with a prescribed interest in the premises or a person connected to the premises licence holder to give an "interim authority notice" to the licensing authority. This has the effect of reinstating the premises licence in the name of the person giving the notice for a maximum period of 7 days, during which time an application for transfer must be made. The chief officer of police may object to an interim authority notice, in which case the licensing authority must hold a hearing to consider his representations: LA 2003, s 48. Even if no interim authority notice is given, any person who could apply for a licence by virtue of s 16 of the LA 2003 can apply within 7 days of the lapse or surrender of the licence for a transfer of the premises licence to him: LA 2003, s 50. Where such an application is made, the premises licence is reinstated from the date of receipt of the application by the licensing authority.
12. Licensing Act 2003, s 34. There is a separate provision in s 37 to apply to vary a premises licence so as to change the name of the premises supervisor. Such an application can have interim effect if requested: LA 2003, s 38. Only the Chief Officer of Police can object to such an application, and only if he is satisfied that the exceptional circumstances of the case are such that granting the application would undermine the crime prevention licensing objective: LA 2003, s 37(5).
13. Licensing Act 2003, s 43.
14. Licensing Act 2003, s 42(6).

8–19829F Reviews of premises licences. An interested party or responsible authority may apply to the licensing authority for a review of a premises licence at any time[1]. Unless the grounds for the application are irrelevant to the licensing objectives, frivolous, vexatious or repetitious, the licensing authority must hold a hearing to consider the application[2], and must, having regard to the application and the relevant representations, take such of a number of steps[3] (if any) as it considers necessary to promote the licensing objectives.

1. Licensing Act 2003, s 51(1). Repeated applications based on the same grounds are prohibited by s 51(4)(*b*)(ii).
2. Licensing Act 2003, s 52(2).
3. The steps are listed at LA 2003, s 52(4).

CLUB PREMISES CERTIFICATES

8–19829G A qualifying club[1] may apply to a licensing authority for a club premises certificate in respect of any premises which are occupied by, and habitually used for the purposes of, the club[2]. A club does not need to specify a premises supervisor, and it is not subject to the same powers of the police to close it[3], but in all other respects the regime for the licensing of clubs is very similar to that of other premises. An application for a club premises certificate must be in a prescribed form and must be advertised correctly[4]. The application must be accompanied by a "club operating schedule"[5] listing, amongst other things, the qualifying club activities (and the times during which they are proposed to take place), whether alcohol is to be supplied for consumption on or off the premises (if applicable), and the steps which the club proposes to take to promote the licensing objectives. A licensing authority receiving a valid application must grant the licence (subject only to such conditions as are consistent with the club operating schedule submitted and any mandatory conditions[6]) unless "relevant representations"[7] have been received. Relevant representations can only be made by an "interested party"[8] or a "responsible authority"[9]. If relevant representations are received, the authority must hold a hearing to consider them (unless all parties to the application agree that a hearing is unnecessary)[10] and, having regard to the representations, must take such of the prescribed steps[11] (if any) as it considers necessary for the promotion of the licensing objectives[12]. The licensing authority may not impose conditions restricting the right of a club to sell alcohol to an associate member[13] or their guest[14]; nor may it impose a condition restricting the nature of plays that may be performed at a club premises that is licensed for that form of regulated entertainment[15]. Once granted a club premises certificate has effect until such time as it is withdrawn (following a review or the club ceasing to be a qualifying club[16]) or it is surrendered[17]. Where a justice of the peace is satisfied, on information on oath, that there are reasonable grounds for believing that a club which holds a club premises certificate does not satisfy the conditions for being a qualifying club in relation to a qualifying club activity to which the certificate relates, and that evidence of that fact is to be obtained at the premises to which the certificate relates, he may issue a warrant authorising a constable to enter the premises, if necessary by force, at any time within one month from the time of issue of the warrant, and to seize and retain any documents relating to the business of the club[18]. Application can be made to vary a club premises certificate[19], and there is power for an interested party or responsible authority to make relevant representations about such an application. An interested party, a responsible authority or a member of the club can apply for a review of the certificate at any time[20]. Unless the grounds for the application are irrelevant to the licensing objectives, frivolous, vexatious or repetitious, the licensing authority must hold a hearing to consider the application[21], and must, having regard to the application and the relevant representations, take such of a number of steps[22] (if any) as it considers necessary to promote the licensing objectives.

---

1. Section 61 of the LA 2003 defines what is a qualifying club. General conditions (listed in LA 2003, s 62) must be satisfied as must additional conditions (listed in LA 2003, s 64) if the club wants to be licensed for the supply of alcohol.
2. Licensing Act 2003, s 71(1).
3. Licensing Act 2003, Part 8. Those powers only exist in relation to premises which have the benefit of a premises licence or a TEN.
4. Licensing Act, s 71.
5. Licensing Act, s 71(5).
6. Licensing Act 2003, s 72(2). Mandatory conditions are those listed in LA 2003, ss 73(2)–(5) and 74.
7. Defined in LA 2003, s 72(7) as those which are about the likely effect of the grant of the premises licence on the promotion of the licensing objectives, and which are, in all other requirements, valid.
8. Defined in LA 2003, s 69(3).
9. Defined in LA 2003, s 69(4).
10. Licensing Act 2003, s 72(3)(*a*).
11. The prescribed steps are listed in s 72(4). The licensing authority has a wide discretion, including modifying or adding to proposed conditions, excluding certain licensable activities, and rejecting the application outright.
12. Licensing Act 2003, s 72(3)(*b*).
13. "Associate member" is defined in LA 2003, s 67.
14. Licensing Act 2003, s 75.
15. Licensing Act 2003, s 76.
16. Licensing Act 2003, s 90. If the licensing authority is of the opinion that this is the case in relation to one or more of its qualifying club activities, it must give a notice to the club withdrawing the certificate so far as it relates to that activity or those activities.
17. Licensing Act 2003, s 80(1).
18. Licensing Act 2003, s 90(5) and (6).
19. Licensing Act 2003, s 84.
20. Licensing Act 2003, s 87(1).
21. Licensing Act 2003, s 88(2).
22. The steps are listed at LA 2003, s 88(4).

Permitted temporary activities

8–19829H Aside from applying for a premises licence, the only other way to receive permission to carry on a licensable activity is for a premises user to apply for a "Temporary Event Notice" ("TEN"). A licensable activity carried out in accordance with a permission given using the TENs procedure is a permitted temporary activity[1]. There are limitations on when the TENs procedure can be used. An activity cannot last more than 96 hours[2]. The maximum number of persons permitted at the event at any one time cannot exceed 499[3]. A TEN is void if the period specified in it starts or ends within 24 hours of another notice given in respect of the same premises by the premises user, or an associate or business colleague of that premises user[4]. A licensing authority must give a "counter notice" (effectively refusing the application for a TEN) if the premises user has already given 50 such notices in the last calendar year (if the premises user is a personal licence holder[5]); or 5 such notices (in the case of anybody else[6]); or if 12 such notices have been given in the last calendar year in respect of the same premises[7]; or if there have been 15 days worth of such events at the premises in the last calendar year[8]. To apply for a permitted temporary activity, the premises user gives a TEN to the licensing authority. The TEN must be in the prescribed form and must contain the prescribed information[9]. A copy of the notice must be served in duplicate on the licensing authority no later than 10 working days before the day on which the event period begins[10], and a copy must be served on the chief officer of police[11]. The chief officer of police must object within 48 hours if he is satisfied that the use of the premises in accordance with the notice would undermine the crime prevention objective[12]. If objection is made the licensing authority must hold a hearing to consider the objection notice[13] and, having regard to the objection notice, must give the premises user a counter notice if it considers it necessary for the promotion of the crime prevention licensing objective[14]. The decision to give or not to give a counter notice under this section can be appealed to the magistrates' court[15], but a decision to give a counter notice because a premises user has exceeded the permitted limits under the TENs procedure cannot.

---

1. Licensing Act 2003, s 98.
2. Licensing Act 2003, s 100(1).
3. Licensing Act 2003, s 100(5)(*d*).
4. Licensing Act 2003, s 101.
5. Licensing Act 2003, s 107(2).

6. Licensing Act 2003, s 107(3).
7. Licensing Act 2003, s 107(4).
8. Licensing Act 2003, s 107(5).
9. Licensing Act 2003, s 100(5).
10. Licensing Act 2003, s 100(7)(*a*).
11. Licensing Act 2003, s 104(1).
12. Licensing Act 2003, s 104(2) and (3). However, there is provision in s 106 for the premises user and the Police to negotiate away any objections by making modifications to the TEN. If this happens the objection notice is treated as withdrawn: LA 2003, s 106(3).
13. Licensing Act 2003, s 105(2)(*a*).
14. Licensing Act 2003, s 105(2)(*b*).
15. Licensing Act 2003, Sch 5, para 16.

PERSONAL LICENCES

8–19829I A personal licence is granted by a licensing authority[1] to an individual and authorises that person to supply (whether by retail or by or on behalf of a club to, or to the order of a member of the club) alcohol, or authorise the supply of alcohol, in accordance with a premises licence[2]. Once granted, it has effect for a period of ten years[3] unless it is surrendered[4], revoked, forfeited or suspended. It must be renewed every 10 years. An application must be made in the prescribed form and must be granted if it appears to the licensing authority that the four prescribed conditions are met[5]. If it appears to the licensing authority that any of the first three prescribed conditions are not met, it must reject the application[6]. If it appears to the authority that the fourth condition is not met (because the applicant has been convicted of a "relevant offence[7]" or "foreign offence[8]") it must give notice to that effect to the chief officer of police. If the chief officer of police is satisfied that, because of those convictions, the grant of a personal licence would undermine the crime prevention objective, he must give the licensing authority an objection notice[9], and the authority must hold a hearing to consider the notice[10]. It must refuse the application if it considers it necessary to promote the crime prevention licensing objective[11]. Similar provisions apply on an application for renewal if the applicant has been convicted of a relevant or foreign offence since the grant of the licence[12]. If the licensing authority becomes aware of a conviction of a personal licence holder for a relevant or foreign offence since that individual was granted a personal licence (whether on first application or renewal), it must give a notice to that effect to the chief officer of police. A process akin to that referred to above (on an application for a grant or renewal of a personal licence) then begins, and the licence must be revoked by a licensing authority after a hearing if it considers this necessary to promote the crime prevention licensing objective[13].

---

1. Application must be made to the licensing authority for the area in which the applicant is ordinarily resident.
2. Licensing Act 2003, s 111(1).
3. Licensing Act 2003, s 115(1).
4. Licensing Act 2003, s 116.
5. The prescribed conditions are listed in LA 2003, s 120(2).
6. Licensing Act 2003, s 120(3).
7. Relevant offences are listed in Sch 4 of the Act. Offences which are spent within the meaning of the Rehabilitation of Offenders Act 1974 must be disregarded: LA 2003, s 114.
8. Defined in LA 2003, s 113(3). Offences which are spent within the meaning of the Rehabilitation of Offenders Act 1974 must be disregarded: LA 2003, s 114.
9. Licensing Act 2003, s 120(5).
10. Licensing Act 2003, s 120(7(*a*).
11. Licensing Act 2003, s 120(7)(*b*)(i).
12. Licensing Act 2003, s 121.
13. Licensing Act 2003, s 124.

8–19829J Personal licence holders appearing before a magistrates' court. Where a personal licence holder is charged with a relevant offence he must, no later than the time he makes his first appearance in a magistrates' court in connection with that offence, produce his personal licence to the court or, if that is not practicable, notify the court of its existence[1]. A similar obligation is placed on a person who is granted a personal licence after a first court appearance but before the matter is dealt with[2]. A personal licence holder in such a situation must also keep the court notified of any changes in the status of his personal licence[3]. Where a personal licence holder is convicted of a relevant offence, the convicting court may order the forfeiture or suspension for up to 6 months of the personal licence[4]. The convicting court may suspend the operation of any such order pending an appeal[5], as may the court to which an appeal is made[6]. A convicting court must also notify the licensing authority that granted the personal licence of the outcome of the prosecution and the sentence imposed[7].

---

1. Licensing Act 2003, s 128(1).
2. Licensing Act 2003, s 128(2) and (3).
3. Licensing Act 2003, s 128(4) and (5).
4. Licensing Act 2003, s 129.
5. Licensing Act 2003, s 129(4).
6. Licensing Act 2003, s 130.
7. Licensing Act 2003, s 130(2).

APPEALS

8–19829K The powers of applicants, interested parties and responsible authorities to appeal against decisions of a licensing authority are wide and varied. Essentially, any party to an original decision of the licensing authority following a hearing may appeal against the decision to grant, vary, impose conditions or refuse an application[1]. Magistrates' courts will sit as a final court of appeal, from which appeals will only be permitted on a point of law[2]. Magistrates' courts hearing an appeal are empowered to dismiss the appeal, substitute the decision of the licensing authority with its own decision, or remit the case to the licensing authority to dispose of in accordance with its direction; and can make such order as to costs as it thinks fit[3]. Appeals must be made to the magistrates' court for the petty sessions area in which the premises concerned are situated[4] and must be commenced by notice of appeal given to the justices' chief executive within the period of 21 days beginning with the day on which the appellant was notified of the decision appealed against[5].

1. This right does not extend to certain decisions that can be made by a licensing authority without the need for a hearing. Such decisions would have to be challenged by way of an application for judicial review. Examples include a decision of the licensing authority that a representation is irrelevant, frivolous, vexatious or repetitious; and a decision of a licensing authority to serve a counter notice to a TEN where the permitted limits have been exceeded: LA 2003, s 107.
2. There is an exception to this rule in the case of closure orders: LA 2003, s 166.
3. Licensing Act 2003, s 181(2). For a more detailed commentary on the award of costs see para **8–19829R**.
4. Licensing Act 2003, para 9, 15, 16(4) and 18(7). In the case of an appeal against a decision in respect of a personal licence, the appeal must be made to the magistrates' court for the petty sessions area which covers the licensing authority that made the original decision.
5. Licensing Act 2003, Sch 5, para 9(2), 15(2), 16(5), 17(7) and 18(5). The Licensing Act (Hearings) Regulations 2005, SI 2005/44 require a notice of determination to be given in writing: reg 34.

8–19829L Appeals in respect of premises licences. Where a licensing authority rejects an application for a premises licence under s 18; rejects an application (in whole or part) to vary a premises licence under s 35; rejects an application under section 35 to vary a premises licence so as to specify a new premises supervisor; or rejects an application to transfer a premises licence under s 44, the applicant may appeal to the magistrates' court[1]. Where a licensing authority grant a premises licence, the applicant may appeal against any decision to impose conditions under s 18(2)(*a*) or (3)(*b*), or to exclude specific licensable activities (s 18(4)(*b*)), or to refuse to specify an individual as the premises supervisor (s 18(4)(*c*))[2]; whilst a person who made relevant representations may appeal on the grounds that the licence ought not to have been granted or that, on granting the licence, different or additional conditions should have been imposed or a decision should have been taken to exclude certain licensable activities or refuse to specify a person as the premises supervisor[3]. Similar rights of appeal exist in relation to the issuing of a provisional statement under s 31[4]; the grant (in whole or part) of an application to vary a premises licence[5]; and a decision on a review of the premises licence under s 52[6]. In addition a chief officer of police may appeal against a decision to vary a premises licence under s 39(2) so as to specify a new premises supervisor[7] or a decision to transfer a licence under s 44[8], so long as, in both cases, he gave a notice objecting to the application in the first place which was not withdrawn. Where an interim authority notice is given under s 47 and a chief officer of police gives a notice under s 48(2), the person given the notice can appeal against a decision to cancel the interim authority and the chief officer of police can appeal against a decision not to cancel it[9]. Where such an appeal is brought, the magistrates' court hearing the appeal may, on such terms as it thinks fit, order the reinstatement of the interim authority notice pending the disposal of the appeal or the expiry of the interim authority period (2 months after the notice was given[10]), whichever occurs first[11].

1. Licensing Act 2003, Sch 5, para 1.
2. Licensing Act 2003, Sch 5, para 2(2).
3. Licensing Act 2003, Sch 5, para 2(3).
4. Licensing Act 2003, Sch 5, para 3.
5. Licensing Act 2003, Sch 5, para 4.
6. Licensing Act 2003, Sch 5, para 8.
7. Licensing Act 2003, Sch 5, para 5(2).
8. Licensing Act 2003, Sch 5, para 6(2).
9. Licensing Act 2003, Sch 5, para 7.
10. Licensing Act 2003, s 47(10).
11. Licensing Act 2003, Sch 5, para 7(4).

8–19829M Appeals in respect of club premises certificates. Where a licensing authority rejects an application for a club premises certificate or rejects (in whole or part) an application to vary a club premises certificate, the club that made the application may appeal against the decision[1]. Where a licensing authority grants a club premises certificate, the club may appeal against any decision to impose conditions under s 72(2) or (3)(*b*), or to exclude specific qualifying club activities (s 72(4)(*b*)); whilst a person who made relevant representations may appeal on the grounds that the certificate ought not to have been granted or that, on granting the certificate, different or additional conditions should have been imposed or a decision should have been taken to exclude certain qualifying club activities[2]. Similar rights of appeal exist in relation to the grant (in whole or part) of an application to vary a certificate[3]; and a decision on a review of the certificate under s 88[4]. A club may also appeal against a decision of a licensing authority to give a notice under s 90 withdrawing the club premises certificate[5].

1. Licensing Act 2003, Sch 5, para 10.
2. Licensing Act 2003, Sch 5, para 11.
3. Licensing Act 2003, Sch 5, para 12.
4. Licensing Act 2003, Sch 5, para 13.
5. Licensing Act 2003, Sch 5, para 14.

8–19829N Appeals in respect of permitted temporary activities. A premises user may appeal against a decision of a licensing authority to give a counter notice[1], and a chief officer of police may appeal against a decision of a licensing authority not to give one[2]. No appeal in respect of a permitted temporary activity may be brought later than 5 working days before the day on which the event period specified in the TEN begins[3].

1. Licensing Act 2003, Sch 5, para 16(2).
2. Licensing Act 2003, Sch 5, para 16(3).
3. Licensing Act 2003, Sch 5, para 16(6).

8–19829O Appeals in respect of personal licences. An applicant may appeal against a decision to reject an application for a personal licence[1], or a decision to revoke a licence[2]. A chief officer of police may appeal against a decision to grant an application for a personal licence where he has served an objection notice to the application[3], and a decision not to revoke a personal licence[4].

1. Whether that decision was made on a first application or on an application for renewal: LA 2003, Sch 5, para 17(1).
2. Licensing Act 2003, Sch 5, para 17(4).
3. Whether that decision was made on a first application or on an application for renewal: LA 2003, Sch 5, para 17(2) and (3).
4. LA 2003, Sch 5, para 17(5).

8–19829P Appeals in respect of closure orders. The licence holder or any person who made representations in respect of a review of a premises licence under s 167 may appeal against the licensing authority's decision[1].

1. Licensing Act 2003, Sch 5, para 18.

8–19829Q Procedure on appeals. Appeals to the magistrates' court are to be by way of a rehearing[1] on both the merits and the law. Although it is a rehearing, justices must pay proper regard to the decision of the local authority and should not exercise their discretion uninfluenced by the local authorities' opinion[2]. Justices will need to be familiar with the scheme of the 2003 Act, the licensing objectives, the DCMS Guidance and the statement of policy of the licensing authority whose decision is being appealed. The court must carry out its appellate function with a view to promoting the licensing objectives[3]. The licensing authority will be a respondent to every appeal, with additional named respondents being specified depending on the decision being appealed against[4]. No guidance has yet been given to magistrates' courts about the giving of directions, but it would seem to be good practice to issue standardised directions covering disclosure, exchange of evidence (lay and expert) and lodging of appeal bundles. If not resolved between the parties, these should be discussed at a pre-trial review. In considering the appeal, the court will be exercising an administrative function. Accordingly, strict rules of evidence do not apply, hearsay evidence is admissible[5] and there is no burden of proof. Although the Licensing Act 2003 does not specify the procedure by which an appeal is brought (referring throughout Sch 5 to "notices of appeal"), r 14 of the Magistrates' Court Rules 1981[6] states that the complainant should present his case first. This may not always be the most appropriate order, since in complex cases it will mean the justices will hear why the decision was allegedly wrong before it hears what the decision was and why it was reached. It is open to a court to vary the order (with the consent of all parties) so that the licensing authority presents its case first. If there is a second respondent then it would be sensible for their case to follow the licensing authority, so that the appellant goes last. Justices are advised to give comprehensive reasons for the decision that they reach.

1. Because of this, fresh evidence may be adduced that was not available at the original hearing (*Rushmoor Borough Council v Richards* (1996) 160 LG Rev 460).
2. *Sagnata Investments v Norwich Corpn* [1971] 2 All ER 1441. The Court of Appeal expressly approved the approach outlined in *Stepney Borough Council v Joffe* [1949] 1 All ER 256, that the appellate court ought "to pay great attention to the fact that the duly constituted and elected local authority have come to an opinion on the matter and ought not lightly to reverse their opinion . . . the function of a court of appeal is to exercise its powers when it is satisfied that the judgment below is wrong, not merely because it is not satisfied that the judgment was right".
3. And, it is submitted, must also have regard to the duty imposed on a licensing authority under s 17 of the Crime and Disorder Act 1998: see para **8–19829C**.
4. Licensing Act 2003, Sch 5, paras 9(4), 15(3), 16(7), 17(8) and 18(6).

5. *Kavanagh v Chief Constable of Devon & Cornwall* [1974] 1QB 624; *Westminster City Council v Zestfair Ltd* (1989) 88 LGR 288.
6. SI 1981/552 as amended: see para **1–5930**.

8–19829R *The role of the DCMS Guidance and the licensing authority's statement of policy in appeal hearings.* Chapter 10 of the DCMS Guidance advises that magistrates' courts must have regard to the Guidance and the licensing authority's statement of licensing policy when hearing an appeal[1]. The Guidance says that the court may depart from either document if it considers that it is justified in doing so because of the individual circumstances of the case; or because it finds any part of either document to be ultra vires[2]. It is submitted that, in this last respect, the Guidance is wrong in law and that a proper method of challenging the validity of a statement of licensing policy is by way of an application for judicial review[3].

1. Guidance issued under s 182 of the Licensing Act 2003, July 2004, para 10.8.
2. Guidance issued under s 182 of the Licensing Act 2003, July 2004, para 10.8. This would appear to run contrary to the decision of the High Court in *R (Westminster City Council) v Middlesex Crown Court & Chorion plc* [2002] LLR 538.
3. For an example of a challenge by way of judicial review to a licensing authority's statement of licensing policy, see *British Beer & Pub Association v Canterbury City Council* [2005] EWHC 1318.

8–19829S Costs on appeal. A magistrates' court hearing an appeal may make such order as to costs as it thinks fit[1]. However, in the absence of any guidance or case law on the subject, it is submitted that existing principles in other areas of administrative law dealt with by magistrates' courts as an appellate body will continue to apply. In the case of *Bradford Metropolitan District Council v Booth*[2] (a case concerning the licensing of a private hire operator) it was held that costs should not be routinely awarded against an authority that acted honestly, reasonably and properly on sound grounds.

1. Licensing Act 2003, s 181(2).
2. TLR, 31/5/2000.

CLOSURE OF PREMISES

8–19829T A police officer of the rank of Superintendent or above may apply to a magistrates' court for an order to close premises licensed under a premises licence or TEN[1] for up to 24 hours if there is or is expected to be disorder in the area and the premises concerned are situated at or near the place of disorder or expected disorder[2]. A magistrates' court may make such an order only if it satisfied that it is necessary to prevent disorder[3]. Once an order has been made a constable may use such force as may be necessary to close premises which have been ordered to close[4]. Additionally, a police officer of the rank of Inspector or above may make a "closure order" in relation to premises licensed under a premises licence or TEN if he reasonably believes that there is, or is likely imminently to be, disorder on, or in the vicinity of and related to, the premises and their closure is necessary in the interests of public safety; or that a public nuisance is being caused by noise coming from the premises and the closure of the premises is necessary to prevent that nuisance[5]. The effect of the closure order is to require the premises to be closed for a period not exceeding 24 hours from the moment that notice of the order is given to an appropriate person[6] who is connected with any of the activities to which the disorder or nuisance relates[7]. It is an offence to permit premises to be open in contravention of an order[8]. As soon as reasonably practicable after a closure order has come into force, the police officer that decided to make the order must apply to a magistrates' court for it to consider the order and any extension of it[9]. If the police officer reasonably believes that a magistrates' court will not have determined whether to exercise its powers under s 165(2) by the end of the initial 24 hour closure period he may, before that initial period expires, extend it by a further period of up to 24 hours if certain conditions are satisfied[10]. Equally, the police officer must cancel the order if he does not reasonably believe that the conditions for it remain.

1. But not a premises that has the benefit of a club premises certificate.
2. Licensing Act 2003, s 160(1).
3. Licensing Act 2003, s 160(3).
4. Licensing Act 2003, s 160(7).
5. Licensing Act 2003, s 161(1).
6. Defined in LA 2003, s 171(5).
7. Licensing Act 2003, s 161(2) and (5).
8. Licensing Act 2003, s 161(6).
9. Licensing Act 2003, s 164(1).
10. Licensing Act 2003, s 162.

8–19829U Consideration of closure order by magistrates' court. As soon as reasonably practicable after receipt of an application under s 164(1) a magistrates' court must hold a hearing to consider whether it is appropriate to exercise any of its powers in relation to the order[1]. The powers are listed in s 164(2) and are wide ranging. In coming to a determination the court must consider, in particular, whether continued closure is necessary for the same reasons as the order was made in the first place[2]. Offences are committed if, without reasonable excuse, a person permits premises to be open in contravention of the magistrates' order. There is a right of appeal to the Crown Court against the decision of a magistrates' court[3]. Once a decision has been made by a magistrates' court in relation to a premises with the benefit of a premises licence, it must notify the licensing authority of that decision[4]. The licensing authority must then review the premises licence[5].

1. Licensing Act 2003, s 165(1). The court does not need to exercise its powers if the premises have ceased to be licensed (for example, because the premises had the benefit of a TEN that has subsequently expired). The hearing is to be by way of a complaint for an order: Licensing Act 2003, s 165(9).
2. Licensing Act 2003, s 165(3).
3. Licensing Act 2003, s 166(1).
4. Licensing Act 2003, s 165(4).
5. Licensing Act 2003, s 167(2).

OFFENCES – INTRODUCTION

8–19829V All offences in the LA 2003 are summary only, but the time limit for instituting proceedings is raised to 12 months[1]. Proceedings for offences may be instituted by a licensing authority, the DPP, or (in the case of offences under ss 146 and 147 by a local weights and measures authority[2]). Offences may be committed by bodies corporate, partnerships and unincorporated associations and by individuals in those organisations if the requirements of s 187 are satisfied.

1. Licensing Act 2003, s 186(3).
2. Licensing Act 2003, s 186(2).

8–19829W "Documentary" offences. Part 7 outlines the substantive offences contained in the Act. However, there are a raft of documentary offences throughout the Act, dealing with such matters as failing to notify a licensing authority of a change in the name or address of a premises licence holder or premises supervisor[1]; a change in the name, rules[2] or address[3] of a club; a conviction of a personal licence holder for a relevant or foreign offence[4]; and the name or address of a personal licence holder[5]. Offences are also committed if a summary of a premises licence or club premises certificate, or a copy of a temporary event notice is not displayed at the premises to which they relate[6]. Furthermore, offences are committed if a premises licence, club premises certificate or personal licence is not provided to the licensing authority to be updated when requested[7]. There are also offences relating to the obstruction of an authorised person who is carrying out his duties in relation to personal licences, club premises certificates or permitted temporary activities[8]; and offences of failing to produce a premises licence, club premises certificate, temporary event notice or personal licence to an authorised officer or police constable[9].

1. Licensing Act 2003, s 33(6).
2. Licensing Act 2003, s 82(6).
3. Licensing Act 2003, s 83(6).
4. Either during the application period for a licence: LA 2003, s 123(2); or after a licence has been granted: LA 2003, s 132(4).
5. Licensing Act 2003, s 127(1).
6. See, for example, Licensing Act 2003, ss 57(4), 94(5), 94(6) and 109(4).
7. See, for example, Licensing Act 2003, s s 41(5), 56(3), 93(3) and 134(5).
8. See, for example, Licensing Act 2003, ss 59(5), 96(5) and 108(3). The offence does not apply to obstruction of a police officer because that is already an offence: Police Act 1996, s 89(2).
9. See, for example, Licensing Act 2003, ss 57(7), 94(9), 109(8) and 135(4).

8–19829X Offences – unauthorised licensable activities. A person commits an offence if he carries on, attempts to carry on or knowingly allows to be carried on a licensable activity on or from any premises otherwise than under and in accordance with a premises licence, club premises certificate or valid temporary event notice[1]. It is also an offence to expose alcohol for sale by retail[2] in circumstances where the sale would be an unauthorised licensable activity[3]; and to keep alcohol in one's possession or under one's control with the intention of selling it by retail or supplying it in circumstances where the sale or supply would be an unauthorised licensable activity[4]. A due diligence defence[5] is available for all of these offences except for one committed under s 136(1)(*b*).

1. Licensing Act 2003, s 136(1). No offence is committed solely by reason of the person being a performer in an unlicensed performance of regulated entertainment: LA 2003, 136(2). Conviction carries a maximum penalty of 6 months' imprisonment and/or a £20,000 fine.
2. "Sale by retail" is defined in Licensing Act 2003, s 192.
3. Licensing Act 2003, s 137(1). Conviction carries a maximum penalty of 6 months imprisonment and/or a £20,000 fine. A convicting court may order forfeiture of the alcohol in question: Licensing Act 2003, s 137(4).
4. Licensing Act 2003, s 138(1). Conviction carries a maximum of a level 2 fine on the standard scale. A convicting court may order forfeiture of the alcohol in question: LA 2003, s 138(5).
5. Licensing Act 2003, s 139.

8–19829Y Offences – drunkenness and disorderly conduct. A large number of people can commit an offence of knowingly[1] allowing disorderly conduct[2] on relevant premises[3]. Those people include any person who works at the premises in a capacity, paid or unpaid, which authorises him to prevent the conduct; the holder of a premises licence; a premises supervisor; any member or officer of a club who is present at the club when the disorder takes place in a capacity which enables him to prevent it; and the premises user in relation to a permitted temporary activity[4]. The same group of people may commit an offence of knowingly[5] selling, attempting to sell or allowing to be sold alcohol to a person who is drunk[6]. It is an offence for a person, on relevant premises[7], to knowingly obtain or attempt to obtain alcohol for consumption on those premises by a person who is drunk[8]; and it is an offence for a drunk or disorderly person, without reasonable excuse, to fail to leave relevant premises[9] when requested to do so by a constable or a person to whom s 143(2) applies[10], or to enter or attempt to enter such premises after that person has requested him not to do so[11].

1. See the case of *R v Winson* [1968] 1 All ER 197. The doctrine of delegation applies to the concept of "knowingly", so that a defendant can be guilty of an offence committed by another if he has delegated responsibility for compliance with the law to that other person who did knowingly allow the offence to occur. See also *Howker v Robinson* [1972] 2 All ER 786.
2. "Disorderly conduct" is not defined.
3. Licensing Act 2003, s 140(1). The offence carries a maximum of a level 3 fine on the standard scale. "Relevant premises" are defined in s 159 and include premises covered by a premises licence, club premises certificate or temporary event notice.
4. Licensing Act 2003, s 140(2).
5. See note 1, above.
6. Licensing Act 2003, 141(1). The offence carries a maximum of a level 3 fine on the standard scale. "Drunk" is not defined, but in the case of *Neale v E (a minor)* (1983) 80 Cr App Rep 20, (a case on the meaning of "drunk" under the offence of drunkenness in a public place, contrary to s 91 of the Criminal Justice Act 1967), it was held that it referred to a person who has taken intoxicating liquor to excess so that he has lost the power of self-control.
7. See note 3, above, for definition of "relevant premises".
8. Licensing Act 2003, s 142(1). The offence carries a maximum of a level 3 fine on the standard scale. See note 6, above, for guidance on the meaning of "drunk".
9. See note 3, above, for definition of "relevant premises".
10. Licensing Act 2003, s 143(1)(*a*). The offence carries a maximum of a level 1 fine on the standard scale.
11. Licensing Act 2003, s 143(1)(*b*). The offence carries a maximum of a level 1 fine on the standard scale.

8–19829Z Offences – smuggled goods. The same group of people who can commit an offence under s 140(1)[1], can also commit an offence of knowingly[2] keeping or allowing to be kept, on any relevant premises[3], any goods which have been imported without payment of duty or which have otherwise been unlawfully imported[4].

1. See para **8–19829Y**, ante.
2. See note 1 to para **8–19829Y**, ante, for discussion of "knowingly". The defendant need only know that the goods are on the premises, not that they are smuggled.
3. See note 3, to para **8–19829Y**, ante, for meaning of "relevant premises".
4. Licensing Act 2003, s 144(1). The offence carries a maximum of a level 3 fine on the standard scale. A convicting court may order forfeiture of the goods in question: LA 2003, s 144(4).

8–19829ZA Offences – children and alcohol – unaccompanied children on certain premises. It is an offence[1] for a person listed in s 145(3) to allow an unaccompanied child under 16 to be on premises that he knows are exclusively or primarily used for the supply of alcohol for consumption there[2] at a time when they are open for that purpose[3]; or to allow an unaccompanied[4] child under 16 to be on those premises between midnight and 5am when the premises[5] are open for the purposes of being used for the supply of alcohol for consumption there[6]. No offence is committed if the child is on the premises solely for the purpose of passing to or from some other place and there is no other convenient means of getting to or from that place[7]. If a person is charged with the offence by reason of his own conduct, it is a defence[8] that the person believed the child to be 16 or over or the accompanying person (if there was one) to be 18 or over, and he had either taken all reasonable steps[9] to establish the individual's age, or nobody could reasonably have suspected from the individual's appearance that he was aged under 16 or under 18, as the case may be. A person charged because of the act or default of another has a defence if he exercised all due diligence to avoid committing it[10].

1. The offences carry a maximum of a level 3 fine on the standard scale: LA 2003, s 145(9).
2. The premises can be licensed by virtue of a premises licence, club premises certificate or temporary event notice: LA 2003, s 145(4) and (10).
3. Licensing Act 2003, s 145(1)(*a*).
4. "Unaccompanied" means not accompanied by an individual aged 18 or over: Licensing Act 2003, s 145(2)(*b*).
5. See note 1 above for definition of premises.
6. Licensing Act 2003, s 145(1)(*b*).
7. Licensing Act 2003, s 145(5).
8. Licensing Act 2003, s 145(6).
9. A person is deemed to have taken all reasonable steps if he asked the individual for evidence of age and the evidence would have convinced a reasonable person: LA 2003, s 145(7).
10. Licensing Act 2003, s 145(8).

8–19829ZB Offences – children and alcohol – sale or supply of alcohol to children. There are numerous offences involving the sale of alcohol to children. A person commits an offence if he sells alcohol to a child under 18[1]. A club commits an offence[2] if alcohol is supplied by it or on its behalf to, or to the order of, a member of the club who is under 18[3]. A person charged with an offence by reason of his own conduct has the same defence as is available in respect of a s 145 charge[4]; and a person charged because of the act or default of another has a due diligence defence available[5]. It is also an offence to knowingly[6] allow the sale of alcohol, on relevant premises[7], to a child under 18[8]. Further, there are offences in relation to the sale or supply liqueur confectionery[9] to children under 16[10].

1. Licensing Act 2003, s 149(1)(*a*). The offence can be committed anywhere, even on unlicensed premises. A similar offence is created if an under 18 member of a club is supplied with, or attempts to be supplied with, alcohol: LA 2003, s 149(1)(*b*).
2. Licensing Act 2003, s 149(2).
3. Licensing Act 2003, s 149(3)(*a*). A similar offence is committed if the person is a member of a club: Licensing Act 2003, s 149(3)(*b*). Both offences carry a defence that the person charged had no reason to suspect that the individual was under 18: LA 2003, s 149(6).
4. Licensing Act 2003, s 149(4)(*a*). A similar offence is committed if the person is a member of a club: LA 2003, s 149(4)(*b*). "Relevant premises" are defined in s 159. Both offences carry a defence that the person charged had no reason to suspect that the individual was under 18: LA 2003, s 149(6).
5. "The table meal exemption": Licensing Act 2003, s 149(5).
6. So the offence would not be committed if the child unwittingly consumed a spiked drink.
7. Licensing Act 2003, s 150(1). No offence is committed if the "table meal exemption" applies: LA 2003, s 150(4). "Relevant premises" are defined in LA 2003, s 159.
8. Licensing Act 2003, s 150(2). No offence is committed if the "table meal exemption" applies: LA 2003, s 150(4). "Relevant premises" are defined in s 159.
9. "Relevant premises" are defined in s 159.
10. Licensing Act 2003, s 151(1).

8–19829ZC Offences – children and alcohol – purchase and consumption of alcohol by children. A child under 18 commits an offence if he buys or attempts to buy alcohol[1], unless that act is committed in the course of him being used for a test purchase operation[2]. A person who acts as an agent for a child under 18 by buying or attempting to buy alcohol on behalf of the child also commits an offence[3], as does a person who acts as agent for a child under 18 and buys or attempts to buy alcohol for him for consumption on relevant premises[4]. However, this last offence does not apply if the person purchasing or attempting to purchase the alcohol is over 18; the child is 16 or 17; the alcohol is beer, wine or cider; the purchase is for consumption at a table meal; and the child is accompanied by an adult[5]. A child also commits an offence if he knowingly[6] consumes alcohol on relevant premises[7], and a person to whom s 150(3) applies commits an offence if he knowingly allows the consumption of alcohol by a child under 18 on relevant premises[8].

1. Licensing Act 2003, s 149(1)(*a*). The offence can be committed anywhere, even on unlicensed premises. A similar offence is created if an under 18 member of a club is supplied with, or attempts to be supplied with, alcohol: Licensing Act 2003, s 149(1)(*b*).
2. Licensing Act 2003, s 149(2).
3. Licensing Act 2003, s 149(3)(*a*). A similar offence is committed if the person is a member of a club: LA 2003, s 149(3)(*b*). Both offences carry a defence that the person charged had no reason to suspect that the individual was under 18: LA 2003, 149(6).
4. Licensing Act 2003, s 149(4)(*a*). A similar offence is committed if the person is a member of a club: Licensing Act 2003, s 149(4)(*b*). "Relevant premises" are defined in s 159. Both offences carry a defence that the person charged had no reason to suspect that the individual was under 18: LA 2003, 149(6).
5. "The table meal exemption": Licensing Act 2003, s 149(5).
6. So the offence would not be committed if the child unwittingly consumed a spiked drink.
7. Licensing Act 2003, s 150(1). No offence is committed if the "table meal exemption" applies: LA 2003, s 150(4). "Relevant premises" are defined in LA 2003, s 159.
8. Licensing Act 2003, s 150(2). No offence is committed if the "table meal exemption" applies: LA 2003, s 150(4)."Relevant premises" are defined in s 159.

8–19829ZD Offences – children and alcohol – delivering alcohol to children and sending children to obtain alcohol. A person who works on relevant premises[1] in any capacity commits an offence if he knowingly delivers to a child under 18 alcohol sold on the premises, or supplied on the premises (in the case of a club)[2]. Similar offences are committed by a person who knowingly allows anybody else to deliver the alcohol[3]. The offences are not committed if the alcohol is delivered to a place where the buyer or person supplied lives or works[4]; if the child under 18 is himself working on relevant premises in a capacity that involves the delivery of alcohol; or if the alcohol is sold or supplied for consumption on relevant premises[5]. It is also an offence to knowingly send a child under 18 to obtain alcohol sold or supplied on relevant premises for consumption off those premises[6].

1. "Relevant premises" are defined in LA 2003, s 159.
2. Licensing Act 2003, s 151(1).
3. Licensing Act 2003, s 151(2) and (4). The person must work in a capacity which authorises him to prevent the delivery: LA 2003, s 151(3) and (5).

4. This would seem to mean that a child can take delivery of the alcohol on behalf of a parent or employer and no offence is committed.
5. Licensing Act 2003, s 151(6).
6. Licensing Act 2003, s 152(1). An example would be a parent sending a child to collect alcohol which had already been paid for from an off licence, although it is immaterial where the alcohol is actually collected from: LA 2003, s 152(2). Exceptions are provided in the case of test purchase operations (LA 2003, s 152(4)) and where the child works on the relevant premises in a capacity that involves the delivery of alcohol (LA 2003, s 152(3)).

8–19829ZE Offences – children and alcohol – unsupervised sales by children. It is an offence for a responsible person[1] on relevant premises[2] to knowingly allow a child under 18 to make a sale or supply of alcohol on the premises unless the sale or supply has been specifically approved by that or another responsible person[3]. However, no offence is committed if the child serves or supplies alcohol to a person for consumption with a table meal in an area set aside for that purpose[4].

1. "Responsible person" is defined in LA 2003, s 153(4).
2. "Relevant premises" are defined in LA 2003, s 159.
3. Licensing Act 2003, s 153(1).
4. Licensing Act 2003, s 153(2).

8–19829ZF Offences – vehicles and trains. A person commits an offence if he sells by retail[1] alcohol on or from a vehicle[2] at a time when the vehicle is not permanently or temporarily parked[3]. A magistrates' court, if it is satisfied that it is necessary to prevent disorder, may, on the application of a police officer of the rank of Inspector or above, make an order prohibiting the sale of alcohol during a specified period on any railway vehicle that is at a station or stations in the petty sessional area of the court, or on any railway vehicle that is travelling between such stations, one of which must be in that petty sessional area[4]. It is an offence to knowingly sell, attempt to sell or allow the sale of alcohol in contravention of such an order[5].

1. "Sale by retail" is defined in LA 2003, s 192.
2. "Vehicle" is defined in LA 2003, s 193 as "a vehicle intended or adapted for use on roads".
3. Licensing Act 2003, s 156(1). The offence carries a maximum penalty of 3 months imprisonment and/or a £20,000 fine. A due diligence defence is available: LA 2003, s 156(3).
4. Licensing Act 2003, s 157(1)–(3). The order must be served by the police officer on the train operator(s) affected by the order. It would seem that this power is designed to compliment the power in LA 2003, s 160 for magistrates to order the closure of premises in an area of ongoing or expected disorder: see para **8–19829T**, ante.
5. Licensing Act 2003, s 157(5). The offence carries a maximum penalty of 3 months' imprisonment and/or a £20,000 fine: LA 2003, s 157(6).

8–19829ZG Offences – false statements. It is an offence for a person to knowingly or recklessly make a false statement[1] in or in connection with any of numerous applications under the Act[2].

1. A person is treated as making a false statement if he produces, furnishes, signs or otherwise makes use of a document that contains a false statement: LA 2003, s 158(2).
2. Licensing Act 2003, s 158(1). The offence carries a maximum of a level 5 fine on the standard scale.

Licensing Act 2003[1]

(2003 c 17)

PART 1[2]

Licensable Activities

8–19830 1. Licensable activities and qualifying club activities. (1) For the purposes of this Act the following are licensable activities[3]—

(*a*) the sale by retail[4] of alcohol[5],
(*b*) the supply of alcohol by or on behalf of a club to, or to the order of, a member of the club,
(*c*) the provision of regulated entertainment, and
(*d*) the provision of late night refreshment.

(2) For those purposes the following licensable activities are also qualifying club activities—

(*a*) the supply of alcohol by or on behalf of a club to, or to the order of, a member of the club,
(*b*) the sale by retail of alcohol by or on behalf of a club to a guest of a member of the club for consumption on the premises where the sale takes place, and
(*c*) the provision of regulated entertainment where that provision is by or on behalf of a club for members of the club or members of the club and their guests.

(3) In this Act references to the supply of alcohol by or on behalf of a club to, or to the order of, a member of the club do not include a reference to any supply which is a sale by retail of alcohol.

(4) Schedule 1 makes provision about what constitutes the provision of regulated entertainment for the purposes of this Act.

(5) Schedule 2 makes provision about what constitutes the provision of late night refreshment for

those purposes (including provision that certain activities carried on in relation to certain clubs or hotels etc, or certain employees, do not constitute provision of late night refreshment and are, accordingly, not licensable activities).

(6) For the purposes of this Act premises are "used" for a licensable activity if that activity is carried on or from the premises.

(7) This section is subject to sections 173 to 175 (which exclude activities from the definition of licensable activity in certain circumstances).

[Licensing Act 2003, s 1.]

---

1. This Act is to be brought into force in accordance with orders made under s 201. At the date of going to press the following commencement orders have been made: SI 2003/1911 (s 199 of and Sch 7 relating to s 66 (Sunday closing in Wales and Monmouthshire) and s 67 (supplementary provisions for Welsh Sunday polls) of and Schedule 8 (polls in Wales and Monmouthshire); (No 2) SI 2003/2100 (s 155 and s 199 relating to the entries in Schedule 7 relating to the Confiscation of Alcohol (Young Persons) Act 1997 and section 12 of the Criminal Justice and Police Act 2001); (No 3) SI 2003/3222 in this PART, post; (No 4) SI 2004/1738 (s 200 and Sch 8 para 34 on 7 July 2004 at 12.25 pm); (No 5) SI 2004/2360 (ss 6, 9(1), (3) on 10 September 2004), (ss 7, 10–23, 25, 29, 31-37, 39, 59 (part), 60–66, 68–77, 79, 82-86, 90, 96, 111–118, 120, 122–132, 134–135, 158, 178, 181(part), 183(2), 184-190, 195, 200 (part), Sch 4, Sch 5 (part), Sch 8 on 7 February 2005); (No 6) 2005/2090 (ss 34-40, 42-46, 84-86, 181 and Sch 5 all so far as not then in force on 7 August 2005); (No 7 and Transitional Provisions) 2005/3056 (Part 5 so far as it is not already in force, on 10th November 2005; except paras 98 and 99(c) of Schedule 6 to the Act and the repeal of s 2(1A) and s 5A of the 1985 Act, the remaining provisions of the Act, so far as they are not already in force, on the second appointed day).

The Licensing Act 2003 (First appointed day and personal licences transitional period) Order 2004, SI 2004/1739 has appointed 7th February 2005 as the "first appointed day". The "second appointed day" was specified as 24th November 2005 by the Licensing Act 2003 (Second appointed day) Order 2005, SI 2005/2091.

Section 200 of the Act in so far as it relates to Sch 8, para 34 and that paragraph of that Schedule came into force on 7 July 2004: Licensing Act 2003 (Commencement No 4) Order 2004, SI 2004/1738.

2. Part 1 comprises ss 1–2 and Schs 1 and 2.

3. For activities in certain locations which are not licensable, see s 173, post and for exemptions for raffles and tombola, etc., see s 175, post..

4. For meaning of "sale by retail", see s 192, post.

5. For meaning of "alcohol", see s 191, post.

8–19831 **2. Authorisation for licensable activities and qualifying club activities.** (1) A licensable activity may be carried on—

(*a*) under and in accordance with a premises licence (see Part 3), or

(*b*) in circumstances where the activity is a permitted temporary activity by virtue of Part 5.

(2) A qualifying club activity may be carried on under and in accordance with a club premises certificate (see Part 4).

(3) Nothing in this Act prevents two or more authorisations having effect concurrently in respect of the whole or a part of the same premises or in respect of the same person.

(4) For the purposes of subsection (3) "authorisation" means—

(*a*) a premises licence;

(*b*) a club premises certificate;

(*c*) a temporary event notice.

[Licensing Act 2003, s 2.]

PART 2[1]
LICENSING AUTHORITIES

The authorities

8–19832 **3. Licensing authorities.** (1) In this Act "licensing authority" means—

(*a*) the council of a district in England,

(*b*) the council of a county in England in which there are no district councils,

(*c*) the council of a county or county borough in Wales,

(*d*) the council of a London borough,

(*e*) the Common Council of the City of London,

(*f*) the Sub-Treasurer of the Inner Temple,

(*g*) the Under-Treasurer of the Middle Temple, or

(*h*) the Council of the Isles of Scilly.

(2) For the purposes of this Act, a licensing authority's area is the area for which the authority acts.

[Licensing Act 2003, s 3.]

---

1. Part 2 comprises ss 3–10 and Sch 3.

Functions of licensing authorities etc

8–19833 **4. General duties of licensing authorities.** (1) A licensing authority must carry out its functions under this Act ("licensing functions") with a view to promoting the licensing objectives.

(2) The licensing objectives are—

(*a*) the prevention of crime and disorder;
(*b*) public safety;
(*c*) the prevention of public nuisance; and
(*d*) the protection of children from harm.

(3) In carrying out its licensing functions, a licensing authority must also have regard to—

(*a*) its licensing statement published under section 5, and
(*b*) any guidance issued by the Secretary of State under section 182.

[Licensing Act 2003, s 4.]

8–19834 5. Statement of licensing policy. *Every licensing authority, in accordance with any regulations published, is required to make in consultation with interested parties, publish and keep under review a Statement of licensing policy in respect of each 3 year period*[1].

1. The Licensing Act 2003 (Licensing statement period) Order 2004, SI 2004/2362 made under s 5(2) appoints 7 January 2005 as the day the first period of three years begins.Part 2 comprises ss 3–10 and Sch 3.

8–19835 6, 7. *Licensing authority must establish a licensing committee; certain functions may be delegated and exercised at various levels of the authority.*

8–19836 8. Requirement to keep a register. *Licensing authority must keep a register containing specified information and such other information as may be prescribed by the Secretary of State*[1].

1. The Licensing Act 2003 (Licensing Authority's Register) (Other Information) Regulations 2005, SI 2005/43 have been made.

Licensing committees

8–19837 9. *Power of licensing committee to establish sub-committees and to regulate its own procedure. Power of Secretary of State to make Regulations regarding the proceedings of licensing committees and sub-committees. The Licensing Act 2003 (Hearings) Regulations 2005, SI 2005/44 have been made.*

PART 3[1]
PREMISES LICENCES

Introductory

8–19838 11. Premises licence. In this Act "premises licence" means a licence granted under this Part, in respect of any premises, which authorises the premises[2] to be used for one or more licensable activities.

[Licensing Act 2003, s 11.]

1. Part 3 comprises ss 11–59.
2. For meaning of "premises", see s 193, post.

8–19839 12. The relevant licensing authority. *Determination of relevant licensing authority for a premises is dependent upon the location of the whole, or greater part of the premises.*

8–19840 13. Authorised persons, interested parties and responsible authorities. (1) In this Part in relation to any premises each of the following expressions has the meaning given to it by this section—

"authorised person",
"interested party",
"responsible authority".

(2) "Authorised person" means any of the following—

(*a*) an officer of a licensing authority in whose area the premises are situated who is authorised by that authority for the purposes of this Act,
(*b*) an inspector appointed by the fire and rescue authority for the area in which the premises are situtated,
(*c*) an inspector appointed under section 19 of the Health and Safety at Work etc Act 1974 (c 37),
(*d*) an officer of a local authority, in whose area the premises are situated, who is authorised by that authority for the purposes of exercising one or more of its statutory functions in relation to minimising or preventing the risk of pollution of the environment or of harm to human health,
(*e*) in relation to a vessel, an inspector, or a surveyor of ships, appointed under section 256 of the Merchant Shipping Act 1995 (c 21),
(*f*) a person prescribed for the purposes of this subsection.

(3) "Interested party" means any of the following—

(*a*) a person living in the vicinity of the premises,
(*b*) a body representing persons who live in that vicinity,
(*c*) a person involved in a business in that vicinity,
(*d*) a body representing persons involved in such businesses.

(4) "Responsible authority" means any of the following—

(*a*) the chief officer of police for any police area in which the premises are situated,
(*b*) the fire and rescue authority for any area in which the premises are situated,
(*c*) the enforcing authority within the meaning given by section 18 of the Health and Safety at Work etc Act 1974 for any area in which the premises are situated,
(*d*) the local planning authority within the meaning given by the Town and Country Planning Act 1990 (c 8) for any area in which the premises are situated,
(*e*) the local authority by which statutory functions are exercisable in any area in which the premises are situated in relation to minimising or preventing the risk of pollution of the environment or of harm to human health,
(*f*) a body which—
  (i) represents those who, in relation to any such area, are responsible for, or interested in, matters relating to the protection of children from harm, and
  (ii) is recognised by the licensing authority for that area for the purposes of this section as being competent to advise it on such matters,
(*g*) any licensing authority (other than the relevant licensing authority) in whose area part of the premises is situated,
(*h*) in relation to a vessel—
  (i) a navigation authority (within the meaning of section 221(1) of the Water Resources Act 1991 (c 57) having functions in relation to the waters where the vessel is usually moored or berthed or any waters where it is, or is proposed to be, navigated at a time when it is used for licensable activities,
  (ii) the Environment Agency,
  (iii) the British Waterways Board, or
  (iv) the Secretary of State,
(i) a person prescribed[1] for the purposes of this subsection.

(5) For the purposes of this section, "statutory function" means a function conferred by or under any enactment.
[Licensing Act 2003, s 13 as amended by the Fire and Rescue Services Act 2004, Sch 1 and SI 2005/1541.]

1. See the Licensing Act 2003 (Premises Licences and Club Premises Certificates) Regulations 2005, SI 2005/42.

8–19841 14. Meaning of "supply of alcohol". For the purposes of this Part the "supply of alcohol" means—

(*a*) the sale by retail of alcohol, or
(*b*) the supply of alcohol by or on behalf of a club to, or to the order of, a member of the club.
[Licensing Act 2003, s 14.]

8–19842 15. Meaning of "designated premises supervisor". (1) In this Act references to the "designated premises supervisor", in relation to a premises licence, are to the individual for the time being specified in that licence as the premises supervisor.

(2) Nothing in this Act prevents an individual who holds a premises licence from also being specified in the licence as the premises supervisor.
[Licensing Act 2003, s 15.]

Grant of premises licence

8–19843 16. Applicant for premises licence. *Prescribes persons or bodies who can apply for a premises licence. Residual power to Secretary of State to prescribe persons of other descriptions who can also apply.*

8–19844 17. Application for premises licence. *Application to be in the prescribed form and accompanied by an Operating Schedule; application to be advertised in accordance with regulations*[1].

1. See the Licensing Act 2003 (Premises Licences and Club Premises Certificates) Regulations 2005, SI 2005/42.

8–19845 18. Determination of application for premises licence[1]. (1) This section applies where the relevant licensing authority—

(*a*) receives an application for a premises licence made in accordance with section 17, and (*b*) is satisfied that the applicant has complied with any requirement imposed on him under subsection (5) of that section.

(2) Subject to subsection (3), the authority must grant the licence in accordance with the application subject only to—

(*a*) such conditions as are consistent with the operating schedule accompanying the application, and

(*b*) any conditions which must under section 19, 20 or 21 be included in the licence.

(3) Where relevant representations are made, the authority must—

(*a*) hold a hearing to consider them, unless the authority, the applicant and each person who has made such representations agree that a hearing is unnecessary, and

(*b*) having regard to the representations, take such of the steps mentioned in subsection (4) (if any) as it considers necessary for the promotion of the licensing objectives.

(4) The steps are—

(*a*) to grant the licence subject to—

(i) the conditions mentioned in subsection (2)(*a*) modified to such extent as the authority considers necessary for the promotion of the licensing objectives, and

(ii) any condition which must under section 19, 20 or 21 be included in the licence;

(*b*) to exclude from the scope of the licence any of the licensable activities to which the application relates;

(*c*) to refuse to specify a person in the licence as the premises supervisor;

(*d*) to reject the application.

(5) For the purposes of subsection (4)(*a*)(i) the conditions mentioned in subsection (2)(*a*) are modified if any of them is altered or omitted or any new condition is added.

(6) For the purposes of this section, "relevant representations" means representations which—

(*a*) are about the likely effect of the grant of the premises licence on the promotion of the licensing objectives,

(*b*) meet the requirements of subsection (7),

(*c*) if they relate to the identity of the person named in the application as the proposed premises supervisor, meet the requirements of subsection (9), and

(*d*) are not excluded representations by virtue of section 32 (restriction on making representations following issue of provisional statement).

(7) The requirements of this subsection are—

(*a*) that the representations were made by an interested party or responsible authority within the period prescribed under section 17(5)(*c*),

(*b*) that they have not been withdrawn, and

(*c*) in the case of representations made by an interested party (who is not also a responsible authority), that they are not, in the opinion of the relevant licensing authority, frivolous or vexatious.

(8) Where the authority determines for the purposes of subsection (7)(*c*) that any representations are frivolous or vexatious, it must notify the person who made them of the reasons for its determination.

(9) The requirements of this subsection are that the representations—

(*a*) were made by a chief officer of police for a police area in which the premises are situated, and

(*b*) include a statement that, due to the exceptional circumstances of the case, he is satisfied that the designation of the person concerned as the premises supervisor under the premises licence would undermine the crime prevention objective.

(10) In discharging its duty under subsection (2) or (3)(*b*), a licensing authority may grant a licence under this section subject to different conditions in respect of—

(*a*) different parts of the premises concerned;

(*b*) different licensable activities.

[Licensing Act 2003, s 18.]

---

1. For appeal to a magistrates' court against a decision of a licensing authority under this section, see s 181 and Sch 5, post.

8–19846 19. Mandatory conditions where licence authorises supply of alcohol. (1) Where a premises licence authorises the supply of alcohol, the licence must include the following conditions.

(2) The first condition is that no supply of alcohol may be made under the premises licence—

(*a*) at a time when there is no designated premises supervisor in respect of the premises licence, or

(*b*) at a time when the designated premises supervisor does not hold a personal licence or his personal licence is suspended.

(3) The second condition is that every supply of alcohol under the premises licence must be made or authorised by a person who holds a personal licence.
[Licensing Act 2003, s 19.]

8–19847 20. Mandatory condition: exhibition of films. (1) Where a premises licence authorises the exhibition of films, the licence must include a condition requiring the admission of children to the exhibition of any film to be restricted in accordance with this section.

(2) Where the film classification body is specified in the licence, unless subsection (3)(*b*) applies, admission of children must be restricted in accordance with any recommendation made by that body.

(3) Where—

(*a*) the film classification body is not specified in the licence, or
(*b*) the relevant licensing authority has notified the holder of the licence that this subsection applies to the film in question,

admission of children must be restricted in accordance with any recommendation made by that licensing authority.

(4) In this section—

"children" means persons aged under 18; and
"film classification body" means the person or persons designated as the authority under section 4 of the Video Recordings Act 1984 (c 39) (authority to determine suitability of video works for classification).

[Licensing Act 2003, s 20.]

8–19848 21. Mandatory condition: door supervision. (1) Where a premises licence includes a condition that at specified times one or more individuals must be at the premises to carry out a security activity, the licence must include a condition that each such individual must be licensed by the Security Industry Authority.

(2) But nothing in subsection (1) requires such a condition to be imposed—

(*a*) in respect of premises within paragraph 8(3)(*a*) of Schedule 2 to the Private Security Industry Act 2001 (c 12)[1] (premises with premises licences authorising plays or films), or
(*b*) in respect of premises in relation to—
   (i) any occasion mentioned in paragraph 8(3)(*b*) or (*c*) of that Schedule (premises being used exclusively by club with club premises certificate, under a temporary event notice authorising plays or films or under a gaming licence), or
   (ii) any occasion within paragraph 8(3)(*d*) of that Schedule (occasions prescribed by regulations under that Act).

(3) For the purposes of this section—

(*a*) "security activity" means an activity to which paragraph 2(1)(*a*) of that Schedule applies, and
(*b*) paragraph 8(5) of that Schedule (interpretation of references to an occasion) applies as it applies in relation to paragraph 8 of that Schedule.

[Licensing Act 2003, s 21.]

1. In PART VIII, INDUSTRY AND COMMERCE, post.

8–19849 22. Prohibited conditions: plays. (1) In relation to a premises licence which authorises the performance of plays, no condition may be attached to the licence as to the nature of the plays which may be performed, or the manner of performing plays, under the licence.

(2) But subsection (1) does not prevent a licensing authority imposing, in accordance with section 18(2)(*a*) or (3)(*b*), 35(3)(*b*) or 52(3), any condition which it considers necessary on the grounds of public safety.

[Licensing Act 2003, s 22.]

8–19850 23. Grant or rejection of application. (1) Where an application is granted under section 18, the relevant licensing authority must forthwith—

(*a*) give a notice to that effect to—
   (i) the applicant,
   (ii) any person who made relevant representations in respect of the application, and
   (iii) the chief officer of police for the police area (or each police area) in which the premises are situated, and
(*b*) issue the applicant with the licence and a summary of it.

(2) Where relevant representations were made in respect of the application, the notice under subsection (1)(*a*) must state the authority's reasons for its decision as to the steps (if any) to take under section 18(3)(*b*).

(3) Where an application is rejected under section 18, the relevant licensing authority must forthwith give a notice to that effect, stating its reasons for the decision, to—

(*a*) the applicant,
(*b*) any person who made relevant representations in respect of the application, and
(*c*) the chief officer of police for the police area (or each police area) in which the premises are situated.

(4) In this section "relevant representations" has the meaning given in section 18(6).
[Licensing Act 2003, s 23.]

8–19851 24. Form of licence and summary. *Licence and summary of it to be in prescribed form*[1].

1. See the Licensing Act 2003 (Premises Licences and Club Premises Certificates) Regulations 2005, SI 2005/42.

8–19852 25. Theft, loss, etc of premises licence or summary. *Power to apply for duplicate licence or summary on payment of fee.*

Duration of licence

8–19853 26. Period of validity of premises licence. *Premises licence to have effect until revoked, lapses, is surrendered, or is for a limited period and comes to an end. Licence of no effect if suspended following a review under s 52.*

8–19854 27. Death, incapacity, insolvency etc of licence holder. (1) A premises licence lapses if the holder of the licence—

(*a*) dies,
(*b*) becomes mentally incapable (within the meaning of section 13(1) of the Enduring Powers of Attorney Act 1985 (c 29)),
(*c*) becomes insolvent,
(*d*) is dissolved, or
(*e*) if it is a club, ceases to be a recognised club.

(2) This section is subject to sections 47 and 50 (which make provision for the reinstatement of the licence in certain circumstances).

(3) For the purposes of this section, an individual becomes insolvent on—

(*a*) the approval of a voluntary arrangement proposed by him,
(*b*) being adjudged bankrupt or having his estate sequestrated, or
(*c*) entering into a deed of arrangement made for the benefit of his creditors or a trust deed for his creditors.

(4) For the purposes of this section, a company becomes insolvent on—

(*a*) the approval of a voluntary arrangement proposed by its directors,
(*b*) the appointment of an administrator in respect of the company,
(*c*) the appointment of an administrative receiver in respect of the company, or
(*d*) going into liquidation.

(5) An expression used in this section and in the Insolvency Act 1986 (c 45) has the same meaning in this section as in that Act.
[Licensing Act 2003, s 27.]

8–19855 28. Surrender of premises licence. *Premises licence holder may surrender licence by giving notice to licensing authority. Licence lapses on receipt of notice.*

Provisional statement

8–19856 29, 30. *Application for provisional statement to be in the prescribed form and accompanied by a Schedule of Works*[1].

1. The Licensing Act 2003 (Premises Licences and Club Premises Certificates) Regulations 2005, SI 2005/42 have been made. Application to be advertised in accordance with Regulations.

8–19857 31. Determination of application for provisional statement[1]**.** (1) This section applies where the relevant licensing authority—

(*a*) receives a provisional statement application, and
(*b*) is satisfied that the applicant has complied with any requirement imposed on him by virtue of section 30.

(2) Where no relevant representations are made, the authority must issue the applicant with a statement to that effect.

(3) Where relevant representations are made, the authority must—

(*a*) hold a hearing to consider them, unless the authority, the applicant and each person who has made such representations agree that a hearing is unnecessary, (*b*) determine whether, on the basis of those representations and the provisional statement application, it would consider it necessary to take any steps under section 18(3)(*b*) if, on the work being satisfactorily completed, it had to decide whether to grant a premises licence in the form described in the provisional statement application, and

(*c*) issue the applicant with a statement which—

(i) gives details of that determination, and

(ii) states the authority's reasons for its decision as to the steps (if any) that it would be necessary to take under section 18(3)(*b*).

(4) The licensing authority must give a copy of the provisional statement to—

(*a*) each person who made relevant representations, and

(*b*) the chief officer of police for each police area in which the premises are situated.

(5) In this section "relevant representations" means representations—

(*a*) which are about the likely effect on the licensing objectives of the grant of a premises licence in the form described in the provisional statement application, if the work at the premises was satisfactorily completed, and

(*b*) which meet the requirements of subsection (6).

(6) The requirements are—

(*a*) that the representations are made by an interested party or responsible authority within the period prescribed under section 17(5)(*c*) by virtue of section 30,

(*b*) that the representations have not been withdrawn, and

(*c*) in the case of representations made by an interested party (who is not also a responsible authority), that they are not, in the opinion of the relevant licensing authority, frivolous or vexatious.

(7) Where the authority determines for the purposes of subsection (6)(*c*) that any representations are frivolous or vexatious, it must notify the person who made them of the reasons for its determination.

(8) In this section "provisional statement application" means an application made in accordance with section 29.

[Licensing Act 2003, s 31.]

---

1. For appeal to a magistrates' court against a decision of a licensing authority under this section, see s 181 and Sch 5, post.

8–19858 32. Restriction on representations following provisional statement. (1) This section applies where a provisional statement has been issued in respect of any premises ("the relevant premises") and a person subsequently applies for a premises licence in respect of—

(*a*) the relevant premises or a part of them, or

(*b*) premises that are substantially the same as the relevant premises or a part of them.

(2) Where—

(*a*) the application for the premises licence is an application for a licence in the same form as the licence described in the application for the provisional statement, and

(*b*) the work described in the schedule of works accompanying the application for that statement has been satisfactorily completed,

representations made by a person ("the relevant person") in respect of the application for the premises licence are excluded representations for the purposes of section 18(6)(*d*) if subsection (3) applies.

(3) This subsection applies if—

(*a*) given the information provided in the application for the provisional statement, the relevant person could have made the same, or substantially the same, representations about that application but failed to do so, without reasonable excuse, and

(*b*) there has been no material change in circumstances relating either to the relevant premises or to the area in the vicinity of those premises since the provisional statement was made.

[Licensing Act 2003, s 32.]

Duty to notify certain changes

8–19859 33. Notification of change of name or address. (1) The holder of a premises licence must, as soon as is reasonably practicable, notify the relevant licensing authority of any change in—

(*a*) his name or address,

(*b*) unless the designated premises supervisor has already notified the authority under subsection (4), the name or address of that supervisor.

(2) Subsection (1) is subject to regulations under section 55(1) (fee to accompany application).

(3) A notice under subsection (1) must also be accompanied by the premises licence (or the

appropriate part of the licence) or, if that is not practicable, by a statement of the reasons for the failure to produce the licence (or part).

(4) Where the designated premises supervisor under a premises licence is not the holder of the licence, he may notify the relevant licensing authority under this subsection of any change in his name or address.

(5) Where the designated premises supervisor gives a notice under subsection (4), he must, as soon as is reasonably practicable, give the holder of the premises licence a copy of that notice.

(6) A person commits an offence if he fails, without reasonable excuse, to comply with this section.

(7) A person guilty of an offence under subsection (6) is liable on summary conviction to a fine not exceeding level 2 on the standard scale.

[Licensing Act 2003, s 33.]

Variation of licences

8–19860 34. Application to vary premises licence. *Application for variation of premises licence to be in the prescribed form and advertised in accordance with regulations*[1].

---

1. See the Licensing Act 2003 (Premises Licences and Club Premises Certificates) Regulations 2005, SI 2005/42.

8–19861 35. Determination of application under section 34[1]**.** (1) This section applies where the relevant licensing authority—

(*a*) receives an application, made in accordance with section 34, to vary a premises licence, and

(*b*) is satisfied that the applicant has complied with any requirement imposed on him by virtue of subsection (5) of that section.

(2) Subject to subsection (3) and section 36(6), the authority must grant the application.

(3) Where relevant representations are made, the authority must—

(*a*) hold a hearing to consider them, unless the authority, the applicant and each person who has made such representations agree that a hearing is unnecessary, and

(*b*) having regard to the representations, take such of the steps mentioned in subsection (4) (if any) as it considers necessary for the promotion of the licensing objectives.

(4) The steps are—

(*a*) to modify the conditions of the licence;

(*b*) to reject the whole or part of the application;

and for this purpose the conditions of the licence are modified if any of them is altered or omitted or any new condition is added.

(5) In this section "relevant representations" means representations which—

(*a*) are about the likely effect of the grant of the application on the promotion of the licensing objectives, and

(*b*) meet the requirements of subsection (6).

(6) The requirements are—

(*a*) that the representations are made by an interested party or responsible authority within the period prescribed under section 17(5)(*c*) by virtue of section 34(5),

(*b*) that they have not been withdrawn, and

(*c*) in the case of representations made by an interested party (who is not also a responsible authority), that they are not, in the opinion of the relevant licensing authority, frivolous or vexatious.

(7) Subsections (2) and (3) are subject to sections 19, 20 and 21 (which require certain conditions to be included in premises licences).

[Licensing Act 2003, s 35.]

---

1. For appeal to a magistrates' court against a decision of a licensing authority under this section, see s 181 and Sch 5, post.

8–19862 36. Supplementary provision about determinations under section 35. (1) Where an application (or any part of an application) is granted under section 35, the relevant licensing authority must forthwith give a notice to that effect to—

(*a*) the applicant,

(*b*) any person who made relevant representations in respect of the application, and

(*c*) the chief officer of police for the police area (or each police area) in which the premises are situated.

(2) Where relevant representations were made in respect of the application, the notice under subsection (1) must state the authority's reasons for its decision as to the steps (if any) to take under section 35(3)(*b*).

(3) The notice under subsection (1) must specify the time when the variation in question takes effect.

That time is the time specified in the application or, if that time is before the applicant is given that notice, such later time as the relevant licensing authority specifies in the notice.

(4) Where an application (or any part of an application) is rejected under section 35, the relevant licensing authority must forthwith give a notice to that effect stating its reasons for rejecting the application to—

(*a*) the applicant,
(*b*) any person who made relevant representations in respect of the application, and
(*c*) the chief officer of police for the police area (or each police area) in which the premises are situated.

(5) Where the relevant licensing authority determines for the purposes of section 35(6)(*c*) that any representations are frivolous or vexatious, it must notify the person who made them of the reasons for that determination.

(6) A licence may not be varied under section 35 so as—

(*a*) to extend the period for which the licence has effect, or
(*b*) to vary substantially the premises to which it relates.

(7) In discharging its duty under subsection (2) or (3)(*b*) of that section, a licensing authority may vary a premises licence so that it has effect subject to different conditions in respect of—

(*a*) different parts of the premises concerned;
(*b*) different licensable activities.

(8) In this section "relevant representations" has the meaning given in section 35(5).
[Licensing Act 2003, s 36.]

8–19863 37. Application to vary licence to specify individual as premises supervisor. (1)–(4) *Application for variation of premises licence to specify individual as premises supervisor to be in the prescribed form and in accordance with regulations*[1].

(5) Where a chief officer of police notified under subsection (4) is satisfied that the exceptional circumstances of the case are such that granting the application would undermine the crime prevention objective, he must give the relevant licensing authority a notice stating the reasons why he is so satisfied.

(6) The chief officer of police must give that notice within the period of 14 days beginning with the day on which he is notified of the application under subsection (4).
[Licensing Act 2003, s 37.]

1. See the Licensing Act 2003 (Premises Licences and Club Premises Certificates) Regulations 2005, SI 2005/42.

8–19864 38. Circumstances in which section 37 application given interim effect. *Section 37 application to have interim effect if requested.*

8–19865 39. Determination of section 37 application[1]**.** (1) This section applies where an application is made, in accordance with section 37, to vary a premises licence so as to specify a new premises supervisor ("the proposed individual").

(2) Subject to subsection (3), the relevant licensing authority must grant the application.

(3) Where a notice is given under section 37(5) (and not withdrawn), the authority must—

(*a*) hold a hearing to consider it, unless the authority, the applicant and the chief officer of police who gave the notice agree that a hearing is unnecessary, and
(*b*) having regard to the notice, reject the application if it considers it necessary for the promotion of the crime prevention objective to do so.

(4) Where an application under section 37 is granted or rejected, the relevant licensing authority must give a notice to that effect to—

(*a*) the applicant,
(*b*) the proposed individual, and
(*c*) the chief officer of police for the police area (or each police area) in which the premises are situated.

(5) Where a chief officer of police gave a notice under subsection (5) of that section (and it was not withdrawn), the notice under subsection (4) of this section must state the authority's reasons for granting or rejecting the application.

(6) Where the application is granted, the notice under subsection (4) must specify the time when the variation takes effect.

That time is the time specified in the application or, if that time is before the applicant is given that notice, such later time as the relevant licensing authority specifies in the notice.
[Licensing Act 2003, s 39.]

1. For appeal to a magistrates' court against a decision of a licensing authority under this section, see s 181 and Sch 5, post.

8–19866 40. Duty of applicant following determination under section 39. (1) Where the holder of a premises licence is notified under section 39(4), he must forthwith—

(*a*) if his application has been granted, notify the person (if any) who has been replaced as the designated premises supervisor of the variation, and
(*b*) if his application has been rejected, give the designated premises supervisor (if any) notice to that effect.

(2) A person commits an offence if he fails, without reasonable excuse, to comply with subsection (1).

(3) A person guilty of an offence under subsection (2) is liable on summary conviction to a fine not exceeding level 3 on the standard scale.
[Licensing Act 2003, s 40.]

8–19867 41. Request to be removed as designated premises supervisor. (1) Where an individual wishes to cease being the designated premises supervisor in respect of a premises licence, he may give the relevant licensing authority a notice to that effect.

(2) Subsection (1) is subject to regulations under section 54 (form etc of notices etc).

(3) Where the individual is the holder of the premises licence, the notice under subsection (1) must also be accompanied by the premises licence (or the appropriate part of the licence) or, if that is not practicable, by a statement of the reasons for the failure to provide the licence (or part).

(4) In any other case, the individual must no later than 48 hours after giving the notice under subsection (1) give the holder of the premises licence—

(*a*) a copy of that notice, and
(*b*) a notice directing the holder to send to the relevant licensing authority within 14 days of receiving the notice—

(i) the premises licence (or the appropriate part of the licence), or
(ii) if that is not practicable, a statement of the reasons for the failure to provide the licence (or part).

(5) A person commits an offence if he fails, without reasonable excuse, to comply with a direction given to him under subsection (4)(*b*).

(6) A person guilty of an offence under subsection (5) is liable on summary conviction to a fine not exceeding level 3 on the standard scale.

(7) Where an individual—

(*a*) gives the relevant licensing authority a notice in accordance with this section, and
(*b*) satisfies the requirements of subsection (3) or (4),

he is to be treated for the purposes of this Act as if, from the relevant time, he were not the designated premises supervisor.

(8) For this purpose "the relevant time" means—

(*a*) the time the notice under subsection (1) is received by the relevant licensing authority, or
(*b*) if later, the time specified in the notice.
[Licensing Act 2003, s 41.]

Transfer of premises licence

8–19868 42. Application for transfer of premises licence. (1)–(4) *Application for transfer of premises licence to be in prescribed form and in accordance with regulations*[1].

(5) The applicant must give notice of his application to the chief officer of police for the police area (or each police area) in which the premises are situated.

(6) Where a chief officer of police notified under subsection (5) is satisfied that the exceptional circumstances of the case are such that granting the application would undermine the crime prevention objective, he must give the relevant licensing authority a notice stating the reasons why he is so satisfied.

(7) The chief officer of police must give that notice within the period of 14 days beginning with the day on which he is notified of the application under subsection (5).
[Licensing Act 2003, s 42.]

1. See the Licensing Act 2003 (Premises Licences and Club Premises Certificates) Regulations 2005, SI 2005/42.

8–19869 43. Circumstances in which transfer application given interim effect. *Transfer application given interim effect if requested and with consent of existing premises licence holder (unless exempted from that requirement by licensing authority).*

8–19870 **44. Determination of transfer application**[1]**.** (1) This section applies where an application for the transfer of a licence is made in accordance with section 42.

(2) Subject to subsections (3) and (5), the authority must transfer the licence in accordance with the application.

(3) The authority must reject the application if none of the conditions in subsection (4) applies.

(4) The conditions are—

(*a*) that section 43(1) (applications given interim effect) applies to the application,
(*b*) that the holder of the premises licence consents to the transfer,
(*c*) that the applicant is exempted under subsection (6) from the requirement to obtain the holder's consent to the transfer.

(5) Where a notice is given under section 42(6) (and not withdrawn), and subsection (3) above does not apply, the authority must—

(*a*) hold a hearing to consider it, unless the authority, the applicant and the chief officer of police who gave the notice agree that a hearing is unnecessary, and
(*b*) having regard to the notice, reject the application if it considers it necessary for the promotion of the crime prevention objective to do so.

(6) The relevant licensing authority must exempt the applicant from the requirement to obtain the holder's consent if the applicant shows to the authority's satisfaction—

(*a*) that he has taken all reasonable steps to obtain that consent, and
(*b*) that, if the application were granted, he would be in a position to use the premises for the licensable activity or activities authorised by the premises licence.

(7) Where the relevant licensing authority refuses to exempt an applicant under subsection (6), it must notify the applicant of its reasons for that decision.
[Licensing Act 2003, s 44.]

---

1. For appeal to a magistrates' court against a decision of a licensing authority under this section, see s 181 and Sch 5, post.

8–19871 **45. Notification of determination under section 44.** (1) Where an application under section 42 is granted or rejected, the relevant licensing authority must give a notice to that effect to—

(*a*) the applicant, and
(*b*) the chief officer of police for the police area (or each police area) in which the premises are situated.

(2) Where a chief officer of police gave a notice under subsection (6) of that section (and it was not withdrawn), the notice under subsection (1) of this section must state the licensing authority's reasons for granting or rejecting the application.

(3) Where the application is granted, the notice under subsection (1) must specify the time when the transfer takes effect.

That time is the time specified in the application or, if that time is before the applicant is given that notice, such later time as the relevant licensing authority specifies in the notice.

(4) The relevant licensing authority must also give a copy of the notice given under subsection (1)—

(*a*) where the application is granted—

(i) to the holder of the licence immediately before the application was granted, or
(ii) if the application was one to which section 43(1) applied, to the holder of the licence immediately before the application was made (if any),

(*b*) where the application is rejected, to the holder of the premises licence (if any).
[Licensing Act 2003, s 45.]

8–19872 **46. Duty to notify designated premises supervisor of transfer.** (1) This section applies where—

(*a*) an application is made in accordance with section 42 to transfer a premises licence in respect of which there is a designated premises supervisor, and
(*b*) the applicant and that supervisor are not the same person.

(2) Where section 43(1) applies in relation to the application, the applicant must forthwith notify the designated premises supervisor of the application.

(3) If the application is granted, the applicant must forthwith notify the designated premises supervisor of the transfer.

(4) A person commits an offence if he fails, without reasonable excuse, to comply with this section.

(5) A person guilty of an offence under subsection (4) is liable on summary conviction to a fine not exceeding level 3 on the standard scale.
[Licensing Act 2003, s 46.]

Interim authority notices

8–19873 47. Interim authority notice following death etc of licence holder. *Power for a person with a prescribed interest to serve an interim authority notice on licensing authority within 7 days of a licence having lapsed because of death, incapacity or insolvency of licence holder. Application to be in prescribed form and in accordance with regulations*[1].

1. See the Licensing Act 2003 (Premises Licences and Club Premises Certificates) Regulations 2005, SI 2005/42.

8–19874 48. Cancellation of interim authority notice following police objections[1]**.** (1) This section applies where—

(*a*) an interim authority notice by a person ("the relevant person") is given in accordance with section 47,

(*b*) the chief officer of police for the police area (or each police area) in which the premises are situated is given a copy of the interim authority notice before the end of the initial seven day period (within the meaning of that section), and

(*c*) that chief officer (or any of those chief officers) is satisfied that the exceptional circumstances of the case are such that a failure to cancel the interim authority notice would undermine the crime prevention objective.

(2) The chief officer of police must no later than 48 hours after he receives the copy of the interim authority notice give the relevant licensing authority a notice stating why he is so satisfied.

(3) Where a notice is given by the chief officer of police (and not withdrawn), the authority must—

(*a*) hold a hearing to consider it, unless the authority, the relevant person and the chief officer of police agree that a hearing is unnecessary, and

(*b*) having regard to the notice given by the chief officer of police, cancel the interim authority notice if it considers it necessary for the promotion of the crime prevention objective to do so.

(4) An interim authority notice is cancelled under subsection (3)(*b*) by the licensing authority giving the relevant person a notice stating that it is cancelled and the authority's reasons for its decision.

(5) The licensing authority must give a copy of a notice under subsection (4) to the chief officer of police for the police area (or each police area) in which the premises are situated.

(6) The premises licence lapses if, and when, a notice is given under subsection (4). This is subject to paragraph 7(5) of Schedule 5 (reinstatement of premises licence where appeal made against cancellation of interim authority notice).

(7) The relevant licensing authority must not cancel an interim authority notice after a relevant transfer application (within the meaning of section 47) is made in respect of the premises licence.
[Licensing Act 2003, s 48.]

1. For appeal to a magistrates' court against a decision of a licensing authority under this section, see s 181 and Sch 5, post.

8–19875 49. Supplementary provision about interim authority notices. (1) On receipt of an interim authority notice, the relevant licensing authority must issue to the person who gave the notice a copy of the licence and a copy of the summary (in each case certified by the authority to be a true copy).

(2) The copies issued under this section must be copies of the premises licence and summary in the form in which they existed immediately before the licence lapsed under section 27, except that they must specify the person who gave the interim authority notice as the person who is the holder.

(3) This Act applies in relation to a copy issued under this section as it applies in relation to an original licence or summary.

(4) Where a person becomes the holder of a premises licence by virtue of section 47, he must (unless he is the designated premises supervisor under the licence) forthwith notify the supervisor (if any) of the interim authority notice.

(5) A person commits an offence if he fails, without reasonable excuse, to comply with subsection (4).

(6) A person guilty of an offence under subsection (5) is liable on summary conviction to a fine not exceeding level 3 on the standard scale.
[Licensing Act 2003, s 49.]

Transfer following death etc of licence holder

8–19876 50. Reinstatement of licence on transfer following death etc of holder. *Power to any person who could apply for a premises licence under s 16(1) to apply for reinstatement of lapsed licence on transfer under s 42.*

Review of licences

8–19877 51. Application for review of premises licence. (1) Where a premises licence has effect, an interested party or a responsible authority may apply to the relevant licensing authority for a review of the licence.

(2) Subsection (1) is subject to regulations[1] under section 54 (form etc of applications etc).

(3) The Secretary of State must by regulations under this section—

(*a*) require the applicant to give a notice containing details of the application to the holder of the premises licence and each responsible authority within such period as may be prescribed;

(*b*) require the authority to advertise the application and invite representations about it to be made to the authority by interested parties and responsible authorities;

(*c*) prescribe the period during which representations may be made by the holder of the premises licence, any responsible authority or any interested party;

(*d*) require any notice under paragraph (*a*) or advertisement under paragraph (*b*) to specify that period.

(4) The relevant licensing authority may, at any time, reject any ground for review specified in an application under this section if it is satisfied—

(*a*) that the ground is not relevant to one or more of the licensing objectives, or

(*b*) in the case of an application made by a person other than a responsible authority, that—

(i) the ground is frivolous or vexatious, or

(ii) the ground is a repetition.

(5) For this purpose a ground for review is a repetition if—

(*a*) it is identical or substantially similar to—

(i) a ground for review specified in an earlier application for review made in respect of the same premises licence and determined under section 52, or

(ii) representations considered by the relevant licensing authority in accordance with section 18, before it determined the application for the premises licence under that section, or

(iii) representations which would have been so considered but for the fact that they were excluded representations by virtue of section 32, and

(*b*) a reasonable interval has not elapsed since that earlier application for review or the grant of the licence (as the case may be).

(6) Where the authority rejects a ground for review under subsection (4)(*b*), it must notify the applicant of its decision and, if the ground was rejected because it was frivolous or vexatious, the authority must notify him of its reasons for making that decision.

(7) The application is to be treated as rejected to the extent that any of the grounds for review are rejected under subsection (4).

Accordingly the requirements imposed under subsection (3)(*a*) and (*b*) and by section 52 (so far as not already met) apply only to so much (if any) of the application as has not been rejected.

[Licensing Act 2003, s 51.]

1. See the Licensing Act 2003 (Premises Licences and Club Premises Certificates) Regulations 2005, SI 2005/42.

8–19878 **52. Determination of application for review[1].** (1) This section applies where—

(*a*) the relevant licensing authority receives an application made in accordance with section 51,

(*b*) the applicant has complied with any requirement imposed on him under subsection (3)(*a*) or (*d*) of that section, and

(*c*) the authority has complied with any requirement imposed on it under subsection (3)(*b*) or (*d*) of that section.

(2) Before determining the application, the authority must hold a hearing to consider it and any relevant representations.

(3) The authority must, having regard to the application and any relevant representations, take such of the steps mentioned in subsection (4) (if any) as it considers necessary for the promotion of the licensing objectives.

(4) The steps are—

(*a*) to modify the conditions of the licence;

(*b*) to exclude a licensable activity from the scope of the licence;

(*c*) to remove the designated premises supervisor;

(*d*) to suspend the licence for a period not exceeding three months;

(*e*) to revoke the licence;

and for this purpose the conditions of the licence are modified if any of them is altered or omitted or any new condition is added.

(5) Subsection (3) is subject to sections 19, 20 and 21 (requirement to include certain conditions in premises licences).

(6) Where the authority takes a step mentioned in subsection (4)(*a*) or (*b*), it may provide that the modification or exclusion is to have effect for only such period (not exceeding three months) as it may specify.

(7) In this section "relevant representations" means representations which—

(*a*) are relevant to one or more of the licensing objectives, and (*b*) meet the requirements of subsection (8).

(8) The requirements are—

(*a*) that the representations are made—

(i) by the holder of the premises licence, a responsible authority or an interested party, and
(ii) within the period prescribed under section 51(3)(*c*),

(*b*) that they have not been withdrawn, and
(*c*) if they are made by an interested party (who is not also a responsible authority), that they are not, in the opinion of the relevant licensing authority, frivolous or vexatious.

(9) Where the relevant licensing authority determines that any representations are frivolous or vexatious, it must notify the person who made them of the reasons for that determination.

(10) Where a licensing authority determines an application for review under this section it must notify the determination and its reasons for making it to—

(*a*) the holder of the licence,
(*b*) the applicant,
(*c*) any person who made relevant representations, and
(*d*) the chief officer of police for the police area (or each police area) in which the premises are situated.

(11) A determination under this section does not have effect—

(*a*) until the end of the period given for appealing against the decision, or
(*b*) if the decision is appealed against, until the appeal is disposed of.

[Licensing Act 2003, s 52.]

1. For appeal to a magistrates' court against a decision of a licensing authority under this section, see s 181 and Sch 5, post.

8–19879 53. Supplementary provision about review. *Licensing authority able to determine review which has been applied for by itself in its separate capacity as a responsible authority under s 13(4).*

Production of licence, rights of entry, etc

8–19880 56. Licensing authority's duty to update licence document. (1) Where—

(*a*) the relevant licensing authority, in relation to a premises licence, makes a determination or receives a notice under this Part,
(*b*) a premises licence lapses under this Part, or
(*c*) an appeal against a decision under this Part is disposed of,

the relevant licensing authority must make the appropriate amendments (if any) to the licence and, if necessary, issue a new summary of the licence.

(2) Where a licensing authority is not in possession of the licence (or the appropriate part of the licence) it may, for the purposes of discharging its obligations under subsection (1), require the holder of a premises licence to produce the licence (or the appropriate part) to the authority within 14 days from the date on which he is notified of the requirement.

(3) A person commits an offence if he fails, without reasonable excuse, to comply with a requirement under subsection (2).

(4) A person guilty of an offence under subsection (3) is liable on summary conviction to a fine not exceeding level 2 on the standard scale.

[Licensing Act 2003, s 56.]

8–19881 57. Duty to keep and produce licence. (1) This section applies whenever premises in respect of which a premises licence has effect are being used for one or more licensable activities authorised by the licence.

(2) The holder of the premises licence must secure that the licence or a certified copy of it is kept at the premises in the custody or under the control of—

(*a*) the holder of the licence, or
(*b*) a person who works at the premises and whom the holder of the licence has nominated in writing for the purposes of this subsection.

(3) The holder of the premises licence must secure that—

(*a*) the summary of the licence or a certified copy of that summary, and
(*b*) a notice specifying the position held at the premises by any person nominated for the purposes of subsection (2),

are prominently displayed at the premises.

(4) The holder of a premises licence commits an offence if he fails, without reasonable excuse, to comply with subsection (2) or (3).

(5) A constable or an authorised person may require the person who, by virtue of arrangements

made for the purposes of subsection (2), is required to have the premises licence (or a certified copy of it) in his custody or under his control to produce the licence (or such a copy) for examination.

(6) An authorised person exercising the power conferred by subsection (5) must, if so requested, produce evidence of his authority to exercise the power.

(7) A person commits an offence if he fails, without reasonable excuse, to produce a premises licence or certified copy of a premises licence in accordance with a requirement under subsection (5).

(8) A person guilty of an offence under this section is liable on summary conviction to a fine not exceeding level 2 on the standard scale.

(9) In subsection (3) the reference to the summary of the licence is a reference to the summary issued under section 23 or, where one or more summaries have subsequently been issued under section 56, the most recent summary to have been so issued.

(10) Section 58 makes provision about certified copies of documents for the purposes of this section.

[Licensing Act 2003, s 57.]

8–19882 58. Provision supplementary to section 57. (1) Any reference in section 57 to a certified copy of any document is a reference to a copy of that document which is certified to be a true copy by—

(*a*) the relevant licensing authority,

(*b*) a solicitor or notary, or

(*c*) a person of a prescribed[1] description.

(2) Any certified copy produced in accordance with a requirement under section 57(5) must be a copy of the document in the form in which it exists at the time.

(3) A document which purports to be a certified copy of a document is to be taken to be such a copy, and to comply with the requirements of subsection (2), unless the contrary is shown.

[Licensing Act 2003, s 58.]

1. I.e. prescribed by regulations, see s 193, post. At the date of going to press no such regulations had been made.

8–19883 59. Inspection of premises before grant of licence etc. (1) In this section "relevant application" means an application under—

(*a*) section 17 (grant of licence),

(*b*) section 29 (provisional statement),

(*c*) section 34 (variation of licence), or

(*d*) section 51 (review of licence).

(2) A constable or an authorised person may, at any reasonable time before the determination of a relevant application, enter the premises to which the application relates to assess—

(*a*) in a case within subsection (1)(*a*), (*b*) or (*c*), the likely effect of the grant of the application on the promotion of the licensing objectives, and

(*b*) in a case within subsection (1)(*d*), the effect of the activities authorised by the premises licence on the promotion of those objectives.

(3) An authorised person exercising the power conferred by this section must, if so requested, produce evidence of his authority to exercise the power.

(4) A constable or an authorised person exercising the power conferred by this section in relation to an application within subsection (1)(*d*) may, if necessary, use reasonable force.

(5) A person commits an offence if he intentionally obstructs an authorised person exercising a power conferred by this section.

(6) A person guilty of an offence under this section is liable on summary conviction to a fine not exceeding level 2 on the standard scale.

[Licensing Act 2003, s 59.]

PART 4[1]
CLUBS

Introductory

8–19884 60. Club premises certificate. (1) In this Act "club premises certificate" means a certificate granted under this Part—

(*a*) in respect of premises[2] occupied by, and habitually used for the purposes of, a club,

(*b*) by the relevant licensing authority, and

(*c*) certifying the matters specified in subsection (2).

(2) Those matters are—

(*a*) that the premises may be used by the club for one or more qualifying club activities[3] specified in the certificate, and

(*b*) that the club is a qualifying club in relation to each of those activities (see section 61).

[Licensing Act 2003, s 60.]

1. Part 4 comprises ss 60–97.
2. For meaning of "premises", see s 193, post.
3. For meaning of "qualifying club activities", see s 1(2), ante.

Qualifying clubs

8–19885 **61. Qualifying clubs.** (1) This section applies for determining for the purposes of this Part whether a club is a qualifying club in relation to a qualifying club activity.

(2) A club is a qualifying club in relation to the supply of alcohol to members or guests[1] if it satisfies both—

(*a*) the general conditions in section 62, and
(*b*) the additional conditions in section 64.

(3) A club is a qualifying club in relation to the provision of regulated entertainment[2] if it satisfies the general conditions in section 62.
[Licensing Act 2003, s 61.]

1. For meaning of "supply of alcohol to members or guests", see s 70, post.
2. For meaning of "regulated entertainment, see Sch 1, post.

8–19886 **62. The general conditions.** (1) The general conditions which a club must satisfy if it is to be a qualifying club in relation to a qualifying club activity are the following.

(2) Condition 1 is that under the rules of the club persons may not—

(*a*) be admitted to membership, or
(*b*) be admitted, as candidates for membership, to any of the privileges of membership,

without an interval of at least two days between their nomination or application for membership and their admission.

(3) Condition 2 is that under the rules of the club persons becoming members without prior nomination or application may not be admitted to the privileges of membership without an interval of at least two days between their becoming members and their admission.

(4) Condition 3 is that the club is established and conducted in good faith as a club (see section 63).

(5) Condition 4 is that the club has at least 25 members.

(6) Condition 5 is that alcohol is not supplied, or intended to be supplied, to members on the premises otherwise than by or on behalf of the club.
[Licensing Act 2003, s 62.]

8–19887 **63. Determining whether a club is established and conducted in good faith.** (1) In determining for the purposes of condition 3 in subsection (4) of section 62 whether a club is established and conducted in good faith as a club, the matters to be taken into account are those specified in subsection (2).

(2) Those matters are—

(*a*) any arrangements restricting the club's freedom of purchase of alcohol;
(*b*) any provision in the rules, or arrangements, under which—
  (i) money or property of the club, or
  (ii) any gain arising from the carrying on of the club,

is or may be applied otherwise than for the benefit of the club as a whole or for charitable, benevolent or political purposes;

(*c*) the arrangements for giving members information about the finances of the club;
(*d*) the books of account and other records kept to ensure the accuracy of that information;
(*e*) the nature of the premises[1] occupied by the club.

(3) If a licensing authority decides for any purpose of this Act that a club does not satisfy condition 3 in subsection (4) of section 62, the authority must give the club notice of the decision and of the reasons for it.
[Licensing Act 2003, s 63.]

1. For meaning of "premises", see s 193, post.

8–19888 **64. The additional conditions for the supply of alcohol.** (1) The additional conditions which a club must satisfy if it is to be a qualifying club in relation to the supply of alcohol to members or guests[1] are the following.

(2) Additional condition 1 is that (so far as not managed by the club in general meeting or otherwise by the general body of members) the purchase of alcohol for the club, and the supply of alcohol by the club, are managed by a committee whose members—

(*a*) are members of the club;
(*b*) have attained the age of 18 years; and

(*c*) are elected by the members of the club.

This subsection is subject to section 65 (which makes special provision for industrial and provident societies, friendly societies etc).

(3) Additional condition 2 is that no arrangements are, or are intended to be, made for any person to receive at the expense of the club any commission, percentage or similar payment on, or with reference to, purchases of alcohol by the club.

(4) Additional condition 3 is that no arrangements are, or are intended to be, made for any person directly or indirectly to derive any pecuniary benefit from the supply of alcohol by or on behalf of the club to members or guests, apart from—

(*a*) any benefit accruing to the club as a whole, or

(*b*) any benefit which a person derives indirectly by reason of the supply giving rise or contributing to a general gain from the carrying on of the club.

[Licensing Act 2003, s 64.]

1. For meaning of "supply of alcohol to members or guests", see s 70, post.

8–19889 **65. Industrial and provident societies, friendly societies etc.** (1) Subsection (2) applies in relation to any club which is—

(*a*) a registered society, within the meaning of the Industrial and Provident Societies Act 1965 (c 12)(see section 74(1) of that Act),

(*b*) a registered society, within the meaning of the Friendly Societies Act 1974 (c 46) (see section 111(1) of that Act), or

(*c*) a registered friendly society, within the meaning of the Friendly Societies Act 1992 (c 40) (see section 116 of that Act).

(2) Any such club is to be taken for the purposes of this Act to satisfy additional condition 1 in subsection (2) of section 64 if and to the extent that—

(*a*) the purchase of alcohol for the club, and

(*b*) the supply of alcohol by the club,

are under the control of the members or of a committee appointed by the members.

(3) References in this Act, other than this section, to—

(*a*) subsection (2) of section 64, or

(*b*) additional condition 1 in that subsection,

are references to it as read with subsection (1) of this section.

(4) Subject to subsection (5), this Act applies in relation to an incorporated friendly society as it applies in relation to a club, and accordingly—

(*a*) the premises[1] of the society are to be treated as the premises of a club,

(*b*) the members of the society are to be treated as the members of the club, and

(*c*) anything done by or on behalf of the society is to be treated as done by or on behalf of the club.

(5) In determining for the purposes of section 61 whether an incorporated friendly society is a qualifying club in relation to a qualifying club activity[2], the society is to be taken to satisfy the following conditions—

(*a*) condition 3 in subsection (4) of section 62,

(*b*) condition 5 in subsection (6) of that section,

(*c*) the additional conditions in section 64.

(6) In this section "incorporated friendly society" has the same meaning as in the Friendly Societies Act 1992 (see section 116 of that Act).

[Licensing Act 2003, s 65.]

1. For meaning of "premises", see s 193, post.
2. For "qualifying club activities", see s 1(2), ante.

8–19890 **66. Miners' welfare institutes.** (1) Subject to subsection (2), this Act applies to a relevant miners' welfare institute as it applies to a club, and accordingly—

(*a*) the premises of the institute are to be treated as the premises of a club,

(*b*) the persons enrolled as members of the institute are to be treated as the members of the club, and

(*c*) anything done by or on behalf of the trustees or managers in carrying on the institute is to be treated as done by or on behalf of the club.

(2) In determining for the purposes of section 61 whether a relevant miners' welfare institute is a qualifying club in relation to a qualifying club activity, the institute is to be taken to satisfy the following conditions—

(*a*) condition 3 in subsection (4) of section 62,
(*b*) condition 4 in subsection (5) of that section,
(*c*) condition 5 in subsection (6) of that section,
(*d*) the additional conditions in section 64.

(3) For the purposes of this section—

(*a*) "miners' welfare institute" means an association organised for the social well-being and recreation of persons employed in or about coal mines (or of such persons in particular), and
(*b*) a miners' welfare institute is "relevant" if it satisfies one of the following conditions.

(4) The first condition is that—

(*a*) the institute is managed by a committee or board, and
(*b*) at least two thirds of the committee or board consists—
  (i) partly of persons appointed or nominated, or appointed or elected from among persons nominated, by one or more licensed operators within the meaning of the Coal Industry Act 1994 (c 21), and
  (ii) partly of persons appointed or nominated, or appointed or elected from among persons nominated, by one or more organisations representing persons employed in or about coal mines.

(5) The second condition is that—

(*a*) the institute is managed by a committee or board, but
(*b*) the making of—
  (i) an appointment or nomination falling within subsection (4)(*b*)(i), or
  (ii) an appointment or nomination falling within subsection (4)(*b*)(ii),

is not practicable or would not be appropriate, and

(*c*) at least two thirds of the committee or board consists—
  (i) partly of persons employed, or formerly employed, in or about coal mines, and
  (ii) partly of persons appointed by the Coal Industry Social Welfare Organisation or a body or person to which the functions of that Organisation have been transferred under section 12(3) of the Miners' Welfare Act 1952 (c 23).

(6) The third condition is that the premises of the institute are held on trusts to which section 2 of the Recreational Charities Act 1958 (c 17) applies.
[Licensing Act 2003, s 66.]

Interpretation

8–19891 67. Associate members and their guests. (1) Any reference in this Act (other than this section) to a guest of a member of a club includes a reference to—

(*a*) an associate member of the club, and
(*b*) a guest of an associate member of the club.

(2) For the purposes of this Act a person is an "associate member" of a club if—

(*a*) in accordance with the rules of the club, he is admitted to its premises as being a member of another club, and
(*b*) that other club is a recognised club (see section 193).

[Licensing Act 2003, s 67.]

8–19892 68. The relevant licensing authority. *Determination of relevant licensing authority for a club dependent on location of whole, or greater part of club premises.*

8–19893 69. Authorised persons, interested parties and responsible authorities. *Authorised persons, interested parties and responsible authorities are the same for club premises as they are for premises licences*[1].

1. See s 13, ante, for full list.

8–19894 70. Other definitions relating to clubs. In this Part—

"secretary", in relation to a club, includes any person (whether or not an officer of the club) performing the duties of a secretary;

"supply of alcohol to members or guests" means, in the case of any club,—

(*a*) the supply of alcohol by or on behalf of the club to, or to the order of, a member of the club, or
(*b*) the sale by retail of alcohol by or on behalf of the club to a guest of a member of the club for consumption on the premises where the sale takes place,

and related expressions are to be construed accordingly.
[Licensing Act 2003, s 70.]

Grant of club premises certificate

8–19895 71. Application for club premises certificate. *Application to be in the prescribed form and accompanied by a Club Operating Schedule; application to be advertised in accordance with regulations*[1].

1. See the Licensing Act 2003 (Premises Licences and Club Premises Certificates) Regulations 2005, SI 2005/42.

8–19896 72. Determination of application for club premises certificate. (1) This section applies where the relevant licensing authority—

(*a*) receives an application for a club premises certificate made in accordance with section 71, and
(*b*) is satisfied that the applicant has complied with any requirement imposed on the applicant under subsection (6) of that section.

(2) Subject to subsection (3), the authority must grant the certificate in accordance with the application subject only to—

(*a*) such conditions as are consistent with the club operating schedule accompanying the application, and
(*b*) any conditions which must under section 73(2) to (5) or 74 be included in the certificate.

(3) Where relevant representations are made, the authority must—

(*a*) hold a hearing to consider them, unless the authority, the applicant and each person who has made such representations agree that a hearing is unnecessary, and
(*b*) having regard to the representations, take such of the steps mentioned in subsection (4) (if any) as it considers necessary for the promotion of the licensing objectives.

(4) The steps are—

(*a*) to grant the certificate subject to—
 (i) the conditions mentioned in subsection (2)(*a*) modified to such extent as the authority considers necessary for the promotion of the licensing objectives, and
 (ii) any conditions which must under section 73(2) to (5) or 74 be included in the certificate;
(*b*) to exclude from the scope of the certificate any of the qualifying club activities to which the application relates;
(*c*) to reject the application.

(5) Subsections (2) and (3)(*b*) are subject to section 73(1) (certificate may authorise off-supplies only if it authorises on-supplies).

(6) For the purposes of subsection (4)(*a*)(4)(*a*) the conditions mentioned in subsection (2)(*a*) are modified if any of them is altered or omitted or any new condition is added.

(7) For the purposes of this section, "relevant representations" means representations which—

(*a*) are about the likely effect of the grant of the certificate on the promotion of the licensing objectives, and
(*b*) meet the requirements of subsection (8).

(8) The requirements are—

(*a*) that the representations were made by an interested party or responsible authority within the period prescribed under section 71(6)(*c*),
(*b*) that they have not been withdrawn, and
(*c*) in the case of representations made by an interested party (who is not also a responsible authority), that they are not, in the opinion of the relevant licensing authority, frivolous or vexatious.

(9) Where the authority determines for the purposes of subsection (8)(*c*) that any representations are frivolous or vexatious, it must notify the person who made them of the reasons for its determination.

(10) In discharging its duty under subsection (2) or (3)(*b*) a licensing authority may grant a club premises certificate subject to different conditions in respect of—

(*a*) different parts of the premises concerned;
(*b*) different qualifying club activities.

[Licensing Act 2003, s 72.]

8–19897 73. Certificate authorising supply of alcohol for consumption off the premises. (1) A club premises certificate may not authorise the supply of alcohol for consumption off the premises unless it also authorises the supply of alcohol to a member of the club for consumption on those premises.

(2) A club premises certificate which authorises the supply of alcohol for consumption off the premises must include the following conditions.

(3) The first condition is that the supply must be made at a time when the premises are open for the purposes of supplying alcohol, in accordance with the club premises certificate, to members of the club for consumption on the premises.

(4) The second condition is that any alcohol supplied for consumption off the premises must be in a sealed container.

(5) The third condition is that any supply of alcohol for consumption off the premises must be made to a member of the club in person.

[Licensing Act 2003, s 73.]

8–19898 74. Mandatory condition: exhibition of films. (1) Where a club premises certificate authorises the exhibition of films, the certificate must include a condition requiring the admission of children to the exhibition of any film to be restricted in accordance with this section.

(2) Where the film classification body is specified in the certificate, unless subsection (3)(*b*) applies, admission of children must be restricted in accordance with any recommendation made by that body.

(3) Where—

(*a*) the film classification body is not specified in the certificate, or

(*b*) the relevant licensing authority has notified the club which holds the certificate that this subsection applies to the film in question,

admission of children must be restricted in accordance with any recommendation made by that licensing authority.

(4) In this section—

"children" means persons aged under 18; and

"film classification body" means the person or persons designated as the authority under section 4 of the Video Recordings Act 1984 (c 39) (authority to determine suitability of video works for classification).

[Licensing Act 2003, s 74.]

8–19899 75. Prohibited conditions: associate members and their guests. (1) Where the rules of a club provide for the sale by retail of alcohol on any premises by or on behalf of the club to, or to a guest of, an associate member[1] of the club, no condition may be attached to a club premises certificate in respect of the sale by retail of alcohol on those premises by or on behalf of the club so as to prevent the sale by retail of alcohol to any such associate member or guest.

(2) Where the rules of a club provide for the provision of any regulated entertainment on any premises by or on behalf of the club to, or to a guest of, an associate member of the club, no condition may be attached to a club premises certificate in respect of the provision of any such regulated entertainment on those premises by or on behalf of the club so as to prevent its provision to any such associate member or guest.

[Licensing Act 2003, s 75.]

1. For "associate members" and "guests", see s 67, ante.

8–19900 76. Prohibited conditions: plays. (1) In relation to a club premises certificate which authorises the performance of plays, no condition may be attached to the certificate as to the nature of the plays which may be performed, or the manner of performing plays, under the certificate.

(2) But subsection (1) does not prevent a licensing authority imposing, in accordance with section 72(2) or (3)(*b*), 85(3)(*b*) or 88(3), any condition which it considers necessary on the grounds of public safety.

[Licensing Act 2003, s 76.]

8–19901 77. Grant or rejection of application for club premises certificate. (1) Where an application is granted under section 72, the relevant licensing authority must forthwith—

(*a*) give a notice to that effect to—

(i) the applicant,

(ii) any person who made relevant representations in respect of the application, and

(iii) the chief officer of police for the police area (or each police area) in which the premises are situated, and

(*b*) issue the club with the club premises certificate and a summary of it.

(2) Where relevant representations were made in respect of the application, the notice under subsection (1)(*a*) must specify the authority's reasons for its decision as to the steps (if any) to take under section 72(3)(*b*).

(3) Where an application is rejected under section 72, the relevant licensing authority must forthwith give a notice to that effect, stating its reasons for that decision, to—

(*a*) the applicant,
(*b*) any person who made relevant representations in respect of the application, and
(*c*) the chief officer of police for the police area (or each police area) in which the premises are situated.

(4) In this section "relevant representations" has the meaning given in section 72(6).
[Licensing Act 2003, s 77.]

8–19902 **78. Form of certificate and summary.** *Licence and summary to be in form prescribed*[1].

1. See the Licensing Act 2003 (Premises Licences and Club Premises Certificates) Regulations 2005, SI 2005/42.

8–19903 **79. Theft, loss, etc of certificate or summary.** *Power to apply for duplicate licence or summary on payment of fee.*

Duration of certificate

8–19904 **80. Period of validity of club premises certificate.** *Club premises certificate to have effect until withdrawn under ss 88 or 90 or until lapses. Certificate of no effect if suspended following a review under s 88.*

8–19905 **81. Surrender of club premises certificate.** *Club may surrender certificate by giving notice to licensing authority. Certificate lapses on receipt of notice.*

Duty to notify certain changes

8–19906 **82. Notification of change of name or alteration of rules of club.** (1) Where a club—
(*a*) holds a club premises certificate, or
(*b*) has made an application for a club premises certificate which has not been determined by the relevant licensing authority,

the secretary[1] of the club must give the relevant licensing authority notice of any change in the name, or alteration made to the rules, of the club.

(2) Subsection (1) is subject to regulations under section 92(1) (power to prescribe fee to accompany application).

(3) A notice under subsection (1) by a club which holds a club premises certificate must be accompanied by the certificate or, if that is not practicable, by a statement of the reasons for the failure to produce the certificate.

(4) An authority notified under this section of a change in the name, or alteration to the rules, of a club must amend the club premises certificate accordingly.

(5) But nothing in subsection (4) requires or authorises the making of any amendment to a club premises certificate so as to change the premises to which the certificate relates (and no amendment made under that subsection to a club premises certificate has effect so as to change those premises).

(6) If a notice required by this section is not given within the 28 days following the day on which the change of name or alteration to the rules is made, the secretary of the club commits an offence.

(7) A person guilty of an offence under subsection (6) is liable on summary conviction to a fine not exceeding level 2 on the standard scale.
[Licensing Act 2003, s 82.]

1. For the secretary of a club, see s 70, ante.

8–19907 **83. Change of relevant registered address of club.** (1) A club which holds a club premises certificate may give the relevant licensing authority notice of any change desired to be made in the address which is to be the club's relevant registered address.

(2) If a club which holds a club premises certificate ceases to have any authority to make use of the address which is its relevant registered address, it must as soon as reasonably practicable give to the relevant licensing authority notice of the change to be made in the address which is to be the club's relevant registered address.

(3) Subsections (1) and (2) are subject to regulations under section 92(1) (power to prescribe fee to accompany application).

(4) A notice under subsection (1) or (2) must also be accompanied by the club premises certificate or, if that is not practicable, by a statement of the reasons for the failure to produce the certificate.

(5) An authority notified under subsection (1) or (2) of a change to be made in the relevant registered address of a club must amend the club premises certificate accordingly.

(6) If a club fails, without reasonable excuse, to comply with subsection (2) the secretary commits an offence.

(7) A person guilty of an offence under subsection (6) is liable on summary conviction to a fine not exceeding level 2 on the standard scale.

(8) In this section "relevant registered address" has the meaning given in section 184(7).
[Licensing Act 2003, s 83.]

Variation of certificates

8–19908 84. Application to vary club premises certificate. *Application for variation of club premises certificate to be in the prescribed form and advertised in accordance with Regulations. The Licensing Act 2003 (Premises Licences and Club Premises Certificates) Regulations 2005, SI 2005/42 have been made.*

8–19909 85. Determination of application under section 84. (1) This section applies where the relevant licensing authority—

(*a*) receives an application, made in accordance with section 84, to vary a club premises certificate, and

(*b*) is satisfied that the applicant has complied with any requirement imposed by virtue of subsection (4) of that section.

(2) Subject to subsection (3) and section 86(6), the authority must grant the application.

(3) Where relevant representations are made, the authority must—

(*a*) hold a hearing to consider them, unless the authority, the applicant and each person who has made such representations agree that a hearing is unnecessary, and

(*b*) having regard to the representations, take such of the steps mentioned in subsection (4) (if any) as it considers necessary for the promotion of the licensing objectives.

(4) The steps are—

(*a*) to modify the conditions of the certificate;

(*b*) to reject the whole or part of the application;

and for this purpose the conditions of the certificate are modified if any of them is altered or omitted or any new condition is added.

(5) In this section "relevant representations" means representations which—

(*a*) are about the likely effect of the grant of the application on the promotion of the licensing objectives, and

(*b*) meet the requirements of subsection (6).

(6) The requirements are—

(*a*) that the representations are made by an interested party or responsible authority within the period prescribed under section 71(6)(*c*) by virtue of section 84(4),

(*b*) that they have not been withdrawn, and

(*c*) in the case of representations made by an interested party (who is not also a responsible authority), that they are not, in the opinion of the relevant licensing authority, frivolous or vexatious.

(7) Subsections (2) and (3) are subject to sections 73 and 74 (mandatory conditions relating to supply of alcohol for consumption off the premises and to exhibition of films).
[Licensing Act 2003, s 85.]

8–19910 86. Supplementary provision about applications under section 84. (1) Where an application (or any part of an application) is granted under section 85, the relevant licensing authority must forthwith give a notice to that effect to—

(*a*) the applicant,

(*b*) any person who made relevant representations in respect of the application, and

(*c*) the chief officer of police for the police area (or each police area) in which the premises are situated.

(2) Where relevant representations were made in respect of the application, the notice under subsection (1) must specify the authority's reasons for its decision as to the steps (if any) to take under section 85(3)(*b*).

(3) The notice under subsection (1) must specify the time when the variation in question takes effect.

That time is the time specified in the application or, if that time is before the applicant is given the notice, such later time as the relevant licensing authority specifies in the notice.

(4) Where an application (or any part of an application) is rejected under section 85, the relevant licensing authority must forthwith give a notice to that effect stating its reasons for rejecting the application to—

(*a*) the applicant,

(*b*) any person who made relevant representations, and

(*c*) the chief officer of police for the police area (or each police area) in which the premises are situated.

(5) Where the relevant licensing authority determines for the purposes of section 85(6)(*c*) that any representations are frivolous or vexatious, it must give the person who made them its reasons for that determination.

(6) A club premises certificate may not be varied under section 85 so as to vary substantially the premises to which it relates.

(7) In discharging its duty under subsection (2) or (3)(*b*) of that section, a licensing authority may vary a club premises certificate so that it has effect subject to different conditions in respect of—

(*a*) different parts of the premises concerned;
(*b*) different qualifying club activities.

(8) In this section "relevant representations" has the meaning given in section 85(5).
[Licensing Act 2003, s 86.]

Review of certificates

8–19911 **87. Application for review of club premises certificate.** (1) Where a club holds a club premises certificate—

(*a*) an interested party,
(*b*) a responsible authority, or
(*c*) a member of the club,

may apply to the relevant licensing authority for a review of the certificate.

(2) Subsection (1) is subject to regulations under section 91 (form etc of applications).

(3) The Secretary of State must by regulations[1] under this section—

(*a*) require the applicant to give a notice containing details of the application to the club and each responsible authority within such period as may be prescribed;
(*b*) require the authority to advertise the application and invite representations relating to it to be made to the authority;
(*c*) prescribe the period during which representations may be made by the club, any responsible authority and any interested party;
(*d*) require any notice under paragraph (*a*) or advertisement under paragraph (*b*) to specify that period.

(4) The relevant licensing authority may, at any time, reject any ground for review specified in an application under this section if it is satisfied—

(*a*) that the ground is not relevant to one or more of the licensing objectives, or
(*b*) in the case of an application made by a person other than a responsible authority, that—
  (i) the ground is frivolous or vexatious, or
  (ii) the ground is a repetition.

(5) For this purpose a ground for review is a repetition if—

(*a*) it is identical or substantially similar to—
  (i) a ground for review specified in an earlier application for review made in respect of the same club premises certificate and determined under section 88, or
  (ii) representations considered by the relevant licensing authority in accordance with section 72, before it determined the application for the club premises certificate under that section, and
(*b*) a reasonable interval has not elapsed since that earlier application or that grant.

(6) Where the authority rejects a ground for review under subsection (4)(*b*), it must notify the applicant of its decision and, if the ground was rejected because it was frivolous or vexatious, the authority must notify him of its reasons for making that decision.

(7) The application is to be treated as rejected to the extent that any of the grounds for review are rejected under subsection (4).

Accordingly, the requirements imposed under subsection (3)(*a*) and (*b*) and by section 88 (so far as not already met) apply only to so much (if any) of the application as has not been rejected.
[Licensing Act 2003, s 87.]

1. See the Licensing Act 2003 (Premises Licences and Club Premises Certificates) Regulations 2005, SI 2005/42.

8–19912 **88. Determination of application for review.** (1) This section applies where—

(*a*) the relevant licensing authority receives an application made in accordance with section 87,
(*b*) the applicant has complied with any requirement imposed by virtue of subsection (3)(*a*) or (*d*) of that section, and
(*c*) the authority has complied with any requirement imposed on it under subsection (3)(*b*) or (*d*) of that section.

(2) Before determining the application, the authority must hold a hearing to consider it and any relevant representations.

(3) The authority must, having regard to the application and any relevant representations, take such of the steps mentioned in subsection (4) (if any) as it considers necessary for the promotion of the licensing objectives.

(4) The steps are—

(*a*) to modify the conditions of the certificate;
(*b*) to exclude a qualifying club activity from the scope of the certificate;
(*c*) to suspend the certificate for a period not exceeding three months;
(*d*) to withdraw the certificate;

and for this purpose the conditions of the certificate are modified if any of them is altered or omitted or any new condition is added.

(5) Subsection (3) is subject to sections 73 and 74 (mandatory conditions relating to supply of alcohol for consumption off the premises and to exhibition of films).

(6) Where the authority takes a step within subsection (4)(*a*) or (*b*), it may provide that the modification or exclusion is to have effect for only such period (not exceeding three months) as it may specify.

(7) In this section "relevant representations" means representations which—

(*a*) are relevant to one or more of the licensing objectives, and
(*b*) meet the requirements of subsection (8).

(8) The requirements are—

(*a*) that the representations are made by the club, a responsible authority or an interested party within the period prescribed under section 87(3)(*c*),
(*b*) that they have not been withdrawn, and
(*c*) if they are made by an interested party (who is not also a responsible authority), that they are not, in the opinion of the relevant licensing authority, frivolous or vexatious.

(9) Where the relevant licensing authority determines that any representations are frivolous or vexatious, it must give the person who made them its reasons for that determination.

(10) Where a licensing authority determines an application for review under this section it must notify the determination and its reasons for making it to—

(*a*) the club,
(*b*) the applicant,
(*c*) any person who made relevant representations, and
(*d*) the chief officer of police for the police area (or each police area) in which the premises are situated.

(11) A determination under this section does not have effect—

(*a*) until the end of the period given for appealing against the decision, or
(*b*) if the decision is appealed against, until the appeal is disposed of.

[Licensing Act 2003, s 88.]

8–19913 89. Supplementary provision about review. *Licensing authority able to determine review which has been applied for by itself in its separate capacity as a responsible authority.*

Withdrawal of certificates

8–19914 90. Club ceasing to be a qualifying club. (1) Where—

(*a*) a club holds a club premises certificate, and
(*b*) it appears to the relevant licensing authority that the club does not satisfy the conditions for being a qualifying club in relation to a qualifying club activity to which the certificate relates (see section 61),

the authority must give a notice to the club withdrawing the certificate, so far as relating to that activity.

(2) Where the only reason that the club does not satisfy the conditions for being a qualifying club in relation to the activity in question is that the club has fewer than the required number of members, the notice withdrawing the certificate must state that the withdrawal—

(*a*) does not take effect until immediately after the end of the period of three months following the date of the notice, and
(*b*) will not take effect if, at the end of that period, the club again has at least the required number of members.

(3) The references in subsection (2) to the required number of members are references to the minimum number of members required by condition 4 in section 62(5) (25 at the passing of this Act).

(4) Nothing in subsection (2) prevents the giving of a further notice of withdrawal under this section at any time.

(5) Where a justice of the peace is satisfied, on information on oath, that there are reasonable grounds for believing—

(*a*) that a club which holds a club premises certificate does not satisfy the conditions for being a qualifying club in relation to a qualifying club activity to which the certificate relates, and (*b*) that evidence of that fact is to be obtained at the premises to which the certificate relates,

he may issue a warrant authorising a constable to enter the premises, if necessary by force, at any time within one month from the time of the issue of the warrant, and search them.

(6) A person who enters premises under the authority of a warrant under subsection (5) may seize and remove any documents relating to the business of the club in question.
[Licensing Act 2003, s 90.]

General provision

8–19915 **91. Form etc of applications and notices under Part 4.** *Applications and notices to be in the form prescribed by regulations*[1].

1. See the Licensing Act 2003 (Premises Licences and Club Premises Certificates) Regulations 2005, SI 2005/42.

Production of certificate, rights of entry, etc

8–19916 **93. Licensing authority's duty to update club premises certificate.** (1) Where—

(*a*) the relevant licensing authority, in relation to a club premises certificate, makes a determination or receives a notice under this Part, or
(*b*) an appeal against a decision under this Part is disposed of,

the relevant licensing authority must make the appropriate amendments (if any) to the certificate and, if necessary, issue a new summary of the certificate.

(2) Where a licensing authority is not in possession of the club premises certificate, it may, for the purpose of discharging its obligations under subsection (1), require the secretary of the club to produce the certificate to the authority within 14 days from the date on which the club is notified of the requirement.

(3) A person commits an offence if he fails, without reasonable excuse, to comply with a requirement under subsection (2).

(4) A person guilty of an offence under subsection (3) is liable on summary conviction to a fine not exceeding level 2 on the standard scale.
[Licensing Act 2003, s 93.]

8–19917 **94. Duty to keep and produce certificate.** (1) This section applies whenever premises in respect of which a club premises certificate has effect are being used for one or more qualifying club activities authorised by the certificate.

(2) The secretary[1] of the club must secure that the certificate, or a certified copy of it, is kept at the premises in the custody or under the control of a person (the "nominated person") who—

(*a*) falls within subsection (3),
(*b*) has been nominated for the purpose by the secretary in writing, and
(*c*) has been identified to the relevant licensing authority in a notice given by the secretary.

(3) The persons who fall within this subsection are—

(*a*) the secretary of the club,
(*b*) any member of the club,
(*c*) any person who works at the premises for the purposes of the club.

(4) The nominated person must secure that—

(*a*) the summary of the certificate or a certified copy of that summary, and
(*b*) a notice specifying the position which he holds at the premises,

are prominently displayed at the premises.

(5) The secretary commits an offence if he fails, without reasonable excuse, to comply with subsection (2).

(6) The nominated person commits an offence if he fails, without reasonable excuse, to comply with subsection (4).

(7) A constable or an authorised person may require the nominated person to produce the club premises certificate (or certified copy) for examination.

(8) An authorised person exercising the power conferred by subsection (7) must, if so requested, produce evidence of his authority to exercise the power.

(9) A person commits an offence if he fails, without reasonable excuse, to produce a club premises certificate or certified copy of a club premises certificate in accordance with a requirement under subsection (7).

(10) A person guilty of an offence under this section is liable on summary conviction to a fine not exceeding level 2 on the standard scale.

(11) In subsection (4) the reference to the summary of the certificate is a reference to the summary issued under section 77 or, where one or more summaries have subsequently been issued under section 93, the most recent summary to be so issued.

(12) Section 95 makes provision about certified copies of club premises certificates and of summaries of club premises certificates for the purposes of this section.
[Licensing Act 2003, s 94.]

1. For the secretary of a club, see s 70, ante.

8–19918 **95. Provision supplementary to section 94.** (1) Any reference in section 94 to a certified copy of a document is a reference to a copy of the document which is certified to be a true copy by—

(*a*) the relevant licensing authority,
(*b*) a solicitor or notary, or
(*c*) a person of a prescribed description.

(2) Any certified copy produced in accordance with a requirement under subsection 94(7) must be a copy of the document in the form in which it exists at the time.

(3) A document which purports to be a certified copy of a document is to be taken to be such a copy, and to comply with the requirements of subsection (2), unless the contrary is shown.
[Licensing Act 2003, s 95.]

8–19919 **96. Inspection of premises before grant of certificate etc.** (1) Subsection (2) applies where—

(*a*) a club applies for a club premises certificate in respect of any premises,
(*b*) a club applies under section 84 for the variation of a club premises certificate held by it, or
(*c*) an application is made under section 87 for review of a club premises certificate.

(2) On production of his authority—

(*a*) an authorised person, or
(*b*) a constable authorised by the chief officer of police,

may enter and inspect the premises.

(3) Any entry and inspection under this section must take place at a reasonable time on a day—

(*a*) which is not more than 14 days after the making of the application in question, and
(*b*) which is specified in the notice required by subsection (4).

(4) Before an authorised person or constable enters and inspects any premises under this section, at least 48 hours' notice must be given to the club.

(5) Any person obstructing an authorised person in the exercise of the power conferred by this section commits an offence.

(6) A person guilty of an offence under subsection (5) is liable on summary conviction to a fine not exceeding level 2 on the standard scale.

(7) The relevant licensing authority may, on the application of a responsible authority, extend by not more than 7 days the time allowed for carrying out an entry and inspection under this section.

(8) The relevant licensing authority may allow such an extension of time only if it appears to the authority that—

(*a*) reasonable steps had been taken for an authorised person or constable authorised by the applicant to inspect the premises in good time, but
(*b*) it was not possible for the inspection to take place within the time allowed.

[Licensing Act 2003, s 96.]

8–19920 **97. Other powers of entry and search.** (1) Where a club premises certificate has effect in respect of any premises, a constable may enter and search the premises if he has reasonable cause to believe—

(*a*) that an offence under section 4(3)(*a*), (*b*) or (*c*) of the Misuse of Drugs Act 1971 (c 38) (supplying or offering to supply, or being concerned in supplying or making an offer to supply, a controlled drug) has been, is being, or is about to be, committed there, or
(*b*) that there is likely to be a breach of the peace there.

(2) A constable exercising any power conferred by this section may, if necessary, use reasonable force.
[Licensing Act 2003, s 97.]

PART 5[1]

PERMITTED TEMPORARY ACTIVITIES

Introductory

8–19921 **98. Meaning of "permitted temporary activity".** (1) A licensable activity[2] is a permitted temporary activity by virtue of this Part if—

(*a*) it is carried on in accordance with a notice given in accordance with section 100, and
(*b*) the following conditions are satisfied.

(2) The first condition is that the requirements of sections 102 (acknowledgement of notice) and 104(1) (notification of police) are met in relation to the notice.

(3) The second condition is that the notice has not been withdrawn under this Part.

(4) The third condition is that no counter notice has been given under this Part in respect of the notice.

[Licensing Act 2003, s 98.]

1. Part 5 comprises ss 98–110.
2. For meaning of "licensable activity", see s 1(1), ante.

8–19922 99. The relevant licensing authority. In this Part references to the "relevant licensing authority", in relation to any premises, are references to—

(*a*) the licensing authority in whose area the premises are situated, or
(*b*) where the premises are situated in the areas of two or more licensing authorities, each of those authorities.

[Licensing Act 2003, s 99.]

Temporary event notices

8–19923 100. Temporary event notice. (1) Where it is proposed to use premises[1] for one or more licensable activities during a period not exceeding 96 hours, an individual may give to the relevant licensing authority notice of that proposal (a "temporary event notice").

(2) In this Act, the "premises user", in relation to a temporary event notice, is the individual who gave the notice.

(3) An individual may not give a temporary event notice unless he is aged 18 or over.

(4) A temporary event notice must be in the prescribed form and contain—

(*a*) a statement of the matters mentioned in subsection (5),
(*b*) where subsection (6) applies, a statement of the condition mentioned in that subsection, and
(*c*) such other information as may be prescribed[2].

(5) Those matters are—

(*a*) the licensable activities to which the proposal mentioned in subsection (1) relates ("the relevant licensable activities"),
(*b*) the period (not exceeding 96 hours) during which it is proposed to use the premises for those activities ("the event period"),
(*c*) the times during the event period when the premises user proposes that those licensable activities shall take place,
(*d*) the maximum number of persons (being a number less than 500) which the premises user proposes should, during those times, be allowed on the premises at the same time,
(*e*) where the relevant licensable activities include the supply of alcohol, whether supplies are proposed to be for consumption on the premises or off the premises, or both, and
(*f*) such other matters as may be prescribed[2].

(6) Where the relevant licensable activities include the supply of alcohol, the notice must make it a condition of using the premises for such supplies that all such supplies are made by or under the authority of the premises user.

(7) The temporary event notice—

(*a*) must be given to the relevant licensing authority (in duplicate) no later than ten working days before the day on which the event period begins, and
(*b*) must be accompanied by the prescribed[3] fee.

(8) The Secretary of State may, by order—

(*a*) amend subsections (1) and (5)(*b*) so as to substitute any period for the period for the time being specified there;
(*b*) amend subsection (5)(*d*) so as to substitute any number for the number for the time being specified there.

(9) In this section "supply of alcohol" means—

(*a*) the sale by retail of alcohol, or
(*b*) the supply of alcohol by or on behalf of a club to, or to the order of, a member of the club.

[Licensing Act 2003, s 100.]

1. For meaning of "premises", see s 193, post.
2. The Licensing Act 2003 (Permitted Temporary Activities) (Notices) Regulations 2005, SI 2005/2918 have been made.
3. The Licensing Act 2003 (Fees) Regulations 2005, SI 2005/79 have been made.

8–19924 101. Minimum of 24 hours between event periods. *Temporary Event Notice void if period specified in it starts or ends within 24 hours of another notice given in respect of the same premises by the premises user, or an associate or business colleague of that premises user.*

8–19925 102. Acknowledgement of notice. *Licensing authority obliged to acknowledge receipt of Temporary Event Notice within one working day of receipt, unless counter notice served under s 107 because permitted limits have been exceeded.*

8–19926 103. Withdrawal of notice. (1) A temporary event notice may be withdrawn by the premises user giving the relevant licensing authority a notice to that effect no later than 24 hours before the beginning of the event period specified in the temporary event notice.

(2) Nothing in section 102 or sections 104 to 107 applies in relation to a notice withdrawn in accordance with this section.

[Licensing Act 2003, s 103.]

Police objections

8–19927 104. Objection to notice by the police. *Copy of Temporary Event Notice to be served on Chief Officer of Police no later than 10 working days before event begins. Police must give objection notice within 48 hours if satisfied that use of premises in accordance with the Temporary Event Notice would undermine the crime prevention licensing objective.*

8–19928 105. Counter notice following police objection. (1) This section applies where an objection notice is given in respect of a temporary event notice.

(2) The relevant licensing authority must—

(*a*) hold a hearing to consider the objection notice, unless the premises user, the chief officer of police who gave the objection notice and the authority agree that a hearing is unnecessary, and

(*b*) having regard to the objection notice, give the premises user a counter notice under this section if it considers it necessary for the promotion of the crime prevention objective to do so.

(3) The relevant licensing authority must—

(*a*) in a case where it decides not to give a counter notice under this section, give the premises user and the relevant chief officer of police notice of the decision, and

(*b*) in any other case—

(i) give the premises user the counter notice and a notice stating the reasons for its decision, and

(ii) give the relevant chief officer of police a copy of both of those notices.

(4) A decision must be made under subsection (2)(*b*), and the requirements of subsection (3) must be met, at least 24 hours before the beginning of the event period specified in the temporary event notice.

(5) Where the premises are situated in the area of more than one licensing authority, the functions conferred on the relevant licensing authority by this section must be exercised by those authorities jointly.

(6) This section does not apply—

(*a*) if the objection notice has been withdrawn (whether by virtue of section 106 or otherwise), or

(*b*) if the premises user has been given a counter notice under section 107.

(7) In this section "objection notice" and "relevant chief officer of police" have the same meaning as in section 104.

[Licensing Act 2003, s 105.]

8–19929 106. Modification of notice following police objection. *Power of Chief Officer of Police, where an objection notice has been given, to modify the Temporary Event Notice with the agreement of the premises user so as to reach agreement with the premises user without the need for a hearing.*

Limits on temporary event notices

8–19930 107. Counter notice where permitted limits exceeded. *Duty of licensing authority to give counter notice if permitted limits exceeded. The giving of a counter notice under this section cannot be appealed to the magistrates' court.*

Rights of entry, production of notice, etc

8–19931 108. Right of entry where temporary event notice given. (1) A constable or an authorised officer may, at any reasonable time, enter the premises to which a temporary event notice relates to assess the likely effect of the notice on the promotion of the crime prevention objective.

(2) An authorised officer exercising the power conferred by this section must, if so requested, produce evidence of his authority to exercise the power.

(3) A person commits an offence if he intentionally obstructs an authorised officer exercising a power conferred by this section.

(4) A person guilty of an offence under this section is liable on summary conviction to a fine not exceeding level 2 on the standard scale.

(5) In this section "authorised officer" means—

(*a*) an officer of the licensing authority in whose area the premises are situated, or
(*b*) if the premises are situated in the area of more than one licensing authority, an officer of any of those authorities,

authorised for the purposes of this Act.
[Licensing Act 2003, s 108.]

8–19932 **109. Duty to keep and produce temporary event notice.** (1) This section applies whenever premises are being used for one or more licensable activities which are or are purported to be permitted temporary activities by virtue of this Part.

(2) The premises user must either—

(*a*) secure that a copy of the temporary event notice is prominently displayed at the premises, or
(*b*) meet the requirements of subsection (3).

(3) The requirements of this subsection are that the premises user must—

(*a*) secure that the temporary event notice is kept at the premises in—

(i) his custody, or
(ii) in the custody of a person who is present and working at the premises and whom he has nominated for the purposes of this section, and

(*b*) where the temporary event notice is in the custody of a person so nominated, secure that a notice specifying that fact and the position held at the premises by that person is prominently displayed at the premises.

(4) The premises user commits an offence if he fails, without reasonable excuse, to comply with subsection (2).

(5) Where—

(*a*) the temporary event notice is not displayed as mentioned in subsection (2)(*a*), and
(*b*) no notice is displayed as mentioned in subsection (3)(*b*),

a constable or authorised officer may require the premises user to produce the temporary event notice for examination.

(6) Where a notice is displayed as mentioned in subsection (3)(*b*), a constable or authorised officer may require the person specified in that notice to produce the temporary event notice for examination.

(7) An authorised officer exercising the power conferred by subsection (5) or (6) must, if so requested, produce evidence of his authority to exercise the power.

(8) A person commits an offence if he fails, without reasonable excuse, to produce a temporary event notice in accordance with a requirement under subsection (5) or (6).

(9) A person guilty of an offence under this section is liable on summary conviction to a fine not exceeding level 2 on the standard scale.

(10) In this section "authorised officer" has the meaning given in section 108(5).
[Licensing Act 2003, s 109.]

Miscellaneous

8–19933 **110. Theft, loss, etc of temporary event notice.** *Power to apply for a duplicate Temporary Event Notice on payment of a fee.*

PART 6[1]
PERSONAL LICENCES

Introductory

8–19934 **111. Personal licence.** (1) In this Act "personal licence" means a licence which—

(*a*) is granted by a licensing authority to an individual, and
(*b*) authorises that individual to supply alcohol, or authorise the supply of alcohol, in accordance with a premises licence.

(2) In subsection (1)(*b*) the reference to an individual supplying alcohol is to him—

(*a*) selling alcohol by retail, or
(*b*) supplying alcohol by or on behalf of a club to, or to the order of, a member of the club.

[Licensing Act 2003, s 111.]

1. Part 6 comprises ss 111–135 and Sch 4.

8–19935 112. The relevant licensing authority. For the purposes of this Part the "relevant licensing authority", in relation to a personal licence, is the licensing authority which granted the licence.
[Licensing Act 2003, s 112.]

8–19936 113. Meaning of "relevant offence" and "foreign offence". (1) In this Part "relevant offence" means an offence listed in Schedule 4.

(2) The Secretary of State may by order amend that list so as to add, modify or omit any entry.

(3) In this Part "foreign offence" means an offence (other than a relevant offence) under the law of any place outside England and Wales.
[Licensing Act 2003, s 113.]

8–19937 114. Spent convictions. For the purposes of this Part a conviction for a relevant offence or a foreign offence must be disregarded if it is spent for the purposes of the Rehabilitation of Offenders Act 1974 (c 53)[1].
[Licensing Act 2003, s 114.]

---

1. In PART III: SENTENCING, ante.

8–19938 115. Period of validity of personal licence. *Personal licence to have effect for 10 years and renewable for 10 year periods thereafter. Personal licence ceases to have effect if surrendered under s 116, revoked under s 119, or forfeited under s 129. Also of no effect during period of any suspension under s 129.*

8–19939 116. Surrender of personal licence. *Personal licence may be surrendered by giving of notice to licensing authority. Licence lapses on receipt of notice.*

Grant and renewal of licences

8–19940 117. Application for grant or renewal of personal licence. *Application for grant of personal licence to be made to licensing authority for the area where the applicant is ordinarily resident and to be in form prescribed by regulations*[1]*. Application for renewal to be made to licensing authority that granted the original licence and may be made during a 2 month period beginning 3 months before the licence is due to expire.*

---

1. The Licensing Act 2003 (Personal Licences) Regulations 2005, SI 200/41 have been made.

8–19941 118, 119. *Individual permitted to hold one personal licence only; personal licence deemed to continue if application for renewal not been determined before the date that the personal licence expires.*

8–19942 120. Determination of application for grant. (1) This section applies where an application for the grant of a personal licence is made to a licensing authority in accordance with section 117.

(2) The authority must grant the licence if it appears to it that—

(*a*) the applicant is aged 18 or over,
(*b*) he possesses a licensing qualification or is a person of a prescribed[1] description,
(*c*) no personal licence held by him has been forfeited in the period of five years ending with the day the application was made, and
(*d*) he has not been convicted of any relevant offence[2] or any foreign offence.

(3) The authority must reject the application if it appears to it that the applicant fails to meet the condition in paragraph (*a*), (*b*) or (*c*) of subsection (2).

(4) If it appears to the authority that the applicant meets the conditions in paragraphs (*a*), (*b*) and (*c*) of that subsection but fails to meet the condition in paragraph (*d*) of that subsection, the authority must give the chief officer of police for its area a notice to that effect.

(5) Where, having regard to—

(*a*) any conviction of the applicant for a relevant offence, and
(*b*) any conviction of his for a foreign offence which the chief officer of police considers to be comparable to a relevant offence,

the chief officer of police is satisfied that granting the licence would undermine the crime prevention objective, he must, within the period of 14 days beginning with the day he received the notice under subsection (4), give the authority a notice stating the reasons why he is so satisfied (an "objection notice").

(6) Where no objection notice is given within that period (or the notice is withdrawn), the authority must grant the application.

(7) In any other case, the authority—

(*a*) must hold a hearing to consider the objection notice, unless the applicant, the chief officer of police and the authority agree that it is unnecessary, and (*b*) having regard to the notice, must—

(i) reject the application if it considers it necessary for the promotion of the crime prevention objective to do so, and

(ii) grant the application in any other case.

(8) In this section "licensing qualification" means—

(*a*) a qualification—

(i) accredited at the time of its award, and

(ii) awarded by a body accredited at that time,

(*b*) a qualification awarded before the coming into force of this section which the Secretary of State certifies is to be treated for the purposes of this section as if it were a qualification within paragraph (*a*), or

(*c*) a qualification obtained in Scotland or Northern Ireland or in an EEA State (other than the United Kingdom) which is equivalent to a qualification within paragraph (*a*) or (*b*).

(9) For this purpose—

"accredited" means accredited by the Secretary of State; and

"EEA State" means a state which is a contracting party to the Agreement on the European Economic Area signed at Oporto on 2nd May 1992, as adjusted by the Protocol signed at Brussels on 17th March 1993.

[Licensing Act 2003, s 120.]

1. See the Licensing Act 2003 (Personal Licences) Regulations 2005, SI 2005/41.
2. For meaning of "relevant offence", see Sch 4, post.

8–19943 121. Determination of application for renewal. (1) This section applies where an application for the renewal of a personal licence is made to the relevant licensing authority in accordance with section 117.

(2) If it appears to the authority that the applicant has been convicted of any relevant offence or foreign offence since the relevant time, the relevant licensing authority must give notice to that effect to the chief officer of police for its area.

(3) Where, having regard to—

(*a*) any conviction of the applicant for a relevant offence, and

(*b*) any conviction of his for a foreign offence which the chief officer of police considers to be comparable to a relevant offence,

the chief officer of police is satisfied that renewing the licence would undermine the crime prevention objective, he must, within the period of 14 days beginning with the day he received the notice under subsection (2), give the authority a notice stating the reasons why he is so satisfied (an "objection notice").

(4) For the purposes of subsection (3)(*a*) and (*b*) it is irrelevant whether the conviction occurred before or after the relevant time.

(5) Where no objection notice is given within that period (or any such notice is withdrawn), the authority must grant the application.

(6) In any other case, the authority—

(*a*) must hold a hearing to consider the objection notice unless the applicant, the chief officer of police and the authority agree that it is unnecessary, and

(*b*) having regard to the notice, must—

(i) reject the application if it considers it necessary for the promotion of the crime prevention objective to do so, and

(ii) grant the application in any other case.

(7) In this section "the relevant time" means—

(*a*) if the personal licence has not been renewed since it was granted, the time it was granted, and

(*b*) if it has been renewed, the last time it was renewed.

[Licensing Act 2003, s 121.]

8–19944 122. Notification of determinations. (1) Where a licensing authority grants an application—

(*a*) it must give the applicant and the chief officer of police for its area a notice to that effect, and

(*b*) if the chief officer of police gave an objection notice (which was not withdrawn), the notice under paragraph (*a*) must contain a statement of the licensing authority's reasons for granting the application.

(2) A licensing authority which rejects an application must give the applicant and the chief officer of police for its area a notice to that effect containing a statement of the authority's reasons for rejecting the application.

(3) In this section—

"application" means an application for the grant or renewal of a personal licence; and
"objection notice" has the meaning given in section 120 or 121, as the case may be.
[Licensing Act 2003, s 122.]

8–19945 123. Duty to notify licensing authority of convictions during application period. (1) Where an applicant for the grant or renewal of a personal licence is convicted of a relevant offence or a foreign offence during the application period, he must as soon as reasonably practicable notify the conviction to the authority to which the application is made.

(2) A person commits an offence if he fails, without reasonable excuse, to comply with subsection (1).

(3) A person guilty of an offence under this section is liable on summary conviction to a fine not exceeding level 4 on the standard scale.

(4) In this section "the application period" means the period that—

(*a*) begins when the application for grant or renewal is made, and
(*b*) ends when the application is determined or withdrawn.

[Licensing Act 2003, s 123.]

8–19946 124. Convictions coming to light after grant or renewal. (1) This section applies where, after a licensing authority has granted or renewed a personal licence, it becomes aware (whether by virtue of section 123(1), 131 or 132 or otherwise) that the holder of a personal licence ("the offender") was convicted during the application period of any relevant offence or foreign offence.

(2) The licensing authority must give a notice to that effect to the chief officer of police for its area.

(3) Where, having regard to—

(*a*) any conviction of the applicant for a relevant offence, and
(*b*) any conviction of his for a foreign offence which the chief officer of police considers to be comparable to a relevant offence,

which occurred before the end of the application period, the chief officer of police is satisfied that continuation of the licence would undermine the crime prevention objective, he must, within the period of 14 days beginning with the day he received the notice under subsection (2), give the authority a notice stating the reasons why he is so satisfied (an "objection notice").

(4) Where an objection notice is given within that period (and not withdrawn), the authority—

(*a*) must hold a hearing to consider the objection notice, unless the holder of the licence, the chief officer of police and the authority agree it is unnecessary, and
(*b*) having regard to the notice, must revoke the licence if it considers it necessary for the promotion of the crime prevention objective to do so.

(5) Where the authority revokes or decides not to revoke a licence under subsection (4) it must notify the offender and the chief officer of police of the decision and its reasons for making it.

(6) A decision under this section does not have effect—

(*a*) until the end of the period given for appealing against the decision, or
(*b*) if the decision is appealed against, until the appeal is disposed of.

(7) In this section "application period", in relation to the grant or renewal of a personal licence, means the period that—

(*a*) begins when the application for the grant or renewal is made, and
(*b*) ends at the time of the grant or renewal.

[Licensing Act 2003, s 124.]

8–19947 125. Form of personal licence. *Form of personal licence prescribed by regulations*[1].

---

1. The Licensing Act 2003 (Personal Licences) Regulations 2005, SI 2005/41 have been made.

8–19948 126. Theft, loss, etc of personal licence. *Power to apply for duplicate personal licence on payment of fee.*

Duty to notify certain changes

8–19949 127. Duty to notify change of name or address. (1) The holder of a personal licence must, as soon as reasonably practicable, notify the relevant licensing authority of any change in his name or address as stated in the personal licence.

(2) Subsection (1) is subject to regulations under section 133(2) (power to prescribe fee to accompany notice).

(3) A notice under subsection (1) must also be accompanied by the personal licence or, if that is not practicable, by a statement of the reasons for the failure to provide the licence.

(4) A person commits an offence if he fails, without reasonable excuse, to comply with this section.

(5) A person guilty of an offence under subsection (4) is liable on summary conviction to a fine not exceeding level 2 on the standard scale.
[Licensing Act 2003, s 127.]

Conviction of licence holder for relevant offence

8–19950 128. Duty to notify court of personal licence. (1) Where the holder of a personal licence is charged with a relevant offence[1], he must, no later than the time he makes his first appearance in a magistrates' court in connection with that offence—

(*a*) produce to the court the personal licence, or
(*b*) if that is not practicable, notify the court of the existence of the personal licence and the identity of the relevant licensing authority and of the reasons why he cannot produce the licence.

(2) Subsection (3) applies where a person charged with a relevant offence is granted a personal licence—

(*a*) after his first appearance in a magistrates' court in connection with that offence, but
(*b*) before—

(i) his conviction, and sentencing for the offence, or his acquittal, or,
(ii) where an appeal is brought against his conviction, sentence or acquittal, the disposal of that appeal.

(3) At his next appearance in court in connection with that offence, that person must—

(*a*) produce to the court the personal licence, or
(*b*) if that is not practicable, notify the court of the existence of the personal licence and the identity of the relevant licensing authority and of the reasons why he cannot produce the licence.

(4) Where—

(*a*) a person charged with a relevant offence has produced his licence to, or notified, a court under subsection (1) or (3), and
(*b*) before he is convicted of and sentenced for, or acquitted of, that offence, a notifiable event occurs in respect of the licence,

he must, at his next appearance in court in connection with that offence, notify the court of that event.

(5) For this purpose a "notifiable event" in relation to a personal licence means any of the following—

(*a*) the making or withdrawal of an application for renewal of the licence;
(*b*) the surrender of the licence under section 116;
(*c*) the renewal of the licence under section 121;
(*d*) the revocation of the licence under section 124.

(6) A person commits an offence if he fails, without reasonable excuse, to comply with this section.

(7) A person guilty of an offence under subsection (6) is liable on summary conviction to a fine not exceeding level 2 on the standard scale.
[Licensing Act 2003, s 128.]

---

1. For meaning of "relevant offence", see Sch 4, post.

8–19951 129. Forfeiture or suspension of licence on conviction for relevant offence. (1) This section applies where the holder of a personal licence is convicted of a relevant offence[1] by or before a court in England and Wales.

(2) The court may—

(*a*) order the forfeiture of the licence, or
(*b*) order its suspension for a period not exceeding six months.

(3) In determining whether to make an order under subsection (2), the court may take account of any previous conviction of the holder for a relevant offence.

(4) Where a court makes an order under this section it may suspend the order pending an appeal against it.

(5) Subject to subsection (4) and section 130, an order under this section takes effect immediately after it is made.
[Licensing Act 2003, s 129.]

---

1. For meaning of "relevant offence", see Sch 4, post.

8–19952 131. Court's duty to notify licensing authority of convictions. (1) This section applies where a person who holds a personal licence ("the relevant person") is convicted, by or before a court in England and Wales, of a relevant offence in a case where—

(*a*) the relevant person has given notice under section 128 (notification of personal licence), or
(*b*) the court is, for any other reason, aware of the existence of that personal licence.

(2) The appropriate officer of the court must (as soon as reasonably practicable)—

(*a*) send to the relevant licensing authority a notice specifying—

(i) the name and address of the relevant person,
(ii) the nature and date of the conviction, and
(iii) any sentence passed in respect of it, including any order made under section 129, and

(*b*) send a copy of the notice to the relevant person.

(3) Where, on an appeal against the relevant person's conviction for the relevant offence or against the sentence imposed on him for that offence, his conviction is quashed or a new sentence is substituted for that sentence, the court which determines the appeal must (as soon as reasonably practicable) arrange—

(*a*) for notice of the quashing of the conviction or the substituting of the sentence to be sent to the relevant licensing authority, and
(*b*) for a copy of the notice to be sent to the relevant person.

(4) Where the case is referred to the Court of Appeal under section 36 of the Criminal Justice Act 1988 (c 33) (review of lenient sentence), the court must cause—

(*a*) notice of any action it takes under subsection (1) of that section to be sent to the relevant licensing authority, and
(*b*) a copy of the notice to be sent to the relevant person.

(5) For the purposes of subsection (2) "the appropriate officer" is—

(*a*) in the case of a magistrates' court, the clerk of the court, and
(*b*) in the case of the Crown Court, the appropriate officer;

and section 141 of the Magistrates' Courts Act 1980 (c 43) (meaning of "clerk of a magistrates' court") applies in relation to this subsection as it applies in relation to that section.
[Licensing Act 2003, s 131.]

8–19953 132. Licence holder's duty to notify licensing authority of convictions. (1) Subsection (2) applies where the holder of a personal licence—

(*a*) is convicted of a relevant offence, in a case where section 131(1) does not apply, or
(*b*) is convicted of a foreign offence.

(2) The holder must—

(*a*) as soon as reasonably practicable after the conviction, give the relevant licensing authority a notice containing details of the nature and date of the conviction, and any sentence imposed on him in respect of it, and
(*b*) as soon as reasonably practicable after the determination of any appeal against the conviction or sentence, or of any reference under section 36 of the Criminal Justice Act 1988 (c 33) in respect of the case, give the relevant licensing authority a notice containing details of the determination.

(3) A notice under subsection (2) must be accompanied by the personal licence or, if that is not practicable, a statement of the reasons for the failure to provide the licence.

(4) A person commits an offence if he fails, without reasonable excuse, to comply with this section.

(5) A person guilty of an offence under subsection (4) is liable on summary conviction to a fine not exceeding level 2 on the standard scale.
[Licensing Act 2003, s 132.]

General provision

8–19954 133. Form etc of applications and notices under Part 6. *Form of application or notice, manner in which it is to be made or give and information and documents to accompany it and any fee payable to be prescribed by regulations[1].*

1. The Licensing Act 2003 (Personal Licences) Regulations 2005, SI 2005/41 and the Licensing Act 2003 (Fees) Regulations 2005, SI 2005/79 have been made.

8–19955 134. Licensing authority's duty to update licence document. (1) Where—

(*a*) the relevant licensing authority makes a determination under section 121 or 124(4),
(*b*) it receives a notice under section 123(1), 127, 131 or 132, or
(*c*) an appeal against a decision under this Part is disposed of,

in relation to a personal licence, the authority must make the appropriate amendments (if any) to the licence.

(2) Where, under section 131, notice is given of the making of an order under section 129, the relevant licensing authority must make an endorsement on the licence stating the terms of the order.

(3) Where, under section 131, notice is given of the quashing of such an order, any endorsement previously made under subsection (2) in respect of it must be cancelled.

(4) Where a licensing authority is not in possession of a personal licence, it may, for the purposes of discharging its obligations under this section, require the holder of the licence to produce it to the authority within 14 days beginning with the day on which he is notified of the requirement.

(5) A person commits an offence if he fails, without reasonable excuse, to comply with a requirement under subsection (4).

(6) A person guilty of an offence under subsection (5) is liable on summary conviction to a fine not exceeding level 2 on the standard scale.

[Licensing Act 2003, s 134.]

Production of licence

8–19956 **135. Licence holder's duty to produce licence.** (1) This section applies where the holder of a personal licence is on premises to make or authorise the supply of alcohol, and such supplies—

(*a*) are authorised by a premises licence in respect of those premises, or

(*b*) are a permitted temporary activity on the premises by virtue of a temporary event notice given under Part 5 in respect of which he is the premises user.

(2) Any constable or authorised officer may require the holder of the personal licence to produce that licence for examination.

(3) An authorised officer exercising the power conferred by subsection (2) must, if so requested, produce evidence of his authority to exercise the power.

(4) A person who fails, without reasonable excuse, to comply with a requirement under subsection (2) is guilty of an offence.

(5) A person guilty of an offence under subsection (4) is liable on summary conviction to a fine not exceeding level 2 on the standard scale.

(6) In this section "authorised officer" means an officer of a licensing authority authorised by the authority for the purposes of this Act.

[Licensing Act 2003, s 135.]

PART 7[1]
OFFENCES

Unauthorised licensable activities

8–19957 **136. Unauthorised licensable activities.** (1) A person commits an offence[2] if—

(*a*) he carries on or attempts to carry on a licensable activity[3] on or from any premises otherwise than under and in accordance with an authorisation, or

(*b*) he knowingly allows a licensable activity[3] to be so carried on.

(2) Where the licensable activity[3] in question is the provision of regulated entertainment, a person does not commit an offence under this section if his only involvement in the provision of the entertainment is that he—

(*a*) performs in a play,

(*b*) participates as a sportsman in an indoor sporting event,

(*c*) boxes or wrestles in a boxing or wrestling entertainment,

(*d*) performs live music,

(*e*) plays recorded music,

(*f*) performs dance, or

(*g*) does something coming within paragraph 2(1)(*h*) of Schedule 1 (entertainment similar to music, dance, etc).

(3) Subsection (2) is to be construed in accordance with Part 3 of Schedule 1.

(4) A person guilty of an offence under this section is liable on summary conviction to imprisonment for a term not exceeding six months or to a fine not exceeding £20,000, or to both.

(5) In this Part "authorisation" means—

(*a*) a premises licence,

(*b*) a club premises certificate, or

(*c*) a temporary event notice in respect of which the conditions of section 98(2) to (4) are satisfied.

[Licensing Act 2003, s 136.]

---

1. Part 7 comprises ss 136–159.
2. For defence of due diligence, see s 139, post.
3. For meaning of "licensing activity", see s 1(1).

8–19958 137. Exposing alcohol for unauthorised sale. (1) A person commits an offence[1] if, on any premises, he exposes for sale by retail any alcohol in circumstances where the sale by retail of that alcohol on those premises would be an unauthorised licensable activity.

(2) For that purpose a licensable activity is unauthorised unless it is under and in accordance with an authorisation.

(3) A person guilty of an offence under this section is liable on summary conviction to imprisonment for a term not exceeding six months or to a fine not exceeding £20,000, or to both.

(4) The court by which a person is convicted of an offence under this section may order the alcohol in question, and any container for it, to be forfeited and either destroyed or dealt with in such other manner as the court may order.

[Licensing Act 2003, s 137.]

1. For defence of due diligence, see s 139, post.

8–19959 138. Keeping alcohol on premises for unauthorised sale etc. (1) A person commits an offence[1] if he has in his possession or under his control alcohol which he intends to sell by retail or supply in circumstances where that activity would be an unauthorised licensable activity.

(2) For that purpose a licensable activity is unauthorised unless it is under and in accordance with an authorisation[2].

(3) In subsection (1) the reference to the supply of alcohol is a reference to the supply of alcohol by or on behalf of a club to, or to the order of, a member of the club.

(4) A person guilty of an offence under this section is liable on summary conviction to a fine not exceeding level 2 on the standard scale.

(5) The court by which a person is convicted of an offence under this section may order the alcohol in question, and any container for it, to be forfeited and either destroyed or dealt with in such other manner as the court may order.

[Licensing Act 2003, s 138.]

1. For defence of due diligence, see s 139, post.
2. For meaning of "authorisation", see s 136(5), post.

8–19960 139. Defence of due diligence. (1) In proceedings against a person for an offence to which subsection (2) applies, it is a defence that—

(*a*) his act was due to a mistake, or to reliance on information given to him, or to an act or omission by another person, or to some other cause beyond his control, and

(*b*) he took all reasonable precautions and exercised all due diligence to avoid committing the offence.

(2) This subsection applies to an offence under—

(*a*) section 136(1)(*a*) (carrying on unauthorised licensable activity),

(*b*) section 137 (exposing alcohol for unauthorised sale), or

(*c*) section 138 (keeping alcohol on premises for unauthorised sale).

[Licensing Act 2003, s 139.]

Drunkenness and disorderly conduct

8–19961 140. Allowing disorderly conduct on licensed premises etc. (1) A person to whom subsection (2) applies commits an offence if he knowingly allows disorderly conduct on relevant premises.

(2) This subsection applies—

(*a*) to any person who works at the premises in a capacity, whether paid or unpaid, which authorises him to prevent the conduct,

(*b*) in the case of licensed premises, to—

(i) the holder of a premises licence in respect of the premises, and

(ii) the designated premises supervisor (if any) under such a licence,

(*c*) in the case of premises in respect of which a club premises certificate has effect, to any member or officer of the club which holds the certificate who at the time the conduct takes place is present on the premises in a capacity which enables him to prevent it, and

(*d*) in the case of premises which may be used for a permitted temporary activity by virtue of Part 5, to the premises user in relation to the temporary event notice in question.

(3) A person guilty of an offence under this section is liable on summary conviction to a fine not exceeding level 3 on the standard scale.

[Licensing Act 2003, s 140.]

8–19962 141. Sale of alcohol to a person who is drunk. (1) A person to whom subsection (2) applies commits an offence if, on relevant premises, he knowingly—

(*a*) sells or attempts to sell alcohol to a person who is drunk, or (*b*) allows alcohol to be sold to such a person.

(2) This subsection applies—

(*a*) to any person who works at the premises in a capacity, whether paid or unpaid, which gives him authority to sell the alcohol concerned,

(*b*) in the case of licensed premises, to—

(i) the holder of a premises licence in respect of the premises, and

(ii) the designated premises supervisor (if any) under such a licence,

(*c*) in the case of premises in respect of which a club premises certificate has effect, to any member or officer of the club which holds the certificate who at the time the sale (or attempted sale) takes place is present on the premises in a capacity which enables him to prevent it, and

(*d*) in the case of premises which may be used for a permitted temporary activity by virtue of Part 5, to the premises user in relation to the temporary event notice in question.

(3) This section applies in relation to the supply of alcohol by or on behalf of a club to or to the order of a member of the club as it applies in relation to the sale of alcohol.

(4) A person guilty of an offence under this section is liable on summary conviction to a fine not exceeding level 3 on the standard scale.

[Licensing Act 2003, s 141.]

8–19963 142. Obtaining alcohol for a person who is drunk. (1) A person commits an offence if, on relevant premises, he knowingly obtains or attempts to obtain alcohol for consumption on those premises by a person who is drunk.

(2) A person guilty of an offence under this section is liable on summary conviction to a fine not exceeding level 3 on the standard scale.

[Licensing Act 2003, s 142.]

8–19964 143. Failure to leave licensed premises etc. (1) A person who is drunk or disorderly commits an offence if, without reasonable excuse—

(*a*) he fails to leave relevant premises when requested to do so by a constable or by a person to whom subsection (2) applies, or

(*b*) he enters or attempts to enter relevant premises after a constable or a person to whom subsection (2) applies has requested him not to enter.

(2) This subsection applies—

(*a*) to any person who works at the premises in a capacity, whether paid or unpaid, which authorises him to make such a request,

(*b*) in the case of licensed premises, to—

(i) the holder of a premises licence in respect of the premises, or

(ii) the designated premises supervisor (if any) under such a licence,

(*c*) in the case of premises in respect of which a club premises certificate has effect, to any member or officer of the club which holds the certificate who is present on the premises in a capacity which enables him to make such a request, and

(*d*) in the case of premises which may be used for a permitted temporary activity by virtue of Part 5, to the premises user in relation to the temporary event notice in question.

(3) A person guilty of an offence under subsection (1) is liable on summary conviction to a fine not exceeding level 1 on the standard scale.

(4) On being requested to do so by a person to whom subsection (2) applies, a constable must—

(*a*) help to expel from relevant premises a person who is drunk or disorderly;

(*b*) help to prevent such a person from entering relevant premises.

[Licensing Act 2003, s 143.]

Smuggled goods

8–19965 144. Keeping of smuggled goods. (1) A person to whom subsection (2) applies commits an offence if he knowingly keeps or allows to be kept, on any relevant premises, any goods which have been imported without payment of duty or which have otherwise been unlawfully imported.

(2) This subsection applies—

(*a*) to any person who works at the premises in a capacity, whether paid or unpaid, which gives him authority to prevent the keeping of the goods on the premises,

(*b*) in the case of licensed premises, to—

(i) the holder of a premises licence in respect of the premises, and

(ii) the designated premises supervisor (if any) under such a licence,

(*c*) in the case of premises in respect of which a club premises certificate has effect, to any member or officer of the club which holds the certificate who is present on the premises at any time when the goods are kept on the premises in a capacity which enables him to prevent them being so kept, and

(*d*) in the case of premises which may be used for a permitted temporary activity by virtue of Part 5, to the premises user in relation to the temporary event notice in question.

(3) A person guilty of an offence under this section is liable on summary conviction to a fine not exceeding level 3 on the standard scale.

(4) The court by which a person is convicted of an offence under this section may order the goods in question, and any container for them, to be forfeited and either destroyed or dealt with in such other manner as the court may order.

[Licensing Act 2003, s 144.]

Children and alcohol

8–19966 145. Unaccompanied children prohibited from certain premises. (1) A person to whom subsection (3) applies commits an offence if—

(*a*) knowing that relevant premises are within subsection (4), he allows an unaccompanied child to be on the premises at a time when they are open for the purposes of being used for the supply of alcohol for consumption there, or

(*b*) he allows an unaccompanied child to be on relevant premises at a time between the hours of midnight and 5 a.m. when the premises are open for the purposes of being used for the supply of alcohol for consumption there.

(2) For the purposes of this section—

(*a*) "child" means an individual aged under 16,

(*b*) a child is unaccompanied if he is not in the company of an individual aged 18 or over.

(3) This subsection applies—

(*a*) to any person who works at the premises in a capacity, whether paid or unpaid, which authorises him to request the unaccompanied child to leave the premises,

(*b*) in the case of licensed premises, to—

(i) the holder of a premises licence in respect of the premises, and

(ii) the designated premises supervisor (if any) under such a licence,

(*c*) in the case of premises in respect of which a club premises certificate has effect, to any member or officer of the club which holds the certificate who is present on the premises in a capacity which enables him to make such a request, and

(*d*) in the case of premises which may be used for a permitted temporary activity by virtue of Part 5, to the premises user in relation to the temporary event notice in question.

(4) Relevant premises are within this subsection if—

(*a*) they are exclusively or primarily used for the supply of alcohol for consumption on the premises, or

(*b*) they are open for the purposes of being used for the supply of alcohol for consumption on the premises by virtue of Part 5 (permitted temporary activities) and, at the time the temporary event notice in question has effect, they are exclusively or primarily used for such supplies.

(5) No offence is committed under this section if the unaccompanied child is on the premises solely for the purpose of passing to or from some other place to or from which there is no other convenient means of access or egress.

(6) Where a person is charged with an offence under this section by reason of his own conduct it is a defence that—

(*a*) he believed that the unaccompanied child was aged 16 or over or that an individual accompanying him was aged 18 or over, and

(*b*) either—

(i) he had taken all reasonable steps to establish the individual's age, or

(ii) nobody could reasonably have suspected from the individual's appearance that he was aged under 16 or, as the case may be, under 18.

(7) For the purposes of subsection (6), a person is treated as having taken all reasonable steps to establish an individual's age if—

(*a*) he asked the individual for evidence of his age, and

(*b*) the evidence would have convinced a reasonable person.

(8) Where a person ("the accused") is charged with an offence under this section by reason of the act or default of some other person, it is a defence that the accused exercised all due diligence to avoid committing it.

(9) A person guilty of an offence under this section is liable on summary conviction to a fine not exceeding level 3 on the standard scale.

(10) In this section "supply of alcohol" means—

(*a*) the sale by retail of alcohol, or
(*b*) the supply of alcohol by or on behalf of a club to, or to the order of, a member of the club.
[Licensing Act 2003, s 145.]

8–19967 146. Sale of alcohol to children. (1) A person commits an offence if he sells alcohol to an individual aged under 18.

(2) A club commits an offence if alcohol is supplied by it or on its behalf—
(*a*) to, or to the order of, a member of the club who is aged under 18, or
(*b*) to the order of a member of the club, to an individual who is aged under 18.

(3) A person commits an offence if he supplies alcohol on behalf of a club—
(*a*) to, or to the order of, a member of the club who is aged under 18, or
(*b*) to the order of a member of the club, to an individual who is aged under 18.

(4) Where a person is charged with an offence under this section by reason of his own conduct it is a defence that—
(*a*) he believed that the individual was aged 18 or over, and
(*b*) either—
(i) he had taken all reasonable steps to establish the individual's age, or
(ii) nobody could reasonably have suspected from the individual's appearance that he was aged under 18.

(5) For the purposes of subsection (4), a person is treated as having taken all reasonable steps to establish an individual's age if—
(*a*) he asked the individual for evidence of his age, and
(*b*) the evidence would have convinced a reasonable person.

(6) Where a person ("the accused") is charged with an offence under this section by reason of the act or default of some other person, it is a defence that the accused exercised all due diligence to avoid committing it.

(7) A person guilty of an offence under this section is liable on summary conviction to a fine not exceeding level 5 on the standard scale.
[Licensing Act 2003, s 146.]

8–19968 147. Allowing the sale of alcohol to children. (1) A person to whom subsection (2) applies commits an offence if he knowingly allows the sale of alcohol on relevant premises to an individual aged under 18.

(2) This subsection applies to a person who works at the premises in a capacity, whether paid or unpaid, which authorises him to prevent the sale.

(3) A person to whom subsection (4) applies commits an offence if he knowingly allows alcohol to be supplied on relevant premises by or on behalf of a club—
(*a*) to or to the order of a member of the club who is aged under 18, or
(*b*) to the order of a member of the club, to an individual who is aged under 18.

(4) This subsection applies to—
(*a*) a person who works on the premises in a capacity, whether paid or unpaid, which authorises him to prevent the supply, and
(*b*) any member or officer of the club who at the time of the supply is present on the relevant premises in a capacity which enables him to prevent it.

(5) A person guilty of an offence under this section is liable on summary conviction to a fine not exceeding level 5 on the standard scale.
[Licensing Act 2003, s 147.]

8–19969 148. Sale of liqueur confectionery to children under 16. (1) A person commits an offence if he—
(*a*) sells liqueur confectionery to an individual aged under 16, or
(*b*) supplies such confectionery, on behalf of a club—
(i) to or to the order of a member of the club who is aged under 16, or
(ii) to the order of a member of the club, to an individual who is aged under 16.

(2) A club commits an offence if liqueur confectionery is supplied by it or on its behalf—
(*a*) to or to the order of a member of the club who is aged under 16, or
(*b*) to the order of a member of the club, to an individual who is aged under 16.

(3) Where a person is charged with an offence under this section by reason of his own conduct it is a defence that—
(*a*) he believed that the individual was aged 16 or over, and
(*b*) either—

(i) he had taken all reasonable steps to establish the individual's age, or
(ii) nobody could reasonably have suspected from the individual's appearance that he was aged under 16.

(4) For the purposes of subsection (3), a person is treated as having taken all reasonable steps to establish an individual's age if—

(*a*) he asked the individual for evidence of his age, and
(*b*) the evidence would have convinced a reasonable person.

(5) Where a person ("the accused") is charged with an offence under this section by reason of the act or default of some other person, it is a defence that the accused exercised all due diligence to avoid committing it.

(6) A person guilty of an offence under this section is liable on summary conviction to a fine not exceeding level 2 on the standard scale.

(7) In this section "liqueur confectionery" has the meaning given in section 191(2).
[Licensing Act 2003, s 148.]

8–19970 **149. Purchase of alcohol by or on behalf of children.** (1) An individual aged under 18 commits an offence if—

(*a*) he buys or attempts to buy alcohol, or
(*b*) where he is a member of a club—
(i) alcohol is supplied to him or to his order by or on behalf of the club, as a result of some act or default of his, or
(ii) he attempts to have alcohol supplied to him or to his order by or on behalf of the club.

(2) But subsection (1) does not apply where the individual buys or attempts to buy the alcohol at the request of—

(*a*) a constable, or
(*b*) a weights and measures inspector,

who is acting in the course of his duty.

(3) A person commits an offence if—

(*a*) he buys or attempts to buy alcohol on behalf of an individual aged under 18, or
(*b*) where he is a member of a club, on behalf of an individual aged under 18 he—
(i) makes arrangements whereby alcohol is supplied to him or to his order by or on behalf of the club, or
(ii) attempts to make such arrangements.

(4) A person ("the relevant person") commits an offence if—

(*a*) he buys or attempts to buy alcohol for consumption on relevant premises by an individual aged under 18, or
(*b*) where he is a member of a club—
(i) by some act or default of his, alcohol is supplied to him, or to his order, by or on behalf of the club for consumption on relevant premises by an individual aged under 18, or
(ii) he attempts to have alcohol so supplied for such consumption.

(5) But subsection (4) does not apply where—

(*a*) the relevant person is aged 18 or over,
(*b*) the individual is aged 16 or 17,
(*c*) the alcohol is beer, wine or cider,
(*d*) its purchase or supply is for consumption at a table meal on relevant premises, and
(*e*) the individual is accompanied at the meal by an individual aged 18 or over.

(6) Where a person is charged with an offence under subsection (3) or (4) it is a defence that he had no reason to suspect that the individual was aged under 18.

(7) A person guilty of an offence under this section is liable on summary conviction—

(*a*) in the case of an offence under subsection (1), to a fine not exceeding level 3 on the standard scale, and
(*b*) in the case of an offence under subsection (3) or (4), to a fine not exceeding level 5 on the standard scale.

[Licensing Act 2003, s 149.]

8–19971 **150. Consumption of alcohol by children.** (1) An individual aged under 18 commits an offence if he knowingly consumes alcohol on relevant premises.

(2) A person to whom subsection (3) applies commits an offence if he knowingly allows the consumption of alcohol on relevant premises by an individual aged under 18.

(3) This subsection applies—

(*a*) to a person who works at the premises in a capacity, whether paid or unpaid, which authorises him to prevent the consumption, and

(*b*) where the alcohol was supplied by a club to or to the order of a member of the club, to any member or officer of the club who is present at the premises at the time of the consumption in a capacity which enables him to prevent it.

(4) Subsections (1) and (2) do not apply where—

(*a*) the individual is aged 16 or 17,

(*b*) the alcohol is beer, wine or cider,

(*c*) its consumption is at a table meal on relevant premises, and

(*d*) the individual is accompanied at the meal by an individual aged 18 or over.

(5) A person guilty of an offence under this section is liable on summary conviction—

(*a*) in the case of an offence under subsection (1), to a fine not exceeding level 3 on the standard scale, and

(*b*) in the case of an offence under subsection (2), to a fine not exceeding level 5 on the standard scale.

[Licensing Act 2003, s 150.]

8–19972 **151. Delivering alcohol to children.** (1) A person who works on relevant premises in any capacity, whether paid or unpaid, commits an offence if he knowingly delivers to an individual aged under 18—

(*a*) alcohol sold on the premises, or

(*b*) alcohol supplied on the premises by or on behalf of a club to or to the order of a member of the club.

(2) A person to whom subsection (3) applies commits an offence if he knowingly allows anybody else to deliver to an individual aged under 18 alcohol sold on relevant premises.

(3) This subsection applies to a person who works on the premises in a capacity, whether paid or unpaid, which authorises him to prevent the delivery of the alcohol.

(4) A person to whom subsection (5) applies commits an offence if he knowingly allows anybody else to deliver to an individual aged under 18 alcohol supplied on relevant premises by or on behalf of a club to or to the order of a member of the club.

(5) This subsection applies—

(*a*) to a person who works on the premises in a capacity, whether paid or unpaid, which authorises him to prevent the supply, and

(*b*) to any member or officer of the club who at the time of the supply in question is present on the premises in a capacity which enables him to prevent the supply.

(6) Subsections (1), (2) and (4) do not apply where—

(*a*) the alcohol is delivered at a place where the buyer or, as the case may be, person supplied lives or works, or

(*b*) the individual aged under 18 works on the relevant premises in a capacity, whether paid or unpaid, which involves the delivery of alcohol, or

(*c*) the alcohol is sold or supplied for consumption on the relevant premises.

(7) A person guilty of an offence under this section is liable on summary conviction to a fine not exceeding level 5 on the standard scale.

[Licensing Act 2003, s 151.]

8–19973 **152. Sending a child to obtain alcohol.** (1) A person commits an offence if he knowingly sends an individual aged under 18 to obtain—

(*a*) alcohol sold or to be sold on relevant premises for consumption off the premises, or

(*b*) alcohol supplied or to be supplied by or on behalf of a club to or to the order of a member of the club for such consumption.

(2) For the purposes of this section, it is immaterial whether the individual aged under 18 is sent to obtain the alcohol from the relevant premises or from other premises from which it is delivered in pursuance of the sale or supply.

(3) Subsection (1) does not apply where the individual aged under 18 works on the relevant premises in a capacity, whether paid or unpaid, which involves the delivery of alcohol.

(4) Subsection (1) also does not apply where the individual aged under 18 is sent by—

(*a*) a constable, or

(*b*) a weights and measures inspector,

who is acting in the course of his duty.

(5) A person guilty of an offence under this section is liable on summary conviction to a fine not exceeding level 5 on the standard scale.

[Licensing Act 2003, s 152.]

8–19974 **153. Prohibition of unsupervised sales by children.** (1) A responsible person commits an offence if on any relevant premises he knowingly allows an individual aged under 18 to make on the premises—

(*a*) any sale of alcohol, or

(*b*) any supply of alcohol by or on behalf of a club to or to the order of a member of the club,

unless the sale or supply has been specifically approved by that or another responsible person.

(2) But subsection (1) does not apply where—

(*a*) the alcohol is sold or supplied for consumption with a table meal,

(*b*) it is sold or supplied in premises which are being used for the service of table meals (or in a part of any premises which is being so used), and

(*c*) the premises are (or the part is) not used for the sale or supply of alcohol otherwise than to persons having table meals there and for consumption by such a person as an ancillary to his meal.

(3) A person guilty of an offence under this section is liable on summary conviction to a fine not exceeding level 1 on the standard scale.

(4) In this section "responsible person" means—

(*a*) in relation to licensed premises—

(i) the holder of a premises licence in respect of the premises,

(ii) the designated premises supervisor (if any) under such a licence, or

(iii) any individual aged 18 or over who is authorised for the purposes of this section by such a holder or supervisor,

(*b*) in relation to premises in respect of which there is in force a club premises certificate, any member or officer of the club present on the premises in a capacity which enables him to prevent the supply in question, and

(*c*) in relation to premises which may be used for a permitted temporary activity by virtue of Part 5—

(i) the premises user, or

(ii) any individual aged 18 or over who is authorised for the purposes of this section by the premises user.

[Licensing Act 2003, s 153.]

8–19975 **154. Enforcement role for weights and measures authorities.** (1) It is the duty of every local weights and measures authority in England and Wales to enforce within its area the provisions of sections 146 and 147, so far as they apply to sales of alcohol made on or from premises to which the public have access.

(2) A weights and measures inspector may make, or authorise any person to make on his behalf, such purchases of goods as appear expedient for the purpose of determining whether those provisions are being complied with.

[Licensing Act 2003, s 154.]

Confiscation of alcohol

8–19976 **155. Confiscation of sealed containers of alcohol.** *Confiscation of Alcohol (Young Persons) Act 1997 amended to remove the requirement for the alcohol to be in a sealed container in certain circumstances.*

Vehicles and trains

8–19977 **156. Prohibition on sale of alcohol on moving vehicles.** (1) A person commits an offence under this section if he sells by retail alcohol on or from a vehicle at a time when the vehicle is not permanently or temporarily parked.

(2) A person guilty of an offence under this section is liable on summary conviction to imprisonment for a term not exceeding three months or to a fine not exceeding £20,000, or to both.

(3) In proceedings against a person for an offence under this section, it is a defence that—

(*a*) his act was due to a mistake, or to reliance on information given to him, or to an act or omission by another person, or to some other cause beyond his control, and

(*b*) he took all reasonable precautions and exercised all due diligence to avoid committing the offence.

[Licensing Act 2003, s 156.]

8–19978 **157. Power to prohibit sale of alcohol on trains.** (1) A magistrates' court acting for a petty sessions area may make an order prohibiting the sale of alcohol, during such period as may be specified, on any railway vehicle—

(*a*) at such station or stations as may be specified, being stations in that area, or

(*b*) travelling between such stations as may be specified, at least one of which is in that area.

(2) A magistrates' court may make an order under this section only on the application of a senior police officer.

(3) A magistrates' court may not make such an order unless it is satisfied that the order is necessary to prevent disorder.

(4) Where an order is made under this section, the responsible senior police officer must, forthwith, serve a copy of the order on the train operator (or each train operator) affected by the order.

(5) A person commits an offence if he knowingly—

(*a*) sells or attempts to sell alcohol in contravention of an order under this section, or
(*b*) allows the sale of alcohol in contravention of such an order.

(6) A person guilty of an offence under this section is liable on summary conviction to imprisonment for a term not exceeding three months or to a fine not exceeding £20,000, or to both.

(7) In this section—

"railway vehicle" has the meaning given by section 83 of the Railways Act 1993;
"responsible senior police officer", in relation to an order under this section, means the senior police officer who applied for the order or, if the chief officer of police of the force in question has designated another senior police officer for the purpose, that other officer;
"senior police officer" means a police officer of, or above, the rank of inspector;
"specified" means specified in the order under this section;
"station" has the meaning given by section 83 of the Railways Act 1993 (c 43); and
"train operator" means a person authorised by a licence under section 8 of that Act to operate railway assets (within the meaning of section 6 of that Act).

[Licensing Act 2003, s 157.]

False statement relating to licensing etc

8–19979 **158. False statements made for the purposes of this Act.** (1) A person commits an offence if he knowingly or recklessly makes a false statement in or in connection with—

(*a*) an application for the grant, variation, transfer or review of a premises licence or club premises certificate,
(*b*) an application for a provisional statement,
(*c*) a temporary event notice, an interim authority notice or any other notice under this Act,
(*d*) an application for the grant or renewal of a personal licence, or
(*e*) a notice within section 178(1) (notice by freeholder etc conferring right to be notified of changes to licensing register).

(2) For the purposes of subsection (1) a person is to be treated as making a false statement if he produces, furnishes, signs or otherwise makes use of a document that contains a false statement.

(3) A person guilty of an offence under this section is liable on summary conviction to a fine not exceeding level 5 on the standard scale.

[Licensing Act 2003, s 158.]

Interpretation

8–19980 **159. Interpretation of Part 7.** In this Part—

"authorisation" has the meaning given in section 136(5);
"relevant premises" means—

(*a*) licensed premises, or
(*b*) premises in respect of which there is in force a club premises certificate, or
(*c*) premises which may be used for a permitted temporary activity by virtue of Part 5;

"table meal" means a meal eaten by a person seated at a table, or at a counter or other structure which serves the purpose of a table and is not used for the service of refreshments for consumption by persons not seated at a table or structure serving the purpose of a table; and
"weights and measures inspector" means an inspector of weights and measures appointed under section 72(1) of the Weights and Measures Act 1985 (c 72).

[Licensing Act 2003, s 159.]

PART 8[1]
CLOSURE OF PREMISES

Closure of premises in an identified area

8–19981 **160. Orders to close premises in area experiencing disorder.** (1) Where there is or is expected to be disorder in any petty sessions area, a magistrates' court acting for the area may make an order requiring all premises—

(*a*) which are situated at or near the place of the disorder or expected disorder, and
(*b*) in respect of which a premises licence or a temporary event notice has effect,

to be closed for a period, not exceeding 24 hours, specified in the order.

(2) A magistrates' court may make an order under this section only on the application of a police officer who is of the rank of superintendent or above.

(3) A magistrates' court may not make such an order unless it is satisfied that it is necessary to prevent disorder.

(4) Where an order is made under this section, a person to whom subsection (5) applies commits an offence if he knowingly keeps any premises to which the order relates open, or allows any such premises to be kept open, during the period of the order.

(5) This subsection applies—

(*a*) to any manager of the premises,

(*b*) in the case of licensed premises, to—

(i) the holder of a premises licence in respect of the premises, and

(ii) the designated premises supervisor (if any) under such a licence, and

(*c*) in the case of premises in respect of which a temporary event notice has effect, to the premises user in relation to that notice.

(6) A person guilty of an offence under subsection (4) is liable on summary conviction to a fine not exceeding level 3 on the standard scale.

(7) A constable may use such force as may be necessary for the purpose of closing premises ordered to be closed under this section.

[Licensing Act 2003, s 160.]

1. Part 8 comprises ss 160–171.

Closure of identified premises

8–19982 161. Closure orders for identified premises. (1) A senior police officer may make a closure order in relation to any relevant premises if he reasonably believes that—

(*a*) there is, or is likely imminently to be, disorder on, or in the vicinity of and related to, the premises and their closure is necessary in the interests of public safety, or

(*b*) a public nuisance is being caused by noise coming from the premises and the closure of the premises is necessary to prevent that nuisance.

(2) A closure order is an order under this section requiring relevant premises to be closed for a period not exceeding 24 hours beginning with the coming into force of the order.

(3) In determining whether to make a closure order in respect of any premises, the senior police officer must have regard, in particular, to the conduct of each appropriate person in relation to the disorder or nuisance.

(4) A closure order must—

(*a*) specify the premises to which it relates,

(*b*) specify the period for which the premises are to be closed,

(*c*) specify the grounds on which it is made, and

(*d*) state the effect of sections 162 to 168.

(5) A closure order in respect of any relevant premises comes into force at the time a constable gives notice of it to an appropriate person who is connected with any of the activities to which the disorder or nuisance relates.

(6) A person commits an offence if, without reasonable excuse, he permits relevant premises to be open in contravention of a closure order or any extension of it.

(7) A person guilty of an offence under subsection (6) is liable on summary conviction to imprisonment for a term not exceeding three months or to a fine not exceeding £20,000, or to both.

(8) In this section—

"relevant premises" means premises in respect of which one or more of the following have effect—

(*a*) a premises licence,

(*b*) a temporary event notice; and

"senior police officer" means a police officer of, or above, the rank of inspector.

[Licensing Act 2003, s 161.]

8–19983 162. Extension of closure order. (1) Where, before the end of the period for which relevant premises are to be closed under a closure order or any extension of it (the "closure period"), the responsible senior police officer reasonably believes that—

(*a*) a relevant magistrates' court will not have determined whether to exercise its powers under section 165(2) in respect of the closure order, and any extension of it, by the end of the closure period, and

(*b*) the conditions for an extension are satisfied,

he may extend the closure period for a further period not exceeding 24 hours beginning with the end of the previous closure period.

(2) The conditions for an extension are that—

(*a*) in the case of an order made by virtue of section 161(1)(*a*), closure is necessary in the interests of public safety because of disorder or likely disorder on, or in the vicinity of and related to, the premises,

(*b*) in the case of an order made by virtue of section 161(1)(*b*), closure is necessary to ensure that no public nuisance is, or is likely to be, caused by noise coming from the premises.

(3) An extension in relation to any relevant premises comes into force when a constable gives notice of it to an appropriate person connected with any of the activities to which the disorder or nuisance relates or is expected to relate.

(4) But the extension does not come into force unless the notice is given before the end of the previous closure period.

[Licensing Act 2003, s 162.]

8–19984 **163. Cancellation of closure order.** (1) The responsible senior police officer may cancel a closure order and any extension of it at any time—

(*a*) after the making of the order, but

(*b*) before a relevant magistrates' court has determined whether to exercise its powers under section 165(2) in respect of the order and any extension of it.

(2) The responsible senior police officer must cancel a closure order and any extension of it if he does not reasonably believe that—

(*a*) in the case of an order made by virtue of section 161(1)(*a*), closure is necessary in the interests of public safety because of disorder or likely disorder on, or in the vicinity of and related to, the premises,

(*b*) in the case of an order made by virtue of section 161(1)(*b*), closure is necessary to ensure that no public nuisance is, or is likely to be, caused by noise coming from the premises.

(3) Where a closure order and any extension of it are cancelled under this section, the responsible senior police officer must give notice of the cancellation to an appropriate person connected with any of the activities related to the disorder (or anticipated disorder) or nuisance in respect of which the closure order was made.

[Licensing Act 2003, s 163.]

8–19985 **164. Application to magistrates' court by police.** (1) The responsible senior police officer must, as soon as reasonably practicable after a closure order comes into force in respect of any relevant premises, apply to a relevant magistrates' court for it to consider the order and any extension of it.

(2) Where an application is made under this section in respect of licensed premises, the responsible senior officer must also notify the relevant licensing authority—

(*a*) that a closure order has come into force,

(*b*) of the contents of the order and of any extension of it, and

(*c*) of the application under subsection (1).

[Licensing Act 2003, s 164.]

8–19986 **165. Consideration of closure order by magistrates' court.** (1) A relevant magistrates' court must as soon as reasonably practicable after receiving an application under section 164(1)—

(*a*) hold a hearing to consider whether it is appropriate to exercise any of the court's powers under subsection (2) in relation to the closure order or any extension of it, and

(*b*) determine whether to exercise any of those powers.

(2) The relevant magistrates' court may—

(*a*) revoke the closure order and any extension of it;

(*b*) order the premises to remain, or to be, closed until such time as the relevant licensing authority has made a determination in respect of the order for the purposes of section 167;

(*c*) order the premises to remain or to be closed until that time subject to such exceptions as may be specified in the order;

(*d*) order the premises to remain or to be closed until that time unless such conditions as may be specified in the order are satisfied.

(3) In determining whether the premises will be, or will remain, closed the relevant magistrates' court must, in particular, consider whether—

(*a*) in the case of an order made by virtue of section 161(1)(*a*), closure is necessary in the interests of public safety because of disorder or likely disorder on the premises, or in the vicinity of and related to, the premises;

(*b*) in the case of an order made by virtue of section 161(1)(*b*), closure is necessary to ensure that no public nuisance is, or is likely to be, caused by noise coming from the premises.

(4) In the case of licensed premises, the relevant magistrates' court must notify the relevant licensing authority of any determination it makes under subsection (1)(*b*).

(5) Subsection (2) does not apply if, before the relevant magistrates' court discharges its functions under that subsection, the premises cease to be relevant premises.

(6) Any order made under subsection (2) ceases to have effect if the premises cease to be relevant premises.

(7) A person commits an offence if, without reasonable excuse, he permits relevant premises to be open in contravention of an order under subsection (2)(*b*), (*c*) or (*d*).

(8) A person guilty of an offence under subsection (7) is liable on summary conviction to imprisonment for a term not exceeding three months or to a fine not exceeding £20,000, or to both.

(9) The powers conferred on a magistrates' court by this section are to be exercised in the place required by the Magistrates' Courts Act 1980 (c 43) for the hearing of a complaint and may be exercised by a single justice.

(10) Evidence given for the purposes of proceedings under this section must be given on oath.

[Licensing Act 2003, s 165.]

8–19987 **166. Appeal from decision of magistrates' court.** *Power to appeal to Crown Court by giving notice of appeal to the officer of the court within 21 days beginning with the day the decision of the magistrates' court was made.*

8–19988 **167. Review of premises licence following closure order.** (1) This section applies where—

(*a*) a closure order has come into force in relation to premises in respect of which a premises licence has effect, and

(*b*) the relevant licensing authority has received a notice under section 165(4) (notice of magistrates' court's determination), in relation to the order and any extension of it.

(2) The relevant licensing authority must review the premises licence.

(3) The authority must reach a determination on the review no later than 28 days after the day on which it receives the notice mentioned in subsection (1)(*b*).

(4) The Secretary of State must by regulations[1]—

(*a*) require the relevant licensing authority to give, to the holder of the premises licence and each responsible authority, notice of—

(i) the review,

(ii) the closure order and any extension of it, and

(iii) any order made in relation to it under section 165(2);

(*b*) require the authority to advertise the review and invite representations about it to be made to the authority by responsible authorities and interested parties;

(*c*) prescribe the period during which representations may be made by the holder of the premises licence, any responsible authority or any interested party;

(*d*) require any notice under paragraph (*a*) or advertisement under paragraph (*b*) to specify that period.

(5) The relevant licensing authority must—

(*a*) hold a hearing to consider—

(i) the closure order and any extension of it,

(ii) any order under section 165(2), and

(iii) any relevant representations, and

(*b*) take such of the steps mentioned in subsection (6) (if any) as it considers necessary for the promotion of the licensing objectives.

(6) Those steps are—

(*a*) to modify the conditions of the premises licence,

(*b*) to exclude a licensable activity from the scope of the licence,

(*c*) to remove the designated premises supervisor from the licence,

(*d*) to suspend the licence for a period not exceeding three months, or

(*e*) to revoke the licence;

and for this purpose the conditions of a premises licence are modified if any of them is altered or omitted or any new condition is added.

(7) Subsection (5)(*b*) is subject to sections 19, 20 and 21 (requirement to include certain conditions in premises licences).

(8) Where the authority takes a step within subsection (6)(*a*) or (*b*), it may provide that the modification or exclusion is to have effect only for a specified period (not exceeding three months).

(9) In this section "relevant representations" means representations which—

(*a*) are relevant to one or more of the licensing objectives, and

(*b*) meet the requirements of subsection (10).

(10) The requirements are—

(*a*) that the representations are made by the holder of the premises licence, a responsible authority or an interested party within the period prescribed under subsection (4)(*c*),

(*b*) that they have not been withdrawn, and

(*c*) if they are made by an interested party (who is not also a responsible authority), that they are not, in the opinion of the relevant licensing authority, frivolous or vexatious.

(11) Where the relevant licensing authority determines that any representations are frivolous or vexatious, it must notify the person who made them of the reasons for that determination.

(12) Where a licensing authority determines a review under this section it must notify the determination and its reasons for making it to—

(*a*) the holder of the licence,

(*b*) any person who made relevant representations, and

(*c*) the chief officer of police for the police area (or each police area) in which the premises are situated.

(13) Section 168 makes provision about when the determination takes effect.

(14) In this section "interested party" and "responsible authority" have the same meaning as in Part 3.

[Licensing Act 2003, s 167.]

---

1. See the Licensing Act 2003 (Premises Licences and Club Premises Certificates) Regulations 2005, SI 2005/42.

8–19989 **168. Provision about decisions under section 167.** (1) Subject to this section, a decision under section 167 does not have effect until the relevant time.

(2) In this section "the relevant time", in relation to any decision, means—

(*a*) the end of the period given for appealing against the decision, or

(*b*) if the decision is appealed against, the time the appeal is disposed of.

(3) Subsections (4) and (5) apply where—

(*a*) the relevant licensing authority decides on a review under section 167 to take one or more of the steps mentioned in subsection (6)(*a*) to (*d*) of that section, and

(*b*) the premises to which the licence relates have been closed, by virtue of an order under section 165(2)(*b*), (*c*) or (*d*), until that decision was made.

(4) The decision by the relevant licensing authority to take any of the steps mentioned in section 167(6)(*a*) to (*d*) takes effect when it is notified to the holder of the licence under section 167(12).

This is subject to subsection (5) and paragraph 18(3) of Schedule 5 (power of magistrates' court to suspend decision pending appeal).

(5) The relevant licensing authority may, on such terms as it thinks fit, suspend the operation of that decision (in whole or in part) until the relevant time.

(6) Subsection (7) applies where—

(*a*) the relevant licensing authority decides on a review under section 167 to revoke the premises licence, and

(*b*) the premises to which the licence relates have been closed, by virtue of an order under section 165(2)(*b*), (*c*) or (*d*), until that decision was made.

(7) The premises must remain closed (but the licence otherwise in force) until the relevant time.

This is subject to paragraph 18(4) of Schedule 5 (power of magistrates' court to modify closure order pending appeal).

(8) A person commits an offence if, without reasonable excuse, he allows premises to be open in contravention of subsection (7).

(9) A person guilty of an offence under subsection (8) is liable on summary conviction to imprisonment for a term not exceeding three months or to a fine not exceeding £20,000, or to both.

[Licensing Act 2003, s 168.]

8–19990 **169. Enforcement of closure order.** A constable may use such force as may be necessary for the purposes of closing premises in compliance with a closure order.

[Licensing Act 2003, s 169.]

Interpretation

8–19991 **171. Interpretation of Part 8.** (1) This section has effect for the purposes of this Part.

(2) Relevant premises are open if a person who is not within subsection (4) enters the premises and—

(*a*) he buys or is otherwise supplied with food, drink or anything usually sold on the premises, or

(*b*) while he is on the premises, they are used for the provision of regulated entertainment.

(3) But in determining whether relevant premises are open the following are to be disregarded—

(*a*) where no premises licence has effect in respect of the premises, any use of the premises for activities (other than licensable activities) which do not take place during an event period specified in a temporary event notice having effect in respect of the premises,

(*b*) any use of the premises for a qualifying club activity under and in accordance with a club premises certificate, and

(*c*) any supply exempted under paragraph 3 of Schedule 2 (certain supplies of hot food and drink by clubs, hotels etc not a licensable activity) in circumstances where a person will neither be admitted to the premises, nor be supplied as mentioned in sub-paragraph (1)(*b*) of that paragraph, except by virtue of being a member of a recognised club or a guest of such a member.

(4) A person is within this subsection if he is—

(*a*) an appropriate person in relation to the premises,

(*b*) a person who usually lives at the premises, or

(*c*) a member of the family of a person within paragraph (*a*) or (*b*).

(5) The following expressions have the meanings given—

"appropriate person", in relation to any relevant premises, means—

(*a*) any person who holds a premises licence in respect of the premises,

(*b*) any designated premises supervisor under such a licence,

(*c*) the premises user in relation to any temporary event notice which has effect in respect of the premises, or

(*d*) a manager of the premises;

"closure order" has the meaning given in section 161(2);

"extension", in relation to a closure order, means an extension of the order under section 162;

"manager", in relation to any premises, means a person who works at the premises in a capacity, whether paid or unpaid, which authorises him to close them;

"relevant licensing authority", in relation to any licensed premises, has the same meaning as in Part 3;

"relevant magistrates' court", in relation to any relevant premises, means a magistrates' court acting for the petty sessions area in which the premises are situated;

"relevant premises" has the meaning given in section 161(8);

"responsible senior police officer", in relation to a closure order, means—

(*a*) the senior police officer who made the order, or

(*b*) if another senior police officer is designated for the purpose by the chief officer of police for the police area in which the premises are situated, that other officer;

"senior police officer" has the meaning given in section 161(8).

(6) A temporary event notice has effect from the time it is given in accordance with Part 5 until—

(*a*) the time it is withdrawn,

(*b*) the time a counter notice is given under that Part, or

(*c*) the expiry of the event period specified in the temporary event notice,

whichever first occurs.

[Licensing Act 2003, s 171.]

PART 9[1]
MISCELLANEOUS AND SUPPLEMENTARY

Special occasions

8–19992 **172. Relaxation of opening hours for special occasions.** *Power of Secretary of State to make a "Licensing Hours Order" for celebration periods marking an occasion of exceptional international, national or local significance.*

1. Part 8 comprises ss 172–201 and Schs 5–8.

Exemptions etc

8–19993 **173. Activities in certain locations not licensable.** (1) An activity is not a licensable activity if it is carried on—

(*a*) aboard an aircraft, hovercraft or railway vehicle engaged on a journey,

(*b*) aboard a vessel engaged on an international journey,

(*c*) at an approved wharf at a designated port or hoverport,

(*d*) at an examination station at a designated airport,

(*e*) at a royal palace,

(*f*) at premises which, at the time when the activity is carried on, are permanently or temporarily occupied for the purposes of the armed forces of the Crown, (*g*) at premises in respect of which a certificate issued under section 174 (exemption for national security) has effect, or

(*h*) at such other place as may be prescribed.

(2) For the purposes of subsection (1) the period during which an aircraft, hovercraft, railway vehicle or vessel is engaged on a journey includes—

(*a*) any period ending with its departure when preparations are being made for the journey, and

(*b*) any period after its arrival at its destination when it continues to be occupied by those (or any of those) who made the journey (or any part of it).

(3) The Secretary of State may by order designate a port, hoverport or airport for the purposes of subsection (1), if it appears to him to be one at which there is a substantial amount of international passenger traffic.

(4) Any port, airport or hoverport where section 86A or 87 of the Licensing Act 1964 (c 26) is in operation immediately before the commencement of this section is, on and after that commencement, to be treated for the purposes of subsection (1) as if it were designated.

(5) But provision may by order be made for subsection (4) to cease to have effect in relation to any port, airport or hoverport.

(6) For the purposes of this section—

"approved wharf" has the meaning given by section 20A of the Customs and Excise Management Act 1979 (c 2);

"designated" means designated by an order under subsection (3);

"examination station" has the meaning given by section 22A of that Act;

"international journey" means—

(*a*) a journey from a place in the United Kingdom to an immediate destination outside the United Kingdom, or

(*b*) a journey from a place outside the United Kingdom to an immediate destination in the United Kingdom; and

"railway vehicle" has the meaning given by section 83 of the Railways Act 1993 (c 43).

[Licensing Act 2003, s 173.]

8–19994 **174. Certifying of premises on grounds of national security.** (1) A Minister of the Crown may issue a certificate under this section in respect of any premises, if he considers that it is appropriate to do so for the purposes of safeguarding national security.

(2) A certificate under this section may identify the premises in question by means of a general description.

(3) A document purporting to be a certificate under this section is to be received in evidence and treated as being a certificate under this section unless the contrary is proved.

(4) A document which purports to be certified by or on behalf of a Minister of the Crown as a true copy of a certificate given by a Minister of the Crown under this section is evidence of that certificate.

(5) A Minister of the Crown may cancel a certificate issued by him, or any other Minister of the Crown, under this section.

(6) The powers conferred by this section on a Minister of the Crown may be exercised only by a Minister who is a member of the Cabinet or by the Attorney General.

(7) In this section "Minister of the Crown" has the meaning given by the Ministers of the Crown Act 1975 (c 26).

[Licensing Act 2003, s 174.]

8–19995 **175. Exemption for raffle, tombola, etc.** (1) The conduct of a lottery which, but for this subsection, would to any extent constitute a licensable activity by reason of one or more of the prizes in the lottery consisting of alcohol, is not (for that reason alone) to be treated as constituting a licensable activity if—

(*a*) the lottery is promoted as an incident of an exempt entertainment,

(*b*) after the deduction of all relevant expenses, the whole proceeds of the entertainment (including those of the lottery) are applied for purposes other than private gain, and

(*c*) subsection (2) does not apply.

(2) This subsection applies if—

(*a*) the alcohol consists of or includes alcohol not in a sealed container,

(*b*) any prize in the lottery is a money prize,

(*c*) a ticket or chance in the lottery is sold or issued, or the result of the lottery is declared, other than at the premises where the entertainment takes place and during the entertainment, or

(*d*) the opportunity to participate in a lottery or in gaming is the only or main inducement to attend the entertainment.

(3) For the purposes of subsection (1)(*b*), the following are relevant expenses—

(*a*) the expenses of the entertainment, excluding expenses incurred in connection with the lottery,

(*b*) the expenses incurred in printing tickets in the lottery,
(*c*) such reasonable and proper expenses as the promoters of the lottery appropriate on account of any expenses they incur in buying prizes in the lottery.

(4) In this section—

"exempt entertainment" has the same meaning as in section 3(1) of the Lotteries and Amusements Act 1976 (c 32)[1];
"gaming" has the meaning given by section 52 of the Gaming Act 1968 (c 65)[1];
"money" and "ticket" have the meaning given by section 23 of the Lotteries and Amusements Act 1976[1]; and
"private gain", in relation to the proceeds of an entertainment, is to be construed in accordance with section 22 of that Act.

[Licensing Act 2003, s 175.]

1. In this PART, ante.

Service areas and garages etc

8–19996 **176. Prohibition of alcohol sales at service areas, garages etc.** (1) No premises licence, club premises certificate or temporary event notice has effect to authorise the sale by retail or supply of alcohol on or from excluded premises.

(2) In this section "excluded premises" means—

(*a*) premises situated on land acquired or appropriated by a special road authority, and for the time being used, for the provision of facilities to be used in connection with the use of a special road provided for the use of traffic of class I (with or without other classes); or
(*b*) premises used primarily as a garage or which form part of premises which are primarily so used.

(3) The Secretary of State may by order amend the definition of excluded premises in subsection (2) so as to include or exclude premises of such description as may be specified in the order.

(4) For the purposes of this section—

(*a*) "special road" and "special road authority" have the same meaning as in the Highways Act 1980 (c 66), except that "special road" includes a trunk road to which (by virtue of paragraph 3 of Schedule 23 to that Act) the provisions of that Act apply as if the road were a special road,
(*b*) "class I" means class I in Schedule 4 to the Highways Act 1980 as varied from time to time by an order under section 17 of that Act, but if that Schedule is amended by such an order so as to add to it a further class of traffic, the order may adapt the reference in subsection (2)(*a*) to traffic of class I so as to take account of the additional class, and
(*c*) premises are used as a garage if they are used for one or more of the following—
  (i) the retailing of petrol,
  (ii) the retailing of derv,
  (iii) the sale of motor vehicles,
  (iv) the maintenance of motor vehicles.

[Licensing Act 2003, s 176.]

Small premises

8–19997 **177. Dancing and live music in certain small premises.** (1) Subsection (2) applies where—

(*a*) a premises licence authorises—
  (i) the supply of alcohol for consumption on the premises, and
  (ii) the provision of music entertainment, and
(*b*) the premises—
  (i) are used primarily for the supply of alcohol for consumption on the premises, and
  (ii) have a permitted capacity of not more than 200 persons.

(2) At any time when—

(*a*) the premises—
  (i) are open for the purposes of being used for the supply of alcohol for consumption on the premises, and
  (ii) are being used for the provision of music entertainment, and
(*b*) subsection (4) does not apply,

any licensing authority imposed condition of the premises licence which relates to the provision of music entertainment does not have effect, in relation to the provision of that entertainment, unless it falls within subsection (5) or (6).

(3) Subsection (4) applies where—

(*a*) a premises licence authorises the provision of music entertainment, and

(*b*) the premises have a permitted capacity of not more than 200 persons.

(4) At any time between the hours of 8 a.m. and midnight when the premises—

(*a*) are being used for the provision of music entertainment which consists of—

(i) the performance of unamplified, live music, or

(ii) facilities for enabling persons to take part in entertainment within sub-paragraph (i), but

(*b*) are not being used for the provision of any other description of regulated entertainment,

any licensing authority imposed condition of the premises licence which relates to the provision of the music entertainment does not have effect, in relation to the provision of that entertainment, unless it falls within subsection (6).

(5) A condition falls within this subsection if the premises licence specifies that the licensing authority which granted the licence considers the imposition of the condition necessary on one or both of the following grounds—

(*a*) the prevention of crime and disorder,

(*b*) public safety.

(6) A condition falls within this subsection if, on a review of the premises licence—

(*a*) it is altered so as to include a statement that this section does not apply to it, or

(*b*) it is added to the licence and includes such a statement.

(7) This section applies in relation to a club premises certificate as it applies in relation to a premises licence except that, in the application of this section in relation to such a certificate, the definition of "licensing authority imposed condition" in subsection (8) has effect as if for "section 18(3)(*b*)" to the end there were substituted "section 72(3)(*b*) (but is not referred to in section 72(2)) or which is imposed by virtue of section 85(3)(*b*) or 88(3)".

(8) In this section—

"licensing authority imposed condition" means a condition which is imposed by virtue of section 18(3)(*b*) (but is not referred to in section 18(2)(*a*)) or which is imposed by virtue of 35(3)(*b*), 52(3) or 167(5)(*b*) or in accordance with section 21;

"music entertainment" means—

(*a*) entertainment of a description falling within, or of a similar description to that falling within, paragraph 2(1)(*e*) or (*g*) of Schedule 1, or

(*b*) facilities enabling persons to take part in entertainment within paragraph (*a*);

"permitted capacity", in relation to any premises, means—

(*a*) *repealed*

(*b*) the limit on the number of persons who may be on the premises at any one time in accordance with a recommendation made by, or on behalf of, the fire authority for the area in which the premises are situated (or, if the premises are situated in the area of more than one fire authority, those authorities); and

"supply of alcohol" means—

(*a*) the sale by retail of alcohol, or

(*b*) the supply of alcohol by or on behalf of a club to, or to the order of, a member of the club.

[Licensing Act 2003, s 177 as amended by SI 2005/1541.]

Rights of freeholders etc

8–19998 **178. Right of freeholder etc to be notified of licensing matters.** *Right of person with a property interest in any premises to notify the licensing authority of that interest and then to be told by the licensing authority of any changes to the licensing register affecting that premises.*

Rights of entry

8–19999 **179. Rights of entry to investigate licensable activities.** (1) Where a constable or an authorised person has reason to believe that any premises are being, or are about to be, used for a licensable activity, he may enter the premises with a view to seeing whether the activity is being, or is to be, carried on under and in accordance with an authorisation.

(2) An authorised person exercising the power conferred by this section must, if so requested, produce evidence of his authority to exercise the power.

(3) A person exercising the power conferred by this section may, if necessary, use reasonable force.

(4) A person commits an offence if he intentionally obstructs an authorised person exercising a power conferred by this section.

(5) A person guilty of an offence under subsection (4) is liable on summary conviction to a fine not exceeding level 3 on the standard scale.

(6) In this section—

"authorisation" means—

(*a*) a premises licence,
(*b*) a club premises certificate, or
(*c*) a temporary event notice in respect of which the conditions of section 98(2) to (4) are satisfied; and

"authorised person" means an authorised person within the meaning of Part 3 or 4 or an authorised officer within the meaning of section 108(5).

(7) Nothing in this section applies in relation to premises in respect of which there is a club premises certificate but no other authorisation.
[Licensing Act 2003, s 179.]

8–20000 180. Right of entry to investigate offences. (1) A constable may enter and search any premises in respect of which he has reason to believe that an offence under this Act has been, is being or is about to be committed.

(2) A constable exercising a power conferred by this section may, if necessary, use reasonable force.
[Licensing Act 2003, s 180.]

Appeals

8–20001 181. Appeals against decisions of licensing authorities. (1) Schedule 5 (which makes provision for appeals against decisions of licensing authorities) has effect.

(2) On an appeal in accordance with that Schedule against a decision of a licensing authority, a magistrates' court may—

(*a*) dismiss the appeal,
(*b*) substitute for the decision appealed against any other decision which could have been made by the licensing authority, or
(*c*) remit the case to the licensing authority to dispose of it in accordance with the direction of the court,

and may make such order as to costs as it thinks fit.
[Licensing Act 2003, s 181.]

Guidance, hearings etc

8–20002 182. Guidance. (1) The Secretary of State must issue guidance ("the licensing guidance") to licensing authorities on the discharge of their functions under this Act.

(2)–(7) *Procedure for Guidance to be approved; power of Secretary of State to revise the Guidance from time to time*[1].

1. The "Guidance issued under s 182 of the Licensing Act 2003 and Guidance to Police Officers on the operation of Closure Powers in Part 8 of the Licensing Act 2003" dated July 2004 has been issued by the Secretary of State.

8–20003 183. Hearings. *Power to make regulations prescribing hearings procedure*[1].

1. The Licensing Act 2003 (Hearings) Regulations 2005, SI 2005/44 have been made. A licensing authority may not award costs in respect of licensing hearings.

8–20004 184. Giving of notices, etc. (1) This section has effect in relation to any document required or authorised by or under this Act to be given to any person ("relevant document").

(2) Where that person is a licensing authority, the relevant document must be given by addressing it to the authority and leaving it at or sending it by post to—

(*a*) the principal office of the authority, or
(*b*) any other office of the authority specified by it as one at which it will accept documents of the same description as that document.

(3) In any other case the relevant document may be given to the person in question by delivering it to him, or by leaving it at his proper address, or by sending it by post to him at that address.

(4) A relevant document may—

(*a*) in the case of a body corporate (other than a licensing authority), be given to the secretary or clerk of that body;
(*b*) in the case of a partnership, be given to a partner or a person having the control or management of the partnership business;
(*c*) in the case of an unincorporated association (other than a partnership), be given to an officer of the association.

(5) For the purposes of this section and section 7 of the Interpretation Act 1978 (c 30) (service of

documents by post) in its application to this section, the proper address of any person to whom a relevant document is to be given is his last known address, except that—

(*a*) in the case of a body corporate or its secretary or clerk, it is the address of the registered office of that body or its principal office in the United Kingdom,
(*b*) in the case of a partnership, a partner or a person having control or management of the partnership business, it is that of the principal office of the partnership in the United Kingdom, and
(*c*) in the case of an unincorporated association (other than a partnership) or any officer of the association, it is that of its principal office in the United Kingdom.

(6) But if a relevant document is given to a person in his capacity as the holder of a premises licence, club premises certificate or personal licence, or as the designated premises supervisor under a premises licence, his relevant registered address is also to be treated, for the purposes of this section and section 7 of the Interpretation Act 1978 (c 30), as his proper address.

(7) In subsection (6) "relevant registered address", in relation to such a person, means the address given for that person in the record for the licence or certificate (as the case may be) which is contained in the register kept under section 8 by the licensing authority which granted the licence or certificate.

(8) The following provisions of the Local Government Act 1972 (c 70)do not apply in relation to the service of a relevant document—

(*a*) section 231 (service of notices on local authorities etc),
(*b*) section 233 (service of notices by local authorities).

[Licensing Act 2003, s 184.]

8–20005 **185. Provision of information.** *Power to share information between responsible authorities and licensing authorities for the purposes of facilitating the exercise of their functions under the Act.*

General provisions about offences

8–20006 **186. Proceedings for offences.** (1) In this section "offence" means an offence under this Act.

(2) Proceedings for an offence may be instituted—

(*a*) by a licensing authority,
(*b*) by the Director of Public Prosecutions, or
(*c*) in the case of an offence under section 146 or 147 (sale of alcohol to children), by a local weights and measures authority (within the meaning of section 69 of the Weights and Measures Act 1985 (c 72)).

(3) In relation to any offence, section 127(1) of the Magistrates' Courts Act 1980 (information to be laid within six months of offence) is to have effect as if for the reference to six months there were substituted a reference to 12 months.

[Licensing Act 2003, s 186.]

8–20007 **187. Offences by bodies corporate etc.** (1) If an offence committed by a body corporate is shown—

(*a*) to have been committed with the consent or connivance of an officer, or
(*b*) to be attributable to any neglect on his part,

the officer as well as the body corporate is guilty of the offence and liable to be proceeded against and punished accordingly.

(2) If the affairs of a body corporate are managed by its members, subsection (1) applies in relation to the acts and defaults of a member in connection with his functions of management as if he were a director of the body.

(3) In subsection (1) "officer", in relation to a body corporate, means—

(*a*) a director, member of the committee of management, chief executive, manager, secretary or other similar officer of the body, or a person purporting to act in any such capacity, or
(*b*) an individual who is a controller of the body.

(4) If an offence committed by a partnership is shown—

(*a*) to have been committed with the consent or connivance of a partner, or
(*b*) to be attributable to any neglect on his part,

the partner as well as the partnership is guilty of the offence and liable to be proceeded against and punished accordingly.

(5) In subsection (4) "partner" includes a person purporting to act as a partner.

(6) If an offence committed by an unincorporated association (other than a partnership) is shown—

(*a*) to have been committed with the consent or connivance of an officer of the association or a member of its governing body, or
(*b*) to be attributable to any neglect on the part of such an officer or member,

that officer or member as well as the association is guilty of the offence and liable to be proceeded against and punished accordingly.

(7) Regulations may provide for the application of any provision of this section, with such modifications as the Secretary of State considers appropriate, to a body corporate or unincorporated association formed or recognised under the law of a territory outside the United Kingdom.

(8) In this section "offence" means an offence under this Act.

[Licensing Act 2003, s 187.]

8–20008 188. Jurisdiction and procedure in respect of offences. (1) A fine imposed on an unincorporated association on its conviction for an offence is to be paid out of the funds of the association.

(2) Proceedings for an offence alleged to have been committed by an unincorporated association must be brought in the name of the association (and not in that of any of its members).

(3) Rules of court relating to the service of documents are to have effect as if the association were a body corporate.

(4) In proceedings for an offence brought against an unincorporated association, section 33 of the Criminal Justice Act 1925 (c 86) and Schedule 3 to the Magistrates' Courts Act 1980 (c 43) (procedure) apply as they do in relation to a body corporate.

(5) Proceedings for an offence may be taken—

(*a*) against a body corporate or unincorporated association at any place at which it has a place of business;

(*b*) against an individual at any place where he is for the time being.

(6) Subsection (5) does not affect any jurisdiction exercisable apart from this section.

(7) In this section "offence" means an offence under this Act.

[Licensing Act 2003, s 188.]

Vessels, vehicles and moveable structures

8–20009 189. Vessels, vehicles and moveable structures. (1) This Act applies in relation to a vessel which is not permanently moored or berthed as if it were premises situated in the place where it is usually moored or berthed.

(2) Where a vehicle which is not permanently situated in the same place is, or is proposed to be, used for one or more licensable activities while parked at a particular place, the vehicle is to be treated for the purposes of this Act as if it were premises situated at that place.

(3) Where a moveable structure which is not permanently situated in the same place is, or is proposed to be, used for one or more licensable activities while set in a particular place, the structure is to be treated for the purposes of this Act as if it were premises situated at that place.

(4) Where subsection (2) applies in relation to the same vehicle, or subsection (3) applies in relation to the same structure, in respect of more than one place, the premises which by virtue of that subsection are situated at each such place are to be treated as separate premises.

(5) Sections 29 to 31 (which make provision in respect of provisional statements relating to premises licences) do not apply in relation to a vessel, vehicle or structure to which this section applies.

[Licensing Act 2003, s 189.]

Interpretation

8–20010 190. Location of sales. (1) This section applies where the place where a contract for the sale of alcohol is made is different from the place where the alcohol is appropriated to the contract.

(2) For the purposes of this Act the sale of alcohol is to be treated as taking place where the alcohol is appropriated to the contract.

[Licensing Act 2003, s 190.]

8–20011 191. Meaning of "alcohol". (1) In this Act, "alcohol" means spirits, wine, beer, cider or any other fermented, distilled or spirituous liquor, but does not include—

(*a*) alcohol which is of a strength not exceeding 0.5% at the time of the sale or supply in question,

(*b*) perfume,

(*c*) flavouring essences recognised by the Commissioners of Customs and Excise as not being intended for consumption as or with dutiable alcoholic liquor,

(*d*) the aromatic flavouring essence commonly known as Angostura bitters,

(*e*) alcohol which is, or is included in, a medicinal product,

(*f*) denatured alcohol,

(*g*) methyl alcohol,

(*h*) naphtha, or

(i) alcohol contained in liqueur confectionery.

(2) In this section—

"denatured alcohol" has the same meaning as in section 5 of the Finance Act 1995 (c 4);

"dutiable alcoholic liquor" has the same meaning as in the Alcoholic Liquor Duties Act 1979 (c 4);

"liqueur confectionery" means confectionery which—

(*a*) contains alcohol in a proportion not greater than 0.2 litres of alcohol (of a strength not exceeding 57%) per kilogram of the confectionery, and

(*b*) either consists of separate pieces weighing not more than 42g or is designed to be broken into such pieces for the purpose of consumption;

"medicinal product" has the same meaning as in section 130 of the Medicines Act 1968 (c 67); and

"strength" is to be construed in accordance with section 2 of the Alcoholic Liquor Duties Act 1979.

[Licensing Act 2003, s 191.]

8–20012 **192. Meaning of "sale by retail".** (1) For the purposes of this Act "sale by retail", in relation to any alcohol, means a sale of alcohol to any person, other than a sale of alcohol that—

(*a*) is within subsection (2),

(*b*) is made from premises owned by the person making the sale, or occupied by him under a lease to which the provisions of Part 2 of the Landlord and Tenant Act 1954 (c 56) (security of tenure) apply, and

(*c*) is made for consumption off the premises.

(2) A sale of alcohol is within this subsection if it is—

(*a*) to a trader for the purposes of his trade,

(*b*) to a club, which holds a club premises certificate, for the purposes of that club,

(*c*) to the holder of a personal licence for the purpose of making sales authorised by a premises licence,

(*d*) to the holder of a premises licence for the purpose of making sales authorised by that licence, or

(*e*) to the premises user in relation to a temporary event notice for the purpose of making sales authorised by that notice.

[Licensing Act 2003, s 192.]

8–20013 **193. Other definitions.** In this Act—

"beer" has the same meaning as in the Alcoholic Liquor Duties Act 1979 (c 4);

"cider" has the same meaning as in that Act;

"crime prevention objective" means the licensing objective mentioned in section 4(2)(*a*) (prevention of crime and disorder);

"licensed premises" means premises in respect of which a premises licence has effect;

"licensing functions" is to be construed in accordance with section 4(1);

"order", except so far as the contrary intention appears, means an order made by the Secretary of State;

"premises" means any place and includes a vehicle, vessel or moveable structure;

"prescribed" means prescribed by regulations;

"recognised club" means a club which satisfies conditions 1 to 3 of the general conditions in section 62;

"regulations" means regulations made by the Secretary of State;

"vehicle" means a vehicle intended or adapted for use on roads;

"vessel" includes a ship, boat, raft or other apparatus constructed or adapted for floating on water;

"wine" means—

(*a*) "wine" within the meaning of the Alcoholic Liquor Duties Act 1979, and

(*b*) "made-wine" within the meaning of that Act;

"working day" means any day other than a Saturday, a Sunday, Christmas Day, Good Friday or a day which is a bank holiday under the Banking and Financial Dealings Act 1971 (c 80) in England and Wales.

[Licensing Act 2003, s 193.]

8–20014 **194. Index of defined expressions.** In this Act the following expressions are defined or otherwise explained by the provisions indicated—

Expression	*Interpretation provision*
alcohol	section 191
associate member	section 67(2)
authorised person, in Part 3	section 13
authorised person, in Part 4	section 69

Expression	*Interpretation provision*
beer	section 193
cider	section 193
club premises certificate	section 60
conviction, in Part 6	section 114
crime prevention objective	section 193
designated premises supervisor	section 15
foreign offence, in Part 6	section 113
given, in relation to a notice, etc	section 184
guest	section 67(1)
interested party, in Part 3	section 13
interested party, in Part 4	section 69
interim authority notice	section 47
late night refreshment	Schedule 2
licensable activity	section 1(1)
licensed premises	section 193
licensing authority	section 3(1)
licensing authority's area	section 3(2)
licensing functions	sections 4(1) and 193
licensing objectives	section 4(2)
order	section 193
permitted temporary activity	section 98
personal licence	section 111(1)
premises	section 193
premises licence	section 11
premises user, in relation to a temporary event notice	section 100(2)
prescribed	section 193
provisional statement	section 29(3)
qualifying club	section 61
qualifying club activity	section 1(2)
recognised club	section 193
regulated entertainment	Schedule 1
regulations	section 193
relevant licensing authority, in Part 3	section 12
relevant licensing authority, in Part 4	section 68
relevant licensing authority, in Part 5	section 99
relevant licensing authority, in Part 6	section 112
relevant offence, in Part 6	section 113
responsible authority, in Part 3	section 13
responsible authority, in Part 4	section 69
sale by retail, in relation to alcohol	section 192
secretary, in Part 4	section 70
supply of alcohol, in Part 3	section 14
supply of alcohol to members or guests, in relation to a club, in Part 4	section 70
temporary event notice	section 100(1)
vehicle	section 193
vessel	section 193
wine	section 193
working day	section 193

[Licensing Act 2003, s 194.]

Supplementary and general

8–20015 195. Crown application. (1) This Act binds the Crown and has effect in relation to land in which there is—

(*a*) an interest belonging to Her Majesty in right of the Crown,
(*b*) an interest belonging to a government department, or
(*c*) an interest held in trust for Her Majesty for the purposes of such a department.

(2) This Act also applies to—

(*a*) land which is vested in, but not occupied by, Her Majesty in right of the Duchy of Lancaster, and
(*b*) land which is vested in, but not occupied by, the possessor for the time being of the Duchy of Cornwall.

(3) No contravention by the Crown of any provision made by or under this Act makes the Crown criminally liable; but the High Court may declare unlawful any act or omission of the Crown which constitutes such a contravention.

(4) Provision made by or under this Act applies to persons in the public service of the Crown as it applies to other persons.

(5) But nothing in this Act affects Her Majesty in Her private capacity.

[Licensing Act 2003, s 195.]

8–20016 **196. Removal of privileges and exemptions.** No privilege or exemption mentioned in section 199(*a*) or (*b*) of the Licensing Act 1964 (c 26) (University of Cambridge and the Vintners of the City of London) operates to exempt any person from the requirements of this Act.

[Licensing Act 2003, s 196.]

8–20017 **197. Regulations and orders**

198. Minor and consequential amendments

199. Repeals

8–20018 **200. Transitional provision etc**

8–20019 **201. Short title, commencement and extent.** (1) This Act may be cited as the Licensing Act 2003.

(2) The preceding provisions (and the Schedules) come into force in accordance with provision made by order[1].

(3) Subject to subsections (4) and (5), this Act extends to England and Wales only.

(4) Section 155(1) also extends to Northern Ireland.

(5) An amendment or repeal contained in Schedule 6 or 7 has the same extent as the enactment to which it relates.

[Licensing Act 2003, s 201.]

---

1. For commencement orders made at the date of going to press, see the note to the title of this Act, ante.

8–20020A

Section 1

SCHEDULE 1
PROVISION OF REGULATED ENTERTAINMENT

8–20020B

PART 1
GENERAL DEFINITIONS

The provision of regulated entertainment

1. (1) For the purposes of this Act the "provision of regulated entertainment" means the provision of—

(*a*) entertainment of a description falling within paragraph 2, or
(*b*) entertainment facilities falling within paragraph 3,

where the conditions in sub-paragraphs (2) and (3) are satisfied.

(2) The first condition is that the entertainment is, or entertainment facilities are, provided—

(*a*) to any extent for members of the public or a section of the public,
(*b*) exclusively for members of a club which is a qualifying club in relation to the provision of regulated entertainment, or for members of such a club and their guests, or
(*c*) in any case not falling within paragraph (*a*) or (*b*), for consideration and with a view to profit.

(3) The second condition is that the premises on which the entertainment is, or entertainment facilities are, provided are made available for the purpose, or for purposes which include the purpose, of enabling the entertainment concerned (whether of a description falling within paragraph 2(1) or paragraph 3(2)) to take place.

To the extent that the provision of entertainment facilities consists of making premises available, the premises are to be regarded for the purposes of this sub-paragraph as premises "on which" entertainment facilities are provided.

(4) For the purposes of sub-paragraph (2)(*c*), entertainment is, or entertainment facilities are, to be regarded as provided for consideration only if any charge—

(*a*) is made by or on behalf of—
  (i) any person concerned in the organisation or management of that entertainment, or
  (ii) any person concerned in the organisation or management of those facilities who is also concerned in the organisation or management of the entertainment within paragraph 3(2) in which those facilities enable persons to take part, and
(*b*) is paid by or on behalf of some or all of the persons for whom that entertainment is, or those facilities are, provided.

(5) In sub-paragraph (4), "charge" includes any charge for the provision of goods or services.

(6) For the purposes of sub-paragraph (4)(*a*), where the entertainment consists of the performance of live

music or the playing of recorded music, a person performing or playing the music is not concerned in the organisation or management of the entertainment by reason only that he does one or more of the following—

(*a*) chooses the music to be performed or played,
(*b*) determines the manner in which he performs or plays it,
(*c*) provides any facilities for the purposes of his performance or playing of the music.

(7) This paragraph is subject to Part 2 of this Schedule (exemptions).

Entertainment

2. (1) The descriptions of entertainment are—

(*a*) a performance of a play,
(*b*) an exhibition of a film,
(*c*) an indoor sporting event,
(*d*) a boxing or wrestling entertainment,
(*e*) a performance of live music,
(*f*) any playing of recorded music,
(*g*) a performance of dance,
(*h*) entertainment of a similar description to that falling within paragraph (*e*), (*f*) or (*g*),

where the entertainment takes place in the presence of an audience and is provided for the purpose, or for purposes which include the purpose, of entertaining that audience.

(2) Any reference in sub-paragraph (1) to an audience includes a reference to spectators.

(3) This paragraph is subject to Part 3 of this Schedule (interpretation).

Entertainment facilities

3. (1) In this Schedule, "entertainment facilities" means facilities for enabling persons to take part in entertainment of a description falling within sub-paragraph (2) for the purpose, or for purposes which include the purpose, of being entertained.

(2) The descriptions of entertainment are—

(*a*) making music,
(*b*) dancing,
(*c*) entertainment of a similar description to that falling within paragraph (*a*) or (*b*).

(3) This paragraph is subject to Part 3 of this Schedule (interpretation).

Power to amend Schedule

4. The Secretary of State may by order amend this Schedule for the purpose of modifying—

(*a*) the descriptions of entertainment specified in paragraph 2, or
(*b*) the descriptions of entertainment specified in paragraph 3,

and for this purpose "modify" includes adding, varying or removing any description.

8–20020C

PART 2
EXEMPTIONS

Film exhibitions for the purposes of advertisement, information, education, etc

5. The provision of entertainment consisting of the exhibition of a film is not to be regarded as the provision of regulated entertainment for the purposes of this Act if its sole or main purpose is to—

(*a*) demonstrate any product,
(*b*) advertise any goods or services, or
(*c*) provide information, education or instruction.

Film exhibitions: museums and art galleries

6. The provision of entertainment consisting of the exhibition of a film is not to be regarded as the provision of regulated entertainment for the purposes of this Act if it consists of or forms part of an exhibit put on show for any purposes of a museum or art gallery.

Music incidental to certain other activities

7. The provision of entertainment consisting of the performance of live music or the playing of recorded music is not to be regarded as the provision of regulated entertainment for the purposes of this Act to the extent that it is incidental to some other activity which is not itself—

(*a*) a description of entertainment falling within paragraph 2, or
(*b*) the provision of entertainment facilities.

Use of television or radio receivers

8. The provision of any entertainment or entertainment facilities is not to be regarded as the provision of regulated entertainment for the purposes of this Act to the extent that it consists of the simultaneous reception and playing of a programme included in a programme service within the meaning of the Broadcasting Act 1990 (c 42).

Religious services, places of worship etc

9. The provision of any entertainment or entertainment facilities—

(*a*) for the purposes of, or for purposes incidental to, a religious meeting or service, or
(*b*) at a place of public religious worship,

is not to be regarded as the provision of regulated entertainment for the purposes of this Act.

Garden fêtes, etc

10. (1) The provision of any entertainment or entertainment facilities at a garden fête, or at a function or event of a similar character, is not to be regarded as the provision of regulated entertainment for the purposes of this Act.

(2) But sub-paragraph (1) does not apply if the fête, function or event is promoted with a view to applying the whole or part of its proceeds for purposes of private gain.

(3) In sub-paragraph (2) "private gain", in relation to the proceeds of a fête, function or event, is to be construed in accordance with section 22 of the Lotteries and Amusements Act 1976 (c 32).

Morris dancing etc

11. The provision of any entertainment or entertainment facilities is not to be regarded as the provision of regulated entertainment for the purposes of this Act to the extent that it consists of the provision of—

(*a*) a performance of morris dancing or any dancing of a similar nature or a performance of unamplified, live music as an integral part of such a performance , or
(*b*) facilities for enabling persons to take part in entertainment of a description falling within paragraph (*a*).

Vehicles in motion

12. The provision of any entertainment or entertainment facilities—

(*a*) on premises consisting of or forming part of a vehicle, and
(*b*) at a time when the vehicle is not permanently or temporarily parked,

is not to be regarded as the provision of regulated entertainment for the purposes of this Act.

8–20020D

PART 3
INTERPRETATION

General

13. This Part has effect for the purposes of this Schedule.

Plays

14. (1) A "performance of a play" means a performance of any dramatic piece, whether involving improvisation or not,—

(*a*) which is given wholly or in part by one or more persons actually present and performing, and
(*b*) in which the whole or a major proportion of what is done by the person or persons performing, whether by way of speech, singing or action, involves the playing of a role.

(2) In this paragraph, "performance" includes rehearsal (and "performing" is to be construed accordingly).

Film exhibitions

15. An "exhibition of a film" means any exhibition of moving pictures.

Indoor sporting events

16. (1) An "indoor sporting event" is a sporting event—

(*a*) which takes place wholly inside a building, and
(*b*) at which the spectators present at the event are accommodated wholly inside that building.

(2) In this paragraph—

"building" means any roofed structure (other than a structure with a roof which may be opened or closed) and includes a vehicle, vessel or moveable structure,
"sporting event" means any contest, exhibition or display of any sport, and
"sport" includes—

(*a*) any game in which physical skill is the predominant factor, and
(*b*) any form of physical recreation which is also engaged in for purposes of competition or display.

Boxing or wrestling entertainments

17. A "boxing or wrestling entertainment" is any contest, exhibition or display of boxing or wrestling.

Music

18. "Music" includes vocal or instrumental music or any combination of the two.

8–20020E

Section 1

SCHEDULE 2
PROVISION OF LATE NIGHT REFRESHMENT

The provision of late night refreshment

1. (1) For the purposes of this Act, a person "provides late night refreshment" if—

(*a*) at any time between the hours of 11.00 p m. and 5.00 a.m., he supplies hot food or hot drink to members of the public, or a section of the public, on or from any premises, whether for consumption on or off the premises, or

(*b*) at any time between those hours when members of the public, or a section of the public, are admitted to any premises, he supplies, or holds himself out as willing to supply, hot food or hot drink to any persons, or to persons of a particular description, on or from those premises, whether for consumption on or off the premises,

unless the supply is an exempt supply by virtue of paragraph 3, 4 or 5.

(2) References in this Act to the "provision of late night refreshment" are to be construed in accordance with sub-paragraph (1).

(3) This paragraph is subject to the following provisions of this Schedule.

Hot food or hot drink

2. Food or drink supplied on or from any premises is "hot" for the purposes of this Schedule if the food or drink, or any part of it,—

(*a*) before it is supplied, is heated on the premises or elsewhere for the purpose of enabling it to be consumed at a temperature above the ambient air temperature and, at the time of supply, is above that temperature, or

(*b*) after it is supplied, may be heated on the premises for the purpose of enabling it to be consumed at a temperature above the ambient air temperature.

Exempt supplies: clubs, hotels etc and employees

3. (1) The supply of hot food or hot drink on or from any premises at any time is an exempt supply for the purposes of paragraph 1(1) if, at that time, a person will neither—

(*a*) be admitted to the premises, nor

(*b*) be supplied with hot food or hot drink on or from the premises,

except by virtue of being a person of a description falling within sub-paragraph (2).

(2) The descriptions are that—

(*a*) he is a member of a recognised club,

(*b*) he is a person staying at a particular hotel, or at particular comparable premises, for the night in question,

(*c*) he is an employee of a particular employer,

(*d*) he is engaged in a particular trade, he is a member of a particular profession or he follows a particular vocation,

(*e*) he is a guest of a person falling within any of paragraphs (*a*) to (*d*).

(3) The premises which, for the purposes of sub-paragraph (2)(*b*), are comparable to a hotel are—

(*a*) a guest house, lodging house or hostel,

(*b*) a caravan site or camping site, or

(*c*) any other premises the main purpose of maintaining which is the provision of facilities for overnight accommodation.

Exempt supplies: premises licensed under certain other Acts

4. The supply of hot food or hot drink on or from any premises is an exempt supply for the purposes of paragraph 1(1) if it takes place during a period for which—

(*a*) the premises may be used for a public exhibition of a kind described in section 21(1) of the Greater London Council (General Powers) Act 1966 (c xxviii) by virtue of a licence under that section, or

(*b*) the premises may be used as near beer premises within the meaning of section 14 of the London Local Authorities Act 1995 (c x) by virtue of a licence under section 16 of that Act.

Miscellaneous exempt supplies

5. (1) The following supplies of hot food or hot drink are exempt supplies for the purposes of paragraph 1(1)—

(*a*) the supply of hot drink which consists of or contains alcohol,

(*b*) the supply of hot drink by means of a vending machine,

(*c*) the supply of hot food or hot drink free of charge,

(*d*) the supply of hot food or hot drink by a registered charity or a person authorised by a registered charity,

(*e*) the supply of hot food or hot drink on a vehicle at a time when the vehicle is not permanently or temporarily parked.

(2) Hot drink is supplied by means of a vending machine for the purposes of sub-paragraph (1)(*b*) only if—

(*a*) the payment for the hot drink is inserted into the machine by a member of the public, and

(*b*) the hot drink is supplied directly by the machine to a member of the public.

(3) Hot food or hot drink is not to be regarded as supplied free of charge for the purposes of sub-paragraph (1)(*c*) if, in order to obtain the hot food or hot drink, a charge must be paid—

(*a*) for admission to any premises, or
(*b*) for some other item.

(4) In sub-paragraph (1)(*d*) "registered charity" means—

(*a*) a charity which is registered under section 3 of the Charities Act 1993 (c 10), or
(*b*) a charity which by virtue of subsection (5) of that section is not required to be so registered.

Clubs which are not recognised clubs: members and guests

6. For the purposes of this Schedule—

(*a*) the supply of hot food or hot drink to a person as being a member, or the guest of a member, of a club which is not a recognised club is to be taken to be a supply to a member of the public, and
(*b*) the admission of any person to any premises as being such a member or guest is to be taken to be the admission of a member of the public.

8–20020G

Section 113

SCHEDULE 4

PERSONAL LICENCE: RELEVANT OFFENCES

(*Amended by SI 2005/2366*)

1. An offence under this Act.

2. An offence under any of the following enactments—

(*a*) Schedule 12 to the London Government Act 1963 (c 33) (public entertainment licensing);
(*b*) the Licensing Act 1964 (c 26);
(*c*) the Private Places of Entertainment (Licensing) Act 1967 (c 19);
(*d*) section 13 of the Theatres Act 1968 (c 54);
(*e*) the Late Night Refreshment Houses Act 1969 (c 53);
(*f*) section 6 of, or Schedule 1 to, the Local Government (Miscellaneous Provisions) Act 1982 (c 30);
(*g*) the Licensing (Occasional Permissions) Act 1983 (c 24);
(*h*) the Cinemas Act 1985 (c 13);
(*i*) the London Local Authorities Act 1990 (c vii).

3. An offence under the Firearms Act 1968 (c 27).

4. An offence under section 1 of the Trade Descriptions Act 1968 (c 29) (false trade description of goods) in circumstances where the goods in question are or include alcohol.

5. An offence under any of the following provisions of the Theft Act 1968 (c 60)—

(*a*) section 1 (theft);
(*b*) section 8 (robbery);
(*c*) section 9 (burglary);
(*d*) section 10 (aggravated burglary);
(*e*) section 11 (removal of articles from places open to the public);
(*f*) section 12A (aggravated vehicle-taking), in circumstances where subsection (2)(*b*) of that section applies and the accident caused the death of any person;
(*g*) section 13 (abstracting of electricity);
(*h*) section 15 (obtaining property by deception);
(*i*) section 15A (obtaining a money transfer by deception);
(*j*) section 16 (obtaining pecuniary advantage by deception);
(*k*) section 17 (false accounting);
(*l*) section 19 (false statements by company directors etc);
(*m*) section 20 (suppression, etc of documents);
(*n*) section 21 (blackmail);
(*o*) section 22 (handling stolen goods);
(*p*) section 24A (dishonestly retaining a wrongful credit);
(*q*) section 25 (going equipped for stealing etc).

6. An offence under section 7(2) of the Gaming Act 1968 (c 65) (allowing child to take part in gaming on premises licensed for the sale of alcohol).

7. An offence under any of the following provisions of the Misuse of Drugs Act 1971 (c 38)—

(*a*) section 4(2) (production of a controlled drug);
(*b*) section 4(3) (supply of a controlled drug);
(*c*) section 5(3) (possession of a controlled drug with intent to supply);
(*d*) section 8 (permitting activities to take place on premises).

8. An offence under either of the following provisions of the Theft Act 1978 (c 31)—

(*a*) section 1 (obtaining services by deception);
(*b*) section 2 (evasion of liability by deception).

9. An offence under either of the following provisions of the Customs and Excise Management Act 1979 (c 2)—

(*a*) section 170 (disregarding subsection (1)(*a*)) (fraudulent evasion of duty etc);
(*b*) section 170B (taking preparatory steps for evasion of duty).

10. An offence under either of the following provisions of the Tobacco Products Duty Act 1979 (c 7)—

(*a*) section 8G (possession and sale of unmarked tobacco);
(*b*) section 8H (use of premises for sale of unmarked tobacco).

11. An offence under the Forgery and Counterfeiting Act 1981 (c 45) (other than an offence under section 18 or 19 of that Act).

12. An offence under the Firearms (Amendment) Act 1988 (c 45).

13. An offence under any of the following provisions of the Copyright, Designs and Patents Act 1988 (c 48)—

(*a*) section 107(1)(*d*)(iii) (public exhibition in the course of a business of article infringing copyright);
(*b*) section 107(3) (infringement of copyright by public performance of work etc);
(*c*) section 198(2) (broadcast etc of recording of performance made without sufficient consent);
(*d*) section 297(1) (fraudulent reception of transmission);
(*e*) section 297A(1) (supply etc of unauthorised decoder).

14. An offence under any of the following provisions of the Road Traffic Act 1988 (c 52)—

(*a*) section 3A (causing death by careless driving while under the influence of drink or drugs);
(*b*) section 4 (driving etc a vehicle when under the influence of drink or drugs);
(*c*) section 5 (driving etc a vehicle with alcohol concentration above prescribed limit).

15. An offence under either of the following provisions of the Food Safety Act 1990 (c 16) in circumstances where the food in question is or includes alcohol—

(*a*) section 14 (selling food or drink not of the nature, substance or quality demanded);
(*b*) section 15 (falsely describing or presenting food or drink).

16. An offence under section 92(1) or (2) of the Trade Marks Act 1994 (c 26) (unauthorised use of trade mark, etc in relation to goods) in circumstances where the goods in question are or include alcohol.

17. An offence under the Firearms (Amendment) Act 1997 (c 5).

18. A sexual offence, being an offence—

(*a*) listed in Part 2 of Schedule 15 to the Criminal Justice Act 2003, other than the offence mentioned in paragraph 95 (an offence under section 4 of the Sexual Offences Act 1967 (procuring others to commit homosexual acts));
(*b*) an offence under section 8 of the Sexual Offences Act 1956 (intercourse with a defective);
(c) an offence under section 18 of the Sexual Offences Act 1956 (fraudulent abduction of an heiress).

19. A violent offence, being any offence which leads, or is intended or likely to lead, to a person's death or to physical injury to a person, including an offence which is required to be charged as arson (whether or not it would otherwise fall within this definition).

20. An offence under section 3 of the Private Security Industry Act 2001 (c 12) (engaging in certain activities relating to security without a licence).

8–20020G

Section 181

SCHEDULE 5
APPEALS

8–20020H

PART 1
PREMISES LICENCES

Rejection of applications relating to premises licences

1. Where a licensing authority—

(*a*) rejects an application for a premises licence under section 18,
(*b*) rejects (in whole or in part) an application to vary a premises licence under section 35,
(*c*) rejects an application to vary a premises licence to specify an individual as the premises supervisor under section 39, or
(*d*) rejects an application to transfer a premises licence under section 44,

the applicant may appeal against the decision.

Decision to grant premises licence or impose conditions etc

2. (1) This paragraph applies where a licensing authority grants a premises licence under section 18.
(2) The holder of the licence may appeal against any decision—

(*a*) to impose conditions on the licence under subsection (2)(*a*) or (3)(*b*) of that section, or
(*b*) to take any step mentioned in subsection (4)(*b*) or (*c*) of that section (exclusion of licensable activity or refusal to specify person as premises supervisor).

(3) Where a person who made relevant representations in relation to the application desires to contend—

(*a*) that the licence ought not to have been granted, or
(*b*) that, on granting the licence, the licensing authority ought to have imposed different or additional conditions, or to have taken a step mentioned in subsection (4)(*b*) or (*c*) of that section,

he may appeal against the decision.
(4) In sub-paragraph (3) "relevant representations" has the meaning given in section 18(6).

Issue of provisional statement

3. (1) This paragraph applies where a provisional statement is issued under subsection (3)(*c*) of section 31.
(2) An appeal against the decision may be made by—

(*a*) the applicant, or
(*b*) any person who made relevant representations in relation to the application.

(3) In sub-paragraph (2) "relevant representations" has the meaning given in subsection (5) of that section.

Variation of licence under section 35

4. (1) This paragraph applies where an application to vary a premises licence is granted (in whole or in part) under section 35.

(2) The applicant may appeal against any decision to modify the conditions of the licence under subsection (4)(*a*) of that section.

(3) Where a person who made relevant representations in relation to the application desires to contend—

(*a*) that any variation made ought not to have been made, or
(*b*) that, when varying the licence, the licensing authority ought not to have modified the conditions of the licence, or ought to have modified them in a different way, under subsection (4)(*a*) of that section,

he may appeal against the decision.

(4) In sub-paragraph (3) "relevant representations" has the meaning given in section 35(5).

Variation of licence to specify individual as premises supervisor

5. (1) This paragraph applies where an application to vary a premises licence is granted under section 39(2) in a case where a chief officer of police gave a notice under section 37(5) (which was not withdrawn).

(2) The chief officer of police may appeal against the decision to grant the application.

Transfer of licence

6. (1) This paragraph applies where an application to transfer a premises licence is granted under section 44 in a case where a chief officer of police gave a notice under section 42(6) (which was not withdrawn).

(2) The chief officer of police may appeal against the decision to grant the application.

Interim authority notice

7. (1) This paragraph applies where—

(*a*) an interim authority notice is given in accordance with section 47, and
(*b*) a chief officer of police gives a notice under section 48(2) (which is not withdrawn).

(2) Where the relevant licensing authority decides to cancel the interim authority notice under subsection (3) of section 48, the person who gave the interim authority notice may appeal against that decision.

(3) Where the relevant licensing authority decides not to cancel the notice under that subsection, the chief officer of police may appeal against that decision.

(4) Where an appeal is brought under sub-paragraph (2), the court to which it is brought may, on such terms as it thinks fit, order the reinstatement of the interim authority notice pending—

(*a*) the disposal of the appeal, or
(*b*) the expiry of the interim authority period,

whichever first occurs.

(5) Where the court makes an order under sub-paragraph (4), the premises licence is reinstated from the time the order is made, and section 47 has effect in a case where the appeal is dismissed or abandoned before the end of the interim authority period as if—

(*a*) the reference in subsection (7)(*b*) to the end of the interim authority period were a reference to the time when the appeal is dismissed or abandoned, and
(*b*) the reference in subsection (9)(*a*) to the interim authority period were a reference to that period disregarding the part of it which falls after that time.

(6) In this paragraph "interim authority period" has the same meaning as in section 47.

Review of premises licence

8. (1) This paragraph applies where an application for a review of a premises licence is decided under section 52.

(2) An appeal may be made against that decision by—

(*a*) the applicant for the review,
(*b*) the holder of the premises licence, or
(*c*) any other person who made relevant representations in relation to the application.

(3) In sub-paragraph (2) "relevant representations" has the meaning given in section 52(7).

General provision about appeals under this Part

9. (1) An appeal under this Part must be made to the magistrates' court for the petty sessions area (or any such area) in which the premises concerned are situated.

(2) An appeal under this Part must be commenced by notice of appeal given by the appellant to the justices' chief executive for the magistrates' court within the period of 21 days beginning with the day on which the appellant was notified by the licensing authority of the decision appealed against.

(3) On an appeal under paragraph 2(3), 3(2)(*b*), 4(3), 5(2), 6(2) or 8(2)(*a*) or (*c*), the holder of the premises licence is to be the respondent in addition to the licensing authority.

(4) On an appeal under paragraph 7(3), the person who gave the interim authority notice is to be the respondent in addition to the licensing authority.

8–20020I

PART 2
CLUB PREMISES CERTIFICATES

Rejection of applications relating to club premises certificates

10. Where a licensing authority—

(*a*) rejects an application for a club premises certificate under section 72, or
(*b*) rejects (in whole or in part) an application to vary a club premises certificate under section 85,

the club that made the application may appeal against the decision.

Decision to grant club premises certificate or impose conditions etc

11. (1) This paragraph applies where a licensing authority grants a club premises certificate under section 72.
(2) The club holding the certificate may appeal against any decision—

(*a*) to impose conditions on the certificate under subsection (2) or (3)(*b*) of that section, or
(*b*) to take any step mentioned in subsection (4)(*b*) of that section (exclusion of qualifying club activity).

(3) Where a person who made relevant representations in relation to the application desires to contend—

(*a*) that the certificate ought not to have been granted, or
(*b*) that, on granting the certificate, the licensing authority ought to have imposed different or additional conditions, or to have taken a step mentioned in subsection (4)(*b*) of that section,

he may appeal against the decision.
(4) In sub-paragraph (3) "relevant representations" has the meaning given in section 72(7).

Variation of club premises certificate

12. (1) This paragraph applies where an application to vary a club premises certificate is granted (in whole or in part) under section 85.
(2) The club may appeal against any decision to modify the conditions of the certificate under subsection (3)(*b*) of that section.
(3) Where a person who made relevant representations in relation to the application desires to contend—

(*a*) that any variation ought not to have been made, or
(*b*) that, when varying the certificate, the licensing authority ought not to have modified the conditions of the certificate, or ought to have modified them in a different way, under subsection (3)(*b*) of that section,

he may appeal against the decision.
(4) In sub-paragraph (3) "relevant representations" has the meaning given in section 85(5).

Review of club premises certificate

13. (1) This paragraph applies where an application for a review of a club premises certificate is decided under section 88.
(2) An appeal may be made against that decision by—

(*a*) the applicant for the review,
(*b*) the club that holds or held the club premises certificate, or
(*c*) any other person who made relevant representations in relation to the application.

(3) In sub-paragraph (2) "relevant representations" has the meaning given in section 88(7).

Withdrawal of club premises certificate

14. Where the relevant licensing authority gives notice withdrawing a club premises certificate under section 90, the club which holds or held the certificate may appeal against the decision to withdraw it.

General provision about appeals under this Part

15. (1) An appeal under this Part must be made to the magistrates' court for the petty sessions area (or any such area) in which the premises concerned are situated.
(2) An appeal under this Part must be commenced by notice of appeal given by the appellant to the justices' chief executive for the magistrates' court within the period of 21 days beginning with the day on which the appellant was notified by the licensing authority of the decision appealed against.
(3) On an appeal under paragraph 11(3), 12(3) or 13(2)(*a*) or (*c*), the club that holds or held the club premises certificate is to be the respondent in addition to the licensing authority.

8–20020J

PART 3
OTHER APPEALS

Temporary event notices

16. (1) This paragraph applies where—

(*a*) a temporary event notice is given under section 100, and
(*b*) a chief officer of police gives an objection notice in accordance with section 104(2).

(2) Where the relevant licensing authority gives a counter notice under section 105(3), the premises user may appeal against that decision.

(3) Where that authority decides not to give such a counter notice, the chief officer of police may appeal against that decision.

(4) An appeal under this paragraph must be made to the magistrates' court for the petty sessions area (or any such area) in which the premises concerned are situated.

(5) An appeal under this paragraph must be commenced by notice of appeal given by the appellant to the justices' chief executive for the magistrates' court within the period of 21 days beginning with the day on which the appellant was notified by the licensing authority of the decision appealed against.

(6) But no appeal may be brought later than five working days before the day on which the event period specified in the temporary event notice begins.

(7) On an appeal under sub-paragraph (3), the premises user is to be the respondent in addition to the licensing authority.

(8) In this paragraph—

"objection notice" has the same meaning as in section 104; and
"relevant licensing authority" has the meaning given in section 99.

Personal licences

17. (1) Where a licensing authority—

(*a*) rejects an application for the grant of a personal licence under section 120, or
(*b*) rejects an application for the renewal of a personal licence under section 121,

the applicant may appeal against that decision.

(2) Where a licensing authority grants an application for a personal licence under section 120(7), the chief officer of police who gave the objection notice (within the meaning of section 120(5)) may appeal against that decision.

(3) Where a licensing authority grants an application for the renewal of a personal licence under section 121(6), the chief officer of police who gave the objection notice (within the meaning of section 121(3)) may appeal against that decision.

(4) Where a licensing authority revokes a personal licence under section 124(4), the holder of the licence may appeal against that decision.

(5) Where in a case to which section 124 (convictions coming to light after grant or renewal) applies—

(*a*) the chief officer of police for the licensing authority's area gives a notice under subsection (3) of that section (and does not later withdraw it), and
(*b*) the licensing authority decides not to revoke the licence,

the chief officer of police may appeal against the decision.

(6) An appeal under this paragraph must be made to the magistrates' court for a petty sessions area in which the licensing authority's area (or any part of it) is situated.

(7) An appeal under this paragraph must be commenced by notice of appeal given by the appellant to the justices' chief executive for the magistrates' court within the period of 21 days beginning with the day on which the appellant was notified by the licensing authority of the decision appealed against.

(8) On an appeal under sub-paragraph (2), (3) or (5), the holder of the personal licence is to be the respondent in addition to the licensing authority.

(9) Sub-paragraph (10) applies where the holder of a personal licence gives notice of appeal against a decision of a licensing authority to refuse to renew it.

(10) The relevant licensing authority, or the magistrates' court to which the appeal has been made, may, on such conditions as it thinks fit—

(*a*) order that the licence is to continue in force until the relevant time, if it would otherwise cease to have effect before that time, or
(*b*) where the licence has already ceased to have effect, order its reinstatement until the relevant time.

(11) In sub-paragraph (10) "the relevant time" means—

(*a*) the time the appeal is dismissed or abandoned, or
(*b*) where the appeal is allowed, the time the licence is renewed.

Closure orders

18. (1) This paragraph applies where, on a review of a premises licence under section 167, the relevant licensing authority decides under subsection (5)(*b*) of that section—

(*a*) to take any of the steps mentioned in subsection (6) of that section, in relation to a premises licence for those premises, or
(*b*) not to take any such step.

(2) An appeal may be made against that decision by—

(*a*) the holder of the premises licence, or
(*b*) any other person who made relevant representations in relation to the review.

(3) Where an appeal is made under this paragraph against a decision to take any of the steps mentioned in section 167(6)(*a*) to (*d*) (modification of licence conditions etc), the appropriate magistrates' court may in a case within section 168(3) (premises closed when decision taken)—

(*a*) if the relevant licensing authority has not made an order under section 168(5) (order suspending operation of decision in whole or part), make any order under section 168(5) that could have been made by the relevant licensing authority, or
(*b*) if the authority has made such an order, cancel it or substitute for it any order which could have been made by the authority under section 168(5).

(4) Where an appeal is made under this paragraph in a case within section 168(6) (premises closed when

decision to revoke made to remain closed pending appeal), the appropriate magistrates' court may, on such conditions as it thinks fit, order that section 168(7) (premises to remain closed pending appeal) is not to apply to the premises.

(5) An appeal under this paragraph must be commenced by notice of appeal given by the appellant to the justices' chief executive for the magistrates' court within the period of 21 days beginning with the day on which the appellant was notified by the relevant licensing authority of the decision appealed against.

(6) On an appeal under this paragraph by a person other than the holder of the premises licence, that holder is to be the respondent in addition to the licensing authority that made the decision.

(7) In this paragraph—

"appropriate magistrates' court" means the magistrates' court for the petty sessions area (or any such area) in which the premises concerned are situated;

"relevant licensing authority" has the same meaning as in Part 3 of this Act; and

"relevant representations" has the meaning given in section 167(9).

Non-Domestic Rating (Collection and Enforcement) (Local Lists) Regulations 1989[1]

(SI 1989/1058 amended by SI 1990/145 and 156, SI 1991/141, SI 1992/474 and 1512, SI 1993/616, 774, 894 and 1493, the Statute Law (Repeals) Act 1995, Sch 1, SI 1996/675 and 1880, SI 1998/3089, SI 2000/2026, SI 2001/362 and 1076 and SI 2003/1714 (W), 2210 (E), 2604 (E) and 3052 (E))

Part I
General

8–20030 **1. Citation, commencement and interpretation.** (1) *Citation, commencement.*

(2) In these Regulations—

"the Act" means the Local Government Finance Act 1988;

"address" in relation to electronic communications, includes any number or address used for the purposes of such communications;

"business day" means any day except a Saturday or Sunday, Christmas Day, Good Friday or a day which is a bank holiday under the Banking and Financial Dealings Act 1971 in England and Wales;

"demand notice regulations" means the Council Tax and Non-Domestic Rating (Demand Notices)(England) Regulations 1993 or, as the case may be, the Council Tax and Non-Domestic Rating (Demand Notices) (England) Regulations 2003;

"electronic communication" means a communication transmitted (whether from one person to another, from one device to another or from a person to a device or vice versa)—

(*a*) by means of a telecommunications system (within the meaning of the Telecommunications Act 1984); or

(*b*) by other means but while in electronic form.

1. These Regulations made under ss 63, 143(1) and (2) and 146(6) of, and paras 1–4 of Sch 9 to, the Local Government Finance Act 1988, are practically identical in form to the Community Charges (Administration and Enforcement) Regulations, ante. So far as non-domestic ratepayers appearing on central lists are concerned, see the Local Government Finance Act 1988, ss 52 to 54, ante in Part IV: Local Government.

8–20031 **2. Service of notices.** (1) *Common Council notices to be served as under s 233 Local Government Act 1972.*

(2) Without prejudice to section 233 of the Local Government Act 1972 and paragraph (1) above, where any notice which is required or authorised by these Regulations to be given to or served on a person relates to a hereditament which is (or, where such a notice relates to more than one hereditament, one or more of which is) a place of business of that person, it may be given or served by leaving it at, or by sending it by post to him at, the place of business (or, as the case may be, one of those places of business).

(3) Without prejudice to section 233 of the Local Government Act 1972 and paragraphs (1) and (2) above and subject to paragraphs (4) to (7) below, any notice required or authorised to be given to or served by a billing authority on any person by a provision of Part II of these Regulations, or any information required by the demand notice regulations to be supplied to any person when a demand notice (within the meaning of Part II of these Regulations) is served:

(*a*) may be so given, served or supplied by sending the notice or information to that person by electronic communication to such address as may be notified by that person for that purpose; or

(*b*) shall be treated as given, served or supplied to that person where—

(i) the billing authority and that person have agreed for that purpose that any documents containing the notice or information may be accessed by that person on a website;

(ii) the document is a document to which that agreement applies;

(iii) the billing authority has published the document on a website; and

(iv) that person is notified, in a manner for the time being agreed for those purposes between him and the billing authority, of—

(*aa*) the publication of the document on a website;
(*bb*) the address of that website; and
(*cc*) the place on the website where the document may be accessed.

(4) For the purpose of any legal proceedings, a notice given by a means described in paragraph (3) shall, unless the contrary is proved, be treated as served on the second business day after—

(*a*) it was sent in accordance with paragraph (3)(a); or
(*b*) notification of its publication was given in accordance with paragraph (3)(*b*)(iv).

(5) A person who has notified an address for the purpose of paragraph (3)(*a*) shall, by notice in writing to the billing authority, advise the billing authority of any change in that address; and the change shall take effect on the third business day after the date on which the notice is received by the billing authority.

(6) A person who has notified an address for the purpose of paragraph (3)(*a*) may, by notice in writing to the billing authority, withdraw that notification; and the withdrawal shall take effect on the third business day after the date on which the notice is received by the billing authority.

(7) A person who has entered into an agreement with the billing authority under paragraph (3)(*b*)(i) may, by notice in writing to the billing authority, inform the authority that he no longer wishes to be a party to the agreement; and where such notice is given, the agreement shall be treated as revoked on the third business day after the date on which the notice is received by the billing authority.

PART II
BILLING

8–20032 **3. Interpretation and application of Part II.** (1) In this Part—

"the amount payable" for a chargeable financial year or part of a chargeable financial year in relation to a ratepayer, a billing authority and a hereditament means—

(*a*) the amount the ratepayer is liable to pay to the authority as regards the hereditament in respect of the year or part under section 43 or 45 of the Act, whether calculated by reference to section 43(4) to (6) or 45(4) to (6) of the Act (as those provisions are amended or substituted in any case by or under Schedule 7A to the Act) or by reference to an amount or rules determined or prescribed under section 47(1)(*a*) or 58(3)(*a*) of the Act; or

(*b*) where an amount falls to be credited by the billing authority against the ratepayer's liability in respect of the year or part, the amount (if any) by which the amount referred to in sub-paragraph (*a*) above exceeds the amount falling to be so credited;

"demand notice" means the notice required to be served by regulation 4(1);

"ratepayer" in relation to a chargeable financial year and a billing authority means a person liable to pay an amount under section 43 or 45 of the Act to the authority in respect of the year; and

"relevant year" in relation to a notice means the chargeable financial year to which the notice relates;

"the 1992 Act" means the Non-Domestic Rating Act 1992;

"the 1993 Act" means the Non-Domestic Rating Act 1993;

"transitional adjustment notice" has the meaning given by paragraph 7A(2)(*b*) of Schedule 1.

(2) For the purposes of this Part the conditions mentioned in section 43(1) or 45(1) of the Act are not to be treated as fulfilled as regards a hereditament on any day on which the chargeable amount for the day in respect of it is 0 by virtue of a determination to that effect under section 47(1)(*a*) of the Act.

(3) Where references are made in this Part to the day on which a notice is issued, they shall be taken to be references—

(*a*) if the notice is served in the manner described in regulation 2(2) or section 233(2) of the Local Government Act 1972 by being left at, or sent by post to, a person's place of business or proper address, to the day on which it is so left or posted, or
(*b*) in any other case, to the day on which it is served.

(4) The provisions of this Part which provide for the repayment or crediting of any amount or the adjustment of payments due under a notice (including in particular paragraph 7 of Schedule 1) shall have effect subject to paragraph 10(4) of Schedule 7 to the Act.

8–20033 **4. The requirement for demand notices.** (1) For each chargeable financial year a billing authority shall, in accordance with regulations 5 to 7, serve a notice in writing on every person who is a ratepayer of the authority in relation to the year.

(2) Different demand notices shall be served for different chargeable financial years.

(3) A demand notice shall be served with respect to the amount payable for every hereditament as regards which a person is a ratepayer of the authority, though a single notice may relate to the amount payable with respect to more than one such hereditament.

(4) If a single demand notice relates to the amount payable with respect to more than one

hereditament, subject to paragraphs 5 and 8 of Schedule 1 the amounts due under it, and the times at which they fall due, shall be determined as if separate notices were issued in respect of each hereditament.

8–20034 **5. Service of demand notices**[1]. (1) Subject to paragraph (2), a demand notice shall be served on or as soon as practicable after—

(*a*) except in a case falling within sub-paragraph (*b*), 1st April in the relevant year, or
(*b*) if the conditions mentioned in section 43(1) or 45(1) of the Act are not fulfilled in respect of that day as regards the ratepayers and the hereditament concerned, the first day after that day in respect of which such conditions are fulfilled as regards them.

(2) Subject to paragraph (3), a demand notice may, if the non-domestic multiplier for the relevant year has been determined or set under Schedule 7 to the Act, be served before the beginning of the relevant year on a person with respect to whom on the day it is issued it appears to the billing authority that the conditions mentioned in section 43(1) or 45(1) of the Act are fulfilled (or would be fulfilled if a list sent under section 41(5) of the Act were in force) as regards the hereditament to which it relates; and if it is so served, references in this Part to a ratepayer shall, in relation to that notice and so far as the context permits, be construed as references to that person.

(3) A demand notice shall not be served before the authority has set amounts for the relevant year under section 30 of the Local Government Finance Act 1992.

1. Where a boundary order changes the charging authority to that of another one, this regulation is modified by SI 1991/242.

8–20035 **6. Payments under demand notices**[1]. (1) If a demand notice is issued before or during the relevant year and it appears to the billing authority that the conditions mentioned in section 43(1) or 45(1) of the Act are fulfilled (or would be fulfilled if a list sent under section 41(5) of the Act were in force) in respect of the day on which the notice is issued as regards the ratepayer and the hereditament to which it relates, the notice shall require payment of an amount equal to the charging authority's estimate of the amount payable for the year, made as respects periods after the issue of the notice on the assumption that the conditions concerned will continue to be fulfilled on every day after that day.

(2) If a demand notice is issued during the relevant year but paragraph (1) does not apply, the notice shall require payment of an amount equal to the amount payable for the period in the year up to the day on which the conditions mentioned in sections 43(1) and 45(1) were last fulfilled as regards the ratepayer and hereditament concerned.

(3) If, after a notice is served to which paragraph (2) applies, the conditions mentioned in section 43(1) or 45(1) of the Act are fulfilled again in the relevant year as regards the ratepayer and the hereditament concerned, a further notice shall be served on him requiring payments with respect to the amount payable in relation to the hereditament for the period in the relevant year beginning with the day in respect of which the conditions are so fulfilled again; and regulations 5 to 8 (and, so far as applicable, Schedule 1) shall apply to the further notice with respect to that period as if it were a demand notice and the conditions had previously not been fulfilled.

(4) If a demand notice is issued after the end of the relevant year, it shall require payment of the amount payable for the year.

1. Where a boundary order changes the charging authority to that of another one, this regulation is modified by SI 1991/242.

8–20036 **7. Payments under demand notices: further provision.** (1) Unless an agreement under paragraph (3) in relation to the relevant year has been reached between the ratepayer and the billing authority before the demand notice is issued, a notice to which regulation 6(1) applies shall require the estimate of the amount payable to be paid by instalments in accordance with Part I of Schedule 1; and where such instalments are required Part II of the Schedule applies for their cessation or adjustment in the circumstances described in that Part.

(2) If an agreement under paragraph (3) in relation to the relevant year has been reached between the billing authority and the ratepayer before the demand notice is issued, a notice to which regulation 6(1) applies shall require the estimate of the amount payable to be paid in accordance with that agreement.

(3) A billing authority and a ratepayer may agree that the estimate of the amount payable which is required to be paid under a notice to which regulation 6(1) applies should be paid in such manner as is provided by the agreement, rather than in accordance with Schedule 1.

(4) Notwithstanding anything in the foregoing provisions of this regulation, such an agreement may be entered into either before or after the demand notice concerned is issued, and may make provision for the cessation or adjustment of payments, and for the making of fresh estimates, in the event of the estimate mentioned in regulation 6(1) turning out to be wrong; and if it is entered into after the demand notice has been issued, it may make provision dealing with the treatment for the purposes of the agreement of any sums paid in accordance with Schedule 1 before it was entered into.

(5) A notice to which regulation 6(2) or (4) applies shall require payment of the amount payable

on the expiry of such period (being not less than 14 days) after the day of issue of the notice as is specified in it.

(6) No payment in respect of the amount payable by a ratepayer in relation to a hereditament for any chargeable financial year (whether interim, final or sole) need be made unless a notice served under this Part requires it.

8–20037 **8. Failure to pay instalments.** (1) Where—

(*a*) a demand notice has been served by a billing authority on a ratepayer,
(*b*) instalments are payable under the notice in accordance with Schedule 1, and
(*c*) any such instalment is not paid in accordance with the Schedule,

the billing authority shall (unless all the instalments have fallen due) serve a further notice on the ratepayer stating the instalments required to be paid.

(2) If, after the service of a further notice under paragraph (1), the ratepayer—

(*a*) fails to pay, before the expiry of the period of 7 days beginning with the day of service of the further notice, any instalments which fall due before the expiry of that period under the demand notice concerned, or
(*b*) fails to pay any instalment which falls due after the expiry of that period under the demand notice concerned on or before the day on which it so falls due,

the unpaid balance of the estimated amount shall become payable by him at the expiry of a further period 7 days beginning with the day of the failure.

(3) If the unpaid balance of the estimated amount has become payable under paragraph (2), and on calculating the amount payable for the relevant year in relation to a hereditament to which the demand notice concerned relates that amount proves to be greater than the estimated amount in relation to the hereditament, an additional sum equal to the difference between the two shall, on the service by the billing authority on the ratepayer of a notice stating the amount payable, be due from the person to the authority on the expiry of such period (being not less than 14 days) after the day of issue of the notice as is specified in it.

(4) If the unpaid balance of the estimated amount has become payable under paragraph (2), and on calculating the amount payable for the relevant year in relation to a hereditament to which the demand notice concerned relates that amount proves to be less than the estimated amount in relation to the hereditament, the billing authority shall notify the ratepayer in writing of the amount payable; and any overpayment in respect of any liability of the ratepayer under this Part—

(*a*) shall be repaid if the ratepayer so requires, or
(*b*) in any other case shall (as the billing authority determines) either be repaid or be credited against any subsequent liability of the ratepayer to pay anything to it by way of non-domestic rate.

(5) If any factor or assumption by reference to which the estimated amount was calculated in relation to a hereditament is shown to be false before the amount payable is capable of final determination for the purposes of paragraphs (3) and (4), the billing authority may, and if so required by the ratepayer shall, make a calculation of the appropriate amount with a view to adjusting the ratepayer's liability in respect of the estimated amount and (as appropriate) to—

(*a*) requiring an interim payment from the ratepayer if the appropriate amount is greater than the estimated amount, or
(*b*) making an interim repayment to the ratepayer if the appropriate amount is less than the amount of the estimated amount paid.

(6) The appropriate amount for the purposes of paragraph (5) is the amount which would be required to be paid under a demand notice if such a notice were issued with respect to the relevant year, the ratepayer and the hereditament on the day that the notice under paragraph (7) is issued or the repayment under paragraph (5)(*b*) is made (as the case may be); and more than one calculation of the appropriate amount and interim payment or repayment may be required or made under paragraph (5) according to the circumstances.

(7) On calculating the appropriate amount the billing authority shall notify the ratepayer in writing of it; and a payment required under paragraph (5)(*a*) shall be due from the ratepayer to the billing authority on the expiry of such period (being not less than 14 days) after the day of issue of the notice as is specified in it.

(8) In this regulation—

"the appropriate amount" has the meaning given in paragraph (6); and

"the estimated amount" means the amount last estimated under regulation 6(1) for the purposes of the demand notice mentioned in paragraph (1)(*a*) or any subsequent notice given under paragraph 7(2) or, as the case may be, paragraph 7A or paragraph 7B of Schedule 1 prior to the failure mentioned in paragraph (2) above, save that if in any case an interim adjustment has been required or made under paragraph (5) in relation to a hereditament, it means as regards the next payment, repayment or interim adjustment in relation to the hereditament under this regulation (if any), the appropriate amount by reference to which the previous interim adjustment was so made.

8–20038 9. Demand notices: final adjustment. (1) This regulation applies where—

(*a*) a notice has been issued by a billing authority under this Part requiring a payment or payments to be made by a ratepayer in respect of the amount payable in relation to a hereditament for a chargeable financial year or part of a chargeable financial year,

(*b*) the payment or payments required to be paid are found to be in excess of or less than the amount payable in relation to the hereditament for the year or the part, and

(*c*) provision for adjusting the amounts required under the notice and (as appropriate) for the making of additional payments or the repaying or crediting of any amount overpaid is not made by any other provision of this Part, of the Act or of any agreement entered into under regulation 7(3).

(2) the billing authority shall as soon as practicable after the expiry of the year or the part of a year serve a further notice on the ratepayer stating the amount payable for the year or part in relation to the hereditament, and adjusting (by reference to that amount) the amounts required to be paid under the notice referred to in paragraph (1)(*a*).

(3) If the amount stated in the further notice is greater than the amount required to be paid under the notice referred to in paragraph (1)(*a*), the amount of the difference for which such other provision as is mentioned in paragraph (1)(*c*) is not made shall be due from the ratepayer to the billing authority on the expiry of such period (being not less than 14 days) after the day of issue of the notice as is specified in it.

(4) If there has been an overpayment in respect of any liability of the ratepayer under this Part, the amount overpaid for which such other provision as is mentioned in paragraph (1)(*c*) is not made—

(*a*) shall be repaid if the ratepayer so requires, or

(*b*) in any other case shall (as the billing authority determines) either be repaid or be credited against any subsequent liability of the ratepayer to pay anything to it by way of non-domestic rate.

8–20039 10. Interpretation and application of Part III. (1) In this Part—

"debtor" means a person against whom a liability order has been made; and

"liability order" means an order under regulation 12.

(2) A sum which has become payable to a billing authority under Part II and which has not been paid shall be recoverable under a liability order, or in a court of competent jurisdiction, in accordance with regulations 11 to 21.

(3) References in this Part to a sum which has become payable and which has not been paid include references to a sum forming part of a larger sum which has become payable and the other part of which has been paid.

8–20040 11. Liability orders: preliminary steps. (1) Subject to paragraph (3), before a billing authority applies for a liability order it shall serve on the person against whom the application is to be made a notice ("reminder notice"), which is to be in addition to any notice required to be served under Part II and which is to state every amount in respect of which the authority is to make the application.

(2) A reminder notice may be served in respect of an amount at any time after it has become due.

(3) A reminder notice need not be served on a person who has been served under regulation 8(1) with a notice in respect of the amount concerned where there has been such a failure as is mentioned in regulation 8(2)(*a*) in relation to the notice.

8–20041 12. Application for liability order. (1) Subject to paragraph (3), if an amount which has fallen due under regulation 8(2) in consequence of such a failure as is mentioned in sub-paragraph (*a*) of that provision is wholly or partly unpaid, or (in a case where a reminder notice is required under regulation 11) the amount stated in the reminder notice is wholly or partly unpaid at the expiry of the period of 7 days beginning with the day on which the notice was served, the billing authority may, in accordance with paragraph (2), apply to a magistrates' court for an order against the person by whom it is payable.

(2) The application is to be instituted by making complaint to a justice of the peace, and requesting the issue of a summons directed to that person to appear before the court to show why he has not paid the sum which is outstanding.

(3) Section 127(1) of the Magistrates' Courts Act 1980 does not apply to such an application; but no application may be instituted in respect of a sum after the period of 6 years beginning with the day on which it became due under Part II.

(4) A warrant shall not be issued under section 55(2) of the Magistrates' Courts Act 1980 in any proceedings under this regulation.

(5) The court shall make the order[1] if it is satisfied that the sum has become payable by the defendant and has not been paid.

(6) An order made pursuant to paragraph (5) shall be made in respect of an amount equal to the aggregate of—

(*a*) the sum payable, and

(*b*) a sum of an amount equal to the costs reasonably incurred by the applicant in obtaining the order.

(7) Where the sum payable is paid after a liability order has been applied for under paragraph (2) but before it is made, the court shall nonetheless (if so requested by the billing authority) make the order in respect of a sum of an amount equal to the costs reasonably incurred by the authority in making the application.

---

1. Justices may reopen their decision to make a liability order made in ignorance of the receipt of an application to adjourn so that they may exercise their judicial discretion whether to grant the order or adjourn (*Liverpool City Council v Pleroma Distribution Ltd* [2003] RA 34, [2003] 04 LS Gaz R 33). The appropriate procedure where liability orders were made as a result of incorrect service would be (i) for the individual to inform the justices and the local authority that he or she had not been properly served; (ii) the authority should determine if that assertion was correct, which would entail some co-operation with the individual; (iii) where it was established that the individual was not liable, but he or she was not content to accept the authority's assurance that liability orders would not be enforced, and wished for them to be set aside, the authority should join in an application to the justices to have the orders set aside; (iv) if such an application was refused, then the justices would be acting unreasonably and would be liable for costs (*R (on the application of Tull) v Camberwell Green Magistrates' Court* (2004) 168 JPN 986).

8–20042 13. Liability orders: further provision. (1) A single liability order may deal with one person and one such amount (or aggregate amount) as is mentioned in regulation 12(6) or (7), or, if the court thinks fit, may deal with more than one person and more than one such amount (or aggregate amount).

(2) A summons issued under regulation 12(2) may be served on a person—

(*a*) by delivering it to him,

(*b*) by leaving it as his usual or last known place of abode, or in the case of a company, at its registered office,

(*c*) by sending it by post to him at his usual or last known place of abode, or in the case of a company, to its registered office,

(*d*) where all or part of the sum to which it relates is payable with respect to a hereditament which is a place of business of the person, by leaving it at, or by sending it by post to him at, the place of business, or

(*e*) by leaving it at, or by sending it by post to him at, an address given by the person as an address at which service of the summons will be accepted.

(2A) No liability order shall be made in pursuance of a summons issued under regulation 12(2) unless fourteen days have elapsed since the day on which the summons was served.

(3) The amount in respect of which a liability order is made is enforceable in accordance with this part; and accordingly for the purposes of any of the provisions of Part III of the Magistrates' Courts Act 1980 (satisfaction and enforcement) it is not to be treated as a sum adjudged to be paid by order of the court.

8–20043 14. Distress. (1) Where a liability order has been made, the authority which applied for the order may levy the appropriate amount by distress and sale of the goods of the debtor against whom the order was made.

(1A) Without prejudice to paragraph (8) below, no person making a distress shall seize any goods of the debtor of the following description—

such clothing, bedding, furniture, household equipment and provisions as are necessary for satisfying the basic domestic needs of the debtor and his family.

(2) The appropriate amount for the purposes of paragraph (1) is the aggregate of—

(*a*) an amount equal to any outstanding sum which is or forms part of the amount in respect of which the liability order was made, and

(*b*) a sum determined in accordance with Schedule 3 in respect of charges connected with the distress.

(3) If, before[1] any goods are seized, the appropriate amount (including charges arising up to the time of the payment or tender) is paid or tendered to the authority, the authority shall accept the amount and the levy shall not be proceeded with.

(4) Where an authority has seized[1] goods of the debtor in pursuance of the distress, but before sale of those goods the appropriate amount (including charges arising up to the time of the payment or tender) is paid or tendered to the authority, the authority shall accept the amount, the sale shall not be proceeded with and the goods shall be made available for collection by the debtor.

(5) The person levying distress on behalf of an authority shall carry with him the written authorisation of the authority, which he shall show to the debtor if so requested; and he shall hand to the debtor or leave at the premises where the distress is levied a copy of this regulation and Schedule 3 and a memorandum setting out the appropriate amount, and shall hand to the debtor a copy of any close or walking possession agreement entered into[2].

(6) A distress may be made anywhere in England and Wales.

(6A) No distress under this regulation may be granted other than by a person who is authorised to act as a bailiff by a general certificate granted under section 7 of the Law of Distress Amendment Act 1888.

(7) A distress shall not be deemed unlawful on account of an defect or want of form in the liability order, and no person making a distress shall be deemed a trespasser on that account;

and no person making a distress shall be deemed a trespasser from the beginning on account of any subsequent irregularity in making the distress, but a person sustaining special damage by reason of the subsequent irregularity may recover full satisfaction for the special damage (and no more) by proceedings in trespass or otherwise.

(8) The provisions of this regulation shall not affect the operation of any enactment which protects goods of any class from distress.

(9) *Revoked.*

---

1. The debtor does not have a continuous opportunity to end the process by appropriate tender, the opportunity only arises *before* seizure of goods (reg 14(3)) and after seizure and before sale (reg 14(4); there is no opportunity to redeem the goods afforded during the period of seizure itself (*Wilson v South Kesteven District Council* [2000] 4 All ER 577, [2001] 1 WLR 387, CA).

2. The memorandum should be handed over to the debtor at the earliest opportunity, ideally when the person levying distress first enters the premises and embarks on the distraint process. Failure to provide the memorandum constitutes a "subsequent irregularity" within the meaning of reg 14(7). Special damage covers all loss occasioned by the irregularity but the distress process itself is not rendered unlawful by such irregularity (*Wilson v South Kesteven District Council* [2000] 4 All ER 577, [2001] 1 WLR 387, CA).

8–20044 15. Appeals in connection with distress. (1) A person aggrieved by the levy of, or an attempt to levy, a distress may appeal to a magistrates' court.

(2) The appeal shall be instituted by making complaint[1] to a justice of the peace, and requesting the issue of a summons directed to the authority which levied or attempted to levy the distress to appear before the court to answer to the matter by which he is aggrieved.

(3) If the court is satisfied that a levy was irregular, it may order these goods distrained to be discharged if they are in the possession of the authority; and it may by order award compensation in respect of any goods distrained and sold of an amount equal to the amount which, in the opinion of the court, would be awarded by way of special damages in respect of the goods if proceedings were brought in trespass or otherwise in connection with the irregularity under regulation 14(7).

(4) If the court is satisfied that an attempted levy was irregular, it may by order require the authority to desist from levying in the manner giving rise to the irregularity.

---

1. If on the hearing of the complaint the justices form the opinion that the case raises complex issues of title, they have a discretion to decline to continue the hearing, leaving the complainant with the right to proceed by way of an action in the High Court or county court (*R v Basildon Justices, ex p Holding and Barnes plc* (1994) 158 JP 980).

8–20045 16. Commitment to prison. (1) Where a charging authority has sought to levy an amount by distress under regulation 14, the debtor is an individual, and the person making the distress reports to the authority that he was unable (for whatever reason) to find any or sufficient goods of the debtor on which to levy the amount, the authority may apply to a magistrates' court for the issue of a warrant committing the debtor to prison.

(2) On such application being made the court shall (in the debtor's presence) inquire as to his means and inquire whether the failure to pay which led to the liability order concerned being made against him was due to his wilful refusal or culpable neglect.

(3) If (and only if) the court is of the opinion that his failure was due to his wilful refusal or culpable neglect it may if it thinks fit—

(*a*) issue a warrant of commitment against the debtor, or

(*b*) fix a term of imprisonment and postpone the issue of the warrant until such time and on such conditions (if any) as the court thinks just.

(4) The warrant shall be made in respect of the relevant amount; and the relevant amount for this purpose is the aggregate of—

(*a*) the appropriate amount mentioned in regulation 14(2), or (as the case may be) so much of it as remains outstanding, and

(*b*) a sum of an amount equal to the costs reasonably incurred by the applicant in respect of the application.

(5) The warrant—

(*a*) shall state the relevant amount mentioned in paragraph (4),

(*b*) may be directed to the authority making the application and to such other persons (if any) as the court issuing it thinks fit, and

(*c*) may be executed anywhere in England and Wales by any person to whom it is directed.

(6) If—

(*a*) before a warrant has been issued, or a term of imprisonment fixed and the issue of a warrant postponed, an amount determined in accordance with paragraph (6A) is paid or tendered to the authority, or

(*b*) after a term of imprisonment has been fixed and the issue of a warrant postponed, any amount the court has ordered the debtor to pay is paid or tendered to the authority, or

(*c*) after a warrant has been issued, the amount stated in it is paid or tendered to the authority, the authority shall accept the amount concerned, no further steps shall be taken as regards its recovery, and the debtor, if committed to prison, shall be released.

(6A) The amount referred to in paragraph (6)(*a*) above is the aggregate of—

(6B) For the purposes of paragraph (6A)(*b*) above, the authority's reasonable costs in respect of any application shall not exceed the amount specified in relation to that application in Schedule 4.]

(7) The order in the warrant shall be that the debtor be imprisoned for a time specified[1] in the warrant which shall not exceed 3 months, unless the amount stated in the warrant is sooner paid; but—

(*a*) where a warrant is issued after a postponement under paragraph (3)(*b*) and, since the term of imprisonment was fixed but before the issue of the warrant, the amount mentioned in paragraph (4)(*a*) with respect to which the warrant would (but for the postponement) have been made has been reduced by a part payment, the period of imprisonment ordered under the warrant shall be the term (a)the appropriate amount mentioned in regulation 14(2) (or so much of it as remains outstanding), and

(b) subject to sub-paragraph (6B) below, the authority's reasonable costs incurred up to the time of payment or tender in making one or more of the applications referred to in Schedule 4.fixed under paragraph (3) reduced by such number of days as bears to the total number of days in that term less one day the same proportion as the part paid bears to that amount, and

(*b*) where, after the issue of a warrant, a part payment of the amount stated in it is made, the period of imprisonment shall be reduced by such number of days as bears to the total number of days in the term of imprisonment specified in the warrant less one day the same proportion as the part paid bears to the amount so stated.

(8) In calculating a reduction required under paragraph (7) any fraction of a day shall be left out of account; and rule 55(1), (2) and (3) of the Magistrates' Courts Rules 1981 applies (so far as is relevant) to a part payment as if the imprisonment concerned were imposed for want of sufficient distress to satisfy a sum adjudged to be paid by a magistrates' court.

---

1. When determining the period of imprisonment to be specified in the warrant, the justices must have regard to the principle of proportionality. The more serious the case, whether in terms of the amount outstanding or in terms of the degree of culpability or blame to be attached to the debtor for his non-payment, the closer will any period imposed approach the maximum. A finding of wilful refusal, in this respect, represents a more serious state of affairs than culpable neglect (*R v Highbury Corner Magistrates' Court, ex p Uchendu* (1994) 158 JP 409).

8–20046 17. Commitment to prison: further provision. (1) A single warrant may not be issued under regulation 16 against more than one person.

(2) Where an application under regulation 16 has been made, and after the making of the inquiries mentioned in paragraph (2) of that regulation no warrant is issued or term of imprisonment fixed, the court may remit all or part of the appropriate amount mentioned in regulation 14(2) to which the application relates.

(3) Where an application under regulation 16 has been made but no warrant is issued or term of imprisonment fixed, the application may be renewed (except so far as regards any sum remitted under paragraph (2)) on the ground that the circumstances of the debtor have changed.

(4) A statement in writing to the effect that wages of any amount have been paid to the debtor during any period, purporting to be signed by or on behalf of his employer, shall in any proceedings under regulation 16 be evidence of the facts there stated.

(5) For the purpose of enabling enquiry to be made as to the debtor's conduct and means under regulation 16(2), a justice of the peace may—

(*a*) issue a summons to him to appear before a magistrates' court and (if he does not obey the summons) issue a warrant for his arrest, or

(*b*) issue a warrant for the debtor's arrest without issuing a summons.

(6) A warrant issued under paragraph (5) may be executed anywhere in England and Wales by any person to whom it is directed or by any constable acting within his police area; and section 125(3) of the Magistrates' Courts Act 1980 applies to such a warrant.

(7) Regulation 16 and this regulation have effect subject to Part I of the Criminal Justice Act 1982 (treatment of young offenders).

8–20047 18. Insolvency. (1) Where a liability order has been made and the debtor against whom it was made is an individual, the amount due shall be deemed to be a debt for the purposes of section 267 of the Insolvency Act 1986 (grounds of creditor's petition).

(2) Where a liability order has been made and the debtor against whom it was made is a company, the amount due shall be deemed to be a debt for the purpose of section 122(1)(*f*) (winding up of companies by the court) or, as the case may be, section 221(5)(*b*) (winding up of unregistered companies) of that Act.

(3) The amount due for the purposes of this regulation is an amount equal to any outstanding sum which is or forms part of the amount in respect of which the liability order was made.

8–20048 19. Relationship between remedies under a liability order. (1) Where a warrant of commitment is issued against (or a term of imprisonment is fixed in the case of) a person under regulation 16(3), no steps, or no further steps, may be taken under this Part by way of distress or bankruptcy in relation to the relevant amount mentioned in regulation 16(4).

(2) Steps under this Part by way of distress, commitment, bankruptcy or winding up may not be taken against a person under a liability order while steps by way of another of those methods are being taken against him under it.

(3) Subject to paragraphs (1) and (2) distress may be resorted to more than once.

(4) Where a step is taken by way of distress for the recovery of an outstanding sum which is or forms part of an amount in respect of which a liability order has been made, any sum recovered thereby which is less than the aggregate of the amount outstanding and any charges arising under Schedule 3 shall be treated as discharging first the charges, the balance (if any) being applied towards the discharge of the outstanding sum.

8–20049 20. Recovery in court of competent jurisdiction. (1) A sum which has become payable to a billing authority under Part II, which has not been paid, and in respect of which a liability order has not been made may (as an alternative to recovery under a liability order) be recovered in the court of competent jurisdiction.

(2) A liability order may not be made in respect of any amount in relation to which proceedings have been instituted under paragraph (1) above.

8–20060 21. Magistrates' courts. (1) Justices of the peace appointed for a commission area within which is situated the area of a billing authority shall have jurisdiction to act under the provisions of this Part as respects that authority.

(1A) Paragraph (1) shall have effect in its application to billing authorities in Wales as if the words "the whole or any part of" were inserted before "the area".

(2) Subject to any other enactment authorising a District Judge (Magistrates' Courts) or other person to act by himself, a magistrates' court shall not under this Part hear a summons, entertain an application for a warrant or hold an inquiry as to means on such an application except when composed of at least two justices.

(3) References to a justice of the peace in regulations 12(2) and 15(2) shall be construed subject to rule 3 of the Justices' Clerks Rules 1970 (which authorises certain matters authorised to be done by a justice of the peace to be done by a justices' clerk).

(4) In any proceedings under regulation 12 (application for liability order), regulation 15 (appeals in connection with distress) or regulation 16 (commitment to prison), a statement contained in a document constituting or forming part of a record compiled by the applicant authority or an authorised person[1] shall be admissible as evidence of any fact stated in it of which direct oral evidence would be admissible.

(5) In proceedings where the applicant authority or an authorised person[1] desires to give a statement in evidence in accordance with paragraph (4), and the document containing that statement is produced by a computer, a certificate—

(*a*) identifying the document containing the statement and the computer by which it was produced;

(*b*) containing a statement that at all material times the computer was operating properly, or if not, that any respect in which it was not operating properly or was out of operation was not such as to affect the production of the document or the accuracy of its contents;

(*c*) giving such explanation as may be appropriate of the content of the document; and

(*d*) purporting to be signed by a person occupying a responsible position in relation to the operation of the computer,

shall be admissible as evidence of anything which is stated in it to the best of the signatory's information and belief.

(6) In paragraph (4) above, "statement" includes any representation of fact, whether made in words or otherwise; and the reference to an application under regulation 16 includes a reference to an application made in the circumstances mentioned in regulation 17(3).

(7) In this regulation and in regulation 23(3), "authorised person" means any person authorised by a billing authority to exercise any functions relating to the collection and enforcement of non-domestic rates[1].

---

1. A billing authority may authorise another person, or that person's employees, to exercise functions relating to the administration and enforcement of non-domestic rates: see the Local Authorities (Contracting Out of Tax Billing, Collection and Enforcement Functions) Order 1996, SI 1996/1880.

8–20061 22. Repayments. A sum which has become payable (by way of repayment) under Part II to a person other than a billing authority but which has not been paid shall be recoverable in a court of competent jurisdiction.

8–20062 23. Miscellaneous provisions. (1) Any matter which could be the subject of an appeal under regulations under section 55 of the Act may not be raised in proceedings under this Part.

(2) The contents of a local non-domestic rating list or an extract from such a list may be proved in proceedings under this Part by production of a copy of the list or relevant part of the list purporting to be certified by the proper officer of the billing authority to which the list or extract relates to be a true copy.

(3) If a liability order has been made and by virtue of—

(*a*) a notification which is given by the charging authority under regulation 8(4) or (7) or 9(2) or paragraph 6(3) or 7(2)(*a*) of Schedule or sub-paragraph (2) of paragraph 7A of that Schedule (including a notification given under that sub-paragraph pursuant to paragraph 7B(2) of that Schedule), or

(*b*) paragraph 10(4) or Schedule 7 to the Act applying in any case,

any part of the amount mentioned in regulation 12(6)(*a*) in respect of which the order was made would (if paid) fall to be repaid or credited against any subsequent liability, that part shall be treated for the purposes of this Part as paid on the day the notification is given or the multiplier in substitution is set under paragraph 10 of Schedule 7 to the Act (as the case may be) and accordingly as no longer outstanding.

(4) If, after a warrant is issued or term of imprisonment is fixed under regulation 16(3), and before the term of imprisonment has begun or been fully served, a charging authority gives such a notification as is mentioned in paragraph (3)(*a*) in the case in question, or sets a multiplier in substitution so that paragraph 10(4) of Schedule 7 to the Act applies in the case in question, it shall forthwith notify accordingly the justices' chief executive for the court which issued the warrant and (if the debtor is detained) the governor or keeper of the prison or place where he is detained or such other person as has lawful custody of him.

PART IV
MISCELLANEOUS

8–20063 24. Outstanding liabilities on death. (1) This regulation applies where a person dies and at any time before his death he was (or is alleged to have been) subject to a non-domestic rate.

(2) Where—

(*a*) before the deceased's death a sum has become payable by him under Part II or by way of relevant costs in respect of a non-domestic rate but has not been paid, or

(*b*) after the deceased's death a sum would, but for his death (and whether or not on the service of a notice) become payable by him under Part II in respect of a non-domestic rate,

his executor or administrator shall, subject to paragraph (3) and to the extent that it is not in excess of the deceased's liability under the Act (including relevant costs payable by him) in respect of the rate, be liable to pay the sum and may deduct out of the assets and effects of the deceased any payments made (or to be made).

(3) Where paragraph (2)(*b*) applies, the liability of the executor or administrator does not arise until the service on him of a notice requiring payment of the sum.

(4) Where before the deceased's death a sum in excess of his liability under the Act (including relevant costs payable by him) in respect of a non-domestic rate has been paid (whether the excess arises because of his death or otherwise) and has not been repaid or credited under Part II, his executor or administrator shall be entitled to the sum.

(5) Costs are relevant costs for the purposes of paragraphs (2) and (4) if—

(*a*) an order or warrant (as the case may be) was made by the court in respect of them under regulation 12(6)(*b*) or (7) or 16(4)(*b*), or in proceedings under regulation 20, or

(*b*) they are charges connected with distress which may be recovered pursuant to regulation 14(2)(*b*).

(6) A sum payable under paragraph (2) shall be enforceable in the administration of the deceased's estate as a debt of the deceased and accordingly—

(*a*) no liability order need be applied for in respect of it after the deceased's death under regulation 12, and

(*b*) the liability of the executor or administrator is a liability in his capacity as such.

(7) Regulation 23(1) and (2) applies to proceedings to enforce a liability arising under this regulation as it applies to proceedings under Part III.

(8) Insofar as is relevant to his liability under this regulation in the administration of the deceased's estate, the executor or administrator may institute, continue or withdraw proceedings (whether by way of appeal under regulations under section 55 of the Act or otherwise).

8–20064

Regulation 7(1)

SCHEDULE 1
NON-DOMESTIC RATE INSTALMENT SCHEME

8–20065

SCHEDULE 2
ENFORCEMENT: PRESCRIBED FORMS

Revoked.

8–20066

Regulation 14(2)(*b*)

SCHEDULE 3
CHARGES CONNECTED WITH DISTRESS

Non-Domestic Rating (Unoccupied Property) Regulations 1989[1]

(SI 1989/2261 amended by SI 1995/549, SI 2000/520 and SI 2004/3146 (E))

8–20067 1. *Citation, commencement and interpretation.*

1. Made under ss 45(1)(*d*), (9) and (10), 143(2) and 146(6) of, and paras 1 and 8(2)(*a*) of Sch 11 to, the Local Government Finance Act 1988.

8–20068 2. Property liable for unoccupied property rates. (1) The class of non-domestic hereditaments prescribed for the purposes of section 45(1) of the Act consists of all relevant non-domestic hereditaments to which none of the conditions in paragraph (2) applies.

(2) The conditions are that—

(*a*) the whole hereditament has, subject to paragraph (3), been unoccupied for a continuous period not exceeding three months;

(*b*) its owner is prohibited by law from occupying it or allowing it to be occupied;

(*c*) it is kept vacant by reason of action taken by or on behalf of the Crown or any local or public authority with a view to prohibiting the occupation of the hereditament or to acquiring it;

(*d*) it is the subject of a building preservation notice as defined by section 58 of the Town and Country Planning Act 1971 or is included in a list compiled under section 54 of that Act;

(*e*) it is included in the Schedule of monuments compiled under section 1 of the Ancient Monuments and Archaeological Areas Act 1979;

(*f*) it is a qualifying industrial hereditament;

(*g*) its rateable value is less than £2,200[1];

(*h*) the owner is entitled to possession only in his capacity as the personal representative of a deceased person;

(*i*) there subsists in respect of the owner's estate a bankruptcy order within the meaning of Parts VIII to XI of the Insolvency Act 1986;

(*j*) the owner is entitled to possession of the hereditament in his capacity as trustee under a deed of arrangement to which the Deeds of Arrangement Act 1914 applies;

(*k*) the owner is a company which is subject to a winding-up order made under the Insolvency Act 1986 or which is being wound up voluntarily under that Act;

(*l*) the owner is entitled to possession of the hereditament in his capacity as liquidator by virtue of an order made under section 112 or section 145 of the Insolvency Act 1986.

(3) Where a hereditament which has been unoccupied becomes occupied on any day and becomes unoccupied again on the expiration of a period of less than six weeks beginning with that day, then for the purposes of ascertaining whether the hereditament has been continuously unoccupied for the period mentioned in paragraph (2)(*a*) it shall be treated as having been unoccupied on that day and throughout the period.

(4) For the purpose of paragraph (2)(*a*), a hereditament which has not previously been occupied shall be treated as becoming unoccupied—

(*a*) on the day determined under paragraph 8 of Schedule 1 to the General Rate Act 1967, or

(*b*) on the day determined under Schedule 4A to the Act, or

(*c*) where neither (*a*) not (*b*) applies, on the day for which the hereditament is first shown in a local rating list.

whichever day first occurs.

(5) (*a*) In paragraph (1), "relevant non-domestic hereditament" means any non-domestic hereditament consisting of, or of part of, any building, together with any land ordinarily used or intended for use for the purposes of the building or part, and

(*b*) in paragraph (2)(*f*)—

"qualifying industrial hereditament" means any hereditament other than a retail hereditament in relation to which all buildings comprised in the hereditament are—

(i) constructed or adapted for use in the course of a trade or business; and

(ii) constructed or adapted for use for one or more of the following purposes, or one or more such purposes and one or more purposes ancillary thereto—

(*a*) the manufacture, repair or adaptation of goods or materials, or the subsection of goods or materials to any process;

(*b*) storage (including the storage or handling of goods in the course of their distribution);

(*c*) the working or processing of minerals;

(*d*) the generation of electricity; and

"retail hereditament" means any hereditament where any building or part of a building comprised in the hereditament is constructed or adapted for the purpose of the retail provision of—

(i) goods, or

(ii) services, other than storage for distribution services, on or from the hereditament.

1. The sum of £2,200 has effect from 1 April 2005; prior to that date the relevant figure was £1,900.

8–20069 3. *Appeals against completion notices: transitional provision.*

Council Tax (Administration and Enforcement) Regulations 1992[1]

(SI 1992/613 amended by SI 1992/3008, SI 1993/196 and 773, SI 1994/505, SI 1995/22, the Statute Law (Repeals) Act 1995, Sch 1, SI 1996/675 and 1880, SI 1997/393, SI 1998/295, SI 1999/534, SI 2000/2026, SI 2001/1076 and 2237, SI 2003/552 (W) and 768 (E), 1715 (W), 2211 (E) and 2604 (E), SI 2004/927 (E), 785 (W) and 1013 (W), SI 2005/2866 (E) and 3302 (W))

PART I

General

8–20075 **1. Citation, commencement and interpretation.** (1) *Citation and commencement.*

(2) In these Regulations—

"the Act" means the Local Government Finance Act 1992;

"address" in relation to electronic communications, includes any number or address used for the purposes of such communications;

"business day" means any day except a Saturday or Sunday, Christmas Day, Good Friday or a day which is a bank holiday under the Banking and Financial Dealings Act 1971 in England and Wales;

"electronic communication" means a communication transmitted (whether from one person to another, from one device to another or from a person to a device or vice versa)—

(*a*) by means of a telecommunications system (within the meaning of the Telecommunications Act 1984); or

(*b*) by other means but while in electronic form;

"Exempt Dwellings Order" means the Council Tax (Exempt Dwellings) Order 1992;

"demand notice regulations" means regulations under paragraph 1(1) of Schedule 2 to the Act making such provision as is mentioned in paragraph 2(4)(*e*) or 2(4)(*j*) of that Schedule; and

"discount" means a discount under section 11 or section 11A of the Act, or a reduction in the amount of council tax payable for a dwelling under section 13A of the Act where the dwelling falls into a class for which the billing authority has determined under section 13A(3) that liability shall be reduced otherwise than to nil;

"exempt dwelling" means a dwelling which is exempt from council tax under the Exempt Dwellings Order or a dwelling which falls into a class for which the billing authority has determined under section 13A(3) of the Act that the amount of council tax payable shall be reduced to nil.

"managing agent", in relation to a dwelling, means any person authorised to arrange lettings of the dwelling.

1. Made by the Secretary of State for the Environment, as respects England, and the Secretary of State for Wales, as respects Wales, in exercise of the powers conferred on them by ss 16(3) and 113(1) and (2) of, and paragraphs 1(1), 2(2), (3), (4)(*a*) to (*c*) and (5), 3–11, 13(1)(*a*) and (3), 16 and 18 of Sch 2, paras 1 and 6 of Sch 3 and paras 1–15, and 17–19 of Schedule 4 to, the Local Government Finance Act 1992.

8–20076 **2. Service of notices.** (1) Where any notice which is required or authorised by these Regulations to be given to or served on any person falls to be given or served by or on behalf of the Common Council it may be given or served in any manner in which it might be given or served under section 233 of the Local Government Act 1972 if the Common Council were a local authority within the meaning of that section.

(2) If the name of any person on whom a notice is to be served in accordance with regulation 3 (information from residents etc) or regulation 12 (information relating to exempt dwellings etc) cannot after reasonable inquiry be ascertained, the notice may be served by addressing it to "The Resident" or, as the case may be, "The Owner" or "The Managing Agent" of the dwelling concerned (naming the dwelling) without further name or description.

(3) If the name of any person to whom a notice is to be given or on whom a notice is to be served in accordance with any provision of Part V (billing) of these Regulations cannot after reasonable inquiry be ascertained, the notice may be given or served by addressing it to "The Council Tax Payer" of the dwelling concerned (naming the dwelling) without further name or description.

(4) Without prejudice to section 233 of the Local Government Act 1972 and paragraphs (1), (2) and (3) above and subject to paragraphs (5) to (8) below, any notice required or authorised to be given to or served by a billing authority on any person by a provision of Part II, III or V of these Regulations, or any information required by the demand notice regulations to be supplied to any person when a demand notice (within the meaning of Part V of these Regulations) is served:

(*a*) may be so given, served or supplied by sending the notice or information to that person by electronic communication to such address as may be notified by that person for that purpose; or

(*b*) shall be treated as given, served or supplied to that person where—

(i) the billing authority and that person have agreed for that purpose that any document containing that notice or information may be accessed by that person on a website;

(ii) the document is a document to which that agreement applies;
(iii) the billing authority has published the document on a website; and
(iv) that person is notified, in a manner for the time being agreed for that purpose between him and the billing authority, of—
(*aa*) the publication of the document on a website;
(*bb*) the address of that website; and
(*cc*) the place on the website where the document may be accessed.

(5) For the purpose of any legal proceedings, a notice given by a means described in paragraph (4), shall, unless the contrary is proved, be treated as served on the second business day after—

(*a*) it was sent in accordance with sub-paragraph (a); or
(*b*) notification of its publication was given in accordance with sub-paragraph (b)(iv).

(6) A person who has notified an address for the purpose of paragraph (4)(a) shall, by notice in writing to the billing authority, advise the billing authority of any change in that address; and the change shall take effect on the third business day after the date on which the notice is received by the billing authority.

(7) A person who has notified an address for the purpose of paragraph (4)(a) may, by notice in writing to the billing authority, withdraw that notification; and the withdrawal shall take effect on the third business day after the date on which the notice is received by the billing authority.

(8) A person who has entered into an agreement with the billing authority under paragraph (4)(b)(i) may, by notice in writing to the billing authority, inform the authority that he no longer wishes to be party to the agreement; and where such notice is given, the agreement shall be treated as revoked on the third business day after the date on which the notice is received by the billing authority.

PART II
Information: General

PART III
Exempt Dwellings, Etc

PART IV
Discounts

PART V
Billing

8–20077 **17. Interpretation and application of Part V.** (1) In this Part—

"demand notice" means the notice required to be served by regulation 18(1);
"joint taxpayers" means two or more persons who are, or in the opinion of the billing authority will be, jointly and severally liable to pay to the authority an amount in respect of council tax in respect of a particular dwelling and a day (whether such liability arises by virtue of section 6(3) or (4)(*b*), 7(4) or (5), 8(4) or (5) or 9(1) of the Act);
"joint taxpayers' notice" means a notice served in accordance with regulation 28;
"Part II scheme" means a scheme for the payment of the chargeable amount by instalments in accordance with a scheme complying with the requirements of Part II of Schedule 1 to these Regulations;
"the relevant year", in relation to a notice, means the financial year to which the notice relates.

(1A) Any reference in this Part to the relevant valuation band in relation to a dwelling is a reference to the valuation band shown as applicable to the dwelling—

(*a*) in the billing authority's valuation list; or
(*b*) if no such list is in force—
(i) except in a case to which paragraph (1B) applies, in the copy of the proposed list supplied to the authority under section 22(5)(*b*) of the Act;
(ii) in a case to which paragraph (1B) applies, in information which for the purposes of this paragraph is relevant information.

(1B) This paragraph applies where the listing officer supplies the authority with information relating to property shown in the proposed list (including information relating to the application to such property of article 3 or 4 of the Council Tax (Chargeable Dwellings) Order 1992); and such information is relevant information for the purposes of paragraph (1A)(*b*)(ii) to the extent that it differs from information contained in the proposed list.

(2) Except where the context otherwise requires, and subject to paragraph (5), any reference in this Part to the liable person (however expressed) is a reference—

(*a*) to a person who is, or in the opinion of the billing authority will be, solely liable to pay to the authority, an amount in respect of council tax in respect of a particular dwelling and a day; or
(*b*) where persons are joint taxpayers, to those persons.

(3) Any reference in this Part to the chargeable amount is a reference to the amount the liable person is or will be liable to pay.

(4) Any reference in this Part to the day on or time at which a notice is issued, is a reference—

(*a*) if the notice is served in the manner described in section 233(2) of the Local Government Act 1972 by being left at, or sent by post to, a person's proper address, to the day on or time at which it is so left or posted, or

(*b*) in any other case, to the day on or time at which the notice is served.

(5) This Part applies (amongst other matters) for the making of payments in relation to the chargeable amount for a financial year; but its application as regards persons who are joint taxpayers is subject to the provisions of regulations 27 to 28A.

(6) The provisions of this Part which provide for the repayment or crediting of any amount or the adjustment of payments due under a notice shall have effect subject to section 31(4) of the Act.

8–20078 18. The requirement for demand notices. (1) Subject to paragraph (2), for each financial year a billing authority shall serve a notice in writing[1] on every liable person in accordance with regulations 19 to 21.

(2) Where, but for this paragraph, notices would fall to be served in accordance with this Part—

(*a*) at the same time; and

(*b*) in respect of the same dwelling,

in relation to a financial year not then ended and any preceding financial year, nothing in paragraph (1) shall require a billing authority to serve more than one notice.

(3) If a person is liable in any financial year to pay to the same billing authority different chargeable amounts in respect of different dwellings, a demand notice shall be served in respect of each chargeable amount.

8–20079 19. Service of demand notices. (1) The demand notice is to be served on or as soon as practicable after the day the billing authority first sets an amount of council tax for the relevant year for the category of dwellings which includes the chargeable dwelling to which the notice relates.

(2) For the purposes of paragraph (1), "category" shall be construed in accordance with section 30(4) of the Act; and where a demand notice is served before 1st April 1993, a dwelling shall be treated as included in the category in which, in the opinion of the billing authority, it will be included on 1st April 1993.

---

1. The Council Tax and Non-Domestic Rating (Demand Notices) (England) Regulations 1993, SI 1993/191 provide for the content of Council Tax notices and for the information to be supplied with such notices in the financial year beginning on 1 April 1993.

8–20080 20. Demand notices: payments required. (1) If the demand notice is issued before or during the relevant year, the notice shall require the making of payments on account of the amount referred to in paragraph (2).

(2) The amount is—

(*a*) the billing authority's estimate of the chargeable amount, made as respects the relevant year or part, as the case may be, on the assumptions referred to in paragraph (3); or

(*b*) where an amount falls to be credited by the billing authority against the chargeable amount, the amount (if any) by which the amount estimated as mentioned in sub-paragraph (*a*) exceeds the amount falling to be so credited.

(3) The assumptions are—

(*a*) that the person will be liable to pay the council tax to which the notice relates on every day after the issue of the notice;

(*b*) that, as regards the dwelling concerned, the relevant valuation band on the day the notice is issued will remain the relevant valuation band for the dwelling as regards every day after the issue of the notice;

(*c*) if on the day the notice is issued the person satisfies conditions prescribed for the purposes of regulations under section 13 of the Act (and consequently the chargeable amount in his case is less than it would otherwise be), that he will continue to satisfy those conditions as regards every day after the issue of the notice;

(*d*) if, by virtue of regulation 9(1), the dwelling to which the notice relates is assumed to be a chargeable dwelling on the day the notice is issued, that it will continue to be a chargeable dwelling as regards every day after the issue of the notice;

(*e*) if, by virtue of regulation 15(1), the chargeable amount is assumed not to be subject to a discount on the day the notice is issued, that it will not be subject to a discount as regards any day after the issue of the notice;

(*f*) if, by virtue of regulation 15(2), the chargeable amount is assumed to be subject to a discount on the day the notice is issued, that it will continue to be subject to the same rate of discount as regards every day after the issue of the notice; and

(*g*) if on the day the notice is issued a determination as to council tax benefit to which the person is entitled is in effect, and by virtue of regulations under section 138(1) of the Social

Security Administration Act 1992 the benefit allowed as regards that day takes the form of a reduction in the amount the person is liable to pay in respect of council tax for the relevant year, that as regards every day after that day he will be allowed the same reduction in that amount.

(4) If the demand notice is issued during the relevant year and the liable person is not liable to pay an amount by way of council tax in respect of the day on which the notice is issued, the demand notice shall require payment of—

(*a*) the chargeable amount for the period in the year up to the last day in respect of which he was so liable; or

(*b*) where an amount falls to be credited by the billing authority against that chargeable amount, an amount equal to the amount (if any) by which that chargeable amount exceeds the amount falling to be so credited.

(5) If the demand notice is issued after the end of the relevant year, it shall require payment of—

(*a*) the chargeable amount; or

(*b*) where an amount falls to be credited by the billing authority against the chargeable amount, an amount equal to the amount (if any) by which the chargeable amount exceeds the amount falling to be so credited.

8–20081 **21. Council tax: payments.** (1) Unless—

(*a*) an agreement under paragraph (5) in relation to the relevant year has been reached between the billing authority and the liable person before the demand notice is issued, or

(*b*) the authority has resolved that a Part II scheme shall have effect for the relevant year as regards dwellings of a class which includes the dwelling in respect of which the chargeable amount falls to be paid,

a notice to which paragraph (1) of regulation 20 applies shall require the amount mentioned in paragraph (2) of that regulation to be paid by instalments in accordance with Part I of Schedule 1 hereto.

(2) Where a billing authority has resolved as mentioned in paragraph (1)(*b*), a notice to which paragraph (1) of regulation 20 applies shall require the amount mentioned in paragraph (2) of that regulation to be paid by instalments in accordance with the provisions of the authority's Part II scheme.

(3) Where instalments are required to be paid in accordance with a Part II scheme or under Part I of Schedule 1, Part III of that Schedule applies for their cessation or adjustment in the circumstances described in that Part (subject, in the case of payments in accordance with a Part II scheme, to provision included in the scheme pursuant to paragraph 8(6) of Part II of that Schedule).

(4) If an agreement under paragraph (5) in relation to the relevant year has been reached between the billing authority and the liable person before the demand notice is issued, a notice to which paragraph (1) of regulation 20 applies shall require the amount mentioned in paragraph (2) of that regulation to be paid in accordance with that agreement.

(5) A billing authority and a liable person may agree that the amount mentioned in regulation 20(2) which is required to be paid under a notice to which regulation 20(1) applies shall be paid in such manner as is provided by the agreement.

(6) Notwithstanding the foregoing provisions of this regulation, such an agreement may be entered into either before or after the demand notice concerned is issued, and may make provision for the cessation or adjustment of payments, and for the making of fresh estimates, in the event of the estimate mentioned in regulation 20(2) turning out to be wrong; and if it is entered into after the demand notice has been issued, it may make provision dealing with the treatment for the purposes of the agreement of any sums paid in accordance with Part I of Schedule 1 or a Part II scheme before it was entered into.

(7) A notice to which regulation 20(4) or (5) applies shall (as the billing authority determines) require payment of the amount concerned—

(*a*) on the expiry of such period (being not less than 14 days) after the day of issue of the notice as is specified in it; or

(*b*) by instalments of such amounts as are specified in the notice, payable at such intervals and on such day in each interval as is so specified.

8–20082 **22. Notices: further provision.** No payment on account of the chargeable amount (whether interim, final or sole) need be made unless a notice served under this Part requires it.

8–20083 **23. Failure to pay instalments.** (1) Subject to paragraph (2), where—

(*a*) a demand notice has been served by a billing authority on a liable person,

(*b*) instalments in respect of the council tax to which the notice relates are payable in accordance with Part I of Schedule 1 or, as the case may be, a Part II scheme or a determination under regulation 21(7), and

(*c*) any such instalment is not paid in accordance with that Schedule or, as the case may be, the relevant scheme or determination

the billing authority shall serve a notice ("reminder notice") on the liable person stating—

(i) the amount which is the aggregate of the instalments which are due under the demand notice or any subsequent notice given under paragraph 10 of Schedule 1 and which are unpaid and the instalments that will become due within the period of seven days beginning with the day on which the reminder notice is issued;

(ii) that the amount mentioned in sub-paragraph (i) above is required to be paid by him within the period mentioned in that sub-paragraph;

(iii) the effect of paragraph (3) below and the amount that will become payable by him in the circumstances mentioned in that paragraph; and

(iv) where the notice is the second such notice as regards the relevant year, the effect of paragraph (4) below.

(2) Nothing in paragraph (1) shall require the service of a reminder notice—

(*a*) where all the instalments have fallen due; or

(*b*) in the circumstances mentioned in paragraphs (3) and (4).

(3) If, within the period of 7 days beginning with the day on which a reminder notice is issued, the liable person fails to pay any instalments which are or will become due before the expiry of that period, the unpaid balance of the estimated amount (or, as the case may be, the chargeable amount) shall become payable by him at the expiry of a further period of 7 days beginning with the day of the failure.

(4) If, after making a payment in accordance with a reminder notice which is the second such notice as regards the relevant year, the liable person fails to pay any subsequent instalment as regards that year on or before the day on which it falls due, the unpaid balance of the estimated amount (or, as the case may be, the chargeable amount) shall become payable by him on the day following the day of the failure.

8–20084 **24.** *Payments: adjustments*

8–20085 **25.** *Lump sum payments*

8–20086 **26.** *Non-cash payments*

8–20087 **27. Joint taxpayers.** (1) This regulation applies in the case of joint taxpayers; but its application to joint taxpayers on whom a joint taxpayers' notice is served is subject to regulation 28A.

(2) In a case to which this regulation applies—

(*a*) regulation 18 (the requirement for demand notices) has effect as if in paragraph (1) for the words "every liable person" there were substituted the words "at least one of the joint taxpayers";

(*b*) regulation 20 (demand notices; payments required) has effect as if—

(i) the assumption referred to in sub-paragraph (*c*) of paragraph (3) is made as regards such of the joint taxpayers as on the day of issue of the demand notice satisfy the conditions referred to in that sub-paragraph;

(ii) the assumption referred to in sub-paragraph (*g*) of paragraph (3) is made as regards such of the joint taxpayers in respect of whom on the day of issue of the demand notice a determination has effect as mentioned in that sub-paragraph;

(*c*) regulation 21 (council tax: payments) has effect as if—

(i) in paragraphs (1) and (4), for the words "the liable person" there were substituted the words "one or more of the joint taxpayers";

(ii) in paragraph (3), for the words after "that Part" there were substituted the following—

"subject—

(*a*) in the case of payments in accordance with a Part II scheme, to provision included in the scheme pursuant to paragraph 8(6) of Part II of that Schedule; and

(*b*) in the case of joint taxpayers, to regulations 28 and 28A.";

(iii) in paragraph (5), for the words "a liable person" there were substituted the words "one or more of the joint taxpayers"; and

(iv) in paragraph (5), there were inserted at the end the words ": but, subject to regulation 28A(1), a billing authority may not enter into an agreement after the issue of the demand notice concerned with a joint taxpayer on whom that notice was not served";

(*d*) regulation 23 (failure to pay instalments) has effect as if references to the liable person and to an amount becoming payable by the liable person were references to such of the joint taxpayers as have been served with a demand notice and to an amount becoming payable by them, respectively;

(*e*) regulation 29 (collection of penalties) has effect as if—

(i) for paragraph (1), there were substituted the following—

"(1) Subject to paragraphs (2) and (3), where a penalty is payable to a billing authority under any of sub-paragraphs (1) to (3) of paragraph 1 of Schedule 3 to the Act by a person who is one of joint taxpayers, it may be collected by the service by the authority on the person of a notice requiring payment of the penalty on the expiry of such period (being not less than 14 days) after the issue of the notice as is specified in it."; and

(ii) paragraph (4) were omitted; and

(*f*) paragraph 9 (cessation of instalments) of Schedule 1 does not apply unless—

(i) every person on whom the demand notice was served has ceased to be a joint taxpayer;

(ii) none of those persons is, as regards any part of the period to which the demand notice relates, solely liable to pay an amount in respect of council tax as regards the dwelling concerned; and

(iii) no other person who, as regards any part of that period, was jointly and severally liable with any of those persons as regards the dwelling concerned, is a liable person (whether his liability is sole or joint and several) as regards the dwelling concerned.

8–20088 **28. Joint taxpayers' notice.** (1) An amount shall not be payable by a person who is one of joint taxpayers and on whom a demand notice has not been served unless a notice ("joint taxpayers' notice") is served on him in accordance with the following provisions of this regulation.

(2) A joint taxpayers' notice may not be served on a person after the expiry of the period of six years beginning with the first day of the financial year to which the notice relates.

(3) Where—

(*a*) a joint taxpayers' notice is served during the relevant year; and

(*b*) the person on whom (as one of the joint taxpayers) a demand notice for that year was served (or, if more than one person was so served, each of them) is not on the day of issue of the notice one of the joint taxpayers; and

(*c*) the unpaid balance of the estimated amount has not become due as mentioned in paragraph (3) or (4) of regulation 23,

the notice shall require the payment of the adjusted amount.

(4) For the purposes of paragraph (3)—

"the adjusted amount" means an amount equal to the lesser of—

(*a*) the billing authority's estimate of the chargeable amount made as respects the period to which the joint taxpayers' notice relates; and regulation 20(3) shall have effect for these purposes as it has effect in a case to which regulation 27 applies and as if references in regulation 27(2)(*b*) to the demand notice were references to the joint taxpayers' notice; and

(*b*) the relevant sum; and

"the relevant sum" means an amount equal to the difference between—

(*a*) the amount estimated or last estimated as regards the dwelling concerned—

(i) for the purposes of an agreement under regulation 21(5); or

(ii) under regulation 20(2) for the purposes of the demand notice or any subsequent notice given under paragraph 10 of Schedule 1; and

(*b*) the aggregate of the amounts paid to the authority under any such agreement or notice before the issue of the joint taxpayers' notice.

(5) Subject to regulation 28A(1), the amount required to be paid under paragraph (3) shall be payable by instalments of such amounts, and at such intervals and on such days in each interval, as are specified in the notice; provided that the number of instalments shall not be less than the number of instalments payable under the agreement, the demand notice or any subsequent notice given under paragraph 10 of Schedule 1, as the case may be, as regards the period beginning on the day on which the joint taxpayers' notice is served and ending on the last day of the relevant year.

(6) A joint taxpayers' notice which is issued after the end of the relevant year, or after the unpaid balance of the estimated amount has become due as mentioned in paragraph (3) or (4) of regulation 23, shall (as the billing authority determines) require payment of the amount concerned—

(*a*) on the expiry of such period (being not less than 14 days) after the issue of the notice as is specified in it; or

(*b*) by instalments of such amounts as are specified in the notice, payable at such intervals and on such day in each interval as is so specified.

8–20088A **28A. Joint taxpayers' notice: further provision.** (1) A billing authority and a person on whom a joint taxpayers' notice is served may agree that the amount required to be paid under the notice shall be paid in such manner as is provided by the agreement; and paragraph (6) of regulation 21 shall apply with the necessary modifications in relation to an agreement under this paragraph as it applies to an agreement under paragraph (5) of that regulation.

(2) Regulation 23 (failure to pay instalments) shall apply with the necessary modifications in relation to instalments payable in accordance with a joint taxpayers' notice as it applies to instalments payable in accordance with Part I of Schedule 1 or a Part II scheme.

(3) If the amount required to be paid under a joint taxpayers' notice is shown to be incorrect, the billing authority shall serve a further notice on every person on whom the joint taxpayers' notice was served stating the revised sum required to be paid.

(4) If the amount stated in the further notice served under paragraph (3) is greater than the amount required to be paid under the joint taxpayers' notice, the further notice shall also state

the revised amount of each remaining instalment or, as the case may be, the period (being not less than 14 days) after the issue of that further notice within which the further sum payable is required to be paid.

(5) If the amount stated in the further notice under paragraph (3) is less than the amount required to be paid under the joint taxpayers' notice, any overpayment—

(*a*) shall be repaid if the person on whom the joint taxpayers' notice was served so requires, or

(*b*) in any other case shall (as the billing authority determines) either be repaid or be credited against any subsequent liability of that person to make a payment in respect of council tax to the authority.

8–20089 **29. Collection of penalties.** (1) Subject to paragraphs (2) to (4), where a penalty is payable by a person to a billing authority under any of sub-paragraphs (1) to (3) of paragraph 1 of Schedule 3 to the Act it may be collected, as the authority to which it is payable determines, either—

(*a*) by treating the penalty for the purposes of regulations 20 and 21 and Schedule 1 as if it were part of the amount that the person is or will be liable to pay in respect of council tax as regards any demand notice issued pursuant to regulation 20(2) after the penalty is imposed, or

(*b*) by the service by the authority on the person of a notice requiring payment of the penalty on the expiry of such period (being not less than 14 days) after the issue of the notice as is specified in it.

(2) Where the imposition of a penalty is subject to an appeal or arbitration, no amount shall be payable in respect of the penalty while the appeal or arbitration is outstanding.

(3) The imposition of a penalty is to be treated as subject to an appeal or arbitration for the purposes of this regulation and regulation 27(6) until such time as the matter is finally disposed of in accordance with regulations under paragraph 4 of Schedule 11 to the Local Government Finance Act 1988 (valuable tribunals) or is abandoned or fails for non-prosecution; and the circumstances in which an appeal is to be treated as failing for non-prosecution include the expiry of any time prescribed under paragraph 8(2)(*a*) of that Schedule in consequence of which any such appeal would be required to be dismissed by a valuation tribunal.

(4) A demand notice making provision for the recovery of a penalty which is subject to appeal or arbitration may not be issued under paragraph (1)(*a*) during the period that the appeal or arbitration concerned is outstanding; and where a penalty becomes subject to appeal or arbitration after the issue of a demand notice which makes such provision, such proportion of the instalments due under it as are attributable to the penalty shall not fall due until the appeal or arbitration is finally disposed of, abandoned or fails for non-prosecution.

(5) Where an amount has been paid by a person in respect of a penalty which is quashed under paragraph 1(6) of Schedule 3 to the Act or pursuant to the order of a valuation tribunal or the High Court, the billing authority which imposed the penalty may allow the amount to him by way of deduction against any other sum which has become due from him under this Part (whether in respect of another penalty or otherwise); and any balance shall be repaid to him.

8–20090 **30. Appeals in relation to estimates.** Section 16(1) of the Act shall not apply where the ground on which the person concerned is aggrieved is that any assumption as to the future that is required by this Part to be made in the calculation of an amount may prove to be inaccurate.

8–20091 **31. Demand notices: final adjustment.** (1) This regulation applies where—

(*a*) a notice has been issued by a billing authority under this Part requiring a payment or payments to be made by a person in respect of his liability to pay council tax for a financial year or part of a financial year,

(*b*) the payment or payments required to be made are found to be in excess of or less than his liability for the year or the part, and

(*c*) provision for adjusting the amounts required under the notice and (as appropriate) for the making of additional payments or the repaying or crediting of any amount overpaid is not made by any other provision of this Part, of the Act or of any agreement entered into under regulation 21(5).

(2) The billing authority shall as soon as practicable after the expiry of the year or the part of a year serve a further notice on the person stating the amount of his liability for the year or the part, and adjusting (by reference to that amount) the amounts required to be paid under the notice referred to in paragraph (1)(*a*).

(3) If the amount stated in the further notice is greater than the amount required to be paid under the notice referred to in paragraph (1)(*a*), the amount of the difference for which such other provision as is mentioned in paragraph (1)(*c*) is not made shall be due from the person to the billing authority on the expiry of such period (being not less than 14 days) after the day of issue of the notice as is specified in it.

(4) If there has been an overpayment, the amount overpaid for which such other provision as is mentioned in paragraph (1)(*c*) is not made—

(*a*) shall be repaid if the person so requires, or

(*b*) in any other case shall (as the billing authority determines) either be repaid or be credited against any subsequent liability of the person to make a payment in respect of any council tax of the authority.

PART VI
Enforcement

8-20092 32. Interpretation and application of Part VI. (1) In this Part—

"attachment of allowances order" means an order under regulation 44;

"attachment of earnings order" means an order under regulation 37;

"authorised person" means any person authorised by a billing authority to exercise any functions relating to the administration and enforcement of the council tax[1];

"charging order" means an order under regulation 50;

"debtor" means a person against whom a liability order has been made;

"earnings" means sums payable to a person—

(*a*) by way of wages or salary (including any fees, bonus, commission, overtime pay or other emoluments payable in addition to wages or salary or payable under a contract of service); or

(*b*) by way of statutory sick pay,

but, in so far as the following would otherwise be treated as earnings, they shall not be treated as such:

(i) sums payable by any public department of the Government of Northern Ireland or of a territory outside the United Kingdom;

(ii) pay or allowances payable to the debtor as a member of Her Majesty's forces other than pay or allowances payable by his employer to him as a special member of a reserve force (within the meaning of the Reserve Forces Act 1996);

(iii) allowances or benefit payable under the Social Security Acts;

(iii*a*) tax credits within the meaning of the Tax Credits Act 2002;

(iv) allowances payable in respect of disablement or disability; and

(v) wages payable to a person as a seaman, other than wages payable to him as a seaman of a fishing boat;

(vi) tax credits within the meaning of the Tax Credits Act 2002.

"the Income Support Regulations" means the Council Tax (Deductions from Income Support) Regulations 1993;

"liability order" means an order under regulation 34 or regulation 36A(5); and

"net earnings" in relation to an employment means the residue of earnings payable under the employment after deduction by the employer of—

(*a*) income tax;

(*b*) primary Class 1 contributions under Part I of the Social Security Contributions and Benefits Act 1992; and

(*c*) amounts deductible under any enactment, or in pursuance of a request in writing by the debtor, for the purposes of a superannuation scheme, namely any enactment, rules, deed or other instrument providing for the payment of annuities or lump sum—

(i) to the persons with respect to whom the instrument has effect on their retirement at a specified age or on becoming incapacitated at some earlier age, or

(ii) to the personal representatives or the widows, widowers, surviving civil partners, relatives or dependants of such persons on their death or otherwise,

whether with or without any further or other benefits; and where an order under regulation 32 (making of attachment of earnings order) of the Community Charges (Administration and Enforcement) Regulations 1989 made before the making of the attachment of earnings order concerned remains in force,

(*d*) any amount required to be deducted in accordance with that order.

(2) In sub-paragraph (v) of the definition of "earnings" in paragraph (1) above expressions used in the Merchant Shipping Act 1894 have the same meanings as in that Act.

(3) Regulations 33 to 53 apply for the recovery of a sum which has become payable to a billing authority under Part V and which has not been paid; but their application in relation to a sum for which persons are jointly and severally liable under that Part is subject to the provisions of regulation 54 (joint and several liability).

(4) References in this Part to a sum which has become payable and which has not been paid include references to a sum forming part of a larger sum which has become payable and the other part of which has been paid.

(5) Any reference in this Part to the day on or time at which a notice is issued, is a reference—

(*a*) if the notice is served in the manner described in section 233(2) of the Local Government Act 1972 by being left at, or sent by post to, a person's proper address, to the day on or time at which it is so left or posted, or

(*b*) in any other case, to the day on or time at which the notice is served.

1. A billing authority may authorise another person, or that person's employees, to exercise functions relating to the administration and enforcement of the council tax: see the Local Authorities (Contracting Out of Tax Billing, Collection and Enforcement Functions) Order 1996, SI 1996/1880.

8–20093 **33. Liability orders: preliminary steps.** (1) Subject to paragraph (3), before a billing authority applies for a liability order it shall serve on the person against whom the application is to be made a notice ("final notice"), and which is to state every amount in respect of which the authority is to make the application.

(2) A final notice may be served in respect of an amount at any time after it has become due.

(3) Nothing in paragraph (1) shall require the service of a final notice in the circumstances mentioned in paragraph (3) of regulation 23 (including that paragraph as applied as mentioned in regulation 28A(2)).

8–20094 **34. Application for liability order.** (1) If an amount which has fallen due under paragraph (3) or (4) of regulation 23 (including those paragraphs as applied as mentioned in regulation 28A(2)) is wholly or partly unpaid, or (in a case where a final notice is required under regulation 33) the amount stated in the final notice is wholly or partly unpaid at the expiry of the period of 7 days beginning with the day on which the notice was issued, the billing authority may, in accordance with paragraph (2), apply to a magistrates' court for an order against the person by whom it is payable.

(2) The application is to be instituted by making complaint to a justice of the peace, and requesting the issue of a summons directed to that person to appear before the court to show why he has not paid the sum which is outstanding.

(3) Section 127(1) of the Magistrates' Courts Act 1980 does not apply to such an application; but no application may be instituted in respect of a sum after the period of six years beginning with the day on which it became due[1] under Part V.

(4) A warrant shall not be issued under section 55(2) of the Magistrates' Courts Act 1980 in any proceedings under this regulation.

(5) If, after a summons has been issued in accordance with paragraph (2) but before the application is heard, there is paid or tendered to the authority an amount equal to the aggregate of—

(*a*) the sum specified in the summons as the sum outstanding or so much of it as remains outstanding (as the case may be); and

(*b*) a sum of an amount equal to the costs reasonably incurred by the authority in connection with the application up to the time of the payment or tender,

the authority shall accept the amount and the application shall not be proceeded with.

(6) The court shall[2] make the order[3] if it is satisfied that the sum has become payable by the defendant and has not been paid.

(7) An order made pursuant to paragraph (6) shall be made in respect of an amount equal to the aggregate of—

(*a*) the sum payable, and

(*b*) a sum of an amount equal to the costs reasonably incurred by the applicant in obtaining the order.

(8) Where the sum payable is paid after a liability order has been applied for under paragraph (2) but before it is made, the court shall nonetheless (if so requested by the billing authority) make the order in respect of a sum of an amount equal to the costs reasonably incurred by the authority in making the application.

1. Liability to pay council tax arises when the demand is service and not when the amount of tax was set by the billing authority (*Regentford v Thanet District Council* [2004] TLR 143 (whether procedural or substantial prejudice precluded a claim did not arise on the facts where the payer had allowed the proceedings to go by default, see also *Encon Insulation Ltd v Nottingham City Council* [1999] RA 382)).

2. Justices may reopen their decision to make a liability order made in ignorance of the receipt of an application to adjourn so that they may exercise their judicial discretion whether to grant the order or adjourn (*Liverpool City Council v Pleroma Distribution Ltd* [2003] 04 LS Gaz R 33, decided under reg 12(5) of the Non-Domestic Rating (Collection and Enforcement) Regs 1989).

3. In a case decided under the Community Charge (Administration and Enforcement) Regulations 1989, a liability order may be made for the full amount of the community charge notwithstanding that an application for benefit under the Community Charge Benefits (General) Regulations 1989 is outstanding, or that the local authority is in breach of its statutory duty under those regulations to determine such an application "within 14 days . . . or as soon as practicable thereafter" (*R v Bristol City Magistrates' Court, ex p Willsman* (1991) 156 JP 409, CA).

8–20095 **35. Liability orders: further provision.** (1) A single liability order may deal with one person and one such amount (or aggregate amount) as is mentioned in regulation 34(7) and (8), or, if the court thinks fit, may deal with more than one person and more than one such amount.

(2) A summons issued under regulation 34(2) may be served on a person—

(*a*) by delivering it to him, or

(*b*) by leaving it at his usual or last known place of abode, or in the case of a company, at its registered office, or (*c*) by sending it by post to him at his usual or last known place of abode, or in the case of a company, to its registered office, or

(*d*) by leaving it at, or by sending it by post to him at, an address given by the person as an address at which service of the summons will be accepted.

(2A) No liability order shall be made in pursuance of a summons issued under regulation 34(2) unless 14 days have elapsed since the day on which the summons was served.

(3) The amount in respect of which a liability order[1] is made is enforceable in accordance with this Part; and accordingly for the purposes of any of the provisions of Part III of the Magistrates' Courts Act 1980 (satisfaction and enforcement) it is not to be treated as a sum adjudged to be paid by order of the court.

---

1. In addition to the remedies available under this Part, where a liability order has been made and the debtor is entitled to income support the billing authority concerned may apply to the Secretary of State asking him to deduct sums from any amounts payable to the debtor by way of income support in order to secure the payment of any outstanding sum which is or forms part of the amount in respect of which the liability order was made (Council Tax (Deductions from Income Support) Regulations 1993, SI 1993/494, reg 2).

8–20096 **36. Duties of debtors subject to liability order.** (1) Where a liability order has been made, the debtor against whom it was made shall, during such time as the amount in respect of which the order was made remains wholly or partly unpaid, be under a duty to supply relevant information to the billing authority on whose application it was made.

(2) For the purposes of paragraph (1), relevant information is such information as fulfils the following conditions—

(*a*) it is in the debtor's possession or control;

(*b*) the billing authority requests him by notice given in writing to supply it; and

(*c*) it falls within paragraph (3).

(3) Information falls within this paragraph if it is specified in the notice mentioned in paragraph (2)(*b*) and it falls within one or more of the following descriptions—

(*a*) information as to the name and address of an employer of the debtor;

(*b*) information as to earnings or expected earnings of the debtor;

(*c*) information as to deductions and expected deductions from such earnings in respect of the matters referred to in paragraphs (*a*) to (*c*) of the definition of "net earnings" in regulation 32 or attachment of earnings orders made under this Part, regulation 32 of the Community Charges (Administration and Enforcement) Regulations 1989, the Attachment of Earnings Act 1971 or the Child Support Act 1991;

(*d*) information as to the debtor's work or identity number in an employment, or such other information as will enable an employer of the debtor to identify him;

(*e*) information as to sources of income of the debtor other than an employer of his;

(*f*) information as to whether another person is jointly and severally liable with the debtor for the whole or any part of the amount in respect of which the order was made.

(4) Information is to be supplied within 14 days of the day on which the request is made.

8–20096A **36A Quashing of liability orders.** (1) Where—

(*a*) a magistrates' court has made a liability order pursuant to regulation 34(6), and

(*b*) the authority on whose application the liability order was made considers that the order should not have been made,

the authority may apply to a magistrates' court to have the liability order quashed.

(2) Where, on an application by an authority in accordance with paragraph (1) above, the magistrates' court is satisfied that the liability order should not have been made, it shall quash the order.

(3) Where an authority makes an application under paragraph (1) for a liability order ("the original order") to be quashed, and a lesser amount than the amount for which the original order was made has fallen due under paragraph (3) or (4) of regulation 23 (including those paragraphs as applied as mentioned in regulation 28A(2)) and is wholly or partly unpaid or (in a case where a final notice is required under regulation 33) the amount stated in the final notice is wholly or partly unpaid at the expiry of the period of seven days beginning with the day on which the notice was issued, the billing authority may also apply to the magistrates' court for an order against the person by whom the lesser amount was payable.

(4) Paragraphs (2) to (5) of regulation 34 shall apply to applications under paragraph (3) above.

(5) Where, having quashed a liability order in accordance with paragraph (2) above, the magistrates' court is satisfied that, had the original application for the liability order been for a liability order in respect of a lesser sum payable, such an order could properly have been made, it shall make a liability order in respect of the aggregate of—

(*a*) that lesser sum payable, and

(*b*) any sum included in the quashed order in respect of the costs reasonably incurred by the authority in obtaining the quashed order.

8–20097 **37. Making of attachment of earnings order.** (1) Where a liability order has been made and the debtor against whom it was made is an individual, the authority which applied for the order may, subject to paragraph (4), make an order under this regulation to secure the payment of the appropriate amount.

(1A) For the purposes of this regulation the appropriate amount is the aggregate of—

(*a*) any outstanding sum which is or forms part of the amount in respect of which the liability order was made; and

(*b*) where the authority concerned has sought to levy an amount by distress and sale of the debtor's goods under regulation 45 and the person making the distress has reported that he was unable (for whatever reason) to find any or sufficient goods of the debtor on which to levy the amount—

(i) a sum determined in accordance with Schedule 5 in respect of charges connected with the distress, and

(ii) if the authority has applied for the issue of a warrant committing the debtor to prison in accordance with regulation 47, the authority's reasonable costs incurred up to the time of the making of the order under regulation 37, in making one or more of the applications referred to in Schedule 6, but not exceeding the amount specified for that application in Schedule 6.

(2) An order under this regulation—

(*a*) shall be in the form specified in (and accordingly contain the matters specified in) Schedule 3; and

(*b*) shall remain in force until discharged under regulation 41(2) or the whole amount to which it relates has been paid (whether by attachment of earnings or otherwise).

(3) The authority may serve a copy of the order on a person who appears to the authority to have the debtor in his employment; and a person on whom it is so served who has the debtor in his employment shall comply with it.

(4) No order may be made under this regulation by an authority if the effect would be that the number of orders for the time being in force made by that authority in relation to the debtor in question exceeded two.

8–20098 **38. Deductions under attachment of earnings order.** (1) Subject to paragraphs (2) and (3), the sum to be deducted by an employer under an attachment of earnings order on any pay-day shall be—

(*a*) where the debtor's earnings from the employer are payable weekly, a sum equal to the appropriate percentage of the net earnings otherwise payable on that pay-day; and for this purpose the appropriate percentage is the percentage (or percentages) specified in column 2 of Table A in Schedule 4 in relation to the band in column 1 of that Table within which the net earnings fall;

(*b*) where his earnings from the employer are payable monthly, a sum equal to the appropriate percentage of the net earnings otherwise payable on that pay-day; and for this purpose the appropriate percentage is the percentage (or percentages) specified in column 2 of Table B in that Schedule 4 in relation to the band in column 1 of Table within which the net earnings fall;

(*c*) where his earnings from the employer are payable at regular intervals of a whole number of weeks or months, the sum arrived at by—

(i) calculating what would be his weekly or monthly net earnings by dividing the net earnings payable to him by the employer on the pay-day by that whole number (of weeks or months, as the case may be),

(ii) ascertaining the percentage (or percentages) specified in column 2 of Table A (if the whole number is of weeks) or of Table B (if the whole number is of months) in Schedule 4 opposite the band in column 1 of that Table within which the notional net earnings calculated under paragraph (i) fall, and

(iii) calculating the sum which equals the appropriate percentage (or percentages) of the notional net earnings for any of those weeks or months and multiplying that sum by the whole number of weeks or months, as appropriate.

(2) Where paragraph (1) applies and the amount to be paid to the debtor on any pay-day includes an advance in respect of future pay, the sum to be deducted on that pay-day shall be the aggregate of the amount which would otherwise fall to be deducted under paragraph (1) and—

(*a*) where the amount advanced would otherwise have been paid on a single pay-day, the sum which would have been deducted on that pay-day in accordance with paragraph (1) if the amount advanced had been the amount of net earnings on that day; or

(*b*) where the amount advanced would otherwise have been paid on more than one pay-day, the sums which would have been deducted on each of the relevant pay-days in accordance with paragraph (1) if—

(i) an equal proportion of the amount advanced had been paid on each of those days; and

(ii) the net earnings of the debtor on each of those days had been an amount equal to that proportion.

(3) Where the amount payable to the debtor on any pay-day is reduced by reason of an earlier

advance of pay, the net earnings of the debtor on that day shall, for the purposes of paragraph (1), be the amount defined in regulation 32(1) less the amount of the deduction.

(4) Subject to paragraphs (5) and (6), where the debtor's earnings from the employer are payable at regular intervals other than at intervals to which paragraph (1) applies, the sum to be deducted on any pay-day shall be arrived at by—

(*a*) calculating what would be his daily net earnings by dividing the net earnings payable to him by the employer on the pay-day by the number of days in the interval,

(*b*) ascertaining the percentage (or percentages) specified in column 2 of Table C in Schedule 4 opposite the band in column 1 of that Table within which the notional net earnings calculated under sub-paragraph (*a*) fall, and

(*c*) calculating the sum which equals the appropriate percentage (or percentages) of the notional daily net earnings and multiplying that sum by the number of days in the interval.

(5) Where the debtor's earnings are payable as mentioned in paragraph (4), and the amount to be paid to the debtor on any pay-day includes an amount advanced in respect of future pay, the amount of the debtor's notional net earnings under sub-paragraph (*a*) of that paragraph shall be calculated in accordance with the formula—

$$\frac{A+B}{C+D}$$

where—

A is the amount of net earnings payable to him on that pay-day (exclusive of the amount advanced);

B is the amount advanced;

C is the number of days in the period for which the amount of net earnings is payable; and

D is the number of days in the period for which, but for the agreement to pay in advance, the amount advanced would have been payable.

(6) Paragraph (3) applies in relation to paragraph (4) as it applies in relation to paragraph (1).

(7) Where earnings are payable to a debtor by the employer by 2 or more series of payments at regular intervals—

(*a*) if some or all of the intervals are of different lengths—

(i) for the purpose of arriving at the sum to be deducted, whichever of paragraphs (1), (2), (3), (4), (5) and (6) is appropriate shall apply to the series with the shortest interval (or, if there is more than one series with the shortest interval, such one of those series as the employer may choose), and

(ii) in relation to the earnings payable in every other series, the sum to be deducted shall be 20 per cent of the net earnings or, where on any pay-day an amount advanced is also paid, 20 per cent of the aggregate of the net earnings and the amount advanced;

(*b*) if all of the intervals are of the same length, whichever of paragraphs (1), (2), (3), (4), (5) and (6) is appropriate shall apply to such series as the employer may choose and sub-paragraph (*a*)(ii) shall apply to every other series,

and paragraph (3) shall apply in relation to sub-paragraph (*a*)(ii) above as it applies in relation to paragraph (1).

(8) Subject to paragraphs (9) and (10), where the debtor's earnings from the employer are payable at irregular intervals, the sums to be deducted on any pay-day shall be arrived at by—

(*a*) calculating what would be his daily net earnings by dividing the net earnings payable to him by the employer on the pay-day—

(i) by the number of days since earnings were last payable by the employer to him, or

(ii) if the earnings are the first earnings to be payable by the employer to him with respect to the employment in question, by the number of days since he began the employment;

(*b*) ascertaining the percentage (or percentages) specified in column 2 of Table C of Schedule 4 opposite the band in column 1 of that Table within which the notional net earnings calculated under sub-paragraph (*a*) fall; and

(*c*) calculating the sum which equals the appropriate percentage (or percentages) of the daily net earnings and multiplying that sum by the same number as that of the divisor for the purposes of the calculation mentioned in sub-paragraph (*a*).

(9) Where on the same pay-day there are payable to the debtor by the employer both earnings payable at regular intervals and earnings payable at irregular intervals, for the purpose of arriving at the sum to be deducted on the pay-day under the foregoing provisions of this regulation all the earnings shall be aggregated and treated as earnings payable at the regular interval.

(10) Where there are earnings payable to the debtor by the employer at regular intervals on the pay-day, and earnings are payable by the employer to him at irregular intervals on a different pay-day, the sum to be deducted on each of the pay-days on which the earnings which are payable at irregular intervals are so payable shall be 20 per cent of the net earnings payable to him on the day.

8–20099 **39. Attachment of earnings orders: ancillary powers and duties of employers and others served.** (1) An employer who deducts and pays amounts under an attachment of earnings order may, on each occasion that he makes such a deduction, also deduct from the debtor's earnings the sum of one pound towards his administrative costs.

(2) An employer who deducts and pays amounts under an attachment of earnings order shall, in accordance with paragraph (3), notify the debtor in writing of—

(*a*) the total amount of the sums (including sums deducted under paragraph (1)) deducted under the order up to the time of the notification; or

(*b*) the total amount of the sums (including sums deducted under paragraph (1)) that will fall to be so deducted after that time.

(3) A notification under paragraph (2) must be given at the time that the pay statement given by the employer to the debtor next after a deduction has been made is so given, or if no such statements are usually issued by the employer, as soon as practicable after a deduction has been made.

(4) A person on whom a copy of an attachment of earnings order has been served shall, in accordance with paragraph (5), notify in writing the authority which made the order if he does not have the debtor against whom it was made in his employment or the debtor subsequently ceases to be in his employment.

(5) A notification under paragraph (4) must be given within 14 days of the day on which the copy of the order was served on him or the debtor ceased to be in his employment (as the case may be).

(6) While an attachment of earnings order is in force, any person who becomes the debtor's employer and knows that the order is in force and by what authority it was made shall notify that authority in writing that he is the debtor's employer.

(7) A notification under paragraph (6) must be given within 14 days of the day on which the debtor became the person's employee or of the day on which the person first knows that the order is in force and the identity of the authority by which it was made, whichever is the later.

8–20100 40. Attachment of earnings orders: duties of debtor. (1) While an attachment of earnings order is in force, the debtor in respect of whom the order has been made shall notify in writing the authority which made it of each occasion when he leaves an employment or becomes employed or re-employed, and (in a case where he becomes so employed or re-employed) shall include in the notification a statement of—

(*a*) his earnings and (so far as he is able) expected earnings from the employment concerned,

(*b*) the deductions and (so far as he is able) expected deductions from such earnings—

(i) in respect of income tax;

(ii) in respect of primary Class 1 contributions under Part I of the Social Security Contributions and Benefits Act 1992;

(iii) for the purposes of such a superannuation scheme as is mentioned in the definition of "net earnings" in regulation 32(1),

(*c*) the name and address of the employer, and—

(*d*) his work or identity number in the employment (if any).

(2) A notification under paragraph (1) must be given within 14 days of the day on which the debtor leaves or commences (or recommences) the employment (as the case may be), or (if later) the day on which he is informed by the authority that the order has been made.

8–20101 41. Attachment of earnings orders: ancillary powers and duties of authority. (1) Where the whole amount to which an attachment of earnings order relates has been paid (whether by attachment of earnings or otherwise), the authority by which it was made shall give notice of the fact to any person who appears to it to have the debtor in his employment and who has been served with a copy of the order.

(2) The authority by which an attachment of earnings order was made may, on its own account or on the application of the debtor or an employer of the debtor, make an order discharging the attachment of earnings order; and if it does so it shall give notice of that fact to any person who appears to it to have the debtor in his employment and who has been served with a copy of the order.

(3) If an authority serves a copy of an attachment of earnings order in accordance with regulation 37(3), it shall (unless it has previously done so) also serve a copy of the order on the debtor.

8–20102 42. Priority as between orders. (1) Where an employer would, but for this paragraph, be obliged to make deductions on any pay-day under more than one attachment of earnings order, he shall—

(*a*) deal with the orders according to the respective dates on which they were made, disregarding any later order until an earlier one has been dealt with; and

(*b*) deal with any later order as if the earnings to which it relates were the residue of the debtor's earnings after the making of any deduction to comply with any earlier order.

(2) Subject to paragraph (3), where an employer would, but for this paragraph, be obliged to comply with one or more attachment of earnings order and with one or more deduction order, he shall deal with the orders according to the respective dates on which they were made in like manner as under paragraph (1).

(3) An employer shall not deal with a deduction order made either wholly or in part in respect

of the payment of a judgment debt or payments under an administration order until he has dealt with the attachment of earnings order or orders and any other deduction order.

(4) In this regulation "deduction order" means an order under the Attachment of Earnings Act 1971 or section 31(2) (deductions from earnings orders) of the Child Support Act 1991.

8–20103 43. Attachment of earnings orders: persons employed under the Crown. (1) Where a debtor is in the employment of the Crown and an attachment of earnings order is made in respect of him, for the purposes of this Part—

(*a*) the chief officer for the time being of the department, office or other body in which the debtor is employed shall be treated as having the debtor in his employment (any transfer of the debtor from one department, office or body to another being treated as a change of employment); and

(*b*) any earnings paid by the Crown or a Minister of the Crown, or out of the public revenue of the United Kingdom, shall be treated as paid by that chief officer.

(2) If any question arises as to what department, office or other body is concerned for the purposes of this regulation, or as to who for those purposes is its chief officer, the question shall be referred to and determined by the Minister for the Civil Service.

(3) A document purporting to set out a determination of the Minister under paragraph (2) and to be signed by an official of the Office of that Minister shall, in any proceedings arising in relation to an attachment of earnings order, be admissible in evidence and be deemed to contain an accurate statement of such a determination unless the contrary is shown.

(4) This Part shall have effect in relation to attachment of earnings orders notwithstanding any enactment passed before 29th May 1970 and preventing or avoiding the attachment or diversion of sums due to a person in respect of services under the Crown; whether by way of remuneration, pension or otherwise.

8–20104 44. Attachment of allowances orders. (1) This regulation applies in relation to an elected member of a relevant billing authority or a relevant precepting authority.

(2) For the purposes of this regulation—

(*a*) a relevant billing authority is a billing authority other than the Common Council;

(*b*) a relevant precepting authority is a major precepting authority other than the Receiver for the Metropolitan Police District;

(*c*) a person is an elected member of a relevant precepting authority other than a county council if he is appointed to the authority by a constituent council of which he is an elected member; and

(*d*) references to attachable allowances are references to the allowances referred to in paragraph (7)(*b*).

(3) Where a liability order has been made and the debtor against whom it was made is a person in relation to whom this regulation applies, the authority which applied for the order may make an order under this regulation to secure the payment of any outstanding sum which is or forms part of the amount in respect of which the liability order was made.

(4) An order under this regulation shall be expressed to be directed to the authority of whom the debtor is an elected member and shall operate as an instruction to the authority to make deductions from attachable allowances payable to the debtor and to pay the sums so deducted to the authority by which the order was made.

(5) An order under this regulation shall remain in force until discharged or the whole sum to which it relates has been paid (whether by attachment of allowances or otherwise).

(6) The sum to be deducted by an authority under an order under this regulation on any day shall be a sum equal to 40 per cent of the aggregate of attachable allowances payable to the debtor on that day.

(7) Paragraph (3) of regulation 37, paragraphs (1) to (5) of regulation 39 and paragraphs (1) and (2) of regulation 41 shall apply to orders under this regulation as they apply to attachment of earnings orders as if any reference in those paragraphs—

(*a*) to an employer or a person having the debtor in his employment, were a reference to such an authority as is mentioned in paragraph (1) above having the debtor as an elected member;

(*b*) to the debtor's earnings, were a reference to allowances—

(i) payable to the debtor in accordance with a scheme under regulations under section 18 (schemes for basic, attendance and special responsibility allowances for local authority members) of the Local Government and Housing Act 1989; or

(ii) in the nature of an attendance allowance, payable to the debtor under section 175 (allowances for attending conferences and meetings) of the Local Government Act 1972;

(*c*) to an attachment of earnings order, were a reference to an order under this regulation.

8–20105 45. Distress. (1) Where a liability order has been made, the authority which applied for the order may, subject to regulation 45A, levy the appropriate amount by distress and sale of the goods of the debtor against whom the order was made.

(1A) Without prejudice to paragraph (8) below, no person making a distress shall seize any goods of the debtor of the following descriptions—

(*a*) such tools, books, vehicles and other items of equipment as are necessary to the debtor for use personally by him in his employment, business or vocation;

(*b*) such clothing, bedding, furniture, household equipment and provisions as are necessary for satisfying the basic domestic needs of the debtor and his family.

(2) The appropriate amount for the purposes of paragraph (1) is the aggregate of—

(*a*) an amount equal to any outstanding sum which is or forms part of the amount in respect of which the liability order was made, and

(*b*) a sum determined in accordance with Schedule 5 in respect of charges connected with the distress.

(3) If, before any goods are seized, the appropriate amount (including charges arising up to the time of the payment or tender) is paid or tendered to the authority, the authority shall accept the amount and the levy shall not be proceeded with.

(4) Where an authority has seized goods of the debtor in pursuance of the distress, but before sale of those goods the appropriate amount (including charges arising up to the time of the payment or tender) is paid or tendered to the authority, the authority shall accept the amount, the sale shall not be proceeded with and the goods shall be made available for collection by the debtor.

(5) The person levying distress on behalf of an authority shall carry with him the written authorisation of the authority, which he shall show to the debtor if so requested; and he shall hand to the debtor or leave at the premises where the distress is levied a copy of this regulation and Schedule 5 and a memorandum setting out the appropriate amount, and shall hand to the debtor a copy of any close or walking possession agreement entered into.

(6) A distress may be made anywhere in England and Wales.

(6A) No distress under this regulation may be made other than by a person who is authorised to act as a bailiff by a general certificate granted under section 7 of the Law of Distress Amendment Act 1888.

(7) A distress shall not be deemed unlawful on account of any defect or want of form in the liability order, and no person making a distress shall be deemed a trespasser on that account; and no person making a distress shall be deemed a trespasser from the beginning on account of any subsequent irregularity in making the distress, but a person sustaining special damage by reason of the subsequent irregularity may recover full satisfaction for the special damage (and no more) by proceedings in trespass or otherwise.

(8) The provisions of this regulation shall not affect the operation of any enactment which protects goods of any class from distress.

(9) *Revoked.*

8–20105A 45A. Information preliminary to distress. (1) No distress shall be made under these regulations unless, no less than 14 days before a visit in connection with the distress is first made to the premises where it is to be levied, the authority have sent to the debtor written notice of the matters specified in paragraph (2) below.

(2) The matters are—

(a) the fact that a liability order has been made against the debtor;

(b) the amount in respect of which the liability order was made and, where this is a different amount, the amount which remains outstanding;

(c) a warning that unless the amount specified has been paid before the expiry of 14 days beginning on the date of the sending of the notice, distress may be levied;

(d) notice that if distress is levied further costs will be incurred by the debtor;

(e) the fees prescribed in Schedule 5 to these Regulations;

(f) the address and telephone number at which the debtor can communicate with the authority.

8–20106 46. Appeals in connection with distress. (1) A person aggrieved by the levy of, or an attempt to levy, a distress may appeal to a magistrates' court.

(2) The appeal shall be instituted by making complaint[1] to a justice of the peace, and requesting the issue of a summons directed to the authority which levied or attempted to levy the distress to appear before the court to answer to the matter by which the person is aggrieved.

(3) If the court is satisfied that a levy was irregular, it may order the goods distrained to be discharged if they are in the possession of the authority; and it may by order award compensation in respect of any goods distrained and sold of an amount equal to the amount which, in the opinion of the court, would be awarded by way of special damages in respect of the goods if proceedings were brought in trespass or otherwise in connection with the irregularity under regulation 45(7).

(4) If the court is satisfied that an attempted levy was irregular, it may by order require the authority to desist from levying in the manner giving rise to the irregularity.

1. If on the hearing of the complaint the justices form the opinion that the case raises complex issues of title, they have a discretion to decline to continue the hearing, leaving the complainant with the right to proceed by

way of an action in the High Court or county court (*R v Basildon Justices, ex p Holding and Barnes plc* (1994) 158 JP 980).

8–20107 47. Commitment to prison[1]. (1) Where a billing authority has sought to levy an amount by distress under regulation 45, the debtor is an individual who has attained the age of 18 years, and the person making the distress reports to the authority that he was unable (for whatever reason) to find any or sufficient goods of the debtor on which to levy the amount[2], the authority may apply to a magistrates' court for the issue of a warrant committing the debtor to prison[3].

(2) On such application being made the court shall (in the debtor's presence) inquire as to his means and inquire whether the failure to pay which has led to the application is due to his wilful refusal or culpable neglect.

(3) If (and only if) the court is of the opinion that his failure is due to his wilful refusal or culpable neglect[4] it may if it thinks fit[5]—

(*a*) issue a warrant of commitment against the debtor, or

(*b*) fix a term of imprisonment and postpone[6] the issue of the warrant until such time and on such conditions[7] (if any) as the court thinks just.

(4) The warrant shall be made in respect of the relevant amount; and the relevant amount for this purpose is the aggregate of—

(*a*) an amount equal to the appropriate amount mentioned in regulation 45(2) or (as the case may be) so much of it as remains outstanding, and

(*b*) a sum of an amount equal to the costs reasonably incurred by the applicant in respect of the application.

(5) The warrant—

(*a*) shall state the relevant amount mentioned in paragraph (4),

(*b*) may be directed to the authority making the application and to such other persons (if any) as the court issuing it thinks fit, and

(*c*) may be executed anywhere in England and Wales by any person to whom it is directed.

(6) If—

(*a*) before a warrant has been issued, or a term of imprisonment fixed and the issue of a warrant postponed, an amount determined in accordance with paragraph (6A) below is paid or tendered to the authority, or

(*b*) after a term of imprisonment has been fixed and the issue of a warrant postponed, the amount (if any) the court has ordered the debtor to pay is paid or tendered to the authority, or

(*c*) after a warrant has been issued, the amount stated in it is paid or tendered to the authority,

the authority shall accept the amount concerned, no further steps shall be taken as regards its recovery, and the debtor, if committed to prison, shall be released.

(6A) The amount referred to in paragraph (6)(*a*) above is the aggregate of—

(*a*) the appropriate amount mentioned in regulation 45(2) (or so much of it as remains outstanding), and

(*b*) subject to paragraph (6B) below, the authority's reasonable costs incurred up to the time of payment or tender in making one or more of the applications referred to in Schedule 6.

(6B) For the purposes of paragraph (6A)(*b*) above, the authority's reasonable costs in respect of any application shall not exceed the amount specified for that application in Schedule 6.

(7) The order in the warrant shall be that the debtor be imprisoned for a time specified[8] in the warrant which shall not exceed 3 months, unless the amount stated in the warrant is sooner paid; but—

(*a*) where a warrant is issued after a postponement under paragraph (3)(*b*) and, since the term of imprisonment was fixed but before the issue of the warrant, the amount mentioned in paragraph (4)(*a*) with respect to which the warrant would (but for the postponement) have been made has been reduced by a part payment, the period of imprisonment ordered under the warrant shall be the term fixed under paragraph (3) reduced by such number of days as bears to the total number of days in that term less one day the same proportion as the part paid bears to that amount, and

(*b*) where, after the issue of a warrant, a part payment of the amount stated in it is made, the period of imprisonment shall be reduced by such number of days as bears to the total number of days in the term of imprisonment specified in the warrant less one day the same proportion as the part paid bears to the amount so stated.

(8) In calculating a reduction required under paragraph (7) any fraction of a day shall be left out of account; and rule 55(1), (2) and (3) of the Magistrates' Courts Rules 1981 applies (so far as is relevant) to a part payment as if the imprisonment concerned were imposed for want of sufficient distress to satisfy a sum adjudged to be paid by a magistrates' court.

---

1. Cases decided under the similarly worded reg 41 of the Community Charge etc Regulations 1989 are still useful sources of reference and have, therefore, been included in the footnotes to this regulation. The power to commit to prison is plainly intended to be used as a weapon to extract payment rather than to punish (*R v Wolverhampton Magistrates' Court, ex p Mould* [1992] RA 309) and is a perfectly proper means of extracting

payment from a person possessed of income or assets who has been guilty of wilful refusal (*R v Oldbury Justices, ex p Smith* (1994) 159 JP 316). Justices retain a discretion and the Regulations do not limit the power to commit to prison to those cases in which every other possibility has been exhaustively explored (*R v Newcastle-under-Lyme Justices, ex p K A Massey* (26 May 1993, unreported). Nevertheless, before committing a debtor to prison, it is incumbent upon justices to consider all available alternatives to effect the recovery of the sum due (*R v Middleton Magistrates, ex p Phillips* (29 October 1993, unreported).

2. It is unnecessary for the justices to determine the existence of these preconditions to the local authority's decision to apply for a warrant of commitment; the procedure adopted by the local authority, however, may be challenged on proceedings for judicial review (*R v Dudley Justices, ex p Blatchford* (1992) 156 JP 846).

3. It is not necessary for the charging authority to call evidence to establish the requirements of sub-s (1); the application need not be by way of complaint and therefore would not be subject to the time limit contained in s 127 of the Magistrates' Court Act 1980 (*R v Wolverhampton Magistrates' Court* (1992) 157 JP 1017).

4. If the basis of the decision is that the defaulter had earning capacity which he chose not to use, there must at least be clear evidence that gainful employment for which he was fit was on offer to the defaulter which he had rejected; the proper date for assessing his means is when the court hears the application for commitment (See *R v Poole Justices, ex p Benham* (1991) 156 JP 177).

5. Justices must consider the issue of wilful refusal or culpable neglect separately from the question of the appropriate disposal. Accordingly, where justices find that the debtor has wilfully refused to pay, it does not follow that the court has no alternative other than to order the immediate issue of the warrant of commitment. It is incumbent on the justices, in such circumstances, to consider any offer to pay and if they deem it inappropriate to fix a term of imprisonment and postpone the issue of the warrant on terms, they must give reasons for so deciding (*R v Middleton Magistrates, ex p Phillips* 29 October 1993, unreported). See also *R v Alfreton Justices, ex p Gratton* (1993) Times, 7 December. However in *R v Oldbury Justices, ex p Smith* (1994) 159 JP 316 Turner J doubted the need to give reasons for making a finding of wilful refusal or culpable neglect given that the appropriate route of appeal was by way of case stated in which the justices' reasons would be made apparent.

6. The court may take into account the attitude of a spouse where the charge payer is financially dependent upon that spouse (*R v Ramsgate Magistrates' Court, ex p Haddow* (1992) 157 JP 545). In proceedings for recovery of the Community Charge under the Community Charges (Administration and Enforcement) Regulations 1989, SI 1989/712, it was held that the principles governing the exercise of discretion under reg 41(3)(*a*) and (b) of the 1989 regs were different; justices were not obliged to exhaust all possibilities of recovering unpaid community charge before making a suspended committal order (*R v Preston Justices, ex p McCosh* (1995) Times, 30 January). We would suggest that this reasoning remains applicable to reg 47(3)(*a*) and (*b*) of the 1992 regulations. Where the court postpones the issue of the warrant of commitment, it will not be lawful for the warrant to be issued without there being a further hearing, on the application of the local authority, of which the debtor must be given notice of the date and purpose of the hearing, and an opportunity of attending. The magistrates must be satisfied that the council tax payer has received notice of the hearing and must carry out an appropriate inquiry to make sure that the notice must have come into his hands. Accordingly the notice should be sent by recorded delivery, see *R v Newcastle upon Tyne Justices, ex p Devine* (1998) 162 JP 602, DC (a case decided under the similarly worded reg 41 of the Community Charge (Administration and Enforcement) Regulations 1989, SI 1989/712). At that hearing the debtor is entitled to put the local authority to proof of non-payment and non-compliance with the conditions of postponement; and to draw the court's attention to any change of circumstances since the decision to fix the terms of imprisonment which renders it inexpedient for the warrant to issue (*R v Faversham and Sittingbourne Magistrates' Court, ex p Ursell* (1992) 156 JP 765). See also *R v Northampton Justices, ex p Newell* (1992) 157 JP 869. Before it can activate the committal order, the court must be satisfied that the debtor has had the ability to pay the instalment order, or otherwise comply with the conditions on which the issue of the warrant was postponed, but has failed to do so; see *R v Felixstowe Justices, ex p Herridge* [1993] RA 83.

7. When postponing the issue of a warrant on terms as to the repayment of the sum due by instalments, the court should be mindful of the principles applicable to the payment of fines in criminal cases. If satisfied that the particular person in front of the court is a person of limited means and if such an order is contemplated, the appropriate course is to remit such part of the arrears as will reduce the total sum in respect of which the order is made to a sum which can be met by the instalments envisaged within a reasonable period and certainly not a period in excess of three years (*R v Newcastle upon Tyne Justices, ex p Devine* (1998) 162 JP 602, DC (a case decided under the similarly worded reg 41 of the Community Charge (Administration and Enforcement) Regulations 1989, SI 1989/712).

8. In an application for judicial review of a decision under reg 16 of the Non-Domestic Rating (Collection etc) Regulations 1989, post, the High Court held that, when determining the period of imprisonment to be specified in the warrant, the justices must have regard to the principle of proportionality. The more serious the case, whether in terms of the amount outstanding or in terms of the degree of culpability or blame to be attached to the debtor for his non-payment, the closer will any period imposed approach the maximum. A finding of wilful refusal, in this respect, represents a more serious state of affairs than culpable neglect; see *R v Highbury Corner Magistrates' Court, ex p Uchendu* (1994) 158 JP 409.

8–20108 **48. Commitment to prison: further provision.** (1) A single warrant may not be issued under regulation 47 against more than one person.

(2) Where an application under regulation 47 has been made, and after the making of the inquiries mentioned in paragraph (2) of that regulation no warrant is issued or term of imprisonment fixed, the court may remit[1] all or part of the appropriate amount mentioned in regulation 45(2) with respect to which the application related.

(3) Where an application under regulation 47 has been made but no warrant is issued or term of imprisonment fixed, the application may be renewed (except so far as regards any sum remitted under paragraph (2)) on the ground that the circumstances of the debtor have changed.

(4) A statement in writing to the effect that wages of any amount have been paid to the debtor during any period, purporting to be signed by or on behalf of his employer, shall in any proceedings under regulation 47 be evidence of the facts there stated.

(5) For the purpose of enabling inquiry to be made as to the debtor's conduct and means under regulation 47, a justice of the peace may—

(*a*) issue a summons to him to appear before a magistrates' court and (if he does not obey the summons) issue a warrant for his arrest, or

(*b*) issue a warrant for the debtor's arrest without issuing a summons.

(6) A warrant issued under paragraph (5) may be executed anywhere in England and Wales by any person to whom it is directed or by any constable acting within his police area; and section 125(3) of the Magistrates' Courts Act 1980 applies to such a warrant.

(7) Regulation 47 and this regulation have effect subject to Part I of the Criminal Justice Act 1982 (treatment of young offenders).

1. In cases decided under the similarly worded reg 42 of the Community Charge etc Regulations 1989 it is maintained that if the court has come to the conclusion that there has been wilful refusal or culpable neglect, then it must proceed accordingly and it is not open to contend that there is a discretion to remit all or part of the appropriate amount (*R v Oldbury Justices, ex p Smith* (1994) 159 JP 316) and that there is no inherent power available to justices to remit a community charge debt once a term of imprisonment has been fixed or a warrant of commitment has been issued (*Harrogate Borough Council v Barker* (1995) 159 JP 809).

8–20109 **49. Insolvency.** (1) Where a liability order has been made and the debtor against whom it was made is an individual, the amount due shall be deemed to be a debt for the purposes of section 267 of the Insolvency Act 1986 (grounds of creditor's petition).

(2) Where a liability order has been made and the debtor against whom it was made is a company, the amount due shall be deemed to be a debt for the purposes of section 122(1)(*f*) (winding up of companies by the court) or, as the case may be, section 221(5)(*b*) (winding up of unregistered companies) of that Act.

(3) For the purposes of this regulation the amount due is an amount equal to any outstanding sum which is or forms part of the amount in respect of which the liability order was made.

8–20110 **50. Charging orders.** (1) An application to the appropriate court may be made under this regulation where—

(*a*) a magistrates' court has made one or more liability orders pursuant to either regulation 34(6) or 36A(5);

(*b*) the amount mentioned in regulation 34(7)(*a*) or 36A(5)(*a*) in respect of which the liability order was made, or, where more than one liability order was made, the aggregate of the amounts mentioned in regulation 34(7)(*a*) or 36A(5)(*a*) in respect of which each such liability order was made, is an amount the debtor is liable to pay under Part V; and

(*c*) at the time that the application under this regulation is made at least £1000 of the amount in respect of which the liability order was made, or, where more than one liability order was made, the aggregate of the amounts in respect of which those liability orders were made, remains outstanding.

(2) The application which may be made to the appropriate court under this regulation is an application by the authority concerned for an order imposing, on any interest held by the debtor beneficially in the relevant dwelling, a charge for securing the due amount; and the court may make such an order on such application.

(3) For the purposes of paragraph (2)—

(*a*) the authority concerned is the authority which applied for the one or more liability orders referred to in paragraph (1)(a);

(*b*) the relevant dwelling is the dwelling in respect of which, at the time the application for the liability order was made, or, where more than one liability order was made, at the time the applications for the liability orders were made, the debtor was liable to pay council tax;

(*c*) the due amount is the aggregate of—

(i) an amount equal to any outstanding sum which is or forms part of the amount in respect of which the one or more liability orders were made; and

(ii) a sum of an amount equal to the costs reasonably incurred by the applicant in obtaining the charging order;

(*d*) the appropriate court is the county court for the area in which the relevant dwelling is situated.

8–20111 **51. Charging orders: further provision.** (1) In deciding whether to make a charging order, the court shall consider all the circumstances of the case, and in particular any evidence before it as to—

(*a*) the personal circumstances of the debtor, and

(*b*) whether any other person would be likely to be unduly prejudiced by the making of the order.

(2) A charging order—

(*a*) shall specify the dwelling concerned and the interest held by the debtor beneficially in it, and

(*b*) may, as the court thinks fit, be made absolutely or subject to conditions as to the time when the charge is to become enforceable or as to other matters.

(3) A charge imposed by a charging order shall have the like effect and shall be enforceable in

the same courts and in the same manner as an equitable charge created by the debtor by writing under his hand.

(4) The court by which a charging order was made may at any time, on the application of the debtor, the authority on whose application the order was made or any person interested in the dwelling, make an order discharging or varying the charging order.

(5) The Land Charges Act 1972 and the Land Registration Act 1925 shall apply in relation to charging orders as they apply in relation to orders or writs issued or made for the purposes of enforcing judgments; and in section 49(1)(*g*) of the Land Registration Act 1925, after the words "Local Government Finance Act 1988" there are inserted the words ", or regulations under paragraph 11 of Schedule 4 to the Local Government Finance Act 1992".

(6) Where a charging order has been protected by an entry registered under the Land Charges Act 1972 or the Land Registration Act 1925, an order under paragraph (4) discharging the charging order may direct that the entry be cancelled.

8–20112 52. Relationship between remedies. (1) Where a warrant of commitment is issued against (or a term of imprisonment is fixed in the case of) a person under regulation 47(3), no steps, or no further steps, may be taken under this Part by way of attachment of allowances, attachment of earnings, distress, bankruptcy or charging, or under the Income Support Regulations in relation to the relevant amount mentioned in regulation 47(4).

(2) Steps under this Part by way of attachment of allowances, attachment of earnings, distress, commitment, bankruptcy, winding up or charging may not be taken in relation to a person against whom a liability order has been made while—

(*a*) steps by way of another of those methods are being taken against him under it; or

(*b*) deductions are being made under the Income Support Regulations from any amount payable to him by way of income support; or

(*c*) an application under regulation 2 of the Income Support Regulations has been made in respect of him to the Secretary of State and remains undetermined.

(2A) An application under regulation 2 of the Income Support Regulations may not be made in respect of a person against whom a liability order has been made while steps under this Part are being taken against him for the recovery of an amount equal to any outstanding sum which is or forms part of the amount in respect of which the liability order was made.

(3) Subject to paragraphs (1) and (2)—

(*a*) attachment of allowances, attachment of earnings, deductions under the Income Support Regulations or distress may be resorted to more than once, and

(*b*) attachment of allowances, attachment of earnings, deductions under the Income Support Regulations or distress may be resorted to in any order or alternately (or both).

(4) Where a step is taken for the recovery of an outstanding sum which is or forms part of an amount in respect of which a liability order has been made and under which additional costs or charges with respect to the step are also recoverable in accordance with this Part, any sum recovered thereby which is less than the aggregate of the amount outstanding and such additional costs and charges shall be treated as discharging first the costs and charges, the balance (if any) being applied towards the discharge of the outstanding sum.

8–20113 53. Magistrates' courts. (1) Justices of the peace for a commission area within which is situated the area of a billing authority shall have jurisdiction to act under the provisions of this Part as respects that authority.

(1A) Paragraph (1) shall have effect in its application to billing authorities in Wales as if the words "the whole or any part of" were inserted before "the area".

(2) Subject to any other enactment authorising a District Judge (Magistrates' Courts) or other person to act by himself, a magistrates' court shall not under this Part hear a summons, entertain an application for a warrant or hold an inquiry as to means on such an application except when composed of at least two justices.

(3) References to a justice of the peace in regulations 34(2) and 46(2) shall be construed subject to rule 3 of the Justices' Clerks Rules 1970 (which authorises certain matters authorised to be done by a justice of the pace to be done by a justices' clerk).

(4) In any proceedings under regulation 34 (application for liability order), regulation 46 (appeals in connection with distress) or regulation 47 (commitment to prison), a statement contained in a document constituting or forming part of a record compiled by the applicant authority or an authorised person[1] shall be admissible as evidence of any fact stated in it of which direct oral evidence would be admissible.

(5) In proceedings where the applicant authority or an authorised person[1] desires to give a statement in evidence in accordance with paragraph (4), and the document containing that statement is produced by a computer, a certificate—

(*a*) identifying the document containing the statement and the computer by which it was produced;

(*b*) containing a statement that at all material times the computer was operating properly, or if not, that any respect in which it was not operating properly or was out of operation was not such as to affect the production of the document or the accuracy of its contents;

(*c*) giving such explanation as may be appropriate of the content of the document; and (*d*) purporting to be signed by a person occupying a responsible position in relation to the operation of the computer,

shall be admissible as evidence of anything which is stated in it to the best of the signatory's information and belief.

(6) In paragraph (4) above, "statement" includes any representation of fact, whether made in words or otherwise; and the reference to an application under regulation 47 includes a reference to an application made in the circumstances mentioned in regulation 48(3).

1. A billing authority may authorise another person, or that person's employees, to exercise functions relating to the administration and enforcement of the council tax: see the Local Authorities (Contracting Out of Tax Billing, Collection and Enforcement Functions) Order 1996, SI 1996/1880.

8–20114 54. Joint and several liability: enforcement. (1) This regulation has effect with respect to the application of regulations 33 to 53 to a sum for which persons are jointly and severally liable under Part V.

(2) In this regulation, "joint taxpayers" means two or more individuals who are jointly and severally liable to pay an amount in respect of council tax.

(3) A final notice served in accordance with regulation 33 on every person against whom the application for a liability order is to be made may be addressed to two or more joint taxpayers in joint names.

(3A) A summons under regulation 34(2) may be addressed to two or more joint taxpayers in joint names.

(4) A liability order may be made against one or more joint taxpayers in respect of an amount for which they are jointly and severally liable.

(5) Where a liability order has been made against two or more joint taxpayers, subject to paragraphs (6) and 6(A)—

(*a*) an attachment of allowances order or an attachment of earnings order may be made against one of them, or different such orders may be made against more than one;

(*b*) a distress may be made against one or more of them;

(*c*) a charging order may be made against one of them, or against more than one jointly, or different such orders may be made against more than one of them (as the circumstances require); and

(*d*) deductions may be made under the Income Support Regulations from any amount payable to one or more of them by way of income support.

(6) Where a liability order has been made against two or more joint taxpayers in respect of an amount, steps by way of any method specified in paragraph (5)—

(*a*) may not be taken under it in respect of one of them while steps by way of that or another of those methods are being taken under it in respect of another of them; and

(*b*) may be taken under it in respect of one of them notwithstanding that no steps by way of that or another of those methods have been taken under it in respect of another of them.

(6A) Where a liability order has been made against two or more joint taxpayers and an amount is payable to one of them by way of income support and—

(*a*) deductions are being made under the Income Support Regulations from any such amount; or

(*b*) an application under regulation 2 of those Regulations has been made in respect of him to the Secretary of State and remains undetermined.

no steps, or no further steps, by way of attachment of allowances or earnings, distress, commitment, bankruptcy or charging may be taken, under that or any other liability order, against him or any other of those joint taxpayers who is a member of his family.

(6B) In paragraph (6A) above—

"income support" means income support within the meaning of the Social Security Contributions and Benefits Act 1992; and

"family" has the same meaning as in section 137(1) of that Act.

(7) Where a distress has been made against two or more joint taxpayers in respect of an amount a warrant of commitment may, subject to paragraph (8), be applied for at any time against one of them or different warrants may be applied for against more than one of them: but no such application may be made in respect of any of them who has not attained the age of 18 years.

(8) Where a liability order has been made against two or more joint taxpayers in respect of an amount, a warrant of commitment may not be applied for unless—

(*a*) distress has been made against all of them; and

(*b*) the person making the distress reports to the authority that, in relation to each of them, he was unable (for whatever reason) to find any or sufficient goods.

(9) Where a liability order has been made against two or more joint taxpayers in respect of an amount, and a warrant of commitment is issued against (or a term of imprisonment is fixed in the case of) one of them under regulation 47(3), no steps, or no further steps, may be taken

against any of them by way of attachment of allowances or earnings, distress, bankruptcy or charging in relation to the amount mentioned in regulation 47(4).

(9A) Where a liability order has been made against persons who are joint taxpayers, and a warrant of commitment is issued against (or a term of imprisonment is fixed in the case of) one of them under regulation 47(3), no steps, or further steps, may be taken under the Income Support Regulations in respect of any of them in relation to the amount mentioned in regulation 47(4).

(10) Where a liability order has been made against two or more joint taxpayers in respect of an amount and in making distress against one of them goods jointly owned by both or all of them are found, distress may be levied against those goods with respect to that amount; but in any subsequent proceedings under regulation 47 (commitment), charges arising under Schedule 5 from such a distress shall be treated as charges relating to the person against whose goods the levy was intended to be made when the joint goods were found, and not as charges relating to the other or others.

(11) Where—

(*a*) a liability order has been made against two or more joint taxpayers in respect of an amount; and

(*b*) a charge has arisen as regards one of them under head B of the Table in paragraph 1 of Schedule 5 in respect of that amount,

no further charge may be aggregated for the purposes of regulation 45(2) under that head or head A of that Table in consequence of any subsequent levy or attempted levy against either in respect of that amount; and a charge under head A(i) or charges under that head and head A(ii) against one of them shall be treated for those purposes as a charge or, as the case may be, charges under that head with respect to the other as well as that one.

8–20115 55. Repayments. A sum which has become payable (by way of repayment) under Part V to a person other than a billing authority but which has not been paid shall be recoverable in a court of competent jurisdiction.

8–20116 56. Offences. (1) A person shall be guilty of an offence if, following a request under paragraph (2)(*b*) of regulation 36, he is under a duty to supply information and—

(*a*) he fails without reasonable excuse to supply the information in accordance with that regulation, or

(*b*) in supplying information in purported compliance with that regulation he makes a statement which is false in a material particular or recklessly makes a statement which is false in a material particular.

(2) Subject to paragraph (3), a person shall be guilty of an offence if, following the service on him of a copy of an attachment of allowances order or an attachment of earnings order, he is under a duty to comply with the order by virtue of regulation 37(3) (including that provision as applied for the purposes of attachment of allowances orders by regulation 44(7)) and he fails to do so.

(3) It shall be a defence for a person charged with an offence under paragraph (2) to prove that he took all reasonable steps to comply with the order.

(4) A person shall be guilty of an offence if he is under a duty to notify another person under regulation 39(2) and (3) or (4) and (5) (including those provisions as applied for the purposes of attachment of allowances orders by regulation 44(7)), regulation 39(6) and (7) or regulation 40 and—

(*a*) he fails without reasonable excuse to notify the other person in accordance with the provision concerned, or

(*b*) in notifying the other person in purported compliance with the provision concerned he makes a statement which he knows to be false in a material particular or recklessly makes a statement which is false in a material particular.

(5) A person guilty of an offence under paragraph (1)(*a*) or (4)(*a*) shall be liable on summary conviction to a fine not exceeding level 2 on the standard scale.

(6) A person guilty of an offence under paragraph (1)(*b*), (2) or (4)(*b*) shall be liable on summary conviction to a fine not exceeding level 3 on the standard scale.

8–20117 57. Miscellaneous provisions. (1) Any matter which could be the subject of an appeal under section 16 of the Act or regulations under section 24 of the Act may not be raised in proceedings under this Part.

(2) If a liability order has been made and by virtue of—

(*a*) a notification which is given by the billing authority or an authorised person[1] under regulation 24(2) or (5), 25(5) or (8), 28(3) or (4) or 31(2), or paragraph 9(3) or 10(2)(*a*) of Schedule 1, or

(*b*) section 31(4) of the Act applying in any case,

any part of the amount mentioned in regulation 34(5)(*a*) in respect of which the order was made would (if paid) fall to be repaid or credited against any subsequent liability, that part shall be treated for the purposes of this Part as paid on the day the notification is given or the amount in substitution is set under section 31(2) of the Act and accordingly is no longer outstanding.

(3) If, after a warrant is issued or term of imprisonment is fixed under regulation 47(3), and before the term of imprisonment has begun or been fully served, a billing authority gives such a notification as is mentioned in paragraph (2)(*a*) in the case in question, or sets an amount in substitution so that section 31(4) of the Act applies in the case in question, it shall forthwith notify accordingly the justices' chief executive for the court which issued the warrant and (if the debtor is detained) the governor or keeper of the prison or place where he is detained or such other person as has lawful custody of him.

(4) If the debtor is treated as having paid an amount under paragraph (2) on any day, and

(*a*) that day falls after the completion of the service of a term of imprisonment imposed under regulation 47 in respect of the amount he is treated as having paid, or

(*b*) the debtor is serving a term of imprisonment imposed under regulation 47 on that day and the amount he is treated as having paid exceeds the amount of any part payment which, if made, would cause the expiry of the term of imprisonment pursuant to paragraph (7)(*b*) of that regulation on that day,

the amount mentioned in sub-paragraph (*a*) or excess mentioned in sub-paragraph (*b*) shall be paid to the debtor or credited against any subsequent liability of his, as the debtor requires.

---

1. A billing authority may authorise another person, or that person's employees, to exercise functions relating to the administration and enforcement of the council tax: see the Local Authorities (Contracting Out of Tax Billing, Collection and Enforcement Functions) Order 1996, SI 1996/1880.

Part VII

Miscellaneous

8–20118 **58. Outstanding liabilities on death.** (1) This regulation applies where a person dies and at any time before his death—

(*a*) he was (or is alleged to have been) liable to pay council tax under section 6, 7 or 8 of the Act, or

(*b*) he was (or is alleged to have been) so liable, as spouse or civil partner, under section 9 of the Act, or

(*c*) a penalty was imposed on him under any of sub-paragraphs (1) to (3) of paragraph 1 of Schedule 3 to the Act.

(2) Where—

(*a*) before the deceased's death a sum has become payable by him under Part V or by way of relevant costs in respect of one of the matters mentioned in paragraph (1) but has not been paid, or

(*b*) after the deceased's death a sum would, but for his death (and whether or not on the service of a notice), become payable by him under Part V in respect of one of those matters,

his executor or administrator shall, subject to paragraph (3) and to the extent that it is not in excess of the deceased's liability under the Act (including relevant costs payable by him) in respect of the matter, be liable to pay the sum and may deduct out of the assets and effects of the deceased any payments made (or to be made).

(3) Where paragraph (2)(*b*) applies, the liability of the executor or administrator does not arise until the service on him of a notice requiring payment of the sum.

(4) Where before the deceased's death a sum in excess of his liability under the Act (including relevant costs payable by him) in respect of one of the matters mentioned in paragraph (1) has been paid (whether the excess arises because of his death or otherwise) and has not been repaid or credited under Part V, his executor or administrator shall be entitled to the sum.

(5) Costs are relevant costs for the purposes of paragraphs (2) and (4) if—

(*a*) an order or warrant (as the case may be) was made by the court in respect of them before the deceased's death under regulation 34(7)(*b*) or (8), 36A(5)(*b*), 47(4)(*b*) or 50(3)(*c*)(ii), or

(*b*) they are charges connected with distress which may be recovered pursuant to regulation 45(2)(*b*).

(6) A sum payable under paragraph (2) shall be enforceable in the administration of the deceased's estate as a debt of the deceased and accordingly—

(*a*) no liability order need be applied for in respect of it after the deceased's death under regulation 34, and

(*b*) the liability of the executor or administrator is a liability in his capacity as such.

(7) Regulation 57(1) applies to proceedings to enforce a liability arising under this regulation as it applies to proceedings under Part VI.

(8) Insofar as is relevant to his liability under this regulation in the administration of the deceased's estate, the executor or administrator may institute, continue or withdraw proceedings (whether by way of appeal under section 16 of the Act or otherwise).

8–20119
Regulation 21

SCHEDULE 1

Council Tax Instalment Schemes

8–20120

SCHEDULE 2

Forms of Liability Order and of Warrant of Commitment

(*Revoked.*)

8-20121

Regulation 37

SCHEDULE 3

FORM OF ATTACHMENT OF EARNINGS ORDER

8-20122

SCHEDULE 4

DEDUCTIONS TO BE MADE UNDER ATTACHMENT OF EARNINGS ORDER

8-20123

Regulation 45(2)(*B*)

SCHEDULE 5

CHARGES CONNECTED WITH DISTRESS

1. The sum in respect of charges connected with the distress which may be aggregated under regulation 45(2) shall be as set out in the following Table—

	(1) Matter connected with distress	(2) Charge
A	For making a visit to premises with a view to levying distress (where no levy is made— (i) where the visit is the first or only such visit: (ii) where the visit is the second such visit	 £22.50. £16.50.
B	For levying distress:	The lesser of— (i) the amount of the costs and fees reasonably incurred; and (ii) the relevant amount calculated under paragraph 2(1) with respect to the levy.
C	For one attendance with a vehicle with a view to the removal of goods (where, following the levy, goods are not removed):	Reasonable costs and fees incurred.
D	For the removal and storage of goods for the purposes of sale:	Reasonable costs and fees incurred.
E	For the possession of goods as described in paragraph 2(2)— (i) for close possession (the man in possession to provide his own board): (ii) for walking possession:	 £14 per day. £11.00.
F	For appraisement of an item distrained, at the request in writing of the debtor:	Reasonable fees and expenses of the broker appraising.
G	For other expenses of, and commission on, a sale by auction— (i) where the sale is held on the auctioneer's premises: (ii) where the sale is held on the debtor's premises:	 The auctioneer's commission fee and out-of-pocket expenses (but not exceeding in aggregate 15 per cent. of the sum realised), together with reasonable costs and fees incurred in respect of advertising. The auctioneer's commission fee (but not exceeding $7\frac{1}{2}$ per cent. of the sum realised), together with the auctioneer's out-of-pocket expenses and reasonable costs and fees incurred in respect of advertising.
H	Where no sale takes place by reason of payment or tender in the circumstances referred to in regulation 45(4):	[Either— (i) £22.50, or (ii) the actual costs incurred, to a maximum of 5 per cent of the amount in respect of which the liability order was made, whichever is greater.]

2. (1) In head B of the Table to paragraph 1, "the relevant amount" with respect to a levy means—

(*a*) where the sum due at the time of the levy does not exceed £100, £22.50;

(*b*) where the sum due at the time of the levy exceeds £100, 22.5 per cent on the first £100 of the sum due, 4 per cent on the next £400, $2^1/_4$ per cent on the next £1,500, 1 per cent on the next £8,000 and $^1/_4$ per cent on any additional sum;

and the sum due at any time for these purposes means so much of the amount in respect of which the liability order concerned was made as is outstanding at the time.

(2) An authority takes close or walking possession of goods for the purposes of head E of the Table to paragraph 1 if it takes such possession in pursuance of an agreement—

(*a*) to which the debtor is a signatory;

(*b*) which is made at the time that the distress is levied; and

(*c*) (without prejudice to such other terms as may be agreed) which is expressed to the effect that, in consideration of the authority not immediately removing the goods distrained upon from the premises occupied by the debtor and delaying its sale of the goods, the authority may remove and sell the goods after a later specified date if the debtor has not by then paid the amount distrained for (including charges under this Schedule),

and an authority takes close possession of goods on any day for those purposes if during the greater part of the day a person is left on the premises in physical possession of the goods on behalf of the authority under such an agreement.

2A. No charge shall be payable under Head F of the Table to paragraph 1 in respect of the appraisement of an item unless the debtor has been advised of the charge, and the manner of its calculation, before the appraisement is made.

3. (1) Where the calculation under this Schedule of a percentage of a sum results in an amount containing a fraction of a pound, that fraction shall be reckoned as a whole pound.

(2) In the case of dispute as to any charge under this Schedule (other than a charge of a prescribed amount), the debtor or the authority may apply to the district judge of the county court for the district in which the distress is or is intended to be levied for the amount of the charge to be taxed.

(3) On any such application, the district judge may give such directions as to the costs of the taxation as he thinks fit; and any such costs directed to be paid by the debtor to the billing authority shall be added to the sum which may be aggregated under regulation 45(2).

(4) References in the Table to paragraph 1 to costs, fees and expenses include references to amounts payable by way of value added tax with respect to the supply of goods or services to which the costs, fees and expenses relate.

8–20124

Regulation 47(6A) and (6B)

SCHEDULE 6
COSTS CONNECTED WITH COMMITTAL

(1) *Application*	(2) *Maximum costs*
For making an application for the issue of a warrant:	£55.00.
For making an application for an arrest warrant with bail:	£55.00.
For making an application for an arrest warrant without bail:	£70.00.

LONDON

8–20210 The following subject matter has been selected as being of most common concern to those practising in the magistrates' courts in and around the Metropolis. It contains the following—

Public Order

Metropolitan Police Act 1839

(2 and 3 Vict c 47)

8–20229 **54. Offences in thoroughfares or public places.** Every person shall be liable to a penalty not more than **level 2** on the standard scale, who, within the limits of the metropolitan police district shall in any thoroughfare or public place[1], commit any of the following offences; (that is to say,)

1. very person who shall, to the annoyance[2] of the inhabitants or passengers expose for show or sale (except in a market lawfully appointed for that purpose) or feed or fodder any horse or other animal, or show any caravan containing any animal or any other show or public entertainment, or shoe, bleed, or farry any horse or animal (except in cases of accident), or clean, dress, exercise, train, or break any horse or animal, or clean, make, or repair any part of any cart or carriage, except in cases of accident where repair on the spot is necessary:
2. Every person who shall turn loose any horse or cattle, or suffer to be at large any unmuzzled ferocious[3] dog, or set on or urge any dog or other animal to attack, worry, or put in fear any person, horse, or other animal:
3. Every person who by negligence or ill-usage in driving cattle shall cause any mischief to be done by such cattle, or who shall in anywise misbehave himself in the driving, care, or management of such cattle, and also every person not being hired or employed to drive such cattle who shall wantonly and unlawfully, pelt, drive, or hunt any such cattle:
4. Every person having the care of any cart or carriage who shall ride on any part thereof, on the shafts, or on any horse or other animal drawing the same, without having and holding the reins, or who shall be at such a distance from such cart or carriage as not to have the complete control over every horse or other animal drawing the same[4]:
5. Every person who shall ride or drive furiously, or so as to endanger the life or limb of any person, or to the common danger of the passengers in any thoroughfare[5]:
6. Every person who shall cause any cart, public carriage, sledge, truck, or barrow, with or without horses, to stand longer than may be necessary for loading or unloading or for taking up or setting down passengers, except hackney carriages standing for hire in any place not forbidden by law, or who, by means of any cart, carriage, sledge, truck, or barrow or any horse or other animal, shall wilfully interrupt[6] any public crossing, or wilfully cause any obstruction in any thoroughfare:
7. Every person who shall lead or ride any horse or other animal, or draw or drive any cart or carriage, sledge, truck, or barrow, upon any footway or curbstone, or fasten any horse or other animal so that it can stand across or upon any footway:
8. Every person who shall roll or carry any cask, tub, hoop, or wheel, or any ladder, plank, pole, showboard, or placard, upon any footway[7], except for the purpose of loading or unloading any cart or carriage, or of crossing the footway:
9. Every person who, after being made acquainted with the regulations or directions which the commissioners of police shall have made for regulating the route of horses, carts, carriages, and persons for preventing obstructions during public processions and on other occasions herein-before specified, shall wilfully disregard or not conform himself thereunto:
10. Every person who, without the consent of the owner or occupier, shall affix any posting bill or other paper against or upon any building, wall, fence, or pale, or write upon, soil, deface, or mark any such building, wall, fence, or pale with chalk or paint, or in any other way whatsoever, or wilfully break, destroy, or damage any part of any such building, wall, fence, or pale, or any fixture or appendage thereunto, or any tree, shrub, or seat in any public walk park, or garden:
11. (*Repealed.*)
12. Every person who shall sell or distribute or offer for sale or distribution, or exhibit to public view, any profane, book, paper, print, drawing, painting or representation, or sing any profane, indecent, or obscene song or ballad, or use any profane, indecent or obscene language to the annoyance[8] of the inhabitants or passengers:
13. (*Repealed*).
14. Every person except the guards and postmen belonging to her Majesty's Post Office in the performance of their duty, who shall blow any horn or use any other noisy instrument[9] for the purpose of calling persons together, or of announcing any show or entertainment, or for the purpose of hawking, selling, distributing, or collecting any article whatsoever, or of obtaining money or alms:
15. Every person who shall wantonly discharge any fire-arm or throw or discharge[10] any stone or other missile, to the damage or danger of any person, or make any bonfire, or throw or set fire to any firework:

16. Every person who shall wilfully and wantonly disturb any inhabitant by pulling or ringing any door-bell[11] or knocking at any door without lawful excuse, or who shall wilfully and unlawfully extinguish the light of any lamp:

17. Every person who shall fly any kite or play at any game to the annoyance of the inhabitants or passengers[12], or who shall make or use any slide upon ice or snow in any street or other thoroughfare, to the common danger of the passengers.

[Metropolitan Police Act 1839, s 54, as amended by Street Offences Act 1959, Criminal Justice Act 1967, Statute Law (Repeals) Act 1973, Criminal Law Act 1977, Sch 6, the Indecent Displays (Control) Act 1981, Sch, the Criminal Justice Act 1982, s 46, the Police and Criminal Evidence Act 1984, Sch 7 and the Public Order Act 1986, Sch 3.]

---

1. There is no definition of "public place" in this Act. However, this section can be compared with the Town Police Clauses Act 1847, s 28, to which the definition of "public place" contained in the Public Health Amendment Act 1907, s 81, as amended (post) is expressly extended. Some of the offences created by the following subsections can, it is submitted, be committed on private property adjacent to public places and in view of persons thereon.

2. To constitute an offence there must have been some annoyance in fact, or something necessarily calculated to be so (*Allen v Baldock* (1867) 31 JP 311). See also *Innes v Newman* [1894] 2 QB 292, 58 JP 543, where it was held, in respect of a prosecution under a byelaw, that as the act complained of was such as was calculated to annoy the inhabitants generally, it was sufficient to prove that one inhabitant was annoyed.

3. It should be noted that there is no necessity for knowledge of the dog's ferocious nature to be proved.

4. A similar provision appears in s 78 of the Highway Act 1835, ante.

5. See also s 35 of the Offences Against the Person Act 1861, and s 28 of the London Hackney Carriages Act 1843.

6. See note 1 to s 28 of the Town Police Clauses Act 1847, post.

7. This subsection is wider in its application than similar provisions in s 72 of the Highway Act 1835, which is restricted to footpaths at the road side; see the words "thoroughfare or public place" in the opening sentence of this section.

8. On a prosecution under s 54(12), where indecent or obscene language is alleged, it is sufficient to show that the words were calculated to annoy; proof of actual annoyance is not required (*Myers v Garrett* [1972] Crim LR 232). See also note 2 to s 54(1), supra.

9. The Control of Pollution Act 1974, s 62 (see title PUBLIC HEALTH, post) prohibits the use of loudspeakers in streets otherwise than for certain specified purposes and between certain specified hours.

10. There is a similar provision in the Explosives Act 1875, s 80, in relation to fireworks.

11. See note 3, to the Town Police Clauses Act 1847, s 28, post.

12. The playing of football or any game on a highway "to the annoyance of a user" is an offence against the Highways Act 1980, s 161, title HIGHWAYS, ante.

8–20230 **58. Indecent behaviour[1].** Every person who shall be guilty of any violent or indecent behaviour in any police station house, shall be liable to a penalty of not more than **level 1** on the standard scale for every such offence or may be committed, if the magistrate[2] before whom he shall be convicted shall think fit instead of inflicting on him any pecuniary penalty, [to a term of imprisonment not exceeding one month].

[Metropolitan Police Act 1839, s 58, as amended by the Penalties for Drunkenness Act 1962, the Criminal Justice Act 1967, Sch 7 and the Criminal Justice Act 1982, ss 38 and 46.]

---

1. The Criminal Justice Act 1967, s 91 in PART I: MAGISTRATES' COURTS, PROCEDURE, ante, has effect in place of this section where a person is guilty whilst drunk of disorderly behaviour (Criminal Justice Act 1967, s 91(2)).

2. Lay justices in the Inner London area have jurisdiction by virtue of the Justices of the Peace Act 1979, s 33, ante.

Licensing

Greater London Council (General Powers) Act 1978

(1978 c xiii)

PART II
PROVISIONS RELATING TO THE COUNCIL

Licensing of public entertainments

8–20360 **3. Licensing of entertainment by way of posing.** *Repealed.*

8–20361 **4.** *Repealed.*

8–20362 **5. Licensing of entertainments booking offices.** (1) No premises in a borough shall, on or after 1st October, 1978, be used as a booking office except under and in accordance with the terms of a licence (hereafter in this section referred to as a "booking office licence") granted by the borough council in pursuance of the provisions of this section.

(2) Subject to the next following subsection, the provisions of sub-paragraphs (2), (3) and (5) of paragraph 1, sub-paragraphs (1) and (2) of paragraph 2 and paragraphs 3, 6A, 6B, 7 to 10, 12, 12A, 12B, 12C and 17 to 20 of Schedule 12[1] to the Act of 1963 shall apply to a booking office licence as they apply in relation to a licence under paragraph 1 of that Schedule and as if the booking office licence had been granted under the said paragraph 1.

(3) For the purposes of the application of the provisions of the said Schedule 12, referred to in the foregoing subsection, to a booking office licence—

(*a*) for sub-paragraph (1) of paragraph 10 of the said Schedule there shall be substituted the following—

"(1) If any premises are used as a booking office, as defined in subsection (4) of section 5 (Licensing of entertainments booking offices) of the Greater London Council (General Powers) Act 1978, without a licence being held in respect thereof under the said section 5, then—

(*a*) any person concerned in the organisation or management of that booking office; and

(*b*) any other person who, knowing or having reasonable cause to suspect that those premises would be so used as a booking office—

(i) allowed the premises to be so used; or

(ii) let the premises, or otherwise made the premises available to any person by whom an offence in connection with that use of the premises has been committed;

shall be guilty of an offence.";

(*b*) in sub-paragraph (2) of the said paragraph 10, for the words "for any entertainment" there shall be substituted the words "as a booking office (as defined in subsection (4) of section 5 of the said Act of 1978)"; and

(*c*) in sub-paragraph (1) of paragraph 12 of the said Schedule 12, for the words "at which he has reason to believe that an entertainment to which either of those paragraphs applies is being given or is about to be given" there shall be substituted the words "which he has reason to believe are being used as a booking office (as defined in subsection (4) of section 5 of the said Act of 1978)" and for the word "entertainment", where it occurs for the second time, there shall be substituted the word "use".

(4)

(*a*) In this section "booking office" means any premises, not being premises exempted in accordance with paragraph (*b*) of this subsection or premises in use at the time in question for any of the following purposes, that is to say—

(i) public dancing or music or any other public entertainment of the like kind;

(ii) repealed

whose principal function at that time is to serve as premises at which members of the public may by the purchase of tickets or vouchers, or, on payment, by any other means, secure admission (whether or not on payment of a further charge) to any other premises (not being premises to which paragraph (*c*) of this subsection applies) used for any of the purposes mentioned in sub-paragraph (i) of this paragraph.

(*b*)

(i) If, in the opinion of the borough council, it is inappropriate that any premises or any class of premises should remain subject as booking offices to the provisions of this section, they may by resolution determine that as from a date to be fixed by the resolution those premises or that class of premises shall be exempted from such provisions.

(ii) If, in the opinion of the borough council, after the date fixed by a resolution passed under the foregoing sub-paragraph and having regard to any relevant circumstances, any premises or any class of premises exempted as booking offices from the provisions of this section by virtue of such a resolution should again become subject to the said provisions, they may by a further resolution determine that those premises or that class of premises shall again become subject as booking offices to the said provisions as from a date to be fixed by such further resolution.

(*c*) This paragraph applies (for the purposes of paragraph (*a*) of this subsection) to—

(i) the Theatre Royal Drury Lane, the Royal Covent Garden Opera House, the Theatre Royal Haymarket and the Royal Albert Hall;

(ii) premises which may be used for the performance of plays without a licence under the Theatres Act 1968 by virtue of any letters patent of the Crown; and

(iii) any other premises specified by resolution of the borough council from time to time for the purposes of this paragraph.

(5) In this section "borough" includes the City of London and "borough council" includes the Common Council.

[Greater London Council (General Powers) Act 1978, s 5 as amended by the Greater London Council (General Powers) Act 1984, s 4 and the Local Government Act 1985, Sch 8 and the Licensing Act 2003, Sch 6.]

1. Ante.

London Local Authorities Act 1990

(1990 c vii)

PART III

STREET TRADING

8–20387 21. Interpretation of Part III. (1) In this Part of this Act—

"grant", unless the context otherwise requires, includes renew and renewal, and cognate words shall be construed accordingly;

"ice cream trading" means the selling, exposing or offering for sale of goods consisting wholly or mainly of ice cream, frozen confectionery or other similar commodities from a vehicle;

"itinerant ice cream trading" means ice cream trading from a vehicle which goes from place to place remaining in any one location in the course of trading for short periods only;

"licence street" means a street designated under section 24 (Designation of licence streets) of this Act;

"receptacle" includes a vehicle or stall and any basket, bag, box, vessel, stand, easel, board, tray or thing which is used (whether or not constructed or adapted for such use) as a container for or for the display of any article or thing or equipment used in the provision of any service;

"street" includes—

(*a*) any road or footway;

(*b*) any other area, not being within permanently enclosed premises, within 7 metres of any road or footway, to which the public have access without payment;

(*c*) any part of such road, footway or area;

(*d*) any part of any housing development provided or maintained by a local authority under Part II of the Housing Act 1985;

"street trading"[1] means subject to subsection (2) below—

(*a*) the selling or the exposure or offer for sale of any article (including a living thing); and

(*b*) the purchasing of or offering to purchase any ticket; and

(*c*) the supplying of or offering to supply any service,

in a street for gain or reward;

"street trading licence" means a licence granted under this Part of this Act and valid for the period specified therein being not less than six months and not more than three years;

"temporary licence" means a licence granted under this Part of this Act valid for a single day or for such period as may be specified in the licence not exceeding six months.

(2) The following are not street trading for the purposes of this Part of this Act—

(*a*) trading by a person acting as a pedlar under the authority of a Pedlar's Certificate granted under the Pedlars Act 1871, if the trading is carried out only be means of visits from house to house;

(*b*) anything done in a market or fair the right to hold which was acquired by virtue of a grant (including a presumed grant) or acquired or established by virtue of any enactment or order;

(*c*) trading in a trunk road picnic area provided by the Secretary of State under section 112 of the Highways Act 1980;

(*d*) trading as a news-vendor provided that the only articles sold or exposed or offered for sale are current newspapers or periodicals and they are sold or exposed or offered for sale without a receptacle for them or, if with a receptacle for them such receptacle does not—

(i) exceed 1 metre in length or width or 2 metres in height; or

(ii) occupy a ground area exceeding 0·25 square metre; or

(iii) stand on the carriageway of a street; or

(iv) cause undue interference or inconvenience to persons using the street;

(*e*) selling articles or things to occupiers of premises adjoining any street, or offering or exposing them for sale from a vehicle which is used only for the regular delivery of milk or other perishable goods to those persons;

(*f*) the use for trading under Part VIIA of the Highways Act 1980 of any object or structure placed on, in or over a highway;

(*g*) the operation of facilities for recreation or refreshment under Part VIIA of the Highways Act 1980;

(*h*) the doing of anything authorised by regulations made under section 5 of the Police, Factories, &c (Miscellaneous Provisions) Act 1916 or by permit or order made under Part III of the Charities Act 1992 (c 41);*

(*i*) trading in a highway in relation to which a control order under section 7 of the Local Government (Miscellaneous Provisions) Act 1976 is in force, other than trading to which the control order does not apply; and

(*j*) the selling or the exposure or offer for sale of articles or the provision of services on private land adjacent to a shop provided that the selling or the exposure or offer for sale of the articles or the provision of the services—

(i) forms part of the business of the owner of the shop or a person assessed for uniform business rate in respect of the shop; and

(ii) takes place during the period during which the shop is open to the public for business.

[London Local Authorities Act 1990, s 21 as amended by the London Local Authorities Act 1994, s 6 and the London Local Authorities Act 2004, Sch 4.]

***Amended by the London Local Authorities Act 1996, s 26, when in force.**

1. Exposing goods for sale on a pavement outside a shop for payment within the shop is street trading for the purposes of this Act (*Wandsworth London Borough Council v Rosenthal* (1996) Times, 28 March).

2. Prior to its amendment, this subsection referred to the "owner or occupier", and the phrase "owner or occupier" did not limit the person concerned to freeholder or possessor of the land; it was a question of fact and degree whether a person was the owner or occupier (*O'Gorman v Brent London Borough Council* (1993) 91 LGR 555).

8–20388 22. Application of Part III. This Part of this Act applies to the borough of a participating council[1] as from the appointed day[2].

[London Local Authorities Act 1990, s 22.]

---

1. The participating councils are listed in Sch 1 to the Act and include Inner and Outer London Boroughs. Subsections 23–33 of the Act make provision for the designation of licence streets, applications for licences, succession on death or retirement, conditions, revocation or variation, appeals, temporary licences, fees and charges, receptacles and containers.

2. See the note to s 5 ante as to appointed day.

8–20388A 30. Part III appeals. (1) Any person aggrieved—

(*aa*) by the refusal of a borough council to renew a licence because they are not satisfied as mentioned in subsection (4)(*b*) of section 25 (Application for street trading licences) of this Act;

(*a*) by the refusal of a borough council to grant or renew a licence on any of the grounds mentioned in subsection (6)(*a*) to (*e*) of section 25 (Application for street trading licences); or

(*b*) by a decision of a borough council under subsection (7) of the said section 25 to grant him a licence either on terms mentioned in that subsection different from those on the licence which he previously held or different from those for which he applied; or

(*c*) by any further condition attached by a borough council under subsection (8) of section 27 (Conditions of street trading licences) of this Act in addition to the standard conditions; or

(*d*) by a decision of the borough council either—

(i) to vary the conditions of a licence under subsection (2) of section 28 (Revocation or variation of licences under Part III) of this Act; or

(ii) to revoke a licence under subsection (1) of the said section 28;* or

(e) by a resolution of a borough council under section 37 (Ice cream trading) of this Act;

may appeal to a magistrates' court acting for the area in which the licence street is situated.

(2) An appeal under subsection (1) above may be brought—

(*a*) in the case of an appeal under paragraph (*aa*), (*a*), (*b*), (*c*) or (*d*) of that subsection, at any time before the expiration of the period of 21 days beginning with the date upon which notification in writing is given of the refusal or decision;

(*b*) in the case of an appeal under paragraph (*e*) of that subsection, at any time before the expiration of the period of 21 days beginning with the date of the second publication of the notice required by subsection (10) of section 24 (Designation of licence streets) as applied by the said section 37.

(3) A person desiring to appeal against such refusal or decision as is mentioned in subsection (1) above shall give a written notice to the magistrates' court and to the borough council specifying the refusal or decision against which he wishes to appeal and the grounds upon which such appeal is made.

(4) An appeal by either party against the decision of the magistrates' court under this section may be brought to the Crown Court.

(5) On an appeal to the magistrates' court or to the Crown Court under this section, the court may make such order as it thinks fit.

(6) subject to subsections (7) to (9) below, it shall be the duty of the borough council to give effect to the order of the magistrates' court or the Crown Court.

(7) A borough council need not give effect to the order of the magistrates' court until the time for bringing an appeal under subsection (4) above has expired and, if such an appeal is duly brought, until the determination or abandonment of the appeal.

(8) Where a licence holder applies for renewal of his licence, his existing licence shall remain valid—

(*a*) until the grant by the borough council of a new licence with the same conditions; or

(*b*) if the borough council refuse renewal of the licence or decide to grant a licence with conditions different from those of the existing licence and he has a right of appeal under this section, until the time for bringing an appeal has expired or where an appeal is duly brought, until the determination or abandonment of the appeal; or

(*c*) if he has no right of appeal under this section until the borough council either grant him a new licence with conditions different from those of the existing licence or notify him of their decision to refuse his application.

(9) Where—

(*a*) a borough council decide

(i) to vary the conditions of a licence under subsection (2) of the said section 28; or

(ii) to revoke a licence under subsection (1) of the said section 28; and

(*b*) a right of appeal is available to the licence holder under this section;

the variation or revocation shall not take effect until the time for bringing an appeal has expired or where an appeal is duly brought, until the determination or abandonment of the appeal.

(10) For the avoidance of doubt, it is hereby declared that an application under section 31 of the Supreme Court Act 1981 (application for judicial review) or under the Rules of the Supreme Court 1965 in respect of any matter which is or could be the subject of an appeal to the magistrates' court or to the Crown Court under this section shall not be treated as an appeal for the purposes of subsection (8) or (9) above.

(11) Any person aggrieved—

(*a*) by a resolution rescinding or varying a designating resolution;

(*b*) by a resolution under subsection (1)(*b*) of section 24 (Designation of licence streets) of this Act;

(*c*) by a standard condition prescribed by regulations under subsection (3) of section 27 (Conditions of street trading licences) of this Act; or

(*d*) by the amount of a fee or charge under section 32 (Fees and charges) of this Act;

may appeal to the Secretary of State whose decision shall be final.

(12) An appeal under subsection (11) above may be brought—

(*a*) in the case of an appeal under paragraph (*a*) or (*b*) of that subsection, at any time before the expiration of the period of three months beginning with the date on which notice of the passing of the resolution is published for the second time in accordance with subsection (10) of section 24 (Designation of licence streets) of this Act;

(*b*) in the case of an appeal under paragraph (*c*) of that subsection, at any time before the expiration of the period of three months beginning with the date upon which the licence holders or a body or bodies representative of them were notified of the making of the regulations;

(*c*) in the case of an appeal under paragraph (*d*) of that subsection—

(i) if it relates to the amount of a fee payable under subsection (1) of section 32 (Fees and charges) of this Act, at any time before the expiration of the period of three months beginning with the date on which the fee payable is notified to the licence holders or a body or bodies representative of them;

(ii) if it relates to the amount of a charge under subsection (2) of section 32 (Fees and charges) of this Act, at any time before the expiration of the period of three months beginning with the date on which notice of the determination of the charge has been given to the licence holders or a body or bodies representative of them.

[London Local Authorities Act 1990, s 30, as amended by the London Local Authorities Act 1994, s 6.]

8–20389 34. Offences. Any person who without reasonable excuse—

(1) contravenes any of the conditions of a street trading licence or a temporary licence; or

(2) in connection with an application for a street trading licence or a temporary licence makes a statement which he knows to be false in a material particular; or

(3) resists or intentionally obstructs any authorised officer of a borough council in the execution of his duties under this Part of this Act; or

(4) fails on demand without reasonable excuse in the case of an individual licence holder to produce his licence duly signed by him and bearing his photograph, and, in the case of an individual carrying on ice cream trading under a licence granted to a company incorporated under the Companies Acts or to a partnership, to produce the photograph required by subsection (2) of section 27 (Conditions of street trading licences) of this Act to an authorised officer of the borough council or to a constable;

shall be guilty of an offence and shall be liable on summary conviction to a fine not exceeding **level 3** on the standard scale.

[London Local Authorities Act 1990, s 34 as amended by the London Local Authorities Act 1994, s 6.]

8–20390 36. Employment of assistants. Subject to the provisions of this section a person holding a street trading licence may employ any other person to assist him in the conduct of street trading authorised by the licence but if any person employed by a licence holder during the temporary

absence of the licence holder fails to comply with the conditions of the street trading licence held by his employer such failure shall be deemed to be a failure by the licence holder.
[London Local Authorities Act 1990, s 36.]

8–20391 **37. Ice cream trading.** (1) Nothing in this Part of this Act shall apply to itinerant ice cream trading in any street unless—

(*a*) that street is a licence street; or
(*b*) the street has been designated as a prohibited street under the following provisions of this section.

(2)–(4) *Designation of prohibited street.*
[London Local Authorities Act 1990, s 37 as amended by the London Local Authorities Act 1994, s 6.]

8–20392 **38. Unlicensed street trading.** (1) A person who—

(*a*) is not the holder of a street trading licence or a temporary licence and who engages in street trading[1] in a borough whether or not from a stationary position; or
(*b*) is the holder of a street trading licence or a temporary licence and who, without the borough council's specific permission in writing engages in street trading[1] in a borough on a day or in a place not specified in that licence;

shall be guilty of an offence and shall be liable on summary conviction to a fine not exceeding **level 3** on the standard scale.(2) In any proceedings for an offence under this section or for an offence of aiding, abetting, counselling or procuring the commission of an offence under this section where it is shown that—

(*a*) any article or thing was displayed (whether or not in or on any receptacle) in any street; or
(*b*) any receptacle or equipment used in the provision of any service was available in any street in such circumstances that a service was being offered;

the article, thing, receptacle or equipment concerned shall be presumed to have been exposed or offered for sale and the receptacle or equipment shall be deemed to have been used for the purposes for which a street trading licence was required unless it can be proved to the satisfaction of the court that the article or thing or receptacle or equipment was brought into that street for some purpose other than street trading.

(3) Where an offence under this section committed by a body corporate is proved to have been committed with the consent or connivance of, or to be attributable to any neglect on the part of, any director, manager, secretary or other similar officer of the body corporate, or any person who was purporting to act in any such capacity, he, as well as the body corporate, shall be guilty of the offence and liable to the same maximum penalty as the body corporate.

(4) If an authorised officer or a constable has reasonable grounds for suspecting that a person has committed an offence under this section he may seize—

(*a*) any article or thing being offered for sale, displayed or exposed for sale; or
(*b*) any other article or thing of a similar nature to that being offered or exposed for sale which is in the possession of or under the control of any person who is displaying an article or thing; or
(*c*) any receptacle or equipment being used by that person,

which may be required to be used in evidence in any proceedings in respect of that offence, or may be the subject of forfeiture under subsection (5) below, provided that no article or thing which is of a perishable nature shall be seized under the provisions of this subsection.

(4A) An authorised officer or constable may also seize, for examination purposes, any article or thing which he has reasonable cause to suspect may be an article or thing which is prohibited by a specifying resolution made under subsection (1)(*b*) of section 24 (Designation of licence streets) of this Act.

Unless the article or thing is required for evidential purposes it shall be returned as soon as possible to the person from whom it was seized.

(4B) An authorised officer shall produce his authority if required to do so by the person having control or possession of anything seized in pursuance of the powers in subsections (4) and (4A) above.

(4C)

(*a*) The following provisions of this subsection shall have effect where any article or thing (including any receptacle or equipment) is seized under subsection (4) above or is seized and retained because it is required for evidential purposes under subsection (4A) above and references in those provisions to proceedings are to proceedings in respect of the alleged offence in relation to which the article or thing is seized.
(*b*) Subject to paragraph (e) below, following the conclusion of the proceedings the article or thing shall be returned to the person from whom it was seized unless—
   (i) the court orders it to be forfeited under subsection (5) below; or

(ii) any award of costs to the council by the court, which may include removal, return and storage costs, have not been paid within 28 days of the making of the order.

(*ba*) Where after 28 days any costs awarded by the court to the council have not been paid to the council in full—

(i) the article or thing may be disposed of in any way the council thinks fit; and

(ii) any sum obtained by the council in excess of the costs awarded by the court shall be returned to the person to whom the article or thing belongs.

(*bb*) When any article or thing is disposed of by the council under this subsection the council shall have a duty to secure the best possible price which can reasonably be obtained for that article or thing.

(*c*) Subject to paragraph (*d*) below, where a receptacle seized under subsection (4) above is a motor vehicle used for ice cream trading, the borough council or the Commissioner of Police of the Metropolis (as the case may be) shall, within three days of the receipt of an application in writing by the owner or registered keeper of the vehicle, permit him to remove it.

(*d*) Paragraph (*c*) above shall not apply where—

(i) the owner or registered keeper of the vehicle has been convicted of an offence under this Part of this Act or under the City of Westmonster Act 1999; or

(ii) the owner or registered keeper of the vehicle is being prosecuted for a previous alleged offence under this Part of this Act or the said Act of 1999; or

(iii) the vehicle has been used in the commission of such an offence or previous alleged offence;

if the offence or previous alleged offence was committed or is alleged to have been committed no more than three years before the seizure and (in the case of an alleged offence) the proceedings are continuing.

(*e*) If no proceedings are instituted before the expiration of a period of 28 days beginning with the date of seizure, or any proceedings instituted within that period are discontinued, at the expiration of that period or, as the case may be, on the discontinuance of the proceedings, the article or thing shall be returned to the person from whom it was seized unless it has not proved possible, after diligent enquiry, to identify that person and ascertain his address.

(*f*) Where the article or thing is not returned because it has not proved possible to identify the person from whom it was seized and ascertain his address the borough council (whether the article or thing was seized by a constable or by an authorised officer) may apply to a magistrates' court for an order as to the manner in which it should be dealt with and in the case of a sum referred to in paragraph (*ba*) above the council shall apply to the court for an order directing the disposal of the proceeds.

(5) Subject to subsection (6) below the court by or before which a person is convicted of an offence under this section or for an offence of aiding, abetting, counselling or procuring the commission of an offence under this section may order anything produced to the court[2], and shown to the satisfaction of the court to relate to the offence, to be forfeited and dealt with in such manner as the court may order.

(6) The court shall not order anything to be forfeited under subsection (5) above where a person claiming to be the owner of or otherwise interested in it applies to be heard by the court, unless an opportunity has been given to him to show cause why the order should not be made and in considering whether to make such an order a court shall have regard—

(i) to the value of the property; and

(ii) to the likely financial and other effects on the offender of the making of the order (taken together with any other order that the court contemplates making).

(7) An authorised officer shall produce his authority if required to do so by the person having care or control of anything seized in pursuance of the powers in subsection (4) above.

(8)

(*a*) This subsection shall have effect where—

(i) an article, thing or receptacle is seized under subsection (4) above; and

(ii)

(A) not less than six months have passed since the date of the seizure and no information has been laid against any person for an offence under this section in respect of the acts or circumstances which occasioned the seizure; or

(B) proceedings for such an offence have been brought and either the person charged has been acquitted (whether or not on appeal) and the time for appealing against or challenging the acquittal (where applicable) has expired without an appeal or challenge being brought, or the proceedings (including any appeal) have been withdrawn by, or have failed for want of prosecution by, the person by whom the original proceedings were brought.

(*b*) When this subsection has effect a person who has or at the time of seizure had a legal interest in the article, thing or receptacle seized may recover compensation from the borough council or (where it is seized by a constable) the Commissioner of Police of the Metropolis by civil action in the County Court in respect of any loss suffered by him as a result of the seizure.

(*c*) The court may not make an order for compensation under paragraph (*b*) above unless it is satisfied that seizure was not lawful under subsection (4) above.

[London Local Authorities Act 1990, s 38 as amended by the London Local Authorities Act 1994, s 6 and the London Local Authorities Act 2004, Sch 4.]

---

1. The term "streeting trading" is apt to cover the sale of one motor vehicle offered for sale in a street with a notice that it was for sale, the price and a telephone number: *Haringey London Borough Council v Michniewicz* [2004] TLR 354.

2. The items must be physically present or treated as being produced by virtue of being exhibited by a statement served under s 9 of the Criminal Justice Act 1967; but if there is a late objection to non-production in either of the aforementioned ways of the items it is open to the justices to adjourn for the items to be produced, or to make arrangements to view the items on some convenient occasion on the same or a future date (*R (on the application of London Borough of Islington) v Jordan* [2002] EWHC 2645 (Admin), (2002) 167 JP 1).

8–20393 **39. Savings.** (1) Nothing in this Part of this Act shall affect—

(*a*) section 13 of the Markets and Fairs Clauses Act 1847 (prohibition of sales elsewhere than in a market or in shops etc) as applied by any other Acts;

(*b*) section 56 of the Food Act 1984 (prohibition of certain sales during market hours);

(*c*) the sale or exposure or offer for sale by Transport for London or any or its subsidiaries (within the meaning of the Greater London Authority Act 1999) of refreshments at any shelter or other accommodation provided by either of them under section 65 (refreshment shelters etc) of the London Passenger Transport Act 1938.

(2) Nothing in this Part of this Act shall afford a defence to a charge in respect of any offence at common law or under an enactment other than this Part of this Act.

[London Local Authorities Act 1990, s 39, as amended by SI 2003/1615.]

Traffic and transport

London Transport Act 1977[1]

(1977 c xii)

8–20394 **12. Increase of fines fixed by enactments.** (1) In their application to London Regional Transport or any subsidiary of theirs (within the meaning of the London Regional Transport Act 1984) to any railway of London Regional Transport or of any such subsidiary or to any train, station or other works or premises connected therewith the enactments specified in column (1) of the Schedule to this Act (being enactments creating the offences broadly described in column (2) of that Schedule) shall each have effect as if the maximum fine which may be imposed on summary conviction of any offence specified in the enactment were a fine not exceeding the amount specified in column (4) of that Schedule instead of a fine of, or not exceeding the amount specified in column (3) of that Schedule[2].

(2) Subsection (1) of this section shall not affect the powers of a court to award imprisonment under any enactment specified in the Schedule to this Act:

Provided that section 17 of the Railway Regulation Act 1842 (which provides for the punishment of persons employed on railways who are guilty of misconduct) shall in its application under subsection (1) of this section have effect as if for the words "two calendar months" in each place where those words occur there were substituted the words "three calendar months".

[London Transport Act 1977, s 12 as amended by the London Regional Transport Act 1984, Sch 6.]

---

1. Offences committed on and in connection with the railways of the London Regional Transport are brought within the scope of the Regulation of Railways Acts by virtue of the London Transport Act 1971, ss 25 and 26. The penalties are, however, amended in their application to London Regional Transport trains by this Act and by the London Transport Act 1980, s 25, post. See also the British Railways Board byelaws in PART VII: TRANSPORT, ante, which are in identical terms with the London Regional Transport Railways byelaws.

2. The offences are thus given maximum penalties which accord with those applicable where British Railways Board property is involved, as indicated in PART VII: TRANSPORT, ante. The statutory provisions are: Railway Regulation Act 1840, s 16; Railway Regulation Act 1842, s 17; Railways Clauses Consolidation Act 1845, s 75; Regulation of Railways Act 1868, s 22; Regulation of Railways 1889, s 5(1) (3); British Transport Commission Act 1949, ss 55 and 56.

8–20395 **13. Increase of fines for contravening byelaws.** (1) (*Repealed*).

(2) Section 25 (Byelaws for road transport premises) of the Act of 1969 shall have effect as if in subsection (2) thereof for the words "twenty-five pounds" there were substituted the words "fifty pounds".

(3) Any byelaws in force immediately before the passing of this Act made under section 67 of the Transport Act 1962 or section 25 of the Act of 1969 shall have effect as if the amount specified in such byelaws as the maximum fine which may be imposed on summary conviction of any offence specified in such byelaws were fifty pounds.

(4) Subsection (3) of this section shall have effect subject to any byelaws made under section 67 of the Transport Act 1962 or section 25 of the Act of 1969 after the passing of this Act.

[London Transport Act 1977, s 13 as amended by the Transport Act 1981, Sch 12.]

Port of London Act 1968

(1968 c xxxii)

8–20400 This Act makes provision for numerous offences relating to the operation of the Port of London. The penalties were substantially increased by the Port of London Act 1982 (c ix), Schedule 1. The 1982 Act also supplied a new s 199 to the 1968 Act which provides for traffic offences on dock roads and applies provisions in the (now) Road Traffic Regulation Act 1984 and the Road Traffic Act 1988 to those roads.

London Transport Act 1980[1]

(1980 c xxxii)

8–20410 25. Increase of fines fixed by enactments. In their application to London Regional Transport or any subsidiary of theirs (within the meaning of the London Regional Transport Act 1984) to any railway of London Regional Transport or of any such subsidiary or any works connected therewith or to any train on such railway, the enactments specified in column (1) of Schedule 3[2] to this Act (being enactments creating the offences broadly described in column (2) of that schedule) shall each have effect as if the maximum fine which may be imposed on summary conviction of any offence specified in the enactment were the amount specified in column (4) of that schedule instead of that specified in column (3) thereof.

[London Transport Act 1980, s 25 as amended by the London Regional Transport Act 1984, Sch 6.]

1. See note 1 to para **8–20394**, to the London Transport Act 1977, ante.

2. The offences specified in the Schedule are thus given maximum penalties which accord with those applicable where Railtrack property is involved, as indicated in title RAILWAYS, post. The statutory provisions concerned are: Railways Clauses Consolidation Act 1845, s 24 (Obstructing construction of railway), in each case an increase from £25 to £50 which would now appear to be a fine of **level 2** on the standard scale (Criminal Justice Act 1982, s 46); s 103 (refusal or neglect to quit carriage at destination), in each case an increase from £25 to £50 which would now appear to be a fine of **level 2** on the standard scale (Criminal Justice Act 1982, s 46).

Road Traffic Act 1991

(1991 c 40)

8–20545 Part II of the Act is concerned with traffic in London. A parking attendant may fix a penalty charge notice to a stationary vehicle in a designated parking place. Person removing or interfering with it, unless owner or person in charge of vehicle, or London authority, guilty of an offence: penalty on summary conviction fine not exceeding **level 2** (s 66). Attendant may fix immobilisation device, person without authority removing or interfering with notice about device fixed to vehicle, guilty of an offence: penalty on summary conviction fine not exceeding **level 2**; unauthorised person removing or attempting to remove device, guilty of an offence: penalty on summary convictions fine not exceeding **level 3** (s 69). Exemptions for disabled persons; misuse of exemption penalty on summary conviction fine not exceeding **level 3** (s 70). Representations may be made in relation to removal or immobilisation of vehicle: if false in a material particular and made recklessly or knowing it to be false, penalty on summary conviction a fine not exceeding **level 5** (s 71). Appeal to parking adjudicator if authority reject representations: penalty for falsehoods as under s 71 (s 72). Person failing without reasonable excuse to attend hearing by parking adjudicator or to produce document, penalty on summary conviction fine not exceeding **level 2** (s 73). Supplementary parking penalty provisions are set out in **Sch 6**.

London Local Authorities and Transport for London Act 2003

(2003 c iii)

PART 1
PRELIMINARY

8–20545A 1. Citation and commencement. (1) This Act may be cited as the London Local Authorities and Transport for London Act 2003 and, except for—

section 4 (Penalty charges for road traffic contraventions);
section 5 (Contraventions of lorry ban order: supplementary);
section 7 (Disapplication of offences); and
section 16 (Vehicle crossings over footways and verges),

shall come into operation at the end of the period of two months beginning with the date on which it is passed.

(2) The said sections 4, 5, 7 and 16 shall come into operation on the appointed day.

(3) This Act and the London Local Authorities Acts 1990 to 2000 may be cited together as the London Local Authorities Acts 1990 to 2003.

[London Local Authorities and Transport for London Act 2003, s 1.]

8–20545B 2. Interpretation. (1) In this Act—

"the Act of 1984" means the Road Traffic Regulation Act 1984 (c 27);

"borough council" means London borough council and includes the Common Council of the City of London in its capacity as a local authority and "borough" and "council" shall be construed accordingly.

(2) Subject to paragraph 1(8) of Schedule 1 to this Act, the owner of a vehicle for the purposes of this Act, shall be taken to be the person by whom the vehicle is kept.

(3) Subject to the said paragraph 1(8), in determining, for the purposes of this Act, who was the owner of a vehicle at any time, it shall be presumed that the owner was the person in whose name the vehicle was at that time registered under the Vehicle Excise and Registration Act 1994 (c 22).

[London Local Authorities and Transport for London Act 2003, s 2.]

8–20545C 3. Appointed day. (1) In subsection (2) of section 1 (Citation and commencement) of this Act "the appointed day" means such day as may be fixed—

(*a*) in relation to a borough by resolution of the borough council; or

(*b*) in relation to a GLA road or a GLA side road by a decision of Transport for London,

subject to and in accordance with the provisions of this section.

(2) Different days may be fixed under this section for the purpose of the application of different provisions of this Act to a borough.

(3) Different days may be fixed under this section for the purpose of the application of the provisions of this Act to different GLA roads or GLA side roads.

(4) But no day fixed under this section may be before the end of the period of two months beginning with the date on which this Act is passed.

(5) The borough council or Transport for London shall cause to be published in a local newspaper circulating in their area and in the London Gazette notice—

(*a*) of the passing of any such resolution or taking of any such decision and of a day fixed thereby; and

(*b*) the general effect of the provisions of this Act coming into operation as from that day,

and the day so fixed shall not be earlier than the expiration of three months from the publication of the said notice.

(6) Either a photostatic or other reproduction certified by the officer appointed for that purpose by the borough council or by Transport for London to be a reproduction of a page or part of a page of any such newspaper or the London Gazette bearing the date of its publication and containing any such notice shall be evidence of the publication of the notice, and of the date of publication.

(7) In subsection (5) above, "their area" in relation to Transport for London means the area of any borough council in which the GLA road or GLA side road to which the resolution or decision relates is situated.

[London Local Authorities and Transport for London Act 2003, s 3.]

PART 2
ROAD TRAFFIC AND HIGHWAYS

Penalty charges

8–20545D 4. Penalty charges for road traffic contraventions. (1) This section applies where—

(*a*) in relation to a GLA road or GLA side road, Transport for London or, subject to subsection (3) below, the relevant borough council; or (*b*) in relation to any other road in the area of a borough council, the relevant borough council or, subject to subsection (4) below, Transport for London,

have reason to believe (whether or not on the basis of information provided by a camera or other device) that a penalty charge is payable under this section with respect to a motor vehicle.

(2) Transport for London or, as the case may be, the relevant borough council may serve a penalty charge notice—

(*a*) in relation to a penalty charge payable by virtue of subsection (5) below, on the person appearing to them to be the owner of the vehicle; and

(*b*) in relation to a penalty charge payable by virtue of subsection (7) below, on either or both of the following—

(i) the person appearing to them to be the operator of the vehicle; and

(ii) the person appearing to them to be the person who was in control of the vehicle at the time of the contravention.

(3) The relevant borough council shall not exercise the power exercisable by virtue of subsection (1)(a) above unless they have obtained the consent in writing of Transport for London.

(4) Transport for London shall not exercise the power exercisable by virtue of subsection (1)(b) above unless they have obtained the consent in writing of the relevant borough council.

(5) Subject to subsection (6) below, for the purposes of this section, a penalty charge is payable with respect to a motor vehicle by the owner of the vehicle if the person driving or propelling the vehicle—

(*a*) acts in contravention of a prescribed order; or

(*b*) fails to comply with an indication given by a scheduled section 36 traffic sign.

(6) No penalty charge shall be payable under subsection (5)(a) above where—

(*a*) the person acting in contravention of the prescribed order also fails to comply with an indication given by a scheduled section 36 traffic sign; or

(*b*) the contravention of the prescribed order would also give rise to a liability to pay a penalty charge under section 77 of the Road Traffic Act 1991 (c 40).

(7) For the purposes of this section, a penalty charge is payable with respect to a vehicle by—

(*a*) the operator of the vehicle; and

(*b*) the person in control of the vehicle,

if the person in control of the vehicle acts in contravention of the lorry ban order.

(8) A penalty charge notice under this section must—

(*a*) state—

(i) the grounds on which the council or, as the case may be, Transport for London believe that the penalty charge is payable with respect to the vehicle;

(ii) the amount of the penalty charge which is payable;

(iii) that the penalty charge must be paid before the end of the period of 28 days beginning with the date of the notice;

(iv) that if the penalty charge is paid before the end of the period of 14 days beginning with the date of the notice, the amount of the penalty charge will be reduced by the specified proportion;

(v) that, if the penalty charge is not paid before the end of the 28 day period, an increased charge may be payable;

(vi) the amount of the increased charge;

(vii) the address to which payment of the penalty charge must be sent; and

(viii) that the person on whom the notice is served may be entitled to make representations under paragraph 1 of Schedule 1 to this Act; and

(*b*) specify the form in which any such representations are to be made.

(9) The Secretary of State may by regulations prescribe additional matters which must be dealt with in any penalty charge notice.

(10) In subsection (8)(*a*)(iv) above, "specified proportion" means such proportion, applicable in all cases, as may be determined for the purposes of this section by the appointing authorities acting through the Joint Committee.

(11) Schedule 1 to this Act shall have effect with respect to representations against penalty charge notices, and other matters supplementary to the provisions of this section.

(12) Subject to subsection (13) below, sections 74 and 74A of the Road Traffic Act 1991 (c 40) shall apply in relation to the levels of penalty charges under this section as they apply in relation to the levels of (among other charges) penalty charges under Part II of that Act.

(13) Before setting the level of any charges under the said section 74 as applied by subsection (12) above, the borough councils and Transport for London shall consult such bodies as in their opinion are sufficiently representative of such road users as would be affected by the imposition of such charges.

(14) No provision in this section shall apply to any vehicle on an occasion when it is being used for fire brigade, ambulance or police purposes.

(15) Schedule 2 to this Act shall have effect with respect to financial provisions relating to the provisions of this section.

(16) In this section—

"Joint Committee" means the Joint Committee established under section 73 of the Road Traffic Act 1991;

"motor vehicle" means a mechanically propelled vehicle intended or adapted for use on roads;

"prescribed order" means an order under section 6 or 9 of the Act of 1984 which makes provision for a relevant traffic control;

"relevant traffic control" means any requirement, restriction or prohibition (other than a requirement, restriction or prohibition under the lorry ban order) which is or may be conveyed by a scheduled traffic sign;

"road" has the same meaning as in the Act of 1984;

"scheduled section 36 traffic sign" means—

(*a*) a scheduled traffic sign of a type to which section 36 (Drivers to comply with traffic signs) of the Road Traffic Act 1988 (c 52) applies by virtue of regulations made under section 64(5) of the Act of 1984; but

(*b*) does not include a traffic sign which indicates any prohibition or restriction imposed by the lorry ban order;

"scheduled traffic sign" means a traffic sign of a type described in Schedule 3 to this Act;

"traffic sign" has the meaning given by section 64(1) of the Act of 1984.

(17) In this section and section 5 (Contraventions of lorry ban order: supplementary) of this Act—

"driver's notice" means a penalty charge notice served under subsection (2)(b)(ii) above on the person appearing to have been the person in control of the vehicle at the time of the alleged contravention of the lorry ban order;

"the lorry ban order" means the Greater London (Restriction of Goods Vehicles) Traffic Order 1985 made by the Greater London Council under section 6 of the Act of 1984, as amended, replaced or substituted by any subsequent order;

"operator of a vehicle" means the holder of any operator's licence in respect of that vehicle under section 2 of the Goods Vehicles (Licensing of Operators) Act 1995 (c 23);

"operator's notice" means a penalty charge notice served under subsection (2)(b)(i) above on the person appearing to be the operator of a vehicle;

"relevant borough council" means the borough council in whose area the alleged contravention or failure occurred.

(18) In determining, for the purposes of any provision of this Act, whether a penalty charge has been paid before the end of a particular period, it shall be taken to be paid when it is received by the council concerned, or as the case may be, Transport for London.

(19) The Secretary of State may, by regulations, amend Schedule 3 to this Act by—

(*a*) adding any traffic signs to the list of traffic signs in the Schedule; or

(*b*) making any other amendments to the Schedule as may be necessary as a consequence of any amendment, replacement or substitution of the Traffic Signs Regulations and General Directions 2002 (SI 2002/3113).*

[London Local Authorities and Transport for London Act 2003, s 4.]

***Repealed by the Traffic Management Act 2004, s 98, Sch 12, Pt 1, from a date to be appointed.**

8–20545E 5. Contraventions of lorry ban order: supplementary. (1) An operator's notice shall state that before the end of the period of 14 days beginning with the date of the notice, the operator of the vehicle must provide the relevant borough council, or as the case may be, Transport for London, with the name and address of the person who was in control of the vehicle when the alleged contravention of the lorry ban order took place.

(2) Any person who in response to a requirement stated in a penalty charge notice by virtue of subsection (1) above fails to comply with the requirement shall be guilty of an offence unless he shows to the satisfaction of the court that—

(*a*) he was not the operator of the vehicle at the time the alleged contravention of the lorry ban order took place; or

(*b*) he did not know, and could not with reasonable diligence have ascertained, who was the person in control of the vehicle.

(3) Any person who in response to a requirement stated in a penalty charge notice by virtue of subsection (1) above gives information which is false in a material particular and does so recklessly or knowing it to be false in that particular shall be guilty of an offence.

(4) Any person guilty of an offence under subsection (2) or (3) above shall be liable on summary conviction—

(*a*) in the case of subsection (2) to a fine not exceeding level 3 on the standard scale; and
(*b*) in the case of subsection (3) to a fine not exceeding level 5 on the standard scale.

(5) In the case where an operator's notice is served on the person appearing to be the operator of the vehicle, the provisions of this Act mentioned below shall have effect as follows—

(*a*) for paragraph 1(4)(*a*) of Schedule 1 there shall be substituted—

"(*a*) that the recipient was not the operator of the vehicle at the time the alleged contravention of the order took place;";

(*b*) paragraph 1(4)(*c*) and (d), (5) and (6) of Schedule 1 shall be omitted; and
(*c*) after paragraph 1(4) of Schedule 1 the following sub-paragraph shall be inserted—

"(4A) Where the ground mentioned in sub-paragraph (4)(a) above is relied on in any representations made under this paragraph, those representations must include a statement of the name and address of the operator of the vehicle at the time of the alleged contravention or failure to comply (if that information is in his possession).".

(6) In the case where a driver's notice is served on the person appearing to have been in control of the vehicle at the time of the alleged contravention, the provisions of this Act mentioned below shall have effect as follows—

(*a*) for paragraph 1(4)(*a*) of Schedule 1 there shall be substituted—

"(*a*) that the recipient was not the person in control of the vehicle at the time the alleged contravention of the lorry ban order took place;";

(*b*) paragraph 1(4)(*c*) and (*d*), (5) and (6) of Schedule 1 shall be omitted; and
(*c*) after paragraph 1(4) of Schedule 1 the following sub-paragraph shall be inserted—

"(4A) Where the ground mentioned in sub-paragraph (4)(*a*) above is relied on in any representations made under this paragraph, those representations must include a statement of the name and address of the person in control of the vehicle at the time of the alleged contravention or failure to comply (if that information is in his possession).".

(7) In the case where, under paragraph 1(4) of Schedule 1 to this Act as so applied and having effect in accordance with subsections (5) or (6) above the relevant borough council or as the case may be Transport for London is provided with the name and address of—

(*a*) the operator of the vehicle; or
(*b*) the person who was in control of the vehicle at the time of the alleged contravention of the lorry ban order,

they may serve a fresh penalty charge notice in accordance with paragraph 2(2) of that Schedule on either of those persons, or both.*
[London Local Authorities and Transport for London Act 2003, s 5.]

***Repealed by the Traffic Management Act 2004, s 98, Sch 12, Pt 1, from a date to be appointed.**

8–20545F 6. Limitation on service of penalty charge notice. (1) Subject to the provisions of this section, no penalty charge notice may be served under this Act after the expiry of the period of 28 days beginning with the date on which the alleged contravention or failure to comply occurred.

(2) Subject to the provisions of this section, where—

(*a*) a penalty charge notice has been cancelled under paragraph 2 of Schedule 1 to this Act; or
(*b*) a penalty charge notice has been cancelled in compliance with a direction given by a traffic adjudicator under paragraph 4(2) of the said Schedule; or
(*c*) a penalty charge notice is deemed to have been cancelled under paragraph 7(8)(*c*) of the said Schedule (deemed cancellation where a statutory declaration under paragraph 7(2)(*a*) of that Schedule is served under paragraph 7(1)(*c*)),

the borough council or Transport for London , as the case may be, may not serve a fresh penalty charge notice after the expiry of the period of 28 days from the date of the cancellation of the penalty charge notice or, in a case falling within paragraph (*c*) above, the date on which that council or body are served with notice under paragraph 7(8)(*d*) of the said Schedule.

(3) Subsection (6) below applies where the following conditions are met.

(4) The first condition is that where a borough council or Transport for London, as the case may be, has before the expiry of 14 days from—

(*a*) the date on which the alleged contravention or failure to comply occurred; or
(*b*) the date of the cancellation of the penalty charge notice in the case where a penalty charge notice has been cancelled—
 (i) under paragraph 2 of the said Schedule; or
 (ii) in compliance with a direction given by a traffic adjudicator under paragraph 4(2) of the said Schedule; or
(*c*) the date on which the borough council or Transport for London, as the case may be, are served with notice under paragraph 7(8)(*d*) of the said Schedule where the penalty charge notice is deemed to have been cancelled under paragraph 7(8)(*c*),

made a request to the Secretary of State for the supply of relevant particulars.

(5) The second condition is that those particulars have not been supplied to the borough council or Transport for London, as the case may be, before the date after which that council or body would not be entitled to serve a penalty charge notice or a fresh penalty charge notice by virtue of subsection (1) or (2) above.

(6) Where this subsection applies, the borough council or Transport for London, as the case may be, shall continue to be entitled to serve a penalty charge notice or a fresh penalty charge notice for a further period of 6 months beginning with the date mentioned in subsection (5) above.

(7) In this section, "relevant particulars" are particulars relating to the identity of the owner of the vehicle contained in the register of mechanically propelled vehicles maintained by the Secretary of State under the Vehicle Excise and Registration Act 1994 (c 22).*

[London Local Authorities and Transport for London Act 2003, s 6.]

***Repealed by the Traffic Management Act 2004, s 98, Sch 12, Pt 1, from a date to be appointed.**

8–20545G 7. Disapplication of offences. (1) This section applies to the following roads—

(*a*) GLA roads and GLA side roads; and

(*b*) any other road in the area of a borough council.

(2) Section 8 of the Act of 1984 shall apply in respect of a road to which this section applies as if after subsection (1A), the following subsection were inserted—

"(1B) Subsection (1) above does not apply in relation to any person who acts in contravention of or fails to comply with—

(*a*) an order under section 6 of this Act; or

(*b*) the lorry ban order within the meaning of section 4 of the London Local Authorities and Transport for London Act 2003 (penalty charges for road traffic contraventions),

if as a result a penalty charge is payable under subsection (5) or, as the case may be, subsection (7) of section 4 of that Act.".

(3) Section 11 of the Act of 1984 shall apply in respect of a road to which this section applies as if after subsection (2), the following subsection were inserted—

"(2A) This section does not apply in relation to any person who acts in contravention of or fails to comply with an experimental traffic order if as a result a penalty charge is payable under section 4(5) of the London Local Authorities and Transport for London Act 2003 (penalty charges for road traffic contraventions).".

(4) Section 36 of the Road Traffic Act 1988 (c 52) shall apply in respect of a road to which this section applies as if after subsection (1), the following subsection were inserted—

"(1A) Subsection (1) above does not apply in relation to any such person who fails to comply with the indication given by the sign if as a result a penalty charge is payable under section 4(5) of the London Local Authorities and Transport for London Act 2003 (penalty charges for road traffic contraventions).".*

[London Local Authorities and Transport for London Act 2003, s 7.]

***Repealed by the Traffic Management Act 2004, s 98, Sch 12, Pt 1, from a date to be appointed.**

Fixed penalties

8–20545H 8. Fixed penalty offences. (1) Where on any occasion an authorised officer of a borough council or Transport for London finds a person who he has reason to believe has on that occasion committed an offence under any of the enactments—

(*a*) mentioned in columns (1) and (2) of the table set out in Schedule 4 to this Act; and

(*b*) described in column (3) of that table;

the officer may give that person a notice offering him the opportunity of discharging any liability to conviction for that offence by payment of a fixed penalty.

(2) The powers of an authorised officer of a borough council under subsection (1) above may be exercised only in relation to offences alleged to have been committed in respect of a highway in respect of which the council is highway authority.

(3) The powers of an authorised officer of Transport for London under subsection (1) above may be exercised only in relation to offences alleged to have been committed in respect of a GLA road or a GLA side road.

(4) Sections 9 (Fixed penalty notices), 10 (Levels of fixed penalties) and 11 (Fixed penalties: reserve powers of Secretary of State) of this Act shall apply in respect of fixed penalty notices under this section.

(5) Schedule 2 to this Act shall have effect with respect to financial provisions relating to the administration and enforcement of this section and sections 9 to 11 (Fixed penalties) of this Act.

(6) The Secretary of State may, by regulations, amend Schedule 4 to this Act by the addition of further offences to the list of offences therein described.
[London Local Authorities and Transport for London Act 2003, s 8.]

8–20545I 9. Fixed penalty notices. (1) The provisions of this section shall have effect in relation to notices ("fixed penalty notices") which may be given under section 8 (Fixed penalty offences) of this Act.

(2) Where a person is given a fixed penalty notice in respect of an offence—

(*a*) no proceedings shall be instituted for that offence before the expiration of 14 days following the date of the notice; and

(*b*) he shall not be convicted of that offence if he pays the fixed penalty before the expiration of that period.

(3) A fixed penalty notice under this section shall give such particulars of the circumstances alleged to constitute the offence as are necessary for giving reasonable information of the offence and shall state—

(*a*) the period during which, by virtue of subsection (2) above, proceedings will not be taken for the offence;

(*b*) the amount of the fixed penalty; and

(*c*) the name of the person to whom and the address at which the fixed penalty may be paid; and, without prejudice to payment by any other method, payment of the fixed penalty may be made by pre-paying and posting to that person at that address a letter containing the amount of the penalty (in cash or otherwise).

(4) Where a letter is sent in accordance with subsection (3) above, payment shall be regarded as having been made at the time at which that letter would be delivered in the ordinary course of post.

(5) The form of notices under this section shall be such as the Secretary of State may by regulations prescribe.

(6) The fixed penalty payable in pursuance of a fixed penalty notice under this section shall be paid to the borough council or Transport for London, as the case may be.

(7) In any proceedings a certificate which—

(*a*) purports to be signed by or on behalf of the chief finance officer of the council, or as the case may be, Transport for London; and

(*b*) states that payment of a fixed penalty was or was not received by a date specified in the certificate,

shall be evidence of the facts stated.
[London Local Authorities and Transport for London Act 2003, s 9.]

8–20545J 10. Levels of fixed penalties

8–20545K 11. Fixed penalties: reserve powers of Secretary of State

Parking

8–20545L 12. *Repealed by the Traffic Management Act 2004, Sch 12.*

8–20545M 13. False applications for parking authorisations. (1) Insofar as subsection (2) of section 115 of the Act of 1984 (mishandling of parking documents and related offences) relates to any authorisation which may be issued by a borough council or by Transport for London—

(*a*) proceedings for an offence under that section may be brought within a period of six months from the date on which evidence sufficient in the opinion of the prosecutor to warrant the proceedings came to his knowledge, but

(*b*) no such proceedings shall be brought by virtue of this section more than three years after the commission of the offence.

(2) For the purposes of subsection (1) above a certificate signed by or on behalf of the prosecutor and stating the date on which evidence such as is mentioned in that subsection came to his knowledge, shall be conclusive evidence of that fact; and a certificate purporting to be so signed shall be deemed to be so signed unless the contrary is proved.
[London Local Authorities and Transport for London Act 2003, s 13.]

8–20545N 14. Parking at dropped footways. (1) This section shall apply to any part of the carriageway of—

(*a*) any GLA road or GLA side road in a special parking area; and

(*b*) any other road in a special parking area in the area of a borough council,

which is adjacent to a dropped footway.

(2) But this section shall not apply in respect of any part of the carriageway during any period in which—

(*a*) an order under section 6 or section 9 of the Act of 1984 (which make provision about road traffic regulation orders) prohibits or permits the waiting of vehicles on it; or

(*b*) an order under section 45 of the Act of 1984 (Designation of parking places on highways) provides for its use as a designated parking place.

(3) A driver of a vehicle shall not at any time cause it to wait on a part of a road to which this section applies and the prohibition under this subsection shall be enforceable as if it had been imposed by an order under the said section 6.

(4) In the case where—

(*a*) residential premises have a driveway which is not shared by other premises; and

(*b*) the purpose of the dropped footway is to assist vehicles to enter or leave the road from or to the driveway,

the relevant borough council or Transport for London, as the case may be, may not issue a penalty charge notice in respect of any breach of the prohibition under subsection (3) above unless requested to do so by the occupier of the premises.

(5) Nothing in subsection (3) above shall require the placing of any traffic signs in connection with the prohibition thereby imposed.

(6) Nothing in this section shall prohibit the driver of a vehicle from causing it to wait in the circumstances mentioned in subsection (3) above—

(*a*) if the vehicle is being used for fire brigade, ambulance or police purposes;

(*b*) if the driver is prevented from proceeding by circumstances beyond his control or it is necessary for him to wait in order to avoid an accident;

(*c*) for so long as may be necessary for the purpose of enabling persons to board or alight from the vehicle;

(*d*) for so long as may be necessary (up to a maximum of 20 minutes) for the delivery or collection of goods or merchandise or the loading or unloading of the vehicle at any premises if that cannot reasonably be carried out as respects those premises without waiting as mentioned in subsection (3) above; or

(*e*) if the vehicle is being used for a purpose to which subsection (7) below applies and cannot be used for that purpose without so waiting.

(7) This subsection applies to any purpose connected with—

(*a*) any building operation, demolition or excavation;

(*b*) the collection of waste by or on behalf of any council;

(*c*) the removal of any obstruction to traffic;

(*d*) the maintenance, improvement or reconstruction of the road; or

(*e*) the laying, erection, alteration, repair or cleaning of—

(i) any traffic sign, traffic light or street light;

(ii) any sewer or any main, pipe, cable or apparatus for the supply of water, gas or electricity; or

(iii) any telegraph or telephone wire, cable, post or support.

(8) In this section—

"dropped footway" means any part of the footway or verge where it has been lowered to meet the level of the carriageway of a road for the purpose of—

(*a*) assisting pedestrians crossing the road; or

(*b*) assisting vehicles to enter or leave the road across the footway or verge;

"special parking area" means a special parking area designated by an order made by the Secretary of State under section 76(1) of the Road Traffic Act 1991 (c 40);

"road" has the same meaning as in section 142(1) of the Act of 1984.*

[London Local Authorities and Transport for London Act 2003, s 14.]

***Repealed by the Traffic Management Act 2004, s 98, Sch 12, Pt 1, from a date to be appointed.**

8–20545O 15. Penalty charges under Road Traffic Act 1991: statutory declarations. (1) Paragraph 8 of Schedule 6 to the Road Traffic Act 1991 applies as follows insofar as it relates to matters arising from the issuing of a penalty charge notice under section 66 (Parking penalties in London) of that Act by a parking attendant employed by—

(*a*) a borough council or Transport for London; or

(*b*) any person with whom a borough council or Transport for London have made arrangements for the purposes of section 63A (Parking attendants) of the Act of 1984.

(2) After sub-paragraph (2) the following sub-paragraphs are inserted—

"(2A) A statutory declaration under this paragraph is invalid and sub-paragraph (5) below shall not apply in relation to the declaration if one or more of the following grounds is met—

(*a*) the person who made the declaration claims that more than one of the grounds mentioned in sub-paragraph (2) above is met;
(*b*) the declaration is not signed by any person purporting to make it;
(*c*) the declaration is not signed by or does not contain an address for a person purporting to be a witness to the signature of the person making it.

(2B) The Secretary of State may by regulations amend sub-paragraph (2A) above by the addition of further grounds for a statutory declaration to be invalid.".

(3) After sub-paragraph (3) the following sub-paragraph is inserted—

"(3A) In considering an application under sub-paragraph (3) above the district judge must take into consideration any representations made by the London authority before the expiry of the period of 14 days beginning on the date on which copies of the application and the statutory declaration are served by the court on the London authority.".

(4) In sub-paragraph (5), at the beginning the words "Subject to sub-paragraphs (2A) above and (5A) below" are inserted.

(5) After sub-paragraph (5) the following sub-paragraph is inserted—

"(5A) Where—
(*a*) sub-paragraph (4) above applies; and
(*b*) the order of the court is deemed to have been revoked under sub-paragraph (5) above,

the London authority concerned shall not be liable to pay the person making the declaration any sums other than the increased charge which was payable under the county court order.".*

[London Local Authorities and Transport for London Act 2003, s 15.]

***Repealed by the Traffic Management Act 2004, s 98, Sch 12, Pt 1, from a date to be appointed.**

Vehicle Crossings

8–20545P 16. Vehicle crossings over footways and verges

Removal notices

8–20545Q 17. Removal of things deposited on the highway. (1) This section applies in respect of any part of—

(*a*) any highway for which Transport for London are the highway authority; and
(*b*) any highway for which a borough council are the highway authority.

(2) If the highway authority are satisfied that—

(*a*) things are deposited unlawfully and persistently on any part of the highway to which this section applies; and
(*b*) the depositing of the things is caused by persons having control of or an interest in a business carried on in premises in the vicinity of the part of the highway concerned,

the highway authority may serve a notice under this subsection ("a subsection (2) removal notice") on any person having control of or an interest in the relevant business.

(3) A subsection (2) removal notice shall—

(*a*) state the date on which it shall come into effect (which shall be no sooner than the date on which the period of 7 days beginning with the date of service of the notice expires);
(*b*) state the date on which it shall expire (which shall be no later than the date on which the period of 28 days beginning with the date on which it comes into effect expires);
(*c*) give a description of the part of the highway to which the notice relates;
(*d*) state that in the period during which the notice has effect, the highway authority may without further notice remove any thing deposited unlawfully on the part of the highway to which the notice relates;
(*e*) state the effect of subsections (5) and (12) below.

(4) Where a subsection (2) removal notice is served under subsection (2) above, a copy of the notice shall be affixed by the highway authority to a conspicuous place in the vicinity of the part of the highway to which the notice relates.

(5) If any thing is deposited unlawfully on any part of the highway to which a subsection (2) removal notice relates, the highway authority may—

(*a*) remove the thing forthwith; and
(*b*) no sooner than the relevant date, dispose of the thing.

(6) If a highway authority remove a thing under section 149(2) of the Highways Act 1980 (c 66) (which makes provision about things deposited on the highway so as to cause a danger), instead of proceeding under subsection (3) of that section, they may proceed in accordance with subsection (7) below.

(7) If the highway authority proceed under this subsection, no sooner than 24 hours after the

removal of the thing under the said section 149(2), they shall issue a notice ("a subsection (7) removal notice") and proceed in the manner described in subsection (9) below.

(8) A subsection (7) removal notice shall—

(*a*) give a description of the thing removed;
(*b*) state the effect of subsections (10) and (12) below.

(9) Where a subsection (7) removal notice is issued, the notice or a copy of the notice shall be affixed by the highway authority to a conspicuous place in the vicinity of the part of the highway from which the thing was removed.

(10) A highway authority may, no sooner than the relevant date, dispose of any thing which they have removed and in respect of which a subsection (7) removal notice has been issued.

(11) Any person who without reasonable excuse removes, alters or damages a notice affixed to any place under subsection (4) or (9) above shall be guilty of an offence and liable on summary conviction to a fine not exceeding level 3 on the standard scale.

(12) The authority by whom a thing is removed in pursuance of this section may recover from the person by whom it was deposited on the highway, or from any person claiming to be entitled to it, any expenses reasonably incurred by the authority in removing, storing or disposing of it.

(13) After payment out of any proceeds arising from the disposal of the thing of the expenses incurred in the removal, storage and disposal of the thing, the highway authority may apply the balance, if any, of the proceeds to the maintenance of the highways maintainable at the public expense by them.

(14) If the thing in question is not of sufficient value to defray the expenses of removing it, the highway authority may recover from the person who deposited it on the highway the expenses, or the balance of the expenses, reasonably incurred by them in removing it.

(15) If, after a thing has been disposed of by a highway authority pursuant to this section, a person claims to have been the owner of the thing at the time when it was removed and the conditions specified in subsection (16) below are fulfilled, there shall be payable to him by the highway authority a sum calculated in accordance with subsection (17) below.

(16) The conditions are that—

(*a*) the person claiming satisfies the highway authority that he was the owner of the thing at the time it was removed; and
(*b*) the claim is made before the expiry of the period of five months beginning with the date on which the thing was removed.

(17) The sum payable under subsection (15) above shall be calculated by deducting from the proceeds of sale the charges reasonably incurred by the highway authority for the removing, storing and disposing of the thing.

(18) In subsections (5) and (10) above, the "relevant date" in respect of a thing is the date on which expires the period of 14 days beginning with the date on which the thing was removed by the highway authority.

(19) For the purposes of this section and section 18 (Removal notices: appeals) of this Act—

(*a*) "the relevant business" means the business referred to in subsection (1) above; and
(*b*) a person having an interest in a relevant business includes a person who—
   (i) owns the business; or
   (ii) manages the business; or
   (iii) employs any person to manage the business; or
   (iv) is involved in the conduct of the business.

[London Local Authorities and Transport for London Act 2003, s 17.]

8-20545R 18. Removal notices: appeals

8-20545S 19. Service of removal notices

PART 3

SUPPLEMENTARY

8-20545T 20. Disclosure of information

8-20545U 21. Authorised officers

8-20545V 22. Obstruction of authorised officer. Any person who intentionally obstructs any authorised officer acting in the exercise of his powers under this Act shall be guilty of an offence and liable on summary conviction to a fine not exceeding level 3 on the standard scale.

[London Local Authorities and Transport for London Act 2003, s 22.]

8-20545W 23. Provision of information to authorised officer of Transport for London.

(1) This section applies where an authorised officer of Transport for London has reasonable grounds

for suspecting that any offence in respect of which that body may prosecute legal proceedings has been committed or attempted, or is being committed or attempted.

(2) If, on being requested by the authorised officer to furnish his name and address for service of a summons or fixed penalty notice the relevant person—

(*a*) fails to furnish a name; or
(*b*) furnishes a false name; or
(*c*) furnishes a false address,

the relevant person shall, unless the authorised officer failed to produce his authorisation on making the request, be guilty of an offence punishable on summary conviction by a fine not exceeding level 5 on the standard scale.

(3) In this section "the relevant person" means any person who the authorised officer has reasonable grounds to suspect of having committed or having attempted to commit the offence or being in the course of committing or attempting to commit it.
[London Local Authorities and Transport for London Act 2003, s 23.]

8–20545X 24. Defence of due diligence. (1) In proceedings for an offence under this Act it shall be a defence for the person charged to prove that he took all reasonable precautions and exercised all due diligence to avoid the commission of the offence.

(2) If in any case the defence provided under subsection (1) above involves the allegation that the commission of the offence was due to the act or default of another person, the person charged shall not, without leave of the court, be entitled to rely on that defence unless, no later than 7 clear days before the hearing, he has served on the prosecutor a notice in writing giving such information as was then in his possession identifying or assisting in the identification of that other person.
[London Local Authorities and Transport for London Act 2003, s 24.]

8–20545Y 25. Liability of directors, etc. (1) Where an offence under this Act committed by a body corporate is proved to have been committed with the consent or connivance of, or to be attributable to any neglect on the part of, a director, manager, secretary or other similar officer of the body corporate or any person who was purporting to act in any such capacity, he, as well as the body corporate, shall be guilty of the offence.

(2) Where the affairs of the body corporate are managed by its members, subsection (1) above shall apply to the acts and defaults of a member in connection with his functions of management as if he were a director of the body corporate.
[London Local Authorities and Transport for London Act 2003, s 25.]

8–20545Z 26. Regulations

8–20546

Section 4

SCHEDULE 1

PENALTY CHARGE NOTICES ETC UNDER SECTION 4 (PENALTY CHARGES FOR ROAD TRAFFIC CONTRAVENTIONS) OF THIS ACT

Representations against penalty charge notice

1. (1) Where it appears to a person on whom a penalty charge notice has been served under section 4 (Penalty charges for road traffic contraventions) of this Act (in this Schedule referred to as "the recipient") that one or other of the grounds mentioned in sub-paragraph (4) below is satisfied, he may make representations to that effect to the enforcing authority.

(2) Any representations under this paragraph must be made in such form as may be specified by the enforcing authority, acting through the Joint Committee (within the meaning of subsection (16) of the said section 4).

(3) The enforcing authority may disregard any such representations which are received by them after the end of the period of 28 days beginning with the date on which the penalty charge notice in question was served.

(4) The grounds referred to in sub-paragraph (1) above are—

(*a*) that the recipient—

(i) never was the owner of the vehicle in question;
(ii) had ceased to be its owner before the date on which the penalty charge was alleged to have become payable; or
(iii) became its owner after that date;

(*b*) that there was no—

(i) contravention of a prescribed order; or
(ii) failure to comply with an indication; or
(iii) contravention of the lorry ban order,

under subsection (5) or (7) of the said section 4 as the case may be;

(*c*) that at the time the alleged contravention or failure took place the person who was in control of the vehicle was in control of the vehicle without the consent of the owner;

(*d*) that the recipient is a vehicle-hire firm and—

(i) the vehicle in question was at the material time hired from that firm under a vehicle hiring agreement; and

(ii) the person hiring it had signed a statement of liability acknowledging his liability in respect of any penalty charge notice issued in respect of the vehicle during the currency of the hiring agreement; or

(*e*) that the penalty charge exceeded the amount applicable in the circumstances of the case.

(5) Where the ground mentioned in sub-paragraph (4)(a)(ii) above is relied on in any representations made under this paragraph, those representations must include a statement of the name and address of the person to whom the vehicle was disposed of by the person making the representations (if that information is in his possession).

(6) Where the ground mentioned in sub-paragraph (4)(a)(iii) above is relied on in any representations made under this paragraph, those representations must include a statement of the name and address of the person from whom the vehicle was acquired by the person making the representations (if that information is in his possession).

(7) It shall be the duty of the enforcing authority to whom representations are duly made under this paragraph—

(*a*) to consider them and any supporting evidence which the person making them provides; and

(*b*) to serve on that person notice of their decision as to whether they accept that the ground in question has been established.

(8) Where the ground that is accepted is that mentioned in sub-paragraph (4)(d) above, the person hiring the vehicle shall be deemed to be its owner for the purposes of this Act.

(9) In this paragraph, "vehicle hiring agreement" and "vehicle-hire firm" have the same meanings as in section 66 of the Road Traffic Offenders Act 1988 (c 53) (Hired vehicles).

Cancellation of penalty charge notice

2. (1) Where representations are made under paragraph 1 above and the enforcing authority accept that the ground in question has been established they shall—

(*a*) cancel the penalty charge notice; and

(*b*) state in the notice served under sub-paragraph (7) of paragraph 1 above that the penalty charge notice has been cancelled.

(2) The cancellation of a penalty charge notice under this paragraph shall not be taken to prevent the enforcing authority serving a fresh penalty charge notice on another person.

Rejection of representations against penalty charge notice

3. Where any representations are made under paragraph 1 above but the enforcing authority do not accept that a ground has been established, the notice served under sub-paragraph (7) of the said paragraph 1 (in this Schedule referred to as "the notice of rejection") must—

(*a*) state that a charge certificate may be served under paragraph 5 below unless before the end of the period of 28 days beginning with the date of service of the notice of rejection—

(i) the penalty charge is paid; or

(ii) the person on whom the notice is served appeals to a traffic adjudicator against the penalty charge; and

(*b*) describe in general terms the form and manner in which such an appeal must be made,

and may contain such other information as the enforcing authority consider appropriate.

Adjudication by traffic adjudicator

4. (1) Where an enforcing authority serve a notice of rejection, the person who made the representations under paragraph 1 above in respect of which that notice was served may, before—

(*a*) the end of the period of 28 days beginning with the date of service of that notice; or

(*b*) such longer period as a traffic adjudicator may allow,

appeal to a traffic adjudicator against the decision of the enforcing authority.

(2) On an appeal under this paragraph, the traffic adjudicator shall consider the representations in question and any additional representations which are made by the appellant on any of the grounds mentioned in paragraph 1(4) above and may give the enforcing authority such directions as he considers appropriate.

(3) It shall be the duty of the enforcing authority to whom a direction is given under sub-paragraph (2) above to comply with it forthwith.

Charge certificates

5. (1) Where a penalty charge notice is served on any person and the penalty charge to which it relates is not paid before the end of the relevant period, the enforcing authority may serve on that person a statement (in this paragraph referred to as a "charge certificate") to the effect that the penalty charge in question is increased by 50 per cent.

(2) The relevant period, in relation to a penalty charge notice is the period of 28 days beginning—

(*a*) where no representations are made under paragraph 1 above, with the date on which the penalty charge notice is served;

(*b*) where such representations are made and a notice of rejection is served by the enforcing authority and no appeal against the notice of rejection is made with the date on which the period within which an appeal could have been made expires; or

(*c*) where there has been an unsuccessful appeal against a notice of rejection, with the date on which notice of the adjudicator's decision is served on the appellant.

(3) Where an appeal against a notice of rejection is made but is withdrawn before the decision of the adjudicator is made the relevant period in relation to a penalty charge notice is the period of 14 days beginning with the date on which the appeal is withdrawn.

Enforcement of charge certificate

6. (1) Where a charge certificate has been served on any person and the increased penalty charge provided for in the certificate is not paid before the end of the period of 14 days beginning with the date on which the certificate is served, the enforcing authority may, if a county court so orders, recover the increased charge as if it were payable under a county court order.

(2) Any notice of any county court order made under this paragraph and being served on any person shall be accompanied by a copy of the penalty charge notice to which the penalty charge relates.

(3) Section 78 of the Road Traffic Act 1991 (c 40) (which makes provision for the recovery of sums that are payable under or by virtue of any provision of Part II of that Act and are recoverable as if they were payable under a county court order) shall have effect as though an increased penalty charge recoverable under sub-paragraph (1) above were a Part II debt for the purposes of that section.

Invalid notices

7. (1) This paragraph applies where—

(*a*) a county court makes an order under paragraph 6 above;

(*b*) the person against whom it is made makes a statutory declaration complying with sub-paragraph (2) below; and

(*c*) that declaration is, before the end of the period of 21 days beginning with the date on which notice of the county court's order is served on him, served on the county court which made the order.

(2) The statutory declaration must state that the person making it—

(*a*) did not receive the penalty charge notice in question;

(*b*) made representations to the enforcing authority under paragraph 1 above but did not receive a notice of rejection from that authority; or

(c) appealed to a traffic adjudicator under paragraph 4 above against the rejection by that authority of representations made by him under paragraph 1 above but had no response to the appeal.

(3) A statutory declaration under this paragraph is invalid and sub-paragraph (8) below shall not apply in relation to the declaration if one or more of the following grounds is met—

(*a*) the person who made the declaration claims that more than one of the grounds mentioned in sub-paragraph (2) above is met;

(*b*) the declaration is not signed by any person purporting to make it;

(*c*) the declaration is not signed by or does not contain an address for a person purporting to be a witness to the signature of the person making it.

(4) The Secretary of State may by regulations amend sub-paragraph (3) above by the addition of further grounds for a statutory declaration to be invalid.

(5) Sub-paragraph (7) below applies where it appears to a district judge, on the application of a person on whom a charge certificate has been served, that it would be unreasonable in the circumstances of his case to insist on him serving his statutory declaration within the period of 21 days allowed for by sub-paragraph (1) above.

(6) In considering an application under sub-paragraph (5) above the district judge must take into consideration any representations made by the enforcing authority before the expiry of the period of 14 days beginning on the date on which copies of the application and the statutory declaration are served by the court on the enforcing authority.

(7) Where this sub-paragraph applies, the district judge may allow such longer period for service of the statutory declaration as he considers appropriate.

(8) Subject to sub-paragraphs (3) above and (10) below, where a statutory declaration is served under sub-paragraph (1)(c) above—

(a) the order of the court shall be deemed to have been revoked;

(*b*) the charge certificate shall be deemed to have been cancelled;

(*c*) in the case of a statutory declaration under sub-paragraph (2)(a) above, the penalty charge notice to which the charge certificate relates shall be deemed to have been cancelled; and

(*d*) the district judge shall serve written notice of the effect of service of the statutory declaration on the person making it and on the enforcing authority.

(9) Service of a declaration under sub-paragraph (2)(a) above shall not prevent the enforcing authority serving a fresh penalty charge notice but if, when it was served, the relevant order under paragraph 6 was accompanied by

a copy of the penalty charge notice to which the charge certificate relates, a fresh penalty charge notice in the same terms shall be deemed to have been served on the person making the declaration on the same day as the declaration was served.

(10) Where—

(*a*) sub-paragraph (7) above applies; and
(*b*) the order of the court is deemed to have been revoked under sub-paragraph (8) above,

the enforcing authority concerned shall not be liable to pay the person making the declaration any sums other than the increased charge which was payable under the county court order.

(11) Where a declaration has been served under sub-paragraph (2)(b) or (c) above, the enforcing authority shall refer the case to the traffic adjudicator who may give such direction as he considers appropriate.

Offence of giving false information

8. (1) A person who, in response to a penalty charge notice served under section 4 (Penalty charges for road traffic contraventions) of this Act makes any representation under paragraph 1 or 4 above which is false in a material particular and does so recklessly or knowing it to be false in that particular is guilty of an offence.

(2) Any person guilty of such an offence shall be liable on summary conviction to a fine not exceeding level 5 on the standard scale.

Service by post

9. Any charge certificate, or notice under section 4 (Penalty charges for road traffic contraventions) of this Act or this Schedule—

(*a*) may be served by post; and
(*b*) where the person on whom it is to be served is a body corporate, is duly served if it is sent by post to the secretary or clerk of that body.

Traffic Adjudicators

10. (1) Functions of traffic adjudicators under this Schedule shall be discharged by the persons who are appointed as parking adjudicators under section 73 of the Road Traffic Act 1991 (c 40).

(2) Regulations under section 73(11) of the said Act of 1991 (provision as to procedure to be followed in relation to proceedings before parking adjudicators) may make provision with respect to proceedings before parking adjudicators when exercising the functions of traffic adjudicators under this Schedule; and any regulations under that subsection in force at the coming into operation of section 4 (Penalty charges for road traffic contraventions) of this Act shall, with any necessary modifications, apply in relation to such proceedings.

(3) The references to a parking adjudicator or parking adjudicators in section 73(13) to (15) and (17) and (18) of the said Act of 1991 shall include references to a parking adjudicator or parking adjudicators exercising the functions of traffic adjudicators under this Schedule but section 73(15) of that Act shall not apply to a penalty charge under the said section 4 which remains payable following an adjudication under this Schedule.

Interpretation

11. In this Schedule "the enforcing authority", in relation to any penalty charge notice or charge certificate, means—

(*a*) where the notice was served by a borough council, or the certificate relates to a notice so served, that council;
(*b*) where the notice was served by Transport for London, or the certificate relates to a notice so served, Transport for London.*

***Repealed by the Traffic Management Act 2004, s 98, Sch 12, Pt 1, from a date to be appointed.**

8–20546A SCHEDULE 2

FINANCIAL PROVISIONS RELATING TO SECTIONS 4 (PENALTY CHARGES FOR ROAD TRAFFIC CONTRAVENTIONS) AND* 8 TO 11 (FIXED PENALTIES) OF THIS ACT

***Words repealed by the Traffic Management Act 2004, s 98, Sch 12, Pt 1, from a date to be appointed.**

8–20546B SCHEDULE 3

SCHEDULED TRAFFIC SIGNS FOR THE PURPOSES OF SECTION 4 (PENALTY CHARGES FOR ROAD TRAFFIC CONTRAVENTIONS) OF THIS ACT*

***Schedule repealed by the Traffic Management Act 2004, s 98, Sch 12, Pt 1, from a date to be appointed.**

8–20546C

Section 8

SCHEDULE 4

OFFENCES IN RESPECT OF WHICH FIXED PENALTY NOTICES MAY BE SERVED UNDER SECTION 8 (FIXED PENALTY OFFENCES) OF THIS ACT

	(1) Act	(2) Section	(3) Description of Offence
1	Highways Act 1980 (c 66)	132(1)	Painting or otherwise inscribing or affixing picture etc upon the surface of a highway or upon a tree, structure or works on or in a highway
2		137(1)	Wilful obstruction of highway
3		138	Erecting a building, fence or hedge on highway
4		139(3)	Depositing builder's skip on highway without permission
5		139(4)(*a*)	Failure to secure lighting or other marking of builder's skip
6		139(4)(*b*)	Failure to secure marking of builder's skip with name and address
7		139(4)(*c*)	Failure to secure removal of builder's skip
8		139(4)(*d*)	Failure to comply with conditions of permission
9		140(3)	Failure to remove or reposition builder's skip
10		141(3)	Failure to comply with notice requiring removal of tree or shrub
11		147A(2)	Using of stall etc for road side sales in certain circumstances
12		148(*a*)	Depositing material etc on a made-up carriageway
13		148(*b*)	Depositing material etc within 15 feet from centre of made-up carriageway
14		148(*c*)	Depositing anything on highway to the interruption of user
15		148(*d*)	Pitching of booths, stalls or stands or encamping on highway
16		151(3)	Failure to comply with notice requiring works to prevent soil or refuse escaping onto street or into sewer
17		152(4)	Failure to comply with notice requiring removal of projection from buildings
18		153(5)	Failure to comply with notice requiring alteration of door, gate or bar opening outwards onto street
19		155(2)	Keeping of animals straying or lying on side of highway
20		161(1)	Depositing things on highway which cause injury or danger
21		169(5)	Erecting scaffolding or other structure without licence or failing to comply with terms of licence or perform duty under subsection (4)

Hackney carriages and private hire vehicles

London Hackney Carriage Act 1831

(1 & 2 Will 4 c 22)

8–20561 **35.** Hackney carriage standing in a street or place and not already hired shall be deemed to be plying for hire; driver refusing hire and unable to adduce evidence to court of hiring shall forfeit a sum not exceeding **level 1** on the standard scale[1].
[London Hackney Carriage Act 1831, s 35, as amended by the Statute Law Revision (No 2) Act 1888, the Criminal Justice Act 1967, Sch 3 and the Criminal Justice Act 1982, ss 38 and 46—summarised.]

---

1. This section, for the purpose of hiring of taxis at separate fares under ss 10 and 11 of the Transport Act 1985, has been disapplied by the Licensed Taxis (Hiring at Separate Fares) (London) Order 1986, SI 1986/1387.

8–20562 **36.** Compensation to be made to drivers improperly summoned for refusing to carry any person.
[London Hackney Carriage Act 1831, s 36, as amended by the Statute Law Revision (No 2) Act 1888, and the Statute Law (Repeals) Act 1976—summarised.]

8–20563 **41. Persons refusing to pay the driver his fare, or in injuring his carriage, to be liable to make compensation, or to be committed to prison.** If any person shall refuse or omit to pay the driver of any hackney carriage the sum justly due to him for the hire of such hackney carriage, or if any person shall deface or in any manner injure any such hackney carriage it shall be lawful for any justice of the peace, upon complaint thereof made to him, to grant a summons, or if it shall appear to him necessary, a warrant, for bringing before him or any other justice such defaulter or defender, and upon proof of the facts made upon oath before any such justice, to award reasonable satisfaction to the party so complaining for his fare or for his damages and costs, and also a reasonable compensation for his loss of time in attending to make and establish such complaint.
[London Hackney Carriage Act 1831, s 41, as amended by the Statute Law (Repeals) Act 1976.]

8–20564 **47.** Driver may demand deposit when required to wait with carriage—penalty on such driver refusing to wait, or to account for the deposit, etc **level 1** on the standard scale.
[London Hackney Carriage Act 1831, s 47 as amended by the Statute Law Revision Act 1974, the Statute Law Revision (No 2) Act 1888, the Criminal Law Act 1977, s 31 and the Criminal Justice Act 1982, s 46—summarised.]

8–20565 **56. Penalty on proprietors or drivers misbehaving.** If the proprietor or driver of any hackney carriage, or any other person having the care thereof, shall, by intoxication, or by wanton and furious driving or by any other wilful misconduct, injure or endanger any person in his life, limbs or property, or if any such proprietor or driver shall make use of any abusive or insulting language, or be guilty of other rude behaviour to or towards any person whatever, or shall assault or obstruct any officer of police, constable, watchman, or patrole, in the execution of his duty, every such proprietor, driver or other person so offending in any of the several cases aforesaid, shall forfeit a sum not exceeding **level 1** on the standard scale[1].
[London Hackney Carriage Act 1831, s 56, as amended by the Summary Jurisdiction Act 1884, s 4, the Statute Law Revision (No 2) Act 1888, the Statute Law (Repeals) Act 1976, the Criminal Law Act 1977, s 31, the Criminal Justice Act 1982, s 46 and the Statute Law (Repeals) Act 2004.]

---

1. The wording of the section has been slightly edited to accord with modern circumstances. A conviction under this section can lead to the proprietor's licence being revoked.

London Hackney Carriages Act 1843[1]

(6 & 7 Vict c 86)

8–20580 **10. Lending etc licence or ticket.** Any person transferring or lending a licence or permitting another person to use or wear a ticket[2], or proprietor knowingly suffering unlicensed person to act as driver: penalty not exceeding **level 3** on the standard scale.
[London Hackney Carriages Act 1843, s 10, as amended by the Statute Law Revision Act 1874 (No 2), the Statute Law Revision Act 1891, the Criminal Justice Act 1967, Sch 3, the Statute Law (Repeals) Act 1976, the Criminal Justice Act 1982, ss 35, 38 and 46 and the Statute Law (Repeals) Act 1993, Sch 1—summarised.]

---

1. A hackney carriage is defined for the purposes of these Acts by the Metropolitan Public Carriage Act 1869, s 4, as meaning any carriage for the conveyance of passengers which plies for hire (within the Metropolitan Police District or the City of London) and is not a stage carriage. A motor vehicle is included within the definition (Road Traffic Act 1988, s 191).

This Act, to the extent that it is part of the taxi code, except ss 3 and 33, shall apply to the use of taxis to provide local services under a special licence under s 12 of the Transport Act 1985 (Local Services (Operation by Taxis) (London) Regulations 1986, SI 1986/566).

2. The word "badge" is now more commonly used.

8–20581 14. Persons applying for licences to sign a requisition for the same, etc—Penalty on applicants or referees making false representations. Before any [hackney carriage driver's licence] shall be granted, a requisition for the same, in such form as Transport for London shall from time to time appoint for that purpose . . ., shall be made and signed by the person by whom such licence shall be required; and in every such requisition all such particulars as Transport for London shall require shall be truly set forth; and every person applying for or attempting to procure any such licence who shall make or cause to be made any false representation in regard to any of the said particulars, or who shall not truly answer all questions which shall be demanded of him in relation to such application for a licence, and also every person to whom reference shall be made who shall, in regard to such application, wilfully and knowingly make any misrepresentation, shall forfeit for every such offence the sum of **level 3** on the standard scale; and it shall be lawful for Transport for London to proceed for recovering of such penalty before any magistrate at any time within one calendar month after the commission of the offence, or during the currency of the licence so improperly obtained.

[London Hackney Carriages Act 1843, s 14, as amended by the Statute Law Revision Act 1891, the Criminal Justice Act 1967, Sch 3, the Forgery and Counterfeiting Act 1981, Sch, the Criminal Justice Act 1982, ss 38 and 46 and the Greater London Authority Act 1999, Sch 20.]

8–20582 17. Tickets to be worn by drivers, etc. Every licensed driver . . . shall at all times during his employment and when he shall be required to attend before any justice of the peace, wear his ticket[1] conspicuously upon his breast in such manner that the whole of the writing thereon shall be distinctly legible; and every driver . . . who shall act as such, or who shall attend when required before any justice of the peace, without wearing such ticket[1] in manner aforesaid, or who, when thereunto required shall refuse to produce such ticket[1] for inspection, or to permit any person to note the writing thereon, shall for every such offence forfeit the sum of **level 1** on the standard scale.

[London Hackney Carriages Act 1843, s 17, as amended by the Statute Law Revision Act 1874 (No 2), the Statute Law Revision Act 1891, the Criminal Justice Act 1967, Sch 3, the Statute Law (Repeals) Act 1976 and the Criminal Justice Act 1982, ss 38 and 46.]

1. That is, a badge: see note 2 to s 10, ante.

8–20583 18. Licences and tickets to be delivered up on the discontinuance of licences. Wilful neglect to deliver up within 3 days, or use or wear false ticket for purposes of deception; maximum fine **level 1** on the standard scale; limitation period 12 months from expiry of licence.

[London Hackney Carriages Act 1843, s 18, as amended by the Statute Law Revision Act 1891, the Criminal Law Act 1977, s 31 and the Criminal Justice Act 1982, s 46—summarised.]

8–20584 19. New tickets to be delivered instead of defaced or lost tickets. . . . Every person licensed under the authority of this Act who shall use or wear the ticket[1] granted to him after the writing thereon shall be obliterated, defaced or obscured so that the same shall not be distinctly legible, shall for every such offence forfeit the sum of **level 1** on the standard scale.

[London Hackney Carriages Act 1843, s 19, as amended by the Statute Law Revision Act 1891, the Criminal Law Act 1977, s 31 and the Criminal Justice Act 1982, s 46—summarised.]

1. That is, a badge: see note 2 to s 10, ante.

8–20585 25. Licences may be revoked or suspended. It shall be lawful for any justice of the peace before whom any [hackney carriage] driver shall be convicted of any offence, whether under this Act or any other Act, if such justice in his discretion shall think fit, to revoke the licence of such driver, and also any other licence he shall hold under the provisions of this Act, or to suspend the same for such time as the justice shall think proper, and for that purpose to require the proprietor (*or*) driver in whose possession such licence and the ticket[1] thereunto belonging shall then be to deliver up the same; and every proprietor, (*or*) driver who, being so required, shall refuse or neglect to deliver up such licence and any such ticket, or either of them, shall forfeit[2] so often as he shall be so required and refuse or neglect as aforesaid the sum of **level 1** on the standard scale; and the justice shall forthwith send such licence and ticket[1] to Transport for London, who shall cancel such licence if it has been revoked by the justice, or, if it has been suspended shall, at the end of the time for which it shall have been suspended, re-deliver such licence with the ticket[1], to the person to whom it was granted.

A magistrates' court that makes an order revoking or suspending any licence under this section may, if the court thinks fit, suspend the effect of the order pending an appeal against the order.

[London Hackney Carriages Act 1843, s 25, as amended by the Statute Law Revision Act 1874 (No 2), the Statute Law Revision Act 1891, the Statute Law (Repeals) Act 1976, the Criminal Law Act 1977, s 31, the Criminal Justice Act 1982, s 46, the Transport Act 1985, Sch 7 and the Greater London Authority Act 1999, Sch 20.]

1. That is, a badge: see note 2 to s 10, ante.
2. Penalty recoverable on summary conviction.

8–20586 27. No person to act as driver etc of any carriage without the consent of the proprietor. The person and any driver suffering him to act liable to fine not exceeding **level 1** on the standard scale; driver not revealing name, address and (any) licence number of person he has allowed to act as driver is liable therefor to further penalty not exceeding **level 1** on the standard scale; police constable may take charge of carriage.
[London Hackney Carriages Act 1843, s 27, as amended by the Statute Law Revision Act (No 2), the Statute Law Revision Act 1891, the Statute Law (Repeals) Act 1976, the Criminal Law Act 1977, s 31, the Criminal Justice Act 1982, s 46 and the Police and Criminal Evidence Act 1984, Sch 6—summarised.]

8–20587 28. Punishment for furious driving, and wilful misbehaviour—Compensation[1] for injury, etc. Proprietor paying compensation may recover from driver, etc.—Every driver of a hackney carriage, who shall be guilty of wanton or furious driving, or who by carelessness or wilful misbehaviour shall cause any hurt or damage to any person or property being in any street or highway, and also every driver, who during his employment shall be drunk, or shall make use of any insulting or abusive language, or shall be guilty of any insulting gesture or any misbehaviour, shall for every such offence forfeit the sum of **level 1** on the standard scale; or it shall be lawful for the justice before whom such complaint shall be brought, if in his discretion he shall think proper, instead of inflicting such penalty, forthwith to commit the offender to prison for any period not exceeding **two calendar months**.
[London Hackney Carriages Act 1843, s 28, as amended by the Statute Law Revision Act 1872 (No 2), the Statute Law Revision Act 1891, the Statute Law (Repeals) Act 1976, the Criminal Law Act 1977, s 31, the Criminal Justice Act 1982, s 46 and the Statute Law (Repeals) Act 1993, Sch 1.]

1. The provision relating to compensation was repealed by the Statute Law (Repeals) Act 1993, Sch 1.

8–20588 33. Penalty on drivers for loitering or causing any obstruction . . . etc[1].— . . . Every driver of a hackney carriage who shall ply for hire elsewhere than at some standing or place appointed for that purpose, or who by loitering or by any wilful misbehaviour shall cause any obstruction in or upon any public street, road or place, and every driver of a hackney carriage, whether hired or unhired, allowing any person beside himself, not being the hirer or a person employed by such hirer, to ride on the driving box, shall for every such offence forfeit a sum not exceeding **level 1** on the standard scale.
[London Hackney Carriages Act 1843, s 33, as amended by the Statute Law Revision Act 1891, the Criminal Justice Act 1967, Sch 3, the Statute Law (Repeals) Act 1976 and the Criminal Justice Act 1982, ss 38 and 46.]

1. As to disapplication of this section to a taxi being used for local services under a special licence, see note 1 to s 10, ante.

8–20589 38. Complaints to be made within seven days. . . . All complaints under the provisions of the London Hackney Carriage Act 1831, or of this Act, or of the orders and regulations made in pursuance of either of them, shall be made within seven days next after the day on which the cause of complaint shall have arisen.
[London Hackney Carriages Act 1843, s 38, as amended by the Statute Law Revision Act 1891, and the Statute Law (Repeals) Act 1976.]

London Hackney Carriages Act 1850

(13 & 14 Vict c 7)

8–20600 This Act is to be construed as one with the 1843 Act and the 1853 Act. Section 4 enables Transport for London to appoint standings for hackney carriages and to make regulations therefor. Breach of regulations is punishable under s 19 of the London Hackney Carriage Act 1853.

London Hackney Carriage Act 1853

(16 & 17 Vict c 33)

8–20610 17. Drivers liable to penalties for certain offences[1]. The driver of any hackney carriage who shall commit any of the following offences within the limits of this Act, shall be liable to a penalty not exceeding **level 3** on the standard scale for each offence:

(1) Every driver of a hackney carriage[2] who shall demand or take more than the proper fare[3], or who shall refuse to admit and carry in his carriage the number of persons painted or marked on such carriage or specified in the certificate granted by Transport for London in respect of such carriage,

or who shall refuse to carry by his carriage a reasonable quantity of luggage for any person hiring or intending to hire such carriage:

(2) Every driver of a hackney carriage who shall refuse to drive such carriage to any place within the limits of the Act, not exceeding six miles[4] to which he shall be required to drive any person hiring or intending to hire such carriage, or who shall refuse to drive any such carriage for any time not exceeding one hour, if so required by any person hiring or intending to hire such carriage, or who shall not drive the same at a reasonable and proper speed, not less than six miles an hour, except in cases of unavoidable delay, or when required by the hirer thereof to drive at any slower pace:

(3) Every driver of a hackney carriage who shall ply for hire with any carriage or horse which shall be at the time unfit for public use.

[London Hackney Carriage Act 1853, s 17, as amended by the Summary Jurisdiction Act 1884, the Statute Law Revision Act 1892, the Criminal Justice Act 1967, Sch 3, the Statute Law (Repeals) Act 1973, the Statute Law (Repeals) Act 1976, the Criminal Justice Act 1982, ss 39, 46 and Sch 3 and the Greater London Authority Act 199, Sch 20.]

---

1. This section, to the extent that it is part of the taxi code, has been disapplied as regards the use of a taxi to provide local services under a special licence under s 12 of the Transport Act 1985 (Local Services (Operation by Taxis) (London) Regulations 1986, SI 1986/566). Moreover, for the purpose of hiring of taxis at separate fares under ss 10 and 11 of the Transport Act 1985, the provisions of this section relating to obligatory hirings, the number of persons to be carried at the instance of the hirer, and the carriage of luggage have been disapplied by the Licensed Taxis (Hiring of Separate Fares) (London) Order 1986, SI 1986/1387.

2. A vehicle licensed and commonly used as a hackney carriage which plies for hire within s 4 of the Metropolitan Public Carriage Act 1869 cannot be divested of the attribute of a hackney carriage (*Bassam v Green* [1981] RTR 362).

3. A driver demands or takes more than the proper fare if he either asks for an excessive fare or asks for the proper fare and in addition for some supplemental payment which is not a fare (*Bassam v Green* [1981] RTR 362).

4. Now twenty miles (London Cab Order 1972, SI 1972 No 1074). A taxi driver commits no offence by refusing to stop when hailed (*Hunt v Morgan* [1949] 1 KB 233, [1948] 2 All ER 1065). The driver must observe the general law despite the requirements of this section (*Levinson v Powell* [1967] 3 All ER 796, 132 JP 10).

Metropolitan Public Carriage Act 1869[1]

(32 & 33 Vict c 115)

8–20620 **6.** *Grant of hackney carriage licences.*

---

1. This Act, to the extent that it is part of the taxi code, except ss 2, 9, and 10, shall apply to the use of a taxi to provide local services under a special licence under s 12 of the Transport Act 1985 (Local Services (Operation by Taxis) (London) Regulations 1986, SI 1986/566).

8–20621 **7. Penalty on use of unlicensed carriage.** If any unlicensed hackney carriage plies for hire[1], the owner of such carriage shall be liable to a penalty not exceeding **level 4** on the standard scale. And if any unlicensed hackney carriage is found on any stand within the limits of this Act[2], the owner of such carriage shall be liable to a penalty not exceeding **level 4** on the standard scale. The driver also shall in every such case be liable to a like penalty unless he proves that he was ignorant of the fact of the carriage being an unlicensed carriage.

Any hackney carriage plying for hire, and any hackney carriage found on any stand without having such distinguishing mark, or being otherwise distinguished in such manner as may for the time being be prescribed shall be deemed to be an unlicensed carriage.

[Metropolitan Public Carriage Act 1869, s 7, as amended by the Criminal Justice Act 1967, Sch 3, the Statute Law (Repeals) Act 1976, Sch 1, the Criminal Justice Act 1982, ss 35, 39, 46 and Sch 3 and the Greater London Authority Act 1999, Schs 20 and 34.]

---

1. As to "plying for hire" see note to the Town Police Clauses Act 1847, s 38, in title TOWNS IMPROVEMENT: TOWN POLICE, post.

2. The Metropolitan Police District and the City of London (Town Police Clauses Act 1847, s 2).

8–20622 **8. Hackney carriage to be driven by licensed drivers.** (1) Transport for London shall have the function of licensing persons to be drivers of hackney carriages.

(2) No hackney carriage shall ply for hire within the limits of this Act unless under the charge of a driver having a licence under this section from Transport for London.

(3) If any hackney carriage plies for hire in contravention of this section—

(*a*) the person driving the carriage, and

(*b*) the owner of the carriage, unless he proves that the driver acted without his privity or consent,

shall each be liable to a penalty not exceeding level 3 on the standard scale.

(4) Transport for London may send to the Commissioner of Police of the Metropolis or the Commissioner of Police for the City of London—

(*a*) details of a person to whom Transport for London is considering granting a licence under this section, and

(*b*) a request for the Commissioner's observations;

and the Commissioner shall respond to the request.

(5) A licence under this section may—

(*a*) be granted on such conditions,
(*b*) be in such form,
(*c*) be subject to revocation or suspension in such event, and
(*d*) generally be dealt with in such manner,

as may be prescribed.

(6) Subsection (5) of this section is subject to the following provisions of this section.

(7) A licence under this section shall, if not revoked or suspended, be in force for three years.

(8) A fee of such amount (if any) as Transport for London may determine shall be paid to Transport for London—

(*a*) by any applicant for a licence under this section, on making the application for the licence;
(*b*) by any applicant for the taking or re-taking of any test or examination, or any part of a test or examination, with respect to any matter of fitness, on making the application for the taking or re-taking of the test, examination or part; and
(*c*) by any person granted a licence under this section, on the grant of the licence.

(9) In paragraph (b) of subsection (8) of this section "matter of fitness" means—

(*a*) any matter as respects which Transport for London must be satisfied before granting a licence under this section; or
(*b*) any matter such that, if Transport for London is not satisfied with respect to the matter, they may refuse to grant a licence under this section.

(10) Different amounts may be determined under subsection (8) of this section for different purposes or different cases.

(11) Transport for London may remit or refund the whole or part of a fee under subsection (8) of this section.

[Metropolitan Public Carriage Act 1869, s 8, as substituted by the Greater London Authority Act 1999, Sch 20.]

8–20623 **9.** *Regulations as to hackney and stage carriages*[1].

1. Various London Cab Orders have been made: see SR & O 1934 No 1346, amended by SI 1955/1853, SI 1962/289, SI 1971/333, SI 1974/601, SI 1980/588, SI 1983/653, SI 1986/857, SI 1987/999, SI 1988/996, SI 1990/1075 and 2003, SI 1992/1169, SI 1993/1093, SI 1994/1087, SI 1995/837 and 1181, SI 1996/960 and 1176, SI 1997/1116, SI 1998/1043, SI 1999/1117 and 3250 and SI 2000/1276. Penalty for contravention is fine not exceeding **£20**.

London Cab Act 1896

(59 & 60 Vict c 27)

8–20640 **1. Penalties for defrauding cabmen.** If any person commits any of the following offences with respect to a cab[1] namely:

(*a*) hires a cab[1] knowing or having reason to believe that he cannot pay the lawful fare, or with intent to avoid payment of the lawful fare; or
(*b*) fraudulently endeavours to avoid payment of a fare lawfully due from him; or
(*c*) having failed or refused to pay a fare lawfully due from him, either refuses to give to the driver an address at which he can be found, or, with intent to deceive, gives a false address,

he shall be liable on summary conviction to pay, in addition to the fare, a fine not exceeding **level 1** on the standard scale, or in the discretion of the court, to be imprisoned for a term not exceeding fourteen days; and the whole or any part of any fine imposed may be applied in compensation to the driver.

[London Cab Act 1896, s 1, as amended by the Criminal Justice Act 1967, Sch 3 and the Criminal Justice Act 1982, ss 38 and 46.]

1. A "cab" means a hackney carriage within the meaning of the Metropolitan Public Carriage Act 1869.

Transport Act 1985

(1985 c 67)

8–20650 **17. London taxi and taxi driver licensing: appeals.** (1) In this section—

"licence" means a licence under section 6 of the Metropolitan Public Carriage Act 1869 (taxi licences) or under section 8 of that Act (taxi driver licences); and
"licensing authority" means the person empowered to grant a licence.

(2) Where the licensing authority has refused to grant, or has suspended or revoked, a licence the

applicant for, or (as the case may be) holder of, the licence may, before the expiry of the designated period—

(*a*) require the authority to reconsider his decision; or

(*b*) appeal to the appropriate court.

(3) Any call for a reconsideration under subsection (2) above must be made to the licensing authority in writing.

(4) On any reconsideration under this section the person calling for the decision to be reconsidered shall be entitled to be heard either in person or by his representative.

(5) If the person calling for a decision to be reconsidered under this section is dissatisfied with the decision of the licensing authority on reconsideration, he may, before the expiry of the designated period, appeal to the appropriate court.

(6) On any appeal to it under this section, the court may make such order as it thinks fit; and any order which it makes shall be binding on the licensing authority.

(7) Where a person holds a licence which is in force when he applies for a new licence in substitution for it, the existing licence shall continue in force until the application for the new licence, or any appeal under this section in relation to that application, is disposed of, but without prejudice to the exercise in the meantime of any power of the licensing authority to revoke the existing licence.

(8) For the purposes of subsection (7) above, where the licensing authority refuses to grant the new licence the application shall not be treated as disposed of—

(*a*) where no call for a reconsideration of the authority's decision is made under subsection (2) above, until the expiry of the designated period;

(*b*) where such a reconsideration is called for, until the expiry of the designated period which begins by reference to the decision of the authority on reconsideration.

(9) Where the licensing authority suspends or revokes a licence, or confirms a decision to do so, he may, if the holder of the licence so requests, direct that his decision shall not have effect until the expiry of the designated period.

(10) In this section

"the appropriate court" means the magistrates' court for the petty sessions area in which the licensing authority has his office or, if he has more than one office, his principal office;

"designated period" means such period as may be specified for the purpose by London cab order;

"London cab order" means an order made by Transport for London.

(11) Any power to make a London cab order under this section includes power to vary or revoke a previous such order.

[Transport Act 1985, s 17, as amended by the Greater London Authority Act 1999, s 254.]

Private Hire Vehicles (London) Act 1998[1]

(1998 c 34)

Introductory

8–20650A 1. Meaning of "private hire vehicle", "operator" and related expressions.

(1) In this Act—

(*a*) "private hire vehicle" means a vehicle constructed or adapted to seat fewer than nine passengers which is made available with a driver to the public for hire for the purpose of carrying passengers, other than a licensed taxi or a public service vehicle[2]; and

(*b*) "operator" means a person who makes provision for the invitation or acceptance of, or who accepts, private hire bookings.

(2) Any reference in this Act to a vehicle being "used as a private hire vehicle" is a reference to a private hire vehicle which—

(*a*) is in use in connection with a hiring for the purpose of carrying one or more passengers; or

(*b*) is immediately available to an operator to carry out a private hire booking.

(3) Any reference in this Act to the operator of a vehicle which is being used as a private hire vehicle is a reference to the operator who accepted the booking for the hiring or to whom the vehicle is immediately available, as the case may be.

(4) In this Act "private hire booking" means a booking for the hire of a private hire vehicle for the purpose of carrying one or more passengers (including a booking to carry out as sub-contractor a private hire booking accepted by another operator).

(5) In this Act "operating centre" means premises at which private hire bookings are accepted by an operator.

[Private Hire Vehicles (London) Act 1998, s 1.]

---

1. This Act is to be brought into force in accordance with orders made under s 40. At the date of going to press, the Private Hire Vehicles (London) Act 1998 (Commencement No 1) Order 2000, SI 2000/3144, had been made bringing

ss 1, 3, 4(1), (3) and (4), 5(5), 15(1) to (3) and (5), 16(1) and (2), 17 to 20, 21(1) and (3), 22(1) and (4), 23 to 29, 32, 33, 34(1) and (2) and 36 to 38, into force on 22 January 2001; and ss 2, 4(5) and (6), 5(1) to (4), 21(4) and 22(5) and (6) on 22 October 2001; the (No 2) Order SI 2003, SI 2003/580 brought into force s 13(1), (2)(*a*) and (4) to (7), s 13(2)(*b*), except so far as it relates to the requirement mentioned in s 13(3), ss14(1), (2) and (4), 15(4), 16(4) and 22(3) on 1 April 2003; ss 12(1) to (6), 14(3) and (5) and 31, so much of s 39(2) as relates to the entries in Sch 2 for s 4 of the London Cab Act 1968, the Broadcasting Act 1990 and the Transport and Works Act 1992 on 1 June 2003; s 13(2)(*b*) of the Act so far as it is not already in force, and s 13(3) on 1 April 2006 in relation to applications for London PHV drivers' licences received by Transport for London on or after that day; the (No 3) Order SI 2004, SI 2004/241 brought into force ss 7 to 11, 22(2), 34(3) and 35 for the purposes of existing private hire vehicles as defined by reg 2 of the Private Hire Vehicles (London) (Transitional Provisions) Regulations 2004, SI 2004/242, on 8 March 2004, and for all other purposes, on 8 April 2004; and with the exception of s 13(2)(*b*) of the Act (so far as it relates to the requirement in s 13(3)) and s 13(3), all other provisions of the Act not yet in force on 8 June 2004.

2. For savings in respect of vehicles used for funerals and weddings, see s 29, post.

Regulation of private hire vehicle operators in London

8–20651 2. Requirement for London operator's licence. (1) No person shall in London make provision for the invitation or acceptance of, or accept, private hire bookings unless he is the holder of a private hire vehicle operator's licence for London (in this Act referred to as a "London PHV operator's licence").

(2) A person who makes provision for the invitation or acceptance of private hire bookings, or who accepts such a booking, in contravention of this section is guilty of an offence and liable on summary conviction to a fine not exceeding level 4 on the standard scale.

[Private Hire Vehicles (London) Act 1998, s 2.]

8–20651A 3. London operator's licences. (1) Any person may apply to the licensing authority for a London PHV operator's licence.

(2) An application under this section shall state the address of any premises in London which the applicant proposes to use as an operating centre.

(3) The licensing authority shall grant a London PHV operator's licence to the applicant if the authority is satisfied that—

(*a*) the applicant is a fit and proper person to hold a London PHV operator's licence; and

(*b*) any further requirements that may be prescribed (which may include requirements relating to operating centres) are met.

(4) A London PHV operator's licence shall be granted subject to such conditions as may be prescribed[1] and such other conditions as the licensing authority may think fit.

(5) A London PHV operator's licence shall be granted for five years or such shorter period as the licensing authority may consider appropriate in the circumstances of the case.

(6) A London PHV operator's licence shall—

(*a*) specify the address of any premises in London which the holder of the licence may use as an operating centre;

(*b*) be in such form and contain such particulars as the licensing authority may think fit.

(7) An applicant for a London PHV operator's licence may appeal[2] to a magistrates' court against—

(*a*) a decision not to grant such a licence;

(*b*) a decision not to specify an address proposed in the application as an operating centre; or

(*c*) any condition (other than a prescribed condition) to which the licence is subject.

[Private Hire Vehicles (London) Act 1998, s 3, as amended by the Greater London Authority Act 1999, s 254.]

---

1. See the Private Hire Vehicles (London) (Operators' Licences) Regulations 2000, SI 2000/3146.

2. For provisions relating to appeals, see ss 25–26, post and the Magistrates' Courts Rules 1991, r 34 in PART 1 MAGISTRATES COURT PROCEDURE, ante.

8–20651B 4. Obligations of London operators. (1) The holder of a London PHV operator's licence (in this Act referred to as a "London PHV operator") shall not in London accept a private hire booking other than at an operating centre specified in his licence.

(2) A London PHV operator shall secure that any vehicle which is provided by him for carrying out a private hire booking accepted by him in London is—

(*a*) a vehicle for which a London PHV licence is in force driven by a person holding a London PHV driver's licence; or

(*b*) a London cab driven by a person holding a London cab driver's licence.

(3) A London PHV operator shall—

(*a*) display a copy of his licence at each operating centre specified in the licence;

(*b*) keep at each specified operating centre a record in the prescribed[1] form of the private hire bookings accepted by him there;

(*c*) before the commencement of each journey booked at a specified operating centre, enter in the record kept under paragraph (*b*) the prescribed[1] particulars of the booking;

(*d*) keep at each specified operating centre such records as may be prescribed[1] of particulars of the private hire vehicles and drivers which are available to him for carrying out bookings accepted by him at that centre;

(*e*) at the request of a constable or authorised officer, produce for inspection any record required by this section to be kept.

(4) If a London PHV operator ceases to use an operating centre specified in his licence he shall preserve any record he was required by this section to keep there for such period as may be prescribed[1].

(5) A London PHV operator who contravenes any provision of this section is guilty of an offence and liable on summary conviction to a fine not exceeding **level 3** on the standard scale.

(6) It is a defence[2] in proceedings for an offence under this section for an operator to show that he exercised all due diligence to avoid committing such an offence.

[Private Hire Vehicles (London) Act 1998, s 4.]

---

1. See the Private Hire Vehicles (London) (Operators' Licences) Regulations 2000, SI 2000/3146.
2. An accused who raises this defence is not required to establish it beyond reasonable doubt, but on the balance of probabilities: see *R v Carr-Briant* [1943] KB 607, [1943] 2 All ER 156, 107 JP 167.

8–20651C 5. Hirings accepted on behalf of another operator. (1) A London PHV operator ("the first operator") who has in London accepted a private hire booking may not arrange for another operator to provide a vehicle to carry out that booking as sub-contractor unless—

(*a*) the other operator is a London PHV operator and the sub-contracted booking is accepted at an operating centre in London;

(*b*) the other operator is licensed under section 55 of the Local Government (Miscellaneous Provisions) Act 1976 (in this Act referred to as "the 1976 Act") by the council of a district and the sub-contracted booking is accepted in that district; or

(*c*) the other operator accepts the sub-contracted booking in Scotland.

(2) A London PHV operator who contravenes subsection (1) is guilty of an offence and liable on summary conviction to a fine not exceeding **level 3** on the standard scale.

(3) It is a defence[1] in proceedings for an offence under this section for an operator to show that he exercised all due diligence to avoid committing such an offence.

(4) It is immaterial for the purposes of subsection (1) whether or not sub-contracting is permitted by the contract between the first operator and the person who made the booking.

(5) For the avoidance of doubt (and subject to any relevant contract terms), a contract of hire between a person who made a private hire booking at an operating centre in London and the London PHV operator who accepted the booking remains in force despite the making of arrangements by that operator for another contractor to provide a vehicle to carry out that booking as sub-contractor.

[Private Hire Vehicles (London) Act 1998, s 5.]

---

1. An accused who raises this defence is not required to establish it beyond reasonable doubt, but on the balance of probabilities: see *R v Carr-Briant* [1943] KB 607, [1943] 2 All ER 156, 107 JP 167.

Regulation of private hire vehicles in London

8–20652 6. Requirement for private hire vehicle licence. (1) A vehicle shall not be used as a private hire vehicle on a road in London unless a private hire vehicle licence is in force for that vehicle.

(2) The driver and operator of a vehicle used in contravention of this section are each guilty of an offence.

(3) The owner[1] of a vehicle who permits it to be used in contravention of this section is guilty of an offence.

(4) It is a defence[2] in proceedings for an offence under subsection (2) for the driver or operator to show that he exercised all due diligence to prevent the vehicle being used in contravention of this section.

(5) A person guilty of an offence under this section is liable on summary conviction to a fine not exceeding **level 4** on the standard scale.

(6) In this section "private hire vehicle licence" means—

(*a*) except where paragraph (*b*) or (*c*) applies, a London PHV licence;

(*b*) if the vehicle is in use for the purposes of a hiring the booking for which was accepted outside London in a controlled district, a licence under section 48 of the 1976 Act issued by the council for that district; and

(*c*) if the vehicle is in use for the purposes of a hiring the booking for which was accepted in Scotland, a licence under section 10 of the Civic Government (Scotland) Act 1982 (in this Act referred to as "the 1982 Act"),

and for the purposes of paragraph (*b*) or (*c*) it is immaterial that the booking in question is a sub-contracted booking.

(7) This section does not apply to a vehicle used for the purposes of a hiring for a journey beginning outside London in an area of England and Wales which is not a controlled district.
[Private Hire Vehicles (London) Act 1998, s 6.]

---

1. For "owner" see s 35, post.
2. An accused who raises this defence is not required to establish it beyond reasonable doubt, but on the balance of probabilities: see *R v Carr-Briant* [1943] KB 607, [1943] 2 All ER 156, 107 JP 167.

8–20652A 7. London PHV licences. (1) The owner[1] of any vehicle constructed or adapted to seat fewer than nine passengers may apply to the licensing authority for a private hire vehicle licence for London (in this Act referred to as a "London PHV licence") for that vehicle.

(2) The licensing authority shall grant a London PHV licence for a vehicle if the authority is satisfied—

(*a*) that the vehicle—

(i) is suitable in type, size and design for use as a private hire vehicle;
(ii) is safe, comfortable and in a suitable mechanical condition for that use; and
(iii) is not of such design and appearance as would lead any person to believe that the vehicle is a London cab;

(*b*) that there is in force in relation to the use of the vehicle a policy of insurance or such security as complies with the requirements of Part VI of the Road Traffic Act 1988; and
(*c*) that any further requirements that may be prescribed are met.

(3) A London PHV licence may not be granted in respect of more than one vehicle.

(4) A London PHV licence shall be granted subject to such conditions as may be prescribed and such other conditions as the licensing authority may think fit.

(5) A London PHV licence shall be in such form and shall contain such particulars as the licensing authority may think fit.

(6) A London PHV licence shall be granted for one year or for such shorter period as the licensing authority may consider appropriate in the circumstances of the case.

(7) An applicant for a London PHV licence may appeal[2] to a magistrates' court against a decision not to grant such a licence or against any condition (other than a prescribed condition) to which the licence is subject.
[Private Hire Vehicles (London) Act 1998, s 7, as amended by the Greater London Authority Act 1999, s 254.]

---

1. For "owner" see s 35, post.
2. For provisions relating to appeals see ss 25–26, post and the Magistrates' Court Rules 1981, r 34 in PART 1: MAGISTRATES' COURTS PROCEDURE ante.

8–20652B 8. Obligations of owners of licensed vehicles. (1) This section applies to the owner of any vehicle to which a London PHV licence relates.

(2) The owner[1] shall present the vehicle for inspection and testing by or on behalf of the licensing authority within such period and at such place as the authority may by notice reasonably require.

The vehicle shall not be required to be presented under this subsection on more than three separate occasions during any one period of 12 months.

(3) The owner shall (without prejudice to section 170 of the Road Traffic Act 1988) report any accident to the vehicle materially affecting—

(*a*) the safety, performance or appearance of the vehicle, or
(*b*) the comfort or convenience of persons carried in the vehicle,

to the licensing authority as soon as reasonably practical and in any case within 72 hours of the accident occurring.

(4) If the ownership of the vehicle changes, the person who was previously the owner shall within 14 days of the change give notice to the licensing authority of that fact and the name and address of the new owner.

(5) A person who, without reasonable excuse, contravenes any provision of this section is guilty of an offence and liable on summary conviction to a fine not exceeding **level 3** on the standard scale.
[Private Hire Vehicles (London) Act 1998, s 8, as amended by the Greater London Authority Act 1999, s 254.]

---

1. For "owner" see s 35, post.

8–20652C 9. Fitness of licensed vehicles. (1) A constable or authorised officer has power at all reasonable times to inspect and test, for the purpose of ascertaining its fitness, any vehicle to which a London PHV licence relates.

(2) If a constable or authorised officer is not satisfied as to the fitness of such a vehicle he may by notice to the owner of the vehicle—

(*a*) require the owner[1] to make the vehicle available for further inspection and testing at such reasonable time and place as may be specified in the notice; and (*b*) if he thinks fit, suspend the London PHV licence relating to that vehicle until such time as a constable or authorised officer is satisfied as to the fitness of the vehicle.

(3) A notice under subsection (2)(*b*) shall state the grounds on which the licence is being suspended and the suspension shall take effect on the day on which it is served on the owner.

(4) A licence suspended under subsection (2)(*b*) shall remain suspended until such time as a constable or authorised officer by notice to the owner directs that the licence is again in force.

(5) If a licence remains suspended at the end of the period of two months beginning with the day on which a notice under subsection (2)(*b*) was served on the owner of the vehicle—

(*a*) a constable or authorised officer may by notice to the owner direct that the licence is revoked; and

(*b*) the revocation shall take effect at the end of the period of 21 days beginning with the day on which the owner is served with that notice.

(6) An owner[1] may appeal[2] against a notice under subsection (2)(*b*) or (5) to a magistrates' court.
[Private Hire Vehicles (London) Act 1998, s 9.]

1. For "owner" see s 35, post.
2. For provisions relating to appeals see ss 25–26, post and the Magistrates' Court Rules 1981, r 34 in PART 1: MAGISTRATES' COURTS PROCEDURE ante.

8–20652D 10. Identification of licensed vehicles. (1) The licensing authority shall issue a disc or plate for each vehicle to which a London PHV licence relates which identifies that vehicle as a vehicle for which such a licence is in force.

(2) No vehicle to which a London PHV licence relates shall be used as a private hire vehicle on a road in London unless the disc or plate issued under this section is exhibited on the vehicle in such manner as may be prescribed.

(3) The licensing authority may by notice exempt a vehicle from the requirement under subsection (2) when it is being used to provide a service specified in the notice if the authority considers it inappropriate (having regard to that service) to require the disc or plate in question to be exhibited.

(4) The driver and operator of a vehicle used in contravention of subsection (2) are each guilty of an offence.

(5) The owner[1] of a vehicle who permits it to be used in contravention of subsection (2) is guilty of an offence.

(6) It is a defence[2] in proceedings for an offence under subsection (4) for the driver or operator to show that he exercised all due diligence to prevent the vehicle being used in contravention of subsection (2).

(7) A person guilty of an offence under this section is liable on summary conviction to a fine not exceeding **level 3** on the standard scale.
[Private Hire Vehicles (London) Act 1998, s 10, as amended by the Greater London Authority Act 1999, s 254.]

1. For "owner" see s 35, post.
2. An accused who raises this defence is not required to establish it beyond reasonable doubt, but on the balance of probabilities: see *R v Carr-Briant* [1943] KB 607, [1943] 2 All ER 156, 107 JP 167.

8–20652E 11. Prohibition of taximeters. (1) No vehicle to which a London PHV licence relates shall be equipped with a taximeter.

(2) If such a vehicle is equipped with a taximeter, the owner[1] of that vehicle is guilty of an offence and liable on summary conviction to a fine not exceeding **level 3** on the standard scale.

(3) In this section "taximeter" means a device for calculating the fare to be charged in respect of any journey by reference to the distance travelled or time elapsed since the start of the journey (or a combination of both).
[Private Hire Vehicles (London) Act 1998, s 11.]

1. For "owner" see s 35, post.

Regulation of drivers of private hire vehicles in London

8–20653 12. Requirement for private hire vehicle driver's licence. (1) No vehicle shall be used as a private hire vehicle on a road in London unless the driver holds a private hire vehicle driver's licence.

(2) The driver and operator of a vehicle used in contravention of this section are each guilty of an offence.

(3) The owner[1] of a vehicle who permits it to be used in contravention of this section is guilty of an offence.

(4) It is a defence[2] in proceedings against the operator of a vehicle for an offence under subsection (2) for the operator to show that he exercised all due diligence to prevent the vehicle being used in contravention of this section.

(5) A person guilty of an offence under this section is liable on summary conviction to a fine not exceeding **level 4** on the standard scale.

(6) In this section "private hire vehicle driver's licence" means—

(*a*) except where paragraph (*b*) or (*c*) applies, a London PHV driver's licence;

(*b*) if the vehicle is in use for the purposes of a hiring the booking for which was accepted outside London in a controlled district in England and Wales, a licence under section 51 of the 1976 Act issued by the council for that district; and

(*c*) if the vehicle is in use for a hiring the booking for which was accepted in Scotland, a licence under section 13 of the 1982 Act,

and for the purposes of paragraph (*b*) or (*c*) it is immaterial that the booking in question is a sub-contracted booking.

(7) This section does not apply to the use of a vehicle for the purposes of a hiring for a journey beginning outside London in an area of England and Wales which is not a controlled district.
[Private Hire Vehicles (London) Act 1998, s 12.]

1. For "owner" see s 35, post.
2. An accused who raises this defence is not required to establish it beyond reasonable doubt, but on the balance of probabilities: see *R v Carr-Briant* [1943] KB 607, [1943] 2 All ER 156, 107 JP 167.

8–20653A 13. London PHV driver's licences. (1) Any person may apply to the licensing authority for a private hire vehicle driver's licence for London (in this Act referred to as a "London PHV driver's licence").

(2) The licensing authority shall grant a London PHV driver's licence to an applicant if the authority is satisfied that—

(*a*) the applicant has attained the age of 21, is (and has for at least three years been) authorised to drive a motor car and is a fit and proper person to hold a London PHV driver's licence; and

(*b*) the requirement mentioned in subsection (3), and any further requirements prescribed by the licensing authority, are met.

(3) The licensing authority shall require applicants to show to the authority's satisfaction (whether by taking a test or otherwise) that they possess a level—

(*a*) of knowledge of London or parts of London; and

(*b*) of general topographical skills,

which appears to the authority to be appropriate.

The licensing authority may impose different requirements in relation to different applicants.

(4) The licensing authority may send a copy of an application to the Commissioner of Police of the Metropolis or the Commissioner of Police for the City of London with a request for the Commissioner's observations; and the Commissioner shall respond to the request.

(5) A London PHV driver's licence—

(*a*) may be granted subject to such conditions as the licensing authority may think fit;

(*b*) shall be in such form and shall contain such particulars as the licensing authority may think fit; and

(*c*) shall be granted for three years or for such shorter period as the Secretary of State may consider appropriate in the circumstances of the particular case.

(6) An applicant may appeal[1] to a magistrates' court against a decision not to grant a London PHV driver's licence or against any condition to which such a licence is subject.

(7) For the purposes of subsection (2), a person is authorised to drive a motor car if—

(*a*) he holds a licence granted under Part III of the Road Traffic Act 1988 (other than a provisional licence) authorising him to drive a motor car; or

(*b*) he is authorised by virtue of section 99A(1) or 109(1) of that Act (Community licences and Northern Ireland licences) to drive a motor car in Great Britain.
[Private Hire Vehicles (London) Act 1998, s 13, as amended by the Greater London Authority Act 1999, s 254.]

1. For provisions relating to appeals see ss 25–26, post and the Magistrates' Court Rules 1981, r 34 in PART 1: MAGISTRATES' COURTS PROCEDURE ante.

8–20653B 14. Issue of driver's badges. (1) The licensing authority shall issue a badge to each person to whom the authority has granted a London PHV driver's licence.

(2) The licensing authority may prescribe the form of badges issued under this section.

(3) A person issued with such a badge shall, when he is the driver of a vehicle being used as a private hire vehicle, wear the badge in such position and manner as to be plainly and distinctly visible.

(4) The licensing authority may by notice exempt a person from the requirement under subsection (3), when he is the driver of a vehicle being used to provide a service specified in the notice if the authority considers it inappropriate (having regard to that service) to require the badge to be worn.

(5) Any person who without reasonable excuse contravenes subsection (3) is guilty of an offence and liable on summary conviction to a fine not exceeding **level 3** on the standard scale.
[Private Hire Vehicles (London) Act 1998, s 14, as amended by the Greater London Authority Act 1999, s 254.]

Licences: general provisions

8–20654 15. Applications for licences. (1) An application for the grant of a licence under this Act shall be made in such form, and include such declarations and information, as the licensing authority may require.

(2) The licensing authority may require an applicant to furnish such further information as the authority may consider necessary for dealing with the application.

(3) The information which an applicant for a London PHV operator's licence may be required to furnish includes in particular information about—

(*a*) any premises in London which he proposes to use as an operating centre;

(*b*) any convictions recorded against him;

(*c*) any business activities he has carried on before making the application;

(*d*) if the applicant is or has been a director or secretary of a company, that company;

(*e*) if the applicant is a company, information about the directors or secretary of that company;

(*f*) if the applicant proposes to act as an operator in partnership with any other person, information about that person.

(4) An applicant for a London PHV driver's licence may be required by the licensing authority—

(*a*) to produce a certificate signed by a registered medical practitioner to the effect that—

(i) he is physically fit to be the driver of a private hire vehicle; and

(ii) if any specific requirements of physical fitness have been prescribed for persons holding London PHV licences, that he meets those requirements; and

(*b*) whether or not such a certificate has been produced, to submit to examination by a registered medical practitioner selected by the licensing authority as to his physical fitness to be the driver of such a vehicle.

(5) The provisions of this Act apply to the renewal of a licence as they apply to the grant of a licence.

[Private Hire Vehicles (London) Act 1998, s 15, as amended by the Greater London Authority Act 1999, s 254.]

8–20654A 16. Power to suspend or revoke licences. (1) The licensing authority may suspend or revoke a licence under this Act for any reasonable cause including (without prejudice to the generality of this subsection) any ground mentioned below.

(2) A London PHV operator's licence may be suspended or revoked where—

(*a*) the licensing authority is no longer satisfied that the licence holder is fit to hold such a licence; or

(*b*) the licence holder has failed to comply with any condition of the licence or any other obligation imposed on him by or under this Act.

(3) A London PHV licence may be suspended or revoked where—

(*a*) the Secretary of State is no longer satisfied that the vehicle to which it relates is fit for use as a private hire vehicle; or

(*b*) the owner has failed to comply with any condition of the licence or any other obligation imposed on him by or under this Act.

(4) A London PHV driver's licence may be suspended or revoked where—

(*a*) the licence holder has, since the grant of the licence, been convicted of an offence involving dishonesty, indecency or violence;

(*b*) the licensing authority is for any other reason no longer satisfied that the licence holder is fit to hold such a licence; or

(*c*) the licence holder has failed to comply with any condition of the licence or any other obligation imposed on him by or under this Act.

[Private Hire Vehicles (London) Act 1998, s 16, as amended by the Greater London Authority Act 1999, s 254.]

8–20654B 17. Suspension and revocation under section 16: procedure. (1) Where the licensing authority has decided to suspend or revoke a licence under section 16—

(*a*) the authority shall give notice of the decision and the grounds for the decision to the licence holder or, in the case of a London PHV licence, the owner of the vehicle to which the licence relates; and

(*b*) the suspension or revocation takes effect at the end of the period of 21 days beginning with the day on which that notice is served on the licence holder or the owner.

(2) If the licensing authority is of the opinion that the interests of public safety require the suspension or revocation of a licence to have immediate effect, and the authority includes a statement of that opinion and the reasons for it in the notice of suspension or revocation, the suspension or revocation takes effect when the notice is served on the licence holder or vehicle owner (as the case may be).

(3) A licence suspended under this section shall remain suspended until such time as the licensing authority by notice directs that the licence is again in force.

(4) The holder of a London PHV operator's or driver's licence, or the owner of a vehicle to which a PHV licence relates, may appeal[1] to a magistrates' court against a decision under section 16 to suspend or revoke that licence.
[Private Hire Vehicles (London) Act 1998, s 17, as amended by the Greater London Authority Act 1999, s 254.]

1. For provisions relating to appeals see ss 25–26, post and the Magistrates' Court Rules 1981, r 34 in PART 1: MAGISTRATES' COURTS PROCEDURE ante.

8–20654C 18. Variation of operator's licence at the request of the operator. (1) The licensing authority may, on the application of a London PHV operator, vary his licence by adding a reference to a new operating centre or removing an existing reference to an operating centre.

(2) An application for the variation of a licence under this section shall be made in such form, and include such declarations and information, as the licensing authority may require.

(3) The licensing authority may require an applicant to furnish such further information as he may consider necessary for dealing with the application.

(4) The licensing authority shall not add a reference to a new operating centre unless the authority is satisfied that the premises in question meet any requirements prescribed under section 3(3)(*b*).

(5) An applicant for the variation of a London PHV operator's licence under this section may appeal[1] to a magistrates' court against a decision not to add a new operating centre to the licence.
[Private Hire Vehicles (London) Act 1998, s 18, as amended by the Greater London Authority Act 1999, s 254.]

1. For provisions relating to appeals see ss 25–26, post and the Magistrates' Court Rules 1981, r 34 in PART 1: MAGISTRATES' COURTS PROCEDURE ante.

8–20654D 19. Variation of operator's licence by the licensing authority. (1) The licensing authority may—

(*a*) suspend the operation of a London PHV operator's licence so far as relating to any operating centre specified in the licence; or
(*b*) vary such a licence by removing a reference to an operating centre previously specified in the licence,

if the authority is no longer satisfied that the operating centre in question meets any requirements prescribed under section 3(3)(*b*) or for any other reasonable cause.

(2) Where the licensing authority has decided to suspend the operation of a licence as mentioned in subsection (1)(*a*) or vary a licence as mentioned in subsection (1)(*b*)—

(*a*) the authority shall give notice of the decision and the grounds for it to the licence holder; and
(*b*) the decision shall take effect at the end of the period of 21 days beginning with the day on which the licence holder is served with that notice.

(3) If the licensing authority is of the opinion that the interests of public safety require his decision to have immediate effect, and the authority includes a statement of that opinion and the reasons for it in the notice, the authority's decision shall take effect when the notice is served on the licence holder.

(4) If a licence is suspended in relation to an operating centre, the premises in question shall not be regarded for the purposes of this Act as premises at which the licence holder is authorised to accept private hire bookings, until such time as the licensing authority by notice states that the licence is no longer suspended in relation to those premises.

(5) The holder of a London PHV operator's licence may appeal[1] to a magistrates' court against a decision under subsection (1).
[Private Hire Vehicles (London) Act 1998, s 19, as amended by the Greater London Authority Act 1999, s 254.]

1. For provisions relating to appeals see ss 25–26, post and the Magistrates' Court Rules 1981, r 34 in PART 1: MAGISTRATES' COURTS PROCEDURE ante.

8–20654DA 20. *Fees for grant of licences, etc*

8–20654E 21. Production of documents. (1) The holder of a London PHV operator's licence or a London PHV driver's licence shall at the request of a constable or authorised officer produce his licence for inspection.

(2) The owner[1] of a vehicle to which a London PHV licence relates shall at the request of a constable or authorised officer produce for inspection—

(*a*) the London PHV licence for that vehicle;
(*b*) the certificate of the policy of insurance or security required in respect of the vehicle by Part VI of the Road Traffic Act 1988.

(3) A document required to be produced under this section shall be produced either forthwith or—

(*a*) if the request is made by a constable, at any police station within London nominated by the licence holder or vehicle owner when the request is made, or (*b*) if the request is made by an authorised officer, at such place as the officer may reasonably require,

before the end of the period of 6 days beginning with the day on which the request is made.

(4) A person who without reasonable excuse contravenes this section is guilty of an offence and liable on summary conviction to a fine not exceeding **level 3** on the standard scale.

[Private Hire Vehicles (London) Act 1998, s 21.]

1. For "owner" see s 35, post.

8–20654F 22. Return of licences, etc. (1) The holder of a London PHV operator's licence shall return the licence to the licensing authority after the expiry or revocation of that licence, within the period of 7 days after the day on which the licence expires or the revocation takes effect.

(2) The owner[1] of a vehicle to which a London PHV licence relates shall return the licence and the plate or disc which was issued for the vehicle under section 10 to the licensing authority after the expiry or revocation of that licence within the period of 7 days after the day on which the licence expires or the revocation takes effect.

(3) The holder of a London PHV driver's licence shall return the licence and his driver's badge to the licensing authority after the expiry or revocation of that licence, within the period of 7 days after the day on which the licence expires or the revocation takes effect.

(4) On the suspension of a licence under this Act, the licensing authority, a constable or an authorised officer may by notice direct the holder of the licence, or the owner of the vehicle, to return the licence to the authority, constable or officer (as the case may be) within the period of 7 days after the day on which the notice is served on that person.

A direction under this subsection may also direct—

(*a*) the return by the vehicle owner of the disc or plate which was issued for the vehicle under section 10 (in the case of a London PHV licence); or

(*b*) the return by the licence holder of the driver's badge (in the case of a London PHV driver's licence).

(5) A person who without reasonable excuse fails to comply with any requirement or direction under this section to return a licence, disc, plate or badge is guilty of an offence.

(6) A person guilty of an offence under this section is liable on summary conviction—

(*a*) to a fine not exceeding **level 3** on the standard scale; and

(*b*) in the case of a continuing offence, to a fine not exceeding **ten pounds for each day** during which an offence continues after conviction.

(7) A constable or authorised officer is entitled to remove and retain the plate or disc from a vehicle to which an expired, suspended or revoked London PHV licence relates following—

(*a*) a failure to comply with subsection (2) or a direction under subsection (4);

(*b*) a suspension or revocation of the licence which has immediate effect by virtue of section 9(3) or 17(2).

[Private Hire Vehicles (London) Act 1998, s 22, amended by the Greater London Authority Act 1999, s 254.]

1. For "owner" see s 35, post.

8–20654G 23. *Register of licences*

8–20654H 24. *Delegation of functions by the Secretary of State*

8–20655 25. Appeals. (1) This section applies to any appeal which lies under this Act to a magistrates' court against a decision of the licensing authority, a constable or an authorised officer in relation to, or to an application for, a licence under this Act.

(2) If the licensing authority has exercised the power to delegate functions under section 24, such an appeal shall be heard by a magistrates' court.

(3) Any such appeal shall be by way of complaint for an order and the Magistrates' Courts Act 1980 shall apply to the proceedings.

(4) The time within which a person may bring such an appeal is 21 days from the date on which notice of the decision appealed against is served on him.

(5) In the case of a decision where an appeal lies, the notice of the decision shall state the right of appeal to a magistrates' court and the time within which an appeal may be brought.

(6) An appeal against any decision of a magistrates' court in pursuance of an appeal to which this section applies shall lie to the Crown Court at the instance of any party to the proceedings in the magistrates' court.

(7) Where on appeal a court varies or reverses any decision of the licensing authority, a constable or an authorised officer, the order of the court shall be given effect to by the licensing authority or, as the case may be, a constable or authorised officer.

[Private Hire Vehicles (London) Act 1998, s 25, as amended by the Greater London Authority Act 1999, s 254 and SI 2005/886.]

8–20655A 26. Effect of appeal on decision appealed against. (1) If any decision of the licensing authority against which a right of appeal is conferred by this Act—

(*a*) involves the execution of any work or the taking of any action;
(*b*) makes it unlawful for any person to carry on a business which he was lawfully carrying on at the time of the decision,

the decision shall not take effect until the time for appealing has expired or (where an appeal is brought) until the appeal is disposed of or withdrawn.

(2) This section does not apply in relation to a decision to suspend, vary or revoke a licence if the notice of suspension, variation or revocation directs that, in the interests of public safety, the decision is to have immediate effect.
[Private Hire Vehicles (London) Act 1998, s 26.]

8–20655B 27. Obstruction of authorised officers etc. (1) A person who wilfully obstructs a constable or authorised officer acting in pursuance of this Act is guilty of an offence and liable on summary conviction to a fine not exceeding **level 3** on the standard scale.

(2) A person who, without reasonable excuse—

(*a*) fails to comply with any requirement properly made to such person by a constable or authorised officer acting in pursuance of this Act; or
(*b*) fails to give a constable or authorised officer acting in pursuance of this Act any other assistance or information which he may reasonably require of such person for the purpose of performing his functions under this Act,

is guilty of an offence and liable on summary conviction to a fine not exceeding **level 3** on the standard scale.

(3) A person who makes any statement which he knows to be false in giving any information to an authorised officer or constable acting in pursuance of this Act is guilty of an offence and liable on summary conviction to a fine not exceeding **level 5** on the standard scale.
[Private Hire Vehicles (London) Act 1998, s 27.]

8–20655C 28. Penalty for false statements. A person who knowingly or recklessly makes a statement or furnishes information which is false or misleading in any material particular for the purpose of procuring the grant or renewal of a licence under this Act, or the variation of an operator's licence under section 18, is guilty of an offence and liable on summary conviction to a fine not exceeding **level 5** on the standard scale.
[Private Hire Vehicles (London) Act 1998, s 28.]

8–20655D 29. Saving for vehicles used for funerals and weddings. Nothing in this Act applies to any vehicle whose use as a private hire vehicle is limited to use in connection with funerals or weddings.
[Private Hire Vehicles (London) Act 1998, s 29.]

Further controls

8–20656 30. Prohibition of certain signs, notices etc. (1) The Secretary of State may make regulations prohibiting the display in London on or from vehicles (other than licensed taxis and public service vehicles) of any sign, notice or other feature of a description specified in the regulations.

(2) Before making the regulations the Secretary of State shall consult such bodies appearing to him to represent the London cab trade and the private hire vehicle trade in London as he considers appropriate.

(3) Any person who—

(*a*) drives a vehicle in respect of which a prohibition imposed by regulations under this section is contravened; or
(*b*) causes or permits such a prohibition to be contravened in respect of any vehicle,

is guilty of an offence and liable on summary conviction to a fine not exceeding **level 4** on the standard scale.
[Private Hire Vehicles (London) Act 1998, s 30.]

8–20656A 31. Prohibition of certain advertisements. (1) This section applies to any advertisement—

(*a*) indicating that vehicles can be hired on application to a specified address in London;
(*b*) indicating that vehicles can be hired by telephone on a telephone number being the number of premises in London; or
(*c*) on or near any premises in London, indicating that vehicles can be hired at those premises.

(2) No such advertisement shall include—

(*a*) any of the following words, namely "taxi", "taxis", "cab" or "cabs", or
(*b*) any word so closely resembling any of those words as to be likely to be mistaken for it,

(whether alone or as part of another word), unless the vehicles offered for hire are London cabs.

(3) An advertisement which includes the word "minicab", "mini-cab" or "mini cab" (whether in the singular or plural) does not by reason only of that fact contravene this section.

(4) Any person who issues, or causes to be issued, an advertisement which contravenes this section is guilty of an offence and liable on summary conviction to a fine not exceeding **level 4** on the standard scale.

(5) It is a defence for a person charged with an offence under this section to prove[1] that—

(*a*) he is a person whose business it is to publish or arrange for the publication of advertisements;
(*b*) he received the advertisement in question for publication in the ordinary course of business; and
(*c*) he did not know and had no reason to suspect that its publication would amount to an offence under this section.

(6) In this section—

"advertisement" includes every form of advertising (whatever the medium) and references to the issue of an advertisement shall be construed accordingly;
"telephone number" includes any number used for the purposes of communicating with another by electronic means; and "telephone" shall be construed accordingly.
[Private Hire Vehicles (London) Act 1998, s 31.]

1. An accused who raises this defence is not required to establish it beyond reasonable doubt, but on the balance of probabilities: see *R v Carr-Briant* [1943] KB 607, [1943] 2 All ER 156, 107 JP 167.

Miscellaneous and supplementary

8–20656B 32. Regulations[1]

1. See the Private Hire Vehicles (London) (Operators' Licences) Regulations 2000, SI 2000/3146.

8–20657 33. Offences due to fault of other person. (1) Where an offence by any person under this Act is due to the act or default of another person, then (whether proceedings are taken against the first mentioned person or not) that other person is guilty of the offence and is liable to be proceeded against and punished accordingly.

(2) Where an offence under this Act committed by a body corporate is proved to have been committed with the consent or connivance of, or attributable to any neglect on the part of, any director, manager, secretary or other similar officer of the body corporate (or any person purporting to act in that capacity), he as well as the body corporate is guilty of the offence is liable to be proceeded against and punished accordingly.
[Private Hire Vehicles (London) Act 1998, s 33.]

8–20657A 34. Service of notices. (1) Any notice authorised or required under this Act to be given to any person may be served by post.

(2) For the purposes of section 7 of the Interpretation Act 1978 any such notice is properly addressed to a London PHV operator if it is addressed to him at any operating centre of his in London.

(3) Any notice authorised or required under this Act to be given to the owner of a vehicle shall be deemed to have been effectively given if it is given to the person who is for the time being notified to the Secretary of State for the purposes of this Act as the owner of the vehicle (or, if more than one person is currently notified as the owner, if it is given to any of them).
[Private Hire Vehicles (London) Act 1998, s 34.]

8–20657B 35. References to the owner of a vehicle. (1) For the purposes of this Act the owner of a vehicle shall be taken to be the person by whom it is kept.

(2) In determining, in the course of any proceedings for an offence under this Act, who was the owner of a vehicle at any time it shall be presumed that the owner was the person who was the registered keeper of the vehicle at that time.

(3) Notwithstanding that presumption—

(*a*) it is open to the defence to show that the person who was the registered keeper of a vehicle at any particular time was not the person by whom the vehicle was kept at that time; and (*b*) it is open to the prosecution to prove that the vehicle was kept at that time by some person other than the registered keeper.

(4) In this section "registered keeper", in relation to a vehicle, means the person in whose name the vehicle was registered under the Vehicle Excise and Registration Act 1994[1].
[Private Hire Vehicles (London) Act 1998, s 35.]

1. In PART VII: TRANSPORT, title ROAD TRAFFIC, ante.

8–20658 36. Interpretation. In this Act, unless the context otherwise requires—

"authorised officer" means an officer authorised in writing by the Secretary of State for the purposes of this Act;
"controlled district" means an area for which Part II of the 1976 Act is in force by virtue of a resolution passed by a district council under section 45 of that Act;
"driver's badge" means the badge issued to the holder of a London PHV driver's licence;
"hackney carriage" means a vehicle licensed under section 37 of the Town Police Clauses Act 1847 or any similar enactment;
"licensed taxi" means a hackney carriage, a London cab or a taxi licensed under Part II of the 1982 Act;
"London" means the area consisting of the metropolitan police district and the City of London (including the Temples);
"London cab" means a vehicle licensed under section 6 of the Metropolitan Public Carriage Act 1869;
"London PHV driver's licence" means a licence under section 13;
"London PHV licence" means a licence under section 7;
"London PHV operator" has the meaning given in section 4(1);
"London PHV operator's licence" means a licence under section 2;
"notice" means notice in writing;
"operating centre" has the meaning given in section 1(5);
"operator" has the meaning given in section 1(1);
"prescribed" means prescribed in regulations under section 32(1);
"private hire vehicle" has the meaning given in section 1(1);
"public service vehicle" has the same meaning as in the Public Passenger Vehicles Act 1981,
"road" means any length of highway or of any other road to which the public has access (including bridges over which a road passes);
"the 1976 Act" means the Local Government (Miscellaneous Provisions) Act 1976;
"the 1982 Act" means the Civic Government (Scotland) Act 1982; and
"vehicle" means a mechanically propelled vehicle (other than a tramcar) intended or adapted for use on roads.
[Private Hire Vehicles (London) Act 1998, s 36.]

8–20659 37. Power to make transitional etc provisions. (1) The Secretary of State may by regulations[1] make such transitional provisions and such savings as he considers necessary or expedient in preparation for, in connection with, or in consequence of—

(*a*) the coming into force of any provision of this Act; or
(*b*) the operation of any enactment repealed or amended by a provision of this Act during any period when the repeal or amendment is not wholly in force.

(2) Regulations under this section may modify any enactment contained in this or in any other Act.

(3) Before making regulations under this section the Secretary of State shall consult the licensing authority.
[Private Hire Vehicles (London) Act 1998, s 37, as amended by the Greater London Authority Act 1999, Sch 21.]

1. See the Private Hire Vehicles (London) (Operators' Licences) Regulations 2000, SI 2000/3146. See also the Private Hire Vehicles (London) (Transitional and Saving Provisions) Regulations 2003, SI 2003/655 amended by SI 2003/3028 and the Private Hire Vehicles (London) (Transitional Provisional) Regulations 2004, SI 2004/242.

8–20659A 39. *Consequential amendments and repeals*

8–20659B 40. *Short title, commencement and extent*

Miscellaneous

Greater London Council (General Powers) Act 1981

(1981 c xvii)

PART I[1]

PRELIMINARY

8–20660 1. Short title. This Act may be cited as the Greater London Council (General Powers) Act 1981.

[Greater London Council (General Powers) Act 1981, s 1.]

1. Part I contains ss 1, 2.

8–20661 2. Interpretation. In this Act, except as otherwise expressly provided or unless the context otherwise requires—

"the Act of 1936" means the Public Health Act 1936;

"borough council" means London borough council and includes the Common Council of the City of London; and "borough" shall be construed accordingly;

"the Council" means the Greater London Council;

"daily fine" means a fine for each day on which an offence is continued after conviction thereof.

[Greater London Council (General Powers) Act 1981, s 2.]

PART II[1]

PROVISIONS RELATING TO THE COUNCIL

8–20662 3–6. *Increased penalties, amendments and other provisions.*

1. Part II contains ss 3–6.

PART IV[1]

PROVISIONS RELATING TO CONTROL BY BOROUGH COUNCILS OF OVERCROWDING IN CERTAIN HOSTELS

8–20663 8. Meaning of "hostel". In this Part of this Act "hostel" means any premises in which there is provided on payment sleeping accommodation, whether with or without the provision of board or facilities for the preparation of food, in one or more common dormitories or other sleeping areas, if in any one of those areas four or more persons, not all being members of the same family or of the same household, are accommodated at the same time.

[Greater London Council (General Powers) Act 1981, s 8.]

1. Part IV contains ss 8–16.

8–20664 9. Overcrowding in hostels. (1) If on or after 1 January 1982 it appears to a borough council that premises in the borough are being used as a hostel and that excessive numbers of persons are being accommodated in the premises having regard to any of the following matters, that is to say:

(*a*) the size and condition of the rooms available;

(*b*) the adequacy of the means of lighting, heating, sanitation, ventilation or (where appropriate) food storage or preparation provided in the premises;

(*c*) the adequacy of the personal washing facilities so provided; the borough council may serve on the occupier of the premises or on any person having the control and management thereof, or on both, a notice—

(i) stating, in relation to any room on the premises, or to any part of the premises not being a room, the maximum number of persons (if any) by whom it may be occupied as sleeping accommodation at any one time, or, as the case may be, that it shall not be occupied as aforesaid; and

(ii) informing him of the effect of section 12 (Part IV penalties) of this Act:

Provided that a notice under this subsection shall not apply limits in relation to the number of persons who may occupy any room on the premises, or any part of the premises not being a room, which are more onerous than any limits for the time being applied to the premises by a registration scheme under section 346 of the Housing Act 1985, a direction under section 354 of that Act, or an overcrowding notice under section 358 of that Act.

(2) For the purposes of the foregoing subsection a notice may, in relation to any room, prescribe special maxima applicable in any case where some or all of the persons occupying the room are under such age as may be specified in the notice.

(3) A notice served under this section shall, if no appeal is brought under section 10 (Part IV appeals) of this Act, become operative in relation to the premises to which it relates on the expiration

of twenty-one days from the date of service of the notice and shall be final and conclusive as to any matters which could have been raised on such an appeal, and any such notice against which an appeal is brought shall, if and so far as it is confirmed by the court, or if the appeal is withdrawn, become operative as from the date of the determination of the appeal, or of the withdrawal thereof, as the case may be.
[Greater London Council (General Powers) Act 1981, s 9, as amended by the Housing (Consequential Provisions) Act 1985, Sch 2.]

8–20665 **10. Part IV appeals.** Any person aggrieved by a notice under section 9 (Overcrowding in hostels) of this Act may, within twenty-one days after the service of the notice, appeal to a magistrates' court, and on any such appeal the court may make such order either confirming or quashing or varying the notice as the court thinks fit.
[Greater London Council (General Powers) Act 1981, s 10.]

8–20666 **11. Exhibition of notice.** Any person occupying or having the control and management of premises in respect of which a notice under section 9 (Overcrowding in hostels) of this Act has become operative shall keep exhibited in a suitable place, to be specified in the notice, in the premises to which the notice relates a copy of the notice in the form in which it has come into effect, and if without reasonable excuse he fails to do so he shall be guilty of an offence and liable on summary conviction to a fine not exceeding **level 2** on the standard scale and to a daily fine not exceeding **£5**.
[Greater London Council (General Powers) Act 1981, s 11, as amended by the Criminal Justice Act 1982, s 46.]

8–20667 **12. Part IV penalties.** (1) Any person who, while a notice is operative in pursuance of the provisions of this Part of this Act, knowingly causes or permits any room or other part of the premises to which the notice relates to be occupied as sleeping accommodation otherwise than in accordance with the notice shall be guilty of an offence:

Provided that a person shall not be convicted of an offence under this section where the facts which would otherwise have given rise to such an offence are, so far as is relevant, the same as the facts giving rise to an offence for which that person has been convicted under section 355(2) or 358(4) of the Housing Act 1985.

(2) Any person committing an offence under this section shall be liable on summary conviction to a fine not exceeding **level 4** on the standard scale.
[Greater London Council (General Powers) Act 1981, s 12, as amended by the Criminal Justice Act 1982, s 46 and the Housing (Consequential Provisions) Act 1985, Sch 2.]

8–20668 **13. Withdrawal of notice.** Where a borough council have served a notice under section 9 (Overcrowding in hostels) of this Act in respect of any premises, they may at any time withdraw the notice, without prejudice to anything done in pursuance thereof or to the service of another notice, or, if there is any material change of circumstances, they may substitute for the notice a further notice under the said section 9.
[Greater London Council (General Powers) Act 1981, s 13.]

8–20669 **14. Powers of entry for inspection, etc.** (1) An authorised officer of a borough council (on producing, if so required, some duly authenticated document showing his authority) may enter upon, inspect and examine any premises used, or which he has reasonable cause to believe are used, or intended to be used, as a hostel and may do all such things as are reasonably necessary for the purpose—

(*a*) of ascertaining whether or not circumstances exist which would authorise the borough council to take any action under this Part of this Act;
(*b*) of preparing a notice under subsection (1) of section 9 (Overcrowding in hostels) of this Act; or
(*c*) of ascertaining whether there is, or has been any contravention of the provisions of this Part of this Act.

(2) Any person who intentionally obstructs any person acting in the exercise of his powers under this section shall be guilty of an offence and liable on summary conviction to a fine not exceeding **level 3** on the standard scale.

(3) The provisions of subsections (2), (3) and (4) of section 287 (which confers powers to enter on premises) of the Act of 1936 shall apply in respect of entry into any premises for the purposes of this section as they apply to entry into premises for the purposes of subsection (1) of that section.
[Greater London Council (General Powers) Act 1981, s 14, as amended by the Criminal Justice Act 1982, s 46.]

8–20670 **15. Evidence in legal proceedings.** If in any proceedings under this Part of this Act it is alleged that persons occupying any premises or part thereof are members of the same family or of the same household, the burden of proving that allegation shall rest upon the person by whom it is made.
[Greater London Council (General Powers) Act 1981, s 15.]

8–20671 **16. Exemption for certain premises.** Nothing in this Part of this Act shall apply to any premises used as a hostel being premises—

(*a*) occupied, used or managed by the Crown, by the Common Council of the City of London or by an authority or body established by or under any enactment or operating under Royal Charter;

(*b*) (not being premises referred to in the foregoing paragraph) occupied, used or managed by a school within the meaning of the Education Act 1996, by a university established by any enactment or operating under Royal Charter or by any college, school or similar institution forming part of, or connected with, such a university;

(*c*) occupied, used or managed by a polytechnic designated by the Secretary of State;

(*d*) (not being premises referred to in paragraph (*a*) or (*b*) above) occupied, used or managed by any college, school or similar institution assisted by a local education authority;

(*e*) (*Repealed*);

(*f*) used as a hospital by virtue of any enactment or under Royal Charter;

(*g*) used as a nursing home or a mental nursing home as defined in the Nursing Homes Act 1975;

(*gg*) used as a children's home as defined in section 63 of the Children Act 1989;

(*h*) used as a voluntary home as defined in section 60 of the Children Act 1989 and which—

(i) are registered under section 60;

(ii) are an assisted community home within the meaning of section 53 of that Act;

(*i*) liable to be inspected under section 67 of the Children Act 1989;

(*j*) (*repealed*);

(*k*) occupied, used or managed by any person who is in receipt of a grant by virtue of regulations made under section 485 of the Education Act 1996;

(*l*) occupied, used or managed by a registered social landlord within the meaning of the Housing Act 1985 (see section 5(4) and (5) of that Act);

(*m*) occupied, used or managed, for the purposes specified in paragraph 4 of Schedule 5 to the Supplementary Benefits Act 1976, by a voluntary organisation which is in receipt of contributions from the Secretary of State under the said paragraph 4;

(*n*) approved by the Secretary of State under section 49(1) of the Powers of Criminal Courts Act 1973; or

(*o*) occupied, used or managed by any society or individual in receipt of a payment in respect of those premises under section 51(3)(*f*) of the said Act of 1973.

[Greater London Council (General Powers) Act 1981, s 16, as amended by the Housing (Consequential Provisions) Act 1985, Sch 2, the Children Act 1989, Sch 13, the Education Act 1996, Sch. 37, SI 1996/2325 and SI 1997/221 and the Care Standards Act 2000, s 116.]

PART V[1]

FURTHER PROVISIONS RELATING TO BOROUGH COUNCILS

8–20673 **18. Stopping up of streets.** (1) Subject to the provisions of this section, if it appears to a magistrates' court, after a view, if the court thinks fit, by any two or more of the justices composing the court, that a street in a borough (other than the City of London or the Royal Borough of Kensington and Chelsea) or any part thereof (not being—

(*a*) a trunk road;

(*b*) a special road;

(*c*) a metropolitan road;

(*d*) a street forming part of the route of a stage carriage or express carriage service; or

(*e*) except with the consent of the British Railways Board, a street belonging to that board);

in respect of which a borough council have made an application to the court under this section—

(i) is temporarily not required to afford either vehicular access or both vehicular and pedestrian access to any premises or to secure the expeditious, convenient and safe movement of, as the case may be, either vehicular traffic or both vehicular traffic and foot passengers; and

(ii) is being used for the unauthorised deposit of refuse;

the court may by order authorise the borough council to stop up the street or that part thereof either to vehicular traffic or to both vehicular traffic and foot passengers, as the case may be, for such period not exceeding two years as may be specified in the order.

(2) Not later than twenty-eight days before the day on which the application is heard the borough council shall—

(*a*) cause a copy of a notice stating their intention to apply for the order, specifying the time and place at which the application is to be made and the terms of the order applied for (embodying a plan showing what will be the effect thereof) to be displayed in a prominent position at the ends of the street or part thereof in respect of which the application is to be made and shall serve a copy of that notice on the Council; and

(*b*) publish in a local newspaper circulating in the borough a copy of the said notice except that there may be substituted for the plan a statement of a place in the borough where the plan may be inspected free of charge at all reasonable hours; and

(*c*) deliver a copy of the said notice together with a copy of the plan to each owner and occupier of land adjoining the street or part thereof in respect of which the application is to be made; and (*d*) deliver a copy of the said notice together with a copy of the plan to the Commissioner of Police of the Metropolis and to the Chief Officer of the London Ambulance Service.

(3) Before implementing an order for stopping up a street or part thereof under this section, the borough council shall serve a copy of the order on the Council, on any statutory undertaker affected and on any universal service provider (within the meaning of the Postal Services Act 2000) who provides a universal postal service (within the meaning of that Act) in an area which includes the street or part thereof to which the order applies.

(4) At any time when an order under this section is in force application may be made to a magistrates' court by the borough council or the Council, if they consider that the street or part thereof is required to secure the expeditious, convenient and safe movement of vehicular traffic or foot passengers, or by any person who wishes to use the street or part thereof to afford vehicular or pedestrian access to any premises, for the order to be rescinded or modified, and if it appears to the court that the street or part thereof is required to afford vehicular or pedestrian access to any premises or to secure the expeditious, convenient and safe movement of vehicular traffic or foot passengers the court shall by order rescind or modify the order made under this section.

(5) On the hearing of an application under this section the borough council, the Council, the applicant, any person who uses the street and any other person who would be aggrieved by the making of the order the subject of the application shall have a right to be heard.

(6) The provisions of section 41 (which imposes duties as to the maintenance of certain highways) of the Highways Act 1980 shall not apply in respect of any street or to any part thereof while that street or that part thereof, as the case may be, is stopped up to both vehicular traffic and foot passengers pursuant to an order of the court under subsection (1) of this section.

(7) Part II of Schedule 12 to the said Act of 1980 shall apply where—

(*a*) in pursuance of an order under this section a street or part of a street is stopped up to traffic; and

(*b*) immediately before the order is made there is in, upon, over, along or across the street any apparatus belonging to or used by any statutory undertakers for the purpose of their undertaking;

as if in that Schedule references to section 116 (which relates to the stopping up or diversion of highways) of the said Act of 1980 were references to this section.

(8) Where any street or part of a street is stopped up either to vehicular traffic or to both vehicular traffic and foot passengers under this section, the borough council shall afford vehicular access thereto to the British Railways Board, any universal service provider (within the meaning of the Postal Services Act 2000) who requires such access in connection with the provision of a universal postal service (within the meaning of that Act) and, without prejudice to paragraphs 18 and 19 of Part III of Schedule 9 to the London Government Act 1963, the Thames Water Authority.

(9) *Consequential provisions relating to the Post Office.*

(10) In this section the expression "telegraphic line" has the same meaning as in the Telegraph Act 1878.

[Greater London Council (General Powers) Act 1981, s 18, as amended by SI 2001/648.]

---

1. Part V contains ss 17–19.

8–20674 **19. Acupuncturists, tattooists and cosmetic piercers.** (1) As from the appointed day in any borough a person shall not in that borough carry on the practice of acupuncture or the business of tattooing or cosmetic piercing unless he is registered by the borough council in respect of that practice or business under this section; and he shall not carry on any such practice or business on premises occupied by him unless the premises are so registered.

(2) Subject to subsection (9)(*b*) of this section, on application for registration under this section the borough council shall register the applicant and, if the application specifies premises, those premises, and shall issue to the applicant a certificate of registration.

(3) The person making an application under this section shall when making the same pay to the borough council such amount as may be determined from time to time by resolution of the borough council as being appropriate and as may be sufficient in the aggregate to cover in whole or in part—

(*a*) the reasonable cost of carrying out inspections of premises for the purpose of determining whether any byelaws made under this section are being complied with; and

(*b*) any reasonable administrative or other cost incurred by the borough council in connection with the registration of persons or premises under this section.

(4) The borough council may make byelaws for the purpose of securing—

(*a*) the cleanliness of premises required to be registered under this section and the sterilising, so far as is appropriate, of the instruments, towels, materials and equipment used in connection with the practice or business;

(*b*) the cleanliness of persons engaged in such practice or business in regard to both themselves and their clothing; and (*c*) that books, cards or forms are kept by persons registered under this section recording their activities in connection with the practice or business in respect of which they are so registered and that appropriate entries are made in such books, cards or forms;

and different provisions may be made by such byelaws as respects the different kinds of practice or business to which this section applies.

(5) Nothing in this section shall extend to the practice of acupuncture or the business of tattooing or cosmetic piercing by or under the supervision of a registered medical practitioner or to the practice of acupuncture by a dentist registered under the Dentists Act [1984] or to premises on which the practice of acupuncture or the business of tattooing or cosmetic piercing, as the case may be, is carried on by or under the supervision of a registered medical practitioner or on which the practice of acupuncture is carried on by or under the supervision of a dentist registered as aforesaid.

(6) Any person who without reasonable excuse contravenes subsection (1) above shall be guilty of an offence and liable on summary conviction to a fine not exceeding **level 3** on the standard scale.

(7) Any person who contravenes any byelaw made under subsection (4) above shall be guilty of an offence and liable on summary conviction to a fine not exceeding **level 2** on the standard scale and, if he is registered under this section, the court by which he is convicted may, instead of, or in addition to, imposing a fine, order the suspension or cancellation of his registration and of the registration of the premises in which the offence was committed if they are occupied by him.

(8) A court ordering the suspension or cancellation of registration under subsection (7) above may suspend the operation of the order until the expiration of the period prescribed under section 14 (which confers powers to make Crown Court rules) of the Courts Act 1971 for giving notice of appeal to the Crown Court:

Provided that if notice of appeal is given within the said period an order made under this subsection shall be suspended until the appeal is finally determined or abandoned.

(9) Where the registration of any person is cancelled by order of a court under subsection (7) above—

(*a*) he shall within seven days deliver up to the borough council the cancelled certificate of registration, and if without reasonable excuse he fails to do so, he shall be guilty of an offence and liable on summary conviction to a fine not exceeding **level 2** on the standard scale and to a daily fine not exceeding **£5**; and

(*b*) he shall not again be registered by a borough council under this section in respect of the practice or business in question except in pursuance of a further order of a magistrates' court made on his application.

(10) The occupier of premises registered under this section shall keep a copy of any byelaw made relating to his practice of acupuncture or business of tattooing or cosmetic piercing, as the case may be, and of the certificate of registration of the premises issued under this section prominently displayed in the premises; and if without reasonable excuse he fails to do so he shall be guilty of an offence and liable on summary conviction to a fine not exceeding **level 2** on the standard scale and to a daily fine not exceeding **£5**.

(11)

(*a*) Section 287 (which confers powers to enter on premises) of the Act of 1936 shall have effect as if references therein to that Act included a reference to this section.

(b) Any person who intentionally obstructs any person acting in the exercise of his powers under this subsection shall be guilty of an offence and liable on summary conviction to a fine not exceeding **level 3** on the standard scale.

(12) In this section "premises" includes a stall and "cosmetic piercing" means the piercing of any part of the body for cosmetic purposes.

(13)

(*a*) In this section "the appointed day" means such day as may be fixed in relation to a borough by resolution of the borough council, subject to and in accordance with the provisions of this subsection.

(*b*) The borough council shall cause to be published in one or more local newspapers circulating in the borough notice—

(i) of the passing of any such resolution and of the day fixed thereby;

(ii) of the general effect of the provisions of this section coming into operation as from that day;

and the day so fixed shall not be earlier than the expiration of twenty-eight days from the date of first publication of the said notice.

(*c*) Either a photostatic or other reproduction certified by the proper officer of the borough to be a true reproduction of a page, or part of a page, of any such newspaper being a page or part bearing the date of its publication and containing any such notice shall be evidence of the publication of the notice and of the date of publication.

(*d*) Different appointed days may be fixed for the different kinds of practice or business to which this section applies.

[Greater London Council (General Powers) Act 1981, s 19, as amended by the Criminal Justice Act 1982, s 46.]

PART VI[1]
MISCELLANEOUS AND SUPPLEMENTAL

8–20675 20. Application of Shops Act 1950 to exhibition and conference premises. (1) Sections 1, 2, 8 and 47 of the Shops Act 1950 shall not apply to—

(*a*) a shop to which this section applies at any of the scheduled premises during the course of an exhibition, trade fair or conference at those premises and in the period when works or facilities in respect of that exhibition, trade fair or conference are being provided or removed; and

(*b*) a stand provided at any of the scheduled premises, whether in a building or in the open, while used for the purposes, and as part, of an exhibition, trade fair or conference at any of the scheduled premises.

(2) A shop to which this section applies is a permanent shop used for the carrying on of any retail trade or business and forming part of any of the scheduled premises if that shop is being used for the purposes of, or in connection with, an exhibition, trade fair or conference at those premises and is being used, as the case may be, either—

(*a*) as part of that exhibition, trade fair or conference; or

(*b*) for the serving of persons engaged in the provision or removal of works or facilities in respect of that exhibition, trade fair or conference.

(3) In this section—

"the scheduled premises" means the premises described in Schedule 3 to this Act; and
"stand" includes any platform, structure, space or other area.

[Greater London Council (General Powers) Act 1981, s 20.]

1. Part VI contains ss 20–23.

8–20676 21. Liability of directors, etc. Where an offence under Part IV or section 19 (Acupuncturists, tattooists and cosmetic piercers) of this Act, or against any byelaw made under the said section 19 committed by a body corporate is proved to have been committed with the consent or connivance of, or to be attributable to any neglect on the part of, a director, manager, secretary or other similar officer of the body corporate or any person who was purporting to act in any such capacity, he, as well as the body corporate, shall be guilty of that offence.

[Greater London Council (General Powers) Act 1981, s 21.]

8–20677

Section 20 SCHEDULE 3

PREMISES IN GREATER LONDON IN RESPECT OF WHICH CERTAIN PROVISIONS OF THE SHOPS ACT 1950 SHALL NOT APPLY DURING EXHIBITIONS, TRADE FAIRS AND CONFERENCES

(*Amended by the Greater London Council (General Powers) Act 1983, s 7.*)

1. Alexandra Palace, Wood Green, London N22.
2. Barbican Centre for Arts and Conferences and North Barbican Exhibition Halls, London EC2.
3. Earl's Court, Warwick Road, London SW5.
4. Olympia, Blythe Road and Hammersmith Road, London W14.
5. Royal Festival Hall, South Bank, London SE1.
6. Wembley Conference Centre and Wembley Arena, Wembley, Middlesex.
7. Premises, forming part of the World Trade Centre, known as International House, St. Katherine's Way, London E1 and Europe House, and Ivory House, East Smithfield, London E1.

Greater London Council (General Powers) Act 1982

(1982 c i)

PART I
PRELIMINARY

8–20781 2. Interpretation. In this Act, except as otherwise expressly provided or unless the context otherwise requires—

"the Act of 1972" means the Greater London Council (General Powers) Act 1972;
"borough council" means London borough council and includes the Common Council of the City of London, and "borough" shall be construed accordingly;
"the Council" means the Greater London Council;
"the Kensington and Chelsea Council" means the council of the Royal Borough of Kensington and Chelsea; and
"local authority" means the Council or a borough council.

[Greater London Council (General Powers) Act 1982, s 2.]

PART II
PROVISIONS RELATING TO THE COUNCIL AND TO BOROUGH COUNCILS

8–20782 **4. Removal of vehicles illegally parked on housing estates.** (1) The powers of a local authority under section 23(1) of the Housing Act 1985 (byelaws for regulation of authority's houses) as extended by section 7 (Byelaws as to parking, etc, on housing estates) of the Greater London Council (General Powers) Act 1975, to make byelaws prohibiting or regulating the parking or use of vehicles on any land held by them for the purposes of Part II of the Housing Act of 1985, not being a highway, shall include power to make byelaws with respect to—

(*a*) the removal from any place on such land (whether to any other such place or to some other place) of any vehicle left there in contravention of the byelaws;
(*b*) the safe custody of any such vehicle so removed;
(*c*) the taking of such steps as are reasonable to find a person appearing to them to be the owner of the vehicle;
(*d*) following the taking of such steps, the disposal (which may include the destruction in the case of a vehicle which in the opinion of the local authority is in such a condition that it ought to be destroyed) of any such vehicle which appears to the local authority to be abandoned in such circumstances as may be prescribed in the byelaws;
(*e*) the imposition of charges for such removal, safe custody or disposal and the recovery of those charges from any person responsible; and
(*f*) the payment to the owner of the vehicle of the balance, if any, of the proceeds of such disposal after deduction of the charges imposed in respect of such removal, safe custody and disposal.

(2) While a vehicle is in the custody of a local authority in pursuance of byelaws made under section 23(1) of the Housing Act 1985, other than a vehicle which in their opinion is in such a condition that it ought to be destroyed, it shall be their duty to take such steps as are reasonably necessary for the safe custody of the vehicle.

(3) In this section—

"person responsible" in relation to a vehicle means—

(*a*) the owner of the vehicle at the time when it was put in the place from which it was removed, unless he shows that he was not concerned in, and did not know of, its being there;
(*b*) any person by whom it was put in the place aforesaid; and

"vehicle" has the same meaning as in section 17 of the Act of 1972.

[Greater London Council (General Powers) Act 1982, s 4, as amended by the Housing (Consequential Provisions) Act 1985, Sch 2.]

8–20783 **5. Repair, etc, of vehicles on highways.** *Repealed.*

Greater London Council (General Powers) Act 1984

(1984 c xxvii)

PART I[1]
PRELIMINARY

8–20801 **2. Interpretation.** In this Act, except as otherwise expressly provided or unless the context otherwise requires—

"the Act of 1963" means the London Government Act 1963;
"the Act of 1968" means the Greater London Council (General Powers) Act 1968;
"the Act of 1971" means the Town and Country Planning Act 1971;
"borough council" means London borough council and includes the Common Council of the City of London; and "borough" shall be construed accordingly; and
"the Council" means the Greater London Council.

[Greater London Council (General Powers) Act 1984, s 2.]

1. Part I contains ss 1, 2.

PART VII[1]
OTHER PROVISIONS RELATING TO BOROUGH COUNCILS

8–20802 **37. Removal of occupants of dangerous buildings in outer London.** (1) If it appears to an outer London borough council that any building in the borough is in such a condition as to be dangerous to its occupants, that council may apply to a magistrates' court and the court may make an order directing that any occupants of the building be removed therefrom by a constable.

(2)

(*a*) Where a magistrates' court has made an order under the foregoing subsection it shall not be lawful for the building to be occupied unless the dangerous state thereof has been remedied to the satisfaction of the outer London borough council or a magistrates' court has revoked the order.

(*b*) Any person who, knowing that an order has been made by a magistrates' court under the foregoing subsection in respect of a building, occupies that building in contravention of this subsection or permits it to be so occupied, shall be liable on summary conviction to a fine not exceeding **level 5** on the standard scale.

(3) In this section—

"building" includes any structure or erection and any part of a building as so defined; and "outer London borough council" means the council of an outer London borough.

[Greater London Council (General Powers) Act 1984, s 37.]

1. Part VII contains ss 36–41.

8–20803 38. Removal of occupants of buildings in vicinity of dangerous structures, etc. (1)

(*a*) This section applies where—

(i) in an inner London borough or the City of London, the district surveyor, or any surveyor required to make a survey under section 61 of the London Building Acts (Amendment) Act 1939, has certified under section 62 of that Act that a structure is in a dangerous state; or

(ii) in an outer London borough, it appears to the council of that borough that any building is in such a condition, or is used to carry such loads, as to be dangerous.

(*b*) In this subsection "structure" has the meaning assigned to it in section 60 of the said Act of 1939.

(2) Where this section applies and it appears to a borough council that the occupants of any building are in danger by reason of—

(*a*) the proximity of that building to any such structure or building as is referred to in the foregoing subsection; or

(*b*) any works being carried out, or proposed to be carried out, to any such structure or building as aforesaid for the purpose of remedying its dangerous state or condition;

the borough council may apply to a magistrates' court and the court may make an order directing that any occupants of the first-mentioned building be removed therefrom by a constable.

(3)

(*a*) Before applying to a magistrates' court for an order under the last foregoing subsection, a borough council shall give notice of the application to the occupants of the building in respect of which the application is made.

(*b*) Notwithstanding subsection (9) of that section, section 233 (which relates to the service of notices by local authorities) of the Local Government Act 1972 shall apply to the giving of notice under this subsection other than by the Common Council of the City of London.

(4)

(*a*) Where a magistrates' court has made an order under subsection (2) of this section it shall not be lawful for the building in respect of which the order was made to be occupied unless the danger has been removed, or the works have been completed, as the case may be, to the satisfaction of the borough council or a magistrates' court has revoked the order.

(*b*) Any person who, knowing that an order has been made by a magistrates' court under subsection (2) of this section in respect of a building, occupies that building in contravention of this subsection or permits it to be so occupied, shall be liable on summary conviction to a fine not exceeding **level 5** on the standard scale.

(5) An application may be made under subsection (2) of this section, and a magistrates' court may make an order under that subsection, in respect of a building in the proximity of such a structure as is referred to in sub-paragraph (*a*)(i) of subsection (1) of this section, or where the works described in paragraph (*b*) of the said subsection (2) are being carried out, or are proposed to be carried out, to such a structure, notwithstanding that the owner of the structure has served on the borough council a written requirement under section 63 of the said Act of 1939.

(6) In this section, "building" includes any structure or erection and any part of a building as so defined.

[Greater London Council (General Powers) Act 1984, s 38.]

8–20804 39. Occupants removed from buildings to have priority housing need. For the purposes of Part VII of the Housing Act 1996 (homelessness) a person who resides in any building in respect of which an order has been made by a magistrates' court under section 37 (Removal of occupants of dangerous buildings in outer London) or section 38 (Removal of occupants of buildings

in vicinity of dangerous structures, etc) of this Act shall be treated as if he were homeless or threatened with homelessness as a result of an emergency such as flood, fire or other disaster.
[Greater London Council (General Powers) Act 1984, s 39, as amended by the Housing (Consequential Provisions) Act 1985, Sch 2 and the Housing Act 1996, Sch 17.]

London Local Authorities Act 1994

(1994 c xii)

8–20810 **1. Short title and commencement.** This Act may be cited as the London Local Authorities Act 1994 and except section 5 (Night café licensing) of this Act shall come into operation at the end of the period of two months beginning with the date on which it is passed[1].
[London Local Authorities Act 1994, s 1.]

1. This Act was passed on 21 July 1994.

8–20811 **2. Interpretation.** In this Act, except as otherwise expressly provided or unless the context otherwise requires—

"the Act of 1990" means the London Local Authorities Act 1990;

Repealed;

"borough council" means London borough council but does not include the Common Council of the City of London; and "borough" shall be construed accordingly.

[London Local Authorities Act 1994, s 2, as amended by the London Local Authorities Act 2004, Sch 4.]

8–20812 **3. Appointed day.** (1) In this Act "the appointed day" means such day as may be fixed in relation to a borough by resolution of the borough council, subject to and in accordance with the provisions of this section.

(2) Different days may be fixed under this section for the purpose of the application of different provisions of this Act to a borough.

(3) The borough council shall cause to be published in a local newspaper circulating in the borough notice—

(*a*) of the passing of any such resolution and of the day fixed thereby; and
(*b*) of the general effect of the provisions of this Act coming into operation as from that day;

and the day so fixed shall not be earlier than the expiration of three months from the publication of the said notice.

(4) Either a photostatic or other reproduction certified by the officer appointed for that purpose by the borough council to be a true reproduction of a page or part of a page of any such newspaper bearing the date of its publication and containing any such notice shall be evidence of the publication of the notice, and of the date of publication.
[London Local Authorities Act 1994, s 3.]

8–20813 **4. Distribution of free literature.** (1) A borough council may designate, in accordance with subsection (9) below, any of the following places, or any part of such places, in the borough as places to which this section applies—

(*a*)

(i) a public off-street car park;
(ii) a recreation ground, park, pleasure ground or open space under the management or control of a local authority; or

(*b*) a street or way to which the public commonly have access, whether or not as of right.

(2) Any person who distributes free literature in a place designated under subsection (1) above without the consent of the borough council or in breach of any condition subject to which the council's consent is given or causes or permits any person so to do shall be guilty of an offence and liable on summary conviction to a fine not exceeding **level 2** on the standard scale.

(3)

(*a*) The reference in subsection (2) above to a person who distributes free literature in a place designated under subsection (1) above shall be deemed to include a reference to a person who distributes free literature on or from land within 7 metres of any designated street who is not—

(i) the owner of that land; or
(ii) the person liable to be assessed to the uniform business rate in respect thereof; or
(iii) on that land with the consent in writing of either of the persons mentioned in sub-paragraphs (i) and (ii) above.

(*b*) Where in any proceedings under this section it is shown that any free literature was distributed by a person on or from land within 7 metres of any street or designated street the burden of proof shall lie on that person to show to the satisfaction of the court that at the relevant time he was a person referred to in sub-paragraph (i) or (ii) of the foregoing paragraph or had the consent referred to in sub-paragraph (iii) thereof.

(4) Where a person is distributing free literature in a place designated under subsection (1) above without the consent of the borough council an authorised officer may seize any supply of that literature which the person has at or near that place.

(5)

(*a*) The following provisions of this subsection shall have effect where any literature is seized under subsection (4) above and references in those provisions to proceedings are to proceedings in respect of the alleged offence in relation to which the literature is seized.

(*b*) Subject to paragraph (*c*) below, at the conclusion of the proceedings the literature shall be returned to the person from whom it was seized unless the court orders it to be forfeited under any enactment.

(*c*) If no proceedings are instituted before the expiration of a period of 28 days beginning with the date of seizure, or any proceedings instituted within that period are discontinued, at the expiration of that period or, as the case may be, on the discontinuance of the proceedings, the literature shall be returned to the person from whom it was seized unless it has not proved possible, after diligent enquiry, to identify that person and ascertain his address.

(*d*) Where the literature is not returned because it has not proved possible to identify the person from whom it was seized and ascertain his address the council may apply to a magistrates' court for an order as to the manner in which they should deal with it.

(6) The conditions of consent referred to in subsection (2) above include, without prejudice to the generality of the power to impose conditions, conditions as to the times or period for which the consent is valid, conditions for the prevention of detriment to the amenities of the area, a condition requiring the person distributing free literature to produce on demand to an authorised officer of the borough council or to a constable documentary evidence of the consent, conditions as to the part of the place designated under subsection (1) above where the consent is to apply and conditions as to the payment for the consent of such reasonable fee to cover the expense of the borough council in dealing with applications for such consents as the borough council may by resolution prescribe; and any such consent may be revoked by notice to the person to whom the consent was given.

(7) The grounds upon which a borough council may withhold consent under subsection (2) above, and may revoke a consent under subsection (6) above are that—

(*a*) the applicant is unsuitable by reason of misconduct;

(*b*) the applicant has within the previous five years been convicted of an offence under this section;

(*c*) there is already a sufficiency of persons to whom consent has been given under this section, carrying out in the designated place the activity in respect of which the consent is requested;

(*d*) there would be a risk of danger or unreasonable inconvenience to users of any highway if the consent is given, or, as the case may be, not revoked;

(*e*) (in the case of a revocation) the applicant has failed to avail himself, or to avail himself to a reasonable extent, of his consent.

(8) A person aggrieved by—

(*a*) the withholding by the borough council of consent referred to in subsection (2) above;

(*b*) the conditions subject to which the borough council give such consent; or

(*c*) the revocation of such consent under subsection (6) above;

may appeal to a magistrates' court by way of complaint for an order and on such an appeal the court may dismiss or allow the appeal or may vary any conditions imposed by the borough council.

(9)

(*a*) Before designating any place under subsection (1) above the borough council shall give notice of their proposal by advertisement in a local newspaper circulating in the borough, and by posting a copy of the notice in the places to which it relates, stating that objections to the proposal may be made to the proper officer of the borough council within a time, not less than 28 days after the giving of the notice, specified in the notice.

(*b*) After taking into consideration any objections made in accordance with paragraph (*a*) above, the borough council may be resolution designate, as places to which this section applies for the purposes of subsection (2) above, all or any, or any part, of the places specified in the notice given under that paragraph.

(10) A resolution under subsection (9)(*b*) above shall come into force on such day as shall be specified by a notice given in the same manner as a notice given under subsection (9)(*a*) above, being a day not less than 28 days after the day on which notice is given under this subsection.

(11) Any resolution under subsection (9)(*b*) above may be rescinded, or varied by the deletion of any place or part of a place, by a subsequent resolution of the borough council.

(12) In proceedings for an offence under section 9 of the Metropolitan Streets Act 1867, it shall be a defence for the accused to show that he was acting with the consent of a borough council under this section and in compliance with any conditions subject to which that consent was given.

(13) This section does not apply to the distribution of free literature—

(*a*) by a charity within the meaning of the Charities Act 1960 where that literature relates to or is for the benefit of that body;

(*b*) by or on behalf of a political organisation;

(*c*) where the person who distributes it does so by putting it into a building or letterbox; or

(*d*) by Transport for London or any or its subsidiaries (within the meaning of the Greater London Authority Act 1999) or any person who provides a service pursuant to—

(i) an agreement made in accordance with section 156 of the Greater London Authority Act 1999, or

(ii) a transport subsidiary's agreement within the meaning of section 169 of that Act.

(14) In this section—

"distribute" means to offer or make available, and includes the placing of free literature on, or affixing it to, a vehicle;

"free literature" means any newspaper, document, card or other literature for which no charge is made to the recipient and which advertises, or contains or comprises an advertisement, for commercial gain.*

[London Local Authorities Act 1994, s 4, as amended by SI 2003/1615.]

***Repealed by the Clean Neighbourhoods and Environment Act 2005, Sch 5 from a date to be appointed.**

8–20815 **10. Liability of directors, etc.** (1) Where an offence under this Act committed by a body corporate is proved to have been committed with the consent or connivance of, or to be attributable to any neglect on the part of, a director, manager, secretary or other similar officer of the body corporate or any person who was purporting to act in any such capacity, he, as well as the body corporate, shall be guilty of the offence.

(2) Where the affairs of a body corporate are managed by its members, subsection (1) above shall apply to the acts and defaults of a member in connection with his functions of management as if he were a director of the body corporate.

[London Local Authorities Act 1994, s 10.]

London Local Authorities Act 1995

(1995 c x)

PART I
PRELIMINARY

8–20816 **1. Citation and commencement.** (1) This Act may be cited as the London Local Authorities Act 1995.

(2) The London Local Authorities Act 1990, the London Local Authorities (No. 2) Act 1990, the London Local Authorities Act 1991, the London Local Authorities Act 1994 and this Act may together be cited as the London Local Authorities Acts 1990 to 1995.

(3) This Act, except Part V (Registration of door supervisors) and, save as otherwise provided by section 15 (Application of Part IV), Part IV (Near beer licensing) shall come into operation at the end of the period of two months beginning with the date on which it is passed.

---

1. Part I contains ss 1–3.

[London Local Authorities Act 1995, s 1.]

8–20817 **2. Interpretation.** In this Act, except as otherwise expressly provided or unless the context otherwise requires—

"the Act of 1984" means the Road Traffic Regulation Act 1984;

"the Act of 1990" means the Town and Country Planning Act 1990;

"the Act of 1991" means the Road Traffic Act 1991;

"authorised officer" means an officer of a participating council authorised by the council in writing to act in relation to the relevant provision of this Act;

"the Commissioner" means the Commissioner of Police of the Metropolis or, in the City of London, the Commissioner of the City Police;

"the fire and rescue authority", in relation to premises, means—

(*a*) where the Regulatory Reform (Fire Safety) Order 2005 applies to the premises, the enforcing authority within the meaning given by article 25 of that Order; or

(*b*) in any other case, the London Fire and Emergency Planning Authority;

"participating council" means the common council of the City of London and the council of any London borough; and "borough" and "council" shall be construed accordingly;

"penalty charge" has the same meaning as in section 66 of the Act of 1991;

"road" has the same meaning as in section 142(1) of the Act of 1984;

"special parking area" means a special parking area designated by an order made by the Secretary of State under section 76(1) of the Act of 1991;*

"traffic sign" has the same meaning as in section 64(1) of the Act of 1984.

[London Local Authorities Act 1995, s 2, as amended by the London Local Authorities Act 1996, s 27, the Greater London Authority Act 1999, Sch 29 and SI 2005/1541.]

***Substituted by definition "special enforcement area" by the Traffic Management Act 2004, Sch 11 from a date to be appointed.**

8–20818 **3. Appointed day.** (1) In this Act "the appointed day" means such day *as may* be fixed in relation to a borough by resolution of the borough council, subject to and in accordance with the provisions of this section.

(2) Different days may be fixed under this section for the purpose of the application of different provisions of this Act to a borough.

(3) The borough council shall cause to be published in a local newspaper circulating in the borough notice—

(*a*) of the passing of any such resolution and of a day fixed thereby; and

(*b*) of the general effect of the provisions of this Act coming into operation as from that day;

and the day so fixed shall not be earlier than the expiration of three months from the publication of the said notice.

(4) Either a photostatic or other reproduction certified by the officer appointed for that purpose by the borough council to be a true reproduction of a page or part of a page of any such newspaper bearing the date of its publication and containing any such notice shall be evidence of the publication of the notice, and of the date of publication.

[London Local Authorities Act 1995, s 3.]

8–20818A

PART II[1]
PARKING

---

1. Part II contains ss 4–9.

8–20818B

PART III[1]
ADVERTISEMENTS, DISPLAYS, ETC.

---

1. Part III contains ss 10–13.

PART IV[1]
NEAR BEER LICENSING

8–20819 **14. Interpretation of Part IV.** In this Part of this Act—

"the Act of 1964" means the Licensing Act 1964;

"near beer premises" means any premises, vehicle, vessel or stall used for a business which—

(*a*) consists to a significant degree in—

(i) the sale to customers for consumption on the premises of liquid refreshments which include in their trade description any of the following words:—beer, lager, pils, shandy, cider, wine, champagne, cocktail, sherry, gin, brandy, whisky, vodka or other words which imply that the liquid refreshment contains or can reasonably be expected to contain alcohol; or

(ii) the sale to customers for consumption on the premises of liquid refreshments which consist of any beverage commonly expected to contain alcohol or calculated to represent any alcoholic beverage; and

(*b*) offers, expressly or by implication, whether on payment of a fee or not, either or both of the following:—

(i) the provision of companions for customers on the premises; or

(ii) the provision of live entertainment on the premises;

but does not include any such premises in which the sale to customers for consumption of alcohol is not a licensable activity under or by virtue of section 173 of the Licensing Act 2003 or in respect of which there is in force—

(A) a premises licence under Part 3 of that Act which authorises the supply of alcohol (within the meaning of section 14 of that Act) for consumption on the premises;

(B) a licence granted by the council under section 21 (Licensing of public exhibitions, etc.) of the Greater London Council (General Powers) Act 1966 or a premises licence granted under Part 3 of the Licensing Act 2003 which authorises the provision of any form of regulated entertainment (within the meaning of Schedule 1 to that Act);

(C) *repealed;*

(D) *repealed;*

(E) *repealed;*

(F) a temporary event notice under the Licensing Act 2003, by virtue of which the premises may be used for the supply of alcohol (within the meaning of section 14 of that Act);

during the hours permitted by such licence or notice:Provided that the premises are in use wholly or mainly and bona fide for the purpose authorised bysuch licence or notice; and does not include any such premises in respect of which there is in force a licence under Part II of the Gaming Act 1968;**

"occupier" in relation to any premises means an occupier who is—

(*a*) the freeholder; or

(*b*) a lessee; or

(*c*) a tenant holding a tenancy of at least one year in duration.

[London Local Authorities Act 1995, s 14 as amended by the Licensing Act 2003, Sch 6.]

***Words substituted by the Gambling Act 2005, Sch 16 from a date to be appointed.**

1. Part IV contains ss 14–28.

8–20820 **15. Application of Part IV.** This Part of this Act applies to the City of Westminster as from the date of commencement and to the boroughs of all other participating councils as from the appointed day.

[London Local Authorities Act 1995, s 15.]

8–20821 **16. Licensing.** (1) No premises shall be used in the borough as near beer premises except under and in accordance with a near beer licence granted under this section by the council.

(2) The council may grant to an applicant and from time to time, renew or transfer a near beer licence on such terms and conditions and subject to such restrictions as may be specified.

(3) Without prejudice to the generality of subsection (2) above, such conditions may relate to—

(*a*) the maintenance of public order and safety;

(*b*) the hours of opening and closing the premises for use as near beer premises to ensure that nuisance is not likely to be caused to residents in the neighbourhood;

(*c*) the display of advertisements on or near the near beer premises and the prohibition of touting in any form;

(*d*) the display of prices of goods and services offered on the premises;

(*e*) the number of persons who may be allowed to be on the premises at any time;

(*f*) the taking of proper precautions against fire, and the maintenance in proper order of means of escape in case of fire, fire-fighting equipment and means of lighting, sanitation and ventilation of the premises;

(*g*) the maintenance in safe condition of means of heating the premises.

(3A) No term, condition or restriction is to be imposed under subsection (2) above in so far as it relates to any matter in relation to which requirements or prohibitions are or could be imposed by or under the Regulatory Reform (Fire Safety) Order 2005 in respect of the premises.

(4) Provided it has not been cancelled or revoked the near beer licence shall remain in force for 18 months or such shorter period specified in the near beer licence as the council may think fit.

[London Local Authorities Act 1995, s 16 as amended by SI 2005/1541.]

8–20821A **17. Applications under Part IV.** (1) The occupier of premises in the borough may apply for the grant, renewal or transfer of a near beer licence, and shall not later than the day the application is made send a copy to the Commissioner and a copy to the fire and rescue authority and, subject to subsection (2) below, no such application shall be considered by the council unless the applicant complies with this subsection.

(2) The council may in such cases as they think fit, after consulting with the Commissioner and the fire and rescue authority, consider an application for the grant, renewal or transfer of a near beer licence notwithstanding that the applicant has failed to comply with subsection (1) above.

(3) In considering any application for the grant, renewal or transfer of a near beer licence the council shall have regard to any observations submitted to them by the Commissioner or by the fire and rescue authority within 28 days of the making of the application and may have regard to any observations submitted by him or them thereafter.

(4) An applicant for the grant, renewal, transfer or variation of a near beer licence shall furnish

such particulars and give such other notices, including the public advertisement of the application, as the council may by regulation prescribe.

(5) Regulations under subsection (4) above may, inter alia, prescribe the procedure for determining applications.

(6) An applicant for the grant, renewal or transfer of a near beer licence shall pay a reasonable fee determined by the council.

(7) Where, before the date of expiry of a near beer licence, an application has been made for its renewal or transfer, the near beer licence shall be deemed to remain in force, or as the case may require, to have effect with any necessary modifications until the determination of the application by the council or the withdrawal of the application.

[London Local Authorities Act 1995, s 17, as amended by the Fire and Rescue Services Act 2004, Sch 1.]

8–20821AA 17A. Renewal and transfer of licence: supplementary. (1) The following provisions of this section shall have effect as respects cases where, before the date of expiry of a licence an application for renewal of the licence has been made ("a renewal case") or an application for transfer of the licence has been made ("a transfer case").

(2) If the application is not determined before the prospective expiry date, the licence shall not be deemed to remain in force under subsection (7) or (8) of section 17 (Applications) of this Act, after that date and the application shall be deemed to be withdrawn on that date, unless before then the applicant pays the council a continuation fee.

(3) Where a continuation fee is paid in pursuance of subsection (2) above in a renewal case, the applicant's application for renewal shall be deemed to be an application for renewal for a period of twelve months starting on the day following the prospective expiry date.

(4) Where a continuation fee is paid in pursuance of subsection (2) above in a transfer case—

(*a*) the applicant shall be deemed to have made an application for the renewal of the licence for a period of twelve months starting on the day following the prospective expiry date;

(*b*) the Council shall determine the application for transfer and deemed application for renewal together; and

(*c*) in the following provisions of this section, references to "the application" in a transfer case are references to the application for transfer and the application for renewal.

(5) If the application is not determined before the date of the expiry of the renewal period under subsection (3) or (4) above, as the case may be, the licence shall not be deemed to remain in force under subsection (7) or (8) of the said section 17, as the case may be, after that date, and the application shall be deemed to be withdrawn on that date, unless before then the applicant pays the council a further continuation fee.

(6) Where a further continuation fee is paid in pursuance of subsection (5) above then—

(*a*) in a renewal case, the applicant's application for renewal shall be deemed to be an application for renewal for a period starting on the day following the date of the expiry of the renewal period under subsection (3) above; and

(*b*) in a transfer case, the applicant's application so far as it is a deemed application for renewal shall be deemed to be an application for renewal for a period starting on the day following the date of the expiry of the renewal period under subsection (4) above.

(7) A deemed application for renewal under subsection (6) shall be for a period expiring—

(*a*) where the application is withdrawn, on the date of withdrawal;

(*b*) where the application is refused, on the date of the refusal;

(*c*) where the application is granted, on one or other of the following:—

(i) the date twelve months after the beginning of the period; or

(ii) such other date as may be specified by the Council when allowing the application.

(8) In this section—

"the prospective expiry date" means—

(*a*) in a transfer case, the date on which the licence would have expired if the application for transfer had not been made; and

(*b*) in a renewal case, the date of the expiry of the period in respect of which the application for renewal of the licence was made;

"a continuation fee" is a fee of the same amount as the fee payable in respect of an application for renewal of a licence.

[London Local Authorities Act 1995, s 17A, as inserted by the London Local Authorities Act 2000, s 29.]

8–20821B 18. Refusal of licence. (1) The council may refuse to grant, renew or transfer a near beer licence on any of the following grounds:—

(*a*) the premises are not structurally suitable for the purpose;

(*b*) there is a likelihood of nuisance being caused by reason of the conduct, management or situation of the premises or the character of the relevant locality or the use to which any premises in the vicinity are put;

(*c*) the persons concerned or intended to be concerned in the conduct or management of the premises as a near beer establishment could be reasonably regarded as not being fit and proper persons to hold such a licence;

(*d*) the premises are not provided with satisfactory means of lighting, sanitation and ventilation;

(*e*) the means of heating the premises are not safe;

(*f*) where the Regulatory Reform (Fire Safety) Order 2005 applies to the premises, that Order or any regulations made under it are not being complied with in respect of the premises;

(*g*) where the Regulatory Reform (Fire Safety) Order 2005 does not apply to the premises—

(i) proper precautions against fire on the premises are not being taken;

(ii) satisfactory means of escape in case of fire and suitable fire-fighting appliances are not provided on the premises; or

(*h*) the applicant has failed to comply with the requirements of subsection (4) or (6) of section 17 (Applications under Part IV) of this Act.

(2) The council shall not refuse an application without giving the applicant an opportunity to appear before the committee or sub-committee determining the application.

(3) The council may not delegate to an officer their function of refusing an application under this Part of this Act.

(4) Where the council refuse to grant, renew or transfer a licence, they shall, if required to do so by the applicant or holder of the licence, give him a statement in writing of the reasons for their decision within 7 days of his requiring them to do so.

[London Local Authorities Act 1995, s 18 as amended by SI 2005/1541.]

8–20822 19. Transmission and cancellation of near beer licences. (1) In the event of the death of the holder of a near beer licence, the person carrying on at the place in respect of which the near beer licence was granted the function to which the near beer licence relates shall be deemed to be the holder of the near beer licence unless and until the near beer licence is transferred to some other person.

(2) The council may, at the written request of the holder of a near beer licence, cancel the near beer licence.

[London Local Authorities Act 1995, s 19.]

8–20822A 20. Power to prescribe standard terms, conditions and restrictions under Part IV. (1) The council may make regulations prescribing standard conditions applicable to all, or any class of near beer licences, that is to say terms, conditions and restrictions on or subject to which such near beer licences, or near beer licences of that class are in general to be granted, renewed or transferred by them.

(1A) No standard condition that is applicable to premises to which the Regulatory Reform (Fire Safety) Order 2005 applies may be prescribed by regulation under subsection (1) above in so far as it relates to any matter in relation to which requirements or prohibitions are or could be imposed by or under that Order.

(2) Where the council have made regulations under this section, every such near beer licence granted, renewed or transferred by them shall be deemed to have been so granted, renewed or transferred subject to any standard conditions applicable to it unless those standard conditions have been expressly excluded or amended.

[London Local Authorities Act 1995, s 20 as amended by SI 2005/1541.]

8–20822B 21. Provisional grant of near beer licences. (1) Where application is made to the council for the grant of a near beer licence in respect of premises which are to be, or are in the course of being constructed, extended or altered or improved and the council are satisfied that the premises would if *completed* in accordance with plans or proposals deposited in pursuance of the requirements of the council be such that they would grant the near beer licence, the council may grant the near beer licence subject to a condition that it shall be of no effect until confirmed by them.

(2) The council shall, on application being made for the appropriate variation of the near beer licence, confirm any near beer licence granted by virtue of subsection (1) above if and when they are satisfied that the premises have been completed in accordance with the plans or proposals referred to in the said subsection (1) or in accordance with those plans or proposals as modified with the approval of the council.

[London Local Authorities Act 1995, s 21.]

8–20823 22. Variation of near beer licences. (1) The holder of a near beer licence may at any time apply to the council for a variation in the terms, conditions or restrictions on or subject to which the near beer licence is held.

(2) The person making an application for such a variation of licence shall on making the application pay to the council such reasonable fee as the council may fix.

(3) The council may, subject to subsection (4) below—

(*a*) make the variation specified in the application;

(*b*) make that variation together with such further variation consequent thereon as the council may determine; or

(*c*) refuse the application:

Provided that no variation relating to fire safety conditions shall be made under this section before the fire and rescue authority have been consulted.

(4) No term, condition or restriction may be varied under this section in so far as the effect of the variation would be that the term, condition or restriction as varied would relate to any matter in relation to which requirements or prohibitions are or could be imposed by or under the Regulatory Reform (Fire Safety) Order 2005.

[London Local Authorities Act 1995, s 22, as amended by the Fire and Rescue Services Act 2004, Sch 1 and SI 2005/1541.]

8–20823A 23. Appeals under Part IV. (1) Any of the following persons, that is to say:—

(*a*) an applicant for the grant, renewal or transfer of a near beer licence whose application is refused;

(*b*) an applicant for the grant, renewal or transfer of a near beer licence who is aggrieved by any term, condition or restriction on or subject to which the near beer licence is granted, renewed or transferred;

(*c*) an applicant for the variation of the terms, conditions or restrictions on or subject to which a near beer licence is held whose application is refused;

(*d*) an applicant for the variation of the terms, conditions or restrictions on or subject to which a near beer licence is held who is aggrieved by any term, condition or restriction contained in a further variation made consequent on the variation applied for;

(*e*) a holder of any such near beer licence whose near beer licence is revoked under section 24 (Enforcement under Part IV) of this Act;

may at any time before the expiration of the period of 21 days beginning with the relevant date appeal to the magistrates' court acting for the petty sessions area in which the premises are situated by way of complaint for an order.

(2) In this section "the relevant date" means the date on which the person in question is notified in writing of the refusal of his application, the imposition of the terms, conditions or restrictions by which he is aggrieved or the revocation of his near beer licence, as the case may be.

(3) An appeal by either party against the decision of the magistrates' court under this section may be brought to the Crown Court.

(4) On an appeal to the magistrates' court or to the Crown Court under this section the court may make such order as it thinks fit and it shall be the duty of the council to give effect to such order.

(5) Where any near beer licence is revoked under the said section 24 of this Act or an application for the renewal of such a near beer licence is refused, the near beer licence shall be deemed to remain in force—

(*a*) until the time for bringing an appeal under this section has expired and, if such an appeal is duly brought, until the determination or abandonment of the appeal; and

(*b*) where an appeal relating to the refusal of an application for such a renewal is successful until the licence is renewed by the council.

(6) Where any near beer licence is renewed under section 16 (Licensing) of this Act and the council specify any term, condition or restriction which was not previously specified in relation to that licence, the near beer licence shall be deemed to be free of it until the time for bringing an appeal under this section has expired and, if such an appeal is duly brought, until the determination or abandonment of the appeal.

(7) Where the holder of a licence makes an application under section 22 (Variation of near beer licences) of this Act and the council make the variation applied for together with a further variation, then the licence shall continue as it was before the application—

(*a*) until the time for bringing an appeal under this section against any term, condition or restriction contained in the further variation has expired; and

(*b*) where any such appeal is brought, until the determination or abandonment of the appeal.

[London Local Authorities Act 1995, s 23.]

8–20823AA 23A. Appeals: supplementary provisions. (1) The following provisions of this section shall have effect as respects cases where an appeal under section 23 (Appeals under Part IV) of this Act is brought, within the period for doing so, against the revocation of a licence ("a revocation case") or against the refusal of an application for renewal of a licence ("a refusal case").

(2) If the appeal is not determined before the prospective expiry date, the licence shall not be deemed to remain in force under subsection (5) of the said section 23 after that date, and the appeal shall be deemed to be abandoned on that date, unless before then—

(*a*) in a revocation case, the appellant makes an application for the renewal of the licence for a period of twelve months starting on the day following the prospective expiry date;

(*b*) in a refusal case the appellant pays the council a continuation fee.

(3) Where a continuation fee is paid in pursuance of subsection (2)(*b*) above, the appellant's refused application for renewal shall be deemed to be an application for renewal for a period of twelve months starting on the day following the prospective expiry date.

(4) If the appeal is not determined before the date of the expiry of the renewal period under subsection (2)(*a*) or (3) above, as the case may be, the licence shall not be deemed to remain in force under subsection (5) of the said section 23 after that date, and the appeal shall be deemed to be abandoned on that date, unless before then the appellant pays the council a continuation fee or, as the case may be, a further continuation fee.

(5) Where a continuation fee or a further continuation fee is paid in pursuance of subsection (4) above, the appellant's application for renewal or, as the case may be, refused application for renewal shall be deemed to be an application for renewal for a period starting on the day following the date of the expiry of the renewal period under subsection (2)(*a*) above or, as the case may be, subsection (3) above.

(6) A deemed application for renewal under subsection (5) shall be for a period expiring—

(*a*) where the appeal is withdrawn, on the date of withdrawal;

(*b*) where the appeal is unsuccessful—

(i) if a further appeal is available but is not made within the period for doing so, on the date of the expiry of that period;

(ii) if no further appeal is available, on the date of the decision of the court;

(*c*) where the appeal is successful, on the day before the date of the next anniversary of the beginning of the period; provided that where the period, at the time of the decision of the court, has been running for more than twelve months, the court may specify an earlier date.

(7) In this section—

"the prospective expiry date" means—

(*a*) in a revocation case, the date on which the licence would have expired if it had not been revoked; and

(*b*) in a refusal case, the date of the expiry of the period in respect of which the refused application for renewal of the licence was made;

"a continuation fee" is a fee of the same amount as the fee payable in respect of an application for renewal of a licence.

[London Local Authorities Act 1995, s 23A, as inserted by the London Local Authorities Act 2000, s 29.]

8–20823B 24. Enforcement under Part IV. (1) If any occupier or other person concerned in the conduct or management of premises in the borough which are not currently licensed by the council under this Part of this Act—

(*a*) uses them as near beer premises; or

(*b*) permits them to be so used knowing or having reasonable cause to suspect that they are not currently so licensed;

he shall be guilty of an offence and shall be liable on summary conviction to a fine not exceeding **level 5** on the standard scale or to imprisonment for a term not exceeding **three months*** or to both.

(2) If any premises in respect of which a near beer licence is in force are used as near beer premises otherwise than in accordance with the terms, conditions or restrictions on or subject to which the near beer licence is held then the holder of the licence or other person concerned in the conduct or management of the premises shall be guilty of an offence and liable on summary conviction to a fine not exceeding **level 5** on the standard scale.

(3) Subject to section 23 (Appeals under Part IV) of this Act, the council may revoke a near beer licence if its holder is convicted of an offence under subsection (2) above.

[London Local Authorities Act 1995, s 24.]

***"51 weeks" substituted by the Criminal Justice Act 2003, Sch 26, from a date to be appointed,**

8–20824 25. Powers of entry under Part IV. (1) Any authorised officer (on production, if so required, of a duly authenticated document of his authority) or any police officer may at all reasonable times enter upon, inspect and examine any premises used, or which he has reasonable cause to believe are—

(*a*) used or intended to be used as a near beer premises either without the requisite near beer licence; or

(*b*) used in contravention of the terms, conditions or restrictions on or subject to which a near beer licence is granted;

and may do all things reasonably necessary for the purpose of ascertaining whether an offence has been committed.

(2) Subsections (2), (3) and (4) of section 287 of the Public Health Act 1936 shall apply in

respect of entry to premises for the purposes of subsection (1) above as they apply to entry to premises for the purposes of subsection (1) of that section.

(3) An officer of the fire and rescue authority authorised by the fire and rescue authority in writing to act in relation to this Part of this Act may at all reasonable times enter upon, inspect and examine premises which are licensed under this Part of this Act to ascertain whether conditions attached to the licence by virtue of section 16(3)(*f*) (Licensing) of this Act are being complied with.

(4) Any person who intentionally obstructs any person acting in the exercise of his powers under this section shall be guilty of an offence and shall be liable on summary conviction to a fine not exceeding **level 3** on the standard scale.

[London Local Authorities Act 1995, s 25, as amended by the Fire and Rescue Services Act 2004, Sch 1.]

8–20824A 26. Seizure. (1) Any police officer who enters any premises by virtue of the powers contained in subsection (1) of section 25 (Powers of entry under Part IV) of this Act or any authorised officer who enters any premises under the authority of a warrant granted under subsection (2) of the said section 25 of this Act may seize and remove any apparatus or equipment or other thing whatsoever found on the premises which he has reasonable cause to believe may be liable to be forfeited under under section 143 of the Powers of Criminal Courts (Sentencing) Act 2000.

(2) (*a*) The following provisions of this subsection shall have effect where any apparatus or equipment or any other thing is seized under subsection (1) above and references in those provisions to proceedings are to proceedings in respect of the alleged offence in relation to which the article or thing is seized.

(*b*) Subject to paragraphs (*c*) and (*d*) below, at the conclusion of the proceedings the apparatus, equipment or thing shall be returned to the premises from which it was seized unless the court orders it to be forfeited under any enactment.

(*c*) If no proceedings are instituted before the expiration of a period of 28 days beginning with the date of seizure, or any proceedings instituted within that period are discontinued, at the expiration of that period or, as the case may be, on the discontinuance of the proceedings, the apparatus, equipment or thing shall, subject to paragraph (*d*) below, he returned to the premises from which it was seized.

(*d*) Where, at the time at which any apparatus, equipment or thing falls to be returned under paragraph (*b*) or (*c*) above, the premises from which it was seized have ceased to be occupied or the occupier of the premises appears to the council to be different from the person who occupied the premises at the time of seizure the council may, instead of returning it to the premises apply to a magistrates' court for an order as to the manner in which it should be dealt with.

[London Local Authorities Act 1995, s 26, as amended by the Powers of Criminal Courts (Sentencing) Act 2000, Sch 9.]

8–20824B 27. Application to existing premises. Where near beer premises exist on the date this Part of this Act comes into force in the borough in which the near beer premises are situated and application for a near beer licence is made in respect of those premises within four weeks of that date those premises may lawfully continue to be used as near beer premises until the determination or withdrawal of that application and if an appeal is lodged until the determination or abandonment of the appeal.

[London Local Authorities Act 1995, s 27.]

PART VI[1]
MISCELLANEOUS

8–20829 48. Offences by bodies corporate. (1) Where an offence under this Act committed by a body corporate is proved to have been committed with the consent or connivance of, or to be attributable to any neglect on the part of, any director, manager, secretary or other similar officer of the body corporate or any person who was purporting to act in any such capacity, he, as well as the body corporate, shall be guilty of that offence and shall be liable to be proceeded against and punished accordingly.

(2) Where the affairs of a body corporate are managed by its members subsection (1) above shall apply to the acts and defaults of a member in connection with his function of management as if he were a director of the body corporate.

[London Local Authorities Act 1995, s 48.]

1. Part VI contains ss 44–48.

London Local Authorities Act 1996

(1996 c ix)

PART I[1]
PRELIMINARY

8–20829A 1. Citation and commencement. (1) This Act may be cited as the London Local Authorities Act 1996 and except where otherwise provided shall come into operation at the end of the period of two months beginning with the date on which it is passed[2].

(2) The London Local Authorities Act 1990, the London Local Authorities (No. 2) Act 1990, the London Local Authorities Act 1991, the London Local Authorities Act 1994, the London Local Authorities Act 1995 and this Act may together be cited as the London Local Authorities Acts 1990 to 1996.

[London Local Authorities Act 1996, s 1.]

1. Part I comprises ss 1 and 2.
2. This Act was passed on 17 October 1996.

8–20829B 2. Interpretation. In this Act, except as otherwise expressly provided or unless the context otherwise requires—

Repealed;

"borough council" means London borough council and includes the Common Council of the City of London; and "borough" and "council" shall be construed accordingly;

"Transport for London" means the body established by section 154 of the Greater London Authority Act 1999.

[London Local Authorities Act 1996, s 2, as amended by SI 2001/690 and the London Local Authorities Act 2004, Sch 4.]

PART II[1]
BUS LANES

8–20829C 3–9. *Penalty charges for offences in relation to bus lanes.*

1. Part II comprises ss 3–9.

PART III[1]
OCCASIONAL SALES

8–20829D 10. Meaning of occasional sale. In this Part of this Act "occasional sale" means a concourse of buyers and sellers of articles held otherwise than on a highway or in a building (except a car park) and comprising not less than five stalls, stands, vehicles (whether movable or not) or pitches from which articles are sold, but does not include—

(*a*) a market or fair the right to hold which was acquired by virtue of a grant (including a presumed grant) or acquired or established by statute;

(*b*) a sale by auction of farm livestock or deadstock;

(*c*) sales of a class which from time to time is by resolution of the borough council excluded from the operation of this Part of this Act;

(*d*) a market held in accordance with a planning permission granted under section 58(1)(b) of the Town and Country Planning Act 1990 (which provides for the granting of planning permission) or under a similar provision of a predecessor to that Act; or

(*e*) a market the holding of which commenced before 1st July 1948 and has continued without extinguishment.

[London Local Authorities Act 1996, s 10.]

1. Part III comprises ss 10–19.

8–20829E 11. Application of Part III. (1) This Part of this Act applies to a borough as from such day as may be fixed in relation to that borough by resolution of the borough council, subject to and in accordance with the provisions of this section.

(2) The borough council shall cause to be published in a local newspaper circulating in the borough notice—

(*a*) of the passing of any such resolution and of a day fixed thereby; and

(*b*) of the general effect of the provisions of this Part of this Act;

and the day so fixed shall not be earlier than the expiration of three months from the publication of the said notice.

(3) Either a photostatic or other reproduction certified by the officer appointed for that purpose by the borough council to be a true reproduction of a page or part of a page of any such newspaper

bearing the date of its publication and containing any such notice shall be evidence of the publication of the notice, and of the date of publication.
[London Local Authorities Act 1996, s 11.]

8–20829F 12. Licensing of occasional sales. (1) Subject to the provisions of this Part of this Act it shall be unlawful for any person to hold an occasional sale within a borough unless that person is authorised to do so by a licence under this Part of this Act.

(2) No licence under this Part of this Act is required if the proceeds of the occasional sale are to be applied solely or principally for charitable, social, sporting, religious or political purposes.

(3) A person holds an occasional sale for the purposes of this Part of this Act if—

(*a*) he receives or is entitled to receive payment for any space or pitch hired or let on the site of the sale to persons wishing to trade at the sale; or

(*b*) as a person promoting the sale, or as the agent, licensee or assignee of a person promoting the sale, he receives or is entitled to receive payment from persons trading at the sale for goods sold or services rendered to persons attending the sale.

[London Local Authorities Act 1996, s 12.]

8–20829G 13. Application for licence. (1) An application for a licence under this Part of this Act shall be made in writing to the borough council, not later than 42 days before the date on which the occasional sale is to be held:

Provided that nothing in this section shall prevent a borough council from granting a licence, notwithstanding that application has been made at a later date than aforesaid if they consider it reasonable in the circumstances so to do.

(2)–(3) *Information to be specified and fees.*
[London Local Authorities Act 1996, s 13.]

8–20829H 14. Grant of licence. (1) The borough council may grant a licence under this Part of this Act and in granting a licence may impose reasonable conditions relating to—

(*a*) the time of commencement of the occasional sale;

(*b*) the duration of the occasional sale;

(*c*) the arrangements to be made for accommodating the vehicles of persons attending the occasional sale;

(*d*) the arrangements to be made for controlling road congestion, litter and noise caused by the occasional sale;

(*e*) a requirement that the names and addresses of persons selling articles at the occasional sale are publicly displayed.

(2) If the borough council have not refused to grant a licence within 21 days of the receipt by them of an application duly made for a licence under subsection (1) of section 13 (Application for licence) of this Act, they shall be deemed to have granted a licence for an occasional sale in accordance with the details specified in the application.

(3) The borough council shall grant an application for a licence under this Part of this Act unless they consider that the application ought to be refused on one or more of the grounds specified in subsection (4) below.

(4) The borough council may refuse an application on any of the following grounds—

(*a*) that inadequate arrangements have been proposed for accommodating the vehicles of persons attending the occasional sale;

(*b*) that inadequate arrangements have been proposed for controlling road congestion, litter or noise caused by the occasional sale; or

(*c*) that the applicant has been granted a licence by any borough council for an occasional sale within three years before the date of the application and failed to comply with conditions imposed in relation to that licence.

[London Local Authorities Act 1996, s 14.]

8–20829I 15. Part III appeals. (1) If the borough council refuse to grant a licence under this Part of this Act they shall notify the applicant in writing—

(*a*) of their decision and of the ground or grounds for such refusal; and

(*b*) of his rights of appeal specified in this section.

(2) Any person aggrieved—

(*a*) by the refusal of a borough council to grant a licence; or

(*b*) by a condition imposed by a borough council under subsection (1) of section 14 (Grant of licence) of this Act;

may appeal[1] to a magistrates' court acting for the area in which the proposed occasional sale is to be held.

(3) A person desiring to appeal against such refusal or condition shall give a written notice to the

magistrates' court and to the borough council specifying the refusal or condition against which he wishes to appeal and the grounds upon which such appeal is made.

(4) On an appeal to the magistrates' court under this section, the court may make such order as it thinks fit and it shall be the duty of the borough council to give effect to the order.
[London Local Authorities Act 1996, s 15.]

1. An appeal shall be brought by way of complaint; see the Magistrates' Courts Rules 1981, r 34 in PART I: MAGISTRATES' COURTS, PROCEDURE, ante.

8–20829J 16. Display of names, etc. (1) Any person who holds an occasional sale shall display his full name and business address and the full name and business address of the person appointed to receive and answer complaints about the occasional sale in a prominent position at the place where the sale is held.

(2) Any person who holds an occasional sale shall display on all notices, leaflets and posters given, distributed or exhibited by him or on his behalf in connection with the sale the full name and business address of—

(*a*) himself; and
(*b*) the person appointed to receive and answer complaints about the occasional sale.
[London Local Authorities Act 1996, s 16.]

8–20829K 17. Powers of entry. An authorised officer on producing if so required a duly authenticated document showing his authority, or any constable, may enter and inspect any premises if he has reasonable cause to believe that they are being, have been or are intended to be, used for or in connection with an occasional sale for the purpose of ascertaining whether there is or has been or is intended to be a contravention of this Part of this Act in, or in connection with, the premises.
[London Local Authorities Act 1996, s 17.]

8–20829L 18. Enforcement. (1) Any person who contravenes section 12 (Licensing of occasional sales) of this Act shall be guilty of an offence and liable on summary conviction to a fine not exceeding **level 4** on the standard scale.

(2) Any person who contravenes a condition imposed under section 14 (Grant of licence) of this Act shall be guilty of an offence and liable on summary conviction to a fine not exceeding **level 3** on the standard scale.

(3) Any person who without reasonable excuse contravenes section 16 (Display of names, etc.) of this Act shall be guilty of an offence and liable on summary conviction to a fine not exceeding **level 2** on the standard scale.
[London Local Authorities Act 1996, s 18.]

8–20829M 19. Restriction on right to prosecute. The written consent of the Director of Public Prosecutions is needed for the laying of an information of an offence created by this Part of this Act by any person other than an authorised officer or a constable.
[London Local Authorities Act 1996, s 19.]

PART V[1]
MISCELLANEOUS

8–20829R 24. Application of Environmental Protection Act 1990. The Environmental Protection Act 1990 shall have effect in a borough as though—

(1) in section 79 (which relates to statutory nuisances and inspections therefor)—

(*a*) in subsection (1), after paragraph (*ga*) there were inserted the following paragraph—

"(*gb*) smoke, fumes or gases emitted from any vehicle, machinery or equipment on a street so as to be prejudicial to health or a nuisance other than from any vehicle, machinery or equipment being used for fire brigade purposes;";

(*b*) after subsection (6A) there were inserted the following subsection—

"(6B) Subsection (1) (*gb*) above does not apply in relation to smoke, fumes or gases emitted from the exhaust system of a vehicle."; and

(*c*) in subsection (7), after the definition of "street" there were inserted—

" 'vehicle' means a mechanically propelled vehicle intended or adapted for use on roads, whether or not it is in a fit state for such use, and includes any trailer intended or adapted for use as an attachment to such a vehicle, any chassis or body, with or without wheels, appearing to have formed part of such a vehicle or trailer and anything attached to such a vehicle or trailer;";

(2) in section 80A (1), after "section 79 (1) (*ga*)" there were inserted "or (*gb*)".
[London Local Authorities Act 1996, s 24.]

1. Part V comprises ss 24–31.

8–20829S **25.** *Amendment of London Local Authorities Act 1991.*

8–20829T **26. Public charitable collections.** *Amends the London Local Authorities Act 1990.*

8–20829U **27. Application of London Local Authorities Act 1995 to Tower Hamlets.** *Amends the London Local Authorities Act 1995.*

8–20829V **28.** Obstruction of authorised officer.—(1) Any person who—

(*a*) internationally obstructs any authorised officer acting in the exercise of his powers under this Act; or

(*b*) without reasonable cause fails to give any authorised officer any assistance or information which the officer may reasonably require of him for the purposes of the exercise of the officer's functions under the provision of this Act;

shall be guilty of an offence and liable on summary conviction to a fine not exceeding **level 3** on the standard scale.

(2) Subsection (1)(*b*) above applies in relation to a constable as it applies in relation to an authorised officer.

(3) A person shall be guilty of an offence if, in giving any information which is required of him by virtue of subsection (1)(*b*) above—

(*a*) he can make any statement which he knows is false in a material particular; or

(*b*) he recklessly makes a statement which is false in a material particular.

(4) A person guilty of an offence under subsection (3) above shall be liable on summary conviction to a fine not exceeding **level 5** on the standard scale.

[London Local Authorities Act 1996, s 28.]

8–20829W **29. Defence of due diligence.** (1) In proceedings for an offence under this Act it shall be a defence for the person charged to prove that he took all reasonable precautions and exercised all due diligence to avoid the commission of the offence.

(2) If in any case the defence provided under subsection (1) above involves the allegation that the commission of the offence was due to the act or default of another person, the person charged shall not, without leave of the court, be entitled to rely on that defence unless, no later than 7 clear days before the hearing, he has served on the prosecutor a notice in writing giving such information as was then in his possession identifying or assisting in the identification of that other person.

[London Local Authorities Act 1996, s 29.]

8–20829X **30. Liability of directors, etc.** (1) Where an offence under this Act committed by a body corporate is provided to have been committed with the consent or connivance of, or to be attributable to any neglect on the part of, a director, manager, secretary or other similar officer of the body corporate or any person who was purporting to act in any such capacity, he, as well as the body corporate, shall be guilty of the offence.

(2) Where the affairs of the body corporate are managed by its members, subsection (1) above shall apply to the acts and defaults of a member in connection with his functions of management as if he were a director of the body corporate.

[London Local Authorities Act 1996, s 30.]

8–20829Y **31.** *Regulations.*

8–20829Z

SCHEDULE 1

ENFORCEMENT NOTICES, ETC. UNDER PART II (BUS LANES) OF THIS ACT[1]

1. Schedule 1 provides that where a penalty charge has been issued under s 4 of the Act but is not paid within 28 days, the Council may serve an enforcement notice on the owner or person in charge of the vehicle. Representations may be made against the charge or notice on grounds prescribed in para 4 which inter alia provides that where it is maintained that the recipient was not in charge of the vehicle, he must include a statement of the name and address of the person whom he believed to be in charge at the material time. Failure to comply is a summary offence punishable by a fine not exceeding **level 3** unless he shows that he did not know, and could not with reasonable diligence have ascertained, who was the driver.

It is also a summary offence under paragraph 11 punishable by a fine not exceeding **level 5** for a person to make any representation to a council or traffic adjudicator under paragraph 2 or 6 which is false in a material particular and who does so recklessly or knowing it to be false in that particular.

Greater London Authority Act 1999[1]

(1999 c 29)

PART II[2]

GENERAL FUNCTIONS AND PROCEDURE

General functions of the Assembly

8–20829ZA **59. Review and investigation.** (1) The Assembly shall keep under review the exercise by the Mayor of the statutory functions exercisable by him.

(2) For the purposes of subsection (1) above, the powers of the Assembly include in particular power to investigate, and prepare reports about,—

(*a*) any actions and decisions of the Mayor,
(*b*) any actions and decisions of any member of staff of the Authority,
(*c*) matters relating to the principal purposes of the Authority,
(*d*) matters in relation to which statutory functions are exercisable by the Mayor, or
(*e*) any other matters which the Assembly considers to be of importance to Greater London.

[Greater London Authority Act 1999, s 59.]

---

1. The Greater London Authority Act 1999 establishes amnd makes provision about the Greater London Authority, the Mayor of London and the London Assembly. The Act makes provision in relation to London borough councils and the common council of the city of London with respect to matters consequential on the establishment of the Greater London Authority. The Act also makes provision with respect to the functioning of other local authorities and statutory bodies exercising functions in Greater London including provision about transport and road traffic.

The Act contains a number of penal provisions, but only those that are thought likely to be of relevance to the work of the magistrates' courts in Greater London are set out in this work.

The Act is to be brought into force in accordance with s 425. At the date of going to press, the following Greater London Authority Act 1999 commencement orders had been made:

Commencement (No 1) Order 1999, SI 1999/3271;
Commencement (No 2) Order 1999, SI 1999/3376;
Commencement (No 3) Order 1999, SI 1999/3434;
Commencement (No 4) Order 1999, SI 2000/801;
Commencement (No 5) Order 2000, SI 2000/1094;
Commencement (No 6) Order 2000, SI 2000./1095;
Commencement (No 7) Order SI 2000/1648;
Commencement (No 8) Order 2000 SI 2000/3145;
Commencement (No 9) Order 2000, SI 2000/3379.

Of the provisions set out in this work, s 63 had not been brought into force.

2. Part II comprises ss 30 to 80.

8–20829ZB 60. Proposals to the Mayor.. *Power of the Assembly to submit a propsal to the Mayor.*
[Greater London Authority Act 1999, s 60.]

Attendance of witnesses and production of documents

8–20829ZC 61. Power to require attendance at Assembly meetings. (1) Subject to section 63 below, the Assembly may require any person to whom subsection (2), (3), (4) or (5) below applies—

(*a*) to attend proceedings of the Assembly for the purpose of giving evidence, or
(*b*) to produce to the Assembly documents in his possession or under his control.

(2) This subsection applies to—

(*a*) any person who is a member of staff of the Authority, or of any functional body, to whom sections 1 to 3 of the Local Government and Housing Act 1989 apply,
(*b*) any person who is the chairman of, or a member of, any functional body, and
(*c*) any person who has within the three years prior to the date of the requirement to be imposed under subsection (1) above been the chairman of, or a member of, any functional body.

(3) This subsection applies to—

(*a*) any person who has within the three years prior to the date of the requirement to be imposed under subsection (1) above had a contractual relationship with the Authority, and
(*b*) any person who is a member of, or a member of staff of, a body which has within the three years prior to the date of the requirement to be imposed under subsection (1) above had such a relationship.

(4) This subsection applies to—

(*a*) any person who has within the three years prior to the date of the requirement to be imposed under subsection (1) above received a grant from the Authority, and
(*b*) any person who is a member of, or a member of staff of, a body which has within the three years prior to the date of the requirement to be imposed under subsection (1) above received such a grant.

(5) This subsection applies to—

(*a*) any person who is an Assembly member,
(*b*) any person who has within the three years prior to the date of the requirement to be imposed under subsection (1) above been an Assembly member, and
(*c*) any person who has within the three years prior to the date of the requirement to be imposed under subsection (1) above been the Mayor.

(6) A requirement imposed under subsection (1) above on a person falling within subsection (2) above—

(*a*) if imposed under paragraph (*a*) of subsection (1) above, is to attend to give evidence in connection with matters in relation to which statutory functions are exercisable by the Authority or any functional body, and

(*b*) if imposed under paragraph (*b*) of subsection (1) above, is to produce documents which relate to those matters.

(7) A requirement imposed under subsection (1) above on a person falling within subsection (3) above—

(*a*) if imposed under paragraph (*a*) of subsection (1) above, is to attend to give evidence in connection with the contractual relationship with the Authority, and

(*b*) if imposed under paragraph (*b*) of subsection (1) above, is to produce documents which relate to that contractual relationship.

(8) A requirement imposed under subsection (1) above on a person falling within subsection (4) above—

(*a*) if imposed under paragraph (*a*) of subsection (1) above, is to attend to give evidence in connection with the grant received from the Authority, and

(*b*) if imposed under paragraph (*b*) of subsection (1) above, is to produce documents which relate to that grant.

(9) A requirement imposed under subsection (1) above on a person falling within subsection (5) above—

(*a*) if imposed under paragraph (*a*) of subsection (1) above, is to attend to give evidence in connection with the exercise by the person attending of the functions of the Authority, and

(*b*) if imposed under paragraph (*b*) of subsection (1) above, is to produce documents which relate to the exercise of those functions by that person.

(10) Nothing in this section shall require a person appointed under section 67(1) or (2) below to—

(*a*) give any evidence, or

(*b*) produce any documents,

which disclose advice given by that person to the Mayor.

(11) Nothing in this section shall require a person who is—

(*a*) a member of a functional body, or

(*b*) a member of staff of a functional body,

to give any evidence, or produce any document, which discloses advice given to the Mayor by that person or, except as provided by subsection (12) below, by that functional body.

(12) Subsection (11) above does not relieve a person from a requirement to give any evidence, or produce any document, which discloses advice given to the Mayor by—

(*a*) the Metropolitan Police Authority, or

(*b*) the London Fire and Emergency Planning Authority,

if or to the extent that the advice falls within subsection (13) below.

(13) Advice given to the Mayor by a functional body falls within this subsection if it has been disclosed—

(*a*) at a meeting of, or of a committee or sub-committee of, the functional body at a time when the meeting was open to members of the public by virtue of Part VA of the Local Government Act 1972 (access to meetings and documents); or

(*b*) in a document which has been open to inspection by members of the public by virtue of that Part of that Act.

(14) For the purposes of this section and sections 62 to 65 below—

(*a*) "document" means anything in which information is recorded in any form (and references to producing a document are to the production of the information in it in a visible and legible form, including the production of a copy of the document or an extract of the relevant part of the document),

(*b*) any reference to a member of staff of a body includes a reference to an officer or employee of that body, and

(*c*) any reference to proceedings is a reference to proceedings at a meeting.

[Greater London Authority Act 1999, s 61.]

8–20829ZD 62. Procedure for requiring attendance. (1) The powers of the Assembly under section 61(1) above may be exercised by and for the purposes of an ordinary committee of the Assembly, if the committee is expressly authorised to exercise those powers by the standing orders or by the Assembly, but may not be exercised by any individual Assembly member or by any member of staff of the Authority.

(2) Except in the case of a committee which is authorised by standing orders to exercise the powers of the Assembly under section 61(1) above, section 54 above shall not apply in relation to—

(*a*) the Assembly's function of deciding to exercise its powers under section 61(1) above; or (*b*) the Assembly's function under subsection (1) above of authorising a committee to exercise those powers.

(3) In order to impose a requirement on a person under section 61(1) above the head of the Authority's paid service must give him notice specifying—

(*a*) the time and place at which he is to attend and the matters about which he is to be required to give evidence, or

(*b*) the documents, or types of documents, which he is to produce, the date by which he is to produce them and the matters to which the document or documents relate.

(4) Where a requirement under section 61(1) above is imposed on a person to attend proceedings or produce documents on behalf of a body, the notice required to be given to him under subsection (3) above must also specify that body.

(5) A notice required by subsection (3) above to be given to a person must be given at least two weeks before the day on which the proceedings are to take place, or by which the documents are to be produced, unless he waives this right.

(6) A notice required by subsection (3) above to be given to a person shall be taken to have been given to him if it is sent by registered post or the recorded delivery service and—

(*a*) if he is a member of staff of the Authority or the chairman of, a member of, or a member of staff of a functional body, it is sent to his normal place of work,

(*b*) if he is a person required to attend proceedings or produce documents on behalf of a body, it is sent to the registered or principal office of the body,

(*c*) if he is any other individual, it is sent to his usual or last known address, or

(*d*) in the case of any person, where that person has given an address for service of the notice, it is sent to that address.

[Greater London Authority Act 1999, s 62.]

8–20829ZE 63. Restriction of information. The Secretary of State may by order—

(*a*) prescribe categories of information which a person who is required under subsection (1)(*a*) of section 61 above to attend proceedings of the Assembly may refuse to give, or

(*b*) prescribe categories of documents which a person who is required under subsection (1)(*b*) of that section to produce documents may refuse to produce.

[Greater London Authority Act 1999, s 63.]

8–20829ZF 64. Failure to attend proceedings etc. (1) A person to whom a notice under section 62(3) above has been given is guilty of an offence if he—

(*a*) refuses or fails, without reasonable excuse, to attend proceedings as required by the notice,

(*b*) refuses to answer any question which is properly put to him when attending any proceedings as required by the notice,

(*c*) refuses or fails, without reasonable excuse, to produce any document required by the notice to be produced by him, or

(*d*) intentionally alters, suppresses, conceals or destroys any document required by the notice to be produced by him.

(2) A person guilty of an offence under subsection (1) above is liable on summary conviction to—

(*a*) a fine not exceeding **level 5** on the standard scale, or

(*b*) imprisonment for a term not exceeding **three months**.

(3) A person is not obliged by section 61 above to answer any question or produce any document which he would be entitled to refuse to answer or produce in or for the purposes of proceedings in a court in England and Wales.

[Greater London Authority Act 1999, s 64.]

8–20829ZG 65. Proceedings under section 61(1): openness. (1) In its application by virtue of section 58 above, Part VA of the Local Government Act 1972 (access to meetings and documents of certain authorities, committees and sub-committees), so far as relating to any proceedings under section 61(1) above ("the evidentiary proceedings"), shall have effect with the following additional modifications.

(2) In section 100B (access to agenda and connected reports) any reference to a report for a meeting includes a reference to any document (other than the agenda) supplied before, and for the purposes of, the evidentiary proceedings (a "relevant document").

(3) If a report or relevant document is supplied less than three clear days before the evidentiary proceedings, copies of the report or document shall be open to inspection by the public under subsection (1) of that section from the time such copies are available to Assembly members, notwithstanding anything in subsection (3) of section 100B.

(4) In section 100C (inspection of minutes and other documents after meetings)—

(*a*) any reference to the minutes of a meeting shall be taken to include a reference to a transcript or other record of evidence given in the course of the evidentiary proceedings; and (*b*) any reference to a report for the meeting includes a reference to a relevant document.

(5) In section 100D (inspection of background papers) any reference in subsections (1) to (4) to background papers for a report (or part of a report) shall be taken as a reference to any additional documents supplied by a witness.

(6) In this section, "additional documents supplied by a witness" means documents supplied, whether before, during or after the evidentiary proceedings,—

(*a*) by a person attending to give evidence at the proceedings, and
(*b*) for the use of Assembly members in connection with the proceedings,

but does not include any document which is a relevant document.

(7) In section 100F (additional rights of access for members) subsections (2) to (4) shall not have effect in relation to documents which contain material relating to any business to be transacted at the evidentiary proceedings.

(8) In section 100H (supplemental provisions and offences) in subsection (6), in the definition of "accessible documents"—

(*a*) the reference in paragraph (*d*) to a report for the meeting includes a reference to a relevant document; and
(*b*) the reference in paragraph (*e*) to background papers for a report for a meeting shall be taken as a reference to any additional documents supplied by a witness.

[Greater London Authority Act 1999, s 65.]

PART IV[1]
TRANSPORT

CHAPTER IX[1]
PENALTY FARES

8–20829ZH 245. Penalty fares. Schedule 17[2] to this Act shall have effect for the purpose of providing for the payment of penalty fares in the circumstances set out in that Schedule.
[Greater London Authority Act 1999, s 245.]

1. Part IV comprises ss 141–303. Chapter IX comprises s 245.
2. See, post.

CHAPTER XI[1]
HACKNEY CARRIAGES AND PRIVATE HIRE VEHICLES

8–20829ZI 253. Hackney carriages. Schedule 20[2] to this Act (which makes provision about hackney carriages) shall have effect.
[Greater London Authority Act 1999, s 253.]

1. Chapter XI comprises ss 253–255.
2. See, post.

8–20829ZJ 254. The Private Hire Vehicles (London) Act 1998. (1) Except as provided by the following provisions of this section, the functions of the Secretary of State under the Private Hire Vehicles (London) Act 1998[1] are transferred by this subsection to Transport for London.

(2) Subsection (1) above does not apply to any functions of the Secretary of State under section 37, 38 or 40 of that Act (transitional provisions, financial provisions and commencement etc).

(3) Schedule 21[2] to this Act (which makes amendments to the Private Hire Vehicles (London) Act 1998 in consequence of subsections (1) and (2) above) shall have effect.

(4) Any regulations made, licence issued, authorisation granted, or other thing done under the Private Hire Vehicles (London) Act 1998, other than section 37, 38 or 40, by or in relation to the Secretary of State before the coming into force of this section shall have effect as from the coming into force of this section as made, issued, granted or done by or in relation to Transport for London.
[Greater London Authority Act 1999, s 254.]

1. See, ante.
2. Schedule 21 is not set out in this work.

8–20829ZK 255. Provisions consequent on alteration of metropolitan police district. (1) Where, by virtue of the coming into force of section 323 below, the whole or any part of the area of a district council ceases to be within the metropolitan police district, the following provisions of this section shall have effect[1].

(2) The provisions of the Town Police Clauses Act 1847[2] with respect to hackney carriages, as incorporated in the Public Health Act 1875, shall apply throughout the council's area.

(3) The council's area shall constitute a single licensing area for the purposes of those provisions, without the passing of any resolution under Part II of Schedule 14 to the Local Government Act 1972 (extension resolutions).

(4) The provisions of Part II of the Local Government (Miscellaneous Provisions) Act 1976[3] (hackney carriages and private hire vehicles) shall also apply throughout the council's area, without the passing of any resolution under section 45 of that Act (application of Part II).

(5) Where an order is made under section 425 below bringing section 323 below into force, the provision that may be made by virtue of section 420 or 425 below includes provision enabling or facilitating—

(*a*) the making of byelaws,
(*b*) the issuing of licences, discs or plates, and
(*c*) the establishment and operation of a licensing system,

in relation to hackney carriages or private hire vehicles by a district council falling within subsection (1) above in preparation for the coming into force of this section.

(6) The provision that may be made by virtue of subsection (5) above includes provision for the application of any enactment with or without modification.

(7) Subsections (5) and (6) above are without prejudice to the provision that may be made by virtue of sections 420 and 425 below.
[Greater London Authority Act 1999, s 255.]

1. See also the Greater London Authority Act 1999 (Hackney Carriages and Private Hire Vehicles) (Transitional and Consequential Provisions) Order 2000, SI 2000/412.
2. See title, TOWNS IMPROVEMENT; TOWN POLICE, post.
3. See title LOCAL GOVERNMENT, ante.

Section 245

SCHEDULE 17
PENALTY FARES

Introductory

8–20829ZL **1.** (1) In this Schedule unless the context otherwise requires—

"authorised person" means, in relation to any purpose, a person authorised for that purpose by Transport for London or by the person providing the service;

"compulsory ticket area" means that part of a station which, under the byelaws of the person providing a train service to which this Schedule applies, passengers are not permitted to enter without a fare ticket, general travel authority or platform ticket;

"fare ticket" means a ticket (including one issued by a third person) showing payment of a fare and authorising the person in respect of whom it is issued to make a single journey covered by that fare on a local service or train service to which this Schedule applies, or to make that journey and a return journey (whether or not it also authorises him to make a journey on a service provided by a third person);

"general travel authority" means any permit (including one issued by a third person), other than a fare ticket, authorising the person in respect of whom it is issued to travel on a local service or train service to which this Schedule applies (whether or not it also authorises him to travel on a service provided by a third person);

"penalty fare" means a penalty fare payable pursuant to paragraph 3 or 4 below;

"the penalty fare provisions" means paragraphs 3 to 8 below;

"person providing the service" means the operator of the service, except that, in the case of a service provided in pursuance of an agreement entered into by Transport for London under section 156(2) or (3)(*a*) of this Act or in pursuance of a transport subsidiary's agreement, means Transport for London;

"platform ticket" means a ticket authorising a person to enter a compulsory ticket area but not to make a journey;

"station" means a station serving a train service to which this Schedule applies;

"third person" means a person other than one referred to in paragraph 2(1)(*a*) or (*b*) below; and

"train service" means a service for the carriage of passengers by rail.

(2) Subject to sub-paragraph (3) below, a person is travelling on a train service to which this Schedule applies at any time when he is on a train forming part of that service or is in a compulsory ticket area.

(3) A person at a station is not to be taken as travelling by reason only of being in a compulsory ticket area or boarding a train at that station if he has entered that area or boards that train otherwise than for the purpose of making a journey and produces, if required to do so by an authorised person, a valid platform ticket.

(4) Any reference in this Schedule to a person producing a fare ticket or general travel authority on being required to do so by an authorised person is a reference to producing, when so required, a fare ticket or general travel authority which, either by itself or together with any other fare ticket or general travel authority produced by that person at the same time, is valid for the journey he has made.

(5) For the purposes of sub-paragraph (4) above—

(*a*) a person who has entered a compulsory ticket area otherwise than by transferring from a train service provided by a third person but has not boarded a train shall be taken to have made a journey for which the minimum fare is payable; and

(*b*) a person who is on a train shall be taken to have made a journey ending at the next station at which the train is scheduled to stop.

(6) In sub-paragraph (5) above "minimum fare" means the minimum fare for which a journey from the station in question could validly be made by the person in question.

(7) For the purposes of this Schedule a person is to be taken as transferring from a service provided by a third person to a service to which this Schedule applies if, but only if, having travelled on a train forming part of the former service, he—

(*a*) goes from that train into a compulsory ticket area and finishes his journey at the station of which that area forms part; or (*b*) goes from that train into a compulsory ticket area and from that area boards a train forming part of a service to which this Schedule applies.

(8) For the purposes of sub-paragraph (7)(b) above, in a case where the transfer takes place at a station controlled by a third person, "compulsory ticket area" means such area at that station as corresponds with a compulsory ticket area within the meaning of this Schedule.

Operation of this Schedule

8–20829ZM **2.** (1) This Schedule applies to any local service or train service provided—

(*a*) by Transport for London or any of its subsidiaries; or

(*b*) by any other person in pursuance of an agreement entered into by Transport for London under section 156(2) or (3)(a) of this Act, or in pursuance of a transport subsidiary's agreement, which provides that this Schedule is to apply to services provided in pursuance of that agreement.

(2) References in the following provisions of this Schedule to a local service or to a train service are, unless the context otherwise requires, references to a local service or a train service to which this Schedule applies.

(3) The penalty fare provisions have effect in relation to travel on any local service or train service or any part of such a service if an order under sub-paragraph (4) below is for the time being in force in respect of such service or part of a service.

(4) The Mayor may by order provide that the penalty fare provisions shall have effect, as from such day as may be specified in the order, with respect to any local service or train service or any part of any local service or train service, and different days may be specified in any such order with respect to different services or different parts of any service.

(5) The revocation by the Mayor of an order made under sub-paragraph (4) above shall be without prejudice to the power of the Mayor to make further orders under that sub-paragraph as respects any service or part of a service dealt with by the order.

(6) Any activating order made by the Secretary of State under section 3(4) of the London Regional Transport (Penalty Fares) Act 1992 and in force immediately before the coming into force of sub-paragraph (4) above shall have effect as from the coming into force of that sub-paragraph as if it were an order made by the Mayor under that sub-paragraph.

(7) For the purposes of this Schedule a reference to an agreement entered into by Transport for London under section 156(2) or (3) of this Act includes a reference to an agreement—

(*a*) which was entered into by London Regional Transport under section 3(2) or (2A) of the London Regional Transport Act 1984, and

(*b*) which by virtue of section 300 or 415 of this Act has effect as if made by Transport for London.

Penalty fares on local services

8–20829ZN **3.** (1) If a person travelling on a ticket bus service who has had a reasonable opportunity to obtain a fare ticket for a journey on that service fails to produce a fare ticket or a general travel authority on being required to do so by an authorised person, he shall be liable to pay a penalty fare if required to do so by an authorised person.

(2) If a person travels on a non-ticket bus service without paying the fare properly payable for a journey on that service and, while so travelling, fails to produce a general travel authority on being required to do so by an authorised person, he shall be liable to pay a penalty fare if required to do so by an authorised person.

(3) In this paragraph a "ticket bus service" means a local service on which fare tickets are issued in return for fares paid by persons travelling on that service, and a "non-ticket bus service" means a local service on which fare tickets are not so issued.

Penalty fares on trains

8–20829ZO **4.** (1) Subject to sub-paragraph (2) below, if a person travelling on a train service fails to produce a fare ticket or a general travel authority on being required to do so by an authorised person, he shall be liable to pay a penalty fare if required to do so by an authorised person.

(2) Subject to sub-paragraph (3) below, a person shall not be liable to pay a penalty fare under this paragraph if at the time when and the station where he started to travel on the train service there were no facilities available for the sale of the necessary fare ticket for his journey.

(3) A person who starts to travel on a train service by transferring to that service from a train service provided by a third person shall not be liable to pay a penalty fare under this paragraph if—

(*a*) on being required to produce a fare ticket or general travel authority he produces a valid deferred fare authority issued by that person; or

(*b*) at the time when and the station where he started to travel on the train service provided by that person there were no facilities for either the sale of the necessary fare ticket for his journey or the sale of deferred fare authorities.

(4) Without prejudice to sub-paragraphs (2) or (3) above, a person shall not be liable to pay a penalty fare under this paragraph if at the time when and the station where his journey began—

(*a*) there was displayed a notice (however expressed) indicating that it was permissible for passengers beginning a journey at that station at that time to do so without having a fare ticket or a general travel authority or (in the case of a station controlled by a third person) a deferred fare authority; or

(*b*) a person in the uniform of the person controlling that station gave permission to the same effect.

(5) In sub-paragraph (3) above, "deferred fare authority" means a ticket or other document described as such on its face; and a deferred fare authority is valid for the purposes of that paragraph if it authorises a person in possession of it to start a journey at the time when and the station where the person producing it started his journey.

(6) Sub-paragraphs (7) and (8) below have effect with respect to the burden of proof in any action for the

recovery of a penalty fare under this paragraph, so far as concerns the question whether the facts of the case fall within sub-paragraphs (2), (3)(*b*) or (4) above.

(7) In any case where the defendant has provided the plaintiff with a relevant statement in due time it shall be for the plaintiff to show that the facts of the case do not fall within sub-paragraph (2), (3)(*b*) or (4) above and in any other case it shall be for the defendant to show that the facts of the case fall within any of those provisions.

(8) For the purposes of sub-paragraph (7) above—

(*a*) a relevant statement is a statement giving an explanation of the defendant's failure to produce a fare ticket, general travel authority or (where relevant) deferred fare authority, together with any information as to his journey relevant to that explanation (including, in every case, an indication of the time when and the station where he started to travel on the train service and also, if he started so to travel when he transferred from a train service provided by a third person, the time when and the station where he started to travel on that service); and

(*b*) a statement is provided in due time if it is provided when the defendant is required to produce a fare ticket or general travel authority, or at any later time before the expiration of the period of 21 days beginning with the day following the day on which the journey is completed.

Amount of penalty fare

8–20829ZP **5.** (1) Subject to sub-paragraph (2) below, a penalty fare shall be—

(*a*) in respect of any journey on a local service, £5;

(*b*) in respect of any train journey, £10;

and shall be payable to the person providing the service on which the requirement to pay the penalty fare is made before the expiration of the period of 21 days beginning with the day following the day on which the journey is completed.

(2) The Mayor may by order prescribe that the amount of the penalty fare in either or both of the cases set out in sub-paragraph (1) above shall be different (whether higher or lower).

(3) No order may be made by the Mayor under sub-paragraph (2) above unless he has consulted the Secretary of State and—

(*a*) such persons or bodies representative of local authorities,

(*b*) such persons or bodies representative of those who travel on local services and train services, and

(*c*) such other persons or bodies,

as the Mayor considers it appropriate to consult.

Documents in connection with penalty fare requirement

8–20829ZQ **6.** (1) An authorised person who requires a person (referred to below as "the passenger") to pay a penalty fare shall give him either a receipt for the payment of the amount of the penalty (where the passenger makes that payment to the authorised person) or a notice stating that the requirement has been made.

(2) A receipt or notice given under sub-paragraph (1) above shall specify the passenger's destination on the local service or train service on which he is travelling when required to pay the penalty fare, and shall operate as an authority to him to complete his journey to or at that destination.

(3) For the purposes of sub-paragraph (2) above, the passenger's destination shall (unless he is at that destination or only one destination is possible in the circumstances) be taken to be the destination stated by the passenger or, in default of any statement by him for that purpose, such destination as may be specified by the authorised person.

Supplementary provision

8–20829ZR **7.** (1) A person who is required to pay a penalty fare shall, unless he pays, immediately and in cash, the amount of the penalty fare to an authorised person requiring such payment, give to that authorised person, if that person requires him to do so, his name and address.

(2) A person failing to give his name and address when required to do so under sub-paragraph (1) above shall be guilty of an offence and liable on summary conviction to a fine not exceeding level 2 on the standard scale.

(3) Transport for London shall secure that the requirements of sub-paragraph (4) or, as the case may be, (5) below with respect to warning notices are met in the case of a local service or train service in relation to travel on which the penalty fare provisions have effect.

(4) In the case of a local service, a warning notice meeting the requirements of sub-paragraphs (6) and (7) below shall be posted in every vehicle used in providing that service or, where any such vehicle has more than one deck, on each deck of that vehicle, in such a position as to be readily visible to persons travelling on the vehicle.

(5) In the case of a train service, a warning notice meeting the requirements of sub-paragraphs (6) and (7) below shall be posted—

(*a*) at every station at which persons may start to travel on that service, in such a position as to be readily visible to prospective passengers; and

(*b*) in every carriage of every train used in providing that service in such a position as to be readily visible to passengers travelling in the carriage.

(6) A warning notice posted pursuant to sub-paragraph (4) or (5) above shall (however expressed) indicate the circumstances (as provided in paragraph 3(1) or (2) above or, as the case may be, paragraph 4(1) above) in which persons travelling on the service in question may be liable to pay a penalty fare.

(7) Every warning notice posted in pursuance of this paragraph shall state the amount of the relevant penalty fare.

(8) Where an authorised person requires any person to do anything pursuant to any provision of this Schedule he shall, if so requested by the person concerned, produce to that person a duly authenticated document showing his authority.

(9) A requirement by an authorised person shall be of no effect if, as respects that requirement, he fails to comply with sub-paragraph (8) above.

Exclusion of double liability

8–20829ZS **8.** (1) Where a person has become liable under paragraph 3 or 4 above to pay a penalty fare in respect of any journey on a local service or any train journey (referred to below as "the relevant journey"), no proceedings may be brought against him for any of the offences specified in sub-paragraph (3) below before the end of the period mentioned in paragraph 5(1) above.

(2) No proceedings may be brought after the end of that period if—

(*a*) before the end of that period, the person who has become liable to pay the penalty fare has paid it to the person providing the service on which the requirement to pay it was made; or

(*b*) an action has been brought against the person who has become liable to pay the penalty fare for the recovery of that fare.

(3) The offences mentioned in sub-paragraph (1) above are—

(*a*) any offence under section 5(3)(*a*) or (*b*) of the Regulation of Railways Act 1889 (travelling without paying the correct fare with intent to avoid payment) arising from the relevant journey;

(*b*) any offence under byelaws made under section 67 of the Transport Act 1962 or paragraph 26 of Schedule 11 to this Act (byelaws for railways, etc) involving a failure to obtain or produce a fare ticket or general travel authority for the relevant journey; and

(*c*) any offence under section 25(3) of the Public Passenger Vehicles Act 1981 of contravening or failing to comply with any provision of regulations for the time being having effect by virtue of that section by failing to pay the fare properly payable for the relevant journey or any part of it.

(4) If proceedings are brought in contravention of this paragraph the person who has become liable to pay the penalty fare shall cease to be liable to pay it, but where that person has paid that fare, the person to whom it is paid shall be liable to repay to that person the amount of that fare.

Power to apply Schedule to certain other train services

8–20829ZT **9.** (1) This paragraph applies to any services for the carriage of passengers by railway which do not fall within paragraph 2(1) above but which—

(*a*) are provided wholly within Greater London; and

(*b*) are services, or services of a class or description, designated in an order made by the Secretary of State as services in relation to which this paragraph is to apply;

and in the following provisions of this paragraph any such services are referred to as "qualifying train services".

(2) The Mayor may, on the application of a person who provides qualifying train services, by order provide that this Schedule shall apply, from such date and with such modifications as may be specified in the order, to qualifying train services provided by that person.

(3) The power to make an order under sub-paragraph (2) above includes power, exercisable in the same manner and subject to the same conditions and limitations, to revoke, amend or re-enact any such order.

(4) Without prejudice to sub-paragraph (3) above, an order under sub-paragraph (2) above may specify circumstances in which the order shall cease to have effect before the expiry of any period specified in such an order.

(5) An order under sub-paragraph (2) above, and any order revoking, amending or re-enacting such an order, may contain such incidental, supplemental, consequential or transitional provision as may appear to the Mayor to be necessary or expedient.

(6) Where a person makes an application for an order under sub-paragraph (2) above, or for an order revoking, amending or re-enacting such an order, the Mayor may recover from that person payments in respect of the administrative costs reasonably incurred in connection with—

(*a*) the application, and

(*b*) if an order is made as a result of the application, the making of the order,

not exceeding £5,000 in the aggregate.

(7) The Mayor shall secure that any order under sub-paragraph (2) above, and any order revoking, amending or re-enacting any such order, is printed and published.

(8) A fee may be charged for the sale of an order printed and published under sub-paragraph (7) above.

(9) Where any services become qualifying services by virtue of an order under sub-paragraph (1)(*b*) above, any order which—

(*a*) is contained in a statutory instrument made by the Secretary of State,

(*b*) makes provision for or in connection with the imposition of penalty fares on passengers travelling on those services, and

(*c*) is in force immediately before this paragraph begins to apply to the services by virtue of the order under sub-paragraph (1)(*b*) above,

may, so far as relating to those services, be revoked under this paragraph as if it were an order under sub-paragraph (2) above.

(10) This paragraph applies in relation to a tramway as it applies in relation to a railway.

(11) In this paragraph "railway" and "tramway" have the meaning given by section 67(1) of the Transport and Works Act 1992.

Appeals

8–20829ZU **10.** (1) If requested to do so by the Mayor, the Secretary of State shall by regulations make provision enabling a person required to pay a penalty fare to appeal against that requirement.

(2) Regulations under this paragraph may include provision—

(*a*) for appeals to be heard and determined by independent adjudicators,
(*b*) for the appointment of such adjudicators,
(*c*) for requiring Transport for London to reconsider, before an appeal is determined, whether the appellant should be required to pay the penalty fare, and
(*d*) for the adjudicator's directions in relation to an appeal to be binding upon Transport for London and the appellant.

8–20829ZV 11 *Repeal of London Regional Transport (Penalty Fares) Act 1992*

Section 253

SCHEDULE 20
HACKNEY CARRIAGES
(Amended by the Statute Law (Repeals) Act 2004.)

PART I
TRANSFERS OF FUNCTIONS AND AMENDMENTS

The London Hackney Carriages Act 1843[1]

8–20829ZW **1.** (1) All the jurisdiction, powers, authorities, privileges, interests and duties which, immediately before the coming into force of this paragraph, were vested in or exercisable by the Commissioners of Police of the Metropolis by virtue of section 2 of the London Hackney Carriages Act 1850 (transfer of functions of registrar of metropolitan public carriages to Commissioners of Police of the Metropolis) are transferred to and vested in Transport for London by this sub-paragraph.

(2) The London Hackney Carriages Act 1843 shall accordingly be amended as follows.

(3) For "the registrar" and "the said registrar", wherever occurring, there shall be substituted "Transport for London".

(4) In section 18 (licences and tickets to be delivered up on discontinuance of licence) for "him" there shall be substituted "Transport for London".

(5) In section 19 (new tickets to be delivered instead of defaced or lost tickets) for "for the use of Her Majesty" there shall be substituted "to Transport for London".

8–20829ZY **2–8 Amendment of other enactments relating to Hackney carriages**[1]

1. These amendments have been incorporated into the relevant enactments contained in this work.

PART II
TRANSITIONAL PROVISIONS

Saving

8–20829ZZ **9.** This Part of this Schedule is without prejudice to the provision that may be made under any power conferred on a Minister of the Crown by this Act to make subordinate legislation, within the meaning of the Interpretation Act 1978.

The London Hackney Carriages Act 1843

8–20829ZZA **10.** (1) Any licence to act as driver of hackney carriages—

(*a*) which was issued under section 8 of the London Hackney Carriages Act 1843 by or on behalf of the Commissioner of Police of the Metropolis, and
(*b*) which is in force immediately before the coming into force of paragraph 1 above,

shall have effect as from the coming into force of that paragraph as if it had been issued by Transport for London.

(2) Any metal ticket—

(*a*) which was issued under that section by or on behalf of the Commissioner of Police of the Metropolis, and
(*b*) which is in force immediately before the coming into force of paragraph 1 above,

shall have effect as from the coming into force of that paragraph as if it had been issued by Transport for London.

The London Hackney Carriages Act 1850

8–20829ZZB **11.** Any regulations made or other thing done under section 4 of the London Hackney Carriages Act 1850 by or on behalf of a Commissioner of Police of the Metropolis and in force or otherwise having effect immediately before the coming into force of paragraph 2 above shall have effect as from the coming into force of that paragraph as if made or done by or, in the case of a signature, by a person authorised for the purpose by, Transport for London.

The London Hackney Carriage Act 1853

8–20829ZZC **12.** Any notice given under section 2 of the London Hackney Carriage Act 1853 and having effect immediately before the coming into force of sub-paragraph (2) of paragraph 3 above shall have effect as from the coming into force of that sub-paragraph as a notice given by Transport for London.

8–20829ZZD **13.** *Repealed.*

The Metropolitan Public Carriage Act 1869

8–20829ZZE 14. (1) Any order—

(*a*) made by or on behalf of the Secretary of State under or by virtue of any enactment contained in the Metropolitan Public Carriage Act 1869, and

(*b*) in force immediately before the coming into force of any provision of paragraph 7 above in relation to that enactment,

shall, to the extent that the provision made by the order could be made by Transport for London, have effect as from the coming into force of that provision in relation to that enactment as a London cab order, but with the substitution for references to the Secretary of State of references to Transport for London.

(2) Any licence granted under section 6 or 8 of that Act and in force immediately before the coming into force of sub-paragraph (3) or (5) of paragraph 5 above in relation to that section shall have effect as from the coming into force of that sub-paragraph in relation to that section as a licence granted under that section by Transport for London.

(3) Any suspension or revocation of a licence under section 6 or 8 of that Act having effect immediately before the coming into force of sub-paragraph (3) or (5) of paragraph 5 above shall have effect as from the coming into force of that sub-paragraph in relation to that section as the suspension or revocation of the licence by Transport for London.

(4) Any appointment made under section 12 of that Act by the Secretary of State and in force immediately before the coming into force of sub-paragraph (9) of paragraph 5 above shall have effect as from the coming into force of that sub-paragraph as an appointment made by Transport for London.

The London Cab and Stage Carriage Act 1907

8–20829ZZF 15. (1) Any regulations made by the Secretary of State by order by virtue of section 1 of the London Cab and Stage Carriage Act 1907 and in force immediately before the coming into force of sub-paragraph (2) of paragraph 6 above shall have effect as from the coming into force of that paragraph as regulations made by London cab order by virtue of that section.

(2) Any sum for the time being allowed by the Secretary of State under subsection (1) of section 2 of that Act immediately before the coming into force of paragraph (*a*) of sub-paragraph (4) of paragraph 6 above shall have effect as from the coming into force of that paragraph as the sum for the time being allowed under that subsection by Transport for London until such time as Transport for London allow a different sum.

(3) Any order made by the Secretary of State under section 2 of that Act and in force immediately before the coming into force of paragraph (*b*) of sub-paragraph (4) of paragraph 6 above shall have effect as from the coming into force of that paragraph as a London cab order.

(4) Any approval given by or on behalf of the Secretary of State for the purposes of the definition of "taximeter" in section 6(1) of that Act and in force immediately before the coming into force of the amendment made by paragraph (*b*) of sub-paragraph (5) of paragraph 6 above shall have effect as from the coming into force of that amendment as an approval given by Transport for London.

The London Cab Act 1968

8–20829ZZG 16. (1) Any order made by the Secretary of State under section 2 of the London Cab Act 1968 and in force immediately before the coming into force of paragraph (*a*) of sub-paragraph (4) of paragraph 7 above shall have effect as from the coming into force of that paragraph as a London cab order.

(2) Any order made by the Secretary of State under section 4A of that Act and in force immediately before the coming into force of paragraph (*a*) of sub-paragraph (5) of paragraph 7 above shall have effect as a London cab order as from the coming into force of that paragraph.

The Transport Act 1985

8–20829ZZH 17. (1) Any scheme made under section 10 of the Transport Act 1985 by the Secretary of State and in force immediately before the coming into force of paragraph (*a*) of sub-paragraph (2) of paragraph 8 above shall have effect as from the coming into force of that paragraph as a scheme made by Transport for London.

(2) Any regulations prescribing a period for the purposes of a provision of that Act specified in paragraph (*a*) of sub-paragraph (3) of paragraph 8 above and in force immediately before the coming into force of that paragraph shall, until such time as a period is specified by London cab order for the purposes of that provision, continue in force and have effect as if the period so prescribed were the period specified for the purposes of that provision by London cab order.

London Local Authorities Act 2000

(2000 c vii)

PART I[1]
PRELIMINARY

8–20829ZZI 1. Citation and commencement. (1) This Act may be cited as the London Local Authorities Act 2000 and except where otherwise provided shall come into force at the end of the period of two months beginning with the date on which it is passed.

(2) The London Local Authorities Acts 1990 to 1996 and this Act may together be cited as the London Local Authorities Acts 1990 to 2000.

[London Local Authorities Act 2000, s 1.]

---

1. Part I contains ss 1–2.

8–20829ZZJ 2. Interpretation. In this Act, except as otherwise expressly provided or unless the context otherwise requires—

Repealed;

"functions" includes powers and duties;

"participating council" means the common council in its capacity as a local authority and the council of any London borough; and "borough", "City" and "council" shall be construed accordingly.

[London Local Authorities Act 2000, s 2, as amended by the London Local Authorities Act 2004, s 27 and Sch 5.]

PART II[1]
PARKING

8–20829ZZK

1. Part II contains ss 3–16.

PART III[1]
PUBLIC HEALTH

8–20829ZZL 17. Interpretation of Part III. (1) In this Part of this Act—

"the Act of 1936" means the Public Health Act 1936[2];

"the Act of 1990" means the Environmental Protection Act 1990[2];

"cleansing notice" means a notice served under subsection (1) of section 19 (Cleansing relevant land of litter and refuse) of this Act;

"relevant land" means any street in the area of a participating council together with any land which is in the open air and is adjacent to such a street otherwise than land comprised in a highway but does not include—

(*a*) any land which a person has a duty to ensure is, so far as is practicable, kept clear of litter and refuse by virtue of section 89 of the Act of 1990; or

(*b*) any canal or inland navigation belonging to or under the control of the British Waterways Board, or any works, lands or premises belonging to or under the control of the British Waterways Board and held or used by them in connection with such canal or inland navigation;

"relevant premises" means—

(*a*) premises which front or abut on relevant land; and

(*b*) premises which are served by the relevant land as a means of access; and

(*c*) where any such premises as are mentioned in paragraph (*a*) above form part of a building in which other premises are situated, those other premises;

"street" has the same meaning as in section 343 (Interpretation) of the Act of 1936 but does not include a highway;

"waste control enactments" means—

(a) the following sections of the Act of 1990:—

(i) section 45 (Collection of controlled waste); and

(ii) section 46 (Receptacles for household waste); and

(iii) section 47 (Receptacles for commercial or industrial waste); and

(*b*) section 19 (Cleansing relevant land of litter and refuse) of this Act.

(2) The definitions in section 75 of the Act of 1990 shall apply for the purposes of this Part of this Act.

[London Local Authorities Act 2000, s 17.]

1. Part III contains ss 17–21.
2. In this PART, title PUBLIC HEALTH, post.

8–20829ZZM 18. Enforcement of waste control enactments. The following sections of the Control of Pollution Act 1974[1] shall have effect as if references therein to that Act included references to the waste control enactments—

(*a*) section 91 (Rights of entry and inspection, etc); and

(*b*) section 92 (Provisions supplementary to s 91).

[London Local Authorities Act 2000, s 18.]

1. In this PART, title PUBLIC HEALTH, post.

8–20829ZZN 19. Cleansing relevant land of litter and refuse. (1) A participating council may by notice specify the standards and frequency at which relevant land requires to be swept and cleansed so as to keep it reasonably clear of litter and refuse and shall serve a copy of such notice on the owner of the relevant land or the owner or occupier of any relevant premises.

(2) If, at any time after the expiration of 42 days from the service of the cleansing notice, the council determine that the relevant land is not being swept and cleansed in accordance with the notice then the council shall give notice of this determination to the person on whom the cleansing notice was served and may cause the relevant land to be swept and cleansed.

(3) At any time the council may decide to revoke any cleansing notice or any determination made under subsection (2) above and shall give notice of any such decision to the person who was served with the cleansing notice or the determination, as the case may be and may serve a fresh cleansing notice or make a fresh determination as the case may be.

(4) A person served with a cleansing notice or a notice under subsection (2) above may appeal to a magistrates' court on any of the following grounds which are appropriate in the circumstances of the particular case:—

(*a*) that the notice or requirement under the notice is not justified by the terms of this section;
(*b*) that there has been some informality, defect or error in, or in connection with, the notice;
(*c*) that the standards and frequency at which the sweeping and cleansing is to be carried out are unreasonable;
(*d*) that it would have been equitable for the notice to have been served on the occupier of the premises in question instead of on the owner, or on the owner instead of on the occupier;
(*e*) where the sweeping and cleansing is for the common benefit of the premises in question and other premises, that some other person, being the owner or occupier of premises to be benefited, ought to contribute towards the expenses of executing any works required.

(5) If and in so far as an appeal under this section is based on the ground of some informality, defect or error in or in connection with the notice, the court shall dismiss the appeal, if it is satisfied that the informality, defect or error was not a material one.

(6) Where the grounds upon which an appeal under this section is brought include a ground specified in paragraph (*d*) or paragraph (*e*) of subsection (4) above, the appellant shall serve a copy of his notice of appeal on each other person referred to, and in the case of any appeal under this section may serve a copy of his notice of appeal on any other person having an estate or interest in the premises in question, and on the hearing of the appeal the court may make such order as it thinks fit with respect to the person by whom any sweeping and cleansing is to be carried out and the contribution to be made by any other person towards the cost of the work, or as to the proportions in which any expenses which may become recoverable by the council are to be borne by the appellant and such other person.

In exercising its powers under this subsection, the court shall have regard—

(*a*) as between an owner and an occupier, to the terms and conditions whether contractual or statutory, of the tenancy and to the nature of the works required; and
(*b*) in any case, to the degree of benefit to be derived by the different persons concerned.

(7) Subject to such right of appeal as aforesaid, where the council causes land to be swept and cleansed under subsection (2) above, they may recover from the person on whom the cleansing notice was served the expenses reasonably incurred by them in so doing.

(8) In proceedings by the council for the recovery of any expenses under subsection (7) above, it shall not be open to the defendant to raise any question which he could have raised on an appeal under this section.

(9) Sections 275, 283(1), 285, 289 and 300 of the Act of 1936 shall apply to a cleansing notice.

(10) Sections 278, 283(1), 285, 291 and 300 of the Act of 1936 shall apply to a notice under subsection (2) above.

(11) The sections of the Act of 1936 mentioned in subsections (9) and (10) above shall apply to notices served under this section as if—

(*a*) references therein to that Act included references to this section; and
(*b*) references therein to the execution of works included references to the carrying out of sweeping and cleansing and cognate terms shall be construed accordingly.

(12) Section 291 of the Act of 1936 shall apply to notices served under subsection (2) above as if references to the owner of the premises in respect of which the expenses were incurred included references to the person on whom the cleansing notice was served.

[London Local Authorities Act 2000, s 19 as amended by SI 2005/886.]

8–20829ZZO 20. Collection and disposal of waste. Where a cleansing notice is served in respect of relevant land—

(*a*) if the land is swept and cleansed in accordance with the notice any resulting litter or refuse left for removal shall be treated as commercial waste; and
(*b*) if the land is swept and cleansed by the council in pursuance of subsection (2) of section 19 (Cleansing relevant land of litter and refuse) of this Act any such litter or refuse shall be treated as household waste.

[London Local Authorities Act 2000, s 20.]

8–20829ZZP 21. Offence of leaving litter. Section 87 of the Act of 1990 (which provides for an offence of leaving litter) shall apply to any relevant land in respect of which a cleansing notice has been served in so far as that land does not constitute a public open place for the purposes of the said section 87.
[London Local Authorities Act 2000, s 21.]

PART IV[1]
LICENSING

8–20829ZZV 27–28. *Special Treatment Premises*

1. Part IV contains ss 27–31.

8–20829ZZW 29. Near beer premises. (1) Part IV (Near Beer Licensing) of the London Local Authorities Act 1995 applies in the area of a participating council in accordance with the following subsections.

(2) In section 14 (Interpretation of Part IV)—

(*a*) in the definition of "near beer premises" paragraph (*a*) is replaced by the following paragraph:—

"(*a*) consists in or includes the sale to customers for consumption on the premises of refreshments; and"

(*b*) the definition of "occupier" is left out.

(3) In section 17 (Applications under Part IV)—

(*a*) in subsection (1) the words from the beginning to "and shall" are replaced by "An applicant for the grant, renewal or transfer of a near beer licence shall";

(*b*) in subsection (7)—

(i) at the beginning, the words "Subject to section 17A (Renewal and transfer of licence: supplementary) of this Act," are inserted;

(ii) the words "or transfer" and the words from "or as the case may require, to have effect with any necessary modifications" are left out;

(*c*) at the end the following subsections are inserted:—

"(8) Subject to section 17A (Renewal and transfer of licence: supplementary) of this Act, where, before the date of expiry of a near beer licence, an application has been made for the transfer of that licence, the licence shall be deemed to remain in force (with any necessary modifications) notwithstanding that the date of expiry of the licence has passed, until the determination of the application by the council or the withdrawal of the application.

(9) Where an applicant for the transfer of a near beer licence is carrying on the functions to which the licence relates, "any necessary modifications" where those words appear in subsection (8) above, means the substitution for the name of the licence holder of the name of the applicant for the transfer of the licence and any other necessary modifications.".

(4) After the said section 17, the following section is inserted:—

"17A. Renewal and transfer of licence: supplementary. (1) The following provisions of this section shall have effect as respects cases where, before the date of expiry of a licence an application for renewal of the licence has been made ("a renewal case") or an application for transfer of the licence has been made ("a transfer case").

(2) If the application is not determined before the prospective expiry date, the licence shall not be deemed to remain in force under subsection (7) or (8) of section 17 (Applications) of this Act, after that date and the application shall be deemed to be withdrawn on that date, unless before then the applicant pays the council a continuation fee.

(3) Where a continuation fee is paid in pursuance of subsection (2) above in a renewal case, the applicant's application for renewal shall be deemed to be an application for renewal for a period of twelve months starting on the day following the prospective expiry date.

(4) Where a continuation fee is paid in pursuance of subsection (2) above in a transfer case—

(*a*) the applicant shall be deemed to have made an application for the renewal of the licence for a period of twelve months starting on the day following the prospective expiry date;

(*b*) the Council shall determine the application for transfer and deemed application for renewal together; and

(*c*) in the following provisions of this section, references to "the application" in a transfer case are references to the application for transfer and the application for renewal.

(5) If the application is not determined before the date of the expiry of the renewal period under subsection (3) or (4) above, as the case may be, the licence shall not be deemed to remain in force under subsection (7) or (8) of the said section 17, as the case may be, after that date, and

the application shall be deemed to be withdrawn on that date, unless before then the applicant pays the council a further continuation fee.

(6) Where a further continuation fee is paid in pursuance of subsection (5) above then—

(a) in a renewal case, the applicant's application for renewal shall be deemed to be an application for renewal for a period starting on the day following the date of the expiry of the renewal period under subsection (3) above; and

(b) in a transfer case, the applicant's application so far as it is a deemed application for renewal shall be deemed to be an application for renewal for a period starting on the day following the date of the expiry of the renewal period under subsection (4) above.

(7) A deemed application for renewal under subsection (6) shall be for a period expiring—

(*a*) where the application is withdrawn, on the date of withdrawal;
(*b*) where the application is refused, on the date of the refusal;
(*c*) where the application is granted, on one or other of the following:—
 (i) the date twelve months after the beginning of the period; or
 (ii) such other date as may be specified by the Council when allowing the application.

(8) In this section—

"the prospective expiry date" means—

(*a*) in a transfer case, the date on which the licence would have expired if the application for transfer had not been made; and
(*b*) in a renewal case, the date of the expiry of the period in respect of which the application for renewal of the licence was made;

"a continuation fee" is a fee of the same amount as the fee payable in respect of an application for renewal of a licence.".

(5) In section 23 (Appeals under Part IV) at the beginning of subsection (5) the words "Subject to section 23A below" are inserted.

(6) After the said section 23, the following section is inserted:—

"23A. Appeals: supplementary provisions. (1) The following provisions of this section shall have effect as respects cases where an appeal under section 23 (Appeals under Part IV) of this Act is brought, within the period for doing so, against the revocation of a licence ("a revocation case") or against the refusal of an application for renewal of a licence ("a refusal case").

(2) If the appeal is not determined before the prospective expiry date, the licence shall not be deemed to remain in force under subsection (5) of the said section 23 after that date, and the appeal shall be deemed to be abandoned on that date, unless before then—

(*a*) in a revocation case, the appellant makes an application for the renewal of the licence for a period of twelve months starting on the day following the prospective expiry date;
(*b*) in a refusal case the appellant pays the council a continuation fee.

(3) Where a continuation fee is paid in pursuance of subsection (2)(*b*) above, the appellant's refused application for renewal shall be deemed to be an application for renewal for a period of twelve months starting on the day following the prospective expiry date.

(4) If the appeal is not determined before the date of the expiry of the renewal period under subsection (2)(*a*) or (3) above, as the case may be, the licence shall not be deemed to remain in force under subsection (5) of the said section 23 after that date, and the appeal shall be deemed to be abandoned on that date, unless before then the appellant pays the council a continuation fee or, as the case may be, a further continuation fee.

(5) Where a continuation fee or a further continuation fee is paid in pursuance of subsection (4) above, the appellant's application for renewal or, as the case may be, refused application for renewal shall be deemed to be an application for renewal for a period starting on the day following the date of the expiry of the renewal period under subsection (2)(*a*) above or, as the case may be, subsection (3) above.

(6) A deemed application for renewal under subsection (5) shall be for a period expiring—

(*a*) where the appeal is withdrawn, on the date of withdrawal;
(*b*) where the appeal is unsuccessful—
 (i) if a further appeal is available but is not made within the period for doing so, on the date of the expiry of that period;
 (ii) if no further appeal is available, on the date of the decision of the court;
(*c*) where the appeal is successful, on the day before the date of the next anniversary of the beginning of the period; provided that where the period, at the time of the decision of the court, has been running for more than twelve months, the court may specify an earlier date.

(7) In this section—

"the prospective expiry date" means—

(*a*) in a revocation case, the date on which the licence would have expired if it had not been revoked; and

(*b*) in a refusal case, the date of the expiry of the period in respect of which the refused application for renewal of the licence was made;

"a continuation fee" is a fee of the same amount as the fee payable in respect of an application for renewal of a licence.".

(7) In subsection (2) of section 24 (Enforcement under Part IV) after the words "holder of the licence" the words ", an applicant for the transfer of a near beer licence where he is carrying out the functions to which the licence relates" are inserted.
[London Local Authorities Act 2000, s 29.]

8–20829ZZX 30. Door supervisors. In its application to the area of a participating council, section 29 (Interpretation of Part V) of the London Local Authorities Act 1995 is amended as follows—

(*a*) in paragraph (*c*) of the definition of "licensed premises" the words "or licensed" are left out;

(*b*) in the definition of "door supervisor"—

(i) before the words "to maintain order" the words "any person employed" are inserted; and

(ii) at the end the words "but, in respect of premises in respect of which there is in force for the time being a justices' on-licence within the meaning of section 1(2) of the Licensing Act 1964 does not include the holder of that licence" are inserted.

[London Local Authorities Act 2000, s 30.]

8–20829ZZY 31. Fees in relation to distribution of free literature. Subsection (6) of section 4 (Distribution of free literature) of the London Local Authorities Act 1994 is amended in its application to the area of a participating council other than the City by the substitution of the words "in whole or in part the reasonable administrative or other costs in connection with their functions under this section" for the words "the expense of the borough council in dealing with applications for such consents".
[London Local Authorities Act 2000, s 31.]

PART V[1]
LICENSING OF BUSKERS

8–20829ZZZ 32. Interpretation of Part V. In this Part of this Act—

"busking" means the provision of entertainment in a street but does not include the provision of entertainment—

(*a*) of a class which from time to time is by resolution of a participating council excluded from the operation of this Part of this Act;

(*b*) under and in accordance with a premises licence under Part 3 of the Licensing Act 2003, or a temporary event notice having effect under Part 5 of that Act, which authorises the provision of regulated entertainment (within paragraph 2(1)(*e*) to (*h*) or 3(2) of Schedule 1 to that Act (music and dancing));

(*c*) which is authorised specifically to take place in a street under any other enactment; or

(*d*) consisting of music performed as an incident of a religious meeting, procession or service;

and "busk" and "busks" shall be construed accordingly;

"licence" means a licence under section 35 (Power to license) of this Act and "licensed" shall be construed accordingly;

"street" includes—

(*a*) any street or way to which the public commonly have access, whether or not as of right;

(*b*) any place, not being within permanently enclosed premises, within 7 metres of any such street or way, to which the public commonly have access;

(*c*) any area in the open air to which the public commonly have access;

(*d*) any street, way or open area within any housing development provided or maintained by a local authority under Part II of the Housing Act 1985;

but does not include any land in respect of which there are byelaws in force which regulate the provision of entertainment and which are made by London Transport Executive or London Regional Transport.

[London Local Authorities Act 2000, s 32 as amended by the Licensing Act 2003, Sch 6.]

1. Part V contains ss 32–44.

8–20829ZZZA 33. Application of Part V. (1) This Part of this Act applies in the area of a participating council as from such day as may be fixed in relation to that council by resolution, and the council may apply this Part to all their area or to any part identified in the resolution and notice under this section.

(2) The council shall not pass a resolution under this section in respect of any part of their area

unless they have reason to believe that there has been, is being or is likely to be caused, as a result of busking—

(*a*) undue interference with or inconvenience to or risk to safety of persons using a street in that part of their area or other streets within the vicinity of that street; or

(*b*) nuisance to the occupiers of property in or in the vicinity of a street in that part of their area.

(3) The council shall cause to be published in a local newspaper circulating in the borough or the City notice—

(*a*) of the passing of any such resolution and of a day fixed thereby; and

(*b*) of the general effect of the provisions of this Act coming into operation as from that day;

and the day so fixed shall not be earlier than the expiration of three months from the publication of the said notice.

(4) Either a photostatic or other reproduction certified by the officer appointed for that purpose by the council to be a true reproduction of a page or part of a page of any such newspaper bearing the date of its publication and containing any such notice shall be evidence of the publication of the notice, and of the date of publication.

[London Local Authorities Act 2000, s 33.]

8–20829ZZZB 34. Designation of licence streets. If a participating council consider that busking should be licensed in their area they may pass any of the following resolutions:—

(*a*) a resolution (in this Part of this Act referred to as a "designating resolution") designating any street or part of a street within the borough or the City as a "licence street";

(*b*) a resolution prescribing in relation to any licence street or any part of a licence street any hours during which busking may take place;

and may by subsequent resolution rescind or vary any such resolution.

[London Local Authorities Act 2000, s 34.]

8–20829ZZZC 35. Power to license. (1) The council may license an applicant for one or more days or such period as may be specified in the licence on such terms and conditions and subject to such restrictions as may be so specified.

(2) Without prejudice to the generality of subsection (1) above, such conditions may relate to—

(*a*) the area in which busking may take place;

(*b*) the hours during which busking may take place;

(*c*) the prevention of obstruction to persons using the street; or

(*d*) the prevention of nuisance to the occupiers of nearby property.

[London Local Authorities Act 2000, s 35.]

8–20829ZZZD 36. Applicants under Part V. (1) An applicant for the grant of a licence shall provide such information as the council may by regulation prescribe.

(2) Regulations under subsection (1) above may, inter alia, prescribe the procedure for determining applications.

(3) An applicant for a licence shall pay such fee determined by the council as may be sufficient to cover in whole or in part the reasonable administrative or other costs incurred in connection with their functions under this Part of this Act.

[London Local Authorities Act 2000, s 36.]

8–20829ZZZE 37. Refusal of licence. (1) The council may refuse to grant a licence on any of the following grounds:—

(*a*) that the applicant could be reasonably regarded as not being a fit and proper person to hold a licence;

(*b*) that there is not enough space in the street in respect of which the application is made for busking to take place without causing undue interference with, or inconvenience to, or risk to the safety of persons using the street, or other streets within the vicinity of the street;

(*c*) that there is a likelihood of nuisance being caused to the occupiers of premises in or in the vicinity of the street in respect of which the application is made.

(2) The council shall refuse to grant a licence in respect of an application which relates to any street other than a licence street.

[London Local Authorities Act 2000, s 37.]

8–20829ZZZF 38. Cancellation of licence. The council may, at the written request of the holder of a licence, cancel that licence.

[London Local Authorities Act 2000, s 38.]

8–20829ZZZG 39. Revocation of licence. The council may revoke a licence on any of the following grounds:—

(*a*) that there has been a breach of the conditions of the licence;

(*b*) that undue interference with, or inconvenience to, or risk to the safety of persons using the street, or other streets within the vicinity of the street, has been caused as a result of the busking;

(*c*) that nuisance has been caused as a result of the busking to occupiers of property in or in the vicinity of the street in respect of which the licence was granted.

[London Local Authorities Act 2000, s 39.]

8–20829ZZZH 40. Power to prescribe standard terms, conditions and restrictions under Part V. (1) The council may make regulations prescribing standard conditions applicable to all licences.

(2) Where the council have made regulations under this section, every licence granted by them shall be deemed to have been so granted subject to the standard conditions except so far as they are expressly excluded or amended in any particular case.

(3) Without prejudice to the generality of subsection (1) above, the standard conditions applied shall include a condition requiring the licence holder to carry his licence with him when busking.

[London Local Authorities Act 2000, s 40.]

8–20829ZZZI 41. Appeals under Part V. (1) Any of the following persons, that is to say:—

(*a*) an applicant for the grant of a licence whose application is refused;

(*b*) a licence holder who is aggrieved by any term, condition or restriction on or subject to which the licence is held; or

(*c*) a licence holder whose licence has been revoked;

may at any time before the expiration of the period of 21 days beginning with the relevant date appeal to the magistrates' court acting for the area in which the licence street is situated by way of complaint for an order.

(2) In subsection (1) above "the relevant date" means either the date on which the person in question or his representative is informed in writing of the refusal of his application, the imposition of the terms, conditions or restrictions by which he is aggrieved or the revocation of his registration, as the case may be, or 7 days after the date when such notification was posted to him by first class pre-paid letter, whichever is the earlier.

(3) An appeal by either party against the decision of the magistrates' court under this section may be made to the Crown Court.

(4) On an appeal to the magistrates' court or to the Crown Court under this section the court may make such order as it thinks fit in relation to the matter which is the subject of the appeal and it shall be the duty of the council to give effect to such order.

[London Local Authorities Act 2000, s 41.]

8–20829ZZZJ 42. Enforcement under Part V. Any person who—

(*a*) busks in any street to which this Part of this Act applies without the authority of a licence; or

(*b*) is concerned with the organisation or management of busking which is not authorised by a licence; or

(*c*) contravenes any condition of his licence; or

(*d*) in connection with his application for a licence makes a statement which he knows to be false in a material particular;

shall be guilty of an offence and shall be liable on summary conviction to a fine not exceeding level 3 on the standard scale.

[London Local Authorities Act 2000, s 42.]

8–20829ZZZK 43. Seizure under Part V. (1) An authorised officer or a constable who has reasonable cause to believe that busking is taking place or is about to take place without a licence or in breach of the terms and conditions of a licence or in a street which is not a licence street to which this Part of this Act applies may require that busking either cease or not take place.

(2) Subject to subsection (3) below if the busking continues or takes place despite the requirement under subsection (1) above the authorised officer or constable may seize and remove any apparatus or equipment used in connection with the busking which may be required to be used in evidence in respect of an offence under section 42 (Enforcement under Part V) of this Act.

(3) An authorised officer or constable shall not seize any apparatus or equipment in pursuance of the powers in subsection (2) above unless the person busking fails to produce, in pursuance of a request by the constable or authorised officer, a licence authorising the busking.

(4) Before exercising any power under this section, an authorised officer shall, if requested to do so by the person busking, produce his authority.

(5)

(*a*) The following provisions of this subsection shall have effect where any apparatus or equipment or any other thing is seized by an authorised officer under subsection (2) above and reference in those provisions to proceedings are to proceedings in respect of the alleged offence in relation to which the apparatus or equipment is seized.

(*b*) Subject to paragraph (*c*) below, after the conclusion of the proceedings, the apparatus or equipment shall be returned to the person from whom it was seized unless—

(i) the court orders it to be forfeited under any enactment;

(ii) any costs awarded to the council by the court, have not been paid within 28 days of the making of the order.

(*c*) Where after 28 days any costs awarded by the court to the council have not been paid to the council in full, the apparatus or equipment may be disposed of in any way the council thinks fit and any sum obtained by the council in excess of the costs awarded by the court shall be returned to the person to whom the apparatus or equipment belongs and when any apparatus or equipment is disposed of by the council under this subsection the council shall have a duty to secure the best possible price which can reasonably be obtained for that apparatus or equipment.

(*d*) If no proceedings are instituted before the expiration of a period of 28 days beginning with the date of seizure, or any proceedings instituted within that period are discontinued, at the expiration of that period or, as the case may be, on the discontinuance of the proceedings, the apparatus or equipment shall, subject to paragraph (*e*) below, be returned to the person from whom it was seized unless it has not proved possible, after diligent enquiry, to identify that person and ascertain his address.

(*e*) Where the apparatus or equipment is not returned because it has not proved possible to identify the person from whom it was seized and ascertain his address, the council (whether the article or thing was seized by an authorised officer or a constable) may apply to a magistrates' court for an order as to the manner in which it should be dealt with.

(6) In this section "authorised officer" includes a person employed by any contractor of the council with whom the council has contracted for the purposes of this section where that person has been authorised in writing by that contractor to act in relation to this section.

(7)

(*a*) This subsection shall have effect where apparatus or equipment is seized under subsection (2) above and either—

(i) not less than six months have passed since the date of the seizure and no information has been laid against any person for an offence under this section in respect of the act or circumstances which occasioned the seizure; or

(ii) proceedings for such an offence have been brought and either the person charged has been acquitted (whether or not on appeal) and the time for appealing against or challenging the acquittal (where applicable) has expired without an appeal or challenge being brought, or the proceedings (including any appeal) have been withdrawn by, or have failed for want of prosecution by, the person by whom the original proceedings were brought.

(*b*) When this subsection has effect a person who has or at the time of seizure had a legal interest in the apparatus or equipment seized may recover compensation from the council or (where it is seized by a constable) the Commissioner by civil action in the County Court in respect of any loss suffered by him as a result of the seizure.

(*c*) The court may only make an order for compensation under paragraph (*b*) above if satisfied that seizure was not lawful under subsection (2) above.

[London Local Authorities Act 2000, s 43.]

8–20829ZZZL 44. *Resolutions under Part V*

8–20829ZZZM

PART VI[1]

MISCELLANEOUS

1. Part VI contains ss 45–52.

MALICIOUS COMMUNICATIONS

Malicious Communications Act 1988

(1988 c 27)

8–20830 1. Offence of sending letters etc with intent to cause distress or anxiety. (1) Any person who sends to another person—

(*a*) a letter, electronic communication or article of any description which conveys—

(i) a message which is indecent or grossly offensive;

(ii) a threat; or

(iii) information which is false and known or believed to be false by the sender; or (*b*) any article or electronic communication which is, in whole or part, of an indecent or grossly offensive nature,

is guilty of an offence if his purpose, or one of his purposes, in sending it is that it should, so far as falling within paragraph (*a*) or (*b*) above, cause distress or anxiety to the recipient or to any other person to whom he intends that it or its contents or nature should be communicated.

(2) A person is not guilty of an offence by virtue of subsection (1)(*a*)(ii) above if he shows—

(a) that the threat was used to reinforce a demand made by him on reasonable grounds; and
(b) that he believed, and had reasonable grounds for believing, that the use of the threat was a proper means of reinforcing the demand.

(2A) In this section 'electronic communication' includes—

(a) any oral or other communication by means of an electronic communications network; and
(b) any communication (however sent) that is in electronic form.

(3) In this section references to sending include references to delivering or transmitting and to causing to be sent, delivered or transmitted and "sender" shall be construed accordingly.

(4) A person guilty of an offence under this section shall be liable on summary conviction to [imprisonment for a term not exceeding six months or to a fine not exceeding level 5 on the standard scale, or to both

[Malicious Communications Act 1988, s 1, as amended by the Criminal Justice and Police Act 2001, s 43 and the Communications Act 2003, Sch 17.]

MEDICINE AND PHARMACY

8–20835 This title contains the following statutes—

The following statutory instrument is also reproduced—

8–20840 European Communities Act 1972: regulations. Within the scope of the title Medicines and Pharmacy would logically fall the subject matter of a number of regulations made under the very wide enabling power provided in section 2(2) of the European Communities Act 1972. Where such regulations create offences they are noted below in chronological order:

Medicines (Administration of Radioactive Substances) Regulations 1978, SI 1978/1066 amended by SI 1995/2147;
Medicines (Stilbenes and Thyrostatic Substances) Regulations 1982, SI 1982/626 amended by SI 1986/1980;
Medicines (Hormone Growth Promoters) (Prohibition on Use) Regulations 1988, SI 1988/705;
Electro-Medical Equipment (EEC Requirements) Regulations 1988, SI 1988/1586;
Controlled Drugs (Substances Useful for Manufacture) Regulations 1991, SI 1991/1285 amended by SI 1992/2814;

Medicines Act 1968 (Application to Radiopharmaceutical Associated Products) Regulations 1992, SI 1992/605 amended by SI 2004/1031;

Controlled Drugs (Substances Useful for Manufacture) (Intra-Community Trade) Regulations 1993, SI 1993/2166 amended by SI 2001/3683 and SI 2004/850;

Medicines (Homeopathic Medicinal Products for Human Use) Regulations 1994, SI 1994/105 amended by SI 1994/899, SI 1995/541, SI 1996/482, SI 1999/566, SI 2000/592, SI 2001/795, SI 2002/236 and 542, SI 2003/2321, SI 2004/1031 and SI 2005/2753;

Medicines (Advertising) Regulations 1994, SI 1994/1932 amended by SI 1996/1552, SI 1999/267 and 784, SI 2002/236, SI 2003/2321, SI 2004/1480 and SI 2005/2787;

Medicines for Human Use (Marketing Authorisation etc) Regulations 1994, SI 1994/3144 amended by SI 1997/2884, SI 1998/3105, SI 1999/1540, SI 2000/292, SI 2001/795, SI 2002/236 and 542, SI 2003/17 and 2321, SI 2004/1031, 2990 and 3224 and SI 2005/50, 768, 1520, 1710 and 2759;

Ionising Radiation (Medical Exposure) Regulations 2000, SI 2000/1059 amended by SI 2004/1031;

Medicines for Human Use (Clinical Trials) Regulations 2004, SI 2004/1031 amended by SI 2004/3224 and SI 2005/2759;

Blood Safety and Quality Regulations 2005, SI 2005/50 amended by SI 2005/1098 and 2898;

Medicines (Traditional Herbal Medicinal Products for Human Use) Regulations 2005, SI 2005/2750;

Veterinary Medicines Regulations 2005, SI 2005/2745;

Medicines for Human Use (Manufacturing, Wholesale Dealing and Miscellaneous Amendments) Regulations 2005, SI 2005/2789.

Cancer Act 1939

(2 & 3 Geo 6 c 13)

8–20870 **4. Prohibition of certain advertisements.** (1) No person shall take any part in the publication of any advertisement[1]—

(*a*) containing an offer to treat any person for cancer, or to prescribe any remedy therefor, or to give any advice in connection with the treatment thereof; or

(*b*) *Repealed.*

(2) If any person contravenes[2] any of the provisions of the foregoing subsection, he shall be liable to summary conviction, in the case of a first conviction, to a fine not exceeding **level 3** on the standard scale or to imprisonment for a term not exceeding **three months**, or to both such a fine and such imprisonment.

(3) *Repealed.*

(4) In any proceedings for a contravention of subsection (1) of this section, it shall be a defence for the person charged to prove—

(*a*) that the advertisement to which the proceedings relate was published only so far as was reasonably necessary to bring it to the notice of persons of the following classes or of one or some of them, that is to say—

(i) members of either House of Parliament or of a local authority or of the governing body of a voluntary hospital[3];

(ii) *Repealed*);

(iii) registered medical practitioners;

(iv) registered nurses;

(v) registered pharmacists and persons lawfully conducting a retail pharmacy business in accordance with s 69 of the Medicines Act 1968;

(vi) persons undergoing training with a view to becoming registered medical practitioners, registered nurses or pharmacists;

(vii) *Repealed*;

(*b*) that the said advertisement was published only in a publication of a technical character intended for circulation mainly amongst persons of the classes mentioned in the last preceding paragraph or one or some of those classes; or

(*c*) that the said advertisement was published in such circumstances that he did not know and had no reason to believe that he was taking part in the publication thereof.

(5) Nothing in this section shall apply in respect of any advertisement published by a local authority or by the governing body of a voluntary hospital or by any person acting with the sanction of the Minister.

[Cancer Act 1939, s 4, as amended by the Medicines Act 1968, Schs 5 and 6, the Criminal Justice Act 1982, ss 35, 38 and 46 and the Statute Law (Repeals) Act 1986, Sch 1.]

1. "Advertisement" includes any notice, circular, label, wrapper or other document and any announcement made orally or by any means of producing or transmitting sounds (sub-s (8)).

2. A prosecution under this section shall not be instituted in England or Wales without the consent of the Attorney-General (sub-s (6)). Subject thereto, it shall be the duty of the council of every county and county borough to institute the proceedings (sub-s (7)).

3. "Hospital" includes a clinic, dispensary or other institution for the reception of the sick, whether as in-patients or out-patients (s 5(1)).

Pharmacy Act 1954

(2 & 3 Eliz 2 c 61)

8–20880 1–5. Qualification, etc.—This consolidating measure provides for the appointment by the Council of the Pharmaceutical Society of Great Britain of a registrar whose duty it is to maintain a register of all persons qualified to be registered as pharmaceutical chemists. Provision is made for qualification by examination, degree or diploma, and for qualification by appropriate European diploma. The registrar shall prepare and publish an Annual Register of Pharmaceutical Chemists. A certificate of registration shall be issued without fee.
[Pharmacy Act 1954, ss 1–5, amended by SI 1987/2202—summarised.]

8–20881 6. Evidence of registration. (1) Any document purporting to be a print of the Annual Register of Pharmaceutical Chemists printed and published by authority of the registrar in any year shall, at any time before the publication of the said Annual Register for the succeeding year, be admissible in any proceedings as evidence that any person named therein is, and that any person not named therein is not, a registered pharmaceutical chemist.

(2) Any such certificate as is mentioned in the last foregoing section (s 5) shall be admissible in any proceedings as evidence that the person named therein as a registered pharmaceutical chemist is a registered pharmaceutical chemist.
[Pharmacy Act 1954, s 6.]

8–20882 7–13. Control of register.—A committee known as "the Statutory Committee" is empowered to direct the removal of a name from the register for prescribed cause and this direction is subject to appeal to the High Court. The registrar must correct the register as required.
[Pharmacy Act 1954, ss 7–13, amended by SI 1987/2202—summarised.]

Offences

8–20883 18. Falsification by the registrar. If the registrar wilfully makes or causes to be made any falsification in any matter relating to the register or the Annual Register of Pharmaceutical Chemists or any such certificate as is mentioned in subsection (5) of section three of this Act, he shall be guilty of a misdemeanour and, in the case of a falsification relating to the said Annual Register, liable to imprisonment for a term not exceeding **twelve months**.
[Pharmacy Act 1954, s 18.]

8–20884 20. Offences relating to certificates. (1) Any person fraudulently exhibits any certificate purporting to be a certificate of membership of the Society, he shall be guilty of a misdemeanour.

(2) If, with intent to deceive, any person—

(*a*) uses, or lends to or allows to be used by any other person any certificate issued under the Pharmacy Acts; or

(*b*) makes or has in his possession any document so closely resembling such a certificate as to be calculated to deceive,

he shall be liable on summary conviction, in respect of each offence, to a fine not exceeding **level 3** on the standard scale and, in the case of a continuing offence, to a further fine not exceeding **£5** for every day subsequent to the day on which he is convicted of the offence during which the contravention continues.

(3) If any person to whom a certificate of registration has been issued in pursuance of section five of this Act ceases to be a registered pharmaceutical chemist he shall, before the expiration of fourteen days from so ceasing, transmit the certificate to the registrar for cancellation, and, if he fails to do so, he shall be liable on summary conviction, in respect of each offence, to a fine not exceeding **level 1** on the standard scale and to a further fine not exceeding **£1** for every day subsequent to the day on which he is convicted of the offence during which the default continues.
[Pharmacy Act 1954, s 20, amended by Criminal Justice Act 1967, 3rd Sch, the Forgery and Counterfeiting Act 1981, Sch and the Criminal Justice Act 1982, ss 38 and 46.]

8–20885 21. Extension of time for certain prosecutions. Notwithstanding anything in the Magistrates' Courts Act 1980, or the Summary Jurisdiction (Scotland) Act 1954, proceedings for an offence under subsection (2) or subsection (3) of the last foregoing section may be commenced at any time within the period of twelve months next after the date of the commission of the offence.
[Pharmacy Act 1954, s 21, as amended by the Magistrates' Courts Act 1980, Sch 7 and the Statute Law (Repeals) Act 1993, Sch 1.]

Medicines Act 1968

(1968 c 67)

PART I
MEDICINES COMMISSION

8–20999 *Part I of the Act (ss 1 to 5) establishes the Medicines Commission to act with respect to medicinal products.*

PART II
LICENCES AND CERTIFICATES RELATING TO MEDICINAL PRODUCTS

General provisions and exemptions

8–21000 7. General provisions as to dealing with medicinal products. (1) The following provisions of this section have effect subject to—

(*a*) any exemption conferred by or under this Part of this Act[1];
(*b*) the provisions of this Part of this Act relating to clinical trials and medicinal tests on animals[2]; and
(*c*) the provisions of section 48[3] of this Act.

(2) Except in accordance with a licence granted[4] for the purposes of this section (in this Act referred to as a "product licence") no person shall[5], in the course of a business carried on by him, and in circumstances to which this subsection applies—

(*a*) sell, supply or export any medicinal product, or
(*b*) procure the sale, supply or exportation of any medicinal product, or
(*c*) procure the manufacture or assembly of any medicinal product for sale, supply or exportation.

(2A) *Repealed.*
(2B) *Repealed.*
(3) No person shall import any medicinal product except in accordance with a product licence.
(3A) The restrictions imposed by subsections (2) and (3) of this section shall not apply where the medicinal product concerned is an investigational medicinal product within the meaning of the Clinical Trials Regulations.
(3B) The restrictions imposed by subsections (2) and (3) of this section shall not apply where the medicinal product concerned is a homoeopathic medicinal product to which the 2001 Directive applies and which fulfils the conditions laid down in Article 14(1) of that Directive.
(4) In relation to an imported medicinal product, subsection (2) of this section applies to circumstances in which the person selling, supplying or exporting the medicinal product in question, or procuring the sale, supply or exportation or the manufacture or assembly for sale, supply or exportation of that product, has himself imported the product or procured its importation.
(5) In relation to any medicinal product which has not been imported, subsection (2) of this section applies to any circumstances in which the person selling, supplying or exporting the medicinal product in question, or procuring the sale, supply or exporting or the manufacture or assembly for sale, supply or exportation of that product,

(*a*) is responsible for the composition of the product, or
(*b*) if that product is a proprietary medicinal product, a ready-made veterinary drug or an industrially produced medicinal product other than a veterinary drug is responsible for the placing of the product on the market in the United Kingdom.

(6) For the purposes of subsection (5) of this section a person shall be taken to be responsible for the composition of a medicinal product if (but only if) in the course of a business carried on by him—

(*a*) he procures the manufacture of the product to his order by another person, where the order specifies, or incorporates by reference to some other document, particulars of the composition of the product ordered, whether those particulars amount to a complete specification or not, or
(*b*) he manufactures the product otherwise than in pursuance of an order which fulfils the conditions specified in the preceding paragraph.

(6A) Where the product which a person is responsible for placing on the market in the United Kingdom is not a veterinary drug, subsection (5)(*b*) of this section shall not apply if the product is—

(*a*) *repealed*
(*b*) a radiopharmaceutical in which the radionuclide is in the form of a sealed source
(*c*) *repealed.*

(6B) Where the product which a person is responsible for placing on the market in the United Kingdom is a veterinary drug, subsection (5)(*b*) of this section shall not apply if the product is—

(*a*) a vaccine, toxin or serum,
(*b*) a product based on radioactive isotopes,

(*c*) a product specially prepared for administration by a veterinary surgeon or veterinary practitioner to a particular animal or herd which is under his care,

(*d*) a homoeopathic medicinal product, or

(*e*) an additive for animal feeding stuffs to which the provisions of Council Directive 70/524/EEC apply.

(7) In this section—

"homoeopathic medicinal product" means any medicinal product (which may contain a number of principles) prepared from substances called homoeopathic stocks in accordance with a homoeopathic manufacturing procedure described by the European Pharmacopoeia or, in the absence thereof, by any pharmacopoeia used officially in a member State;

"proprietary medicinal product" means a ready-prepared medicinal product placed on the market in the United Kingdom under a special name and in a special pack;

"radiopharmaceutical" means a ready-prepared medicinal product which, when ready for use, contains one or more radionuclides included for a medicinal purpose; and

"ready-made veterinary drug" means a ready-prepared veterinary drug placed on the market in the United Kingdom in a pharmaceutical form in which it may be used without further processing, not being a drug placed on the market under a special name and in a special pack;

(i) vaccines, toxins or serums,

(ii) veterinary drugs based on radioactive isotopes,

(iii) veterinary drugs specially prepared for administration by a veterinary surgeon or veterinary practitioner to a particular animal or herd which is under his care,

(iv) homoeopathic veterinary drugs, or

(v) additives for animal feeding stuffs to which the provisions of Council Directive 70/524/EEC apply.

[Medicines Act 1968, s 7, as amended by SI 1977/1050, SI 1983/1724, SI 1992/604, SI 1994/276, SI 2004/1031, SI 2005/50 and SI 2005/2753.]

---

1. Sections 9–14 contain exemptions for doctors, dentists, veterinary surgeons and practitioners, pharmacists, nurses and midwives, herbal remedies, imports, and re-exports; s 16 contains transitional exemptions. A number of orders have been made giving exemption either from s 7 alone, or from some or all of Part II; the following include exemption from s 7:

the Medicines (Importation of Medicinal Products for Re-Exportation) Order 1971, SI 1971/1326 amended by SI 1977/640 and SI 2005/2745;

the Medicines (Exemption from Licences) (Food and Cosmetics) Order 1971, SI 1971/1410 amended by SI 1973/2079;

the Medicines (Exemption from Licences) (Special and Transitional Cases) Order 1971, SI 1971/1450 amended by SI 1972/1200, SI 1978/1139, SI 1979/1585, SI 1989/1184, SI 1989/2323 and SI 2005/2745;

the Medicines (Exemption from Licences) (Special Cases and Miscellaneous Provisions) Order 1972, SI 1972/1200 amended by SI 1974/498, SI 1978/1139, SI 1979/1585, SI 1989/2323,SI 2004/1031 and SI 2005/2745;

the Medicines (Exemption from Licences) (Emergency Importation) Order 1974, SI 1974/316 amended by SI 2005/2745;

the Medicines (Exemption from Licences) (Ingredients) Order 1974, SI 1974/1150 amended by SI 2005/2745;

the Medicines (Exemption from Licences) (Importation) Order 1984, SI 1984/763;

the Medicines (Exemption from Licences) (Intermediate Medicated Feeding Stuffs) Order 1990, SI 1990/567;

the Medicines (Exemption from Licensing) (Radiopharmaceuticals) Order 1992, SI 1992/2844.

2. See ss 31 and 32, post.

3. Section 48 provides for the postponement of restrictions in relation to exports.

4. The licensing authority is the body of Ministers for health and agriculture for England, Scotland and Northern Ireland as specified in s 1(1) of the Act (s 6). Sections 18–30 and Sch 2 of the Act deal with the procedure, etc on an application for a licence, and s 107 states the validity of decisions and the right to apply to the High Court for a decision to be quashed.

5. These restrictions do not apply to anything done before the "first appointed day", being a day to be appointed by order: s 16(1).

8–21001 **8. Provisions as to manufacture and wholesale dealing.** (1) The following provisions of this section shall have effect without prejudice to the operation of section 7 of this Act, but subject to the exemptions and provisions referred to in paragraphs (*a*) to (*c*) of subsection (1) of that section.

(2) Subject to subsections (2A) and (2C) of this section no person shall, in the course of a business carried on by him, manufacture, assemble or import from a third country any medicinal product except in accordance with a licence granted for the purposes of this subsection (in this Act referred to as a "manufacturer's licence")[1].

(2A) In the case of a medicinal product that is an investigational medicinal product, the restrictions imposed by subsection (2) of this section only apply—

(*a*) if the product has a product licence or marketing authorization, and

(*b*) to the extent that the manufacture or assembly of the product is in accordance with the terms and conditions of that licence or authorization.

(2B) In subsection (2A) of this section—

"investigational medicinal product" has the meaning given by the Clinical Trials Regulations; and

"marketing authorization" means—

(*a*) a marketing authorization issued by a competent authority in accordance with Directive 2001/83/EC, or
(*b*) a marketing authorization granted by the European Commission under Council Regulation (EEC) 2309/93.

(2C) The prohibition in subsection (2) does not apply to a person who, in connection with the importation of a medicinal product from a third country—

(*a*) provides facilities solely for transporting the product, or
(*b*) in the course of a business carried on by him as an import agent, imports the medicinal product solely to the order of another person who holds a manufacturer's licence authorising the importation of the product.

(2D) The Ministers may prescribe requirements (either generally or in relation to a prescribed class of medicinal product or activity)—

(*a*) with which the holder of a manufacturer's licence must comply, and
(*b*) which are to have effect as if they were provisions of the licence.

(3) Subject to subsections (3C) and (3D) of this section no person shall, in the course of a business carried on by him—

(*a*) sell, or offer for sale, any medicinal product by way of wholesale dealing, or
(*b*) distribute, otherwise than by way of sale, any proprietary medicinal product, ready-made veterinary drug or industrially produced medicinal product other than a veterinary drug which has been imported, but was not consigned from a member State,

except in accordance with a wholesale dealer's licence[1].

(3A) Without prejudice to the generality of subsection (3) of this section but subject to subsections (3C) and (3D), no person shall, in the course of a business carried on by him, distribute by way of wholesale dealing a product to which the 2001 Directive applies except in accordance with a wholesale dealer's licence.

(3B) Distribution of such a product by way of wholesale dealing shall not be taken to be in accordance with a wholesale dealer's licence unless, in particular, it occurs in the course of a business which is carried on at a place or places specified in the licence.

(3C) The restrictions imposed by subsections (3) and (3A) of this section do not apply to anything done in relation to a product to which the 2001 Directive applies by the holder of a manufacturer's licence in respect of it.

(3D) The restrictions imposed by subsections (3) and (3A) of this section shall not apply where the medicinal product concerned is a homeopathic medicinal product with the meaning of the Clinical Trials Regulations.

(3E) The Ministers may prescribe requirements (either generally or in relation to a prescribed class of medicinal product or activity)—

(*a*) with which the holder of a wholesale dealer's licence must comply, and
(*b*) which are to have effect as if they were provisions of the licence.

(4) Where the product which a person distributes is not a veterinary drug subsection (3)(*b*) of this section shall not apply if the product is–

(*a*) *repealed*
(*b*) a radiopharmaceutical in which the radionuclide is in the form of a sealed source,
(*c*) *repealed*.

(5) Where the product which a person distributes is a veterinary drug, subsection (3)(*b*) of this section shall not apply if the product is—

(*a*) a vaccine, toxin or serum,
(*b*) a product based on radioactive isotopes,
(*c*) a product specially prepared for administration by a veterinary surgeon or veterinary practitioner to a particular animal or herd which is under his care.
(*d*) a homoeopathic medicinal product, or
(*e*) an additive for animal feeding stuffs to which the provisions of Council Directive 70/524/EEC apply.

(6) In this section, "homoeopathic medicinal product", "proprietary medicinal product", "radiopharmaceutical" and "ready-made veterinary drug" have the same meanings as in section 7 of this Act.

(7) In this section any reference to distribution of a product by way of wholesale dealing is a reference to—

(*a*) selling or supplying it, or
(*b*) procuring, holding or exporting it for the purposes of sale or supply, to a person who receives it for the purposes of—
   (i) selling or supplying it, or
   (ii) administering it or causing it to be administered to one or more human beings,

in the course of a business carried on by that person.

(8) In this Act any reference to a wholesale dealer's licence is a reference to a licence granted for the purposes of subsection (3) or (3A) of this section.

[Medicines Act 1968, s 8, as amended by SI 1977/1050, SI 1983/1724, SI 1992/604, SI 1993/834, SI 1994/276, SI 2002/236, SI 2004/1031, 2005/50 and SI 2005/2789.]

---

1. A number of orders have been made giving exemption either from s 8 alone or from some or all of Pt II; the following include exemption from s 8 generally:

the Medicines (Exemption from Licences) (Food and Cosmetics) Order 1971, SI 1971/1410 amended by SI 1973/2079;

the Medicines (Exemption from Licences) (Special and Transitional Cases) Order 1971, SI 1971/1450 amended by SI 1972/1200. SI 1978/1139, SI 1979/1585, SI 1989/1184, SI 1989/2323 and SI 2005/2745;

the Medicines (Exemption from Licences) (Special Cases and Miscellaneous Provisions) Order 1972, SI 1972/1200 amended by SI 1974/498, SI 1978/1139, SI 1979/1585, SI 1989/2323, SI 2004/1031 and SI 2005/2745;

the Medicines (Exemption from Licences) (Ingredients) Order 1974, SI 1974/1150 amended by SI 2005/2745;

Exemption from the restrictions of s 8(2) alone are contained in:

the Medicines (Exemption from Licences) (Assembly) Order 1979, SI 1979/1114;

the Medicines (Contact Lens Fluids and other Substances) (Exemption from Licences) Order 1979, SI 1979/1585 amended by SI 1979/1745.

Exemption from the restrictions of s 8(3) are contained in:

the Medicines (Exemption from Licences) (Wholesale Dealing in Confectionery) Order 1975, SI 1975/762;

the Medicines (Exemption from Licences) (Wholesale Dealing) Order 1990, SI 1990/566 amended by SI 2005/2745.

Clinical trials and medicinal tests on animals

8–21002 31. Clinical trials. (1) In this Act "clinical trial" means an investigation or series of investigations consisting of the administration of one or more medicinal products of a particular description—

(*a*) by, or under the direction of, a doctor or dentist to one or more patients of his, or

(*b*) by, or under the direction of, two or more doctors or dentists, each product being administered by, or under the direction of, one or other of those doctors or dentists to one or more patients of his,

where (in any such case) there is evidence that medicinal products of that description have effects which may be beneficial to the patient or patients in question and the administration of the product or products is for the purpose of ascertaining whether, or to what extent, the product has, or the products have, those or any other effects, whether beneficial or harmful.

(2) Subject to the following provisions of this Act, no person shall, in the course of a business carried on by him—

(*a*) sell or supply any medicinal product for the purposes of a clinical trial, or

(*b*) procure the sale or supply of any medicinal product for the purposes of a clinical trial, or

(*c*) procure the manufacture or assembly of any medicinal product for sale or supply for the purposes of a clinical trial,

unless one or other of the conditions specified in the next following subsection is fulfilled.

(3) Those conditions, in relation to a person doing any of the things specified in the preceding subsection, are—

(*a*) that he is the holder of a product licence[1] which authorises the clinical trial in question, or does it to the order of the holder of such a licence, and (in either case) he does it in accordance with that licence;

(*b*) that a certificate for the purposes of this section (in this Act referred to as a "clinical trial certificate"[2]) has been issued certifying that, subject to the provisions of the certificate, the licensing authority have consented to the clinical trial in question and that certificate is for the time being in force and the trial is to be carried out in accordance with that certificate.

(4) Subject to the following provisions of this Act, no person shall import any mechanical product for the purposes of a clinical trial unless either—

(*a*) he is the holder of a product licence which authorises that clinical trial or imports the product to the order of the holder of such a licence, and (in either case) he imports it in accordance with that licence, or

(*b*) a clinical trial certificate has been issued certifying as mentioned in subsection (3)(*b*) of this section and that certificate is for the time being in force and the trial is to be carried out in accordance with that certificate.

(5) Subject to the next following subsection, the restrictions imposed by the preceding provisions of this section do not apply to a doctor or dentist in respect of his selling or supplying, or procuring the sale or supply of, a medicinal product, or procuring the manufacture or assembly of a medicinal product specially prepared to his order, or specially importing a medicinal product, where (in any such case) he is, or acts at the request of, the doctor or dentist by whom, or under whose direction, the product is to be administered.

(6) The exemptions conferred by the last preceding subsection do not apply in a case where the

clinical trial in question is to be carried out under arrangements made by, or at the request of, a third party (that is to say, a person who is not the doctor or dentist, or one of the doctors or dentists, by whom, or under whose direction, one or more medicinal products are to be administered in that trial).

(7) The restrictions imposed by subsection (2) of this section do not apply to anything which is done in a registered pharmacy, a hospital or a health centre and is done there by or under the supervision of a pharmacist in accordance with a prescription given by a doctor or dentist; and those restrictions do not apply to anything done by or under the supervision of a pharmacist which consists of procuring the preparation or dispensing of a medicinal product in accordance with a prescription given by a doctor or dentist, or of procuring the assembly of a medicinal product.

(8) The restrictions imposed by subsection (2) of this section also do not apply to anything done in relation to a medicinal product where—

(*a*) it is done by the person who, in the course of a business carried on by him, has manufactured or assembled the product, where he has manufactured or assembled it to the order of a doctor or dentist who has stated that it is required for administration to a patient of his or is required, at the request of another doctor or dentist, for administration to a patient of that other doctor or dentist, or

(*b*) it is done by the person who, in the course of a business carried on by him, has manufactured or assembled the product to the order of a pharmacist in accordance with a prescription given by a practitioner, or

(*c*) it consists of selling the product by way of wholesale dealing where it has been manufactured or assembled on the circumstances specified in paragraph (*a*) or paragraph (*b*) of this subsection.

(9) For the purposes of this section a product licence shall be taken to be a licence which authorises a particular clinical trial if—

(*a*) the trial is to be a trial of medicinal products of a description to which the licence relates, and

(*b*) the uses of medicinal products of that description which are referred to in the licence are such as to include their use for the purposes of that trial.

(10) A clinical trial certificate may certify as mentioned in subsection (3)(*b*) of this section without specifying the doctor or dentist (or, if there is to be more than one, any of the doctors or dentists) by whom, or under whose direction, any medicinal product is to be administered, or the patient or patients to whom any medicinal product is to be administered.

[Medicines Act 1968, s 31.]

1. See s 7, ante.
2. Sections 36–39 of the Act deal with the procedure, etc on an application for a certificate.

8–21003 32. Medicinal tests on animals. (1) Subject to the following provisions of this Act[1], no person shall, in the course of a business carried on by him—

(*a*) sell or supply any medicinal product for the purposes of a medicinal test on animals, or

(*b*) procure the sale or supply of any medicinal product for the purposes of such a test, or

(*c*) procure the manufacture or assembly of any medicinal product for sale or supply for the purposes of such a test,

unless one or other of the conditions specified in the next following subsection is fulfilled.

(2) Those conditions, in relation to a person doing any of the things specified in the preceding subsection, are—

(*a*) that he is the holder of a product licence which authorises the test in question, or he does it to the order of the holder of such a licence, and (in either case) he does it in accordance with that licence;

(*b*) that a certificate for the purposes of this section (in this Act referred to as an "animal test certificate") has been issued certifying that, subject to the provisions of the certificate, the licensing authority have consented to the test in question and that certificate is for the time being in force and the test is to be carried out in accordance with that certificate.

(3) Subject to the following provisions of this Act, no person shall import any medicinal product for the purposes of a medicinal test on animals unless either—

(*a*) he is the holder of a product licence which authorises that test, or imports the product to the order of the holder of such a licence, and (in either case) he imports it in accordance with that licence, or

(*b*) an animal test certificate has been issued certifying as mentioned in subsection (2)(*b*) of this section and that certificate is for the time being in force and the test is to be carried out in accordance with that certificate.

(4) Subject to the following provisions of this Act, no person shall, in the course of a business carried on by him, administer any substance or article to an animal by way of a medicinal test on animals, or procure any substance or article to be so administered, unless either—

(*a*) in the case of a medicinal product, there is in force a product licence (whether held by him or by another person) which authorises that test and the product is administered in accordance with that licence or in accordance with any instructions required by the licence to be communicated to the person carrying out the test, or

(*b*) whether the substance or article is a medicinal product or not, an animal test certificate has been issued certifying as mentioned in subsection (2)(*b*) of this section and that certificate is for the time being in force and the substance or article is administered in accordance with that certificate.

(5) For the purposes of this section a product licence shall be taken to be a licence which authorises a particular medicinal test on animals if—

(*a*) the substance or article to be administered in the test is a medicinal product of a description to which the licence relates, and

(*b*) the uses of medicinal products of that description which are referred to in the licence are such as to include their test for the purposes of that test.

(6) In this Act "medicinal test on animals" means an investigation or series of investigations consisting of any of the following, that is to say—

(*a*) the administration of a medicinal product of a particular description to one or more animals, where there is evidence that medicinal products of that description have effects which may be beneficial to, or otherwise advantageous in relation to, that animal or those animals, and the product is administered for the purpose of ascertaining whether, or to what extent, it has those or any other effects, whether advantageous or otherwise;

(*b*) the administration of a medicinal product to one or more animals in circumstances where there is no such evidence as is mentioned in the preceding paragraph, and the product is administered for the purpose of ascertaining whether, or to what extent, it has any effects relevant to a medicinal purpose;

(*c*) the administration of any substance or article, other than a medicinal product, to one or more animals for the purpose of ascertaining whether it has any effects relevant to a medicinal purpose, whether there is evidence that it has effects which may be beneficial to, or otherwise advantageous in relation to, that animal or those animals or not.

[Medicines Act 1968, s 32.]

1. Section 33 provides certain exemptions in respect of medicinal tests on animals, and s 35 contains supplementary provisions as to clinical trials and medicinal tests on animals.

8–21004 **34. Restrictions as to animals on which medicinal test have been carried out.** (1) Subject of the following provisions of this Act, no person shall in the course of a business carried on by him sell or supply for human consumption an animal to which in the course of that business a substance or article has been administered by way of a test to which this section applies, or the carcase or any part of the carcase or any produce of such an animal, unless—

(*a*) at the time when the substance or article was so administered there was in force an animal test certificate issued in respect of that test, and

(*b*) all the provisions of that certificate relating to the carrying out of the test and the disposal of the animal or its carcase or produce are, and have at all material times been, complied with.

(2) This section applies to any medicinal test on animals which is carried out in the course of the business of the person who has manufactured the substance or article administered in the test, or is carried out on his behalf in the course of the business of a laboratory or research establishment carried on by another person, and (in either case) is so carried out on one or more animals kept in the course of the business of the person carrying out the test.

[Medicines Act 1968, s 34.]

Medicated animal feeding stuffs

8–21005 **40. Medicated animal feeding stuffs.** (1) The Agriculture Ministers[1] may by regulations[2] prohibit the incorporation by any person, in the course of a business carried on by him, of a medicinal product of any description in an animal feeding stuff unless such of the conditions mentioned in subsection (2) of this section as may be specified in the regulations are satisfied.

(2) The conditions referred to in subsection (1) of this section are—

(*a*) that it is incorporated in accordance with provisions relating to the incorporation of the medicinal product in animal feeding stuffs contained in a product licence or animal test certificate (whether held by him or by another person);

(*b*) that it is incorporated in accordance with a written direction given by a veterinary surgeon or veterinary practitioner, being a written direction complying with such requirements as may be specified in the regulations;

(*c*) that the person concerned is for the time being entered in a register kept for the purposes of the regulations by the registrar or the Northern Ireland enforcement authority.

(3) A condition imposed by virtue of subsection (2)(*a*) of this section shall be taken to be satisfied if the person incorporating the medicinal product in the animal feeding stuff—

(*a*) is not the holder of a product licence or animal test certificate containing such provisions as are mentioned in that paragraph,

(*b*) believes, on reasonable grounds, that another person is the holder of such a licence or certificate containing such provisions and that the medicinal product is incorporated in accordance with those provisions.

(4) The Agriculture Ministers may by regulations[1] prohibit—

(*a*) the sale, offer for sale, supply or export by any person in the course of a business carried on by him of any animal feeding stuff in which a medicinal product has been incorporated, or

(*b*) the importation by any person of any animal feeding stuff in which a medicinal product has been incorporated,

unless such of the conditions mentioned in subsection (5) of this section as may be specified in the regulations are satisfied.

(5) The conditions referred to in subsection (4) of this section are—

(*a*) that the medicinal product was not incorporated in the animal feeding stuff in contravention of any prohibition imposed by virtue of subsection (1) of this section;

(*b*) that the feeding stuff is sold, offered for sale, supplied, exported or imported (as the case may be) in accordance with a written direction given by a veterinary surgeon or veterinary practitioner, being a written direction complying with such requirements as may be specified in the regulations;

(*c*) that the person concerned is for the time being entered in a register kept for the purposes of the regulations by the registrar or the Northern Ireland enforcement authority.

(6) A condition imposed by virtue of subsection (5)(*a*) of this section shall be taken to be satisfied if the person selling, offering for sale, supplying, exporting or importing the animal feeding stuff—

(*a*) did not incorporate the medicinal product in it, and

(*b*) had no reasonable grounds to believe that it was incorporated in contravention of any prohibition imposed by virtue of subsection (1) of this section.

(7) Regulations under this section may impose such conditions as the Agriculture Ministers[3] think fit in respect of the inclusion or retention of persons in a register kept for the purposes of the regulations, including conditions requiring the payment to the registrar or the Northern Ireland enforcement authority of fees of such amounts as the Agriculture Ministers may with the consent of the Treasury determine.

(8)–(9) *Supplementary provisions as to fees.*

(10) A person contravenes this section if he contravenes any prohibition imposed by virtue of subsection (1) or (4) of this section.

(11) References in this Act to the incorporation of a medicinal product in an animal feeding stuff do not include a reference to it being so incorporated in the course of making a medicinal product; but, subject to that, they include a reference to the incorporation—

(*a*) for a medicinal purpose of a substance or article other than a medicinal product, or

(*b*) of a substance in which a medicinal product has been incorporated,

in an animal feeding stuff.

(12) In this section—

"the Northern Ireland enforcement authority" means any Northern Ireland Department having a duty to enforce any provision of this section or of regulations under it; and

"the registrar" means any person appointed under section 1 of the Pharmacy Act 1954 as registrar for the purposes of that Act.

[Medicines Act 1968, s 40, as substituted by the Animal Health and Welfare Act 1984, s 13.]

---

1. Now the Secretary of State for Environment, Food and Rural Affairs, see the Ministry of Agriculture, Fisheries and Food (Dissolution) Order 2002, SI 2002/794.

2. See now the Veterinary Medicines Regulations 2005, SI 2005/2745, made under s 2(2) of the European Communities Act 1972 and listed ante.

3. Now the Secretary of State for Environment, Food and Rural Affairs, see the Ministry of Agriculture, Fisheries and Food (Dissolution) Order 2002, SI 2002/794.

Supplementary provisions

8–21006 43. Extension of s 7 to certain special circumstances. (1) Where in the course of a business carried on by him a person sells, supplies or exports a substance or article for use wholly or mainly in either or both of the ways specified in section 130(1) of this Act, and the substance or article not having been—

(*a*) manufactured or imported for such use, or

(*b*) previously sold or supplied for such use,

does not constitute a medicinal product before that person so sells, supplies or exports it, then (subject to subsection (2) of this section) subsection (2) of section 7 of this Act, if apart from this subsection it would not so have effect, shall have effect in relation to the sale, supply or exportation or the substance or article as if he were selling, supplying or exporting it in circumstances to which that subsection applies.

(2) Subsection (1) of this section shall not have effect in relation to a transaction whereby a person, in the course of a business carried on by him, sells a substance or article or supplies a substance or article in circumstances corresponding to retail sale unless in the course of that business the substance or article has been assembled for the purpose of being sold or supplied by him.

(3) In any reference in this Part of this Act to the provisions of, or the restrictions imposed, by section 7 of this Act, the reference to that section shall be construed as including a reference to subsection (2) of that section as extended by the preceding subsections.

(4) Where in the course of a business carried on by him a person proposes to sell, supply or export a substance or article for use as mentioned in subsection (1) of this section, where the substance or article will not constitute a medicinal product before he so sells, supplies or exports it and he will not be selling, supplying or exporting it in circumstances to which section 7(2) of this Act applies, he may, if he so desires, apply for a product licence in respect of that substance or article, and the licensing authority (subject to the provisions of sections 19 to 22* of this Act) may grant to him a product licence in respect of it, as if he were proposing to sell, supply or export it in circumstances to which section 7(2) of this Act applies; and a product licence so granted may be renewed, suspended, revoked or varied accordingly.

(5) In subsection (2) of this section the reference to assembling a substance or article in the course of a business carried on by a person is a reference to doing in the course of that business anything which (in accordance with section 132(1) of this Act) would constitute assembling if it had been a medicinal product when sold or supplied to him.

[Medicines Act 1968, s 43.]

***"22A" substituted by SI 2005/1094 from 30 October 2005.**

8–21007 **44. Provision of information to licensing authority.** (1) Where an application has been made to the licensing authority for a licence under this Part of this Act (including a licence of right) or for a clinical trial certificate or animal test certificate (including a certificate to which a person is entitled by virtue of section 37(4) of this Act) the licensing authority, before determining the application, may request the applicant to furnish to the licensing authority such information relating to the application as the licensing authority may consider requisite; and, where any such request has been made, the licensing authority shall not be required to determine the application until either—

(*a*) the information requested has been furnished to them, or
(*b*) it has been shown to their reasonable satisfaction that the applicant is unable to furnish the information.

(2) The licensing authority may serve on the holder of a licence under this Part of this Act, or of a clinical trial certificate or animal test certificate, a notice requiring him, within such time as may be specified in the notice, to furnish to the licensing authority information of any description specified in the notice in accordance with the following provisions of this section.

(3) Except as provided by subsection (4) of this section, a notice under subsection (2) of this section shall not be served unless it appears to the licensing authority, or it is represented to them by the appropriate committee, that circumstances exist by reason of which it is necessary to consider whether the licence or certificate should be varied, suspended or revoked; and the information required by such a notice shall be such as appears to the licensing authority, or is represented to them by the committee, to be requisite for considering that question.

(4) Subsection (3) of this section shall not have effect in the case of a licence of right, or of a certificate issued in pursuance of section 37(4) of this Act, whether the licence or certificate has been renewed or not; and in the case of such a licence or certificate, a notice under this section may be served at any time and may require any information which, in the opinion of the licensing authority, would be relevant if—

(*a*) sections 25 and 37(4) of this Act had not been enacted, and
(*b*) the licensing authority were then dealing with an application, by the person who is the holder of the licence or certificate, for the grant or issue of a licence or certificate containing the same provisions as those contained in the licence or certificate in question.

(5) Before the end of the period of two years from the date on which a product licence, other than a licence of right, is granted, the holder of the licence shall, in respect of each description of medicinal products to which the licence relates which is effectively on the market in the United Kingdom within that period, notify to the licensing authority a date on which medicinal products of that description were effectively on that market.

[Medicines Act 1968, s 44 as amended by SI 2005/1094.]

8–21008 45. Offences under Part II[1].—(1) Subject to the next following section, any person who contravenes any of the provisions of section 7, section 8, section 31, section 32, section 34 or section 40 of this Act, or who is in possession of any medicinal product or animal feeding stuff for the purpose of selling, supplying or exporting it in contravention of any of those sections, shall be guilty of an offence.

(2) Where any medicinal product or animal feeding stuff is imported in contravention of section 7, section 31, section 32 or section 40 of this Act, any person who, otherwise than for the purpose of performing or exercising a duty or power imposed or conferred by or under this Act or any other enactment, is in possession of the product or feeding stuff knowing or having reasonable cause to suspect that it was so imported shall be guilty of an offence.

(3) Any person who, being the holder of a product licence or of a clinical trial certificate or animal test certificate, procures another person to carry out a process in the manufacture or assembly or medicinal products of a description to which the licence or certificate relates, and—

(*a*) does not communicate to that person the provisions of the licence or certificate which are applicable to medicinal products of that description, or

(*b*) in a case where any of those provisions has been varied by a decision of the licensing authority, does not communicate the variation to that person within fourteen days after notice of the decision has been served on him,

shall be guilty of an offence.

(4) Any person who, being the holder of a product licence or of an animal test certificate, sells or supplies a substance or article to which the licence or certificate relates to another person for the purpose of its being incorporated in any animal feeding stuff, and does not communicate to that person any provisions of the licence or certificate which relate to the incorporation of that substance or article in animal feeding stuffs, or any instructions required by the licence to be communicated by him to persons to whom the substance or article is sold or supplied for that purpose, shall be guilty of an offence.

(5) Where any such provisions of a product licence or animal test certificate as are mentioned in subsection (4) of this section are varied by the licensing authority, and on varying those provisions the licensing authority serve on the holder of the licence or certificate a notice requiring him, within such time (not being less than fourteen days from the date of service of the notice) as may be specified in the notice, to take such steps as may be so specified for making the variation known, either generally or to persons or classes of persons specified in the notice, then if the holder of the licence or certificate does not comply with the requirements of that notice he shall be guilty of an offence.

(6) Any person who, in giving any information which he is required to give under section 44 of this Act, makes a statement which he knows to be false in a material particular shall be guilty of an offence.

(7) Any person who without reasonable excuse fails to comply with a requirement imposed on him by a notice under section 44(2) of this Act shall be guilty of an offence.

(8) Any person guilty of an offence under any of subsections (1) to (6) of this section shall be liable[2]—

(*a*) on summary conviction, to a fine not exceeding **the statutory maximum**;

(*b*) on conviction on indictment, to a **fine** or to imprisonment for a term not exceeding **two years** or to **both**.

(9) Any person guilty of an offence under subsection (7) of this section shall be liable on summary conviction to a fine not exceeding **level 3** on the standard scale.

[Medicines Act 1968, s 45, as amended by the Criminal Law Act 1977, s 28 and the Criminal Justice Act 1982, ss 38 and 46.]

1. A number of orders have been made giving exemption from ss 7 or 8 and these are noted to those sections, the following orders have given exemption more generally from Part II of the Act:
the Medicines (Exemption from Licences) (Special and Transitional Cases) Order 1971, SI 1971/1450 amended by SI 1972/1200, SI 1978/1139, SI 1979/1585, SI 1989/1184, SI 1989/2323 and SI 2005/2745;
the Medicines (Exemption from Licences) (Special Cases and Miscellaneous Provisions) Order 1972, SI 1972/1200 amended by SI 1974/498, SI 1978/1139, SI 1979/1585, SI 1989/2323, SI 2004/1031 and SI 2005/2745;
the Medicines (Exemption from Licences) (Ingredients) Order 1974, SI 1974/1150 amended by SI 2005/2745;
2. For procedure in respect of this offence, triable either way, see Magistrates' Courts Act 1980, ss 17A–21 in PART I: MAGISTRATES' COURTS, PROCEDURE.

8–21009 46. Special defences under s 45. (1) Where the holder of a product licence or of a clinical trial certificate or animal test certificate is charged with an offence under the last preceding section in respect of any substance or article which has been manufactured (or, in the case of a medicinal product, manufactured or assembled) to his order by another person and has been so manufactured or assembled as not to comply with the provisions to that licence or certificate which are applicable to it, shall be a defence for him to prove—

(*a*) that he had communicated those provisions to that other person, and

(*b*) that he did not know, and could not by the exercise of reasonable care have discovered, that those provisions had not been complied with.

(2) Where the holder of a manufacturer's licence is charged with an offence under the last preceding section in respect of any medicinal products which have been manufactured or assembled by him, in circumstances where he is not the holder of a product licence or of a clinical trial certificate or animal test certificate which is applicable to those products, but the products were manufactured or assembled to the order of another person, it shall be a defence for him to prove that he believed, and had reasonable grounds for believing—

(*a*) that the other person in question was the holder of a product licence applicable to those products, or of a clinical trial certificate or animal test certificate applicable to them, and
(*b*) that the products were manufactured or assembled in accordance with that product licence or certificate.

(3)–(4) *Repealed.*
[Medicines Act 1968, s 46, as amended by the Animal Health and Welfare Act 1984, Sch 1 and 2.]

8–21010 **47.** *Regulations to prescribe standard provisions.*

PART III[1]
FURTHER PROVISIONS RELATING TO DEALINGS WITH MEDICINAL PRODUCTS

Provisions as to sale or supply of medicinal products

8–21011 **51. General sale lists.** (1) The appropriate Ministers[2] may by order[3] specify descriptions or classes of medicinal products, as being products which in their opinion can with reasonable safety be sold or supplied otherwise than by, or under the supervision of, a pharmacist.

(2) In this Act any reference to a medicinal product on a general sale list is a reference to a medicinal product of a description, or falling within a class, specified in an order under this section which is for the time being in force.

(3) An order under this section may designate any description or class of medicinal products specified in the order as being medicinal products which, in the opinion of the appropriate Ministers, can with reasonable safety be sold by means of automatic machines; and any reference in this Act to a medicinal product in the automatic machines section of a general sale list is a reference to a medicinal product of a description, or falling within a class, so designated by any such order which is for the time being in force.
[Medicines Act 1968, s 51.]

---

1. This part of the Act shall have effect as if all relevant medicinal products were medicinal products for the purposes of the Act (whether or not they would otherwise be so). See the Medicines for Human Use (Marketing Authorisations etc) Regulations 1994, SI 1994/3144 made under s 2 of the European Communities Act 1972 and listed, ante.

2. Now the Secretary of State for Health, see the Transfer of Functions (Medicines and Poisons) Order 1999, SI 1999/3142 and the Secretary of State for Environment, Food and Rural Affairs, see the Ministry of Agriculture, Fisheries and Food (Dissolution) Order 2002, SI 2002/794.

3. The Medicines (Veterinary Drugs) (General Sale List) Order 1984, SI 1984/768, and the Medicines (Products Other Than Veterinary Drugs) (General Sale List) Order 1984, SI 1984/769, amended by SI 1985/1540, SI 1987/910, SI 1989/969, SI 1990/1129, SI 1992/1535, SI 1994/2410, SI 1995/3216, SI 1997/2043, SI 1998/2170, SI 1999/852 and 2535, SI 2000/1092 and 2526, SI 2001/2068 and 4111 and SI 2002/933 and SI 2005/2750.

8–21012 **52. Sale or supply of medicinal products not on general sale list.** Subject to any exemption conferred by or under this Part of this Act[1], on and after such day as the Minister may by order[2] appoint for the purposes of this section (in this Part of this Act referred to as "the appointed day") no person shall, in the course of a business carried on by him, sell by retail, offer or expose for sale by retail, or supply in circumstances corresponding to retail sale, any medicinal product which is not a medicinal product on a general sale list, unless—

(*a*) that person is, in respect of that business, a person lawfully conducting a retail pharmacy business;
(*b*) the product is sold, offered or exposed for sale, or supplied, on premises which are a registered pharmacy; and
(*c*) that person, or, if the transaction is carried out on his behalf by another person, then that other person, is, or acts under the supervision of, a pharmacist.

[Medicines Act 1968, s 52.]

---

1. Sections 55 and 56 contain exemptions for doctors, dentists, veterinary surgeons and practitioners, and herbal remedies; and s 57 gives power for these exemptions to be extended or modified by order. See the Medicines (Pharmacy and General Sale—Exemption) Order 1980, SI 1980/1924, amended by SI 1982/27, SI 1989/1852, SI 1994/2409 and 3142, SI 1997/1350, SI 1998/107 and 2368, SI 2000/2469, SI 2002/880, SI 2003/697, SI 2004/1, 1190 and 1771 and SI 2005/766, 848, 1507, 2745, 2750, 2759 and 3324; the Medicines (Retail Sale or Supply of Herbal Remedies) Order 1977, SI 1977/2130 amended by SI 2005/2745 and 2750; the Medicines (Collection and Delivery Arrangements-—Exemption) Order 1978, SI 1978/1421.

2. The day appointed for the purposes of this section was 1 February 1978 (SI 1977/2126).

8–21013 **53. Sale or supply of medicinal products on general sale list.** (1) Subject to any exemption conferred by or under this Part of this Act[1], on and after the appointed day no person shall, in the course of a business carried on by him, sell by retail, or offer or expose for sale by retail, or supply in circumstances corresponding to retail sale, any medicinal product on a general sale list elsewhere than at a registered pharmacy, unless the conditions specified in the following provisions of this section are fulfilled.

(2) The place at which the medicinal product is sold, offered, exposed or supplied as mentioned in the preceding subsection must be premises of which the person carrying on the business in question is the occupier and which he is able to close so as to exclude the public, unless either—

(*a*) the product is sold, offered, exposed for sale or supplied by means of an automatic machine and the product is a medicinal product in the automatic machines section of a general sale list, or

(*b*) the product is a veterinary drug.

(3) The medicinal product must have been made up for sale in a container elsewhere than at the place at which it is sold, offered, exposed for sale or supplied as mentioned in subsection (1) of this section and the container must not have been opened since the product was made up for sale in it.

(4) The business, so far as concerns the sale or supply of medicinal products, must be carried on in accordance with such conditions (if any) as may be prescribed[2] for the purposes of this section.
[Medicines Act 1968, s 53.]

---

1. See note 1 to s 52 above.
2. The Medicines (Sale or Supply) (Miscellaneous Provisions) Regulations 1980, SI 1980/1923 amended by SI 1982/28, SI 1990/1124 and 2487, SI 1992/2938, SI 1994/2411 and 3142, SI 1995/3215, SI 1997/1831 and 2045, SI 1998/1045, SI 1999/644 and 2510, SI 2000/7, 1070, 1918, SI 2001/3849, SI 2002/2469, SI 2003/698, SI 2004/1771 and SI 2005/764, 1520, 2745 and 2750 provides controls for the safekeeping of veterinary drugs, the location of automatic machines, the persons to be supplied and records; offences are created punishable on summary conviction with a maximum fine of **£400**.

8–21014 **54. Sale of medicinal products from automatic machines.** (1) On and after th appointed day no person shall sell, or offer or expose for sale, any medicinal product by means of automatic machine unless it is a medicinal product in the automatic machines section of a ger sale list.

(2) The appropriate Ministers may by order provide that no person shall by means of an auton machine sell, or offer or expose for sale, any medicinal product to which the order applies unless container in which it is sold, or offered or exposed for sale, complies with such restrictions as to the quantity of the medicinal product, or the number of medicinal product, or the number of medicinal products, which it contains as may be specified in the order.

(3) An order under subsection (2) of this section may be made either in respect of medicinal products generally or in respect of medicinal products of a particular description or falling within a particular class specified in the order.
[Medicines Act 1968, s 54.]

Additional provisions

8–21015 **58. Medicinal products on prescription only.** (1) The appropriate Ministers may by order[1] specify descriptions or classes of medicinal products[2] for the purposes of this section; and, in relation to any description or class so specified, the order shall state which of the following, that is to say—

(*a*) doctors,
(*b*) dentists, and
(*c*) veterinary surgeons and veterinary practitioners,
(*d*) registered nurses or midwives who are of such a description and comply with such conditions as may be specified in the order, and
(*e*) other persons who are of such a description and comply with such conditions as may be specified in the order.

are to be appropriate practitioners for the purposes of this section.★

(1A) The descriptions of persons which may be specified in an order by virtue of subsection (1)(*e*) are the following, or any sub-category of such a description—

(*a*) persons who are registered in the register maintained under article 5 of the Health Professions Order 2001;
(*b*) persons who are pharmacists;
(*c*) persons whose names are entered in a roll or record established by the General Dental Council by virtue of section 45 of the Dentists Act 1984 (c 24) (dental auxiliaries);
(*d*) persons who are registered in either of the registers of ophthalmic opticians kept under section 7(*a*) of the Opticians Act 1989 (c 44); and
(*e*) persons who are registered osteopaths within the meaning of the Osteopaths Act 1993 (c 21);
(*f*) persons who are registered chiropractors within the meaning of the Chiropractors Act 1994 (c 17);
(*g*) persons who are registered in any register established, continued or maintained under an Order in Council under section 60(1) of the Health Act 1999 (c 8);

(*h*) any other description of persons which appears to the appropriate Ministers to be a description of persons whose profession is regulated by or under a provision of, or made under, an Act of the Scottish Parliament or Northern Ireland legislation and which the appropriate Ministers consider it appropriate to specify.

(1B) Where an order under this section includes provision by virtue of subsection (1)(*e*), the order shall specify such conditions as are necessary to secure that any person who is an appropriate practitioner by virtue of the provision may prescribe, give directions or administer only in respect of human use.

(2) Subject to the following provisions of this section—

(*a*) no person[3] shall sell by retail, or supply in circumstances corresponding to retail sale, a medicinal product[4] of a description, or falling within a class, specified in an order under this section except in accordance with a prescription given by an appropriate practitioner; and

(*b*) no person shall administer (otherwise than to himself) any such medicinal product unless he is an appropriate practitioner or a person acting in accordance with the directions[5] of an appropriate practitioner.

(3) Subsection (2)(*a*) of this section shall not apply—

(*a*) to the sale or supply of a medicinal product to a patient of his by a doctor or dentist who is an appropriate practitioner, or

(*b*) to the sale or supply of a medicinal product, for administration to an animal or herd under his care, by a veterinary surgeon or veterinary practitioner who is an appropriate practitioner.

(4) Without prejudice to the last preceding subsection, any order[1] made by the appropriate Ministers for the purposes of this section may provide—

(*a*) that paragraph (*a*) or subsection (*b*) of subsection (2) of this section, or both those paragraphs, shall have effect subject to such exemptions as may be specified in the order or, where the appropriate practitioner is a registered nurse or midwife, or is an appropriate practitioner by virtue or provision made under subsection (1)(*e*) of this section, such modifications as may be so specified;

(*b*) that, for the purpose of paragraph (*a*) of that subsection, a medicinal product shall not be taken to be sold or supplied in accordance with a prescription given by an appropriate practitioner unless such conditions as are prescribed by the order are fulfilled.

(4A) An order under this section may provide, in relation to a person who is an appropriate practitioner by virtue of subsection (1)(*d*) or (*e*), that such a person may—

(*a*) give a prescription for a medicinal product falling within a description or class specified in the order;

(*b*) administer any such medicinal product; or

(*c*) give directions for the administration of any such medicinal product,

only where he complies with such conditions as may be specified in the order in respect of the cases or circumstances in which he may do so.

(4B) An order under this section may provide, in relation to a condition specified by virtue of subsection (4A), for the condition to have effect subject to such exemptions as may be specified in the order.

(4C) Where a condition is specified by virtue of subsection (4A), any prescription or direction given by a person in contravention of the condition is not (subject to such exemptions or modifications as may be specified in the order by virtue of subsection (4)(*a*) of this section) given by an appropriate practitioner for the purposes of subsection (2)(*a*) or (*b*) of this section.

(5) Any exemption conferred or modification made by an order in accordance with subsection (4)(*a*) of this section may be conferred or made subject to such conditions or limitations as may be specified in the order.

(6) Before making an order under this section the appropriate Ministers shall consult the appropriate committee.

[Medicines Act 1968, s 58, as amended by the Medicinal Products: Prescription by Nurses etc Act 1994, s 1, the Health and Social Care Act 2001, s 63, SI 2002/253, SI 2003/1590 and SI 2005/1094.]

---

1. See the Prescription Only Medicines (Human Use) Order 1997, SI 1997/1830 amended by SI 1997/2044, SI 1998/108, 1178 and 2081, SI 1999/1044 and 3463, SI 2000/1917, 2899 and 3231, SI 2001/2777 and 3942, SI 2002/549 and 2469, SI 2003/696 and 2915, SI 2004/2, 1031, 1189, 1771 and 2693 and SI 2005/765, 848, 1507, 2759 and 3324; Medicines for Human Use (Prescribing) Order 2005, SI 2005/765 amended by SI 2005/1507.

2. Sections 58A and 58B lay down the criteria to be applied in specifying which products are to be supplied on prescription only, s 59 contains special provisions relating to new products, and ss 60–62 give power to control sale or supply by regulations or order. The Medicines (Aristolochia and Mu Tong etc) (Prohibition) Order 2001, SI 2001/1841 amended by SI 2005/2750 and the Medicines for Human Use (Kava-kava) (Prohibition) Order 2002, SI 2002/3170 amended by SI 2005/2750 have been made.

3. This is an offence of strict liability hence there is no requirement to prove mens rea (*Pharmaceutical Society of Great Britain v Storkwain Ltd* [1986] 2 All ER 635, [1986] 1 WLR 903, 150 JP 385, HL).

4. Labels are prima facie admissible evidence under s 24 of the Criminal Justice Act 1988 as to the contents of the containers that bear them; furthermore, having regard to the special meaning of the phrase "medicinal product" in EC law, because a product may be medicinal by presentation and not necessarily by function, it is unnecessary for the

prosecution to adduce evidence of its ingredients (*Department for the Environment, Food and Rural Affairs v Atkinson* [2002] EWHC 2028 (Admin), [2002] JPN 802).

5. A person making up a prescription of a qualified practitioner, eg when acting as a shopkeeper, does not act in accordance with the directions of that practitioner (*Roberts v Coombs* [1949] 2 KB 221, [1949] 2 All ER 37, 113 JP 339).

8–21016 63. Adulteration of medicinal products. No person shall—

(*a*) add any substance to, or abstract[1] any substance from, a medicinal product so as to affect injuriously the composition of the product, with intent that the product shall be sold or supplied in that state, or

(*b*) sell or supply, or offer or expose for sale or supply, or have in his possession for the purpose of sale or supply, any medicinal product whose composition has been injuriously affected by the addition or abstraction of any substance.

[Medicines Act 1968, s 63.]

1. The dilution of a substance so as to reduce the percentage of an ingredient is not abstraction (*Dearden v Whiteley* (1916) 80 JP 215).

8–21017 64. Protection of purchasers of medicinal products. (1) No person shall, to the prejudice of the purchaser, sell any medicinal product which is not of the nature or quality demanded by the purchaser.

(2) For the purposes of this section the sale of a medicinal product shall not be taken to be otherwise than to the prejudice of the purchaser by reason only that the purchaser buys the product for the purpose of analysis or examination.

(3) Subsection (1) of this section shall not be taken to be contravened by reason only that a medicinal product contains some extraneous matter, if it is proved that the presence of that matter was an inevitable consequence of the process of manufacture of the product.

(4) Subsection (1) of this section shall not be taken to be contravened by reason only that a substance has been added to, or abstracted from, the medicinal product, if it is proved that—

(*a*) the addition or abstraction was not carried out fraudulently, and did not injuriously affect the composition of the product, and

(*b*) the product was sold having attached to it, or to a container or package in which it was sold, a conspicuous notice of adequate size and legibly printed, specifying the substance added or abstracted.

(5) Where a medicinal product is sold or supplied in pursuance of a prescription given by a practitioner, the preceding provisions of this section shall have effect as if—

(*a*) in those provisions any reference to sale included a reference to supply and (except as provided by the following paragraph) any reference to the purchaser included a reference to the person (if any) for whom the product was prescribed by the practitioner, and

(*b*) in subsection (1) of this section, for the words "demanded by the purchaser", there were substituted the words "specified in the prescription".

[Medicines Act 1968, s 64.]

8–21018 65. Compliance with standards specified in monographs in certain publications. (1) No person shall, in the course of a business carried on by him—

(*a*) sell a medicinal product which has been demanded by the purchaser by, or by express reference to, a particular name, or

(*b*) sell or supply a medicinal product in pursuance of a prescription given by a practitioner in which the product required is described by, or by express reference, to a particular name,

if that name is a name at the head of the relevant monograph and the product does not comply with the standard specified in that monograph.

(2) No person shall, in the course of a business carried on by him, sell or supply a medicinal product which, in the course of that business, has been offered or exposed for sale and has been so offered or exposed for sale by, or by express reference to, a particular name, if that name is a name at the head of the relevant monograph and the product does not comply with the standard specified in that monograph.

(3) Where a medicinal product is sold or supplied in the circumstances specified in subsection (1) or subsection (2) of this section, and the name in question is the name, not of the product itself, but of an active ingredient of the product, then for the purposes of the subsection in question the product shall be taken not to comply with the standard specified in the relevant monograph if, in so far as it consists of that ingredient, it does not comply with the standard so specified.

(4) Subject to subsection (7) of this section, in this section "publication" means one of the following, that is to say, the British Pharmacopoeia, the British Pharmaceutical Codex, the British Veterinary Codex and any compendium published under Part VII of this Act; "the relevant monograph", in relation to the sale or supply of a medicinal product which has been demanded, described in a prescription, or offered or exposed for sale, by or by express reference to a particular name—

(*a*) if, together with that name, there was specified a particular edition of a particular publication, means the monograph (if any) headed by that name in that edition of the publication, or, if there is no such monograph in that edition, means the appropriate current monograph (if any) headed by that name;

(*b*) if, together with that name, there was specified a particular publication, but not a particular edition of that publication, means the monograph (if any) headed by that name in the current edition of that publication, or, if there is no such monograph in that edition, means the appropriate current monograph (if any) headed by that name, or, in default of such a monograph, means the monograph headed by that name in the latest edition of the specified publication which contained a monograph so headed;

(*c*) if no publication was specified together with that name, means the appropriate current monograph (if any);

and "current" means current at the time when the medicinal product in question is demanded, described in a prescription, or offered or exposed for sale, as mentioned in subsection (1) or subsection (2) of this section.

(5) In this section "the appropriate current monograph", in relation to a particular name, means—

(*a*) the monograph (if any) headed by that name in the current edition of the British Pharmacopoeia, or

(*b*) if there is no such monograph, then the monograph (if any) headed by that name in the current edition of a compendium published under Part VII of this Act, or

(*c*) if there is no such monograph, then the monograph (if any) headed by that name in the current edition of the British Pharmaceutical Codex or the British Veterinary Codex.

(6) Subject to subsection (8) of this section, for the purposes of this section an edition of a publication—

(*a*) if it is the current edition of that publication, shall be taken as it is for the time being in force (that is to say, together with any amendments, additions and deletions made to it up to the time referred to in subsection (4) of this section), or

(*b*) if it is an edition previous to the current edition of that publication, shall be taken as it was immediately before the time when it was superseded by a subsequent edition of that publication (that is to say, together with any amendments, additions and deletions made to it up to that time),

and any monograph in an edition of a publication shall be construed in accordance with any general monograph or notice or any appendix, note or other explanatory material which is contained in that edition and is applicable to that monograph, and any reference in this section to compliance with the standard specified in a monograph shall be construed accordingly.

(7) In relation to any time on or after the date on which, by notice published in the Gazette by or on behalf of the Health Ministers[1], it is declared that the European Pharmacopoeia prepared in pursuance of the Convention in that behalf done at Strasbourg on 22nd July 1964 is to have effect for the purposes of this section, subsections (1) and (2) of this section shall have effect as if, after the words "that name is", in each place where those words occur, there were inserted the words "or is an approved synonym for," subsection (4) of this section shall have effect as if, before the words "the British Pharmacopoeia", there were inserted the words "the European Pharmacopoeia", and after the words "headed by that name", in each place where those words occur, there were inserted the words "or by a name for which it is an approved synonym", and subsection (5) of this section shall have effect as if for paragraph (*a*) of that subsection there were substituted the following paragraphs—

"(*a*) the monograph (if any) headed by that name, or by a name for which it is an approved synonym, in the current edition of the European Pharmacopoeia, or

(*aa*) if there is no such monograph, then the monograph (if any) headed by that name in the current edition of the British Pharmacopoeia, or".

(8) For the purposes of this section, an edition of the European Pharmacopoeia—

(*a*) if it is the current edition of that Pharmacopoeia at the time in question, shall be taken as it is for the time being in force in the United Kingdom (that is to say, together with any amendments, additions and deletions made to it which, by notice published as mentioned in subsection (7) of this section before the time referred to in subsection (4) of this section, have been declared to have effect for the purposes of this section), and

(*b*) if it is an edition previous to the current edition of that Pharmacopoeia, shall be taken as it was immediately before the time when it was superseded by a subsequent edition of that Pharmacopoeia in force in the United Kingdom (that is to say, together with any amendments, additions and deletions made to it which, by notice so published before that time, had been declared so to have effect),

and a name shall be taken to be an approved synonym for a name at the head of a monograph in the European Pharmacopoeia if, by a notice so published and not withdrawn by any subsequent notice so published, it has been declared to be approved by the Medicines Commission* as a synonym for that name.

[Medicines Act 1968, s 65 as amended by SI 2005/1094.]

1. Now the Secretary of State for Health, see the Transfer of Functions (Medicines and Poisons) Order 1999, SI 1999/3142 and the Secretary of State for Environment, Food and Rural Affairs, see the Ministry of Agriculture, Fisheries and Food (Dissolution) Order 2002, SI 2002/794.

8–21019 **66.** *Power to make regulations to control dealings with medicinal Products.*

Offences, and provision for disqualification

8–21030 **67. Offences under Part III.** (1) The following provisions of this section shall have effect subject to sections 121 and 122 of this Act[1].

(1A) Any person who gives a prescription or directions or administers a medicinal product in contravention of a condition imposed by an order under section 58 of this Act by virtue of subsection (4A) of that section shall be guilty of an offence.

(1B) Any person who—

(*a*) is an appropriate practitioner by virtue of provision made under section 58(1) of this Act; and
(*b*) gives a prescription or directions in respect of a medicinal product of a description or class in relation to which he is not an appropriate practitioner,

shall be guilty of an offence.

(2) Any person who contravenes any of the following provisions of this Part of this Act, that is to say, sections 52, 58, 63, 64 and 65, or who contravenes any regulations made under section 60 or section 61 or any order[2] made under section 62 of this Act, shall be guilty of an offence.

(3) Where a medicinal product is sold, supplied or imported in contravention of an order made under section 62 of this Act, any person who, otherwise than for the purpose of performing or exercising a duty or power imposed or conferred by or under this Act or any other enactment, is in possession of the medicinal product, knowing or having reasonable cause to suspect that it was sold, supplied or imported in contravention of the order, shall be guilty of an offence.

(3A) A person who has in his possession a medicinal product to which paragraph (*a*) of section 58(2) applies, with the intention of supplying it otherwise than in accordance with the requirements of that paragraph, is guilty of an offence.

(4) Any person guilty of an offence under subsection (1A), (1B), (2), (3) or (3A) of this section shall be liable[3]—

(*a*) on summary conviction, to a fine not exceeding **the statutory maximum**;
(*b*) on conviction on indictment, to a **fine** or to imprisonment for a term not exceeding **two years** or to **both**.

(5) Any person who contravenes section 53 or section 54(1) or an order made under section 54(2) of this Act shall be guilty of an offence and liable on summary conviction to a fine not exceeding **level 3** on the standard scale.

(6) Any regulations made under section 66 of this Act may provide that any person who contravenes the regulations shall be guilty of an offence and liable on summary conviction to a fine not exceeding **level 5** on the standard scale or such lesser sum as may be specified in the regulations.
[Medicines Act 1968, s 67, as amended by the Criminal Law Act 1977, ss 28 and 31, the Criminal Justice Act 1982, ss 38 and 46, the Health and Social Care Act 2001, s 63 and SI 2005/2789.]

1. These sections deal with the liability of another person and the defence of warranty.
2. The following Orders have been made: the Medicines (Bal Jivan Chamcho Prohibition) (No 2) Order 1977, SI 1977/670 amended by SI 1990/2487, the Medicines (Prohibition of Non Medical Anti-Microbial Substances) Order 1977, SI 1977/2131, amended by SI 1990/2487, SI 1992/2684 and SI 2005/2745, the Medicines (Chloroform Prohibition) Order 1979, 1979/382 amended by SI 1980/263 and SI 1989/1184, the Medicines (Phenacetin Prohibition) Order 1979, SI 1979/1181, the Medicine (Carbadox, Prohibition) Order 1986 SI 1986/1368.
3. For procedure in respect of this offence, triable either way, see Magistrates' Courts Act 1980, ss 17A–21 in PART I: MAGISTRATES' COURTS, PROCEDURE.

8–21031 **68. Disqualification on conviction of certain offences.** (1) Where in proceedings brought by an enforcement authority a person is convicted of an offence under section 67(6) of this Act in respect of any premises used for carrying on a retail pharmacy business, then on the application of that authority the court by or before which he was convicted may (subject to the following provisions of this section) make an order disqualifying him from using those premises for the purposes of such a business for such period, not exceeding two years, as may be specified in the order.

(2) The court shall not make an order under this section disqualifying a person in respect of any premises unless the court thinks it expedient to do so having regard—

(*a*) to the gravity of the offence of which he has been convicted as mentioned in the preceding subsection, or
(*b*) to the unsatisfactory nature of the premises, or
(*c*) to any offences under section 67(6) of this Act of which he has previously been convicted.

(3) No order under this section shall be made against a person on the application of an enforcement

authority unless the authority have, not less than fourteen days before the date of the hearing, given him notice in writing of their intention to apply for such an order to be made against him.

(4) If, while an order under this section disqualifying a person in respect of any premises is in force, the premises are used for the purposes of a retail pharmacy business carried on by him, he shall be guilty of an offence and liable on summary conviction to a fine not exceeding **level 5** on the standard scale.

(5) Subject to the next following subsection, at any time after the end of the period of six months from the date on which an order under this section comes into force, the person to whom the order relates may apply to the court by which the order was made to revoke the order or to vary it by reducing the period of disqualification.

(6) On any application made under subsection (5) of this section the court may revoke or vary the order as mentioned in that subsection if it thinks it proper to do so having regard to all the circumstances of the case, including in particular the conduct of the applicant and any improvement in the state of the premises to which the order relates; but, if on any such application the court refuses to revoke or vary the order, no further application made by the applicant under that subsection shall be entertained if it is made within three months from the date of the refusal.

(7) The court to which an application under subsection (5) of this section is made shall have power to order the applicant to pay the whole or any part of the costs of the application.

(8) In the application of this section to Scotland, for references to an enforcement authority and to costs there shall be substituted respectively references to the procurator fiscal and to expenses.

[Medicines Act 1968, s 68, as amended by the Criminal Justice Act 1982, ss 38 and 46.]

PART IV
PHARMACIES

8–21032 **77. Annual return of premises to registrar.** Every person who carried on a retail pharmacy business[1] shall, in the month of January in each year, send to the registrar—

(*a*) a list of all premises at which his business, so far as it consists of the retail sale of medicinal products, is carried on, and

(*b*) in the case of any premises where medicinal products, other than medicinal products on a general sale list, are sold by retail, or are supplied in circumstances corresponding to retail sale, the name of the pharmacist under whose personal control the business, so far as concerns the retail sale or supply of medicinal products at those premises, is carried on.

[Medicines Act 1968, s 77.]

1. Under provisions contained in ss 69–76 every retail pharmacy business, as defined in s 132(1), must be registered; and ss 80–83 contain provisions whereby the "Statutory Committee" of the Pharmaceutical Society may direct disqualification and removal from the register.

Provisions as to use of certain titles, descriptions and emblems

8–21033 **78. Restrictions on use of titles, descriptions and emblems.** (1) The provisions of this section shall have effect subject to section 79[1] of this Act.

(2) No person shall—

(*a*) take or use any of the following titles, that is to say, chemist and druggist, druggist, dispensing chemist, and dispensing druggist, or

(*b*) take or use the title of chemist in connection with the sale of any goods by retail or the supply of any goods in circumstances corresponding to retail sale[2],

unless the conditions specified in the next following subsection are fulfilled.

(3) Those conditions are—

(*a*) in the case of an individual, that he is a person lawfully conducting a retail pharmacy business (either alone or as a member of a partnership) and that he does not take or use the title in question in connection with any premises at which any goods are sold by retail, or are supplied in circumstances corresponding to retail sale, unless these premises are a registered pharmacy, and

(*b*) in the case of a body corporate, that the body is a person lawfully conducting a retail pharmacy business and that the title in question is not taken or used by that body in connection with any premises at which any goods are sold by retail, or are supplied in circumstances corresponding to retail sale, unless those premises are a registered pharmacy, and that the pharmacist who, in relation to that business, is such a superintendent as is referred to in section 71(1) of this Act is a member of the board of the body corporate.

(4) No person shall, in connection with a business carried on by him which consists of or includes the retail sale of any goods, or the supply of any goods in circumstances corresponding to retail sale, use the description "pharmacy" except in respect of a registered pharmacy or in respect of the pharmaceutical department of a hospital or a health centre.

(5) (*a*) No person who is not a pharmacist shall take or use any of the following titles, that is to say, pharmaceutical chemist, pharmaceutist, pharmacist, member of the Pharmaceutical Society, and Fellow of the Pharmaceutical Society, and

(*b*) without prejudice to the preceding paragraph, no person shall take or use any of those titles in connection with a business carried on (whether by him or by some other person) at any premises which consists of or includes the retail sale of any goods, or the supply of any goods in circumstances corresponding to retail sale, unless those premises are a registered pharmacy or a hospital or health centre.

(6) No person shall, in connection with any business, use any title, description or emblem likely to suggest—

(*a*) that he possesses any qualification with respect to the sale, manufacture or assembly of medicinal products which he does not in fact possess, or

(*b*) that any person employed in the business possesses any such qualification which that person does not in fact possess.

(7) For the purposes of the last preceding subsection the use of the description "pharmacy", in connection with a business carried on at any premises, shall be taken to be likely to suggest that the person carrying on the business (where that person is not a body corporate) is a pharmacist and that any other person, under whose personal control the business (so far as concerns the retail sale of medicinal products or the supply of such products in circumstances corresponding to retail sale) is carried on at those premises, is also a pharmacist.

(8) Where a person is lawfully conducting a retail pharmacy business as being a representative of a pharmacist in the circumstances specified in section 69(1)(*e*) of this Act, subsections (5) to (7) of this section shall not have effect so as to prevent the representative from taking or using, in connection with that business, any title, description or emblem which the pharmacist himself could have used in accordance with those subsections.

[Medicines Act 1968, s 78 amended by the Statute Law (Repeals) Act 1993, Sch 1.]

---

1. Section 79 gives the Minister power to modify or extend the restrictions under s 78.

2. A business name on a shop sign incorporating the word "chemist" was held not to be conclusive if there is another notice displayed denying that a qualified chemist is in charge of the shop under a previous enactment, see *Denerley v Spink* [1947] KB 768, [1947] 1 All ER 835, 111 JP 318; this case would seem to apply to this provision, provided the premises were a registered pharmacy.

8–21034 **84. Offences under Part IV.** (1) Any person who contravenes section 77 of this Act shall be guilty of an offence and liable on summary conviction to a fine not exceeding **level 3** on the standard scale.

(2) Any person who contravenes section 78 of this Act or who contravenes any regulations made under section 79(2) of this Act shall be guilty of an offence and liable on summary conviction to a fine not exceeding **level 3** on the standard scale.

[Medicines Act 1968, s 84, as amended by the Criminal Justice Act 1982, ss 38 and 46.]

PART V

CONTAINERS, PACKAGES AND IDENTIFICATION OF MEDICINAL PRODUCTS

8–21035 **85. Labelling and marking of containers and packages.** (1) The appropriate Ministers may make regulations[1] imposing such requirements as, for any of the purposes specified in subsection (2) of this section, they consider necessary or expedient with respect to any of the following matters, that is to say—

(*a*) the labelling of containers of medicinal products;

(*b*) the labelling of packages of medicinal products;

(*c*) the display of distinctive marks on containers and packages of medicinal products.

(2) The purposes referred to in the preceding subsection are—

(*a*) securing that medicinal products are correctly described and readily identifiable;

(*b*) securing that any appropriate warning or other appropriate information or instruction is given, and that false or misleading information is not given, with respect to medicinal products;

(*c*) promoting safety in relation to medicinal products.

(3) No person shall, in the course of a business carried on by him, sell or supply, or have in his possession for the purpose of sale or supply, any medicinal product in such circumstances as to contravene any requirements imposed by regulations under this section which are applicable to that product.

(4) In so far as any such requirements relate to the labelling or marking of containers of medicinal products, a person who, in the course of a business carried on by him, sells or supplies a medicinal product to which the requirements are applicable without its being enclosed in a container shall, except in so far as the regulations otherwise provide, be taken to contravene those requirements as if he had sold or supplied it in a container not complying with those requirements.

(5) Without prejudice to the preceding provisions of this section, no person shall, in the course of

a business carried on by him, sell or supply, or have in his possession for the purpose of sale or supply, a medicinal product of any description in a container or package which is labelled or marked in such a way that the container or package—

(*a*) falsely describes the product, or
(*b*) is likely to mislead as to the nature or quality of the product or as to the uses or effects of medicinal products of that description.

[Medicines Act 1968, s 85.]

1. The Medicines (Labelling) Regulations 1976, SI 1976/1726, as amended by SI 1977/996 and 2168, SI 1978/41, SI 1981/1791, SI 1983/1729, SI 1985/1558 and 2008, SI 1992/3273, SI 1994/104 and 3142, SI 1996/2194, SI 2002/236, SI 2004/1031 and SI 2005/2745 and 2753 have been made; the penalty for contravention of the Regulations is the same as that set out in s 91(2), post. See also the Medicines (Contact Lens Fluids and Other Substances) (Labelling) Regulations 1979, SI 1979/1759, amended by SI 1981/1689.

8–21036 86. Leaflets. (1) The appropriate Ministers may make regulations[1] imposing such requirements as, for any of the purposes specified in section 85(2) of this Act, they consider necessary or expedient with respect to leaflets relating to medicinal products which are supplied, or are intended to be supplied, with the products, whether by being enclosed in containers or packages of the product or otherwise.

(2) No person shall, in the course of a business carried on by him, supply with any medicinal product, or have in his possession for the purpose of so supplying, a leaflet which contravenes any requirements imposed by regulations under this section which are applicable to that leaflet.

(3) Without prejudice to the preceding provisions of this section, no person shall, in the course of a business carried on by him, supply with a medicinal product of any description, or have in his possession for the purpose of so supplying, a leaflet which—

(*a*) falsely describes the product, or
(*b*) is likely to mislead as to the nature or quality of the product or as to the uses or effects of medicinal products of that description.

(4) No person shall, in the course of a business carried on by him supply a product to which the 2001 Directive applies, unless—

(*a*) a leaflet enclosed in, or supplied with, the container or package of the product, or
(*b*) the container or package itself,

contains the particulars which a leaflet relating to the product is required by regulations under subsection (1) of this section to contain, and does so in the manner required by such regulations.

[Medicines Act 1968, s 86 amended by SI 1994/276 and SI 2002/236.]

1. See note 1 to s 85, ante. The Medicines (Leaflets) Regulations 1977, SI 1977/1055 amended by SI 1992/3274, SI 1994/104 and SI 2005/2753 and the Medicines (Leaflets for Veterinary Drugs) Regulations 1983, SI 1983/1727, amended by SI 1985/2008, have also been made under s 86(1).

8–21037 87. Requirements as to containers. (1) The appropriate Ministers may make regulations[1] prohibiting the sale or supply of medicinal products otherwise than in containers which comply with such requirements as those Ministers consider necessary or expedient for any of the purposes specified in section 85(2) of this Act, or for the purpose of preserving the quality of the products, and in particular, may by the regulations require such containers to be of such strength, to be made of such materials, and to be of shapes or patterns, as may be prescribed.

(2) No person shall, in the course of a business carried on by him, sell or supply, or have in his possession for the purpose of sale or supply, any medicinal product in such circumstances as to contravene any requirements imposed by regulations under this section which are applicable to that product.

[Medicines Act 1968, s 87.]

1. The Medicines (Fluted Bottles) Regulations 1978, SI 1978/40, amended by SI 1994/3142, SI 2004/1031 and SI 2005/2745, and the Medicines (Child Safety) Regulations 2003, SI 2003/2317 amended by SI 2004/1771 and SI 2005/1520 have been made.

8–21038 88. Distinctive colours, shapes and markings of medicinal products. (1) Regulations[1] made by the appropriate Ministers may impose such requirements as, for any of the purposes specified in section 85(2) of this Act, those Ministers consider necessary or expedient with respect to any one or more of the following matters, that is to say—

(*a*) the colour of the products;
(*b*) the shape of the products; and
(*c*) distinctive marks to be displayed on the products.

(2) Regulations[1] made under this section may provide that medicinal products of any such description, or falling within any such class, as may be specified in the regulations shall not except in

such circumstances (if any) as may be so specified, be of any such colour or shape, or display any such mark, as may be so specified.

(3) No person shall, in the course of a business carried on by him, sell or supply, or have in his possession for the purpose of sale or supply, any medicinal product which contravenes any requirements imposed by regulations under this section.
[Medicines Act 1968, s 88.]

1. The Medicines (Child Safety) Regulations 2003, SI 2003/2317 amended by SI 2004/1771 and SI 2005/1520 have been made.

8–21039 **89. Display of information on automatic machines.** (1) Regulations made by the appropriate Ministers may impose such requirements as they consider necessary or expedient with respect to the display on automatic machines of information relating to medicinal products offered or exposed for sale by means of such machines.

(2) No person shall offer or expose for sale any medicinal product by means of an automatic machine in such circumstances as to contravene any requirements imposed by regulations under this section which are applicable to that product.
[Medicines Act 1968, s 89.]

8–21040 **90. Provisions as to medicated animal feeding stuffs.** (1) The provisions of subsections (1) to (4) of section 85, subsections (1) and (2) of section 86, and section 87 of this Act shall have effect in relation to animal feeding stuffs in which medicinal products have been incorporated as if in those provisions any reference to the appropriate Ministers were a reference to the Agriculture Ministers[1] and any reference to medicinal products were a reference to animal feeding stuffs in which medicinal products have been incorporated.

(2) Without prejudice to the preceding subsection, but subject to the next following subsection, no person shall, in the course of a business carried on by him, sell or supply, or have in his possession for the purpose of sale or supply, any animal feeding stuff in which a medicinal product of any description has been incorporated, which is in a container or package labelled or marked in such a way that the container or package—

(*a*) falsely describes the animal feeding stuff in so far as its composition results from the incorporation of the medicinal product in it, or
(*b*) is likely to mislead as to the nature or quality of the animal feeding stuff in so far as its composition so results, or
(*c*) is likely to mislead as to the uses or effects of animal feeding stuffs in which medicinal products of the description in question have been incorporated, in so far as any uses or effects are attributable to the incorporation of such medicinal products;

and no person shall, in the course of a business carried on by him, supply with any such animal feeding stuff, or have in his possession for the purpose of so supplying, a leaflet which falsely describes the animal feeding stuff, or is likely to mislead, as mentioned in paragraph (*a*), paragraph (*b*) or paragraph (*c*) of this subsection.

(3) For the purposes of subsection (2) of this section no account shall be taken—

(*a*) of any mark which is made on a container or package in pursuance of Part IV of the Agriculture Act 1970; or
(*b*) of any statement which, in pursuance of that Part is made in any leaflet supplied, or intended to be supplied, with any material.

(4) Section 130(10) of this Act shall have effect with the necessary modifications for the purpose of subsection (2)(*e*) of this section.
[Medicines Act 1968, s 90, as amended by the Agriculture Act 1970.]

1. Now the Secretary of State for Environment, Food and Rural Affairs, see the Ministry of Agriculture, Fisheries and Food (Dissolution) Order 2002, SI 2002/794.

8–21041 **91. Offences under Part V, and supplementary provisions.** (1) Subject to sections 121 and 122 of this Act, any person who contravenes the provisions of section 85(5), section 86(3) or (4) or section 90(2) of this Act shall be guilty of an offence and liable[1]—

(*a*) on summary conviction, to a fine not exceeding **the statutory maximum**;
(*b*) on conviction on indictment, to a **fine** or to imprisonment for a term not exceeding **two years** or to **both**.

(2) Any regulations made under this Part of this Act may provide that any person who contravenes the regulations, or who contravenes the provisions of section 85(3), section 86(2) or section 87(2) of this Act or any of those provisions as applied by section 90(1) of this Act, shall be guilty of an offence and—

(*a*) shall be liable on summary conviction to a fine not exceeding **£2,000**; or such lesser sum as may be specified in the regulations, and (*b*) if the regulations so provide, shall be liable on conviction on indictment to a fine or to imprisonment for a term not exceeding **two years** or to both.

(3) Without prejudice to the application of section 129(5) of this Act, any power to make regulations conferred by sections 85 to 87 of this Act may be exercised so as to impose requirements either in relation to medicinal products generally or in relation to medicinal products of a particular description, or falling within a particular class, specified in the regulations, and any power to make regulations conferred by those sections as applied by section 90(1) of this Act shall be exercisable in a corresponding way.

(4) In this Part of this Act "requirements" includes restrictions.

[Medicines Act 1968, s 91, as amended by the Criminal Law Act 1977, s. 28.]

1. For procedure in respect of this offence, triable either way, see Magistrates' Courts Act 1980, ss 17A–21 in PART I: MAGISTRATES' COURTS, PROCEDURE.

PART VI[1]
PROMOTION OF SALES OF MEDICINAL PRODUCTS

8–21042 **92. Scope of Part VI.** (1) Subject to the following provisions of this section, in this Part of this Act "advertisement" includes every form of advertising, whether in a publication, or by the display of any notice, or by means of any catalogue, price list, letter (whether circular or addressed to a particular person) or other document, or by words inscribed on any article, or by means of a photograph, film, sound recording, broadcast or cable programme, or in any other way, and any reference to the issue of an advertisement shall be construed accordingly.

(2) Notwithstanding anything in the preceding subsection, in this Part of this Act "advertisement" does not include spoken words except—

(*a*) words forming part of a sound recording, and
(*b*) words broadcast or included in a cable programme service.

(3) Except as provided by section 95 of this Act, for the purposes of this Part of this Act neither of the following shall be taken to constitute the issue of an advertisement, that is to say—

(*a*) the sale or supply, or offer or exposure for sale or supply, of a medicinal product in a labelled container or package;
(*b*) the supply, with a medicinal product of any description, of a leaflet relating solely to medicinal products of that description.

(4) In this Part of this Act "commercially interested party", in relation to medicinal products of any description, means any person who—

(*a*) is the holder of a licence under Part II[2] of this Act which is applicable to medicinal products of that description, or
(*b*) not being the holder of such a licence, is a person who, in the course of a business carried on by him, is engaged[3], in relation to medicinal products of that description, in any such activities as are mentioned in subsection (2) or subsection (3) of section 7 or in subsection (2) or subsection (3) or (3A) of section 8 of this Act, or
(*c*) sells by retail any medicinal products of that description in the course of a business carried on by him,

and any reference to the request or consent of a commercially interested party includes a reference to any request made or consent given by a person acting on behalf of a commercially interested party; and "relevant business" means any business which consists of or includes the sale or supply of medicinal products.

(5) In this Part of this Act "representation" means any statement or undertaking (whether constituting a condition or a warranty or not) which consists of spoken words other than words falling within paragraph (*a*) or paragraph (*b*) of subsection (2) of this section, and any reference to making a representation shall be construed accordingly.

(6) In this section "film", "sound recording", "broadcast", "cable programme", "cable programme service", and related expressions, have the same meaning as in Part I of the Copyright Designs and Patents Act 1988 (copyright).

[Medicines Act 1968, s 92, as amended by the Cable and Broadcasting Act 1984, Schs 5 and 6, the Copyright, Designs and Patents Act 1988, Schs 7 and 8 and SI 1993/834 and the Medicines of Human Use (Marketing Authorisation etc) Regulations 1994, SI 1994/3144.]

1. This part of the Act shall have effect as if all relevant medicinal products were medicinal products for the purposes of the Act (whether or not they would otherwise be so). See the Medicines for Human Use (Marketing Authorisations etc) Regulations 1994, SI 1994/3144.

2. A licence under Part II of the Act includes a reference to a marketing authorisation. See the Medicines for Human Use (Marketing Authorisations etc) Regulations 1994, SI 1994/3144, reg 9(7).

3. The reference to being engaged, in relation to medicinal products of the description in question, in any such activities as are referred to in this subsection include a reference to being engaged in putting medicinal products of that description on the market. See the Medicines for Human Use (Marketing Authorisation etc) Regulations 1994, SI 1994/3144, reg 9(7).

8–21043 **93. False or misleading advertisements and representations.** (1) Subject to the following provisions of this section, any person who, being a commercially interested party, or at the request or with the consent of a commercially interested party, issues, or causes another person to issue, a false or misleading advertisement relating to medicinal products of any description shall be guilty of an offence.

(2) Where a licence under Part II of this Act is in force which is applicable to medicinal products of a particular description, and, in accordance with the provisions of the licence, the purposes for which medicinal products of that description may be recommended to be used are limited to those specified in the licence, then, subject to the following provisions of this section, any person who, being a commercially interested party, or at the request or with the consent of a commercially interested party, issues, or causes another person to issue, an advertisement relating to medicinal products of that description which consists of or includes unauthorised recommendations shall be guilty of an offence.

(3) Subject to the following provisions of this section, any person who in the course of a relevant business carried on by him, or while acting on behalf of a person carrying on such a business, makes a false or misleading representation relating to a medicinal product in connection with the sale, or offer for sale, of that product shall be guilty of an offence; and any person who, in the course of such a business or while acting on behalf of a person carrying on such a business, makes a false or misleading representation relating to medicinal products of a particular description—

(*a*) to a practitioner for the purpose of inducing him to prescribe or supply medicinal products of that description, or

(*b*) to a patient or client of a practitioner for the purpose of inducing him to request the practitioner to prescribe medicinal products of that description, or

(*c*) to a person for the purpose of inducing him to purchase medicinal products of that description from a person selling them by retail,

shall be guilty of an offence.

(4) Where in the circumstances specified in subsection (2) of this section any person, in the course of a relevant business carried on by him, or while acting on behalf of a person carrying on such a business—

(*a*) in connection with the sale, or offer for sale, of a medicinal product of the description in question, makes a representation relating to the product which consists of or includes unauthorised recommendations, or

(*b*) for any such purpose as is specified in paragraphs (*a*) to (*c*) of subsection (3) of this section makes a representation relating to medicinal products of that description which consists of or includes unauthorised recommendations,

that person, subject to the following provisions of this section, shall be guilty of an offence.

(5) Where a person is charged with an offence under this section, it shall be a defence for him to prove—

(*a*) where the offence charged is under subsection (1) or subsection (3) of this section, that he did not know, and could not with reasonable diligence have discovered, that the advertisement or representation was false or misleading;

(*b*) where the offence charged is under subsection (2) or subsection (4) of this section, that he did not know, and could not with reasonable diligence have discovered, that the recommendations made by the advertisement or representation were unauthorised recommendations.

(6) Without prejudice to the last preceding subsection, where a person is charged with an offence under this section in respect of the issue of an advertisement, it shall be a defence for him to prove that he is a person whose business it is to issue or arrange for the issue of advertisements, and that either—

(*a*) he received the advertisement for issue in the ordinary course of business and issued it, or arranged for it to be issued, either unaltered or without any alteration except in respect of lettering or lay-out, or

(*b*) not being a commercially interested party, he received from a commercially interested party the information on which the advertisement was based and in the ordinary course of business prepared the advertisement in accordance with that information for issue at the request of that party,

and (in either case) that he did not know and had no reason to suspect that the issue of the advertisement would amount to an offence under this section.

(7) For the purposes of this section an advertisement (whether it contains an accurate statement of the composition of medicinal products of the description in question or not) shall be taken to be false or misleading if (but only if)—

(*a*) it falsely describes the description of medicinal products to which it relates, or

(*b*) it is likely to mislead as to the nature[1] or quality[1] of medicinal products of that description or as to their uses[1] or effects[1], and any reference in this section to a false or misleading representation shall be construed in a corresponding way.

(8) The preceding provisions of this section shall have effect subject to section 121 of this Act.

(9) Any person guilty of an offence under this section shall be liable[2]—

(*a*) on summary conviction, to a fine not exceeding **the statutory maximum**;

(*b*) on conviction on indictment, to a **fine** or to imprisonment for a term not exceeding **two years** or to **both**.

(10) In this section "unauthorised recommendations", in relation to the circumstances specified in subsection (2) of this section, means recommendations whereby medicinal products of a description to which the licence in question is applicable are recommended to be used for purposes other than those specified in the licence.

[Medicines Act 1968, s 93, as amended by the Criminal Law Act 1977, s 28.]

---

1. It is desirable that the particulars of the offence should show which words in s 93(7)(*b*) are relied on in the circumstances; the restricted meaning of "quality" in s 2 of the Food Act 1984 (now s 14 of the Food Safety Act 1990) does not apply here (*R v Roussel Laboratories and Good* (1988) 153 JP 298, CA).

2. For procedure in respect of this offence, triable either way, see Magistrates' Courts Act 1980, ss 17A–21 in PART I: MAGISTRATES' COURTS, PROCEDURE.

8–21044 94. Advertisements requiring consent of holder of product licence. (1) Where a product licence under this Act is in force which is applicable to medicinal products of a particular description, then, except with the consent of the holder of the licence—

(*a*) no commercially interested party (other than the holder of the licence) shall issue, or cause another person to issue, any advertisement relating to medicinal products of that description; and

(*b*) no person who is not a commercially interested party shall, at the request or with the consent of a commercially interested party, issue, or cause another person to issue, any such advertisement.

(2) Subject to section 121 of this Act, any person who contravenes the preceding subsection shall be guilty of an offence and liable on summary conviction to a fine not exceeding **level 3** on the standard scale.

[Medicines Act 1968, s 94, as amended by the Criminal Justice Act 1982, ss 38 and 46.]

8–21045 95. Powers to regulate advertisements and representations. (1) The appropriate Ministers may by regulations[1] prohibit any one or more of the following, that is to say—

(*a*) the issue of advertisements relating to medicinal products of a description, or falling within a class, specified in the regulations;

(*b*) the issue of advertisements likely to lead to the use of any medicinal product, or any other substance or article, for the purpose of treating or preventing a disease specified in the regulations or for the purpose of diagnosis of a disease so specified or of ascertaining the existence, degree or extent of a physiological condition so specified or of permanently or temporarily preventing or otherwise interfering with the normal operation of a physiological function so specified, or for the purpose of artificially inducing a condition of body or mind so specified;

(*c*) the issue of advertisements likely to lead to the use of medicinal products of a particular description or falling within a particular class specified in the regulations, or the use of any other substance or article of a description or class so specified, for any such purpose as is mentioned in paragraph (*b*) of this subsection;

(*d*) the issue of advertisements relating to medicinal products and containing a word or phrase specified in the regulations, as being a word or phrase which, in the opinion of the appropriate Ministers, is likely to mislead the public as to the nature or effects of the products or as to any condition of body or mind in connection with which the products might be used.

(2) Where any regulations are made in accordance with paragraph (*b*), paragraph (*c*) or paragraph (*d*) of the preceding subsection, the regulations may prohibit the making of any representation likely to lead to the use of a medicinal product or other substance or article to which the regulations apply for a purpose specified in the regulations in accordance with paragraph (*b*) of that subsection, or containing a word or phrase specified in the regulations in accordance with paragraph (*d*) of that subsection, if the representation—

(*a*) is made in connection with the sale or supply, or offer for sale or supply, of a medicinal product or other substance or article to which the regulations apply, or

(*b*) is made to a person for the purpose of inducing him to purchase such a medicinal product, substance or article from a person selling by retail medicinal products or other substances or articles to which the regulations apply, or

(*c*) in the case of medicinal products of a description to which the regulations apply, is made to a practitioner for the purpose of inducing him to prescribe or supply medicinal products of that description or is made to a patient or client of a practitioner for the purpose of inducing him to request the practitioner to prescribe medicinal products of that description.

(3) Without prejudice to the preceding provisions of this section, the appropriate Ministers may by regulations[2] impose such requirements as, for any of the purposes specified in the next following subsection, they consider necessary or expedient with respect to any one or more of the following matters, that is to say—

(*a*) the particulars which advertisements relating to medicinal products must contain;
(*b*) the form of any such advertisement; and
(*c*) in the case of advertisements by way of cinematograph films or television, the duration for which, and the manner in which, any part of such an advertisement which contains particulars of a description specified in the regulations must be exhibited;

and any such regulations may prohibit the use, in relation to medicinal products of a description specified in the regulations, of advertisements of any particular kind so specified.

(4) The purposes referred to in subsection (3) of this section are—

(*a*) securing that adequate information is given with respect to medicinal products;
(*b*) preventing the giving of misleading information with respect to such products;
(*c*) promoting safety in relation to such products.

(5) Without prejudice to the application of section 129(5) of this Act, any prohibition imposed by regulations under this section may be a total prohibition or may be imposed subject to such exceptions as may be specified in the regulations.

(6) Any regulations made under this section may provide that any person who contravenes the regulations shall be guilty of an offence and—

(*a*) shall be liable on summary conviction to a fine not exceeding **£2,000** or such lesser sum as may be specified in the regulations, and
(*b*) if the regulations so provide, shall be liable on conviction on indictment to a fine or to imprisonment for a term not exceeding **two years** or to both.

(7) Section 92(3) of this Act shall not have effect for the purposes of paragraphs (*b*) to (*d*) of subsection (1) of this section.
[Medicines Act 1968, s 95, as amended by the Criminal Law Act 1977, s 28.]

1. The Medicine (Advertising of Medicinal Products) Regulations 1975, SI 1975/298, the Medicines (Advertising of Medicinal Products) (No 2) Regulations 1975, SI 1975/1326 amended by SI 1979/1760 and SI 1994/1932 and SI 2002/880, the Medicines (Labelling and Advertising to the Public) Regulations 1978, SI 1978/41 amended by SI 1994/1932, SI 2002/880 and SI 2004/1771, the Medicines (Contact Lens Fluids and Other Substances) (Advertising and Miscellaneous Amendments) Regulations 1979, SI 1979/1760 amended by SI 2005/848 and the Medicines (Advertising) Regulations 1994, SI 1994/1932 amended by SI 1996/1552, SI 1999/267 and 784, SI 2002/236, SI 2003/2321, SI 2004/1480 and SI 2005/2787 have been made and create offences which are triable either way but on summary conviction punishable with a fine not exceeding the statutory maximum.

2. See the Medicines (Advertising of Medicinal Products) (No 2) Regulations 1975, SI 1975/1326 amended by SI 1979/1760 and SI 1994/1932. See also the Medicines (Labelling and Advertising to the Public) Regulations 1978, SI 1978/41 amended by SI 1994/1932, SI 2002/880 and SI 2004/1771.

8–21046 **96. Advertisements and representations directed to practitioners.** (1) On and after the relevant date, no advertisement relating to medicinal products of a particular description, other than a data sheet, shall be sent or delivered to a practitioner—

(*a*) by any commercially interested party, or
(*b*) by any person at the request or with the consent of a commercially interested party,

unless the conditions specified in subsection (3) of this section are fulfilled.

(2) On and after the relevant date, no representation likely to promote the use of medicinal products of a particular description referred to in the representation shall be made to a practitioner by a person carrying on a relevant business, or by a person acting on behalf of a person carrying on such a business, unless the conditions specified in subsection (3) of this section are fulfilled.

(3) Those conditions are—

(*a*) that a data sheet relating to medicinal products of the description in question is sent or delivered to the practitioner with the advertisement, or is delivered to him at the time when the representation is made, or that such a data sheet has been sent or delivered to him not more than fifteen months before the date on which the advertisement is sent or delivered or the representation is made, and
(*b*) that the advertisement or representation is not inconsistent with the particulars contained in the data sheet.

(4) For the purposes of this section the relevant date—

(*a*) in relation to medicinal products of any description to which neither subsection (2) nor subsection (3) of section 16 of this Act is applicable, is the first appointed day, and
(*b*) in relation to medicinal products of any description to which either of those subsections is applicable, is the date of expiry of the period of six months from the date (or, if more than

one, the latest date) on which, by virtue of one or more orders under section 17 of this Act, those subsections cease (or, if only one of them is applicable, that subsection ceases) to have effect in relation to them.

(5) Subject to section 121 of this Act, any person who contravenes subsection (1) or subsection (2) of this section shall be guilty of an offence, and, if he contravenes that subsection by not complying with the condition specified in paragraph (*b*) of subsection (3) of this section, shall be liable[1]—

(*a*) on summary conviction, to a fine not exceeding **the statutory maximum**, or

(*b*) on conviction on indictment, to a **fine** or to imprisonment for a term not exceeding **two years** or to **both**.

and, in any other case, shall be liable on summary conviction to a fine not exceeding **level 3** on the standard scale.

(6) In this and the next following section "data sheet" means a document relating to medicinal products of a particular description, which is prepared by or on behalf of the holder of a product licence which is applicable to medicinal products of that description and which—

(*a*) complies with such requirements as to dimensions and form, as to the particulars to be contained in it, and as to the manner (whether in respect of type, size, colour or disposition of lettering or otherwise) in which any such particulars are to be so contained, as may be prescribed[2] for the purposes of this subsection, and

(*b*) does not contain any information relating to medicinal products of that description except the particulars so prescribed.

(7) Nothing in this section applies in relation to a relevant medicinal product, as defined by paragraph (1) of regulation 2 of the Medicines (Advertising) Regulations 1994, in respect of which there is required to exist a summary of product characteristics as defined by that paragraph.

[Medicines Act 1968, s 96, as amended by the Criminal Law Act 1977, s 28, the Criminal Justice Act 1982, ss 38 and 46 and SI 1995/2321.]

---

1. For procedure in respect of this offence, triable either way, see Magistrates' Courts Act 1980, ss 17A–21 in PART I: MAGISTRATES' COURTS, PROCEDURE.

2. See the Medicines (Data Sheet) Regulations 1972, SI 1972/2076, as amended by SI 1981/1633, SI 1989/1183, SI 1996/2420, SI 2000/2386 and SI 2005/2787.

8–21047 97. Power for licensing authority to require copies of advertisements. (1) The licensing authority may serve on any person a notice requiring him, within such time as may be specified in the notice, to furnish to the licensing authority such number of copies (not exceeding twelve) as may be so specified of any advertisement (including any data sheet) relating to medicinal products, or to medicinal products of a description or falling within a class so specified, which he has issued, or has caused to be issued, within the period of twelve months ending with the date of service of the notice, and which he has so issued, or caused to be issued—

(*a*) being a commercially interested party, or

(*b*) at the request or with the consent of a commercially interested party.

(2) Any person who without reasonable excuse fails to comply with any requirement imposed on him by a notice under this section shall be guilty of an offence, and shall be liable on summary conviction to a fine not exceeding **level 3** on the standard scale.

[Medicines Act 1968, s 97, as amended by the Criminal Justice Act 1982, ss 38 and 45.]

PART VII[1]

British Pharmacopoeia and other publications

8–21047A 99–103. *Relates to the British Pharmacopoeia and other publications*

---

1. This part of the Act shall have effect as if all relevant medicinal products were medicinal products for the purposes of the Act (whether or not they would otherwise be so). See the Medicines for Human Use (Marketing Authorisations etc) Regulations 1994, SI 1994/3144.

PART VIII

MISCELLANEOUS AND SUPPLEMENTARY PROVISIONS

8–21047B 104–106. *Power to apply Act by order[1] to other substances and to activities other than carrying on a business.*

---

1. See the Medicines (Cyanogenetic Substances) Order 1984, SI 1984/187.

8–21048 108. Enforcement in England and Wales. (1) It shall be the duty of the appropriate Minister to enforce in England and Wales, or to secure the enforcement in England and Wales of, the provisions of this Act and any regulations and orders made under it.

(2) For the purposes of performing that duty in relation to—

(*a*) the provision of any order made under paragraph (*a*) of section 62(1) of this Act and of section 63(*b*), sections 64 and 65, subsections (3) to (5) of section 85, and sections 87(2), 88(3) and 89(2) of this Act, in the application of any of those provisions to the retail sale, offer or exposure for retail sale, or possession for the purpose of retail sale, of medicinal products and to the supply, offer or exposure for supply, or possession for the purpose of supply, of medicinal products in circumstances corresponding to retail sale;

(*b*) the provisions of subsections (2) and (3) of section 86 of this Act, in their application to the supply, or possession for the purpose of supply, of leaflets with medicinal products sold or to be sold by retail, or supplied or to be supplied in circumstances corresponding to retail sale; and

(*c*) the provisions of section 93 and 94 of this Act and any regulations made under section 95 of this Act,

the appropriate Minister shall, in respect of each area for which there is a drugs authority, make arrangements or give directions whereby the Pharmaceutical Society, or the drugs authority for that area, or both the Society and that authority, to such extent as, in the case of that Society or authority, the arrangements or directions may provide, shall have power concurrently with the appropriate Minister, or shall be under a duty concurrently with him, to enforce the provisions specified in paragraphs (*a*) and (*b*) of this subsection, in their application as mentioned in those paragraphs, and the provisions and regulations specified in paragraph (*c*) of this subsection.

(3) Any arrangements made with, or directions given to, the Pharmaceutical Society under subsection (2) of this section, in so far as they relate to the provisions and regulations specified in paragraph (*c*) of that subsection, shall be limited to the enforcement of those provisions and regulations in respect of—

(*a*) any advertisement issued or representation made on or in any premises, ship, aircraft, vehicle, stall or place where medicinal products are sold by retail or are supplied in circumstances corresponding to retail sale, and

(*b*) any advertisement displayed on, or in close proximity to, an automatic machine in which medicinal products are offered or exposed for sale.

(4) Regulations made jointly by the Minister of Health and the Minister of Agriculture, Fisheries and Food may provide that any such body to which this subsection applies as may be specified in the regulations shall, to such extent as in the case of that body may be so specified, and either—

(*a*) in respect of England and Wales generally, or

(*b*) in respect of such area in England or Wales as may be so specified,

have power concurrently with the appropriate Minister, or be under a duty concurrently with him, to enforce any regulations made under section 66 of this Act.

(5) Subsection (4) of this section applies to the following bodies, that is to say, the Pharmaceutical Society, any drugs authority, the council of any county district which is not a drugs authority, and the overseers of the Inner Temple and the Middle Temple.

(6) The Pharmaceutical Society shall be under a duty, concurrently with the appropriate Minister—

(*a*) to enforce the provisions of sections 40, 52 and 58 of this Act and of any regulations made under section 40 of this Act in their application to England and Wales;

(*b*) to enforce the provisions of any regulations made under section 60 or section 61 of this Act in their application to premises in England and Wales at which medicinal products are sold by retail or are supplied in circumstances corresponding to retail sale; and

(*c*) to enforce the provisions of sections 77 and 78 of this Act, and of any regulations made under section 79(2) of this Act, in their application to England and Wales.

(7) Regulations made jointly by the Minister of Health and the Minister of Agriculture, Fisheries and Food may provide that, in respect of, each area in England or Wales for which there is a drugs authority, the Pharmaceutical Society, or the drugs authority for that area, or both the Society and that authority, to such extent as, in the case of that Society or authority, the regulations may provide, shall have power concurrently with the appropriate Minister, or shall be under a duty concurrently with him, to enforce the provisions of sections 53 and 54 of this Act.

(8) The council of every county or county borough and of every metropolitan district in England and Wales, the council of every London borough and the Common Council of the City of London shall be under a duty, concurrently with the appropriate Minister, to enforce in their area—

(*a*) any order made under paragraph (*b*) of section 62(1) of this Act, and

(*b*) the provisions of section 90 of this Act and any regulations made by virtue of that section.

(9) Notwithstanding anything in subsections (2) to (8) of this section, no duty or power conferred or imposed by or under any of those subsections shall be performed or be exercisable in relation to—

(*a*) any hospital, or

(*b*) so much of any premises as is used by a practitioner for carrying on his practice, or

(*c*) so much of any premises (not falling within either of the preceding paragraphs) as is used for veterinary medicine or veterinary surgery for the purposes of any institution.

(10) If the appropriate Minister is satisfied, after making such inquiry as he thinks fit, that the Pharmaceutical Society or any other body on whom a duty to enforce any provisions is imposed by or under subsections (4) to (8) of this section have in relation to any matter failed to perform that duty, and that the public interest requires that the provisions in question should be enforced in relation to it, he may determine that he will himself enforce those provisions in relation to that matter.

(11) In this section "the appropriate Minister"—

(*a*) in relation to the performances of any function under this section (whether by making any arrangements or giving any direction or otherwise) where the function is or is to be performed exclusively in relation to veterinary drugs, or to section 90 of this Act or any regulations made by virtue of that section, means the Minister of Agriculture, Fisheries and Food, and

(*b*) in all other respects, means the Minister of Health[1].

(12) In this section "drugs authority" means—

(*a*) as respects each London borough, metropolitan district, county borough or non-metropolitan county, the council of that borough, district, county borough or county; and

(*b*) as respects the City of London (including the Temples), the Common Council of that City.

[Medicines Act 1968, s 108, as amended by the Local Government Act 1972, Sch 30, Animal Health and Welfare Act 1984, Sch 1, SI 1988/1955, the Food Safety Act 1990, Sch 3, and the Local Government (Wales) Act 1994, Sch 16.]

---

1. Now the Secretary of State for Health, see the Transfer of Functions (Medicines and Poisons) Order 1999, SI 1999/3142.

8–21049 **111. Rights of entry.** (1) Subject to the following provisions of this section, any person duly authorised in writing by an enforcement authority shall, on production, if required, of his credentials, have a right at any reasonable time to enter any premises—

(*a*) for the purpose of ascertaining whether there is or has been, on or in connection with those premises, any contravention of any provisions of this Act or of any regulations or order made under this Act which, by or under any provisions of sections 108 to 110 of this Act, that authority is required or empowered to enforce,

(*aa*) for the purpose specified in the third sub-paragraph of Article 111(1) of the 2001 Directive, or

(*b*) generally for the purposes of the performance by the authority of their functions under this Act or under any such regulations or order.

(2) Any person duly authorised in writing by an enforcement authority shall, on production, if required, of his credentials, have a right at any reasonable time—

(*a*) to enter any ship, aircraft or hover vehicle for the purpose of ascertaining whether there is in the shop, aircraft or vehicle any substance or article imported in contravention of any provisions of this Act or of any regulations or order made under this Act which, by or under any provisions of sections 108 to 110 of this Act, that authority is required or empowered to enforce;

(*b*) to enter any vehicle other than a hover vehicle, any stall or place other than premises, or any home-going ship, for any purpose for which under subsection (1) of this section, the person so authorised would have a right to enter any premises.

(3) Without prejudice to subsection (1) of this section, any person duly authorised in writing by the licensing authority shall, on production, if required, of his credentials, have a right at any reasonable time to enter any premises occupied by an applicant for a licence or certificate under Part II of this Act for the purposes of verifying any statement contained in the application for the licence or certificate.

(4) Admission to any premises used only as a private dwelling-house shall not be demanded as of right by virtue of the preceding provisions of this section unless twenty-four hours' notice of the intended entry has been given to the occupier.

(5) If a justice of the peace, on sworn information in writing, is satisfied that there are reasonable grounds for entering any premises for any purposes for which a person authorised by an enforcement authority has a right to enter them in accordance with the preceding provisions of this section, and is also satisfied—

(*a*) that admission to the premises has been refused, or that a refusal is apprehended, and (in either case) that notice of the intention to apply for a warrant has been given to the occupier, or

(*b*) that an application for admission, or the giving of such a notice, would defeat the object of the entry, or

(*c*) that the case is one of urgency, or

(*d*) that the premises are unoccupied or the occupier is temporarily absent,

the justice may by warrant under his hand authorise the enforcement authority, or any person duly authorised by them, to enter the premises, if need be by force.

(6) The last preceding subsection shall have effect in relation to entering any ship, aircraft, vehicle,

stall or place which may be entered under subsection (2) of this section as it has effect in relation to entering any premises, as if in the last preceding subsection any reference to the occupier were a reference to the master, commander or other person in charge of the ship, aircraft, vehicle, stall or place.

(7) Any warrant granted under this section shall continue in force for a period of one month.

(8) In this section "home-going-ship" means a ship plying exclusively in inland waters or engaged exclusively in coastal voyages; and for the purposes of this subsection "inland waters" means any canal, river, lake, loch, navigation or estuary and "coastal voyage" means a voyage which starts and ends in the United Kingdom and does not involve calling at any place outside the United Kingdom.

(9) In the application of this section to Scotland, references to a justice of the peace include references to the sheriff and a magistrate.

[Medicines Act 1968, s 111 as amended by SI 2005/2789.]

8–21050 **112. Power to inspect, take samples and seize goods and documents.** (1) For the purpose of ascertaining whether there is or has been a contravention of this Act or of any regulations or order made thereunder which, by or under any provisions of sections 108 to 110 of this Act an enforcement authority is required or empowered to enforce, any person duly authorised in writing by that authority shall have a right to inspect—

(*a*) any substance or article appearing to him to be a medicinal product;

(*b*) any article appearing to him to be a container or package used or intended to be used to contain any medicinal product or to be a label or leaflet used or intended to be used in connection with a medicinal product; or

(*c*) any plant or equipment appearing to him to be used or intended to be used in connection with the manufacture or assembly of medicinal products, and any process of manufacture or assembly of any medicinal products and the means employed, at any stage in the processes of manufacture or assembly, for testing the materials after they have been subjected to those processes.

(2) Where for the purpose specified in the preceding subsection a person authorised as mentioned in that subsection requires a sample of any substance or article appearing to him to be—

(*a*) a medicinal product sold or supplied or intended to be sold or supplied, or

(*b*) a substance or article used or intended to be used in the manufacture of a medicinal product,

he shall (if he does not obtain the sample by purchase) have a right to take a sample of that substance or article.

(3) For the purpose specified in subsection (1) of this section, any person authorised as mentioned in that subsection shall have a right—

(*a*) to require any person carrying on a business which consists of or includes the manufacture, assembly, sale or supply of medicinal products, and any person employed in connection with such a business, to produce any books or documents relating to the business which are in his possession or under his control;

(*b*) to take copies of, or of any entry in, any book or document produced in pursuance of the preceding paragraph.

(4) Any person so authorised shall have a right to seize and detain any substance or article which he has reasonable cause to believe to be a substance or article in relation to which, or by means of which, an offence under this Act is being or has been committed, and any document which he has reasonable cause to believe to be a document which may be required as evidence in proceedings under this Act.

(5) For the purpose of exercising any such right as is specified in subsection (4) of this section the person having that right may, so far as is reasonably necessary in order to secure that the provisions of this Act and any regulations or order made thereunder are duly observed, require any person having authority to do so to break open any container or package or open any vending machine, or to permit him to do so.

(6) Where a person seizes any substance or article (including any document) in the exercise of such a right as is specified in subsection (4) of this section, he shall inform the person from whom it is seized, and, in the case of anything seized from a vending machine, the person whose name and address are stated on the machine as being those of the owner of the machine, or, if no name and address are so stated, the occupier of the premises on which the machine stands or to which it is affixed.

(7) Without prejudice to the preceding provisions of this section, any person duly authorised in writing by the licensing authority shall have the rights conferred by those provisions in relation to things belonging to, or any business carried on by, an applicant for a licence or certificate under Part II of this Act, and may exercise those rights for the purpose of verifying any statement contained in the application for the licence or certificate; and, where by virtue of this subsection a person exercises any such right as is specified in subsection (4) of this section, he shall be subject to the duty imposed by subsection (6) of this section.

(8) Notwithstanding anything in the preceding provisions of this section, where a person claiming

to exercise a right by virtue of this section is required to produce his credentials, the right shall not be exercisable by him except on production of those credentials.

(9) The provisions of Schedule 3 to this Act shall have effect with respect to samples obtained on behalf of enforcement authorities for the purposes of this Act.
[Medicines Act 1968, s 112.]

8–21051 113. Application of sampling procedure to substance or article seized under s 112. (1) The provisions of this section shall have effect where a person (in this section referred to as an "authorised officer") seizes a substance or article (other than a document) in the exercise of such a right as is specified in subsection (4) of section 112 of this Act (including that subsection as applied by subsection (7) of that section).

(2) If any person who in accordance with subsection (6) of that section is entitled to be informed of the seizure so requests, either at the time of the seizure or at any subsequent time, not being later than twenty-one days after he is informed of the seizure, then, subject to the next following subsection, the authorised officer shall either—

(*a*) set aside a sample of the substance or article seized, or

(*b*) treat that substance or article as a sample,

whichever he considers more appropriate having regard to the nature of that substance or article.

(3) An authorised officer shall not be required by virtue of subsection (2) of this section to set aside a sample, or to treat a substance or article as a sample, if the nature of the substance or article is such that it is not reasonably practical to do either of those things.

(4) Where in accordance with subsection (2) of this section an authorised officer sets aside a sample, or treats a substance or article as a sample, he shall divide it into three parts, each part to be marked and sealed or fastened up in such manner as its nature will permit, and shall supply one part of it to the person who made the request under subsection (2) of this section.

(5) Paragraphs 10, 11 and 12 and paragraphs 15 to 27 of Schedule 3 to this Act shall have effect in relation to a sample set aside, or a substance or article treated as a sample, in accordance with subsection (2) of this section as they have effect in relation to a sample obtained as mentioned in paragraph 1 of that Schedule, but as if in those paragraphs—

(*a*) any reference to a sampling officer were a reference to an authorised officer;

(*b*) any reference to a sample included a reference to a substance or article treated as a sample;

(*c*) any reference to the preceding provisions of that Schedule were a reference to the preceding provisions of this section; and

(*d*) any reference to the relevant enforcement authority were a reference to the authority by whom the authorised officer is authorised for the purposes of section 112 of this Act,

and as if in paragraph 24(1) of that Schedule the reference to a substance or article obtained as mentioned in paragraph 1 of that Schedule were a reference to a substance or article of which a sample has been set aside, or which has been treated as a sample, in accordance with subsection (2) of this section.
[Medicines Act 1968, s 113.]

8–21052 114. Supplementary provisions as to rights of entry and related rights. (1) Any person entering any property (that is to say, any premises, ship, aircraft, vehicle, stall or place) by virtue of section 111 of this Act (whether in pursuance of a warrant or not) may take with him such other persons and such equipment as may appear to him to be necessary; and on leaving any such property which he has entered in pursuance of a warrant under that section he shall, if the property is unoccupied or the occupier (or, in the case of a ship, aircraft, vehicle, stall or place, the master, commander or other person in charge of it) is temporarily absent, leave it as effectively secured against trespass as he found it.

(2) Any person who—

(*a*) wilfully obstructs a person acting in pursuance of this Act and duly authorised so to act by an enforcement authority, or

(*b*) wilfully fails to comply with any requirement properly made to him by a person so acting under section 112 of this Act, or

(*c*) without reasonable cause fails to give to a person so acting any other assistance or information which that person may reasonably require of him for the purpose of the performance of his functions under this Act,

shall be guilty of an offence and shall be liable on summary conviction to a fine not exceeding **level 3** on the standard scale.

(3) If any person, in giving any such information as is mentioned in subsection (2)(*c*) of this section, makes any statement which he knows to be false, he shall be guilty of an offence and shall be liable[1]—

(*a*) on summary conviction, to a fine not exceeding **the statutory maximum**;

(*b*) on conviction on indictment, to a **fine** or to imprisonment for a term not exceeding **two years** or to **both**.

(4) Nothing in this section shall be construed as requiring a person to answer any question or give any information if to do so might incriminate that person or (where that person is married or a civil partner) the spouse or civil partner of that person.
[Medicines Act 1968, s 114, as amended by the Criminal Law Act 1977, s 28 and the Criminal Justice Act 1982, ss 38 and 46 and the Civil Partnership Act 2004, Sch 27.]

---

1. For procedure in respect of this offence, triable either way, see Magistrates' Courts Act 1980, ss 17A–21 in PART I: MAGISTRATES' COURTS, PROCEDURE.

8–21053 **115. Analysis of samples in other cases.** (1) A person who, not being a person authorised in that behalf by an enforcement authority, has purchased a medicinal product may submit a sample of it for analysis to the public analyst for the area in which the product was purchased, or, if for the time being there is no public analyst for that area, then to the public analyst for some other area.

(2) Paragraphs 2 to 13 of Schedule 3 to this Act shall have effect in relation to a person proposing to submit a sample in pursuance of the preceding subsection, as if in those paragraphs any reference to the sampling officer were a reference to that person.

(3) Subject to the following provisions of this section, a public analyst to whom a sample is submitted under subsection (1) of this section shall as soon as practicable analyse the sample or cause it to be analysed by some other person under his direction.

(4) If the public analyst to whom a sample is submitted under subsection (1) of this section determines that for any reason an effective analysis of the sample cannot be performed by him or under his direction, he shall send it to the public analyst for some other area, and (subject to the next following subsection) that other public analyst shall as soon as practicable analyse the sample or cause it to be analysed by some other person under his direction.

(5) A public analyst to whom a sample is submitted or sent under this section may demand payment in advance of the prescribed fee, and, if he demands such payment, he shall not be required to analyse the sample or cause it to be analysed until the fee has been paid.

(6) A public analyst who has analysed a sample or caused a sample to be analysed under this section shall issue a certificate specifying the results of the analysis to the person by whom the sample was originally submitted.

(7) Any certificate issued under subsection (5) of this section shall be in a form prescribed[1] by the Ministers and shall be signed by the public analyst who issues the certificate.

(8) Paragraphs 21 to 23 of Schedule 3 to this Act shall have effect in relation to a certificate issued under subsection (6) of this section as they have effect in relation to a certificate issued under paragraph 19 of that Schedule.

(9) Any regulations prescribing a fee for the purposes of this section shall be made by the Ministers.

(10) In this section "public analyst" has the meaning assigned to it by paragraph 1(2) of Schedule 3 to this Act.
[Medicines Act 1968, s 115.]

---

1. The Medicines (Certificates of Analysis) Regulations 1977, SI 1977/1399 amended by SI 2005/2745, have been made.

8–21054 **115A. Facilities for microbiological examinations.** A drugs authority or the council of a non-metropolitan district may provide facilities for microbiological examinations of drugs.
[Medicines Act 1968, s 115A, as inserted by the Food Safety Act 1990, Sch 3.]

8–21064 **116. Liability to forfeiture under Customs and Excise Act 1952.** (1) For the purposes of section 49 of the Customs and Excise Management Act 1979 (forfeiture of goods improperly imported) any imported goods shall be deemed to be imported contrary to a restriction for the time being in force with respect to them under this Act if—

(*a*) they are goods falling within a class specified in an order made by the Ministers for the purposes of this subsection, and
(*b*) they are imported in such circumstances as are specified in that order.

(2) For the purposes of section 68 of the Customs and Excise Management Act 1979 (offences in relation to exportation of prohibited or restricted goods) any goods shall be deemed to be exported contrary to a restriction for the time being in force with respect to them under this Act if—

(*a*) they are goods falling within a class specified in an order made by the Ministers for the purposes of this subsection, and
(*b*) they are exported in such circumstances as are specified in that order.

(3) Any class of goods specified in an order under subsection (1) or subsection (2) of this section shall be so specified as to consist exclusively of goods appearing to the Ministers to be goods which are, or normally are, medicinal products or are, or normally are, animal feeding stuffs in which medicinal products have been incorporated.
[Medicines Act 1968, s 116, as amended by the Customs and Excise Management Act 1979, Sch 4.]

8–21065 117. Special enforcement and sampling provisions relating to animal feeding stuffs. (1) For the purposes of the application of the provisions of sections 112, 113 and 115 of this Act in relation to animal feeding stuffs, regulations[1] made by the Agriculture Ministers may provide that any of those provisions specified in the regulations shall have effect subject to such modifications as may be so specified.

(2) Regulations[1] made by the Agriculture Ministers[2]—

(*a*) may make provisions as to the manner in which samples may be taken by virtue of the provisions of section 112 of this Act as modified by any regulations made under the preceding subsection, as to the manner in which samples may be set aside, or substances or articles may be treated as samples, by virtue of the provisions of section 113 of this Act as so modified, or as to the manner in which samples may be submitted for analysis by virtue of the provisions of section 115 of this Act as so modified, and

(*b*) in relation to samples so taken, set aside or submitted for analysis, or substances or articles so treated as samples, may make provision (either in substitution for, or by way of modification of or addition to, any of the provisions of Schedule 3 to this Act) as to the manner in which such samples, substances and articles are to be dealt with.

(3) For the purposes of proceedings for such offences under this Act relating to animal feeding stuffs as may be prescribed by regulations[1] made under subsection (2) of this section, the regulations may—

(*a*) prescribe a method of analysis to be used in analysing samples of animal feeding stuffs in order to determine what quantity or proportion (if any) of a substance or article of a description or class specified in the regulations has been incorporated in them, and

(*b*) provide that, on production in the proceedings of such evidence as may be so prescribed of the results of an analysis of a sample performed by the method so prescribed, evidence of the results of any analysis of any part of the sample performed by any other method shall not be admissible in those proceedings.

(4) In relation to the incorporation in animal feeding stuffs of substances or articles of any description or class specified in an order[3] made under this subsection by the Agriculture Ministers, so much of any licence granted or animal test certificate issued under Part II of this Act as imposes any restriction or requirement by reference to the quantity to be incorporated, or the proportion in which any substance or article may be incorporated, in any animal feeding stuff shall not be taken to be contravened in any particular case if the discrepancy does not exceed such limit as may be specified by the order in relation to substances or articles of that description or class.

(5) Where a label or mark on a container or package containing any animal feeding stuff, or a leaflet supplied or to be supplied with any animal feeding stuff, specifies a quantity or proportion of a medicinal product of a particular description as being incorporated in the animal feeding stuff, section 90(2) of this Act shall not be taken to be contravened by reason only that the quantity or proportion actually incorporated in the animal feeding stuff is greater or less than so specified, if the discrepancy does not exceed such limit as the Agriculture Ministers may by order[3] specify in relation to medicinal products of that description, or in relation to a class of medicinal products which includes medicinal products of that description.

(5A) The power conferred by subsection (1) of this section to provide for the purposes there mentioned that any of the provisions of section 115 of this Act shall have effect (with or without modifications) in relation to animal feeding stuffs that, in place of all or any of those provisions, provisions specified in the regulations shall have effect, being provisions corresponding to any of those made by sections 75 and 78 of the Agriculture Act 1970.

(6) In section 114(2)(*b*) of this Act the reference to section 112 of this Act shall be construed as including a reference to the provisions of that section as modified by any regulations made under this section and the reference in subsection (2) of this section to the provisions of section 115 of this act as modified by any such regulations shall be construed as including a reference to any provisions specified in the regulations in place of any of the provisions of section 115 of this Act.

(7) The powers conferred by subsection (2) of this section shall be exercisable in addition to any power exercisable by virtue of paragraph 27 of Schedule 3 to this Act.

(8) References in subsections (1), (3) and (5A) of this section to animal feeding stuffs include a reference to any medicated feeding stuff, within the meaning of section 130(3A) of this Act.

[Medicines Act 1968, s 117, as amended by the Animal Health and Welfare Act 1984, s 15 and Sch 1.]

1. The Medicines (Animal Feeding Stuffs) (Enforcement) Regulations 1985, SI 1985/273 amended by SI 1989/2324 and SI 1996/1261, have been made.

2. Now the Secretary of State for Environment, Food and Rural Affairs, see the Ministry of Agriculture, Fisheries and Food (Dissolution) Order 2002, SI 2002/794.

3. The Medicines (Feeding Stuffs Additives) Order 1975, SI 1975/1349, and the Medicines (Feeding Stuffs Limits of Variation) Order 1976, SI 1976/31, have been made.

8–21066 118. Restrictions on disclosure of information. (1) If any person discloses to any other person—

(*a*) any information with respect to any manufacturing process or trade secret obtained by him in premises which he has entered by virtue of section 111 of this Act, or (*b*) any information obtained by or furnished to him in pursuance of this Act,

he shall, unless the disclosure was made in the performance of his duty, be guilty of an offence.

(1A) Subsection (1) of this section does not apply if—

(*a*) the person making the disclosure referred to in that section is, or is acting on behalf of a person who is, a public authority for the purposes of the Freedom of Information Act 2000, and

(*b*) the information is not held by the authority on behalf of another person.

(2) Any person guilty of an offence under this section shall be liable[1]—

(*a*) on summary conviction, to a fine not exceeding **the statutory maximum**;

(*b*) on conviction on indictment, to a **fine** or to imprisonment for a term not exceeding **two years** or to **both**.

[Medicines Act 1968, s 118, as amended by the Criminal Law Act 1977, s 28 and SI 2004/3363.]

1. For procedure in respect of this offence, triable either way, see Magistrates' Courts Act 1980, ss 17A–21 in PART I: MAGISTRATES' COURTS, PROCEDURE.

8–21067 121. Contravention due to default of other person. (1) Where a contravention by any person of any provision to which this section applies constitutes an offence under this Act, and is due to an act or default of another person, then, whether proceedings are taken against the first-mentioned person or not, that other person may be charged with and convicted of that offence, and shall be liable on conviction to the same punishment as might have been imposed on the first-mentioned person if he had been convicted of the offence.

(2) Where a person who is charged with an offence under this Act in respect of a contravention of a provision to which this section applies proves to the satisfaction of the court—

(*a*) that he exercised all due diligence to secure that the provision in question would not be contravened, and

(*b*) that the contravention was due to the act or default of another person,

the first-mentioned person shall, subject to the next following subsection be acquitted of the offence.

(3) A person shall not, without the leave of the court, be entitled to rely on the defence provided by subsection (2) of this section unless, not later than seven clear days before the date of the hearing, he has served on the prosecutor a notice in writing giving such information identifying, or assisting in the identification of, the other person in question as was then in his possession.

(4) This section applies to the following provisions, that is to say, sections 63 to 65, 85 to 90, and 93 to 96, and the provisions of any regulations made under any of those sections.

[Medicines Act 1968, s 121.]

8–21068 122. Warranty as defence. (1) Subject to the following provisions of this section, in any proceedings for an offence under this Act in respect of a contravention of a provision to which this section applies, it shall be a defence for the defendant to prove—

(*a*) that he purchased the substance or article to which the contravention relates in the United Kingdom as being a substance or article which could be lawfully sold, supplied, or offered or exposed for sale, or could be lawfully sold, supplied, or offered or exposed for sale under the name or description or for the purpose under or for which he sold, supplied, or offered or exposed it for sale, and with a written warranty to that effect;

(*b*) that at the time of the commission of the alleged offence he had no reason to believe that it was otherwise; and

(*c*) that the substance or article was then in the same state as when he purchased it.

(2) This section applies to the following provisions, that is to say, section 63(*b*), sections 64 and 65, sections 85 to 88 and section 90 and the provisions of any regulations made under any of those sections.

(3) A warranty shall not be a defence by virtue of this section unless the defendant has, not later than three clear days before the date of the hearing, sent to the prosecutor a copy of the warranty with a notice stating that he intends to rely on it and specifying the name and address of the person from whom he received it, and has also sent a like notice to that person.

(4) Where the defendant is a servant of the person who purchased the substance or article under the warranty, he shall be entitled to rely on the provisions of this section in the same way as his employer would have been entitled to do if he had been the defendant.

(5) The person by whom the warranty is alleged to have been given shall be entitled to appear at the hearing and to give evidence, and the court may, if it thinks fit, adjourn the hearing to enable him to do so.

(6) For the purposes of this section a name or description entered in an invoice shall be deemed to be a written warranty that the article or substance to which the name or description applies can be sold, supplied, or offered or exposed for sale under that name or description by any person without contravening any provision to which this section applies.

(7) In the application of this and the next following section to Scotland, any reference to the defendant shall be construed as a reference to the accused.
[Medicines Act 1968, s 122.]

8–21069 123. Offences in relation to warranties and certificates of analysis. (1) If a defendant in any such proceedings as are mentioned in section 122(1) of this Act wilfully applies to any substance or article—

(*a*) a warranty given in relation to a different substance or article, or
(*b*) a certificate issued under section 115 of this Act, or under paragraph 19 of Schedule 3 to this Act, which related to a sample of a different substance or article,

he shall be guilty of an offence.

(2) A person who, in respect of any substance or article sold by him in respect of which a warranty might be pleaded under section 122 of this Act, gives to the purchaser a false warranty in writing shall be guilty of an offence, unless he proves that when he gave the warranty he had reason to believe that the statement or description contained in it was accurate.

(3) Where the defendant in any such proceedings as are mentioned in section 122(1) of this Act relies successfully on a warranty given to him or to his employer, any proceedings for an offence under subsection (2) of this section in respect of the warranty may, at the option of the prosecutor, be taken either before a court having jurisdiction in the place where a sample of the substance or article to which the warranty relates was procured, or before a court having jurisdiction in the place where the warranty was given.

(4) Any person guilty of an offence under this section shall be liable[1]—

(*a*) on summary conviction, to a fine not exceeding **the statutory maximum**;
(*b*) on conviction on indictment, to a **fine** or to imprisonment for a term not exceeding **two years** or to **both**.

[Medicines Act 1968, s 123, as amended by the Criminal Law Act 1977, s 28.]

1. For procedure in respect of this offence, triable either way, see Magistrates' Courts Act 1980, ss 17A–21 in PART I: MAGISTRATES' COURTS, PROCEDURE.

8–21070 124. Offences by bodies corporate. (1) Where an offence under this Act which is committed by a body corporate is proved to have been committed with the consent and connivance of, or to be attributable to any neglect on the part of, any director, manager, secretary or other similar officer of the body corporate, or any person who was purporting to act in any such capacity, he as well as the body corporate shall be guilty of that offence and shall be liable to be proceeded against and punished accordingly.

(2) In relation to a body corporate carrying on a retail pharmacy business as mentioned in subsection (1) of section 71 of this Act, the preceding subsection shall have effect in relation to a person who (not being such an officer of the body corporate as is mentioned in the preceding subsection)—

(*a*) is the superintendent referred to in subsection (1) of that section, or
(*b*) at any premises where the business is carried on, is the pharmacist referred to in subsection (1)(*a*) of that section who acts under the directions of the superintendent,

as if he were such an officer of the body corporate as is mentioned in the preceding subsection.

(3) In this section "director", in relation to a body corporate established by or under any enactment for the purpose of carrying on under national ownership any industry or part of an industry or undertaking, being a body corporate whose affairs are managed by its members, means a member of that body corporate.
[Medicines Act 1968, s 124.]

8–21071 125. Prosecutions. (1) Notwithstanding anything in section 127(1) of the Magistrates' Courts Act 1980, a magistrates' court in England or Wales may try an information for an offence under this Act if the information was laid at any time within twelve months from the commission of the offence.

(2) *Relates to Scotland.*

(3) *Relates to Northern Ireland.*

(4) Neither the Pharmaceutical Society nor any other body referred to in subsection (2) or subsection (8) of section 108 of this Act shall institute proceedings for an offence under this Act in respect of a contravention of a provision which, by virtue of either of those subsections, that Society or body have a power or duty to enforce, unless they have given to the appropriate Minister not less than twenty-eight days' notice of their intention to institute proceedings, together with a summary of the facts upon which the charges are founded.

(5) For the purposes of subsection (4) of this section the appropriate Minister, in relation to a contravention of any provision, is the Minister who in accordance with section 108 of this Act had a concurrent duty to enforce that provision.

(6) A health authority (as defined by section 110 of this Act) shall not prosecute for an offence

under this Act in respect of a contravention of any provision which, by virtue of subsection (2) of that section, the authority have a power or duty to enforce, unless the authority have given to the Minister of Health and Social Services for Northern Ireland not less than twenty-eight days' notice of their intentions to begin the prosecution, together with a summary of the facts upon which the charges are founded.

(7) A certificate of the Minister who is the appropriate Minister for the purposes of subsection (4) of this section that the requirements of that subsection have been complied with in relation to any proceedings, and a certificate of the Minister of Health and Social Services for Northern Ireland that the requirements of subsection (6) of this section have been complied with in relation to any prosecution, shall be conclusive evidence that those requirements have been so complied with; and any document purporting to be such a certificate and to be signed by or on behalf of that Minister shall be presumed to be such a certificate unless the contrary is proved.

[Medicines Act 1968, s 125, as amended by the Magistrates' Courts Act 1980, Sch 7.]

8–21072 126. Presumptions. (1) For the purposes of any proceedings under this Act for an offence consisting of—

(*a*) offering any animal feeding stuff for sale in contravention of section 40 of this Act, or

(*b*) offering a medicinal product for sale by retail in contravention of section 52 or section 53 of this Act, or

(*c*) offering a medicinal product for sale in contravention of section 63(*b*) of this Act,

where it is proved that the animal feeding stuff or medicinal product in question was found on a vehicle from which animal feeding stuffs or medicinal products are sold, it shall be presumed, unless the contrary is proved, that the person in charge of the vehicle offered that animal feeding stuff or medicinal product for sale and, in a case falling within paragraph (*b*) of this subsection, that he offered it for sale by retail.

(2) For the purposes of any proceedings under this Act for an offence consisting of a contravention of so much of any provision to which this subsection applies as relates to a person's having any medicinal product or animal feeding stuff in his possession for the purpose of sale or supply, where it is proved that the medicinal product or animal feeding stuff in question was found on premises at which the person charged with the offence carries on a business consisting of or including the sale or supply of medicinal products or of animal feeding stuffs in which medicinal products have been incorporated, it shall be presumed, unless the contrary is proved, that he had that medicinal product or animal feeding stuff in his possession for the purpose of sale or supply.

(3) Subsection (2) of this section applies to the following provisions of this Act, that is to say, section 63(*b*), subsections (3) and (5) of section 85, subsection (2) of section 87 and subsection (3) of section 88, to any of those provisions as applied by subsection (1) of section 90, and to subsection (2) of section 90 except in so far as it relates to leaflets.

(4) For the purposes of any proceedings under this Act for an offence consisting of a contravention of subsection (2) or subsection (3) of section 86 of this Act, or of so much of subsection (2) of section 90 of this Act as relates to leaflets, where it is proved that the leaflet in question was found on premises at which the person charged with the offence carries on a business consisting of or including the sale or supply of medicinal products or of animal feeding stuffs in which medicinal products have been incorporated, it shall be presumed, unless the contrary is proved, that he had the leaflet in his possession—

(*a*) where the offence charged relates to section 86 of this Act, for the purpose of supplying it with a medicinal product, or

(*b*) where the offence charged relates to section 90 of this Act, for the purpose of supplying it with animal feeding stuff in which a medicinal product has been incorporated.

[Medicines Act 1968, s 126, as amended by the Animal Health and Welfare Act 1984, Sch 1.]

8–21073 127. Service of documents. Any notice or other document required or authorised by any provision of this Act to be served on any person, or to be given or sent to any person, may be served, given or sent—

(*a*) by delivering it to him; or

(*b*) by sending it by post[1] to him at his usual or last-known residence or place of business in the United Kingdom; or

(*c*) in the case of a body corporate, by delivering it to the secretary or clerk of the body corporate at its registered or principal office or sending it by post[1] to the secretary or clerk of that body corporate at that office.

[Medicines Act 1968, s 127.]

1. See presumption of due delivery in s 7 of the Interpretation Act 1978, in PART II: EVIDENCE, ante.

8–21074 129. *General power to make orders and regulations*

8–21075 130. Meaning of "medicinal product" and related expressions. (1) Subject to the following provisions of this section, in this Act "medicinal product" means any substance or article (not being an instrument, apparatus or appliance) which is manufactured, sold, supplied, imported or exported for use wholly or mainly in either or both of the following ways, that is to say—

(*a*) use by being administered to one or more human beings or animals for a medicinal purpose;
(*b*) use, in circumstances to which this paragraph applies, as an ingredient in the preparation of a substance or article which is to be administered to one or more human beings or animals for a medicinal purpose.

(2) In this Act "a medicinal purpose" means any one or more of the following purposes, that is to say—

(*a*) treating or preventing disease;
(*b*) diagnosing disease or ascertaining the existence, degree or extent of a physiological condition;
(*c*) contraception;
(*d*) inducing anaesthesia;
(*e*) otherwise preventing or interfering with the normal operation of a physiological function, whether permanently or temporarily, and whether by way of terminating, reducing or postponing, or increasing or accelerating, the operation of that function or in any other way.

(3) In paragraph (*b*) of subsection (1) of this section the reference to use in circumstances to which that paragraph applies is a reference to any one or more of the following, that is to say—

(*a*) use in a pharmacy or in a hospital;
(*b*) use by a practitioner;
(*c*) use in the course of business which consists of or includes the retail sale, or the supply in circumstances corresponding to retail sale, of herbal remedies.

(3A) An order made by the Agriculture Ministers[1] may provide that, for the purposes of this Act, any specified description or class of medicated feeding stuff—

(*a*) is to be treated as a medicinal product (subject to the following provisions of this section), or
(*b*) is not to be so treated (notwithstanding anything in subsection (1) of this section).

(3B) In subsection (3A) of this section "medicated feeding stuff" means any substance which is manufactured, sold, supplied, imported or exported for use wholly or mainly in either or both of the following ways, that is to say—

(*a*) use by being fed to one or more animals for a medicinal purpose or for purposes that include that purpose, or
(*b*) use as an ingredient in the preparation of a substance which is to be fed to one or more animals for a medicinal purpose or for purposes that include that purpose.

(3C) No order shall be made under subsection (3A) of this section unless a draft of the order has been laid before Parliament and approved by resolution of each House of Parliament.

(4) Notwithstanding anything in subsection (1) or (3A) of this section, in this Act "medicinal product" does not include any substance or article which is manufactured for use wholly or mainly by being administered to one or more human beings or animals, where it is to be administered to them—

(*a*) in the course of the business of the person who has manufactured it (in this subsection referred to as "the manufacturer"), or on behalf of the manufacturer in the course of the business of a laboratory or research establishment carried on by another person, and
(*b*) solely by way of a test for ascertaining what effects it has when so administered, and
(*c*) in circumstances where the manufacturer has no knowledge of any evidence that those effects are likely to be beneficial to those human beings, or beneficial to, or otherwise advantageous in relation to, those animals, as the case may be,

and which (having been so manufactured) is not sold, supplied or exported for use wholly or mainly in any way not fulfilling all the conditions specified in paragraphs (*a*) to (*c*) of this subsection.

(5) In this Act "medicinal product" shall also be taken not to include—

(*a*) substances used in dental surgery for filling dental cavities;
(*b*) bandages and other surgical dressings, except medicated dressings within subsection (5A) below;
(*ba*) whole human blood and human blood components;
(*c*) substances and articles of such other descriptions or classes, as may be specified by an order made by the Ministers, the Health Ministers or the Agriculture Ministers for the purposes of this subsection.

(5A) Medicated dressings are within this subsection (and accordingly are not excluded from the definition of "medicinal product" by subsection (5)(*b*) above) if—

(*a*) their medication has a curative function which is not limited to sterilising the dressing; and
(*b*) they are not dressings of a kind to which the requirements of Article 2 of Council Directive 93/42/EEC (placing medical devices on the market and putting them into service) apply or would apply but for Article 4 (devices intended for special purposes) or 22 (transitional provisions) of that Directive.

(5B) For the purposes of this section, "human blood component" means any of the following constituents of human blood: red cells, white cells, platelets and plasma.

(6) Where in accordance with the preceding provisions of this section a substance or article is a medicinal product immediately after it has been manufactured, imported or exported as mentioned in subsection (1) or (3B) of this section, or immediately after the first occasion on which it has been sold or supplied as mentioned in the relevant subsection, then it shall not cease to be a medicinal product for the purposes of this Act by reason only that, at any subsequent time, it is sold, supplied, imported or exported for use wholly or mainly in a way other than those specified in the relevant subsection.

(7) *Repealed.*

(8) For the purposes of this Act medicinal products are of the same description if (but only if)—

(*a*) they are manufactured to the same specification, and

(*b*) they are, or are to be, sold, supplied, imported or exported in the same pharmaceutical form,

and in this Act "description", in relation to medicinal products, shall be construed accordingly.

(9) In this Act "administer" means administer to a human being or an animal, whether orally, by injection or by introduction into the body in any other way, or by external application, whether by direct contact with the body or not; and any reference in this Act to administering (or feeding) a substance or article is a reference to administering (or feeding) it either in its existing state or after it has been dissolved or dispersed in, or diluted or mixed with, some other substance used as a vehicle.

(10) For the purposes of this Act a document, advertisement or representation shall be taken to be likely to mislead as to the uses or effects of medicinal products of a particular description if it is likely to mislead as to any of the following matters, that is to say—

(*a*) any purposes for which medicinal products of that description can with reasonable safety be used;

(*b*) any purposes for which such products cannot be so used; and

(*c*) any effects which such products when used, or when used in any particular way referred to in the document, advertisement or representation, produce or are intended to produce.

[Medicines Act 1968, s 130, as amended by the Animal Health and Welfare Act 1984, s 13 and Schs 1 and 2, SI 1994/3119 and SI 2005/50 and SI 2005/2789.]

---

1. Now the Secretary of State for Environment, Food and Rural Affairs, see the Ministry of Agriculture, Fisheries and Food (Dissolution) Order 2002, SI 2002/794.

8–21076 131. Meaning of "wholesale dealing", "retail sale" and related expressions. (1) In this Act any reference to selling anything by way of wholesale dealing is a reference to selling it to a person as being a person who buys it for one or more of the purposes specified in subsection (2) of this section, except that it does not include any such sale by the person who manufactured it.

(2) The purposes referred to in the preceding subsection, in relation to a person to whom anything is sold, are the purposes of—

(*a*) selling or supplying it, or

(*b*) administering it or causing it to be administered to one or more human beings,

in the course of a business carried on by that person.

(3) In this Act any reference to selling by retail, or to retail sale, is a reference to selling a substance or article to a person as being a person who buys it otherwise than for a purpose specified in subsection (2) of this section.

(4) In this Act any reference to supplying anything in circumstances corresponding to retail sale is a reference to supplying it, otherwise than by way of sale, to a person as being a person who receives it for a purpose other than that of—

(*a*) selling or supplying it, or

(*b*) administering it or causing it to be administered to one or more human beings,

in the course of a business carried on by that person.

(5) For the purposes of this section the provision of services by or on behalf of the Minister of Health, the Secretary of State or the Ministry of Health and Social Services for Northern Ireland under the National Health Service Act 1977, the National Health Service (Scotland) Act 1978 or the Health and Personal Social Services (Northern Ireland) Order 1972 shall be treated as the carrying on of a business by that Minister, the Secretary of State or that Ministry, as the case may be.

[Medicines Act 1968, s 131, as amended by the National Health Service Reorganisation Act 1973, Sch 4, the National Health Service Act 1977, Sch 15 and the National Health Service (Scotland) Act 1978, Sch 16.]

8–21077 132. General interpretation provisions. (1) In this Act, except in so far as the context otherwise requires, the following expressions have the meanings hereby assigned to them respectively, that is to say:*

"Advisory Body" has the meaning given to it by paragraph 1 of Schedule 1A to this Act;

"analysis" includes micro-biological assay but no other form of biological assay, and "analyse" has a corresponding meaning;

"animal" includes any bird, fish or reptile;

"animal feeding stuff" means any substance which is intended for use either by being fed to one or more animals or as an ingredient in the preparation of such a substance, not being in either case a medicinal product;

"animal test certificate" has the meaning assigned to it by section 32 of this Act;

"the appropriate committee" has the meaning assigned to it by section 4(6) of this Act;

"the appropriate Ministers" shall be construed in accordance with section 1(2) of this Act[1];

"assemble", in relation to a medicinal product, means enclosing the product (with or without other medicinal products of the same description) in a container which is labelled before the product is sold or supplied, or, where the product (with or without other medicinal products of the same description) is already enclosed in the container in which it is to be sold or supplied, labelling the container before the product is sold or supplied in it, and "assembly" has a corresponding meaning;

"business" includes a professional practice and includes any activity carried on by a body of persons, whether corporate or unincorporate;

"clinical trial" and "clinical trial certificate" have the meanings assigned to them by section 31 of this Act;

"the Commission" means the Commission for Human Medicines established under this Act;

"composition", in relation to a medicinal product, means the ingredients of which it consists and the proportions, and the degrees of strength, quality and purity, in which those ingredients are contained in it respectively;

"container", in relation to a medicinal product, means the bottle, jar, box, packet, or other receptacle which contains or is to contain it, not being a capsule, cachet or other article in which the product is or is to be administered, and where any such receptacle is or is to be contained in another such receptacle, includes the former but does not include the latter receptacle;

"contravention" includes failure to comply and "contravene" has a corresponding meaning;

"dentist" means a person registered in the dentists register under the Dentists Act 1984 or entered in the list of visiting EEA practitioners under Schedule 4 to that Act;

"the 1981 Directive" means Council Directive 81/851/EEC of 28th September 1981 on the approximation of the laws of Member States relating to veterinary medicinal products (as amended by Council Directive 90/676/EEC).

"the 2001 Directive" means Directive 2001/83/EC of the European Parliament and of the Council on the Community code relating to medicinal products for human use, as amended, by—

(*a*) Directive 2002/98/EC of the European Parliament and of the Council of 27 January 2003 setting standards of quality and safety for the collection, testing, processing, storage and distribution of human blood and blood components,

(*b*) Commission Directive 2003/63/EC amending Directive 2001/83/EC on the Community code relating to medicinal products for human use,

(*c*) Directive 2004/24/EC of the European Parliament and of the Council amending, as regards traditional herbal medicinal products, Directive 2001/83/EC on the Community code relating to medicinal products for human use; and

(*d*) Directive 2004/27/EC of the European Parliament and of the Council amending Directive 2001/83/EC on the Community code relating to medicinal products for human use;

"disease" includes any injury, ailment or adverse condition, whether of body or mind;

"doctor" means a registered medical practitioner within the meaning of Schedule 1 to the Interpretation Act 1978;

"drugs authority" has the meaning assigned to it by section 108(12) of this Act;

"EEA State" means a Member State, Norway, Iceland or Liechtenstein;

"enforcement authority" means any Minister or body on whom a duty or power to enforce any provisions of this Act or of any regulations or order made thereunder is imposed or conferred by or under sections 108 to 110 of this Act;*

"Expert Advisory Group" means an Expert Advisory Group established under paragraph 3 or 4 of Schedule 1A to this Act;

"export" means export from the United Kingdom, whether by land, sea or air, and "import" has a corresponding meaning;

"the first appointed day" has the meaning assigned to it by section 16(1) of this Act;

"the Gazette" means the London, Edinburgh and Belfast Gazettes;

"health centre" means a health centre maintained under section 2 or 3 of the National Health Service Act 1977, section 15 of the National Health Service (Scotland) Act 1947 or article 5 of the Health and Personal Social Services (Northern Ireland) Order 1972;

"the Herbal Regulations" means the Medicines (Traditional Herbal Medicinal Products for Human Use) Regulations 2005;

"herbal remedy" means a medicinal product consisting of a substance produced by subjecting a plant or plants to drying, crushing or any other process, or of a mixture whose sole ingredients are two or more substances so produced, or of a mixture whose sole ingredients are one or more substances so produced and water or some other inert substance;

"herd" includes a flock;*

"the Homoeopathic Regulations" means the Medicines (Homoeopathic Medicinal Products for Human Use) Regulations 1994;

"hospital" includes a clinic, nursing home or similar institution;

"hover vehicle" means a vehicle designed to be supported on a cushion of air;

"import from a third country" means import from any country other than an EEA State;

"ingredient", in relation to the manufacture or preparation of a substance, includes anything which is the sole active ingredient of that substance as manufactured or prepared;

"labelling", in relation to a container or package of medicinal products, means affixing to or otherwise displaying on it a notice describing or otherwise relating to the contents, and "label" has a corresponding meaning;

"leaflet" includes any written information;

"the licensing authority" has the meaning assigned to it by section 6 of this Act;

"licence of right" has the meaning assigned to it by section 25(4) of this Act;

"manufacture", in relation to a medicinal product, includes any process carried out in the course of making the product, but does not include dissolving or dispersing the product in, or diluting or mixing it with, some other substance used as a vehicle for the purpose of administering it and does not include the incorporation of the product in any animal feeding stuff;

"the Marketing Authorisation Regulations" means the Medicines for Human Use (Marketing Authorisations Etc.) Regulations 1994;

"medicinal test on animals" has the meaning assigned to it by section 32 of this Act;

"offence under this Act" includes an offence under any regulations or order made under this Act;

"package", in relation to any medicinal products, means any box, packet or other article in which one or more containers of the products are or are to be enclosed, and, where any such box, packet or other article is or is to be itself enclosed in one or more other boxes, packets or other articles, includes each of the boxes, packets or articles in question;

"Pharmaceutical Society" in relation to Great Britain means the Pharmaceutical Society of Great Britain, and in relation to Northern Ireland means the Pharmaceutical Society of Northern Ireland;

"pharmacist" in relation to Great Britain means a person registered in the register of pharmaceutical chemists established in pursuance of the Pharmacy Act 1852 and maintained in pursuance of section 2(1) of the Pharmacy Act 1954, and in relation to Northern Ireland (subject to any order made under paragraph 1 of Schedule 4 to this Act) means a person registered in the register of pharmaceutical chemists for Northern Ireland made out and maintained under section 9 of the Pharmacy and Poisons Act (Northern Ireland) 1925;

"plant" includes any part of a plant;

"poultry" means a domestic fowls, turkeys, geese, ducks, guinea-fowls, pigeons, pheasants and partridges;

"practitioner" (except where the word occurs as part of the expression "veterinary practitioner") means a doctor, dentist, veterinary surgeon or veterinary practitioner;

"prescribed" means prescribed by regulations under this Act;

"product licence", "manufacturer's licence" and "wholesale dealer's licence" have the meanings assigned to them by sections 7 and 8 of this Act;

"registered pharmacy" has the meaning assigned to it by section 74 of this Act;

"retail pharmacy business" means a business (not being a professional practice carried on by a practitioner) which consists of or includes the retail sale of medicinal products other than medicinal products on a general sale list (whether medicinal products on such a list are sold in the course of that business or not);

"substance" means any natural or artificial substance, whether in solid or liquid form or in the form of a gas or vapour;

"the time allowed", in Part II of, and Schedule 2 to, this Act has the meaning assigned to it by section 21(12) of this Act;

"treatment", in relation to disease, includes anything done or provided for alleviating the effects of the disease, whether it is done or provided by way of cure or not;

"veterinary drug" means a medicinal product which is manufactured, sold, supplied, imported or exported for the purposes of being administered to animals, but not for the purpose of being administered to human beings;

"veterinary practitioner" means a person registered in the supplementary veterinary register kept under section 8 of the Veterinary Surgeons Act 1966;

"veterinary surgeon" means a person registered in the register of veterinary surgeons kept under section 2 of the Veterinary Surgeons Act 1966;

"writing" includes any form of notation, whether by hand or by printing, typewriting or any similar process, and "written" has a corresponding meaning;

(2) For the purposes of this Act considerations of safety, in relation to any substance or article, shall be taken to include consideration of the extent (if any) to which the substance or article—

(*a*) if used without proper safeguards, is capable of causing danger to the health of the community, or of causing danger to the health of animals generally or of one or more species of animals, or (*b*) if administered to an animal, may be harmful to the animal or may induce disease in other animals or may leave a residue in the carcase or produce of the animal which may be harmful to human beings, or

(*c*) may interfere with the treatment, prevention or diagnosis of disease, or

(*d*) may be harmful to the person administering it or (in the case of an instrument, apparatus or appliance) the person operating it,

and any reference in this Act to safety or to the interests of safety shall be construed accordingly.

(3) In this Act any reference to doing anything in accordance with a licence under Part II of this Act shall be construed as a reference to doing it in pursuance of such a licence and in compliance with any conditions and any limitations (whether as to area or otherwise) to which the licence is subject, and so as not to fall within any exceptions to which it is subject, and any reference to doing anything in accordance with an animal test certificate shall be construed in a corresponding way.

(4) Any reference in this Act to the holder of a licence or certificate shall be construed as a reference to the holder of a licence or certificate which is for the time being in force.

(5) For the purposes of this Act medicinal products of any description shall be taken to be effectively on the market in the United Kingdom at a particular time if (but only if) during the whole of the period of one month ending with that time adequate stocks of medicinal products of that description were available, or could within a reasonable time be made available, for sale or supply to such persons in the United Kingdom as were likely to require them.

(6) Except in so far as the context otherwise requires, any reference in this Act to an enactment shall be construed as a reference to that enactment as amended or extended by or under any other enactment, including this Act.

[Medicines Act 1968, s 132, as amended by the Local Government Act 1972, s 198, the Dentists Act 1984, Sch 5, the Food Act 1984, Sch 10, the Animal Health and Welfare Act 1984, s 13, the Food Safety Act 1990, Schs 3 and 5, the Medicines Act 1968 (Amendment) (No 2) Regulations 1992, SI 1992/3271, SI 1996/1496, SI 2002/236, SI 2003/2321, SI 2005/1094, SI 2005/2754 and SI 2005/2789.]

1. "The Health Ministers" means the Secretary of State concerned with health in England and the "Agriculture Ministers" means the Secretary of State for Environment, Food and Rural Affairs, see the Transfer of Functions (Medicines and Poisons) Order 1999, SI 1999/3142 and the Ministry of Agriculture, Fisheries and Food (Dissolution) Order 2002, SI 2002/794.

8–21078 **133. General provisions as to operation of Act.** (1) The provisions of this Act, and of any regulations or orders made under it, shall operate cumulatively; and any exemption or exception from any of those provisions shall not be construed as conferring any exemption or exception in relation to any other of those provisions.

(2) Except in so far as this Act otherwise expressly provides, and subject to the provisions of section 33 of the Interpretation Act 1889[1] (which relates to offences under two or more laws), the provisions of this Act shall not be construed as—

(*a*) conferring a right of action in any civil proceedings (other than proceedings for the recovery of a fine) in respect of any contravention of this Act or of any regulations or orders made under this Act, or

(*b*) affecting any restriction imposed by or under any other enactment, whether contained in a public general Act or in a local or private Act, or

(*c*) derogating from any right of action or other remedy (whether civil or criminal) in proceedings instituted otherwise than under this Act.

(3) No exemption conferred by or under any provision of this Act shall be construed as derogating from any exemption or immunity of the Crown.

[Medicines Act 1968, s 133, as amended by the National Health Service Reorganisation Act 1973, Sch 4, the National Health Service Act 1977, Sch 15 and the Medical Act 1983, Sch 5.]

1. Now s 18 of the Interpretation Act 1978 in PART II: EVIDENCE, ante.

Sections 112 and 115

SCHEDULE 3[1]

SAMPLING

(As amended by the Food Act 1984, Sch 10 and the Food Safety Act 1990, Sch 3 and SI 1994/3144.)

Introductory

8–21079 **1.** (1) The provisions of this Schedule shall have effect where a person authorised in that behalf by an enforcement authority (in this Schedule referred to as a "sampling officer") obtains a sample of any substance or article—

(*a*) for the purpose of ascertaining whether there is or has been, in connection with that substance or article, any contravention of any provisions of this Act or of any regulations or order made thereunder which, by or under any provisions of sections 108 to 110 of this Act, that authority (in this Schedule referred to as "the relevant enforcement authority") is required or empowered to enforce, or

(*b*) otherwise for any purpose connected with the performance by that authority of their functions under this Act or under any such regulations or order, and the sampling officer obtains the sample by purchase or in the exercise of any power conferred by section 112 of this Act.

(2) In this Schedule "public analyst", except in relation to Northern Ireland, has the meaning assigned to it by section 27 of the Food Safety Act 1990, and in relation to Northern Ireland has the meaning assigned to it by section 31 of the Food and Drugs Act (Northern Ireland) 1958.

1. This Schedule shall have effect to create certain criminal offences in connection with obligations of applicants for marketing authorisations and other persons arising under the relevant community provisions. It shall also have effect as if all relevant medicinal products were medicinal products for the purposes of the Act (whether or not they would otherwise have been so). See the Medicines for Human Use (Marketing Authorisation etc) Regulations 1994, SI 1994/3144.

Division of sample

8–21090 **2.** The sampling officer shall forthwith divide the sample into three parts, each part to be marked and sealed or fastened up in such manner as its nature will permit.

3. If the sample was purchased by the sampling officer, otherwise than from an automatic machine, he shall supply one part of the sample to the seller.

4. If the sampling officer obtained the sample from an automatic machine, then—

(*a*) if a person's name, and an address in the United Kingdom, are stated on the machine as being the name and address of the owner of the machine, the sampling officer shall supply one part of the sample to that person;

(*b*) in any other case, the sampling officer shall supply one part of the sample to the occupier of the premises on which the machine stands or to which it is affixed.

5. If the sample is of goods consigned from outside the United Kingdom and was taken by the sampling officer before delivery to the consignee, the sampling officer shall supply one part of the sample to the consignee.

6. If, in a case not falling within any of paragraphs 3 to 5 of this Schedule, the sample was obtained by the sampling officer at the request or with the consent of a purchaser, the sampling officer shall supply one part of the sample to the seller.

7. If, in a case not falling within any of paragraphs 3 to 6 of this Schedule, the sample was taken in transit, the sampling officer shall supply one part of the sample to the consignor.

8. In any case not falling within any of paragraphs 3 to 7 of this Schedule the sampling officer shall supply one part of the sample to the person appearing to him to be the owner of the substance or article from which the sample was taken.

9. In every case falling within any of paragraphs 3 to 8 of this Schedule the sampling officer shall inform the person to whom the part of the sample in question is supplied that the sample has been obtained for the purpose of analysis or other appropriate examination.

10. Of the remaining parts of the sample into which the sample is divided in accordance with paragraph 2 of this Schedule, the sampling officer, unless he decides not to submit the sample for analysis or other appropriate examination, shall—

(*a*) retain one part for future comparison, and

(*b*) submit the other part for analysis or examination in accordance with the following provisions of this Schedule.

11. Where a sample consists of substances or articles enclosed in unopened containers, and it appears to the sampling officer that to open the containers and divide the contents into parts—

(*a*) is not reasonably practicable, or

(*b*) might affect the composition or impede the proper analysis or other examination of the contents,

the sampling officer may divide the sample into parts by dividing the containers into three lots without opening them.

12. Section 127 of this Act shall have effect in relation to supplying any part of a sample in pursuance of the preceding paragraphs as it has effect in relation to the service of a document.

13. If after reasonable inquiry the sampling officer is unable to ascertain the name of a person to whom, or the address at which, a part of a sample ought to be supplied in pursuance of the preceding paragraphs, he may retain that part of the sample instead of supplying it.

Notice to person named on container

8–21091 **14.** (1) Where it appears to the sampling officer that a substance or article of which he has obtained a sample was manufactured or assembled by a person whose name and address in the United Kingdom are stated on its container, and who is not a person to whom a part of the sample is required to be supplied under the preceding provisions of this Schedule, the sampling officer, unless he decides not to submit the sample for analysis or other appropriate examination, shall serve notice on that person—

(*a*) stating that the sample has been obtained by the sampling officer, and

(*b*) specifying the person from whom the sampling officer purchased it, or, if he obtained it otherwise than by purchase, the place from which he obtained it.

(2) The notice required to be served under the preceding sub-paragraph shall be served before the end of the period of three days beginning with the day on which the sample was obtained.

Analysis or other examination of sample

8–21092 **15.** If the sampling officer decides to submit the sample for analysis or other appropriate examination, he shall—

(*a*) submit it for analysis to the public analyst for the area in which the sample was obtained, or, if for the time being there is no public analyst for that area, then to the public analyst for some other area, or (*b*) submit it for other appropriate examination to the person having the management or control of any laboratory available for the purpose in accordance with any arrangements made in that behalf by the relevant enforcement authority.

16. Where the relevant enforcement authority is a Minister or the Pharmaceutical Society, and the sampling officer decides to have the sample analysed, he may (instead of submitting it to a public analyst) submit it for analysis to the person having the management or control of any laboratory available for the purpose in accordance with any arrangements made in that behalf by the relevant enforcement authority.

17. Any such arrangements as are mentioned in paragraph 15(*b*) or paragraph 16 of this Schedule—

(*a*) if they relate exclusively to the examination or analysis of veterinary drugs and are made by an enforcement authority in England and Wales other than the Minister of Agriculture, Fisheries and Food, shall be arrangements approved by that Minister;

(*b*) if in any other case they are made by an enforcement authority in England and Wales other than the Minister of Health, shall be arrangements approved by the Minister of Health;

(*c*) if they are made by an enforcement authority in Scotland other than the Secretary of State, shall be arrangements approved by the Secretary of State;

and any such arrangements as are mentioned in paragraph 15(*b*) of this Schedule, if made by a health authority in Northern Ireland, shall be arrangements approved by the Minister of Health and Social Services for Northern Ireland.

18. (1) Subject to the following sub-paragraph, the person to whom the sample is submitted under paragraph 15 or paragraph 16 of this Schedule shall analyse or examine the sample (as the case may be), or cause the sample to be analysed or examined by some other person under his direction, as soon as practicable.

(2) If the person to whom the sample is so submitted is a public analyst, and that analyst determines that for any reason an effective analysis of the sample cannot be performed by him or under his direction, he shall send it to the public analyst for some other area, and that other public analyst shall as soon as practicable analyse the sample or cause it to be analysed by some other person under his direction.

19. (1) A public analyst who has analysed a sample submitted to him under the preceding provisions of this Schedule, or who has caused such a sample to be analysed by some other person under his direction, shall issue and send to the sampling officer a certificate specifying the result of the analysis.

(2) A person having the management or control of a laboratory in which a sample submitted to him under the preceding provisions of this Schedule has been analysed or examined, or a person appointed by him for the purpose, shall issue and send to the sampling officer a certificate specifying the result of the analysis or examination.

(3) Any certificate issued under this paragraph shall be in a form prescribed by the Ministers and shall be signed by the person who issues the certificate.

20. (1) Any person to whom, in accordance with paragraphs 2 to 8 of this Schedule, a part of the sample is required to be supplied shall, on payment of the prescribed fee to the relevant enforcement authority, be entitled to be supplied with a copy of any certificate as to the result of an analysis or examination which is sent to the sampling officer under paragraph 19 of this Schedule.

(2) Any regulations prescribing a fee for the purposes of this paragraph shall be made by the Ministers.

Provisions as to evidence

8–21093 **21.** In any proceedings for an offence under this Act a document produced by one of the parties to the proceedings and purporting to be a certificate issued under paragraph 19 of this Schedule shall be sufficient evidence of the facts stated in the document, unless the other party requires that the person who issued the certificate shall be called as a witness; and, in any proceedings in Scotland, if that person is called as a witness, his evidence shall be sufficient evidence of those facts.

22. In any proceedings for an offence under this Act a document produced by one of the parties to the proceedings, which has been supplied to him by the other party as being a copy of such a certificate, shall be sufficient evidence of the facts stated in the document.

23. (1) If in any such proceedings before a magistrates' court a defendant intends to produce such a certificate, or to require that the person by whom such a certificate was issued shall be called as a witness, a notice of his intention, and (where he intends to produce such a certificate) a copy of the certificate, shall be given to the other party at least three clear days before the day on which the summons is returnable.

(2) If the preceding sub-paragraph is not complied with, the court may, if it thinks fit, adjourn the hearing on such terms as it thinks proper.

(3) and (4) *Relate to Scotland.*

Analysis under direction of court

8–21094 **24.** (1) In any proceedings for an offence under this Act, where the proceedings relate to a substance or article of which a sample has been obtained as mentioned in paragraph 1 of this Schedule, the part of the sample retained in pursuance of paragraph 10(*a*) of this Schedule shall be produced as evidence; and the court—

(*a*) at the request of either party to the proceedings shall, and

(*b*) in the absence of any such request may if it thinks fit,

cause that part of the sample to be sent for analysis to the Government Chemist (or, in Northern Ireland, the Government Chemist for Northern Ireland) or to be sent for other appropriate examination to the person having the management or control of a laboratory specified by the court.

(2) If, in a case where an appeal is brought, no action has been taken under the preceding sub-paragraph, the provisions of that sub-paragraph shall have effect in relation to the court by which the appeal is heard.

(3) A person to whom a part of a sample is sent under this paragraph for analysis or other examination shall analyse or examine it, or cause it to be analysed or examined on his behalf, and shall transmit to the court a certificate specifying the result of the analysis or examination.

(4) Any such certificate shall be signed by that person, or signed on his behalf by the person who made the analysis or examination or a person under whose direction it was made.

(5) Any such certificate shall be evidence (and, in Scotland, shall be sufficient evidence) of the facts stated in

the certificate unless any party to the proceedings requires that the person by whom it was signed shall be called as a witness; and, in any proceedings in Scotland, if that person is called as a witness, his evidence shall be sufficient evidence of those facts.

25. The costs of any analysis or examination under paragraph 24 of this Schedule shall be paid by the prosecutor or the defendant (or, in Scotland, the accused) as the court may order.

Proof by written statement

8–21095 **26.** In relation to England and Wales section 9 of the Criminal Justice Act 1967, and in relation to Northern Ireland any corresponding enactments which may be passed by the Parliament of Northern Ireland, shall not have effect with respect to any document produced as mentioned in paragraph 21 or paragraph 22 of this Schedule or with respect to any certificate transmitted to a court under paragraph 24 of this Schedule.

Power to modify sampling provisions

8–21096 **27.** The Ministers may by order provide that, in relation to substances or articles of any such description as may be specified in the order, the preceding provisions of this Schedule shall have effect subject to such exceptions and modifications as may be specified in the order.

Payment for sample taken under compulsory powers

8–21097 **28.** (1) Where a sampling officer takes a sample in the exercise of any power conferred by section 112 of this Act he shall, if payment is demanded, pay the value of the sample to the person to whom a part of the sample is required under paragraph 5, paragraph 7 or paragraph 8 of this Schedule (as the case may be) to be supplied.

(2) In default of agreement between the sampling officer and the person mentioned in the preceding sub-paragraph, the value of the sample shall be determined by the arbitration of a single arbitrator appointed by the sampling officer and the other person in question or, if they are unable to agree on the appointment of an arbitrator, shall be determined by the county court for the district (or, in Northern Ireland, the division) in which the sample was taken.

(3) In the application of this paragraph to Scotland, for references to an arbitrator there shall be substituted references to an arbiter and for the reference to the county court there shall be substituted a reference to the sheriff.

Application of s 64 to samples

8–21098 **29.** Where a medicinal product is taken as a sample by a sampling officer in the exercise of any power conferred by section 112 of this Act, the provisions of subsections (1) to (4) of section 64 of this Act shall have effect as if the taking of the product as a sample were a sale of it to the sampling officer by the person from whom it is taken; and, if the product was prepared in pursuance of a prescription given by a practitioner, those provisions shall so have effect as if, in subsection (1) of that section, for the words "demanded by the purchaser", there were substituted the words "specified in the prescription".

Misuse of Drugs Act 1971[1]

(1971 c 38)

8–21200 **1.** *Advisory Council on the Misuse of Drugs*

1. This Act, together with Orders made thereunder, regulates all matters concerning the use and abuse of controlled drugs. Only those parts of the Act which relate to proceedings in criminal courts are included in this work.

Controlled drugs and their classification

8–21201 **2. Controlled drugs and their classification for purposes of this Act.** (1) In this Act—

(*a*) the expression "controlled drug" means any substance[1] or product for the time being specified in Part I, II, or III of Schedule 2 to this Act; and

(*b*) the expressions "Class A drug", "Class B drug" and "Class C drug" mean any of the substances and products for the time being specified respectively in Part I, Part II and Part III of that Schedule;

and the provisions of Part IV of that Schedule shall have effect with respect to the meanings of expressions used in that Schedule.

(2) Her Majesty may by Order in Council make such amendments in Schedule 2 to this Act as may be requisite for the purpose of adding any substance or product to, or removing any substance or product from, any of Parts I to III of that Schedule, including amendments for securing that no substance or product is for the time being specified in a particular one of those Parts or for inserting any substance or product into any of those Parts in which no substance or product is for the time being specified.

(3) An Order in Council under this section may amend Part IV of Schedule 2 to this Act, and may do so whether or not it amends any other Part of that Schedule.

(4) An Order in Council under this section may be varied or revoked by a subsequent Order in Council thereunder.

(5) No recommendation shall be made to Her Majesty in Council to make an Order under this

section unless a draft of the Order has been laid before Parliament and approved by a resolution of each House of Parliament; and the Secretary of State shall not lay a draft of such an Order before Parliament except after consultation with or on the recommendation of the Advisory Council.
[Misuse of Drugs Act 1971, s 2.]

1. "Substance" has a wider meaning than "product". Any kind of matter comes within the meaning of substance, whereas product envisages the result of some kind of process (*R v Greensmith* [1983] 3 All ER 444, [1983] 1 WLR 1124, 147 JP 730, CA).

Restrictions relating to controlled drugs etc

8–21202 **3. Restriction of importation and exportation of controlled drugs.** (1) Subject to subsection (2) below—

(*a*) the importation of a controlled drug[1]; and
(*b*) the exportation of a controlled[1] drug,

are hereby prohibited[2].

(2) Subsection (1) above does not apply—

(*a*) to the importation or exportation of a controlled drug which is for the time being excepted from paragraph (*a*) or, as the case may be, paragraph (*b*) of subsection (1) above by regulations under section 7 of this Act; or
(*b*) to the importation or exportation of a controlled drug under and in accordance with the terms of a licence[3] issued by the Secretary of State and in compliance with any conditions attached thereto.

[Misuse of Drugs Act 1971, s 3.]

1. See s 2, ante.
2. These are offences punishable under the Customs and Excise Management Act 1979; see s 50 (improper importation), s 68 (improper exportation), and s 170 (fraudulent evasion of a prohibition or restriction affecting goods); also s 147 for time limit on prosecution.
3. It is the defendant's responsibility to prove (on a balance of probabilities (*R v Oliver* [1944] KB 68, [1943] 2 All ER 800, 108 JP 30)) that he has a licence; *R v Ewens* [1967] 1 QB 322, [1966] 2 All ER 470. See also Magistrates' Courts Act 1980, s 101, ante, for onus of proving exceptions, etc.

8–21203 **4. Restriction of production and supply of controlled drugs.** (1) Subject to any regulations[1] under section 7 of this Act for the time being in force, it shall not be lawful for a person—

(*a*) to produce[2] a controlled drug[3]; or
(*b*) to supply[2] or offer[4] to supply a controlled drug to another.

(2) Subject to section 28 of this Act[5], it is an offence[6] for a person—

(*a*) to produce[2] a controlled drug in contravention of subsection (1) above; or
(*b*) to be concerned in[7] the production[2] of such a drug in contravention of that subsection by another.

(3) Subject to section 28 of this Act[5], it is an offence[6] for a person—

(*a*) to supply[8] or offer to supply a controlled drug to another[9] in contravention of subsection (1) above; or
(*b*) to be concerned in[7] the supplying[8] of such a drug to another in contravention of that subsection; or
(*c*) to be concerned in[7] the making to another in contravention of that subsection of an offer to supply[5] such a drug.

[Misuse of Drugs Act 1971, s 4.]

1. For exceptions to the restriction in this section, see the Misuse of Drugs Regulations 2001, post.
2. See s 37(1), post, for definition of the terms "produce" and "supplying".
3. In *R v Harris* (1979) 69 Cr App Rep 122, it was held that co-defendants who had acquainted themselves with the proper process to produce amphetamine and had entered into an agreement to produce such a drug were properly convicted of conspiracy to produce a controlled drug, notwithstanding that the attempt failed because one ingredient was wrong and a further knowledge of the process was required; *DPP v Nock and DPP v Alsford* [1980] AC 979, [1978] 2 All ER 654, 67 Cr App Rep 116, HL, distinguished. There must be established some identifiable participation in the process of producing a controlled drug before a person can be convicted (*R v Farr* [1982] Crim LR 745, CA).
4. It is an offence to *offer* to supply a controlled drug even though the substance in the defendant's possession is *not* such a drug (*aliter* if the offence charged is supplying) (*Haggard v Mason* [1976] 1 All ER 337, 140 JP 198). Cf *Mieras v Rees* (1975) 139 JP 549 (alleged attempt under s 19, post.) The offence is complete when the offer to supply a controlled drug is made, regardless of whether the offerer intends to carry the offer into effect by actually supplying the drug (*R v Goddard* [1992] Crim LR 588). Whether the words spoken and the circumstances in which they were uttered amounted to an offer is a question of fact having regard to the effect of the words and any relevant circumstances apparent to the offeree. An offer once made cannot be withdrawn, any attempt to withdraw may only be relevant to the issue whether there was an offer in the first place. There is no need for the offer to meet the specificity as to date and time of delivery of the civil law and it does not matter whether the offeror or the offeree took the initiative (*R v Prior* [2004] EWCA Crim 1147, [2004] Crim LR 849).
5. Section 28 relates to the availability of the defence of lack of knowledge.
6. For method of trial, penalty, etc see s 25 and Sch 4, post. Anything shown to relate to the offence may be forfeited (see s 27, post). An information may be laid at any time within twelve months from the commission of the offence (see

s 25(4), post). On a plea of guilty the prosecution is not bound to call scientific evidence to prove the nature of the drug: *R v Wells* [1976] Crim LR 518.

7. This is designed to provide a means of proceeding against the "trafficker", and individuals who have connived rather than contrived, and so have escaped prosecution for aiding and abetting the commission of an offence; for example someone assisting in the injection of a drug into someone else. It is also sufficient to involve people who may be at some distance from the actual making of the offer (*R v Blake* (1979) 68 Cr App Rep 1). To prove an offence under subs (3)(*b*) or (*c*), the prosecution has to prove (1) the supply of a drug to another or, as the case may be, the making of an offer to supply a drug to another in contravention of s 4(1); (2) participation by the defendant in an enterprise involving such supply, or as the case may be, such offer to supply; and (3) knowledge by the defendant of the nature of the enterprise, ie that it involved supply of a drug or, as the case may be, offering to supply a drug (*R v Hughes* (1985) 81 Cr App Rep 344).

8. See s 37(1), post, for definition of the term "supplying". The word "supply" in s 4(3)(*a*) implies an act designed to benefit the recipient and does not cover the deposit of a controlled drug with another for safe keeping (*R v Dempsey* (1985) 82 Cr App Rep 291, 150 JP 213).

9. The "another" cannot be someone who is also charged in the indictment (*R v Adepoju* [1988] Crim LR 378, CA).

8–21203A **4A. Aggravation of offence of supply of controlled drug.** (1) This section applies if—

(*a*) a court is considering the seriousness of an offence under section 4(3) of this Act, and
(*b*) at the time the offence was committed the offender had attained the age of 18.

(2) If either of the following conditions is met the court—

(*a*) must treat the fact that the condition is met as an aggravating factor (that is to say, a factor that increases the seriousness of the offence), and
(*b*) must state in open court that the offence is so aggravated.

(3) The first condition is that the offence was committed on or in the vicinity of school premises at a relevant time.

(4) The second condition is that in connection with the commission of the offence the offender used a courier who, at the time the offence was committed, was under the age of 18.

(5) In subsection (3), a relevant time is—

(a) any time when the school premises are in use by persons under the age of 18;
(b) one hour before the start and one hour after the end of any such time.

(6) For the purposes of subsection (4), a person uses a courier in connection with an offence under section 4(3) of this Act if he causes or permits another person (the courier)—

(*a*) to deliver a controlled drug to a third person, or
(*b*) to deliver a drug related consideration to himself or a third person.

(7) For the purposes of subsection (6), a drug related consideration is a consideration of any description which—

(*a*) is obtained in connection with the supply of a controlled drug, or
(*b*) is intended to be used in connection with obtaining a controlled drug.

(8) In this section—

"school premises" means land used for the purposes of a school excluding any land occupied solely as a dwelling by a person employed at the school; and

"school" has the same meaning—

(*a*) in England and Wales, as in section 4 of the Education Act 1996;
(*b*) in Scotland, as in section 135(1) of the Education (Scotland) Act 1980;
(*c*) in Northern Ireland, as in Article 2(2) of the Education and Libraries (Northern Ireland) Order 1986.

[Misuse of Drugs Act 1971, s 4A as inserted by the Drugs Act, s 1.]

8–21204 **5. Restriction of possession of controlled drugs.** (1) Subject to any regulations[1] under section 7 of this Act for the time being in force, it shall not be lawful for a person to have a controlled drug in his possession[2].

(2) Subject to section 28 of this Act[3] and to subsection (4) below, it is an offence[4] for a person to have a controlled drug[5] in his possession[2] in contravention of subsection (1) above.

(3) Subject to section 28 of this Act[3], it is an offence[4] for a person to have a controlled drug[6] in his possession[2], whether lawfully or not, with intent to supply[7] it to another in contravention of section 4(1) of this Act.

(4) In any proceedings for an offence under subsection (2) above in which it is proved that the accused had a controlled drug in his possession[2], it shall be a defence for him to prove—

(*a*) that, knowing or suspecting it to be a controlled drug, he took possession of it for the purpose of preventing another from committing or continuing to commit an offence in connection with that drug and that as soon as possible after taking possession of it he took all such steps as were reasonably open to him to destroy[8] the drug or to deliver it into the custody of a person lawfully entitled to take custody of it; or
(*b*) that, knowing or suspecting it to be a controlled drug, he took possession of it for the purpose of delivering it into the custody of a person lawfully entitled to take custody of it and that as

soon as possible after taking possession of it he took all such steps as were reasonably open to him to deliver it into the custody of such a person.

(5) *Repealed.*

(6) Nothing in subsection (4) above shall prejudice any defence which it is open to a person charged with an offence under this section to raise apart from that subsection.

[Misuse of Drugs Act 1971, s 5, as amended by the Criminal Attempts Act 1981, Sch.]

---

1. The Misuse of Drugs Regulations 2001, post, set out the persons authorised to supply and possess various classes of controlled drugs (see in particular reg 10 thereof) and except specified drugs from the prohibition on the possession of controlled drugs (see reg 4 thereof).

2. The Act does not contain a definition of 'possession' but the nature of possession has received extensive consideration in case law, in particular by the House of Lords in *R v Lambert* [2001] UKHL 37, [2002] 2 AC 545, [2001] 3 All ER 577, [2001] 3 WLR 206.

Possession embraces both a factual and a mental element.

Control The factual element is control. Section 37(3) provides that for the purposes of the Act the things which a person has in his possession shall be taken to include any thing subject to his control which is in the custody of another.

In *R v Wright* (1975) 119 Sol Jo 825 (following *Warner v Metropolitan Police Comr* [1969] 2 AC 256, [1968] 2 All ER 356, HL) a distinction was made between mere physical custody of an object, and its possession for the commission of an offence. The defendant was given a container and told to throw it away, which he did instantly: he could not be convicted although he suspected it might contain drugs. A person having given directions to a supplier following which he receives a parcel containing a drug through his letter-box, becomes the possessor of the drug once the parcel is put through the letter-box (*R v Peaston* [1979] Crim LR 183).

If a person smokes cannabis resin he must have cannabis resin in his possession at the time of smoking (*Chief Constable of Cheshire Constabulary v Hunt* (1983) 147 JP 567). Once a controlled drug has been consumed and has changed in character, the consumer could not then be said to be 'in possession' of it, though it might be evidence of possession immediately before he consumed it (*Hambleton v Callinan* [1968] 2 QB 427, [1968] 2 All ER 943, 132 JP 461.

Possession does not depend on the powers of memory of the alleged possessor and does not come and go as memory revives or fades; accordingly, a defendant who placed a drug knowing it was cannabis in his wallet was held to be in possession of it even though his memory of its presence had faded (*R v Martindale* [1986] 3 All ER 25, [1986] 1 WLR 1042, CA).

Mental element The mental element in offences contrary to section 5 was exhaustively considered by the House of Lords in *R v Lambert*, supra from which the following propositions are derived.

The prosecution must prove:

(*a*) the defendant was in possession of something;
(*b*) the defendant knew he was in possession of that something; and
(*c*) the thing which the defendant possessed was a controlled drug.

Lack of knowledge The prosecution is not required to prove that the defendant knew that the thing which he possessed was a controlled drug but if the prosecution have adduced sufficient evidence to prove (*a*)–(*c*), section 28(2), (3) post, stipulates the way in which lack of knowledge etc can be a defence in proceedings. To bring himself within the provisions of section 28 (2), (3) the defendant must satisfy an evidential burden of adducing evidence which is sufficient to raise the issue of knowledge. If sufficient evidence is adduced to raise the issue, it will be for the prosecution to show beyond reasonable doubt that the defence is not made out by the evidence.

Quantity is of importance in two respects when determining whether or not an accused person has a controlled drug in his possession. First, is the quantity sufficient to enable a court to find as a matter of fact that it amounts to something? If it is visible, tangible and measurable, it is certainly something. The question is one of fact for the commonsense of the tribunal. Secondly, quantity may be relevant to the issue of knowledge. If the quantity in custody or control is minute, the question arises – was it so minute that it cannot be proved that the accuse knew he had it? If knowledge cannot be proved, possession is not established (*R v Boyeson* [1982] AC 768, [1982] 2 All ER 161, 146 JP 217, HL). See also *R v Colyer* [1974] Crim LR 243 (minute quantity) and *R v Ashton Rickardt* [1977] Crim LR 424. As to aggregating several amounts of a drug, see *R v Bayliss and Oliver* [1978] Crim LR 361. As to conviction for possessing a lesser amount than charged, see *R v Peevey* (1973) 579 Cr App Rep 554.

Mere presence in the same vehicle as cannabis, even if someone had said there was cannabis in the car, is not sufficient to prove possession (*R v Strong* and *R v Berry* [1989] 10 LS Gaz R 41, CA).

Once the prosecution prove that the defendant had control of a box which he was delivering on his motor cycle and knew it contained something, which was in fact the drug alleged, he has the onus of bringing himself within the provisions of s 28(3); see *R v McNamara* (1988) 87 Cr App Rep 246, 152 JP 390 approved in *R v Lambert*, supra.

Controlled drug Where an experienced drug user admits possession of a substance which he himself identifies as a controlled drug, that admission and identification are sufficient to provide *prima facie* evidence of the nature of the substance and of unlawful possession of a controlled drug; see *R v Chatwood* [1980] 1 All ER 467, [1980] 1 WLR 874. It is important that the prosecution should prove possession of the drug as charged; see *Muir v Smith* [1978] Crim LR 293 where the prosecution failed as it could not be ascertained whether the substance was cannabis or herbal cannabis.

3. Section 28 relates to the availability of the defence of lack of knowledge.

4. For prosecution and punishment of offences, see s 25 and Sch 4, post.

5. The burden is on the prosecution to prove not only that the substance was a controlled drug within the meaning of the Act, but also that it was not in a form permitted by the Misuse of Drugs Regulations 1985, reg 4 and Sch 5, post (*R v Hunt* [1987] AC 352, [1987] 1 All ER 1). Prosecuting authorities must heed the observations in *R v Hunt, supra*, as to the desirability of clarity in the terms of the analyst's certificate (*R v Jones* (1997) 161 JP 597, [1998] Crim LR 56). As to raising objection to the admissibility of evidence of analysis during a trial, see *A-G for the Cayman Islands v Roberts* [2002] UKPC 18, [2002] 2 Cr App Rep 388.

6. The prosecution only has to establish that the accused was in possession of the controlled drug as charged with the necessary intent; the accused will not be able to avail himself of the defences in s 28(2) or 28(3)(*b*)(ii) where he believed the substance to be a different drug from that alleged by the prosecution as it is not necessary for the prosecution to prove which controlled drug it was in order to obtain a conviction. The only purpose of specifying the class of drug in the particulars of the offence is that that factor affects the sentence which can be passed on conviction (*R v Leeson* [2000] 1 Cr App Rep 233, 164 JP 224, [2000] Crim LR 195).

7. "Supply" covers a wide range of transactions, of which a feature common to all of those transactions is a transfer of physical control of a drug from one person to another (*R v Delgado* [1984] 1 All ER 449, [1984] 1 WLR 89, 148 JP 431, CA); but the transfer must be for the purposes of the transferee (*R v Maginnis* [1987] AC 303, [1987] 1 All ER 907). A

person in unlawful possession of a controlled drug which has been deposited with him for safe keeping has the intent to supply that drug to another if his intention is to return the drug to the person who deposited it with him (*R v Maginnis*, supra). Evidence of large amounts of money in the possession of the defendant or an extravagant life style *prima facie* explicable only if derived from drug dealing is admissible in cases of possession of drugs with intent to supply if it is of probative significance to an issue in the case (*R v Morris* [1995] 2 Cr App Rep 69, 159 JP 1 and see *R v Lucas* [1995] Crim LR 400, CA). Moreover, the finding of money, whether in the home of the defendant or perhaps, more cogently, in the possession of the defendant when away from his home, and in conjunction with a substantial quantity of drugs, is capable of being relevant to the issue of whether there is proved an intent to supply (*R v Grant* [1996] 1 Cr App Rep 73).

8. The act of destruction must be that of the defendant and relying on the forces of nature ultimately to destroy the drugs by burying the drugs them in the ground is not sufficient (*R v Murphy* [2002] EWCA Crim 1587, [2003] 1 Cr App Rep 276, [2002] Crim LR 819).

8–21205 **6. Restriction of cultivation of cannabis plant.** (1) Subject to any regulations under section 7 of this Act for the time being in force, it shall not be lawful for a person to cultivate any plant of the genus *Cannabis*[1].

(2) Subject to section 28 of this Act[2], it is an offence[3] to cultivate any such plant in contravention of subsection (1) above.

[Misuse of Drugs Act 1971, s 6.]

1. See s 37, post, for definition and reg 12 of the Misuse of Drugs Regulations 2001, post.
2. See note 3 to s 5, ante.
3. See note 5 to s 4, ante.

8–21206 **7. Authorisation of activities otherwise unlawful.** (1) The Secretary of State may by regulations[1]—

(*a*) except from section 3(1)(*a*) or (*b*), 4(1)(*a*) or (*b*) or 5(1) of this Act such controlled drugs as may be specified in the regulations; and

(*b*) make such other provision as he thinks fit for the purpose of making it lawful for persons to do things which under any of the following provisions of this Act, that is to say sections 4(1), 5(1) and 6(1), it would otherwise be unlawful for them to do.

(2) Without prejudice to the generality of paragraph (*b*) of subsection (1) above, regulations under that subsection authorising the doing of any such thing as is mentioned in that paragraph may in particular provide for the doing of that thing to be lawful—

(*a*) if it is done under and in accordance with the terms of a licence or other authority issued by the Secretary of State and in compliance with any conditions attached thereto; or

(*b*) if it is done in compliance with such conditions as may be prescribed.

(3) Subject to subsection (4) below, the Secretary of State shall so exercise his power to make regulations under subsection (1) above as to secure—

(*a*) that it is not unlawful under section 4(1) of this Act for a doctor, dentist, veterinary practitioner or veterinary surgeon[2], acting in his capacity as such, to prescribe, administer, manufacture, compound or supply a controlled drug, or for a pharmacist or a person lawfully conducting a retail pharmacy business[3], acting in either case in his capacity as such, to manufacture, compound or supply a controlled drug; and

(*b*) that it is not unlawful under section 5(1) of this Act for a doctor, dentist, veterinary practitioner, veterinary surgeon[2], pharmacist or person lawfully conducting a retail pharmacy business[3] to have a controlled drug in his possession for the purpose of acting in his capacity as such.

(4) If in the case of any controlled drug the Secretary of State is of the opinion that it is in the public interest—

(*a*) for production, supply and possession of that drug to be either wholly unlawful or unlawful except for purposes of research or other special purposes; or

(*b*) for it to be unlawful for practitioners, pharmacists and persons lawfully conducting retail pharmacy businesses to do in relation to that drug any of the things mentioned in subsection (3) above except under a licence or other authority issued by the Secretary of State,

he may by order designate that drug as a drug to which this subsection applies[4]; and while there is in force an order under this subsection designating a controlled drug as one to which this subsection applies, subsection (3) above shall not apply as regards that drug.

(5) Any order under subsection (4) above may be varied or revoked by a subsequent order thereunder.

(6) The power to make orders under subsection (4) above shall be exercisable by statutory instrument, which shall be subject to annulment in pursuance of a resolution of either House of Parliament.

(7) The Secretary of State shall not make any order under subsection (4) above except after consultation with or on the recommendation of the Advisory Council.

(8) References in this section to a person's "doing" things include references to his having things in his possession.

(9) *Application to Northern Ireland.*
[Misuse of Drugs Act 1971, s 7.]

1. The Misuse of Drugs Regulations 2001, have been made, in this title, post.
2. For meaning of "doctor", "dentist", "veterinary practitioner" and "veterinary surgeon", see s 37(1), post.
3. For meaning of a "person lawfully conducting a retail pharmacy business", see s 37(1), post.
4. The Misuse of Drugs (Designation) Order 2001, SI 2001/3997 amended by SI 2005/1652, has been made.

Miscellaneous offences involving controlled drugs etc

8–21207 **8. Occupiers etc of premises to be punishable for permitting certain activities to take place there.** A person commits an offence[1] if, being the occupier[2] or concerned in the management of any premises[3], he knowingly[4] permits[5] or suffers any of the following activities to take place on those premises, that is to say—

(*a*) producing or attempting to produce a controlled drug in contravention of section 4(1) of this Act;
(*b*) supplying or attempting to supply a controlled drug to another in contravention of section 4(1) of this Act, or offering to supply a controlled drug to another in contravention of section 4[6];
(*c*) preparing opium for smoking;
(*d*) smoking[7] cannabis[8], cannabis resin[8] or prepared opium[8].*

[Misuse of Drugs Act 1971, s 8.]

***Paragraph (d) prospectively substituted by the Criminal Justice and Court Services Act 2001, s 38.**

1. See note 5 to s 4, ante. For possible duplicity in informations under this section, see *Ware v Fox, Fox v Dingley* [1967] 1 All ER 100, 131 JP 113 (a case under the repealed Dangerous Drugs Act 1965).
2. "Occupier" includes anyone in occupation of premises whose degree of occupation was such that he could exclude anyone likely to commit an offence under the Act (*R v Tao* [1977] QB 141, [1976] 3 All ER 65, 140 JP 596). The fact that one person can be identified as an occupier, even if enjoying a legal title or tenancy, does not preclude the application of that description to another person (*R v Coid* [1998] Crim LR 199).
3. If a person is exercising control over premises, running them or managing them, the fact that he is not lawfully in possession of them is irrelevant (*R v Josephs and R v Christie* (1977) 65 Cr App Rep 253.
4. That is, with *mens rea*; suspicion by itself is not enough to constitute permission (*R v Thomas*, (1976) 63 Cr App Rep 65, [1976] Crim LR 517). On a charge of permitting premises to be used for supplying a controlled drug, it is not necessary for the Crown to prove more than knowledge of the supply of a controlled drug, even where the particular drug is specified in the charge (*R v Bett* [1999] 1 All ER 600, [1999] 1 Cr App Rep 361, 163 JP 65).
5. To establish the offence of permitting under s 8(*b*) the prosecution must prove: (i) knowledge, actual or by closing eyes to the obvious, that dealing in controlled drugs is taking place; and (ii) unwillingness to prevent it, which can be inferred from failure to take steps readily available to prevent it. A defendant's belief that the steps he has taken are reasonable is irrelevant; it is not for a defendant to judge his own conduct: *R v Brock* [2001] 1 WLR 1159, 165 JP 331, CA.
6. See note 4 to s 4, ante.
7. The commission of this offence requires the actual smoking of cannabis; mere tentative permission to smoke cannabis is insufficient (*R v Auguste* [2003] EWCA Crim 3929, [2004] 1 WLR 917, [2004] 4 All ER 373, [2004] 2 Cr App Rep 173 (*d*)).
8. For definition, see s 37, post.

8–21208 **9. Prohibition of certain activities etc relating to opium.** Subject to section 28 of this Act[1], it is an offence[2] for a person—

(*a*) to smoke or otherwise use prepared opium[3]; or
(*b*) to frequent a place used for the purpose of opium smoking; or
(*c*) to have in his possession—
 (i) any pipes or other utensils made or adapted for use in connection with the smoking of opium, being pipes or utensils which have been used by him or with his knowledge and permission in that connection or which he intends to use or permit others to use in that connection; or
 (ii) any utensils which have been used by him or with his knowledge and permission in connection with the preparation of opium for smoking.

[Misuse of Drugs Act 1971, s 9.]

1. See note 5 to s 4, ante.
2. See note 4 to s 4, ante.
3. For definition, see s 37, post.

8–21209 **9A. Prohibition of supply etc, of articles for administering or preparing controlled drugs.** (1) A person who supplies or offers to supply any article which may be used or adapted to be used (whether by itself or in combination with another article or other articles) in the administration by any person of a controlled drug to himself or another, believing that the article (or the article as adapted) is to be so used in circumstances where the administration is unlawful, is guilty of an offence.

(2) It is not an offence under subsection (1) above to supply or offer to supply a hypodermic syringe, or any part of one.

(3) A person who supplies or offers to supply any article which may be used to prepare a controlled drug for administration by any person to himself or another believing that the article is to be used in circumstances where the administration is unlawful is guilty of an offence.

(4) For the purposes of this section, any administration of a controlled drug is unlawful except—

(*a*) the administration by any person of a controlled drug to another in circumstances where the administration of the drug is not unlawful under section 4(1) of this Act, or

(*b*) the administration by any person of a controlled drug to himself in circumstances where having the controlled drug in his possession is not unlawful under section 5(1) of this Act.

(5) In this section, references to administration by any person of a controlled drug to himself include a reference to his administering it to himself with the assistance of another.
[Misuse of Drugs Act 1971, s 9A, as inserted by the Drug Trafficking Offences Act 1986, s 34.]

Powers of Secretary of State for preventing misuse of controlled drugs

8–21210 10. Power to make regulations for preventing misuse of controlled drugs. (1) Subject to the provisions of this Act, the Secretary of State may by regulations make such provision as appears to him necessary or expedient for preventing the misuse of controlled drugs[1].

(2) Without prejudice to the generality of subsection (1) above, regulations under this section may in particular make provision—

(*a*) for requiring precautions to be taken for the safe custody of controlled drugs[2];

(*b*) for imposing requirements as to the documentation of transactions involving controlled drugs, and for requiring copies of documents relating to such transactions to be furnished to the prescribed authority;

(*c*) for requiring the keeping of records and the furnishing of information with respect to controlled drugs in such circumstances and in such manner as may be prescribed;

(*d*) for the inspection of any precautions taken or records kept in pursuance of regulations under this section;

(*e*) as to the packaging and labelling of controlled drugs;

(*f*) for regulating the transport of controlled drugs and the methods used for destroying or otherwise disposing of such drugs when no longer required;

(*g*) for regulating the issue of prescriptions containing controlled drugs and the supply of controlled drugs on prescriptions, and for requiring persons issuing or dispensing prescriptions containing such drugs to furnish to the prescribed authority such information relating to those prescriptions as may be prescribed;

(*h*) for requiring any doctor who attends a person who he considers, or has reasonable grounds to suspect, is addicted (within the meaning of the regulations) to controlled drugs of any description to furnish to the prescribed authority such particulars with respect to that person as may be prescribed;

(*i*) for prohibiting any doctor from administering, supplying and authorising the administration and supply to persons so addicted and from prescribing for such persons, such controlled drugs as may be prescribed, except under and in accordance with the terms of a licence issued by the Secretary of State in pursuance of the regulations

[Misuse of Drugs Act 1971, s 10.]

1. The following have been made; the Misuse of Drugs (Safe Custody) Regulations 1973, SI 1973/798 amended by SI 1974/1449, SI 1975/294, SI 1984/1146, SI 1985/2067, SI 1986/2332 and SI 1999/1403, the Misuse of Drugs (Supply to Addicts) Regulations 1997, SI 1997/1001 amended by SI 2005/2864 and the Misuse of Drugs Regulations 2001, this title, post.

2. The Misuse of Drugs (Safe Custody) Regulations 1973, SI 1973/798 amended by SI 1974/1449, SI 1975/294, SI 1984/1146, SI 1985/2067, SI 1986/2332 and SI 1999/1403 have been made. Regulation 5(1) which requires drugs to be kept "in a locked receptacle" would not be complied with by leaving them in an unlocked case in a locked motor car (*Kameswara Rao v Wyles* [1949] 2 All ER 685, 113 JP 516).

8–21211 11. Power to direct special precautions for safe custody of controlled drugs to be taken at certain premises. (1) Without prejudice to any requirement imposed by regulations made in pursuance of section 10(2)(*a*) of this Act, the Secretary of State may by notice in writing served on the occupier of any premises on which controlled drugs are or are proposed to be kept give directions as to the taking of precautions or further precautions for the safe custody of any controlled drugs of a description in the notice which are kept on those premises.

(2) It is an offence[1] to contravene any directions given under subsection (1) above.
[Misuse of Drugs Act 1971, s 11.]

1. See note 5 to s 4, ante.

8–21212 12. Directions prohibiting prescribing, supply etc of controlled drugs by practitioners etc convicted of certain offences. (1) Where a person who is a practitioner or pharmacist[1] has after the coming into operation of this subsection been convicted—

(*a*) of an offence[2] under this Act or under the Dangerous Drugs Act 1965 or any enactment repealed by that Act; or

(*b*) of an offence under sections 45, 56 or 304 of the Customs and Excise Act 1952 or under sections 50, 68 or 170 of the Customs and Excise Management Act 1979 in connection with a prohibition of or restriction on importation or exportation of a controlled drug having effect by virtue of section 3 of this Act or which had effect by virtue of any provision contained in or repealed by the Dangerous Drugs Act 1965,

(*c*) of an offence under section 12 or 13 of the Criminal Justice (International Co-operation) Act 1990;

the Secretary of State may give a direction under subsection (2) below in respect of that person.

(2) A direction under this subsection in respect of a person shall—

(*a*) if that person is a practitioner, be a direction prohibiting him from having in his possession, prescribing, administering, manufacturing, compounding and supplying and from authorising the administration and supply of such controlled drugs as may be specified in the direction;

(*b*) if that person is a pharmacist, be a direction prohibiting him from having in his possession, manufacturing, compounding and supplying and from supervising and controlling the manufacture, compounding and supply of such controlled drugs as may be specified in the direction.

(3) The Secretary of State may at any time give a direction cancelling or suspending any direction given by him under subsection (2) above, or cancelling any direction of his under this subsection by which a direction so given is suspended.

(4) The Secretary of State shall cause a copy of any direction given by him under this section to be served on the person to whom it applies, and shall cause notice of any such direction to be published in the London, Edinburgh and Belfast Gazettes.

(5) A direction under this section shall take effect when a copy of it is served on the person to whom it applies.

(6) It is an offence[3] to contravene a direction given under subsection (2) above.

(7) *Amendment of s* 80 *of the Medicines Act* 1968.

[Misuse of Drugs Act 1971, s 12, as amended by the Customs and Excise Management Act 1979, Sch 4 and the Criminal Justice (International Co-operation) Act 1990, s 23.]

1. For meaning of "practitioner", see s 37(1) of this Act, and for meaning of "pharmacist" see s 132(1) of the Medicines Act 1968.
2. This includes an offence under s 1 of the Criminal Attempts Act 1981 of attempting to commit an offence under the Misuse of Drugs Act 1971 (Criminal Attempts Act 1981, s 7 (3)).
3. See note 5 to s 4, ante.

8–21213 13. Directions prohibiting prescribing, supply etc of controlled drugs by practitioners in other cases. (1) In the event of a contravention by a doctor of regulations made in pursuance of paragraph (*h*) or (*i*) of section 10(2) of this Act, or of the terms of a licence issued under regulations made in pursuance of the said paragraph (*i*), the Secretary of State may, subject to and in accordance with section 14[1] of this Act, give a direction in respect of the doctor concerned prohibiting him from prescribing, administering and supplying and from authorising the administration and supply of such controlled drugs as may be specified in the direction.

(2) If the Secretary of State is of the opinion that a practitioner is or has after the coming into operation of this subsection been prescribing, administering or supplying or authorising the administration or supply of any controlled drugs in an irresponsible manner, the Secretary of State may, subject to and in accordance with section 14 or 15 of this Act, give a direction in respect of the practitioner concerned prohibiting him from prescribing, administering and supplying and from authorising administration and supply of such controlled drugs as may be specified in the direction.

(3) A contravention[2] such as is mentioned in subsection (1) above does not as such constitute an offence, but it is an offence[3] to contravene a direction given under subsection (1) or (2) above.

[Misuse of Drugs Act 1971, s 13.]

1. Section 14 provides for the investigation of an alleged contravention, by a tribunal set up in accordance with s 16 and Sch 3 to this Act. It is following such investigation that the Secretary of State may give a direction, contravention of which will be an offence by virtue of sub-s (3) of this section.
2. "Contravention" includes failure to comply (s 37(1)).
3. See note 5 to s 4, ante.

8–21214 17. Power to obtain information from doctors, pharmacists etc in certain circumstances. (1) If it appears to the Secretary of State that there exists in any area in Great Britain a social problem caused by the extensive misuse of dangerous or otherwise harmful drugs in that area, he may by notice in writing served on any doctor or pharmacist practising in the vicinity of that area, or on any person carrying on a retail pharmacy business within the meaning of the Medicines Act 1968 at any premises situated in or in the vicinity of that area, require him to furnish to the Secretary of State, with respect to any such drugs specified in the notices and as regards any period so specified, such particulars as may be so specified relating to the quantities in which and the number and frequency of the occasions on which those drugs—

(*a*) in the case of a doctor, were prescribed, administered or supplied by him;
(*b*) in the case of a pharmacist, were supplied by him; or
(*c*) in the case of a person carrying on a retail pharmacy business, were supplied in the course of that business at any premises so situated which may be specified in the notice.

(2) A notice under this section may require any such particulars to be furnished in such manner and within such time as may be specified in the notice and, if served on a pharmacist or person carrying on a retail pharmacy business, may require him to furnish the names and addresses of doctors on whose prescriptions any dangerous or otherwise harmful drugs to which the notice relates were supplied, but shall not require any person to furnish any particulars relating to the identity of any person for or to whom any such drug has been prescribed, administered or supplied.

(3) A person commits an offence[1] if without reasonable excuse (proof of which shall lie on him) he fails to comply with any requirement to which he is subject by virtue of subsection (1) above.

(4) A person commits an offence[1] if in purported compliance with a requirement imposed under this section he gives any information which he knows to be false in a material particular or recklessly gives any information which is so false.

(5) *Application to Northern Ireland.*

[Misuse of Drugs Act 1971, s 17.]

1. See note 5 to s 4, ante.

Miscellaneous offences and powers

8–21215 **18. Miscellaneous offences.** (1) It is an offence[1] for a person to contravene any regulations made under this Act other than regulations made in pursuance of section 10(2)(*h*) or (*i*).

(2) It is an offence[1] for a person to contravene a condition or other term of a licence issued under section 3 of this Act or of a licence or other authority issued under regulations made under this Act, not being a licence issued under regulations made in pursuance of section 10(2)(*i*).

(3) A person commits an offence[1] if, in purported compliance with any obligation to give information to which he is subject under or by virtue of regulations made under this Act, he gives any information which he knows to be false in a material particular or recklessly gives any information which is so false.

(4) A person commits an offence[1] if, for the purpose of obtaining, whether for himself or another, the issue or renewal of a licence or other authority under this Act or under any regulations made under this Act, he—

(*a*) makes any statement or gives any information which he knows to be false in a material particular or recklessly gives any information which is so false; or
(*b*) produces or otherwise makes use of any book, record or other document which to his knowledge contains any statement or information which he knows to be false in a material particular.

[Misuse of Drugs Act 1971, s 18.]

1. See note 5 to s 4, ante.

8–21216 **19. Attempts etc to commit offences.** It is an offence[1] for a person to incite another to commit such an offence[2].

[Misuse of Drugs Act 1971, s 19, as amended by the Criminal Attempts Act 1981, Sch]

1. The method of trial and penalty for an offence under this section depends on the nature of the substantive offence. See s 25(3), post. Anything shown to relate to the offence may be forfeited. See s 27, post.

2. The Criminal Attempts Act 1981 is directed to the law of attempt and conspiracy and does not amend the law of incitement so that s 19 refers not only to the offences under s 18 but also to offences elsewhere in the 1971 Act (*R v Marlow* [1997] Crim LR 897, CA.)

8–21217 **20. Assisting in or inducing commission outside United Kingdom of offence punishable under a corresponding law.** A person commits an offence[1] if in the United Kingdom he assists in or induces the commission in any place outside the United Kingdom[2] of an offence punishable under the provisions of a corresponding law[3] in force in that place.

[Misuse of Drugs Act 1971, s 20.]

1. See note 5 to s 4, ante.

2. This section repeats in a modified form, provisions in earlier legislation to deal with a person in this country who organises the smuggling of drugs, for instance from the Continent to the United States of America, but does not himself handle any of the drugs in this country. For power of search, see s 23(3). For a conviction, see *R v Yasukichi Miyagawa* [1924] 1 KB 614, 88 JP 44. The words "assist in the commission of an offence" are not to be narrowly construed; see *R v Vickers* [1975] 2 All ER 945, 139 JP 623 and *R v Evans* [1977] 1 All ER 228, 141 JP 141. The offence outside the UK must be committed: the provision will not apply where a yacht carrying cannabis from Spain to Holland is arrested in the

UK (*R v Panayi and Karte* (1987) 86 Cr App Rep 261, [1987] Crim LR 764, CA); subsequent proceedings [1989] 1 WLR 187, CA.

3. For meaning of "corresponding law", see s 36, post.

8–21218 **21. Offences by corporations.** Where any offence under this Act or Part II of the Criminal Justice (International Co-operation) Act 1990 committed by a body corporate is proved to have been committed with the consent or connivance of, to be attributable to any neglect on the part of, any director, manager, secretary or other similar officer of the body corporate, or any person purporting to act in any such capacity, he as well as the body corporate shall be guilty of that offence and shall be liable to be proceeded against accordingly.

[Misuse of Drugs Act 1971, s 21, as amended by the Criminal Justice (International Co-operation) Act 1990, s 23, the Drug Trafficking Act 1994, Sch 1, and the Proceeds of Crime Act 2002, s 457.]

8–21219 **22. Further powers to make regulations.** The Secretary of State may by regulations[1] make provision—

(*a*) for excluding in such cases as may be prescribed—

(i) the application of any provision of this Act which creates an offence; or

(ii) the application of any of the following provisions of the Customs and Excise Management Act 1979, that is to say, sections 50(1) to (4), 68(2) and (3) and 170, in so far as they apply in relation to a prohibition or restriction of importation or exportation having effect by virtue of section 3 of this Act;

(*b*) for applying any of the provisions of sections 14 to 16 of this Act and Schedule 3 thereto, with such modifications (if any) as may be prescribed—

(i) in relation to any proposal by the Secretary of State to give a direction under section 12(2) of this Act; or

(ii) for such purposes of regulations under this Act as may be prescribed;

(*c*) for the application of any of the provisions of this Act or regulations or orders thereunder to servants or agents of the Crown, subject to such exceptions, adaptations and modifications as may be prescribed.

[Misuse of Drugs Act 1971, s 22, as amended by the Customs and Excise Management Act 1979, Sch 4.]

1. The Misuse of Drugs (Supply to Addicts) Regulations 1997, SI 1997/1001 amended by SI 2005/2864 and the Misuse of Drugs 2001, in this title, post, have been made.

Law enforcement and punishment of offences

8–21230 **23. Powers to search and obtain evidence.** A constable or other person authorised in that behalf by a general or special order of the Secretary of State (or in Northern Ireland either of the Secretary of State or the Ministry of Home Affairs for Northern Ireland) shall, for the purposes of the execution of this Act, have power to enter the premises of a person carrying on business as a producer or supplier of any controlled drugs[1] and to demand the production of, and to inspect[2] any books or documents relating to dealings in any such drugs and to inspect any stocks of any such drugs.

(2) If a constable has reasonable grounds to suspect that any person is in possession of a controlled drug in contravention of this Act or of any regulations made thereunder, the constable may—

(*a*) search that person, and detain him for the purpose of searching him;

(*b*) search any vehicle or vessel in which the constable suspects that the drug may be found, and for that purpose require the person in control of the vehicle or vessel to stop it;

(*c*) seize and detain, for the purposes of proceedings under this Act, anything found in the course of the search which appears to the constable to be evidence of an offence under this Act.

In this subsection "vessel" includes a hovercraft within the meaning of the Hovercraft Act 1968; and nothing in this subsection shall prejudice any power of search or any power to seize or detain property which is exercisable by a constable apart from this subsection.

(3) If a justice of the peace (or in Scotland a justice of the peace, a magistrate or a sheriff) is satisfied by information on oath that there is reasonable ground for suspecting—

(*a*) that any controlled drugs are, in contravention of this Act or of any regulations made thereunder, in the possession of a person on any premises; or

(*b*) that a document directly or indirectly relating to, or connected with, a transaction or dealing which was, or an intended transaction or dealing which would if carried out be, an offence under this Act, or in the case of a transaction or dealing carried out or intended to be carried out in a place outside the United Kingdom, an offence against the provisions of a corresponding law in force in that place, is in the possession of a person on any premises,

he may grant a warrant[3] authorising any constable acting for the police area in which the premises are situated at any time or times within one month from the date of the warrant, to enter, if need by force, the premises named in the warrant, and to search the premises and any persons found therein[4] and, if there is reasonable ground for suspecting that an offence under this Act has been committed in relation to any controlled drugs found on the premises or in the possession of any such persons, or that a document so found is such a document as is mentioned in paragraph (*b*) above, to seize and detain those drugs or that document, as the case may be.

(3A) The powers conferred by subsection (1) above shall be exercisable also for the purposes of the execution of Part II of the Criminal Justice (International Co-operation) Act 1990 and subsection (3) above (excluding paragraph (*a*)) shall apply also to offences under section 12 or 13 of that Act of 1990, taking references in those provisions to controlled drugs as references to scheduled substances within the meaning of that Part.

(4) A person commits an offence[5] if he—

(*a*) intentionally obstructs a person in the exercise of his powers under this section; or

(*b*) conceals from a person acting in the exercise of his powers under subsection (1) above any such books, documents, stocks or drugs as are mentioned in that subsection; or

(*c*) without reasonable excuse (proof of which shall lie on him) fails to produce any such books or documents as are so mentioned where their production is demanded by a person in the exercise of his powers under that subsection.

(5) *Application to Northern Ireland.*

[Misuse of Drugs Act 1971, s 23, as amended by the Criminal Justice (International Co-operation) Act 1990, s 23, the Drug Trafficking Act 1994, Sch 1 and the Proceeds of Crime Act 2002, s 457.]

1. The power to enter and search premises is also exercisable for the purposes of arts 4, 5 and 5a of Council Regulation (EEC) 3677/90 as amended: the Controlled Drugs (Substances Useful for Manufacture) Regulations 1991, SI 1991/1285 amended by SI 1992/2914.

2. This includes the right to take notes of the entries therein. Cf *Hart v Cohen and Van der Laan* (1902) 4 F 445.

3. The warrant will authorise entry only to the premises described in the warrant, see *R v Atkinson* [1976] Crim LR 307 (wrong flat number applied for and stated in warrant), though misspellings or trivial errors will not necessarily invalidate the warrant.

4. Where a warrant provides for a search of premises and persons therein, the police may detain a person in one room while they search another room (*DPP v Meaden* [2003] EWHC 3005 (Admin), [2004] 4 All ER 75, [2004] 1 WLR 945, [2004] Crim LR 587).

5. See note 5 to s 4, ante.

8–21231 24. *Repealed.*

8–21232 **25. Prosecution[1] and punishment of offences.** (1) Schedule 4[2] to this Act shall have effect, in accordance with subsection (2) below, with respect to the way in which offences under this Act are punishable on conviction.

(2) In relation to an offence under a provision of this Act specified in the first column of the Schedule (the general nature of the offence being described in the second column)—

(*a*) the third column shows whether an offence is punishable on summary conviction or on indictment or in either way;

(*b*) the fourth, fifth and sixth columns show respectively the punishments which may be imposed on a person convicted of the offence in the way specified in relation thereto in the third column (that is to say, summarily or on indictment) according to whether the controlled drug in relation to which the offence was committed was a Class A drug, a Class B drug or a Class C drug[3]; and

(*c*) the seventh column shows the punishments which may be imposed on a person convicted of the offence in the way specified in relation thereto in the third column (that is to say, summarily or on indictment), whether or not the offence was committed in relation to a controlled drug and, if it was so committed, irrespective of whether the drug was a Class A drug, a Class B drug or a Class C drug[3];

and in the fourth, fifth, sixth and seventh columns a reference to a period gives the maximum term of imprisonment and a reference to a sum of money the maximum fine.

(3) An offence under section 19 of this Act shall be punishable on summary conviction, on indictment or in either way according to whether, under Schedule 4 to this Act, the substantive offence is punishable on summary conviction, on indictment or in either way; and the punishments which may be imposed on a person convicted of an offence under that section are the same as those which, under that Schedule, may be imposed on a person convicted of the substantive offence.

In this subsection "the substantive offence" means the offence under this Act to which, the incitement mentioned in section 19 was directed.

(4) Notwithstanding anything in section 127(1) of the Magistrates' Courts Act 1980, a magistrates' court in England and Wales may try an information for an offence under this Act if the information was laid at any time within twelve months from the commission of the offence.

(5) *Application to Scotland.*

(6) *Application to Northern Ireland.*

[Misuse of Drugs Act 1971, s 25, as amended by the Magistrates' Courts Act 1980, Sch 7 and the Criminal Attempts Act 1981, Schedule.]

1. There is no provision similar to that in earlier legislation whereby proceedings on indictment either required the consent of the Attorney General or had to be instituted by the Director of Public Prosecutions. Parliament has however expressed the hope that prosecutors will not proceed by way of indictment where summary proceedings are adequate.

2. See post.
3. See Sch 2, post, and s 2, ante.

8–21233 27. Forfeiture. (1) Subject to subsection (2) below, the court by or before which a person is convicted of an offence[1] under this Act or an offence falling within subsection (3) below or an offence to which section 1 of the Criminal Justice (Scotland) Act 1987 relates may order anything[2] shown to the satisfaction[3] of the court to relate to the offence, to be forfeited and either destroyed or dealt with[4] in such other manner as the court may order.

(2) The court shall not order anything to be forfeited under this section, where a person claiming to be the owner of or otherwise interested in it applies to be heard by the court, unless an opportunity has been given to him to show cause why the order should not be made.

(3) An offence falls within this subsection if it is an offence specified in—

(*a*) paragraph 1 of Schedule 2 to the Proceeds of Crime Act 2002 (drug trafficking offences), or

(*b*) so far as it relates to that paragraph, paragraph 10 of that Schedule.

[Misuse of Drugs Act 1971, s 27, as amended by the Criminal Justice Act 1988, s 70, the Criminal Justice (International Co-operation) Act 1990, Sch 4, the Drug Trafficking Act 1994, Sch 1 and the Proceeds of Crime Act 2002, s 456.]

---

1. The power of forfeiture applies only to property shown to be connected with the offence of which the offender is convicted; the proceeds of the sale of drugs, not the subject of the charge, which the offender had in his possession prior to his being searched cannot therefore be forfeited (*R v Llewellyn* [1985] Crim LR 750) and see *R v Simms* (1988) 9 Cr App Rep (S) 417, CA.

2. In *R v Beard* [1974] 1 WLR 1549, Caulfield J held that "anything" includes money but would not include a house; but cf *Haggard v Mason* [1976] 1 All ER 337, 140 JP 198. The power of forfeiture applies only to tangible things capable of being destroyed or dealt with in some other manner as the court thinks fit, and not to choses in action or other intangibles (*R v Cuthbertson* [1980] 2 All ER 401, 144 JP 366). Cash seized by the police and placed in a deposit account does not cease to be a tangible asset and still be the subject of a forfeiture order (*R v Marland and Jones* (1985) 82 Cr App Rep 134).

Where a motor vehicle is used as a means of transport on the journey in the course of which the defendant is arrested and on other trips to purchase drugs, the vehicle may be the subject of a forfeiture order (*R v Bowers* (1993) 15 Cr App Rep (S) 315, [1994] Crim LR 230, CA (forfeiture order upheld notwithstanding the fact that the motor vehicle had been purchased with money provided by the defendant's elderly mother and the vehicle was used to take his mother to visit his mentally handicapped brother)).

3. The court must make a proper investigation to ensure that the statutory requirements are fulfilled before making a forfeiture order. Where the court is minded to make such an order, it should first allow the offender to put before the court any material tending the show that the thing in question is not related to the offence (*R v Churcher* (1986) 8 Cr App Rep (S) 94).

4. Disposal of forfeited articles should not be carried out until the time for appeal has expired.

Miscellaneous and supplementary provisions

8–21234 28. Proof of lack of knowledge etc to be a defence in proceedings for certain offences[1]. (1) This section applies to offences under any of the following provisions of this Act, that is to say section 4(2) and (3), section 5 (2) and (3), section 6(2) and section 9[2].

(2) Subject to subsection (3) below, in any proceedings for an offence to which this section applies it shall be a defence for the accused to prove[3] that he neither knew of nor suspected nor had reason to suspect the existence of some fact[4] alleged by the prosecution which it is necessary for the prosecution to prove if he is to be convicted of the offence charged.

(3) Where in any proceedings for an offence to which this section applies it is necessary, if the accused is to be convicted of the offence charged, for the prosecution to prove that some substance or product involved in the alleged offence was the controlled drug which the prosecution alleges it to have been, and it is proved that the substance or product in question was that controlled drug, the accused[5]—

(*a*) shall not be acquitted[6] of the offence charged by reason only of proving that he neither knew nor suspected nor had reason to suspect that the substance or product in question was the particular controlled drug alleged; but

(*b*) shall be acquitted thereof—

(i) if he proves[3] that he neither believed nor suspected nor had reason to suspect[7] that the substance or product in question was a controlled drug; or

(ii) if he proves[3] that he believed the substance or product in question to be a controlled drug, or a controlled drug of a description, such that, if it had in fact been that controlled drug or a controlled drug of that description, he would not at the material time have been committing any offence to which this section applies.

(4) Nothing in this section shall prejudice any defence which it is open to a person charged with an offence to which this section applies to raise apart from this section.

[Misuse of Drugs Act 1971, s 28.]

---

1. The presumption of innocence given effect in article of the European Convention of Human Rights, is not breached by this provision which places an evidential burden on the defendant (*R v Lambert* [2001] UKHL 37, [2002] 2 AC 545, [2001] 3 All ER 577, [2001] 3 WLR 206).

2. These offences are production and supply (s 4), possession (s 5), cultivation of the cannabis plant (s 6), smoking using prepared opium (s 9) and allied offences.

3. This places an evidential burden on the defendant to raise certain issues which amount to a defence and which the prosecution must disprove beyond a reasonable doubt. The words 'to prove' in sub-ss (2) and (3) must be read as "to give sufficient evidence". The effect is that the burden of proof remains on the prosecution throughout. If sufficient evidence is adduced to raise the issue, it will be for the prosecution to show beyond reasonable doubt that the defence is not made out by the evidence. What the accused must do is put evidence before the court which, if believed, could be taken by a reasonable jury or magistrates' court to support his defence. (*R v Lambert* [2001] UKHL 37, [2002] 2 AC 545, [2001] 3 All ER 577, [2001] 3 WLR 206).

4. For example, that he possessed some substance. The onus remains on the prosecution to prove the defendant knew he had something which was in fact a dangerous drug; once this is proved, it is open for the defendant to try and raise the issue of lack of knowledge under s 28; see note 2 to s 5, ante.

5. Once the prosecution prove that the defendant had control of a box which he was delivering on his motor cycle and knew it contained something, which was in fact the drug alleged, he has the onus of bringing himself within the provisions of s 28(3); see *R v McNamara* (1988) 152 JP 390, 87 Cr App Rep 246, CA, followed in *R v Matrix* [1997] Crim LR 901, CA (possession of obscene video film depicting children.).

6. This does not prevent a court from taking into account, in deciding sentence, the defendant's genuine belief that the drug in question was a different controlled drug.

7. The words "neither knew nor suspected nor had reason to suspect" are not to be read as one when considering whether self-induced intoxication could act as a defence. It was a factor to be considered, and could eliminate the knowledge or suspicion of the first two tests, being subjective. But the third test "reason to suspect" called for an objective appraisal (*R v Young* [1984] 2 All ER 164, [1984] 1 WLR 654, 148 JP 492).

8–21235 **29. Service of documents.** (1) Any notice or other document required or authorised by any provisions of this Act to be served on any person may be served on him either by delivering it to him or by leaving it at his proper address or by sending it by post.

(2) Any notice or other document so required or authorised to be served on a body corporate shall be duly served if it is served on the secretary or clerk of that body.

(3) For the purposes of this section, and of section 26 of the Interpretation Act 1889[1] in its application to this section, the proper address of any person shall, in the case of the secretary or clerk of a body corporate, be that of the registered or principal office of that body, and in any other case shall be the last address of the person to be served which is known to the Secretary of State.

(4) Where any of the following documents, that is to say—

(*a*) a notice under section 11(1) or section 15(6) of this Act; or

(*b*) a copy of a direction given under section 12(2), section 13(1) or (2) or section 16(3) of this Act,

is served by sending it by registered post or by the recorded delivery service, service thereof shall be deemed to have been affected at the time when the letter containing it would be delivered in the ordinary course of post; and so much of section 26 of the Interpretation Act 1889[1] as relates to the time when service by post is deemed to have been effected shall not apply to such a document if it is served by so sending it.

[Misuse of Drugs Act 1971, s 29.]

1. Now s 7 of the Interpretation Act 1978.

8–21236 **31. General provisions as to regulations.** (1) Regulations made by the Secretary of State under any provisions of this Act—

(*a*) may make different provision in relation to different controlled drugs, different classes of persons, different provisions of this Act or other different cases or circumstances; and

(*b*) may make the opinion, consent or approval of a prescribed authority or of any person authorised in a prescribed manner material for purposes of any provision of the regulations; and

(*c*) may contain such supplementary, incidental and transitional provisions as appear expedient to the Secretary of State.

(2) Any power of the Secretary of State to make regulations under this Act shall be exercisable by statutory instrument, which shall be subject to annulment in pursuance of a resolution of either House of Parliament.

(3) The Secretary of State shall not make any regulations under this Act except after consultation with the Advisory Council.

(4) *Application to Northern Ireland.*

[Misuse of Drugs Act 1971, s 31.]

8–21237 **36. Meaning of "corresponding law", and evidence of certain matters by certificate.** (1) In this Act the expression "corresponding law" means a law stated in a certificate purporting to be issued by or on behalf of the government of a country outside the United Kingdom to be a law providing for the control and regulation in that country of the production, supply, use, export and import of drugs and other substances in accordance with the provisions of the Single Convention on Narcotic Drugs signed at New York on 30th March 1961 or a law providing for the control and regulation in that country of the production, supply, use, export and import of dangerous or otherwise harmful drugs in pursuance of any treaty, convention or other agreement or arrangement to which the government of that country and Her Majesty's Government in the United Kingdom are for the time being parties.

(2) A statement in any such certificate as aforesaid to the effect that any facts constitute an offence against the law mentioned in the certificate shall be evidence, and in Scotland sufficient evidence, of the matters stated.

[Misuse of Drugs Act 1971, s 36.]

8–21238 37. Interpretation. (1) In this Act, except in so far as the context otherwise requires, the following expressions have the meanings hereby assigned to them respectively, that is to say—

"the Advisory Council" means the Advisory Council on the Misuse of Drugs established under this Act;

"cannabis" (except in the expression "cannabis resin") means any plant of the genus *Cannabis* or any part of any such plant (by whatever name designated)[1] except that it does not include cannabis resin or any of the following products after separation from the rest of the plant, namely—

(*a*) mature stalk of any such plant,

(*b*) fibre produced from mature stalk of any such plant, and

(*c*) seed of any such plant[2];

"cannabis resin" means the separated resin, whether crude or purified, obtained from any plant of the genus *Cannabis*[3];

"contravention" includes failure to comply, and "contravene" has a corresponding meaning;

"controlled drug" has the meaning assigned by section 2 of this Act;

"corresponding law" has the meaning assigned by section 36(1) of this Act;

"dentist" means a person registered in the dentists' register under the Dentists Act 1984 or entered in the list of visiting EEA practitioners under Schedule 4 to that Act;

"doctor" means a registered medical practitioner within the meaning of Schedule 1 to the Interpretation Act 1978;

"enactment" includes an enactment of the Parliament of Northern Ireland;

"person lawfully conducting retail pharmacy business" means a person lawfully conducting such a business in accordance with section 69 of the Medicines Act 1968;

"pharmacist" has the same meaning as in the Medicines Act 1968;

"practitioner" (except in the expression "veterinary practitioner") means a doctor, dentist, veterinary practitioner or veterinary surgeon;

"prepared opium" means opium prepared for smoking and includes dross and any other residues remaining after opium has been smoked;

"prescribed" means prescribed by regulations made by the Secretary of State under this Act;

"produce", where the reference is to producing a controlled drug, means producing it by manufacture, cultivation or any other method[4], and "production" has a corresponding meaning;

"supplying" includes distributing[5];

"veterinary practitioner" means a person registered in the supplementary veterinary register kept under section 8 of the Veterinary Surgeons Act 1966;

"veterinary surgeon" means a person registered in the register of veterinary surgeons kept under section 2 of the Veterinary Surgeons Act 1966.

(2) References in this Act to misusing a drug are references to misusing it by taking it; and the reference in the foregoing provision to the taking of a drug is a reference to the taking of it by a human being by way of any form of self-administration, whether or not involving assistance by another.

(3) For the purposes of this Act the things which a person has in his possession shall be taken to include any thing subject to his control which is in the custody of another.

(4) Except in so far as the context otherwise requires, any reference in this Act to an enactment shall be construed as a reference to that enactment as amended or extended by or under any other enactment.

(5) *Repealed.*

[Misuse of Drugs Act 1971, s 37, as amended by SI 1976/1213, the Criminal Law Act 1977, s 52, the Medical Act 1983, Sch 5, the Dentists Act 1984, Sch 5, SI 1996/1496 and the Statute Law (Repeals) Act 2004.]

---

1. Eg, hashish, gunjah, bhang, marijuana.
2. For consideration of the effect the amendment of this definition by s 52 of the Criminal Law Act 1977 has had, see *Taylor v Chief Constable of Kent* [1981] 1 WLR 606, 72 Cr App Rep 318.
3. Leaves and stalk which have been removed from a cannabis plant do not amount to "cannabis resin", since the separation contemplated by the section is a serious and deliberate removal of resin from the plant, see *R v Goodchild (No 2), A-G's Reference (No 1 of 1977)* [1978] 1 All ER 649, [1977] 1 WLR 1213, 65 Cr App Rep 165, CA. Compacted shakings or scrapings of part of a cannabis plant which on microscopic examination were seen to contain intact cannabis oil-bearing glandular trichomes nevertheless came within the definition of cannabis resin (*R v Janet Thomas* [1981] Crim LR 496.)
4. Conversion from one form of a drug to another can amount to production (*R v Russell* (1991) 94 Cr App Rep 351, CA). The preparation of plants so as to discard the parts which are not usable for the drug and to put together those which are amounts to "production" of cannabis (*R v Harris* [1996] 1 Cr App Rep 369.

5. A person who purchased drugs for himself and others could supply the drugs to the others (*Holmes v Chief Constable Merseyside Police* [1976] Crim LR 125), followed in *R v Buckley* (1979) 69 Cr App Rep 371).

6. These sections were repealed with effect from 1st February 1978.

8–21239

SCHEDULES

SCHEDULE 1

CONSTITUTION OF ADVISORY COUNCIL ON THE MISUSE OF DRUGS

8–21240

Section 2

SCHEDULE 2

CONTROLLED DRUGS[1]

(As amended by SI 1973/771, SI 1975/421, SI 1977/1243, SI 1979/299, SI 1983/765, SI 1984/859, SI 1985/1995, SI 1986/2230, SI 1989/1340, SI 1990/2589, SI 1995/1966, SI 1996/1300, SI 1998/750, SI 2001/3932, SI 2003/1243 and 3201, the Drugs Act 2005, s 21, SI 2005/1650 and 3178.)

PART I

CLASS A DRUGS

1. The following substances and products, namely—

(*a*)

Acetorphine.
Alfentanil.
Allylprodine.
Alphacetylmethadol.
Alphameprodine.
Alphamethadol.
Alphaprodine.
Anileridine.
Benzethidine.
Benzylmorphine (3-benzylmorphine).
Betacetylmethadol.
Betameprodine.
Betamethadol.
Betaprodine.
Bezitramide.
Bufotenine.
Carfentanil
Clonitazene.
Coca leaf.
Cocaine.
Desomorphine.
Dextromoramide.
Diamorphine.
Diampromide.
Diethylthiambutene.
Difenoxin (1-(3-cyano-3,3-diphenylpropyl) -4-phenylpiperidine-4-carboxylic acid)
Dihydrocodeinone *O*-carboxymethyloxime.
Dihydroetorphine.
Dihydromorphine.
Dimenoxadole.
Dimepheptanol.
Dimethylthiambutene.
Dioxaphetyl butyrate.
Diphenoxylate.
Dipipanone.
(Drotebanol (3,4-dimethoxy-17-methylmorphinan-6 beta, 14-diol).
Egonine, and any derivative of ecgonine which is convertible to ecgonine or to cocaine.
Ethylmethylthiambutene.
Eticyclidine
Etonitazene.
Etorphine.
Etoxeridine.
Etryptamine
Fentanyl.
Fungus (of any kind) which contains psilocin or an ester of psilocin.
Furethidine.
Hydrocodone.
Hydromorphinol.
Hydromorphone.
Hydroxypethidine.
Isomethadone.
Ketobemidone.
Levomethorphan.
Levomoramide.

Levophenacylmorphan.
Levorphanol.
Lofentanil.
Lysergamide.
Lysergide and other *N*-alkyl derivatives of lysergamide.
Mescaline.
Metazocine.
Methadone.
Methadyl acetate.
Methyldesorphine.
Methyldihydromorphine (6-methyldihydromorphine).
Metopon.
Morpheridine.
Morphine.
Morphine methobromide, morphine *N*-oxide and other pentavalent nitrogen morphine derivatives.
Myrophine.
Nicomorphine (3,6-dinicotinoyl-morphine).
Noracymethadol.
Norlevorphanol.
Normethadone.
Normorphine.
Norpipanone.
Opium, whether raw, prepared or medicinal.
Oxycodone.
Oxymorphone.
Pethidine.
Phenadoxone.
Phenampromide.
Phenazocine.
Phencyclidine.
Phenomorphan.
Phenoperidine.
Piminodine.
Piritramide.
Poppy-straw and concentrate of poppy-straw.
Proheptazine.
Properidine (1-methyl-4-phenyl-piperidine-4-carboxylic acid isopropyl ester).
Psilocin.
Racemethorphan.
Racemoramide.
Racemorphan.
Remifentanil.
Rolicyclidine.
Sufentanil.
Tenocyclidine.
Thebacon.
Thebaine.
Tilidate
Trimeperidine.
4-Bromo-2,5-dimethoxy-alpha-methylphenethylamine
4-Cyano-2-dimethylamino-4, 4-diphenylbutane
4-Cyano-1-methyl-4-phenyl-piperidine.
N,N-Diethyltryptamine.
N,N-Dimethyltryptamine.
2,5-Dimethoxy-alpha,4-dimethylphenethylamine.
N-Hydroxy-tenamphetamine.
1-Methyl-4-phenylpiperidine-4-carboxylic acid.
2-Methyl-3-morpholino-1, 1-diphenylpropanecarboxylic acid.
4-Methyl-aminorex.
4-Phenylpiperidine-4-carboxylic acid ethyl ester.

(*b*) any compound (not being a compound for the time being specified in sub-paragraph (*a*) above) structurally derived from tryptamine or from a ringhydroxy tryptamine by substitution at the nitrogen atom of the sidechain with one or more alkyl substituents but no other substituent;

(*ba*) the following phenethylamine derivatives, namely:—

Allyl(α-methyl-3,4-methylenedioxyphenethyl)amine
2-Amino-1-(2,5-dimethoxy-4-methylphenyl)ethanol
2-Amino-1-(3,4-dimethoxyphenyl)ethanol
Benzyl(α-methyl-3,4-methylenedioxyphenethyl)amine
4-Bromo-β,2,5-trimethoxyphenethylamine
N-(4-*sec*-Butylthio-2,5-dimethoxyphenethyl)hydroxylamine
Cyclopropylmethyl(α-methyl-3,4-methylenedioxyphenethyl)amine
2-(4,7-Dimethoxy-2,3-dihydro-1*H*-indan-5-yl)ethylamine
2-(4,7-Dimethoxy-2,3-dihydro-1*H*-indan-5-yl)-1-methylethylamine
2-(2,5-Dimethoxy-4-methylphenyl)cyclopropylamine
2-(1,4-Dimethoxy-2-naphthyl)ethylamine

2-(1,4-Dimethoxy-2-naphthyl)-1-methylethylamine
N-(2,5-Dimethoxy-4-propylthiophenethyl)hydroxylamine
2-(1,4-Dimethoxy-5,6,7,8-tetrahydro-2-naphthyl)ethylamine
2-(1,4-Dimethoxy-5,6,7,8-tetrahydro-2-naphthyl)-1-methylethylamine
α,,α-Dimethyl-3,4-methylenedioxyphenethylamine
α,,α-Dimethyl-3,4-methylenedioxyphenethyl(methyl)amine
Dimethyl(*α*-methyl-3,4-methylenedioxyphenethyl)amine
N-(4-Ethylthio-2,5-dimethoxyphenethyl)hydroxylamine
4-Iodo-2,5-dimethoxy-*α*-methylphenethyl(dimethyl)amine
2-(1,4-Methano-5,8-dimethoxy-1,2,3,4-tetrahydro-6-naphthyl)ethylamine
2-(1,4-Methano-5,8-dimethoxy-1,2,3,4-tetrahydro-6-naphthyl)-1-methylethylamine
2-(5-Methoxy-2,2-dimethyl-2,3-dihydrobenzo[*b*]furan-6-yl)-1-methylethylamine
2-Methoxyethyl(*a*-methyl-3,4-methylenedioxyphenethyl)amine
2-(5-Methoxy-2-methyl-2,3-dihydrobenzo[*b*]furan-6-yl)-1-methylethylamine
ß;-Methoxy-3,4-methylenedioxyphenethylamine
1-(3,4-Methylenedioxybenzyl)butyl(ethyl)amine
1-(3,4-Methylenedioxybenzyl)butyl(methyl)amine
2-(*α*-Methyl-3,4-methylenedioxyphenethylamino)ethanol
α-Methyl-3,4-methylenedioxyphenethyl(prop-2-ynyl)amine
N-Methyl-*N*-(*α*-methyl-3,4-methylenedioxyphenethyl)hydroxylamine
O-Methyl-*N*-(*α*-methyl-3,4-methylenedioxyphenethyl)hydroxylamine
α-Methyl-4-(methylthio)phenethylamine
ß,3,4,5-Tetramethoxyphenethylamine
ß,2,5-Trimethoxy-4-methylphenethylamine;

(*c*) any compound (not being methoxyphenamine or a compound for the time being specified in sub-paragraph (*a*) above) structurally derived from phenethylamine, an *N*-alkylphenethylamine, alpha-methylphenethylamine, an *N*-alkyl-alpha-methylphenethylamine, alpha -ethylphenethylamine, or an *N*-alkyl-alpha-ethylphenethylamine by substitution in the ring to any extent with alkyl, alkoxy, alkylene- dioxy or halide substituents, whether or not further substituted in the ring by one or more other univalent substituents.

(*d*) any compound (not being a compound for the time being specified in sub-paragraph (*a*) above) structurally derived from fentanyl by modification in any of the following ways, that is to say,

(i) by replacement of the phenyl portion of the phenethyl group by any heteromonocycle whether or not further substituted in the heterocycle;
(ii) by substitution in the phenethyl group with alkyl, alkenyl, alkoxy, hydroxy, halogeno, haloalkyl, amino or nitro groups;
(iii) by substitution in the piperidine ring with alkyl or alkenyl groups;
(iv) by substitution in the aniline ring with alkyl, alkoxy, alkylenedioxy, halogeno or haloalkyl groups;
(v) by substitution at the 4-position of the piperidine ring with any alkoxycarbonyl or alkoxyalkyl or acyloxy group;
(vi) by replacement of the *N*-propionyl group by another acyl group;

(*e*) any compound (not being a compound for the time being specified in sub-paragraph (*a*) above) structurally derived from pethidine by modification in any of the following ways, that is to say,

(i) by replacement of the 1-methyl group by an acyl, alkyl whether or not unsaturated, benzyl or phenethyl group, whether or not further substituted;
(ii) by substitution in the piperidine ring with alkyl or alkenyl groups or with a propano bridge, whether or not further substituted;
(iii) by substitution in the 4-phenyl ring with alkyl, alkoxy, aryloxy, halogeno or haloalkyl groups;
(iv) by replacement of the 4-ethoxycarbonyl by any other alkoxycarbonyl or any alkoxyalkyl or acyloxy group;
(v) by formation of an *N*-oxide or of a quaternary base.

2. Any stereoisomeric form of a substance for the time being specified in paragraph 1 above not being dextromethorphan or dextrophan.

3. Any ester or ether of a substance for the time being specified in paragraph 1 or 2 above, not being a substance for the time being specified in Part II of this Schedule.

4. Any salt of a substance for the time being specified in any of paragraphs 1 to 3 above.

5. Any preparation[4] or other product containing a substance or product for the time being specified in any of paragraphs 1 to 4 above.

6. Any preparation designed for administration by injections which includes a substance or product for the time being specified in any of paragraphs 1 to 3 of Part II of this Schedule.

---

1. Schedule 2 classifies drugs for penalties for misuse and not for regimes of control; for the latter classification see the Schedules to the Misuse of Drugs Regulations 1985, post. The offence of lawful possession of any controlled drug described in Sch 2 by its scientific name is not established by proof of possession of naturally occurring material of which the described drug is one of the constituents unseparated from the others. This is so whether or not the naturally occurring material is also included as another item in the list of controlled drugs (*DPP v Goodchild*) [1978] 2 All ER 161, [1978] 1 WLR 578, 142 JP 338, HL).

2. A charge alleging possession of "cannabis *or* cannabis resin" is not necessarily bad for duplicity; see *R v Newcastle-under-Lyme Justices, ex p Hemmings* [1987] Crim LR 416.

3. "Cocaine" can be a natural substance or a substance resulting from a chemical transformation and the word 'cocaine' in para 1 of Part I of the Schedule is a generic word which includes both direct extracts from the coca leaf and whatever results from a chemical transformation (*R v Greensmith* [1983] 3 All ER 444, [1983] 1 WLR 1124, and see *A-G for the Cayman Islands v Roberts* [2002] UKPC 18, [2002] 2 Cr App Rep 388).

4. "Preparation" has its ordinary and natural meaning and is not intended to have a technical meaning; *R v Stevens* [1981] Crim LR 568 (mushrooms altered by the hand of man to become a powder containing psilocybin). In *R v Cunliffe*

[1986] Crim LR 547, CA, it was held that the defendant who had picked and allowed to dry a quantity of psilocybin mushrooms (Mexican magic mushrooms) was in possession of a *preparation* containing psilocybin an ester of psilocin. Similarly, in *Hodder v DPP* [1990] Crim LR 261, psilocybin mushrooms which were picked, separated into packages and then frozen, were held to be a *preparation* containing psilocybin.

PART II
CLASS B DRUGS

8–21241 **1.** The following substances and products, namely—

(*a*)

Acetyldihydrocodeine.
Amphetamine.
Codeine.
Dihydrocodeine.
Ethylmorphine (3-ethylmorphine).
Glutethimide
Lefetamine
Mecloqualone.
Methaqualone.
Methcathinone
Methylamphetamine.
a-Methylphenethylhydroxylamine;
Methylphenidate.
Methylphenobarbitone.
Nicodine.
Nicodicodine (6-nicotinoyldihydrocodeine)
Norcodeine.
Pentazocine
Phenmetrazine.
Pholcodine
Propiram
Zipeprol

(*b*)

any 5, 5 distributed barbituric acid.

2. Any stereoisomeric form of a substance for the time being specified in paragraph 1 of this Part of this Schedule.

3. Any salt of a substance for the time being specified in paragraph 1 or 2 of this Part of this Schedule.

4. Any preparation or other product containing a substance or product for the time being specified in any of paragraphs 1 to 3 of this Part of this Schedule, but not being a preparation falling within paragraph 6 of Part I of this Schedule.

PART III
CLASS C DRUGS

8–21242 **1.** The following substances, namely—

(*a*)

Alprazolam
Aminorex
Benzphetamine.
Bromazepam
Brotizolam
Buprenorphine
Camazepam
Cannabinol
Cannabinol derivatives
Cannabis and cannabis resin
Cathine
Cathinone
Chlordiazepoxide
Chlorphentermine.
Clobazam
Clonazepam
Clorazepic acid
Clotiazepam
Cloxazolam
Delorazepam
Dextropropoxyphene
Diazepam
Diethylpropion
Estazolam
Ethchlorvynol
Ethinamate
Ethyl loflazepate
Fencamfamin
Fenethylline
Fenproporex

Fludiazepam
Flunitrazepam
Flurazepam
Halazepam
Haloxazolam
4-Hydroxy-n-butyric acid
Ketamine
Ketazolam
Loprazolam
Lorazepam
Lormetazepam
Mazindol
Medazepam
Mefenorex
Mephentermine.
Meprobamate
Mesocarb
Methyprylone
Midazolam
Nimetazepam
Nitrazepam
Nordazepam
Oxazepam
Oxazolam
Pemoline
Phendimetrazine.
Phentermine
Pinazepam
Pipradrol.
Prazepam
Pyrovalerone
Temazepam
Tetrazepam
Triazolam
N-Ethylamphetamine
Zolpidem

(*b*)

4-Androstene-3, 17-dione
5-Androstene-3, 17-diol
Atamestane.
Bolandiol.
Bolasterone.
Bolazine.
Boldenone.
Bolenol.
Bolmantalate.
Calusterone.
4-Chloromethandienone.
Clostebol.
Drostanolone.
Enestebol.
Epitiostanol.
Ethyloestrenol.
Fluoxymesterone.
Formebolone.
Furazabol.
Mebolazine.
Mepitiostane.
Mesabolone.
Mestanolone.
Mesterolone.
Methandienone.
Methandriol.
Methenolone.
Methyltestosterone.
Metribolone.
Mibolerone.
Nandrolone.
19-Nor-4-Androstene-3, 17-dione
19-Nor-5-Androstene-3, 17-diol
Norboletone.
Norclostebol.
Norethandrolone.
Ovandrotone.
Oxabolone.

Oxandrolone.
Oxymesterone.
Oxymetholone.
Prasterone.
Propetandrol.
Quinbolone.
Roxibolone.
Silandrone.
Stanolone.
Stanozolol.
Stenbolone.
Testosterone.
Thiomesterone.
Trenbolone.

(*c*) any compound (not being Trilostane or a compound for the time being specified in sub-paragraph (*b*) above) structurally derived from 17-hydroxyandrostan-3-one or from 17-hydroxyestran-3-one by modification in any of the following ways, that is to say,

(i) by further substitution at position 17 by a methyl or ethyl group;
(ii) by substitution to any extent at one or more of positions 1, 2, 4, 6, 7, 9, 11 or 16, but at no other position;
(iii) by unsaturation in the carbocyclic ring system to any extent, provided that there are no more than two ethylenic bonds in any one carbocyclic ring;
(iv) by fusion of ring A with a heterocyclic system

(*d*) any substances which is an ester or ether (or, where more than one hydroxyl function is available, both an ester and an ether) of a substance specified in sub-paragraph (*b*) or described in sub-paragraph (*c*) above or of cannabinol or a cannabinol derivative;

(*e*) Chorionic Gonadotrophin (HCG).

Clenbuterol.
Non-human chorionic gonadotrophin
Somatotropin
Somatrem.
Somatropin.

2. Any stereoisomeric form of a substance for the time being specified in paragraph 1 of this Part of this Schedule not being phenylpropanolamine.

3. Any salt of a substance for the time being specified in paragraph 1 or 2 of this Part of this Schedule.

4. Any preparation or other product containing a substance for the time being specified in any of paragraphs 1 to 3 of this Part of this Schedule.

8–21243

PART IV

MEANING OF CERTAIN EXPRESSIONS USED IN THIS SCHEDULE

For the purposes of this Schedule the following expressions (which are not among those defined in section 37(1) of this Act) have the meanings hereby assigned to them respectively, that is to say—

"cannabinol derivatives" means the following substances, except where contained in cannabis or cannabis resin, namely tetrahydro derivatives of cannabinol and 3-alkyl homologues of cannabinol or of its tetrahydro derivatives;

"coca leaf" means the leaf of any plant of the genus *Erythroxylon* from whose leaves cocaine can be extracted either directly or by chemical transformation;

"concentrate of poppy-straw" means the material produced when poppy-straw has entered into a process for the concentration of its alkaloids;

"medicinal opium" means raw opium which has undergone the process necessary to adapt it for medicinal use in accordance with the requirements of the British Pharmacopoeia, whether it is in the form of powder or is granulated or is in any other form, and whether it is or is not mixed with natural substances;

"opium poppy" means the plant of the species *Papaver somniferum* L;

"poppy straw" means all parts, except the seeds, of the opium poppy, after mowing;

"raw opium" includes powdered or granulated opium but does not include medicinal opium.

SCHEDULE 3

8–21244

TRIBUNALS ADVISORY BODIES AND PROFESSIONAL PANELS

SCHEDULE 4

(Amended by the Criminal Law Act 1977, ss 27 and 28 and Schs 5 and 6, the Criminal Justice Act 1982, s 46, the Controlled Drugs (Penalties) Act 1985, s 1, the Drug Trafficking Offences Act 1986, s 34 and the Criminal Justice and Public Order Act 1994, Sch 8.)

8–21245 PROSECUTION AND PUNISHMENT OF OFFENCES[1] Section 25

Section creating Offence	General Nature of Offence	Mode of Prosecution	Punishment			
			Class A drug[2] involved	Class B drug[2] involved	Class C drug[2] involved	General
Section 4 (2)	Production, or being concerned in the production, of a controlled drug.	(*a*) Summary.	6 months or the statutory maximum, or both.	6 months or the statutory maximum, or both.	3 months or £2,500, or both.	
		(*b*) On indictment.	Life, or a fine, or both.	14 years or a fine, or both.	14 years or a fine, or both.	
Section 4(3)	Supplying or offering to supply a controlled drug or being concerned in the doing of either activity by another	(*a*) Summary.	6 months or the statutory maximum, or both.	6 months or the statutory maximum, or both.	3 months or £2,500, or both.	
		(*b*) On indictment.	Life or a fine, or both	14 years or a fine, or both	14 years or a fine, or both	
Section 5(2)	Having possession of a controlled drug.	(*a*) Summary.	6 months or the statutory maximum, or both.	3 months or £2,500, or both.	3 months or £1,000 or both.	
		(*b*) On indictment.	7 years or a fine, or both.	5 years or a fine, or both.	2 years or a fine, or both.	
Section 5(3)	Having possession of a controlled drug with intent to supply it to another.	(*a*) Summary	6 months or the statutory maximum, or both.	6 months or the statutory maximum, or both.	3 months or £2,500, or both.	
		(*b*) On indictment	Life, or a fine, or both.	14 years or a fine, or both.	14 years or a fine, or both.	
Section 6(2)	Cultivation of a cannabis plant.	(*a*) Summary.	—	—	—	6 months or the statutory maximum, or both
		(*b*) On indictment.	—	—	—	14 years or a fine, or both.

1. For procedure in respect of the offences which are triable either way, see the Magistrates' Courts Act 1980, ss 17A–21, in PART I, MAGISTRATES' COURTS, PROCEDURE, ante.
2. See Sch 2, ante. The penalties expressed in money rather than levels, were specifically altered by Sch 5 to the Criminal Law Act 1977 to these amounts. The "standard scale" introduced by the Criminal Justice Act 1982 applies by s 46 thereof to summary offences only, and not to offences triable either way, like these; nor, by virtue of s 32 of the Magistrates' Courts Act 1980 does the "prescribed sum" apply.

Section creating Offence	General Nature of Offence	Mode of Prosecution	Punishment			
			Class A drug[3] involved	Class B drug[3] involved	Class C drug[3] involved	General
Section 8	Being the occupier, or concerned in the management, of premises and permitting or suffering certain activities to take place there.	(*a*) Summary.	6 months or the statutory maximum, or both.	6 months or the statutory maximum, or both.	3 months or £2,500, or both.	.
		(*b*) On indictment	14 years or a fine, or both.	14 years or a fine, or both.	14 years or a fine, or both.	
Section 9	Offences relating to opium.	(*a*) Summary.	—	—	—	6 months or the statutory maximum, or both.
		(*b*) On indictment	—	—	—	14 years or a fine, or both.
Section 9A	Prohibition of supply etc of articles for administering or preparing controlled drugs.	Summary.	—	—	—	6 months or level 5 on the standard scale, or both
Section 11(2)	Contravention of directions relating to safe custody of controlled drugs.	(*a*) Summary.	—	—	—	6 months or the statutory maximum, or both.
		(*b*) On indictment.	—	—	—	2 years or a fine, or both.
Section 12(6)	Contravention of direction prohibiting practitioner etc. from possessing, supplying etc. controlled drugs.	(*a*) Summary	6 months or the statutory maximum, or both.	6 months or the statutory maximum, or both.	3 months or £2,500, or both.	
		(*b*) On indictment.	14 years or a fine, or both.	14 years or a fine, or both.	14 years or a fine, or both.	
Section 13(3)	Contravention of direction prohibiting practitioner etc. from prescribing, supplying etc. controlled drugs.	(*a*) Summary	6 months or the statutory maximum, or both.	6 months or the statutory maximum, or both.	3 months or £2,500, or both	
		(*b*) On indictment.	14 years or a fine, or both.	14 years or a fine, or both.	14 years or a fine, or both.	
Section 17(3)	Failure to comply with notice requiring information relating to prescribing, supply etc. of drugs.	Summary	—	—	—	**Level 3** on the standard scale.
Section 17(4)	Giving false information in purported compliance, supply etc. of drugs.	(*a*) Summary	—	—	—	6 months or the statutory maximum, or both.
		(*b*) On indictment.	—	—	—	2 years or a fine, or both.
Section 18(1)	Contravention of regulating (other than regulations relating to addicts).	(*a*) Summary	—	—	—	6 months or the statutory maximum, or both.
		(*b*) On indictment.	—	—	—	2 years or a fine, or both.

Section creating Offence	General Nature of Offence	Mode of Prosecution	Punishment			
			Class A drug[3] involved	Class B drug[3] involved	Class C drug[3] involved	General
Section 18 (2)	Contravention of terms of licence or other authority (other than licence issued under regulations relating to addicts).	(*a*) Summary	—	—	—	6 months or the statutory maximum, or both.
		(*b*) On indictment.	—	—	—	2 years or a fine, or both.
Section 18(3)	Giving false information in purported compliance with obligation to give information imposed under or by virtue of regulations.	(*a*) Summary	—	—	—	6 months or the statutory maximum, or both.
		(*b*) On indictment.	—	—	—	2 years or a fine, or both.
Section 18(4)	Giving false information, or producing document etc., for purposes of obtaining issue or renewal of a licence or other authority.	(*a*) Summary.	—	—	—	6 months or the statutory maximum, or both.
		(*b*) On indictment.	—	—	—	2 years or a fine, or both.
Section 20	Assisting in or inducing commission outside United Kingdom of an offence punishable under a corresponding law.	(*a*) Summary.	—	—	—	6 months or the statutory maximum, or both.
		(*b*) On indictment.	—	—	—	14 years or a fine, or both.
Section 23(4)	Obstructing exercise of powers of search etc. or concealing books, drugs, etc.	(*a*) Summary.	—	—	—	6 months or the statutory maximum, or both.
		(*b*) On indictment.	—	—	—	2 years or a fine, or both.

3. See Sch 2, ante.

Poisons Act 1972

(1972 c 66)

8–21350 2. Poisons List[1]**.** (1) The list of substances treated as poisons for the purposes of the Pharmacy and Poisons Act 1933 shall continue to have effect for the purposes of this Act.

(2) *Power to amend the list referred to in subs.* (1); *in this Act referred to as "the Poisons List".*

(3), (4) *Division of Poisons List into two parts.*

[Poisons Act 1972, s 2.]

1. See the Poisons List Order 1982, SI 1982/217 amended by SI 1985/1077, SI 1986/10 and 1704 and SI 1992/2293.

8–21351 3. Regulation of sale of poisons. (1) Subject to the provisions of this Act, it shall not be lawful—

(*a*) for a person to sell any non-medicinal poison which is a substance included in Part I of the Poisons List, unless—

(i) he is a person lawfully conducting a retail pharmacy business, and
(ii) the sale is effected on premises which are a registered pharmacy, and
(iii) the sale is effected by, or under the supervision of, a pharmacist;

(*b*) for a person to sell any non-medicinal poison which is a substance included in Part II of the Poisons List, unless—

(i) he is a person lawfully conducting a retail pharmacy business and the sale is effected on premises which are a registered pharmacy, or
(ii) his name is entered in a local authority's list in respect of the premises on which the poison is sold;

(*c*) for a person to sell any non-medicinal poison, whether it is a substance included in Part I or in Part II of the Poisons List, unless the container of the poison is labelled in the prescribed manner—

(i) with the name of the poison, and
(ii) in the case of a preparation which contains a poison as one of its ingredients, with the prescribed particulars as to the proportion which the poison contained in the preparation bears to the total ingredients, and
(iii) with the word "poison" or other prescribed indication of the character of the article, and
(iv) with the name of the seller of the poison and the address of the premises on which it is sold.

(2) Subject to the provisions of this Act—

(*a*) it shall not be lawful to sell any non-medicinal poison which is a substance included in Part I of the Poisons List to any person unless that person is either—

(i) certified in writing in the prescribed manner by a person authorised by the Poisons Rule to give a certificate for the purposes of this section, or
(ii) known by the seller or by a pharmacist in the employment of the seller at the premises where the sale is effected,

to be a person to whom the poison may properly be sold;

(*b*) the seller of any such poison shall not deliver it until—

(i) he has made or caused to be made an entry in a book to be kept for that purpose stating in the prescribed form the date of the sale, the name and address of the purchaser and of the person (if any) by whom the certificate required under paragraph (*a*) above was given, the name and quantity of the article sold, and the purposes for which it is stated by the purchaser to be required, and
(ii) the purchaser has signed the entry.

(3) Subject to the provisions of this Act, it shall not be lawful for a non-medicinal poison to be exposed for sale in, or to be offered for sale by means of, an automatic machine.

[Poisons Act 1972, s 3.]

8–21352 4. Exclusion of sales by wholesale and certain other sales. Except as provided by the Poisons Rules, nothing in subsections (1) and (2) of section 3 of this Act shall extend to or interfere with—

(*a*) the sale of poisons by way of wholesale dealing;
(*b*) the sale of poisons to be exported to purchasers outside the United Kingdom;
(*c*) the sale of an article to a doctor, dentist, veterinary surgeon or veterinary practitioner for the purpose of his profession;

(*d*) the sale of an article for use in or in connection with any hospital, infirmary, dispensary or similar institution approved by an order, whether general or special, of the Secretary of State; or

(*e*) the sale of an article by a person carrying on a business in the course of which poisons are regularly sold either by way of wholesale dealing or for use by the purchasers in their trade or business to—

(i) a person who requires the article for the purpose of his trade or business, or

(ii) a person who requires the article for the purpose of enabling him to comply with any requirements made by or in pursuance of any enactment with respect to the medical treatment of persons employed by him in any trade or business carried on by him, or

(iii) a government department or an officer of the Crown requiring the article for the purposes of the public service, or any local authority (whether a local authority as defined in this Act or not) requiring the article in connection with the exercise by the authority of any statutory powers, or

(iv) a person or institution concerned with scientific education or research, if the article is required for the purposes of that education or research.

[Poisons Act 1972, s 4.]

8–21353 5. *List of persons entitled to sell poisons to be kept by local authority*

8–21354 **6. Supplementary provisions as to local authorities' lists.** (3) If any person whose name is entered in a local authority's list is convicted before any court of any offence which, in the opinion of the court, renders him unfit to have his name on the list, the court may, as part of the sentence, order his name to be removed from the list and direct that he shall, for such period as may be specified in the order, be disqualified for having his name entered in any local authority's list.

(4) It shall not be lawful for any person whose name is entered in a local authority's list to use in connection with his business any title, emblem or description reasonably calculated to suggest that he is entitled to sell any poison which he is not entitled to sell; and if any person acts in contravention of this subsection he shall be liable on summary conviction, in respect of each offence, to a fine not exceeding **level 2** on the standard scale and, in the case of a continuing offence, to a further fine not exceeding **£5** for every day subsequent to the day on which he is convicted of the offence during which the contravention continues.

[Poisons Act 1972, s 6, as amended by the Criminal Law Act 1977, Sch 6, the Local Government, Planning and Land Act 1980, Sch 6 and the Criminal Justice Act 1982, s 46.]

8–21355 7. *Power of Secretary of State to make rules*[1]

1. The Poisons Rules 1982, SI 1982/218 amended by SI 1985/1077, SI 1986/10 and 1704 and SI 1992/2293, have been made.

8–21356 **8. Penalties.** (1) A person who acts in contravention of or fails to comply with any of the preceding provisions of this Act (other than section 6(4)) or with the Poisons Rules shall, on summary conviction, be liable in respect of each offence to a fine not exceeding **level 4** on the standard scale, and, in the case of a continuing offence, to a further fine not exceeding **£10** for every day subsequent to the day on which he is convicted of the offence during which the contravention or default continues.

(2) In the case of proceedings against a person under this section for or in connection with the sale, exposure for sale or supply of a non-medicinal poison effected by an employee—

(*a*) it shall not be a defence that the employee acted without the authority of the employer, and

(*b*) any material fact known to the employee shall be deemed to have been known to the employer.

(3) Notwithstanding any provision in any Act prescribing the period within which summary proceedings may be commenced, proceedings for an offence under this Act may be commenced at any time within the period of twelve months next after the date of the commission of the offence or, in the case of proceedings instituted by, or by the direction of, the Secretary of State, either within that period or within the period of three months next after the date on which evidence sufficient in the opinion of the Secretary of State to justify a prosecution for the offence comes to his knowledge, whichever period ends on the later date.

For the purposes of this subsection, a certificate purporting to be signed by the Secretary of State as to the date on which such evidence came to his knowledge shall be conclusive evidence thereof.

(4) A document purporting to be a certificate signed by—

(*a*) a public analyst appointed under section 27 of the Food Safety Act 1990, or

(*b*) a person appointed by the Secretary of State to make analyses for the purposes of this Act,

stating the result of an analysis made by him, shall be admissible in any proceedings under this Act as evidence of the matters stated therein; but either party may require the person by whom the analysis was made to be called as a witness.

(5) *Scotland.*

[Poisons Act 1972, s 8, as amended by the Criminal Law Act 1977, Sch 6, the Criminal Justice Act 1982, s 46, the Food Act 1984, Sch 10 and the Food Safety Act 1990, Sch 3.]

8–21357 9. Inspection and enforcement. (1) It shall be the duty of the Pharmaceutical Society of Great Britain (in this section referred to as "the Society") to take all reasonable steps by means of inspection and otherwise—

(*a*) to enforce the provisions of subsections (2) and (3) of section 20 of the Pharmacy Act 1954 (offences relating to certificates), and

(*b*) to secure compliance by pharmacists and persons carrying on a retail pharmacy business with the preceding provisions of this Act and with the Poisons Rules;

and the Society shall for that purpose appoint such number of inspectors as the Privy Council may direct.

(2) A person shall not be qualified for appointment by the Society as inspector under this section unless he is a pharmacist, and every such appointment shall be subject to the approval of the Privy Council.

(3) A person appointed by the Society as inspector under this section shall hold office subject to such conditions with respect to salary and otherwise as the Council of the Society may with the approval of the Privy Council determine.

(4) An inspector appointed by the Society under this section—

(*a*) shall, for the purpose of enforcing the provisions of subsections (2) and (3) of section 20 of the Pharmacy Act 1954 and for securing compliance by pharmacists and persons carrying on a retail pharmacy business with the preceding provisions of this Act and with the Poisons Rules, have power at all reasonable times to enter any registered pharmacy, and

(*b*) shall, for the purpose of securing compliance by other persons with the preceding provisions of this Act and with the Poisons Rules, so far as those provisions and Rules relate to substances included in Part I of the Poisons List, have power to enter any premises in which he has reasonable cause to suspect that a breach of the law has been committed in relation to any such substances,

and in either case shall have power to make such examination and inquiry and to do such other things (including the taking, on payment, of samples) as may be necessary for ascertaining whether those provisions and Rules are being complied with.

(5) It shall be the duty of every local authority by means of inspection and otherwise to take all reasonable steps—

(*a*) to secure compliance by persons, not being persons lawfully conducting a retail pharmacy business, with the preceding provisions of this Act and with the Poisons Rules so far as those provisions and Rules relate to substances included in Part II of the Poisons List, and

(*b*) to secure compliance with those provisions and Rules by persons lawfully conducting a retail pharmacy business, in so far as that business is carried on at premises which are not a registered pharmacy,

and for those purposes to appoint inspectors; and an inspector appointed by the Society in pursuance of subsection (1) above may, with the consent of the Society, be appointed by a local authority to be also an inspector for the purposes of this subsection.

(6) An inspector appointed by the local authority shall, for the purposes of subsection (5) above, have power at all reasonable times to enter any premises on which any person whose name is entered in a local authority's list carries on business, and any premises on which the inspector has reasonable cause to suspect that a breach of the law has been committed in respect of any substances included in Part II of the Poisons List, and in either case shall have power to make such examination and inquiry and to do such other things (including the taking, on payment, of samples) as may be necessary for the purposes of the inspection.

(7) An inspector appointed by a local authority in England or Wales for the purposes of subsection (5) above shall have power with the consent of the local authority to institute proceedings under this Act before a court of summary jurisdiction in the name of the authority, and to conduct any proceedings so instituted by him notwithstanding that he is not of counsel or a solicitor.

(8) If a person—

(*a*) wilfully delays or obstructs an inspector in the exercise of any powers under this section, or

(*b*) refuses to allow any sample to be taken in accordance with the provisions of this section, or

(*c*) fails without reasonable excuse to give any information which he is duly required under this section to give,

he shall in respect of each offence be liable on summary conviction to a fine not exceeding **level 2** on the standard scale.

(9) Nothing in this section shall authorise any inspector to enter or inspect the premises, not being a shop, of a doctor, a dentist, a veterinary surgeon or a veterinary practitioner.

[Poisons Act 1972, s 9, as amended by the Criminal Law Act 1977, Sch 6 and the Criminal Justice Act 1982, s 46.]

8–21358 **11. Interpretation.** (1) In this Act "non-medicinal poison" means a substance which is included in Part I or Part II of the Poisons List and is neither—

(*a*) a medicinal product as defined by section 130 of the Medicines Act 1968, nor

(*b*) a substance in relation to which, by virtue of an order under section 104 or section 105 of that Act for the time being in force (and whether, in the case of an order under section 104 of that Act, it is referred to in the order as a substance or as an article), the provisions of sections 51 to 54 and sections 69 to 77 of that Act (whether subject to exceptions and modifications or not and with or without other provisions of that Act) have effect in relation to medicinal products as so defined.

(2) In this Act, unless the context otherwise requires, the following expressions have the following meanings, that is to say—

"the board" means, in relation to a body corporate, the persons controlling that body, by whatever name called;

"dentist" means a person registered in the dentists register kept under the Dentists Act 1984 or a person entered in the list of visiting EEA practitioners under Schedule 4 to that Act;

"doctor" means a registered medical practitioner within the meaning of Schedule 1 to the Interpretation Act 1978;

"local authority" means—

(*a*) in relation to England, the Council of a county, metropolitan district or London borough or the Common Council of the City of London,

(*aa*) in relation to Wales, the council of a county or county borough, and

(*b*) *Scotland*;

"local authority's list" means a list kept by a local authority under section 5 of this Act;

"person lawfully conducting a retail pharmacy business" shall be construed in accordance with section 69 of the Medicines Act 1968;

"pharmacist" means a person registered in the register of pharmaceutical chemists established in pursuance of the Pharmacy Act 1852 and maintained in pursuance of section 2(1) of the Pharmacy Act 1954;

"Poisons Rules" means rules made by the Secretary of State under section 7 of this Act;

"prescribed" means prescribed by the Poisons Rules;

"registered pharmacy" has the meaning assigned to it by section 74 of the Medicines Act 1968;

"retail pharmacy business" has the meaning assigned to it by section 132(1) of the Medicines Act 1968;

"sale by way of wholesale dealing" means sale to a person who buys for the purpose of selling again;

"veterinary practitioner" means a person registered in the supplementary veterinary register kept under section 8 of the Veterinary Surgeons Act 1966;

"veterinary surgeon" means a person registered in the register of veterinary surgeons kept under section 2 of the Veterinary Surgeons Act 1966.

[Poisons Act 1972, s 11, as amended by the Local Government Act 1972, Sch 29, the Medical Act 1983, Sch 5, the Dentists Act 1984, Sch 5, the Local Government Act 1985, Sch 8, the Local Government (Wales) Act 1994, Sch 16 and SI 1996/1496.]

8–21359 **13.** *Commencement and transitional provisions*

National Health Service Act 1977

(1977 c 49)

PART II[1]

Other provisions supplementary to Part II

8–21501 **54. Sale of medical practices.** (1) It is unlawful to sell the goodwill of the medical practice of a person who has at any time—

(*a*) provided general medical services under arrangements made with any Council, Committee or Authority under the National Health Service Act 1946, the National Health Service Reorganisation Act 1973 or this Act, or

(*b*) provided or performed personal medical services in accordance with section 28C arrangements[1],

unless that person no longer provides or performs such services and has never carried on the practice in a relevant area.

(2) In this section—

"goodwill" includes any part of goodwill and, in relation to a person practising in partnership, means his share of the goodwill of the partnership practice;

"medical practice" includes any part of a medical practice; and

"relevant area", in relation to any Council, Committee or Authority by arrangement with whom a person has at any time—

(*a*) provided general medical services, or

(*b*) provided or performed personal medical services in accordance with section 28C arrangements[1],

means the area, district or locality of that Council, Committee or Authority (at that time).

(3) Schedule 10 supplements the provisions of this section.*

[National Health Service Act 1977, s 54 as substituted by the Health Service (Primary Care) Act 1997, s 34.]

***Section substituted by the National Health Service (Primary Care) Act 1997, s 34(1), from a date to be appointed. Further amended by the Health and Social Care (Community Health and Standards) Act 2003, Sch 11, from a date to be appointed.**

1. The reference to arrangements made under s 28C of the 1977 Act is to be taken as referring only to a pilot scheme under Part 1 of the Act under which personal medical services are to be provided: National Health Service (Primary Care) Act 1997 (Commencement No 4) Order 1998, SI 1998/631 art 3(2).

PART III[1]

OTHER POWERS OF THE SECRETARY OF STATE AS TO THE HEALTH SERVICE

Control of maximum prices for medical supplies

8–21502 57. Maximum price of medical supplies may be controlled. (1) The Secretary of State may by order provide for controlling maximum prices to be charged for any medical supplies required for the purposes of this Act.

(2) The Secretary of State may by direction given with respect to any undertaking, or by order made with respect to any class or description of undertakings, being an undertaking or class or description of undertakings concerned with medical supplies required for the purposes of this Act, require persons carrying on the undertaking or undertakings of that class or description—

(*a*) to keep such books, accounts and records relating to the undertaking as may be prescribed by the direction or, as the case may be, by the order or a notice served under the order;

(*b*) to furnish at such times, in such manner and in such form as may be so prescribed such estimates, returns or information relating to the undertaking as may be so prescribed.

(3) The additional provisions set out in Schedule 11[2] to this Act have effect in relation to this section; and

"medical supplies" in this section includes surgical, dental and optical materials and equipment; and

"undertaking" in this section and that Schedule means any public utility undertaking or any undertaking by way of trade or business.

[National Health Service Act 1977, s 57.]

---

1. Part III contains ss 57–86.
2. Post.

Inquiries, and default and emergency powers

8–21503 84. Inquiries. *Repealed.*

PART VI[1]

MISCELLANEOUS AND SUPPLEMENTARY

General provisions as to charges

8–21504 122. Recovery of charges. (1) All charges[2] recoverable under this Act by the Secretary of State, a local social services authority[3], or any body constituted under this Act or Part I of the National Health Service and Community Care Act 1990 or Part 1 of the Health and Social Care (Community Health and Standards) Act 2003, may, without prejudice to any other method of recovery, be recovered summarily as a civil debt[4].

(2) If any person, for the purpose of evading the payment of any charge under this Act, or of reducing the amount of any such charge—

(*a*) knowingly makes any false statement or false representation, or

(*b*) produces or furnishes, or causes or knowingly allows to be produced or furnished, any document or information which he knows to be false in a material particular,

the charge, or as the case may be the balance of the charge, may be recovered from him by the person by whom the cost of the service in question was defrayed.

[National Health Service Act 1977, s 122, as amended by the National Health Service and Community Care Act 1990, Sch 9, the Health Act 1999, Schs 4 and 5 and Health and Social Care (Community Health and Standards) Act 2003, Sch 4.]

1. Part VI contains ss 121–130.

2. Charges may be for accommodation or services provided under the Act (s 58); in respect of part of the cost of accommodation in single rooms or small wards where an undertaking to pay is given (s 63); for accommodation and services for private resident patients (s 65) and for care of mothers and young children; prevention, care and after-care services and home help and laundry facilities provided by local social services authorities (Sch 8).

3. "Local social services authority" means the council of a non-metropolitan county, of a county borough or of a metropolitan district or London borough, or the Common Council of the City of London (National Health Service Act 1977, s 128(1)).

4. For procedure for recovery of a civil debt summarily, see s 58 of the Magistrates' Courts Act 1980 in PART I: MAGISTRATES' COURTS, PROCEDURE, ante.

8–21504A 122A. Recovery of other charges and payments[1]. (1) Where goods or services to which this section applies are provided and either—

(*a*) any charge payable by any person under this Act in respect of the provision of the goods or services is reduced, remitted or repaid, but that person is not entitled to the reduction, remission or repayment, or

(*b*) any payment under this Act is made to, or for the benefit of, any person in respect of the cost of obtaining the goods or services, but that person is not entitled to, or to the benefit of, the payment,

the amount mentioned in subsection (2) below is recoverable summarily as a civil debt[2] from the person in question by the responsible authority.

(2) That amount—

(*a*) in a case within subsection (1)(*a*) above, is the amount of the charge or (where it has been reduced) reduction,

(*b*) in a case within subsection (1)(*b*) above, is the amount of the payment.

(3) Where two or more persons are liable under section 122(1) above or this section to pay an amount in respect of the same charge or payment, those persons shall be jointly and severally liable.

(4) For the purposes of this section, the circumstances in which a person is to be treated as not entitled to a reduction, remission or repayment of a charge, or to (or to the benefit of) a payment, include in particular those in which it is received (wholly or partly)—

(*a*) on the ground that he or another is a person of a particular description, where the person in question is not in fact of that description,

(*b*) on the ground that he or another holds a particular certificate, when the person in question does not in fact hold such a certificate or does hold such a certificate but is not entitled to it,

(*c*) on the ground that he or another has made a particular statement, when the person in question has not made such a statement or the statement made by him is false.

(5) In this section and section 122B below, "responsible authority" means—

(*a*) in relation to the recovery of any charge under section 122(1) above in respect of the provision of goods or services to which this section applies, the person by whom the charge is recoverable,

(*b*) in relation to the recovery by virtue of this section of the whole or part of the amount of any such charge, the person by whom the charge would have been recoverable,

(*c*) in a case within subsection (1)(*b*) above, the person who made the payment.

(6) But the Secretary of State may by directions provide for—

(*a*) the functions of any responsible authority of recovering any charges under this Act in respect of the provision of goods or services to which this section applies,

(*b*) the functions of any responsible authority under this section and section 122B below,

to be exercised on behalf of the authority by another health service body.

(7) This section applies to the following goods and services—

(*a*) dental treatment and appliances provided in pursuance of this Act,

(*b*) drugs and medicines provided in pursuance of this Act,

(*c*) the testing of sight,

(*d*) optical appliances,

(*e*) any other appliances provided in pursuance of this Act.

[National Health Service Act 1977, s 122A, as inserted by the Health Act 1999, s 39.]

1. Sections 122A to 122C of this Act also apply to charges which may be made and recovered under s 20 of the national Health Service (Primary Care) Act 1997 as they apply to charges under the 1977 Act which may be recovered under s 122(1)(*a*) to the 1977 Act includes a reference to a pilot scheme (within the meaning of the 1977 Act) (Health Act 1999, s 39(3)).

8–21504B 122B. Penalties[1]. (1) Regulations may provide that, where a person fails to pay—

(*a*) any amount recoverable from him under section 122(1) above in respect of the provision of goods or services to which section 122A above applies, or

(*b*) any amount recoverable from him under section 122A above, a notice (referred to in this section as a penalty notice) may be served on the person by the responsible authority requiring him to pay to the authority, within a prescribed period, that amount together with a charge (referred to in this section as a penalty charge) of an amount determined in accordance with the regulations.

(2) The regulations may not provide for the amount of the penalty charge to exceed whichever is the smaller of—

(*a*) £100,
(*b*) the amount referred to in subsection (1)(*a*) or (*b*) above multiplied by 5.

(3) The Secretary of State may by order provide for subsection (2) above to have effect as if, for the sum specified in paragraph (*a*) or the multiplier specified in paragraph (*b*) (including that sum or multiplier as substituted by a previous order), there were substituted a sum or (as the case may be) multiplier specified in the order.

(4) Regulations may provide that, if a person fails to pay the amount he is required to pay under a penalty notice within the period in question, he must also pay to the responsible authority by way of penalty a further sum determined in accordance with the regulations.

(5) The further sum must not exceed 50 per cent of the amount of the penalty charge.

(6) Any sum payable under the regulations (including the amount referred to in subsection (1)(*a*) or (*b*) above) may be recovered by the responsible authority summarily as a civil debt[2].

(7) But a person is not liable by virtue of a penalty notice—

(*a*) to pay at any time so much of any amount referred to in subsection (1)(*a*) or (*b*) above for which he is jointly and severally liable with another as at that time has been paid, or ordered by a court to be paid, by that other, or
(*b*) to a penalty charge, or a further sum by way of penalty, if he shows that he did not act wrongfully, or with any lack of care, in respect of the charge or payment in question.

(8) In spite of section 126(1) below, no order is to be made under subsection (3) above unless a draft has been laid before, and approved by resolution of, each House of Parliament.
[National Health Service Act 1977, s 122B as inserted by the Health Act 1999, s 39.]

1. See note 1 to s 122A in paragraph **8–21504A**, ante.
2. For procedure for recovery of a civil debt summarily, see s 58 of the Magistrates' Court Act 1980 in PART 1: MAGISTRATES' COURTS, PROCEDURE, ante.

8–21504C 122C. Offences[1]. (1) A person is guilty of an offence if he does any act mentioned in subsection (2) below with a view to securing for himself or another—

(*a*) the evasion of the whole or part of any charge under this Act in respect of the provision of goods or services to which section 122A above applies,
(*b*) the reduction, remission or repayment of any such charge, where he or (as the case may be) the other is not entitled to the reduction, remission or repayment,
(*c*) a payment under this Act (whether to, or for the benefit of, himself or the other) in respect of the cost of obtaining such goods or services, where he or (as the case may be) the other is not entitled to, or to the benefit of, the payment.

(2) The acts referred to in subsection (1) above are—

(*a*) knowingly making, or causing or knowingly allowing another to make, a false statement or representation, or
(*b*) in the case of any document or information which he knows to be false in a material particular, producing or providing it or causing or knowingly allowing another to produce or provide it.

(3) A person guilty of an offence under this section is liable on summary conviction to a fine not exceeding level 4 on the standard scale.

(4) A person, although he is not a barrister or solicitor, may conduct any proceedings under this section before a magistrates' court if he is authorised to do so by the Secretary of State.

(5) Proceedings for an offence under this section may be begun within either of the following periods—

(*a*) the period of three months beginning with the date on which evidence, sufficient in the opinion of the Secretary of State to justify a prosecution for the offence, comes to his knowledge,
(*b*) the period of 12 months beginning with the commission of the offence.

(6) For the purposes of subsection (5) above, a certificate purporting to be signed by or on behalf of the Secretary of State as to the date on which such evidence as is mentioned in paragraph (*a*) of that subsection came to his knowledge is conclusive evidence of that date.

(7) Where, in respect of any charge or payment under this Act—

(*a*) a person is convicted of an offence under this section, or
(*b*) a person pays any penalty charge, and any further sum by way of penalty, recoverable from him under section 122B above,

he shall not, in a case within paragraph (*a*) above, be liable to pay any such penalty charge or further sum by way of penalty or, in a case within paragraph (*b*) above, be convicted of such an offence.

(8) Subsection (4) of section 122A above applies for the purposes of this section as it applies for the purposes of that.

[National Health Service Act 1977, s 122C, as inserted by the Health Act 1999, s 39.]

---

1. See note 1 to s 122A in para **8–21504A**, ante.

8–21505 124. Special notices of births and deaths. (1) The requirements of this section with respect to the notification of births and deaths are in addition to, and not in substitution for, the requirements of any Act relating to the registration of births and deaths.

(2)–(3) *Duty of registrar of births and deaths to furnish particulars.*

(4) In the case of every child born, it is the duty—

(*a*) of the child's father, if at the time of the birth he is actually residing on the premises where the birth takes place, and

(*b*) of any person in attendance upon the mother at the time of, or within six hours after, the birth,

to give notice of the birth (as provided in subsection (5) below) to the prescribed Health Authority for the area in which the birth takes place.

This subsection applies to any child which has issued forth from its mother after the expiry of the twenty-eighth week of pregnancy whether alive or dead.

(5) Notice under subsection (4) above shall be given either—

(*a*) by posting within 36 hours after the birth a prepaid letter or postcard addressed to the prescribed Health Authority at their offices and containing the required information, or

(*b*) by delivering within that period at that officer's office a written notice containing the required information,

and a Health Authority shall, upon application to them, supply without charge to any medical practitioner or midwife residing or practising within their area prepaid addressed envelopes together with the forms of notice.

(6) Any person who fails to give notice of a birth in accordance with subsection (4) above is liable on summary conviction to a fine not exceeding **level 1** on the standard scale, unless he satisfies the court that he believed, and had reasonable grounds for believing, that notice had been duly given by some other person.

Proceedings in respect of this offence shall not, without the Attorney-General's written consent, be taken by any person other than a party aggrieved or the Health Authority concerned.

(7) A registrar of births and deaths shall, for the purpose of obtaining information concerning births which have occurred in his sub-district, have access at all reasonable times to notices of births received by a Health Authority under this section, or to any book in which those notices may be recorded.

[National Health Service Act 1977, s 124, amended by the Criminal Law Act 1977, s 31, the Health Services Act 1980, Sch 1, the Criminal Justice Act 1982, s 46 and the Health Authorities Act 1995, Schs 1 and 3.]

Section 54

SCHEDULE 10

ADDITIONAL PROVISIONS AS TO PROHIBITION OF SALE OF MEDICAL PRACTICES

(Amended by the Criminal Law Act 1977, s 32, the National Health Service (Primary Care) Act 1997, Sch 2, the Health and Social Care Act 2001, s 14(3) and the Health and Social Care (Community Health and Standards) Act 2003, Sch 11.)

Prohibition, and certificate of the Secretary of State

8–21506 1. (1) Any person who sells or buys the goodwill of a medical practice which it is unlawful to sell by virtue of section 54(1) above is guilty of an offence and liable on conviction on indictment to a fine not exceeding—

(*a*) such amount as will in the court's opinion secure that he derives no benefit from the offence, and

(*b*) the further amount of £500,

or to imprisonment for a term not exceeding **three months**, or to both such fine and such imprisonment.

(2) Any person proposing to be a party to a transaction or a series of transactions which he thinks might amount to a sale of the goodwill of a medical practice in contravention of section 54(1) may ask the Secretary of State for a certificate under this paragraph.

(3) The Secretary of State shall consider any such application, and, if he is satisfied that the transaction or series of transactions does not involve the giving of valuable consideration in respect of the goodwill of such a medical practice, he shall issue to the applicant a certificate to that effect, which shall be in the prescribed form and shall set out all material circumstances disclosed to the Secretary of State.

(4) Where any person is charged with an offence under this paragraph in respect of any transaction or series of transactions, it shall be a defence to the charge to prove that the transaction or series of transactions was certified by the Secretary of State under sub-paragraph (3) above.

(5) Any document purporting to be such a certificate shall be admissible in evidence and shall be deemed to be such a certificate unless the contrary is proved.

(6) If it appears to the court that the applicant for any such certificate failed to disclose to the Secretary of State

all the material circumstances, or made any misrepresentation with respect thereto, the court may disregard the certificate, and sub-paragraph (4) shall not apply thereto.

(7) A prosecution for an offence under this paragraph shall only be instituted by or with the consent of the Director of Public Prosecutions, and the Secretary of State shall, at the request of the Director, furnish him with a copy of any certificate issued by the Secretary of State under sub-paragraph (3), and with copies of any documents produced to him in connection with the application for that certificate.

(8) *Repealed.*

2. *Certain transactions deemed sale of goodwill.*

Carried-over goodwill

3. The fact that a person's medical practice was previously carried on by another person who at any time provided or performed services as specified in section 54(1)does not, by itself, make it unlawful under section 54(1) for the goodwill of his practice to be sold.

Section 57

SCHEDULE 11[1]

ADDITIONAL PROVISIONS AS TO THE CONTROL OF MAXIMUM PRICES FOR MEDICAL SUPPLIES

(Amended by the Criminal Law Act 1977, ss 28–32, the British Nationality Act 1981, Sch 7, the Criminal Justice Act 1982, ss 38 and 46 and SI 2004/3363.)

Orders and directions

8–21507 **1.** (1) Any power of making orders under section 57 above includes power to provide for any incidental and supplementary provisions which the Secretary of State thinks it expedient for the purposes of the order to provide.

(2) An order under section 57 may make such provisions (including provision for requiring any person to furnish any information) as the Secretary of State thinks necessary or expedient for facilitating the introduction or operation of a scheme of control for which provision has been made, or for which, in his opinion, it will or may be found necessary or expedient that provision should be made, under that section.

(3) An order under section 57 may prohibit the doing of anything regulated by the order except under the authority of a licence granted by such authority or person as may be specified in the order, and may be made so as to apply either to persons or undertakings generally or to any particular person or undertaking or class of persons or undertakings, and so as to have effect either generally or in any particular area.

(4) The Interpretation Act 1889 shall apply to the interpretation of any order made under section 57 as it applies to the interpretation of an Act of Parliament and for the purposes of section 38 of that Act any such order shall be deemed to be an Act of Parliament.

---

1. Schedule 11 repealed in relation to health service medicines by the Health Act 1999, s 38 and Sch 5.

Notices, authorisations and proof of documents

8–21508 **2.** (1) A notice to be served on any person for the purposes of section 57 above, or of any order or direction made or given under that section, shall be deemed to have been duly served on the person to whom it is directed if—

(*a*) it is delivered to him personally; or

(*b*) it is sent by registered post or the recorded delivery service addressed to him at his last or usual place of abode or place of business.

(2) Where under section 57 and this Schedule a person has power to authorise other persons to act thereunder, the power may be exercised so as to confer the authority either on particular persons or on a specified class of persons.

(3) Any permit, licence, permission or authorisation granted for the purposes of section 57 may be revoked at any time by the authority or person empowered to grant it.

(4) Every document purporting to be an instrument made or issued by the Secretary of State or other authority or person in pursuance of section 57 and this Schedule or any provisions so having effect and to be signed by or on behalf of the Secretary of State, or that authority or person, shall be received in evidence and shall until the contrary is proved, be deemed to be an instrument made or issued by the Secretary of State, or that authority or person.

(5) Prima facie evidence of any such instrument as is described in sub-paragraph (4) above may in any legal proceedings (including arbitrations) be given by the production of a document purporting to be certified to be a true copy of the instrument by or on behalf of the Secretary of State or other authority or person having power to make or issue the instrument.

Territorial extent

8–21509 **3.** So far as any provisions contained in or having effect under section 57 above and this Schedule impose prohibitions, restrictions or obligations on persons, those provisions apply to all persons in the United Kingdom and all persons on board any British ship or aircraft, not being an excepted ship or aircraft, and to all other persons, wherever they may be, who are ordinarily resident in the United Kingdom and who are citizens of the United Kingdom and Colonies or British protected persons.

In this paragraph—

"British aircraft" means an aircraft registered in—

(*a*) any part of Her Majesty's dominions;

(*b*) any country outside Her Majesty's dominions in which for the time being Her Majesty has jurisdiction;

(*c*) any country consisting partly of one or more colonies and partly of one or more such countries as are mentioned in paragraph (*b*) above;

"British protected person" means the same as in the British Nationality Act 1981;

"excepted ship or aircraft" means a ship or aircraft registered in any country for the time being listed in Schedule 3 to the British Nationality Act 1981 or in any territory administered by the government of any such country, not being a ship or aircraft for the time being placed at the disposal of, or chartered by or on behalf of, Her Majesty's Government in the United Kingdom.

False documents and false statements

8–21510 **4.** (1) A person shall not, with intent to deceive—

(*a*) use any document issued for the purpose of section 57 above and this Schedule or of any order made under that section;

(*b*) have in his possession any document so closely resembling such a document as is described in paragraph (*a*) above as to be calculated to deceive;

(*c*) produce, furnish, send or otherwise make use of for purposes connected with that section and this Schedule or any order or direction made or given under that section, any book, account, estimate, return, declaration or other document which is false in a material particular.

(2) A person shall not, in furnishing any information for the purposes of section 57 and this Schedule or of any order made under that section, make a statement which he knows to be false in a material particular or recklessly make a statement which is false in a material particular.

Restrictions on disclosing information

8–21511 **5.** No person who obtains any information by virtue of section 57 above and this Schedule shall, otherwise than in connection with the execution of that section and this Schedule or of an order made under that section, disclose that information except for the purposes of any criminal proceedings, or of a report of any criminal proceedings, or with permission granted by or on behalf of a Minister of the Crown.

8–21511A **5A.** Paragraph 5 above does not apply if—

(*a*) the person making the disclosure referred to in that section is, or is acting on behalf of a person who is, a public authority for the purposes of the Freedom of Information Act 2000, and

(*b*) the information is not held by the authority on behalf of another person.

Offences by corporations

8–21512 **6.** Where an offence under this Schedule committed by a body corporate is proved to have been committed with the consent or connivance of, or to be attributable to any neglect on the part of, any director, manager, secretary or other similar officer of the body corporate or any person who was purporting to act in any such capacity, he, as well as the body corporate, shall be guilty of that offence and shall be liable to be proceeded against and punished accordingly.

In this paragraph, the expression "director", in relation to a body corporate established by or under any enactment for the purpose of carrying on under national ownership any industry or part of an industry or undertaking, being a body corporate whose affairs are managed by its members, means a member of that body corporate.

Penalties

8–21513 **7.** (1) If any person contravenes or fails to comply with any order made under section 57 above, or any direction given or requirement imposed under that section, or contravenes or fails to comply with this Schedule (except for paragraph 8(3) or paragraph 9(4) below) he is, save as otherwise expressly provided, guilty of an offence.

(2) Subject to any special provisions contained in this Schedule, a person guilty of such an offence, shall[1]—

(*a*) on summary conviction, be liable to imprisonment for a term not exceeding **three months** or to a fine not exceeding **the statutory maximum**, or to **both**; or

(*b*) on conviction on indictment be liable to imprisonment for a term not exceeding **two years** or to a **fine**, or to **both**.

(3) Where a person convicted on indictment of such an offence is a body corporate, no provision limiting the amount of the fine which may be imposed shall apply, and the body corporate shall be liable to a fine of such amount as the court thinks just.

---

1. For procedure in respect of this offence, triable either way, see the Magistrates' Courts Act 1980, ss 17A–21, in PART I: MAGISTRATES' COURTS, PROCEDURE, ante.

Production of documents

8–21514 **8.** (1) for the purposes—

(*a*) of securing compliance with any order made or direction given under section 57 above by or on behalf of the Secretary of State, or

(*b*) of verifying any estimates, returns or information furnished to the Secretary of State in connection with section 57 or any order made or direction given under that section,

an officer of the Secretary of State duly authorised in that behalf has power, on producing (if required to do so) evidence of his authority, to require any person carrying on an undertaking or employed in connection with an undertaking to produce to that officer forthwith any documents relating to the undertaking which that officer may reasonably require for the purpose set out above.

(2) The power conferred by this paragraph to require any person to produce documents includes power—

(*a*) if the documents are produced, to take copies of them or extracts from them and to require that person, or where that person is a body corporate, any other person who is a present or past officer of, or is employed by, the body corporate, to provide an explanation of any of them;

(*b*) if the documents are not produced, to require the person who was required to produce them to state, to the best of his knowledge and belief, where they are.

(3) If any requirement to produce documents or provide an explanation or make a statement which is imposed by virtue of this paragraph is not complied with, the person on whom the requirement was so imposed is guilty of an offence and liable on summary conviction to imprisonment for a term not exceeding **three months** or to a fine not exceeding **level 3** on the standard scale, or to both.

Where a person is charged with such an offence in respect of a requirement to produce any document, it shall be a defence to prove that they were not in his possession or under his control and that it was not reasonably practicable for him to comply with the requirements.

9. (1) If a justice of the peace is satisfied, on information on oath laid on the Secretary of State's behalf, that there are any reasonable grounds for suspecting that there are on any premises any documents of which production has been required by virtue of paragraph 8 above and which have not been produced in compliance with that requirement, he may issue a warrant under this paragraph.

A warrant so issued may authorise any constable, together with the other persons named in the warrant and any other constables—

(*a*) to enter the premises specified in the information (using such force as is reasonably necessary for the purpose); and

(*b*) to search the premises and take possession of any documents appearing to be such documents as are mentioned above, or to take in relation to any documents so appearing any other steps which may appear necessary for preserving them and preventing interference with them.

(2) Every warrant issued under this paragraph shall continue in force until the end of the period of one month after the date on which it is issued.

(3) Any documents of which possession is taken under this paragraph may be retained for a period of three months or, if within that period there are commenced any proceedings for an offence under section 57 above and this Schedule to which they are relevant, until the conclusion of those proceedings.

(4) Any person who obstructs the exercise of any right of entry or search conferred by virtue of a warrant under this paragraph, or who obstructs the exercise of any rights so conferred to take possession of any documents, is guilty of an offence and liable on summary conviction to imprisonment for a term not exceeding **three months** or to a fine not exceeding **level 3** on the standard scale, or to both.

Medical Act 1983[1]

(1983 c 54)

PART II[2]

MEDICAL EDUCATION AND REGISTRATION: PERSONS QUALIFYING IN THE UNITED KINGDOM AND ELSEWHERE IN THE EEA

8–21517 **18. Visiting EEA practitioners.** (1) If he complies with the requirements of this section it shall be lawful for a person who is a national[3] of any EEA State and lawfully established in medical practice in an EEA State other than the United Kingdom on visiting the United Kingdom to render medical services there temporarily without first being registered under the foregoing provisions of this Part or under Part III of this Act.

(2) Such a person intending so to render services shall provide the Registrar with—

(*a*) a declaration in writing giving particulars of the services to be rendered and the period or periods in which he expects to render them; and

(*b*) a certificate or certificates issued by the competent authority or body and bearing a date not less recent than 12 months prior to the date on which it is provided, which shows—

(i) that he is lawfully practising medicine in an EEA State other than the United Kingdom, and

(ii) that he holds medical qualifications which EEA States are required by the Directive 93/16/EEC to recognise;

and for the purposes of this subsection "the competent authority or body" means the authority or body designated by the EEA State concerned as competent for the purposes of Article 17(3) of that Directive.

(3) In an urgent case the documents to be provided under subsection (2) above may be provided after the services have been rendered, but where they are so provided they shall be provided as soon as possible thereafter and in any event not more than 15 days after the date on which the practitioner first rendered such services.

(4) Where a person complies with the requirements of subsection (2) above, the Registrar shall register him under this section in the register of medical practitioners as a visiting EEA practitioner for such period or periods as, having regard to the particulars given in the declaration referred to in subsection (2)(*a*) above, he considers appropriate.

(5) Registration of a person as a visiting EEA practitioner shall cease if—

(*a*) he becomes established in medical practice in the United Kingdom; or (*b*) he renders, save in a case of urgency, medical services in the United Kingdom otherwise than in accordance with a declaration made by him under subsection (2)(*a*) above.

(6) Any person who—

(*a*) is not a national of an EEA State; but

(*b*) is, by virtue of a right conferred by article 11 of Regulation (EEC) No. 1612/68, or any other enforceable Community right, entitled to be treated, for the purposes of access to the medical profession, no less favourably than a national of such a State,

shall be treated for the purposes of this section as if he were such a national.
[Medical Act 1983, s 18, as amended by SI 1996/1591.]

1. This Act consolidates the Medical Acts 1956 to 1978. The Act provides for the continuance of the General Medical Council (referred to in the Act as "the General Council") and its constitution. The General Council is responsible for the registration of medical practitioners, and the Registrar of the General Council is required to keep two registers of medical practitioners registered under the Act containing the names of those registered and the qualifications they are entitled to have registered. The two registers are "the register of medical practitioners", consisting of four lists, namely (*a*) the principal list, (*b*) the overseas list, (*c*) the visiting overseas doctors list, and (*d*) the visiting EEA practitioners list, and "the register of medical practitioners with limited registration". Medical practitioners shall be registered as fully registered medical practitioners, or provisionally or with limited registration as provided in Parts II and III of the Act and in the appropriate list of the register (s 2). Recognition of primary European qualifications and entitlement to full registration is provided by amendments to the Act by the European Primary Medical Qualifications Regulations 1996, SI 1996/1591.

2. Part II contains ss 3–18.

3. For meaning of "national", in relation to an EEA State, see s 55, post.

PART VI[1]

PRIVILEGES OF REGISTERED PRACTITIONERS

8–21518 **48. Certificates invalid if not signed by fully registered practitioner.** A certificate required by any enactment, whether passed before or after the commencement of this Act, from any physician, surgeon, licentiate in medicine and surgery or other medical practitioner[2] shall not be valid unless the person signing it is fully registered.
[Medical Act 1983, s 48.]

1. Part VI contains ss 46–49.

2. Reference in any enactment to a "registered medical practitioner" means a fully registered person within the meaning of the Medical Act 1983 (Interpretation Act 1978, Sch 1, in PART II: EVIDENCE, ante).

8–21519 **49. Penalty for pretending to be registered[1].** (1) Subject to subsection (2) below, any person who wilfully and falsely pretends to be or takes or uses the name or title of physician, doctor of medicine, licentiate in medicine and surgery, bachelor of medicine, surgeon, general practitioner or apothecary, or any name, title, addition or description implying that he is registered[2] under any provision of this Act[3], or that he is recognised by law as a physician or surgeon or licentiate in medicine and surgery or a practitioner in medicine or an apothecary, shall be liable on summary conviction to a fine not exceeding **level 5** on the standard scale.

(2) Subsection (1) above shall not apply to anything done by a person who is a national[4] of any EEA State for the purposes of or in connection with the lawful rendering of medical services by him without first being registered under this Act if he has previously complied with the requirements of subsection (2) of section 18[5] above or subsequently complies with its requirements as modified in respect of urgent cases by subsection (3) of that section.

(3)–(4) *Scotland.*
[Medical Act 1983, s 49, as amended by the Statute Law (Repeals) Act 1993, Sch 1 and SI 1996/1591.]

1. Reference in any enactment to a "registered medical practitioner" means a fully registered person within the meaning of the Medical Act 1983 (Interpretation Act 1978, Sch 1, in PART II: EVIDENCE, ante).

2. The Registrar is required by s 34 of the Act to cause to be printed, published and sold, under the direction of the General Council, a publication called "the Medical Register", being a register of all persons appearing in the principal list in the register of medical practitioners, as existing on the 1st January in that year except those whose registration is suspended or subject to conditions. The General Council may also direct publication of "the Overseas Medical Register". A copy of either publication purporting to be printed and published in accordance with s 34 shall be evidence that the persons specified therein are registered fully or provisionally in the principal list or the overseas list in the register of medical practitioners, as appears from the publication; and the absence of the name of any person from such a copy shall be evidence that he is not registered under ss 3, 15, 19 or 21 of the Act (s 34).

3. A person on whom the degree of doctor of medicine has been conferred by a genuine, and not a bogus, university, is entitled to describe himself as a doctor of medicine in circumstances which, as the justices may find, do not imply that he is registered under the Act (*Younghusband v Luftig* [1942] 2 KB 354, [1949] 2 All ER 72, 113 JP 366, in which all previous relevant decisions were reviewed; applied in *Wilson v Inyang* [1951] 2 KB 799, [1952] 2 All ER 237, 115 JP 411).

4. For the meaning of "national", in relation to an EEA State, see s 55, post.

5. Ante.

8–21519A **49. Penalty for pretending to hold a licence to practise.** (1) If a person who does not hold a licence to practise—

(*a*) holds himself out as having such a licence; or

(*b*) engages in conduct calculated to suggest that he has such a licence,

shall be liable on summary conviction to a fine not exceeding **level 5** on the standard scale.

(2)–(3) *Scotland.*

[Medical Act 1983, s 49A, as inserted by SI 2002/3135.]

PART VII[1]

MISCELLANEOUS AND GENERAL

8–21520 **54. Saving for certain occupations.** Nothing in this Act shall prejudice or in any way affect the lawful occupation, trade, or business of chemists and druggists and dentists, or the rights, privileges or employment of duly licensed apothecaries in Northern Ireland, so far as the occupation, trade or business extends to selling, compounding or dispensing medicines.

[Medical Act 1983, s 54.]

1. Part VII contains ss 50–57.

8–21521 **55. Interpretation[1].** (1) In this Act—

"fully registered person" means a person for the time being registered under section 3, 19 or 27 above as a fully registered medical practitioner, or under section 18 above as a visiting EEA practitioner, and—

(*a*) so far as mentioned in subsection (3) of section 15 (including that subsection as applied by section 15A(4)) or 21 above, but not further, includes a person for the time being provisionally registered;

(*b*) in relation to such employment and such things as are mentioned in paragraphs (*a*), (*b*) and (*c*) of subsection (7) of section 22 above, but not in relation to other matters, includes a person for the time being registered under that section with limited registration;

and "fully registered" shall be construed accordingly;

"the General Council" means the General Medical Council;

"limited registration" has the meaning given by section 22(2) above;

"national", in relation to a EEA State, has the same meaning as in the Community Treaties, but does not include a person who by virtue of Article 2 of Protocol No 3 (Channel Islands and Isle of Man) to the Treaty of Accession is not to benefit from Community provisions relating to the free movement of persons and services;

"provisionally registered" means provisionally registered under section 15, 15A or 21 above;

"the register" means the register of medical practitioners, except that, in relation to a person registered with limited registration, it means the register of medical practitioners with limited registration;

"the Registrar" has the meaning given by section 2(1) above but subject to sub-paragraph (3) of paragraph 16 of Schedule 1 to this Act;

(2) *Repealed.*

[Medical Act 1983, s 55, as amended by SI 1996/1591, SI 2000/3041 and SI 2002/3135—abridged.]

1. Only those definitions which are likely to be relevant to the work of magistrates' courts are included in this work.

Anatomy Act 1984

(1984 c 14)

Introductory

8–21620 **1. Definitions, and scope of Act.** (1) In this Act "anatomical examination" means the examination by dissection of a body for purposes of teaching or studying, or researching into, morphology; and where parts of a body are separated in the course of its anatomical examination, such examination includes the examination by dissection of the parts for those purposes.

(2) In this Act "anatomical specimen" means—

(*a*) a body to be used for anatomical examination, or

(*b*) a body in course of being used for anatomical examination (including separated parts of such a body).

(3) In this Act "body" means the body of a deceased person.

(4) Nothing in this Act applies to anything done for the purposes of a post-mortem examination requested or required or directed to be made by a competent legal authority or carried out for the purpose of establishing or confirming the causes of death or of investigating the existence or nature of abnormal conditions.

(5) If part of a body is authorised under section 1 of the Human Tissue Act 1961 to be removed for purposes of medical education or research, that section (and not this Act) applies to the removal

and use of the part, even if the education or research consists of or involves anatomical examination; but the preceding provisions of this subsection do not prevent this Act applying as regards the body after such removal or where no such removal is made.*
[Anatomy Act 1984, s 1.]

***Repealed, in relation to England and Wales, by the Human Tissue Act 2004, Sch 7 from a date to be appointed.**

Anatomical examination

8–21621 **2. Control of examinations and possession.** (1) No person shall carry out an anatomical examination unless—

(*a*) he carries it out on premises which at the time of the examination are licensed under section 3(1),
(*b*) he is authorised to carry it out under section 3(3),
(*c*) at the time the examination is carried out it is lawful by virtue of section 4, and
(*d*) death has been registered, in the case of the body concerned, under section 15 of the 1953 Act or section 22 of the 1965 Act.

(2) Subject to subsection (3), no person shall have an anatomical specimen in his possession unless—

(*a*) he is authorised to have possession under section 3(4),
(*b*) anatomical examination of the specimen is at the time concerned lawful by virtue of section 4, and
(*c*) a certificate of cause of death has been signed, in the case of the body concerned, in accordance with section 22(1) of the 1953 Act or section 24 of the 1965 Act.

(3) Subsection (2) does not apply where a person came into lawful possession of a body immediately after death and retained possession prior to its removal to the place where anatomical examination is to take place.

(4) In this section "the 1953 Act" means the Births and Deaths Registration Act 1953 and "the 1965 Act" means the Registration of Births, Deaths and Marriages (Scotland) Act 1965.*
[Anatomy Act 1984, s 2.]

***Repealed, in relation to England and Wales, by the Human Tissue Act 2004, Sch 7 from a date to be appointed.**

8–21622 **3. Licences.** (1) The Secretary of State may grant a licence for the use of premises for carrying out anatomical examinations.

(2) The Secretary of State may grant a licence to a person to do one or both of the following:—

(*a*) carry out anatomical examinations;
(*b*) have possession of anatomical specimens.

(3) A person is authorised under this subsection to carry out an anatomical examination if—

(*a*) at the time of the examination he is licensed to carry it out under subsection (2)(*a*), or
(*b*) he carries out the examination in the course of teaching or studying, or researching into, morphology and has permission (general or particular) to carry out the examination from a person who is so licensed at the time of the examination.

(4) A person is authorised under this subsection to have possession of an anatomical specimen if—

(*a*) at the time he has possession he is licensed to do so under subsection (2)(*b*), or
(*b*) he has, from a person who is so licensed at that time, permission (general or particular) to have such possession.

(5) A person to whom a licence has been granted under subsection (2) shall—

(*a*) compile such records in relation to anatomical examinations and anatomical specimens as may be specified by regulations[1] made by the Secretary of State, and
(*b*) retain for such period as may be so specified any records compiled in accordance with paragraph (*a*).

(6) The power to make regulations under subsection (5) shall be exercisable by statutory instrument subject to annulment in pursuance of a resolution of either House of Parliament. *
[Anatomy Act 1984, s 3.]

***Repealed, in relation to England and Wales, by the Human Tissue Act 2004, Sch 7 from a date to be appointed.**

1. See reg 2 of the Anatomy Regulations 1988, SI 1988/44 amended by SI 1988/198.

8–21623 **4. Lawful examinations.** (1) Subsection (2) applies if a person, either in writing at any time or orally in the presence of two or more witnesses during his last illness, has expressed a request that his body be used after his death for anatomical examination.

(2) If the person lawfully in possession of the body after death has no reason to believe that the request was withdrawn, he may authorise the use of the body in accordance with the request.

(3) Without prejudice to subsection (2), the person lawfully in possession of a body may authorise it to be used for anatomical examination if, having made such reasonable inquiry as may be practicable, he has no reason to believe—

(*a*) that the deceased, either in writing at any time or orally in the presence of two or more witnesses during his last illness, had expressed an objection to his body being so used after his death, and had not withdrawn it, or

(*b*) that the surviving spouse, *surviving civil partner** or any surviving relative of the deceased objects to the body being so used.

(4) Subject to subsections (5) to (8), the anatomical examination of a body in accordance with an authority given in pursuance of this section is lawful by virtue of this section.

(5) Where a person has reason to believe that an inquest may be required to be held on any body or that a post-mortem examination of any body may be required by the coroner, he shall not, except with the coroner's consent—

(*a*) give an authority under this section in respect of the body, or

(*b*) act on such an authority given by any other person.

This subsection does not apply to Scotland.

(6) *Applies to Scotland.*)

(7) No authority shall be given under this section in respect of a body by a person entrusted with the body for the purpose only of its interment or cremation.

(8) Authority under this section expires at the end of the statutory period (even if the person lawfully in possession of the body concerned authorises its use under subsection (2) or (3) for a longer or shorter period or for no particular period).

(9) In the case of a body lying in

(*a*) a hospital, nursing home** or other institution; or

(*b*) *accommodation provided by a care home service (as defined by section 2(3) of the Regulation of Care (Scotland) Act 2001 (asp 8)****, any authority under this section may be given on behalf of the person having the control and management of the institution *or accommodation*** by any officer or person designated for that purpose by the first-mentioned person.

(10) In subsection (8) "the statutory period" means the period of 3 years (or such other period as the Secretary of State may from time to time by order specify for the purposes of this subsection) beginning with the date of the deceased's death.

(11) The power to make an order under subsection (10) shall be exercisable by statutory instrument subject to annulment in pursuance of a resolution of either House of Parliament; and no such order shall apply in relation to the body of a person who died before the coming into force of the order.****

[Anatomy Act 1984, s 4.]

***Words in italics inserted in relation to Scotland only by SSI 2005/623.**

****Repealed in relation to Scotland by the Regulation of Care (Scotland) Act 2001, Sch 3, from a date to be appointed.**

*****Words in italics inserted in relation to Scotland only by the Regulation of Care (Scotland) Act 2001, Sch 3.**

******Section repealed, in relation to England and Wales, by the Human Tissue Act 2004, Sch 7 from a date to be appointed.**

Possession after examination

8–21624 **5. Control of possession after examination.** (1) This section applies where—

(*a*) authority under section 4 to use a body for anatomical examination has expired, or

(*b*) the anatomical examination of a body has been concluded before the expiry of such authority.

(2) Subject to subsections (3) and (4), no person shall have the body or part of the body in his possession.

(3) Subsection (2) does not apply where a person has possession of the body or part for the purpose only of its decent disposal.

(4) Subsection (2) does not apply where—

(*a*) a person has possession of part of a body whose anatomical examination has been concluded before the expiry of authority under section 4,

(*b*) the part is such that the person from whose body it came cannot be recognised simply by examination of the part,

(*c*) the person with possession is authorised to have possession under subsection (5), and

(*d*) possession of the part is lawful by virtue of section 6.

(5) If the Secretary of State thinks it desirable to do so in the interests of education or research, he

may grant a licence to a person to have possession of parts of bodies, and a person is authorised under this subsection to have possession of a part of a body if—

(*a*) at the time he has possession he is licensed to do so under this subsection, or

(*b*) he has, from a person who is so licensed at that time, permission (general or particular) to have such possession.

(6) A person to whom a licence has been granted under subsection (5) shall—

(*a*) compile such records in relation to parts of bodies as may be specified by regulations[1] made by the Secretary of State, and

(*b*) retain for such period as may be so specified any records compiled in accordance with paragraph (*a*).

(7) The power to make regulations under subsection (6) shall be exercisable by statutory instrument subject to annulment in pursuance of a resolution of either House of Parliament.*

[Anatomy Act 1984, s 5.]

***Repealed, in relation to England and Wales, by the Human Tissue Act 2004, Sch 7 from a date to be appointed.**

1. See reg 3 of the Anatomy Regulations 1988, SI 1988/44 amended by SI 1988/198.

8–21625 6. Lawful possession. (1) Subsection (2) applies if a person, in expressing a request as mentioned in section 4(1), has given permission for possession of parts (or any specified parts) of his body to be held after its anatomical examination is concluded.

(2) If the person lawfully in possession of the body after death has no reason to believe that the permission was withdrawn, he may, in giving authority under section 4(2), give authority for possession to be held in accordance with the permission.

(3) Without prejudice to subsection (2), the person lawfully in possession of a body may, in giving authority under section 4(3), give authority for possession of parts (or any specified parts) of the body to be held after its anatomical examination is concluded if, having made such reasonable inquiry as may be practicable, he has no reason to believe—

(*a*) that the deceased, either in writing at any time or orally in the presence of two or more witnesses during his last illness, had expressed an objection to such possession being held, and had not withdrawn it, or

(*b*) that the surviving spouse, *surviving civil partner** or any surviving relative of the deceased objects to such possession being held.

(4) It is lawful by virtue of this section to have possession of part of a body if possession is held in accordance with an authority given in pursuance of this section.**

[Anatomy Act 1984, s 6.]

***Words in italics inserted in relation to Scotland only by SSI 2005/623.**
****Repealed, in relation to England and Wales, by the Human Tissue Act 2004, Sch 7 from a date to be appointed.**

Miscellaneous

8–21626 7. Licences: general provisions. (1) Applications for licences under this Act shall be made in such manner as the Secretary of State may decide.

(2) A licence under this Act may be granted to such person as the Secretary of State thinks suitable, and a licence under section 3(1) may be granted in respect of such premises as he thinks suitable.

(3) The Secretary of State may require the payment of such fee as he thinks fit in respect of any application for a licence under this Act.

(4) Where the Secretary of State decides not to grant a licence under this Act he shall take reasonable steps to secure that the applicant is notified in writing of his decision and of the reasons for it.

(5) A licence under this Act may be granted subject to such conditions as the Secretary of State thinks necessary or desirable, but no condition may be imposed in relation to a matter dealt with by regulations under section 8.

(6) A licence under this Act shall be effective for such period as the Secretary of State may stipulate when he grants it, except that—

(*a*) he may (subject to subsection (7)) revoke a licence if he thinks it reasonable to do so;

(*b*) he may at any time accept the surrender of a licence from the person to whom it was granted;

(*c*) if the person to whom the licence was granted dies the licence shall then expire (subject to subsection (9)).

(7) Where the Secretary of State decides to revoke a licence under this Act the revocation shall be ineffective unless he gives to the person to whom the licence was granted a written notice stating—

(*a*) that he proposes to revoke the licence on a date which is specified in the notice and is at least 28 days after the date of the notice, and (*b*) the reasons for his decision.

(8) A notice under subsection (7) may be given by post.

(9) Where a person holding a licence under this Act dies, any permission given by him under section 3(3)(*b*) or (4)(*b*) or 5(5)(*b*) (as the case may be), and effective immediately before his death, shall continue to be effective for a period of 21 days commencing with the date of his death; but if the period for which the licence was granted would have expired before the expiry of the 21 days, the permission shall expire when the licence would have expired.*

[Anatomy Act 1984, s 7.]

***Repealed, in relation to England and Wales, by the Human Tissue Act 2004, Sch 7 from a date to be appointed.**

8–21627 **8. Regulations.** (1) The Secretary of State may make regulations[1]—

(*a*) in relation to bodies the anatomical examination of which is lawful by virtue of section 4, with a view to securing their efficient and orderly examination and the decent disposal of the bodies (and parts of them) after their examination has been concluded;

(*b*) in relation to parts of bodies the possession of which is lawful by virtue of section 6, with a view to securing that they are decently cared for.

(2) The regulations may make different provision for different cases or descriptions of case, including different provision for different areas.

(3) No regulations under this section shall apply in relation to the body of a person who died before the coming into force of the regulations.

(4) The power to make regulations under this section shall be exercisable by statutory instrument subject to annulment in pursuance of a resolution of either House of Parliament.*

[Anatomy Act 1984, s 8.]

***Repealed, in relation to England and Wales, by the Human Tissue Act 2004, Sch 7 from a date to be appointed.**

1. See reg 4 of the Anatomy Regulations 1988, SI 1988/44 amended by SI 1988/198.

8–21628 **9. Inspectors of anatomy.** (1) The Secretary of State may appoint such persons as he thinks fit to be inspectors, each to be known as Her Majesty's Inspector of Anatomy or (if the terms of the appointment so provide) Her Majesty's Inspector of Anatomy for Scotland.

(2) An inspector shall be appointed—

(*a*) to advise the Secretary of State on the exercise of his functions under this Act;

(*b*) for the purpose mentioned in paragraph (*a*), to inspect premises in respect of which licences are sought under section 3(1), in order to ascertain whether the premises are suitable;

(*c*) for the purpose mentioned in paragraph (*a*), to examine applications for licences under this Act, in order to ascertain whether the applicants are suitable;

(*d*) to inspect premises, in order to ascertain whether any offence has been or is being committed under section 11(1) or (2) or against regulations under section 8 (as mentioned in section 11(4)).

(3) The Secretary of State shall pay to an inspector such remuneration as the Secretary of State may decide.

(4) An inspector shall be appointed on such other terms and conditions as the Secretary of State may determine.

(5) The Secretary of State may in the case of such of the inspectors as he may determine—

(*a*) pay such pensions, allowances or gratuities to or in respect of them as may be so determined,

(*b*) make such payments towards the provision of pensions, allowances or gratuities to or in respect of any of them as may be so determined, or

(*c*) provide and maintain such schemes (whether contributory or not) for the payment of pensions, allowances or gratuities to or in respect of them as may be so determined.*

[Anatomy Act 1984, s 9.]

***Repealed, in relation to England and Wales, by the Human Tissue Act 2004, Sch 7 from a date to be appointed.**

8–21629 **10. Power to inspect records and premises.** (1) An inspector duly authorised in writing by the Secretary of State may (subject to subsections (3) and (4)) require the production of, and inspect and take copies of, any records which a person is required to retain by virtue of section 3(5) or 5(6).

(2) Where—

(*a*) an inspector has reasonable cause to believe that an offence under section 11(1)(*a*) or (2) or against regulations under section 8 (as mentioned in section 11(4)) has been or is being committed on any premises, and (*b*) he is duly authorised in writing by the Secretary of State to enter and inspect the premises with a view to ascertaining whether the offence has been or is being committed,

he may (subject to subsections (3) to (5)) enter and inspect the premises for that purpose.

(3) An inspector who proposes to require the production of records or enter premises in exercise of a power under this section shall, if so required, produce evidence of his authority before making the requirement or entering.

(4) A power under this section may only be exercised at a reasonable time.

(5) The power to enter premises under subsection (2) may only be exercised if a licence under section 3(1) is effective in respect of the premises both at the time of the suspected offence and at the time of the entry.

(6) Information (including information in records) obtained by any person in pursuance of this section shall not be disclosed except—

(*a*) with the written consent of the person by whom the information was provided, or

(*b*) to any Minister of the Crown, or

(*c*) in the form of a summary of similar information obtained from a number of persons, where the summary is so framed as not to enable particulars relating to any one person or undertaking to be ascertained from it, or

(*d*) with a view to the institution of, or otherwise for the purposes of, any criminal proceedings, or

(*e*) for the purposes of a report of any criminal proceedings.

(7) In this section "inspector" means a person appointed under section 9.★

[Anatomy Act 1984, s 10.]

★Repealed, in relation to England and Wales, by the Human Tissue Act 2004, Sch 7 from a date to be appointed.

8–21630 **11. Offences.** (1) A person who—

(*a*) carries out an anatomical examination in contravention of section 2(1), or

(*b*) has in his possession an anatomical specimen in contravention of section 2(2), or

(*c*) has in his possession a body or part of a body in contravention of section 5(2),

shall be guilty of an offence.

(2) A person who contravenes a condition attached to a licence granted to him under this Act shall be guilty of an offence.

(3) Where a person is charged with an offence under subsection (1) or (2), it shall be a defence to prove that he took all reasonable precautions and exercised all due diligence to avoid the commission of the offence.

(4) Regulations[1] under section 8 may provide that a person who without reasonable excuse contravenes any specified provision of the regulations shall be guilty of an offence against the regulations; and references in this section to an offence against the regulations shall be construed accordingly.

(5) A person who—

(*a*) fails without reasonable excuse to comply with section 3(5) or 5(6), or

(*b*) in purported compliance with section 3(5) or 5(6) compiles a record which he knows is false in a material particular, or

(*c*) alters a record compiled in compliance with section 3(5) or 5(6) so that the record becomes to his knowledge false in a material particular, or

(*d*) fails without reasonable excuse to comply with a requirement imposed by virtue of section 10(1), or

(*e*) intentionally obstructs an inspector in the exercise of his powers under section 10(1) or (2), or

(*f*) discloses information in contravention of section 10(6),

shall be guilty of an offence.

(6) A person guilty of an offence under subsection (1) or (2) shall be liable on summary conviction to a fine not exceeding **level 3** on the standard scale or to imprisonment for a term not exceeding **3 months★**.

(7) Regulations[1] under section 8 may provide that a person guilty of an offence against the regulations shall be liable on summary conviction to a fine not exceeding an amount which is specified in the regulations in relation to the offence concerned and which does not exceed level 3 on the standard scale; and they may further provide that he may instead be liable on summary conviction to imprisonment for a term not exceeding 3 months★.

(8) A person guilty of an offence under subsection (5) shall be liable on summary conviction to a fine not exceeding **level 3** on the standard scale.

(9) Where an offence under this section or against regulations under section 8 is committed by a body corporate and is proved to have been committed with the consent or connivance of or to be attributable to any neglect on the part of any director, manager, secretary or other similar officer of

the body corporate, or any person who was purporting to act in any such capacity, he as well as the body corporate shall be guilty of the offence and shall be liable to be proceeded against and punished accordingly.

(10) If a person carries out an anatomical examination or has possession of an anatomical specimen or of a body falling within section 5(1) or part of such a body, and the circumstances are such that he commits no offence under subsection (1) or (2) above or against regulations under section 8, he shall be guilty of no other offence of carrying out such examination or having such possession.**

[Anatomy Act 1984, s 11, as amended by the Statute Law (Repeals) Act 1993, Sch 1.]

***Words substituted and new sub-s (7) inserted by the Criminal Justice Act 2003, Schs 26 and 27, from a date to be appointed.**

****Repealed, in relation to England and Wales, by the Human Tissue Act 2004, Sch 7 from a date to be appointed.**

1. Regulation 5 of the Anatomy Regulations 1988, SI 1988/44 amended by SI 1988/198 provides that a person who without reasonable cause contravenes any provision of reg 4 (dealing with the examination and disposal of bodies) shall be guilty of an offence punishable on summary conviction with a fine not exceeding **level 3** on the standard scale.

Dentists Act 1984[1]

(1984 c 24)

PART I[2]
THE GENERAL DENTAL COUNCIL

8–21739 **1–2.** *Constitution and general duties of the Council; Committees of the Council.*

1. This Act consolidates the Dentists Acts 1957 to 1983 and was extensively amended by the Dentists Act 1984 (Amendment) Order 2005, SI 2005/2011. The Act provides for the continuance of the General Dental Council (referred to in the Act as "the Council") and its constitution. It shall be the general concern of the Council (*a*) to promote high standards of education at all its stages in all aspects of dentistry; and (*b*) to promote high standards of professional conduct, performance and practice among persons registered under this Act (s 1). The Council is responsible for the registration of dentists, and the Registrar is required to keep the register. Subject to the provisions of the Act, the following persons are entitled to be registered in the dentists register, namely (*a*) any person who is a graduate or licentiate in dentistry of a dental authority; (*b*) any person who is a national of a member State and holds an appropriate European diploma; and (*c*) any person who holds a recognised overseas diploma (s 15).

The European Primary and Specialist Dental Qualification Regulations 1998, SI 1998/811 amended by SI 2003/3148 implement European obligations relating to the training of dentists and specialist dentists contained in the Council Directive 78/678/EEC. Under the regulations the General Dental Council is specified as the competent authority for the United Kingdom in relation to specified functions under those Directives.

The Professional Conduct Committee of the Council has power to erase the name of a dentist from the register or direct suspension of his registration where it is satisfied that a registered dentist has been convicted in the UK of a criminal offence or has been convicted elsewhere of an offence which, if committed in England and Wales, would constitute a criminal offence, or has been guilty of serious professional misconduct (s 27). Where the fitness of a registered dentist to practise is judged by the Health Committee of the Council to be seriously impaired by reason of his physical or mental condition the Committee may direct that his registration be suspended or that his registration be made conditional on compliance with specified requirements (s 28).

2. Part I contains ss 1, 2.

8–21740

PART II[1]
DENTAL EDUCATION

1. Part II contains ss 3–13.

PART III[1]
THE DENTAL PROFESSION

Use of titles and descriptions

8–21741 **26. Use of titles and descriptions.** (1) A registered[2] dentist shall by virtue of being registered be entitled to take and use the description of dentist, dental surgeon or dental practitioner.

(2) A registered dentist shall not take or use, or affix to or use in connection with his premises, any title or description reasonably calculated to suggest that he possesses any professional status or qualification other than a professional status or qualification which he in fact possesses and which is indicated by particulars entered in the register in respect of him.

(3) If the Council are of opinion that any branch of dentistry has become so distinctive that it would be for the convenience of the public or of the dental profession that registered dentists qualified to practise, or practising, in that branch of dentistry should use a distinctive title, they may by regulations prescribe appropriate titles and conditions under which they may be used; and the use of a prescribed title under the prescribed conditions shall not constitute a contravention of subsection (2) above.

(4) In the case of any prescribed title regulations under subsection (3) above may provide—

(*a*) for a list to be kept by the Council of the names of registered dentists who are qualified under such regulations to use that title; and

(*b*) for any registered dentist who is so qualified to be entitled to have his name entered in the list;

and where regulations so provide as aforesaid nothing in that subsection shall permit that title to be used by any such dentist unless his name has been entered in the list.

(4A) The Council may make regulations—

(*a*) prescribing a fee to be charged on the entry of a name in a list for the time being kept by them under subsection (4), or on the restoration of any entry to such a list;

(*b*) prescribing a fee to be charged in respect of the retention of the name of a person in such a list.

(4B) Regulations under subsection (4A) may in particular authorise the registrar—

(*a*) to refuse to make in or restore to a list for the time being kept by the Council under subsection (4) any entry until a fee prescribed by the regulations has been paid; and

(*b*) to erase from such a list the name of a person who, after such notices and warnings as may be prescribed by the regulations, fails to pay a fee prescribed by the regulations in respect of the retention of a person's name in that list.

(5) *Repealed.*

(6) Any person who contravenes subsection (2) above shall be liable on summary conviction to a fine not exceeding the **third level** on the standard scale.

(7) The Council shall from time to time publish any list for the time being kept by them under subsection (4).

[Dentists Act 1984, s 26 as amended by SI 2005/2011.]

---

1. Part III contains ss 14–36.
2. A certificate purporting to be signed by the registrar, certifying that a person— (*a*) is registered in the register, (*b*) is not registered in the register, (*c*) was registered in the register at a specified date or during a specified period, (*d*) was not registered in the register at a specified date or during a specified period, or (*e*) has never been registered in the register, shall be prima facie evidence in all courts of law of the facts stated in the certificate (s 14(6)).

8–21741A 26A–26B. *Insurance and Guidance*

Visiting EEA practitioners

8–21742 36. Visiting EEA practitioners. Schedule 4[1] to this Act (which makes provision for persons established in dental practice in other EEA States to render dental services during a visit to the United Kingdom without being registered under this Act) shall have effect.

[Dentists Act 1984, s 36, as amended by SI 1996/1496.]

---

1. See, post.

PART IIIA

PROFESSIONS COMPLEMENTARY TO DENTISTRY

36A–36R. *Regulation of professions complementary to Dentistry*

PART IV[1]

RESTRICTIONS ON PRACTICE OF DENTISTRY AND ON CARRYING ON BUSINESS OF DENTISTRY

The practice of dentistry

8–21743 37. Definition of practice of dentistry. (1) Subject to subsection (1A), for the purposes of this Act, the practice of dentistry shall be deemed to include the performance of any such operation and the giving of any such treatment, advice[2] or attendance[2] as is usually performed or given by dentists; and any person who performs any operation or gives any treatment, advice or attendance on or to any person as preparatory to or for the purpose of or in connection with the fitting, insertion or fixing of dentures, artificial teeth or other dental appliances shall be deemed to have practised dentistry within the meaning of this Act.

"(1A) For the purposes of this Act, the practice of dentistry shall be deemed not to include the performance of any medical task by a person who—

(a) is qualified to carry out such a task; and

(b) is a member of a profession regulated by a regulatory body (other than the Council) listed in section 25(3) of the National Health Service Reform and Health Care Professions Act 2002."; and

(c) for subsection (2) substitute—

(2) Dental work to which subsection (2A) or (2B) applies shall not be treated for the purposes

of this Act as amounting to the practice of dentistry if it is undertaken under the direct personal supervision of—

(*a*) a registered dentist; or

(*b*) a registered dental care professional of a kind authorised in rules under this section to carry out such supervision.

(2A) This subsection applies to dental work if it is undertaken—

(*a*) by a person recognised by a dental authority as a student of dentistry or by a medical authority as a medical student; and

(*b*) as part of a course of instruction or training approved by that authority for students of that kind or as part of an examination so approved.

(2B) This subsection applies to dental work if it is undertaken by a person as part of—

(*a*) a course of instruction or training which he is following in order to qualify for registration in the dental care professionals register under a particular title or titles; or

(*b*) an examination which he must pass in order to satisfy the requirements for registration in that register under a particular title or titles.

(3) In this section "medical authority" means one of the universities and other bodies who choose appointed members of the General Medical Council.
[Dentists Act 1984, s 37 as amended by SI 2005/2011.]

1. Part IV contains ss 37–44.

2. "Advice" means advice in connection with the fitting of the mouth itself; not as to the supply of new teeth to an existing denture (*Twyford v Puntschart* [1947] 1 All ER 773, 111 JP 315). The construction of these expressions was considered in *Almy v Thomas* [1953] 2 All ER 1050, 117 JP 561.

8–21744 **38. Prohibition on practice of dentistry by laymen.** (1) A person who is not a registered[1] dentist, a visiting EEC practitioner entered in the list of such practitioners, or a registered medical practitioner[2] shall not practise or hold himself out, whether directly or by implication, as practising or as being prepared to practise dentistry.

(2) Any person who acts in contravention of subsection (1) above shall be liable on summary conviction to a fine not exceeding the **fifth level** on the standard scale.

(3) Summary proceedings for an offence under this section may be brought within the period of six months beginning with the date on which evidence sufficient in the opinion of the prosecutor to warrant the proceedings came to his knowledge; but no such proceedings shall be brought by virtue of this subsection more than two years after the commission of the offence.

(4) For the purposes of subsection (3) above a certificate signed by or on behalf of the prosecutor and stating the date on which such evidence as is mentioned in that subsection came to his knowledge shall be conclusive evidence of that date, and any certificate purporting to be so signed shall be taken to have been so signed unless the contrary is proved.
[Dentists Act 1984, s 38.]

1. See note 2 to s 26, ante.

2. "Registered medical practitioner" means a fully registered person within the meaning of the Medical Act 1983 (Interpretation Act 1978, Sch 1, in PART II: EVIDENCE, ante).

8–21745 **39. Prohibition on use of practitioners' titles by laymen.** (1) A person who is not a registered dentist, a visiting EEC practitioner entered in the list of such practitioners or a registered medical practitioner shall not take or use the title of dentist, dental surgeon or dental practitioner, either alone or in combination with any other word.

(2) No person shall take or use any title or description implying that he is a registered dentist unless he is a registered dentist.

(3) Any person who acts in contravention of this section shall be liable on summary conviction to a fine not exceeding the **fifth level** on the standard scale.
[Dentists Act 1984, s 39.]

Restrictions on carrying on the business of dentistry

8–21746 **40. Definition of business of dentistry.** (1) For the purposes of this Act a person shall be treated as carrying on the business of dentistry if, and only if, he or a partnership of which he is a member receives payment for services rendered in the course of the practice of dentistry by him or by a partner of his, or by an employee of his or of all or any of the partners.

(2) Notwithstanding subsection (1) above, the receipt of payments—

(*a*) by an authority providing national health services, or*

(*ab*) by a person (other than one falling within paragraph (*a*) above) providing personal dental services under section 28C of the National Health Service Act 1977 or section 17C of the National Health Service (Scotland) Act 1978, or

(*b*) by a person providing dental treatment for his employees without a view to profit, or (*c*) by a person providing dental treatment without a view to profit under conditions approved by the Secretary of State or the Department of Health and Social Services for Northern Ireland,

shall not constitute the carrying on of the business of dentistry for the purposes of this Act.
[Dentists Act 1984, s 40, as amended by SI 1998/1546.]

***New para (2)(*ab*) inserted by the Health and Social Care (Community Health and Standards) Act 2003, from a date to be appointed.**

8–21747 **41. Restriction on individuals.** (1) Subject to the provisions of this section, an individual who is not a registered dentist or a registered medical practitioner shall not carry on the business of dentistry unless he was engaged in carrying on the business of dentistry on 21st July 1955, and any individual who contravenes this section shall be liable on summary conviction to a fine not exceeding the **fifth level** on the standard scale.

(2) The exemption conferred by subsection (1) above on persons who were carrying on the business of dentistry on the date there mentioned shall not extend to any person who has at any time ceased to be a registered dentist in consequence of his name being erased from the register, or his registration in it being suspended, under section 27 above.

(3) This section shall not operate to prevent a person from carrying on the business of dentistry during any period for which his registration in the register is suspended by virtue of a direction under Part III of this Act or by virtue of an order under section 30(3)(*b*) or section 32 above; and subsections (4) and (6) below shall apply in relation to a person whose registration is so suspended as they apply in relation to a registered dentist.

(4) Where a registered dentist or registered medical practitioner who died after 3rd July 1956 was at his death carrying on a business or practice constituting the business of dentistry, this section shall not operate to prevent his personal representatives or his surviving spouse or his surviving civil partner or any of his children, or trustees on behalf of his surviving spouse or his surviving civil partner or any of his children, from carrying on the business of dentistry in continuance of that business or practice during the three years beginning with his death.

(5) Where a registered dentist or a registered medical practitioner who died before 4th July 1956 was at his death carrying on a business or practice constituting the business of dentistry, this section shall not operate to prevent his widow, or trustees on behalf of his widow, from carrying on the business of dentistry in continuance of that business or practice at any time during her life.

(6) Where a registered dentist or registered medical practitioner becomes bankrupt at a time when he is carrying on a business or practice constituting the business of dentistry, this section shall not operate to prevent his trustee in bankruptcy, or in Northern Ireland the official assignee, from carrying on the business of dentistry in continuance of that business or practice during the three years beginning with the bankruptcy.
[Dentists Act 1984, s 41 as amended by the Civil Partnership Act 2004, Sch 27.]

8–21749 **43. Bodies corporate entitled to carry on business of dentistry.** (1) A body corporate may, subject to the following provisions of this Part of this Act, carry on the business of dentistry if—

(*a*) it was carrying on the business of dentistry on 21st July 1955, and
(*b*) it carries on no business other than dentistry or some business ancillary to the business of dentistry, and
(*c*) a majority of the directors are registered dentists, and
(*d*) all its operating staff are either registered dentists or dental auxiliaries.

(2) Paragraph (*a*) of subsection (1) above shall not apply—

(*a*) to a society registered under the Industrial and Provident Societies Act 1965 or the Industrial and Provident Societies Act (Northern Ireland) 1969, or
(*b*) to a body corporate coming into existence on the reconstruction of a body corporate carrying on business on the date mentioned in that paragraph, or coming into existence on the amalgamation of two or more such bodies.

(3) Paragraph (*b*) of subsection (1) above shall not apply to a body corporate which was carrying on the business of dentistry before 28th July 1921 so as to prevent it from carrying on any business which that body was at that date lawfully entitled to carry on.

(4) Every body corporate carrying on the business of dentistry shall in every year transmit to the registrar a statement in the prescribed form containing the names and addresses of all persons who are its directors or managers or who perform dental operations in connection with its business, and if any such body corporate fails to do so, it shall be deemed to be carrying on the business of dentistry in contravention of the provisions of section 42 above.

(5) If a body corporate exempted by this section ceases at any time to carry on the business of dentistry, the exemption conferred by this section shall not extend to that body on any subsequent occasion when it carries on the business of dentistry.

(6) Nothing in this section shall prevent a body corporate from carrying on the business of

dentistry in the circumstances mentioned in subsections (4), (5) and (6) of section 41 above, and subsection (4) above shall not apply in those circumstances.

(7) In this section "prescribed" means prescribed by regulations made by the Council.
[Dentists Act 1984, s 43.]

PART VI[1]
MISCELLANEOUS AND SUPPLEMENTARY

8–21753 **52. Regulations and other documents.** (1) The Statutory Instruments Act 1946 shall apply to a statutory instrument containing regulations made by the Council under this Act in like manner as if the regulations had been made by a Minister of the Crown.

(2) Prima facie evidence of any document issued by the Council may be given in all legal proceedings by the production of a copy or extract purporting to be certified to be a true copy or extract by the registrar or some other officer of the Council authorised to give a certificate for the purposes of this subsection.

(3) No proof shall be required of the handwriting or official position or authority of any person certifying in pursuance of this section to the truth of any copy of, or extract from, any regulations or other document.
[Dentists Act 1984, s 52.]

1. Part VI contains ss 49–56.

8–21754 **53. Interpretation.** (1) In this Act—

"the Council" means the General Dental Council;
"dental authority" shall be construed in accordance with section 3(4) above.
"diploma" means any diploma, degree, fellowship, membership, licence, authority to practise, letters testimonial, certificate or other status or document granted by any university, corporation, college or other body or by any department of, or persons acting under the authority of, the government of any country or place (whether within or without Her Majesty's dominions);
"the EEA Agreement" and "EEA State" have the meanings given by section 15(7) above;
"recognised overseas diploma" has the meaning given by section 15(2) above;
"the register" means the dentists register;
"registered dentist" means (subject to section 17(4) above) a person for the time being registered in the register;
"the registrar" means the person for the time being appointed under section 14(3) above;
"visiting EEA practitioner entered in the list of such practitioners" means a person entered in the list of EEA practitioners under Schedule 4 to this Act.

(2) In this Act references to the practice of dentistry shall be construed in accordance with section 37 above, and references to carrying on the business of dentistry shall be construed in accordance with section 40 above.

(3) References in this Act to the provision of national health services are references to the provision of—

(*a*) services under

(i) section 2, 3, 5(1)(*a*) or 28C of, Schedule 1 to, the National Health Service Act 1977;
(ii) section 17C, 36, 38 or 39 of the National Health Service (Scotland) Act 1978; or
(iii) Article 5, 8 or 9 of the Health and Personal Social Services (Northern Ireland) Order 1972; and

(*b*) services at health centres provided under the said sections 2, 3 or 36 or the said Article 5.

(4) *Repealed.*
[Dentists Act 1984, s 53, as amended by the Statute Law (Repeals) Act 1993, Sch 1, SI 1996/1496 and the National Health Service (Primary Care) Act 1997, Sch 2.]

Section 36

SCHEDULE 4
VISITING EEA PRACTITIONERS

(Amended by SI 1996/1496.)

Preliminary

8–21755 **1.** (1) This Schedule has effect for the purpose of enabling a person to whom it applies to render dental services during a visit to the United Kingdom without being registered under this Act.

(2) This Schedule applies to any national of an EEA State who is established in dental practice in an EEA State other than the United Kingdom.

(2A) Any person who—

(*a*) is not a national of an EEA State, but

(*b*) is, by virtue of a right conferred by Article 11 of Council Regulation (EEC) No 1612/68 or any other enforceable Community right, entitled to be treated, for the purposes of access to the profession of dentistry, no less favourably than a national of such a State,

shall be treated for the purposes of sub-paragraph (2) above as if he were such a national.

(3) In this Schedule—

"national", in relation to an EEA State, means the same as in the Community Treaties, but does not include a person who by virtue of Article 2 of Protocol No 3 (Channel Islands and Isle of Man) to the Treaty of Accession is not to benefit from Community provisions relating to the free movement of persons and services; and

"the Recognition Directive" has the meaning which "Community Council Directive No 78/686/EEC" has in Schedule 2 to this Act.

---

1. See OJ No L 233/1.

Declarations and certificates to be provided by visiting EEA practitioners

8–21756 **2.** (1) A person to whom this Schedule applies who intends to render dental services as mentioned in paragraph 1(1) above shall provide the registrar with—

(*a*) a declaration in writing giving particulars of the services to be rendered and the period or periods in which he expects to render them; and

(*b*) a certificate or certificates issued by the authority or body designated by the EEA State concerned as competent for the purposes of Article 15(3) of the Recognition Directive (provision of services) showing—

(i) that he is lawfully practising dentistry in an EEA State other than the United Kingdom, and

(ii) that he holds a diploma in dentistry which EEA States are required by that Directive to recognise.

(2) For the purposes of sub-paragraph (1) above—

(*a*) in an urgent case the declaration to be provided under paragraph (*a*) may be provided after the services have been rendered, but, if so, it shall be provided as soon as possible thereafter and in any event not more than fifteen days after the date on which the practitioner has rendered the services, and

(*b*) every certificate to be provided under paragraph (*b*) shall bear a date not less recent than twelve months prior to the date on which the certificate was provided.

List of EEA practitioners

8–21757 **3.** (1) The registrar shall continue to keep a list known as the list of visiting EEA practitioners.

(2) Where a person to whom this Schedule applies complies with the requirements of paragraph 2(1) above, the registrar shall, subject to paragraph 4 below, enter his name, together with particulars of any diplomas held by him, in the list of EEA practitioners.

(3) Subject to paragraph 4 below, that entry shall have effect for the period specified in the list against the entry, being the period which appears to the registrar to be appropriate having regard to the particulars given in the declaration referred to in paragraph 2(1)(*a*) above.

Persons not entitled to be included in the list of visiting EEA practitioners

8–21758 **4.** A person to whom this Schedule applies shall not be entitled to have his name included in the list of visiting EEA practitioners if—

(*a*) he is subject to a disqualifying decision (within the meaning of section 35 of this Act) taken in relation to him in an EEA State; or

(*b*) he is subject to a prohibition imposed on him under paragraph 5 below;

and any entry in the list relating to a practitioner shall not have effect or shall cease to have effect if he is or becomes subject to such a decision or prohibition or if he becomes established in dental practice in the United Kingdom or renders, save in cases of urgency, dental services in the United Kingdom which fall outside those specified in the declaration made by him under paragraph 2(1)(*a*) above.

Disciplinary provisions affecting practitioners who render services while visiting the United Kingdom

8–21759 **5.** (1) If a person who is or has been entered in the list of visiting EEA practitioners—

(*a*) has been convicted of a criminal offence, whether in an EEA State or elsewhere, or

(*b*) has been guilty of any serious professional misconduct,

the Professional Conduct Committee may, if they think fit, impose on him a prohibition in respect of the rendering of dental services in the United Kingdom in the future.

(2) A prohibition imposed under this paragraph shall be for an indefinite period.

(3) A person may apply to the Council for termination of a prohibition imposed on him under this paragraph and the Council may, on any such application, terminate the prohibition; but no application shall be made under this paragraph—

(*a*) earlier than ten months from the date on which the prohibition was imposed; or

(*b*) in the period of ten months following a decision made on an earlier application.

Intoxicating Substances (Supply) Act 1985

(1985 c 26)

8–21870 1. Offence of supply of intoxicating substance. (1) It is an offence for a person to supply or offer to supply a substance other than a controlled drug—

(*a*) to a person under the age of eighteen whom he knows or has reasonable cause to believe, to be under that age; or

(*b*) to a person—

(i) who is acting on behalf of a person under that age; and

(ii) whom he knows, or has reasonable cause to believe, to be so acting,

if he knows or has reasonable cause to believe that the substance is, or its fumes are, likely to be inhaled by the person under the age of eighteen for the purpose of causing intoxication.

(2) In proceedings against any person for an offence under subsection (1) above it is a defence for him to show that at the time he made the supply or offer he was under the age of eighteen and was acting otherwise than in the course or furtherance of a business.

(3) A person guilty of an offence under this section shall be liable on summary conviction to imprisonment for a term not exceeding **six months** or to a fine not exceeding **level 5** on the standard scale, or to **both**.

(4) In this section "controlled drug" has the same meaning as in the Misuse of Drugs Act 1971[1].

[Intoxicating Substances (Supply) Act 1985, s 1, as amended by the Statute Law (Repeals) Act 1993, Sch 1.]

1. See this title, ante.

8–21871 2. *Short title, commencement and extent*

Health and Medicines Act 1988

(1988 c 49)

HIV testing kits and services

8–22000 23. HIV testing kits and services. (1) The Secretary of State may provide by regulations[1] that a person—

(*a*) who sells or supplies to another on HIV testing kit or any component part of such a kit;

(*b*) who provides another with HIV testing services; or

(*c*) who advertises such kits or component parts or such services,

shall be guilty of an offence.

(2) The power to make regulations conferred by this section shall be exercisable by statutory instrument, and a statutory instrument made by virtue of this section shall be subject to annulment in pursuance of a resolution of either House of Parliament.

(3) The power may be exercised—

(*a*) either in relation to all cases to which the power extends, or in relation to all those cases subject to specified exceptions, or in relation to any specified cases or classes of case; and

(*b*) so as to make, as respects the cases in relation to which it is exercised—

(i) the full provision to which the power extends or any less provision (whether by way of exception or otherwise);

(ii) the same provision for all cases in relation to which the power is exercised, or different provision for different cases or different classes of case, or different provision as respects the same case or class of case for different purposes;

(iii) any such provision either unconditionally, or subject to any specified condition,

and includes power to make such incidental or supplemental provision as the Secretary of State considers appropriate.

(4) If any person contravenes regulations under this section, he shall be liable[2]—

(*a*) on summary conviction to a fine not exceeding **the statutory maximum**; and

(*b*) on conviction on indictment to a **fine** or to imprisonment for a term of not more than **two years**, or to **both**.

(5) Where an offence under this section which is committed by a body corporate is proved to have been committed with the consent or connivance of, or to be attributable to any neglect on the part of, any director, manager, secretary or other similar officer of the body corporate, or any person who was purporting to act in any such capacity, he as well as the body corporate shall be guilty of that offence and shall be liable to be proceeded against and punished accordingly.

(6) In this section—

"HIV" means Immunodeficiency Virus of any type;

"HIV testing kit" means a diagnostic kit the purpose of which is to detect the presence of HIV or HIV antibodies; and

"HIV testing services" means diagnostic services the purpose of which is to detect the presence of HIV or HIV antibodies in identifiable individuals.

[Health and Medicines Act 1988, s 23.]

1. The HIV Testing Kits and Services Regulations 1992, SI 1992/460 have been made.

2. For procedure in respect of an offence which is triable either way, see the Magistrates' Courts Act 1980, ss 17A–21, in PART I: MAGISTRATES' COURTS, PROCEDURE, ante.

Human Organ Transplants Act 1989

(1989 c 31)

8–22001 **1. Prohibition of commercial dealings in human organs.** (1) A person is guilty of an offence if he—

(*a*) makes or receives any payment for the supply of, or for an offer to supply, an organ which has been or is to be removed from a dead or living person and is intended to be transplanted into another person whether in Scotland or elsewhere;

(*b*) seeks to find a person willing to supply for payment such an organ as is mentioned in paragraph (*a*) above or offers to supply such an organ for payment;

(*c*) initiates or negotiates any arrangement involving the making of any payment for the supply of, or for an offer to supply, such an organ; or

(*d*) takes part in the management or control of a body of persons corporate or unincorporate whose activities consist of or include the initiation or negotiation of such arrangements.

(2) Without prejudice to paragraph (*b*) of subsection (1) above, a person is guilty of an offence if he causes to be published or distributed, or knowingly publishes or distributes, an advertisement—

(*a*) inviting persons to supply for payment any such organs as are mentioned in paragraph (*a*) of that subsection or offering to supply any such organs for payment; or

(*b*) indicating that the advertiser is willing to initiate or negotiate any such arrangement as is mentioned in paragraph (*c*) of that subsection.

(3) In this section "payment" means payment in money or money's worth but does not include any payment for defraying or reimbursing—

(*a*) the cost of removing, transporting or preserving the organ to be supplied; or

(*b*) any expenses or loss of earnings incurred by a person so far as reasonably and directly attributable to his supplying an organ from his body.

(4) In this section "advertisement" includes any form of advertising whether to the public generally, to any section of the public or individually to selected persons.

(5) A person guilty of an offence under subsection (1) above is liable on summary conviction to imprisonment for a term not exceeding **three months*** or a fine not exceeding **level 5** on the standard scale or **both;** and a person guilty of an offence under subsection (2) above is liable on summary conviction to a fine not exceeding **level 5** on that scale.**

[Human Organ Transplants Act 1989, s 1 as amended by the Human Tissue Act 2004, Sch 7.]

***"51 weeks" substituted by the Criminal Justice Act 2003, Sch 26, from a date to be appointed.**

****Repealed, in relation to England and Wales, and in part in relation to Scotland, by the Human Tissue Act 2004, Sch 7 from a date to be appointed.**

8–22002 **2. Restriction on transplants between persons not genetically related[1].** (1) Subject to subsection (3) below, a person is guilty of an offence if in Great Britain he—

(*a*) removes from a living person an organ intended to be transplanted into another person; or

(*b*) transplants an organ removed from a living person into another person,

unless the person into whom the organ is to be or, as the case may be, is transplanted is genetically related to the person from whom the organ is removed.

(2) for the purposes of this section a person is genetically related to—

(*a*) his natural parents and children;

(*b*) his brothers and sisters of the whole or half blood;

(*c*) the brothers and sisters of the whole or half blood of either of his natural parents; and

(*d*) the natural children of his brothers and sisters of the whole or half blood or of the brothers and sisters of the whole or half blood of either of his natural parents;

but persons shall not in any particular case be treated as related in any of those ways unless the fact of the relationship has been established by such means as are specified by regulations[2] made by the Secretary of State.

(3) The Secretary of State may by regulations[3] provide that the prohibition in subsection (1) shall not apply in cases where—

(*a*) such authority as is specified in or constituted by the regulations is satisfied—

(i) that no payment has been or is to be made in contravention of section 1 above; and

(ii) that such other conditions as are specified in the regulations are satisfied; and

(*b*) that such other requirements as may be specified in the regulations are complied with

(4) The expenses of any such authority shall be defrayed by the Secretary of State out of money provided by Parliament.

(5) A person guilty of an offence under this section is liable on summary conviction to imprisonment for a term not exceeding **three months** or a fine not exceeding **level 5** on the standard scale or **both**.

(6) The power to make regulations under this section shall be exercisable by statutory instrument.

(7) Regulations under subsection (2) above shall be subject to annulment in pursuance of a resolution of either House of Parliament; and no regulations shall be made under subsection (3) above unless a draft of them has been laid before and approved by a resolution of each House of Parliament.*

[Human Organ Transplants Act 1989, s 2.]

***Repealed, in relation to England and Wales, and in part in relation to Scotland, by the Human Tissue Act 2004, Sch 7 from a date to be appointed.**

1. Sections 27–29 of the Human Fertilisation and Embryology Act 1990 (which confer the status of "mother" and "father" in relation to a child who is being or has been carried by a woman as the result of the placing in her of an embryo or of sperm and eggs for her artificial insemination), in PART IV: FAMILY LAW, ante, have no application for the purposes of s 2 of this Act (Human Fertilisation and Embryology Act 1990, Sch 4).

2. The Human Organ Transplants (Establishment of Relationships) Regulations 1998, SI 1998/1428 have been made.

3. The Human Organ Transplants (Unrelated Persons) Regulations 1989, SI 1989/3448 have been made.

8–22003 **3. Information about transplant operations.** (1) The Secretary of State may make regulations[1] requiring such persons as are specified in the regulations to supply to such authority as is so specified such information as may be so specified with respect to transplants that have been or are proposed to be carried out in Great Britain using organs removed from dead or living persons.

(2) Any such authority shall keep a record of information supplied to it in pursuance of the regulations made under this section.

(3) Any person who without reasonable excuse fails to comply with those regulations is guilty of an offence and liable on summary conviction to a fine not exceeding **level 3** on the standard scale; and any person who, in purported compliance with those regulations, knowingly or recklessly supplies information which is false or misleading in a material respect is guilty of an offence and liable on summary conviction to a fine not exceeding **level 5** on the standard scale.

(4) The power to make regulations under this section shall be exercisable by statutory instrument subject to annulment in pursuance of a resolution of either House of Parliament.*

[Human Organ Transplants Act 1989, s 3.]

***Repealed, in relation to England and Wales, and in part in relation to Scotland, by the Human Tissue Act 2004, Sch 7 from a date to be appointed.**

1. The Human Organ Transplants (Supply of Information) Regulations 1989, SI 1989/2108 have been made.

8–22004 **4. Offences by bodies corporate.** (1) Where an offence under this Act committed by a body corporate is proved to have been committed with the consent or connivance of, or to be attributable to any neglect on the part of, any director, manager, secretary or other similar officer of the body corporate or any person who was purporting to act in any such capacity, he as well as the body corporate is guilty of the offence and is liable to be proceeded against and punished accordingly.

(2) Where the affairs of a body corporate are managed by its members, subsection (1) above shall apply to the acts and defaults of a member in connection with his functions of management as if he were a director of the body corporate.*

[Human Organ Transplants Act 1989, s 4.]

***Repealed, in relation to England and Wales, and in part in relation to Scotland, by the Human Tissue Act 2004, Sch 7 from a date to be appointed.**

8–22005 **5. Prosecutions.** No proceedings for an offence under section 1 or 2 above shall be instituted in England and Wales except by or with the consent of the Director of Public Prosecutions.*

[Human Organ Transplants Act 1989, s 5.]

***Repealed by the Human Tissue Act 2004, Sch 7 from a date to be appointed.**

8–22006 **6.** *Northern Ireland**

***Repealed by the Human Tissue Act 2004, Sch 7 from a date to be appointed.**

8–22007 **7. Short title interpretation commencement and extent.** (1) *Citation.*

(2) In this Act "organ" means any part of a human body consisting of a structured arrangement of tissues which, if wholly removed, cannot be replicated by the body.

(3) Section 1 above shall not come into force until the day after that on which this Act is passed[1] and section 2(1) above shall not come into force until such day as the Secretary of State may appoint by an order[2] made by statutory instrument.

(4) *Northern Ireland.**

[Human Organ Transplants Act 1989, s 7.]

***Repealed, in relation to England and Wales, by the Human Tissue Act 2004, Sch 7 from a date to be appointed.**

1. This Act was passed on 27 July 1989.
2. The day appointed for the coming into force of s 2(1) was the 1 April 1990 (SI 1989/2106).

Opticians Act 1989

(1989 c 44)

PART IV

RESTRICTIONS ON TESTING OF SIGHT, FITTING OF CONTACT LENSES, SALE AND SUPPLY OF OPTICAL APPLIANCES AND USE OF TITLES AND DESCRIPTIONS

8–22008 **24. Testing of sight.** (1) Subject to the following provisions of this section, a person who is not a registered medical practitioner or registered optometrist[2] shall not test[2] the sight of another person.

(2) Subsection (1) above shall not apply to the testing of sight by a person recognised by a medical authority[2] as a medical student, if carried out as part of a course of instruction approved by that authority for medical students or as part of an examination so approved.

(3) The Council[2] may by rules[3] exempt from subsection (1) above the testing of sight by persons training as optometrists[2], or any prescribed class of such persons, in such cases and subject to compliance with such conditions as may be prescribed by the rules.

(4) Any person who contravenes subsection (1) above shall be liable on summary conviction to a fine of an amount not exceeding **level 5** on the standard scale.

[Opticians Act 1989, s 24 as amended by SI 2005/848.]

1. Part IV contains ss 24–30.
2. Defined in s 36.
3. The General Optical Council (Testing of Sight by Persons Training as Ophthalmic Opticians Rules) Order of Council 1994, SI 1994/70 amended by SI 1999/2897 has been made.

8–22009 **25. Fitting of contact lenses.** (1) Subject to the following provisions of this section a person who is not a registered medical practitioner, a registered optometrist or a registered dispensing optician must not fit a contact lens for an individual.

(1A) A registered medical practitioner, a registered optometrist, a registered dispensing optician or a person to whom, by virtue of subsection (2) or (3) below, subsection (1) above does not apply, must not fit a contact lens for an individual unless—

(*a*) where the duty to give an individual a signed written prescription under section 26(2) below arises, he has the particulars of such a prescription given to the individual within the period of two years ending on the date the fitting begins; and

(*b*) the fitting begins before any re-examination date specified in that prescription.

(2) Subsection (1) above shall not apply to the fitting of contact lenses by a person recognised by a medical authority as a medical student, if carried out as part of a course of instruction approved by that authority for medical students or as part of an examination so approved.

(3) The Council may by rules exempt from subsection (1) above the fitting of contact lenses by persons training as optometrists or dispensing opticians, or any prescribed class of such persons, in such cases and subject to compliance with such conditions as may be prescribed by the rules.

(4) Any person who contravenes subsection (1) or (1A) above shall be liable on summary conviction to a fine of an amount not exceeding **level 5** on the standard scale.

(5) A person to whom this subsection applies who fits a contact lens to an individual must—

(*a*) on completion of the fitting, provide the individual with a signed, written specification of each lens fitted sufficient to enable the lens to be replicated unless, having carried out the assessment referred to in subsection (9)(*a*) below, he is of the view that a contact lens is not appropriate; and (*b*) provide the individual with instructions and information on the care, wearing, treatment, cleaning and maintenance of the lens.

(6) The obligation to provide a specification or instructions or information under subsection (5) above applies—

(*a*) if only one person took part in fitting a contact lens for the individual, to that person;
(*b*) if a series of persons took part in fitting a contact lens for an individual, to the last person to fit a lens.

(7) A specification issued in accordance with subsection (5) above must—

(*a*) state the period during which the specification remains valid and its expiry date; and
(*b*) in the case of a specification provided by a registered medical practitioner, contain such particulars as the Secretary of State may specify in regulations[1].

(8) A specification becomes invalid after its expiry date.

(9) For the purposes of this section and section 27(3A) below, "fitting" a contact lens means—

(*a*) assessing whether a contact lens meets the needs of the individual; and, where appropriate
(*b*) providing the individual with one or more contact lenses for use during a trial period,

and "fit" and "fitted" shall be construed accordingly.

(10) In the application of this section to Northern Ireland, for any reference to the Secretary of State there shall be substituted a reference to the Department of Health, Social Services and Public Safety in Northern Ireland.
[Opticians Act 1989, s 25 as amended by SI 2005/848.]

1. See the Contact Lens (Specification) and Miscellaneous Amendments Regulations 2005, SI 2005/1481.

8–22010 **26. Duties to be performed on sight testing.** *Secretary of State may make Regulations.*
[Opticians Act 1989, s 26—summarised.]

8–22011 **27. Sale and supply of optical appliances.** (1) A person shall not sell—

(*a*) any contact lens for use by any person who does not have a valid specification provided pursuant to section 25(5) above; or
(*b*) subject to the following provisions of this section, any optical appliance or zero powered contact lens unless the sale is effected by or under the supervision of a registered medical practitioner, a registered optometrist or a registered dispensing optician.

(2) Subsection (1) above shall not apply to any of the following sales—

(*a*) a sale for a person who has attained the age of sixteen of spectacles which have two single vision lenses of the same positive spherical power not exceeding 4 dioptres where the sale is wholly for the purpose of correcting, remedying or relieving presbyopia;
(*b*) a sale of an optical appliance intended for use as protection or cover for the eyes in sports if—
  (i) neither lens fitted to the appliance has a positive or negative spherical power exceeding 8 dioptres;
  (ii) the appliance is an appliance with a single vision lens or single visions lenses; and
  (iii) the appliance falls within any category of appliance specified in an order made by the Privy Council for the purposes of this section; or
(*c*) a sale of a contact lens for a person who has attained the age of sixteen where the sale satisfies the requirements of subsection (3) below.

(3) Those requirements are that—

(*a*) the seller has—
  (i) the original specification;
  (ii) a copy of the original specification which he verifies with the person who provided it; or
  (iii) an order from the purchaser, submitted either in writing or electronically, which contains the particulars of the specification of the person who intends to wear the contact lens ("the wearer"), and the seller verifies those particulars with the person who provided the specification;
(*b*) the seller is reasonably satisfied that the goods ordered are for use by the person named in the specification;
(*c*) the sale is made before the expiry date mentioned in the specification;
(*d*) the seller is, or is under the general direction of, a registered medical practitioner, a registered optometrist or a registered dispensing optician; and
(*e*) the wearer—
  (i) is not, so far as the seller knows, registered as blind or registered as partially sighted in a register compiled by a local authority under section 29(4)(g) of the National Assistance Act 1948 (welfare services);

(ii) has not been certified as blind or as partially sighted and in consequence registered as blind or partially sighted in a register maintained by or on behalf of a council constituted under the Local Government (Scotland) Act 1994; or

(iii) has not been certified as blind and in consequence registered as blind in a register maintained by or on behalf of a Health and Social Services Board in Northern Ireland.

(3A) In this section—

(*a*) "seller"—

(i) includes any person who supplies the optical appliance or, as the case may be, the zero powered contact lens whether or not payment is made to him for the supply; and

(ii) does not include a person who supplies the contact lens as part of the assessment process in the course of fitting the lenses to the individual; and

(*b*) lenses are to be taken to have the same positive spherical power if the difference between them is within the tolerances relating to the power of such lenses specified from time to time by the British Standard Specification.

(3B) The seller must make arrangements, except in such cases or classes of cases as may be prescribed in rules made by the Council, for the individual for whom the optical appliance or, as the case may be, the zero powered contact lens is supplied to receive aftercare in so far as, and for so long as, may be reasonable in his particular case.

(3C) The Council may by rules specify the arrangements which are to be made or may be made under subsection (3B) above.

(4) Subsection (1) above shall apply to the supply of an optical appliance or zero powered contact lens in the course of the practice or business of an optometrist or dispensing optician, whether by the person carrying on the practice or business or by a person employed by him, if the supply was effected in pursuance of arrangements made—

(*a*) with a Minister of the Crown or Government Department (including a Northern Ireland department); or

(*b*) with any body on whom functions are conferred by or by virtue of—

(i) the National Health Service 1977 or the National Health Service and Community Care Act 1990;

(ii) the National Health Service (Scotland) Act 1978; or

(iii) the Health and Personal Social Services (Northern Ireland) Order 1972, or the Health and Personal Social Services (Northern Ireland) Order 1991,

as it applies to the sale of an optical appliance or zero powered contact lens.

(5) Subsection (1) above shall not apply to the sale of an optical appliance or zero powered contact lens—

(*a*) to a registered medical practitioner, registered optician or enrolled body corporate for the purposes of his practice or of his or its business;

(*b*) to a manufacturer of or dealer in optical appliances for the purposes of his business;

(*c*) to any authority or person carrying on a hospital, clinic, nursing home or other institution providing medical or surgical treatment;

(*cc*) to any authority or person providing a care home service (as defined by section 2(3) of the Regulation of Care (Scotland) Act 2001 (asp 8)), which includes the provision of medical or surgical treatment;

(*d*) to a Minister of the Crown or government department (including a Northern Ireland department);

(*e*) for the purpose of its export; or

(*f*) in accordance with an order under subsection (6) below.

(6) An order under this subsection is an order made by the Privy Council and specifying—

(*a*) optical appliances to which it applies; and

(*b*) conditions subject to which their sale is exempted from the requirements of subsection (1) above.

(7) Any such order relating to optical appliances consisting of or including one or more lenses shall specify, as a condition subject to which the sale of any such appliance is so exempted, the condition that the appliance must be in accordance with a written prescription which—

(*a*) has been given by a registered medical practitioner or registered optometrist following a testing of sight by him; and

(*b*) bears a date not more than such time as is specified in the order before the prescription is presented to the proposed seller of the appliance.

(8) An order under subsection (6) above may not specify as appliances to which it applies—

(*a*) contact lenses; or

(*b*) any optical appliance for a person under 16 years of age

(9) On any prosecution for selling an optical appliance or zero powered contact lens in contravention of subsection (1) above it shall be a defence for the defendant to prove—

(*a*) that he sold the appliance or lens as an antique or secondhand article; and

(*b*) that he did not know, and had no reason to believe, that the appliance was bought for the purpose of being used for correcting, remedying or relieving a defect of sight.

(10) A person who contravenes subsection (1) above shall be liable on summary conviction to a fine of an amount not exceeding **level 5** on the standard scale.

[Opticians Act 1989, s 27, as amended by the Regulation of Care (Scotland) Act 2001, s 79, the National Health Service and Community Care Act 1990, Sch 9 and SI 2005/848.]

8–22012 **28. Penalty for pretending to be registered etc.** (1) Any individual—

(*a*) who takes or uses the title of ophthalmic optician or the title of optometrist when he is not registered in the register of optometrists; or

(*b*) who takes or uses the title of dispensing optician when he is not registered in the register of dispensing opticians; or

(*c*) who takes or uses the title of registered optometrist when he is not registered in the register of optometrists maintained under section 7 above;

(*cc*) who holds himself out as being a student registrant when he is not registered in the register of those undertaking training as optometrists or dispensing opticians maintained under section 8A above;

(*ccc*) who holds himself out as having a specialty or proficiency which qualifies for entry in the appropriate register in accordance with rules made under section 10(1A) above but for whom no entry is extant;

(*d*) who takes or uses any name, title, addition or description falsely implying that he is registered in any of the registers; or

(*e*) who otherwise pretends that he is registered in any of the registers,

shall be liable on summary conviction to a fine of an amount not exceeding **level 5** on the standard scale.

(2) On any prosecution for an offence under subsection (1)(*d*) or (*e*) above, the taking or use of the title of optician by a person to whom this subsection applies is to be taken to imply that he is registered in one of the registers, but the implication may be rebutted if the defendant proves that he took or, as the case may be, used the title in circumstances where it would have been unreasonable for people to believe, in consequence of his taking or, as the case may be, use of it, that he was in fact registered in one of the registers.

(3) Subject to subsection (4) below, subsection (2) above applies to a person who carries on the business—

(*a*) of selling optical appliances; or

(*b*) of supplying optical appliances in pursuance of arrangements made as mentioned in section 27(4) above.

(4) Subsection (2) above does not apply to a person who sells or supplies only optical appliances or zero powered contact lenses or both as mentioned in section 27(5)(*a*) to (*e*) above.

(5) Any body corporate which—

(*a*) takes or uses the title of ophthalmic optician, the title of optometrist, the title of dispensing optician or the title of registered optician when it is not registered;

(*b*) takes or uses any name, title, addition or description falsely implying that it is registered;

(*c*) otherwise pretends that it is registered,

shall be liable on summary conviction to a fine of an amount not exceeding level 5 on the standard scale.

(6) On any prosecution for an offence under subsection (5)(*b*) or (*c*) above, the taking or using of the title of optician by a body corporate to which this subsection applies is to be taken to imply that it is registered, but the implication may be rebutted if the body corporate took or, as the case may be, used the title in circumstances where it would have been unreasonable for people to believe, in consequence of its taking or, as the case may be, use of it, that it was in fact registered.

(7) Subject to subsection (8) below, subsection (6) above applies to a body corporate which carries on the business—

(*a*) of selling optical appliances; or

(*b*) of supplying optical appliances or zero powered contact lenses in pursuance of arrangements made as mentioned in section 27(4) above.

(8) Subsection (6) above does not apply to a body corporate which sells or supplies optical appliances or zero powered contact lenses only as mentioned in section 27(5)(*a*) to (*e*) above.

(9) It is immaterial for the purposes of this section whether a title was used alone or in combination with any other words.

[Opticians Act 1989, s 28 as amended by SI 2005/848.]

8–22013 **29. Provision as to death or bankruptcy of registered optician.** (1) Where a registered optometrist or registered dispensing optician dies at a time when he is carrying on business or is in practice as an optometrist or dispensing optician, then during the three years beginning with his death or such longer period as the Council may in any particular case allow, section 28 above shall not operate to prevent—

(*a*) his executors or administrators;
(*b*) his surviving spouse or his surviving civil partner;
(*c*) any of his children; or
(*d*) trustees on behalf of his surviving spouse or his surviving civil partner or any of his children,

from taking or using in relation to that business or practice, but in conjunction with the name in which he carried it on, any title which he was entitled to take or use immediately before his death.

(2) Where a registered optometrist or registered dispensing optician becomes bankrupt at a time when he is carrying on business or is in practice as an optometrist or dispensing optician, then, during the three years beginning with the bankruptcy, section 28 above shall not operate to prevent his trustee in bankruptcy from taking or using in relation to that business or practice, but in conjunction with the name in which he carried it on, any title which he was entitled to take or use immediately before the bankruptcy.

(3) Where—

(*a*) a person by virtue of subsection (1) or (2) above takes or uses any title in relation to the business or practice—
  (i) of a deceased optometrist or dispensing optician; or
  (ii) of an optometrist or dispensing optician who has become bankrupt; and
(*b*) an offence under section 24, 25 or 27 above is committed in the course of that business or practice,

the Fitness to Practice Committee may, if they think fit, direct that subsection (1) or (2) above shall cease to apply in relation to that business or practice.

(4) This Act shall have effect in relation to any case in which it is alleged that there has been a conviction of any such offence and to any direction under subsection (3) above as it has effect in relation to a case in which it is alleged that a registrant's fitness to practise or as the case may be a business registrant's fitness to carry on business as an optometrist or a dispensing optician or both, is impaired and the making of an order under Part 2A above.

(5) *Scotland.*

(6) *Northern Ireland.*

[Opticians Act 1989, s 29 as amended by the Civil Partnership Act 2004, Sch 27 and SI 2005/848.]

8–22014 **30. Offences by bodies corporate.** (1) Where an offence under this Act which has been committed by a body corporate is proved to have been committed with the consent or connivance of, or to be attributable to any neglect on the part of, any responsible officer of the body corporate, he, as well as the body corporate, shall be deemed to be guilty of that offence and shall be liable to be proceeded against and punished accordingly.

(2) In subsection (1) above, "responsible officer" means any director, manager, secretary or other similar officer of the body corporate, or of a branch or department of the body corporate, or any person purporting to act in any such capacity.

[Opticians Act 1989, s 30 as amended by SI 2005/848.]

8–22014A **30A. Legal proceedings.** (1) Notwithstanding anything in any enactment, proceedings for an offence under this Part of this Act may be begun at any time within the period of six months beginning with the date on which evidence sufficient in the opinion of the Council to justify a prosecution for the offence comes to the Council's knowledge, or within a period of two years beginning with the date of the commission of the offence, whichever period first expires.

(2) In this section, "enactment" means—

(a) an Act of Parliament;
(b) an Act of the Scottish Parliament;
(c) any Northern Ireland legislation; or
(d) any instrument made under or having effect by virtue of an Act of Parliament, an Act of the Scottish Parliament or any Northern Ireland legislation.

[Opticians Act 1989, s 30A as inserted by SI 2005/848.]

PART V[1]
MISCELLANEOUS AND SUPPLEMENTARY

Supplementary

8–22015 **36. Interpretation.** (1) In this Act, unless the context otherwise requires—

"approved training establishment" means an establishment approved by the Council under section 12(7)(*a*) above;

"approved qualification" means any qualification approved by the Council under section 12(7)(*b*) above;

"body corporate" includes a limited liability partnership and, in Scotland, a partnership; and in relation to such partnerships, a reference to a director or other officer of a body corporate is a reference to a member;

"business registrant" means a body corporate registered in the register maintained by the Council under section 9 above;

"the Council" means the General Optical Council;

"dispensing optician" means a person engaged or proposing to engage in the fitting and supply of optical appliances;

"electronic communication" has the same meaning as in the Electronic Communications Act 2000;

"financial penalty order" means an order under Part 2A above that a registrant shall pay to the Council a sum specified in the order;

"functions" includes powers and duties;

"Hearings Panel" means the panel of persons appointed under section 5D(1) above;

"individual registrant" means any person whose name is in a register maintained by the Council under section 7 or 8A above;

"medical authority" means one of the universities and other bodies who choose appointed members of the General Medical Council;

"optometrist" means a person engaged or proposing to engage in the testing of sight (otherwise than as a registered medical practitioner or a person recognised by a medical authority as a medical student), whether or not he is also engaged or proposing to engage in the fitting and supply of optical appliances;

"optical appliance" means an appliance designed to correct, remedy or relieve a defect of sight;

"prescribed" means prescribed by rules under this Act;

"register" means, unless the context otherwise requires, any one of the following registers—

(*a*) the register of optometrists maintained under section 7 above;
(*b*) the register of dispensing opticians maintained under section 7 above;
(*c*) the registers of students maintained under section 8A above;
(*d*) the register of bodies corporate under section 9 above,

and, except where used in relation to medical practitioners, "registered" and "registration" have corresponding meanings;

"registrant", except in the expressions "individual registrant", "business registrant" and "student registrant", means a person whose name is in the appropriate register;

"student registrant" means a person whose name is in one of the registers maintained by the Council under section 8A above;

(2) References in this Act to testing sight are references to testing sight with the object of determining whether there is any and, if so, what defect of sight and of correcting, remedying or relieving any such defect of an anatomical or physiological nature by means of an optical appliance prescribed on the basis of the determination.

[Opticians Act 1989, s 36 as amended by SI 2005/848.]

1. Part V includes ss 31–38.
2. Only relevant definitions are printed here.

Criminal Justice (International Co-operation) Act 1990[1]

(1990 c 5)

PART II[2]

THE VIENNA CONVENTION

Substances useful for manufacture of controlled drugs

8–22016 12. Manufacture and supply of scheduled substances. (1) It is an offence for a person—

(*a*) to manufacture a scheduled substance; or
(*b*) to supply such a substance to another person,

knowing or suspecting that the substance is to be used in or for the unlawful production of a controlled drug.

(1A) A person does not commit an offence under subsection (1) above if he manufactures or, as the case may be, supplies the scheduled substance with the express consent of a constable.

(2) A person guilty of an offence under subsection (1) above is liable[3]—

(*a*) on summary conviction, to imprisonment for a term not exceeding **six months** or a fine not exceeding **the statutory maximum** or **both;**

(*b*) on conviction on indictment, to imprisonment for a term not exceeding **fourteen years** or a **fine** or **both**.

(3) In this section "a controlled drug" has the same meaning as in the Misuse of Drugs Act 1971 and "unlawful production of a controlled drug" means the production of such a drug which is unlawful by virtue of section 4(1)(*a*) of that Act.

(4) In this section and elsewhere in this Part of this Act "a scheduled substance" means a substance for the time being specified in Schedule 2 to this Act.

(5) Her Majesty may by Order in Council amend that Schedule (whether by addition, deletion or transfer from one Table to the other) but—

(*a*) no such Order shall add any substance to the Schedule unless—

(i) it appears to Her Majesty to be frequently used in or for the unlawful production of a controlled drug; or

(ii) it has been added to the Annex to the Vienna Convention under Article 12 of that Convention; and

(*b*) no such Order shall be made unless a draft of it has been laid before and approved by a resolution of each House of Parliament*.

[Criminal Justice (International Co-operation) Act 1990, s 12, as amended by the Criminal Justice (International Co-operation) Act 1998, s 1.]

***The Criminal Justice (International Co-operation) Act 1990, Part II, is printed as prospectively amended by the Criminal Justice Act 1993, s 25 and Sch 6. For Commencement Orders made at the date of going to press under the Criminal Justice Act 1993, see PART I: MAGISTRATES' COURTS, PROCEDURE, ANTE.**

1. Part I of this Act (Criminal Proceedings and Investigations) is printed in PART I: MAGISTRATES' COURTS, PROCEDURE, ante.

2. Part II contains ss 12–14.

3. For procedure in respect of an offence which is triable either way, see the Magistrates' Courts Act 1980, ss 17A–21, in PART I: MAGISTRATES' COURT, PROCEDURE, ante.

8–22017 **13. Regulations about scheduled substances.** (1) The Secretary of State may by regulations[1] make provision—

(*a*) imposing requirements as to the documentation of transactions involving scheduled substances;

(*b*) requiring the keeping of records and the furnishing of information with respect to such substances;

(*c*) for the inspection of records kept pursuant to the regulations;

(*d*) for the labelling of consignments of scheduled substances.

(2) Regulations made by virtue of subsection (1)(*b*) may, in particular, require—

(*a*) the notification of the proposed exportation of substances specified in Table I in Schedule 2 to this Act to such countries as may be specified in the regulations; and

(*b*) the production, in such circumstances as may be so specified, of evidence that the required notification has been given;

and for the purposes of section 68 of the Customs and Excise Management Act 1979 (offences relating to exportation of prohibited or restricted goods) any such substance shall be deemed to be exported contrary to a restriction for the time being in force with respect to it under this Act if it is exported without the requisite notification having been given.

(3) Regulations under this section may make different provision in relation to the substances specified in Table I and Table II in Schedule 2 to this Act respectively and in relation to different cases or circumstances.

(4) The power to make regulations under this section shall be exercisable by statutory instrument subject to annulment in pursuance of a resolution of either House of Parliament.

(5) Any person who fails to comply with any requirement imposed by the regulations or, in purported compliance with any such requirement, furnishes information which he knows to be false in a material particular or recklessly furnishes information which is false in a material particular is guilty of an offence and liable[2]—

(*a*) on summary conviction, to imprisonment for a term not exceeding **six months** or a fine not exceeding the **statutory maximum** or **both;**

(*b*) on conviction on indictment, to imprisonment for a term not exceeding **two years** or a **fine** or **both**.

(6) No information obtained pursuant to the regulations shall be disclosed except for the purposes of criminal proceedings or of proceedings under the provisions of the Criminal Justice (Scotland) Act 1987 relating to the confiscation of the proceeds of drug trafficking or corresponding provisions in force in Northern Ireland or of proceedings under Part 2, 3 or 4 of the Proceeds of Crime Act 2002.

[Criminal Justice (International Co-operation) Act 1990, s 13, as amended by the Drug Trafficking Act 1994, Sch 1, the Proceeds of Crime Act 2002, Sch 11.]

1. See the Controlled Drugs (Substances Useful for Manufacture) Regulations 1991, SI 1991/1285. See also the Controlled Drugs (Substances Useful for Manufacture) (Intra-Community Trade) Regulations 1993, SI 1993/2166 made under the European Communities Act 1972, s 2(2).

2. For procedure in respect of an offence which is triable either way, see the Magistrates' Courts Act 1980, ss 17A–21, in PART I: MAGISTRATES' COURTS, PROCEDURE, ante.

Proceeds of drug trafficking

8–22019 **15. Interest on sums unpaid under confiscation orders.** (1) If any sum required to be paid by a person under a confiscation order is not paid when it is required to be paid (whether forthwith on the making of the order or at a time specified under section 396(1) of the Criminal Procedure (Scotland) Act 1975) that person shall be liable to pay interest on that sum for the period for which it remains unpaid and the amount of the interest shall for the purposes of enforcement be treated as part of the amount to be recovered from him under the confiscation order.

(2) The sheriff may, on the application of the prosecutor, increase the term of imprisonment or detention fixed in respect of the confiscation order under section 396(2) of the said Act of 1975 (imprisonment in default of payment) if the effect of subsection (1) above is to increase the maximum period applicable in relation to the order under section 407(1A) of the said Act of 1975.

(3) The rate of interest under subsection (1) above shall be the rate payable under a decree of the Court of Session.

[Criminal Justice (International Co-operation) Act 1990, s 15, as amended by the Drug Trafficking Act 1994, Schs 1 and 3 and the Criminal Justice (Scotland) Act 1995, Sch 6.]

Offences at sea

8–22022 **18. Offences on British ships.** Anything which would constitute a drug trafficking offence if done on land in any part of the United Kingdom shall constitute that offence if done on a British ship.

[Criminal Justice (International Co-operation) Act 1990, s 18.]

8–22023 **19. Ships used for illicit traffic.** (1) This section applies to a British ship, a ship registered in a state other than the United Kingdom which is a party to the Vienna Convention (a "Convention state") and a ship not registered[1] in any country or territory.

(2) A person is guilty of an offence if on a ship to which this section applies, wherever it may be, he—

(*a*) has a controlled drug in his possession; or

(*b*) is in any way knowingly concerned in the carrying or concealing of a controlled drug on the ship,

knowing or having reasonable grounds to suspect that the drug is intended to be imported or has been exported contrary to section 3(1) of the Misuse of Drugs Act 1971 or the law of any state other than the United Kingdom.

(3) A certificate purporting to be issued by or on behalf of the government of any state to the effect that the importation or export of a controlled drug is prohibited by the law of that state shall be evidence, and in Scotland sufficient evidence, of the matters stated.

(4) A person guilty of an offence under this section is liable[2]—

(*a*) in a case where the controlled drug is a Class A drug—

(i) on summary conviction, to imprisonment for a term not exceeding **six months** or a fine not exceeding **the statutory maximum** or **both**;

(ii) on conviction on indictment, to imprisonment for **life** or a **fine** or **both**;

(*b*) in a case where the controlled drug is a Class B drug—

(i) on summary conviction, to imprisonment for a term not exceeding **six months** or a fine not exceeding **the statutory maximum** or **both**;

(ii) on conviction on indictment, to imprisonment for a term not exceeding **fourteen years** or **fine** or **both**;

(*c*) in a case where the controlled drug is a Class C drug—

(i) on summary conviction, to imprisonment for a term not exceeding **three months** or a fine not exceeding **the statutory maximum** or **both**;

(ii) on conviction on indictment, to imprisonment for a term not exceeding **five years*** or a **fine** or **both**.

(5) In this section "a controlled drug" and the references to controlled drugs of a specified Class have the same meaning as in the said Act of 1971; and an offence under this section shall be included in the offences to which section 28 of that Act (defences) applies.

[Criminal Justice (International Co-operation) Act 1990, s 19.]

***Words substituted by the Criminal Justice Act 2003, Sch 28, from a date to be appointed,**

1. Evidence of searches of US computer databases which contained documentation information on all United States

documented vessels was held to be both admissible and sufficient to establish that the defendants' yacht was not registered as a vessel of the United States; accordingly, the judge was entitled to reach the conclusion that if the yacht was not so registered there was an overwhelming inference that she was not registered anywhere (*R v Dean* [1998] 2 Cr App Rep 171).

2. For procedure in respect of an offence which is triable either way, see the Magistrates' Courts Act 1980, ss 17A–21, in PART I: MAGISTRATES' COURTS, PROCEDURE, ante.

8–22024 20. Enforcement powers. (1) The powers conferred on an enforcement officer by Schedule 3 to this Act shall be exercisable in relation to any ship to which section 18 or 19 above applies for the purpose of detecting and the taking of appropriate action in respect of the offences mentioned in those sections.

(2) Those powers shall not be exercised outside the landward limits of the territorial sea of the United Kingdom in relation to a ship registered in a Convention state except with the authority of the Commissioners of Customs and Excise; and they shall not give his authority unless that state has in relation to that ship—

(*a*) requested the assistance of the United Kingdom for the purpose mentioned in subsection (1) above; or

(*b*) authorised the United Kingdom to act for that purpose.

(3) In giving their authority pursuant to a request or authorisation from a Convention state the Commissioners of Customs and Excise shall impose such conditions or limitations on the exercise of the powers as may be necessary to give effect to any conditions or limitations imposed by that state.

(4) The Commissioners of Customs and Excise may, either of their own motion or in response to a request from a Convention state, authorise a Convention state to exercise, in relation to a British ship, powers corresponding to those conferred on enforcement officers by Schedule 3 to this Act but subject to such conditions or limitations, if any, as they may impose.

(5) Subsection (4) above is without prejudice to any agreement made, or which may be made, on behalf of the United Kingdom whereby the United Kingdom undertakes not to object to the exercise by any other state in relation to a British ship of powers corresponding to those conferred by that Schedule.

(6) The powers conferred by that Schedule shall not be exercised in the territorial sea of any state other than the United Kingdom without the authority of the Commissioners of Customs and Excise and they shall not give their authority unless that state has consented to the exercise of those powers.

[Criminal Justice (International Co-operation) Act 1990, s 20, as amended by the Criminal Justice Act 1993, s 23.]

8–22025 21. Jurisdiction and prosecutions. (1) Proceedings under this Part of this Act or Schedule 3 in respect of an offence on a ship may be taken, and the offence may for all incidental purposes be treated as having been committed, in any place in the United Kingdom.

(2) No such proceedings shall be instituted—

(*a*) in England or Wales except by or with the consent of the Director of Public Prosecutions or the Commissioners of Customs and Excise;

(*b*) *Northern Ireland.*

(3) Without prejudice to subsection (2) above no proceedings for an offence under section 19 above alleged to have been committed outside the landward limits of the territorial sea of the United Kingdom on a ship registered in a Convention state shall be instituted except in pursuance of the exercise with the authority of the Commissioners of Customs and Excise of the powers conferred by Schedule 3 to this Act; and section 3 of the Territorial Waters Jurisdiction Act 1878 (consent of Secretary of State for certain prosecutions) shall not apply to those proceedings.

[Criminal Justice (International Co-operation) Act 1990, s 21, as amended by the Criminal Justice Act 1993, s 23.]

Supplementary

8–22026 22. Extradition. *Repealed.*

8–22028 24. Interpretation of Part II. (1) In this Part of this Act—

"British ship" means a ship registered in the United Kingdom or a colony;

"Convention state" has the meaning given in section 19(1) above;

"scheduled substance" has the meaning given in section 12(4) above;

"ship" includes any vessel used in navigation;

"the territorial sea of the United Kingdom" includes the territorial sea adjacent to any of the Channel Islands, the Isle of Man or any colony;

"the Vienna Convention" means the United Nations Convention against Illicit Traffic in Narcotic Drugs and Psychotropic Substances which was signed in Vienna on 20th December 1988.

(2) Any expression used in this Part of this Act which is also used in the Drug Trafficking Act 1994 has the same meaning as in that Act.

(3) In relation to Scotland, any expression used in this Part of this Act which is also used in the Criminal Justice (Scotland) Act 1987 has the same meaning as in that Act and "drug trafficking offence" means an offence to which section 1 of that Act relates.

(4) If in any proceedings under this Part of this Act any question arises whether any country or territory is a state or is a party to the Vienna Convention, a certificate issued by or under the authority of the Secretary of State shall be conclusive evidence on that question.
[Criminal Justice (International Co-operation) Act 1990, s 24, as amended by the Drug Trafficking Act 1994, Sch 1.]

PART IV[1]
GENERAL

8–22036 **30. Expenses and receipts.** (1) Any expenses incurred by the Secretary of State under this Act shall be defrayed out of money provided by Parliament.*

(2)–(3) *Repealed.*

[Criminal Justice (International Co-operation) Act 1990, s 30, as amended by the Criminal Justice Act 1993, s 25 and the Drug Trafficking Act 1994, Sch 3.]

***The Criminal Justice (International Co-operation) Act 1990, Part IV, is printed as prospectively amended by the Criminal Justice Act 1993, s 25 and Sch 6. For Commencement Orders made at the date of going to press under the Criminal Justice Act 1993, see PART I: MAGISTRATES' COURTS, PROCEDURE, ANTE.**

1. Part IV contains ss 30–32.

8–22037 **31. Consequential and other amendments, repeals and revocation.** (1) *Consequential amendments.*

(2) *Repealed.*

(3)–(4) *Repeals, revocation.*

[Criminal Justice (International Co-operation) Act 1990, s 31, as amended by the Drug Trafficking Act 1994, Sch 3.]

8–22038 **32. Short title, commencement and extent.** (1) This Act may be cited as the Criminal Justice (International Co-operation) Act 1990.

(2) This Act shall come into force on such day as may be appointed by the Secretary of State by an order[1] made by statutory instrument and different days may be appointed for different provisions and different purposes and for different parts of the United Kingdom.

(3) This Act extends to Northern Ireland.

(4) Her Majesty may by Order in Council direct that the provisions of this Act and those provisions of the Drug Trafficking Act 1994 which re-enact provisions of this Act shall extend, with such exceptions and modifications as appear to Her Majesty to be appropriate, to any of the Channel Islands, the Isle of Man or any colony.

[Criminal Justice (International Co-operation) Act 1990, s 32, as amended by the Drug Trafficking Act 1994, Sch 1.]

1. The Criminal Justice (International Co-operation) Act 1980 (Commencement No 1) Order 1991, SI 1991/1072, and (Commencement No 2) Order 1991, SI 1991/2108, have been made.

8–22039

Sections 12 and 13

SCHEDULE 2
SUBSTANCES USEFUL FOR MANUFACTURING CONTROLLED DRUGS

(Amended by SI 1992/2873 and SI 2001/3933.)

TABLE I

N-ACETYLANTHRANILIC ACID
EPHEDRINE
EROGOMETRINE
ERGOTAMINE
ISOSAFROLE
LYSERGIC ACID
3, 4-METHYLENE DIOXYPHENYL-2-PROPANONE
NOREPHEDRINE
1-PHENYL-2-PROPANONE
PIPERONAL
PSEUDOEPHEDRINE
SAFROLE

The salts of the substances listed in this Table whenever the existence of such salts is possible.

TABLE II

ACETIC ANHYDRIDE
ACETONE
ANTHRANILIC ACID
ETHYL ETHER
HYDROCHLORIC ACID
METHYL ETHYL KETONE (also referred to as 2- BUTANONE or M.E.K.)

PHENYLACETIC ACID
PIPERIDINE
POTASSIUM PERMANGANATE
SULPHURIC ACID
TOLUENE

The salts of the substances listed in this Table whenever the existence of such salts is possible.

Section 20

SCHEDULE 3

ENFORCEMENT POWERS IN RESPECT OF SHIPS

Preliminary

8–22040 **1.** (1) In this Schedule "an enforcement officer"[1] means—

(*a*) a constable;
(*b*) an officer commissioned by the Commissioners of Customs and Excise under section 6(3) of the Customs and Excise Management Act 1979; and
(*c*) any other person of a description specified in an order[1] made for the purposes of this Schedule by the Secretary of State.

(2) The power to make an order under sub-paragraph (1)(*c*) above shall be exercisable by statutory instrument subject to annulment in pursuance of a resolution of either House of Parliament.

(3) In this Schedule "the ship" means the ship in relation to which the powers conferred by this Schedule are exercised.

1. The Criminal Justice (International Co-operation) Act 1990 (Enforcement Officers) Order 1992, SI 1992/77, has been made and provides that the following descriptions of persons, in addition to those specified in paras (*a*) and (*b*), shall be enforcement officers under this Schedule—

(*a*) commissioned officers of any of Her Majesty's ships;
(*b*) officers of the sea-fishery inspectorate of the Ministry of Agriculture, Fisheries and Food;
(*c*) officers of the fishery protection service of the Secretary of State for Scotland holding the rank of commander, first officer or second officer.

Power to stop, board, divert and detain[1]

8–22041 **2.** (1) An enforcement officer may stop the ship, board it and, if he thinks it necessary for the exercise of his functions, require it to be taken to a port in the United Kingdom and detain it there.

(2) Where an enforcement officer is exercising his powers with the authority of the Commissioners of Customs and Excise given under section 20(2) of this Act the officer may require the ship to be taken to a port in the Convention state in question or, if that state has so requested, in any other country or territory willing to receive it.

(3) For any of those purposes he may require the master or any member of the crew to take such action as may be necessary.

(4) If an enforcement officer detains a vessel he shall serve on the master a notice in writing stating that it is to be detained until the notice is withdrawn by the service on him of a further notice in writing signed by an enforcement officer.

1. As amended by the Criminal Justice Act 1993, s 23.

Power to search and obtain information

8–22042 **3.** (1) An enforcement officer may search the ship, anyone on it and anything on it including its cargo.

(2) An enforcement officer may require any person on the ship to give information concerning himself or anything on the ship.

(3) Without prejudice to the generality of those powers an enforcement officer may—

(*a*) open any containers;
(*b*) make tests and take samples of anything on the ship;
(*c*) require the production of documents, books or records relating to the ship or anything on it;
(*d*) make photographs or copies of anything whose production he has power to require.

Powers in respect of suspected offence

8–22043 **4.** If an enforcement officer has reasonable grounds to suspect that an offence mentioned in section 18 or 19 of this Act has been committed on a ship to which that section applies he may—

(*a*) arrest without warrant anyone whom he has reasonable grounds for suspecting to be guilty of the offence; and
(*b*) seize and detain anything found on the ship which appears to him to be evidence of the offence.

Assistants

8–22044 **5.** (1) An enforcement officer may take with him, to assist him in exercising his powers—

(*a*) any other persons; and
(*b*) any equipment or materials.

(2) A person whom an enforcement officer takes with him to assist him may perform any of the officer's functions but only under the officer's supervision.

Use of reasonable force

8–22045 **6.** An enforcement officer may use reasonable force, if necessary, in the performance of his functions.

Evidence of authority

8–22046 **7.** An enforcement officer shall, if required, produce evidence of his authority.

Protection of officers

8–22047 **8.** An enforcement officer shall not be liable in any civil or criminal proceedings for anything done in the purported performance of his functions under this Schedule if the court is satisfied that the act was done in good faith and that there were reasonable grounds for doing it.

Offences

8–22048 **9.** (1) A person is guilty of an offence if he—

(*a*) intentionally obstructs an enforcement officer in the performance of any of his functions under this Schedule;
(*b*) fails without reasonable excuse to comply with a requirement made by an enforcement officer in the performance of those functions; or
(*c*) in purporting to give information required by an officer for the performance of those functions—
  (i) makes a statement which he knows to be false in a material particular or recklessly makes a statement which is false in a material particular; or
  (ii) intentionally fails to disclose any material particular.

(2) A person guilty of an offence under this paragraph is liable on summary conviction to a fine not exceeding **level 5** on the standard scale.

Osteopaths Act 1993[1]

(1993 c 21)

The General Council and its committees

8–22050 **1. The General Osteopathic Council and its committees.** (1) There shall be a body corporate to be known as the General Osteopathic Council (referred to in this Act as "the General Council").

(2) It shall be the duty of the General Council to develop, promote and regulate the profession of osteopathy.

(3) The General Council shall have such other functions as are conferred on it by this Act.

(4) Part I of the Schedule shall have effect with respect to the constitution of the General Council.

(5) There shall be four committees of the General Council, to be known as—

(*a*) the Education Committee;
(*b*) the Investigating Committee;
(*c*) the Professional Conduct Committee; and
(*d*) the Health Committee.

(6) The four committees are referred to in this Act as "the statutory committees".

(7) Each of the statutory committees shall have the functions conferred on it by or under this Act.

(8) The General Council may establish such other committees as it considers appropriate in connection with the discharge of its functions.

(9)–(12) *Supplementary provisions as to committees; Orders in Council with respect to matters dealt with by Schedule 1 to the Act.*

[Osteopaths Act 1993, s 1.]

---

1. This Act establishes a body to be known as the General Osteopathic Council; provides for the regulation of the profession of osteopathy, including making provision as to the registration of osteopaths and as to their professional education and conduct.

For commencement provisions, see s 42, post.

8–22051 **32. Offences.** (1) A person who (whether expressly or by implication) describes himself as an osteopath, osteopathic practitioner, osteopathic physician, osteopathist, osteotherapist, or any other kind of osteopath, is guilty of an offence unless he is a registered osteopath.

(2) A person who, without reasonable excuse, fails to comply with any requirement imposed by—

(*a*) the Professional Conduct Committee,
(*b*) the Health Committee, or
(*c*) an appeal tribunal hearing an appeal under section 30[1],

under rules made by virtue of section 26(2)(*h*)[2] or under any corresponding rules made by virtue of section 30(4) is guilty of an offence.

(3) A person guilty of an offence under this section shall be liable on summary conviction to a fine not exceeding **level five** on the standard scale.
[Osteopaths Act 1993, s 32.]

1. Section 30 provides for a right of appeal to an appeal tribunal against decisions of the Health Committee.
2. Section 26(2)(*h*) of the Act empowers the General Council to make rules as to the procedure to be followed by the Professional Conduct Committee or the Health Committee in considering any allegation under s 22 (consideration of allegations by the Professional Conduct Committee) or 23 (consideration of allegations by the Health Committee), and under s 26(2)(*h*) the rules shall, in particular, include provision empowering the Committee to require persons to attend and give evidence or to produce documents.

Supplemental

8–22052 41. Interpretation[1]. In this Act—

"conditionally registered osteopath" means a person who is registered with conditional registration;
"fully registered osteopath" means a person who is registered with full registration;
"the General Council" means the General Osteopathic Council;
"prescribed" means prescribed by rules made by the General Council;
"provisionally registered osteopath" means a person who is registered with provisional registration;
"recognised qualification" has the meaning given by section 14(1);
"the register" means the register of osteopaths maintained by the Registrar under section 2;
"registered" means registered in the register;
"registered address", in relation to a registered osteopath, means the address which is entered in the register;
"registered osteopath" means a person who is registered as a fully registered osteopath, as a conditionally registered osteopath or as a provisionally registered osteopath;
"the Registrar" has the meaning given in section 2(2);
"the statutory committees" has the meaning given by section 1(6).
[Osteopaths Act 1993, s 41.]

1. Only those definitions which are relevant to this work are printed here.

8–22053 42. Short title, commencement, transitional provisions and extent. (1) This Act may be cited as the Osteopaths Act 1993.

(2) This Act shall come into force on such day as the Secretary of State may by order[1] appoint.

(3) The power conferred by subsection (2) shall be exercisable by statutory instrument.

(4) Different days may be appointed by an order under subsection (2) for different purposes and different provisions.

(5) Any order under subsection (2) may make such transitional provision as the Secretary of State considers appropriate.

(6)–(7) *Transitional provisions; extent.*
[Osteopaths Act 1993, s 42.]

1. At the date of going to press the following commencement orders have been made: Commencement (No 1 and Transitional Provision) Order 1997, SI 1997/34; Commencement (No 2) Order 1998, SI 1998/872; Commencement (No 3) Order 1998, SI 1998/1138; Commencement (No 4) Order 1999, SI 1999/1767; Commencement (No 5) Order 2000, SI 2000/217; Commencement (No 6 and Transitional Provisions) Order 2000, SI 2000/1065; Commencement (No 7) Order 2002, SI 2002/500. All the provisions of the Act are in force with the following exceptions: s 1(4) in so far as it relates to paras 3, 9, 10, 12, 14(1), 14(3)(*d*), 14(4) and 14(5)(*a*).

Chiropractors Act 1994[1]

(1994 c 17)

The General Council and its committees

8–22060 1. The General Chiropractic Council and its committees. (1) There shall be a body corporate to be known as the General Chiropractic Council (referred to in this Act as "the General Council").

(2) It shall be the duty of the General Council to develop, promote and regulate the profession of chiropractic.

(3) The General Council shall have such other functions as are conferred on it by this Act.

(4) Part I of Schedule 1 shall have effect with respect to the constitution of the General Council.

(5) There shall be four committees of the General Council, to be known as—

(*a*) the Education Committee;
(*b*) the Investigating Committee;
(*c*) the Professional Conduct Committee; and
(*d*) the Health Committee.

(6) The four committees are referred to in this Act as "the statutory committees".

(7) Each of the statutory committees shall have the functions conferred on it by or under this Act.

(8) The General Council may establish such other committees as it considers appropriate in connection with the discharge of its functions.

(9)–(12) *Supplementary provisions as to committees; Orders in Council with respect to matters dealt with by Schedule 1 to the Act.*

[Chiropractors Act 1994, s 1.]

1. This Act establishes a body to be known as the General Chiropractic Council; provides for the regulation of the chiropractic profession, including making provision as to the registration of chiropractors and as to their professional education and conduct.

The Act is to be brought into force in accordance with s 44, post.

8–22060A 3–10. *Registration of chiropractors.*

Offences

8–22061 32. Offences. (1) A person who (whether expressly or by implication) describes himself as a chiropractor, chiropractic practitioner, chiropractitioner, chiropractic physician, or any other kind of chiropractor, is guilty of an offence unless he is a registered chiropractor.

(2) A person who, without reasonable excuse, fails to comply with any requirement imposed by—

(*a*) the Professional Conduct Committee,

(*b*) the Health Committee, or

(*c*) an appeal tribunal hearing an appeal under section 30[1],

under rules made by virtue of section 26(2)(*h*)[2] or under any corresponding rules made by virtue of section 30(4) is guilty of an offence.

(3) A person guilty of an offence under this section shall be liable on summary conviction to a fine not exceeding **level five** on the standard scale.

[Chiropractors Act 1994, s 32.]

1. Section 30 provides for a right of appeal to an appeal tribunal against decisions of the Health Committee. See the General Chiropractic Council (Health Appeal Tribunal) Rules Order 2000, SI 2000/3214.

2. Section 26(2)(*h*) of the Act empowers the General Council to make rules as to the procedure to be followed by the Professional Conduct Committee or the Health Committee in considering any allegation under s 22 (consideration of allegations by the Professional Conduct Committee) or 23 (consideration of allegations by the Health Committee), and under s 26(2)(*h*) the rules shall, in particular, include provision empowering the Committee to require persons to attend and give evidence or to produce documents. See the General Chiropractic Council (Professional Conduct Committee) Rules Order of Council 2000, SI 2000/3290 amended by SI 2005/2114. See also the General Chiropractic Council (Health Committee) Rules Order of Council 2000, SI 2000/3291 made under s 26.

Supplemental

8–22062 43. Interpretation[1]. In this Act—

"conditionally registered chiropractor" means a person who is registered with conditional registration;

"fully registered chiropractor" means a person who is registered with full registration;

"the General Council" means the General Chiropractic Council;

"prescribed" means prescribed by rules made by the General Council;

"provisionally registered chiropractor" means a person who is registered with provisional registration;

"recognised qualification" has the meaning given by section 14(1);

"the register" means the register of chiropractors maintained by the Registrar under section 2;

"registered" means registered in the register;

"registered address" means the address which is entered in the register, in relation to the chiropractor in question, in accordance with the requirements of section 6(1) and does not include any other address which may be entered in the register, in relation to him, by virtue of rules made under section 6(2);

"registered chiropractor" means a person who is registered as a fully registered chiropractor, as a conditionally registered chiropractor or as a provisionally registered chiropractor;

"the Registrar" has the meaning given in section 2(2);

"the statutory committees" has the meaning given by section 1(6).

[Chiropractors Act 1994, s 43.]

1. Only those definitions which are relevant to this work are printed here.

8–22063 44. Short title, commencement, transitional provisions and extent. (1) This Act may be cited as the Chiropractors Act 1994.

(2) Section 42 and Schedule 2 shall come into force on the passing of this Act.

(3) The other provisions of this Act shall come into force on such day as the Secretary of State may by order[1] appoint.

(4) The power conferred by subsection (3) shall be exercisable by statutory instrument.

(5) Different days may be appointed by an order under subsection (3) for different purposes and different provisions.

(6) Any order under subsection (3) may make such transitional provision as the Secretary of State considers appropriate.

(7)–(8) *Transitional provisions; extent.*

[Chiropractors Act 1994, s 44.]

---

1. At the date of going to press, the Chiropractors Act 1994 (Commencement No 1 and Transitional Provision) Order 1998, SI 1998/2031, had been made bringing into force on 14 August 1998 certain provisions of the Act for the purpose of establishing the General Chiropractic Council; and the Chiropractors Act 1999 (Commencement No 2) Order 1999, SI 1999/1309 and the Chiropractors Act 1999 (Commencement No 3) Order 1999, SI 1999/1496 and the Chiropractors Act 1994 (Commencement No 4) Order 2000, SI 2000/2388, have been made. Of the provisions reproduced in this work, s 32(1) had not been brought into force when we went to press.

Drug Trafficking Act 1994

(1994 c 37)

PART IV[1]

MISCELLANEOUS AND SUPPLEMENTAL

Investigations into drug trafficking

8–22065U 55. Order to make material available. (1) A constable may, for the purpose of an investigation into drug trafficking, apply[2] to a Circuit judge for an order under subsection (2) below in relation to particular material or material of a particular description.

(2) If on such an application the judge is satisfied that the conditions in subsection (4) below are fulfilled, he may make an order that the person who appears to him in possession of the material to which the application relates shall—

(*a*) produce it to a constable for him to take away, or
(*b*) give a constable access to it,

within such period as the order may specify.

This subsection has effect subject to section 59(11) of this Act.

(3) The period to be specified in an order under subsection (2) above shall be seven days unless it appears to the judge that a longer or shorter period would be appropriate in the particular circumstances of the application.

(4) The conditions referred to in subsection (2) above are—

(*a*) that there are reasonable grounds for suspecting that a specified person has carried on drug trafficking;
(*b*) that there are reasonable grounds for suspecting that the material to which the application relates—
 (i) is likely to be of substantial value (whether by itself or together with other material) to the investigation for the purpose of which the application is made; and
 (ii) does not consist of or include items subject to legal privilege or excluded material; and
(*c*) that there are reasonable grounds for believing that it is in the public interest, having regard—
 (i) to the benefit likely to accrue to the investigation if the material is obtained, and
 (ii) to the circumstances under which the person in possession of the material holds it,

that the material should be produced or that access to it should be given.

(5) Where the judge makes an order under subsection (2)(*b*) above in relation to material on any premises he may, on the application of a constable, order any person who appears to him to be entitled to grant entry to the premises to allow a constable to enter the premises to obtain access to the material.

(6) An application under subsection (1) or (5) above may be made ex parte to a judge in chambers.

(7) Provision may be made by Criminal Procedure Rules as to—

(*a*) the discharge and variation of orders under this section; and
(*b*) proceedings relating to such orders.

(8) An order of a Circuit judge under this section shall have effect as if it were an order of the Crown Court.

(9) Where the material to which an application under subsection (1) above relates consists of information contained in a computer—

(*a*) an order under subsection 2(*a*) above shall have effect as an order to produce the material in a form in which it can be taken away and in which it is visible and legible; and (*b*) an order under subsection 2(*b*) above shall have effect as an order to give access to the material in a form in which it is visible and legible.

(10) An order under subsection (2) above—

(*a*) shall not confer any right to production of, or access to, items subject to legal privilege or excluded material;

(*b*) shall have effect notwithstanding any obligation as to secrecy or other restriction upon the disclosure of information imposed by statute or otherwise; and

(*c*) may be made in relation to material in the possession of an authorised government department;

and in this subsection "authorised government department" means a government department which is an authorised department for the purposes of the Crown Proceedings Act 1947.

[Drug Trafficking Act 1994, s 55, as amended by the Proceeds of Crime Act 2002, Sch 11 and the Courts Act 2003, Sch 8.]

---

1. Part IV contains ss 55–69.

2. An application under s 55 should be made ex p (*R v Central Criminal Court, ex p Francis & Francis* [1989] AC 346, [1988] 1 All ER 677, 87 Cr App Rep 104, DC); however, the recipient of an order has the opportunity to apply to discharge or vary the order before it takes effect (Criminal Procedure Rules 2005, Part 30, in PART I: MAGISTRATES' COURTS, PROCEDURE, ante). The power to make an order is not limited to investigations in the UK, but the information must show that the intention is to assist a foreign law enforcement agency. Only exceptionally will the judge require undertakings from the applicant before making the order (*R v Crown Court at Southwark, ex p Customs and Excise Comrs* [1990] 1 QB 650, [1989] 3 All ER 673, DC). Application may be made for an order for the production of material solely or partly for the purpose of assisting an investigation by a law enforcement agency of another country into drug trafficking, as well as for the purpose of an investigation by UK customs officers. Nevertheless, if the application is made in order to assist an investigation by a foreign law enforcement agency this must be made clear on the face of the information in support of the application (*R v Crown Court at Southwark, ex p Customs and Excise Comrs* [1990] 1 QB 650, [1989] 3 All ER 673).

8–22066 56. Authority for search. (1) A constable may, for the purpose of an investigation into drug trafficking, apply to a Circuit judge for a warrant under this section in relation to specified premises.

(2) On such application the judge may issue a warrant authorising a constable to enter and search the premises if the judge is satisfied—

(*a*) that an order made under section 55 of this Act in relation to material on the premises has not been complied with;

(*b*) that the conditions in subsection (3) below are fulfilled; or

(*c*) that the conditions in subsection (4) below are fulfilled.

(3) The conditions referred to in subsection (2)(*b*) above are—

(*a*) that there are reasonable grounds for suspecting that a specified person has carried on drug trafficking;

(*b*) that the conditions in subsection (4)(*b*) and (*c*) of section 55 of this Act are fulfilled in relation to any material on the premises; and

(*c*) that it would not be appropriate to make an order under that section in relation to the material because—

(i) it is not practicable to communicate with any person entitled to produce the material;

(ii) it is not practicable to communicate with any person entitled to grant access to the material or entitled to grant entry to the premises in which the material is situated; or

(iii) the investigation for the purpose of which the application is made might be seriously prejudiced unless a constable could secure immediate access to the material.

(4) The conditions referred to in subsection (2)(*c*) above are—

(*a*) that there are reasonable grounds for suspecting that a specified person has carried on drug trafficking;

(*b*) that there are reasonable grounds for suspecting that there is on the premises material relating to the specified person or to drug trafficking which is likely to be of substantial value (whether by itself or together with other material) to the investigation for the purpose of which the application is made, but that the material cannot at the time of the application be particularised; and

(*c*) that—

(i) it is not practicable to communicate with any person entitled to grant entry to the premises;

(ii) entry to the premises will not be granted unless a warrant is produced; or

(iii) the investigation for the purpose of which the application is made might be seriously prejudiced unless a constable arriving at the premises could secure immediate entry to them.

(5) Where a constable has entered premises in the execution of a warrant issued under this section, he may seize and retain any material, other than items subject to legal privilege and excluded material,

which is likely to be of substantial value (whether by itself or together with other material) to the investigation for the purpose of which the warrant was issued[1].
[Drug Trafficking Act 1994, s 56, as amended by the Proceeds of Crime Act 2002, Sch 11.]

1. The Criminal Justice and Police Act 2001, Part 2 (see PART 1, ante) conferred additional powers of seizure. Section 55 of that Act (obligation to return excluded and special procedure material) has effect, in relation to the power of seizure conferred by s 56(5), with the omission of every reference to special procedure material: the Criminal Justice and Police Act 2001, s 55(5).

8–22066A 57. Provisions supplementary to sections 55 and 56. (1) For the purposes of sections 21 and 22 of the Police and Criminal Evidence Act 1984 (access to, and copying and retention of, seized material)—

(*a*) an investigation into drug trafficking shall be treated as if it were an investigation of or in connection with an offence; and

(*b*) material produced in pursuance of an order under section 55(2)(*a*) of this Act shall be treated as if it were material seized by a constable.

(2) In sections 55 and 56 of this Act "excluded material", "items subject to legal privilege" and "premises" have the same meaning as in the 1984 Act.
[Drug Trafficking Act 1994, s 57.]

8–22066B 58. Offence of prejudicing investigation. (1) Where, in relation to an investigation into drug trafficking—

(*a*) an order under section 55 of this Act has been made or has been applied for and has not been refused, or

(*b*) a warrant under section 56 of this Act has been issued,

a person is guilty of an offence if, knowing or suspecting that the investigation is taking place, he makes any disclosure which is likely to prejudice the investigation.

(2) In proceedings against a person for an offence under this section, it is a defence to prove—

(*a*) that he did not know or suspect that the disclosure was likely to prejudice the investigation; or

(*b*) that he had lawful authority or reasonable excuse for making the disclosure.

(3) Nothing in subsection (1) above makes it an offence for a professional legal adviser to disclose any information or other matter—

(*a*) to, or to a representative of, a client of his in connection with the giving by the adviser of legal advice to the client; or

(*b*) to any person—

(i) in contemplation of, or in connection with, legal proceedings; and

(ii) for the purpose of those proceedings.

(4) Subsection (3) above does not apply in relation to any information or other matter which is disclosed with a view to furthering any criminal purpose.

(5) A person guilty of an offence under this section shall be liable—

(*a*) on summary conviction, to imprisonment for a term not exceeding **six months** or to a fine not exceeding **the statutory maximum** or to **both**; and

(*b*) on conviction on indictment, to imprisonment for a term not exceeding **five years** or to a **fine** or to **both**.
[Drug Trafficking Act 1994, s 58.]

1. For procedure in respect of this offence which is triable either way, see the Magistrates' Courts Act 1980, ss 17A-21, in PART I: MAGISTRATES' COURTS, PROCEDURE, ante.

8–22066C 59. Disclosure of information held by government departments(1)–(10) *Repealed*.

. (11) In the case of material in the possession of an authorised government department, an order under section 55(2) of this Act may require any officer of the department (whether named in the order or not) who may for the time being be in possession of the material concerned to comply with it, and such an order shall be served as if the proceedings were civil proceedings against the department.

(12) The person on whom such an order is served—

(*a*) shall take all reasonable steps to bring it to the attention of the officer concerned; and

(*b*) if the order is not brought to that officer's attention within the period specified in an order under section 55(2), shall report the reasons for the failure to the court;

and it shall also be the duty of any other officer of the department in receipt of the order to take such steps as are mentioned in paragraph (*a*) above.

(13) In this section "authorised government department" means a government department which is an authorised department for the purposes of the Crown Proceedings Act 1947.
[Drug Trafficking Act 1994, s 59, as amended by the Proceeds of Crime Act 2002, Sch 11.]

8–22066D 59A. Construction of sections 55 to 59. (1) This section has effect for the purposes of sections 55 to 59.

(2) A reference to constable includes a reference to a customs officer.

(3) A customs officer is a person commissioned by the Commissioners of Customs and Excise under section 6(3) of the Customs and Excise Management Act 1979 (c 2).

(4) Drug trafficking means doing or being concerned in any of the following (whether in England and Wales or elsewhere)—

(*a*) producing or supplying a controlled drug where the production or supply contravenes section 4(1) of the Misuse of Drugs Act 1971 or a corresponding law,

(*b*) transporting or storing a controlled drug where possession of the drug contravenes section 5(1) of that Act or a corresponding law;

(*c*) importing or exporting a controlled drug where the importation or exportation is prohibited by section 3(1) of that Act or a corresponding law;

(*d*) manufacturing or supplying a scheduled substance within the meaning of section 12 of the Criminal Justice (International Co-operation) Act 1990 where the manufacture or supply is an offence under that section or would be such an offence if it took place in England and Wales;

(*e*) using any ship for illicit traffic in controlled drugs in circumstances which amount to the commission of an offence under section 19 of that Act.

(5) In this section "corresponding law" has the same meaning as in the Misuse of Drugs Act 1971.*

[Drug Trafficking Act 1994, s 59A as inserted by the Proceeds of Crime Act 2002, s 456.]

Prosecution of offences etc

8–22066E 60. Revenue and Customs prosecutions. (1) Proceedings for a specified offence may be instituted by the Director of Revenue and Customs Prosecutions or by order of the Commissioners for Her Majesty's Revenue and Customs ("the Commissioners").

(2) Any proceedings for a specified offence which are instituted by order of the Commissioners shall be commenced in the name of an officer of Revenue and Customs.

(3) *Repealed.*

(4) Where the Commissioners investigate, or propose to investigate, any matter with a view to determining—

(*a*) whether there are grounds for believing that a specified offence has been committed, or

(*b*) whether a person should be prosecuted for a specified offence,

that matter shall be treated as an assigned matter within the meaning of the Customs and Excise Management Act 1979.

(5) Nothing in this section shall be taken—

(*a*) to prevent any person (including any officer) who has power to arrest, detain or prosecute any person for a specified offence from doing so; or

(*b*) to prevent a court from proceeding to deal with a person brought before it following his arrest by an officer for a specified offence, even though the proceedings have not been instituted in accordance with this section.

(6) In this section—

"specified offence" means—

(*a*) an offence under section 58 of this Act;*

(*b*) attempting to commit, conspiracy to commit or incitement to commit any such offence;

(*c*) *repealed.*

(6A) Proceedings for an offence are instituted—

(*a*) when a justice of the peace issues a summons or warrant under section 1 of the Magistrates' Courts Act 1980 (issue of summons to, or warrant for arrest of, accused) in respect of the offence;

(*b*) when a person is charged with the offence after being taken into custody without a warrant;

(*c*) when a bill of indictment is preferred under section 2 of the Administration of Justice (Miscellaneous Provisions) Act 1933 in a case falling within paragraph (*b*) of subsection (2) of that section (preferment by direction of the criminal division of the Court of Appeal or by direction, or with the consent, of a High Court judge).

(6B) Where the application of subsection (6A) would result in there being more than one time for the institution of proceedings they must be taken to have been instituted at the earliest of those times.

(7) *Repealed.*

(8) *Repealed.*

[Drug Trafficking Act 1994, s 60, as amended by the Proceeds of Crime Act 2002, Sch 11 and the Commissioners for Revenue and Customs Act 2005, Sch 4.]

***Paragraph (6A)(*aa*) inserted by the Criminal Justice Act 2003, Sch 36 from a date to be appointed.**

8–22066F 61. Extension of certain offences to Crown servants and exemptions for regulators etc. (1) The Secretary of State may by regulations[1] provide that, in such circumstances as may be prescribed, section 58 of this Act shall apply to such persons in the public service of the Crown, or such categories of person in that service, as may be prescribed.

(2) *Repealed.*

(3) *Repealed.*

(4) *Repealed.*

(5) In this section—

"the Crown" includes the Crown in right of Her Majesty's Government in Northern Ireland; and

"prescribed" means prescribed by regulations made by the Secretary of State.

(6) Any power to make regulations under this section shall be exercisable by statutory instrument.

(7) Any such instrument shall be subject to annulment in pursuance of a resolution of either House of Parliament.

[Drug Trafficking Act 1994, s 61, as amended by the Proceeds of Crime Act 2002, Sch 11.]

1. The Drug Trafficking Offences Act 1986 (Crown Servants and Regulators etc) Regulations 1994, SI 1994/1757 amended by SI 2001/3649, have been made and have effect as if made under this Act by virtue of Sch 2.

Interpretation of Act

8–22066G 62. *Repealed.*

8–22066H 63. General interpretation. (1) *Repealed.*

(2) *Repealed.*

(3) Subject to section 66(2) and (6) of this Act—

(*a*) *repealed*);

(*b*) any reference in this Act to "drug trafficking" includes a reference to drug trafficking carried out before the commencement of this Act.

[Drug Trafficking Act 1994, s 63, as amended by the Proceeds of Crime Act 2002, Sch 11.]

8–22066I 64. *Repealed.*

Supplemental

8–22066J 65. Consequential amendments and modifications of other Acts. (1) The enactments mentioned in Schedule 1 to this Act shall have effect subject to the amendments there specified (being amendments consequential upon the provisions of this Act).

(2) In section 1(2)(*a*) of the Rehabilitation of Offenders Act 1974 (failure to pay fines etc not to prevent person becoming rehabilitated) the reference to a fine or other sum adjudged to be paid by or imposed on a conviction does not include a reference to an amount payable under a confiscation order.

(3) Section 281(4) of the Insolvency Act 1986 (discharge of bankrupt not to release him from liabilities in respect of fines, etc) shall have effect as if the reference to a fine included a reference to a confiscation order.

(4) Section 55(2) of the Bankruptcy (Scotland) Act 1985 (discharge of debtor not to release him from liabilities in respect of fines etc) shall have effect as if the reference to a fine included a reference to a confiscation order.

[Drug Trafficking Act 1994, s 65.]

8–22066K 66. Transitional provisions and savings. (1) The transitional provisions and savings set out in Schedule 2 to this Act shall have effect.

(2) Part I and section 59 of this Act shall not apply—

(*a*) in relation to any proceedings for, or in respect of, an offence if the person accused (or, as the case may be, convicted) of that offence was charged with the offence (whether by the laying of an information or otherwise) before the date on which this Act comes into force, or

(*b*) in relation to any proceedings not within paragraph (*a*) above instituted before that date,

and references in this subsection to proceedings include a reference to any order made by a court in the proceedings.

(3) Accordingly (and without prejudice to section 16 of the Interpretation Act 1978), the relevant enactments and any instrument made under any of those enactments shall continue to apply in relation to any proceedings within subsection (2)(*a*) or (*b*) above (and, in particular, in relation to any confiscation order, within the meaning of the Drug Trafficking Offences Act 1986, made in any such proceedings) as if this Act had not been passed.

(4) In subsection (3) above "the relevant enactments" are—

(*a*) the enactments reproduced in Part I and section 59 of this Act,

(*b*) any other enactment reproduced by this Act, so far as applicable in relation to any of the enactments reproduced in that Part or that section, and (*c*) any enactment amended by this Act,

but do not include any enactment which, immediately before the date on which this Act comes into force, had not come into force.

(5) Subsection (2) above is without prejudice to section 4(7), 7(4), 26(3) or 29(7) of this Act.

(6) Nothing in section 19(3) or (4) of this Act shall apply to any proceedings—

(*a*) for an offence committed before the commencement of this Act; or

(*b*) for one or more offences, any one of which was so committed.

[Drug Trafficking Act 1994, s 66.]

8–22066L 67. Repeals etc. (1) The enactments mentioned in Schedule 3 to this Act are repealed to the extent specified in the third column of that Schedule.

(2) Paragraph 9 of Schedule 2 to the Criminal Justice (Confiscation) (Northern Ireland) Order 1990 (which amends section 29(1) of the Criminal Justice (International Co-operation) Act 1990) is hereby revoked.

[Drug Trafficking Act 1994, s 67.]

8–22066M 68. Extent. (1) Subject to the following provisions of this section, this Act extends to England and Wales only.

(2) The following provisions of this Act also extend to Scotland—

(*a*) *repealed*);

(*b*) *repealed*);

(*c*) *repealed*);

(*d*) section 59(11) to (13);

(*e*) this section;

(*f*) section 69;

(*g*) sections 63, 65(1), 66 and 67(1), so far as they relate to provisions which extend to Scotland; and

(*h*) Schedule 2.*

(3) The following provisions of this Act also extend to Northern Ireland—

(*a*) *repealed*);

(*b*) this section;

(*c*) section 69;

(*d*) sections 63, 65(1), 66 and 67(1), so far as they relate to provisions which extend to Northern Ireland; and

(*e*) Schedule 2.*

(4) Section 67(2) of this Act extends to Northern Ireland only.

(5) The modifications of other enactments specified in section 65(2) to (4) of this Act, and the amendments specified in Schedule 1 to this Act, have the same extent as the enactments to which they relate.

(6) Subject to subsection (7) below, the repeals contained in Schedule 3 to this Act have the same extent as the provisions to which they relate.

(7) The repeals of—

(*a*) sections 14 and 23A of the Criminal Justice (International Co-operation) Act 1990, and

(*b*) paragraph 5 of Schedule 4 to the Criminal Justice Act 1993,

extend to England and Wales only.

[Drug Trafficking Act 1994, s 68, as amended by the Proceeds of Crime Act 2002, Sch 11.]

8–22066N 69. *Short title and commencement*

Health Act 1999[1]

(1999 c 8)

PART I[2]

THE NATIONAL HEALTH SERVICE

Quality etc

8–22068 18–24

Repealed.

2. Part I comprises ss 1 to 44.

PART III[1]

MISCELLANEOUS AND SUPPLEMENTARY

Miscellaneous

8–22068FA 60. *Regulation of health care and associated professions*

1. Part III comprises ss 60 to 69.

Supplementary

8–22068G 62. *Regulations and orders*[1]

1. The Nursing and Midwifery Order 2001, SI 2002/253 amended by SI 2004/1947 provides for the regulation of nurses and midwives and creates a regulatory body, the Nursing and Midwifery Council, which is required to set standards of education, training, conduct and performance and to put in place arrangements to ensure that they are met. Certain offences are created by arts 44 and 45 punishable on summary conviction by a fine not exceeding **level 3** on the standard scale. These are, principally, where a person falsely represents himself as being registered or having professional qualifications or uses a title to which he is not entitled; or, although not falling within the specified categories, attends a woman in childbirth. Transitional provisions are made by the Nursing and Midwifery Order 2001 (Transitional Provisions) Order 2002, SI 2002/1125 and the Nursing and Midwifery Order 2001 (Transitional Provisions) Order 2004, SI 2004/1762. A number of Orders of Council have been made under SI 2002/253 which regulate the professions of nursing and midwifery, the subject matter of which is outside the scope of this Manual.

The Health Professions Order 2001, SI 2002/254 amended by SI 2004/1947 provides for the regulation of a number of health professions (arts therapists; chiropodists; clinical scientists; dietitians; medical laboratory technicians; occupational therapists; orthoptists; paramedics; physiotherapists; prosthetists and orthotists; radiographers; and speech and language therapists) it creates a regulatory body, the Health Professions Council, which is required to set standards of education, training, conduct and performance and to put in place arrangements to ensure that they are met. Article 39 provides for certain actions to be offences punishable on summary conviction by a fine not exceeding **level 5** on the standard scale. These are, principally, where a person falsely represents himself as being registered or having professional qualifications or uses a title to which he is not entitled. Transitional provisions are made by the Health Professions Order 2001 (Transitional Provisions) Order 2002, SI 2002/1124.

8–22068GA 63. Supplementary and consequential provision etc. (1) The Secretary of State may by order[1] make—

(*a*) such supplementary, incidental or consequential provision, or
(*b*) such transitory, transitional or saving provision,

as he considers necessary or expedient for the purposes of, in consequence of or for giving full effect to any provision of this Act.

(2) The provision which may be made under subsection (1) includes provision amending or repealing any enactment, instrument or document.
[Health Act 1999, s 63.]

1. The Health Authorities Act 1995 (Rectification of Transitional Arrangements) Order 2000, SI 2000/179 has been made.

Final provisions

8–22068H 65. Amendments and repeals. (1) Schedule 4 (amendments of enactments) is to have effect.

(2) The repeals set out in Schedule 5 (which include the repeal of an enactment which is spent) are to have effect.
[Health Act 1999, s 65.]

8–22068HA 66. Devolution

8–22068I 67. Commencement. (1) The preceding provisions of this Act (including the Schedules) are to come into force on such day as the Secretary of State may by order[1] appoint.

(2) Different days may be appointed under this section for different purposes.

(3) Subsection (1) does not apply to the repeal of section 10 of the Professions Supplementary to Medicine Act 1960 (power to extend or restrict application of Act), which comes into force on 1st July 1999 or, if later, on the day on which this Act is passed.

(4) Subsection (1) does not apply to section 66, of which—

(*a*) subsections (1) and (3) to (6) come into force on the day on which this Act is passed,
(*b*) subsection (2) comes into force on 1st July 1999 or, if later, the day on which this Act is passed.

[Health Act 1999, s 67.]

1. At the date of going to press the following commencement orders had been made: Health Act 1999 (Commencement No 1) Order 1999, SI 1999/2177, Health Act 1999 (Commencement No 2) Order 1999, SI 1999/2342, Health Act 1999

(Commencement No 3) Order 1999, SI 1999/2540, Health Act 1999 (Commencement No 4) Order 1999, SI 1999/90, Health Act 1999 (Commencement No 5) Order 1999, SI 1999/2793, the Health Act 1999 (Commencement No 6) (Scotland) Order 1999, SSI 1999/115, the Health Act 1999 (Commencement No 8) Order 2000, SI 2000/779, and the Health Act 1999 (Commencement No 9) Order 2000, SI 2000/1041. All the provisions set out in this work were brought into force no later than 4 January 2000.

8–22068J 68. Extent. (1) Subject to the following provisions—

(*a*) Part I extends only to England and Wales,
(*b*) Part II extends only to Scotland, and
(*c*) this Part extends to Northern Ireland (as well as to England and Wales and Scotland).

(2) The amendment or repeal of an enactment, or a power to amend or repeal an enactment, which extends to any part of the United Kingdom extends also to that part.

(3) Sections 22 and 25 extend to Scotland and Northern Ireland.

(4) Sections 33 to 38 extend to Scotland and Northern Ireland.

(5) The Secretary of State may by order provide that so much of this Act as extends to England and Wales is to apply to the Isles of Scilly with such modifications (if any) as are specified in the order; but otherwise this Act does not extend there.
[Health Act 1999, s 68.]

8–22068K 69. Short title. This Act may be cited as the Health Act 1999.
[Health Act 1999, s 69.]

National Health Service Reform and Health Care Professions Act 2002[1]

Part 1
National Health Service, etc

Joint working

8–22070 23. Joint working with the prison service. (1) In exercising their respective functions, NHS bodies (on the one hand) and the prison service (on the other) shall co-operate with one another with a view to improving the way in which those functions are exercised in relation to securing and maintaining the health of prisoners.

(2) The appropriate authority may by regulations make provision for or in connection with enabling prescribed NHS bodies (on the one hand) and the prison service (on the other) to enter into prescribed arrangements in relation to the exercise of—

(*a*) prescribed functions of the NHS bodies, and
(*b*) prescribed health-related functions of the prison service,

if the arrangements are likely to lead to an improvement in the way in which those functions are exercised in relation to securing and maintaining the health of prisoners.

(3) The arrangements which may be prescribed include arrangements—

(*a*) for or in connection with the establishment and maintenance of a fund—
  (i) which is made up of contributions by one or more NHS bodies and by the prison service, and
  (ii) out of which payments may be made towards expenditure incurred in the exercise of both prescribed functions of the NHS body or bodies and prescribed health-related functions of the prison service,
(*b*) for or in connection with the exercise by an NHS body on behalf of the prison service of prescribed health-related functions of the prison service in conjunction with the exercise by the NHS body of prescribed functions of theirs,
(*c*) for or in connection with the exercise by the prison service on behalf of an NHS body of prescribed functions of the NHS body in conjunction with the exercise by the prison service of prescribed health-related functions of the prison service,
(*d*) as to the provision of staff, goods, services or accommodation in connection with any arrangements mentioned in paragraph (*a*), (*b*) or (*c*),
(*e*) as to the making of payments by the prison service to an NHS body in connection with any arrangements mentioned in paragraph (*b*),
(*f*) as to the making of payments by an NHS body to the prison service in connection with any arrangements mentioned in paragraph (*c*).

(4) Any arrangements made by virtue of this section do not affect the liability of NHS bodies, or of the prison service, for the exercise of any of their functions.

(5) In this section—

"appropriate authority" means—

(*a*) the Secretary of State, in relation to England, and
(*b*) the National Assembly for Wales, in relation to Wales,

"NHS bodies" means Strategic Health Authorities, Primary Care Trusts, NHS trusts, Special Health Authorities, Health Authorities and Local Health Boards,

"prison service" means the Minister of the Crown exercising functions in relation to prisons (within the meaning of the Prison Act 1952 (c 52)),

"Minister of the Crown" has the same meaning as in the Ministers of the Crown Act 1975 (c 26).

[National Health Service Reform and Health Care Professions Act 2002, s 23.]

1. With the exception of ss 38–42 this Act is to be brought into force in accordance with commencement orders made under s 42. At the date of going to press no commencement order had been made with respect to s 23.

Human Tissue Act 2004[1]

(2004 c 30)

PART 1[2]

REMOVAL, STORAGE AND USE OF HUMAN ORGANS AND OTHER TISSUE FOR SCHEDULED PURPOSES

8–22070A **1. Authorisation of activities for scheduled purposes.** (1) The following activities shall be lawful if done with appropriate consent—

(*a*) the storage of the body of a deceased person for use for a purpose specified in Schedule 1, other than anatomical examination;
(*b*) the use of the body of a deceased person for a purpose so specified, other than anatomical examination;
(*c*) the removal from the body of a deceased person, for use for a purpose specified in Schedule 1, of any relevant material of which the body consists or which it contains;
(*d*) the storage for use for a purpose specified in Part 1 of Schedule 1 of any relevant material which has come from a human body;
(*e*) the storage for use for a purpose specified in Part 2 of Schedule 1 of any relevant material which has come from the body of a deceased person;
(*f*) the use for a purpose specified in Part 1 of Schedule 1 of any relevant material which has come from a human body;
(*g*) the use for a purpose specified in Part 2 of Schedule 1 of any relevant material which has come from the body of a deceased person.

(2) The storage of the body of a deceased person for use for the purpose of anatomical examination shall be lawful if done—

(*a*) with appropriate consent, and
(*b*) after the signing of a certificate—
  (i) under section 22(1) of the Births and Deaths Registration Act 1953 (c 20), or
  (ii) under Article 25(2) of the Births and Deaths Registration (Northern Ireland) Order 1976 (SI 1976/1041 (NI 14)),

of the cause of death of the person.

(3) The use of the body of a deceased person for the purpose of anatomical examination shall be lawful if done—

(*a*) with appropriate consent, and
(*b*) after the death of the person has been registered—
  (i) under section 15 of the Births and Deaths Registration Act 1953, or
  (ii) under Article 21 of the Births and Deaths Registration (Northern Ireland) Order 1976.

(4) Subsections (1) to (3) do not apply to an activity of a kind mentioned there if it is done in relation to—

(*a*) a body to which subsection (5) applies, or
(*b*) relevant material to which subsection (6) applies.

(5) This subsection applies to a body if—

(*a*) it has been imported, or
(*b*) it is the body of a person who died before the day on which this section comes into force and at least one hundred years have elapsed since the date of the person's death.

(6) This subsection applies to relevant material if—

(*a*) it has been imported,
(*b*) it has come from a body which has been imported, or

(*c*) it is material which has come from the body of a person who died before the day on which this section comes into force and at least one hundred years have elapsed since the date of the person's death.

(7) Subsection (1)(*d*) does not apply to the storage of relevant material for use for the purpose of research in connection with disorders, or the functioning, of the human body if—

(*a*) the material has come from the body of a living person, and
(*b*) the research falls within subsection (9).

(8) Subsection (1)(*f*) does not apply to the use of relevant material for the purpose of research in connection with disorders, or the functioning, of the human body if—

(*a*) the material has come from the body of a living person, and
(*b*) the research falls within subsection (9).

(9) Research falls within this subsection if—

(*a*) it is ethically approved in accordance with regulations made by the Secretary of State, and
(*b*) it is to be, or is, carried out in circumstances such that the person carrying it out is not in possession, and not likely to come into possession, of information from which the person from whose body the material has come can be identified.

(10) The following activities shall be lawful—

(*a*) the storage for use for a purpose specified in Part 2 of Schedule 1 of any relevant material which has come from the body of a living person;
(*b*) the use for such a purpose of any relevant material which has come from the body of a living person;
(*c*) an activity in relation to which subsection (4), (7) or (8) has effect.

(11) The Secretary of State may by order—

(*a*) vary or omit any of the purposes specified in Part 1 or 2 of Schedule 1, or
(*b*) add to the purposes specified in Part 1 or 2 of that Schedule.

(12) Nothing in this section applies to—

(*a*) the use of relevant material in connection with a device to which Directive 98/79/EC of the European Parliament and of the Council on *in vitro* diagnostic medical devices applies, where the use falls within the Directive, or
(*b*) the storage of relevant material for use falling within paragraph (*a*).

(13) In this section, the references to a body or material which has been imported do not include a body or material which has been imported after having been exported with a view to its subsequently being re-imported.
[Human Tissue Act 2004, s 1.]

1. The Act provides a legislative framework for body donation and the taking, storage and use of human organs and tissue, and makes consent the fundamental principle underpinning these activities.

The Act sets up an authority the aim of which is to rationalise such activities as transplantation and anatomical examination, and it will regulate other activities such as post mortem examinations and the storage of human material for education, training and research.

The Act is in 3 Parts and has 7 Schedules.

The Act will be brought into force in accordance with commencement orders made under s 60. At the time of going to press no commencement orders had been made.

2. Part 1 contains ss 1–12.

8–22070B 2. "Appropriate consent": children. (1) This section makes provision for the interpretation of "appropriate consent" in section 1 in relation to an activity involving the body, or material from the body, of a person who is a child or has died a child ("the child concerned").

(2) Subject to subsection (3), where the child concerned is alive, "appropriate consent" means his consent.

(3) Where—

(*a*) the child concerned is alive,
(*b*) neither a decision of his to consent to the activity, nor a decision of his not to consent to it, is in force, and
(*c*) either he is not competent to deal with the issue of consent in relation to the activity or, though he is competent to deal with that issue, he fails to do so,

"appropriate consent" means the consent of a person who has parental responsibility for him.

(4) Where the child concerned has died and the activity is one to which subsection (5) applies, "appropriate consent" means his consent in writing.

(5) This subsection applies to an activity involving storage for use, or use, for the purpose of—

(*a*) public display, or
(*b*) where the subject-matter of the activity is not excepted material, anatomical examination.

(6) Consent in writing for the purposes of subsection (4) is only valid if—

(*a*) it is signed by the child concerned in the presence of at least one witness who attests the signature, or

(*b*) it is signed at the direction of the child concerned, in his presence and in the presence of at least one witness who attests the signature.

(7) Where the child concerned has died and the activity is not one to which subsection (5) applies, "appropriate consent" means—

(*a*) if a decision of his to consent to the activity, or a decision of his not to consent to it, was in force immediately before he died, his consent;

(*b*) if paragraph (*a*) does not apply—

(i) the consent of a person who had parental responsibility for him immediately before he died, or

(ii) where no person had parental responsibility for him immediately before he died, the consent of a person who stood in a qualifying relationship to him at that time.

[Human Tissue Act 2004, s 2.]

8–22070C 3. "Appropriate consent": adults. (1) This section makes provision for the interpretation of "appropriate consent" in section 1 in relation to an activity involving the body, or material from the body, of a person who is an adult or has died an adult ("the person concerned").

(2) Where the person concerned is alive, "appropriate consent" means his consent.

(3) Where the person concerned has died and the activity is one to which subsection (4) applies, "appropriate consent" means his consent in writing.

(4) This subsection applies to an activity involving storage for use, or use, for the purpose of—

(*a*) public display, or

(*b*) where the subject-matter of the activity is not excepted material, anatomical examination.

(5) Consent in writing for the purposes of subsection (3) is only valid if—

(*a*) it is signed by the person concerned in the presence of at least one witness who attests the signature,

(*b*) it is signed at the direction of the person concerned, in his presence and in the presence of at least one witness who attests the signature, or

(*c*) it is contained in a will of the person concerned made in accordance with the requirements of—

(i) section 9 of the Wills Act 1837 (c 26), or

(ii) Article 5 of the Wills and Administration Proceedings (Northern Ireland) Order 1994 (SI 1994/1899 (NI 13)).

(6) Where the person concerned has died and the activity is not one to which subsection (4) applies, "appropriate consent" means—

(*a*) if a decision of his to consent to the activity, or a decision of his not to consent to it, was in force immediately before he died, his consent;

(*b*) if—

(i) paragraph (*a*) does not apply, and

(ii) he has appointed a person or persons under section 4 to deal after his death with the issue of consent in relation to the activity,

consent given under the appointment;

(*c*) if neither paragraph (*a*) nor paragraph (*b*) applies, the consent of a person who stood in a qualifying relationship to him immediately before he died.

(7) Where the person concerned has appointed a person or persons under section 4 to deal after his death with the issue of consent in relation to the activity, the appointment shall be disregarded for the purposes of subsection (6) if no one is able to give consent under it.

(8) If it is not reasonably practicable to communicate with a person appointed under section 4 within the time available if consent in relation to the activity is to be acted on, he shall be treated for the purposes of subsection (7) as not able to give consent under the appointment in relation to it.

[Human Tissue Act 2004, s 3.]

8–22070D 4. Nominated representatives. (1) An adult may appoint one or more persons to represent him after his death in relation to consent for the purposes of section 1.

(2) An appointment under this section may be general or limited to consent in relation to such one or more activities as may be specified in the appointment.

(3) An appointment under this section may be made orally or in writing.

(4) An oral appointment under this section is only valid if made in the presence of at least two witnesses present at the same time.

(5) A written appointment under this section is only valid if—

(*a*) it is signed by the person making it in the presence of at least one witness who attests the signature, (*b*) it is signed at the direction of the person making it, in his presence and in the presence of at least one witness who attests the signature, or

(*c*) it is contained in a will of the person making it, being a will which is made in accordance with the requirements of—

(i) section 9 of the Wills Act 1837 (c 26), or

(ii) Article 5 of the Wills and Administration Proceedings (Northern Ireland) Order 1994 (SI 1994/1899 (NI 13)).

(6) Where a person appoints two or more persons under this section in relation to the same activity, they shall be regarded as appointed to act jointly and severally unless the appointment provides that they are appointed to act jointly.

(7) An appointment under this section may be revoked at any time.

(8) Subsections (3) to (5) apply to the revocation of an appointment under this section as they apply to the making of such an appointment.

(9) A person appointed under this section may at any time renounce his appointment.

(10) A person may not act under an appointment under this section if—

(*a*) he is not an adult, or

(*b*) he is of a description prescribed for the purposes of this provision by regulations made by the Secretary of State.

[Human Tissue Act 2004, s 4.]

8–22070E 5. Prohibition of activities without consent etc. (1) A person commits an offence if, without appropriate consent, he does an activity to which subsection (1), (2) or (3) of section 1 applies, unless he reasonably believes—

(*a*) that he does the activity with appropriate consent, or

(*b*) that what he does is not an activity to which the subsection applies.

(2) A person commits an offence if—

(*a*) he falsely represents to a person whom he knows or believes is going to, or may, do an activity to which subsection (1), (2) or (3) of section 1 applies—

(i) that there is appropriate consent to the doing of the activity, or

(ii) that the activity is not one to which the subsection applies, and

(*b*) he knows that the representation is false or does not believe it to be true.

(3) Subject to subsection (4), a person commits an offence if, when he does an activity to which section 1(2) applies, neither of the following has been signed in relation to the cause of death of the person concerned—

(*a*) a certificate under section 22(1) of the Births and Deaths Registration Act 1953 (c 20), and

(*b*) a certificate under Article 25(2) of the Births and Deaths Registration (Northern Ireland) Order 1976 (SI 1976/1041 (NI 14)).

(4) Subsection (3) does not apply—

(*a*) where the person reasonably believes—

(i) that a certificate under either of those provisions has been signed in relation to the cause of death of the person concerned, or

(ii) that what he does is not an activity to which section 1(2) applies, or

(*b*) where the person comes into lawful possession of the body immediately after death and stores it prior to its removal to a place where anatomical examination is to take place.

(5) Subject to subsection (6), a person commits an offence if, when he does an activity to which section 1(3) applies, the death of the person concerned has not been registered under either of the following provisions—

(*a*) section 15 of the Births and Deaths Registration Act 1953, and

(*b*) Article 21 of the Births and Deaths Registration (Northern Ireland) Order 1976.

(6) Subsection (5) does not apply where the person reasonably believes—

(*a*) that the death of the person concerned has been registered under either of those provisions, or

(*b*) that what he does is not an activity to which section 1(3) applies.

(7) A person guilty of an offence under this section shall be liable—

(*a*) on summary conviction to a fine not exceeding the statutory maximum;

(*b*) on conviction on indictment—

(i) to imprisonment for a term not exceeding 3 years, or

(ii) to a fine, or

(iii) to both.

(8) In this section, "appropriate consent" has the same meaning as in section 1.
[Human Tissue Act 2004, s 5.]

8–22070F **6. Activities involving material from adults who lack capacity to consent.** Where—

(*a*) an activity of a kind mentioned in section 1(1)(*d*) or (*f*) involves material from the body of a person who—

(i) is an adult, and
(ii) lacks capacity to consent to the activity, and

(*b*) neither a decision of his to consent to the activity, nor a decision of his not to consent to it, is in force,

there shall for the purposes of this Part be deemed to be consent of his to the activity if it is done in circumstances of a kind specified by regulations made by the Secretary of State.
[Human Tissue Act 2004, s 6.]

8–22070G **7. Powers to dispense with need for consent.** (1) If the Authority is satisfied—

(*a*) that relevant material has come from the body of a living person,
(*b*) that it is not reasonably possible to trace the person from whose body the material has come ("the donor"),
(*c*) that it is desirable in the interests of another person (including a future person) that the material be used for the purpose of obtaining scientific or medical information about the donor, and
(*d*) that there is no reason to believe—

(i) that the donor has died,
(ii) that a decision of the donor to refuse to consent to the use of the material for that purpose is in force, or
(iii) that the donor lacks capacity to consent to the use of the material for that purpose,

it may direct that subsection (3) apply to the material for the benefit of the other person.

(2) If the Authority is satisfied—

(*a*) that relevant material has come from the body of a living person,
(*b*) that it is desirable in the interests of another person (including a future person) that the material be used for the purpose of obtaining scientific or medical information about the person from whose body the material has come ("the donor"),
(*c*) that reasonable efforts have been made to get the donor to decide whether to consent to the use of the material for that purpose,
(*d*) that there is no reason to believe—

(i) that the donor has died,
(ii) that a decision of the donor to refuse to consent to the use of the material for that purpose is in force, or
(iii) that the donor lacks capacity to consent to the use of the material for that purpose, and

(*e*) that the donor has been given notice of the application for the exercise of the power conferred by this subsection,

it may direct that subsection (3) apply to the material for the benefit of the other person.

(3) Where material is the subject of a direction under subsection (1) or (2), there shall for the purposes of this Part be deemed to be consent of the donor to the use of the material for the purpose of obtaining scientific or medical information about him which may be relevant to the person for whose benefit the direction is given.

(4) The Secretary of State may by regulations enable the High Court, in such circumstances as the regulations may provide, to make an order deeming there for the purposes of this Part to be appropriate consent to an activity consisting of—

(*a*) the storage of the body of a deceased person for use for the purpose of research in connection with disorders, or the functioning, of the human body,
(*b*) the use of the body of a deceased person for that purpose,
(*c*) the removal from the body of a deceased person, for use for that purpose, of any relevant material of which the body consists or which it contains,
(*d*) the storage for use for that purpose of any relevant material which has come from a human body, or
(*e*) the use for that purpose of any relevant material which has come from a human body.

[Human Tissue Act 2004, s 7.]

8–22070H **8. Restriction of activities in relation to donated material.** (1) Subject to subsection (2), a person commits an offence if he—

(*a*) uses donated material for a purpose which is not a qualifying purpose, or (*b*) stores donated material for use for a purpose which is not a qualifying purpose.

(2) Subsection (1) does not apply where the person reasonably believes that what he uses, or stores, is not donated material.

(3) A person guilty of an offence under this section shall be liable—

(*a*) on summary conviction to a fine not exceeding the statutory maximum;
(*b*) on conviction on indictment—

(i) to imprisonment for a term not exceeding 3 years, or
(ii) to a fine, or
(iii) to both.

(4) In subsection (1), references to a qualifying purpose are to—

(*a*) a purpose specified in Schedule 1,
(*b*) the purpose of medical diagnosis or treatment,
(*c*) the purpose of decent disposal, or
(*d*) a purpose specified in regulations made by the Secretary of State.

(5) In this section, references to donated material are to—

(*a*) the body of a deceased person, or
(*b*) relevant material which has come from a human body,

which is, or has been, the subject of donation.

(6) For the purposes of subsection (5), a body, or material, is the subject of donation if authority under section 1(1) to (3) exists in relation to it.
[Human Tissue Act 2004, s 8.]

8–22070I 9. Existing holdings. (1) In its application to the following activities, section 1(1) shall have effect with the omission of the words "if done with appropriate consent"—

(*a*) the storage of an existing holding for use for a purpose specified in Schedule 1;
(*b*) the use of an existing holding for a purpose so specified.

(2) Subsection (1) does not apply where the existing holding is a body, or separated part of a body, in relation to which section 10(3) or (5) has effect.

(3) Section 5(1) and (2) shall have effect as if the activities mentioned in subsection (1) were not activities to which section 1(1) applies.

(4) In this section, "existing holding" means—

(*a*) the body of a deceased person, or
(*b*) relevant material which has come from a human body,

held, immediately before the day on which section 1(1) comes into force, for use for a purpose specified in Schedule 1.
[Human Tissue Act 2004, s 9.]

8–22070J 10. Existing anatomical specimens. (1) This section applies where a person dies during the three years immediately preceding the coming into force of section 1.

(2) Subsection (3) applies where—

(*a*) before section 1 comes into force, authority is given under section 4(2) or (3) of the Anatomy Act 1984 (c 14) for the person's body to be used for anatomical examination, and
(*b*) section 1 comes into force before anatomical examination of the person's body is concluded.

(3) During so much of the relevant period as falls after section 1 comes into force, that authority shall be treated for the purposes of section 1 as appropriate consent in relation to—

(*a*) the storage of the person's body, or separated parts of his body, for use for the purpose of anatomical examination, and
(*b*) the use of his body, or separated parts of his body, for that purpose.

(4) Subsection (5) applies where—

(*a*) before section 1 comes into force, authority is given under section 6(2) or (3) of the Anatomy Act 1984 for possession of parts (or any specified parts) of the person's body to be held after anatomical examination of his body is concluded, and
(*b*) anatomical examination of the person's body is concluded—

(i) after section 1 comes into force, but
(ii) before the end of the period of three years beginning with the date of the person's death.

(5) With effect from the conclusion of the anatomical examination of the person's body, that authority shall be treated for the purposes of section 1 as appropriate consent in relation to—

(*a*) the storage for use for a qualifying purpose of a part of the person's body which—

(i) is a part to which that authority relates, and
(ii) is such that the person cannot be recognised simply by examination of the part, and

(*b*) the use for a qualifying purpose of such a part of the person's body.

(6) Where for the purposes of section 1 there would not be appropriate consent in relation to an activity but for authority given under the Anatomy Act 1984 (c 14) being treated for those purposes as appropriate consent in relation to the activity, section 1(1) to (3) do not authorise the doing of the activity otherwise than in accordance with that authority.

(7) In subsection (3), "the relevant period", in relation to a person, means whichever is the shorter of—

(*a*) the period of three years beginning with the date of the person's death, and
(*b*) the period beginning with that date and ending when anatomical examination of the person's body is concluded.

(8) In subsection (5), "qualifying purpose" means a purpose specified in paragraph 6 or 9 of Schedule 1.

(9) The Secretary of State may by order amend subsection (8).
[Human Tissue Act 2004, s 10.]

8–22070K 11. Coroners. (1) Nothing in this Part applies to anything done for purposes of functions of a coroner or under the authority of a coroner.

(2) Where a person knows, or has reason to believe, that—

(*a*) the body of a deceased person, or
(*b*) relevant material which has come from the body of a deceased person,

is, or may be, required for purposes of functions of a coroner, he shall not act on authority under section 1 in relation to the body, or material, except with the consent of the coroner.
[Human Tissue Act 2004, s 11.]

8–22070L 12. Interpretation of Part 1. In this Part, "excepted material" means material which has—

(*a*) come from the body of a living person, or
(*b*) come from the body of a deceased person otherwise than in the course of use of the body for the purpose of anatomical examination.

[Human Tissue Act 2004, s 12.]

PART 2[1]

REGULATION OF ACTIVITIES INVOLVING HUMAN TISSUE

The Human Tissue Authority

8–22070M 13. The Human Tissue Authority. (1) There shall be a body corporate to be known as the Human Tissue Authority (referred to in this Act as "the Authority").

(2) Schedule 2 (which makes further provision about the Authority) has effect.
[Human Tissue Act 2004, s 13.]

1. Part 2 contains ss 13–41. Part 2 creates a body corporate known as the Human Tissue Authority and a licensing regime to regulate: anatomical and post mortem examinations; the removal of material and organs from deceased bodies; the storage of anatomical specimens, bodies and relevant material; and the use for public display of deceased persons and material from the bodies of deceased persons.

8–22070N 14. Remit. (1) The following are the activities within the remit of the Authority—

(*a*) the removal from a human body, for use for a scheduled purpose, of any relevant material of which the body consists or which it contains;
(*b*) the use, for a scheduled purpose, of—
  (i) the body of a deceased person, or
  (ii) relevant material which has come from a human body;
(*c*) the storage of an anatomical specimen or former anatomical specimen;
(*d*) the storage (in any case not falling within paragraph (*c*)) of—
  (i) the body of a deceased person, or
  (ii) relevant material which has come from a human body,

  for use for a scheduled purpose;
(*e*) the import or export of—
  (i) the body of a deceased person, or
  (ii) relevant material which has come from a human body,

  for use for a scheduled purpose;
(*f*) the disposal of the body of a deceased person which has been—
  (i) imported for use,
  (ii) stored for use, or

(iii) used,

for a scheduled purpose;

(*g*) the disposal of relevant material which—

(i) has been removed from a person's body for the purposes of his medical treatment,
(ii) has been removed from the body of a deceased person for the purposes of an anatomical, or post-mortem, examination,
(iii) has been removed from a human body (otherwise than as mentioned in sub-paragraph (ii)) for use for a scheduled purpose,
(iv) has come from a human body and been imported for use for a scheduled purpose, or
(v) has come from the body of a deceased person which has been imported for use for a scheduled purpose.

(2) Without prejudice to the generality of subsection (1)(*a*) and (*b*), the activities within the remit of the Authority include, in particular—

(*a*) the carrying-out of an anatomical examination, and
(*b*) the making of a post-mortem examination.

(3) An activity is excluded from the remit of the Authority if—

(*a*) it relates to the body of a person who died before the day on which this section comes into force or to material which has come from the body of such a person, and
(*b*) at least one hundred years have elapsed since the date of the person's death.

(4) The Secretary of State may by order amend this section for the purpose of adding to the activities within the remit of the Authority.

(5) In this section, "relevant material", in relation to use for the scheduled purpose of transplantation, does not include blood or anything derived from blood.
[Human Tissue Act 2004, s 14.]

8–22070O 15. General functions. The Authority shall have the following general functions—

(*a*) maintaining a statement of the general principles which it considers should be followed—

(i) in the carrying-on of activities within its remit, and
(ii) in the carrying-out of its functions in relation to such activities;

(*b*) providing in relation to activities within its remit such general oversight and guidance as it considers appropriate;
(*c*) superintending, in relation to activities within its remit, compliance with—

(i) requirements imposed by or under Part 1 or this Part, and
(ii) codes of practice under this Act;

(*d*) providing to the public, and to persons carrying on activities within its remit, such information and advice as it considers appropriate about the nature and purpose of such activities;
(*e*) monitoring developments relating to activities within its remit and advising the Secretary of State, the National Assembly for Wales and the relevant Northern Ireland department on issues relating to such developments;
(*f*) advising the Secretary of State, the National Assembly for Wales or the relevant Northern Ireland department on such other issues relating to activities within its remit as he, the Assembly or the department may require.

[Human Tissue Act 2004, s 15.]

Licensing

8–22070P 16. Licence requirement. (1) No person shall do an activity to which this section applies otherwise than under the authority of a licence granted for the purposes of this section.

(2) This section applies to the following activities—

(*a*) the carrying-out of an anatomical examination;
(*b*) the making of a post-mortem examination;
(*c*) the removal from the body of a deceased person (otherwise than in the course of an activity mentioned in paragraph (*a*) or (*b*)) of relevant material of which the body consists or which it contains, for use for a scheduled purpose other than transplantation;
(*d*) the storage of an anatomical specimen;
(*e*) the storage (in any case not falling within paragraph (*d*)) of—

(i) the body of a deceased person, or
(ii) relevant material which has come from a human body,

for use for a scheduled purpose;

(*f*) the use, for the purpose of public display, of—

(i) the body of a deceased person, or
(ii) relevant material which has come from the body of a deceased person.

(3) The Secretary of State may by regulations specify circumstances in which storage of relevant material by a person who intends to use it for a scheduled purpose is excepted from subsection (2)(*e*)(ii).

(4) An activity is excluded from subsection (2) if—

(*a*) it relates to the body of a person who died before the day on which this section comes into force or to material which has come from the body of such a person, and
(*b*) at least one hundred years have elapsed since the date of the person's death.

(5) The Secretary of State may by regulations amend this section for the purpose of—

(*a*) adding to the activities to which this section applies,
(*b*) removing an activity from the activities to which this section applies, or
(*c*) altering the description of an activity to which this section applies.

(6) Schedule 3 (which makes provision about licences for the purposes of this section) has effect.

(7) In subsection (2)—

(*a*) references to storage do not include storage which is incidental to transportation, and
(*b*) "relevant material", in relation to use for the scheduled purpose of transplantation, does not include blood or anything derived from blood.

[Human Tissue Act 2004, s 16.]

8–22070Q 17. Persons to whom licence applies. The authority conferred by a licence extends to—

(*a*) the designated individual,
(*b*) any person who is designated as a person to whom the licence applies by a notice given to the Authority by the designated individual, and
(*c*) any person acting under the direction of—

(i) the designated individual, or
(ii) a person designated as mentioned in paragraph (*b*).

[Human Tissue Act 2004, s 17.]

8–22070R 18. Duty of the designated individual. It shall be the duty of the individual designated in a licence as the person under whose supervision the licensed activity is authorised to be carried on to secure—

(*a*) that the other persons to whom the licence applies are suitable persons to participate in the carrying-on of the licensed activity,
(*b*) that suitable practices are used in the course of carrying on that activity, and
(*c*) that the conditions of the licence are complied with.

[Human Tissue Act 2004, s 18.]

8–22070S 19. Right to reconsideration of licensing decisions

8–22070T 20. Appeals committees

8–22070U 21. Procedure on reconsideration

8–22070V 22. Appeal on point of law

8–22070W 23. Conduct of licensed activities

8–22070X 24. Changes of licence circumstance

8–22070Y 25. Breach of licence requirement. (1) A person who contravenes section 16(1) commits an offence, unless he reasonably believes—

(*a*) that what he does is not an activity to which section 16 applies, or
(*b*) that he acts under the authority of a licence.

(2) A person guilty of an offence under subsection (1) shall be liable—

(*a*) on summary conviction to a fine not exceeding the statutory maximum;
(*b*) on conviction on indictment—

(i) to imprisonment for a term not exceeding 3 years, or
(ii) to a fine, or
(iii) to both.

[Human Tissue Act 2004, s 25.]

Codes of practice

8–22070Z 26. Preparation of codes

8–22071 27. Provision with respect to consent

8–22071A 28. Effect of codes

8–22071B 29. Approval of codes

Anatomy

8–22071C 30. Possession of anatomical specimens away from licensed premises. (1) Subject to subsections (2) to (6), a person commits an offence if—

(*a*) he has possession of an anatomical specimen, and
(*b*) the specimen is not on premises in respect of which an anatomy licence is in force.

(2) Subsection (1) does not apply where—

(*a*) the specimen has come from premises in respect of which a storage licence is in force, and
(*b*) the person—

(i) is authorised in writing by the designated individual to have possession of the specimen, and
(ii) has possession of the specimen only for a purpose for which he is so authorised to have possession of it.

(3) Subsection (1) does not apply where—

(*a*) the specimen is the body of a deceased person which is to be used for the purpose of anatomical examination,
(*b*) the person who has possession of the body has come into lawful possession of it immediately after the deceased's death, and
(*c*) he retains possession of the body prior to its removal to premises in respect of which an anatomy licence is in force.

(4) Subsection (1) does not apply where the person has possession of the specimen only for the purpose of transporting it to premises—

(*a*) in respect of which an anatomy licence is in force, or
(*b*) where the specimen is to be used for the purpose of education, training or research.

(5) Subsection (1) does not apply where the person has possession of the specimen for purposes of functions of, or under the authority of, a coroner.

(6) Subsection (1) does not apply where the person reasonably believes—

(*a*) that what he has possession of is not an anatomical specimen,
(*b*) that the specimen is on premises in respect of which an anatomy licence is in force, or
(*c*) that any of subsections (2) to (5) applies.

(7) A person guilty of an offence under subsection (1) shall be liable—

(*a*) on summary conviction to a fine not exceeding the statutory maximum;
(*b*) on conviction on indictment—

(i) to imprisonment for a term not exceeding 3 years, or
(ii) to a fine, or
(iii) to both.

(8) In this section—

"anatomy licence" means a licence authorising—

(*a*) the carrying-out of an anatomical examination, or
(*b*) the storage of anatomical specimens;

"storage licence" means a licence authorising the storage of anatomical specimens.
[Human Tissue Act 2004, s 30.]

8–22071D 31. Possession of former anatomical specimens away from licensed premises. (1) Subject to subsections (2) to (5), a person commits an offence if—

(*a*) he has possession of a former anatomical specimen, and
(*b*) the specimen is not on premises in respect of which a storage licence is in force.

(2) Subsection (1) does not apply where—

(*a*) the specimen has come from premises in respect of which a storage licence is in force, and
(*b*) the person—

(i) is authorised in writing by the designated individual to have possession of the specimen, and
(ii) has possession of the specimen only for a purpose for which he is so authorised to have possession of it.

(3) Subsection (1) does not apply where the person has possession of the specimen only for the purpose of transporting it to premises—

(*a*) in respect of which a storage licence is in force, or
(*b*) where the specimen is to be used for the purpose of education, training or research.

(4) Subsection (1) does not apply where the person has possession of the specimen—

(*a*) only for the purpose of its decent disposal, or
(*b*) for purposes of functions of, or under the authority of, a coroner.

(5) Subsection (1) does not apply where the person reasonably believes—

(*a*) that what he has possession of is not a former anatomical specimen,
(*b*) that the specimen is on premises in respect of which a storage licence is in force, or
(*c*) that any of subsections (2) to (4) applies.

(6) A person guilty of an offence under subsection (1) shall be liable—

(*a*) on summary conviction to a fine not exceeding the statutory maximum;
(*b*) on conviction on indictment—
  (i) to imprisonment for a term not exceeding 3 years, or
  (ii) to a fine, or
  (iii) to both.

(7) In this section, "storage licence" means a licence authorising the storage, for use for a scheduled purpose, of relevant material which has come from a human body.
[Human Tissue Act 2004, s 31.]

Trafficking

8–22071E 32. Prohibition of commercial dealings in human material for transplantation.
(1) A person commits an offence if he—

(*a*) gives or receives a reward for the supply of, or for an offer to supply, any controlled material;
(*b*) seeks to find a person willing to supply any controlled material for reward;
(*c*) offers to supply any controlled material for reward;
(*d*) initiates or negotiates any arrangement involving the giving of a reward for the supply of, or for an offer to supply, any controlled material;
(*e*) takes part in the management or control of a body of persons corporate or unincorporate whose activities consist of or include the initiation or negotiation of such arrangements.

(2) Without prejudice to subsection (1)(*b*) and (*c*), a person commits an offence if he causes to be published or distributed, or knowingly publishes or distributes, an advertisement—

(*a*) inviting persons to supply, or offering to supply, any controlled material for reward, or
(*b*) indicating that the advertiser is willing to initiate or negotiate any such arrangement as is mentioned in subsection (1)(*d*).

(3) A person who engages in an activity to which subsection (1) or (2) applies does not commit an offence under that subsection if he is designated by the Authority as a person who may lawfully engage in the activity.

(4) A person guilty of an offence under subsection (1) shall be liable—

(*a*) on summary conviction—
  (i) to imprisonment for a term not exceeding 12 months, or
  (ii) to a fine not exceeding the statutory maximum, or
  (iii) to both;
(*b*) on conviction on indictment—
  (i) to imprisonment for a term not exceeding 3 years, or
  (ii) to a fine, or
  (iii) to both.

(5) A person guilty of an offence under subsection (2) shall be liable on summary conviction—

(*a*) to imprisonment for a term not exceeding 51 weeks, or
(*b*) to a fine not exceeding level 5 on the standard scale, or
(*c*) to both.

(6) For the purposes of subsections (1) and (2), payment in money or money's worth to the holder of a licence shall be treated as not being a reward where—

(*a*) it is in consideration for transporting, removing, preparing, preserving or storing controlled material, and
(*b*) its receipt by the holder of the licence is not expressly prohibited by the terms of the licence.

(7) References in subsections (1) and (2) to reward, in relation to the supply of any controlled material, do not include payment in money or money's worth for defraying or reimbursing—

(*a*) any expenses incurred in, or in connection with, transporting, removing, preparing, preserving or storing the material,

(*b*) any liability incurred in respect of—

(i) expenses incurred by a third party in, or in connection with, any of the activities mentioned in paragraph (*a*), or

(ii) a payment in relation to which subsection (6) has effect, or

(*c*) any expenses or loss of earnings incurred by the person from whose body the material comes so far as reasonably and directly attributable to his supplying the material from his body.

(8) For the purposes of this section, controlled material is any material which—

(*a*) consists of or includes human cells,
(*b*) is, or is intended to be removed, from a human body,
(*c*) is intended to be used for the purpose of transplantation, and
(*d*) is not of a kind excepted under subsection (9).

(9) The following kinds of material are excepted—

(*a*) gametes,
(*b*) embryos, and
(*c*) material which is the subject of property because of an application of human skill.

(10) Where the body of a deceased person is intended to be used to provide material which—

(*a*) consists of or includes human cells, and
(*b*) is not of a kind excepted under subsection (9),

for use for the purpose of transplantation, the body shall be treated as controlled material for the purposes of this section.

(11) In this section—

"advertisement" includes any form of advertising whether to the public generally, to any section of the public or individually to selected persons;

"reward" means any description of financial or other material advantage.

[Human Tissue Act 2004, s 32.]

Transplants

8–22071F 33. Restriction on transplants involving a live donor. (1) Subject to subsections (3) and (5), a person commits an offence if—

(*a*) he removes any transplantable material from the body of a living person intending that the material be used for the purpose of transplantation, and

(*b*) when he removes the material, he knows, or might reasonably be expected to know, that the person from whose body he removes the material is alive.

(2) Subject to subsections (3) and (5), a person commits an offence if—

(*a*) he uses for the purpose of transplantation any transplantable material which has come from the body of a living person, and

(*b*) when he does so, he knows, or might reasonably be expected to know, that the transplantable material has come from the body of a living person.

(3) The Secretary of State may by regulations provide that subsection (1) or (2) shall not apply in a case where—

(*a*) the Authority is satisfied—

(i) that no reward has been or is to be given in contravention of section 32, and

(ii) that such other conditions as are specified in the regulations are satisfied, and

(*b*) such other requirements as are specified in the regulations are complied with.

(4) Regulations under subsection (3) shall include provision for decisions of the Authority in relation to matters which fall to be decided by it under the regulations to be subject, in such circumstances as the regulations may provide, to reconsideration in accordance with such procedure as the regulations may provide.

(5) Where under subsection (3) an exception from subsection (1) or (2) is in force, a person does not commit an offence under that subsection if he reasonably believes that the exception applies.

(6) A person guilty of an offence under this section is liable on summary conviction—

(*a*) to imprisonment for a term not exceeding 51 weeks, or
(*b*) to a fine not exceeding level 5 on the standard scale, or
(*c*) to both.

(7) In this section—

"reward" has the same meaning as in section 32;

"transplantable material" means material of a description specified by regulations made by the Secretary of State.

[Human Tissue Act 2004, s 33.]

8–22071G 34. Information about transplant operations. (1) The Secretary of State may make regulations requiring such persons as may be specified in the regulations to supply to such authority as may be so specified such information as may be so specified with respect to transplants that have been or are proposed to be carried out using transplantable material removed from a human body.

(2) Any such authority shall keep a record of information supplied to it in pursuance of regulations under this section.

(3) A person commits an offence if—

(*a*) he fails without reasonable excuse to comply with regulations under this section, or

(*b*) in purported compliance with such regulations, he knowingly or recklessly supplies information which is false or misleading in a material respect.

(4) A person guilty of an offence under subsection (3)(*a*) is liable on summary conviction to a fine not exceeding level 3 on the standard scale.

(5) A person guilty of an offence under subsection (3)(*b*) is liable on summary conviction to a fine not exceeding level 5 on the standard scale.

(6) In this section, "transplantable material" has the same meaning as in section 33.

[Human Tissue Act 2004, s 34.]

General

8–22071H 35. Agency arrangements and provision of services

8–22071I 36. Annual report

8–22071J 37. Directions

8–22071K 38. Duties in relation to carrying out functions

Exceptions

8–22071L 39. Criminal justice purposes. (1) Subject to subsection (2), nothing in section 14(1) or 16(2) applies to anything done for purposes related to—

(*a*) the prevention or detection of crime, or

(*b*) the conduct of a prosecution.

(2) Subsection (1) does not except from section 14(1) or 16(2) the carrying-out of a post-mortem examination for purposes of functions of a coroner.

(3) The reference in subsection (2) to the carrying-out of a post-mortem examination does not include the removal of relevant material from the body of a deceased person, or from a part of the body of a deceased person, at the first place where the body or part is situated to be attended by a constable.

(4) For the purposes of subsection (1)(*a*), detecting crime shall be taken to include—

(*a*) establishing by whom, for what purpose, by what means and generally in what circumstances any crime was committed, and

(*b*) the apprehension of the person by whom any crime was committed;

and the reference in subsection (1)(*a*) to the detection of crime includes any detection outside the United Kingdom of any crime or suspected crime.

(5) In subsection (1)(*b*), the reference to a prosecution includes a prosecution brought in respect of any crime in a country or territory outside the United Kingdom.

(6) In this section, references to crime include a reference to any conduct which—

(*a*) constitutes one or more criminal offences (whether under the law of a part of the United Kingdom or of a country or territory outside the United Kingdom),

(*b*) is, or corresponds to, any conduct which, if it all took place in any one part of the United Kingdom, would constitute one or more criminal offences, or

(*c*) constitutes one or more offences of a kind triable by court-martial under the Army Act 1955 (3 & 4 Eliz. 2 c. 18), the Air Force Act 1955 (3 & 4 Eliz. 2 c. 19) or the Naval Discipline Act 1957 (c 53).

[Human Tissue Act 2004, s 39.]

8–22071M 40. Religious relics. (1) This section applies—

(*a*) to the use of—

(i) the body of a deceased person, or

(ii) relevant material which has come from a human body,

for the purpose of public display at a place of public religious worship or at a place associated with such a place, and

(*b*) to the storage of—

(i) the body of a deceased person, or

(ii) relevant material which has come from a human body,

for use for the purpose mentioned in paragraph (*a*).

(2) An activity to which this section applies is excluded from sections 14(1) and 16(2) if there is a connection between—

(*a*) the body or material to which the activity relates, and

(*b*) the religious worship which takes place at the place of public religious worship concerned.

(3) For the purposes of this section, a place is associated with a place of public religious worship if it is used for purposes associated with the religious worship which takes place there.

[Human Tissue Act 2004, s 40.]

Supplementary

8–22071N 41. Interpretation of Part 2. (1) In this Part—

"anatomical specimen" means—

(*a*) the body of a deceased person to be used for the purpose of anatomical examination, or

(*b*) the body of a deceased person in the course of being used for the purpose of anatomical examination (including separated parts of such a body);

"appeals committee" has the meaning given by section 20(2);

"designated individual", in relation to a licence, means the individual designated in the licence as the person under whose supervision the licensed activity is authorised to be carried on;

"export" means export from England, Wales or Northern Ireland to a place outside England, Wales and Northern Ireland;

"import" means import into England, Wales or Northern Ireland from a place outside England, Wales and Northern Ireland;

"scheduled purpose" means a purpose specified in Schedule 1.

(2) In this Part, references to the carrying-out of an anatomical examination are to the carrying-out of a macroscopic examination by dissection for anatomical purposes of the body of a deceased person, and, where parts of the body of a deceased person are separated in the course of such an examination, include the carrying-out of a macroscopic examination by dissection of the parts for those purposes.

(3) In this Part, references to a person to whom a licence applies are to a person to whom the authority conferred by the licence extends (as provided by section 17).

[Human Tissue Act 2004, s 41.]

PART 3[1]

MISCELLANEOUS AND GENERAL

Miscellaneous

8–22071O 42. Power of Human Tissue Authority to assist other public authorities

8–22071P 43. Preservation for transplantation. (1) Where part of a body lying in a hospital, nursing home or other institution is or may be suitable for use for transplantation, it shall be lawful for the person having the control and management of the institution—

(*a*) to take steps for the purpose of preserving the part for use for transplantation, and

(*b*) to retain the body for that purpose.

(2) Authority under subsection (1)(*a*) shall only extend—

(*a*) to the taking of the minimum steps necessary for the purpose mentioned in that provision, and

(*b*) to the use of the least invasive procedure.

(3) Authority under subsection (1) ceases to apply once it has been established that consent making removal of the part for transplantation lawful has not been, and will not be, given.

(4) Authority under subsection (1) shall extend to any person authorised to act under the authority by—

(*a*) the person on whom the authority is conferred by that subsection, or

(*b*) a person authorised under this subsection to act under the authority.

(5) An activity done with authority under subsection (1) shall be treated—

(*a*) for the purposes of Part 1, as not being an activity to which section 1(1) applies;

(*b*) for the purposes of Part 2, as not being an activity to which section 16 applies.

(6) In this section, "body" means the body of a deceased person.
[Human Tissue Act 2004, s 43.]

---

1. Part 3 contains ss 42–61.

8–22071Q 44. Surplus tissue. (1) It shall be lawful for material to which subsection (2) or (3) applies to be dealt with as waste.

(2) This subsection applies to any material which consists of or includes human cells and which has come from a person's body in the course of his—

(*a*) receiving medical treatment,
(*b*) undergoing diagnostic testing, or
(*c*) participating in research.

(3) This subsection applies to any relevant material which—

(*a*) has come from a human body, and
(*b*) ceases to be used, or stored for use, for a purpose specified in Schedule 1.

(4) This section shall not be read as making unlawful anything which is lawful apart from this section.
[Human Tissue Act 2004, s 44.]

8–22071R 45. Non-consensual analysis of DNA. (1) A person commits an offence if—

(*a*) he has any bodily material intending—
 (i) that any human DNA in the material be analysed without qualifying consent, and
 (ii) that the results of the analysis be used otherwise than for an excepted purpose,
(*b*) the material is not of a kind excepted under subsection (2), and
(*c*) he does not reasonably believe the material to be of a kind so excepted.

(2) Bodily material is excepted if—

(*a*) it is material which has come from the body of a person who died before the day on which this section comes into force and at least one hundred years have elapsed since the date of the person's death,
(*b*) it is an existing holding and the person who has it is not in possession, and not likely to come into possession, of information from which the individual from whose body the material has come can be identified, or
(*c*) it is an embryo outside the human body.

(3) A person guilty of an offence under this section—

(*a*) is liable on summary conviction to a fine not exceeding the statutory maximum;
(*b*) is liable on conviction on indictment—
 (i) to imprisonment for a term not exceeding 3 years, or
 (ii) to a fine, or
 (iii) to both.

(4) Schedule 4 (which makes provision for the interpretation of "qualifying consent" and "use for an excepted purpose" in subsection (1)(*a*)) has effect.

(5) In this section (and Schedule 4)—

"bodily material" means material which—
 (*a*) has come from a human body, and
 (*b*) consists of or includes human cells;

"existing holding" means bodily material held immediately before the day on which this section comes into force.
[Human Tissue Act 2004, s 45.]

8–22071S 46. Power to give effect to Community obligations

8–22071T 47. Power to de-accession human remains

General

8–22071U 48. Powers of inspection, entry, search and seizure. Schedule 5 (which makes provision about powers of inspection, entry, search and seizure for the purposes of this Act) has effect.
[Human Tissue Act 2004, s 48.]

8–22071V 49. Offences by bodies corporate. (1) Where an offence under this Act is committed by a body corporate and is proved to have been committed with the consent or connivance of or to be attributable to any neglect on the part of—

(*a*) any director, manager, secretary or other similar officer of the body corporate, or
(*b*) any person who was purporting to act in any such capacity,

he (as well as the body corporate) commits the offence and shall be liable to be proceeded against and punished accordingly.

(2) Where the affairs of a body corporate are managed by its members, subsection (1) applies in relation to the acts and defaults of a member in connection with his functions of management as if he were a director of the body corporate.

(3) Where an offence under this Act is committed by a Scottish partnership and is proved to have been committed with the consent or connivance of a partner, or to be attributable to any neglect on the part of a partner, he (as well as the partnership) commits the offence and shall be liable to be proceeded against and punished accordingly.

(4) In subsection (3), "partner" includes a person purporting to act as a partner.
[Human Tissue Act 2004, s 49.]

8–22071W 50. Prosecutions. No proceedings for an offence under section 5, 32 or 33 shall be instituted—

(*a*) in England and Wales, except by or with the consent of the Director of Public Prosecutions;
(*b*) in Northern Ireland, except by or with the consent of the Director of Public Prosecutions for Northern Ireland.

[Human Tissue Act 2004, s 50.]

8–22071X 51. Offences: Northern Ireland

8–22071Y 52. Orders and regulations

8–22071Z 53. "Relevant material". (1) In this Act, "relevant material" means material, other than gametes, which consists of or includes human cells.

(2) In this Act, references to relevant material from a human body do not include—

(*a*) embryos outside the human body, or
(*b*) hair and nail from the body of a living person.

[Human Tissue Act 2004, s 53.]

8–22072 54. General interpretation. (1) In this Act—

"adult" means a person who has attained the age of 18 years;
"anatomical examination" means macroscopic examination by dissection for anatomical purposes;
"anatomical purposes" means purposes of teaching or studying, or researching into, the gross structure of the human body;
"the Authority" has the meaning given by section 13(1);
"child", except in the context of qualifying relationships, means a person who has not attained the age of 18 years;
"licence" means a licence under paragraph 1 of Schedule 3;
"licensed activity", in relation to a licence, means the activity which the licence authorises to be carried on;
"parental responsibility"—

(*a*) in relation to England and Wales, has the same meaning as in the Children Act 1989 (c 41), and
(*b*) in relation to Northern Ireland, has the same meaning as in the Children (Northern Ireland) Order 1995 (SI 1995/755 (NI 2));

"relevant Northern Ireland department" means the Department of Health, Social Services and Public Safety.

(2) In this Act—

(*a*) references to material from the body of a living person are to material from the body of a person alive at the point of separation, and
(*b*) references to material from the body of a deceased person are to material from the body of a person not alive at the point of separation.

(3) In this Act, references to transplantation are to transplantation to a human body and include transfusion.

(4) In this Act, references to decent disposal include, in relation to disposal of material which has come from a human body, disposal as waste.

(5) In this Act, references to public display, in relation to the body of a deceased person, do not include—

(*a*) display for the purpose of enabling people to pay their final respects to the deceased, or
(*b*) display which is incidental to the deceased's funeral.

(6) Subsections (1) and (4) of section 1 of the Human Fertilisation and Embryology Act 1990 (c

37) (definitions of "embryo" and "gametes") have effect for the purposes of this Act as they have effect for the purposes of that Act (other than that section).

(7) For the purposes of this Act, material shall not be regarded as from a human body if it is created outside the human body.

(8) For the purposes of this Act, except section 49, a person is another's partner if the two of them (whether of different sexes or the same sex) live as partners in an enduring family relationship.

(9) The following are qualifying relationships for the purposes of this Act, spouse, civil partner, partner, parent, child, brother, sister, grandparent, grandchild, child of a brother or sister, stepfather, stepmother, half-brother, half-sister and friend of long standing.

(10) The Secretary of State may by order amend subsection (9).

[Human Tissue Act 2004, s 54 as amended by SI 2005/3129.]

8–22072A 55. Financial provisions

8–22072B 56. Consequential amendments

8–22072C 57. Repeals and revocations

8–22072D 58. Transition. (1) In relation to an offence committed before the commencement of section 154(1) of the Criminal Justice Act 2003 (c 44), the reference in section 32(4)(*a*)(i) to 12 months is to be read as a reference to 6 months.

(2) In relation to an offence committed before the commencement of section 281(5) of the Criminal Justice Act 2003, the reference in each of sections 32(5)(*a*) and 33(6)(*a*) to 51 weeks is to be read as a reference to 6 months.

(3) The Secretary of State may by order made by statutory instrument make in connection with the coming into force of any provision of this Act such transitional provision or savings as he considers necessary or expedient.

(4) The power under subsection (3) includes power to make different provision for different cases.

(5) Before making provision under subsection (3) in connection with the coming into force in England and Wales of any provision of this Act, except section 47, the Secretary of State shall consult the National Assembly for Wales.

(6) Before making provision under subsection (3) in connection with the coming into force in Northern Ireland of any provision of this Act, except section 47, the Secretary of State shall consult the relevant Northern Ireland department.

(7) Before making provision under subsection (3) in connection with the coming into force in Scotland of any provision of this Act, except section 47, the Secretary of State shall consult the Scottish Ministers.

[Human Tissue Act 2004, s 58.]

8–22072E 59. Extent. (1) Subject to the following provisions, this Act extends to England and Wales and Northern Ireland only.

(2) Sections 58(1), (2) and (5) and 60(3) extend to England and Wales only.

(3) Sections 51(1) to (3), 58(6) and 60(4) extend to Northern Ireland only.

(4) The following provisions also extend to Scotland—

(*a*) sections 45(1) to (3) and (5) and 47,
(*b*) section 49 so far as having effect for the purposes of section 45,
(*c*) section 52 so far as relating to orders under section 54(10) or paragraph 13 of Schedule 4 or regulations under paragraph 6(2) or 12(2) of that Schedule,
(*d*) section 54(2)(*a*), (3), (8) and (9) so far as having effect for the purposes of Schedule 4,
(*e*) section 54(6) and (7) so far as having effect for the purposes of section 45 or Schedule 4,
(*f*) sections 54(10) and 58(3) and (4), this section and sections 60(1) and (2) and 61, and
(*g*) Schedule 4, except paragraphs 3 and 9(2) to (5), and section 45(4) so far as relating thereto.

(5) The following provisions extend to Scotland only—

(*a*) sections 58(7) and 60(5),
(*b*) paragraphs 3 and 9(4) and (5) of Schedule 4, and section 45(4) so far as relating thereto, and
(*c*) paragraphs 2 and 4 of Schedule 6, and section 56 so far as relating thereto.

(6) Subject to subsection (5), any amendment made by this Act has the same extent as the enactment to which it relates.

(7) Subject to subsection (8), any repeal or revocation made by this Act has the same extent as the enactment or instrument to which it relates.

(8) Except as provided by subsection (9), the repeals of the following do not extend to Scotland—

(*a*) the Human Tissue Act 1961 (c 54),
(*b*) the Anatomy Act 1984 (c 14),
(*c*) the Corneal Tissue Act 1986 (c 18), and
(*d*) the Human Organ Transplants Act 1989 (c 31).

(9) The repeals of the following provisions do extend to Scotland—

(*a*) in section 1(4A)(*b*) of the Human Tissue Act 1961, the words ", Primary Care Trust";
(*b*) in section 1(10) of that Act—

(i) paragraph (*a*) of the definition of "health authority",
(ii) in the definition of "NHS trust", the words "the National Health Service and Community Care Act 1990 or", and
(iii) the words after the definition of that expression;

(*c*) section 4(5) of the Anatomy Act 1984;
(*d*) in the Human Organ Transplants Act 1989—

(i) in section 1, the words "in Great Britain", in the first and third places where they occur,
(ii) in sections 2 and 3, the words "in Great Britain", in each place, and
(iii) sections 5 and 6.

[Human Tissue Act 2004, s 59.]

8–22072F 60. Commencement. (1) The following provisions shall come into force on the day on which this Act is passed—

this section, and
sections 58(3) to (7), 59 and 61.

(2) The remaining provisions of this Act shall come into force on such day as the Secretary of State may appoint by order made by statutory instrument, and different days may be so appointed for different purposes.

(3) Before exercising the power under subsection (2) in relation to the coming into force in England and Wales of any provision of this Act, except section 47, the Secretary of State shall consult the National Assembly for Wales.

(4) Before exercising the power under subsection (2) in relation to the coming into force in Northern Ireland of any provision of this Act, except section 47, the Secretary of State shall consult the relevant Northern Ireland department.

(5) Before exercising the power under subsection (2) in relation to the coming into force in Scotland of any provision of this Act, except section 47, the Secretary of State shall consult the Scottish Ministers.

(6) No day may be appointed under subsection (2) for the coming into force of section 5 or 8 which is earlier than the end of the period of three months beginning with the day on which the Authority first issues a code of practice dealing with the matters mentioned in section 26(2)(*h*) and (*i*).

(7) If the Authority first issues a code of practice dealing with one of the matters mentioned in subsection (6) before it first issues a code of practice dealing with the other, that subsection shall have effect as if the three month period were one beginning with the later of—

(*a*) the day on which the Authority first issues a code of practice dealing with the matter mentioned in section 26(2)(*h*), and
(*b*) the day on which the Authority first issues a code of practice dealing with the matter mentioned in section 26(2)(i).

[Human Tissue Act 2004, s 60.]

1. At the time of going to press no commencement orders had been made.

8–22072G 61. Short title

8–22072H

Section 1

SCHEDULE 1
SCHEDULED PURPOSES

PART 1
PURPOSES REQUIRING CONSENT: GENERAL

1 Anatomical examination.
2 Determining the cause of death.
3 Establishing after a person's death the efficacy of any drug or other treatment administered to him.
4 Obtaining scientific or medical information about a living or deceased person which may be relevant to any other person (including a future person).
5 Public display.
6 Research in connection with disorders, or the functioning, of the human body.
7 Transplantation.

PART 2
PURPOSES REQUIRING CONSENT: DECEASED PERSONS

8 Clinical audit.
9 Education or training relating to human health.

10 Performance assessment.
11 Public health monitoring.
12 Quality assurance.

8–22072I

Section 13

SCHEDULE 2
THE HUMAN TISSUE AUTHORITY

Instruments

18. A document purporting—

(*a*) to be duly executed under the seal of the Authority, or
(*b*) to be signed on its behalf,

shall be received in evidence and be taken, without further proof, to be so executed or signed unless the contrary is shown.

Application of Statutory Instruments Act 1946

22. The Statutory Instruments Act 1946 (c 36) shall apply to any power to make orders or regulations conferred by an Act on the Authority as if the Authority were a Minister of the Crown.

Public records

23. In Schedule 1 to the Public Records Act 1958 (c 51) (definition of public records), in Part 2 of the Table at the end of paragraph 3 the following entry is inserted at the appropriate place—

"Human Tissue Authority."

Investigation by Parliamentary Commissioner

8–22072J

Section 16

SCHEDULE 3
LICENCES FOR THE PURPOSES OF SECTION 16

Power to grant licence

1. The Authority may on application grant a licence for the purposes of section 16.

Characteristics of licence

2. (1) A licence shall not authorise the carrying-on of more than one activity to which section 16 applies.
(2) A licence shall—

(*a*) specify the premises where the licensed activity is authorised to be carried on, and
(*b*) designate an individual as the person under whose supervision the licensed activity is authorised to be carried on.

(3) A licence shall not authorise the licensed activity to be carried on—

(*a*) on premises at different places, or
(*b*) under the supervision of more than one individual.

(4) It shall be a condition of a licence—

(*a*) that the licensed activity shall be carried on only on the premises specified in the licence;
(*b*) that the licensed activity shall be carried on only under the supervision of the individual designated in the licence as the person under whose supervision it is authorised to be carried on;
(*c*) that such information about such matters relating to the carrying-on of the licensed activity as may be specified in directions shall be recorded in such form as may be so specified;
(*d*) that any record made for the purposes of the condition in paragraph (*c*) shall be kept until the end of such period as may be specified in directions;
(*e*) that there shall be provided to such person and at such intervals as may be specified in directions—

(i) such copies of, or extracts from, any record to which the condition in paragraph (*d*) relates, and
(ii) such other information,

as may be so specified;

(*f*) that there shall be paid to the Authority at such times as may be specified in directions sums of such amount as may be so specified in respect of its costs in connection with superintending compliance with the terms of licences.

(5) Directions for the purposes of sub-paragraph (4) may be given in relation to licences generally, licences of a particular description or a particular licence.

3. (1) This paragraph applies to a licence authorising the storage of anatomical specimens.

(2) It shall be a condition of a licence to which this paragraph applies that storage at the premises specified in the licence of the body of a deceased person for use for the purpose of anatomical examination shall not begin before that body's storage there for use for that purpose has been authorised in writing by—

(*a*) the designated individual, or
(*b*) an individual who has the Authority's permission to give such authorisation (see paragraph 12).

(3) It shall be a condition of a licence to which this paragraph applies that any anatomical specimen which is stored at the premises specified in the licence shall be released from storage at the premises only into the possession of a person who is authorised in writing by the designated individual to have the specimen in his possession.

(4) It shall be a condition of a licence to which this paragraph applies that the designated individual shall give authority for the purposes of the condition in sub-paragraph (3) only if he is satisfied—

(*a*) that the person to whom authority is given is a suitable person to have the specimen in his possession, and
(*b*) that that person intends to use the specimen only for the purpose of education, training or research.

(5) It shall be a condition of a licence to which this paragraph applies that any authority given for the purposes of the condition in sub-paragraph (3) shall specify—

(*a*) the person to whom the authority is given,
(*b*) the specimen to which the authority relates,
(*c*) the purpose for which the specimen may be used, and
(*d*) the duration of the authority.

(6) It shall be a condition of a licence to which this paragraph applies that the designated individual shall give such notice of any authorisation for the purposes of the condition in sub-paragraph (3) as may be specified in directions.

(7) It shall be a condition of a licence to which this paragraph applies that such information about authorisations for the purposes of the condition in sub-paragraph (3) as may be specified in directions shall be recorded in such form as may be so specified.

4. (1) This paragraph applies to a licence authorising the activity mentioned in section 16(2)(*e*).

(2) It shall be a condition of a licence to which this paragraph applies that any former anatomical specimen which is stored at the premises specified in the licence shall be released from storage at the premises only into the possession of a person who is authorised in writing by the designated individual to have the specimen in his possession.

(3) The condition in sub-paragraph (2) does not apply to the release from storage of a specimen for the purpose of its decent disposal.

(4) It shall be a condition of a licence to which this paragraph applies that the designated individual shall give authority for the purposes of the condition in sub-paragraph (2) only if he is satisfied—

(*a*) that the person to whom authority is given is a suitable person to have the specimen in his possession, and
(*b*) that that person intends to use the specimen only for the purpose of education, training or research.

(5) It shall be a condition of a licence to which this paragraph applies that any authority given for the purposes of the condition in sub-paragraph (2) shall specify—

(*a*) the person to whom the authority is given,
(*b*) the specimen to which the authority relates,
(*c*) the purpose for which the specimen may be used, and
(*d*) the duration of the authority.

(6) It shall be a condition of a licence to which this paragraph applies that the designated individual shall give such notice of any authorisation for the purposes of the condition in sub-paragraph (2) as may be specified in directions.

(7) It shall be a condition of a licence to which this paragraph applies that such information about authorisations for the purposes of the condition in sub-paragraph (2) as may be specified in directions shall be recorded in such form as may be so specified.

Power to impose conditions

5. The Authority may grant a licence subject to such further conditions as it thinks fit.

Pre-conditions to grant of licence

6. (1) The Authority may not grant a licence in pursuance of an application unless the following requirements are met.

(2) The proposed designated individual must—

(*a*) be the applicant for the licence, or
(*b*) consent to the application for the licence.

(3) The Authority must be satisfied that the proposed designated individual—

(*a*) is a suitable person to supervise the activity to be authorised by the licence, and
(*b*) will perform the duty under section 18.

(4) Where the applicant for the licence is not the proposed designated individual, the Authority must be satisfied that the applicant is a suitable person to be the holder of the licence.

(5) The Authority must be satisfied that the premises in respect of which the licence is to be granted are suitable for the activity to be authorised by the licence.

(6) A copy of the conditions to be imposed by the licence must have been shown to, and acknowledged in writing by—

(*a*) the applicant for the licence, and
(*b*) where different, the proposed designated individual.

(7) In this paragraph, references to the proposed designated individual are to the individual whom the application proposes the licence designate as the person under whose supervision the activity to be authorised by the licence is to be carried on.

Power to revoke licence

7. (1) The Authority may revoke a licence on application by—

(*a*) the holder of the licence, or
(*b*) the designated individual.

(2) The Authority may revoke a licence otherwise than on an application under sub-paragraph (1) if—

(*a*) it is satisfied that any information given for the purposes of the application for the licence was in any material respect false or misleading,
(*b*) it is satisfied that the designated individual has failed to discharge, or is unable because of incapacity to discharge, the duty under section 18,
(*c*) it ceases to be satisfied that the premises specified in the licence are suitable for the licensed activity,
(*d*) it ceases to be satisfied that the person to whom the licence is granted is a suitable person to be the holder of the licence,
(*e*) it ceases to be satisfied that the designated individual is a suitable person to supervise the licensed activity,
(*f*) the designated individual dies, or
(*g*) it is satisfied that there has been any other material change of circumstances since the licence was granted.

Power to vary licence

8. (1) The Authority may on application by the holder of a licence vary the licence so as to substitute another individual for the designated individual if—

(*a*) the application is made with the consent of the other individual, and
(*b*) the authority is satisfied that the other individual is a suitable person to supervise the licensed activity.

(2) The Authority may vary a licence on application by—

(*a*) the holder of the licence, or
(*b*) the designated individual.

(3) The Authority may vary a licence without an application under sub-paragraph (2) if it has power to revoke the licence under paragraph 7(2).

(4) The powers under sub-paragraphs (2) and (3) do not extend to making the kind of variation mentioned in sub-paragraph (1).

(5) The Authority may vary a licence without an application under sub-paragraph (2) by—

(*a*) removing or varying a condition of the licence, or
(*b*) adding a condition to the licence.

(6) The powers conferred by this paragraph do not extend to the conditions required by paragraphs 2(4), 3 and 4.

Power to suspend licence

9. (1) Where the Authority—

(*a*) has reasonable grounds to suspect that there are grounds for revoking a licence, and
(*b*) is of the opinion that the licence should immediately be suspended,

it may by notice suspend the licence for such period not exceeding three months as may be specified in the notice.

(2) The Authority may continue suspension under sub-paragraph (1) by giving a further notice under that sub-paragraph.

(3) Notice under sub-paragraph (1) shall be given to the designated individual or, where the designated individual has died or appears to the Authority to be unable because of incapacity to discharge the duty under section 18—

(*a*) to the holder of the licence, or
(*b*) to some other person to whom the licence applies.

(4) Subject to sub-paragraph (5), a licence shall be of no effect while a notice under sub-paragraph (1) is in force.

(5) An application may be made under paragraph 7(1) or 8(1) or (2) notwithstanding the fact that a notice under sub-paragraph (1) is in force.

Procedure in relation to licensing decisions

10. (1) Before making a decision—

(*a*) to refuse an application for the grant, revocation or variation of a licence, or
(*b*) to grant an application for a licence subject to a condition under paragraph 5,

the Authority shall give the applicant notice of the proposed decision and of the reasons for it.

(2) Before making a decision under paragraph 7(2) or 8(3) or (5), the Authority shall give notice of the proposed decision and of the reasons for it to—

(*a*) the holder of the licence, and
(*b*) where different, the designated individual.

(3) A person to whom notice under sub-paragraph (1) or (2) is given has the right to require the Authority to give him an opportunity to make representations of one of the following kinds about the proposed decision, namely—

(*a*) oral representations by him, or a person acting on his behalf;
(*b*) written representations by him.

(4) The right under sub-paragraph (3) is exercisable by giving the Authority notice of exercise of the right before the end of the period of 28 days beginning with the day on which the notice under sub-paragraph (1) or (2) was given.

(5) The Authority may by regulations make such additional provision about procedure in relation to the carrying-out of functions under this Schedule as it thinks fit.

Notification of licensing decisions

11. (1) In the case of a decision to grant a licence, the Authority shall give notice of the decision to—

(*a*) the applicant, and
(*b*) the person who is to be the designated individual.

(2) In the case of a decision to revoke a licence, the Authority shall give notice of the decision to—

(*a*) the holder of the licence, and
(*b*) the designated individual.

(3) In the case of a decision to vary a licence on an application under paragraph 8(1), the Authority shall give notice of the decision to—

(*a*) the holder of the licence, and
(*b*) the person who is to be the designated individual.

(4) In the case of any other decision to vary a licence, the Authority shall give notice of the decision to—

(*a*) the holder of the licence, and
(*b*) the designated individual.

(5) In the case of a decision to refuse an application for the grant, revocation or variation of a licence, the Authority shall give notice of the decision to the applicant.

(6) Subject to sub-paragraph (7), a notice under sub-paragraph (2), (4) or (5) shall include a statement of the reasons for the decision.

(7) In the case of a notice under sub-paragraph (2) or (4), the notice is not required to include a statement of the reasons for the decision if the decision is made on an application under paragraph 7(1) or 8(2).

Permission for the purposes of the licence condition required by paragraph 3(2)

12. (1) This paragraph applies to a licence authorising the storage of anatomical specimens.

(2) The reference to the Authority's permission in the condition of the licence required by paragraph 3(2) ("the authorisation condition") is to—

(*a*) permission granted by the Authority on an application made, in conjunction with the application for the licence, by—

(i) the applicant for the licence, or
(ii) the person who, within the meaning of paragraph 6, is the proposed designated individual, or

(*b*) permission granted by the Authority on application by—

(i) the holder of the licence, or
(ii) the designated individual.

(3) The Authority may grant permission to an individual for the purposes of the authorisation condition only if it is satisfied that the individual is a suitable person to give authorisation under that condition.

(4) The Authority may revoke permission granted to an individual for the purposes of the authorisation condition—

(*a*) on application by the individual, the designated individual or the holder of the licence, or
(*b*) if it ceases to be satisfied that the individual is a suitable person to give authorisation under that condition.

(5) Before refusing an application for the grant or revocation of permission, the Authority shall give the applicant notice of the proposed refusal and of the reasons for it.

(6) Before revoking permission under sub-paragraph (4)(*b*), the Authority shall give notice of the proposed revocation and of the reasons for it—

(*a*) to the individual concerned, and
(*b*) to the designated individual and, where different, the holder of the licence.

(7) Paragraph 10(3) and (4) shall apply in relation to notice under sub-paragraph (5) or (6) as to notice under paragraph 10(1).

(8) In the case of a decision to refuse an application for the grant or revocation of permission, the Authority shall give notice of the decision to the applicant.

(9) In the case of a decision to grant or revoke permission, the Authority shall give notice of the decision—

(*a*) to the individual concerned, and
(*b*) to the designated individual and, where different, the holder of the licence.

(10) Notice under sub-paragraph (8), and notice under sub-paragraph (9) of revocation under sub-paragraph (4)(*b*), shall include a statement of the reasons for the refusal or revocation.

(11) Where the Authority—

(*a*) has reasonable grounds to suspect that there are grounds for revoking permission granted to an individual for the purposes of the authorisation condition, and
(*b*) is of the opinion that the permission should immediately be suspended,

it may by notice suspend the permission for such period not exceeding three months as may be specified in the notice.

(12) The Authority may continue suspension under sub-paragraph (11) by giving a further notice under that sub-paragraph.

(13) Notice under sub-paragraph (11) shall be given to—

(*a*) the individual concerned, and
(*b*) the designated individual and, where different, the holder of the licence.

Applications under this Schedule

13. (1) The Authority may by regulations make provision about applications under this Schedule and may, in particular, make provision about—

(*a*) the form and content of such an application,
(*b*) the information to be supplied with such an application, and
(*c*) procedure in relation to the determination of such an application.

(2) An application under this Schedule shall be accompanied by such fee (if any) as the Authority may determine.

8–22072K

Section 45

SCHEDULE 4
SECTION 45: SUPPLEMENTARY
PART 1
QUALIFYING CONSENT

Introductory

1. This Part of this Schedule makes provision for the interpretation of "qualifying consent" in section 45(1)(*a*)(i).

Qualifying consent

2. (1) In relation to analysis of DNA manufactured by the body of a person who is alive, "qualifying consent" means his consent, except where sub-paragraph (2) applies.

(2) Where—

(*a*) the person is a child,
(*b*) neither a decision of his to consent, nor a decision of his not to consent, is in force, and
(*c*) either he is not competent to deal with the issue of consent or, though he is competent to deal with that issue, he fails to do so,

"qualifying consent" means the consent of a person who has parental responsibility for him.

(3) In relation to analysis of DNA manufactured by the body of a person who has died an adult, "qualifying consent" means—

(*a*) if a decision of his to consent, or a decision of his not to consent, was in force immediately before he died, his consent;
(*b*) if paragraph (*a*) does not apply, the consent of a person who stood in a qualifying relationship to him immediately before he died.

(4) In relation to analysis of DNA manufactured by the body of a person who has died a child, "qualifying consent" means—

(*a*) if a decision of his to consent, or a decision of his not to consent, was in force immediately before he died, his consent;
(*b*) if paragraph (*a*) does not apply—

(i) the consent of a person who had parental responsibility for him immediately before he died, or
(ii) where no person had parental responsibility for him immediately before he died, the consent of a person who stood in a qualifying relationship to him at that time.

PART 2
USE FOR AN EXCEPTED PURPOSE

Introductory

4. This Part of this Schedule makes provision for the interpretation of "use for an excepted purpose" in section 45(1)(*a*)(ii).

Purposes of general application

5. (1) Use of the results of an analysis of DNA for any of the following purposes is use for an excepted purpose—

(*a*) the medical diagnosis or treatment of the person whose body manufactured the DNA;
(*b*) purposes of functions of a coroner;
(*c*) purposes of functions of a procurator fiscal in connection with the investigation of deaths;
(*d*) the prevention or detection of crime;
(*e*) the conduct of a prosecution;
(*f*) purposes of national security;
(*g*) implementing an order or direction of a court or tribunal, including one outside the United Kingdom.

(2) For the purposes of sub-paragraph (1)(*d*), detecting crime shall be taken to include—

(*a*) establishing by whom, for what purpose, by what means and generally in what circumstances any crime was committed, and (*b*) the apprehension of the person by whom any crime was committed;

and the reference in sub-paragraph (1)(*d*) to the detection of crime includes any detection outside the United Kingdom of any crime or suspected crime.

(3) In sub-paragraph (1)(*e*), the reference to a prosecution includes a prosecution brought in respect of a crime in a country or territory outside the United Kingdom.

(4) In this paragraph, a reference to a crime includes a reference to any conduct which—

(*a*) constitutes one or more criminal offences (whether under the law of a part of the United Kingdom or a country or territory outside the United Kingdom),
(*b*) is, or corresponds to, conduct which, if it all took place in any one part of the United Kingdom, would constitute one or more criminal offences, or
(*c*) constitutes one or more offences of a kind triable by court-martial under the Army Act 1955 (3 & 4 Eliz. 2 c 18), the Air Force Act 1955 (3 & 4 Eliz. 2 c 19) or the Naval Discipline Act 1957 (c 53).

(5) Sub-paragraph (1)(*g*) shall not be taken to confer any power to make orders or give directions.

Purpose of research in connection with disorders, or functioning, of the human body

6. (1) Use of the results of an analysis of DNA for the purpose of research in connection with disorders, or the functioning, of the human body is use for an excepted purpose if the bodily material concerned is the subject of an order under sub-paragraph (2).

(2) The Secretary of State may by regulations specify circumstances in which the High Court or the Court of Session may order that this paragraph apply to bodily material.

Purposes relating to existing holdings

7. Use of the results of an analysis of DNA for any of the following purposes is use for an excepted purpose if the bodily material concerned is an existing holding—

(*a*) clinical audit;
(*b*) determining the cause of death;
(*c*) education or training relating to human health;
(*d*) establishing after a person's death the efficacy of any drug or other treatment administered to him;
(*e*) obtaining scientific or medical information about a living or deceased person which may be relevant to any other person (including a future person);
(*f*) performance assessment;
(*g*) public health monitoring;
(*h*) quality assurance;
(*i*) research in connection with disorders, or the functioning, of the human body;
(*j*) transplantation.

Purposes relating to material from body of a living person

8. Use of the results of an analysis of DNA for any of the following purposes is use for an excepted purpose if the bodily material concerned is from the body of a living person—

(*a*) clinical audit;
(*b*) education or training relating to human health;
(*c*) performance assessment;
(*d*) public health monitoring;
(*e*) quality assurance.

9. (1) Use of the results of an analysis of DNA for the purpose of obtaining scientific or medical information about the person whose body manufactured the DNA is use for an excepted purpose if—

(*a*) the bodily material concerned is the subject of a direction under sub-paragraph (2) or (3) or an order under sub-paragraph (4) or (5), and
(*b*) the information may be relevant to the person for whose benefit the direction is given or order is made.

(2) If the Authority is satisfied—

(*a*) that bodily material has come from the body of a living person,
(*b*) that it is not reasonably possible to trace the person from whose body the material has come ("the donor"),
(*c*) that it is desirable in the interests of another person (including a future person) that DNA in the material be analysed for the purpose of obtaining scientific or medical information about the donor, and
(*d*) that there is no reason to believe—
  (i) that the donor has died,
  (ii) that a decision of the donor to refuse consent to the use of the material for that purpose is in force, or
  (iii) that the donor lacks capacity to consent to the use of the material for that purpose,

it may direct that this paragraph apply to the material for the benefit of the other person.

(3) If the Authority is satisfied—

(*a*) that bodily material has come from the body of a living person,
(*b*) that it is desirable in the interests of another person (including a future person) that DNA in the material be analysed for the purpose of obtaining scientific or medical information about the person from whose body the material has come ("the donor"),
(*c*) that reasonable efforts have been made to get the donor to decide whether to consent to the use of the material for that purpose,

(*d*) that there is no reason to believe—

(i) that the donor has died,
(ii) that a decision of the donor to refuse to consent to the use of the material for that purpose is in force, or
(iii) that the donor lacks capacity to consent to the use of the material for that purpose, and

(*e*) that the donor has been given notice of the application for the exercise of the power conferred by this sub-paragraph,

it may direct that this paragraph apply to the material for the benefit of the other person.

(4) If the Court of Session is satisfied—

(*a*) that bodily material has come from the body of a living person,
(*b*) that it is not reasonably possible to trace the person from whose body the material has come ("the donor"),
(*c*) that it is desirable in the interests of another person (including a future person) that DNA in the material be analysed for the purpose of obtaining scientific or medical information about the donor, and
(*d*) that there is no reason to believe—

(i) that the donor has died,
(ii) that a decision of the donor to refuse consent to the use of the material for that purpose is in force, or
(iii) that the donor is an incapable adult within the meaning of the Adults with Incapacity (Scotland) Act 2000 (asp 4),

it may order that this paragraph apply to the material for the benefit of the other person.

(5) If the Court of Session is satisfied—

(*a*) that bodily material has come from the body of a living person,
(*b*) that it is desirable in the interests of another person (including a future person) that DNA in the material be analysed for the purpose of obtaining scientific or medical information about the person from whose body the material has come ("the donor"),
(*c*) that reasonable efforts have been made to get the donor to decide whether to consent to the use of the material for that purpose,
(*d*) that there is no reason to believe—

(i) that the donor has died,
(ii) that a decision of the donor to refuse to consent to the use of the material for that purpose is in force, or
(iii) that the donor is an incapable adult within the meaning of the Adults with Incapacity (Scotland) Act 2000, and

(*e*) that the donor has been given notice of the application for the exercise of the power conferred by this sub-paragraph,

it may order that this paragraph apply to the material for the benefit of the other person.

10. Use of the results of an analysis of DNA for the purpose of research in connection with disorders, or the functioning, of the human body is use for an excepted purpose if—

(*a*) the bodily material concerned is from the body of a living person,
(*b*) the research is ethically approved in accordance with regulations made by the Secretary of State, and
(*c*) the analysis is to be carried out in circumstances such that the person carrying it out is not in possession, and not likely to come into possession, of information from which the individual from whose body the material has come can be identified.

Purpose authorised under section 1

11. Use of the results of an analysis of DNA for a purpose specified in paragraph 7 is use for an excepted purpose if the use in England and Wales, or Northern Ireland, for that purpose of the bodily material concerned is authorised by section 1(1) or (10)(*c*).

Purposes relating to DNA of adults who lack capacity to consent

12. (1) Use of the results of an analysis of DNA for a purpose specified under sub-paragraph (2) is use for an excepted purpose if—

(*a*) the DNA has been manufactured by the body of a person who—

(i) has attained the age of 18 years and, under the law of England and Wales or Northern Ireland, lacks capacity to consent to analysis of the DNA, or
(ii) under the law of Scotland, is an adult with incapacity within the meaning of the Adults with Incapacity (Scotland) Act 2000 (asp 4), and

(*b*) neither a decision of his to consent to analysis of the DNA for that purpose, nor a decision of his not to consent to analysis of it for that purpose, is in force.

(2) The Secretary of State may by regulations specify for the purposes of this paragraph purposes for which DNA may be analysed.

8–22072L

Section 48

SCHEDULE 5

POWERS OF INSPECTION, ENTRY, SEARCH AND SEIZURE

Inspection of statutory records

1. (1) A duly authorised person may require a person to produce for inspection any records which he is required to keep by, or by virtue of, this Act.

(2) Where records which a person is so required to keep are stored in any electronic form, the power under sub-paragraph (1) includes power to require the records to be made available for inspection—

(*a*) in a visible and legible form, or
(*b*) in a form from which they can readily be produced in a visible and legible form.

(3) A duly authorised person may inspect and take copies of any records produced for inspection in pursuance of a requirement under this paragraph.

Entry and inspection of licensed premises

2. (1) A duly authorised person may at any reasonable time enter and inspect any premises in respect of which a licence is in force.

(2) The power in sub-paragraph (1) is exercisable for purposes of the Authority's functions in relation to licences.

Entry and search in connection with suspected offence

3. (1) If a justice of the peace is satisfied on sworn information or, in Northern Ireland, on a complaint on oath that there are reasonable grounds for believing—

(*a*) that an offence under Part 1 or 2 is being, or has been, committed on any premises, and
(*b*) that any of the conditions in sub-paragraph (2) is met in relation to the premises,

he may by signed warrant authorise a duly authorised person to enter the premises, if need be by force, and search them.

(2) The conditions referred to are—

(*a*) that entry to the premises has been, or is likely to be, refused and notice of the intention to apply for a warrant under this paragraph has been given to the occupier;
(*b*) that the premises are unoccupied;
(*c*) that the occupier is temporarily absent;
(*d*) that an application for admission to the premises or the giving of notice of the intention to apply for a warrant under this paragraph would defeat the object of entry.

(3) A warrant under this paragraph shall continue in force until the end of the period of 31 days beginning with the day on which it is issued.

Execution of warrants

4. (1) Entry and search under a warrant under paragraph 3 is unlawful if any of sub-paragraphs (2) to (4) and (6) is not complied with.

(2) Entry and search shall be at a reasonable time unless the person executing the warrant thinks that the purpose of the search may be frustrated on an entry at a reasonable time.

(3) If the occupier of the premises to which the warrant relates is present when the person executing the warrant seeks to enter them, the person executing the warrant shall—

(*a*) produce the warrant to the occupier, and
(*b*) give him—

(i) a copy of the warrant, and
(ii) an appropriate statement.

(4) If the occupier of the premises to which the warrant relates is not present when the person executing the warrant seeks to enter them, but some other person is present who appears to the person executing the warrant to be in charge of the premises, the person executing the warrant shall—

(*a*) produce the warrant to that other person,
(*b*) give him—

(i) a copy of the warrant, and
(ii) an appropriate statement, and

(*c*) leave a copy of the warrant in a prominent place on the premises.

(5) In sub-paragraphs (3)(*b*)(ii) and (4)(*b*)(ii), the references to an appropriate statement are to a statement in writing containing such information relating to the powers of the person executing the warrant and the rights and obligations of the person to whom the statement is given as may be prescribed by regulations made by the Secretary of State.

(6) If the premises to which the warrant relates are unoccupied, the person executing the warrant shall leave a copy of it in a prominent place on the premises.

(7) Where the premises in relation to which a warrant under paragraph 3 is executed are unoccupied or the occupier is temporarily absent, the person executing the warrant shall, when leaving the premises, leave them as effectively secured as he found them.

Seizure in the course of inspection or search

5. (1) A duly authorised person entering and inspecting premises under paragraph 2 may seize anything on the premises which he has reasonable grounds to believe may be required for purposes of the Authority's functions relating to the grant, revocation, variation or suspension of licences.

(2) A duly authorised person entering and searching premises under a warrant under paragraph 3 may seize anything on the premises which he has reasonable grounds to believe may be required for the purpose of being used in evidence in any proceedings for an offence under Part 1 or 2.

(3) Where a person has power under sub-paragraph (1) or (2) to seize anything, he may take such steps as appear to be necessary for preserving the thing or preventing interference with it.

(4) The power under sub-paragraph (1) or (2) includes power to retain anything seized in exercise of the power for so long as it may be required for the purpose for which it was seized.

(5) Where by virtue of sub-paragraph (1) or (2) a person seizes anything, he shall leave on the premises from which the thing was seized a statement giving particulars of what he has seized and stating that he has seized it.

Powers: supplementary

6. (1) Power under this Schedule to enter and inspect or search any premises includes power to take such other persons and equipment as the person exercising the power reasonably considers necessary.

(2) Power under this Schedule to inspect or search any premises includes, in particular—

(*a*) power to inspect any equipment found on the premises,

(*b*) power to inspect and take copies of any records found on the premises, and

(*c*) in the case of premises in respect of which a licence is in force, power to observe the carrying-on on the premises of the licensed activity.

(3) Any power under this Schedule to enter, inspect or search premises includes power to require any person to afford such facilities and assistance with respect to matters under that person's control as are necessary to enable the power of entry, inspection or search to be exercised.

7. (1) A person's right to exercise a power under this Schedule is subject to his producing evidence of his entitlement to exercise it, if required.

(2) As soon as reasonably practicable after having exercised a power under this Schedule to inspect or search premises, the duly authorised person shall—

(*a*) prepare a written report of the inspection or search, and

(*b*) if requested to do so by the appropriate person, give him a copy of the report.

(3) In sub-paragraph (2), the "appropriate person" means—

(*a*) in relation to premises in respect of which a licence is in force, the designated individual (as defined in section 41);

(*b*) in relation to any other premises, the occupier.

Enforcement

8. (1) A person commits an offence if—

(*a*) he fails without reasonable excuse to comply with a requirement under paragraph 1(1) or 6(3), or

(*b*) he intentionally obstructs the exercise of any right under this Schedule.

(2) A person guilty of an offence under this paragraph is liable on summary conviction to a fine not exceeding level 5 on the standard scale.

Interpretation

9. In this Schedule, "duly authorised person", in the context of any provision, means a person authorised by the Authority to act for the purposes of that provision.

8–22072M SCHEDULE 6

CONSEQUENTIAL AMENDMENTS

1. Where these concern provisions that appear in this work their effect will be noted when they come into force.

8–22072N SCHEDULE 7

REPEALS AND REVOCATIONS

1. Where these concern provisions that appear in this work their effect will be noted when they come into force.

Drugs Act 2005[1]

(2005 c 17)

PART 1[2]

SUPPLY OF CONTROLLED DRUGS

8–22073 1. Aggravated supply of controlled drug. *Inserts s 4A into the Misuse of Drugs Act 1971.*

1. This Act received the Royal Assent on 7 April 2005. The Act is in four parts:

Part 1 makes provision for the aggravated supply of controlled drugs, and proof of intention to supply a controlled drug.

Part 2 amends police powers in relation to drugs searches, testing for the presence of drugs and extended detention for suspected drug offenders.

Part 3 provides for assessment following testing for presence of Class A drugs.

Part 4 provides for intervention orders to accompany anti-social behaviour orders in certain cases.

The Act will be brought into force in accordance with commencement orders made under s 24. At the time of going to press the following commencement orders had been made: Drugs Act 2005 (Commencement No 1) Order 2005, SI 2005/1650; Drugs Act 2005 (Commencement No 2) Order 2005, SI 2005/2223; and Drugs Act

2005 (Commencement No 3) Order 2005, SI 2005/3053. The provisions reproduced below are in force unless otherwise stated.

2. Part 1 contains ss 1 and 2.

8–22073A 2. Proof of intention to supply a controlled drug[1]. (1) The Misuse of Drugs Act 1971 is amended as follows.

(2) In section 5 (restriction of possession of controlled drugs), after subsection (4) insert—

"(4A) In any proceedings for an offence under subsection (3) above, if it is proved that the accused had an amount of a controlled drug in his possession which is not less than the prescribed amount, the court or jury must assume that he had the drug in his possession with the intent to supply it as mentioned in subsection (3).

(4B) Subsection (4A) above does not apply if evidence is adduced which is sufficient to raise an issue that the accused may not have had the drug in his possession with that intent.

(4C) Regulations under subsection (4A) above have effect only in relation to proceedings for an offence committed after the regulations come into force."

(3) In section 31 (general provisions as to regulations)—

(*a*) in subsection (2), after "which shall" insert ", except as provided by subsection (2A),";

(*b*) after subsection (2) insert—

"(2A) A statutory instrument containing regulations under section 5(4A) of this Act shall not be made unless a draft of the instrument has been laid before, and approved by a resolution of, each House of Parliament.";

(*c*) after subsection (4) insert—

"(4A) Subsection (4) does not apply in relation to regulations under section 5(4A) of this Act."

(4) In section 38 (special provisions as to Northern Ireland) after subsection (1) insert—

"(1A) Subsection (1) does not apply, in relation to regulations under section 5(4A) of this Act, to the reference to the Secretary of State in the definition of "prescribed" in section 37(1) of this Act."

[Drugs Act 2005, s 2.]

1. At the time of going to press, s 2 was not in force.

PART 2[1]

POLICE POWERS RELATING TO DRUGS

8–22073B 3. Drug offence searches: England and Wales. *Section 3 amends s 55 of the Police and Criminal Evidence Act 1984.*

1. Part 2 contains ss 3–8.

4. *Northern Ireland.*

5. X-rays and ultrasound scans: England and Wales. *Inserts s 55 into the Police and Criminal Evidence Act 1984.*

6. *Northern Ireland.*

7. Testing for presence of Class A drugs. *Amends s 63B of the Police and Criminal Evidence Act 1984.*

8. Extended detention of suspected drug offenders. *Amends s 152 of the Criminal Justice Act 1988.*

PART 3[1]

ASSESSMENT OF MISUSE OF DRUGS

8–22073C 9. Initial assessment following testing for presence of Class A drugs. (1) This section applies if—

(*a*) a sample is taken under section 63B of PACE (testing for presence of Class A drug) from a person detained at a police station,

(*b*) an analysis of the sample reveals that a specified Class A drug may be present in the person's body,

(*c*) the age condition is met, and

(*d*) the notification condition is met.

(2) A police officer may, at any time before the person is released from detention at the police station, require him to attend an initial assessment and remain for its duration.

(3) An initial assessment is an appointment with a suitably qualified person (an "initial assessor")—

(*a*) for the purpose of establishing whether the person is dependent upon or has a propensity to misuse any specified Class A drug,

(*b*) if the initial assessor thinks that he has such a dependency or propensity, for the purpose of establishing whether he might benefit from further assessment, or from assistance or treatment (or both), in connection with the dependency or propensity, and

(*c*) if the initial assessor thinks that he might benefit from such assistance or treatment (or both), for the purpose of providing him with advice, including an explanation of the types of assistance or treatment (or both) which are available.

(4) The age condition is met if the person has attained the age of 18 or such different age as the Secretary of State may by order made by statutory instrument specify for the purposes of this section.

(5) In relation to a person ("A") who has attained the age of 18, the notification condition is met if—

(*a*) the relevant chief officer has been notified by the Secretary of State that arrangements for conducting initial assessments for persons who have attained the age of 18 have been made for persons from whom samples have been taken (under section 63B of PACE) at the police station in which A is detained, and

(*b*) the notice has not been withdrawn.

(6) In relation to a person ("C") who is of an age which is less than 18, the notification condition is met if—

(*a*) the relevant chief officer has been notified by the Secretary of State that arrangements for conducting initial assessments for persons of that age have been made for persons from whom samples have been taken (under section 63B of PACE) at the police station in which C is detained, and

(*b*) the notice has not been withdrawn.

(7) In subsections (5) and (6), "relevant chief officer" means the chief officer of police of the police force for the police area in which the police station is situated.

[Drugs Act 2005, s 9.]

1. Part 3 contains ss 9–19. At the time of going to press, ss 9, 12, 18 and 19 were in force; ss 11 and 15–17 were in force in so far as they relate to an initial assessment required under s 9: see Drugs Act 2005 (Commencement No 3) Order 2005, SI 2005/3053.

8–22073D 10. Follow-up assessment. (1) This section applies if—

(*a*) a police officer requires a person to attend an initial assessment and remain for its duration under section 9(2),

(*b*) the age condition is met, and

(*c*) the notification condition is met.

(2) The police officer must, at the same time as he imposes the requirement under section 9(2)—

(*a*) require the person to attend a follow-up assessment and remain for its duration, and

(*b*) inform him that the requirement ceases to have effect if he is informed at the initial assessment that he is no longer required to attend the follow-up assessment.

(3) A follow-up assessment is an appointment with a suitably qualified person (a "follow-up assessor")—

(*a*) for any of the purposes of the initial assessment which were not fulfilled at the initial assessment, and

(*b*) if the follow-up assessor thinks it appropriate, for the purpose of drawing up a care plan.

(4) A care plan is a plan which sets out the nature of the assistance or treatment (or both) which may be most appropriate for the person in connection with any dependency upon, or any propensity to misuse, a specified Class A drug which the follow-up assessor thinks that he has.

(5) The age condition is met if the person has attained the age of 18 or such different age as the Secretary of State may by order made by statutory instrument specify for the purposes of this section.

(6) In relation to a person ("A") who has attained the age of 18, the notification condition is met if—

(*a*) the relevant chief officer has been notified by the Secretary of State that arrangements for conducting follow-up assessments for persons who have attained the age of 18 have been made for persons from whom samples have been taken (under section 63B of PACE) at the police station in which A is detained, and

(*b*) the notice has not been withdrawn.

(7) In relation to a person ("C") who is of an age which is less than 18, the notification condition is met if—

(*a*) the relevant chief officer has been notified by the Secretary of State that arrangements for conducting follow-up assessments for persons of that age have been made for persons from whom samples have been taken (under section 63B of PACE) at the police station in which C is detained, and

(*b*) the notice has not been withdrawn.

(8) In subsections (6) and (7), "relevant chief officer" means the chief officer of police of the police force for the police area in which the police station is situated.
[Drugs Act 2005, s 10.]

8–22073E 11. Requirements under sections 9 and 10: supplemental. (1) This section applies if a person is required to attend an initial assessment and remain for its duration by virtue of section 9(2).

(2) A police officer must—

(*a*) inform the person of the time when, and the place at which, the initial assessment is to take place, and

(*b*) explain that this information will be confirmed in writing.

(3) A police officer must warn the person that he may be liable to prosecution if he fails without good cause to attend the initial assessment and remain for its duration.

(4) If the person is also required to attend a follow-up assessment and remain for its duration by virtue of section 10(2), a police officer must also warn the person that he may be liable to prosecution if he fails without good cause to attend the follow-up assessment and remain for its duration.

(5) A police officer must give the person notice in writing which—

(*a*) confirms that he is required to attend and remain for the duration of an initial assessment or both an initial assessment and a follow-up assessment (as the case may be),

(*b*) confirms the information given in pursuance of subsection (2), and

(*c*) repeats the warning given in pursuance of subsection (3) and any warning given in pursuance of subsection (4).

(6) The duties imposed by subsections (2) to (5) must be discharged before the person is released from detention at the police station.

(7) A record must be made, as part of the person's custody record, of—

(*a*) the requirement imposed on him by virtue of section 9(2),

(*b*) any requirement imposed on him by virtue of section 10(2),

(*c*) the information and explanation given to him in pursuance of subsection (2) above,

(*d*) the warning given to him in pursuance of subsection (3) above and any warning given to him in pursuance of subsection (4) above, and

(*e*) the notice given to him in pursuance of subsection (5) above.

(8) If a person is given a notice in pursuance of subsection (5), a police officer or a suitably qualified person may give the person a further notice in writing which—

(*a*) informs the person of any change to the time when, or to the place at which, the initial assessment is to take place, and

(*b*) repeats the warning given in pursuance of subsection (3) and any warning given in pursuance of subsection (4).
[Drugs Act 2005, s 11.]

8–22073F 12. Attendance at initial assessment. (1) This section applies if a person is required to attend an initial assessment and remain for its duration by virtue of section 9(2).

(2) The initial assessor must inform a police officer or a police support officer if the person—

(*a*) fails to attend the initial assessment at the specified time and place, or

(*b*) attends the assessment at the specified time and place but fails to remain for its duration.

(3) A person is guilty of an offence if without good cause—

(*a*) he fails to attend an initial assessment at the specified time and place, or

(*b*) he attends the assessment at the specified time and place but fails to remain for its duration.

(4) A person who is guilty of an offence under subsection (3) is liable on summary conviction to imprisonment for a term not exceeding 51 weeks, or to a fine not exceeding level 4 on the standard scale, or to both.

(5) If a person fails to attend an initial assessment at the specified time and place, any requirement imposed on him by virtue of section 10(2) ceases to have effect.

(6) In this section—

(*a*) the specified time, in relation to the person concerned, is the time specified in the notice given to him in pursuance of subsection (5) of section 11 or, if a further notice specifying a different time has been given to him in pursuance of subsection (8) of that section, the time specified in that notice, and

(*b*) the specified place, in relation to the person concerned, is the place specified in the notice given to him in pursuance of subsection (5) of section 11 or, if a further notice specifying a different place has been given to him in pursuance of subsection (8) of that section, the place specified in that notice.

(7) In relation to an offence committed before the commencement of section 281(5) of the Criminal Justice Act 2003 (c 44) (alteration of penalties for summary offences), the reference in subsection (4) to 51 weeks is to be read as a reference to 3 months.
[Drugs Act 2005, s 12.]

8–22073G **13. Arrangements for follow-up assessment.** (1) This section applies if—

(*a*) a person attends an initial assessment in pursuance of section 9(2), and

(*b*) he is required to attend a follow-up assessment and remain for its duration by virtue of section 10(2).

(2) If the initial assessor thinks that a follow-up assessment is not appropriate, he must inform the person concerned that he is no longer required to attend the follow-up assessment.

(3) The requirement imposed by virtue of section 10(2) ceases to have effect if the person is informed as mentioned in subsection (2).

(4) If the initial assessor thinks that a follow-up assessment is appropriate, the assessor must—

(*a*) inform the person of the time when, and the place at which, the follow-up assessment is to take place, and

(*b*) explain that this information will be confirmed in writing.

(5) The assessor must also warn the person that, if he fails without good cause to attend the follow-up assessment and remain for its duration, he may be liable to prosecution.

(6) The initial assessor must also give the person notice in writing which—

(*a*) confirms that he is required to attend and remain for the duration of the follow-up assessment,

(*b*) confirms the information given in pursuance of subsection (4), and

(*c*) repeats the warning given in pursuance of subsection (5).

(7) The duties mentioned in subsections (2) and (4) to (6) must be discharged before the conclusion of the initial assessment.

(8) If a person is given a notice in pursuance of subsection (6), the initial assessor or another suitably qualified person may give the person a further notice in writing which—

(*a*) informs the person of any change to the time when, or to the place at which, the follow-up assessment is to take place, and

(*b*) repeats the warning mentioned in subsection (5).
[Drugs Act 2005, s 13.]

8–22073H **14. Attendance at follow-up assessment.** (1) This section applies if a person is required to attend a follow-up assessment and remain for its duration by virtue of section 10(2).

(2) The follow-up assessor must inform a police officer or a police support officer if the person—

(*a*) fails to attend the follow-up assessment at the specified time and place, or

(*b*) attends the assessment at the specified time and place but fails to remain for its duration.

(3) A person is guilty of an offence if without good cause—

(*a*) he fails to attend a follow-up assessment at the specified time and place, or

(*b*) he attends the assessment at the specified time and place but fails to remain for its duration.

(4) A person who is guilty of an offence under subsection (3) is liable on summary conviction to imprisonment for a term not exceeding 51 weeks, or to a fine not exceeding level 4 on the standard scale, or to both.

(5) In this section—

(*a*) the specified time, in relation to the person concerned, is the time specified in the notice given to him in pursuance of subsection (6) of section 13 or, if a further notice specifying a different time has been given to him in pursuance of subsection (8) of that section, the time specified in that notice, and

(*b*) the specified place, in relation to the person concerned, is the place specified in the notice given to him in pursuance of subsection (6) of section 13 or, if a further notice specifying a different place has been given to him in pursuance of subsection (8) of that section, the place specified in that notice.

(6) In relation to an offence committed before the commencement of section 281(5) of the Criminal Justice Act 2003 (c 44) (alteration of penalties for summary offences), the reference in subsection (4) to 51 weeks is to be read as a reference to 3 months.
[Drugs Act 2005, s 14.]

8–22073I **15. Disclosure of information about assessments.** (1) An initial assessor may disclose information obtained as a result of an initial assessment to any of the following—

(*a*) a person who is involved in the conduct of the assessment;

(*b*) a person who is or may be involved in the conduct of any follow-up assessment.

(2) A follow-up assessor may disclose information obtained as a result of a follow-up assessment to a person who is involved in the conduct of the assessment.

(3) Subject to subsections (1) and (2), information obtained as a result of an initial or a follow-up assessment may not be disclosed by any person without the written consent of the person to whom the assessment relates.

(4) Nothing in this section affects the operation of section 17(4).

[Drugs Act 2005, s 15.]

8–22073J 16. Samples submitted for further analysis. (1) A requirement imposed on a person by virtue of section 9(2) or 10(2) ceases to have effect if at any time before he has fully complied with the requirement—

(*a*) a police officer makes arrangements for a further analysis of the sample taken from him as mentioned in section 9(1)(*a*), and

(*b*) the analysis does not reveal that a specified Class A drug was present in the person's body.

(2) If a requirement ceases to have effect by virtue of subsection (1), a police officer must so inform the person concerned.

(3) Nothing in subsection (1) affects the validity of anything done in connection with the requirement before it ceases to have effect.

(4) If a person fails to attend an assessment which he is required to attend by virtue of section 9(2) or fails to remain for the duration of such an assessment but, at any time after his failure, the requirement ceases to have effect by virtue of subsection (1) above—

(*a*) no proceedings for an offence under section 12(3) may be brought against him, and

(*b*) if any such proceedings were commenced before the requirement ceased to have effect, those proceedings must be discontinued.

(5) If a person fails to attend an assessment which he is required to attend by virtue of section 10(2) or fails to remain for the duration of such an assessment but, at any time after his failure, the requirement ceases to have effect by virtue of subsection (1) above—

(*a*) no proceedings for an offence under section 14(3) may be brought against him, and

(*b*) if any such proceedings were commenced before the requirement ceased to have effect, those proceedings must be discontinued.

[Drugs Act 2005, s 16.]

8–22073K 17. Relationship with Bail Act 1976 etc. (1) A requirement imposed on a person by virtue of section 9(2) or 10(2) ceases to have effect if at any time before he has fully complied with the requirement—

(*a*) he is charged with the related offence, and

(*b*) a court imposes on him a condition of bail under section 3(6D) of the Bail Act 1976 (c 63) (duty to impose condition to undergo relevant assessment etc).

(2) For the purposes of section 3(6D) of the 1976 Act, a relevant assessment (within the meaning of that Act) is to be treated as having been carried out if—

(*a*) a person attends an initial assessment and remains for its duration, and

(*b*) the initial assessor is satisfied that the initial assessment fulfilled the purposes of a relevant assessment.

(3) For the purposes of paragraph 6B(2)(*b*) of Schedule 1 to the 1976 Act (exceptions to right to bail for drug users in certain areas), a person is to be treated as having undergone a relevant assessment (within the meaning of that Act) if—

(*a*) the person attends an initial assessment and remains for its duration, and

(*b*) the initial assessor is satisfied that the initial assessment fulfilled the purposes of a relevant assessment.

(4) An initial assessor may disclose information relating to an initial assessment for the purpose of enabling a court considering an application for bail by the person concerned to determine whether subsection (2) or (3) applies.

(5) Nothing in subsection (1) affects—

(*a*) the validity of anything done in connection with the requirement before it ceases to have effect, or

(*b*) any liability which the person may have for an offence under section 12(3) or 14(3) committed before the requirement ceases to have effect.

(6) In subsection (1), "the related offence" is the offence in respect of which the condition specified in subsection (1A) or (2) of section 63B of PACE is satisfied in relation to the taking of the sample mentioned in section 9(1)(*a*) of this Act.

[Drugs Act 2005, s 17.]

8–22073L **18. Orders under this Part and guidance.** (1) A statutory instrument containing an order under section 9(4) or 10(5) must not be made unless a draft of the instrument has been laid before, and approved by a resolution of, each House of Parliament.

(2) Any such order may—

(*a*) make different provision for different police areas;

(*b*) make such provision as the Secretary of State considers appropriate in connection with requiring persons who have not attained the age of 18 to attend and remain for the duration of an initial assessment or a follow-up assessment (as the case may be), including provision amending this Part.

(3) In exercising any functions conferred by this Part, a police officer and a suitably qualified person must have regard to any guidance issued by the Secretary of State for the purposes of this Part.

[Drugs Act 2005, s 18.]

8–22073M **19. Interpretation.** (1) This section applies for the purposes of this Part.

(2) "Class A drug" and "misuse" have the same meanings as in the Misuse of Drugs Act 1971 (c 38).

(3) "Specified", in relation to a Class A drug, has the same meaning as in Part 3 of the Criminal Justice and Court Services Act 2000 (c 43).

(4) "Initial assessment" and "initial assessor" must be construed in accordance with section 9(3).

(5) "Follow-up assessment" and "follow-up assessor" must be construed in accordance with section 10(3).

(6) "Suitably qualified person" means a person who has such qualifications or experience as are from time to time specified by the Secretary of State for the purposes of this Part.

(7) "Police support officer" means a person who is employed by a police authority under section 15(1) of the Police Act 1996 (c 16) and who is under the direction and control of the chief officer of police of the police force maintained by that authority.

(8) "PACE" means the Police and Criminal Evidence Act 1984 (c 60).

[Drugs Act 2005, s 19.]

PART 4[1]
MISCELLANEOUS AND GENERAL

8–22073N **20. Anti-social behaviour orders: intervention orders.** (1) After section 1F of the Crime and Disorder Act 1998 (c 37) (inserted by section 142(1) of the Serious Organised Crime and Police Act 2005 (c 15)) insert—

"**1G. Intervention orders.** (1) This section applies if, in relation to a person who has attained the age of 18, a relevant authority—

(*a*) makes an application for an anti-social behaviour order or an order under section 1B above (the behaviour order),

(*b*) has obtained from an appropriately qualified person a report relating to the effect on the person's behaviour of the misuse of controlled drugs or of such other factors as the Secretary of State by order prescribes, and

(*c*) has engaged in consultation with such persons as the Secretary of State by order prescribes for the purpose of ascertaining that, if the report recommends that an order under this section is made, appropriate activities will be available.

(2) The relevant authority may make an application to the court which is considering the application for the behaviour order for an order under this section (an intervention order).

(3) If the court—

(*a*) makes the behaviour order, and

(*b*) is satisfied that the relevant conditions are met,

it may also make an intervention order.

(4) The relevant conditions are—

(*a*) that an intervention order is desirable in the interests of preventing a repetition of the behaviour which led to the behaviour order being made (trigger behaviour);

(*b*) that appropriate activities relating to the trigger behaviour or its cause are available for the defendant;

(*c*) that the defendant is not (at the time the intervention order is made) subject to another intervention order or to any other treatment relating to the trigger behaviour or its cause (whether on a voluntary basis or by virtue of a requirement imposed in pursuance of any enactment);

(*d*) that the court has been notified by the Secretary of State that arrangements for implementing intervention orders are available in the area in which it appears that the defendant resides or will reside and the notice has not been withdrawn.

(5) An intervention order is an order which—

(*a*) requires the defendant to comply, for a period not exceeding six months, with such requirements as are specified in the order, and

(*b*) requires the defendant to comply with any directions given by a person authorised to do so under the order with a view to the implementation of the requirements under paragraph (*a*) above.

(6) An intervention order or directions given under the order may require the defendant—

(*a*) to participate in the activities specified in the requirement or directions at a time or times so specified;

(*b*) to present himself to a person or persons so specified at a time or times so specified.

(7) Requirements included in, or directions given under, an intervention order must, as far as practicable, be such as to avoid—

(*a*) any conflict with the defendant's religious beliefs, and

(*b*) any interference with the times (if any) at which he normally works or attends an educational establishment.

(8) If the defendant fails to comply with a requirement included in or a direction given under an intervention order, the person responsible for the provision or supervision of appropriate activities under the order must inform the relevant authority of that fact.

(9) The person responsible for the provision or supervision of appropriate activities is a person of such description as is prescribed by order made by the Secretary of State.

(10) In this section—

"appropriate activities" means such activities, or activities of such a description, as are prescribed by order made by the Secretary of State for the purposes of this section;

"appropriately qualified person" means a person who has such qualifications or experience as the Secretary of State by order prescribes;

"controlled drug" has the same meaning as in the Misuse of Drugs Act 1971;

"relevant authority" means a relevant authority for the purposes of section 1 above.

(11) An order under this section made by the Secretary of State may make different provision for different purposes.

(12) This section and section 1H below apply to a person in respect of whom a behaviour order has been made subject to the following modifications—

(*a*) in subsection (1) above paragraph (*a*) must be ignored;

(*b*) in subsection (2) above, for "is considering the application for" substitute "made";

(*c*) in subsection (3) above paragraph (*a*), the word "and" following it and the word "also" must be ignored.

1H. Intervention orders: explanation, breach, amendment etc. (1) Before making an intervention order the court must explain to the defendant in ordinary language—

(*a*) the effect of the order and of the requirements proposed to be included in it,

(*b*) the consequences which may follow (under subsection (3) below) if he fails to comply with any of those requirements, and

(*c*) that the court has power (under subsection (5) below) to review the order on the application either of the defendant or of the relevant authority.

(2) The power of the Secretary of State under section 174(4) of the Criminal Justice Act 2003 includes power by order to—

(*a*) prescribe cases in which subsection (1) does not apply, and

(*b*) prescribe cases in which the explanation referred to in that subsection may be made in the absence of the defendant, or may be provided in written form.

(3) If a person in respect of whom an intervention order is made fails without reasonable excuse to comply with any requirement included in the order he is guilty of an offence and liable on summary conviction to a fine not exceeding level 4 on the standard scale.

(4) If the behaviour order as a result of which an intervention order is made ceases to have effect, the intervention order (if it has not previously ceased to have effect) ceases to have effect when the behaviour order does.

(5) On an application made by—

(*a*) a person subject to an intervention order, or

(*b*) the relevant authority,

the court which made the intervention order may vary or discharge it by a further order.

(6) An application under subsection (5) made to a magistrates' court must be made by complaint.

(7) If the behaviour order as a result of which an intervention order was made is varied, the court varying the behaviour order may by a further order vary or discharge the intervention order.

(8) Expressions used in this section and in section 1G have the same meaning in this section as in that section."

(2) In section 114(2) of that Act (procedure for subordinate legislation) after "1A" insert ", 1G".

1. Part 4 contains ss 20–24. At the time of going to press, ss 21 and 23 were in force (s 22 came into force on the day the Act was passed).

[Drugs Act 2005, s 20.]

8–22073O 21. Inclusion of mushrooms containing psilocin etc as Class A drugs. In Part 1 of Schedule 2 to the Misuse of Drugs Act 1971 (c 38) (Class A drugs), in paragraph 1, insert at the appropriate place—

"Fungus (of any kind) which contains psilocin or an ester of psilocin."

[Drugs Act 2005, s 21.]

8–22073P 22. Financial provision. There shall be paid out of money provided by Parliament—

(*a*) any expenditure incurred by the Secretary of State by virtue of this Act, and

(*b*) any increase attributable to this Act in the sums payable out of money so provided under any other Act.

[Drugs Act 2005, s 22.]

8–22073Q 23. Amendments and repeals. (1) Schedule 1 (which contains amendments) has effect.

(2) Schedule 2 (which contains repeals) has effect.

[Drugs Act 2005, s 23.]

8–22073R 24. Short title, commencement and extent. (1) This Act may be cited as the Drugs Act 2005.

(2) This section and section 22 come into force on the day on which this Act is passed.

(3) Otherwise, this Act comes into force on such day as the Secretary of State may by order[1] made by statutory instrument appoint.

(4) Different days may be appointed for different purposes.

(5) An order under subsection (3) may make—

(*a*) any supplementary, incidental or consequential provision, and

(*b*) any transitory, transitional or saving provision,

as the Secretary of State considers necessary or expedient in connection with the order.

(6) Subject to subsection (7), this Act (except this section and sections 22 and 23) extends to England and Wales only.

(7) So far as it amends or repeals any enactment, this Act has the same extent as the enactment amended or repealed.

[Drugs Act 2005, s 24.]

1. The following commencement orders have been made: Drugs Act 2005 (Commencement No 1) Order 2005, SI 2005/1650; Drugs Act 2005 (Commencement No 2) Order 2005, SI 2005/2223; and Drugs Act 2005 (Commencement No 3) Order 2005, SI 2005/3053.

Misuse of Drugs Regulations 2001[1]

(SI 2001/3998 amended by SI 2003/1432, 1653 and 2429, SI 2004/1031 and 1771 and SI 2005/271, 1653, 2864 and 3372)

8–22080 1. ***Citation and commencement***

1. Made by the Secretary of State in pursuance of ss 7, 10, 22 and 31 of the Misuse of Drugs Act 1971. Contravention of the regulations is made an offence by s 18(1) of the Misuse of Drugs Act 1971; such offences are triable either way: Sch 4 to the Act. For procedure in respect of an offence triable either way see ss 17A–22 to the Magistrates' Courts Act 1980 in PART I: MAGISTRATES' COURTS, PROCEDURE.

8–22081 2. Interpretation. (1) In these Regulations, unless the context otherwise requires—

"the Act" means the Misuse of Drugs Act 1971;

"authorised as a member of a group" means authorised by virtue of being a member of a class as respects which the Secretary of State has granted an authority under and for the purposes of regulation 8(3), 9(3) or 10(3) which is in force, and "his group authority", in relation to a person who is a member of such a class, means the authority so granted to that class;

"clinical management plan" has the same meaning as in the Prescription Only Medicines (Human Use) Order 1997;

"document" has the same meaning as in Part I of the Civil Evidence Act 1968

"exempt product" means a preparation or other product consisting of one or more component parts, any of which contains a controlled drug, where—

(*a*) the preparation or other product is not designed for administration of the controlled drug to a human being or animal;

(*b*) the controlled drug in any component part is packaged in such a form, or in combination with other active or inert substances in such a manner, that it cannot be recovered by readily applicable means or in a yield which constitutes a risk to health; and

(*c*) no one component part of the product or preparation contains more than one milligram of the controlled drug or one microgram in the case of lysergide or any other *N*-alkyl derivative of lysergamide;

"extended formulary nurse prescriber" has the same meaning as in the Prescription Only Medicines (Human Use) Order 1997, and such a person may only prescribe controlled drugs in accordance with regulation 6B;

"health prescription" means a prescription issued by a doctor or a dentist under the National Health Service Act 1977, the National Health Service (Scotland) Act 1978, the Health and Personal Social Services (Northern Ireland) Order 1972 or the National Health Service (Isle of Man) Acts 1948 to 1979 (Acts of Tynwald) or upon a form issued by a local authority for use in connection with the health service of that authority;

"installation manager" and "offshore installation" have the same meanings as in the Mineral Workings (Offshore Installations) Act 1971;

"master" and "seamen" have the same meanings as in the Merchant Shipping Act 1995;

"medicinal product" has the same meaning as in the Medicines Act 1968;

"officer of customs and excise" means an officer within the meaning of the Customs and Excise Management Act 1979;

"patient group direction" has the same meaning as in the Prescription Only Medicines (Human Use) Order 1997;

"prescription" means a prescription issued by a doctor for the medical treatment of a single individual, by a supplementary presciber for the medical treatment of a single individual, by an extended formulary nurse prescirber for the medical treatment of a single individual, by a dentist for the dental treatment of a single individual or by a veterinary surgeon or veterinary practitioner for the purposes of animal treatment;

"professional register" means the register maintained by the Nursing and Midwifery Council under article 5 of the Nursing and Midwifery Order 2001;

"register" means either a bound book, which does not include any form of loose leaf register or card index, or a computerised system which is in accordance with best practice guidance endorsed by the Secretary of State under section 2 of the National Health Service Act 1977;

"registered midwife" has the same meaning as in the Prescription Only Medicines (Human Use) Order 1997;

"registered nurse" has the same meaning as in the Prescription Only Medicines (Human Use) Order 1997;

"registered ophthalmic optician" has the same meaning as in the Prescription Only Medicines (Human Use) Order 1997;

"registered pharmacy" has the same meaning as in the Medicines Act 1968;

"retail dealer" means a person lawfully conducting a retail pharmacy business or a pharmacist engaged in supplying drugs to the public at a health centre within the meaning of the Medicines Act 1968;

"specialist community public health nurse" means a registered nurse or midwife who is also registered in the Specialist Community Public Health Nurses' Part of the professional register and against whose name in that Part of the register there is an annotation that she has a qualification in health visiting;

"sister or acting sister" includes any male nurse occupying a similar position;

"state registered chiropodist" has the same meaning as in the Prescription Only Medicines (Human Use) Order 1997;

"state registered paramedic" has the same meaning as in the Prescription Only Medicines (Human Use) Order 1997;

"supplementary prescriber" has the same meaning as in the Prescription Only Medicines (Human Use) Order 1997;

"wholesale dealer" means a person who carries on the business of selling drugs to persons who buy to sell again.

(2) In these Regulations any reference to a regulation or schedule shall be construed as a reference to a regulation contained in these Regulations or, as the case may be, to a schedule to these Regulations, and any reference in a regulation or schedule to a paragraph shall be construed as a reference to a paragraph of that regulation or schedule.

(3) Nothing in these Regulations shall be construed as derogating from any power or immunity of the Crown, its servants or agents.

8–22082 **3. Specification of controlled drugs for purposes of Regulations.** Schedules 1 to 5 shall have effect for the purpose of specifying the controlled drugs to which certain provisions of these Regulations apply.

8–22083 **4. Exceptions for drugs in Schedules 4 and 5 and poppy-straw.** (1) Section 3(1) of the Act (which prohibits the importation and exportation of controlled drugs) shall not have effect in relation to the drugs specified in Schedule 5.

(2) The application of section 3(1) of the Act, in so far as it creates an offence, and the application of sections 50(1) to (4), 68(2) and (3) or 170 of the Customs and Excise Management Act 1979, in so far as they apply in relation to a prohibition or restriction on importation or exportation having effect by virtue of section 3 of the Act, are hereby excluded in the case of importation or exportation by any person for administration to himself of any drug specified in Part II of Schedule 4 which is contained in a medicinal product.

(3) Section 5(1) of the Act (which prohibits the possession of controlled drugs) shall not have effect in relation to—

(*a*) any drug specified in Part II of Schedule 4 which is contained in a medicinal product;
(*b*) the drugs specified in Schedule 5[1].

(4) Sections 4(1) (which prohibits the production and supply of controlled drugs) and 5(1) of the Act shall not have effect in relation to poppy-straw.

(5) Sections 3(1), 4(1) and 5(1) of the Act shall not have effect in relation to any exempt product.

1. On a prosecution for unlawful possession of a controlled drug, contrary to s 5(2) of the Misuse of Drugs Act 1971, the burden is on the prosecution to prove that the controlled drug was not in a form permitted by Sch 5, post (*R v Hunt* [1987] AC 352, [1987] 1 All ER 1, 82 Cr App Rep 173).

8–22083A **4A. Exceptions for drugs in Schedule 1.** (1) Section 5(1) of the Act (which prohibits the possession of controlled drugs) shall not have effect in relation to a fungus (of any kind) which contains psilocin or an ester of psilocin where that fungus—

(*a*) is growing uncultivated;
(*b*) is picked by a person already in lawful possession of it for the purpose of delivering it as soon as is reasonably practicable into the custody of a person lawfully entitled to take custody of it and it remains in that person's possession for and in accordance with that purpose;
(*c*) is picked for either of the purposes specified in paragraph (2) and is held for and in accordance with the purpose specified in paragraph (2)(*b*), either by the person who picked it or by another person; or
(*d*) is picked for the purpose specified in paragraph (2)(*b*) and is held for and in accordance with the purpose in paragraph (2)(*a*), either by the person who picked it or by another person.

(2) The purposes specified for the purposes of this paragraph are—

(*a*) the purpose of delivering the fungus as soon as is reasonably practicable into the custody of a person lawfully entitled to take custody of it; and
(*b*) the purpose of destroying the fungus as soon as is reasonably practicable.

8–22084 **5. Licences to produce etc controlled drugs.** Where any person is authorised by a licence of the Secretary of State issued under this regulation and for the time being in force to produce, supply, offer to supply or have in his possession any controlled drug, it shall not by virtue of section 4(1) or 5(1) of the Act be unlawful for that person to produce, supply, offer to supply or have in his possession that drug in accordance with the terms of the licence and in compliance with any conditions attached to the licence.

8–22085 **6. General authority to supply and possess.** (1) Notwithstanding the provisions of section 4(1)(*b*) of the Act, any person who is lawfully in possession of a controlled drug may supply that drug to the person from whom he obtained it.

(2) Notwithstanding the provisions of section 4(1)(*b*) of the Act, any person who has in his possession a drug specified in Schedule 2, 3, 4 or 5 which has been supplied by or on the prescription of a practitioner, a registered nurse, a supplementary prescriber or a person specified in Schedule 8 for the treatment of that person, or of a person whom he represents, may supply that drug to any doctor, dentist or pharmacist for the purpose of destruction.

(3) Notwithstanding the provisions of section 4(1)(*b*) of the Act, any person who is lawfully in possession of a drug specified in Schedule 2, 3, 4 or 5 which has been supplied by or on the prescription of a veterinary practitioner or veterinary surgeon for the treatment of animals may supply that drug to any veterinary practitioner, veterinary surgeon or pharmacist for the purpose of destruction.

(4) It shall not by virtue of section 4(1)(*b*) or 5(1) of the Act be unlawful for any person in respect of whom a licence has been granted and is in force under section 16(1) of the Wildlife and Countryside Act 1981 to supply, offer to supply or have in his possession any drug specified in Schedule 2 or 3 for the purposes for which that licence was granted.

(5) Notwithstanding the provisions of section 4(1)(*b*) of the Act, any of the persons specified in paragraph (7) may supply any controlled drug to any person who may lawfully have that drug in his possession.

(6) Notwithstanding the provisions of section 5(1) of the Act, any of the persons so specified may have any controlled drug in his possession.

(7) The persons referred to in paragraphs (5) and (6) are

(*a*) a constable when acting in the course of his duty as such;
(*b*) a person engaged in the business of a carrier when acting in the course of that business;
(*c*) a person engaged in the business of the Post Office when acting in the course of that business;
(*d*) an officer of customs and excise when acting in the course of his duty as such;
(*e*) a person engaged in the work of any laboratory to which the drug has been sent for forensic examination when acting in the course of his duty as a person so engaged;
(*f*) a person engaged in conveying the drug to a person who may lawfully have that drug in his possession.

8–22085A **6A. Supply of articles for administering or preparing controlled drugs.** (1) Notwithstanding the provisions of section 9A(1) and (3) of the Act, any of the persons specified in paragraph (2) may, when acting in their capacity as such, supply or offer to supply the following articles—

(*a*) a swab;
(*b*) utensils for the preparation of a controlled drug;
(*c*) citric acid;
(*d*) a filter;
(*e*) ampoules of water for injection, only when supplied or offered for supply in accordance with the Medicines Act 1968 and of any instrument which is in force thereunder;
(*f*) ascorbic acid

(2) The persons referred to in paragraph (1) are—

(*a*) a practitioner;
(*b*) a pharmacist;
(*c*) a person employed or engaged in the lawful provision of drug treatment services;
(*d*) a supplementary prescriber acting under and in accordance with the terms of a clinical management plan.

8–22085B **6B. Authority for Extended Formulary Nurse Prescribers to prescribe.** An extended formulary nurse prescriber may only prescribe—

(*a*) diamorphine, diazepam, lorazepam, midazolam, morphine or oxycodone for use in palliative care;
(*b*) buprenorphine or fentanyl for transdermal use in palliative care;
(*c*) diamorphine or morphine for pain relief in respect of suspected myocardial infarction or for relief of acute or severe pain after trauma including in either case post-operative pain relief;
(*d*) chlordiazepoxide hydrochloride or diazepam for treatment of initial or acute withdrawal symptoms caused by the withdrawal of alcohol from persons habituated to it;
(*e*) codeine phosphate, dihydrocodeine tartrate or co-phenotrope.

8–22086 **7. Administration of drugs in Schedules 2, 3, 4 and 5.** (1) Any person may administer to another any drug specified in Schedule 5.

(2) A doctor or dentist may administer to a patient any drug specified in Schedule 2, 3 or 4.

(3) Any person other than a doctor or dentist may administer to a patient, in accordance with the directions of a doctor or dentist, any drug specified in Schedule 2, 3 or 4.

(4) Notwithstanding the provisions of paragraph (3), an extended formulary nurse prescriber may administer to a patient, without the directions of a doctor or dentist, any controlled drug which she may prescribe under regulation 6B provided it is administered for a purpose for which it may be prescribed under that regulation.

(5) Notwithstanding the provisions of paragraph (3), any person may administer to a patient in accordance with the specific directions of an extended formulary nurse prescriber any controlled drug which the extended formulary nurse prescriber may prescribe under regulation 6B provided it is administered for a purpose for which it may be prescribed under that regulation.

(6) Notwithstanding the provisions of paragraph (3), a supplementary prescriber acting under and in accordance with the terms of a clinical management plan may administer to a patient, without the directions of a doctor or dentist, any drug specified in Schedule 2, 3 or 4.

(7) Notwithstanding the provisions of paragraph (3), any person may administer to a patient, in accordance with the directions of a supplementary prescriber acting under and in accordance with the terms of a clinical management plan, any drug specified in Schedule 2, 3 or 4.

8–22087 **8. Production and supply of drugs in Schedules 2 and 5.** (1) Notwithstanding the provisions of section 4(1)(*a*) of the Act—

(*a*) a practitioner or pharmacist, acting in his capacity as such, may manufacture or compound any drug specified in Schedule 2 or 5;
(*b*) a person lawfully conducting a retail pharmacy business and acting in his capacity as such may, at the registered pharmacy at which he carries on that business, manufacture or compound any drug specified in Schedule 2 or 5.

(2) Notwithstanding the provisions of section 4(1)(*b*) of the Act, any of the following persons, that is to say—

(*a*) a practitioner;
(*b*) a pharmacist;
(*c*) a person lawfully conducting a retail pharmacy business;
(*d*) the person in charge or acting person in charge of a hospital or nursing home which is wholly or mainly maintained by a public authority out of public funds or by a charity or by voluntary subscriptions;
(*e*) in the case of such a drug supplied to her by a person responsible for the dispensing and supply of medicines at the hospital or nursing home, the sister or acting sister for the time being in charge of a ward, theatre or other department in such a hospital or nursing home as aforesaid;
(*f*) a person who is in charge of a laboratory the recognised activities of which consist in, or include, the conduct of scientific education or research and which is attached to a university, university college or such a hospital as aforesaid or to any other institution approved for the purpose under this sub-paragraph by the Secretary of State;
(*g*) a public analyst appointed under section 27 of the Food Safety Act 1990;
(*h*) a sampling officer within the meaning of Schedule 3 to the Medicines Act 1968;
(*i*) a person employed or engaged in connection with a scheme for testing the quality or amount of the drugs, preparations and appliances supplied under the National Health Service Act 1977 or the National Health Service (Scotland) Act 1978 and the regulations made thereunder;
(*j*) a person authorised by the Pharmaceutical Society of Great Britain for the purposes of section 108 or 109 of the Medicines Act 1968,
(*k*) a supplementary prescriber acting under and in accordance with the terms of a clinical management plan,

may, when acting in his capacity as such, supply or offer to supply any drug specified in Schedule 2 or 5 to any person who may lawfully have that drug in his possession, except that nothing in this paragraph authorises—

(i) the person in charge or acting person in charge of a hospital or nursing home, having a pharmacist responsible for the dispensing and supply of medicines, to supply or offer to supply any drug; or
(ii) a sister or acting sister for the time being in charge of a ward, theatre or other department to supply any drug otherwise than for administration to a patient in that ward, theatre or department in accordance with the directions of a doctor or dentist.

(3) Notwithstanding the provisions of section 4(1)(*b*) of the Act, a person who is authorised as a member of a group may, under and in accordance with the terms of his group authority and in compliance with any conditions attached thereto, supply or offer to supply any drug specified in Schedule 2 or 5 to any person who may lawfully have that drug in his possession.

(4) Notwithstanding the provisions of section 4(1)(*b*) of the Act, a person who is authorised by a written authority issued by the Secretary of State under and for the purposes of this paragraph and for the time being in force may, at the premises specified in that authority and in compliance with any conditions so specified, supply or offer to supply any drug specified in Schedule 5 to any person who may lawfully have that drug in his possession.

(5) Notwithstanding the provisions of section 4(1)(*b*) of the Act—

(*a*) the owner of a ship, or the master of a ship which does not carry a doctor among the seamen employed in it; or
(*b*) the installation manager of an offshore installation,

may supply or offer to supply any drug specified in Schedule 2 or 5—

(i) for the purpose of compliance with any of the provisions specified in paragraph (6), to any person on that ship or installation;
(ii) to any person who may lawfully supply that drug to him;
(iii) to any constable for the purpose of the destruction of that drug.

(6) The provisions referred to in paragraph (5) are any provision of, or of any instrument which is in force under—

(*a*) the Mineral Workings (Offshore Installations) Act 1971;
(*b*) the Health and Safety at Work etc Act 1974 or
(*c*) the Merchant Shipping Act 1995.

(7) Notwithstanding the provisions of section 4(1)(*b*) of the Act, an extended formulary nurse prescriber may, when acting in her capacity as such, supply or offer to supply—

(*a*) codeine phosphate, dihydrocodeine tartrate and co-phenotrope;
(*b*) diamorphine and morphine for pain relief in respect of suspected myocardial infarction or for relief of acute or severe pain after trauma including in either case post-operative pain relief;
(*c*) diamorphine, morphine and oxycodone for use in palliative care; and
(*d*) fentanyl for transdermal use in palliative care,

to any person who may lawfully have any of these drugs in his possession.

(8) Notwithstanding the provisions of section 4(1)(*b*) of the Act—

(*a*) a registered nurse, when acting in her capacity as such, may supply or offer to supply, under and in accordance with the terms of a patient group direction, diamorphine for the treatment of cardiac pain to a person admitted as a patient to a coronary care unit or an accident and emergency department of a hospital;

(*b*) a registered nurse or a person specified in Schedule 8 may, when acting in their capacity as such, supply or offer to supply, under and in accordance with the terms of a patient group direction, any drug specified in Schedule 5 to any person who may lawfully have that drug in his possession.

8–22088 **9. Production and supply of drugs in Schedules 3 and 4.** (1) Notwithstanding the provisions of section 4(1)(*a*) of the Act—

(*a*) a practitioner or pharmacist, acting in his capacity as such, may manufacture or compound any drug specified in Schedule 3 or 4;

(*b*) a person lawfully conducting a retail pharmacy business and acting in his capacity as such may, at the registered pharmacy at which he carries on that business, manufacture or compound any drug specified in Schedule 3 or 4;

(*c*) a person who is authorised by a written authority issued by the Secretary of State under and for the purposes of this sub-paragraph and for the time being in force may, at the premises specified in that authority and in compliance with any conditions so specified, produce any drug specified in Schedule 3 or 4.

(2) Notwithstanding the provisions of section 4(1)(*b*) of the Act, any of the following persons, that is to say—

(*a*) a practitioner;

(*b*) a pharmacist;

(*c*) a person lawfully conducting a retail pharmacy business;

(*d*) a person in charge of a laboratory the recognised activities of which consist in, or include, the conduct of scientific education or research;

(*e*) a public analyst appointed under section 27 of the Food Safety Act 1990;

(*f*) a sampling officer within the meaning of Schedule 3 to the Medicines Act 1968;

(*g*) a person employed or engaged in connection with a scheme for testing the quality or amount of the drugs, preparations and appliances supplied under the National Health Service Act 1977 or the National Health Service (Scotland) Act 1978 and the regulations made thereunder;

(*h*) a person authorised by the Pharmaceutical Society of Great Britain for the purposes of section 108 or 109 of the Medicines Act 1968,

(*i*) a supplementary prescriber acting under and in accordance with the terms of a clinical management plan,

may, when acting in his capacity as such, supply or offer to supply any drug specified in Schedule 3 or 4 to any person who may lawfully have that drug in his possession.

(3) Notwithstanding the provisions of section 4(1)(*b*) of the Act—

(*a*) a person who is authorised as a member of a group, under and in accordance with the terms of his group authority and in compliance with any conditions attached thereto;

(*b*) the person in charge or acting person in charge of a hospital or nursing home;

(*c*) in the case of such a drug supplied to her by a person responsible for the dispensing and supply of medicines at that hospital or nursing home, the sister or acting sister for the time being in charge of a ward, theatre or other department in a hospital or nursing home,

may, when acting in his capacity as such, supply or offer to supply any drug specified in Schedule 3, or any drug specified in Schedule 4 which is contained in a medicinal product, to any person who may lawfully have that drug in his possession, except that nothing in this paragraph authorises—

(i) the person in charge or acting person in charge of a hospital or nursing home, having a pharmacist responsible for the dispensing and supply of medicines, to supply or offer to supply any drug;

(ii) a sister or acting sister for the time being in charge of a ward, theatre or other department to supply any drug otherwise than for administration to a patient in that ward, theatre or department in accordance with the directions of a doctor or dentist.

(4) Notwithstanding the provisions of section 4(1)(*b*) of the Act—

(*a*) a person who is authorised by a written authority issued by the Secretary of State under and for the purposes of this sub-paragraph and for the time being in force may, at the premises specified in that authority and in compliance with any conditions so specified, supply or offer to supply any drug specified in Schedule 3 or 4 to any person who may lawfully have that drug in his possession;

(*b*) a person who is authorised under paragraph (1)(c) may supply or offer to supply any drug which he may, by virtue of being so authorised, lawfully produce to any person who may lawfully have that drug in his possession.

(5) Notwithstanding the provisions of section 4(1)(*b*) of the Act—

(*a*) the owner of a ship, or the master of a ship which does not carry a doctor among the seamen employed in it;
(*b*) the installation manager of an offshore installation,

may supply or offer to supply any drug specified in Schedule 3, or any drug specified in Schedule 4 which is contained in a medicinal product—

(i) for the purpose of compliance with any of the provisions specified in regulation 8(6), to any person on that ship or installation; or
(ii) to any person who may lawfully supply that drug to him.

(6) Notwithstanding the provisions of section 4(1)(*b*) of the Act, a person in charge of a laboratory may, when acting in his capacity as such, supply or offer to supply any drug specified in Schedule 3 which is required for use as a buffering agent in chemical analysis to any person who may lawfully have that drug in his possession.

(7) Notwithstanding the provisions of section 4(1)(*b*) of the Act, an extended formulary nurse prescriber may, when acting in her capacity as such, supply or offer to supply—

(*a*) diazepam, lorazepam and midazolam for use in palliative care;
(*b*) buprenorphine for transdermal use in palliative care; and
(*c*) chlordiazepoxide hydrochloride and diazepam for treatment of initial or acute withdrawal symptoms caused by the withdrawal of alcohol from persons habituated to it,

to any person who may lawfully have any of these drugs in his possession.

(8) Notwithstanding the provisions of section 4(1)(*b*) of the Act, a registered nurse or a person specified in Schedule 8, when acting in their capacity as such, may supply or offer to supply, under and in accordance with the terms of a patient group direction, any drug specified in Schedule 4 to any person who may lawfully have that drug in his possession, except that this paragraph shall not have effect in the case of—

(*a*) the supply or offer to supply of any of the anabolic steroid drugs specified in Part II of Schedule 4; and
(*b*) any drug or preparation which is designed for administration by injection and which is to be used for the purpose of treating a person who is addicted to a drug;
(*c*) for the purposes of paragraph (*b*) above, a person shall be regarded as being addicted to a drug if, and only if, he has as a result of repeated administration become so dependent upon the drug that he has an overpowering desire for the administration of it to be continued.

8–22089 **10. Possession of drugs in Schedules 2, 3 and 4.** (1) Notwithstanding the provisions of section 5(1) of the Act—

(*a*) a person specified in one of sub-paragraphs (*a*) to (k) of regulation 8(2) may have in his possession any drug specified in Schedule 2;
(*b*) a person specified in one of sub-paragraphs (*a*) to (i) of regulation 9(2) may have in his possession any drug specified in Schedule 3 or 4;
(*c*) a person specified in regulation 9(3)(*b*) or (c) or (6) may have in his possession any drug specified in Schedule 3,

for the purpose of acting in his capacity as such a person[1], except that nothing in this paragraph authorises—

(i) a person specified in sub-paragraph (*e*) of regulation 8(2);
(ii) a person specified in sub-paragraph (c) of regulation 9(3); or
(iii) a person specified in regulation 9(6),

to have in his possession any drug other than such a drug as is mentioned in the paragraph or sub-paragraph in question specifying him.

(2) Notwithstanding the provisions of section 5(1) of the Act, a person may have in his possession any drug specified in Schedule 2, 3 or Part I of Schedule 4 for administration for medical, dental or veterinary purposes in accordance with the directions of a practitioner, a supplementary prescriber acting under and in accordance with the terms of a clinical management plan or an extended formulary nurse prescriber, except that this paragraph shall not have effect in the case of a person to whom the drug has been supplied by or on the prescription of a doctor, a supplementary prescriber or an extended formulary nurse prescriber if—

(*a*) that person was then being supplied with any controlled drug by or on the prescription of another doctor, another supplementary prescriber or another extended formulary nurse prescriber and failed to disclose that fact to the first mentioned doctor, supplementary prescriber or extended formulary nurse prescriber before the supply by him or on his prescription; or
(*b*) that or any other person on his behalf made a declaration or statement, which was false in any particular, for the purpose of obtaining the supply or prescription.

(3) Notwithstanding the provisions of section 5(1) of the Act, a person who is authorised as a member of a group may, under and in accordance with the terms of his group authority and in compliance with any conditions attached thereto, have any drug specified in Schedule 2, 3 or Part I of Schedule 4 in his possession.

(4) Notwithstanding the provisions of section 5(1) of the Act—

(*a*) a person who is authorised by a written authority issued by the Secretary of State under and for the purposes of this sub-paragraph and for the time being in force may, at the premises specified in that authority and in compliance with any conditions so specified, have in his possession any drug specified in Schedule 3 or 4;

(*b*) a person who is authorised under regulation 9(1)(c) may have in his possession any drug which he may, by virtue of being so authorised, lawfully produce;

(*c*) a person who is authorised under regulation 9(4)(*a*) may have in his possession any drug which he may, by virtue of being so authorised, lawfully supply or offer to supply.

(5) Notwithstanding the provisions of section 5(1) of the Act—

(*a*) any person may have in his possession any drug specified in Schedule 2, 3 or Part I of Schedule 4 for the purpose of compliance with any of the provisions specified in regulation 8(6);

(*b*) the master of a foreign ship which is in a port in Great Britain may have in his possession any drug specified in Schedule 2, 3 or Part I of Schedule 4 so far as necessary for the equipment of the ship.

(6) The foregoing provisions of this regulation are without prejudice to the provisions of regulation 4(3)(*a*).

---

1. A doctor bona fide treating himself is acting inhis capacity as a doctor although he himself is receiving the benefit of the drug (*R v Dunbar* [1982] 1 All ER 188, [1981] 1 WLR 1536, 74 Cr App Rep 88).

8–22090 **11. Exemption for midwives.** (1) Notwithstanding the provisions of sections 4(1)(*b*) and 5(1) of the Act, a registered midwife who has, in accordance with the provisions of rules made under article 42 of the Order, notified to the local supervising authority her intention to practise may, subject to the provisions of this regulation—

(*a*) so far as necessary to her professional practice, have in her possession;

(*b*) so far as necessary as aforesaid, administer; and

(*c*) surrender to the appropriate medical officer such stocks in her possession as are no longer required by her of,

any controlled drug which she may, under and in accordance with the provisions of the Medicines Act 1968 and of any instrument which is in force thereunder, lawfully administer.

(2) Nothing in paragraph (1) authorises a midwife to have in her possession any drug which has been obtained otherwise than on a midwife's supply order signed by the appropriate medical officer.

(3) In this regulation—

"appropriate medical officer" means—

(*a*) a doctor who is for the time being authorised in writing for the purposes of this regulation by the local supervising authority for the region or area in which the drug was, or is to be, obtained; or

(*b*) for the purposes of paragraph (2), a person appointed under and in accordance with article 43 of the Order by that authority to exercise supervision over registered midwives within their area, who is for the time being authorised as aforesaid;

"local supervising authority" has the meaning it is given by Schedule 4 of the Order;

"midwife's supply order" means an order in writing specifying the name and occupation of the midwife obtaining the drug, the purpose for which it is required and the total quantity to be obtained;

"the Order" means the Nursing and Midwifery Order 2001.

8–22091 **12. Cultivation under licence of cannabis plant.** Where any person is authorised by a licence of the Secretary of State issued under this regulation and for the time being in force to cultivate plants of the genus Cannabis, it shall not by virtue of section 6 of the Act be unlawful for that person to cultivate any such plant in accordance with the terms of the licence and in compliance with any conditions attached to the licence.

8–22092 **13. Approval of premises for cannabis smoking for research purposes.** Section 8 of the Act (which makes it an offence for the occupier of premises to permit certain activities there) shall not have effect in relation to the smoking of cannabis or cannabis resin for the purposes of research on any premises for the time being approved for the purpose under this regulation by the Secretary of State.

8–22093 **14. Documents to be obtained by supplier of controlled drugs.** (1) Where a person (hereafter in this paragraph referred to as "the supplier"), not being a practitioner, supplies a controlled drug otherwise than on a prescription, the supplier shall not deliver the drug to a person who—

(*a*) purports to be sent by or on behalf of the person to whom it is supplied (hereafter in this paragraph referred to as "the recipient"); and

(*b*) is not authorised by any provision of these Regulations other than the provisions of regulation 6(6) and (7)(*f*) to have that drug in his possession, unless that person produces to the supplier a statement in writing signed by the recipient to the effect that he is empowered by the recipient to receive that drug on behalf of the recipient, and the supplier is reasonably satisfied that the document is a genuine document.

(2) Where a person (hereafter in this paragraph referred to as "the supplier") supplies a controlled drug, otherwise than on a prescription or by way of administration, to any of the persons specified in paragraph (4), the supplier shall not deliver the drug—

(*a*) until he has obtained a requisition in writing which—

(i) is signed by the person to whom the drug is supplied (hereafter in this paragraph referred to as "the recipient");

(ii) states the name, address and profession or occupation of the recipient;

(iii) specifies the purpose for which the drug supplied is required and the total quantity to be supplied; and

(iv) where appropriate, satisfies the requirements of paragraph (5);

(*b*) unless he is reasonably satisfied that the signature is that of the person purporting to have signed the requisition and that that person is engaged in the profession or occupation specified in the requisition,

except that where the recipient is a practitioner and he represents that he urgently requires a controlled drug for the purpose of his profession, the supplier may, if he is reasonably satisfied that the recipient so requires the drug and is, by reason of some emergency, unable before delivery to furnish to the supplier a requisition in writing duly signed, deliver the drug to the recipient on an undertaking by the recipient to furnish such a requisition within the twenty-four hours next following.

(3) A person who has given such an undertaking as aforesaid shall deliver to the person by whom the controlled drug was supplied a signed requisition in accordance with the undertaking.

(4) The persons referred to in paragraph (2) are—

(*a*) a practitioner;

(*b*) the person in charge or acting person in charge of a hospital or nursing home;

(*c*) a person who is in charge of a laboratory;

(*d*) the owner of a ship, or the master of a ship which does not carry a doctor among the seamen employed in it;

(*e*) the master of a foreign ship in a port in Great Britain;

(*f*) the installation manager of an offshore installation

(*g*) a supplementary presciber.

(5) A requisition furnished for the purposes of paragraph (2) shall—

(*a*) where furnished by the person in charge or acting person in charge of a hospital or nursing home, be signed by a doctor or dentist employed or engaged in that hospital or nursing home;

(*b*) where furnished by the master of a foreign ship, contain a statement, signed by the proper officer of the port health authority, or, in Scotland, the medical officer designated under section 14 of the National Health Service (Scotland) Act 1978 by the Health Board, within whose jurisdiction the ship is, that the quantity of the drug to be supplied is the quantity necessary for the equipment of the ship.

(6) Where the person responsible for the dispensing and supply of medicines at any hospital or nursing home supplies a controlled drug to the sister or acting sister for the time being in charge of any ward, theatre or other department in that hospital or nursing home (hereafter in this paragraph referred to as "the recipient") he shall—

(*a*) obtain a requisition in writing, signed by the recipient, which specifies the total quantity of the drug to be supplied; and

(*b*) mark the requisition in such manner as to show that it has been complied with,

and any requisition obtained for the purposes of this paragraph shall be retained in the dispensary at which the drug was supplied and a copy of the requisition or a note of it shall be retained or kept by the recipient.

(7) Nothing in this regulation shall have effect in relation to—

(*a*) the drugs specified in Schedules 4 and 5 or poppy-straw;

(*b*) any drug specified in Schedule 3 contained in or comprising a preparation which—

(i) is required for use as a buffering agent in chemical analysis;

(ii) has present in it both a substance specified in paragraph 1 or 2 of that Schedule and a salt of that substance; and

(iii) is pre-mixed in a kit;

(*c*) any exempt product.

8–22094 **15. Form of prescriptions.** (1) Subject to the provisions of this regulation, a person shall not issue a prescription containing a controlled drug other than a drug specified in Schedule 4 or 5 or temazepam unless the prescription complies with the following requirements, that is to say, it shall—

(*a*) be written so as to be indelible, be dated and be signed by the person issuing it with his usual signature;
(*b*) *revoked*;
(*c*) except in the case of a health prescription, specify the address of the person issuing it;
(*d*) if issued by a dentist, have the words "for dental treatment only" written on it and, if issued by a veterinary surgeon or a veterinary practitioner, have a declaration written on it that the controlled drug is prescribed for an animal or herd under his care;
(*e*) specify the name and address of the person for whose treatment it is issued or, if it is issued by a veterinary surgeon or veterinary practitioner, of the person to whom the controlled drug prescribed is to be delivered;
(*f*) specify the dose to be taken and—
   (i) in the case of a prescription containing a controlled drug which is a preparation, the form and, where appropriate, the strength of the preparation, and either the total quantity (in both words and figures) of the preparation or the number (in both words and figures) of dosage units, as appropriate, to be supplied;
   (ii) in any other case, the total quantity (in both words and figures) of the controlled drug to be supplied;
(*g*) in the case of a prescription for a total quantity intended to be supplied by instalments, contain a direction specifying the amount of the instalments of the total amount which may be supplied and the intervals to be observed when supplying.

(2) *Revoked.*

(3) In the case of a prescription issued for the treatment of a patient in a hospital or nursing home, it shall be a sufficient compliance with paragraph (1)(*e*) if the prescription is written on the patient's bed card or case sheet.

8–22095 **16. Provisions as to supply on prescription.** (1) A person shall not supply a controlled drug other than a drug specified in Schedule 4 or 5 on a prescription—

(*a*) unless the prescription complies with the provisions of regulation 15;
(*b*) unless the address specified in the prescription as the address of the person issuing it is an address within the United Kingdom;
(*c*) unless he either is acquainted with the signature of the person by whom it purports to be issued and has no reason to suppose that it is not genuine, or has taken reasonably sufficient steps to satisfy himself that it is genuine;
(*d*) before the date specified in the prescription;
(*e*) subject to paragraph (3), later than thirteen weeks after the date specified in the prescription.

(2) Subject to paragraphs (3) and (4), a person supplying on prescription a controlled drug other than a drug specified in Schedule 4 or 5 shall, at the time of the supply, mark on the prescription the date on which the drug is supplied and, unless it is a health prescription, shall retain the prescription on the premises from which the drug was supplied.

(3) A person supplying temazepam on prescription in accordance with a prescription form of a kind specified in regulation 2A(1)(*a*)(i) of the National Health Service (Pharmaceutical Services) Regulations 1992 shall, at the time of the supply, enter on the form by electronic means the date on which the drug is supplied.

(4) In the case of a prescription containing a controlled drug other than a drug specified in Schedule 4 or 5, which contains a direction that specified instalments of the total amount may be supplied at stated intervals, the person supplying the drug shall not do so otherwise than in accordance with that direction, and—

(*a*) paragraph (1) shall have effect as if for the requirement contained in sub-paragraph (*e*) thereof there were substituted a requirement that the occasion on which the first instalment is supplied shall not be later than thirteen weeks after the date specified in the prescription;
(*b*) paragraph (2) shall have effect as if for the words "at the time of the supply" there were substituted the words "on each occasion on which an instalment is supplied".

8–22096 **17. Exemption for certain prescriptions.** Nothing in regulations 15 and 16 shall have effect in relation to a prescription issued for the purposes of a scheme for testing the quality or amount of the drugs, preparations and appliances supplied under the National Health Service Act 1977 or the National Health Service (Scotland) Act 1978 and the regulations made thereunder or to any prescriptions issued for the purposes of the Medicines Act 1968 to a sampling officer within the meaning of that Act.

8–22097 **18. Marking of bottles and other containers.** (1) Subject to paragraph (2), no person shall supply a controlled drug otherwise than in a bottle, package or other container which is plainly marked—

(*a*) in the case of a controlled drug other than a preparation, with the amount of the drug contained therein;
(*b*) in the case of a controlled drug which is a preparation—

(i) made up into tablets, capsules or other dosage units, with the amount of each component (being a controlled drug) of the preparation in each dosage unit and the number of dosage units in the bottle, package or other container;

(ii) not made up as aforesaid, with the total amount of the preparation in the bottle, package or other container and the percentage of each of its components which is a controlled drug.

(2) Nothing in this regulation shall have effect in relation to—

(*a*) the drugs specified in Schedules 4 and 5 or poppy-straw;

(*b*) any drug specified in Schedule 3 contained in or comprising a preparation which—

(i) is required for use as a buffering agent in chemical analysis;

(ii) has present in it both a substance specified in paragraph 1 or 2 of that Schedule and a salt of that substance; and

(iii) is premixed in a kit;

(*c*) any exempt product;

(*d*) the supply of a controlled drug by or on the prescription of a practitioner or supplementary presciber;

(*e*) the supply of a controlled drug for administration in a clinical trial or a medicinal test on animals.

(3) In this regulation—

"clinical trial" has the same meaning as in the Medicines for Human Use (Clinical Trials) Regulations 2003;

"medicinal test on animals" has the same meaning as in the Medicines Act 1968.

8–22098 **19. Record-keeping requirements in respect of drugs in Schedules 1 and 2.** (1) Subject to paragraph (3) and regulation 21, every person authorised by or under regulation 5 or 8 to supply any drug specified in Schedule 1 or 2 shall comply with the following requirements, that is to say—

(*a*) he shall, in accordance with the provisions of this regulation and of regulation 20, keep a register and shall enter therein in chronological sequence in the form specified in Part I or Part II of Schedule 6, as the case may require, particulars of every quantity of a drug specified in Schedule 1 or 2 obtained by him and of every quantity of such a drug supplied (whether by way of administration or otherwise) by him whether to persons within or outside Great Britain;

(*b*) he shall use a separate register or separate part of the register for entries made in respect of each class of drugs, and each of the drugs specified in paragraphs 1 and 3 of Schedule 1 and paragraphs 1, 3 and 6 of Schedule 2 together with its salts and any preparation or other product containing it or any of its salts shall be treated as a separate class, so however that any stereoisomeric form of a drug or its salts shall be classed with that drug.

(2) Nothing in paragraph (1) shall be taken as preventing the use of a separate section within a register or separate part of a register in respect of different drugs or strengths of drugs comprised within the class of drugs to which that register or separate part relates.

(3) The foregoing provisions of this regulation shall not have effect in relation to—

(*a*) in the case of a drug supplied to him for the purpose of destruction in pursuance of regulation 6(2) or (3), a practitioner or pharmacist;

(*b*) a person licensed under regulation 5 to supply any drug, where the licence so directs; or

(*c*) the sister or acting sister for the time being in charge of a ward, theatre or other department in a hospital or nursing home.

8–22099 **20. Requirements as to registers.** Any person required to keep a register under regulation 19 shall comply with the following requirements, that is to say—

(*a*) the class of drugs to which the entries on any page of any such register relate shall be specified at the head of that page;

(*b*) every entry required to be made under regulation 19 in such a register shall be made on the day on which the drug is obtained or, as the case may be, on which the transaction in respect of the supply of the drug by the person required to make the entry takes place or, if that is not reasonably practicable, on the day next following that day;

(*c*) no cancellation, obliteration or alteration of any such entry shall be made, and a correction of such an entry shall be made only by way of marginal note or footnote which shall specify the date on which the correction is made;

(*d*) every such entry and every correction of such an entry shall be made in ink or otherwise so as to be indelible or shall be in a computerised form in which every such entry is attributable and capable of being audited and which is in accordance with best practice guidance endorsed by the Secretary of State under section 2 of the National Health Service Act 1977;

(*e*) such a register shall not be used for any purpose other than the purposes of these Regulations;

(*f*) a separate register shall be kept in respect of each premises at which the person required to keep the register carries on his business or occupation, but subject to that not more than one register shall be kept at one time in respect of each class of drugs in respect of which he is required to keep a separate register, so, however, that a separate register may, with the approval of the Secretary of State, be kept in respect of each department of the business carried on by him;

(*g*) every such register in which entries are currently being made shall be kept at the premises to which it relates and, where the register is in computerised form, be accessible from those premises.

8–22100 21. Record-keeping requirements in respect of drugs in Schedule 2 in particular cases. (1) Where a drug specified in Schedule 2 is supplied in accordance with regulation 8(5)(*a*)(i) to any person on a ship, an entry in the official log book required to be kept under the Merchant Shipping Act 1995 or, in the case of a ship which is not required to carry such an official logbook, a report signed by the master of the ship, shall, notwithstanding anything in these Regulations, be a sufficient record of the supply if the entry or report specifies the drug supplied and, in the case of a report, it is delivered as soon as may be to a superintendent at a Marine Office established and maintained under the Merchant Shipping Act 1995.

(2) Where a drug specified in Schedule 2 is supplied in accordance with regulation 8(5)(*b*)(i) to a person on an offshore installation, an entry in the installation logbook required to be maintained under the Offshore Installations (Logbooks and Registration of Death) Regulations 1972 which specifies the drug supplied shall, notwithstanding anything in these Regulations, be a sufficient record of the supply.

(3) A midwife authorised by regulation 11(1) to have any drug specified in Schedule 2 in her possession shall—

(*a*) on each occasion on which she obtains a supply of such a drug, enter in a book kept by her and used solely for the purposes of this paragraph the date, the name and address of the person from whom the drug was obtained, the amount obtained and the form in which it was obtained; and

(*b*) on administering such a drug to a patient, enter in the said book as soon as practicable the name and address of the patient, the amount administered and the form in which it was administered.

8–22101 22. Record-keeping requirements in respect of drugs Schedules 3 and 4. (1) Every person who is authorised under regulation 5 or 9(1)(c) to produce any drug specified in Schedule 3 or 4 shall make a record of each quantity of such a drug produced by him.

(2) Every person who is authorised by or under any provision of the Act to import or export any drug specified in Schedule 3 shall make a record of each quantity of such a drug imported or exported by him.

(3) Every person who is authorised under regulation 9(4) to supply any drug specified in Schedule 4 shall make a record of each quantity of such a drug imported or exported by him.

(4) Paragraph (2) shall not have effect in relation to a person licensed under the Act to import or export any drug where the licence so directs.

8–22102 23. Preservation of registers, books and other documents. (1) All registers and books kept in pursuance of regulation 19 or 21(3) shall be preserved for a period of two years from the date on which the last entry therein is made.

(2) Every record made in pursuance of regulation 22 shall be preserved for a period of two years from the date on which the record was made.

(3) Every requisition, order or prescription (other than a health prescription) on which a controlled drug is supplied in pursuance of these regulations shall be preserved for a period of two years from the date on which the last delivery under it was made.

8–22103 24. Preservation of records relating to drugs in Schedules 3 and 5. (1) A producer of any drug specified in Schedule 3 or 5 and a wholesale dealer in any such drug shall keep every invoice or other like record issued in respect of each quantity of such a drug obtained by him and in respect of each quantity of such a drug supplied by him.

(2) A person who is authorised under regulation 9(4)(*a*) to supply any drug specified in Schedule 3 shall keep every invoice or other like record issued in respect of each quantity of such a drug obtained by him and in respect of each quantity of such a drug supplied by him.

(3) A retail dealer in any drug specified in Schedule 3, a person in charge or acting person in charge of a hospital or nursing home and a person in charge of a laboratory shall keep every invoice or other like record issued in respect of each quantity of such a drug obtained by him and in respect of each quantity of such a drug supplied by him.

(4) A retail dealer in any drug specified in Schedule 5 shall keep every invoice or other like record issued in respect of each quantity of such a drug obtained by him.

(5) Every invoice or other record which is required by this regulation to be kept in respect of a drug specified in Schedule 3 shall contain information sufficient to identify the date of the transaction and the person by whom or to whom the drug was supplied.

(6) Every document kept in pursuance of this regulation (other than a health prescription) shall be preserved for a period of two years from the date on which it is issued, except that the keeping

of a copy of the document made at any time during the said period of two years shall be treated for the purposes of this paragraph as if it were the keeping of the original document.

8–22103A **24A. Preservation of records: supplementary].** For the purposes of regulations 23 and 24(6), "preserved" means kept in its original form, or copied and kept in a computerised form which is in accordance with best practice guidance endorsed by the Secretary of State under section 2 of the National Health Service Act 1977.

8–22104 **25. Exempt products.** Nothing in regulations 19 to 24 shall have effect in relation to any exempt product.

8–22105 **26. Furnishing of information with respect to controlled drugs.** (1) The persons specified in paragraph (2) shall on demand made by the Secretary of State or by any person authorised in writing by the Secretary of State in that behalf—

(*a*) furnish such particulars as may be requested in respect of the producing, obtaining or supplying by him of any controlled drug or in respect of any stock of such drugs in his possession;

(*b*) for the purpose of confirming any such particulars, produce any stock of such drugs in his possession;

(*c*) produce any register, book or document required to be kept under these Regulations relating to any dealings in controlled drugs which is in his possession.

(1A) For the purposes of paragraph (1)(*c*), the Secretary of State or any person authorised in writing by the Secretary of State in that behalf may request that a register which is kept in computerised form be produced by sending a copy of it, in computerised or other form, to the appropriate person.

(2) The persons referred to in paragraph (1) are—

(*a*) any person authorised by or under these Regulations to produce any controlled drug;

(*b*) any person authorised by or under any provision of the Act to import or export any controlled drug;

(*c*) a wholesale dealer;

(*d*) a retail dealer;

(*e*) a practitioner;

(*f*) the person in charge or acting person in charge of a hospital or nursing home;

(*g*) a person who is in charge of a laboratory;

(*h*) a person who is authorised under regulation 9(4)(*a*) to supply any controlled drug;

(*i*) a supplementary prescriber.

(3) Nothing in this regulation shall require the furnishing of personal records which a person has acquired or created in the course of his profession or occupation and which he holds in confidence; and in this paragraph "personal records" means documentary and other records concerning an individual (whether living or dead) who can be identified from them and relating to his physical or mental health.

8–22106 **27. Destruction of controlled drugs.** (1) No person who is required by any provision of, or by any term or condition of a licence having effect under, these Regulations to keep records with respect to a drug specified in Schedule 1, 2, 3 or 4 shall destroy such a drug or cause such a drug to be destroyed except in the presence of and in accordance with any directions given by a person authorised (whether personally or as a member of a class) for the purposes of this paragraph by the Secretary of State (hereafter in this regulation referred to as an "authorised person").

(2) An authorised person may, for the purposes of analysis, take a sample of a drug specified in Schedule 1, 2, 3 or 4 which is to be destroyed.

(3) Where a drug specified in Schedule 1, 2, 3 or 4 is destroyed in pursuance of paragraph (1) by or at the instance of a person who is required by any provision of, or by any term or condition of a licence having effect under, these Regulations to keep a record in respect of the obtaining or supply of that drug, that record shall include particulars of the date of destruction and the quantity destroyed and shall be signed by the authorised person in whose presence the drug is destroyed.

(4) Where the master or owner of a ship or installation manager of an offshore installation has in his possession a drug specified in Schedule 2 which he no longer requires, he shall not destroy the drug or cause it to be destroyed but shall dispose of it to a constable, or to a person who may lawfully supply that drug to him.

(5) Nothing in paragraph (1) or (3) shall apply to any person who is required to keep records only by virtue of regulation 22(2) or (3) or 24(3).

(6) Nothing in paragraph (1) or (3) shall apply to the destruction of a drug which has been supplied to a practitioner or pharmacist for that purpose in pursuance of regulation 6(2) or (3).

8–22107 **28. Revocations.** (1) The regulations specified in Schedule 7 are hereby revoked.

(2) Notwithstanding paragraph (1), any register, record, book, prescription or other document required to be preserved under regulation 23 or 24 of the Misuse of Drugs Regulations 1985 shall be preserved for the same period of time as if these Regulations had not been made.

(3) In the case of a prescription issued before the coming into force of these Regulations, regulation 16(1) shall have effect as if—

(*a*) in the case of a prescription containing a controlled drug other than a drug to which the provisions of regulation 15 of the Misuse of Drugs Regulations 1985 applied at the time the prescription was issued, sub-paragraphs (*a*) and (*b*) of that paragraph were omitted; and

(*b*) in any other case, for the said sub-paragraphs (*a*) and (*b*) there were substituted the words "unless the prescription complies with the provisions of the Misuse of Drugs Regulations 1985 relating to prescriptions".

8–22108

Regulation 3

SCHEDULE 1

CONTROLLED DRUGS SUBJECT TO THE REQUIREMENTS OF REGULATIONS 14, 15, 16, 18, 19, 20, 23, 26 AND 27[1]

1. The following substances and products, namely -

(*a*) Bufotenine
Cannabinol
Cannabinol derivatives not being dronabinol or its stereoisomers
Cannabis and cannabis resin
Cathinone
Coca leaf
Concentrate of poppy-straw
Eticyclidine
Etryptamine
Fungus (of any kind) which contains psilocin or an ester of psilocin
Lysergamide
Lysergide and other *N*-alkyl derivatives of lysergamide
Mescaline
Methcathinone
Psilocin
Raw opium
Rolicyclidine
Tenocyclidine
4-Bromo-2,5-dimethoxy-α-methylphenethylamine
N,N-Diethyltryptamine
N,N-Dimethyltryptamine
2,5-Dimethoxy-α,4-dimethylphenethylamine
N-Hydroxy-tenamphetamine
4-Methyl-aminorex

(*b*) any compound (not being a compound for the time being specified in sub-paragraph (*a*) above) structurally derived from tryptamine or from a ring-hydroxy tryptamine by substitution at the nitrogen atom of the sidechain with one or more alkyl substituents but no other substituent;

(*c*) the following phenethylamine derivatives, namely—
Allyl(α-methyl-3,4-methylenedioxyphenethyl)amine
2-Amino-1-(2,5-dimethoxy-4-methylphenyl)ethanol
2-Amino-1-(3,4-dimethoxyphenyl)ethanol
Benzyl(α-methyl-3,4-methylenedioxyphenethyl)amine
4-Bromo-α,2,5-trimethoxyphenethylamine
N-(4-*sec*-Butylthio-2,5-dimethoxyphenethyl)hydroxylamine
Cyclopropylmethyl(α-methyl-3,4-methylenedioxyphenethyl)amine
2-(4,7-Dimethoxy-2,3-dihydro-1*H*-indan-5-yl)ethylamine
2-(4,7-Dimethoxy-2,3-dihydro-1*H*-indan-5-yl)-1-methylethylamine
2-(2,5-Dimethoxy-4-methylphenyl)cyclopropylamine
2-(1,4-Dimethoxy-2-naphthyl)ethylamine
2-(1,4-Dimethoxy-2-naphthyl)-1-methylethylamine
N-(2,5-Dimethoxy-4-propylthiophenethyl)hydroxylamine
2-(1,4-Dimethoxy-5,6,7,8-tetrahydro-2-naphthyl)ethylamine
2-(1,4-Dimethoxy-5,6,7,8-tetrahydro-2-naphthyl)-1-methylethylamine
α,α-Dimethyl-3,4-methylenedioxyphenethylamine
α,α-Dimethyl-3,4-methylenedioxyphenethyl(methyl)amine
Dimethyl(α-methyl-3,4-methylenedioxyphenethyl)amine
N-(4-Ethylthio-2,5-dimethoxyphenethyl)hydroxylamine
4-Iodo-2,5-dimethoxy-α-methylphenethyl(dimethyl)amine
2-(1,4-Methano-5,8-dimethoxy-1,2,3,4-tetrahydro-6-naphthyl)ethylamine
2-(1,4-Methano-5,8-dimethoxy-1,2,3,4-tetrahydro-6-naphthyl)-1-methylethylamine
2-(5-Methoxy-2,2-dimethyl-2,3-dihydrobenzo[*b*]furan-6-yl)-1-methylethylamine
2-Methoxyethyl(α-methyl-3,4-methylenedioxyphenethyl)amine
2-(5-Methoxy-2-methyl-2,3-dihydrobenzo[*b*]furan-6-yl)-1-methylethylamine
ß-Methoxy-3,4-methylenedioxyphenethylamine
1-(3,4-Methylenedioxybenzyl)butyl(ethyl)amine
1-(3,4-Methylenedioxybenzyl)butyl(methyl)amine
2-(α-Methyl-3,4-methylenedioxyphenethylamino)ethanol
α-Methyl-3,4-methylenedioxyphenethyl(prop-2-ynyl)amine
N-Methyl-*N*-(α-methyl-3,4-methylenedioxyphenethyl)hydroxylamine
O-Methyl-*N*-(α-methyl-3,4-methylenedioxyphenethyl)hydroxylamine
α-Methyl-4-(methylthio)phenethylamine
ß,3,4,5-Tetramethoxyphenethylamine
ß,2,5-Trimethoxy-4-methylphenethylamine

(*d*) any compound (not being methoxyphenamine or a compound for the time being specified in sub-paragraph (*a*) above) structurally derived from phenethylamine, an *N*-alkylphenethylamine, α-methylphenethylamine, an *N*-alkyl-α-methylphenethylamine, α-ethylphenethylamine, or an *N*-alkyl-α-ethylphenethylamine by substitution in the ring to any extent with alkyl, alkoxy, alkylenedioxy or halide substitutents, whether or not further substituted in the ring by one or more other univalent substituents;

(*e*) any compound (not being a compound for the time being specified in Schedule 2) structurally derived from fentanyl by modification in any of the following ways, that is to say -

(i) by replacement of the phenyl portion of the phenethyl group by any heteromonocycle whether or not further substituted in the heterocycle;

(ii) by substitution in the phenethyl group with alkyl, alkenyl, alkoxy, hydroxy, halogeno, haloalkyl, amino or nitro groups;

(iii) by substitution in the piperidine ring with alkyl or alkenyl groups;

(iv) by substitution in the aniline ring with alkyl, alkoxy, alkylenedioxy, halogeno or haloalkyl groups;

(v) by substitution at the 4-position of the piperidine ring with any alkoxycarbonyl or alkoxyalkyl or acyloxy group;

(vi) by replacement of the *N*-propionyl group by another acyl group;

(*f*) any compound (not being a compound for the time being specified in Schedule 2) structurally derived from pethidine by modification in any of the following ways, that is to say—

(i) by replacement of the l-methyl group by an acyl, alkyl whether or not unsaturated, benzyl or phenethyl group, whether or not further substituted;

(ii) by substitution in the piperidine ring with alkyl or alkenyl groups or with a propano bridge, whether or not further substituted;

(iii) by substitution in the 4-phenyl ring with alkyl, alkoxy, aryloxy, halogeno or haloalkyl groups;

(iv) by replacement of the 4-ethoxycarbonyl by any other alkoxycarbonyl or any alkoxyalkyl or acyloxy group;

(v) by formation of an *N*-oxide or of a quaternary base.

2. Any stereoisomeric form of a substance specified in paragraph 1.

3. Any ester or ether of a substance specified in paragraph 1 or 2.

4. Any salt of a substance specified in any of paragraphs 1 to 3.

5. Any preparation or other product containing a substance or product specified in any of paragraphs 1 to 4, not being a preparation specified in Schedule 5.

---

1. These Schedules classify drugs for regime of control and not for penalties for misuse. For the latter classifications, see Sch 2 to the Misuse of Drugs Act 1971, ante.

8–22109

Regulation 3

SCHEDULE 2

CONTROLLED DRUGS SUBJECT TO THE REQUIREMENTS OF REGULATIONS 14, 15, 16, 18, 19, 20, 21, 23, 26 AND 27[1]

(*As amended by SI 2003/1432.*)

1. The following substances and products, namely—

Acetorphine
Alfentanil
Allylprodine
Alphacetylmethadol
Alphameprodine
Alphamethadol
Alphaprodine
Anileridine
Benzethidine
Benzylmorphine (3-benzylmorphine)
Betacetylmethadol
Betameprodine
Betamethadol
Betaprodine
Bezitramide
Carfentanil
Clonitazene
Cocaine
Desomorphine
Dextromoramide
Diamorphine
Diampromide
Diethylthiambutene
Difenoxin
Dihydrocodeinone *O*-carboxymethyloxime
Dihydroetorphine
Dihydromorphine
Dimenoxadole
Dimepheptanol
Dimethylthiambutene
Dioxaphetyl butyrate
Diphenoxylate
Dipipanone
Dronabinol
Drotebanol
Ecgonine, and any derivative of ecgonine which is convertible to ecgonine or to cocaine
Levomoramide
Levophenacylmorphan
Levorphanol
Lofentanil
Medicinal opium
Metazocine
Methadone
Methadyl acetate
Methyldesorphine
Methyldihydromorphine (6-methyldihydromorphine)
Metopon
Morpheridine
Morphine
Morphine methobromide, morphine N-oxide and other pentavalent nitrogen morphine derivatives
Myrophine
Nicomorphine
Noracymethadol
Norlevorphanol
Normethadone
Normorphine
Norpipanone
Oxycodone
Oxymorphone
Pethidine
Phenadoxone
Phenampromide
Phenazocine
Phencyclidine
Phenomorphan
Phenoperidine
Piminodine
Piritramide
Proheptazine
Properidine
Racemethorphan
Racemoramide

Ethylmethylthiambutene
Etonitazene
Etorphine
Etoxeridine
Fentanyl
Furethidine
Hydrocodone
Hydromorphinol
Hydromorphone
Hydroxypethidine
Isomethadone
Ketobemidone
Levomethorphan
Racemorphan
Remifentanil
Sufentanil
Thebacon
Thebaine
Tilidate
Trimeperidine
Zipeprol
4-Cyano-2-dimethylamino-4,4-diphenylbutane
4-Cyano-1-methyl-4-phenylpiperidine
2-Methyl-3-morpholino-1,1-diphenylpropane-carboxylic acid
α-Methylphenethylhydroxylamine
1-Methyl-4-phenylpiperidine-4-carboxylicacid
4-Phenylpiperidine-4-carboxylicacid ethyl ester

2. Any stereoisomeric form of a substance specified in paragraph 1 not being dextromethorphan or dextrorphan.

3. Any ester or ether of a substance specified in paragraph 1 or 2, not being a substance specified in paragraph 6.

4. Any salt of a substance specified in any of paragraphs 1 to 3.

5. Any preparation or other product containing a substance or product specified in any of paragraphs 1 to 4, not being a preparation specified in Schedule 5.

6. The following substances and products, namely—

Acetyldihydrocodeine
Amphetamine
Codeine
Dextropropoxyphene
Dihydrocodeine
Ethylmorphine (3-ethylmorphine)
Fenethylline
Glutethimide
Lefetamine
Mecloqualone
Methaqualone
Methylamphetamine
Methylphenidate
Nicocodine
Nicodicodine (6-nicotinoyldihydrocodeine)
Norcodeine
Phenmetrazine
Pholcodine
Propiram
Quinalbarbitone

7. Any stereoisomeric form of a substance specified in paragraph 6.

8. Any salt of a substance specified in paragraph 6 or 7.

9. Any preparation or other product containing a substance or product specified in any of paragraphs 6 to 8, not being a preparation specified in Schedule 5.

1. See note 1 to Sch 1 to these Regulations, ante.

8–22110

Regulation 3

SCHEDULE 3

CONTROLLED DRUGS SUBJECT TO THE REQUIREMENTS OF REGULATIONS 14, 15 (EXCEPT TEMAZEPAM), 16, 18, 22, 23, 24, 26 AND 27[1]

1. The following substances, namely—

(*a*)

Benzphetamine
Buprenorphine
Cathine
Chlorphentermine
Diethylpropion
Ethchlorvynol
Ethinamate
Flunitrazepam
Mazindol
Mephentermine
Meprobamate
Methylphenobarbitone
Methyprylone
Pentazocine
Phendimetrazine
Phentermine
Pipradrol
Temazepam

(*b*) any 5, 5 disubstituted barbituric acid not being quinalbarbitone.

2. Any stereoisomeric form of a substance specified in paragraph 1 not being phenylpropanolamine.

3. Any salt of a substance specified in paragraph 1 or 2.

4. Any preparation or other product containing a substance specified in any of paragraphs 1 to 3, not being a preparation specified in Schedule 5.

1. See note 1 to Sch 1 to these Regulations, ante.

8–22111

Regulation 3

SCHEDULE 4[1]

(*As amended by SI 2003/1432 and SI 2005/3372.*)

PART I

CONTROLLED DRUGS SUBJECT TO THE REQUIREMENTS OF REGULATIONS 22, 23, 26 AND 27

1. The following substances and products, namely—

Alprazolam
Aminorex
Bromazepam
Brotizolam
Camazepam
Chlordiazepoxide
Clobazam
Ketazolam
Loprazolam
Lorazepam
Lormetazepam
Medazepam
Mefenorex
Mesocarb

Clonazepam
Clorazepic acid
Clotiazepam
Cloxazolam
Delorazepam
Diazepam
Estazolam
Ethyl loflazepate
Fencamfamin
Fenproporex
Fludiazepam
Flurazepam
Halazepam
Haloxazolam
4-Hydroxy-n-butyric acid
Ketamine
Midazolam
Nimetazepam
Nitrazepam
Nordazepam
Oxazepam
Oxazolam
Pemoline
Pinazepam
Prazepam
Pyrovalerone
Tetrazepam
Triazolam
N-Ethylamphetamine
Zolpidem

2. Any stereoisomeric form of a substance specified in paragraph 1.

3. Any salt of a substance specified in paragraph 1 or 2.

4. Any preparation or other product containing a substance or product specified in any of paragraphs 1 to 3, not being a preparation specified in Schedule 5.

PART II

CONTROLLED DRUGS EXCEPTED FROM THE PROHIBITION ON POSSESSION WHEN IN THE FORM OF A MEDICINAL PRODUCT; EXCLUDED FROM THE APPLICATION OF OFFENCES ARISING FROM THE PROHIBITION ON IMPORTATION AND EXPORTATION WHEN IMPORTED OR EXPORTED IN THE FORM OF A MEDICINAL PRODUCT BY ANY PERSON FOR ADMINISTRATION TO HIMSELF; AND SUBJECT TO THE REQUIREMENTS OF REGULATIONS 22, 23, 26 AND 27

1. The following substances, namely—

4-Androstene-3, 17-dione
5-Androstene-3, 17 diol
Atamestane
Bolandiol
Bolasterone
Bolazine
Boldenone
Bolenol
Bolmantalate
Calusterone
4-Chloromethandienone
Clostebol
Drostanolone
Enestebol
Epitiostanol
Ethyloestrenol
Fluoxymesterone
Formebolone
Furazabol
Mebolazine
Mepitiostane
Mesabolone
Mestanolone
Mesterolone
Methandienone
Methandriol
Methenolone
Methyltestosterone
Metribolone
Mibolerone
Nandrolone
19-Nor-4-Androstene-3, 17-dione
19-Nor-5-Androstene-3, 17-diol
Norboletone
Norclostebol
Norethandrolone
Ovandrotone
Oxabolone
Oxandrolone
Oxymesterone
Oxymetholone
Prasterone
Propetandrol
Quinbolone
Roxibolone
Silandrone
Stanolone
Stanozolol
Stenbolone
Testosterone
Thiomesterone
Trenbolone

2. Any compound (not being Trilostane or a compound for the time being specified in paragraph 1 of this Part of this Schedule) structurally derived from 17-hydroxyandrostan-3-one or from 17-hydroxyestran-3-oneby modification in any of the following ways, that is to say -

(*a*) by further substitution at position 17 by a methyl or ethyl group;
(*b*) by substitution to any extent at one or more of positions 1, 2, 4, 6, 7, 9, 11 or 16, but at no other position;
(*c*) by unsaturation in the carbocyclic ring system to any extent, provided that there are no more than two ethylenic bonds in any one carbocyclic ring;
(*d*) by fusion of ring A with a heterocyclic system.

3. Any substance which is an ester or ether (or, where more than one hydroxyl function is available, both an ester and an ether) of a substance specified in paragraph 1 or described in paragraph 2 of this Part of this Schedule.

4. The following substances, namely—

Chorionic Gonadotrophin (HCG)
Clenbuterol
Non-human chorionic gonadotrophin
Somatotropin
Somatrem
Somatropin

5. Any stereoisomeric form of a substance specified or described in any of paragraphs 1 to 4 of this Part of this Schedule.

6. Any salt of a substance specified or described in any of paragraphs 1 to 5 of this Part of this Schedule.

7. Any preparation or other product containing a substance or product specified or described in any of paragraphs 1 to 6 of this Part of this Schedule, not being a preparation specified in Schedule 5.

---

1. See note 1 to Sch 1 to these Regulations, ante.

8–22112

Regulation 3

SCHEDULE 5

CONTROLLED DRUGS EXCEPTED[2] FROM THE PROHIBITION ON IMPORTATION, EXPORTATION AND POSSESSION AND SUBJECT TO THE REQUIREMENTS OF REGULATIONS 24 AND 26[1]

(*As amended by SI 2005/2864.*)

1. (1) Any preparation of one or more of the substances to which this paragraph applies, not being a preparation designed for administration by injection, when compounded with one or more other active or inert ingredients and containing a total of not more than 100 milligrams of the substance or substances (calculated as base) per dosage unit or with a total concentration of not more than 2.5% (calculated as base) in undivided preparations.

(2) The substances to which this paragraph applies are acetyldihydrocodeine, codeine, dihydrocodeine, ethylmorphine, nicocodine, nicodicodine (6-nicotinoyldihydrocodeine), norcodeine and pholcodine and their respective salts.

2. *Revoked.*

3. Any preparation of medicinal opium or of morphine containing (in either case) not more than 0.2% of morphine calculated as anhydrous morphine base, being a preparation compounded with one or more other active or inert ingredients in such a way that the opium or, as the case may be, the morphine cannot be recovered by readily applicable means or in a yield which would constitute a risk to health.

4. Any preparation of dextropropoxyphene, being a preparation designed for oral administration, containing not more than 135 milligrams of dextropropoxyphene (calculated as base) per dosage unit or with a total concentration of not more than 2.5% (calculated as base) in undivided preparations.

5. Any preparation of difenoxin containing, per dosage unit, not more than 0.5 milligrams of difenoxin and a quantity of atropine sulphate equivalent to at least 5% of the dose of difenoxin.

6. Any preparation of diphenoxylate containing, per dosage unit, not more than 2.5 milligrams of diphenoxylate calculated as base, and a quantity of atropine sulphate equivalent to at least 1% of the dose of diphenoxylate.

7. Any preparation of propiram containing, per dosage unit, not more than 100 milligrams of propiram calculated as base and compounded with at least the same amount (by weight) of methylcellulose.

8. Any powder of ipecacuanha and opium comprising—

10% opium, in powder,
10% ipecacuanha root, in powder, well mixed with
80% of any other powdered ingredient containing no controlled drug.

9. Any mixture containing one or more of the preparations specified in paragraphs 1 to 8, being a mixture of which none of the other ingredients is a controlled drug.

---

1. See note 1 to Sch 1 to these Regulations, ante.
2. Unlike the exceptions contained in these Regulations permitting possession of controlled drugs specified in Schs 2 and 3, ante, in the case of controlled drugs in Sch 5, by virtue of reg 4, ante, the general exception referred to here is not restricted to any particular class of person; see reg 4, ante, and *R v Hunt* [1986] QB 125, [1986] 1 All ER 184, 150 JP 83, CA.

8–22113

Regulation 19

SCHEDULE 6

FORM OF REGISTER

Regulation 28

SCHEDULE 7

REGULATIONS REVOKED

MENTAL HEALTH

8–22200 This title contains the following statutes—

Mental Health Act 1983[1]

(1983 c 20)

PART I[2]

APPLICATION OF ACT

8–22229 **1. Application of Act: "mental disorder".** (1) The provisions of this Act shall have effect with respect to the reception, care and treatment of mentally disordered patients, the management of their property and other related matters.

(2) In this Act—

"mental disorder" means mental illness, arrested or incomplete development of mind, psychopathic disorder and any other disorder or disability of mind and "mentally disordered" shall be construed accordingly;

"severe mental impairment" means a state of arrested or incomplete development of mind which includes severe impairment of intelligence and social functioning and is associated with abnormally aggressive or seriously irresponsible conduct on the part of the person concerned and "severely mentally impaired" shall be construed accordingly;

"mental impairment" means a state of arrested or incomplete development of mind (not amounting to severe mental impairment) which includes significant impairment of intelligence and social functioning and is associated with abnormally aggressive or seriously irresponsible conduct on the part of the person concerned and "mentally impaired" shall be construed accordingly;

"psychopathic disorder" means a persistent disorder or disability of mind (whether or not including significant impairment of intelligence) which results in abnormally aggressive or seriously irresponsible conduct on the part of the person concerned;

and other expressions shall have the meanings assigned to them in section 145 below.

(3) Nothing in subsection (2) above shall be construed as implying that a person may be dealt with under this Act as suffering from mental disorder, or from any form of mental disorder described in this section, by reason only of promiscuity or other immoral conduct, sexual deviancy or dependence on alcohol or drugs.

[Mental Health Act 1983, s 1.]

---

1. This Act consolidates the law relating to mentally disordered persons which was previously contained in the Mental Health Act 1959 as amended by the Mental Health (Amendment) Act 1982.

Parts I to VI, VIII and X of the Act are described in a Memorandum entitled, "The Mental Health Act 1983", published by the Department of Health and Social Security (HMSO 1983).

2. Part I contains section 1.

PART II[1]
COMPULSORY ADMISSION TO HOSPITAL AND GUARDIANSHIP

Procedure for hospital admission

8–22229A 2. Admission for assessment. (1) A patient may be admitted to a hospital and detained there for the period allowed by subsection (4) below in pursuance of an application (in this Act referred to as "an application for admission for assessment") made in accordance with subsections (2) and (3) below.

(2) An application for admission for assessment may be made in respect of a patient on the grounds that—

(*a*) he is suffering from mental disorder of a nature or degree which warrants the detention of the patient in a hospital for assessment (or for assessment followed by medical treatment) for at least a limited period; and

(*b*) he ought to be so detained in the interests of his own health or safety or with a view to the protection of other persons.

(3) An application for admission for assessment shall be founded on the written recommendations in the prescribed form of two registered medical practitioners, including in each case a statement that in the opinion of the practitioner the conditions set out in subsection (2) above are complied with.

(4) Subject to the provisions of section 29(4) below, a patient admitted to hospital in pursuance of an application for admission for assessment may be detained for a period not exceeding 28 days beginning with the day on which he is admitted, but shall not be detained after the expiration of that period unless before it has expired he has become liable to be detained by virtue of a subsequent application, order or direction under the following provisions of this Act.

[Mental Health Act 1983, s 2.]

---

1. Part II contains ss 2–34. Part II of the Act deals with the circumstances in which, and procedures through which, patients may be compulsorily admitted to and detained in hospital or received into guardianship, otherwise than through the courts, or on transfer from prison or other institutions or on return to the United Kingdom. See also the Mental Health (Hospital, Guardianship and Consent to Treatment) Regulations 1983, SI 1983/893 amended by SI 1993/2156, SI 1997/801, SI 1998/2624 and SI 2005/2078.

8–22229B 3. Admission for treatment. (1) A patient may be admitted to a hospital and detained there for the period allowed by the following provisions of this Act in pursuance of an application (in this Act referred to as "an application for admission for treatment") made in accordance with this section.

(2) An application for admission for treatment may be made in respect of a patient on the grounds that—

(*a*) he is suffering from mental illness, severe mental impairment, psychopathic disorder or mental impairment and his mental disorder is of a nature or degree which makes it appropriate for him to receive medical treatment in a hospital; and

(*b*) in the case of psychopathic disorder or mental impairment, such treatment is likely to alleviate or prevent a deterioration of his condition; and

(*c*) it is necessary for the health or safety of the patient or for the protection of other persons that he should receive such treatment and it cannot be provided unless he is detained under this section.

(3) An application for admission for treatment shall be founded on the written recommendations in the prescribed form of two registered medical practitioners, including in each case a statement that in the opinion of the practitioner the conditions set out in subsection (2) above are complied with; and each such recommendation shall include—

(*a*) such particulars as may be prescribed of the grounds for that opinion so far as it relates to the conditions set out in paragraphs (*a*) and (*b*) of that subsection; and

(*b*) a statement of the reasons for that opinion so far as it relates to the conditions set out in paragraph (*c*) of that subsection, specifying whether other methods of dealing with the patient are available and, if so, why they are not appropriate.

[Mental Health Act 1983, s 3.]

8–22229C 4. Admission for assessment in cases of emergency. (1) In any case of urgent necessity, an application for admission for assessment may be made in respect of a patient in accordance with the following provisions of this section, and any application so made is in this Act referred to as "an emergency application".

(2) An emergency application may be made either by an approved social worker or by the nearest relative of the patient; and every such application shall include a statement that it is of urgent necessity for the patient to be admitted and detained under section 2 above, and that compliance with the provisions of this Part of this Act relating to applications under that section would involve undesirable delay.

(3) An emergency application shall be sufficient in the first instance if founded on one of the medical recommendations required by section 2 above, given, if practicable, by a practitioner who has previous acquaintance with the patient and otherwise complying with the requirements of section 12 below so far as applicable to a single recommendation, and verifying the statement referred to in subsection (2) above.

(4) An emergency application shall cease to have effect on the expiration of a period of 72 hours from the time when the patient is admitted to the hospital unless—

(*a*) the second medical recommendation required by section 2 above is given and received by the managers within that period; and

(*b*) that recommendation and the recommendation referred to in subsection (3) above together comply with all the requirements of section 12 below (other than the requirement as to the time of signature of the second recommendation).

(5) In relation to an emergency application, section 11 below shall have effect as if in subsection (5) of that section for the words "the period of 14 days ending with the date of the application" there were substituted the words "the previous 24 hours".

[Mental Health Act 1983, s 4.]

8–22229D 5. Application in respect of patient already in hospital. (1) An application for the admission of a patient to a hospital may be made under this Part of this Act notwithstanding that the patient is already an in-patient in that hospital or, in the case of an application for admission for treatment, that the patient is for the time being liable to be detained in the hospital in pursuance of an application for admission for assessment; and where an application is so made the patient shall be treated for the purposes of this Part of this Act as if he had been admitted to the hospital at the time when that application was received by the managers.

(2) If, in the case of a patient who is an in-patient in a hospital, it appears to the registered medical practitioner in charge of the treatment of the patient that an application ought to be made under this Part of this Act for the admission of the patient to hospital, he may furnish to the managers a report in writing to that effect; and in any such case the patient may be detained in the hospital for a period of 72 hours from the time when the report is so furnished.

(3) The registered medical practitioner in charge of the treatment of a patient in a hospital may nominate one (but not more than one) other registered medical practitioner on the staff of that hospital to act for him under subsection (2) above in his absence.

(4) If, in the case of a patient who is receiving treatment for mental disorder as an in-patient in a hospital, it appears to a nurse of the prescribed class—

(*a*) that the patient is suffering from mental disorder to such a degree that it is necessary for his health or safety or for the protection of others for him to be immediately restrained from leaving the hospital; and

(*b*) that it is not practicable to secure the immediate attendance of a practitioner for the purpose of furnishing a report under subsection (2) above,

the nurse may record that fact in writing; and in that event the patient may be detained in the hospital for a period of six hours from the time when that fact is so recorded or until the earlier arrival at the place where the patient is detained of a practitioner having power to furnish a report under that subsection.

(5) A record made under subsection (4) above shall be delivered by the nurse (or by a person authorised by the nurse in that behalf) to the managers of the hospital as soon as possible after it is

made; and where a record is made under that subsection the period mentioned in subsection (2) above shall begin at the time when it is made.

(6) The reference in subsection (1) above to an in-patient does not include an in-patient who is liable to be detained in pursuance of an application under this Part of this Act and the references in subsections (2) and (4) above do not include an in-patient who is liable to be detained in a hospital under this Part of this Act.

(7) In subsection (4) above "prescribed" means prescribed by an order made by the Secretary of State.

[Mental Health Act 1983, s 5.]

8–22229E 6. Effect of application for admission. (1) An application for the admission of a patient to a hospital under this Part of this Act, duly completed in accordance with the provisions of this Part of this Act, shall be sufficient authority for the applicant, or any person authorised by the applicant, to take the patient and convey him to the hospital at any time within the following period, that is to say—

(*a*) in the case of an application other than an emergency application, the period of 14 days beginning with the date on which the patient was last examined by a registered medical practitioner before giving a medical recommendation for the purposes of the application;

(*b*) in the case of an emergency application, the period of 24 hours beginning at the time when the patient was examined by the practitioner giving the medical recommendation which is referred to in section 4(3) above, or at the time when the application is made, whichever is the earlier.

(2) Where a patient is admitted within the said period to the hospital specified in such an application as is mentioned in subsection (1) above, or, being within that hospital, is treated by virtue of section 5 above as if he had been so admitted, the application shall be sufficient authority for the managers to detain the patient in the hospital in accordance with the provisions of this Act.

(3) Any application for the admission of a patient under this Part of this Act which appears to be duly made and to be founded on the necessary medical recommendations may be acted upon without further proof of the signature or qualification of the person by whom the application or any such medical recommendation is made or given or of any matter of fact or opinion stated in it.

(4) Where a patient is admitted to a hospital in pursuance of an application for admission for treatment, any previous application under this Part of this Act by virtue of which he was liable to be detained in a hospital or subject to guardianship shall cease to have effect.

[Mental Health Act 1983, s 6.]

Guardianship

8–22229F 7. Application for guardianship. (1) A patient who has attained the age of 16 years may be received into guardianship, for the period allowed by the following provisions of this Act, in pursuance of an application (in this Act referred to as "a guardianship application") made in accordance with this section.

(2) A guardianship application may be made in respect of a patient on the grounds that—

(*a*) he is suffering from mental disorder, being mental illness, severe mental impairment, psychopathic disorder or mental impairment and his mental disorder is of a nature or degree which warrants his reception into guardianship under this section; and

(*b*) it is necessary in the interests of the welfare of the patient or for the protection of other persons that the patient should be so received.

(3) A guardianship application shall be founded on the written recommendations in the prescribed form of two registered medical practitioners, including in each case a statement that in the opinion of the practitioner the conditions set out in subsection (2) above are complied with; and each such recommendation shall include—

(*a*) such particulars as may be prescribed of the grounds for that opinion so far as it relates to the conditions set out in paragraph (*a*) of that subsection; and

(*b*) a statement of the reasons for that opinion so far as it relates to the conditions set out in paragraph (*b*) of that subsection.

(4) A guardianship application shall state the age of the patient or, if his exact age is not known to the applicant, shall state (if it be the fact) that the patient is believed to have attained the age of 16 years.

(5) The person named as guardian in a guardianship application may be either a local social services authority or any other person (including the applicant himself); but a guardianship application in which a person other than a local social services authority is named as guardian shall be of no effect unless it is accepted on behalf of that person by the local social services authority for the area in which he resides, and shall be accompanied by a statement in writing by that person that he is willing to act as guardian.

[Mental Health Act 1983, s 7.]

8–22229G 8. Effect of guardianship application, etc. (1) Where a guardianship application, duly made under the provisions of this Part of this Act and forwarded to the local social services authority within the period allowed by subsection (2) below is accepted by that authority, the application shall, subject to regulations made by the Secretary of State, confer on the authority or person named in the application as guardian, to the exclusion of any other person—

(*a*) the power to require the patient to reside at a place specified by the authority or person named as guardian;
(*b*) the power to require the patient to attend at places and times so specified for the purpose of medical treatment, occupation, education or training;
(*c*) the power to require access to the patient to be given, at any place where the patient is residing, to any registered medical practitioner, approved social worker or other person so specified.

(2) The period within which a guardianship application is required for the purposes of this section to be forwarded to the local social services authority is the period of 14 days beginning with the date on which the patient was last examined by a registered medical practitioner before giving a medical recommendation for the purposes of the application.

(3) A guardianship application which appears to be duly made and to be founded on the necessary medical recommendations may be acted upon without further proof of the signature or qualification of the person by whom the application or any such medical recommendation is made or given, or of any matter of fact or opinion stated in the application.

(4) If within the period of 14 days beginning with the day on which a guardianship application has been accepted by the local social services authority the application, or any medical recommendation given for the purposes of the application, is found to be in any respect incorrect or defective, the application or recommendation may, within that period and with the consent of that authority, be amended by the person by whom it was signed; and upon such amendment being made the application or recommendation shall have effect and shall be deemed to have had effect as if it had been originally made as so amended.

(5) Where a patient is received into guardianship in pursuance of a guardianship application, any previous application under this Part of this Act by virtue of which he was subject to guardianship or liable to be detained in a hospital shall cease to have effect.
[Mental Health Act 1983, s 8.]

8–22229H 9. Regulations as to guardianship. (1) Subject to the provisions of this Part of this Act, the Secretary of State may make regulations—

(*a*) for regulating the exercise by the guardians of patients received into guardianship under this Part of this Act of their powers as such; and
(*b*) for imposing on such guardians, and upon local social services authorities in the case of patients under the guardianship of persons other than local social services authorities, such duties as he considers necessary or expedient in the interests of the patients.

(2) Regulations under this section may in particular make provision for requiring the patients to be visited, on such occasions or at such intervals as may be prescribed by the regulations, on behalf of such local social services authorities as may be so prescribed, and shall provide for the appointment, in the case of every patient subject to the guardianship of a person other than a local social services authority, of a registered medical practitioner to act as the nominated medical attendant of the patient.
[Mental Health Act 1983, s 9.]

8–22229I 10. Transfer of guardianship in case of death, incapacity, etc of guardian. (1) If any person (other than a local social services authority) who is the guardian of a patient received into guardianship under this Part of this Act—

(*a*) dies; or
(*b*) gives notice in writing to the local social services authority that he desires to relinquish the functions of guardian,

the guardianship of the patient shall thereupon vest in the local social services authority, but without prejudice to any power to transfer the patient into the guardianship of another person in pursuance of regulations under section 19 below.

(2) If any such person, not having given notice under subsection (1)(*b*) above, is incapacitated by illness or any other cause from performing the functions of guardian of the patient, those functions may, during his incapacity, be performed on his behalf by the local social services authority or by any other person approved for the purposes by that authority.

(3) If it appears to the county court, upon application made by an approved social worker, that any person other than a local social services authority having the guardianship of a patient received into guardianship under this Part of this Act has performed his functions negligently or in a manner contrary to the interests of the welfare of the patient, the court may order that the guardianship of the patient be transferred to the local social services authority or to any other person approved for the purpose by that authority.

(4) Where the guardianship of a patient is transferred to a local social services authority or other

person by or under this section, subsection (2)(*c*) of section 19 below shall apply as if the patient had been transferred into the guardianship of that authority or person in pursuance of regulations under that section.
[Mental Health Act 1983, s 10.]

General provisions as to applications and recommendations

8–22229J **11. General provisions as to applications.** (1) Subject to the provisions of this section, an application for admission for assessment, an application for admission for treatment and a guardianship application may be made either by the nearest relative of the patient or by an approved social worker; and every such application shall specify the qualification of the applicant to make the application.

(2) Every application for admission shall be addressed to the managers of the hospital to which admission is sought and every guardianship application shall be forwarded to the local social services authority named in the application as guardian, or, as the case may be, to the local social services authority for the area in which the person so named resides.

(3) Before or within a reasonable time after an application for the admission of a patient for assessment is made by an approved social worker, that social worker shall take such steps as are practicable to inform the person (if any) appearing to be the nearest relative of the patient that the application is to be or has been made and of the power of the nearest relative under section 23(2)(*a*) below.

(4) Neither an application for admission for treatment nor a guardianship application shall be made by an approved social worker if the nearest relative of the patient has notified that social worker, or the local social services authority by whom that social worker is appointed, that he objects to the application being made and, without prejudice to the foregoing provision, no such application shall be made by such a social worker except after consultation with the person (if any) appearing to be the nearest relative of the patient unless it appears to that social worker that in the circumstances such consultation is not reasonably practicable or would involve unreasonable delay.

(5) None of the applications mentioned in subsection (1) above shall be made by any person in respect of a patient unless that person has personally seen the patient within the period of 14 days ending with the date of the application.

(6) An application for admission for treatment or a guardianship application, and any recommendation given for the purposes of such an application, may describe the patient as suffering from more than one of the following forms of mental disorder, namely mental illness, severe mental impairment, psychopathic disorder or mental impairment; but the application shall be of no effect unless the patient is described in each of the recommendations as suffering from the same form of mental disorder, whether or not he is also described in either of those recommendations as suffering from another form.

(7) Each of the applications mentioned in subsection (1) above shall be sufficient if the recommendations on which it is founded are given either as separate recommendations, each signed by a registered medical practitioner, or as a joint recommendation signed by two such practitioners.
[Mental Health Act 1983, s 11.]

8–22229K **12. General provisions as to medical recommendations.** (1) The recommendations required for the purposes of an application for the admission of a patient under this Part of this Act (in this Act referred to as "medical recommendations") shall be signed on or before the date of the application, and shall be given by practitioners who have personally examined the patient either together or separately, but where they have examined the patient separately not more than five days must have elapsed between the days on which the separate examinations took place.

(2) Of the medical recommendations given for the purposes of any such application, one shall be given by a practitioner approved for the purposes of this section by the Secretary of State as having special experience in the diagnosis or treatment of mental disorder; and unless that practitioner has previous acquaintance with the patient, the other such recommendation shall, if practicable, be given by a registered medical practitioner who has such previous acquaintance.

(3) Subject to subsection (4) below, where the application is for the admission of the patient to a hospital which is not a registered establishment, one (but not more than one) of the medical recommendations may be given by a practitioner on the staff of that hospital, except where the patient is proposed to be accommodated under section 18A(4), 65 or 66 of the National Health Service Act 1977 or paragraph 14 of Schedule 2 to the National Health Service and Community Care Act 1990 (which relate to accommodation for private patients) or otherwise to be accomodated, by virtue of an undertaking to pay in respect of the accommodation, in a hospital vested in an NHS trust.

(4) Subsection (3) above shall not preclude both the medical recommendations being given by practitioners on the staff of the hospital in question if—

(*a*) compliance with that subsection would result in delay involving serious risk to the health or safety of the patient; and

(*b*) one of the practitioners giving the recommendations works at the hospital for less than half of the time which he is bound by contract to devote to work in the health service; and (*c*) where one of those practitioners is a consultant, the other does not work (whether at the hospital or elsewhere) in a grade in which he is under that consultant's directions.

(5) A medical recommendation for the purposes of an application for the admission of a patient under this Part of this Act shall not be given by—

(*a*) the applicant;

(*b*) a partner of the applicant or of a practitioner by whom another medical recommendation is given for the purposes of the same application;

(*c*) a person employed as an assistant by the applicant or by any such practitioner;

(*d*) a person who receives or has an interest in the receipt of any payments made on account of the maintenance of the patient; or

(*e*) except as provided by subsection (3) or (4) above, a practitioner on the staff of the hospital to which the patient is to be admitted,

or by the husband, wife, civil partner , father, father-in-law, mother, mother-in-law, son, son-in-law, daughter, daughter-in-law, brother, brother-in-law, sister or sister-in-law of the patient, or of any person mentioned in paragraphs (*a*) to (*e*) above, or of a practitioner by whom another medical recommendation is given for the purposes of the same application.

(6) A general practitioner who is employed part-time in a hospital shall not for the purposes of this section be regarded as a practitioner on its staff.

(7) Subsections (1), (2) and (5) above shall apply to applications for guardianship as they apply to applications for admission but with the substitution for paragraph (*e*) of subsection (5) above of the following paragraph—

"(*e*) the person named as guardian in the application.".

[Mental Health Act 1983, s 12, as amended by the National Health Service and Community Care Act 1990, s 66, Sch 9, SI 2000/90, the Care Standards Act 2000, s 116, the Health and Social Care (Community Health and Standards) Act 2003, Sch 4 and the Civil Partnership Act 2004, Sch 27.]

8–22229L 13. Duty of approved social workers to make applications for admission or guardianship. (1) It shall be the duty of an approved social worker to make an application for admission to hospital or a guardianship application in respect of a patient within the area of the local social services authority by which that officer is appointed in any case where he is satisfied that such an application ought to be made and is of the opinion, having regard to any wishes expressed by relatives of the patient or any other relevant circumstances, that it is necessary or proper for the application to be made by him.

(2) Before making an application for the admission of a patient to hospital an approved social worker shall interview the patient in a suitable manner and satisfy himself that detention in a hospital is in all the circumstances of the case the most appropriate way of providing the care and medical treatment of which the patient stands in need.

(3) An application under this section by an approved social worker may be made outside the area of the local social services authority by which he is appointed.

(4) It shall be the duty of a local social services authority, if so required by the nearest relative of a patient residing in their area, to direct an approved social worker as soon as practicable to take the patient's case into consideration under subsection (1) above with a view to making an application for his admission to hospital; and if in any such case that approved social worker decides not to make an application he shall inform the nearest relative of his reasons in writing.

(5) Nothing in this section shall be construed as authorising or requiring an application to be made by an approved social worker in contravention of the provisions of section 11(4) above, or as restricting the power of an approved social worker to make any application under this Act.

[Mental Health Act 1983, s 13.]

8–22229M 14. Social reports. Where a patient is admitted to a hospital in pursuance of an application (other than an emergency application) made under this Part of this Act by his nearest relative, the managers of the hospital shall as soon as practicable give notice of that fact to the local social services authority for the area in which the patient resided immediately before his admission; and that authority shall as soon as practicable arrange for a social worker of their social services department* to interview the patient and provide the managers with a report on his social circumstances.

[Mental Health Act 1983, s 14.]

***Words repealed by the Children Act 2004, Sch 5 from a date to be appointed.**

8–22229N 15. Rectification of applications and recommendations. (1) If within the period of 14 days beginning with the day on which a patient has been admitted to a hospital in pursuance of an application for admission for assessment or for treatment the application, or any medical recommendation given for the purposes of the application, is found to be in any respect incorrect or defective, the application or recommendation may, within that period and with the consent of the managers of the hospital, be amended by the person by whom it was signed; and upon such amendment being made the application or recommendation shall have effect and shall be deemed to have had effect as if it had been originally made as so amended.

(2) Without prejudice to subsection (1) above, if within the period mentioned in that subsection it appears to the managers of the hospital that one of the two medical recommendations on which an application for the admission of a patient is founded is insufficient to warrant the detention of the patient in pursuance of the application, they may, within that period, give notice in writing to that effect to the applicant; and where any such notice is given in respect of a medical recommendation, that recommendation shall be disregarded, but the application shall be, and shall be deemed always to have been, sufficient if—

(*a*) a fresh medical recommendation complying with the relevant provisions of this Part of this Act (other than the provisions relating to the time of signature and the interval between examinations) is furnished to the managers within that period; and

(*b*) that recommendation, and the other recommendation on which the application is founded, together comply with those provisions.

(3) Where the medical recommendations upon which an application for admission is founded are, taken together, insufficient to warrant the detention of the patient in pursuance of the application, a notice under subsection (2) above may be given in respect of either of those recommendations; but this subsection shall not apply in a case where the application is of no effect by virtue of section 11(6) above.

(4) Nothing in this section shall be construed as authorising the giving of notice in respect of an application made as an emergency application, or the detention of a patient admitted in pursuance of such an application, after the period of 72 hours referred to in section 4(4) above, unless the conditions set out in paragraphs (*a*) and (*b*) of that section are complied with or would be complied with apart from any error or defect to which this section applies.

[Mental Health Act 1983, s 15.]

Position of patients subject to detention or guardianship

8–22229O 16. Reclassification of patients. (1) If in the case of a patient who is for the time being detained in a hospital in pursuance of an application for admission for treatment, or subject to guardianship in pursuance of a guardianship application, it appears to the appropriate medical officer that the patient is suffering from a form of mental disorder other than the form or forms specified in the application, he may furnish to the managers of the hospital, or to the guardian, as the case may be, a report to that effect; and where a report is so furnished, the application shall have effect as if that other form of mental disorder were specified in it.

(2) Where a report under subsection (1) above in respect of a patient detained in a hospital is to the effect that he is suffering from psychopathic disorder or mental impairment but not from mental illness or severe mental impairment the appropriate medical officer shall include in the report a statement of his opinion whether further medical treatment in hospital is likely to alleviate or prevent a deterioration of the patient's condition; and if he states that in his opinion such treatment is not likely to have that effect the authority of the managers to detain the patient shall cease.

(3) Before furnishing a report under subsection (1) above the appropriate medical officer shall consult one or more other persons who have been professionally concerned with the patient's medical treatment.

(4) Where a report is furnished under this section in respect of a patient, the managers or guardian shall cause the patient and the nearest relative to be informed.

(5) In this section "appropriate medical officer" means—

(*a*) in the case of a patient who is subject to the guardianship of a person other than a local social services authority, the nominated medical attendant of the patient; and

(*b*) in any other case, the responsible medical officer.

[Mental Health Act 1983, s 16.]

8–22229P 17. Leave of absence from hospital. (1) The responsible medical officer may grant to any patient who is for the time being liable to be detained in a hospital under this Part of this Act leave to be absent from the hospital subject to such conditions (if any) as that officer considers necessary in the interests of the patient or for the protection of other persons.

(2) Leave of absence may be granted to a patient under this section either indefinitely or on specified occasions or for any specified period; and where leave is so granted for a specified period, that period may be extended by further leave granted in the absence of the patient.

(3) Where it appears to the responsible medical officer that it is necessary so to do in the interests of the patient or for the protection of other persons, he may, upon granting leave of absence under this section, direct that the patient remain in custody during his absence; and where leave of absence is so granted the patient may be kept in the custody of any officer on the staff of the hospital, or of any other person authorised in writing by the managers of the hospital or, if the patient is required in accordance with conditions imposed on the grant of leave of absence to reside in another hospital, of any officer on the staff of that other hospital.

(4) In any case where a patient is absent from a hospital in pursuance of leave of absence granted

under this section, and it appears to the responsible medical officer that it is necessary so to do in the interests of the patient's health or safety or for the protection of other persons, that officer may, subject to subsection (5) below, by notice in writing given to the patient or to the person for the time being in charge of the patient, revoke the leave of absence and recall the patient to the hospital.

(5) A patient to whom leave of absence is granted under this section shall not be recalled under subsection (4) above after he has ceased to be liable to be detained under this Part of this Act.

[Mental Health Act 1983, s 13, as amended by the Mental Health (Patients in the Community) Act 1995, s 3.]

8–22229Q 18. Return and readmission of patients absent without leave. (1) Where a patient who is for the time being liable to be detained under this Part of this Act in a hospital—

(*a*) absents himself from the hospital without leave granted under section 17 above; or

(*b*) fails to return to the hospital on any occasion on which, or at the expiration of any period for which, leave of absence was granted to him under that section, or upon being recalled under that section; or

(*c*) absents himself without permission from any place where he is required to reside in accordance with conditions imposed on the grant of leave of absence under that section,

he may, subject to the provisions of this section, be taken into custody and returned to the hospital or place by any approved social worker, by any officer on the staff of the hospital, by any constable, or by any person authorised in writing by the managers of the hospital.

(2) Where the place referred to in paragraph (*c*) of subsection (1) above is a hospital other than the one in which the patient is for the time being liable to be detained, the references in that subsection to an officer on the staff of the hospital and the managers of the hospital shall respectively include references to an officer on the staff of the first-mentioned hospital and the managers of that hospital.

(3) Where a patient who is for the time being subject to guardianship under this Part of this Act absents himself without the leave of the guardian from the place at which he is required by the guardian to reside, he may, subject to the provisions of this section, be taken into custody and returned to that place by any officer on the staff of a local social services authority, by any constable, or by any person authorised in writing by the guardian or a local social services authority.

(4) patient shall not be taken into custody under this section after the later of—

(*a*) the end of the period of six months beginning with the first day of his absence without leave; and

(*b*) the end of the period for which (apart from section 21 below) he is liable to be detained or subject to guardianship;

and, in determining for the purposes of paragraph (*b*) above or any other provision of this Act whether a person who is or has been absent without leave is at any time liable to be detained or subject to guardianship, a report furnished under section 20 or 21B below before the first day of his absence without leave shall not be taken to have renewed the authority for his detention or guardianship unless the period of renewal began before that day.

(5) A patient shall not be taken into custody under this section if the period for which he is liable to be detained is that specified in section 2(4), 4(4) or 5(2) or (4) above and that period has expired.

(6) In this Act "absent without leave" means absent from any hospital or other place and liable to be taken into custody and returned under this section, and related expressions shall be construed accordingly.

[Mental Health Act 1983, s 18, as amended by the Mental Health (Patients in the Community) Act 1995, s 2.]

8–22229R 19. Regulations as to transfer of patients. (1) In such circumstances and subject to such conditions as may be prescribed by regulations made by the Secretary of State—

(*a*) a patient who is for the time being liable to be detained in a hospital by virtue of an application under this Part of this Act may be transferred to another hospital or into the guardianship of a local social services authority or of any person approved by such an authority;

(*b*) a patient who is for the time being subject to the guardianship of a local social services authority or other person by virtue of an application under this Part of this Act may be transferred into the guardianship of another local social services authority or person, or be transferred to a hospital.

(2) Where a patient is transferred in pursuance of regulations under this section, the provisions of this Part of this Act (including this subsection) shall apply to him as follows, that is to say—

(*a*) in the case of a patient who is liable to be detained in a hospital by virtue of an application for admission for assessment or for treatment and is transferred to another hospital, as if the application were an application for admission to that other hospital and as if the patient had been admitted to that other hospital at the time when he was originally admitted in pursuance of the application;

(*b*) in the case of a patient who is liable to be detained in a hospital by virtue of such an application and is transferred into guardianship, as if the application were a guardianship application duly accepted at the said time;

(*c*) in the case of a patient who is subject to guardianship by virtue of a guardianship application and is transferred into the guardianship of another authority or person, as if the application were for his reception into the guardianship of that authority or person and had been accepted at the time when it was originally accepted;

(*d*) in the case of a patient who is subject to guardianship by virtue of a guardianship application and is transferred to a hospital, as if the guardianship application were an application for admission to that hospital for treatment and as if the patient had been admitted to the hospital at the time when the application was originally accepted.

(3) Without prejudice to subsections (1) and (2) above, any patient who is for the time being liable to be detained under this Part of this Act in a hospital vested in the Secretary of State for the purposes of his functions under the National Health Service Act 1977 or any accommodation used under Part I of that Act by the managers of such a hospital or in a hospital vested in a National Health Service trust, NHS foundation trust or Primary Care Trust, may at any time be removed to any other such hospital or accommodation which is managed by the managers of, or is vested in the National Health Service trust, NHS foundation trust or Primary Care Trust for, the first-mentioned hospital; and paragraph (*a*) of subsection (2) above shall apply in relation to a patient so removed as it applies in relation to a patient transferred in pursuance of regulations made under this section.

(4) Regulations made under this section may make provision for regulating the conveyance to their destination of patients authorised to be transferred or removed in pursuance of the regulations or under subsection (3) above.

[Mental Health Act 1983, s 19, as amended by the National Health Service and Community Care Act 1990, s 66, Sch 9, SI 2000/90 and the Health and Social Care (Community Health and Standards) Act 2003, Sch 4.]

Duration of detention or guardianship and discharge

8–22229S 20. Duration of authority. (1) Subject to the following provisions of this Part of this Act, a patient admitted to hospital in pursuance of an application for admission for treatment, and a patient placed under guardianship in pursuance of a guardianship application, may be detained in a hospital or kept under guardianship for a period not exceeding six months beginning with the day on which he was so admitted, or the day on which the guardianship application was accepted, as the case may be, but shall not be so detained or kept for any longer period unless the authority for his detention or guardianship is renewed under this section.

(2) Authority for the detention or guardianship of a patient may, unless the patient has previously been discharged, be renewed—

(*a*) from the expiration of the period referred to in subsection (1) above, for a further period of six months;

(*b*) from the expiration of any period of renewal under paragraph (*a*) above, for a further period of one year,

and so on for periods of one year at a time.

(3) Within the period of two months ending on the day on which a patient who is liable to be detained in pursuance of an application for admission for treatment would cease under this section to be so liable in default of the renewal of the authority for his detention, it shall be the duty of the responsible medical officer—

(*a*) to examine the patient; and

(*b*) if it appears to him that the conditions set out in subsection (4) below are satisfied, to furnish to the managers of the hospital where the patient is detained a report to that effect in the prescribed form;

and where such a report is furnished in respect of a patient the managers shall, unless they discharge the patient, cause him to be informed.

(4) The conditions referred to in subsection (3) above are that—

(*a*) the patient is suffering from mental illness, severe mental impairment, psychopathic disorder or mental impairment, and his mental disorder is of a nature or degree which makes it appropriate for him to receive medical treatment in a hospital; and

(*b*) such treatment is likely to alleviate or prevent a deterioration of his condition; and

(*c*) it is necessary for the health or safety of the patient or for the protection of other persons that he should receive such treatment and that it cannot be provided unless he continues to be detained;

but, in the case of mental illness or severe mental impairment, it shall be an alternative to the condition specified in paragraph (*b*) above that the patient, if discharged, is unlikely to be able to care for himself, to obtain the care which he needs or to guard himself against serious exploitation.

(5) Before furnishing a report under subsection (3) above the responsible medical officer shall consult one or more other persons who have been professionally concerned with the patient's medical treatment.

(6) Within the period of two months ending with the day on which a patient who is subject to guardianship under this Part of this Act would cease under this section to be so liable in default of the renewal of the authority for his guardianship, it shall be the duty of the appropriate medical officer—

(*a*) to examine the patient; and

(*b*) if it appears to him that the conditions set out in subsection (7) below are satisfied, to furnish to the guardian and, where the guardian is a person other than a local social services authority, to the responsible local social services authority a report to that effect in the prescribed form;

and where such a report is furnished in respect of a patient, the local social services authority shall, unless they discharge the patient, cause him to be informed.

(7) The conditions referred to in subsection (6) above are that—

(*a*) the patient is suffering from mental illness, severe mental impairment, psychopathic disorder or mental impairment and his mental disorder is of a nature or degree which warrants his reception into guardianship; and

(*b*) it is necessary in the interests of the welfare of the patient or for the protection of other persons that the patient should remain under guardianship.

(8) Where a report is duly furnished under subsection (3) or (6) above, the authority for the detention or guardianship of the patient shall be thereby renewed for the period prescribed in that case by subsection (2) above.

(9) Where the form of mental disorder specified in a report furnished under subsection (3) or (6) above is a form of disorder other than that specified in the application for admission for treatment or, as the case may be, in the guardianship application, that application shall have effect as if that other form of mental disorder were specified in it; and where on any occasion a report specifying such a form of mental disorder is furnished under either of those subsections the appropriate medical officer need not on that occasion furnish a report under section 16 above.

(10) In this section "appropriate medical officer" has the same meaning as in section 16(5) above.

[Mental Health Act 1983, s 20.]

8–22229T 21. Special provisions as to patients absent without leave. (1) Where a patient is absent without leave—

(*a*) on the day on which (apart from this section) he would cease to be liable to be detained or subject to guardianship under this Part of this Act; or

(*b*) within the period of one week ending with that day,

he shall not cease to be so liable or subject until the relevant time.

(2) For the purposes of subsection (1) above the relevant time—

(*a*) where the patient is taken into custody under section 18 above, is the end of the period of one week beginning with the day on which he is returned to the hospital or place where he ought to be;

(*b*) where the patient returns himself to the hospital or place where he ought to be within the period during which he can be taken into custody under section 18 above, is the end of the period of one week beginning with the day on which he so returns himself; and

(*c*) otherwise, is the end of the period during which he can be taken into custody under section 18 above.

[Mental Health Act 1983, s 21, as substituted by the Mental Health (Patients in the Community) Act 1995, s 2.]

8–22229U 21A. Patients who are taken into custody or return within 28 days. (1) This section applies where a patient who is absent without leave is taken into custody under section 18 above, or returns himself to the hospital or place where he ought to be, not later than the end of the period of 28 days beginning with the first day of his absence without leave.

(2) Where the period for which the patient is liable to be detained or subject to guardianship is extended by section 21 above, any examination and report to be made and furnished in respect of the patient under section 20(3) or (6) above may be made and furnished within the period as so extended.

(3) Where the authority for the detention or guardianship of the patient is renewed by virtue of subsection (2) above after the day on which (apart from section 21 above) that authority would have expired, the renewal shall take effect as from that day.

[Mental Health Act 1983, s 21A, as inserted by the Mental Health (Patients in the Community) Act 1995, s 2.]

8–22229V 21B. Patients who are taken into custody or return after more than 28 days. (1) This section applies where a patient who is absent without leave is taken into custody under section 18 above, or returns himself to the hospital or place where he ought to be, later than the end of the period of 28 days beginning with the first day of his absence without leave.

(2) It shall be the duty of the appropriate medical officer, within the period of one week beginning with the day on which the patient is returned or returns himself to the hospital or place where he ought to be—

(*a*) to examine the patient; and

(*b*) if it appears to him that the relevant conditions are satisfied, to furnish to the appropriate body a report to that effect in the prescribed form;

and where such a report is furnished in respect of the patient the appropriate body shall cause him to be informed.

(3) Where the patient is liable to be detained (as opposed to subject to guardianship), the appropriate medical officer shall, before furnishing a report under subsection (2) above, consult—

(*a*) one or more other persons who have been professionally concerned with the patient's medical treatment; and

(*b*) an approved social worker.

(4) Where the patient would (apart from any renewal of the authority for his detention or guardianship on or after the day on which he is returned or returns himself to the hospital or place where he ought to be) be liable to be detained or subject to guardianship after the end of the period of one week beginning with that day, he shall cease to be so liable or subject at the end of that period unless a report is duly furnished in respect of him under subsection (2) above.

(5) Where the patient would (apart from section 21 above) have ceased to be liable to be detained or subject to guardianship on or before the day on which a report is duly furnished in respect of him under subsection (2) above, the report shall renew the authority for his detention or guardianship for the period prescribed in that case by section 20(2) above.

(6) Where the authority for the detention or guardianship of the patient is renewed by virtue of subsection (5) above—

(*a*) the renewal shall take effect as from the day on which (apart from section 21 above and that subsection) the authority would have expired; and

(*b*) if (apart from this paragraph) the renewed authority would expire on or before the day on which the report is furnished, the report shall further renew the authority, as from the day on which it would expire, for the period prescribed in that case by section 20(2) above.

(7) Where the authority for the detention or guardianship of the patient would expire within the period of two months beginning with the day on which a report is duly furnished in respect of him under subsection (2) above, the report shall, if it so provides, have effect also as a report duly furnished under section 20(3) or (6) above; and the reference in this subsection to authority includes any authority renewed under subsection (5) above by the report.

(8) Where the form of mental disorder specified in a report furnished under subsection (2) above is a form of disorder other than that specified in the application for admission for treatment or guardianship application concerned (and the report does not have effect as a report furnished under section 20(3) or (6) above), that application shall have effect as if that other form of mental disorder were specified in it.

(9) Where on any occasion a report specifying such a form of mental disorder is furnished under subsection (2) above the appropriate medical officer need not on that occasion furnish a report under section 16 above.

(10) In this section—

"appropriate medical officer" has the same meaning as in section 16(5) above;

"the appropriate body" means—

(*a*) in relation to a patient who is liable to be detained in a hospital, the managers of the hospital; and

(*b*) in relation to a patient who is subject to guardianship, the responsible local social services authority; and

"the relevant conditions" means—

(*a*) in relation to a patient who is liable to be detained in a hospital, the conditions set out in subsection (4) of section 20 above; and

(*b*) in relation to a patient who is subject to guardianship, the conditions set out in subsection (7) of that section.

[Mental Health Act 1983, s 21B, as inserted by the Mental Health (Patients in the Community) Act 1995, s 2.]

8–22229W 22. Special provisions as to patients sentenced to imprisonment, etc. (1) Where a patient who is liable to be detained by virtue of an application for admission for treatment or is subject to guardianship by virtue of a guardianship application is detained in custody in pursuance of any sentence or order passed or made by a court in the United Kingdom (including an order committing or remanding him in custody), and is so detained for a period exceeding, or for successive periods exceeding in the aggregate, six months, the application shall cease to have effect at the expiration of that period.

(2) Where any such patient is so detained in custody but the application does not cease to have effect under subsection (1) above, then—

(*a*) if apart from this subsection the patient would have ceased to be liable to be so detained or subject to guardianship on or before the day on which he is discharged from custody, he shall not cease and shall be deemed not to have ceased to be so liable or subject until the end of that day; and (*b*) in any case, sections 18, 21 and 21A above, shall apply in relation to the patient as if he had absented himself without leave on that day.

(3) In its application by virtue of subsection (2) above section 18(4) above shall have effect with the substitution of the words "end of the period of 28 days beginning with the first day of his absence without leave." for the words from "later of" onwards.

[Mental Health Act 1983, s 22, as amended by the Mental Health (Patients in the Community) Act 1995, s 2.]

8–22229X 23. Discharge of patients. (1) Subject to the provisions of this section and section 25 below, a patient who is for the time being liable to be detained or subject to guardianship under this Part of this Act shall cease to be so liable or subject if an order in writing discharging him from detention or guardianship (in this Act referred to as "an order for discharge") is made in accordance with this section.

(2) An order for discharge may be made in respect of a patient—

(*a*) where the patient is liable to be detained in a hospital in pursuance of an application for admission for assessment or for treatment by the responsible medical officer, by the managers or by the nearest relative of the patient;

(*b*) where the patient is subject to guardianship, by the responsible medical officer, by the responsible local social services authority or by the nearest relative of the patient.

(3) Where the patient is liable to be detained in a registered establishment in pursuance of an application for admission for assessment or for treatment, an order for his discharge may, without prejudice to subsection (2) above, be made by the Secretary of State and, if the patient is maintained under a contract with a National Health Service trust, NHS foundation trust, Health Authority, Special Health Authority or Primary Care Trust, by that National Health Service trust, NHS foundation trust, Health Authority, Special Health Authority or Primary Care Trust.

(4) The powers conferred by this section on any authority trust (other than a NHS foundation trust) or body of persons may be exercised subject to subsection (3) below by any three or more members of that authority trust or body authorised by them in that behalf or by three or more members of a committee or sub-committee of that authority trust or body which has been authorised by them in that behalf.

(5) The reference in subsection (4) above to the members of an authority, trust or body or the members of a committee or sub-committee of an authority, trust or body,—

(*a*) in the case of a Health Authority, Special Health Authority or Primary Care Trust or a committee or sub-committee of a Health Authority, Special Health Authority or Primary Care Trust, is a reference only to the chairman of the authority or trust and such members (of the authority, trust, committee or sub-committee, as the case may be) as are not also officers of the authority or trust, within the meaning of the National Health Service Act 1977; and

(*b*) in the case of a National Health Service trust or a committee or sub-committee of such a trust, is a reference only to the chairman of the trust and such directors or (in the case of a committee or sub-committee) members as are not also employees of the trust.

(6) The powers conferred by this section on any NHS foundation trust may be exercised by any three or more non-executive directors of the board of the trust authorised by the board in that behalf.

[Mental Health Act 1983, s 23, as amended by the National Health Service and Community Care Act 1990, s 66, Sch 9, the Health Authorities Act 1995 s 2, Sch 1, SI 2000/90, the Care Standards Act 2000, s 116 and the Health and Social Care (Community Health and Standards) Act 2003, Sch 4.]

8–22229Y 24. Visiting and examination of patients. (1) For the purpose of advising as to the exercise by the nearest relative of a patient who is liable to be detained or subject to guardianship under this Part of this Act of any power to order his discharge, any registered medical practitioner authorised by or on behalf of the nearest relative of the patient may, at any reasonable time, visit the patient and examine him in private.

(2) Any registered medical practitioner authorised for the purposes of subsection (1) above to visit and examine a patient may require the production of and inspect any records relating to the detention or treatment of the patient in any hospital or to any after-care services provided for the patient under section 117 below.

(3) Where application is made by the Secretary of State or a Health Authority, Special Health Authority, Primary Care Trust, National Health Service trust or NHS foundation trust to exercise, in respect of a patient liable to be detained in a registered establishment, any power to make an order for his discharge, the following persons, that is to say—

(*a*) any registered medical practitioner authorised by the Secretary of State or, as the case may be, that Health Authority, Special Health Authority, Primary Care Trust, National Health Service trust or NHS foundation trust; and

(*b*) any other person (whether a registered medical practitioner or not) authorised under Part II of the Care Standards Act 2000 to inspect the home;

may at any reasonable time visit the patient and interview him in private.

(4) Any person authorised for the purposes of subsection (3) above to visit a patient may require

the production of and inspect any documents constituting or alleged to constitute the authority for the detention of the patient under this Part of this Act; and any person so authorised, who is a registered medical practitioner, may examine the patient in private, and may require the production of and inspect any other records relating to the treatment of the patient in the home or to any after-care services provided for the patient under section 117 below.

[Mental Health Act 1983, s 24, as amended by the Registered Homes Act 1984, s 57, Sch 1, the Health Authorities Act 1995, s 2, Sch 1, the Mental Health (Patients in the Community) Act 1995, s 1, Sch 1, SI 2000/90, the Care Standards Act 2000, s 116 and the Health and Social Care (Community Health and Standards) Act 2003, Sch 4.]

8–22229Z 25. Restrictions on discharge by nearest relative. (1) An order for the discharge of a patient who is liable to be detained in a hospital shall not be made by his nearest relative except after giving not less than 72 hours' notice in writing to the managers of the hospital; and if, within 72 hours after such notice has been given, the responsible medical officer furnishes to the managers a report certifying that in the opinion of that officer the patient, if discharged, would be likely to act in a manner dangerous to other persons or to himself,—

(*a*) any order for the discharge of the patient made by that relative in pursuance of the notice shall be of no effect; and

(*b*) no further order for the discharge of the patient shall be made by that relative during the period of six months beginning with the date of the report.

(2) In any case where a report under subsection (1) above is furnished in respect of a patient who is liable to be detained in pursuance of an application for admission for treatment the managers shall cause the nearest relative of the patient to be informed.

[Mental Health Act 1983, s 25.]

After-care under supervision

8–22229ZA 25A. Application for supervision. (1) Where a patient—

(*a*) is liable to be detained in a hospital in pursuance of an application for admission for treatment; and

(*b*) has attained the age of 16 years,

an application may be made for him to be supervised after he leaves hospital, for the period allowed by the following provisions of this Act, with a view to securing that he receives the after-care services provided for him under section 117 below.

(2) In this Act an application for a patient to be so supervised is referred to as a "supervision application"; and where a supervision application has been duly made and accepted under this Part of this Act in respect of a patient and he has left hospital, he is for the purposes of this Act "subject to after-care under supervision" (until he ceases to be so subject in accordance with the provisions of this Act).

(3) A supervision application shall be made in accordance with this section and sections 25B and 25C below.

(4) A supervision application may be made in respect of a patient only on the grounds that—

(*a*) he is suffering from mental disorder, being mental illness, severe mental impairment, psychopathic disorder or mental impairment;

(*b*) there would be a substantial risk of serious harm to the health or safety of the patient or the safety of other persons, or of the patient being seriously exploited, if he were not to receive the after-care services to be provided for him under section 117 below after he leaves hospital; and

(*c*) his being subject to after-care under supervision is likely to help to secure that he receives the after-care services to be so provided.

(5) A supervision application may be made only by the responsible medical officer.

(6) A supervision application in respect of a patient shall be addressed to the Health Authority which will have the duty under section 117 below to provide after-care services for the patient after he leaves hospital.

(7) Before accepting a supervision application in respect of a patient a Health Authority shall consult the local social services authority which will also have that duty.

(8) Where a Health Authority accept a supervision application in respect of a patient the Health Authority shall—

(*a*) inform the patient both orally and in writing—

(i) that the supervision application has been accepted; and

(ii) of the effect in his case of the provisions of this Act relating to a patient subject to after-care under supervision (including, in particular, what rights of applying to a Mental Health Review Tribunal are available);

(*b*) inform any person whose name is stated in the supervision application in accordance with sub-paragraph (i) of paragraph (*e*) of section 25B(5) below that the supervision application has been accepted; and (*c*) inform in writing any person whose name is so stated in accordance with sub-paragraph (ii) of that paragraph that the supervision application has been accepted.

(9) Where a patient in respect of whom a supervision application is made is granted leave of absence from a hospital under section 17 above (whether before or after the supervision application is made), references in—

(*a*) this section and the following provisions of this Part of this Act; and
(*b*) Part V of this Act,

to his leaving hospital shall be construed as references to his period of leave expiring (otherwise than on his return to the hospital or transfer to another hospital).

[Mental Health Act 1983, s 25A, as inserted by the Mental Health (Patients in the Community) Act 1995, s 1.]

8–22229ZB 25B. Making of supervision application. (1) The responsible medical officer shall not make a supervision application unless—

(*a*) subsection (2) below is complied with; and
(*b*) the responsible medical officer has considered the matters specified in subsection (4) below.

(2) This subsection is complied with if—

(*a*) the following persons have been consulted about the making of the supervision application—
 (i) the patient;
 (ii) one or more persons who have been professionally concerned with the patient's medical treatment in hospital;
 (iii) one or more persons who will be professionally concerned with the after-care services to be provided for the patient under section 117 below; and
 (iv) any person who the responsible medical officer believes will play a substantial part in the care of the patient after he leaves hospital but will not be professionally concerned with any of the after-care services to be so provided;
(*b*) such steps as are practicable have been taken to consult the person (if any) appearing to be the nearest relative of the patient about the making of the supervision application; and
(*c*) the responsible medical officer has taken into account any views expressed by the persons consulted.

(3) Where the patient has requested that paragraph (*b*) of subsection (2) above should not apply, that paragraph shall not apply unless—

(*a*) the patient has a propensity to violent or dangerous behaviour towards others; and
(*b*) the responsible medical officer considers that it is appropriate for steps such as are mentioned in that paragraph to be taken.

(4) The matters referred to in subsection (1)(*b*) above are—

(*a*) the after-care services to be provided for the patient under section 117 below; and
(*b*) any requirements to be imposed on him under section 25D below.

(5) A supervision application shall state—

(*a*) that the patient is liable to be detained in a hospital in pursuance of an application for admission for treatment;
(*b*) the age of the patient or, if his exact age is not known to the applicant, that the patient is believed to have attained the age of 16 years;
(*c*) that in the opinion of the applicant (having regard in particular to the patient's history) all of the conditions set out in section 25A(4) above are complied with;
(*d*) the name of the person who is to be the community responsible medical officer, and of the person who is to be the supervisor, in relation to the patient after he leaves hospital; and
(*e*) the name of—
 (i) any person who has been consulted under paragraph (*a*)(iv) of subsection (2) above; and
 (ii) any person who has been consulted under paragraph (*b*) of that subsection.

(6) A supervision application shall be accompanied by—

(*a*) the written recommendation in the prescribed form of a registered medical practitioner who will be professionally concerned with the patient's medical treatment after he leaves hospital or, if no such practitioner other than the responsible medical officer will be so concerned, of any registered medical practitioner; and
(*b*) the written recommendation in the prescribed form of an approved social worker.

(7) A recommendation under subsection (6)(*a*) above shall include a statement that in the opinion of the medical practitioner (having regard in particular to the patient's history) all of the conditions set out in section 25A(4) above are complied with.

(8) A recommendation under subsection (6)(*b*) above shall include a statement that in the opinion of the social worker (having regard in particular to the patient's history) both of the conditions set out in section 25A(4)(*b*) and (*c*) above are complied with.

(9) A supervision application shall also be accompanied by—

(*a*) a statement in writing by the person who is to be the community responsible medical officer in relation to the patient after he leaves hospital that he is to be in charge of the medical treatment provided for the patient as part of the after-care services provided for him under section 117 below;

(*b*) a statement in writing by the person who is to be the supervisor in relation to the patient after he leaves hospital that he is to supervise the patient with a view to securing that he receives the after-care services so provided;

(*c*) details of the after-care services to be provided for the patient under section 117 below; and

(*d*) details of any requirements to be imposed on him under section 25D below.

(10) On making a supervision application in respect of a patient the responsible medical officer shall—

(*a*) inform the patient both orally and in writing;

(*b*) inform any person who has been consulted under paragraph (*a*)(iv) of subsection (2) above; and

(*c*) inform in writing any person who has been consulted under paragraph (*b*) of that subsection,

of the matters specified in subsection (11) below.

(11) The matters referred to in subsection (10) above are—

(*a*) that the application is being made;

(*b*) the after-care services to be provided for the patient under section 117 below;

(*c*) any requirements to be imposed on him under section 25D below; and

(*d*) the name of the person who is to be the community responsible medical officer, and of the person who is to be the supervisor, in relation to the patient after he leaves hospital.

[Mental Health Act 1983, s 25B, as inserted by the Mental Health (Patients in the Community) Act 1995, s 1.]

8–22229ZC 25C. Supervision applications: supplementary. (1) Subject to subsection (2) below, a supervision application, and the recommendation under section 25B(6)(*a*) above accompanying it, may describe the patient as suffering from more than one of the following forms of mental disorder, namely, mental illness, severe mental impairment, psychopathic disorder and mental impairment.

(2) A supervision application shall be of no effect unless the patient is described in the application and the recommendation under section 25B(6)(*a*) above accompanying it as suffering from the same form of mental disorder, whether or not he is also described in the application or the recommendation as suffering from another form.

(3) A registered medical practitioner may at any reasonable time visit a patient and examine him in private for the purpose of deciding whether to make a recommendation under section 25B(6)(*a*) above.

(4) An approved social worker may at any reasonable time visit and interview a patient for the purpose of deciding whether to make a recommendation under section 25B(6)(*b*) above.

(5) For the purpose of deciding whether to make a recommendation under section 25B(6) above in respect of a patient, a registered medical practitioner or an approved social worker may require the production of and inspect any records relating to the detention or treatment of the patient in any hospital or to any after-care services provided for the patient under section 117 below.

(6) If, within the period of 14 days beginning with the day on which a supervision application has been accepted, the application, or any recommendation accompanying it, is found to be in any respect incorrect or defective, the application or recommendation may, within that period and with the consent of the Health Authority which accepted the application, be amended by the person by whom it was made or given.

(7) Where an application or recommendation is amended in accordance with subsection (6) above it shall have effect, and shall be deemed to have had effect, as if it had been originally made or given as so amended.

(8) A supervision application which appears to be duly made and to be accompanied by recommendations under section 25B(6) above may be acted upon without further proof of—

(*a*) the signature or qualification of the person by whom the application or any such recommendation was made or given; or

(*b*) any matter of fact or opinion stated in the application or recommendation.

(9) A recommendation under section 25B(6) above accompanying a supervision application in respect of a patient shall not be given by—

(*a*) the responsible medical officer;

(*b*) a person who receives or has an interest in the receipt of any payments made on account of the maintenance of the patient; or

(*c*) a close relative of the patient, of any person mentioned in paragraph (*a*) or (*b*) above or of a person by whom the other recommendation is given under section 25B(6) above for the purposes of the application.

(10) In subsection (9)(*c*) above "close relative" means husband, wife, civil partner, father, father-in-law, mother, mother-in-law, son, son-in-law, daughter, daughter-in-law, brother, brother-in-law, sister or sister-in-law.

[Mental Health Act 1983, s 25C, as inserted by the Mental Health (Patients in the Community) Act 1995, s 1 and amended by the Civil Partnership Act 2004, Sch 27.]

8–22229ZD 25D. Requirements to secure receipt of after-care under supervision. (1) Where a patient is subject to after-care under supervision (or, if he has not yet left hospital, is to be so subject after he leaves hospital), the responsible after-care bodies have power to impose any of the requirements specified in subsection (3) below for the purpose of securing that the patient receives the after-care services provided for him under section 117 below.

(2) In this Act "the responsible after-care bodies", in relation to a patient, means the bodies which have (or will have) the duty under section 117 below to provide after-care services for the patient.

(3) The requirements referred to in subsection (1) above are—

(*a*) that the patient reside at a specified place;

(*b*) that the patient attend at specified places and times for the purpose of medical treatment, occupation, education or training; and

(*c*) that access to the patient be given, at any place where the patient is residing, to the supervisor, any registered medical practitioner or any approved social worker or to any other person authorised by the supervisor.

(4) A patient subject to after-care under supervision may be taken and conveyed by, or by any person authorised by, the supervisor to any place where the patient is required to reside or to attend for the purpose of medical treatment, occupation, education or training.

(5) A person who demands—

(*a*) to be given access to a patient in whose case a requirement has been imposed under subsection (3)(*c*) above; or

(*b*) to take and convey a patient in pursuance of subsection (4) above,

shall, if asked to do so, produce some duly authenticated document to show that he is a person entitled to be given access to, or to take and convey, the patient.

[Mental Health Act 1983, s 25D, as inserted by the Mental Health (Patients in the Community) Act 1995, s 1.]

8–22229ZE 25E. Review of after-care under supervision etc. (1) The after-care services provided (or to be provided) under section 117 below for a patient who is (or is to be) subject to after-care under supervision, and any requirements imposed on him under section 25D above, shall be kept under review, and (where appropriate) modified, by the responsible after-care bodies.

(2) This subsection applies in relation to a patient who is subject to after-care under supervision where he refuses or neglects—

(*a*) to receive any or all of the after-care services provided for him under section 117 below; or

(*b*) to comply with any or all of any requirements imposed on him under section 25D above.

(3) Where subsection (2) above applies in relation to a patient, the responsible after-care bodies shall review, and (where appropriate) modify—

(*a*) the after-care services provided for him under section 117 below; and

(*b*) any requirements imposed on him under section 25D above.

(4) Where subsection (2) above applies in relation to a patient, the responsible after-care bodies shall also—

(*a*) consider whether it might be appropriate for him to cease to be subject to after-care under supervision and, if they conclude that it might be, inform the community responsible medical officer; and

(*b*) consider whether it might be appropriate for him to be admitted to a hospital for treatment and, if they conclude that it might be, inform an approved social worker.

(5) The responsible after-care bodies shall not modify—

(*a*) the after-care services provided (or to be provided) under section 117 below for a patient who is (or is to be) subject to after-care under supervision; or

(*b*) any requirements imposed on him under section 25D above,

unless subsection (6) below is complied with.

(6) This subsection is complied with if—

(*a*) the patient has been consulted about the modifications;

(*b*) any person who the responsible after-care bodies believe plays (or will play) a substantial part in the care of the patient but is not (or will not be) professionally concerned with the after-care services provided for the patient under section 117 below has been consulted about the modifications;

(*c*) such steps as are practicable have been taken to consult the person (if any) appearing to be the nearest relative of the patient about the modifications; and (*d*) the responsible after-care bodies have taken into account any views expressed by the persons consulted.

(7) Where the patient has requested that paragraph (*c*) of subsection (6) above should not apply, that paragraph shall not apply unless—

(*a*) the patient has a propensity to violent or dangerous behaviour towards others; and
(*b*) the community responsible medical officer (or the person who is to be the community responsible medical officer) considers that it is appropriate for steps such as are mentioned in that paragraph to be taken.

(8) Where the responsible after-care bodies modify the after-care services provided (or to be provided) for the patient under section 117 below or any requirements imposed on him under section 25D above, they shall—

(*a*) inform the patient both orally and in writing;
(*b*) inform any person who has been consulted under paragraph (*b*) of subsection (6) above; and
(*c*) inform in writing any person who has been consulted under paragraph (*c*) of that subsection,

that the modifications have been made.

(9) Where—

(*a*) a person other than the person named in the supervision application becomes the community responsible medical officer when the patient leaves hospital; or
(*b*) when the patient is subject to after-care under supervision, one person ceases to be, and another becomes, the community responsible medical officer,

the responsible after-care bodies shall comply with subsection (11) below.

(10) Where—

(*a*) a person other than the person named in the supervision application becomes the supervisor when the patient leaves hospital; or
(*b*) when the patient is subject to after-care under supervision, one person ceases to be, and another becomes, the supervisor,

the responsible after-care bodies shall comply with subsection (11) below.

(11) The responsible after-care bodies comply with this subsection if they—

(*a*) inform the patient both orally and in writing;
(*b*) inform any person who they believe plays a substantial part in the care of the patient but is not professionally concerned with the after-care services provided for the patient under section 117 below; and
(*c*) unless the patient otherwise requests, take such steps as are practicable to inform in writing the person (if any) appearing to be the nearest relative of the patient,

of the name of the person who becomes the community responsible medical officer or the supervisor.
[Mental Health Act 1983, s 25E, as inserted by the Mental Health (Patients in the Community) Act 1995, s 1.]

8–22229ZF 25F. Reclassification of patient subject to after-care under supervision. (1) If it appears to the community responsible medical officer that a patient subject to after-care under supervision is suffering from a form of mental disorder other than the form or forms specified in the supervision application made in respect of the patient, he may furnish a report to that effect to the Health Authority which have the duty under section 117 below to provide after-care services for the patient.

(2) Where a report is so furnished the supervision application shall have effect as if that other form of mental disorder were specified in it.

(3) Unless no-one other than the community responsible medical officer is professionally concerned with the patient's medical treatment, he shall consult one or more persons who are so concerned before furnishing a report under subsection (1) above.

(4) Where a report is furnished under subsection (1) above in respect of a patient, the responsible after-care bodies shall—

(*a*) inform the patient both orally and in writing; and
(*b*) unless the patient otherwise requests, take such steps as are practicable to inform in writing the person (if any) appearing to be the nearest relative of the patient,

that the report has been furnished.
[Mental Health Act 1983, s 25F, as inserted by the Mental Health (Patients in the Community) Act 1995, s 1.]

8–22229ZG 25G. Duration and renewal of after-care under supervision. (1) Subject to sections 25H and 25I below, a patient subject to after-care under supervision shall be so subject for the period—

(*a*) beginning when he leaves hospital; and
(*b*) ending with the period of six months beginning with the day on which the supervision application was accepted,

but shall not be so subject for any longer period except in accordance with the following provisions of this section.

(2) A patient already subject to after-care under supervision may be made so subject—

(*a*) from the end of the period referred to in subsection (1) above, for a further period of six months; and

(*b*) from the end of any period of renewal under paragraph (*a*) above, for a further period of one year,

and so on for periods of one year at a time.

(3) Within the period of two months ending on the day on which a patient who is subject to after-care under supervision would (in default of the operation of subsection (7) below) cease to be so subject, it shall be the duty of the community responsible medical officer—

(*a*) to examine the patient; and

(*b*) if it appears to him that the conditions set out in subsection (4) below are complied with, to furnish to the responsible after-care bodies a report to that effect in the prescribed form.

(4) The conditions referred to in subsection (3) above are that—

(*a*) the patient is suffering from mental disorder, being mental illness, severe mental impairment, psychopathic disorder or mental impairment;

(*b*) there would be a substantial risk of serious harm to the health or safety of the patient or the safety of other persons, or of the patient being seriously exploited, if he were not to receive the after-care services provided for him under section 117 below;

(*c*) his being subject to after-care under supervision is likely to help to secure that he receives the after-care services so provided.

(5) The community responsible medical officer shall not consider whether the conditions set out in subsection (4) above are complied with unless—

(*a*) the following persons have been consulted—

(i) the patient;

(ii) the supervisor;

(iii) unless no-one other than the community responsible medical officer is professionally concerned with the patient's medical treatment, one or more persons who are so concerned;

(iv) one or more persons who are professionally concerned with the after-care services (other than medical treatment) provided for the patient under section 117 below; and

(v) any person who the community responsible medical officer believes plays a substantial part in the care of the patient but is not professionally concerned with the after-care services so provided;

(*b*) such steps as are practicable have been taken to consult the person (if any) appearing to be the nearest relative of the patient; and

(*c*) the community responsible medical officer has taken into account any relevant views expressed by the persons consulted.

(6) Where the patient has requested that paragraph (*b*) of subsection (5) above should not apply, that paragraph shall not apply unless—

(*a*) the patient has a propensity to violent or dangerous behaviour towards others; and

(*b*) the community responsible medical officer considers that it is appropriate for steps such as are mentioned in that paragraph to be taken.

(7) Where a report is duly furnished under subsection (3) above, the patient shall be thereby made subject to after-care under supervision for the further period prescribed in that case by subsection (2) above.

(8) Where a report is furnished under subsection (3) above, the responsible after-care bodies shall—

(*a*) inform the patient both orally and in writing—

(i) that the report has been furnished; and

(ii) of the effect in his case of the provisions of this Act relating to making a patient subject to after-care under supervision for a further period (including, in particular, what rights of applying to a Mental Health Review Tribunal are available);

(*b*) inform any person who has been consulted under paragraph (*a*)(v) of subsection (5) above that the report has been furnished; and

(*c*) inform in writing any person who has been consulted under paragraph (*b*) of that subsection that the report has been furnished.

(9) Where the form of mental disorder specified in a report furnished under subsection (3) above is a form of disorder other than that specified in the supervision application, that application shall have effect as if that other form of mental disorder were specified in it.

(10) Where on any occasion a report specifying such a form of mental disorder is furnished under

subsection (3) above the community responsible medical officer need not on that occasion furnish a report under section 25F above.
[Mental Health Act 1983, s 25G, as inserted by the Mental Health (Patients in the Community) Act 1995, s 1.]

8–22229ZH 25H. Ending of after-care under supervision. (1) The community responsible medical officer may at any time direct that a patient subject to after-care under supervision shall cease to be so subject.

(2) The community responsible medical officer shall not give a direction under subsection (1) above unless subsection (3) below is complied with.

(3) This subsection is complied with if—

(*a*) the following persons have been consulted about the giving of the direction—

(i) the patient;
(ii) the supervisor;
(ii) unless no-one other than the community responsible medical officer is professionally concerned with the patient's medical treatment, one or more persons who are so concerned;
(iv) one or more persons who are professionally concerned with the after-care services (other than medical treatment) provided for the patient under section 117 below; and
(v) any person who the community responsible medical officer believes plays a substantial part in the care of the patient but is not professionally concerned with the after-care services so provided;

(*b*) such steps as are practicable have been taken to consult the person (if any) appearing to be the nearest relative of the patient about the giving of the direction; and
(*c*) the community responsible medical officer has taken into account any views expressed by the persons consulted.

(4) Where the patient has requested that paragraph (*b*) of subsection (3) above should not apply, that paragraph shall not apply unless—

(*a*) the patient has a propensity to violent or dangerous behaviour towards others; and
(*b*) the community responsible medical officer considers that it is appropriate for steps such as are mentioned in that paragraph to be taken.

(5) A patient subject to after-care under supervision shall cease to be so subject if he—

(*a*) is admitted to a hospital in pursuance of an application for admission for treatment; or
(*b*) is received into guardianship.

(6) Where a patient (for any reason) ceases to be subject to after-care under supervision the responsible after-care bodies shall—

(*a*) inform the patient both orally and in writing;
(*b*) inform any person who they believe plays a substantial part in the care of the patient but is not professionally concerned with the after-care services provided for the patient under section 117 below; and
(*c*) take such steps as are practicable to inform in writing the person (if any) appearing to be the nearest relative of the patient,

that the patient has ceased to be so subject.

(7) Where the patient has requested that paragraph (*c*) of subsection (6) above should not apply, that paragraph shall not apply unless subsection (3)(*b*) above applied in his case by virtue of subsection (4) above.
[Mental Health Act 1983, s 25H, as inserted by the Mental Health (Patients in the Community) Act 1995, s 1.]

8–22229ZI 25I. Special provisions as to patients sentenced to imprisonment etc. (1) This section applies where a patient who is subject to after-care under supervision—

(*a*) is detained in custody in pursuance of any sentence or order passed or made by a court in the United Kingdom (including an order committing or remanding him in custody); or
(*b*) is detained in hospital in pursuance of an application for admission for assessment.

(2) At any time when the patient is detained as mentioned in subsection (1)(*a*) or (*b*) above he is not required—

(*a*) to receive any after-care services provided for him under section 117 below; or
(*b*) to comply with any requirements imposed on him under section 25D above.

(3) If the patient is detained as mentioned in paragraph (*a*) of subsection (1) above for a period of, or successive periods amounting in the aggregate to, six months or less, or is detained as mentioned in paragraph (*b*) of that subsection, and, apart from this subsection, he—

(*a*) would have ceased to be subject to after-care under supervision during the period for which he is so detained; or (*b*) would cease to be so subject during the period of 28 days beginning with the day on which he ceases to be so detained,

he shall be deemed not to have ceased, and shall not cease, to be so subject until the end of that period of 28 days.

(4) Where the period for which the patient is subject to after-care under supervision is extended by subsection (3) above, any examination and report to be made and furnished in respect of the patient under section 25G(3) above may be made and furnished within the period as so extended.

(5) Where, by virtue of subsection (4) above, the patient is made subject to after-care under supervision for a further period after the day on which (apart from subsection (3) above) he would have ceased to be so subject, the further period shall be deemed to have commenced with that day.

[Mental Health Act 1983, s 25I, as inserted by the Mental Health (Patients in the Community) Act 1995, s 1.]

8–22229ZJ 25J. Patients moving from Scotland to England and Wales. (1) *Repealed.*

(2) Sections 25A to 25I above, section 117 below and any other provision of this Act relating to supervision applications or patients subject to after-care under supervision shall apply in relation to a patient in respect of whom a supervision application is or is to be made by virtue of this section subject to such modifications as the Secretary of State may by regulations prescribe.

[Mental Health Act 1983, s 25J, as inserted by the Mental Health (Patients in the Community) Act 1995, s 1 and amended by SI 2005/2078.]

Functions of relatives of patients

8–22229ZK 26. Definition of "relative" and "nearest relative". (1) In this Part of this Act "relative" means any of the following persons:—

(*a*) husband or wife;
(*b*) son or daughter;
(*c*) father or mother;
(*d*) brother or sister;
(*e*) grandparent;
(*f*) grandchild;
(*g*) uncle or aunt;
(*h*) nephew or niece.

(2) In deducing relationships for the purposes of this section, any relationship of the half-blood shall be treated as a relationship of the whole blood, and an illegitimate person shall be treated as the legitimate child of

(*a*) his mother, and
(*b*) if his father has parental responsibility for him within the meaning of section 3 of the Children Act 1989, his father.

(3) In this Part of this Act, subject to the provisions of this section and to the following provisions of this Part of this Act, the "nearest relative" means the person first described in subsection (1) above who is for the time being surviving, relatives of the whole blood being preferred to relatives of the same description of the half-blood and the elder or eldest of two or more relatives described in any paragraph of that subsection being preferred to the other or others of those relatives, regardless of sex.

(4) Subject to the provisions of this section and to the following provisions of this Part of this Act, where the patient ordinarily resides with or is cared for by one or more of his relatives (or, if he is for the time being an in-patient in a hospital, he last ordinarily resided with or was cared for by one or more of his relatives) his nearest relative shall be determined—

(*a*) by giving preference to that relative or those relatives over the other or others; and
(*b*) as between two or more such relatives, in accordance with subsection (3) above.

(5) Where the person who, under subsection (3) or (4) above, would be the nearest relative of a patient—

(*a*) in the case of a patient ordinarily resident in the United Kingdom, the Channel Islands or the Isle of Man, is not so resident; or
(*b*) is the husband or wife of the patient, but is permanently separated from the patient, either by agreement or under an order of a court, or has deserted or has been deserted by the patient for a period which has come to an end; or
(*c*) is a person other than the husband, wife, father or mother of the patient, and is for the time being under 18 years of age;
(*d*) (*Repealed*).

the nearest relative of the patient shall be ascertained as if that person were dead.

(6) In this section "husband" and "wife" include a person who is living with the patient as the patient's husband or wife, as the case may be (or, if the patient is for the time being an in-patient in a hospital, was so living until the patient was admitted), and has been or had been so living for a period of not less than six months; but a person shall not be treated by virtue of this subsection as the nearest

relative of a married patient unless the husband or wife of the patient is disregarded by virtue of paragraph (*b*) of subsection (5) above.

(7) A person, other than a relative, with whom the patient ordinarily resides (or, if the patient is for the time being an in-patient in a hospital, last ordinarily resided before he was admitted), and with whom he has or had been ordinarily residing for a period of not less than five years, shall be treated for the purposes of this Part of this Act as if he were a relative but—

(*a*) shall be treated for the purposes of subsection (3) above as if mentioned last in subsection (1) above; and

(*b*) shall not be treated by virtue of this subsection as the nearest relative of a married patient unless the husband or wife of the patient is disregarded by virtue of paragraph (*b*) of subsection (5) above.

[Mental Health Act 1983, s 26, as amended by SI 1991/1881 and the Children Act 1989, s 108, Schs 14 and 15.]

8–22229ZL 27. Children and young persons in care. Where—

(*a*) a patient who is a child or young person is in the care of a local authority by virtue of a care order within the meaning of the Children Act 1989; or

(*b*) the rights and powers of a parent of a patient who is a child or young person are vested in a local authority by virtue of section 16 of the Social Work (Scotland) Act 1968,

the authority shall be deemed to be the nearest relative of the patient in preference to any person except the patient's husband or wife (if any).

[Mental Health Act 1983, s 27, as substituted by the Children Act 1989, s 108, Sch 14.]

8–22229ZM 28. Nearest relative of minor under guardianship, etc. (1) Where—

(*a*) a guardian has been appointed for a person who has not attained the age of eighteen years; or

(*b*) a residence order (as defined by section 8 of the Children Act 1989) is in force with respect to such a person,

the guardian (or guardians, where there is more than one) or the person named in the residence order shall, to the exclusion of any other person, be deemed to be his nearest relative.

(2) Subsection (5) of section 26 above shall apply in relation to a person who is, or who is one of the persons, deemed to be the nearest relative of a patient by virtue of this section as it applies in relation to a person who would be the nearest relative under subsection (3) of that section.

(3) In this section "guardian" includes a special guardian (within the meaning of the Children Act 1989), but does not include a guardian under this Part of this Act.

(4) In this section "court" includes a court in Scotland or Northern Ireland, and "enactment" includes an enactment of the Parliament of Northern Ireland, a Measure of the Northern Ireland Assembly and an Order in Council under Schedule 1 of the Northern Ireland Act 1974.

[Mental Health Act 1983, s 28, as amended by the Children Act 1989, s 108, Schs 13 and 14 and the Adoption and Children Act 2002, Sch 3.]

8–22229ZN 29. Appointment by court of acting nearest relative. (1) The county court may, upon application made in accordance with the provisions of this section in respect of a patient, by order direct that the functions of the nearest relative of the patient under this Part of this Act and sections 66 and 69 below shall, during the continuance in force of the order, be exercisable by the applicant, or by any other person specified in the application, being a person who, in the opinion of the court, is a proper person to act as the patient's nearest relative and is willing to do so.

(2) An order under this section may be made on the application of—

(*a*) any relative of the patient;

(*b*) any other person with whom the patient is residing (or, if the patient is then an in-patient in a hospital, was last residing before he was admitted); or

(*c*) an approved social worker;

but in relation to an application made by such a social worker, subsection (1) above shall have effect as if for the words "the applicant" there were substituted the words "the local social services authority".

(3) An application for an order under this section may be made upon any of the following grounds, that is to say—

(*a*) that the patient has no nearest relative within the meaning of this Act, or that it is not reasonably practicable to ascertain whether he has such a relative, or who that relative is;

(*b*) that the nearest relative of the patient is incapable of acting as such by reason of mental disorder or other illness;

(*c*) that the nearest relative of the patient unreasonably objects to the making of an application for admission for treatment or a guardianship application in respect of the patient; or

(*d*) that the nearest relative of the patient has exercised without due regard to the welfare of the patient or the interests of the public his power to discharge the patient from hospital or guardianship under this Part of this Act, or is likely to do so.

(4) If, immediately before the expiration of the period for which a patient is liable to be detained

by virtue of an application for admission for assessment, an application under this section, which is an application made on the ground specified in subsection (3)(*c*) or (*d*) above, is pending in respect of the patient, that period shall be extended—

(*a*) in any case, until the application under this section has been finally disposed of; and

(*b*) if an order is made in pursuance of the application under this section, for a further period of seven days;

and for the purposes of this subsection an application under this section shall be deemed to have been finally disposed of at the expiration of the time allowed for appealing from the decision of the court or, if notice of appeal has been given within that time, when the appeal has been heard or withdrawn, and "pending" shall be construed accordingly.

(5) An order made on the ground specified in subsection (3)(*a*) or (*b*) above may specify a period for which it is to continue in force unless previously discharged under section 30 below.

(6) While an order made under this section is in force, the provisions of this Part of this Act (other than this section and section 30 below) and sections 66, 69, 132(4) and 133 below shall apply in relation to the patient as if for any reference to the nearest relative of the patient there were substituted a reference to the person having the functions of that relative and (without prejudice to section 30 below) shall so apply notwithstanding that the person who was the patient's nearest relative when the order was made is no longer his nearest relative; but this subsection shall not apply to section 66 below in the case mentioned in paragraph (h) of subsection (1) of that section.
[Mental Health Act 1983, s 29.]

8–22229ZO 30. Discharge and variation of orders under s 29. (1) An order made under section 29 above in respect of a patient may be discharged by the county court upon application made—

(*a*) in any case, by the person having the functions of the nearest relative of the patient by virtue of the order;

(*b*) where the order was made on the ground specified in paragraph (*a*) or paragraph (*b*) of section 29(3) above, or where the person who was the nearest relative of the patient when the order was made has ceased to be his nearest relative, on the application of the nearest relative of the patient.

(2) An order made under section 29 above in respect of a patient may be varied by the county court, on the application of the person having the functions of the nearest relative by virtue of the order or on the application of an approved social worker, by substituting for the first-mentioned person a local social services authority or any other person who in the opinion of the court is a proper person to exercise those functions, being an authority or person who is willing to do so.

(3) If the person having the functions of the nearest relative of a patient by virtue of an order under section 29 above dies—

(*a*) subsections (1) and (2) above shall apply as if for any reference to that person there were substituted a reference to any relative of the patient, and

(*b*) until the order is discharged or varied under those provisions the functions of the nearest relative under this Part of this Act and sections 66 and 69 below shall not be exercisable by any person.

(4) An order under section 29 above shall, unless previously discharged under subsection (1) above, cease to have effect at the expiration of the period, if any, specified under subsection (5) of that section or, where no such period is specified—

(*a*) if the patient was on the date of the order liable to be detained in pursuance of an application for admission for treatment or by virtue of an order or direction under Part III of this Act (otherwise than under section 35, 36 or 38) or was subject to guardianship under this Part of this Act or by virtue of such an order or direction, or becomes so liable or subject within the period of three months beginning with that date, when he ceases to be so liable or subject (otherwise than on being transferred in pursuance of regulations under section 19 above);

(*b*) if the patient was not on the date of the order, and has not within the said period become, so liable or subject, at the expiration of that period.

(5) The discharge or variation under this section of an order made under section 29 above shall not affect the validity of anything previously done in pursuance of the order.
[Mental Health Act 1983, s 30.]

Supplemental

8–22229ZP 31. Procedure on applications to county court. County court rules which relate to applications authorised by this Part of this Act to be made to a county court may make provision—

(*a*) for the hearing and determination of such applications otherwise than in open court;

(*b*) for the admission on the hearing of such applications of evidence of such descriptions as may be specified in the rules notwithstanding anything to the contrary in any enactment or rule of law relating to the admissibility of evidence;

(*c*) for the visiting and interviewing of patients in private by or under the directions of the court.
[Mental Health Act 1983, s 31.]

8–22229ZQ 32. Regulations for purposes of Part II. (1) The Secretary of State may make regulations for prescribing anything which, under this Part of this Act, is required or authorised to be prescribed, and otherwise for carrying this Part of this Act into full effect.

(2) Regulations under this section may in particular make provision—

(*a*) for prescribing the form of any application, recommendation, report, order, notice or other document to be made or given under this Part of this Act;

(*b*) for prescribing the manner in which any such application, recommendation, report, order, notice or other document may be proved, and for regulating the service of any such application, report, order or notice;

(*c*) for requiring such bodies as may be prescribed by the regulations to keep such registers or other records as may be so prescribed in respect of patients liable to be detained or subject to guardianship or to after-care under supervision under this Part of this Act, and to furnish or make available to those patients, and their relatives, such written statements of their rights and powers under this Act as may be so prescribed;

(*d*) for the determination in accordance with the regulations of the age of any person whose exact age cannot be ascertained by reference to the registers kept under the Births and Deaths Registration Act 1953; and

(*e*) for enabling the functions under this Part of this Act of the nearest relative of a patient to be performed, in such circumstances and subject to such conditions (if any) as may be prescribed by the regulations, by any person authorised in that behalf by that relative;

and for the purposes of this Part of this Act any application, report or notice the service of which is regulated under paragraph (*b*) above shall be deemed to have been received by or furnished to the authority or person to whom it is authorised or required to be furnished, addressed or given if it is duly served in accordance with the regulations.

(3) Without prejudice to subsections (1) and (2) above, but subject to section 23(4) above, regulations under this section may determine the manner in which functions under this Part of this Act of the managers of hospitals, local social services authorities, Health Authorities, Special Health Authorities, Primary Care Trusts, National Health Service trusts or NHS foundation trusts are to be exercised, and such regulations may in particular specify the circumstances in which, and the conditions subject to which, any such functions may be performed by officers of or other persons acting on behalf of those managers authorities and trusts.
[Mental Health Act 1983, s 32, as amended by the National Health Service and Community Care Act 1990, s 66, Sch 9, the Health Authorities Act 1995, s 2, Sch 1, the Mental Health (Patients in the Community) Act 1995, s 1, Sch 1, SI 2000/90 and the Health and Social Care (Community Health and Standards) Act 2003, Sch 4.]

8–22229ZR 33. Special provisions as to wards of court. (1) An application for the admission to hospital of a minor who is a ward of court may be made under this Part of this Act with the leave of the court; and section 11(4) above shall not apply in relation to an application so made.

(2) Where a minor who is a ward of court is liable to be detained in a hospital by virtue of an application for admission under this Part of this Act, any power exercisable under this Part of this Act or under section 66 below in relation to the patient by his nearest relative shall be exercisable by or with the leave of the court.

(3) Nothing in this Part of this Act shall be construed as authorising the making of a guardianship application in respect of a minor who is a ward of court, or the transfer into guardianship of any such minor.

(4) Where a supervision application has been made in respect of a minor who is a ward of court, the provisions of this Part of this Act relating to after-care under supervision have effect in relation to the minor subject to any order which the court may make in the exercise of its wardship jurisdiction.
[Mental Health Act 1983, s 33, as amended by the Mental Health (Patients in the Community) Act 1995, s 1, Sch 1.]

8–22229ZS 34. Interpretation of Part II. (1) In this Part of this Act—

"the community responsible medical officer", in relation to a patient subject to after-care under supervision, means the person who, in accordance with section 117(2A)(*a*) below, is in charge of medical treatment provided for him;

"the nominated medical attendant", in relation to a patient who is subject to the guardianship of a person other than a local social services authority, means the person appointed in pursuance of regulations made under section 9(2) above to act as the medical attendant of the patient;

"registered establishment" means an establishment—

(*a*) which would not, apart from subsection (2) below, be a hospital for the purposes of this Part; and

(*b*) in respect of which a person is registered under Part II of the Care Standards Act 2000 as an independent hospital in which treatment or nursing (or both) are provided for persons liable to be detained under this Act;

"the responsible medical officer" means (except in the phrase "the community responsible medical officer")—

(*a*) in relation to a patient who is liable to be detained by virtue of an application for admission for assessment or an application for admission for treatment or who is to be subject to after-care under supervision after leaving hospital, the registered medical practitioner in charge of the treatment of the patient;

(*b*) in relation to a patient subject to guardianship, the medical officer authorised by the local social services authority to act (either generally or in any particular case or for any particular purpose) as the responsible medical officer.

"the supervisor", in relation to a patient subject to after-care under supervision, means the person who, in accordance with section 117(2A)(*b*) below, is supervising him.

(1A) Nothing in this Act prevents the same person from acting as more than one of the following in relation to a patient, that is—

(*a*) the responsible medical officer;

(*b*) the community responsible medical officer; and

(*c*) the supervisor.

(2) Except where otherwise expressly provided, this Part of this Act applies in relation to a registered establishment, being a home in respect of which the particulars of registration are for the time being entered in the separate part of the register kept for the purposes of section 23(5)(*b*) of the Registered Homes Act 1984, as it applies in relation to a hospital, and references in this Part of this Act to a hospital, and any reference in this Act to a hospital to which this Part of this Act applies, shall be construed accordingly.**

(3) In relation to a patient who is subject to guardianship in pursuance of a guardianship application, any reference in this Part of this Act to the responsible local social services authority is a reference—

(*a*) where the patient is subject to the guardianship of a local social services authority, to that authority;

(*b*) where the patient is subject to the guardianship of a person other than a local social services authority, to the local social services authority for the area in which that person resides.

[Mental Health Act 1983, s 34, as amended by the Registered Homes Act 1984, s 57, Sch 1, the Mental Health (Patients in the Community) Act 1995, s 1, Sch 1 and the Care Standards Act 2000, s 116.]

PART III[1]

PATIENTS CONCERNED IN CRIMINAL PROCEEDINGS OR UNDER SENTENCE

Remands to hospital

8–22230 **35. Remand to hospital for report on accused's mental condition.** (1) Subject to the provisions of this section, the Crown Court or a magistrates' court may remand[2] an accused person to a hospital specified by the court for a report on his mental condition.

(2) For the purposes of this section an accused person is—

(*a*) in relation to the Crown Court, any person who is awaiting trial before the court for an offence punishable with imprisonment or who has been arraigned before the court for such an offence and has not yet been sentenced or otherwise dealt with for the offence on which he has been arraigned;

(*b*) in relation to a magistrates' court, any person who has been convicted by the court of an offence punishable on summary conviction with imprisonment and any person charged with such an offence if the court is satisfied that he did the act or made the omission charged or he has consented to the exercise by the court of the powers conferred by this section.

(3) Subject to subsection (4) below, the powers conferred by this section may be exercised if—

(*a*) the court is satisfied, on the written or oral evidence of a registered medical practitioner, that there is reason to suspect that the accused person is suffering from mental illness, psychopathic disorder, severe mental impairment or mental impairment; and

(*b*) the court is of the opinion that it would be impracticable for a report on his mental condition to be made if he were remanded on bail;

but those powers shall not be exercised by the Crown Court in respect of a person who has been convicted before the court if the sentence for the offence of which he has been convicted is fixed by law.

(4) The court shall not remand an accused person to a hospital under this section unless satisfied, on the written or oral evidence of the registered medical practitioner who would be responsible for making the report or of some other person representing the managers of the hospital, that arrangements have been made for his admission to that hospital and for his admission to it within the period of seven days beginning with the date of the remand; and if the court is so satisfied it may, pending his admission, give directions for his conveyance to and detention in a place of safety.

(5) Where a court has remanded an accused person under this section it may further remand him

if it appears to the court, on the written or oral evidence of the registered medical practitioner responsible for making the report, that a further remand is necessary for completing the assessment of the accused person's mental condition.

(6) The power of further remanding an accused person under this section may be exercised by the court without his being brought before the court if he is represented by counsel or a solicitor and his counsel or solicitor is given an opportunity of being heard.

(7) An accused person shall not be remanded or further remanded under this section for more than 28 days at a time or for more than 12 weeks in all; and the court may at any time terminate the remand if it appears to the court that it is appropriate to do so.

(8) An accused person remanded to hospital under this section shall be entitled to obtain at his own expense an independent report on his mental condition from a registered medical practitioner chosen by him and to apply to the court on the basis of it for his remand to be terminated under subsection (7) above.

(9) Where an accused person is remanded under this section—

(*a*) a constable or any other person directed to do so by the court shall convey the accused person to the hospital specified by the court within the period mentioned in subsection (4) above; and

(*b*) the managers of the hospital shall admit him within that period and thereafter detain him in accordance with the provisions of this section.

(10) If an accused person absconds from a hospital to which he has been remanded under this section, or while being conveyed to or from that hospital, he may be arrested[3] without warrant by any constable and shall, after being arrested, be brought as soon as practicable before the court that remanded him; and the court may thereupon terminate the remand and deal with him in any way in which it could have dealt with him if he had not been remanded under this section.

[Mental Health Act 1983, s 35.]

1. Part III contains ss 35–55.

2. A general power to remand on bail or in custody for medical examination is given under s 30 of the Magistrates' Courts Act 1980 in PART I: MAGISTRATES' COURTS, PROCEDURE, ante.

3. This power of arrest is preserved by the Police and Criminal Evidence Act 1984, s 26 and Sch 2.

8–22231 **36. Remand of accused person to hospital for treatment.** (1) Subject to the provisions of this section, the Crown Court may, instead of remanding an accused person in custody, remand him to a hospital specified by the court if satisfied, on the written or oral evidence of two registered medical practitioners, that he is suffering from mental illness or severe mental impairment of a nature or degree which makes it appropriate for him to be detained in a hospital for medical treatment.

(2) For the purposes of this section an accused person is any person who is in custody awaiting trial before the Crown Court for an offence punishable with imprisonment (other than an offence the sentence for which is fixed by law) or who at any time before sentence is in custody in the course of a trial before that court for such an offence.

(3) The court shall not remand an accused person under this section to a hospital unless it is satisfied, on the written or oral evidence of the registered medical practitioner who would be in charge of his treatment or of some other person representing the managers of the hospital, that arrangements have been made for his admission to that hospital and for his admission to it within the period of seven days beginning with the date of the remand; and if the court is so satisfied it may, pending his admission, give directions for his conveyance to and detention in a place of safety.

(4) Where a court has remanded an accused person under this section it may further remand him if it appears to the court, on the written or oral evidence of the responsible medical officer, that a further remand is warranted.

(5) The power of further remanding an accused person under this section may be exercised by the court without his being brought before the court if he is represented by counsel or a solicitor and his counsel or solicitor is given an opportunity of being heard.

(6) An accused person shall not be remanded or further remanded under this section for more than 28 days at a time or for more than 12 weeks in all; and the court may at any time terminate the remand if it appears to the court that it is appropriate to do so.

(7) An accused person remanded to hospital under this section shall be entitled to obtain at his own expense an independent report on his mental condition from a registered medical practitioner chosen by him and to apply to the court on the basis of it for his remand to be terminated under subsection (6) above.

(8) Subsections (9) and (10) of section 35 above shall have effect in relation to a remand under this section as they have effect in relation to a remand under that section.

[Mental Health Act 1983, s 36.]

Hospital and guardianship orders

8–22232 **37. Powers[1] of courts to order hospital admission or guardianship.** (1) Where a person is convicted before the Crown Court of an offence punishable with imprisonment other than an offence the sentence for which is fixed by law or falls to be imposed under section 109(2) of the Powers of Criminal Courts (Sentencing) Act 2000[4], or is convicted by a magistrates' court[2] of an offence punishable on summary conviction with imprisonment, and the conditions mentioned in subsection (2) below are satisfied, the court may by order authorise his admission to and detention in such hospital as may be specified in the order or, as the case may be, place him under the guardianship of a local social services authority or of such other person approved by a local social services authority as may be so specified[3].

(1A) In the case of an offence the sentence for which would otherwise fall to be imposed under subsection (2) of section 110 or 111 of the Powers of Criminal Courts (Sentencing) Act 2000[4], nothing in that subsection shall prevent a court from making an order under subsection (1) above for the admission of the offender to a hospital.

(1B) For the purposes of subsections (1) and (1A) above, a sentence fails to be imposed under section 109(2), 110(2) or 111(2) of the Powers of Criminal Courts (Sentencing) Act 2000 if it is required by that provision and the court is not of the opinion there mentioned.

(2) The conditions referred to in subsection (1) above are that—

(*a*) the court is satisfied, on the written or oral evidence of two registered medical practitioners, that the offender is suffering from mental illness, psychopathic disorder[3], severe mental impairment[5] or mental impairment[5] and that either—

(i) the mental disorder[5] from which the offender is suffering is of a nature or degree which makes it appropriate for him to be detained in a hospital for medical treatment and, in the case of psychopathic disorder or mental impairment, that such treatment is likely to alleviate or prevent a deterioration of his condition; or

(ii) in the case of an offender who has attained the age of 16 years, the mental disorder is of a nature or degree which warrants his reception into guardianship under this Act; and

(*b*) the court is of the opinion, having regard to all the circumstances including the nature of the offence and the character and antecedents of the offender, and to the other available methods of dealing with him, that the most suitable method of disposing of the case is by means of an order under this section.

(3) Where a person is charged before a magistrates' court[6] with any act or omission as an offence and the court would have power, on convicting him of that offence, to make an order under subsection (1) above in his case as being a person suffering from mental illness or severe mental impairment, then, if the court is satisfied that the accused did the act or made the omission charged, the court may, if it thinks fit, make such an order without convicting[7] him.

(4) An order for the admission of an offender to a hospital (in this Act referred to as "a hospital order") shall not be made under this section unless the court is satisfied on the written or oral evidence of the registered medical practitioner who would be in charge of his treatment or of some other person representing the managers of the hospital that arrangements have been made for his admission to that hospital, and for his admission to it within the period of 28 days beginning with the date of the making of such an order; and the court may, pending his admission within that period, give such directions as it thinks fit for his conveyance to and detention in a place of safety[8].

(5) If within the said period of 28 days it appears to the Secretary of State that by reason of an emergency or other special circumstances it is not practicable for the patient to be received into the hospital specified in the order, he may give directions for the admission of the patient to such other hospital as appears to be appropriate instead of the hospital so specified; and where such directions are given—

(*a*) the Secretary of State shall cause the person having the custody of the patient to be informed, and

(*b*) the hospital order shall have effect as if the hospital specified in the directions were substituted for the hospital specified in the order.

(6) An order placing an offender under the guardianship of a local social services authority or of any other person (in this Act referred to as "a guardianship order") shall not be made under this section unless the court is satisfied that that authority or person is willing to receive the offender into guardianship.

(7) A hospital order or guardianship order shall specify the form or forms of mental disorder referred to in subsection (2)(*a*) above from which, upon the evidence taken into account under that subsection, the offender is found by the court to be suffering; and no such order shall be made unless the offender is described by each of the practitioners whose evidence is taken into account under that subsection as suffering from the same one of those forms of mental disorder, whether or not he is also described by either of them as suffering from another of them.

(8) Where an order is made under this section, the court shall not—

(*a*) pass sentence of imprisonment or impose a fine or make a probation order in respect of the offence,

(*b*) if the order under this section is a hospital order, make a referral order (within the meaning of the Powers of Criminal Courts (Sentencing) Act 2000) in respect of the offence, or

(*b*) make in respect of the offender a supervision order (within the meaning of that Act) or an order under section 150 of that Act (binding over of parent or guardian), but the court may make any other order which it has power to make apart from this section; and for the purposes of this subsection "sentence of imprisonment" includes any sentence or order for detention.

[Mental Health Act 1983, s 37, as amended by the Crime (Sentences) Act 1997, Schs 4 and 6, the Crime and Disorder Act 1998, Sch 8, Youth Justice and Criminal Evidence Act 1999, Sch 4 and the Powers of Criminal Courts (Sentencing) Act 2000, Sch 9.]

1. See PART III: SENTENCING, para **3–491** for guidance on the making of orders under s 37 and consideration of restriction orders under s 41.

2. See Criminal Procedure Rules 2005, Part 49, in PART I: MAGISTRATES' COURTS, PROCEDURE, post.

A mentally disordered person guilty of an offence not punishable by imprisonment, may be remanded for report in accordance with ss 10 and 128 of the Magistrates' Courts Act 1980. See Home Office Circular No 151/1961, dated 25th August 1961.

Payment for a report may be made out of central funds; see the Criminal Justice Act 1967, s 32(2) in PART I: MAGISTRATES' COURTS, PROCEDURE, and the Prosecution of Offences Act 1985, s 19 in PART I: MAGISTRATES' COURTS, PROCEDURE, ante.

3. This power to specify a hospital includes power to specify a hospital unit (Crime (Sentences) Act 1997, s 47, in PART III: SENTENCING, ante).

4. See PART III: SENTENCING, ante.

5. For the meaning of "mental disorder", "severe mental impairment", "mental impairment" and "psychopathic disorder", see s 1, ante.

6. This includes a youth court *(R (on the application of P) v Barking Youth Court* [2002] EWHC 734 (Admin), [2002] 2 Cr App Rep 294, 166 JP 641, [2002] Crim LR 657.

7. It follows that as there is no requirement for a trial, the provisions of s 20 of the Magistrates' Courts Act 1980 (procedure where summary trial appears more suitable for an offence triable either way) do not apply. However, the circumstances in which it will be appropriate to exercise this power will be very rare and will usually require the consent of those acting for the accused if he is under a disability so that he cannot be tried *(R v Lincolnshire (Kesteven) Justices, ex p O'Connor* [1983] 1 All ER 901, [1983] 1 WLR 335). Magistrates may still proceed to act under sub-s (3) even where the defendant has elected to go for trial by jury *(R v Ramsgate Justices, ex p Kazmarek* (1984) 149 JP 16). However, a magistrates' court has no jurisdiction under s 37(3) to make an order under sub-s (1) in respect of a defendant who is charged with an offence that is triable only on indictment *(R v Chippenham Magistrates' Court, ex p Thompson* (1995) 160 JP 207). As regards s 4A of the Criminal Procedure (Insanity) Act 1964 which makes analogous provisions relating to trial on indictment, it has been held that there is no incompatibility between procedures for determining whether the defendant 'did the act' and Article 6 of the European Convention on Human Rights. The criminal charge provisions of Article 6 do not apply as these proceedings cannot result in a conviction: *R v M* [2001] EWCA Crim 2024, [2002] 1 Cr App Rep 25.

8. For meaning of "place of safety", see s 55(1), post.

9. See PART V: YOUTH COURTS, ante.

8–22233 **38. Interim hospital orders.** (1) Where a person is convicted before the Crown Court of an offence punishable with imprisonment (other than an offence the sentence for which is fixed by law) or is convicted by a magistrates' court of an offence punishable on summary conviction with imprisonment and the court before or by which he is convicted is satisfied, on the written or oral evidence of two registered medical practitioners—

(*a*) that the offender is suffering from mental illness, psychopathic disorder, severe mental impairment or mental impairment; and

(*b*) that there is reason to suppose that the mental disorder from which the offender is suffering is such that it may be appropriate for a hospital order to be made in his case,

the court may, before making a hospital order or dealing with him in some other way, make an order (in this Act referred to as "an interim hospital order") authorising his admission to such hospital as may be specified in the order and his detention there in accordance with this section.

(2) In the case of an offender who is subject to an interim hospital order the court may make a hospital order without his being brought before the court if he is represented by counsel or a solicitor and his counsel or solicitor is given an opportunity of being heard.

(3) At least one of the registered medical practitioners whose evidence is taken into account under subsection (1) above shall be employed at the hospital which is to be specified in the order.

(4) An interim hospital order shall not be made for the admission of an offender to a hospital unless the court is satisfied, on the written or oral evidence of the registered medical practitioner who would be in charge of his treatment or of some other person representing the managers of the hospital, that arrangements have been made for his admission to that hospital and for his admission to it within the period of 28 days beginning with the date of the order; and if the court is so satisfied the court may, pending his admission, give directions for his conveyance to and detention in a place of safety.

(5) An interim hospital order—

(*a*) shall be in force for such period, not exceeding 12 weeks, as the court may specify when making the order; but

(*b*) may be renewed for further periods of not more than 28 days at a time if it appears to the court, on the written or oral evidence of the responsible medical officer, that the continuation of the order is warranted;

but no such order shall continue in force for more than 12 months in all and the court shall terminate the order if it makes a hospital order in respect of the offender or decides after considering the written or oral evidence of the responsible medical officer to deal with the offender in some other way.

(6) The power of renewing an interim hospital order may be exercised without the offender being brought before the court if he is represented by counsel or a solicitor and his counsel or solicitor is given an opportunity of being heard.

(7) If an offender absconds from a hospital in which he is detained in pursuance of an interim hospital order, or while being conveyed to or from such a hospital, he may be arrested[1] without warrant by a constable and shall, after being arrested, be brought as soon as practicable before the court that made the order; and the court may thereupon terminate the order and deal with him in any way in which it could have dealt with him if no such order had been made.

[Mental Health Act 1983, s 38, as amended by the Crime (Sentences) Act 1997, s 49.]

1. This power of arrest is preserved by the Police and Criminal Evidence Act 1984, s 26 and Sch 2.

8–22234 39. Information as to hospitals. (1) Where a court is minded to make a hospital order or interim hospital order in respect of any person it may request—

(*a*) the Health Authority for the area in which that person resides or last resided; or

(*b*) any other Health Authority that appears to the court to be appropriate,

to furnish[1] the court with such information as that Health Authority have or can reasonably obtain with respect to the hospital or hospitals (if any) in their area or elsewhere at which arrangements could be made for the admission of that person in pursuance of the order, and that Health Authority shall comply with any such request.

(2) *Repealed.*

[Mental Health Act 1983, s 39, as amended by the Health Authorities Act 1995, Schs 1 and 3.]

1. In cases where it is desired to make use of this provision, the Clerk to the Justices should contact the Regional Medical Officer for the Regional Health Authority covering the area from which the offender appears to come; see Home Office Circular No 69/1983, dated 19th August 1983.

8–22235 39A. Information to facilitate guardianship orders. Where a court is minded to make a guardianship order in respect of any offender, it may request the local social services authority for the area in which the offender resides or last resided, or any other local social services authority that appears to the court to be appropriate—

(*a*) to inform the court whether it or any other person approved by it is willing to receive the offender into guardianship; and

(*b*) if so, to give such information as it reasonably can about how it or the other person could be expected to exercise in relation to the offender the powers conferred by section 40(2) below;

and that authority shall comply with any such request.

[Mental Health Act 1983, s 39A added by the Criminal Justice Act 1991, s 27(1).]

8–22236 40. Effect of hospital orders, guardianship orders and interim hospital orders. (1) A hospital order shall be sufficient authority—

(*a*) for a constable, an approved social worker[1] or any other person directed to do so by the court to convey the patient to the hospital specified in the order within a period of 28 days; and

(*b*) for the managers of the hospital to admit him at any time within that period and thereafter detain him in accordance with the provisions of this Act.

(2) A guardianship order shall confer on the authority or person named in the order as guardian the same powers as a guardianship application made and accepted under Part II[2] of this Act.

(3) Where an interim hospital order is made in respect of an offender—

(*a*) a constable or any other person directed to do so by the court shall convey the offender to the hospital specified in the order within the period mentioned in section 38(4) above; and

(*b*) the managers of the hospital shall admit him within that period and thereafter detain him in accordance with the provisions of section 38 above.

(4) A patient who is admitted to a hospital in pursuance of a hospital order, or placed under guardianship by a guardianship order, shall, subject to the provisions of this subsection, be treated for the purposes of the provisions of this Act mentioned in Part I of Schedule 1 to this Act as if he had been so admitted or placed on the date of the order in pursuance of an application for admission for treatment or a guardianship application, as the case may be, duly made under Part II[2] of this Act, but subject to any modifications of those provisions specified in that Part of that Schedule.

(5) Where a patient is admitted to a hospital in pursuance of a hospital order, or placed under guardianship by a guardianship order, any previous application, hospital order or guardianship order by virtue of which he was liable to be detained in a hospital or subject to guardianship shall cease to have effect; but if the first-mentioned order, or the conviction on which it was made, is quashed on appeal, this subsection shall not apply and section 22 above shall have effect as if during any period for which the patient was liable to be detained or subject to guardianship under the order, he had been detained in custody as mentioned in that section.

(6) Where—

(*a*) a patient admitted to a hospital in pursuance of a hospital order is absent without leave;
(*b*) a warrant to arrest him has been issued under section 72 of the Criminal Justice Act 1967;
(*c*) he is held pursuant to the warrant in any country or territory other than the United Kingdom, any of the Channel Islands and the Isle of Man,

he shall be treated as having been taken into custody under section 18 above on first being so held.
[Mental Health Act 1983, s 40, as amended by the Mental Health (Patients in the Community) Act 1995, s 2.]

1. For the meaning of "approved social worker", see s 145, post.
2. The provisions of Pt II of the Act are not included in this work.

Restriction orders

8–22237 **41. Power[1] of higher courts to restrict discharge from hospital.** (1) Where a hospital order is made in respect of an offender by the Crown Court, and it appears to the court, having regard to the nature of the offence, the antecedents of the offender and the risk of his committing further offences if set at large, that it is necessary for the protection of the public from serious harm so to do[2], the court may, subject to the provisions of this section, further order that the offender shall be subject to the special restrictions set out in this section, either without limit of time or during such period as may be specified in the order; and an order under this section shall be known as "a restriction order".

(2) A restriction order shall not be made in the case of any person unless at least one of the registered medical practitioners whose evidence is taken into account by the court under section 37(2)(*a*) above has given evidence orally before the court.

(3) The special restrictions applicable to a patient in respect of whom a restriction order is in force are as follows—

(*a*) none of the provisions of Part II[3] of this Act relating to the duration, renewal and expiration of authority for the detention of patients shall apply, and the patient shall continue to be liable to be detained by virtue of the relevant hospital order until he is duly discharged under the said Part II[3] or absolutely discharged under section 42, 73, 74 or 75 below;
(*aa*) none of the provisions of Part II of this Act relating to after-care under supervision shall apply;
(*b*) no application shall be made to a Mental Health Review Tribunal in respect of a patient under section 66 or 69(1) below;
(*c*) the following powers shall be exercisable only with the consent of the Secretary of State, namely—
   (i) power to grant leave of absence to the patient under section 17 above;
   (ii) power to transfer the patient in pursuance of regulations under section 19 above or in pursuance of subsection (3) of that section; and
   (iii) power to order the discharge of the patient under section 23 above;

   and if leave of absence is granted under the said section 17 power to recall the patient under that section shall vest in the Secretary of State as well as the responsible medical officer; and
(*d*) the power of the Secretary of State to recall the patient under the said section 17 and power to take the patient into custody and return him under section 18 above may be exercised at any time;

and in relation to any such patient section 40(4) above shall have effect as if it referred to Part II of Schedule 1 to this Act instead of Part I of that Schedule.

(4) A hospital order shall not cease to have effect under section 40(5) above if a restriction order in respect of the patient is in force at the material time.

(5) Where a restriction order in respect of a patient ceases to have effect while the relevant hospital order continues in force, the provisions of section 40 above and Part I of Schedule 1 to this Act shall apply to the patient as if he had been admitted to the hospital in pursuance of a hospital order (without a restriction order) made on the date on which the restriction order ceased to have effect.

(6) While a person is subject to a restriction order the responsible medical officer shall at such intervals (not exceeding one year) as the Secretary of State may direct examine and report to the Secretary of State on that person; and every report shall contain such particulars as the Secretary of State may require.

[Mental Health Act 1983, s 41, as amended by the Mental Health (Patients in the Community) Act 1995, Sch 1 and the Crime (Sentences) Act 1997, s 49.]

1. The provisions of Pt II of the Act are not included in this work. See also *R v Birch* (1989) 90 Cr App Rep 78, where the principles applicable to the imposition of a restriction order were considered.

2. Before a restriction order can be made there must be evidence which points to the likely fact that if the offender were released in the relatively near future he would constitute a danger to other members of the public (*R v Courtney* [1988] Crim LR 130). See also *R v Kearney* [2002] EWCA Crim 2772, [2003] 2 Cr App Rep (S) 85 (it is not part of the justification for a restriction order that it might help or add to the protection of the offender himself).

3. See PART III: SENTENCING, para **3–491** for guidance on the making of orders under s 37 and consideration of restriction orders under s 41.

8–22238 42. Powers of Secretary of State in respect of patients subject to restriction orders. (1) If the Secretary of State is satisfied that in the case of any patient a restriction order is no longer required for the protection of the public from serious harm, he may direct that the patient shall cease to be subject to the special restrictions set out in section 41(3) above; and where the Secretary of State so directs, the restriction order shall cease to have effect, and section 41(5) above shall apply accordingly.

(2) At any time while a restriction order is in force in respect of a patient, the Secretary of State may, if he thinks fit, by warrant discharge the patient from hospital, either absolutely or subject to conditions; and where a person is absolutely discharged under this subsection, he shall thereupon cease to be liable to be detained by virtue of the relevant hospital order, and the restriction order shall cease to have effect accordingly.

(3) The Secretary of State may at any time during the continuance in force of a restriction order in respect of a patient who has been conditionally discharged under subsection (2) above by warrant recall[1] the patient to such hospital as may be specified in the warrant.

(4) Where a patient is recalled as mentioned in subsection (3) above—

(*a*) if the hospital specified in the warrant is not the hospital from which the patient was conditionally discharged, the hospital order and the restriction order shall have effect as if the hospital specified in the warrant were substituted for the hospital specified in the hospital order;

(*b*) in any case, the patient shall be treated for the purposes of section 18 above as if he had absented himself without leave from the hospital specified in the warrant, and, if the restriction order was made for a specified period, that period shall not in any event expire until the patient returns to the hospital or is returned to the hospital under that section.

(5) If a restriction order in respect of a patient ceases to have effect after the patient has been conditionally discharged under this section, the patient shall, unless previously recalled under subsection (3) above, be deemed to be absolutely discharged on the date when the order ceases to have effect, and shall cease to be liable to be detained by virtue of the relevant hospital order accordingly.

(6) The Secretary of State may, if satisfied that the attendance at any place in Great Britain of a patient who is subject to a restriction order is desirable in the interests of justice or for the purposes of any public inquiry, direct him to be taken to that place; and where a patient is directed under this subsection to be taken to any place he shall, unless the Secretary of State otherwise directs, be kept in custody while being so taken, while at that place and while being taken back to the hospital in which he is liable to be detained.

[Mental Health Act 1983, s 42.]

---

1. "Recall" may refer not only to a physical recall to hospital but also to the reinstatement of a regime of control under s 41 such as in respect of a patient previously discharged conditionally by a Mental Health Review Tribunal but subsequently readmitted under s 3 of the Act (*R v Secretary of State for the Home Department, ex p D* (1996) Times, 10 May, CA).

8–22239 43. Power of magistrates' courts to commit for restriction order. (1) If in the case of a person of or over the age of 14 years who is convicted by a magistrates' court of an offence punishable on summary conviction with imprisonment[1]—

(*a*) the conditions which under section 37(1) above are required to be satisfied for the making of a hospital order are satisfied in respect of the offender; but

(*b*) it appears to the court, having regard to the nature of the offence, the antecedents[2] of the offender and the risk of his committing further offences if set at large, that if a hospital order is made a restriction order should also be made[3],

the court may, instead of making a hospital order or dealing with him in any other manner, commit him in custody to the Crown Court[4] to be dealt with in respect of the offence[5].

(2) Where an offender is committed to the Crown Court under this section, the Crown Court shall inquire into the circumstances of the case and may—

(*a*) if that court would have power so to do under the foregoing provisions of this Part of this Act upon the conviction of the offender before that court of such an offence as is described in section 37(1) above, make a hospital order in his case, with or without a restriction order;

(*b*) if the court does not make such an order, deal with the offender in any other manner in which the magistrates' court might have dealt with him.

(3) The Crown Court shall have the same power to make orders under sections 35, 36 and 38 above in the case of a person committed to the court under this section as the Crown Court has under those sections in the case of an accused person within the meaning of section 35 or 36 above or of a person convicted before that court as mentioned in section 38 above.

(4) The power of a magistrates' court under section 3 of the Powers of Criminal Courts (Sentencing) Act 2000 (which enables such a court to commit an offender to the Crown Court where the court is of the opinion that greater punishment should be inflicted for the offence than the court has power to inflict) shall also be exercisable by a magistrates' court where it is of the opinion that

greater punishment should be inflicted as aforesaid on the offender unless a hospital order is made in his case with a restriction order.

(5) The power of the Crown Court to make a hospital order, with or without a restriction order, in the case of a person convicted before that court of an offence may, in the same circumstances and subject to the same conditions, be exercised by such a court in the case of a person committed to the court under section 5 of the Vagrancy Act 1824 (which provides for the committal to the Crown Court of persons who are incorrigible rogues within the meaning of that section).

[Mental Health Act 1983, s 43, as amended by the Powers of Criminal Courts (Sentencing) Act 2000, Sch 9.]

1. This means, so punishable in the case of an adult. Statutory restrictions imposed on the imprisonment of young offenders have no application in construing this expression (s 54(2), post).

2. Under s 38 of the Magistrates' Courts Act 1980 before it was substituted by the Criminal Justice Act 1991, "antecedents" was not limited to previous convictions.

3. The provisions of this section supply the only means whereby a magistrates' court can secure that an order is made restricting an offender's discharge.

4. For selection of the most convenient location of the Crown Court, see the Directions of the Lord Chief Justice, paras 8 and 9, in PART I: MAGISTRATES' COURTS, PROCEDURE, ante.

5. See Criminal Procedure Rules 2005, r 43.2, in PART I: MAGISTRATES' COURTS, PROCEDURE, ante.

8–22240 44. Committal to hospital under s 43. (1) Where an offender is committed under section 43(1) above and the magistrates' court by which he is committed is satisfied on written or oral evidence that arrangements have been made for the admission of the offender to a hospital in the event of an order being made under this section, the court may, instead of committing him in custody, by order direct him to be admitted to that hospital, specifying it, and to be detained there until the case is disposed of by the Crown Court, and may give such directions as it thinks fit for his production from the hospital to attend the Crown Court by which his case is to be dealt with[1].

(2) The evidence required by subsection (1) above shall be given by the registered medical practitioner who would be in charge of the offender's treatment or by some other person representing the managers of the hospital in question.

(3) The power to give directions under section 37(4) above, section 37(5) above and section 40(1) above shall apply in relation to an order under this section as they apply in relation to a hospital order, but as if references to the period of 28 days mentioned in section 40(1) above were omitted; and subject as aforesaid an order under this section shall, until the offender's case is disposed of by the Crown Court, have the same effect as a hospital order together with a restriction order, made without limitation of time.

[Mental Health Act 1983, s 44.]

1. See the Criminal Procedure Rules 2005, Part 49 in PART I: MAGISTRATES' COURTS, PROCEDURE, ante.

8–22241 45. Appeals from magistrates' courts. (1) Where on the trial of an information charging a person with an offence a magistrates' court makes a hospital order or guardianship order in respect of him without convicting him, he shall have the same right of appeal against the order as if it had been made on his conviction[1]; and on any such appeal the Crown Court shall have the same powers as if the appeal had been against both conviction and sentence.

(2) An appeal by a child or young person with respect to whom any such order has been made, whether the appeal is against the order or against the finding upon which the order was made, may be brought by him or by his parent or guardian on his behalf.

[Mental Health Act 1983, s 45.]

1. See Magistrates' Courts Act 1980, ss 108–114 and Criminal Procedure Rules 2005, Part 63, in PART I: MAGISTRATES' COURTS, PROCEDURE, ante.

Hospital and limitation directions

8–22241A 45A. Power of higher courts to direct hospital admission. (1) This section applies where, in the case of a person convicted before the Crown Court of an offence the sentence for which is not fixed by law—

(*a*) the conditions mentioned in subsection (2) below are fulfilled; and

(*b*) except where the offence is one the sentence for which falls to be imposed under section 2 of the Crime (Sentences) Act 1997, the court considers making a hospital order in respect of him before deciding to impose a sentence of imprisonment ("the relevant sentence") in respect of the offence.

(2) The conditions referred to in subsection (1) above are that the court is satisfied, on the written or oral evidence of two registered medical practitioners—

(*a*) that the offender is suffering from psychopathic disorder;

(*b*) that the mental disorder from which the offender is suffering is of a nature or degree which makes it appropriate for him to be detained in a hospital for medical treatment; and

(*c*) that such treatment is likely to alleviate or prevent a deterioration of his condition.

(3) The court may give both of the following directions, namely—

(*a*) a direction that, instead of being removed to and detained in a prison, the offender be removed to and detained in such hospital[1] as may be specified in the direction (in this Act referred to as a "hospital direction"); and

(*b*) a direction that the offender be subject to the special restrictions set out in section 41 above (in this Act referred to as a "limitation direction").

(4) A hospital direction and a limitation direction shall not be given in relation to an offender unless at least one of the medical practitioners whose evidence is taken into account by the court under subsection (2) above has given evidence orally before the court.

(5) A hospital direction and a limitation direction shall not be given in relation to an offender unless the court is satisfied on the written or oral evidence of the registered medical practitioner who would be in charge of his treatment, or of some other person representing the managers of the hospital that arrangements have been made—

(*a*) for his admission to that hospital; and

(*b*) for his admission to it within the period of 28 days beginning with the day of the giving of such directions;

and the court may, pending his admission within that period, give such directions as it thinks fit for his conveyance to and detention in a place of safety.

(6) If within the said period of 28 days it appears to the Secretary of State that by reason of an emergency or other special circumstances it is not practicable for the patient to be received into the hospital specified in the hospital direction, he may give instructions for the admission of the patient to such other hospital as appears to be appropriate instead of the hospital so specified.

(7) Where such instructions are given—

(*a*) the Secretary of State shall cause the person having the custody of the patient to be informed, and

(*b*) the hospital direction shall have effect as if the hospital specified in the instructions were substituted for the hospital specified in the hospital direction.

(8) Section 38(1) and (5) and section 39 above shall have effect as if any reference to the making of a hospital order included a reference to the giving of a hospital direction and a limitation direction.

(9) A hospital direction and a limitation direction given in relation to an offender shall have effect not only as regards the relevant sentence but also (so far as applicable) as regards any other sentence of imprisonment imposed on the same or a previous occasion.

(10) The Secretary of State may by order provide that this section shall have effect as if the reference in subsection (2) above to psychopathic disorder included a reference to a mental disorder of such other description as may be specified in the order.

(11) An order made under this section may—

(*a*) apply generally, or in relation to such classes of offenders or offences as may be specified in the order;

(*b*) provide that any reference in this section to a sentence of imprisonment, or to a prison, shall include a reference to a custodial sentence, or to an institution, of such description as may be so specified; and

(*c*) include such supplementary, incidental or consequential provisions as appear to the Secretary of State to be necessary or expedient.

[Mental Health Act 1983, s 45A, as inserted by the Crime (Sentences) Act 1997, s 46.]

---

1. This power to specify a hospital includes power to specify a hospital unit (Crime (Sentences) Act 1997, s 47, in PART III: SENTENCING, ante).

8–22241B 45B. Effect of hospital and limitation directions. (1) A hospital direction and a limitation direction shall be sufficient authority—

(*a*) for a constable or any other person directed to do so by the court to convey the patient to the hospital specified in the hospital direction within a period of 28 days; and

(*b*) for the managers of the hospital to admit him at any time within that period and thereafter detain him in accordance with the provisions of this Act.

(2) With respect to any person—

(*a*) a hospital direction shall have effect as a transfer direction; and

(*b*) a limitation direction shall have effect as a restriction direction.

(3) While a person is subject to a hospital direction and a limitation direction the responsible medical officer shall at such intervals (not exceeding one year) as the Secretary of State may direct examine and report to the Secretary of State on that person; and every report shall contain such particulars as the Secretary of State may require.

[Mental Health Act 1983, s 45B, as inserted by the Crime (Sentences) Act 1997, s 46.]

Detention during Her Majesty's pleasure

8–22242 **46. Persons ordered to be kept in custody during Her Majesty's pleasure.** (1) The Secretary of State may by warrant direct that any person who, by virtue of any enactment to which this subsection applies, is required to be kept in custody during Her Majesty's pleasure or until the directions of Her Majesty are known shall be detained in such hospital (not being a registered establishment) as may be specified in the warrant and, where that person is not already detained in the hospital, give directions for his removal there.

(2) The enactments to which subsection (1) above applies are section 16 of the Courts-Martial (Appeals) Act 1968, section 116 of the Army Act 1955, section 116 of the Air Force Act 1955 and section 63 of the Naval Discipline Act 1957.

(3) A direction under this section in respect of any person shall have the same effect as a hospital order together with a restriction order, made without limitation of time; and where such a direction is given in respect of a person while he is in the hospital, he shall be deemed to be admitted in pursuance of, and on the date of, the direction.*

[Mental Health Act 1983, s 46, as amended by the Care Standards Act 2000, s 116.]

***Repealed by the Armed Forces Act 1996, Sch 7, when in force.**

Transfer to hospital of prisoners, etc

8–22243 **47. Removal to hospital of persons serving sentences of imprisonment, etc.** (1) If in the case of a person serving a sentence of imprisonment the Secretary of State is satisfied, by reports from at least two registered medical practitioners—

(*a*) that the said person is suffering from mental illness, psychopathic disorder, severe mental impairment or mental impairment; and

(*b*) that the mental disorder from which that person is suffering is of a nature or degree which makes it appropriate for him to be detained in a hospital for medical treatment and, in the case of psychopathic disorder or mental impairment, that such treatment is likely to alleviate or prevent a deterioration of his condition;

the Secretary of State may, if he is of the opinion having regard to the public interest and all the circumstances that it is expedient so to do, by warrant direct that that person be removed to and detained in such hospital[1] as may be specified in the direction; and a direction under this section shall be known as "a transfer direction".

(2) A transfer direction shall cease to have effect at the expiration of the period of 14 days beginning with the date on which it is given unless within that period the person with respect to whom it was given has been received into the hospital specified in the direction.

(3) A transfer direction with respect to any person shall have the same effect as a hospital order made in his case.

(4) A transfer direction shall specify the form or forms of mental disorder referred to in paragraph (*a*) of subsection (1) above from which, upon the reports taken into account under that subsection, the patient is found by the Secretary of State to be suffering; and no such direction shall be given unless the patient is described in each of those reports as suffering from the same form of disorder, whether or not he is also described in either of them as suffering from another form.

(5) References in this Part of this Act to a person serving a sentence[2] of imprisonment include references—

(*a*) to a person detained in pursuance of any sentence or order for detention made by a court in criminal proceedings (other than an order made in consequence of a finding of insanity or unfitness to stand trial);

(*b*) to a person committed to custody under section 115(3) of the Magistrates' Courts Act 1980[4] (which relates to persons who fail to comply with an order to enter into recognisances to keep the peace or be of good behaviour); and

(*c*) to a person committed by a court to a prison or other institution to which the Prison Act 1952 applies in default of payment of any sum adjudged to be paid on his conviction.

[Mental Health Act 1983, s 47, as amended by the Crime (Sentences) Act 1997, s 49 and Sch 6 and the Domestic Violence, Crime and Victims Act 2004, Sch 10.]

1. This power to specify a hospital includes power to specify a hospital unit (Crime (Sentences) Act 1997, s 47, in PART III: SENTENCING, ante).

2. This shall not be construed as references to a person subject to an order of the Court of Appeal under ss 6 and 14 of the Criminal Appeal Act 1968.

3. This exception extends to orders made under the Criminal Procedure (Insanity) Act 1964, s 5(1)(*a*) or (*c*) (Criminal Procedure (Insanity) Act 1964, s 5(6)).

4. See PART I: MAGISTRATES' COURTS, PROCEDURE, ante.

8–22244 **48. Removal to hospital of other prisoners.** (1) If in the case of a person to whom this section applies the Secretary of State is satisfied by the same reports as are required for the purposes of section 47 above that that person is suffering from mental illness or severe mental impairment of a nature or degree which makes it appropriate for him to be detained in a hospital for medical treatment and that he is in urgent need of such treatment, the Secretary of State shall have the same power of giving a transfer direction in respect of him under that section as if he were serving a sentence of imprisonment.

(2) This section applies to the following persons, that is to say—

(*a*) persons detained in a prison or remand centre*, not being persons serving a sentence of imprisonment or persons falling within the following paragraphs of this subsection;

(*b*) persons remanded in custody by a magistrates' court[1];

(*c*) civil prisoners, that is to say, persons committed by a court to prison for a limited term, who are not persons falling to be dealt with under section 47 above;

(*d*) persons detained under the Immigration Act 1971 or under section 62 of the Nationality, Immigration and Asylum Act 2002 (detention by the Secretary of State).

(3) Subsections (2) to (4) of section 47 above shall apply for the purposes of this section and of any transfer direction given by virtue of this section as they apply for the purposes of that section and of any transfer direction under that section.

[Mental Health Act 1983, s 48, as amended by the Nationality, Immigration and Asylum Act 2002, s 62 and the Statute Law (Repeals) Act 2004.]

***Repealed by the Criminal Justice and Court Services Act 2000, Sch 7 from a date to be appointed.**

1. Where a transfer direction is made under this section in respect of a person remanded in custody by a magistrates' court, and, during its currency, that person is committed for trial, prescribed notice shall be sent to the hospital where he is detained and to the governor of the prison to which he could normally have been committed (Criminal Procedure Rules 2005, Part 19, in PART I: MAGISTRATES' COURTS, PROCEDURE, ante).

8–22245 **49. Restriction on discharge of prisoners removed to hospital.** (1) Where a transfer direction is given in respect of any person, the Secretary of State, if he thinks fit, may by warrant further direct that that person shall be subject to the special restrictions set out in section 41 above; and where the Secretary of State gives a transfer direction in respect of any such person as is described in paragraph (*a*) or (*b*) of section 48(2) above, he shall also give a direction under this section applying those restrictions to him.

(2) A direction under this section shall have the same effect as a restriction order made under section 41 above and shall be known as "a restriction direction".

(3) While a person is subject to a restriction direction the responsible medical officer shall at such intervals (not exceeding one year) as the Secretary of State may direct examine and report to the Secretary of State on that person; and every report shall contain such particulars as the Secretary of State may require.

[Mental Health Act 1983, s 49.]

8–22246 **50. Further provisions as to prisoners under sentence.** (1) Where a transfer direction and a restriction direction have been given in respect of a person serving a sentence of imprisonment and before the expiration of that person's sentence the Secretary of State is notified by the responsible medical officer[1], any other registered medical practitioner or a Mental Health Review Tribunal that that person no longer requires treatment in hospital for mental disorder or that no effective treatment for his disorder can be given in the hospital to which he has been removed, the Secretary of State may—

(*a*) by warrant direct that he be remitted to any prison or other institution in which he might have been detained if he had not been removed to hospital, there to be dealt with as if he had not been so removed; or

(*b*) exercise any power of releasing him on licence or discharging him under supervision which could have been exercisable if he had been remitted to such a prison or institution as aforesaid,

and on his arrival in the prison or other institution or, as the case may be, his release or discharge as aforesaid, the transfer direction and the restriction direction shall cease to have effect.

(2) A restriction direction in the case of a person serving a sentence of imprisonment shall cease to have effect on the expiration of the sentence.

(3) Subject to subsection (4) below, references in this section to the expiration of a person's sentence are references to the expiration of the period during which he would have been liable to be detained in a prison or other institution if the transfer direction had not been given.

(3A)[1] In applying subsection (3) above account shall be taken of any early release days awarded to the person under section 11 of the Crime (Sentences) Act 1997 (read with section 22 of that Act).

(4) For the purposes of section 49(2) of the Prison Act 1952 (which provides for discounting from the sentences of certain prisoners periods while they are unlawfully at large) a patient who, having been transferred in pursuance of a transfer direction from any such institution as is referred to in that section, is at large in circumstances in which he is liable to be taken into custody under any provision of this Act, shall be treated as unlawfully at large and absent from that institution.

(5) The preceding provisions of this section shall have effect as if—

(*a*) the reference in subsection (1) to a transfer direction and a restriction direction having been given in respect of a person serving a sentence of imprisonment included a reference to a hospital direction and a limitation direction having been given in respect of a person sentenced to imprisonment;

(*b*) the reference in subsection (2) to a restriction direction included a reference to a limitation direction; and

(*c*) references in subsections (3) and (4) to a transfer direction included references to a hospital direction.

[Mental Health Act 1983, s 50, as amended by the Criminal Justice Act 1991, Sch 13 and the Crime (Sentences) Act 1997, Sch 4.]

---

1. When applying the "treatability" test, the clinical judgment is that of the RMO who is not under a duty to disclose reports on individual components of the patient's medical regime or to present contrary views expressed by some members of the inter-disciplinary team, although he is under a duty to make proper inquiries and consider views expressed: *R (Morley) v Nottinghamshire Health Care NHS Trust* [2002] EWCA Civ 1728, [2003] 1 All ER 784.

2. At the date of going to press, subsection (3A) which is to be inserted by the Crime (Sentences) Act 1997, Sch 4, para 12, had not been brought into force.

8–22247 **51. Further provisions as to detained persons.** (1) This section has effect where a transfer direction has been given in respect of any such person as is described in paragraph (*a*) of section 48(2) above and that person is in this section referred to as "the detainee".

(2) The transfer direction shall cease to have effect when the detainee's case is disposed of by the court having jurisdiction to try or otherwise deal with him, but without prejudice to any power of that court to make a hospital order or other order under this Part of this Act in his case.

(3) If the Secretary of State is notified by the responsible medical officer, any other registered medical practitioner or a Mental Health Review Tribunal at any time before the detainee's case is disposed of by that court—

(*a*) that the detainee no longer requires treatment in hospital for mental disorder; or

(*b*) that no effective treatment for his disorder can be given at the hospital to which he has been removed,

the Secretary of State may by warrant direct that he be remitted to any place where he might have been detained if he had not been removed to hospital, there to be dealt with as if he had not been so removed, and on his arrival at the place to which he is so remitted the transfer direction shall cease to have effect.

(4) If (no direction having been given under subsection (3) above) the court having jurisdiction to try or otherwise deal with the detainee is satisfied on the written or oral evidence of the responsible medical officer—

(*a*) that the detainee no longer requires treatment in hospital for mental disorder; or

(*b*) that no effective treatment for his disorder can be given at the hospital to which he has been removed,

the court may order him to be remitted to any such place as is mentioned in subsection (3) above or, subject to section 25 of the Criminal Justice and Public Order Act 1994, released on bail and on his arrival at that place or, as the case may be, his release on bail the transfer direction shall cease to have effect.

(5) If (no direction or order having been given or made under subsection (3) or (4) above) it appears to the court having jurisdiction to try or otherwise deal with the detainee—

(*a*) that it is impracticable or inappropriate[1] to bring the detainee before the court; and

(*b*) that the conditions set out in subsection (6) below are satisfied,

the court may make a hospital order (with or without a restriction order) in his case in his absence and, in the case of a person awaiting trial, without convicting him.

(6) A hospital order may be made in respect of a person under subsection (5) above if the court—

(*a*) is satisfied, on the written or oral evidence of at least two registered medical practitioners, that the detainee is suffering from mental illness or severe mental impairment of a nature or degree which makes it appropriate for the patient to be detained in a hospital for medical treatment; and

(*b*) is of the opinion, after considering any depositions or other documents required to be sent to the proper officer of the court, that it is proper to make such an order.

(7) Where a person committed to the Crown Court to be dealt with under section 43 above is admitted to a hospital in pursuance of an order under section 44 above, subsections (5) and (6) above shall apply as if he were a person subject to a transfer direction.

[Mental Health Act 1983, s 51, as amended by the Criminal Justice and Public Order Act 1994, Sch 10.]

---

1. Where the defendant is in the court building no question of impracticability for the purposes of s 51(5)(a) arises and "inappropriate" must be construed restrictively as to pass sentence, without convicting, is a drastic step; although it is not necessary to construe "inappropriate" as meaning "physically impossible" a high degree of disablement or physical disorder needs to be present: *R (on the application of Kenneally) v Crown Court at Snaresbrook* [2001] EWHC Admin 968, [2002] QB 1169, [2002] 2 WLR 1430..

8–22248 52. Further provisions as to persons remanded by magistrates' courts. (1) This section has effect where a transfer direction has been given in respect of any such person as is described in paragraph (*b*) of section 48(2) above; and that person is in this section referred to as "the accused".

(2) Subject to subsection (5) below, the transfer direction shall cease to have effect on the expiration of the period of remand unless the accused is committed in custody to the Crown Court for trial or to be otherwise dealt with.

(3) Subject to subsection (4) below, the power of further remanding[1] the accused under section 128 of the Magistrates' Courts Act 1980 may be exercised by the court without his being brought before the court; and if the court further remands the accused in custody (whether or not he is brought before the court) the period of remand shall, for the purposes of this section, be deemed not to have expired.

(4) The court shall not under subsection (3) above further remand the accused in his absence unless he has appeared before the court within the previous six months.

(5) If the magistrates' court is satisfied, on the written or oral evidence of the responsible medical officer—

(*a*) that the accused no longer requires treatment in hospital for mental disorder; or

(*b*) that no effective treatment for his disorder can be given in the hospital to which he has been removed,

the court may direct that the transfer direction shall cease to have effect notwithstanding that the period of remand has not expired or that the accused is committed to the Crown Court as mentioned in subsection (2) above.

(6) If the accused is committed to the Crown Court as mentioned in subsection (2) above and the transfer direction has not ceased to have effect under subsection (5) above, section 51 above shall apply as if the transfer direction given in his case were a direction given in respect of a person falling within that section.

(7) The magistrates' court may, in the absence of the accused, inquire as examining justices into an offence alleged to have been committed by him and commit him for trial in accordance with section 6 of the Magistrates' Courts Act 1980 if—

(*a*) the court is satisfied, on the written or oral evidence of the responsible medical officer, that the accused is unfit to take part in the proceedings; and

(*b*) where the court proceeds under subsection (1) of that section, the accused is represented by counsel or a solicitor.

[Mental Health Act 1983, s 52.]

1. Notice of the further remand must be sent by the court to the managers of the hospital (Criminal Procedure Rules 2005, Part 19, in PART I: MAGISTRATES' COURTS, PROCEDURE, ante).

8–22249 53. Further provisions as to civil prisoners and persons detained under the Immigration Acts. (1) Subject to subsection (2) below, a transfer direction given in respect of any such person as is described in paragraph (*c*) or (*d*) of section 48(2) above shall cease to have effect on the expiration of the period during which he would, but for his removal to hospital, be liable to be detained in the place from which he was removed.

(2) Where a transfer direction and a restriction direction have been given in respect of any such person as is mentioned in subsection (1) above, then, if the Secretary of State is notified by the responsible medical officer, any other registered medical practitioner or a Mental Health Review Tribunal at any time before the expiration of the period there mentioned—

(*a*) that that person no longer requires treatment in hospital for mental disorder; or

(*b*) that no effective treatment for his disorder can be given in the hospital to which he has been removed,

the Secretary of State may by warrant direct that he be remitted to any place where he might have been detained if he had not been removed to hospital, and on his arrival at the place to which he is so remitted the transfer direction and the restriction direction shall cease to have effect.

[Mental Health Act 1983, s 53, as amended by the Nationality, Immigration and Asylum Act 2002, s 62.]

Supplemental

8–22259 54. Requirements as to medical evidence. (1) The registered medical practitioner whose evidence is taken into account under section 35(3)(*a*) above and at least one of the registered medical practitioners whose evidence is taken into account under sections 36(1), 37(2)(*a*), 38(1), 45A(2) and 51(6)(*a*) above and whose reports are taken into account under sections 47(1) and 48(1) above shall be a practitioner approved for the purposes of section 12 above by the Secretary of State as having special experience in the diagnosis or treatment of mental disorder.

(2) For the purposes of any provision of this Part of this Act under which a court may act on the written evidence of—

(*a*) a registered medical practitioner or a registered medical practitioner of any description; or (*b*) a person representing the managers of a hospital,

a report in writing purporting to be signed by a registered medical practitioner or a registered medical practitioner of such a description or by a person representing the managers of a hospital may, subject to the provisions of this section, be received in evidence without proof of the signature of the practitioner or that person and without proof that he has the requisite qualifications or authority or is of the requisite description; but the court may require the signatory of any such report to be called to give oral evidence.

(3) Where, in pursuance of a direction of the court, any such report is tendered in evidence otherwise than by or on behalf of the person who is the subject of the report, then—

(*a*) if that person is represented by counsel or a solicitor, a copy of the report shall be given to his counsel or solicitor;

(*b*) if that person is not so represented, the substance of the report shall be disclosed to him or, where he is a child or young person, to his parent or guardian if present in court[1]; and

(*c*) except where the report relates only to arrangements for his admission to a hospital, that person may require the signatory of the report to be called to give oral evidence, and evidence to rebut the evidence contained in the report may be called by or on behalf of that person[1].

[Mental Health Act 1983, s 54, as amended by the Crime (Sentences) Act 1997, Sch 4.]

1. In relation to children and young persons, these provisions override the Criminal Procedure Rules 2005, Part 44 in PART I: MAGISTRATES' COURTS, PROCEDURE, ante, in so far as those Rules are inconsistent with them.

8–22260 54A. Reduction of period for making hospital orders. Secretary of State may by order reduce periods in ss 37(4), (5) and 38(4) and make consequential amendments.

[Mental Health Act 1983, s 54A added by the Criminal Justice Act 1991, s 27(2)—summarised.]

8–22261 55. Interpretation of Part III. (1) In this Part of this Act—

"child" and "young person" have the same meaning as in the Children and Young Persons Act 1933[1];

"civil prisoner" has the meaning given to it by section 48(2)(*c*) above;

"guardian", in relation to a child or young person, has the same meaning as in the Children and Young Persons Act 1933[1];

"place of safety", in relation to a person who is not a child or young person, means any police station, prison or remand centre, or any hospital the managers of which are willing temporarily to receive him, and in relation to a child or young person has the same meaning as in the Children and Young Persons Act 1933[1];

"responsible medical officer", in relation to a person liable to be detained in a hospital within the meaning of Part II of this Act, means the registered medical practitioner in charge of the treatment of the patient.

(2) Any reference in this Part of this Act to an offence punishable on summary conviction with imprisonment shall be construed without regard to any prohibition or restriction imposed by or under any enactment relating to the imprisonment of young offenders.

(3) Where a patient who is liable to be detained in a hospital in pursuance of an order or direction under this Part of this Act is treated by virtue of any provision of this Part of this Act as if he had been admitted to the hospital in pursuance of a subsequent order or direction under this Part of this Act or a subsequent application for admission for treatment under Part II of this Act, he shall be treated as if the subsequent order, direction or application had described him as suffering from the form or forms of mental disorder specified in the earlier order or direction or, where he is treated as if he had been so admitted by virtue of a direction under section 42(1) above, such form of mental disorder as may be specified in the direction under that section.

(4) Any reference to a hospital order, a guardianship order or a restriction order in section 40(2), (4) or (5), section 41(3) to (5), or section 42 above or section 69(1) below shall be construed as including a reference to any order or direction under this Part of this Act having the same effect as the first-mentioned order; and the exceptions and modifications set out in Schedule 1 to this Act in respect of the provisions of this Act described in that Schedule accordingly include those which are consequential on the provisions of this subsection.

(5) Section 34(2) above shall apply for the purposes of this Part of this Act as it applies for the purposes of Part II of this Act.

(6) References in this Part of this Act to persons serving a sentence of imprisonment shall be construed in accordance with section 47(5) above.

(7) Section 99[2] of the Children and Young Persons Act 1933 (which relates to the presumption and determination of age) shall apply for the purposes of this Part of this Act as it applies for the purposes of that Act.

[Mental Health Act 1983, s 55.]

1. See s 107, thereof, in PART V: YOUTH COURTS, ante.
2. See PART V: YOUTH COURTS, ante.

8–22262

PART IV[1]

CONSENT TO TREATMENT

1. Part IV contains ss 56–64.

8–22263

PART V[1]

MENTAL HEALTH REVIEW TRIBUNALS

1. Part V contains ss 65–79.

8–22264

PART VI[1]

REMOVAL AND RETURN OF PATIENTS WITHIN UNITED KINGDOM, ETC

1. Part VI contains ss 80–92.

8–22265

PART VII[1]

MANAGEMENT OF PROPERTY AND AFFAIRS OF PATIENTS

1. Part VII contains ss 93–113.

PART VIII[1]

MISCELLANEOUS FUNCTIONS OF LOCAL AUTHORITIES AND THE SECRETARY OF STATE

Approved social workers

8–22266 **114. Appointment of approved social workers.** (1) A local social services authority shall appoint a sufficient number of approved social workers[2] for the purpose of discharging the functions conferred on them by this Act.

(2) No person shall be appointed by a local social services authority as an approved social worker unless he is approved by the authority as having appropriate competence in dealing with persons who are suffering from mental disorder.

(3) In approving a person for appointment as an approved social worker a local social services authority shall have regard to such matters as the Secretary of State may direct.
[Mental Health Act 1983, s 114.]

1. Part VIII contains ss 114–125.
2. For the meaning of "approved social worker", see s 145, post.

8–22267 **115. Powers of entry and inspection.** An approved social worker[1] of a local social services authority may at all reasonable times after producing, if asked to do so, some duly authenticated document showing that he is such a social worker, enter and inspect[2] any premises (not being a hospital) in the area of that authority in which a mentally disordered patient is living, if he has reasonable cause to believe that the patient is not under proper care.
[Mental Health Act 1983, s 115.]

1. For the meaning of "approved social worker", see s 145, post.
2. Any person who without reasonable excuse refuses to allow the inspection of any premises is guilty of an offence; see s 129, post.

Visiting patients

8–22268 **116. Welfare of certain hospital patients.** (1) Where a patient to whom this section applies is admitted to a hospital, independent hospital or care home in England and Wales (whether for treatment for mental disorder or for any other reason) then, without prejudice to their duties in relation to the patient apart from the provisions of this section, the authority shall arrange for visits to be made to him on behalf of the authority, and shall take such other steps in relation to the patient while in the hospital, independent hospital or care home as would be expected to be taken by his parents.

(2) This section applies to—

(*a*) a child or young person—

(i) who is in the care of a local authority by virtue of a care order within the meaning of the Children Act 1989, or

(ii) in respect of whom the rights and powers of a parent are vested in a local authority by virtue of section 16 of the Social Work (Scotland) Act 1968.

(*b*) a person who is subject to the guardianship of a local social services authority under the provisions of this Act; or

(*c*) a person the functions of whose nearest relative under this Act are for the time being transferred to a local social services authority.

[Mental Health Act 1983, s 116, as amended by the Mental Health (Scotland) Act 1984, Sch 3, the Care Standards Act 2000, s 116, SI 2005/2078 and SSI 20005/465.]

After-care

8-22269 **117. After-care.** (1) This section applies to persons who are detained under section 3 above, or admitted to a hospital in pursuance of a hospital order made under section 37 above, or transferred to a hospital in pursuance of a hospital direction made under section 45A above or a transfer direction made under section 47 or 48 above, and then cease to be detained and (whether or not immediately after so ceasing) leave hospital.

(2) It shall be the duty of the Health Authority and of the local social services authority to provide, in co-operation with relevant voluntary agencies, after-care services for any person to whom this section applies until such time as the Health Authority and the local social services authority are satisfied that the person concerned is no longer in need of such services; but they shall not be so satisfied in the case of a patient who is subject to after-care under supervision at any time while he remains so subject.

(2A) It shall be the duty of the Primary Care Trust or Health Authority to secure that at all times while a patient is subject to after-care under supervision—

(*a*) a person who is a registered medical practitioner approved for the purposes of section 12 above by the Secretary of State as having special experience in the diagnosis or treatment of mental disorder is in charge of the medical treatment provided for the patient as part of the after-care services provided for him under this section; and

(*b*) a person professionally concerned with any of the after-care services so provided is supervising him with a view to securing that he receives the after-care services so provided.

(2B) Section 32 above shall apply for the purposes of this section as it applies for the purposes of Part II of this Act.

(3) In this section "the Primary Care Trust or Health Authority" means the Primary Care Trust or Health Authority, and "the local social services authority" means the local social services authority, for the area in which the person concerned is resident or to which he is sent on discharge by the hospital in which he was detained.

[Mental Health Act 1983, s 117, as amended by the Health Authorities Act 1995, Sch 1, the Mental Health (Patients in the Community) Act 1995, Sch 1, the Crime (Sentences) Act 1997, Sch 4 and the National Health Services and Community Care Act 1990, Sch 9.]

Functions of the Secretary of State

8-22270 **118.** *Code of practice.*

8-22271 **123. Transfers to and from special hospitals.** (1) Without prejudice to any other provisions of this Act with respect to the transfer of patients, any patient who is for the time being liable to be detained under this Act (other than under section 35, 36 or 38 above) in a hospital at which high security psychiatric services are provided may, upon the directions of the Secretary of State, at any time be removed into any other hospital at which those services are provided.

(2) Without prejudice to any such provision, the Secretary of State may give directions for the transfer of any patient who is for the time being liable to be so detained into a hospital at which those services are not provided.

(3) Subsections (2) and (4) of section 19 above shall apply in relation to the transfer or removal of a patient under this section as they apply in relation to the transfer or removal of a patient from one hospital to another under that section.

[Mental Health Act 1983, s 123, as amended by the Health Act 1999, Schs 4 and 5.]

8-22273 **125.** *Repealed.*

PART IX[1]

Offences

8-22274 **126. Forgery, false statements, etc.** (1) Any person who without lawful authority or excuse has in his custody or under his control any document to which this subsection applies, which is, and which he knows or believes to be, false within the meaning of Part I of the Forgery and Counterfeiting Act 1981, shall be guilty of an offence.

(2) Any person who without lawful authority or excuse makes, or has in his custody or under his control, any document so closely resembling a document to which subsection (1) above applies as to be calculated to deceive shall be guilty of an offence.

(3) The documents to which subsection (1) above applies are any documents purporting to be—

(*a*) an application under Part II of this Act;
(*b*) a medical or other recommendation or report under this Act; and
(*c*) any other document required or authorised to be made for any of the purposes of this Act.

(4) Any person who—

(*a*) wilfully makes a false entry or statement in application, recommendation, report, record or other document required or authorised to be made for any of the purposes of this Act; or
(*b*) with intent to deceive, makes use of any such entry or statement which he knows to be false,

shall be guilty of an offence.

(5) Any person guilty of an offence under this section shall be liable[2]—

(*a*) on summary conviction, to imprisonment for a term not exceeding **six months** or to a fine not exceeding **the statutory maximum**, or to **both**;
(*b*) on conviction on indictment, to imprisonment for a term not exceeding **two years** or to a **fine** of any amount, or to **both**.

[Mental Health Act 1983, s 126, as amended by the Mental Health (Patients in the Community) Act 1995, Sch 1.]

---

1. Part IX contains ss 126–130.
2. For procedure in respect of this offence which is triable either way, see the Magistrates' Courts Act 1980, ss 17A–21, in PART I: MAGISTRATES' COURTS, PROCEDURE, ante.

8–22275 127. Ill-treatment of patients. (1) It shall be an offence for any person who is an officer on the staff of or otherwise employed in, or who is one of the managers of, a hospital, an independent hospital or care home—

(*a*) to ill-treat or wilfully to neglect[1] a patient for the time being receiving treatment for mental disorder as an in-patient in that hospital or home; or
(*b*) to ill-treat or wilfully to neglect[1], on the premises of which the hospital or home forms part, a patient for the time being receiving such treatment there as an out-patient.

(2) It shall be an offence for any individual to ill-treat or wilfully to neglect[1] a mentally disordered patient who is for the time being subject to his guardianship under this Act or otherwise in his custody or care (whether by virtue of any legal or moral obligation or otherwise).

(2A) It shall be an offence for any individual to ill-treat or wilfully to neglect[1] a mentally disordered patient who is for the time being subject to after-care under supervision.

(3) Any person guilty of an offence under this section shall be liable[2]—

(*a*) on summary conviction, to imprisonment for a term not exceeding **six months** or to a fine not exceeding **the statutory maximum**, or to **both**;
(*b*) on conviction on indictment, to imprisonment for a term not exceeding **two years** or to a **fine** of any amount, or to **both**.

(4) No proceedings shall be instituted for an offence under this section except by or with the consent of the Director of Public Prosecutions.

[Mental Health Act 1983, s 127, as amended by the Mental Health (Patients in the Community) Act 1995, Sch 1 and the Care Standards Act 2000, s 116.]

---

1. Ill-treatment and wilful neglect are not the same, although ill-treatment can cover most, if not all, forms of neglect. For ill-treatment it must be proved that there was deliberate conduct which could properly be described as ill-treatment whether or not it damaged or threatened to damage the victim's health, plus a guilty mind involving an appreciation or recklessness of inexcusable ill-treatment (*R v Newington* (1990) 91 Cr App Rep 247, [1990] Crim LR 593, CA).
2. For procedure in respect of this offence which is triable either way, see the Magistrates' Courts Act 1980, ss 17A–21, in PART I: MAGISTRATES' COURTS, PROCEDURE, ante.

8–22276 128. Assisting patients to absent themselves without leave, etc. (1) Where any person induces or knowingly[1] assists another person who is liable to be detained in a hospital within the meaning of Part II of this Act or is subject to guardianship under this Act to absent himself without leave he shall be guilty of an offence.

(2) Where any person induces or knowingly assists another person who is in legal custody by virtue of section 137 below to escape from such custody he shall be guilty of an offence.

(3) Where any person knowingly harbours a patient who is absent without leave or is otherwise at large and liable to be retaken under this Act or gives him any assistance with intent to prevent, hinder or interfere with his being taken into custody or returned to the hospital or other place where he ought to be he shall be guilty of an offence.

(4) Any person guilty of an offence under this section shall be liable[2]—

(*a*) on summary conviction, to imprisonment for a term not exceeding **six months** or to a fine not exceeding **the statutory maximum**, or to **both**;
(*b*) on conviction on indictment, to imprisonment for a term not exceeding **two years** or to a **fine** of any amount, or to **both**.

[Mental Health Act 1983, s 128.]

1. A person may act "knowingly" if, intending what is happening, he deliberately looks the other way (*Ross v Moss* [1965] 2 QB 396, [1965] 3 All ER 145, 129 JP 537).
2. For procedure in respect of this offence which is triable either way, see the Magistrates' Courts Act 1980, ss 17A–21, in PART I: MAGISTRATES' COURTS, PROCEDURE, ante.

8–22277 **129. Obstruction.** (1) Any person who without reasonable cause—

(*a*) refuses to allow the inspection of any premises; or

(*b*) refuses to allow the visiting, interviewing or examination of any person by a person authorised in that behalf by or under this Act or to give access to any person to a person so authorised; or

(*c*) refuses to produce for the inspection of any person so authorised any document or record the production of which is duly required by him; or

(*d*) otherwise obstructs any such person in the exercise of his functions,

shall be guilty of an offence.

(2) Without prejudice to the generality of subsection (1) above, any person who insists on being present when required to withdraw by a person authorised by or under this Act to interview or examine a person in private shall be guilty of an offence.

(3) Any person guilty of an offence under this section shall be liable on summary conviction to imprisonment for a term not exceeding **three months** or to a fine not exceeding **level 4** on the standard scale or to **both**.

[Mental Health Act 1983, s 129, as amended by the Mental Health (Patients in the Community) Act 1995, Sch 1.]

8–22278 **130. Prosecutions by local authorities.** A local social services authority may institute proceedings for any offence under this Part of this Act, but without prejudice to any provision this Part of this Act requiring the consent of the Director of Public Prosecutions for the institution of such proceedings[1].

[Mental Health Act 1983, s 130.]

1. This consent is required for the institution of proceedings under s 127, ante.

PART X[1]

MISCELLANEOUS AND SUPPLEMENTARY

Miscellaneous provisions

8–22279 **131. Informal admission of patients[2].** (1) Nothing in this Act shall be construed as preventing a patient who requires treatment for mental disorder from being admitted to any hospital or registered establishment in pursuance of arrangements made in that behalf and without any application, order or direction rendering him liable to be detained under this Act, or from remaining in any hospital or registered establishment in pursuance of such arrangements after he has ceased to be so liable to be detained.

(2) In the case of a minor who has attained the age of 16 years and is capable of expressing his own wishes, any such arrangements as are mentioned in subsection (1) above may be made, carried out and determined even though there are one or more persons who have parental responsibility for him (within the meaning of the Children Act 1989).

[Mental Health Act 1983, s 131, as amended by the Children Act 1989, Sch 13 and the Care Standards Act 2000, s 116.]

1. Part X contains ss 131–149.
2. Where a child is not competent (within the terms of *Gillick v West Norfolk and Wisbech Area Health Authority* [1986] AC 112, [1985] 3 All ER 402, HL, [1986] 1 FLR 224) and the child is in the care of the local authority that authority was in the same position as a parent and could use its powers under the Child Care Act 1980, s 10 to arrange voluntary admission (*R v Kirklees Metropolitan Borough Council, ex p C* [1993] 2 FCR 381, [1993] 2 FLR 187, CA).

8–22290 **132. Duty of managers of hospitals to give information to detained patients.** (1) The managers of a hospital or registered establishment in which a patient is detained under this Act shall take such steps as are practicable to ensure that the patient understands—

(*a*) under which of the provisions of this Act he is for the time being detained and the effect of that provision; and

(*b*) what rights of applying to a Mental Health Review Tribunal are available to him in respect of his detention under that provision;

and those steps shall be taken as soon as practicable after the commencement of the patient's detention under the provision in question.

(2) The managers of a hospital or mental nursing home* in which a patient is detained as aforesaid shall also take such steps as are practicable to ensure that the patient understands the effect, so far as relevant in his case, of sections 23, 25, 56 to 64, 66(1)(*g*), 118 and 120 above and section 134 below; and those steps shall be taken as soon as practicable after the commencement of the patient's detention in the hospital or nursing home.

(3) The steps to be taken under subsections (1) and (2) above shall include giving the requisite information both orally and in writing.

(4) The managers of a hospital or registered establishment in which a patient is detained as aforesaid shall, except where the patient otherwise requests, take such steps as are practicable to furnish the person (if any) appearing to them to be his nearest relative with a copy of any information given to him in writing under subsections (1) and (2) above; and those steps shall be taken when the information is given to the patient or within a reasonable time thereafter.

[Mental Health Act 1983, s 132, as amended by the Care Standards Act 2000, s 116.]

8–22291 **133. Duty of managers of hospitals to inform nearest relatives of discharge.** (1) Where a patient liable to be detained under this Act in a hospital or registered establishment is to be discharged otherwise than by virtue of an order for discharge made by his nearest relative, the managers of the hospital or registered establishment shall, subject to subsection (2) below, take such steps as are practicable to inform the person (if any) appearing to them to be the nearest relative of the patient; and that information shall, if practicable, be given at least seven days before the date of discharge.

(2) Subsection (1) above shall not apply if the patient or his nearest relative has requested that information about the patient's discharge should not be given under this section.

[Mental Health Act 1983, s 133, as amended by the Care Standards Act 2000, s 116.]

8–22292 **134. Correspondence of patients.** (1) A postal packet addressed to any person by a patient detained in a hospital under this Act and delivered by the patient for dispatch may be withheld from the postal operator—

(*a*) if that person has requested that communications addressed to him by the patient should be withheld; or

(*b*) subject to subsection (3) below, if the hospital is one at which high security psychiatric services are provided and the managers of the hospital consider that the postal packet is likely—

(i) to cause distress to the person to whom it is addressed or to any other person (not being a person on the staff of the hospital); or

(ii) to cause danger to any person;

and any request for the purposes of paragraph (*a*) above shall be made by a notice in writing given to the managers of the hospital, the registered medical practitioner in charge of the treatment of the patient or the Secretary of State.

(2) Subject to subsection (3) below, a postal packet addressed to a patient detained under this Act in a hospital at which high security psychiatric services are provided may be withheld from the patient if, in the opinion of the managers of the hospital, it is necessary to do so in the interests of the safety of the patient or for the protection of other persons.

(3) Subsections (1)(*b*) and (2) above do not apply to any postal packet addressed by a patient to, or sent to a patient by or on behalf of—

(*a*) any Minister of the Crown or Member of either House of Parliament;

(*b*) the Master or any other officer of the Court of Protection or any of the Lord Chancellor's Visitors;*

(*c*) the Parliamentary Commissioner for Administration, the Socttish Public Services Ombudsman, the Public Service Ombudsman for Wales, the Health Service Commissioner for England, the Health Service Commissioner for Wales, the Health Service Commissioner for Wales or a Local Commissioner within the meaning of Part III of the Local Government Act 1974;

(*d*) a Mental Health Review Tribunal;

(*e*) a Strategic Health Authority, Health Authority, Special Health Authority or Primary Care Trust, a local social services authority, a Community Health Council, a Patients' Forum or a local probation board established under section 4 of the Criminal Justice and Court Services Act 2000;

(*ea*) a provider of a patient advocacy and liaison service for the assistance of patients at the hospital and their families and carers;

(*eb*) a provider of independent advocacy services for the patient;

(*f*) the managers of the hospital in which the patient is detained;

(*g*) any legally qualified person instructed by the patient to act as his legal adviser; or

(*h*) the European Commission of Human Rights or the European Court of Human Rights.

(3A) In subsection (3) above—

(*a*) "patient advocacy and liaison service" means a service of a description prescribed by regulations made by the Secretary of State, and

(*b*) "independent advocacy services" means services provided under arrangements under section 19A of the National Health Service Act 1977.

(4) The managers of a hospital may inspect and open any postal packet for the purposes of determining—

(*a*) whether it is one to which subsection (1) or (2) applies, and

(*b*) in the case of a postal packet to which subsection (1) or (2) above applies, whether or not it should be withheld under that subsection;

and the power to withhold a postal packet under either of those subsections includes power to withhold anything contained in it.

(5) Where a postal packet or anything contained in it is withheld under subsection (1) or (2) above the managers of the hospital shall record that fact in writing.

(6) Where a postal packet or anything contained in it is withheld under subsection (1)(*b*) or (2) above the managers of the hospital shall within seven days give notice of that fact to the patient and, in the case of a packet withheld under subsection (2) above, to the person (if known) by whom the postal packet was sent; and any such notice shall be given in writing and shall contain a statement of the effect of section 121(7) and (8) above.

(7) The functions of the managers of a hospital under this section shall be discharged on their behalf by a person on the staff of the hospital appointed by them for that purpose and different persons may be appointed to discharge different functions.

(8) The Secretary of State may make regulations[1] with respect to the exercise of the powers conferred by this section.

(9) In this section "hospital" has the same meaning as in Part II of this Act and "postal operator" and "postal packet" have the same meaning as in the Postal Services Act 2000.

[Mental Health Act 1983, s 134 amended by the Probation Service Act 1993, Sch 3, the Health Authorities Act 1995, Sch 1, the Government of Wales Act 1998, Sch 12, the Health Act 1999, Sch 4, SI 2000/90, the Postal Services Act 2000, Sch 8, the Criminal Justice and Court Services Act 2000, Sch 7, the Health and Social Care Act 2001, s 67(1), the National Health Service Reform and Health Care Professions Act 2002, s 19, SI 2002/2469, SI 2004/1823 and the Public Services Ombudsman (Wales) Act 2005, Sch 6.]

***Substituted by the Mental Capacity Act 2005, Sch 6 from a date to be appointed.**

1. See the Mental Health (Hospital, Guardianship and Consent to Treatment) Regulations 1983, SI 1983/893 amended by SI 1993/2156, SI 1997/801, SI 1998/2624 and SI 2005/2078.

8–22293 **135. Warrant to search for and remove patients.** (1) If it appears to a justice of the peace, on information on oath laid by an approved social worker, that there is reasonable cause to suspect that a person believed to be suffering from mental disorder—

(*a*) has been, or is being, ill-treated, neglected or kept otherwise than under proper control, in any place within the jurisdiction of the justice, or

(*b*) being unable to care for himself, is living alone in any such place,

the justice may issue a warrant[1] authorising any constable to enter, if need be by force, any premises specified in the warrant in which that person is believed to be, and, if thought fit, to remove him to a place of safety with a view to the making of an application in respect of him under Part II of this Act, or of other arrangements for his treatment or care.

(2) If it appears to a justice of the peace, on information on oath laid by any constable or other person who is authorised by or under this Act or under article 8 of the Mental Health (Care and Treatment) Scotland) Act 2003 (Consequential Provisions) Order 2005 to take a patient to any place, or to take into custody or retake a patient who is liable under this Act or under the said article 8 to be so taken or retaken—*

(*a*) that there is reasonable cause to believe that the patient is to be found on premises within the jurisdiction of the justice; and

(*b*) that admission to the premises has been refused or that a refusal of such admission is apprehended,

the justice may issue a warrant authorising any constable to enter the premises, if need be by force, and remove the patient.

(3) A patient who is removed to a place of safety in the execution of a warrant issued under this section may be detained there for a period not exceeding 72 hours.

(4) In the execution of a warrant issued under subsection (1) above, a constable shall be accompanied by an approved social worker[2] and by a registered medical practitioner[2], and in the execution of a warrant issued under subsection (2) above a constable may be accompanied—

(*a*) by a registered medical practitioner[2];

(*b*) by any person authorised by or under this Act or under article 8 of the Mental Health (Care and Treatment) Scotland) Act 2003 (Consequential Provisions) Order 2005 to take or retake the patient.*

(5) It shall not be necessary in any information or warrant under subsection (1) above to name the patient concerned.

(6) In this section "place of safety" means residential accommodation provided by a local social services authority under Part III of the National Assistance Act 1948, a hospital as defined by this

Act, a police station, an independent hospital or care home for mentally disordered persons or any other suitable place the occupier of which is willing temporarily to receive the patient.
[Mental Health Act 1983, s 135, as amended by the Police and Criminal Evidence Act 1984, Schs 6 and 7, the Mental Health (Scotland) Act 1984, Sch 3 and the National Health Service and Community Care Act 1990, Sch 10, the Care Standards Act 2000, s 116 and SI 2005/2078.]

***Reproduced as in force in England and Wales.**

1. See precedent, in PART IX: PRECEDENTS AND FORMS, post. It is not permissible to imply into s 135 of the Mental Health Act 1983 a power to insist that named professionals are there when the police officer executes the warrant, and the inclusion of such names in a warrant is surplusage and has no effect on its legality or its execution: *Ward v Metropolitan Police Comr* [2005] UKHL 32, [2006] 1 AC 23, [2005] 3 All ER 1013, [2005] 2 WLR 1114.

2. Although the purpose of the attendance of professionals is, in part, to ensure that a person is not removed when they judge that the basis upon which the warrant was granted is not made out, and this purpose is assisted if either of them knows the case well or the doctor has specialist knowledge in mental health, there is no power for a magistrate to identify the professionals who are to accompany the constable (*Ward v Metropolitan Police Comr* [2005] UKHL 32, [2006] 1 AC 23, [2005] 3 All ER 1013, [2005] 2 WLR 1114).

8–22294 **136. Mentally disordered persons found in public places.** (1) If a constable finds in a place to which the public have access a person who appears to him to be suffering from mental disorder and to be in immediate need of care or control, the constable may, if he thinks it necessary to do so in the interests of that person or for the protection of other persons, remove[1] that person to a place of safety within the meaning of section 135 above.

(2) A person removed to a place of safety under this section may be detained there for a period not exceeding 72 hours[2] for the purpose of enabling him to be examined by a registered medical practitioner and to be interviewed by an approved social worker and of making any necessary arrangements for his treatment or care.
[Mental Health Act 1983, s 136.]

1. This power of removal is preserved by the Police and Criminal Evidence Act 1984, s 26 and Sch 2.

2. During this period, arrangements can be made for admission to hospital for observation and, if necessary treatment, in accordance with Pt II of the Act which is not detailed in this work.

8–22295 **137. Provisions as to custody, conveyance and detention.** (1) Any person required or authorised by or by virtue of this Act to be conveyed to any place or to be kept in custody or detained in a place of safety or at any place to which he is taken under section 42(6) above shall, while being so conveyed, detained or kept, as the case may be, be deemed to be in legal custody[1].

(2) A constable or any other person required or authorised by or by virtue of this Act to take any person into custody, or to convey or detain any person shall, for the purposes of taking him into custody or conveying or detaining him, have all the powers, authorities, protection and privileges which a constable has within the area for which he acts as constable.

(3) In this section "convey" includes any other expression denoting removal from one place to another.
[Mental Health Act 1983, s 137.]

1. It will therefore be an offence to induce or knowingly assist such a person to escape (see s 128, ante).

8–22296 **138. Retaking of patients escaping from custody.** (1) If any person who is in legal custody by virtue of section 137 above escapes, he may, subject to the provisions of this section, be retaken[1]—

(*a*) in any case, by the person who had his custody immediately before the escape, or by any constable or approved social worker;

(*b*) if at the time of the escape he was liable to be detained in a hospital within the meaning of Part II of this Act, or subject to guardianship under this Act, by any other person who could take him into custody under section 18 above if he had absented himself without leave[2].

(2) A person to whom paragraph (*b*) of subsection (1) above applies shall not be retaken under this section after the expiration of the period within which he could be retaken under section 18 above if he had absented himself without leave on the day of the escape unless he is subject to a restriction order under Part III of this Act or an order or direction having the same effect as such an order; and subsection (4) of the said section 18 shall apply with the necessary modifications accordingly.

(3) A person who escapes while being taken to or detained in a place of safety under section 135 or 136 above shall not be retaken under this section after the expiration of the period of 72 hours beginning with the time when he escapes or the period during which he is liable to be so detained, whichever expires first.

(4) This section, so far as it relates to the escape of a person liable to be detained in a hospital within the meaning of Part II of this Act, shall apply in relation to a person who escapes—

(*a*) while being taken to or from such a hospital in pursuance of regulations under section 19 above, or of any order, direction or authorisation under Part III or VI of this Act (other than under section 35, 36, 38, 53, 83 or 85) or under section 123 above; or (*b*) while being taken to or detained in a place of safety in pursuance of an order under Part III of this Act (other than under section 35, 36 or 38 above) pending his admission to such a hospital,

as if he were liable to be detained in that hospital and, if he had not previously been received in that hospital, as if he had been so received.

(5) In computing for the purposes of the power to give directions under section 37(4) above and for the purposes of sections 37(5) and 40(1) above the period of 28 days mentioned in those sections, no account shall be taken of any time during which the patient is at large and liable to be retaken by virtue of this section.

(6) Section 21[3] above shall, with any necessary modifications, apply in relation to a patient who is at large and liable to be retaken by virtue of this section as it applies in relation to a patient who is absent without leave and references in that section to section 18 above shall be construed accordingly.

[Mental Health Act 1983, s 138]

---

1. This power to retake is preserved by the Police and Criminal Evidence Act 1984, s 26 and Sch 2.
2. For power of magistrate to issue a warrant in respect of a person liable to be retaken, see Criminal Justice Act 1967, s 72, in this PART: title PRISONS, post.
3. By this section if a patient is absent without leave at the time when he would otherwise cease to be liable to be detained or subject to guardianship under Pt II of the Act, this liability shall not cease, but the special provisions contained in this section shall apply.

8–22297 **139. Protection for acts done in pursuance of this Act[1].** (1) No person shall be liable, whether on the ground of want of jurisdiction or on any other ground, to any civil or criminal proceedings to which he would have been liable apart from this section in respect of any act purporting to be done in pursuance of this Act or any regulations or rules made under this Act, or in, or in pursuance of anything done in, the discharge of functions conferred by any other enactment on the authority having jurisdiction under Part VII of this Act, unless the act was done in bad faith or without reasonable care[2].

(2) No civil proceedings shall be brought against any person in any court in respect of any such act without the leave of the High Court; and no criminal proceedings shall be brought against any person in any court in respect of any such act except by or with the consent of the Director of Public Prosecutions.

(3) This section does not apply to proceedings for an offence under this Act, being proceedings which, under any other provision of this Act, can be instituted only by or with the consent of the Director of Public Prosecutions.

(4) This section does not apply to proceedings against the Secretary of State or against a Strategic Health Authority, Health Authority, Special Health Authority or Primary Care Trust or against a National Health Service trust established under the National Health Service and Community Care Act 1990*.

(5) *Northern Ireland.*

[Mental Health Act 1983, s 139, as amended by the National Health Service and Community Care Act 1990, Sch 9, the Health Authorities Act 1995, Sch 1, SI 2000/90 and SI 2002/2469.]

***Amended by the Health and Social Care (Community Health and Standards) Act 2003, Sch 4, from a date to be appointed.**

1. For a consideration of the scope of this section, see *Pountney v Griffiths* [1975] 2 All ER 881, 139 JP 590.
2. See *Kynaston v Secretary of State for Home Affairs* (1981) 73 Cr App Rep 281, CA.

8–22298 **140. Notification of hospitals having arrangements for reception of urgent cases.** It shall be the duty of every Health Authority to give notice to every local social services authority for an area wholly or partly comprised within the Health Authority's area specifying the hospital or hospitals administered by or otherwise available to the Health Authority in which arrangements are from time to time in force for the reception, in case of special urgency, of patients requiring treatment for mental disorder.

[Mental Health Act 1983, s 140, as amended by the National Health Service and Community Care Act 1990, Sch 9 and the Health Authorities Act 1995, Sch 1.]

8–22299 **141. Members of Parliament suffering from mental illness.** (1) Where a member of the House of Commons is authorised to be detained on the ground (however formulated) that he is suffering from mental illness, it shall be the duty of the court, authority or person on whose order or application, and of any registered medical practitioner upon whose recommendation or certificate, the detention was authorised, and of the person in charge of the hospital or other place in which the member is authorised to be detained, to notify the Speaker of the House of Commons that the detention has been authorised.

(2)–(7) *Powers of the Speaker of the House of Commons.*

(8) *Scotland.*

(9) *This section to have effect with modifications in relation to members of the National Assembly for Wales.*

(10) *Northern Ireland.*

[Mental Health Act 1983, s 141, amended by the Government of Wales Act 1998, Sch 12.]

8–22300 142. *Pay, pensions, etc, of mentally disordered persons.*

Supplemental

8–22301 143. *General provisions as to regulations, orders and rules.*

8–22302 144. *Power to amend local Acts.*

8–22303 145. Interpretation. (1) In this Act, unless the context otherwise requires—

"absent without leave" has the meaning given to it by section 18 above and related expressions shall be construed accordingly;

"application for admission for assessment" has the meaning given in section 2 above;

"application for admission for treatment" has the meaning given in section 3 above;

"approved social worker" means an officer of a local social services authority appointed to act as an approved social worker for the purposes of this Act;

"care home" has the same meaning as in the Care Standards Act 2000;

"Health Authority" means a Health Authority established under section 8 of the National Health Service Act 1977;

"high security psychiatric services" has the same meaning as in the National health Service Act 1977,*

"hospital" means—

(*a*) any health service hospital within the meaning of the National Health Service Act 1977; and

(*b*) any accommodation provided by a local authority and used as a hospital by or on behalf of the Secretary of State under that Act;

and "hospital within the meaning of Part II of this Act" has the meaning given in section 34 above;

"hospital direction" has the meaning given in section 45A(3)(*a*) above;

"hospital order" and "guardianship order" have the meanings respectively given in section 37 above;

"independent hospital" has the same meaning as in the Care Standards Act 2000;

"interim hospital order" has the meaning given in section 38 above;

"limitation direction" has the meaning given in section 45A(3)(*b*) above;

"local social services authority" means a council which is a local authority for the purpose of the Local Authority Social Services Act 1970;

"the managers" means—

(*a*) in relation to a hospital vested in the Secretary of State for the purposes of his functions under the National Health Service Act 1977, and in relation to any accommodation provided by a local authority and used as a hospital by or on behalf of the Secretary of State under that Act, the Strategic Health Authority, Health Authority or Special Health Authority responsible for the administration of the hospital;

(*b*) *Repealed*;

(*bb*) in relation to a hospital vested in a Primary Care Trust or a National Health Service trust, the trust;

(*bc*) in relation to a hospital vested in an NHS foundation trust, the trust;

(*c*) in relation to a mental nursing home registered in pursuance of the Registered Homes Act 1984, the person or persons registered in respect of the home;

and in this definition " hospital" means a hospital within the meaning of Part II of this Act;

"medical treatment" includes nursing, and also includes care, habilitation and rehabilitation under medical supervision;

"mental disorder", "severe mental impairment", "mental impairment" and "psychopathic disorder" have the meanings given in section 1 above;

"nearest relative", in relation to a patient, has the meaning given in Part II of this Act;

"patient" (except in Part VII of this Act) means a person suffering or appearing to be suffering from mental disorder;

"Primary Care Trust" means a Primary Care Trust established under section 16A of the National Health Service Act 1977;

"registered establishment" has the meaning given in section 34 above;

"the responsible after-care bodies" has the meaning given in section 25D above;

"restriction direction" has the meaning given to it by section 49 above;

"restriction order" has the meaning given to it by section 41 above;

"Special Health Authority" means a Special Health Authority established under section 11 of the National Health Service Act 1977;

"Strategic Health Authority means a Strategic Health Authority established under section 8 of the National Health Service Act 1977;
"supervision application" has the meaning given in section 25A above;
"transfer direction" has the meaning given to it by section 47 above.

(1AA) Where high security psychiatric services and other services are provided at a hospital, the part of the hospital at which high security psychiatric services are provided and the other part shall be treated as separate hospitals for the purposes of this Act.

(1A) References in this Act to a patient being subject to after-care under supervision (or to after-care under supervision) shall be construed in accordance with section 25A above.

(2) (*Repealed*).

(3) In relation to a person who is liable to be detained or subject to guardianship by virtue of an order or direction under Part III of this Act (other than under section 35, 36 or 38), any reference in this Act to any enactment contained in Part II of this Act or in section 66 or 67 above shall be construed as a reference to that enactment as it applies to that person by virtue of Part III of this Act.
[Mental Health Act 1983, s 145, as amended by the Registered Homes Act 1984, Sch 1, the National Health Service and Community Care Act 1990, Sch 9, the Statute Law (Repeals) Act 1993, Sch 1, the Mental Health (Amendment) Act 1994, s 1, the Health Authorities Act 1995, Sch 1, the Mental Health (Patients in the Community) Act 1995, Sch 1, the Crime (Sentences) Act 1997, Sch 4, the Health Act 1999, Schs 4 and 5, SI 2000/90, the Care Standards Act 2000, s 116, SI 2002/2469 and the Health and Social Care (Community Health and Standards) Act 2003, Sch 4.]

8–22304 146–147. *Application to Scotland and Northern Ireland.*

8–22305 148. Consequential and transitional provisions and repeals. (1) Schedule 4 (consequential amendments) and Schedule 5 (transitional and saving provisions) to this Act shall have effect but without prejudice to the operation of sections 15 to 17 of the Interpretation Act 1978 (which relate to the effect of repeals).

(2) Where any amendment in Schedule 4 to this Act affects an enactment amended by the Mental Health (Amendment) Act 1982 the amendment in Schedule 4 shall come into force immediately after the provision of the Act of 1982 amending that enactment.

(3) The enactments specified in Schedule 6 to this Act are hereby repealed to the extent mentioned in the third column of that Schedule.
[Mental Health Act 1983, s 148.]

8–22306 149. Short title, commencement and application to Scilly Isles. (1) This Act may be cited as the Mental Health Act 1983.

(2) Subject to subsection (3) below and Schedule 5 to this Act, this Act shall come into force on 30th September 1983.

(3) *Repealed.*

(4) Section 130(4) of the National Health Service Act 1977 (which provides for the extension of that Act to the Isles of Scilly) shall have effect as if the references to that Act included references to this Act.
[Mental Health Act 1983, s 149, as amended by the Statute Law (Repeals) Act 2004.]

1. The day appointed for the coming into force of ss 35, 36, 38 and 40(3) of the Act was the 1st October 1984 (SI 1984/1357).

Enduring Powers of Attorney Act 1985[1]*

(1985 c 29)

Enduring powers of attorney

***Repealed by the Mental Capacity Act 2005, Sch 7 from a date to be appointed.**

1. This Act enables powers of attorney to be created which will survive any subsequent mental incapacity of the donor. The Act thereby provides a simpler method for dealing with the affairs of the mentally ill and an alternative to applying to the Court of Protection for a receiver to be appointed. The Act was brought into force on 10 March 1986 (Enduring Powers of Attorney Act 1985 (Commencement) Order 1986, SI 1986/125).

8–22410 1. Enduring power of attorney to survive mental incapacity of donor. A power of attorney which is an enduring power within the meaning of the Act shall not be revoked by any subsequent mental incapacity of the donor, but upon such incapacity supervening the donee of the power may not, subject to certain exceptions, do anything under the authority of the power until the instrument creating the power is registered by the court under section 6 of the Act.*
[Enduring Powers of Attorney Act 1985, s 1—summarised.]

***Repealed by the Mental Capacity Act 2005, Sch 7 from a date to be appointed.**

8–22411 2. Characteristics of an enduring power. An instrument creating an enduring power must be in a prescribed form[1], and be executed in the prescribed manner by the donor and the attorney; the instrument must contain a statement to the effect by the donor that he intends the power to continue in spite of any supervening mental incapacity of his, and that he has read or has had read to him information explaining the effect of creating the power.*
[Enduring Powers of Attorney Act 1985, s 2—summarised.]

***Repealed by the Mental Capacity Act 2005, Sch 7 from a date to be appointed.**
1. See the Enduring Powers of Attorney (Prescribed Form) Regulations 1986, SI 1986/126.

8–22412 3. Scope of authority etc of attorney under enduring power. The scope of authority of an attorney under an enduring power shall be regulated by conditions and restrictions.*
[Enduring Powers of Attorney Act 1985, s 3—summarised.]

***Repealed by the Mental Capacity Act 2005, Sch 7 from a date to be appointed.**

Action on actual or impending incapacity of donor

8–22413 4. Duties of attorney in event of actual or impending incapacity of donor. (1) If the attorney under an enduring power has reason to believe that the donor is or is becoming mentally incapable subsections (2) to (6) below shall apply.

(2) The attorney shall, as soon as practicable, make an application to the court for the registration of the instrument creating the power.

(3) Before making an application for registration the attorney shall comply with the provisions as to notice set out in Schedule 1.

(4) An application for registration shall be made in the prescribed form[1] and shall contain such statements as may be prescribed.

(5) The attorney may, before making an application for the registration of the instrument, refer to the court for its determination any question as to the validity of the power and he shall comply with any direction given to him by the court on that determination.

(6) No disclaimer of the power shall be valid unless and until the attorney gives notice of it to the court.

(7) Any person who, in an application for registration, makes a statement which he knows to be false in a material particular shall be liable[2]—

(*a*) on conviction on indictment, to imprisonment for a term not exceeding **two years** or to a **fine**, or **both**; and

(*b*) on summary conviction, to imprisonment for a term not exceeding **six months** or to a fine not exceeding the **statutory maximum**, or **both**.

(8) In this section and Schedule 1[3] "prescribed" means prescribed by rules of the court.*
[Enduring Powers of Attorney Act 1985, s 4.]

***Repealed by the Mental Capacity Act 2005, Sch 7 from a date to be appointed.**
1. See the Court of Protection (Enduring Powers of Attorney) Rules 1986, SI 1986/127.
2. For procedure in respect of an offence triable either way, see the Magistrates' Courts Act 1980, ss 17A–21, in PART I: MAGISTRATES' COURTS, PROCEDURE, ante.
3. Sch 1 is not printed in this work.

8–22414 5–6. *Functions of court prior to registration and on application for registration.**

***Repealed by the Mental Capacity Act 2005, Sch 7 from a date to be appointed.**

Legal position after registration

8–22415 7. Effect and proof of registration. (1)–(2) *Effect of registration.*

(3) A document purporting to be an office copy of an instrument registered under this Act shall, in any part of the United Kingdom, be evidence of the contents of the instrument and of the fact that it has been so registered.

(4) Subsection (3) above is without prejudice to section 3 of the Powers of Attorney Act 1971 (proof by certified copies) and to any other method of proof authorised by law.*
[Enduring Powers of Attorney Act 1985, s 7.]

***Repealed by the Mental Capacity Act 2005, Sch 7 from a date to be appointed.**

8–22416 13. Interpretation. (1) In this Act—

"the court", in relation to any functions under this Act, means the authority having jurisdiction under Part VII of the Mental Health Act 1983;

"enduring power" is to be construed in accordance with section 2;

"mentally incapable" or "mental incapacity", except where it refers to revocation at common law, means, in relation to any person, that he is incapable by reason of mental disorder of managing and administering his property and affairs and "mentally capable" and "mental capacity" shall be construed accordingly;

"mental disorder" has the same meaning as it has in the Mental Health Act 1983;

"notice" means notice in writing;

"rules of the court" means rules under Part VII of the Mental Health Act 1983 as applied by section 10;

"*trust corporation*".

(2) Any question arising under or for the purposes of this Act as to what the donor of the power might at any time be expected to do shall be determined by assuming that he had full mental capacity at the time but otherwise by reference to the circumstances existing at that time.*

[Enduring Powers of Attorney Act 1985, s 13, as amended by the Statute Law (Repeals) Act 1993, Sch 1.]

***Repealed by the Mental Capacity Act 2005, Sch 7 from a date to be appointed.**

8–22417 **14.** *Short title, commencement and extent.**

***Repealed by the Mental Capacity Act 2005, Sch 7 from a date to be appointed.**

Mental Capacity Act 2005[1]

(2005 c 9)

8–22418 **1. The principles.** (1) The following principles apply for the purposes of this Act.

(2) A person must be assumed to have capacity unless it is established that he lacks capacity.

(3) A person is not to be treated as unable to make a decision unless all practicable steps to help him to do so have been taken without success.

(4) A person is not to be treated as unable to make a decision merely because he makes an unwise decision.

(5) An act done, or decision made, under this Act for or on behalf of a person who lacks capacity must be done, or made, in his best interests.

(6) Before the act is done, or the decision is made, regard must be had to whether the purpose for which it is needed can be as effectively achieved in a way that is less restrictive of the person's rights and freedom of action.

[Mental Capacity Act 2005, s 1.]

---

1. This Act repeals the Enduring Powers of Attorney Act 1985 and makes new provision relating to persons who lack capacity; establishes a superior court of record called the Court of Protection and makes provision in connection with the Convention on the International Protection of Adults signed at the Hague on 13 January 2000. The Act is to be brought into force by commencement orders made under s 68. At the date of going to press no such orders had been made.

8–22419 **2. People who lack capacity.** (1) For the purposes of this Act, a person lacks capacity in relation to a matter if at the material time he is unable to make a decision for himself in relation to the matter because of an impairment of, or a disturbance in the functioning of, the mind or brain.

(2) It does not matter whether the impairment or disturbance is permanent or temporary.

(3) A lack of capacity cannot be established merely by reference to—

(*a*) a person's age or appearance, or

(*b*) a condition of his, or an aspect of his behaviour, which might lead others to make unjustified assumptions about his capacity.

(4) In proceedings under this Act or any other enactment, any question whether a person lacks capacity within the meaning of this Act must be decided on the balance of probabilities.

(5) No power which a person ("D") may exercise under this Act—

(*a*) in relation to a person who lacks capacity, or

(*b*) where D reasonably thinks that a person lacks capacity,

is exercisable in relation to a person under 16.

(6) Subsection (5) is subject to section 18(3).

[Mental Capacity Act 2005, s 2.]

8–22420 **3. Inability to make decisions.** (1) For the purposes of section 2, a person is unable to make a decision for himself if he is unable—

(*a*) to understand the information relevant to the decision,

(*b*) to retain that information,

(*c*) to use or weigh that information as part of the process of making the decision, or

(*d*) to communicate his decision (whether by talking, using sign language or any other means).

(2) A person is not to be regarded as unable to understand the information relevant to a decision if he is able to understand an explanation of it given to him in a way that is appropriate to his circumstances (using simple language, visual aids or any other means).

(3) The fact that a person is able to retain the information relevant to a decision for a short period only does not prevent him from being regarded as able to make the decision.

(4) The information relevant to a decision includes information about the reasonably foreseeable consequences of—

(*a*) deciding one way or another, or
(*b*) failing to make the decision.

[Mental Capacity Act 2005, s 3.]

8–22421 **4. Best interests.** (1) In determining for the purposes of this Act what is in a person's best interests, the person making the determination must not make it merely on the basis of—

(*a*) the person's age or appearance, or
(*b*) a condition of his, or an aspect of his behaviour, which might lead others to make unjustified assumptions about what might be in his best interests.

(2) The person making the determination must consider all the relevant circumstances and, in particular, take the following steps.

(3) He must consider—

(*a*) whether it is likely that the person will at some time have capacity in relation to the matter in question, and
(*b*) if it appears likely that he will, when that is likely to be.

(4) He must, so far as reasonably practicable, permit and encourage the person to participate, or to improve his ability to participate, as fully as possible in any act done for him and any decision affecting him.

(5) Where the determination relates to life-sustaining treatment he must not, in considering whether the treatment is in the best interests of the person concerned, be motivated by a desire to bring about his death.

(6) He must consider, so far as is reasonably ascertainable—

(*a*) the person's past and present wishes and feelings (and, in particular, any relevant written statement made by him when he had capacity),
(*b*) the beliefs and values that would be likely to influence his decision if he had capacity, and
(*c*) the other factors that he would be likely to consider if he were able to do so.

(7) He must take into account, if it is practicable and appropriate to consult them, the views of—

(*a*) anyone named by the person as someone to be consulted on the matter in question or on matters of that kind,
(*b*) anyone engaged in caring for the person or interested in his welfare,
(*c*) any donee of a lasting power of attorney granted by the person, and
(*d*) any deputy appointed for the person by the court,

as to what would be in the person's best interests and, in particular, as to the matters mentioned in subsection (6).

(8) The duties imposed by subsections (1) to (7) also apply in relation to the exercise of any powers which—

(*a*) are exercisable under a lasting power of attorney, or
(*b*) are exercisable by a person under this Act where he reasonably believes that another person lacks capacity.

(9) In the case of an act done, or a decision made, by a person other than the court, there is sufficient compliance with this section if (having complied with the requirements of subsections (1) to (7)) he reasonably believes that what he does or decides is in the best interests of the person concerned.

(10) "Life-sustaining treatment" means treatment which in the view of a person providing health care for the person concerned is necessary to sustain life.

(11) "Relevant circumstances" are those—

(*a*) of which the person making the determination is aware, and
(*b*) which it would be reasonable to regard as relevant.

[Mental Capacity Act 2005, s 4.]

8–22422 **5. Acts in connection with care or treatment.** (1) If a person ("D") does an act in connection with the care or treatment of another person ("P"), the act is one to which this section applies if—

(*a*) before doing the act, D takes reasonable steps to establish whether P lacks capacity in relation to the matter in question, and
(*b*) when doing the act, D reasonably believes—

(i) that P lacks capacity in relation to the matter, and
(ii) that it will be in P's best interests for the act to be done.

(2) D does not incur any liability in relation to the act that he would not have incurred if P—

(*a*) had had capacity to consent in relation to the matter, and
(*b*) had consented to D's doing the act.

(3) Nothing in this section excludes a person's civil liability for loss or damage, or his criminal liability, resulting from his negligence in doing the act.

(4) Nothing in this section affects the operation of sections 24 to 26 (advance decisions to refuse treatment).

[Mental Capacity Act 2005, s 5.]

8–22423 **6. Section 5 acts: limitations.** (1) If D does an act that is intended to restrain P, it is not an act to which section 5 applies unless two further conditions are satisfied.

(2) The first condition is that D reasonably believes that it is necessary to do the act in order to prevent harm to P.

(3) The second is that the act is a proportionate response to—

(*a*) the likelihood of P's suffering harm, and
(*b*) the seriousness of that harm.

(4) For the purposes of this section D restrains P if he—

(*a*) uses, or threatens to use, force to secure the doing of an act which P resists, or
(*b*) restricts P's liberty of movement, whether or not P resists.

(5) But D does more than merely restrain P if he deprives P of his liberty within the meaning of Article 5(1) of the Human Rights Convention (whether or not D is a public authority).

(6) Section 5 does not authorise a person to do an act which conflicts with a decision made, within the scope of his authority and in accordance with this Part, by—

(*a*) a donee of a lasting power of attorney granted by P, or
(*b*) a deputy appointed for P by the court.

(7) But nothing in subsection (6) stops a person—

(*a*) providing life-sustaining treatment, or
(*b*) doing any act which he reasonably believes to be necessary to prevent a serious deterioration in P's condition,

while a decision as respects any relevant issue is sought from the court.

[Mental Capacity Act 2005, s 6.]

8–22424 **44. Ill-treatment or neglect.** (1) Subsection (2) applies if a person ("D")—

(*a*) has the care of a person ("P") who lacks, or whom D reasonably believes to lack, capacity,
(*b*) is the donee of a lasting power of attorney, or an enduring power of attorney (within the meaning of Schedule 4), created by P, or
(*c*) is a deputy[1] appointed by the court for P.

(2) D is guilty of an offence if he ill-treats or wilfully neglects P.

(3) A person guilty of an offence under this section is liable[2]—

(*a*) on summary conviction, to imprisonment for a term not exceeding 12 months or a fine not exceeding the statutory maximum or both;
(*b*) on conviction on indictment, to imprisonment for a term not exceeding 5 years or a fine or both.

[Mental Capacity Act 2005, s 44.]

1. "Deputy" has the meaning given in s 16(2)(*b*) ie where a person lacks capacity in relation to a matter or matters concerning his personal welfare, or his property and affairs and the court may make the decision or decisions on his behalf in relation to the matter or matters, or appoint a person (a "deputy") to make decisions on P's behalf in relation to the matter or matters.

2. For procedure in respect of this offence which is triable either way, see the Magistrates' Courts Act 1980, s 17A–21 in PART I: MAGISTRATES' COURTS, PROCEDURE, ante.

NUISANCES

8–22430 **Public nuisances.** A person is guilty of a public nuisance who does an unlawful act or fails to discharge a legal duty and thereby— (*a*) endangers the lives, safety, health, property or comfort of the public; or (*b*) obstructs the public in the exercise or enjoyment of any right that is common to all the subjects of Her Majesty[1]. The offence of public nuisance is sufficiently clear to enable a person, with appropriate legal advice if necessary, to regulate his behaviour and meets the certainty requirement of art 7 of the European Convention on Human Rights and also meets the requirements of arts 8 and 10. Unless there is good reason for doing otherwise, where the conduct falls within the definition of a statutory offence, it is ordinarily proper that conduct falling within that definition should be prosecuted for the statutory offence and not for a common law offence. Nor is it in the ordinary way a reason for resorting to the common law offence that the prosecutor is freed from mandatory time limits or restrictions on penalty. It must rather be assumed that Parliament imposed such restrictions. Accordingly, the circumstances in which, in future, there can properly be resort to the common law crime of public nuisance will be relatively rare[1]. Earlier authorities, cited below, must be read in the light of this approach. A nuisance which materially affects the reasonable comfort and convenience of persons within its sphere, may be a public nuisance (*A-G v P Y A Quarries Ltd* [1957] 2 QB 169, [1957] 1 All ER 894, 121 JP 323). See also *R v Madden* [1973] 3 All ER 155. As injury is caused to separate individuals rather than to the community or a significant section of it, whatever other offence may have constituted, the crime of public nuisance does not extend to separate and individual telephone calls, however persistent and vexatious, or postal communications[2]. An offensive trade, either from the noise or smell, carried on to the annoyance or discomfort of all persons in the neighbourhood, is a nuisance; so is every unauthorised obstruction of the highway to the annoyance of the public (see *R v Train* (1862) 2 B & S 640, 26 JP 469).

It is sufficient if the inconvenience result as an immediate consequence of the act, as the erection of a booth for rope-dancing, or exhibiting effigies in a shop window, so as to attract crowds, and thereby causing the footway to be obstructed. In *R v Graham and Burns* (1888) 4 TLR 212, Charles J, ruled that there is no right to hold public meetings in Trafalgar Square, or in any other public place, but that such places are "for people to pass along," a use which is directly in conflict with that for public meeting; and in *Ex p Lewis* (1888) 21 QBD 191, 52 JP 773, the Court of Appeal acquiesced in this ruling. Keeping ferocious animals without proper control is a public nuisance (3 Burn's Justice, 30th ed, 1032); and exposing a person in public having a contagious disease (see also Public Health (Control of Diseases) Act 1984 in title Public Health, post). Prior to the Obscene Publications Act 1959, selling obscene prints or books was an indictable offence but by s 2(4) of that Act, a person publishing an obscene article (as therein defined) shall no longer be proceeded against at common law[3]. Exposing a horse in a fair which has the glanders, is an indictable offence. So is an indecent exposure of the person in a public omnibus, in the view of persons travelling therein (*R v Holmes* (1853) Dears CC 207, 17 JP 390); or on the roof of a back of a house, so as to be visible to the persons in the back premises of many other houses (*R v Thallman* (1863) Le & Ca 326, 27 JP 790); and it is not necessary that the exposure should be on a[4] public highway (id). It may be at a spot where the public are in the habit of trespassing without interference, although not a public place (*R v Wellard* (1884) 14 QBD 63, 49 JP 296). Showing and keeping a booth on Epsom Downs for an indecent performance to anyone desirous of seeing it were held to constitute a common law offence (*R v Saunders* (1875) 1 QBD 15). More than one person must at least have been able to see the act of indecency complained of, but actual disgust or annoyance on the part of an observer need not be proved (*R v Mayling* [1963] 2 QB 717, [1963] 1 All ER 687, 127 JP 269; *R v Lunderbech* [1991] Crim LR 784).

Drawing a crowd of noisy and disorderly people close to a dwelling-house by music and fireworks is a nuisance which will be restrained by injunction (*Walker v Brewster* (1867) LR 5 Eq 25, 32 JP 87, and Treat. 115). Defendants, the manager and proprietors of a theatre, were held liable for obstruction to access to plaintiff's premises by reason of the assembling of a large crowd or queue in the street previously to opening of theatre (Cozens-Hardy MR and Swinfen-Eady LJ; Phillimore LJ *diss*) (*Lyons, Sons & Co v Gulliver* [1914] 1 Ch 631, 78 JP 98).

If the nuisance is stopped before the hearing an injunction may not be granted (*Barber v Penley* [1893] 2 Ch 447, 57 JP 562). But if an injunction would have been granted in the first instance, costs may be given (*Wagstaff v Edison Bell Phonograph Co* (1893) 10 TLR 80). Chitty J, granted an *interim* injunction restraining two defendants, one of whom had a "merry-go-round", from playing organs at a place resorted to by excursionists, sixty yards from a dwelling-house. It was held that what each did might not amount to a nuisance in law, yet if the aggregate noise caused by the two did amount to a legal nuisance, the plaintiff was entitled to the protection of the court (*Lambton v Mellish, Lambton v Cox* [1894] 3 Ch 163, 58 JP 835). As to the nuisance created by a circus, see *Inchbald v Robinson, Inchbald v Barrington* (1869) 4 Ch App 388, 38 JP 484. See also *Phillips v Thomas* (1890) 62 LT 793, and *Bedford v Leeds Corpn* (1913) 77 JP 430. Similar nuisances may be dealt with summarily under bye-laws. A bye-law made under the Municipal Corpns Act 1882, provided that no person should to the annoyance or disturbance of residents or passengers keep or manage a shooting gallery, swing-boat, roundabout, or other like thing on any street or public place or on land adjoining or near to such street or public place, provided that the bye-law should not apply to any fair lawfully held. The Queen's Bench Division upheld the bye-law (*Teale v Harris* (1896) 60 JP 744). No length of time will legalise a public nuisance (*R v Cross* (1812) 3 Camp 224, and Treat. 36 JP 242). Collecting crowds round a shop by exhibiting attractive objects and thus creating an obstruction on the highway is an indictable nuisance (*R v Lewis* (1881) 72 LT Jo 117, Treat, 46 JP 20). Nothing short of absolute necessity will justify a person in obstructing the highway. An encroachment on or enclosure of a town or village green, also any erection thereon, or disturbance, or interference or occupation of the soil thereof, which is made otherwise than with a view to the better enjoyment of such town or village green, or recreation ground, is a public nuisance (Commons

Act 1876, 39 & 40 Vict c 56, s 29). A gipsy encampment may in certain circumstances be a public nuisance, and an injunction will be granted against the owner of the land restraining him from allowing his land to be used for such a purpose (*A-G v Stone* (1895) 60 JP 168).

A defendant is guilty if he knew or ought to have known that as a result of his actions a public nuisance would be committed; actual knowledge need not be established[5]

Procedure.—Offences at common law of public nuisance are triable either way (Magistrates' Courts Act 1980, s 17 and Sch 1); for procedure see ibid, ss 17A–21 in PART I: MAGISTRATES' COURTS, PROCEDURE, ante. Punishable on summary conviction by imprisonment not exceeding **six months** and/or a fine not exceeding **the statutory maximum** (ibid, s 32). For other summary proceedings see the Environmental Protection Act 1990, ss 80 et seq in this PART: title PUBLIC HEALTH, post.

1. *R v Rimmington; R v Goldstein* [2005] UKHL 63, [2005] 3 WLR 982, [2006] Crim LR 153.
2. *R v Rimmington* [2005] UKHL 63, [2005] 3 WLR 982, [2006] Crim LR 153 (sending 538 separate postal packages containing racially offensive material to members of the public).
3. See this PART: title OBSCENE PUBLICATIONS, post.
4. A urinal adjoining a public footway in a public park is a public place, so as to subject parties committing gross indecencies there to an indictment for a nuisance (*R v Harris* (1871) LR 1 CCR 282, 35 JP 185). Where the indecency consists of an exposure of person with intent to insult any female, see the Vagrancy Act 1824, s 4, title VAGRANTS, post.
5. *R v Shorrock* [1993] 3 All ER 917, 98 Cr App R 67, approved in *R v Rimmington; R v Goldstein* [2005] UKHL 63, [2005] 3 WLR 982, [2006] Crim LR 153 (in *Goldstein* conviction quashed for causing nuisance to the public by posting or causing to be posted to a friend, an envelope containing salt which leaked causing an anthrax scare at the sorting office as no evidence that it was foreseeable by him).

OBSCENE PUBLICATIONS

8–22444 This title contains the following statutes—

Children and Young Persons (Harmful Publications) Act 1955

(3 & 4 Eliz 2 c 28)

8–22445 1. Works to which this Act applies. This Act applies to any book, magazine or other like work which is of a kind likely to fall into the hands of children or young persons[1] and consists wholly or mainly of stories told in pictures (with or without the addition of written matter), being stories portraying—

(*a*) the commission of crimes; or
(*b*) acts of violence or cruelty; or
(*c*) incidents of a repulsive or horrible nature;

in such a way that the work as a whole would tend to corrupt a child or young person into whose hands it might fall.
[Children and Young Persons (Harmful Publications) Act 1955, s 1.]

1. "Child" means a person under the age of fourteen years: "young person" means a person who has attained the age of fourteen years and is under the age of eighteen years (Children and Young Persons Act 1933, s 107, applied by Children and Young Persons (Harmful Publications) Act 1955, s 5(2)).

8–22446 2. Penalty for printing, publishing, selling, &c, works to which this Act applies. (1) A person who prints, publishes, sells or lets on hire a work to which this Act applies, or has any such work in his possession for the purpose of selling it or letting it on hire, shall be guilty of an offence and liable, on summary conviction, to imprisonment for a term not exceeding **four months*** or to a fine not exceeding **level 3** on the standard scale or to both:

Provided that, in any proceedings taken under this subsection against a person in respect of selling or letting on hire a work or of having it in his possession for the purpose of selling it or letting it on hire, it shall be a defence for him to prove that he had not examined the contents of the work and had no reasonable cause to suspect that it was one to which this Act applies.

(2) A prosecution for an offence under this section shall not, in England or Wales, be instituted[1] except by, or with the consent of, the Attorney-General[2].
[Children and Young Persons (Harmful Publications) Act 1955, s 2 as amended by the Criminal Justice Act 1982, ss 38 and 46.]

***"51 weeks" substituted by the Criminal Justice Act 2003, Sch 26, from a date to be appointed.**

1. The prosecution is "instituted" on the laying of an information for a summons or a warrant (*Willace's Case* (1797) 1 East PC 186; *Brooks v Bagshaw* [1904] 2 KB 798, 68 JP 514).

2. Any function of the Attorney-General may be discharged by the Solicitor-General if (*a*) the office of Attorney-General is vacant; (*b*) he is unable to act owing to absence or illness; or (*c*) he authorises the Solicitor-General to act in any particular case (Law Officers Act 1944, s 1).

8–22447 **3. Power to search for, and dispose of, works to which this Act applies and articles for printing them.** (1) Where, upon an information being laid before a justice of the peace that a person has, or is suspected of having, committed an offence under the last foregoing section with respect to a work (thereafter in this subsection referred to as "the relevant work"), the justice issues a summons directed to that person requiring him to answer to the information or issues a warrant to arrest that person, that or any other justice, if satisfied by written information[1] substantiated on oath that there is reasonable ground for suspecting that the said person has in his possession or under his control—

(*a*) any copies of the relevant work or any other work to which this Act applies; or
(*b*) any plate[2] prepared for the purpose of printing copies of the relevant work or any other work to which this Act applies or any photographic film prepared for that purpose;

may grant a search warrant authorising any constable to enter (if necessary by force) any premises specified in the warrant and any vehicle or stall used by the said person for the purposes of trade or business and to search the premises, vehicle or stall and seize any of the following things which the constable finds therein or thereon, that is to say:

(i) any copies of the relevant work and any copies of any other work which the constable has reasonable cause to believe to be one to which this Act applies; and
(ii) any plate[2] which the constable has reasonable cause to believe to have been prepared for the purpose of printing copies of any such work as is mentioned in paragraph (i) of this subsection and any photographic film[3] which he has reasonable cause to believe to have been prepared for that purpose.

(2) The court by or before which a person is convicted of an offence under the last foregoing section with respect to a work may order any copies of that work and any plate[2] prepared for the purpose of printing copies of that work or photographic film[3] prepared for that purpose, being copies which have, or a plate or film which has, been found in his possession or under his control, to be forfeited:

Provided that an order made under this subsection by a magistrates' court or, on appeal from a magistrates' court, by a court of quarter sessions shall not take effect until the expiration of the ordinary time[4] within which an appeal in the matter of the proceedings in which the order was made may be lodged (whether by giving notice of appeal or applying for a case to be stated for the opinion of the High Court) or, where such an appeal is duly lodged, until the appeal is finally decided or abandoned.

(3) *Application to Scotland.*

[Children and Young Persons (Harmful Publications) Act 1955, s 3 as amended by the Police and Criminal Evidence Act 1984, Sch 7.]

1. Note that this "written information" may not be submitted except at the same time or after a prosecution has been "instituted" by the issue of a summons or a warrant for an offence under s 2, supra, and this may only be with the consent of the Attorney-General (see s 2, supra).
2. "Plate" includes block, mould, matrix and stencil (s 5(2)).
3. "Photographic film" includes photographic plate (s 5(2)).
4. This will be 21 days in respect of an appeal to the Crown Court (Criminal Procedure Rules 2005, Part 63) or an application for a case stated (Magistrates' Courts Act 1980, s 111).

8–22448 **4. Prohibition of importation of works to which this Act applies and articles for printing them.** The importation of—

(*a*) any work to which this Act applies; and
(*b*) any plate prepared for the purpose of printing copies of any such work and any photographic film prepared for that purpose;

is hereby prohibited[1].

[Children and Young Persons (Harmful Publications) Act 1955, s 4.]

1. Importation will be an offence under the Customs and Excise Management Act 1979; see ss 49(1)(*b*) and 50 thereof.

Obscene Publications Act 1959[1]

(7 & 8 Eliz 2 c 66)

8–22449 **1. Test of obscenity.** (1) For the purposes of this Act an article shall be deemed to be obscene if its effect or (where the article comprises two or more distinct items) the effect of any one of its items[2] is, if taken as a whole, such as to tend to deprave and corrupt[3] persons[4] who are likely, having regard to all relevant circumstances, to read, see or hear the matter contained or embodied in it[5].

(2) In this Act "article"[6] means any description of article containing or embodying matter to be read or looked at or both, any sound record, and any film or other record of a picture or pictures.

(3) For the purposes of this Act a person publishes[7] an article who—

(*a*) [8] distributes, circulates, sells, lets on hire, gives, or lends it, or who offers[9] it for sale or for letting on hire; or

(*b*) in the case of an article containing or embodying matter to be looked at or a record, shows, plays or projects it, or, where the matter is data stored electronically, transmits that data:

(4) For the purposes of this Act a person also publishes an article to the extent that any matter recorded on it is included by him in a programme included in a programme service[10].

(5) Where the inclusion of any matter in a programme so included would, if that matter were recorded matter, constitute the publication of an obscene article for the purposes of this Act by virtue of subsection (4) above, this Act shall have effect in relation to the inclusion of that matter in that programme as if it were recorded matter.

(6) In this section "programme" and "programme service" have the same meaning as in the Broadcasting Act 1990[10].

[Obscene Publications Act 1959, s 1, as amended by the Criminal Law Act 1977, s 53, the Broadcasting Act 1990, s 162 and Sch 21 and the Criminal Justice and Public Order Act 1994, Sch 9.]

---

1. For the application of this Act to television and sound programmes, reference should be made to the Broadcasting Act 1990, Sch 15, title TELECOMMUNICATIONS AND BROADCASTING, post.

2. Where an article, such as a magazine, comprises a number of distinct items, the test has to be applied to the individual items and if it shows one item to be obscene that is enough to make the whole article obscene (*R v Anderson* [1972] 1 QB 304, [1971] 3 All ER 1152, 136 JP 97).

3. The words "deprave and corrupt" refer to the effect on the mind, including the emotions, and it is not necessary that any physical (or "overt") sexual activity should result: see *DPP v Whyte* [1972] AC 849, [1972] 3 All ER 12, 136 JP 686; in which case Lord WILBERFORCE and Lord CROSS also stated that the proposition that likely readers of the books, being addicts of that type of material whose morals were already in a state of depravity or corruption, were incapable of being further depraved or corrupted, was fallacious.

4. In relation to a book "persons" cannot mean all readers, nor any one reader, nor, necessarily, the majority of readers or the average reader: the question is whether the effect of the book is to tend to deprave and corrupt a significant proportion; what is a significant proportion being a matter for the jury (or magistrates) to decide: *R v Calder & Boyars Ltd* [1968] 3 All ER 644, 133 JP 20; but it is not appropriate for justices to consider what is the largest category of "most likely" readers and then to exclude persons falling within other categories from consideration, for it does not follow that the latter are not also "likely" readers: see *DPP v Whyte*, supra. For consideration of the position where obscene articles are intended for publication outside the jurisdiction of the English courts, see *Gold Star Publications v DPP* [1981] 2 All ER 257, [1981] 1 WLR 732.

5. The test for obscenity depends upon the publication itself and the intention of the publisher is irrelevant (*R v Shaw* [1961] 1 All ER 330). (This was a decision of the Court of Criminal Appeal, on which issue there was no appeal to the House of Lords in the later state of this prosecution.) Obscenity and its tendency to deprave and corrupt are not limited to matters of sex (*John Calder (Publications) Ltd v Powell* [1965] 1 All ER 159, 129 JP 136, concerning a book relating to drug taking). In *DPP v A & BC Chewing Gum Ltd* [1968] 1 QB 159, [1967] 2 All ER 504, 131 JP 373, a Divisional Court of the Queen's Bench Division remitted a case for rehearing on the ground that a magistrates' court had wrongly refused to hear evidence of a psychiatrist about the likely effect on the minds of children of cards (sold with chewing gum) alleged by the prosecution to be obscene; but in *R v Anderson*, supra, the Court of Appeal held that that case should be regarded as highly exceptional in that the alleged obscene matter was (*a*) directed at very young children, and (*b*) was itself of a somewhat unusual kind; normally the issue "obscene or no" must be tried by the jury (or magistrates) without the assistance of expert evidence on that issue. See also *R v Staniforth* [1975] Crim LR 291, and *DPP v Jordan* [1977] AC 699, [1976] 3 All ER 775.

Proceedings at common law are now considerably restricted by s 2(4) of the Obscene Publications Act 1959.

See also s 28 of the Town Police Clauses Act 1847, in this PART: title TOWNS IMPROVEMENT; TOWN POLICE, post; Children and Young Persons Act 1933 s 39 in PART V: YOUTH COURTS, ante; Judicial Proceedings (Regulation of Reports) Act 1926, title LIBEL, ante.

6. A video cassette is an article within the meaning of s 1 (2) (*A-G's Reference (No 5 of 1980)* [1980] 3 All ER 816). Expert evidence may be necessary to act as guidance where the effects of potentially corrupting material was outside the experience of the ordinary man or woman; *R v Skirving, R v Grossman* [1985] QB 819, [1985] 2 All ER 705 (book containing instructions and recipes on how to make best use of the drug cocaine).

7. The act of developing and printing a photographic film depicting obscene acts, of which a print was then returned to the customer, is capable of constituting an act of publication within the meaning of s 1(3) (*R v Taylor* [1995] 1 Cr App Rep 131, 158 JP 317, [1994] Crim LR 527).

8. Forms of publication fall into three distinct groups: (*i*) "sells, lets on hire, gives or lends" means publication to an individual; (*ii*) "distributes, circulates" involves more than one person; (*iii*) a mere "offer for sale or letting on hire" constitutes publication: discussed by the Court of Criminal Appeal in *R v Barker* [1962] 1 All ER 748, [1962] 1 WLR 349, 126 JP 274. Whether the article will tend to deprave and corrupt may depend upon the persons to whom it is published (*R v Barker*, supra; *R v Clayton and Halsey* [1963] 1 QB 163, [1962] 3 All ER 500, 127 JP 7 (purchase made by police officers)). See now Obscene Publications Act 1964, post.

9. Display in a shop window may be merely "an invitation to treat" and not "an offer for sale", *cf Fisher v Bell* [1961] 1 QB 394, [1960] 3 All ER 731, 125 JP 101; applied to this Act by the Queen's Bench Divisional Court in *Mella v Monahan* [1961] Crim LR 175. See now the Obscene Publications Act 1964, post.

10. For the meaning of "programme" and "programme service", see ss 202 and 201 of the Broadcasting Act 1990, in this PART: title WIRELESS TELEGRAPHY AND BROADCASTING, post. For the application of the Obscene Publications Act 1959 to television and sound programmes, see the Broadcasting Act 1990, Sch 15, in this PART: title TELECOMMUNICATIONS AND BROADCASTING, post.

8–22450 **2. Prohibition on publication of obscene matter**[1]**.** (1) Subject as hereinafter provided, any person who, whether for gain or not, publishes an obscene article or who has an obscene article for publication for gain (whether gain to himself or gain to another)[2] shall be liable[3]—

(*a*) on summary conviction to a fine not exceeding **the statutory maximum** or to imprisonment for a term not exceeding **six months**;

(*b*) on conviction on indictment to a **fine** or to imprisonment for a term not exceeding **three years** or **both**.

(2) *Repealed.*

(3) A prosecution for an offence against this section shall not be commenced more than two years after the commission of the offence.

(3A) Proceedings for an offence under this section shall not be instituted except by or with the consent of the Director of Public Prosecutions in any case where the article in question is a moving picture film of a width of not less than sixteen millimetres and the relevant publication or the only other publication which followed or could reasonably have been expected to follow from the relevant publication took place or (as the case may be) was to take place in the course of an exhibition of a film and in this subsection "the relevant publication" means—

(*a*) in the case of any proceedings under this section for publishing an obscene article, the publication in respect of which the defendant would be charged if the proceedings were brought; and

(*b*) in the case of any proceedings under this section for having an obscene article for publication for gain, the publication which, if the proceedings were brought, the defendant would be alleged to have had in contemplation.

(4) A person publishing an article shall not be proceeded against for an offence at common law consisting of the publication of any matter contained or embodied in the article where it is of the essence of the offence that the matter is obscene[4].

(4A) Without prejudice to subsection (4) above, a person shall not be proceeded against for an offence at common law—

(*a*) in respect of an exhibition of a film or anything said or done in the course of an exhibition of a film, where it is of the essence of the common law offence that the exhibition or, as the case may be, what was said or done was obscene, indecent, offensive, disgusting or injurious to morality; or

(*b*) in respect of an agreement to give an exhibition of a film or to cause anything to be said or done in the course of such an exhibition where the common law offence consists of conspiring to corrupt public morals or to do any act contrary to public morals or decency.

(5) A person shall not be convicted of an offence against this section if he proves[5] that he had not examined the article in respect of which he is charged and had no reasonable cause to suspect that it was such that his publication of it would make him liable to be convicted of an offence against this section.

(6) In any proceedings against a person under this section the question whether an article is obscene shall be determined without regard to any publication by another person unless it could reasonably have been expected that the publication by the other person would follow from publication by the person charged.

(7) In this section, "exhibition of a film" has the meaning given in paragraph 15 of Schedule 1 to the Licensing Act 2003.

[Obscene Publications Act 1959, s 2, as amended by the Criminal Law Act 1977, ss 28, 53 and Sch 13, the Cinematograph (Amendment) Act 1982, Sch 1, the Cinemas Act 1985, Sch 2 and the Licensing Act 2003, Sch 6.]

1. For the application of the Act to television and sound programmes see the Broadcasting Act 1990, Sch 15 in this PART, title TELECOMMUNICATIONS AND BROADCASTING post.

2. The alternative offence was added by the Obscene Publications Act 1964, post, to which reference should be made, particularly with regard to modifications of sub-ss. (5) and (6) of this section.

3. For procedure in respect of an offence triable either way, see Magistrates' Courts Act 1980, ss 17A–21, ante.

4. A prosecution for the common law offence of outraging public decency is not barred by s 2(4) (*R v Gibson* [1990] 2 QB 619, [1991] 1 All ER 439, 155 JP 126, CA).

5. If the defendant avails himself of this statutory defence, the onus of proof is on him (*Cant v Harley & Sons Ltd* [1938] 2 All ER 768); but less so than on the prosecution in proving a case beyond reasonable doubt and the onus may be discharged by evidence of probability (*R v Carr-Briant* [1943] KB 607, [1943] 2 All ER 156, 107 JP 167). Note also the special defence that the publication was for the public good created by s 4, post.

6. See title THEATRE, CINEMATOGRAPH AND VIDEO, in this PART: post.

8–22451 **3. Powers of search and seizure.** (1) If a justice of the peace is satisfied by information[1] on oath that there is reasonable ground for suspecting that, in any premises in the petty sessions area for which he acts, or on any stall or vehicle in that area, being premises or a stall or vehicle specified in the information, obscene articles are, or are from time to time, kept for publication[2] for gain, the justice may issue a warrant[1] under his hand empowering any constable to enter[3] (if need be by force) and search the premises, or to search the stall or vehicle, and to seize and remove any articles found therein or thereon which the constable has reason to believe to be obscene articles and to be kept for publication for gain.

(2) A warrant under the foregoing subsection shall, if any obscene articles are seized under the warrant, also empower the seizure and removal of any documents found in the premises or, as the case may be, on the stall or vehicle which relate to a trade or business carried on at the premises or from the stall or vehicle.

(3) Subject to subsection (3A) of this section, any articles seized under subsection (1) of this section shall be brought before a justice of the peace acting for the same petty sessions area as the justice who issued the warrant, and the justice before whom the articles are brought may thereupon issue a summons[4] to the occupier of the premises or, as the case may be, the user of the stall or vehicle to appear on a day specified in the summons before a magistrates' court[5] for that petty sessions area to show cause why the articles or any of them should not be forfeited; and if the court is satisfied[6], as respects any of the articles, that at the time when they were seized they were obscene articles[7] kept for publication for gain, the court shall order[8] those articles to be forfeited[9];

Provided that if the person summoned does not appear, the court shall not make an order unless service of the summons is proved[10].

Provided also that this subsection does not apply in relation to any article seized under subsection (1) of this section which is returned to the occupier of the premises or, as the case may be, to the user of the stall or vehicle in or on which it was found.

(3A) Without prejudice to the duty of a court to make an order for the forfeiture of an article where section 1(4) of the Obscene Publications Act 1964 applies (orders made on conviction), in a case where by virtue of subsection (3A) of section 2 of this Act proceedings under the said section 2 for having an article for publication for gain could not be instituted except by or with the consent of the Director of Public Prosecutions, no order for the forfeiture of the article shall be made under this section unless the warrant under which the article was seized was issued on an information laid by or on behalf of the Director of Public Prosecutions.

(4) In addition to the person summoned, any other person being the owner, author or maker of any of the articles brought before the court, or any other person through whose hands they had passed before being seized, shall be entitled[11] to appear before the court on the day specified in the summons to show cause why they should not be forfeited.

(5) Where an order is made under this section for the forfeiture of any articles, any person who appeared, or was entitled[12] to appear, to show cause against the making of the order may appeal to the Crown Court; and no such order shall take effect until the expiration of the period within which notice of appeal to the Crown Court may be given against the order[13], or, if before the expiration thereof notice of appeal is duly given or application is made for the statement of a case for the opinion of the High Court, until the final determination or abandonment of the proceedings on the appeal or case.

(6) If as respects any articles brought before it the court does not order forfeiture, the court may if it thinks fit order the person on whose information the warrant for the seizure of the articles was issued to pay such costs as the court thinks reasonable to any person who has appeared before the court to show cause why those articles should not be forfeited; and costs ordered to be paid under this subsection shall be enforceable as a civil debt[14].

(7) For the purposes of this section the question whether an article is obscene shall be determined on the assumption that copies of it would be published in any manner likely having regard to the circumstances in which it was found, but in no other manner[15].

[Obscene Publications Act 1959, s 3, as amended by the Courts Act 1971, Schs 8 and 9, the Criminal Law Act 1977, s 53 and Sch 12 and the Police and Criminal Evidence Act 1984, Sch 7.]

---

1. A warrant under this subsection shall not be issued except on an information laid by or on behalf of the Director of Public Prosecutions or by a constable (Criminal Justice Act 1967, s 25). As to television and sound programmes, see also the Broadcasting Act 1990, Sch 15, title TELECOMMUNICATIONS AND BROADCASTING, post.

2. Section 2 of the Obscene Publications Act 1964, post, provides in effect, that photographic negatives kept for the reproduction of photographs therefrom are articles kept for publication, thereby overriding the contrary decision in *Straker v DPP* [1963] 1 QB 926, [1963] 1 All ER 697, 127 JP 260.

3. The issue and execution of the warrant must be in conformity with the Police and Criminal Evidence Act 1984, ss 15 and 16, ante in PART I: MAGISTRATES' COURTS, PROCEDURE.

4. The summons will be issued on the information previously made on oath upon which the warrant was found: it is unnecessary to have a fresh information as a preliminary to the issue of a summons. It has been said by the High Court *obiter* that the summons must be issued within a reasonable time after the execution of the warrant (*Cox v Stinton* [1951] 2 KB 1021, [1951] 2 All ER 637, 115 JP 490).

5. The court need not necessarily consist of justices different from the justices who examined the articles before the summons was issued (*Morgan v Bowker* [1964] 1 QB 507, [1963] 1 All ER 691, 127 JP 264).

6. The Queen's Bench Divisional Court has upheld a direction of a judge hearing an appeal from justices by which appellant and respondent were enabled either to agree or to submit representative items of each of three degrees of obscenity for the court to consider; it would however have preferred a division into categories of pornographic behaviour or sexual perversions (*R v Crown Court at Snaresbrook, ex p Metropolitan Police Comr* (1984) 148 JP 449.

7. An English court is both competent and entitled to hold that articles are obscene, notwithstanding that they are intended for publication outside the jurisdiction of the English courts (*Gold Star Publications v DPP* [1981] 2 All ER 257, [1981] 1 WLR 732).

8. The order that the articles shall be forfeited relates to the "whole" articles even if parts only are obscene: thus where illustrations on the inside covers of a book were obscene, the whole book, and not the covers only, are required to be forfeited (*Paget Publications Ltd v Watson* [1952] 1 All ER 1256, 116 JP 320). Note the special defence that the publication

was for the public good created by s 4, post. If articles are seized under this section and a person is convicted of having them for publication for gain (s 2 (as amended) ante), the court on conviction shall order forfeiture (Obscene Publications Act 1964, s 1(4), post).

9. Where an order had been made for forfeiture of some only of many articles seized, it was held that appeal by way of case stated was appropriate in respect of the articles not ordered to be forfeited: but the court expressed the hope that such a course would be taken only in extreme cases (*Burke v Copper* [1962] 2 All ER 14, [1962] 1 WLR 700, 126 JP 319).

10. For service of summons, see for proof of service, see Criminal Procedure Rules 2005, Part 4, in PART I: MAGISTRATES' COURTS, PROCEDURE, ante.

11. There is no duty to issue separate summonses to persons so entitled although each of them is entitled to "show cause" separately: their knowledge of the proceedings will be obtained from the summons issued to the occupier of the premises or user of the stall or vehicle.

12. Note that the right of appeal is not restricted to persons who appeared before the magistrates' court: appeal is available to all who are entitled to appear by virtue of sub-s (4), supra.

13. This is 21 days: see the Criminal Procedure Rules 2005, Part 63, in PART I: MAGISTRATES' COURTS, PROCEDURE, ante.

14. See Magistrates' Courts Act 1980, s 58, in PART I, ante.

15. The court must hear evidence tendered by the defence of the circumstances in which the articles were found, eg the nature of the business carried on, the methods employed in it, and then determine whether the articles would tend to deprave or corrupt persons to whom publication would be so made (*Morgan v Bowker* [1964] 1 QB 507, [1963] 1 All ER 691, 127 JP 264).

8–22452 **4. Defence of public good**[1]. (1) Subject to subsection (1A) of this section, a person shall not be convicted of an offence against section two of this Act, and an order for forfeiture shall not be made under the foregoing section, if it is proved that publication of the article in question is justified as being for the public good on the ground that it is in the interests of science, literature, art or learning[2], or of other objects of general concern[3].

(1A) Subsection (1) of this section shall not apply where the article in question is a moving picture film or soundtrack, but—

(*a*) a person shall not be convicted of an offence against section 2 of this Act in relation to any such film or soundtrack, and

(*b*) an order for forfeiture of any such film or soundtrack shall not be made under section 3 of this Act,

if it is proved that publication of the film or soundtrack is justified as being for the public good on the ground that it is in the interests of drama, opera, ballet or any other art, or of literature or learning.

(2) It is hereby declared that the evidence of experts as to the literary, artistic, scientific or other merits of an article may be admitted in any proceedings under this Act either to establish or to negative the said ground[4].

(3) In this section "moving picture soundtrack" means any sound record designed for playing with a moving picture film, whether incorporated with the film or not.

[Obscene Publications Act 1959, s 4, as amended by the Criminal Law Act 1977, s 53.]

1. On a charge under s 2(1) the proper course is for the court to determine the issues (i) whether the article is obscene and (ii) whether it was published by the defendant, before considering whether the defendant has succeeded in establishing the defence under s 4(1) (*DPP v Jordan* [1977] AC 699, [1976] 3 All ER 775, 141 JP 13).

2. "Learning" means a product of scholarship: *A-G's Reference* (*No* 3 *of* 1977) [1978] 3 All ER 1166, [1978] 1 WLR 1123.

3. These other objects must be such as not only conduce to the public good but are of concern to members of the public in general. The words "other objects of general concern" fall within the same area as "science, literature, art or learning". Expert evidence, in support of a defence under s 4, that obscene material is of therapeutic benefit to persons with certain sexual tendencies is, accordingly, inadmissible (*DPP v Jordan*, supra.)

4. The court is not bound by the evidence of such experts even though it is not contradicted by counter-evidence (*John Calder* (*Publications*) *Ltd v Powell* [1965] 1 QB 509, [1965] 1 All ER 159, 129 JP 136). The onus is on the defence to make out this defence on the balance of probabilities, but the court may require the defence witnesses on this defence to be heard first and the prosecution witnesses in rebuttal (*R v Calder & Boyars Ltd* [1968] 3 All ER 644).

Obscene Publications Act 1964

(1964 c 74)

8–22560 The Obscene Publications Act 1964 amends s 2(1) of the Act of 1959, by creating the offence of *having* an obscene article for publication for gain (s 1(1)).

A person shall be deemed to have an article for publication for gain if with a view to such publication he has the article in his ownership, possession or control (s 1(2)).

By this amendment, a conviction may be obtained in circumstances where a prosecution for publishing would fail by reason of the decisions in *R v Clayton and Halsey*, and *Mella v Monahan*, ante[1].

In proceedings brought under this amendment, the following provisions apply in place of sub-ss (5) and (6) of s 2 of the Act of 1959—

(*a*) he shall not be convicted of that offence if he proves that he had not examined the article and had no reasonable cause to suspect that it was such that his having it would make him liable to be convicted of an offence against that section; and (*b*) the question whether the article is obscene shall be determined by reference to such publication for gain of the article as in the circumstances may reasonably be inferred he had in contemplation and to any further publication that could reasonably be expected to follow from it, but not to any other publication (s 1(3)).

1. See notes 7 and 8 to s 1 of the Obscene Publications Act 1959.

8–22561 **2. Negatives, etc for production of obscene articles.** (1) The Obscene Publications Act 1959 (as amended by this Act) shall apply in relation to anything which is intended to be used, either alone or as one of a set, for the reproduction or manufacture therefrom of articles containing or embodying matter to be read, looked at or listened to, as if it were an article containing or embodying that matter so far as that matter is to be derived from it or from the set.

(2) For the purposes of the Obscene Publications Act 1959 (as so amended) an article shall be deemed to be had or kept for publication if it is had or kept for the reproduction or manufacture therefrom of articles for publication; and the question whether an article so had or kept is obscene shall—

(*a*) for purposes of s 2 of the Act be determined in accordance with s 1(3)(*b*) above as if any reference there to publication of the article were a reference to publication of articles reproduced or manufactured from it; and

(*b*) for purposes of s 3 of the Act be determined on the assumption that articles reproduced or manufactured from it would be published in any manner likely having regard to the circumstances in which it was found, but in no other manner.

[Obscene Publications Act 1964, s 2.]

Indecent Displays (Control) Act 1981

(1981 c 42)

8–22600 **1. Indecent displays.** (1) If any indecent matter is publicly displayed the person making the display and any person causing or permitting the display to be made shall be guilty of an offence.

(2) Any matter which is displayed in or so as to be visible from any public place shall, for the purposes of this section, be deemed to be publicly displayed.

(3) In subsection (2) above, "public place", in relation to the display of any matter, means any place to which the public have or are permitted to have access (whether on payment or otherwise) while that matter is displayed except—

(*a*) a place to which the public are permitted to have access only on payment which is or includes payment for that display; or

(*b*) a shop or any part of a shop to which the public can only gain access by passing beyond an adequate warning notice;

but the exclusions contained in paragraphs (*a*) and (*b*) above shall only apply where persons under the age of 18 years are not permitted to enter while the display in question is continuing.

(4) Nothing in this section applies in relation to any matter—

(*a*) included by any person in a television broadcasting service or other television programme service (within the meaning of Part I of the Broadcasting Act 1990);

(*b*) included in the display of an art gallery or museum and visible only from within the gallery or museum; or

(*c*) displayed by or with the authority of, and visible only from within a building occupied by, the Crown or any local authority; or

(*d*) included in a performance of a play (within the meaning of paragraph 14(1) of Schedule 1 to the Licensing Act 2003) in England and Wales or of a play (within the meaning of the Theatres Act 1968) in Scotland;

(*e*) included in an exhibition of a film, within the meaning of paragraph 15 of Schedule 1 to the Licensing Act 2003, in England and Wales, or a film exhibition, as defined in the Cinemas Act 1985, in Scotland—

(i) given in a place which as regards that exhibition is required to be licensed under section 1 of that Act or by virtue only of section 5, 7 or 8 of that Act is not required to be so licensed; or

(ii) which is an exhibition to which section 6 of that Act applies given by an exempted organisation as defined in subsection (6) of that section.

(5) In this section "matter" includes anything capable of being displayed, except that it does not include an actual human body or any part thereof; and in determining for the purpose of this section whether any displayed matter is indecent—

(*a*) there shall be disregarded any part of that matter which is not exposed to view; and

(*b*) account may be taken of the effect of juxtaposing one thing with another.

(6) A warning notice shall not be adequate for the purposes of this section unless it complies with the following requirements—

(*a*) The warning notice must contain the following words, and no others—

"WARNING

Persons passing beyond this notice will find material on display which they may consider indecent No admittance to persons under 18 years of age."

(*b*) The word "WARNING" must appear as a heading.

(*c*) No pictures or other matter shall appear on the notice.

(*d*) The notice must be so situated that no one could reasonably gain access to the shop or part of the shop in question without being aware of the notice and it must be easily legible by any person gaining such access.

[Indecent Displays (Control) Act 1981, s 1 as amended by the Cinematograph (Amendment) Act 1982, Sch 1, the Cable and Broadcasting Act 1984, Sch 5, the Cinemas Act 1985, Sch 2, the Broadcasting Act 1990, Sch 20 and the Licensing Act 2003, Sch 6.]

8–22601 2. Powers of arrest, seizure and entry. (1) *Repealed.*

(2) A constable may seize any article which he has reasonable grounds for believing to be or to contain indecent matter and to have been used in the commission of an offence under this Act.

(3) In England and Wales, a justice of the peace if satisfied on information on oath that there are reasonable grounds for suspecting that an offence under this Act has been or is being committed on any premises and, in Scotland, a sheriff or justice of the peace on being so satisfied on evidence on oath, may issue a warrant[1] authorising any constable to enter the premises specified in the information or, as the case may be, evidence (if need be by force) to seize any article which the constable has reasonable grounds for believing to be or to contain indecent matter and to have been used in the commission of an offence under this Act.

[Indecent Displays (Control) Act 1981, s 2 as amended by the Police and Criminal Evidence Act 1984, Sch 7.]

1. The issue and execution of this warrant must conform to the Police and Criminal Evidence Act 1984, ss 15 and 16 in PART I: MAGISTRATES' COURTS, PROCEDURE, ante.

8–22602 3. Offences by corporations. (1) Where a body corporate is guilty of an offence under this Act and it is proved that the offence occurred with the consent or connivance of, or was attributable to any neglect on the part of, any director, manager, secretary or other officer of the body, or any person who was purporting to act in any such capacity he, as well as the body corporate, shall be deemed to be guilty of that offence and shall be liable to be proceeded against and punished accordingly.

(2) Where the affairs of a body corporate are managed by its members, subsection (1) shall apply in relation to the acts and defaults of a member in connection with his functions of management as if he were a director of the body corporate.

[Indecent Displays (Control) Act 1981, s 3.]

8–22603 4. Penalties. (1) In England and Wales, any person guilty of an offence under this Act shall be liable[1]—

(*a*) on summary conviction, to a fine not exceeding **the statutory maximum**; or

(*b*) on conviction on indictment, to imprisonment for a term not exceeding **two years** or a **fine** or **both**.

(2) *Scotland.*

(3) *Repealed.*

[Indecent Displays (Control) Act 1981, s 4 amended by the Statute Law (Repeals) Act 1993, Sch 1.]

1. For procedure in respect of a triable either way offence, see the Magistrates' Courts Act 1980, ss 17A–21, in PART I, ante.

OFFENSIVE WEAPONS

8–22629 This title contains the following statutes—

8–22630 PREVENTION OF CRIME ACT 1953
8–22649 RESTRICTION OF OFFENSIVE WEAPONS ACT 1959
8–22650 BIOLOGICAL WEAPONS ACT 1974
8–22660 CROSSBOWS ACT 1987
8–22680 CRIMINAL JUSTICE ACT 1988
8–22690 CHEMICAL WEAPONS ACT 1996
8–22728 KNIVES ACT 1997

8–22740 LANDMINES ACT 1998
8–22742 NUCLEAR EXPLOSIONS (PROHIBITION AND INSPECTIONS) ACT 1998

and the following statutory instruments—

8–22744 Criminal Justice Act 1988 (Offensive Weapons) Order 1988
8–22746 Knives (Forfeited Property) Regulations 1997

Prevention of Crime Act 1953

(1 & 2 Eliz 2 c 14)

8–22630 **1. Prohibition of the carrying of offensive weapons without lawful authority or reasonable excuse.** (1) Any person who without lawful authority or reasonable excuse[1], the proof whereof shall lie on him, has with[2] him in any public place any offensive weapon[3] shall be guilty of an offence, and shall be liable[4]—

(*a*) on summary conviction, to imprisonment for a term not exceeding **six months** or a fine not exceeding **the statutory maximum**, or **both**;

(*b*) on conviction on indictment, to imprisonment for a term not exceeding **four years** or a **fine** or **both**.

(2) Where any person is convicted of an offence under subsection (1) of this section the court may make an order for the forfeiture[5] or disposal of any weapon in respect of which the offence was committed.

(3) *Repealed.*

(4) In this section "public place"[6] includes any highway and any other premises or place to which at the material time the public have or are permitted to have access, whether on payment or otherwise[3]; and "offensive weapon" means any article made or adapted[7] for use for causing injury to the person, or intended[8] by the person having it with him for such use by him[9] or by some other person.

[Prevention of Crime Act 1953, s 1, as amended by the Criminal Justice Act 1967, Sch 3, the Criminal Law Act 1977, ss 28 and 32, the Police and Criminal Evidence Act 1984, Sch 7, the Public Order Act 1986, Sch 2, the Criminal Justice Act 1988, s 46 and the Offensive Weapons Act 1996 s 2.]

---

1. This saving is identified with the carrying of the weapon, not with the manner of its use (*R v Jura* [1954] 1 QB 503, [1954] 1 All ER 696, 118 JP 280). Apart therefrom, injury caused by the weapon is evidence that it was carried for that use: see sub-s (4), infra; but if an article (possessed lawfully or for good reason) is used offensively to cause injury, this does not necessarily prove the intent required (ie to use for causing injury) which the prosecution must show in respect of articles which are not offensive weapons per se (*R v Dayle* [1973] 3 All ER 1151, 138 JP 65). The prosecution must prove, in the case of an article which is not an offensive weapon per se, e.g. a domestic knife (or an ordinary sheath knife, *R v Williamson* [1978] Crim LR 229), that at the time and place alleged it was the defendant's intention to use it for causing injury (*R v Allamby* [1974] 3 All ER 126, 138 JP 659: in *Bates v Bulman* (1979) 68 Cr App Rep 21 it was held that, as the purport of the Act was to prevent the carrying of offensive weapons, an offence was not committed by a defendant who seized a clasp knife, which he had not been carrying, for instant use on his victim. See also *C v DPP* [2002] Crim LR 322, where a dog was released from its lead and the lead was then used violently against police officers; it was held that the evidence had not been capable of sustaining the justices' conclusion that the intent to cause injury, which made the lead an offensive weapon, had been formed prior to the occasion of its actual use. A flick knife is an offensive weapon per se (*R v Simpson* [1983] 3 All ER 789, [1983] 1 WLR 1494, 48 JP 33, CA. See also *Ohlson v Hylton* [1975] Crim LR 292, *R v Giles* [1976] Crim LR 253 and *R v Veasey* [1999] Crim LR 158, CA). "Injury" includes intimidation of a sort which is capable of producing injury through the operation of shock (*Woodward v Koessler* [1958] 3 All ER 557, 123 JP 14, as explained in *R v Edmonds* [1963] 2 QB 142, [1963] 1 All ER 828, 127 JP 283). Self protection from imminent attack may be a reasonable excuse (*Evans v Hughes* [1972] 3 All ER 412, 136 JP 725) but not the carrying of a knife on the off chance of being attacked (*R v Peacock* [1973] Crim LR 639), nor to repel unlawful violence which the defendant had knowingly and deliberately brought about by creating a situation in which violence was liable to be inflicted (*Malnik v DPP* [1989] Crim LR 451). See also *Bradley v Moss* [1974] Crim LR 430, and *Pittard v Mahoney* [1977] Crim LR 169. Security guards at dance halls who each carried a truncheon "as a deterrent and as part of the uniform" had no reasonable excuse in law (*R v Spanner, Poulter, Ward* [1973] Crim LR 704).

In *Bryan v Mott* [1976] Crim LR 64 it was held that it was not a "reasonable excuse" to have an offensive weapon for the purpose of committing suicide.

2. The onus is on the prosecution to prove that the accused knowingly had the weapon with him (*R v Cugullere* [1961] 2 All ER 343, 125 JP 414), and, where two or more are jointly charged, that each knew of weapons that another had with him and that there was a common purpose (*R v Edmonds* [1963] 2 QB 142, [1963] 1 All ER 828, 127 JP 283). The fact that the accused forgot he had the weapon is not in itself a reasonable excuse (*R v McCalla* (1988) 152 JP 481, 87 Cr App Rep 372, CA). However, depending on the circumstances of a particular case, forgetfulness may be relevant to whether or not a defendant has a reasonable excuse for possession of an offensive weapon (*R v Glidewell* (1999) 163 JP 557, CA). The question of "lawful authority or reasonable excuse" does not arise until the prosecutor has established that the accused had with him an "offensive weapon" as alternatively defined by s 1(4) of the Act (*R v Petrie* [1961] 1 All ER 466, 125 JP 198).

3. Defined in s 1(4), post. See also note to the definition of 'public place' in s 139 of the Criminal Justice Act 1988 and note thereto, post.

4. For procedure in respect of an offence triable either way, see Magistrates' Courts Act 1980, ss 17A–21, in PART I: MAGISTRATES' COURTS, PROCEDURE, ante.

5. For disposal of forfeited weapons, see Magistrates' Courts Act 1980, s 140, in PART I: MAGISTRATES' COURTS, PROCEDURE, ante.

6. In *Knox v Anderton* (1983) 147 JP 340, [1983] Crim LR 114, the upper landing of a block of flats on a housing estate was held to be a public place.

7. A machete in a scabbard and "Black Widow" catapult (a powerful catapult made of 2 strong pieces of rubber tubing, a leather sling and a forearm rest) were held not to be made or adapted for use for causing injury to the person (*Southwell v Chadwick* (1987) 85 Cr App Rep 235).

8. "Recklessness" as to whether the article will cause injury is insufficient: *R v Byrne* [2003] EWCA Crim 3253, [2004] Crim LR 582.

9. A flick knife as defined in s 1(1)(*a*) of the Restriction of Offensive Weapons Act 1959 is an offensive weapon per se (*Gibson v Wales* [1983] 1 All ER 869, [1983] 1 WLR 393, 76 Cr App Rep 60.

Restriction of Offensive Weapons Act 1959

(7 & 8 Eliz 2 c 37)

8–22649 Penalties for offences in connection with dangerous weapons. (1) Any person who manufactures, sells or hires or offers for sale or hire or exposes or has in his possession for the purpose of sale or hire[1] or lends or gives to any other person—

(*a*) any knife which has a blade which opens automatically by hand pressure applied to a button, spring or other device in or attached to the handle of the knife, sometimes known as a "flick knife" or "flick gun"; or

(*b*) any knife which has a blade which is released from the handle or sheath thereof by the force of gravity or the application of centrifugal force and which, when released, is locked in place by means of a button, spring, lever, or other device, sometimes known as a "gravity knife",

shall be guilty of an offence and shall be liable on summary conviction to imprisonment for a term not exceeding **six months** or to a fine not exceeding **level 5** on the standard scale or to **both** such imprisonment and fine.

(2) The importation of any such knife as is described in the foregoing subsection is hereby prohibited[2].

[Restriction of Offensive Weapons Act 1959, s 1, amended by the Restriction of Offensive Weapons Act 1961, s 1, the Criminal Justice Act 1982, ss 35, 38 and 46 and the Criminal Justice Act 1988, s 46.]

---

1. The inclusion of these words by the Act of 1961, meets the decision in *Fisher v Bell* [1961] 1 QB 394, [1960] 3 All ER 781, 125 JP 101.

2. Non-compliance with this prohibition is an offence within s 170 of the Customs and Excise Management Act 1979, in this PART: title CUSTOMS AND EXCISE, ante.

Biological Weapons Act 1974

(1974 c 6)

8–22650 1. Restriction on development etc of certain biological agents and toxins and biological weapons. (1) No person shall develop, produce, stockpile, acquire or retain—

(*a*) any biological agent or toxin of a type and in a quantity that has no justification for prophylactic, protective or other peaceful purposes; or

(*b*) any weapon, equipment or means of delivery designed to use biological agents or toxins for hostile purposes or in armed conflict.

(1A) A person shall not—

(a) transfer any biological agent or toxin to another person or enter into an agreement to do so, or

(b) make arrangements under which another person transfers any biological agent or toxin or enters into an agreement with a third person to do so,

if the biological agent or toxin is likely to be kept or used (whether by the transferee or any other person) otherwise than for prophylactic, protective or other peaceful purposes and he knows or has reason to believe that that is the case.

(2) In this section—

"biological agent" means any microbial or other biological agent; and

"toxin" means any toxin, whatever its origin or method of production.

(3) Any person contravening this section shall be guilty of an offence and shall, on conviction on indictment, be liable to imprisonment for **life**.

[Biological Weapons Act 1974, s 1, as amended by the Anti-terrorism, Crime and Security Act 2001, s 43.]

8–22650A 1A. Extraterritorial application of section 1. (1) Section 1 applies to acts done outside the United Kingdom, but only if they are done by a United Kingdom person.

(2) Proceedings for an offence committed under section 1 outside the United Kingdom may be taken, and the offence may for incidental purposes be treated as having been committed, in any place in the United Kingdom.

(3) Her Majesty may by Order in Council extend the application of section 1, so far as it applies to acts done outside the United Kingdom, to bodies incorporated under the law of any of the Channel Islands, the Isle of Man or any colony.

(4) In this section "United Kingdom person" means a United Kingdom national, a Scottish partnership or a body incorporated under the law of a part of the United Kingdom.

(5) For this purpose a United Kingdom national is an individual who is—

(a) a British citizen, a British overseas territories citizen, a British National (Overseas) or a British Overseas citizen;

(b) a person who under the British Nationality Act 1981 (c 61) is a British subject; or

(c) a British protected person within the meaning of that Act.

(6) Nothing in this section affects any criminal liability arising otherwise than under this section.

[Biological Weapons Act 1974, s 1A, as inserted by the Anti-territorism, Crime and Security Act 2001, s 44 and amended by the British Overseas Territories Act 2002, s 2(3).]

8–22650B 1B. Revenue and Customs prosecutions. (1) Proceedings for a biological weapons offence may be instituted by the Director of Revenue and Customs Prosecutions or by order of the Commissioners for Her Majesty's Revenue and Customs if it appears to the Director or to the Commissioners that the offence has involved—

(a) the development or production outside the United Kingdom of any thing mentioned in section 1(1)(a) or (b) above;

(b) the movement of any such thing into or out of any country or territory;

(c) any proposal or attempt to do anything falling within paragraph (a) or (b) above.

(2) In this section "biological weapons offence" means an offence under section 1 of this Act or section 50 of the Anti-terrorism, Crime and Security Act 2001 (including an offence of aiding, abetting, counselling, procuring or inciting the commission of, or attempting or conspiring to commit, such an offence).

(3) Any proceedings for an offence which are instituted by order of the Commissioners under subsection (1) above shall be commenced in the name of an officer of Revenue and Customs, but may be continued by another officer.

(4) Where the Commissioners investigate, or propose to investigate, any matter with a view to determining—

(a) whether there are grounds for believing that a biological weapons offence has been committed, or

(b) whether a person should be prosecuted for such an offence,

that matter shall be treated as an assigned matter within the meaning of the Customs and Excise Management Act 1979.

(5) Nothing in this section affects any power of any person (including any officer) apart from this section.

(6) *Repealed.*

(7) This section does not apply to the institution of proceedings in Scotland.]

[Biological Weapons Act 1974, s 1B, as inserted by the Anti-terrorism, Crime and Security Act 2001, s 45 and amended by the Commissioners fo5r Revenue and Customs Act 2005, Sch 4.]

8–22651 2. Prosecution of offences. (1) Proceedings for an offence under section 1 above shall not be instituted—

(*a*) in England or Wales, except by or with the consent of the Attorney General; or

(*b*) *Northern Ireland.*

(2) *Northern Ireland.*

[Biological Weapons Act 1974, s 2, as amended by the Criminal Jurisdiction Act 1975, Sch 6.]

8–22652 3. Offences by bodies corporate. Where an offence under section 1 of this Act which is committed by a body corporate is proved to have been committed with the consent and connivance of, or to be attributable to any negligence on the part of, any director, manager, secretary or other similar officer of the body corporate, or any person who was purporting to act in any such capacity, he as well as the body corporate shall be guilty of that offence and shall be liable to be proceeded against and punished accordingly.

[Biological Weapons Act 1974, s 3.]

8–22653 4. Powers to search and obtain evidence. (1) If a justice of the peace is satisfied by information on oath, or in Scotland the sheriff or a magistrate or justice of the peace is satisfied by evidence on oath, that there is reasonable ground for suspecting that an offence under section 1 of this Act has been, or is about to be, committed, he may grant a search warrant[1] authorising a constable—

(*a*) to enter, at any time within three months from the date of the warrant, any premises or place named therein, if necessary by force, and to search the premises or place and every person found therein;

(*b*) to inspect any document found in the premises or place or in the possession of any person found therein, and to take copies of, or seize or detain any such document;
(*c*) to inspect, seize and detain any equipment so found; and
(*d*) to inspect, sample, seize and detain any substance so found.

(2) A warrant issued under subsection (1) above, authorising a constable to take the steps mentioned in that subsection, may also authorise any person named in the warrant to accompany the constable and assist him in taking any of those steps.
[Biological Weapons Act 1974, s 4 as amended by the Police and Criminal Evidence Act 1984, Sch 7 and the Serious Organised Crime and Police Act 2005, Sch 16.]

---

1. The issue and execution of this warrant must conform to the Police and Criminal Evidence Act 1984, ss 15 and 16 in PART I: MAGISTRATES' COURTS, PROCEDURE, ante.

Crossbows Act 1987

(1987 c 32)

8–22660 **1. Sale and letting on hire.** A person who sells or lets on hire a crossbow or a part of a crossbow to a person under the age of seventeen is guilty of an offence, unless he believes him to be seventeen years of age or older and has reasonable ground for the belief.
[Crossbows Act 1987, s 1.]

8–22661 **2. Purchase and hiring.** A person under the age of seventeen who buys or hires a crossbow or a part of a crossbow is guilty of an offence.
[Crossbows Act 1987, s 2.]

8–22662 **3. Possession.** A person under the age of seventeen who has with him—

(*a*) a crossbow which is capable of discharging a missile, or
(*b*) parts of a crossbow which together (and without any other parts) can be assembled to form a crossbow capable of discharging a missile,

is guilty of an offence, unless he is under the supervision of a person who is twenty-one years of age or older.
[Crossbows Act 1987, s 3.]

8–22663 **4. Powers of search and seizure etc.** (1) If a constable suspects with reasonable cause that a person is committing or has committed an offence under section 3, the constable may—

(*a*) search that person for a crossbow or part of a crossbow;
(*b*) search any vehicle, or anything in or on a vehicle, in or on which the constable suspects with reasonable cause there is a crossbow, or part of a crossbow, connected with the offence.

(2) A constable may detain a person or vehicle for the purpose of a search under subsection (1).

(3) A constable may seize and retain for the purpose of proceedings for an offence under this Act anything discovered by him in the course of a search under subsection (1) which appears to him to be a crossbow or part of a crossbow.

(4) For the purpose of exercising the powers conferred by this section a constable may enter any land other than a dwelling-house.
[Crossbows Act 1987, s 4.]

8–22664 **5. Exception.** This Act does not apply to crossbows with a draw weight of less than 1·4 kilograms.
[Crossbows Act 1987, s 5.]

8–22665 **6. Punishments.** (1) A person guilty of an offence under section 1 shall be liable, on summary conviction, to imprisonment for a term not exceeding **six months**, to a fine not exceeding **level 5** on the standard scale, or to **both**.

(2) A person guilty of an offence under section 2 or 3 shall be liable, on summary conviction, to a fine not exceeding **level 3** on the standard scale.

(3) The court by which a person is convicted of an offence under this Act may make such order as it thinks fit as to the forfeiture or disposal of any crossbow or part of a crossbow in respect of which the offence was committed.
[Crossbows Act 1987, s 6.]

8–22666 **7.** *Northern Ireland.*

8–22667 **8.** *Short title, commencement and extent.*

Criminal Justice Act 1988[1]

(1988 c 33)

PART XI[2]

MISCELLANEOUS

Articles with blades or points and offensive weapons

8–22680 **139. Offence of having article with blade or point in public place.** (1) Subject to subsections (4) and (5) below, any person who has an article to which this section applies with him in a public place[3] shall be guilty of an offence[4].

(2) Subject to subsection (3) below, this section applies to any article which has a blade or is sharply pointed except a folding pocketknife[5].

(3) This section applies to a folding pocketknife if the cutting edge of its blade exceeds 3 inches.

(4) It shall be a defence for a person charged with an offence under this section to prove[6] that he had good reason[7] or lawful authority[8] for having the article with him in a public place.

(5) Without prejudice to the generality of subsection (4) above, it shall be a defence for a person charged with an offence under this section to prove that he had the article with him—

(*a*) for use at work[9];
(*b*) for religious reasons[10]; or
(*c*) as part of any national costume.

(6) A person guilty of an offence under subsection (1) above shall be liable[11]

(*a*) on summary conviction, to imprisonment for a term not exceeding **six months**, or a fine not exceeding the **statutory maximum** or **both;**
(*b*) on conviction on indictment, to imprisonment for a term not exceeding **two years**, or a **fine**, or **both**.

(7) In this section "public place" includes any place to which at the material time the public have or are permitted access, whether on payment or otherwise[12].

(8) This section shall not have effect in relation to anything done before it comes into force.

[Criminal Justice Act 1988, s 139 as amended by the Offensive Weapons Act 1996, s 3.]

---

1. Sections 139–142 of the Criminal Justice Act 1988 which are printed here came into force on the 29 September 1988. For other provisions of the Criminal Justice Act 1988, see in particular PART I: MAGISTRATES' COURTS, PROCEDURE, ante.
2. Part XI contains ss 133–167.
3. Whether the place is actually a public place is a question of fact; whether a place is capable of being a public place is a question of law (*R v Hanrahan* (2004) 168 JPN 947).
4. For an offence to be proved the prosecution must establish that the accused knew that he was in possession of the article in question. Accordingly, a direction to a jury that a mere belief by the accused that the knife was somewhere in his van would suffice to establish the offence was held to be wrong because there was neither sufficient knowledge, nor sufficient control or proximity to the article for the offence to be established (*R v Daubney* (2000) 164 JP 519, CA).
5. For a knife to be a folding pocket-knife within the meaning of this section, it must be readily and immediately foldable at all times, simply by the folding process. A lock-knife, which required a further process, namely activating a trigger mechanism to fold the blade back into the handle, was held not to be a folding pocket-knife (*Harris v DPP* [1993] 1 All ER 562); followed in *R v Deegan* [1998] Crim LR 562, [1998] 2 Cr App Rep 121. The section applies to articles which have a blade or are sharply pointed, falling into the same broad category as a knife or sharply pointed instrument; it does not apply to a screwdriver just because it has a blade (*R v Davis* [1998] Crim LR 564). It is unnecessary for the blade to be sharp; the words of the statute, namely "any article that has a blade" are unqualified and will, thus, include a blunt butter knife: *Brooker v DPP* [2005] EWHC Admin 1132, (2005) 169 JP 368.
6. This reverse burden of proof does not conflict with art 6 of the Convention, since it is a proportionate measure and well within reasonable limits: *L v DPP* [2001] EWHC Admin 882, [2003] QB 137, [2002] 3 WLR 863, [2003] 2 WLR 693, [2002] 1 Cr App Rep 420, 166 JP 113, followed in *R v Matthews* [2003] EWCA Crim 813, [2003] 2 Cr App Rep 302. Once the prosecution has discharged the burden of proving the ingredients of the offence against s 139(1), the defendant is guilty unless he can discharge the burden imposed by s 139(4) of the Act; see *Godwin v DPP* (1993) 96 Cr App Rep 244.
7. Forgetfulness is not sufficient to prevent the state of possession from continuing, but there may be circumstances in which forgetfulness can be relevant to the "good reason" defence: for instance, if the reason that the defendant forgot that a bladed instrument, usually used for his work, was in his possession was a relevant illness or was occasioned by medication for such an illness: *Bayliss v DPP* (2003) 167 JPN, 103. See also: *R v McCalla* (1988) 87 Cr App Rep; (*DPP v Gregson* (1992) 157 JP 201). In *R v Jolie* [2003] EWCA Crim 1543, [2004] Cr App Rep 44, (2003) 167 JP 313, [2003] Crim LR 730 it was affirmed that forgetfulness does not bring possession to an end; that forgetfulness cannot be a good reason, though it can be part of a good reason; and that the words "good reason" do not require a judicial gloss. As to when forgetfulness might assist a defendant the court gave the example (in para 16) of a parent who, having bought a kitchen knife and put in the glove compartment of a car out of reach of a child then forgot to retrieve it when he got home; it seemed to the court contrary to Parliament's intention that such a person would be committing an offence the next time he drove the vehicle on a public road.

A reason may be capable of being a good reason, but fail to amount to a good reason on the facts of the case (see *Mohammed v Chief Constable of South Yorkshire Police* [2002] EWHC 406 (Admin), [2002] All ER (D) 374 (Feb), where the defendant took a meat cleaver to sharpen it but had it in his possession for that purpose for longer than he needed to). It cannot be a good reason to possess a knife that you may wish to commit self harm with it at some time the following day (*R v Bown* [2003] EWCA Crim 1989, [2003] 33 LS Gaz R 27, (2003) 167 JP 429, [2004] Crim LR 67).

8. The fact that a blade may be used for other functions than as a weapon does not mean it is not prima facie a blade for the purposes of the statute, and for a defendant to prove he had a lawful purpose for having the bladed article he would have to have a specific good reason for having it in his possession at that moment: *R v Giles* (2003) 167 JPN 103.

9. Interpretation of the ordinary everyday use of "for use at work" is not a matter of law but it is for the justices to decide for themselves what the phrase means in the context of the case. Therefore possession of a bladed article by an unemployed mechanic to do some repairs on his car that was parked in the road could come within this defence, see *R v Manning* [1998] Crim LR 198, CA.

10. The religious reasons must constitute the predominant, if not only the only motivation for the accused being in possession of the bladed article in a public place; and it must also be shown that the religious reason specifically motivated the accused to have the article with him on the occasion in question: *R v Wang* [2003] EWCA Crim 3228, (2004) 168 JP 224.

11. For procedure in respect of this offence which is triable either way, see the Magistrates' Courts Act 1980, ss 17A-21, in PART I: MAGISTRATES' COURTS, PROCEDURE, ante.

12. "Public place" should not be construed so as to include land adjacent to areas where the public has access from which harm against which the section was designed to provide protection could be inflicted (*R v Roberts* [2003] EWCA Crim 2753, [2004] 1 WLR 181, 167 JP 675, [2004] Crim LR 141). See also the definition of "public place" in s 1 of the Prevention of Crime Act 1953 and note thereto, ante.

8–22681 **139A. Offence of having article with blade or point (or offensive weapon) on school premises.** (1) Any person who has an article to which section 139 of this Act applies with him on school premises shall be guilty of an offence.

(2) Any person who has an offensive weapon within the meaning of section 1 of the Prevention of Crime Act 1953 with him on school premises shall be guilty of an offence.

(3) It shall be defence for a person charged with an offence under subsection (1) or (2) above to prove that he had good reason or lawful authority for having the article or weapon with him on the premises in question.

(4) Without prejudice to the generality of subsection (3) above, it shall be a defence for a person charged with an offence under subsection (1) or (2) above to prove that he had the article or weapon in question with him—

(*a*) for use at work,
(*b*) for educational purposes,
(*c*) for religious reasons, or
(*d*) as part of any national costume.

(5) A person guilty of an offence—

(*a*) under subsection (1) above shall be liable[1]—

(i) on summary conviction to imprisonment for a term not exceeding **six months**, or a fine not exceeding the **statutory maximum**, or **both;**
(ii) on conviction on indictment, to imprisonment for a term not exceeding **two years**, or a **fine**, or **both;**

(*b*) under subsection (2) above shall be liable—

(i) on summary conviction to imprisonment for a term not exceeding **six months**, or a fine not exceeding the **statutory maximum**, or **both;**
(ii) on conviction on indictment, to imprisonment for a term not exceeding **four years**, or a **fine**, or **both**.

(6) In this section and section 139B, "school premises" means land used for the purposes of a school excluding any land occupied solely as a dwelling by a person employed at the school; and "school" has the meaning given by section 4 of the Education Act 1996.

(7) *Northern Ireland.*

[Criminal Justice Act 1988, s 139A as inserted by the Offensive Weapons Act 1996, s 4 and amended by the Education Act 1996, Sch 37.]

---

1. For procedure in respect of this offence which is triable either way, see the Magistrates' Courts Act 1980, ss 17A-21, in PART I: MAGISTRATES' COURTS, PROCEDURE, ante.

8–22682 **139B. Power of entry to search for articles with a blade or point and offensive weapons.** (1) A constable may enter school premises and search those premises and any person on those premises for—

(*a*) any article to which section 139 of this Act applies, or
(*b*) any offensive weapon within the meaning of section 1 of the Prevention of Crime Act 1953,

if he has reasonable grounds for believing that an offence under section 139A of this Act is being, or has been, committed.

(2) If in the course of a search under this section a constable discovers an article or weapon which he has reasonable grounds for suspecting to be an article or weapon of a kind described in subsection (1) above, he may seize and retain it.

(3) The constable may use reasonable force, if necessary, in the exercise of the power of entry conferred by this section.

(4) *Northern Ireland.*

[Criminal Justice Act 1988, s 139B as inserted by the Offensive Weapons Act 1996, s 4.]

8–22683 140. Extension of constable's power to stop and search. *Amendment of the Police and Criminal Evidence Act 1984.*

8–22684 141. Offensive weapons. (1) Any person who manufactures, sells or hires or offers for sale or hire, exposes or has in his possession for the purpose of sale or hire, or lends or gives to any other person, a weapon to which this section applies shall be guilty of an offence and liable on summary conviction to imprisonment for a term not exceeding **six months** or to a fine not exceeding **level 5** on the standard scale or both.

(2) The Secretary of State may by order[1] made by statutory instrument direct that this section shall apply to any description of weapon specified in the order except—

(*a*) any weapon subject to the Firearms Act 1968; and
(*b*) crossbows.

(3) A statutory instrument containing an order under this section shall not be made unless a draft of the instrument has been laid before Parliament and has been approved by a resolution of each House of Parliament.

(4) The importation of a weapon to which this section applies is hereby prohibited.

(5) It shall be a defence for any person charged in respect of any conduct of his relating to a weapon to which this section applies—

(*a*) with an offence under subsection (1) above; or
(*b*) with an offence under section 50(2) or (3) of the Customs and Excise Management Act 1979 (improper importation),

to prove that his conduct was only for the purposes of functions carried out on behalf of the Crown or of a visiting force.

(6) In this section the reference to the Crown includes the Crown in right of Her Majesty's Government in Northern Ireland; and

"visiting force" means any body, contingent or detachment of the forces of a country—

(*a*) mentioned in subsection (1)(*a*) of section 1 of the Visiting Forces Act 1952; or
(*b*) designated for the purposes of any provision of that Act by Order in Council under subsection (2) of that section,

which is present in the United Kingdom (including United Kingdom territorial waters) or in any place to which subsection (7) below applies on the invitation of Her Majesty's Government in the United Kingdom.

(7) This subsection applies to any place on, under or above an installation in a designated area within the meaning of section 1(7) of the Continental Shelf Act 1964 or any waters within 500 metres of such an installation.

(8) It shall be a defence for any person charged in respect of any conduct of his relating to a weapon to which this section applies—

(*a*) with an offence under subsection (1) above; or
(*b*) with an offence under section 50(2) or (3) of the Customs and Excise Management Act 1979,

to prove that the conduct in question was only for the purposes of making the weapon available to a museum or gallery to which this subsection applies.

(9) If a person acting on behalf of a museum or gallery to which subsection (8) above applies is charged with hiring or lending a weapon to which this section applies, it shall be a defence for him to prove that he had reasonable grounds for believing that the person to whom he lent or hired it would use it only for cultural, artistic or educational purposes.

(10) Subsection (8) above applies to a museum or gallery only if it does not distribute profits.

(11) In this section "museum or gallery" includes any institution which has as its purpose, or one of its purposes, the preservation, display and interpretation of material of historical, artistic or scientific interest and gives the public access to it.

(12) This section shall not have effect in relation to anything done before it comes into force.

(13) *Northern Ireland.*

[Criminal Justice Act 1988, s 141.]

1. See the Criminal Justice Act 1988 (Offensive Weapons) Order 1988, post.

8–22685 141A. Sale of knives and certain articles with blade or point to persons under sixteen. (1) Any person who sells to a person under the age of sixteen years an article to which this section applies shall be guilty of an offence and liable on summary conviction to imprisonment for a term not exceeding **six months**, or a fine not exceeding **level 5** on the standard scale, or both.

(2) Subject to subsection (3) below, this section applies to—

(*a*) any knife, knife blade or razor blade,
(*b*) any axe, and
(*c*) any other article which has a blade or which is sharply pointed and which is made or adapted for use for causing injury to the person.

(3) This section does not apply to any article described in—

(*a*) section 1 of the Restriction of Offensive Weapons Act 1959,
(*b*) an order made under section 141(2) of this Act, or
(*c*) an order[1] made by the Secretary of State under this section.

(4) It shall be a defence for a person charged with an offence under subsection (1) above to prove that he took all reasonable precautions and exercised all due diligence to avoid the commission of the offence.

(5) The power to make an order under this section shall be exercisable by statutory instrument which shall be subject to annulment in pursuance of a resolution of either House of Parliament.
[Criminal Justice Act 1988, s 141A as inserted by the Offensive Weapons Act 1996, s 6.]

1. The Criminal Justice Act 1988 (Offensive Weapons) (Exemption) Order 1996, SI 1996/3064, has been made.

8–22686 **142. Power of justice of the peace to authorise entry and search of premises for offensive weapons.** (1) If on an application made by a constable a justice of the peace (including, in Scotland, the sheriff) is satisfied that there are reasonable grounds for believing—

(*a*) that there are on premises specified in the application—
(i) knives such as are mentioned in section 1(1) of the Restriction of Offensive Weapons Act 1959; or
(ii) weapons to which section 141 above applies; and
(*b*) that an offence under section 1 of the Restriction of Offensive Weapons Act 1959 or section 141 above has been or is being committed in relation to them; and
(*c*) that any of the conditions specified in subsection (3) below applies,

he may issue a warrant authorising a constable to enter and search the premises.

(2) A constable may seize and retain anything for which a search has been authorised under subsection (1) above.

(3) The conditions mentioned in subsection (1)(*b*)[1] above are—

(*a*) that it is not practicable to communicate with any person entitled to grant entry to the premises;
(*b*) that it is practicable to communicate with a person entitled to grant entry to the premises but it is not practicable to communicate with any person entitled to grant access to the knives or weapons to which the application relates;
(*c*) that entry to the premises will not be granted unless a warrant is produced;
(*d*) that the purpose of a search may be frustrated or seriously prejudiced unless a constable arriving at the premises can secure immediate entry to them.

(4) *Northern Ireland,*
[Criminal Justice Act 1988, s 142.]

1. The Act refers to subsection (1)(*b*), but clearly this reference should be to subsection (1)(*c*).

Chemical Weapons Act 1996[1]

(1996 c 6)

Introduction

8–22690 **1. General interpretation.** (1) Chemical weapons are—

(*a*) toxic chemicals and their precursors;
(*b*) munitions and other devices designed to cause death or harm through the toxic properties of toxic chemicals released by them;
(*c*) equipment designed for use in connection with munitions and devices falling within paragraph (*b*).

(2) Subsection (1) is subject to sections 2(2) and (3), 10(1) and 11(2) (by virtue of which an object is not a chemical weapon if the use or intended use is only for permitted purposes).

(3) Permitted purposes are—

(*a*) peaceful purposes;
(*b*) purposes related to protection against toxic chemicals;
(*c*) legitimate military purposes;
(*d*) purposes of enforcing the law.

(4) Legitimate military purposes except those which depend on the use of the toxic properties of chemicals as a method of warfare in circumstances where the main object is to cause death, permanent harm or temporary incapacity to humans or animals.

(5) A toxic chemical is a chemical which through its chemical action on life processes can cause

death, permanent harm or temporary incapacity to humans or animals; and the origin, method of production and place of production are immaterial.

(6) A precursor is a chemical reactant which takes part at any stage in the production (by whatever method) of a toxic chemical.

(7) References to an object include references to a substance.

(8) The Convention is the Convention on the Prohibition of the Development, Production, Stockpiling and Use of Chemical Weapons and on their Destruction, signed at Paris on 13 January 1993.

(9) This section applies for the purposes of this Act.
[Chemical Weapons Act 1996, s 1.]

---

1. This Act promotes the control of chemical weapons and of certain toxic chemicals and precursors. The Act implements in the UK the Convention on the Prohibition of the Development, Production, Stockpiling and Use of Chemical Weapons and on their Destruction, which was signed in Paris on 13 January 1993. The Chemical Weapons Act 1996 was brought fully into force on 16 September 1996 by the Chemical Weapons Act 1996 (Commencement) Order 1996, SI 1996/2054.

Chemical weapons

8–22691 **2. Use etc. of chemical weapons.** (1) No person shall—

(*a*) use a chemical weapon;
(*b*) develop or produce a chemical weapon;
(*c*) have a chemical weapon in his possession;
(*d*) participate in the transfer of a chemical weapon;
(*e*) engage in military preparations, or in preparations of a military nature, intending to use a chemical weapon.

(2) For the purposes of subsection (1)(*a*) an object is not a chemical weapon if the person uses the object only for permitted purposes; and in deciding whether permitted purposes are intended the types and quantities of objects shall be taken into account.

(3) For the purposes of subsection (1)(*b*), (*c*), (*d*) or (*e*) an object is not a chemical weapon if the person does the act there mentioned with the intention that the object will be used only for permitted purposes; and in deciding whether permitted purposes are intended the types and quantities of objects shall be taken into account.

(4) For the purposes of subsection (1)(*d*) a person participates in the transfer of an object if—

(*a*) he acquires or disposes of the object or enters into a contract to acquire or dispose of it, or
(*b*) he makes arrangements under which another person acquires or disposes of the object or another person enters into a contract to acquire or dispose of it.

(5) For the purposes of subsection (4)—

(*a*) to acquire an object is to buy it, hire it, borrow it or accept it as a gift;
(*b*) to dispose of an object is to sell it, let it on hire, lend it or give it.

(6) In proceedings for an offence under section (1)(*a*), (*c*) or (*d*) relating to an object it is a defence for the accused to prove—

(*a*) that he neither knew nor suspected nor had reason to suspect that the object was a chemical weapon, or
(*b*) that he knew or suspected it to be a chemical weapon and as soon as reasonably practicable after he first so knew or suspected he took all reasonable steps to inform the Secretary of State or a constable of his knowledge or suspicion.

(7) Nothing in subsection (6) prejudices any defence which it is open to a person charged with an offence under this section to raise apart from that subsection.

(8) A person contravening this section is guilty of an offence and liable on conviction on indictment to imprisonment for life.
[Chemical Weapons Act 1996, s 2.]

8–22692 **3. Application of section 2.** (1) Section 2 applies to acts done in the United Kingdom or elsewhere.

(2) So far as it applies to acts done outside the United Kingdom, section 2 applies to United Kingdom nationals, Scottish partnerships, and bodies incorporated under the law of any part of the United Kingdom.

(3) Her Majesty may by Order[1] in Council extend the application of section 2, so far as it applies to acts done outside the United Kingdom, to bodies incorporated under the law of any of the Channel Islands, the Isle of Man or any colony.

(4) For the purposes of this section a United Kingdom national is an individual who is—

(*a*) British citizen, a British overseas territories citizen, a British National (Overseas) or a British Overseas citizen,
(*b*) a person who under the British Nationality Act 1981 is a British subject, or
(*c*) a British protected person within the meaning of that Act.

(5) Proceedings for an offence committed under section 2 outside the United Kingdom may be taken, and the offence may for incidental purposes be treated as having been committed, in any place in the United Kingdom.
[Chemical Weapons Act 1996, s 3, as amended by the British Overseas Territories Act 2002, s 2(3).]

---

1. The following Chemical Weapons Act 1996 Orders have been made: Jersey, SI 1998/2565; Isle of Man, SI 1998/2794; Guernsey, SI 2000/743.

8–22693 **4. Suspicious objects.** (1) If—

(*a*) the Secretary of State has grounds to suspect that an object is a chemical weapon, and
(*b*) at least one person falls within subsection (2),

the Secretary of State may serve on any person falling within that subsection a copy of a notice falling within subsection (3).

(2) The person falling within this subsection are—

(*a*) any person who appears to the Secretary of State to have the object in his possession, and
(*b*) any person not falling within paragraph (*a*) and who appears to the Secretary of State to have an interest which the Secretary of State believes is materially affected by the notice.

(3) A notice falling within this subsection is a notice which—

(*a*) describes the object and states its location;
(*b*) states that the Secretary of State suspects that the object is a chemical weapon and gives the reasons for his suspicion;
(*c*) states that he is considering whether to secure its destruction under sections 5 to 7;
(*d*) states that any person may make representations that the object is not a chemical weapon;
(*e*) states that a person on whom the notice is served and who has the object in his possession must not relinquish possession before a date specified in the notice.

[Chemical Weapons Act 1996, s 4.]

8–22694 **5. Power to remove or immobilise objects.** (1) If the Secretary of State has reasonable cause to believe that—

(*a*) an object is on premises to which the public has access or which are occupied by a person who consents to action being taken under this subsection, and
(*b*) the object is a chemical weapon,

the Secretary of State may authorise a person to enter the premises and to search them.

(2) If—

(*a*) a justice of the peace is satisfied on information on oath that there is reasonable cause to believe that an object is on premises (of whatever nature) and that it is a chemical weapon, or
(*b*) in Scotland a justice, within the meaning of section 307 of the Criminal Procedure (Scotland) Act 1995, is satisfied by evidence on oath as mentioned in paragraph (a),

he may issue a warrant in writing authorising a person acting under the authority of the Secretary of State to enter the premises, if necessary by force, at any time within one month from the time of the issue of the warrant and to search them.

(3) A person who acts under an authorisation given under subsection (1) or (2) may take with him such other persons and such equipment as appear to him to be necessary.

(4) If a person enters premises under an authorisation given under subsection (1) or (2) and the object is found there he may make the object safe and—

(*a*) he may seize and remove it if it is reasonably practicable to do so, or
(*b*) he may in any other case affix a warning to the object or to something in a conspicuous position near the object, stating that the object is not to be moved or interfered with before a date specified in the warning)

(5) For the purposes of subsection (4) an object is made safe if, without being destroyed, it is prevented from being an immediate danger (as where a fuse is neutralised or the object is smothered in foam).

(6) The powers conferred on an authorised person under this section shall only be exercisable, if the authorisation under subsection (1) or the warrant so provides, in the presence of a constable.

(7) This section applies whether or not any copy of a notice has been served under section 4.

[Chemical Weapons Act 1996, s 5.]

8–22695 **6. Power to destroy removed objects.** (1) This section applies if an object is removed from premises under section 5, and for the purposes of this section—

(*a*) the first six-month period is the period of six months beginning with the day after the removal;
(*b*) the second six-month period is the period of six months beginning with the day after the first six-month period ends.

(2) If at any time in the second six-month period the Secretary of State decides that the object

should be destroyed he may authorise a person to destroy it; but this is subject to subsection (3) to (5).

(3) If at any time in the first six-month period—

(*a*) any person appears to the Secretary of State to have had the object in his possession immediately before its removal, or

(*b*) any person not falling within paragraph (*a*) appears to the Secretary of State to have an interest which the Secretary of State believes would be materially affected by the object's destruction,

the Secretary of State must serve on such a person a copy of a notice falling within subsection (4).

(4) A notice falling within this subsection is a notice which—

(*a*) describes the object and states its location;

(*b*) states that the Secretary of State proposes to secure its destruction and gives the reasons for his proposal;

(*c*) states that the person on whom the copy of the notice is served may object to the Secretary of State's proposal;

(*d*) states than an objection (if made) must be made in writing to the Secretary of State before such date as is specified in the notice and must state why the object should not be destroyed.

(5) Before he reaches a decision under subsection (2) the Secretary of State must—

(*a*) allow any person on whom a copy of a notice has been served under subsection (3) time to respond, and

(*b*) take into account any objections to the object's proposed destruction (whether made in response to a notice or otherwise).

(6) If an object is removed from premises under section 5 and destroyed under this section the Secretary of State may recover from a responsible person any costs reasonably incurred by the Secretary of State in connection with the removal and destruction; and a responsible person is any person who had possession of the object immediately before its removal.

(7) If—

(*a*) an object is removed from premises under section 5,

(*b*) at the end of the second six-month period the Secretary of State has not authorised the destruction of the object, and

(*c*) a person had possession of the object immediately before its removal,

the Secretary of State must return the object to the person mentioned in paragraph (c) or, if there is more than one, to such of them as the Secretary of State thinks appropriate.

[Chemical Weapons Act 1996, s 6.]

8–22696 7. Power to enter premises and destroy objects. (1) This section applies if a warning has been affixed under section 5, and for the purposes of this section—

(*a*) the first six-month period is the period of six months beginning with the day after the warning was affixed;

(*b*) the second six-month period is the period of six months beginning with the day after the first six-month period ends.

(2) If at any time in the second six-month period the Secretary of State decides that the object should be destroyed it may be destroyed as provided by subsections (6) to (9); but this is subject to subsection (3) to (5).

(3) If at any time in the first six-month period—

(*a*) any person appears to the Secretary of State to have had the object in his possession immediately before the warning was affixed, or

(*b*) any person not falling within paragraph (*a*) appears to the Secretary of State to have an interest which the Secretary of State believes would be materially affected by the object's destruction,

the Secretary of State must serve on such a person a copy of a notice falling within subsection (4).

(4) A notice falling within this subsection is a notice which—

(*a*) describes the object and states its location;

(*b*) states that the Secretary of State proposes to secure its destruction and gives the reasons for his proposal;

(*c*) states that the person on whom the copy of the notice is served may object to the Secretary of State's proposal;

(*d*) states that an objection (if made) must be made in writing to the Secretary of State before such date as is specified in the notice and must state why the object should not be destroyed.

(5) Before he reaches a decision under subsection (2) the Secretary of State must—

(*a*) allow any person on whom a copy of a notice has been served under subsection (3) time to respond, and (*b*) take into account any objections to the object's proposed destruction (whether made in response to a notice or otherwise).

(6) If—

(*a*) at any time in the second six-month period the Secretary of State decides that the object should be destroyed, and

(*b*) the object is on premises to which the public has access or which are occupied by a person who consents to action being taken under this subsection,

the Secretary of State may authorise a person to enter the premises and to destroy the object if it is found there.

(7) If (whatever the nature of the premises concerned)—

(*a*) a justice of the peace is satisfied on information on oath that a warning has been affixed under section 5, and that the Secretary of State has decided at any time in the second six-month period that the object should be destroyed, or

(*b*) in Scotland a justice, within the meaning of section 307 of the Criminal Procedure (Scotland) Act 1995, is satisfied by evidence on oath as mentioned in paragraph (*a*),

he may issue a warrant in writing authorising a person acting under the authority of the Secretary of State to enter the premises, if necessary by force, at any time within one month from the time of the issue of the warrant and to destroy the object if it is found there.

(8) A person who acts under an authorisation given under subsection (6) or (7) may take with him such other persons and such equipment as appear to him to be necessary.

(9) The powers conferred on an authorised person under this section shall only be exercisable, if the authorisation under subsection (6) or the warrant so provides, in the presence of a constable.

(10) Where an object is destroyed under this section the Secretary of State may recover from a responsible person any costs reasonably incurred by the Secretary of State in connection with the destruction; and a responsible person is any person who had possession of the object immediately before the warning was affixed under section 5.

[Chemical Weapons Act 1996, s 7.]

8–22697 8. Compensation for destruction. (1) This section applies if a person claims that—

(*a*) an object has been destroyed under section 6 or 7,

(*b*) he had an interest which was materially affected by the destruction and he sustained loss as a result, and

(*c*) no copy of a notice was served on him under the section concerned (whether or not one was served on any other person).

(2) If the person concerned makes an application under this section to the High Court or in Scotland the Court of Session, and the Court finds that his claim is justified, the Court may order the Secretary of State to pay to the applicant such amount (if any) by way of compensation as the Court considers just.

(3) If the Court believes that the object would have been destroyed even if a copy of a notice had been served on the applicant under the section concerned the Court must not order compensation to be paid under this section.

[Chemical Weapons Act 1996, s 8.]

8–22698 9. Offences relating to destruction etc. (1) If—

(*a*) a copy of a notice is served on a person under section 4,

(*b*) the notice relates to an object in his possession at the time the copy is served,

(*c*) he relinquishes possession before the date specified under section 4(3)(*e*), and;

(*d*) he has no reasonable excuse for so relinquishing possession,

he is guilty of an offence.

(2) If a person wilfully obstructs a person in—

(*a*) entering or searching premises under an authorisation given under section 5(1) or (2) or 7(6) or (7),

(*b*) making an object safe, seizing or removing an object, or affixing a warning, under section 5(4),

(*c*) destroying an object under an authorisation given under section 6(2) or 7(6) or (7), or

(*d*) attempting to do anything mentioned in paragraphs (*a*) to (*c*), the person so obstructing is guilty of an offence.

(3) If—

(*a*) a warning is affixed under section 5(4),

(*b*) a person interferes with the warning, or moves or interferes with the object before the date specified in the warning, and

(*c*) he has no reasonable excuse for doing so,

he is guilty of an offence.

(4) A person guilty of an offence under any of the preceding provisions of this section is liable[1].

(*a*) on summary conviction, to a fine of an amount not exceeding **the statutory maximum;**

(*b*) on conviction on indictment, to a **fine**.

(5) A person who knowingly makes a false or misleading statement in response to a copy of a notice served under section 4, 6 or 7 is guilty of an offence and liable[1]—

(*a*) on summary conviction, to a fine of an amount not exceeding **the statutory maximum;**

(*b*) on conviction on indictment, to imprisonment for a term not exceeding **two years** or to a **fine** or to **both**.

[Chemical Weapons Act 1996, s 9.]

---

1. For procedure in respect of this offence which is triable either way, see the Magistrates' Courts Act 1980, ss 17A–21, in PART I: MAGISTRATES' COURTS PROCEDURE, ante.

8–22699 **10. Destruction etc. supplementary.** (1) If an object is in the possession of a person who intends that it will be used only for permitted purposes, it is not a chemical weapon for the purposes of sections 4(1) and (3) and 5(1) and (2); and in deciding whether permitted purposes are intended the types and quantities of objects shall be taken into account.

(2) For the purposes of sections 4 to 9—

(*a*) to the extent that an object consists of a toxic chemical or precursor, it is destroyed if it is permanently prevented from being used other than for permitted purposes;

(*b*) to the extent that an object consists of a munition or other device designed to cause death or harm through toxic chemicals released by it, it is destroyed if it is permanently prevented from doing so;

(*c*) to the extent that an object consists of equipment designed for use in connection with a munition or other device, it is destroyed if it is permanently prevented from being so used.

(3) In sections 5 to 9 "premises" includes land (including buildings), moveable structures, vehicles, vessels, aircraft and hovercraft.

(4) Nothing in sections 4 to 7 affects any power arising otherwise than by virtue of those sections (such as a power to dispose of property in police possession in connection with the investigation of a suspected offence).

[Chemical Weapons Act 1996, s 10.]

Premises for producing chemical weapons etc.

8–22700 **11. Premises or equipment for producing chemical weapons.** (1) No person shall—

(*a*) construct premises he intends to be used to produce chemical weapons;

(*b*) alter premises in circumstances where he intends that they will be used to produce chemical weapons;

(*c*) install or construct equipment he intends to be used to produce chemical weapons;

(*d*) alter equipment in circumstances where he intends that it will be used to produce chemical weapons;

(*e*) permit the construction on land he occupies of premises he intends to be used to produce chemical weapons;

(*f*) permit premises on land he occupies to be altered in circumstances where he intends that they will be used to produce chemical weapons;

(*g*) permit the installation or construction on land he occupies of equipment he intends to be used to produce chemical weapons;

(*h*) permit equipment on land he occupies to be altered in circumstances where he intends that it will be used to produce chemical weapons.

(2) For the purposes of subsection (1) an object is not a chemical weapon if the person intends that the object will be used only for permitted purposes; and in deciding whether permitted purposes are intended the types and quantities of objects shall be taken into account.

(3) A person contravening this section is guilty of an offence and liable on conviction on indictment to imprisonment for life.

[Chemical Weapons Act 1996, s 11.]

8–22701 **12. Suspicious equipment or buildings.** (1) If—

(*a*) the Secretary of State has grounds to suspect that any equipment or building is a chemical weapons production facility, and

(*b*) at least one person falls within subsection (2),

the Secretary of State may serve on any person falling within that subsection a copy of a notice falling within subsection (3).

(2) The persons falling within this subsection are—

(*a*) any person who appears to the Secretary of State to occupy the land on which the equipment or building is situated, (*b*) if the Secretary of State's suspicion relates to equipment, any person not falling within paragraph (*a*) and who appears to the Secretary of State to have the equipment in his possession, and

(*c*) any person not falling within paragraph (*a*) or (*b*) and who appears to the Secretary of State to have an interest which the Secretary of State believes is materially affected by the notice.

(3) A notice falling within this subsection is a notice which—

(*a*) describes the equipment or building and states its location;

(*b*) states that the Secretary of State suspects that the equipment or building is a chemical weapons production facility and gives the reasons for his suspicion;

(*c*) states that he is considering whether to require the equipment or building to be destroyed or altered;

(*d*) states that any person may make representations that the equipment or building is not a chemical weapons production facility.

(4) If the notice relates to equipment it must state that a person on whom the notice is served and who has the equipment in his possession must not relinquish possession of, or alter or use, the equipment before a date specified in the notice.
[Chemical Weapons Act 1996, s 12.]

8–22702 13. Notice requiring destruction or alteration. (1) If—

(*a*) the secretary of State has reasonable cause to believe that any equipment or building is a chemical weapons production facility, and

(*b*) at least one person falls within subsection (2),

the Secretary of State may serve on each person falling within that subsection a copy of a notice falling within subsection (3).

(2) The persons falling within this subsection are—

(*a*) any person who appears to the Secretary of State to occupy the land on which the equipment or building is situated,

(*b*) if the Secretary of State's belief relates to equipment, any person not falling within paragraph (*a*) and who appears to the Secretary of State to have the equipment in his possession, and

(*c*) any person not falling within paragraph (*a*) or (*b*) and who appears to the Secretary of State to have an interest which the Secretary of State believes would be materially affected by the destruction or alteration of the equipment or building.

(3) A notice falling within this subsection is a notice which—

(*a*) describes the equipment or building and states its location;

(*b*) states that the Secretary of State believes the equipment or building is a chemical weapons production facility;

(*c*) requires the equipment or building to be destroyed or altered (as the case may be) in a manner, and before a date, specified in the notice.

(4) If a notice under this section requires any equipment or building to be altered, a further notice under this section may—

(*a*) revoke the first notice, and

(*b*) require the equipment or building to be destroyed;

and the preceding provisions of this section shall apply to the further notice accordingly.

(5) This section applies whether or not any copy of a notice has been served under section 12.
[Chemical Weapons Act 1996, s 13.]

8–22703 14. Power where notice not complied with. (1) For the purposes of this section the qualifying condition is that—

(*a*) a notice has been prepared under section 13,

(*b*) the provisions of section 13(1) to (3) have been complied with in relation to the notice,

(*c*) the notice has not been revoked, and

(*d*) any requirement set out in the notice has not been complied with.

(2) If—

(*a*) a justice of the peace is satisfied on information on oath that the qualifying condition is fulfilled, or

(*b*) in Scotland a justice, within the meaning of section 307 of the Criminal Procedure (Scotland) Act 1995, is satisfied by evidence on oath that the qualifying condition is fulfilled,

he may issue a warrant in writing authorising a person acting under the authority of the Secretary of State to take remedial action under this section.

(3) If a person is authorised by a warrant to take remedial action under this section he may—

(*a*) enter the land on which the equipment or building is situated, if necessary by force;

(*b*) do whatever is required to secure that the equipment or building is destroyed or altered in a manner specified in the notice;

(*c*) take with him such other persons and such equipment as appear to him to be necessary to help him to exercise the powers mentioned in paragraphs (*a*) and (*b*).

(4) The powers conferred on an authorised person under this section shall only be exercisable, if the warrant so provides, in the presence of a constable.

(5) If anything is done in exercise of the powers mentioned in this section, the Secretary of State may recover from a responsible person any costs reasonably incurred by the Secretary of State in connection with the exercise of those powers; and a responsible person is—

(*a*) in the case of equipment, any person in possession of the equipment at the time the land is entered;

(*b*) in the case of a building, any person occupying the land at the time it is entered.

[Chemical Weapons Act 1996, s 14.]

8–22704 15. Position where no notice can be served. (1) For the purposes of this section the qualifying condition is that—

(*a*) the Secretary of State has reasonable cause to believe that any equipment or building is a chemical weapons production facility,

(*b*) in the period of six months beginning with the day after he formed his belief it has not been possible to serve a copy of a notice under section 13 because of the circumstances mentioned in subsection (2), and

(*c*) the Secretary of State has drawn up proposals for the destruction or alteration of the equipment or building in a manner specified in the proposals.

(2) The circumstances are that—

(*a*) no person appeared to the Secretary of State to occupy the land on which the equipment or building is situated,

(*b*) if the Secretary of State's belief relates to equipment, no person appeared to the Secretary of State to have the equipment in his possession, and

(*c*) no person appeared to the Secretary of State to have an interest which the Secretary of State believed would be materially affected by the destruction or alteration of the equipment or building.

(3) If—

(*a*) a justice of the peace is satisfied on information on oath that the qualifying condition is fulfilled, or

(*b*) in Scotland a justice, within the meaning of section 307 of the Criminal Procedure (Scotland) Act 1995, is satisfied by evidence on oath that the qualifying condition is fulfilled,

he may issue a warrant in writing authorising a person acting under the authority of the Secretary of State to take remedial action under this section.

(4) If a person is authorised by a warrant to take remedial action under this section he may—

(*a*) enter the land on which the equipment or building is situated, if necessary by force;

(*b*) do whatever is required to secure that the equipment or building is destroyed or altered in a manner specified in the proposals drawn up by the Secretary of State;

(*c*) take with him such other persons and such equipment as appear to him to be necessary to help him to exercise the powers mentioned in paragraphs (*a*) and (*b*).

(5) The powers conferred on an authorised person under this section shall only be exercisable, if the warrant so provides, in the presence of a constable.

(6) If anything is done in exercise of the powers mentioned in this section, the Secretary of State may recover from a responsible person any costs reasonably incurred by the Secretary of State in connection with the exercise of those powers; and a responsible person is—

(*a*) in the case of equipment, any person in possession of the equipment at the time the land is entered;

(*b*) in the case of a building, any person occupying the land at the time it is entered.

[Chemical Weapons Act 1996, s 15.]

8–22705 16. Compensation for destruction or alteration. (1) This section applies if a person claims that—

(*a*) any equipment or building has been destroyed or altered in compliance with a notice falling within section 13(3) or has been destroyed or altered under section 14,

(*b*) he had an interest which was materially affected by the destruction or alteration and he sustained loss as a result, and

(*c*) no copy of a notice was served on him under section 13.

(2) This section also applies if a person claims that—

(*a*) any equipment or building has been destroyed or altered under section 15, and (*b*) he had an interest which was materially affected by the destruction or alteration and he sustained loss as a result.

(3) If a person concerned makes an application under this section to the High Court or in Scotland the Court of Session, and the Court finds that his claim is justified, the Court may order the Secretary of State to pay to the applicant such amount (if any) by way of compensation as the Court considers just.

(4) If the Court believes that the equipment or building would have been destroyed or altered even if a copy of a notice had been served on the application under section 13 the Court must not order compensation to be paid under this section.
[Chemical Weapons Act 1996, s 16.]

8–22706 **17. Offences relating to destruction etc.** (1) If—

(*a*) a copy of a notice is served on a person under section 12,
(*b*) the notice relates to equipment in his possession at the time the copy is served,
(*c*) he relinquishes possession of, or alters or uses, the equipment before the date specified under section 12(4), and
(*d*) he has no reasonable excuse for doing so,

he is guilty of an offence.

(2) If—

(*a*) a copy of a notice is served on a person under section 13,
(*b*) the notice relates to equipment in his possession at the time the copy is served or to a building situated on land he occupies at that time,
(*c*) any requirement set out in the notice is not fulfilled, and
(*d*) he has no reasonable excuse for the requirement not being fulfilled,

he is guilty of an offence.

(3) If a person wilfully obstructs—

(*a*) a person exercising, or attempting to exercise, the powers mentioned in section 14(3)(*a*) or (*b*) or 15(4)(*a*) or (*b*), or
(*b*) any other person taken with him as mentioned in section 14(3)(*c*) or 15(4)(*c*) and helping him, or attempting to help him, to exercise those powers,

the person so obstructing is guilty of an offence.

(4) A person guilty of an offence under any of the preceding provisions of this section is liable[1]

(*a*) on summary conviction, to a fine of an amount not exceeding **the statutory maximum;**
(*b*) on conviction on indictment, to a **fine.**

(5) A person who knowingly makes a false or misleading statement in response to a notice served under section 12 is guilty of an offence and liable[1]—

(*a*) on summary conviction, to a fine of an amount not exceeding **the statutory maximum;**
(*b*) on conviction on indictment, to imprisonment for a term not exceeding **two years** or to a **fine** or to **both**.

[Chemical Weapons Act 1996, s 17.]

1. For procedure in respect of this offence which is triable either way, see the Magistrates' Courts Act 1980, ss 17A–21, in PART I: MAGISTRATES' COURTS, PROCEDURE, ante.

8–22707 **18. Destruction etc: supplementary.** (1) In sections 12 to 15 "chemical weapons production facility" has the meaning given by the definition of that expression in the Convention, and for this purpose—

(*a*) expressions used in the definition in the Convention shall be construed in accordance with the Convention, and
(*b*) section 1 shall be ignored.

(2) For the purposes of sections 12 to 16 "destroyed" and "destruction", in relation to a building, mean demolished and demolition.

(3) Nothing in sections 12 to 15 affects any power arising otherwise than by virtue of those sections (such as a power to dispose of property in police possession in connection with the investigation of a suspected offence).
[Chemical Weapons Act 1996, s 18.]

Chemicals for permitted purposes

8–22708 **19. Restriction on use etc.** (1) Subject to section 20 (which relates to licences) no person shall—

(*a*) use a Schedule 1 toxic chemical or precursor for a permitted purpose, or
(*b*) produce or have in his possession a Schedule 1 toxic chemical or precursor with the intention that it will be used for a permitted purpose.

(2) A Schedule 1 toxic chemical or precursor is a toxic chemical or precursor listed in Schedule 1 to the annex on chemicals to the Convention; and for ease of reference that Schedule is set out in the Schedule to this Act.

(3) A person contravening this section is guilty of an offence and liable[1]—

(*a*) on summary conviction, to a fine of an amount not exceeding **the statutory maximum;**

(*b*) on conviction on indictment, to a **fine**.

[Chemical Weapons Act 1996, s 19.]

1. For procedure in respect of this offence which is triable either way, see the Magistrates' Courts Act 1980, ss 17A–21, in PART I: MAGISTRATES' COURTS, PROCEDURE, ante.

8–22709 **20. Licences.** (1) Section 19 does not apply to anything done in accordance with the terms of a licence granted by the Secretary of State and having effect at the time it is done.

(2) The Secretary of State may—

(*a*) grant a licence in such circumstances and on such terms as he thinks fits;

(*b*) vary or revoke a licence by serving a notice to that effect on the person to whom the licence was granted.

(3) A variation or revocation shall take effect at such reasonable time as is specified in the notice served under subsection (2)(*b*).

(4) The Secretary of State may by order make provision with respect to appealing against a refusal to grant, renew or vary a licence or against a variation or revocation of a licence.

(5) An order under subsection (4) shall be made by statutory instrument subject to annulment in pursuance of a resolution of either House of Parliament.

(6) A person who knowingly makes a false or misleading statement for the purpose of obtaining a licence or a renewal or variation of a licence, or of opposing a variation or revocation of a licence, is guilty of an offence and liable[1]—

(*a*) on summary conviction, to a fine of an amount not exceeding **the statutory maximum;**

(*b*) on conviction on indictment, to imprisonment for a term not exceeding **two years** or to a **fine** or to **both**.

[Chemical Weapons Act 1996, s 20.]

1. For procedure in respect of this offence which is triable either way, see the Magistrates' Courts Act 1980, ss 17A–21, in PART I: MAGISTRATES' COURTS, PROCEDURE, ante.

Information and records

8–22710 **21. Information for purposes of Act.** (1) If the Secretary of State has grounds to suspect that a person is committing or has committed an offence under this Act the Secretary of State may by notice served on the person require him to give in such form as is specified in the notice, and within such reasonable period as is so specified, such information as—

(*a*) the Secretary of State has reasonable cause to believe will help to establish whether the person is committing or has committed such an offence, and

(*b*) is specified in the notice.

(2) A person who without reasonable excuse fails to comply with a notice served on him under subsection (1) is guilty of an offence and liable[1]—

(*a*) on summary conviction, to a fine of an amount not exceeding **the statutory maximum;**

(*b*) on conviction on indictment, to a **fine**.

(3) A person on whom a notice is served under subsection (1) and who knowingly makes a false or misleading statement in response to it is guilty of an offence and liable[1]—

(*a*) a summary conviction, to a fine of an amount not exceeding the **statutory maximum**;

(*b*) on conviction on indictment, to imprisonment for a term not exceeding **two years** or to a **fine** or to **both**.

[Chemical Weapons Act 1996, s 21.]

1. For procedure in respect of this offence which is triable either way, see the Magistrates' Courts Act 1980, ss 17A–21, in PART I: MAGISTRATES' COURTS, PROCEDURE, ante.

8–22711 **22. Information and records for purposes of Convention.** (1) The Secretary of State may by notice served on any person require him to give in such form as is specified in the notice, and within such reasonable period as is so specified, such information as—

(*a*) the Secretary of State has reasonable cause to believe is or will be needed in connection with anything to be done for the purposes of the Convention, and

(*b*) is specified in the notice;

and the information required by a notice may relate to a state of affairs subsisting before the coming into force of this Act or of the Convention.

(2) The Secretary of State may by notice served on any person require him to keep such records as—

(*a*) the Secretary of State has reasonable cause to believe will facilitate the giving of information the person may at any time be required to give under subsection (1), and
(*b*) are specified in the notice.

(3) A person who without reasonable excuse fails to comply with a notice served on him under subsection (1) or (2) is guilty of an offence and liable[1]—

(*a*) on summary conviction, to a fine of an amount not exceeding **the statutory maximum;**
(*b*) on conviction on indictment, to a **fine**.

(4) A person on whom a notice is served under subsection (1) and who knowingly makes a false or misleading statement in response to it is guilty of an offence and liable[1]—

(*a*) on summary conviction, to a fine of an amount not exceeding **the statutory maximum;**
(*b*) on conviction on indictment, to imprisonment for a term not exceeding **two years** or to a **fine** or to **both**

[Chemical Weapons Act 1996, s 22.]

1. For procedure in respect of this offence which is triable either way, see the Magistrates' Courts Act 1980, ss 17A–21, in PART I: MAGISTRATES' COURTS, PROCEDURE, ante.

8–22712 **23. Identifying persons who have information.** (1) The Secretary of State may make regulations[1] requiring persons of any description specified in the regulations to inform him that they are of such a description.

(2) Any such description must be so framed that persons within it are persons on whom the Secretary of State is likely to want to serve a notice under section 22.

(3) If regulations are made under this section the Secretary of State shall arrange for a statement of the fact that they have been made to be published in such manner as is likely to bring them to the attention of persons affected by them.

(4) A person who without reasonable excuse fails to comply with a requirement imposed by the regulations is guilty of an offence and liable[2]—

(*a*) on summary conviction, to a fine of an amount not exceeding **the statutory maximum;**
(*b*) on conviction on indictment, to a **fine.**

(5) A person who knowingly makes a false or misleading statement in response to a requirement imposed by the regulations is guilty of an offence and liable[1]—

(*a*) a summary conviction, to a fine of an amount not exceeding **the statutory maximum;**
(*b*) on conviction on indictment, to imprisonment for a term not exceeding **two years** or to a **fine** or to **both.**

(6) The regulations shall be made by statutory instrument subject to annulment in pursuance of a resolution of either House of Parliament.

[Chemical Weapons Act 1996, s 23.]

1. See the Chemical Weapons (Notification) Regulations 1996, SI 1996/2503, amended by SI 1996/2669 and SI 2004/2406.

2. For procedure in respect of this offence which is triable either way, see the Magistrates' Courts Act 1980, ss 17A–21, in PART I: MAGISTRATES' COURTS, PROCEDURE, ante.

Inspections under Convention

8–22713 **24. Inspections: interpretation.** For the purposes of sections 25 to 28—

(*a*) the verification annex is the annex on implementation and verification to the Convention;
(*b*) a routine inspection is an inspection conducted pursuant to Parts II to IX of that annex;
(*c*) a challenge inspection is an inspection conducted pursuant to Parts II and X of that annex;
(*d*) an assistance inspection is an inspection conducted pursuant to Parts II and XI of that annex;
(*e*) "in-country escort," "inspector", "inspection team" and "observer" have the meanings given by Part I of that annex.

[Chemical Weapons Act 1996, s 24.]

8–22714 **25. Rights of entry etc. for purposes of inspections.** (1) If it is proposed to conduct a routine inspection, a challenge inspection or an assistance inspection in the United Kingdom, the Secretary of State may issue an authorisation under this section in respect of that inspection.

(2) An authorisation under this section shall—

(*a*) contain a description of the area (the specified area) in which the inspection is to be conducted,
(*b*) specify the type of inspection concerned,
(*c*) state the name of the members of the inspection team by whom the inspection is to be carried out, and

(*d*) in the case of a challenge inspection, state the name of any observer who may accompany the team.

(3) Such an authorisation shall have the effect of authorising the inspection team—

(*a*) to exercise within the specified area such rights of access, entry and unobstructed inspection as are conferred on them by the verification annex, and

(*b*) to do such other things within that area in connection with the inspection as they are entitled to do by virtue of the verification annex (including things concerning the maintenance, replacement or adjustment of any instrument or other object).

(4) such an authorisation shall in addition have the effect of—

(*a*) authorising an in-country escort to accompany the inspection team in accordance with the provisions of the verification annex, and

(*b*) authorising any constable to give such assistance as the in-country escort may request for the purpose of facilitating the conduct of the inspection in accordance with the verification annex;

and the name of the person in charge of the in-country escort shall be stated in the authorisation.

(5) An authorisation under this section in the case of a challenge inspection shall in addition have the effect of authorising the observer to exercise within the specified area such rights of access and entry as are conferred on him by the verification annex.

(6) Any constable giving assistance in accordance with subsection (4)(b) may use such reasonable force as he considers necessary for the purpose mentioned in that provision.

(7) The occupier of any premises—

(*a*) in relation to which it is proposed to exercise a right of entry in reliance on an authorisation under this section, or

(*b*) on which an inspection is being carried out in reliance on such an authorisation,

or a person acting on behalf of the occupier of any such premises, shall be entitled to require a copy of the authorisation to be shown to him by a member of the in-country escort.

(8) The validity of any authorisation purporting to be issued under this section in respect of any inspection shall not be called in question in any court of law at any time before the conclusion of that inspection.

(9) Accordingly, where an authorisation purports to be issued under this section in respect of any inspection, no proceedings (of whatever nature) shall be brought at any time before the conclusion of the inspection if they would, if successful, have the effect of preventing, delaying or otherwise affecting the carrying out of the inspection.

(10) If in any proceedings any question arises whether a person at any time was or was not, in relation to any routine, challenge or assistance inspection, a member of the inspection team or a member of the in-country escort or the observer, a certificate issued by or under the authority of the Secretary of State stating any fact relating to that question shall be conclusive evidence of that fact.

(11) If an authorisation is issued under this section the Secretary of State may issue an amendment varying the specified area, and—

(*a*) from the time when the amendment is expressed to take effect this section shall apply as if the specified area were the area as varied;

(*b*) subsection (8) shall apply to the amendment as it applies to the authorisation;

(*c*) the Secretary of State may issue further amendments varying the specified area and in such a case paragraphs (*a*) and (*b*) shall apply.

[Chemical Weapons Act 1996, s 24.]

8–22715 **26. Offences in connection with inspections.** (1) If an authorisation has been issued under section 25 in respect of any inspection, a person is guilty of an offence if he—

(*a*) refuses without reasonable excuse to comply with any request made by any constable or a member of the in-country escort for the purpose of facilitating the conduct of that inspection in accordance with the verification annex,

(*b*) interferes without reasonable excuse with any container, instrument or other object installed in the course of that inspection in accordance with the verification annex, or

(*c*) wilfully obstructs any member of the inspection team or of the in-country escort, or the observer, in the conduct of that inspection in accordance with the verification annex.

(2) Subsection (1)(*b*) applies to interference which occurs at any time while the container, instrument or other objects is retained in accordance with the verification annex.

(3) A person guilty of an offence under this section is liable[1]—

(*a*) on summary conviction, to a fine of an amount not exceeding **the statutory maximum;**

(*b*) on conviction on indictment, to a **fine.**

[Chemical Weapons Act 1996, s 26.]

---

1. For procedure in respect of this offence which is triable either way, see the Magistrates' Courts Act 1980, ss 17A–21, in PART I: MAGISTRATES' COURTS, PROCEDURE, ante.

8–22716 27. Privileges and immunities in connection with inspections. (1) Members of inspection teams and observers shall enjoy the same privileges and immunities as are enjoyed by diplomatic agents in accordance with the following provisions of the 1961 Articles, namely—

(*a*) Article 29
(*b*) paragraphs 1 and 2 of the Article 30,
(*c*) paragraphs 1, 2 and 3 of Article 31, and
(*d*) Article 34.

(2) Such persons shall, in addition, enjoy the same privileges as are enjoyed by diplomatic agents in accordance with paragraph 1(*b*) of Article 36 of the 1961 Articles, except in relation to articles the importing or exporting of which is prohibited by law or controlled by the enactments relating to quarantine.

(3) Samples and approved equipment carried by members of an inspection team shall be inviolable and exempt from customs duties.

(4) The privileges and immunities accorded to members of inspection teams and observers by virtue of this section shall be enjoyed by them at any time when they are in the United Kingdom—

(*a*) in connection with the carrying out there of a routine inspection, a challenge inspection or an assistance inspection, or
(*b*) while in transit to or from the territory of another party to the Convention in connection with the carrying out of such an inspection there.

(5) If—

(*a*) immunity from jurisdiction of a member of an inspection team is waived in accordance with the verification annex, and
(*b*) a notice made by the Secretary of State and informing the member of the waiver is delivered to him in person,

then, from the time the notice is so delivered, this section shall not have effect to confer that immunity on the member.

(6) If in any proceedings any question arises whether a person is or is not entitled to any privilege or immunity by virtue of this section, a certificate issued by or under the authority of the Secretary of State stating any fact relating to that question shall be conclusive evidence of that fact.

(7) In this section—

"the 1961 Articles" means the Articles which are set out in Schedule 1 to the Diplomatic Privileges Act 1964 (Articles of Vienna Convention on Diplomatic Relations of 1961 having force of law in United Kingdom);

"approved equipment" and "samples" shall be construed in accordance with the verification annex;

"enactment" includes an enactment comprised in subordinate legislation (within the meaning of the Interpretation Act 1978.

[Chemical Weapons Act 1996, s 27.]

8–22717 28. *Reimbursement of expenditure*

Offences: miscellaneous

8–22718 29. Power to search and obtain evidence. (1) If—

(*a*) a justice of the peace is satisfied on information on oath that there is reasonable ground for suspecting that an offence under this Act is being, has been or is about to be committed on any premises or that evidence of the commission of such an offence is to be found there, or
(*b*) in Scotland a justice, within the meaning of section 307 of the Criminal Procedure (Scotland) Act 1995, is satisfied by evidence on oath as mentioned in paragraph (*a*) above,

he may issue a warrant in writing authorising a person acting under the authority of the Secretary of State to enter the premises, if necessary by force, at any time within one month form the time of the issue of the warrant and to search them.

(2) A person who enters the premises under the authority of the warrant may—

(*a*) take with him such other persons and such equipment as appear to him to be necessary;
(*b*) inspect any document found on the premises which he has reasonable cause to believe may be required as evidence for the purposes of proceedings in respect of an offence under this Act;
(*c*) take copies of, or seize and remove, any such document;
(*d*) inspect, seize and remove any device or equipment found on the premises which he has reasonable cause to believe may be required as such evidence;
(*e*) inspect, sample, seize and remove any substance found on the premises which he has reasonable cause to believe may be required as such evidence;
(*f*) search or cause to be searched any person found on the premises whom he has reasonable cause to believe to be in possession of any document, device, equipment or substance;

but no woman or girl shall be searched except by a woman.

(3) The powers conferred by a warrant under this section shall only be exercisable, if the warrant so provides, in the presence of a constable.

[Chemical Weapons Act 1996, s 29.]

8–22719 **30. Forfeiture in case of conviction.** (1) The court by or before which a person is convicted of an offence under this Act may order that anything shown to the court's satisfaction to relate to the offence shall be forfeited, and either destroyed or otherwise dealt with in such manner as the court may order.

(2) In particular, the court may order the thing to be dealt with as the Secretary of State may see fit; and in such a case the Secretary of State may direct that it be destroyed or otherwise dealt with.

(3) Where—

(*a*) the court proposes to order anything to be forfeited under this section, and

(*b*) a person claiming to have an interest in it applies to be heard by the court,

the court must not order it to be forfeited unless he has been given an opportunity to show cause why the order should not be made.

[Chemical Weapons Act 1996, s 30.]

8–22719A **30A. Revenue and Customs prosecutions.** (1) Proceedings for a chemical weapons offence may be instituted by the Director of Revenue and Customs Prosecutions or by order of the Commissioners for Her Majesty's Revenue and Customs if it appears to the Director or to the Commissioners that the offence has involved—

(a) the development or production outside the United Kingdom of a chemical weapon;

(b) the movement of a chemical weapon into or out of any country or territory;

(c) any proposal or attempt to do anything falling within paragraph (a) or (b).

(2) In this section "chemical weapons offence" means an offence under section 2 above or section 50 of the Anti-terrorism, Crime and Security Act 2001 (including an offence of aiding, abetting, counselling, procuring or inciting the commission of, or attempting or conspiring to commit, such an offence).

(3) Any proceedings for an offence which are instituted by order of the Commissioners under subsection (1) above shall be commenced in the name of an officer of Revenue and Customs, but may be continued by another officer.

(4) Where the Commissioners investigate, or propose to investigate, any matter with a view to determining—

(a) whether there are grounds for believing that a chemical weapons offence has been committed, or

(b) whether a person should be prosecuted for such an offence,

that matter shall be treated as an assigned matter within the meaning of the Customs and Excise Management Act 1979.

(5) Nothing in this section affects any power of any person (including any officer) apart from this section.

(6) *Repealed.*

(7) This section does not apply to the institution of proceedings in Scotland.]

[Chemical Weapons Act 1996, s 30A, as inserted by the Anti-terrorism, Crime and Security Act 2001, s 46 and amended by the Commissioners for Revenue and Customs Act 2005, Sch 4.]

8–22720 **31. Offences: other provisions.** (1) Proceedings for an offence under section 2 or 11 shall not be instituted—

(*a*) in England and Wales, except by or with the consent of the Attorney General;

(*b*) in Northern Ireland, except by or with the consent of the Attorney General for Northern Ireland.*

(2) Proceedings for an offence under any provision of this Act other than section 2 or 11 shall not be instituted except by or with the consent of the Secretary of State; but the preceding provisions of this section do not apply to Scotland.

(3) Where an offence under this Act is committed by a body corporate and is proved to have been committed with the consent or connivance of, or to be attributable to any neglect on the part of—

(*a*) a director, manager, secretary or other similar officer of the body corporate, or

(*b*) any person who was purporting to act in any such capacity,

he as well as the body corporate shall be guilty of that offence and shall be liable to be proceeded against and punished accordingly.

(4) In subsection (3) "director", in relation to a body corporate whose affairs are managed by its members, means a member of the body corporate.

(5) Where an offence under this Act is committed by a Scottish partnership and is proved to have

been committed with the consent or connivance of a partner, he as well as the partnership shall be guilty of that offence and shall be liable to be proceeded against and punished accordingly.
[Chemical Weapons Act 1996, s 31.]

***Sub-section (1) words repealed and substituted by the Justice (Northern Ireland) Act 2002, s 28, from a date to be appointed.**

Other miscellaneous provisions

8–22721 32. Disclosure of information. (1) This section applies to information if—

(*a*) it was obtained under, or in connection with anything done under, this Act or the Convention, and
(*b*) it relates to a particular business or other activity carried on by any person.

(2) So long as the business or activity continues to be carried on the information shall not be disclosed except—

(*a*) with the consent of the person for the time being carrying on the business or activity,
(*b*) in connection with anything done for the purposes of the Convention,
(*c*) in connection with anything done for the purposes of this Act,
(*d*) in connection with the investigation of any criminal offence or for the purposes of any criminal proceedings,
(*e*) in connection with the enforcement of any restriction on imports or exports,
(*f*) in dealing with an emergency involving danger to the public,
(*g*) with a view to ensuring the security of the United Kingdom, or
(*h*) to the International Court of Justice for the purpose of enabling that Court do deal with any dispute referred to it under the Convention.

(3) The reference to this Act in subsection (2)(*c*) does not include a reference to section 33.

(4) A person who discloses information in contravention of this section is guilty of an offence and liable[1]—

(*a*) on summary conviction, to a fine of an amount not exceeding **the statutory maximum;**
(*b*) on conviction on indictment, to imprisonment for a term not exceeding **two years** or to a **fine** or to **both**.

(5) Where a person proposes to disclose information to which this section applies in circumstances where the disclosure would by virtue of paragraphs (*b*) to (*h*) or subsection (2) not contravene this section, he may disclose the information notwithstanding any obligation not to disclose it that would otherwise apply.
[Chemical Weapons Act 1996, s 32.]

1. For procedure in respect of this offence which is triable either way, see the Magistrates' Courts Act 1980, ss 17A–21, in PART I: MAGISTRATES' COURTS, PROCEDURE, ante.

8–22722 33. *Annual reports by the Secretary of State.*

8–22723 34. Service of notices. A notice under any provision of this Act, or a copy of a notice under any such provision, may be served on a person—

(*a*) by delivering it to him in person,
(*b*) by sending it by post to him at his usual or last-known residence or place of business in the United Kingdom, or
(*c*) in the case of a body corporate, by delivering it to the secretary or clerk of the body corporate at its registered or principal office or sending it by post to the secretary or clerk of that body corporate at that office.

[Chemical Weapons Act 1996, s 34.]

8–22724 36. Power to amend this Act. (1) The Secretary of State may by order make such additions to, omissions from or other modifications to this Act as he considers necessary or desirable to give effect to any amendment of the Convention made in pursuance of its provisions.

(2) The power to make an order under this section shall, if the order solely modifies the Schedule to this Act, be exercisable by statutory instrument subject to annulment in pursuance of a resolution of either House of Parliament.

(3) The power to make any other order under this section shall be exercisable by statutory instrument, and no such order shall be made unless a draft of it has been laid before and approved by resolution of each House of Parliament.
[Chemical Weapons Act 1996, s 36.]

8–22725 37. The Crown. (1) Subject to the following provisions of this section, this Act binds the Crown.

(2) No contravention by the Crown of a provision made by or under this Act shall make the

Crown criminally liable; but the High Court or in Scotland the Court of Session may, on the application of a person appearing to the Court to have an interest, declare unlawful any act or omission of the Crown which constitutes such a contravention.

(3) Notwithstanding subsection (2), the provisions made by or under this Act apply to persons in the public service of the Crown as they apply to other persons.

(4) Nothing in this section affects Her Majesty in her private capacity; and this subsection shall be construed as if section 38(3) of the Crown Proceedings Act 1947 (meaning of Her Majesty in her private capacity) were contained in this Act.
[Chemical Weapons Act 1996, s 37.]

General

8–22726 **39. Commencement, extent and citation.** (1) This Act (except this section) shall come into force on such day as the Secretary of State may appoint by order[1] made by statutory instrument.

(2) It is hereby declared that this Act extends to Northern Ireland.

(3) Her Majesty may by Order in Council make provision for extending any of the provisions of this Act, with such exceptions, adaptations or modifications as may be specified in the Order[2], to any of the Channel Islands, the Isle of Man or any colony.

(4) This Act may be cited as the Chemical Weapons Act 1996.
[Chemical Weapons Act 1996, s 39.]

---

1. The Chemical Weapons Act 1996 (Commencement) Order 1996, SI 1996/2054, appointed the 16 September 1996 for the coming into force of this Act.
2. The following Chemical Weapons Act 1996 Orders have been made under this provision: Jersey, SI 1998/2565; Isle of Man, SI 1998/2794; Guernsey, SI 2000/743; Overseas Territories SI 2005/854.

8–22727 SCHEDULE

SCHEDULED TOXIC CHEMICALS AND PRECURSORS

A TOXIC CHEMICALS: **(CAS registry number)**

(1)	O-Alkyl (less than or equal to C10, incl cycloalkyl) alkyl (Me, Et, n-Pr or i-Pr)-phosphonofluoridates	
	eg Sarin: O-Isopropyl methylphosphonofluoridate	(107-44-8)
	Soman: O-Pinacolyl methylphosphonofluoridate	(96-64-0)
(2)	O-Alkyl (less than or equal to C10, incl cycloalkyl) N,N-dialkyl (Me, Et, n-Pr or i-Pr) phosphoramidocyanidates	
	eg Tabun: 0-Ethyl N,N-dimethyl phosphoramidocyanidate	(77-81-6)
(3)	O-Alkyl (H or less than or equal to C10, incl cycloalkyl) S-2-dailkyl (Me, Et, n-Pr or i-Pr)-aminoethyl alkyl (Me, Et, n-Pr or i-Pr) phosphonothiolates and corresponding alkylated or protonated salts	
	eg VX: 0-Ethyl S-2-diisopropylaminoethyl methyl phosphonothiolate	(50782-69-9)
(4)	Sulfur mustards:	
	2-Chloroethylchloromethylsulfide	(2625-76-5)
	Mustard gas: Bis (2-chloroethyl) sulfide	(505-60-2)
	Bis (2-chloroethylthio) methane	(63869-13-6)
	Sesquimustard: 1,2-Bis (2-chloroethylthio) ethane	(3563-36-8)
	1,3-Bis (2-chloroethylthio)-n-propane	(63905-10-2)
	1,4-Bis (2-chloroethylthio)-n-butane	(142868-93-7)
	1,5-Bis (2-chloroethylthio)-n-pentane	(142868-94-8)
	Bis (2-chloroethylthiomethyl) ether	(63918-90-1)
	O-Mustard: Bis (2-chloroethylthioethy) ether	(63918-89-8)
(5)	Lewisites:	
	Lewisite 1: 2-Chlorovinyldichloroarsine	(541-25-3)
	Lewisite 2: Bis (2-chlorovinyl) chloroarsine	(40334-69-8)
	Lewisite 3: Tris (2-chlorovinyl) arsine	(40334-70-1)
(6)	Nitrogen mustards:	
	HN1: Bis (2-chloroethyl) ethylamine	(538-07-8)
	HN2: Bis (2-chloroethyl) methylamine	(51-75-2)
	HN3: Tris (2-chloroethyl) amine	(555-77-1)
(7)	Saxitoxin	(35523-89-8)
(8)	Ricin	(9009-86-3)

B PRECURSORS:

(9)	Alkyl (Me, Et, n-Pr or i-Pr) phosphonyldifluorides	
	eg DF: Methylphosphonyldifluoride	(676-99-3)
(10)	O-Alkyl (H or less than or equal to C10, incl cycloalkyl) O-2-dialkyl (Me, Et, n-Pr or i-Pr)-aminoethyl alkyl (Me, Et, n-Pr or i-Pr) phosphonites and corresponding alkylated or protonated salts	

B PRECURSORS:

	eg QL: O-Ethyl O-2 diisopropylaminoethyl methylphosphonite	(57856-11-8)
(11)	Chlorosarin: O-Isopropyl methylphosphonochloridate	(1445-76-7)
(12)	Chlorosoman: O-Pinacolyl methylphosphonochloridate	(7040-57-5)

Notes:

1. This Schedule sets out Schedule 1 to the annex on chemicals to the Convention as corrected.

2. In this Schedule the reference to the CAS registry is to the chemical abstract service registry.

3. This Schedule must be read subject to the following proposition, which is based on a note in the Convention: where reference is made to groups of dialkylated chemicals, followed by a list of alkyl groups in parentheses, all chemicals possible by all possible combinations of alkyl groups listed in the parentheses must be taken to be listed in the Schedule.

Knives Act 1997

(1997 c 21)

The offences

8–22728 **1. Unlawful marketing of knives.** (1) A person is guilty of an offence if he markets a knife in a way which—

(*a*) indicates, or suggests, that it is suitable for combat; or

(*b*) is otherwise likely to stimulate or encourage violent behaviour involving the use of the knife as a weapon.

(2) "Suitable for combat" and "violent behaviour" are defined in section 10.

(3) For the purposes of this Act, an indication or suggestion that a knife is suitable for combat may, in particular, be given or made by a name or description—

(*a*) applied to the knife;

(*b*) on the knife or on any packaging in which it is contained; or

(*c*) included in any advertisement which, expressly or by implication, relates to the knife.

(4) For the purposes of this Act, a person markets a knife if—

(*a*) he sells or hires it;

(*b*) he offers, or exposes, it for sale or hire; or

(*c*) he has it in his possession for the purpose of sale or hire.

(5) A person who is guilty of an offence under this section is liable[2]—

(*a*) on summary conviction to imprisonment for a term not exceeding **six months** or to a fine not exceeding the **statutory maximum**, or to **both**;

(*b*) on conviction on indictment to imprisonment for a term not exceeding **two years** or to a **fine**, or to **both**.

[Knives Act 1997, s 1.]

---

1. With the exception of s 11, the provisions of this Act have been brought into force by orders made under s 11: the Knives Act 1997 (Commencement) (No 1) Order 1997, SI 1997/1906, bringing into force sections 1 to 7, 9 and 10 on 1 September 1997, and the Knives Act 1997 (Commencement) (No 2) Order 1999, SI 1999/5, bringing into force s 8 on 1 March 1999.

2. For procedure in respect of this offence which is triable either way, see the Magistrates' Courts Act 1980, ss 17A-21, in PART I: MAGISTRATES' COURTS, PROCEDURE, ante.

8–22729 **2. Publications.** (1) A person is guilty of an offence if he publishes any written, pictorial or other material in connection with the marketing of any knife and that material—

(*a*) indicates, or suggests, that the knife is suitable for combat; or

(*b*) is otherwise likely to stimulate or encourage violent behaviour involving the use of the knife as a weapon.

(2) A person who is guilty of an offence under this section is liable[1]—

(*a*) on summary conviction to imprisonment for a term not exceeding **six months** or to a fine not exceeding the **statutory maximum**, or to **both**;

(*b*) on conviction on indictment to imprisonment for a term not exceeding **two years** or to a **fine**, or to **both**.

[Knives Act 1997, s 2.]

---

1. For procedure in respect of this offence which is triable either way, see the Magistrates' Courts Act 1980, ss 17A-21, in PART I: MAGISTRATES' COURTS, PROCEDURE, ante.

The defences

8–22730 **3. Exempt trades.** (1) It is a defence for a person charged with an offence under section 1 to prove[1] that—

(*a*) the knife was marketed—

(i) for use by the armed forces of any country;
(ii) as an antique or curio; or
(iii) as falling within such other category (if any) as may be prescribed;

(*b*) it was reasonable for the knife to be marketed in that way; and
(*c*) there were no reasonable grounds for suspecting that a person into whose possession the knife might come in consequence of the way in which it was marketed would use it for an unlawful purpose.

(2) It is a defence for a person charged with an offence under section 2 to prove that—

(*a*) the material was published in connection with marketing a knife—

(i) for use by the armed forces of any country;
(ii) as an antique or curio; or
(iii) as falling within such other category (if any) as may be prescribed;

(*b*) it was reasonable for the knife to be marketed in that way; and
(*c*) there were no reasonable grounds for suspecting that a person into whose possession the knife might come in consequence of the publishing of the material would use it for an unlawful purpose.

(3) In this section "prescribed" means prescribed by regulations made by the Secretary of State.
[Knives Act 1997, s 3.]

1. The standard of proof is on a preponderance of probabilities, less onerous than on the prosecution; *R v Carr-Briant* [1943] KB 607, [1943] 2 All ER 156, 107 JP 167, *R v Dunbar* [1958] 1 QB 1, [1957] 2 All ER 737, [1957] 3 WLR 330.

8–22731 **4. Other defences.** (1) It is a defence for a person charged with an offence under section 1 to prove[1] that he did not know or suspect, and had no reasonable grounds for suspecting, that the way in which the knife was marketed—

(*a*) amounted to an indication or suggestion that the knife was suitable for combat; or
(*b*) was likely to stimulate or encourage violent behaviour involving the use of the knife as a weapon.

(2) It is a defence for a person charged with an offence under section 2 to prove[1] that he did not know or suspect, and had no reasonable grounds for suspecting, that the material—

(*a*) amounted to an indication or suggestion that the knife was suitable for combat; or
(*b*) was likely to stimulate or encourage violent behaviour involving the use of the knife as a weapon.

(3) It is a defence for a person charged with an offence under section 1 or 2 to prove[1] that he took all reasonable precautions and exercised all due diligence to avoid committing the offence.
[Knives Act 1997, s 4.]

1. The standard of proof is on a preponderance of probabilities, less onerous than on the prosecution; *R v Carr-Briant* [1943] KB 607, [1943] 2 All ER 156, 107 JP 167, *R v Dunbar* [1958] 1 QB 1, [1957] 2 All ER 737, [1957] 3 WLR 330.

Supplementary powers

8–22732 **5. Supplementary powers of entry, seizure and retention.** (1) If, on an application made by a constable, a justice of the peace or sheriff is satisfied that there are reasonable grounds for suspecting—

(*a*) that a person ("the suspect") has committed an offence under section 1 in relation to knives of a particular description, and
(*b*) that knives of that description and in the suspect's possession or under his control are to be found on particular premises,

the justice or sheriff may issue a warrant authorising a constable to enter those premises, search for the knives and seize and remove any that he finds.

(2) If, on an application made by a constable, a justice of the peace or sheriff is satisfied that there are reasonable grounds for suspecting—

(*a*) that a person ("the suspect") has committed an offence under section 2 in relation to particular material, and
(*b*) that publications consisting of or containing that material and in the suspect's possession or under his control are to be found on particular premises,

the justice or sheriff may issue a warrant authorising a constable to enter those premises, search for the publications and seize and remove any that he finds.

(3) A constable, in the exercise of his powers under a warrant issued under this section, may if necessary use reasonable force.

(4) Any knives or publications which have been seized and removed by a constable under a warrant issued under this section may be retained until the conclusion of proceedings against the suspect[1].

(5) For the purposes of this section, proceedings in relation to a suspect are concluded if—

(*a*) he is found guilty and sentenced or otherwise dealt with for the offence;
(*b*) he is acquitted;
(*c*) proceedings for the offence are discontinued; or
(*d*) it is decided not to prosecute him.

(6) In this section "premises" includes any place and, in particular, any vehicle, vessel, aircraft or hovercraft and any tent or movable structure.

[Knives Act 1997, s 5.]

1. See the Criminal Justice and Police Act 2001, Part 2 (PART I, ante). These provisions confer, by ss 50 and 51, additional powers of seizure of property in relation to searches carried out under existing powers. However, s 57 (retention of seized items) does not authorise the retention of any property which could not be retained under the provisions listed in s 57(1), which include s 5(4) of the Knives Act 1997, if the property was seized under the new powers (ie those conferred by ss 50 and 51) in reliance on one of those powers (ie those conferred by the provisions listed in s 57(1)). Section 57(4) further provides that nothing in any of the provisions listed in s 57(1) authorises the retention of anything after an obligation to return it has arisen under Part 2.

8–22733 **6. Forfeiture of knives and publications.** (1) If a person is convicted of an offence under section 1 in relation to a knife of a particular description, the court may make an order for forfeiture in respect of any knives of that description—

(*a*) seized under a warrant issued under section 5; or
(*b*) in the offender's possession or under his control at the relevant time.

(2) If a person is convicted of an offence under section 2 in relation to particular material, the court may make an order for forfeiture in respect of any publications consisting of or containing that material which—

(*a*) have been seized under warrant issued under section 5; or
(*b*) were in the offender's possession or under his control at the relevant time.

(3) The court may make an order under subsection (1) or (2)—

(*a*) whether or not it also deals with the offender in respect of the offence in any other way; and
(*b*) without regard to any restrictions on forfeiture in any enactment.

(4) In considering whether to make an order, the court must have regard—

(*a*) to the value of the property; and
(*b*) to the likely financial and other effects on the offender of the making of the order (taken together with any other order that the court contemplates making).

(5) In this section "relevant time"—

(*a*) in relation to a person convicted in England and Wales or Northern Ireland of an offence under section 1 or 2, means the time of his arrest for the offence or of the issue of a summons in respect of it;
(*b*) in relation to a person so convicted in Scotland, means the time of his arrest for the offence or of his being cited as an accused in respect of it.

[Knives Act 1997, s 6.]

8–22734 **7. Effect of a forfeiture order.** (1) An order under section 6 (a "forfeiture order") operates to deprive the offender of his rights, if any, in the property to which it relates.

(2) The property to which a forfeiture order relates must be taken into the possession of the police (if it is not already in their possession).

(3) The court may, on an application made by a person who—

(*a*) claims property to which a forfeiture order applies, but
(*b*) is not the offender from whom it was forfeited,

make an order (a "recovery order") for delivery of the property to the applicant if it appears to the court that he owns it.

(4) An application to a sheriff must be made in such manner as may be prescribed by act of adjournal.

(5) No application may be made after the end of the period of 6 months beginning with the date on which the forfeiture order was made.

(6) No application may succeed unless the claimant satisfies the court—

(*a*) that he had not consented to the offender having possession of the property; or (*b*) that he did not know, and had no reason to suspect, that the offence was likely to be committed.

(7) If a person has a right to recover property which is in the possession of another in pursuance of a recovery order, that right—

(*a*) is not affected by the making of the recovery order at any time before the end of the period of 6 months beginning with the date on which the order is made; but

(*b*) is lost at the end of that period.

(8) The Secretary of State may make regulations[1], in relation to property forfeited under this section, for disposing of the property and dealing with the proceeds in cases where—

(*a*) no application has been made before the end of the period of 6 months beginning with the date on which the forfeiture order was made; or

(*b*) no such application has succeeded.

(9) The regulations[1] may also provide for investing money and auditing accounts.

(10) In this section, "application" means an application under subsection (3).

[Knives Act 1997, s 7.]

1. The Knives (Forfeited Property) Regulations 1997 have been made, in this TITLE, post.

8–22735 8. Powers to stop and search for knives or offensive weapons. *Amendment of the Criminal Justice and Public Order Act 1994.*

Miscellaneous

8–22736 9. Offences by bodies corporate. (1) If an offence under this Act committed by a body corporate is proved—

(*a*) to have been committed with the consent or connivance of an officer, or

(*b*) to be attributable to any neglect on his part,

he as well as the body corporate is guilty of the offence and liable to be proceeded against and punished accordingly.

(2) In subsection (1) "officer", in relation to a body corporate, means a director, manager, secretary or other similar office of the body, or a person purporting to act in any such capacity.

(3) If the affairs of a body corporate are managed by its members, subsection (1) applies in relation to the acts and defaults of a member in connection with his functions of management as if he were a director of the body corporate.

(4) *Scotland.*

[Knives Act 1997, s 9.]

8–22737 10. Interpretation. In this Act—

"the court" means—

(*a*) in relation to England and Wales or Northern Ireland, the Crown Court or a magistrates' court;

(*b*) in relation to Scotland, the sheriff;

"knife" means an instrument which has a blade or is sharply pointed;

"marketing" and related expressions are to be read with section 1(4);

"publication" includes a publication in electronic form and, in the case of a publication which is, or may be, produced from electronic data, any medium on which the data are stored;

"suitable for combat" means suitable for use as a weapon for inflicting injury on a person or causing a person to fear injury;

"violent behaviour" means an unlawful act inflicting injury on a person or causing a person to fear injury.

[Knives Act 1997, s 10.]

8–22738 11. Short title, commencement, extent etc. (1) This Act may be cited as the Knives Act 1997.

(2) This section comes into force on the passing of this Act.

(3) The other provisions of this Act come into force on such date as may be appointed by order[1] made by the Secretary of State; but different dates may be appointed for different provisions and for different purposes.

(4)–(6) *Regulations and orders.*

(7) *Extent*

[Knives Act 1997, s 11.]

1. As to commencement orders which has been made at the date of going to press, see note 1 to the short title of this Act, ante.

Landmines Act 1998[1]

(1998 c 33)

8–22740 The Landmines Act 1998 implements obligations under the Ottawa Convention[2] and promotes the control of anti-personnel landmines. The use, development or production, acquisition, possession or transfer of an anti personnel mine defined in s 1, is an offence punishable on indictment by imprisonment not exceeding **14 years** or a **fine** or **both** (s 2). Prohibitions may apply to conduct by UK nationals outside the UK (s 3). Provision is made for defences including possession etc for the purpose of developing techniques for mine detection, clearance and destruction or other lawful purposes as defined (s 4) and for certain international military operations (s 5) or where the accused proves lack of the requisite knowledge (s 6). The Secretary of State may take steps to secure the destruction of anti-personnel mines by serving a notice on a person suspected of having a prohibited object in his possession giving him the opportunity to make representations (s 7) and a justice may issue a warrant authorising entry within one month of issue to search premises (s 8) for prohibited objects which may subsequently be ordered by the Secretary of State to be destroyed (s 9). Various offences are created in relation to failure to comply with or frustrating the procedures for searching for and destroying prohibited items which are punishable on summary conviction by a fine not exceeding the **statutory maximum** or on indictment by a **fine** or (in the case of an offence of knowingly making a false or misleading statement in response to a notice served by the Secretary of State under ss 7, 9 or 10) a term of imprisonment not exceeding **2 years** (s 12).

Provision is made for rights of entry for fact finding missions under the Ottawa Convention (ss 13–16); information and records (s 17) including power for a justice to issue a search warrant where there are reasonable grounds for suspecting an offence under the Act is being, has been or is about to be committed on any premises or that evidence of the commission of such an offence is to be found there (s 18). Proceedings for an offence under section 2 may not be instituted except by or with the consent of the Attorney General (s 20) and in certain circumstances may be conducted by Revenue and Customs (s 21). On conviction of an offence under the Act, the court may order forfeiture of anything relating to the offence (s 22).

1. This Act was brought fully into force on 1 March 1999 by the Landmines Act 1998 (Commencement) Order 1999, SI 1999/448. See also the Landmines Act 1998 (Guernsey) Order 2000, SI 2000/2769, the Landmines Act (Isle of Man) Order 2000, SI 2000/2770, the Landmines Act 1998 (Overseas Territories) Order 2001, SI 2001/3499 and the Landmines Act 1998 (Jersey) Order 2001, SI 2001/3930.

2. Convention on the Prohibition of the Use, Stockpiling, Production and Transfer of Anti-Personnel Mines and on their Destruction, which was signed by the United Kingdom at Ottawa on 3 December 1997.

Nuclear Explosions (Prohibition and Inspections) Act 1998

(1998 c 7)

8–22742 This Act gives effect to certain provisions of the Comprehensive Nuclear-Test-Ban Treaty adopted in New York on 10 September 1996 and the Protocol to that treaty.

Except where carried out in the course of an armed conflict any person who knowingly causes a nuclear weapons test explosion or other nuclear explosion is guilty of an offence triable only on indictment and is liable on conviction to imprisonment for **life** (s 1) and the offence may be committed by a United Kingdom national outside the United Kingdom (s 2). Proceedings may only be commenced with the consent of the Attorney General (s 3). Inspection teams may conduct on-site inspections in accordance with the Treaty and the Secretary of State may issue an authorisation granting rights of access, entry and unobstructed inspection and may authorise the police to assist such inspection (ss 4–5). A person is guilty of an offence punishable on summary conviction by a fine not exceeding **the statutory maximum** or on indictment by a fine if he fails without reasonable excuse to comply with a request to facilitate such an inspection or wilfully obstructs a member of the inspection team (s 7). A justice who is satisfied there are reasonable grounds for suspecting that an offence under this Act has been, is or is about to be committed on any premises or that evidence of such an offence is to be found there may issue a warrant to enter, by force if necessary, and search the premises (s 10).

Criminal Justice Act 1988 (Offensive Weapons) Order 1988[1]

(SI 1988/2019 amended by SI 2002/1668 and SI 2004/1271)

8–22744 **1.** *Citation and Commencement.*

1. Made by the Secretary of State under section 141(2) of the Criminal Justice Act 1988. Revoked in relation to Scotland by SSI 2005/483.

2. The Schedule to this Order shall have effect.

SCHEDULE

(*Amended by SSI 2002/323 and SI 2004/1271.*)

Article 2

8–22745 **1.** Section 141 of the Criminal Justice Act 1988 (offensive weapons) shall apply to the following descriptions of weapons, other than weapons of those descriptions which are antiques for the purposes of this Schedule:

(*a*) a knuckleduster, that is, a band of metal or other hard material worn on one or more fingers, and designed to cause injury, and any weapon incorporating a knuckleduster;

(*b*) a swordstick, that is, a hollow walking-stick or cane containing a blade which may be used as a sword;

(*c*) the weapon sometimes known as a "handclaw", being a band of metal or other hard material from which a number of sharp spikes protrude, and worn around the hand;

(*d*) the weapon sometimes known as a "belt buckle knife", being a buckle which incorporates or conceals a knife;

(*e*) the weapon sometimes known as a "push dagger", being a knife the handle of which fits within a clenched fist and the blade of which protrudes from between two fingers;

(*f*) the weapon sometimes known as a "hollow kubatan", being a cylindrical container containing a number of sharp spikes;

(*g*) the weapon sometimes known as a "footclaw", being a bar of metal or other hard material from which a number of sharp spikes protrude, and worn strapped to the foot;

(*h*) the weapon sometimes known as a "shuriken", "shaken" or "death star", being a hard non-flexible plate having three or more sharp radiating points and designed to be thrown;

(*i*) the weapon sometimes known as a "balisong" or "butterfly knife", being a blade enclosed by its handle, which is designed to split down the middle, without the operation of a spring or other mechanical means, to reveal the blade;

(*j*) the weapon sometimes known as a "telescopic truncheon", being a truncheon which extends automatically by hand pressure applied to a button, spring or other device in or attached to its handle;

(*k*) the weapon sometimes known as a "blowpipe" or "blow gun", being a hollow tube out of which hard pellets or darts are shot by the use of breath;

(*l*) the weapon sometimes known as a "kusari gama", being a length of rope, cord, wire or chain fastened at one end to a sickle;

(*m*) the weapon sometimes known as a "kyoketsu shoge", being a length of rope, cord, wire or chain fastened at one end to a hooked knife;

(*n*) the weapon sometimes known as a "manrikgusari" or "kusari", being a length of rope, cord, wire or chain fastened at each end to a hard weight or hand grip;

(*o*) a disguised knife, that is any knife which has a concealed blade or concealed sharp point and is designed to appear to be an everyday object of a kind commonly carried on the person or in a handbag, briefcase, or other hand luggage (such as a comb, brush, writing instrument, cigarette lighter, key, lipstick or telephone).*

(*p*) a stealth knife, that is a knife or spike, which has a blade, or sharp point, made from a material that is not readuily detectable by apparatus used for detecting metal and which is not designed for domestic use or for use in the processing, preparatn or consumption of food or as a toy;**

(*q*) a straight, side-handled or friction-lock truncheon (sometimes known as a baton).**

***Sub-paragraph (*o*) inserted in relation to Scotland only by SSI 2002/323.**

****Sub-paragraphs (*p*) and (*q*) inserted in relation to England, Wales and Northern Ireland by SI 2004/1271.**

2. For the purposes of this Schedule, a weapon is an antique if it was manufactured more than 100 years before the date of any offence alleged to have been committed in respect of that weapon under subsection (1) of the said section 141 or section 50(2) or (3) of the Customs and Excise Management Act 1979 (improper importation).

Knives (Forfeited Property) Regulations 1997[1]

(SI 1997/1907 amended by SI 2000/1549)

8–22746 **1.** *Citation and commencement.*

---

1. Made by the Secretary of State, in exercise of the powers conferred on him by s 7(8) and (9) of the Knives Act 1997.

Interpretation

2. In these Regulations,

"museum or similar institution" means any institution which has as its purpose, or one of its purposes, the preservation and display of material of historical, aesthetic or technical interest to which the public are given access.

"the relevant authority" means

(*a*) in relation to a police area in England and Wales listed in Schedule 1 to the Police Act 1996 or the City of London police area, the police authority (within the meaning of that Act);

(*b*) in relation to the metropolitan police district, the Metropolitan Police Authority;

(*c*) *Scotland.*

"the 1997 Act" means the Knives Act 1997.

Property to which Regulations apply

3. (1) Subject to paragraph (2) below, these Regulations apply to property which is in the possession of the police by virtue of a forfeiture order under section 6 of the 1997 Act and in respect of which—

(*a*) no application under section 7(3) of the 1997 Act has been made before the end of the period of 6 months beginning with the date on which the forfeiture order was made; or
(*b*) no such application has succeeded.

(2) Where, within the period specified in paragraph (1) above, an application by a claimant of the property has been made under section 7(3) of the 1997 Act or the person upon whose conviction the court ordered the forfeiture of the property under section 6 of that Act has appealed against the conviction or sentence, these Regulations shall not apply to the property until that application or appeal has been determined.

Disposal of property

4. (1) Subject to paragraph (2) below, property to which these Regulations apply shall be destroyed.

(2) Where the relevant authority are satisfied that property to which these Regulations apply which would otherwise fall to be destroyed is of particular rarity, aesthetic quality or technical or historical interest, they may, instead of arranging for its destruction, give or sell it to a museum or similar institution.

(3) The proceeds of disposals under these Regulations (if any) shall be paid to the relevant authority and

(*a*) in relation to authorities in England and Wales shall be subject to the regulations governing the application of the proceeds of sale of property made under section 2 of the Police (Property) Act 1897; and
(*b*) in relation to authorities in Scotland shall vest in the relevant authority.

OFFICIAL SECRETS

8–22750 This title contains the following statutes—

8–22751 Official Secrets Act 1911
8–22770 Official Secrets Act 1920
8–22790 Official Secrets Act 1989

Official Secrets Act 1911

(1 & 2 Geo 5 c 28)

8–22751 **1. Penalties for spying.** (1) If any person for any purpose[2] prejudicial to the safety or interests of the State—

(*a*) approaches, inspects, passes over, or is in the neighbourhood of, or enters any prohibited place[3] within the meaning of this Act, or
(*b*) makes any sketch, plan, model[4], or note which is calculated to be or might be or is intended to be directly or indirectly useful to an enemy[5]; or
(*c*) obtains, collects, records or publishes or communicates[6] to any other person any secret official code word or pass word, or any sketch, plan, model, article, or note, or other document or information which is calculated to be or might be or is intended to be directly or indirectly useful to an enemy,

shall be guilty of an offence[7].

(2) On a prosecution under this section it shall not be necessary to show that the accused person was guilty of any particular act tending to show a purpose prejudicial to the safety or interests of the State, and, notwithstanding that no such act is proved against him, he may be convicted if, from the circumstances of the case, or his conduct, or his known character as proved, it appears that his purpose was a purpose prejudicial to the safety or interests of the State; and if any sketch, plan, model, article, note, document, or information relating to or used in any prohibited place[8] within the meaning of this Act, or anything is such a place, or any secret official code word or pass word, is made, obtained, collected, recorded, published or communicated by any person other than a person acting under lawful authority, it shall be deemed to have been made, obtained, collected, recorded, published, or communicated for a purpose prejudicial to the safety or interests of the State unless the contrary is proved.

[Official Secrets Act 1911, s 1, as amended by Official Secrets Act 1920, First and Second Schedules.]

1. The Official Secrets Acts 1911, 1920 and 1939 shall be construed as one (Official Secrets Act 1939, s 2(1)). The Official Secrets Acts apply to acts done by a diplomatic agent in respect of the archives of the diplomatic mission in which he is employed (*R v AB* [1941] 1 KB 454). The communication of classified information in the UK or elsewhere by any

person now or in the past a member of or having dealings with any Euratom institution is an offence by s 11(2) of the European Communities Act 1972, construed with these Acts.

2. The purpose is not limited by the reference to "spying" in the marginal note (*R v Chandler* [1962] 2 All ER 314; affd sub nom *Chandler v DPP* [1964] AC 763, [1962] 3 All ER 142, HL, where the meanings of phrases used in this section were considered in detail). See also *R v Bettaney* [1985] Crim LR 104, CA.

3. See 1911 Act, s 3, post.

4. "Sketch" includes any photograph or other mode of representing any plan or thing; "model" includes design, pattern, and specimen; and "document" includes part of a document (1911 Act, s 12).

5. The word "enemy" does not necessarily mean someone with whom this country is at war, but a potential enemy (*R v Parrott* (1913) 8 Cr App Rep 186).

6. Expressions referring to communicating include any communicating, whether in whole or in part, and whether the sketch, plan, model, article, note, document, or information itself or the substance, effect or description thereof only to be communicated; and expressions referring to the communication of any sketch, plan, model, article, note or document include the transfer or transmission of the sketch, plan, model, article, note or document (1911 Act, s 12 as amended by the Official Secrets Act 1989, Sch 2). The communication is an offence, even if made without any corruption (*R v Crisp and Homewood* (1919) 83 JP 121).

7. "Offence" is substituted for "felony" to accord with Criminal Law Act 1967, s 12(5). For punishment, see 1920 Act, s 8, post.

8. See 1911 Act, s 3, post.

8–22752 **3. Definition of prohibited place.** For the purposes of this Act, the expression "prohibited place" means—

(*a*) any work of defence, arsenal, naval or air force establishment or station, factory, dockyard, mine, mine-field, camp, ship, or aircraft belonging to or occupied by or on behalf of Her Majesty, or any telegraph, telephone, wireless or signal station, or office so belonging[1] or occupied and any place belonging to or occupied by or on behalf of Her Majesty and used for the purpose of building, repairing, making, or storing any munitions of war, or any sketches, plans, models, or documents, relating thereto, or for the purpose of getting any metals, oil, or minerals of use in time of war, [substituted by Official Secrets Act 1920, First Schedule].

(*b*) any place not belonging to Her Majesty where any munitions of war or any sketches, models, plans or documents relating thereto, are being made, repaired, gotten, or stored under contract with, or with any person on behalf of, Her Majesty, or otherwise on behalf of Her Majesty; and

(*c*) [2] any place belonging to or used for the purposes of Her Majesty which is for the time being declared by order[3] of a Secretary of State to be a prohibited place for the purposes of this section on the ground that information with respect thereto, or damage thereto, would be useful to an enemy; and

(*d*) any railway, road, way or channel, or other means of communication by land or water (including any works or structures being part thereof or connected therewith) or any place used for gas, water, electricity works or other works for the purposes of a public character, or any place where munitions of war, or any sketches, models, plans or documents relating thereto are being made, repaired, or stored otherwise than on behalf of Her Majesty, which is for the time being declared by order of a Secretary of State to be a prohibited place for the purposes of this section, on the ground that information with respect thereto, or the destruction or obstruction thereof, or interference therewith, would be useful to an enemy[4].

[Official Secrets Act 1911, s 3, as amended by Official Secrets Act 1920, First Schedule.]

1. Any reference to a place belonging to Her Majesty includes a place belonging to any department of the Government of the United Kingdom or of any British possessions, whether the place is or is not actually vested in Her Majesty (1911 Act, s 12).

2. For application of this paragraph to any place belonging to or used for the purposes of the United Kingdom Atomic Energy Authority, see Atomic Energy Authority Act 1954, s 6(3). A place belonging to or used for the purposes of the Civil Aviation Authority shall be deemed to be a place belonging to Her Majesty (Civil Aviation Act 1982, s 18(2)).

3. Places have been prescribed by the Official Secrets (Prohibited Places) Order 1994, SI 1994/968.

4. See note to "enemy" in s 1(1)(*b*), ante.

8–22753 **6. Power to arrest.** Any person who is found committing[1] an offence under this Act, or who is reasonably suspected of having committed, or having attempted to commit, or being about to commit such an offence, may be apprehended and detained.*

[Official Secrets Act 1911, s 6, as amended by Criminal Law Act 1967, Sch 3.]

*. **Repealed by the Serious Organised Crime and Police Act 2005, s 178 from a date to be appointed.**

1. See *Roberts v Orchard* (1863) 2 H & C 769; *Horley v Rogers* (1860) 2 E & E 674, 24 JP 582, and *Leete v Hart* (1868) LR 3 CP 322, 32 JP 407.

8–22754 **7. Penalty for harbouring spies.** If any person, knowingly harbours any person whom he knows, or has reasonable grounds for supposing, to be a person who is about to commit or who has committed an offence under this Act, or knowingly permits to meet or assemble in any premises in his occupation or under his control any such persons, or if any person having harboured any such person, or permitted to meet or assemble in any premises in his occupation or under his control any

such persons, wilfully omits or refuses to disclose to a superintendent of police any information which it is in his power to give in relation to any such person he shall be guilty of a misdemeanour.
[Official Secrets Act 1911, s 7, as amended by Official Secrets Act 1920, First and Second Schedules.]

8–22755 8. Restriction on prosecution. A prosecution for an offence under this Act[1] shall not be instituted except by or with the consent of the Attorney-General[2].
[Official Secrets Act 1911, s 8, as amended by the Criminal Jurisdiction Act 1975, Sch 6.]

1. The expression "offence under this Act" includes any act, omission or other thing which is punishable under this Act (1911 Act, s 12).
2. The expression "Attorney-General" means the Attorney-General for England (1911 Act, s 12, amended by the Law Officers Act 1997, Schedule). Nothing in s 2 of the Administration of Justice (Miscellaneous Provisions) Act 1933, shall affect this provision (Administration of Justice (Miscellaneous Provisions) Act 1933, s 2(7)).

8–22756 9. Search warrants. (1) If a justice of the peace is satisfied by information on oath that there is reasonable ground for suspecting that an offence under this Act[1] has been or is about to be committed, he may grant a search warrant authorising any constable to enter at any time any premises or place named in the warrant, if necessary by force, and to search the premises or place and every person found therein; and to seize any sketch, plan, model, article, note or document, or anything of a like nature or anything which is evidence of an offence under this Act[1] having been or being about to be committed, which he may find on the premises or place or on any such person, and with regard to or in connection with which he has reasonable ground for suspecting that an offence under this Act[1] has been or is about to be committed.

(2) Where it appears to a superintendent of police[2] that the case is one of great emergency and that in the interest of the State immediate action is necessary, he may by a written order under his name give to any constable the like authority as may be given by the warrant of a justice under this section.
[Official Secrets Act 1911, s 9 as amended by the Police and Criminal Evidence Act 1984, Sch 7.]

1. This includes provisions under the Official Secrets Act 1989 other than s 8(1), (4) or (5); Official Secrets Act 1989, s 11 (3); the Police and Criminal Evidence Act 1984, s 9(2) (exclusion of legal privilege items etc) and Sch 1, para 3(*b*) (access conditions for special procedure) apply to s 9(1) of the 1911 Act; Official Secrets Act 1989, s 11(3).
2. The expression "superintendent of police" includes any police officer of a like or superior rank and any person upon whom the powers of a superintendent of police are for the purposes of this Act conferred by a Secretary of State (1911 Act, s 12 as amended by 1920 Act, Sch 1).

Official Secrets Act 1920

(1920 c 75)

8–22770 1–4. Unauthorised use of uniforms, falsification of reports, personation and false documents [s 1 amended by the Forgery and Counterfeiting Act 1981, Sch.] Communications with foreign agents to be evidence of commission of certain offences [s 2]. Interfering with officers of the police or members of Her Majesty's forces [s 3][1].

1. This section relates to such interference "in the vicinity of" any prohibited place. In *Adler v George* [1964] 2 QB 7, [1964] 1 All ER 628, 128 JP 251, it was held that these words extended to the place itself.

8–22772 6. Duty of giving information as to commission of offences. (1) Where a chief officer of police[1] is satisfied that there is reasonable ground for suspecting that an offence under section one of the principal Act has been committed and for believing that any person is able to furnish information as to the offence or suspected offence, he may apply to a Secretary of State for permission to exercise the powers conferred by this subsection and, if such permission is granted, he may authorise a superintendent of police[2], or any police officer not below the rank of inspector, to require the person believed to be able to furnish information to give any information in his power relating to the offence or suspected offence[3], and, if so required and on tender of his reasonable expenses, to attend at such reasonable time and place as may be specified by the superintendent or other officer; and if a person required in pursuance of such an authorisation to give information, or to attend as aforesaid, fails to comply with any such requirement or knowingly gives false information, he shall be guilty of a misdemeanour.

(2) Where a chief officer of police has reasonable ground to believe that the case is one of great emergency and that in the interest of the State immediate action is necessary, he may exercise the powers conferred by the last foregoing subsection without applying for or being granted the permission of a Secretary of State, but if he does so shall forthwith report the circumstances to the Secretary of State.
[Official Secrets Act 1920, s 6, as substituted by the Official Secrets Act 1939, s 1.]

1. "Chief officer of police" includes any other officer of police expressly authorised by a chief officer of police to act on his behalf for the purposes of this section when by reason of illness, absence, or other cause he is unable to do so (sub-s (3)). As to the meaning of "chief officer of police", see the Official Secrets Act 1920, s 11(3).

2. See note to s 9 of the 1911 Act, supra.

3. This extends to an unauthorised person having received confidential police information (*Lewis v Cattle* [1938] 2 KB 454, [1938] 3 All ER 368, 102 JP 239).

8–22773 **7. Attempts, incitement, etc.** Any person who attempts to commit any offence under the principal Act of this Act, or solicits or incites or endeavours to persuade another person to commit an offence, or aids or abets and[1] does any act preparatory to the commission of an offence under the principal Act or this Act, shall be guilty of an offence[2], and on conviction shall be liable to the same punishment, and to be proceeded against in the same manner as if he had committed the offence.
[Official Secrets Act 1920, s 7.]

1. The word "and" should be read as "or" to give an intelligible meaning to the succeeding phrase (*R v Oakes* [1959] 2 QB 350, [1959] 2 All ER 92, 123 JP 290).

2. "Offence" is substituted for "felony or misdemeanour or summary offence" to accord with Criminal Law Act 1967, s 12(5).

8–22774 **8. Provision as to trial and punishment of offences.** (1) Any person who is guilty of an offence[1] under the principal Act or this Act shall be liable to imprisonment for a term not exceeding **fourteen years**.

(2) Any person who is guilty of a misdemeanour under the principal Act or this Act shall be liable[2] on conviction on indictment to imprisonment, for a term not exceeding **two years**[3], or, on conviction under the [Magistrates' Courts Act 1980] to imprisonment, for a term not exceeding **three months** or to a fine not exceeding **the statutory maximum**, or to **both** such imprisonment and fine: Provided that no misdemeanour under the principal Act or this Act shall be dealt with summarily except with the consent of the Attorney-General[4].

(3) For the purposes of the trial of a person for an offence under the principal Act or this Act, the offence shall be deemed to have been committed either at the place in which the same was actually committed, or at any place in the United Kingdom in which the offender may be found.

(4) In addition and without prejudice to any powers which a court may possess to order the exclusion of the public from any proceedings if, in the course of proceedings before a court against any person for an offence under the principal Act or this Act or the proceedings on appeal, or in the course of the trial of a person for an offence[1] under the principal Act or this Act, application is made by the prosecution, on the ground that the publication of any evidence to be given or of any statement to be made in the course of the proceedings would be prejudicial to the national safety, that all or any portion of the public shall be excluded during any part of the hearing, the court may make an order to that effect, but the passing of the sentence shall in any case take place in public.

(5) Where the person guilty of an offence under the principal Act or this Act is a company or corporation, every director[5] and officer of the company or corporation shall be guilty of the like offence unless he proves that the act or omission constituting the offence took place without his knowledge or consent.
[Official Secrets Act 1920, s 8, as amended by the Criminal Law Act 1977, s 28.]

1. "Offence" is substituted for "felony or misdemeanour or summary offence" to accord with Criminal Law Act 1967, s 12(5).

2. For procedure in respect of an offence triable either way, see the Magistrates' Courts Act 1980, ss 17A–21, in PART I: MAGISTRATES' COURTS, PROCEDURE, ante.

3. Offences under this Act, which are not arrestable offences by virtue of the term of imprisonment for which a person may be sentenced in respect of them are arrestable offences by virtue of Sch 1A to the Police and Criminal Evidence Act 1984.

4. See PART I: MAGISTRATES' COURTS, PROCEDURE, para **1–410 Criminal prosecutions**, ante.

5. See *Dean v Hiesler* [1942] 2 All ER 340, 106 JP 282.

Official Secrets Act 1989[1]

(1989 c 6)

8–22790 **1. Security and intelligence.** (1) A person who is or has been—

(*a*) a member of the security and intelligence services; or

(*b*) a person notified that he is subject to the provisions of this subsection,

is guilty of an offence[2] if without lawful authority he discloses any information, document or other article relating to security or intelligence which is or has been in his possession by virtue of his position as a member of any of those services or in the course of his work while the notification is or was in force.

(2) The reference in subsection (1) above to disclosing information relating to security or intelligence includes a reference to making any statement which purports to be a disclosure of such information or is intended to be taken by those to whom it is addressed as being such a disclosure.

(3) A person who is or has been a Crown servant or government contractor is guilty of an offence[2] if without lawful authority he makes a damaging disclosure of any information, document or other article relating to security or intelligence which is or has been in his possession by virtue of his position as such but otherwise than as mentioned in subsection (1) above.

(4) For the purposes of subsection (3) above a disclosure is damaging if—

(*a*) it causes damage to the work of, or of any part of, the security and intelligence services; or

(*b*) it is of information or a document or other article which is such that its unauthorised disclosure would be likely to cause such damage or which falls within a class or description of information, documents or articles the unauthorised disclosure of which would be likely to have that effect.

(5) It is a defence for a person charged with an offence under this section to prove that at the time of the alleged offence he did not know, and had no reasonable cause to believe, that the information, document or article in question related to security or intelligence or, in the case of an offence under subsection (3), that the disclosure would be damaging within the meaning of that subsection.

(6) Notification that a person is subject to subsection (1) above shall be effected by a notice in writing served on him by a Minister of the Crown; and such a notice may be served if, in the Minister's opinion, the work undertaken by the person in question is or includes work connected with the security and intelligence services and its nature is such that the interests of national security require that he should be subject to the provisions of that subsection.

(7) Subject to subsection (8) below, a notification for the purposes of subsection (1) above shall be in force for the period of five years beginning with the day on which it is served but may be renewed by further notices under subsection (6) above for periods of five years at a time.

(8) A notification for the purposes of subsection (1) above may at any time be revoked by a further notice in writing served by the Minister on the person concerned; and the Minister shall serve such a further notice as soon as, in his opinion, the work undertaken by that person ceases to be such as is mentioned in subsection (6) above.

(9) In this section "security or intelligence" means the work of, or in support of, the security and intelligence services or any part of them, and references to information relating to security or intelligence include references to information held or transmitted by those services or by persons in support of, or of any part of, them.

[Official Secrets Act 1989, s 1.]

1. The effect of this Act is to replace s 2 of the Official Secrets Act 1911 by provisions protecting more limited classes of official information.

2. For prosecution, trial and penalties, see ss 9–11 post. A defendant prosecuted under ss 1(1)(a) and 4(1) and (3)(a) of this Act is not entitled to put forward a defence of disclosure in the national interest or belief that such disclosure was in the national interest: *R v Shayler* [2002] UKHL 11, [2003] 1 AC 247, [2002] 2 All ER 477, [2002] 2 WLR 754.

8–22791 **2. Defence.** (1) A person who is or has been a Crown servant or government contractor is guilty of an offence[1] if without lawful authority he makes a damaging disclosure of any information, document or other article relating to defence which is or has been in his possession by virtue of his position as such.

(2) For the purposes of subsection (1) above a disclosure is damaging if—

(*a*) it damages the capability of, or of any part of, the armed forces of the Crown to carry out their tasks or leads to loss of life or injury to members of those forces or serious damage to the equipment or installations of those forces; or

(*b*) otherwise than as mentioned in paragraph (*a*) above, it endangers the interests of the United Kingdom abroad, seriously obstructs the promotion or protection by the United Kingdom of those interests or endangers the safety of British citizens abroad; or

(*c*) it is of information or of a document or article which is such that its unauthorised disclosure would be likely to have any of those effects.

(3) It is a defence for a person charged with an offence under this section to prove that at the time of the alleged offence he did not know, and had no reasonable cause to believe, that the information, document or article in question related to defence or that its disclosure would be damaging within the meaning of subsection (1) above.

(4) In this section "defence" means—

(*a*) the size, shape, organisation, logistics, order of battle, deployment, operations, state of readiness and training of the armed forces of the Crown;

(*b*) the weapons, stores or other equipment of those forces and the invention, development, production and operation of such equipment and research relating to it;

(*c*) defence policy and strategy and military planning and intelligence;

(*d*) plans and measures for the maintenance of essential supplies and services that are or would be needed in time of war.

[Official Secrets Act 1989, s 2.]

1. For prosecution, trial and penalties, see ss 9–11 post.

8–22792 **3. International relations.** (1) A person who is or has been a Crown servant or government contractor is guilty of an offence[1] if without lawful authority he makes a damaging disclosure of—

(*a*) any information, document or other article relating to international relations; or
(*b*) any confidential information, document or other article which was obtained from a State other than the United Kingdom or an international organisation,

being information or a document or article which is or has been in his possession by virtue of his position as a Crown servant or government contractor.

(2) For the purposes of subsection (1) above a disclosure is damaging if—

(*a*) it endangers the interests of the United Kingdom abroad, seriously obstructs the promotion or protection by the United Kingdom of those interests or endangers the safety of British citizens abroad; or
(*b*) it is of information or of a document or article which is such that its unauthorised disclosure would be likely to have any of those effects.

(3) In the case of information or a document or article within subsection (1)(*b*) above—

(*a*) the fact that it is confidential, or
(*b*) its nature or contents,

may be sufficient to establish for the purposes of subsection (2)(*b*) above that the information, document or article is such that its unauthorised disclosure would be likely to have any of the effects there mentioned.

(4) It is a defence for a person charged with an offence under this section to prove that at the time of the alleged offence he did not know, and had no reasonable cause to believe, that the information, document or article in question was such as is mentioned in subsection (1) above or that its disclosure would be damaging within the meaning of that subsection.

(5) In this section "international relations" means the relations between States, between international organisations or between one or more States and one or more such organisations and includes any matter relating to a State other than the United Kingdom or to an international organisation which is capable of affecting the relations of the United Kingdom with another State or with an international organisation.

(6) For the purposes of this section any information, document or article obtained from a State or organisation is confidential at any time while the terms on which it was obtained require it to be held in confidence or while the circumstances in which it was obtained make it reasonable for the State or organisation to expect that it would be so held.
[Official Secrets Act 1989, s 3.]

---

1. For prosecution, trial and penalties, see ss 9–11 post.

8–22793 **4. Crime and special investigation powers.** (1) A person who is or has been a Crown servant or government contractor is guilty of an offence[1] if without lawful authority he discloses any information, document or other article to which this section applies and which is or has been in his possession by virtue of his position as such.

(2) This section applies to any information, document or other article—

(*a*) the disclosure of which—
  (i) results in the commission of an offence; or
  (ii) facilitates an escape from legal custody or the doing of any other act prejudicial to the safekeeping of persons in legal custody; or
  (iii) impedes the prevention or detection of offences or the apprehension or prosecution of suspected offenders; or
(*b*) which is such that its unauthorised disclosure would be likely to have any of those effects.

(3) This section also applies to—

(*a*) any information obtained by reason of the interception of any communication in obedience to a warrant issued under section 2 of the Interception of Communications Act 1985 or under the authority of an interception warrant under section 5 of the Regulation of Investigatory Powers Act 2000, any information relating to the obtaining of information by reason of any such interception and any document or other article which is or has been used or held for use in, or has been obtained by reason of, any such interception; and
(*b*) any information obtained by reason of action authorised by a warrant issued under section 3 of the Security Service Act 1989 or under section 5 of the Intelligence Services Act 1994 or by an authorisation given under section 7 of that Act, any information relating to the obtaining of information by reason of any such action and any document or other article which is or has been used or held for use in, or has been obtained by reason of, any such action.

(4) It is a defence for a person charged with an offence under this section in respect of a disclosure falling within subsection (2)(*a*) above to prove that at the time of the alleged offence he did not know,

and had no reasonable cause to believe, that the disclosure would have any of the effects there mentioned.

(5) It is a defence for a person charged with an offence under this section in respect of any other disclosure to prove that at the time of the alleged offence he did not know, and had no reasonable cause to believe, that the information, document or article in question was information or a document or article to which this section applies.

(6) In this section "legal custody" includes detention in pursuance of any enactment or any instrument made under an enactment.

[Official Secrets Act 1989, s 4, as amended by the Intelligence Services Act 1994, Sch 4 and the Regulation of Investigatory Powers Act 2000, Sch 4.]

1. For prosecution, trial and penalties see ss 9–11 post. A defendant prosecuted under ss 1(1)(a) and 4(1) and (3)(a) of this Act is not entitled to put forward a defence of disclosure in the national interest or belief that such disclosure was in the national interest: *R v Shayler* [2002] UKHL 11, [2003] 1 AC 247, [2002] 2 All ER 477, [2002] 2 WLR 754.

8–22794 5. Information resulting from unauthorised disclosures or entrusted in confidence. (1) Subsection (2) below applies where—

(*a*) any information, document or other article protected against disclosure by the foregoing provisions of this Act has come into a person's possession as a result of having been—

(i) disclosed (whether to him or another) by a Crown servant or government contractor without lawful authority; or

(ii) entrusted to him by a Crown servant or government contractor on terms requiring it to be held in confidence or in circumstances in which the Crown servant or government contractor could reasonably expect that it would be so held; or

(iii) disclosed (whether to him or another) without lawful authority by a person to whom it was entrusted as mentioned in sub-paragraph (ii) above; and

(*b*) the disclosure without lawful authority of the information, document or article by the person into whose possession it has come is not an offence under any of those provisions.

(2) Subject to subsections (3) and (4) below, the person into whose possession the information, document or article has come is guilty of an offence[1] if he discloses it without lawful authority knowing, or having reasonable cause to believe, that it is protected against disclosure by the foregoing provisions of this Act and that it has come into his possession as mentioned in subsection (1) above.

(3) In the case of information or a document or article protected against disclosure by sections 1 to 3 above, a person does not commit an offence under subsection (2) above unless—

(*a*) the disclosure by him is damaging; and

(*b*) he makes it knowing, or having reasonable cause to believe, that it would be damaging;

and the question whether a disclosure is damaging shall be determined for the purposes of this subsection as it would be in relation to a disclosure of that information, document or article by a Crown servant in contravention of section 1(3), 2(1) or 3(1) above.

(4) A person does not commit an offence under subsection (2) above in respect of information or a document or other article which has come into his possession as a result of having been disclosed—

(*a*) as mentioned in subsection (1)(*a*)(i) above by a government contractor; or

(*b*) as mentioned in subsection (1)(*a*)(iii) above,

unless that disclosure was by a British citizen or took place in the United Kingdom, in any of the Channel Islands or in the Isle of Man or a colony.

(5) For the purposes of this section information or a document or article is protected against disclosure by the foregoing provisions of this Act if—

(*a*) it relates to security or intelligence, defence or international relations within the meaning of section 1, 2 or 3 above or is such as is mentioned in section 3(1)(*b*) above; or

(*b*) it is information or a document or article to which section 4 above applies;

and information or a document or article is protected against disclosure by sections 1 to 3 above if it falls within paragraph (*a*) above.

(6) A person is guilty of an offence[1] if without lawful authority he discloses any information, document or other article which he knows, or has reasonable cause to believe, to have come into his possession as a result of a contravention of section 1 of the Official Secrets Act 1911.

[Official Secrets Act 1989, s 5.]

1. For prosecution, trial and penalties, see ss 9–11 post.

8–22795 6. Information entrusted in confidence to other States or international organisations. (1) This section applies where—

(*a*) any information, document or other article which—

(i) relates to security or intelligence, defence or international relations; and

(ii) has been communicated in confidence by or on behalf of the United Kingdom to another State or to an international organisation,

has come into a person's possession as a result of having been disclosed (whether to him or another) without the authority of that State or organisation or, in the case of an organisation, of a member of it; and

(*b*) the disclosure without lawful authority of the information, document or article by the person into whose possession it has come is not an offence under any of the foregoing provisions of this Act.

(2) Subject to subsection (3) below, the person into whose possession the information, document or article has come is guilty of an offence[1] if he makes a damaging disclosure of it knowing, or having reasonable cause to believe, that it is such as is mentioned in subsection (1) above, that it has come into his possession as there mentioned and that its disclosure would be damaging.

(3) A person does not commit an offence under subsection (2) above if the information, document or article is disclosed by him with lawful authority or has previously been made available to the public with the authority of the State or organisation concerned or, in the case of an organisation, of a member of it.

(4) For the purposes of this section "security or intelligence", "defence" and "international relations" have the same meaning as in sections 1, 2 and 3 above and the question whether a disclosure is damaging shall be determined as it would be in relation to a disclosure of the information, document or article in question by a Crown servant in contravention of section 1(3), 2(1) and 3(1) above.

(5) For the purposes of this section information or a document or article is communicated in confidence if it is communicated on terms requiring it to be held in confidence or in circumstances in which the person communicating it could reasonably expect that it would be so held.
[Official Secrets Act 1989, s 6.]

1. For prosecution, trial and penalties, see ss 9–11 post.

8–22796 7. **Authorised disclosures.** (1) For the purposes of this Act a disclosure by—

(*a*) a Crown servant; or
(*b*) a person, not being a Crown servant or government contractor, in whose case a notification for the purposes of section 1(1) above is in force,

is made with lawful authority if, and only if, it is made in accordance with his official duty.

(2) For the purposes of this Act a disclosure by a government contractor is made with lawful authority if, and only if, it is made—

(*a*) in accordance with an official authorisation; or
(*b*) for the purposes of the functions by virtue of which he is a government contractor and without contravening an official restriction.

(3) For the purposes of this Act a disclosure made by any other person is made with lawful authority if, and only if, it is made—

(*a*) to a Crown servant for the purposes of his functions as such; or
(*b*) in accordance with an official authorisation.

(4) It is a defence for a person charged with an offence under any of the foregoing provisions of this Act to prove that at the time of the alleged offence he believed that he had lawful authority to make the disclosure in question and had no reasonable cause to believe otherwise.

(5) In this section "official authorisation" and "official restriction" mean, subject to subsection (6) below, an authorisation or restriction duly given or imposed by a Crown servant or government contractor or by or on behalf of a prescribed[1] body or a body of a prescribed[1] class.

(6) In relation to section 6 above "official authorisation" includes an authorisation duly given by or on behalf of the State or organisation concerned or, in the case of an organisation, a member of it.
[Official Secrets Act 1989, s 7.]

1. The Official Secrets Act 1989 (Prescription) Order 1990, SI 1990/200, amended by SI 1993/847 and SI 2003/1918, has been made; Sch 3 to the order lists the prescribed bodies.

8–22797 8. **Safeguarding of information.** (1) Where a Crown servant or government contractor, by virtue of his position as such, has in his possession or under his control any document or other article which it would be an offence under any of the foregoing provisions of this Act for him to disclose without lawful authority he is guilty of an offence[1] if—

(*a*) being a Crown servant, he retains the document or article contrary to his official duty; or
(*b*) being a government contractor, he fails to comply with an official direction for the return or disposal of the document or article,

or if he fails to take such care to prevent the unauthorised disclosure of the document or article as a person in his position may reasonably be expected to take.

(2) It is a defence for a Crown servant charged with an offence under subsection (1)(*a*) above to prove that at the time of the alleged offence he believed that he was acting in accordance with his official duty and had no reasonable cause to believe otherwise.

(3) In subsections (1) and (2) above references to a Crown servant include any person, not being a Crown servant or government contractor, in whose case a notification for the purposes of section 1(1) above is in force.

(4) Where a person has in his possession or under his control any document or other article which it would be an offence under section 5 above for him to disclose without lawful authority, he is guilty of an offence[1] if—

(*a*) he fails to comply with an official direction for its return or disposal; or

(*b*) where he obtained it from a Crown servant or government contractor on terms requiring it to be held in confidence or in circumstances in which that servant or contractor could reasonably expect that it would be so held, he fails to take such care to prevent its unauthorised disclosure as a person in his position may reasonably be expected to take.

(5) Where a person has in his possession or under his control any document or other article which it would be an offence under section 6 above for him to disclose without lawful authority, he is guilty of an offence[1] if he fails to comply with an official direction for its return or disposal.

(6) A person is guilty of an offence[1] if he discloses any official information, document or other article which can be used for the purpose of obtaining access to any information, document of other article protected against disclosure by the foregoing provisions of this Act and the circumstances in which it is disclosed are such that it would be reasonable to expect that it might be used for that purpose without authority.

(7) For the purposes of subsection (6) above a person discloses information or a document or article which is official if—

(*a*) he has or has had it in his possession by virtue of his position as a Crown servant or government contractor; or

(*b*) he knows or has reasonable cause to believe that a Crown servant or government contractor has or has had it in his possession by virtue of his position as such.

(8) Subsection (5) of section 5 above applies for the purposes of subsection (6) above as it applies for the purposes of that section.

(9) In this section "official direction" means a direction duly given by a Crown servant or government contractor or by or on behalf of a prescribed[2] body or a body of a prescribed[2] class.
[Official Secrets Act 1989, s 8.]

1. For prosecution, trial and penalties, see ss 9–11 post.
2. The Official Secrets Act 1989 (Prescription) Order 1990, SI 1990/200, amended by SI 1993/847 and SI 2003/1918, has been made; Sch 3 prescribes only the Civil Aviation Authority for the purposes of s 8(9).

8–22798 9. Prosecutions. (1) Subject to subsection (2) below, no prosecution for an offence under this Act shall be instituted in England and Wales or in Northern Ireland except by or with the consent of the Attorney General or, as the case may be, the Attorney General for Northern Ireland.

(2) Subsection (1) above does not apply to an offence in respect of any such information, document or article as is mentioned in section 4(2) above but no prosecution for such an offence shall be instituted in England and Wales or in Northern Ireland except by or with the consent of the Director of Public Prosecutions or, as the case may be, the Director of Public Prosecutions for Northern Ireland.
[Official Secrets Act 1989, s 9.]

8–22799 10. Penalties. (1) A person guilty of an offence under any provision of this Act other than section 8(1), (4) or (5) shall be liable[1]—

(*a*) on conviction on indictment, to imprisonment for a term not exceeding **two years** or a **fine** or **both**;

(*b*) on summary conviction, to imprisonment for a term not exceeding **six months** or a fine not exceeding the **statutory maximum** or **both**.

(2) A person guilty of an offence under section 8(1), (4) or (5) above shall be liable on summary conviction to imprisonment for a term not exceeding **three months*** or a fine not exceeding **level 5** on the standard scale or both.
[Official Secrets Act 1989, s 10.]

***"51 weeks" substituted by the Criminal Justice Act 2003, Sch 26, from a date to be appointed.**
1. For procedure in respect of an offence triable either way, see Magistrates' Courts Act 1980, ss 17A–21, in PART I: MAGISTRATES' COURTS, PROCEDURE, ante.

8–22800 11. Arrest[1], search and trial. (1)–(3) *Application to Police and Criminal Evidence Act 1984, s 24(2); s 9(2) of, and para 3(b) of Sch 1 to, that Act to apply to s 9(1) of the Official Secrets Act 1911; Criminal Law Act (Northern Ireland) Act 1967, s 2.*

(4) Section 8(4) of the Official Secrets Act 1920 (exclusion of public from hearing on grounds of national safety) shall have effect as if references to offences under that Act included references to offences under any provision of this Act other than section 8(1), (4) or (5).

(5) Proceedings for an offence under this Act may be taken in any place in the United Kingdom.

[Official Secrets Act 1989, s 11.]

---

1. Offences under this Act, other than offences contrary to s 8(1), (4) or (5) are arrestable offences by virtue of Sch 1A to the Police and Criminal Evidence Act 1984.

8–22801 12. "Crown servant" and "government contractor". (1) In this Act "Crown servant" means—

(*a*) a Minister of the Crown;

(*aa*) a member of the Scottish Executive or a junior Scottish Minister;

(b) *Repealed.*

(*c*) any person employed in the civil service of the Crown, including Her Majesty's Diplomatic Service, Her Majesty's Overseas Civil Service, the civil service of Northern Ireland and the Northern Ireland Court Service;

(*d*) any member of the naval, military or air forces of the Crown, including any person employed by an association established for the purposes of Part XI of the Reserve Forces Act 1996;

(e) any constable and any other person employed or appointed in or for the purposes of any police force (including a police force within the meaning of the Police (Northern Ireland) Act 1998 or the National Intelligence Service or National Crime Squad);*

(*f*) any person who is a member or employee of a prescribed body or a body of a prescribed[1] class and either is prescribed[1] for the purposes of this paragraph or belongs to a prescribed[1] class of members or employees of any such body;

(*g*) any person who is the holder of a prescribed[2] office or who is an employee of such a holder and either is prescribed[2] for the purposes of this paragraph or belongs to a prescribed[2] class of such employees.

(2) In this Act "government contractor" means, subject to subsection (3) below, any person who is not a Crown servant but who provides, or is employed in the provision of, goods or services—

(*a*) for the purposes of any Minister or person mentioned in paragraph (*a*) or (*b*) of subsection (1) above, of any office-holder in the Scottish Administration, of any of the services, forces or bodies mentioned in that subsection or of the holder of any office prescribed under that subsection;

(*aa*) for the purposes of the National Assembly for Wales; or

(*b*) under an agreement or arrangement certified by the Secretary of State as being one to which the government of a State other than the United Kingdom or an international organisation is a party or which is subordinate to, or made for the purposes of implementing, any such agreement or arrangement.

(3) Where an employee or class of employees of any body, or of any holder of an office, is prescribed by an order made for the purposes of subsection (1) above—

(*a*) any employee of that body, or of the holder of that office, who is not prescribed or is not within the prescribed class; and

(*b*) any person who does not provide, or is not employed in the provision of, goods or services for the purposes of the performance of those functions of the body or the holder of the office in connection with which the employee or prescribed class of employees is engaged,

shall not be a government contractor for the purposes of this Act.

(4) In this section "office-holder in the Scottish Administration" has the same meaning as in section 126(7)(*a*) of the Scotland Act 1998.*

(4A) In this section the reference to a police force includes a reference to the Civil Nuclear Constabulary.

(5) This Act shall apply to the following as it applies to persons falling within the definition of Crown servant—

(*a*) the First Minister and deputy First Minister in Northern Ireland; and

(*b*) Northern Ireland Ministers and junior Ministers.

[Official Secrets Act 1989, s 12, as amended by the Reserve Forces Act 1996, Sch 10, the Police Act 1997, Sch 9, the Government of Wales Act 1998, Sch 12, the Scotland Act 1998, Sch 8, the Government of Wales 1998, Sch 12, the Northern Ireland Act 1998, Sch 13 and the Police (Northern Ireland) Act 1998, Sch 4 and the Energy Act 2004, s 198.]

***Words substituted by the Serious Organised Crime and Police Act 2005, Sch 4 from a date to be appointed.**

1. See Sch 1 of the Official Secrets Act 1989 (Prescription) Order 1990, SI 1990/200, amended by SI 1993/847 and SI 2003/1918.

2. See Sch 2 of the Official Secrets Act 1989 (Prescription) Order 1990, SI 1990/200, amended by SI 1993/847 and SI 2003/1918.

8–22802 13. Other interpretation provisions. (1) In this Act—

"disclose" and "disclosure", in relation to a document or other article, include parting with possession of it;

"international organisation" means, subject to subsections (2) and (3) below, an organisation of which only States are members and includes a reference to any organ of such an organisation;

"prescribed" means prescribed by an order made by the Secretary of State;

"State" includes the government of a State and any organ of its government and references to a State other than the United Kingdom include references to any territory outside the United Kingdom.

(2) In section 12(2)(*b*) above the reference to an international organisation includes a reference to any such organisation whether or not one of which only States are members and includes a commercial organisation.

(3) In determining for the purposes of subsection (1) above whether only States are members of an organisation, any member which is itself an organisation of which only States are members, or which is an organ of such an organisation, shall be treated as a State.

[Official Secrets Act 1989, s 13.]

8–22803 15. Acts done abroad and extent. (1) Any act—

(*a*) done by a British citizen or Crown servant; or

(*b*) done by any person in any of the Channel Islands or the Isle of Man or any colony,

shall, if it would be an offence by that person under any provision of this Act other than section 8(1), (4) or (5) when done by him in the United Kingdom, be an offence under that provision.

(2)–(3) Northern Ireland, Channel Islands, Isle of Man, any colony.

[Official Secrets Act 1989, s 15.]

PEDLARS

Pedlars Act 1871

(34 & 35 Vict c 96)

Preliminary

8–22910 1. *Short title.*

8–22911 2. (*Repealed*).

8–22912 3. Interpretation. In this Act, if not inconsistent with the context, the following terms have the meanings herein-after respectively assigned to them; that is to say,—

The term "pedlar" means any hawker, pedlar[1], pretty chapman, tinker, caster of metals, mender of chairs, or other person who, without any horse or other beast bearing or drawing burden, travels and trades on foot and goes from town to town or to other men's houses,[2], carrying to sell or exposing for sale[3] any goods, wares, or merchandise, or procuring orders for goods, wares, or merchandise immediately to be delivered, or selling or offering for sale his skill in handicraft:

[Pedlars Act 1871, s 23 as amended by the Statute Law Revision (No 2) Act 1893, the Police Act 1964, Sch 10 and the Statute Law (Repeal) Act 1993, s 1.]

---

1. A person need not derive his entire living or even a substantial part of it from acting as pedlar for him to be a pedlar for the purposes of s 3 (*Murphy v Duke* [1985] QB 905, [1985] 2 All ER 274, [1985] 2 WLR 773.)

2. Persons who travelled from town to town by conveyance and then walked from house to house were travelling on foot and were pedlars (*Sample v Hulme* [1956] 3 All ER 447n, 120 JP 564). A pedlar trades as he travels as distinct from someone who merely travels to trade; thus a street trader who sold Christmas paper from a portable stand in a street could not claim to be a pedlar (*Watson v Malloy* [1988] 3 All ER 459, [1989] 1 WLR 1026, 86 LGR 766, DC). However, to be a pedlar a person does not have to travel and trade simultaneously; he does not have to be in motion while trading. A pedlar is an itinerant or peripatetic seller who is travelling when not trading. The use of a stall or stand might indicate an intention to remain longer than is necessary to effect a sale to an individual but is not determinative of the issue whether a person is a pedlar or not and in determining the nature of a seller's trading practices and the nature of his conduct while stationary for the purpose of selling it is necessary to consider the length of time for which a person is in one place and what he does in that place. A person who stood in one place for an hour selling goods from a bag at his feet and attracting people's attention to come to him to buy was not acting as a pedlar (*Stevenage Borough Council v Wright* (1996) Times, 10 April).

3. Ladies making up wearing apparel and offering the same for sale on behalf of a charity do not come within the definition of pedlar (*Gregg v Smith* (1873) LR 8 QB 302, 42 LJMC 121). Selling within the meaning of this section is to include bartering or exchanging goods for other goods so that a person bartering needles and thread for rags, bones, etc. was held to be a hawker and pedlar, and to require a hawker's licence (*Druce v. Gabb* (1858) 31 LTOS 98, & WR 479). A person soliciting orders for goods but having no goods with him and subsequently delivering the goods for which he had taken orders is not a person "carrying to sell" or "exposing for sale" within the definition of pedlar (*R v M'Knight* (1830) 10 B & C 734, 5 Man & Ry KB 644).

Certificates to be obtained by Pedlars

8–22913 **4. No one to act as a pedlar without certificate.** No Person shall act as a pedlar without such certificate as in this Act mentioned, or in any district where he is not authorised by his certificate so to act.

Any person who—

(1) acts as a pedlar without having obtained a certificate under this Act authorising him so to act;
(2) (*Repealed*),

shall be liable to a penalty not exceeding **level 1** on the standard scale.

[Pedlars Act 1871, s 4 as amended by the Pedlars Act 1881, s 2, the Criminal Law Act 1977, s 31 and the Criminal Justice Act 1982, ss 38 and 46.]

8–22914 **5. Grant of Certificate.** The following regulations shall made with respect to the grant of pedlar certificates:

1. Subject as in this Act mentioned, a pedlar's certificate shall be granted to any person by the chief officer of police for the police area in which the person applying for a certificate has, during one month previous to such application, resided, on such officer being satisfied that the applicant is above seventeen years of age, is a person of good character, and in good faith intends to carry on the trade of a pedlar:
2. An application for a pedlar's certificate shall be in the form specified in schedule two to this Act, or as near thereto as circumstances admit:
3. There shall be paid for a pedlar's certificate previously to the delivery thereof to the applicant a fee of £12.25[1]
4. A pedlar's certificate shall be in the form specified in schedule two to this Act, or as near thereto as circumstances admit;
5 A pedlar's certificate shall remain in force for one year from the date of the issue thereof, and no longer:
6. On the delivery up of the old certificate, or on sufficient evidence being produced to the satisfaction of the chief officer of police that the old certificate has been lost, that officer may, either at the expiration of the current year, or during the currency of any year grant a new certificate in the same manner as upon a first application for a pedlar's certificate. In Great Britain one of Her Majesty's Principal Secretaries of State, and in Ireland the Lord Lieutenant may from time to time provide for the expiration of all pedlars certificates at the same period of each year, and in doing so shall provide for the apportionment of the fees payable in respect of any such certificate.*

[Pedlars Act 1871, s 5 as amended by the Police Act 1996, Sch 7.]

***Paragraph 6 amended by SI 1999/663, Sch 1 when in force.**

1. Pedlar's Certificates (Variation of Fee) Order 1985, SI 1985/2027.

8–22915 **6. Effect of certificate.** For the purpose of the Markets and Fairs Clauses Act 1874[1] and any Act incorporating the same, a certificate under this Act shall have the same effect, within the district[2] for which it is granted, as a hawker's licence, and the term "licensed hawker" in the first-mentioned Act shall be construed to include a pedlar holding such a certificate.

[Pedlars Act 1871, s 6 as amended by the Pedlars Act 1881, Schedule.]

---

1. A pedlar selling tollable articles, such as vegetables and fruit, within the limits of a market, is exempted from the penalty imposed by s 13 of that statute (*Howard v Lupton* (1875) LR 10 QB 598, 40 JP 7). But so long only as he acts as a pedlar within the definition of s 3 of the Pedlars Act 1871 (*Woolwich Local Board of Health v Gardiner* [1895] 2 QB 497, 59 JP 597, 659). See also *Lee v Wallocks* (1914) 78 JP 365.

2. "A pedlar's certificate granted under the Pedlars Act 1871 shall during the time for which it continues in force authorise the person to whom it is granted to act as a pedlar within any part of the United Kingdom." (Pedlars Act 1881, s 2).

8–22916 **7.** (*Repealed*).

8–22917 **8. Register of certificates to be kept in each area.** There shall be kept in each police area a register of the certificates granted in such area under this Act, in such form and with such particulars as may from time to time be directed in Great Britain by one of Her Majesty's Principal Secretaries of State, and in Ireland by the Lord Lieutenant.*

The entries in such register, and any copy of any such entries, certified by the chief officer of police to be a true copy, shall be evidence of the facts stated therein.

[Pedlars Act 1871, s 8 as amended by the Pedlars Act 1881, Sch and the Police Act 1996, Sch 7.]

***Amended by SI 1999/663, Sch 1 when in force.**

8–22918 **9. Forms of application to be kept at chief police office.** Forms of applications for certificates shall be kept at every police office in every police area, and shall be given gratis to any person applying for the same; and all applications for certificates shall be delivered at the police office

of the division or subdivision of the police area within which the applicant resides, and certificates, when duly signed by the chief officer of police, shall be issued at such office.
[Pedlars Act 1871, s 9 as amended by the Police Act 1996, Sch 7.]

8–22919 10. Certificate not to be assigned. A person to whom a pedlar's certificate is granted under this Act shall not lend, transfer, or assign the same to any other person, and any person who lends, transfers, or assigns such certificate to any other person shall for each offence be liable to a penalty not exceeding **level 1** on the standard scale.
[Pedlars Act 1871, s 10 as amended by the Criminal Law Act 1977, s 41 and the Criminal Justice Act 1982, ss 38 and 46.]

8–22920 11. Certificate not to be borrowed. No person shall borrow or make use of a pedlar's certificate granted to any other person, and any person who borrows or makes use of such certificate shall for each offence be liable to a penalty not exceeding **level 1** on the standard scale.
[Pedlars Act 1871, s 11 as amended by Criminal Law Act 1977, s 41 and the Criminal Justice Act 1982, ss 38 and 46.]

8–22921 12. Penalty for forging certificate. Any person who commits any of the following offences; (that is to say,)

1 Makes false representations with a view to obtain a pedlar's certificate under this Act;
2–5 (*Repealed*),

shall be liable to imprisonment for a term not exceeding **six months** or to a fine not exceeding **level 2** on the standard scale, or to **both** such imprisonment and fine.
[Pedlars Act 1871, s 12 as amended by the Pedlars Act 1881, Schedule, the Criminal Law Act 1977, s 41, the Forgery and Counterfeiting Act 1981, Schedule and the Criminal Justice Act 1982, ss 38 and 46.]

8–22922 13. (*Repealed*).

8–22923 14. Convictions to be indorsed on certificate. If any pedlar is convicted of any offence under this Act, the court, before which he is convicted shall indorse or cause to be indorsed on his certificate a record of such conviction.

The indorsements made under this Act on a pedlar's certificate shall be evidence of the facts stated therein.
[Pedlars Act 1871, s 14.]

8–22924 15. Appeal against refusal of certificate by chief officer of police. If the chief officer of police refuses to grant a certificate, the applicant may appeal to a court of summary jurisdiction having jurisdiction in the place where such grant was refused, in accordance with the following provisions:

1. The applicant shall, within one week after the refusal, give to the chief officer of police notice in writing of the appeal:
2. The appeal shall be heard at the sitting of the court which happens next after the expiration of the said week, but the court may, on the application of either party, adjourn the case:
3. The court shall hear and determine the matter of the appeal, and make such order thereon, with or without costs to either party, as to the court seems just:
4. An appeal under this Act to a court of summary jurisdiction in England or Ireland shall be deemed to be a matter on which that court has authority by law to make an order in pursuance of the Summary Jurisdiction Acts, and in Scotland the court may adjudicate on matters arising under this section, in accordance with the enactments relating to the exercise of their ordinary jurisdiction:
5 Any certificate granted in pursuance of an order of the court, shall have the same effect as if it had been originally granted by the chief officer of police.

[Pedlars Act 1871, s 15 as amended by the Pedlars Act 1881, s 2.]

8–22925 16. Deprivation of pedlars of certificates by court. Any court before which any pedlar is convicted for any offence, whether under this or any other Act, or otherwise, may, if he or they think fit, deprive such pedlar of his certificate; and any such court shall deprive such pedlar of his certificate; and any such court shall deprive such pedlar of his certificate if he is convicted of begging.

Any court of summary jurisdiction may summon a pedlar holding a certificate under this Act to appear before them, and if he fail to appear, or on appearance to satisfy the court that he is in good faith carrying on the business of a pedlar, shall deprive him of his certificate.
[Pedlars Act 1871, s 16.]

Duties of Pedlars

8–22926 17. Pedlar to show certificate to certain persons on demand. Any pedlar shall at all times, on demand, produce and show his certificate to any of the following persons; (that is to say,)

1. Any justice of the peace; or

2. Any constable or officer of police; or
3. Any person to whom such pedlar offers his goods for sale; or
4. Any person in whose private grounds of premises such pedlar is found:

And any pedlar who refuses, on demand, to show his certificate to, and allow it to be read and a copy thereof to be taken by, any of the persons hereby authorised to demand it, shall or each offence be liable to a penalty not exceeding **level 1** on the standard scale.
[Pedlars Act 1871, s 17 as amended by the Criminal Law Act 1977, s 41 and the Criminal Justice Act 1982, ss 38 and 46.]

8–22927 18–19. (*Repealed*).

Legal Proceedings

8–22928 20. *Summary proceedings for offences, etc*[1].

1. Superseded for practical purposes by the Magistrates' Courts Act 1980 and Rules made thereunder.

8–22929 21. Application of fees. All fees received under this Act in England and Ireland shall be applied in manner in which penalties recoverable under this Act are applicable.
[Pedlars Act 1871, s 21.]

8–22930 22. Deputy of chief officer of police. Any act or thing by this Act authorised to be done by the chief officer of police may be done by any police officer under his command authorised by him in that behalf, and the term "chief officer of police" in this Act includes in relation to any such act or thing, the police officer so authorised.
[Pedlars Act 1871, s 22.]

8–22931 23. Certificate not required by commercial travellers, sellers of fish, or sellers in fairs. Nothing in this Act shall render it necessary for a certificate to be obtained by the following persons as such; (that is to say,)

1. Commercial travellers or other persons selling or seeking orders for goods, wares, or merchandise to or from persons who are dealers therein, and who buy to sell again, or selling or seeking orders for books as agents authorised in writing by the publishers of such books:
2. Sellers of vegetables[1], fish, fruit, or victuals:
3. Persons selling or exposing to sale goods, wares, or merchandise in any public mart, market, or fair legally established.

[Pedlars Act 1871, s 23.]

1. In a case under the Prevention of Crimes Act tried at Chester Assizes, COLERIDGE J, held that lavender was a vegetable within this exemption (see 77JP Jo 610).

8–22932 24. Reservation of powers of local authority. Nothing in this Act shall take away or diminish any of the powers vested in any local authority by any general or local Act in force in the district of such local authority.
[Pedlars Act 1871, s 24.]

8–22933 25. (*Repealed*).

8–22934

SCHEDULES

SCHEDULE 1

(*Repealed by the Police Act 1964, s 64(3), Sch 10, Pt I.*)

Section 5

SCHEDULE 2

FORM A

(*Sch 1 repealed by the Police Act 1964, s 64(3), Sch 10, Pt I.*)

8–22935

FORM OF APPLICATION FOR PEDLAR'S CERTIFICATE

1. I, *A.B.* (*Christian and surname of applicant in full*) have during the last calendar month resided at .... in the parish of...............in the county of ....

2. I am by trade and occupation a (*here state trade and occupation of applicant, eg, that he is a hawker, pedlar, etc*)

3. I am ....years of age.

4. I apply for a certificate under the Pedlars Act 1871 authorizing me to act as a pedlar within the .... police area.

Dated this .... day of ....

(Signed) .... *A.B.* .... *(Here insert Christian and surname of applicant.)*

FORM B
FORM OF PEDLAR'S CERTIFICATE[1]

In pursuance of the Pedlars Act, 1871, I certify that *A.B.* (*name of applicant*) of .... in the county of .... aged .... years, is hereby authorized to act as a pedlar within the .... police area for a year from the date of this certificate. (*To be altered, if necessary, to correspond to any order of the Secretary of State or* Department for Social Development* *as to time of expiration of licenses.*)

Certified this .... day of ...... A.D. ......

.... (Signed) (*Here insert name and description of the officer signing the certificate.*)

The certificate will expire on the .... day of ...., A.D.

***Form B prospectively amended by SI 1999/663, Sch 1, para 6(3) when in force.**

1. Authorises the person to whom it is granted to act as a pedlar within any part of the United Kingdom (Pedlars Act 1881, s 2).

PERJURY

Perjury Act 1911

(1 & 2 Geo 5 c 6)

8–22936 **1. Perjury—Judicial proceedings**[1]. (1) If any person[2] lawfully sworn as a witness or as an interpreter in a judicial proceeding wilfully[3] makes a statement material[4] in that proceeding, which he knows to be false or does not believe to be true, he shall be guilty of perjury, shall, on conviction thereof on indictment, be liable to penal servitude for a term not exceeding **seven years**,[5], or to imprisonment with or without hard labour for a term not exceeding two years, or to a fine or to both such penal servitude or imprisonment and fine.

(2) The expression "judicial proceedings" includes a proceeding before any court[6], tribunal[7], or person[8] having by law power to hear, receive, and examine evidence on oath.

(3) Where a statement made for the purposes of a judicial proceeding is not made before the tribunal itself, but is made on oath before a person authorised by law to administer an oath to the person who makes the statement, and to record or authenticate the statement, it shall, for the purpose of this section, be treated as having been made in a judicial proceeding.

(4) A statement made by a person lawfully sworn in England for the purposes of a judicial proceeding—

(*a*) in another part of Her Majesty's dominions; or

(*b*) in a British tribunal lawfully constituted in any place by sea or land outside Her Majesty's dominions; or

(*c*) in a tribunal of any foreign state,

shall, for the purposes of this section, be treated as a statement made in a judicial proceeding in England.

(5) Where, for the purposes of a judicial proceeding in England, a person is lawfully sworn under the authority of an Act of Parliament—

(*a*) in any other part of Her Majesty's dominions; or

(*b*) before a British tribunal or a British officer in a foreign country, or within the jurisdiction[9] of the Admiralty of England;

a statement made by such person so sworn as aforesaid (unless the Act of Parliament under which it was made otherwise specifically provides) shall be treated for the purposes of this section as having need made in the judicial proceeding in England for the purposes whereof it was made.

(6) The question whether a statement on which perjury is assigned was material is a question of law to be determined by the court of trial.

[Perjury Act 1911, s 1.]

1. A person who, in sworn evidence before the European Court, makes any statement which he knows to be false or does not believe to be true shall, whether he is a British subject or not, be guilty of an offence and may be proceeded against and punished as for an offence under s 1(1) of the Perjury Act 1911 (European Communities Act 1972, s 11(1)). The report by the European Court leading to a bill of indictment is not admissible before the court in England or Wales.

2. A person not a competent witness, but sworn by mistake, cannot be indicted for perjury (per HANNEN J, *R v Clegg* (1868) 19 LT 47).

3. "Wilfully" requires the prosecution to prove that the defendant who made the statement did so deliberately and not inadvertently or by mistake (*R v Millward* [1985] QB 519, [1985] 1 All ER 859, 149 JP 545, CA).

4. The question of materiality is one of law to be determined by the court of trial (s 1(6)). This subsection settles a point as to which some doubt attached. As to materiality, see *R v Philpotts* (1851) 3 Car & Kir 135; *R v Gibbon* (1862) Le & Ca 109; *R v Mullany* (1865) Le & Ca 593; *R v Shaw* (1865) Le & Ca 579, 29 JP 339; *R v Tyson* (1867) LR 1 CCR 107, 32 JP 53; *R v Smith* (1867) LR 1 CCR 110, 32 JP 405; *R v Alsop* (1869) 33 JP 485; *R v Hadfield* (1886) 51 JP 344; *R v Baker* [1895] 1 QB 797; *R v Hewitt* (1913) 9 Cr App Rep 192; *R v Wheeler* [1917] 1 KB 283, 81 JP 75.

The defendant's belief as to the materiality of the statement is irrelevant. The materiality of the statement is a matter which by virtue of s 1(6) is to be decided objectively by the judge (*R v Millward* [1985] QB 519, [1985] 1 All ER 859, 149 JP 545, CA).

5. Imprisonment with hard labour was abolished by the Criminal Justice Act 1948, s 1(2); the punishment is now imprisonment for a term not exceeding 7 years or a fine or both; see the Criminal Justice Act 1948, s 1(1) and (2).

6. For consideration of the release, for the purposes of committal proceedings, of confidential papers in wardship proceedings in which perjury is alleged, see *Re H (a minor)* [1985] 3 All ER 1, [1985] 1 WLR 1164, CA.

7. Two special commissioners acting under the Income Tax Acts, constitute a tribunal (*R v Hood-Barrs* [1943] 1 KB 455, [1943] 1 All ER 665).

8. As to perjury on an inquisition held before a deputy coroner, see *R v Johnson* (1873) LR 2 CCR 15, 37 JP 181. A witness, summoned under s 27 of the Bankruptcy Act 1883, was sworn before a registrar in bankruptcy, and was examined by the solicitor for the official receiver in the presence of his own solicitor, but not in the presence of the registrar, who sat in an adjoining room:—*Held:* the examination was not taken before a court of competent jurisdiction, and a conviction for perjury was quashed (*R v Lloyd* (1887) 19 QBD 213, 52 JP 86). The power of justices to administer oaths is limited; they must be acting under authority at the time (*R v Shaw* (1911) 75 JP 191). A witness was properly convicted for giving false evidence on the hearing of a charge against a prisoner who had been apprehended on a warrant improperly issued (*R v Hughes* (1879) 4 QBD 614, 43 JP 556). Where perjury was committed in an affidavit filed in an action against a non-existent person, it was held that the affidavit had been sworn in a "judicial proceeding" (*R v Castiglione* (1912) 76 JP 351).

9. This will cover the case of depositions taken on oath on a British steamship on the high seas, or in a foreign port, for use at a trial in this country.

8–22937 **1A. False unsworn statements under Evidence (Proceedings in Other Jurisdictions) Act 1975.** If any person, in giving any testimony (either orally or in writing) otherwise than on oath, where required to do so by an order under s 2 of the Evidence (Proceedings in Other Jurisdictions) Act 1975, makes a statement—

(*a*) which he knows to be false in a material particular; or
(*b*) which is false in a material particular and which he does not believe to be true,

he shall be guilty of an offence[1] and shall be liable on conviction on indictment to imprisonment for a term not exceeding **two years** or a **fine** or **both**.

[Perjury Act 1911, s 1A, as inserted by the Evidence (Proceedings in Other Jurisdictions) Act 1975, Sch 1.]

1. Triable either way; see Magistrates' Courts Act 1980, s 17 and Sch 1, also ss 17A–21 (procedure) and s 32 (penalty), in PART I: MAGISTRATES' COURTS, PROCEDURE, ante.

8–22938 **2. False statement on oath not in judicial proceeding.** If any person—

(1) being required or authorised by law to make any statement on oath for any purpose, and being lawfully sworn (otherwise than in a judicial proceeding) wilfully makes a statement which is material for that purpose and which he knows to be false or does not believe to be true; or

(2) wilfully uses any false affidavit for the purposes of the Bills of Sale Act 1878, as amended by any subsequent enactment,

he shall be guilty of a misdemeanour, and, on conviction thereof on indictment, shall be liable to penal servitude for a term not exceeding **seven years**,[1], or to imprisonment with or without hard labour, for a term not exceeding two years, or to a fine or to both such penal servitude or imprisonment and fine[2]

[Perjury Act 1911, s 2.]

1. Imprisonment with hard labour was abolished by the Criminal Justice Act 1948, s 1(2); the punishment is now imprisonment for a term not exceeding 7 years or a fine or both; see the Criminal Justice Act 1948, s 1(1) and (2).

2. Triable either way; see Magistrates' Courts Act 1980, s 17 and Sch 1, also ss 17A–21 (procedure) and s 32 (penalty), in PART I: MAGISTRATES' COURTS, PROCEDURE, ante.

8–22939 **3. False statements, etc. with reference to marriage.** (1) If any person—

(*a*) for the purpose of procuring a marriage, or a certificate or licence for marriage, knowingly and wilfully makes a false oath, or makes or signs a false[1] declaration, notice or certificate required under any Act of Parliament for the time being in force relating to marriage; or
(*b*) knowingly and wilfully makes, or knowingly and wilfully causes to be made, for the purpose of being inserted in any register of marriage, a false statement as to any particular required by law to be known and registered relating to any marriage; or
(*c*) forbids the issue of any certificate or licence for marriage by falsely representing himself to be a person whose consent to the marriage is required by law knowing such representation to be false, or
(*d*) with respect to a declaration made under section 16(1A) or 27B(2) of the Marriage Act 1949—
 (i) enters a caveat under subsection (2) of the said section 16, or
 (ii) makes a statement mentioned in subsection (4) of the said section 27B,

 which he knows to be false in a material particular,

he shall be guilty of a misdemeanour, and, on conviction thereof on indictment, shall be liable to penal servitude for a term not exceeding **seven years**,[1], or to imprisonment, with or without hard labour, for a term not exceeding two years, or to a **fine** or to **both** such penal servitude or imprisonment and fine and on summary conviction thereof shall be liable to a penalty not exceeding **the statutory maximum**[2].

(2) No prosecution for knowingly and wilfully making a false declaration for the purpose of procuring any marriage out of the district in which the parties or one of them dwell shall take place after the expiration of eighteen months form the solemnization of the marriage to which the declaration refers.

[Perjury Act 1911, s 3 amended by the Criminal Justice Act 1925, s 28(1), the Criminal Justice Act 1967, Sch 3, Criminal Law Act 1977, s 28 and the Marriage (Prohibited Degrees of Relationship) Act 1986, s 4.]

---

1. Imprisonment with hard labour was abolished by the Criminal Justice Act 1948, s 1(2); the punishment is now imprisonment for a term not exceeding 7 years or a fine or both; see the Criminal Justice Act 1948, s 1(1) and (2).

2. For procedure in respect of an offence triable either way, see the Magistrates' Courts Act 1980, ss 17A–21, in PART I: MAGISTRATES' COURTS, PROCEDURE, ante. Offences under ss 3 and 4 remain triable either way despite Sch 1, para 14 to the Magistrates' Courts Act 1980 because of the saving provision of s 17(2) of that Act.

8–22940 **4. False statements, etc. Births or deaths**.—(1) If any[1] person—

(*a*) wilfully makes any false answer to any question put to him by any registrar of births or deaths relating to the particulars required to be registered concerning any birth or death, or, wilfully gives to any such registrar any false information concerning any birth or death or the cause of any death; or

(*b*) wilfully makes any false certificate or declaration under or for the purposes of any Act relating to the registration of births or deaths, or, knowing any such certificate or declaration to be false, uses the same as true or gives or sends the same as true to any person; or

(*c*) wilfully makes, gives or uses any false statement or declaration as to a child born alive as having been still-born, or as to the body of a deceased person or a still-born child in any coffin, or falsely pretends that any child born alive was still-born; or

(*d*) makes any false statement with intent to have the same inserted in any register of births or deaths:

he shall be guilty of a misdemeanour and shall be liable—

(i) on conviction thereof on indictment, to penal servitude for a term not exceeding **seven years**,[2], or to imprisonment, with or without hard labour, for a term not exceeding two years, or to a **fine** instead of either of the said punishments; and

(ii) on summary conviction thereof, to a penalty not exceeding **the statutory maximum**[3].

(2) A prosecution on indictment for an offence against this section shall not be commenced more than three years after the commission of the offence.

[Perjury Act 1911, s 4, as amended by Criminal Justice Act 1925, s 28(2), Criminal Justice Act 1967, Sch 3 and Criminal Law Act 1977, s 20.]

---

1. The falsity of a statement by a woman that her husband is the father of her child may not be proved by regimental records disclosing that her husband was serving abroad when the child was conceived, for regimental records are not public documents (*Pettit v Lilley* [1946] 1 All ER 593, 110 JP 218).

2. Imprisonment with hard labour was abolished by the Criminal Justice Act 1948, s 1(2); the punishment is now imprisonment for a term not exceeding 7 years or a fine or both; see the Criminal Justice Act 1948, s 1(1) and (2).

3. For procedure in respect of an offence triable either way, see the Magistrates' Courts Act 1980, ss 17A–21, in PART I: MAGISTRATES' COURTS, PROCEDURE, ante. Offences under ss 3 and 4 remain triable either way despite Sch 1, para 14 to the Magistrates' Courts Act 1980 because of the saving provision of s 17(2) of that Act.

8–22941 **5. False statutory declarations, etc, without oath.** If any person knowingly and wilfully[1] makes (otherwise than on oath) a statement[2] false in a material particular, and the statement is made—

(*a*) in a statutory[3] declaration; or

(*b*) in an abstract, account, balance, sheet, book, certificate[4], declaration, entry, estimate, inventory, notice, report, return, or other document which he is authorised or required to make, attest, or verify, by any public general Act of Parliament for the time being in force; or

(*c*) in any oral declaration or oral answer which he is required to make by, under, or in pursuance of any public general Act of Parliament for the time being in force,

he shall be guilty of a misdemeanour and shall be liable[5] on conviction thereof on indictment to imprisonment, with or without hard labour[6], for any term not exceeding **two years**, or to a **fine** or to **both** such imprisonment and fine.

[Perjury Act 1911, s 5.]

---

1. This means an intention to do a particular act proscribed with the knowledge of the material circumstances which render it an offence. There is no further requirement to establish some further or ulterior intention on the part of the accused (*R v Sood* [1998] 2 Cr App Rep 355, [1999] Crim LR 85, CA).

2. See s 16(3), post; *R v Bradbury, R v Edlin* [1921] 1 KB 562, 85 JP 128. False statements made with intent to defraud the Crown, but not coming within the scope of this section, may constitute a common law misdemeanour (*R v Hudson* [1956] 2 QB 252, [1956] 1 All ER 814, 120 JP 216).

3. Justices are competent to take these declarations by virtue of the Statutory Declarations Act 1835, s 18, in PART II: EVIDENCE, ante. A personal representative (defined by s 55(xi)) making a false statement in writing that he has not given or made an assent or conveyance of a legal estate shall be liable in like manner as if the statement had been contained in a statutory declaration (Administration of Estates Act 1925, s 36(6)). Making a false declaration for the purpose of receiving

payment out of a grant in pursuance of the Appropriation Act 1946, for half-pay or Navy, Army, Air, or Civil non-effective services is a misdemeanour (Appropriation Act 1946, s 7(2)).

4. It is an offence for a person to give a certificate under an Act relating to the registration of births and deaths, and which can be used under such an Act, and it is not necessary for the prosecution to prove that the accused gave the certificate with the intention that it should be so used (*R v Ryan* (1914) 78 JP 192).

5. Triable either way: see Magistrates' Courts Act 1980, s 17 and Sch 1, also ss 17A–21 (procedure) and s 32 (penalty) in PART I: MAGISTRATES' COURTS, PROCEDURE, ante.

6. Imprisonment with hard labour was abolished by the Criminal Justice Act 1948, s 1(2).

8–22942 6. False declarations, etc to obtain registration, etc. If any person—

(*a*) procures or attempts to procure himself to be registered on any register[1] or roll kept under or in pursuance of any public general Act of Parliament for the time being in force of persons qualified by law to practise any vocation or calling; or

(*b*) procures or attempts to procure a certificate of the registration of any person on any such register or roll as aforesaid,

by wilfully making or producing or causing to be made or produced either verbally or in writing, any declaration, certificate, or representation which he knows to be false or fraudulent, he shall be guilty of a misdemeanour and shall be liable[2] on conviction thereof on indictment to imprisonment for any term not exceeding **twelve months**, or to a fine, or to both such imprisonment and fine.
[Perjury Act 1911, s 6.]

1. This will apply to existing registers under the Medical Act 1983; the Dentists Act 1984; the Veterinary Surgeons Act 1966; the Pharmacy Act 1954; the Nurses, Midwives and Health Visitors Act 1997; and also to professional registers which may be established in the future.

2. Triable either way; see Magistrates' Courts Act 1980, s 17 and Sch 1, also ss 17A–21 (procedure) and s 32 (penalty) in PART I: MAGISTRATES' COURTS, PROCEDURE, ante.

8–22943 7. Aiders, abettors, suborners, etc. (1) Every person who aids, abets, counsels, procures, or suborns another person to commit an offence against this Act shall be liable to be proceeded against, indicted, tried and punished as if he were a principal offender.

(2) Every person who incites another person to commit an offence against this Act shall be guilty of a misdemeanour, and, on conviction thereof on indictment, shall be liable[1] to imprisonment, or to a fine, or to both such imprisonment and fine.
[Perjury Act 1911, s 7, as amended by the Criminal Law Act 1967, s 7 and the Criminal Attempts Act 1981, Sch.]

1. On conviction on indictment this offence is punishable by a term of imprisonment for not more than 2 years (Powers of Criminal Courts Act 1973, s 18(1)). Triable either way; see Magistrates' Courts Act 1980, s 17 and Sch 1, also ss 17A–21 (procedure) and s 32 (penalty) in PART I: MAGISTRATES' COURTS, PROCEDURE, ante.

8–22944 8. Venue. Where an offence against this Act or any offence punishable as perjury or as subornation of perjury under any other Act of Parliament is committed in any place either on sea or land outside the United Kingdom, the offender may be proceeded against, indicted, tried, and punished . . . in England . . .
[Perjury Act 1911, s 8, as amended by the Criminal Law 1967, s 10 and Sch 3.]

8–22945 12. *Form of indictment*[1].

1. As to preferring a bill of indictment under this section, see the Administration of Justice (Miscellaneous Provisions) Act 1933, s 2(2)(*b*).

Separate counts may be laid in the same indictment where the perjury has been repeated at different times and places, and the prisoner may be sentenced on each count for an aggregate term exceeding the maximum punishment which can be adjudged for one offence (*Castro v R* (1881) 6 App Cas 229, 45 JP 452). On prosecution for perjury, etc, alleged to have been committed on trial of an indictment, fact of former trial to be proved by production of certificate signed by clerk of court or other person having custody of records, or his deputy (s 14). On a trial for perjury in a summary proceeding before justices, either the information should be produced or some evidence given of the precise nature of the charge before the justices (*R v Carr* (1867) 31 JP 789).

8–22946 13. Corroboration. A person shall not be liable to be convicted of[1] any offence against this Act, or of any offence declared by any other Act to be perjury or subornation of perjury, or to be punishable as perjury or subornation of perjury solely upon the evidence of one witness[2] as to the falsity of any statement alleged to be false.
[Perjury Act 1911, s 13.]

1. It will be observed that this section applies not only to perjury and offences punishable as perjury, but also to false statements not on oath. The offence must be proved either by two witnesses, or by one witness and proof of other material and relevant facts in confirmation. See *R v Threlfall* (1914) 111 LT 168. A general direction by the Judge on the need of corroboration of the evidence of an accomplice is sufficient, without a direction as to this section (*R v Saldanha* (1920) 85 JP 47). The warning must be the strongest possible (*R v Atkinson* (1934) 24 Cr App Rep 123). See heading *Corroboration* in title EVIDENCE, PART II, ante.

2. Evidence of a confession that a sworn statement was false is evidence of the statement's falsity (*R v Peach* [1990] 2 All ER 966, [1990] 1 WLR 976, CA).

8–22947 14. Proof of certain proceedings on which perjury is assigned. On a prosecution—

(*a*) for perjury alleged to have been committed on the trial of an indictment for ... misdemeanour; or

(*b*) for procuring a suborning the commission of perjury on any such trial,

the fact of the former trial shall be sufficiently proved by the production of a certificate containing the substance and effect (omitting the formal parts) of the indictment and trial purporting to be signed by the clerk of the court, or other person having the custody of the records of the court where the indictment was tried, or by the deputy of that clerk or other person, without proof of the signature or official character of the clerk or person appearing to have signed the certificate.

[Perjury Act 1911, s 14, as amended by the Criminal Law Act 1967, s 10 and Sch 3.]

8–22948 15. Interpretation. (1) For the purposes of this Act, the forms and ceremonies used in administering an oath are immaterial, if the court or person before whom the oath is taken has power to administer an oath for the purpose of verifying the statement in question, and if the oath has been administered in a form and with ceremonies which the person taking the oath has accepted without objection, or has declared to be binding on him.

(2) The expression "oath" includes "affirmation" and "declaration", and the expression "swear" includes "affirm" and "declare"; the expression "statutory declaration" means a declaration made by virtue of the Statutory Declaration Act 1835[1], or of any Act, Order in Council, rule or regulation applying or extending the provisions thereof.

[Perjury Act 1911, s 15, as amended by the Administration of Justice Act 1977, Sch 5.]

1. See PART II: EVIDENCE, ante.

8–22949 16. Savings. (1) Where the making of a false statement is not only an offence under this Act, but also by virtue of some other Act is a corrupt practice or subjects the offender to any forfeiture or disqualification or to any penalty other than imprisonment, or fine, the liability of the offender under this Act shall be in addition to and not in substitution for his liability under such other Act.

(2) Nothing in this Act shall apply to a statement made without oath by a child under the provisions of the Prevention of Cruelty to Children Act 1904, and the[1] Children Act 1908.

(3) Where the making of a false statement is by any other Act, whether passed before or after the commencement of this Act, made punishable on[2] summary conviction, proceedings may be taken either under such other Act or under this Act:

Provided that where such an offence is by any Act passed before the commencement of this Act, as originally enacted, made punishable[3] only on summary conviction, it shall remain only so punishable.

[Perjury Act 1911, s 16.]

1. See the Criminal Justice Act 1988, s 33A in Part III, ante, and the Children and Young Persons Act 1933, s 38, ante.
2. See note 4 to s 5, ante.
3. The Court of Criminal Appeal held that these words mean that the offence cannot, under any circumstances, be punished otherwise than on summary conviction, and therefore exclude an offence triable either way under what is now ss 17A–21 of the Magistrates' Courts Act 1980 (*R v Bradbury, R v Edlin* [1921] 1 KB 562, 85 JP 128).

PERSONS, OFFENCES AGAINST

8–23050 This title contains the following statutes—

8–23079 OFFENCES AGAINST THE PERSON ACT 1861
8–23230 INFANT LIFE (PRESERVATION) ACT 1929
8–23240 INFANTICIDE ACT 1938
8–23250 HOMICIDE ACT 1957
8–23270 SUICIDE ACT 1961
8–23290 ABORTION ACT 1967
8–23330 TATTOOING OF MINORS ACT 1969
8–23350 INTERNATIONALLY PROTECTED PERSONS ACT 1978
8–23360 TAKING OF HOSTAGES ACT 1982
8–23400 CRIMINAL JUSTICE ACT 1988
8–23456 UNITED NATIONS PERSONNEL ACT 1997
8–23466 PROTECTION FROM HARASSMENT ACT 1997
8–23485 TERRORISM ACT 2000
8–23559P ANTI-TERRORISM, CRIME AND SECURITY ACT 2001
8–23559ZZZJ FEMALE GENITAL MUTILATION ACT 2003
8–23559ZZZR PREVENTION OF TERRORISM ACT 2005

and the following statutory instrument—

8–23560 Abortion Regulations 1991

For statutes relating to abduction of child by parent or other person, see the Child Abduction Act 1984, ss 1 and 2 in PART IV: FAMILY LAW, ante; assaults on police officers, see the Police Act 1996, s 89 in this PART title, POLICE, post; cruelty to persons under 16, see the Children and Young Persons Act 1933, s 1 in PART V: YOUTH COURTS, ante; sexual offences, see this PART title, SEXUAL OFFENCES, post; causing death by dangerous driving of mechanically propelled vehicle, see the Road Traffic Act 1988, s 1 in PART VII: TRANSPORT, title, ROAD TRAFFIC, ante.

8–23060 Common assault and battery. Common assault and battery are separate statutory offences and a person guilty of either is liable to a fine not exceeding **level 5** on the standard scale, or to imprisonment for a term not exceeding **six months** or to **both**[1].

An assault is any intentional or reckless act which causes a person to apprehend immediate unlawful force or personal violence. A battery is any intentional or reckless infliction of unlawful force or personal violence. A battery therefore, often (but not always) includes an assault. As a result, the term "assault" tends to be used in a broad sense to cover both assault and battery[2]. Nevertheless, a clear distinction should be made between the two offences, particularly when laying an information. An information alleging "assault and battery" is bad for duplicity and where there is actual as well as apprehended unlawful violence the appropriate wording in the information is "assault by beating"[3].

Common assault and battery are summary offences but either may, in certain circumstances, be included in an indictment[4] or committed to the Crown Court for trial[5].

Although assault and battery are discrete offences for the purposes of s 39 of the Criminal Justice Act 1988, the term "assault" encompasses the offence of battery for the purposes of s 40 of the Criminal Justice Act 1988 (the power to join in an indictment the summary offence of assault)[2].

1. Criminal Justice Act 1988, s 39, see this title, post.
2. See *R v Lynsey* [1995] 3 All ER 654, [1995] 2 Cr App Rep 667, 159 JP 437, CA.
3. *DPP v Taylor and Little* [1992] 1 All ER 299, [1991] Crim LR 904, 155 JP 713.
4. Criminal Justice Act 1988, s 40; see PART I: MAGISTRATES' COURTS, PROCEDURE, ante.
5. Criminal Justice Act 1988, s 41; see PART I: MAGISTRATES' COURTS, PROCEDURE, ante.

8–23061 Apprehension or infliction of unlawful force or violence. Common assault involves causing a person to apprehend immediate unlawful violence. Physical injury or contact is not necessary[1]. The emphasis is on the reaction of the victim. Actions meant as a joke may be an assault if the victim is sufficiently frightened[2]. Words or gestures alone, depending on the circumstances, may constitute an assault[3]. Where the making of a silent telephone call causes fear of immediate and unlawful violence, the caller will be guilty of an assault[3]. On the other hand words can negative actions which would otherwise be an assault[4]. The victim must perceive the unlawful violence as being "immediate" but this tends to be interpreted widely. So, where a man terrified a woman by staring at her through her window it was held that she apprehended some immediate violence even though he was outside[5]. It has also been held to be sufficient to prove a fear of violence at some time not excluding the immediate future[6].

The infliction of unlawful force or personal violence constitutes a battery. "Force" has been defined as the least touching of another person in anger[7] but it is recognised that a certain degree of physical contact is inevitable in everyday life[8]. Most batteries involve the direct infliction of force or violence but there are cases which illustrate that a battery may be committed indirectly[9]. The offence of battery may be committed even though there is no direct physical contact between the assailant and the victim, provided the direct application of force is established through the use of another person as a medium or through the use of a weapon as a medium[10].

Although an omission cannot constitute an assault[11], an assault occasioning actual bodily harm is committed where the injury is the natural result of what the assailant said and did, ie that it was something that could reasonably have been foreseen as the consequence[12], or as being "the result of" what was said and done[13]. The cause must be more than *de minimis* for which a convenient term is "a substantial cause"[14] although this may imply a larger meaning and reference to "more than a slight or trifling" link is a useful way to avoid the term '*de minimis*'[15]. Accordingly, where someone (by act or word or a combination of the two) creates a danger and thereby exposes another to a reasonably foreseeable risk of injury which materializes, there is an evidential basis for the *actus reus* of an assault occasioning actual bodily harm (it remains for the prosecution to prove an intention to assault or appropriate recklessness)[16]. Therefore a person who created a dangerous situation by depositing acid in a hand-face drying machine and took the risk of someone using the machine before he could get back and render it harmless was guilty of assault occasioning actual bodily harm[17] as was a suspect the subject of a body search who had given a dishonest assurance to a police officer about the contents of his pockets where the officer was injured by an exposed needle of a hypodermic syringe in his pocket[18].

1. *R v Mansfield Justices, ex p Sharkey* [1985] 1 All ER 193, 149 JP 129, [1985] Crim LR 148.
2. *Logdon v DPP* [1976] Crim LR 121.
3. *R v Ireland* [1997] 4 All ER 225, [1997] 3 WLR 534, 161 JP 569, HL.
4. *Tuberville v Savage* (1669) 1 Mod Rep 3.
5. *Smith v Chief Superintendent, Woking Police Station* [1983] Crim LR 323.

6. *R v Constanza* [1997] 2 Cr App Rep 492 (defendant sending threatening letters to victim who suffered psychological damage from fear of violence).
7. *Cole v Turner* (1704) 6 Mod Rep 149.
8. *Wilson v Pringle* [1987] QB 237.
9. *R v Martin* (1881) 8 QBD 54; *DPP v K (a minor)* [1990] 1 All ER 331, 154 JP 192, 91 Cr App Rep 23.
10. *Haystead v Chief Constable of Derbyshire* [2000] 3 All ER 890, 164 JP 396, [2000] 2 Cr App Rep 339, DC.
11. *Fagan v Metropolitan Police Comr* [1968] 3 All ER 442, 133 JP 16, 52 Cr App Rep 700; *DPP v K (a minor)* [1990] 1 All ER 331, 154 JP 192, 91 Cr App Rep 23.
12. *R v Roberts* (1971) 56 Cr App Rep 95, CA.
13. See *R v Notman* [1994] Crim LR 518, CA.
14. *R v Hennigan* [1971] 3 All ER 133, 55 Cr App Rep 262, 135 JP 504; *R v Notman* [1994] Crim LR 518, CA.
15. *R v Kimsey* [1996] Crim LR 35.
16. *R v Roberts* (1971) 56 Cr App R 95, [1972] Crim LR 27, CA, *DPP v K (a minor)* [1990] 1 All ER 331, 154 JP 192, 91 Cr App R 23, *DPP v Santa-Bermudez* [2004] EWHC 2908 (Admin), 168 JP 373, [2004] Crim LR 471.
17. *DPP v K (a minor)* [1990] 1 All ER 331, 154 JP 192, 91 Cr App Rep 23.
18. *DPP v Santa-Bermudez* [2004] EWHC 2908 (Admin), 168 JP 373, [2004] Crim LR 471.

8–23062 Intention or recklessness. In order to constitute an assault or battery punishable by the criminal law, it must be established that the defendant acted intentionally or recklessly[1]. After some confusion, it now seems accepted that subjective, *Cunningham* recklessness is required (ie it must be established that the accused has foreseen that the particular kind of harm might be done and yet has gone on to take the risk of it)[2].

1. *R v Venna* [1976] QB 421, [1975] 3 All ER 788, 140 JP 31.
2. *R v Savage; R v Parmenter* [1991] 4 All ER 698, 155 JP 935, HL. See para **1–290, Criminal Responsibility, Guilty mind (mens rea)**; PART I: MAGISTRATES' COURTS, PROCEDURE, ante.

8–23063 Consent. Generally speaking, in order to prove a charge of assault, the prosecution must establish that the victim did not consent to the defendant's actions. If the victim consented to the assault the defendant is not guilty unless the public interest requires otherwise. It has been held that it was not in the public interest for people to cause or to try to cause each other actual bodily harm and a fight between two persons would be unlawful, whether in public or private, if actual bodily harm was intended or caused[1]. Furthermore, convictions under s 47 and s 20 of the Offences against the Person Act 1861 were upheld in respect of members of a sado-masochistic group who inflicted pain on each other for mutual sexual pleasure because public policy required that society be protected against a cult of violence[2]. Less extreme cases must be considered on a case by case basis so that, for example, public policy did not require that consensual activity between husband and wife which involved burning the husband's initials on the wife's buttocks where there was no aggressive intent should attract criminal sanctions[3].

Consent to sexual intercourse does not include consent to the risk of contracting a sexually transmitted disease. Thus, where a person, knowing that he is suffering a serious sexual disease, recklessly transmits it to another through consensual sexual intercourse he can be guilty of inflicting grievous bodily harm, contrary to s 20 of the Offences Against the Person Act 1861; the victim's consent to sexual intercourse is not, of itself, to be regarded as consent to the risk of consequent disease; but that if the victim does consent to such a risk that will provide a defence to a charge under s 20[4].

Nevertheless, in charges of common assault and battery, if the facts or the defence raise the issue of consent, the prosecution must prove the absence of consent[5], or if there was consent that it was given through ignorance[6] or fraudulent misrepresentation[7]. Fraud will only negative consent if it deceived the victim as to the identity of the person or the nature of the act[8]. The concept of the "identity of the person" is not extended to the qualifications or attributes of the defendant[9].

A blow struck in sport, and not likely or intended to cause bodily harm, is not an assault[10], nor is rough horseplay provided it is innocent of anger or intention to cause bodily harm[11]. However, an injury inflicted on an opponent by deliberately flouting the rules of the game may form the basis of a criminal prosecution[12]. Most organised sports have their own disciplinary procedures to uphold their rules and standards of play; criminal prosecutions should, therefore, be brought only in cases that are so grave as to be properly categorised as criminal[13]. If what occurs goes beyond what a player can reasonably be regarded as having accepted by taking part in the sport, this indicates that the conduct will not be covered by the defence of consent; on the other hand, the fact that the play is within the rules and practice of the game and does not go beyond them, will be a firm indication that what has happened is not criminal [13]. "Prize fights" have been held to amount to batteries. A mere exhibition of skill in sparring is not illegal; but if parties meet intending to fight until one gives in from exhaustion or injury received it is a prize-fight, whether the combatants fight in gloves or not[14].

As distinct from the civil law, the maxim ex turpi causa non oritur actio does not apply to criminal proceedings and the criminal law will act to prevent serious injury or death even when the persons subject to such injury or death consented to or willingly accepted the risk of actual injury or death. Accordingly, it was no defence to manslaughter that there was no duty of care to the victims who were illegal immigrants engaged in the same enterprise as the defendant lorry driver[15].

1. *A–G's Reference (No 6 of 1980)* [1981] QB 715, [1981] 2 All ER 1057.
2. *R v Brown* [2004] 1 AC 212, [1993] 2 All ER 75, 157 JP 337, HL.

3. *R v Wilson* [1996] 3 WLR 125, [1996] 2 Cr App Rep 241, [1996] Crim LR 573, CA.

4. *R v Dica* [2004] EWCA Crim 1103, [2004] QB 1257, [2004] 3 All ER 593, [2003] 3 WLR 213. However, their lordships made clear that they were not considering an allegation of deliberate infection or spreading HIV with intent to cause grievous bodily harm; and in such circumstances the principle in *Brown* (see infra) meant that the agreement of the participants would provide no defence to a charge under section 18 of the 1861 Act.

See also *R v Konzani* [2005] EWCA Crim 706, [2005] 2 Cr App R 14,169 JPN 227, in which it was affirmed that, for a complainant's consent to the risks of contracting the HIV virus to provide a defence, her consent had to be an informed consent and, in that regard, there was a critical distinction between taking a risk of the various, potentially adverse consequences of sexual intercourse, and giving an informed consent the risk of infection with a fatal disease. Moreover, a complainant could not give consent to something of which she was ignorant and, in such circumstances, silence was not consistent with honest or with a genuine behalf that there was informed consent.

5. *R v May* [1912] 3 KB 572, 77 JP 31; *R v Donovan* [1934] 2 KB 498, 98 JP 409.

6. *R v Lock* (1872) LR 2 CCR 10.

7. *R v Rosinski* (1824) 1 Mood CC 19; *R v Williams* (1838) C & P 286; *R v Bennett* (1866) 4 F & F 105.

8. *R v Williams* [1923] KB 340 rape where victim was fraudulently induced to consent to sexual intercourse in the belief that the defendant had to perform an operation to enable her to produce her voice properly).

9. *R v Richardson* [1998] 3 WLR 1292, [1998] 2 Cr App Rep 200, CA, [1999] Crim LR 62. But see *R v Tabassum* [2000] 2 Cr App Rep 328, [2000] Crim LR 686, CA (defendant examined breasts of his female victims who believed he was medically qualified and working for a hospital. Although they consented to the nature of the act, they did not consent to the quality of the act ie that it was done by a person without medical qualifications).

10. *R v Coney* (1882) 8 QBD 534, 46 JP 404.

11. *R v Bruce* (1847) 2 Cox CC 262.

12. *R v Billinghurst* [1978] Crim LR 553.

13. *R v Barnes* [2004] EWCA Crim 3246. [2005] 2 All ER 113, [2005] 1 Cr App R 30, [2005] Crim LR 381 in which the following guidance was given. It must be borne in mind that in highly competitive sports conduct outside the rules could be expected to occur in the heat of the moment and even if conduct justified not only being penalised but also a warning or even a sending off it still might not reach the threshold level required for it to be criminal. The type of sport, the level at which it was played, the nature of the act, the degree of force used, the extent of the risk of injury and the state of mind of the defendant were all likely to be relevant in determining whether the defendant's actions went beyond the threshold and warranted criminal proceedings.

14. *R v Orton* (1878) 43 JP 72; See Treatise on "Boxing Matches", 61 JP 802, where the various authorities are cited and discussed.

15. *R v Wacker* [2002] EWCA Crim 1944, [2003] QB 1207, [2003] 4 All ER 295, [2003] 1 Cr App Rep 329.

8–23064 Moderate chastisement. *Parents may inflict moderate and reasonable chastisement on their children, but standards of reasonableness change over the years. The current state of the law is that, in considering the reasonableness or otherwise of the chastisement, regard should be paid to the nature and context of the defendant's behaviour, its duration, its physical and mental consequences in relation to the child, the age and personal characteristics of the child and the reasons given by the defendant for administering punishment*[1]. *Where a defence of reasonable chastisement might be available, it is for the prosecution to prove that the accused did more than inflict moderate and reasonable chastisement on the child*[2].

By virtue of the Education Act 1996, s 548[3], *the giving of corporal punishment to a child cannot be justified in proceedings on the ground that it was done in pursuance of a right exercisable by a member of staff at a school by virtue of his position. "Child" for this purpose means a child for whom education is provided at any school; or for whom education is provided, otherwise than at school, under any arrangements made by a local education authority; or for whom specified nursery education is provided otherwise than at school.*

Section 58 of the Children Act 2004, which came into force on 15 January 2005, removes the justification of battery on the ground that it constituted reasonable punishment where the prosecution is brought under ss 18, 20 and 47 of the Offences Against the Person Act 1861 or s 1 of the Children and Young Persons Act 1933.

1. *R v H (assault of child: reasonable chastisement)* [2001] EWCA Crim 1024, [2001] 3 FCR 144, [2001 2 FLR 431, [2002] 1 Cr App Rep 59.

2. *R v Smith* [1985] Crim LR 42.

3. In this PART: title EDUCATION, ante.

8–23065 Self-defence, justification, provocation. A person is entitled to use reasonable force to defend himself, his property[1] or another person[2]. In addition, a person may use "such force as is reasonable in the circumstances in the prevention of crime"[3]. Where a defendant puts forward a justification for the infliction of violence, such as self-defence, provocation, resistance to violence, the onus is on the prosecution to disprove these matters if a verdict of guilty is to be justified[4].

The degree of force permissible depends on whether the defendant's actions were reasonable in the circumstances. When the issue of self-defence is raised it is an important consideration that the accused should have demonstrated by his actions that he did not want to fight. It has been said that a person must have shown that he was prepared to temporise and disengage and perhaps make some physical withdrawal[5] but it was subsequently made clear that a failure to retreat is only an *element* in the considerations upon which the reasonableness of an accused's conduct is to be judged; in some circumstances a person might act in self-defence and have a good defence without temporising, disengaging or withdrawing[6]. However, the test of reasonableness is not entirely objective[7] and the state of mind of the accused should not be overlooked completely. As a result, when assessing the reasonableness of the force used, it has been said:

"It is both good law and good sense that a man who is attacked may defend himself . . . but may only do what is reasonably necessary . . . If there has been an attack so that defence is reasonably necessary, it will be recognised that a person defending himself cannot weigh to a nicety the exact measure of his necessary defensive action. If . . . in a moment of unexpected anguish a person had only done what he honestly and instinctively thought was necessary, that would be most potent evidence that only reasonable defensive action had been taken"[8].

As mere words probably do not amount to an assault, insulting words, however gross, do not justify blows. A breach of the peace can only be justified when used to prevent a breach of the peace, although the circumstances of the provocation may be taken into consideration in awarding the punishment. Provocation does not alter the nature of the offence, but it is allowed for in the sentence[9].

Nevertheless, the test of the appropriate degree of force a person is entitled to use in self-defence is not any degree of force which he believed was reasonable, however well founded the belief. The court must first decide whether a defendant honestly believed that the circumstances were such as required him to use force to defend himself from an attack or threatened attack. The court must then decide whether the force used was reasonable in the circumstances as the defendant believed them to be[10] including, it would seem, the danger he believed to be involved[11].

It is inappropriate, except in exceptional circumstances which would make the evidence especially probative, in deciding whether excessive force has been used, to take into account whether the defendant is suffering from some psychiatric condition[12].

1. *A–G's Reference (No 2 of 1983)* [1983] 1 All ER 988, [1984] Crim LR 289, 149 JP 104.
2. *R v Rose* (1884) 15 Cox CC 540; *R v Duffy* [1967] 1 QB 63, [1966] 1 All ER 62, 130 JP 137.
3. Criminal Law Act 1967, s 3 in PART I: MAGISTRATES' COURTS, PROCEDURE, ante.
4. *R v Wheeler* [1967] 3 All ER 829, 132 JP 41; *R v Abraham* [1973] 3 All ER 694, 137 JP 826.
5. *R v Julien* [1969] 2 All ER 856, 133 JP 489.
6. *R v Whyte* [1987] 3 All ER 416, 85 Cr App Rep 283.
7. *Palmer v R* [1971] AC 814, [1971] 1 All ER 1077, 55 Cr App Rep 223; *R v McInnes* [1971] 3 All ER 295, 55 Cr App Rep 551.
8. Per Lord Morris in *Palmer v R* [1971] AC 814, [1971] 1 All ER 1077, 55 Cr App Rep 223.
9. Per Viscount Simon in *Holmes v DPP* [1946] AC 588, [1946] 2 All ER 124; *R v Cunningham* [1959] 1 QB 288, [1958] 3 All ER 711, 123 JP 134.
10. *R v Owino* [1996] 2 Cr App Rep 128; *DPP v Armstrong-Braun* (1998) 163 JP 271, [1999] Crim LR 416.
11. See *Shaw (Norman) v R* [2001] UKPC 26, [2002] Crim LR 140 and commentary thereto.
12. *R v Martin (Anthony)* [2001] EWCA Crim 2245, [2003] QB 1, [2002] 2 WLR 1, [2002] 1 Cr App Rep 323, [2002] Crim LR 136.

8–23066 Mistake. If a person believed mistakenly that the victim was consenting or that a crime was being committed which he intended to prevent, he must be judged against the mistaken facts or circumstances as he believed them to be[1]. If the belief was in fact held, its unreasonableness in objective terms is irrelevant so far as guilt or innocence is concerned[2]. A genuine belief in facts which if true would justify self-defence is a defence to a crime of personal violence as negativing intent to act unlawfully[3]. However, it would appear that an honest and reasonable belief that a constable is acting outside his duty will not always constitute a defence[4]. Nevertheless, a defendant is not entitled to rely on a mistake of fact induced by self-intoxication[5].

1. *R v Williams (Gladstone)* (1983) 78 Cr App Rep 276.
2. *R v Kimber* [1983] 3 All ER 316, [1983] 1 WLR 1118.
3. *Beckford v R* [1988] AC 130, [1987] 3 All ER 425, 85 Cr App Rep 378.
4. *R v Fennel* [1971] 1 QB 428, [1970] 3 All ER 215, [1970] Crim LR 581, 134 JP 678; *R v Ball* (1989) 90 Cr App Rep 378, [1989] Crim LR 581.
5. *Re O'Grady* [1987] QB 995, [1987] 3 All ER 420, 85 Cr App Rep 315.

8–23067 Aggravated assaults. Some assaults are regarded as being of a more serious nature and specific statutory provisions cater for these in the Offences against the Person Act. The more common offences are wounding or causing grievous bodily harm with intent[1], wounding or inflicting grievous bodily harm[2], assault with intent to resist or prevent arrest[3] and assault occasioning actual bodily harm[4].

1. Offences against the Person Act 1861, s 18, post.
2. Offences against the Person Act 1861, s 20, post.
3. Offences against the Person Act 1861, s 38, post.
4. Offences against the Person Act 1861, s 47, post.

8–23067A Harassment. Conduct which is less than a threat of immediate unlawful violence may amount to harassment[1]. A person who pursues a course of conduct which amounts to harassment of another and who knows or ought to know that it amounts to such harassment is, with certain exceptions, guilty of an offence contrary to section 2 of the Protection from Harassment Act 1997[1]. He may also (in civil proceedings) be liable for damages and be made subject to an injunction. Breach of such an injunction is an offence triable either way (s 3). Further, a person whose conduct causes another to fear on at least two occasions, that violence will be used against him is guilty of an offence if he knows or ought to have known that his course of conduct will cause the other so to fear on each of those occasions (s 4). A court may, when sentencing or dealing with a person convicted of an offence under section 2 or 4, make a restraining order to protect the victim of any other person named in the order from further conduct amounting to harassment or which will cause a fear of violence (s 5).

1. Protection from Harassment Act 1997, s 7(2), is this PART, post. See also *Chambers and Edwards v DPP* [1995] Crim LR 896 and see also s 5 of the Public Order Act 1986, this PART: title PUBLIC MEETINGS AND PUBLIC ORDER, post.

8–23068 Kidnapping. The common law offence of kidnapping is an attack on, and infringement of, the personal liberty of an individual. The offence contains four ingredients: the taking away of one person by another, by force or fraud, without the consent of the person so taken or carried away and without lawful excuse[1]. The offence may be committed by a man against his wife[2] and where only a short distance is involved[3]. A father may be guilty of kidnapping his child[1] but in such cases it is the absence of the child's consent which is material. In the case of a very young child the absence of consent would be a necessary inference from its age, but in the case of an older child it is a question of fact for the jury whether the child concerned has sufficient understanding and intelligence to give its consent, and, if the jury considers that it has these qualities, it must then consider whether it has been proved that the child did give its consent[1]. The intent required is basic intent and self-induced intoxication is no defence[4].

The offence is punishable on indictment by a fine and imprisonment. See also the Child Abduction Act 1984, in PART V: YOUTH COURTS, ante.

1. *R v D* [1984] AC 778, [1984] 2 All ER 449. See also *R v Cort* [2003] EWCA Crim 2149, [2004] QB 388, [2003] 3 WLR 1300, 167 JP 504, [2004] Cr App R 18 (the defendant falsely stated to women waiting at a bus stop that their bus had broken down and offered them a lift; it was held that what they were consenting to was a lift and not being taken away by fraud and that their consent was vitiated by that fraudulently induced mistake).
2. *R v Reid* [1973] QB 299, [1972] 2 All ER 1350.
3. *R v Wellard* [1978] 3 All ER 161, [1978] 1 WLR 921, 67 Cr App Rep 364.
4. *R v Hutchins* [1988] Crim LR 379.

8–23069 False imprisonment. The common law offence of false imprisonment comprises unlawful detention, compulsion, restraint of personal liberty[1] but is not committed merely by preventing someone from proceeding along a particular way[2]. A parent may be guilty of false imprisonment of a child where the facts take the circumstances outside reasonable parental discipline[3].

1. See *Mee v Cruikshank* (1902) 86 LT 708, 66 JP 89, 20 Cox 210; *R v Linsberg and Leies* (1905) 69 JP 107.
2. *Bird v Jones* (1845) 7 QB 742, 15 LJQB 82, 10 JP 4.
3. See *R v Rahman* (1985) 120 Sol Jo 431, CA.

Offences Against the Person Act 1861

(24 & 25 Vict c 100)

Homicide

8–23079 1–3. *Repealed (see Homicide Act 1957, post).*

8–23080 4. Soliciting to commit murder. Whosoever shall solicit[1], encourage, persuade, or endeavour to persuade, or shall propose to any person, to murder any other person, whether he be a subject of Her Majesty or not, and whether he be within the Queen's Dominions or not, shall be guilty of [an offence] and being convicted thereof shall be liable to imprisonment for life.
[Offences Against the Person Act 1861, s 4, as amended by the Statute Law Revision Act 1892, and the Criminal Law Act 1977, s 5.]

1. As to conspiracy to murder, see now ss 1–5 of the Criminal Law Act 1977, in title CONSPIRACY, ante. A person who solicits a pregnant woman to murder her child after its birth commits an offence, at all events if the child is born alive (*R v Shephard* [1919] 2 KB 125, 83 JP 131). The offence may be completed by the publication of an article in a newspaper not addressed to a particular individual (*R v Most* (1881) 7 QBD 244, 45 JP 696). But the offence is not complete unless there has been some actual communication between the accused and the person solicited, etc, though it is not necessary to show that the mind of the person solicited was affected thereby; proof of posting will suffice (*R v Krause* (1902) 66 JP 121). An indictment charging a person with encouraging persons unknown to murder the sovereigns and rulers of Europe was held good as a sufficiently well defined class was referred to by the words "sovereigns of Europe" (*R v Antonelli and Barberi* (1906) 70 JP 4).

8–23081 5. Manslaughter.—Whosoever shall be convicted of manslaughter[1] shall be liable, at the discretion of the court, to imprisonment for life.
[Offences Against the Person Act 1861, s 5.]

1. Manslaughter is based mainly, though not exclusively, on the **absence of the intention to kill**, but with the presence of an element of unlawfulness which is the elusive factor (*Andrews v DPP* [1937] AC 576, [1937] 2 All ER 552, 101 JP 386, HL): in order to establish criminal liability the facts must be such that in the opinion of the jury the negligence of the

accused went beyond a mere matter of compensation between subjects and showed such disregard for the life and safety of others as to amount to a crime against the State and conduct deserving punishment (*per* Lord HEWART CJ, in *R v Bateman* (1925) 89 JP 162). An accused is guilty of manslaughter if it is proved that he intentionally did an act which was unlawful and dangerous and that it inadvertently caused death; but it is unnecessary to prove that he knew the act was unlawful or dangerous (*DPP v Newbury* [1977] AC 500, [1976] 2 All ER 365, 140 JP 370, HL). Approval was given in the case of *R v Watson* [1989] 2 All ER 865, [1989] 1 WLR 684, CA, to manslaughter being defined as the offence committed when one person causes the death of another by an act which is unlawful and which is also dangerous, dangerous in the sense that it is an act which all sober and reasonable people would inevitably realise must subject the victim to the risk of some harm resulting whether the defendant realised that or not. A jury must be satisfied that the unlawful act was such that all reasonable people would be bound to recognise that it exposed the victim to the risk of harm (*R v Mahal* [1991] Crim LR 632, CA). Where the victim died as the result of injuries sustained from jumping from a speeding car in which he was threatened with robbery, the considerations were whether it was reasonably foreseeable that some physical harm, albeit not serious, was likely to result from the threat of robbery, and whether the victim's response was within the range which might be expected (*R v Williams and Davis* [1992] Crim LR 198, CA).

Where the charge of manslaughter is based on an unlawful and dangerous act, it must be an **act directed at the victim** and likely to cause him immediate injury (*R v Dalby* [1982] 1 All ER 916, [1982] 1 WLR 425), but in that case the court was concerned with the quality of the act rather than the identity of the person at whom it was aimed. Therefore, it does not matter that the act has been aimed at some person other than the victim or that the death has not arisen due to some immediate impact on, or physical contact with, the victim since the primary question is one of causation; i.e. whether the defendant's act caused the victim's death (*R v Mitchell* [1983] QB 741, [1983] 2 All ER 427, 76 Cr App Rep 293, CA). In cases where the defendant supplies the victim with drugs the defendant will not be guilty of manslaughter where the victim had voluntarily injected himself with a fatal dose but it will be otherwise where the defendant is assisting or encouraging the victim to inject himself (*R v Kennedy* [1999] Crim LR 65, CA) but this broad approach was not followed in *R v Rogers* [2003] EWCA Crim 945, [2003] 2 Cr App Rep 160, [2003] Crim LR 555 where the application of a tourniquet to the deceased's arm was culpable because it was "part and parcel" of the administration of the heroin. However, the reference by the Criminal Cases Review Commission of *Kennedy* was subsequently dismissed by the Court of Appeal (*R v Kennedy (No 2)* [2005] EWCA Crim 685, [2005] 1 WLR 2159, [2005] 2 Cr App R 23). An armed person who fires at the police and holds a woman by force in front of him as a shield when the police might well fire shots at him in self-defence commits two such unlawful and dangerous acts (*R v Pagett* (1983) 76 Cr App Rep 279, CA). Common sense standards apply when considering the defence of self-defence, in deciding whether more force was used than was necessary in the circumstances; see *R v Shannon* [1980] Crim LR 438. The act which caused death and the necessary mental state do not have to coincide in point of time; the mens rea may be contained in an initial unlawful assault and the actus reus may be the eventual act causing death (*R v Le Brun* [1992] QB 61, [1991] 4 All ER 673, CA).

Particular circumstances—A person may be convicted of manslaughter after a summary conviction of an assault (*R v Morris* (1867) LR 1 CCR 90, 31 JP 516). Evidence that death was due to a combination of physical exertion and fright or strong emotion, caused by an illegal act of the accused, is sufficient to support a conviction for manslaughter without proof of actual violence (*per* RIDLEY, J, in *R v Hayward* (1908) 21 Cox, CC 692; see also *R v Reid* [1976] Crim LR 570—joint possession of revolver intended to frighten; contrast *R v Perman* [1996] 1 Cr App Rep 24 where the defendant believed the gun in possession of the co-accused was unloaded.): also if death was connected with the state of health (*status lymphaticus*) of the deceased (*R v Woods* (1921) 85 JP 272). Where a number of people participate in the commission of a dangerous act, all may be convicted; as where three men fired off cartridges at a board in private grounds, one of which killed a boy, all were equally guilty although it was not shown which shot caused the death (*R v Salmon* (1880) 6 QBD 79, 45 JP 270; and see *R v Baldessare* (1930) 144 LT 185; *R v Wesley Smith* [1963] 3 All ER 597, 128 JP 13). Any person, whether licensed or unlicensed, who deals with the life or health of another person is bound to use competent skill and sufficient attention: if the patient dies for the want of either, there is manslaughter (*R v Burdee* (1916) 86 LJKB 871). One act of carelessness by a doctor in preparing too strong a mixture for injection whereby the patient dies does not amount to manslaughter: the negligence to be imputed depends upon the probable, not the actual, result (*Akerele v R* [1943] AC 255, [1943] 1 All ER 367). The death of a sick child accelerated by the refusal of a parent to procure medical assistance, even though the refusal is due to religious scruples, may lead to a conviction for manslaughter (*R v Senior* [1899] 1 QB 283, 63 JP 8). Where the allegation is neglect of a duty assumed to care for an infirm person, a reckless disregard of the infirm person's health and welfare must be shown; mere inadvertence is not enough (*R v Stone, R v Dobinson* [1977] QB 354, [1977] 2 All ER 341, 141 JP 354). It is clear from *R v Stanley Smith* [1979] 3 All ER 605, [1979] 1 WLR 1445, that the test of the recklessness is subjective, that a deliberate decision has been taken to run the risk involved in not getting medical attention, and in all the circumstances that was a wholly unjustified risk to take.

Involuntary manslaughter has been held to involve the following ingredients: (1) the existence of a duty; (2) a breach of the duty causing death; (3) gross negligence justifying criminal conviction. Gross negligence might properly be found based upon any of the following states of mind: *(a)* indifference to an obvious risk of injury to health; *(b)* actual foresight of the risk coupled with the determination nevertheless to run it; *(c)* an appreciation of the risk coupled with an intention to avoid it but also coupled with such a high degree of negligence in the attempted avoidance as the jury considered justified a conviction; *(d)* inattention or failure to avert to a serious risk which went beyond "mere inadvertence" in respect of an obvious and important matter which the defendant's duty demanded he should address (*R v Prentice* [1993] 4 All ER 935, CA, *R v Sullman* [1994] QB 302, CA, *R v Adomako* [1995] 1 AC 171, [1994] 3 All ER 79, HL, *R v Holloway* [1994] QB 302, [1993] 4 All ER 935, CA). The maxim ex turpi causa non oritur actio does not apply to criminal proceedings to preclude a duty of care to participants involved in an unlawful activity, even when the persons subject to such injury or death, consented to or willingly accepted the risk of actual injury or death (*R v Wacker* [2002] EWCA Crim 1944, [2003] QB 1207, [2003] 4 All ER 295, [2003] 1 Cr App Rep 329). The ingredients of the offence of gross negligent manslaughter have sufficient certainty to meet the requirements of art 7 of the European Convention on Human Rights (*R v Misra and Srivastava* [2004] EWCA Crim 2375, [2005] 1 Cr App R 21, [2005] Crim LR 324).

Procedure—For requirement for consent of Attorney-General to institute proceedings in certain circumstances see note to the Homicide Act 1957, s 1, post. Manslaughter by the driver of a motor vehicle involves compulsory disqualification for holding a driving licence (Road Traffic Offenders Act 1988, Sch 2).

For the obligation placed on the clerk to the justices to notify the coroner, who is responsible for holding an inquest, of the making of a charge of murder, manslaughter or infanticide and of the result of the proceedings before the court, see the Coroners Act 1988, s 17, in this PART, title CORONERS, ante.

A coroner's inquest is not to find a person guilty of manslaughter; Criminal Law Act 1977, s 56.

As to corporate manslaughter, see *R v P & O European Ferries (Dover) Ltd* [1991] Crim LR 695.

8–23082 **9.** *Murder or manslaughter abroad*[1].

8–23083 **10.** *Provision for the trial of murder and manslaughter where the death or cause of death only happens in England or Ireland*[1].

1. Sections 9 and 10 give English courts jurisdiction where acts were committed abroad.

Letters threatening to murder

8–23084 16. Threats to kill. A person who without lawful excuse[1] makes to another a threat, intending that that other would fear it would be carried out, to kill that other or a third person[2] shall be guilty of an offence[3] and liable on conviction on indictment to imprisonment for a term not exceeding **ten years**.

[Offences against the Person Act 1861, s 16, as amended by the Criminal Law Act 1977, Sch 12.]

1. A lawful excuse can exist if a threat to kill is made for the prevention of crime or for self-defence, provided that it is reasonable in the circumstances to make such a threat; the onus is on the prosecution to prove that there was no lawful excuse for making the threat (*R v Cousins* [1982] QB 526, [1982] 2 All ER 115, CA).

2. A foetus in utero is not a person distinct from its mother and therefore a threat to cause the mother to have a miscarriage is not an offence under s 16; however a threat to kill a child after its birth when it was still a foetus is an offence under s 16 (*R v Tait* [1990] 1 QB 290, [1989] 3 All ER 682, CA).

3. Triable either way; see Magistrates' Courts Act 1980, s 17 and Sch 1, also ss 17A–21 (procedure) and s 32 (penalty) in PART I: MAGISTRATES' COURTS, PROCEDURE, ante.

Acts causing or tending to cause danger to Life or Bodily Harm

8–23085 17. Impeding a person endeavouring to save himself from shipwreck. Whosoever shall unlawfully and maliciously[1] prevent or impede any person, being on board of, or having quitted any ship or vessel which shall be in distress or wrecked, stranded, or cast on shore, in his endeavour to save his life, or shall unlawfully and maliciously prevent or impede any person in his endeavour to save the life of any such person as in this section first aforesaid shall be guilty of [an offence] and being convicted thereof shall be liable to imprisonment for life.

[Offences Against the Person Act 1861, s 17 as amended by the Statute Law Revision Act 1892, the Statute Law Revision (No 2) Act 1893 and the Criminal Law Act 1967, s 1.]

1. For meaning of "maliciously", see para **1–302 Criminal responsibility—Guilty mind (mens rea)** in PART I: MAGISTRATES' COURTS, PROCEDURE, ante.

8–23086 18. Wounding with intent to do grievous bodily harm. Whosoever shall unlawfully and maliciously[1] by any means whatsoever, wound[2] or cause[3] any grievous bodily harm[4] to any person with intent[5] to do some grievous bodily harm to any person, or with intent to resist or prevent the lawful[6] apprehension or detainer of any person—shall be guilty of [an offence] and being convicted thereof shall be liable to imprisonment for **life**.

[Offences Against the Person Act 1861, s 18, as amended by the Statute Law Revision Act 1892, the Statute Law Revision (No 2) Act 1983, the Criminal Law Act 1967, s 1 and Sch 3.]

1. For meaning of "maliciously", see para **1–290 Criminal responsibility—Guilty mind (mens rea)** in PART I: MAGISTRATES' COURTS, PROCEDURE, ante.

2. To constitute a "wound" there must be a break in the continuity of the whole skin; accordingly, an injury where there has merely been internal rupturing of blood vessels is not a "wound" (*C (a minor) v Eisenhower* [1984] QB 331, [1983] 3 All ER 230).

3. The test of causation is an objective one, and separate from the accused's intention. To establish that the defendant caused the victim's injuries, the prosecution must prove that the defendant's conduct caused or materially contributed to those injuries, ie were they reasonably foreseeable as a consequence by a reasonable person in the defendant's shoes. It is not necessary for the reasonable man to be taken to be of the same age and sex as the defendant (*R v Marjoram* [2000] Crim LR 373, CA (defendant caused victim's injuries sustained when she jumped through a window when the defendant accompanied by a large number of people shouting abuse and kicking at her door forced open the door to her room)).

4. To constitute grievous bodily harm, really serious bodily harm must be caused (*R v Metharam* [1961] 3 All ER 200, 125 JP 578; *DPP v Smith* [1961] AC 290, [1960] 3 All ER 161, 124 JP 473); "grievous" means no more and no less than "really serious", and there is no distinction between the phrases "serious bodily harm" and "really serious bodily harm"; see *R v Saunders* [1985] LS Gaz R 1005, CA. A modified interpretation applied in *R v Ashman* (1858) 1 F & F 88, identifying the expression with serious interference with health or comfort, is no longer appropriate. In *R v Bollom* [2003] EWCA Crim 2846, [2004] 2 Cr App Rep 50, the question arose as to whether the degree of a harm had to be considered with or without reference to the health or other particular factors relating to the person harmed (in this case a 17-month-old baby who had suffered extensive bruising and some abrasions). It was held that it was necessary to consider the injuries in their real context and there was no pre-condition to a finding that the injuries amounted to grievous bodily harm that the victim should require treatment or that the harm would have lasting consequences; however, where it is alleged that the injuries collectively, though not individually, amount to grievous bodily harm the court must be satisfied that they were inflicted in a single assault and not in a series of assaults.

5. Where intent is an ingredient of the offence, there is no onus on the defendant to prove that the alleged act was accidental. A person may be taken to intend the consequence only of his intentional acts (*R v Davies* (1913) 29 TLR 350). Recklessness cannot amount to the specific intent required (*R v Belfon* [1976] 3 All ER 46, 140 JP 523). In determining this intention, the court is not bound to draw an inference by reason only of the result being a natural and probable consequence of the defendant's actions. It shall decide upon his intent by reference to all the evidence, drawing such inferences there-from as appear proper. See Criminal Justice Act 1967, s 8, ante. The approved direction to a jury is "You must feel sure that the defendant intended to cause serious bodily harm to the victim. You can only decide what his intention was by considering all the relevant circumstances and in particular what he did and what he said about it" (*R v Purcell* (1986) 83 Cr App Rep 45, CA).

If any person fire a pistol into a group of people, not aiming at any one in particular, but intending generally to do grievous bodily harm, the offender may be indicted for shooting at the person with intent to do grievous bodily harm (*R v Fretwell* (1864) Le & Ca 443, 28 JP 344; see *R v Ward* (1872) LR 1 CCR 356, 36 JP 453).

Provocation does not alter the nature of the offence, but it is allowed for in the sentence (per Viscount SIMON in *Holmes v DPP* [1946] AC 588, [1946] 2 All ER 124; *R v Cunningham* [1959] 1 QB 288, [1958] 3 All ER 711, 123 JP 134). For form of charge where a blow misses and hits another person, see *R v Monger* [1973] Crim LR 301. Drunkenness as a defence has to be very extreme before it should influence the prosecution to accept a plea of guilty to a charge under s 20 instead (*R v Stubbs* (1988) 88 Cr App Rep 53, CA).

6. If the apprehension would not have been lawful an indictment under this section cannot be sustained (*R v Marsden* (1868) LR 1 CCR 131, 32 JP 436).

8–23087 20. Inflicting bodily injury, with or without weapon[1]. Whosoever shall unlawfully and maliciously[2] wound[3] or inflict any grievous bodily harm[3] upon any other person, either with or without any weapon or instrument shall be guilty of [an offence] and being convicted thereof shall be liable to imprisonment not exceeding **five years**[4].*

[Offences Against the Person Act 1861, s 20 as amended by the Statute Law Revision Act 1892, the Criminal Justice Act 1948, s 1 and the Criminal Law Act 1967, s 1.]

***Amended in relation to Northern Ireland by SI 2004/1991.**

1. As to having in possession any firearm or imitation firearm at the time of committing or at the time of apprehension for offences under ss 20–22, 30, 32, 38, 47 and 56 of this Act, aiding and abetting or attempting to commit any ch offence, see the Firearms Act, 1968, s 17, and Sch 1, ante.

2. For the meaning of "maliciously" see para **1–302 Criminal responsibility—Guilty mind (mens rea)** in PART I: MAGISTRATES' COURTS, PROCEDURE, ante. It is neither limited to, nor does it indeed require, any ill will towards the persons injured. (*R v Savage, R v Parmenter* [1992] 1 AC 699, [1991] 4 All ER 698, HL).The word "maliciously" in this statute was satisfied by a malice which had a different object for the blow. L had a quarrel with C and aimed a blow at him, but accidentally struck and wounded E. The CCR confirmed the conviction, and distinguished the case from *R v Pembliton* (1874) LR 2 CCR 119, 38 JP 454 (*R v Latimer* (1886) 17 QBD 359, 51 JP 184). B extinguished the gaslights on the staircase of a theatre, and placed a bar across the passage; the darkness caused a panic, and two persons were seriously injured. He was rightly convicted under this section; personal malice need not be proved (*R v Martin* (1881) 8 QBD 54, 46 JP 228). This case was followed in *R v Chapin* (1909) 74 JP 71. A's wife being frightened by his threats, tried to get out of a window to escape, and fell and broke her leg. The conviction was affirmed (*R v Halliday* (1890) 54 JP 312; followed in *R v Beech* (1912) 76 JP 287; and *R v Coleman* (1920) 84 JP 112). An intention to frighten is not a sufficient *mens rea* (*Flack v Hunt* [1980] Crim LR 44; *R v Sullivan* [1981] Crim LR 46).

In order to establish that a defendant has acted maliciously it has to be shown that, on the facts known to him at the time, he actually foresaw that some bodily harm, not necessarily amounting to grievous bodily harm or wounding, might occur: *R v Parmenter* and *R v Savage* [1992] AC 699, [1991] 4 All ER 698, HL. Accordingly, a defendant who believed his gun to be unloaded, when in fact it contained pellets, and fired at another person thereby causing injury, was held not to have acted maliciously (*W (a minor) v Dolbey* [1983] Crim LR 681); and see *R v Rainbird* [1989] Crim LR 505.

3. See notes 2 and 4 to s 18, ante. An offence contrary to s 20 of this Act may be committed where no physical violence is applied directly or indirectly to the body of the victim, and in this context "grievous bodily harm" may include psychiatric injury (*R v Ireland* [1997] 4 All ER 225, [1997] 3 WLR 534, 161 JP 569, HL).

4. Triable either way; see Magistrates' Courts Act 1980, s 17 and Sch 1, also ss 17A–21 (procedure) and s 32 (penalty) in PART I: MAGISTRATES' COURTS, PROCEDURE, ante. See criticism by Lord GODDARD, CJ, of justices who permitted a charge under s 18 to be reduced to one under this section, at the request of both prosecution and defence, so as to empower them to deal with the case summarily (*R v Bodmin Justices, ex p McEwen* [1947] KB 321, [1947] 1 All ER 109, 111 JP 47).

8–23088 21. Attempting to choke etc in order to commit indictable offence. Whosoever shall by any means whatsoever attempt to choke, suffocate, or strangle any other person, or shall by any means calculated to choke, suffocate, or strangle, attempt to render any other person insensible, unconscious, or incapable of resistance, with intent in any of such cases thereby to enable himself or any other person to commit or with intent in any of such cases thereby to assist any other person in committing any indictable offence shall be guilty of an [offence][1] and being convicted thereof shall be liable to imprisonment for **life**.

[Offences Against the Person Act 1861, s 21 as amended by the Statute Law Revision Act 1892, the Criminal Justice Act 1948, s 1 and the Criminal Law Act 1967, s 1.]

8–23089 22. Using chloroform etc to commit indictable offence. Whosoever shall unlawfully apply or administer to or cause to be taken by, or attempt to apply or administer to, or attempt to cause to be administered to or taken by, any person, any chloroform, laudanum, or other stupefying or overpowering drug, matter, or thing, with intent in any of such cases thereby to enable himself or any other person to commit, or with intent in any of such cases thereby to assist any other person in committing any indictable offence shall be guilty of [an offence] and being convicted thereof shall be liable to imprisonment for **life**[1].

[Offences Against the Person Act 1861, s 22 as amended by the Statute Law Revision Act 1892, the Criminal Justice Act 1948, s 1 and the Criminal Law Act 1967, s 1.]

1. Where firearms were involved, see note 1 to s 20, ante.

8–23090 23. Maliciously administering poison etc so as to endanger life etc. Whosoever shall unlawfully and maliciously[1] administer to, or cause to be administered to, or taken by, any other person[2], any poison, or other destructive or noxious thing, so as thereby to endanger the life of such person, or so as thereby to inflict upon any such person any grievous bodily harm shall be guilty of [an offence][3], and being convicted thereof shall be liable to imprisonment for any term not exceeding **ten years**.

[Offences Against the Person Act 1861, s 23 as amended by the Statute Law Revision Act 1892, the Criminal Justice Act 1948 s 1 and the Criminal Law Act 1967, s 1.]

---

1. For meaning of "maliciously", see para **1–290 Criminal responsibility—Guilty mind (mens rea)** in PART I: MAGISTRATES' COURTS, PROCEDURE, ante. For "administer" see note to s 24, post.

2. The consent of the person to the administration to him of a noxious substance for the purpose of committing suicide is no defence to a charge under this section (*R v McShane* (1977) 66 Cr App Rep 97).

3. A person charged under this section may be convicted of an offence against s 24, infra (Offences Against the Person Act 1861, s 25).

8–23091 24. Maliciously administering poison etc with intent to injure, aggrieve or annoy. Whosoever shall unlawfully and maliciously[1] administer[2] to, or cause to be administered to or taken by any other person, any poison or other destructive or noxious thing[3], with intent to injure[4], aggrieve, or annoy[5] such person shall be guilty of [an offence], and being convicted thereof shall be liable to imprisonment not exceeding **five years**.

[Offences Against the Person Act 1861, s 24 as amended by the Statute Law Revision Act 1892, the Statute Law Revision (No 2) Act 1893, the Criminal Justice Act 1948, s 1 and the Criminal Law Act 1967, s 1.]

---

1. For meaning of "maliciously", see para **1–302 Criminal responsibility—Guilty mind (mens rea)** in PART I: MAGISTRATES' COURTS, PROCEDURE, ante.

2. "Administer" includes conduct which, not being the application of direct physical force to the victim, nevertheless brought the noxious thing into contract with the victim's body (*R v Gillard* (1988) 87 Cr App Rep 189). A person who applied a tourniquet to the arm of an addict who was injecting himself with heroin which caused a cardiac arrest, was playing a part in the mechanics of injection that caused death and had no defence to an offence under s 23, or to unlawful act manslaughter: *R v Rogers* [2003] EWCA Crim 945, [2003] Crim LR 555.

3. Administering to a woman a noxious drug (cantharides) with intent to excite sexual passion, in order that the prisoner might have connection with her, will be an offence under this section (*R v Wilkins* (1861) Le & Ca 89, 25 JP 773); but not if the quantity administered is incapable of producing any effect, for it is not in that form noxious (*R v Hennah* (1877) 41 JP 171). See also *R v Wood* [1975] Crim LR 236 (sleeping tablets). The concept of the "noxious thing" involves not only the quality or nature of the substance, but also the quantity administered or sought to be administered; "noxious" means something less in importance than, and different in quality from, poison or other destructive things (*R v Marcus* [1981] 2 All ER 833, [1981] 1 WLR 774, 145 JP 380, CA). See also the Sexual Offences Act 2003, s 61 (administering a substance with the intention of stupefying or overpowering a person to facilitate sexual activity) in PART VIII: title SEXUAL OFFENCES, post.

4. There must be an intent to injure in the sense of causing physical harm; see *R v Hill* (1986) 83 Cr App Rep 386, [1986] Crim LR 815.

5. Although the administration of the poison with intent to annoy is only a misdemeanour, if the effects are such as to cause grievous bodily harm the offence will amount to felony (*Tully v Corrie* (1867) 17 LT 140).

8–23092 26. Not providing apprentices etc with food etc whereby life endangered. Whosoever being legally liable, either as a master or mistress, to provide for any apprentice[1] or servant necessary food, clothing, or lodging, shall wilfully and without lawful excuse refuse or neglect to provide the same, or shall unlawfully and maliciously do or cause to be done any bodily harm to any such apprentice or servant, so that the life of such apprentice or servant shall be endangered or the health of such apprentice of servant shall have been or shall be likely to be permanently injured shall be guilty of an offence[2] and being convicted thereof shall be liable to imprisonment not exceeding **five years**.

[Offences Against the Person Act 1861, s 26 as amended by the Statute Law Revision Act 1892, the Statute Law Revision (No 2) Act 1893, the Criminal Justice Act 1948, s 1 and the Criminal Law Act 1967, s 1.]

---

1. See also Conspiracy, and Protection of Property Act 1875, s 6, in title EMPLOYMENT, ante.

2. Triable either way; see Magistrates' Courts Act 1980, s 17 and Sch 1, also ss. 18–21 (procedure) and s 32 (penalty).

8–23093 27. Exposing child whereby life is in danger. Whosoever shall unlawfully abandon[1] or expose any child, being under the age of two years, whereby the life of such child shall be endangered, or the health of such child shall have been or shall be likely to be permanently injured shall be guilty of an offence[2] and being convicted hereof shall be liable to imprisonment not exceeding **five years**.

[Offences Against the Person Act 1861, s 27 as amended by the Statute Law Revision Act 1892, the Statute Law Revision (No 2) Act 1893, the Criminal Justice Act 1948, s 1 and the Criminal Law Act 1967, s 1.]

---

1. A father knowingly leaving his child for some hours outside his house, after it has been left there by his wife, with whom he was not living, is guilty of abandonment (*R v White* (1871) LR 1 CCR 331, 36 JP 134). See also *R v Falkingham* (1870) LR 1 CCR 222, 34 JP 149; Treat 35 JP 417. For general offence of abandoning a child, see Children and Young Persons Act 1933, s 1 in PART V: YOUTH COURTS.

2. Triable either way; see Magistrates' Courts Act 1980, s 17 and Sch 1, also ss 17A–21 (procedure) and s 32 (penalty) in PART I: MAGISTRATES' COURTS, PROCEDURE, ante.

8–23094 28. Causing bodily injury by gunpowder. Whosoever shall unlawfully and maliciously[1], by the explosion of gunpowder or other explosive substance, burn, maim, disfigure, disable, or do any grievous bodily harm to any person shall be guilty of [an offence] and being convicted thereof shall be liable to imprisonment for **life**.

[Offences Against the Person Act 1861, s 28 as amended by the Statute Law Revision Act 1892, the Statute Law Revision (No 2) Act 1893, the Criminal Justice Act 1948, s 1 and Sch 10, and the Criminal Law Act 1967, s 1.]

summons for an assault was no bar to a civil action for the same assault (*Reed v Nutt* (1890) 24 QBD 669, 54 JP 599). The certificate will be a bar to an indictment for unlawfully wounding (*R v Elrington* (1861) 26 JP 117). The certificate will not prevent justices ordering the defendant to enter into a recognisance to keep the peace (*Ex p Davis* (1871) 35 JP 551).

8–23115 45. **Release**[1]. If any person against whom any such complaint as is mentioned in section 44 of this Act shall have been preferred by or on behalf of the party aggrieved shall have obtained such a certificate, or having been[2] convicted, shall have paid the whole amount adjudged to be paid, or shall have suffered the imprisonment, in every such case he shall be released[3] from all further or other proceedings, civil[4] or criminal, for the[5] same cause.

[Offences Against the Person Act 1861, s 45 as amended by the Criminal Justice Act 1948, s 1 and the Criminal Justice Act 1988, Sch 15.]

1. Notwithstanding the provisions of this section, proceedings may be taken against the acquitted person for the offence of which he was acquitted where an order is made under s 54(3) of the Criminal Procedure and Investigations Act 1996 (acquittals tainted by intimidation etc), in PART I: MAGISTRATES' COURTS, PROCEDURE, ante (Criminal Procedure and Investigations Act 1996, s 57(1), in PART I: MAGISTRATES' COURTS, PROCEDURE, ante).

2. A second conviction after a conviction under a separate enactment, but upon the same facts, will be quashed (*Wemyss v Hopkins* (1875) LR 10 QB 378, 39 JP 549; and see PART I: MAGISTRATES' COURTS, PROCEDURE, para **1–448 Res judicata, estoppel, autrefois convict/acquit, functus officio** ante and Treat 40 JP 17, 61 JP 610).

3. These words include all proceedings arising out of the same assault, whether taken by the informant or by any other person consequently aggrieved. A certificate of dismissal under s 44 supersedes the necessity for other proof, but if such certificate is not produced, it will be for the defendant to prove by other evidence, not only that the former information was for the same matter with which he is charged a second time, but that it was dismissed upon the merits, and the decision was intended to be final. If this be done, the plea of autrefois acquit will, it is conceived, be available in like manner as in indictments (*R v Newbury Justices* (1851) 15 JP Jo 321). So conviction, with payment of the fine, is an answer to an action for injuries to business occasioned by the assault (*Masper v Brown* (1876) 1 CPD 97, 40 JP 265; *Solomon v Frinigan* (1866) 30 JP Jo 756; *Holden v King* (1876) 41 JP 25). The conviction of a servant or agent does not operate to release the person by whom he was employed (*Dyer v Munday* [1895] 1 QB 742, 59 JP 276). If there be neither a conviction nor a dismissal with a certificate thereof, but merely an order for the defendant to enter into a recognisance to keep the peace and pay the costs thereof, no release can be pleaded (*Hartley v Hindmarsh* (1866) LR 1 CP 553). But where a prisoner was convicted and discharged conditionally on giving security to be of good behaviour, under the repealed s 16 of the Summary Jurisdiction Act 1879, it was held the conviction was a bar at common law, apart from the statute, to a subsequent indictment upon the same facts for unlawfully wounding, unlawfully inflicting grievous bodily harm, assault occasioning actual bodily harm, and common assault (*R v Miles* (1890) 24 QBD 423, 54 JP 549).

4. If justices desire to give a defendant the protection afforded by this Act they should found their proceedings and judgment upon s 44, inasmuch as the common law defence to an indictment would be no defence to civil proceedings (*R v Miles*, supra).

5. A was convicted for assault and sentenced to imprisonment and underwent the punishment. He was afterwards convicted of manslaughter for same assault. The CCR held the conviction for assault was no bar, as the subsequent indictment for manslaughter was not for the "same cause" as the assault (*R v Morris* (1867) LR 1 CCR 90, 31 JP 516, Treat 60 JP 18). So a conviction for a common assault could not be pleaded in bar to an indictment for rape, though possibly it might be for an assault with intent to commit rape; for the essence of the crime of rape is a felonious assault by penetration of the person of the prosecutrix, although evidence may be given which, if true, would constitute a rape, and justices may disbelieve that evidence, but believe that an assault had been committed, and convict the defendant (per HAWKINS, J: *R v Miles*, supra). The ground for this decision seems to be that the aggravating circumstances, unless coupled with the assault, amount to no crime. In *Masper v Brown*, supra, it was held that the "same cause" meant the same assault; but *R v Morris* does not seem to have been cited or referred to in that case.

8–23116 47. Assault occasioning bodily harm —Whosoever shall be convicted upon an indictment of any assault[1] occasioning actual bodily harm[2] shall be liable[3] to be imprisoned for any term not exceeding **5 years**.*

[Offences Against the Person Act 1861, s 47, as amended by the Statute Law Revision Act 1892, the Criminal Justice Act 1948, s 1 and the Criminal Justice Act 1988, Sch 16.]

***Amended in relation to Northern Ireland by SI 2004/1991.**

1. The mental element of assault is an intention to cause the victim to apprehend immediate and unlawful violence, or recklessness whether such apprehension be caused; proof is required of an assault which occasioned actual bodily harm; the prosecution are not obliged to prove that the defendant intended to cause some actual bodily harm or was reckless as to whether such harm would be caused (*R v Savage, R v Parmenter* [1992] 1 AC 699, [1991] 4 All ER 698, HL). For the offence of common assault see the Criminal Justice Act 1988, s 39, post.

2. "Actual" means that the bodily harm should not be so trivial or trifling as to be effectively without significance. "Bodily" means "concerned with the body". "Harm" is not limited to "injury" but extends to "hurt" and "damage". "Actual bodily harm" is not limited to 'harm to the skin, flesh and bones of the victim'; it applies to all parts of the body including the victim's organs, his nervous system and his brain but not excluding other parts of the body. Physical pain consequent on an assault is not a necessary ingredient of this offence.

Hair is an attribute and part of the human body, even if the hair above the surface of the scalp is no more than dead tissue. Therefore the cutting off a substantial part of the victims' hair in the course of an assault is capable of amounting to an assault which occasions actual bodily harm (*DPP v Smith* [2006] EWHC 94 (Admin), [2006] 2 All ER 16, 170 JP 45).

Loss of consciousness falls within the meaning of "actual bodily harm" since it involves an injurious impairment of the victim's sensory functions and it is axiomatic that the harm is "actual" (*R (on the application of T) v Director of Public Prosecutions* [2003] EWHC 266 (Admin), [2003] Crim LR 622).

The phrase "actual bodily harm" is capable of including psychiatric injury. But it does not include mere emotions such as fear or distress or panic, nor does it include, as such, states of mind that are not themselves evidence of some identifiable clinical condition (*R v Chan-Fook* [1994] 2 All ER 552, [1994] 1 WLR 689, [1994] Crim LR 432). The making of a telephone call followed by silence, or a series of telephone calls, is capable of amounting to an assault occasioning actual bodily harm if the calls make the victims apprehensive and cause them psychological damage (*R v Ireland* [1997] 4 All ER 225, [1997] 3 WLR 534, 161 JP 569 HL). Where the victim claims to have suffered physical pain as a result of the defendant's non-physical assault the court must have the benefit of psychiatric evidence as to whether such injury could be caused by the defendant's conduct (*R v Morris* [1998] 1 Cr App Rep 386).

3. This offence is triable either way (Magistrates' Courts Act 1980, Sch 1). For procedure, see ibid, ss 17A–21, in PART I: MAGISTRATES' COURTS, PROCEDURE, ante.

Bigamy

8–23117 **57. Bigamy.** Whosoever, being married[1], shall marry[2] any other person during the life of the former husband or wife, whether the second marriage shall have taken place in England or Ireland or[3] elsewhere shall be guilty of [an offence], and being convicted thereof shall be liable to imprisonment for any term not exceeding **seven years**[8];

Provided that nothing in this section contained shall extend to any second marriage contracted elsewhere than in England and Ireland by any other than a subject of Her Majesty[4], or to any person marrying a second time, whose husband or wife shall have been continually absent from such person for the space of seven years[5] then last past, and shall not have been known[6] by such person to be living within that time[7] or shall extend to any person who, at the time of such second marriage, shall have been divorced from the bond of the first marriage, or to any person whose former marriage shall have been declared void by the sentence of any court of competent jurisdiction.

[Offences Against the Person Act 1861, s 57 as amended by the Criminal Justice Act 1925, Sch 3, the Criminal Justice Act 1948, s 1 and the Criminal Law Act 1967, s 1 and Sch 3.]

---

1. W was convicted of bigamy in marrying B, he subsequently married C, and in her lifetime married D, and was again indicted for marrying D in the lifetime of C. For the defence the previous conviction was proved, and the judge ruled that it lay on the prisoner to prove that his first wife was alive when he married D and C. The CCR held that the onus of proof that the first wife was dead at the time of the marriage with C was on the prosecution, and quashed the conviction (*R v Willshire* (1881) 6 QBD 366, 45 JP 375). Where a prisoner charged with bigamy alleged that his first marriage was invalid on the ground that when he married, his first wife had a husband living, the Common Sergeant held that it was for the prisoner, after the prosecution had proved his two marriages, to prove that the first husband was alive at the time of his (the prisoner's) first marriage (*R v Thomson* (1905) 70 JP 6), or for the accused to prove as a defence that at the time of the second marriage he had reasonable cause to believe, and honestly believed, that his first marriage was void on the ground that the woman he then married was already married (*R v Dolman* [1949] 1 All ER 813); applied, *R v King* [1964] 1 QB 285, [1963] 3 All ER 561. The relevant time for determining whether a person was married within the meaning of s 57 is the time of the alleged bigamous marriage (*R v Sagoo* [1975] QB 885, [1975] 2 All ER 926, 139 JP 604, CA).

The first marriage must be strictly proved by production of the certificate of the registrar of marriages; an admission by the prisoner is insufficient (*R v Lindsay* (1902) 66 JP 505). The wife or husband of a person charged with bigamy may be called as a witness either for the prosecution or defence and without the consent of the person charged (Criminal Justice Administration Act 1914, s 28(3)), but as he or she at the trial may elect not to give evidence, it is advisable to call another witness to prove the first marriage.

2. When a married man went through the form of a marriage with his wife's niece, the offence was held to be bigamy, although such marriage would have been void as being within the prohibited degree of affinity (*R v Allen* (1872) LR 1 CCR 367, 36 JP 820). The validity of the second marriage is immaterial (*R v Robinson* [1938] 1 All ER 301). So also when a married man married a woman under a false Christian name, and there was no evidence whether the woman knew of the name being false, a conviction was affirmed (*R v Rea* (1872) LR 1 CCR 365, 36 JP 422).

Where a prisoner alleges that, at the time of his second marriage, he *bona fide* believed that his first marriage was invalid, he must prove that he had such a belief and circumstances justify it (*R v Thomson* (1905) 70 JP 6). This decision was followed in *R v Connatty* (1919) 83 JP 292 and applied by the Court of Criminal Appeal in *R v King* [1964] 1 QB 285, [1963] 3 All ER 561, *R v Wheat, infra*, distinguished, An erroneous, but *bona fide*, belief on reasonable grounds, that the accused had been divorced is no defence. Dictum in *R v Thomson, supra*, doubted (*R v Stocks* [1921] 2 KB 119, 85 JP 203).

3. The English courts have jurisdiction to try a British subject for bigamy where the bigamous marriage takes place in a foreign country (*R v Earl Russell* [1901] AC 446). In order to prove a foreign marriage (other than in civil cases (*Spivack v Spivack* (1930) 94 JP 91)), expert evidence—by a professional lawyer, or a person peritus virtute officii (*R v Moscovitch* (1927) 138 LT 183)—must be adduced, whether the prisoner relies on it for his defence or the Crown relies on it in a prosecution for bigamy (*R v Naguib* [1917] 1 KB 359, 81 JP 116); Scotland is a foreign country (*R v Povey* (1852) Dears CC 32, 16 JP 745). As to proof of irregular marriages in Scotland, see 172 LTN 246. An Irish marriage, celebrated prior to 1922, may be proved by certified copies of the register (Marriages (Ireland) Act 1844; Registration of Marriages (Ireland) Act 1863), but, if since 1922, it must be proved as a foreign marriage (*Todd v Todd* [1961] 2 All ER 881). A Colonial marriage should be proved by an expert in the law of the colony, unless celebrated according to the rites of the Church of England (*Perry v Perry* [1920] P 361). By Orders made under the Evidence (Foreign, Dominion and Colonial Documents) Act 1933 (amended by the Oaths and Evidence (Overseas Authorities and Countries) Act 1963, s 5), duly authenticated certificates of entries in public registers in Belgium, France and Australia may be admitted in evidence (see *Practice Direction* [1955] 2 All ER 465, [1955] 1 WLR 668, *Motture v Motture* [1955] 3 All ER 242n, [1955] 1 WLR 1066). Similar Orders in respect of other parts of the Commonwealth are listed in Halsbury's Statutory Instruments, Vol 7, EVIDENCE, and Supplement.

4. It is not necessary to aver in the indictment that the prisoner is a subject of Her Majesty (*R v Audley* [1907] 1 KB 383, 71 JP 101).

5. The defence of seven years' absence of the lawful husband or wife continues to be available in relation to a third or subsequent "marriage" (*R v Taylor* [1950] 2 KB 368, [1950] 2 All ER 170).

6. *Bona fide* belief on reasonable grounds in the death of the husband or wife before the second marriage is a good defence although the seven years have not expired. This case was reserved for the consideration of all the judges (*R v Tolson* (1889) 23 QBD 168, 54 JP 4): and an honest and reasonable belief that at the time of the second ceremony the first marriage had been dissolved is a defence to bigamy (*R v Gould* [1968] 2 QB 65, [1968] 1 All ER 849, 132 JP 209).

7. The husband had not been heard of for seventeen years, but it was incumbent on the prosecution to prove that he was alive at the date of the second marriage, it being a question of fact (*R v Lumley* (1869) LR 1 CCR 196, 33 JP 326). The burden of proof as to the knowledge of the prisoner that his first wife was alive within seven years of the second marriage, where the parties had separated *by consent*, was in *R v Curgerwen* (1865) LR 1 CCR 1, 29 JP 820 (followed in *R v Lund* (1921) 16 Cr App Rep 31; and *R v Peake* (1922) 17 Cr App Rep 22), held to be on the prosecution. Cf *Parkinson v Parkinson* [1939] 3 All ER 108. Also when the absence is caused through wilful desertion and such absence is proved, it

lies on the prosecution to show not merely that the person charged had the means of knowledge, but that he or she knew that the first wife or husband, as the case may be, was living (per KENNEDY, J, *R v Faulkes* (1903) 19 TLR 250). But in *R v Jones* (1883) 11 QBD 118, 47 JP 535, where prisoner was married in 1865, and went through a ceremony of marriage with another woman in 1882, and there was no evidence how long the married parties lived together or when they last saw each other, it was held not necessary to prove affirmatively that at the time of the second marriage the prisoner knew his first wife was alive, and prisoner was rightly convicted.

8. Triable either way; see Magistrates' Courts Act 1980, s 17 and Sch 1, also ss 17A–21 (procedure) and s 32 (penalty) in PART I: MAGISTRATES' COURTS, PROCEDURE, ante. In *R v Crowhurst* [1979] Crim LR 399, the Court of Appeal held that sentences for bigamy must vary in accordance with the circumstances of the case; where there was deception of the innocent party, with some injury resulting, an immediate custodial sentence was necessary, the length depending on the gravity of the injury inflicted. In other cases a non-custodial sentence might be appropriate. Justices' clerks have been asked by Home Office Circular Letter of 17th February 1981 to notify the General Register Office of all convictions in magistrates' courts of bigamy. Notification by way of a copy of the certificate of conviction or finding of guilt should be sent, together with, if available, the addresses of the defendant and the person with whom the bigamous marriage was contracted to the Marriage Section, General Register Office, St Catherine's House, 10 Kingsway, London, WC2B 6JP.

Attempts to procure Abortion[1]

8–23118 **58. Administering drugs or using instruments to procure abortion.** Every woman being with child who, with intent to procure her own[2] miscarriage, shall unlawfully administer to herself any poison or other noxious[3] thing, or shall unlawfully use any instrument or other means whatsoever with the like intent, and whosoever with intent[4] to procure the miscarriage[5] of any woman, whether she be or be not with child, shall unlawfully administer to her or cause to be taken by her any poison or other noxious thing, or shall unlawfully[6] use any instrument or other means whatsoever with the like intent[7] shall be guilty of [an offence], and being convicted thereof shall be liable to imprisonment for life.

[Offences Against the Person Act 1861, s 58 as amended by the Statute Law Revision Act 1892, the Statute Law Revision (No 2) Act 1893,the Criminal Justice Act 1948, s 1 and the Criminal Law Act 1967, s 1.

---

1. These sections should be read in conjunction with the Abortion Act 1967, post.

2. When the woman is charged it is necessary to show that she was actually with child, which is not necessary where another person is charged with the offence, but she may be charged with conspiring with others to commit the offence although not in fact pregnant (see *R v Whitchurch* (1890) 24 QBD 420, 54 JP 472). A person who consents to another using an instrument upon her with intent to procure miscarriage can be convicted of aiding and abetting the felony under the second part of the section, although there is no allegation in the indictment that the accused was "with child" at the time of the offence (*R v Sockett* (1908) 72 JP 428). A conviction may be affirmed, although there is no proof that the stuff given was noxious otherwise than from its effects (*R v Hollis* (1873) 37 JP 582).

3. The offence is complete if the thing is noxious "as administered", although innoxious if differently administered (*R v Cramp* (1880) 5 QBD 307, 44 JP 411). Taking a thing in the belief that it is capable of procuring abortion, though in fact it is not, is an attempt to commit the crime (*R v Brown* (1899) 63 JP 790). Inciting a woman to take the thing believing it to be capable of procuring abortion is inciting her to commit the offence, although the commission of the offence in the manner proposed is impossible (*id.*). Where the accused was indicted for attempting to administer noxious things to a pregnant woman, and for inciting her to attempt to administer to herself noxious things with intent to procure her own miscarriage, ROWLATT, J, directed the jury that the substantial question was whether the things were noxious in the sense of being abortives to the knowledge of the accused (*R v Osborn* (1919) 84 JP 63).

4. Evidence of the use of instruments with intent to procure abortion on previous occasions was admitted to prove a systematic course of conduct on the part of the prisoner, and the intent with which the prisoner used the instruments (*R v Bond* (1906) 2 KB 389, 70 JP 424). An accomplice's evidence of a previous operation (*R v Lovegrove* [1920] 3 KB 643, 85 JP 75), and also, on a charge of administering under this section, of the use of instruments on another occasion, has been admitted (*R v Starkie* [1922] 2 KB 275, 86 JP 74).

5. The 'morning-after pill' is not an abortificiant and does not procure a miscarriage as it prevents fertilisation or implantation and the word 'miscarriage' presupposes that the fertilized ovum has become implanted in the uterus (*R (Smeaton) v Secretary of State for Health* [2002] EWHC 610 (Admin), [2002] 2 FCR 193, [2002] 2 FLR 146).

6. If a doctor using his best judgment comes to the opinion that the continuance of the pregnancy will endanger the life of the mother or make her a physical or mental wreck, he is not only entitled, but it is his duty, to perform the operation, and the operation will not be unlawful. The onus is on the prosecution to prove the negative beyond reasonable doubt. The desire of the woman to be relieved of her pregnancy is no justification (charge of MACNAGHTEN, J, to the jury in *R v Bourne* [1939] 1 KB 687, [1938] 3 All ER 615).

7. Upon the trial for murder or manslaughter of any child or for infanticide or for abortion, the jury may find the accused guilty of child destruction (Infant Life (Preservation) Act 1929, s 2(2)).

8–23119 **59. Procuring drugs etc to cause abortion.** Whosoever shall unlawfully supply or procure[1] any poison or other noxious thing, or any instrument or thing whatsoever, knowing that the same is intended[2] to be unlawfully used or employed with intent to procure the miscarriage[3] of any woman, whether she be or be not with child shall be guilty of [an offence], and being convicted thereof shall be liable to imprisonment not exceeding **five years**.

[Offences Against the Person Act 1861, s 59 as amended by the Statute Law Revision Act 1892, the Criminal Justice Act 1948 s 1 and the Criminal Law Act 1967, s 1.]

---

1. In this context, the word "procure" has its ordinary meaning of getting possession of something from another person (*R v Mills* [1963] 1 QB 522, [1963] 1 All ER 202, 127 JP 176).

2. It is not necessary that the woman herself whose miscarriage it is intended to procure should intend to use the drug, or that any other person than the one who procured the drug should intend it to be used for the purpose of procuring a miscarriage (*R v Hillman* (1863) Le & Ca 343, 27 JP 805).

3. See note to 'miscarriage' in s 58, ante.

Concealing the Birth of a Child

8–23120 **60. Concealing the birth of a child.** If any woman[1] shall be delivered of a child, every person who shall by any secret disposition of the dead body[2] of the said child, whether such child died before, at, or after its birth, endeavour to conceal the birth[3] thereof shall be guilty of [an offence] and being convicted thereof shall be liable[4] to be imprisoned for any term not exceeding **two years**.

[Offences Against the Person Act 1861, s 60 as amended by the Criminal Justice Act 1948, s 1 and the Criminal Law Act 1967, s 1 and Schs 2 and 3.]

1. There is no authority to order surgical examination of a woman's person. An action was successfully brought upon such an order against a justice and two doctors (*Agnew v Jobson* (1877) 42 JP 424, Treat 434). But if the woman submit to the examination, although reluctantly, it must be shown that what was done was against her will, in the absence of evidence of force, violence, or coercion (*Latter v Braddell* (1881) 45 JP 520).

2. The concealment must be from a desire to keep the world at large in ignorance of the birth, and not from a desire to escape individual anger (*R v Morris* (1848) 2 Cox CC 489). There must be a concealment of the fact of birth, and that concealment must be carried out by the secret disposition of the dead body (*R v Rosenberg* (1906) 70 JP 264). The place of concealment need not be intended as the final deposit. Placing the dead body between the bed and the mattress was held under the repealed statutes to be a sufficient disposition of the body (see *R v Goldthorpe* (1841) Car & M 335, and *R v Perry* (1855) Dears CC 471). Throwing the dead body over a wall into a field, such wall forming the boundary of the yard of a public-house, was held to be evidence of "secret disposition" (*R v Brown* (1870) LR 1 CCR 244, 34 JP 436, 22 LT 484). Although placing the dead body in an unlocked box is not of itself sufficient evidence of concealment, all the attendant circumstances may be taken into consideration (*R v Cook* (1870) 22 LT 216). Under the present statute any "secret disposition" is sufficient, and this section is so framed as to include every person who uses any endeavours to conceal the birth, and it is immaterial whether "there be any evidence against the mother or not". A woman who endeavours to conceal the birth by depositing the child, while alive, in a field, leaving the infant to die from exposure, cannot be convicted under this section, which relates to the secret disposition of the *dead* body of a child (*R v May* (1867) 31 JP 356).

3. An indictment for endeavouring to conceal the birth failed for want of proof of the child's death (*R v Bell* (1874) Ir R 8 CL 542); also for insufficient evidence to identify the body found as the child of which the woman was said to have been delivered (*R v Williams* (1871) 11 Cox CC 684). The confession of the accused is sufficient evidence to convict for concealment of birth, although no dead body is found (per RIDLEY, J, *R v Kersey* (1908) 21 Cox CC 690).

4. Triable either way; see Magistrates' Courts Act 1980, s 17 and Sch 1, also ss 17A–21 (procedure) and s 32 (penalty) in PART I: MAGISTRATES' COURTS, PROCEDURE, ante.

Making Gunpowder to commit offences and searching for the same

8–23121 **64. Making or having gunpowder etc with intent to commit offence.** Whosoever shall knowingly have in his possession, or make or manufacture[1] any gunpowder, explosive substance, or any dangerous or noxious thing, or any machine, engine, instrument, or thing, with intent, by means thereof, to commit, or for the purpose of enabling any other person to commit, any offence mentioned in this Act[2] shall be guilty of an offence and on being convicted thereof shall be liable, at the discretion of the court, to be imprisoned for any term not exceeding **two years**.

[Offences Against the Person Act 1861, s 64 as amended by the Statute Law Revision (No 2) Act 1893, the Criminal Justice Act 1948, Sch 10, the Sexual Offences Act 1956, Sch 4 and the Criminal Law Act 1967, s 10 and Sch 2.]

1. See also Explosive Substances Act 1883, ss 3, 4, in this PART: title HEALTH AND SAFETY, ante.

2. S 65 empowers a justice to grant a search warrant for the purposes of s 64.

Infant Life (Preservation) Act 1929

(19 & 20 Geo 5 c 34)

8–23230 **1. Punishment for child destruction**[1]. (1) Subject as hereinafter in this subsection provided, any person who, with intent to destroy the life of a child capable of being born alive[2], by any wilful act causes a child to die before it has an existence independent of its mother, shall be guilty of child destruction and shall be liable on conviction thereof on indictment to imprisonment for **life:** Provided that no person shall be found guilty of an offence under this section unless it is proved that the act which caused the death of the child was not done in good faith for the purpose only of preserving the life of the mother[3].

(2) For the purposes of this Act, evidence that a woman had at any material time been pregnant for a period of twenty-eight weeks or more shall be *prima facie* proof that she was at that time pregnant of a child capable of being born alive.

[Infant Life (Preservation) Act 1929, s 1.]

1. See also the Infanticide Act 1938, post, and the Offences Against the Person Act 1861 ss 58, 59 (abortion). On the trial of a person charged with murder or manslaughter of a child or with infanticide there may be a verdict of guilty of child destruction (Infant Life (Preservation) Act 1929 s 2(2), and on a trial for child destruction there may be a verdict of guilty under s 58 of the 1861 Act (Infant Life (Preservation) Act 1929, s 2(3)).

2. A foetus of between 18 and 21 weeks which if delivered by hysterotomy would never be capable of breathing either naturally or artificially, is not a "child capable of being born alive"; abortion thereof would not constitute an offence under this section (*C v S* [1988] QB 135, [1987] 1 All ER 1230, [1987] 2 FLR 505, CA).

3. See *R v Bourne* [1939] 1 KB 687, [1938] 3 All ER 615, noted to Offences Against the Person Act 1861, s 58, ante.

Infanticide Act 1938

(1 & 2 Geo 6 c 36)

8–23240 1. Offence of infanticide. (1) Where a woman by any wilful act or omission causes the death of her child being a child under the age of twelve months, but at the time of the act or omission the balance of her mind was disturbed by reason of her not having fully recovered from the effect of giving birth to the child or by reason of the effect of lactation consequent upon the birth of the child, then, notwithstanding that the circumstances were such that but for this Act the offence would have amounted to murder, she shall be guilty of infanticide[1], and may for such offence be dealt with and punished as if she had been guilty of the offence of manslaughter of the child.

(2) Where upon the trial of a woman for the murder of her child, being a child under the age of twelve months, the jury are of opinion that she by any wilful act or omission caused its death, but at the time of the act or omission the balance of her mind was disturbed by reason of her not having fully recovered from the effect of giving birth to the child or by reason of the effect of lactation consequent upon the birth of the child, then the jury may, notwithstanding that the circumstances were such that but for the provisions of this Act they might have returned a verdict of murder, return in lieu thereof a verdict of infanticide[1].

[Infanticide Act 1938, s 1(1), (2).]

1. On a trial of a person for infanticide there may be a verdict of child destruction; see the Infant Life (Preservation) Act 1929, s 2(2). A coroner's inquest is not to find a person guilty of infanticide; Criminal Law Act 1977, s 56. The Consent of the Attorney-General will be required to institute proceedings where the mother has previously been convicted of an offence committed in circumstances alleged to be connected with the death (Law Reform (Year and a Day Rule) Act 1996, s 2(2)*(b)*.

Homicide Act 1957

(5 & 6 Eliz 2 c 11)

Murder[1]

8–23250 1. Abolition of "constructive malice". (1) Where a person kills another in the course of furtherance of some other offence, the killing shall not amount to murder unless done with the same malice aforethought (express or implied[2]) as is required for a killing to amount to murder when not done in the course or furtherance of another offence.

(2) For the purposes of the foregoing subsection, a killing done in the course or for the purpose of resisting an officer of justice, or of resisting or avoiding or preventing a lawful arrest, or of effecting or assisting an escape or rescue from legal custody, shall be treated as a killing in the course or furtherance of an offence.

[Homicide Act 1957, s 1.]

1. **Murder** is an offence at common law, For manslaughter, see the Offences Against the Person Act 1861 s 5 ante.

Death may be proved by circumstantial evidence, although no body is found (*R v Onufrejczyk* [1955] 1 QB 388, [1955] 1 All ER 247). In charges of murder, the Crown must prove *(a)* death as a result of the voluntary act of the accused, and *(b)* malice of the accused; malice is a question for the jury, and, if the jury are satisfied with the prisoner's explanation, or, on a review of all the evidence, are left in reasonable doubt whether, even if his explanation is not accepted, the act was unintentional or provoked, the prisoner is entitled to be acquitted (*Woolmington v DPP* [1935] AC 462, HL; explained in *Mancini v DPP* [1942] AC 1, [1941] 3 All ER 272, HL). The defence of duress is not available to a person charged with murder whether as principal in the first degree (the actual killer) or as a principal in the second degree (the aider and abettor) (*R v Howe* [1987] AC 417, [1987] 1 All ER 771). Common sense standards apply when considering the defence of self-defence, in deciding whether more force was used than was necessary in the circumstances; see *R v Shannon* [1980] Crim LR 438 and *R Oatridge* [1992] Crim LR 205 (which also deals with mistaken belief). In order to reduce a charge of murder to manslaughter, it has to be shown that the provocative conduct relied on had suddenly and temporarily deprived the accused of the power of self-control (*R v Thornton* [1992] 1 All ER 306), 96 Cr App Rep 112).

Manslaughter may be committed where unlawful injury is deliberately inflicted either to a child in utero or to a mother carrying a child in utero. The fact that the death of the child is caused solely in consequence of injury to the mother rather than as a consequence of injury to the foetus does not negative any liability for manslaughter (*A-G's Reference (No 3 of 1994)* [1998] 1 Cr App Rep 91, [1997] Crim LR 829, HL).

If the injury caused by the accused causes death, it matters not that the victim might have survived had he not refused a blood transfusion; persons who use violence must take their victims as they find them (*R v Blaue* [1975] 3 All ER 446, 139 JP 841). Where supervening events occur which may have had some causative effect leading to the victim's death, the prosecution must prove that the injuries inflicted by the defendant were a significant cause of death (*R v Mellor* [1996] 2 Cr App Rep 245, [1996] Crim LR 743, CA).

Intent: Before an act can be murder, it must be "aimed at someone" and in addition must be committed with (1) intention to cause death or (2) intention to cause grievous bodily harm or (3) intention to expose someone to a known serious risk of death or grievous bodily harm resulting from acts committed deliberately and without lawful excuse. It does not matter whether the defendant desired those consequences or not, nor that the act and intention were aimed at someone other than the eventual victim. Without one of the three types of intention, however, the mere fact that the defendant acts in the knowledge that grievous bodily harm is likely, or highly likely to ensue is not by itself enough to constitute murder (*Hyam v DPP* [1975] AC 55, [1974] 2 All ER 41, 138 JP 374, HL). Knowledge or foresight of consequences is at best material from which the jury, properly directed, may infer intention when considering a crime of specific intent, such as murder (*R v Moloney* [1985] AC 905, [1985] 1 All ER 1025, 149 JP 369, HL; considered in *R v Hancock and R v Shankland*) [1986] AC 455, [1986] 1 All ER 641, 150 JP 33). For proof of criminal intent, see the Criminal Law Act 1967, s 8 in PART I: MAGISTRATES' COURTS, PROCEDURE, ante. A coroner's inquest is not to find a person guilty of murder; Criminal Law Act 1977, s 56. In the case of a joint enterprise, proof is necessary that the principal party intended to kill or do serious harm at the time he killed; the secondary party must be proved to have lent himself to a criminal enterprise involving the inflicting, if necessary, of serious harm or death or have had an express or tacit understanding with the principal party that such harm or death should, if necessary, be inflicted (*R v Slack* [1989] QB 775, [1989] 3 All ER 90, CA). See also *R v Roberts* [1993] 1 All ER 583, (1993) Cr App Rep 291. As to withdrawal from a joint enterprise *R v Rook* [1993] 2 All ER 955.

Procedure: The former common law rule that for the purposes of offences involving death and of suicide, an act or omission was conclusively presumed not to have caused a person's death if more than a year and a day elapsed before he died has been abolished (Law Reform (Year and a Day Rule) Act 1996, s 1). Proceedings in respect of an allegation of murder, manslaughter, infanticide or any other offence of which one of the elements is causing a person's death or aiding, abetting, counselling or procuring a person's suicide where the injury alleged to have caused the death was sustained more than three years before the death occurred or the person has previously been convicted of an offence committed in circumstances alleged to be connected with the death, may only be instituted by or with the consent of the Attorney General (s 2).

For the obligation placed on the clerk to the justices to notify the coroner, who is responsible for holding an inquest, or the making of a charge of murder, manslaughter or infanticide and of the result of the proceedings before the court, see the Coroners Act 1988, s 17, in this PART, title CORONERS, ante. If it appears to the court from a written statement of means furnished by the accused that his means are such that he requires assistance in meeting the costs of legal representation, he must be granted representation on committal for trial for murder (Legal Aid Act 1988, s 21); and he may be granted representation (which may include representation by counsel) for the committal proceedings; see the Legal Aid in Criminal and Care Proceedings (General) Regulations 1989, regs 40, 44 and 48 in PART I: MAGISTRATES' COURTS, PROCEDURE, ante.

In *R v Vernege* [1982] 1 All ER 403, [1982] 1 WLR 293 the Court of Appeal stated that in committal proceedings for murder, a proper consideration for the magistrates to take into account when considering bail is that in his own interests the accused should be examined by a prison doctor so that the various relevant matters affecting his state of mind at the time of the offence may be considered by the doctor, and in particular the possibility of a defence of diminished responsibility.

2. Implied malice will arise where the act of the accused which causes death is voluntary and done with intent to cause grievous bodily harm. A court is not bound to infer that a person intended or foresaw a result of his actions by reason only of its being a natural or probable consequence thereof, but shall decide whether he did intend or foresee that result from all the evidence, drawing from the evidence such inferences as appear to be proper: see Criminal Justice Act 1967, s 8, ante.

8–23251 **2. Persons suffering from diminished responsibility.** (1) Where a person kills or is a party to the killing of another, he shall not be convicted of murder if he was suffering from such abnormality of mind (whether arising from a condition of arrested or retarded development of mind or any inherent causes or induced by disease or injury) as substantially impaired his mental responsibility[1] for his acts and omissions in doing or being a party to the killing.

(2) On a charge of murder, it shall be for the defence to prove[2] that the person charged is by virtue of this section not liable to be convicted of murder.

(3) A person who but.for this section would be liable, whether as principal or as accessory, to be convicted of murder shall be liable instead to be convicted of manslaughter.

(4) The fact that one party to a killing is by virtue of this section not liable to be convicted of murder shall not affect the question whether the killing amounted to murder in the case of any other party to it.

[Homicide Act 1957, s 2.]

---

1. It is not appropriate to consider only partial or borderline insanity as amounting to diminished responsibility (*R v Seers* (1984) 149 JP 124, [1985] Crim LR 315, CA).

2. The presumption of innocence given effect in article of the European Convention of Human Rights, is not breached by this provision which places the burden on the defendant to prove certain facts to establish a defence (*R v Lambert* [2001] UKHL 37, [2002] 2 AC 545, [2001] 3 All ER 577, [2001] 3 WLR 206).

8–23252 **3. Provocation.** Where on a charge of murder there is evidence on which the jury can find that the person charged was provoked (whether by things done or by things said or by both together) to lose his self-control, the question whether the provocation was enough to make a reasonable man do as he did shall be left to be determined by the jury; and in determining the question the jury shall take into account everything both done and said according to the effect which, in their opinion, it would have on a reasonable man[1].

[Homicide Act 1957, s 3.]

---

1. For the purposes of s 3 the jury is allowed to take into account not only those characteristics of the accused which are relevant to the gravity of the provocation but also those which affect his powers of self-control. However, not everything which causes loss of self-control is necessarily capable of being an acceptable reason for such loss of control. The law expects people to exercise control over their emotions and a tendency to violent rages or childish tantrums is a defect in character rather than an excuse. Before a defence of provocation can be made out, the jury has to think that the circumstances were such as to make the loss of self-control sufficiently excusable to reduce the gravity of the offence from murder to manslaughter. In deciding what should count as a sufficient excuse, the jury has to apply what they consider to be appropriate standards of behaviour; on the one hand making allowance for human nature and the power of the emotions but, on the other hand, not allowing someone to rely on his own violent disposition. The general principle is that the same standards of behaviour are expected of everyone, regardless of their individual psychological make-up. But this is a principle not a rigid rule and so where the jury think there was some characteristic of the accused, whether temporary or permanent, which affected the degree of control which society could reasonably have expected of *him* and which it would be unjust not to take into account, they may give effect to it (*R v Smith* [2000] 4 All ER 289, [2000] 3 WLR 654, [2001] 1 Cr App Rep 31, HL). As the jury may take into account all matters relating to whether the defendant should reasonably

have controlled himself, they may consider the kind of man the defendant was and his mental state (*R v Weller* [2003] EWCA Crim 815, [2004] 1 Cr App Rep 1, [2003] Crim LR 724).

8–23253 **4. Suicide pacts.** (1) It shall be manslaughter, and shall not be murder, for a person acting in pursuance of a suicide pact between him and another to kill the other or be a party to the other being killed by a third person.

(2) Where it is shown that a person charged with the murder of another killed the other or was a party to his being killed, it shall be for the defence to prove that the person charged was acting in pursuance of a suicide pact between him and the other.

(3) For the purposes of this section "suicide pact" means a common agreement between two or more persons having for its object the death of all of them, whether or not each is to take his own life, but nothing done by a person who enters into a suicide pact shall be treated as done by him in pursuance of the pact unless it is done while he has the settled intention of dying in pursuance of the pact.

[Homicide Act 1957, s 4, as amended by Suicide Act 1961, s 3(2) and 2nd Sch.]

Suicide Act 1961

(9 & 10 Eliz 2 c 60)

8–23270 **1. Suicide to cease to be a crime.** The rule of law whereby it is a crime for a person to commit suicide is hereby abrogated.

[Suicide Act 1961, s 1.]

8–23271 **2. Criminal liability for complicity in another's suicide.** (1) A person[1] who aids, abets, counsels or procures the suicide of another, or an attempt by another to commit suicide, shall be liable on conviction on indictment to imprisonment for a term not exceeding fourteen years[2].

(2) If on the trial of an indictment for murder or manslaughter it is proved that the accused aided, abetted, counselled or procured the suicide of the person in question, the jury may find him guilty of that offence.

(3) The enactments mentioned in the first column of the First Schedule to this Act shall have effect subject to the amendments provided for in the second column (which preserve in relation to offences under this section the previous operation of those enactments in relation to murder or manslaughter)[3].

(4) No proceedings shall be instituted for an offence under this section except by or with the consent of the Director of Public Prosecutions[4].

[Suicide Act 1961, s 2, as amended by the Criminal Jurisdiction Act 1975, Sch 6.]

---

1. As every attempt to commit an offence is an offence at common law, a person may be properly charged with attempting to aid, abet, counsel or procure the suicide (*R v McShane* (1977) 66 Cr App Rep 97). For consideration as to the circumstances when distribution of a booklet containing advice on committing suicide may constitute an offence, see *A-G v Able* [1984] QB 795, [1984] 1 All ER 277.

2. For the obligation placed on the clerk to the justices to notify the coroner, who is responsible for holding an inquest where a death has occurred, of a charge under s 2(1) and of the result of the proceedings before the magistrates' court, see the Coroners Act 1988, 17, title Coroners, ante.

3. So far as is relevant to this work, the Act has been noted to the enactments affected by the First Schedule.

4. The consent of the Attorney General will be required instead of that of the Director of Public Prosecutions in the circumstances prescribed in s 2 of the Law Reform (Year and a Day Rule) Act 1996, see note to the Homicide Act 1957, s 1, ante.

Section 2(4) does not give the Director power to give an undertaking that he will not prosecute an offence under s 2 yet to be committed; his discretion can only be exercised in respect of past events giving rise to a suspicion of the commission of an offence under the section (*R (on the application of Pretty) v DPP* [2001] UKHL 61, [2002] 1 AC 800, [2002] 1 All ER 1, [2002] 1 FCR 1).

Abortion Act 1967

(1967 c 87)

8–23290 **1. Medical termination of pregnancy.** (1) Subject to the provisions of this section, a person shall not be guilty of an offence under the law relating to abortion[1], when a pregnancy is terminated by a registered medical practitioner[2] if two registered medical practitioners are of the opinion, formed in good faith[3]—

(*a*) that the pregnancy has not exceeded its twenty-fourth week and that the continuance of the pregnancy would involve risk, greater than if the pregnancy were terminated, of injury to the physical or mental health of the pregnant woman or any existing children of her family; or

(*b*) that the termination is necessary to prevent grave permanent injury to the physical or mental health of the pregnant woman; or

(*c*) that the continuance of the pregnancy would involve risk to the life of the pregnant woman, greater than if the pregnancy were terminated; or (*d*) that there is a substantial risk that if the child were born it would suffer from such physical or mental abnormalities as to be seriously handicapped.

(2) In determining whether the continuance of a pregnancy would involve such risk of injury to health as is mentioned in paragraph (*a*) or (*b*) of subsection (1) of this section, account may be taken of the pregnant woman's actual or reasonably foreseeable environment.

(3) Except as provided by subsection (4) of this section, any treatment for the termination of pregnancy must be carried out in a hospital vested in the Secretary of State for the purposes of his functions under the National Health Service Act 1977 or the National Health Service (Scotland) Act 1978 or in a hospital vested in a Primary Care Trust or a National Health Service trust or in a place approved for the purposes of this section by the Secretary of State.*

(3A) The power under subsection (3) of this section to approve a place includes power, in relation to treatment consisting primarily in the use of such medicines as may be specified in the approval and carried out in such manner as may be so specified, to approve a class of places.

(4) Subsection (3) of this section, and so much of subsection (1) as relates to the opinion of two registered medical practitioners, shall not apply to the termination of a pregnancy by a registered medical practitioner in a case where he is of the opinion, formed in good faith, that the termination is immediately necessary to save the life or to prevent grave permanent injury to the physical or mental health of the pregnant woman.

[Abortion Act 1967, s 1, as amended by the Health Services Act 1980, Sch 1, the National Health Service and Community Care Act 1990, Sch 9, the Human Fertilisation and Embryology Act 1990, s 37 and SI 2000/90.]

***Amended by the Health and Social Care (Community Health and Standards) Act 2003, Sch 4, from a date to be appointed.**

1. Ie, ss 58 and 50 of the Offences Against the Person Act 1861, ante, and any rule of law relating to the procurement of abortion (s 6).

2. A pregnancy is "terminated by a registered medical practitioner" when the treatment prescribed and initiated by that practitioner, who remains in charge of it throughout, is carried out in accordance with his directions by qualified nursing staff entrusted with its execution in accordance with accepted medical practice (*Royal College of Nursing v Department of Health and Social Security* [1982] AC 800, [1981] 1 All ER 545.

3. The question of good faith must be determined on the total evidence and not just on the views of medical experts (*R v John Smith* [1974] 1 All ER 376, 138 JP 175).

8–23291 **2. Notification.** (1) The Minister of Health in respect of England and Wales, and the Secretary of State in respect of Scotland, shall by statutory instrument make regulations[1] to provide—

(*a*) for requiring any such opinion as is referred to in s 1 of this Act to be certified by the practitioners or practitioner concerned in such form and at such time as may be prescribed by the regulations, and for requiring the preservation and disposal of certificates made for the purposes of the regulations;

(*b*) for requiring any registered medical practitioner who terminates a pregnancy to give notice of the termination and such other information relating to the termination as may be so prescribed;

(*c*) for prohibiting the disclosure, except to such persons or for such purposes as may be so prescribed, of notices given or information furnished pursuant to the regulations.

(2) The information furnished in pursuance of regulations made by virtue of paragraph (*b*) of subsection (1) of this section shall be notified solely to the Chief Medical Officers of the Ministry of Health and the Scottish Administration respectively.

(3) Any person who wilfully contravenes or wilfully fails to comply with the requirements of regulations under subsection (1) of this section shall be liable on summary conviction to a fine not exceeding **level 5** on the standard scale.

(4) Any statutory instrument made by virtue of this section shall be subject to annulment in pursuance of a resolution of either House of Parliament.

[Abortion Act 1967, s 2, as amended by the Criminal Law Act 1977, Sch 6, the Criminal Justice Act 1982, s 46 and SI 1999/1042, Sch 3.]

1. See the Abortion Regulations 1991, post.

8–23292 **3. Application of Act to visiting forces, etc.** (1) In relation to the termination of a pregnancy in a case where the following conditions are satisfied, that is to say—

(*a*) the treatment for termination of the pregnancy was carried out in a hospital controlled by the proper authorities of a body to which this section applies; and

(*b*) the pregnant woman had at the time of the treatment a relevant association with that body; and

(*c*) the treatment was carried out by a registered medical practitioner or a person who at the time of the treatment was a member of that body appointed as a medical practitioner for that body by the proper authorities of that body,

this Act shall have effect as if any reference in s 1 to a registered medical practitioner and to a hospital vested in the Secretary of State included respectively a reference to such a person as is mentioned in paragraph *(c)* of this subsection and to a hospital controlled as aforesaid, and as if s 2 were omitted.

(2) The bodies to which this section applies are any force which is a visiting force within the meaning of any of the provisions of Part I of the Visiting Forces Act 1952 and any headquarters within the meaning of the Schedule to the International Headquarters and Defence Organisations Act 1964[1]; and for the purposes of this section—

(*a*) a woman shall be treated as having a relevant association at any time with a body to which this section applies if at that time—

(i) in the case of such a force as aforesaid, she had a relevant association within the meaning of the said Part I with the force; and

(ii) in the case of such a headquarters as aforesaid, she was a member of the headquarters or a dependant within the meaning of the Schedule aforesaid of such a member; and

(*b*) any reference to a member of a body to which this section applies shall be construed—

(i) in the case of such a force as aforesaid, as a reference to a member of or of a civilian component of that force within the meaning of the said Part I; and

(ii) in the case of such a headquarters as aforesaid, as a reference to a member of that headquarters within the meaning of the Schedule aforesaid.

[Abortion Act 1967, s 3, as amended by the Health Services Act 1980, Sch 1.]

1. See title ARMED FORCES, ante.

8–23293 **4. Conscientious objection to participation in treatment.** (1) Subject to subsection (2) of this section, no person shall be under any duty, whether by contract or by any statutory or other legal requirement, to participate in any treatment authorised by this Act to which he has a conscientious objection:

Provided that in any legal proceedings the burden of proof of conscientious objection shall rest on the person claiming to rely on it.

(2) Nothing in subsection (1) of this section shall affect any duty to participants in treatment which is necessary to save the life or to prevent grave permanent injury to the physical or mental health of a pregnant woman.

(3) (*Applies to Scotland.*)

[Abortion Act 1967, s 4.]

8–23294 **5. Supplementary provisions.** (1) No offence under the Infant Life (Preservation) Act 1929 shall be committed by a registered medical practitioner who terminates a pregnancy in accordance with the provisions of this Act.

(2) For the purposes of the law relating to abortion, anything done with intent to procure a woman's miscarriage (or, in the case of a woman carrying more than one foetus, her miscarriage of any foetus) is unlawfully done unless authorised by section 1 of this Act and, in the case of a woman carrying more than one foetus, anything done with intent to procure her miscarriage of any foetus is authorised by that section if—

(*a*) the ground for termination of the pregnancy specified in subsection (1)(*d*) of that section applies in relation to any foetus and the thing is done for the purpose of procuring the miscarriage of that foetus, or

(*b*) any of the other grounds for termination of the pregnancy specified in that section applies.

[Abortion Act 1967, s 5 as amended by the Human Fertilisation and Embryology Act 1990, s 37.]

Tattooing of Minors Act 1969

(1969 c 24)

8–23330 **1. Prohibition of tattooing of minors.** It shall be an offence to tattoo[1] a person under the age of eighteen except when the tattoo is performed for medical reasons by a qualified medical practitioner or by a person working under his direction, but it shall be a defence for a person charged to show that at the time the tattoo was performed he had reasonable cause to believe that the person tattooed was of or over the age of eighteen and did in fact so believe.

[Tattooing of Minors Act 1969, s 1.]

1. "Tattoo" means the insertion into the skin of any colouring material designed to leave a permanent mark (Tattooing of Minors Act, s 3).

8–23331 **2. Penalties.** Any person committing such an offence shall be liable to a fine not exceeding **level 3** on the standard scale.

[Tattooing of Minors Act 1969, s 2 as amended by the Criminal Justice Act 1982, ss 35, 38 and 46.]

Internationally Protected Persons Act 1978

(1978 c 17)

8–23350 This Act[1] implements the Convention on the prevention and punishment of crimes against Internationally Protected Persons adopted by the United Nations General Assembly in 1973. The Act provides that if a person, whether a citizen of the United Kingdom and Colonies or not, outside the United Kingdom—

(*a*) does any act in relation to a protected person (defined to include a Head of State, a Head of Government and an official representative of a State) which if done in the United Kingdom would have made him guilty of murder, manslaughter, rape, assault occasioning actual bodily harm or causing injury, kidnapping, abduction[2], false imprisonment, or certain offences under the Offences against the Person Act 1861 or s 2 of the Explosive Substances Act 1883, or

(*b*) in connection with an attack on premises or a vehicle, ordinarily used by a protected person, does any act which if done in the United Kingdom would have made him guilty of an offence under s 2 of the Explosive Substances Act 1883, or s 1 of the Criminal Damage Act 1971,

he shall in any part of the United Kingdom be guilty of the offences aforesaid of which the Act would have made him guilty if he had done it there. A person shall similarly be guilty of attempting or aiding, abetting, counselling or procuring the commission of such an offence. A person who threatens to commit, or attempts to threaten or aids, abets, counsels or procures the making of such a threat to commit such an offence shall be liable on conviction on indictment to imprisonment for a term not exceeding **ten years** and not exceeding the term of imprisonment to which a person would be liable for the offence constituted by doing the act threatened at the place where the contravention occurs[3].
[Internationally Protected Persons Act 1978, s 1—summarised.]

Proceedings for an offence which would not be an offence apart from the provisions of section 1 of the Act shall not be begun in England and Wales except by or with the consent of the Attorney General.
[Internationally Protected Persons Act 1978, s 2—summarised.]

1. Provision is also made by the Suppression of Terrorism Act 1978, title Extradition etc, ante, for giving United Kingdom courts jurisdiction with respect to offences committed outside the United Kingdom but in a convention country, and in particular offence against a protected person.

2. This reference to "abduction" shall be construed as not including an offence under s 1 of the Child Abduction Act 1984 (Child Abduction Act 1984, s 11(3)).

3. By virtue of the Extradition (Internationally Protected Persons) Order 1979, SI 1979/453 amended by SI 1982/147, SI 1985/1990, SI 1986/2013, SI 1987/454 and 2042 and SI 1988/2244 offences against internationally protected persons which are mentioned in s 1 are made extraditable offences for the purposes of the Extradition Act 1989 in the case of foreign States which are parties to the Convention.

Taking of Hostages Act 1982[1]

(1982 c 28)

8–23360 1. Hostage taking. (1) A person, whatever his nationality, who, in the United Kingdom or elsewhere,—

(*a*) detains any other person ("the hostage"), and

(*b*) in order to compel a State, international governmental organisation or person to do or abstain from doing any act, threatens to kill, injure or continue to detain the hostage,

commits an offence.

(2) A person guilty of an offence under this Act shall be liable, on conviction on indictment, to imprisonment for **life**.
[Taking of Hostages Act 1982, s 1.]

1. This Act came into force on 26th November 1982. The Extradition (Taking of Hostages) Order 1985, SI 1985/751 amended by SI 1985/1992, SI 1986/2015, SI 1987/455 and 2044 and SI 1988/2246, applies the Extradition Act 1989 so as to make extraditable the offences described in this Act and attempts to commit such offences, in the case of States Parties to the International Convention against the Taking of Hostages.

8–23361 2. Prosecution of offences. (1) Proceedings for an offence under this Act shall not be instituted—

(*a*) in England and Wales, except by or with the consent of the Attorney General; and

(*b*) *Northern Ireland.*

(2) *Scotland.*

(3) *Northern Ireland.*

[Taking of Hostages Act, 1982, s 2.]

8–23362 5. Application to Channel Islands, Isle of Man, etc[1].

1. The Taking of Hostages Act 1982 (Overseas Territories) Order 1982, SI 1992/1540 amended by SI 1987/455 applies the Act to certain named territories. See also SI 1982/1533 (Jersey), SI 1982/1539 (Guernsey) and SI 1982/1839 (Isle of Man).

Criminal Justice Act 1988[1]

(1988 c 33)

PART V[2]

JURISDICTION, IMPRISONMENT, FINES, ETC

Jurisdiction

8–23400 **39. Common assault and battery[3] to be summary offences[4].** Common assault and battery shall be summary offences and a person guilty of either of them shall be liable to a fine not exceeding **level 5** on the standard scale, to imprisonment for a term not exceeding **six months**, or to **both**[5].

[Criminal Justice Act 1988, s 39.]

1. For other provisions of the Criminal Justice Act 1988, see in particular PART I: MAGISTRATES' COURTS, PROCEDURE, ante.
2. Part V contains ss 37–40.
3. There are two offences, assault by threats and assault by beating (*DPP v Taylor, DPP v Little* [1992] QB 645, [1992] 1 All ER 299, 155 JP 713, DC). The threat of physical contact or the actual physical contact as the case may be, requires a mental element which is an intention, or recklessness causing another person to apprehend immediate and unlawful violence; see *R v Venna* [1976] QB 421, [1976] 3 All ER 788, CA.
4. An alternative verdict of guilty of common assault on an indictment charging assault occasioning actual bodily harm may not be brought unless the terms of s 40 of this Act (ante, PART I: MAGISTRATES' COURTS, PROCEDURE) are followed (*R v Mearns* [1991] 1 QB 82, [1990] 3 All ER 989, 154 JP 447).
5. Although it is not a necessary ingredient of an offence of common assault that the victim suffer injury, nevertheless the court should take into account, when considering the gravity of the offence and the appropriate sentence, the consequences to the victim. It is not necessary to prefer a more serious charge provided the court's sentencing powers are adequate to reflect the actual gravity of the offending (*R v Nottingham Crown Court, ex p DPP* [1996] 1 Cr App Rep (S) 283, [1995] Crim LR 902).

PART XI[1]

MISCELLANEOUS

Torture

8–23401 **134. Torture.** (1) A public official or person acting in an official capacity, whatever his nationality, commits the offence of torture if in the United Kingdom or elsewhere he intentionally inflicts severe pain or suffering on another in the performance or purported performance of his official duties.

(2) A person not falling within subsection (1) above commits the offence of torture, whatever his nationality, if—

(*a*) in the United Kingdom or elsewhere he intentionally inflicts severe pain or suffering on another at the instigation or with the consent or acquiescence—

(i) of a public official; or
(ii) of a person acting in an official capacity; and

(*b*) the official or other person is performing or purporting to perform his official duties when he instigates the commission of the offence or consents to or acquiesces in it.

(3) It is immaterial whether the pain or suffering is physical or mental and whether it is caused by an act or an omission.

(4) It shall be a defence for a person charged with an offence under this section in respect of any conduct of his to prove that he had lawful authority, justification or excuse for that conduct.

(5) For the purposes of this section "lawful authority, justification or excuse" means—

(*a*) in relation to pain or suffering inflicted in the United Kingdom, lawful authority, justification or excuse under the law of the part of the United Kingdom where it was inflicted;

(*b*) in relation to pain or suffering inflicted outside the United Kingdom—

(i) if it was inflicted by a United Kingdom official acting under the law of the United Kingdom or by a person acting in an official capacity under that law, lawful authority, justification or excuse under that law;
(ii) if it was inflicted by a United Kingdom official acting under the law of any part of the United Kingdom or by a person acting in an official capacity under such law, lawful authority, justification or excuse under the law of the part of the United Kingdom under whose law he was acting; and
(iii) in any other case, lawful authority, justification or excuse under the law of the place where it was inflicted.

(6) A person who commits the offence of torture shall be liable on conviction on indictment to imprisonment for **life**.
[Criminal Justice Act 1988, s 134.]

1. Part XI contains ss 133–167.

8–23402 **135. Requirement of Attorney General's consent for prosecutions.** Proceedings for an offence under section 134 above shall not be begun—

(*a*) in England and Wales, except by, or with the consent of, the Attorney General; or
(*b*) *Northern Ireland.*
[Criminal Justice Act 1988, s 135.]

8–23403 **138. Application to Channel Islands, Isle of Man and colonies.** (1) Her Majesty may by Order[1] in Council make provision for extending sections 134 and 135 above, with such modifications and exceptions as may be specified in the Order, to any of the Channel Islands, the Isle of Man or any colony.

(2)–(3) *Repealed.*
[Criminal Justice Act 1988, s 138 as amended by the Extradition Act 1989, Sch 2.]

1. See the Criminal Justice Act 1988 (Torture) (Overseas Territories) Order 1988, SI 1988/2242, amended by SI 1992/1715.

United Nations Personnel Act 1997

(1997 c 13)

8–23456 **1. Attacks on UN workers.** (1) If a person does outside the United Kingdom any act to or in relation to a UN worker which, if he had done it in any part of the United Kingdom, would have made him guilty of any of the offences mentioned in subsection (2), he shall in that part of the United Kingdom be guilty of that offence.

(2) The offences referred to in subsection (1) are—

(*a*) murder, manslaughter, culpable homicide, rape, assault causing injury, kidnapping, abduction and false imprisonment;
(*b*) an offence under section 18, 20, 21, 22, 23, 24, 28, 29, 30 or 47 of the Offences against the Person Act 1861; and
(*c*) an offence under section 2 of the Explosive Substances Act 1883.
[United Nations Personnel Act 1997, s 1.]

8–23457 **2. Attacks in connection with premises and vehicles.** (1) If a person does outside the United Kingdom any act, in connection with an attack on relevant premises or on a vehicle ordinarily used by a UN worker which is made when a UN worker is on or in the premises or vehicle, which, if he had done it in any part of the United Kingdom, would have made him guilty of any of the offences mentioned in subsection (2), he shall in that part of the United Kingdom be guilty of that offence.

(2) The offences referred to in subsection (1) are—

(*a*) an offence under section 2 of the Explosive Substances Act 1883;
(*b*) an offence under section 1 of the Criminal Damage Act 1971;
(*c*) an offence under article 3 of the Criminal Damage (Northern Ireland) Order 1977; and
(*d*) wilful fire-raising.

(3) In this section—

"relevant premises" means premises at which a UN worker resides or is staying or which a UN worker uses for the purpose of carrying out his functions as such a worker; and
"vehicle" includes any means of conveyance.
[United Nations Personnel Act 1997, s 2.]

8–23458 **3. Threats of attacks on UN workers.** (1) If a person in the United Kingdom or elsewhere contravenes subsection (2) he shall be guilty of an offence.

(2) A person contravenes this subsection if, in order to compel a person to do or abstain from doing any act, he—

(*a*) makes to a person a threat that any person will do an act which is—
  (i) an offence mentioned in section 1(2) against a UN worker, or
  (ii) an offence mentioned in subsection (2) of section 2 in connection with such an attack as is mentioned in subsection (1) of that section, and
(*b*) intends that the person to whom he makes the threat shall fear that it will be carried out.

(3) A person guilty of an offence under this section shall be liable on conviction on indictment to imprisonment for a term—

(*a*) not exceeding **ten years**, and

(*b*) not exceeding the term of imprisonment to which a person would be liable for the offence constituted by doing the act threatened at the place where the conviction occurs and at the time of the offence to which the conviction relates.

[United Nations Personnel Act 1997, s 3.]

8–23459 **4. Meaning of UN worker.** (1) For the purposes of this Act a person is a UN worker, in relation to an alleged offence, if at the time of the alleged offence—

(*a*) he is engaged or deployed by the Secretary-General of the United Nations as a member of the military, police or civilian component of a UN operation,

(*b*) he is, in his capacity as an official or expert on mission of the United Nations, a specialised agency of the United Nations or the International Atomic Energy Agency, present in an area where a UN operation is being conducted,

(*c*) he is assigned, with the agreement of an organ of the United Nations, by the Government of any State or by an international governmental organisation to carry out activities in support of the fulfilment of the mandate of a UN operation,

(*d*) he is engaged by the Secretary-General of the United Nations, a specialised agency or the International Atomic Energy Agency to carry out such activities, or

(*e*) he is deployed by a humanitarian non-governmental organisation or agency under an agreement with the Secretary-General of the United Nations, with a specialised agency or with the International Atomic Energy Agency to carry out such activities.

(2) Subject to subsection (3), in this section "UN operation" means an operation—

(*a*) which is established, in accordance with the Charter of the United Nations, by an organ of the United Nations,

(*b*) which is conducted under the authority and control of the United Nations, and

(*c*) which—

(i) has as its purpose the maintenance or restoration of international peace and security, or

(ii) has, for the purposes of the Convention, been declared by the Security Council or the General Assembly of the United Nations to be an operation where there exists an exceptional risk to the safety of the participating personnel.

(3) In this section "UN operation" does not include any operation—

(*a*) which is authorised by the Security Council of the United Nations as an enforcement action under Chapter VII of the Charter of the United Nations,

(*b*) in which UN workers are engaged as combatants against organised armed forces, and

(*c*) to which the law of international armed conflict applies.

(4) In this section—

"the Convention" means the Convention on the Safety of United Nations and Associated Personnel adopted by the General Assembly of the United Nations on 9 December 1994; and

"specialised agency" has the meaning assigned to it by Article 57 of the Charter of the United Nations.

(5) If, in any proceedings, a question arises as to whether—

(*a*) a person is or was a UN worker, or

(*b*) an operation is or was a UN operation,

a certificate issued by or under the authority of the Secretary of State and stating any fact relating to the question shall be conclusive evidence of that fact.

[United Nations Personnel Act 1997, s 4.]

8–23460 **5. Provisions supplementary to sections 1 to 3.** (1) Proceedings for an offence which (disregarding the provisions of the Internationally Protected Persons Act 1978, the Suppression of Terrorism Act 1978, the Nuclear Material (Offences) Act 1983 and the Terrorism Act 2000) would not be an offence apart from section 1, 2 or 3 above shall not be begun—

(*a*) in England and Wales, except by or with the consent of the Attorney General;

(*b*) in Northern Ireland, except by or with the consent of the Attorney General for Northern Ireland.

(2) Without prejudice to any jurisdiction exercisable apart from this subsection, every sheriff court in Scotland shall have jurisdiction to entertain proceedings for an offence which (disregarding the provisions of the Internationally Protected Persons Act 1978, the Suppression of Terrorism Act 1978, the Nuclear Material (Offences) Act 1983 and the Terrorism Act 2000) would not be an offence in Scotland apart from section 1, 2 or 3 above.

(3) A person is guilty of an offence under, or by virtue of, section 1, 2 or 3 regardless of his nationality.

(4) For the purposes of those sections, it is immaterial whether a person knows that another person is a UN worker.
[United Nations Personnel Act 1997, s 5 as amended by the Crime (International Co-operation) Act 2003, Sch 5.]

8–23461 6. *Repealed.*

8–23462 7. *Consequential amendments.*

8–23463 8. **Interpretation.** In this Act—

"act" includes omission; and

"UN worker" has the meaning given in section 4.

[United Nations Personnel Act 1997, s 8.]

8–23464 9. *Extent*[1].

1. The United Nations Personnel (Guernsey) Order 1998, SI 1998/1075 has been made under s 9(2). This act has been extended with modifications, to the Bailiwick of Jersey by the United Nations Personnel (Jersey) Order 1998, SI 1998/1267 and to the Isle of Man by the United Nations Personnel (Isle of Man) Order 1998, SI 1998/1509.

8–23465 10. *Short title and commencement.*

Protection from Harassment Act 1997[1]

(1997 c 40)

England and Wales

8–23466 1. **Prohibition of harassment.** (1) A person must not pursue a course of conduct[2]—

(*a*) which amounts to harassment[3] of another[4], and

(*b*) which he knows or ought to know amounts to harassment[3] of the other.

(1A) A person must not pursue a course of conduct—

(*a*) which involves harassment of two or more persons, and

(*b*) which he knows or ought to know involves harassment of those persons, and

(*c*) by which he intends to persuade any person (whether or not one of those mentioned above)—

(i) not to do something that he is entitled or required to do, or

(ii) to do something that he is not under any obligation to do.

(2) For the purposes of this section, the person whose course of conduct is in question ought to know that it amounts to or involves harassment[3] of another if a reasonable person[5] in possession of the same information would think the course of conduct amounted to or involved harassment[3] of the other.

(3) Subsection (1) or (1A) does not apply to a course of conduct if the person who pursued it shows[6]—

(*a*) that it was pursued for the purpose of preventing or detecting crime,

(*b*) that it was pursued under any enactment or rule of law or to comply with any condition or requirement imposed by any person under any enactment, or

(*c*) that in the particular circumstances the pursuit of the course of conduct was reasonable[7].

[Protection from Harassment Act 1997, s 1 as amended by the Serious Organised Crime and Police Act 2005, s 125.]

1. With the exception of ss 13–16, the provisions of this Act are to be brought into force by orders made under s 15. For commencement orders made at the time of going to press, see note to section 15, post.

2. A "course of conduct" must involve conduct on at least two occasions and "conduct" includes speech (s 7(1)(2), post). While proof of two incidents can be sufficient to constitute an offence, the fewer the occasions and the wider they are spread the less likely it will be that a finding of harassment can reasonably be made (*Lau v DPP* [2000] 1 FLR 799, [2000] Crim LR 580, DC). See also *R v Hills* [2001] 1 FLR 580, [2001] Crim LR 318, CA (2 incidents, 6 months apart, held to be separate with no appropriate or sensible causal connection that could justify the conclusion that they amounted to a course of conduct); and *Pratt v DPP* [2001] EWHC 483 (Admin), 165 JP 800 (where the 2 incidents, almost 3 months apart, did amount to a course of conduct, but the case was "borderline".) The court ought to be alert to this where the evidence of some of the incidents is accepted but not others (see for a trial on indictment: *R v Patel* [2004] EWCA Crim 3284, 169 JP 93, [2005] 1 FLR 803, [2006] Crim LR 649). The fact that the victim was informed of the course of conduct (the contents of 2 telephone calls to her employer) by a third party rather than by the defendant himself did not mean that no offence was committed once she had been so informed, even in circumstances where the defendant had asked that she should not be so informed, provided there was evidence on the basis of which the court could properly conclude that the defendant was pursuing a course of conduct which he knew or ought to have known amounted to harassment of the victim: *Kellett v DPP* [2001] EWHC Admin 107.

Three threatening and abusive telephone calls made within the space of 5 minutes can constitute "a course of conduct", and a conviction can follow even though the complainant was distressed only once (because the calls were recorded and played back on a single occasion) (*Kelly v DPP* [2002] EWHC Admin 1428, (2002) 166 JP 621.

A "course of conduct" may include acts that occurred more than 6 months before the date on which the information was laid; this does not violate s 127 of the Magistrates' Courts Act 1980 if the final event relied on occurred within the 6-month limitation period: *DPP v Baker* [2004] EWHC Admin 2792, (2005) 169 JP 140.

3. References to harassing a person include alarming the person or causing the person distress (s 7(2), post). See also *Chambers and Edwards v DPP* [1995] Crim LR 896 decided under the Public Order Act 1986, this PART: title PUBLIC MEETINGS AND PUBLIC ORDER, post. This Act is directed at the prevention of stalking, anti-social behaviour by neighbours and racial harassment and its ambit does not extend to an alleged aggressive conduct of litigation (*Tuppen v Microsoft Corpn Ltd* (2000) Times, 15 November, QBD).

4. Two or more complainants may be named in one charge under s 1of the Protection from Harassment Act 1997; and, if the complainants were "a close knit definable group" and the acts complained of constitute pursuing a single course of conduct aimed at the group, there is no unfairness to the defendant and such a charge is not bad for duplicity merely because only one of the complainants was present on a particular occasion: *DPP v Dunn* [2001] 1 Cr App Rep 352, 165 JP 130, [2001] Crim LR 130, DC. (Cf the narrower interpretation of s 4, post.)

5. The defendant's mental disorder (paranoid schizophrenia) was not to be considered as a relevant condition of the hypothetical reasonable man under s 1(2) or to be taken into account when assessing whether the defendant's conduct was reasonable under s 1(3)(*c*); both s 1(2) and s 1(3) involved objective tests and it did not assist to consider the law relating to duress or provocation since their aims were different: *R v Colohan* [2001] EWCA Crim 1251, [2001] Crim LR 845.

6. The standard of proof is on a preponderance of probabilities, less onerous than on the prosecution; *R v Carr-Briant* [1943] KB 607, [1943] 2 All ER 156, 107 JP 167, *R v Dunbar* [1958] 1 QB 1, [1957] 2 All ER 737, [1957] 3 WLR 330.

7. It is not reasonable to pursue a course of conduct which is in breach of a court injunction designed to prevent it (*DPP v Selvanayagam* (1999) Times, 23 June, DC).

8–23467 2. Offence of harassment. (1) A person who pursues a course of conduct in breach of section 1(1) or (1A) is guilty of an offence.

(2) A person guilty of an offence under this section is liable on summary conviction to imprisonment for a term not exceeding **six months**, or a fine not exceeding **level 5** on the standard scale, or **both**.

(3) *Repealed.*

[Protection from Harassment Act 1997, s 2 as amended by the Police Reform Act 2002. S 107(2) and the Serious Organised Crime and Police Act 2005, s 125.]

8–23468 3. Civil remedy. (1) An actual or apprehended breach of section 1(1) may be the subject of a claim in civil proceedings by the person[1] who is or may be the victim of the course of conduct in question.

(2) On such a claim, damages may be awarded for (among other things) any anxiety caused by the harassment and any financial loss resulting from the harassment.

(3) Where—

(*a*) in such proceedings the High Court or a county court grants an injunction for the purpose of restraining the defendant from pursuing any conduct which amounts to harassment, and

(*b*) the plaintiff considers that the defendant has done anything which he is prohibited from doing by the injunction.

the plaintiff may apply for the issue of a warrant for the arrest of the defendant.

(4) An application under subsection (3) may be made—

(*a*) where the injunction was granted by the High Court, to a judge of that court, and

(*b*) where the injunction was granted by a county court, to a judge or district judge of that or any other county court.

(5) The judge or district judge to whom an application under subsection (3) is made may only issue a warrant if—

(*a*) the application is substantiated on oath, and

(*b*) the judge or district judge has reasonable grounds for believing that the defendant has done anything which he is prohibited from doing by the injunction.

(6) Where—

(*a*) the High Court or a county court grants an injunction for the purpose mentioned in subsection (3)(*a*), and

(*b*) without reasonable excuse the defendant does anything which he is prohibited from doing by the injunction,

he is guilty of an offence.

(7) Where a person is convicted of an offence under subsection (6) in respect of any conduct, that conduct is not punishable as a contempt of court.

(8) A person cannot be convicted of an offence under subsection (6) in respect of any conduct which has been punished as a contempt of court.

(9) A person guilty of an offence under subsection (6) is liable[2]—

(*a*) on conviction on indictment, to imprisonment for a term not exceeding **five years**, or a **fine**, or **both**, or

(*b*) on summary conviction, to imprisonment for a term not exceeding **six months**, or a fine not exceeding the **statutory maximum**, or **both**.

[Protection from Harassment Act 1997, s 3 as amended by the Serious Organised Crime and Police Act 2005, s 125.]

1. This does not include a company which cannot be the subject of harassment and cannot bring proceedings under the Act (*Daiichi UK Ltd v Stop Huntingdon Animal Cruelty*) (2003) Times, 22 October, QBD).

2. For procedure in respect of this offence which is triable either way, see the Magistrates' Courts Act 1980, ss 17A–21, in PART I: MAGISTRATES' COURTS, PROCEDURE, ante.

8–23468A 3A. Injunctions to protect persons from harassment within section 1(1A). (1) This section applies where there is an actual or apprehended breach of section 1(1A) by any person ("the relevant person").

(2) In such a case—

(*a*) any person who is or may be a victim of the course of conduct in question, or

(*b*) any person who is or may be a person falling within section 1(1A)(*c*),

may apply to the High Court or a county court for an injunction restraining the relevant person from pursuing any conduct which amounts to harassment in relation to any person or persons mentioned or described in the injunction.

(3) Section 3(3) to (9) apply in relation to an injunction granted under subsection (2) above as they apply in relation to an injunction granted as mentioned in section 3(3)(*a*).

[Protection from Harassment Act 1997, s 3A as inserted by the Serious Organised Crime and Police Act 2005, s 125.]

8–23469 4. Putting people in fear of violence. (1) A person whose course of conduct causes another to fear, on at least two occasions, that violence will be used against him[1] is guilty of an offence if he knows or ought to know that his course of conduct will cause the other so to fear on each of those occasions.

(2) For the purposes of this section, the person whose course of conduct is in question ought to know that it will cause another to fear that violence will be used against him on any occasion if a reasonable person in possession of the same information would think the course of conduct would cause the other so to fear on that occasion.

(3) It is a defence for a person charged with an offence under this section to show[2] that—

(*a*) his course of conduct was pursued for the purpose of preventing or detecting crime.

(*b*) his course of conduct was pursued under any enactment or rule of law or to comply with any condition or requirement imposed by any person under any enactment, or

(*c*) the pursuit of his course of conduct was reasonable for the protection of himself or another or for the protection of his or another's property.

(4) A person guilty of an offence under this section is liable[3]—

(*a*) on conviction on indictment, to imprisonment for a term not exceeding **five years**, or a **fine**, or **both**, or

(*b*) on summary conviction, to imprisonment for a term not exceeding **six months**, or a fine not exceeding the **statutory maximum**, or **both**.

(5) If on the trial on indictment of a person charged with an offence under this section the jury find him not guilty of the offence charged, they may find him guilty of an offence under section 2.

(6) The Crown Court has the same powers and duties in relation to a person who is by virtue of subsection (5) convicted before it of an offence under section 2 as a magistrates' court would have on convicting him of the offence.

[Protection from Harassment Act 1997, s 4.]

1. Where, in relation to one of the 2 occasions relied on by the prosecution, the evidence was that the defendant threatened to blow the victim's dogs' brains out and the victim was not asked whether she had been caused to fear violence to herself on that occasion, the court was entitled to convict; words or conduct ostensibly directed to something or someone other than the victim did not, because so directed, fall outside conduct that could support a conviction: *R v DPP* [2001] EWHC Admin 17, [2001] Crim LR 397, 165 JP 349. However, it is not possible to read "others" for "another" or "them" rather than "him" in s 4; although there can be cases where the requirements of s 4 are met in relation to 2 persons, the course of conduct must cause 1 complainant to fear, on at least 2 occasions, that violence will be used against him, as opposed to another: *Caurti v DPP* [2002] Crim LR 131.

2. The standard of proof is on a preponderance of probabilities, less onerous than on the prosecution; *R v Carr-Briant* [1943] KB 607, [1943] 2 All ER 156, 107 JP 167, *R v Dunbar* [1958] 1 QB 1, [1957] 2 All ER 737, [1957] 3 WLR 330.

3. For procedure in respect of this offence which is triable either way, see the Magistrates' Courts Act 1980, ss 17A–21, in PART I: MAGISTRATES' COURTS, PROCEDURE, ante.

8–23470 5. Restraining orders★. (1) A court sentencing or otherwise dealing with a person ("the defendant") convicted of an offence under section 2 or 4★ may (as well as sentencing him or dealing with him in any other way) make an order[1] under this section.

(2) The order may, for the purpose of protecting the victim or victims of the offence, or any other person mentioned in the order, from further★ conduct which—

(*a*) amounts to harassment, or

(*b*) will cause a fear of violence,

prohibit the defendant from doing anything described[2] in the order.

(3) The order may have effect for a specified period or until further order.★

(4) The prosecutor, the defendant or any other person mentioned in the order may apply to the court which made the order for it to be varied or discharged by a further order.*

(5) If without reasonable excuse the defendant does anything which he is prohibited from doing[2] by an order under this section, he is guilty of an offence.

(6) A person guilty of an offence under this section is liable—

(*a*) on conviction on indictment, to imprisonment for a term not exceeding **five years**, or a **fine**, or **both**, or

(*b*) on summary conviction, to imprisonment for a term not exceeding **six months**, or a fine not exceeding the **statutory maximum**, or **both**.*

[Protection from Harassment Act 1997, s 5 as amended by the Serious Organised Crime and Police Act 2005, s 125.]

***Section heading amended, words in sub-ss (1) and (2) repealed, new sub-ss (3A), (4A) and (7) and new s 5A inserted by the Domestic Violence, Crime and Victims Act 2004, Sch 12 from a date to be appointed.**

1. An order under this section must identify by name those who are protected by it. Accordingly it was not sufficient to make an order in the terms not to "contact or communicate with any member of staff" of a hostel; the staff had to be referred to by name (*R v Mann* (2000) Times, 11 April, CA).

2. The interpretation of ordinary words in a court order is a question of fact; the criminal context is not a reason for giving a narrow or strained meaning to words which bear their ordinary meaning, and the application of that meaning to the facts is a matter for the fact-finding tribunal: *R v Evans* [2004] EWCA Crim 3102, (2005) 169 JP 129, [2005] 1 Cr App R 32, [2005] Crim LR 654 (parking a car so that it blocked in the van of somebody visiting the complainants' property was held to breach a restraining order that prohibited the defendant from "abusive action" towards the complainants).

8–23471 6. Limitation. *Amendment to section 11 of the Limitation Act 1980 (special time limit for actions in respect of personal injuries).*

8–23472 7. Interpretation of this group of sections. (1) This section applies for the interpretation of sections 1 to 5*.

(2) References to harassing a person include alarming the person or causing the person distress.

(3) A "course of conduct" must involve—

(*a*) in the case of conduct in relation to a single person (section 1(1)), conduct on at least two occasions in relation to that person, or

(*b*) in the case of conduct in relation to two or more persons (section 1(1A)), conduct on at least one occasion in relation to each of those persons.

(3A) A person's conduct on any occasion shall be taken, if aided, abetted, counselled or procured by another—

(*a*) to be conduct on that occasion of the other (as well as conduct of the person whose conduct it is); and

(*b*) to be conduct in relation to which the other's knowledge and purpose, and what he ought to have known, are the same as they were in relation to what was contemplated or reasonably foreseeable at the time of the aiding, abetting, counselling or procuring.

(4) "Conduct" includes speech.

(5) References to a person, in the context of the harassment of a person, are references to a person who is an individual.

[Protection from Harassment Act 1997, s 7 amended by the Criminal Justice and Police Act 2001, s 44(1) and the Criminal Justice and Police Act 2001, s 44 and the Serious Organised Crime and Police Act 2005, s 125.]

***Words substituted by the Domestic Violence, Crime and Victims Act 2004, Sch 10 from a date to be appointed.**

Scotland

8–23472A 8–11. *Scottish provisions.*

General

8–23473 12. National security etc. (1) If the Secretary of State certifies that in his opinion anything done by a specified person on a specified occasion related to—

(*a*) national security,

(*b*) the economic well-being of the United Kingdom, or

(*c*) the prevention or detection of serious crime,

and was done on behalf of the Crown, the certificate is conclusive evidence that this Act does not apply to any conduct of that person on that occasion.

(2) In subsection (1), "specified" means specified in the certificate in question.

(3) A document purporting to be a certificate under subsection (1) is to be received in evidence and, unless the contrary is proved, be treated as being such a certificate.

[Protection from Harassment Act 1997, s 12.]

8–23474 **13.** *Northern Ireland.*

8–23475 **14.** *Extent.*

8–23476 **15. Commencement.** (1) Sections 1, 2, 4, 5 and 7 to 12 are to come into force on such day as the Secretary of State may by order made by statutory instrument appoint[1].

(2) Sections 3 and 6 are to come into force on such day as the Lord Chancellor may by order made by statutory instrument appoint[1].

(3) Different days may be appointed under this section for different purposes.

[Protection from Harassment Act 1997, s 15.]

---

1. Sections 13–16 came into force at Royal Assent on 21 March 1997; the remaining provisions except section 3(3)–(9) (injunctions) were brought into force on 16 June 1997 by the following commencement orders made under s 15: Commencement Order (No 1), SI 1997/1418 and Commencement Order (No 2), SI 1997/1498. Section 3(3)–(9) was brought into force on 1 September 1998 by Commencement Order (No 3), SI 1998/1902.

8–23477 **16.** *Short title.*

Terrorism Act 2000

(2000 c 11)

PART I[1]

INTRODUCTORY

8–23485 **1. Terrorism: interpretation.** (1) In this Act "terrorism" means the use or threat of action where—

(*a*) the action falls within subsection (2),
(*b*) the use or threat is designed to influence the government or to intimidate the public or a section of the public, and
(*c*) the use or threat is made for the purpose of advancing a political, religious or ideological cause.

(2) Action falls within this subsection if it—

(*a*) involves serious violence against a person,
(*b*) involves serious damage to property,
(*c*) endangers a person's life, other than that of the person committing the action,
(*d*) creates a serious risk to the health or safety of the public or a section of the public, or
(*e*) is designed seriously to interfere with or seriously to disrupt an electronic system.

(3) The use or threat of action falling within subsection (2) which involves the use of firearms or explosives is terrorism whether or not subsection (1)(*b*) is satisfied.

(4) In this section—

(*a*) "action" includes action outside the United Kingdom,
(*b*) a reference to any person or to property is a reference to any person, or to property, wherever situated,
(*c*) a reference to the public includes a reference to the public of a country other than the United Kingdom, and
(*d*) "the government" means the government of the United Kingdom, of a Part of the United Kingdom or of a country other than the United Kingdom.

(5) In this Act a reference to action taken for the purposes of terrorism includes a reference to action taken for the benefit of a proscribed organisation.

[Terrorism Act 2000, s 1.]

---

1. Part I contains ss 1–2 and Sch 1. With the exception of ss 2(1)(*b*) and (2) and 118, Sch 1 and 128–131, the provisions of this Act are to be brought into force by orders made unders 128. For orders made at the time of going to press, see note to s 128, post.

8–23486 **2.** *Repeal of temporary legislation*

PART II[1]

PROSCRIBED ORGANISATIONS

Procedure

8–23487 **3. Proscription.** (1) For the purposes of this Act an organisation is proscribed if—

(*a*) it is listed in Schedule 2, or
(*b*) it operates under the same name as an organisation listed in that Schedule.

(2) Subsection (1)(*b*) shall not apply in relation to an organisation listed in Schedule 2 if its entry is the subject of a note in that Schedule.

(3) The Secretary of State may by order—

(*a*) add an organisation to Schedule 2;
(*b*) remove an organisation from that Schedule;
(*c*) amend that Schedule in some other way.

(4) The Secretary of State may exercise his power under subsection (3)(*a*) in respect of an organisation only if he believes that it is concerned in terrorism.

(5) For the purposes of subsection (4) an organisation is concerned in terrorism if it—

(*a*) commits or participates in acts of terrorism,
(*b*) prepares for terrorism,
(*c*) promotes or encourages terrorism, or
(*d*) is otherwise concerned in terrorism.

[Terrorism Act 2000, s 3.]

---

1. Part II contains ss 3–13 and Schs 2 and 3.

8–23488 **4.** *Deproscription: application*

8–23489 **5.** *Deproscription: appeal*

8–23490 **6.** *Further appeal*

8–23491 **7. Appeal: effect on conviction, &c.** (1) This section applies where—

(*a*) an appeal under section 5 has been allowed in respect of an organisation,
(*b*) an order has been made under section 3(3)(*b*) in respect of the organisation in accordance with an order of the Commission under section 5(4) (and, if the order was made in reliance on section 123(5), a resolution has been passed by each House of Parliament under section 123(5)(*b*)),
(*c*) a person has been convicted of an offence in respect of the organisation under any of sections 11 to 13, 15 to 19 and 56, and
(*d*) the activity to which the charge referred took place on or after the date of the refusal to deproscribe against which the appeal under section 5 was brought.

(2) If the person mentioned in subsection (1)(*c*) was convicted on indictment—

(*a*) he may appeal against the conviction to the Court of Appeal, and
(*b*) the Court of Appeal shall allow the appeal.

(3) A person may appeal against a conviction by virtue of subsection (2) whether or not he has already appealed against the conviction.

(4) An appeal by virtue of subsection (2)—

(*a*) must be brought within the period of 28 days beginning with the date on which the order mentioned in subsection (1)(*b*) comes into force, and
(*b*) shall be treated as an appeal under section 1 of the Criminal Appeal Act 1968 (but does not require leave).

(5) If the person mentioned in subsection (1)(*c*) was convicted by a magistrates' court—

(*a*) he may appeal against the conviction to the Crown Court, and
(*b*) the Crown Court shall allow the appeal.

(6) A person may appeal against a conviction by virtue of subsection (5)—

(*a*) whether or not he pleaded guilty,
(*b*) whether or not he has already appealed against the conviction, and
(*c*) whether or not he has made an application in respect of the conviction under section 111 of the Magistrates' Courts Act 1980 (case stated).

(7) An appeal by virtue of subsection (5)—

(*a*) must be brought within the period of 21 days beginning with the date on which the order mentioned in subsection (1)(*b*) comes into force, and
(*b*) shall be treated as an appeal under section 108(1)(*b*) of the Magistrates' Courts Act 1980[1].

(8) In section 133(5) of the Criminal Justice Act 1988 (compensation for miscarriage of justice) after paragraph (*b*) there shall be inserted—

"or

(*c*) on an appeal under section 7 of the Terrorism Act 2000."

[Terrorism Act 2000, s 7.]

---

1. PART I: MAGISTRATES' COURTS, PROCEDURE, ante.

8–23492 8. *Section 7: Scotland and Northern Ireland*

8–23493 9. *Application of Human Rights Act 1998 to appeals before the Proscribed Organisations Appeals Commission*

8–23494 10. Immunity. (1) The following shall not be admissible as evidence in proceedings for an offence under any of sections 11 to 13, 15 to 19 and 56—

(*a*) evidence of anything done in relation to an application to the Secretary of State under section 4,
(*b*) evidence of anything done in relation to proceedings before the Proscribed Organisations Appeal Commission under section 5 above or section 7(1) of the Human Rights Act 1998,
(*c*) evidence of anything done in relation to proceedings under section 6 (including that section as applied by section 9(2)), and
(*d*) any document submitted for the purposes of proceedings mentioned in any of paragraphs (*a*) to (*c*).

(2) But subsection (1) does not prevent evidence from being adduced on behalf of the accused.
[Terrorism Act 2000, s 10.]

Offences

8–23495 11. Membership. (1) A person commits an offence if he belongs or professes to belong to a proscribed organisation[1].

(2) It is a defence for a person charged with an offence under subsection (1) to prove[2]—

(*a*) that the organisation was not proscribed on the last (or only) occasion on which he became a member or began to profess to be a member, and
(*b*) that he has not taken part in the activities of the organisation at any time while it was proscribed.

(3) A person guilty of an offence under this section shall be liable[3]—

(*a*) on conviction on indictment, to imprisonment for a term not exceeding ten years, to a fine or to both, or
(*b*) on summary conviction, to imprisonment for a term not exceeding six months, to a fine not exceeding the statutory maximum or to both.

(4) In subsection (2) "proscribed" means proscribed for the purposes of any of the following—

(*a*) this Act;
(*b*) the Northern Ireland (Emergency Provisions) Act 1996;
(*c*) the Northern Ireland (Emergency Provisions) Act 1991;
(*d*) the Prevention of Terrorism (Temporary Provisions) Act 1989;
(*e*) the Prevention of Terrorism (Temporary Provisions) Act 1984;
(*f*) the Northern Ireland (Emergency Provisions) Act 1978;
(*g*) the Prevention of Terrorism (Temporary Provisions) Act 1976;
(*h*) the Prevention of Terrorism (Temporary Provisions) Act 1974;
(*i*) the Northern Ireland (Emergency Provisions) Act 1973.

[Terrorism Act 2000, s 11.]

---

1. In *R v Hundal and R v Dhaliwal* [2004] EWCA Crim 389, [2004] 2 Cr App Rep 307 the question arose as to whether persons resident abroad and visiting and UK, who belonged to a foreign branch of an organisation proscribed in the UK but not where they were resident, and who had not participated in any of the activities of the organisation inside United Kingdom, were guilty of this offence. It was held that: (1) The court could take into count the joining of an organisation outside the jurisdiction and activities outside the jurisdiction to determine whether the person was a member of the proscribed organisation; (2) what is required is for there to be someone who is in this country, and therefore subject to its jurisdiction who at the time that he is in this country is a member of the proscribed organisation; (3) To establish that the person concerned is a member of the proscribed organisation, evidence can be given that the person joined the organisation from abroad or when abroad, but he would only be guilty of an offence when he was in this country. Either he would have to travel to this country in order to commit an offence after he became a member or he would already have had to be in this country and joined the local foreign branch of the proscribed organisation while in this country.

Their lordships further held that evidence of membership of a proscribed organisation obtained as a result of a compulsory search under Sch 7 could be used in a prosecution under s 11; following the decision in *R v Kearns* [2002] EWCA 748, [2002] 1 WLR 2815, 1 Cr App Rep 111 this was not in breach of art 6.

2. It was held in *A-G's Reference (No 4 of 2002)* [2004] UKHL 43, [2005] 1 AC 264, [2004] 1 All ER 1, [2004] 3 WLR 976 (reversing the decision of the Court of Appeal) that since s 11(2) impermissibly infringed the presumption of innocence, it was appropriate, pursuant to s 3 of the 1998 Act, to read down s 11(2) so as to impose on the defendant an evidential burden only, even though that was not Parliament's intention when enacting the subsection.

3. For procedure in respect of this offence which is triable either way, see the Magistrates' Courts Act 1980, ss 17A–21, in PART I: MAGISTRATES' COURTS, PROCEDURE, ante.

8–23496 12. Support. (1) A person commits an offence if—

(*a*) he invites support for a proscribed organisation, and

(*b*) the support is not, or is not restricted to, the provision of money or other property (within the meaning of section 15).

(2) A person commits an offence if he arranges, manages or assists in arranging or managing a meeting which he knows is—

(*a*) to support a proscribed organisation,
(*b*) to further the activities of a proscribed organisation, or
(*c*) to be addressed by a person who belongs or professes to belong to a proscribed organisation.

(3) A person commits an offence if he addresses a meeting and the purpose of his address is to encourage support for a proscribed organisation or to further its activities.

(4) Where a person is charged with an offence under subsection (2)(*c*) in respect of a private meeting it is a defence for him to prove[1] that he had no reasonable cause to believe that the address mentioned in subsection (2)(*c*) would support a proscribed organisation or further its activities.

(5) In subsections (2) to (4)—

(*a*) "meeting" means a meeting of three or more persons, whether or not the public are admitted, and
(*b*) a meeting is private if the public are not admitted.

(6) A person guilty of an offence under this section shall be liable—

(*a*) on conviction on indictment, to imprisonment for a term not exceeding ten years, to a fine or to both, or
(*b*) on summary conviction, to imprisonment for a term not exceeding six months, to a fine not exceeding the statutory maximum or to both[2].

[Terrorism Act 2000, s 12.]

---

1. For this defence, see s 118, post.
2. For procedure in respect of this offence which is triable either way, see the Magistrates' Courts Act 1980, ss 17A–21, in PART I: MAGISTRATES' COURTS, PROCEDURE, ante

8–23497 **13. Uniform.** (1) A person in a public place commits an offence if he—

(*a*) wears an item of clothing, or
(*b*) wears, carries or displays an article,

in such a way or in such circumstances as to arouse reasonable suspicion that he is a member or supporter of a proscribed organisation.

(2) A constable in Scotland may arrest a person without a warrant if he has reasonable grounds to suspect that the person is guilty of an offence under this section.

(3) A person guilty of an offence under this section shall be liable on summary conviction to—

(*a*) imprisonment for a term not exceeding six months,
(*b*) a fine not exceeding level 5 on the standard scale, or
(*c*) both.

[Terrorism Act 2000, s 13.]

PART III[1]
TERRORIST PROPERTY

Interpretation

8–23498 **14. Terrorist property.** (1) In this Act "terrorist property" means—

(*a*) money or other property which is likely to be used for the purposes of terrorism (including any resources of a proscribed organisation),
(*b*) proceeds of the commission of acts of terrorism, and
(*c*) proceeds of acts carried out for the purposes of terrorism.

(2) In subsection (1)—

(*a*) a reference to proceeds of an act includes a reference to any property which wholly or partly, and directly or indirectly, represents the proceeds of the act (including payments or other rewards in connection with its commission), and
(*b*) the reference to an organisation's resources includes a reference to any money or other property which is applied or made available, or is to be applied or made available, for use by the organisation.

[Terrorism Act 2000, s 14.]

---

1. Part III contains ss 14–31 and Schs 3 and 4.

Offences

8–23499 **15. Fund-raising.** (1) A person commits an offence[1] if he—

(*a*) invites another to provide money or other property, and (*b*) intends that it should be used, or has reasonable cause to suspect that it may be used, for the purposes of terrorism.

(2) A person commits an offence[1] if he—

(*a*) receives money or other property, and
(*b*) intends that it should be used, or has reasonable cause to suspect that it may be used, for the purposes of terrorism.

(3) A person commits an offence[1] if he—

(*a*) provides money or other property, and
(*b*) knows or has reasonable cause to suspect that it will or may be used for the purposes of terrorism.

(4) In this section a reference to the provision of money or other property is a reference to its being given, lent or otherwise made available, whether or not for consideration.
[Terrorism Act 2000, s 15.]

1. For mode of trial and punishment, see s 22, post.

8–23500 **16. Use and possession.** (1) A person commits an offence[1] if he uses money or other property for the purposes of terrorism.

(2) A person commits an offence[1] if he—

(*a*) possesses money or other property, and
(*b*) intends that it should be used, or has reasonable cause to suspect that it may be used, for the purposes of terrorism.

[Terrorism Act 2000, s 16.]

1. For mode of trial and punishment, see s 22, post.

8–23501 **17. Funding arrangements.** A person commits an offence[1] if—

(*a*) he enters into or becomes concerned in an arrangement as a result of which money or other property is made available or is to be made available to another, and
(*b*) he knows or has reasonable cause to suspect that it will or may be used for the purposes of terrorism.

[Terrorism Act 2000, s 17.]

1. For mode of trial and punishment, see s 22, post.

8–23502 **18. Money laundering.** (1) A person commits an offence[1] if he enters into or becomes concerned in an arrangement which facilitates the retention or control by or on behalf of another person of terrorist property—

(*a*) by concealment,
(*b*) by removal from the jurisdiction,
(*c*) by transfer to nominees, or
(*d*) in any other way.

(2) It is a defence for a person charged with an offence under subsection (1) to prove[2] that he did not know and had no reasonable cause to suspect that the arrangement related to terrorist property.
[Terrorism Act 2000, s 18.]

1. For mode of trial and punishment, see s 22, post.
2. On the balance of probabilities, see *R v Carr-Briant* [1943] KB 607, [1943] 2 All ER 156, 107 JP 167.

8–23503 **19. Disclosure of information: duty.** (1) This section applies where a person—

(*a*) believes or suspects that another person has committed an offence under any of sections 15 to 18, and
(*b*) bases his belief or suspicion on information which comes to his attention in the course of a trade, profession, business or employment.

(1A) But this section does not apply if the information came to the person in the course of a business in the regulated sector.

(2) The person commits an offence[1] if he does not disclose to a constable as soon as is reasonably practicable—

(*a*) his belief or suspicion, and
(*b*) the information on which it is based.

(3) It is a defence for a person charged with an offence under subsection (2) to prove[2] that he had a reasonable excuse for not making the disclosure.

(4) Where—

(*a*) a person is in employment,
(*b*) his employer has established a procedure for the making of disclosures of the matters specified in subsection (2), and
(*c*) he is charged with an offence under that subsection,

it is a defence for him to prove[2] that he disclosed the matters specified in that subsection in accordance with the procedure.

(5) Subsection (2) does not require disclosure by a professional legal adviser of—

(*a*) information which he obtains in privileged circumstances, or
(*b*) a belief or suspicion based on information which he obtains in privileged circumstances.

(6) For the purpose of subsection (5) information is obtained by an adviser in privileged circumstances if it comes to him, otherwise than with a view to furthering a criminal purpose—

(*a*) from a client or a client's representative, in connection with the provision of legal advice by the adviser to the client,
(*b*) from a person seeking legal advice from the adviser, or from the person's representative, or
(*c*) from any person, for the purpose of actual or contemplated legal proceedings.

(7) For the purposes of subsection (1)(*a*) a person shall be treated as having committed an offence under one of sections 15 to 18 if—

(*a*) he has taken an action or been in possession of a thing, and
(*b*) he would have committed an offence under one of those sections if he had been in the United Kingdom at the time when he took the action or was in possession of the thing.

(7A) The reference to a business in the regulated sector must be construed in accordance with Schedule 3A.

(7B) The reference to a constable includes a reference to a member of the staff of the Serious Organised Crime Agency authorised for the purposes of this section by the Director General of that Agency.

(8) A person guilty of an offence under this section shall be liable[3]—

(*a*) on conviction on indictment, to imprisonment for a term not exceeding five years, to a fine or to both, or
(*b*) on summary conviction, to imprisonment for a term not exceeding six months, or to a fine not exceeding the statutory maximum or to both.

[Terrorism Act 2000, s 19, as amended by the Anti-terrorism, Crime and Security Act, 2001, Sch 2 and the Serious Organised Crime And Police Act 2005, Sch 4.]

1. For mode of trial and punishment, see s 22, post.
2. On the balance of probabilities, see *R v Carr-Briant* [1943] KB 607, [1943] 2 All ER 156, 107 JP 167.
3. For procedure in respect of this offence which is triable either way, see the Magistrates' Courts Act 1980, ss 17A–21, in PART I: MAGISTRATES' COURTS, PROCEDURE, ante.

8–23504 20. Disclosure of information: permission. (1) A person may disclose to a constable—

(*a*) a suspicion or belief that any money or other property is terrorist property or is derived from terrorist property;
(*b*) any matter on which the suspicion or belief is based.

(2) A person may make a disclosure to a constable in the circumstances mentioned in section 19(1) and (2).

(3) Subsections (1) and (2) shall have effect notwithstanding any restriction on the disclosure of information imposed by statute or otherwise.

(4) Where—

(*a*) a person is in employment, and
(*b*) his employer has established a procedure for the making of disclosures of the kinds mentioned in subsection (1) and section 19(2),

subsections (1) and (2) shall have effect in relation to that person as if any reference to disclosure to a constable included a reference to disclosure in accordance with the procedure.

(5) References to a constable includes a reference to a member of the staff of the Serious Organised Crime Agency authorised for the purposes of this section by the Director General of that Agency.

[Terrorism Act 2000, s 20, as amended by the Anti-terrorism, Crime and Security Act 2001, Sch 2 as amended by the Serious Organised Crime And Police Act 2005, Sch 4.]

8–23505 21. Cooperation with police. (1) A person does not commit an offence under any of sections 15 to 18 if he is acting with the express consent of a constable.

(2) Subject to subsections (3) and (4), a person does not commit an offence under any of sections 15 to 18 by involvement in a transaction or arrangement relating to money or other property if he discloses to a constable—

(*a*) his suspicion or belief that the money or other property is terrorist property, and
(*b*) the information on which his suspicion or belief is based.

(3) Subsection (2) applies only where a person makes a disclosure—

(*a*) after he becomes concerned in the transaction concerned,
(*b*) on his own initiative, and
(*c*) as soon as is reasonably practicable.

(4) Subsection (2) does not apply to a person if—

(*a*) a constable forbids him to continue his involvement in the transaction or arrangement to which the disclosure relates, and
(*b*) he continues his involvement.

(5) It is a defence for a person charged with an offence under any of sections 15(2) and (3) and 16 to 18 to prove[1] that—

(*a*) he intended to make a disclosure of the kind mentioned in subsections (2) and (3), and
(*b*) there is reasonable excuse for his failure to do so.

(6) Where—

(*a*) a person is in employment, and
(*b*) his employer has established a procedure for the making of disclosures of the same kind as may be made to a constable under subsection (2),

this section shall have effect in relation to that person as if any reference to disclosure to a constable included a reference to disclosure in accordance with the procedure.

(7) A reference in this section to a transaction or arrangement relating to money or other property includes a reference to use or possession.
[Terrorism Act 2000, s 21.]

1. On the balance of probabilities, see *R v Carr-Briant* [1943] KB 607, [1943] 2 All ER 156, 107 JP 167.

8–23505A **21A. Failure to disclose: regulated sector.** (1) A person commits an offence if each of the following three conditions is satisfied.

(2) The first condition is that he—

(*a*) knows or suspects, or
(*b*) has reasonable grounds for knowing or suspecting,

that another person has committed an offence under any of sections 15 to 18.

(3) The second condition is that the information or other matter—

(*a*) on which his knowledge or suspicion is based, or
(*b*) which gives reasonable grounds for such knowledge or suspicion,

came to him in the course of a business in the regulated sector.

(4) The third condition is that he does not disclose the information or other matter to a constable or a nominated officer as soon as is practicable after it comes to him.

(5) But a person does not commit an offence under this section if—

(*a*) he has a reasonable excuse for not disclosing the information or other matter;
(*b*) he is a professional legal adviser and the information or other matter came to him in privileged circumstances.

(6) In deciding whether a person committed an offence under this section the court must consider whether he followed any relevant guidance which was at the time concerned—

(*a*) issued by a supervisory authority or any other appropriate body,
(*b*) approved by the Treasury, and
(*c*) published in a manner it approved as appropriate in its opinion to bring the guidance to the attention of persons likely to be affected by it.

(7) A disclosure to a nominated officer is a disclosure which—

(*a*) is made to a person nominated by the alleged offender's employer to receive disclosures under this section, and
(*b*) is made in the course of the alleged offender's employment and in accordance with the procedure established by the employer for the purpose.

(8) Information or other matter comes to a professional legal adviser in privileged circumstances if it is communicated or given to him—

(*a*) by (or by a representative of) a client of his in connection with the giving by the adviser of legal advice to the client,
(*b*) by (or by a representative of) a person seeking legal advice from the adviser, or
(*c*) by a person in connection with legal proceedings or contemplated legal proceedings.

(9) But subsection (8) does not apply to information or other matter which is communicated or given with a view to furthering a criminal purpose.

(10) Schedule 3A has effect for the purpose of determining what is—

(*a*) a business in the regulated sector;
(*b*) a supervisory authority.

(11) For the purposes of subsection (2) a person is to be taken to have committed an offence there mentioned if—

(*a*) he has taken an action or been in possession of a thing, and
(*b*) he would have committed the offence if he had been in the United Kingdom at the time when he took the action or was in possession of the thing.

(12) A person guilty of an offence under this section is liable—

(a) on conviction on indictment, to imprisonment for a term not exceeding five years or to a fine or to both;
(b) on summary conviction, to imprisonment for a term not exceeding six months or to a fine not exceeding the statutory maximum or to both.

(13) An appropriate body is any body which regulates or is representative of any trade, profession, business or employment carried on by the alleged offender.

(14) The reference to a constable includes a reference to a member of the staff of the Serious Organised Crime Agency authorised for the purposes of this section by the Director General of that Agency.

[Terrorism Act 2000, s 21A, as inserted by the Anti-terrorism, Crime and Security Act 2001, Sch 2 as amended by the Serious Organised Crime And Police Act 2005, Sch 4.]

8–23505B 21B. Protected disclosures. (1) A disclosure which satisfies the following three conditions is not to be taken to breach any restriction on the disclosure of information (however imposed).

(2) The first condition is that the information or other matter disclosed came to the person making the disclosure (the discloser) in the course of a business in the regulated sector.

(3) The second condition is that the information or other matter—

(*a*) causes the discloser to know or suspect, or
(*b*) gives him reasonable grounds for knowing or suspecting,

that another person has committed an offence under any of sections 15 to 18.

(4) The third condition is that the disclosure is made to a constable or a nominated officer as soon as is practicable after the information or other matter comes to the discloser.

(5) A disclosure to a nominated officer is a disclosure which—

(*a*) is made to a person nominated by the discloser's employer to receive disclosures under this section, and
(*b*) is made in the course of the discloser's employment and in accordance with the procedure established by the employer for the purpose.

(6) The reference to a business in the regulated sector must be construed in accordance with Schedule 3A.

(7) The reference to a constable includes a reference to a member of the staff of the Serious Organised Crime Agency authorised for the purposes of this section by the Director General of that Agency.

[Terrorism Act 2000, s 21B, as inserted by the Anti-terrorism, Crime and Security Act 2001, Sch 2 as amended by the Serious Organised Crime And Police Act 2005, Sch 4.]

8–23506 22. Penalties. A person guilty of an offence under any of sections 15 to 18 shall be liable[1]—

(*a*) on conviction on indictment, to imprisonment for a term not exceeding 14 years, to a fine or to both, or
(*b*) on summary conviction, to imprisonment for a term not exceeding six months, to a fine not exceeding the statutory maximum or to both.

[Terrorism Act 2000, s 22.]

---

1. For procedure in respect of this offence which is triable either way, see the Magistrates' Courts Act 1980, ss 17A–21, in PART I: MAGISTRATES' COURTS, PROCEDURE, ante.

8–23507 23. Forfeiture. (1) The court by or before which a person is convicted of an offence under any of sections 15 to 18 may make a forfeiture order in accordance with the provisions of this section.

(2) Where a person is convicted of an offence under section 15(1) or (2) or 16 the court may order the forfeiture of any money or other property—

(*a*) which, at the time of the offence, he had in his possession or under his control, and
(*b*) which, at that time, he intended should be used, or had reasonable cause to suspect might be used, for the purposes of terrorism.

(3) Where a person is convicted of an offence under section 15(3) the court may order the forfeiture of any money or other property—

(*a*) which, at the time of the offence, he had in his possession or under his control, and
(*b*) which, at that time, he knew or had reasonable cause to suspect would or might be used for the purposes of terrorism.

(4) Where a person is convicted of an offence under section 17 the court may order the forfeiture of the money or other property—

(*a*) to which the arrangement in question related, and
(*b*) which, at the time of the offence, he knew or had reasonable cause to suspect would or might be used for the purposes of terrorism.

(5) Where a person is convicted of an offence under section 18 the court may order the forfeiture of the money or other property to which the arrangement in question related.

(6) Where a person is convicted of an offence under any of sections 15 to 18, the court may order the forfeiture of any money or other property which wholly or partly, and directly or indirectly, is received by any person as a payment or other reward in connection with the commission of the offence.

(7) Where a person other than the convicted person claims to be the owner of or otherwise interested in anything which can be forfeited by an order under this section, the court shall give him an opportunity to be heard before making an order.

(8) A court in Scotland shall not make an order under this section except on the application of the prosecutor—

(*a*) in proceedings on indictment, when he moves for sentence, and
(*b*) in summary proceedings, before the court convicts the accused,

and for the purposes of any appeal or review, an order under this section made by a court in Scotland is a sentence.

(9) Schedule 4 (which makes further provision in relation to forfeiture orders under this section) shall have effect.

[Terrorism Act 2000, s 23.]

PART IV[1]

TERRORIST INVESTIGATIONS

Interpretation

8–23516 **32. Terrorist investigation.** In this Act "terrorist investigation" means an investigation of—

(*a*) the commission, preparation or instigation of acts of terrorism,
(*b*) an act which appears to have been done for the purposes of terrorism,
(*c*) the resources of a proscribed organisation,
(*d*) the possibility of making an order under section 3(3), or
(*e*) the commission, preparation or instigation of an offence under this Act.

[Terrorism Act 2000, s 32.]

1. Part IV contains ss 32–39 and Schs 5 and 6.

Cordons

8–23517 **33. Cordoned areas.** (1) An area is a cordoned area for the purposes of this Act if it is designated under this section.

(2) A designation may be made only if the person making it considers it expedient for the purposes of a terrorist investigation.

(3) If a designation is made orally, the person making it shall confirm it in writing as soon as is reasonably practicable.

(4) The person making a designation shall arrange for the demarcation of the cordoned area, so far as is reasonably practicable—

(*a*) by means of tape marked with the word "police", or
(*b*) in such other manner as a constable considers appropriate.

[Terrorism Act 2000, s 33.]

8–23518 **34. Power to designate.** (1) Subject to subsections (1A), (1B) and (2) a designation under section 33 may only be made—

(*a*) where the area is outside Northern Ireland and is wholly or partly within a police area, by an officer for the police area who is of at least the rank of superintendent, and
(*b*) where the area is in Northern Ireland, by a member of the Royal Ulster Constabulary who is of at least the rank of superintendent.

(1A) A designation under section 33 may be made in relation to an area (outside Northern Ireland) which is ina place specified in section 31(1)(*a*) to (*f*) of the Railways and Transport Safety Act, by a member of the British Transport Police Force who is of at least the rank of superintendent.

(1B) A designation under section 33 may be made by a member of the Ministry of Defence Police who is of at least the rank of superintendent in relation to an area outside or in Northern Ireland—

(*a*) if it is a place to which subsection (2) of section 2 of the Ministry of Defence Police Act 1987 (c 4) applies,

(*b*) if a request has been made under paragraph (*a*), (*b*) or (*d*) of subsection (3A) of that section in relation to a terrorist investigation and it is a place where he has the powers and privileges of a constable by virtue of that subsection as a result of the request, or

(*c*) if a request has been made under paragraph (*c*) of that subsection in relation to a terrorist investigation and it is a place described in subsection 1A of this section.

(1C) But a designation under section 33 may not be made by—

(*a*) a member of the British Transport Police Force, or

(*b*) a member of the Ministry of Defence Police,

in any other case.

(2) A constable who is not of the rank required by subsection (1) may make a designation if he considers it necessary by reason of urgency.

(3) Where a constable makes a designation in reliance on subsection (2) he shall as soon as is reasonably practicable—

(*a*) make a written record of the time at which the designation was made, and

(*b*) ensure that a police officer of at least the rank of superintendent is informed.

(4) An officer who is informed of a designation in accordance with subsection (3)(*b*)—

(*a*) shall confirm the designation or cancel it with effect from such time as he may direct, and

(*b*) shall, if he cancels the designation, make a written record of the cancellation and the reason for it.

[Terrorism Act 2000, s 34, as amended by the Anti-terrorism, Crime and Security Act 2001, Sch 7 and SI 2004/1573.]

8–23519 35. Duration. (1) A designation under section 33 has effect, subject to subsections (2) to (5), during the period—

(*a*) beginning at the time when it is made, and

(*b*) ending with a date or at a time specified in the designation.

(2) The date or time specified under subsection (1)(*b*) must not occur after the end of the period of 14 days beginning with the day on which the designation is made.

(3) The period during which a designation has effect may be extended in writing from time to time by—

(*a*) the person who made it, or

(*b*) a person who could have made it (otherwise than by virtue of section 34(2)).

(4) An extension shall specify the additional period during which the designation is to have effect.

(5) A designation shall not have effect after the end of the period of 28 days beginning with the day on which it is made.

[Terrorism Act 2000, s 35.]

8–23520 36. Police powers. (1) A constable in uniform may—

(*a*) order a person in a cordoned area to leave it immediately;

(*b*) order a person immediately to leave premises which are wholly or partly in or adjacent to a cordoned area;

(*c*) order the driver or person in charge of a vehicle in a cordoned area to move it from the area immediately;

(*d*) arrange for the removal of a vehicle from a cordoned area;

(*e*) arrange for the movement of a vehicle within a cordoned area;

(*f*) prohibit or restrict access to a cordoned area by pedestrians or vehicles.

(2) A person commits an offence if he fails to comply with an order, prohibition or restriction imposed by virtue of subsection (1).

(3) It is a defence for a person charged with an offence under subsection (2) to prove[1] that he had a reasonable excuse for his failure.

(4) A person guilty of an offence under subsection (2) shall be liable on summary conviction to—

(*a*) imprisonment for a term not exceeding three months,

(*b*) a fine not exceeding level 4 on the standard scale, or

(*c*) both.

[Terrorism Act 2000, s 36.]

---

1. On the balance of probabilities, see *R v Carr-Briant* [1943] KB 607, [1943] 2 All ER 156, 107 JP 167.

Information and evidence

8–23521 37. Powers. Schedule 5 (power to obtain information, &c) shall have effect.
[Terrorism Act 2000, s 37.]

8–23522 38. Financial information. Schedule 6 (financial information) shall have effect.
[Terrorism Act 2000, s 38.]

8–23522A 38A. Account monitoring orders. Schedule 6A (account monitoring orders) shall have effect.
[Terrorism Act 2000, s 38A, as inserted by the Anti-terrorism, Crime and Security Act 2001, Sch 2.]

8–23522B 38B. Information about acts of terrorism. (1) This section applies where a person has information which he knows or believes might be of material assistance—

(*a*) in preventing the commission by another person of an act of terrorism, or
(*b*) in securing the apprehension, prosecution or conviction of another person, in the United Kingdom, for an offence involving the commission, preparation or instigation of an act of terrorism.

(2) The person commits an offence if he does not disclose the information as soon as reasonably practicable in accordance with subsection (3).

(3) Disclosure is in accordance with this subsection if it is made—

(*a*) in England and Wales, to a constable,
(*b*) in Scotland, to a constable, or
(*c*) in Northern Ireland, to a constable or a member of Her Majesty's forces.

(4) It is a defence for a person charged with an offence under subsection (2) to prove that he had a reasonable excuse for not making the disclosure.

(5) A person guilty of an offence under this section shall be liable—

(*a*) on conviction on indictment, to imprisonment for a term not exceeding five years, or to a fine or to both, or
(*b*) on summary conviction, to imprisonment for a term not exceeding six months, or to a fine not exceeding the statutory maximum or to both.

(6) Proceedings for an offence under this section may be taken, and the offence may for the purposes of those proceedings be treated as having been committed, in any place where the person to be charged is or has at any time been since he first knew or believed that the information might be of material assistance as mentioned in subsection (1).
[Terrorism Act 2000, s 38B, as inserted by the Anti-terrorism, Crime and Security Act 2001, Sch 2.]

8–23523 39. Disclosure of information, &c. (1) Subsection (2) applies where a person knows or has reasonable cause to suspect that a constable is conducting or proposes to conduct a terrorist investigation.

(2) The person commits an offence if he—

(*a*) discloses to another anything which is likely to prejudice the investigation, or
(*b*) interferes with material which is likely to be relevant to the investigation.

(3) Subsection (4) applies where a person knows or has reasonable cause to suspect that a disclosure has been or will be made under any of sections 19 to 21 or 38B.

(4) The person commits an offence if he—

(*a*) discloses to another anything which is likely to prejudice an investigation resulting from the disclosure under that section, or
(*b*) interferes with material which is likely to be relevant to an investigation resulting from the disclosure under that section.

(5) It is a defence for a person charged with an offence under subsection (2) or (4) to prove[1]—

(*a*) that he did not know and had no reasonable cause to suspect that the disclosure or interference was likely to affect a terrorist investigation, or
(*b*) that he had a reasonable excuse for the disclosure or interference.

(6) Subsections (2) and (4) do not apply to a disclosure which is made by a professional legal adviser—

(*a*) to his client or to his client's representative in connection with the provision of legal advice by the adviser to the client and not with a view to furthering a criminal purpose, or
(*b*) to any person for the purpose of actual or contemplated legal proceedings and not with a view to furthering a criminal purpose.

(7) A person guilty of an offence under this section shall be liable[2]—

(*a*) on conviction on indictment, to imprisonment for a term not exceeding five years, to a fine or to both, or (*b*) on summary conviction, to imprisonment for a term not exceeding six months, to a fine not exceeding the statutory maximum or to both.

(8) For the purposes of this section—

(*a*) a reference to conducting a terrorist investigation includes a reference to taking part in the conduct of, or assisting, a terrorist investigation, and

(*b*) a person interferes with material if he falsifies it, conceals it, destroys it or disposes of it, or if he causes or permits another to do any of those things.

[Terrorism Act 2000, s 39, as amended by the Anti-terrorism, Crime and Security Act 2001, s 117(1), (3).]

1. On the balance of probabilities, see *R v Carr-Briant* [1943] KB 607, [1943] 2 All ER 156, 107 JP 167 and for the defence under sub-s (5)(*a*) see s 118, post.

2. For procedure in respect of this offence which is triable either way, see the Magistrates' Courts Act 1980, ss 17A–21, in PART I: MAGISTRATES' COURTS, PROCEDURE, ante.

PART V[1]
COUNTER-TERRORIST POWERS

Suspected terrorists

8–23524 40. Terrorist: interpretation. (1) In this Part "terrorist" means a person who—

(*a*) has committed an offence under any of sections 11, 12, 15 to 18, 54 and 56 to 63, or

(*b*) is or has been concerned in the commission, preparation or instigation of acts of terrorism.

(2) The reference in subsection (1)(*b*) to a person who has been concerned in the commission, preparation or instigation of acts of terrorism includes a reference to a person who has been, whether before or after the passing of this Act, concerned in the commission, preparation or instigation of acts of terrorism within the meaning given by section 1.

[Terrorism Act 2000, s 40.]

1. Part V contains ss 40–53 and Schs 7 and 8.

8–23525 41. Arrest without warrant. (1) A constable may arrest without a warrant a person whom he reasonably suspects to be a terrorist.

(2) Where a person is arrested under this section the provisions of Schedule 8 (detention: treatment, review and extension) shall apply.

(3) Subject to subsections (4) to (7), a person detained under this section shall (unless detained under any other power) be released not later than the end of the period of 48 hours beginning—

(*a*) with the time of his arrest under this section, or

(*b*) if he was being detained under Schedule 7 when he was arrested under this section, with the time when his examination under that Schedule began.

(4) If on a review of a person's detention under Part II of Schedule 8 the review officer does not authorise continued detention, the person shall (unless detained in accordance with subsection (5) or (6) or under any other power) be released.

(5) Where a police officer intends to make an application for a warrant under paragraph 29 of Schedule 8 extending a person's detention, the person may be detained pending the making of the application.

(6) Where an application has been made under paragraph 29 or 36 of Schedule 8 in respect of a person's detention, he may be detained pending the conclusion of proceedings on the application.

(7) Where an application under paragraph 29 or 36 of Schedule 8 is granted in respect of a person's detention, he may be detained, subject to paragraph 37 of that Schedule, during the period specified in the warrant.

(8) The refusal of an application in respect of a person's detention under paragraph 29 or 36 of Schedule 8 shall not prevent his continued detention in accordance with this section.

(9) A person who has the powers of a constable in one Part of the United Kingdom may exercise the power under subsection (1) in any Part of the United Kingdom.

[Terrorism Act 2000, s 41.]

8–23526 42. Search of premises. (1) A justice of the peace may on the application of a constable issue a warrant in relation to specified premises if he is satisfied that there are reasonable grounds for suspecting that a person whom the constable reasonably suspects to be a person falling within section 40(1)(*b*) is to be found there.

(2) A warrant under this section shall authorise any constable to enter and search the specified premises for the purpose of arresting the person referred to in subsection (1) under section 41.

(3) In the application of subsection (1) to Scotland—

(*a*) "justice of the peace" includes the sheriff, and

(*b*) the justice of the peace or sheriff can be satisfied as mentioned in that subsection only by having heard evidence on oath.

[Terrorism Act 2000, s 42.]

8–23527 **43. Search of persons.** (1) A constable may stop and search a person whom he reasonably suspects to be a terrorist to discover whether he has in his possession anything which may constitute evidence that he is a terrorist.

(2) A constable may search a person arrested under section 41 to discover whether he has in his possession anything which may constitute evidence that he is a terrorist.

(3) A search of a person under this section must be carried out by someone of the same sex.

(4) A constable may seize and retain anything which he discovers in the course of a search of a person under subsection (1) or (2) and which he reasonably suspects may constitute evidence that the person is a terrorist.

(5) A person who has the powers of a constable in one Part of the United Kingdom may exercise a power under this section in any Part of the United Kingdom.

[Terrorism Act 2000, s 43.]

Power to stop and search[1]

8–23528 **44. Authorisations.** (1) An authorisation under this subsection authorises any constable in uniform to stop a vehicle in an area or at a place specified in the authorisation and to search—

(*a*) the vehicle;
(*b*) the driver of the vehicle;
(*c*) a passenger in the vehicle;
(*d*) anything in or on the vehicle or carried by the driver or a passenger.

(2) An authorisation under this subsection authorises any constable in uniform to stop a pedestrian in an area or at a place specified in the authorisation and to search—

(*a*) the pedestrian;
(*b*) anything carried by him.

(3) An authorisation under subsection (1) or (2) may be given only if the person giving it considers it expedient for the prevention of acts of terrorism.

(4) An authorisation may be given—

(*a*) where the specified area or place is the whole or part of a police area outside Northern Ireland other than one mentioned in paragraph (*b*) or (*c*), by a police officer for the area who is of at least the rank of assistant chief constable;
(*b*) where the specified area or place is the whole or part of the metropolitan police district, by a police officer for the district who is of at least the rank of commander of the metropolitan police;
(*c*) where the specified area or place is the whole or part of the City of London, by a police officer for the City who is of at least the rank of commander in the City of London police force;
(*d*) where the specified area or place is the whole or part of Northern Ireland, by a member of the Police Service of Northern Ireland who is of at least the rank of assistant chief constable.

(4A) In a case (within subsection (4)(*a*), (*b*) or (*c*)) in which the specified area or place is in a place described in section 34(1A), an authorisation may also be given by a member of the British Transport Police Force who is of at least the rank of assistant chief constable.

(4B) In a case in which the specified area or place is a place to which section 2(2) of the Ministry of Defence Police Act 1987 applies, an authorisation may also be given by a member of the Ministry of Defence Police who is of at least the rank of assistant chief constable.

(4BA) In a case in which the specified area or place is a place in which memebers of the Civil Nuclear Constabulary have the powers and privileges of a constable, an authorisation may also be given by a member of that Constabulary who is of at least the rank of assistant chief constable.

(4C) But an authorisation may not be given by—

(*a*) a member of the British Transport Police Force,
(*b*) a member of the Civil Nuclear Constabulary,

in any other case.

(5) If an authorisation is given orally, the person giving it shall confirm it in writing as soon as is reasonably practicable.

[Terrorism Act 2000, s 44, as amended by the Anti-terrorism, Crime and Security Act 2001, Sch 7 and SI 2004/1573 and the Energy Act 2004, ss 57 and 197.]

---

1. In *R (on the application of Gillan) v Metropolitan Police Comr and R (on the application of Quinton) v Same* [2004] EWCA Civ 1067, [2005] QB 388, [2005] 1 All ER 970, [2004] 3 WLR 1144, [2005] Crim LR 414 it was held: (*a*) while this legislation, which conferred a random power of stop and search backed up by sanctions, accordingly had to be restrictively construed there was no justification for not giving the statutory language its ordinary meaning; ss 44 and 45 did not conflict with the provisions of the Convention for the Protection of Human Rights and Fundamental Freedoms, although the manner in which the power thereunder were exercised might do so; (*b*) the powers created by the Act and the authorisation given under it were limited to searching for articles of a kind which could be used in connection with terrorism and, so exercised, there was nothing that threatened the rights of freedom of expression under article 10 or freedom of assembly under art 11 of the Convention; (*c*) the stop and search process did involve an interference with the right to respect for private life under art 8(1) but it was in accordance with the law and art 8(2) could be relied upon; and

(*d*) on the facts, the programme of successive authorisations (which covered the whole of the Metropolitan District and were in each case for the maximum period of 28 days) was justified.

8–23529 45. Exercise of power. (1) The power conferred by an authorisation under section 44(1) or (2)—

(*a*) may be exercised only for the purpose of searching for articles of a kind which could be used in connection with terrorism, and
(*b*) may be exercised whether or not the constable has grounds for suspecting the presence of articles of that kind.

(2) A constable may seize and retain an article which he discovers in the course of a search by virtue of section 44(1) or (2) and which he reasonably suspects is intended to be used in connection with terrorism.

(3) A constable exercising the power conferred by an authorisation may not require a person to remove any clothing in public except for headgear, footwear, an outer coat, a jacket or gloves.

(4) Where a constable proposes to search a person or vehicle by virtue of section 44(1) or (2) he may detain the person or vehicle for such time as is reasonably required to permit the search to be carried out at or near the place where the person or vehicle is stopped.

(5) Where—

(*a*) a vehicle or pedestrian is stopped by virtue of section 44(1) or (2), and
(*b*) the driver of the vehicle or the pedestrian applies for a written statement that the vehicle was stopped, or that he was stopped, by virtue of section 44(1) or (2),

the written statement shall be provided.

(6) An application under subsection (5) must be made within the period of 12 months beginning with the date on which the vehicle or pedestrian was stopped.
[Terrorism Act 2000, s 45.]

8–23530 46. Duration of authorisation. (1) An authorisation under section 44 has effect, subject to subsections (2) to (7), during the period—

(*a*) beginning at the time when the authorisation is given, and
(*b*) ending with a date or at a time specified in the authorisation.

(2) The date or time specified under subsection (1)(*b*) must not occur after the end of the period of 28 days beginning with the day on which the authorisation is given.

(2A) An authorisation under section 44(4BA) does not have effect except in relation to times when the specified area or place where members of the Civil Nuclear Constabulary have the powers and privileges of a constable.

(3) The person who gives an authorisation shall inform the Secretary of State as soon as is reasonably practicable.

(4) If an authorisation is not confirmed by the Secretary of State before the end of the period of 48 hours beginning with the time when it is given—

(*a*) it shall cease to have effect at the end of that period, but
(*b*) its ceasing to have effect shall not affect the lawfulness of anything done in reliance on it before the end of that period.

(5) Where the Secretary of State confirms an authorisation he may substitute an earlier date or time for the date or time specified under subsection (1)(*b*).

(6) The Secretary of State may cancel an authorisation with effect from a specified time.

(7) An authorisation may be renewed in writing by the person who gave it or by a person who could have given it; and subsections (1) to (6) shall apply as if a new authorisation were given on each occasion on which the authorisation is renewed.
[Terrorism Act 2000, s 46 as amended by the Energy Act 2004, s 57.]

8–23531 47. Offences. (1) A person commits an offence if he—

(*a*) fails to stop a vehicle when required to do so by a constable in the exercise of the power conferred by an authorisation under section 44(1);
(*b*) fails to stop when required to do so by a constable in the exercise of the power conferred by an authorisation under section 44(2);
(*c*) wilfully obstructs a constable in the exercise of the power conferred by an authorisation under section 44(1) or (2).

(2) A person guilty of an offence under this section shall be liable on summary conviction to—

(*a*) imprisonment for a term not exceeding six months,
(*b*) a fine not exceeding level 5 on the standard scale, or
(*c*) both.

[Terrorism Act 2000, s 47.]

Parking

8–23532 **48. Authorisations.** (1) An authorisation under this section authorises any constable in uniform to prohibit or restrict the parking of vehicles on a road specified in the authorisation.

(2) An authorisation may be given only if the person giving it considers it expedient for the prevention of acts of terrorism.

(3) An authorisation may be given—

(*a*) where the road specified is outside Northern Ireland and is wholly or partly within a police area other than one mentioned in paragraphs (*b*) or (*c*), by a police officer for the area who is of at least the rank of assistant chief constable;

(*b*) where the road specified is wholly or partly in the metropolitan police district, by a police officer for the district who is of at least the rank of commander of the metropolitan police;

(*c*) where the road specified is wholly or partly in the City of London, by a police officer for the City who is of at least the rank of commander in the City of London police force;

(*d*) where the road specified is in Northern Ireland, by a member of the Royal Ulster Constabulary who is of at least the rank of assistant chief constable.

(4) If an authorisation is given orally, the person giving it shall confirm it in writing as soon as is reasonably practicable.

[Terrorism Act 2000, s 48.]

8–23533 **49. Exercise of power.** (1) The power conferred by an authorisation under section 48 shall be exercised by placing a traffic sign on the road concerned.

(2) A constable exercising the power conferred by an authorisation under section 48 may suspend a parking place.

(3) Where a parking place is suspended under subsection (2), the suspension shall be treated as a restriction imposed by virtue of section 48—

(*a*) for the purposes of section 99 of the Road Traffic Regulation Act 1984 (removal of vehicles illegally parked, &c) and of any regulations in force under that section, and

(*b*) for the purposes of Articles 47 and 48 of the Road Traffic Regulation (Northern Ireland) Order 1997 (in relation to Northern Ireland).

[Terrorism Act 2000, s 49.]

8–23534 **50. Duration of authorisation.** (1) An authorisation under section 48 has effect, subject to subsections (2) and (3), during the period specified in the authorisation.

(2) The period specified shall not exceed 28 days.

(3) An authorisation may be renewed in writing by the person who gave it or by a person who could have given it; and subsections (1) and (2) shall apply as if a new authorisation were given on each occasion on which the authorisation is renewed.

[Terrorism Act 2000, s 50.]

8–23535 **51. Offences.** (1) A person commits an offence if he parks a vehicle in contravention of a prohibition or restriction imposed by virtue of section 48.

(2) A person commits an offence if—

(*a*) he is the driver or other person in charge of a vehicle which has been permitted to remain at rest in contravention of any prohibition or restriction imposed by virtue of section 48, and

(*b*) he fails to move the vehicle when ordered to do so by a constable in uniform.

(3) It is a defence for a person charged with an offence under this section to prove[1] that he had a reasonable excuse for the act or omission in question.

(4) Possession of a current disabled person's badge shall not itself constitute a reasonable excuse for the purposes of subsection (3).

(5) A person guilty of an offence under subsection (1) shall be liable on summary conviction to a fine not exceeding level 4 on the standard scale.

(6) A person guilty of an offence under subsection (2) shall be liable on summary conviction to—

(*a*) imprisonment for a term not exceeding three months,

(*b*) a fine not exceeding level 4 on the standard scale, or

(*c*) both.

[Terrorism Act 2000, s 51.]

---

1. On the balance of probabilities, see *R v Carr-Briant* [1943] KB 607, [1943] 2 All ER 156, 107 JP 167.

8–23536 **52. Interpretation.** In sections 48 to 51—

"disabled person's badge" means a badge issued, or having effect as if issued, under any regulations for the time being in force under section 21 of the Chronically Sick and Disabled Persons Act 1970 (in relation to England and Wales and Scotland) or section 14 of the Chronically Sick and Disabled Persons (Northern Ireland) Act 1978 (in relation to Northern Ireland);

"driver" means, in relation to a vehicle which has been left on any road, the person who was driving it when it was left there;

"parking" means leaving a vehicle or permitting it to remain at rest;

"traffic sign" has the meaning given in section 142(1) of the Road Traffic Regulation Act 1984 (in relation to England and Wales and Scotland) and in Article 28 of the Road Traffic Regulation (Northern Ireland) Order 1997 (in relation to Northern Ireland);

"vehicle" has the same meaning as in section 99(5) of the Road Traffic Regulation Act 1984 (in relation to England and Wales and Scotland) and Article 47(4) of the Road Traffic Regulation (Northern Ireland) Order 1997 (in relation to Northern Ireland).

[Terrorism Act 2000, s 52.]

Port and border controls

8–23537 53. Port and border controls. (1) Schedule 7 (port and border controls) shall have effect.

(2) The Secretary of State may by order repeal paragraph 16 of Schedule 7.

(3) The powers conferred by Schedule 7 shall be exercisable notwithstanding the rights conferred by section 1 of the Immigration Act 1971 (general principles regulating entry into and staying in the United Kingdom).

[Terrorism Act 2000, s 53.]

PART VI[1]
MISCELLANEOUS

Terrorist offences

8–23538 54. Weapons training. (1) A person commits an offence if he provides instruction or training in the making or use of—

(*a*) firearms,

(*aa*) radioactive material or weapons designed or adapted for the discharge of any radioactive material,

(*b*) explosives, or

(*c*) chemical, biological or nuclear weapons.

(2) A person commits an offence if he receives instruction or training in the making or use of—

(*a*) firearms,

(*aa*) radioactive material or weapons designed or adapted for the discharge of any radioactive material

(*b*) explosives, or

(*c*) chemical, biological or nuclear weapons.

(3) A person commits an offence if he invites another to receive instruction or training and the receipt—

(*a*) would constitute an offence under subsection (2), or

(*b*) would constitute an offence under subsection (2) but for the fact that it is to take place outside the United Kingdom.

(4) For the purpose of subsections (1) and (3)—

(*a*) a reference to the provision of instruction includes a reference to making it available either generally or to one or more specific persons, and

(*b*) an invitation to receive instruction or training may be either general or addressed to one or more specific persons.

(5) It is a defence[2] for a person charged with an offence under this section in relation to instruction or training to prove that his action or involvement was wholly for a purpose other than assisting, preparing for or participating in terrorism.

(6) A person guilty of an offence under this section shall be liable[3]—

(*a*) on conviction on indictment, to imprisonment for a term not exceeding ten years, to a fine or to both, or

(*b*) on summary conviction, to imprisonment for a term not exceeding six months, to a fine not exceeding the statutory maximum or to both.

(7) A court by or before which a person is convicted of an offence under this section may order the forfeiture of anything which the court considers to have been in the person's possession for purposes connected with the offence.

(8) Before making an order under subsection (7) a court must give an opportunity to be heard to any person, other than the convicted person, who claims to be the owner of or otherwise interested in anything which can be forfeited under that subsection.

(9) An order under subsection (7) shall not come into force until there is no further possibility of

it being varied, or set aside, on appeal (disregarding any power of a court to grant leave to appeal out of time).
[Terrorism Act 2000, s 54, as amended by the Anti-terrorism, Crime and Security Act 2001, s 120(1).]

1. Part VI contains ss 54–64.
2. For defences to this offence, see further s 118, post
3. For procedure in respect of this offence which is triable either way, see the Magistrates' Courts Act 1980, ss 17A–21, in PART I: MAGISTRATES' COURTS, PROCEDURE, ante.

8–23539 **55. Weapons training: interpretation.** In section 54—

"biological weapon" means a biological agent or toxin (within the meaning of the Biological Weapons Act 1974) in a form capable of use for hostile purposes or anything to which section 1(1)(*b*) of that Act applies,
"chemical weapon" has the meaning given by section 1 of the Chemical Weapons Act 1996, and
"radioactive material" means radioactive material capable of endangering life or causing harm to human health.
[Terrorism Act 2000, s 55, as amended by the Anti-terrorism, Crime and Security Act 2001, s 120(2).]

8–23540 **56. Directing terrorist organisation.** (1) A person commits an offence if he directs, at any level, the activities of an organisation which is concerned in the commission of acts of terrorism.
(2) A person guilty of an offence under this section is liable on conviction on indictment to imprisonment for life.
[Terrorism Act 2000, s 56.]

8–23541 **57. Possession for terrorist purposes.** (1) A person commits an offence if he possesses an article in circumstances which give rise to a reasonable suspicion that his possession is for a purpose connected with the commission, preparation or instigation of an act of terrorism.
(2) It is a defence[1] for a person charged with an offence under this section to prove that his possession of the article was not for a purpose connected with the commission, preparation or instigation of an act of terrorism.
(3) In proceedings for an offence under this section, if it is proved that an article—

(*a*) was on any premises at the same time as the accused, or
(*b*) was on premises of which the accused was the occupier or which he habitually used otherwise than as a member of the public,

the court may assume that the accused possessed the article, unless he proves that he did not know of its presence on the premises or that he had no control over it.
(4) A person guilty of an offence under this section shall be liable[2]—

(*a*) on conviction on indictment, to imprisonment for a term not exceeding 10 years, to a fine or to both, or
(*b*) on summary conviction, to imprisonment for a term not exceeding six months, to a fine not exceeding the statutory maximum or to both.

[Terrorism Act 2000, s 57.]

1. For defences to this offence, see further s 118, post.
2. For procedure in respect of this offence which is triable either way, see the Magistrates' Courts Act 1980, ss 17A–21, in PART I: MAGISTRATES' COURTS, PROCEDURE, ante.

8–23542 **58. Collection of information.** (1) A person commits an offence if—

(*a*) he collects or makes a record of information of a kind likely to be useful to a person committing or preparing an act of terrorism, or
(*b*) he possesses a document or record containing information of that kind.

(2) In this section "record" includes a photographic or electronic record.
(3) It is a defence[1] for a person charged with an offence under this section to prove that he had a reasonable excuse for his action or possession.
(4) A person guilty of an offence under this section shall be liable[2]—

(*a*) on conviction on indictment, to imprisonment for a term not exceeding 10 years, to a fine or to both, or
(*b*) on summary conviction, to imprisonment for a term not exceeding six months, to a fine not exceeding the statutory maximum or to both.

(5) A court by or before which a person is convicted of an offence under this section may order the forfeiture of any document or record containing information of the kind mentioned in subsection (1)(*a*).
(6) Before making an order under subsection (5) a court must give an opportunity to be heard to any person, other than the convicted person, who claims to be the owner of or otherwise interested in anything which can be forfeited under that subsection.
(7) An order under subsection (5) shall not come into force until there is no further possibility of

it being varied, or set aside, on appeal (disregarding any power of a court to grant leave to appeal out of time).
[Terrorism Act 2000, s 58.]

1. For defences to this offence, see further s 118, post.
2. For procedure in respect of this offence which is triable either way, see the Magistrates' Courts Act 1980, ss 17A–21, in PART I: MAGISTRATES' COURTS, PROCEDURE, ante.

Inciting terrorism overseas

8–23543 59. England and Wales. (1) A person commits an offence if—

(*a*) he incites another person to commit an act of terrorism wholly or partly outside the United Kingdom, and
(*b*) the act would, if committed in England and Wales, constitute one of the offences listed in subsection (2).

(2) Those offences are—

(*a*) murder,
(*b*) an offence under section 18 of the Offences against the Person Act 1861 (wounding with intent),
(*c*) an offence under section 23 or 24 of that Act (poison),
(*d*) an offence under section 28 or 29 of that Act (explosions), and
(*e*) an offence under section 1(2) of the Criminal Damage Act 1971 (endangering life by damaging property).

(3) A person guilty of an offence under this section shall be liable to any penalty to which he would be liable on conviction of the offence listed in subsection (2) which corresponds to the act which he incites.

(4) For the purposes of subsection (1) it is immaterial whether or not the person incited is in the United Kingdom at the time of the incitement.

(5) Nothing in this section imposes criminal liability on any person acting on behalf of, or holding office under, the Crown.
[Terrorism Act 2000, s 59.]

8–23544 60–61. *Northern Ireland and Scotland*

Terrorist bombing and finance offences

8–23545 62. Terrorist bombing: jurisdiction. (1) If—

(*a*) a person does anything outside the United Kingdom as an act of terrorism or for the purposes of terrorism, and
(*b*) his action would have constituted the commission of one of the offences listed in subsection (2) if it had been done in the United Kingdom,

he shall be guilty of the offence.

(2) The offences referred to in subsection (1)(*b*) are—

(*a*) an offence under section 2, 3 or 5 of the Explosive Substances Act 1883 (causing explosions, &c),
(*b*) an offence under section 1 of the Biological Weapons Act 1974 (biological weapons), and
(*c*) an offence under section 2 of the Chemical Weapons Act 1996 (chemical weapons).

[Terrorism Act 2000, s 62.]

8–23546 63. Terrorist finance: jurisdiction. (1) If—

(*a*) a person does anything outside the United Kingdom, and
(*b*) his action would have constituted the commission of an offence under any of sections 15 to 18 if it had been done in the United Kingdom,

he shall be guilty of the offence.

(2) For the purposes of subsection (1)(*b*), section 18(1)(*b*) shall be read as if for "the jurisdiction" there were substituted "a jurisdiction".
[Terrorism Act 2000, s 63.]

8–23546A 63A. Other terrorist offences under this Act: jurisdiction. (1) If—

(*a*) a United Kingdom national or a United Kingdom resident does anything outside the United Kingdom, and
(*b*) his action, if done in any part of the United Kingdom, would have constituted an offence under section 54 or any of sections 56 to 61,

he shall be guilty in that part of the United Kingdom of the offence.

(2) For the purposes of this section and sections 63B and 63C a "United Kingdom national" means an individual who is—

(*a*) a British citizen, a British overseas territories citizen, a British National (Overseas) or a British Overseas citizen,

(*b*) a person who under the British Nationality Act 1981 is a British subject, or

(*c*) a British protected person within the meaning of that Act.

(3) For the purposes of this section and sections 63B and 63C a "United Kingdom resident" means an individual who is resident in the United Kingdom.

[Terrorism Act 2000, s 63A, inserted by the Crime (International Co-operation) Act 2003, s 52.]

8–23546B **63B. Terrorist attacks abroad by UK nationals or residents: jurisdiction.** (1) If—

(*a*) a United Kingdom national or a United Kingdom resident does anything outside the United Kingdom as an act of terrorism or for the purposes of terrorism, and

(*b*) his action, if done in any part of the United Kingdom, would have constituted an offence listed in subsection (2),

he shall be guilty in that part of the United Kingdom of the offence.

(2) These are the offences—

(*a*) murder, manslaughter, culpable homicide, rape, assault causing injury, assault to injury, kidnapping, abduction or false imprisonment,

(*b*) an offence under section 4, 16, 18, 20, 21, 22, 23, 24, 28, 29, 30 or 64 of the Offences against the Person Act 1861,

(*c*) an offence under any of sections 1 to 5 of the Forgery and Counterfeiting Act 1981,

(*d*) the uttering of a forged document or an offence under section 46A of the Criminal Law (Consolidation) (Scotland) Act 1995,

(*e*) an offence under section 1 or 2 of the Criminal Damage Act 1971,

(*f*) an offence under Article 3 or 4 of the Criminal Damage (Northern Ireland) Order 1977,

(*g*) malicious mischief,

(*h*) wilful fire-raising.

[Terrorism Act 2000, s 63B, inserted by the Crime (International Co-operation) Act 2003, s 52.]

8–23546C **63C. Terrorist attacks abroad on UK nationals, residents and diplomatic staff etc: jurisdiction.** (1) If—

(*a*) a person does anything outside the United Kingdom as an act of terrorism or for the purposes of terrorism,

(*b*) his action is done to, or in relation to, a United Kingdom national, a United Kingdom resident or a protected person, and

(*c*) his action, if done in any part of the United Kingdom, would have constituted an offence listed in subsection (2),

he shall be guilty in that part of the United Kingdom of the offence.

(2) These are the offences—

(*a*) murder, manslaughter, culpable homicide, rape, assault causing injury, assault to injury, kidnapping, abduction or false imprisonment,

(*b*) an offence under section 4, 16, 18, 20, 21, 22, 23, 24, 28, 29, 30 or 64 of the Offences against the Person Act 1861,

(*c*) an offence under section 1, 2, 3, 4 or 5(1) or (3) of the Forgery and Counterfeiting Act 1981,

(*d*) the uttering of a forged document or an offence under section 46A(1) of the Criminal Law (Consolidation) (Scotland) Act 1995.

(3) For the purposes of this section and section 63D a person is a protected person if—

(*a*) he is a member of a United Kingdom diplomatic mission within the meaning of Article 1(*b*) of the Vienna Convention on Diplomatic Relations signed in 1961 (as that Article has effect in the United Kingdom by virtue of section 2 of and Schedule 1 to the Diplomatic Privileges Act 1964),

(*b*) he is a member of a United Kingdom consular post within the meaning of Article 1(*g*) of the Vienna Convention on Consular Relations signed in 1963 (as that Article has effect in the United Kingdom by virtue of section 1 of and Schedule 1 to the Consular Relations Act 1968),

(*c*) he carries out any functions for the purposes of the European Medicines Agency, or

(*d*) he carries out any functions for the purposes of a body specified in an order made by the Secretary of State.

(4) The Secretary of State may specify a body under subsection (3)(*d*) only if—

(*a*) it is established by or under the Treaty establishing the European Community or the Treaty on European Union, and

(*b*) the principal place in which its functions are carried out is a place in the United Kingdom.

(5) If in any proceedings a question arises as to whether a person is or was a protected person, a certificate—

(*a*) issued by or under the authority of the Secretary of State, and
(*b*) stating any fact relating to the question,

is to be conclusive evidence of that fact.

[Terrorism Act 2000, s 63C, inserted by the Crime (International Co-operation) Act 2003, s 52 and amended by SI 2004/3224.]

8–23546D 63D. Terrorist attacks or threats abroad in connection with UK diplomatic premises etc: jurisdiction. (1) If—

(*a*) a person does anything outside the United Kingdom as an act of terrorism or for the purposes of terrorism,
(*b*) his action is done in connection with an attack on relevant premises or on a vehicle ordinarily used by a protected person,
(*c*) the attack is made when a protected person is on or in the premises or vehicle, and
(*d*) his action, if done in any part of the United Kingdom, would have constituted an offence listed in subsection (2),

he shall be guilty in that part of the United Kingdom of the offence.

(2) These are the offences—

(*a*) an offence under section 1 of the Criminal Damage Act 1971,
(*b*) an offence under Article 3 of the Criminal Damage (Northern Ireland) Order 1977,
(*c*) malicious mischief,
(*d*) wilful fire-raising.

(3) If—

(*a*) a person does anything outside the United Kingdom as an act of terrorism or for the purposes of terrorism,
(*b*) his action consists of a threat of an attack on relevant premises or on a vehicle ordinarily used by a protected person,
(*c*) the attack is threatened to be made when a protected person is, or is likely to be, on or in the premises or vehicle, and
(*d*) his action, if done in any part of the United Kingdom, would have constituted an offence listed in subsection (4),

he shall be guilty in that part of the United Kingdom of the offence.

(4) These are the offences—

(*a*) an offence under section 2 of the Criminal Damage Act 1971,
(*b*) an offence under Article 4 of the Criminal Damage (Northern Ireland) Order 1977,
(*c*) breach of the peace (in relation to Scotland only).

(5) "Relevant premises" means—

(*a*) premises at which a protected person resides or is staying, or
(*b*) premises which a protected person uses for the purpose of carrying out his functions as such a person.

[Terrorism Act 2000, s 63D, inserted by the Crime (International Co-operation) Act 2003, s 52.]

8–23546E 63E. Sections 63B to 63D: supplementary. (1) Proceedings for an offence which (disregarding the Acts listed in subsection (2)) would not be an offence apart from section 63B, 63C or 63D are not to be started—

(*a*) in England and Wales, except by or with the consent of the Attorney General,
(*b*) in Northern Ireland, except by or with the consent of the Advocate General for Northern Ireland.

(2) These are the Acts—

(*a*) the Internationally Protected Persons Act 1978,
(*b*) the Suppression of Terrorism Act 1978,
(*c*) the Nuclear Material (Offences) Act 1983,
(*d*) the United Nations Personnel Act 1997.

(3) For the purposes of sections 63C and 63D it is immaterial whether a person knows that another person is a United Kingdom national, a United Kingdom resident or a protected person.

(4) In relation to any time before the coming into force of section 27(1) of the Justice (Northern Ireland) Act 2002, the reference in subsection (1)(*b*) to the Advocate General for Northern Ireland is to be read as a reference to the Attorney General for Northern Ireland.

[Terrorism Act 2000, s 63E, inserted by the Crime (International Co-operation) Act 2003, s 52.]

8–23547 64. *Repealed.*

PART VII[1]
NORTHERN IRELAND

8–23548

1. Part VII contains ss 65–113 and Schs 9–13.

PART VIII[1]
GENERAL

8–23549 114. Police powers. (1) A power conferred by virtue of this Act on a constable—

(*a*) is additional to powers which he has at common law or by virtue of any other enactment, and
(*b*) shall not be taken to affect those powers.

(2) A constable may if necessary use reasonable force for the purpose of exercising a power conferred on him by virtue of this Act (apart from paragraphs 2 and 3 of Schedule 7).

(3) Where anything is seized by a constable under a power conferred by virtue of this Act, it may (unless the contrary intention appears) be retained for so long as is necessary in all the circumstances.
[Terrorism Act 2000, s 114.]

1. Part VIII contains ss 114–131 and Schs 14–16.

8–23550 115. Officers' powers. Schedule 14 (which makes provision about the exercise of functions by authorised officers for the purposes of sections 25 to 31 and examining officers for the purposes of Schedule 7) shall have effect.
[Terrorism Act 2000, s 115.]

8–23551 116. Powers to stop and search. (1) A power to search premises conferred by virtue of this Act shall be taken to include power to search a container.

(2) A power conferred by virtue of this Act to stop a person includes power to stop a vehicle (other than an aircraft which is airborne).

(3) A person commits an offence if he fails to stop a vehicle when required to do so by virtue of this section.

(4) A person guilty of an offence under subsection (3) shall be liable on summary conviction to—

(*a*) imprisonment for a term not exceeding six months,
(*b*) a fine not exceeding level 5 on the standard scale, or
(*c*) both.
[Terrorism Act 2000, s 116.]

8–23552 117. Consent to prosecution. (1) This section applies to an offence under any provision of this Act other than an offence under—

(*a*) section 36,
(*b*) section 51,
(*c*) paragraph 18 of Schedule 7,
(*d*) paragraph 12 of Schedule 12, or
(*e*) Schedule 13.

(2) Proceedings for an offence to which this section applies—

(*a*) shall not be instituted in England and Wales without the consent of the Director of Public Prosecutions, and
(*b*) shall not be instituted in Northern Ireland without the consent of the Director of Public Prosecutions for Northern Ireland.

(3) Where it appears to the Director of Public Prosecutions or the Director of Public Prosecutions for Northern Ireland that an offence to which this section applies is committed for a purpose connected with the affairs of a country other than the United Kingdom—

(*a*) subsection (2) shall not apply, and
(*b*) proceedings for the offence shall not be instituted without the consent of the Attorney General or the Attorney General for Northern Ireland.
[Terrorism Act 2000, s 117.]

8–23553 118. Defences. (1) Subsection (2) applies where in accordance with a provision mentioned in subsection (5) it is a defence for a person charged with an offence to prove a particular matter.

(2) If the person adduces evidence which is sufficient to raise an issue with respect to the matter the court or jury shall assume that the defence is satisfied unless the prosecution proves beyond reasonable doubt that it is not.

(3) Subsection (4) applies where in accordance with a provision mentioned in subsection (5) a court—

(*a*) may make an assumption in relation to a person charged with an offence unless a particular matter is proved, or

(*b*) may accept a fact as sufficient evidence unless a particular matter is proved.

(4) If evidence is adduced which is sufficient to raise an issue with respect to the matter mentioned in subsection (3)(*a*) or (*b*) the court shall treat it as proved unless the prosecution disproves it beyond reasonable doubt.

(5) The provisions in respect of which subsections (2) and (4) apply are—

(*a*) sections 12(4), 39(5)(*a*), 54, 57, 58, 77 and 103 of this Act, and

(*b*) sections 13, 32 and 33 of the Northern Ireland (Emergency Provisions) Act 1996 (possession and information offences) as they have effect by virtue of Schedule 1 to this Act.

[Terrorism Act 2000, s 118.]

8–23554 **119. Crown servants, regulators, &c.** (1) The Secretary of State may make regulations[1] providing for any of sections 15 to 23 and 39 to apply to persons in the public service of the Crown.

(2) The Secretary of State may make regulations providing for section 19 not to apply to persons who are in his opinion performing or connected with the performance of regulatory, supervisory, investigative or registration functions of a public nature.

(3) Regulations—

(*a*) may make different provision for different purposes,

(*b*) may make provision which is to apply only in specified circumstances, and

(*c*) may make provision which applies only to particular persons or to persons of a particular description.

[Terrorism Act 2000, s 119.]

1. See the Terrorism Act 2000 (Crown Servants and Regulators) Regulations 2001, SI 2001/192 amended by SI 2003/3075.

8–23555 **120. Evidence.** (1) A document which purports to be—

(*a*) a notice or direction given or order made by the Secretary of State for the purposes of a provision of this Act, and

(*b*) signed by him or on his behalf,

shall be received in evidence and shall, until the contrary is proved, be deemed to have been given or made by the Secretary of State.

(2) A document bearing a certificate which—

(*a*) purports to be signed by or on behalf of the Secretary of State, and

(*b*) states that the document is a true copy of a notice or direction given or order made by the Secretary of State for the purposes of a provision of this Act,

shall be evidence (or, in Scotland, sufficient evidence) of the document in legal proceedings.

(3) In subsections (1) and (2) a reference to an order does not include a reference to an order made by statutory instrument.

(4) The Documentary Evidence Act 1868 shall apply to an authorisation given in writing by the Secretary of State for the purposes of this Act as it applies to an order made by him.

[Terrorism Act 2000, s 120.]

8–23556 **121. Interpretation.** In this Act—

"act" and "action" include omission,

"article" includes substance and any other thing,

"British Transport Police Force" means the constables appointed under section 53 of the British Transport Commission Act 1949 (c xxix),

"customs officer" means an officer of Revenue and Customs,

"dwelling" means a building or part of a building used as a dwelling, and a vehicle which is habitually stationary and which is used as a dwelling,

"explosive" means—

(*a*) an article or substance manufactured for the purpose of producing a practical effect by explosion,

(*b*) materials for making an article or substance within paragraph (*a*),

(*c*) anything used or intended to be used for causing or assisting in causing an explosion, and

(*d*) a part of anything within paragraph (*a*) or (*c*),

"firearm" includes an air gun or air pistol,

"immigration officer" means a person appointed as an immigration officer under paragraph 1 of Schedule 2 to the Immigration Act 1971,

"the Islands" means the Channel Islands and the Isle of Man,

"organisation" includes any association or combination of persons,
(*repealed*)
"premises", except in section 63D, includes any place and in particular includes—

(*a*) a vehicle,
(*b*) an offshore installation within the meaning given in section 44 of the Petroleum Act 1998, and
(*c*) a tent or moveable structure,

"property" includes property wherever situated and whether real or personal, heritable or moveable, and things in action and other intangible or incorporeal property,
"public place" means a place to which members of the public have or are permitted to have access, whether or not for payment,
"road" has the same meaning as in the Road Traffic Act 1988 (in relation to England and Wales), the Roads (Scotland) Act 1984 (in relation to Scotland) and the Road Traffic Regulation (Northern Ireland) Order 1997 (in relation to Northern Ireland), and includes part of a road, and
"vehicle", except in sections 48 to 52 and Schedule 7, includes an aircraft, hovercraft, train or vessel.
[Terrorism Act 2000, s 121, as amended by the Anti-terrorism, Crime and Security Act 2001, Sch 7, the Crime International Co-operation Act 2003, Sch 5, SI 2004/1573 and the Commissioners for Revenue and Customs Act 2005, Sch 4.]

8–23557 122. Index of defined expressions. In this Act the expressions listed below are defined by the provisions specified.

Expression	*Interpretation provision*
Act	Section 121
Action	Section 121
Action taken for the purposes of terrorism	Section 1(5)
Article	Section 121
British Transport Police Force	Section 121
Cordoned area	Section 33
Customs officer	Section 121
Dwelling	Section 121
Examining officer	Schedule 7, paragraph 1
Explosive	Section 121
Firearm	Section 121
Immigration officer	Section 121
The Islands	Section 121
Organisation	Section 121
Premises	Section 121
Property	Section 121
Proscribed organisation	Section 3(1)
Public place	Section 121
Road	Section 121
Scheduled offence (in Part VII)	Section 65
Terrorism	Section 1
Terrorist (in Part V)	Section 40
Terrorist investigation	Section 32

Expression	*Interpretation provision*
Terrorist property	Section 14
Vehicle	Section 121
Vehicle (in sections 48 to 51)	Section 52

[Terrorism Act 2000, s 122, as amended by the Anti-terrorism, Crime and Security Act 2001, Sch 7.]

8–23558 **123.** *Orders and regulations*

8–23559 **124.** *Directions*

8–23559A **125.** *Amendments and repeals*

8–23559B **126.** *Report to Parliament*

8–23559C **127.** *Money*

8–23559D **128. Commencement.** The preceding provisions of this Act, apart from sections 2(1)(*b*) and (2) and 118 and Schedule 1, shall come into force in accordance with provision made by the Secretary of State by order[1].
[Terrorism Act 2000, s 128.]

1. With the exception of s 100, the whole of the Act has been brought into force by the following orders: Commencement (No 1) Order 2000, SI 2000/2800; Commencement (No 2) Order 2001, SI 2001/2944; Commencement (No 3) Order 2001, SI 2001/421.

8–23559E **129.** *Transitional provisions*

8–23559F **130.** *Extent*

8–23559G **131.** *Short title*

SCHEDULE 2
Proscribed Organisations
(*As amended by SI 2001/1261, SI 2002/2724 and SI 2005/2892.*)

Section 3

8–23559H The Irish Republican Army[1].
Cumann na mBan.
Fianna na hEireann.
The Red Hand Commando.
Saor Eire.
The Ulster Freedom Fighters.
The Ulster Volunteer Force.
The Irish National Liberation Army.
The Irish People's Liberation Organisation.
The Ulster Defence Association.
The Loyalist Volunteer Force.
The Continuity Army Council.
The Orange Volunteers.
The Red Hand Defenders.
Al-Qa'ida
Egyptian Islamic Jihad
Al-Gama'at al-Islamiya
Armed Islamic Group (Groupe Islamique Armée) (GIA)
Salafist Group for Call and Combat (Groupe Salafiste pour la Prédication et le Combat) (GSPC)
Babbar Khalsa
International Sikh Youth Federation
Harakat Mujahideen
Jaish e Mohammed
Lashkar e Tayyaba
Liberation Tigers of Tamil Eelam (LTTE)
Hizballah External Security Organisation
Hamas-Izz al-Din al-Qassem Brigades

Palestinian Islamic Jihad—Shaqaqi
Abu Nidal Organisation
Islamic Army of Aden
Mujaheddin e Khalq
Kurdistan Workers' Party (Partiya Karkeren Kurdistan) (PKK)
Revolutionary Peoples' Liberation Party—Front (Devrimci Halk Kurtulus Partisi-Cephesi) (DHKP-C)
Basque Homeland and Liberty (Euskadi ta Askatasuna) (ETA)
17 November Revolutionary Organisation (N17)
Abu Sayyaf Group
Asbat Al-Ansar
Islamic Movement of Uzbekistan
Jemaah Islamiyah
Al Ittihad Al Islamia
Ansar Al Islam
Ansar Al Sunna
Groupe Islamique Combattant Marocain
Harakat-ul-Jihad-ul-Islami
Harakat-ul-Jihad-ul-Islami (Bangladesh)
Harakat-ul-Mujahideen/Alami
Hezb-e Islami Gulbuddin
Islamic Jihad Union
Jamaat ul-Furquan
Jundallah
Khuddam ul-Islam
Lashkar-e Jhangvi
Libyan Islamic Fighting Group
Sipah-e Sahaba Pakistan*Note*

The entry for The Orange Volunteers refers to the organisation which uses that name and in the name of which a statement described as a press release was published on 14th October 1998.

The entry for Jemaah Islamiyah refers to the organisation using that name that is based in south-east Asia, members of which were arrested by the Singapore authorities in December 2001 in connection with a plot to attack US and other Western targets in Singapore.

---

1. This is an umbrella term capable of describing all manifestations or splinter groups (*R v Z* [2005] UKHL 35, [2005] 2 AC 645, [2005] 3 All ER 95, [2005] Crim LR 985).

SCHEDULE 3A
REGULATED SECTOR AND SUPERVISORY AUTHORITIES

(*Substituted by SI 2003/3076, the Pensions Act 2004, Sch 12 and the Gambling Act 2005, Sch 16.*)

PART 1
REGULATED SECTOR

Business in the regulated sector

8–23559HA **1.** (1) A business is in the regulated sector to the extent that it engages in any of the following activities in the United Kingdom—

- (*a*) a regulated activity specified in sub-paragraph (2);
- (*b*) the activities of the National Savings Bank;
- (*c*) any activity carried on for the purpose of raising money authorised to be raised under the National Loans Act 1968 (c 13) under the auspices of the Director of Savings;
- (*d*) the business of operating a bureau de change, transmitting money (or any representation of monetary value) by any means or cashing cheques which are made payable to customers;
- (*e*) any of the activities in points 1 to 12 or 14 of Annex 1 to the Banking Consolidation Directive when carried on by way of business, ignoring an activity falling within any of paragraphs (a) to (d);
- (*f*) estate agency work;
- (*g*) operating a casino by way of business;
- (*h*) the activities of a person appointed to act as an insolvency practitioner within the meaning of section 388 of the Insolvency Act 1986 (c 45) or Article 3 of the Insolvency (Northern Ireland) Order 1989 (SI 1989/2405 (NI 19));
- (*i*) the provision by way of business of advice about the tax affairs of another person by a body corporate or unincorporate or, in the case of a sole practitioner, by an individual;
- (*j*) the provision by way of business of accountancy services by a body corporate or unincorporate or, in the case of a sole practitioner, by an individual;
- (*k*) the provision by way of business of audit services by a person who is eligible for appointment as a company auditor under section 25 of the Companies Act 1989 (c 40) or Article 28 of the Companies (Northern Ireland) Order 1990 (SI 1990/593 (NI 5));
- (*l*) the provision by way of business of legal services by a body corporate or unincorporate or, in the case of a sole practitioner, by an individual and which involves participation in a financial or real property transaction (whether by assisting in the planning or execution of any such transaction or otherwise by acting for, or on behalf of, a client in any such transaction);
- (*m*) the provision by way of business of services in relation to the formation, operation or management of a company or a trust;
- (*n*) the activity of dealing in goods of any description by way of business (including dealing as an auctioneer) whenever a transaction involves accepting a total cash payment of 15,000 euro or more.

(2) These are the regulated activities—

(*a*) accepting deposits;
(*b*) effecting or carrying out contracts of long-term insurance when carried on by a person who has received official authorisation pursuant to Article 4 or 51 of the Life Assurance Consolidation Directive;
(*c*) dealing in investments as principal or as agent;
(*d*) arranging deals in investments;
(e) managing investments;
(*f*) safeguarding and administering investments;
(*g*) sending dematerialised instructions;
(*h*) establishing (and taking other steps in relation to) collective investment schemes;
(*i*) advising on investments;
(*j*) issuing electronic money.

Excluded activities

2. A business is not in the regulated sector to the extent that it engages in any of the following activities—

(*a*) the issue of withdrawable share capital within the limit set by section 6 of the Industrial and Provident Societies Act 1965 (c 12) by a society registered under that Act;
(*b*) the acceptance of deposits from the public within the limit set by section 7(3) of that Act by such a society;
(*c*) the issue of withdrawable share capital within the limit set by section 6 of the Industrial and Provident Societies Act (Northern Ireland) 1969 (c 24 (NI)) by a society registered under that Act;
(*d*) the acceptance of deposits from the public within the limit set by section 7(3) of that Act by such a society;
(*e*) activities carried on by the Bank of England;
(*f*) any activity in respect of which an exemption order under section 38 of the Financial Services and Markets Act 2000 (c 8) has effect if it is carried on by a person who is for the time being specified in the order or falls within a class of persons so specified;
(*g*) the regulated activities of arranging deals in investments or advising on investments, in so far as the investment consists of rights under a regulated mortgage contract;[1]
(*h*) the regulated activities of dealing in investments as agent, arranging deals in investments, managing investments or advising on investments, in so far as the investment consists of rights under, or any right to or interest in, a contract of insurance which is not a qualifying contract of insurance.[2]

3. (1) This paragraph has effect for the purposes of paragraphs 1 and 2.

(2) Paragraphs 1(1)(*a*) and 2(*g*)[1] and (*h*)[2] must be read with section 22 of the Financial Services and Markets Act 2000, any relevant order under that section and Schedule 2 to that Act.

(3) The Banking Consolidation Directive is the Directive of the European Parliament and Council relating to the taking up and pursuit of the business of credit institutions (No 2000/12/EC), as amended.

(4) The Life Assurance Consolidation Directive is the Directive of the European Parliament and Council concerning life assurance (No 2002/83/EC).

(5) "Estate agency work" has the meaning given by section 1 of the Estate Agents Act 1979 (c 38) save for the omission of the words " (including a business in which he is employed)" in subsection (1) and includes a case where, in relation to a disposal or acquisition, the person acts as principal.

(6) References to amounts in euro include references to equivalent amounts in another currency.

(7) "Cash" means notes, coins or travellers' cheques in any currency.

(8) For the purpose of the application of this Part to Scotland, "real property" means "heritable property".

Part 2
Supervisory Authorities

8–23559HB **4.** (1) Each of the following is a supervisory authority—

(*a*) the Bank of England;
(*b*) the Financial Services Authority;
(*c*) the Council of Lloyd's;
(*d*) the Director General of Fair Trading;
(*e*) a body which is a designated professional body for the purposes of Part 20 of the Financial Services and Markets Act 2000;
(*f*) the Pensions Regulator;
(*g*) the Gambling Commission.

(2) The Secretary of State is also a supervisory authority in the exercise, in relation to a person carrying on a business in the regulated sector, of his functions under the enactments relating to companies or insolvency or under the Financial Services and Markets Act 2000.

(3) The Treasury are also a supervisory authority in the exercise, in relation to a person carrying on a business in the regulated sector, of their functions under the enactments relating to companies or insolvency or under the Financial Services and Markets Act 2000.

Part 3
Power To Amend

8–23559HC **5.** (1) The Treasury may by order amend Part 1 or 2 of this Schedule.

(2) An order under sub-paragraph (1) must be made by statutory instrument subject to annulment in pursuance of a resolution of either House of Parliament.

SCHEDULE 4

FORFEITURE ORDERS

(*As amended by the Anti-terrorism, Crime and Security Act 2001, Sch 2 and the Land Registration Act 2002, ss 133 and 135.*)

Section 23

PART I

ENGLAND AND WALES

Interpretation

8–23559I 1. In this Part of this Schedule—

"forfeiture order" means an order made by a court in England and Wales under section 23, and

"forfeited property" means the money or other property to which a forfeiture order applies.

Implementation of forfeiture orders

2. (1) Where a court in England and Wales makes a forfeiture order it may make such other provision as appears to it to be necessary for giving effect to the order, and in particular it may—

(*a*) require any of the forfeited property to be paid or handed over to the proper officer or to a constable designated for the purpose by the chief officer of police of a police force specified in the order;

(*b*) direct any of the forfeited property other than money or land to be sold or otherwise disposed of in such manner as the court may direct and the proceeds (if any) to be paid to the proper officer;

(*c*) appoint a receiver to take possession, subject to such conditions and exceptions as may be specified by the court, of any of the forfeited property, to realise it in such manner as the court may direct and to pay the proceeds to the proper officer;

(*d*) direct a specified part of any forfeited money, or of the proceeds of the sale, disposal or realisation of any forfeited property, to be paid by the proper officer to a specified person falling within section 23(7).

(2) A forfeiture order shall not come into force until there is no further possibility of it being varied, or set aside, on appeal (disregarding any power of a court to grant leave to appeal out of time).

(3) In sub-paragraph (1)(*b*) and (*d*) a reference to the proceeds of the sale, disposal or realisation of property is a reference to the proceeds after deduction of the costs of sale, disposal or realisation.

(4) Section 140 of the Magistrates' Courts Act 1980 (disposal of non-pecuniary forfeitures) shall not apply.

3. (1) A receiver appointed under paragraph 2 shall be entitled to be paid his remuneration and expenses by the proper officer out of the proceeds of the property realised by the receiver and paid to the proper officer under paragraph 2(1)(*c*).

(2) If and so far as those proceeds are insufficient, the receiver shall be entitled to be paid his remuneration and expenses by the prosecutor.

(3) A receiver appointed under paragraph 2 shall not be liable to any person in respect of any loss or damage resulting from action—

(*a*) which he takes in relation to property which is not forfeited property, but which he reasonably believes to be forfeited property,

(*b*) which he would be entitled to take if the property were forfeited property, and

(*c*) which he reasonably believes that he is entitled to take because of his belief that the property is forfeited property.

(4) Sub-paragraph (3) does not apply in so far as the loss or damage is caused by the receiver's negligence.

4. (1) In paragraphs 2 and 3 "the proper officer" means—

(*a*) where the forfeiture order is made by a magistrates' court, the designated officer for that court,

(*b*) where the forfeiture order is made by the Crown Court and the defendant was committed to the Crown Court by a magistrates' court, the designated officer for the magistrates' court, and

(*c*) where the forfeiture order is made by the Crown Court and the proceedings were instituted by a bill of indictment preferred by virtue of section 2(2)(*b*) of the Administration of Justice (Miscellaneous Provisions) Act 1933, the designated officer for the magistrates' court for the place where the trial took place.

(2) The proper officer shall issue a certificate in respect of a forfeiture order if an application is made by—

(*a*) the prosecutor in the proceedings in which the forfeiture order was made,

(*b*) the defendant in those proceedings, or

(*c*) a person whom the court heard under section 23(7) before making the order.

(3) The certificate shall state the extent (if any) to which, at the date of the certificate, effect has been given to the forfeiture order.

Restraint orders

5. (1) The High Court may make a restraint order under this paragraph where—

(*a*) proceedings have been instituted in England and Wales for an offence under any of sections 15 to 18,

(*b*) the proceedings have not been concluded,

(*c*) an application for a restraint order is made to the High Court by the prosecutor, and

(*d*) a forfeiture order has been made, or it appears to the High Court that a forfeiture order may be made, in the proceedings for the offence.

(2) The High Court may also make a restraint order under this paragraph where—

(*a*) a criminal investigation has been started in England and Wales with regard to an offence under any of sections 15 to 18, (*b*) an application for a restraint order is made to the High Court by the person who the High Court is satisfied will have the conduct of any proceedings for the offence, and

(*c*) it appears to the High Court that a forfeiture order may be made in any proceedings for the offence.

(3) A restraint order prohibits a person to whom notice of it is given, subject to any conditions and exceptions specified in the order, from dealing with property in respect of which a forfeiture order has been or could be made in any proceedings referred to in sub-paragraph (1) or (2).

(4) An application for a restraint order may be made to a judge in chambers without notice.

(5) In this paragraph a reference to dealing with property includes a reference to removing the property from Great Britain.

(6) In this paragraph "criminal investigation" means an investigation which police officers or other persons have a duty to conduct with a view to it being ascertained whether a person should be charged with an offence.

6. (1) A restraint order shall provide for notice of it to be given to any person affected by the order.

(2) A restraint order may be discharged or varied by the High Court on the application of a person affected by it.

(3) A restraint order made under paragraph 5(1) shall in particular be discharged on an application under sub-paragraph (2) if the proceedings for the offence have been concluded.

(4) A restraint order made under paragraph 5(2) shall in particular be discharged on an application under sub-paragraph (2)—

(*a*) if no proceedings in respect of offences under any of sections 15 to 18 are instituted within such time as the High Court considers reasonable, and

(*b*) if all proceedings in respect of offences under any of sections 15 to 18 have been concluded.

7. (1) A constable may seize any property subject to a restraint order for the purpose of preventing it from being removed from Great Britain.

(2) Property seized under this paragraph shall be dealt with in accordance with the High Court's directions.

8. (1) The Land Charges Act 1972 and the Land Registration Act 2002—

(*a*) shall apply in relation to restraint orders as they apply in relation to orders affecting land made by the court for the purpose of enforcing judgments or recognizances, except that no notice may be entered in the register of title under the Land Registration Act 2002 in respect of such orders, and

(*b*) shall apply in relation to applications for restraint orders as they apply in relation to other pending land actions.

(2) *Repealed.*

(3) *Repealed.*

Compensation

9. (1) This paragraph applies where a restraint order is discharged under paragraph 6(4)(*a*).

(2) This paragraph also applies where a forfeiture order or a restraint order is made in or in relation to proceedings for an offence under any of sections 15 to 18 which—

(*a*) do not result in conviction for an offence under any of those sections,

(*b*) result in conviction for an offence under any of those sections in respect of which the person convicted is subsequently pardoned by Her Majesty, or

(*c*) result in conviction for an offence under any of those sections which is subsequently quashed.

(3) A person who had an interest in any property which was subject to the order may apply to the High Court for compensation.

(4) The High Court may order compensation to be paid to the applicant if satisfied—

(*a*) that there was a serious default on the part of a person concerned in the investigation or prosecution of the offence,

(*b*) that the person in default was or was acting as a member of a police force, or was a member of the Crown Prosecution Service or was acting on behalf of the Service,

(*c*) that the applicant has suffered loss in consequence of anything done in relation to the property by or in pursuance of the forfeiture order or restraint order, and

(*d*) that, having regard to all the circumstances, it is appropriate to order compensation to be paid.

(5) The High Court shall not order compensation to be paid where it appears to it that proceedings for the offence would have been instituted even if the serious default had not occurred.

(6) Compensation payable under this paragraph shall be paid—

(*a*) where the person in default was or was acting as a member of a police force, out of the police fund out of which the expenses of that police force are met, and

(*b*) where the person in default was a member of the Crown Prosecution Service, or was acting on behalf of the Service, by the Director of Public Prosecutions.

10. (1) This paragraph applies where—

(*a*) a forfeiture order or a restraint order is made in or in relation to proceedings for an offence under any of sections 15 to 18, and

(*b*) the proceedings result in a conviction which is subsequently quashed on an appeal under section 7(2) or (5).

(2) A person who had an interest in any property which was subject to the order may apply to the High Court for compensation.

(3) The High Court may order compensation to be paid to the applicant if satisfied—

(*a*) that the applicant has suffered loss in consequence of anything done in relation to the property by or in pursuance of the forfeiture order or restraint order, and

(*b*) that, having regard to all the circumstances, it is appropriate to order compensation to be paid.

(4) Compensation payable under this paragraph shall be paid by the Secretary of State.

Proceedings for an offence: timing

11. (1) For the purposes of this Part of this Schedule proceedings for an offence are instituted—

(*a*) when a justice of the peace issues a summons or warrant under section 1 of the Magistrates' Courts Act 1980 in respect of the offence;
(*b*) when a person is charged with the offence after being taken into custody without a warrant;
(*c*) when a bill of indictment charging a person with the offence is preferred by virtue of section 2(2)(*b*) of the Administration of Justice (Miscellaneous Provisions) Act 1933.

(2) Where the application of sub-paragraph (1) would result in there being more than one time for the institution of proceedings they shall be taken to be instituted at the earliest of those times.

(3) For the purposes of this Part of this Schedule proceedings are concluded—

(*a*) when a forfeiture order has been made in those proceedings and effect has been given to it in respect of all the forfeited property, or
(*b*) when no forfeiture order has been made in those proceedings and there is no further possibility of one being made as a result of an appeal (disregarding any power of a court to grant leave to appeal out of time).

Enforcement of orders made elsewhere in the British Islands

12. In the following provisions of this Part of this Schedule—

"a Scottish order" means—

(*a*) an order made in Scotland under section 23 ("a Scottish forfeiture order"),
(*b*) an order made under paragraph 18 ("a Scottish restraint order"), or
(*c*) an order made under any other provision of Part II of this Schedule in relation to a Scottish forfeiture or restraint order;

"a Northern Ireland order" means—

(*a*) an order made in Northern Ireland under section 23 ("a Northern Ireland forfeiture order"),
(*b*) an order made under paragraph 33 ("a Northern Ireland restraint order"), or
(*c*) an order made under any other provision of Part III of this Schedule in relation to a Northern Ireland forfeiture or restraint order;

"an Islands order" means an order made in any of the Islands under a provision of the law of that Island corresponding to—

(*a*) section 23 ("an Islands forfeiture order"),
(*b*) paragraph 5 ("an Islands restraint order"), or
(*c*) any other provision of this Part of this Schedule.

13. (1) Subject to the provisions of this paragraph, a Scottish, Northern Ireland or Islands order shall have effect in the law of England and Wales.

(2) But such an order shall be enforced in England and Wales only in accordance with—

(*a*) the provisions of this paragraph, and
(*b*) any provision made by rules of court as to the manner in which, and the conditions subject to which, such orders are to be enforced there.

(3) On an application made to it in accordance with rules of court for registration of a Scottish, Northern Ireland or Islands order, the High Court shall direct that the order shall, in accordance with such rules, be registered in that court.

(4) Rules of court shall also make provision—

(*a*) for cancelling or varying the registration of a Scottish, Northern Ireland or Islands forfeiture order when effect has been given to it, whether in England and Wales or elsewhere, in respect of all or, as the case may be, part of the money or other property to which the order applies;
(*b*) for cancelling or varying the registration of a Scottish, Northern Ireland or Islands restraint order which has been discharged or varied by the court by which it was made.

(5) If a Scottish, Northern Ireland or Islands forfeiture order is registered under this paragraph the High Court shall have, in relation to that order, the same powers as a court has under paragraph 2(1) to give effect to a forfeiture order made by it and—

(*a*) paragraph 3 shall apply accordingly,
(*b*) any functions of a justices' chief executive shall be exercised by the appropriate officer of the High Court, and
(*c*) after making any payment required by virtue of paragraph 2(1)(*d*) or 3, the balance of any sums received by the appropriate officer of the High Court by virtue of an order made under this sub-paragraph shall be paid by him to the Secretary of State.

(6) If a Scottish, Northern Ireland or Islands restraint order is registered under this paragraph—

(*a*) paragraphs 7 and 8 shall apply as they apply to a restraint order under paragraph 5, and
(*b*) the High Court shall have power to make an order under section 33 of the Supreme Court Act 1981* (extended power to order inspection of property, &c) in relation to proceedings brought or likely to be brought for a Scottish, Northern Ireland or Islands restraint order as if those proceedings had been brought or were likely to be brought in the High Court.

(7) In addition, if a Scottish, Northern Ireland or Islands order is registered under this paragraph—

(*a*) the High Court shall have, in relation to its enforcement, the same power as if the order had originally been made in the High Court,
(*b*) proceedings for or with respect to its enforcement may be taken as if the order had originally been made in the High Court, and

(*c*) proceedings for or with respect to contravention of such an order, whether before or after such registration, may be taken as if the order had originally been made in the High Court.

(8) The High Court may also make such orders or do otherwise as seems to it appropriate for the purpose of—

(*a*) assisting the achievement in England and Wales of the purposes of a Scottish, Northern Ireland or Islands order, or

(*b*) assisting a receiver or other person directed by a Scottish, Northern Ireland or Islands order to sell or otherwise dispose of property.

(9) The following documents shall be received in evidence in England and Wales without further proof—

(*a*) a document purporting to be a copy of a Scottish, Northern Ireland or Islands order and to be certified as such by a proper officer of the court by which it was made, and

(*b*) a document purporting to be a certificate for purposes corresponding to those of paragraph 4(2) and (3) and to be certified by a proper officer of the court concerned.

*

Enforcement of orders made in designated countries

14. (1) Her Majesty may by Order[1] in Council make provision for the purpose of enabling the enforcement in England and Wales of external orders.

(2) An "external order" means an order—

(*a*) which is made in a country or territory designated for the purposes of this paragraph by the Order in Council, and

(*b*) which makes relevant provision.

(3) "Relevant provision" means—

(*a*) provision for the forfeiture of terrorist property ("an external forfeiture order"), or

(*b*) provision prohibiting dealing with property which is subject to an external forfeiture order or in respect of which such an order could be made in proceedings which have been or are to be instituted in the designated country or territory ("an external restraint order").

(4) An Order in Council under this paragraph may, in particular, include provision—

(*a*) which, for the purpose of facilitating the enforcement of any external order that may be made, has effect at times before there is an external order to be enforced;

(*b*) for matters corresponding to those for which provision is made by, or can be made under, paragraph 13(1) to (8) in relation to the orders to which that paragraph applies;

(*c*) for the proof of any matter relevant for the purposes of anything falling to be done in pursuance of the Order in Council.

(5) An Order in Council under this paragraph may also make provision with respect to anything falling to be done on behalf of the United Kingdom in a designated country or territory in relation to proceedings in that country or territory for or in connection with the making of an external order.

(6) An Order in Council under this paragraph—

(*a*) may make different provision for different cases, and

(*b*) shall not be made unless a draft of it has been laid before and approved by resolution of each House of Parliament.

---

1. The Terrorism Act 2000 (Enforcement of External Orders) Order 2001, SI 2001/3927 has been made.

8–23559IA

SCHEDULE 5

TERRORIST INVESTIGATIONS: INFORMATION

(*As amended by the Anti-terrorism, Crime and Security Act 2001, s 121(1) and SI 2003/427.*)

Section 37

PART I
ENGLAND AND WALES AND NORTHERN IRELAND

Searches

1. (1) A constable may apply to a justice of the peace for the issue of a warrant under this paragraph for the purposes of a terrorist investigation.

(2) A warrant under this paragraph shall authorise any constable—

(*a*) to enter the premises specified in the warrant,

(*b*) to search the premises and any person found there, and

(*c*) to seize and retain any relevant material which is found on a search under paragraph (*b*).

(3) For the purpose of sub-paragraph (2)(*c*) material is relevant if the constable has reasonable grounds for believing that—

(*a*) it is likely to be of substantial value, whether by itself or together with other material, to a terrorist investigation, and

(*b*) it must be seized in order to prevent it from being concealed, lost, damaged, altered or destroyed.

(4) A warrant under this paragraph shall not authorise—

(*a*) the seizure and retention of items subject to legal privilege, or

(*b*) a constable to require a person to remove any clothing in public except for headgear, footwear, an outer coat, a jacket or gloves.

(5) Subject to paragraph 2, a justice may grant an application under this paragraph if satisfied—

(*a*) that the warrant is sought for the purposes of a terrorist investigation,

(*b*) that there are reasonable grounds for believing that there is material on premises specified in the application which is likely to be of substantial value, whether by itself or together with other material, to a terrorist investigation and which does not consist of or include excepted material (within the meaning of paragraph 4 below), and

(*c*) that the issue of a warrant is likely to be necessary in the circumstances of the case.

2. (1) This paragraph applies where an application is made under paragraph 1 and—

(*a*) the application is made by a police officer of at least the rank of superintendent,

(*b*) the application does not relate to residential premises, and

(*c*) the justice to whom the application is made is not satisfied of the matter referred to in paragraph 1(5)(*c*).

(2) The justice may grant the application if satisfied of the matters referred to in paragraph 1(5)(*a*) and (*b*).

(3) Where a warrant under paragraph 1 is issued by virtue of this paragraph, the powers under paragraph 1(2)(*a*) and (*b*) are exercisable only within the period of 24 hours beginning with the time when the warrant is issued.

(4) For the purpose of sub-paragraph (1) "residential premises" means any premises which the officer making the application has reasonable grounds for believing are used wholly or mainly as a dwelling.

3. (1) Subject to sub-paragraph (2), a police officer of at least the rank of superintendent may by a written authority signed by him authorise a search of specified premises which are wholly or partly within a cordoned area.

(2) A constable who is not of the rank required by sub-paragraph (1) may give an authorisation under this paragraph if he considers it necessary by reason of urgency.

(3) An authorisation under this paragraph shall authorise any constable—

(*a*) to enter the premises specified in the authority,

(*b*) to search the premises and any person found there, and

(*c*) to seize and retain any relevant material (within the meaning of paragraph 1(3)) which is found on a search under paragraph (*b*).

(4) The powers under sub-paragraph (3)(*a*) and (*b*) may be exercised—

(*a*) on one or more occasions, and

(*b*) at any time during the period when the designation of the cordoned area under section 33 has effect.

(5) An authorisation under this paragraph shall not authorise—

(*a*) the seizure and retention of items subject to legal privilege;

(*b*) a constable to require a person to remove any clothing in public except for headgear, footwear, an outer coat, a jacket or gloves.

(6) An authorisation under this paragraph shall not be given unless the person giving it has reasonable grounds for believing that there is material to be found on the premises which—

(*a*) is likely to be of substantial value, whether by itself or together with other material, to a terrorist investigation, and

(*b*) does not consist of or include excepted material.

(7) A person commits an offence if he wilfully obstructs a search under this paragraph.

(8) A person guilty of an offence under sub-paragraph (7) shall be liable on summary conviction to—

(*a*) imprisonment for a term not exceeding three months*,

(*b*) a fine not exceeding level 4 on the standard scale, or

(*c*) both.

Excepted material

4. In this Part—

(*a*) "excluded material" has the meaning given by section 11 of the Police and Criminal Evidence Act 1984,

(*b*) "items subject to legal privilege" has the meaning given by section 10 of that Act, and

(*c*) "special procedure material" has the meaning given by section 14 of that Act;

and material is "excepted material" if it falls within any of paragraphs *(a)* to *(c)*.

Excluded and special procedure material: production & access

5. (1) A constable may apply to a Circuit judge** for an order under this paragraph for the purposes of a terrorist investigation.

(2) An application for an order shall relate to particular material, or material of a particular description, which consists of or includes excluded material or special procedure material.

(3) An order under this paragraph may require a specified person—

(*a*) to produce to a constable within a specified period for seizure and retention any material which he has in his possession, custody or power and to which the application relates;

(*b*) to give a constable access to any material of the kind mentioned in paragraph (*a*) within a specified period;

(*c*) to state to the best of his knowledge and belief the location of material to which the application relates if it is not in, and it will not come into, his possession, custody or power within the period specified under paragraph (*a*) or (*b*).

(4) For the purposes of this paragraph—

(*a*) an order may specify a person only if he appears to the Circuit judge** to have in his possession, custody or power any of the material to which the application relates, and

(*b*) a period specified in an order shall be the period of seven days beginning with the date of the order unless it appears to the judge that a different period would be appropriate in the particular circumstances of the application.

(5) Where a Circuit judge** makes an order under sub-paragraph (3)(*b*) in relation to material on any premises, he may, on the application of a constable, order any person who appears to the judge to be entitled to grant entry to the premises to allow any constable to enter the premises to obtain access to the material.

6. (1) A Circuit judge** may grant an application under paragraph 5 if satisfied—

(*a*) that the material to which the application relates consists of or includes excluded material or special procedure material,

(*b*) that it does not include items subject to legal privilege, and

(*c*) that the conditions in sub-paragraphs (2) and (3) are satisfied in respect of that material.

(2) The first condition is that—

(*a*) the order is sought for the purposes of a terrorist investigation, and

(*b*) there are reasonable grounds for believing that the material is likely to be of substantial value, whether by itself or together with other material, to a terrorist investigation.

(3) The second condition is that there are reasonable grounds for believing that it is in the public interest that the material should be produced or that access to it should be given having regard—

(*a*) to the benefit likely to accrue to a terrorist investigation if the material is obtained, and

(*b*) to the circumstances under which the person concerned has any of the material in his possession, custody or power.

7. (1) An order under paragraph 5 may be made in relation to—

(*a*) material consisting of or including excluded or special procedure material which is expected to come into existence within the period of 28 days beginning with the date of the order;

(*b*) a person who the Circuit judge** thinks is likely to have any of the material to which the application relates in his possession, custody or power within that period.

(2) Where an order is made under paragraph 5 by virtue of this paragraph, paragraph 5(3) shall apply with the following modifications—

(*a*) the order shall require the specified person to notify a named constable as soon as is reasonably practicable after any material to which the application relates comes into his possession, custody or power,

(*b*) the reference in paragraph 5(3)(*a*) to material which the specified person has in his possession, custody or power shall be taken as a reference to the material referred to in paragraph (*a*) above which comes into his possession, custody or power, and

(*c*) the reference in paragraph 5(3)(*c*) to the specified period shall be taken as a reference to the period of 28 days beginning with the date of the order.

(3) Where an order is made under paragraph 5 by virtue of this paragraph, paragraph 5(4) shall not apply and the order—

(*a*) may only specify a person falling within sub-paragraph (1)(*b*), and

(*b*) shall specify the period of seven days beginning with the date of notification required under sub-paragraph (2)(*a*) unless it appears to the judge that a different period would be appropriate in the particular circumstances of the application.

8. (1) An order under paragraph 5—

(*a*) shall not confer any right to production of, or access to, items subject to legal privilege, and

(*b*) shall have effect notwithstanding any restriction on the disclosure of information imposed by statute or otherwise.

(2) Where the material to which an application under paragraph 5 relates consists of information contained in a computer—

(*a*) an order under paragraph 5(3)(*a*) shall have effect as an order to produce the material in a form in which it can be taken away and in which it is visible and legible, and

(*b*) an order under paragraph 5(3)(*b*) shall have effect as an order to give access to the material in a form in which it is visible and legible.

9. (1) An order under paragraph 5 may be made in relation to material in the possession, custody or power of a government department.

(2) Where an order is made by virtue of sub-paragraph (1)—

(*a*) it shall be served as if the proceedings were civil proceedings against the department, and

(*b*) it may require any officer of the department, whether named in the order or not, who may for the time being have in his possession, custody or power the material concerned, to comply with the order.

(3) In this paragraph "government department" means an authorised government department for the purposes of the Crown Proceedings Act 1947.

10. (1) An order of a Circuit judge** under paragraph 5 shall have effect as if it were an order of the Crown Court.

(2) Criminal Procedure Rules may make provision about proceedings relating to an order under paragraph 5.

(3) In particular, the rules may make provision about the variation or discharge of an order.

Excluded or special procedure material: search

11. (1) A constable may apply to a Circuit judge** for the issue of a warrant under this paragraph for the purposes of a terrorist investigation.

(2) A warrant under this paragraph shall authorise any constable—

(*a*) to enter the premises specified in the warrant,
(*b*) to search the premises and any person found there, and
(*c*) to seize and retain any relevant material which is found on a search under paragraph (*b*).

(3) A warrant under this paragraph shall not authorise—

(*a*) the seizure and retention of items subject to legal privilege;
(*b*) a constable to require a person to remove any clothing in public except for headgear, footwear, an outer coat, a jacket or gloves.

(4) For the purpose of sub-paragraph (2)(*c*) material is relevant if the constable has reasonable grounds for believing that it is likely to be of substantial value, whether by itself or together with other material, to a terrorist investigation.

12. (1) A Circuit judge** may grant an application under paragraph 11 if satisfied that an order made under paragraph 5 in relation to material on the premises specified in the application has not been complied with.

(2) A Circuit judge** may also grant an application under paragraph 11 if satisfied that there are reasonable grounds for believing that—

(*a*) there is material on premises specified in the application which consists of or includes excluded material or special procedure material but does not include items subject to legal privilege, and
(*b*) the conditions in sub-paragraphs (3) and (4) are satisfied.

(3) The first condition is that—

(*a*) the warrant is sought for the purposes of a terrorist investigation, and
(*b*) the material is likely to be of substantial value, whether by itself or together with other material, to a terrorist investigation.

(4) The second condition is that it is not appropriate to make an order under paragraph 5 in relation to the material because—

(*a*) it is not practicable to communicate with any person entitled to produce the material,
(*b*) it is not practicable to communicate with any person entitled to grant access to the material or entitled to grant entry to the premises on which the material is situated, or
(*c*) a terrorist investigation may be seriously prejudiced unless a constable can secure immediate access to the material.

Explanations

13. (1) A constable may apply to a Circuit judge** for an order under this paragraph requiring any person specified in the order to provide an explanation of any material—

(*a*) seized in pursuance of a warrant under paragraph 1 or 11, or
(*b*) produced or made available to a constable under paragraph 5.

(2) An order under this paragraph shall not require any person to disclose any information which he would be entitled to refuse to disclose on grounds of legal professional privilege in proceedings in the High Court.

(3) But a lawyer may be required to provide the name and address of his client.

(4) A statement by a person in response to a requirement imposed by an order under this paragraph—

(*a*) may be made orally or in writing, and
(*b*) may be used in evidence against him only on a prosecution for an offence under paragraph 14.

(5) Paragraph 10 shall apply to orders under this paragraph as it applies to orders under paragraph 5.

14. (1) A person commits an offence if, in purported compliance with an order under paragraph 13, he—

(*a*) makes a statement which he knows to be false or misleading in a material particular, or
(*b*) recklessly makes a statement which is false or misleading in a material particular.

(2) A person guilty of an offence under sub-paragraph (1) shall be liable—

(*a*) on conviction on indictment, to imprisonment for a term not exceeding two years, to a fine or to both, or
(*b*) on summary conviction, to imprisonment for a term not exceeding six months, to a fine not exceeding the statutory maximum or to both.

Urgent cases

15. (1) A police officer of at least the rank of superintendent may by a written order signed by him give to any constable the authority which may be given by a search warrant under paragraph 1 or 11.

(2) An order shall not be made under this paragraph unless the officer has reasonable grounds for believing—

(*a*) that the case is one of great emergency, and
(*b*) that immediate action is necessary.

(3) Where an order is made under this paragraph particulars of the case shall be notified as soon as is reasonably practicable to the Secretary of State.

(4) A person commits an offence if he wilfully obstructs a search under this paragraph.

(5) A person guilty of an offence under sub-paragraph (4) shall be liable on summary conviction to—

(*a*) imprisonment for a term not exceeding three months*,
(*b*) a fine not exceeding level 4 on the standard scale, or
(*c*) both.

16. (1) If a police officer of at least the rank of superintendent has reasonable grounds for believing that the case is one of great emergency he may by a written notice signed by him require any person specified in the notice to provide an explanation of any material seized in pursuance of an order under paragraph 15.

(2) Sub-paragraphs (2) to (4) of paragraph 13 and paragraph 14 shall apply to a notice under this paragraph as they apply to an order under paragraph 13.

(3) A person commits an offence if he fails to comply with a notice under this paragraph.

(4) It is a defence for a person charged with an offence under sub-paragraph (3) to show that he had a reasonable excuse for his failure.

(5) A person guilty of an offence under sub-paragraph (3) shall be liable on summary conviction to—

(*a*) imprisonment for a term not exceeding six months,
(*b*) a fine not exceeding level 5 on the standard scale, or
(*c*) both.

Supplementary

17. For the purposes of sections 21 and 22 of the Police and Criminal Evidence Act 1984 (seized material: access, copying and retention)—

(*a*) a terrorist investigation shall be treated as an investigation of or in connection with an offence, and
(*b*) material produced in pursuance of an order under paragraph 5 shall be treated as if it were material seized by a constable.

Northern Ireland

18. In the application of this Part to Northern Ireland—

(*a*) the reference in paragraph 4(*a*) to section 11 of the Police and Criminal Evidence Act 1984 shall be taken as a reference to Article 13 of the Police and Criminal Evidence (Northern Ireland) Order 1989,
(*b*) the reference in paragraph 4(*b*) to section 10 of that Act shall be taken as a reference to Article 12 of that Order,
(*c*) the reference in paragraph 4(*c*) to section 14 of that Act shall be taken as a reference to Article 16 of that Order,
(*d*) the references in paragraph 9(1) and (2) to "government department" shall be taken as including references to an authorised Northern Ireland department for the purposes of the Crown Proceedings Act 1947,
(*dd*) the reference in paragraph 10(2) to "Criminal Procedure Rules" shall be taken as a reference to Crown Court Rules,
(*e*) *repealed*
(*f*) the reference in paragraph 17 to sections 21 and 22 of the Police and Criminal Evidence Act 1984 shall be taken as a reference to Articles 23 and 24 of the Police and Criminal Evidence (Northern Ireland) Order 1989, and
(*g*) references to "a Circuit judge" shall be taken as references to a Crown Court judge.

19–21. *Repealed.*

Section 38

SCHEDULE 6
Financial Information

(*As amended by SI 2000/2952, the Anti-terrorism, Crime and Security Act 2001, Sch 2, SI 2001/3649, the Courts Act 2003, Sch 8 and 2004/3379.*)

Orders

8–23559J **1.** (1) Where an order has been made under this paragraph in relation to a terrorist investigation, a constable named in the order may require a financial institution to which the order applies to provide customer information for the purposes of the investigation.

(1A) The order may provide that it applies to—

(*a*) all financial institutions,
(*b*) a particular description, or particular descriptions, of financial institutions, or
(*c*) a particular financial institution or particular financial institutions.

(2) The information shall be provided—

(*a*) in such manner and within such time as the constable may specify, and
(*b*) notwithstanding any restriction on the disclosure of information imposed by statute or otherwise.

(3) An institution which fails to comply with a requirement under this paragraph shall be guilty of an offence.

(4) It is a defence for an institution charged with an offence under sub-paragraph (3) to prove—

(*a*) that the information required was not in the institution's possession, or
(*b*) that it was not reasonably practicable for the institution to comply with the requirement.

(5) An institution guilty of an offence under sub-paragraph (3) shall be liable on summary conviction to a fine not exceeding level 5 on the standard scale.

Procedure

2. An order under paragraph 1 may be made only on the application of—

(*a*) in England and Wales or Northern Ireland, a police officer of at least the rank of superintendent, or
(*b*) in Scotland, the procurator fiscal.

3. An order under paragraph 1 may be made only by—

(*a*) in England and Wales, a Circuit judge,*
(*b*) in Scotland, the sheriff, or
(*c*) in Northern Ireland, a Crown Court judge.

***Amended by the Courts Act 2003, Sch 4 from a date to be appointed.**

4. (1) Crown Court Rules may make provision about the procedure for an application under paragraph 1.

(2) The High Court of Justiciary may, by Act of Adjournal, make provision about the procedure for an application under paragraph 1.

(3) Crown Court Rules may make provision about the procedure for an application under paragraph 1.

Criteria for making order

5. An order under paragraph 1 may be made only if the person making it is satisfied that—

(*a*) the order is sought for the purposes of a terrorist investigation,
(*b*) the tracing of terrorist property is desirable for the purposes of the investigation, and
(*c*) the order will enhance the effectiveness of the investigation.

Financial institution

6. (1) In this Schedule "financial institution" means—

(*a*) a person who has permission under Part 4 of the Financial Services and Markets Act 2000 to accept deposits,
(*b*) (*repealed*),
(*c*) a credit union (within the meaning of the Credit Unions Act 1979 or the Credit Unions (Northern Ireland) Order 1985),
(*d*) a person carrying on a relevant regulated activity,
(*e*) the National Savings Bank,
(*f*) a person who carries out an activity for the purposes of raising money authorised to be raised under the National Loans Act 1968 under the auspices of the Director of National Savings,
(*g*) a European institution carrying on a home regulated activity (within the meaning of Directive 2000/12/EC of the European Parliament and of the Council] relating to the taking up and pursuit of the business of credit institutions),
(*h*) a person carrying out an activity specified in any of points 1 to 12 and 14 of Annex 1 to that Directive, and
(*i*) a person who carries on an insurance business in accordance with an authorisation pursuant to Article 4 or 51 of Directive 2002/83/EC of the European Parliament and of the Council of 5th November 2002 concerning life assurance.

(1A) For the purposes of sub-paragraph (1)(*d*), a relevant regulated activity means—

(*a*) dealing in investments as principal or as agent,
(*b*) arranging deals in investments,
(*c*) managing investments,
(*d*) safeguarding and administering investments,
(*e*) sending dematerialised instructions,
(*f*) establishing etc collective investment schemes,
(*g*) advising on investments.

(1B) Sub-paragraphs (1)(*a*) and (1A) must be read with—

(*a*) section 22 of the Financial Services and Markets Act 2000;
(*b*) any relevant order under that section; and
(*c*) Schedule 2 to that Act.

(2) The Secretary of State may by order provide for a class of person—

(*a*) to be a financial institution for the purposes of this Schedule, or
(*b*) to cease to be a financial institution for the purposes of this Schedule.

(3) An institution which ceases to be a financial institution for the purposes of this Schedule (whether by virtue of sub-paragraph (2)(*b*) or otherwise) shall continue to be treated as a financial institution for the purposes of any requirement under paragraph 1 to provide customer information which relates to a time when the institution was a financial institution.

Customer information

7. (1) In this Schedule "customer information" means (subject to sub-paragraph (3))—

(*a*) information whether a business relationship exists or existed between a financial institution and a particular person ("a customer"),
(*b*) a customer's account number,
(*c*) a customer's full name,
(*d*) a customer's date of birth,
(*e*) a customer's address or former address,
(*f*) the date on which a business relationship between a financial institution and a customer begins or ends,
(*g*) any evidence of a customer's identity obtained by a financial institution in pursuance of or for the purposes of any legislation relating to money laundering, and
(*h*) the identity of a person sharing an account with a customer.

(2) For the purposes of this Schedule there is a business relationship between a financial institution and a person if (and only if)—

(*a*) there is an arrangement between them designed to facilitate the carrying out of frequent or regular transactions between them, and
(*b*) the total amount of payments to be made in the course of the arrangement is neither known nor capable of being ascertained when the arrangement is made.

(3) The Secretary of State may by order provide for a class of information—

(*a*) to be customer information for the purposes of this Schedule, or
(*b*) to cease to be customer information for the purposes of this Schedule.

Offence by body corporate, &c

8. (1) This paragraph applies where an offence under paragraph 1(3) is committed by an institution and it is proved that the offence—

(*a*) was committed with the consent or connivance of an officer of the institution, or
(*b*) was attributable to neglect on the part of an officer of the institution.

(2) The officer, as well as the institution, shall be guilty of the offence.

(3) Where an individual is convicted of an offence under paragraph 1(3) by virtue of this paragraph, he shall be liable on summary conviction to—

(*a*) imprisonment for a term not exceeding six months,
(*b*) a fine not exceeding level 5 on the standard scale, or
(*c*) both.

(4) In the case of an institution which is a body corporate, in this paragraph "officer" includes—

(*a*) a director, manager or secretary,
(*b*) a person purporting to act as a director, manager or secretary, and
(*c*) if the affairs of the body are managed by its members, a member.

(5) In the case of an institution which is a partnership, in this paragraph "officer" means a partner.

(6) In the case of an institution which is an unincorporated association (other than a partnership), in this paragraph "officer" means a person concerned in the management or control of the association.

Self-incrimination

9. (1) Customer information provided by a financial institution under this Schedule shall not be admissible in evidence in criminal proceedings against the institution or any of its officers or employees.

(2) Sub-paragraph (1) shall not apply in relation to proceedings for an offence under paragraph 1(3) (including proceedings brought by virtue of paragraph 8).

SCHEDULE 6A
Account Monitoring Orders

Introduction

8–23559JA **1.** (1) This paragraph applies for the purposes of this Schedule.

(2) A judge is—

(a) a Circuit judge, in England and Wales;
(b) the sheriff, in Scotland;
(c) a Crown Court judge, in Northern Ireland.

(3) The court is—

(a) the Crown Court, in England and Wales or Northern Ireland;
(b) the sheriff, in Scotland.

(4) An appropriate officer is—

(a) a police officer, in England and Wales or Northern Ireland;
(b) the procurator fiscal, in Scotland.

(5) "Financial institution" has the same meaning as in Schedule 6.

Account monitoring orders

2. (1) A judge may, on an application made to him by an appropriate officer, make an account monitoring order if he is satisfied that—

(*a*) the order is sought for the purposes of a terrorist investigation,
(*b*) the tracing of terrorist property is desirable for the purposes of the investigation, and
(*c*) the order will enhance the effectiveness of the investigation.

(2) The application for an account monitoring order must state that the order is sought against the financial institution specified in the application in relation to information which—

(*a*) relates to an account or accounts held at the institution by the person specified in the application (whether solely or jointly with another), and
(*b*) is of the description so specified.

(3) The application for an account monitoring order may specify information relating to—

(*a*) all accounts held by the person specified in the application for the order at the financial institution so specified,
(*b*) a particular description, or particular descriptions, of accounts so held, or
(*c*) a particular account, or particular accounts, so held.

(4) An account monitoring order is an order that the financial institution specified in the application for the order must—

(*a*) for the period specified in the order,
(*b*) in the manner so specified,
(*c*) at or by the time or times so specified, and
(*d*) at the place or places so specified,

provide information of the description specified in the application to an appropriate officer.

(5) The period stated in an account monitoring order must not exceed the period of 90 days beginning with the day on which the order is made.

Applications

3. (1) An application for an account monitoring order may be made ex parte to a judge in chambers.

(2) The description of information specified in an application for an account monitoring order may be varied by the person who made the application.

(3) If the application was made by a police officer, the description of information specified in it may be varied by a different police officer.

Discharge or variation

4. (1) An application to discharge or vary an account monitoring order may be made to the court by—

(*a*) the person who applied for the order;
(*b*) any person affected by the order.

(2) If the application for the account monitoring order was made by a police officer, an application to discharge or vary the order may be made by a different police officer.

(3) The court—

(*a*) may discharge the order;
(*b*) may vary the order.

Rules of court

5. (1) Rules of court may make provision as to the practice and procedure to be followed in connection with proceedings relating to account monitoring orders.

(2) In Scotland, rules of court shall, without prejudice to section 305 of the Criminal Procedure (Scotland) Act 1995 (c 46), be made by Act of Adjournal.

Effect of orders

6. (1) In England and Wales and Northern Ireland, an account monitoring order has effect as if it were an order of the court.

(2) An account monitoring order has effect in spite of any restriction on the disclosure of information (however imposed).

Statements

7. (1) A statement made by a financial institution in response to an account monitoring order may not be used in evidence against it in criminal proceedings.

(2) But sub-paragraph (1) does not apply—

(*a*) in the case of proceedings for contempt of court;
(*b*) in the case of proceedings under section 23 where the financial institution has been convicted of an offence under any of sections 15 to 18;
(*c*) on a prosecution for an offence where, in giving evidence, the financial institution makes a statement inconsistent with the statement mentioned in sub-paragraph (1).

(3) A statement may not be used by virtue of sub-paragraph (2)(c) against a financial institution unless—

(*a*) evidence relating to it is adduced, or
(*b*) a question relating to it is asked,

by or on behalf of the financial institution in the proceedings arising out of the prosecution.

SCHEDULE 7
Port and Border Controls

(*As amended by the Anti-terrorism, Crime and Security Act 2001, ss 118(1), 119(1).*)

Section 53

Interpretation

8–23559K **1.** (1) In this Schedule "examining officer" means any of the following—

(*a*) a constable,
(*b*) an immigration officer, and
(*c*) a customs officer who is designated for the purpose of this Schedule by the Secretary of State and the Commissioners of Customs and Excise.

(2) In this Schedule—

"the border area" has the meaning given by paragraph 4,
"captain" means master of a ship or commander of an aircraft,
"port" includes an airport and a hoverport,
"ship" includes a hovercraft, and
"vehicle" includes a train.

(3) A place shall be treated as a port for the purposes of this Schedule in relation to a person if an examining officer believes that the person—

(*a*) has gone there for the purpose of embarking on a ship or aircraft, or
(*b*) has arrived there on disembarking from a ship or aircraft.

Power to stop, question and detain

2. (1) An examining officer may question a person to whom this paragraph applies for the purpose of determining whether he appears to be a person falling within section 40(1)(*b*).

(2) This paragraph applies to a person if—

(*a*) he is at a port or in the border area, and
(*b*) the examining officer believes that the person's presence at the port or in the area is connected with his entering or leaving Great Britain or Northern Ireland or his travelling by air within Great Britian or within Northern Ireland.

(3) This paragraph also applies to a person on a ship or aircraft which has arrived at any place in Great Britain or Northern Ireland (whether from within ir outside Great Britain or Northern Ireland).

(4) An examining officer may exercise his powers under this paragraph whether or not he has grounds for suspecting that a person falls within section 40(1)(*b*).

3. An examining officer may question a person who is in the border area for the purpose of determining whether his presence in the area is connected with his entering or leaving Northern Ireland.

4. (1) A place in Northern Ireland is within the border area for the purposes of paragraphs 2 and 3 if it is no more than one mile from the border between Northern Ireland and the Republic of Ireland.

(2) If a train goes from the Republic of Ireland to Northern Ireland, the first place in Northern Ireland at which it stops for the purpose of allowing passengers to leave is within the border area for the purposes of paragraphs 2 and 3.

5. A person who is questioned under paragraph 2 or 3 must—

(*a*) give the examining officer any information in his possession which the officer requests;
(*b*) give the examining officer on request either a valid passport which includes a photograph or another document which establishes his identity;
(*c*) declare whether he has with him documents of a kind specified by the examining officer;
(*d*) give the examining officer on request any document which he has with him and which is of a kind specified by the officer.

6. (1) For the purposes of exercising a power under paragraph 2 or 3 an examining officer may—

(*a*) stop a person or vehicle;
(*b*) detain a person.

(2) For the purpose of detaining a person under this paragraph, an examining officer may authorise the person's removal from a ship, aircraft or vehicle.

(3) Where a person is detained under this paragraph the provisions of Part I of Schedule 8 (treatment) shall apply.

(4) A person detained under this paragraph shall (unless detained under any other power) be released not later than the end of the period of nine hours beginning with the time when his examination begins.

Searches

7. For the purpose of satisfying himself whether there are any persons whom he may wish to question under paragraph 2 an examining officer may—

(*a*) search a ship or aircraft;
(*b*) search anything on a ship or aircraft;
(*c*) search anything which he reasonably believes has been, or is about to be, on a ship or aircraft.

8. (1) An examining officer who questions a person under paragraph 2 may, for the purpose of determining whether he falls within section 40(1)(*b*)—

(*a*) search the person;
(*b*) search anything which he has with him, or which belongs to him, and which is on a ship or aircraft;
(*c*) search anything which he has with him, or which belongs to him, and which the examining officer reasonably believes has been, or is about to be, on a ship or aircraft;
(*d*) search a ship or aircraft for anything falling within paragraph (*b*).

(2) Where an examining officer questions a person in the border area under paragraph 2 he may (in addition to the matters specified in sub-paragraph (1)), for the purpose of determining whether the person falls within section 40(1)(*b*)—

(*a*) search a vehicle;
(*b*) search anything in or on a vehicle;
(*c*) search anything which he reasonably believes has been, or is about to be, in or on a vehicle.

(3) A search of a person under this paragraph must be carried out by someone of the same sex.

9. (1) An examining officer may examine goods to which this paragraph applies for the purpose of determining whether they have been used in the commission, preparation or instigation of acts of terrorism.

(2) This paragraph applies to—

(*a*) goods which have arrived in or are about to leave Great Britain or Northern Ireland on a ship or vehicle, and
(*b*) goods which have arrived at or are about to leave any place in Great Britain or Northern Ireland on an aircraft (whether the place they have come from or are going to is within or outside Great Britain or Northern Ireland).

(3) In this paragraph "goods" includes—

(*a*) property of any description, and
(*b*) containers.

(4) An examining officer may board a ship or aircraft or enter a vehicle for the purpose of determining whether to exercise his power under this paragraph.

10. (1) An examining officer may authorise a person to carry out on his behalf a search or examination under any of paragraphs 7 to 9.

(2) A person authorised under this paragraph shall be treated as an examining officer for the purposes of—

(*a*) paragraphs 9(4) and 11 of this Schedule, and
(*b*) paragraphs 2 and 3 of Schedule 14.

Detention of property

11. (1) This paragraph applies to anything which—

(*a*) is given to an examining officer in accordance with paragraph 5(*d*),
(*b*) is searched or found on a search under paragraph 8, or
(*c*) is examined under paragraph 9.

(2) An examining officer may detain the thing—

(*a*) for the purpose of examination, for a period not exceeding seven days beginning with the day on which the detention commences,
(*b*) while he believes that it may be needed for use as evidence in criminal proceedings, or
(*c*) while he believes that it may be needed in connection with a decision by the Secretary of State whether to make a deportation order under the Immigration Act 1971.

Designated ports

12. (1) This paragraph applies to a journey—

(*a*) to Great Britain from the Republic of Ireland, Northern Ireland or any of the Islands,
(*b*) from Great Britain to any of those places,
(*c*) to Northern Ireland from Great Britain, the Republic of Ireland or any of the Islands, or
(*d*) from Northern Ireland to any of those places.

(2) Where a ship or aircraft is employed to carry passengers for reward on a journey to which this paragraph applies the owners or agents of the ship or aircraft shall not arrange for it to call at a port in Great Britain or Northern Ireland for the purpose of disembarking or embarking passengers unless—

(*a*) the port is a designated port, or
(*b*) an examining officer approves the arrangement.

(3) Where an aircraft is employed on a journey to which this paragraph applies otherwise than to carry passengers for reward, the captain of the aircraft shall not permit it to call at or leave a port in Great Britain or Northern Ireland unless—

(*a*) the port is a designated port, or
(*b*) he gives at least 12 hours' notice in writing to a constable for the police area in which the port is situated (or, where the port is in Northern Ireland, to a member of the Royal Ulster Constabulary*).

(4) A designated port is a port which appears in the Table at the end of this Schedule.

(5) The Secretary of State may by order—

(*a*) add an entry to the Table;
(*b*) remove an entry from the Table.

***Amended by the Anti-terrorism, Crime and Security Act 2001, s 121(1), from a date to be appointed.**

Embarkation and disembarkation

13. (1) The Secretary of State may by notice in writing to the owners or agents of ships or aircraft—

(*a*) designate control areas in any port in the United Kingdom;

(*b*) specify conditions for or restrictions on the embarkation or disembarkation of passengers in a control area.

(2) Where owners or agents of a ship or aircraft receive notice under sub-paragraph (1) in relation to a port they shall take all reasonable steps to ensure, in respect of the ship or aircraft—

(*a*) that passengers do not embark or disembark at the port outside a control area, and

(*b*) that any specified conditions are met and any specified restrictions are complied with.

14. (1) The Secretary of State may by notice in writing to persons concerned with the management of a port in the United Kingdom ("the port managers")—

(*a*) designate control areas in the port;

(*b*) require the port managers to provide at their own expense specified facilities in a control area for the purposes of the embarkation or disembarkation of passengers or their examination under this Schedule;

(*c*) require conditions to be met and restrictions to be complied with in relation to the embarkation or disembarkation of passengers in a control area;

(*d*) require the port managers to display, in specified locations in control areas, notices containing specified information about the provisions of this Schedule in such form as may be specified.

(2) Where port managers receive notice under sub-paragraph (1) they shall take all reasonable steps to comply with any requirement set out in the notice.

15. (1) This paragraph applies to a ship employed to carry passengers for reward, or an aircraft, which—

(*a*) arrives in Great Britain from the Republic of Ireland, Northern Ireland or any of the Islands,

(*b*) arrives in Northern Ireland from Great Britain, the Republic of Ireland or any of the Islands,

(*c*) leaves Great Britain for the Republic of Ireland, Northern Ireland or any of the Islands, or

(*d*) leaves Northern Ireland for Great Britain, the Republic of Ireland or any of the Islands.

(2) The captain shall ensure—

(*a*) that passengers and members of the crew do not disembark at a port in Great Britain or Northern Ireland unless either they have been examined by an examining officer or they disembark in accordance with arrangements approved by an examining officer;

(*b*) that passengers and members of the crew do not embark at a port in Great Britain or Northern Ireland except in accordance with arrangements approved by an examining officer;

(*c*) where a person is to be examined under this Schedule on board the ship or aircraft, that he is presented for examination in an orderly manner.

(3) Where paragraph 27 of Schedule 2 to the Immigration Act 1971 (disembarkation requirements on arrival in the United Kingdom) applies, the requirements of sub-paragraph (2)(*a*) above are in addition to the requirements of paragraph 27 of that Schedule.

Carding

16. (1) The Secretary of State may by order[1] make provision requiring a person to whom this paragraph applies, if required to do so by an examining officer, to complete and produce to the officer a card containing such information in such form as the order may specify.

(2) An order under this paragraph may require the owners or agents of a ship or aircraft employed to carry passengers for reward to supply their passengers with cards in the form required by virtue of sub-paragraph (1).

(3) This paragraph applies to a person—

(*a*) who disembarks in Great Britain from a ship or aircraft which has come from the Republic of Ireland, Northern Ireland or any of the Islands,

(*b*) who disembarks in Northern Ireland from a ship or aircraft which has come from Great Britain, the Republic of Ireland, or any of the Islands,

(*c*) who embarks in Great Britain on a ship or aircraft which is going to the Republic of Ireland, Northern Ireland or any of the Islands, or

(*d*) who embarks in Northern Ireland on a ship or aircraft which is going to Great Britain, the Republic of Ireland, or any of the Islands.

---

1. The Terrorism Act 2000 (Carding) Order 2001, SI 2001/426 has been made.

Provision of passenger information

17. (1) This paragraph applies to a ship or aircraft which—

(a) arrives or is expected to arrive in any place in the United Kingdom (whether from another place in the United Kingdom or from outside the United Kingdom), or

(b) leaves or is expected to leave the United Kingdom.

(2) If an examining officer gives the owners or agents of a ship or aircraft to which this paragraph applies a written request to provide specified information, the owners or agents shall comply with the request as soon as is reasonably practicable.

(3) A request to an owner or agent may relate—

(*a*) to a particular ship or aircraft,

(*b*) to all ships or aircraft of the owner or agent to which this paragraph applies, or

(*c*) to specified ships or aircraft.

(4) Information may be specified in a request only if it is of a kind which is prescribed by order[1] of the Secretary of State and which relates—

(*a*) to passengers,

(*b*) to crew,

(*c*) to vehicles belonging to passengers or crew, or
(*d*) to goods.

(5) A passenger or member of the crew on a ship or aircraft shall give the captain any information required for the purpose of enabling the owners or agents to comply with a request under this paragraph.

(6) Sub-paragraphs (2) and (5) shall not require the provision of information which is required to be provided under or by virtue of paragraph 27(2) or 27B of Schedule 2 to the Immigration Act 1971.

1. See Sch 7 to the Terrorism Act 2000 (Information) Order 2002, SI 2002/1945.

Offences

18. (1) A person commits an offence if he—

(*a*) wilfully fails to comply with a duty imposed under or by virtue of this Schedule,
(*b*) wilfully contravenes a prohibition imposed under or by virtue of this Schedule, or
(*c*) wilfully obstructs, or seeks to frustrate, a search or examination under or by virtue of this Schedule.

(2) A person guilty of an offence under this paragraph shall be liable on summary conviction to—

(*a*) imprisonment for a term not exceeding three months,
(*b*) a fine not exceeding level 4 on the standard scale, or
(*c*) both.

TABLE
DESIGNATED PORTS
Great Britain

8–23559L

Seaports	*Airports*
Ardrossan	Aberdeen
Cairnryan	Biggin Hill
Campbeltown	Birmingham
Fishguard	Blackpool
Fleetwood	Bournemouth (Hurn)
Heysham	Bristol
Holyhead	Cambridge
Pembroke Dock	Cardiff
Plymouth	Carlisle
Poole Harbour	Coventry
Port of Liverpool	East Midlands
Portsmouth Continental Ferry Port	Edinburgh
Southampton	Exeter
Stranraer	Glasgow
Swansea	Gloucester/Cheltenham (Staverton)
Torquay	Humberside
Troon	Leeds/Bradford
Weymouth	Liverpool
	London-City
	London-Gatwick
	London-Heathrow
	Luton
	Lydd
	Manchester
	Manston
	Newcastle
	Norwich
	Plymouth
	Prestwick
	Sheffield City
	Southampton
	Southend
	Stansted
	Teesside

Northern Ireland

Seaports	*Airports*
Ballycastle	Belfast City
Belfast	Belfast International
Larne	City of Derry
Port of Londonderry	
Warrenpoint	

Section 41 and Schedule 7, para 6

SCHEDULE 8
DETENTION

(Amended by the Criminal Justice and Police Act 2001, ss 75 and 84(4), the Anti-terrorism, Crime and Security Act 2001, s 127(2), the Proceeds of Crime Act 2002, s 456 and the Serious Organised Crime and Police Act 2005, Sch 7.)

PART I
TREATMENT OF PERSONS DETAINED UNDER SECTION 41 OR SCHEDULE 7

Place of detention

8–23559M 1. (1) The Secretary of State shall designate places at which persons may be detained under Schedule 7 or section 41.

(2) In this Schedule a reference to a police station includes a reference to any place which the Secretary of State has designated under sub-paragraph (1) as a place where a person may be detained under section 41.

(3) Where a person is detained under Schedule 7, he may be taken in the custody of an examining officer or of a person acting under an examining officer's authority to and from any place where his attendance is required for the purpose of—

(*a*) his examination under that Schedule,
(*b*) establishing his nationality or citizenship, or
(*c*) making arrangements for his admission to a country or territory outside the United Kingdom.

(4) A constable who arrests a person under section 41 shall take him as soon as is reasonably practicable to the police station which the constable considers the most appropriate.

(5) In this paragraph "examining officer" has the meaning given in Schedule 7.

(6) Where a person is arrested in one Part of the United Kingdom and all or part of his detention takes place in another Part, the provisions of this Schedule which apply to detention in a particular Part of the United Kingdom apply in relation to him while he is detained in that Part.

Identification

2. (1) An authorised person may take any steps which are reasonably necessary for—

(*a*) photographing the detained person,
(*b*) measuring him, or
(*c*) identifying him.

(2) In sub-paragraph (1) "authorised person" means any of the following—

(*a*) a constable,
(*b*) a prison officer,
(*c*) a person authorised by the Secretary of State, and
(*d*) in the case of a person detained under Schedule 7, an examining officer (within the meaning of that Schedule).

(3) This paragraph does not confer the power to take—

(*a*) fingerprints, non-intimate samples or intimate samples (within the meaning given by paragraph 15 below), or
(*b*) relevant physical data or samples as mentioned in section 18 of the Criminal Procedure (Scotland) Act 1995 as applied by paragraph 20 below.

Audio and video recording of interviews

3. (1) The Secretary of State shall—

(*a*) issue a code of practice about the audio recording of interviews to which this paragraph applies, and
(*b*) make an order[1] requiring the audio recording of interviews to which this paragraph applies in accordance with any relevant code of practice under paragraph (*a*).

(2) The Secretary of State may make an order requiring the video recording of—

(*a*) interviews to which this paragraph applies;
(*b*) interviews to which this paragraph applies which take place in a particular Part of the United Kingdom.

(3) An order under sub-paragraph (2) shall specify whether the video recording which it requires is to be silent or with sound.

(4) Where an order is made under sub-paragraph (2)—

(*a*) the Secretary of State shall issue a code of practice about the video recording of interviews to which the order applies, and
(*b*) the order shall require the interviews to be video recorded in accordance with any relevant code of practice under paragraph (*a*).

(5) Where the Secretary of State has made an order under sub-paragraph (2) requiring certain interviews to be video recorded with sound—

(*a*) he need not make an order under sub-paragraph (1)(*b*) in relation to those interviews, but
(*b*) he may do so.

(6) This paragraph applies to any interview by a constable of a person detained under Schedule 7 or section 41 if the interview takes place in a police station.

(7) A code of practice under this paragraph—

(*a*) may make provision in relation to a particular Part of the United Kingdom;
(*b*) may make different provision for different Parts of the United Kingdom.

1. The Terrorism Act 2000 (Code of Practice on Audio Recording of Interviews) (No 2) Order 2001, SI 2001/189 requires interviews of persons detained under s 41 or Sch 7 which are conducted by a police constable at a police station, to be audio recorded in accordance with the audio code of practice.

4. (1) This paragraph applies to a code of practice under paragraph 3.
(2) Where the Secretary of State proposes to issue a code of practice he shall—

(*a*) publish a draft,
(*b*) consider any representations made to him about the draft, and
(*c*) if he thinks it appropriate, modify the draft in the light of any representations made to him.

(3) The Secretary of State shall lay a draft of the code before Parliament.
(4) When the Secretary of State has laid a draft code before Parliament he may bring it into operation by order[1].
(5) The Secretary of State may revise a code and issue the revised code; and sub-paragraphs (2) to (4) shall apply to a revised code as they apply to an original code.
(6) The failure by a constable to observe a provision of a code shall not of itself make him liable to criminal or civil proceedings.
(7) A code—

(*a*) shall be admissible in evidence in criminal and civil proceedings, and
(*b*) shall be taken into account by a court or tribunal in any case in which it appears to the court or tribunal to be relevant.

1. The 19 February 2001 was appointed by the Terrorism Act 2000 (Code of Practice on Audio Recording of Interviews) Order 2001, SI 2001/159.

Status

5. A detained person shall be deemed to be in legal custody throughout the period of his detention.

Rights: England, Wales and Northern Ireland

6. (1) Subject to paragraph 8, a person detained under Schedule 7 or section 41 at a police station in England, Wales or Northern Ireland shall be entitled, if he so requests, to have one named person informed as soon as is reasonably practicable that he is being detained there.
(2) The person named must be—

(*a*) a friend of the detained person,
(*b*) a relative, or
(*c*) a person who is known to the detained person or who is likely to take an interest in his welfare.

(3) Where a detained person is transferred from one police station to another, he shall be entitled to exercise the right under this paragraph in respect of the police station to which he is transferred.

7. (1) Subject to paragraphs 8 and 9, a person detained under Schedule 7 or section 41 at a police station in England, Wales or Northern Ireland shall be entitled, if he so requests, to consult a solicitor as soon as is reasonably practicable, privately and at any time.
(2) Where a request is made under sub-paragraph (1), the request and the time at which it was made shall be recorded.

8. (1) Subject to sub-paragraph (2), an officer of at least the rank of superintendent may authorise a delay—

(*a*) in informing the person named by a detained person under paragraph 6;
(*b*) in permitting a detained person to consult a solicitor under paragraph 7.

(2) But where a person is detained under section 41 he must be permitted to exercise his rights under paragraphs 6 and 7 before the end of the period mentioned in subsection (3) of that section.
(3) Subject to sub-paragraph (5), an officer may give an authorisation under sub-paragraph (1) only if he has reasonable grounds for believing—

(*a*) in the case of an authorisation under sub-paragraph (1)(*a*), that informing the named person of the detained person's detention will have any of the consequences specified in sub-paragraph (4), or
(*b*) in the case of an authorisation under sub-paragraph (1)(*b*), that the exercise of the right under paragraph 7 at the time when the detained person desires to exercise it will have any of the consequences specified in sub-paragraph (4).

(4) Those consequences are—

(*a*) interference with or harm to evidence of a serious offence,
(*b*) interference with or physical injury to any person,
(*c*) the alerting of persons who are suspected of having committed a serious offence but who have not been arrested for it,
(*d*) the hindering of the recovery of property obtained as a result of a serious offence or in respect of which a forfeiture order could be made under section 23,
(*e*) interference with the gathering of information about the commission, preparation or instigation of acts of terrorism,
(*f*) the alerting of a person and thereby making it more difficult to prevent an act of terrorism, and
(*g*) the alerting of a person and thereby making it more difficult to secure a person's apprehension, prosecution or conviction in connection with the commission, preparation or instigation of an act of terrorism.

(5) An officer may also give an authorisation under sub-paragraph (1) if he has reasonable grounds for believing that—

(*a*) the detained person has benefited from his criminal conduct, and
(*b*) the recovery of the value of the property constituting the benefit will be hindered by—
(i) informing the named person of the detained person's detention (in the case of an authorisation under sub-paragraph (1)(*a*)), or
(ii) the exercise of the right under paragraph 7 (in the case of an authorisation under sub-paragraph (1)(*b*)).

(5A) For the purposes of sub-paragraph (5) the question whether a person has benefited from his criminal conduct is to be decided in accordance with Part 2 of the Proceeds of Crime Act 2002.

(6) If an authorisation under sub-paragraph (1) is given orally, the person giving it shall confirm it in writing as soon as is reasonably practicable.

(7) Where an authorisation under sub-paragraph (1) is given—

(*a*) the detained person shall be told the reason for the delay as soon as is reasonably practicable, and
(*b*) the reason shall be recorded as soon as is reasonably practicable.

(8) Where the reason for authorising delay ceases to subsist there may be no further delay in permitting the exercise of the right in the absence of a further authorisation under sub-paragraph (1).

(9) In this paragraph, references to a "serious offence" are (in relation to England and Wales) to an indictable offence, and (in relation to Northern Ireland) to a serious arrestable offence within the meaning of Article 87 of the Police and Criminal Evidence (Northern Ireland) Order 1989; but it also include—

(*a*) an offence under any of the provisions mentioned in section 40(1)(*a*) of this Act, and
(*b*) an attempt or conspiracy to commit an offence under any of the provisions mentioned in section 40(1)(*a*).

9. (1) A direction under this paragraph may provide that a detained person who wishes to exercise the right under paragraph 7 may consult a solicitor only in the sight and hearing of a qualified officer.

(2) A direction under this paragraph may be given—

(*a*) where the person is detained at a police station in England or Wales, by an officer of at least the rank of Commander or Assistant Chief Constable, or
(*b*) where the person is detained at a police station in Northern Ireland, by an officer of at least the rank of Assistant Chief Constable.

(3) A direction under this paragraph may be given only if the officer giving it has reasonable grounds for believing that, unless the direction is given, the exercise of the right by the detained person will have any of the consequences specified in paragraph 8(4) or the consequence specified in paragraph 8(5)(*c*).

(4) In this paragraph "a qualified officer" means a police officer who—

(*a*) is of at least the rank of inspector,
(*b*) is of the uniformed branch of the force of which the officer giving the direction is a member, and
(*c*) in the opinion of the officer giving the direction, has no connection with the detained person's case.

(5) A direction under this paragraph shall cease to have effect once the reason for giving it ceases to subsist.

10. (1) This paragraph applies where a person is detained in England, Wales or Northern Ireland under Schedule 7 or section 41.

(2) Fingerprints may be taken from the detained person only if they are taken by a constable—

(*a*) with the appropriate consent given in writing, or
(*b*) without that consent under sub-paragraph (4).

(3) A non-intimate sample may be taken from the detained person only if it is taken by a constable—

(*a*) with the appropriate consent given in writing, or
(*b*) without that consent under sub-paragraph (4).

(4) Fingerprints or a non-intimate sample may be taken from the detained person without the appropriate consent only if—

(*a*) he is detained at a police station and a police officer of at least the rank of superintendent authorises the fingerprints or sample to be taken, or
(*b*) he has been convicted of a recordable offence and, where a non-intimate sample is to be taken, he was convicted of the offence on or after 10th April 1995 (or 29th July 1996 where the non-intimate sample is to be taken in Northern Ireland).

(5) An intimate sample may be taken from the detained person only if—

(*a*) he is detained at a police station,
(*b*) the appropriate consent is given in writing,
(*c*) a police officer of at least the rank of superintendent authorises the sample to be taken, and
(*d*) subject to paragraph 13(2) and (3), the sample is taken by a constable.

(6) Subject to sub-paragraph (6A) an officer may give an authorisation under sub-paragraph (4)(*a*) or (5)(*c*) only if—

(*a*) in the case of a person detained under section 41, the officer reasonably suspects that the person has been involved in an offence under any of the provisions mentioned in section 40(1)(*a*), and the officer reasonably believes that the fingerprints or sample will tend to confirm or disprove his involvement, or
(*b*) in any case, the officer is satisfied that the taking of the fingerprints or sample from the person is necessary in order to assist in determining whether he falls within section 40(1)(*b*).

(6A) An officer may also give an authorisation under sub-paragraph (4)(*a*) for the taking of fingerprints if—

(*a*) he is satisfied that the fingerprints of the detained person will facilitate the ascertainment of that person's identity; and (*b*) that person has refused to identify himself or the officer has reasonable grounds for suspecting that that person is not who he claims to be.

(6B) In this paragraph references to ascertaining a person's identity include references to showing that he is not a particular person.

(7) If an authorisation under sub-paragraph (4)(*a*) or (5)(*c*) is given orally, the person giving it shall confirm it in writing as soon as is reasonably practicable.

11. (1) Before fingerprints or a sample are taken from a person under paragraph 10, he shall be informed—

(*a*) that the fingerprints or sample may be used for the purposes of paragraph 14(4), section 63A(1) of the Police and Criminal Evidence Act 1984 and Article 63A(1) of the Police and Criminal Evidence (Northern Ireland) Order 1989 (checking of fingerprints and samples), and

(*b*) where the fingerprints or sample are to be taken under paragraph 10(2)(*a*), (3)(*a*) or (4)(*b*), of the reason for taking the fingerprints or sample.

(2) Before fingerprints or a sample are taken from a person upon an authorisation given under paragraph 10(4)(*a*) or (5)(*c*), he shall be informed—

(*a*) that the authorisation has been given,

(*b*) of the grounds upon which it has been given, and

(*c*) where relevant, of the nature of the offence in which it is suspected that he has been involved.

(3) After fingerprints or a sample are taken under paragraph 10, there shall be recorded as soon as is reasonably practicable any of the following which apply—

(*a*) the fact that the person has been informed in accordance with sub-paragraphs (1) and (2),

(*b*) the reason referred to in sub-paragraph (1)(*b*),

(*c*) the authorisation given under paragraph 10(4)(*a*) or (5)(*c*),

(*d*) the grounds upon which that authorisation has been given, and

(*e*) the fact that the appropriate consent has been given.

12. (1) This paragraph applies where—

(*a*) two or more non-intimate samples suitable for the same means of analysis have been taken from a person under paragraph 10,

(*b*) those samples have proved insufficient, and

(*c*) the person has been released from detention.

(2) An intimate sample may be taken from the person if—

(*a*) the appropriate consent is given in writing,

(*b*) a police officer of at least the rank of superintendent authorises the sample to be taken, and

(*c*) subject to paragraph 13(2) and (3), the sample is taken by a constable.

(3) Paragraphs 10(6) and (7) and 11 shall apply in relation to the taking of an intimate sample under this paragraph; and a reference to a person detained under section 41 shall be taken as a reference to a person who was detained under section 41 when the non-intimate samples mentioned in sub-paragraph (1)(*a*) were taken.

13. (1) Where appropriate written consent to the taking of an intimate sample from a person under paragraph 10 or 12 is refused without good cause, in any proceedings against that person for an offence—

(*a*) the court, in determining whether to commit him for trial or whether there is a case to answer, may draw such inferences from the refusal as appear proper, and

(*b*) the court or jury, in determining whether that person is guilty of the offence charged, may draw such inferences from the refusal as appear proper.

(2) An intimate sample other than a sample of urine or a dental impression may be taken under paragraph 10 or 12 only by a registered medical practitioner acting on the authority of a constable.

(3) An intimate sample which is a dental impression may be taken under paragraph 10 or 12 only by a registered dentist acting on the authority of a constable.

(4) Where a sample of hair other than pubic hair is to be taken under paragraph 10 the sample may be taken either by cutting hairs or by plucking hairs with their roots so long as no more are plucked than the person taking the sample reasonably considers to be necessary for a sufficient sample.

14. (1) This paragraph applies to—

(*a*) fingerprints or samples taken under paragraph 10 or 12, and

(*b*) information derived from those samples.

(2) The fingerprints and samples may be retained but shall not be used by any person except for the purposes of a terrorist investigation or for purposes related to the prevention or detection of crime, the investigation of an offence or the conduct of a prosecution.

(3) In particular, a check may not be made against them under—

(*a*) section 63A(1) of the Police and Criminal Evidence Act 1984 (checking of fingerprints and samples), or

(*b*) Article 63A(1) of the Police and Criminal Evidence (Northern Ireland) Order 1989 (checking of fingerprints and samples),

except for the purpose of a terrorist investigation or for purposes related to the prevention or detection of crime, the investigation of an offence or the conduct of a prosecution.

(4) The fingerprints, samples or information may be checked, subject to sub-paragraph (2), against—

(*a*) other fingerprints or samples taken under paragraph 10 or 12 or information derived from those samples,

(*b*) relevant physical data or samples taken by virtue of paragraph 20,

(*c*) any of the fingerprints, samples and information mentioned in section 63A(1)(*a*) and (*b*) of the Police and Criminal Evidence Act 1984 (checking of fingerprints and samples),

(*d*) any of the fingerprints, samples and information mentioned in Article 63A(1)(*a*) and (*b*) of the Police and Criminal Evidence (Northern Ireland) Order 1989 (checking of fingerprints and samples), and (*e*) fingerprints or samples taken under section 15(9) of, or paragraph 7(5) of Schedule 5 to, the Prevention of Terrorism (Temporary Provisions) Act 1989 or information derived from those samples.

(4A) In this paragraph—

(*a*) a reference to crime includes a reference to any conduct which—

(i) constitutes one or more criminal offences (whether under the law of a part of the United Kingdom or of a country or territory outside the United Kingdom); or

(ii) is, or corresponds to, any conduct which, if it all took place in any one part of the United Kingdom, would constitute one or more criminal offences;

and

(*b*) the references to an investigation and to a prosecution include references, respectively, to any investigation outside the United Kingdom of any crime or suspected crime and to a prosecution brought in respect of any crime in a country or territory outside the United Kingdom.

(5) This paragraph (other than sub-paragraph (4)) shall apply to fingerprints or samples taken under section 15(9) of, or paragraph 7(5) of Schedule 5 to, the Prevention of Terrorism (Temporary Provisions) Act 1989 and information derived from those samples as it applies to fingerprints or samples taken under paragraph 10 or 12 and the information derived from those samples.

15. (1) In the application of paragraphs 10 to 14 in relation to a person detained in England or Wales the following expressions shall have the meaning given by section 65 of the Police and Criminal Evidence Act 1984 (Part V definitions)—

(*a*) "appropriate consent",
(*b*) "fingerprints",
(*c*) "insufficient",
(*d*) "intimate sample",
(*e*) "non-intimate sample",
(*f*) "registered dentist", and
(*g*) "sufficient".

(2) In the application of paragraphs 10 to 14 in relation to a person detained in Northern Ireland the expressions listed in sub-paragraph (1) shall have the meaning given by Article 53 of the Police and Criminal Evidence (Northern Ireland) Order 1989 (definitions).

(3) In paragraph 10 "recordable offence" shall have—

(*a*) in relation to a person detained in England or Wales, the meaning given by section 118(1) of the Police and Criminal Evidence Act 1984 (general interpretation), and

(*b*) in relation to a person detained in Northern Ireland, the meaning given by Article 2(2) of the Police and Criminal Evidence (Northern Ireland) Order 1989 (definitions).

Rights: Scotland

16. (1) A person detained under Schedule 7 or section 41 at a police station in Scotland shall be entitled to have intimation of his detention and of the place where he is being detained sent without delay to a solicitor and to another person named by him.

(2) The person named must be—

(*a*) a friend of the detained person,
(*b*) a relative, or
(*c*) a person who is known to the detained person or who is likely to take an interest in his welfare.

(3) Where a detained person is transferred from one police station to another, he shall be entitled to exercise the right under sub-paragraph (1) in respect of the police station to which he is transferred.

(4) A police officer not below the rank of superintendent may authorise a delay in making intimation where, in his view, the delay is necessary on one of the grounds mentioned in paragraph 17(3) or where paragraph 17(4) applies.

(5) Where a detained person requests that the intimation be made, there shall be recorded the time when the request is—

(*a*) made, and
(*b*) complied with.

(6) A person detained shall be entitled to consult a solicitor at any time, without delay.

(7) A police officer not below the rank of superintendent may authorise a delay in holding the consultation where, in his view, the delay is necessary on one of the grounds mentioned in paragraph 17(3) or where paragraph 17(4) applies.

(8) Subject to paragraph 17, the consultation shall be private.

(9) Where a person is detained under section 41 he must be permitted to exercise his rights under this paragraph before the end of the period mentioned in subsection (3) of that section.

17. (1) An officer not below the rank of Assistant Chief Constable may direct that the consultation mentioned in paragraph 16(6) shall be in the presence of a uniformed officer not below the rank of inspector if it appears to the officer giving the direction to be necessary on one of the grounds mentioned in sub-paragraph (3).

(2) A uniformed officer directed to be present during a consultation shall be an officer who, in the opinion of the officer giving the direction, has no connection with the case.

(3) The grounds mentioned in paragraph 16(4) and (7) and in sub-paragraph (1) are—

(*a*) that it is in the interests of the investigation or prevention of crime;
(*b*) that it is in the interests of the apprehension, prosecution or conviction of offenders;
(*c*) that it will further the recovery of property obtained as a result of the commission of an offence or in respect of which a forfeiture order could be made under section 23;

(*d*) that it will further the operation of Part 2 or 3 of the Proceeds of Crime Act 2002 or the Proceeds of Crime (Northern Ireland) Order 1996 (confiscation of the proceeds of an offence).

(4) This sub-paragraph applies where an officer mentioned in paragraph 16(4) or (7) has reasonable grounds for believing that—

(*a*) the detained person has benefited from his criminal conduct, and
(*b*) the recovery of the value of the property constituting the benefit will be hindered by—
 (i) informing the named person of the detained person's detention (in the case of an authorisation under paragraph 16(4)), or
 (ii) the exercise of the entitlement under paragraph 16(6) (in the case of an authorisation under paragraph 16(7)).

(4A) For the purposes of sub-paragraph (4) the question whether a person has benefited from his criminal conduct is to be decided in accordance with Part 3 of the Proceeds of Crime Act 2002.

(5) Where delay is authorised in the exercising of any of the rights mentioned in paragraph 16(1) and (6)—

(*a*) if the authorisation is given orally, the person giving it shall confirm it in writing as soon as is reasonably practicable,
(*b*) the detained person shall be told the reason for the delay as soon as is reasonably practicable, and
(*c*) the reason shall be recorded as soon as is reasonably practicable.

18. (1) Paragraphs 16 and 17 shall have effect, in relation to a person detained under section 41 or Schedule 7, in place of any enactment or rule of law under or by virtue of which a person arrested or detained may be entitled to communicate or consult with any other person.

(2) But, where a person detained under Schedule 7 or section 41 at a police station in Scotland appears to a constable to be a child—

(*a*) the other person named by the person detained in pursuance of paragraph 16(1) shall be that person's parent, and
(*b*) section 15(4) of the Criminal Procedure (Scotland) Act 1995 shall apply to the person detained as it applies to a person who appears to a constable to be a child who is being detained as mentioned in paragraph (*b*) of section 15(1) of that Act,

and in this sub-paragraph "child" and "parent" have the same meaning as in section 15(4) of that Act.

19. The Secretary of State shall, by order, make provision to require that—

(*a*) except in such circumstances, and
(*b*) subject to such conditions,

as may be specified in the order, where a person detained has been permitted to consult a solicitor, the solicitor shall be allowed to be present at any interview carried out in connection with a terrorist investigation or for the purposes of Schedule 7.

20. (1) Subject to the modifications specified in sub-paragraphs (2) and (3), section 18 of the Criminal Procedure (Scotland) Act 1995 (procedure for taking certain prints and samples) shall apply to a person detained under Schedule 7 or section 41 at a police station in Scotland as it applies to a person arrested or a person detained under section 14 of that Act.

(2) For subsection (2) of section 18 there shall be substituted—

"(2) Subject to subsection (2A), a constable may take from a detained person or require a detained person to provide relevant physical data only if—

(*a*) in the case of a person detained under section 41 of the Terrorism Act 2000, he reasonably suspects that the person has been involved in an offence under any of the provisions mentioned in section 40(1)(*a*) of that Act and he reasonably believes that the relevant physical data will tend to confirm or disprove his involvement; or
(*b*) in any case, he is satisfied that it is necessary to do so in order to assist in determining whether the person falls within section 40(1)(*b*).

(2A) A constable may also take fingerprints from a detained person or require him to provide them if—

(*a*) he is satisfied that the fingerprints of that person will facilitate the ascertainment of that person's identity; and
(*b*) that person has refused to identify himself or the constable has reasonable grounds for suspecting that that person is not who he claims to be.

(2B) In this section references to ascertaining a person's identity include references to showing that he is not a particular person."

(3) Subsections (3) to (5) shall not apply, but any relevant physical data or sample taken in pursuance of section 18 as applied by this paragraph may be retained but shall not be used by any person except for the purposes of a terrorist investigation or for purposes related to the prevention or detection of crime, the investigation of an offence or the conduct of a prosecution.

(4) In this paragraph—

(*a*) a reference to crime includes a reference to any conduct which—
 (i) constitutes one or more criminal offences (whether under the law of a part of the United Kingdom or of a country or territory outside the United Kingdom); or
 (ii) is, or corresponds to, any conduct which, if it all took place in any one part of the United Kingdom, would constitute one or more criminal offences; and
(*b*) the references to an investigation and to a prosecution include references, respectively, to any investigation outside the United Kingdom of any crime or suspected crime and to a prosecution brought in respect of any crime in a country or territory outside the United Kingdom.

PART II
REVIEW OF DETENTION UNDER SECTION 41

Requirement

8–23559N **21.** (1) A person's detention shall be periodically reviewed by a review officer.

(2) The first review shall be carried out as soon as is reasonably practicable after the time of the person's arrest.

(3) Subsequent reviews shall, subject to paragraph 22, be carried out at intervals of not more than 12 hours.

(4) No review of a person's detention shall be carried out after a warrant extending his detention has been issued under Part III.

Postponement

22. (1) A review may be postponed if at the latest time at which it may be carried out in accordance with paragraph 21—

(*a*) the detained person is being questioned by a police officer and an officer is satisfied that an interruption of the questioning to carry out the review would prejudice the investigation in connection with which the person is being detained,

(*b*) no review officer is readily available, or

(*c*) it is not practicable for any other reason to carry out the review.

(2) Where a review is postponed it shall be carried out as soon as is reasonably practicable.

(3) For the purposes of ascertaining the time within which the next review is to be carried out, a postponed review shall be deemed to have been carried out at the latest time at which it could have been carried out in accordance with paragraph 21.

Grounds for continued detention

23. (1) A review officer may authorise a person's continued detention only if satisfied that it is necessary—

(*a*) to obtain relevant evidence whether by questioning him or otherwise,

(*b*) to preserve relevant evidence,

(*c*) pending a decision whether to apply to the Secretary of State for a deportation notice to be served on the detained person,

(*d*) pending the making of an application to the Secretary of State for a deportation notice to be served on the detained person,

(*e*) pending consideration by the Secretary of State whether to serve a deportation notice on the detained person, or

(*f*) pending a decision whether the detained person should be charged with an offence.

(2) The review officer shall not authorise continued detention by virtue of sub-paragraph (1)(*a*) or (*b*) unless he is satisfied that the investigation in connection with which the person is detained is being conducted diligently and expeditiously.

(3) The review officer shall not authorise continued detention by virtue of sub-paragraph (1)(*c*) to (*f*) unless he is satisfied that the process pending the completion of which detention is necessary is being conducted diligently and expeditiously.

(4) In sub-paragraph (1)(*a*) and (*b*) "relevant evidence" means evidence which—

(*a*) relates to the commission by the detained person of an offence under any of the provisions mentioned in section 40(1)(*a*), or

(*b*) indicates that the detained person falls within section 40(1)(*b*).

(5) In sub-paragraph (1) "deportation notice" means notice of a decision to make a deportation order under the Immigration Act 1971.

Review officer

24. (1) The review officer shall be an officer who has not been directly involved in the investigation in connection with which the person is detained.

(2) In the case of a review carried out within the period of 24 hours beginning with the time of arrest, the review officer shall be an officer of at least the rank of inspector.

(3) In the case of any other review, the review officer shall be an officer of at least the rank of superintendent.

25. (1) This paragraph applies where—

(*a*) the review officer is of a rank lower than superintendent,

(*b*) an officer of higher rank than the review officer gives directions relating to the detained person, and

(*c*) those directions are at variance with the performance by the review officer of a duty imposed on him under this Schedule.

(2) The review officer shall refer the matter at once to an officer of at least the rank of superintendent.

Representations

26. (1) Before determining whether to authorise a person's continued detention, a review officer shall give either of the following persons an opportunity to make representations about the detention—

(*a*) the detained person, or

(*b*) a solicitor representing him who is available at the time of the review.

(2) Representations may be oral or written.

(3) A review officer may refuse to hear oral representations from the detained person if he considers that he is unfit to make representations because of his condition or behaviour.

Rights

27. (1) Where a review officer authorises continued detention he shall inform the detained person—

(*a*) of any of his rights under paragraphs 6 and 7 which he has not yet exercised, and
(*b*) if the exercise of any of his rights under either of those paragraphs is being delayed in accordance with the provisions of paragraph 8, of the fact that it is being so delayed.

(2) Where a review of a person's detention is being carried out at a time when his exercise of a right under either of those paragraphs is being delayed—

(*a*) the review officer shall consider whether the reason or reasons for which the delay was authorised continue to subsist, and
(*b*) if in his opinion the reason or reasons have ceased to subsist, he shall inform the officer who authorised the delay of his opinion (unless he was that officer).

(3) In the application of this paragraph to Scotland, for the references to paragraphs 6, 7 and 8 substitute references to paragraph 16.

(4) The following provisions (requirement to bring an accused person before the court after his arrest) shall not apply to a person detained under section 41—

(*a*) section 135(3) of the Criminal Procedure (Scotland) Act 1995, and
(*b*) Article 8(1) of the Criminal Justice (Children) (Northern Ireland) Order 1998.

(5) Section 22(1) of the Criminal Procedure (Scotland) Act 1995 (interim liberation by officer in charge of police station) shall not apply to a person detained under section 41.

Record

28. (1) A review officer carrying out a review shall make a written record of the outcome of the review and of any of the following which apply—

(*a*) the grounds upon which continued detention is authorised,
(*b*) the reason for postponement of the review,
(*c*) the fact that the detained person has been informed as required under paragraph 27(1),
(*d*) the officer's conclusion on the matter considered under paragraph 27(2)(*a*),
(*e*) the fact that he has taken action under paragraph 27(2)(*b*), and
(*f*) the fact that the detained person is being detained by virtue of section 41(5) or (6).

(2) The review officer shall—

(*a*) make the record in the presence of the detained person, and
(*b*) inform him at that time whether the review officer is authorising continued detention, and if he is, of his grounds.

(3) Sub-paragraph (2) shall not apply where, at the time when the record is made, the detained person is—

(*a*) incapable of understanding what is said to him,
(*b*) violent or likely to become violent, or
(*c*) in urgent need of medical attention.

PART III
EXTENSION OF DETENTION UNDER SECTION 41

Warrants of further detention

8–23559O **29.** (1) A police officer of at least the rank of superintendent may apply to a judicial authority for the issue of a warrant of further detention under this Part.

(2) A warrant of further detention—

(*a*) shall authorise the further detention under section 41 of a specified person for a specified period, and
(*b*) shall state the time at which it is issued.

(3) The specified period in relation to a person shall end not later than the end of the period of seven days beginning—

(*a*) with the time of his arrest under section 41, or
(*b*) if he was being detained under Schedule 7 when he was arrested under section 41, with the time when his examination under that Schedule began.

(4) In this Part "judicial authority" means—

(*a*) in England and Wales, the Senior District Judge (Chief Magistrate) or his deputy, or a District Judge (Magistrates' Courts) who is designated for the purpose of this Part by the Lord Chancellor,
(*b*) in Scotland, the sheriff, and
(*c*) in Northern Ireland, a county court judge, or a resident magistrate who is designated for the purpose of this Part by the Lord Chancellor.

Time limit

30. (1) An application for a warrant shall be made—

(*a*) during the period mentioned in section 41(3), or
(*b*) within six hours of the end of that period.

(2) The judicial authority hearing an application made by virtue of sub-paragraph (1)(*b*) shall dismiss the application if he considers that it would have been reasonably practicable to make it during the period mentioned in section 41(3).

(3) For the purposes of this Schedule, an application for a warrant is made when written or oral notice of an intention to make the application is given to a judicial authority.

Notice

31. An application for a warrant may not be heard unless the person to whom it relates has been given a notice stating—

(*a*) that the application has been made,
(*b*) the time at which the application was made,
(*c*) the time at which it is to be heard, and
(*d*) the grounds upon which further detention is sought.

Grounds for extension

32. (1) A judicial authority may issue a warrant of further detention only if satisfied that—

(*a*) there are reasonable grounds for believing that the further detention of the person to whom the application relates is necessary to obtain relevant evidence whether by questioning him or otherwise or to preserve relevant evidence, and
(*b*) the investigation in connection with which the person is detained is being conducted diligently and expeditiously.

(2) In sub-paragraph (1) "relevant evidence" means, in relation to the person to whom the application relates, evidence which—

(*a*) relates to his commission of an offence under any of the provisions mentioned in section 40(1)(*a*), or
(*b*) indicates that he is a person falling within section 40(1)(*b*).

Representation

33. (1) The person to whom an application relates shall—

(*a*) be given an opportunity to make oral or written representations to the judicial authority about the application, and
(*b*) subject to sub-paragraph (3), be entitled to be legally represented at the hearing.

(2) A judicial authority shall adjourn the hearing of an application to enable the person to whom the application relates to obtain legal representation where—

(*a*) he is not legally represented,
(*b*) he is entitled to be legally represented, and
(*c*) he wishes to be so represented.

(3) A judicial authority may exclude any of the following persons from any part of the hearing—

(*a*) the person to whom the application relates;
(*b*) anyone representing him.

(4) A judicial authority may, after giving an opportunity for representations to be made by or on behalf of the applicant and the person to whom the application relates, direct—

(a) that the hearing of the application must be conducted, and
(b) that all representations by or on behalf of a person for the purposes of the hearing must be made,

by such means (whether a live television link or other means) falling within sub-paragraph (5) as may be specified in the direction and not in the presence (apart from by those means) of the applicant, of the person to whom the application relates or of any legal representative of that person.

(5) A means of conducting the hearing and of making representations falls within this sub-paragraph if it allows the person to whom the application relates and any legal representative of his (without being present at the hearing and to the extent that they are not excluded from it under sub-paragraph (3))—

(a) to see and hear the judicial authority and the making of representations to it by other persons; and
(b) to be seen and heard by the judicial authority.

(6) If the person to whom the application relates wishes to make representations about whether a direction should be given under sub-paragraph (4), he must do so by using the facilities that will be used if the judicial authority decides to give a direction under that sub-paragraph.

(7) Sub-paragraph (2) applies to the hearing of representations about whether a direction should be given under sub-paragraph (4) in the case of any application as it applies to a hearing of the application.

(8) A judicial authority shall not give a direction under sub-paragraph (4) unless—

(a) it has been notified by the Secretary of State that facilities are available at the place where the person to whom the application relates is held for the judicial authority to conduct a hearing by means falling within sub-paragraph (5); and
(b) that notification has not been withdrawn.

(9) If in a case where it has power to do so a judicial authority decides not to give a direction under sub-paragraph (4), it shall state its reasons for not giving it.*

***Sub-paragraphs (4)–(9) inserted in relation to England, Wales and Northern Ireland only, by the Criminal Justice and Police Act 2001, s 75.**

Information

34. (1) The officer who has made an application for a warrant may apply to the judicial authority for an order that specified information upon which he intends to rely be withheld from—

(*a*) the person to whom the application relates, and
(*b*) anyone representing him.

(2) Subject to sub-paragraph (3), a judicial authority may make an order under sub-paragraph (1) in relation to specified information only if satisfied that there are reasonable grounds for believing that if the information were disclosed—

(*a*) evidence of an offence under any of the provisions mentioned in section 40(1)(*a*) would be interfered with or harmed,
(*b*) the recovery of property obtained as a result of an offence under any of those provisions would be hindered,
(*c*) the recovery of property in respect of which a forfeiture order could be made under section 23 would be hindered,
(*d*) the apprehension, prosecution or conviction of a person who is suspected of falling within section 40(1)(*a*) or (*b*) would be made more difficult as a result of his being alerted,
(*e*) the prevention of an act of terrorism would be made more difficult as a result of a person being alerted,
(*f*) the gathering of information about the commission, preparation or instigation of an act of terrorism would be interfered with, or
(*g*) a person would be interfered with or physically injured.

(3) A judicial authority may also make an order under sub-paragraph (1) in relation to specified information if satisfied that there are reasonable grounds for believing that—

(*a*) the detained person has benefited from his criminal conduct, and
(*b*) the recovery of the value of the property constituting the benefit would be hindered if the information were disclosed.

(3A) For the purposes of sub-paragraph (3) the question whether a person has benefited from his criminal conduct is to be decided in accordance with Part 2 or 3 of the Proceeds of Crime Act 2002.

(4) The judicial authority shall direct that the following be excluded from the hearing of the application under this paragraph—

(*a*) the person to whom the application for a warrant relates, and
(*b*) anyone representing him.

Adjournments

35. (1) A judicial authority may adjourn the hearing of an application for a warrant only if the hearing is adjourned to a date before the expiry of the period mentioned in section 41(3).

(2) This paragraph shall not apply to an adjournment under paragraph 33(2).

Extensions of warrants

36. (1) A police officer of at least the rank of superintendent may apply to a judicial authority for the extension or further extension of the period specified in a warrant of further detention.

(2) Where the period specified is extended, the warrant shall be endorsed with a note stating the new specified period.

(3) The specified period shall end not later than the end of the period of seven days beginning—

(*a*) with the time of the person's arrest under section 41, or
(*b*) if he was being detained under Schedule 7 when he was arrested under section 41, with the time when his examination under that Schedule began.

(4) Paragraphs 30(3) and 31 to 34 shall apply to an application under this paragraph as they apply to an application for a warrant of further detention.

(5) A judicial authority may adjourn the hearing of an application under sub-paragraph (1) only if the hearing is adjourned to a date before the expiry of the period specified in the warrant.

(6) Sub-paragraph (5) shall not apply to an adjournment under paragraph 33(2).

Detention—conditions

37. A person detained by virtue of a warrant issued under this Part shall (unless detained in accordance with section 41(5) or (6) or under any other power) be released immediately if the officer having custody of him becomes aware that any of the grounds under paragraph 32(1)(*a*) and (*b*) upon which the judicial authority authorised his further detention have ceased to apply.

8–23559OA

Section 115

SCHEDULE 14
EXERCISE OF OFFICERS' POWERS

(Amended by the Anti-terrorism, Crime and Security Act 2001, s 2.)

General

1. In this Schedule an "officer" means—

(*a*) an authorised officer within the meaning given by [the terrorist cash provisions], and
(*b*) an examining officer within the meaning of Schedule 7

and "the terrorist cash provisions" means Schedule 1 to the Anti-terrorism, Crime and Security Act 2001.

2. An officer may enter a vehicle (within the meaning of section 121) for the purpose of exercising any of the functions conferred on him by virtue of this Act or the terrorist cash provisions.

3. An officer may if necessary use reasonable force for the purpose of exercising a power conferred on him by virtue of this Act (apart from paragraphs 2 and 3 of Schedule 7) or the terrorist cash provisions.

Information

4. (1) Information acquired by an officer may be supplied—

(*a*) to the Secretary of State for use in relation to immigration;
(*b*) to the Commissioners of Customs and Excise or a customs officer;
(*c*) to a constable;
(*d*) to the Director General of the National Criminal Intelligence Service or of the National Crime Squad;
(*e*) to a person specified by order of the Secretary of State for use of a kind specified in the order.

(2) Information acquired by a customs officer or an immigration officer may be supplied to an examining officer within the meaning of Schedule 7.

Code of practice

5. An officer shall perform functions conferred on him by virtue of this Act or the terrorist cash provisions in accordance with any relevant code of practice in operation under paragraph 6.

6. (1) The Secretary of State shall issue codes of practice[1] about the exercise by officers of functions conferred on them by virtue of this Act or the terrorist cash provisions.

(2) The failure by an officer to observe a provision of a code shall not of itself make him liable to criminal or civil proceedings.

(3) A code—

(*a*) shall be admissible in evidence in criminal and civil proceedings, and
(*b*) shall be taken into account by a court or tribunal in any case in which it appears to the court or tribunal to be relevant.

(4) The Secretary of State may revise a code and issue the revised code.

7. (1) Before issuing a code of practice the Secretary of State shall—

(*a*) publish a draft code,
(*b*) consider any representations made to him about the draft, and
(*c*) if he thinks it appropriate, modify the draft in the light of any representations made to him.

(2) The Secretary of State shall lay a draft of the code before Parliament.

(3) When the Secretary of State has laid a draft code before Parliament he may bring it into operation by order.

(4) This paragraph has effect in relation to the issue of a revised code as it has effect in relation to the first issue of a code.

---

1. By the Terrorism Act 2000 (Code of Practice for Authorised Officers) Order 2001, SI 2001/425 the code of practice in connection with the exercise of functions conferred on authorised officers laid before Parliament in draft on 15 January 2001, came into operation on 19 February 2001 and by the Terrorism Act 2000 (Code of Practice for Examining Officers) Order 2001, SI 2001/427 the code of practice in connection with the exercise of functions conferred on examining officers laid before Parliament in draft on 15 January 2001, came into operation on 19 February 2001.

Anti-terrorism, Crime and Security Act 2001[1]

(2001 c 24)

PART 1[2]
TERRORIST PROPERTY

8–23559P 1. Forfeiture of terrorist cash. (1) Schedule 1 (which makes provision for enabling cash which—

(*a*) is intended to be used for the purposes of terrorism,
(*b*) consists of resources of an organisation which is a proscribed organisation, or
(*c*) is, or represents, property obtained through terrorism,

to be forfeited in civil proceedings before a magistrates' court or (in Scotland) the sheriff) is to have effect.

(2) The powers conferred by Schedule 1 are exercisable in relation to any cash whether or not any proceedings have been brought for an offence in connection with the cash.

(3) Expressions used in this section have the same meaning as in Schedule 1.

(4) Sections 24 to 31 of the Terrorism Act 2000 (c 11) (seizure of terrorist cash) are to cease to have effect.

(5) An order under section 127 bringing Schedule 1 into force may make any modifications of any code of practice then in operation under Schedule 14 to the Terrorism Act 2000 (exercise of officers' powers) which the Secretary of State thinks necessary or expedient.
[Anti-terrorism, Crime and Security Act 2001, s 1.]

---

1. This Act was passed in response to the terrorist attack on New York on 11 September 2001. The Act amends the Terrorism Act 2000; makes further provision about terrorism and security; makes provision about immigration and asylum; amends or extends the criminal law and powers for preventing crime and enforcing that law; makes provision about the control of pathogens and toxins; provides for the retention of communications data; provides for the implementation of Title VI of the Treaty on European Union; and provides for certain connected purposes.

Part 1 of the Act, together with Sch 1, makes provision for the forfeiture of terrorist cash; Part 2 is concerned with freezing orders; Part 3 is concerned with the disclosure of information; Part 4 is concerned with immigration and asylum; Part 5 is concerned with race and religion; Part 6 is concerned with weapons of mass destruction; Part 7 is concerned with the security of pathogens and toxins; Part 8 is concerned with the security of the nuclear industry; Part 9 is concerned with aviation security; Part 10 is concerned with police powers; Part 11 is concerned with the retention of communications data; Part 12 is concerned with bribery and corruption; Part 13 makes miscellaneous provisions; Part 14 contains supplemental provisions.

As to commencement, see s 127, post. The majority of the Act's provisions came into force on, or soon, the date the Act received the Royal Assent. As to the remaining provisions, the following commencement orders have been made: Anti-terrorism, Crime and Security Act 2001 (Commencement No 1 and Consequential Provisions) Order 2001, SI 2001/4019; Anti-terrorism, Crime and Security Act 2001 (Commencement No 2) (Scotland) Order 2001, SI 2001/4014; Anti-terrorism, Crime and Security Act 2001 (Commencement No 3) Order 2001, SI 2002/228; Anti-terrorism, Crime and Security Act 2001 (Commencement No 4 and Consequential Provisions) Order 2001, SI 2002/1279; and Anti-terrorism, Crime and Security Act 2001 (Commencement No 5 and Consequential Provisions) Order 2001, SI 2002/1558.

2. Part 1 contains ss 1–3.

8–23559Q 2. *This section amends Sch 2 to the Access to Justice Act 1999*[1]

1. See PART I: MAGISTRATES' COURTS, PROCEDURE, para **1–3982**.

8–23559R 3. *This section, with Sch 2, amends the Terrorism Act 2000*[1]

1. See this PART, ante.

PART 2[1]

FREEZING ORDERS

Orders

8–23559S 4. Power to make order. (1) The Treasury may make a freezing order if the following two conditions are satisfied.

(2) The first condition is that the Treasury reasonably believe that—

(*a*) action to the detriment of the United Kingdom's economy (or part of it) has been or is likely to be taken by a person or persons, or

(*b*) action constituting a threat to the life or property of one or more nationals of the United Kingdom or residents of the United Kingdom has been or is likely to be taken by a person or persons.

(3) If one person is believed to have taken or to be likely to take the action the second condition is that the person is—

(*a*) the government of a country or territory outside the United Kingdom, or

(*b*) a resident of a country or territory outside the United Kingdom.

(4) If two or more persons are believed to have taken or to be likely to take the action the second condition is that each of them falls within paragraph (*a*) or (*b*) of subsection (3); and different persons may fall within different paragraphs.

[Anti-terrorism, Crime and Security Act 2001, s 4.]

1. Part 2 contains ss 4–16.

8–23559T 5. Contents of order. (1) A freezing order is an order which prohibits persons from making funds available to or for the benefit of a person or persons specified in the order.

(2) The order must provide that these are the persons who are prohibited—

(*a*) all persons in the United Kingdom, and

(*b*) all persons elsewhere who are nationals of the United Kingdom or are bodies incorporated under the law of any part of the United Kingdom or are Scottish partnerships.

(3) The order may specify the following (and only the following) as the person or persons to whom or for whose benefit funds are not to be made available—

(*a*) the person or persons reasonably believed by the Treasury to have taken or to be likely to take the action referred to in section 4;

(*b*) any person the Treasury reasonably believe has provided or is likely to provide assistance (directly or indirectly) to that person or any of those persons.

(4) A person may be specified under subsection (3) by—

(*a*) being named in the order, or

(*b*) falling within a description of persons set out in the order.

(5) The description must be such that a reasonable person would know whether he fell within it.

(6) Funds are financial assets and economic benefits of any kind.

[Anti-terrorism, Crime and Security Act 2001, s 5.]

8–23559W 6. Contents: further provisions. Schedule 3 contains further provisions about the contents of freezing orders.
[Anti-terrorism, Crime and Security Act 2001, s 6.]

8–23559X 7. Review of order. The Treasury must keep a freezing order under review.
[Anti-terrorism, Crime and Security Act 2001, s 7.]

8–23559Y 8. Duration of order. A freezing order ceases to have effect at the end of the period of 2 years starting with the day on which it is made.
[Anti-terrorism, Crime and Security Act 2001, s 8.]

Interpretation

8–23559Z 9. Nationals and residents. (1) A national of the United Kingdom is an individual who is—

(*a*) a British citizen, a British overseas territories citizen, a British National (Overseas) or a British Overseas citizen,
(*b*) a person who under the British Nationality Act 1981 (c 61) is a British subject, or
(*c*) a British protected person within the meaning of that Act.

(2) A resident of the United Kingdom is—

(*a*) an individual who is ordinarily resident in the United Kingdom,
(*b*) a body incorporated under the law of any part of the United Kingdom, or
(*c*) a Scottish partnership.

(3) A resident of a country or territory outside the United Kingdom is—

(*a*) an individual who is ordinarily resident in such a country or territory, or
(*b*) a body incorporated under the law of such a country or territory.

(4) For the purposes of subsection (3)(*b*) a branch situated in a country or territory outside the United Kingdom of—

(*a*) a body incorporated under the law of any part of the United Kingdom, or
(*b*) a Scottish partnership,

is to be treated as a body incorporated under the law of the country or territory where the branch is situated.

(5) This section applies for the purposes of this Part.
[Anti-terrorism, Crime and Security Act 2001, s 9, as amenedd by the British Overseas Territories Act 2002, s 2(3).]

Orders: procedure etc

8–23559ZA 10. Procedure for making freezing orders. (1) A power to make a freezing order is exercisable by statutory instrument.

(2) A freezing order—

(*a*) must be laid before Parliament after being made;
(*b*) ceases to have effect at the end of the relevant period unless before the end of that period the order is approved by a resolution of each House of Parliament (but without that affecting anything done under the order or the power to make a new order).

(3) The relevant period is a period of 28 days starting with the day on which the order is made.

(4) In calculating the relevant period no account is to be taken of any time during which Parliament is dissolved or prorogued or during which both Houses are adjourned for more than 4 days.

(5) If the Treasury propose to make a freezing order in the belief that the condition in section 4(2)(*b*) is satisfied, they must not make the order unless they consult the Secretary of State.
[Anti-terrorism, Crime and Security Act 2001, s 10.]

8–23559ZB 11. Procedure for making certain amending orders. (1) This section applies if—

(*a*) a freezing order is made specifying by description (rather than by name) the person or persons to whom or for whose benefit funds are not to be made available,
(*b*) it is proposed to make a further order which amends the freezing order only so as to make it specify by name the person or persons (or any of the persons) to whom or for whose benefit funds are not to be made available, and
(*c*) the Treasury reasonably believe that the person or persons named fall within the description contained in the freezing order and the further order contains a statement of the Treasury's belief.

(2) This section also applies if—

(*a*) a freezing order is made specifying by name the person or persons to whom or for whose benefit funds are not to be made available, (*b*) it is proposed to make a further order which amends the freezing order only so as to make it specify by name a further person or further persons to whom or for whose benefit funds are not to be made available, and

(*c*) the Treasury reasonably believe that the further person or persons fall within the same description as the person or persons specified in the freezing order and the further order contains a statement of the Treasury's belief.

(3) This section also applies if—

(*a*) a freezing order is made, and

(*b*) it is proposed to make a further order which amends the freezing order only so as to make it specify (whether by name or description) fewer persons to whom or for whose benefit funds are not to be made available.

(4) If this section applies, a statutory instrument containing the further order is subject to annulment in pursuance of a resolution of either House of Parliament.

[Anti-terrorism, Crime and Security Act 2001, s 11.]

8–23559ZC 12. Procedure for revoking orders. A statutory instrument containing an order revoking a freezing order (without re-enacting it) is subject to annulment in pursuance of a resolution of either House of Parliament.

[Anti-terrorism, Crime and Security Act 2001, s 12.]

8–23559ZD 13. De-hybridisation. If apart from this section an order under this Part would be treated for the purposes of the standing orders of either House of Parliament as a hybrid instrument, it is to proceed in that House as if it were not such an instrument.

[Anti-terrorism, Crime and Security Act 2001, s 13.]

8–23559ZE 14. Orders: supplementary. (1) Where this Part confers a power to make provision, different provision may be made for different purposes.

(2) An order under this Part may include supplementary, incidental, saving or transitional provisions.

(3) Nothing in this Part affects the generality of subsection (2).

[Anti-terrorism, Crime and Security Act 2001, s 14.]

Miscellaneous

8–23559ZF 15. The Crown. (1) A freezing order binds the Crown, subject to the following provisions of this section.

(2) No contravention by the Crown of a provision of a freezing order makes the Crown criminally liable; but the High Court or in Scotland the Court of Session may, on the application of a person appearing to the Court to have an interest, declare unlawful any act or omission of the Crown which constitutes such a contravention.

(3) Nothing in this section affects Her Majesty in her private capacity; and this is to be construed as if section 38(3) of the Crown Proceedings Act 1947 (c 44) (meaning of Her Majesty in her private capacity) were contained in this Act.

[Anti-terrorism, Crime and Security Act 2001, s 15.]

8–23559ZG 16. Repeals. (1) These provisions shall cease to have effect—

(*a*) section 2 of the Emergency Laws (Re-enactments and Repeals) Act 1964 (c 60) (Treasury's power to prohibit action on certain orders as to gold etc);

(*b*) section 55 of the Finance Act 1968 (c 44) (meaning of security in section 2 of 1964 Act).

(2) Subsection (1) does not affect a reference which—

(*a*) is to a provision referred to in that subsection, and

(*b*) is contained in a provision made under an Act.

[Anti-terrorism, Crime and Security Act 2001, s 16.]

PART 3[1]

DISCLOSURE OF INFORMATION

8–23559ZH 17. Extension of existing disclosure powers. (1) This section applies to the provisions listed in Schedule 4, so far as they authorise the disclosure of information.

(2) Each of the provisions to which this section applies shall have effect, in relation to the disclosure of information by or on behalf of a public authority, as if the purposes for which the disclosure of information is authorised by that provision included each of the following—

(*a*) the purposes of any criminal investigation whatever which is being or may be carried out, whether in the United Kingdom or elsewhere;

(*b*) the purposes of any criminal proceedings whatever which have been or may be initiated, whether in the United Kingdom or elsewhere;

(*c*) the purposes of the initiation or bringing to an end of any such investigation or proceedings;

(*d*) the purpose of facilitating a determination of whether any such investigation or proceedings should be initiated or brought to an end.

(3) The Treasury may by order made by statutory instrument add any provision contained in any subordinate legislation to the provisions to which this section applies.

(4) The Treasury shall not make an order under subsection (3) unless a draft of it has been laid before Parliament and approved by a resolution of each House.

(5) No disclosure of information shall be made by virtue of this section unless the public authority by which the disclosure is made is satisfied that the making of the disclosure is proportionate to what is sought to be achieved by it.

(6) Nothing in this section shall be taken to prejudice any power to disclose information which exists apart from this section.

(7) The information that may be disclosed by virtue of this section includes information obtained before the commencement of this section.

[Anti-terrorism, Crime and Security Act 2001, s 17.]

---

1. Part 3 contains ss 17–20.

8–23559ZI 18. Restriction on disclosure of information for overseas purposes. (1) Subject to subsections (2) and (3), the Secretary of State may give a direction which—

(*a*) specifies any overseas proceedings or any description of overseas proceedings; and

(*b*) prohibits the making of any relevant disclosure for the purposes of those proceedings or, as the case may be, of proceedings of that description.

(2) In subsection (1) the reference, in relation to a direction, to a relevant disclosure is a reference to a disclosure authorised by any of the provisions to which section 17 applies which—

(*a*) is made for a purpose mentioned in subsection (2)(*a*) to (*d*) of that section; and

(*b*) is a disclosure of any such information as is described in the direction.

(3) The Secretary of State shall not give a direction under this section unless it appears to him that the overseas proceedings in question, or that overseas proceedings of the description in question, relate or would relate—

(*a*) to a matter in respect of which it would be more appropriate for any jurisdiction or investigation to be exercised or carried out by a court or other authority of the United Kingdom, or of a particular part of the United Kingdom;

(*b*) to a matter in respect of which it would be more appropriate for any jurisdiction or investigation to be exercised or carried out by a court or other authority of a third country; or

(*c*) to a matter that would fall within paragraph (*a*) or (*b*)—

(i) if it were appropriate for there to be any exercise of jurisdiction or investigation at all; and

(ii) if (where one does not exist) a court or other authority with the necessary jurisdiction or functions existed in the United Kingdom, in the part of the United Kingdom in question or, as the case may be, in the third country in question.

(4) A direction under this section shall not have the effect of prohibiting—

(*a*) the making of any disclosure by a Minister of the Crown or by the Treasury; or

(*b*) the making of any disclosure in pursuance of a Community obligation.

(5) A direction under this section—

(*a*) may prohibit the making of disclosures absolutely or in such cases, or subject to such conditions as to consent or otherwise, as may be specified in it; and

(*b*) must be published or otherwise issued by the Secretary of State in such manner as he considers appropriate for bringing it to the attention of persons likely to be affected by it.

(6) A person who, knowing of any direction under this section, discloses any information in contravention of that direction shall be guilty of an offence and liable—

(*a*) on conviction on indictment, to imprisonment for a term not exceeding two years or to a fine or to both;

(*b*) on summary conviction, to imprisonment for a term not exceeding three months or to a fine not exceeding the statutory maximum or to both[1].

(7) The following are overseas proceedings for the purposes of this section—

(*a*) criminal proceedings which are taking place, or will or may take place, in a country or territory outside the United Kingdom;

(*b*) a criminal investigation which is being, or will or may be, conducted by an authority of any such country or territory.

(8) References in this section, in relation to any proceedings or investigation, to a third country are references to any country or territory outside the United Kingdom which is not the country or territory where the proceedings are taking place, or will or may take place or, as the case may be, is

not the country or territory of the authority which is conducting the investigation, or which will or may conduct it.

(9) In this section "court" includes a tribunal of any description.

[Anti-terrorism, Crime and Security Act 2001, s 18.]

---

1. For procedure in respect of this offence, which is triable either way, see the Magistrates' Courts Act 1980, ss 17A–21, in PART 1: MAGISTRATES' COURTS, PROCEDURE, ante.

8–23559ZJ 19. Disclosure of information held by revenue departments. (1) This section applies to information which is held by or on behalf of the Commissioners of Inland Revenue or by or on behalf of the Commissioners of Customs and Excise, including information obtained before the coming into force of this section.

(2) No obligation of secrecy imposed by statute or otherwise prevents the disclosure, in accordance with the following provisions of this section, of information to which this section applies if the disclosure is made—

(*a*) for the purpose of facilitating the carrying out by any of the intelligence services of any of that service's functions;

(*b*) for the purposes of any criminal investigation whatever which is being or may be carried out, whether in the United Kingdom or elsewhere;

(*c*) for the purposes of any criminal proceedings whatever which have been or may be initiated, whether in the United Kingdom or elsewhere;

(*d*) for the purposes of the initiation or bringing to an end of any such investigation or proceedings; or

(*e*) for the purpose of facilitating a determination of whether any such investigation or proceedings should be initiated or brought to an end.

(3) No disclosure of information to which this section applies shall be made by virtue of this section unless the person by whom the disclosure is made is satisfied that the making of the disclosure is proportionate to what is sought to be achieved by it.

(4) Information to which this section applies shall not be disclosed by virtue of this section except by the Commissioners by or on whose behalf it is held or with their authority.

(5) Information obtained by means of a disclosure authorised by subsection (2) shall not be further disclosed except—

(*a*) for a purpose mentioned in that subsection; and

(*b*) with the consent of the Commissioners by whom or with whose authority it was initially disclosed;

and information so obtained otherwise than by or on behalf of any of the intelligence services shall not be further disclosed (with or without such consent) to any of those services, or to any person acting on behalf of any of those services, except for a purpose mentioned in paragraphs (*b*) to (*e*) of that subsection.

(6) A consent for the purposes of subsection (5) may be given either in relation to a particular disclosure or in relation to disclosures made in such circumstances as may be specified or described in the consent.

(7) Nothing in this section authorises the making of any disclosure which is prohibited by any provision of the Data Protection Act 1998 (c 29).

(8) References in this section to information which is held on behalf of the Commissioners of Inland Revenue or of the Commissioners of Customs and Excise include references to information which—

(*a*) is held by a person who provides services to the Commissioners of Inland Revenue or, as the case may be, to the Commissioners of Customs and Excise; and

(*b*) is held by that person in connection with the provision of those services.

(9) In this section "intelligence service" has the same meaning as in the Regulation of Investigatory Powers Act 2000 (c 23).

(10) Nothing in this section shall be taken to prejudice any power to disclose information which exists apart from this section.

[Anti-terrorism, Crime and Security Act 2001, s 19.]

8–23559ZK 20. Interpretation of Part 3. (1) In this Part—

"criminal investigation" means an investigation of any criminal conduct, including an investigation of alleged or suspected criminal conduct and an investigation of whether criminal conduct has taken place;

"information" includes—

(*a*) documents; and

(*b*) in relation to a disclosure authorised by a provision to which section 17 applies, anything that falls to be treated as information for the purposes of that provision;

"public authority" has the same meaning as in section 6 of the Human Rights Act 1998 (c 42); and

"subordinate legislation" has the same meaning as in the Interpretation Act 1978 (c 30).

(2) Proceedings outside the United Kingdom shall not be taken to be criminal proceedings for the purposes of this Part unless the conduct with which the defendant in those proceedings is charged is criminal conduct or conduct which, to a substantial extent, consists of criminal conduct.

(3) In this section—

"conduct" includes acts, omissions and statements; and

"criminal conduct" means any conduct which—

(*a*) constitutes one or more criminal offences under the law of a part of the United Kingdom; or

(*b*) is, or corresponds to, conduct which, if it all took place in a particular part of the United Kingdom, would constitute one or more offences under the law of that part of the United Kingdom.

[Anti-terrorism, Crime and Security Act 2001, s 20.]

PART 4[1]
IMMIGRATION AND ASYLUM[2]

8–23559ZL

1. Part 4 contains ss 21–36.
2. This part contains provisions in relation to suspected international terrorists. The Anti-terrorism, Crime and Security Act 2001 (Continuance in force of sections 21 to 23) Order 2004, SI 2004/751 provides that these provisions continue in force until 14 March 2005. In anticipation of the possible incompatibility of these provisions with art 5(1) of the Convention for the Protection of Human Rights and Fundamental Freedoms the UK made a derogation from art 5(1): see The Human Rights Act 1998 (Designation Derogation) Order, SI 2001/4032. There is a right of appeal against certification to the Special Immigration Appeals Commission, which is established by the Act as a superior court of record whose decisions can be questioned only in accordance with specified provisions, and that body must hold a review as soon as it is reasonably practicable after the expiry of 6 months from the date the certificate was issued or the determination of any appeal. Further reviews must be held as soon as is reasonably practicable after the expiry of 3 months from the date of the previous review.

The certification and detention provisions will expire on March 14. The Anti-terrorism, Crime and Security Act 2001 (Continuance in force of sections 21 to 23) Order 2004, SI 2004/751 provides that these provisions continue in force for a period of one year commencing on 14 March 2004.

Detention under these provisions may not be compatible with art 5(1) of the Convention for the Protection of Human Rights and Fundamental Freedoms. Consequently, the UK had made a derogation from art 5(1): see The Human Rights Act 1998 (Amendment No 2) Order 2001, SI 2001/4032. In *A v Secretary of State for the Home Department* [2002] EWCA Civ 1502, [2002] JPN 862, the Special Immigration Appeals Commission's decision to quash the Human Rights Act 1998 (Designated Derogation) Order 2001 and to declare incompatible with the Convention s 21 of the Anti-terrorism, Crime and Security Act 2001, on the grounds that these provisions permitted the detention of non UK nationals resident in the UK but not UK nationals and, consequently, were discriminatory, was overturned by the Court of Appeal: *A v Secretary of State for the Home Department* [2002] EWCA Civ 1502, [2003] 1 All ER 816. The decision of the Court of Appeal was in turn reversed by the House of Lords on the basis that these provisions were disproportionate and discriminatory: *A v Secretary of State for the Home Department* [2004] UKHL 56, [2005] 2 AC 68, [2005] 3 All ER 169, [2005] 2 WLR 87.

The Special Immigration Appeals Commission is expected to behave like a court and therefore in considering an appeal under s 25, it must apply the standards of justice which have traditionally characterised the proceedings of English courts. This excludes the use of evidence obtained by torture, whatever might be its source as there is a general rule that evidence obtained by torture is inadmissible in judicial proceedings: *A v Secretary of State for the Home Department (No 2)* [2005] UKHL 71, [2005] 3 WLR 1249.

PART 5[1]
RACE AND RELIGION[2]

8–23559ZM

1. Part 5 contains ss 37–42.
2. Part 5 amends various provisions of the Public Order Act 1986, the Crime and Disorder Act 1998, the Police and Criminal Evidence Act 1984, the Powers of Criminal Courts (Sentencing) Act 2000 and correlative provisions relating to Northern Ireland. The main changes are that the offence of racial hatred in s 17 of the Public Order Act 1986 now extends to racial hatred towards groups outside Great Britain and the maximum penalty is now 7 years' imprisonment, and the racially aggravated offences created by the Crime and Disorder Act 1998 have become "racially *or religiously* aggravated" offences. Part 5 does not apply to anything done before it came into force (s 42).

PART 6[1]
WEAPONS OF MASS DESTRUCTION[2]

8–23559ZMA

1. Part 6 contains ss 43–50.
2. Sections 43–46 amend the Biological Weapons Act 1974 and the Chemical Weapons Act 1996.

Nuclear weapons

8–23559ZN 47. Use etc of nuclear weapons. (1) A person who—

(*a*) knowingly causes a nuclear weapon explosion;

(*b*) develops or produces, or participates in the development or production of, a nuclear weapon;

(*c*) has a nuclear weapon in his possession;

(*d*) participates in the transfer of a nuclear weapon; or

(*e*) engages in military preparations, or in preparations of a military nature, intending to use, or threaten to use, a nuclear weapon, is guilty of an offence.

(2) Subsection (1) has effect subject to the exceptions and defences in sections 48 and 49.

(3) For the purposes of subsection (1)(*b*) a person participates in the development or production of a nuclear weapon if he does any act which—

(*a*) facilitates the development by another of the capability to produce or use a nuclear weapon, or

(*b*) facilitates the making by another of a nuclear weapon,

knowing or having reason to believe that his act has (or will have) that effect.

(4) For the purposes of subsection (1)(*d*) a person participates in the transfer of a nuclear weapon if—

(*a*) he buys or otherwise acquires it or agrees with another to do so;

(*b*) he sells or otherwise disposes of it or agrees with another to do so; or

(*c*) he makes arrangements under which another person either acquires or disposes of it or agrees with a third person to do so.

(5) A person guilty of an offence under this section is liable on conviction on indictment to imprisonment for life.

(6) In this section "nuclear weapon" includes a nuclear explosive device that is not intended for use as a weapon.

(7) This section applies to acts done outside the United Kingdom, but only if they are done by a United Kingdom person.

(8) Nothing in subsection (7) affects any criminal liability arising otherwise than under that subsection.

(9) Paragraph (*a*) of subsection (1) shall cease to have effect on the coming into force of the Nuclear Explosions (Prohibition and Inspections) Act 1998 (c 7).

[Anti-terrorism, Crime and Security Act 2001, s 47.]

8–23559ZO 48. Exceptions. (1) Nothing in section 47 applies—

(*a*) to an act which is authorised under subsection (2); or

(*b*) to an act done in the course of an armed conflict.

(2) The Secretary of State may—

(*a*) authorise any act which would otherwise contravene section 47 in such manner and on such terms as he thinks fit; and

(*b*) withdraw or vary any authorisation given under this subsection.

(3) Any question arising in proceedings for an offence under section 47 as to whether anything was done in the course of an armed conflict shall be determined by the Secretary of State.

(4) A certificate purporting to set out any such determination and to be signed by the Secretary of State shall be received in evidence in any such proceedings and shall be presumed to be so signed unless the contrary is shown.

[Anti-terrorism, Crime and Security Act 2001, s 48.]

8–23559ZP 49. Defences. (1) In proceedings for an offence under section 47(1)(*c*) or (*d*) relating to an object it is a defence for the accused to show that he did not know and had no reason to believe that the object was a nuclear weapon.

(2) But he shall be taken to have shown that fact if—

(*a*) sufficient evidence is adduced to raise an issue with respect to it; and

(*b*) the contrary is not proved by the prosecution beyond reasonable doubt.

(3) In proceedings for such an offence it is also a defence for the accused to show that he knew or believed that the object was a nuclear weapon but, as soon as reasonably practicable after he first knew or believed that fact, he took all reasonable steps to inform the Secretary of State or a constable of his knowledge or belief.

[Anti-terrorism, Crime and Security Act 2001, s 49.]

Assisting or inducing weapons-related acts overseas

8–23559ZQ 50. Assisting or inducing certain weapons-related acts overseas. (1) A person who aids, abets, counsels or procures, or incites, a person who is not a United Kingdom person to do a relevant act outside the United Kingdom is guilty of an offence.

(2) For this purpose a relevant act is an act that, if done by a United Kingdom person, would contravene any of the following provisions—

(*a*) section 1 of the Biological Weapons Act 1974 (offences relating to biological agents and toxins);
(*b*) section 2 of the Chemical Weapons Act 1996 (offences relating to chemical weapons); or
(*c*) section 47 above (offences relating to nuclear weapons).

(3) Nothing in this section applies to an act mentioned in subsection (1) which—

(*a*) relates to a relevant act which would contravene section 47; and
(*b*) is authorised by the Secretary of State;

and section 48(2) applies for the purpose of authorising acts that would otherwise constitute an offence under this section.

(4) A person accused of an offence under this section in relation to a relevant act which would contravene a provision mentioned in subsection (2) may raise any defence which would be open to a person accused of the corresponding offence ancillary to an offence under that provision.

(5) A person convicted of an offence under this section is liable on conviction on indictment to imprisonment for life.

(6) This section applies to acts done outside the United Kingdom, but only if they are done by a United Kingdom person.

(7) Nothing in this section prejudices any criminal liability existing apart from this section.
[Anti-terrorism, Crime and Security Act 2001, s 50.]

Supplemental provisions relating to sections 47 and 50

8–23559ZR 51. Extraterritorial application. (1) Proceedings for an offence committed under section 47 or 50 outside the United Kingdom may be taken, and the offence may for incidental purposes be treated as having been committed, in any part of the United Kingdom.

(2) Her Majesty may by Order in Council extend the application of section 47 or 50, so far as it applies to acts done outside the United Kingdom, to bodies incorporated under the law of any of the Channel Islands, the Isle of Man or any colony.
[Anti-terrorism, Crime and Security Act 2001, s 51.]

8–23559ZS 52. Powers of entry. (1) If—

(*a*) a justice of the peace is satisfied on information on oath that there are reasonable grounds for suspecting that evidence of the commission of an offence under section 47 or 50 is to be found on any premises; or
(*b*) in Scotland the sheriff is satisfied by evidence on oath as mentioned in paragraph (*a*),

he may issue a warrant authorising an authorised officer to enter the premises, if necessary by force, at any time within one month from the time of the issue of the warrant and to search them.

(2) The powers of a person who enters the premises under the authority of the warrant include power—

(*a*) to take with him such other persons and such equipment as appear to him to be necessary;
(*b*) to inspect, seize and retain any substance, equipment or document found on the premises;
(*c*) to require any document or other information which is held in electronic form and is accessible from the premises to be produced in a form—

(i) in which he can read and copy it; or
(ii) from which it can readily be produced in a form in which he can read and copy it;

(*d*) to copy any document which he has reasonable cause to believe may be required as evidence for the purposes of proceedings in respect of an offence under section 47 or 50.

(3) A constable who enters premises under the authority of a warrant or by virtue of subsection (2)(*a*) may—

(*a*) give such assistance as an authorised officer may request for the purpose of facilitating the exercise of any power under this section; and
(*b*) search or cause to be searched any person on the premises who the constable has reasonable cause to believe may have in his possession any document or other thing which may be required as evidence for the purposes of proceedings in respect of an offence under section 47 or 50.

(4) No constable shall search a person of the opposite sex.

(5) The powers conferred by a warrant under this section shall only be exercisable, if the warrant so provides, in the presence of a constable.

(6) A person who—

(*a*) wilfully obstructs an authorised officer in the exercise of a power conferred by a warrant under this section; or
(*b*) fails without reasonable excuse to comply with a reasonable request made by an authorised officer or a constable for the purpose of facilitating the exercise of such a power,

is guilty of an offence.

(7) A person guilty of an offence under subsection (6) is liable—

(*a*) on summary conviction, to a fine not exceeding the statutory maximum; and

(*b*) on conviction on indictment, to imprisonment for a term not exceeding two years or a fine (or both)[1].

(8) In this section "authorised officer" means an authorised officer of the Secretary of State.
[Anti-terrorism, Crime and Security Act 2001, s 52.]

1. For procedure in respect of this offence, which is triable either way, see the Magistrates' Courts Act 1980, ss 17A–21, in PART I: MAGISTRATES' COURTS, PROCEDURE, ante.

8–23559ZT 53. Customs and Excise prosecutions. (1) Proceedings for a nuclear weapons offence may be instituted by order of the Commissioners of Customs and Excise if it appears to them that the offence has involved—

(*a*) the development or production outside the United Kingdom of a nuclear weapon;

(*b*) the movement of a nuclear weapon into or out of any country or territory;

(*c*) any proposal or attempt to do anything falling within paragraph (*a*) or (*b*).

(2) In this section "nuclear weapons offence" means an offence under section 47 or 50 (including an offence of aiding, abetting, counselling, procuring or inciting the commission of, or attempting or conspiring to commit, such an offence).

(3) Any proceedings for an offence which are instituted under subsection (1) shall be commenced in the name of an officer, but may be continued by another officer.

(4) Where the Commissioners of Customs and Excise investigate, or propose to investigate, any matter with a view to determining—

(*a*) whether there are grounds for believing that a nuclear weapons offence has been committed, or

(*b*) whether a person should be prosecuted for such an offence,

that matter shall be treated as an assigned matter within the meaning of the Customs and Excise Management Act 1979 (c 2).

(5) Nothing in this section affects any powers of any person (including any officer) apart from this section.

(6) In this section "officer" means a person commissioned by the Commissioners of Customs and Excise.

(7) This section does not apply to the institution of proceedings in Scotland.
[Anti-terrorism, Crime and Security Act 2001, s 53.]

8–23559ZU 54. Offences. (1) A person who knowingly or recklessly makes a false or misleading statement for the purpose of obtaining (or opposing the variation or withdrawal of) authorisation for the purposes of section 47 or 50 is guilty of an offence.

(2) A person guilty of an offence under subsection (1) is liable—

(*a*) on summary conviction, to a fine of an amount not exceeding the statutory maximum;

(*b*) on conviction on indictment, to imprisonment for a term not exceeding two years or a fine (or both)[1].

(3) Where an offence under section 47, 50 or subsection (1) above committed by a body corporate is proved to have been committed with the consent or connivance of, or to be attributable to any neglect on the part of—

(*a*) a director, manager, secretary or other similar officer of the body corporate; or

(*b*) any person who was purporting to act in any such capacity,

he as well as the body corporate shall be guilty of that offence and shall be liable to be proceeded against and punished accordingly.

(4) In subsection (3) "director", in relation to a body corporate whose affairs are managed by its members, means a member of the body corporate.
[Anti-terrorism, Crime and Security Act 2001, s 54.]

1. For procedure in respect of this offence, which is triable either way, see the Magistrates' Courts Act 1980, ss 17A–21, in PART I: MAGISTRATES' COURTS, PROCEDURE, ante.

8–23559ZV 55. Consent to prosecutions. Proceedings for an offence under section 47 or 50 shall not be instituted—

(*a*) in England and Wales, except by or with the consent of the Attorney General;

(*b*) in Northern Ireland, except by or with the consent of the Attorney General for Northern Ireland.*
[Anti-terrorism, Crime and Security Act 2001, s 55.]

***Paragraph (*b*) words repealed and substituted by the Justice (Northern Ireland) Act 2002, s 28(2) from a date to be appointed.**

8–23559ZW 56. Interpretation of Part 6. (1) In this Part "United Kingdom person" means a United Kingdom national, a Scottish partnership or a body incorporated under the law of a part of the United Kingdom.

(2) For this purpose a United Kingdom national is an individual who is—

(*a*) a British citizen, a British overseas territories citizen, a British National (Overseas) or a British Overseas citizen;

(*b*) a person who under the British Nationality Act 1981 (c 61) is a British subject; or

(*c*) a British protected person within the meaning of that Act.

[Anti-terrorism, Crime and Security Act 2001, s 56, as amended by the British Overseas Territories Act 2002, s 2(3).]

Extension of Part 6 to dependencies

8–23559ZX 57. Power to extend Part 6 to dependencies. Her Majesty may by Order in Council[1] direct that any of the provisions of this Part shall extend, with such exceptions and modifications as appear to Her Majesty to be appropriate, to any of the Channel Islands, the Isle of Man or to any British overseas territory.

[Anti-terrorism, Crime and Security Act 2001, s 57.]

1. The Chemical Weapons (Overseas Territories) Order 2005, SI 2005/854 has been made.

PART 7[1]
SECURITY OF PATHOGENS AND TOXINS

8–23559ZY

1. Part 7 contains ss 58–75.

PART 8[1]
SECURITY OF NUCLEAR INDUSTRY

8–23559ZYA 76. Atomic Energy Authority special constables. *Repealed.*

8–23559ZZ 77. Regulation of security of civil nuclear industry. (1) The Secretary of State may make regulations[1] for the purpose of ensuring the security of—

(*a*) nuclear sites and other nuclear premises;

(*b*) nuclear material used or stored on nuclear sites or other nuclear premises and equipment or software used or stored on such sites or premises in connection with activities involving nuclear material;

(*c*) other radioactive material used or stored on nuclear sites and equipment or software used or stored on nuclear sites in connection with activities involving other radioactive material;

(*ca*) equipment or software in the United Kingdom which—

(i) is capable of being used in, or in connection with, the enrichment of uranium; and

(ii) is in the possession or control of a person involved in uranium enrichment activities;

(*d*) sensitive nuclear information which is in the possession or control in the United Kingdom of—

(i) a person who is involved in activities on or in relation to a nuclear site or nuclear premises or who is proposing or likely to become so involved;

(ii) a person involved in uranium enrichment activities; or

(iii) a person who is storing, transporting or transmitting the information for or on behalf of a person falling within sub-paragraph (i) or (ii);

(*e*) nuclear material which is being (or is expected to be)—

(i) transported within the United Kingdom or its territorial sea;

(ii) transported (outside the United Kingdom and its territorial sea) to or from any nuclear site or other nuclear premises in the United Kingdom; or

(iii) carried on board a United Kingdom ship;

(*f*) information relating to the security of anything mentioned in paragraphs (*a*) to (*e*).

(2) The regulations may, in particular—

(*a*) require a person to produce for the approval of the Secretary of State a plan for ensuring the security of anything mentioned in subsection (1) and to comply with the plan as approved by the Secretary of State;

(*b*) require compliance with any directions given by the Secretary of State;

(*c*) impose requirements in relation to any activities by reference to the approval of the Secretary of State;

(*d*) create summary offences or offences triable either way;

(*e*) make provision for the purposes mentioned in subsection (1) corresponding to any provision which may be made for the general purposes of Part 1 of the Health and Safety at Work etc Act 1974 (c 37) by virtue of section 15(2), (3)(*c*) and (4) to (8) of that Act (health and safety regulations);

(*f*) make provision corresponding to any provision which may be made by virtue of section 43(2) to (5), (8) and (9) of that Act (fees), in connection with the performance by or on behalf of the Secretary of State or any other specified body or person of functions under the regulations; and

(*g*) apply (with or without modifications), or make provision corresponding to, any provision contained in sections 19 to 42 and 44 to 47 of that Act.

(3) An offence under the regulations may be made punishable—

(*a*) in the case of an offence triable either way—

(i) on conviction on indictment, with imprisonment for a term not exceeding two years or a fine (or both); and

(ii) on summary conviction, with imprisonment for a term not exceeding six months or a fine not exceeding the statutory maximum (or both); or

(*b*) in the case of a summary offence, with imprisonment for a term not exceeding six months or a fine not exceeding level 5 on the standard scale (or both)[2].

(4) The regulations may make—

(*a*) provision applying to acts done outside the United Kingdom by United Kingdom persons;

(*b*) different provision for different purposes; and

(*c*) such incidental, supplementary and transitional provision as the Secretary of State considers appropriate.

(5) Before making the regulations the Secretary of State shall consult—

(*a*) the Health and Safety Commission; and

(*b*) such other persons as he considers appropriate.

(6) The power to make the regulations is exercisable by statutory instrument subject to annulment in pursuance of a resolution of either House of Parliament.

(6A) References in this section to a person involved in uranium enrichment activities are references to a person who is or is proposing to become involved in any of the following activities (whether in the United Kingdom or elsewhere)—

(*a*) the enrichment of uranium;

(*b*) activities carried on with a view to, or in connection with, the enrichment of uranium;

(*c*) the production, storage, transport or transmission of equipment or software for or on behalf of persons involved in uranium enrichment activities; or

(*d*) activities that make it reasonable to assume that he will become involved in something mentioned in paragraphs (*a*) to (*c*).

(7) In this section—

"enrichment of uranium" means a treatment of uranium that increases the proportion of isotope 235 contained in the uranium;

"equipment" includes equipment that has not been assembled and its components;

"nuclear material" has the same meaning as in Chapter 3 of Part 1 of the Energy Act 2004;

"nuclear site" means a licensed nuclear site within the meaning of that Chapter;

"other nuclear premises" means premises other than a nuclear site on which nuclear material is used or stored;

"sensitive nuclear information" means—

(*a*) information relating to, or capable of use in connection with, the enrichment of uranium; or

(*b*) information relating to activities carried out on or in relation to nuclear sites or other nuclear premises which appears to the Secretary of State to be information which needs to be protected in the interests of national security;

"United Kingdom ship" means a ship registered in the United Kingdom under Part 2 of the Merchant Shipping Act 1995 (c 21)

(8) Any sums received by virtue of provision made under subsection (2)(*f*) shall be paid into the Consolidated Fund.

[Anti-terrorism, Crime and Security Act 2001, s 77, as amended by the Energy Act 2004, s 77 and the Energy Act 2004, Sch 14.]

1. The Nuclear Industries Security Regulations 2003, SI 2003/403, have been made.

2. For procedure in respect of this offence, which is triable either way, see the Magistrates' Courts Act, ss 17A-21, in PART 1: MAGISTRATES' COURTS, PROCEDURE, ante.

8–23559ZZA 78. *Repeals relating to security of civil nuclear installations*[1]

1. At the date of going to press, s 78 had not been brought into force.

8–23559ZZB 79. Prohibition of disclosures relating to nuclear security. (1) A person is guilty of an offence if he discloses any information or thing the disclosure of which might prejudice the security of any nuclear site or of any nuclear material—

(*a*) with the intention of prejudicing that security; or
(*b*) being reckless as to whether the disclosure might prejudice that security.

(2) The reference in subsection (1) to nuclear material is a reference to—

(*a*) nuclear material which is being held on any nuclear site, or
(*b*) nuclear material anywhere in the world which is being transported to or from a nuclear site or carried on board a British ship,

(including nuclear material which is expected to be so held, transported or carried).

(3) A person guilty of an offence under subsection (1) is liable—

(*a*) on conviction on indictment, to imprisonment for a term not exceeding seven years or a fine (or both); and
(*b*) on summary conviction, to imprisonment for a term not exceeding six months or a fine not exceeding the statutory maximum (or both)[1].

(4) In this section—

"British ship" means a ship (including a ship belonging to Her Majesty) which is registered in the United Kingdom;
"disclose" and "disclosure", in relation to a thing, include parting with possession of it;
"nuclear material" has the same meaning as in Chapter 3 of Part 1 of the Energy Act 2004; and
"nuclear site" means a site in the United Kingdom (including a site occupied by or on behalf of the Crown) which is (or is expected to be) used for any purpose mentioned in section 1(1) of the Nuclear Installations Act 1965 (c 57).

(5) This section applies to acts done outside the United Kingdom, but only if they are done by a United Kingdom person.

(6) Proceedings for an offence committed outside the United Kingdom may be taken, and the offence may for incidental purposes be treated as having been committed, in any place in the United Kingdom.

(7) Nothing in subsection (5) affects any criminal liability arising otherwise than under that subsection.

[Anti-terrorism, Crime and Security Act 2001, s 79 as amended by the Energy Act 2004, Sch 14.]

1. For procedure in respect of this offence, which is triable either way, see the Magistrates' Courts Act 1980, ss 17A–21, in PART I: MAGISTRATES' COURTS, PROCEDURE, ante.

8–23559ZZC 80. Prohibition of disclosures of uranium enrichment technology. (1) This section applies to—

(*a*) any information about the enrichment of uranium; or
(*b*) any information or thing which is, or is likely to be, used in connection with the enrichment of uranium;

and for this purpose "the enrichment of uranium" means any treatment of uranium that increases the proportion of the isotope 235 contained in the uranium.

(2) The Secretary of State may make regulations[1] prohibiting the disclosure of information or things to which this section applies.

(3) A person who contravenes a prohibition is guilty of an offence and liable—

(*a*) on conviction on indictment, to imprisonment for a term not exceeding seven years or a fine (or both); and
(*b*) on summary conviction, to imprisonment for a term not exceeding six months or a fine not exceeding the statutory maximum (or both)[2].

(4) The regulations may, in particular, provide for—

(*a*) a prohibition to apply, or not to apply—
  (i) to such information or things; and
  (ii) in such cases or circumstances,

  as may be prescribed;
(*b*) the authorisation by the Secretary of State of disclosures that would otherwise be prohibited; and
(*c*) defences to an offence under subsection (3) relating to any prohibition.

(5) The regulations may—

(*a*) provide for any prohibition to apply to acts done outside the United Kingdom by United Kingdom persons;

(*b*) make different provision for different purposes; and

(*c*) make such incidental, supplementary and transitional provision as the Secretary of State thinks fit.

(6) The power to make the regulations is exercisable by statutory instrument.

(7) The regulations shall not be made unless a draft of the regulations has been laid before and approved by each House of Parliament.

(8) In this section—

"disclosure", in relation to a thing, includes parting with possession of it;

"information" includes software; and

"prescribed" means specified or described in the regulations.

[Anti-terrorism, Crime and Security Act 2001, s 80.]

1. The Uranium Enrichment Technology (Prohibition on Disclosure) Regulations 2004, SI 2004/1818 have been made.

2. For procedure in respect of this offence, which is triable either way, see the Magistrates' Courts Act 1980, ss 17A–21, in PART I: MAGISTRATES' COURTS, PROCEDURE, ante.

8–23559ZZD 81. Part 8: supplementary. (1) Proceedings for an offence under section 79 or 80 shall not be instituted—

(*a*) in England and Wales, except by or with the consent of the Attorney General; or

(*b*) in Northern Ireland, except by or with the consent of the Attorney General for Northern Ireland.*

(2) In this Part "United Kingdom person" means a United Kingdom national, a Scottish partnership or a body incorporated under the law of any part of the United Kingdom.

(3) For this purpose a United Kingdom national is an individual who is—

(*a*) a British citizen, a British overseas territories citizen, a British National (Overseas) or a British Overseas citizen;

(*b*) a person who under the British Nationality Act 1981 (c 61) is a British subject; or

(*c*) a British protected person within the meaning of that Act.

[Anti-terrorism, Crime and Security Act 2001, s 81, as amended by the British Overseas Territories Act 2002, s 2(3).]

***Sub-section (1), para (*b*), words repealed and substituted by the Justice (Northern Ireland) Act 2002, s 28(2) from a date to be appointed.**

PART 9[1]

AVIATION SECURITY[2]

8–23559ZZE 88. Extent outside United Kingdom. (1) The powers in section 108(1) and (2) of the Civil Aviation Act 1982 (c 16) (extension outside United Kingdom) apply to provisions of this Part which amend that Act.

(2) The powers in section 39(3) of the Aviation Security Act 1982 (extension outside United Kingdom) apply to provisions of this Part which amend that Act.

[Anti-terrorism, Crime and Security Act 2001, s 88.]

1. Part 9 contains ss 82–88.

2. Sections 82–87 amend or add provisions to the Police and Criminal Evidence Act 1984 (new arrest without warrant powers) and the Civil Aviation Act 1982 (increased penalty for trespass on aerodrome) and the Aviation Security Act 1982 (approved providers of aviation security services; detention of aircraft; and offence relating to air cargo agent documents). Section 88 provides that the jurisdiction extending powers contained in s 108(1) and (2) of the Civil Aviation Act 1982 and s 39(3) of the Aviation Security Act 1982 apply to the provisions of Part 9 of the Anti-terrorism, Crime and Security Act 2001 that amend those Acts.

PART 10[1]

POLICE POWERS[2]

MoD and transport police

8–23559ZZF 100. Jurisdiction of transport police. (1) Where a member of the British Transport Police Force has been requested by a constable of—

(*a*) the police force for any police area,

(*b*) the Ministry of Defence Police, or

(*c*) the Civil Nuclear Constabulary,

("the requesting force") to assist him in the execution of his duties in relation to a particular incident, investigation or operation, members of the British Transport Police Force have for the purposes of that incident, investigation or operation the same powers and privileges as constables of the requesting force.

(2) Members of the British Transport Police Force have in any police area the same powers and privileges as constables of the police force for that police area—

(*a*) in relation to persons whom they suspect on reasonable grounds of having committed, being in the course of committing or being about to commit an offence, or

(*b*) if they believe on reasonable grounds that they need those powers and privileges in order to save life or to prevent or minimise personal injury.

(3) But members of the British Transport Police Force have powers and privileges by virtue of subsection (2) only if—

(*a*) they are in uniform or have with them documentary evidence that they are members of that Force, and

(*b*) they believe on reasonable grounds that a power of a constable which they would not have apart from that subsection ought to be exercised and that, if it cannot be exercised until they secure the attendance of or a request under subsection (1) by a constable who has it, the purpose for which they believe it ought to be exercised will be frustrated or seriously prejudiced.

(4) In this section—

"British Transport Police Force" means the constables appointed under section 53 of the British Transport Commission Act 1949 (c xxix)

[Anti-terrorism, Crime and Security Act 2001, s 100 as amended by the Energy Act 2004, Sch 14.]

---

1. Part 10 contains ss 89–101.

2. Part 10 amends Sch 8 to the Terrorism Act 2000 (fingerprinting, etc); the Police and Criminal Evidence Act 1984 (as to searches and examination to establish identity and photographing of suspects); the Criminal Justice and Public Order Act 1994 (powers to require removal of disguises); and the Ministry of Defence Police Act 1987 (as to the jurisdiction of MoD police and the provision of assistance to other forces).

8–23559ZZG 101. Further provisions about transport police and MoD police. Schedule 7 contains amendments relating to the British Transport Police Force and the Ministry of Defence Police.

[Anti-terrorism, Crime and Security Act 2001, s 101.]

PART 11[1]

RETENTION OF COMMUNICATIONS DATA[2]

8–23559ZZH 102. Codes and agreements about the retention of communications data.

(5) A code of practice or agreement under this section which is for the time being in force shall be admissible in evidence in any legal proceedings in which the question arises whether or not the retention of any communications data is justified on the grounds that a failure to retain the data would be likely to prejudice national security, the prevention or detection of crime or the prosecution of offenders.

[Anti-terrorism, Crime and Security Act 2001, s 102.]

---

1. Part 11 contains ss 102–107.

2. Part 11 requires the Security of State, following publication of a draft before which he must consult the Information Commissioner and affected communications providers, to issue a code of practice relating to the retention by communications providers of communications data obtained by or held by them. The code shall be brought into force by an order made by statutory instrument, a draft of which must be approved by resolution of each House of Parliament. The code may be revised from time to time, subject to the procedures stated above. The draft code of practice entitled "Voluntary Retention of Communications Data under Part 11: Anti-terrorism, Crime and Security Act 2001—Voluntary Code of Practice", laid before each House of Parliament on 11 September 2003 came into force on 5 December 2003 by the Retention of Communications Data (Code of Practice) Order 2003, SI 2003/3175.

The Security of State may also enter into agreements with communications providers as to the practices the latter are to follow in relation to the retention of communications data obtained by or held by them.

The Secretary of State may also by order made by statutory instrument (subject to the same Parliamentary approval) authorize himself to give directions about the retention of communications data. Before giving such directions the Secretary of State must consult affected communications providers. The duty of communications providers to comply with directions is enforceable by civil proceedings. The period within which the Secretary of State may give such directions has been extended for two years commencing on 14 December 2003 by the Retention of Communications Data (Extension of Initial Period) Order 2003, SI 2003/3173 and extended for a further two years commencing on 14 December 2005 by the Retention of Communications Data (Further Extension of Initial Period) Order 2005, SI 2005/3335.

8–23559ZZI 107. Interpretation of Part 11. (1) In this Part—

"communications data" has the same meaning as in Chapter 2 of Part 1 of the Regulation of Investigatory Powers Act 2000 (c 23);

"communications provider" means a person who provides a postal service or a telecommunications service;

"legal proceedings", "postal service" and "telecommunications service" each has the same meaning as in that Act;

and any reference in this Part to the prevention or detection of crime shall be construed as if contained in Chapter 2 of Part 1 of that Act.

(2) References in this Part, in relation to any code of practice, agreement or direction, to the retention by a communications provider of any communications data include references to the retention of any data obtained by that provider before the time when the code was issued, the agreement made or the direction given, and to data already held by that provider at that time.
[Anti-terrorism, Crime and Security Act 2001, s 107.]

PART 12[1]

BRIBERY AND CORRUPTION[2]

8–23559ZZJ

1. Part 12 contains ss 108–110

2. Part 12 amends the common law offence of bribery by making it immaterial whether the briber or recipient of the bribe has any functions connected with or carried out in the UK. Similar amendments are made to the offences under s 1 of the Prevention of Corruption Act 1906; s 7 of the Public Bodies Corrupt Practices Act 1889; and s 4(2) of the Prevention of Corruption Act 1916.

Part 12 also makes the offences listed above (save the last) extra-territorial when committed by a UK national (as defined).

PART 13[1]

MISCELLANEOUS

Third pillar of the European Union

8–23559ZZK 111. *Implementation of the third pillar*

1. Part 13 contains ss 111–121.

8–23559ZZL 112. *Third pillar: supplemental*

Dangerous substances

8–23559ZZM 113. Use of noxious substances or things to cause harm and intimidate. (1) A person who takes any action which—

(*a*) involves the use of a noxious substance or other noxious thing;
(*b*) has or is likely to have an effect falling within subsection (2); and
(*c*) is designed to influence the government or to intimidate the public or a section of the public,

is guilty of an offence.

(2) Action has an effect falling within this subsection if it—

(*a*) causes serious violence against a person anywhere in the world;
(*b*) causes serious damage to real or personal property anywhere in the world;
(*c*) endangers human life or creates a serious risk to the health or safety of the public or a section of the public; or
(*d*) induces in members of the public the fear that the action is likely to endanger their lives or create a serious risk to their health or safety;

but any effect on the person taking the action is to be disregarded.

(3) A person who—

(*a*) makes a threat that he or another will take any action which constitutes an offence under subsection (1); and
(*b*) intends thereby to induce in a person anywhere in the world the fear that the threat is likely to be carried out,

is guilty of an offence.

(4) A person guilty of an offence under this section is liable—

(*a*) on summary conviction, to imprisonment for a term not exceeding six months or a fine not exceeding the statutory maximum (or both); and
(*b*) on conviction on indictment, to imprisonment for a term not exceeding fourteen years or a fine (or both)[1].

(5) In this section—

"the government" means the government of the United Kingdom, of a part of the United Kingdom or of a country other than the United Kingdom; and

"the public" includes the public of a country other than the United Kingdom.

[Anti-terrorism, Crime and Security Act 2001, s 113.]

1. For procedure in respect of this offence, which is triable either way, see the Magistrates' Courts Act 1980, ss 17A–21, in PART I: MAGISTRATES' COURTS, PROCEDURE, ante.

8–23559ZZMA 113A. Application of section 113. (1) Section 113 applies to conduct done—

(a) in the United Kingdom; or
(b) outside the United Kingdom which satisfies the following two conditions.

(2) The first condition is that the conduct is done for the purpose of advancing a political, religious or ideological cause.

(3) The second condition is that the conduct is—

(a) by a United Kingdom national or a United Kingdom resident;
(b) by any person done to, or in relation to, a United Kingdom national, a United Kingdom resident or a protected person; or
(c) by any person done in circumstances which fall within section 63D(1)(b) and (c) or (3)(b) and (c) of the Terrorism Act 2000.

(4) The following expressions have the same meaning as they have for the purposes of sections 63C and 63D of that Act—

(a) "United Kingdom national";
(b) "United Kingdom resident";
(c) "protected person".

(5) For the purposes of this section it is immaterial whether a person knows that another is a United Kingdom national, a United Kingdom resident or a protected person.

[Anti-terrorism, Crime and Security Act 2001, s 113A as inserted by the Criminal Justice (International Co-operation) Act 2003, s 53.]

8–23559ZZMB 113B. Consent to prosecution for offence under section 113. (1) Proceedings for an offence committed under section 113 outside the United Kingdom are not to be started—

(a) in England and Wales, except by or with the consent of the Attorney General;
(b) in Northern Ireland, except by or with the consent of the Advocate General for Northern Ireland.

(2) Proceedings for an offence committed under section 113 outside the United Kingdom may be taken, and the offence may for incidental purposes be treated as having been committed, in any part of the United Kingdom.

(3) In relation to any time before the coming into force of section 27(1) of the Justice (Northern Ireland) Act 2002, the reference in subsection (1)(b) to the Advocate General for Northern Ireland is to be read as a reference to the Attorney General for Northern Ireland.

[Anti-terrorism, Crime and Security Act 2001, s 113B as inserted by the Criminal Justice (International Co-operation) Act 2003, s 53.]

8–23559ZZN 114. Hoaxes involving noxious substances or things. (1) A person is guilty of an offence if he—

(*a*) places any substance or other thing in any place; or
(*b*) sends any substance or other thing from one place to another (by post, rail or any other means whatever);

with the intention of inducing in a person anywhere in the world a belief that it is likely to be (or contain) a noxious substance or other noxious thing and thereby endanger human life or create a serious risk to human health.

(2) A person is guilty of an offence if he communicates any information which he knows or believes to be false with the intention of inducing in a person anywhere in the world a belief that a noxious substance or other noxious thing is likely to be present (whether at the time the information is communicated or later) in any place and thereby endanger human life or create a serious risk to human health.

(3) A person guilty of an offence under this section is liable—

(*a*) on summary conviction, to imprisonment for a term not exceeding six months or a fine not exceeding the statutory maximum (or both); and
(*b*) on conviction on indictment, to imprisonment for a term not exceeding seven years or a fine (or both)[1].

[Anti-terrorism, Crime and Security Act 2001, s 114.]

1. For procedure in respect of this offence, which is triable either way, see the Magistrates' Courts Act 1980, ss 17A–21, in PART I: MAGISTRATES' COURTS, PROCEDURE, ante.

8–23559ZZO 115. Sections 113 and 114: supplementary. (1) For the purposes of sections 113 and 114 "substance" includes any biological agent and any other natural or artificial substance (whatever its form, origin or method of production).

(2) For a person to be guilty of an offence under section 113(3) or 114 it is not necessary for him

to have any particular person in mind as the person in whom he intends to induce the belief in question.
[Anti-terrorism, Crime and Security Act 2001, s 115.]

Intelligence Services Act 1994

8–23559ZZP 116. *Amendments of Intelligence Services Act 1994*

Terrorism Act 2000

8–23559ZZQ 117–120. *Information about acts of terrorism*[1]

1. These provisions amend the Terrorism Act 2000.

8–23559ZZR 121. *Crown Court judges: Northern Ireland*

PART 14[1]
SUPPLEMENTAL

8–23559ZZS 122–124. *Review of Act, etc*

1. Part 14 contains 122–129.

8–23559ZZT 125. *Repeals and revocation*

8–23559ZZU 126. *Expenses*

8–23559ZZV 127. Commencement[1]. (1) Except as provided in subsections (2) to (4), this Act comes into force on such day as the Secretary of State may appoint by order.

(2) The following provisions come into force on the day on which this Act is passed—

(*a*) Parts 2 to 6,
(*b*) Part 8, except section 78,
(*c*) Part 9, except sections 84 and 87,
(*d*) sections 89 to 97,
(*e*) sections 98 to 100, except so far as they extend to Scotland,
(*f*) section 101 and Schedule 7, except so far as they relate to the entries in respect of the Police (Scotland) Act 1967,
(*g*) Part 11,
(*h*) Part 13, except section 121,
(i) this Part, except section 125 and Schedule 8 so far as they relate to the entries—
  (i) in Part 1 of Schedule 8,
  (ii) in Part 5 of Schedule 8, in respect of the Nuclear Installations Act 1965,
  (iii) in Part 6 of Schedule 8, in respect of the British Transport Commission Act 1962 and the Ministry of Defence Police Act 1987, so far as those entries extend to Scotland,
  (iv) in Part 7 of Schedule 8, in respect of Schedule 5 to the Terrorism Act 2000.

(3) The following provisions come into force at the end of the period of two months beginning with the day on which this Act is passed—

(*a*) section 84,
(*b*) section 87.

(4) The following provisions come into force on such day as the Secretary of State and the Scottish Ministers, acting jointly, may appoint by order—

(*a*) sections 98 to 100, so far as they extend to Scotland,
(*b*) section 101 and Schedule 7, so far as they relate to the entries in respect of the Police (Scotland) Act 1967, and
(*c*) section 125 and Schedule 8, so far as they relate to the entries in Part 6 of Schedule 8 in respect of the British Transport Commission Act 1962 and the Ministry of Defence Police Act 1987, so far as those entries extend to Scotland.

(5) Different days may be appointed for different provisions and for different purposes.

(6) An order under this section—

(*a*) must be made by statutory instrument, and
(*b*) may contain incidental, supplemental, consequential or transitional provision.

[Anti-terrorism, Crime and Security Act 2001, s 127.]

1. The following commencement orders have been made: Anti-terrorism, Crime and Security Act 2001 (Commencement No 1 and Consequential Provisions) Order 2001, SI 2001/4019; Anti-terrorism, Crime and Security Act 2001 (Commencement No 2) (Scotland) Order 2001, SI 2001/4014; Anti-terrorism, Crime and Security Act 2001 (Commencement No 3) Order 2001, SI 2002/228; Anti-terrorism, Crime and Security Act 2001 (Commencement No 4

and Consequential Provisions) Order 2001, SI 2002/1279; and Anti-terrorism, Crime and Security Act 2001 (Commencement No 5 and Consequential Provisions) Order 2001, SI 2002/1558. All the provisions of the Act, with the exceptions of s 78 and some of the repeals specified in Schedule 8, are now in force.

8–23559ZZW 128. Extent. (1) The following provisions do not extend to Scotland—

(*a*) Part 5,
(*b*) Part 12,
(*c*) in Part 6 of Schedule 8, the repeals in the Criminal Justice and Police Order Act 1994 and in the Crime and Disorder Act 1998.

(2) The following provisions do not extend to Northern Ireland—

(*a*) section 76,
(*b*) section 100.

(3) Except as provided in subsections (1) and (2), an amendment, repeal or revocation in this Act has the same extent as the enactment amended, repealed or revoked.
[Anti-terrorism, Crime and Security Act 2001, s 128.]

8–23559ZZX 129. Short title. This Act may be cited as the Anti-terrorism, Crime and Security Act 2001.
[Anti-terrorism, Crime and Security Act 2001, s 129.]

Section 1

SCHEDULE 1
FORFEITURE OF TERRORIST CASH

PART 1
INTRODUCTORY

8–23559ZZY 1. Terrorist cash. (1) This Schedule applies to cash ("terrorist cash") which—

(*a*) is within subsection (1)(*a*) or (*b*) of section 1, or
(*b*) is property earmarked as terrorist property.

(2) "Cash" means—

(*a*) coins and notes in any currency,
(*b*) postal orders,
(*c*) cheques of any kind, including travellers' cheques,
(*d*) bankers' drafts,
(*e*) bearer bonds and bearer shares,

found at any place in the United Kingdom.

(3) Cash also includes any kind of monetary instrument which is found at any place in the United Kingdom, if the instrument is specified by the Secretary of State by order.

(4) The power to make an order under sub-paragraph (3) is exercisable by statutory instrument, which is subject to annulment in pursuance of a resolution of either House of Parliament.

PART 2
SEIZURE AND DETENTION

8–23559ZZZ 2. Seizure of cash. (1) An authorised officer may seize any cash if he has reasonable grounds for suspecting that it is terrorist cash.

(2) An authorised officer may also seize cash part of which he has reasonable grounds for suspecting to be terrorist cash if it is not reasonably practicable to seize only that part.

3. Detention of seized cash. (1) While the authorised officer continues to have reasonable grounds for his suspicion, cash seized under this Schedule may be detained initially for a period of 48 hours.

(2) The period for which the cash or any part of it may be detained may be extended by an order made by a magistrates' court or (in Scotland) the sheriff; but the order may not authorise the detention of any of the cash—

(*a*) beyond the end of the period of three months beginning with the date of the order, and
(*b*) in the case of any further order under this paragraph, beyond the end of the period of two years beginning with the date of the first order.

(3) A justice of the peace may also exercise the power of a magistrates' court to make the first order under sub-paragraph (2) extending the period.

(4) An order under sub-paragraph (2) must provide for notice to be given to persons affected by it.

(5) An application for an order under sub-paragraph (2)—

(*a*) in relation to England and Wales and Northern Ireland, may be made by the Commissioners of Customs and Excise or an authorised officer,
(*b*) *Scotland*,

and the court, sheriff or justice may make the order if satisfied, in relation to any cash to be further detained, that one of the following conditions is met.

(6) The first condition is that there are reasonable grounds for suspecting that the cash is intended to be used for the purposes of terrorism and that either—

(*a*) its continued detention is justified while its intended use is further investigated or consideration is given to bringing (in the United Kingdom or elsewhere) proceedings against any person for an offence with which the cash is connected, or (*b*) proceedings against any person for an offence with which the cash is connected have been started and have not been concluded.

(7) The second condition is that there are reasonable grounds for suspecting that the cash consists of resources of an organisation which is a proscribed organisation and that either—

(*a*) its continued detention is justified while investigation is made into whether or not it consists of such resources or consideration is given to bringing (in the United Kingdom or elsewhere) proceedings against any person for an offence with which the cash is connected, or

(*b*) proceedings against any person for an offence with which the cash is connected have been started and have not been concluded.

(8) The third condition is that there are reasonable grounds for suspecting that the cash is property earmarked as terrorist property and that either—

(*a*) its continued detention is justified while its derivation is further investigated or consideration is given to bringing (in the United Kingdom or elsewhere) proceedings against any person for an offence with which the cash is connected, or

(*b*) proceedings against any person for an offence with which the cash is connected have been started and have not been concluded.

4. Payment of detained cash into an account. (1) If cash is detained under this Schedule for more than 48 hours, it is to be held in an interest-bearing account and the interest accruing on it is to be added to it on its forfeiture or release.

(2) In the case of cash seized under paragraph 2(2), the authorised officer must, on paying it into the account, release so much of the cash then held in the account as is not attributable to terrorist cash.

(3) Sub-paragraph (1) does not apply if the cash is required as evidence of an offence or evidence in proceedings under this Schedule.

5. Release of detained cash. (1) This paragraph applies while any cash is detained under this Schedule.

(2) A magistrates' court or (in Scotland) the sheriff may direct the release of the whole or any part of the cash if satisfied, on an application by the person from whom it was seized, that the conditions in paragraph 3 for the detention of cash are no longer met in relation to the cash to be released.

(3) A authorised officer or (in Scotland) a procurator fiscal may, after notifying the magistrates' court, sheriff or justice under whose order cash is being detained, release the whole or any part of it if satisfied that the detention of the cash to be released is no longer justified.

(4) But cash is not to be released—

(*a*) if an application for its forfeiture under paragraph 6, or for its release under paragraph 9, is made, until any proceedings in pursuance of the application (including any proceedings on appeal) are concluded,

(*b*) if (in the United Kingdom or elsewhere) proceedings are started against any person for an offence with which the cash is connected, until the proceedings are concluded.

PART 3
FORFEITURE

8–23559ZZZA 6. Forfeiture. (1) While cash is detained under this Schedule, an application for the forfeiture of the whole or any part of it may be made—

(*a*) to a magistrates' court by the Commissioners of Customs and Excise or an authorised officer,

(*b*) *Scotland.*

(2) The court or sheriff may order the forfeiture of the cash or any part of it if satisfied that the cash or part is terrorist cash.

(3) In the case of property earmarked as terrorist property which belongs to joint tenants one of whom is an excepted joint owner, the order may not apply to so much of it as the court or sheriff thinks is attributable to the excepted joint owner's share.

(4) An excepted joint owner is a joint tenant who obtained the property in circumstances in which it would not (as against him) be earmarked; and references to his share of the earmarked property are to so much of the property as would have been his if the joint tenancy had been severed.

7. Appeal against forfeiture. (1) Any party to proceedings in which an order is made under paragraph 6 ("a forfeiture order") who is aggrieved by the order may appeal—

(*a*) in relation to England and Wales, to the Crown Court,

(*b*) *Scotland,*

(*c*) *Northern Ireland.*

(2) An appeal under sub-paragraph (1) must be made—

(*a*) within the period of 30 days beginning with the date on which the order is made, or

(*b*) if sub-paragraph (6) applies, before the end of the period of 30 days beginning with the date on which the order under section 3(3)(*b*) of the Terrorism Act 2000 (c 11) referred to in that sub-paragraph comes into force.

(3) The appeal is to be by way of a rehearing.

(4) The court hearing the appeal may make any order it thinks appropriate.

(5) If the court upholds the appeal, it may order the release of the cash.

(6) Where a successful application for a forfeiture order relies (wholly or partly) on the fact that an organisation is proscribed, this sub-paragraph applies if—

(*a*) a deproscription appeal under section 5 of the Terrorism Act 2000 is allowed in respect of the organisation,

(*b*) an order is made under section 3(3)(*b*) of that Act in respect of the organisation in accordance with an order of the Proscribed Organisations Appeal Commission under section 5(4) of that Act (and, if the order is made in reliance on section 123(5) of that Act, a resolution is passed by each House of Parliament under section 123(5)(*b*)), and

(*c*) the forfeited cash was seized under this Schedule on or after the date of the refusal to deproscribe against which the appeal under section 5 of that Act was brought.

8. Application of forfeited cash. (1) Cash forfeited under this Schedule, and any accrued interest on it—

(*a*) if forfeited by a magistrates' court in England and Wales or Northern Ireland, is to be paid into the Consolidated Fund,

(*b*) *Scotland.*

(2) But it is not to be paid in—

(*a*) before the end of the period within which an appeal under paragraph 7 may be made, or

(*b*) if a person appeals under that paragraph, before the appeal is determined or otherwise disposed of.

PART 4
MISCELLANEOUS

8–23559ZZZB **9. Victims.** (1) A person who claims that any cash detained under this Schedule, or any part of it, belongs to him may apply to a magistrates' court or (in Scotland) the sheriff for the cash or part to be released to him.

(2) The application may be made in the course of proceedings under paragraph 3 or 6 or at any other time.

(3) If it appears to the court or sheriff concerned that—

(*a*) the applicant was deprived of the cash claimed, or of property which it represents, by criminal conduct,

(*b*) the property he was deprived of was not, immediately before he was deprived of it, property obtained by or in return for criminal conduct and nor did it then represent such property, and

(*c*) the cash claimed belongs to him,

the court or sheriff may order the cash to be released to the applicant.

10. Compensation. (1) If no forfeiture order is made in respect of any cash detained under this Schedule, the person to whom the cash belongs or from whom it was seized may make an application to the magistrates' court or (in Scotland) the sheriff for compensation.

(2) If, for any period after the initial detention of the cash for 48 hours, the cash was not held in an interest-bearing account while detained, the court or sheriff may order an amount of compensation to be paid to the applicant.

(3) The amount of compensation to be paid under sub-paragraph (2) is the amount the court or sheriff thinks would have been earned in interest in the period in question if the cash had been held in an interest-bearing account.

(4) If the court or sheriff is satisfied that, taking account of any interest to be paid under this Schedule or any amount to be paid under sub-paragraph (2), the applicant has suffered loss as a result of the detention of the cash and that the circumstances are exceptional, the court or sheriff may order compensation (or additional compensation) to be paid to him .

(5) The amount of compensation to be paid under sub-paragraph (4) is the amount the court or sheriff thinks reasonable, having regard to the loss suffered and any other relevant circumstances.

(6) If the cash was seized by a customs officer, the compensation is to be paid by the Commissioners of Customs and Excise.

(7) If the cash was seized by a constable, the compensation is to be paid as follows—

(*a*) in the case of a constable of a police force in England and Wales, it is to be paid out of the police fund from which the expenses of the police force are met,

(*b*) *Scotland,*

(*c*) *Northern Ireland.*

(8) If the cash was seized by an immigration officer, the compensation is to be paid by the Secretary of State.

(9) If a forfeiture order is made in respect only of a part of any cash detained under this Schedule, this paragraph has effect in relation to the other part.

(10) This paragraph does not apply if the court or sheriff makes an order under paragraph 9.

PART 5
PROPERTY EARMARKED AS TERRORIST PROPERTY

8–23559ZZZC **11. Property obtained through terrorism.** (1) A person obtains property through terrorism if he obtains property by or in return for acts of terrorism, or acts carried out for the purposes of terrorism.

(2) In deciding whether any property was obtained through terrorism—

(*a*) it is immaterial whether or not any money, goods or services were provided in order to put the person in question in a position to carry out the acts,

(*b*) it is not necessary to show that the act was of a particular kind if it is shown that the property was obtained through acts of one of a number of kinds, each of which would have been an act of terrorism, or an act carried out for the purposes of terrorism.

12. Property earmarked as terrorist property. (1) Property obtained through terrorism is earmarked as terrorist property.

(2) But if property obtained through terrorism has been disposed of (since it was so obtained), it is earmarked as terrorist property only if it is held by a person into whose hands it may be followed.

(3) Earmarked property obtained through terrorism may be followed into the hands of a person obtaining it on a disposal by—

(*a*) the person who obtained the property through terrorism, or
(*b*) a person into whose hands it may (by virtue of this sub-paragraph) be followed.

13. Tracing property. (1) Where property obtained through terrorism ("the original property") is or has been earmarked as terrorist property, property which represents the original property is also earmarked.

(2) If a person enters into a transaction by which—

(*a*) he disposes of earmarked property, whether the original property or property which (by virtue of this Part) represents the original property, and
(*b*) he obtains other property in place of it,

the other property represents the original property.

(3) If a person disposes of earmarked property which represents the original property, the property may be followed into the hands of the person who obtains it (and it continues to represent the original property).

14. Mixing property. (1) Sub-paragraph (2) applies if a person's property which is earmarked as terrorist property is mixed with other property (whether his property or another's).

(2) The portion of the mixed property which is attributable to the property earmarked as terrorist property represents the property obtained through terrorism.

(3) Property earmarked as terrorist property is mixed with other property if (for example) it is used—

(*a*) to increase funds held in a bank account,
(*b*) in part payment for the acquisition of an asset,
(*c*) for the restoration or improvement of land,
(*d*) by a person holding a leasehold interest in the property to acquire the freehold.

15. Accruing profits. (1) This paragraph applies where a person who has property earmarked as terrorist property obtains further property consisting of profits accruing in respect of the earmarked property.

(2) The further property is to be treated as representing the property obtained through terrorism.

16. General exceptions. (1) If—

(*a*) a person disposes of property earmarked as terrorist property, and
(*b*) the person who obtains it on the disposal does so in good faith, for value and without notice that it was earmarked,

the property may not be followed into that person's hands and, accordingly, it ceases to be earmarked.

(2) If—

(*a*) in pursuance of a judgment in civil proceedings (whether in the United Kingdom or elsewhere), the defendant makes a payment to the claimant or the claimant otherwise obtains property from the defendant,
(*b*) the claimant's claim is based on the defendant's criminal conduct, and
(*c*) apart from this sub-paragraph, the sum received, or the property obtained, by the claimant would be earmarked as terrorist property,

the property ceases to be earmarked.

In relation to Scotland, "claimant" and "defendant" are to be read as "pursuer" and "defender"; and, in relation to Northern Ireland, "claimant" is to be read as "plaintiff".

(3) If—

(*a*) a payment is made to a person in pursuance of a compensation order under Article 14 of the Criminal Justice (Northern Ireland) Order 1994 (SI 1994/2795 (NI 15)), section 249 of the Criminal Procedure (Scotland) Act 1995 (c 46) or section 130 of the Powers of Criminal Courts (Sentencing) Act 2000 (c 6), and
(*b*) apart from this sub-paragraph, the sum received would be earmarked as terrorist property,

the property ceases to be earmarked.

(4) If—

(*a*) a payment is made to a person in pursuance of a restitution order under section 27 of the Theft Act (Northern Ireland) 1969 (c 16 (NI)) or section 148(2) of the Powers of Criminal Courts (Sentencing) Act 2000 or a person otherwise obtains any property in pursuance of such an order, and
(*b*) apart from this sub-paragraph, the sum received, or the property obtained, would be earmarked as terrorist property,

the property ceases to be earmarked.

(5) If—

(*a*) in pursuance of an order made by the court under section 382(3) or 383(5) of the Financial Services and Markets Act 2000 (c 8) (restitution orders), an amount is paid to or distributed among any persons in accordance with the court's directions, and
(*b*) apart from this sub-paragraph, the sum received by them would be earmarked as terrorist property,

the property ceases to be earmarked.

(6) If—

(*a*) in pursuance of a requirement of the Financial Services Authority under section 384(5) of the Financial Services and Markets Act 2000 (c 8) (power of authority to require restitution), an amount is paid to or distributed among any persons, and
(*b*) apart from this sub-paragraph, the sum received by them would be earmarked as terrorist property,

the property ceases to be earmarked.

(7) Where—

(*a*) a person enters into a transaction to which paragraph 13(2) applies, and
(*b*) the disposal is one to which sub-paragraph (1) applies,

this paragraph does not affect the question whether (by virtue of paragraph 13(2)) any property obtained on the transaction in place of the property disposed of is earmarked.

PART 6
INTERPRETATION

8–23559ZZZD 17. Property. (1) Property is all property wherever situated and includes—

(*a*) money,
(*b*) all forms of property, real or personal, heritable or moveable,
(*c*) things in action and other intangible or incorporeal property.

(2) Any reference to a person's property (whether expressed as a reference to the property he holds or otherwise) is to be read as follows.
(3) In relation to land, it is a reference to any interest which he holds in the land.
(4) In relation to property other than land, it is a reference—

(*a*) to the property (if it belongs to him), or
(*b*) to any other interest which he holds in the property.

18. Obtaining and disposing of property. (1) References to a person disposing of his property include a reference—

(*a*) to his disposing of a part of it, or
(*b*) to his granting an interest in it,

(or to both); and references to the property disposed of are to any property obtained on the disposal.
(2) If a person grants an interest in property of his which is earmarked as terrorist property, the question whether the interest is also earmarked is to be determined in the same manner as it is on any other disposal of earmarked property.
(3) A person who makes a payment to another is to be treated as making a disposal of his property to the other, whatever form the payment takes.
(4) Where a person's property passes to another under a will or intestacy or by operation of law, it is to be treated as disposed of by him to the other.
(5) A person is only to be treated as having obtained his property for value in a case where he gave unexecuted consideration if the consideration has become executed consideration.

19. General interpretation. (1) In this Schedule—

"authorised officer" means a constable, a customs officer or an immigration officer,
"cash" has the meaning given by paragraph 1,
"constable", in relation to Northern Ireland, means a police officer within the meaning of the Police (Northern Ireland) Act 2000 (c 32),
"criminal conduct" means conduct which constitutes an offence in any part of the United Kingdom, or would constitute an offence in any part of the United Kingdom if it occurred there,
"customs officer" means an officer commissioned by the Commissioners of Customs and Excise under section 6(3) of the Customs and Excise Management Act 1979 (c 2),
"forfeiture order" has the meaning given by paragraph 7,
"immigration officer" means a person appointed as an immigration officer under paragraph 1 of Schedule 2 to the Immigration Act 1971 (c 77),
"interest", in relation to land—

(*a*) in the case of land in England and Wales or Northern Ireland, means any legal estate and any equitable interest or power,
(*b*) *Scotland*,

"interest", in relation to property other than land, includes any right (including a right to possession of the property),
"part", in relation to property, includes a portion,
"property obtained through terrorism" has the meaning given by paragraph 11,
"property earmarked as terrorist property" is to be read in accordance with Part 5,
"proscribed organisation" has the same meaning as in the Terrorism Act 2000 (c 11),
"terrorism" has the same meaning as in the Terrorism Act 2000,
"terrorist cash" has the meaning given by paragraph 1,
"value" means market value.

(2) Paragraphs 17 and 18 and the following provisions apply for the purposes of this Schedule.
(3) For the purpose of deciding whether or not property was earmarked as terrorist property at any time (including times before commencement), it is to be assumed that this Schedule was in force at that and any other relevant time.
(4) References to anything done or intended to be done for the purposes of terrorism include anything done or intended to be done for the benefit of a proscribed organisation.
(5) An organisation's resources include any cash which is applied or made available, or is to be applied or made available, for use by the organisation.

(6) Proceedings against any person for an offence are concluded when—

(*a*) the person is convicted or acquitted,
(*b*) the prosecution is discontinued or, in Scotland, the trial diet is deserted simpliciter, or
(*c*) the jury is discharged without a finding.

Section 3

SCHEDULE 2[1]

TERRORIST PROPERTY: AMENDMENTS

8–23559ZZZE

---

1. Schedule 2 makes amendments to the Terrorism Act 2000.

Section 6

SCHEDULE 3

FREEZING ORDERS

8–23559ZZZF 1. Interpretation. References in this Schedule to a person specified in a freezing order as a person to whom or for whose benefit funds are not to be made available are to be read in accordance with section 5(4).

2. Funds. A freezing order may include provision that funds include gold, cash, deposits, securities (such as stocks, shares and debentures) and such other matters as the order may specify.

3. Making funds available. (1) A freezing order must include provision as to the meaning (in relation to funds) of making available to or for the benefit of a person.

(2) In particular, an order may provide that the expression includes—

(*a*) allowing a person to withdraw from an account;
(*b*) honouring a cheque payable to a person;
(*c*) crediting a person's account with interest;
(*d*) releasing documents of title (such as share certificates) held on a person's behalf;
(*e*) making available the proceeds of realisation of a person's property;
(*f*) making a payment to or for a person's benefit (for instance, under a contract or as a gift or under any enactment such as the enactments relating to social security);
(*g*) such other acts as the order may specify.

4. Licences. (1) A freezing order must include—

(*a*) provision for the granting of licences authorising funds to be made available;
(*b*) provision that a prohibition under the order is not to apply if funds are made available in accordance with a licence.

(2) In particular, an order may provide—

(*a*) that a licence may be granted generally or to a specified person or persons or description of persons;
(*b*) that a licence may authorise funds to be made available to or for the benefit of persons generally or a specified person or persons or description of persons;
(*c*) that a licence may authorise funds to be made available generally or for specified purposes;
(*d*) that a licence may be granted in relation to funds generally or to funds of a specified description;
(*e*) for a licence to be granted in pursuance of an application or without an application being made;
(*f*) for the form and manner in which applications for licences are to be made;
(*g*) for licences to be granted by the Treasury or a person authorised by the Treasury;
(*h*) for the form in which licences are to be granted;
(i) for licences to be granted subject to conditions;
(*j*) for licences to be of a defined or indefinite duration;
(*k*) for the charging of a fee to cover the administrative costs of granting a licence;
(*l*) for the variation and revocation of licences.

5. Information and documents. (1) A freezing order may include provision that a person—

(*a*) must provide information if required to do so and it is reasonably needed for the purpose of ascertaining whether an offence under the order has been committed;
(*b*) must produce a document if required to do so and it is reasonably needed for that purpose.

(2) In particular, an order may include—

(*a*) provision that a requirement to provide information or to produce a document may be made by the Treasury or a person authorised by the Treasury;
(*b*) provision that information must be provided, and a document must be produced, within a reasonable period specified in the order and at a place specified by the person requiring it;
(*c*) provision that the provision of information is not to be taken to breach any restriction on the disclosure of information (however imposed);
(*d*) provision restricting the use to which information or a document may be put and the circumstances in which it may be disclosed;
(*e*) provision that a requirement to provide information or produce a document does not apply to privileged information or a privileged document;
(*f*) provision that information is privileged if the person would be entitled to refuse to provide it on grounds of legal professional privilege in proceedings in the High Court or (in Scotland) on grounds of confidentiality of communications in proceedings in the Court of Session;

(*g*) provision that a document is privileged if the person would be entitled to refuse to produce it on grounds of legal professional privilege in proceedings in the High Court or (in Scotland) on grounds of confidentiality of communications in proceedings in the Court of Session;

(*h*) provision that information or a document held with the intention of furthering a criminal purpose is not privileged.

6. Disclosure of information. (1) A freezing order may include provision requiring a person to disclose information as mentioned below if the following three conditions are satisfied.

(2) The first condition is that the person required to disclose is specified or falls within a description specified in the order.

(3) The second condition is that the person required to disclose knows or suspects, or has grounds for knowing or suspecting, that a person specified in the freezing order as a person to whom or for whose benefit funds are not to be made available—

(*a*) is a customer of his or has been a customer of his at any time since the freezing order came into force, or

(*b*) is a person with whom he has dealings in the course of his business or has had such dealings at any time since the freezing order came into force.

(4) The third condition is that the information—

(*a*) on which the knowledge or suspicion of the person required to disclose is based, or

(*b*) which gives grounds for his knowledge or suspicion,

came to him in the course of a business in the regulated sector.

(5) The freezing order may require the person required to disclose to make a disclosure to the Treasury of that information as soon as is practicable after it comes to him.

(6) The freezing order may include—

(*a*) provision that Schedule 3A to the Terrorism Act 2000 (c 11) is to have effect for the purpose of determining what is a business in the regulated sector;

(*b*) provision that the disclosure of information is not to be taken to breach any restriction on the disclosure of information (however imposed);

(*c*) provision restricting the use to which information may be put and the circumstances in which it may be disclosed by the Treasury;

(*d*) provision that the requirement to disclose information does not apply to privileged information;

(*e*) provision that information is privileged if the person would be entitled to refuse to disclose it on grounds of legal professional privilege in proceedings in the High Court or (in Scotland) on grounds of confidentiality of communications in proceedings in the Court of Session;

(*f*) provision that information held with the intention of furthering a criminal purpose is not privileged.

7. Offences. (1) A freezing order may include any of the provisions set out in this paragraph.

(2) A person commits an offence if he fails to comply with a prohibition imposed by the order.

(3) A person commits an offence if he engages in an activity knowing or intending that it will enable or facilitate the commission by another person of an offence under a provision included under sub-paragraph (2).

(4) A person commits an offence if—

(*a*) he fails without reasonable excuse to provide information, or to produce a document, in response to a requirement made under the order;

(*b*) he provides information, or produces a document, which he knows is false in a material particular in response to such a requirement or with a view to obtaining a licence under the order;

(*c*) he recklessly provides information, or produces a document, which is false in a material particular in response to such a requirement or with a view to obtaining a licence under the order;

(*d*) he fails without reasonable excuse to disclose information as required by a provision included under paragraph 6.

(5) A person does not commit an offence under a provision included under sub-paragraph (2) or (3) if he proves that he did not know and had no reason to suppose that the person to whom or for whose benefit funds were made available, or were to be made available, was the person (or one of the persons) specified in the freezing order as a person to whom or for whose benefit funds are not to be made available.

(6) A person guilty of an offence under a provision included under sub-paragraph (2) or (3) is liable—

(*a*) on summary conviction, to imprisonment for a term not exceeding 6 months or to a fine not exceeding the statutory maximum or to both;

(*b*) on conviction on indictment, to imprisonment for a term not exceeding 2 years or to a fine or to both[1].

(7) A person guilty of an offence under a provision included under sub-paragraph (4) is liable on summary conviction to imprisonment for a term not exceeding 6 months or to a fine not exceeding level 5 on the standard scale or to both.

8. Offences: procedure. (1) A freezing order may include any of the provisions set out in this paragraph.

(2) Proceedings for an offence under the order are not to be instituted in England and Wales except by or with the consent of the Treasury or the Director of Public Prosecutions.

(3) Proceedings for an offence under the order are not to be instituted in Northern Ireland except by or with the consent of the Treasury or the Director of Public Prosecutions for Northern Ireland.

(4) Despite anything in section 127(1) of the Magistrates' Courts Act 1980 (c 43) (information to be laid within 6 months of offence) an information relating to an offence under the order which is triable by a magistrates' court in England and Wales may be so tried if it is laid at any time in the period of one year starting with the date of the commission of the offence.

(5) *Scotland.*

(6) *Northern Ireland.*

9. Offences by bodies corporate etc. (1) A freezing order may include any of the provisions set out in this paragraph.

(2) If an offence under the order—

(*a*) is committed by a body corporate, and

(*b*) is proved to have been committed with the consent or connivance of an officer, or to be attributable to any neglect on his part,

he as well as the body corporate is guilty of the offence and liable to be proceeded against and punished accordingly.

(3) These are officers of a body corporate—

(*a*) a director, manager, secretary or other similar officer of the body;

(*b*) any person purporting to act in any such capacity.

(4) If the affairs of a body corporate are managed by its members sub-paragraph (2) applies in relation to the acts and defaults of a member in connection with his functions of management as if he were an officer of the body.

(5) If an offence under the order—

(*a*) is committed by a Scottish partnership, and

(*b*) is proved to have been committed with the consent or connivance of a partner, or to be attributable to any neglect on his part,

he as well as the partnership is guilty of the offence and liable to be proceeded against and punished accordingly.

10. Compensation. (1) A freezing order may include provision for the award of compensation to or on behalf of a person on the grounds that he has suffered loss as a result of—

(*a*) the order;

(*b*) the fact that a licence has not been granted under the order;

(*c*) the fact that a licence under the order has been granted on particular terms rather than others;

(*d*) the fact that a licence under the order has been varied or revoked.

(2) In particular, the order may include—

(*a*) provision about the person who may make a claim for an award;

(*b*) provision about the person to whom a claim for an award is to be made (which may be provision that it is to be made to the High Court or, in Scotland, the Court of Session);

(*c*) provision about the procedure for making and deciding a claim;

(*d*) provision that no compensation is to be awarded unless the claimant has behaved reasonably (which may include provision requiring him to mitigate his loss, for instance by applying for a licence);

(*e*) provision that compensation must be awarded in specified circumstances or may be awarded in specified circumstances (which may include provision that the circumstances involve negligence or other fault);

(*f*) provision about the amount that may be awarded;

(*g*) provision about who is to pay any compensation awarded (which may include provision that it is to be paid or reimbursed by the Treasury);

(*h*) provision about how compensation is to be paid (which may include provision for payment to a person other than the claimant).

11. Treasury's duty to give reasons. A freezing order must include provision that if—

(*a*) a person is specified in the order as a person to whom or for whose benefit funds are not to be made available, and

(*b*) he makes a written request to the Treasury to give him the reason why he is so specified,

as soon as is practicable the Treasury must give the person the reason in writing.

---

1. For procedure in respect of this offence, which is triable either way, see the Magistrates' Courts Act 1980, ss 17A–21, in PART I: MAGISTRATES' COURTS, PROCEDURE, ante.

Section 17

SCHEDULE 4
EXTENSION OF EXISTING DISCLOSURE POWERS

(*Amended by the Enterprise Act 2002, Sch 26, the Communications Act 2003, Sch 19, the Health and Social Care (Community Health and Standards) Act 2003, Sch 4 and the Companies (Audit, Investigations and Community Enterprise) Act 2002, Sch 2.*)

PART 1
ENACTMENTS TO WHICH SECTION 17 APPLIES

8–23559ZZZG **1. Agricultural Marketing Act 1958 (c 47).** Section 47(2) of the Agricultural Marketing Act 1958.

2. Harbours Act 1964 (c 40). Section 46(1) of the Harbours Act 1964.

3. Cereals Marketing Act 1965 (c 14). Section 17(2) of the Cereals Marketing Act 1965.

4. Agriculture Act 1967 (c 22). Section 24(1) of the Agriculture Act 1967.

5. *Repealed.*

6. Sea Fish Industry Act 1970 (c 11). Section 14(2) of the Sea Fish Industry Act 1970.

7. National Savings Bank Act 1971 (c 29). Section 12(2) of the National Savings Bank Act 1971.

8. Employment Agencies Act 1973 (c 35). Section 9(4) of the Employment Agencies Act 1973.

9. *Repealed.*

10. *Repealed.*

11. *Repealed.*

12. Health and Safety at Work etc Act 1974 (c 37). Section 28(7) of the Health and Safety at Work etc Act 1974.

13. Sex Discrimination Act 1975 (c 65). Section 61(1) of the Sex Discrimination Act 1975.

14. Race Relations Act 1976 (c 74). Section 52(1) of the Race Relations Act 1976.

15. Energy Act 1976 (c 76). Paragraph 7 of Schedule 2 to the Energy Act 1976.

16. National Health Service Act 1977 (c 49). Paragraph 5 of Schedule 11 to the National Health Service Act 1977.

17. *Repealed.*

18. Public Passenger Vehicles Act 1981 (c 14). Section 54(8) of the Public Passenger Vehicles Act 1981.

19. Fisheries Act 1981 (c 29). Section 12(2) of the Fisheries Act 1981.

20. Merchant Shipping (Liner Conferences) Act 1982 (c 37). Section 10(2) of the Merchant Shipping (Liner Conferences) Act 1982.

21. Civil Aviation Act 1982 (c 16). Section 23(4) of the Civil Aviation Act 1982.

22. Diseases of Fish Act 1983 (c 30). Section 9(1) of the Diseases of Fish Act 1983.

23. Telecommunications Act 1984 (c 12). Section 101(2) of the Telecommunications Act 1984.

24. Companies Act 1985 (c 6). Section 449 of the Companies Act 1985.

25. Airports Act 1986 (c 31). Section 74(2) of the Airports Act 1986.

26. Legal Aid (Scotland) Act 1986 (c 47). Section 34(2) of the Legal Aid (Scotland) Act 1986.

27. *Repealed.*

28. Companies Act 1989 (c 40). Section 87(1) of the Companies Act 1989.

29. *Repealed.*

30. *Repealed.*

31. Water Industry Act 1991 (c 56). Section 206(3) of the Water Industry Act 1991.

32. Water Resources Act 1991 (c 57). Section 204(2) of the Water Resources Act 1991.

33. *Repealed.*

34. Railways Act 1993 (c 43). Section 145(2) of the Railways Act 1993.

35. Coal Industry Act 1994 (c 21). Section 59(2) of the Coal Industry Act 1994.

36. Shipping and Trading Interests (Protection) Act 1995 (c 22). Section 3(4) of the Shipping and Trading Interests (Protection) Act 1995.

37. Pensions Act 1995 (c 26). (1) Section 105(2) of the Pensions Act 1995.
(2) Section 108(2) of that Act.

38. Goods Vehicles (Licensing of Operators) Act 1995 (c 23). Section 35(4) of the Goods Vehicles (Licensing of Operators) Act 1995.

39. Chemical Weapons Act 1996 (c 6). Section 32(2) of the Chemical Weapons Act 1996.

40. Bank of England Act 1998 (c 11). (1) Paragraph 5 of Schedule 7 to the Bank of England Act 1998.
(2) Paragraph 2 of Schedule 8 to that Act.

41. Audit Commission Act 1998 (c 18). Section 49(1) of the Audit Commission Act 1998.

42. Data Protection Act 1998 (c 29). Section 59(1) of the Data Protection Act 1998.

43. Police (Northern Ireland) Act 1998 (c 32). Section 63(1) of the Police (Northern Ireland) Act 1998.

44. Landmines Act 1998 (c 33). Section 19(2) of the Landmines Act 1998.

45. Health Act 1999 (c 8). Section 24 of the Health Act 1999.

46. Disability Rights Commission Act 1999 (c 17). Paragraph 22(2)(*f*) of Schedule 3 to the Disability Rights Commission Act 1999.

47. Access to Justice Act 1999 (c 22). Section 20(2) of the Access to Justice Act 1999.

48. Nuclear Safeguards Act 2000 (c 5). Section 6(2) of the Nuclear Safeguards Act 2000.

49. Finance Act 2000 (c 21). Paragraph 34(3) of Schedule 22 to the Finance Act 2000.

50. Local Government Act 2000 (c 22). Section 63(1) of the Local Government Act 2000.

51. Postal Services Act 2000 (c 26). Paragraph 3(1) of Schedule 7 to the Postal Services Act 2000.

52. Utilities Act 2000 (c 27). Section 105(4) of the Utilities Act 2000.

53. Transport Act 2000 (c 38). (1) Section 143(5)(*b*) of the Transport Act 2000.
(2) Paragraph 13(3) of Schedule 10 to that Act.

53A. Paragraph 8(1) of Schedule 5 to the Health and Social Care (Community Health and Standards) Act 2003,

SCHEDULES 5–7[1]

8–23559ZZZH

1. Schedules 5 and 6 make various provisions as to pathogens and toxins.
Schedule 7 contains amendments to various legislation, including: the Firearms Act 1968; the Police and Criminal Evidence Act 1984; the Criminal Justice and Public Order Act 1994; the Police Act 1996; and the Terrorism Act 2000.

8–23559ZZZI
Section 125

SCHEDULE 8
REPEALS AND REVOCATION

Female Genital Mutilation Act 2003[1]

(2003 c 31)

8–23559ZZZJ 1. Offence of female genital mutilation. (1) A person is guilty of an offence if he excises, infibulates or otherwise mutilates the whole or any part of a girl's labia majora, labia minora or clitoris.

(2) But no offence is committed by an approved person who performs—

(*a*) a surgical operation on a girl which is necessary for her physical or mental health, or
(*b*) a surgical operation on a girl who is in any stage of labour, or has just given birth, for purposes connected with the labour or birth.

(3) The following are approved persons—

(*a*) in relation to an operation falling within subsection (2)(a), a registered medical practitioner,
(*b*) in relation to an operation falling within subsection (2)(b), a registered medical practitioner, a registered midwife or a person undergoing a course of training with a view to becoming such a practitioner or midwife.

(4) There is also no offence committed by a person who—

(*a*) performs a surgical operation falling within subsection (2)(a) or (b) outside the United Kingdom, and
(*b*) in relation to such an operation exercises functions corresponding to those of an approved person.

(5) For the purpose of determining whether an operation is necessary for the mental health of a girl it is immaterial whether she or any other person believes that the operation is required as a matter of custom or ritual.
[Female Genital Mutilation Act 2003, s 1.]

1. This Act restates in amended form the law relating to female genital mutilation. The whole of the Act came into force on 3 March 2004 (see Female Genital Mutilation Act 2003 (Commencement) Order 2004, SI 2004/286)

8–23559ZZZK 2. Offence of assisting a girl to mutilate her own genitalia. A person is guilty of an offence if he aids, abets, counsels or procures a girl to excise, infibulate or otherwise mutilate the whole or any part of her own labia majora, labia minora or clitoris.
[Female Genital Mutilation Act 2003, s 2.]

8–23559ZZZL 3. Offence of assisting a non-UK person to mutilate overseas a girl's genitalia. (1) A person is guilty of an offence if he aids, abets, counsels or procures a person who is not a United Kingdom national or permanent United Kingdom resident to do a relevant act of female genital mutilation outside the United Kingdom.

(2) An act is a relevant act of female genital mutilation if—

(*a*) it is done in relation to a United Kingdom national or permanent United Kingdom resident, and

(*b*) it would, if done by such a person, constitute an offence under section 1.

(3) But no offence is committed if the relevant act of female genital mutilation—

(*a*) is a surgical operation falling within section 1(2)(a) or (b), and

(*b*) is performed by a person who, in relation to such an operation, is an approved person or exercises functions corresponding to those of an approved person.

[Female Genital Mutilation Act 2003, s 3.]

8–23559ZZZM 4. Extension of sections 1 to 3 to extra-territorial acts. (1) Sections 1 to 3 extend to any act done outside the United Kingdom by a United Kingdom national or permanent United Kingdom resident.

(2) If an offence under this Act is committed outside the United Kingdom—

(*a*) proceedings may be taken, and

(*b*) the offence may for incidental purposes be treated as having been committed,

in any place in England and Wales or Northern Ireland.
[Female Genital Mutilation Act 2003, s 4.]

8–23559ZZZN 5. Penalties for offences. A person guilty of an offence under this Act is liable—

(*a*) on conviction on indictment[1], to imprisonment for a term not exceeding 14 years or a fine (or both),

(*b*) on summary conviction, to imprisonment for a term not exceeding six months or a fine not exceeding the statutory maximum (or both).

[Female Genital Mutilation Act 2003, s 5.]

1. For procedure in respect of offences triable either way see the Magistrates' Courts' Act 1980, s 17A–21 in PART 1: MAGISTRATES' COURTS, PROCEDURE, ante.

8–23559ZZZO 6. Definitions. (1) Girl includes woman.

(2) A United Kingdom national is an individual who is—

(*a*) a British citizen, a British overseas territories citizen, a British National (Overseas) or a British Overseas citizen,

(*b*) a person who under the British Nationality Act 1981 (c 61) is a British subject, or

(*c*) a British protected person within the meaning of that Act.

(3) A permanent United Kingdom resident is an individual who is settled in the United Kingdom (within the meaning of the Immigration Act 1971 (c 77)).

(4) This section has effect for the purposes of this Act.
[Female Genital Mutilation Act 2003, s 6.]

8–23559ZZZP 7. Consequential provision. (1) The Prohibition of Female Circumcision Act 1985 (c 38) ceases to have effect.

(2) In paragraph 1(b) of the Schedule to the Visiting Forces Act 1952 (c 67) (offences against the person in respect of which a member of a visiting force may in certain circumstances not be tried by a United Kingdom court), for paragraph (xi) there is substituted—

"(xi)the Female Genital Mutilation Act 2003;".

[Female Genital Mutilation Act 2003, s 7.]

8–23559ZZZQ 8. Short title, commencement, extent and general saving. (1) This Act may be cited as the Female Genital Mutilation Act 2003.

(2) This Act comes into force on such day as the Secretary of State may by order made by statutory instrument appoint.

(3) An order under subsection (2) may include transitional or saving provisions.

(4) This Act does not extend to Scotland.

(5) Nothing in this Act affects any criminal liability arising apart from this Act.

[Female Genital Mutilation Act 2003, s 8.]

Prevention of Terrorism Act 2005

(2005 c 2)

Control orders

8–23559ZZZR 1. Power to make control orders. (1) In this Act "control order" means an order against an individual that imposes obligations on him for purposes connected with protecting members of the public from a risk of terrorism.

(2) The power to make a control order against an individual shall be exercisable—

(*a*) except in the case of an order imposing obligations that are incompatible with the individual's right to liberty under Article 5 of the Human Rights Convention, by the Secretary of State; and

(*b*) in the case of an order imposing obligations that are or include derogating obligations, by the court on an application by the Secretary of State.

(3) The obligations that may be imposed by a control order made against an individual are any obligations that the Secretary of State or (as the case may be) the court considers necessary for purposes connected with preventing or restricting involvement by that individual in terrorism-related activity.

(4) Those obligations may include, in particular—

(*a*) a prohibition or restriction on his possession or use of specified articles or substances;

(*b*) a prohibition or restriction on his use of specified services or specified facilities, or on his carrying on specified activities;

(*c*) a restriction in respect of his work or other occupation, or in respect of his business;

(*d*) a restriction on his association or communications with specified persons or with other persons generally;

(*e*) a restriction in respect of his place of residence or on the persons to whom he gives access to his place of residence;

(*f*) a prohibition on his being at specified places or within a specified area at specified times or on specified days;

(*g*) a prohibition or restriction on his movements to, from or within the United Kingdom, a specified part of the United Kingdom or a specified place or area within the United Kingdom;

(*h*) a requirement on him to comply with such other prohibitions or restrictions on his movements as may be imposed, for a period not exceeding 24 hours, by directions given to him in the specified manner, by a specified person and for the purpose of securing compliance with other obligations imposed by or under the order;

(*i*) a requirement on him to surrender his passport, or anything in his possession to which a prohibition or restriction imposed by the order relates, to a specified person for a period not exceeding the period for which the order remains in force;

(*j*) a requirement on him to give access to specified persons to his place of residence or to other premises to which he has power to grant access;

(*k*) a requirement on him to allow specified persons to search that place or any such premises for the purpose of ascertaining whether obligations imposed by or under the order have been, are being or are about to be contravened;

(*l*) a requirement on him to allow specified persons, either for that purpose or for the purpose of securing that the order is complied with, to remove anything found in that place or on any such premises and to subject it to tests or to retain it for a period not exceeding the period for which the order remains in force;

(*m*) a requirement on him to allow himself to be photographed;

(*n*) a requirement on him to co-operate with specified arrangements for enabling his movements, communications or other activities to be monitored by electronic or other means;

(*o*) a requirement on him to comply with a demand made in the specified manner to provide information to a specified person in accordance with the demand;

(*p*) a requirement on him to report to a specified person at specified times and places.

(5) Power by or under a control order to prohibit or restrict the controlled person's movements includes, in particular, power to impose a requirement on him to remain at or within a particular place or area (whether for a particular period or at particular times or generally).

(6) The reference in subsection (4)(n) to co-operating with specified arrangements for monitoring includes a reference to each of the following—

(*a*) submitting to procedures required by the arrangements;

(*b*) wearing or otherwise using apparatus approved by or in accordance with the arrangements;

(*c*) maintaining such apparatus in the specified manner;

(*d*) complying with directions given by persons carrying out functions for the purposes of those arrangements.

(7) The information that the controlled person may be required to provide under a control order includes, in particular, advance information about his proposed movements or other activities.

(8) A control order may provide for a prohibition, restriction or requirement imposed by or under the order to apply only where a specified person has not given his consent or approval to what would otherwise contravene the prohibition, restriction or requirement.

(9) For the purposes of this Act involvement in terrorism-related activity is any one or more of the following—

(*a*) the commission, preparation or instigation of acts of terrorism;

(*b*) conduct which facilitates the commission, preparation or instigation of such acts, or which is intended to do so;

(*c*) conduct which gives encouragement to the commission, preparation or instigation of such acts, or which is intended to do so;

(*d*) conduct which gives support or assistance to individuals who are known or believed to be involved in terrorism-related activity;

and for the purposes of this subsection it is immaterial whether the acts of terrorism in question are specific acts of terrorism or acts of terrorism generally.

(10) In this Act—

"derogating obligation" means an obligation on an individual which—

(*a*) is incompatible with his right to liberty under Article 5 of the Human Rights Convention; but

(*b*) is of a description of obligations which, for the purposes of the designation of a designated derogation, is set out in the designation order;

"designated derogation" has the same meaning as in the Human Rights Act 1998 (c 42) (see section 14(1) of that Act);

"designation order", in relation to a designated derogation, means the order under section 14(1) of the Human Rights Act 1998 by which the derogation is designated.

[Prevention of Terrorism Act 2005, s 1.]

2. Making of non-derogating control orders. *Secretary of State may make a non-derogating control order which has effect for a period of twelve months beginning on the day it was made and which may renewed on one or more occasions.*

3. Supervision by court of making of non-derogating control orders. *Permission of the High Court required with provision for the making of orders in cases of urgency until the permission of the court has been obtained.*

4. Power of court to make derogating control orders. *Application to the High Court for an order which has effect for a period of 6 months beginning on the day it was made and which may be renewed on further application.*

8–23559ZZZS 5. Arrest and detention pending derogating control order. (1) A constable may arrest and detain an individual if—

(*a*) the Secretary of State has made an application to the court for a derogating control order to be made against that individual; and

(*b*) the constable considers that the individual's arrest and detention is necessary to ensure that he is available to be given notice of the order if it is made.

(2) A constable who has arrested an individual under this section must take him to the designated place that the constable considers most appropriate as soon as practicable after the arrest.

(3) An individual taken to a designated place under this section may be detained there until the end of 48 hours from the time of his arrest.

(4) If the court considers that it is necessary to do so to ensure that the individual in question is available to be given notice of any derogating control order that is made against him, it may, during the 48 hours following his arrest, extend the period for which the individual may be detained under this section by a period of no more than 48 hours.

(5) An individual may not be detained under this section at any time after—

(*a*) he has become bound by a derogating control order made against him on the Secretary of State's application; or

(*b*) the court has dismissed the application.

(6) A person who has the powers of a constable in one part of the United Kingdom may exercise the power of arrest under this section in that part of the United Kingdom or in any other part of the United Kingdom.

(7) An individual detained under this section—

(*a*) shall be deemed to be in legal custody throughout the period of his detention; and

(*b*) after having been taken to a designated place shall be deemed—

(i) in England and Wales, to be in police detention for the purposes of the Police and Criminal Evidence Act 1984 (c 60); and

(ii) in Northern Ireland, to be in police detention for the purposes of the Police and Criminal Evidence (Northern Ireland) Order 1989 (SI 1989/1341 (NI 12));

but paragraph (b) has effect subject to subsection (8).

(8) Paragraphs 1(6), 2, 6 to 9 and 16 to 19 of Schedule 8 to the Terrorism Act 2000 (c 11) (powers and safeguards in the case of persons detained under section 41 of that Act) apply to an individual detained under this section as they apply to a person detained under section 41 of that Act, but with the following modifications—

(*a*) the omission of paragraph 2(2)(*b*) to (*d*) (which confers powers on persons specified by the Secretary of State, prison officers and examining officers);

(*b*) the omission of paragraph 8(2), (5) and (5A) (which relates to the postponement of a person's rights in England and Wales or Northern Ireland); and

(*c*) the omission of paragraphs 16(9) and 17(4) and (4A) (which make similar provision for Scotland).

(9) The power to detain an individual under this section includes power to detain him in a manner that is incompatible with his right to liberty under Article 5 of the Human Rights Convention if, and only if—

(*a*) there is a designated derogation in respect of the detention of individuals under this section in connection with the making of applications for derogating control orders; and

(*b*) that derogation and the designated derogation relating to the power to make the orders applied for are designated in respect of the same public emergency.

(10) In this section "designated place" means any place which the Secretary of State has designated under paragraph 1(1) of Schedule 8 to the Terrorism Act 2000 (c 11) as a place at which persons may be detained under section 41 of that Act.

[Prevention of Terrorism Act 2005, s 5.]

6. Duration of derogating control orders

7. Modification, notification and proof of orders etc

8. Criminal investigations after making of control order

8–23559ZZZT 9. Offences. (1) A person who, without reasonable excuse, contravenes an obligation imposed on him by a control order is guilty of an offence.

(2) A person is guilty of an offence if—

(*a*) a control order by which he is bound at a time when he leaves the United Kingdom requires him, whenever he enters the United Kingdom, to report to a specified person that he is or has been the subject of such an order;

(*b*) he re-enters the United Kingdom after the order has ceased to have effect;

(*c*) the occasion on which he re-enters the United Kingdom is the first occasion on which he does so after leaving while the order was in force; and

(d) on that occasion he fails, without reasonable excuse, to report to the specified person in the manner that was required by the order.

(3) A person is guilty of an offence if he intentionally obstructs the exercise by any person of a power conferred by section 7(9).

(4) A person guilty of an offence under subsection (1) or (2) shall be liable[1]—

(*a*) on conviction on indictment, to imprisonment for a term not exceeding 5 years or to a fine, or to both;

(*b*) on summary conviction in England and Wales, to imprisonment for a term not exceeding 12 months or to a fine not exceeding the **statutory maximum**, or to **both**;

(*c*) on summary conviction in Scotland or Northern Ireland, to imprisonment for a term not exceeding 6 months or to a fine not exceeding the statutory maximum, or to both.

(5) In relation to an offence committed before the commencement of section 154(1) of the Criminal Justice Act 2003 (c 44), the reference in subsection (4)(b) to 12 months is to be read as a reference to 6 months.

(6) Where a person is convicted by or before any court of an offence under subsection (1) or (2), it is not to be open to the court, in respect of that offence—

(*a*) to make an order under section 12(1)(b) of the Powers of Criminal Courts (Sentencing) Act 2000 (c 6) (conditional discharge);

(*b*) to make an order under section 228(1) of the Criminal Procedure (Scotland) Act 1995 (c 46) (probation orders); or

(*c*) to make an order under Article 4(1)(b) of the Criminal Justice (Northern Ireland) Order 1996 (SI 1996/3160 (NI 24)) (conditional discharge in Northern Ireland).

(7) A person guilty of an offence under subsection (3) shall be liable—

(*a*) on summary conviction in England and Wales, to imprisonment for a term not exceeding 51 weeks or to a fine not exceeding level 5 on the standard scale, or to both;

(*b*) on summary conviction in Scotland or Northern Ireland, to imprisonment for a term not exceeding 6 months or to a fine not exceeding level 5 on the standard scale, or to both.

(8) In relation to an offence committed before the commencement of section 281(5) of the Criminal Justice Act 2003, the reference in subsection (7)(*a*) to 51 weeks is to be read as a reference to 6 months.

(9) In Schedule 1A to the Police and Criminal Evidence Act 1984 (c 60) (arrestable offences), at the end insert—

"27A. Prevention of Terrorism Act 2005. An offence under section 9(3) of the Prevention of Terrorism Act 2005."

(10) In Article 26(2) of the Police and Criminal Evidence (Northern Ireland) Order 1989 (SI 1989/1341 (NI 12)) (offences for which an arrest may be made without a warrant in Northern Ireland), at the end insert—

"(*o*) an offence under section 9(3) of the Prevention of Terrorism Act 2005."

[Prevention of Terrorism Act 2005, s 9.]

1. For mode of trial of this offence which is triable either way, see the Magistrates' Courts Act 1980, ss 17–21 in PART I: MAGISTRATES' COURTS, PROCEDURE, ante.

Appeals and other proceedings

10. Appeals relating to non-derogating control orders

11. Jurisdiction and appeals in relation to control order decisions etc

8–23559ZZZU 12. Effect of court's decisions on convictions. (1) This section applies where—

(*a*) a control order, a renewal of a control order or an obligation imposed by a control order is quashed by the court in control order proceedings, or on an appeal from a determination in such proceedings; and

(*b*) before it was quashed a person had been convicted by virtue of section 9(1) or (2) of an offence of which he could not have been convicted had the order, renewal or (as the case may be) obligation been quashed before the proceedings for the offence were brought.

(2) The person convicted may appeal against the conviction—

(*a*) in the case of a conviction on indictment in England and Wales or Northern Ireland, to the Court of Appeal;

(*b*) in the case of a conviction on indictment or summary conviction in Scotland, to the High Court of Justiciary;

(*c*) in the case of a summary conviction in England and Wales, to the Crown Court; and

(*d*) in the case of a summary conviction in Northern Ireland, to the county court.

(3) On an appeal under this section to any court, that court must allow the appeal and quash the conviction.

(4) An appeal under this section to the Court of Appeal against a conviction on indictment—

(*a*) may be brought irrespective of whether the appellant has previously appealed against his conviction;

(*b*) may not be brought more than 28 days after the date of the quashing of the order, renewal or obligation; and

(*c*) is to be treated as an appeal under section 1 of the Criminal Appeal Act 1968 (c 19) or, in Northern Ireland, under section 1 of the Criminal Appeal (Northern Ireland) Act 1980 (c 47), but does not require leave in either case.

(5) An appeal under this section to the High Court of Justiciary against a conviction on indictment—

(*a*) may be brought irrespective of whether the appellant has previously appealed against his conviction;

(*b*) may not be brought more than two weeks after the date of the quashing of the order, renewal or obligation; and

(*c*) is to be treated as an appeal under section 106 of the Criminal Procedure (Scotland) Act 1995 (c 46) for which leave has been granted.

(6) An appeal under this section to the High Court of Justiciary against a summary conviction—

(*a*) may be brought irrespective of whether the appellant pleaded guilty;
(*b*) may be brought irrespective of whether the appellant has previously appealed against his conviction;
(*c*) may not be brought more than two weeks after the date of the quashing of the order, renewal or obligation;
(*d*) is to be by note of appeal, which shall state the ground of appeal;
(*e*) is to be treated as an appeal for which leave has been granted under Part 10 of the Criminal Procedure (Scotland) Act 1995; and
(*f*) must be in accordance with such procedure as the High Court of Justiciary may, by Act of Adjournal, determine.

(7) An appeal under this section to the Crown Court or to the county court in Northern Ireland against a summary conviction—

(*a*) may be brought irrespective of whether the appellant pleaded guilty;
(*b*) may be brought irrespective of whether he has previously appealed against his conviction or made an application in respect of the conviction under section 111 of the Magistrates' Courts Act 1980 (c 43) or Article 146 of the Magistrates' Courts (Northern Ireland) Order 1981 (SI 1981/1675 (NI 26)) (case stated);
(*c*) may not be brought more than 21 days after the date of the quashing of the order, renewal or obligation; and
(*d*) is to be treated as an appeal under section 108(1)(b) of that Act or, in Northern Ireland, under Article 140(1)(b) of that Order.

(8) In section 133(5) of the Criminal Justice Act 1988 (c 33) (compensation for miscarriages of justice), at the end of paragraph (*c*) insert

"or
(*d*) on an appeal under section 12 of the Prevention of Terrorism Act 2005."

[Prevention of Terrorism Act 2005, s 12.]

Supplemental

8–23559ZZZV 13. Duration of sections 1 to 9. (1) Except so far as otherwise provided under this section, sections 1 to 9 expire at the end of the period of 12 months beginning with the day on which this Act is passed.

(2) The Secretary of State may, by order made by statutory instrument—

(*a*) repeal sections 1 to 9;
(*b*) at any time revive those sections for a period not exceeding one year; or
(*c*) provide that those sections—
   (i) are not to expire at the time when they would otherwise expire under subsection (1) or in accordance with an order under this subsection; but
   (ii) are to continue in force after that time for a period not exceeding one year.

(3) Before making an order under this section the Secretary of State must consult—

(*a*) the person appointed for the purposes of section 14(2);
(*b*) the Intelligence Services Commissioner; and
(*c*) the Director-General of the Security Service.

(4) No order may be made by the Secretary of State under this section unless a draft of it has been laid before Parliament and approved by a resolution of each House.

(5) Subsection (4) does not apply to an order that contains a declaration by the Secretary of State that the order needs, by reason of urgency, to be made without the approval required by that subsection.

(6) An order under this section that contains such a declaration—

(*a*) must be laid before Parliament after being made; and
(*b*) if not approved by a resolution of each House before the end of 40 days beginning with the day on which the order was made, ceases to have effect at the end of that period.

(7) Where an order ceases to have effect in accordance with subsection (6), that does not—

(*a*) affect anything previously done in reliance on the order; or
(*b*) prevent the making of a new order to the same or similar effect.

(8) Where sections 1 to 9 expire or are repealed at any time by virtue of this section, that does not prevent or otherwise affect—

(*a*) the court's consideration of a reference made before that time under subsection (3)(*a*) of section 3;
(*b*) the holding or continuation after that time of any hearing in pursuance of directions under subsection (2)(*c*) or (6)(*b*) or (*c*) of that section;

(*c*) the holding or continuation after that time of a hearing to determine whether to confirm a derogating control order (with or without modifications); or

(*d*) the bringing or continuation after that time of any appeal, or further appeal, relating to a decision in any proceedings mentioned in paragraphs (*a*) to (*c*) of this subsection;

but proceedings may be begun or continued by virtue of this subsection so far only as they are for the purpose of determining whether a certificate of the Secretary of State, a control order or an obligation imposed by such an order should be quashed or treated as quashed.

(9) Nothing in this Act about the period for which a control order is to have effect or is renewed enables such an order to continue in force after the provision under which it was made or last renewed has expired or been repealed by virtue of this section.

(10) In subsection (6) "40 days" means 40 days computed as provided for in section 7(1) of the Statutory Instruments Act 1946 (c 36).

[Prevention of Terrorism Act 2005, s 12.]

14. Reporting and review

8–23559ZZZW 15. General interpretation. (1) In this Act—

"act" and "conduct" include omissions and statements;

"act of terrorism" includes anything constituting an action taken for the purposes of terrorism, within the meaning of the Terrorism Act 2000 (c 11) (see section 1(5) of that Act);

"apparatus" includes any equipment, machinery or device and any wire or cable, together with any software used with it;

"article" and "information" include documents and other records, and software;

"contravene" includes fail to comply, and cognate expressions are to be construed accordingly;

"control order" has the meaning given by section 1(1);

"control order proceedings" has the meaning given by section 11(6);

"the controlled person", in relation to a control order, means the individual on whom the order imposes obligations;

"the court"—

(*a*) in relation to proceedings relating to a control order in the case of which the controlled person is a person whose principal place of residence is in Scotland, means the Outer House of the Court of Session;

(*b*) in relation to proceedings relating to a control order in the case of which the controlled person is a person whose principal place of residence is in Northern Ireland, means the High Court in Northern Ireland; and

(*c*) in any other case, means the High Court in England and Wales;

"derogating control order" means a control order imposing obligations that are or include derogating obligations;

"derogating obligation", "designated derogation" and "designation order" have the meanings given by section 1(10);

"the Human Rights Convention" means the Convention within the meaning of the Human Rights Act 1998 (c 42) (see section 21(1) of that Act);

"modification" includes omission, addition or alteration, and cognate expressions are to be construed accordingly;

"non-derogating control order" means a control order made by the Secretary of State;

"passport" means—

(*a*) a United Kingdom passport (within the meaning of the Immigration Act 1971 (c 77));

(*b*) a passport issued by or on behalf of the authorities of a country or territory outside the United Kingdom, or by or on behalf of an international organisation;

(*c*) a document that can be used (in some or all circumstances) instead of a passport;

"premises" includes any vehicle, vessel, aircraft or hovercraft;

"the public" means the public in the whole or a part of the United Kingdom or the public in another country or territory, or any section of the public;

"specified", in relation to a control order, means specified in that order or falling within a description so specified;

"terrorism" has the same meaning as in the Terrorism Act 2000 (c 11) (see section 1(1) to (4) of that Act);

"terrorism-related activity" and, in relation to such activity, "involvement" are to be construed in accordance with section 1(9).

(2) A power under this Act to quash a control order, the renewal of such an order or an obligation imposed by such an order includes power—

(*a*) in England and Wales or Northern Ireland, to stay the quashing of the order, renewal or obligation pending an appeal, or further appeal, against the decision to quash; and

(*b*) in Scotland, to determine that the quashing is of no effect pending such an appeal or further appeal.

(3) Every power of the Secretary of State or of the court to revoke a control order or to modify the obligations imposed by such an order—

(*a*) includes power to provide for the revocation or modification to take effect from such time as the Secretary of State or (as the case may be) the court may determine; and

(*b*) in the case of a revocation by the court (including a revocation in pursuance of section 7(7)) includes power to postpone the effect of the revocation either pending an appeal or for the purpose of giving the Secretary of State an opportunity to decide whether to exercise his own powers to make a control order against the individual in question.

(4) For the purposes of this Act a failure by the Secretary of State to consider an application by the controlled person for—

(*a*) the revocation of a control order, or

(*b*) the modification of an obligation imposed by such an order,

is to be treated as a decision by the Secretary of State not to revoke or (as the case may be) not to modify the order.

[Prevention of Terrorism Act 2005, s 15.]

8–23559ZZZX 16. Other supplemental provisions. (1) This Act may be cited as the Prevention of Terrorism Act 2005.

(2) The following provisions are repealed—

(*a*) sections 21 to 32 of the Anti-terrorism, Crime and Security Act 2001 (c 24) (suspected international terrorists);

(*b*) in section 1(4) of the Special Immigration Appeals Commission Act 1997 (c 68), paragraph (b) (which refers to section 30 of the 2001 Act) and the word "or" immediately preceding it;

(*c*) section 62(15) and (16) of the Nationality, Immigration and Asylum Act 2002 (c 41) and paragraph 30 of Schedule 7 to that Act (which amended sections 23, 24 and 27 of the 2001 Act); and

(*d*) section 32 of the Asylum and Immigration (Treatment of Claimants, etc) Act 2004 (c 19) (which amended sections 24 and 27 of the 2001 Act).

(3) Subsection (2) comes into force on 14th March 2005.

(4) The repeals made by this Act do not prevent or otherwise affect—

(*a*) the continuation of any appeal to the Special Immigration Appeals Commission under section 25(1) of the Anti-terrorism, Crime and Security Act 2001 that has been brought but not concluded before the commencement of those repeals;

(*b*) the bringing or continuation of a further appeal relating to a decision of that Commission on such an appeal or on any other appeal brought under section 25(1) of that Act before the commencement of those repeals; or

(*c*) any proceedings resulting from a decision on a further appeal from such a decision;

but no other proceedings before that Commission under Part 4 of that Act, nor any appeal or further appeal relating to any such other proceedings, may be brought or continued at any time after the commencement of the repeals.

(5) The Secretary of State may enter into such contracts and other arrangements with other persons as he considers appropriate for securing their assistance in connection with any monitoring, by electronic or other means, that he considers needs to be carried out in connection with obligations that have been or may be imposed by or under control orders.

(6) There shall be paid out of money provided by Parliament—

(*a*) any expenditure incurred by the Secretary of State by virtue of this Act; and

(*b*) any increase attributable to this Act in the sums payable out of such money under any other Act.

(7) This Act extends to Northern Ireland.

(8) Her Majesty may by Order in Council direct that this Act shall extend, with such modifications as appear to Her Majesty to be appropriate, to any of the Channel Islands or the Isle of Man.

[Prevention of Terrorism Act 2005, s 16.]

Section 11

SCHEDULE

CONTROL ORDER PROCEEDINGS ETC

Abortion Regulations 1991[1]

(SI 1991/499 amended by SI 2002/887, 2879 and 3135)

8–23560 1. *Citation and commencement.*

(2) These Regulations extend to England and Wales only.

1. Made by the Secretary of State for Health, in exercise of the powers conferred by s 2 of the Abortion Act 1967.

Interpretation

8-23561 2. In these Regulations—

"the Act" means the Abortion Act 1967;

"electronic communication" has the same meaning as in section 15 of the Electronic Communications Act 2000;

"practitioner" means a registered medical practitioner;

"solicitor" means a person who is qualified to act as a solicitor as provided by section 1 of the Solicitors Act 1974.

Certificate of opinion

8-23562 3. (1) Any opinion to which section 1 of the Act refers shall be certified—

(a) in the case of a pregnancy terminated in accordance with section 1(1) of the Act, either—

(i) in the form set out in Part I of Schedule 1 to these Regulations; or

(ii) in a certificate signed and dated by both practitioners jointly or in separate certificates signed and dated by each practitioner stating:—

(*a*) the full name and address of each practitioner;

(*b*) the full name and address of the pregnant woman;

(*c*) whether or not each practitioner has seen or examined, or seen and examined, the pregnant woman; and

(*d*) that each practitioner is of the opinion formed in good faith that at least one and the same ground mentioned in paragraph (*a*) to (*d*) of section 1(1) of the Act is fulfilled.

(*b*) in the case of a pregnancy terminated in accordance with section 1(4) of the Act, either—

(i) in the form set out in Part II of Schedule 1 to these Regulations; or

(ii) in a certificate giving the full name and address of the practitioner and containing the full name and address of the pregnant woman and stating that the practitioner is of the opinion formed in good faith that one of the grounds mentioned in section 1(4) of the Act is fulfilled.

(2) Any certificate of an opinion referred to in section 1(1) of the Act shall be given before the commencement of the treatment for the termination of the pregnancy to which it relates.

(3) Any certificate of an opinion referred to in section 1(4) of the Act shall be given before the commencement of the treatment for the termination of the pregnancy to which it relates or, if that is not reasonably practicable, not later than 24 hours after such termination.

(4) Any such certificate as is referred to in paragraphs (2) and (3) of this regulation shall be preserved by the practitioner who terminated the pregnancy to which it relates for a period of not less than three years beginning with the date of the termination.

(5) A certificate which is no longer to be preserved shall be destroyed by the person in whose custody it then is.

Notice of termination of pregnancy and information relating to the termination

8-23563 4. (1) Any practitioner who terminates a pregnancy in England or Wales shall give to the appropriate Chief Medical Officer—

(*a*) notice of the termination, and

(*b*) such other information relating to the termination as is specified in Schedule 2 to these Regulations,

and shall do so by sending them to him within 14 days of the termination either in a sealed envelope or by an electronic communication transmitted by an electronic communications system used solely for the transfer of confidential information to him.

(2) The appropriate Chief Medical Officer is—

(*a*) where the pregnancy was terminated in England, the Chief Medical Officer of the Department of Health, Richmond House, Whitehall, London SW1A 2NS; or

(*b*) where the pregnancy was terminated in Wales, the Chief Medical Officer of the Welsh Office, Cathays Park, Cardiff CF1 3NQ.

Restriction on disclosure of information

8-23564 5. A notice given or any information furnished to a Chief Medical Officer in pursuance of these Regulations shall not be disclosed except that disclosure may be made—

(*a*) for the purposes of carrying out their duties—

(i) to an officer of the Department of Health authorised by the Chief Medical Officer of that Department, or to an officer of the Welsh Office authorised by the Chief Medical Officer of that Office, as the case may be, or

(ii) to the Registrar General or a member of his staff authorised by him; or

(iii) to an individual authorised by the Chief Medical Officer who is engaged in setting up, maintaining and supporting a computer system used for the purpose of recording, processing and holding such notice or information; or

(*b*) for the purposes of carrying out his duties in relation to offences against the Act or the law relating to abortion, to the Director of Public Prosecutions or a member of his staff authorised by him; or

(*c*) for the purposes of investigating whether an offence has been committed under the Act or the law relating to abortion, to a police officer not below the rank of superintendent or a person authorised by him; or

(*d*) pursuant to a court order, for the purposes of proceedings which have begun; or

(*e*) for the purposes of bona fide scientific research; or

(*f*) to the practitioner who terminated the pregnancy; or

(*g*) to a practitioner, with the consent in writing of the woman whose pregnancy was terminated; or

(*h*) when requested by the President of the General Medical Council for the purpose of investigating whether the fitness to practise of the practitioner is impaired, there has been serious professional misconduct by a practitioner, to the President of the General Medical Council or a member of its staff authorised by him.

(*i*) to the woman whose pregnancy was terminated, on her supplying to the Chief Medical Officer written details of her date of birth, the date and place of the termination and a copy of the certificate of registration of her birth certified as a true copy of the original by a solicitor or a practitioner.

8–23565 6. *Revocations.*

PERVERTING JUSTICE

8–23567 The common law offence of perverting, or attempting to pervert the course of justice, is triable only on indictment. See *R v Vreones* [1891] 1 QB 360; *R v Grimes* [1968] 3 All ER 179; *R v Andrews* [1973] QB 422, [1973] 1 All ER 857; *R v Panayiotou* [1973] 3 All ER 112, [1973] 1 WLR 1032; *R v Britton* [1973] Crim LR 375 (motorist drank beer and told mother to obstruct police, instead of giving specimen of breath); *R v Kellett* [1976] QB 372, [1975] 3 All ER 468, CA (attempt to dissuade potential witnesses from giving evidence offence if intention or means improper); *R v Thomas and R v Ferguson* [1979] 1 All ER 577 (assisting someone wanted by police as suspect to evade lawful arrest). It is not a necessary element of the offence that there should be an unlawful means (*R v Toney* [1993] 2 All ER 409, [1993] Crim LR 397). The prosecution must prove either an intent to pervert the course of justice or an in tent to do something which, if achieved, would pervert the course of justice (*R v Lalani* [1999] 1 Cr App Rep 481, CA, juror communicating with defendant acquitted as no evidence adduced of her state of mind). The offence should not be charged where the prosecution can only present its case on the alternative basis that the defendant must either have committed perjury or have given false information to the police (*Tsang Ping-nam v R* [1982] Crim LR 46). It is only right to charge perverting the course of justice where there are seriously aggravating features such as wasted police time and where members of the public, have been detained (*R v Sookoo* (2002) Times, 10 April, CA). Inaction is not an act or a course of conduct (*R v Headley* [1996] RTR 173 (defendant ignored summons in his name and allowed informations alleging contraventions of the Road Traffic Acts by his brother to be proved in his own name)). Nor is driving home after an accident and not reporting it until the following day because the accused knew he would have been in difficulty with the breathalyser; the actus reus of the offence requires more than driving off and waiting for alcohol to dissipate from the body (*R v Clark (Mark)* [2003] EWCA Crim 991, [2003] 2 Cr App Rep 63, [2003] RTR 27, [2003] Crim LR 558).

The "course of justice" is distinct from the "ends of justice"; an intention to pervert the course of justice can exist even though the motive is to further the ends of justice (*A-G's Reference (No 1 of 2002)* [2002] EWCA Crim 2392, [2003] Crim LR 410). A course of justice must have been embarked upon, and the defendant must be shown to have intended to interfere with the administration of justice (*R v Selvage and R v Morgan* [1982] Crim LR 47). It is sufficient for a conviction if the defendant intended to mislead a judicial tribunal in any or all of the possible judicial proceedings which might ensue (*R v Sinha* [1995] Crim LR 68). It is not necessary for a police investigation to have commenced when the acts in question occurred (*R v Rafique, R v Sajid, R v Rajah* [1993] 4 All ER 1, [1993] 3 WLR 617). The offence of attempting to pervert the course of justice is in itself a substantive common law offence, reference to the Criminal Attempts Act 1981 would therefore be wrong; see *R v Williams* [1991] Crim LR 205.

The scope of the offence of perverting the course of justice is sufficiently clear so as not be incompatible with art 7 of the Convention; the article permits the gradual clarification of the rules of criminal liability from case to case through judicial interpretation provided that the development is consistent with the essence of the offence and could have been foreseen: *R v Cotter, Clair and Wynn* [2002] EWCA Crim 1033, [2003] QB 951, [2003] 2 WLR 115, [2002] 2 Cr App Rep 405.

The essence of the offence (in contrast to the offence of wasting police time) is not a risk of an innocent person being subjected to wrongful arrest, so that if the innocent person targeted was not alive at that time there could be no such risk; the essence is that a defendant has put in train the machinery of public justice which, if the matter were carried through in a way he wished or foresaw, would cause a risk to an innocent person, and if that person has in fact died it is a classic case of impossible attempt: *R v Brown* [2004] EWCA Crim 744, [2004] Crim LR 665.

POLICE

8–23580 The title contains the following statutes—

and also the following statutory instruments—

8–23585 This title is concerned with constables, being mainly police officers appointed under the Police Act 1996, the British Transport Commission Act 1949[1] and the Ministry of Defence Police Act 1987. The appointment and jurisdiction of constables[2] are dealt with by s 53(1)(*b*) of the 1949 Act and s 30 of the 1996 Act; their powers are largely defined by the Police and Criminal Evidence Act 1984 in PART I: MAGISTRATES' COURTS, PROCEDURE, ante; see also "Investigation of Offences", paras **1–220** to **1–244**, ante. Police complaints and discipline are provided for in Part IX, ss 83–105, of the Police and Criminal Evidence Act 1984 (not printed in this Manual), and ss 50 and 84 of the 1996 Act enables the making of discipline regulations; some current regulations are printed post.

The Police Act 1997 establishes the National Criminal Intelligence Service and the National Crime Squad and creates offences of causing disaffection among members of these services. This Act further provides for authorisation of action to interfere with property and for the provision of certificates of criminal records.

1. Note however the following appointments of police for limited purposes: airport police (Civil Aviation Act 1982, s 57); fishery officers (Sea Fisheries Regulation Act 1966, s 10); harbour, docks or pier police (Harbours, Docks and Piers Clauses Act 1847, ss 79, 80); nominated special constables (Special Constables Act 1923, s 3, Emergency Laws (Miscellaneous Provisions) Act 1947, Sch 2, Atomic Energy Authority Act 1954, ss 6, 9, Sch 3, Atomic Energy Authority Act 1971, Sch, Atomic Energy Authority (Special Constables) Act 1976, Visiting Forces and International Headquarters (Application of Law) Order 1965 (SI 1965/1536), art 6); Port of London Police (Port of London Act 1968, s 154); university police (Universities Act 1825, s 1); water bailiffs (Salmon and Freshwater Fisheries Act 1975, s 36).
2. That is, a person holding the *office* of constable, and not just the rank: see Police Act 1996, s 29.

8–23590 Constables, execution of warrant of commitment. The person apprehended on a warrant issued in England or Wales may be conveyed either to the prison mentioned in the warrant, or to any other prison (Criminal Procedure Rules 2005, r 18.6, in PART I: MAGISTRATES' COURTS, PROCEDURE, post).

A warrant of commitment issued by a justice of the peace may be executed anywhere in England and Wales by any person to whom it is directed or by any constable acting within his police area[1]. A sentence of imprisonment imposed on an offender shall be treated as reduced by any period during which the offender was in police detention in connection with the offence for which the sentence was passed. Therefore, any period spent by an offender in police detention prior to his conveyance to prison will be treated as part of the term of imprisonment[2].

1. Magistrates' Courts Act 1980, s 125(2), in PART I: MAGISTRATES' COURTS, PROCEDURE, ante.
2. See Criminal Justice Act 1967, s 67, in PART I: MAGISTRATES' COURTS, PROCEDURE, ante.

8–23591 Refusing to assist a constable. It is an indictable misdemeanour at common law punishable by fine or imprisonment or both to refuse to aid and assist a constable in the execution of his duty when duly called on to do so, if the person so called upon is physically capable of helping, and has no lawful excuse for refusing.

To support an indictment for refusing to aid in quelling a riot it was held that it was necessary to prove, first, that the constable saw a breach of the peace committed; secondly, that there was reasonable necessity for calling on the defendant for his assistance; and, thirdly, that the defendant refused without any physical impossibility or lawful excuse (*R v Brown* (1841) Car & M 314, Treat 34 JP 129). As to the indictment for refusing to assist, see *R v Sherlock* (1866) LR 1 CCR 20, 30 JP 85. A person assaulting the party charged to assist the constable may be punished for the assault (Police Act 1996, s 89); and if he rescues the prisoner, may be indicted for the rescue. Where a person is in custody of a private party, he should give notice to the rescuer of the cause for which he is in custody; where in that of a constable, the rescuer must take notice of it himself at his peril (6 JP 319).

Police (Property) Act 1897

(60 & 61 Vict c 30)

8-23610 **1. Power to make orders with respect to property in possession of police.** (1) Where any property has come into the possession of the police in connection with their investigation of a suspected offence, a court of summary jurisdiction may, on application either by an officer of police[1] or by a claimant of the property, make an order[2] for the delivery of the property to the person appearing to the magistrate or court to be the owner[3] thereof, or, if the owner cannot be ascertained, make such order with respect to the property as to the magistrate or court may seem meet.

(2) An order under this section shall not affect the right of any person to take within six months from the date of the order legal proceedings against any person in possession of property delivered by virtue of the order for the recovery of the property, but on the expiration of those six months the right shall cease.

(3) *Repealed.*

[Police (Property) Act 1897, s 1, as amended by Theft Act 1968, the Criminal Justice Act 1972, s 58 and the Consumer Credit Act 1974, Sch 5 and the Statute Law (Repeals) Act 1989, Sch 1.]

---

1. The police should apply for an order under this section before parting with the property. The plaintiff having lost a gig, the person in whose possession it was found was tried for larceny and acquitted. A police officer who handed it over to the person so acquitted was liable in trover to the plaintiff (*Winter v Bancks* (1901) 65 JP 468). For consideration of a successful claimant's title to property after the making of an order, see *Irving v National Provincial Bank Ltd* [1902] 2 QB 73, [1962] 1 All ER 157, 126 JP 76.

2. Proceedings are appropriately to be brought by way of complaint and there is power to award costs under s 64 of the Magistrates' Courts Act 1980 (*R v Uxbridge Justices, ex p Metropolitan Police Comr* [1981] QB 829, [1981] 3 All ER 129, 146 JP 42, CA; and in appropriate circumstances this includes making an order for costs against the police (*Mercer v Oldham* [1984] Crim LR 232). However, where the chief constable brought an application to determine to whom cash should be returned – the person from whom it was seized or the company that was the victim of that person's offending – and the court made an order in favour of the former, there was no power, having regard to the terms of s 64(1)(*b*) of the MCA 1980, to order the chief constable to pay that person's costs, since the complaint had not been dismissed; moreover, the order was wholly unreasonable: *R (on the application of the Chief Constable of Northamptonshire) v Daventry Justices* [2001] Admin 446). Justices are to be discouraged from using the procedure of this Act in cases which involve a real issue of law or any real difficulty in determining whether a particular person is or is not the owner; see dicta in *Raymond Lyons & Co v Metropolitan Police Comr*, infra.

3. The innkeeper's lien attaches to stolen property received by an innkeeper from a guest as a security for payment of his bill. The meaning of "owner" was not decided (*Marsh v Police Comr* [1945] KB 43, [1944] 2 All ER 392, 109 JP 45). In *Raymond Lyons & Co Ltd v Metropolitan Police Comr* [1975] QB 321, [1975] 1 All ER 335, 139 JP 213 it was held that "owner" is to be given its ordinary popular meaning. A court may make an order in favour of an offender despite the property having passed under an illegal contract (*Chief Constable of West Midlands v White* (1992) 157 JP 222). Where police officers seized a stolen vehicle then in the possession of C, who was its registered keeper, but C, though aware that the car was stolen, was not prosecuted, and the police were unable to trace anybody with a better title to the vehicle than C, C was entitled to the return of the vehicle once the purposes of s 22 of PACE had been exhausted: *Costello v Chief Constable of Derbyshire Constabulary* [2001] EWCA Civ 381, [2001] 3 All ER 150, [2001] 1 WLR 1437.

Costello was not dealing with the 1897 Act; however, it was held in *R (on the application of Ian Carter) v Ipswich Magistrates' Court* [2002] EWHC 332 (Admin), [2002] All ER (*d*) 110 (Feb) that the same principles apply both to civil actions in the county court and to applications under the 1897 Act.

Where claimants had paid for vehicles and, though they had been stolen, they had not been the thieves or been concerned in the thefts, those were significant facts and the justices had been wrong to order destruction of the vehicles on the grounds that they could never have become "legal", the significance of which, whatever it meant, was difficult to see where the court was endeavouring to determine ownership for the purposes of s 1 (*Haley v Chief Constable of Northamptonshire Police* [2002] EWHC 1492 (Admin), (2002) 166 JP 719).

8-23611 **2. Regulations with respect to unclaimed property.** (1) A Secretary of State may make regulations[1] (limited by sub-s (2)) for the disposal of property which has come into the possession of the police under the circumstances mentioned in this Act in cases where the owner of the property has not been ascertained, and no order of a competent court has been made with respect thereto.

(2)–(2B) *Regulations.*

(3) Where the property is a perishable article or its custody involves unreasonable expense or inconvenience, it may be sold at any time, but the proceeds of sale shall not be disposed of until they have remained in the possession of the police for a year. In any other case the property shall not be sold until it has remained in the possession of the police for a year.

(4) Regulations[1] may be made by the Secretary of State as to the investment of money and audit of accounts.*

[Police (Property) Act 1897, s 2 as amended by the Statute Law Repeals Act 1908 and the Police Property Act 1997, s 1.]

***Prospectively repealed by the Police (Northern Ireland) Act 1998, Sch 6, as from a day to be appointed.**

1. See the Police (Property) Regulations 1997, in this title, post.

8–23612 2A. *Application to SOCA*

Police Pensions Act 1976

(1976 c 35)

8–23780 Regulations[1] by the Secretary of State may make detailed provision for police pensions. They may enable pensions to be varied, suspended, terminated or forfeited or applied otherwise than by being paid to the persons to whom they were awarded [s 1—summarised.]

1. Section 12 provides savings for existing regulations, see the Police Pensions Regulations, SI 1971/232 as amended and SI 1973/428 as amended with supplementary provisions made by SI 1987/256 as amended; there are also transitional savings (by s 12(2)) for the provisions of ss 4(1) and (2) and 5(1) and (5) of the Police Pensions Act 1948 as amended by the Criminal Justice Act 1948, Sch 9 and the Superannuation Act 1972, s 15 and Sch 8 (forfeiture of pensions and appeals). The current provision is the Police Pensions Regulations 1987, SI 1987/257 as amended by SI 1987/341 and 2215, SI 1988/1339, SI 1989/733, SI 1990/805, SI 1991/1517, 1992/1343 and 2349, SI 1994/641, SI 1996/867, SI 1997/2852, SI 1998/577, SI 2000/843 and 1549, SI 2001/3649 and 3888, SI 2002/2529 and 3202, SI 2003/27, 535 and 2716, SI 2004/1491, 1760 and 2354 and SI 2005/1439. See also: the Police Pensions (Purchase of Increased Benefits) Regulations 1987, SI 1987/2215 amended by SI 2004/2354 and SI 2005/1439; Police Pensions (Additional Voluntary Contributions) Regulations 1991, SI 1991/1304 amended by SI 2003/27, 535 and 2717; and the Police Pensions (Part-time Service) Regulations 2005, SI 2005/1439.

8–23781 10. Obtaining pension by self-inflicted injury etc. If any person obtains or attempts to obtain for himself or any other person any pension under any regulations made under section 1 above by maiming or injuring himself, or causing himself to be maimed or injured, or otherwise producing disease or infirmity, he shall be liable[1]—

(*a*) on conviction on indictment, to imprisonment for a term not exceeding **two years;** or

(*b*) on summary conviction, to imprisonment for a term not exceeding **three months** or to a fine not exceeding the **statutory maximum**.

[Police Pensions Act 1976, s 10, as amended by the Criminal Law Act 1977, s. 28.]

1. For procedure in respect of an offence triable either way, see the Magistrates' Courts Act 1980, ss 17A–21, ante.

SCHEDULE 1

PENSIONS UNDER REPEALED ENACTMENTS

8–23782 This Schedule makes provision for pensions excluded from the operation of regulations under this Act and the forfeiture of pensions under repealed enactments. [Sch 1—summarised.]

Ministry of Defence Police Act 1987

(1987 c 4)

8–23800 1. The Ministry of Defence Police. (1) There shall be a police force to be known as the Ministry of Defence Police and consisting—

(*a*) of persons nominated by the Secretary of State; and

(*b*) of persons who at the coming into force of this Act are special constables by virtue of appointment under section 3 of the Special Constables Act 1923 on the nomination of the Defence Council.

(2) A person nominated under subsection (1) above shall—

(*a*) in England and Wales be attested as a constable by making the declaration required of a member of a police force maintained under the Police Act 1996 before a justice of the peace;

(*b*)–(*c*) Scotland; Northern Ireland.

(3)–(6) *Power of the Secretary of State to appoint a chief constable for the Ministry of Defence Police; to suspend a member of the Police from duty; to appoint the Ministry of Defence Police Committee, and to make regulations*[1].

[Ministry of Defence Police Act 1987, s 1 as amended by the Police Act 1996, Sch 7.]

1. The following regulations have been made under this provision: Ministry of Defence Police Appeal Tribunals Regulations 2004, SI 2004/652; Ministry of Defence Police (Conduct) Regulations 2004, SI 2004/653 amended by SI 2005/3389; Ministry of Defence Police (Conduct) (Senior Officers) Regulations 2004, SI 2004/654.

8–23801 **2. Jurisdiction.** (1) In any place in the United Kingdom to which subsection (2) below for the time being applies, members of the Ministry of Defence Police shall have the powers and privileges of constables.

(2)[1] The places to which this subsection applies are—

(*a*) land, vehicles, vessels, aircraft and hovercraft in the possession, under the control or used for the purposes of—

(i) the Secretary of State for Defence;
(ii) the Defence Council;
(iii) a headquarters or defence organisation; or
(iv) the service authorities of a visiting force;

(*b*) land, vehicles, vessels, aircraft and hovercraft which are—

(i) in the possession, under the control or used for the purposes of an ordnance company; and
(ii) used for the purpose of, or for purposes which include, the making or development of ordnance or otherwise for naval, military or air force purposes;

(*c*) land, vehicles, vessels, aircraft and hovercraft which are—

(i) in the possession, under the control or used for the purposes of a dockyard contractor; and
(ii) used for the purpose of, or for purposes which include, providing designated services or otherwise for naval, military or air force purposes;

(*d*) (*repealed*) and
(*e*) land where the Secretary of State has agreed to provide the services of the Ministry of Defence Police under an agreement notice of which has been published in the appropriate Gazette.

(3) Members of the Ministry of Defence Police shall also have the powers and privileges of constables in any place in the United Kingdom to which subsection (2) above does not for the time being apply—

(*a*) in relation to Crown property[2], international defence property, ordnance property and dockyard property;
(*b*) in relation to persons—

(i) subject to the control of the Defence Council;
(ii) employed under or for the purposes of the Ministry of Defence or the Defence Council; or
(iii) in respect of whom the service courts and service authorities of any country may exercise powers by virtue of section 2 of the Visiting Forces Act 1952;

(*ba*) in connection with offences against persons within paragraph (*b*) above, with the incitement of such persons to commit offences and with offences under the Prevention of Corruption Acts 1889 to 1916 in relation to such persons;
(*c*) in relation to matters connected with anything done under a contract entered into by the Secretary of State for Defence for the purposes of his Department or the Defence Council; and
(*d*) for the purpose of securing the unimpeded passage of any such property as is mentioned in paragraph (*a*) above.

(3A) Where a member of the Ministry of Defence Police has been requested by a constable of—

(*a*) the police force for any police area;
(*b*) the Police Service of Northern Ireland;
(*c*) the British Transport Police Force; or
(*d*) the Civil Nuclear Constabulary,

to assist him in the execution of his duties in relation to a particular incident, investigation or operation, members of the Ministry of Defence Police shall have the powers and privileges of constables for the purposes of that incident, investigation or operation but subject to subsection (3B) below.

(3B) Members of the Ministry of Defence Police have the powers and privileges of constables for the purposes of an incident, investigation or operation by virtue of subsection (3A) above—

(*a*) if the request was made under paragraph (*a*) of that subsection by a constable of the police force for a police area, only in that police area;
(*b*) if it was made under paragraph (*b*) of that subsection, only in Northern Ireland;
(*c*) if it was made under paragraph (*c*) of that subsection, only to the extent that those powers and privileges would in the circumstances be exercisable for those purposes by a constable of the British Transport Police Force by virtue of subsection (1A) or, in Scotland, subsection (4) of section 53 of the British Transport Commission Act 1949 (c xxix); or
(*d*) if it was made under paragraph (*d*) of that subsection, only to the extent that those powers and privileges would in the circumstances be exercisable for those purposes by a constable of the Civil Nuclear Constabulary.

(3C) Members of the Ministry of Defence Police shall have in any police area the same powers and privileges as constables of the police force for that police area, and in Northern Ireland the same powers and privileges as constables of the Police Service of Northern Ireland,—

(*a*) in relation to persons whom they suspect on reasonable grounds of having committed, being in the course of committing or being about to commit an offence; or

(*b*) if they believe on reasonable grounds that they need those powers and privileges in order to save life or to prevent or minimise personal injury.

(3D) But members of the Ministry of Defence Police have powers and privileges by virtue of subsection (3C) above only if—

(*a*) they are in uniform or have with them documentary evidence that they are members of the Ministry of Defence Police; and

(*b*) they believe on reasonable grounds that a power of a constable which they would not have apart from that subsection ought to be exercised and that, if it cannot be exercised until they secure the attendance of or a request under subsection (3A) above by a constable who has it, the purpose for which they believe it ought to be exercised will be frustrated or seriously prejudiced.

(4) Subsections (1) to (3D) above shall have effect in the territorial waters adjacent to the United Kingdom, but as if the references in those subsections to the powers and privileges of constables were references in those subsections to the powers and privileges of constables in the nearest part of the United Kingdom.

(5) In this section—

"appropriate Gazette" means—

(i) in relation to land in England or Wales, the London Gazette;
(ii) in relation to land in Scotland, the Edinburgh Gazette, and
(iii) in relation to land in Northern Ireland, the Belfast Gazette;

"British Transport Police Force" means the constables appointed under section 53 of the British Transport Commission Act 1949 (c xxix);

"Crown property" includes property in the possession or under the control of the Crown and property which has been unlawfully removed from its possession or control;

"designated services" means services designated under subsection (1) of section 1 of the Dockyard Services Act 1986;

"dockyard contractor" means a company which is a dockyard contractor as defined by subsection (13) of that section;

"dockyard property" means property which—

(*a*) belongs to a dockyard contractor, is in its possession or under its control or has been unlawfully removed from its possession or control; and

(*b*) is (or was immediately before its removal) used to any extent for the purpose of providing designated services or otherwise for naval, military or air force purposes;

"headquarters", "defence organisation" and "visiting force" mean respectively a headquarters, defence organisation or visiting force to which the Visiting Forces and International Headquarters (Application of Law) Order 1965, or any order replacing that order, applies;

"international defence property" means property which belongs to, is in the possession or under the control of or has been unlawfully removed from the possession or control of a headquarters, a defence organisation or the service authorities of a visiting force;

"ordnance company" means a company in which there is for the time being vested any property, right or liability which has at some time been the subject of a transfer by virtue of a provision made under section 1(1)(*a*) of the Ordnance Factories and Military Services Act 1984;

"ordnance property" means property which—

(*a*) belongs to an ordnance company, is in its possession or under its control or has been unlawfully removed from its possession or control; and

(*b*) is (or was immediately before its removal) used to any extent for the purpose of, or for purposes including, the making or development of ordnance or otherwise for naval, military or air force purposes;

"service authorities" means naval, military or air force authorities; and

"vessel" includes any ship or boat or any other description of vessel used in navigation.

[Ministry of Defence Police Act 1987, s 2, as amended by the Anti-terrorism, Crime and Security Act 2001, Sch 8 and the Energy Act 2004, Schs 14 and 23.]

---

1. The places to which subsection (2) applies shall also include land, vehicles, vessels, aircraft and hovercraft which are (*a*) in the possession, under the control or used for the purposes of a contractor within the meaning of the Atomic Weapons Establishment Act 1991, s 1(4); and (*b*) used for the purposes of, or for purposes which include, carrying on designated activities within the meaning of s 1, Ministry of Defence Police Act 1987 (Atomic Weapons Establishment Act 1991, s 4(1)).

2. The reference in subsection (3) to Crown property includes a reference to property which (*a*) belongs to a contractor, within the meaning of s 1(4) of the Atomic Weapons Establishment Act 1991, is in its possession or under its control or

has been unlawfully removed from its possession or control; and (*b*) is (or was immediately before its removal) used to any extent for the purpose of carrying on designated activities within the meaning of s 1, Ministry of Defence Police Act 1987 (Atomic Weapons Establishment Act 1991, s 4).

8–23801A **2A. Provision of assistance to other forces.** (1) The Chief Constable of the Ministry of Defence Police may, on the application of the chief officer of any relevant force, provide constables or other assistance for the purpose of enabling that force to meet any special demand on its resources.

(2) Where a member of the Ministry of Defence Police is provided for the assistance of a relevant force under this section—

(*a*) he shall be under the direction and control of the chief officer of that force; and
(*b*) he shall have the same powers and privileges as a member of that force.

(3) Constables are not to be regarded as provided for the assistance of a relevant force under this section in a case where assistance is provided under section 2 above.

(4) In this section—

"British Transport Police Force" has the same meaning as in section 2 above;
"chief officer" means—

(*a*) the chief officer of the police force for any police area;
(*b*) the Chief Constable of the Police Service of Northern Ireland;
(*c*) the Chief Constable of the British Transport Police Force; or
(*d*) the Chief Constable of the Civil Nuclear Constabulary

"relevant force" means—

(*a*) the police force for any police area;
(*b*) the Police Service of Northern Ireland;
(*c*) the British Transport Police Force; or
(*d*) the Civil Nuclear Constabulary

[Ministry of Defence Police Act 1987, s 2A, as inserted by the Anti-Terrorism, Crime and Security Act 2001, s 99 and amended by the Energy Act 2004, Schs 14 and 23.]

8–23801B **2B. Constables serving with other forces.** (1) This section applies where a member of the Ministry of Defence Police serves with a relevant force under arrangements made between the chief officer of that force and the chief constable of the Ministry of Defence Police.

(2) The member of the Ministry of Defence Police—

(*a*) shall be under the direction and control of the chief officer of the relevant force; and
(*b*) shall have the same powers and privileges as a member of that force.

(3) In this section—

"British Transport Police Force" has the same meaning as in section 2 above;
"chief officer" means—

(*a*) any chief officer of police of a police force for a police area in Great Britain;
(*b*) the chief constable of the Police Service of Northern Ireland;
(*c*) *repealed*;
(*d*) *repealed*;
(*e*) the chief constable of the British Transport Police Force; or
(*f*) the chief constable of the Civil Nuclear Constabulary;

"relevant force" means—

(*a*) any police force for a police area in Great Britain;
(*b*) the Police Service of Northern Ireland;
(*c*) *repealed*;
(*d*) *repealed*;
(*e*) the British Transport Police Force; or
(*f*) Civil Nuclear Constabulary

[Ministry of Defence Police Act 1987, s 2B, as inserted by the Police Reform Act 2002, s 78 and amended by the Energy Act 2004, Schs 14 and 23.]

8–23802 **3–4.** *Defence Police Federation; representation at disciplinary hearings.*

8–23803 **5. Impersonation etc.** (1) Any person who with intent to deceive impersonates a member of the Ministry of Defence Police, or makes any statement or does any act calculated falsely to suggest that he is such a member, shall be guilty of an offence and liable on summary conviction to imprisonment for a term not exceeding **six months** or to a fine not exceeding **level 5** on the standard scale, or to both.

(2) Any person who, not being a member of the Ministry of Defence Police, wears any article of the uniform of the Ministry of Defence Police in circumstances where it gives him an appearance so nearly resembling that of a member as to be calculated to deceive shall be guilty of an offence and liable on summary conviction to a fine not exceeding **level 3** on the standard scale.

(3) Any person who, not being a member of the Ministry of Defence Police, has in his possession any article of uniform of the Ministry of Defence Police shall, unless he proves that he obtained possession of that article lawfully and has possession of it for a lawful purpose, be guilty of an offence and liable on summary conviction to a fine not exceeding **level 1** on the standard scale.

(4) In this section "article of uniform" means any article of uniform or any distinctive badge or mark or document of identification usually issued to members of the Ministry of Defence Police, or any thing having the appearance of such an article, badge, mark or document.

[Ministry of Defence Police Act 1987, s 5.]

8–23804 6. Causing disaffection. Any person who causes, or attempts to cause, or does any act calculated to cause, disaffection amongst the members of the Ministry of Defence Police, or induces or attempts to induce, or does any act calculated to induce, any member of the Ministry of Defence Police to withhold his services or to commit breaches of discipline, shall be guilty of an offence and liable[1]—

(*a*) on summary conviction, to imprisonment for a term not exceeding **six months** or to a fine not exceeding the **statutory maximum**, or to **both;**

(*b*) on conviction on indictment, to imprisonment for a term not exceeding **two years** or to a **fine** or to **both**.

[Ministry of Defence Police Act 1987, s 6.]

1. For procedure in respect of this offence which is triable either way, see the Magistrates' Courts Act 1980, ss 17A–21, in PART I: MAGISTRATES' COURTS, PROCEDURE, ante.

8–23804A 6A. Causing disaffection. Any power of the Secretary of State under this Act to make regulations shall include power to make different provision for different purposes.

[Ministry of Defence Police Act 1987, s 6A as inserted by the Police Reform Act 2002, s 79.]

8–23805 7–8. *Consequential amendments and repeals; short title, commencement and extent.*

Police Act 1996[1]

(1996 c 16)

PART I[2]

ORGANISATION OF POLICE FORCES

Police areas

8–23806 1. Police areas. (1) England and Wales shall be divided into police areas.

(2) The police areas referred to in subsection (1) shall be—

(*a*) those listed in Schedule 1 (subject to any amendment made to that Schedule by an order under section 32 below, section 58 of the Local Government Act 1972, or section 17 of the Local Government Act 1992),

(*b*) the metropolitan police district, and

(*c*) the City of London police area.

(3) References in Schedule 1 to any local government area are to that area as it is for the time being.

[Police Act 1996, s 1, as amended by the Greater London Authority Act 1999, Schs 27 and 34.]

1. The Police Act 1996 shall come into force in accordance with the provisions of s 104, post. All the provisions reproduced here are in force.
2. Part I comprises ss 1–35.

Forces outside London

8–23807 2. Maintenance of police forces. A police force shall be maintained for every police area for the time being listed in Schedule 1.

[Police Act 1996, s 2.]

8–23808 3. Establishment of police authorities. (1) There shall be a police authority for every police area for the time being listed in Schedule 1.

(2) A police authority established under this section for any area shall be a body corporate to be known by the name of the area with the addition of the words "Police Authority".

[Police Act 1996, s 3.]

8–23809 4. Membership of police authorities etc. (1) Subject to subsection (2), each police authority established under section 3 shall consist of seventeen members.

(2) The Secretary of State may by order provide in relation to a police authority specified in the order that the number of its members shall be a specified odd number greater than seventeen.

(3) A statutory instrument containing an order made under subsection (2) shall be laid before Parliament after being made.

(4) Schedules 2 and 3 shall have effect in relation to police authorities established under section 3 and the appointment of their members.

[Police Act 1996, s 4.]

8–23810 **5. Reductions in size of police authorities.** (1) This section applies to any order under subsection 4(2) which varies or revokes an earlier order so as to reduce the number of a police authority's members.

(2) Before making an order to which this section applies, the Secretary of State shall consult—

(*a*) the authority,

(*b*) the councils which are relevant councils in relation to the authority for the purposes of Schedule 2, and

(*c*) any selection panel, constituted under regulations made in accordance with section 29(2) of the Justices of the Peace Act 1997, which is responsible, or is represented on a joint committee which is responsible, for the appointment of members of the authority.

(3) An order to which this section applies may include provision as to the termination of the appointment of the existing members of the authority and the making of new appointments or re-appointments.

[Police Act 1996, s 5 as amended by the Justices of the Peace Act 1997, Sch 5.]

8–23810A **5A. Maintenance of the metropolitan police force.** A police force shall be maintained for the metropolitan police district.

[Police Act 1996, s 5A, as inserted by the Greater London Authority Act 1999, s 310(1).]

8–23810B **5B. Establishment of the Metropolitan Police Authority.** (1) There shall be a police authority for the metropolitan police district.

(2) The police authority established under this section shall be a body corporate to be known as the Metropolitan Police Authority.

[Police Act 1996, s 5B, as inserted by the Greater London Authority Act 1999, s 310(1).]

8–23810C **5C. Membership etc of the Metropolitan Police Authority.** (1) The Metropolitan Police Authority shall consist of twenty-three members (subject to subsection (2)).

(2) The Secretary of State may by order provide that the number of members of the Metropolitan Police Authority shall be a specified odd number not less than seventeen.

(3) Before making an order under subsection (2) which reduces the number of members of the Metropolitan Police Authority, the Secretary of State shall consult—

(*a*) the Greater London Authority;

(*b*) the Metropolitan Police Authority; and

(*c*) the person or body responsible for the appointment of members of the Greater London Magistrates' Courts Authority under regulations made under section 30B of the Justices of the Peace Act 1997 (which, by virtue of paragraph 5(*b*) of Schedule 2A to this Act, appoints magistrates to be members of the Metropolitan Police Authority).

(4) An order under subsection (2) which reduces the number of members of the Metropolitan Police Authority may include provision as to the termination of the appointment of the existing members of the Metropolitan Police Authority and the making of new appointments or re-appointments.

(5) A statutory instrument containing an order under subsection (2) shall be laid before Parliament after being made.

(6) Schedules 2A and 3 shall have effect in relation to the Metropolitan Police Authority and the appointment of its members.]

[Police Act 1996, s 5C, as inserted by the Greater London Authority Act 1999, s 310(1).]

8–23811 **6. General functions of police authorities.** (1) Every police authority established under section 3 shall secure the maintenance of an efficient and effective police force for its area[1].

(2) In discharging its functions, every police authority established under section 3 shall have regard to—

(*a*) any objectives determined by the Secretary of State under section 37,

(*b*) any objectives determined by the authority under section 7,

(*c*) any performance targets established by the authority, whether in compliance with a direction under section 38 or otherwise, and

(*d*) any local policing plan issued by the authority under section 8.

(3) In discharging any function to which a code of practice issued under section 39 relates, a police authority established under section 3 shall have regard to the code.

(4) A police authority shall comply with any direction given to it by the Secretary of State under section 38 or 40.

(5) This section shall apply in relation to the Metropolitan Police Authority as it applies in relation to a police authority established under section 3.

[Police Act 1996, s 6, as amended by the Greater London Authority Act 1999, s 311.]

1. Police constables are not servants or agents of the police authority but public servants and officers of the Crown (*Fisher v Oldham Corpn* [1930] 2 KB 364, 94 JP 132). The police authority does not have a monopoly power to supply equipment, the Secretary of State retains the prerogative power to keep the peace (*R v Secretary of State for the Home Department, ex p Northumbria Police Authority* [1989] QB 26, [1988] 1 All ER 556, CA) (supply of riot equipment to Chief Constable without consent of the local police authority).

8–23811A **6. General functions of police authorities.** (1) Every police authority maintaining a police force for a police area in England and Wales shall, before the beginning of every relevant three-year period, issue a plan ("a three-year strategy plan") which sets out the authority's medium and long term strategies for the policing of that area during that period.

(2) Before a three-year strategy plan for any period is issued by a police authority, a draft of a plan setting out medium and long term strategies for the policing of the authority's area during that period must have been—

(*a*) prepared by the chief officer of police of the police force maintained by that authority; and

(*b*) submitted by him to the police authority for its consideration.

(3) In preparing the draft plan, the chief officer of police of a police force shall have regard to the views, obtained in accordance with arrangements under section 96, of people in the police area in question.

(4) A police authority which has issued a three-year strategy plan for any period may modify that plan at any time during that period.

(5) It shall be the duty, in issuing, preparing or modifying a three-year strategy plan or a draft of such a plan, of every police authority or chief officer of police to have regard to the National Policing Plan in force at that time.

(6) The Secretary of State—

(*a*) shall issue guidance to police authorities and chief officers of police as to the matters to be contained in any three-year strategy plan, and as to the form to be taken by any such plan; and

(*b*) may from time to time revise and modify that guidance;

and it shall be the duty of every police authority and chief officer of police to take account of any guidance under this subsection when issuing, preparing or modifying any such plan or any draft plan prepared for the purposes of subsection (2).

(7) Before issuing or revising any guidance under subsection (6) the Secretary of State shall consult with—

(*a*) persons whom he considers to represent the interests of police authorities;

(*b*) persons whom he considers to represent the interests of chief officers of police; and

(*c*) such other persons as he thinks fit.

(8) A police authority which is proposing to issue or modify any plan under this section shall submit that plan, or the modifications, to the Secretary of State.

(9) Where a police authority issues a three-year strategy plan or modifies such a plan, it shall—

(*a*) send a copy of the plan or the modified plan to the Secretary of State; and

(*b*) cause the plan or modified plan to be published;

and the copy of any modified plan sent to the Secretary of State and the publication of any modified plan must show the modifications, or be accompanied by or published with a document which sets them out or describes them.

(10) If the Secretary of State considers that there are grounds for thinking that—

(*a*) a police authority's three-year strategy plan, or

(*b*) any proposals by a police authority for such a plan, or for the modification of such a plan,

may not be consistent with any National Policing Plan applicable to a financial year wholly or partly comprised in the period to which the strategy plan applies, he shall, before informing the police authority of his conclusions on whether or not it is in fact so inconsistent, consult with the persons mentioned in subsection (11).

(11) Those persons are—

(*a*) the police authority in question;

(*b*) the chief officer of police of the police force maintained by that authority;

(*c*) persons whom the Secretary of State considers to represent the interests of police authorities; and

(*d*) persons whom the Secretary of State considers to represent the interests of chief officers of police.

(12) Before a police authority—

(*a*) issues a three-year strategy plan that differs in any material respect from the draft submitted to it by the chief officer of police of the force maintained by that authority, or

(*b*) modifies its three-year strategy plan,

it shall consult with that chief officer.

(13) Any best value performance plan prepared by a police authority under section 6 of the Local Government Act 1999 (c 27) for any financial year must be consistent with any three-year strategy plan which sets out the authority's current strategies for policing its area during any period which includes the whole or any part of that financial year.

(14) The Secretary of State may by regulations make provision for—

(*a*) the procedure to be followed on the submission to him of any plan or modifications for the purposes of this section; and

(*b*) the periods which are to constitute relevant three-year periods for the purposes of this section;

and those regulations may provide for a period of less than three years to be the first period treated as a relevant three-year period for the purposes of this section.

(15) A statutory instrument containing regulations under this section shall be subject to annulment in pursuance of a resolution of either House of Parliament.

[Police Act 1996, s 6A, as inserted by the Police Reform Act 2002, s 92(1).]

8–23812 7–9. *Duty of Police Authority to determine local policing objectives, issue local policing plan, issue local policing summary and issue annual report*

8–23812A 9A–9H. *Commissioners, Commanders and other members of the Police of the Metropolis*

8–23813 20. *Questions on police matters at council meetings*

General provisions

8–23814 23–25. *Collaboration agreements, aid of one police force by another and provision of special services*

8–23815 29. Attestation of constables[1]**.** Every member of a police force maintained for a police area and every special constable appointed for a police area shall, on appointment, be attested as a constable by making a declaration in the form set out in Schedule 4—

(*a*) (*Repealed*),

(*b*) before a justice of the peace having jurisdiction within the police area.

[Police Act 1996, s 29, as amended by the Greater London Authority Act 1999, Schs 27 and 34.]

1. This section applies to a constable or special constable of the British Transport Police Force with the omission of the words in paragraph (*b*) "having jurisdiction within the police area" (Railways and Transport Safety Act 2003, ss 24 and 25).

8–23816 30. Jurisdiction of constables. (1) A member of a police force shall have all the powers and privileges of a constable throughout England and Wales and the adjacent United Kingdom waters.

(2) A special constable shall have all the powers and privileges of a constable in the police area for which he is appointed[1] and, where the boundary of that area includes the coast, in the adjacent United Kingdom waters.

(3) Without prejudice to subsection (2), a special constable appointed for a police area shall have all the powers and privileges of a constable—

(*a*) in the case of a special constable appointed for a police area other than the City of London police area, in any other police area which is contiguous to his own police area; and

(*b*) in the case of a special constable appointed for the City of London police area, in the metropolitan police district and in any police area which is contiguous to that district.

(3A) A member of the British Transport Police Force who is for the time being required by virtue of section 23 or 24 to serve with a police force maintained by a police authority shall have all the powers and privileges of a member of that police force.

(4) A special constable who is for the time being required by virtue of section 23 or 24[2] to serve with another police force shall have all the powers and privileges of a constable in any area in which special constables appointed for the area for which that force is maintained have those powers and privileges under this section.

(5) In this section—

"powers" includes powers under any enactment, whenever passed or made;

"United Kingdom waters" means the sea and other waters within the seaward limits of the territorial sea;

and this section, so far as it relates to powers under any enactment, makes them exercisable throughout the United Kingdom waters whether or not the enactment applies to those waters apart from this provision.

(6) This section is without prejudice to—

(*a*) sections 98 and 99 below[3]; and

(*b*) to any other enactment conferring powers on constables for particular purposes.

[Police Act 1996, s 30, as amended by the Anti-terrorism, Crime and Security Act 2001, Sch 7.]

1. By ss 1 and 2 of the Metropolitan Police Act 1860 (as amended by the Defence (Transfer of Functions) (No 1) Order 1964) constables of the Metropolitan Police Force could be employed in HM yards (which by s 6 of the Air Force (Application of Enactments) (No 2) Order 1918, includes steam factory yards and aircraft factories) or at HM principal military or air force stations in England and Wales and within 15 miles of such yards or stations. Any two justices may appoint persons nominated by the Minister of Aviation to be special constables on any premises vested in the Minister or under his control (Civil Aviation Act 1982, s 57). Any two justices may appoint persons nominated by the Defence Council, who will exclusively control them with power to suspend their employment, to be special constables within the yards and stations and limits within which constables of the Metropolitan Police Force may by the Metropolitan Police Act 1860, both as originally enacted and as applied to the Air Force, be employed (Special Constables Act 1923, s 3 (as amended)). The Metropolitan Police Act 1860 is repealed by the Police Act 1964, Sch 10, but not so far as it is applied by the Special Constables Act 1923 (for transitional provisions and savings, see Police Act 1996, Sch 8). The power conferred by s 8 of the 1923 Act shall extend to the appointment of persons so nominated to be special constables in, and within 15 miles of, any other premises in Great Britain which are for the time being in the possession or under the control of the Defence Council, the Secretary of State for Defence or the Minister of Aviation, or are for the time being used for or in connection with naval, military or air force purposes, and the said s 3 shall have effect accordingly (Emergency Laws (Miscellaneous Provisions) Act 1947, Sch 2, para 1 (as amended)). These powers are related to the property of service authorities of a visiting force and to persons subject to the service law of any such force by the Visiting Forces and International Headquarters (Application of Law) Order 1965, SI 1965/1536, art 6. The Order extends to the international headquarters and defence organisations specified therein. For application of these provisions to premises in the possession or under the control of the United Kingdom Atomic Energy Authority, see Atomic Energy Authority 1954, Sch 3. As to the effect of change in police authority areas, see the Transfer of Police Officers Order 1974, SI 1974/551.

2. These sections provide for collaboration agreements and mutual aid as between two or more police forces.

3. These sections provide for cross border aid of one police force by another and for jurisdiction of metropolitan police officers on particular duties in Scotland or Northern Ireland. See note to the Magistrates' Courts Act 1980, s 125(2), in PART I: MAGISTRATES' COURTS, PROCEDURE, ante.

PART II[1]

CENTRAL SUPERVISION, DIRECTION AND FACILITIES

Functions of Secretary of State

8–23817 36. General duty of Secretary of State. (1) The Secretary of State shall exercise his powers[2] under the provisions of this Act referred to in subsection (2) in such manner and to such extent as appears to him to be best calculated to promote the efficiency and effectiveness of the police.

(2) The provisions of this Act mentioned in subsection (1) are—

(*a*) Part I;

(*b*) this Part;

(*c*) Part III (other than section 61 and 62);

(*d*) in Chapter II of Part IV, section 85 and Schedule 6; and

(*e*) in Part V, section 95.

[Police Act 1996, s 36.]

1. Part II comprises ss 36–58.

2. These include in respect of police authorities, the setting of objectives, performance targets and directions to take remedial measures after an adverse inspection report, the submissions of reports, the setting of a minimum budget and the issue of a Code of Practice by the Secretary of State; in respect of Chief Constables their retirement in the interest of efficiency or effectiveness and the submission of reports; the provision of criminal statistics; the making of grants for police purposes.

8–23817A 36A. National Policing Plan. (1) It shall be the duty of the Secretary of State, before the beginning of each financial year, to prepare a National Policing Plan for that year.

(2) The Secretary of State shall lay the National Policing Plan for a financial year before Parliament.

(3) Subject to subsection (4), any such plan must be laid before Parliament not later than 30th November in the preceding financial year.

(4) If there are exceptional circumstances, any such plan may be laid before Parliament after the date mentioned in subsection (3); but it must be so laid before the beginning of the financial year to which it relates.

(5) If a plan is laid before Parliament after the date mentioned in subsection (3), the plan must contain a statement of the exceptional circumstances that gave rise to its being so laid.

(6) The National Policing Plan for a financial year—

(*a*) must set out whatever the Secretary of State considers to be the strategic policing priorities generally for the police forces maintained for police areas in England and Wales for the period of three years beginning with that year;

(*b*) must describe what, in relation to that period, the Secretary of State is intending or proposing so far as each of the following is concerned—

(i) the setting of objectives under section 37 and the giving of general directions in relation to any objective so set;

(ii) the specification, under section 4 of the Local Government Act 1999 (c 27) (performance indicators), of performance indicators (within the meaning of that section) for police authorities;

(iii) the making of regulations under the powers conferred by this Act, by Part 4 of the Criminal Justice and Police Act 2001 (c 16) (police training) and by Part 2 of the Police Reform Act 2002 (c 30) (complaints etc);

(iv) the issuing of guidance under any provision of this Act or of Part 2 of the Police Reform Act 2002 (c 30); and

(v) the issuing and revision of codes of practice under this Act and under Chapter 1 of Part 4 of the Police Reform Act 2002 (powers exercisable by civilians);

(*c*) may contain such other information, plans and advice as the Secretary of State considers relevant to the priorities set out in the plan.

(7) Before laying the National Policing Plan for a financial year before Parliament, the Secretary of State shall consult with—

(*a*) persons whom he considers to represent the interests of police authorities;
(*b*) persons whom he considers to represent the interests of chief officers of police; and
(*c*) such other persons as he thinks fit.

(8) In this section—

"financial year" means the period of twelve months ending with 31st March; and
"general direction" means a direction under section 38 establishing performance targets for all police authorities to which section 37 applies.

[Police Act 1996, s 36A as inserted by the Police Reform Act 2002, s 1.]

8–23818 50. *Regulations for police forces*[1].

1. The following regulations have been made: Police (Promotion) Regulations 1996, SI 1996/1685 amended by SI 2002/767, SI 2003/2595 and SI 2005/178; Police (Efficiency) Regulations 1999, SI 1999/732 amended by SI 2000/1549, SI 2001/3888 and SI 2003/528; Police Appeals Tribunal Rules 1999, SI 1999/818 and SI 2003/527 and 2597; Police Regulations 2003, SI 2003/527 amended by SI 2003/2594, SI 2004/3216 and SI 2005/2834; Police (Conduct) Regulations 2004, in this title, post.

8–23819 51. *Regulations for special constables*[1].

1. The Special Constables Regulations 1965, SI 1965/536 amended by SI 1968/899 (revoked), SI 1992/1526 (revoked) and 1641, SI 2002/3180 and SI 2004/645 have been made.

8–23820 52. *Regulations for police cadets*[1].

1. The Police Cadets Regulations 1979, SI 1979/1727 amended by SI 1982/350 and 1487, SI 1983/161, SI 1984/1633, SI 1985/131 and 686, SI 1987/1754, SI 1988/728, 1992/276 and SI 1993/2528 have been made.

8–23821 53. *Regulations as to standard of equipment.*

8–23822 54–56. *Inspectorate of Constabulary.*

8–23823 57. *Secretary of State may provide or contribute to common services to promote the efficiency or effectiveness of the police.*

PART V[1]

MISCELLANEOUS AND GENERAL

Offences

8–23824 89. Assaults on constables[2]**.** (1) Any person who assaults a constable in the execution of his duty[3], or a person assisting a constable in the execution of his duty[4], shall be guilty of an offence and liable on summary conviction to imprisonment for a term not exceeding **six months** or to a fine not exceeding **level 5** on the standard scale, or to **both**.

(2) Any person who resists or wilfully[5] obstructs[6] a constable in the execution of his duty, or a person assisting a constable in the execution of his duty[7], shall be guilty of an offence[8] and liable on summary conviction to imprisonment for a term not exceeding **one month*** or to a fine not exceeding **level 3** on the standard scale, or to **both**.

(3) This section also applies to a constable who is a member of a police force maintained in

Scotland or Northern Ireland when he is executing a warrant, or otherwise acting in England or Wales, by virtue of any enactment conferring powers on him in England and Wales.

(4) In this section references to a person assisting a constable in the execution of his duty include references to any person who is neither a constable nor in the company of a constable but who—

(*a*) is a member of an international joint investigation team that is led by a member of a police force; and

(*b*) is carrying out his functions as a member of that team.

(5) In this section "international joint investigation team" means any investigation team formed in accordance with—

(*a*) any framework decision on joint investigation teams adopted under Article 34 of the Treaty on European Union;

(*b*) the Convention on Mutual Assistance in Criminal Matters between the Member States of the European Union, and the Protocol to that Convention, established in accordance with that Article of that Treaty; or

(*c*) any international agreement to which the United Kingdom is a party and which is specified for the purposes of this section in an order[9] made by the Secretary of State.

(6) A statutory instrument containing an order under subsection (5) shall be subject to annulment in pursuance of a resolution of either House of Parliament.

[Police Act 1996, s 89 as amended by the Police Reform Act 2002, s 104 and the Serious Organised Crime and Police Act 2005, Sch.]

***"51 weeks" substituted by the Criminal Justice Act 2003, Sch 26, from a date to be appointed.**

1. Part V comprises ss 89–106.

2. Subsections (1) and (2) apply in relation to a constable of the British Transport Police (Railways and Transport Safety Act 2003, s 68).

3. It is not always clear how far this duty extends. It is sufficient in the case of all peace officers to prove that they acted in that character, without producing their appointment (*Berryman v Wise* (1791) 4 Term Rep 366); and in *Butler v Ford* (1833) 1 Cr & M 662, the court held that proof of acting was sufficient, although the constable was appointed under a local Act. In order to substantiate an offence of assaulting a police officer in the execution of his duty by a person who had been arrested for obstruction of police officers when engaged in the arrest of a third party, it is necessary for the justices to find that the arrest of the third party was lawful, which it is not open to them to do if they are not told of the reason for the arrest: *Riley v DPP* (1989) 154 JP 453, 91 Cr App Rep 14; followed in *R (on the application of Odewale) v DPP* CO/1381/2000 where it was held that justices were not entitled to infer that a police officer was acting in the course of his duty in carrying out a search pursuant to s 18 of PACE from his bare, albeit unchallenged, assertion in evidence that he was carrying out such a search. (*Riley v DPP* (1989) 154 JP 453, 91 Cr App Rep 14). In *R v Forbes* (1865) 10 Cox CC 362, the defendant was convicted before the Recorder of London for assaulting two police officers who were in plain clothes, although the prisoner contended that he did not know the men were constables. This decision was approved by the Court of Criminal Appeal in *R v Maxwell and Clanchy* (1909) 73 JP 176 (see Treat 31 JP 225). It is not a defence to a charge of assault if the defendant honestly and mistakenly disbelieved the identity of an officer and believed that his actions were justified in self-defence, unless there were reasonable grounds for that belief (*Albert v Lavin* [1982] AC 546, [1981] 1 All ER 628, 145 JP 184, CA; affd [1982] AC 546, [1981] 3 All ER 878, 146 JP 78, HL). In *R v Mark* [1961] Crim LR 173, MAXWELL TURNER, J, ruled that if it were found as a fact that the defendant acted under a genuine belief, honestly and reasonably held, that the constable assaulted was committing a crime or breach of the peace this would be a good defence. In *R v Fennell* [1971] 1 QB 428, [1970] 3 All ER 215, 134 JP 678, the Court of Appeal reserved the question, whether an assault would be justifiable to release another person wrongfully arrested, but held that if the arrest is, in fact, lawful an assault is not justifiable even if it is honestly believed on reasonable grounds that the arrest was unlawful. A person charged in the information with assaulting a constable in the execution of his duty cannot be convicted of a common assault on the hearing of such information (*R v Brickill* (1860) 28 JP 359); but a fresh information may be laid. Where a constable is empowered at common law or by statute to search a person on reasonable suspicion, he acts when so doing in the execution of his duty, and an assault upon him is not excused by the fact that the search does not confirm the reasonable suspicion (*Willey v Peace* [1951] 1 KB 94, [1950] 2 All ER 724, 114 JP 502). A custody sergeant is entitled to remove obstructive or abusive persons from his custody suite and provided that, in the course of that, he uses no more force than is reasonable he is acting in the course of his duty (*R (on the application of Bucher) v DPP* [2003] EWHC 580 (Admin), CO/4484/2002, (2003) 167 JPN 182). Where, however, a constable took hold of a missing 14-year-old girl by her elbow and told her that she had to come with him, he had exceeded his duty; he should have told her that he had spoken to her father, her father wanted her home and he proposed to take her home (*C v DPP* [2003] All ER (D) 37 (Nov), 167 JPN 864).

If a constable apprehends on reasonable grounds that a breach of the peace may be committed, he is not only entitled, but is under a duty, to take reasonable steps to prevent that breach occurring. Provided he honestly and reasonably forms the opinion that there is a real risk of a breach of the peace in the sense that it is in close proximity both in place and time, then the conditions exist for reasonable preventive action. Accordingly, where police officers stopped a convoy of striking miners whom they believed were intending to demonstrate and form a mass picket at one or more of four collieries in the area, it was held that the police officers acted reasonably and in the execution of their duty by preventing the striking miners from passing through the police cordon and, when they did attempt to force their way through the cordon, were justified in arresting them on the ground that if they proceeded it was feared a breach of the peace would occur at one of the collieries (*Moss v McLachlan* (1984) 149 JP 167, [1985] IRLR 76). Officers who have helped a youth leader eject persons from a youth club and who are subsequently assaulted, may be acting in the execution of their duty (*Coffin v Smith* (1980) 71 Cr App Rep 221). Where a police officer genuinely suspects on reasonable grounds that a breach of the peace is likely to occur inside private premises he is entitled to exercise his common law power to arrest for breach of the peace without a warrant (*McConnell v Chief Constable of the Greater Manchester Police* [1990] 1 All ER 423, [1990] 1 WLR 364, CA).

The test of the reasonableness of a constable's action is objective in the sense that it is for the court to decide not whether the view taken by the constable fell within the broad band of rational decisions but whether in the light of what he knew and perceived at the time the court is satisfied that it was reasonable to fear an imminent breach of the peace. Accordingly, although reasonableness of belief is a question for the court, it is to be evaluated without the qualifications of hindsight. The next and critical question for the constable, and in turn for the court, is where the threat is coming from, because it is there that the preventative action must be directed. If there is no real threat, no question of intervention for breach of the peace arises. If the defendant is being so provocative that someone in the crowd, without behaving wholly unreasonably, might be moved to violence, the constable is entitled to ask him to stop and arrest him if he will not. If the threat of disorder or violence is coming from passers-by who are taking that opportunity to react so as to cause trouble, then it is they and not the defendant who should be asked to desist and arrested if they will not (*Redmond-Bate v DPP* (1999) 163 JP 789, [1999] Crim LR 998 – constable held not to be acting in the execution of his duty when he required three women preachers to stop preaching from the steps of a cathedral because some of those in the crowd that had gathered were showing hostility towards the preachers and he feared a breach of the peace).

A constable is not acting in the execution of his duty if he commits an illegal act, for example when trying to restrain a person using force to resist an unlawful search (see *McBean v Parker* (1983) 147 JP 205, [1983] Crim LR 399). But not every trivial interference with a citizen's liberties will take a matter outside an officer's duty (*Donnelly v Jackman* [1970] 1 All ER 987, [1970] 1 WLR 562, 134 JP 352; *Bentley v Brudzinski* (1982) 75 Cr App Rep 217, [1982] Crim LR 825; *Weight v Long* [1986] Crim LR 746). A police officer who took hold of a man's arm, not intending to detain or arrest him but in order to draw his attention to the content of what was being said to him was held to be acting within the execution of his duty (*Mepstead v DPP* (1995) 160 JP 475). A person might be interfering with the exercise of a power of entry without physically impeding an officer; therefore, where police officers responded to a 999 call that had been cut off before it had ended, and found the defendant outside the address shouting and banging the door, and he refused to move away from the door, the officer was acting in the execution of his duty when he took the defendant by the arm, not intending to arrest him but to lead him away, and the defendant's violent reaction to that made out a prima facie case of police assault: *Smith v DPP* [2001] EWHC Admin 55, [2001] Crim LR 735, 165 JP 432, DC. A police officer who detains a person against their will in the honest and reasonable, but mistaken, belief that the person has already been arrested by another officer, is not acting in the execution of his duty (*Kerr v DPP* (1994) 158 JP 1048).

When a constable enters private premises found insecure at night in order to protect private property therein, he is not acting in the execution of his duty (*Great Central Rly Co v Bates* [1921] 3 KB 578; as explained by DU PARCQ, J, in *Davis v Lisle*, infra). Nor when he is assaulted after being requested by the occupier to leave his garage that he has entered without a warrant in order to make inquiries; but if the assault occurred when he is acting on a request to leave the premises or while he was where he was entitled to be by implied licence, eg, in the pathway leading to the door of the premises, an offence would be committed (*Davis v Lisle* [1936] 2 KB 434, [1936] 2 All ER 213, 100 JP 280; *Robson v Hallett* [1967] 2 QB 939, [1967] 2 All ER 407, 131 JP 333). A police officer is entitled to remain on premises to prevent a breach of the peace even though he is there as a trespasser. Where an officer visited a house and told one of the occupiers (D) that he had come to speak to a member of the household (S) and the officer was allowed entry by D, and the officer then told S that he was under arrest, the justices were entitled to conclude that D had given informed consent to the officer to enter; the officer had not acted covertly and, given the family's previous dealings with the police, it would have been obvious why the officer wanted to speak to S: *Hobson v Chief Constable of Cheshire Constabulary* [2003] EWHC 3011 (Admin), (2003) 168 JP 111. The officer is not obliged to nullify his trespass by leaving the premises before returning to deal with the breach of the peace (*Lamb v DPP* (1989) 154 JP 381). The activation of a burglar alarm in a police station gives a constable an implied authority to enter the premises to investigate the matter, and having entered as a licensee, a reasonable time must be allowed for investigation before the licence is revoked (*Kay v Hibbert* [1977] Crim LR 226). In *Great Central Rly Co v Bates*, supra, ATKIN, L J, said: "It appears to be very important that it should be established that nobody has a right to enter premises except strictly in accordance with authority." It is the duty of a constable to stop a breach of the peace and to take the necessary steps to prevent one that he reasonably apprehends is likely to take place. Accordingly, if he reasonably apprehends that a breach of the peace in the vicinity will be caused by the holding of a public meeting in a street, he is acting in the execution of his duty in requesting the promoter to desist and in taking all requisite steps to stop the meeting (*Duncan v Jones* [1936] 1 KB 218, 99 JP 399; See also *Thomas v Sawkins* [1935] 2 KB 249, [1935] All ER Rep 655, 99 JP 295; cf *Davies v Griffiths* [1937] 2 All ER 671, 101 JP 247). The Sessional Orders of the House of Commons requiring metropolitan police constables to prevent obstruction of streets leading to that House are binding on them, and therefore those constables are in the execution of their duty when taking steps to prevent that obstruction (*Pankhurst v Jarvis* (1910) 74 JP 64; *Despard v Wilcox* (1910) 74 JP 115).

Powers to stop and search, enter premises, arrest etc are now extensively defined by the Police and Criminal Evidence Act 1984. See generally paras **1–170** to **1–190**, ante, PART I: MAGISTRATES' COURTS, PROCEDURE.

4. Where a constable, acting in the execution of his duty by questioning the defendant, goes outside his duty by catching hold of that person to detain him, the defence of justification of self-defence to an offence under this section will succeed if the defendant did not use unreasonable force to resist the detention (*Kenlin v Gardiner* [1967] 2 QB 510, [1966] 3 All ER 931, 131 JP 91). The fact that a defendant mistakenly believes he is being arrested when in fact he is not and the restraint is unlawful, does not impact on his entitlement to resist such unlawful restraint (*R v McKoy* (2002) Times, 17 June, CA).

5. A person wilfully obstructs a police constable in the execution of his duty if he deliberately does an act which, though not necessarily "aimed at" or "hostile to" the police, in fact prevents a constable from carrying out his duty or makes it more difficult for him to do so, and if he knows and intends (whether or not that is his predominant intention) that his conduct will have that effect; the motive with which the act is committed is irrelevant unless it constitutes a lawful excuse for the obstruction (*Lewis v Cox* [1985] QB 509, [1984] 3 All ER 672, 148 JP 601). It is immaterial that the defendant does not appreciate that his action amounted to obstruction (*Moore v Green* [1983] 1 All ER 663). A person cannot obstruct a police officer in the execution of his duty when he reasonably believes that he is not a police officer (*Ostler v Elliott* [1980] Crim LR 584).

6. A person who simply gave drivers of motor cars notice of a "police trap" was held not guilty of obstruction under an enactment replaced by this sub-section (*Bastable v Little* [1907] 1 KB 59, 71 JP 52). The obstruction, however, is not limited to physical obstruction, so where cars when warned of a police trap are being driven at an illegal speed, the person so warning may be convicted of obstruction (*Betts v Stevens* [1910] 1 KB 1, 73 JP 486; *Bastable v Little*, supra distinguished). But see *Green v Moore* [1982] 1 All ER 428, 146 JP 142, where the Divisional Court criticised the decision in *Bastable v Little*, supra, and expressed the view that it should be strictly confined to its own facts. In *Green v Moore*, supra, the court was unable to find any distinction between a warning given in order that the commission of a crime might be suspended whilst there is a danger of detection and one which is given in order that the commission of a crime may be postponed until after the danger of detection has passed. In *R (on the application of DPP) v Glendinning* [2005] EWHC Admin 2333, (2005) 169 JP 649, however, it was re-affirmed that a conviction for obstruction required evidence that there were vehicles that were speeding or were likely to speed at the location of the speed trap. A person's mere refusal to answer a constable's questions which, in the circumstances, he was not legally obliged to answer, is not caught by the section (*Rice v Connolly* [1966] 2 QB 414, [1966] 2 All ER 649, 130 JP 322), but in *Ricketts v Cox* (1981) 74 Cr App Rep 298, [1982] Crim LR 184, it was held that a defendant who was abusive, unco-operative and positively hostile to police officers, using obscene language calculated to provoke and antagonise the officers, amounted to obstruction. While it is lawful for a third party to advise a suspect of his right not to answer questions put to him by a police officer, if the third party by his abusive, persistent and unruly behaviour, acts in a way that goes well beyond the exercise of his legal rights and prevents communication between the officer and the suspect, or makes it more difficult, he will be guilty of obstructing the police;

see *Green v DPP* (1991) 155 JP 816, DC. In *Ingleton v Dibble* [1972] 1 QB 480, [1972] 1 All ER 275, 136 JP 155, it was held that there was a distinction between a refusal to act (as in *Rice v Connolly*, supra) and the doing of some positive act, and that it was not necessary to show, where the obstruction consists of a positive act, that it must be unlawful independently. It was held that the driver of a motor car who drank whisky after being asked to take a breath test with the object and effect of frustrating the procedure under ss 2 and 3 of the Road Safety Act 1967 was guilty of obstructing the police, and in *R v Britton* [1973] Crim LR 375 a similar action with a bottle of beer led to a conviction for the common law misdemeanour of attempting to defeat the due course of justice. A private citizen can never have a lawful excuse for interfering with an arrest by a police officer which is lawful (*Hills v Ellis* [1983] QB 680, [1983] 1 All ER 667).

A person who shouted, outside a public house, outside "permitted hours", that the police were waiting to enter, was rightly convicted (*Hinchliffe v Sheldon* [1955] 3 All ER 406, 120 JP 13). Failure to accord entry to police officers acting under s 4 of the Road Traffic Act 1988 may be a wilful obstruction (*Lunt v DPP* [1993] Crim LR 534). Persons waiting outside the residence of the Prime Minister to present a petition, and refusing to go away when requested by the police, were held rightly convicted under an enactment replaced by this subsection (*Despard v Wilcox* (1910) 74 JP 115; see also *Pankhurst v Jarvis* (1910) 74 JP 64); so also were persons acting as pickets in connection with a trade dispute who refused to move when requested by a police officer who was limiting the number of pickets to what was reasonable because of an anticipated breach of the peace (*Piddington v Bates, Robson v Ribton-Turner* [1960] 3 All ER 660). An offence was committed under this section where an excessive number of pickets carried on a circling manœuvre and obstructed the highway causing vehicles to stop, although there was no anticipated breach of the peace (*Tynan v Balmar* [1967] 1 QB 91, [1966] 2 All ER 133). Striking miners, intending to join a mass picket at a local colliery, who attempted to force their way through a police cordon which had been set up to prevent a breach of the peace occurring at one or more of four collieries, were held to have been properly convicted (*Moss v McLachlan* (1984) 149 JP 167, [1985] IRLR 76). A person shooting by "firing wide" is guilty of resisting or wilfully obstructing a constable in the execution of his duty (*R v Hufflett* (1919) 84 JP 24). A police officer can require other persons to break traffic regulations if it is reasonably necessary to protect life or property; refusal to comply is an obstruction (*Johnson v Phillips* [1975] 3 All ER 682, 140 JP 37). Where the police have removed the driver of a motor car, they have a duty to see that the vehicle is properly looked after; that might be done where the passenger shows the capacity and right to do so but not where he appears unfit. If the passenger then prevents the constable from taking the car he will be guilty of obstruction: *Liepens v Spearman* [1985] Crim LR 229.

7. See note 2, ante.

8. Unless one of the general arrest conditions under s 25 of the Police and Criminal Evidence Act 1984 applies, there is no statutory power of arrest for the offence of obstructing a police officer in the execution of his duties. While there is no common law power to arrest for obstruction per se, there is a common law power to arrest for such an obstruction where its nature was such that it actually caused, or was likely to cause, a breach of the peace, or was calculated to prevent the lawful arrest or detention of another (*Wershof v Metropolitan Police Comr* [1978] 3 All ER 540; *R v Redman* [1994] Crim LR 914).

9. The International Joint Investigation Teams (International Agreement) Order 2004, SI 2004/1127 has been made which specifies the Convention implementing the Schengen Agreement of 14 June 1985.

8–23825 90. Impersonation, etc. (1) Any person who with intent to deceive impersonates a member of a police force[1] or special constable, or makes any statement or does any act calculated falsely to suggest that he is such a member or constable, shall be guilty of an offence and liable on summary conviction to imprisonment for a term not exceeding **six months** or to a fine not exceeding **level 5** on the standard scale, or to **both**.

(2) Any person who, not being a constable, wears any article of police uniform in circumstances where it gives him an appearance so nearly resembling that of a member of a police force[1] as to be calculated to deceive[2] shall be guilty of an offence and liable on summary conviction to a fine not exceeding **level 3** on the standard scale.

(3) Any person who, not being a member of a police force[1] or special constable, has in his possession any article of police uniform shall, unless he proves that he obtained possession of that article lawfully and has possession of it for a lawful purpose, be guilty of an offence and liable on summary conviction to a fine not exceeding **level 1** on the standard scale.

(4) In this section—

(*a*) "article of police uniform" means any article of uniform or any distinctive badge or mark or document of identification usually issued to members of police forces or special constables, or anything having the appearance of such an article, badge, mark or document,

(*aa*) "member of a police force" includes a member of the British Transport Police Force, and

(*b*) "special constable" means a special constable appointed for a police area.

[Police Act 1996, s 90, as amended by the Anti-terrorism, Crime and Security Act 2001, Sch 7.]

1. This includes constables and special constables of the British Transport Police (Railways and Transport Safety Act 2003, s 68).

2. The words "calculated to deceive" mean "likely (or reasonably likely) to deceive" and do not involve that there should be an intention to deceive (*Turner v Shearer* [1973] 1 All ER 397, 137 JP 191).

8–23826 91. Causing disaffection. (1) Any person who causes, or attempts to cause, or does any act calculated to cause, disaffection amongst the members of any police force, or induces or attempts to induce, or does any act calculated to induce, any member of a police force to withhold his services, shall be guilty of an offence and liable[1]—

(*a*) on summary conviction, to imprisonment for a term not exceeding **six months** or to a fine not exceeding the **statutory maximum**, or to **both**;

(*b*) on conviction on indictment, to imprisonment for a term not exceeding **two years** or to a **fine**, or to **both**.

(2) This section applies in the case of—

(*a*) special constables appointed for a police area,

(*b*) members of the Civil Nuclear Constabulary, and

(*c*) members of the British Transport police force,

as it applies in the case of members of a police force.

[Police Act 1996, s 91, as amended by the Anti-terrorism, Crime and Security Act 2001, Sch 7 and the Energy Act 2004, s 68.]

1. For procedure in respect of an offence triable either way, see the Magistrates' Courts Act 1980, ss 17A–21, in PART I: MAGISTRATES' COURTS PROCEDURE, ante.

Supplemental

8–23827 **101. Interpretation.** (1) Except where the context otherwise requires, in this Act—

"British Transport Police Force" means the constables appointed under section 53 of the British Transport Commission Act 1949 (c xxix);

"chief officer of police" means—

(*a*) In relation to a police force maintained under section 2, the chief constable,

(*b*) in relation to the metropolitan police force, the Commissioner of Police of the Metropolis, and

(*c*) in relation to the City of London police force, the Commissioner of Police for the City of London;

"City of London police area" means the City of London as defined for the purposes of the Acts relating to the City of London police force;

"metropolitan police district" means that district as defined in section 76 of the London Government Act 1963;

"police area" means a police area provided for by section 1;

"police authority" means—

(*a*) in relation to a police area listed in Schedule 1, the authority established under section 3,

(*b*) in relation to the metropolitan police district, the Metropolitan Police Authority, and

(*c*) in relation to the City of London police area, the Common Council;

"police force" means a force maintained by a police authority;

"police fund" means—

(*a*) in relation to a force maintained under section 2 or the metropolitan police fund, the fund kept by that force's police authority under section 14,

(*b*) (*Repealed*), and

(*c*) in relation to the City of London police force, the fund out of which the expenses of that force are paid.

(2) In this Act "police purposes", in relation to a police area, includes the purposes of—

(*a*) special constables appointed for that area,

(*b*) police cadets undergoing training with a view to becoming members of the police force maintained for that area, and

(*c*) civilians employed for the purposes of that force or of any such special constables or cadets.

[Police Act 1996, s 101, as amended by the Greater Police Authority Act 1999, s 312 and Sch 34 and the Anti-terrorism, Crime and Security Act 2001, Sch 7.]

8–23828 **102.** *Orders, rules and regulations.*

8–23829 **103.** *Consequential amendments, transitional provisions, repeals, etc.*

8–23830 **104. Commencement.** (1) Except as provided by subsection (2), this Act shall come into force at the end of the period of three months beginning with the day on which it is passed.

(2) The following provisions of this Act—

section 50(3),
Part IV (including Schedules 5 and 6) other than section 88,
paragraphs 43, 45 and 46 of Schedule 7,
paragraph 12 of Schedule 8, and
Part II of Schedule 9,

shall come into force on such day as the Secretary of State may by order[1] appoint.

(3) An order under this section may appoint different days for different purposes or different areas.

(4) The power to make order under this section includes power to make such transitional provisions and savings as appear to the Secretary of State to be necessary or expedient.

(5) Where an order under this section contains provisions made by virtue of subsection (4), the

statutory instrument containing that order shall be subject to annulment in pursuance of a resolution of either House of Parliament.
[Police Act 1996, s 104.]

---

1. These remaining provisions of this Act were brought fully into force on 1 April 1999 by the Police Act 1996 (Commencement and Transitional Provisions) Order 1999, SI 1999/533

8–23831 **105.** *Extent.*

8–23832 **106.** *Citation.*

SCHEDULES

Section 4

SCHEDULE 2

POLICE AUTHORITIES ESTABLISHED UNDER SECTION 3

(*Amended by the Justices of the Peace Act 1997, Sch 5, and the Greater London Authority Act 1999, Schs 27 and 34, the Criminal Justice and Police Act 2001, s 107 and Sch 7 and the Police Reform Act 2002, s 94.*)

Membership of police authorities

8–23833 **1.** (1) Where, by virtue of section 4, a police authority is to consist of seventeen members—

(*a*) nine of those members shall be members of a relevant council appointed under paragraph 2,
(*b*) five shall be persons appointed under paragraph 5, and
(*c*) three shall be magistrates appointed under paragraph 8.

(2) Where, by virtue of an order under subsection (2) of that section, a police authority is to consist of more than seventeen members—

(*a*) a number which is greater by one than the number of members provided for in paragraphs (*b*) and (*c*) below shall be members of a relevant council appointed under paragraph 2,
(*b*) such number as may be prescribed by the order, not exceeding one third of the total membership, shall be persons appointed under paragraph 5, and
(*c*) the remainder shall be magistrates appointed under paragraph 8.

Appointment of members by relevant councils

8–23834 **2.** (1) In the case of a police authority in relation to which there is only one relevant council, the members of the police authority referred to in paragraph 1(1)(*a*) or (2)(*a*) shall be appointed by that council.

(2) In any other case, those members shall be appointed by a joint committee consisting of persons appointed by the relevant councils from among their own members.

8–23835 **3.** The number of members of the joint committee, and the number of those members to be appointed by each relevant council, shall be such as the councils may agree or, in the absence of agreement, as may be determined by the Secretary of State.

8–23836 **4.** (1) A council or joint committee shall exercise its power to appoint members of a police authority under paragraph 2 so as to ensure that, so far as practicable, in the case of the members for whose appointment it is responsible, the proportion who are members of any given party—

(*a*) where it is a council that is responsible for their appointment, is the same as the proportion of the members of the council who are members of that party; and
(*b*) where it is a joint committee that is so responsible, is the same as the proportion of the members of the relevant councils taken as a whole who are members of that party.

(2) (*Repealed*).

Appointment of independent members

8–23837 **5.** The members of a police authority referred to in paragraph 1(1)(*b*) or (2)(*b*) shall be appointed—

(*a*) by the members of the police authority appointed under paragraph 2 or 8,
(*b*) from among persons on a short-list prepared by the Secretary of State in accordance with Schedule 3.

8–23838 **6.** (1) Every police authority shall arrange for a notice stating—

(*a*) the name of each of its members appointed under paragraph 5, and
(*b*) such other information relating to him as the authority considers appropriate,

to be published in such manner as appears to it to be appropriate.

(2) A police authority shall send to the Secretary of State a copy of any notice which it has arranged to be published under sub-paragraph (1).

Appointment of magistrates

8–23839 **7.** The members of a police authority referred to in paragraph 1(1)(*c*) or (2)(*c*)—

(*a*) must be magistrates for an area all or part of which constitutes or forms part of the authority's area, and
(*b*) shall be appointed in accordance with paragraph 8;

and in that paragraph references to a panel are references to a selection panel constituted under regulations made in accordance with section 29(2) of the Justices of the Peace Act 1997.

8–23840 **8.** (1) Where there is a panel for an area which constitutes or includes the police authority's area, that panel shall make the appointment.

(2) Where the area of more than one panel falls wholly or partly within the police authority's area, the appointment shall be made by a joint committee consisting of representatives from the panels concerned.

(3) The number of members of a joint committee, and the number of those members to be appointed by each panel, shall be such as the panels may agree or, in the absence of agreement, as may be determined by the Lord Chancellor.

Chairman

8–23841 **9.** (1) A police authority shall at each annual meeting appoint a chairman from among its members.

(2) The appointment under sub-paragraph (1) shall be the first business transacted at the meeting.

(3) On a casual vacancy occurring in the office of chairman, an appointment to fill the vacancy shall be made—

(*a*) at the next meeting of the authority (other than an extraordinary meeting), or
(*b*) if that meeting is held within fourteen days after the date on which the vacancy occurs and is not an annual meeting, not later than the next following meeting.

Vice-chairmen

8–23841A **9A.** (1) At an annual meeting a police authority may appoint one or more vice-chairmen from among its members.

(2) The making of appointments under sub-paragraph (1) shall be the first business transacted at the meeting after the appointment of the chairman.

(3) Where a vice-chairman ceases to hold office at any time between annual meetings, a police authority may make an appointment to fill the vacancy at any meeting of the authority held more than fourteen days after the occurrence of the vacancy.

(4) Subject to any standing orders made by a police authority, anything authorised or required to be done by, to or before their chairman may be done by, to or before any vice-chairman of the authority.

Disqualification

8–23842 **10.** (*Repealed*).

8–23843 **11.** (1) Subject to sub-paragraphs (3) and (4), a person shall be disqualified for being appointed as or being a member of a police authority if—

(*a*) he holds any paid office or employment appointments to which are or may be made or confirmed by the police authority or any committee or sub-committee of the authority, or by a joint committee on which the authority are represented, or by any person holding any such office or employment;
(*b*) a bankruptcy order has been made against him or his estate has been sequestrated or he has made a composition or arrangement with, or granted a trust deed for, his creditors;
(*c*) he is subject to a disqualification order or disqualification undertaking under the Company Directors Disqualification Act 1986 to a disqualification order under Part II of the Companies (Northern Ireland) Order 1989, or to an order made under section 429(2)(*b*) of the Insolvency Act 1986 (failure to pay under county court administration order); or
(*d*) he has within five years before the date of his appointment or since his appointment been convicted in the United Kingdom, the Channel Islands or the Isle of Man of an offence, and has had passed on him a sentence of imprisonment (whether suspended or not) for a period of not less than three months.

(2) A paid employee of a police authority who is employed under the direction of a joint board, joint authority or joint committee on which the authority is represented and any member of which is appointed on the nomination of some other police authority shall be disqualified for being appointed as or being a member of that other police authority.

(3) Where a person is disqualified under sub-paragraph (1)(*b*) by reason that a bankruptcy order has been made against him or his estate has been sequestrated, the disqualification shall cease—

(*a*) unless the bankruptcy order is previously annulled or the sequestration of his estate is recalled or reduced, on his obtaining a discharge; and
(*b*) if the bankruptcy order is annulled or the sequestration of his estate is recalled or reduced, on the date of that event.

(4) Where a person is disqualified under sub-paragraph (1)(*b*) by reason of his having made a composition or arrangement with, or granted a trust deed for, his creditors and he pays his debts in full, the disqualification shall cease on the date on which the payment is completed, and in any other case it shall cease at the end of the period of five years beginning with the date on which the terms of the deed of composition or arrangement or trust deed are fulfilled.

(5) For the purposes of sub-paragraph (1)(*d*), the date of a conviction shall be taken to be the ordinary date on which the period allowed for making an appeal or application expires or, if an appeal or application is made, the date on which the appeal or application is finally disposed of or abandoned or fails by reason of its non-prosecution.

8–23844 **12.** (*Repealed*).

8–23845 **13.** (1) Without prejudice to paragraph 11, a person shall be disqualified for being appointed as a member of a police authority under paragraph 5 if—

(*a*) he has not yet attained the age of twenty-one years, or

(*b*) neither his principal or only place of work, nor his principal or only place of residence, has been in the area of the authority during the whole of the period of twelve months ending with the day of appointment.

(2) Without prejudice to paragraph 11, a person shall be disqualified for being a member so appointed if, at any time, neither his principal or only place of work, nor his principal or only place of residence, is within that area.

8–23846 **14.** (1) Without prejudice to paragraph 11, a person shall be disqualified for being appointed as a member of a police authority under paragraph 5, and for being a member so appointed, if he is—

(*a*) a member of the council for a county, district, county borough or London borough which is wholly or partly within the area of the police authority;

(*b*) a magistrate eligible for appointment to the police authority under paragraph 8;

(*c*) a member of the selection panel for the police authority's area established under Schedule 3;

(*d*) a member of a police force;

(*e*) an officer or employee of a police authority; or

(*f*) an officer or employee of a relevant council.

(2) A person shall not be regarded for the purposes of sub-paragraph (1)(*f*) as an employee of a relevant council by reason of his holding—

(*a*) the post of head teacher or principal of a school, college or other educational institution or establishment which is maintained or assisted by a local education authority; or

(*b*) any other post as a teacher or lecturer in any such school, college, institution or establishment.

Tenure of office

8–23847 **15.** Subject to the following paragraphs (and to the provisions of any order under section 4(2)) a person shall hold and vacate office as a member of a police authority in accordance with the terms of his appointment.

8–23848 **16.** (1) A person shall be appointed to hold office as a member for—

(*a*) a term of four years, or

(*b*) such shorter term as the body appointing him may determine in any particular case.

(2) A person shall not, by virtue of sub-paragraph (1)(*b*), be appointed under paragraph 5 for a term shorter than four years without the approval of the Secretary of State.

8–23849 **17.** (1) A person may at any time resign his office as a member, or as chairman or vice-chairman, by notice in writing to the police authority.

(2) Where a member appointed under paragraph 5 resigns his office as a member under sub-paragraph (1) of this paragraph, he shall send a copy of the notice to the Secretary of State.

8–23850 **18.** (1) A member of a relevant council appointed to be a member of a police authority under paragraph 2 shall cease to be a member of the authority if he ceases to be a member of the council (and does not on the same day again become a member of the council).

(2) A magistrate appointed to be a member of a police authority under paragraph 8 shall cease to be a member of the authority if he ceases to be a magistrate for an area all or part of which constitutes or forms part of the authority's area.

8–23851 **19.** (1) A police authority may remove a member from office by notice in writing if—

(*a*) he has been absent from meetings of the police authority for a period longer than three consecutive months without the consent of the authority,

(*b*) he has been convicted of a criminal offence (but is not disqualified for being a member under paragraph 11),

(*c*) the police authority is satisfied that the member is incapacitated by physical or mental illness, or

(*d*) the police authority is satisfied that the member is otherwise unable or unfit to discharge his functions as a member.

(2) Where a police authority removes a member under sub-paragraph (1), it shall give notice of that fact—

(*a*) in the case of a member appointed under paragraph 2 or 8, to the body which appointed him, and

(*b*) in the case of a member appointed under paragraph 5, to the Secretary of State.

8–23852 **20.** A council or joint committee may remove from office a member of a police authority appointed by it under paragraph 2 with a view to appointing another in his place if it considers that to do so would further the object provided for by paragraph 4.

8–23853 **21.** If a chairman or vice-chairman of a police authority ceases to be a member, he shall also cease to be chairman or vice-chairman.

Eligibility for re-appointment

8–23854 **22.** A person who ceases to be a member, otherwise than by virtue of paragraph 19, or ceases to be chairman or vice-chairman, may (if otherwise eligible) be re-appointed.

Validity of acts

8–23855 **23.** The acts and proceedings of any person appointed to be a member or chairman or vice-chairman of a police authority and acting in that office shall, notwithstanding his disqualification or want of qualification, be as valid and effectual as if he had been qualified.

24. The proceedings of a police authority shall not be invalidated by a vacancy in the membership of the authority or in the office of chairman, by a vacancy for a vice-chairman or by any defect in the appointment of a person as a member or as chairman or vice-chairman.

Allowances

8–23856 **25.** (1) A police authority may make to its chairman, vice-chairman and other members such payments by way of reimbursement of expenses as the Secretary of State may, with the approval of the Treasury, determine.

(2) Payments made under sub-paragraph (1) may differ according to whether the recipient is a chairman, a vice-chairman or other member or was appointed under paragraph 2, 5 or 8.

Allowances for members etc

8–23856A **25A.** (1) Subject to the following provisions of this paragraph, a police authority may make to its chairman, vice-chairmen and other members such payments by way of reimbursement of expenses and allowances as the authority may determine.

(2) Subject to sub-paragraph (6), no payment shall be made under this paragraph except in accordance with arrangements published by the authority not more than twelve months before the making of the payment.

(3) A police authority may from time to time revise any arrangements made for the purposes of this paragraph; but, no revisions shall take effect until published by the authority.

(4) It shall be the duty of a police authority, when making or revising any arrangements made for the purposes of this paragraph, to have regard to any guidance given by the Secretary of State about the reimbursement of expenses or about the payment of allowances.

(5) Payments made under this paragraph may differ according to whether the recipient is the chairman, a vice chairman or other member or is appointed under paragraph 2, 5 or 8.

(6) The Secretary of State may by regulations impose such limits as may be provided for by or under the regulations on the payments that may be made under this paragraph.

(7) A statutory instrument containing regulations under sub-paragraph (6) shall be subject to annulment in pursuance of a resolution of either House of Parliament.

Members of standards committees

25B. Paragraphs 25 and 25A shall have effect in relation to a police authority as if references to members of the authority included references to persons who are not members of the authority but are members of the authority's standards committee; and the power to make different payments according to the recipient shall include power to make different payments to persons who are not members of the authority but are members of the authority's standards committee.

Interpretation

8–23857 **26.** (1) For the purposes of this Schedule, a council is a "relevant council"[1] in relation to a police authority if—

(*a*) it is the council for a county, district, or county borough which constitutes, or is wholly within, the authority's police area, and

(*b*) in the case of a district council, the district is not in a county having a county council within paragraph (*a*).

(2) (*Repealed*).

27. In this Schedule "magistrate" has the same meaning as in the Justices of the Peace Act 1997.

---

1. Various Police Area and Authority Orders have been made under ss 17 and 26 of the Local Government Act 1992 in consequence of the reorganization of local government which affect the definition of 'relevant council' in relation to their respective Police Authorities.

Section 5C

SCHEDULE 2A

THE METROPOLITAN POLICE AUTHORITY

(*Inserted by the Greater London Authority Act 1999, Sch 26, amended by the Insolvency Act 2000, s 8, the Criminal Justice and Police Act 2001, ss 104 and 107 and Sch 7 and the Police Reform Act 2002, s 94.*)

Membership

8–23857A **1.** (1) Where the Metropolitan Police Authority is to consist of twenty-three members—

(*a*) twelve of those members shall be members of the London Assembly appointed under paragraph 2,

(*b*) seven shall be persons appointed under paragraph 3, and

(*c*) four shall be magistrates appointed under paragraph 5.

(2) Where, by virtue of an order under section 5C(2), the Metropolitan Police Authority is to consist of a number of members other than twenty-three—

(*a*) a number which is greater by one than the number of members provided for in paragraphs (*b*) and (*c*) shall be members of the London Assembly appointed under paragraph 2,

(*b*) such number as may be prescribed by the order, not exceeding one third of the total membership, shall be persons appointed under paragraph 3, and

(*c*) the remainder shall be magistrates appointed under paragraph 5.

Appointment of members by the Mayor

8–23857B **2.** (1) The members of the Metropolitan Police Authority referred to in paragraph 1(1)(*a*) or (2)(*a*) shall be appointed by the Mayor of London in accordance with this paragraph.

(2) One of those members must be the Deputy Mayor, except as provided by paragraphs 9(2)(*b*) and 17(*b*) of Schedule 4 to the Greater London Authority Act 1999 or unless the Deputy Mayor is disqualified for being appointed as or being a member of the Metropolitan Police Authority under paragraph 7 below.

(3) The Mayor (or, where paragraph 9(2)(*b*) or 17(*b*) of Schedule 4 to that Act applies, the Chair of the London Assembly) shall ensure that, so far as practicable, in the case of the members of the Authority who are members of the London Assembly appointed under this paragraph, the proportion who are members of any given party is the same as the proportion of the members of the London Assembly who are members of that party.

Appointment of independent members

8–23857C **3.** (1) The members of the Metropolitan Police Authority referred to in paragraph 1(1)(*b*) or (2)(*b*) shall be appointed in accordance with this paragraph.

(2) One shall be appointed by the Secretary of State.

(3) The remainder shall be appointed—

(*a*) by the members of the Metropolitan Police Authority appointed under paragraph 2 or 5,

(*b*) from among persons on a short-list prepared by the Secretary of State in accordance with Schedule 3.

(4) In the application of Schedule 3 in relation to the appointment of the first members of the Metropolitan Police Authority, the selection panel referred to in paragraph 1(1)(*b*) of that Schedule shall, instead of being constituted in accordance with sub-paragraphs (2) and (3) of that paragraph, be constituted in accordance with sub-paragraph (5) below.

(5) The selection panel shall consist of three members, of whom—

(*a*) one shall be appointed by the Secretary of State;

(*b*) one shall be appointed by the Secretary of State after consultation with persons whom, or organisations which, he considers represent the interests of local government in Greater London; and

(*c*) one shall be appointed by the two members of the panel appointed by virtue of paragraphs (*a*) and (*b*).

(6) Notwithstanding paragraph 3(1A) of Schedule 3, the persons appointed under paragraphs (*b*) and (*c*) of sub-paragraph (5) shall cease to hold office when all the first members of the Metropolitan Police Authority have been appointed (but shall be eligible for further appointment under Schedule 3); but an appointment under paragraph (*a*) of that sub-paragraph shall have effect thereafter as if it had been an appointment under paragraph 1(2)(*b*) of that Schedule.

4. (1) The Metropolitan Police Authority shall arrange for a notice stating—

(*a*) the name of each of its members appointed under paragraph 3(2) or (3), and

(*b*) such other information relating to any such member as the Metropolitan Police Authority considers appropriate,

to be published in such manner as appears to it to be appropriate.

(2) The Metropolitan Police Authority shall send to the Secretary of State a copy of any notice which it has arranged to be published under sub-paragraph (1).

Appointment of magistrates

8–23857D **5.** The members of the Metropolitan Police Authority referred to in paragraph 1(1)(*c*) or (2)(*c*)—

(*a*) must be magistrates for commission areas which are wholly or partly within the metropolitan police district, and

(*b*) shall be appointed by the person or body responsible for the appointment of members of the Greater London Magistrates' Courts Authority under regulations made under section 30B of the Justices of the Peace Act 1997.

Chairman

8–23857E **6.** (1) The Metropolitan Police Authority shall at each annual meeting appoint a chairman from among its members.

(2) The appointment under sub-paragraph (1) shall be the first business transacted at the meeting.

(3) On a casual vacancy occurring in the office of chairman, an appointment to fill the vacancy shall be made—

(*a*) at the next meeting of the Metropolitan Police Authority (other than an extraordinary meeting), or

(*b*) if that meeting is held within fourteen days after the date on which the vacancy occurs and is not an annual meeting, not later than the next following meeting.

Vice-chairmen

8–23857EA **6A.** (1) At an annual meeting the Metropolitan Police Authority may appoint one or more vice-chairmen from among its members.

(2) The making of appointments under sub-paragraph (1) shall be the first business transacted at the meeting after the appointment of the chairman.

(3) Where a vice-chairman ceases to hold office at any time between annual meetings, the Metropolitan Police Authority may make an appointment to fill the vacancy at any meeting of the Authority held more than fourteen days after the occurrence of the vacancy.

(4) Subject to any standing orders made by the Metropolitan Police Authority, anything authorised or required to be done by, to or before their chairman may be done by, to or before any vice-chairman of the authority.]

Disqualification

8–23857F **7.** (1) Subject to sub-paragraphs (3) and (4), a person shall be disqualified for being appointed as or being a member of the Metropolitan Police Authority if—

(*a*) he holds any paid office or employment appointments to which are or may be made or confirmed by the Metropolitan Police Authority or any committee or sub-committee of the Metropolitan Police Authority, or by a joint committee on which the Metropolitan Police Authority is represented, or by a person holding any such office or employment;

(*b*) a bankruptcy order has been made against him, or his estate has been sequestrated or he has made a composition or arrangement with, or granted a trust deed for, his creditors;

(*c*) he is subject to a disqualification order or disqualification undertaking under the Company Directors Disqualification Act 1986 to a disqualification order under Part II of the Companies (Northern Ireland) Order 1989, or to an order made under section 429(2)(*b*) of the Insolvency Act 1986 (failure to pay under county court administration order); or

(*d*) he has within five years before the date of his appointment or since his appointment been convicted in the United Kingdom, the Channel Islands or the Isle of Man of an offence, and has had passed on him a sentence of imprisonment (whether suspended or not) for a period of not less than three months.

(2) A paid employee of a police authority who is employed under the direction of a joint board, joint authority or joint committee—

(*a*) on which that police authority is represented, and

(*b*) any member of which is appointed on the nomination of some other police authority,

shall be disqualified for being appointed as, or being, a member of that other police authority if either of those police authorities is the Metropolitan Police Authority.

(3) Where a person is disqualified under sub-paragraph (1)(*b*) by reason that a bankruptcy order has been made against him or his estate has been sequestrated, the disqualification shall cease—

(*a*) unless the bankruptcy order is previously annulled or the sequestration of his estate is recalled or reduced, on his obtaining a discharge; and

(*b*) if the bankruptcy order is annulled or the sequestration of his estate is recalled or reduced, on the date of that event.

(4) Where a person is disqualified under sub-paragraph (1)(*b*) by reason of his having made a composition or arrangement with, or granted a trust deed for, his creditors and he pays his debts in full, the disqualification shall cease on the date on which the payment is completed, and in any other case it shall cease at the end of the period of five years beginning with the date on which the terms of the deed of composition or arrangement or trust deed are fulfilled.

(5) For the purposes of sub-paragraph (1)(*d*), the date of a conviction shall be taken to be the ordinary date on which the period allowed for making an appeal or application expires or, if an appeal or application is made, the date on which the appeal or application is finally disposed of or abandoned or fails by reason of its non-prosecution.

8. (1) Without prejudice to paragraph 7, a person shall be disqualified for being appointed as a member of the Metropolitan Police Authority under paragraph 3 if—

(*a*) he has not yet attained the age of twenty-one years, or

(*b*) neither his principal or only place of work, nor his principal or only place of residence, has been in the metropolitan police district during the whole of the period of twelve months ending with the day of appointment.

(2) Without prejudice to paragraph 7, a person shall be disqualified for being a member so appointed if, at any time, neither his principal or only place of work, nor his principal or only place of residence, is within the metropolitan police district.

9. (1) Without prejudice to paragraph 7, a person shall be disqualified for being appointed as a member of the Metropolitan Police Authority under paragraph 3, and for being a member so appointed, if he is—

(*a*) a member of a London borough council;

(*b*) the Mayor of London;

(*c*) a member of the London Assembly;

(*d*) a magistrate for a commission area which is wholly or partly within the metropolitan police district;

(*e*) a member of the selection panel for the metropolitan police district established under Schedule 3;

(*f*) a member of a police force;

(*g*) an officer or employee of a police authority; or

(*h*) an officer or employee of the Greater London Authority or of a London borough council.

(2) A person shall not be regarded for the purposes of sub-paragraph (1)(*h*) as an employee of a London borough council by reason of his holding—

(*a*) the post of head teacher or principal of a school, college or other educational institution or establishment which is maintained or assisted by a local education authority; or

(*b*) any other post as a teacher or lecturer in any such school, college, institution or establishment.

Tenure of office

8–23857G **10.** Subject to the following paragraphs (and to the provision of any order under section 5C(2)) a person shall hold and vacate office as a member of the Metropolitan Police Authority in accordance with the terms of his appointment.

11. (1) A person shall be appointed to hold office as a member for—

(*a*) a term of four years, or

(*b*) such shorter term as the person or body appointing him may determine in any particular case.

(2) A person shall not, by virtue of sub-paragraph (1)(*b*), be appointed under paragraph 3(3) for a term shorter than four years without the approval of the Secretary of State.

12. (1) A person may at any time resign his office as a member, or as chairman or vice-chairman, by notice in writing to the Metropolitan Police Authority.

(2) Where a member appointed under paragraph 3 resigns his office as a member under sub-paragraph (1) of this paragraph, he shall send a copy of the notice to the Secretary of State.

13. (1) A member of the London Assembly appointed to be a member of the Metropolitan Police Authority under paragraph 2 shall cease to be a member of the Metropolitan Police Authority if he ceases to be a member of the London Assembly (and does not immediately again become a member of the London Assembly).

(2) The Deputy Mayor appointed to be a member of the Metropolitan Police Authority under paragraph 2 shall cease to be a member of that Authority if he ceases to be Deputy Mayor.

(3) A magistrate appointed to be a member of the Metropolitan Police Authority under paragraph 5 shall cease to be a member of that Authority if he ceases to be one of the magistrates for commission areas which are wholly or partly within the metropolitan police district.

14. (1) The Metropolitan Police Authority may remove a member from office by notice in writing if—

(*a*) he has been absent from meetings of the Metropolitan Police Authority for a period longer than three consecutive months without the consent of the Metropolitan Police Authority,

(*b*) he has been convicted of a criminal offence (but is not disqualified for being a member under paragraph 7),

(*c*) the Metropolitan Police Authority is satisfied that the member is incapacitated by physical or mental illness, or

(*d*) the Metropolitan Police Authority is satisfied that the member is otherwise unable or unfit to discharge his functions as a member.

(2) Where the Metropolitan Police Authority removes a member under sub-paragraph (1), it shall give notice of that fact—

(*a*) in the case of a member appointed under paragraph 2 or 5, to the body or person which appointed him, and

(*b*) in the case of a member appointed under paragraph 3, to the Secretary of State.

15. The Mayor of London may remove from office a member of the Metropolitan Police Authority appointed by him under paragraph 2 with a view to appointing another in his place if he considers that to do so would further the object provided for by paragraph 2(3).

16. If the chairman or vice-chairman of the Metropolitan Police Authority ceases to be a member, he shall also cease to be chairman or vice-chairman.

Eligibility for re-appointment

8–23857H **17.** A person who ceases to be a member, otherwise than by virtue of paragraph 14, or ceases to be chairman or vice-chairman may (if otherwise eligible) be re-appointed.

Validity of acts

8–23857I **18.** The acts and proceedings of any person appointed to be a member or chairman or vice-chairman of the Metropolitan Police Authority and acting in that office shall, notwithstanding his disqualification or want of qualification, be as valid and effectual as if he had been qualified.

19. The proceedings of the Metropolitan Police Authority shall not be invalidated by a vacancy in the membership of the Metropolitan Police Authority or in the office of chairman, by a vacancy for a vice-chairman or by any defect in the appointment of a person as a member or as chairman or vice-chairman.

Allowances

8–23857J **20.** (1) The Metropolitan Police Authority may make to its chairman, vice-chairmen and other members such payments by way of reimbursement of expenses as the Secretary of State may determine.

(2) (*Repealed*).

(3) Payments made under sub-paragraph (1) may differ according to whether the recipient is the chairman, a vice-chairman or one of the other members of the Metropolitan Police Authority or was appointed under paragraph 2, 3 or 5.

Allowances for members etc

8–23857JA **20A.** (1) Subject to the following provisions of this paragraph, the Metropolitan Police Authority may make to its chairman, vice-chairmen and other members such payments by way of reimbursement of expenses and allowances as that Authority may determine.

(2) Subject to sub-paragraphs (6) and (7), no payment shall be made under this paragraph except in accordance with arrangements published by the Metropolitan Police Authority not more than twelve months before the making of the payment.

(3) The Metropolitan Police Authority may from time to time revise any arrangements made for the purposes of this paragraph; but, no revisions shall take effect until published by that Authority.

(4) It shall be the duty of the Metropolitan Police Authority, when making or revising any arrangements made for the purposes of this paragraph, to have regard to any guidance given by the Secretary of State about the reimbursement of expenses or about the payment of allowances.

(5) Payments made under this paragraph may differ according to whether the recipient is the chairman, a vice chairman or one of the other members of the Metropolitan Police Authority, or is appointed under paragraph 3 or 5.

(6) No payment by way of an allowance shall be made under this paragraph to any member of the Metropolitan Police Authority who is also a member of the London Assembly.

(7) The Secretary of State may by regulations impose such limits as may be provided for by or under the regulations on the payments that may be made under this paragraph.

(8) A statutory instrument containing regulations under sub-paragraph (7) shall be subject to annulment in pursuance of a resolution of either House of Parliament.

Members of standards committees

20B. Paragraphs 20 and 20A shall have effect in relation to the Metropolitan Police Authority as if references to the members of that Authority included references to persons who are not members of that Authority but are members of the Authority's standards committee; and the power to make different payments according to the recipient shall include power to make different payments to persons who are not members of that Authority but are members of the Authority's standards committee.

Mayor's functions to be exercised by him personally

8–23857K **21.** Any functions exercisable by the Mayor of London under this Schedule may only be exercised by him personally.

Interpretation

8–23857L **22.** In this Schedule—

"commission area" has the same meaning as in the Justices of the Peace Act 1997;
"magistrate" has the same meaning as in the Justices of the Peace Act 1997.

Section 4

SCHEDULE 3

POLICE AUTHORITIES: SELECTION OF INDEPENDENT MEMBERS

(Amended by the Criminal Justice and Police Act 2001, Sch 7.)

Selection panels

8–23858 **1.** (1) There shall be a selection panel

(*a*) for each police area for the time being listed in Schedule 1; and
(*b*) for the police area constituted by the metropolitan police district.

(2) Each selection panel shall consist of three members, one of whom shall be appointed by each of the following—

(*a*) the designated members of the police authority for the area;
(*b*) the Secretary of State;
(*c*) the two members of the panel appointed by virtue of paragraphs (*a*) and (*b*).

(3) A designated member may be appointed as a member of a selection panel by virtue of paragraph (*a*) (but not paragraph (*b*) or (*c*)) of sub-paragraph (2).

(4) In this Schedule "designated member" means a member appointed under paragraph 2 or 8 of Schedule 2 or paragraph 2 or 5 of Schedule 2A.

8–23859 **2.** A person shall be disqualified for being appointed as or being a member of a selection panel if, by virtue of paragraph 11, 13 or 14(1)(*d*) to (*f*) of Schedule 2 or paragraph 7, 8 or 9(1)(*b*) or (*f*) to (*h*) of Schedule 2A, he is disqualified—

(*a*) for being appointed under paragraph 5 of Schedule 2 or paragraph 3(2) or (3) of Schedule 2A as a member of the police authority for the panel's area, or
(*b*) for being a member so appointed.

8–23860 **3.** (1) A person shall be appointed to hold office as a member of a selection panel for a term of two years,

(1A) (*Repealed*)

(2) A person may at any time resign his office as a member by notice in writing to the persons who under paragraph 1 would be required to appoint his successor.

(3) A person shall not cease to be a member by reason only that any of the persons appointing him cease to hold the positions by virtue of which they appointed him.

8–23861 **4.** A member of a selection panel may be removed from office by notice in writing by the persons who, under paragraph 1, would be required to appoint his successor ("the appointer") if—

(*a*) the member has been absent from two consecutive meetings of the selection panel without the consent of the panel,
(*b*) the member has been convicted of a criminal offence (but is not disqualified for being a member under paragraph 2),
(*c*) the appointer is satisfied that the member is incapacitated by physical or mental illness, or
(*d*) the appointer is satisfied that the member is otherwise unable or unfit to discharge his functions as a member.

8–23862 **5.** A person who ceases to be a member of a selection panel, otherwise than by virtue of paragraph 4, may (if otherwise eligible) be re-appointed.

8–23863 **6.** (1) The acts and proceedings of any person appointed to be a member of a selection panel and acting in that office shall, notwithstanding his disqualification or want of qualification, be as valid and effectual as if he had been qualified.

(2) Subject to the provisions of any regulations made under paragraph 11, the proceedings of a selection panel shall not be invalidated by—

(*a*) a vacancy in the membership of the panel, or
(*b*) a defect in the appointment of a person as a member.

8–23864 **7.** (1) A police authority shall make to members of the selection panel for the authority's area such payments by way of reimbursement of expenses and allowances as it may determine.

(2) A police authority shall—

(*a*) provide the selection panel for the authority's area with such accommodation, and such secretarial and other assistance, as they may reasonably require, and
(*b*) meet any expenses incurred by the panel in the exercise of their functions.

Functions of selection panel

8–23865 **8.** (1) Where appointments to a police authority are to be made under paragraph 5 of Schedule 2 [or paragraph 3(3) of Schedule 2A], the selection panel for the authority's area shall nominate persons willing to be candidates for appointment.

(2) Unless the selection panel are able to identify only a smaller number, the number of persons to be nominated by a selection panel under this paragraph on any occasion shall be a number four times greater than the number of appointments to be made under paragraph 5 of Schedule 2 or paragraph 3(3) of Schedule 2A (as the case may be).

(3) A selection panel shall notify the Secretary of State of—

(*a*) the name of each person nominated by it under this paragraph, and
(*b*) such other information regarding those persons as it considers appropriate.

8–23865A **9.** A person shall not be nominated under paragraph 8 in relation to an authority

(*a*) if, by virtue of paragraph 11, 13 or 14 of Schedule 2, he is disqualified for being appointed as a member of the authority under paragraph 5 of that Schedule; or
(*b*) if, by virtue of paragraph 7, 8 or 9 of Schedule 2A, he is disqualified for being appointed as a member of the authority under paragraph 3(3) of that Schedule.

8–23866 **10.** In exercising their functions a selection panel shall have regard to the desirability of ensuring that, so far as reasonably practicable, the persons nominated by them under paragraph 8—

(*a*) represent the interests of a wide range of people within the community in the police area, and
(*b*) include persons with skills, knowledge or experience in such fields as may be specified for the purposes of this paragraph in regulations made under paragraph 11.

8–23867 **11.** (1) The Secretary of State may make regulations as to—

(*a*) the procedures to be followed in relation to the selection of persons for nomination under paragraph 8, and
(*b*) the conduct of the proceedings of selection panels.

(2) Without prejudice to the generality of sub-paragraph (1), regulations under this paragraph may—

(*a*) make provision (including provision imposing time limits) as to the procedures to be adopted when inviting applications or suggestions for nomination under paragraph 8, and for dealing with applications and suggestions received;
(*b*) make provision specifying the fields referred to in paragraph 10;
(*c*) prescribe matters, in addition to those mentioned in paragraph 10, to which a selection panel is to have regard in carrying out any of its functions;
(*d*) provide for decisions of a selection panel to be taken by a majority of the members.

(3) Regulations[1] under this paragraph may make different provision for different cases and circumstances.

(4) A statutory instrument containing regulations under this paragraph shall be subject to annulment in pursuance of a resolution of either House of Parliament.

---

1. See the Police Authorities (Selection Panel) Regulations 1994, SI 1994/2023 amended by SI 2000/1549 and SI 2002/1282.

Secretary of State's short-list

8–23868 **12.** (1) Where the Secretary of State receives a notice under paragraph 8(3), he shall as soon as practicable prepare a short-list of candidates and send it to the police authority concerned.

(2) Subject to paragraph 13, the candidates on the short-list prepared by the Secretary of State shall be persons nominated by the selection panel, and their number shall be one half of the number of those persons.

(3) Where the number of persons nominated by the panel is an odd number, the number to be short-listed by the Secretary of State shall be one half of the number nominated reduced by one.

8–23869 **13.** (1) This paragraph has effect where the number of persons nominated by the selection panel is less than twice the number of vacancies to be filled by appointments under paragraph 5 of Schedule 2 or paragraph 3(3) of Schedule 2A (as the case may be).

(2) The Secretary of State may himself nominate such number of candidates as, when added to the number nominated by the selection panel, equals twice the number of vacancies; and if he does so, paragraph 12 shall have effect as if the selection panel had nominated the Secretary of State's nominees as well as their own.

8–23870 **14.** The Secretary of State shall give to the designated members any information regarding the persons on his short-list which they request and which he has received under paragraph 8.

8–23871
Section 29

SCHEDULE 4
FORM OF DECLARATION

(*Substituted by the Police Reform Act 2002, s 83.*)

['I . . . . . of . . . . . do solemnly and sincerely declare and affirm that I will well and truly serve the Queen in the office of constable, with fairness, integrity, diligence and impartiality, upholding fundamental human rights and according equal respect to all people; and that I will, to the best of my power, cause the peace to be kept and preserved and prevent all offences against people and property; and that while I continue to hold the said office I will, to the best of my skill and knowledge, discharge all the duties thereof faithfully according to law.']

Police Act 1997[1]

(1997 c 50)

PART I[2]
THE NATIONAL CRIMINAL INTELLIGENCE SERVICE

8–23872 This part establishes the Service Authority for the National Criminal Intelligence Service. Membership comprises eleven members but may be such odd number exceeding eleven as may be specified by Order made by the Secretary of State (s 1 and Sch I). The NCIS Service Authority shall maintain a body known as the National Criminal Intelligence Service whose functions are:

(*a*) to gather, store and analyse information in order to provide criminal intelligence,
(*b*) to provide criminal intelligence to police forces in Great Britain, the Royal Ulster Constabulary, the National Crime Squad and other law enforcement agencies, and
(*c*) to act in support of such police forces, the Royal Ulster Constabulary, the National Crime Squad and other law enforcement agencies carrying out their criminal intelligence activities (s 2).

The NCIS Service Authority is required to ensure that the NCIS is effective and efficient and to set objectives, to prepare a service plan and annual reports (ss 3–5). Provision is made for the appointment of a Director General and a Deputy Director General (s 6–8).

1. This Act is to be brought into force in accordance with orders made under s 135. At the date of going to press the following commencement orders have been made: Commencement Order (No 1) SI 1997/1377; Commencement Order (No 2) SI 1997/1696; Commencement Order (No 3) SI 1997/1930; Commencement Order (No 4) SI 1997/2390; Commencement (No 5) and Transitional Provisions Order 1998, SI 1998/354; Commencement Order (No 6) 1999, SI 1999/151; Commencement Order (No 6) 2001, SI 2001/1097; Commencement Order (No 7) 2002, SI 2002/413. Of the provisions reproduced in this Manual Pts I, II, III and IV and Part V (except s 112), ss 134 (partly), 135–138 have been brought into force.
2. Part I comprises ss 1–46.

Miscellaneous

8–23873 43. Causing disaffection. *Repealed.*

PART II[1]
THE NATIONAL CRIME SQUAD

8–23874 This Part establishes the Service Authority for the National Crime Squad. The NCS Service Authority shall maintain a body known as the National Crime Squad whose functions are to prevent and detect serious crime which is of relevance to more than one police area in England and Wales (s 48). It may also:

(*a*) at the request of a chief officer of police of a police force in England and Wales, act in support of the activities of his force in the prevention and detection of serious crime;
(*b*) at the request of the Director General of NCIS, act in support of the activities of NCIS;
(*c*) institute criminal proceedings;
(*d*) co-operate with other police forces in the United Kingdom in the prevention and detection of serious crime;
(*e*) act in support of other law enforcement agencies in the prevention and detection of serious crime (s 48).

The NCS Service Authority is required to ensure that the NCS is effective and efficient and to set objectives, to prepare a service plan and annual reports (ss 49–51). Provision is made for the appointment of a Director General and a Deputy Director General (s 52–54). As to changes made by the Criminal Justice and Police Act 2001, see para **8–23872**, supra.

1. Part II comprises ss 47–90.

Miscellaneous

8–23875 87. Causing disaffection. *Repealed.*

Part III[1]
Authorisations in Respect of Property

8–23876 This Part provides that no entry on or interference with property or with wireless telegraphy shall be unlawful if it is authorised in accordance with an authorisation having effect under this Part (s 92). An "authorising officer" i.e. a chief constable, a police commissioner, the Director Generals of the National Criminal Intelligence Service and the National Crime Squad or an officer designated by the Commissioners for Customs and Excise may authorise such action as he may specify, where he believes that it is necessary for the action to be taken on the ground that it is likely to be of substantial value in the prevention or detection of serious crime, and what is sought to be achieved cannot reasonably be achieved by other means (s 93). In cases of urgency such powers may be exercised by the next officer in line of command (s 94 amended by the Crime and Disorder Act 1998, s 113 and Sch 10). Except in cases of urgency, authorisations must be in writing (s 95)[2].

Authorisations must be notified to Commissioners appointed by the Prime Minister under s 91 and must be approved by them where the authorisation relates to circumstances where the person who gives the authorisation believes that any of the property specified in the authorisation is used wholly or mainly as a dwelling or as a bedroom in a hotel or constitutes office premises; or the action authorised is likely to result in a person acquiring knowledge of matters subject to legal privilege, confidential personal information, or confidential journalistic material (ss 97–100). Provision is made for the Secretary of State to issue a Code of Practice (s 101)[3]; for dealing with complaints (s 102) and for quashing an authorisation (s 103). Appeals may be made by authorising officers and complaints to the Chief Commissioner (ss 104–106).

1. Part III comprises ss 91–108.
2. The Police Act 1997 (Notification of Authorisations, etc) Order 1998, SI 1998/3241 specifies the particulars to be included in an authorisation to interfere with property and a renewal or cancellation of such authorisation.
3. The Police Act 1997 (Authorisation of Action in Respect of Property) (Code of Practice) Order 1998, SI 1998/3240 has been made which makes provision for a Code of Practice applying to operations involving interference with property or wireless telegraphy carried out by the police, Customs and Excise, NCIS and NCS.

Part IV[1]
Police Information Technology Organisation

1. Part IV comprises ss 109–111.

Part V[1]
Certificates of Criminal Records, &c.

8–23877 **112. Criminal conviction certificates.** (1) The Secretary of State shall issue a criminal conviction certificate to any individual who—

(*a*) makes an application in the prescribed[2] form, and
(*b*) pays any fee that is payable in relation to the application under regulations[2] made by the Secretary of State.

(2) A criminal conviction certificate is a certificate which—

(*a*) gives the prescribed details of every conviction of the applicant which is recorded in central records, or
(*b*) states that there is no such conviction.

(3) In this section—

"central records" means such records of convictions held for the use of police forces generally as may be prescribed;

"conviction" means a conviction within the meaning of the Rehabilitation of Offenders Act 1974, other than a spent conviction.

(4) Where an applicant has received a criminal conviction certificate, the Secretary of State may refuse to issue another certificate to that applicant during such period as may be prescribed.
[Police Act 1997, s 112.]

1. Part V comprises ss 112–127.
2. The Police Act 1997 (Criminal Records) Regulations 2002 have been made, in this Part, post.

8–23878 **113. Criminal record certificates.** (1) The Secretary of State shall issue a criminal record certificate to any individual who—

(*a*) makes an application under this section in the prescribed[1] form countersigned by a registered person, and
(*b*) pays any fee that is payable in relation to the application under regulations[1] made by the Secretary of State.

(2) An application under this section must be accompanied by a statement by the registered person that the certificate is required for the purposes of an exempted question.

(3) A criminal record certificate is a certificate which—

(*a*) gives the prescribed details of every relevant matter relating to the applicant which is recorded in central records, or

(*b*) states that there is no such matter.

(3A) If an application under this section is accompanied by a statement by the registered person that the certificate is required for the purpose of considering the applicant's [suitability to be employed, supplied to work, found work or given work in] a position (whether paid or unpaid) within subsection (3B), or the suitability of the applicant, or of a person living in the same household as the applicant, to be a foster parent or to adopt a child, the criminal record certificate shall also state—

(*a*) whether the applicant is included in—

(i) the list kept under section 1 of the Protection of Children Act 1999;

(ia) the list kept under section 1(1) of the Protection of Children (Scotland) Act 2003 (asp 5);

(ii) (*repealed*)

(iii) (*repealed*) and

(*b*) if he is included in the list kept under section 1 of the Protection of Children Act 1999 (c 14), such details of his inclusion as may be prescribed;

(*c*) whether he is subject to a direction under section 142 of the Education Act 2002; and

(*d*) If he is subject to a direction under that section, such details of the circumstances in which it was given as may be prescribed, including the grounds on which it was given.

(3B) A position is within this subsection if it is—

(*a*) a child care position within the meaning of the Protection of Children Act 1999;

(*aa*) a child care position within the meaning of the Protection of Children (Scotland) Act 2003 (asp 5);

(*b*) a position which involves work to which section 142 of the Education Act 2002 applies;

(*c*) (*repealed*) or

(*d*) a position of such other description as may be prescribed;

(*repealed*).

(3C) If an application under this section is accompanied by a statement by the registered person that the certificate is required for the purpose of considering the applicant's suitability to be employed, supplied to work, found work or given work in a position (whether paid or unpaid) within subsection (3D), the criminal record certificate shall also state—

(*a*) whether the applicant is included in the list kept under section 81 of the Care Standards Act 2000; and

(*b*) if he is included in that list, such details of his inclusion as may be prescribed.

(3D) A position is within this subsection if it is—

(*a*) a care position within the meaning of Part VII of the Care Standards Act 2000; or

(*b*) a position of such other description as may be prescribed.

(3E) The references in subsections (3A) and (3C) to considering the applicant's suitability to be employed, supplied to work, found work or given work in a position falling within subsection (3B) or (3D) include references to—

(*a*) considering the applicant's suitability to be registered—

(i) under Part II of the Care Standards Act 2000 (establishments and agencies);

(ii) under Part IV of that Act (social care workers); or

(iii) under Part 3 of the Regulation of Care (Scotland) Act 2001 (asp 8) (social workers); or

(iv) for child minding or providing day care under section 71 of the Children Act 1989 or Article 118 of the Children (Northern Ireland) Order 1995 (child minding and day care); and

(*b*) considering the applicant's application to have a care service, consisting of the provision of child minding or the day care of children, registered under Part 1 of the Regulation of Care (Scotland) Act 2001 (asp 8) (care services).

(3A) If an application under this section is accompanied by a statement by the registered person that the certificate is required for the purpose of considering the applicant's suitability to be employed, supplied to work, found work or given work in a position (whether paid or unpaid) within subsection (3B), or the suitability of the applicant, or of a person living in the same household as the applicant, to be a foster parent or to adopt a child, the criminal record certificate shall also state—

(*a*) whether the applicant is included in—

(i) the list kept under section 1 of the Protection of Children Act 1999;

(ii) (*repealed*)

(iii) (*repealed*)

(*b*) if he is included in the list kept under section 1 of the Protection of Children Act 1999 (c 14), such details of his inclusion as may be prescribed;

(*c*) whether he is subject to a direction under section 142 of the Education Act 2002; and

(*d*) If he is subject to a direction under that section, such details of the circumstances in which it was given as may be prescribed, including the grounds on which it was given.

(3B) A position is within this subsection if it is—

(*a*) a child care position within the meaning of the Protection of Children Act 1999;*

(*b*) a position which involves work to which section 142 of the Education Act 2002 applies;

(*c*) (*repealed*)

(*d*) a position of such other description as may be prescribed;

(*repealed*).

(3C) If an application under this section is accompanied by a statement by the registered person that the certificate is required for the purpose of considering the applicant's suitability to be employed, supplied to work, found work or given work in a position (whether paid or unpaid) within subsection (3D), the criminal record certificate shall also state—

(*a*) whether the applicant is included in the list kept under section 81 of the Care Standards Act 2000; and

(*b*) if he is included in that list, such details of his inclusion as may be prescribed.**

(3D) A position is within this subsection if it is—

(*a*) a care position within the meaning of Part VII of the Care Standards Act 2000; or

(*b*) a position of such other description as may be prescribed.**

(3E) The references in subsections (3A) and (3C) to suitability to be employed, supplied to work, found work or given work in a position falling within subsection (3B) or (3D) include references to suitability to be registered—

(*a*) under Part II of the Care Standards Act 2000 (establishments and agencies);

(*b*) under Part IV of that Act (social care workers); or

(*c*) for child minding or providing day care under section 71 of the Children Act 1989 or Article 118 of the Children (Northern Ireland) Order 1995 (child minding and day care).***

(3F) The references in subsections (3A) and (3C) to considering the applicant's suitability to be employed, supplied to work, found work or given work in a position falling within subsection (3B) or (3D) include references to considering, for the purposes of Part 10A of the Children Act 1989 (child minding and day care in England and Wales), his suitability—

(*a*) to look after or be in regular contact with children under the age of eight, or

(*b*) in the case of an applicant for or holder of a certificate under section 79W of that Act, or a person prescribed under subsection (4) of that section, to look after children within the meaning of that section.****

(3G) The references in subsections (3A) and (3C) to considering the applicant's suitability to be employed, supplied to work, found work or given work in a position falling within subsection (3B) or (3D) include references to considering, for the purposes of section 3 of the Teaching and Higher Education Act 1998 (registration of teachers within the General Teaching Council for England or the General Teaching Council for Wales), his suitability to be a teacher.*****

(4) The Secretary of State shall send a copy of a criminal record certificate to the registered person who countersigned the application.

(5) In this section—

"central records" means such records of convictions and cautions held for the use of police forces generally as may be prescribed;

"exempted question" means a question in relation to which section 4(2)(*a*) or (*b*) of the Rehabilitation of Offenders Act 1974 (effect of rehabilitation) has been excluded by an order of the Secretary of State under section 4(4);

"relevant matter" means—

(i) a conviction within the meaning of the Rehabilitation of Offenders Act 1974, including a spent conviction, and

(ii) a caution.******

[Police Act 1997, s 113, as amended by the Protection of Children Act 1999, s 8(1), the Care Standards Act 2000, ss 102 and 104, SI 2002/2953 and the Education Act 2002, s 152.]

***Section reproduced as in force in England and Wales (certain amendments not yet in force in Scotland).**

****Sub-sections (3C), (3D) printed as prospectively inserted by the Care Standards Act 2000, s 90(1).**

*****Sub-section (3E), para (*b*) printed as prospectively inserted by the Care Standards Act 2000, s 104(1), (2)(*b*) and para (c) as amended in relation to England by SI 2002/2953 from 20 January 2003. Sub-sections (3EA)–(3ED) inserted in relation to Northern Ireland by SI 2003/417, from a date to be appointed.**

******Sub-section (3F) in force in relation to England from 1 October 2002, as regards Wales from 19 December 2002 and in force in Scotland from a date to be appointed.**

*******Sub-section (3G) printed as prospectively inserted by the Education Act 2002, s 148.**
********Sub-section 113 repealed and new sub-ss 113A–113F inserted by the Serious Organised Crime and Police Act 2005, s 163 from a date to be appointed.**
1. The Police Act 1997 (Criminal Records) Regulations 2002 have been made, in this PART, post.

8–23878A 113A. Criminal record certificates. (1) The Secretary of State must issue a criminal record certificate to any individual who—

(a) makes an application in the prescribed manner and form, and
(b) pays in the prescribed manner any prescribed fee.

(2) The application must—

(a) be countersigned by a registered person, and
(b) be accompanied by a statement by the registered person that the certificate is required for the purposes of an exempted question.

(3) A criminal record certificate is a certificate which—

(a) gives the prescribed details of every relevant matter relating to the applicant which is recorded in central records, or
(b) states that there is no such matter.

(4) The Secretary of State must send a copy of a criminal record certificate to the registered person who countersigned the application.

(5) The Secretary of State may treat an application under this section as an application under section 113B if—

(a) in his opinion the certificate is required for a purpose prescribed under subsection (2) of that section,
(b) the registered person provides him with the statement required by that subsection, and
(c) the applicant consents and pays to the Secretary of State the amount (if any) by which the fee payable in relation to an application under that section exceeds the fee paid in relation to the application under this section.

(6) In this section—

"central records" means such records of convictions and cautions held for the use of police forces generally as may be prescribed;

"exempted question" means a question in relation to which section 4(2)(a) or (b) of the Rehabilitation of Offenders Act 1974 (effect of rehabilitation) has been excluded by an order of the Secretary of State under section 4(4) of that Act;

"relevant matter" means—

(a) a conviction within the meaning of the Rehabilitation of Offenders Act 1974, including a spent conviction, and
(b) a caution.*

[Police Act 1997, s 113A as inserted by the Serious Organised Crime and Police Act 2005, s 163.]

***Reproduced as in force in England and Wales.**

8–23878B 113B. Enhanced criminal record certificates. (1) The Secretary of State must issue an enhanced criminal record certificate to any individual who—

(a) makes an application in the prescribed manner and form, and
(b) pays in the prescribed manner any prescribed fee.

(2) The application must—

(a) be countersigned by a registered person, and
(b) be accompanied by a statement by the registered person that the certificate is required for a prescribed purpose.

(3) An enhanced criminal record certificate is a certificate which—

(a) gives the prescribed details of every relevant matter relating to the applicant which is recorded in central records and any information provided in accordance with subsection (4), or
(b) states that there is no such matter or information.

(4) Before issuing an enhanced criminal record certificate the Secretary of State must request the chief officer of every relevant police force to provide any information which, in the chief officer's opinion—

(a) might be relevant for the purpose described in the statement under subsection (2), and
(b) ought to be included in the certificate.

(5) The Secretary of State must also request the chief officer of every relevant police force to provide any information which, in the chief officer's opinion—

(a) might be relevant for the purpose described in the statement under subsection (2),

(b) ought not to be included in the certificate, in the interests of the prevention or detection of crime, and

(c) can, without harming those interests, be disclosed to the registered person.

(6) The Secretary of State must send to the registered person who countersigned the application—

(a) a copy of the enhanced criminal record certificate, and

(b) any information provided in accordance with subsection (5).

(7) The Secretary of State may treat an application under this section as an application under section 113A if in his opinion the certificate is not required for a purpose prescribed under subsection (2).

(8) If by virtue of subsection (7) the Secretary of State treats an application under this section as an application under section 113A, he must refund to the applicant the amount (if any) by which the fee paid in relation to the application under this section exceeds the fee payable in relation to an application under section 113A.

(9) In this section—

"central records", "exempted question", and "relevant matter" have the same meaning as in section 113A;

"relevant police force", in relation to an application under this section, means a police force which is a relevant police force in relation to that application under regulations made by the Secretary of State.

(10) For the purposes of this section references to a police force include any of the following—

(a) the Royal Navy Regulating Branch;
(b) the Royal Marines Police;
(c) the Royal Military Police;
(d) the Royal Air Force Police;
(e) the Ministry of Defence Police;
(f) the National Criminal Intelligence Service;
(g) the National Crime Squad;
(h) the British Transport Police;
(i) the Civil Nuclear Constabulary;
(j) the States of Jersey Police Force;
(k) the salaried police force of the Island of Guernsey;
(l) the Isle of Man Constabulary;
(m) a body with functions in any country or territory outside the British Islands which correspond to those of a police force in any part of the United Kingdom,

and any reference to the chief officer of a police force includes the person responsible for the direction of a body mentioned in this subsection.

(11) For the purposes of this section each of the following must be treated as if it were a police force—

(a) the Commissioners for Her Majesty's Revenue and Customs (and for this purpose a reference to the chief officer of a police force must be taken to be a reference to any one of the Commissioners);

(b) the Serious Organised Crime Agency (and for this purpose a reference to the chief officer of a police force must be taken to be a reference to the Director General of the Agency);

(c) such other department or body as is prescribed (and regulations may prescribe in relation to the department or body the person to whom a reference to the chief officer is to be taken to be).*

[Police Act 1997, s 113B as inserted by the Serious Organised Crime and Police Act 2005, s 163.]

***Reproduced as in force in England and Wales.**

8–23878C 113C. Criminal record certificates: suitability relating to children. (1) If an application under section 113A or 113B is accompanied by a children's suitability statement the criminal record certificate or enhanced criminal record certificate (as the case may be) must also state—

(a) whether the applicant is included in a specified children's list;

(b) if he is included in such a list, such details of his inclusion as may be prescribed;

(c) whether he is subject to a specified children's direction;

(d) if he is subject to such a direction, the grounds on which it was given and such details as may be prescribed of the circumstances in which it was given.

(2) A children's suitability statement is a statement by the registered person that the certificate is required for the purpose of considering—

(a) the applicant's suitability to be employed, supplied to work, found work or given work in a position (whether paid or unpaid) within subsection (5),

(b) the applicant's suitability to be a foster parent or to adopt a child,

(c) the applicant's suitability to be a child's special guardian for the purposes of sections 14A and 14C of the Children Act 1989,
(d) the applicant's suitability to have a child placed with him by virtue of section 70 of the Children (Scotland) Act 1995 or by virtue of section 5(2), (3) and (4) of the Social Work (Scotland) Act 1968, or
(e) the suitability of a person living in the same household as the applicant to be a person mentioned in paragraph (b) or (c) or to have a child placed with him as mentioned in paragraph (d).

(3) Each of the following is a specified children's list—

(a) the list kept under section 1 of the Protection of Children Act 1999;
(b) the list kept under section 1(1) of the Protection of Children (Scotland) Act 2003;
(c) the list kept under Article 3 of the Protection of Children and Vulnerable Adults (Northern Ireland) Order 2003;
(d) any list kept for the purposes of regulations under Article 70(2)(e) or 88A(2)(b) of the Education and Libraries (Northern Ireland) Order 1986;
(e) any such other list as the Secretary of State specifies by order if he thinks that the list corresponds to a list specified in paragraphs (a) to (c) and is kept in pursuance of the law of a country or territory outside the United Kingdom.

(4) Each of the following is a specified children's direction—

(a) a direction under section 142 of the Education Act 2002;
(b) anything which the Secretary of State specifies by order which he thinks corresponds to such a direction and which is done for the purposes of the law of Scotland or of Northern Ireland or of a country or territory outside the United Kingdom.

(5) A position falls within this subsection if it is any of the following—

(a) a child care position within the meaning of the Protection of Children Act 1999;
(b) a child care position within the meaning of the Protection of Children (Scotland) Act 2003;
(c) a child care position within the meaning of Chapter 1 of Part 2 of the Protection of Children and Vulnerable Adults (Northern Ireland) Order 2003;
(d) a position, employment or further employment in which may be prohibited or restricted by regulations under Article 70(2)(e) or 88A(2)(b) of the Education and Libraries (Northern Ireland) Order 1986;
(e) a position which involves work to which section 142 of the Education Act 2002 applies;
(f) a position of such other description as may be prescribed.

(6) An order under subsection (4)(b) may make such modifications of subsection (1)(d) as the Secretary of State thinks necessary or expedient in consequence of the order.*

[Police Act 1997, s 113C as inserted by the Serious Organised Crime and Police Act 2005, s 163 and SI 2005/3496.]

***Reproduced as in force in England and Wales.**

8–23878D 113D. Criminal record certificates: suitability relating to adults. (1) If an application under section 113A or 113B is accompanied by an adults' suitability statement the criminal record certificate or enhanced criminal record certificate (as the case may be) must also state—

(a) whether the applicant is included in a specified adults' list;
(b) if he is included in such a list, such details of his inclusion as may be prescribed.

(2) An adults' suitability statement is a statement by the registered person that the certificate is required for the purpose of considering the applicant's suitability to be employed, supplied to work, found work or given work in a position (whether paid or unpaid) falling within subsection (4).

(3) Each of the following is a specified adults' list—

(a) the list kept under section 81 of the Care Standards Act 2000;
(b) the list kept under Article 35 of the Protection of Children and Vulnerable Adults (Northern Ireland) Order 2003;
(c) any such other list as the Secretary of State specifies by order if he thinks that the list corresponds to a list specified in paragraph (a) or (b) and is kept in pursuance of the law of Scotland or of a country or territory outside the United Kingdom.

(4) A position falls within this subsection if it is any of the following—

(a) a care position within the meaning of Part 7 of the Care Standards Act 2000;
(b) a care position within the meaning of Part 3 of the Protection of Children and Vulnerable Adults (Northern Ireland) Order 2003;
(c) a position concerned with providing a care service (as defined by section 2(1) of the Regulation of Care (Scotland) Act 2001);
(d) a position of such other description as may be prescribed.*

[Police Act 1997, s 113D as inserted by the Serious Organised Crime and Police Act 2005, s 163.]

***Reproduced as in force in England and Wales.**

8–23878E 113E. Criminal record certificates: specified children's and adults' lists: urgent cases. (1) Subsection (2) applies to an application under section 113A or 113B if—

(a) it is accompanied by a children's suitability statement,
(b) the registered person requests an urgent preliminary response, and
(c) the applicant pays in the prescribed manner such additional fee as is prescribed in respect of the application.

(2) The Secretary of State must notify the registered person—

(a) if the applicant is not included in a specified children's list, of that fact;
(b) if the applicant is included in such a list, of the details prescribed for the purposes of section 113C(1)(b) above;
(c) if the applicant is not subject to a specified children's direction, of that fact;
(d) if the applicant is subject to such a direction, of the grounds on which the direction was given and the details prescribed for the purposes of section 113C(1)(d) above.

(3) Subsection (4) applies to an application under section 113A or 113B if—

(a) it is accompanied by an adults' suitability statement,
(b) the registered person requests an urgent preliminary response, and
(c) the applicant pays in the prescribed manner such additional fee as is prescribed in respect of the application.

(4) The Secretary of State must notify the registered person either—

(a) that the applicant is not included in a specified adults' list, or
(b) that a criminal record certificate or enhanced criminal record certificate will be issued in due course.

(5) In this section—

"criminal record certificate" has the same meaning as in section 113A;
"enhanced criminal record certificate" has the same meaning as in section 113B;
"children's suitability statement", "specified children's direction" and "specified children's list" have the same meaning as in section 113C;
"adults' suitability statement" and "specified adults' list" have the same meaning as in section 113D.*

[Police Act 1997, s 113E as inserted by the Serious Organised Crime and Police Act 2005, s 163.]

***Reproduced as in force in England and Wales.**

8–23878F 113F. Criminal record certificates: supplementary. (1) References in sections 113C(2) and 113D(2) to considering the applicant's suitability to be employed, supplied to work, found work or given work in a position falling within section 113C(5) or 113D(4) include references to considering—

(a) for the purposes of Part 10A of the Children Act 1989 (child minding and day care in England and Wales), the applicant's suitability to look after or be in regular contact with children under the age of eight;
(b) for the purposes of that Part of that Act, in the case of an applicant for or holder of a certificate under section 79W of that Act, or a person prescribed under subsection (4) of that section, his suitability to look after children within the meaning of that section;
(c) the applicant's suitability to be registered for child minding or providing day care under section 71 of the Children Act 1989 or Article 118 of the Children (Northern Ireland) Order 1995 (child minding and day care);
(d) for the purposes of section 3 of the Teaching and Higher Education Act 1998 (registration of teachers with the General Teaching Council for England or the General Teaching Council for Wales) or of section 6 of the Teaching Council (Scotland) Act 1965 (registration of teachers with the General Teaching Council for Scotland), the applicant's suitability to be a teacher;
(e) the applicant's suitability to be registered under Part 2 of the Care Standards Act 2000 (establishments and agencies);
(f) the applicant's suitability to be registered under Part 4 of that Act (social care workers);
(g) the applicant's suitability to be registered under Part 1 of the Regulation of Care (Scotland) Act 2001 (applications by persons seeking to provide a care service);
(h) the applicant's suitability to be registered under Part 3 of that Act (social workers and other social service workers);
(i) the applicant's application to have a care service, consisting of the provision of child minding or the day care of children, registered under Part 1 of that Act (care services);
(j) the applicant's suitability to be registered under Part 1 of the Health and Personal Social Services Act (Northern Ireland) 2001 (social care workers);

(k) the applicant's suitability to be registered under Part 3 of the Health and Personal Social Services (Quality, Improvement and Regulation) (Northern Ireland) Order 2003 (regulation of establishments and agencies).

(2) The power to make an order under section 113C or 113D is exercisable by statutory instrument, but no such order may be made unless a draft of the order has been laid before and approved by a resolution of each House of Parliament.

(3) If the power mentioned in subsection (2) is exercised by the Scottish Ministers, the reference in that subsection to each House of Parliament must be construed as a reference to the Scottish Parliament.*

[Police Act 1997, s 113F as inserted by the Serious Organised Crime and Police Act 2005, s 163.]

***Reproduced as in force in England and Wales.**

8–23879 114. Criminal record certificates: Crown employment

8–23880 115. Enhanced criminal record certificates. (1) The Secretary of State shall issue an enhanced criminal record certificate to any individual who—

(*a*) makes an application under this section in the prescribed[1] manner and form countersigned by a registered person, and

(*b*) pays in the prescribed manner any fee that is payable in relation to the application under regulations[1] made by the Secretary of State.

(2) An application under this section must be accompanied by a statement by the registered person that the certificate is required for the purposes of an exempted question asked—

(*a*) in the course of considering the applicant's suitability for a position (whether paid or unpaid) within subsection (3) or (4),

(*b*) for a purpose relating to any of the matters listed in subsection (5), or

(*c*) in relation to an individual whom subsection (6C), (6D) or (6E) applies.

for such purposes as may be prescribed under this subsection.

(3) A position is within this subsection if it involves regularly caring for, training, supervising or being in sole charge of persons aged under 18.

(4) A position is within this subsection if—

(*a*) it is of a kind specified in regulations[2] made by the Secretary of State, and

(*b*) it involves regularly caring for, training, supervising or being in sole charge of persons aged 18 or over.

(5) The matters referred to in subsection (2)(*b*) are

(*a*) a certificate for the purposes of sections 19 or 27(1) or (5) of the Gaming Act 1968 (gaming);

(*b*) a certificate of consent, or a licence, for any purpose of Schedule 2 to that Act (licences);

(*c*) registration or certification in accordance with Schedule 1A, 2 or 2A to the Lotteries and Amusements Act 1976 (societies, schemes and lottery managers);

(*d*) a licence under section 5 or 6 of the National Lottery etc. Act 1993 (running or promoting lotteries);

(*da*) a personal licence under the Licensing Act 2003;

(*e*) registration under section 71 of the Children Act 1989* or registration for child minding or providing day care under Part XA of that Act, or the holding of a certificate under section 79W of that Act, or registration under Article 118 of the Children (Northern Ireland) Order 1995 (child minding and day care);**

(*ee*) registration under the Regulation of Care (Scotland) Act 2001 (asp 8) of a care service (as defined in section 2(1) of that Act);***

(*ef*) registration under Part 3 of that Act of a social worker or other social service worker ("social worker" and "social service worker" having the same meanings as in that Act);***

(*ea*) registration under Part II of the Care Standards Act 2000 (establishments and agencies);****

(*eb*) registration under Part IV of that Act (social care workers);**

(*f*) the placing of children with foster parents in accordance with any provision of, or made by virtue of, the Children Act 1989 or the Children (Northern Ireland) Order 1995 or the exercise of any duty under or by virtue of section 67 of that Act or Article 108 of that Order (welfare of privately fostered children);

(*g*) the approval of any person as a foster carer by virtue of section 5(2), (3) and (4) of the Social Work (Scotland) Act 1968, the exercise by a local authority of their functions under the Foster Children (Scotland) Act 1984 or the placing of children with foster parents by virtue of section 70 of the Children (Scotland) Act 1995 (disposal of referral by children's hearing);

(*ga*) a licence under the Private Security Industry Act 2001 to engage in any such licensable conduct (within the meaning of that Act) as will or may involve, or relate to, activities to which paragraph 8 of Schedule 2 to that Act applies (door supervisors etc for public houses and clubs and comparable venues).****

(*h*) a decision made by an adoption agency within the meaning of section 2 of the Adoption and Children Act 2002 as to a person's suitability to adopt a child.

(*i*) an assessment, investigation or review by an adoption agency or local authority as to the suitability of a person, whether or not the person in respect of whom the certificate is sought, to adopt a child (this paragraph being construed in accordance with sections 1(3A) and (4) and 65(1) of the Adoption (Scotland) Act 1978 (c 28) and as if it were one of the provisions of that Act listed in the definition of "adoption agency" in the said section 65(1)).

(6) An enhanced criminal record certificate is a certificate which—

(*a*) gives—

(i) the prescribed details of every relevant matter relating to the applicant which is recorded in central records, and

(ii) any information provided in accordance with subsection (7), or

(*b*) states that there is no such matter or information.

(6A) If an application under this section is accompanied by a statement by the registered person that the certificate is required for the purpose of considering the applicant's suitability to be employed, supplied to work, found work or given work in a position (whether paid or unpaid) falling within subsection (3B) of section 113, the suitability of the applicant, or of a person living in the same household as the applicant, to be a foster parent or to adopt a child, the enhanced criminal record certificate shall also state—

(*a*) whether the applicant is included in—

(i) the list kept under section 1 of the Protection of Children Act 1999;

(ii) the list kept for the purposes of regulations made under section 218(6) of the Education Reform Act 1988 ("the 1988 Act list"); or*****

(iii) any list kept by the Secretary of State or the National Assembly for Wales of persons disqualified under section 470 or 471 of the Education Act 1996 ("the 1996 Act list"); and*****

(*b*) if he is included in the list kept under section 1 of the Protection of Children Act 1999 (c 14), such details of his inclusion as may be prescribed;

(*c*) whether he is subject to a direction under section 142 of the Education Act 2002; and

(*d*) If he is subject to a direction under that section, such details of the circumstances in which it was given as may be prescribed, including the grounds on which it was given.

(6B) If an application under this section is accompanied by a statement by the registered person that the certificate is required for the purpose of considering the applicant's suitability to be employed, supplied to work, found work or given work in a position (whether paid or unpaid) falling within subsection (3D) of section 113, the enhanced criminal record certificate shall also state—

(*a*) whether the applicant is included in the list kept under section 81 of the Care Standards Act 2000; and

(*b*) if he is included in that list, such details of his inclusion as may be prescribed.******

(6BA) The references in subsections (6A) and (6B) to considering the applicant's suitability to be employed, supplied to work, found work or given work in a position falling within section 113(3B) or (3D) include references to considering, for the purposes of Part 10A of the Children Act 1989 (child minding and day care in England and Wales) his suitability—

(*a*) to look after or be in regular contact with children under the age of eight, or

(*b*) in the case of an applicant for or holder of a certificate under section 79W of that Act, or a person prescribed under subsection (4) of that section, to look after children within the meaning of that section.

(6BB) The references in subsections (6A) and (6B) to considering the applicant's suitability to be employed, supplied to work, found work or given work in a position falling within section 113(3B) or (3D) include references to considering, for the purposes of section 3 of the Teaching and Higher Education Act 1998, his suitability to be a teacher. *******

(6C) This subsection applies to an individual included or seeking inclusion in any list prepared for the purposes of Part 2 of the National Health Service Act 1977 (c 49) of—

(*a*) medical practitioners undertaking to provide general medical services,

(*b*) persons undertaking to provide general dental services,

(*c*) persons undertaking to provide general ophthalmic services, or

(*d*) persons undertaking to provide pharmaceutical services.

(6D) This subsection applies to an individual who is—

(*a*) a director of a body corporate included or seeking inclusion in a list referred to in subsection (6C)(*b*) or (*c*),

(*b*) a member of a limited liability partnership included or seeking inclusion in a list referred to in subsection (6C)(*c*), (*c*) a member of the body of persons controlling a body corporate (whether or not a limited liability partnership) included or seeking inclusion in a list referred to in subsection (6C)(*d*).

(6E) This subsection applies to an individual included or seeking inclusion in any list prepared by a Primary Care Trust or Health Authority under—

(*a*) section 28DA of the National Health Service Act 1977 or section 8ZA of the National Health Service (Primary Care) Act 1997 (lists of persons who may perform personal medical services or personal dental services), or

(*b*) section 43D of the 1977 Act (supplementary lists),

and to an individual included or seeking inclusion in any list corresponding to a list referred to in paragraph (*a*) prepared by a Primary Care Trust or Health Authority by virtue of regulations made under section 41 of the Health and Social Care Act 2001 (which provides for the application of enactments in relation to local pharmaceutical services).********

(7) Before issuing an enhanced criminal record certificate the Secretary of State shall request the chief officer of every relevant police force to provide any information which, in the chief officer's opinion—

(*a*) might be relevant for the purpose described in the statement under subsection (2), and

(*b*) ought to be included in the certificate[3].

(8) The Secretary of State shall also request the chief officer of every relevant police force to provide any information which, in the chief officer's opinion—

(*a*) might be relevant for the purpose described in the statement under subsection (2),

(*b*) ought not to be included in the certificate, in the interests of the prevention of detection of crime, and

(*c*) can, without harming those interests, be disclosed to the registered person.

(9) The Secretary of State shall send to the registered person who countersigned an application under this section—

(*a*) a copy of the enhanced criminal record certificate, and

(*b*) any information provided in accordance with subsection (8). *********

(10) In this section—

"central records", "exempted question" and "relevant matter" have the same meaning as in section 113; and

"relevant police force", in relation to an application under this section, means a police force which is a relevant police force in relation to that application under regulations made by the Secretary of State.†

[Police Act 1997, s 115, as amended by the Care Standards Act 2000, s 90, the Health and Social Care Act 2001, s 19 and the National Health Service Reform, the Health Care Professions Act 2002, s 2, the Education Act 2002, Sch 13 and the Licensing Act 2003, Sch 6.]

---

†Repealed by the Serious Organised Crime and Police Act 2005, Sch 17 from a date to be appointed.

***Sub-section (5), para (*e*) words "registration under section 71 of the Children Act 1989" repealed, in relation to Scotland, by the Regulation of Care (Scotland) Act 2001, s 79.**

****Sub-section (5)(*ec*) inserted by the Education Act 2002, Sch 12, from a date to be appointed.**

*****Sub-sections (5)(*ee*) and (*ef*) relate to Scotland only by virtue of the Regulation of Care (Scotland) Act 2001, s 79.**

******Sub-section (*ga*) is reproduced as inserted by the Private Security Act 2001, s 21, from a date to be appointed.**

*******Sub-paragraphs (a)(ii) and (iii) repealed by the Education Act 2002, Sch 21. In force in Wales and Scotland; in force in relation to England from a date to be appointed.**

********Sub-section (6B) relates to England and Wales.**

*********Sub-section (6BB) reproduced as inserted by the Education Act 2002, s 148 from a date to be appointed.**

**********Sub-sections (6EA) and (6EB) inserted in relation to Northern Ireland by SI 2003/417, from a date to be appointed.**

***********Sub-sections (9A) and (9B) inserted by the Criminal Justice Act 2003, Sch 35 from a date to be appointed.**

1. The Police Act 1997 (Criminal Records) Regulations 2002 have been made, in this PART, post.

2. The Police Act 1997 (Enhanced Criminal Record Certificates) (Protection of Vulnerable Adults) Regulations 2002, SI 2002/446 have been made and apply this provision to certain adults with disabilities receiving nursing or care in a care home, in his own home or a hospital or clinic and a position is specified for the purposes of this subsection if it is of a kind which enables a person to have regular contact in the course of his duties with a vulnerable adult.

3. In *R (on the application of X) v Chief Constable of the West Midlands Police* [2004] EWCA Civ 1068, [2005] 1 WLR 65, it was held that the Chief Constable was under a duty to disclose information which might be relevant (here, that a charge of indecent exposure had been brought against the complainant and then discontinued) unless there was some good reason for not doing so, and that it imposed too heavy an obligation on the Chief Constable to require him to give an opportunity for a person to make representations prior to performing his statutory duty of disclosure.

8–23881 116. Enhanced criminal record certificates: judicial appointments and Crown employment. Enhanced criminal record certificates: judicial appointments and Crown employment.

8–23882 117. Disputes about accuracy of certificates. (1) Where an applicant for a certificate under any of sections 112 to 116 believes that the information contained in the certificate is inaccurate he may make an application in writing to the Secretary of State for a new certificate.

(2) The Secretary of State shall consider any application under this section; and where he is of the opinion that the information in the certificate is inaccurate he shall issue a new certificate.

[Police Act 1997, s 117.]

8–23883 118. Evidence of identity. *Secretary of State may require evidence of identity including fingerprint.*

8–23884 119. Sources of information. *Any person who holds records of convictions or cautions for the use of police forces generally shall make those records available to the Secretary of State.*

8–23885 120. Registered persons. (1) For the purposes of this Part a registered person is a person who is listed in a register to be maintained by the Secretary of State for the purposes of this Part.

(2)–(3) *Regulations*[1].

(4) A person applying for registration under this section must be—

(*a*) a body corporate or unincorporate,
(*b*) a person appointed to an office by virtue of any enactment, or
(*c*) an individual who employs others in the course of a business.

(5) A body applying for registration under this section must satisfy the Secretary of State that it—

(*a*) is likely to ask exempted questions, or
(*b*) is likely to countersign applications under section 113 or 115★ at the request of bodies or individuals asking exempted questions.

(6) A person, other than a body, applying for registration under this section must satisfy the Secretary of State that he is likely to ask exempted questions.

(7) In this section "exempted question" has the same meaning as in section 113★.

[Police Act 1997, s 120.]

★Substituted by the Serious Organised Crime and Police Act 2005, Sch 14 from a date to be appointed.

1. The Police Act 1997 (Criminal Records) (Registration) Regulations 2001, SI 2001/1194 amended by SI 2001/2498 have been made.

8–23885A 120A. Refusal and cancellation of registration★. (1) The Secretary of State may refuse to include a person in the register maintained for the purposes of this Part if it appears to him that the registration of that person is likely to make it possible for information to become available to an individual who, in the Secretary of State's opinion, is not a suitable person to have access to that information.

(2) The Secretary of State may remove a person from the register if it appears to the Secretary of State—

(*a*) that the registration of that person is likely to make it possible for information to become available to an individual who, in the Secretary of State's opinion, is not a suitable person to have access to that information; or
(*b*) that the registration of that person has resulted in information becoming known to such an individual.

(3) In determining for the purposes of this section whether an individual is a suitable person to have access to any information, the Secretary of State may have regard, in particular, to—

(*a*) any information relating to that person which concerns a relevant matter;
(*b*) whether that person is included in any list mentioned in section 113(3A) or (3C); and★★ ★★★
(*c*) any information provided to the Secretary of State under subsection (4).★

(4) It shall be the duty of the chief officer of any police force to comply, as soon as practicable after receiving it, with any request by the Secretary of State to provide the Secretary of State with information which—

(*a*) is available to the chief officer;
(*b*) relates to—

  (i) an applicant for registration;
  (ii) a registered person; or
  (iii) an individual who is likely to have access to information in consequence of the countersigning of applications by a particular applicant for registration or by a particular registered person;

and

(*c*) concerns a matter which the Secretary of State has notified to the chief officer to be a matter which, in the opinion of the Secretary of State, is relevant to the determination of the suitability of individuals for having access to the information that may be provided in consequence of the countersigning of applications under this Part.

(5) In this section 'relevant matter' has the same meaning as in section 113.***
[Police Act 1997, s 120A as inserted by the Criminal Justice and Police Act 2001, s 134(1).]

***Amended by the Criminal Justice Act 2003, s 336 from a date to be appointed,**
****Amended in relation to Northern Ireland by SI 2003/417, from a date to be appointed.**
*****Amended and new sub-s (6) inserted by the Serious Organised Crime and Police Act 2005, s 163 from a date to be appointed.**

8–23886 121. *Scotland.*

8–23887 122. *Code of practice*

8–23888 123. Offences: falsification, &c. (1) A person commits an offence if, with intent to deceive, he—

(*a*) makes a false certificate under this Part,
(*b*) alters a certificate under this Part,
(*c*) uses a certificate under this Part which relates to another person in a way which suggests that it relates to himself, or
(*d*) allows a certificate under this Part which relates to him to be used by another person in a way which suggests that it relates to that other person.

(2) A person commits an offence if he knowingly makes a false statement for the purpose of obtaining, or enabling another person to obtain, a certificate under this Part.

(3) A person who is guilty of an offence under this section shall be liable on summary conviction to imprisonment for a term not exceeding **six months** or to a fine not exceeding **level 5** on the standard scale, or to **both**.
[Police Act 1997, s 123.]

8–23889 124. Offences: disclosure. (1) A member, officer or employee of a body registered under section 120 commits an offence if he discloses information provided following an application under section 113 or 115 unless he discloses it, in the course of his duties—

(*a*) to another member, officer or employee of the registered body,
(*b*) to a member, officer or employee of a body at the request of which the registered body countersigned the application, or
(*c*) to an individual at whose request the registered body countersigned the relevant application.

(2) When information is provided under section 113 or 115 following an application countersigned at the request of a body which is not registered under section 120, a member, officer or employee of the body commits an offence if he discloses the information unless he discloses it, in the course of his duties, to another member, officer or employee of that body.

(3) Where information is provided under section 113 or 115 following an application countersigned by or at the request of an individual—

(*a*) the individual commits an offence if he discloses the information unless he discloses it to an employee of his for the purpose of the employee's duties, and
(*b*) an employee of the individual commits an offence if he discloses the information unless he discloses it, in the course of his duties, to another employee of the individual.

(4) Where information provided under section 113 or 115 is disclosed to a person and the disclosure—

(*a*) is an offence under this section, or
(*b*) would be an offence under this section but for subsection (5) or (6)(*a*), (*d*), (*e*) or (*f*),

the person to whom the information is disclosed commits an offence (subject to subsections (5) and (6)) if he discloses it to any other person.

(5) Subsections (1) to (4) do not apply to a disclosure of information provided in accordance with section 115(8) which is made with the written consent of the chief officer who provided the information.

(6) Subsections (1) to (4) do not apply to a disclosure of information contained in a certificate under section 113 or 115 which is made—

(*a*) with a written consent of the applicant for the certificate, or
(*b*) to a government department, or
(*c*) to a person appointed to an office by virtue of any enactment, or
(*d*) in accordance with an obligation to provide information under or by virtue of any enactment, or
(*e*) for the purposes of answering an exempted question (within the meaning of section 113) of a kind specified in regulations made by the Secretary of State, or
(*f*) for some other purpose specified in regulations made by the Secretary of State.

(7) A person who is guilty of an offence under this section shall be liable on summary conviction to imprisonment for a term not exceeding **six months** or to a fine not exceeding **level 3** on the standard scale, or to **both**.*
[Police Act 1997, s 124.]

8–23889A 124A. Further offences: disclosure of information obtained in connection with delegated function. (1) Any person who is engaged in the discharge of functions conferred by this Part on the Secretary of State commits an offence if he discloses information which has been obtained by him in connection with those functions and which relates to a particular person unless he discloses the information, in the course of his duties,—

(*a*) to another person engaged in the discharge of those functions,
(*b*) to the chief officer of a police force in connection with a request under this Part to provide information to the Secretary of State, or
(*c*) to an applicant or registered person who is entitled under this Part to the information disclosed to him.

(2) Where information is disclosed to a person and the disclosure—
(*a*) is an offence under subsection (1), or
(*b*) would be an offence under subsection (1) but for subsection (3)(a), (d) or (e),

the person to whom the information is disclosed commits an offence if he discloses it to any other person.

(3) Subsection (1) does not apply to a disclosure of information which is made—
(*a*) with the written consent of the person to whom the information relates,
(*b*) to a government department,
(*c*) to a person appointed to an office by virtue of any enactment,
(*d*) in accordance with an obligation to provide information under or by virtue of any enactment, or
(*e*) for some other purpose specified in regulations made by the Secretary of State.

(4) A person who is guilty of an offence under this section shall be liable on summary conviction to imprisonment for a term not exceeding 51 weeks or to a fine not exceeding level 3 on the standard scale, or to both.

(5) In relation to an offence committed before the commencement of section 281(5) of the Criminal Justice Act 2003, the reference in subsection (4) to 51 weeks is to be read as a reference to 6 months.

(6) For the purposes of this section the reference to a police force includes any body mentioned in subsections (10)(*a*) to (i) and (11) of section 113B and the reference to a chief officer must be construed accordingly. *
[Police Act 1997, s 124A as inserted by the Criminal Justice Act 2003, Sch 35 and amended by the Serious Organised Crime and Police Act 2005, s 165.]

***Section 124B inserted in relation to Scotland by the Criminal Justice (Scotland) Act 2003, s 70, from a date to be appointed.**

8–23890 125. *Regulations*

8–23891 126. Interpretation of Part V. (1) In this Part—

"caution" means a caution given to a person in England and Wales or Northern Ireland in respect of an offence which, at the time when the caution is given, he has admitted;
"certificate" means any one or more documents issued in response to a particular application;
"chief officer" means—
(i) a chief officer of police of a police force in England and Wales.
(ii) a chief constable of a police force in Scotland, and
(iii) the Chief Constable of the Royal Ulster Constabulary;
"government department" includes a Northern Ireland department;
"Minister of the Crown" includes a Northern Ireland department;
"police authority" means—
(i) a police authority for an area in Great Britain or a joint police board (within the meaning of the Police (Scotland) Act 1967), and
(ii) the Police Authority for Northern Ireland;
"police force" means—
(i) a police force in Great Britain, and
(ii) the Royal Ulster Constabulary and the Royal Ulster Constabulary Reserve;
"prescribed" shall be construed in accordance with section 125(1).

(2) *Northern Ireland.*

(3)–(4) *Scotland.*
[Police Act 1997, s 126 as amended by the Serious Organised Crime and Police Act 2005, s 166.]

8–23892 127. Saving: disclosure of information and records. Nothing in sections 112 to 119 shall be taken to prejudice any power which exists apart from this Act to disclose information or to make records available.
[Police Act 1997, s 127.]

PART VII[1]
GENERAL

8–23893 134. *Amendments and repeals*

1. Part VII comprises ss 134–138.

8–23894 135. Commencement. (1) The preceding provisions of this Act shall come into force on such day as the Secretary of State may by order made by statutory instrument appoint.
(2)–(5) *Further provisions.*
[Police Act 1997, s 135.]

1. For commencement orders made at the date of going to press, see the note to the short title to this Act, ante.

8–23895 136. *Police: co-operation and implementation*

8–23896 137. *Extent*

8–23897 138. *Short title*

Police Reform Act 2002[1]

(2000 c 30)

PART 2
COMPLAINTS AND MISCONDUCT[2]

The Independent Police Complaints Commission

Application of Part 2

8–23897A This Part (ss 9–29) establishes an Independent Police Complaints Commission which consists of a Chairman appointed by the Queen and not less than 10 other members appointed by the Secretary of State (s 9). The functions of the Commission include handling complaints about the conduct of persons serving with the police and the recording of conduct which constitutes or involves the commission of a criminal offence or which justifies disciplinary proceedings and the manner in which such matters are investigated (s 11). The Commission must make a report to the Secretary of State at the end of each financial year (s 11).

1. With the exception of s 100 and related amendments in Sch 8 which came into force on 24 July 2002, this Act is to be brought into force in accordance with commencement orders made under s 108. At the date of going to press the following commencement orders had been made: (No 1) SI 2002/2306; (No 2) SSI 2002/420 (Scotland); (No 3) SI 2002/2750; (No 4) SI 2003/808; (No 5) SI 2003/2593; (No 6) SI 2004/119; (No 7) SI 2004/636; (No 8) SI 2004/913; (No 9) SI 2004/1319; (No 10) SI 2004/3338.
2. Part 2 comprises ss 9–29 and Schs 2 and 3.

8–23897B 12. Complaints, matters and persons to which Part 2 applies. (1) In this Part references to a complaint are references (subject to the following provisions of this section) to any complaint about the conduct of a person serving with the police which is made (whether in writing or otherwise) by—

(*a*) a member of the public who claims to be the person in relation to whom the conduct took place;
(*b*) a member of the public not falling within paragraph (*a*) who claims to have been adversely affected by the conduct;
(*c*) a member of the public who claims to have witnessed the conduct;
(*d*) a person acting on behalf of a person falling within any of paragraphs (*a*) to (*c*).

(2) In this Part "conduct matter" means (subject to the following provisions of this section, paragraph 2(4) of Schedule 3 and any regulations made by virtue of section 23(2)(*d*)) any matter which is not and has not been the subject of a complaint but in the case of which there is an indication (whether from the circumstances or otherwise) that a person serving with the police may have—

(*a*) committed a criminal offence; or

(*b*) behaved in a manner which would justify the bringing of disciplinary proceedings.

(2A) In this Part "death or serious injury matter" (or "DSI matter" for short) means any circumstances (other than those which are or have been the subject of a complaint or which amount to a conduct matter)—

(*a*) in or in consequence of which a person has died or has sustained serious injury; and

(*b*) in relation to which the requirements of either subsection (2B) or subsection (2C) are satisfied.

(2B) The requirements of this subsection are that at the time of the death or serious injury the person—

(*a*) had been arrested by a person serving with the police and had not been released from that arrest; or

(*b*) was otherwise detained in the custody of a person serving with the police.

(2C) The requirements of this subsection are that—

(*a*) at or before the time of the death or serious injury the person had contact (of whatever kind, and whether direct or indirect) with a person serving with the police who was acting in the execution of his duties; and

(*b*) there is an indication that the contact may have caused (whether directly or indirectly) or contributed to the death or serious injury.

(2D) In subsection (2A) the reference to a person includes a person serving with the police, but in relation to such a person "contact" in subsection (2C) does not include contact that he has whilst acting in the execution of his duties.

(3) The complaints that are complaints for the purposes of this Part by virtue of subsection (1)(*b*) do not, except in a case falling within subsection (4), include any made by or on behalf of a person who claims to have been adversely affected as a consequence only of having seen or heard the conduct, or any of the alleged effects of the conduct.

(4) A case falls within this subsection if—

(*a*) it was only because the person in question was physically present, or sufficiently nearby, when the conduct took place or the effects occurred that he was able to see or hear the conduct or its effects; or

(*b*) the adverse effect is attributable to, or was aggravated by, the fact that the person in relation to whom the conduct took place was already known to the person claiming to have suffered the adverse effect.

(5) For the purposes of this section a person shall be taken to have witnessed conduct if, and only if—

(*a*) he acquired his knowledge of that conduct in a manner which would make him a competent witness capable of giving admissible evidence of that conduct in criminal proceedings; or

(*b*) he has in his possession or under his control anything which would in any such proceedings constitute admissible evidence of that conduct.

(6) For the purposes of this Part a person falling within subsection 1(*a*) to (*c*) to shall not be taken to have authorised another person to act on his behalf unless—

(*a*) that other person is for the time being designated for the purposes of this Part by the Commission as a person through whom complaints may be made, or he is of a description of persons so designated; or

(*b*) the other person has been given, and is able to produce, the written consent to his so acting of the person on whose behalf he acts.

(7) For the purposes of this Part, a person is serving with the police if—

(*a*) he is a member of a police force;

(*b*) he is an employee of a police authority who is under the direction and control of a chief officer; or

(*c*) he is a special constable who is under the direction and control of a chief officer.

[Police Reform Act 2002, s 12 as amended by the Serious Organised Crime and Police Act 2005, Sch 12.]

Handling of complaints and conduct matters etc

8–23897C 13. Handling of complaints, conduct matters and DSI mattersetc. Schedule 3 (which makes provision for the handling of complaints, conduct matters and DSI matters and for the carrying out of investigations) shall have effect subject to section 14(1).

[Police Reform Act 2002, s 13 as amended by the Serious Organised Crime and Police Act 2005, Sch 12.]

8–23897D 14. Direction and control matters. (1) Nothing in Schedule 3 shall have effect with respect to so much of any complaint as relates to the direction and control of a police force by—

(*a*) the chief officer of police of that force; or

(*b*) a person for the time being carrying out the functions of the chief officer of police of that force.

(2) The Secretary of State may issue guidance to chief officers and to police authorities about the handling of so much of any complaint as relates to the direction and control of a police force by such a person as is mentioned in subsection (1).

(3) It shall be the duty of a chief officer and of a police authority when handling any complaint relating to such a matter to have regard to any guidance issued under subsection (2).
[Police Reform Act 2002, s 14.]

Co-operation, assistance and information

Sections 15–29 make provision for the co-operation of police forces with the Commission in the investigation of complaints and for funding of investigations, provision of information to the Commission, inspection of police premises and use of investigatory powers, and a duty to keep the complainant informed. The Commission may also issue guidance to police authorities and chief officers concerning the exercise of their functions under this Part and the Secretary of State may make regulations.

PART 4
POLICE POWERS ETC[1]

CHAPTER 1
EXERCISE OF POLICE POWERS ETC BY CIVILIANS[2]

8–23897E 38. Police powers for police authority employees. (1) The chief officer of police of any police force may designate any person who—

(*a*) is employed by the police authority maintaining that force, and
(*b*) is under the direction and control of that chief officer,

as an officer of one or more of the descriptions specified in subsection (2).

(2) The description of officers are as follows—

(*a*) community support officer;
(*b*) investigating officer;
(*c*) detention officer;
(*d*) escort officer.

(3) A Director General may designate any person who—

(*a*) is an employee of his Service Authority, and
(*b*) is under the direction and control of that Director General,

as an investigating officer.

(4) A chief officer of police or a Director General shall not designate a person under this section unless he is satisfied that that person—

(*a*) is a suitable person to carry out the functions for the purposes of which he is designated;
(*b*) is capable of effectively carrying out those functions; and
(*c*) has received adequate training in the carrying out of those functions and in the exercise and performance of the powers and duties to be conferred on him by virtue of the designation.

(5) A person designated under this section shall have the powers and duties conferred or imposed on him by the designation.

(6) Powers and duties may be conferred or imposed on a designated person by means only of the application to him by his designation of provisions of the applicable Part of Schedule 4 that are to apply to the designated person; and for this purpose the applicable Part of that Schedule is—

(*a*) in the case of a person designated as a community support officer, Part 1;
(*b*) in the case of a person designated as an investigating officer, Part 2;
(*c*) in the case of a person designated as a detention officer, Part 3; and
(*d*) in the case of a person designated as an escort officer, Part 4.

(7) An employee of a police authority or of a Service Authority authorised or required to do anything by virtue of a designation under this section—

(*a*) shall not be authorised or required by virtue of that designation to engage in any conduct otherwise than in the course of that employment; and
(*b*) shall be so authorised or required subject to such restrictions and conditions (if any) as may be specified in his designation.

(8) Where any power exercisable by any person in reliance on his designation under this section is a power which, in the case of its exercise by a constable, includes or is supplemented by a power to use reasonable force, any person exercising that power in reliance on that designation shall have the same entitlement as a constable to use reasonable force.

(9) Where any power exercisable by any person in reliance on his designation under this section

includes power to use force to enter any premises, that power shall not be exercisable by that person except—

(*a*) in the company, and under the supervision, of a constable; or

(*b*) for the purpose of saving life or limb or preventing serious damage to property.

[Police Reform Act 2002, s 38.]

1. Part 4 comprises ss 38–77 and Sch 4–6.
2. Chapter 1 comprises ss 38–47 and Schs 4 and 5.

8–23897F 39. Police powers for contracted-out staff. (1) This section applies if a police authority has entered into a contract with a person ("the contractor") for the provision of services relating to the detention or escort of persons who have been arrested or are otherwise in custody.

(2) The chief officer of police of the police force maintained by that police authority may designate any person who is an employee of the contractor as either or both of the following—

(*a*) a detention officer; or

(*b*) an escort officer.

(3) A person designated under this section shall have the powers and duties conferred or imposed on him by the designation.

(4) A chief officer of police shall not designate a person under this section unless he is satisfied that that person—

(*a*) is a suitable person to carry out the functions for the purposes of which he is designated;

(*b*) is capable of effectively carrying out those functions; and

(*c*) has received adequate training in the carrying out of those functions and in the exercise and performance of the powers and duties to be conferred on him by virtue of the designation.

(5) A chief officer of police shall not designate a person under this section unless he is satisfied that the contractor is a fit and proper person to supervise the carrying out of the functions for the purposes of which that person is designated.

(6) Powers and duties may be conferred or imposed on a designated person by means only of the application to him by his designation of provisions of the applicable Part of Schedule 4 that are to apply to the designated person; and for this purpose the applicable Part of that Schedule is—

(*a*) in the case of a person designated as a detention officer, Part 3; and

(*b*) in the case of a person designated as an escort officer, Part 4.

(7) An employee of the contractor authorised or required to do anything by virtue of a designation under this section—

(*a*) shall not be authorised or required by virtue of that designation to engage in any conduct otherwise than in the course of that employment; and

(*b*) shall be so authorised or required subject to such restrictions and conditions (if any) as may be specified in his designation.

(8) Where any power exercisable by any person in reliance on his designation under this section is a power which, in the case of its exercise by a constable, includes or is supplemented by a power to use reasonable force, any person exercising that power in reliance on that designation shall have the same entitlement as a constable to use reasonable force.

(9) The Secretary of State may by regulations[1] make provision for the handling of complaints relating to, or other instances of misconduct involving, the carrying out by any person designated under this section of the functions for the purposes of which any power or duty is conferred or imposed by his designation.

(10) Regulations under subsection (9) may, in particular, provide that any provision made by Part 2 of this Act with respect to complaints against persons serving with the police is to apply, with such modifications as may be prescribed by them, with respect to complaints against persons designated under this section.

(11) Before making regulations under this section, the Secretary of State shall consult with—

(*a*) persons whom he considers to represent the interests of police authorities;

(*b*) persons whom he considers to represent the interests of chief officers of police;

(*c*) the Independent Police Complaints Commission; and

(*d*) such other persons as he thinks fit.

(12) A designation under this section, unless it is previously withdrawn or ceases to have effect in accordance with subsection (13), shall remain in force for such period as may be specified in the designation; but it may be renewed at any time with effect from the time when it would otherwise expire.

(13) A designation under this section shall cease to have effect—

(*a*) if the designated person ceases to be an employee of the contractor; or

(*b*) if the contract between the police authority and the contractor is terminated or expires.

[Police Reform Act 2002, s 39.]

1. The Police (Complaints and Misconduct) Regulations 2004, SI 2004/643 amended by SI 2005/3389 have been made.

8–23897G 40. Community safety accreditation schemes. (1) The chief officer of police of any police force may, if he considers that it is appropriate to do so for the purposes specified in subsection (3), establish and maintain a scheme ("a community safety accreditation scheme").

(2) A community safety accreditation scheme is a scheme for the exercise in the chief officer's police area by persons accredited by him under section 41 of the powers conferred by their accreditations under that section.

(3) Those purposes are—

(*a*) contributing to community safety and security; and

(*b*) in co-operation with the police force for the area, combatting crime and disorder, public nuisance and other forms of anti-social behaviour.

(4) Before establishing a community safety accreditation scheme for his police area, a chief officer of any police force (other than the Commissioner of Police of the Metropolis) must consult with—

(*a*) the police authority maintaining that force, and

(*b*) every local authority any part of whose area lies within the police area.

(5) Before establishing a community safety accreditation scheme for the metropolitan police district, the Commissioner of Police of the Metropolis must consult with—

(*a*) the Metropolitan Police Authority;

(*b*) the Mayor of London; and

(*c*) every local authority any part of whose area lies within the metropolitan police district.

(6) In subsections (4)(*b*) and (5)(*c*) "local authority" means—

(*a*) in relation to England, a district council, a London borough council, the Common Council of the City of London or the Council of the Isles of Scilly; and

(*b*) in relation to Wales, a county council or a county borough council.

(7) Every police plan under section 8 of the 1996 Act which is issued after the commencement of this section, and every draft of such a plan which is submitted by a chief officer of police to a police authority after the commencement of this section, must set out—

(*a*) whether a community safety accreditation scheme is maintained for the police area in question;

(*b*) if not, whether there is any proposal to establish such a scheme for that area during the period to which the plan relates;

(*c*) particulars of any such proposal or of any proposal to modify during that period any community safety accreditation scheme that is already maintained for that area;

(*d*) the extent (if any) of any arrangements for provisions specified in Schedule 4 to be applied to designated persons employed by the police authority; and

(*e*) the respects in which any community safety accreditation scheme that is maintained or proposed will be supplementing those arrangements during the period to which the plan relates.

(8) A community safety accreditation scheme must contain provision for the making of arrangements with employers who—

(*a*) are carrying on business in the police area in question, or

(*b*) are carrying on business in relation to the whole or any part of that area or in relation to places situated within it,

for those employers to supervise the carrying out by their employees of the community safety functions for the purposes of which powers are conferred on those employees by means of accreditations under section 41.

(9) It shall be the duty of a chief officer of police who establishes and maintains a community safety accreditation scheme to ensure that the employers of the persons on whom powers are conferred by the grant of accreditations under section 41 have established and maintain satisfactory arrangements for handling complaints relating to the carrying out by those persons of the functions for the purposes of which the powers are conferred.

[Police Reform Act 2002, s 40.]

8–23897H 41. Accreditation under community safety accreditation schemes. (1) This section applies where a chief officer of police has, for the purposes of a community safety accreditation scheme, entered into any arrangements with any employer for or with respect to the carrying out of community safety functions by employees of that employer.

(2) The chief officer of police may, on the making of an application for the purpose by such person and in such manner as he may require, grant accreditation under this section to any employee of the employer.

(3) Schedule 5 (which sets out the powers that may be conferred on accredited persons) shall have effect.

(4) A chief officer of police shall not grant accreditation to a person under this section unless he is satisfied—

(*a*) that that person's employer is a fit and proper person to supervise the carrying out of the functions for the purposes of which the accreditation is to be granted;

(*b*) that the person himself is a suitable person to exercise the powers that will be conferred on him by virtue of the accreditation;

(*c*) that that person is capable of effectively carrying out the functions for the purposes of which those powers are to be conferred on him; and

(*d*) that that person has received adequate training for the exercise of those powers.

(5) A chief officer of police may charge such fee as he considers appropriate for one or both of the following—

(*a*) considering an application for or for the renewal of an accreditation under this section;

(*b*) granting such an accreditation.

(6) A person authorised or required to do anything by virtue of an accreditation under this section—

(*a*) shall not be authorised or required by virtue of that accreditation to engage in any conduct otherwise than in the course of his employment by the employer with whom the chief officer of police has entered into the arrangements mentioned in subsection (1); and

(*b*) shall be so authorised or required subject to such other restrictions and conditions (if any) as may be specified in his accreditation.

(7) An accreditation under this section, unless it is previously withdrawn or ceases to have effect in accordance with subsection (8), shall remain in force for such period as may be specified in the accreditation; but it may be renewed at any time with effect from the time when it would otherwise expire.

(8) An accreditation under this section shall cease to have effect—

(*a*) if the accredited person ceases to be an employee of the person with whom the chief officer of police has entered into the arrangements mentioned in subsection (1); or

(*b*) if those arrangements are terminated or expire.

[Police Reform Act 2002, s 41.]

8–23897I 42. Supplementary provisions relating to designations and accreditations. (1) A person who exercises or performs any power or duty in relation to any person in reliance on his designation under section 38 or 39 or his accreditation under section 41, or who purports to do so, shall produce that designation or accreditation to that person, if requested to do so.

(2) A power exercisable by any person in reliance on his designation by a chief officer of police under section 38 or 39 or his accreditation under section 41 shall, subject to subsection (2A), be exercisable only by a person wearing such uniform as may be—

(*a*) determined or approved for the purposes of this Chapter by the chief officer of police who granted the designation or accreditation; and

(*b*) identified or described in the designation or accreditation;

and, in the case of an accredited person, such a power shall be exercisable only if he is also wearing such badge as may be specified for the purposes of this subsection by the Secretary of State, and is wearing it in such manner, or in such place, as may be so specified.

(2A) A police officer of or above the rank of inspector may direct a particular investigating officer not to wear a uniform for the purposes of a particular operation; and if he so directs, subsection (2) shall not apply in relation to that investigating officer for the purposes of that operation.

(2B) In subsection (2A), "investigating officer" means a person designated as an investigating officer under section 38 by the chief officer of police of the same force as the officer giving the direction.

(3) A chief officer of police who has granted a designation or accreditation to any person under section 38, 39 or 41 may at any time, by notice to the designated or accredited person, modify or withdraw that designation or accreditation.

(4) *Repealed.*

(5) Where any person's designation under section 39 is modified or withdrawn, the chief officer giving notice of the modification or withdrawal shall send a copy of the notice to the contractor responsible for supervising that person in the carrying out of the functions for the purposes of which the designation was granted.

(6) Where any person's accreditation under section 41 is modified or withdrawn, the chief officer giving notice of the modification or withdrawal shall send a copy of the notice to the employer responsible for supervising that person in the carrying out of the functions for the purposes of which the accreditation was granted.

(7) For the purposes of determining liability for the unlawful conduct of employees of a police authority, conduct by such an employee in reliance or purported reliance on a designation under

section 38 shall be taken to be conduct in the course of his employment by the police authority; and, in the case of a tort, that authority shall fall to be treated as a joint tortfeasor accordingly.

(8) *Repealed.*

(9) For the purposes of determining liability for the unlawful conduct of employees of a contractor (within the meaning of section 39), conduct by such an employee in reliance or purported reliance on a designation under that section shall be taken to be conduct in the course of his employment by that contractor; and, in the case of a tort, that contractor shall fall to be treated as a joint tortfeasor accordingly.

(10) For the purposes of determining liability for the unlawful conduct of employees of a person with whom a chief officer of police has entered into any arrangements for the purposes of a community safety accreditation scheme, conduct by such an employee in reliance or purported reliance on an accreditation under section 41 shall be taken to be conduct in the course of his employment by that employer; and, in the case of a tort, that employer shall fall to be treated as a joint tortfeasor accordingly.

[Police Reform Act 2002, s 42 as amended by the Serious Organised Crime and Police Act 2005, s 122 and the Serious Organised Crime and Police Act 2005, Schs 4 and 17.]

8–23897J 43. Railway safety accreditation scheme. (1) The Secretary of State may make regulations[1] for the purpose of enabling the chief constable of the British Transport Police Force to establish and maintain a scheme ("a railway safety accreditation scheme").

(2) A railway safety accreditation scheme is a scheme for the exercise, within a place specified in section 21(1)(*a*) to (*f*) of the Railways and Transport Safety Act 2003 in England and Wales, by persons accredited by the chief constable of the British Transport Police Force under the scheme, of the powers conferred on those persons by their accreditation under that scheme.

(3)–(9) *Regulations*

(10) In this section—

"local authorities" means district councils, London borough councils, county councils in Wales, county borough councils and the Common Council of the City of London; and

"policed premises" has the meaning given by section 53(3) of the British Transport Commission Act 1949.

[Police Reform Act 2002, s 43 as amended by SI 2004.1573.]

1. The Railway Safety Accreditation Scheme Regulations 2004, SI 2004/915 amended by SI 2004/1573 have been made.

8–23897K 45. *Code of practice relating to chief officers' powers under Chapter 1*

8–23897L 46. Offences against designated and accredited persons etc. (1) Any person who assaults—

(*a*) a designated person in the execution of his duty,
(*b*) an accredited person in the execution of his duty, or
(*c*) a person assisting a designated or accredited person in the execution of his duty,

is guilty of an offence and shall be liable, on summary conviction, to imprisonment for a term not exceeding six months or to a fine not exceeding level 5 on the standard scale, or to both.

(2) Any person who resists or wilfully obstructs—

(*a*) a designated person in the execution of his duty,
(*b*) an accredited person in the execution of his duty, or
(*c*) a person assisting a designated or accredited person in the execution of his duty,

is guilty of an offence and shall be liable, on summary conviction, to imprisonment for a term not exceeding one month* or to a fine not exceeding level 3 on the standard scale, or to both.

(3) Any person who, with intent to deceive—

(*a*) impersonates a designated person or an accredited person,
(*b*) makes any statement or does any act calculated falsely to suggest that he is a designated person or that he is an accredited person, or
(*c*) makes any statement or does any act calculated falsely to suggest that he has powers as a designated or accredited person that exceed the powers he actually has,

is guilty of an offence and shall be liable, on summary conviction, to imprisonment for a term not exceeding six months or to a fine not exceeding level 5 on the standard scale, or to both.

(4) In this section references to the execution by a designated person or accredited person of his duty are references to his exercising any power or performing any duty which is his by virtue of his designation or accreditation.

[Police Reform Act 2002, s 46.]

***"51 weeks" substituted by the Criminal Justice Act 2003, Sch 26, from a date to be appointed.**

8–23897M 47. Interpretation of Chapter 1. (1) In this Chapter—

"accredited person" means a person in relation to whom an accreditation under section 41 is for the time being in force;

"community safety functions" means any functions the carrying out of which would be facilitated by the ability to exercise one or more of the powers mentioned in Schedule 5;

"conduct" includes omissions and statements;

"designated person" means a person in relation to whom a designation under section 38 or 39 is for the time being in force;

"Director General" means—

(*a*) the Director General of the National Criminal Intelligence Service; or

(*b*) the Director General of the National Crime Squad;

"Service Authority" means—

(*a*) in relation to employment with the National Criminal Intelligence Service or to its Director General, the Service Authority for the National Criminal Intelligence Service; and

(*b*) in relation to employment with the National Crime Squad or to its Director General, the Service Authority for the National Crime Squad.

(2) In this Chapter—

(*a*) references to carrying on business include references to carrying out functions under any enactment; and

(*b*) references to the employees of a person carrying on business include references to persons holding office under a person, and references to employers shall be construed accordingly.

[Police Reform Act 2002, s 47.]

CHAPTER 2
PROVISIONS MODIFYING AND SUPPLEMENTING POLICE POWERS[1]

Power to require name and address

8–23897N 50. Persons acting in an anti-social manner. (1) If a constable in uniform has reason to believe that a person has been acting, or is acting, in an anti-social manner (within the meaning of section 1 of the Crime and Disorder Act 1998 (c 37) (anti-social behaviour orders)), he may require that person to give his name and address to the constable.

(2) Any person who—

(*a*) fails to give his name and address when required to do so under subsection (1), or

(*b*) gives a false or inaccurate name or address in response to a requirement under that subsection,

is guilty of an offence and shall be liable, on summary conviction, to a fine not exceeding level 3 on the standard scale.

[Police Reform Act 2002, s 50.]

1. Chapter 2 comprises ss 48–77 and Sch 6.

Persons in police detention

8–23897O 51. Independent custody visitors for places of detention. (1) Every police authority shall—

(*a*) make arrangements for detainees to be visited by persons appointed under the arrangements ("independent custody visitors"); and

(*b*) keep those arrangements under review and from time to time revise them as they think fit.

(2) The arrangements must secure that the persons appointed under the arrangements are independent of both—

(*a*) the police authority; and

(*b*) the chief officer of police of the police force maintained by that authority.

(3) The arrangements may confer on independent custody visitors such powers as the police authority considers necessary to enable them to carry out their functions under the arrangements and may, in particular, confer on them powers—

(*a*) to require access to be given to each police station;

(*b*) to examine records relating to the detention of persons there;

(*c*) to meet detainees there for the purposes of a discussion about their treatment and conditions while detained; and

(*d*) to inspect the facilities there including in particular, cell accommodation, washing and toilet facilities and the facilities for the provision of food.

(4) The arrangements may include provision for access to a detainee to be denied to independent custody visitors if—

(*a*) it appears to an officer of or above the rank of inspector that there are grounds for denying access at the time it is requested;
(*b*) the grounds are grounds specified for the purposes of paragraph (*a*) in the arrangements; and
(*c*) the procedural requirements imposed by the arrangements in relation to a denial of access are complied with.

(5) Grounds shall not be specified in any arrangements for the purposes of subsection (4)(*a*) unless they are grounds for the time being set out for the purposes of this subsection in the code of practice issued by the Secretary of State under subsection (6).

(6) The Secretary of State shall issue, and may from time to time revise, a code of practice as to the carrying out by police authorities and independent custody visitors of their functions under the arrangements.

(7) Before issuing or revising a code of practice under this section, the Secretary of State shall consult with—

(*a*) persons whom he considers to represent the interests of police authorities;
(*b*) persons whom he considers to represent the interests of chief officers of police; and
(*c*) such other persons as he thinks fit.

(8) The Secretary of State shall lay any code of practice issued by him under this section, and any revisions of any such code, before Parliament.

(9) Police authorities and independent custody visitors shall have regard to the code of practice for the time being in force under subsection (6) in the carrying out of their functions under the preceding provisions of this section.

(10) In this section "detainee", in relation to arrangements made under this section, means a person detained in a police station in the police area of the police authority.
[Police Reform Act 2002, s 51.]

Seizure of motor vehicles

8–23897P 59. Vehicles used in manner causing alarm, distress or annoyance. (1) Where a constable in uniform has reasonable grounds for believing that a motor vehicle is being used on any occasion in a manner which—

(*a*) contravenes section 3 or 34 of the Road Traffic Act 1988 (c 52) (careless and inconsiderate driving and prohibition of off-road driving), and
(*b*) is causing, or is likely to cause, alarm, distress or annoyance to members of the public,

he shall have the powers set out in subsection (3).

(2) A constable in uniform shall also have the powers set out in subsection (3) where he has reasonable grounds for believing that a motor vehicle has been used on any occasion in a manner falling within subsection (1).

(3) Those powers are—

(*a*) power, if the motor vehicle is moving, to order the person driving it to stop the vehicle;
(*b*) power to seize and remove the motor vehicle;
(*c*) power, for the purposes of exercising a power falling within paragraph (*a*) or (*b*), to enter any premises on which he has reasonable grounds for believing the motor vehicle to be;
(*d*) power to use reasonable force, if necessary, in the exercise of any power conferred by any of paragraphs to (*a*) to (*c*).

(4) A constable shall not seize a motor vehicle in the exercise of the powers conferred on him by this section unless—

(*a*) he has warned the person appearing to him to be the person whose use falls within subsection (1) that he will seize it, if that use continues or is repeated; and
(*b*) it appears to him that the use has continued or been repeated after the warning.

(5) Subsection (4) does not require a warning to be given by a constable on any occasion on which he would otherwise have the power to seize a motor vehicle under this section if—

(*a*) the circumstances make it impracticable for him to give the warning;
(*b*) the constable has already on that occasion given a warning under that subsection in respect of any use of that motor vehicle or of another motor vehicle by that person or any other person;
(*c*) the constable has reasonable grounds for believing that such a warning has been given on that occasion otherwise than by him; or
(*d*) the constable has reasonable grounds for believing that the person whose use of that motor vehicle on that occasion would justify the seizure is a person to whom a warning under that subsection has been given (whether or not by that constable or in respect the same vehicle or the same or a similar use) on a previous occasion in the previous twelve months.

(6) A person who fails to comply with an order under subsection (3)(*a*) is guilty of an offence and shall be liable, on summary conviction, to a fine not exceeding level 3 on the standard scale.

(7) Subsection (3)(*c*) does not authorise entry into a private dwelling house.

(8) The powers conferred on a constable by this section shall be exercisable only at a time when regulations under section 60 are in force.

(9) In this section—

"driving" has the same meaning as in the Road Traffic Act 1988 (c 52);

"motor vehicle" means any mechanically propelled vehicle, whether or not it is intended or adapted for use on roads; and

"private dwelling house" does not include any garage or other structure occupied with the dwelling house, or any land appurtenant to the dwelling house.

[Police Reform Act 2002, s 59.]

8–23897Q 60. Retention etc of vehicles seized under section 59. (1) The Secretary of State may by regulations[1] make provision as to—

(*a*) the removal and retention of motor vehicles seized under section 59; and

(*b*) the release or disposal of such motor vehicles.

(2) *Regulations*

[Police Reform Act 2002, s 60.]

1. The Police (Retention and Disposal of Motor Vehicles) Regulations 2002, SI 2002/3049 amended by SI 2005/2702 have been made.

PART 6

MISCELLANEOUS[1]

Appointment and attestation of police officers etc

8–23897R 82. Nationality requirements applicable to police officers etc

Subject to regulations, a person of any nationality can hold ofice as a constable.

1. Part 6 comprises ss 82–104.

PART 7

SUPPLEMENTAL[1]

8–23897S 105. Powers of Secretary of State to make orders and regulations

1. Part 7 comprises ss 105–108 and Schs 7 and 8.

8–23897T 106. General interpretation. In this Act—

"the 1984 Act" means the Police and Criminal Evidence Act 1984 (c 60);

"the 1996 Act" means the Police Act 1996 (c 16);

"the 1997 Act" means the Police Act 1997 (c 50);

"the British Transport Police Force" means the force of constables appointed under section 53 of the British Transport Commission Act 1949 (c xxix);

"modifications" includes omissions, alterations and additions, and cognate expressions shall be construed accordingly.

[Police Reform Act 2002, s 106.]

8–23897U 107. *Consequential amendments and repeals*

8–23897V 108. Short title, commencement and extent. (1) This Act may be cited as the Police Reform Act 2002.

(2) This Act, except—

(*a*) the provisions specified in subsection (3) (which come into force on the day on which this Act is passed), and

(*b*) the provisions to which subsections (4) and (5) apply,

shall come into force on such day as the Secretary of State may by order[1] appoint; and different days may be appointed under this subsection for different purposes or different areas.

(3) The provisions coming into force on the day on which this Act is passed are—

(*a*) section 100, the entries in Schedule 8 relating to the Housing Act 1985 (c 68), the Housing Act 1988 (c 50), paragraphs 51 and 59 of Schedule 27 to the Greater London Authority Act 1999 (c 29) and paragraph 74 of Schedule 6 to the Criminal Justice and Police Act 2001 (c 16) and section 107(2) (so far as relating to those entries); and

(*b*) sections 105 and 106 and this section.

(4) The provisions of sections 97 and 98, so far as they relate to local government areas in Wales,

shall come into force on such day as the National Assembly for Wales may by order made by statutory instrument appoint; and different days may be appointed under this subsection for different purposes or different areas.

(5) Sections 70 and 71, and sections 102 to 104 so far as they amend the Police (Scotland) Act 1967 (c 77), shall come into force on such day as the Scottish Ministers may by order appoint; and different days may be appointed under this subsection for different purposes or different areas.

(6) Subject to subsections (7) to (9), this Act extends to England and Wales only.

(7) This Act extends to the United Kingdom so far as it makes the following provision—

(*a*) the provision contained in Part 5;

(*b*) the provision contained in section 82;

(*c*) the provision contained in section 99;

(*d*) the provision contained in section 103(6);

(*e*) any provision (other than one contained in Chapter 1 of Part 4) relating to the National Criminal Intelligence Service.

(8) Section 96 also extends to Northern Ireland.

(9) Subject to subsection (10), this Act, so far as it amends or repeals any enactment (other than one that extends to England and Wales only), has the same extent as the enactment amended or repealed.

(10) The amendments and repeals made by this Act—

(*a*) in section 96 of the Road Traffic Regulation Act 1984 (c 27) (traffic wardens),

(*b*) in sections 103 and 183 of the Road Traffic Act 1988 (c 52) (driving while disqualified), and

(*c*) Part 3 of the Road Traffic Offenders Act 1988 (c 53) (fixed penalties),

do not extend to Scotland.

[Police Reform Act 2002, s 108.]

1. For commencement orders made under this provision see note to title of this Act, ante.

SCHEDULES

8–23897W

Section 8

SCHEDULE 1
POWERS OF THE SECRETARY OF STATE IN RELATION TO NCIS AND NCS

8–23897X

Section 9

SCHEDULE 2
THE INDEPENDENT POLICE COMPLAINTS COMMISSION

Section 13

SCHEDULE 3
HANDLING OF COMPLAINTS AND CONDUCT MATTERS ETC

(*Amended by the Serious Organised Crime and Police Act 2005, Sch 12.*)

PART 1
HANDLING OF COMPLAINTS

Duties to preserve evidence relating to complaints

8–23897Y **1.** (1) Where a complaint is made about the conduct of a chief officer, it shall be the duty of the police authority maintaining his force to secure that all such steps as are appropriate for the purposes of Part 2 of this Act are taken, both initially and from time to time after that, for obtaining and preserving evidence relating to the conduct complained of.

(2) Where—

(*a*) a complaint is made to a chief officer about the conduct of a person under his direction and control, or

(*b*) a chief officer becomes aware that a complaint about the conduct of a person under his direction or control has been made to the Commission or to a police authority,

the chief officer shall take all such steps as appear to him to be appropriate for the purposes of Part 2 of this Act for obtaining and preserving evidence relating to the conduct complained of.

(3) The chief officer's duty under sub-paragraph (2) must be performed as soon as practicable after the complaint is made or, as the case may be, he becomes aware of it.

(4) After that, he shall be under a duty, until he is satisfied that it is no longer necessary to do so, to continue to take the steps from time to time appearing to him to be appropriate for the purposes of Part 2 of this Act for obtaining and preserving evidence relating to the conduct complained of.

(5) It shall be the duty of a police authority to comply with all such directions as may be given to it by the Commission in relation to the performance of its duty under sub-paragraph (1).

(6) It shall be the duty of a chief officer to take all such specific steps for obtaining or preserving evidence relating to any conduct that is the subject-matter of a complaint as he may be directed to take for the purposes of this paragraph by the police authority maintaining his force or by the Commission.

Initial handling and recording of complaints

2. (1) Where a complaint is made to the Commission—

(*a*) it shall ascertain whether the complainant is content for the police authority or chief officer who is the appropriate authority to be notified of the complaint; and (*b*) it shall give notification of the complaint to the appropriate authority if, and only if, the complainant is so content.

(2) Where a complaint is made to a police authority, it shall—

(*a*) determine whether or not it is itself the appropriate authority; and
(*b*) if it determines that it is not, give notification of the complaint to the person who is.

(3) Where a complaint is made to a chief officer, he shall—

(*a*) determine whether or not he is himself the appropriate authority; and
(*b*) if he determines that he is not, give notification of the complaint to the person who is.

(4) Where the Commission—

(*a*) is prevented by sub-paragraph (1)(*b*) from notifying any complaint to the appropriate authority, and
(*b*) considers that it is in the public interest for the subject-matter of the complaint to be brought to the attention of the appropriate authority and recorded under paragraph 11,

the Commission may bring that matter to the appropriate authority's attention under that paragraph as if it were a recordable conduct matter, and (if it does so) the following provisions of this Schedule shall have effect accordingly as if it were such a matter.

(5) Where the Commission, a police authority or a chief officer gives notification of a complaint under any of sub-paragraphs (1) to (3) or the Commission brings any matter to the appropriate authority's attention under sub-paragraph (4), the person who gave the notification or, as the case may be, the Commission shall notify the complainant—

(*a*) that the notification has been given and of what it contained; or
(*b*) that the matter has been brought to the appropriate authority's attention to be dealt with otherwise than as a complaint.

(6) Where—

(*a*) a police authority determines, in the case of any complaint made to the authority, that it is itself the appropriate authority,
(*b*) a chief officer determines, in the case of any complaint made to that chief officer, that he is himself the appropriate authority, or
(*c*) a complaint is notified to a police authority or chief officer under this paragraph,

the authority or chief officer shall record the complaint.

(7) Nothing in this paragraph shall require the notification or recording by any person of any complaint about any conduct if—

(*a*) that person is satisfied that the subject-matter of the complaint has been, or is already being, dealt with by means of criminal or disciplinary proceedings against the person whose conduct it was; or
(*b*) the complaint has been withdrawn.

Failures to notify or record a complaint

3. (1) This paragraph applies where anything which is or purports to be a complaint in relation to which paragraph (2) has effect is received by a police authority or chief officer (whether in consequence of having been made directly or of a notification under that paragraph).

(2) If the police authority or chief officer decides not to take action under paragraph (2) for notifying or recording the whole or any part of what has been received, the authority or chief officer shall notify the complainant of the following matters—

(*a*) the decision to take no action and, if that decision relates to only part of what was received, the part in question;
(*b*) the grounds on which the decision was made; and
(*c*) that complainant's right to appeal against that decision under this paragraph.

(3) The complainant shall have a right of appeal to the Commission against any failure by the police authority or chief officer to make a determination under paragraph 2 or to notify or record anything under that paragraph.

(4) On an appeal under this paragraph, the Commission shall—

(*a*) determine whether any action under paragraph 2 should have been taken in the case in question; and
(*b*) if the Commission finds in the complainant's favour, give such directions as the Commission considers appropriate to the police authority or chief officer as to the action to be taken for making a determination, or for notifying or recording what was received;

and it shall be the duty of a police authority or chief officer to comply with any directions given under paragraph (*b*).

(5) Directions under sub-paragraph (4)(*b*) may require action taken in pursuance of the directions to be treated as taken in accordance with any such provision of paragraph 2 as may be specified in the direction.

(6) The Commission—

(*a*) shall give notification both to the police authority or, as the case may be, the chief officer and to the complainant of any determination made by it under this paragraph; and
(*b*) shall give notification to the complainant of any direction given by it under this paragraph to the police authority or chief officer.

(7) The Secretary of State may by regulations[1] make provision—

(*a*) for the form and manner in which appeals under this paragraph are to be brought;
(*b*) for the period within which any such appeal must be brought; and
(*c*) for the procedure to be followed by the Commission when dealing with or disposing of any such appeal.

Reference of complaints to the Commission

4. (1) It shall be the duty of the appropriate authority to refer a complaint to the Commission if—

(*a*) the complaint is one alleging that the conduct complained of has resulted in death or serious injury;
(*b*) the complaint is of a description specified for the purposes of this sub-paragraph in regulations[1] made by the Secretary of State; or
(*c*) the Commission notifies the appropriate authority that it requires the complaint in question to be referred to the Commission for its consideration.

(2) In a case where there is no obligation under sub-paragraph (1) to make a reference, the appropriate authority may refer a complaint to the Commission if that authority considers that it would be appropriate to do so by reason of—

(*a*) the gravity of the subject-matter of the complaint; or
(*b*) any exceptional circumstances.

(3) In a case in which a reference under sub-paragraph (1) or (2) is neither made nor required to be made, a police authority may refer a complaint to the Commission if—

(*a*) it is one in relation to which the chief officer of police of the police force maintained by that authority is the appropriate authority; and
(*b*) the police authority considers that it would be appropriate to do so reason of—
(i) the gravity of the subject-matter of the complaint; or
(ii) any exceptional circumstances.

(4) Where there is an obligation under this paragraph to refer a complaint to the Commission, it must be so referred within such period as may be provided for by regulations[1] made by the Secretary of State.

(5) Subject to sub-paragraph (7), the following powers—

(*a*) the power of the Commission by virtue of sub-paragraph (1)(*c*) to require a complaint to be referred to it, and
(*b*) the power of a police authority or chief officer to refer a complaint to the Commission under sub-paragraph (2) or (3),

shall each be exercisable at any time irrespective of whether the complaint is already being investigated by any person or has already been considered by the Commission.

(6) A police authority or chief officer which refers a complaint to the Commission under this paragraph shall give a notification of the making of the reference—

(*a*) to the complainant, and
(*b*) except in a case where it appears to that authority or chief officer that to do so might prejudice a possible future investigation of the complaint, to the person complained against.

(7) A complaint that has already been referred to the Commission under this paragraph on a previous occasion—

(*a*) shall not be required to be referred again under this paragraph unless the Commission so directs; and
(*b*) shall not be referred in exercise of any power conferred by this paragraph unless the Commission consents.

Duties of Commission on references under paragraph 4

5. (1) It shall be the duty of the Commission in the case of every complaint referred to it by a police authority or chief officer, to determine whether or not it is necessary for the complaint to be investigated.

(2) Where the Commission determines under this paragraph that it is not necessary for a complaint to be investigated, it may, if it thinks fit, refer the complaint back to the appropriate authority to be dealt with by that authority in accordance with paragraph 6.

(3) Where the Commission refers a complaint back under sub-paragraph (2), it shall give a notification of the making of the reference back—

(*a*) to the complainant, and
(*b*) except in a case where it appears to the Commission that to do so might prejudice a possible future investigation of the complaint, to the person complained against.

Handling of complaints by the appropriate authority

6. (1) This paragraph applies where a complaint has been recorded by the appropriate authority unless the complaint—

(*a*) is one which has been, or must be, referred to the Commission under paragraph 4; and
(*b*) is not for the time being either referred back to the authority under paragraph 5 or the subject of a determination under paragraph 15.

(2) Subject to paragraph 7, the appropriate authority shall determine whether or not the complaint is suitable for being subjected to local resolution, and—

(*a*) if it determines that it is so suitable and the complainant consents, it shall make arrangements for it to be so subjected; and
(*b*) in any other case, it shall make arrangements for the complaint to be investigated by that authority on its own behalf.

(3) A determination that a complaint is suitable for being subjected to local resolution shall not be made unless either—

(*a*) the appropriate authority is satisfied that the conduct complained of (even if it were proved) would not justify the bringing of any criminal or disciplinary proceedings; or (*b*) the Commission, in a case falling within sub-paragraph (4), has approved the use of local resolution.

(4) The Commission may approve the use of local resolution in the case of any complaint if, on an application by the appropriate authority, the Commission is satisfied—

(*a*) that the following two conditions are fulfilled—

(i) that the conduct complained of (even if it were proved) would not justify the bringing of any criminal proceedings; and

(ii) that any disciplinary proceedings the bringing of which would be justified in respect of that conduct (even if it were proved) would be unlikely to result in a dismissal, a requirement to resign or retire, a reduction in rank or other demotion or the imposition of a fine;

or

(*b*) that it will not be practicable (even if the complaint is thoroughly investigated) for either of the following to be brought—

(i) criminal proceedings in respect of the conduct to which it relates that would be likely to result in a conviction; or

(ii) disciplinary proceedings in respect of that conduct that would be likely to result in a dismissal, a requirement to resign or retire, a reduction in rank or other demotion or the imposition of a fine.

(5) No more than one application may be made to the Commission for the purposes of sub-paragraph (4) in respect of the same complaint.

(6) Before a complainant can give his consent for the purposes of this paragraph to the local resolution of his complaint he must have been informed of his rights of appeal under paragraph 9.

(7) A consent given for the purposes of this paragraph shall not be capable of being withdrawn at any time after the procedure for the local resolution of the complaint has been begun.

Dispensation by the Commission from requirements of Schedule

7. (1) If, in a case in which paragraph (6) applies, the appropriate authority considers—

(*a*) that it should handle the complaint otherwise than in accordance with this Schedule or should take no action in relation to it, and

(*b*) that the complaint falls within a description of complaints specified in regulations made by the Secretary of State for the purposes of this paragraph,

the appropriate authority may apply to the Commission, in accordance with the regulations[1], for permission to handle the complaint in whatever manner (if any) that authority thinks fit.

(2) The appropriate authority shall notify the complainant about the making of the application under this paragraph.

(3) Where such an application is made to the Commission, it shall, in accordance with regulations[1] made by the Secretary of State—

(*a*) consider the application and determine whether to grant the permission applied for; and

(*b*) notify its decision to the appropriate authority and the complainant.

(4) Where an application is made under this paragraph in respect of any complaint, the appropriate authority shall not, while the application is being considered by the Commission, take any action in accordance with the provisions of this Schedule (other than under paragraph 1) in relation to that complaint.

(5) Where the Commission gives permission under this paragraph to handle the complaint in whatever manner (if any) the appropriate authority thinks fit, the authority—

(*a*) shall not be required by virtue of any of the provisions of this Schedule (other than paragraph 1) to take any action in relation to the complaint; but

(*b*) may handle the complaint in whatever manner it thinks fit, or take no action in relation to the complaint, and for the purposes of handling the complaint may take any step that it could have taken, or would have been required to take, but for the permission.

(6) Where the Commission determines that no permission should be granted under this paragraph—

(*a*) it shall refer the matter back to the appropriate authority for the making of a determination under paragraph 6(2); and

(*b*) the authority shall then make that determination.

(7) No more than one application may be made to the Commission under this paragraph in respect of the same complaint.

Local resolution of complaints

8. (1) The arrangements made by the appropriate authority for subjecting any complaint to local resolution may include the appointment of a person who—

(*a*) is serving with the police, and

(*b*) is under the direction and control of the chief officer of police of the relevant force,

to secure the local resolution of the complaint.

(2) The Secretary of State may by regulations[1] make provision—

(*a*) for the different descriptions of procedures that are to be available for dealing with a complaint where it is decided it is to be subjected to local resolution;

(*b*) for requiring a person complained against in a case in which the complaint is subjected to local resolution to be given an opportunity of commenting, in such manner as may be provided for in the regulations, on the complaint;

(*c*) for requiring that, on the making of an application in accordance with the regulations, a record of the outcome of any procedure for the local resolution of any complaint is to be given to the complainant.

(3) A statement made by any person for the purposes of the local resolution of any complaint shall not be admissible in any subsequent criminal, civil or disciplinary proceedings except to the extent that it consists of an admission relating to a matter that has not been subjected to local resolution.

(4) If, after attempts have been made to resolve a complaint using local resolution, it appears to the appropriate authority—

(*a*) that the resolution of the complaint in that manner is impossible, or

(*b*) that the complaint is, for any other reason, not suitable for such resolution,

it shall make arrangements for the complaint to be investigated by that authority on its own behalf.

(5) The local resolution of any complaint shall be discontinued if—

(*a*) any arrangements are made under sub-paragraph (4);

(*b*) the Commission notifies the appropriate authority that it requires the complaint to be referred to the Commission under paragraph 4; or

(*c*) the complaint is so referred otherwise than in pursuance of such a notification.

(6) A person who has participated in any attempt to resolve a complaint using local resolution shall be disqualified for appointment under any provision of this Schedule to investigate that complaint, or to assist with the carrying out of the investigation of that complaint.

Appeals relating to local resolution

9. (1) Subject to sub-paragraph (2), a complainant whose complaint has been subjected to local resolution shall have a right of appeal to the Commission against the conduct of the local resolution of that complaint.

(2) The only matter that shall fall to be determined on an appeal under this paragraph is whether there have been any contraventions of the procedural requirements relating to the local resolution of the complaint.

(3) Where an appeal is brought under this paragraph, it shall be the duty of the Commission to give both—

(*a*) the person complained against, and

(*b*) the appropriate authority,

an opportunity of making representations about the matters to which the appeal relates.

(4) On an appeal under this paragraph, the Commission shall determine whether there have been any contraventions of the procedural requirements relating to the local resolution of the complaint.

(5) Where the Commission finds in the complainant's favour on an appeal under this paragraph—

(*a*) it shall give such directions as the Commission considers appropriate to the appropriate authority as to the future handling of the complaint; and

(*b*) it shall be the duty of the appropriate authority to comply with any directions given to it under this sub-paragraph.

(6) Where the Commission determines for the purposes of sub-paragraph (5) that the future handling of the complaint should include an investigation, paragraph 15 shall apply as it applies in the case of a determination mentioned in sub-paragraph (1) of that paragraph.

(7) The Commission—

(*a*) shall give notification to the appropriate authority, to the complainant and to the person complained against of any determination made by it under this paragraph; and

(*b*) shall give notification to the complainant and to the person complained against of any direction given by it under this paragraph to the appropriate authority.

(8) The Secretary of State may by regulations[1] make provision—

(*a*) for the form and manner in which appeals under this paragraph are to be brought;

(*b*) for the period within which any such appeal must be brought; and

(*c*) for the procedure to be followed by the Commission when dealing with or disposing of any such appeal.

---

1. The Police (Complaints and Misconduct) Regulations 2004, SI 2004/643 amended by SI 2005/3389 have been made.

PART 2
HANDLING OF CONDUCT MATTERS

Conduct matters arising in civil proceedings

8–23897Z **10.** (1) This paragraph applies where—

(*a*) a police authority or chief officer has received notification (whether or not under this paragraph) that civil proceedings relating to any matter have been brought by a member of the public against that authority or chief officer, or it otherwise appears to a police authority or chief officer that such proceedings are likely to be so brought; and

(*b*) it appears to that authority or chief officer (whether at the time of the notification or at any time subsequently) that those proceedings involve or would involve a conduct matter.

(2) The authority or chief officer—

(*a*) shall consider whether it or, as the case may be, he is the appropriate authority in relation to the conduct matter in question; and

(*b*) if it or he is not, shall notify the person who is the appropriate authority about the proceedings, or the proposal to bring them, and about the circumstances that make it appear as mentioned in sub-paragraph (1)(*b*).

(3) Where a police authority or chief officer determines for the purposes of this paragraph that it or, as the case may be, he is the appropriate authority in relation to any conduct matter, it or he shall record that matter.

(4) Where the appropriate authority records any matter under this paragraph it—

(*a*) shall first determine whether the matter is one which it is required to refer to the Commission under paragraph 13 or is one which it would be appropriate to so refer; and

(*b*) if it is not required so to refer the matter and does not do so, may deal with the matter in such other manner (if any) as it may determine.

(5) Nothing in sub-paragraph (3) shall require the appropriate authority to record any conduct matter if it is satisfied that the matter has been, or is already being, dealt with by means of criminal or disciplinary proceedings against the person to whose conduct the matter relates.

(6) For the purposes of this paragraph civil proceedings involve a conduct matter if—

(*a*) they relate to such a matter; or

(*b*) they are proceedings that relate to a matter in relation to which a conduct matter, or evidence of a conduct matter, is or may be relevant.

(7) The Secretary of State may by regulations provide for the times at which, or the periods within which, any requirement of this paragraph is to be complied with; and the period from which any such period is to run shall be such time as may be specified in those regulations or as may be determined in a manner set out in the regulations.

Recording etc of conduct matters in other cases

11. (1) Where—

(*a*) a conduct matter comes (otherwise than as mentioned in paragraph 10) to the attention of the police authority or chief officer who is the appropriate authority in relation to that matter, and

(*b*) it appears to the appropriate authority that the conduct involved in that matter falls within sub-paragraph (2),

it shall be the duty of the appropriate authority to record that matter.

(2) Conduct falls within this sub-paragraph if (assuming it to have taken place)—

(*a*) it appears to have resulted in the death of any person or in serious injury to any person;

(*b*) a member of the public has been adversely affected by it; or

(*c*) it is of a description specified for the purposes of this sub-paragraph in regulations[1] made by the Secretary of State.

(3) Where the appropriate authority records any matter under this paragraph it—

(*a*) shall first determine whether the matter is one which it is required to refer to the Commission under paragraph (13) or is one which it would be appropriate to so refer; and

(*b*) if it is not required so to refer the matter and does not do so, may deal with the matter in such other manner (if any) as it may determine.

(4) Nothing in sub-paragraph (1) shall require the appropriate authority to record any conduct matter if it is satisfied that the matter has been, or is already being, dealt with by means of criminal or disciplinary proceedings against the person to whose conduct the matter relates.

(5) If it appears to the Commission—

(*a*) that any matter that has come to its attention is a recordable conduct matter, but

(*b*) that that matter has not been recorded by the appropriate authority,

the Commission may direct the appropriate authority to record that matter; and it shall be the duty of that authority to comply with the direction.

Duties to preserve evidence relating to conduct matters

12. (1) Where a recordable conduct matter that relates to the conduct of a chief officer comes to the attention of the police authority maintaining his force, it shall be the duty of that authority to secure that all such steps as are appropriate for the purposes of Part 2 of this Act are taken, both initially and from time to time after that, for obtaining and preserving evidence relating to that matter.

(2) Where a chief officer becomes aware of any recordable conduct matter relating to the conduct of a person under his direction and control, it shall be his duty to take all such steps as appear to him to be appropriate for the purposes of Part 2 of this Act for obtaining and preserving evidence relating to that matter.

(3) The chief officer's duty under sub-paragraph (2) must be performed as soon as practicable after he becomes aware of the matter in question.

(4) After that, he shall be under a duty, until he is satisfied that it is no longer necessary to do so, to continue to take the steps from time to time appearing to him to be appropriate for the purposes of Part 2 of this Act for obtaining and preserving evidence relating to the matter.

(5) It shall be the duty of a police authority to comply with all such directions as may be given to it by the Commission in relation to the performance of any duty imposed on it by virtue of sub-paragraph (1).

(6) It shall be the duty of the chief officer to take all such specific steps for obtaining or preserving evidence relating to any recordable conduct matter as he may be directed to take for the purposes of this paragraph by the police authority maintaining his force or by the Commission.

Reference of conduct matters to the Commission

13. (1) It shall be the duty of a police authority or a chief officer to refer a recordable conduct matter to the Commission if, in a case (whether or not falling within paragraph 10) in which the authority or chief officer is the appropriate authority—

(*a*) that matter relates to any incident or circumstances in or in consequence of which any person has died or suffered serious injury;

(*b*) that matter is of a description specified for the purposes of this sub-paragraph in regulations made by the Secretary of State; or (*c*) the Commission notifies the appropriate authority that it requires that matter to be referred to the Commission for its consideration.

(2) In any case where there is no obligation under sub-paragraph (1) to make a reference, the appropriate authority may refer a recordable conduct matter to the Commission if that authority considers that it would be appropriate to do so by reason of—

(*a*) the gravity of the matter; or
(*b*) any exceptional circumstances.

(3) In a case in which a reference under sub-paragraph (1) or (2) is neither made nor required to be made, a police authority maintaining any police force may refer any recordable conduct matter to the Commission if—

(*a*) it is one in relation to which the chief officer of police of that force is the appropriate authority; and
(*b*) the police authority considers that it would be appropriate to do so by reason of—

(i) the gravity of the matter; or
(ii) any exceptional circumstances.

(4) Where there is an obligation under this paragraph to refer any matter to the Commission, it must be so referred within such period as may be provided for by regulations[1] made by the Secretary of State.

(5) Subject to sub-paragraph (7), the following powers—

(*a*) the power of the Commission by virtue of sub-paragraph (1)(*c*) to require a matter to be referred to it, and
(*b*) the power of a police authority or chief officer to refer any matter to the Commission under sub-paragraph (2) or (3),

shall each be exercisable at any time irrespective of whether the matter is already being investigated by any person or has already been considered by the Commission.

(6) Where—

(*a*) a police authority or chief officer refers a matter to the Commission under this paragraph, and
(*b*) that authority or chief officer does not consider that to do so might prejudice a possible future investigation of that matter,

that authority or chief officer shall give a notification of the making of the reference to the person to whose conduct that matter relates.

(7) A matter that has already been referred to the Commission under this paragraph on a previous occasion—

(*a*) shall not be required to be referred again under this paragraph unless the Commission so directs; and
(*b*) shall not be referred in exercise of any power conferred by this paragraph unless the Commission consents.

Duties of Commission on references under paragraph 13

14. (1) It shall be the duty of the Commission, in the case of every recordable conduct matter referred to it by a police authority or chief officer under paragraph 13, to determine whether or not it is necessary for the matter to be investigated.

(2) Where the Commission determines under this paragraph that it is not necessary for a recordable conduct matter to be investigated, it may if it thinks fit refer the matter back to the appropriate authority to be dealt with by that authority in such manner (if any) as that authority may determine.

(3) Where—

(*a*) the Commission refers a matter back to the appropriate authority under this paragraph, and
(*b*) the Commission does not consider that to do so might prejudice a possible future investigation of that matter,

the Commission shall give a notification of the making of the reference to the person to whose conduct that matter relates.

1. The Police (Complaints and Misconduct) Regulations 2004, SI 2004/643 amended by SI 2005/3389 have been made.

PART 2A

HANDLING OF DEATH AND SERIOUS INJURY (DSI) MATTERS

Duty to record DSI matters

14A. (1) Where a DSI matter comes to the attention of the police authority or chief officer who is the appropriate authority in relation to that matter, it shall be the duty of the appropriate authority to record that matter.

(2) If it appears to the Commission—

(*a*) that any matter that has come to its attention is a DSI matter, but
(*b*) that that matter has not been recorded by the appropriate authority,

the Commission may direct the appropriate authority to record that matter; and it shall be the duty of that authority to comply with the direction.

Duty to preserve evidence relating to DSI matters

14B. (1) Where—

(*a*) a DSI matter comes to the attention of a police authority, and
(*b*) the relevant officer in relation to that matter is the chief officer of the force maintained by that authority,

it shall be the duty of that authority to secure that all such steps as are appropriate for the purposes of Part 2 of this Act are taken, both initially and from time to time after that, for obtaining and preserving evidence relating to that matter.

(2) Where—

(*a*) a chief officer becomes aware of a DSI matter, and
(*b*) the relevant officer in relation to that matter is a person under his direction and control,

it shall be his duty to take all such steps as appear to him to be appropriate for the purposes of Part 2 of this Act for obtaining and preserving evidence relating to that matter.

(3) The chief officer's duty under sub-paragraph (2) must be performed as soon as practicable after he becomes aware of the matter in question.

(4) After that, he shall be under a duty, until he is satisfied that it is no longer necessary to do so, to continue to take the steps from time to time appearing to him to be appropriate for the purposes of Part 2 of this Act for obtaining and preserving evidence relating to the matter.

(5) It shall be the duty of a police authority to comply with all such directions as may be given to it by the Commission in relation to the performance of any duty imposed on it by virtue of sub-paragraph (1).

(6) It shall be the duty of the chief officer to take all such specific steps for obtaining or preserving evidence relating to any DSI matter as he may be directed to take for the purposes of this paragraph by the police authority maintaining his force or by the Commission.

Reference of DSI matters to the Commission

14C. (1) It shall be the duty of the appropriate authority to refer a DSI matter to the Commission.

(2) The appropriate authority must do so within such period as may be provided for by regulations made by the Secretary of State.

(3) A matter that has already been referred to the Commission under this paragraph on a previous occasion shall not be required to be referred again under this paragraph unless the Commission so directs.

Duties of Commission on references under paragraph 14C

14D. (1) It shall be the duty of the Commission, in the case of every DSI matter referred to it by a police authority or a chief officer, to determine whether or not it is necessary for the matter to be investigated.

(2) Where the Commission determines under this paragraph that it is not necessary for a DSI matter to be investigated, it may if it thinks fit refer the matter back to the appropriate authority to be dealt with by that authority in such manner (if any) as that authority may determine.

PART 3
INVESTIGATIONS AND SUBSEQUENT PROCEEDINGS

Power of the Commission to determine the form of an investigation

8–23897ZA **15.** (1) This paragraph applies where—

(*a*) a complaint, recordable conduct matter or DSI matter is referred to the Commission; and
(*b*) the Commission determines that it is necessary for the complaint or matter to be investigated.

(2) It shall be the duty of the Commission to determine the form which the investigation should take.

(3) In making a determination under sub-paragraph (2) the Commission shall have regard to the following factors—

(*a*) the seriousness of the case; and
(*b*) the public interest.

(4) The only forms which the investigation may take in accordance with a determination made under this paragraph are—

(*a*) an investigation by the appropriate authority on its own behalf;
(*b*) an investigation by that authority under the supervision of the Commission;
(*c*) an investigation by that authority under the management of the Commission;
(*d*) an investigation by the Commission.

(5) The Commission may at any time make a further determination under this paragraph to replace an earlier one.

(6) Where a determination under this paragraph replaces an earlier determination under this paragraph, or relates to a complaint or matter in relation to which the appropriate authority has already begun an investigation on its own behalf, the Commission may give—

(*a*) the appropriate authority, and
(*b*) any person previously appointed to carry out the investigation,

such directions as it considers appropriate for the purpose of giving effect to the new determination.

(7) It shall be the duty of a person to whom a direction is given under sub-paragraph (6) to comply with it.

(8) The Commission shall notify the appropriate authority of any determination that it makes under this paragraph in relation to a particular complaint, recordable conduct matter or DSI matter.

Investigations by the appropriate authority on its own behalf

16. (1) This paragraph applies if the appropriate authority is required by virtue of—

(*a*) any determination made by that authority under paragraph 6(2) (whether following the recording of a complaint or on a reference back under paragraph 5(2)) or under paragraph 8(4), or
(*b*) any determination made by the Commission under paragraph 15,

to make arrangements for a complaint, recordable conduct matter or DSI matter to be investigated by the appropriate authority on its own behalf.

(2) This paragraph also applies if—

(*a*) a determination falls to be made by that authority under paragraph 10(4)(*b*), or 11(3)(*b*) or 14(2) in relation to any recordable conduct matter or under paragraph 14D(2) in relation to any DSI matter; and

(*b*) the appropriate authority determine that it is necessary for the matter to be investigated by the authority on its own behalf.

(3) Subject to sub-paragraph (4) or (5), it shall be the duty of the appropriate authority to appoint—

(*a*) a person serving with the police (whether under the direction and control of the chief officer of police of the relevant force or of the chief officer of another force), or

(*b*) a member of the National Criminal Intelligence Service or the National Crime Squad,

to investigate the complaint or matter.

(4) The person appointed under this paragraph to investigate any complaint or conduct matter—

(*a*) in the case of an investigation relating to any conduct of a chief officer, must not be a person under that chief officer's direction and control; and

(*b*) in the case of an investigation relating to any conduct of the Commissioner of Police of the Metropolis or of the Deputy Commissioner of Police of the Metropolis, must be the person nominated by the Secretary of State for appointment under this paragraph.

(5) The person appointed under this paragraph to investigate any DSI matter—

(*a*) in relation to which the relevant officer is a chief officer, must not be a person under that chief officer's direction and control;

(*b*) in relation to which the relevant officer is the Commissioner of Police of the Metropolis or the Deputy Commissioner of Police of the Metropolis, must be the person nominated by the Secretary of State for appointment under this paragraph.

Investigations supervised by the Commission

17. (1) This paragraph applies where the Commission has determined that it should supervise the investigation by the appropriate authority of any complaint, recordable conduct matter or DSI matter.

(2) On being given notice of that determination, the appropriate authority shall, if it has not already done so, appoint—

(*a*) a person serving with the police (whether under the direction and control of the chief officer of police of the relevant force or of the chief officer of another force), or

(*b*) a member of the National Criminal Intelligence Service or the National Crime Squad,

to investigate the complaint or matter.

(3) The Commission may require that no appointment is made under sub-paragraph (2) unless it has given notice to the appropriate authority that it approves the person whom that authority proposes to appoint.

(4) Where a person has already been appointed to investigate the complaint or matter, or is selected under this sub-paragraph for appointment, and the Commission is not satisfied with that person, the Commission may require the appropriate authority, as soon as reasonably practicable after being required to do so—

(*a*) to select another person falling within sub-paragraph (2)(*a*) or (*b*) to investigate the complaint or matter; and

(*b*) to notify the Commission of the person selected.

(5) Where a selection made in pursuance of a requirement under sub-paragraph (4) has been notified to the Commission, the appropriate authority shall appoint that person to investigate the complaint or matter if, but only if, the Commission notifies the authority that it approves the appointment of that person.

(6) A person appointed under this paragraph to investigate any complaint or conduct matter—

(*a*) in the case of an investigation relating to any conduct of a chief officer, must not be a person under that chief officer's direction and control; and

(*b*) in the case of an investigation relating to any conduct of the Commissioner of Police of the Metropolis or of the Deputy Commissioner of Police of the Metropolis, must be the person nominated by the Secretary of State for appointment under this paragraph.

(6A) The person appointed under this paragraph to investigate any DSI matter—

(*a*) in relation to which the relevant officer is a chief officer, must not be a person under that chief officer's direction and control;

(*b*) in relation to which the relevant officer is the Commissioner of Police of the Metropolis or the Deputy Commissioner of Police of the Metropolis, must be the person nominated by the Secretary of State for appointment under this paragraph.

(7) The person appointed to investigate the complaint or matter shall comply with all such requirements in relation to the carrying out of that investigation as may, in accordance with regulations made for the purposes of this sub-paragraph by the Secretary of State, be imposed by the Commission in relation to that investigation.

Investigations managed by the Commission

18. (1) This paragraph applies where the Commission has determined that it should manage the investigation by the appropriate authority of any complaint, recordable conduct matter or DSI matter.

(2) Sub-paragraphs (2) to (6A) of paragraph 17 shall apply as they apply in the case of an investigation which the Commission has determined is one that it should supervise.

(3) The person appointed to investigate the complaint or matter shall, in relation to that investigation, be under the direction and control of the Commission.

Investigations by the Commission itself

19. (1) This paragraph applies where the Commission has determined that it should itself carry out the investigation of a complaint, recordable conduct matter or DSI matter.

(2) The Commission shall designate both—

(*a*) a member of the Commission's staff to take charge of the investigation on behalf of the Commission, and

(*b*) all such other members of the Commission's staff as are required by the Commission to assist him.

(3) The person designated under sub-paragraph (2) to be the person to take charge of an investigation relating to any conduct of the Commissioner of Police of the Metropolis or of the Deputy Commissioner of Police of the Metropolis must be the person nominated by the Secretary of State to be so designated under that sub-paragraph.

(3A) The person designated under sub-paragraph (2) to be the person to take charge of an investigation of a DSI matter in relation to which the relevant officer is the Commissioner of Police of the Metropolis or the Deputy Commissioner of Police of the Metropolis must be the person nominated by the Secretary of State to be so designated under that sub-paragraph.

(4) A member of the Commission's staff who—

(*a*) is designated under sub-paragraph (2) in relation to any investigation, but

(*b*) does not already, by virtue of section 97(8) of the 1996 Act, have all the powers and privileges of a constable throughout England and Wales and the adjacent United Kingdom waters,

shall, for the purposes of the carrying out of the investigation and all purposes connected with it, have all those powers and privileges throughout England and Wales and those waters.

(5) A member of the Commission's staff who is not a constable shall not, as a result of sub-paragraph (4), be treated as being in police service for the purposes of—

(*a*) section 280 of the Trade Union and Labour Relations (Consolidation) Act 1992 (c 52) (person in police service excluded from definitions of "worker" and "employee"); or

(*b*) section 200 of the Employment Rights Act 1996 (c 18) (certain provisions of that Act not to apply to persons in police service).

(6) The Secretary of State may by order provide that such provisions of the 1984 Act relating to investigations of offences conducted by police officers as may be specified in the order shall apply, subject to such modifications as may be so specified, to investigations of offences conducted by virtue of this paragraph by members of the Commission's staff designated under sub-paragraph (2).

(7) References in this paragraph to the powers and privileges of a constable—

(*a*) are references to any power or privilege conferred by or under any enactment (including one passed after the passing of this Act) on a constable; and

(*b*) shall have effect as if every such power were exercisable, and every such privilege existed, throughout England and Wales and the adjacent United Kingdom waters (whether or not that is the case apart from this sub-paragraph).

(8) In this paragraph "United Kingdom waters" means the sea and other waters within the seaward limits of the United Kingdom's territorial sea.

Restrictions on proceedings pending the conclusion of an investigation

20. (1) No criminal or disciplinary proceedings shall be brought in relation to any matter which is the subject of an investigation in accordance with the provisions of this Schedule until—

(*a*) the appropriate authority has certified the case as a special case under paragraph 20B(3) or 20E(3), or]

(*b*) a report on that investigation has been submitted to the Commission or to the appropriate authority under paragraph 22 or 24A.

(2) Nothing in this paragraph shall prevent the bringing of criminal or disciplinary proceedings in respect of any conduct at any time after the discontinuance of the investigation in accordance with the provisions of this Schedule which relates to that conduct.

(3) The restrictions imposed by this paragraph in relation to the bringing of criminal proceedings shall not apply to the bringing of criminal proceedings by the Director of Public Prosecutions in any case in which it appears to him that there are exceptional circumstances which make it undesirable to delay the bringing of such proceedings.

Accelerated procedure in special cases

20A. (1) If, at any time before the completion of his investigation, a person appointed or designated to investigate a complaint or recordable conduct matter believes that the appropriate authority would, on consideration of the matter, be likely to consider that the special conditions are satisfied, he shall proceed in accordance with the following provisions of this paragraph.

(2) If the person was appointed under paragraph 16, he shall submit to the appropriate authority—

(*a*) a statement of his belief and the grounds for it; and

(*b*) a written report on his investigation to that point;

and if he was appointed following a determination made by the Commission under paragraph 15 he shall send a copy of the statement and the report to the Commission.

(3) If the person was appointed under paragraph 17 or 18 or designated under paragraph 19, he shall submit to the appropriate authority—

(*a*) a statement of his belief and the grounds for it; and

(*b*) a written report on his investigation to that point;

and shall send a copy of the statement and the report to the Commission.

(4) A person submitting a report under this paragraph shall not be prevented by any obligation of secrecy imposed by any rule of law or otherwise from including all such matters in his report as he thinks fit.

(5) A statement and report may be submitted under this paragraph whether or not a previous statement and

report have been submitted; but a second or subsequent statement and report may be submitted only if the person submitting them has grounds to believe that the appropriate authority will reach a different determination under paragraph 20B(2) or 20E(2).

(6) After submitting a report under this paragraph, the person appointed or designated to investigate the complaint or recordable conduct matter shall continue his investigation to such extent as he considers appropriate.

(7) The special conditions are that—

(*a*) the person whose conduct is the subject matter of the investigation may have committed an imprisonable offence and that person's conduct is of a serious nature;

(*b*) there is sufficient evidence, in the form of written statements or other documents, to establish on the balance of probabilities that conduct justifying dismissal took place; and

(*c*) it is in the public interest for the person whose conduct is the subject matter of the investigation to cease to be a member of a police force, or to be a special constable, without delay.

(8) In sub-paragraph (7)—

(*a*) in paragraph (*a*), "imprisonable offence" means an offence which is punishable with imprisonment in the case of a person aged 21 or over; and

(*b*) in paragraph (*b*), "conduct justifying dismissal" means conduct which is so serious that disciplinary proceedings brought in respect of it would be likely to result in a dismissal.

(9) In paragraphs 20B to 20H "special report" means a report submitted under this paragraph.

Investigations managed or carried out by Commission: action by appropriate authority

20B. (1) This paragraph applies where—

(*a*) a statement and special report on an investigation carried out under the management of the Commission, or

(*b*) a statement and special report on an investigation carried out by a person designated by the Commission,

are submitted to the appropriate authority under paragraph 20A(3).

(2) The appropriate authority shall determine whether the special conditions are satisfied.

(3) If the appropriate authority determines that the special conditions are satisfied then, unless it considers that the circumstances are such as to make it inappropriate to do so, it shall—

(*a*) certify the case as a special case for the purposes of Regulation 11 of the Police (Conduct) Regulations 2004 (SI 2004/645); and

(*b*) subject to any request made under paragraph 20G(1), take such steps as are required by that Regulation in relation to a case so certified.

(4) The reference in sub-paragraph (3) to Regulation 11 includes a reference to any corresponding provision replacing that Regulation.

(5) If the appropriate authority determines that the special conditions are satisfied then it shall notify the Director of Public Prosecutions of its determination and send him a copy of the special report.

(6) The appropriate authority shall notify the Commission of a certification under sub-paragraph (3).

(7) If the appropriate authority determines—

(*a*) that the special conditions are not satisfied, or

(*b*) that, although those conditions are satisfied, the circumstances are such as to make it inappropriate at present to bring disciplinary proceedings,

it shall submit to the Commission a memorandum under this sub-paragraph.

(8) The memorandum required to be submitted under sub-paragraph (7) is one which—

(*a*) notifies the Commission of its determination that those conditions are not satisfied or (as the case may be) that they are so satisfied but the circumstances are such as to make it inappropriate at present to bring disciplinary proceedings; and

(*b*) (in either case) sets out its reasons for so determining.

(9) In this paragraph "special conditions" has the meaning given by paragraph 20A(7).

Investigations managed or carried out by Commission: action by Commission

20C. (1) On receipt of a notification under paragraph 20B(6), the Commission shall give a notification—

(*a*) in the case of a complaint, to the complainant and to every person entitled to be kept properly informed in relation to the complaint under section 21; and

(*b*) in the case of a recordable conduct matter, to every person entitled to be kept properly informed in relation to that matter under that section.

(2) The notification required by sub-paragraph (1) is one setting out—

(*a*) the findings of the special report;

(*b*) the appropriate authority's determination under paragraph 20B(2); and

(*c*) the action that the appropriate authority is required to take as a consequence of that determination.

(3) Subsections (5) to (7) of section 20 shall have effect in relation to the duties imposed on the Commission by sub-paragraph (1) as they have effect in relation to the duties imposed on the Commission by that section.

(4) Except so far as may be otherwise provided by regulations made by virtue of sub-paragraph (3), the Commission shall be entitled (notwithstanding any obligation of secrecy imposed by any rule of law or otherwise) to discharge the duty to give a person mentioned in sub-paragraph (1) notification of the findings of the special report by sending that person a copy of that report.

20D. (1) On receipt of a memorandum under paragraph 20B(7), the Commission shall—

(*a*) consider the memorandum;

(*b*) determine, in the light of that consideration, whether or not to make a recommendation under paragraph 20H; and

(*c*) if it thinks fit to do so, make a recommendation under that paragraph.

(2) If the Commission determines not to make a recommendation under paragraph 20H, it shall notify the appropriate authority and the person appointed under paragraph 18 or designated under paragraph 19 of its determination.

Other investigations: action by appropriate authority

20E. (1) This paragraph applies where—

(*a*) a statement and a special report on an investigation carried out by an appropriate authority on its own behalf, or

(*b*) a statement and a special report on an investigation carried out under the supervision of the Commission,

are submitted to the appropriate authority under paragraph 20A(2) or (3).

(2) The appropriate authority shall determine whether the special conditions are satisfied.

(3) If the appropriate authority determines that the special conditions are satisfied then, unless it considers that the circumstances are such as to make it inappropriate to do so, it shall—

(*a*) certify the case as a special case for the purposes of Regulation 11 of the Police (Conduct) Regulations 2004 (SI 2004/645); and

(*b*) subject to any request made under paragraph 20G(1), take such steps as are required by that Regulation in relation to a case so certified.

(4) The reference in sub-paragraph (3) to Regulation 11 includes a reference to any corresponding provision replacing that Regulation.

(5) If the appropriate authority determines that the special conditions are satisfied then it shall notify the Director of Public Prosecutions of its determination and send him a copy of the special report.

(6) Where the statement and report were required under paragraph 20A(2) to be copied to the Commission, the appropriate authority shall notify the Commission of a certification under sub-paragraph (3).

(7) If the appropriate authority determines—

(*a*) that the special conditions are not satisfied, or

(*b*) that, although those conditions are satisfied, the circumstances are such as to make it inappropriate at present to bring disciplinary proceedings,

it shall notify the person appointed under paragraph 16 or 17 of its determination.

(8) In this paragraph "special conditions" has the meaning given by paragraph 20A(7).

20F. (1) If the appropriate authority certifies a case under paragraph 20E(3), it shall give a notification—

(*a*) in the case of a complaint, to the complainant and to every person entitled to be kept properly informed in relation to the complaint under section 21; and

(*b*) in the case of a recordable conduct matter, to every person entitled to be kept properly informed in relation to that matter under that section.

(2) The notification required by sub-paragraph (1) is one setting out—

(*a*) the findings of the report;

(*b*) the authority's determination under paragraph 20E(2); and

(*c*) the action that the authority is required to take in consequence of that determination.

(3) Subsections (5) to (7) of section 20 shall have effect in relation to the duties imposed on the appropriate authority by sub-paragraph (1) as they have effect in relation to the duties imposed on the appropriate authority by that section.

(4) Except so far as may be otherwise provided by regulations made by virtue of sub-paragraph (3), the appropriate authority shall be entitled (notwithstanding any obligation of secrecy imposed by any rule of law or otherwise) to discharge the duty to give a person mentioned in sub-paragraph (1) notification of the findings of the special report by sending that person a copy of that report.

Special cases: Director of Public Prosecutions

20G. (1) On receiving a copy of a special report under paragraph 20B(5) or 20E(5), the Director of Public Prosecutions may request the appropriate authority not to bring disciplinary proceedings without his prior agreement, if the Director considers that bringing such proceedings might prejudice any future criminal proceedings.

(2) The Director of Public Prosecutions—

(*a*) shall notify the appropriate authority of any decision of his to take, or not to take, action in respect of the matters dealt with in a special report copied to him under paragraph 20B(5) or 20E(5); and

(*b*) where the special report was copied to him under paragraph 20B(5), shall send a copy of that notification to the Commission.

(3) It shall be the duty of the Commission to notify the persons mentioned in sub-paragraph (5) if criminal proceedings are brought against any person by the Director of Public Prosecutions in respect of any matters dealt with in a special report copied to him under paragraph 20B(5).

(4) It shall be the duty of the appropriate authority to notify the persons mentioned in sub-paragraph (5) if criminal proceedings are brought against any person by the Director of Public Prosecutions in respect of any matters dealt with in a special report copied to him under paragraph 20E(5).

(5) Those persons are—

(*a*) in the case of a complaint, the complainant and every person entitled to be kept properly informed in relation to the complaint under section 21; and (*b*) in the case of a recordable conduct matter, every person entitled to be kept properly informed in relation to that matter under that section.

Special cases: recommendation or direction of Commission

20H. (1) Where the appropriate authority has submitted, or is required to submit, a memorandum to the Commission under paragraph 20B(7), the Commission may make a recommendation to the appropriate authority that it should certify the case under paragraph 20B(3).

(2) If the Commission determines to make a recommendation under this paragraph, it shall give a notification—

(*a*) in the case of a complaint, to the complainant and to every person entitled to be kept properly informed in relation to the complaint under section 21; and

(*b*) in the case of a recordable conduct matter, to every person entitled to be kept properly informed in relation to that matter under that section.

(3) The notification required by sub-paragraph (2) is one setting out—

(*a*) the findings of the special report; and

(*b*) the Commission's recommendation under this paragraph.

(4) Subsections (5) to (7) of section 20 shall have effect in relation to the duties imposed on the Commission by sub-paragraph (2) as they have effect in relation to the duties imposed on the Commission by that section.

(5) Except so far as may be otherwise provided by regulations made by virtue of sub-paragraph (4), the Commission shall be entitled (notwithstanding any obligation of secrecy imposed by any rule of law or otherwise) to discharge the duty to give a person mentioned in sub-paragraph (2) notification of the findings of the special report by sending that person a copy of the report.

(6) It shall be the duty of the appropriate authority to notify the Commission whether it accepts the recommendation and (if it does) to certify the case and proceed accordingly.

(7) If, after the Commission has made a recommendation under this paragraph, the appropriate authority does not certify the case under paragraph 20B(3)—

(*a*) the Commission may direct the appropriate authority so to certify it; and

(*b*) it shall be the duty of the appropriate authority to comply with the direction and proceed accordingly.

(8) Where the Commission gives the appropriate authority a direction under this paragraph, it shall supply the appropriate authority with a statement of its reasons for doing so.

(9) The Commission may at any time withdraw a direction given under this paragraph.

(10) The appropriate authority shall keep the Commission informed of whatever action it takes in response to a recommendation or direction.

20I. (1) Where—

(*a*) the Commission makes a recommendation under paragraph 20H in the case of an investigation of a complaint, and

(*b*) the appropriate authority notifies the Commission that the recommendation has been accepted,

the Commission shall notify the complainant and every person entitled to be kept properly informed in relation to the complaint under section 21 of that fact and of the steps that have been, or are to be, taken by the appropriate authority to give effect to it.

(2) Where in the case of an investigation of a complaint the appropriate authority—

(*a*) notifies the Commission that it does not accept the recommendation made by the Commission under paragraph 20H, or

(*b*) fails to certify the case under paragraph 20B(3) and to proceed accordingly,

it shall be the duty of the Commission to determine what (if any) further steps to take under paragraph 20H.

(3) It shall be the duty of the Commission to notify the complainant and every person entitled to be kept properly informed in relation to the complaint under section 21—

(*a*) of any determination under sub-paragraph (2) not to take further steps under paragraph 20H; and

(*b*) where it determines under that sub-paragraph to take further steps under that paragraph, of the outcome of the taking of those steps.

Power of the Commission to discontinue an investigation

21. (1) If it any time appears to the Commission (whether on an application by the appropriate authority or otherwise) that a complaint or matter that is being investigated—

(*a*) by the appropriate authority on its own behalf, or

(*b*) under the supervision or management of the Commission,

is of a description of complaint or matter specified in regulations made by the Secretary of State for the purposes of this sub-paragraph, the Commission may by order require the discontinuance of the investigation.

(2) The Commission shall not discontinue any investigation that is being carried out in accordance with paragraph 19 except in such cases as may be authorised by regulations made by the Secretary of State.

(3) Where the Commission makes an order under this paragraph or discontinues an investigation being carried out in accordance with paragraph 19, it shall give notification of the discontinuance—

(*a*) to the appropriate authority;

(*b*) to every person entitled to be kept properly informed in relation to the subject matter of the investigation under section 21; and

(*c*) in a case where the investigation that is discontinued is an investigation of a complaint, to the complainant.

(4) Where an investigation of a complaint, recordable conduct matter or DSI matter is discontinued in accordance with this paragraph—

(*a*) the Commission may give the appropriate authority directions to do any such things as it is authorised to direct by regulations made by the Secretary of State;
(*b*) the Commission may itself take any such steps of a description specified in regulations so made as it considers appropriate for purposes connected with the discontinuance of the investigation; and
(*c*) subject to the preceding paragraphs, neither the appropriate authority nor the Commission shall take any further action in accordance with the provisions of this Schedule in relation to that complaint or matter.

(5) The appropriate authority shall comply with any directions given to it under sub-paragraph (4).

Procedure where conduct matter is revealed during investigation of DSI matter

21A. (1) If during the course of an investigation of a DSI matter it appears to a person appointed under paragraph 18 or designated under paragraph 19 that there is an indication that a person serving with the police ("the person whose conduct is in question") may have—

(*a*) committed a criminal offence, or
(*b*) behaved in a manner which would justify the bringing of disciplinary proceedings,

he shall make a submission to that effect to the Commission.

(2) If, after considering a submission under sub-paragraph (1), the Commission determines that there is such an indication, it shall—

(*a*) notify the appropriate authority in relation to the DSI matter and (if different) the appropriate authority in relation to the person whose conduct is in question of its determination; and
(*b*) send to it (or each of them) a copy of the submission under sub-paragraph (1).

(3) If during the course of an investigation of a DSI matter it appears to a person appointed under paragraph 16 or 17 that there is an indication that a person serving with the police ("the person whose conduct is in question") may have—

(*a*) committed a criminal offence, or
(*b*) behaved in a manner which would justify the bringing of disciplinary proceedings,

he shall make a submission to that effect to the appropriate authority in relation to the DSI matter.

(4) If, after considering a submission under sub-paragraph (3), the appropriate authority determines that there is such an indication, it shall—

(*a*) if it is not the appropriate authority in relation to the person whose conduct is in question, notify that other authority of its determination and send to that authority a copy of the submission under sub-paragraph (3); and
(*b*) notify the Commission of its determination and send to it a copy of the submission under sub-paragraph (3).

(5) Where the appropriate authority in relation to the person whose conduct is in question—

(*a*) is notified of a determination by the Commission under sub-paragraph (2),
(*b*) (in a case where it is also the appropriate authority in relation to the DSI matter) makes a determination under sub-paragraph (4), or
(*c*) (in a case where it is not the appropriate authority in relation to the DSI matter) is notified by that other authority of a determination by it under sub-paragraph (4),

it shall record the matter under paragraph 11 as a conduct matter (and the other provisions of this Schedule shall apply in relation to that matter accordingly).

Final reports on investigations: complaints, conduct matters and certain DSI matters

22. (1) This paragraph applies on the completion of an investigation of—

(*a*) a complaint,
(*b*) a conduct matter, or
(*c*) a DSI matter in respect of which the Commission or the appropriate authority has made a determination under paragraph 21A(2) or (4).

(2) A person appointed under paragraph 16 shall submit a report on his investigation to the appropriate authority.

(3) A person appointed under paragraph 17 or 18 shall—

(*a*) submit a report on his investigation to the Commission; and
(*b*) send a copy of that report to the appropriate authority.

(4) In relation to a DSI matter in respect of which a determination has been made under paragraph 21A(2) or (4), the references in sub-paragraphs (2) and (3) of this paragraph to the appropriate authority are references to—

(*a*) the appropriate authority in relation to the DSI matter; and
(*b*) (where different) the appropriate authority in relation to the person whose conduct is in question.

(5) A person designated under paragraph 19 as the person in charge of an investigation by the Commission itself shall submit a report on it to the Commission.

(6) A person submitting a report under this paragraph shall not be prevented by any obligation of secrecy imposed by any rule of law or otherwise from including all such matters in his report as he thinks fit.

Action by the Commission in response to an investigation report under paragraph 22

23. (1) This paragraph applies where—

(*a*) a report on an investigation carried out under the management of the Commission is submitted to it under sub-paragraph (3) of paragraph 22; or (*b*) a report on an investigation carried out by a person designated by the Commission is submitted to it under sub-paragraph (5) of that paragraph.

(2) On receipt of the report, the Commission—

(*a*) if it appears that the appropriate authority has not already been sent a copy of the report, shall send a copy of the report to that authority;
(*b*) shall determine whether the report indicates that a criminal offence may have been committed by the person whose conduct was the subject-matter of the investigation;
(*c*) if it determines that the report does so indicate, shall notify the Director of Public Prosecutions of the determination and send him a copy of the report; and
(*d*) shall notify the appropriate authority of its determination under paragraph (*b*) and of any action taken by it under paragraph (*c*).

(3) The Director of Public Prosecutions shall notify the Commission of any decision of his to take, or not to take, action in respect of the matters dealt with in any report a copy of which has been sent to him under sub-paragraph (2)(*c*).

(4) It shall be the duty of the Commission to notify the persons mentioned in sub-paragraph (5) if criminal proceedings are brought against any person by the Director of Public Prosecutions in respect of any matters dealt with in a report copied to him under sub-paragraph (2)(*c*).

(5) Those persons are—

(*a*) in the case of a complaint, the complainant and every person entitled to be kept properly informed in relation to the complaint under section 21; and
(*b*) in the case of a recordable conduct matter, every person entitled to be kept properly informed in relation to that matter under that section.

(6) Where the Commission—

(*a*) has determined under sub-paragraph (2)(*b*) that there is no indication in the report that a criminal offence may have been committed,
(*b*) is notified by the Director of Public Prosecutions, in any case in which it has sent him a copy of the report, that the Director proposes to take no action in respect any of the matters dealt with in the report, or
(*c*) is satisfied that all criminal proceedings brought or likely to be brought in respect of matters dealt with in the report have been brought to a conclusion (apart from the bringing and determination of any appeal),

the Commission shall give a notification to the appropriate authority requiring it to determine what action (if any) it will itself take in respect of the matters dealt with in the report.

(7) On being required under sub-paragraph (6) to determine what action it will take in respect of the matters dealt with in the report the appropriate authority shall make that determination and submit a memorandum to the Commission which—

(*a*) sets out whether the appropriate authority is proposing to take any action in respect of the matters dealt with in the report;
(*b*) if the appropriate authority is proposing to take any action, sets out what action it is proposing to take; and
(*c*) if the appropriate authority has decided in relation to any person whose conduct is the subject-matter of the report that disciplinary proceedings should not be brought against that person, sets out its reasons for so deciding.

(8) On receipt of a memorandum under sub-paragraph (7), the Commission shall—

(*a*) consider the memorandum and whether the appropriate authority is proposing to take the action that the Commission considers appropriate in respect of the matters dealt with in the report;
(*b*) determine, in the light of its consideration of those matters, whether or not to make recommendations under paragraph 27; and
(*c*) make such recommendations (if any) under that paragraph as it thinks fit.

(9) On the making of a determination under sub-paragraph (8)(*b*) the Commission shall give a notification—

(*a*) in the case of a complaint, to the complainant and to every person entitled to be kept properly informed in relation to the complaint under section 21; and
(*b*) in the case of a recordable conduct matter, to every person entitled to be kept properly informed in relation to that matter under that section.

(10) The notification required by sub-paragraph (9) is one setting out—

(*a*) the findings of the report;
(*b*) the Commission's determination under sub-paragraph (8)(*b*); and
(*c*) the action which the appropriate authority is to be recommended to take as a consequence of the determination.

(11) Subsections (5) to (7) of section 20 shall have effect in relation to the duties imposed on the Commission by sub-paragraph (9) of this paragraph as they have effect in relation to the duties imposed on the Commission by that section.

(12) Except so far as may be otherwise provided by regulations made by virtue of sub-paragraph (11), the Commission shall be entitled (notwithstanding any obligation of secrecy imposed by any rule of law or otherwise) to discharge the duty to give a person mentioned in sub-paragraph (9) notification of the findings of the report by sending that person a copy of the report.

(13) In relation to a DSI matter in respect of which a determination has been made under paragraph 21A(2) or (4), the references in this paragraph to the appropriate authority are references to the appropriate authority in relation to the person whose conduct is in question.

Action by the appropriate authority in response to an investigation report under paragraph 22

24. (1) This paragraph applies where—

(*a*) a report of an investigation is submitted to the appropriate authority in accordance with paragraph 22(2); or

(*b*) a copy of a report on an investigation carried out under the supervision of the Commission is sent to the appropriate authority in accordance with paragraph 22(3).

(2) On receipt of the report or (as the case may be) of the copy, the appropriate authority—

(*a*) shall determine whether the report indicates that a criminal offence may have been committed by a person whose conduct was the subject-matter of the investigation; and

(*b*) if it determines that the report does so indicate, shall notify the Director of Public Prosecutions of the determination and send him a copy of the report.

(3) The Director of Public Prosecutions shall notify the appropriate authority of any decision of his to take, or not to take, action in respect of the matters dealt with in any report a copy of which has been sent to him under sub-paragraph (2).

(4) It shall be the duty of the appropriate authority to notify the persons mentioned in sub-paragraph (5) if criminal proceedings are brought against any person by the Director of Public Prosecutions in respect of any matters dealt with in a report copied to him under sub-paragraph (2)(*b*).

(5) Those persons are—

(*a*) in the case of a complaint, the complainant and every person entitled to be kept properly informed in relation to the complaint under section 21; and

(*b*) in the case of a recordable conduct matter, every person entitled to be kept properly informed in relation to that matter under that section.

(6) Where the appropriate authority—

(*a*) has determined under sub-paragraph (2) that there is no indication in the report that a criminal offence may have been committed,

(*b*) is notified by the Director of Public Prosecutions, in any case in which it has sent him a copy of the report, that the Director proposes to take no action in respect any of the matters dealt with in the report, or

(*c*) is satisfied that all criminal proceedings brought or likely to be brought in respect of matters dealt with in the report have been brought to a conclusion (apart from the bringing and determination of any appeal),

the appropriate authority shall determine what action (if any) it will itself take in respect of the matters dealt with in the report.

(7) On the making of a determination under sub-paragraph (6) the appropriate authority shall give a notification—

(*a*) in the case of a complaint, to the complainant and to every person entitled to be kept properly informed in relation to the complaint under section 21; and

(*b*) in the case of a recordable conduct matter, to every person entitled to be kept properly informed in relation to that matter under that section.

(8) The notification required by sub-paragraph (7) is one setting out—

(*a*) the findings of the report;

(*b*) whether the authority has determined under sub-paragraph (6) to take any action;

(*c*) the action (if any) which that authority has decided to take; and

(*d*) the complainant's right of appeal under paragraph 25.

(9) Subsections (5) to (7) of section 20 shall have effect in relation to the duties imposed on the appropriate authority by sub-paragraph (7) of this paragraph as they have effect in relation to the duties imposed on the appropriate authority by that section.

(10) Except so far as may be otherwise provided by regulations made by virtue of sub-paragraph (9), the appropriate authority shall be entitled (notwithstanding any obligation of secrecy imposed by any rule of law or otherwise) to discharge the duty to give a person mentioned in sub-paragraph (7) notification of the findings of the report by sending that person a copy of the report.

(11) In relation to a DSI matter in respect of which a determination has been made under paragraph 21A(2) or (4), the references in this paragraph to the appropriate authority are references to the appropriate authority in relation to the person whose conduct is in question.

Final reports on investigations: other DSI matters

24A. (1) This paragraph applies on the completion of an investigation of a DSI matter in respect of which neither the Commission nor the appropriate authority has made a determination under paragraph 21A(2) or (4).

(2) A person appointed under paragraph 16, 17 or 18 or designated under paragraph 19 shall—

(*a*) submit a report on the investigation to the Commission; and

(*b*) send a copy of that report to the appropriate authority.

(3) A person submitting a report under this paragraph shall not be prevented by any obligation of secrecy imposed by any rule of law or otherwise from including all such matters in his report as he thinks fit.

(4) On receipt of the report, the Commission shall determine whether the report indicates that a person serving with the police may have—

(*a*) committed a criminal offence, or

(*b*) behaved in a manner which would justify the bringing of disciplinary proceedings.

Action by the Commission in response to an investigation report under paragraph 24A

24B. (1) If the Commission determines under paragraph 24A(4) that the report indicates that a person serving with the police may have—

(*a*) committed a criminal offence, or

(*b*) behaved in a manner which would justify the bringing of disciplinary proceedings,

it shall notify the appropriate authority in relation to the person whose conduct is in question of its determination and, if it appears that that authority has not already been sent a copy of the report, send a copy of the report to that authority.

(2) Where the appropriate authority in relation to the person whose conduct is in question is notified of a determination by the Commission under sub-paragraph (1), it shall record the matter under paragraph 11 as a conduct matter (and the other provisions of this Schedule shall apply in relation to that matter accordingly).

24C. (1) If the Commission determines under paragraph 24A(4) that there is no indication in the report that a person serving with the police may have—

(*a*) committed a criminal offence, or

(*b*) behaved in a manner which would justify the bringing of disciplinary proceedings,

it shall make such recommendations or give such advice under section 10(1)(*e*) (if any) as it considers necessary or desirable.

(2) Sub-paragraph (1) does not affect any power of the Commission to make recommendations or give advice under section 10(1)(*e*) in other cases (whether arising under this Schedule or otherwise).

Appeals to the Commission with respect to an investigation

25. (1) This paragraph applies where a complaint has been subjected to—

(*a*) an investigation by the appropriate authority on its own behalf; or

(*b*) an investigation under the supervision of the Commission.

(2) The complainant shall have the following rights of appeal to the Commission—

(*a*) a right to appeal on the grounds that he has not been provided with adequate information—

(i) about the findings of the investigation; or

(ii) about any proposals of the appropriate authority to take, or not to take, action in consequence of the report;

(*b*) a right to appeal against the findings of the investigation; and

(*c*) a right of appeal against any proposal of the appropriate authority to take, or not to take, action in respect of any of the matters dealt with in the report of the investigation;

and it shall be the duty of the Commission to notify the appropriate authority, every person entitled to be kept properly informed in relation to the complaint under section 21 and the person complained against of any appeal brought under this paragraph.

(2A) In sub-paragraph (2)—

(*a*) references to the findings of an investigation do not include a reference to findings on a report submitted under paragraph 20A; and

(*b*) references to the report of an investigation do not include a reference to a report submitted under that paragraph.

(3) On the bringing of an appeal under this paragraph, the Commission may require the appropriate authority to submit a memorandum to the Commission which—

(*a*) sets out whether the appropriate authority is proposing to take any action in respect of the matters dealt with in the report;

(*b*) if the appropriate authority is proposing to take any action, sets out what action it is proposing to take; and

(*c*) if the appropriate authority has decided in relation to any person whose conduct is the subject-matter of the report that disciplinary proceedings should not be brought against that person, sets out its reasons for so deciding;

and it shall be the duty of the appropriate authority to comply with any requirement under this sub-paragraph.

(4) Where the Commission so requires on the bringing of any appeal under this paragraph in the case of an investigation by the appropriate authority on its own behalf, the appropriate authority shall provide the Commission with a copy of the report of the investigation.

(5) On an appeal under this paragraph, the Commission shall determine—

(*a*) whether the complainant has been provided with adequate information about the matters mentioned in sub-paragraph (2)(*a*);

(*b*) whether the findings of the investigation need to be reconsidered; and

(*c*) whether the appropriate authority is proposing to take the action that the Commission considers appropriate in consequence of the report.

(6) If, on an appeal under this paragraph, the Commission determines that the complainant has not been provided with adequate information about any matter, the Commission shall give the appropriate authority all such directions as the Commission considers appropriate for securing that the complainant is properly informed.

(7) Nothing in sub-paragraph (6) shall authorise the Commission to require the disclosure of any information the disclosure of which to the appellant has been or is capable of being withheld by virtue of regulations made under section 20(5).

(8) If, on an appeal under this paragraph, the Commission determines that the findings of the investigation need to be reconsidered, it shall either—

(*a*) review those findings without an immediate further investigation; or
(*b*) direct that the complaint be re-investigated.

(9) If, on an appeal under this paragraph, the Commission determines that the appropriate authority is not proposing to take the action in consequence of the report that the Commission considers appropriate, the Commission shall—

(*a*) determine, in the light of that determination, whether or not to make recommendations under paragraph 27; and
(*b*) make such recommendations (if any) under that paragraph as it thinks fit.

(10) The Commission shall give notification of any determination under this paragraph—

(*a*) to the appropriate authority,
(*b*) to the complainant;
(*c*) to every person entitled to be kept properly informed in relation to the complaint under section 21; and
(*d*) except in a case where it appears to the Commission that to do so might prejudice any proposed review or re-investigation of the complaint, to the person complained against.

(11) The Commission shall also give notification of any directions given to the appropriate authority under this paragraph—

(*a*) to the complainant;
(*b*) to every person entitled to be kept properly informed in relation to the complaint under section 21; and
(*c*) except in a case where it appears to the Commission that to do so might prejudice any proposed review or re-investigation of the complaint, to the person complained against.

(12) It shall be the duty of the appropriate authority to comply with any directions given to it under this paragraph.

(13) The Secretary of State may by regulations[1] make provision—

(*a*) for the form and manner in which appeals under this paragraph are to be brought;
(*b*) for the period within which any such appeal must be brought; and
(*c*) for the procedure to be followed by the Commission when dealing with or disposing of any such appeal.

Reviews and re-investigations following an appeal

26. (1) On a review under paragraph 25(8)(*a*) of the findings of an investigation the powers of the Commission shall be, according to its determination on that review, to do one or more of the following—

(*a*) to uphold the findings in whole or in part;
(*b*) to give the appropriate authority such directions—
  (i) as to the carrying out by the appropriate authority of its own review of the findings,
  (ii) as to the information to be provided to the complainant, and
  (iii) generally as to the handling of the matter in future,
  as the Commission thinks fit;
(*c*) to direct that the complaint be re-investigated.

(2) Where the Commission directs under paragraph 25 or sub-paragraph (1) that a complaint be re-investigated, it shall make a determination of the form that the re-investigation should take.

(3) Sub-paragraphs (3) to (7) of paragraph 15 shall apply in relation to a determination under sub-paragraph (2) as they apply in the case of a determination under that paragraph.

(4) The other provisions of this Schedule (including this paragraph) shall apply in relation to any re-investigation in pursuance of a direction under paragraph 25(8) or sub-paragraph (1) of this paragraph as they apply in relation to any investigation in pursuance of a determination under paragraph 15.

(5) The Commission shall give notification of any determination made by it under this paragraph—

(*a*) to the appropriate authority;
(*b*) to the complainant;
(*c*) to every person entitled to be kept properly informed in relation to the complaint under section 21; and
(*d*) except in a case where it appears to the Commission that to do so might prejudice any proposed re-investigation of the complaint, to the person complained against.

(6) The Commission shall also give notification of any directions given to the appropriate authority under this paragraph—

(*a*) to the complainant;
(*b*) to every person entitled to be kept properly informed in relation to the complaint under section; and
(*c*) except in a case where it appears to the Commission that to do so might prejudice any proposed review or re-investigation of the complaint, to the person complained against.

Duties with respect to disciplinary proceedingsf

27. (1) This paragraph applies where, in the case of any investigation, the appropriate authority—

(*a*) has given, or is required to give, a notification under paragraph 24(7) of the action it is proposing to take in relation to the matters dealt with in any report of the investigation; or
(*b*) has submitted, or is required to submit, a memorandum to the Commission under paragraph 23 or 25 setting out the action that it is proposing to take in relation to those matters.

(2) Subject to paragraph 20 and to any recommendations or directions under the following provisions of this paragraph, it shall be the duty of the appropriate authority—

(*a*) to take the action which has been or is required to be notified or, as the case may be, which is or is required to be set out in the memorandum; and (*b*) in a case where that action consists of or includes the bringing of disciplinary proceedings, to secure that those proceedings, once brought, are proceeded with to a proper conclusion.

(3) Where this paragraph applies by virtue of sub-paragraph (1)(*b*), the Commission may make a recommendation to the appropriate authority in respect of any person serving with the police—

(*a*) that disciplinary proceedings, or such disciplinary proceedings as may be specified in the recommendation, are brought against that person in respect of the conduct which was the subject-matter of the investigation; or

(*b*) that any disciplinary proceedings brought against that person are modified so as to include such charges as may be so specified;

and it shall be the duty of the appropriate authority to notify the Commission whether it accepts the recommendation and (if it does) to set out in the notification the steps that it is proposing to take to give effect to it.

(4) If, after the Commission has made a recommendation under this paragraph, the appropriate authority does not take steps to secure that full effect is given to the recommendation—

(*a*) the Commission may direct the appropriate authority to take steps for that purpose; and

(*b*) it shall be the duty of the appropriate authority to comply with the direction.

(5) A direction under sub-paragraph (4) may, to such extent as the Commission thinks fit, set out the steps to be taken by the appropriate authority in order to give effect to the recommendation.

(6) Where the Commission gives the appropriate authority a direction under this paragraph, it shall supply the appropriate authority with a statement of its reasons for doing so.

(7) Where disciplinary proceedings have been brought in accordance with a recommendation or direction under this paragraph, it shall be the duty of the authority to ensure that they are proceeded with to a proper conclusion.

(8) The Commission may at any time withdraw a direction given under this paragraph; and sub-paragraph (7) shall not impose any obligation in relation to any time after the withdrawal of the direction.

(9) The appropriate authority shall keep the Commission informed—

(*a*) in a case in which this paragraph applies by virtue of sub-paragraph (1)(*b*), of whatever action it takes in pursuance of its duty under sub-paragraph (2); and

(*b*) in every case of a recommendation or direction under this paragraph, of whatever action it takes in response to that recommendation or direction.

Information for complainant about disciplinary recommendations

28. (1) Where—

(*a*) the Commission makes recommendations under paragraph 27 in the case of an investigation of a complaint, and

(*b*) the appropriate authority notify the Commission that the recommendations have been accepted,

the Commission shall notify the complainant and every person entitled to be kept properly informed in relation to the complaint under section 21 of that fact and of the steps that have been, or are to be taken, by the appropriate authority to give effect to it.

(2) Where in the case of an investigation of a complaint the appropriate authority—

(*a*) notify the Commission that it does not (either in whole or in part) accept recommendations made by the Commission under paragraph 27, or

(*b*) fails to take steps to give full effect to any such recommendations,

it shall be the duty of the Commission to determine what if any further steps to take under that paragraph.

(3) It shall be the duty of the Commission to notify the complainant and every person entitled to be kept properly informed in relation to the complaint under section 21—

(*a*) of any determination under sub-paragraph (2) not to take further steps under paragraph 27; and

(*b*) where they determine under that sub-paragraph to take further steps under that paragraph, of the outcome of the taking of those steps.

---

1. The Police (Complaints and Misconduct) Regulations 2004, SI 2004/643 amended by SI 2005/3389 have been made.

Section 38

SCHEDULE 4
POWERS EXERCISABLE BY POLICE CIVILIANS

(*Amended by the Anti-social behaviour Act 2003, s 93, the Criminal Justice Act 2003, Sch 1, the Serious Organised Crime and Police Act 2005, Sch 8, the Drugs Act 2005, s 5 and the Anti-social Behaviour Act 2003, s 93, the Criminal Justice Act 2003, Sch 1 and the Serious Organised Crime and Police Act, Sch 8.*)

PART 1
COMMUNITY SUPPORT OFFICERS

Powers to issue fixed penalty notices

8–23897ZB **1.** (1) Where a designation applies this paragraph to any person, that person shall have the powers specified in sub-paragraph (2) in relation to any individual who he has reason to believe has committed a relevant fixed penalty offence at a place within the relevant police area.

(2) Those powers are the following powers so far as exercisable in respect of a relevant fixed penalty offence—

(*a*) the powers of a constable in uniform and of an authorised constable to give a penalty notice under Chapter 1 of Part 1 of the Criminal Justice and Police Act 2001 (c 16) (fixed penalty notices in respect of offences of disorder[1]);

(*aa*) the power of a constable to give a penalty notice under section 444A of the Education Act 1996 (penalty notice in respect of failure to secure regular attendance at school of registered pupil);

(*b*) the power of a constable in uniform to give a person a fixed penalty notice under section 54 of the Road Traffic Offenders Act 1988 (c 53) (fixed penalty notices) in respect of an offence under section 72 of the Highway Act 1835 (c 50) (riding on a footway) committed by cycling;

(c) the power of an authorised officer of a local authority to give a notice under section 4 of the Dogs (Fouling of Land) Act 1996 (c 20) (fixed penalty notices in respect of dog fouling);★

(*ca*) the power of an authorised officer of a local authority to give a notice under section 43(1) of the Anti-social Behaviour Act 2003 (penalty notices in respect of graffiti or fly-posting); and

(*d*) the power of an authorised officer of a litter authority to give a notice under section 88 of the Environmental Protection Act 1990 (c 43) (fixed penalty notices in respect of litter).★

(2A) The reference to the powers mentioned in sub-paragraph (2)(*a*) does not include those powers so far as they relate to an offence under the provisions in the following list—

section 1 of the Theft Act 1968,
section 87 of the Environmental Protection Act 1990.

(3) In this paragraph "relevant fixed penalty offence", in relation to a designated person, means an offence which—

(*a*) is an offence by reference to which a notice may be given to a person in exercise of any of the powers mentioned in sub-paragraph 1(2)(*a*) to (*d*); and

(*b*) is specified or described in that person's designation as an offence he has been designated to enforce under this paragraph.

(4) In its application to an offence which is an offence by reference to which a notice may be given to a person in exercise of the power mentioned in sub-paragraph (2)(*aa*), sub-paragraph (1) shall have effect as if for the words from "who he has reason to believe" to the end there were substituted "in the relevant police area who he has reason to believe has committed a relevant fixed penalty offence".

★Sub-para (2)(*c*) repealed and sub-para (2)(*e*) inserted by the Clean Neighbourhoods and Environment Act 2005, ss 62 and Sch 3 from a date to be appointed.

1. This paragraph is to have effect as if the reference to the powers there mentioned did not include those powers so far as they relate to an offence under any of the following provisions: (*a*) s 1 of the Theft Act 1968; (*b*) s 87 of the Environmental Protection Act 1990 (Criminal Justice and Police Act 2001 (Amendment) and Police Reform Act 2002 (Modification) Order 2004, SI 2004/2540).

Power to require name and address

1A. (1) This paragraph applies if a designation applies it to any person.

(2) Such a designation may specify that, in relation to that person, the application of sub-paragraph (3) is confined to one or more only (and not to all) relevant offences or relevant licensing offences, being in each case specified in the designation.

(3) Subject to sub-paragraph (4), where that person has reason to believe that another person has committed a relevant offence in the relevant police area, or a relevant licensing offence (whether or not in the relevant police area), he may require that other person to give him his name and address.

(4) The power to impose a requirement under sub-paragraph (3) in relation to an offence under a relevant byelaw is exercisable only in a place to which the byelaw relates.

(5) A person who fails to comply with a requirement under sub-paragraph (3) is guilty of an offence and shall be liable, on summary conviction, to a fine not exceeding level 3 on the standard scale.

(6) In its application to an offence which is an offence by reference to which a notice may be given to a person in exercise of the power mentioned in paragraph 1(2)(aa), sub-paragraph (3) of this paragraph shall have effect as if for the words "has committed a relevant offence in the relevant police area" there were substituted "in the relevant police area has committed a relevant offence".

(7) In this paragraph, "relevant offence", "relevant licensing offence" and "relevant byelaw" have the meaning given in paragraph 2 (reading accordingly the references to "this paragraph" in paragraph 2(6)).

Power to detain etc

2. (1) This paragraph applies if a designation applies it to any person.

(2) A designation may not apply this paragraph to any person unless a designation also applies paragraph 1A to him.

(3) Where, in a case in which a requirement under paragraph 1A(3) has been imposed on another person—

(*a*) that other person fails to comply with the requirement, or

(*b*) the person who imposed the requirement has reasonable grounds for suspecting that the other person has given him a name or address that is false or inaccurate,

the person who imposed the requirement may require the other person to wait with him, for a period not exceeding thirty minutes, for the arrival of a constable.

This sub-paragraph does not apply if the requirement was imposed in connection with a relevant licensing offence mentioned in paragraph (a), (c) or (f) of sub-paragraph (6A) believed to have been committed on licensed premises (within the meaning of the Licensing Act 2003).

(3A) Where—

(*a*) a designation applies this paragraph to any person ("the CSO"); and

(*b*) by virtue of a designation under paragraph 1A the CSO has the power to impose a requirement under sub-paragraph (3) of that paragraph in relation to an offence under a relevant byelaw,

the CSO shall also have any power a constable has under the relevant byelaw to remove a person from a place.

(3B) Where a person to whom this paragraph applies ("the CSO") has reason to believe that another person is committing an offence under section 3 or 4 of the Vagrancy Act 1824, and requires him to stop doing whatever gives rise to that belief, the CSO may, if the other person fails to stop as required, require him to wait with the CSO, for a period not exceeding thirty minutes, for the arrival of a constable.

(4) A person who has been required under sub-paragraph (3) or (3B) to wait with a person to whom this Part of this Schedule applies may, if requested to do so, elect that (instead of waiting) he will accompany the person imposing the requirement to a police station in the relevant police area.

(4A) If a person has imposed a requirement under sub-paragraph (3) or (3B) on another person ("P"), and P does not make an election under sub-paragraph (4), the person imposing the requirement shall, if a constable arrives within the thirty-minute period, be under a duty to remain with the constable and P until he has transferred control of P to the constable.

(4B) If, following an election under sub-paragraph (4), the person imposing the requirement under sub-paragraph (3) or (3B) ("the CSO") takes the person upon whom it is imposed ("P") to a police station, the CSO—

(*a*) shall be under a duty to remain at the police station until he has transferred control of P to the custody officer there;

(*b*) until he has so transferred control of P, shall be treated for all purposes as having P in his lawful custody; and

(*c*) for so long as he is at the police station, or in its immediate vicinity, in compliance with, or having complied with, his duty under paragraph (a), shall be under a duty to prevent P's escape and to assist in keeping P under control.

(5) A person who—

(*a*) *repealed,*

(*b*) makes off while subject to a requirement under sub-paragraph (3) or (3B), or

(*c*) makes off while accompanying a person to a police station in accordance with an election under sub-paragraph (4),

is guilty of an offence and shall be liable, on summary conviction, to a fine not exceeding level 3 on the standard scale.

(6) In this paragraph "relevant offence", in relation to a person to whom this paragraph applies, means any offence which is—

(*a*) a relevant fixed penalty offence for the purposes of the application of paragraph 1 to that person; or

(*aa*) an offence under section 32(2) of the Anti-social Behaviour Act 2003; or

(*ab*) an offence committed in a specified park which by virtue of section 2 of the Parks Regulation (Amendment) Act 1926 is an offence against the Parks Regulation Act 1872; or]

(*ac*) an offence under section 3 or 4 of the Vagrancy Act 1824; or

(*ad*) an offence under a relevant byelaw; or

(*b*) an offence the commission of which appears to that person to have caused—

(i) injury, alarm or distress to any other person; or

(ii) the loss of, or any damage to, any other person's property;

but a designation applying this paragraph to any person may provide that an offence is not to be treated as a relevant offence by virtue of paragraph (*b*) unless it satisfies such other conditions as may be specified in the designation.

(6A) In this paragraph "relevant licensing offence" means an offence under any of the following provisions of the Licensing Act 2003—

(*a*) section 141 (otherwise than by virtue of subsection (2)(c) or (3) of that section);

(*b*) section 142;

(*c*) section 146(1);

(*d*) section 149(1)(a), (3)(a) or (4)(a);

(*e*) section 150(1);

(*f*) section 150(2) (otherwise than by virtue of subsection (3)(b) of that section);

(*g*) section 152(1) (excluding paragraph (b)).

(6B) In this paragraph "relevant byelaw" means a byelaw included in a list of byelaws which—

(*a*) have been made by a relevant body with authority to make byelaws for any place within the relevant police area; and

(*b*) the chief officer of the police force for the relevant police area and the relevant body have agreed to include in the list.

(6C) The list must be published by the chief officer in such a way as to bring it to the attention of members of the public in localities where the byelaws in the list apply.

(6D) A list of byelaws mentioned in sub-paragraph (6B) may be amended from time to time by agreement between the chief officer and the relevant body in question, by adding byelaws to it or removing byelaws from it, and the amended list shall also be published by the chief officer as mentioned in sub-paragraph (6C).

(6E) A relevant body for the purposes of sub-paragraph (6B) is—

(*a*) in England, a county council, a district council, a London borough council or a parish council; or in Wales, a county council, a county borough council or a community council;

(*b*) the Greater London Authority;

(*c*) Transport for London;

(*d*) a metropolitan county passenger transport authority established under section 28 of the Local Government Act 1985;

(*e*) any body specified in an order made by the Secretary of State.

(6F) An order under sub-paragraph (6E)(*e*) may provide, in relation to any body specified in the order, that the agreement mentioned in sub-paragraph (6B)(*b*) and (6D) is to be made between the chief officer and the Secretary of State (rather than between the chief officer and the relevant body).

(7) *Repealed.*

(8) The application of any provision of this paragraph by paragraph 3(2), 3A(2) or 7A(8) has no effect unless a designation under this paragraph has applied this paragraph to the CSO in question.

Powers to search individuals and to seize and retain items

2A. (1) Where a designation applies this paragraph to any person, that person shall (subject to sub-paragraph (3)) have the powers mentioned in sub-paragraph (2) in relation to a person upon whom he has imposed a requirement to wait under paragraph 2(3) or (3B) (whether or not that person makes an election under paragraph 2(4)).

(2) Those powers are the same powers as a constable has under section 32 of the 1984 Act in relation to a person arrested at a place other than a police station—

(*a*) to search the arrested person if the constable has reasonable grounds for believing that the arrested person may present a danger to himself or others; and to seize and retain anything he finds on exercising that power, if the constable has reasonable grounds for believing that the person being searched might use it to cause physical injury to himself or to any other person;

(*b*) to search the arrested person for anything which he might use to assist him to escape from lawful custody; and to seize and retain anything he finds on exercising that power (other than an item subject to legal privilege) if the constable has reasonable grounds for believing that the person being searched might use it to assist him to escape from lawful custody.

(3) If in exercise of the power conferred by sub-paragraph (1) the person to whom this paragraph applies seizes and retains anything by virtue of sub-paragraph (2), he must—

(*a*) tell the person from whom it was seized where inquiries about its recovery may be made; and

(*b*) comply with a constable's instructions about what to do with it.

Power to require name and address of person acting in an anti-social manner

3. (1) Where a designation applies this paragraph to any person, that person shall, in the relevant police area, have the powers of a constable in uniform under section 50 to require a person whom he has reason to believe to have been acting, or to be acting, in an anti-social manner (within the meaning of section 1 of the Crime and Disorder Act 1998 (c 37) (anti-social behaviour orders)) to give his name and address.

(2) Sub-paragraphs (3) to (5) of paragraph 2 apply in the case of a requirement imposed by virtue of sub-paragraph (1) as they apply in the case of a requirement under paragraph 1A(3).

Power to require name and address: road traffic offences

3A. (1) Where a designation applies this paragraph to any person, that person shall, in the relevant police area, have the powers of a constable—

(*a*) under subsection (1) of section 165 of the Road Traffic Act 1988 to require a person mentioned in paragraph (*c*) of that subsection who he has reasonable cause to believe has committed, in the relevant police area, an offence under subsection (1) or (2) of section 35 of that Act (including that section as extended by paragraphs 11B(4) and 12(2) of this Schedule) to give his name and address; and

(*b*) under section 169 of that Act to require a person committing an offence under section 37 of that Act (including that section as extended by paragraphs 11B(4) and 12(2) of this Schedule) to give his name and address.

(2) Sub-paragraphs (3) to (5) of paragraph 2 apply in the case of a requirement imposed by virtue of sub-paragraph (1) as they apply in the case of a requirement under paragraph 1A(3).

(3) The reference in section 169 of the Road Traffic Act 1988 to section 37 of that Act is to be taken to include a reference to that section as extended by paragraphs 11B(4) and 12(2) of this Schedule.

Power to use reasonable force to detain person

4. (1) This paragraph applies where a designation—

(*a*) applies this paragraph to a person to whom any or all of paragraphs 1 to 3 are also applied; and

(*b*) sets out the matters in respect of which that person has the power conferred by this paragraph.

(2) The matters that may be set out in a designation as the matters in respect of which a person has the power conferred by this paragraph shall be confined to—

(*a*) offences that are relevant penalty notice offences for the purposes of the application of paragraph 1 to the designated person;

(*b*) offences that are relevant offences or relevant licensing offences for the purposes of the application of paragraph 1A or 2 to the designated person; and

(*c*) behaviour that constitutes acting in an anti-social manner (within the meaning of section 1 of the Crime and Disorder Act 1998 (c 37) (anti-social behaviour orders)).

(3) In any case in which a person to whom this paragraph applies has imposed a requirement on any other person under paragraph 1A(3) or 3(1) in respect of anything appearing to him to be a matter set out in the designation, he may use reasonable force to prevent that other person from making off and to keep him under control while he is either—

(*a*) subject to a requirement imposed in that case by the designated person under sub-paragraph (3) of paragraph 2; or

(*b*) accompanying the designated person to a police station in accordance with an election made in that case under sub-paragraph (4) of that paragraph.

4ZA. Where a designation applies this paragraph to any person, that person may, if he has imposed a requirement on any person to wait with him under paragraph 2(3B) or by virtue of paragraph 7A(8) or 7C(2)(*a*), use reasonable force to prevent that other person from making off and to keep him under control while he is either—

(*a*) subject to that requirement; or
(b) accompanying the designated person to a police station in accordance with an election made under paragraph 2(4).

4ZB. Where a designation applies this paragraph to any person, that person, if he is complying with any duty under sub-paragraph (4A) or (4B) of paragraph 2, may use reasonable force to prevent P (as identified in those sub-paragraphs) from making off (or escaping) and to keep him under control.

Power to disperse groups and remove young persons to their place of residence

4A. Where a designation applies this paragraph to any person, that person shall, within the relevant police area, have the powers which, by virtue of an authorisation under section 30 of the Anti-social Behaviour Act 2003, are conferred on a constable in uniform by section 30(3) to (6) of that Act (power to disperse groups and remove persons under 16 to their place of residence).

4B. (1) Where a designation applies this paragraph to any person, that person shall, within the relevant police area, have the power of a constable under section 15(3) of the Crime and Disorder Act 1998 (power to remove child to their place of residence).

(2) Section 15(1) of that Act shall have effect in relation to the exercise of that power by that person as if the reference to a constable in that section were a reference to that person.

(3) Where that person exercises that power, the duty in section 15(2) of that Act (duty to inform local authority of contravention of curfew notice) is to apply to him as it applies to a constable.

Alcohol consumption in designated public places

5. Where a designation applies this paragraph to any person, that person shall, within the relevant police area, have the powers of a constable under section 12 of the Criminal Justice and Police Act 2001 (c 16) (alcohol consumption in public places)—

(*a*) to impose a requirement under subsection (2) of that section; and
(*b*) to dispose under subsection (3) of that section of anything surrendered to him;

and that section shall have effect in relation to the exercise of those powers by that person as if the references to a constable in subsections (1) and (5) were references to that person.

Confiscation of alcohol

6. Where a designation applies this paragraph to any person, that person shall, within the relevant police area, have the powers of a constable under section 1 of the Confiscation of Alcohol (Young Persons) Act 1997 (c 33) (confiscation of intoxicating liquor)—

(*a*) to impose a requirement under subsection (1) of that section; and
(*b*) to dispose under subsection (2) of that section of anything surrendered to him;

and that section shall have effect in relation to the exercise of those powers by that person as if the references to a constable in subsections (1) and (4) (but not the reference in subsection (5) (arrest)) were references to that person.

Confiscation of tobacco etc

7. Where a designation applies this paragraph to any person, that person shall, within the relevant police area, have—

(*a*) the power to seize anything that a constable in uniform has a duty to seize under subsection (3) of section 7 of the Children and Young Persons Act 1933 (c 12) (seizure of tobacco etc from young persons); and
(*b*) the power to dispose of anything that a constable may dispose of under that subsection;

and the power to dispose of anything shall be a power to dispose of it in such manner as the police authority may direct.

Search and seizure powers: alcohol and tobacco

7A. (1) Where a designation applies this paragraph to any person ("the CSO"), the CSO shall have the powers set out below.

(2) Where—

(*a*) in exercise of the powers referred to in paragraph 5 or 6 the CSO has imposed, under section 12(2) of the Criminal Justice and Police Act 2001 or under section 1 of the Confiscation of Alcohol (Young Persons) Act 1997, a requirement on a person to surrender alcohol or a container for alcohol;
(*b*) that person fails to comply with that requirement; and
(*c*) the CSO reasonably believes that the person has alcohol or a container for alcohol in his possession,

the CSO may search him for it.

(3) Where—

(*a*) in exercise of the powers referred to in paragraph 7 the CSO has sought to seize something which by virtue of that paragraph he has a power to seize;
(*b*) the person from whom he sought to seize it fails to surrender it; and
(*c*) the CSO reasonably believes that the person has it in his possession,

the CSO may search him for it.

(4) The power to search conferred by sub-paragraph (2) or (3)—

(*a*) is to do so only to the extent that is reasonably required for the purpose of discovering whatever the CSO is searching for; and (*b*) does not authorise the CSO to require a person to remove any of his clothing in public other than an outer coat, jacket or gloves.

(5) A person who without reasonable excuse fails to consent to being searched is guilty of an offence and shall be liable, on summary conviction, to a fine not exceeding level 3 on the standard scale.

(6) A CSO who proposes to exercise the power to search a person under sub-paragraph (2) or (3) must inform him that failing without reasonable excuse to consent to being searched is an offence.

(7) If the person in question fails to consent to being searched, the CSO may require him to give the CSO his name and address.

(8) Sub-paragraph (3) of paragraph 2 applies in the case of a requirement imposed by virtue of sub-paragraph (7) as it applies in the case of a requirement under paragraph 1A(3); and sub-paragraphs (4) to (5) of paragraph 2 also apply accordingly.

(9) If on searching the person the CSO discovers what he is searching for, he may seize it and dispose of it.

Powers to seize and detain: controlled drugs

7B. (1) Where a designation applies this paragraph to any person ("the CSO"), the CSO shall, within the relevant police area, have the powers set out in sub-paragraphs (2) and (3).

(2) If the CSO—

(*a*) finds a controlled drug in a person's possession (whether or not he finds it in the course of searching the person by virtue of a designation under any paragraph of this Schedule); and

(*b*) reasonably believes that it is unlawful for the person to be in possession of it,

the CSO may seize it and retain it.

(3) If the CSO—

(*a*) finds a controlled drug in a person's possession (as mentioned in sub-paragraph (2)); or

(*b*) reasonably believes that a person is in possession of a controlled drug,

and reasonably believes that it is unlawful for the person to be in possession of it, the CSO may require him to give the CSO his name and address.

(4) If in exercise of the power conferred by sub-paragraph (2) the CSO seizes and retains a controlled drug, he must—

(*a*) if the person from whom it was seized maintains that he was lawfully in possession of it, tell the person where inquiries about its recovery may be made; and

(*b*) comply with a constable's instructions about what to do with it.

(5) A person who fails to comply with a requirement under sub-paragraph (3) is guilty of an offence and shall be liable, on summary conviction, to a fine not exceeding level 3 on the standard scale.

(6) In this paragraph, "controlled drug" has the same meaning as in the Misuse of Drugs Act 1971.

7C. (1) Sub-paragraph (2) applies where a designation applies this paragraph to any person ("the CSO").

(2) If the CSO imposes a requirement on a person under paragraph 7B(3)—

(*a*) sub-paragraph (3) of paragraph 2 applies in the case of such a requirement as it applies in the case of a requirement under paragraph 1A(3); and

(*b*) sub-paragraphs (4) to (5) of paragraph 2 also apply accordingly.

Entry to save life or limb or prevent serious damage to property

8. Where a designation applies this paragraph to any person, that person shall have the powers of a constable under section 17 of the 1984 Act to enter and search any premises in the relevant police area for the purpose of saving life or limb or preventing serious damage to property.

Entry to investigate licensing offences

8A. (1) Where a designation applies this paragraph to any person, that person shall have the powers of a constable under section 180 of the Licensing Act 2003 to enter and search premises other than clubs in the relevant police area, but only in respect of a relevant licensing offence (as defined for the purposes of paragraph 2).

(2) Except as mentioned in sub-paragraph (3), a person to whom this paragraph applies shall not, in exercise of the power conferred by sub-paragraph (1), enter any premises except in the company, and under the supervision, of a constable.

(3) The prohibition in sub-paragraph (2) does not apply in relation to premises in respect of which the person to whom this paragraph applies reasonably believes that a premises licence under Part 3 of the Licensing Act 2003 authorises the sale of alcohol for consumption off the premises.

Seizure of vehicles used to cause alarm etc

9. (1) Where a designation applies this paragraph to any person—

(*a*) that person shall, within the relevant police area, have all the powers of a constable in uniform under section 59 of this Act which are set out in subsection (3) of that section; and

(*b*) references in that section to a constable, in relation to the exercise of any of those powers by that person, are references to that person.

(2) A person to whom this paragraph applies shall not enter any premises in exercise of the power conferred by section 59(3)(*c*) except in the company, and under the supervision, of a constable.

Abandoned vehicles

10. Where a designation applies this paragraph to any person, that person shall have any such powers in the relevant police area as are conferred on persons designated under that section by regulations under section 99 of the Road Traffic Regulation Act 1984 (c 27) (removal of abandoned vehicles).

Power to stop vehicle for testing

11. Where a designation applies this paragraph to any person, that person shall, within the relevant police area, have the power of a constable in uniform to stop a vehicle under subsection (3) of section 67 of the Road Traffic Act 1988 (c 52) for the purposes of a test under subsection (1) of that section.

Power to stop cycles

11A. (1) Subject to sub-paragraph (2), where a designation applies this paragraph to any person, that person shall, within the relevant police area, have the power of a constable in uniform under section 163(2) of the Road Traffic Act 1988 to stop a cycle.

(2) The power mentioned in sub-paragraph (1) may only be exercised by that person in relation to a person who he has reason to believe has committed an offence under section 72 of the Highway Act 1835 (riding on a footway) by cycling.

Power to control traffic for purposes other than escorting a load of exceptional dimensions

11B. (1) Where a designation applies this paragraph to any person, that person shall have, in the relevant police area—

(*a*) the power of a constable engaged in the regulation of traffic in a road to direct a person driving or propelling a vehicle to stop the vehicle or to make it proceed in, or keep to, a particular line of traffic;

(*b*) the power of a constable in uniform engaged in the regulation of vehicular traffic in a road to direct a person on foot to stop proceeding along or across the carriageway.

(2) The purposes for which those powers may be exercised do not include the purpose mentioned in paragraph 12(1).

(3) Where a designation applies this paragraph to any person, that person shall also have, in the relevant police area, the power of a constable, for the purposes of a traffic survey, to direct a person driving or propelling a vehicle to stop the vehicle, to make it proceed in, or keep to, a particular line of traffic, or to proceed to a particular point on or near the road.

(4) Sections 35 and 37 of the Road Traffic Act 1988 (offences of failing to comply with directions of constable engaged in regulation of traffic in a road) shall have effect in relation to the exercise of the powers mentioned in sub-paragraphs (1) and (3), for the purposes for which they may be exercised and by a person whose designation applies this paragraph to him, as if the references to a constable were references to him.

(5) A designation may not apply this paragraph to any person unless a designation also applies paragraph 3A to him.

Power to control traffic for purposes of escorting a load of exceptional dimensions

12. (1) Where a designation applies this paragraph to any person, that person shall have, for the purpose of escorting a vehicle or trailer carrying a load of exceptional dimensions either to or from the relevant police area, the power of a constable engaged in the regulation of traffic in a road—

(*a*) to direct a vehicle to stop;

(*b*) to make a vehicle proceed in, or keep to, a particular line of traffic; and

(*c*) to direct pedestrians to stop.

(2) Sections 35 and 37 of the Road Traffic Act 1988 (offences of failing to comply with directions of constable engaged in regulation of traffic in a road) shall have effect in relation to the exercise of those powers for the purpose mentioned in sub-paragraph (1) by a person whose designation applies this paragraph to him as if the references to a constable engaged in regulation of traffic in a road were references to that person.

(3) The powers conferred by virtue of this paragraph may be exercised in any police area in England and Wales.

(4) In this paragraph "vehicle or trailer carrying a load of exceptional dimensions" means a vehicle or trailer the use of which is authorised by an order made by the Secretary of State under section 44(1)(*d*) of the Road Traffic Act 1988.

Carrying out of road checks

13. Where a designation applies this paragraph to any person, that person shall have the following powers in the relevant police area—

(*a*) the power to carry out any road check the carrying out of which by a police officer is authorised under section 4 of the 1984 Act (road checks); and

(*b*) for the purpose of exercising that power, the power conferred by section 163 of the Road Traffic Act 1988 (c 52) (power of police to stop vehicles) on a constable in uniform to stop a vehicle.

Power to place traffic signs

13A. (1) Where a designation applies this paragraph to any person, that person shall have, in the relevant police area, the powers of a constable under section 67 of the Road Traffic Regulation Act 1984 to place and maintain traffic signs.

(2) Section 36 of the Road Traffic Act 1988 (drivers to comply with traffic directions) shall apply to signs placed in the exercise of the powers conferred by virtue of sub-paragraph (1).

Cordoned areas

14. Where a designation applies this paragraph to any person, that person shall, in relation to any cordoned area in the relevant police area, have all the powers of a constable in uniform under section 36 of the Terrorism Act 2000 (c 11) (enforcement of cordoned area) to give orders, make arrangements or impose prohibitions or restrictions.

Power to stop and search vehicles etc in authorised areas

15. (1) Where a designation applies this paragraph to any person—

(*a*) that person shall, in any authorised area within the relevant police area, have all the powers of a constable in uniform by virtue of section 44(1)(*a*) and (*d*) and (2)(*b*) and 45(2) of the Terrorism Act 2000 (powers of stop and search)—

(i) to stop and search vehicles;

(ii) to search anything in or on a vehicle or anything carried by the driver of a vehicle or any passenger in a vehicle;

(iii) to search anything carried by a pedestrian; and

(iv) to seize and retain any article discovered in the course of a search carried out by him or by a constable by virtue of any provision of section 44(1) or (2) of that Act;

and

(*b*) the references to a constable in subsections (1) and (4) of section 45 of that Act (which relate to the exercise of those powers) shall have effect in relation to the exercise of any of those powers by that person as references to that person.

(2) A person shall not exercise any power of stop, search or seizure by virtue of this paragraph except in the company, and under the supervision, of a constable.

Photographing of persons arrested, detained or given fixed penalty notices

15ZA. Where a designation applies this paragraph to any person, that person shall, within the relevant police area, have the power of a constable under section 64A(1A) of the 1984 Act (photographing of suspects etc) to take a photograph of a person elsewhere than at a police station.

Power to modify paragraph 1(2A)

15A. (1) The Secretary of State may by order amend paragraph 1(2A) so as to remove a provision from the list or add a provision to the list; but the list must contain only provisions mentioned in the first column of the Table in section 1(1) of the Criminal Justice and Police Act 2001.

(2) The Secretary of State shall not make an order containing (with or without any other provision) any provision authorised by this paragraph unless a draft of that order has been laid before Parliament and approved by a resolution of each House.

PART 2
INVESTIGATING OFFICERS

Search warrants

8–23897ZC **16.** Where a designation applies this paragraph to any person—

(*a*) he may apply as if he were a constable for a warrant under section 8 of the 1984 Act (warrants for entry and search) in respect of any premises whether in the relevant police area or not;

(*b*) the persons to whom a warrant to enter and search any such premises may be issued under that section shall include that person;

(*c*) that person shall have the power of a constable under section 8(2) of that Act in any premises in the relevant police area to seize and retain things for which a search has been authorised under subsection (1) of that section;

(*d*) section 15 of that Act (safeguards) shall have effect in relation to the issue of such a warrant to that person as it has effect in relation to the issue of a warrant under section 8 of that Act to a constable;

(*e*) section 16 of that Act (execution of warrants) shall have effect in relation to any warrant to enter and search premises that is issued (whether to that person or to any other person) , but in respect of premises in the relevant police area only, as if references in that section to a constable included references to that person;

(*f*) section 19(6) of that Act (protection for legally privileged material from seizure) shall have effect in relation to the seizure of anything by that person by virtue of sub-paragraph (*c*) as it has effect in relation to the seizure of anything by a constable;

(*g*) section 20 of that Act (extension of powers of seizure to computerised information) shall have effect in relation the power of seizure conferred on that person by virtue of sub-paragraph (*c*) as it applies in relation to the power of seizure conferred on a constable by section 8(2) of that Act;

(*h*) section 21(1) and (2) of that Act (provision of record of seizure) shall have effect in relation to the seizure of anything by that person in exercise of the power conferred on him by virtue of sub-paragraph (*c*) as if the references to a constable and to an officer included references to that person; and

(i) sections 21(3) to (8) and 22 of that Act (access, copying and retention) shall have effect in relation to anything seized by that person in exercise of that power, or taken away by him following the imposition of a requirement by virtue of sub-paragraph (*g*)—

(i) as they have effect in relation to anything seized in exercise of the power conferred on a constable by section 8(2) of that Act or taken away by a constable following the imposition of a requirement by virtue of section 20 of that Act; and

(ii) as if the references to a constable in subsections (3), (4) and (5) of section 21 included references to a person to whom this paragraph applies.

16A. Where a designation applies this paragraph to any person—

(*a*) the persons to whom a warrant may be addressed under section 26 of the Theft Act 1968 (search for stolen goods) shall, in relation to persons or premises in the relevant police area, include that person; and (*b*) in relation to such a warrant addressed to him, that person shall have the powers under subsection (3) of that section.

16B. Where a designation applies this paragraph to any person, subsection (3), and (to the extent that it applies subsection (3)) subsection (3A), of section 23 of the Misuse of Drugs Act 1971 (powers to search and obtain evidence) shall have effect as if, in relation to premises in the relevant police area, the reference to a constable included a reference to that person.

Access to excluded and special procedure material

17. Where a designation applies this paragraph to any person—

(*a*) he shall have the powers of a constable under section 9(1) of the 1984 Act (special provisions for access) to obtain access, in accordance with Schedule 1 to that Act and the following provisions of this paragraph, to excluded material and special procedure material;

(*b*) that Schedule shall have effect for the purpose of conferring those powers on that person as if—

(i) the references in paragraphs 1, 4, 5, 12 and 13 of that Schedule to a constable were references to that person; and

(ii) the references in paragraphs 12 and 14 of that Schedule to premises were references to premises in the relevant police area (in the case of a specific premises warrant) or any premises, whether in the relevant police area or not (in the case of an all premises warrant);

(*bb*) section 15 of that Act (safeguards) shall have effect in relation to the issue of any warrant under paragraph 12 of that Schedule to that person as it has effect in relation to the issue of a warrant under that paragraph to a constable;

(*bc*) section 16 of that Act (execution of warrants) shall have effect in relation to any warrant to enter and search premises that is issued under paragraph 12 of that Schedule (whether to that person or to any other person), but in respect of premises in the relevant police area only, as if references in that section to a constable included references to that person;

(*c*) section 19(6) of that Act (protection for legally privileged material from seizure) shall have effect in relation to the seizure of anything by that person in exercise of the power conferred on him by paragraph 13 of Schedule 1 to that Act as it has effect in relation to the seizure of anything under that paragraph by a constable;

(*d*) section 20 of that Act (extension of powers of seizure to computerised information) shall have effect in relation the power of seizure conferred on that person by paragraph 13 of Schedule 1 to that Act as it applies in relation to the power of seizure conferred on a constable by that paragraph;

(*e*) section 21(1) and (2) of that Act (provision of record of seizure) shall have effect in relation to the seizure of anything by that person in exercise of the power conferred on him by paragraph 13 of Schedule 1 to that Act as if the references to a constable and to an officer included references to that person; and

(*f*) sections 21(3) to (8) and 22 of that Act (access, copying and retention) shall have effect in relation to anything seized by that person in exercise of that power or taken away by him following the imposition of a requirement by virtue of sub-paragraph (*d*), and to anything produced to him under paragraph 4(*a*) of Schedule 1 to that Act—

(i) as they have effect in relation to anything seized in exercise of the power conferred on a constable by paragraph 13 of that Schedule or taken away by a constable following the imposition of a requirement by virtue of section 20 of that Act or, as the case may be, to anything produced to a constable under paragraph 4(*a*) of that Schedule; and

(ii) as if the references to a constable in subsections (3), (4) and (5) of section 21 included references to a person to whom this paragraph applies.

Entry and search after arrest

18. Where a designation applies this paragraph to any person—

(*a*) he shall have the powers of a constable under section 18 of the 1984 Act (entry and search after arrest) to enter and search any premises in the relevant police area and to seize and retain anything for which he may search under that section;

(*b*) subsections (5) and (6) of that section (power to carry out search before arrested person taken to police station and duty to inform senior officer) shall have effect in relation to any exercise by that person of those powers as if the references in those subsections to a constable were references to that person;

(*c*) section 19(6) of that Act (protection for legally privileged material from seizure) shall have effect in relation to the seizure of anything by that person by virtue of sub-paragraph (*a*) as it has effect in relation to the seizure of anything by a constable;

(*d*) section 20 of that Act (extension of powers of seizure to computerised information) shall have effect in relation the power of seizure conferred on that person by virtue of sub-paragraph (*a*) as it applies in relation to the power of seizure conferred on a constable by section 18(2) of that Act;

(*e*) section 21(1) and (2) of that Act (provision of record of seizure) shall have effect in relation to the seizure of anything by that person in exercise of the power conferred on him by virtue of sub-paragraph (*a*) as if the references to a constable and to an officer included references to that person; and

(*f*) sections 21(3) to (8) and 22 of that Act (access, copying and retention) shall have effect in relation to anything seized by that person in exercise of that power or taken away by him following the imposition of a requirement by virtue of sub-paragraph (*d*)—

(i) as they have effect in relation to anything seized in exercise of the power conferred on a constable by section 18(2) of that Act or taken away by a constable following the imposition of a requirement by virtue of section 20 of that Act; and

(ii) as if the references to a constable in subsections (3), (4) and (5) of section 21 included references to a person to whom this paragraph applies.

General power of seizure

19. Where a designation applies this paragraph to any person—

(*a*) he shall, when lawfully on any premises in the relevant police area, have the same powers as a constable under section 19 of the 1984 Act (general powers of seizure) to seize things;

(*b*) he shall also have the powers of a constable to impose a requirement by virtue of subsection (4) of that section in relation to information accessible from such premises;

(*c*) subsection (6) of that section (protection for legally privileged material from seizure) shall have effect in relation to the seizure of anything by that person by virtue of sub-paragraph (*a*) as it has effect in relation to the seizure of anything by a constable;

(*d*) section 21(1) and (2) of that Act (provision of record of seizure) shall have effect in relation to the seizure of anything by that person in exercise of the power conferred on him by virtue of sub-paragraph (*a*) as if the references to a constable and to an officer included references to that person; and

(*e*) sections 21(3) to (8) and 22 of that Act (access, copying and retention) shall have effect in relation to anything seized by that person in exercise of that power or taken away by him following the imposition of a requirement by virtue of sub-paragraph (*b*)—

(i) as they have effect in relation to anything seized in exercise of the power conferred on a constable by section 19(2) or (3) of that Act or taken away by a constable following the imposition of a requirement by virtue of section 19(4) of that Act; and

(ii) as if the references to a constable in subsections (3), (4) and (5) of section 21 included references to a person to whom this paragraph applies.

Access and copying in the case of things seized by constables

20. Where a designation applies this paragraph to any person, section 21 of the 1984 Act (access and copying) shall have effect in relation to anything seized in the relevant police area by a constable or by a person authorised to accompany him under section 16(2) of that Act as if the references to a constable in subsections (3), (4) and (5) of section 21 (supervision of access and photographing of seized items) included references to a person to whom this paragraph applies.

Arrest at a police station for another offence

21. (1) Where a designation applies this paragraph to any person, he shall have the power to make an arrest at any police station in the relevant police area in any case where an arrest—

(*a*) is required to be made under section 31 of the 1984 Act (arrest for a further offence of a person already at a police station); or

(*b*) would be so required if the reference in that section to a constable included a reference to a person to whom this paragraph applies.

(2) Section 36 of the Criminal Justice and Public Order Act 1994 (c 33) (consequences of failure by arrested person to account for objects etc) shall apply (without prejudice to the effect of any designation applying paragraph 23) in the case of a person arrested in exercise of the power exercisable by virtue of this paragraph as it applies in the case of a person arrested by a constable.

Power to transfer persons into custody of investigating officers

22. (1) Where a designation applies this paragraph to any person, the custody officer for a designated police station in the relevant police area may transfer or permit the transfer to him of a person in police detention for an offence which is being investigated by the person to whom this paragraph applies.

(2) A person into whose custody another person is transferred under sub-paragraph (1)—

(*a*) shall be treated for all purposes as having that person in his lawful custody;

(*b*) shall be under a duty to keep that person under control and to prevent his escape; and

(*c*) shall be entitled to use reasonable force to keep that person in his custody and under his control.

(3) Where a person is transferred into the custody of a person to whom this paragraph applies, in accordance with sub-paragraph (1), subsections (2) and (3) of section 39 of the 1984 Act shall have effect as if—

(*a*) references to the transfer of a person in police detention into the custody of a police officer investigating an offence for which that person is in police detention were references to that person's transfer into the custody of the person to whom this paragraph applies; and

(*b*) references to the officer to whom the transfer is made and to the officer investigating the offence were references to the person to whom this paragraph applies.

Powers in respect of detained persons

22A. Where a designation applies this paragraph to any person, he shall be under a duty, when in the course of his employment he is present at a police station—

(*a*) to assist any officer or other designated person to keep any person detained at the police station under control; and

(*b*) to prevent the escape of any such person,

and for those purposes shall be entitled to use reasonable force.

Power to require arrested person to account for certain matters

23. Where a designation applies this paragraph to any person—

(*a*) he shall have the powers of a constable under sections 36(1)(*c*) and 37(1)(*c*) of the Criminal Justice and Public Order Act 1994 (c 33) to request a person who—

(i) has been arrested by a constable, or by any person to whom paragraph 21 applies, and
(ii) is detained at any place in the relevant police area,

to account for the presence of an object, substance or mark or for the presence of the arrested person at a particular place; and

(*b*) the references to a constable in sections 36(1)(*b*) and (*c*) and (4) and 37(1)(*b*) and (*c*) and (3) of that Act shall have effect accordingly as including references to the person to whom this paragraph is applied.

Extended powers of seizure

24. Where a designation applies this paragraph to any person—

(*a*) the powers of a constable under Part 2 of the Criminal Justice and Police Act 2001 (c 16) (extension of powers of seizure) that are exercisable in the case of a constable by reference to a power of a constable that is conferred on that person by virtue of the provisions of this Part of this Schedule shall be exercisable by that person by reference to that power to the same extent as in the case of a constable but in relation only to premises in the relevant police area and things found on any such premises; and

(*b*) section 56 of that Act (retention of property seized by a constable) shall have effect as if the property referred to in subsection (1) of that section included property seized by that person at any time when he was lawfully on any premises in the relevant police area.

Persons accompanying investigating officers

24A. (1) This paragraph applies where a person ("an authorised person") is authorised by virtue of section 16(2) of the 1984 Act to accompany an investigating officer designated for the purposes of paragraph 16 (or 17) in the execution of a warrant.

(2) The reference in paragraph 16(h) (or 17(e)) to the seizure of anything by a designated person in exercise of a particular power includes a reference to the seizure of anything by the authorised person in exercise of that power by virtue of section 16(2A) of the 1984 Act.

(3) In relation to any such seizure, paragraph 16(h) (or 17(e)) is to be read as if it provided for the references to a constable and to an officer in section 21(1) and (2) of the 1984 Act to include references to the authorised person.

(4) The reference in paragraph 16(i) (or 17(f)) to anything seized by a designated person in exercise of a particular power includes a reference to anything seized by the authorised person in exercise of that power by virtue of section 16(2A) of the 1984 Act.

(5) In relation to anything so seized, paragraph 16(i)(ii) (or 17(f)(ii)) is to be read as if it provided for—

(a) the references to the supervision of a constable in subsections (3) and (4) of section 21 of the 1984 Act to include references to the supervision of a person designated for the purposes of paragraph 16 (or paragraph 17), and

(b) the reference to a constable in subsection (5) of that section to include a reference to such a person or an authorised person accompanying him.

(6) Where an authorised person accompanies an investigating officer who is also designated for the purposes of paragraph 24, the references in sub-paragraphs (a) and (b) of that paragraph to the designated person include references to the authorised person.

PART 3
DETENTION OFFICERS

Attendance at police station for fingerprinting

8–23897ZD **25.** Where a designation applies this paragraph to any person, he shall, in respect of police stations in the relevant police area, have the power of a constable under section 27(1) of the 1984 Act (fingerprinting of suspects) to require a person to attend a police station in order to have his fingerprints taken.

Non-intimate searches of detained persons

26. (1) Where a designation applies this paragraph to any person, he shall have the powers of a constable under section 54 of the 1984 Act (non-intimate searches of detained persons)—

(*a*) to carry out a search under that section of any person at a police station in the relevant police area or of any other person otherwise in police detention in that area; and

(*b*) to seize or retain, or cause to be seized or retained, anything found on such a search.

(2) Subsections (6C) and (9) of section 54 of that Act (restrictions on power to seize personal effects and searches to be carried out by a member of the same sex) shall apply to the exercise by a person to whom this paragraph is applied of any power exercisable by virtue of this paragraph as they apply to the exercise of the power in question by a constable.

Searches and examinations to ascertain identity

27. Where a designation applies this paragraph to any person, he shall have the powers of a constable under section 54A of the 1984 Act (searches and examinations to ascertain identity)—

(*a*) to carry out a search or examination at any police station in the relevant police area; and

(*b*) to take a photograph at any such police station of an identifying mark.

Intimate searches of detained persons

28. (1) Where a designation applies this paragraph to any person, he shall have the powers of a constable by virtue of section 55(6) of the 1984 Act (intimate searches) to carry out an intimate search of a person at any police station in the relevant police area.

(2) Subsection (7) of section 55 of that Act (no intimate search to be carried out by a constable of the opposite sex) shall apply to the exercise by a person to whom this paragraph applies of any power exercisable by virtue of this paragraph as it applies to the exercise of the power in question by a constable.

Fingerprinting without consent

29. Where a designation applies this paragraph to any person—

(*a*) he shall have, at any police station in the relevant police area, the power of a constable under section 61 of the 1984 Act (fingerprinting) to take fingerprints without the appropriate consent; and

(*b*) the requirement by virtue of subsection (7A)(*a*) of that section that a person must be informed by an officer that his fingerprints may be the subject of a speculative search shall be capable of being discharged, in the case of a person at such a station, by his being so informed by the person to whom this paragraph applies.

Warnings about intimate samples

30. Where a designation applies this paragraph to any person, the requirement by virtue of section 62(7A)(*a*) of the 1984 Act (intimate samples) that a person must be informed by an officer that a sample taken from him may be the subject of a speculative search shall be capable of being discharged, in the case of a person in a police station in the relevant police area, by his being so informed by the person to whom this paragraph applies.

Non-intimate samples

31. Where a designation applies this paragraph to any person—

(*a*) he shall have the power of a constable under section 63 of the 1984 Act (non-intimate samples), in the case of a person in a police station in the relevant police area, to take a non-intimate sample without the appropriate consent;

(*b*) the requirement by virtue of subsection (6) of that section (information about authorisation) that a person must be informed by an officer of the matters mentioned in that subsection shall be capable of being discharged, in the case of an authorisation in relation to a person in a police station in the relevant police area, by his being so informed by the person to whom this paragraph applies; and

(*c*) the requirement by virtue of subsection (8B)(*a*) of that section that a person must be informed by an officer that a sample taken from him may be the subject of a speculative search shall be capable of being discharged, in the case of a person in such a police station, by his being so informed by the person to whom this paragraph applies.

Attendance at police station for the taking of a sample

32. Where a designation applies this paragraph to any person, he shall, as respects any police station in the relevant police area, have the power of a constable under subsection (4) of section 63A of the 1984 Act (supplementary provisions relating to fingerprints and samples) to require a person to attend a police station in order to have a sample taken.

Photographing persons in police detention

33. Where a designation applies this paragraph to any person, he shall, at police stations in the relevant police area, have the power of a constable under section 64A of the 1984 Act (photographing of suspects etc) to take a photograph of a person detained at a police station.

Taking of impressions of footwear

33A. Where a designation applies this paragraph to any person—

(*a*) he shall, at any police station in the relevant police area, have the powers of a constable under section 61A of the 1984 Act (impressions of footwear) to take impressions of a person's footwear without the appropriate consent; and

(*b*) the requirement by virtue of section 61A(5)(a) of the 1984 Act that a person must be informed by an officer that an impression of his footwear may be the subject of a speculative search shall be capable of being discharged, in the case of a person at such a station, by his being so informed by the person to whom this paragraph applies.

Powers in respect of detained persons

33B. Where a designation applies this paragraph to any person, he shall be under a duty, when in the course of his employment he is present at a police station—

(*a*) to keep under control any person detained at the police station and for whom he is for the time being responsible;

(*b*) to assist any officer or other designated person to keep any other person detained at the police station under control; and

(*c*) to prevent the escape of any such person as is mentioned in paragraph (*a*) or (*b*),

and for those purposes shall be entitled to use reasonable force.

33C. Where a designation applies this paragraph to any person, he shall be entitled to use reasonable force when—

(*a*) securing, or assisting an officer or another designated person to secure, the detention of a person detained at a police station in the relevant police area, or

(*b*) escorting within a police station in the relevant police area, or assisting an officer or another designated person to escort within such a police station, a person detained there.

33D. Where a designation applies this paragraph to any person, he is authorised to carry out the duty under—

(*a*) section 55 of the Police and Criminal Evidence Act 1984 of informing a person who is to be subject to an intimate search under that section of the matters of which he is required to be informed in pursuance of subsection (3B) of that section;

(*b*) section 55A of that Act of informing a person who is to be subject to x-ray or ultrasound (as the case may be) under that section of the matters of which he is required to be informed in pursuance of subsection (3) of that section.

PART 4
ESCORT OFFICERS

Power to take an arrested person to a police station

8–23897ZE **34.** (1) Where a designation applies this paragraph to any person—

(*a*) the persons who, in the case of a person arrested by a constable in the relevant police area, are authorised for the purposes of subsection (1A) of section 30 of the 1984 Act (procedure on arrest of person elsewhere than at a police station) to take the person arrested to a police station in that area shall include that person;

(*b*) that section shall have effect in relation to the exercise by that person of the power conferred by virtue of paragraph (*a*) as if the references to a constable in subsections (3), (4)(*a*) and (10) (but not the references in subsections (5) to (9)) included references to that person; and

(*c*) a person who is taking another person to a police station in exercise of the power conferred by virtue of paragraph (*a*)—

(i) shall be treated for all purposes as having that person in his lawful custody;
(ii) shall be under a duty to keep the person under control and to prevent his escape; and
(iii) shall be entitled to use reasonable force to keep that person in his charge and under his control;

(*d*) a person who has taken another person to a police station in exercise of the power conferred by virtue of paragraph (*a*)—

(i) shall be under a duty to remain at the police station until he has transferred control of the other person to the custody officer at the police station;
(ii) until he has so transferred control of the other person, shall be treated for all purposes as having that person in his lawful custody;
(iii) for so long as he is at the police station or in its immediate vicinity in compliance with, or having complied with, his duty under sub-paragraph (i), shall be under a duty to prevent the escape of the other person and to assist in keeping him under control; and

(2) Without prejudice to any designation under paragraph 26, where a person has another in his lawful custody by virtue of sub-paragraph (1) of this paragraph—

(*a*) he shall have the same powers under subsections (6A) and (6B) of section 54 of the 1984 Act (non-intimate searches) as a constable has in the case of a person in police detention—

(i) to carry out a search of the other person; and
(ii) to seize or retain, or cause to be seized or retained, anything found on such a search;

(*b*) subsections (6C) and (9) of that section (restrictions on power to seize personal effects and searches to be carried out by a member of the same sex) shall apply to the exercise by a person to whom this paragraph is applied of any power exercisable by virtue of this sub-paragraph as they apply to the exercise of the power in question by a constable.

Escort of persons in police detention

35. (1) Where a designation applies this paragraph to any person, that person may be authorised by the custody officer for any designated police station in the relevant police area to escort a person in police detention—

(*a*) from that police station to another police station in that or any other police area; or
(*b*) from that police station to any other place specified by the custody officer and then either back to that police station or on to another police station in that area or in another police area.

(2) Where a designation applies this paragraph to any person, that person may be authorised by the custody officer for any designated police station outside the relevant police area to escort a person in police detention—

(*a*) from that police station to a designated police station in that area; or
(*b*) from that police station to any place in that area specified by the custody officer and either back to that police station or on to another police station (whether in that area or elsewhere).

(3) A person who is escorting another in accordance with an authorisation under sub-paragraph (1) or (2)—

(*a*) shall be treated for all purposes as having that person in his lawful custody;
(*b*) shall be under a duty to keep the person under control and to prevent his escape; and
(*c*) shall be entitled to use reasonable force to keep that person in his charge and under his control.

(3A) A person who has escorted another person to a police station or other place in accordance with an authorisation under sub-paragraph (1) or (2)—

(*a*) shall be under a duty to remain at the police station or other place until he has transferred control of the other person to a custody officer or other responsible person there;

(b) until he has so transferred control of the other person, shall be treated for all purposes as having that person in his lawful custody;

(c) for so long as he is at the police station or other place, or in its immediate vicinity, in compliance with, or having complied with, his duty under paragraph (a), shall be under a duty to prevent the escape of the other person and to assist in keeping him under control; and

(d) shall be entitled to use reasonable force for the purpose of complying with his duty under paragraph (c).

(4) Without prejudice to any designation under paragraph 26, where a person has another in his lawful custody by virtue of sub-paragraph (3) of this paragraph—

(a) he shall have the same powers under subsections (6A) and (6B) of section 54 the 1984 Act (non-intimate searches) as a constable has in the case of a person in police detention—

(i) to carry out a search of the other person; and
(ii) to seize or retain, or cause to be seized or retained, anything found on such a search;

(b) subsections (6C) and (9) of that section (restrictions on power to seize personal effects and searches to be carried out by a member of the same sex) shall apply to the exercise by a person to whom this paragraph is applied of any power exercisable by virtue of this sub-paragraph as they apply to the exercise of the power in question by a constable.

(5) Section 39(2) of that Act (responsibilities of custody officer transferred to escort) shall have effect where the custody officer for any police station transfers or permits the transfer of any person to the custody of a person who by virtue of this paragraph has lawful custody outside the police station of the person transferred as it would apply if the person to whom this paragraph applies were a police officer.*

PART 4A
STAFF CUSTODY OFFICERS

Exercise of functions of custody officers

35A. (1) Where a designation applies this paragraph to any person, he may (subject to sub-paragraph (2)) perform all the functions of a custody officer under the 1984 Act (except those under section 45A(4) of that Act) and under any other enactment which confers functions on such a custody officer.

(2) But in relation to a police station designated under section 35(1) of the 1984 Act, the person must first also be appointed a custody officer for that police station under section 36(2) of that Act.

(3) A person performing the functions of a custody officer by virtue of a designation under this paragraph (together with, if appropriate, an appointment as such) shall have all the powers and duties of a custody officer.

(4) Except in sections 36 and 45A(4) of the 1984 Act, references in any enactment to a custody officer within the meaning of that Act include references to a person performing the functions of a custody officer by virtue of a designation under this paragraph.*

***Reproduced as inserted by the Serious Organised Crime and Police Act 2005, s 120 from a date to be appointed.**

35C. Where a designation applies this paragraph to any person, he is authorised to carry out the duty under—

(a) section 55 of the Police and Criminal Evidence Act 1984 of informing a person who is to be subject to an intimate search under that section of the matters of which he is required to be informed in pursuance of subsection (3B) of that section;

(b) section 55A of that Act of informing a person who is to be subject to x-ray or ultrasound (as the case may be) under that section of the matters of which he is required to be informed in pursuance of subsection (3) of that section.

PART 5
INTERPRETATION OF SCHEDULE

8–23897ZF **36.** (1) In this Schedule "the relevant police area"—

(a) in relation to a designation under section 38 or 39 by the chief officer of any police force, means the police area for which that force is maintained; and

(b) in relation to a designation under section 38 by a Director General, means England and Wales.

(2) In this Schedule "a designation" means a designation under section 38.

(3) In Parts 3 and 4 of this Schedule "a designation" also includes a designation under section 39.

(3A) In this Schedule "specified park" has the same meaning as in section 162 of the Serious Organised Crime and Police Act 2005.

(4) Expressions used in this Schedule and in the 1984 Act have the same meanings in this Schedule as in that Act.

Section 41

SCHEDULE 5
POWERS EXERCISABLE BY ACCREDITED PERSONS

Power to issue fixed penalty notices

8–23897ZG **1.** (1) An accredited person whose accreditation specifies that this paragraph applies to him shall have the powers specified in sub-paragraph (2) in relation to any individual who he has reason to believe has committed or is committing a relevant fixed penalty offence at a place within the relevant police area.

(2) Those powers are the following powers so far as exercisable in respect of a relevant offence—

(a) the power of a constable in uniform to give a person a fixed penalty notice under section 54 of the Road Traffic Offenders Act 1988 (c 53) (fixed penalty notices) in respect of an offence under section 72 of the Highway Act 1835 (c 50) (riding on a footway) committed by cycling;*

(*aa*) the powers of a constable in uniform to give a penalty notice under Chapter 1 of Part 1 of the Criminal Justice and Police Act 2001 (fixed penalty notices in respect of offences of disorder);[1]

(*ab*) the power of a constable to give a penalty notice under section 444A of the Education Act 1996 (penalty notice in respect of failure to secure regular attendance at school of registered pupil);

(*b*) the power of an authorised officer of a local authority to give a notice under section 4 of the Dogs (Fouling of Land) Act 1996 (c 20) (fixed penalty notices in respect of dog fouling); and*

(*c*) the power of an authorised officer of a litter authority to give a notice under section 88 of the Environmental Protection Act 1990 (c 43) (fixed penalty notices in respect of litter).

(2A) The reference to the powers mentioned in sub-paragraph (2)(*aa*) does not include those powers so far as they relate to an offence under the provisions in the following list—

section 12 of the Licensing Act 1872,
section 91 of the Criminal Justice Act 1967,
section 1 of the Theft Act 1968,
section 1(1) of the Criminal Damage Act 1971,
section 87 of the Environmental Protection Act 1990.

(3) In this paragraph "relevant fixed penalty offence", in relation to an accredited person, means an offence which—

(*a*) is an offence by reference to which a notice may be given to a person in exercise of any of the powers mentioned in sub-paragraph (2)(*a*) to (*c*); and

(*b*) is specified or described in that person's accreditation as an offence he has been accredited to enforce.

(4) In its application to an offence which is an offence by reference to which a notice may be given to a person in exercise of the power mentioned in sub-paragraph (2)(*ab*), sub-paragraph (1) shall have effect as if for the words from "who he has reason to believe" to the end there were substituted "in the relevant police area who he has reason to believe has committed or is committing a relevant fixed penalty offence".

***Sub-paragraphs (2)(*aa*) and (*ba*) inserted by the Anti-social Behaviour Act 2003, s 89, from a date to be appointed.**

1. This paragraph is to have effect as if the reference to the powers there mentioned did not include those powers so far as they relate to an offence under any of the following provisions: (*a*) s 1 of the Theft Act 1968; (*b*) s 1(1) of the Criminal Damage Act 1971; (*c*) s 87 of the Environmental Protection Act 1990 (Amendment) and Police Reform Act 2002 (Modification) Order 2004, SI 2004/2540).

Power to require giving of name and address

2. (1) Where an accredited person whose accreditation specifies that this paragraph applies to him has reason to believe that another person has committed a relevant offence in the relevant police area, he may require that other person to give him his name and address.

(2) A person who fails to comply with a requirement under sub-paragraph (1) is guilty of an offence and shall be liable, on summary conviction, to a fine not exceeding level 3 on the standard scale.

(3) In this paragraph "relevant offence", in relation to any accredited person, means any offence which is—

(*a*) a relevant fixed penalty offence for the purposes of any powers exercisable by the accredited person by virtue of paragraph 1; or

(*aa*) an offence under section 3 or 4 of the Vagrancy Act 1824; or

(*b*) an offence the commission of which appears to the accredited person to have caused—

(i) injury, alarm or distress to any other person; or
(ii) the loss of, or any damage to, any other person's property;

but the accreditation of an accredited person may provide that an offence is not to be treated as a relevant offence by virtue of paragraph (*b*) unless it satisfies such other conditions as may be specified in the accreditation.

(4) In its application to an offence which is an offence by reference to which a notice may be given to a person in exercise of the power mentioned in paragraph 1(2)(*ab*), sub-paragraph (1) of this paragraph shall have effect as if for the words "has committed a relevant offence in the relevant police area" there were substituted "in the relevant police area has committed a relevant offence".

Power to require name and address of person acting in an anti-social manner

3. An accredited person whose accreditation specifies that this paragraph applies to him shall, in the relevant police area, have the powers of a constable in uniform under section 50 to require a person whom he has reason to believe to have been acting, or to be acting, in an anti-social manner (within the meaning of section 1 of the Crime and Disorder Act 1998 (c 37) (anti-social behaviour orders)) to give his name and address.

Power to require name and address: road traffic offences

3A. (1) An accredited person whose accreditation specifies that this paragraph applies to him shall, in the relevant police area, have the powers of a constable—

(*a*) under subsection (1) of section 165 of the Road Traffic Act 1988 to require a person mentioned in paragraph (c) of that subsection who he has reasonable cause to believe has committed, in the relevant police area, an offence under subsection (1) or (2) of section 35 of that Act (including that section as extended by paragraphs 8B(4) and 9(2) of this Schedule) to give his name and address; and

(*b*) under section 169 of that Act to require a person committing an offence under section 37 of that Act (including that section as extended by paragraphs 8B(4) and 9(2) of this Schedule) to give his name and address.

(2) The reference in section 169 of the Road Traffic Act 1988 to section 37 of that Act is to be taken to include a reference to that section as extended by paragraphs 8B(4) and 9(2) of this Schedule.

Power to control traffic for purposes other than escorting a load of exceptional dimensions

8B. (1) A person whose accreditation specifies that this paragraph applies to him shall have, in the relevant police area—

(*a*) the power of a constable engaged in the regulation of traffic in a road to direct a person driving or propelling a vehicle to stop the vehicle or to make it proceed in, or keep to, a particular line of traffic;

(*b*) the power of a constable in uniform engaged in the regulation of vehicular traffic in a road to direct a person on foot to stop proceeding along or across the carriageway.

(2) The purposes for which those powers may be exercised do not include the purpose mentioned in paragraph 9(1).

(3) A person whose accreditation specifies that this paragraph applies to him shall also have, in the relevant police area, the power of a constable, for the purposes of a traffic survey, to direct a person driving or propelling a vehicle to stop the vehicle, to make it proceed in, or keep to, a particular line of traffic, or to proceed to a particular point on or near the road.

(4) Sections 35 and 37 of the Road Traffic Act 1988 (offences of failing to comply with directions of constable engaged in regulation of traffic in a road) shall have effect in relation to the exercise of the powers mentioned in sub-paragraphs (1) and (3), for the purposes for which they may be exercised and by a person whose accreditation specifies that this paragraph applies to him, as if the references to a constable were references to him.

(5) A person's accreditation may not specify that this paragraph applies to him unless it also specifies that paragraph 3A applies to him.

Alcohol consumption in designated public places

4. An accredited person whose accreditation specifies that this paragraph applies to him shall, within the relevant police area, have the powers of a constable under section 12 of the Criminal Justice and Police Act 2001 (c 16) (alcohol consumption in public places)—

(*a*) to impose a requirement under subsection (2) of that section; and

(*b*) to dispose under subsection (3) of that section of anything surrendered to him;

and that section shall have effect in relation to the exercise of those powers by that person as if the references to a constable in subsections (1) and (5) were references to the accredited person.

Confiscation of alcohol

5. An accredited person whose accreditation specifies that this paragraph applies to him shall, within the relevant police area, have the powers of a constable under section 1 of the Confiscation of Alcohol (Young Persons) Act 1997 (c 33) (confiscation of intoxicating liquor)—

(*a*) to impose a requirement under subsection (1) of that section; and

(*b*) to dispose under subsection (2) of that section of anything surrendered to him;

and that section shall have effect in relation to the exercise of those powers by that person as if the references to a constable in subsections (1) and (4) (but not the reference in subsection (5) (arrest)) were references to the accredited person.

Confiscation of tobacco etc

6. (1) An accredited person whose accreditation specifies that this paragraph applies to him shall, within the relevant police area, have—

(*a*) the power to seize anything that a constable in uniform has a duty to seize under subsection (3) of section 7 of the Children and Young Persons Act 1933 (c 12) (seizure of tobacco etc from young persons); and

(*b*) the power to dispose of anything that a constable may dispose of under that subsection;

and the power to dispose of anything shall be a power to dispose of it in such manner as the relevant employer of the accredited person may direct.

(2) In this paragraph "relevant employer", in relation to an accredited person, means the person with whom the chief officer of police for the relevant police area has entered into arrangements under section 40.

Abandoned vehicles

7. An accredited person whose accreditation specifies that this paragraph applies to him shall have all such powers in the relevant police area as are conferred on accredited persons by regulations under section 99 of the Road Traffic Regulation Act 1984 (c 27) (removal of abandoned vehicles).

Power to stop vehicle for testing

8. A person whose accreditation specifies that this paragraph applies to him shall, within the relevant police area, have the power of a constable in uniform to stop a vehicle under subsection (3) of section 67 of the Road Traffic Act 1988 (c 52) for the purposes of a test under subsection (1) of that section.

Power to stop cycles

8A. (1) Subject to sub-paragraph (2), a person whose accreditation specifies that this paragraph applies to him shall, within the relevant police area, have the power of a constable in uniform under section 163(2) of the Road Traffic Act 1988 to stop a cycle.

(2) The power mentioned in sub-paragraph (1) may only be exercised by that person in relation to a person who he has reason to believe has committed an offence under section 72 of the Highway Act 1835 (riding on a footway) by cycling.

Power to control traffic for purposes of escorting a load of exceptional dimensions

9. (1) A person whose accreditation specifies that this paragraph applies to him shall have, for the purpose of escorting a vehicle or trailer carrying a load of exceptional dimensions either to or from the relevant police area, the power of a constable engaged in the regulation of traffic in a road—

(*a*) to direct a vehicle to stop;
(*b*) to make a vehicle proceed in, or keep to, a particular line of traffic; and
(*c*) to direct pedestrians to stop.

(2) Sections 35 and 37 of the Road Traffic Act 1988 (offences of failing to comply with directions of constable engaged in regulation of traffic in a road) shall have effect in relation to the exercise of those powers for the purpose mentioned in sub-paragraph (1) by a person whose accreditation specifies that this paragraph applies to him as if the references to a constable engaged in regulation of traffic in a road were references to that person.

(3) The powers conferred by virtue of this paragraph may be exercised in any police area in England and Wales.

(4) In this paragraph "vehicle or trailer carrying a load of exceptional dimensions" means a vehicle or trailer the use of which is authorised by an order made by the Secretary of State under section 44(1)(*d*) of the Road Traffic Act 1988.

Photographing of persons given fixed penalty notices

9ZA. An accredited person whose accreditation specifies that this paragraph applies to him shall, within the relevant police area, have the power of a constable under section 64A(1A) of the 1984 Act (photographing of suspects etc) to take a photograph, elsewhere than at a police station, of a person to whom the accredited person has given a penalty notice (or as the case may be a fixed penalty notice) in exercise of any power mentioned in paragraph 1(2).

Power to modify paragraph 1(2A)

9A. (1) The Secretary of State may by order amend paragraph 1(2A) so as to remove a provision from the list or add a provision to the list; but the list must contain only provisions mentioned in the first column of the Table in section 1(1) of the Criminal Justice and Police Act 2001.

(2) The Secretary of State shall not make an order containing (with or without any other provision) any provision authorised by this paragraph unless a draft of that order has been laid before Parliament and approved by a resolution of each House.

Meaning of "relevant police area"

10. In this Schedule "the relevant police area", in relation to an accredited person, means the police area for which the police force whose chief officer granted his accreditation is maintained.

8–23897ZH SCHEDULE 6
SPECIFIC OFFENCES WHICH ARE ARRESTABLE OFFENCES

Repealed.

Railways and Transport Safety Act 2003[1]

(2003 c 20)

PART 3
BRITISH TRANSPORT POLICE

Police Authority

8–23897ZI 18–19. *British Transport Police Authority and its functions.*

---

1. This Act makes provision about railways, including tramways and transport safety. Reproduced in this title are those provisions relating to the British Transport Police, Part 1 relating to railways is reproduced in PART VII: TRANSPORT, title RAILWAYS, Part 4 relating to shipping, alcohol and drugs is reproduced in PART VII: TRANSPORT, title MERCHANT SHIPPING and Part 5 relating to aviation, alcohol and drugs is reproduced in PART VII: TRANSPORT, title AVIATION.

Sections 104 and 114 came into force on the passing of the Act (10 July 2003) and ss 105 and 112 came into force on 10 September 2003. The remaining provisions come into force in accordance with orders made under s 120. The following commencement orders have been made: (No 1) SI 2003/2681; (No 2) SI 2004/827; (No 3) SI 2004/1572; (No 4) SI 2004/2759; (No 5) 2005/1991. Part 3 was brought into force on 1 July 2004, except ss 34(1) and s 74 (in force 19 June 2004).

2. Part 3 comprises ss 18–77 and Schs 4 and 5.

Police Force

8–23897ZJ 20–23. *Establishment of police force, Chief Constables, Deputy Chief Constables and Assistant Chief Constables.*

8–23897ZK 24. Constables. *Appointment and attestation of Constables (modifies the Police Act 1996, s 29).*

8–23897ZL 25. Special Constables. *Appointment and attestation of Special Constables (modifies the Police Act 1996, s 29).*

8–23897ZM 26–30. *Cadets, civilian employees, terms of employment and trade union membership.*

Jurisdiction

8–23897ZN 31. Jurisdiction. (1) A constable of the Police Force shall have all the powers and privileges of a constable—

(*a*) on track,
(*b*) on network,
(*c*) in a station,
(*d*) in a light maintenance depot,
(*e*) on other land used for purposes of or in relation to a railway,
(*f*) on other land in which a person who provides railway services has a freehold or leasehold interest, and
(*g*) throughout Great Britain for a purpose connected to a railway or to anything occurring on or in relation to a railway.

(2) A constable of the Police Force may enter property which is or forms part of anything specified in subsection (3)—

(*a*) without a warrant,
(*b*) using reasonable force if necessary, and
(*c*) whether or not an offence has been committed.

(3) Those things are—

(*a*) track,
(*b*) a network,
(*c*) a station,
(*d*) a light maintenance depot, and
(*e*) a railway vehicle.

(4) In this section "powers" includes powers under an enactment whenever passed or made.
[Railways and Transport Safety Act 2003, s 31.]

8–23897ZO 32. Prosecution. Where the Police Force investigates an offence in the course of the exercise of its functions, the Chief Constable may institute criminal proceedings in England and Wales in respect of the offence.
[Railways and Transport Safety Act 2003, s 32.]

Police Services Agreements

8–23897ZP 33–35. *Arrangements with those who provide railway services.*

Regulation of Police Force

8–23897ZQ 36–49. *Regulations and Codes of Practice.*

Planning

8–23897ZR 50–55. *Policing objectives, policing plans, performance targets, directions and three-year strategy plans.*

Information,&c

8–23897ZS 56–62. *Reports, inquiries and public consultation.*

Inspection

8–23897ZT 63–67. *Inspections, directions and action plans.*

Miscellaneous

8–23897ZU 68. Offences. (1) Subsections (1) and (2) of section 89 of the Police Act 1996 (c 16) (assault on constable, &c) shall apply in relation to a constable of the Police Force as they apply in relation to other constables in England and Wales.

(2) Section 90 of that Act (impersonation of constable) shall apply as if—

(*a*) a reference to a member of a police force included a reference to a constable of the Police Force, and
(*b*) a reference to a special constable appointed for a police area included a reference to a special constable of the Police Force.

(3) In their application in relation to the Police Force by virtue of this section, sections 89 and 90 of that Act shall have effect throughout England and Wales and Scotland.
[Railways and Transport Safety Act 2003, s 68.]

General

8–23897ZV 75. Interpretation. (1) For the purposes of this Part (including, except where the context requires otherwise, subsections (2) to (5) below) "railway" means—

(*a*) a railway within the meaning given by section 67(1) of the Transport and Works Act 1992 (c 42) (interpretation), and
(*b*) a tramway within the meaning given by that section.

(2) For the purposes of this Part "railway services" means the management or control, or participation in the management or control, of all or any part or aspect of a railway or railway property.

(3) For the purposes of this Part "railway property" means—

(*a*) a track,
(*b*) a network,
(*c*) a station,
(*d*) a light maintenance depot,
(*e*) a railway vehicle on a network or tramway,
(*f*) rolling stock on a network or tramway,
(*g*) a train used on a network, and
(*h*) a vehicle used on a tramway.

(4) For the purposes of this Part (including subsections (1)(b) and (3) above) "tramway" has the meaning given by section 67(1) of the Transport and Works Act 1992 (c 42).

(5) For the purposes of this Part the following expressions have the meaning given by section 82 or 83 of the Railways Act 1993 (c 43) (interpretation) (or, where appropriate, an equivalent meaning in relation to a tramway)—

(*a*) light maintenance depot,
(*b*) network,
(*c*) railway vehicle,
(*d*) rolling stock,
(*e*) station,
(*f*) track, and
(*g*) train.

(6) In this Part unless the context requires otherwise a reference to a constable of the Police Force includes a reference to a constable of any rank.

(7) In this Part a reference to the National Policing Plan is a reference to the plan provided for in section 36A of the Police Act 1996 (c 16).

(8) This section is subject to section 77(2).
[Railways and Transport Safety Act 2003, s 75.]

8–23897ZW 76. Index of defined expressions. The following expressions are defined for the purposes of this Part by the provisions specified.

Expression	*Provision*
The Authority	Section 18
British Transport Police Federation	Section 39
The Chief Constable	Section 21
Constable	Sections 25(6) and 75
Light maintenance depot	Section 75
National Policing Plan	Section 75
Network	Section 75
Police services agreement	Section 33
The Police Force	Section 20
Railway	Section 75
Railway property	Section 75
Railway services	Section 75
Railway vehicle	Section 75
Rolling stock	Section 75
Station	Section 75
Track	Section 75
Train	Section 75
Tramway	Section 75

[Railways and Transport Safety Act 2003, s 76.]

8–23897ZX 77. *Extent*

8–23897ZY SCHEDULE 4
BRITISH TRANSPORT POLICE AUTHORITY

8–23897ZZ SCHEDULE 5
BRITISH TRANSPORT POLICE: CONSEQUENTIAL AMENDMENTS

Police (Property) Regulations 1997

(SI 1997/1908 amended by SI 2000/1549 and SI 2002/2313)

8–23898 **1.** *Citation and commencement.*

1. Made by the Secretary of State, in exercise of the powers conferred on him by s 2 of the Police (Property) Act 1897, and section 43(5), (6) and (7) of the Powers of Criminal Courts Act 1973.

8–23899 **2.** *Revocation.*

8–23900 **3.** In these Regulations:

"the relevant authority" means

(*a*) in relation to a police area in England and Wales listed in Schedule 1 to the Police Act 1996 or the City of London police area, the police authority (within the meaning of that Act);

(*ab*) in relation to the National Crime Squad, the National Crime Squad Service Authority

(*b*) in relation to the metropolitan police district, the Receiver for the Metropolitan Police Authority;

"the 1897 Act" means the Police (Property) Act 1897.

8–23900A **4.** (1) Subject to regulation 5 below, this regulation applies to property in the possession of the police to which the 1897 Act applies in respect of which the owner has not been ascertained and no order of a competent court has been made.

(2) Subject to section 2(3) of the 1897 Act (which provides for the sale of property which is perishable or the custody of which involves unreasonable expense or inconvenience) property to which this regulation applies shall not be disposed of until it has remained in the possession of the police for a year.

8–23900B **5.** (1) This regulation applies to property which is in the possession of the police by virtue of section 143 of the Powers of Criminal Courts (Sentencing) Act 2000 and in respect of which no application by a claimant has been made within six months of the making of the order under that section or no such application has succeeded.

(2) Subject to section 2(3) of the 1897 Act, property to which this regulation applies shall not be disposed of until the expiration of six months from the date on which the order in respect of the property was made under that section on the conviction of an offender or, if an application by a claimant of the property has been made within that period or the offender has appealed against the conviction or sentence, until that application or appeal has been determined.

8–23900C **6.** (1) After the expiration of the period referred to in regulation 4(2) or 5(2) above, as applicable, property to which these regulations apply (other than money) may be sold.

(2) The proceeds of all sales under these Regulations and any money to which these Regulations apply shall be paid to the relevant authority and shall be kept in a separate account to be called the Police Property Act Fund ("the Fund").

(3) The Fund or any part thereof, may be invested as the relevant authority think fit and the income derived from the investments shall be added to and become part of the Fund.

(4) The moneys, including income from investments standing to the credit of the Fund shall be applicable—

(*a*) to defray expenses incurred in the conveyance, storage and safe custody of the property and in connection with its sale and otherwise in executing these Regulations;

(*b*) to pay reasonable compensation, the amount of which shall be fixed by the relevant authority, to persons by whom property has been delivered to the police;

(*c*) to make payments of such amounts as the relevant authority may determine for such charitable purposes as they may select.

(5) The Chief Officer of Police, or in the case of property in the possession of the National Crime Squad the Director General of that Squad, may, at the request of the relevant authority, exercise the powers and perform the duties of the authority under the foregoing paragraphs of this regulation.

(6) The Fund shall be audited by an auditor nominated for that purpose by the relevant authority.

8–23900D **7.** (1) After the expiration of the period referred to in regulation 4(2) or 5(2) above, as applicable, if in the opinion of the relevant authority to which these Regulations apply (other than money) can be used for police purposes, the relevant authority may determine that the property is to be retained by the authority and the property shall vest in them on the making of the determination.

(2) A determination under paragraph (1) above shall be recorded in writing and published in such manner as the authority think fit and that record shall include the date on which the determination is made.

(3) No determination under paragraph (1) above may be made in relation to any property in relation to which an order has been made under section 145 of the Powers of Criminal Courts (Sentencing) Act 2000.

8–23900E **8.** If the Chief Officer of Police, or in the case of property in the possession of the National Crime Squad the Director General of that Squad, is satisfied that the nature of any property to which these Regulations apply is such that it is not in the public interest that it should be sold or retained, it shall be destroyed or otherwise disposed of in accordance with his directions.

Police Act 1997 (Criminal Records) Regulations 2002[1]

(SI 2002/233 amended by SI 2003/137, 520 and 1418, SI 2004/367, 1759 and 2592 and SI 2005/347)

8–23900T **1. Citation, commencement and extent.** (1) These Regulations may be cited as the Police Act 1997 (Criminal Records) Regulations 2002 and shall come into force on 1st March 2002.

(2) These Regulations extend to England and Wales.

1. Made by the Secretary of State under:
   (a) ss 113(1)(b); 114(1)(b); 115(1)(b) and (10); 116(1)(b); 118(3) and 125(5); and
   (b) having regard to the meaning of "prescribed" in ss 113(1)(a), (3)(a), (3A)(b) and (5); 114(1)(a); 115(1)(a), (6)(a)(i) and (6A)(b); 116(1)(a); 118(2)(a) and 119(3). See also, the Police Act 1997 (Criminal Records) (Welsh Language) Regulations 2003, SI 2003/117.

8–23900U **2. Interpretation.** In these Regulations—

"the Act" means the Police Act 1997;

"reprimand" means a reprimand given to a child or young person in accordance with section 65 of the Crime and Disorder Act 1998;

"volunteer" means a person engaged in an activity which involves spending time, unpaid (except for travel and other approved out-of-pocket expenses), doing something which aims to benefit some third party other than or in addition to a close relative;

"warning" means a warning given to a child or young person in accordance with section 65 of the Crime and Disorder Act 1998.

8–23900V **3. Application form.** The form set out in Schedule 2 to these Regulations, or a form to the like effect, is hereby prescribed for the purposes of sections 113(1)(*a*) (criminal record certificate), 114(1)(*a*) (criminal record certificate: Crown employment), 115(1)(*a*) (enhanced criminal record certificate) and 116(1)(*a*) (enhanced criminal record certificate: judicial appointment and Crown employment) of the Act.

8–23900W **4. Fees for criminal record certificates .** The fee payable in relation to an application for the issue of a criminal record certificate is hereby prescribed as £28 save that no fee is payable in relation to an application made by a volunteer.

8–23900WA **4A. Fees for enhanced criminal record certificates.** The fee payable in relation to an application for the issue of an enhanced criminal record certificate is hereby prescribed as £33 save that no fee is payable in relation to an application made by a volunteer.

8–23900X **5. Relevant matters: prescribed details.** The following details of a relevant matter for the purposes of sections 113(3)(*a*) and 115(6)(*a*)(i) of the Act (including those provisions as applied by sections 114(3) and 116(3), respectively) are hereby prescribed—

(*a*) in the case of a conviction within the meaning of the Rehabilitation of Offenders Act 1974, including a spent conviction—
  (i) the date of conviction;
  (ii) the convicting court;
  (iii) the offence; and
  (iv) the method of disposal for the offence including details of any order made under Part 2 of the Criminal Justice and Court Services Act 2000,

(*b*) in the case of a caution, reprimand or warning—
  (i) the date of caution, reprimand or warning;

(ii) the place where the caution, reprimand or warning was issued; and
(iii) the offence which the person issued with a caution, reprimand or warning had admitted.

8–23900Y 6. List kept under section 1 of the Protection of Children Act 1999: prescribed details. (1) In the case of an applicant included in the list kept under section 1 of the Protection of Children Act 1999 the following details are hereby prescribed for the purposes of sections 113(3A)(*b*) and 115(6A)(*b*) of the Act—

(*a*) the fact that he is included in the list;
(*b*) whether the person is disqualified from working with children for the purposes of section 35 of the Criminal Justice and Court Services Act 2000;
(*c*) whether any appeal against inclusion in the list is pending;
(*d*) whether the inclusion in the list is provisional; and
(*e*) whether or not he may not be employed or, as the case may be, should cease to be employed in a childcare position with a childcare organisation in accordance with section 7 of the Protection of Children Act 1999.

(2) In this regulation "childcare position" and "childcare organisation" have the same meanings as in section 12 of the Protection of Children Act 1999.

8–23900Z 7. Directions made under section 142 of the Education Act 2002: prescribed details. In the case of an applicant subject to a direction made under section 142 of the Education Act 2002 the following details are hereby prescribed for the purposes of sections 113(3A)(d) and 115(6A)(d) of the Act—

(*a*) the fact that he is subject to such a direction;
(*b*) the date the direction was given;
(*c*) details of any prohibition or restriction on his employment; and
(*d*) the grounds on which the direction was made, and, where the grounds are misconduct, details of the misconduct.

8–23900ZA 8. List kept under section 81 of the Care Standards Act 2000: prescribed details. (1) In the case of an applicant included in the list kept under section 81 of the Care Standards Act 2000 the following details are hereby prescribed for the purposes of sections 113(3C)(*b*) and 115(6B)(*b*) of the Act—

(*a*) the fact that he is included in the list;
(*b*) whether the inclusion in the list is provisional;
(*c*) whether any appeal against inclusion in the list is pending; and
(*d*) the fact that the person included in the list is prohibited from working in a care position.

(2) In this regulation "care position" has the same meaning as in Part VII of the Care Standards Act 2000.

8–23900ZB 9. Central records: prescribed details. Information in any form relating to convictions, cautions, reprimands and warnings on a names index held by the Police Information Technology Organisation for the use of constables is hereby prescribed as "central records" for the purposes of section 113(5) of the Act (including that provision as applied by sections 114(3), 115(6) and 116(3)).

8–23900ZC 10. Enhanced criminal record certificates: relevant police forces. For the purposes of an application for an enhanced criminal record certificate "relevant police force" means—

(*a*) the police force maintained for the police area in England and Wales or Scotland within which the applicant resides or has resided within the period of 5 years preceding the date of the application;
(*b*) the Police Service of Northern Ireland if the applicant resides or has resided within the period of 5 years preceding the date of the application within Northern Ireland;
(*c*) such other police force as the chief officer of police of a police force identified as a relevant police force by virtue of paragraphs (*a*) or (*b*) above determines;
(*d*) any police force that the Secretary of State determines to be relevant to the application.

8–23900ZD 11. Evidence of identity: fingerprinting. (1) Where the Secretary of State requires an application under Part V of the Act to be supported by evidence of identity in the form of fingerprints then the place at which they are to be taken is to be determined in accordance with paragraphs (2) and (3) below and he shall notify the applicant—

(*a*) of his requirement; and
(*b*) of the fact that any fingerprints taken from the applicant and provided to the Secretary of State in pursuance of the requirement may be the subject of a speculative search.

(2) Any applicant in receipt of such notification shall notify the Secretary of State of whether he wishes to proceed with his application and, if so, notify the Secretary of State—

(*a*) that he consents to the taking of his fingerprints; and (*b*) of the police station ("the specified police station") that he proposes to attend at for the purposes of having his fingerprints taken.

(3) The Secretary of State may require the police officer in charge of the specified police station, or any other police station he reasonably determines, to take the applicant's fingerprints at the specified station at such reasonable time as the officer may direct and notify to the applicant.

(4) Fingerprints taken in connection with an application under Part V of the Act must be destroyed as soon as is practicable after the identity of the applicant is established to the satisfaction of the Secretary of State.

(5) If fingerprints are destroyed—

(*a*) any copies of the fingerprints shall also be destroyed; and
(*b*) any chief officer of police controlling access to computer data relating to the fingerprints shall make access to the data impossible, as soon as it is practicable to do so.

(6) Any applicant who asks to be allowed to witness the destruction of his fingerprints or copies of them shall have a right to witness it.

(7) If—

(*a*) paragraph (5)(*b*) above falls to be complied with; and
(*b*) the applicant to whose fingerprints the data relates asks for a certificate that it has been complied with,

such a certificate shall be issued to him, not later than the end of the period of three months beginning with the day on which he asks for it, by the responsible chief officer of police or a person authorised by him or on his behalf for the purposes of this regulation.

(8) In the case of an applicant under the age of 18 years the consent of the applicant's parent or guardian to the taking of the applicant's fingerprints is also required.

(9) In this regulation—

"speculative search" has the same meaning as in Part V of the Police and Criminal Evidence Act 1984; and

"responsible chief officer of police" means the chief officer of police in whose area the computer data were put on to the computer.

8–23900ZE 12. Fees payable to police authorities for information provided to the Secretary of State. The Secretary of State shall pay to the appropriate police authority the fee shown in Schedule 3 to these Regulations in respect of each request he makes to the chief officer of a police force for the provision of information under section 115, 116 or 120A(4)of the Act.

SCHEDULE 1
ENABLING POWERS

8–23900ZF These Regulations are made under the following provisions of the Police Act 1997—

(*a*) sections 113(1)(*b*); 114(1)(*b*); 115(1)(*b*) and (10); 116(1)(*b*); 118(3) and 125(5); and
(*b*) having regard to the meaning of "prescribed" in sections 113(1)(*a*), (3)(*a*), (3A)(*b*) and (5); 114(1)(*a*); 115(1)(*a*), (6)(*a*)(i) and (6A)(*b*); 116(1)(*a*); 118(2)(*a*) and 119(3).

SCHEDULE 2

SCHEDULE 3
FEES PAYABLE TO POLICE AUTHORITIES

8–23900ZG

Police Force	*Fee per request*
Avon & Somerset	**£5.00**
Bedfordshire	£4.38
Cambridgeshire	£4.07
Cheshire	£5.70
City of London	£3.99
Cleveland	£5.41
Cumbria	£3.64
Derbyshire	£4.39
Devon & Cornwall	£3.38
Dorset	£3.22
Durham	£3.23
Dyfed-Powys	£2.85
Essex	£2.54
Gloucestershire	£1.27
Greater Manchester	£3.36
Gwent	£6.51
Hampshire	£1.06
Hertfordshire	£4.03
Humberside	£4.53
Kent	£5.86
Lancashire	£3.41
Leicestershire	£3.48

Police Force	Fee per request
Lincolnshire	£1.90
Merseyside	£2.69
Metropolitan	£9.75
Norfolk	£4.07
North Wales	£5.90
North Yorkshire	£2.99
Northamptonshire	£5.74
Northumbria	£1.93
Nottinghamshire	£2.73
South Wales	£2.49
South Yorkshire	£2.37
Staffordshire	£2.91
Suffolk	£2.62
Surrey	£2.77
Sussex	£1.65
Thames Valley	£2.15
Warwickshire	£2.63
West Mercia	£2.60
West Midlands	£1.51
West Yorkshire	£2.54
Wiltshire	£2.95
Police Service of Northern Ireland	£6.94
Central Scotland	£4.83
Dumfries & Galloway	£4.83
Fife	£4.83
Grampian	£4.83
Lothian & Borders	£4.83
Northern	£4.83
Strathclyde	£4.83
Tayside	£4.83

Police Act 1997 (Enhanced Criminal Record Certificates) (Protection of Vulnerable Adults) Regulations 2002

(SI 2002/446)

8–23900ZH 1. Citation, commencement and extent. (1) These Regulations may be cited as the Police Act 1997 (Enhanced Criminal Record Certificates) (Protection of Vulnerable Adults) Regulations 2002 and shall come into force on 1st March 2002.

(2) These Regulations extend to England and Wales.

8–23900ZI 2. Definition of vulnerable adult. (1) In these Regulations "vulnerable adult" means a person aged 18 or over who is receiving services of a type listed in paragraph (2) below and in consequence of a condition of a type listed in paragraph (3) below has a disability of a type listed in paragraph (4) below.

(2) The services are—

(*a*) accommodation and nursing or personal care in a care home;

(*b*) personal care or nursing or support to live independently in his own home;

(*c*) any services provided by an independent hospital, independent clinic, independent medical agency or National Health Service body;

(*d*) social care services; or

(*e*) any services provided in an establishment catering for a person with learning difficulties.

(3) The conditions are—

(*a*) a learning or physical disability;

(*b*) a physical or mental illness, chronic or otherwise, including an addiction to alcohol or drugs; or

(*c*) a reduction in physical or mental capacity.

(4) The disabilities are—

(*a*) a dependency upon others in the performance of, or a requirement for assistance in the performance of, basic physical functions;

(*b*) severe impairment in the ability to communicate with others; or

(*c*) impairment in a person's ability to protect himself from assault, abuse or neglect.

(5) In this regulation "care home", "independent clinic", "independent hospital", "independent medical agency" and "National Health Service body" have the same meanings as in the Care Standards Act 2000.

8–23900ZJ 3. Positions specified for the purposes of section 115(4) of the Police Act 1997. A position is specified for the purposes of section 115(4) of the Police Act 1997 if it is of a kind which enables a person to have regular contact in the course of his duties with a vulnerable adult.

Police (Conduct) Regulations 2004[1]

(SI 2004/645)

8–23900ZK These regulations deal with the conduct of members of police forces, including senior officers, the maintenance of discipline, and procedures where conduct fails to meet the appropriate standard which is defined in Sch 1 to the regulations. Only the Code of Conduct set out in Sch 1 is printed here. The Regulations relate to matters to be dealt with internally by the police, and not by the courts.

---

1. Made by the Secretary of State, in exercise of the powers conferred on him by sections 50 and 51 of the Police Act 1996 and section 81 of the Police Act 1997.

8–23900ZL

Regulation 3

SCHEDULE 1
CODE OF CONDUCT

Honesty and integrity

1. It is of paramount importance that the public has faith in the honesty and integrity of police officers. Officers should therefore be open and truthful in their dealings; avoid being improperly beholden to any person or institution; and discharge their duties with integrity.

Fairness and impartiality

2. Police officers have a particular responsibility to act with fairness and impartiality in all their dealings with the public and their colleagues.

Politeness and tolerance

3. Officers should treat members of the public and colleagues with courtesy and respect, avoiding abusive or deriding attitudes or behaviour. In particular, officers must avoid: favouritism of an individual or group; all forms of harassment, victimisation or unreasonable discrimination; and overbearing conduct to a colleague, particularly to one junior in rank or service.

Use of force and abuse of authority

4. Officers must never knowingly use more force than is reasonable, nor should they abuse their authority.

Performance of duties

5. Officers should be conscientious and diligent in the performance of their duties. Officers should attend work promptly when rostered for duty. If absent through sickness or injury, they should avoid activities likely to retard their return to duty.

Lawful orders

6. The police service is a disciplined body. Unless there is good and sufficient cause to do otherwise, officers must obey all lawful orders and abide by the provisions of legislation applicable to the police. Officers should support their colleagues in the execution of their lawful duties, and oppose any improper behaviour, reporting it where appropriate.

Confidentiality

7. Information which comes into the possession of the police should be treated as confidential. It should not be used for personal benefit and nor should it be divulged to other parties except in the proper course of police duty. Similarly, officers should respect, as confidential, information about force policy and operations unless authorised to disclose it in the course of their duties.

Criminal offences

8. Officers must report any proceedings for a criminal offence taken against them. Conviction of a criminal offence or the administration of a caution may of itself result in further action being taken.

Property

9. Officers must exercise reasonable care to prevent loss or damage to property (excluding their own personal property but including police property).

Sobriety

10. Whilst on duty officers must be sober. Officers should not consume alcohol when on duty unless specifically authorised to do so or it becomes necessary for the proper discharge of police duty.

Appearance

11. Unless on duties which dictate otherwise, officers should always be well turned out, clean and tidy whilst on duty in uniform or in plain clothes.

General conduct

12. Whether on or off duty, police officers should not behave in a way which is likely to bring discredit upon the police service.

Notes

(*a*) The primary duties of those who hold the office of constable are the protection of life and property, the preservation of the Queen's peace, and the prevention and detection of criminal offences. To fulfil these duties they are granted extraordinary powers; the public and the police service therefore have the right to expect the highest standards of conduct from them.

(*b*) This Code sets out the principles which guide police officers' conduct. It does not seek to restrict officers' discretion: rather it aims to define the parameters of conduct within which that discretion should be exercised. However, it is important to note that any breach of the principles in this Code may result in action being taken by the organisation, which, in serious cases, could involve dismissal.

(*c*) Police behaviour, whether on or off duty, affects public confidence in the police service. Any conduct which brings or is likely to bring discredit to the police service may be the subject of sanction. Accordingly, any allegation of conduct which could, if proved, bring or be likely to bring discredit to the police service should be investigated in order to establish whether or not a breach of the Code has occurred and whether formal disciplinary action is appropriate. No investigation is required where the conduct, if proved, would not bring or would not be likely to bring, discredit to the police service.

Police Authorities (Lay Justices Selection Panel) Regulations 2005[1]

(SI 2005/584)

8–23900ZM 1. Citation and commencement. These Regulations may be cited as the Police Authorities (Lay Justices Selection Panel) Regulations 2005 and shall come into force on 1st April 2005.

1. Made by the Secretary of State, in exercise of the powers conferred upon him by para 5 of Sch 3A to the Police Act 1996.

8–23900ZN 2. Interpretation. In these Regulations—

"the 1996 Act" means the Police Act 1996;

"panel" means a selection panel established under Schedule 3A to the 1996 Act;

"lay justice member" means a member of a police authority appointed (or to be appointed) under paragraph 8 of Schedule 2 to the 1996 Act or paragraph 5 of Schedule 2A to that Act.

8–23900ZO 3. Notifications by clerk. (1) Not less than four months before the term of office of a lay justice member is due to expire, the clerk to the police authority shall notify the members of the panel of this fact.

(2) Where-

(a) a person ceases to be a lay justice member otherwise than on the expiry of his term of office, or

(b) the term of office of a lay justice member is due to expire less than four months after these Regulations come into force,

the clerk to the police authority shall notify the members of the panel of this fact.

8–23900ZP 4. Requirement to issue notice. (1) Subject to paragraph (3), where a panel are required to prepare a short-list of candidates to be appointed as lay justice members of a police authority, they shall issue a notice stating the matters referred to in paragraph (2) and shall cause that notice to be disseminated to all lay justices who are assigned to a local justice area wholly or partly within the authority's area.

(2) The matters to be included in a notice referred to in paragraph (1) are—

(a) the name of the police authority and police area;

(b) that a vacancy exists, or will exist, amongst those members of that authority to which lay justices are eligible for appointment;

(c) that the duties of such a member may include—

(i) attendance at meetings of the police authority and its committees;

(ii) keeping abreast of developments in both local and national policing;

(iii) representing the police authority in discussions with interested parties;

(iv) attendance at local police consultative groups, and

(v) liaising with representatives of the local community on policing issues;

(d) that persons are only eligible for appointment if—

(i) in accordance with paragraph 7 of Schedule 2 to the 1996 Act they are assigned to a local justice area wholly or partly within the authority's area; and

(ii) they are not otherwise disqualified;

(e) that, if a person wishes to have his name put forward, he must apply to the panel for an application form, and

(f) the date, not being less than one month after the date when the notice is issued, by which the application form must be completed and returned to the panel if it is to be considered by them in connection with a particular vacancy.

(3) This regulation shall not apply where—

(a) either of the conditions specified in paragraph (4) is satisfied, and

(b) the panel have decided to exercise the discretion conferred on them by regulation 8(1), and

(c) on completion of the procedure required by regulation 8(2), the panel have the names of a sufficient number of persons willing to be included on a short-list for appointment as lay justice members.

(4) The conditions referred to in paragraph (3)(a) are that, at the date when the vacancy occurred or, as the case may be, is expected to occur—

(a) less than two years have passed since the coming into force of this regulation;

(b) less than two years have passed since the date of the issue of the last notice previously issued in accordance with paragraph (1).

(5) In paragraph (3) "sufficient number" means a number four times greater than the number of appointments that are to be made under paragraph 8 of Schedule 2 or paragraph 5 of Schedule 2A (as the case may be) to the 1996 Act.

8–23900ZQ 5. Applications to be considered for appointment of lay justices to police authority. (1) A person who wishes to be considered for appointment as a lay justice member shall submit an application to the panel setting out—

(a) his name and address;
(b) his age;
(c) his current occupation, if any, and any positions held by him up to ten years before the date of the application;
(d) his relevant skills and experience;
(e) his academic, professional and vocational qualifications, if any; and
(f) the reasons why he wishes to be so considered.

(2) The panel shall supply free of charge to any person not disqualified for membership a form for the purposes of an application under paragraph (1).

(3) Together with a form supplied under paragraph (2) there shall be supplied information about the office of lay justice member including a statement setting out paragraphs 11, 13 and 14 of Schedule 2 or paragraphs 7, 8 and 9 of Schedule 2A to the 1996 Act (disqualification) as they apply to such members.

(4) An application made before the coming into force of this regulation which satisfies the requirements of paragraph (1) shall have effect as if made under that paragraph.

8–23900ZR 6. Consideration of applications by panel. (1) A panel shall consider any application for appointment as a lay justice member which has been duly made under regulation 5.

(2) In considering any such application the panel—

(a) shall have regard to guidance produced jointly by the Home Office and the Association of Police Authorities;
(b) may interview any candidate who has submitted an application.

(3) Where an application has been received at a time when no appointment under paragraph 8 of Schedule 2 or paragraph 5 of Schedule 2A (as the case may be) to the 1996 Act is required to be made, the panel may delay considering it until such time as the panel are required to prepare a short-list of candidates for appointment.

(4) Subject to paragraph (6), a panel may consider applications under paragraph (1), may interview candidates under paragraph (2)(b) and may prepare a short-list under paragraph 4 of Schedule 3A to the 1996 Act only if all of their members are present.

(5) A decision of a panel to include a candidate in a short-list under paragraph 4 of Schedule 3A to the 1996 Act may be taken by a majority of their members.

(6) A panel may act if two of their three members are present if—

(a) not less than one week's notice was given of the meeting in question; or
(b) the member of the panel who is not present has previously consented in writing to the other members acting in his absence; or
(c) the member of the panel who is not present has died; or
(d) the meeting is held for the purpose of making the appointment referred to in paragraph 1(2)(c) of Schedule 3A to the 1996 Act.

8–23900ZS 7. Record maintained by panel. (1) The members of a panel shall maintain a record of the persons who have applied to be considered for appointment as lay justice members.

(2) The record maintained under this regulation shall state—

(a) the name and address of every applicant;
(b) such details about the application as the members of the panel consider appropriate;
(c) in the case of a person included on a short-list under paragraph 4 of Schedule 3A to the 1996 Act, that fact; and
(d) in the case of a person who is disqualified as a lay justice, the grounds of the disqualification.

(3) An entry in the record maintained under this regulation may be deleted on the expiry of four years from the date when it was made.

8–23900ZT 8. Inclusion on short-list by panel from names listed in record. (1) Where—

(a) a panel are required to prepare a short-list of candidates to be appointed as lay justice members, and
(b) either of the conditions in regulation 4(4) is satisfied,

the panel may consider the names of the persons previously listed in the record maintained under regulation 7, except those disqualified, with a view to including on the short-list persons included in that record without complying with regulation 4(1).

(2) Where a panel propose to include on a short-list any such person they shall give that person a notice—

(a) stating their proposal, and
(b) requiring him to reply not later than three weeks after the date of that notice stating whether or not he continues to be willing to be included on a short-list for appointment as a lay justice member.

POSTAL SERVICES

8–23901 This title contains references to the following statute—

8–24234 POSTAL SERVICES ACT 2000

Postal Services Act 2000[1]

(2000 c 26)

PART II[2]

LICENCES FOR POSTAL SERVICES

Restriction on provision of postal services

8–24234 6. Restriction on provision of postal services. (1) Subject to section 7, no person shall convey a letter from one place to another unless—

(*a*) he holds a licence authorising him to do so, or
(*b*) he is acting as an employee or agent of a person who is authorised by a licence to do so.

(2) A person who contravenes subsection (1) commits an offence and shall be liable[3]—

(*a*) on summary conviction, to a fine not exceeding the statutory maximum,
(*b*) on conviction on indictment, to a fine.

(3) No proceedings shall be instituted in England and Wales or Northern Ireland in respect of an offence under subsection (2) except by or on behalf of the Commission or the Secretary of State.

(4) Without prejudice to subsection (2), compliance with subsection (1) shall be enforceable by civil proceedings by or on behalf of the Commission or the Secretary of State for an injunction or interdict or for any other appropriate relief or remedy.

(5) Without prejudice to subsections (2) and (4)—

(*a*) the obligation to comply with subsection (1) shall be a duty owed to any person who may be affected by a contravention of subsection (1), and
(*b*) where a duty is owed by virtue of paragraph (a) to any person, any breach of that duty which causes that person to sustain loss or damage shall be actionable at the suit or instance of that person.

(6) Any reference in this section and section 7(1) or (1A) to conveying a letter from one place to another, or the conveyance of a letter, includes a reference to performing, or the performance of, any of the incidental services of receiving, collecting and delivering a letter.

(7) For the purposes of this Part references to a licence are to a licence under this Part and references to a licence holder shall be construed accordingly.

[Postal Services Act 2000, s 6, as amended by SI 2002/3050.]

---

1. Parts I to VI, sections 101 to 114, sections 116 to 119 (including Schedule 7) and section 127(4) and (6) (including Schedules 8 and 9) are to come into force on such day as the Secretary of State may by order appoint. At the date of going to press the following orders had been made: Commencement (No 1 and Transitional Provisions) Order 2000, SI 2000/2957; Commencement (No 2) Order 2001, SI 2001/3111; Commencement (No 3 and Transitional and Savings Provisions) Order 2001, SI 2001/878; Commencement (No 4 and Transitional and Savings Provisions) Order 2001, SI 2001/1148.[2]Part II contains ss 6 - 41. This Act which implements the Postal Services Directive establishes the Postal Services Commission which has the duty to ensure provision of a universal postal service (defined in s 4) and to promote effective competition between postal operators (s 5) and may grant licences to postal operators authorising the conveyance of letters (s 6). The Consumer Council for Postal Services is also established. The Post Office is dissolved (s 75).

3. For mode of trial of this offence which is triable either way, see the Magistrates' Courts Act 1980, ss 17A–21 in PART I: MAGISTRATES' COURTS, PROCEDURE, ANTE.

8–24235 7. Exceptions from section 6. (1) Section 6(1) is not contravened by the conveyance of a letter—

(*a*) which is conveyed in consideration of a payment of not less than £1 made by or on behalf of the person for whom it is conveyed, or
(*b*) which weighs not less than 350 grams.

(1A) Section 6(1) is not contravened by the conveyance of a letter in circumstances where the service of conveying the letter is outside the scope of the universal postal service in the United Kingdom.

(2) Section 6(1) is not contravened by—

(*a*) the conveyance and delivery of a letter personally by the sender,
(*b*) the conveyance and delivery of a letter by a personal friend of the sender,
(*c*) the conveyance and delivery of a single letter by a messenger sent for the purpose by either correspondent,

(*d*) the conveyance of an overseas letter out of the United Kingdom, and the collection of letters for that purpose,

(*e*) the conveyance and delivery of any documents in respect of which a method of service other than by post is required or authorised by law,

(*f*) the conveyance of letters from merchants who are the owners of a merchant ship or commercial aircraft, or of goods carried in such a ship or aircraft, by means of that ship or aircraft, and the delivery of the letters to the addressees by any person employed for the purpose by those merchants, provided that no payment or reward, profit or advantage of any kind is given or received for the conveyance or delivery of those letters,

(*g*) the conveyance and delivery of letters by any person which are letters concerning, and for delivery with, goods carried by that person, provided that no payment or reward, profit or advantage of any kind is given or received for the conveyance or delivery of those letters,

(*h*) the conveyance and delivery to a licence holder of pre-paid letters for conveyance and delivery by that person to the addressees, and the collection of such letters for that purpose,

(*i*) the conveyance and delivery of letters by a person who has a business interest in those letters, and the collection of letters for that purpose,

(*ia*) the conveyance and delivery of letters, and the collection of letters for that purpose, by a person who is not a licence holder, who provides those services under a contract for services where the other party to the contract is the sender and who does not provide those services to any person other than the sender,

(*j*) the conveyance and delivery of banking instruments from one bank to another or from a bank to a government department, and the collection of such instruments for that purpose,

(*k*) the collection, conveyance and delivery of coupons or other entry forms issued by authorised promoters,

(*l*) the collection, conveyance and delivery of Christmas cards by a charity, provided that the activity concerned takes place during the period starting with 25th November in any year and ending with 1st January in the following year,

(*m*) the conveyance and delivery of letters from one government department to another or within the same government department, and the collection of letters for that purpose,

(*n*) the conveyance of letters of members of a document exchange from a departure facility for that exchange to an arrival facility for another document exchange by persons who are not members of either exchange, and the collection and delivery by such persons for that purpose of letters delivered to the departure facility concerned,

(*o*) the conveyance and delivery of brokers' research, during the relevant period and by any person who has printed it, from the business premises where it is printed to the premises of any person who is to convey it onwards,

(*p*) the conveyance and delivery by any person of brokers' research within the period of 24 hours starting with its delivery to his premises or its collection by him during the relevant period from a collection point, and any such collection.

(3) Nothing in paragraphs (*a*) to (*c*) and (*e*) to (*g*) of subsection (2) shall authorise any person to make a collection of letters for the purpose of their being conveyed in any manner authorised by those paragraphs.

(4) For the purposes of paragraph (*i*) of subsection (2) a person has a business interest in a letter if, and only if—

(*a*) he is an employee of one of the correspondents or of a member of the same group as one of the correspondents and the letter relates to the business affairs of that correspondent, or

(*b*) he and one of the correspondents are employees of the same person or of different members of the same group and the letter relates to the business affairs of that person or (as the case may be) the employer of that correspondent.

(5) In this section—

"arrival facility", in relation to a document exchange, means any box, receptacle or other facility associated with that exchange which is provided for the receipt of letters from members of another document exchange which are conveyed to the facility from a departure facility for that other exchange for collection by members of the first exchange,

"authorised promoter" means—

(*a*) a registered pool promoter, or

(*b*) a person who is or has at any time been an associate (within the meaning of section 184 of the Consumer Credit Act 1974) of such a promoter,*

"bank" means—

(*a*) the Bank of England,

(*b*) a deposit taker,

(*c*) an EEA firm of the kind mentioned in paragraph 5(*b*) of Schedule 3 to the Financial Services and Markets Act 2000 who has permission under paragraph 15 of that Schedule (as a result of qualifying for authorisation under paragraph 12(1) of that Schedule) to accept deposits, or (*d*) the central bank of an EEA State other than the United Kingdom,

"banking instrument" means—

(*a*) any cheque or other instrument to which section 4 of the Cheques Act 1957 applies,
(*b*) any document issued by a public officer which is intended to enable a person to obtain payment from a government department of the sum mentioned in the document,
(*c*) any bill of exchange not falling within paragraph (a) or (b) or any promissory note,
(*d*) any postal order or money order,
(*e*) any credit transfer, credit advice or debit advice, or
(*f*) any list of items, or any copy of an item, falling within paragraphs (*a*) to (*e*),

"brokers' research" means any printed documentation prepared by persons licensed or authorised to trade on any regulated stock, share, futures, foreign exchange or commodities market which contains research, analysis and information relating to items traded on that market and which has not been prepared for or on the instructions of any particular person to whom it is addressed or delivered,

"charity" means a body, or the trustees of a trust, established for charitable purposes only,

"collection point" means any business premises where brokers' research is printed or an international airport,

"departure facility", in relation to a document exchange, means any box, receptacle or other facility associated with that exchange which is provided for the collection of letters of members of that exchange which are delivered to the facility by those members for conveyance to an arrival facility for another document exchange for collection by members of that other exchange,

"deposit taker" means a person who has permission under Part 4 of the Financial Services and Markets Act 2000 to accept deposits, but does not include—

(*a*) a credit union, within the meaning of the Credit Unions Act 1979 or the Credit Unions (Northern Ireland) Order 1985,
(*b*) a specially authorised society within the meaning of section 7(1)(*f*) of the Friendly Societies Act 1974,
(*c*) a person who has permission to accept deposits only for the purpose of carrying on another regulated activity in accordance with that permission, "document exchange" means a system involving at least three members for the exchange of letters between members of the system,

"EEA State" means a State which is a contracting party to the Agreement on the European Economic Area signed at Oporto on 2nd May 1992 as adjusted by the Protocol signed at Brussels on 17th March 1993,

"government department" includes any Minister of the Crown, any part of the Scottish Administration, the National Assembly for Wales, the Northern Ireland Assembly, any Northern Ireland Minister or Northern Ireland junior Minister and any Northern Ireland department,

"group" means a body corporate and all of its wholly owned subsidiaries taken together,

"overseas letter" means a letter which is directed to a specific person or address outside the United Kingdom,

"pre-paid letter" includes any letter which, in pursuance of arrangements made with a licence holder, does not require to be pre-paid,

"registered pool promoter" has the meaning given by section 4(2) of the Betting, Gaming and Lotteries Act 1963, and

"relevant period" means—

(*a*) in the case of a collection from an international airport, the period starting with 6.00 pm on any day other than Friday or Saturday and ending with 10.00 am on the next day and the period starting with 6.00 pm on any Friday or Saturday and ending with noon on the next day, and
(*b*) in any other case, the period starting with 6.00 pm on any day and ending with 6.00 am on the next day.

(6) In subsection (5), paragraph (*c*) of the definition of "bank" and the definition of "deposit taker" must be read with—

(*a*) section 22 of the Financial Services and Markets Act 2000;
(*b*) any relevant order under that section; and
(*c*) Schedule 2 to that Act.

[Postal Services Act 2000, s 7, as amended by SI 2001/3649, SI 2002/200 and 3050.]

***Definition substituted by the Gambling Act 2005, Sch 16 from a date to be appointed.**

8–24236 **8.** *Power of Secretary of State to modify section 7 by order*

8–24237 **9.** *General power of Secretary of State to suspend the operation of section 6 by order*

8–24238 **10.** *Emergency supervision by the Secretary of State of the operation of section 6*

Licences

8–24239 **11. Licences: general.** (1) The Commission may, on an application by a person under section 12, grant a licence to that person authorising him to do anything which—

(*a*) would otherwise contravene section 6(1), and
(*b*) is specified in the licence or determined by or under it.

(2) A licence shall not be valid unless it is in writing.

(3) A licence shall not be transferred.

(4) A licence shall, unless it previously ceases to have effect in accordance with its provisions, continue in force for the period specified in it or determined by or under it.

[Postal Services Act 2000, s 11.]

PART III[1]

OTHER FUNCTIONS OF THE COMMISSION AND THE COUNCIL

The Commission

8–24240 **47. Power of the Commission to require information.** (1) The Commission may, for any relevant purpose, serve notice on any person requiring him—

(*a*) to produce any documents which are specified or described in the notice and are in that person's custody or under his control, and
(*b*) to produce them at a time and place so specified and to a person so specified.

(2) The Commission may, for any relevant purpose, serve notice on any person who carries on any business requiring him—

(*a*) to supply to the Commission such information as may be specified or described in the notice, and
(*b*) to supply it at a time and place and in a form and manner so specified and to a person so specified.

(3) The person to whom any document is produced in accordance with a notice under this section may, for any relevant purpose, copy the document so produced.

(4) No person shall be required under this section—

(*a*) to produce any documents which he could not be compelled to produce in civil proceedings before the court, or
(*b*) to supply any information which he could not be compelled to supply in evidence in such proceedings.

(5) Any reference in this section to the production of a document includes a reference to the production of a legible and intelligible copy of information recorded otherwise than in legible form.

(6) In this section—

"the court"—

(*a*) in relation to England and Wales or Northern Ireland, means the High Court, and
(*b*) in relation to Scotland, means the Court of Session,

"relevant purpose" means any purpose connected with—

(*a*) the investigation of an offence under section 6 or any proceedings for such an offence, or
(*b*) the exercise of the Commission's functions under section 22, 23, 24, 30, 42 or 44(4) or (5).

[Postal Services Act 2000, s 47.]

1. Part III contains ss 42–61.

8–24241 **48. Information powers: enforcement.** (1) A person commits an offence if, without reasonable excuse, he fails to do anything required of him by a notice under section 47.

(2) A person commits an offence if he intentionally obstructs or delays any person in the exercise of his powers under section 47(3).

(3) A person who commits an offence under subsection (1) or (2) shall be liable on summary conviction to a fine not exceeding level 5 on the standard scale.

(4) A person commits an offence if he—

(*a*) intentionally alters, suppresses or destroys any document which he has been required to produce by a notice under section 47, or
(*b*) in supplying any information required of him by a notice under section 47, makes any statement which he knows to be false in a material particular or recklessly makes any statement which is false in a material particular.

(5) A person who commits an offence under subsection (4) shall be liable[1]—

(*a*) on summary conviction, to a fine not exceeding the statutory maximum,
(*b*) on conviction on indictment, to a fine.

(6) If a person makes default in complying with a notice under section 47, the court may, on the application of the Commission, make such order as the court considers appropriate for requiring the default to be made good.

(7) Any such order may, in particular, provide that all the costs or expenses of and incidental to the application shall be borne—

(*a*) by the person in default, or
(*b*) if officers of a company or other association are responsible for its default, by those officers.

(8) The reference in this section to the production of a document includes a reference to the production of a legible and intelligible copy of information recorded otherwise than in legible form; and the reference to suppressing a document includes a reference to destroying the means of reproducing information recorded otherwise than in legible form.

(9) In this section "the court"—

(*a*) in relation to England and Wales or Northern Ireland, means the High Court, and
(*b*) in relation to Scotland, means the Court of Session.

[Postal Services Act 2000, s 48.]

1. For mode of trial of this offence which is triable either way, see the Magistrates' Courts Act 1980, ss 17A–21 in PART I: MAGISTRATES' COURTS, PROCEDURE, ante.

8–24242 49. Powers of entry and seizure. (1) Subsection (2) applies where, on an application made by a constable or the Commission, a justice of the peace or, in Scotland, a sheriff is satisfied that there are reasonable grounds for suspecting—

(*a*) that a person has committed an offence under section 6 ("the suspect"), and
(*b*) that articles or documents of a particular description which are required for the purposes of an investigation of the offence are on particular premises.

(2) The justice or sheriff may issue a warrant authorising a person appointed by him ("the appointed person") to enter the premises concerned, search for the articles or documents and, subject to subsection (3), seize and remove any that he may find.

(3) A warrant issued under subsection (2) shall not authorise the seizure and removal of any postal packet, mail-bag or document to which section 104(2) applies; but any such warrant may authorise the appointed person to take copies of the cover of any such packet, bag or document that he finds.

(4) The appointed person, in the exercise of his powers under a warrant issued under this section, may if necessary use reasonable force.

(5) The appointed person, in seeking to enter any premises in the exercise of his powers under the warrant, shall, if required by or on behalf of the owner or occupier or person in charge of the premises, produce evidence of his identity, and of the warrant, before entering.

(6) Any articles or documents which have been seized and removed under a warrant issued under this section may be retained until the conclusion of proceedings against the suspect.

(7) For the purposes of this section, proceedings in relation to a suspect are concluded if—

(*a*) he is found guilty and sentenced or otherwise dealt with for the offence,
(*b*) he is acquitted,
(*c*) proceedings for the offence are discontinued, or
(*d*) it is decided not to prosecute him.

(8) In this section "premises" includes any vehicle, ship or aircraft.

[Postal Services Act 2000, s 49.]

PART V[1]

OFFENCES IN RELATION TO POSTAL SERVICES

Offences of interfering with the mail

8–24243 83. Interfering with the mail: postal operators. (1) A person who is engaged in the business of a postal operator commits an offence if, contrary to his duty and without reasonable excuse, he—

(*a*) intentionally delays or opens a postal packet in the course of its transmission by post, or
(*b*) intentionally opens a mail-bag.

(2) Subsection (1) does not apply to the delaying or opening of a postal packet or the opening of a mail-bag under the authority of—

(*a*) this Act or any other enactment (including, in particular, in pursuance of a warrant issued under any other enactment), or
(*b*) any directly applicable Community provision.

(3) Subsection (1) does not apply to the delaying or opening of a postal packet in accordance with any terms and conditions applicable to its transmission by post.

(4) Subsection (1) does not apply to the delaying of a postal packet as a result of industrial action in contemplation or furtherance of a trade dispute.

(5) In subsection (4) "trade dispute" has the meaning given by section 244 of the Trade Union and Labour Relations (Consolidation) Act 1992 or Article 127 of the Trade Union and Labour Relations (Northern Ireland) Order 1995; and the reference to industrial action shall be construed in accordance with that Act or (as the case may be) that Order.

(6) A person who commits an offence under subsection (1) shall be liable[2]—

(*a*) on summary conviction, to a fine not exceeding the statutory maximum or to imprisonment for a term not exceeding six months or to both,

(*b*) on conviction on indictment, to a fine or to imprisonment for a term not exceeding two years or to both.

[Postal Services Act 2000, s 83.]

---

1. Part V contains ss 83–88.
2. For mode of trial of this offence which is triable either way, see the Magistrates' Courts Act 1980, ss 17A–21 in PART I: MAGISTRATES' COURTS, PROCEDURE, ante.

8–24244 **84. Interfering with the mail: general.** (1) A person commits an offence if, without reasonable excuse, he—

(*a*) intentionally delays or opens a postal packet in the course of its transmission by post, or

(*b*) intentionally opens a mail-bag.

(2) Subsections (2) to (5) of section 83 apply to subsection (1) above as they apply to subsection (1) of that section.

(3) A person commits an offence if, intending to act to a person's detriment and without reasonable excuse, he opens a postal packet which he knows or reasonably suspects has been incorrectly delivered to him.

(4) Subsections (2) and (3) of section 83 (so far as they relate to the opening of postal packets) apply to subsection (3) above as they apply to subsection (1) of that section.

(5) A person who commits an offence under subsection (1) or (3) shall be liable on summary conviction to a fine not exceeding level 5 on the standard scale or to imprisonment for a term not exceeding six months or to both.

[Postal Services Act 2000, s 84.]

Prohibition on sending certain articles by post

8–24245 **85. Prohibition on sending certain articles by post.** (1) A person commits an offence if he sends by post a postal packet which encloses any creature, article or thing of any kind which is likely to injure other postal packets in course of their transmission by post or any person engaged in the business of a postal operator.

(2) Subsection (1) does not apply to postal packets which enclose anything permitted (whether generally or specifically) by the postal operator concerned.

(3) A person commits an offence if he sends by post a postal packet which encloses—

(*a*) any indecent or obscene print, painting, photograph, lithograph, engraving, cinematograph film or other record of a picture or pictures, book, card or written communication, or

(*b*) any other indecent or obscene article (whether or not of a similar kind to those mentioned in paragraph (*a*)).

(4) A person commits an offence if he sends by post a postal packet which has on the packet, or on the cover of the packet, any words, marks or designs which are of an indecent or obscene character.

(5) A person who commits an offence under this section shall be liable[1]—

(*a*) on summary conviction, to a fine not exceeding the statutory maximum,

(*b*) on conviction on indictment, to a fine or to imprisonment for a term not exceeding twelve months or to both.

[Postal Services Act 2000, s 85.]

---

1. For mode of trial of this offence which is triable either way, see the Magistrates' Courts Act 1980, ss 17A–21 in PART I: MAGISTRATES' COURTS, PROCEDURE, ante.

Additional protection for universal postal service

8–24246 **86. Prohibition on affixing advertisements on certain letter boxes etc.** (1) A person commits an offence if, without due authority, he affixes any advertisement, document, board or thing in or on any universal postal service post office, universal postal service letter box or other property belonging to, or used by, a universal service provider in connection with the provision of a universal postal service.

(2) A person commits an offence if, without due authority, he paints or in any way disfigures any such office, box or property.

(3) A person who commits an offence under subsection (1) or (2) shall be liable on summary conviction to a fine not exceeding level 3 on the standard scale.

(4) In this Act—

"universal postal service letter box" means any box or receptacle provided by a universal service provider for the purpose of receiving postal packets, or any class of postal packets, for onwards transmission in connection with the provision of a universal postal service, and

"universal postal service post office" includes any house, building, room, vehicle or place used for the provision of any postal services in connection with the provision of a universal postal service or a part of such a service.

[Postal Services Act 2000, s 86.]

8–24247 **87. Prohibition on misleading descriptions.** (1) A person commits an offence if, without the authority of the universal service provider concerned, he places or maintains in or on any house, wall, door, window, box, post, pillar or other place belonging to him or under his control, any of the following words, letters or marks—

(*a*) the words "letter box" accompanied with words, letters or marks which signify or imply, or may reasonably lead the public to believe, that it is a universal postal service letter box, or

(*b*) any words, letters or marks which signify or imply or may reasonably lead the public to believe that any house, building, room, vehicle or place is a universal postal service post office, or that any box or receptacle is a universal postal service letter box.

(2) A person commits an offence if, without the authority of the universal service provider concerned, he—

(*a*) places or maintains in or on any ship, vehicle, aircraft or premises belonging to him or under his control, or

(*b*) uses in any document in relation to himself or any other person or in relation to any ship, vehicle, aircraft or premises,

any words, letters or marks which signify or imply, or may reasonably lead the public to believe, any of the things mentioned in subsection (3).

(3) The things are—

(*a*) that he or that other person is authorised by the universal service provider concerned to collect, receive, sort, deliver or convey postal packets in connection with the provision of a universal postal service,

(*b*) that the ship, vehicle, aircraft or premises are used by the universal service provider concerned for the purpose of collecting, receiving, sorting, delivering or conveying postal packets in connection with the provision of a universal postal service.

(4) A person commits an offence if, without reasonable excuse, he fails to comply with a notice given to him by the universal service provider concerned requiring him—

(*a*) to remove or efface any words, letters or marks which fall within subsection (1) or (2), or

(*b*) to remove or close up any letter box belonging to him or under his control which has ceased to be a universal postal service letter box.

(5) A person who commits an offence under this section shall be liable on summary conviction to a fine not exceeding level 3 on the standard scale.

[Postal Services Act 2000, s 87.]

8–24248 **88. Obstruction of business of universal service providers.** (1) A person commits an offence if, without reasonable excuse, he—

(*a*) obstructs a person engaged in the business of a universal service provider in the execution of his duty in connection with the provision of a universal postal service, or

(*b*) obstructs, while in any universal postal service post office or related premises, the course of business of a universal service provider.

(2) A person who commits an offence under subsection (1) shall be liable on summary conviction to a fine not exceeding level 2 on the standard scale.

(3) A person commits an offence if, without reasonable excuse, he fails to leave a universal postal service post office or related premises when required to do so by a person who—

(*a*) is engaged in the business of a universal service provider, and

(*b*) reasonably suspects him of committing an offence under subsection (1).

(4) A person who commits an offence under subsection (3)—

(*a*) shall be liable on summary conviction to a fine not exceeding level 2 on the standard scale, and

(*b*) may be removed by any person engaged in the business of a universal service provider.

(5) Any constable shall on demand remove, or assist in removing, any such person.

(6) In this section "related premises" means any premises belonging to a universal postal service post office or used together with any such post office.
[Postal Services Act 2000, s 88.]

PART VI[1]
UNIVERSAL POSTAL SERVICE: SUPPLEMENTARY

Articles in transit

8–24249 **96. Immunity from prosecution.** (1) A universal service provider and a person who is engaged in the business of such a provider shall be entitled to the same immunity from prosecution for conduct in the provision of a universal postal service and falling within subsection (2) as the provider and that person would be entitled to if the provider were a government department.

(2) The following conduct falls within this subsection—

(*a*) possession of anything contained in a postal packet which is in the course of transmission by post where possession of it is prohibited by virtue of any enactment, and

(*b*) failure to comply, in relation to anything contained in a postal packet which is in the course of transmission by post, with any condition or restriction imposed by virtue of any enactment in relation to its possession, conveyance or delivery.

[Postal Services Act 2000, s 96.]

1. Part VI contains ss 89–100 and Schs 5 and 6.

PART VII[1]
MISCELLANEOUS AND SUPPLEMENTARY

Supplementary powers of the Secretary of State

8–24250 **101. Directions in interests of national security etc.** (1) The Secretary of State may give such directions as he considers appropriate to the Commission in relation to the exercise of its functions if he considers it necessary or expedient to do so—

(*a*) in the interests of national security or in the interests of encouraging or maintaining the United Kingdom's relations with another country or territory,

(*b*) in order—

(i) to discharge, or facilitate the discharge of, an international obligation,

(ii) to attain, or facilitate the attainment of, any other object which the Secretary of State considers it necessary or expedient to attain in view of Her Majesty's Government in the United Kingdom being a member of an international organisation or a party to an international agreement, or

(iii) to enable Her Majesty's Government in the United Kingdom to become a member of such an organisation or a party to such an agreement.

(2) Directions under subsection (1) may, in particular, require the Commission—

(*a*) to do or not to do a particular thing, or

(*b*) to secure that a particular thing is done or not done.

(3) The Secretary of State may, if he considers it necessary or expedient to do so for any of the purposes mentioned in subsection (1)(*a*) or (*b*), give such directions as he considers appropriate to licence holders under Part II, or to any particular licence holder under that Part, in connection with anything authorised or required by the licence or licences concerned.

(4) Directions under subsection (3) may, in particular, require a licence holder—

(*a*) to do or not to do a particular thing, or

(*b*) to secure that a particular thing is done or not done.

(5) Before giving a direction under subsection (1), the Secretary of State shall consult the Commission.

(6) Before giving a direction under subsection (3) to a particular licence holder (as opposed to licence holders generally or any description of licence holders), the Secretary of State shall consult the licence holder concerned.

(7) The Secretary of State—

(*a*) shall send to the Commission a copy of any direction given under subsection (3), and

(*b*) shall lay before each House of Parliament a copy of any direction given under this section.

(8) Subsection (7)(*b*) does not apply if the Secretary of State considers that the disclosure of the direction would be against the interests of national security or the interests of the United Kingdom's relations with another country or territory or against the commercial interests of any person who has not consented to the disclosure.

(9) A person shall not disclose, and is not required by any enactment or otherwise to disclose, a direction given or other thing done or omitted to be done by virtue of this section if the Secretary of State notifies him that he considers that—

(*a*) disclosure would be against the interests of national security or the interests of the United Kingdom's relations with another country or territory, or
(*b*) disclosure would be against the commercial interests of any person (other than the person notified) who has not consented to the disclosure.

(10) A person commits an offence if—

(*a*) without reasonable excuse he contravenes a direction under this section, or
(*b*) he makes a disclosure in contravention of subsection (9).

(11) A person who commits an offence under this section shall be liable[2]—

(*a*) on summary conviction, to a fine not exceeding the statutory maximum,
(*b*) on conviction on indictment, to a fine or to imprisonment for a term not exceeding two years or to both.

[Postal Services Act 2000, s 101.]

---

1. Part VII contains ss 101–131 and Schs 7–9.
2. For mode of trial of this offence which is triable either way, see the Magistrates' Courts Act 1980, ss 17A–21 in PART I: MAGISTRATES' COURTS, PROCEDURE, ante.

Inviolability of mails etc

8–24251 **104. Inviolability of mails.** (1) Subsection (2) applies to—

(*a*) a postal packet,
(*b*) anything contained in a postal packet, and
(*c*) a mail-bag containing a postal packet,

which is not the property of the Crown but which is in the course of transmission by post.

(2) Anything to which this subsection applies shall have the same immunity from—

(*a*) examination, or seizure or detention, under a relevant power conferred by virtue of this Act or any other enactment,
(*b*) seizure under distress or in execution,
(*c*) in Scotland, any diligence, and
(*d*) retention by virtue of a lien,

as it would have if it were the property of the Crown.

(3) In subsection (2) "relevant power" means any power other than—

(*a*) a power conferred by section 47 so far as it is exercised for any purpose connected with the investigation of an offence under section 6 or any proceedings for such an offence,
(*b*) a power conferred under section 49,
(*c*) a power conferred by an enactment relating to customs or excise in its application, by virtue of section 105 or any regulations made under that section, to goods contained in postal packets, or
(*d*) a power conferred by section 106 or 107.

(4) The Secretary of State may by order modify subsection (3).

[Postal Services Act 2000, s 104.]

8–24252 **105. Application of customs and excise enactments to certain postal packets.** (1) Subject as follows, the enactments for the time being in force in relation to customs or excise shall apply in relation to goods contained in postal packets to which this section applies which are brought into or sent out of the United Kingdom by post from or to any place outside the United Kingdom as they apply in relation to goods otherwise imported, exported or removed into or out of the United Kingdom from or to any such place.

(2) The Treasury, on the recommendation of the Commissioners of Customs and Excise and the Secretary of State, may make regulations for—

(*a*) specifying the postal packets to which this section applies,
(*b*) making modifications or exceptions in the application of the enactments mentioned in subsection (1) to such packets,
(*c*) enabling persons engaged in the business of a postal operator to perform for the purposes of those enactments and otherwise all or any of the duties of the importer, exporter or person removing the goods,
(*d*) carrying into effect any arrangement with the government or postal administration of any country or territory outside the United Kingdom with respect to foreign postal packets,
(*e*) securing the observance of the enactments mentioned in subsection (1),
(*f*) without prejudice to any liability of any person under those enactments, punishing any contravention of the regulations.

(3) Duties (whether of customs or excise) charged on imported goods or other charges payable in respect of postal packets to which this section applies (whether payable to a postal operator or to a

foreign administration) may be recovered by the postal operator concerned and in England and Wales and Northern Ireland may be so recovered as a civil debt due to him.

(4) In any proceedings for the recovery of any charges payable as mentioned in subsection (3), a certificate of the postal operator concerned of the amount of the charges shall be evidence (and, in Scotland, sufficient evidence) of that fact.

(5) In this section "foreign postal packet" means any postal packet either posted in the United Kingdom and sent to a place outside the United Kingdom, or posted in a place outside the United Kingdom and sent to a place within the United Kingdom, or in transit through the United Kingdom to a place outside the United Kingdom.

[Postal Services Act 2000, s 105.]

8–24253 **106. Power to detain postal packets containing contraband.** (1) A postal operator may—

(*a*) detain any postal packet if he suspects that it may contain relevant goods,
(*b*) forward any packet so detained to the Commissioners of Customs and Excise.

(2) In this section "relevant goods" means—

(*a*) any goods chargeable with any duty charged on imported goods (whether a customs or an excise duty) which has not been paid or secured, or
(*b*) any goods in the course of importation, exportation or removal into or out of the United Kingdom contrary to any prohibition or restriction for the time being in force by virtue of any enactment.

(3) Subsection (1) is without prejudice to section 105.

(4) The Commissioners may open and examine any postal packet forwarded to them under this section—

(*a*) in the presence of the person to whom the packet is addressed, or
(*b*) where the address on the packet is outside the United Kingdom or where subsection (5) applies, in the absence of that person.

(5) This subsection applies where—

(*a*) the Commissioners have—
  (i) left at the address on the packet notice requiring the attendance of the person concerned, or
  (ii) forwarded such notice by post to that address, and
(*b*) the addressee fails to attend.

(6) If the Commissioners find any relevant goods on opening and examining a postal packet under this section, they may detain the packet and its contents for the purpose of taking proceedings in relation to them.

(7) If the Commissioners do not find any relevant goods on opening and examining a postal packet under this section, they shall—

(*a*) deliver the packet to the addressee upon his paying any postage and other sums chargeable on it, or
(*b*) if he is absent, forward the packet to him by post.

[Postal Services Act 2000, s 106.]

8–24254 **107. Conditions of transit of postal packets.** (1) If a postal operator knows or reasonably suspects that a postal packet is being sent by post in contravention of section 85, he may—

(*a*) refuse the transmission of the packet,
(*b*) detain the packet and open it,
(*c*) subject to any requirements as to additional postage or charges, return the packet to its sender or forward it to its destination,
(*d*) destroy or otherwise dispose of the packet.

(2) Subsection (1) is without prejudice to any other powers which the postal operator may have in relation to the packet (whether under the terms and conditions applicable to its transmission by post or otherwise).

(3) The detention or disposal by a postal operator of any postal packet on the grounds of a contravention of section 85 or of any terms and conditions applicable to its transmission by post shall not exempt the sender from any proceedings which might have been taken if the packet had been delivered in due course of post.

[Postal Services Act 2000, s 107.]

Evidential provisions

8–24255 **108. Evidence of amount of postage etc.** (1) The mark of—

(*a*) a universal service provider in connection with the provision of a universal postal service, or (*b*) a foreign postal administration,

of any sum on any postal packet as due in respect of that packet shall, unless the contrary is shown, be sufficient proof in any legal proceedings of the liability of the packet to the sum so marked.

(2) Subsections (3) to (5) apply in relation to any legal proceedings for the recovery of postage or other sums due in respect of postal packets.

(3) In any such proceedings, the production of the packet concerned with a stamp or other endorsement on it of a universal service provider (and made in connection with the provision of a universal postal service) or of a foreign postal administration indicating that the packet—

(*a*) has been refused or rejected,
(*b*) is unclaimed, or
(*c*) cannot for any other reason be delivered,

shall, unless the contrary is shown, be sufficient proof of the fact indicated.

(4) In any such proceedings, a certificate of a universal service provider that any mark, stamp or endorsement is such a mark, stamp or endorsement as is mentioned in subsection (1) or (3) shall, unless the contrary is shown, be sufficient proof of that fact.

(5) In any such proceedings, the person from whom the packet concerned purports to have come shall, unless the contrary is shown, be taken to be the sender of the packet.
[Postal Services Act 2000, s 108.]

8–24256 **109. Evidence of thing being a postal packet.** (1) On the prosecution of an offence under this Act (whether summarily or on indictment), evidence that any article is in the course of transmission by post, or has been accepted by a postal operator for transmission by post, shall be sufficient evidence that the article is a postal packet.

(2) In any proceedings in England and Wales for an offence under section 83 or 84 of this Act, section 27(4) of the Theft Act 1968 shall apply as it applies to proceedings for the theft of anything in the course of transmission by post.

(3) In any proceedings in Northern Ireland for an offence under section 83 or 84 of this Act, section 26(5) of the Theft Act (Northern Ireland) 1969 shall apply as it applies to proceedings for the theft of anything in the course of transmission by post.
[Postal Services Act 2000, s 109.]

8–24257 **110. Certificates in relation to universal postal service letter boxes.** A certificate given by or on behalf of a universal service provider to the effect that any box or receptacle is or was provided by the provider concerned for the purpose of receiving postal packets, or any class of postal packets, for onwards transmission in connection with the provision of a universal postal service, shall, unless the contrary is shown, be sufficient proof in any legal proceedings of the facts stated.
[Postal Services Act 2000, s 110.]

General

8–24258 **120. Offences by bodies corporate.** (1) Where an offence under this Act committed by a body corporate is proved to have been committed with the consent or connivance of, or to be attributable to any neglect on the part of—

(*a*) a director, manager, secretary or other similar officer of the body corporate, or
(*b*) a person purporting to act in such a capacity,

he as well as the body corporate commits the offence and shall be liable to be proceeded against and punished accordingly.

(2) Where the affairs of a body corporate are managed by its members, subsection (1) applies in relation to the acts and defaults of a member in connection with his functions of management as if he were a director of the body corporate.

(3) Where an offence under this Act is committed by a Scottish partnership and is proved to have been committed with the consent or connivance of a partner, he as well as the partnership commits the offence and shall be liable to be proceeded against and punished accordingly.
[Postal Services Act 2000, s 120.]

8–24259 **121. Service of documents.** (1) Any document required or authorised by virtue of this Act to be served on any person may be served—

(*a*) by delivering it to him or by leaving it at his proper address or by sending it by post to him at that address,
(*b*) if the person is a body corporate, by serving it in accordance with paragraph (a) on the secretary of the body, or
(*c*) if the person is a partnership, by serving it in accordance with paragraph (*a*) on a partner or a person having the control or management of the partnership business.

(2) For the purposes of this section and section 7 of the Interpretation Act 1978 (service of documents by post) in its application to this section, the proper address of any person on whom a document is to be served shall be his last known address, except that—

(*a*) in the case of service on a body corporate or its secretary, it shall be the address of the registered or principal office of the body,

(*b*) in the case of service on a partnership or a partner or a person having the control or management of a partnership business, it shall be the address of the principal office of the partnership.

(3) For the purposes of subsection (2) the principal office of a company constituted under the law of a country or territory outside the United Kingdom or of a partnership carrying on business outside the United Kingdom is its principal office within the United Kingdom.

(4) Subsection (5) applies if a person to be served under this Act with any document by another has specified to that other an address within the United Kingdom other than his proper address (as determined under subsection (2)) as the one at which he or someone on his behalf will accept documents of the same description as that document.

(5) In relation to that document, that address shall be treated as his proper address for the purposes of this section and section 7 of the Interpretation Act 1978 in its application to this section, instead of that determined under subsection (2).

(6) This section does not apply to any document if rules of court make provision about its service.

(7) In this section references to serving include references to similar expressions (such as giving or sending).

[Postal Services Act 2000, s 121.]

8–24260 **122.** *Orders and regulations*

8–24261 **125. Interpretation.** (1) In this Act, unless the context otherwise requires—

"body" includes an unincorporated association,

"contravention", in relation to any requirement, condition, direction, order or regulations, includes any failure to comply with it and cognate expressions shall be construed accordingly,

"correspondent", in relation to a postal packet, means the sender or the person to whom it is addressed,

"employee", in relation to a body corporate, includes any officer or director of the body corporate and any other person taking part in its management, and "employer" and other related expressions shall be construed accordingly,

"enactment" includes an Act of the Scottish Parliament, Northern Ireland legislation (within the meaning of the Northern Ireland Act 1998) and an enactment comprised in subordinate legislation, and includes an enactment whenever passed or made,

"financial year" means a year ending with 31st March,

"foreign postal administration" means a postal administration outside the United Kingdom,

"hovercraft" has the same meaning as in the Hovercraft Act 1968,

"letter" means any communication in written form on any kind of physical medium to be conveyed and delivered otherwise than electronically to the person or address indicated by the sender on the item itself or on its wrapping (excluding any book, catalogue, newspaper or periodical); and includes a postal packet containing any such communication,

"mail-bag" includes any form of container or covering in which postal packets in the course of transmission by post are enclosed by a postal operator in the United Kingdom or a foreign postal administration for the purpose of conveyance by post, whether or not it contains any such packets,

"modify" includes amend or repeal,

"Northern Ireland junior Minister" means a member of the Northern Ireland Assembly appointed as a junior Minister under section 19 of the Northern Ireland Act 1998,

"Northern Ireland Minister" includes the First Minister and the deputy First Minister in Northern Ireland,

"notice" means notice in writing,

"post office" includes any house, building, room, vehicle or place used for the provision of any postal services,

"post office letter box" includes any pillar box, wall box, or other box or receptacle provided by a postal operator for the purpose of receiving postal packets, or any class of postal packets, for onwards transmission by post,

"postal operator" means a person who provides the service of conveying postal packets from one place to another by post or any of the incidental services of receiving, collecting, sorting and delivering such packets,

"postal packet" means a letter, parcel, packet or other article transmissible by post,

"postal services" means the service of conveying postal packets from one place to another by post, the incidental services of receiving, collecting, sorting and delivering such packets and any other service which relates to any of those services and is provided in conjunction with any of them,

"the Postal Services Directive" means the Directive of the European Parliament and the Council of the European Union of 15th December 1997 (No 97/67/EC) on common rules for the development of the internal market of Community postal services and the implementation of quality of service as amended by the Directive of the European Parliament and the Council of the European Union of 10th June 2002 (No 2002/39/EC) with regard to the further opening to competition of Community postal services,

"public holiday" means Christmas Day, Good Friday or a day which is a bank holiday under the Banking and Financial Dealings Act 1971 in any part of the United Kingdom,

"registered post service" means a postal service which provides for the registration of postal packets in connection with their transmission by post and for the payment of compensation for any loss or damage,

"sender", in relation to any letter or other communication, means the person whose communication it is,

"ship" includes any boat, vessel or hovercraft,

"subordinate legislation" has the same meaning as in the Interpretation Act 1978 and also includes an instrument made under an Act of the Scottish Parliament and an instrument made under Northern Ireland legislation (within the meaning of section 98(1) of the Northern Ireland Act 1998),

"users", in relation to postal services, includes users as addressees and potential users,

"vehicle" includes a railway vehicle, and

"working day" means—

(*a*) in relation to the collection and delivery of letters, any day which is not a Sunday or a public holiday,

(*b*) in relation to the collection and delivery of postal packets other than letters, any day which is not a Saturday, a Sunday or a public holiday.

(2) For the purposes of the definition of "letter" in subsection (1) the reference to a communication to be conveyed and delivered otherwise than electronically shall be construed as a reference to a communication to be conveyed and delivered otherwise than—

(*a*) by means of an electronic communications network, or

(*b*) by other means but while in electronic form.

(3) For the purposes of this Act—

(*a*) a postal packet shall be taken to be in course of transmission by post from the time of its being delivered to any post office or post office letter box to the time of its being delivered to the addressee,

(*b*) the delivery of a postal packet of any description to a letter carrier or other person authorised to receive postal packets of that description for the post or to a person engaged in the business of a postal operator to be dealt with in the course of that business shall be a delivery to a post office, and

(*c*) the delivery of a postal packet—

(i) at the premises to which it is addressed or redirected, unless they are a post office from which it is to be collected,

(ii) to any box or receptacle to which the occupier of those premises has agreed that postal packets addressed to persons at those premises may be delivered, or

(iii) to the addressee's agent or to any other person considered to be authorised to receive the packet,

shall be a delivery to the addressee.

(4) Any reference in this Act to a subsidiary or wholly owned subsidiary shall be construed in accordance with section 736 of the Companies Act 1985 or Article 4 of the Companies (Northern Ireland) Order 1986.

[Postal Services Act 2000, s 125, as amended by SI 2002/3050 and the Communications Act 2003, Sch 17.]

Final

8–24262 **130. Commencement.** (1) Parts I to VI, sections 101 to 114, sections 116 to 119 (including Schedule 7) and section 127(4) and (6) (including Schedules 8 and 9) shall come into force on such day as the Secretary of State may by order appoint; and different days may be appointed for different purposes or different areas.

(2) Section 115 shall come into force at the end of the period of two months beginning with the day on which this Act is passed.

[Postal Services Act 2000, s 130.]

8–24263 **131.** *Short title and commencement*

Section 95

SCHEDULE 6

FURTHER PROVISIONS RELATING TO LAND

Power to place post-boxes etc in streets

8–24264 **1.** (1) A universal service provider may, for any purpose in connection with the provision of a universal postal service, execute in a street works of any of the kinds mentioned in sub-paragraph (2).

(2) The kinds of works are—

(*a*) placing a universal postal service letter box or a universal postal service pouch-box in a street,

(*b*) inspecting, maintaining, adjusting, repairing, altering or renewing such apparatus which has been so placed, changing its position or removing it,

(*c*) works needed for, or incidental to, the purposes of any works falling within paragraph (*a*) or (*b*) (including, in particular, breaking up or opening a street).

(3) Accordingly, Part III of the New Roads and Street Works Act 1991 (street works in England and Wales), and the Street Works (Northern Ireland) Order 1995, apply in relation to undertakers' works in exercise of a power conferred by this paragraph.

(4) For the avoidance of doubt, references in Part III of the Act of 1991 or the Order of 1995 to apparatus shall be construed as including universal postal service letter boxes and universal postal service pouch-boxes.

(5) Subject to sub-paragraphs (6) and (7), sub-paragraph (1) authorises the universal service provider concerned to execute works of any of the kinds mentioned in sub-paragraph (2) without obtaining any consent which would otherwise be required to be given by the street authority in its capacity as such and, in the case of a maintainable highway, in its capacity as owner.

(6) Sub-paragraph (5) is without prejudice to—

(*a*) the provisions of Part III of the Act of 1991, or the provisions of the Order of 1995, as to the making of requirements by the street authority or as to the settlement of a plan and section and the execution of the works in accordance with them,

(*b*) section 61 of the Act of 1991 or Article 21 of the Order of 1995 (consent required for protected streets).

(7) Sub-paragraph (1) does not free the universal service provider concerned from obtaining any other consent, licence or permission which may be required.

(8) This paragraph binds the Crown.

(9) In this paragraph references to doing anything in a street shall be construed as including references to doing anything under, over, across, along or upon the street.

(10) In this paragraph—

"maintainable highway"—

(*a*) in England and Wales, has the same meaning as in Part III of the Act of 1991 and includes a street in respect of which a declaration has been made under section 87 of that Act (prospectively maintainable highways), and

(*b*) in Northern Ireland, means a road (within the meaning of the Order of 1995) and includes a street in respect of which a declaration has been made under Article 46 of that Order (prospective roads),

"street" and "street authority"—

(*a*) in England and Wales, have the same meaning as in Part III of the Act of 1991, and

(*b*) in Northern Ireland, have the same meaning as in the Order of 1995, and

"universal postal service pouch-box" means any box or receptacle provided by a universal service provider for the temporary storage of postal packets in the course of transmission by post pending their collection for immediate delivery by a person who is in the course of delivering postal packets in connection with the provision of a universal postal service.

(11) In the application of this paragraph to Scotland—

(*a*) references to streets shall be construed as references to roads and references to street authority shall be construed as references to road works authority,

(*b*) "maintainable highway" means a public road within the meaning of Part IV of the Act of 1991 and includes a road in respect of which a declaration has been made under section 146 of that Act (prospective public roads),

(*c*) "road" and "road works authority" have the same meaning as in Part IV of the Act of 1991,

(*d*) in sub-paragraph (3) for the words from "Part III" to "apply" there shall be substituted "Part IV of the New Roads and Street Works Act 1991 (road works in Scotland) applies",

(*e*) in sub-paragraph (4) for the words from "Part III" to "1995" there shall be substituted "Part IV of the Act of 1991",

(*f*) in sub-paragraph (6)(*a*) for the words from "Part III" to "1995," there shall be substituted "Part IV of the Act of 1991", and

(*g*) in sub-paragraph (6)(*b*) for the words from "61" to "of 1995" there shall be substituted "120 of the Act of 1991".

Entry on land for exploratory purposes

2. (1) A person authorised in writing by a universal service provider may, at any reasonable time, enter upon and survey any land for the purpose of ascertaining whether the land would be suitable for use for any purpose in connection with the provision of a universal postal service.

(2) The power to survey land conferred by this paragraph includes power to search and bore for the purpose of ascertaining the nature of the subsoil.

(3) The powers conferred by this paragraph shall not be exercisable in relation to land which is covered by a building or will be so covered on the assumption that any planning permission which is in force is acted on.

(4) In this paragraph "building" includes any garden, yard, outhouses and appurtenances belonging to or usually enjoyed with a building.

3. (1) A person authorised to enter upon any land under paragraph 2 shall not demand to do so as of right unless—

(*a*) 28 days notice of the intended entry has been given to the occupier, and

(*b*) if required to do so, he has produced evidence of his authority and has stated the purpose of his entry.

(2) No person may carry out works authorised by paragraph 2(2) unless notice of the proposed works was included in the notice given under sub-paragraph (1).

(3) If the land in question is held by statutory undertakers and they object to the works on the ground that the carrying out of the works would be seriously detrimental to the carrying on of their undertaking, the authority of the appropriate Minister shall be required for the carrying out of works authorised by paragraph 2(2).

(4) In sub-paragraph (3) as it relates to England and Wales—

"appropriate Minister" means the person indicated by section 265 of the Town and Country Planning Act 1990,

"statutory undertakers" means any persons who, by virtue of section 262 of the Town and Country Planning Act 1990, are or are treated as statutory undertakers for the purposes of that Act or any provision of that Act.

(5) In that sub-paragraph as it relates to Scotland—

"appropriate Minister" means—

(*a*) in relation to any function which, by virtue of section 53 of the Scotland Act 1998, is exercisable by them as the appropriate Minister within the meaning of section 217 of the Town and Country Planning (Scotland) Act 1997, the Scottish Ministers,

(*b*) in any other case, the Minister indicated by that section,

"statutory undertakers" means any persons who, by virtue of section 214 of the Town and Country Planning (Scotland) Act 1997, are or are treated as statutory undertakers for the purposes of that Act or any provision of that Act.

and this sub-paragraph has effect notwithstanding the repeal of section 217 of the Town and Country Planning (Scotland) Act 1997 by paragraph 127(3) of Schedule 2 to the Scotland Act 1998 (Consequential Modifications) (No 2) Order 1999.

(6) In that sub-paragraph as it relates to Northern Ireland—

"appropriate Minister" means—

(*a*) in relation to a statutory undertaker carrying on any railway, road transport or dock or harbour undertaking or the airport operator (within the meaning of the Airports (Northern Ireland) Order 1994) of any airport to which Article 25 of that Order applies, the Minister for Regional Development,

(*b*) in relation to a statutory undertaker carrying on any water transport or inland navigation, the Minister of Culture, Arts and Leisure,

(*c*) in any other case, the Minister of Enterprise, Trade and Investment,

"statutory undertaker" has the same meaning as in Article 2(2) of the Planning (Northern Ireland) Order 1991.

4. (1) Any person who intentionally obstructs a person acting in the exercise of any power conferred by paragraph 2 shall be guilty of an offence.

(2) A person who commits an offence under sub-paragraph (1) shall be liable on summary conviction to a fine not exceeding level 3 on the standard scale.

5. (1) If in the exercise of any power conferred by paragraph 2 any damage is caused to land or moveables, any person interested in the land or moveables may recover compensation in respect of that damage from the universal service provider on whose behalf the power is exercised; and if in consequence of the exercise of such a power a person is disturbed in his enjoyment of any land or moveables, he may recover compensation from the universal service provider in respect of that disturbance.

(2) In relation to England and Wales, any question of disputed compensation under sub-paragraph (1) shall be referred to and determined by the Lands Tribunal; and sections 2 and 4 of the Land Compensation Act 1961 shall apply in relation to the determination subject to any necessary modifications.

(3) In relation to Scotland, any question of disputed compensation under sub-paragraph (1) shall be referred to and determined by the Lands Tribunal for Scotland; and sections 9 and 11 of the Land Compensation (Scotland) Act 1963 shall apply in relation to the determination subject to any necessary modifications.

(4) In relation to Northern Ireland, any question of disputed compensation under sub-paragraph (1) shall be referred to and determined by the Lands Tribunal for Northern Ireland; and the determination shall be deemed to be a determination to which section 31 of the Land Development Values (Compensation) Act (Northern Ireland) 1965 applies.

(5) In this paragraph "moveables" means—

(*a*) in relation to England and Wales and Northern Ireland, chattels, and

(*b*) in relation to Scotland, corporeal moveables.

Acquisition of land by agreement

6. For the purpose of the acquisition by agreement by a universal service provider for any purpose in connection with the provision of a universal postal service of land in England and Wales, the provisions of Part I of the Compulsory Purchase Act 1965 (so far as applicable), other than sections 4 to 8 and section 31, shall apply.

7. For the purpose of the acquisition by agreement by a universal service provider for any purpose in connection with the provision of a universal postal service of land in Scotland, section 188(2) of the Town and Country Planning (Scotland) Act 1997 (incorporation of Lands Clauses Acts) shall, with any necessary modifications, apply for the purposes of this Act as it applies for the purposes of that Act.

8. For the purpose of the acquisition by agreement by a universal service provider for any purpose in connection with the provision of a universal postal service of land in Northern Ireland, the Lands Clauses Acts shall be incorporated with this Act except for sections 127 to 133 (sale of superfluous land) and sections 150 and 151 (access to the special Act) of the Lands Clauses Consolidation Act 1845.

Power to sell Duchy of Lancaster land

9. If a universal service provider proposes to acquire by agreement any land belonging to Her Majesty in right of the Duchy of Lancaster for any purpose in connection with the provision of a universal postal service, the Chancellor and Council of the Duchy of Lancaster may sell that land to him.

Supplementary

10. Any land acquired by agreement by a universal service provider by virtue of any of paragraphs 6 to 9 shall be deemed for all purposes to have been acquired by him for the purposes of his undertaking as a universal service provider.

Section 119

SCHEDULE 7
DISCLOSURE OF INFORMATION

(*Amended by SI 2001/3617, the Water Act 2003, Sch the Communications Act 2003, Sch 17, the Railways Act 2005, Sch 12 and the Water Act 2003, Sch 7.*)

Prohibition on disclosure

8–24265 **1.** (1) This Schedule applies to information if—

(*a*) it was obtained by virtue of this Act (other than section 62 or 118), and

(*b*) it relates to the affairs of an individual or to a particular business.

(2) The information shall not be disclosed during the lifetime of the individual or so long as the business is carried on, except as provided below.

Disclosure with consent

2. Paragraph 1(2) does not apply to a disclosure made with the consent of the individual or the person for the time being carrying on the business.

Other permitted disclosures

3. (1) Paragraph 1(2) does not apply to a disclosure made—

(*a*) for the purpose of facilitating the carrying out by the Secretary of State, the Treasury, the Commission, the Competition Commission or the Council of any of his or their functions under this Act,

(*b*) for the purpose of facilitating the carrying out by a person or body mentioned in sub-paragraph (2) of any of his or its functions under an enactment or instrument specified in sub-paragraph (3),

(*c*) for the purpose of enabling or assisting the Secretary of State, the Treasury, the Department for Enterprise, Trade and Investment in Northern Ireland or the Department of Finance and Personnel in Northern Ireland to exercise any powers conferred by the Financial Services and Markets Act 2000 or by the enactments relating to companies, insurance companies or insolvency,

(*d*) for the purpose of enabling or assisting an inspector appointed under the enactments relating to companies to carry out his functions,

(*e*) for the purpose of enabling or assisting an official receiver to carry out his functions under the enactments relating to insolvency or for the purpose of enabling or assisting a recognised professional body for the purposes of section 391 of the Insolvency Act 1986 or Article 350 of the Insolvency (Northern Ireland) Order 1989 to carry out its functions,

(*f*) for the purpose of facilitating the carrying out by the Health and Safety Commission or the Health and Safety Executive of any of its functions under any enactment or of facilitating the carrying out by any enforcing authority (within the meaning of Part I of the Health and Safety at Work etc Act 1974) of any functions under a relevant statutory provision (within the meaning of that Act),

(*g*) for the purpose of facilitating the carrying out by the Health and Safety Executive for Northern Ireland of any of its functions under any enactment or of facilitating the carrying out by any enforcing authority (within the meaning of Part I of the Health and Safety at Work (Northern Ireland) Order 1978) of any function under a relevant statutory provision (within the meaning of that Order),

(*h*) for the purpose of facilitating the carrying out by the Comptroller and Auditor General, or the Comptroller and Auditor General for Northern Ireland, of any of his functions under any enactment,

(*i*) in connection with the investigation of any criminal offence or for the purposes of any criminal proceedings,

(*j*) for the purposes of any civil proceedings brought by virtue of this Act or any enactment or instrument specified in sub-paragraph (3),

(*k*) in pursuance of a Community obligation,

(*l*) by the Secretary of State, or with his consent, to an international organisation of which the United Kingdom is a member,

(*m*) in connection with negotiations conducted by officers of the Secretary of State with representatives of the government of a country or territory outside the United Kingdom,

(*n*) in connection with the discharge of an obligation of the United Kingdom under international arrangements.

(2) The persons and bodies are—

(*a*) any Minister of the Crown,

(*b*) any Northern Ireland department,

(*c*) any Northern Ireland Minister,

(*d*) the Director General of Fair Trading,

(*e*) the Competition Commission,

(*f*) the Office of Communications,

(*g*) the Independent Television Commission,*

(*h*) *repealed,*

(*i*) the Director General of Gas for Northern Ireland,

(*j*) the water Services Regulation Authority,

(*k*) the Water Appeals Commission for Northern Ireland,

(*l*) *repealed,*

(*m*) the Director General of Electricity Supply for Northern Ireland,

(*n*) the Coal Authority,
(*o*) the Civil Aviation Authority,
(*p*) the Office of Rail Regulation,
(*q*) the Insolvency Practitioners Tribunal,
(*r*) a local weights and measures authority in Great Britain,
(*s*) the Financial Services Authority,
(*t*) the Gas and Electricity Markets Authority,
(*u*) the Gas and Electricity Consumer Council.

(3) The enactments and instruments are—

(*a*) the Industrial and Provident Societies Act 1965,
(*b*) the Industrial and Provident Societies Act 1967,
(*c*) the Trade Descriptions Act 1968,
(*d*) the Friendly and Industrial and Provident Societies Act 1968,
(*e*) the Fair Trading Act 1973,
(*f*) the Consumer Credit Act 1974,
(*g*) the Friendly Societies Act 1974,
(*h*) the Industrial and Provident Societies Act 1975,
(*i*) the Industrial and Provident Societies Act 1978,
(*j*) the Estate Agents Act 1979,
(*k*) the Credit Unions Act 1979,
(*l*) the Competition Act 1980,
(*m*) the Telecommunications Act 1984,
(*n*) the Airports Act 1986,
(*o*) the Gas Act 1986,
(*p*) the Insolvency Act 1986,
(*q*) the Building Societies Act 1986,
(*r*) the Consumer Protection Act 1987,
(*s*) the Electricity Act 1989,
(*t*) the Broadcasting Act 1990,
(*u*) the Property Misdescriptions Act 1991,
(*v*) the Water Industry Act 1991,
(*w*) the Water Resources Act 1991,
(*x*) the Friendly Societies Act 1992,
(*y*) the Railways Act 1993,
(*z*) the Coal Industry Act 1994,
(*aa*) the Broadcasting Act 1996,
(*bb*) the Competition Act 1998,
(*cc*) the Financial Services and Markets Act 2000,
(*dd*) the Regulation of Investigatory Powers Act 2000,
(*ee*) the Utilities Act 2000,
(*ff*) Part I of the Transport Act 2000,
(*gg*) the Insolvency Act 2000,
(*gh*) the Enterprise Act 2002,
(*gi*) the Communications Act 2003,
(*gj*) the Water Act 2003,
(*gk*) the Railways Act 2005,
(*hh*) the Water and Sewerage Services (Northern Ireland) Order 1973,
(*ii*) the Audit (Northern Ireland) Order 1987,
(*jj*) the Consumer Protection (Northern Ireland) Order 1987,
(*kk*) the Insolvency (Northern Ireland) Order 1989,
(*ll*) the Electricity (Northern Ireland) Order 1992,
(*mm*) Part IV of the Airports (Northern Ireland) Order 1994,
(*nn*) the Gas (Northern Ireland) Order 1996,
(*oo*) the Water (Northern Ireland) Order 1999,
(*pp*) the EC Competition Law (Articles 84 and 85) Enforcement Regulations 2001,
(*qq*) any subordinate legislation made for the purpose of securing compliance with the Directive of the Council of the European Communities of 10th September 1984 (No 84/450/EEC) on the approximation of the laws, regulations and administrative provisions of the member States concerning misleading advertising. 4

The Secretary of State may by order modify paragraph 3.

***Sub-paragraph (2)(*g*) repealed by the Communications Act 2003, Sch 17 from a date to be appointed.**

Other exceptions

5. (1) Paragraph 1(2) does not limit the information which may be—

(*a*) included in, or made public as a part of, a report on a reference under section 15,
(*b*) included in, or made public as part of, a report under section 45, 55 or 57,
(*c*) published by the Commission under section 46, or
(*d*) made available by the Council under section 52, 53 or 59 or the Commission under section 58.

(2) Sub-paragraph (1) is without prejudice to any other exception to paragraph 1(2).

(3) Paragraph 1(2) does not apply to information which has been made available to the public by being disclosed in circumstances in which, or for a purpose for which, disclosure is not precluded by this Schedule.

Offence

6. (1) A person commits an offence if he discloses information in contravention of this Schedule.

(2) A person who commits an offence under sub-paragraph (1) shall be liable—

(*a*) on summary conviction, to a fine not exceeding the statutory maximum,

(*b*) on conviction on indictment, to a fine or to imprisonment for a term not exceeding two years or to both.

POUND BREACH

8–24280 Offence at common law. Breaking the pound for the purpose of rescuing cattle, etc, distrained for rent or damage feasant, and which have been actually impounded in a public pound, is a misdemeanour, punishable by fine or imprisonment, or both. Ignorance of the distraint is not a defence to a civil action (*Lavell & Co v O'Leary* [1933] 2 KB 200).

It is a misdemeanour to rescue cattle found in the parish lanes, and which the officer appointed by the leet is in the act of driving to the pound (*R v Bradshaw* (1835) 7 C & P 233). The cattle may be retaken without a breach of the peace, wherever found in fresh pursuit and the jury will judge as to the reasonableness of the time; whether the recapture must be on fresh pursuit, where it does not take place by breaking or entering a close, is not quite clear, but it must be within a reasonable time. The offender may be required to find sureties for answering an indictment at the [Crown Court] (see *Russell v Rider* (1934) 6 C &. P 416). If a sum greater than the damage be demanded and paid under protest, the difference may be recovered back (*Green v Duckett* (1883) 11 QBD 275, 47 JP 487).

8–24231 Cattle straying on highways. See title HIGHWAYS, in PART VII.—TRANSPORT.

PRINTERS

8–24285 Note: See also the Newspaper Libel and Registration Act 1881 in title Libel, ante; also the Children and Young Persons (Harmful Publications) Act 1955, s 2 in title Obscene Publications, ante, and the Representation of the People Act 1983, s 110.

This title contains the following Acts—

Newspapers, Printers and Reading Rooms Repeal Act 1869

(32 & 22 Vict c 24)

SECOND SCHEDULE[1]

8–24286 Penalty[2] upon printers for not publishing their name and residence on every book, and on persons publishing the same. Every person who shall print any paper or book whatsoever[3] which shall be meant to be published or dispersed, and who shall not print upon the front of every such paper, if the same shall be printed on one side only, or upon the first or last leaf of every paper or book which shall consist of more than one leaf, in legible characters, his or her name and usual place of abode or business, and every person who shall publish or disperse, or assist in publishing or dispersing, any printed paper or book on which the name and place of abode of the person printing the same shall not be printed as aforesaid, shall for every copy of such paper so printed by him[4] or her forfeit a sum not more than **level 1** on the standard scale[5];

Provided always that nothing herein contained shall be construed to impose any penalty upon any person for printing any paper excepted out of the operation of the Unlawful Societies Act 1799[1] either in the said Act or by any Act made for the amendment thereof.

---

1. The Newspapers, Printers and Reading Rooms Repeal Act 1869 consolidated provisions in a number of previous Acts, including the Unlawful Societies Act 1799, the Printers and Publishers Acts 1811 and 1839 and the Seditious Meetings Act 1846. They are here reproduced in, and have force as, the Second Schedule to the 1869 Act (amended by the Criminal Justice Act 1982, s 46).

2. The Second Schedule also requires that the information shall not be prosecuted except *in the name of* the Attorney General (see also *Key v Bastin* [1925] 1 KB 650, 89 JP 74). The provision about publishing name and residence on books originated in 2 & 3 Vict, c 12 of which a repealed provision said that 39 Geo III, c 79 was to be construed as one Act with it. That earlier provision stated that prosecutions should be commenced within three months after the offence, and this limitation still applies to the provision printed here about keeping a copy of every paper etc, but arguably no longer applies to the provision about publishing name and residence on books, as there is now no specific requirement to construe together the different enactments now comprising the Second Schedule to the 1869 Act. Prosecutors may however wish to be prepared to justify using the six month limit under the Magistrates' Courts Act 1980, s 127.

3. Exceptions are made by the next paragraph, *infra*, and the second Schedule also specifically excludes papers printed by authority of Parliament, and makes special provision for books or papers printed at the Oxford University Press and the Pitt Press, Cambridge. It also exempts the printing of the name or the name and address, or business or profession of any

person and the articles in which he deals, as well as any papers for the sale of estates or goods by auction or otherwise. See also the Printers Imprint Act 1961, post, which further relaxes the requirements.

4. Despite the wording of the section, it is established that the publisher may be liable to penalties under this section, even though he is not the printer (*A-G v Beauchamp* [1920] 1 KB 650, 84 JP 41; *R v Oakes* [1959] 2 QB 350, [1959] 2 All ER 92.

5. Maximum penalty as amended by the Criminal Law Act 1977, s 31 and the Criminal Justice Act 1982, s 46.

8–24287 Name and residence of printers not required to be put to bank notes, bills, etc, or to any paper printed by authority of any public office. Nothing in the Unlawful Societies Act 1799[1], or in this Act contained shall extend or be construed to extend to require the name and residence of the printer to be printed upon any bank note of the . . . Bank of England, upon any bill of exchange or promissory note, or upon any bond or other security for payment of money, or upon any bill of lading, policy of insurance, letter of attorney, deed, or agreement, or upon any transfer or assignment of any public stocks, funds, or other securities, or upon any transfer or assignment of the stocks of any public corporation or company authorised or sanctioned by Act of Parliament, or upon any dividend warrant of or for any such public or other stocks, funds, or securities, or upon any receipt for money or goods, or upon any proceeding in any court of law or equity, or in any inferior court, warrant, order, or other papers printed by the authority of any public board or public officer in the execution of the duties of their respective offices, notwithstanding the whole of any part of the said several securities, instruments, proceedings, matters, and things aforesaid shall have been or shall be printed. (Amended by the Statute Law Repeals Acts 1893 and 1973.)

1. The Newspapers, Printers and Reading Rooms Repeal Act 1869 consolidated provisions in a number of previous Acts, including the Unlawful Societies Act 1799, the Printers and Publishers Acts 1811 and 1839 and the Seditious Meetings Act 1846. They are here reproduced in, and have force as, the Second Schedule to the 1869 Act (amended by the Criminal Justice Act 1982, s 46).

8–24288 Printers to keep a copy of every paper they print and write thereon the name and abode of their employer. Penalty[1] **of level 2 on the standard scale for neglect or refusing to produce the copy within six months**.—Every person who shall print any paper for hire, reward, gain, or profit, shall carefully preserve and keep one copy (at least) of every paper so printed by him or her, on which he or she shall write, or cause to be written or printed, in fair and legible characters, the name and place of abode of the person or persons by whom he or she shall be employed to print the same; and every person printing any paper for hire, reward, gain, or profit who shall omit or neglect to write, or cause to be written or printed as aforesaid, the name and place of his or her employer on one of such printed papers, or to keep or preserve the same for the space of six calendar months next after the printing thereof, or to produce and show the same to any justice of the peace who within the said space of six calendar months shall require to see the same, maximum fine for omission, neglect, refusal **level 2** on the standard scale[2].

1. The Second Schedule also requires that the information shall not be prosecuted except *in the name of* the Attorney General (see also *Key v Bastin* [1925] 1 KB 650, 89 JP 74). The provision about publishing name and residence on books originated in 2 & 3 Vict, c 12 of which a repealed provision said that 39 Geo III, c 79 was to be construed as one Act with it. That earlier provision stated that prosecutions should be commenced within three months after the offence, and this limitation still applies to the provision printed here about keeping a copy of every paper etc, but arguably no longer applies to the provision about publishing name and residence on books, as there is now no specific requirement to construe together the different enactments now comprising the Second Schedule to the 1869 Act. Prosecutors may however wish to be prepared to justify using the six month limit under the Magistrates' Courts Act 1980, s 127.

2. Maximum penalty as amended by the Criminal Law Act 1977, s 31 and the Criminal Justice Act 1982, s 46.

Printer's Imprint Act 1961

(9 & 10 Eliz 2 c 31)

8–24290 1. Relaxation of requirements as to printer's imprint, etc. (1) Nothing in the Newspapers, Printers, and Reading Rooms Repeal Act 1869, shall require a printer to print a statement of his name and usual place of abode or business (in this Act referred to as the "printer's imprint") on any paper or book unless the matter printed by him therein comprises either—

(*a*) words grouped together in a manner calculated to convey a message, other than words calculated to convey only a greeting, invitation or other message in a conventional form; or

(*b*) a drawing, illustration or other picture, other than a picture representing only a geometrical, floral, or other design or a registered trademark[1] or any combination thereof.

(2) Nothing in the said Act of 1869 shall require a printer to preserve or keep, or prohibit any person from publishing or dispersing or assisting in publishing or dispersing a copy of any paper or book which by virtue of that Act or this Act is not required to bear the printer's imprint.

(3) The exemption conferred by section 31 of the Unlawful Societies Act 1799, as set out in the Second Schedule to the said Act of 1869 (which exempts the printing from engravings or by letterpress of the paper's and particulars there mentioned from requirements as to the printer's imprint and the preservation of copies) shall extend to the printing by any process of those papers

and particulars and of particulars of the services offered by any person; and accordingly in that section the words "to the impression of any engraving or" and the words "by letter-press" are hereby repealed.

(4) The exemptions conferred by this section shall not prejudice any exemption conferred by the said Act of 1869.

[Printer's Imprint Act 1961, s 1.]

1. To be construed as a registered trademark within the meaning of the Trademarks Act 1994 (Sch 4).

PRISONS

8–24291 This title contains the following statutes—

and the following statutory instruments—

Prison Act 1952

(15 & 16 Geo 6 & 1 Eliz 2 c 52)

8–24295 This Act[1] consolidates enactments relating to prisons and other institutions for offenders. The Secretary of State has complete responsibility for such establishments[2]. Only the parts of the Act of relevance to magistrates' courts are set out here.

See also the Prison Rules in this title, post.

1. For application of any enactment with respect to the treatment of persons detained in prisons or other establishments, to persons sentenced by service courts of visiting forces, see Visiting Forces and International Headquarters (Application of Law) Order 1965 (SI 1965/1536), Sch 5, para 5. The Act is applied to other institutions for offenders to the extent prescribed by s 43 thereof.

2. Transferred to him by the Prison Commissioners Dissolution Order 1963, SI 1963/597 made under s 24 of the Criminal Justice Act 1961.

Visiting committees[1] and boards of visitors

8–24296 6. Visiting committees[1] and boards of visitors. (1) *Repealed.*

(2) The Secretary of State shall appoint for every prison a board of visitors of whom not less than two shall be justices of the peace.

(3) Rules made as aforesaid shall prescribe the functions of boards of visitors and shall among other things require members to pay frequent visits to the prison and hear any complaints which may be made by the prisoners and report to the Secretary of State any matter which they consider it expedient to report; and any member of a board of visitors may at any time enter the prison and shall have free access to every part of it and to every prisoner.

(4) (*Repealed*).

[Prison Act 1952, s 6, as amended by the Courts Act 1971, ss 53 and 56, and Sch 7 and 11.]

1. The words "visiting committees" are now obsolete in view of amendments to this section.

Prison Officers

8–24300 8. Powers of prison officers. Every prison officer while acting as such shall have all the powers, authority, protection and privileges of a constable.

[Prison Act 1952, s 8.]

8–24301 8A. Powers of search by authorised employees. (1) An authorised employee at a prison shall have the power to search any prisoner for the purpose of ascertaining whether he has any unauthorised property on his person.

(2) An authorised employee searching a prisoner by virtue of this section—

(*a*) shall not be entitled to require a prisoner to remove any of his clothing other than an outer coat, jacket, headgear, gloves and footwear;

(*b*) may use reasonable force where necessary; and

(*c*) may seize and detain any unauthorised property found on the prisoner in the course of the search.

(3) In this section "authorised employee" means an employee of a description for the time being authorised by the governor to exercise the powers conferred by this section.

(4) The governor of a prison shall take such steps as he considers appropriate to notify to prisoners the descriptions of persons who are for the time being authorised to exercise the powers conferred by this section.

(5) In this section "unauthorised property", in relation to a prisoner, means property which the prisoner is not authorised by prison rules or by the governor to have in his possession or, as the case may be, in his possession in a particular part of the prison.

[Prison Act 1952, s 8A, as inserted by the Criminal Justice and Public Order Act 1994, s 152.]

8–24301A 11. Ejectment of prison officers and their families refusing to quit. (1) Where any living accommodation is provided for a prison officer or his family by virtue of his office, then, if he ceases to be a prison officer or is suspended from office or dies, he, or as the case may be, his family, shall quit the accommodation when required to do so by notice of the Secretary of State.

(2) Where a prison officer or the family of a prison officer refuses or neglects to quit the accommodation forty-eight hours after the giving of such notice as aforesaid, any two justices of the peace, on proof made to them of the facts authorising the giving of the notice and of the service of the notice and of the neglect or refusal to comply therewith, may, by warrant under their hands and seals, direct any constable, within a period specified in the warrant, to enter by force, if necessary, into the accommodation and deliver possession of it to a person acting on behalf of the Secretary of State.

[Prison Act 1952, s 11, as amended by SI 1963/597.]

Confinement and treatment of prisoners

8–24302 13. Legal custody of prisoner. (1) Every prisoner shall be deemed to be in the legal custody of the governor of the prison.

(2) A prisoner shall be deemed to be in legal custody while he is confined in, or is being taken to or from, any prison and while he is working, or is for any other reason, outside the prison in the custody or under the control of an officer of the prison and while he is being taken to any place to which he is required or authorised by or under this Act or section 95, 98, 99 or 108(5) of the Powers of Criminal Courts (Sentencing) Act 2000* to be taken, or is kept in custody in pursuance of any such requirement or authorisation.

[Prison Act 1952, s 13, as amended by Criminal Justice Act 1961, 4th Sch and the Powers of Criminal Courts (Sentencing) Act 2000, Sch 9.]

***Amended by the Criminal Justice and Court Services Act 2000, Sch 7 from a date to be appointed.**

8–24303 16. Photographing and measuring of prisoners. The Secretary of State may make regulations[1].

[Prison Act 1952, s 16.]

1. This section applies to remand centres, young offenders institutions (Prison Act 1952, s 43(1) as amended). Regulations still in force are SR & O 1896 No 762, saved by s 54(3) of the Act. They enable the prisoner to be photographed at any time during imprisonment, in prison dress or any other dress suitable to his position in life, and also to be measured. Finger prints may be taken; so may palm prints (Criminal Justice Act 1967, s 33). The Prison Rules 1999, r 42(2) prohibit the giving of a photograph to a person not authorised to receive it; similar provision is made for young offender institutions.

An untried prisoner may have his photograph, measurements and finger prints taken by order of the Secretary of State, or on written application (stating the purposes of justice for which the records are required) by a police officer of not lower rank than Superintendent, to a magistrate or (in the London metropolitan area) to the commissioner or assistant commissioner of police. An acquitted prisoner without previous convictions shall have all records handed to him, or they will be destroyed.

The above does not apply to prisoners; records can be made before a person is committed to prison provided he does not object.

See also powers contained in the Police and Criminal Evidence Act 1984, s 61 and under the Immigration Act 1971, Sch 2, para 18(2).

8–24304 16A. Testing prisoners for drugs. (1) If an authorisation is in force for the prison, any prison officer may, at the prison, in accordance with prison rules, require any prisoner who is confined in the prison to provide a sample of urine for the purpose of ascertaining whether he has any drug in his body.

(2) If the authorisation so provides, the power conferred to subsection (1) above shall include power to require a prisoner to provide a sample of any other description specified in the authorisation, not being an intimate sample, whether instead of or in addition to a sample of urine.

(3) In this section—

"authorisation" means an authorisation by the governor;

"drug" means any drug which is a controlled drug for the purposes of the Misuse of Drugs Act 1971;

"intimate sample" has the same meaning as in Part V of the Police and Criminal Evidence Act 1984;

"prison officer" includes a prisoner custody officer within the meaning of Part IV of the Criminal Justice Act 1991; and

"prison rules" means rules under section 47 of this Act.

[Prison Act 1952, s 16A, as inserted by the Criminal Justice and Public Order Act 1994, s 151.]

8–24304A 16B. Power to test prisoners for alcohol. (1) If an authorisation is in force for the prison, any prison officer may, at the prison, in accordance with prison rules, require any prisoner who is confined in the prison to provide a sample of breath for the purpose of ascertaining whether he has alcohol in his body.

(2) If the authorisation so provides, the power conferred by subsection (1) above shall include power—

(*a*) to require a prisoner to provide a sample of urine, whether instead of or in addition to a sample of breath, and

(*b*) to require a prisoner to provide a sample of any other description specified in the authorisation, not being an intimate sample, whether instead of or in addition to a sample of breath, a sample of urine or both.

(3) In this section—

"authorisation" means an authorisation by the governor;

"intimate sample" has the same meaning as in Part V of the Police and Criminal Evidence Act 1984;

"prison officer" includes a prisoner custody officer within the meaning of Part IV of the Criminal Justice Act 1991;

"prison rules" means rules under section 47 of this Act.

[Prison Act 1952, s 16B, as inserted by the Prisons (Alcohol Testing) Act 1997, s 1.]

8–24305 19. Right of justice to visit prison. (1) A justice of the peace[1] for any commission area may at any time visit any prison in that area and any prison in which a prisoner is confined in respect of an offence committed in that area, and may examine the condition of the prison and of the prisoners and enter in the visitors' book, to be kept by the governor of the prison, any observations on the condition of the prison or any abuses.

(2) Nothing in the preceding subsection shall authorise a justice of the peace to communicate with any prisoner except on the subject of his treatment in the prison, or to visit any prisoner under sentence of death.

(3) The governor of every prison shall bring any entry in the visitors' book to the attention of the visiting committee or the board of visitors at their next visit.

[Prison Act 1952, s 19, as amended by the Local Government Act 1972, Sch 30 and the Access to Justice Act 1999, Sch 10.]

1. This reference to a justice of the peace shall be construed in relation to any area in England (outside Greater London) or Wales as meaning a justice of the peace for a commission area (as defined in the Justices of the Peace Act 1997, s1 in PART I: MAGISTRATES' COURTS, PROCEDURE, ante) (Local Government Changes for England Regulations 1996, SI 1996/674 and the Magistrates' Courts (Wales) (Consequences of Local Government Changes) Order 1996, SI 1996/675).

8–24306 23. Power of constable, etc, to act outside his jurisdiction. For the purpose of taking a person to or from any prison under the order of any authority competent to give the order a constable or other officer may act outside the area of his jurisdiction and shall notwithstanding that he is so acting have all the powers, authority, protection and privileges of his office.

[Prison Act 1952, s 23.]

Length of sentence, release on licence and temporary discharge

8–24307 24. Calculation of term of sentence. (1) In any sentence of imprisonment the word "month" shall, unless the contrary is expressed, be construed as meaning calendar month[1].

[Prison Act 1952, s 24, as amended by the Criminal Justice Act 1961, 5th Sch.]

1. A prisoner who would be discharged on Sunday, Christmas Day, Good Friday or any Bank Holiday or (in the case of a person serving a term of more than one month) any Saturday, is discharged on the preceding day (Criminal Justice Act 1961, s 23(3)).

Offences

8–24309 39. Assisting prisoner to escape. Any person who aids any prisoner in escaping or attempting to escape from a prison[1] or who, with intent to facilitate the escape of any prisoner, conveys any thing into a prison or to a prisoner, sends any thing (by post or otherwise) into a prison

or to a prisoner or places any thing anywhere outside a prison with a view to its coming into the possession of a prisoner, shall be guilty of [an offence][2] and liable to imprisonment for a term not exceeding **ten years**.
[Prison Act 1952, s 39, amended by Criminal Justice Act 1961, 4th Sch and the Prison Security Act 1992, s 2.]

1. Escape from prison is a common law misdemeanour (Arch CP). See also *R v Frascati* (1981) 73 Cr App Rep 28. "Prison" is confined to premises contemplated by s 42, post, and does not extend to a police room in a magistrates' court in which a person remanded in custody is held pending transport to prison (*R v Moss and Harte* (1985) 150 JP 26, 82 Cr App Rep 116, [1985] Crim LR 659).
2. "Offence" is substituted for "felony" to accord with Criminal Law Act 1967, s 12(5).

8–24310 **40. Unlawful conveyance of spirits or tobacco into prisons, etc.** Any person who contrary to the regulations of a prison brings or attempts to bring into the prison or to a prisoner any spirituous or fermented liquor or tobacco, or places any such liquor or any tobacco anywhere outside the prison with intent that it shall come into the possession of a prisoner, and any officer who contrary to those regulations allows any such liquor or any tobacco to be sold or used in the prison, shall be liable on summary conviction to imprisonment for a term not exceeding **six months** or a fine not exceeding **level 3** on the standard scale or **both**.
[Prison Act 1952, s 40, amended by Criminal Justice Act 1967, 3rd Sch and the Criminal Justice Act 1982, ss 38 and 46.]

8–24311 **41. Unlawful introduction of other articles.** Any person who contrary to the regulations of a prison conveys or attempts to convey any letter or any other thing into or out of the prison or to a prisoner or places it anywhere outside the prison with intent that it shall come into the possession of a prisoner shall, where he is not thereby guilty of an offence under either of the last two preceding sections, be liable on summary conviction to a fine not exceeding **level 3** on the standard scale.
[Prison Act 1952, s 41, as amended by Criminal Justice Act 1967, 3rd Sch and the Criminal Justice Act 1982, ss 38 and 46.]

8–24312 **42. Display of notice of penalties.** The Prison Comrs[1] shall cause to be affixed in a conspicuous place outside every prison a notice of the penalties to which persons committing offences under the three last preceding sections are liable.
[Prison Act 1952, s 42.]

1. Section 42 has not been specifically amended by the Prison Commissioners Dissolution Order 1963 (see Headnote to this Act) but presumably the responsibility for the display of notices has passed to the Secretary of State.

Remand centres, detention centres and [youth custody centres]

8–24313 **43. Remand centres, detention centres and youth custody centres.** (1) The Secretary of State may provide—

(*a*) remand centres, that is to say places for the detention of persons not less than 14 but under 21 years of age who are remanded or committed in custody for trial or sentence*;

(*aa*) young offender institutions, that is to say places for the detention of offenders sentenced to detention in a young offender institution or to custody for life;

(*b*), (*c*) (*Repealed*), and

(*d*) secure training centres, that is to say places in which offenders in respect of whom detention and training orders have been made under section 100 of the Powers of Criminal Courts (Sentencing) Act 2000 may be detained and given training and education and prepared for their release.

(2) The Secretary of State may from time from time direct—

(*a*) that a woman aged 21* years or over who is serving a sentence of imprisonment or who has been committed to prison for default shall be detained in a remand centre or* a youth custody centre instead of a prison;

(*b*) that a woman aged 21 years or over who is remanded in custody or committed in custody for trial or sentence shall be detained in a remand centre instead of a prison;*

(*c*) that a person under 21 but less than 17 years of age who is remanded in custody or committed in custody for trial or sentence shall be detained in a prison instead of a remand centre or a remand centre instead of a prison, notwithstanding anything in section 27 of the Criminal Justice Act 1948 or section 23(3) of the Children and Young Persons Act 1969.**

(3) Notwithstanding subsection (1) above, any person required to be detained in an institution to which this Act applies may be detained in a remand centre for any temporary purpose and a person aged 18 years or over may be detained in such a centre for the purpose of providing maintenance and domestic services for that centre.**

(4) Sections 5A, 6(2) and (3), 16, 22, 25 and 36 of this Act shall apply to remand centres*, detention centres and youth custody centres and to persons detained in them as they apply to prisons and prisoners.

(4A) Sections 16, 22 and 36 of this Act shall apply to secure training centres and to persons detained in them as they apply to prisons and prisoners.

(5) The other provisions of this Act preceding this section, except sections 28 and 37(2) above, shall apply to centres of the descriptions specified in subsection (4) above and to persons detained in them as they apply to prisons and prisoners, but subject to such adaptations and modifications as may be specified in rules made by the Secretary of State.

(5A) The other provisions of this Act preceding this section, except sections 5, 5A, 6(2) and (3), 12, 14, 19, 25, 28 and 37(2) and (3) above, shall apply to secure training centres and to persons detained in them as they apply to prisons and prisoners, but subject to such adaptations and modifications as may be specified in rules made by the Secretary of State.

(6) References in the preceding provisions of this Act to imprisonment shall, so far as those provisions apply to institutions provided under this section, be construed as including references to detention in those institutions.

(7) Nothing in this section shall be taken to prejudice the operation of section 108(5) of the Powers of Criminal Courts (Sentencing) Act 2000.**

[Prison Act 1952, s 43, as substituted by the Criminal Justice Act 1982, s 11 and amended by the Criminal Justice Act 1988, Schs 15 and 16, the Criminal Justice Act 1991, Sch 8, the Criminal Justice and Public Order Act 1994, s 11, the Crime and Disorder Act 1998, Sch 8 and the Powers of Criminal Courts (Sentencing) Act 2000, Sch 9.]

*. **Amended by the Criminal Justice and Court Services Act 2000, Sch 7 from a date to be appointed.**
****Repealed by the Criminal Justice and Court Services Act 2000, s 59 and Sch 7 from a date to be appointed.**

8–24314 **47.** *Power of Secretary of State to make Rules for the regulation and management of prisons etc*[1].

1. The Prison Rules 1999, and the Young Offenders Institution Rules 2000, post, have been made.

Miscellaneous

8–24315 **49. Persons unlawfully at large.** (1) Any person who, having been sentenced to imprisonment[1] or custody for life or ordered to be detained in secure accommodation or in a young offenders institution, or having been committed to a prison or remand centre, is unlawfully at large, may be arrested by a constable without warrant[2] and taken to the place in which he is required in accordance with law to be detained[3].

(2) Where any person sentenced to imprisonment, or ordered to be detained in secure accommodation or in a young offenders institution, is unlawfully at large[4] at any time during the period for which he is liable to be detained in pursuance of the sentence or order, then, unless the Secretary of State otherwise directs, no account shall be taken, in calculating the period for which he is liable to be so detained, of any time during which he is absent from the place in which he is required in accordance with law to be detained:

Provided that—

(*a*) this subsection shall not apply to any period during which any such person as aforesaid is detained in pursuance of the sentence or order or in pursuance of any other sentence of any court in the United Kingdom in a prison or remand centre, in secure accommodation or in a young offenders institution;

(*b*), (*c*) (*Repealed*).

(3) The provisions of the last preceding subsection shall apply to a person who is detained in custody in default of payment of any sum of money as if he were sentenced to imprisonment.

(4) For the purposes of this section a person who, after being temporarily released in pursuance of rules made under subsection (5) of section forty-seven of this Act, is at large at any time during the period for which he is liable to be detained in pursuance of his sentence shall be deemed to be unlawfully at large if the period for which he was temporarily released has expired or if an order recalling him has been made by the Secretary of State in pursuance of the rules[5].

(5) In this section "secure accommodation" means—

(*a*) a young offender institution;
(*b*) a secure training centre; or
(*c*) any other accommodation that is secure accommodation within the meaning given by section 107(1) of the Powers of Criminal Courts (Sentencing) Act 2000 (detention and training orders).

[Prison Act 1952, s 49, as amended by the Criminal Justice Act 1961, ss 30 and 41, and Sch 4, SI 1963/597, the Criminal Justice Act 1967, s 103 and Sch 7, the Children and Young Persons Act 1969, s 72 and Sch 6, the Criminal Justice Act 1982, ss 77 and 78, and Schs 14 and 16, the Criminal Justice Act 1988, s 123 and Sch 8, the Criminal Justice and Public Order Act 1994, Sch 10, the Crime and Disorder Act 1998, Sch 8 and the Powers of Criminal Courts (Sentencing) Act 2000, Sch 9.]

1. This expression is extended to a child or young person detained in accordance with the directions of the Secretary of State (Criminal Justice Act 1967, s 67).
2. This power of arrest is preserved by the Police and Criminal Evidence Act 1984, s 26 and Sch 2.
3. See Criminal Justice Act 1967, s 72, post, for power to issue a warrant.

4. This includes a prisoner compulsorily detained in hospital under s 3 of the Mental Health Act 1983 on the date when the licence is revoked (*R (S) v Secretary of State for the Home Department* [2003] 25 LS Gaz R 46, CA).

5. For further provisions relating to the punishment and return to lawful custody of persons unlawfully at large, see the Prisoners (Return to Custody) Act 1995, this PART, post.

Criminal Justice Act 1961

(9 to 10 Eliz 2 c 39)

PART II
TREATMENT AND SUPERVISION OF PRISONERS AND OTHER DETAINED PERSONS

8–24330 22. Harbouring escaped prisoner. (1) (*Repealed*).

(2) If any person knowingly harbours[1] a person who has escaped from a prison or other institution[2] to which s 39 of the Prison Act 1952 applies, or who having been sentenced in any part of the United Kingdom or in any of the Channel Islands or the Isle of Man to imprisonment or detention, is otherwise unlawfully at large, or gives to any such person any assistance with intent to prevent, hinder or interfere with his being taken into custody, he shall be liable

(*a*) on summary conviction, to imprisonment for a term not exceeding **six months** or to a fine not exceeding **the statutory maximum**, or to **both**;

(*b*) on conviction on indictment, to imprisonment for a term not exceeding **ten years** or to a **fine** or to **both**[3].

(3) In the following enactments (which make provision for the application of sections thirty-nine to forty-two of the Prison Act 1952) that is to say, subsection (3) of section one hundred and twenty-two of the Army Act 1955, subsection (3) of section one hundred and twenty-two of the Air Force Act 1955 and subsection (3) of section eighty-two of the Naval Discipline Act 1957, references to the said section thirty-nine shall be construed as including references to subsection (2) of this section.

(4) (*Repealed*).

[Criminal Justice Act 1961, s 22, as amended by the Children and Young Persons Act 1969, s 72 and Sch 6, Criminal Law Act 1977, s 28 and the Prison Security Act 1992, s 2.]

---

1. "Harbours" means to shelter or provide refuge, but not merely to assist or support (*Darch v Weight* [1984] 2 All ER 245, [1984] 1 WLR 659, 148 JP 588).

2. This does not extend to an escape from a police yard of a prisoner under escort to a remand centre (*Nicoll v Catron* (1985) 149 JP 424, 81 Cr App Rep 339, [1985] Crim LR 223).

3. For procedure in respect of an offence triable either way, see the Magistrates' Courts Act 1980, ss 17A–21, ante.

8–24331 23. Prison rules. (1) For the purposes of rules under section forty-seven of the Prison Act 1952 (which authorises the making of rules for the regulation and management of prisons and the discipline and control of persons required to be detained therein) any offence against the rules committed by a prisoner may be treated as committed in the prison in which he is for the time being confined.

(2) Without prejudice to any power to make provision by rules under the said section forty-seven for the confiscation of money or articles conveyed or deposited in contravention of the said Act or of the rules, provision may be made by such rules for the withholding from prisoners (subject to such exceptions as may be prescribed by the rules) of any money or other article sent to them by post, and for the disposal of any such money or article either by returning it to the sender (where the sender's name and address are known) or in such other manner as may be prescribed by or determined under the rules:

Provided that in relation to a prisoner committed to prison in default of payment of any sum of money, the rules shall provide for the application of any money withheld as aforesaid in or towards the satisfaction of the amount due from him unless, upon being informed of the receipt of the money, he objects to its being so applied.

(3) A prisoner who would, apart from this subsection, be discharged on any of the days to which this subsection applies in his case shall be discharged on the next preceding day which is not one of those days.

Subject to subsection (3A), the days to which this subsection applies are Sunday, Christmas Day, Good Friday and any day which under the Bank Holidays Act 1871 is a bank holiday in England and Wales and, in the case of a person who is serving a term of more than five days, any Saturday.

(3A) In relation to a prisoner to whom an intermittent custody order under section 183 of the Criminal Justice Act 2003 relates, the only days to which subsection (3) applies are Christmas Day, Good Friday and any day which under the Banking and Financial Dealings Act 1971 is a bank holiday in England and Wales.

(4) In this section the references to prisons and prisoners include references respectively to a young offender institution, secure training centres and remand centres** and to persons detained therein.

[Criminal Justice Act 1961, s 23, as amended by the Banking and Financial Dealings Act 1971, s 4 and Sch 2, the

Criminal Justice Act 1982, s 77 and Sch 14, the Criminal Justice and Public Order Act 1994, Sch 10, the Criminal Justice Act 2003, s 186 and SI 2001/1149.]

***Subsection (3) reproduced as amended, and sub-s (3A) as inserted by the Criminal Justice Act 2003, s 186. In force for the purposes of the passing of a sentence of imprisonment to which an intermittent custody order relates and the release on licence of a person serving such a sentence.**

****Amended by the Criminal Justice and Court Services Act 2000, Sch 7 from a date to be appointed.**

PART IV
SUPPLEMENTAL

8–24339A 35. Legal custody. (1) Any person required or authorised by or under this Act to be taken to any place or to be kept in custody shall, while being so taken or kept, be deemed to be in legal custody.

(2) A constable, or any other person required or authorised by or under this Act to take any person to or keep him at any place shall, while taking or keeping him there have all the powers, authorities, protection and privileges which a constable has within the area for which he acts as constable.
[Criminal Justice Act 1961, s 35.]

8–24339B 37. Secretary of State's report. In any case where a court is required by this Act to consider a report made by or on behalf of the Secretary of State in respect of an offender, the court shall cause a copy of the report to be given to the offender or his counsel or solicitor.
[Criminal Justice Act 1961, s 37.]

8–24339C 38. Construction of references to sentence of imprisonment, etc. (1) Except as provided by subsection (3) of this section, the expression "sentence" in this Act does not include a committal for default or the fixing of a term to be served in the event of default, or a committal or attachment for contempt of court.

(2) For the purposes of any provisions of this Act referring to a person who is serving or has served a sentence of any description, the expression "sentence" includes—

(*a*) in any case, a sentence of that description passed by a court in Scotland, Northern Ireland, any of the Channel Islands or the Isle of Man; and

(*b*) in the case of imprisonment, a sentence passed by a court-martial on a person found guilty of a civil offence (within the meaning of the Naval Discipline Act 1957, the Army Act 1955, or the Air Force Act 1955), and a sentence which is treated by virtue of the Colonial Prisoners Removal Act 1884, as a sentence passed by a court in England and Wales.

(3) For the purposes of sections twenty-two and thirty-four of this Act—

(*a*) the expression "imprisonment or detention" means imprisonment, custody for life, detention in a young offenders institution or in a secure training centre or detention under an equivalent sentence passed by a court in the Channel Islands or the Isle of Man;

(*b*) the expression "sentence" includes a sentence passed by a court-martial for any offence, and any order made by any court imposing imprisonment or detention, and "sentenced" shall be construed accordingly;

(*c*) any reference to a person serving a sentence of, or sentenced to, imprisonment or detention shall be construed as including a reference to a person who, under any enactment relating to children and young persons in force in any part of the United Kingdom or any of the Channel Islands or the Isle of Man, has been sentenced by a court to be detained for an offence and is liable to be detained in accordance with directions given by the Secretary of State, . . . or by the Governor of the Isle of Man with the concurrence of the Secretary of State, and any other reference to a sentence of imprisonment or detention shall be construed accordingly.

(4) For the purposes of any reference in this Act to a term of imprisonment or of detention in a young offender institution or to a term of imprisonment or detention, consecutive terms and terms which are wholly or partly concurrent shall be treated as a single term.

(5) (*Repealed*).

(6) The Secretary of State may by order[1] designate as equivalent sentences for the purposes of this Act a description of sentence which a court with jurisdiction in one part of the United Kingdom or in the Channel Islands or the Isle of Man may pass and a description of sentence which a court elsewhere in the United Kingdom or in those Islands may pass.
[Criminal Justice Act 1961, s 38, amended by the Criminal Justice (Scotland) Act 1963, Sch 5, the Criminal Justice Act 1982, Schs 14 and 16, the Criminal Justice Act 1988, Sch 8, the Criminal Justice and Public Order Act 1994, Sch 10 and the Crime (Sentences) Act 1997, Sch 6.]

---

1. Transfer of Offenders (Designation of Equivalent Sentences) Order 1983, SI 1983/1314, amended by SI 1988/1654, has been made.

8–24339D 39. Interpretation. (1) In this Act, unless the context otherwise requires the following expressions have the meanings hereby assigned to them, that is to say—

"court-martial" includes the Courts-Martial Appeal Court and any officer exercising jurisdiction under s 49 of the Naval Discipline Act 1957;

"default" means failure to pay, or want of sufficient distress to satisfy, any fine or other sum of money, or failure to do or abstain from doing any thing required to be done or left undone;

"enactment" includes an enactment of the Parliament of Northern Ireland;

"prison" does not include a naval, military or air force prison;

(1A) *Repealed.*

(1B) Any reference in this Act to a sentence being equivalent to another sentence is to be construed as a reference to its having been so designated under section 38(6) of this Act.

(2) Except as otherwise expressly provided, references in this Act to a court do not include references to a court-martial; and nothing in this Act shall be construed as affecting the punishment which may be awarded by a court-martial under the Naval Discipline Act 1957, the Army Act 1955, or the Air Force Act 1955, for a civil offence within the meaning of those Acts.

(3) Where the age of any person at any time is material for the purposes of any provision of this Act regulating the powers of a court or justice of the peace, his age at the material time shall be deemed to be or to have been that which appears to the court or justice, after considering any available evidence, to be or to have been his age at that time.

(4) Any reference in this Act to any other enactment is a reference thereto as amended, and includes a reference thereto as extended or applied, by or under any other enactment, including this Act.

[Criminal Justice Act 1961, s 39, amended by Criminal Justice (Scotland) Act 1963, Sch 5, Powers of Criminal Courts Act 1973, Sch 5, Criminal Law Act 1977, Sch 12, the Criminal Justice Act 1982, Schs 14 and 16 and the Crime (Sentences) Act 1997, Sch 6.]

8–24339E 44. *Commencement.*

8–24339F 45. *Short title.*

Criminal Justice Act 1967

(1967 c 80)

8–24340 72. Power of magistrates to issue warrants for arrest of escaped prisoners and mental patients. (1) On an information in writing being laid before a justice of the peace for any area in England and Wales or Northern Ireland and substantiated on oath, or alleging that any person is—

(*a*) an offender unlawfully at large from a prison or other institution to which the Prison Act applies in which he is required to be detained after being convicted of an offence; or

(*b*) a convicted mental patient liable to be retaken under section 18, 38(7) or 138 of the Mental Health Act 1983, s 36 or 106 of the Mental Health (Scotland) Act 1960 or s 30 or 108 of the Mental Health Act (Northern Ireland) 1961 (retaking of mental patients who are absent without leave or have escaped from custody)[1];

the justice may issue a warrant to arrest him and bring him before a magistrates' court for that area.

(2) Where a person is brought before a magistrates' court in pursuance of a warrant for his arrest under this section, the court shall, if satisfied that he is the person named in the warrant and if satisfied as to the facts mentioned in paragraph (*a*) or (*b*) of the foregoing subsection, order him to be returned to the prison or other institution where he is required or liable to be detained or, in the case of a convicted mental patient, order him to be kept in custody or detained in a place of safety pending his admission to hospital.

(3) Section 137 of the Mental Health Act 1983[1], s 105 of the Mental Health (Scotland) Act 1960 and s 107 of the Mental Health Act (Northern Ireland) 1961 (custody, conveyance and detention of certain mental patients) shall apply to a convicted mental patient required by this section to be conveyed to any place or to be kept in custody or detained in a place of safety as they apply to a person required by or by virtue of the said Act of 1983, 1960 or 1961, as the case may be, to be so conveyed or kept.

(4) In this section—

"convicted mental patient" means a person liable after being convicted of an offence to be detained under Part III of the Mental Health Act 1983, Part V of the Mental Health (Scotland) Act 1960 or Part III of the Mental Health Act (Northern Ireland) 1961 in pursuance of a hospital order or transfer direction together with an order or direction restricting his discharge or in pursuance of a hospital direction and a limitation direction or a person liable to be detained under section 38 of the said Act of 1983;

"place of safety" has the same meaning as in Part III of the said Act of 1983 or 1960 or Part III of the said Act of 1961, as the case may be;

"Prison Act" means the Prison Act 1952, the Prisons (Scotland) Act [1989] or the Prison Act (Northern Ireland) 1953, as the case may be.

(5) Section 27 of the Criminal Justice Administration Act 1914 (power to issue warrants for the arrest of persons who may be arrested without a warrant) shall cease to have effect.

[Criminal Justice Act 1967, s 72 as amended by the Mental Health (Amendment) Act 1982, Sch 3, the Mental Health Act 1983, Sch 4 and the Crime (Sentences) Act 1997, Sch 4.]

---

1. See title MENTAL HEALTH, ante.

Prison Security Act 1992

(1992 c 25)

8–24341 1. Offence of prison mutiny. (1) Any prisoner who takes part in a prison mutiny shall be guilty of an offence[1] and liable, on conviction on indictment, to imprisonment for a term not exceeding **ten years** or to a **fine** or to **both**.

(2) For the purposes of this section there is a prison mutiny where two or more prisoners, while on the premises of any prison, engage in conduct which is intended to further a common purpose of overthrowing[2] lawful authority in that prison.

(3) For the purposes of this section the intentions and common purpose of prisoners may be inferred from the form and circumstances of their conduct and it shall be immaterial that conduct falling within subsection (2) above takes a different form in the case of different prisoners.

(4) Where there is a prison mutiny, a prisoner who has or is given a reasonable opportunity of submitting to lawful authority[2] and fails, without reasonable excuse, to do so shall be regarded for the purposes of this section as taking part in the mutiny.

(5) Proceedings for an offence under this section shall not be brought except by or with the consent of the Director of Public Prosecutions.

(6) In this section—

"conduct" includes acts and omissions;

"prison" means any prison, young offender institution or remand centre* which is under the general superintendence of, or is provided by, the Secretary of State under the Prison Act 1952, including a contracted out prison within the meaning of Part IV of the Criminal Justice Act 1991;

"prisoner" means any person for the time being in a prison as a result of any requirement imposed by a court or otherwise that he be detained in legal custody.

[Prison Security Act 1992, s 1.]

***Amended by the Criminal Justice and Court Services Act 2000, Sch 7 from a date to be appointed.**

1. This provision creates only one offence although it may be committed in distinct ways which involve different levels of wrongdoing. Accordingly, any indictment should make clear which type of conduct is alleged (*R v Mason* [2004] EWCA Crim 2173, [2005] 1 Cr App R 11, [2005] Crim LR 140).

2. The concept of "overthrowing" is a stronger one than "subverting" and is not synonymous with a refusal to obey lawful orders and for the offence described in sub-s (4) to be committed, there must already be a mutiny occurring (*R v Mason* supra).

Prisoners (Return to Custody) Act 1995

(1995 c 16)

8–24342 1. Remaining at large after temporary release. (1) Subject to subsection (2) below, a person who has been temporarily released in pursuance of rules made under section 47(5) of the Prison Act 1952 (rules for temporary release) is guilty of an offence if—

(*a*) without reasonable excuse, he remains unlawfully at large at any time after becoming so at large by virtue of the expiry of the period for which he was temporarily released; or

(*b*) knowing or believing an order recalling him to have been made and while unlawfully at large by virtue of such an order, he fails, without reasonable excuse, to take all necessary steps for complying as soon as reasonably practicable with that order.

(2) Subsection (1) above shall not apply in the case of a person temporarily released from a secure training centre.

(3) A person guilty of any offence under this section shall be liable, on summary conviction, to imprisonment for a term not exceeding **six months** or to a fine not exceeding **level 5** on the standard scale, or to **both**.

(4) An offence under this section shall be taken to be committed at the place where the offender was required to be detained immediately before being temporarily released.

(5) A person shall be deemed for the purposes of this section to be unlawfully at large whenever he is deemed to be so at large for the purposes of section 49 of the Prison Act 1952 (which confers powers of arrest).

(6) This section shall not apply where the period of temporary release expired, or the order of recall was made, before the commencement of this section.
[Prisoners (Return to Custody) Act 1995, s 1.]

8–24343 **3.** *Short title, commencement and extent.*

Prisoners' Earnings Act 1996[1]

(1996 c 33)

8–24344 **1. Power to make deductions and impose levies.** (1) This section applies where—

(*a*) a prisoner is paid for enhanced wages work done by him; and
(*b*) his net weekly earnings in respect of the work exceed such amount as may be prescribed.

(2) Where the prisoner's net weekly earnings fall to be paid by the governor on behalf of the Secretary of State, the governor may make a deduction from those earnings of an amount not exceeding the prescribed percentage of the excess.

(3) Where those earnings fall to be paid otherwise than as mentioned in subsection (2) above, the governor may impose a levy on those earnings of an amount not exceeding that percentage of the excess.

(4) In this section—

"enhanced wages work", in relation to a prisoner, means any work—

(*a*) which is not directed work, that is to say, work which he is directed to do in pursuance of prison rules; and
(*b*) to which the rates of pay and productivity applicable are higher than those that would be applicable if it were directed work;

"net weekly earnings" means weekly earnings after deduction of such of the following as are applicable, namely—

(*a*) income tax;
(*b*) national insurance contributions;
(*c*) payments required to be made by an order of a court; and
(*d*) payments required to be made by virtue of a maintenance calculation within the meaning of the Child Support Act 1991.*

[Prisoners' Earnings Act 1996, s 1as amended by the Child Support, Pensions and Social Security Act 2000, Sch 3.]

***Reproduced as amended by the Child Support, Pensions and Social Security Act 2000, Sch 3 and in force in relation to certain cases: see SI 2003/192.**

1. The Prisoners Earnings Act 1996 shall come into force on such day or days as the Secretary of State may by order made by statutory instrument appoint (s 5(2), post). At the date of going to press no order has been made.

8–24345 **2. Application of amounts deducted or levied.** (1) Amounts deducted or levied under section 1 above shall be applied, in such proportions as may be prescribed, for the following purposes, namely—

(*a*) the making of payments (directly or indirectly) to such voluntary organisations concerned with victim support or crime prevention or both as may be prescribed;
(*b*) the making of payments into the Consolidated Fund with a view to contributing towards the cost of the prisoner's upkeep;
(*c*) the making of payments to or in respect of such persons (if any) as may be determined by the governor to be dependants of the prisoner in such proportions as may be so determined; and
(*d*) the making of payments into an investment account of a prescribed description with a view to capital and interest being held for the benefit of the prisoner on such terms as may be prescribed.

(2) Where the governor determines under paragraph (*c*) of subsection (1) above that the prisoner has no dependants, any amount which would otherwise have been applied for the purpose mentioned in that paragraph shall be applied for the purpose mentioned in paragraph (*d*) of that subsection.

(3) Where the prisoner is aggrieved by a determination of the governor under subsection (1)(*c*) above, he may appeal against the determination to the Secretary of State.

(4) On such appeal, the Secretary of State may confirm the governor's determination or direct the governor to vary it, so far as relating to amounts deducted or levied after the after the giving of the direction, in such manner as may be specified in the direction.
[Prisoners' Earnings Act 1996, s 2.]

8–24346 **3. Statements of account.** (1) The governor shall, for each week in which an amount is deducted or levied under section 1 above, furnish the prisoner with a statement—

(*a*) showing that amount; and
(*b*) giving details of the manner in which the prescribed proportion of that amount is to be applied for the purpose mentioned in section 2(1)(*c*) above.

(2) Where amounts have been deducted or levied under section 1 above, the governor shall, on a request which is neither frivolous nor vexatious, furnish the prisoner with a statement showing the amount for the time being standing to the credit of the investment account mentioned in section 2(1)(*d*) above.
[Prisoners' Earnings Act 1996, s 3.]

8–24347 **4. Interpretation.** (1) In the application of this Act to a contracted out prison—

(*a*) any reference to the governor shall be construed as a reference to the director; and
(*b*) the reference to the Secretary of State in section 1 above shall be construed as a reference to the person running the prison.

(2) In the application of this Act to England and Wales—

"contracted out prison" has the meaning given by section 92(1) of the Criminal Justice Act 1991;
"prescribed" means prescribed by prison rules;
"prisoner" includes a prisoner on temporary release and a person required to be detained in a young offender institution or remand centre;*
"prison rules" means rules made under section 47 of the Prison Act 1952.

(3) Scotland
[Prisoners' Earnings Act 1996, s 4.]

***Repealed by the Criminal Justice and Court Services Act 2000, Sch 8 from a date to be appointed.**

8–24348 **5. Short title, commencement and extent.** (1) This Act may be cited as the Prisoners' Earnings Act 1996

(2) This Act shall come into force on such day as the Secretary of State may by order made by statutory instrument appoint; and different days may be appointed for different purposes[1].

(3) this Act does not extend to Northern Ireland.
[Prisoners' Earnings Act 1996, s 5.]

---

1. As to commencement orders which had been made at the date of going to press, see note 1 to the short title of this Act, ante.

Secure Training Centre Rules 1998[1]

(SI 1998/472 amended by SI 2003/3005)

8–24410 **1. Citation and commencement.** These Rules may be cited as the Secure Training Centre Rules 1998 and shall come into force on 16th April 1998.

---

1. Made by the Secretary of State, in pursuance of s 47 of the Prison Act 1952 and s 7 of the Criminal Justice and Public Order Act 1994. Security Training Orders made under the 1994 Act have been replaced by the Detention and Training Orders made under the Crime and Disorder Act 1998 with effect from 1 April 2000.

8–24411 **2. Interpretation.** In these Rules unless the contrary intention appears the expression:
"centre" means a secure training centre;
"compulsory school age" has the meaning assigned to it in section 8 of the Education Act 1996;
"convicted trainee" means a trainee who has been ordered to be detained in consequence of his conviction for an offence, and the expression "unconvicted trainee" shall be construed accordingly;
"governor" includes an officer for the time being in charge of a centre;
"independent person" means a person appointed under rule 44 to visit centres and to whom representations may be made by trainees;
"legal adviser" means, in relation to a trainee, his counsel or solicitor, and includes a clerk acting on behalf of his solicitor;
"officer" means an officer of a centre; and
"trainee" means a person detained in a centre.

8–24412 **3. Statement of purpose.** (1) The aims of a centre shall be—

(*a*) to accommodate trainees in a safe environment within secure conditions; and
(*b*) to help trainees prepare for their return to the outside community.

(2) The aim mentioned in paragraph (1)(*b*) above shall be achieved, in particular, by—

(*a*) providing a positive regime offering high standards of education and training;
(*b*) in the case of convicted trainees, establishing a programme designed to tackle the offending behaviour of each trainee and to assist in his development;
(*c*) fostering links between the trainee and the outside community; and
(*d*) in the case of convicted trainees, co-operating with the services responsible for the trainee's supervision after release.

(3) A statement of the aims mentioned in paragraph (1) above and how they are to be achieved shall be prepared and displayed in each centre and shall be made available on request—

(*a*) to trainees;
(*b*) to any person visiting the centre; and
(*c*) to any person inspecting the centre.

8–24413 **4. Classification.** Trainees may be classified, in accordance with any direction of the Secretary of State, taking into account their ages, characters and circumstances.

8–24414 **5. Temporary release.** (1) A trainee may be temporarily released for any period or periods and subject to any conditions.

(2) A trainee released under this rule may be recalled at any time whether any conditions of his release have been broken or not.

8–24415 **6. Privileges.** (1) There shall be established at every centre systems of privileges, incentives and sanctions approved by the Secretary of State and appropriate to the classes of trainees and their ages, characters and circumstances.

(2) Records shall be kept in writing of any privileges or incentives earned and sanctions awarded.

8–24415A **7.** *Information to trainees*

8–24416 **8. Grievance procedure.** (1) There shall be established and administered at each centre a comprehensive grievance procedure, approved by the Secretary of State, to which each trainee and his parent shall have access.

(2) Every request by a trainee to see the governor or an independent person shall be recorded by the officer to whom it is made and promptly passed on to the governor.

(3) On every day, the governor shall hear any requests to see him that are made under paragraph (2) above.

(4) Where a trainee has asked to see an independent person, the governor shall ensure that that person is told of the request as soon as possible.

(5) A written request or complaint under the grievance procedure established under this rule may be made in confidence.

8–24417 **9. Visits generally.** (1) There shall be established at every centre arrangements, approved by the Secretary of State, for trainees to receive visits.

(2) Arrangements established under paragraph (1) above shall take account of—

(*a*) the importance of contact by a trainee with his family, and
(*b*) the need to keep to a minimum any disruption of his education and training.

(3) Subject to the provisions of these Rules, the governor may give such directions as he thinks fit for the supervision of visits to trainees, either generally or in a particular case:

Provided that such directions shall be designed to secure that supervision is not unnecessarily intrusive.

8–24418 **10. Letters generally.** (1) The Secretary of State may, with a view to securing discipline and good order or the prevention of crime or in the interests of any persons, impose restrictions, either generally or in a particular case, upon the communications to be permitted between a trainee and other persons.

(2) Except as provided by these Rules, a trainee shall not be permitted to communicate with any outside person, or that person with him, without the leave of the Secretary of State.

(3) Except as provided by these Rules, every letter or communication to or from a trainee may be read or examined by the governor or any officer deputed by him and the governor may, at his discretion, stop any communication on the ground that its contents are objectionable or of inordinate length.

8–24419 **11. Personal letters, telephone calls and visits.** (1) A trainee shall be entitled—

(*a*) to send three letters a week, the cost of which shall be met by the centre; and
(*b*) to receive a visit once a week.

(2) Subject to the provisions of these Rules a trainee shall in addition to his entitlement under paragraph (1) above be entitled to send any number of letters at his own expense, to receive any

number of letters, to make and receive any number of telephone calls at his own expense and to receive visits.

(3) The normal duration of a visit to which a trainee is entitled by virtue of paragraph (1)(*b*) above shall be one hour.

8–24420 **12. Police interviews.** A police officer may, on production of an order issued by or on behalf of a chief officer of police, interview any trainee willing to see him.

8–24421 **13. Legal advisers.** (1) The legal adviser of a trainee in any legal proceedings, civil or criminal, to which the trainee is a party shall be afforded reasonable facilities for interviewing him in connection with those proceedings and may do so out of hearing of an officer.

(2) A trainee's legal adviser may, with the leave of the Secretary of State, interview the trainee in connection with any other legal business.

8–24422 **14. Correspondence with legal advisers and courts.** (1) A trainee may correspond with his legal adviser and any court and such correspondence may only be opened, read or stopped by the governor in accordance with the provisions of this rule.

(2) Correspondence to which this rule applies may be opened if the governor has reasonable cause to believe that it contains an illicit enclosure and any such enclosure shall be dealt with in accordance with the other provisions of these Rules.

(3) Correspondence to which this rule applies may be opened, read and stopped if the governor has reasonable cause to believe its contents endanger security in the centre or the safety of others or are otherwise of a criminal nature.

(4) A trainee shall be given the opportunity to be present when any correspondence to which this rule applies is opened and shall be informed if it or any enclosure is to be read or stopped.

(5) A trainee shall on request be provided with any writing materials necessary for the purposes of paragraph (1) of this rule.

(6) In this rule, "court" includes the European Commission of Human Rights, the European Court of Human Rights and the European Court of Justice; and "illicit enclosure" includes any article possession of which has not been authorised in accordance with the other provisions of these Rules and any correspondence to or from a person other than the trainee concerned, his legal adviser or a court.

8–24423 **15.** *Clothing*

8–24424 **16.** *Food*

8–24425 **17.** *Alcohol and tobacco*

8–24426 **18.** *Accommodation*

8–24427 **19.** *Beds and bedding*

8–24428 **20.** *Hygiene*

8–24429 **21.** *Library books*

8–24430 **22.** *Medical attendance*

8–24431 **23. Self-harm and suicide assessment.** (1) Every trainee shall, as soon as possible after his reception into the centre and in any case within 24 hours, be interviewed by a social worker and by a member of the healthcare staff with a view to assessing whether and, if so, the extent to which he has suicidal intentions or a propensity to harm himself.

(2) A written assessment of the trainee shall be prepared as soon as practicable after such an interview has concluded.

(3) The assessment prepared under paragraph (2) above shall be reviewed at regular intervals throughout the period of the trainee's detention in the centre and each trainee shall be monitored by a social worker or member of healthcare staff for that purpose.

8–24432 **24. Special illnesses and conditions.** (1) The medical officer shall report to the governor on the case of any trainee whose health is likely to be injuriously affected by continued detention or any conditions of detention. The governor shall send the report to the Secretary of State without delay together with his own recommendations.

(2) The medical officer shall pay special attention to any trainee whose mental condition appears to require it, and make any special arrangements which appear necessary for his supervision or care.

(3) The medical officer shall inform the governor immediately if he suspects any trainee of having suicidal intentions or a propensity to harm himself, and the trainee shall be placed under special observation.

8–24433 **25. Notification of illness or death.** (1) If a trainee dies or becomes seriously ill, sustains any serious injury or is removed to hospital on account of mental disorder, the governor shall at once inform the trainee's parent or guardian, and also any person who the trainee may reasonably have asked should be informed.

(2) If a trainee dies, the governor shall give notice immediately to the coroner having jurisdiction, to the Secretary of State and to the person authorised under rule 43(1) to inspect the centre.

8–24433A **26.** *Religious observance*

8–24434 **27. Regime activities.** (1) A trainee shall be occupied in education, training, physical education and, in the case of a convicted trainee, programmes designed to tackle offending behaviour provided in accordance with rule 3 of these Rules.

(2) For the purpose of determining the appropriate activities under this rule for individual trainees, each trainee shall be assessed as soon as practicable after the date of his reception into the centre and, within 2 weeks of that date, a training plan shall be prepared.

(3) The training plan for each trainee shall be reviewed—

(*a*) in the case of a trainee who is ordered to be detained for a period of 6 months or less or an unconvicted trainee, every two months; and

(*b*) in the case of a trainee who is ordered to be detained for a period of more than 6 months, every three months.

(4) The preparation and reviewing of a trainee's training plan shall be undertaken in consultation with—

(*a*) in the case of a convicted trainee, the services responsible for the trainee's supervision after release;

(*b*) in the case of an unconvicted trainee, an officer of the local authority which is looking after the trainee (within the meaning of section 22(1) of the Children Act 1989); and

(*c*) in all cases, the trainee's parent or guardian.

(5) An officer of the centre shall be nominated by the governor for the purposes of preparing, supervising and reviewing the training plan of each trainee and carrying out the consultation referred to in paragraph (4) above.

(6) The medical officer or a member of the healthcare staff may excuse a trainee from any activity on medical grounds; and no trainee shall be set to participate in any activity for which he is considered by the medical officer or, as the case may be, member of healthcare staff, to be unfit.

8–22435 **28.** *Education and training*

8–24436 **29.** *Outside contacts*

8–24437 **30. After care.** (1) From the beginning of his period of detention, consideration shall be given to a trainee's future and the help to be given to him in preparation for and after his return to the community, in consultation with the appropriate supervising service, in the case of a convicted trainee, or an officer of the local authority which is looking after the trainee (within the meaning of section 22(1) of the Children Act 1989), in the case of an unconvicted trainee.

(2) Every convicted trainee shall be given a careful explanation of his liability to supervision after release and the requirements to which he will be subject while under supervision.

(3) The training plan prepared for a trainee under rule 27 of these Rules shall have regard to the need to help the trainee in preparation for and after his return to the community and, in the case of a trainee who will be of compulsory school age at the date of that return, to education in the community.

8–24438 **31. Maintenance of order and discipline.** (1) Order and discipline shall be maintained in a centre, but with no more restriction than is required in the interests of security and well-ordered community life.

(2) In the control of trainees, officers shall seek to influence them through their own example and leadership, and to enlist their willing co-operation.

8–24439 **32. Custody outside a centre.** (1) A trainee being taken to or from a centre in custody shall be exposed as little as possible to public observation and proper care shall be taken to protect him from curiosity and insult.

(2) A trainee required to be taken in custody anywhere outside a centre shall be kept in the custody of a custody officer or of a police officer.

8–24440 **33. Search.** (1) Every trainee shall be searched on his reception into a centre and subsequently as the governor thinks necessary.

(2) A trainee shall be searched in as seemly a manner as is consistent with discovering anything concealed.

(3) No trainee shall be stripped and searched—

(*a*) without the authority of the governor;
(*b*) in the presence of more than two officers; and
(*c*) in the sight of another trainee or in the sight or presence of an officer not of the same sex.

(4) A written record shall be kept of any search to which paragraph (3) above applies which shall specify—

(*a*) the name of the trainee;
(*b*) the reason for the search;
(*c*) when the search was carried out;
(*d*) who authorised the search and who carried it out; and
(*e*) what, if anything, was found as a result of the search.

8-24441 **34. Record and photograph.** (1) A personal record of each trainee shall be prepared, maintained and preserved in such manner and for such period as the Secretary of State may direct, but no part of the record shall be disclosed to any person not authorised to receive it.

(2) Every trainee may be photographed on reception and subsequently, but no copy of the photograph shall be given to any person not authorised to receive it.

8-24442 **35. Trainees' property.** (1) Anything, other than cash, which a trainee has at a centre and which he is not allowed to retain for his own use shall be taken into the governor's custody and shall be listed in an inventory.

(2) Any cash which a trainee has at a centre shall be paid into an account under the control of the governor and the trainee shall be credited with the amount in the books of the centre.

(3) The governor may confiscate any unauthorised article found in the possession of a trainee after his reception into a centre, or concealed or deposited within a centre.

8-24443 **36. Removal from association.** (1) Where it appears to be necessary in the interests of preventing him from causing significant harm to himself or to any other person or significant damage to property that a trainee should not associate with other trainees, either generally or for particular purposes, the governor may arrange for the trainee's removal from association accordingly.

(2) A trainee shall not be removed under this rule unless all other appropriate methods of control have been applied without success.

(3) A trainee who is placed in his own room during normal waking hours in accordance with arrangements made under this rule shall—

(*a*) be observed at least once in every period of 15 minutes;
(*b*) not be left unaccompanied during normal waking hours for a continuous period of more than 3 hours nor for periods which total in aggregate more than 3 hours in any period of 24 hours;
(*c*) be released from the room as soon as it is no longer necessary for the purposes mentioned in paragraph (1) above that he be removed from association; and
(*d*) be informed both orally and in writing of the reasons for such placement.

(4) A record shall be kept of each occasion on which a trainee is removed from association under this rule which shall specify—

(*a*) the name of the trainee;
(*b*) the date and time removal commenced and finished;
(*c*) who authorised it;
(*d*) the reasons for it and that the trainee was informed in accordance with paragraph (3)(*d*) above; and
(*e*) any observations made in accordance with paragraph (3)(*a*) above;

and the record kept in accordance with this paragraph shall be made available, upon request, to the person authorised under rule 43(1) of these Rules to inspect the centre.

8-24444 **37. Use of force.** (1) An officer in dealing with a trainee shall not use force unnecessarily and, when the application of force to a trainee is necessary, no more force than is necessary shall be used.

(2) No officer shall act deliberately in a manner calculated to provoke a trainee.

8-24445 **38. Physical restraint.** (1) No trainee shall be physically restrained save where necessary for the purpose of preventing him from—

(*a*) escaping from custody;
(*b*) injuring himself or others;
(*c*) damaging property; or
(*d*) inciting another trainee to do anything specified in paragraph (*b*) or (*c*) above,

and then only where no alternative method of preventing the event specified in any of paragraphs (*a*) to (*d*) above is available.

(2) No trainee shall be physically restrained under this rule except in accordance with methods

approved by the Secretary of State and by an officer who has undergone a course of training which is so approved.

(3) Particulars of every occasion on which a trainee is physically restrained under this rule shall be recorded within 12 hours of its occurrence.

8–24446 **39.** *Officers of secure training centres*

8–24447 **40.** *Prohibited articles*

8–24448 **41.** *Control of persons and vehicles*

8–24449 **42. Viewing of secure training centres.** (1) No outside person shall be permitted to view a centre unless authorised by the Secretary of State.

(2) No person viewing a centre shall be permitted to take a photograph, make a sketch or communicate with a trainee unless authorised by the Secretary of State.

8–24450 **43. Inspection of centres.** (1) The Secretary of State may cause any centre to be inspected by persons who are for the time being authorised to conduct inspections under section 80 of the Children Act 1989.

(2) A person conducting an inspection under this rule may be accompanied by Her Majesty's Chief Inspector of Prisons or a person designated by him and by one or more of Her Majesty's Inspectors of Schools in England.

(3) Any person conducting an inspection under this rule or accompanying him in accordance with paragraph (2) above may for that purpose—

(*a*) enter any part of the premises of the centre;
(*b*) conduct an interview with any officer or trainee; and
(*c*) examine any records relating to the centre.

(4) A person who has conducted an inspection under this rule shall report in writing to the Secretary of State and the report shall be published in such manner as the Secretary of State may direct.

8–24451 **44. Appointment of independent persons.** (1) The Secretary of State may appoint independent persons to visit a centre.

(2) Any trainee may make representations to a person appointed under this rule; and for that purpose the governor shall make arrangements for such a person to interview the trainee and to receive representations from him.

(3) A person appointed under this rule shall be entitled to have access to any records relating to the centre except that the medical records relating to any trainee or the personal records of any officer shall not be made available to him without the consent of the trainee or, as the case may be, officer concerned.

(4) A person appointed under this rule shall draw to the attention of the Secretary of State any matter which is of concern to him.

8–24452 **45.** *Delegation by governor*

8–24453 **46. Contracted-out secure training centres.** (1) In their application to a centre which is a contracted-out secure training centre these Rules shall have effect with the following modifications.

(2) For any reference to the governor there shall be substituted a reference to the director.

(3) For any reference to an officer there shall be substituted a reference to a custody officer.

(4) In rule 6(2), at the end there shall be added the words "and the monitor shall be entitled to have access to such records".

(5) In rule 8, at the end there shall be added the following paragraph:

"(6) Where a person is dissatisfied with the outcome of any request or complaint made by him under the grievance procedure established under this rule he may appeal to the monitor, who shall thereupon consider the request or complaint, and any such appeal may be made in confidence."

(6) In rule 10, at the end there shall be added the following paragraph:

"(4) No letter or communication shall be read or examined, and no communication shall be stopped, under paragraph (3) above without the approval of the monitor.".

(7) In rule 15(2), at the end there shall be added the words "and the trainee may appeal from that refusal to the monitor".

(8) In rule 24, at the end there shall be added the following paragraph:

"(4) The monitor shall be informed as soon as practicable and in any event within 12 hours of any trainee having been placed under special observation under paragraph (3) above.".

(9) In rule 25—

(*a*) in paragraph (1) after the word "inform" there shall be inserted the words "the monitor,"; and
(*b*) at the end there shall be added the following paragraph:

"(3) If a trainee in respect of whom notification is given under paragraph (1) above has suffered serious harm, or it is alleged that he has been the subject of any form of abuse, notification shall also be given to a constable and, if in the opinion of the director such harm or abuse is caused by the conduct of any custody officer or other member of the staff of the centre, the monitor.".

(10) In the rule 29(3), at the end there shall be added the words "and subject to the approval of the monitor".

(11) In rule 33, at the end there shall be added the following paragraph:

"(5) The monitor shall be informed within 24 hours of any search to which paragraph (3) above applies and he shall be provided with a copy of the record kept under paragraph (4) above of that search.".

(12) In rule 36, at the end there shall be added the following paragraph:

"(5) The monitor shall be informed within 24 hours of the commencement of any removal from association under this rule and he shall be provided with a copy of the record kept under paragraph (4) above in relation to that removal.".

(13) In rule 38(3), after the word "recorded" there shall be inserted the words "and notified to the monitor".

(14) After rule 45 there shall be inserted the following rule:

"**45A.** (1) The monitor appointed by the Secretary of State in relation to a contracted-out centre shall have the functions specified in respect of him in the foregoing provisions of these Rules as they have effect in accordance with rule 46 of these Rules.

(2) The director appointed by the contractor in relation to a contracted-out centre shall have—

(*a*) the functions specified in respect of him in the foregoing provisions of these Rules as they have effect in accordance with rule 46 of these Rules; and

(*b*) the following additional functions, namely—

(*i*) to promote and safeguard the welfare of the trainees detained in that centre;

(ii) to co-operate with the monitor appointed in relation to that centre and to facilitate the discharge by him of his duties and functions; and

(iii) to issue a notice to each convicted trainee prior to his release from the centre which specifies the requirements with which he must comply following his release.".

Prison Rules 1999[1]

(SI 1999/728 amended by SI 2000/1149, 1794 and 2641, SI 2001/1149, SI 2002/2116, SI 2003/3301 and SI 2005/869 and 3437)

PART I

INTERPRETATION

GENERAL

8–24454 1. Citation and commencement. These Rules may be cited as the Prison Rules 1999 and shall come into force on 1st April 1999.

1. Made by the Secretary of State under the Prison Act 1962, s 47.

8–24455 2. Interpretation. (1) In these Rules, where the context so admits, the expression—

"adjudicator" means a District Judge (Magistrates' Courts) or Deputy District Judge (Magistrates' Courts) approved[1] by the Lord Chancellor for the purpose of inquiring into a charge which has been referred to him;

"communication" includes any written or drawn communication from a prisoner to any other person, whether intended to be transmitted by means of a postal service or not, and any communication from a prisoner to any other person transmitted by means of a telecommunications system;

"controlled drug" means any drug which is a controlled drug for the purposes of the Misuse of Drugs Act 1971;

"convicted prisoner" means, subject to the provisions of rule 7(3), a prisoner who has been convicted or found guilty of an offence or committed or attached for contempt of court or for failing to do or abstain from doing anything required to be done or left undone, and the expression "unconvicted prisoner" shall be construed accordingly;

"fixed term prisoner has the meaning assigned to it by section 237(1) of the Criminal Justice Act 2003";

"governor" includes an officer for the time being in charge of a prison;

"health care professional" means a person who is a member of a profession regulated by a body mentioned in section 25(3) of the National Health Service Reform and Health Care Professions Act 2002 and who is working within the prison pursuant to rule 20(3);

"intercepted material" means the contents of any communication intercepted pursuant to these Rules;

"intermittent custody order" has the meaning assigned to it by section 183 of the Criminal Justice Act 2003;

"legal adviser" means, in relation to a prisoner, his counsel or solicitor, and includes a clerk acting on behalf of his solicitor;

"officer" means an officer of a prison and, for the purposes of rule 40(2), includes a prisoner custody officer who is authorised to perform escort functions in accordance with section 89 of the Criminal Justice Act 1991;

"prison minister" means, in relation to a prison, a minister appointed to that prison under section 10 of the Prison Act 1952;

"registered medical practitioner" and "registered nurse" mean a practitioner or nurse who is working within the prison pursuant to rule 20(3);

"short-term prisoner" and "long-term prisoner" have the meanings assigned to them by section 33(5) of the Criminal Justice Act 1991, as extended by sections 43(1) and 45(1) of that Act;

"telecommunications system" means any system (including the apparatus comprised in it) which exists for the purpose of facilitating the transmission of communications by any means involving the use of electrical or electro-magnetic energy;"the 2003 Act" means the Criminal Justice Act 2003.

(2) In these Rules—

(a) a reference to an award of additional days means additional days awarded under these Rules by virtue of section 42 of the Criminal Justice Act 1991 or by virtue of section 257 of the 2003 Act;

(b) a reference to the Church of England includes a reference to the Church in Wales; and

(c) a reference to a numbered rule is, unless otherwise stated, a reference to the rule of that number in these Rules and a reference in a rule to a numbered paragraph is, unless otherwise stated, a reference to the paragraph of that number in that rule.

---

1. The requirement of the approval of the Lord Chancellor for the appointment of a District Judge (Magistrates' Courts) or Deputy District Judge (Magistrates' Courts) as an adjudicator does not apply to a person who is approved to act as an adjudicator on 18 April 2005, and such a person may continue to act as an adjudicator for so long as he holds office as a District Judge (Magistrates' Courts) or Deputy District Judge (Magistrates' Courts): Prison (Amendment) Rules 2005, SI 2005/789, r 1(2).

Part II
Prisoners
General

8–24456 3. Purpose of prison training and treatment. The purpose of the training and treatment of convicted prisoners shall be to encourage and assist them to lead a good and useful life.

8–24457 4. Outside contacts. (1) Special attention shall be paid to the maintenance of such relationships between a prisoner and his family as are desirable in the best interests of both.

(2) A prisoner shall be encouraged and assisted to establish and maintain such relations with persons and agencies outside prison as may, in the opinion of the governor, best promote the interests of his family and his own social rehabilitation.

8–24458 5. After care. From the beginning of a prisoner's sentence, consideration shall be given, in consultation with the appropriate after-care organisation, to the prisoner's future and the assistance to be given him on and after his release.

8–24459 6. Maintenance of order and discipline. (1) Order and discipline shall be maintained with firmness, but with no more restriction than is required for safe custody and well ordered community life.

(2) In the control of prisoners, officers shall seek to influence them through their own example and leadership, and to enlist their willing co-operation.

(3) At all times the treatment of prisoners shall be such as to encourage their self-respect and a sense of personal responsibility, but a prisoner shall not be employed in any disciplinary capacity.

8–24460 7. Classification of prisoners. (1) Prisoners shall be classified, in accordance with any directions of the Secretary of State, having regard to their age, temperament and record and with a view to maintaining good order and facilitating training and, in the case of convicted prisoners, of furthering the purpose of their training and treatment as provided by rule 3.

(2) Unconvicted prisoners:

(a) shall be kept out of contact with convicted prisoners as far as the governor considers it can reasonably be done, unless and to the extent that they have consented to share residential accommodation or participate in any activity with convicted prisoners; and

(b) shall under no circumstances be required to share a cell with a convicted prisoner.

(3) Prisoners committed or attached for contempt of court, or for failing to do or abstain from doing anything required to be done or left undone:

(*a*) shall be treated as a separate class for the purposes of this rule;
(*b*) notwithstanding anything in this rule, may be permitted to associate with any other class of prisoners if they are willing to do so; and
(*c*) shall have the same privileges as an unconvicted prisoner under rules 20(5), 23(1) and 35(1).

(4) Nothing in this rule shall require a prisoner to be deprived unduly of the society of other persons.

8–24461 8. Privileges. (1) There shall be established at every prison systems of privileges approved by the Secretary of State and appropriate to the classes of prisoners there, which shall include arrangements under which money earned by prisoners in prison may be spent by them within the prison.

(2) Systems of privileges approved under paragraph (1) may include arrangements under which prisoners may be allowed time outside their cells and in association with one another, in excess of the minimum time which, subject to the other provisions of these Rules apart from this rule, is otherwise allowed to prisoners at the prison for this purpose.

(3) Systems of privileges approved under paragraph (1) may include arrangements under which privileges may be granted to prisoners only in so far as they have met, and for so long as they continue to meet, specified standards in their behaviour and their performance in work or other activities.

(4) Systems of privileges which include arrangements of the kind referred to in paragraph (3) shall include procedures to be followed in determining whether or not any of the privileges concerned shall be granted, or shall continue to be granted, to a prisoner; such procedures shall include a requirement that the prisoner be given reasons for any decision adverse to him together with a statement of the means by which he may appeal against it.

(5) Nothing in this rule shall be taken to confer on a prisoner any entitlement to any privilege or to affect any provision in these Rules other than this rule as a result of which any privilege may be forfeited or otherwise lost or a prisoner deprived of association with other prisoners.

8–24462 9. Temporary release. (1) The Secretary of State may, in accordance with the other provisions of this rule, release temporarily a prisoner to whom this rule applies.

(2) A prisoner may be released under this rule for any period or periods and subject to any conditions.

(3) A prisoner may only be released under this rule:

(*a*) on compassionate grounds or for the purpose of receiving medical treatment;
(*b*) to engage in employment or voluntary work;
(*c*) to receive instruction or training which cannot reasonably be provided in the prison;
(*d*) to enable him to participate in any proceedings before any court, tribunal or inquiry;
(*e*) to enable him to consult with his legal adviser in circumstances where it is not reasonably practicable for the consultation to take place in the prison;
(*f*) to assist any police officer in any enquiries;
(*g*) to facilitate the prisoner's transfer between prisons;
(*h*) to assist him in maintaining family ties or in his transition from prison life to freedom; or
(*i*) *revoked.*

(4) A prisoner shall not be released under this rule unless the Secretary of State is satisfied that there would not be an unacceptable risk of his committing offences whilst released or otherwise failing to comply with any condition upon which he is released.

(5) The Secretary of State shall not release under this rule a prisoner serving a sentence of imprisonment if, having regard to:

(*a*) the period or proportion of his sentence which the prisoner has served or, in a case where paragraph (10) does not apply to require all the sentences he is serving to be treated as a single term, the period or proportion of any such sentence he has served; and
(*b*) the frequency with which the prisoner has been granted temporary release under this rule,

the Secretary of State is of the opinion that the release of the prisoner would be likely to undermine public confidence in the administration of justice.

(6) If a prisoner has been temporarily released under this rule during the relevant period and has been sentenced to imprisonment for a criminal offence committed whilst at large following that release, he shall not be released under this rule unless his release, having regard to the circumstances of this conviction, would not, in the opinion of the Secretary of State, be likely to undermine public confidence in the administration of justice.

(7) For the purposes of paragraph (6), "the relevant period":

(*a*) in the case of a prisoner serving a determinate sentence of imprisonment, is the period he has served in respect of that sentence, unless, notwithstanding paragraph (10), the sentences he is serving do not fall to be treated as a single term, in which case it is the period since he was last released in relation to one of those sentences under Part II of the Criminal Justice Act 1991 ("the 1991 Act") or Chapter 6 of Part 12 of the 2003 Act;
(*b*) in the case of a prisoner serving an indeterminate sentence of imprisonment, is, if the prisoner has previously been released on licence under Part II of the Crime (Sentences) Act 1997 or Part II of the 1991 Act or Chapter 6 of Part 12 of the 2003 Act, the period since the

date of his last recall to prison in respect of that sentence or, where the prisoner has not been so released, the period he has served in respect of that sentence; or

(c) in the case of a prisoner detained in prison for any other reason, is the period for which the prisoner has been detained for that reason;

save that where a prisoner falls within two or more of sub-paragraphs *(a)* to *(c)*, the "relevant period", in the case of that prisoner, shall be determined by whichever of the applicable sub-paragraphs produces the longer period.

(8) A prisoner released under this rule may be recalled to prison at any time whether the conditions of his release have been broken or not.

(9) This rule applies to prisoners other than persons committed in custody for trial or to be sentenced or otherwise dealt with before or by any Crown Court or remanded in custody by any court.

(10) For the purposes of any reference in this rule to an inmate's sentence, consecutive terms and terms which are wholly or partly concurrent shall be treated as a single term.

(11) In this rule:

(a) any reference to a sentence of imprisonment shall be construed as including any sentence to detention or custody; and

(b) any reference to release on licence or otherwise under Part II of the 1991 Act includes any release on licence under any legislation providing for early release on licence.

8–24464 **10. Information to prisoners.** (1) Every prisoner shall be provided, as soon as possible after his reception into prison, and in any case within 24 hours, with information in writing about those provisions of these Rules and other matters which it is necessary that he should know, including earnings and privileges, and the proper means of making requests and complaints.

(2) In the case of a prisoner aged less than 18, or a prisoner aged 18 or over who cannot read or appears to have difficulty in understanding the information so provided, the governor, or an officer deputed by him, shall so explain it to him that he can understand his rights and obligations.

(3) A copy of these Rules shall be made available to any prisoner who requests it.

8–24465 **11. Requests and complaints.** (1) A request or complaint to the governor or board of visitors relating to a prisoner's imprisonment shall be made orally or in writing by the prisoner.

(2) On every day the governor shall hear any requests and complaints that are made to him under paragraph (1).

(3) A written request or complaint under paragraph (1) may be made in confidence.

Women Prisoners

8–24466 **12. Women prisoners.** (1) Women prisoners shall normally be kept separate from male prisoners.

(2) The Secretary of State may, subject to any conditions he thinks fit, permit a woman prisoner to have her baby with[1] her in prison, and everything necessary for the baby's maintenance and care may be provided there.

1. For procedural requirements to ensure fairness in any decision whether to transfer a prisoner to a mother and baby unit and the application of article 8 of the European Convention on Human Rights, see *R (on the application of CD) v Secretary of State for the Home Department* [2003] EWHC 155 (Admin), [2003] 1 FLR 979. As the primary decision-maker as to the separation of mother and child is the Secretary of State not the court, any challenge to his decision raises issues of public law and is to be determined whether in the Family Division or the Divisional Court by reference to principles of public law not private law *(CF v Secretary of State for the Home Department* [2004] EWHC 111 (Fam), [2004] 1 FCR 577, [2004] 2 FLR 517).

Religion

8–24467 **13. Religious denomination.** A prisoner shall be treated as being of the religious denomination stated in the record made in pursuance of section 10(5) of the Prison Act 1952 but the governor may, in a proper case and after due enquiry, direct that record to be amended.

8–24468 **14. Special duties of chaplains and prison ministers.** (1) The chaplain or a prison minister of a prison shall—

(a) interview every prisoner of his denomination individually soon after the prisoner's reception into that prison and shortly before his release; and

(b) if no other arrangements are made, read the burial service at the funeral of any prisoner of his denomination who dies in that prison.

(2) The chaplain shall visit daily all prisoners belonging to the Church of England who are sick, under restraint or undergoing cellular confinement; and a prison minister shall do the same, as far as he reasonably can, for prisoners of his denomination.

(3) The chaplain shall visit any prisoner not of the Church of England who is sick, under restraint or undergoing cellular confinement, and is not regularly visited by a minister of his denomination, if the prisoner is willing.

8–24469 **15. Regular visits by ministers of religion.** (1) The chaplain shall visit the prisoners belonging to the Church of England.

(2) A prison minister shall visit the prisoners of his denomination as regularly as he reasonably can.

(3) Where a prisoner belongs to a denomination for which no prison minister has been appointed, the governor shall do what he reasonably can, if so requested by the prisoner, to arrange for him to be visited regularly by a minister of that denomination.

8–24470 **16. Religious services.** (1) The chaplain shall conduct Divine Service for prisoners belonging to the Church of England at least once every Sunday, Christmas Day and Good Friday, and such celebrations of Holy Communion and weekday services as may be arranged.

(2) Prison ministers shall conduct Divine Service for prisoners of their denominations at such times as may be arranged.

8–24471 **17. Substitute for chaplain or prison minister.** (1) A person approved by the Secretary of State may act for the chaplain in his absence.

(2) A prison minister may, with the leave of the Secretary of State, appoint a substitute to act for him in his absence.

8–24472 **18. Sunday work.** Arrangements shall be made so as not to require prisoners of the Christian religion to do any unnecessary work on Sunday, Christmas Day or Good Friday, or prisoners of other religions to do any such work on their recognised days of religious observance.

8–24473 **19. Religious books.** There shall, so far as reasonably practicable, be available for the personal use of every prisoner such religious books recognised by his denomination as are approved by the Secretary of State for use in prisons.

MEDICAL ATTENTION

8–24474 **20. Medical attendance.** (1) The medical officer of a prison shall have the care of the health, mental and physical, of the prisoners in that prison.

(2) Every request by a prisoner to see a registered medical practitioner, a registered nurse or other health care professional such as is mentioned in paragraph (3) officer shall be recorded by the officer to whom it is made and promptly passed on to the medical officer.

(3) The medical officer may consult—

(*a*) a registered medical practitioner,
(*b*) a registered nurse, or
(*c*) any other health care professional,

and such a person may work within the prison under the general supervision of the medical officer.

(4) *Revoked.*

(5) If an unconvicted prisoner desires the attendance of a registered medical practitioner or dentist, and will pay any expense incurred, the governor shall, if he is satisfied that there are reasonable grounds for the request and unless the Secretary of State otherwise directs, allow him to be visited and treated by that practitioner or dentist in consultation with a registered medical practitioner such as is mentioned in paragraph (3).

(6) Subject to any directions given in the particular case by the Secretary of State, a registered medical practitioner selected by or on behalf of a prisoner who is a party to any legal proceedings shall be afforded reasonable facilities for examining him in connection with the proceedings, and may do so out of hearing but in the sight of an officer.

8–24475 **21. Special illnesses and conditions.** (1) A registered medical practitioner such as is mentioned in rule 20(3) shall report to the governor on the case of any prisoner whose health is likely to be injuriously affected by continued imprisonment or any conditions of imprisonment. The governor shall send the report to the Secretary of State without delay, together with his own recommendations.

(2) *Revoked.*

8–24476 **22. Notification of illness or death.** (1) If a prisoner dies, becomes seriously ill, sustains any severe injury or is removed to hospital on account of mental disorder, the governor shall, if he knows his or her address, at once inform the prisoner's spouse or next of kin, and also any person who the prisoner may reasonably have asked should be informed.

(2) If a prisoner dies, the governor shall give notice immediately to the coroner having jurisdiction, to the board of visitors and to the Secretary of State.

PHYSICAL WELFARE AND WORK

8–24477 **23. Clothing.** (1) An unconvicted prisoner may wear clothing of his own if and in so far as it is suitable, tidy and clean, and shall be permitted to arrange for the supply to him from outside prison of sufficient clean clothing:

Provided that, subject to rule 40(3):

(a) he may be required, if and for so long as there are reasonable grounds to believe that there is a serious risk of his attempting to escape, to wear items of clothing which are distinctive by virtue of being specially marked or coloured or both; and

(b) he may be required, if and for so long as the Secretary of State is of the opinion that he would, if he escaped, be highly dangerous to the public or the police or the security of the State, to wear clothing provided under this rule.

(2) Subject to paragraph (1) above, the provisions of this rule shall apply to an unconvicted prisoner as to a convicted prisoner.

(3) A convicted prisoner shall be provided with clothing adequate for warmth and health in accordance with a scale approved by the Secretary of State.

(4) The clothing provided under this rule shall include suitable protective clothing for use at work, where this is needed.

(5) Subject to rule 40(3), a convicted prisoner shall wear clothing provided under this rule and no other, except on the directions of the Secretary of State or as a privilege under rule 8.

(6) A prisoner may be provided, where necessary, with suitable and adequate clothing on his release.

8–24478 **24. Food.** (1) Subject to any directions of the Secretary of State, no prisoner shall be allowed, except as authorised by a health care professional such as is mentioned in rule 20(3), to have any food other than that ordinarily provided.

(2) The food provided shall be wholesome, nutritious, well prepared and served, reasonably varied and sufficient in quantity.

(3) Any person deemed by the governor to be competent, shall from time to time inspect the food both before and after it is cooked and shall report any deficiency or defect to the governor.

(4) In this rule "food" includes drink.

8–24479 **25. Alcohol and tobacco.** (1) No prisoner shall be allowed to have any intoxicating liquor.

(2) No prisoner shall be allowed to smoke or to have any tobacco except as a privilege under rule 8 and in accordance with any orders of the governor.

8–24480 **26. Sleeping accommodation.** (1) No room or cell shall be used as sleeping accommodation for a prisoner unless it has been certified in the manner required by section 14 of the Prison Act 1952 in the case of a cell used for the confinement of a prisoner.

(2) A certificate given under that section or this rule shall specify the maximum number of prisoners who may sleep or be confined at one time in the room or cell to which it relates, and the number so specified shall not be exceeded without the leave of the Secretary of State.

8–24481 **27. Beds and bedding.** Each prisoner shall be provided with a separate bed and with separate bedding adequate for warmth and health.

8–24482 **28. Hygiene.** (1) Every prisoner shall be provided with toilet articles necessary for his health and cleanliness, which shall be replaced as necessary.

(2) Every prisoner shall be required to wash at proper times, have a hot bath or shower on reception and thereafter at least once a week.

(3) A prisoner's hair shall not be cut without his consent.

8–24483 **29. Physical education.** (1) If circumstances reasonably permit, a prisoner aged 21 years or over shall be given the opportunity to participate in physical education for at least one hour a week.

(2) The following provisions shall apply to the extent circumstances reasonably permit to a prisoner who is under 21 years of age—

(a) provision shall be made for the physical education of such a prisoner within the normal working week, as well as evening and weekend physical recreation; the physical education activities will be such as foster personal responsibility and the prisoner's interests and skills and encourage him to make good use of his leisure on release; and

(b) arrangements shall be made for each such prisoner who is a convicted prisoner to participate in physical education for two hours a week on average.

(3) In the case of a prisoner with a need for remedial physical activity, appropriate facilities will be provided.

(4) *Revoked.*

8–24484 **30. Time in the open air.** If the weather permits and subject to the need to maintain good order and discipline, a prisoner shall be given the opportunity to spend time in the open air at least once every day, for such period as may be reasonable in the circumstances.

8–24485 **31. Work.** (1) A convicted prisoner shall be required to do useful work for not more than 10 hours a day, and arrangements shall be made to allow prisoners to work, where possible, outside the cells and in association with one another.

(2) A registered medical practitioner or registered nurse such as is mentioned in rule 20(3) may

excuse a prisoner from work on medical grounds, and no prisoner shall be set to do work which is not of a class for which he has been passed by a registered medical practitioner or registered nurse such as is mentioned in rule 20(3) as being fit.

(3) No prisoner shall be set to do work of a kind not authorised by the Secretary of State.

(4) No prisoner shall work in the service of another prisoner or an officer, or for the private benefit of any person, without the authority of the Secretary of State.

(5) An unconvicted prisoner shall be permitted, if he wishes, to work as if he were a convicted prisoner.

(6) Prisoners may be paid for their work at rates approved by the Secretary of State, either generally or in relation to particular cases.

EDUCATION AND LIBRARY

8–24486 **32. Education.** (1) Every prisoner able to profit from the education facilities provided at a prison shall be encouraged to do so.

(2) Educational classes shall be arranged at every prison and, subject to any directions of the Secretary of State, reasonable facilities shall be afforded to prisoners who wish to do so to improve their education by training by distance learning, private study and recreational classes, in their spare time.

(3) Special attention shall be paid to the education and training of prisoners with special educational needs, and if necessary they shall be taught within the hours normally allotted to work.

(4) In the case of a prisoner of compulsory school age as defined in section 8 of the Education Act 1996, arrangements shall be made for his participation in education or training courses for at least 15 hours a week within the normal working week.

8–24487 **33. Library.** A library shall be provided in every prison and, subject to any directions of the Secretary of State, every prisoner shall be allowed to have library books and to exchange them.

COMMUNICATIONS

8–24488 **34. Communications generally.** (1) Without prejudice to sections 6 and 19 of the Prison Act 1952 and except as provided by these Rules, a prisoner[1] shall not be permitted to communicate with any person outside the prison, or such person with him, except with the leave of the Secretary of State or as a privilege under rule 8.

(2) Notwithstanding paragraph (1) above, and except as otherwise provided in these Rules, the Secretary of State may impose any restriction or condition, either generally or in a particular case, upon the communications to be permitted between a prisoner and other persons if he considers that the restriction or condition to be imposed—

(*a*) Does not interfere with the convention rights of any person; or

(*b*)

(i) is necessary on grounds specified in paragraph (3) below;

(ii) reliance on the grounds is compatible with the convention right to be interfered with; and

(iii) the restriction or condition is proportionate to what is sought to be achieved.

(3) The grounds referred to in paragraph (2) above are—

(*a*) the interests of national security;

(*b*) the prevention, detection, investigation or prosecution of crime;

(*c*) the interests of public safety;

(*d*) securing or maintaining prison security or good order and discipline in prison;

(*e*) the protection of health or morals;

(*f*) the protection of the reputation of others;

(*g*) maintaining the authority and impartiality of the judiciary; or

(*h*) the protection of the rights and freedoms of any person.

(4) Subject to paragraph (2) above, the Secretary of State may require that any visit, or class of visits, shall be held in facilities which include special features restricting or preventing physical contact between a prisoner and a visitor.

(5) Every visit to a prisoner shall take place within the sight of an officer or employee of the prison authorised for the purposes of this rule by the governor (in this rule referred to as an "authorised employee"), unless the Secretary of State otherwise directs, and for the purposes of this paragraph a visit to a prisoner shall be taken to take place within the sight of an officer or authorised employee if it can be seen by an officer or authorised employee by means of an overt closed circuit television system.

(6) Subject to rule 38, every visit to a prisoner shall take place within the hearing of an officer or authorised employee, unless the Secretary of State otherwise directs.

(7) The Secretary of State may give directions, either generally or in relation to any visit or class of visits, concerning the day and times when prisoners may be visited.

(8) In this rule—

(*a*) references to communications include references to communications during visits;

(*b*) references to restrictions and conditions upon communications include references to restrictions and conditions in relation to the length, duration and frequency of communications; and

(*c*) references to convention rights are to the convention rights within the meaning of the Human Rights Act 1998.

---

1. Prisoners must have unimpeded access to a solicitor in order to receive advice and assistance regarding possible civil proceedings, without for example being required by Standing Orders to make an internal complaint first (*R v Secretary of State for the Home Department, ex p Anderson* [1984] QB 778, [1984] 1 All ER 920). "Unimpeded access" does not preclude a closed regime for visitors of exceptional escape risk prisoners whereby physical contact between prisoner and visitor is prevented by an interposed physical barrier (*R v Secretary of State for the Home Department, ex p O'Dhuibhir* (1995) Times, 26 October). A convicted prisoner has no right to communicate orally with the media through a journalist as the loss of that "right" is part and parcel of a sentence of imprisonment. He can no longer speak to those outside prison or receive visits from anyone other than his lawyer and his relatives and friends, If a friend is a journalist the prison is entitled to require an undertaking from the journalist that the material obtained during the visit will not be used for professional purposes (*R v Secretary of State for the Home Department, ex p Simms* [1998] 2 All ER 491, [1998] 3 WLR 1169, CA).

8–24489 35. Personal letters and visits. (1) Subject to paragraph (8), an unconvicted prisoner may send and receive as many letters and may receive as many visits as he wishes within such limits and subject to such conditions as the Secretary of State may direct, either generally or in a particular case.

(2) Subject to paragraphs (2A) and (8), a convicted prisoner shall be entitled—

(*a*) to send and to receive a letter on his reception into a prison and thereafter once a week; and

(*b*) to receive a visit twice in every period of four weeks, but only once in every such period if the Secretary of State so directs.

(2A) A prisoner serving a sentence of imprisonment to which an intermittent custody order relates shall be entitled to receive a visit only where the governor considers that desirable having regard to the extent to which he has been unable to meet with his friends and family in the periods during which he has been temporarily released on licence.

(3) The governor may allow a prisoner an additional letter or visit as a privilege under rule 8 or where necessary for his welfare or that of his family.

(4) The governor may allow a prisoner entitled to a visit to send and to receive a letter instead.

(5) The governor may defer the right of a prisoner to a visit until the expiration of any period of cellular confinement.

(6) The board of visitors may allow a prisoner an additional letter or visit in special circumstances, and may direct that a visit may extend beyond the normal duration.

(7) The Secretary of State may allow additional letters and visits in relation to any prisoner or class of prisoners.

(8) A prisoner shall not be entitled under this rule to receive a visit from:

(*a*) any person, whether or not a relative or friend, during any period of time that person is the subject of a prohibition imposed under rule 73; or

(*b*) any other person, other than a relative or friend, except with the leave of the Secretary of State.

(9) Any letter or visit under the succeeding provisions of these Rules shall not be counted as a letter or visit for the purposes of this rule.

8–24489A 35A. Interception of communications. (1) The Secretary of State may give directions to any governor concerning the interception in a prison of any communication by any prisoner or class of prisoners if the Secretary of State considers that the directions are—

(*a*) necessary on grounds specified in paragraph (4) below; and

(*b*) proportionate to what is sought to be achieved.

(2) Subject to any directions given by the Secretary of State, the governor may make arrangements for any communication by a prisoner or class of prisoners to be intercepted in a prison by an officer or an employee of the prison authorised by the governor for the purposes of this rule (referred to in this rule as an "authorised employee") if he considers that the arrangements are—

(*a*) necessary on grounds specified in paragraph (4) below; and

(*b*) proportionate to what is sought to be achieved.

(3) Any communication by a prisoner may, during the course of its transmission in a prison, be terminated by an officer or an authorised employee if he considers that to terminate the communication is—

(*a*) necessary on grounds specified in paragraph (4) below; and

(*b*) proportionate to what is sought to be achieved by the termination.

(4) The grounds referred to in paragraphs (1)(*a*),(2)(*a*) and (3)(*a*) above are—

(*a*) the interests of national security;

(*b*) the prevention, detection, investigation or prosecution of crime;
(*c*) the interests of public safety;
(*d*) securing or maintaining prison security or good order and discipline in prison;
(*e*) the protection of health or morals; or
(*f*) the protection of the rights and freedoms of any person.

(5) Any reference to the grounds specified in paragraph (4) above in relation to the interception of a communication by means of a telecommunications system in a prison, or the disclosure or retention of intercepted material from such a communication, shall be taken to be a reference to those grounds with the omission of sub-paragraph (*f*).

(6) For the purposes of this rule "interception"—

(*a*) in relation to a communication by means of a telecommunications system, means any action taken in relation to the system or its operation so as to make some or all of the contents of the communications available, while being transmitted, to a person other than the sender or intended recipient of the communication; and the contents of a communication are to be taken to be made available to a person while being transmitted where the contents of the communication, while being transmitted, are diverted or recorded so as to be available to a person subsequently; and
(*b*) in relation to any written or drawn communication, includes opening, reading, examining and copying the communication.

8–24489B **35B. Permanent log of communications.** (1) The governor may arrange for a permanent log to be kept of all communications by or to a prisoner.

(2) The log referred to in paragraph (1) above may include, in relation to a communication by means of a telecommunications system in a prison, a record of the destination, duration and cost of the communication and, in relation to any written or drawn communication, a record of the sender and addressee of the communication.

8–24489C **35C. Disclosure of material.** The governor may not disclose to any person who is not an officer of a prison or of the Secretary of State or an employee of the prison authorised by the governor for the purposes of this rule any intercepted material, information retained pursuant to rule 35B or material obtained by means of an overt closed circuit television system used during a visit unless—

(*a*) he considers that such disclosure is—
  (i) necessary on grounds specified in rule 35A(4); and
  (ii) proportionate to what is sought to be achieved by the disclosure; or

(*b*)
  (i) in the case of intercepted material or material obtained by means of an overt closed circuit television system used during a visit, all parties to the communication or visit consent to the disclosure; or
  (ii) in the case of information retained pursuant to rule 35B, the prisoner to whose communication the information relates, consents to the disclosure.

8–24489D **35D. Retention of material.** (1) The governor shall not retain any intercepted material or material obtained by means of an overt closed circuit television system used during a visit for a period longer than 3 months beginning with the day on which the material was intercepted or obtained unless he is satisfied that continued retention of it is—

(*a*) necessary on grounds specified in rule 35A(4); and
(*b*) proportionate to what is sought to be achieved by the continued retention.

(2) Where such material is retained for longer than 3 months pursuant to paragraph (1) above the governor shall review its continued retention at periodic intervals until such time as it is no longer held by the governor.

(3) The first review referred to in paragraph (2) above shall take place not more than 3 months after the decision to retain the material taken pursuant to paragraph (1) above, and subsequent reviews shall take place not more than 3 months apart thereafter.

(4) If the governor, on a review conducted pursuant to paragraph (2) above or at any other time, is not satisfied that the continued retention of the material satisfies the requirements set out in paragraph (1) above, he shall arrange for the material to be destroyed.

8–24490 **36. Police interviews.** A police officer may, on production of an order issued by or on behalf of a chief officer of police, interview any prisoner willing to see him.

8–24491 **37. Securing release.** A person detained in prison in default of finding a surety, or of payment of a sum of money, may communicate with and be visited at any reasonable time on a weekday by any relative or friend to arrange for a surety or payment in order to secure his release from prison.

8–24492 **38. Legal advisers.** (1) The legal adviser of a prisoner in any legal proceedings, civil or criminal, to which the prisoner is a party shall be afforded reasonable facilities for interviewing him in connection with those proceedings, and may do so out of hearing but in the sight of an officer.

(2) A prisoner's legal adviser may, subject to any directions given by the Secretary of State, interview the prisoner in connection with any other legal business out of hearing but in the sight of an officer.

8–24493 **39. Correspondence with legal advisers and courts.** (1) A prisoner may correspond with his legal adviser and any court and such correspondence may only be opened, read or stopped by the governor in accordance with the provisions of this rule[1].

(2) Correspondence to which this rule applies may be opened if the governor has reasonable cause to believe that it contains an illicit enclosure and any such enclosures shall be dealt with in accordance with the other provision of these Rules.

(3) Correspondence to which this rule applies may be opened, read and stopped if the governor has reasonable cause to believe its contents endanger prison security or the safety of others or are otherwise of a criminal nature.

(4) A prisoner shall be given the opportunity to be present when any correspondence to which this rule applies is opened and shall be informed if it or any enclosure is to be read or stopped.[2]

(5) A prisoner shall on request be provided with any writing materials necessary for the purposes of paragraph (1).

(6) In this rule, "court" includes the European Commission of Human Rights, the European Court of Human Rights and the European Court of Justice; and "illicit enclosure" includes any article possession of which has not been authorised in accordance with the other provisions of these Rules and any correspondence to or from a person other than the prisoner concerned, his legal adviser or a court.

---

1. Although legal professional privilege attaches to correspondence with legal advisers must be protected from unnecessary interference by prison staff, considerations of security may require searches periodically and without notice of cells and everything in them which necessarily will involve examining correspondence so far as it is necessary to ensure that it is bona fide correspondence between a prisoner and a legal adviser and it does not contain anything else (*R v Governor of Whitemoor Prison, ex p Main* [1998] 2 All ER 491, [1998] 3 WLR 1169, CA). Where there is malicious infringement of this rule, a cause of action for misfeasance in public office is complete without proof of special damage (*Watkins v Secretary of State* [2004] EWCA Civ 966, [2004] 4 All ER 1158).

2. For the general right of a prisoner to be present when legal correspondence received or made by a prisoner and kept in his cell is searched and the application of art 8 of the European Convention on Human Rights, see *R v Secretary of State for the Home Department, ex p Daly* [2001] UKHL 26, [2001] 3 All ER 433, [2001] 2 WLR 1622.

Removal, Search, Record and Property

8–24494 **40. Custody outside prison.** (1) A person being taken to or from a prison in custody shall be exposed as little as possible to public observation, and proper care shall be taken to protect him from curiosity and insult.

(2) A prisoner required to be taken in custody anywhere outside a prison shall be kept in the custody of an officer appointed or a police officer.

(3) A prisoner required to be taken in custody to any court shall, when he appears before the court, wear his own clothing or ordinary civilian clothing provided by the governor.

8–24495 **41. Search.** (1) Every prisoner shall be searched when taken into custody by an officer, on his reception into a prison and subsequently as the governor thinks necessary or as the Secretary of State may direct.

(2) A prisoner shall be searched in as seemly a manner as is consistent with discovering anything concealed.

(3) No prisoner shall be stripped and searched in the sight of another prisoner, or in the sight of a person of the opposite sex.

8–24496 **42. Record and photograph.** (1) A personal record of each prisoner shall be prepared and maintained in such manner as the Secretary of State may direct.

(2) Every prisoner may be photographed on reception and subsequently, but no copy of the photograph or any other personal record shall be given to any person not authorised to receive it.

(2A) In this rule "personal record" may include personal information and biometric records (such as fingerprints or other physical measurements).

8–24497 **43. Prisoners' property.** (1) Subject to any directions of the Secretary of State, an unconvicted prisoner may have supplied to him at his expense and retain for his own use books, newspapers, writing materials and other means of occupation, except any that appears objectionable to the board of visitors or, pending consideration by them, to the governor.

(2) Anything, other than cash, which a prisoner has at a prison and which he is not allowed to retain for his own use shall be taken into the governor's custody. An inventory of a prisoner's property shall be kept, and he shall be required to sign it, after having a proper opportunity to see that it is correct.

(2A) Where a prisoner is serving a sentence of imprisonment to which an intermittent custody order relates, an inventory as referred to in paragraph (2) shall only be kept where the value of that property is estimated by the governor to be in excess of £100.

(3) Any cash which a prisoner has at a prison shall be paid into an account under the control of the governor and the prisoner shall be credited with the amount in the books of the prison[1].

(4) Any article belonging to a prisoner which remains unclaimed for a period of more than 3 years after he leaves prison, or dies, may be sold or otherwise disposed of; and the net proceeds of any sale shall be paid to the National Association for the Care and Resettlement of Offenders, for its general purposes.

(5) The governor may confiscate any unauthorised article found in the possession of a prisoner after his reception into prison, or concealed or deposited anywhere within a prison.

1. The governor does not hold the cash on trust for the prisoner with an obligation to invest it in an interest bearing account; the relationship created is one of debtor and creditor. There is no specific rule which prevents the prisoner from requesting the cash to be transferred to an interest-bearing account outside the prison (*Duggan v Governor of Full Sutton Prison* [2003] EWHC 361 (Ch), [2003] 2 All ER 678).

8–24498 **44. Money and articles received by post.** (1) Any money or other article (other than a letter or other communication) sent to a convicted prisoner by post shall be dealt with in accordance with the provisions of this rule, and the prisoner shall be informed of the manner in which it is dealt with.

(2) Any cash shall, at the discretion of the governor, be—

(a) dealt with in accordance with rule 43(3);

(b) returned to the sender; or

(c) in a case where the sender's name and address are not known, paid to the National Association for the Care and Resettlement of Offenders, for its general purposes:

Provided that in relation to a prisoner committed to prison in default of payment of any sum of money, the prisoner shall be informed of the receipt of the cash and, unless he objects to its being so applied, it shall be applied in or towards the satisfaction of the amount due from him.

(3) Any security for money shall, at the discretion of the governor, be—

(a) delivered to the prisoner or placed with his property at the prison;

(b) returned to the sender; or

(c) encashed and the cash dealt with in accordance with paragraph (2).

(4) Any other article to which this rule applies shall, at the discretion of the governor, be—

(a) delivered to the prisoner or placed with his property at the prison;

(b) returned to the sender; or

(c) in a case where the sender's name and address are not known or the article is of such a nature that it would be unreasonable to return it, sold or otherwise disposed of, and the net proceeds of any sale applied in accordance with paragraph (2).

Special Control, Supervision and Restraint and Drug Testing

8–24499 **45. Removal from association.** (1) Where it appears desirable, for the maintenance of good order or discipline or in his own interests, that a prisoner should not associate with other prisoners, either generally or for particular purposes, the governor may arrange for the prisoner's removal from association accordingly.

(2) A prisoner shall not be removed under this rule for a period of more than 72 hours without the authority of the Secretary of State and authority given under this paragraph shall be for a period not exceeding 14 days but it may be renewed from time to time for a like period.

(3) The governor may arrange at his discretion for a prisoner removed under this rule to resume association with other prisoners at any time, and in exercising that discretion the governor must fully consider any recommendation that the prisoner resumes association on medical grounds made by a registered medical practitioner or registered nurse such as is mentioned in rule 20(3).

(4) This rule shall not apply to a prisoner the subject of a direction given under rule 46(1).

8–24500 **46. Close supervision centres.** (1) Where it appears desirable, for the maintenance of good order or discipline or to ensure the safety of officers, prisoners or any other person, that a prisoner should not associate with other prisoners, either generally or for particular purposes, the Secretary of State may direct the prisoner's removal from association accordingly and his placement in a close supervision centre of a prison.

(2) A direction given under paragraph (1) shall be for a period not exceeding one month, but may be renewed from time to time for a like period, and shall continue to apply notwithstanding any transfer of a prisoner from one prison to another.

(3) The Secretary of State may direct that such a prisoner as aforesaid shall resume association with other prisoners, either within a close supervision centre or elsewhere.

(4) In exercising any discretion under this rule, the Secretary of State shall take account of any relevant medical considerations which are known to him.

(5) A close supervision centre is any cell or other part of a prison designated by the Secretary of State for holding prisoners who are subject to a direction given under paragraph (1).

8–24501 **47. Use of force.** (1) An officer in dealing with a prisoner shall not use force unnecessarily and, when the application of force to a prisoner is necessary, no more force than is necessary shall be used.

(2) No officer shall act deliberately in a manner calculated to provoke a prisoner.

8–24502 **48. Temporary confinement.** (1) The governor may order a refractory or violent prisoner to be confined temporarily in a special cell, but a prisoner shall not be so confined as a punishment, or after he has ceased to be refractory or violent.

(2) A prisoner shall not be confined in a special cell for longer than 24 hours without a direction in writing given by an officer of the Secretary of State. Such a direction shall state the grounds for the confinement and the time during which it may continue.

8–24503 **49. Restraints.** (1) The governor may order a prisoner to be put under restraint where this is necessary to prevent the prisoner from injuring himself or others, damaging property or creating a disturbance.

(2) Notice of such an order shall be given without delay to a member of the board of visitors, and to a registered medical practitioner or to a registered nurse such as is mentioned in rule 20(3).

(3) On receipt of the notice, the registered medical practitioner or registered nurse referred to in paragraph (2), shall inform the governor whether there are any medical reasons why the prisoner should not be put under restraint. The governor shall give effect to any recommendation which may be made under this paragraph.

(4) A prisoner shall not be kept under restraint longer than necessary, nor shall he be so kept for longer than 24 hours without a direction in writing given by a member of the board of visitors or by an officer of the Secretary of State (not being an officer of a prison). Such a direction shall state the grounds for the restraint and the time during which it may continue.

(5) Particulars of every case of restraint under the foregoing provisions of this rule shall be forthwith recorded.

(6) Except as provided by this rule no prisoner shall be put under restraint otherwise than for safe custody during removal, or on medical grounds by direction of a registered medical practitioner or of a registered nurse such as is mentioned in rule 20(3). No prisoner shall be put under restraint as a punishment.

(7) Any means of restraint shall be of a pattern authorised by the Secretary of State, and shall be used in such manner and under such conditions as the Secretary of State may direct.

8–24504 **50. Compulsory testing for controlled drugs.** (1) This rule applies where an officer, acting under the powers conferred by section 16A of the Prison Act 1952 (power to test prisoners for drugs), requires a prisoner to provide a sample for the purpose of ascertaining whether he has any controlled drug in his body.

(2) In this rule "sample" means a sample of urine or any other description of sample specified in the authorisation by the governor for the purposes of section 16A of the Prison Act 1952.

(3) When requiring a prisoner to provide a sample, an officer shall, so far as is reasonably practicable, inform the prisoner:

(a) that he is being required to provide a sample in accordance with section 16A of the Prison Act 1952; and

(b) that a refusal to provide a sample may lead to disciplinary proceedings being brought against him.

(4) An officer shall require a prisoner to provide a fresh sample, free from any adulteration.

(5) An officer requiring a sample shall make such arrangements and give the prisoner such instructions for its provision as may be reasonably necessary in order to prevent or detect its adulteration or falsification.

(6) A prisoner who is required to provide a sample may be kept apart from other prisoners for a period not exceeding one hour to enable arrangements to be made for the provision of the sample.

(7) A prisoner who is unable to provide a sample of urine when required to do so may be kept apart from other prisoners until he has provided the required sample, save that a prisoner may not be kept apart under this paragraph for a period of more than 5 hours.

(8) A prisoner required to provide a sample of urine shall be afforded such degree of privacy for the purposes of providing the sample as may be compatible with the need to prevent or detect any adulteration or falsification of the sample; in particular a prisoner shall not be required to provide such a sample in the sight of a person of the opposite sex.

8–24504A **50A. Observation of prisoners by means of an overt closed circuit television system.** (1) Without prejudice to his other powers to supervise the prison, prisoners and other persons in the prison, whether by use of an overt closed circuit television system or otherwise, the governor may make arrangements for any prisoner to be placed under constant observation by means of an overt closed circuit television system while the prisoner is in a cell or other place in the prison if he considers that—

(*a*) such supervision is necessary for—

(i) the health and safety of the prisoner or any other person;

(ii) the prevention, detection, investigation or prosecution of crime; or
(iii) securing or maintaining prison security or good order and discipline in the prison; and

(*b*) it is proportionate to what is sought to be achieved.

(2) If an overt closed circuit television system is used for the purposes of this rule, the provisions of rules 35C and 35D shall apply to any material obtained.

8–24504B **50B. Compulsory testing for alcohol.** (1) This rule applies where an officer, acting under an authorisation in force under section 16B of the Prison Act 1952 (power to test prisoners for alcohol), requires a prisoner to provide a sample for the purpose of ascertaining whether he has alcohol in his body.

(2) When requiring a prisoner to provide a sample an officer shall, so far as is reasonably practicable, inform the prisoner—

(*a*) that he is being required to provide a sample in accordance with section 16B of the Prison Act 1952; and
(*b*) that a refusal to provide a sample may lead to disciplinary proceedings being brought against him.

(3) An officer requiring a sample shall make such arrangements and give the prisoner such instructions for its provision as may be reasonably necessary in order to prevent or detect its adulteration or falsification.

(4) Subject to paragraph (5) a prisoner who is required to provide a sample may be kept apart from other prisoners for a period not exceeding one hour to enable arrangements to be made for the provision of the sample.

(5) A prisoner who is unable to provide a sample of urine when required to do so may be kept apart from other prisoners until he has provided the required sample, except that a prisoner may not be kept apart under this paragraph for a period of more than 5 hours.

(6) A prisoner required to provide a sample of urine shall be afforded such degree of privacy for the purposes of providing the sample as may be compatible with the need to prevent or detect any adulteration or falsification of the sample; in particular a prisoner shall not be required to provide such a sample in the sight of a person of the opposite sex.

OFFENCES AGAINST DISCIPLINE

8–24505 **51. Offences against discipline.** A prisoner is guilty of an offence against discipline if he—

(1) commits any assault;
(1A) commits any racially aggravated assault;
(2) detains any person against his will;
(3) denies access to any part of the prison to any officer or any person (other than a prisoner) who is at the prison for the purpose of working there;
(4) fights with any person;
(5) intentionally endangers the health or personal safety of others or, by his conduct, is reckless whether such health or personal safety is endangered;
(6) intentionally obstructs an officer in the execution of his duty, or any person (other than a prisoner) who is at the prison for the purpose of working there, in the performance of his work;
(7) escapes or absconds from prison or from legal custody;
(8) fails to comply with any condition upon which he is temporarily released under rule 9;
(9) is found with any substance in his urine which demonstrates that a controlled drug has, whether in prison or while on temporary release under rule 9, been administered to him by himself or by another person (but subject to rule 52);;
(10) is intoxicated as a consequence of consuming any alcoholic beverage (but subject to rule 52A);
(11) consumes any alcoholic beverage whether or not provided to him by another person (but subject to rule 52A);
(12) has in his possession—

(*a*) any unauthorised article, or
(*b*) a greater quantity of any article than he is authorised to have;

(13) sells or delivers to any person any unauthorised article;
(14) sells or, without permission, delivers to any person any article which he is allowed to have only for his own use;
(15) takes improperly any article belonging to another person or to a prison;
(16) intentionally or recklessly sets fire to any part of a prison or any other property, whether or not his own;
(17) destroys or damages any part of a prison or any other property, other than his own;
(17A) causes racially aggravated damage to, or destruction of, any part of a prison or any other property, other than his own;
(18) absents himself from any place he is required to be or is present at any place where he is not authorised to be;
(19) is disrespectful to any officer, or any person (other than a prisoner) who is at the prison for the purpose of working there, or any person visiting a prison;
(20) uses threatening, abusive or insulting words or behaviour;

(20A) uses threatening, abusive or insulting racist words or behaviour;

(21) intentionally fails to work properly or, being required to work, refuses to do so;

(22) disobeys any lawful order;

(23) disobeys or fails to comply with any rule or regulation applying to him;

(24) receives any controlled drug, or, without the consent of an officer, any other article, during the course of a visit (not being an interview such as is mentioned in rule 38);

(24A) displays, attaches or draws on any part of a prison, or on any other property, threatening, abusive or insulting racist words, drawings, symbols or other material;

(25)

(a) attempts to commit,
(b) incites another prisoner to commit, or
(c) assists another prisoner to commit or to attempt to commit, any of the foregoing offences.

8–24505A 51A. Interpretation of rule 51. (2) For the purposes of rule 51 words, behaviour or material are racist if they demonstrate, or are motivated (wholly or partly) by, hostility to members of a racial group (whether identifiable or not) based on their membership (or presumed membership) of a racial group, and "membership", "presumed", "racial group" and "racially aggravated", shall have the meanings assigned to them by section 28 of the Crime and Disorder Act 1998.

8–24506 52. Defences to rule 51(9). It shall be a defence for a prisoner charged with an offence under rule 51(9) to show that:

(a) the controlled drug had been, prior to its administration, lawfully in his possession for his use or was administered to him in the course of a lawful supply of the drug to him by another person;
(b) the controlled drug was administered by or to him in circumstances in which he did not know and had no reason to suspect that such a drug was being administered; or
(c) the controlled drug was administered by or to him under duress or to him without his consent in circumstances where it was not reasonable for him to have resisted.

8–24506A

52A Defences to rule 51(10) and rule 51(11) It shall be a defence for a prisoner charged with an offence under rule 51(10) or (11) to show that—

(*a*) the alcohol was consumed by him in circumstances in which he did not know and had no reason to suspect that he was consuming alcohol;
(*b*) the alcohol was consumed by him without his consent in circumstances where it was not reasonable for him to have resisted; or
(*c*) revoked.

8–24507 53. Disciplinary charges[1]. (1) Where a prisoner is to be charged with an offence against discipline, the charge shall be laid as soon as possible and, save in exceptional circumstances, within 48 hours of the discovery of the offence.

(2) Every charge shall be inquired into by the governor[2] or, as the case may be, the adjudicator.

(3) Every charge shall be first inquired into not later, save in exceptional circumstances or in accordance with rule 55A(5), than:

(*a*) where it is inquired into by the governor, the next day, not being a Sunday or public holiday, after it is laid
(*b*) where it is referred to the adjudicator under rule 53A(2), 28 days after it is so referred.

(4) A prisoner who is to be charged with an offence against discipline may be kept apart from other prisoners pending the governor's first inquiry or determination under rule 53A.

1. Where disciplinary proceedings may result in the award of additional days, they are criminal proceedings for the purpose of the European Convention on Human Rights and art 6 applies. Therefore the refusal to allow a prisoner to be legally represented is a breach of art 6(3)(*b*) (*Ezeh v United Kingdom* (Application 39665/98); and *Connors v United Kingdom* (Application 40086/98) [2004] Crim LR 472).

2. An informed and fair-minded observer would regard prison governors, or their deputies, as being quite capable of interpreting and applying the prison rules fairly and independently. However, in the unusual case where a deputy governor had been present when the governor approved a general order for a squat search which the prisoner refused to obey and had not dissented from that approval, an informed and fair-minded observer could infer that he had thereby tacitly accepted that the order was lawful and there was a real possibility that he would be biased if he later had to adjudicate on the defendant's challenge to the validity of the order (*R (Al-Hasan) v Secretary of State for the Home Department* [2005] UKHL 13, [2005] 1 All ER 927, [2005]1 WLR 688). See also *R (Greenfield) v Secretary of State for the Home Department* [2005] UKHL 14, [2005] 1 WLR 673 (no damages awarded for breach of art 6 where on the facts the adjudication should not have been by a deputy controller).

8–24507A 53A. Determination of mode of inquiry. (1) Before inquiring into a charge the governor shall determine whether it is so serious that additional days should be awarded for the offence, if the prisoner is found guilty.

(2) Where the governor determines:

(*a*) that it is so serious, he shall:

(i) refer the charge to the adjudicator forthwith for him to inquir into it;
(ii) refer any other charge arising out of the same incident to the adjudicator forthwith for him to inquire into it; and
(iii) inform the prisoner who has been charged that he has done so;

(*b*) that it is not so serious, he shall proceed to inquire into the charge.

(3) If:

(*a*) at any time during an inquiry into a charge by the governor; or
(*b*) following such an inquiry, after the governor has found the prisoner guilty of an offence but before he has imposed a punishment for that offence,

it appears to the governor that the charge is so serious that additional days should be awarded for the offence if (where sub-paragraph (*a*) applies) the prisoner is found guilty, the governor shall act in accordance with paragraph (2)(*a*)(i) to (iii) and the adjudicator shall first inquire into any charge referred to him under this paragraph not later than, save in exceptional circumstances, 28 days after the charge was referred.

8–24508 **54. Rights of prisoners charged.** (1) Where a prisoner is charged with an offence against discipline, he shall be informed of the charge as soon as possible and, in any case, before the time when it is inquired into by the governor or, as the case may be, the adjudicator.

(2) At an inquiry into a charge against a prisoner he shall be given a full opportunity of hearing what is alleged against him and of presenting his own case.

(3) At an inquiry into a charge which has been referred to the adjudicator, the prisoner who has been charged shall be given the opportunity to be legally represented.

8–24509 **55. Governor's punishments.** (1) If he finds a prisoner guilty of an offence against discipline the governor may, subject to paragraph (2) and to rule 57, impose one or more of the following punishments:

(*a*) caution;
(*b*) forfeiture for a period not exceeding 42 days of any of the privileges under rule 8;
(*c*) exclusion from associated work for a period not exceeding 21 days;
(*d*) stoppage of or deduction from earnings for a period not exceeding 84 days and of an amount not exceeding 42 days earnings;
(*e*) cellular confinement for a period not exceeding 21 days;
(*f*) (*revoked*);
(*g*) in the case of a prisoner otherwise entitled to them, forfeiture for any period of the right, under rule 43(1), to have the articles there mentioned;
(*h*) removal from his wing or living unit for a period of 28 days.

(2) A caution shall not be combined with any other punishment for the same charge.

(3) If a prisoner is found guilty of more than one charge arising out of an incident, punishments under this rule may be ordered to run consecutively but in the case of a punishment of cellular confinement, the total period shall not exceed 21 days.

(4) In imposing a punishment under this rule, the governor shall take into account any guidelines that the Secretary of State may from time to time issue as to the level of punishment that should normally be imposed for a particular offence against discipline.

8–24509A **55A. Adjudicator's punishment.** (1) If he finds a prisoner guilty of an offence against discipline the adjudicator may, subject to paragraph (2) and to rule 57, impose one or more of the following punishments:

(*a*) any of the punishments mentioned in rule 55(1);
(*b*) in the case of a short-term prisoner or long-term prisoner or fixed-term prisoner, an award of additional days not exceeding 42 days.

(2) A caution shall not be combined with any other punishment for the same charge.

(3) If a prisoner is found guilty of more than one charge arising out of an incident, punishments under this rule may be ordered to run consecutively but, in the case of an award of additional days, the total period added shal not exceed 42 days and, in the case of a punishment of cellular confinement, the total period shall not exceed 21 days.

(4) This rule applies to a prisoner who has been charged with having committed an offence against discipline before the date on which the rule came into force, in the same way as it applies to a prisoner who has been charged with having committed an offence against discipline on or after that date, provided the charge is referred to the adjudicator no later than 60 days after that date.

(5) Rule 53(3) shall not apply to a charge where, by virtue of paragraph (4), this rule applies to the prisoner who has been charged.

8–24509A **55B. Review of adjudicator's punishment.** (1) A reviewer means a Senior District Judge (Chief Magistrate) approved by the Lord Chancellor for the purposes of conducting a review under this rule or any deputy of such a judge as nominated by that judge.

(2) Where a punishment is imposed by an adjudicator under rule 55A(1), a prisoner may, within 14 days of receipt of the punishment, request in writing that a reviewer conducts a review.

(3) The review must be commenced within 14 days of receipt of the request and must be conducted on the papers alone.

(4) The review must only be of the punishment imposed and must not be a review of the finding of guilt under rule 55A.

(5) On completion of the review, if it appears to the reviewer that the punishment imposed was manifestly unreasonable he may—

(*a*) reduce the number of any additional days awarded;
(*b*) for whatever punishment has been imposed by the adjudicator, substitute another punishment which is, in his opinion, less severe; or
(*c*) quash the punishment entirely.

(6) A prisoner requesting a review shall serve any additional days awarded under rule 55A(1)(*b*) unless and until they are reduced.

8–24510 56. Forfeiture of remission to be treated as an award of additional days. (1) In this rule, "existing prisoner" and "existing licensee" have the meanings assigned to them by paragraph 8(1) of Schedule 12 to the Criminal Justice Act 1991.

(2) In relation to any existing prisoner or existing licensee who has forfeited any remission of his sentence, the provisions of Part II of the Criminal Justice Act 1991 shall apply as if he had been awarded such number of additional days as equals the numbers of days of remission which he has forfeited.

8–24511 57. Offences committed by young persons. (1) In the case of an offence against discipline committed by an inmate who was under the age of 21 when the offence was committed (other than an offender in relation to whom the Secretary of State has given a direction under section 13(1) of the Criminal Justice Act 1982 that he shall be treated as if he had been sentenced to imprisonment) rule 55 or, as the case may be, rule 55A shall have effect, but—

(*a*) the maximum period of forfeiture of privileges under rule 8 shall be 21 days;
(*b*) the maximum period of stoppage of or deduction from earnings shall be 42 days and the maximum amount shall be 21 days;
(*c*) the maximum period of cellular confinement shall be ten days
(*d*) the maximum period of removal from his cell or living unit shall be 21 days.

(2) In the case of an inmate who has been sentenced to a term of youth custody or detention in a young offender institution, and by virtue of a direction of the Secretary of State under section 99 of the Powers of Criminal Courts (Sentencing) Act 2000, is treated as if he had been sentenced to imprisonment for that term, any punishment imposed on him for an offence against discipline before the said direction was given shall, if it has not been exhausted or remitted, continue to have effect:

(*a*) if imposed by a governor, as if made pursuant to rule 55
(*b*) if imposed by an adjudicator, as if made pursuant to rule 55A.

8–24512 58. Cellular confinement. Before deciding whether to impose a punishment of cellular confinement the governor, adjudicator or reviewer shall first enquire of a registered medical practitioner or registered nurse, such as is mentioned in rule 20(3), as to whether there are any medical reasons why the punishment is unsuitable and shall take this advice into account when making his decision.

8–24513 59. Prospective award of additional days. (1) Subject to paragraph (2), where an offence against discipline is committed by a prisoner who is detained only on remand, additional days may be awarded by the adjudicator notwithstanding that the prisoner has not (or had not at the time of the offence) been sentenced.

(2) An award of additional days under paragraph (1) shall have effect only if the prisoner in question subsequently becomes a short-term or long-term prisoner or fixed-term prisoner whose sentence is reduced, under section 67 of the Criminal Justice Act 1967 or section 240 of the 2003 Act, by a period which includes the time when the offence against discipline was committed.

8–24513A 59A. Removal from a cell or living unit. Following the imposition of a punishment of removal from his cell or living unit, a prisoner shall be accommodated in a separate part of the prison under such restrictions of earnings and activities as the Secretary of State may direct.

8–24514 60. Suspended punishments. (1) Subject to any directions given by the Secretary of State, the power to impose a disciplinary punishment (other than a caution) shall include power to direct that the punishment is not to take effect unless, during a period specified in the direction (not being more than six months from the date of the direction), the prisoner commits another offence against discipline and a direction is given under paragraph (2).

(2) Where a prisoner commits an offence against discipline during the period specified in a direction given under paragraph (1) the person dealing with that offence may—

(*a*) direct that the suspended punishment shall take effect;

(*b*) reduce the period or amount of the suspended punishment and direct that it shall take effect as so reduced;

(*c*) vary the original direction by substituting for the period specified a period expiring not later than six months from the date of variation; or

(*d*) give no direction with respect to the suspended punishment.

(3) Where an award of additional days has been suspended under paragraph (1) and a prisoner is charged with committing an offence against discipline during the period specified in a direction given under that paragraph, the governor shall either:

(*a*) inquire into the charge and give no direction with respect to the suspended award; or

(*b*) refer the charge to the adjudicator for him to inquire into it.

8–24515 **61. Remission and mitigation of punishments and quashing of findings of guilt.** (1) Except in the case of a finding of guilt made, or a punishment imposed, by an adjudicator under rule 55A(1), the Secretary of State may quash any finding of guilt and may remit any punishment or mitigate it either by reducing it or by substituting another award which is, in his opinion, less severe.

(2) Subject to any directions given by the Secretary of State, the governor may, on the grounds of good behaviour, remit or mitigate any punishment already imposed by an adjudicator, governor or the board of visitors.

PART III
OFFICERS OF PRISONS

8–24516 **62. General duty of officers.** (1) It shall be the duty of every officer to conform to these Rules and the rules and regulations of the prison, to assist and support the governor in their maintenance and to obey his lawful instructions.

(2) An officer shall inform the governor promptly of any abuse or impropriety which comes to his knowledge.

8–24517 **63. Gratuities forbidden.** No officer shall receive any unauthorised fee, gratuity or other consideration in connection with his office.

8–24518 **64. Search of officers.** An officer shall submit himself to be searched in the prison if the governor so directs. Any such search shall be conducted in as seemly a manner as is consistent with discovering anything concealed.

8–24519 **65. Transactions with prisoners.** (1) No officer shall take part in any business or pecuniary transaction with or on behalf of a prisoner without the leave of the Secretary of State.

(2) No officer shall without authority bring in or take out, or attempt to bring in or take out, or knowingly allow to be brought in or taken out, to or for a prisoner, or deposit in any place with intent that it shall come into the possession of a prisoner, any article whatsoever.

8–24520 **66. Contact with former prisoners.** No officer shall, without the knowledge of the governor, communicate with any person whom he knows to be a former prisoner or a relative or friend of a prisoner or former prisoner.

8–24521 **67. Communications to the press.** (1) No officer shall make, directly or indirectly, any unauthorised communication to a representative of the press or any other person concerning matters which have become known to him in the course of his duty.

(2) No officer shall, without authority, publish any matter or make any public pronouncement relating to the administration of any institution to which the Prison Act 1952 applies or to any of its inmates.

8–24522 **68. Code of discipline.** The Secretary of State may approve a code of discipline to have effect in relation to officers, or such classes of officers as it may specify, setting out the offences against discipline, the awards which may be made in respect of them and the procedure for dealing with charges.

8–24523 **69. Emergencies.** Where any constable or member of the armed forces of the Crown is employed by reason of any emergency to assist the governor of a prison by performing duties ordinarily performed by an officer of a prison, any reference in Part II of these Rules to such an officer (other than a governor) shall be construed as including a reference to a constable or a member of the armed forces of the Crown so employed.

PART IV
PERSONS HAVING ACCESS TO A PRISON

8–24524 **70. Prohibited articles.** No person shall, without authority, convey into or throw into or deposit in a prison, or convey or throw out of a prison, or convey to a prisoner, or deposit in any place with intent that it shall come into the possession of a prisoner, any money, clothing, food, drink, tobacco, letter, paper, book, tool, controlled drug, firearm, explosive, weapon or other article whatever. Anything so conveyed, thrown or deposited may be confiscated by the governor.

8–24525 71. Control of persons and vehicles. (1) Any person or vehicle entering or leaving a prison may be stopped, examined and searched and in addition any such person may be photographed, fingerprinted or required to submit to other physical measurement.

(1A) Any such search of a person shall be carried out in as seemly a manner as is consistent with discovering anything concealed about the person or their belongings.

(2) The governor may direct the removal from a prison of any person who does not leave on being required to do so.

8–24526 72. Viewing of prisons. (1) No outside person shall be permitted to view a prison unless authorised by statute or the Secretary of State.

(2) No person viewing the prison shall be permitted to take a photograph, make a sketch or communicate with a prisoner unless authorised by statute or the Secretary of State.

8–24527 73. Visitors. (1) Without prejudice to any other powers to prohibit or restrict entry to prisons, or his powers under rules 34 and 35, the Secretary of State may prohibit visits by a person to a prison or to a prisoner in a prison for such periods of time as he considers necessary if the Secretary of State considers that such a prohibition is—

(*a*) necessary on grounds specified in rule 35A(4); and
(*b*) is proportionate to what is sought to be achieved by the prohibition.

(2) Paragraph (1) shall not apply in relation to any visit to a prison or prisoner by a member of the board of visitors of the prison, or justice of the peace, or to prevent any visit by a legal adviser for the purposes of an interview under rule 38 or visit allowed by the board of visitors under rule 35(6).

PART V
BOARDS OF VISITORS

8–24528 74. Disqualification for membership. Any person, directly or indirectly interested in any contract for the supply of goods or services to a prison, shall not be a member of the board of visitors for that prison and any member who becomes so interested in such a contract shall vacate office as a member.

8–24529 75. Board of visitors. (1) A member of the board of visitors for a prison appointed by the Secretary of State under section 6(2) of the Prison Act 1952 shall subject to paragraphs (3) and (4) hold office for three years, or such lesser period as the Secretary of State may appoint.

(2) A member—

(*a*) appointed for the first time to the board of visitors for a particular prison; or
(*b*) reappointed to the board following a gap of a year or more in his membership of it,

shall, during the period of 12 months following the date on which he is so appointed or (as the case may be) reappointed, undertake such training as may reasonably be required by the Secretary of State.

(3) The Secretary of State may terminate the appointment of a member if he is satisfied that—

(*a*) he has failed satisfactorily to perform his duties;
(*b*) he has failed to undertake training he has been required to undertake under paragraph (2), by the end of the period specified in that paragraph;
(*c*) he is by reason of physical or mental illness, or for any other reason, incapable of carrying out his duties;
(*d*) he has been convicted of such a criminal offence, or his conduct has been such, that it is not in the Secretary of State's opinion fitting that he should remain a member; or
(*e*) there is, or appears to be or could appear to be, any conflict of interest between the member performing his duties as a member and any interest of that member, whether personal, financial or otherwise.

(4) Where the Secretary of State:

(*a*) has reason to suspect that a member of the board of visitors for a prison may have so conducted himself that his appointment may be liable to be terminated under paragraph (3)*(a)* or *(d)*; and
(*b*) is of the opinion that the suspected conduct is of such a serious nature that the member cannot be permitted to continue to perform his functions as a member of the board pending the completion of the Secretary of State's investigations into the matter and any decision as to whether the member's appointment should be terminated,

he may suspend the member from office for such period or periods as he may reasonably require in order to complete his investigations and determine whether or not the appointment of the member should be so terminated; and a member so suspended shall not, during the period of his suspension, be regarded as being a member of the board, other than for the purposes of this paragraph and paragraphs (1) and (3).

(5) A board shall have a chairman and a vice chairman who shall be members of the board.

(6) The Secretary of State shall—

(*a*) upon the constitution of a board for the first time, appoint a chairman and a vice chairman to hold office for a period not exceeding twelve months;

(*b*) thereafter appoint, before the date of the first meeting of the board in any year of office of the board, a chairman and vice chairman for that year, having first consulted the board; and

(*c*) promptly fill, after first having consulted the board, any casual vacancy in the office of chairman or vice chairman.

(7) The Secretary of State may terminate the appointment of a member as chairman or vice chairman of the board if he is satisfied that the member has—

(*a*) failed satisfactorily to perform his functions as chairman (or as the case may be) vice chairman;

(*b*) has grossly misconducted himself while performing those functions.

8–24530 **76. Proceedings of boards.** (1) The board of visitors for a prison shall meet at the prison once a month or, if they resolve for reasons specified in the resolution that less frequent meetings are sufficient, not fewer than eight times in twelve months.

(2) The board may fix a quorum of not fewer than three members for proceedings.

(3) The board shall keep minutes of their proceedings.

(4) The proceedings of the board shall not be invalidated by any vacancy in the membership or any defect in the appointment of a member.

8–24531 **77. General duties of boards.** (1) The board of visitors for a prison shall satisfy themselves as to the state of the prison premises, the administration of the prison and the treatment of the prisoners.

(2) The board shall inquire into and report upon any matter into which the Secretary of State asks them to inquire.

(3) The board shall direct the attention of the governor to any matter which calls for his attention, and shall report to the Secretary of State any matter which they consider it expedient to report.

(4) The board shall inform the Secretary of State immediately of any abuse which comes to their knowledge.

(5) Before exercising any power under these Rules the board and any member of the board shall consult the governor in relation to any matter which may affect discipline.

8–24532 **78. Particular duties.** (1) The board of visitors for a prison and any member of the board shall hear any complaint or request which a prisoner wishes to make to them or him.

(2) The board shall arrange for the food of the prisoners to be inspected by a member of the board at frequent intervals.

(3) The board shall inquire into any report made to them, whether or not by a member of the board, that a prisoner's health, mental or physical, is likely to be injuriously affected by any conditions of his imprisonment.

8–24533 **79. Members visiting prisons.** (1) The members of the board of visitors for a prison shall visit the prison frequently, and the board shall arrange a rota whereby at least one of its members visits the prison between meetings of the board.

(2) A member of the board shall have access at any time to every part of the prison and to every prisoner, and he may interview any prisoner out of the sight and hearing of officers.

(3) A member of the board shall have access to the records of the prison.

8–24534 **80. Annual report.** (1) The board of visitors for a prison shall, in accordance with paragraphs (2) and (3) below, from time to time make a report to the Secretary of State concerning the state of the prison and its administration, including in it any advice and suggestions they consider appropriate.

(2) The board shall comply with any directions given to them from time to time by the Secretary of State as to the following matters:

(*a*) the period to be covered by a report under paragraph (1);

(*b*) the frequency with which such a report is to be made; and

(*c*) the length of time from the end of the period covered by such a report within which it is to be made;

either in respect of a particular report or generally; providing that no directions may be issued under this paragraph if they would have the effect of requiring a board to make or deliver a report less frequently than once in every 12 months.

(3) Subject to any directions given to them under paragraph (2), the board shall, under paragraph (1), make an annual report to the Secretary of State as soon as reasonably possible after 31st December each year, which shall cover the period of 12 months ending on that date or, in the case of a board constituted for the first time during that period, such part of that period during which the board has been in existence.

PART VI
SUPPLEMENTAL

8–24535 **81. Delegation by governor.** The governor of a prison may, with the leave of the Secretary of State, delegate any of his powers and duties under these Rules to another officer of that prison.

8–24536 **82. Contracted out prisons.** (1) Where the Secretary of State has entered into a contract for the running of a prison under section 84 of the Criminal Justice Act 1991 ("the 1991 Act") these Rules shall have effect in relation to that prison with the following modifications—

(a) references to an officer in the Rules shall include references to a prisoner custody officer certified as such under section 89(1) of the 1991 Act and performing custodial duties;
(b) references to a governor in the Rules shall include references to a director approved by the Secretary of State for the purposes of section 85(1)*(a)* of the 1991 Act except—
  (i) in rules 45, 48, 49, 53, 53A, 54, 55, 57, 60, 61 and 81 where references to a governor shall include references to a controller appointed by the Secretary of State under section 85(1)*(b)* of the 1991 Act, and
  (ii) in rules 62(1), 66 and 77 where references to a governor shall include references to the director and the controller;
(c) rule 68 shall not apply in relation to a prisoner custody officer certified as such under section 89(1) of the 1991 Act and performing custodial duties.

(2) Where a director exercises the powers set out in section 85(3)*(b)* of the 1991 Act (removal from association, temporary confinement and restraints) in cases of urgency, he shall notify the controller of that fact forthwith.

8–24537 **83. Contracted out parts of prisons.** Where the Secretary of State has entered into a contract for the running of part of a prison under section 84(1) of the Criminal Justice Act 1991, that part and the remaining part shall each be treated for the purposes of Parts II to IV and Part VI of these Rules as if they were separate prisons.

8–24538 **84. Contracted out functions at directly managed prisons.** (1) Where the Secretary of State has entered into a contract under section 88A(1) of the Criminal Justice Act 1991 ("the 1991 Act") for any functions at a directly managed prison to be performed by prisoner custody officers who are authorised to perform custodial duties under section 89(1) of the 1991 Act, references to an officer in these Rules shall, subject to paragraph (2), include references to a prisoner custody officer who is so authorised and who is performing contracted out functions for the purposes of, or for purposes connected with, the prison.

(2) Paragraph (1) shall not apply to references to an officer in rule 68.

(3) In this rule, "directly managed prison" has the meaning assigned to it by section 88A(5) of the 1991 Act.

8–24539 **85. Revocations and savings.** (1) Subject to paragraphs (2) and (3) below, the Rules specified in the Schedule to these Rules are hereby revoked.

(2) Without prejudice to the Interpretation Act 1978, where a prisoner committed an offence against discipline contrary to rule 47 of the Prison Rules 1964 prior to the coming into force of these Rules, those rules shall continue to have effect to permit the prisoner to be charged with such an offence, disciplinary proceedings in relation to such an offence to be continued, and the governor to impose punishment for such an offence.

(3) Without prejudice to the Interpretation Act 1978, any award of additional days or other punishment or suspended punishment for an offence against discipline awarded or imposed under any provision of the rules revoked by this rule, or those rules as saved by paragraph (2), or treated by any such provision as having been awarded or imposed under the rules revoked by this rule, shall have effect as if awarded or imposed under the corresponding provision of these Rules.

Rule 85 SCHEDULE

8–24540 (*Revocations*)

Young Offender Institution Rules 2000[1]

(SI 2000/3371 amended by SI 2002/2117 and SI 2005/897 and 3438)

PART I
PRELIMINARY

8–24550 **1. Citation and commencement.** (a) These Rules may be cited as the Young Offender Institution Rules 2000 and shall come into force on 1st April 2001.

(b) The Rules set out in the Schedule to this Order are hereby revoked.

1. These rules were made by the Secretary of State under s 47 of the Prison Act 1952.

8–24551 **2. Interpretation.** (1) In these Rules, where the context so admits, the expression-

"adjudicator" means a District Judge (Magistrates' Courts) or Deputy District Judge (Magistrates' Courts) approved[1] by the Lord Chancellor for the purpose of inquiring into a charge which has been referred to him;

"communication" includes any written or drawn communication from an inmate to any other person, whether intended to be transmitted by means of a postal service or not, and any communication from an inmate to any other person transmitted by means of a telecommunications system;

"compulsory school age" has the same meaning as in the Education Act 1996;

"controlled drug" means any drug which is a controlled drug for the purposes of the Misuse of Drugs Act 1971;

"fixed-term prisoner" has the meaning assigned to it by section 237(1) of the Criminal Justice Act 2003;

"governor" includes an officer for the time being in charge of a young offender institution;

"health care professional" means a person who is a member of a profession regulated by a body mentioned in section 25(3) of the National Health Service Reform and Health Care Professions Act 2002 and who is working within the young offender institution pursuant to rule 27(3);

"inmate" means a person who is required to be detained in a young offender institution;

"intercepted material" means the contents of any communication intercepted pursuant to these Rules;

"legal adviser" means, in relation to an inmate, his counsel or solicitor, and includes a clerk acting on behalf of his solicitor;

"minister appointed to a young offender institution" means a minister so appointed under section 10 of the Prison Act 1952;

"officer" means an officer of a young offender institution;

"registered medical practitioner" and "registered nurse" mean a practitioner or nurse who is working within the young offender institution pursuant to rule 27(3);

"short-term prisoner" and "long-term prisoner" have the meanings assigned to them by section 33(5) of the Criminal Justice Act 1991, as extended by sections 43(1) and 45(1) of that Act;

"telecommunications system" means any system (including the apparatus comprised in it) which exists for the purpose of facilitating the transmission of communications by any means involving the use of electrical or electro-magnetic energy;

"the 2003 Act" means the Criminal Justice Act 2003.

(2) In these Rules a reference to—

(a) an award of additional days means additional days awarded under these Rules by virtue of section 42 of the Criminal Justice Act 1991 or by virtue of section 257 of the 2003 Act".;

(b) the Church of England includes a reference to the Church of Wales; and

(c) a reference to a numbered rule is, unless otherwise stated, a reference to the rule of that number in these Rules and a reference to a numbered paragraph is in a rule, unless otherwise stated, a reference to the paragraph of that number in that rule.

1. The requirement of the approval of the Lord Chancellor for the appointment of a District Judge (Magistrates' Courts) or Deputy District Judge (Magistrates' Courts) as an adjudicator does not apply to a person who is approved to act as an adjudicator on 18 April 2005, and such a person may continue to act as an adjudicator for so long as he holds office as a District Judge (Magistrates' Courts) or Deputy District Judge (Magistrates' Courts): Young Offender Institution (Amendment) Rules 2005, SI 2005/897, r 1(2).

PART II
INMATES

General

8–24552 **3. Aims and general principles of young offender institutions.** (1) The aim of a young offender institution shall be to help offenders to prepare for their return to the outside community.

(2) The aim mentioned in paragraph (1) shall be achieved, in particular, by—

(a) providing a programme of activities, including education, training and work designed to assist offenders to acquire or develop personal responsibility, self-discipline, physical fitness, interests and skills and to obtain suitable employment after release;

(b) fostering links between the offender and the outside community; and

(c) co-operating with the services responsible for the offender's supervision after release.

8–24553 **4. Classification of inmates.** Inmates may be classified, in accordance with any directions of the Secretary of State, taking into account their ages, characters and circumstances.

Release

8–24554 **5. Temporary release.** (1) The Secretary of State may, in accordance with the other provisions of this rule, release temporarily an inmate to whom this rule applies.

(2) An inmate may be released under this rule for any period or periods and subject to any conditions.

(3) An inmate may only be released under this rule:

(a) on compassionate grounds or for the purpose of receiving medical treatment;
(b) to engage in employment or voluntary work;
(c) to receive instruction or training which cannot reasonably be provided in the young offender institution;
(d) to enable him to participate in any proceedings before any court, tribunal or inquiry;
(e) to enable him to consult with his legal adviser in circumstances where it is not reasonably practicable for the consultation to take place in the young offender institution;
(f) to assist any police officer in any enquiries;
(g) to facilitate the inmate's transfer between the young offender institution and another penal establishment;
(h) to assist him in maintaining family ties or in his transition from life in the young offender institution to freedom; or
(i) *revoked.*

(4) An inmate shall not be released under this rule unless the Secretary of State is satisfied that there would not be an unacceptable risk of his committing offences whilst released or otherwise of his failing to comply with any condition upon which he is released.

(5) Where at any time an offender is subject concurrently:

(a) to a detention and training order; and
(b) to a sentence of detention in a young offender institution,

he shall be treated for the purposes of paragraphs (6) and (7) as if he were subject only to the one of them that was imposed on the later occasion.

(6) The Secretary of State shall not release under this rule an inmate if, having regard to:

(a) the period or proportion of his sentence which the inmate has served or, in a case where paragraph (10) does not apply to require all the sentences he is serving to be treated as a single term, the period or proportion of any such sentence he has served; and
(b) the frequency with which the inmate has been granted temporary release under this rule,

the Secretary of State is of the opinion that the release of the inmate would be likely to undermine public confidence in the administration of justice.

(7) If an inmate has been temporarily released under this rule during the relevant period and has been sentenced to any period of detention, custody or imprisonment for a criminal offence committed whilst at large following that release, he shall not be released under this rule unless his release, having regard to the circumstances of his conviction, would not, in the opinion of the Secretary of State, be likely to undermine public confidence in the administration of justice; and for this purpose "the relevant period":

(a) in the case of an inmate serving a determinate sentence of imprisonment, detention or custody, is the period he has served in respect of that sentence, unless, notwithstanding paragraph (10), the sentences he is serving do not fall to be treated as a single term, in which case it is the period since he was last released in relation to one of those sentences under Part II of the Criminal Justice Act 1991 ("the 1991 Act") or section 100 of the Powers of the Criminal Courts (Sentencing) Act 2000 ("the 2000 Act") or Chapter 6 of Part 12 of the 2003 Act; or
(b) in the case of an inmate serving an indeterminate sentence of imprisonment, detention or custody, is, if the inmate has previously been released on licence under Part II of the 1991 Act or Part II of the Crime (Sentences) Act 1997 or Chapter 6 of Part 12 of the 2003 Act, the period since the date of his last recall to a penal establishment in respect of that sentence or, where the inmate has not been so released, the period he has served in respect of that sentence,

save that where an inmate falls within both of sub-paragraphs (a) and (b) above, the "relevant period", in the case of that inmate, shall be determined by whichever of the applicable sub-paragraphs that produces the longer period.

(8) An inmate released under this rule may be recalled at any time whether the conditions of his release have been broken or not.

(9) This rule applies to inmates other than persons committed in custody for trial or to be sentenced or otherwise dealt with before or by the Crown Court or remanded in custody by any court.

(10) For the purposes of any reference in this rule to an inmate's sentence, consecutive terms and terms which are wholly or partly concurrent shall be treated as a single term.

(11) In this rule, any reference to release on licence under Part II of the 1991 Act includes any release on licence under any earlier legislation providing for early release on licence.

Conditions

8–24555 **6. Privileges.** (1) There shall be established at every young offender institution systems of privileges approved by the Secretary of State and appropriate to the classes of inmates thereof and their ages, characters and circumstances, which shall include arrangements under which money earned by inmates may be spent by them within the young offender institution.

(2) Systems of privileges approved under paragraph (1) may include arrangements under which inmates may be allowed time outside the cells and in association with one another, in excess of the minimum time which, subject to the other provisions of these Rules apart from this rule, is otherwise allowed to inmates at the young offender institution for this purpose.

(3) Systems of privileges approved under paragraph (1) may include arrangements under which privileges may be granted to inmates only in so far as they have met, and for so long as they continue to meet, specified standards in their behaviour and their performance in work or other activities.

(4) Systems of privileges which include arrangements of the kind referred to in paragraph (3) shall include procedures to be followed in determining whether or not any of the privileges concerned shall be granted, or shall continue to be granted, to an inmate; such procedures shall include a requirement that the inmate be given reasons for any decision adverse to him together with a statement of the means by which he may appeal against it.

(5) Nothing in this rule shall be taken to confer on an inmate any entitlement to any privilege or to affect any provision in these Rules other than this rule as a result of which any privilege may be forfeited or otherwise lost or an inmate deprived of association with other inmates.

8–24556 **7. Information to inmates.** (1) Every inmate shall be provided, as soon as possible after his reception into the young offender institution, and in any case within 24 hours, with information in writing about those provisions of these Rules and other matters which it is necessary that he should know, including earnings and privileges, and the proper method of making requests and complaints.

(2) In the case of an inmate aged under 18, or an inmate aged 18 or over who cannot read or appears to have difficulty in understanding the information so provided, the governor, or an officer deputed by him, shall so explain it to him that he can understand his rights and obligations.

(3) A copy of these Rules shall be made available to any inmate who requests it.

8–24557 **8. Requests and complaints.** (1) A request or complaint to the governor or Board of Visitors relating to an inmate's detention shall be made orally or in writing by that inmate.

(2) On every day the governor shall hear any oral requests and complaints that are made to him under paragraph (1).

(3) A written request or complaint under paragraph (1) may be made in confidence.

8–24558 **9. Communications generally.** (1) Without prejudice to sections 6 and 19 of the Prison Act 1952 and except as provided by these Rules, an inmate shall not be permitted to communicate with any person outside the young offender institution, or such person with him, except with the leave of the Secretary of State or as a privilege under rule 7.

(2) Notwithstanding paragraph (1), and except as otherwise provided in these Rules, the Secretary of State may impose any restriction or condition, either generally or in a particular case, upon the communications to be permitted between an inmate and other persons if he considers that the restriction or condition to be imposed—

(a) does not interfere with the Convention rights of any person; or

(b) is necessary on grounds specified in paragraph (3) below, provided that:

(i) reliance on the grounds is compatible with the Convention right to be interfered with; and

(ii) the restriction or condition is proportionate to what is sought to be achieved.

(3) The grounds referred to in paragraph (2) are—

(a) the interests of national security;

(b) the prevention, detection, investigation or prosecution of crime;

(c) the interests of public safety;

(d) securing or maintaining security or good order and discipline in the young offender institution;

(e) the protection of health or morals;

(f) the protection of the reputation of others;

(g) maintaining the authority and impartiality of the judiciary; or

(h) the protection of the rights and freedoms of any person.

(4) Subject to paragraph (2), the Secretary of State may require that any visit, or class of visits, shall be held in facilities which include special features restricting or preventing physical contact between an inmate and a visitor.

(5) Every visit to an inmate shall take place within the sight of an officer or employee of the young offender institution authorised for the purposes of this rule by the governor (in this rule referred to as an "authorised employee"), unless the Secretary of State otherwise directs, and for the purposes of this paragraph a visit to an inmate shall be taken to take place within the sight of an officer or authorised employee if it can be seen by an officer or authorised employee by means of an overt closed circuit television system.

(6) Subject to rule 13, every visit to an inmate shall take place within the hearing of an officer or authorised employee, unless the Secretary of State otherwise directs.

(7) The Secretary of State may give directions, either generally or in relation to any visit or class of visits, concerning the day and times when inmates may be visited.

(8) In this rule—

(a) references to communications include references to communications during visits;

(b) references to restrictions and conditions upon communications include references to restrictions and conditions in relation to the length, duration and frequency of communications; and

(c) references to Convention rights are to the Convention rights within the meaning of the Human Rights Act 1998.

8–24559 **10. Personal letters and visits.** (1) Subject to paragraph (7) an inmate shall be entitled—

(a) to send and to receive a letter on his reception into a young offender institution and thereafter once a week; and

(b) to receive a visit twice in every period of four weeks, but only once in every such period if the Secretary of State so directs.

(2) The governor may allow an inmate an additional letter or visit as a privilege under rule 6 or when necessary for his welfare or that of his family.

(3) The governor may allow an inmate entitled to a visit to send and to receive a letter instead.

(4) The governor may defer the right of an inmate to a visit until the expiration of any period of confinement to a cell or room.

(5) The board of visitors may allow an inmate an additional letter or visit in special circumstances, and may direct that a visit may extend beyond the normal duration.

(6) The Secretary of State may allow additional letters and visits in relation to any inmate or class of inmates.

(7) An inmate shall not be entitled under this rule to receive a visit from—

(a) any person, whether or not a relative or friend, during any period of time that person is the subject of a prohibition imposed under rule 77; or

(b) any other person, other than a relative or friend, except with the leave of the Secretary of State.

(8) Any letter or visit under the succeeding provisions of these Rules shall not be counted as a letter or visit for the purposes of this rule.

8–24560 **11. Interception of communications.** (1) The Secretary of State may give directions to any governor concerning the interception in a young offender institution of any communication by any inmate or class of inmates if the Secretary of State considers that the directions are—

(a) necessary on grounds specified in paragraph (4); and

(b) proportionate to what is sought to be achieved.

(2) Subject to any directions given by the Secretary of State, the governor may make arrangements for any communication by an inmate or class of inmates to be intercepted in a young offender institution by an officer or an employee of the young offender institution authorised by the governor for the purposes of this rule (referred to in this rule as an "authorised employee") if he considers that the arrangements are—

(a) necessary on grounds specified in paragraph (4); and

(b) proportionate to what is sought to be achieved.

(3) Any communication by an inmate may, during the course of its transmission in a young offender institution, be terminated by an officer or an authorised employee if he considers that to terminate the communication is—

(a) necessary on grounds specified in paragraph (4); and

(b) proportionate to what is sought to be achieved by the termination.

(4) The grounds referred to in paragraphs (1)(a), (2)(a) and (3)(a) are—

(a) the interests of national security;

(b) the prevention, detection, investigation or prosecution of crime;

(c) the interests of public safety;

(d) securing or maintaining security or good order and discipline in the young offender institution;

(e) the protection of health or morals; or

(f) the protection of the rights and freedoms of any person.

(5) Any reference to the grounds specified in paragraph (4) in relation to the interception of a communication by means of a telecommunications system in a young offender institution, or the disclosure or retention of intercepted material from such a communication, shall be taken to be a reference to those grounds with the omission of sub-paragraph (f).

(6) For the purposes of this rule "interception"—

(a) in relation to a communication by means of a telecommunications system, means any action taken in relation to the system or its operation so as to make some or all of the contents of the communications available, while being transmitted, to a person other than the sender or intended recipient of the communication; and the contents of a communication are to be taken to be made available to a person while being transmitted where the contents of the communication, while being transmitted, are diverted or recorded so as to be available to a person subsequently; and

(b) in relation to any written or drawn communication, includes opening, reading, examining and copying the communication.

8–24561 **12. Permanent log of communications.** (1) The governor may arrange for a permanent log to be kept of all communications by or to an inmate.

(2) The log referred to in paragraph (1) may include, in relation to a communication by means of a telecommunications system in a young offender institution, a record of the destination, duration and cost of the communication and, in relation to any written or drawn communication, a record of the sender and addressee of the communication.

8–24562 **13. Disclosure of material.** (1) The governor may not disclose to any person who is not an officer of a young offender institution or of the Secretary of State or an employee of the young offender institution authorised by the governor for the purposes of this rule any intercepted material, information retained pursuant to rule 12 or material obtained by means of an overt closed circuit television system used during a visit unless—

(a) he considers that such disclosure is—

(i) necessary on grounds specified in rule 11(4); and

(ii) proportionate to what is sought to be achieved by the disclosure;

(b) in the case of intercepted material or material obtained by means of an overt closed circuit television system used during a visit, all parties to the communication or visit consent to the disclosure; or

(c) in the case of information retained pursuant to rule 12, the inmate to whose communication the information relates, consents to the disclosure.

8–24563 **14. Retention of material.** (1) The governor shall not retain any intercepted material or material obtained by means of an overt closed circuit television system used during a visit for a period longer than 3 months beginning with the day on which the material was intercepted or obtained unless he is satisfied that continued retention of it is—

(a) necessary on grounds specified in rule 11(4); and

(b) proportionate to what is sought to be achieved by the continued retention.

(2) Where such material is retained for longer than three months pursuant to paragraph (1) the governor shall review its continued retention at periodic intervals until such time as it is no longer held by the governor.

(3) The first review referred to in paragraph (2) shall take place not more than three months after the decision to retain the material taken pursuant to paragraph (1) and subsequent reviews shall take place not more than three months apart thereafter.

(4) If the governor, on a review conducted pursuant to paragraph (2) or at any other time, is not satisfied that the continued retention of the material satisfies the requirements set out in paragraph (1), he shall arrange for the material to be destroyed.

8–24564 **15. Police interviews.** A police officer may, on production of an order issued by or on behalf of a chief officer of police, interview any inmate willing to see him.

8–24565 **16. Legal advisers.** (1) The legal adviser of an inmate in any legal proceedings, civil or criminal, to which the inmate is a party shall be afforded reasonable facilities for interviewing him in connection with those proceedings, and may do so out of hearing of an officer.

(2) An inmate's legal adviser may, with the leave of the Secretary of State, interview the inmate in connection with any other legal business.

8–24566 **17. Correspondence with legal advisers and courts.** (1) An inmate may correspond with his legal adviser and any court and such correspondence may only be opened, read or stopped by the governor in accordance with the provisions of this rule.

(2) Correspondence to which this rule applies may be opened if the governor has reasonable cause to believe that it contains an illicit enclosure and any such enclosure shall be dealt with in accordance with the other provisions of these Rules.

(3) Correspondence to which this rule applies may be opened, read and stopped if the governor has reasonable cause to believe its contents endanger prison or young offender institution security or the safety of others or are otherwise of a criminal nature.

(4) An inmate shall be given the opportunity to be present when any correspondence to which this rule applies is opened and shall be informed if it or any enclosure is to be read or stopped.

(5) An inmate shall on request be provided with any writing materials necessary for the purposes of paragraph (1).

(6) In this rule, "court" includes the European Court of Human Rights and the European Court of Justice; and "illicit enclosure" includes any article possession of which has not been authorised in accordance with the other provisions of these Rules and any correspondence to or from a person other than the inmate concerned, his legal adviser or a court.

8–24567 **18. Securing release of defaulters.** An inmate detained in a young offender institution in default of payment of a fine or any other sum of money may communicate with, and be visited at any reasonable time on a weekday by, any relative or friend for payment in order to secure his release.

8–24568 **19.** *Clothing*

8–24569 **20.** *Food*

8–24570 **21.** *Alcohol and tobacco*

8–24571 **22.** *Sleeping accommodation*

8–24572 **23.** *Beds and bedding*

8–24573 **24.** *Hygiene*

8–24574 **25.** *Female inmates*

8–24575 **26.** *Library books*

Medical Attention

8–24576 **27–29.** *Medical attention*

Religion

8–24577 **30–36.** *Religion*

Occupation and Links with the Community

8–24578 **37–42.** *Occupation and Links with the Community*

8–24579 **43. After-care.** (1) From the beginning of his sentence, consideration shall be given, in consultation with the appropriate supervising service, to an inmate's future and the help to be given to him in preparation for and after his return to the community.

(2) Every inmate who is liable to supervision after release shall be given a careful explanation of his liability and the requirements to which he will be subject while under supervision.

Discipline and Control

8–24580 **44. Maintenance of order and discipline.** (1) Order and discipline shall be maintained, but with no more restriction than is required in the interests of security and well-ordered community life.

(2) Notwithstanding paragraph (1), regimes may be established at young offender institutions under which stricter order and discipline are maintained and which emphasise strict standards of dress, appearance and conduct; provided that no inmate shall be required to participate in such a regime unless he has been first assessed as being suitable for it and no inmate shall be required to continue with such a regime if at any time it appears that he is no longer suitable for it.

(3) For the purposes of paragraph (2), whether an inmate is suitable for a stricter regime is to be assessed by reference to whether he is sufficiently fit in mind and body to undertake it and whether, in the opinion of the Secretary of State, experience of the regime will further his rehabilitation.

(4) In the control of inmates, officers shall seek to influence them through their own example and leadership, and to enlist their willing co-operation.

8–24581 **45. Custody outside a young offender institution.** (1) A person being taken to or from a young offender institution in custody shall be exposed as little as possible to public observation and proper care shall be taken to protect him from curiosity and insult.

(2) An inmate required to be taken in custody anywhere outside a young offender institution shall be kept in the custody of an officer appointed under section 3 of the Prison Act 1952 or of a police officer.

(3) An inmate required to be taken in custody to any court shall, when he appears before the court, wear his own clothing or ordinary civilian clothing provided by the governor.

8–24582 **46. Search.** (1) Every inmate shall be searched when taken into custody by an officer, on his reception into a young offender institution and subsequently as the governor thinks necessary or as the Secretary of State may direct.

(2) An inmate shall be searched in as seemly a manner as is consistent with discovering anything concealed.

(3) No inmate shall be stripped and searched in the sight of another inmate or in the sight of a person of the opposite sex.

8–24583 **47. Record and photograph.** (1) A personal record of each inmate shall be prepared and maintained in such manner as the Secretary of State may direct, but no part of the record shall be disclosed to any person not authorised to receive it.

(2) Every inmate may be photographed on reception and subsequently, but no copy of the photograph or any other personal record shall be given to any person not authorised to receive it.

(2A) In this rule "personal record" may include personal information and biometric records (such as fingerprints or other physical measurements).

8–24584 **48. Inmates' property.** (1) Anything, other than cash, which an inmate has at a young offender institution and which he is not allowed to retain for his own use shall be taken into the governor's custody.

(2) Any case which an inmate has at a young offender institution shall be paid into an account under the control of the governor and the inmate shall be credited with the amount in the books of the institution.

(3) Any article belonging to an inmate which remains unclaimed for a period of more than three years after he is released, or dies, may be sold or otherwise disposed of; and the net proceeds of any sale shall be paid to the National Association for the Care and Resettlement of Offenders, for its general purposes.

(4) The governor may confiscate any unauthorised article found in the possession of an inmate after his reception into a young offender institution, or concealed or deposited within a young offender institution.

8–24585 **49. Removal from association.** (1) Where it appears desirable[1], for the maintenance of good order or discipline or in his own interests, that an inmate should not associate with other inmates, either generally or for particular purposes, the governor may arrange for the inmate's removal from association accordingly.

(2) An inmate shall not be removed under this rule for a period of more than 72 hours without the authority of the Secretary of State and authority given under this paragraph shall be for a period not exceeding 14 days but it may be renewed from time to time for a like period.

(3) The governor may arrange at his discretion for an inmate removed under this rule to resume association with other inmates at any time, and in exercising that discretion the governor must fully consider any recommendation that the inmate resumes association on medical grounds made by a registered medical practitioner or registered nurse such as is mentioned in rule 27(3).

1. Contemporary standards of fairness require that before any order is made, young offenders should be given an opportunity to make representations although this need be no more than providing an opportunity to comment on the tentative reasons for making an order (*R (P) v Secretary of State for the Home Department* (2005) Times 21 January, CA).

8–24586 **50. Use of force.** (1) An officer in dealing with an inmate shall not use force unnecessarily and, when the application of force to an inmate is necessary, no more force than is necessary shall be used.

(2) No officer shall act deliberately in a manner calculated to provoke an inmate.

8–24587 **51. Temporary confinement.** (1) The governor may order an inmate who is refractory or violent to be confined temporarily in a special cell or room, but an inmate shall not be so confined as a punishment, or after he has ceased to be refractory or violent.

(2) A cell or room shall not be used for the purpose of this rule unless it has been certified by an officer of the Secretary of State (not being an officer of a young offender institution) that it is suitable for the purpose, that its size, lighting, heating, ventilation and fittings are adequate for health, and that it allows the inmate to communicate at any time with an officer.

(3) In relation to any young offender institution, section 14(6) of the Prison Act 1952 shall have effect so as to enable the provision of special rooms instead of special cells for the temporary confinement of refractory or violent inmates.

(4) An inmate shall not be confined under this rule for longer than 24 hours without a direction in writing given by an officer of the Secretary of State.

8–24588 **52. Restraints.** (1) The governor may order an inmate to be put under restraint where this is necessary to prevent the inmate from injuring himself or others, damaging property or creating a disturbance.

(2) The governor may not order an inmate aged under 17 to be put under restraint, except that he may order such an inmate be placed in handcuffs where this is necessary to prevent the inmate from injuring himself or others, damaging property or creating a disturbance.

(3) Notice of such an order shall be given without delay to a member of the board of visitors and to the registered medical practitioner or registered nurse such as is mentioned in rule 27(3).

(4) On receipt of the notice, the registered medical practitioner or registered nurse referred to in paragraph (3), shall inform the governor whether there are any reasons why the inmate should not be put under restraint. The governor shall give effect to any recommendation which may be made under this paragraph.

(5) An inmate shall not be kept under restraint longer than necessary, nor shall he be so kept for longer than 24 hours without a direction in writing given by a member of the board of visitors or by an officer of the Secretary of State (not being an officer of a young offender institution). Such a direction shall state the grounds for the restraint and the time during which it may continue.

(6) Particulars of every case of restraint under the foregoing provisions of this rule shall be forthwith recorded.

(7) Except as provided by this rule no inmate shall be put under restraint otherwise than for safe custody during removal, or on medical grounds by direction of the registered medical practitioner or registered nurse such as is mentioned in rule 27(3). No inmate shall be put under restraint as a punishment.

(8) Any means of restraint shall be of a pattern authorised by the Secretary of State, and shall be used in such manner and under such conditions as the Secretary of State may direct.

8–24589 53. Compulsory Testing for controlled drugs. (1) This rule applies where an officer, acting under the powers conferred by section 16A of the Prison Act 1952 (power to test inmates for drugs), requires an inmate to provide a sample for the purposes of ascertaining whether he has any controlled drug in his body.

(2) In this rule "sample" means a sample of urine or any other description of sample specified in the authorisation by the governor for the purposes of section 16A.

(3) When requiring an inmate to provide a sample, an officer shall, so far as is reasonably practicable, inform the inmate:

(a) that he is being required to provide a sample in accordance with section 16A of the Prison Act 1952; and

(b) that a refusal to provide a sample may lead to disciplinary proceedings being brought against him.

(4) An officer shall require an inmate to provide a fresh sample, free from any adulteration.

(5) An officer requiring a sample shall make such arrangements and give the inmate such instructions for its provision as may be reasonably necessary in order to prevent or detect its adulteration or falsification.

(6) An inmate who is required to provide a sample may be kept apart from other inmates for a period not exceeding one hour to enable arrangements to be made for the provision of the sample.

(7) An inmate who is unable to provide a sample of urine when required to do so may be kept apart from other inmates until he has provided the required sample, save that an inmate may not be kept apart under this paragraph for a period of more than five hours.

(8) An inmate required to provide a sample of urine shall be afforded such degree of privacy for the purposes of providing the sample as may be compatible with the need to prevent or detect any adulteration or falsification of the sample; in particular an inmate shall not be required to provide such a sample in the sight of a person of the opposite sex.

8–24590 54. Supervision of inmates by means of an overt closed circuit television system. (1) Without prejudice to his powers to make arrangements for the supervision of inmates in his custody, the governor may make arrangements for any inmate to be placed under constant supervision by means of an overt closed circuit television system placed in a cell, dormitory or other place in the young offender institution if he considers that—

(a) such supervision is necessary for—

(i) the health and safety of the inmate or any other person;

(ii) the prevention, detection or prosecution of crime; or

(iii) securing or maintaining security or good order and discipline in the young offender institution; and

(b) it is proportionate to what is sought to be achieved.

(2) If an overt closed circuit television system is used for the purposes of this rule, the provisions of rules 13 and 14 shall apply to any material obtained.

8–24590A 54A. Compulsory testing for alcohol. (1) This rule applies where an officer, acting under an authorisation in force under section 16B of the Prison Act 1952 (power to test prisoners for alcohol), requires an inmate to provide a sample for the purpose of ascertaining whether he has alcohol in his body.

(2) When requiring an inmate to provide a sample an officer shall, so far as is reasonably practicable, inform the inmate—

(*a*) that he is being required to provide a sample in accordance with section 16B of the Prison Act 1952; and

(*b*) that a refusal to provide a sample may lead to disciplinary proceedings being brought against him.

(3) An officer requiring a sample shall make such arrangements and give the inmate such instructions for its provision as may be reasonably necessary in order to prevent or detect its adulteration or falsification.

(4) Subject to paragraph (5) an inmate who is required to provide a sample may be kept apart from other inmates for a period not exceeding one hour to enable arrangements to be made for the provision of the sample.

(5) An inmate who is unable to provide a sample of urine when required to do so may be kept apart from other inmates until he has provided the required sample, except that an inmate may not be kept apart under this paragraph for a period of more than 5 hours.

(6) An inmate required to provide a sample of urine shall be afforded such degree of privacy for the purposes of providing the sample as may be compatible with the need to prevent or detect any adulteration or falsification of the sample; in particular an inmate shall not be required to provide such a sample in the sight of a person of the opposite sex.

8–24591 **55. Offences against discipline.** An inmate is guilty of an offence against discipline if he—

(1) commits any assault;
(2) commits any racially aggravated assault;
(3) detains any person against his will;
(4) denies access to any part of the young offender institution to any officer or any person (other than an inmate) who is at the young offender institution for the purpose of working there;
(5) fights with any person;
(6) intentionally endangers the health or personal safety of others or, by his conduct, is reckless whether such health or personal safety is endangered;
(7) intentionally obstructs an officer in the execution of his duty, or any person (other than an inmate) who is at the young offender institution for the purpose of working there, in the performance of his work;
(8) escapes or absconds from a young offender institution or from legal custody;
(9) fails to comply with any condition upon which he was temporarily released under rule 5 of these rules;
(10) is found with any substance in his urine which demonstrates that a controlled drug has, whether in prison or while on temporary release under rule 5, been administered to him by himself or by another person (but subject to rule 56);
(11) is intoxicated as a consequence of consuming any alcoholic beverage (but subject to rule 56A);
(12) consumes any alcoholic beverage whether or not provided to him by another person (but subject to rule 56A);
(13) has in his possession—
 (a) any unauthorised article, or
 (b) a greater quantity of any article than he is authorised to have;
(14) sells or delivers to any person any unauthorised article;
(15) sells or, without permission, delivers to any person any article which he is allowed to have only for his own use;
(16) takes improperly any article belonging to another person or to a young offender institution;
(17) intentionally or recklessly sets fire to any part of a young offender institution or any other property, whether or not his own;
(18) destroys or damages any part of a young offender institution or any other property other than his own;
(19) causes racially aggravated damage to, or destruction of, any part of a young offender institution or any other property, other than his own;
(20) absents himself from any place where he is required to be or is present at any place where he is not authorised to be;
(21) is disrespectful to any officer, or any person (other than an inmate) who is at the young offender institution for the purpose of working there, or any person visiting a young offender institution;
(22) uses threatening, abusive or insulting words or behaviour;
(23) uses threatening, abusive or insulting racist words or behaviour;
(24) intentionally fails to work properly or, being required to work, refuses to do so;
(25) disobeys any lawful order;
(26) disobeys or fails to comply with any rule or regulation applying to him;
(27) receives any controlled drug or, without the consent of an officer, any other article, during the course of a visit (not being an interview such as is mentioned in rule 16);
(28) displays, attaches or draws on any part of a young offender institution, or on any other property, threatening, abusive, or insulting racist words, drawings, symbols or other material;
(29)
 (a) attempts to commit,
 (b) incites another inmate to commit, or
 (c) assists another inmate to commit or to attempt to commit,

 any of the foregoing offences.

8–24592 **56. Defences to rule 55(10).** It shall be a defence for an inmate charged with an offence under rule 55(10) to show that—

(a) the controlled drug had been, prior to its administration, lawfully in his possession for his use or was administered to him in the course of a lawful supply of the drug to him by another person;
(b) the controlled drug was administered by or to him in circumstances in which he did not know and had no reason to suspect that such a drug was being administered; or
(c) the controlled drug was administered by or to him under duress or to him without his consent in circumstances where it was not reasonable for him to have resisted.

8–24592A **56A Defences to rule 55(11) and rule 55(12).** It shall be a defence for an inmate charged with an offence under rule 55(11) or (12) to show that—
(*a*) the alcohol was consumed by him in circumstances in which he did not know and had no reason to suspect that he was consuming alcohol; or
(*b*) the alcohol was consumed by him without his consent in circumstances where it was not reasonable for him to have resisted; or
(*c*) *revoked.*

8–24593 **57. Interpretation of rule 55.** For the purposes of rule 55 words, behaviour or material shall be racist if they demonstrate or are motivated (wholly or partly) by hostility to members of a racial group (whether identifiable or not) based on their membership (or presumed membership) of a racial group, and "membership", "presumed", "racial group" and "racially aggravated", shall have the meanings assigned to them by section 28 of the Crime and Disorder Act 1998

8–24594 **58. Disciplinary charges.** (1) Where an inmate is to be charged with an offence against discipline, the charge shall be laid as soon as possible and, save in exceptional circumstances, within 48 hours of the discovery of the offence.

(2) Every charge shall be inquired into by the governor.

(3) Every charge shall be first inquired into not later, save in exceptional circumstances, than the next day, not being a Sunday or public holiday, after it is laid.

(4) An inmate who is to be charged with an offence against discipline may be kept apart from other inmates pending the governor's first inquiry.

8–24595 **59. Rights of inmates charged.** (1) Where an inmate is charged with an offence against discipline, he shall be informed of the charge as soon as possible and, in any case, before the time when it is inquired into by the governor.

(2) At an inquiry into charge against an inmate he shall be given a opportunity of hearing what is alleged against him and of presenting his own case.

8–24596 **60. Governor's punishments.** (1) If he finds an inmate guilty of an offence against discipline the governor may, subject to paragraph (3) and rule 64, impose one or more of the following punishments:
(a) caution;
(b) forfeiture for a period not exceeding 21 days of any of the privileges under rule 6;
(c) removal for a period not exceeding 21 days from any particular activity or activities of the young offender institution, other than education, training courses, work and physical education in accordance with rules 37, 38, 39, 40 and 41;
(d) extra work outside the normal working week for a period not exceeding 21 days and for not more than two hours on any day;
(e) stoppage of or deduction from earnings for a period not exceeding 42 days of an amount not exceeding 21 days' earnings;
(f) in the case of an offence against discipline committed by an inmate who was aged 18 or over at the time of commission of the offence, other than an inmate who is serving the period of detention and training under a detention and training order pursuant to section 100 of the Powers of Criminal Courts (Sentencing) Act 2000, confinement to a cell or room for a period not exceeding seven days;
(g) removal from his wing or living unit for a period not exceeding 21 days;
(h) in the case of an inmate who is a short-term or long-term prisoner, an award of additional days not exceeding 42 days.

(2) If an inmate is found guilty of more than one charge arising out of an incident punishments under this rule may be ordered to run consecutively, but, in the case of an award of additional days, the total period shall not exceed 42 days and in the case of an award of cellular confinement the total period shall not exceed seven days.

(3) An award of a caution shall not be combined with any other punishment for the same charge.

(4) In imposing a punishment under this rule, the governor shall take into account any guidelines that the Secretary of State may from time to time issue as to the level of punishment that should normally be imposed for a particular offence against discipline.

8–24596A **60A. Adjudicator's punishments.** (1) If he finds a inmate guilty of an offence against discipline the adjudicator may, subject to paragraph (2) and to rule 65, impose one or more of the following punishments:

(*a*) any of the punishments mentioned in rule 60(1);
(*b*) in the case of an inmate who is a short-term prisoner or long-term prisoner or fixed-term prisoner, an award of additional days not exceeding 42 days.

(2) A caution shall not be combined with any other punishment for the same charge.

(3) If an inmate is found guilty of more than one charge arising out of an incident, punishments under this rule may be ordered to run consecutively but, in the case of an award of additional days, the total period added shall not exceed 42 days and, in the case of a punishment of cellular confinement, the total period shall not exceed ten days.

(4) This rule applies to an inmate who has been charged with having committed an offence against discipline before the date on which the rule came into force, in the same way as it applies to an inmate who has been charged with having committed an offence against discipline on or after that date, provided the charge is referred to the adjudicator no later than 60 days after that date.

(5) Rule 58(3) shall not apply to a charge where, by virtue of paragraph (4), this rule applies to the inmate who has been charged.

8–24596B 60B. Review of adjudicator's punishment. (1) A reviewer means a Senior District Judge (Chief Magistrate) approved by the Lord Chancellor for the purposes of conducting a review under this rule or any deputy of such a judge as nominated by that judge.

(2) Where a punishment is imposed by an adjudicator under rule 60A(1) or rule 65(1A) an inmate may, within 14 days of receipt of the punishment, request in writing that a reviewer conducts a review.

(3) The review must be commenced within 14 days of receipt of the request and must be conducted on the papers alone.

(4) The review must only be of the punishment imposed and must not be a review of the finding of guilt.

(5) On completion of the review, if it appears to the reviewer that the punishment imposed was manifestly unreasonable, he may—

(*a*) reduce the number of any additional days awarded;
(*b*) for whatever punishment has been imposed by the adjudicator, substitute another punishment which is, in his opinion, less severe; or
(*c*) quash the punishment entirely.

(6) An inmate requesting a review shall serve any additional days awarded under rule 60A(1)(*b*) or 65(1A)(*b*) unless and until they are reduced.

8–24597 61. Confinement to a cell or room. (1) Before deciding whether to impose a punishment of confinement to a cell or room, the governor, adjudicator or reviewer shall first enquire of a registered medical practitioner or registered nurse, such as is mentioned in rule 27(3), as to whether there are any medical reasons why the punishment is unsuitable and shall take this into account when making his decision.

(2) No cell or room shall be used as a detention cell or room for the purpose of a punishment of confinement to a cell or room unless it has been certified by an officer of the Secretary of State (not being an officer of a young offender institution) that it is suitable for the purpose; that its size, lighting, heating, ventilation and fittings are adequate for health; and that it allows the inmate to communicate at any time with an officer.

8–24598 62. Removal from wing or living unit. Following the imposition of a punishment of removal from his wing or living unit, an inmate shall be accommodated in a separate part of the young offender institution under such restrictions of earnings and activities as the Secretary of State may direct.

8–24599 63. Suspended punishments. (1) Subject to any directions of the Secretary of State, the power to impose a disciplinary punishment (other than a caution) shall include a power to direct that the punishment is not to take effect unless, during a period specified in the direction (not being more than six months from the date of the direction), the inmate commits another offence against discipline and a direction is given under paragraph (2).

(2) Where an inmate commits an offence against discipline during the period specified in a direction given under paragraph (1), the person dealing with that offence may—

(a) direct that the suspended punishment shall take effect; or
(b) reduce the period or amount of the suspended punishment and direct that it shall take effect as so reduced; or
(c) vary the original direction by substituting for the period specified therein a period expiring not later than six months from the date of variation; or
(d) give no direction with respect to the suspended punishment.

8–24600 64. Remission and mitigation of punishments and quashing of findings of guilt. (1) Except in the case of a finding of guilt made, or a punishment imposed, by an adjudicator under rule 60A(1)(*b*) or rule 65(1A)(*b*) the Secretary of State may quash any findings of guilt and may remit a disciplinary punishment or mitigate it either by reducing it or by substituting a punishment which is, in his opinion, less severe.

(2) Subject to any directions of the Secretary of State, the governor may remit or mitigate any punishment imposed by a governor.

8–24601 **65. Adult female inmates: disciplinary punishments.** (1) In the case of a female inmate aged 21 years or over, rule 60 shall not apply, but the governor may, if he finds the inmate guilty of an offence against discipline, impose one or more of the following punishments:

(a) caution;
(b) forfeiture for a period not exceeding 42 days of any of the privileges under rule 6;
(c) removal for a period not exceeding 21 days from any particular activity or activities of the young offender institution, other than education, training courses, work and physical education in accordance with rules 37, 38, 39, 40 and 41;
(d) stoppage of or deduction from earnings for a period not exceeding 84 days of an amount not exceeding 42 days' earnings;
(e) confinement to a cell or room for a period not exceeding 14 days;
(f) in the case of an inmate who is a short-term or long-term prisoner, an award of additional days not exceeding 42 days.

(1A) In the case of a female inmate aged 21 years or over, where a charge has been referred to the adjudicator, rule 60A shall not apply, but the adjudicator may if he finds the inmate guilty of an offence against discipline, impose one or more of the following punishments:

(*a*) any of the punishments mentioned in paragraph (1);
(*b*) in the case of an inmate who is a short-term or long-term prisoner or fixed-term prisoner, an award of additional days not exceeding 42 days.

(2) Subject to any directions given by the Secretary of State, the governor may, on the grounds of good behaviour, remit or mitigate any punishment already imposed by an adjudicator, governor or the board of visitors.

8–24602 **66. Forfeiture of remission to be treated as an award of additional days.** (1) In this rule, "existing prisoner" and "existing licensee" have the meanings assigned to them by paragraph 8(1) of Schedule 12 to the Criminal Justice Act 1991.

(2) In relation to any existing prisoner or existing licensee who has forfeited any remission of his sentence, the provisions of Part II of the Criminal Justice Act 1991 shall apply as if he had been awarded such number of additional days as equals the number of days of remission which he has forfeited.

8–24603

PART III
OFFICERS OF YOUNG OFFENDER INSTITUTIONS

PART IV
PERSONS HAVING ACCESS TO A YOUNG OFFENDER INSTITUTION

PART V
BOARDS OF VISITORS

8–24604 **78. Disqualification for membership.** Any person directly or indirectly interested in any contract for the supply of goods or services to a young offender institution shall not be a member of the board of visitors for that institution and any member who becomes so interested in such a contract shall vacate office as a member.

8–24605 **79. Appointment.** (1) A member of the board of visitors for a young offender institution appointed by the Secretary of State under section 6(2) of the Prison Act 1952 shall subject to paragraphs (3) and (4) hold office for three years or such shorter period as the Secretary of State may appoint.

(2) A member—

(a) appointed for the first time to the board of visitors for a particular young offender institution; or
(b) re-appointed to the board following a gap of a year or more in his membership of it,

shall, during the period of 12 months following the date on which he is so appointed or (as the case may be) re-appointed, undertake such training as may reasonably be required by the Secretary of State.

(3) The Secretary of State may terminate the appointment of a member if satisfied that—

(a) he has failed satisfactorily to perform his duties;
(b) he has failed to undertake training he has been required to undertake under paragraph (2), by the end of the period specified in that paragraph;
(c) he is by reason of physical or mental illness, or for any other reason, incapable of carrying out his duties;

(d) he has been convicted of such a criminal offence, or his conduct has been such, that it is not in the Secretary of State's opinion fitting that he should remain a member; or

(e) there is, or appears to be, or could appear to be, any conflict of interest between the member performing his duties as a member and any interest of that member, whether personal, financial or otherwise.

(4) Where the Secretary of State:

(a) has reason to suspect that a member of the board of visitors for a young offender institution may have so conducted himself that his appointment may be liable to be terminated under paragraph (3)(a) or (d); and

(b) is of the opinion that the suspected conduct is of such a serious nature that the member cannot be permitted to continue to perform his functions as a member of the board pending the completion of the Secretary of State's investigations into the matter and any decision as to whether the member's appointment should be terminated,

he may suspend the member from office for such period or periods as he may reasonably require in order to complete his investigations and determine whether or not the appointment of the member should be so terminated; and a member so suspended shall not, during the period of the suspension, be regarded as being a member of the board, other than for the purposes of this paragraph and paragraphs (1) and (2).

(5) A board shall have a chairman and a vice chairman, who shall be members of the board.

(6) The Secretary of State shall—

(a) upon the constitution of a board for the first time, appoint a chairman and a vice chairman to hold office for a period not exceeding 12 months;

(b) thereafter appoint, before the date of the first meeting of the board in any year of office of the board, a chairman and a vice chairman for that year, having first consulted the board; and

(c) promptly fill, after having first consulted the board, any casual vacancy in the office of chairman or vice chairman.

(7) The Secretary of State may terminate the appointment of a member as chairman or vice chairman of the board if he is satisfied that the member has—

(a) failed satisfactorily to perform his functions as chairman or (as the case may be) vice-chairman; or

(b) has grossly misconducted himself whilst performing those functions.

8–24606 **80. Proceedings of boards.** (1) The board of visitors for a young offender institution shall meet at the institution at least once a month.

(2) The board may fix a quorum of not fewer than three members for proceedings.

(3) The board shall keep minutes of their proceedings.

(4) The proceedings of the board shall not be invalidated by any vacancy in the membership or any defect in the appointment of a member.

8–24607 **81. General duties of boards.** (1) The board of visitors for a young offender institution shall satisfy themselves as to the state of the premises, the administration of the institution and the treatment of the inmates.

(2) The board shall inquire into and report upon any matter into which the Secretary of State asks them to inquire.

(3) The board shall direct the attention of the governor to any matter which calls for his attention, and shall report to the Secretary of State any matters which they consider it expedient to report.

(4) The board shall inform the Secretary of State immediately of any abuse which comes to their knowledge.

(5) Before exercising any power under these Rules, the board and any member of the board shall consult the governor in relation to any matter which may affect discipline.

8–24608 **82. Particular duties.** (1) The board of visitors for a young offender institution and any member of the board shall hear any complaint or request which an inmate wishes to make to them or him.

(2) The board shall arrange for the food of the inmates to be inspected by a member of the board at frequent intervals.

(3) The board shall inquire into any report made to them, whether or not by a member of the board, that an inmate's health, mental or physical, is likely to be injuriously affected by any conditions of his detention.

8–24609 **83. Members visiting young offender institutions.** (1) The members of the board of visitors for a young offender institution shall visit the institution frequently, and the board shall arrange a rota for the purpose.

(2) A member of the board shall have access at any time to every part of the institution and to every inmate, and he may interview any inmate out of the sight and hearing of officers.

(3) A member of the board shall have access to the records of the young offender institution.

8–24610 84. *Annual report*

PART VI
SUPPLEMENTAL

8–24611 85. *Delegation by governor*

8–24612 86. Contracted out young offender institutions. (1) Where the Secretary of State has entered into a contract for the running of a young offender institution under section 84 of the Criminal Justice Act 1991 (in this rule "the 1991 Act") these Rules shall have effect in relation to that young offender institution with the following modifications—

(a) references to an officer shall include references to a prisoner custody officer certified as such under section 89(1) of the 1991 Act;

(b) references to a governor shall include references to a director approved by the Secretary of State for the purposes of section 85(1)(a) of the 1991 Act except—

(i) in rules 49, 51, 52, 58, 60, 64, 65 and 85 where references to a governor shall include references to a controller appointed by the Secretary of State under section 85(1)(b) of the 1991 Act; and

(ii) in rules 67(1), 71 and 81 where references to a governor shall include references to a director and a controller;

(c) rule 73 shall not apply in relation to a prisoner custody officer certified as such under section 89(1) of the 1991 Act and performing custodial duties.

(2) Where a director exercises the powers set out in section 85(3)(b) of the 1991 Act (removal from association, temporary confinement and restraints) in cases of urgency, he shall notify the controller of that fact forthwith.

8–24613 87. Contracted out parts of young offender institutions. Where the Secretary of State has entered into a contract for the running of part of a young offender institution under section 84(1) of the Criminal Justice Act 1991, that part and the remaining part shall each be treated for the purposes of Parts I to IV and Part VI of these Rules as if they were separate young offender institutions.

8–24614 88. Contracted out functions at directly managed young offender institutions. (1) Where the Secretary of State has entered into a contract under section 88A(1) of the Criminal Justice Act 1991 for any functions at a directly managed young offender institution too be performed by prisoner custody officers who are authorised to perform custodial duties under section 89(1) of that Act, references to an officer in these Rules shall, subject to paragraph (2), include references to a prisoner custody officer who is so authorised and who is performing contracted out functions for the purposes of, or for purposes connected with, the young offender institution.

(2) Paragraph (1) shall not apply to references to an officer in rule 73.

(3) In this rule "directly managed young offender institution" means a young offender institution which is not a contracted out young offender institution.

8–24615 89. *Revocations and savings*

PROPERTY, OFFENCES AGAINST

8–24670 This title comprises the following statutes—

This title also contains the following statutory instruments—

Inclosure Act 1857

(1857 c 31)

8–24671 12. Proceedings for prevention of nuisances in town and village greens and allotments for exercise and recreation. And whereas it is expedient to provide summary means of preventing nuisances in town greens and village greens, and on land allotted and awarded upon

any inclosure under the said Acts as a place for exercise and recreation[1]. If any person wilfully cause any injury or damage to any fence of any such town or village green or land, or wilfully and without lawful authority lead or drive any cattle or animal thereon, or wilfully lay any manure, soil, ashes, or rubbish, or other matter or thing thereon, or do any other act whatsoever to the injury of such town or village green or land, or to the interruption of the use or enjoyment thereof as a place for exercise and recreation, such person shall for every such offence, upon a summary conviction thereof before two justices, upon the information of any churchwarden or overseer[2] of the parish in which such town or village green or land is situate, or of the person in whom the soil of such town or village green or land may be vested, forfeit and pay, in any of the cases aforesaid, and for each and every such offence, over and above the damages occasioned thereby, any sum not exceeding **level 1** on the standard scale; and it shall be lawful for any such churchwarden or overseer[2] or other person as aforesaid to sell and dispose of any such manure, soil, ashes, and rubbish, or other matter or thing as aforesaid; and the proceeds arising from the sale thereof, and every such penalty[3] as aforesaid, shall, as regards any such town, or village green not awarded under the said Acts or any of them to be used as a place for exercise and recreation, be applied in aid of the rates for the repair of the public highways in the parish, and shall, as regards the land so awarded, be applied by the persons or person in whom the soil thereof may be vested in the due maintenance of such land as a place for exercise and recreation; and if any manure, soil, ashes, or rubbish be not of sufficient value to defray the expense of removing the same, the person who laid or deposited such manure, soil, ashes, or rubbish shall repay to such churchwarden or overseer[2] or other person as aforesaid the money necessarily expended in the removal thereof; and every such penalty as aforesaid shall be recovered in manner provided by the [Magistrates' Courts Act 1980]; and the amount of damage occasioned by any such offence as aforesaid shall, in case of dispute, be determined by the justices by whom the offender is convicted; and the payment of the amount of such damage, and the repayments of the money necessarily expended in the removal of any manure, soil, ashes, or rubbish, shall be enforced in like manner as any such penalty.
[Inclosure Act 1857, s 12, as amended by Criminal Justice Act 1967, Sch 3 and the Criminal Justice Act 1982, ss 38 and 46.]

1. Section 30 of the Inclosure Act 1845 makes provision for such allotment.
2. By s 189(3) of the Local Government Act 1972, references in this section to a churchwarden or overseer shall be construed with respect to a green or land (*a*) in a parish as reference to the parish council or if there is none, to the parish meeting; (*b*) in a community where there is a community council, to that council; (*c*) otherwise to the council of the district in which the green or land is situated. Any inhabitant of the parish may lay an information (Commons Act 1876, s 29).
3. For application of penalties, see now Justices of the Peace Act 1979, s 61, but note in particular sub-s (2) thereof.

Malicious Damage Act 1861

(24 & 25 Vict c 97)

8–24672 **47. Exhibiting false signals.** Whosoever shall unlawfully mask, alter, or remove any light or signal, or unlawfully exhibit any false light or signal, with intent to bring any ship, vessel, or boat into danger, or unlawfully and maliciously do anything tending to the immediate loss or destruction of any ship, vessel, or boat, and for which no punishment is hereinbefore provided.—PUN., imprisonment (**life**).
[Malicious Damage Act 1861, s 47.]

8–24673 **48. Removing buoys, etc.** Whosoever shall unlawfully and maliciously cut away, cast adrift, remove, alter, deface, sink, or destroy, or shall unlawfully and maliciously do any act with such intent, or shall in any other manner unlawfully and maliciously injure or conceal any boat, buoy, buoy-rope, perch or mark, used or intended for the guidance of seamen or for the purpose of navigation.—PUN., imprisonment (**seven years**).
[Malicious Damage Act 1861, s 48.]

8–24674 **58. Malice against owner unnecessary.** Every punishment and forfeiture by this Act imposed on any person maliciously[1] committing any offence, whether the same be punishable upon indictment or upon summary conviction, shall equally apply and be enforced whether the offence shall be committed from malice conceived against the owner of the property in respect of which it shall be committed or otherwise[2].
[Malicious Damage Act 1861, s 58.]

1. For meaning of "maliciously", see *R v Cunningham* [1957] 2 QB 396, [1957] 2 All ER 412, 121 JP 451.
2. See *R v Pembliton* (1874) LR 2 CCR 119, 38 JP 454, and cf *R v Latimer* (1886) 17 QBD 359, 51 JP 184.

8–24675 **72. Offences committed within the jurisdiction of the Admiralty.** All indictable offences mentioned in this Act which shall be committed within the jurisdiction of the Admiralty of

England or Ireland shall be liable to the same punishments as if they had been committed upon the land in England or Ireland.
[Malicious Damage Act 1861, s 72, as amended by the Criminal Law Act 1967, Sch 3.]

Town Gardens Protection Act 1863[1]

(26 Vict c 13)

8–24676 5. Penalty for injuring garden. Any person who throws any rubbish into any such garden, or trespasses therein, or gets over the railings or fence, or steals or damages the flowers or plants, or commits any nuisance therein, shall be guilty of an offence and shall be liable on summary conviction for each and every offence aforesaid to a penalty not exceeding **level 1** on the standard scale or to imprisonment for not exceeding **fourteen days**; and in case it shall be necessary to state in any proceedings the ownership of the property of such garden, flowers, or plants, it shall be sufficient to describe the same as the property of the committee by the name A B and others.
[Town Gardens Protection Act 1863, s 5, as amended by the Criminal Law Act 1977, s 31, the Criminal Justice Act 1982, s 46, the Police and Criminal Evidence Act 1984, Sch 6 and the Statute Law (Repeals) Act 1993, Sch 2.]

1. Section 7 provides that nothing in this Act shall extend to or include any garden, ornamental ground or other land belonging to the Crown or under the management of (now) the Secretary of State for the Environment or for which special provision is made for the due care and protection thereof by any public or private Act of Parliament. Apart from this, it has been held that this act applies in any city or borough to any enclosed garden or ornamental garden set apart in any public square, crescent, circus, street or other public place for the use or enjoyment of the inhabitants, not being Crown property or under the protection of any public or private Act. See *Tulk v Metropolitan Board of Works* (1868) LR 3 QB 682, 32 JP 548.

Public Stores Act 1875

(38 & 39 Vict c 25)

8–24677 4. Marks in schedule appropriated for public stores. The marks described in the First Schedule to this Act may be applied in or on stores in order to denote Her Majesty's property in stores so marked; and it shall be lawful for any public department, and the contractors, officers and workmen of such department, to apply those marks, or any of them, in or on any such stores[1]; and if any person without lawful authority (proof of which authority shall lie on the party accused) applies any of those marks in or on any such stores he shall be guilty of a misdemeanour, and shall on conviction thereof be liable to be imprisoned for any term not exceeding **two years**.
[Public Stores Act 1875, s 4 amended by the Statute Law (Repeals) Act 1993, Sch 1.]

1. "Stores" includes all goods and chattels, and any single store or article (s 2).

8–24678 5. Obliteration with intent to concealment. If any person with intent to conceal Her Majesty's property in any stores takes out, destroys, or obliterates, wholly or in part, any such mark as aforesaid, or any mark whatsoever denoting the property of Her Majesty in any stores, he shall be guilty of [an offence][1], and on conviction thereof be liable, in the discretion of the court before which he is convicted, to imprisonment for any term not exceeding **seven years**.
[Public Stores Act 1875, s 5.]

1. "Offence" is substituted for "felony" to accord with Criminal Law Act 1967, s 12(5). Triable either way; see the Magistrates' Courts Act 1980, s 17A and Sch 1, also ss 17A–21 (procedure) and s 32 (penalty).

8–24679 6. Power to stop suspected boats, persons, etc. A constable of the metropolitan police force may, within the limits for which he is constable, and any constable, if deputed[1] by a public department, may, within the limits for which he is constable, stop, search, and detain any vessel, boat or vehicle in or on which there is reason to suspect that any of Her Majesty's stores stolen or unlawfully obtained may be found, or any person reasonably suspected of having or conveying in any manner any of Her Majesty's stores stolen or unlawfully obtained.

A constable shall be deemed to be deputed by a public department within the meaning of this section if he is deputed by any writing signed by the person who is the head of such department, or who is authorised to sign documents on behalf of such a department.
[Public Stores Act 1875, s 6.]

1. A special constable, within premises in the possession or control of the United Kingdom Atomic Energy Authority, is deemed to be so deputed (Atomic Energy Authority Act 1954, Sch 3).

8–24680 8. *Prohibition of sweeping, etc, near dockyards, artillery ranges, etc.*

8–24681 **12. Power of arrest and issue of search warrant.** (1) *Repealed.*

(2) If it is made to appear by information on oath before a justice of the peace that there is reasonable cause to believe that any person has in his custody or possession or on his premises any stores in respect of which an offence against section 5 of this Act has been committed, the justice may issue a warrant to a constable to search for and seize the stores as in the case of stolen goods, and the Police (Property) Act 1897, shall apply as if this subsection were among the enactments mentioned in section 1(1) of that Act.

[Public Stores Act 1875, s 12, as substituted by the Theft Act 1968, Sch 2 and amended by the Serious Organised Crime and Police Act 2005, Sch 7.]

8–24682 **13. Provisions for regimental necessaries, etc.** The provisions of this Act relative to the taking out, destroying, or obliterating of marks, not apply to stores issued as regimental necessaries or otherwise for any soldier, or volunteer[1]; but nothing herein shall relieve any person from any obligation or liability to which he may be subject under any other Act in respect of such stores.

[Public Stores Act 1875, s 13 amended by the Statute Law (Repeals) Act 1993, Sch 1.]

1. By Orders in Council made under the Territorial and Reserve Forces Acts, all volunteers have been transferred to the Territorial Army.

Criminal Damage Act 1971

(1971 c 48)

8–24740 **1. Destroying or damaging property.** (1) A person who without lawful excuse[1] destroys or damages[2] any property[3] belonging to another[4] intending to destroy or damage any such property or being reckless[5] as to whether any such property would be destroyed or damaged shall be guilty of an offence.

(2) A person who without lawful excuse destroys or damages any property, whether belonging to himself or another—

(*a*) intending to destroy or damage any property or being reckless[5] as to whether any property would be destroyed or damaged; and

(*b*) intending by the destruction or damage[6] to endanger the life[7] of another or being reckless[5] as to whether the life of another would be thereby endangered[8];

shall be guilty of an offence.

(3) An offence committed under this section by destroying or damaging property by fire shall be charged as arson[9].

[Criminal Damage Act 1971, s 1.]

1. See s 5, post, for defence of "lawful excuse". A person does not commit an offence under s 1(1) and (3) if he destroys or damages his own property, even though he does so with the intent later to commit a fraud by dishonestly claiming against his insurers, see *R v Denton* [1982] 1 All ER 65, [1981] 1 WLR 1446, 146 JP 138, CA; distinguished in *R v Appleyard* (1985) 81 Cr App Rep 319 (managing director setting fire to company premises). A defendant who damaged padlocks in order to remove a clamp on his car which he had unlawfully parked in a private car park, was held not to have a lawful excuse and, therefore, no defence to a charge of criminal damage (*Lloyd v DPP* [1992] 1 All ER 982, [1991] Crim LR 904). Although the scope of the ancient self-help remedy of recaption was unclear it appeared to apply when a person entered private land to reclaim a chattel that had been wrongly taken on to that land but did not appear to apply where the chattel had come on to the land by consensual means such as the lawful parking of a car (*R v Mitchell* [2003] EWCA Crim 2188, [2004] RTR 14, [2004] Crim LR 139, where on the facts the car was not parked in accordance with the instructions for people who wished to park lawfully). As to whether self-help could apply for the immediate protection from clamping of a car lawfully parked, see the commentary to [2004] Crim LR 139. A person did not have a "lawful excuse" for damaging the outer perimeter fence at an atomic weapons establishment on the grounds that the possession of nuclear weapons was contrary to customary international law; nor did her belief that she was acting out of necessity, self-defence, in the public interest or in order to prevent a nuisance provide a lawful justification or excuse for her action: *Hutchinson v Newbury Magistrates' Court* CO/663/2000. DC.

2. What constitutes criminal damage is a matter of fact and degree; the damage need not be permanent (*Roe v Kingerlee* [1986] Crim LR 735). It can include permanent or temporary impairment of value or usefulness (*Morphitis v Salmon* (1989) 154 JP 365—removal of scaffold clip and bar from upright).

3. A computer "hacker" who obtains unauthorised entry to a computer system and makes alterations impairing its proper use can be convicted of criminal damage, although the damage to the magnetic particles in the disk are not perceptible without using the computer. Tangible property has been damaged even though the damage itself is not tangible. Impairment of usefulness does not require breaking, cutting or removal of a part (*R v Whiteley* [1991] Crim LR 436).

4. Informant need not be a person who actually saw the offence committed, and if ownership be incorrectly described the information should be amended or the hearing adjourned, but not dismissed (*Ralph v Hurrell* (1875) 40 JP 119). No offence is committed if done in the honest though mistaken belief that the property is one's own (*R v David Smith* [1974] 1 All ER 632, [1974] QB 354, 138 JP 236). Where the charge alleges damage to property belonging to the defendant's wife or husband, the prior consent of the Director of Public Prosecutions is necessary: see the Theft Act 1968, s 30(4), post, and *R v Withers* [1975] Crim LR 647. Section 30(3) of the Theft Act 1968 also regulates the presentation of evidence as between husband and wife in such proceedings.

5. It was held in *Metropolitan Police Comr v Caldwell* [1982] AC 341, [1981] 1 All ER 961, [1981] 2 WLR 509 that "reckless" here meant (1) doing an act which in fact creates an obvious risk that property will be destroyed or damaged and (2) when so acting the doer either has not given any thought to the possibility of there being any such risk or has

recognised that there was some risk involved and has none the less gone on to do it. In *R v G* [2003] UKHL 50, [2003] 4 All ER 765, [2003] 3 WLR 1060, 167 JP 621, however, the House of Lords departed from its earlier decision in *Caldwell* and held that that foresight of consequences remained an essential ingredient of recklessness in the context of the offence of criminal damage. Therefore, it had to be shown that the defendant's state of mind was culpable in that he acted recklessly in respect of a circumstance if he was aware of a risk which did or would exist, or in respect of a result if he was aware of a risk that it would occur, and it was, in the circumstances known to him, unreasonable to take the risk. Accordingly, a defendant could not be convicted of the offence if, due to his age or personal characteristics, he genuinely did not appreciate or foresee the risks involved in his actions.

If a defendant closes his mind to a risk he must realise that there is a risk and, on the evidence, that will usually be decisive as to whether he was "reckless". (This was the view of Lord Edmund Davies, who dissented in *Caldwell*, and it was cited approvingly in *R v G*.) Where, however, a defendant realises there is a risk but dismisses it as negligible it cannot be said that he is taking an obvious and significant risk; the court must consider his subjective perception of the risk: *R v Cooper* [2004] EWCA Crim 1382, [2004] All ER (D) 180 (Jun), (2004) 168 JPN 507.

It is submitted that self-induced intoxication, in cases that are brought on the basis of recklessness rather than specific intent, continues to be irrelevant.

If the relevant awareness was not present when the defendant did the act by which the risk of damage was created, he is nonetheless guilty if he subsequently gained that awareness before the risk materialised but failed to do anything to prevent it (*R v Miller* [1983] 2 AC 161, [1983] 1 All ER 978 (which in this respect, it is submitted, remains good law post *R v G*, supra)).

6. The words "destruction or damage" in s 1(2)(*b*) refer back to the destruction or damage intended, or as to which there was recklessness, in s 1(2)(*a*); the words do not refer to the destruction or damage actually caused (*R v Dudley* [1989] Crim LR 57, CA followed in *R v Webster* [1995] 2 All ER 168, CA).

7. It is not necessary to establish that a life was in fact endangered (*R v Parker* [1993] Crim LR 856).

8. Although there are two elements of the offence in paragraphs (a) and (b), the court is concerned with the defendant's state of mind at one stage only, namely when he does the relevant act. The word "thereby" refers to the damage to the property and not to the act which caused the damage; the intention of recklessness must be with regard to the dangers caused by the destroyed or damaged property and not those inherent in the method of causing the destruction or damage (*R v Steer* [1988] AC 111, [1987] 2 All ER 833, 85 Cr App Rep 352, HL followed in *R v Webster* [1995] 2 All ER 168, CA).

On a charge of *attempted* arson in the aggravated form contemplated by s 1(2), in addition to establishing a specific intent to cause damage by fire, it is sufficient to prove that the defendant was reckless as to whether life would thereby be endangered (*A-G's Reference (No 3 of 1992)* [1994] 2 All ER 121, [1994] 1 WLR 409, [1994] RTR 122, 98 Cr App Rep 383).

9. Where the charge states "damage by fire" rather than "arson" it is nonetheless a valid charge: *R v Drayton* [2005] EWCA Crim 2013, (2005) 169 JP 593.

8–24741 2. Threats to destroy or damage property[1]**.** A person who without lawful excuse makes to another a threat, intending that that other would fear it would be carried out—

(*a*) to destroy or damage any property belonging to that other or a third person; or

(*b*) to destroy or damage his own property in a way which he knows is likely to endanger the life of that other or a third person;

shall be guilty of an offence.

[Criminal Damage Act 1971, s 2.]

---

1. The gist of the offence under both parts of s 2 is the threat; the nature of the threat has to be considered objectively so that it does not matter what the person threatened thought was embraced within the threat or whether he feared the threat would be carried out, though the prosecution must prove that the defendant intended that the person threatened would fear that the threat would be carried out (*R v Cakmak* [2002] EWCA Crim 500, [2002] 2 Cr App Rep 158, [2002] Crim LR 581).

8–24742 3. Possessing anything with intent to destroy or damage property. A person who has anything in his custody or under his control intending[1] without lawful excuse to use it or cause or permit another to use it—

(*a*) to destroy or damage any property belonging to some other person; or

(*b*) to destroy or damage his own or the user's property in a way which he knows is likely to endanger the life of some other person;

shall be guilty of an offence.

[Criminal Damage Act 1971, s 3.]

---

1. It is not enough that the defendant realises that the thing may be so used; he must intend or permit such use. But it is unnecessary that the defendant should intend an immediate use of the thing (*R v Buckingham* (1975) 63 Cr App Rep 159).

8–24743 4. Punishment of offences. (1) A person guilty of arson under section 1 above or of an offence[1] under section 1(2) above (whether arson or not) shall on conviction on indictment be liable to imprisonment for **life**.

(2) A person guilty of any other offence[1] under this Act shall on conviction on indictment be liable to imprisonment for a term not exceeding **ten years**.

[Criminal Damage Act 1971, s 4.]

---

1. Offences under ss 1(1) and (3), 2 and 3 are triable either way; see Magistrates' Courts Act 1980, s 17 and Sch 1, also ss 17A–21 (procedure) and s 32 (penalty) in PART I: MAGISTRATES' COURTS, PROCEDURE, ante. Offences under s 1(2) are not triable summarily. As to having in possession any firearm at the time of committing or at the time of apprehension

for an offence under s 1 of this Act, or aiding and abetting or attempting to commit any such offence, see the Firearms Act 1968, s 17 and Sch 1, ante.

8–24744 **5. "Without lawful excuse".** (1) This section applies to any offence under section 1(1) above and any offence under section 2 or 3 above other than one involving a threat by the person charged to destroy or damage property in a way which he knows is likely to endanger the life of another or involving an intent by the person charged to use or cause or permit the use of something in his custody or under his control so to destroy or damage property.

(2) A person charged with an offence to which this section applies shall, whether or not he would be treated for the purposes of this Act as having a lawful excuse apart from this subsection[1], be treated for those purposes as having a lawful excuse—

(*a*) if at the time of the act or acts alleged to constitute the offence he believed that the person or persons whom he believed to be entitled to consent to the destruction of or damage to the property in question had so consented, or would have so consented to it if he or they had known of the destruction or damage and its circumstances[2]; or

(*b*) if he destroyed or damaged or threatened to destroy or damage the property in question or, in the case of a charge of an offence under section 3 above, intended to use or cause or permit the use of something to destroy or damage it, in order to protect[3] property belonging to himself or another or a right or interest[4] in property which was or which he believed to be vested in himself or another, and at the time of the act or acts alleged to constitute the offence he believed—

(i) that the property, right or interest was in immediate need of protection; and

(ii) that the means of protection adopted or proposed to be adopted were or would be reasonable having regard to all the circumstances.

(3) For the purposes of this section it is immaterial whether a belief is justified or not if it is honestly held[2].

(4) For the purposes of subsection (2) above a right or interest in property includes any right or privilege in or over land, whether created by grant, licence or otherwise.

(5) This section shall not be construed as casting doubt on any defence recognised by law as a defence to criminal charges.

[Criminal Damage Act 1971, s 5.]

---

1. In *Stear v Scott* [1992] RTR 226 the Divisional Court was unable to find any authority suggesting a right to use force and cause damage in order to recover property from land upon which property was trespassing (damage to a wheel clamp used to immobilise a vehicle parked on private land without permission).

2. A woman suffering from self-induced intoxication was held to be entitled to the defence under s 5(2) when charged with damaging a house which she mistook for another (*Jaggard v Dickinson* [1981] QB 527, [1980] 3 All ER 716. But a vicar who had a genuine belief in the consent of God and thence the law of England to damage property was held not to have had a lawful excuse (*Blake v DPP* [1993] Crim LR 586).

3. The question whether or not a particular act was done in order to protect property must be an objective test (*R v Hunt* (1977) 66 Cr App Rep 105). The court has to decide first what was in the defendant's mind—a subjective test, and secondly whether it can be said as a matter of law that, on the facts as believed by him, the act was done in order to protect property—an objective test (*R v Hill* [1989] Crim LR 136, CA; applied in *Johnson v DPP* [1994] Crim LR 673). See also *Chamberlain v Lindon* [1998] 2 All ER 538, [1998] 1 WLR 1252, DC (defendant had a lawful excuse to demolish a wall which restricted his right of way as he had an honest belief that it was necessary to do so to protect his right or interest in property. The fact that he chose abatement because he hoped to avoid litigation did not convert the avoidance of litigation into his purpose). See further *R v Jones* [2004] EWCA Crim 1981, [2005] QB 259, [2004] 4 ALL ER 955, [2005] 1 Cr App R 12 (damage to military airbase to prevent allegedly unlawful warfare being waged against Iraq: held that the only objective element in the defence in s 5(2)(*b*) was whether it could be said that on the facts as believed by the defendant the criminal damage alleged could amount to something done to protect property).

4. Every man has a right at common law by any means he pleases to protect his own land or property, provided he does not invade or interfere with the legal rights of his neighbour (*Deane v Clayton* (1817) 7 Taunt 489; *Jordin v Crump* (1841) 8 M & W 782. See also article at 41 JP 737. The test is whether he acted reasonably (*Goodway v Becher* [1951] 2 All ER 349, 115 JP 435). The defence does not arise in circumstances where damage is caused in order to recover a child (*R v Baker and Wilkins* [1997] Crim LR 497).

See s 7(2), post, for jurisdiction of magistrates' courts to try offences where a dispute of title to property is involved.

8–24745 **6. Search for things intended for use in committing offences of criminal damage.** (1) If it is made to appear by information on oath before a justice of the peace that there is reasonable cause to believe that any person has in his custody or under his control or on his premises anything which there is reasonable cause to believe has been used or is intended for use without lawful excuse—

(*a*) to destroy or damage property belonging to another; or

(*b*) to destroy or damage any property in a way likely to endanger the life of another,

the justice may grant a warrant authorising any constable to search for and seize that thing.

(2) A constable who is authorised under this section to search premises for anything, may enter (if need be by force) and search the premises accordingly and may seize anything which he believes to have been used or to be intended to be used as aforesaid.

(3) The Police (Property) Act 1897 (disposal of property in the possession of the police) shall apply to property which has come into the possession of the police under this section as it applies to

property which has come into the possession of the police in the circumstances mentioned in that Act.
[Criminal Damage Act 1971, s 6.]

8–24746 **7. Jurisdiction of magistrates' courts.** (1) *Amendment* (*noted in text*).

(2) No rule of law ousting the jurisdiction of magistrates' courts to try offences where a dispute of title to property is involved shall preclude magistrates' courts from trying offences under this Act, or any other offences of destroying or damaging property.
[Criminal Damage Act 1971, s 7.]

8–24747 **9. Evidence in connection with offences under this Act.** A person shall not be excused, by reason that to do so may incriminate that person or the spouse or civil partner of that person of an offence under this Act—

(*a*) from answering any question put to that person in proceedings for the recovery of administration or any property, for the execution of any trust or for an account of any property or dealings with property; or
(*b*) from complying with any order made in any such proceedings;

but no statement or admission made by a person in answering a question put or complying with an order made as aforesaid shall, in proceedings for an offence under this Act, be admissible in evidence against that person or (unless they married or became civil partners after the making of the statement or admission) against the spouse or civil partner of that person.
[Criminal Damage Act 1971, s 9 as amended by the Civil Partnership Act 2004, Sch 27.]

8–24748 **10. Interpretation.** (1) In this Act "property" means property of a tangible nature[1], whether real or personal, including money and—

(*a*) including wild creatures which have been tamed or are ordinarily[2] kept in captivity, and any other wild creatures or their carcasses if, but only if, they have been reduced into possession which has not been lost or abandoned or are in the course of being reduced into possession; but
(*b*) not including mushrooms growing wild on any land or flowers, fruit or foliage of a plant growing wild on any land.

For the purposes of this subsection "mushroom" includes any fungus and "plant" includes any shrub or tree.

(2) Property shall be treated for the purposes of this Act as belonging to any person—

(*a*) having the custody of control of it;
(*b*) having in it any proprietary right or interest (not being an equitable interest arising only from an agreement to transfer or grant an interest); or
(*c*) having a charge on it.

(3) Where property is subject to a trust, the persons to whom it belongs shall be so treated as including any person having a right to enforce the trust.

(4) Property of a corporation sole shall be so treated as belonging to the corporation notwithstanding a vacancy in the corporation.
[Criminal Damage Act 1971, s 10.]

---

1. This can include a plastic circuit card from which the accused has erased a computer program (*Cox v Riley* [1986] Crim LR 460).

2. It is not necessary for the prosecution to prove that the particular animal was so kept; it is sufficient if the particular animal belonged to a class of animals ordinarily so kept, eg cats (*Nye v Niblett* [1918] 1 KB 23, 82 JP 57).

Protection of Wrecks Act 1973

(1973 c 33)

8–24760 **1. Protection of sites of historic wrecks.** (1) If the Secretary of State is satisfied with respect to any site in United Kingdom waters[1] that—

(*a*) it is, or may prove to be, the site of a vessel lying wrecked on or in the sea bed[1]; and
(*b*) on account of the historical, archaeological or artistic importance of the vessel, or of any objects contained or formerly contained in it which may be lying on the sea bed[1] in or near the wreck, the site ought to be protected from unauthorised interference,

he may by order[2] designate an area round the site as a restricted area.

(2) An order[2] under this section shall identify the site where the vessel lies or formerly lay, or is supposed to lie or have lain, and—

(*a*) the restricted area shall be all within such distance of the site (so identified) as is specified in the order, but excluding any area above high water mark of ordinary spring tides; and (*b*) the distance specified for the purposes of paragraph (*a*) above shall be whatever the Secretary of State thinks appropriate to ensure protection for the wreck.

(3) Subject to section 3(3) below, a person commits an offence[3], if, in a restricted area[4], he does any of the following things otherwise than under the authority of a licence granted by the Secretary of State—

(*a*) he tampers with, damages or removes any part of a vessel lying wrecked on or in the sea bed[1], or any object formerly contained in such a vessel; or
(*b*) he carries out diving or salvage operations directed to the exploration of any wreck or to removing objects from it or from the sea bed[1], or uses equipment constructed or adapted for any purpose of diving or salvage operations; or
(*c*) he deposits, so as to fall and lie abandoned on the sea bed[1], anything which, if it were to fall on the site of a wreck (whether it so falls or not), would wholly or partly obliterate the site or obstruct access to it, or damage any part of the wreck;

and also commits an offence[3] if he causes or permits any of those things to be done by others in a restricted area, otherwise than under the authority of such a licence.

(4) Before making an order under this section, the Secretary of State shall consult with such persons as he considers appropriate having regard to the purposes of the order; but this consultation may be dispensed with if he is satisfied that the case is one in which an order should be made as a matter of immediate urgency.

(5) A licence granted by the Secretary of State for the purposes of subsection (3) above shall be in writing and—

(*a*) the Secretary of State shall in respect of a restricted area grant licences only to persons who appear to him either—
    (i) to be competent, and properly equipped, to carry out salvage operations in a manner appropriate to the historical, archaeological or artistic importance of any wreck which may be lying in the area and of any objects contained or formerly contained in a wreck, or
    (ii) to have any other legitimate reason for doing in the area that which can only be done under the authority of a licence;
(*b*) a licence may be granted subject to conditions or restrictions, and may be varied or revoked by the Secretary of State at any time after giving not less than one week's notice to the licensee; and
(*c*) anything done contrary to any condition or restriction of a licence shall be treated for purposes of subsection (3) above as done otherwise than under the authority of the licence.

(6) Where a person is authorised, by a licence of the Secretary of State granted under this section, to carry out diving or salvage operations, it is an offence for any other person to obstruct him, or cause or permit him to be obstructed, in doing anything which is authorised by the licence, subject however to section 3(3) below.
[Protection of Wrecks Act 1973, s 1.]

1. Defined in s 3, post.
2. A number of Orders have been made.
3. For penalty, see s 3(4), and note also defences under s 3(3).
4. See s 1, ante.

8–24761 2. Prohibition on approaching dangerous wrecks. (1) If the Secretary of State is satisfied with respect to a vessel lying wrecked in United Kingdom waters[1] that—

(*a*) because of anything contained in it, the vessel is in a condition which makes it a potential danger to life or property; and
(*b*) on that account it ought to be protected from unauthorised interference,

he may by order designate an area round the vessel as a prohibited area.

(2) An order under this section shall identify the vessel and the place where it is lying and—

(*a*) the prohibited area shall be all within such distance of the vessel as is specified by the order, excluding any area above high water mark of ordinary spring tides; and
(*b*) the distance specified for the purpose of paragraph (*a*) above shall be whatever the Secretary of State thinks appropriate to ensure that unauthorised persons are kept away from the vessel.

(3) Subject to section 3(3) below, a person commits an offence[2] if, without authority in writing granted by the Secretary of State, he enters a prohibited area, whether on the surface or under water.
[Protection of Wrecks Act 1973, s 2.]

1. Defined in s 3 post.
2. For penalties and defences see s 3 below.

8–24762 3. Supplementary provisions. (1) In this Act—

"United Kingdom waters" means any part of the sea within the seaward limits of United Kingdom territorial waters and includes any part of a river within the ebb and flow of ordinary spring tides;

"the sea" includes any estuary or arm of the sea; and references to the sea bed include any area submerged at high water of ordinary spring tides.

(2) An order under section 1 or section 2 above shall be made by statutory instrument subject to annulment in pursuance of a resolution of either House of Parliament and may be varied or revoked by a subsequent order under the section; and the Secretary of State shall revoke any such order if—

(*a*) in the case of an order under section 1 designating a restricted area, he is of opinion that there is not, or is no longer, any wreck in the area which requires protection under this Act;

(*b*) in the case of an order under section 2 designating a prohibited area, he is satisfied that the vessel is no longer in a condition which makes it a potential danger to life or property.

(3) Nothing is to be regarded as constituting an offence under this Act where it is done by a person—

(*a*) in the course of any action taken by him for the sole purpose of dealing with an emergency of any description; or

(*b*) in exercising, or seeing to the exercise of, functions conferred by or under an enactment (local or other) on him or a body for which he acts; or

(*c*) out of necessity due to stress of weather or navigational hazards.

(4) A person guilty of an offence[1] under section 1 or section 2 above shall be liable on summary conviction to a fine of not more than **the statutory maximum** or on conviction on indictment to a **fine**; and proceedings for such an offence may be taken, and the offence may for all incidental purposes be treated as having been committed, at any place in the United Kingdom where he is for the time being.

[Protection of Wrecks Act 1973, s 3, as amended by the Criminal Law Act 1977, s 28.]

---

1. For procedure in respect of an offence triable either way, see the Magistrates' Courts Act 1980, ss 17A–21, in PART I: MAGISTRATES' COURTS, PROCEDURE, ante.

Supply Powers Act 1975

(1975 c 9)

8–24763 Note.—This Act consolidates provisions of the Ministry of Supply Act 1939 and amendments thereto, giving the Secretary of State power to deal with public service articles. He is enabled to make grants or loans to induce the augmentation of stocks or to improve storage facilities (s 3). He can require returns of stocks, and production and storage facilities (s 4). Information gained as to an individual business can only be disclosed with the consent of the person carrying on that business (s 5).

8–24764 6. Offences and penalties. (1) If any person knowingly or recklessly makes any untrue statement or untrue representation for the purpose of obtaining a payment under section 3 above, either for himself or for any other person, or discloses any information in contravention of section 5 above, he shall be guilty of an offence and liable[1]—

(*a*) on summary conviction, to imprisonment for a term not exceeding **three months** or to a fine not exceeding the **statutory maximum**, or to **both**; or

(*b*) on conviction on indictment, to imprisonment for a term not exceeding **two years** or to a **fine**, or to **both**.

(2) If any person—

(*a*) fails to make any return which he is required to make under section 4 above; or

(*b*) knowingly or recklessly makes any untrue statement in any such return,

he shall be guilty of an offence and liable on summary conviction to a fine not exceeding **level 3** on the standard scale, and, if he is convicted in respect of a failure to make a return and the failure continues after the conviction, he shall be guilty of a further offence and liable on summary conviction to a fine not exceeding **£50** for each day on which the failure continues.

(3) Where any offence under this section committed by a body corporate is proved to have been committed with the consent or connivance of any director, manager, secretary or other officer of the body corporate, he, as well as the body corporate, shall be guilty of the offence and shall be liable to be proceeded against and punished accordingly.

[Supply Powers Act 1975, s 6, as amended by the Criminal Law Act 1977, s 28 and the Criminal Justice Act 1982, ss 38 and 46.]

1. For procedure in respect of an offence triable either way, see the Magistrates' Courts Act 1980, ss 17A–21, in PART I: MAGISTRATES' COURTS, PROCEDURE, ante.

Criminal Law Act 1977

(1977 c 45)

PART II

OFFENCES RELATING TO ENTERING AND REMAINING ON PROPERTY

8–24780 **6. Violence for securing entry.** (1) Subject to the following provisions of this section, any person who, without lawful authority, uses or threatens violence for the purpose of securing entry into any premises for himself or for any other person is guilty of an offence, provided that—

(*a*) there is someone present on those premises at the time who is opposed to the entry which the violence is intended to secure; and

(*b*) the person using or threatening the violence knows that that is the case.

(1A) Subsection (1) above does not apply to a person who is a displaced residential occupier or a protected intending occupier of the premises in question or who is acting on behalf of such an occupier; and if the accused adduces sufficient evidence that he was, or was acting on behalf of, such an occupier he shall be presumed to be, or to be acting on behalf of, such an occupier unless the contrary is proved by the prosecution.

(2) Subject to subsection (1A) above, the fact that a person has any interest in or right to possession or occupation of any premises shall not for the purposes of subsection (1) above constitute lawful authority for the use or threat of violence by him or anyone else for the purpose of securing his entry into those premises.

(3) (*Repealed*).

(4) It is immaterial for the purposes of this section—

(*a*) whether the violence in question is directed against the person or against property; and

(*b*) whether the entry which the violence is intended to secure is for the purpose of acquiring possession of the premises in question or for any other purpose.

(5) A person guilty of an offence under this section shall be liable on summary conviction to imprisonment for a term not exceeding **six months** or to a fine not exceeding **level 5** on the standard scale or to **both**.

(6) A constable in uniform may arrest[1] without warrant anyone who is, or whom he, with reasonable cause, suspects to be, guilty of an offence under this section.

(7) Section 12 below contains provisions which apply for determining when any person is to be regarded for the purposes of this Part of this Act as a displaced residential occupier of any premises or of any access to any premises and section 12A below contains provisions which apply for determining when any person is to be regarded for the purposes of this Part of this Act as a protected intending occupier of any premises or of any access to any premises.

[Criminal Law Act 1977, s 6 as amended by the Criminal Justice Act 1982, s 46 and the Criminal Justice and Public Order Act 1994, s 72 and Sch 11.]

1. This power of arrest is preserved by the Police and Criminal Evidence Act 1984, s 26 and Sch 2.

8–24781 **7. Adverse occupation of residential premises.** (1) Subject to the following provisions of this section and to section 12A(9) below, any person who is on any premises as a trespasser after having entered as such is guilty of an offence if he fails to leave those premises on being required to do so by or on behalf of—

(*a*) a displaced residential occupier of the premises; or

(*b*) an individual who is a protected intending occupier of the premises.

(2) In any proceedings for an offence under this section it shall be a defence for the accused to prove that he believed that the person requiring him to leave the premises was not a displaced residential occupier or protected intending occupier of the premises or a person acting on behalf of a displaced residential occupier or protected intending occupier.

(3) In any proceedings for an offence under this section it shall be a defence for the accused to prove—

(*a*) that the premises in question are or form part of premises used mainly for non-residential purposes; and

(*b*) that he was not on any part of the premises used wholly or mainly for residential purposes.

(4) Any reference in the preceding provisions of this section to any premises includes a reference to any access to them, whether or not any such access itself constitutes premises, within the meaning of this Part of this Act.

(5) A person guilty of an offence under this section shall be liable on summary conviction to

imprisonment for a term not exceeding **six months** or to a fine not exceeding **level 5** on the standard scale or to **both**.

(6) A constable in uniform may arrest[1] without warrant anyone who is, or whom he, with reasonable cause, suspects to be, guilty of an offence under this section.

(7) Section 12 below contains provisions which apply for determining when any person is to be regarded for the purposes of this Part of this Act as a displaced residential occupier of any premises or of any access to any premises and section 12A below contains provisions which apply for determining when any person is to be regarded for the purposes of this Part of this Act as a protected intending occupier of any premises or of any access to any premises.

[Criminal Law Act 1977, s 7, as substituted by the Criminal Justice and Public Order Act 1994, s 73.]

1. This power of arrest is preserved by the Police and Criminal Evidence Act 1984, s 26 and Sch 2.

8–24782 **8. Trespassing with a weapon of offence.** (1) A person who is on any premises as a trespasser, after having entered as such, is guilty of an offence if, without lawful authority or reasonable excuse, he has with him on the premises any weapon of offence.

(2) In subsection (1) above "weapon of offence" means any article made or adapted for use for causing injury to or incapacitating a person, or intended by the person having it with him for such use.

(3) A person guilty of an offence under this section shall be liable on summary conviction to imprisonment for a term not exceeding **three months*** or to a fine not exceeding **level 5** on the standard scale or to **both**.

(4) A constable in uniform may arrest[1] without warrant anyone who is, or whom he, with reasonable cause, suspects to be, in the act of committing an offence under this section.

[Criminal Law Act 1977, s 8 as amended by the Criminal Justice Act 1982, s 46.]

***"51 weeks" substituted by the Criminal Justice Act 2003, Sch 26, from a date to be appointed.**

1. This power of arrest is preserved by the Police and Criminal Evidence Act 1984, s 26 and Sch 2.

8–24783 **9. Trespassing on premises of foreign missions, etc.** (1) Subject to subsection (3) below, a person who enters or is on any premises to which this section applies as a trespasser is guilty of an offence.

(2) This section applies to any premises which are or form part of—

(*a*) the premises of a diplomatic mission within the meaning of the definition in Article 1(*i*) of the Vienna Convention on Diplomatic Relations signed in 1961 as that Article has effect in the United Kingdom by virtue of section 2 of and Schedule 1 to the Diplomatic Privileges Act 1964;

(*aa*) the premises of a closed diplomatic mission; and

(*b*) consular premises within the meaning of the definition in paragraph 1(*j*) of Article 1 of the Vienna Convention on Consular Relations signed in 1963 as that Article has effect in the United Kingdom by virtue of section 1 of and Schedule 1 to the Consular Relations Act 1968;

(*bb*) the premises of a closed consular post;

(*c*) any other premises in respect of which any organisation or body is entitled to inviolability by or under any enactment; and

(*d*) any premises which are the private residence of a diplomatic agent (within the meaning of Article 1(*e*) of the Convention mentioned in paragraph (*a*) above) or of any other person who is entitled to inviolability of residence by or under any enactment.

(2A) In subsection (2) above—

"the premises of a closed diplomatic mission" means premises which fall within Article 45 of the Convention mentioned in subsection 2(*a*) above (as that Article has effect in the United Kingdom by virtue of the section and Schedule mentioned in that paragraph); and

"the premises of a closed consular post" means premises which fall within Article 27 of the Convention mentioned in subsection (2)(*b*) above (as that Article has effect in the United Kingdom by virtue of the section and Schedule mentioned in that paragraph);

(3) In any proceedings for an offence under this section it shall be a defence for the accused to prove that he believed that the premises in question were not premises to which this section applies.

(4) In any proceedings for an offence under this section a certificate issued by or under the authority of the Secretary of State stating that any premises were or formed part of premises of any description mentioned in paragraphs (*a*) to (*d*) of subsection (2) above at the time of the alleged offence shall be conclusive evidence that the premises were or formed part of premises of that description at that time.

(5) A person guilty of an offence under this section shall be liable on summary conviction to imprisonment for a term not exceeding **six months** or to a fine not exceeding **level 5** on the standard scale or to **both**.

(6) Proceedings for an offence under this section shall not be instituted against any person except by or with the consent of the Attorney General.

(7) A constable in uniform may arrest[1] without warrant anyone who is, or whom he, with reasonable cause, suspects to be, in the act of committing an offence under this section.
[Criminal Law Act 1977, s 9 as amended by the Criminal Justice Act 1982, s 46 and the Diplomatic and Consular Premises Act 1987, s 7.]

1. This power of arrest is preserved by the Police and Criminal Evidence Act 1984, s 26 and Sch 2.

8–24784 **10. Obstruction of court officers executing process for possession against unauthorised occupiers.** (1) Without prejudice to section 8(2) of the Sheriffs Act 1887 but subject to the following provisions of this section, a person is guilty of an offence if he resists or intentionally obstructs any person who is in fact an officer of a court engaged in executing any process issued by the High Court or by any county court for the purpose of enforcing any judgment or order for the recovery of any premises or for the delivery of possession of any premises.

(2) Subsection (1) above does not apply unless the judgment or order in question was given or made in proceedings brought under any provisions of rules of court applicable only in circumstances where the person claiming possession of any premises alleges that the premises in question are occupied solely by a person or persons (not being a tenant or tenants holding over after the termination of the tenancy) who entered into or remained in occupation of the premises without the licence or consent of the person claiming possession or any predecessor in title of his.

(3) In any proceedings for an offence under this section it shall be a defence for the accused to prove that he believed that the person he was resisting or obstructing was not an officer of a court.

(4) A person guilty of an offence under this section shall be liable on summary conviction to imprisonment for a term not exceeding **six months** or to a fine not exceeding **level 5** on the standard scale or to **both**.

(5) A constable in uniform or any officer of a court may arrest[1] without warrant anyone who is, or whom he, with reasonable cause, suspects to be, guilty of an offence under this section.

(6) In this section "officer of a court" means—

(*a*) any sheriff, under sheriff, deputy sheriff, bailiff or officer of a sheriff; and

(*b*) any bailiff or other person who is an officer of a county court within the meaning of the County Courts Act 1959.

[Criminal Law Act 1977, s 10 as amended by the Criminal Justice Act 1982, s 46.]

1. This power of arrest is preserved by the Police and Criminal Evidence Act 1984, s 26 and Sch 2.

8–24785 **12. Supplementary provisions.** (1) In this Part of this Act—

(*a*) "premises" means any building, any part of a building under separate occupation, any land ancillary to a building, the site comprising any building or buildings together with any land ancillary thereto, and (for the purposes only of sections 10 and 11 above) any other place; and

(*b*) "access" means, in relation to any premises, any part of any site or building within which those premises are situated which constitutes an ordinary means of access to those premises (whether or not that is its sole or primary use).

(2) References in this section to a building shall apply also to any structure other than a movable one, and to any movable structure, vehicle or vessel designed or adapted for use for residential purposes; and for the purposes of subsection (1) above—

(*a*) part of a building is under separate occupation if anyone is in occupation or entitled to occupation of that part as distinct from the whole; and

(*b*) land is ancillary to a building if it is adjacent to it and used (or intended for use) in connection with the occupation of that building or any part of it.

(3) Subject to subsection (4) below, any person who was occupying any premises as a residence immediately before being excluded from occupation by anyone who entered those premises, or any access to those premises, as a trespasser is a displaced residential occupier of the premises for the purposes of this Part of this Act so long as he continues to be excluded from occupation of the premises by the original trespasser or by any subsequent trespasser.

(4) A person who was himself occupying the premises in question as a trespasser immediately before being excluded from occupation shall not by virtue of subsection (3) above be a displaced residential occupier of the premises for the purposes of this Part of this Act.

(5) A person who by virtue of subsection (3) above is a displaced residential occupier of any premises shall be regarded for the purposes of this Part of this Act as a displaced residential occupier also of any access to those premises.

(6) Anyone who enters or is on or in occupation of any premises by virtue of—

(*a*) any title derived from a trespasser; or

(*b*) any licence or consent given by a trespasser or by a person deriving title from a trespasser,

shall himself be treated as a trespasser for the purposes of this Part of this Act (without prejudice to whether or not he would be a trespasser apart from this provision); and references in this Part of this

Act to a person's entering or being on or occupying any premises as a trespasser shall be construed accordingly.

(7) Anyone who is on any premises as a trespasser shall not cease to be a trespasser for the purposes of this Part of this Act by virtue of being allowed time to leave the premises, nor shall anyone cease to be a displaced residential occupier of any premises by virtue of any such allowance of time to a trespasser.

(8) No rule of law ousting the jurisdiction of magistrates' courts to try offences where a dispute of title to property is involved shall preclude magistrates' courts from trying offences under this Part of this Act.

[Criminal Law Act 1977, s 12.]

8–24786 12A. Protected intending occupiers: supplementary provisions. (1) For the purposes of this Part of this Act an individual is a protected intending occupier of any premises at any time if at that time he falls within subsection (2), (4) or (6) below.

(2) An individual is a protected intending occupier of any premises if—

(*a*) he has in those premises a freehold interest or a leasehold interest with not less than two years still to run;

(*b*) he requires the premises for his own occupation as a residence;

(*c*) he is excluded from occupation of the premises by a person who entered them, or any access to them, as a trespasser; and

(*d*) he or a person acting on his behalf holds a written statement—

(i) which specifies his interest in the premises;

(ii) which states that he requires the premises for occupation as a residence for himself; and

(iii) with respect to which the requirements in subsection (3) below are fulfilled.

(3) The requirements referred to in subsection (2)(*d*)(iii) above are—

(*a*) that the statement is signed by the person whose interest is specified in it in the presence of a justice of the peace or commissioner for oaths; and

(*b*) that the justice of the peace or commissioner for oaths has subscribed his name as a witness to the signature.

(4) An individual is also a protected intending occupier of any premises if—

(*a*) he has a tenancy of those premises (other than a tenancy falling within subsection (2)(*a*) above or (6)(*a*) below) or a licence to occupy those premises granted by a person with a freehold interest or a leasehold interest with not less than two years still to run in the premises;

(*b*) he requires the premises for his own occupation as a residence;

(*c*) he is excluded from occupation of the premises by a person who entered them, or any access to them, as a trespasser; and

(*d*) he or a person acting on his behalf holds a written statement—

(i) which states that he has been granted a tenancy of those premises or a licence to occupy those premises;

(ii) which specifies the interest in the premises of the person who granted that tenancy or licence to occupy ("the landlord");

(iii) which states that he requires the premises for occupation as a residence for himself; and

(iv) with respect to which the requirements in subsection (5) below are fulfilled.

(5) The requirements referred to in subsection (4)(*d*)(iv) above are—

(*a*) that the statement is signed by the landlord and by the tenant or licensee in the presence of a justice of the peace or commissioner for oaths;

(*b*) that the justice of the peace or commissioner for oaths has subscribed his name as a witness to the signatures.

(6) An individual is also a protected intending occupier of any premises if—

(*a*) he has a tenancy of those premises (other than a tenancy falling within subsection (2)(*a*) or (4)(*a*) above) or a licence to occupy those premises granted by an authority to which this subsection applies;

(*b*) he requires the premises for his own occupation as a residence;

(*c*) he is excluded from occupation of the premises by a person who entered the premises, or any access to them, as a trespasser; and

(*d*) there has been issued to him by or on behalf of the authority referred to in paragraph (*a*) above a certificate stating that—

(i) he has been granted a tenancy of those premises or a licence to occupy those premises as a residence by the authority; and

(ii) the authority which granted that tenancy or licence to occupy is one to which this subsection applies, being of a description specified in the certificate.

(7) Subsection (6) above applies to the following authorities—

(*a*) any body mentioned in section 14 of the Rent Act 1977 (landlord's interest belonging to local authority etc);
(*b*) the Housing Corporation;
(*c*) (*Revoked*); and
(*d*) a registered social landlord within the meaning of the Housing Act 1985 (see section 5(4) and (5) of that Act).

(7A) Subsection (6) also applies to the Secretary of State if the tenancy or licence is granted by him under Part III of the Housing Associations Act 1985.

(8) A person is guilty of an offence if he makes a statement for the purposes of subsection (2)(*d*) or (4)(*d*) above which he knows to be false in a material particular or if he recklessly makes such a statement which is false in a material particular.

(9) In any proceedings for an offence under section 7 of this Act where the accused was requested to leave the premises by a person claiming to be or to act on behalf of a protected intending occupier of the premises—

(*a*) it shall be a defence for the accused to prove that, although asked to do so by the accused at the time the accused was requested to leave, that person failed at that time to produce to the accused such a statement as is referred to in subsection (2)(*d*) or (4)(*d*) above or such a certificate as is referred to in subsection (6)(*d*) above; and
(*b*) any document purporting to be a certificate under subsection (6)(*d*) above shall be received in evidence and, unless the contrary is proved, shall be deemed to have been issued by or on behalf of the authority stated in the certificate.

(10) A person guilty of an offence under subsection (8) above shall be liable on summary conviction to imprisonment for a term not exceeding **six months** or to a fine not exceeding **level 5** on the standard scale or to **both**.

(11) A person who is a protected intending occupier of any premises shall be regarded for the purposes of this Part of this Act as a protected intending occupier also of any access to those premises.
[Criminal Law Act 1977, s 12A, as inserted by the Criminal Justice and Public Order Act 1994, s 74 and amended by SI 1996/2325, and the Government of Wales Act 1998, Schs 16 and 18.]

8–24787 **13. Abolitions and repeals.** *Common law offences of forcible entry and forcible detainer, and forcible entry enactments abolished and repealed.*
[Criminal Law Act 1977, s 13.]

Protection of Military Remains Act 1986

(1986 c 35)

8–24890 **1. Application of Act.** (1) This Act applies to any aircraft which has crashed (whether before or after the passing of this Act) while in military service.

(2)–(5) Secretary of State may by Order designate vessels, controlled sites[1].

(6) For the purposes of this Act a place (whether in the United Kingdom, in United Kingdom waters or in international waters) is a protected place if—

(*a*) it comprises the remains of, or of a substantial part of, an aircraft, or vessel to which this Act applies; and
(*b*) it is on or in the sea bed or is the place, or in the immediate vicinity of the place, where the remains were left by the crash, sinking or stranding of that aircraft or vessel;

but no place in international waters shall be a protected place by virtue of its comprising remains of an aircraft or vessel which has crashed, sunk or been stranded while in service with, or while being used for the purposes of, any of the armed forces of a country or territory outside the United Kingdom.

(7) Powers apply to Crown land.

(8) Secretary of State may by Order substitute references to a date later than 4 August 1914 in sub-s (3).
[Protection of Military Remains Act 1986, s 1 with sub-ss (2)–(5), (7), (8)—summarised.]

1. These subsections impose limits on the extent of effect of such Orders.

8–24891 **2. Offences in relation to remains and prohibited operations.** (1) Subject to the following provisions of this section and to section 3 below, a person shall be guilty of an offence—

(*a*) if he contravenes subsection (2) below in relation to any remains of an aircraft or vessel which are comprised in a place which is part of a controlled site;
(*b*) if, believing or have reasonable grounds for suspecting that any place comprises any remains of an aircraft or vessel which has crashed, sunk or been stranded while in military service, he

contravenes that subsection in relation to any remains by virtue of which that place is a protected place.

(*c*) if he knowingly takes part in, or causes or permits any other person to take part in, the carrying out of any excavation or diving or salvage operation which is prohibited by subsection (3) below; or

(*d*) if he knowingly uses, or causes or permits any other person to use, any equipment in connection with the carrying out of any such excavation or operation.

(2) A person contravenes this subsection in relation to any remains—

(*a*) if he tampers with, damages, moves, removes or unearths the remains;

(*b*) if he enters any hatch or other opening in any of the remains which enclose any part of the interior of an aircraft or vessel; or

(*c*) if he causes or permits any other person to do anything falling within paragraph (*a*) or (*b*) above.

(3) An excavation or diving or salvage operation is prohibited by this subsection—

(*a*) if it is carried out at a controlled site for the purpose of investigating or recording details of any remains of an aircraft or vessel which are comprised in a place which is part of that site; or

(*b*) if it is carried out for the purpose of doing something that constitutes, or is likely to involve, a contravention of subsection (2) above in relation to any remains of an aircraft or vessel which are comprised in a protected place or in a place which is part of such a site; or

(*c*) in the case of an excavation, if it is carried out for the purpose of discovering whether any place in the United Kingdom or United Kingdom waters comprises any remains of an aircraft or vessel which has crashed, sunk or been stranded while in military service.

(4) In proceedings against any person for an offence under this section, it shall be a defence for that person to show that what he did or, as the case may be, what he caused or permitted to be done was done under and in accordance with a licence under section 4 below.

(5) In proceedings against any person for an offence under this section in respect of anything done at or in relation to a place which is not part of a controlled site it shall be a defence for that person to show that he believed on reasonable grounds that the circumstances were such that (if those had been the circumstances) the place would not have been a protected place.

(6) In proceedings against any person for an offence under this section it shall be a defence for that person to show that what he did or, as the case may be, what he caused or permitted to be done was urgently necessary in the interests of safety or health or to prevent or avoid serious damage to property.

(7) A person who is guilty of an offence under this section shall be liable[1]—

(*a*) on summary conviction, to a fine not exceeding the **statutory maximum**;

(*b*) on conviction on indictment, to a **fine**.

(8) Nothing in this section shall be construed as restricting any power to carry out works which is conferred by or under any enactment.

(9) References in this section to any remains which are comprised in a protected place or to any remains which are comprised in a place which is part of a controlled site include references to remains other than those by virtue of which that place is a protected place or, as the case may be, to remains other than those in respect of which that site was or could have been designated.

[Protection of Military Remains Act 1986, s 2.]

1. For procedure in respect of an offence triable either way, see Magistrates' Courts Act 1980, ss 17A–21, in PART I: MAGISTRATES' COURTS, PROCEDURE, ante.

8–24892 **3. Extraterritorial jurisdiction.** (1) Where a contravention of subsection (2) of section 2 above occurs in international waters or an excavation or operation prohibited by subsection (3) of that section is carried out in international waters, a person shall be guilty of an offence under that section in respect of that contravention, excavation or operation only—

(*a*) if the acts or omissions which constitute the offence are committed in the United Kingdom, in United Kingdom waters or on board a British-controlled ship; or

(*b*) in a case where those acts or omissions are committed in international waters but not on board a British-controlled ship, if that person is—

(i) a British citizen, a British overseas territories citizen or a British Overseas citizen; or

(ii) a person who under the British Nationality Act 1981 is a British subject; or

(iii) a British protected person (within the meaning of that Act); or

(iv) a company within the meaning of the Companies Act 1985 or the Companies Act (Northern Ireland) 1960.

(2) Subject to subsection (1) above, an offence under section 2 above shall, for the purpose only of conferring jurisdiction on any court, be deemed to have been committed in any place where the offender may for the time being be.

(3) Where subsection (1) above applies in relation to any contravention, excavation or operation, no proceedings for an offence under section 2 above in respect of that contravention, excavation or operation shall be instituted—

(*a*) in England and Wales, except by or with the consent of the Director of Public Prosecutions;
(*b*) *Northern Ireland.*

[Protection of Military Remains Act 1986, s 3, as amended by the British Overseas Territories Act 2002, s 2(3).]

8–24893 4, 5. *Secretary of State has power to grant licences to carry out otherwise prohibited operations; it is an offence triable either way to make false or reckless statements to obtain a licence.*

8–24894 6. *Powers of boarding by authorised persons.*

8–24895 7. *Section 43 of the Powers of Criminal Courts Act 1973 (power to deprive offenders of property used, or intended for use for purposes of crime, to apply; director manager, secretary etc of body corporate liable as well as body corporate.*

8–24896 9. Interpretation. (1) In this Act, except in so far as the context otherwise requires—

"aircraft" includes a hovercraft, glider or balloon;
"British-controlled ship" means a ship registered in the United Kingdom or a ship exempted from such registration under the Merchant Shipping Act 1995;
"controlled site" means any area which is designated as such a site under section 1 above;
"Crown land" has the same meaning as in section 50 of the Ancient Monuments and Archaeological Areas Act 1979;
"international waters" means any part of the sea outside the seaward limits of the territorial waters adjacent to any country or territory;
"military service" shall be construed in accordance with subsection (2) below;
"nautical miles" means international nautical miles of 1,852 metres;
"protected place" shall be construed in accordance with section 1(6) above;
"remains", in relation to, or to part of, an aircraft or vessel which has crashed, sunk or been stranded, includes any cargo, munitions, apparel or personal effects which were on board the aircraft or vessel during its final flight or voyage (including, in the case of a vessel, any aircraft which were on board) and any human remains associated with the aircraft or vessel;
"sea" includes the sea bed and, so far as the tide flows at mean high water springs, any estuary or arm of the sea and the waters of any channel, creek, bay or river;
"sea bed" includes any area submerged at mean high water springs;
"United Kingdom waters" means any part of the sea within the seaward limits of the territorial waters adjacent to the United Kingdom.

(2) For the purposes of this Act an aircraft or vessel shall be regarded as having been in military service at a particular time if at that time it was—

(*a*) in service with, or being used for the purposes of, any of the armed forces of the United Kingdom or any other country or territory; or
(*b*) in the case of an aircraft, being taken from one place to another for delivery into service with any of the armed forces of the United Kingdom.

(3) Where a place comprising the remains of, or of a substantial part of, an aircraft or vessel which has crashed, sunk or been stranded while in military service is situated only partly in United Kingdom waters, that place shall be treated for the purposes of this Act as if the part which is situated in United Kingdom waters and the part which is situated in the United Kingdom or in international waters were separate places each of which comprised the remains of a substantial part of the aircraft or vessel.

[Protection of Military Remains Act 1986, s 9 as amended by the Merchant Shipping Act 1995, Sch 13.]

Criminal Justice and Public Order Act 1994[1]

(1994 c 33)

PART V[2]

PUBLIC ORDER: COLLECTIVE TRESPASS OR NUISANCE ON LAND

Powers to remove trespassers on land

8–24900 61. Power to remove trespassers on land[3]. (1) If the senior police officer present at the scene reasonably believes that two or more persons are trespassing on land and are present there with the common purpose of residing there for any period, that reasonable steps have been taken by or on behalf of the occupier to ask them to leave[4] and—

(*a*) that any of those persons has caused damage to the land or to property on the land or used threatening, abusive or insulting words or behaviour towards the occupier, a member of his family or an employee or agent of his, or

(*b*) that those persons have between them six or more vehicles on the land,

he may direct those persons, or any of them, to leave the land and to remove any vehicles or other property they have with them on the land.

(2) Where the persons in question are reasonably believed by the senior police officer to be persons who were not originally trespassers but have become trespassers on the land, the officer must reasonably believe that the other conditions specified in subsection (1) are satisfied after those persons became trespassers before he can exercise the power conferred by that subsection.

(3) A direction under subsection (1) above, if not communicated to the persons referred to in subsection (1) by the police officer giving the direction, may be communicated to them by any constable at the scene.

(4) If a person knowing that a direction under subsection (1) above has been given which applies to him—

(*a*) fails to leave the land as soon as reasonably practicable, or

(*b*) having left again enters the land as a trespasser within the period of three months beginning with the day on which the direction was given,

he commits an offence and is liable on summary conviction to imprisonment for a term not exceeding **three months*** or a fine not exceeding **level 4** on the standard scale, or **both**.

(4A) *Scotland.*

(4B) *Scotland.*

(5) *Repealed.*

(6) In proceedings for an offence under this section it is a defence for the accused to show—

(*a*) that he was not trespassing on the land, or

(*b*) that he had a reasonable excuse for failing to leave the land as soon as reasonably practicable or, as the case may be, for again entering the land as a trespasser.

(7) In its application in England and Wales to common land this section has effect as if in the preceding subsections of it—

(*a*) references to trespassing or trespassers were references to acts and persons doing acts which constitute either a trespass as against the occupier or an infringement of the commoners' rights; and

(*b*) references to "the occupier" included the commoners or any of them or, in the case of common land to which the public has access, the local authority as well as any commoner.

(8) Subsection (7) above does not—

(*a*) require action by more than one occupier; or

(*b*) constitute persons trespassers as against any commoner or the local authority if they are permitted to be there by the other occupier.

(9) In this section—

"common land" means common land, as defined in section 22 of the Commons Registration Act 1965;

"commoner" means a person with rights of common as defined in section 22 of the Commons Registration Act 1965;

"land" does not include—

(*a*) buildings other than—

(i) agricultural buildings within the meaning of, in England and Wales, paragraphs 3 to 8 of Schedule 5 to the Local Government Finance Act 1988 or, in Scotland, section 7(2) of the Valuation and Rating (Scotland) Act 1956, or

(ii) scheduled monuments within the meaning of the Ancient Monuments and Archaeological Areas Act 1979;

(*b*) land forming part of—

(i) a highway unless it falls within the classifications in section 54 of the Wildlife and Countryside Act 1981 (footpath, bridleway or byway open to all traffic or road used as a public path) or is a cycle track under the Highways Act 1980 or the Cycle Tracks Act 1984; or**

(ii) a road within the meaning of the Roads (Scotland) Act 1984 unless it falls within the definitions in section 151(2)(*a*)(ii) or (*b*) (footpaths and cycle tracks) of that Act or is a bridleway within the meaning of section 47 of the Countryside (Scotland) Act 1967;

"the local authority", in relation to common land, means any local authority which has powers in relation to the land under section 9 of the Commons Registration Act 1965;

"occupier" (and in subsection (8) "the other occupier") means—

(*a*) in England and Wales, the person entitled to possession of the land by virtue of an estate or interest held by him; and (*b*) in Scotland, the person lawfully entitled to natural possession of the land;

"property", in relation to damage to property on land, means—

(*a*) in England and Wales, property within the meaning of section 10(1) of the Criminal Damage Act 1971; and

(*b*) in Scotland, either—

(i) heritable property other than land; or

(ii) corporeal moveable property,

and "damage" includes the deposit of any substance capable of polluting the land;

"trespass" means, in the application of this section—

(*a*) in England and Wales, subject to the extensions effected by subsection (7) above, trespass as against the occupier of the land;

(*b*) in Scotland, entering, or as the case may be remaining on, land without lawful authority and without the occupier's consent; and

"trespassing" and "trespasser" shall be construed accordingly;

"vehicle" includes—

(*a*) any vehicle, whether or not it is in a fit state for use on roads, and includes any chassis or body, with or without wheels, appearing to have formed part of such a vehicle, and any load carried by, and anything attached to, such a vehicle; and

(*b*) a caravan as defined in section 29(1) of the Caravan Sites and Control of Development Act 1960;

and a person may be regarded for the purposes of this section as having a purpose of residing in a place notwithstanding that he has a home elsewhere.

[Criminal Justice and Public Order Act 1994, s 61 as amended by the Land Reform (Scotland) Act 2003, Sch 2 and the Serious Organised Crime and Police Act 2005, Sch 17.]

***"51 weeks" substituted by the Criminal Justice Act 2003, Sch 26, from a date to be appointed.**

****Para (*b*)(i) is amended by the Countryside and Rights of Way Act 2000, Sch 5, from a date to be appointed.**

1. The Criminal Justice and Public Order Act 1994 is reproduced partly in PART VIII under this title, and partly in PARTS I, II AND V of this Manual.

2. PART V contains ss 61–80.

3. The police are entitled to assume, in the absence of material to the contrary, that a local authority seeking the assistance of the police under s 61 is not acting in breach of human rights; the right to a fair trial under art 6 is not engaged by making it an offence to fail to comply with a s 61 direction, nor is there any infringement of the right to peaceful enjoyment of possessions under art 1 of the First Protocol to the Convention (*R (on the application of Fuller) v Chief Constable of Dorset* [2001] EWHC 1057, [2003] QB 480, [2002] 3 All ER 57, [2002] 3 WLR 1133.

4. The power to issue a direction under s 61 cannot lawfully be exercised until trespassers have failed to comply with steps taken by the occupier to ask them to leave, and the direction must require the trespassers to leave the land and to remove their vehicles immediately (*R (on the application of Fuller) v Chief Constable of Dorset*, supra).

8–24901 62. Supplementary powers of seizure. (1) If a direction has been given under section 61 and a constable reasonably suspects that any person to whom the direction applies has, without reasonable excuse—

(*a*) failed to remove any vehicle on the land which appears to the constable to belong to him or to be in his possession or under his control; or

(*b*) entered the land as a trespasser with a vehicle within the period of three months beginning with the day on which the direction was given,

the constable may seize and remove that vehicle.

(2) In this section, "trespasser" and "vehicle" have the same meaning as in section 61.*

[Criminal Justice and Public Order Act 1994, s 62.]

8–24901A 62A. Power to remove trespassers: alternative site available. (1) If the senior police officer present at a scene reasonably believes that the conditions in subsection (2) are satisfied in relation to a person and land, he may direct the person—

(*a*) to leave the land;

(*b*) to remove any vehicle and other property he has with him on the land.

(2) The conditions are—

(*a*) that the person and one or more others ("the trespassers") are trespassing on the land;

(*b*) that the trespassers have between them at least one vehicle on the land;

(*c*) that the trespassers are present on the land with the common purpose of residing there for any period;

(*d*) if it appears to the officer that the person has one or more caravans in his possession or under his control on the land, that there is a suitable pitch on a relevant caravan site for that caravan or each of those caravans;

(*e*) that the occupier of the land or a person acting on his behalf has asked the police to remove the trespassers from the land.

(3) A direction under subsection (1) may be communicated to the person to whom it applies by any constable at the scene.

(4) Subsection (5) applies if—

(*a*) a police officer proposes to give a direction under subsection (1) in relation to a person and land, and

(*b*) it appears to him that the person has one or more caravans in his possession or under his control on the land.

(5) The officer must consult every local authority within whose area the land is situated as to whether there is a suitable pitch for the caravan or each of the caravans on a relevant caravan site which is situated in the local authority's area.

(6) In this section—

"caravan" and "caravan site" have the same meanings as in Part 1 of the Caravan Sites and Control of Development Act 1960;

"relevant caravan site" means a caravan site which is—

(*a*) situated in the area of a local authority within whose area the land is situated, and

(*b*) managed by a relevant site manager;

"relevant site manager" means—

(*a*) a local authority within whose area the land is situated;

(*b*) a registered social landlord;

"registered social landlord" means a body registered as a social landlord under Chapter 1 of Part 1 of the Housing Act 1996.

(7) The Secretary of State may by order amend the definition of "relevant site manager" in subsection (6) by adding a person or description of person.

(8) An order under subsection (7) must be made by statutory instrument and is subject to annulment in pursuance of a resolution of either House of Parliament.

[Criminal Justice and Public Order Act 1994, s 62A as inserted by the Anti-social Behaviour Act 2003, s 60.]

8–24901B 62B. Failure to comply with direction under section 62A: offences. (1) A person commits an offence if he knows that a direction under section 62A(1) has been given which applies to him and—

(*a*) he fails to leave the relevant land as soon as reasonably practicable,or

(*b*) he enters any land in the area of the relevant local authority as a trespasser before the end of the relevant period with the intention of residing there.

(2) The relevant period is the period of 3 months starting with the day on which the direction is given.

(3) A person guilty of an offence under this section is liable on summary conviction to imprisonment for a term not exceeding 3 months* or a fine not exceeding level 4 on the standard scale or both.

(4) *Repealed.*

(5) In proceedings for an offence under this section it is a defence for the accused to show—

(*a*) that he was not trespassing on the land in respect of which he is alleged to have committed the offence, or

(*b*) that he had a reasonable excuse—

(i) for failing to leave the relevant land as soon as reasonably practicable, or

(ii) for entering land in the area of the relevant local authority as a trespasser with the intention of residing there, or

(*c*) that, at the time the direction was given, he was under the age of 18 years and was residing with his parent or guardian.

[Criminal Justice and Public Order Act 1994, s 62B as inserted by the Anti-social Behaviour Act 2003, s 61 and amended by the Serious Organised Crime and Police Act 2005, Sch 7.]

***Substituted by the Criminal Justice Act 2003, Sch 26 from a date to be appointed.**

8–24901C 62C. Failure to comply with direction under section 62A: seizure. (1) This section applies if a direction has been given under section 62A(1) and a constable reasonably suspects that a person to whom the direction applies has, without reasonable excuse—

(*a*) failed to remove any vehicle on the relevant land which appears to the constable to belong to him or to be in his possession or under his control; or

(*b*) entered any land in the area of the relevant local authority as a trespasser with a vehicle before the end of the relevant period with the intention of residing there.

(2) The relevant period is the period of 3 months starting with the day on which the direction is given.

(3) The constable may seize and remove the vehicle.
[Criminal Justice and Public Order Act 1994, s 62C as inserted by the Anti-social Behaviour Act 2003, s 62.]

8–24901D **62D. Common land: modifications.** (1) In their application to common land sections 62A to 62C have effect with these modifications.

(2) References to trespassing and trespassers have effect as if they were references to acts, and persons doing acts, which constitute—

(*a*) a trespass as against the occupier, or
(*b*) an infringement of the commoners' rights.

(3) References to the occupier—

(*a*) in the case of land to which the public has access, include the local authority and any commoner;
(*b*) in any other case, include the commoners or any of them.

(4) Subsection (1) does not—

(*a*) require action by more than one occupier, or
(*b*) constitute persons trespassers as against any commoner or the local authority if they are permitted to be there by the other occupier.

(5) In this section "common land", "commoner" and "the local authority" have the meanings given by section 61.
[Criminal Justice and Public Order Act 1994, s 62D as inserted by the Anti-social Behaviour Act 2003, s 63.]

8–24901E **62E. Sections 62A to 62D: interpretation.** (1) Subsections (2) to (8) apply for the interpretation of sections 62A to 62D and this section.

(2) "Land" does not include buildings other than—

(*a*) agricultural buildings within the meaning of paragraphs 3 to 8 of Schedule 5 to the Local Government Finance Act 1988, or
(*b*) scheduled monuments within the meaning of the Ancient Monuments and Archaeological Areas Act 1979.

(3) "Local authority" means—

(*a*) in Greater London, a London borough or the Common Council of the City of London;
(*b*) in England outside Greater London, a county council, a district council or the Council of the Isles of Scilly;
(*c*) in Wales, a county council or a county borough council.

(4) "Occupier", "trespass", "trespassing" and "trespasser" have the meanings given by section 61 in relation to England and Wales.

(5) "The relevant land" means the land in respect of which a direction under section 62A(1) is given.

(6) "The relevant local authority" means—

(*a*) if the relevant land is situated in the area of more than one local authority (but is not in the Isles of Scilly), the district council or county borough council within whose area the relevant land is situated;
(*b*) if the relevant land is situated in the Isles of Scilly, the Council of the Isles of Scilly;
(*c*) in any other case, the local authority within whose area the relevant land is situated.

(7) "Vehicle" has the meaning given by section 61.

(8) A person may be regarded as having a purpose of residing in a place even if he has a home elsewhere.
[Criminal Justice and Public Order Act 1994, s 62E as inserted by the Anti-social Behaviour Act 2003, s 64.]

Powers in relation to raves

8–24902 **63. Powers to remove persons attending or preparing for a rave.** (1) This section applies to a gathering on land in the open air of 20 or more persons (whether or not trespassers) at which amplified music is played during the night (with or without intermissions) and is such as, by reason of its loudness and duration and the time at which it is played, is likely to cause serious distress to the inhabitants of the locality; and for this purpose—

(*a*) such a gathering continues during intermissions in the music and, where the gathering extends over several days, throughout the period during which amplified music is played at night (with or without intermissions); and
(*b*) "music" includes sounds wholly or predominantly characterised by the emission of a succession of repetitive beats.*

(1A) This section also applies to a gathering if—

(*a*) it is a gathering on land of 20 or more persons who are trespassing on the land; and (*b*) it would be a gathering of a kind mentioned in subsection (1) above if it took place on land in the open air.

(2) If, as respects any land, a police officer of at least the rank of superintendent reasonably believes that—

(*a*) two or more persons are making preparations for the holding there of a gathering to which this section applies,

(*b*) ten or more persons are waiting for such a gathering to begin there, or

(*c*) ten or more persons are attending such a gathering which is in progress,

he may give a direction that those persons and any other persons who come to prepare or wait for or to attend the gathering are to leave the land and remove any vehicles or other property which they have with them on the land.*

(3) A direction under subsection (2) above, if not communicated to the persons referred to in subsection (2) by the police officer giving the direction, may be communicated to them by any constable at the scene.

(4) Persons shall be treated as having had a direction under subsection (2) above communicated to them if reasonable steps have been taken to bring it to their attention.

(5) A direction under subsection (2) above does not apply to an exempt person.

(6) If a person knowing that a direction has been given which applies to him—

(*a*) fails to leave the land as soon as reasonably practicable, or

(*b*) having left again enters the land within the period of 7 days beginning with the day on which the direction was given,

he commits an offence and is liable on summary conviction to imprisonment for a term not exceeding **three months**** or a fine not exceeding **level 4** on the standard scale, or **both**.

(7) In proceedings for an offence under this section** it is a defence for the accused to show that he had a reasonable excuse for failing to leave the land as soon as reasonably practicable or, as the case may be, for again entering the land.

(7A)A person commits an offence if—(*a*)he knows that a direction under subsection (2), and

(*b*) he makes preparations for or attends a gathering to which this section applies within the period of 24 hours starting when the direction was given.

(8) *Repealed.*

(9) This section does not apply—

(*a*) in England and Wales, to a gathering in relation to a licensable activity within section 1(1)(*c*) of the Licensing Act 2003 (provision of certain forms of entertainment) carried on under and in accordance with an authorisation within the meaning of section 136 of that Act; or

(*b*) in Scotland, to a gathering in premises which, by virtue of section 41 of the Civic Government (Scotland) Act 1982, are licensed to be used as a place of public entertainment.

(10) In this section—

"exempt person", in relation to land (or any gathering on land), means the occupier, any member of his family and any employee or agent of his and any person whose home is situated on the land;

"land in the open air" includes a place partly open to the air;

and

"occupier", "trespasser" and "vehicle" have the same meaning as in section 61.

(11) *Repealed.*

[Criminal Justice and Public Order Act 1994, s 63 as amended the Anti-social Behaviour Act 2003, s 58, the Licensing Act 2003, Sch 7 and the Serious Organised Crime And Police Act 2005, Sch 7.]

***Reproduced as in force in England and Wales.**

****Words in sub-ss (6) and (7) substituted by the Criminal Justice act 2003, s 336, from a date to be appointed.**

8–24903 **64. Supplementary powers of entry and seizure.** (1) If a police officer of at least the rank of superintendent reasonably believes that circumstances exist in relation to any land which would justify the giving of a direction under section 63 in relation to a gathering to which that section applies he may authorise any constable to enter the land for any of the purposes specified in subsection (2) below.

(2) Those purposes are—

(*a*) to ascertain whether such circumstances exist; and

(*b*) to exercise any power conferred on a constable by section 63 or subsection (4) below.

(3) A constable who is so authorised to enter land for any purpose may enter the land without a warrant.

(4) If a direction has been given under section 63 and a constable reasonably suspects that any person to whom the direction applies has, without reasonable excuse—

(*a*) failed to remove any vehicle or sound equipment on the land which appears to the constable to belong to him or to be in his possession or under his control; or

(*b*) entered the land as a trespasser with a vehicle or sound equipment within the period of 7 days beginning with the day on which the direction was given,

the constable may seize and remove that vehicle or sound equipment.

(5) Subsection (4) above does not authorise the seizure of any vehicle or sound equipment of an exempt person.

(5A) Entering land in Scotland with sound equipment in the circumstances mentioned in subsection (4)(*b*) above is not an exercise of access rights within the meaning of the Land Reform (Scotland) Act 2003 (asp 2).

(6) In this section—

"exempt person" has the same meaning as in section 63;

"sound equipment" means equipment designed or adapted for amplifying music and any equipment suitable for use in connection with such equipment, and "music" has the same meaning as in section 63; and

"vehicle" has the same meaning as in section 61.

[Criminal Justice and Public Order Act 1994, s 64 as amended by the Land Reform (Scotland) Act 2003, Sch 2.]

8–24904 **65. Raves: power to stop persons from proceeding.** (1) If a constable in uniform reasonably believes that a person is on his way to a gathering to which section 63 applies in relation to which a direction under section 63(2) is in force, he may, subject to subsections (2) and (3) below—

(*a*) stop that person, and

(*b*) direct him not to proceed in the direction of the gathering.

(2) The power conferred by subsection (1) above may only be exercised at a place within 5 miles of the boundary of the site of the gathering.

(3) No direction may be given under subsection (1) above to an exempt person.

(4) If a person knowing that a direction under subsection (1) above has been given to him fails to comply with that direction, he commits an offence and is liable on summary conviction to a fine not exceeding **level 3** on the standard scale.

(5) *Repealed.*

(6) In this section, "exempt person" has the same meaning as in section 63.

[Criminal Justice and Public Order Act 1994, s 65 as amended by the Serious Organised Crime And Police Act 2005, Sch 7.]

8–24905 **66. Power of court to forfeit sound equipment.** (1) Where a person is convicted of an offence under section 63 in relation to a gathering to which that section applies and the court is satisfied that any sound equipment which has been seized from him under section 64(4), or which was in his possession or under his control at the relevant time, has been used at the gathering the court may make an order for forfeiture under this subsection in respect of that property.

(2) The court may make an order under subsection (1) above whether or not it also deals with the offender in respect of the offence in any other way and without regard to any restrictions on forfeiture in any enactment.

(3) In considering whether to make an order under subsection (1) above in respect of any property a court shall have regard—

(*a*) to the value of the property; and

(*b*) to the likely financial and other effects on the offender of the making of the order (taken together with any other order that the court contemplates making).

(4) An order under subsection (1) above shall operate to deprive the offender of his rights, if any, in the property to which it relates, and the property shall (if not already in their possession) be taken into the possession of the police.

(5) Except in a case to which subsection (6) below applies, where any property has been forfeited under subsection (1) above, a magistrates' court may, on application by a claimant of the property, other than the offender from whom it was forfeited under subsection (1) above, make an order for delivery of the property to the applicant if it appears to the court that he is the owner of the property.

(6) In a case where forfeiture under subsection (1) above has been by order of a Scottish court, a claimant such as is mentioned in subsection (5) above may, in such manner as may be prescribed by act of adjournal, apply to that court for an order for the return of the property in question.

(7) No application shall be made under subsection (5), or by virtue of subsection (6), above by any claimant of the property after the expiration of 6 months from the date on which an order under subsection (1) above was made in respect of the property.

(8) No such application shall succeed unless the claimant satisfies the court either that he had not consented to the offender having possession of the property or that he did not know, and had no reason to suspect, that the property was likely to be used at a gathering to which section 63 applies.

(9) An order under subsection (5), or by virtue of subsection (6), above shall not affect the right of any person to take, within the period of 6 months from the date of an order under subsection (5),

or as the case may be by virtue of subsection (6), above, proceedings for the recovery of the property from the person in possession of it in pursuance of the order, but on the expiration of that period the right shall cease.

(10) The Secretary of State may make regulations[1] for the disposal of property, and for the application of the proceeds of sale of property, forfeited under subsection (1) above where no application by a claimant of the property under subsection (5), or by virtue of subsection (6), above has been made within the period specified in subsection (7) above or no such application has succeeded.

(11) The regulations[1] may also provide for the investment of money and for the audit of accounts.

(12) The power to make regulations under subsection (10) above shall be exercisable by statutory instrument which shall be subject to annulment in pursuance of a resolution of either House of Parliament.

(13) In this section—

"relevant time", in relation to a person—

(*a*) convicted in England and Wales of an offence under section 63, means the time of his arrest for the offence or of the issue of a summons in respect of it;

(*b*) so convicted in Scotland, means the time of his arrest for, or of his being cited as an accused in respect of, the offence;

"sound equipment" has the same meaning as in section 64.

[Criminal Justice and Public Order Act 1994, s 66.]

---

1. See the Police (Disposal of Sound Equipment) Regulations 1995, this title, post.

Retention and charges for seized property

8–24906 67. Retention and charges for seized property. (1) Any vehicles which have been seized and removed by a constable under section 62(1)* or 64(4) may be retained in accordance with regulations made by the Secretary of State under subsection (3) below.

(2) Any sound equipment which has been seized and removed by a constable under section 64(4) may be retained until the conclusion of proceedings against the person from whom it was seized for an offence under section 63.

(3) The Secretary of State may make regulations[1]—

(*a*) regulating the retention and safe keeping and the disposal and the destruction in prescribed circumstances of vehicles; and

(*b*) prescribing charges in respect of the removal, retention, disposal and destruction of vehicles.

(4) Any authority shall be entitled to recover from a person from whom a vehicle has been seized such charges as may be prescribed in respect of the removal, retention, disposal and destruction of the vehicle by the authority.

(5) Regulations under subsection (3) above may make different provisions for different classes of vehicles or for different circumstances.

(6) Any charges under subsection (4) above shall be recoverable as a simple contract debt.

(7) Any authority having custody of vehicles under regulations under subsection (3) above shall be entitled to retain custody until any charges under subsection (4) are paid.

(8) The power to make regulations under subsection (3) above shall be exercisable by statutory instrument which shall be subject to annulment in pursuance of a resolution of either House of Parliament.

(9) In this section—

"conclusion of proceedings" against a person means—

(*a*) his being sentenced or otherwise dealt with for the offence or his acquittal;

(*b*) the discontinuance of the proceedings; or

(*c*) the decision not to prosecute him,

whichever is the earlier;

"sound equipment" has the same meaning as in section 64; and

"vehicle" has the same meaning as in section 61.

[Criminal Justice and Public Order Act 1994, s 67.]

***Words inserted by the Anti-social Behaviour Act 2003, s 62, from a date to be appointed.**

1. See the Police (Retention and Disposal of Vehicles) Regulations 1995, this title, post.

Disruptive trespassers

8–24907 68. Offence of aggravated trespass. (1) A person commits the offence of aggravated trespass[1] if he trespasses on land and, in relation to any lawful activity[2] which persons are engaging in or are about to engage in on that or adjoining land, does there anything which is intended by him to have the effect[3]—

(*a*) of intimidating those persons or any of them so as to deter them or any of them from engaging in that activity,

(*b*) of obstructing that activity, or

(*c*) of disrupting that activity[4].

(1A) The refernces in subsection (1) above to trespassing includes, in Scotland, the exercise of access rights (within the meaning of the Land Reform (Scotland) Act 2003 (asp 2)) up to the point when they cease to be exercisable by virtue of the commisssion of the offence under that subsection.

(2) Activity on any occasion on the part of a person or persons on land is "lawful" for the purposes of this section if he or they may engage in the activity on the land on that occasion without committing an offence or trespassing on the land[5].

(3) A person guilty of an offence under this section is liable on summary conviction to imprisonment for a term not exceeding **three months*** or a fine not exceeding **level 4** on the standard scale, or **both**.

(4) *Repealed.*

(5) In this section "land" does not include—

(*a*) the highways and roads excluded from the application of section 61 by paragraph (*b*) of the definition of "land" in subsection (9) of that section; or

(*b*) a road within the meaning of the Roads (Northern Ireland) Order 1993.

[Criminal Justice and Public Order Act 1994, s 68, as amended by the Anti-social Behaviour Act 2003, s 59, the Land Reform (Scotland) Act 2003, Sch 2 and the Serious Organised Crime And Police Act 2005, Sch 7.]

***Words substituted by the Criminal Justice Act 2003, Sch 26, from a date to be appointed.**

1. Where the common law private defence of property is raised the court must first ask itself whether the defendants are contending that they used reasonable force in order to defend property from actual or imminent damage, which constituted or would constitute an unlawful or criminal act. If the answer to that is "no" then the defence is not available. If the answer is "yes" then the court has to go on to consider the facts as the defendants honestly believed them to be and then has to determine objectively whether the force that was used was reasonable in all the circumstances. Thus, in a case where it was clear that the defendants knew quite well that there was nothing unlawful about the drilling of GM maize on the land, even if the seed might be transferred by one means or another to the neighbouring land; they acted as they had because they believed strongly that the seed represented a danger to neighbouring property and they knew that the law would not help them because what was going on was not unlawful or criminal, then, as a matter of law that the private defence of property simply was not available to the defendants on the facts (*DPP v Bayer* [2003] EWHC 2567 (Admin), (2003) 167 JP 666).

2. "Activity" means that something is being done or about to be done by a person and is a more particular definition than "carry on" eg of an enterprise such as farming. Accordingly, the persons engaged in the "lawful activity" must be physically present on the land so that persons who had trespassed on a field and damaged genetically modified crops were not guilty of an offence contrary to s 68(1) where neither the farmer nor anyone responsible for cultivation was present (*Tilly v DPP* [2001] EWCA Admin 821, 166 JP 22, [2002] Crim LR 128).

Conduct which might amount to crimes against peace or to crimes of aggression is not unlawful activity within s 68 of the 1994 Act: *Ayliffe v DPP, Swain v DPP* and *Percy v DPP* [2005] EWHC 684 (Admin), [2005] 3 All ER 330 (which concerned trespasser disrupting activities at military bases during the Iraq war).

3. Since s 68(1) has criminalised an *actus reus* with three effects, the three effects do not need to be the subject of three separate charges (*Nelder v DPP* (1998) Times, 11 June). Where there is no allegation of any second distinct act beyond the trespass itself an information alleging aggravated trespass will be defective (*DPP v Barnard* [2000] Crim LR 371, DC).

4. Defendants who, having taken part in a mass protest against fox hunting, as trespassers, were running towards a hunt with the intention of disrupting it, were held to have been properly convicted of an offence under s 68(1) because the running after the hunt was sufficiently closely connected to the intended disruption as to be more than merely preparatory within the meaning of the Criminal Attempts Act 1981 (*Winder v DPP* (1996) 160 JP 713).

5. This means simply that the activity was lawful when it was being carried out. Parliament cannot be presumed to have intended to make it an offence for a person to disrupt an activity being carried on unlawfully, simply because, if carried on in another way, the activity could be carried on lawfully. Further, if a defendant raises an issue that his or her intention was to disrupt an unlawful activity, it will not assist the prosecution to limit the description in the charge to some lawful aspect of what was occurring on the land; the person must intend to disrupt the specified activity: *Ayliffe v DPP, Swain v DPP* and *Percy v DPP* [2005] EWHC 684 (Admin), [2005] 3 All ER 330.

8–24908 69. Powers to remove persons committing or participating in aggravated trespass.
(1) If the senior police officer present at the scene reasonably believes—

(*a*) that a person is committing, has committed or intends to commit the offence of aggravated trespass on land; or

(*b*) that two or more persons are trespassing on land and are present there with the common purpose of intimidating persons so as to deter them from engaging in a lawful activity or of obstructing or disrupting a lawful activity,

he may direct that person or (as the case may be) those persons (or any of them) to leave the land.

(2) A direction under subsection (1) above, if not communicated to the persons referred to in subsection (1) by the police officer giving the direction may be communicated to them by any constable at the scene.

(3) If a person knowing that a direction under subsection (1) above has been given which applies to him—

(*a*) fails to leave the land as soon as practicable, or

(*b*) having left again enters the land as a trespasser within the period of three months beginning with the day on which the direction was given, he commits an offence and is liable on summary conviction to imprisonment for a term not exceeding **three months*** or a fine not exceeding **level 4** on the standard scale, or both.

(4) In proceedings for an offence under subsection (3) it is a defence for the accused to show—

(*a*) that he was not trespassing on the land, or

(*b*) that he had a reasonable excuse for failing to leave the land as soon as practicable or, as the case may be, for again entering the land as a trespasser.

(5) *Repealed.*

(6) In this section "lawful activity" and "land" have the same meaning as in section 68.

[Criminal Justice and Public Order Act 1994, s 69, as amended by the Anti-social Behaviour Act 2003, s 59 and the Serious Organised Crime And Police Act 2005, Sch 7.]

***Words substituted by the Criminal Justice Act 2003, Sch 26, from a date to be appointed.**

Squatters

8–24909 75. Interim possession orders: false or misleading statements. (1) A person commits an offence if, for the purpose of obtaining an interim possession order, he—

(*a*) makes a statement which he knows to be false or misleading in a material particular; or

(*b*) recklessly makes a statement which is false or misleading in a material particular.

(2) A person commits an offence if, for the purpose of resisting the making of an interim possession order, he—

(*a*) makes a statement which he knows to be false or misleading in a material particular; or

(*b*) recklessly makes a statement which is false or misleading in a material particular.

(3) A person guilty of an offence under this section shall be liable[1]—

(*a*) on conviction on indictment, to imprisonment for a term not exceeding **two years** or a **fine** or **both**;

(*b*) on summary conviction, to imprisonment for a term not exceeding **six months** or a fine not exceeding **the statutory maximum** or **both**.

(4) In this section—

"interim possession order" means an interim possession order (so entitled) made under rules of court for the bringing of summary proceedings for possession of premises which are occupied by trespassers;

"premises" has the same meaning as in Part II of the Criminal Law Act 1977 (offences relating to entering and remaining on property); and

"statement", in relation to an interim possession order, means any statement, in writing or oral and whether as to fact or belief, made in or for the purposes of the proceedings.

[Criminal Justice and Public Order Act 1994, s 75.]

1. For procedure in respect of this offence which is triable either way, see the Magistrates' Courts Act 1980, ss 17A–21, in PART I: MAGISTRATES' COURTS, PROCEDURE, ante.

8–24910 76. Interim possession orders: trespassing during currency of order. (1) This section applies where an interim possession order has been made in respect of any premises and served in accordance with rules of court; and references to "the order" and "the premises" shall be construed accordingly.

(2) Subject to subsection (3), a person who is present on the premises as a trespasser at any time during the currency of the order commits an offence.

(3) No offence under subsection (2) is committed by a person if—

(*a*) he leaves the premises within 24 hours of the time of service of the order and does not return; or

(*b*) a copy of the order was not fixed to the premises in accordance with rules of court.

(4) A person who was in occupation of the premises at the time of service of the order but leaves them commits an offence if he re-enters the premises as a trespasser or attempts to do so after the expiry of the order but within the period of one year beginning with the day on which it was served.

(5) A person guilty of an offence under this section shall be liable on summary conviction to imprisonment for a term not exceeding **six months** or a fine not exceeding **level 5** on the standard scale or both.

(6) A person who is in occupation of the premises at the time of service of the order shall be treated for the purposes of this section as being present as a trespasser.

(7) *Repealed.*

(8) In this section—

"interim possession order" has the same meaning as in section 75 above and "rules of court" is to be construed accordingly; and "premises" has the same meaning as in that section, that is to say, the same meaning as in Part II of the Criminal Law Act 1977 (offences relating to entering and remaining on property).

[Criminal Justice and Public Order Act 1994, s 76 as amended by the Serious Organised Crime And Police Act 2005, Sch 7.]

Powers to remove unauthorised campers

8–24911 **77. Power of local authority to direct unauthorised campers to leave land**[1]**.** (1) If it appears to a local authority that persons are for the time being residing in a vehicle or vehicles within that authority's area—

(*a*) on any land forming part of a highway;
(*b*) on any other unoccupied land; or
(*c*) on any occupied land without the consent of the occupier,

the authority may give a direction that those persons and any others with them[2] are to leave the land and remove the vehicle or vehicles and any other property they have with them on the land.

(2) Notice of a direction under subsection (1) must be served on the persons to whom the direction applies, but it shall be sufficient for this purpose for the direction to specify the land and (except where the direction applies to only one person) to be addressed to all occupants of the vehicles on the land, without naming them.

(3) If a person knowing that a direction under subsection (1) above has been given which applies to him—

(*a*) fails, as soon as practicable, to leave the land or remove from the land any vehicle or other property which is the subject of the direction, or
(*b*) having removed any such vehicle or property again enters the land with a vehicle within the period of three months beginning with the day on which the direction was given,

he commits an offence and is liable on summary conviction to a fine not exceeding **level 3** on the standard scale.

(4) A direction under subsection (1) operates to require persons who re-enter the land within the said period with vehicles or other property to leave and remove the vehicles or other property as it operates in relation to the persons and vehicles or other property on the land when the direction was given.

(5) In proceedings for an offence under this section it is a defence for the accused to show that his failure to leave or to remove the vehicle or other property as soon as practicable or his re-entry with a vehicle was due to illness, mechanical breakdown or other immediate emergency.

(6) In this section—

"land" means land in the open air;

"local authority" means—

(*a*) in Greater London, a London borough or the Common Council of the City of London;
(*b*) in England outside Greater London, a county council, a district council or the Council of the Isles of Scilly;
(*c*) in Wales, a county council or a county borough council;

"occupier" means the person entitled to possession of the land by virtue of an estate or interest held by him;

"vehicle" includes—

(*a*) any vehicle, whether or not it is in a fit state for use on roads, and includes any body, with or without wheels, appearing to have formed part of such a vehicle, and any load carried by, and anything attached to, such a vehicle; and
(*b*) a caravan as defined in section 29(1) of the Caravan Sites and Control of Development Act 1960;

and a person may be regarded for the purposes of this section as residing on any land notwithstanding that he has a home elsewhere.

(7) Until 1st April 1996, in this section "local authority" means, in Wales, a county council or a district council.

[Criminal Justice and Public Order Act 1994, s 77.]

---

1. When deciding whether to make a removal order under this section, the local authority must consider the relationship of its proposed action to the various statutory provisions and humanitarian considerations that would arise, such as those outlined in the Departmental Circular *Gypsy Sites and Unauthorised Camping* DOE 18/94, Welsh Office 76/94). These considerations should be kept under review so far as there are any changes in circumstances after a removal order has been made, when deciding whether to make a complaint to the justices under s 78 of the Act (*R v Wealden District Council, ex p Wales* (1995) Times, 22 September).

The local authority should make inquiries into personal circumstances before and not after making the order. Magistrates are restricted to considering whether the formalities under the Act have been carried out and it is not part of their function to review the merits of the local authority's decision (*R v Wolverhampton Metropolitan Borough Council, ex p Dunne* (1996) 29 HLR 745, DC).

2. A removal notice applies only to persons who were on the land at the time when the direction was made and can be contravened only by such persons (*R v Wealden District Council, ex p Wales* (1995) Times, 22 September).

8–24912 **78. Orders for removal of persons and their vehicles unlawfully on land.** (1) A magistrates' court may[1], on a complaint made by a local authority, if satisfied that persons and vehicles in which they are residing are present on land within that authority's area in contravention of a direction[2] given under section 77, make an order requiring the removal of any vehicle or other property which is so present on the land and any person residing in it.

(2) An order under this section may authorise the local authority to take such steps as are reasonably necessary to ensure that the order is complied with and, in particular, may authorise the authority, by its officers and servants—

(*a*) to enter upon the land specified in the order; and

(*b*) to take, in relation to any vehicle or property to be removed in pursuance of the order, such steps for securing entry and rendering it suitable for removal as may be so specified.

(3) The local authority shall not enter upon any occupied land unless they have given to the owner and occupier at least 24 hours notice of their intention to do so or unless after reasonable inquiries they are unable to ascertain their names and addresses.

(4) A person who wilfully obstructs any person in the exercise of any power conferred on him by an order under this section commits an offence and is liable on summary conviction to a fine not exceeding **level 3** on the standard scale.

(5) Where a complaint is made under this section, a summons issued by the court requiring the person or persons to whom it is directed to appear before the court to answer to the complaint may be directed—

(*a*) to the occupant of a particular vehicle on the land in question; or

(*b*) to all occupants of vehicles on the land in question, without naming him or them.

(6) Section 55(2) of the Magistrates' Courts Act 1980 (warrant for arrest of defendant failing to appear) does not apply to proceedings on a complaint made under this section.

(7) Section 77(6) of this Act applies also for the interpretation of this section.

[Criminal Justice and Public Order Act 1994, s 78.]

---

1. Where a local authority has made a direction under s 77, the question of reasonableness is a matter for the local authority to decide and there is no discretion for magistrates to review the reasonableness of the council's action. Only a limited discretion exists to refuse to make an order in special circumstances, for example when it is unnecessary to do so because the occupier has made an acceptable undertaking to leave by a certain time (*Shropshire County Council v Wynne* (1997) 96 LGR 689, DC). See also the reference to *R v Wolverhampton Metropolitan Borough Council, ex p Dunne* in note 1 to section 77, ante).

2. We would suggest that the legality of any direction is not to be challenged before the justices but by way of judicial review of the local authority's decision (see, for example, *R v Wealden District Council, ex p Wales* (1995) Times, 22 September).

8–24913 **79. Provisions as to directions under s 77 and orders under s 78.** (1) The following provisions apply in relation to the service of notice of a direction under section 77 and of a summons under section 78, referred to in those provisions as a "relevant document".

(2) Where it is impracticable to serve a relevant document on a person named in it, the document shall be treated as duly served on him if a copy of it is fixed in a prominent place to the vehicle concerned; and where a relevant document is directed to the unnamed occupants of vehicles, it shall be treated as duly served on those occupants if a copy of it is fixed in a prominent place to every vehicle on the land in question at the time when service is thus effected.

(3) A local authority shall take such steps as may be reasonably practicable to secure that a copy of any relevant document is displayed on the land in question (otherwise than by being fixed to a vehicle) in a manner designed to ensure that it is likely to be seen by any person camping on the land.

(4) Notice of any relevant document shall be given by the local authority to the owner of the land in question and to any occupier of that land unless, after reasonable inquiries, the authority is unable to ascertain the name and address of the owner or occupier; and the owner of any such land and any occupier of such land shall be entitled to appear and to be heard in the proceedings.

(5) Section 77(6) applies also for the interpretation of this section.

[Criminal Justice and Public Order Act 1994, s 79.]

8–24914 **80.** *Repeal of certain provisions relating to gipsy sites.*

Police (Disposal of Sound Equipment) Regulations 1995[1]

(SI 1995/722 amended by SI 2000/1549)

Extent, citation and commencement

8–24915 **1.** These Regulations, which extend to England and Wales and Scotland, may be cited as the Police (Disposal of Sound Equipment) Regulations 1995 and shall come into force on 10th April 1995.

---

1. Made by the Secretary of State in exercise of the powers conferred on him by s 66(10) and (11) of the Criminal Justice and Public Order Act 1994.

Property to which Regulations apply

8–24916 **2.** (1) Subject to paragraph (2) below, these Regulations apply to property in the possession of the police which has been forfeited by order under section 66(1) of the Criminal Justice and Public Order Act 1994 ("the 1994 Act") provided that—

(*a*) not less than six months have expired from the date on which the order was made, and

(*b*) either—

(i) no application by a claimant of the property has been made under section 66(5) of the 1994 Act, or by virtue of section 66(6); or

(ii) no such application has succeeded.

(2) Where, within the period specified in paragraph (1)(*a*) above—

(*a*) an application by a claimant of the property has been made under section 66(5) of the 1994 Act or by virtue of section 66(6), or

(*b*) the person upon whose conviction the court ordered the forfeiture of the property under section 66(1) of that Act has appealed against his conviction or sentence,

these Regulations shall not apply to the property until the application or appeal has been determined.

Disposal of property

8–24917 **3.** Property to which these Regulations apply shall be disposed of by sale or, if a police officer not below the rank of superintendent is satisfied that the nature of the property is such that it is not in the public interest that it should be sold, by other means in accordance with his directions.

Application of proceeds of sale

8–24918 **4.** (1) The proceeds of any sale under regulation 3 above shall be paid to the police authority and shall be kept in a separate account (referred to in this regulation as "the Fund").

(2) The Fund, or any part thereof, may be invested as the police authority think fit and the income derived from the investments shall be added to and become part of the Fund.

(3) The money, including income from investments, standing to the credit of the Fund shall be applicable—

(*a*) to defray expenses incurred in the conveyance, storage and safe custody of the property to which these Regulations apply and in connection with its sale and otherwise in executing these Regulations;

(*b*) to make such payments of such amounts as the police authority may determine for such charitable purposes as they may select.

(4) The Fund shall be audited by an auditor nominated for that purpose by the police authority.

(5) (*Revoked*).

Police (Retention and Disposal of Vehicles) Regulations 1995[1]

(SI 1995/723)

Extent, citation and commencement

8–24919 **1.** These Regulations, which extend to England and Wales and Scotland, may be cited as the Police (Retention and Disposal of Vehicles) Regulations 1995 and shall come into force on 10th April 1995.

1. Made by the Secretary of State in exercise of the powers conferred on him by s 67(3) of the Criminal Justice and Public Order Act 1994.

Application and interpretation

8–24920 **2.** (1) These Regulations apply to vehicles which have been seized and removed by a constable under section 62(1) or 64(4) of the 1994 Act.

(2) In these Regulations—

"the 1994 Act" means the Criminal Justice and Public Order Act 1994;

"the authority" means a police officer or other person authorised by the chief officer under regulation 3(1);

"G.B. registration mark" means a registration mark issued in relation to a vehicle under the Vehicle Excise and Registration Act 1994;

"local authority" means—

(*a*) in relation to England—

(i) a county council or, in a county where there is no county council, a district council;

(ii) a London borough council, or the Common Council of the City of London; or

(iii) the Council of the Isles of Scilly;

(*b*) in relation to Scotland—

(i) until 1st April 1996, a regional or islands or district council;
(ii) on or after that date, a council constituted under section 2 of the Local Government (Scotland) Act 1994;

(*c*) in relation to Wales—

(i) until 1st April 1996, a county council;
(ii) on or after that date, a county council or county borough council;

"owner" includes—

(*a*) the person by whom, according to the records maintained by the Secretary of State for Transport in connection with any functions exercisable by him by virtue of the Vehicle Excise and Registration Act 1994, the vehicle is kept and used;
(*b*) in relation to a vehicle which is the subject of a hiring agreement or a hire-purchase agreement, the person entitled to possession of the vehicle under the agreement;

"removal notice" means a notice complying with regulation 4;

"specified information", in relation to a vehicle, means such of the following information as can be or could have been ascertained from an inspection of the vehicle, or has been ascertained from any other source, that is to say:

(*a*) in the case of a vehicle which carries a G.B. registration mark, or a mark indicating registration in a place outside Great Britain, particulars of that mark; and
(*b*) the make of the vehicle.

Retention and safe keeping of vehicles

8–24921 **3.** (1) After a vehicle has been seized and removed under section 62(1) or 64(4) of the 1994 Act, it shall be passed into and remain in the custody of a police officer or other person authorised under this regulation by the chief officer of the police force for the area in which the vehicle was seized ("the authority") until—

(*a*) the authority permit it to be removed from their custody by a person appearing to them to be the person from whom the vehicle was seized or the owner of the vehicle; or
(*b*) it has been disposed of or destroyed under these Regulations.

(2) While the vehicle is in the custody of the authority, they shall be under a duty to take such steps as are reasonably necessary for its safe keeping.

Service of removal notice

8–24922 **4.** (1) The authority shall, as soon as they are able after the vehicle has been taken into their custody, take such steps as are practicable to serve a removal notice on the person from whom the vehicle was seized, except where the vehicle has been removed from their custody under regulation 5 below.

(2) A removal notice required to be served under this regulation or under regulation 6(3) below shall comply with, and shall be served in accordance with, the following provisions of this regulation.

(3) The removal notice shall, in respect of the vehicle to which it relates, contain the specified information and shall state:

(*a*) the place where the vehicle was seized;
(*b*) the place where it is now being kept;
(*c*) that the person to whom the notice is directed is required to claim the vehicle from the authority on or before the date specified in the notice, being a date not less than 21 days from the day when the notice is served on him;
(*d*) that unless the vehicle is claimed on or before that date the authority intend to destroy or dispose of it;
(*e*) that charges are payable under these Regulations by the person from whom the vehicle was seized in respect of the removal and retention of the vehicle, and that the vehicle may be retained until such charges are paid.

(4) The removal notice shall be served—

(*a*) by delivering it to the person to whom it is directed;
(*b*) by leaving it at his usual or last known place of abode;
(*c*) by sending it in a prepaid registered letter, or by the recorded delivery service, addressed to him at his usual or last known place of abode; or
(*d*) if the person is—

(i) a body corporate, by delivering it to the secretary or clerk of the body at its registered or principal office, or sending it in a prepaid registered letter, or by the recorded delivery service, addressed to the secretary or clerk of the body at that office;
(ii) a Scottish partnership, by delivering it to any member of, or manager employed by, the partnership at the usual place of business of the partnership, or sending it in a prepaid registered letter, or by the recorded delivery service, addressed to such a person at that place.

Removal of vehicles from custody

8–24923 **5.** (1) Subject to section 67(4) and (7) of the 1994 Act and the following provisions of these Regulations, if at any time a person satisfies the authority that he is the person from whom the vehicle was seized the authority shall permit him to remove the vehicle from their custody.

(2) Paragraph (1) above does not—

(*a*) impose a duty on the authority where they reasonably believe that the person referred to is not the owner of the vehicle or authorised by the owner to remove the vehicle; or

(*b*) prevent the authority, in those circumstances, from returning the vehicle to its owner.

Disposal and destruction of vehicles

8–24924 **6.** (1) Where the authority have been unable to serve a removal notice on the person from whom the vehicle was seized or, following the service of a removal notice, the vehicle has not been removed from their custody under these Regulations, the authority may dispose of or destroy the vehicle in accordance with the following provisions of this regulation.

(2) If the authority are satisfied that the person on whom they have served or attempted to serve a removal notice is the owner of the vehicle, they may dispose of or destroy the vehicle at any time, subject to paragraph (5) below.

(3) Where the authority are not so satisfied, they may, after taking steps under paragraph (4) below to find a person who may be the owner of the vehicle and any other steps for that purpose which appear to them to be practicable, in such manner as they think fit dispose of or destroy the vehicle at any time, subject to paragraph (5) below, if—

(*a*) they fail to find such a person, allowing a reasonable time for any person or body from whom they have requested information to respond to the request; or

(*b*) they find such a person but he fails to comply with a removal notice served on him under this paragraph but complying with, and served in accordance with, regulation 4 above; or

(*c*) they find such a person but he is a person on whom the authority have already served or attempted to serve a removal notice under regulation 4 above.

(4) The steps to be taken under this paragraph to find a person who may be the owner of the vehicle shall be such of the following as are applicable to the vehicle—

(*a*) if the vehicle carries a G.B. registration mark—

(i) the authority shall ascertain from the records maintained by the Secretary of State for Transport in connection with any functions exercisable by him by virtue of the Vehicle Excise and Registration Act 1994 the name and address of the person by whom the vehicle is kept and used; and

(ii) they shall give, where practicable, the specified information to a relevant agency and shall enquire of them whether they can make any enquiries to find the owner of the vehicle;

(*b*) if the vehicle carries a mark indicating registration in Northern Ireland, the authority shall give the specified information and a description of the place where the vehicle was seized to the Secretary of State for Transport and, where practicable, the specified information to a relevant agency shall enquire of them whether they can make any enquiries to find the owner of the vehicle;

(*c*) if the vehicle carries a mark indicating registration in the Republic of Ireland, the authority shall give the specified information and a description of the place where the vehicle was seized to the Secretary of State for Transport, and shall enquire of him whether he can make any enquiries to find the owner of the vehicle;

(*d*) if the vehicle carries a registration mark other than one mentioned in sub-paragraphs (*a*) to (*c*) above, the authority shall, where practicable, give the specified information to a relevant agency and shall enquire of them whether they can make any enquiries to find the owner of the vehicle.

(5) The authority may not destroy or dispose of the vehicle under this regulation—

(*a*) during the period of 3 months starting with the date on which the vehicle was seized;

(*b*) if the period in sub-paragraph (*a*) above has expired, until after the date specified by virtue of regulation 4(3)(*c*) above; or

(*c*) if not otherwise covered by sub-paragraph (*a*) or (*b*) above, during the period of 7 days starting with the date on which the vehicle is claimed under regulation 5 above

(6) In this regulation "relevant agency" means such agency maintaining records of hire purchase agreements about vehicles as the authority considers appropriate.

Information to be given relating to the disposal of a vehicle

8–24925 **7.** (1) Where the authority dispose of or destroy a vehicle pursuant to these Regulations they shall, where it is possible to do so, give information relating to the disposal or destruction of the vehicle to the person from whom the vehicle was seized, to any person who appears to the authority to have been the owner of the vehicle immediately before it was disposed of, and—

(*a*) if the vehicle carried a GB registration mark, to the Secretary of State for Transport;

(*b*) if the vehicle carried a mark indicating registration in Northern Ireland, to the Secretary of State for Transport and to the Secretary of State for Northern Ireland;
(*c*) if the vehicle carried a mark indicating registration in the Republic of Ireland, to the Secretary of State for Transport and to the Commissioners of Customs and Excise;
(*d*) if the vehicle carried a registration mark other than one mentioned in sub-paragraphs (*a*) to (*c*) above, to the Commissioners of Customs and Excise.

(2) In this regulation "information relating to the disposal or destruction of a vehicle" means—

(*a*) any information which is sufficient to relate the information now being given to any information previously given to the same person in respect of the removal, retention, disposal or destruction of the vehicle; and
(*b*) such of the specified information as has not been previously given to the same person in respect of the removal, retention, disposal or destruction of the vehicle.

Payment of proceeds of sale to owner of vehicle

8–24926 8. (1) Where the authority dispose of a vehicle in pursuance of these Regulations by means of sale, they shall pay the net proceeds of sale to any person who, before the end of the period of one year beginning with the date on which the vehicle is sold, satisfies the authority that at the time of the sale he was the owner of the vehicle.

(2) If it appears to the authority that more than one person is the owner of a particular vehicle, such one of them as the authority think fit shall be treated as its owner for the purposes of paragraph (1) above.

(3) In this regulation, "the net proceeds of sale" means any sum by which the proceeds of sale exceed the aggregate of such sums as may be payable under these Regulations in respect of the removal and retention of the vehicle.

Charges for removal, retention and disposal of vehicles

8–24927 9. (1) The prescribed sums for the purpose of section 67(3) of the 1994 Act shall, for any vehicle, be—

(*a*) in respect of removal, £105;
(*b*) in respect of retention, £12 for each period of 24 hours or a part thereof during which the vehicle is in the custody of the authority.

(2) For the purposes of paragraph (1)(*b*) above, each period of 24 hours shall be reckoned from noon on the first day after removal during which the place at which the vehicle is stored is open for the claiming of vehicles before noon.

PUBLIC HEALTH

8–24940 This title contains the following statutes—

Other public health Acts which appear elsewhere in this work are the Town Improvement Clauses Act

1847, the Town Police Clauses Act 1847, title TOWN IMPROVEMENT, TOWNS POLICE, the Hydrogen Cyanide (Fumigation) Act 1937, title HEALTH AND SAFETY. See also the title WATER, post.

This title also contains the following statutory instruments—

8–27160 Control of Noise (Appeals) Rules 1975
8–27171 Litter (Statutory Undertakers) (Designation and Relevant Land) Order 1991
8–27180 Statutory Nuisance (Appeals) Regulations 1995
8–27184 Pollution Prevention and Control (England and Wales) Regulations 2000

8–24950 European Communities Act 1972: regulations. Within the scope of the title Public Health would logically fall the subject matter of a number of regulations made under the very wide enabling power provided in section 2(2) of the European Communities Act 1972. Where such regulations create offences they are noted below in chronological order.

Sludge (Use in Agriculture) Regulations 1989, SI 1989/1263 amended by SI 1990/880 and SI 1996/593;
Household Appliances (Noise Emission) Regulations 1990, SI 1990/161 amended by SI 1994/1386 and SI 2004/693;
Construction Products Regulations 1991, SI 1991/1620;
Environmental Protection (Controls on Injurious Substances) (No 2) Regulation 1993, SI 1993/1643;
Transfrontier Shipment of Waste Regulations 1994, SI 1994/1137 amended by SI 1996/593 and 972 and SI 2005/187;
Notification of Existing Substances (Enforcement) Regulations 1994, SI 1994/1806 amended by SI 1996/1373;
Protection of Water Against Agricultural Nitrate Pollution (England and Wales) Regulations 1996, SI 1996/888 amended by SI 2002/2297 (Wales);
Offshore Petroleum Production and Pipe-lines (Assessment of Environmental Effects) Regulations 1998, SI 1998/968;
Non-Road Mobile Machinery (Emission of Gaseous and Particulate Pollutants) Regulations 1999, SI 1999/1053 amended by SI 2002/1649, SI 2004/693 and 2034 and SI 2006/29;
Groundwater Regulations 1998, SI 1998/2746 amended by SI 2000/1973;
Environmental Protection (Controls on Injurious Substances) Regulations 1999, SI 1999/3244 amended by SI 2003/721;
Environmental Protection (Disposal of Polychlorinated Biphenyls and other Dangerous Substances) (England and Wales) Regulations 2000, SI 2000/1043 amended by SI 2000/3359 and SI 2005/894 and 1806 (W);
Sulphur Content of Liquid Fuels (England and Wales) Regulations 2000, SI 2000/1460;
Noise Emission in the Environment by Equipment for use Outdoors Regulations 2001, SI 2001/1701 amended by SI 2001/3958 and SI 2005/3525;
Environmental Protection (Controls on Ozone-depleting Substances) Regulations 2002, SI 2002/528;
Agricultural or Forestry Tractors and Tractor (Emission of Gaseous and Particulate Pollutants) Regulations 2002, SI 2002/1891;
Packaging (Essential Requirements) Regulations 2003, SI 2003/1941 amended by SI 2004/693 and 1188 and SI 2005/984 and 1806 (W);
End-of-Life Vehicles Regulations 2003, SI 2003/2635 amended by SI 2005/263;
Environmental Protection (Controls on Dangerous Substances) Regulations 2003, SI 2003/3274;
Controls on Nonylphenol and Nonylphenol Ethozylate Regulations 2004, SI 2004/1816;
Genetically Modified Organisms (Traceability and Labelling) (England) Regulations 2004, SI 2004/2412;
Genetically Modified Organisms (Transboundary Movements) (England) Regulations 2004, SI 2004/2692;
Controls on Pentabromodiphenyl Ether and Octabromodiphenyl Ether (No 2) Regulations 2004, SI 2004/3278;
End-of Life Vehicles (Producer Responsibility) Regulations 2005, SI 2005/263;
Greenhouse Gas Emissions Trading Scheme Regulations 2005, SI 2005/925 amended by SI 2005/2903;
Hazardous Waste (England and Wales) Regulations 2005, SI 2005/894;
List of Wastes (England) Regulations 2005, SI 2005/895 amended by SI 2005/1673;
Hazardous Waste (Wales) Regulations 2005, SI 2005/1806;
List of Wastes (Wales) Regulations 2005, SI 2005/1820;
Genetically Modified Organisms (Transboundary Movement) (Wales) Regulations 2005, SI 2005/1912;
Genetically Modified Organisms (Traceability and Labelling) (Wales) Regulations 2005, SI 2005/1914;
Detergents Regulations 2005, SI 2005/2469;
Volatile Organic Compounds in Paints, Varnishes and Vehicle Refinishing Products Regulations 2005, SI 2005/2773;

8–25014 10. Compensation, how determined. Where any compensation, costs, damages or expenses is or are by this Act directed to be paid, and the method for determining the amount thereof is not otherwise provided for, such amount shall in case of dispute be ascertained in the manner provided[1] by the Public Health Acts.

[Public Health Acts Amendment Act 1907, s 10.]

---

1. This section is repealed, except for the purposes of any unrepealed enactment (Public Health Act 1936, Sch 3). See now s 276 thereof, post.

8–25015 12. Crown rights. Nothing in this Act affects prejudicially any estate, right, power, privilege, or exemption of the Crown[1], and in particular nothing herein contained authorises any local authority to take, use, or in any manner interfere with any portion of the shore or bed of the sea or of any river, channel, creek, bay, or estuary, or any land, hereditaments, subjects, or right of whatsoever description belonging to Her Majesty in right of Her Crown, and under the management of the Commissioners of Woods[2] or of the Board of Trade respectively, without the consent in writing of the Commissioners of Woods[2] or the Board of Trade, as the case may be, on behalf of Her Majesty first had and obtained for that purpose (which consent the said Commissioners and Board are hereby respectively authorised to give).

[Public Health Acts Amendment Act 1907, s 12.]

---

1. Extended to any works or apparatus belonging to the Post Office authority or any power conferred on the Minister of Transport by the London Traffic Act 1924 (*repealed and replaced by the Road Traffic Act* 1960) (Public Health Act 1925, ss 10 and 1(3), as amended by Public Health Act 1936, Sch 3).

2. Now the Commissioners of Crown Lands (SR & O 1924, No 1370).

PART II
STREETS AND BUILDINGS

8–25019 21. Power to alter names of streets[1]. The local authority[2] may, with the consent of two-thirds in number of the ratepayers and persons who are liable to pay an amount in respect of council tax in any street, alter the name of such street or any part of such street. The local authority may cause the name of any street or of any part of any street to be painted or otherwise marked on a conspicuous part of any building or other erection.

Any person who shall wilfully and without the consent of the local authority, obliterate, deface, obscure, remove, or alter any such name, shall be liable to a penalty not exceeding **level 1** on the standard scale.

[Public Health Acts Amendment Act 1907, s 21, as amended by the Criminal Law Act 1977, s 31, the Criminal Justice Act 1982, s 46, SI 1990/776 and the Local Government Finance Act 1982, Sch 13.]

---

1. Upon the coming into operation in an area of s 18 of the Public Health Act 1925, post, this section will cease to have effect therein. Section 21 does not apply to Greater London.

2. "Local authority" means the council or a district of London borough, the Common Council of the City of London, the Sub-Treasurer of the Inner Temple and the Under Treasurer of the Middle Temple (Local Government Act 1972, s 180). For application to local government areas, see Local Government Act 1972, Sch 14, paras 24–26.

8–25020 31. Fencing lands adjoining streets. If any land (other than land forming part of any common) adjoining any street is allowed to remain unfenced or if the fences of any such land are allowed to be or remain out of repair, and such land is used for any immoral or indecent purposes, or for any purpose, causing inconvenience or annoyance to the public, in that case, at any time after the expiration of fourteen days from the service upon the owner or occupier of notice in writing by the local authority requiring the land to be fenced or any fence of the land to be repaired, the local authority may cause the land to be fenced or may cause the fences to be repaired in such manner as they think fit, and the reasonable expenses thereby incurred shall be recoverable from such owner or occupier summarily as a civil debt.

[Public Health Acts Amendment Act 1907, s 31, as amended by the Highways Act 1959, 25th Sch and the Local Government Act 1972, Sch 30.]

PART VI
RECREATION GROUNDS[1]

8–25021 76. Parks and pleasure gardens. (1) The local authority[2] shall, in addition to any powers under any general Act, have the powers detailed in this section with respect to any public park or pleasure ground provided by them or under their management and control.

(4) No power given by this section shall be exercised in such a manner as to contravene any convenant or condition subject to which a gift or lease of a public park or pleasure ground has been accepted or made, without the consent of the donor, grantor, lessor, or other person or persons entitled in law to the benefit of such covenant or condition.

[Public Health Acts Amendment Act 1907, s 76, as amended by the Local Government Act 1972, Sch 30 (summarised).]

1. Sections 76, 77 shall be in force throughout the district of every local authority (Public Health Act 1961, s 52(1)). These sections are extended by Pt VI of the Public Health Act 1925 and s 52(2), (3) of the Public Health Act 1961. Section 54 of the 1961 Act contains provisions relating to boating pools and lakes in parks and pleasure gardens. See also s 164 of the Public Health Act 1875 (public pleasure grounds, etc), ante.

2. For definition of "local authority", see footnote 2 to s 21, ante.

8–25022 **77. Power to appoint officers.** The local authority may appoint officers for securing the observance of this Part of this Act, and of the regulations and bye-laws made thereunder, and may procure such officers to be sworn in as constables for that purpose, but any such officer shall not act as a constable unless in uniform or provided with a warrant.
[Public Health Acts Amendment Act 1907, s 77.]

PART VII
POLICE

8–25023 **80. Leading or driving animals.** The local authority may, by order, prescribe the streets in which, and the manner according to which, the leading or driving of animals shall be permitted within their district, provided that the route or routes which it shall be lawful for the local authority so to prescribe shall not be such as would prevent the passage of cattle between any market on the one hand, and any railway station or landing wharf in the district, or any place beyond the district, on the other hand, when such animals are merely passing between such market and railway station, landing wharf, or other place aforesaid, and the local authority shall be bound to allow at all times a reasonably short and efficient route or routes for the passage of such animals. Provided also that any such order shall only operate between the hours of nine in the morning and nine in the evening, and shall not prevent the owner of any animals driving the same to or from his own premises, and nothing in this enactment contained shall authorise the local authority to interfere with the leading or driving of any animals to any duly licensed slaughter-house.
[Public Health Acts Amendment Act 1907, s 80.]

8–25024 **81. Definition of public place and street.** Any place of public resort or recreation ground belonging to, or under the control of the local authority[1], and any unfenced ground adjoining or abutting upon any street in an urban district[2] shall for the purpose of the Vagrancy Act 1824, and of any Act for the time being in force altering or amending the same, be deemed to be an open and public place, and shall be deemed to be a street for the purposes of section twenty-nine of the Town Police Clauses Act 1847, and also for the purposes of so much of section twenty-eight of that Act as relates to the following offences:

Every person who suffers to be at large any unmuzzled ferocious dog, or urges any dog or other animal to attack, worry, or put in fear any person or animal:

Every person who rides or drives furiously any horse or carriage, or drives furiously any cattle:

Every person who wilfully and indecently exposes his person:

Every person who publicly offers for sale or distribution, or exhibits to public view, any profane book, paper, print, drawing, painting, or representation, or sings any profane or obscene song or ballad, or uses any profane or obscene language:

Every person who wantonly discharges any firearm or discharges any missile or makes any bonfire:

Every person who throws or lays any dirt, litter, ashes, or night soil, or any carrion, fish, offal, or rubbish on any street.

[Public Health Acts Amendment Act 1907, s 81, as amended by the Street Offences Act 1959, Sch and the Indecent Displays (Control) Act 1981, Sch.]

1. For definition of "local authority", see footnote 2 to s 21, ante.

2. The Local Government Act 1972, Sch 14, para 23 provides that, with the qualifications set out in that Schedule, all the provisions of the Public Health Acts 1875–1925 extend throughout England and Wales. By para 26 so much of s 81 as relates to the Town Police Clauses Act 1847 does not extend to Greater London.

8–25024A **82. Byelaws as to sea-shore[1].** *The local authority for the prevention of danger, obstruction or annoyance to persons using the sea-shore may make and enforce byelaws[2].*

1. This section was repealed by the Public Health Act 1936, s 346 and Sch 3, so far as regards matters with respect to which byelaws can be made under Part VIII of that Act.

2. For considerations to be applied in the interpretation of byelaws under this section, such as their extent, the meaning of "low water line", and the public right to take fish or dig for worms from the sea-shore, see *Anderson v Alnwick District Council* [1993] 3 All ER 613.

8–25025 **83. Bye-laws as to promenades.** The local authority[1] may, for the prevention of danger, obstruction, or annoyance to persons using the esplanades or promenades within the district, make bye-laws prescribing the nature of the traffic for which they may be used, regulating the selling and hawking of any article, commodity, or thing thereon, and for the preservation of order and good conduct among the persons using the same.
[Public Health Acts Amendment Act 1907, s 83.]

1. For definition of "local authority", see footnote 2 to s 21, ante.

PART X

MISCELLANEOUS

8–25026 **94. Power to license pleasure boats[1].** (1) The local authority[2] may grant upon such terms and conditions as they may think fit licences for pleasure boats and pleasure vessels to be let for hire or to be used for carrying passengers for hire, and to the persons in charge of or navigating such boats and vessels, and may charge for each type of licence such annual fee as appears to them to be appropriate.

(2) Any such licence may be granted for such period as the local authority may think fit, and may be suspended or revoked by the local authority whenever they shall deem such suspension or revocation to be necessary or desirable in the interests of the public:

Provided that the existence of the power to suspend or revoke the licence shall be plainly set forth in the licence itself.

(3) No person shall let for hire any pleasure boat or pleasure vessel not so licensed or at any time during the suspension of the licence for the boat or vessel, nor shall any person carry or permit to be carried passengers for hire in any pleasure boat or vessel unless—

(*a*) the boat or vessel is so licensed and the licence is not suspended; and

(*b*) the person in charge of the boat or vessel and any other person navigating it is so licensed and his licence is not suspended and the conditions of his licence are complied with.

(4) A licence under this section shall not be required for any boat or vessel duly licensed by or under any regulations of the Board of Trade or for a person in charge of or navigating such a boat or vessel.

(5) No person shall carry or permit to be carried in any pleasure boat or pleasure vessel a greater number of passengers for hire than shall be specified in the licence applying to such boat or vessel, and every owner of any such boat or vessel shall, before permitting the same to be used for carrying passengers for hire, paint or cause to be painted, in letters and figures not less than one inch in height and three quarters of an inch in breadth, on a conspicuous part of the said boat or vessel, his own name and also the number of persons which it is licensed to carry in the form "Licensed to carry . . . . persons."

(6) Every person who shall act in contravention of the provisions of this section shall for each offence be liable to a penalty not exceeding **level 3** on the standard scale; but a person shall not be guilty of an offence under this subsection by reason of a failure to comply with such conditions as are mentioned in subsection (3)(*b*) of this section if it is shown that there is a reasonable excuse for the failure.

(7) Any person deeming himself aggrieved by the withholding, suspension, or revocation of any licence under the provisions of this section may appeal to a petty sessional court held after the expiration of two clear days after such withholding, suspension, or revocation:

Provided that the person so aggrieved shall give twenty-four hours' written notice of such appeal, and the ground thereof, to the justices' chief executive for the court, and the court shall have power to make such order as they see fit and to award costs, such costs to be recoverable summarily as a civil debt[3].

(8) No licence under this section shall be required in respect of pleasure boats and pleasure vessels on any inland waterway owned or managed by the British Waterways Board.

(9) In subsections (1) and (3) of this section "let for hire" means let for hire to the public.

[Public Health Acts Amendment Act 1907, s 94, amended by the Criminal Justice Act 1967, 3rd Sch, the Local Government Act 1974, Sch 6, the Local Government (Miscellaneous Provisions) Act 1976, s 18, the Local Government, Planning and Land Act 1980, s 186, the Criminal Justice Act 1982, ss 38 and 46, the Access to Justice Act 1999, s 90 and Sch 13 and SI 1997/1187.]

1. This section extends the power under s 172 of the Public Health Act 1875 as amended: proceedings if taken under the 1875 Act carry a maximum penalty not exceeding **level 2** on the standard scale (Criminal Law Act 1977, s 31(2) and the Criminal Justice Act 1982, s 46.)

2. For definition of "local authority", see footnote 2 to s 21, ante.

3. The procedure is regulated by Magistrates' Courts Rules 1981, r 34, in PART I: MAGISTRATES' COURTS, PROCEDURE, ante.

Public Health Act 1925[1]

(15 & 16 Geo 5 c 71)

PART I[2]

8–25130 **8. Appeals to petty sessional court.** Where any enactment, in this Act provides for an appeal[3] to a petty sessional court against a notice, determination, requirement, order or intended order of a local authority[4] under this Act.

(1) Notice in writing of the appeal and of the grounds thereof shall be given by the appellant[3] to the clerk to the local authority;

(2) The court may make such order in the matter as they consider reasonable, and may award costs to be recoverable as a civil debt[5];

(3) No proceeding shall be taken by the local authority, or work executed, until after the determination or abandonment of the appeal;

(4) Notice of the right of appeal should be endorsed on the order of the local authority and on any notice communicating their determination, requirement or intended order.

[Public Health Act 1925, s 8.]

---

1. Parts I to VIII of this Act and the Public Health Acts 1875–1907 may be cited together as the Public Health Acts 1875 to 1925 (s1(2)). Parts I to VIII of this Act shall be construed as one with the Public Health Acts 1875 to 1907 (s 1(3)). Accordingly, the right of appeal to the Crown Court under s 7 of the Public Health Acts Amendment Act 1907, ante, will also apply to any conviction or order of a magistrates' court under this Act. The National Rivers Authority, every water undertaker and every sewerage undertaker is deemed to be a statutory undertaker for the purposes of this Act (Water Act 1989, Sch 25, para 1). As to the persons who can prosecute, see the Local Government Act 1972, s 223, ante.
2. Part I is not adoptive.
3. "Local authority" or "urban authority" shall be the council of a district or London borough, the Common Council of the City of London, the Sub-Treasurer of the Inner Temple and the Under Treasurer of the Middle Temple (Local Government Act 1972, s 180). For application to local government areas, see Local Government Act 1972, Sch 14, paras 24–26.
4. The procedure shall be by way of complaint for an order (Magistrates' Courts Rules 1981, r 34, in PART I: MAGISTRATES' COURTS, PROCEDURE, ante).
5. See Magistrates' Courts Act 1980, s 58 in PART I: MAGISTRATES' COURTS, PROCEDURE, ante.

PART II[1]

8–25131 17. Notice to urban authority before street is named. Before any street is given a name, notice of the proposed name shall be sent to the urban authority[2] by the person proposing to name the street.

(2) The urban authority,[2]within one month after the receipt of such notice, may, by notice in writing served on the person by whom notice of the proposed name of the street was sent, object to the proposed name.

(3) It shall not be lawful to set up in any street an inscription of the name thereof

(*a*) until the expiration of one month after notice of the proposed name has been sent to the urban authority[2] under this section; and

(*b*) where the urban authority have objected to the proposed name, unless and until such objection has been withdrawn by the urban authority or overruled on appeal; and any person acting in contravention of this provision shall be liable to a penalty not exceeding **level 1** on the standard scale, and to a daily penalty not exceeding **£1**.

(4) Where the urban authority[2] serve a notice of objection under this section, the person proposing to name the street may, within twenty-one days after the serving of the notice, appeal against the objection to a petty sessional court[3].

[Public Health Act 1925, s 17, as amended by the Criminal Law Act 1977, s 31 and the Criminal Justice Act 1982, s 46.]

---

1. Part II extends throughout England and Wales, with the exception of ss 17 to 19 which are adoptive (but do not apply to Greater London) under the Local Government Act 1972, Sch 14, Pt II.
2. "Local authority" or "urban authority" shall be the council of a district or London borough, the Common Council of the City of London, the Sub-Treasurer of the Inner Temple and the Under Treasurer of the Middle Temple (Local Government Act 1972, s 180). For application to local government areas, see Local Government Act 1972, Sch 14, paras 24–26.
3. For procedure on such appeal, see the Public Health Act 1925, s 8, supra, and notes thereto.

8–25132 18. Alteration of name of street. (1) The urban authority[1] by order may alter the name of any street, or part of a street, or may assign a name to any street, or part of a street, to which a name has not been given.

(2) Not less than one month before making an order under this section, the urban authority[1] shall cause notice of the intended order to be posted at each end of the street, or part of the street, or in some conspicuous position in the street or part affected.

(3) Every such notice shall contain a statement that the intended order may be made by the urban authority[1] on or at any time after the day named in the notice, and that an appeal will lie under this Act to a petty sessional court against the intended order at the instance of any person aggrieved.

(4) Any person aggrieved by the intended order of the local authority may, within twenty-one days after the posting of the notice, appeal[2] to a petty sessional court.

[Public Health Act 1925, s 18, as amended by the Local Government Act 1972, Sch 30.]

---

1. See note to "local authority" in s 8, ante.
2. For procedure on such appeal, see the Public Health Act 1925, s 8, supra, and notes thereto.

8–25133 **19. Indication of name of street.** The urban authority[1] shall cause the name of every street to be painted, or otherwise marked, in a conspicuous position on any house, building or erection in or near the street and shall from time to time alter or renew such inscription of the name of any street; if and when the name of the street is altered or the inscription becomes illegible.

(2) If any person destroys, pulls down or defaces any inscription of the name of a street, which has lawfully been set up, or sets up in any street any name different from the name lawfully given to the street, or places or affixes any notice or advertisement within twelve inches of any name of a street marked on a house, building, or erection in pursuance of this section, he shall be liable to a penalty not exceeding **level 1** on the standard scale, and to a daily penalty not exceeding [**£1**].

[Public Health Act 1925, s 19, as amended by the Criminal Law Act 1977, s 31 and the Criminal Justice Act 1982, s 46.]

1. See note to "local authority" in s 8, ante.

8–25134 **26. Bye-laws as to wires, etc, connected with wireless installations.** (1) The local authority may make bye-laws[1] for the prevention of danger or obstruction to persons using any street or public place from posts, wires, tubes, aerials or, any other apparatus, in connection with or for the purposes of wireless telegraphy or telephony installations, stretched or placed, whether before or after the commencement of this section, on or over any premises and liable to fall on to any street or public place. In this section the expression "public place" includes any public park or garden, and any ground to which the public have or are permitted to have access, whether on payment or otherwise.

(2) Nothing in any bye-laws made under this section shall extend to any apparatus belonging to any statutory undertakings[2].

[Public Health Act 1925, s 26.]

1. Penalties may be imposed under the Local Government Act 1972, s 237, in this PART: title LOCAL GOVERNMENT, ante.

2. For the purposes of this section the holder of a licence under s 6 of the Electricity Act 1989 who is entitled to exercise any power conferred by para 1 of Sch 4 to that Act (street works, etc) shall be deemed to be a statutory undertaker and his undertaking a statutory undertaking (Electricity Act 1989, Sch 16, para 2(4)).

PART VIII[1]

8–25135 **75. Bye-laws as to persons waiting to enter public vehicles.** (1) The local authority may make bye-laws[1] for regulating the conduct of persons waiting in the streets[2] to enter public vehicles, and the priority of entry into such vehicles, and may by such bye-laws require queues[3] or lines to be formed and kept by such persons.

[Public Health Act 1925, s 75.]

1. The bye-laws may impose fines. If they do not, the maximum fine is at **level 3** on the standard scale (Local Government Act 1972, s 237, the Criminal Law Act 1977, s 31(2) and the Criminal Justice Act 1982, s 46).

2. For definition, see the Public Health Act 1875, s 4.

3. As to the power to erect in a street barriers and posts for such queues, see Public Health Act 1875, s 75(2), (3).

Public Health Act 1936[1]

(26 Geo 5 & Edw 8 c 49)

PART I.—LOCAL ADMINISTRATION

8–25150 **1. Local authorities[2] under a duty to carry the Act into execution.** (1) (*Duty of local authority to carry this Act, excluding Part VI except* s 198, *into execution.*)

(2) In this Act—

"community", in relation to a common community council acting for two or more grouped communities, means those communities;

"district", in relation to a local authority in Greater London, means a London Borough, the City of London, the Inner Temple or the Middle Temple, as the case may be and, in relation to a local authority in Wales, means a county or (as the case may be) county borough;

"local authority" means the council of a district or London borough, the Common Council of the City of London, the Sub-Treasurer of the Inner Temple and the Under Treasurer of the Middle Temple but, in relation to Wales, means the council of a county or county borough;

"parish", in relation to a common parish council acting for two or more grouped parishes, means those parishes.

[Public Health Act 1936, s 1, as substituted by the Local Government Act 1972, Sch 14 and amended by the National Health Service Reorganisation Act 1973, Sch 4 and the Local Government (Wales) Act 1994, Sch 9.]

1. For application of this and other public health Acts to London, see the London Government Act 1963, s 40 and Sch 11. The Environment Agency, every water undertaker and every sewerage undertaker is deemed to be a statutory undertaker for the purposes of this Act (Water Act 1989, Sch 25, para 1).

2. Any reference to an urban authority or rural authority in the 1936 Act shall be construed as a reference to a local authority (Local Government Act 1972, Sch 14, para 2). Sections 2–10 of the 1936 Act constitute Port Health Authorities and joint boards (incorporated). See the Port Health Authorities (England) Order 1974, SI 1974/215 and note also s 263 of the Local Government Act 1972.

PART II.—SANITATION AND BUILDINGS[1]

1. The Public Health Act 1961, s 1(1) provides that Pt II of that Act (post) shall be construed as one with Pt II of this Act.

SANITARY CONVENIENCES FOR BUILDINGS

8–25155 **45. Buildings having defective closets capable of repair[1].** (1) If it appears to a local authority that any closets provided for or in connection with a building are in such a state as to be prejudicial to health or a nuisance, but that they can without reconstruction be put into a satisfactory condition, the authority shall by notice require the owner or the occupier of the building to execute such works, or to take such steps by cleansing the closets or otherwise, as may be necessary for that purpose.

(2) In so far as a notice under this section requires a person to execute works, the provisions of Part XII of this Act with respect to appeals against, and the enforcement of, notices requiring the execution of works shall apply in relation to the notice.

(3) In so far as such a notice requires a person to take any steps other than the execution of works, he shall, if he fails to comply with the notice, be liable to a fine not exceeding **level 1** on the standard scale and to a further fine not exceeding [£2] for each day on which the offence continues after conviction therefor:

Provided that in any proceedings under this subsection it shall be open to the defendant to question the reasonableness of the authority's requirements or of their decision to address their notice to him and not to the occupier or, as the case may be, the owner of the building.

(4) This section shall not apply to a factory, or to a building to which the next succeeding section applies.

[Public Health Act 1936, s 45, as amended by the Factories Act 1937, Sch 4, the Offices, Shops and Railway Premises Act 1963, Sch 2, the Criminal Law Act 1977, s 31, the Criminal Justice Act 1982, s 46 and the Statute Law (Repeals) Act 1993, Sch 1.]

1. This section does not apply to premises to which the Offices, Shops and Railway Premises Act 1963, applies (Offices, Shops and Railway Premises Act 1963, s 9(6)).

SUPPLEMENTAL PROVISIONS AS TO DRAINS, SANITARY CONVENIENCES, CESSPOOLS, ETC

8–25156 **48. Power of relevant authority to examine and test drains, etc, believed to be defective.** (1) Where it appears to an authority that there are reasonable grounds for believing that a sanitary convenience[1], drain, private sewer or cesspool is in such a condition as to be prejudicial to health[2] or a nuisance, they may examine its condition, and for that purpose may apply any test, other than a test by water under pressure, and, if they deem it necessary, open the ground.

(1A) (*Repealed*).

(2) If on examination the convenience, drain, sewer, or cesspool is found to be in proper condition[3], the authority shall, as soon as possible, reinstate any ground which has been opened by them and make good any damage done by them.

[Public Health Act 1936, s 48, as amended by the Water Act 1973, Sch 8, the Water Act 1989, Sch 8 and the Water Consolidation (Consequential Provisions) Act 1991, Schs 1 and 3.]

1. "Sanitary conveniences" mean closets and urinals (s 90(1)).
2. "Prejudicial to health" means injurious, or likely to cause injury to health (s 343(1)).
3. For remedying defects found on examination, the authority will act under s 39, ante, or s 17 of the Public Health Act 1961, post.

8–25157 **49. Rooms over closets of certain types, or over ashpits, etc, not to be used as living, sleeping or workrooms.** (1) A room which, or any part of which, is immediately over a closet, other than a watercloset or earthcloset, or immediately over a cesspool, midden or ashpit, shall not be occupied as a living room, sleeping room or workroom.

(2) Any person who, after seven days' notice from the local authority, occupies any room in contravention of the provisions of this section, or who permits any room to be so occupied, shall be liable to a fine not exceeding **level 1** on the standard scale, and to a further fine not exceeding [£2] for each day on which the offence continues after conviction therefor.

[Public Health Act 1936, s 49, as amended by the Criminal Law Act 1977, s 31 and the Criminal Justice Act 1982, s 46.]

8–25158 **50. Overflowing and leaking cesspools.** (1) If the contents of any cesspool soak therefrom or overflow, the local authority may by notice require the person by whose act, default or sufferance the soakage or overflow occurred or continued to execute such works, or to take such steps by periodically emptying the cesspool or otherwise, as may be necessary for preventing the soakage or overflow:

Provided that this subsection shall not apply in relation to the effluent from a properly constructed tank for the reception and treatment of sewage, if that effluent is of such a character, and is so conveyed away and disposed of, as not to be prejudicial to health[1] or a nuisance.

(2) In so far as notice under this section requires a person to execute works, the provisions of Part XII[2] of this Act with respect to appeals against, and the enforcement of, notices requiring the execution of works shall apply in relation to the notice.

(3) In so far as such a notice requires a person to take any steps other than the execution of works, he shall, if he fails to comply with the notice, be liable to a fine not exceeding **level 1** on the standard scale, and to a further fine not exceeding [**£2**] for each day on which the offence continues after conviction therefor:

Provided that in any proceeding under this subsection it shall be open to the defendant to question the reasonableness of the authority's requirements.

[Public Health Act 1936, s 50, as amended by the Water Act 1973, Sch 8, the Criminal Law Act 1977, s 31, the Criminal Justice Act 1982, s 46 and the Water Act 1989, Sch 8.]

1. See note 2 to s 48, ante.
2. See ss 290 and 300, post.

8–25159 51. Care of closets. (1) The occupier of every building in, or in connection with, which a watercloset[1] or an earth-closet[2] is provided shall, in the case of a watercloset, cause the flushing apparatus thereof to be kept supplied with water sufficient for flushing and where necessary to be properly protected against frost, and shall, in the case of an earth-closet, cause it to be kept supplied with dry earth or other suitable deodorising material.

(2) A person who fails to comply with any of the provisions of this section shall be liable to a fine not exceeding **level 1** on the standard scale.

[Public Health Act 1936, s 51, as amended by the Criminal Law Act 1977, s 31 and the Criminal Justice Act 1982, s 46.]

1. "Watercloset" means a closet which has a separate fixed receptacle connected to a drainage system and separate provision for flushing from a supply of clean water either by the operation of mechanism or by automatic action (s 90(1)).
2. "Earth closet" means a closet having a movable receptacle for the reception of faecal matter and its deodorisation by the use of earth, ashes or chemicals, or by other methods (s 90(1)).

8–25160 52. Care of sanitary conveniences used in common. Where a sanitary convenience[1] is used in common by the members of two or more families, the following provisions shall have effect—

(*a*) if any person injures or improperly fouls the convenience, or anything used in connection therewith, or wilfully or by negligence causes an obstruction in the drain therefrom, he shall be liable to a fine not exceeding **level 1** on the standard scale;

(*b*) if the convenience, or the approach thereto, is, for want of proper cleansing or attention, in such a condition as to be insanitary, such of the persons having the use thereof in common as are in default, or, in the absence of satisfactory proof as to which of them is in default, each of them, shall be liable to a fine not exceeding **level 1** on the standard scale, and to a further fine not exceeding [**25p**] for each day on which the offence continues after conviction therefor.

[Public Health Act 1936, s 52, as amended by the Criminal Law Act 1977, s 31 and the Criminal Justice Act 1982, s 46.]

1. See note 1 to s 48, ante.

Removal of Refuse, Scavenging, Keeping of Animals, etc

8–25161 78. Scavenging of common courts and passages. (1) If any court, yard or passage which is used in common by the occupants of two or more buildings, but is not a highway repairable by the inhabitants at large, is not regularly swept and kept clean and free from rubbish or other accumulation to the satisfaction of the local authority, the authority may cause it to be swept and cleansed.

(2) The local authority may recover any expenses reasonably incurred by them under this section from the occupiers of the buildings which front or abut on the court or yard, or to which the passage affords access, in such proportions as may be determined[1] by the authority, or, in case of dispute, by a court of summary jurisdiction.

[Public Health Act 1936, s 78.]

1. See ss 300–302, post.

8–25162 79. Power to require removal of noxious matter by occupier of premises in urban district. (1) If in a borough or urban district, or in a rural district or contributory place[1] in which section 49 of the Public Health Act 1875, was in force immediately before the commencement[2] of this Act[3] it appears to the public health inspector that any accumulation of noxious matter ought to be removed, he shall serve notice on the owner[4] thereof, or on the occupier of the premises on which it is found, requiring him to remove it, and, if the notice is not complied with within twenty-four hours after service thereof, the inspector may remove the matter referred to.

(2) A local authority may recover[5] the expenses of any action reasonably taken by their inspector under the preceding subsection from the owner or occupier in default.*

[Public Health Act 1936, s 79.]

***Repealed by the Control of Pollution Act 1974, post, when in force.**

1. For definition of "contributory place", see note 2 to s 46.
2. 1st October, 1937 (s 347(1)).
3. This section applies throughout the district of every local authority (Local Government Act 1972, Sch 14, para 4).
4. That is, the owner of the accumulation.
5. Under s 293, post.

8–25163 80. Power to require periodical removal of manure, etc, from stables, etc, in urban district. (1) In a borough or urban district, and in a rural district or contributory place in which section 50 of the Public Health Act 1875, was in force immediately before the commencement[1] of this Act,[2] the local authority may by public or other notice require the periodical removal, at such intervals as may be specified in the notice, of manure or refuse from mews, stables or other premises.

(2) If a person on whom a notice has been served under this section fails to comply therewith, he shall be liable to a fine not exceeding level 1 on the standard scale.*

[Public Health Act 1936, s 80, as amended by the Criminal Law Act 1977, s 31 and the Criminal Justice Act 1982, s 46.]

***Repealed by the Control of Pollution Act 1974, post, when in force.**

1. 1st October 1937 (s 347(1)).
2. This section applies throughout the district of every local authority (Local Government Act 1972, Sch 14, para 4).

8–25164 81. Bye-laws for the prevention of certain nuisances. A local authority may make bye-laws for preventing—

(*a*) the occurrence of nuisance from snow[1], filth, dust, ashes and rubbish;

(*b*) the keeping[2] of animals so as to be prejudicial to health.

[Public Health Act 1936, s 81.]

1. The accumulation of snow on a roof of premises overhanging a street is a nuisance. The occupier is liable for any danger due to falling snow if, with knowledge, nothing is done within a reasonable time to abate the nuisance (*Slater v Worthington's Cash Stores (1930) Ltd* [1941] 1 KB 488, [1941] 3 All ER 28).
2. This is a statutory nuisance under s 79(1)(*f*) of the Environmental Protection Act 1990, post.

8–25165 82. Bye-laws as to removal through streets of offensive matter or liquid. (1) A local authority may make bye-laws—

(*a*) prescribing the times for the removal or carriage through the streets, of any fæcal or offensive or noxious matter or liquid, whether that matter or liquid is in course of removal or carriage from within, or from without, or through, their district;

(*b*) requiring that the receptacle or vehicle used for the removal or carriage of any such matter or liquid shall be properly constructed and covered so as to prevent the escape of any such matter or liquid;

(*c*) requiring the cleansing of any place whereon any such matter or liquid has been dropped or spilt in the course of removal or carriage.

(2) If and so far as a bye-law made under the preceding subsection is inconsistent with an order under section 6 of the Road Traffic Regulation Act 1984, the order shall prevail.

[Public Health Act 1936, s 82, as amended by the London Government Act 1963, 11th Sch.]

FILTHY OR VERMINOUS PREMISES OR ARTICLES, AND VERMINOUS PERSONS

8–25166 83. Cleansing of filthy or verminous premises[1]. (1) Where a local authority upon consideration of a report from any of their officers or other information in their possession are satisfied that any premises[2]—

(*a*) are in such a filthy or unwholesome condition as to be prejudicial to health[3]; or

(*b*) are verminous[4],

the local authority shall give notice to the owner or occupier of the premises requiring him to take such steps as may be specified in the notice to remedy the condition of the premises by cleansing and disinfecting them and the notice may require among other things the removal of wallpaper or other covering of the walls, or, in the case of verminous premises, the taking of such steps as may be necessary for the purpose of destroying or removing vermin.

(1A) A notice under the foregoing subsection may require—

(*a*) the interior surface of premises used for human habitation or as shops or offices to be papered, painted or distempered, and

(*b*) the interior surface of any other premises to be painted, distempered or whitewashed,

and shall allow the person on whom the notice is served, or the local authority acting in his default, to choose, in a case under paragraph (*a*) of this subsection, between papering, painting and distempering and, in a case under paragraph (*b*) of this subsection, between painting, distempering and whitewashing.

(2) If a person on whom a notice under this section is served fails to comply with the requirements thereof, the authority may themselves carry out the requirements and recover[5] from him the expenses reasonably incurred by them in so doing, and, without prejudice to the right of the authority to exercise that power, he shall be liable to a fine not exceeding **level 1** on the standard scale and to a further fine not exceeding [**£**2] for each day on which the offence continues after conviction therefor:

Provided that in any proceedings under this subsection it shall be open to the defendant to question the reasonableness of the authority's requirements or of their decision to address their notice to him and not to the occupier or, as the case may be, the owner of the premises.

(3) Where a local authority take action under paragraph (*b*) of subsection (1) of this section, their notice may require that they shall be allowed to employ gas for the purpose of destroying vermin on the premises[6] but in that case the notice shall be served both on the owner and on the occupier of the premises, and the authority shall bear the cost of their operations and may provide temporary shelter or house accommodation for any person compelled to leave the premises by reason of their operations.

(4) This section shall not apply to any premises forming part of a factory or a mine or quarry within the meaning of the Mines and Quarries Act 1954.

[Public Health Act 1936, s 83, as amended by the Public Health Act 1961, s 35, the Criminal Justice Act 1967, 3rd Sch and the Criminal Justice Act 1982, ss 38 and 46.]

---

1. This section is applied to ships and boats and to tents, vans, sheds, etc, by ss 267, 268, post. See also the Hydrogen Cyanide (Fumigation) Act 1937, in this PART: title HEALTH AND SAFETY, ante.
2. "Premises" includes messuages, buildings, lands, easements and hereditaments of any tenure (s 343(1)).
3. "Prejudicial to health" means injurious, or likely to cause injury to health (s 343(1)). See also s 92, post.
4. "Vermin" in its application to insects and parasites, include their eggs, larvæ and pupæ, and "verminous" shall be construed accordingly (s 90(1)).
5. Under s 293, post.
6. For extended powers when this requirement is contained in the notice, see Public Health Act 1961, s 36, post.

8–25167 **85. Cleansing of verminous persons and their clothing.** (1) Upon the application of any person, a county council or a local authority may take such measures as are, in their opinion, necessary to free him and his clothing[1] from vermin[2].

(2) Where it appears to a county council or a local authority, upon a report from their medical officer of health or, in the case of a local authority, from their public health inspector, that any person, or the clothing of any person, is verminous, then, if that person consents to be removed to a cleansing station, they may cause him to be removed to such a station, and, if he does not so consent, they may apply to a court of summary jurisdiction, and the court, if satisfied that it is necessary that he or his clothing should be cleansed, may make an order[3] for his removal to such a station and for his detention therein for such period and subject to such conditions as may be specified in the order.

(3) Where a person has been removed to a cleansing station in pursuance of the last preceding subsection, the county council or local authority shall take such measures as may, in their opinion, be necessary to free him and his clothing from vermin.

(4) The cleansing of females under this section shall be carried out only by a registered medical practitioner, or by a woman duly authorised by the medical officer of health.

(5) Any consent required to be given for the purposes of this section may, in the case of a person under the age of sixteen years, be given on his behalf by his parent or guardian.

(6) No charge shall be made in respect of the cleansing of a person or his clothing, or in respect of his removal to, or maintenance in, a cleansing station under this section.

(7) The powers conferred on a county council or local authority by this section shall be in addition to, and not in derogation of, any power[4] in relation to the cleansing of children which may be exercisable by them as a local education authority.

[Public Health Act 1936, s 85.]

---

1. As to cleansing or destruction of filthy or verminous articles, see s 84. A county council or local authority may provide cleansing stations (s 86). The sale of verminous household articles (including clothing) is prohibited (Public Health Act 1961, s 37, post).
2. For definition of "vermin", see note 4 to s 83, supra.
3. As to enforcement of this order, see Magistrates' Courts Act 1980, s 63 in PART I: MAGISTRATES' COURTS, PROCEDURE, ante. This section is applied to ships and boats, and to tents, vans, sheds, etc, by ss 267, 268, post.
4. See Education Act 1996, ss 521–526, in this PART: title EDUCATION.

PART IV—WATER SUPPLY

PROVISIONS FOR THE PROTECTION OF PUBLIC FROM POLLUTED WATER

8–25187 **140. Power to close, or restrict water from, polluted source of supply.** (1) If a local authority are of opinion that the water in or obtained from any well, tank, or other source of supply not vested in them, being water which is, or is likely to be, used for domestic purposes, or in the preparation of food or drink for human consumption, is, or is likely to become, so polluted as to be prejudicial to health[1], the authority may apply to a court of summary jurisdiction and thereupon a summons may be issued to the owner or occupier of the premises to which the source of supply belongs or[2] to any other person alleged in the application to have control thereof.

(2) Upon the hearing of the summons, the court may make an order directing the source of supply to be permanently or temporarily closed or cut off, or the water therefrom to be used for certain purposes only, or such other order as appears to the court to be necessary to prevent injury or danger to the health of persons using the water, or consuming food or drink prepared therewith or therefrom.

The court shall hear any user of the water who claims to be heard, and may cause the water to be analysed at the cost of the local authority.

(3) If a person on whom an order is made under this section fails to comply therewith, the court may, on the application of the local authority, authorise them to do whatever may be necessary for giving effect to the order, and any expenses reasonably incurred by the authority in so doing may be recovered[3] by them from the person in default.

[Public Health Act 1936, s 140.]

1. See note 3 to s 83, ante.
2. The court may select, after considering the local authority's views.
3. See s 293, post.

8–25188 **141. Power to deal with insanitary cisterns, etc.** Any well, tank, cistern, or water-butt used for the supply of water for domestic purposes which is so placed, constructed or kept as to render the water therein liable to contamination prejudicial to health, shall be a statutory nuisance for the purpose of Part III of the Environmental Protection Act 1990.

[Public Health Act 1936, s 141, as amended by the Environmental Protection Act 1990, Sch 151.]

1. For the purposes of the operation of this provision and the exercise or performance of any power or duty conferred or imposed by this provision, no account shall be taken of any radioactivity possessed by any substance or article or by any part of any premises (Radioactive Substances Act 1960, s 9(1), Sch 1).

PART V—PREVENTION, NOTIFICATION AND TREATMENT OF DISEASE[1]

8–25189 **143. (Power of Minister[2] to make regulations with a view to the treatment of certain diseases[3] and for preventing the spread of such diseases.)**

[Public Health Act 1936, s 143, amended by the London Government Act 1963, Sch 18, the National Health Service Reorganisation Act 1973, ss 57, 58, Schs 4 and 5, the Health Services Act 1980, ss 1, 2, and Sch 1, the Civil Aviation Act 1982, s 36, the Criminal Justice Act 1982, ss 39 and 46, and Sch 3, the Health and Social Services and Social Security Adjudications Act 1983, Schs 9 and 10 and the Public Health (Control of Disease) Act 1984 Sch 3.]

1. The Public Health Act 1961, s 1(2) provides that Pt III of that Act, post, shall be construed as one with Pt V of this Act.
2. For Ministerial responsibility, see now the Secretary of State for Social Services Order 1968, SI 1968/1699, and the Transfer of Functions (Wales) Order 1969, SI 1969/388. Additional provisions are contained in Part III of the Public Health Act 1961, post. Section 143(1)–(7) and (10) is repealed by the Public Health (Control of Disease) Act 1984 Sch 3 and replaced by s 13 thereof.
3. The maximum penalty which may be provided by regulations is a fine at level 5 on the standard scale. The Public Health (Infectious Diseases) Regulations 1968 (SI 1968/1366, SI 1969/844, SI 1974/274, SI 1976/1226 and 1955), the Public Health (Aircraft) Regulations 1979, SI 1979/1434 and the Public Health (Ships) Regulations 1979, SI 1979/1435, have been made. For notifiable diseases see post the Health Services and Public Health Act 1968, s 48, listing diseases covered by these regulations.

PART VI—HOSPITALS, NURSING HOMES, ETC

8–25190 **198. Bye-laws as to mortuaries and post-mortem rooms.** A local authority, or a parish council, may make bye-laws[1] with respect to the management, and charges for the use of a mortuary or post-mortem room, provided by them.

[Public Health Act 1936, s 198.]

1. The bye-laws may prescribe the fines; if they do not, the penalty is not exceeding **level 2** on the standard scale (Local Government Act 1972, s 237, the Criminal Law Act 1977, s 31(2) and the Criminal Justice Act 1982, s 46, ante). Ministerial functions under s 198 were transferred to the Minister of Local Government and Planning by the Transfer of Functions (Minister of Health and Minister of Local Government and Planning) (No 2) Order 1951, SI 1951/753. The name of the Minister of Local Government and Planning has now been changed to the Secretary of State for the Environment.

PART VII—NOTIFICATION OF BIRTHS

8–25191 **205. Women not to be employed in factories or workshops within four weeks after birth of a child.** If the occupier of a factory[1] knowingly allows a woman to be employed therein within four weeks after she has given birth to a child, he shall be liable to a fine not exceeding **level 1** on the standard scale.

[Public Health Act 1936, s 205, as amended by the Criminal Law Act 1977, s 31, the Criminal Justice Act 1982, ss 35, 38 and 46 and the Statute Law (Repeals) Act 1993, Sch 1.]

---

1. "Factory" means a factory within the meaning of the Factory and Workshop Acts 1901–1929. This Act was repealed by, and re-enacted in, the Factories Act 1937, and the division has ceased. See now s 175 of the Factories Act 1961, in this PART: TITLE HEALTH AND SAFETY, ante.

PART VIII—BATHS, WASHHOUSES, BATHING PLACES, ETC
PROVISION OF BATHS, ETC

Bye-laws for regulation of baths, etc, with respect to public bathing[1] *and with respect to swimming baths and bathing pools not under the management of a local authority, and for use of baths and bathing places during winter months.*—The local authority may make these bye-laws.
[Public Health Act 1936, ss 223, 226(2), 231, and 233.]

8–25192 234. Baths, etc, to be public places for certain purposes. Any baths, washhouses, swimming bath or bathing place under the management of a local authority shall be deemed to be a public and open place for the purposes of any enactment relating to offences against decency.
[Public Health Act 1936, s 234.]

---

1. For extension of power to make bye-laws about bathing, see s 17 of the Local Government (Miscellaneous Provisions) Act 1976, post.

PART XI—MISCELLANEOUS
WATERCOURSES, DITCHES, PONDS, ETC

8–25193 259. Nuisances in connection with watercourses, ditches, ponds, etc. (1) The following matters shall be statutory nuisances for the purposes of Part III[1] of the Environmental Protection Act 1990, that is to say—

(*a*) any pond, pool, ditch, gutter or watercourse[2] which is so foul or in such a state as to be prejudicial to health[3] or a nuisance;

(*b*) any part of a watercourse, not being a part ordinarily navigated by vessels employed in the carriage of goods by water, which is so choked or silted up as to obstruct or impede the proper flow of water and thereby to cause a nuisance, or give rise to conditions prejudicial to health:

Provided that in the case of an alleged nuisance under paragraph (*b*) nothing in this subsection shall be deemed to impose any liability on any person other than the person by whose act or default[4] the nuisance arises or continues.

(2) (*Repealed*).

[Public Health Act 1936, s 259, as amended by the Criminal Law Act 1977, s 31, the Control of Pollution Act 1974, Sch 4, the Criminal Justice Act 1982, s 46 and the Environmental Protection Act 1990, Sch 15.]

---

1. As to statutory nuisances, see s 79 of the Environmental Protection Act 1990, post.
2. "Watercourse" does not include estuaries or tidal waters (*R v Falmouth and Truro Port Health Authority, ex p South West Water Ltd* [2001] QB 445, [2000] 3 All ER 306, [2000] 3 WLR 1464, CA).
3. "Prejudicial to health" means injurious, or likely to cause injury to health (s 343(1)). As to power of local authority to obtain an order from a court of summary jurisdiction for cleansing offensive ditches lying near to, or forming, boundary of district, see s 261.
4. The owner of land is under no duty at common law to remove obstructions arising by natural causes in a natural watercourse; therefore, such an obstruction, not arising or contained by his act or default, is not a statutory nuisance under s 93, ante (*Neath RDC v Williams* [1951] 1 KB 115, [1950] 2 All ER 625, 114 JP 464).

8–25194 262. Power of local authority to require culverting of watercourses and ditches where building operations in prospect. (1) If a local authority consider that any watercourse or ditch[1] situate upon land[2] laid out for building, or on which any land laid out for building abuts[3], should be wholly or partially filled up or covered over, they may by notice require the owner[4] of the land laid out for building, before any building operations are begun or while any such operations are in progress, wholly or partially to fill up the watercourse or ditch, or to substitute therefore a pipe, drain or culvert with all necessary gullies and other means of conveying surface water into and through it.

(2) Any question arising under this section between a local authority and an owner as to the reasonableness of any works which the authority require to be executed may, on the application of either party, be determined[5] by a court of summary jurisdiction.

(3) Any person who, on any land to which a notice given by a local authority under this section applies begins or proceeds with any building operations before executing the works required by the notice, shall be liable[6] to a fine not exceeding **level 1** on the standard scale and to a further fine not exceeding [**£2**] for each day on which the offence continues after conviction therefor.

(4) Nothing in this section shall empower an authority to require the execution of works upon the land of any person other than the owner of the land laid out for building, without the consent of that person, or prejudicially to affect the rights of any person not being the owner of the land so laid out.

[Public Health Act 1936, s 262, as amended by the Criminal Law Act 1977, s 31 and the Criminal Justice Act 1982, s 46.]

1. As to savings from this section, see s 266, post.
2. "Land" includes any interest in land and any easement or right into or over land (s 343 (1)).
3. See *A-G v Rowley Bros and Oxley* (1910) 75 JP 81.
4. The local authority may contribute to the cost (s 265).
5. See s 300(1)(*b*), post.
6. As to continuing offences and penalties, see s 297, post.

8–25195 **263. Watercourses in urban district not to be culverted except in accordance with approved plans.** (1) It shall not be lawful within [a borough or urban district, or a rural district][1] or contributory place in which section 52 of the Public Health Act 1925, was in force immediately before the commencement[2] of this Act, to culvert or cover any stream or watercourse except in accordance with plans and sections to be submitted to and approved by the local authority, but such approval shall not be withheld unreasonably and, if the authority, within six weeks after plans and sections have been submitted to them, fail to notify their determination to the person by whom the plans and sections were submitted, they shall be deemed to have approved them.

(2) Any question arising under this section between a local authority and an owner as to the reasonableness of any works which the authority require to be executed as a condition of their approval, or as to the reasonableness of their refusal to give approval may, on the application of either party, be determined by a court of summary jurisdiction.

(3) A local authority shall not, as a condition of approving plans or sections under this section, require an owner to receive upon his land, or to make provision for the passage of, a greater quantity of water than he is otherwise obliged to receive or to permit to pass, and, if the owner at the request of the authority makes provision for the passage of a larger quantity of water than he is obliged to permit to pass at the time of the commencement of any work under this section, any additional cost reasonably incurred by him in complying with the request of the authority shall be borne by them.

(4) Any person who contravenes this section shall be liable[3] to a fine not exceeding **level 1** on the standard scale and to a further fine not exceeding [**£2**] for each day on which the offence continues after conviction therefor.

[Public Health Act 1936, s 263, as amended by the Criminal Law Act 1977, s 31 and the Criminal Justice Act 1982, s 46.]

1. This section applies throughout the district of every local authority (Local Government Act 1972, Sch 14, para 4).
2. 1st October 1937 (s 347(1)). Section 52 of the Public Health Act 1925 is repealed by this Act.
3. As to continuing offences, see s 297, post.

8–25196 **264. Urban authority may require repair and cleansing of culverts.** The owner or occupier of any land within [a borough or urban district, or a rural district or contributory place[1] in which section 53[2] of the Public Health Act 1925, was in force immediately before the commencement[3] of this Act][4], shall repair, maintain and cleanse any culvert in, on or under that land, and, if it appears to the local authority that any person has failed to fulfil his obligations under this section they may by notice require him to execute such works of repair, maintenance or cleansing as may be necessary.

The provisions of Part XII of this Act with respect to appeal against, and the enforcement of, notices requiring the execution of works[5] shall apply in relation to any notice given under this section.

[Public Health Act 1936, s 264.]

1. "Contributory place" means a rating district within the meaning of the General Rate Act 1967 (s 343(1)). The 1967 Act has been repealed with effect from 31 March 1990.
2. This section is replaced by this Act.
3. 1st October 1937 (s.347(1)).
4. This section applies throughout the district of every local authority (Local Government Act 1972, Sch 14, para 4).
5. See ss 290, 300, post. The local authority may contribute to the cost (s 265).

8–25197 **266. Saving for land drainage authorities, . . . railway companies and dock undertakers.** (1) The powers conferred by the foregoing provisions of this Part of this Act shall not be exercised—(i) with respect to any stream, watercourse, ditch or culvert within the jurisdiction of a land drainage authority[1], except after consultation with that authority; (ii) . . .

Provided that nothing in this subsection shall apply in relation to the taking of proceedings in respect of a statutory nuisance.

(2) Nothing in the foregoing provisions of this Part of this Act shall prejudice or affect the powers of any railway company[2] or dock undertakers to culvert or cover in any stream or watercourse, or, without the consent of the railway company or dock undertakers concerned, extend to any culvert or covering of a stream or watercourse constructed by a railway company and used by them for the purposes of their railway, or constructed by dock undertakers and used by them for the purposes of their undertaking.

[Public Health Act 1936, s 266, amended by London Government Act 1963, 18th Sch.]

1. Under s 343 as amended by the Water Consolidation (Consequential Provisions) Act 1991, Sch 1, "land drainage authority" means the National Rivers Authority or an internal drainage board.
2. "Railway company" means persons who are statutory undertakers in respect of a railway undertaking (s 343(1)).

SHIPS AND BOATS

8–25198 267. Application to ships and boats of certain provisions of this Act[1]. (1) For the purposes of such of the provisions of this Act specified in subsection (4) of this section as are provisions for the execution of which local authorities are responsible, a vessel[2] lying in any inland or coastal water[3] shall—

(*a*) if those waters are within a port health district, be subject to the jurisdiction of the port health authority for that district;
(*b*) if those waters are within the district of a local authority but not within a port health district, be subject to the jurisdiction of that local authority;
(*c*) if those waters are not within the district of any local authority or any port health district, be subject to the jurisdiction of such local authority as the Minister[4] may from time to time by order direct or, if no such direction is given, within the jurisdiction of the local authority whose district includes that point on land which is nearest to the spot where the vessel is lying.

(2) For the purposes of such of the said provisions as are provisions for the execution of which county councils are responsible, a vessel when lying in any inland or coastal waters not within a county shall be subject to the jurisdiction of the council of the county which includes that point on land which is nearest to the spot where the vessel is lying.

(2A) Subsection (2) of this section does not apply if the point on land which is nearest to the spot where the vessel is lying is Wales.

(3) In relation to any vessel the said provisions shall have effect as if—

(*a*) the vessel were a house, building or premises within the district, or, as the case may be, the county, of the port health authority or local authority or county council to whose jurisdiction it is subject; and
(*b*) the master, or other officer or person in charge, of the vessel were the occupier.

(4) The provisions of this Act referred to in the preceding subsections are Part VI and XII[5] and, so far as regards boats used for human habitation, the provisions of Part II relating to filthy or verminous premises or articles and verminous persons[6].

(5) This section does not apply to any vessel belonging to His Majesty or under the command or charge of an officer holding His Majesty's commission, or to any vessel belonging to a foreign government.

(6) In determining for the purposes of subsection (1) above what provisions of this Act specified in subsection (4) above are provisions for the execution of which local authorities are responsible, no account shall be taken of any enactment (whether contained in this Act or not) relating to port health authorities or joint boards or to any particular port health authority or joint board or of any instrument made under any such enactment.

[Public Health Act 1936, s 267, as amended by the Clean Air Act 1956, 4th Sch, the Local Government (Miscellaneous Provisions) Act 1982, Sch 6, the Public Health (Control of Disease) Act 1984, Sch 3 the Environmental Protection Act 1990, Sch 16, and the Local Government (Wales) Act 1994, Sch 9.]

1. In its application to a council which is a local health authority, this section shall be construed as applying to that council in their capacity of local health authority as well as in other capacities (National Health Service Act 1946, Sch 10).
2. "Vessel" has the same meaning as "ship" in the Merchant Shipping Act 1995 (s 343(1)), see s 313 thereof in PART VII: TRANSPORT, ante.
3. "Inland waters" include rivers, harbours and creeks; "Coastal waters" mean waters within a distance of three nautical miles from any point on the coast measured from low-water mark of ordinary spring tides (s 343(1)).
4. Now the Secretary of State for the Environment.
5. Part VI, ss 181–199, deals with hospitals, nursing homes, etc, and Pt XII, ss 271–347, is headed "General". Many of the sections mentioned were repealed by National Health Service Act 1946, Sch 10.
6. See ss 83–86, ante.

TENTS, VANS, SHEDS, ETC

8–25199 268. Nuisances arising from, and bye-laws and other matters relating to, tents, vans, etc. (1) The provisions of Part III of the Environmental Protection Act 1990 and Parts VII[1] and XII of this Act, and the provisions of Part II relating to filthy or verminous premises or articles and verminous persons, shall apply in relation to tents, vans, sheds and similar structures used for human habitation as they apply in relation to other premises and as if a tent, van, shed or similar structure used for human habitation were a house or a building so used.

(2) For the purposes of Part III of the Environmental Protection Act 1990, a tent, van, shed or similar structure used for human habitation—

(*a*) which is in such a state, or so overcrowded, as to be prejudicial to the health of the inmates; or
(*b*) the use of which, by reason of the absence of proper sanitary accommodation or otherwise, gives rise, whether on the site or on other land, to a nuisance or to conditions prejudicial to health,

shall be a statutory nuisance[2], and the expression "occupier" in relation to a tent, van, shed or similar structure shall include any person for the time being in charge thereof.

(3) Where such a nuisance as is mentioned in paragraph (*b*) of the preceding subsection is alleged to arise, wholly or in part, from the use for human habitation of any tent, van, shed or similar structure, then, without prejudice to the liability of the occupants or other users thereof, an abatement notice[3] may be served on, and proceedings under Part III of the Environmental Protection Act 1990 may be taken against the occupier of the land on which the tent, van, shed or other structure is erected or stationed:

Provided that it shall be a defence for him to prove that he did not authorise the tent, van, shed, or other structure to be stationed or erected on the land.

(4) A local authority may make bye-laws for promoting cleanliness in, and the habitable condition of, tents, vans, sheds and similar structures used for human habitation, and generally for the prevention of nuisances in connection therewith.

(5) The powers of a court before which proceedings are brought—

(*a*) in respect of a statutory nuisance caused by, or arising in connection with, a tent, van, shed or similar structure used for human habitation; or

(*b*) in respect of any contravention of bye-laws made under this section,

shall include power to make an order prohibiting the use for human habitation of the tent, van, shed or other structure in question at such places, or within such area, as may be specified in the order.
[Public Health Act 1936, s 268, as amended by the Public Health (Control of Disease) Act 1984, Sch 3 and the Environmental Protection Act 1990, Sch 15.]

---

1. As to Pt XII, see note 5 to s 267, supra. Part VII, ss 200–205, deals with notification of births.
2. As to statutory nuisances, see s 79 of the Environmental Protection Act 1990, post.
3. See s 80 of the Environmental Protection Act 1990, post.

8–25210 269. Power of local authority to control use of moveable dwellings[1]. (1) For the purpose of regulating in accordance with the provisions of this section[2] the use of moveable dwellings within their district, a local authority may grant—

(i) licences authorising persons to allow land occupied by them within the district to be used as sites for moveable dwellings; and

(ii) licences authorising persons to erect or station, and use, such dwellings within the district;

and may attach to any such licence such conditions as they think fit—

(*a*) in the case of a licence authorising the use of land, with respect to the number and classes of moveable dwellings which may be kept thereon at the same time, and the space to be kept free between any two such dwellings, with respect to water supply, and for securing sanitary conditions;

(*b*) in the case of a licence authorising the use of a moveable dwelling, with respect to the use of that dwelling (including the space to be kept free between it and any other such dwelling) and its removal at the end of a specified period, and for securing sanitary conditions.

(2) Subject to the provisions of this section, a person shall not allow any land occupied by him to be used for camping purposes on more than 42 consecutive days or more than 60 days in any 12 consecutive months, unless either he holds in respect of the land so used such a licence from the local authority of the district as is mentioned in paragraph (i) of the preceding subsection, or each person using the land as a site for a moveable dwelling holds in respect of that dwelling such a licence from that authority as is mentioned in paragraph (ii) of the said subsection.

For the purposes of this subsection, land which is in the occupation of the same person as, and within 100 yards of, a site on which there is during any part of any day a moveable dwelling shall be regarded as being used for camping purposes on that day.

(3) Subject to the provisions of this section, a person shall not keep a moveable dwelling on any one site, or on two or more sites in succession, if any one of those sites is within 100 yards of another of them, on more than 42 consecutive days, or 60 days in any 12 consecutive months, unless either he holds in respect of that dwelling such a licence from the local authority of the district as is mentioned in paragraph (ii) of subsection (1) of this section, or the occupier of each piece of land on which the dwelling is kept holds in respect of that land such a licence from that authority as is mentioned in paragraph (i) of the said subsection.

(4) Where under this section an application for a licence is made to a local authority, the authority shall be deemed to have granted it unconditionally, unless within 4 weeks from the receipt thereof they give notice to the applicant stating that his application is refused, or stating the conditions subject to which a licence is granted, and, if an applicant is aggrieved by the refusal of the authority to grant him a licence, or by any condition attached to a licence granted, he may appeal[3] to a court of summary jurisdiction.

(5) Nothing in this section applies—(i) to a moveable dwelling which—(*a*) is kept by its owner on land occupied by him in connection with his dwelling-house and is used for habitation only by him or by members of his household; or (*b*) is kept by its owner on agricultural land occupied by him and is used for habitation only at certain seasons and only by persons employed in farming operations on

that land; or (ii) . . . (iii) to a moveable dwelling while it is not in use for human habitation and is being kept on premises the occupier of which permits no moveable dwellings to be kept thereon except such as are for the time being not in use for human habitation.

(6) If an organisation satisfies the Minister[4] that it takes reasonable steps for securing—(*a*) that camping sites belonging to or provided by it, or used by its members, are properly managed and kept in good sanitary condition; and (*b*) that moveable dwellings used by its members are so used as not to give rise to any nuisance, the Minister may grant to that organisation a certificate of exemption.

A certificate so granted may be withdrawn at any time, but while in force shall for the purpose of this section have the effect of a licence—(i) authorising the use as a site for moveable dwellings of any camping ground belonging to, provided by or used by members of, the organisation; (ii) authorising any member of the organisation to erect or station on any site, and use, a moveable dwelling.

In this subsection the expression "member" in relation to an organisation includes a member of any branch or unit of, or formed by, the organisation.

(7) A person who contravenes any of the provisions of this section or fails to comply with any condition attached to a licence granted to him under this section, shall be liable to a fine not exceeding **level 1** on the standard scale, and to a further fine not exceeding [**£**2] for each day on which the offence continues after conviction therefor.

(8) For the purposes of this section—

(i) the expression "moveable dwelling" includes any tent, any van or other conveyance whether on wheels or not, and, subject as hereinafter provided, any shed or similar structure, being a tent, conveyance or structure which is used either regularly, or at certain seasons only, or intermittently, for human habitation:

Provided that it does not include a structure to which building regulations apply;

(ii) the owner of land which is not let shall be deemed to be the occupier thereof;

(iii) if a moveable dwelling is removed from the site on which it stands, but within 48 hours is brought back to the same site or to another site within 100 yards thereof, then, for the purpose of reckoning any such period of 42 consecutive days as is mentioned in subsection (2) or subsection (3) of this section, it shall be deemed not to have been removed or, as the case may be, to have been moved direct from the one site to the other.

(9) Subject as hereinafter provided, this section shall not apply to any district in which at the commencement of this Act there was in force a local Act containing provisions enabling the local authority to regulate, by means of bye-laws or licences or otherwise, the use of moveable dwellings or camping grounds:

Provided that, on the application of the local authority, the Minister may declare this section to be in force in their district, and upon the declaration taking effect, such of the provisions of the local Act as may be specified in the declaration shall be repealed or, as the case may be, shall be repealed as respects the district of that authority.

[Public Health Act 1936, s 269, as amended by the Caravan Sites and Control of Development Act 1960, Fourth Sch, the Public Health Act 1961, Sch 1, Part III, the Criminal Justice Act 1967, 3rd Sch, the Criminal Justice Act 1982, ss 38 and 46 and the Building Act 1984, Sch 67.]

1. Subject to certain transitional provisions, this section has ceased to apply to caravans (Caravan Sites and Control of Development Act 1960, s 30). See title TOWN AND COUNTRY PLANNING, post for relevant provisions of that Act.

2. The section deals with public health and sanitary conditions at the site; the local authority may not take into account any question of local amenities in refusing to grant a licence under this section (*Pilling v Abergele UDC* [1950] 1 KB 636, [1950] 1 All ER 76, 114 JP 69).

3. See s 300, post.

HOP-PICKERS, ETC

8–25211 **270. Bye-laws as to hop-pickers and persons engaged in similar work.** A local authority may make bye-laws for securing the decent lodging and accommodation of hop-pickers and other persons engaged temporarily in picking, gathering or lifting fruit, flowers, bulbs, roots or vegetables within their district.

[Public Health Act 1936, s 270.]

PART XII—GENERAL[1]

SUPPLEMENTAL AS TO POWERS OF COUNCILS

8–25212 **278. Compensation to individuals for damage resulting from exercise of powers under this Act.** A local authority shall make compensation[2], and in case of dispute the amount shall be determined by arbitration. If not exceeding **£50** be claimed, all questions may on the application of either party be determined by and the amount recovered before a court of summary jurisdiction.

[Public Health Act 1936, s 278, as amended by the Water Consolidation (Consequential Provisions) Act 1991, Sch 3 (summarised).]

1. For application of certain sections in this Part to Pts IV and VI of the Public Health Act 1961, post, see s 1(4) thereof. In its application to a council which is a local health authority, this Part of the Act shall be construed as applying to that

council in their capacity of local health authority as well as in other capacities (National Health Service Act 1946, Sch 10). Part XII of this Act shall have effect as if so much of Pt II of the Public Health Act 1961 (sanitation and buildings) as does not relate to building regulations were contained in Pt II of the Public Health Act 1936 (Housing and Building Control Act 1984, s 60(1)). This section may apply to a sewerage undertaker; see the Water Industry Act 1991, s 115.

2. This section may be applied for the purposes of the Town and Country Planning Act 1990, ss 178(3), (4), 209(3), (4) and 219(3), (4) and the Planning (Listed Buildings and Conservation Areas) Act 1990, s 42(3).

NOTICES, ETC

8–25213 **283. Notices to be in writing; forms of notices, etc.** (1) All notices, orders, consents, demands and other documents authorised or required by or under this Act to be given, made or issued by a council[1], and all notices and applications authorised or required by or under this Act to be given or made to, or to any officer of, a council shall be in writing[2].

(2) The Minister[3] may by regulations prescribe the form of any notice, advertisement, certificate or other document to be used for any of the purposes of this Act and, if forms are so prescribed, those forms or forms to the like effect may be used in all cases to which those forms are applicable. [Public Health Act 1936, s 2834.]

1. This section may apply to a sewerage undertaker; see the Water Industry Act 1991, s 115.
2. See the Interpretation Act 1978, Sch 1, in PART II: EVIDENCE, ante.
3. By the Transfer of Functions (Minister of Health and Minister of Local Government and Planning) (No 1) Order 1951, SI 1951/142, the majority of the functions under the Public Health Act 1936, formerly exercised by the Minister of Health were transferred to the Minister of Local Government and Planning (now the Secretary of State for the Environment). Certain functions have been retained by the Minister of Health. In this section and others that follow the expression "Minister" means whichever of these two Ministers is appropriate having regard to the functions that are being discharged. Ministerial functions relating to the control of building are exercised by the Minister of Public Building and Works.
4. Section 266 and Sch 4 of the Public Health Act 1875 (which contain similar provisions), are not repealed for the purposes of any unrepealed enactment (Public Health Act 1936, Sch 3).

8–25214 **284. Authentication of documents.** (1) Any notice, order, consent, demand or other document which a council are authorised or required by or under this Act to give, make or issue may be signed on behalf of the council—(*a*) by the clerk of the council; (*b*) by the surveyor, the medical officer of health, the public health inspector or the chief financial officer, of the council as respects documents relating to matters within their respective provinces; (*c*) by any officer of the council authorised by them in writing to sign documents of the particular kind or, as the case may be, the particular document.

(2) Any document purporting to bear the signature of an officer expressed to hold an office by virtue of which he is under this section empowered to sign such a document, or expressed to be duly authorised by the council to sign such a document or the particular document, shall for the purposes of this Act, and of any building regulations and orders made thereunder, be deemed, until the contrary is proved, to have been duly given, made or issued by authority of the council.

In this subsection the expression "signature" includes a facsimile of a signature by whatever process reproduced.
[Public Health Act 1936, s 284, as amended by the Public Health Act 1961, Sch 1, Part III1.]

1. The authentication provided by this section is permissive and not imperative: it does not invalidate any other method of signing a document; cf *Tennant v LCC* (1957) 121 JP 428. Section 266 of the Public Health Act 1875 is not repealed for the purposes of any unrepealed enactment (Public Health Act 1936, Sch 3).

8–25215 **285. Service of notices, etc.** Any notice, order, consent, demand or other document[1] which is required or authorised by or under this Act to be given to or served on any person may, in any case for which no other provision is made by this Act, be given or served[2] either—

(*a*) by delivering it to that person; or
(*b*) in the case of a coroner, or a medical officer of health, by leaving it or sending it in a prepaid[3] letter addressed to him at either his residence or his office and, in the case of any other officer of a council, by leaving it or sending it in a prepaid letter addressed to him, at his office; or
(*c*) in the case of any other person, by leaving it or sending it in a prepaid letter addressed to him, at his usual or last known residence[4]; or
(*d*) in the case of an incorporated company or body, by delivering it to their secretary or clerk at their registered or principal office, or by sending it in a prepaid letter addressed to him at that office; or
(*e*) in the case of a document to be given to or served on a person as being the owner of any premises by virtue of the fact that he receives the rackrent thereof as agent for another, or would so receive it if the premises were let at a rackrent, by leaving it, or sending it in a prepaid letter addressed to him, at his place of business; or
(*f*) in the case of a document to be given to or served on the owner or the occupier of any premises, if it is not practicable after reasonable inquiry to ascertain the name and address of the person to or on whom it should be given or served, or if the premises are unoccupied, by addressing it to the person concerned by the description of "owner" or "occupier" of the

premises (naming them) to which it relates, and delivering it to some person on the premises, or, if there is no person on the premises to whom it can be delivered, by affixing it, or a copy of it, to some conspicuous[5] part of the premises.

[Public Health Act 1936, s 285.]

1. This has been held to include a summons (*R v Braithwaite, ex p Dowling* [1918] 2 KB 319, 82 JP 242—for non-payment of rates; *R v Hastings Justices, ex p Mitchell* (1925) 89 JP JO 86—for employing an unlicensed hackney carriage driver). Inasmuch as s 296, post, requires that prosecutions shall be in accordance with (what is now) the Magistrates' Courts Act 1980, we think it safer that summonses for *offences* should be served and service proved in accordance with the Criminal Procedure Rules 2005, Part 4, in PART I: MAGISTRATES' COURTS, PROCEDURE, ante. This section does not apply to county court summonses (*Wealdstone UDC v Evershed* (1905) 69 JP 258), nor to High Court writs (*Friern Barnet UDC v Adams* [1927] 2 Ch 25, 91 JP 60).

2. Notices duly served under this section are deemed to have been duly served, although in point of fact they never reach the person to whom they are addressed (*Woodford UDC v Henwood* (1900) 64 JP 148). Cf *Re Levy* [1924] 68 Sol Jo 419.

3. It is a condition precedent that the postage should be prepaid. Where there was no evidence of prepayment an action in the Chancery Division failed (*Walthamstow UDC v Henwood* [1897] 1 Ch 41, 61 JP 23).

4. In *R v Braithwaite, ex p Dowling* note 1, supra, residence was held to include his place of business.

5. See *R v Mead* [1894] 2 QB 124, 58 JP 448; *Butler v Gravesend Urban Authority* (1894) 58 JP 446, and *West Ham Corpn v Thomas* (1908) 73 JP 65.

6. Section 267 of the Public Health Act 1875 (which contains similar provisions), is not repealed for the purposes of any unrepealed enactment (Public Health Act 1936, Sch 3).

ENTRY AND OBSTRUCTION

8-25216 287. Power to enter premises. (1) Subject to the provisions of this section, any authorised officer[1] of a council shall, on producing, if so required, some duly authenticated document showing his authority, have a right to enter any premises[2] at all reasonable hours—

(*a*) for the purpose of ascertaining whether there is, or has been, on or in connection with the premises any contravention of the provisions of this Act or of any bye-laws or building regulations made thereunder, being provisions which it is the duty of the council to enforce;

(*b*) for the purpose of ascertaining whether or not circumstances exist which would authorise or require the council to take any action, or execute any work, under this Act or any such bye-laws or building regulations;

(*c*) for the purpose of taking any action, or executing any work, authorised or required by this Act or any such bye-laws or building regulations, or any order made under this Act, to be taken, or executed, by the council;

(*d*) generally, for the purpose of the performance by the council of their functions under this Act or any such bye-laws or building regulations:

Provided that admission to any premises not being a factory or workplace, shall not be demanded as of right unless twenty-four hours' notice[3] of the intended entry has been given to the occupier.

(2) If it is shown to the satisfaction of a justice of the peace on sworn information in writing—

(*a*) that admission to any premises has been refused, or that refusal is apprehended, or that the premises are unoccupied or the occupier is temporarily absent, or that the case is one of urgency, or that an application for admission would defeat the object of the entry; and

(*b*) that there is reasonable ground for entry into the premises for any such purpose as aforesaid,

the justice may by warrant[4] under his hand authorise the council by any authorised officer to enter the premises, if need be by force:

Provided that such a warrant shall not be issued unless the justice is satisfied either that notice of the intention to apply for a warrant has been given to the occupier, or that the premises are unoccupied, or that the occupier is temporarily absent, or that the case is one of urgency, or that the giving of such notice would defeat the object of the entry.

(3) An authorised officer entering any premises by virtue of this section, or of a warrant issued thereunder, may take with him such other persons as may be necessary and on leaving any unoccupied premises which he has entered by virtue of such a warrant shall leave them as effectually secured against trespassers as he found them.

(4) Every warrant granted under this section shall continue in force until the purpose for which the entry is necessary has been satisfied.

(5) If any person who in compliance with the provisions of this section or of a warrant issued thereunder is admitted into a factory or workplace discloses to any person any information obtained by him in the factory or workplace with regard to any manufacturing process or trade secret, he shall, unless such disclosure was made in the performance of his duty, be liable to a fine not exceeding **level 3** on the standard scale or to imprisonment for a term not exceeding **three months**.

(6) (*Repealed*).

[Public Health Act 1936, s 287, as amended by the Public Health Act 1961, Sch 1, Part III, the Criminal Justice Act 1982, ss 38 and 46, the Statute Law (Repeals) Act 1989, Sch 1 and the Statute Law (Repeals) Act 1993, Sch 1.]

1. A like power is given to any member of a fire brigade duly authorised in writing by the authority maintaining the brigade to enter premises for the purpose of obtaining information required for fire-fighting purposes, with respect to the

character of the buildings and other property and available water supplies and the means of access thereto (Fire Service Act 1947, s 1(2)). Section 287 applies in relation to a sewerage undertaker for the purposes of provisions of this Act 1989 and of s 27 of this Act as it applies in relation to a local authority; the words "if so required" in s 287(1) are, however, omitted.

2. In *Senior v Twelves* (1958) 122 JP Jo 379, the Divisional Court held that the right of entry conferred by paras (*b*) and (*c*) of this subsection are not limited to those premises where there may have been a contravention of the Act or bye-laws (see para (*a*)), but may extend, in appropriate cases, to adjoining property. Presumably, this decision would apply to the right conferred by para (*d*).

3. The notice of intended entry must be certain in its terms (cf *Stroud v Bradbury* [1952] 2 All ER 76, 116 JP 386).

4. Note also the power to issue a warrant under s 61 of the Public Health (Control of Disease) Act 1984, post.

8–25217 **288. Penalty for obstructing execution of Act.** A person who wilfully obstructs any person acting in the execution of this Act or of any bye-law, building regulation, order or warrant made or issued thereunder shall, in any case for which no other provision is made by this Act, be liable[1] to a fine not exceeding **level 1** on the standard scale.

[Public Health Act 1936, s 288, as amended by the Public Health Act 1961, Sch 1, Part III, and the Criminal Justice Act 1967, 3rd Sch and the Criminal Justice Act 1982, ss 35, 38 and 46[2].]

1. See ss 296 and 297, post.

2. Section 306 of the Public Health Act 1875 (which contains similar provisions to this section) is not repealed for the purposes of any unrepealed enactment (Public Health Act 1936, Sch 3).

8–25218 **289. Power to require occupier to permit works to be executed by owner.** If on a complaint made by the owner of any premises[1], it appears to a court of summary jurisdiction that the occupier of those premises prevents the owners from executing any work which he is by or under this Act required to execute, the court may order the occupier to permit the execution of the work.

[Public Health Act 1936, s 289[2].]

1. See note 1 to s 73, ante.

2. Section 306 of the Public Health Act 1875 (which contains similar provisions to this section) is not repealed for the purposes of any unrepealed enactment (Public Health Act 1936, Sch 3).

NOTICES REQUIRING THE EXECUTION OF WORKS

8–25219 **290. Provisions as to appeals against, and enforcement of, notices requiring execution of works[1].** (1) The following provisions of this section shall, subject to any express modifications specified in the section under which the notice is given, apply in relation to any notice given under this Act which is expressly declared to be a notice in relation to which the provisions of this Part of this Act with respect to appeals against, and the enforcement of, notices requiring the execution of works are to apply[2].

(2) Any such notice shall indicate[3] the nature of the works to be executed, and state the time within which they are to be executed.

(3) A person served with such a notice as aforesaid may appeal[4] to a court of summary jurisdiction on any of the following grounds which are appropriate in the circumstances of the particular case:

(*a*) that the notice or requirement is not justified by the terms of the section under which it purports to have been given or made;

(*b*) that there has been some informality, defect or error in, or in connection with, the notice;

(*c*) that the authority have refused unreasonably to approve the execution of alternative works, or that the works required by the notice to be executed are otherwise unreasonable in character or extent, or are unnecessary;

(*d*) that the time within which the works are to be executed is not reasonably sufficient[5] for the purpose;

(*e*) that the notice might lawfully have been served on the occupier of the premises in question instead of on the owner, or on the owner instead of on the occupier, and that it would have been equitable for it to have been so served;

(*f*) where the work is work for the common benefit of the premises in question and other premises, that some other person, being the owner or occupier of premises to be benefited, ought to contribute towards the expenses of executing any works required.

(4) If and in so far as an appeal under this section is based on the ground of some informality, defect or error in or in connection with the notice, the court shall dismiss the appeal, if it is satisfied that the informality, defect or error was not a material one.

(5) Where the grounds upon which an appeal under this section is brought include a ground specified in paragraph (*e*) or paragraph (*f*) of subsection (3) of this section, the appellant shall serve a copy of his notice of appeal on each other person referred to, and in the case of any appeal under this section may serve a copy of his notice of appeal on any other person having an estate or interest in the premises in question, and on the hearing of the appeal the court may make such order as it thinks fit with respect to the person by whom any work is to be executed and the contribution to be made by any other person towards the cost of the work, or as to the proportions in which any expenses which may become recoverable by the local authority are to be borne by the appellant and such other person.

In exercising its powers under this subsection, the court shall have regard—

(*a*) as between an owner and an occupier, to the terms and conditions, whether contractual or statutory, of the tenancy and to the nature of the works required; and

(*b*) in any case, to the degree of benefit to be derived by the different persons concerned.

(6) Subject to such right of appeal as aforesaid, if the person required by the notice to execute the works fails to execute the works indicated within the time thereby limited, the local authority may themselves execute the works and recover from that person the expenses reasonably incurred by them in so doing and, without prejudice to their right to exercise that power, he shall be liable[6] to a fine not exceeding **level 4** on the standard scale, and to a further fine not exceeding [**£**2] for each day on which the default continues after conviction thereof.

(7) In proceedings by the local authority against the person served with the notice for the recovery of any expenses which the authority are entitled to recover from him, it shall not be open to him to raise any question which he could have raised on an appeal under this section.

[Public Health Act 1936, s 290, as amended by the Criminal Law Act 1977, Sch 6 and the Criminal Justice Act 1982, s 46.]

---

1. Subsections (2) to (7) of this section are applied, subject to certain modifications, to the service of a notice under s 167(5) of the Highways Act 1980 (powers relating to retaining walls near streets); see Highways Act 1980, s 167, in PART VII: TRANSPORT title HIGHWAYS, ante.
2. The sections are ss 25, 39(1), 40, 44(2), 45(2), 46(3), 47(5), 50(2), 56(1), 59(2), 60(2), 88(4) and 264.
3. This is less precise than the word "specify".
4. See s 300, post.
5. See *Bristol Corpn v Sinnott* [1917] 2 Ch 340, 81 JP 258; *Macclesfield Corpn v Macclesfield Grammar School* [1921] 2 Ch 189, and *Ryall v Cubitt Heath* [1922] 1 KB 275, 86 JP 15.
6. See ss 296 and 297, post.

PROVISIONS AS TO RECOVERY OF EXPENSES, ETC

8–25220 **291. Certain expenses recoverable from owners to be a charge on the premises; power to order payment by instalments.** (1) Where a local authority[1] have incurred expenses for the repayment of which the owner of the premises[2] in respect of which the expenses were incurred is liable, either under this Act or under any enactment repealed thereby, or by agreement with the authority, those expenses, together with interest from the date of service of a demand for the expenses, may be recovered by the authority from the person who is the owner of the premises at the date when the works are completed, or, if he has ceased to be the owner of the premises before the date when a demand for the expenses is served, either from him or from the person who is the owner at the date when the demand is served, and, as from the date of the completion of the works, the expenses and interest accrued due thereon shall, until recovered, be a charge[3] on the premises and on all estates and interests therein.

(2) A local authority may by order declare any expenses recoverable by them under this section to be payable with interest by instalments within a period not exceeding thirty years, until the whole amount is paid; and any such instalments and interest, or any part thereof, may be recovered from the owner or occupier for the time being of the premises in respect of which the expenses were incurred, and, if recovered from the occupier, may be deducted by him from the rent of the premises:

Provided that an occupier shall not be required to pay at any one time any sum in excess of the amount which was due from him on account of rent at, or has become due from him on account of rent since, the date on which he received a demand from the local authority together with a notice requiring him not to pay rent to his landlord without deducting the sum so demanded.

An order may be made under this subsection at any time with respect to any unpaid balance of expenses and accrued interest so, however, that the period for repayment shall not in any case extend beyond thirty years from the service of the first demand for the expenses.

(3) The rate of interest chargeable under subsection (1) or subsection (2) of this section shall be such reasonable rate as the authority may determine.

(4) A local authority shall, for the purpose of enforcing a charge under this section, have all the same powers and remedies under the Law of Property Act 1925, and otherwise as if they were mortgagees by deed having powers of sale and lease, of accepting surrenders of leases and of appointing a receiver.

[Public Health Act 1936, s 291, as amended by the Local Government, Planning and Land Act 1980, Schs 6 and 34.]

---

1. For definition of "local authority", see s 1(2), ante. This section may apply to a sewerage undertaker; see the Water Industry Act 1991, ss 107 and 109.
2. For definition of "premises", see note 1 to s 73, ante.
3. The charge is on the property (see *Altrincham UDC v O'Brien* (1927) 91 JP 149), and not on the interest of any particular owner, but on the total ownership, and it overrides all other proprietary interests (*Birmingham Corpn v Baker* (1881) 17 Ch D 782; *Paddington Borough Council v Finucane* [1928] Ch 567, 92 JP 68; *Bristol Corpn v Virgin* [1928] 2 KB 622, 92 JP 145). The local authority cannot sell free from restrictive covenants (*Tendring Union v Dowton* [1891] 3 Ch 265). The charge is enforced by writ for foreclosure or sale, or by originating summons. For summary proceedings, see s 293, post.

8–25221 **293. Recovery of expenses, etc.** (1) Any sum which a council[1] are entitled to recover under this Act, and with respect to the recovery of which provision is not made by any other section of this Act, may be recovered as a simple contract debt in any court of competent jurisdiction.

(2) *Repealed.*

[Public Health Act 1936, s 293, as amended by the Local Government (Miscellaneous Provisions) Act 1976, s 27.]

1. This section may apply to a sewerage undertaker; see the Water Industry Act 1991, ss 107 and 109.

8–25222 **294. Limitation of liability of agents or trustees for other persons.** Where a council[1] claim to recover any expenses under this Act from a person as being the owner of the premises in respect of which the expenses were incurred and that person proves that he—

(*a*) is receiving the rent of those premises merely as agent or trustee for some other person; and

(*b*) has not, and since the date of the service on him of a demand for payment has not had, in his hands on behalf of that other person sufficient money to discharge the whole demand of the authority,

his liability shall be limited to the total amount of the money which he has or has had in his hands as aforesaid, but a council who are, or would be, debarred by the foregoing provisions from recovering the whole of any such expenses from an agent or trustee may recover the whole or any unpaid balance thereof from the person on whose behalf the agent or trustee receives the rent.

[Public Health Act 1936, s 294[2].]

1. This section may apply to a sewerage undertaker; see the Water Industry Act 1991, ss 107 and 109.
2. This meets the case of *St Helen's Corpn v Kirkham* (1885) 16 QBD 403, 50 JP 647. As to power of the local authority to grant charging orders, see s 295.

PROSECUTION OF OFFENCES, ETC

8–25223 **296. Summary proceedings for offences.** All offences under this Act may be prosecuted under the Summary Jurisdiction Acts.

[Public Health Act 1936, s 296[1].]

1. The Summary Jurisdiction Acts are consolidated in the Magistrates' Courts Act 1980 in PART I: MAGISTRATES' COURTS, PROCEDURE, ante. The corresponding s 251 of the Public Health Act 1875 is not repealed for the purposes of any unrepealed enactment (Public Health Act 1936, Sch 3).

8–25224 **297. Continuing offences and penalties.** Where provision is made by or under this Act for the imposition of a daily penalty in respect of a continuing offence, the court by which a person is convicted of the original offence may fix a reasonable period from the date of conviction for compliance by the defendant with any directions given by the court and, where a court has fixed such a period, the daily penalty shall not be recoverable in respect of any day before the expiration thereof.

[Public Health Act 1936, s 297.]

8–25225 **298. Restriction on right to prosecute[1].** Proceedings in respect of an offence created by or under this Act shall not, without the written consent of the Attorney-General[2], be taken by any person other than a party aggrieved[3], or a council or a body whose function it is to enforce the provisions or bye-laws in question, or by whom or by whose predecessors the bye-law in question was made.

[Public Health Act 1936, s 298.]

1. For a relaxation of the provisions of this section in relation to proceedings brought by a constable in respect of an offence against a bye-law, see the Local Government (Miscellaneous Provisions) Act 1982, s 12, in this PART, title LOCAL GOVERNMENT, ante.
2. See PART I: MAGISTRATES' COURTS, PROCEDURE, para **1–380 Criminal prosecutions**, ante.
3. A person is not a party aggrieved by merely being a ratepayer (*Boyce v Higgins* (1853) 14 CB 1, 17 JP 808), nor by having been a defeated candidate at a local election (*Hollis v Marshall* (1858) 2 H & N 755, 22 JP 210). See also *R v Blanshard* (1866) 30 JP 280, and *Fletcher v Hudson* (1881) 7 QBD 611, 46 JP 372. A candidate against whom votes are fabricated is such a party (*Verdin v Wray* (1877) 2 QBD 608, 41 JP 484). A person who has the same interest in land as the person convicted is a party aggrieved (*Drapers' Co v Hadder* (1892) 57 JP 200). A rival omnibus company is not aggrieved by a local authority running unlicensed omnibus on another route (*Sheffield Corpn v Kitson* [1929] 2 KB 322, 93 JP 135). This section may apply to a sewerage undertaker; see the Water Industry Act 1991, s 115.

8–25226 **299.** *Repealed.*

8–25227 **300. Appeals and applications to courts of summary jurisdiction.** (1) Where any enactment in this Act provides—

(*a*) for an appeal to a court of summary jurisdiction against a requirement, refusal or other decision of a council[1]; or (*b*) for any matter to be determined by, or an application in respect of any matter to be made to, a court of summary jurisdiction,

the procedure shall be by way of complaint for an order[2], and the Summary Jurisdiction Acts[3] shall apply to the proceedings.

(2) The time within which any such appeal may be brought shall be twenty-one days[4] from the date on which notice of the council's requirement, refusal or other decision was served upon the person desiring to appeal, and for the purpose of this subsection the making of the complaint[5] shall be deemed to be the bringing of the appeal.

(3) In any case where such an appeal lies, the document notifying to the person concerned the decision of the council in the matter shall state[6] the right of appeal to a court of summary jurisdiction and the time within which such an appeal may be brought.

[Public Health Act 1936, s 300.]

1. This section may apply to a sewerage undertaker; see the Water Industry Act 1991, ss 106 and 113.
2. See also Magistrates' Courts Rules 1981, r 34, in PART I: MAGISTRATES' COURTS, PROCEDURE, ante.
3. Now the Magistrates' Courts Act 1980.
4. But note however different limitations in s 138(2A) ante and in s 36(3) of the Public Health Act 1961, post.
5. This section does not also require the service of a notice containing the grounds of appeal, as is required by the Public Health Act 1925, s 8.
6. See *Rayner v Stepney Corpn* [1911] 2 Ch 312, 75 JP 468; *Nalder v Ilford Corpn* [1951] 1 KB 822, [1950] 2 All ER 908, 114 JP 594.

8–25228 **301. Appeals to the Crown Court against decisions of justices[1].** Subject as hereinafter provided, where a person aggrieved[2] by any order, determination or other decision of a court of summary jurisdiction under this Act is not by any other enactment authorised to appeal to the Crown Court, he may appeal to such a court:

Provided that nothing in this section shall be construed as conferring a right of appeal from the decision of a court of summary jurisdiction in any case if each of the parties concerned might under this Act have required that the dispute should be determined by arbitration instead of by such a court.

[Public Health Act 1936, s 301, as amended by the Courts Act 1971, Sch 9.]

1. This section applies to an appeal against the refusal to grant a music etc licence under the Public Health Acts (Amendment) Act 1890, s 51 (*R v East Riding of Yorkshire Quarter Sessions, ex p Newton* [1968] 1 QB 32, [1967] 3 All ER 118).
2. This expression includes a successful party wrongly deprived of his costs (*R v Lancashire Quarter Sessions Appeal Committee, ex p Huyton-with-Roby UDC* [1955] 1 QB 52, [1954] 3 All ER 225, 118 JP 526). Normally a public authority is entitled to be treated as a "person aggrieved"; see *Cook v Southend Borough Council* [1990] 2 QB 1, [1990] 1 All ER 243, 154 JP 145, CA. This section may apply to a sewerage undertaker; see the Water Industry Act 1991, ss 106 and 113.

8–25229 **302. Effect of decision of court upon appeal.** Where upon an appeal under this Act a court varies or reverses any decision of a council[1], it shall be the duty of the council to give effect to the order of the court and, in particular, to grant or issue any necessary consent, certificate or other document, and to make any necessary entry in any register.

[Public Health Act 1936, s 302.]

1. This section may apply to a sewerage undertaker; see the Water Industry Act 1991, ss 106 and 113.

8–25240 **304. Judges and justices not to be disqualified by liability to rates.** A judge of any court or a justice of the peace shall not be disqualified from acting in cases arising under this Act by reason only of his being as one of several ratepayers, or as one of any other class of persons, liable in common with the others to contribute to, or be benefited by, any rate or fund out of which any expenses of a council are to be defrayed.

[Public Health Act 1936, s 304[1].]

1. Section 258 of the Public Health Act 1875 (which contains similar provisions), is not repealed for the purposes of any unrepealed enactment (Public Health Act 1936, 3rd Sch).

SAVINGS

8–25241 **328. Powers of Act to be cumulative.** All powers and duties conferred or imposed by this Act shall be deemed to be in addition to, and not in derogation of, any other powers and duties conferred or imposed by Act of Parliament, law or custom, and, subject to any repeal effected by, or other express provision of, this Act, all such other powers and duties may be exercised and shall be performed in the same manner as if this Act had not been passed.

[Public Health Act 1936, s 328.]

Prevention of Damage by Pests Act 1949

(12, 13 & 14 Geo 6 c 55)

PART I

RATS AND MICE

8–25351 **1. Local authorities for the purposes of Part I.** (1) The local authorities for the purposes of this Part of this Act in England and Wales shall be the Common Council of the City of London and the councils of London boroughs and county districts:

Provided that

(*a*) the local authority for any port health district, whether constituted before or after the commencement of this Act, shall be the port health authority; and

(*b*) in relation to sewers vested in the council of any county or in the Greater London Council, the functions of the local authority under this Part of this Act shall be exercisable by that council and not by any other authority.

(2) (*Application to Scotland*).

(3) Section 6 of the Public Health Act 1936 (which provides for the constitution of united districts for any of the purposes of that Act) shall have effect as if the purposes of this Part of this Act were purposes of that Act.

[Prevention of Damage by Pests Act 1949, s 1, amended by London Government Act 1963, Sch 17, and the Local Government Act 1972, Sch 30.]

8–25352 **2. Duties of local authorities.** (1) It shall be the duty of every local authority to take such steps as may be necessary to secure so far as practicable that their district is kept free from rats and mice, and in particular—

(*a*) from time to time carry out such inspections as may be necessary for the purpose aforesaid;

(*b*) to destroy rats and mice on land of which they are the occupier and otherwise to keep such land so far as practicable free from rats and mice;

(*c*) to enforce the duties of owners and occupiers of land under the following provisions of this Part of this Act, and to carry out such operations as are authorised by those provisions.

(2) *Repealed.*

[Prevention of Damage by Pests Act 1949, s 2, as amended by the Local Government, Planning and Land Act 1980, Sch 34.]

8–25353 **3. Obligation of occupiers of land to notify local authority of rats and mice.** (1) Subject to the provisions of this section, the occupier of any land shall give to the local authority forthwith notice in writing if it comes to his knowledge that rats or mice are living on or resorting to the land in substantial numbers.

(2) The foregoing subsection shall not apply to agricultural land, and the Minister may make regulations providing that that subsection shall not apply to such other land as may be prescribed by or under the regulations, or shall apply thereto subject to such modifications as may be so prescribed*.

(3) A person shall not be required to give notice under this section to the local authority of any matter of which notice is given to the Minister in pursuance of Part II of this Act.

(4) Any person who fails to give a notice which he is required to give under this section shall be liable on summary conviction to a fine not exceeding **level 1** on the standard scale.

[Prevention of Damage by Pests Act 1949, s 3, as amended by the Criminal Justice Act 1982, ss 38 and 46.]

***Repealed in relation to England and Wales by the Statute Law (Repeals) Act 2004.**

8–25354 **4. Power of local authority to require action.** (1) If in the case of any land it appears to the local authority, whether in consequence of a notice given in respect of the land under the last foregoing section or otherwise, that steps should be taken for the destruction of rats or mice on the land or otherwise for keeping the land free from rats and mice, they may serve on the owner[1] or occupier of the land a notice[2] requiring him to take, within such reasonable period as may be specified in the notice, such reasonable steps[3] for the purpose aforesaid as may be so specified; and where the owner of any land is not also the occupier thereof separate notices may be served under this section on the owner and on the occupier.

(2) Any such notice may in particular require—

(*a*) the application to the land of any form of treatment specified in the notice;

(*b*) the carrying out on the land of any structural repairs or other works so specified,

and may prescribe the times at which any treatment required by the notice is to be carried out.

(3) *Repealed.*

(4) If on a complaint made by the owner of any land it appears to a court of summary jurisdiction that the occupier of the land prevents the owner from carrying out any work which he is required to carry out by a notice under this section, the court may order the occupier to permit the carrying out of the work.

(5) Subsections (3) to (5) of section 290 of the Public Health Act 1936 (which provides for an appeal to a court of summary jurisdiction against certain notices requiring the execution of works under that Act) shall apply to any notice served under this section requiring the carrying out of any structural works as they apply to any such notice as is mentioned in subsection (1) of that section; and sections 300 to 302 of that Act (which contain supplementary provisions relating to such appeals) shall have effect accordingly.

[Prevention of Damage by Pests Act 1949, s 4, as amended by the Agriculture (Miscellaneous Provisions) Act 1972, Sch 6.]

---

1. "Owner" has the same meaning as in the Public Health Act 1936, s 28. See s 343 of that Act, post. As to notices, see s 10, post.

2. There are no statutory provisions prescribing the form of the notice so that even though the signature on the notice is not that of a local authority's environmental officer but that of another member of staff on his behalf the notice is valid. So long as the source and authenticity of the notice are apparent to the recipient, the notice need not be signed at all, see *Basildon District Council v Railtrack plc* (1998) Times, 27 February, DC.

3. The notice must specify the thing required to be done: a notice to apply poison treatment to the land or to carry out "other work of a not less effectual character" was held not to comply with the section (*Perry v Garner* [1953] 1 QB 335, [1953] 1 All ER 285, 117 JP 104).

8–25355 **5. Remedies for failure to comply with notice under section 4.** (1) Subject to the provisions of the last foregoing section with respect to appeals, if any person on whom a notice is served by the local authority under that section fails to take any steps required by the notice at the time or within the period prescribed by the notice, the local authority may themselves take those steps and recover from him any expenses reasonably incurred by them in doing so.

(2) Without prejudice to the provisions of subsection (1) of this section, but subject to the provisions of the last foregoing section with respect to appeals, a person who fails to take any such steps as aforesaid shall be guilty of an offence and liable on summary conviction to a fine not exceeding **level 3** on the standard scale.

[Prevention of Damage by Pests Act 1949, s 5, as amended by the Criminal Justice Act 1982, s 35, 38 and 46.]

8–25356 **6. Additional powers of local authorities in relation to groups of premises.** (1) If it appears to the local authority that rats or mice are found in substantial numbers on any land comprising premises in the occupation of different persons and that it is expedient to deal with the land as one unit for the purpose of destroying rats or mice or keeping the land so far as practicable free from rats and mice, they may, without serving notices under s 4 of this Act on the occupiers or owners of those premises, themselves take in relation to the land such steps as they consider necessary or expedient for the purpose aforesaid:

Provided that the steps taken by the local authority under this section shall not include the carrying out of any structural work.

(2) Without prejudice to the provisions of section 22 of this Act requiring notice to be given before entry upon land under that section, a local authority shall, before taking any steps under this section in relation to any premises, give to the occupier at least seven days' notice of their intention to do so, specifying the steps proposed to be taken.

(3) Any expenses reasonably incurred by a local authority in taking steps under this section in relation to any land may be recovered by that authority from the several occupiers of the premises comprised in that land in such proportion as may be just having regard to the cost of the work done on the several premises.

(4) For the purposes of this section, any premises which are unoccupied shall be deemed to be in the occupation of the owner, and references in this section to the occupier shall be construed accordingly.

[Prevention of Damage by Pests Act 1949, s 6.]

8–25357 **7. Recovery of expenses under section 5 or section 6.** (1) Any expenses recoverable by a local authority under section 5 or section 6 of this Act may be recovered as a simple contract debt in any court of competent[1] jurisdiction.

(2) Sections 291 and 294 of the Public Health Act 1936 (which provide respectively for charging on the premises expenses recoverable under that Act from the owner, and for limiting the liability for expenses recoverable under that Act of owner receiving rent as agent or trustee) shall so far as applicable apply to expenses recoverable by a local authority under section 5 or section 6 of this Act as they apply to expenses recoverable under that Act by a local authority within the meaning of that Act.

(3) In proceedings under this section by a local authority for the recovery of any expenses incurred by them under section 5 of this Act, it shall not be open to the defendant to raise by way of defence any question which he could have raised on an appeal under section 4 of this Act.

[Prevention of Damage by Pests Act 1949, s 7, as amended by the Local Government Act 1974, Sch 8.]

---

1. Note that this debt is not recoverable summarily as a civil debt.

8–25358 **8. Provisions as to threshing and dismantling of ricks.** (1) The Minister may make regulations for securing that such steps will be taken in connection with the threshing or dismantling of any rick of corn or other crops specified in the regulations as to ensure the destruction of rats or mice escaping from the rick.

(2) Regulations under this section may impose such requirements on the owner of any such rick, and on any person engaged in or concerned with the threshing or dismantling, as may appear to the Minister necessary for the purpose aforesaid; and any person who fails to comply with any of those requirements shall be liable on summary conviction to a fine not exceeding **level 3** on the standard scale or such less amount, if any, as may be prescribed by the regulations.*

[Prevention of Damage by Pests Act 1949, s. 8, as amended by the Criminal Justice Act 1982, ss 38 and 46.]

***Repealed in relation to England and Wales by the Statute Law (Repeals) Act 2004.**

8–25359 **10. Authentication of documents, service of notices, etc.** (1) Sections 284 to 286 of the Public Health Act 1936 (which relate to the authentication of documents, the service of notices and the proof of proceedings of local authorities) shall apply to documents, notices and proceedings of local authorities in England and Wales under this Part of this Act (whether or not they are local authorities within the meaning of that Act) as they apply to documents, notices and proceedings of local authorities under that Act.

[Prevention of Damage by Pests Act 1949, s 10.]

PART II
INFESTATION[1] OF FOOD[2]

8–25360 **13. Obligation of certain undertakers to give notice of occurrence of infestation[3].** (1) Subject to the provisions of this section, every person whose business consists of or includes the manufacture[4], storage, transport or sale of food, shall give to the Minister[5] forthwith notice in writing if it comes to his knowledge that any infestation is present—

(*a*) in any premises or vehicles, or any equipment belonging to any premises or vehicle, used or likely to be used in the course of that business for the manufacture, storage, transport or sale of food;

(*b*) in any food manufactured, stored, transported or sold in the course of that business, or in any other goods for the time being in his possession which are in contact or likely to come into contact with food so manufactured, stored, transported or sold.

(2) Subject to the provisions of this section, every person whose business consists of or includes the manufacture, sale, repair or cleaning of containers[6] shall forthwith give notice in writing to the Minister if it comes to his knowledge that any infestation is present in any container for the time being in his possession which is to be used for the reception of food in the course of any such business as is mentioned in subsection (1) of this section.

(3) The Minister may after consultation with such associations or bodies (if any) as appear to him to be representative of persons affected, make regulations—

(*a*) for relaxing or excluding the requirements of this section in such cases and subject to such conditions (if any) as may be prescribed by or under the regulations;

(*b*) for prohibiting or restricting the delivery in the course of business of any food or other goods in respect of which notice is or is required to be given to the Minister under this section.

[Prevention of Damage by Pests Act 1949, s 13.]

1. "Infestation" means the presence of rats, mice, insects or mites in numbers or under conditions which involve an immediate or potential risk of substantial loss of or damage to food, and "infested" shall be construed accordingly (s 28).
2. "Food" includes any substance ordinarily used in the composition or preparation of food, the seeds of any cereal or vegetable, and any feeding stuffs for animals, but does not include growing crops (s 28).
3. For penalty for contravention, etc, see s 17, post.
4. "Manufacture" includes processing (s 28).
5. "Minister" means the Minister of Agriculture and Fisheries (s 28), now the Minister of Agriculture, Fisheries and Food (SI 1955/554) or the Secretary of State for Wales (SI 1978/272).
6. "Container" includes sacks, boxes, tins and other similar articles (s 28).

8–25361 **14. Power of Minister to give directions to certain undertakers for preventing or mitigating infestation.** (1) Without prejudice to the provisions of any regulations made under the last foregoing section, the Minister may, if he is satisfied, whether in consequence of a notice under the last foregoing section or otherwise, that it is necessary to do so for the purpose of preventing or mitigating damage to food, give such directions[1] under the following provisions of this section as he thinks expedient.

(2) Directions may be given under this section to any person whose business consists of or includes the manufacture, storage, transport or sale of food—

(*a*) prohibiting or restricting the use for the manufacture, storage, transport or sale of food in the course of that business of any premises or vehicle, or any equipment belonging to any premises or vehicles, which is or is likely to become infested;

(*b*) prohibiting or restricting the acceptance, delivery, retention or removal in the course of that business of any infested food or of any other infested goods which are likely to come into contact with food manufactured, stored, transported or sold as aforesaid;

(*c*) requiring the carrying out, within such time as may be specified in the directions, of any structural works, or the application of any form of treatment, being works or treatment appearing to the Minister to be necessary for preventing or remedying infestation in any such premises, vehicles, equipment, food or other goods as aforesaid.

(3) Directions may be given under this section to any person whose business consists of or includes the manufacture, sale, repair or cleaning of containers, requiring the treatment of any infested container, or of any infested premises in which the business is carried on, in such manner as may be specified in the directions, and prohibiting the removal of any such container until it has been so treated.

(4) Where the Minister is satisfied that any food or container in the possession of a person carrying on any such business as is mentioned in subsection (2) or subsection (3) of this section is so infested that the infestation cannot reasonably be remedied by any form of treatment, he may give directions under this section to that person requiring him to destroy it within such time and by such means as may be specified in the directions.

[Prevention of Damage by Pests Act 1949, s 14.]

1. For penalty for non-compliance with directions, see s 17, post.

8–25362 15. Appeal against directions under section 14. (1) Where directions are given under the last foregoing section requiring the carrying out of any structural works, or the destruction of any food or container, any person who is aggrieved thereby may—

(*a*) in the case of directions requiring the carrying out of any structural works, within twenty-one days from the service of the directions;

(*b*) in the case of directions requiring the destruction of any food or container, within seven days from the service of the directions,

appeal[1] to a court of summary jurisdiction for the petty sessions area or place in which the works are required to be carried out or, as the case may be, in which the food or container is for the time being situated.

(2) Upon any such appeal the court, if satisfied that the directions are for any reason invalid, or that any requirement thereof is excessive or unreasonable, may quash or amend the directions, as the case may be, but in any other case shall dismiss the appeal:

Provided that if and so far as the appeal is based on the ground of some informality, defect or error in or in connection with the directions, the court shall dismiss the appeal if satisfied that the informality, defect or error was not a material one.

(3) Any directions given under the last foregoing section requiring the carrying out of any structural works, or the destruction of any food or container, shall include a statement of the right of appeal under this section, and of the time within which such an appeal may be brought.

(4) An appeal shall lie to the Crown Court from the decision of a court of summary jurisdiction under this section in respect of directions requiring the carrying out of any structural works.

[Prevention of Damage by Pests Act 1949, s 15, as amended by the Courts Act 1971, Sch 9 and the Access to Justice Act 1999, Sch 10.]

1. See Magistrates' Courts Rules 1981, r 34, in PART I: MAGISTRATES' COURTS, PROCEDURE, ante.

8–25363 16. Powers of Minister in case of failure to comply with directions. (1) Subject to the provisions of the last foregoing section with respect to appeals, if any person to whom directions are given by the Minister under section 14 of this Act fails to comply with any requirement of the directions within the period prescribed thereby, then, without prejudice to any proceedings which may be taken against him in respect of an offence under this Part of this Act, the Minister may by order authorise any person named in the order to take, on behalf of the person in default, such steps as the Minister considers necessary for securing compliance with that requirement.

(2) The amount of any expenses reasonably incurred by a person authorised as aforesaid in carrying out works under this section may be recovered by the Minister from the person in default.

(3) In proceedings for the recovery of any expenses under this section, it shall not be open to the defendant to raise by way of defence any question which he could have raised on an appeal under the last foregoing section.

[Prevention of Damage by Pests Act 1949, s 16.]

8–25364 17. Offences against Part II. Subject to the provisions of this Part of this Act with respect to appeals, any person who contravenes or fails to comply with this Part of this Act or any directions given thereunder shall be guilty of an offence and liable on summary conviction to a fine not exceeding **level 4** on the standard scale.

[Prevention of Damage by Pests Act 1949, s 17, as amended by the Criminal Justice Act 1982, ss 35, 38 and 46.]

8–25365 **18. Power of Minister to delegate to local authorities.** (1) The Minister may with the consent of any local authority for the purposes of Part I of this Act by order delegate to that authority any of his functions under this Part of this Act (except sub-section (3) of s 13 of this Act), subject to such restrictions and conditions as may be specified in the order.

(2) An order made under this section delegating functions to a local authority may direct that in such cases as may be prescribed by the order any notice of infestation required to be given under section 13 of this Act shall be given to the local authority instead of being given to the Minister.

(3) Any order under this section shall provide for the repayment by the Minister to the local authority of any expenses incurred by them in the performance of functions delegated by the order so far as those expenses are not otherwise recoverable under this Act.

(4) An order under this section may be revoked or varied by a subsequent order.*

[Prevention of Damage by Pests Act 1949, s 18.]

***Repealed in relation to England and Wales by the Statute Law (Repeals) Act 2004.**

PART III
SUPPLEMENTAL

8–25366 **19. Control of methods of destruction of pests, etc.** (1) The Minister may make regulations for controlling the methods for keeping down or destroying rats, mice, insects or mites which may be used by persons carrying on business in the provision of services for that purpose; and such regulations may be particular—

(*a*) approve different methods for use in different circumstances;

(*b*) prohibit the use by persons to whom the regulations apply of any method other than a method so approved.

(2) Any person who fails to comply with regulations made under this section shall be guilty of an offence and liable on summary conviction to a fine not exceeding **level 4** on the standard scale.*

[Prevention of Damage by Pests Act 1949, s 19, as amended by the Criminal Justice Act 1982, ss 35, 38 and 46.]

***Repealed in relation to England and Wales by the Statute Law (Repeals) Act 2004.**

8–25367 **22. Powers of entry.** (1) Any person duly authorised in writing by a local authority[1] for the purposes of Part I of this Act, or by a person empowered by the Minister[2] to exercise functions of a local authority under that Part, may, at any reasonable time, enter upon any land—

(*a*) for the purpose of carrying out any inspection required by the said Part I to be carried out by the local authority;

(*b*) for the purpose of ascertaining whether there is or has been, on or in connection with the land, any failure to comply with any requirement of the said Part I or of any notice served thereunder;

(*c*) for the purpose of taking any steps authorised by section 5 or section 6 of this Act to be taken by the local authority on or in relation to the land.

(2) Any person duly authorised in writing by the Minister, or by a local authority to whom functions of the Minister under Part II of this Act are delegated, may, at any reasonable time, enter upon any land—

(*a*) for the purpose of ascertaining whether there is or has been, on or in connection with the land or any vehicle thereon, any failure to comply with any requirement of the said Part II or of any directions given thereunder;

(*b*) for the purpose of taking any steps authorised to be taken on or in relation to the land under the said Part II by a person named in an order made by the Minister or by that authority thereunder,

and where any such person has entered on any premises for the purposes specified in paragraph (*a*) of this subsection, he may take samples of any food found on those premises.

(3) Any person authorised under this section to enter upon any land shall, if so required, produce evidence of his authority before so entering, and shall not demand admission as of right to any land which is occupied unless twenty-four hours' notice of the intended entry has been given to the occupier.

(4) Any person who wilfully obstructs the exercise of powers conferred by this section or by section 5, section 6(1) or section 16(1) of this Act shall be liable on summary conviction, to a fine not exceeding **level 1** on the standard scale.

(5) If any person who, in compliance with the provisions of this section, is admitted into a factory, workshop or work place, discloses to any person any information obtained by him therein as to any manufacturing process or trade secret, he shall, unless the disclosure is made in the course of performing his duty in connection with the purpose for which he was authorised to enter the premises, be liable on summary conviction to a fine not exceeding **level 3** on the standard scale or to imprisonment for a term not exceeding **three months**.

(6) If any land is damaged in the exercise of a power of entry conferred under this section,

compensation in respect of that damage may be recovered by any person interested in the land from the local authority on whose behalf the entry was effected, or from the Minister, as the case may be.
[Prevention of Damage by Pests Act 1949, s 22, as amended by the Pests Act 1954, s 5(3) and the Criminal Justice Act 1982, ss 35, 38 and 46.]

1. See s 1, ante.
2. "The Minister" means the Minister of Agriculture and Fisheries (s 28), now the Minister of Agriculture, Fisheries and Food (SI 1955/554) or the Secretary of State for Wales (SI 1978/272).

8–25368 26. Legal proceedings. (1) Proceedings for an offence under this Act shall not, in England and Wales, be instituted except by or with the consent of the Minister[1] or the local authority.

(2) Where an offence under this Act is committed by a body corporate, every person who, at the time of the commission of the offence, was a director, general manager, secretary or other similar officer of the body corporate, or was purporting to act in any such capacity, shall be deemed to be guilty of that offence unless he proves that it was committed without his consent or connivance and that he exercised any such diligence to prevent its commission as he ought to have exercised having regard to the nature of his functions in that capacity and to all the circumstances.

(3) For the purposes of the last foregoing subsection, the expression "director", in relation to any body corporate established by or under any enactment for the purpose of carrying on under national ownership any industry or part of an industry or undertaking, being a body corporate whose affairs are managed by the members thereof, means a member of that body.
[Prevention of Damage by Pests Act 1949, s 26.]

1. "The Minister" means the Minister of Agriculture and Fisheries (s 28), now the Minister of Agriculture, Fisheries and Food (SI 1955/554) or the Secretary of State for Wales (SI 1978/272).

Public Health Act 1961[1]

(9 & 10 Eliz 2 c 64)

PART II[2]
SANITATION AND BUILDINGS

Sewers, drains and sanitary conveniences

8–25570 17. Powers to repair drains etc and to remedy stopped-up drains etc. (1) If it appears to a local authority that a drain, private sewer, water-closet, waste pipe or soil pipe—

(*a*) is not sufficiently maintained and kept in good repair, and
(*b*) can be sufficiently repaired at a cost not exceeding £250,

the local authority may, after giving not less than seven days notice to the person or persons concerned, cause the drain, private sewer, water-closet or pipe to be repaired and, subject to subsections (7) and (8) below, recover[1] the expenses reasonably incurred in so doing, so far as they do not exceed £250, from the person or persons concerned, in such proportions, if there is more than one such person, as the local authority may determine.

(2) In subsection (1) above "person concerned" means—

(*a*) in relation to a water-closet, waste pipe or soil pipe, the owner or occupier of the premises on which it is situated, and
(*b*) in relation to a drain or private sewer, any person owning any premises drained by means of it and also, in the case of a sewer, the owner of the sewer.

(3) If it appears to a local authority that on any premises a drain, private sewer, water-closet, waste pipe or soil pipe is stopped up, they may by notice in writing require the owner or occupier of the premises to remedy the defect within forty-eight hours from the service of the notice.

(4) If a notice under subsection (3) of this section is not complied with, the local authority may themselves carry out the work necessary to remedy the defect and, subject to subsections (7) and (8) below, may recover the expenses reasonably incurred in so doing from the person on whom the notice was served.

(5) Where the expenses recoverable by a local authority under subsection (1) or (4) of this section do not exceed £10, the local authority may, if they think fit, remit the payment of the expenses.

(6) In proceedings to recover expenses under this section—

(*a*) where the expenses were incurred under subsection (1) of this section, the court—
  (i) shall inquire whether the local authority were justified in concluding that the drain, private sewer, water-closet, waste pipe or soil pipe was not sufficiently maintained and kept in good repair; and
  (ii) may inquire whether any apportionment of expenses by the local authority under that subsection was fair;
(*b*) where the expenses were incurred under subsection (4) of this section, the court may inquire—

(i) whether any requirement contained in a notice served under subsection (3) of this section was reasonable; and

(ii) whether the expenses ought to be borne wholly or in part by some person other than the defendant in the proceedings.

(7) Subject to subsection (8) below, the court may make such order concerning the expenses or their apportionment as appears to the court to be just.

(8) Where the court determines that the local authority were not justified in concluding that a drain, private sewer, water-closet, waste pipe or soil pipe was not sufficiently maintained and kept in good repair, the local authority shall not recover expenses incurred by them under subsection (1) of this section.

(9) The court shall not revise an apportionment unless it is satisfied that all persons affected by the apportionment or by an order made by virtue of subsection (6)(*b*)(ii) above have had notice of the proceedings and an opportunity of being heard.

(10) Subject to subsection (11) of this section, the provisions of subsection (1) of this section shall not authorise a local authority to carry out works on land which belongs to any statutory undertakers[2] and is held or used by them for the purposes of their undertaking.

(11) Subsection (10) of this section does not apply to houses, or to buildings used as offices or showrooms, other than buildings so used which form part of a railway station.

(12) The Secretary of State may by order made by statutory instrument increase any amount specified in this section.

(13) Nothing in an order made under subsection (12) of this section shall apply to a notice given under this section before the commencement of the order.

(14) A statutory instrument containing an order under subsection (12) of this section shall be subject to annulment in pursuance of a resolution of either House of Parliament.

(15) The provisions of this section shall be without prejudice to section 59 of the Building Act 1984 (which empowers a local authority to serve notices as regards defective drains).

[Public Health Act 1961, s 17, as substituted by the Local Government (Miscellaneous Provisions) Act 1982, s 27 and amended by the Building Act 1984, Sch 6.]

---

1. In accordance with the Public Health Act 1936, s 293, ante.
2. The National Rivers Authority, every water undertaker and every sewerage undertaker is deemed to be a statutory undertaker for the purposes of this Act (Water Act 1989, Sch 25, para 1).

8–25571 **22. Power to cleanse or repair drains.** A local authority may, on the application of the owner or occupier of any premises, undertake the cleansing or repair of any drains, water closets, sinks or gullies in or connected with the premises, and may recover[1] from the applicant such reasonable charge, if any, for so doing as they think fit.

[Public Health Act 1961, s 22.]

1. In accordance with the Public Health Act 1936, s 293, ante.

Accumulations of rubbish

8–25572 **34. Accumulations of rubbish.** (1) If it appears to a local authority that there is on any land in the open air in their area any rubbish which is seriously detrimental to the amenities of the neighbourhood, the local authority may, subject to the provisions of this section, take such steps for removing the rubbish as they may consider necessary in the interests of amenity.

(2) Not less than twenty-eight days before taking any action under this section, the local authority shall serve on the owner and occupier of the land a notice stating the steps which they propose to take and giving particulars of the following provisions of this subsection; and a person on whom the notice is served and any other person having an interest in the land may within twenty-eight days from the service of the notice—

(*a*) serve a counter-notice on the local authority stating that he intends to take those steps himself; or

(*b*) appeal to a magistrates' court[1] on the ground that the local authority were not justified in concluding that action should be taken under this section, or that the steps proposed to be taken are unreasonable.

(3) If a counter-notice is served under the last foregoing subsection, the local authority shall take no further action in the matter under this section unless the person who served the counter-notice either—

(*a*) fails within what seems to the local authority a reasonable time to begin to take the steps stated in the notice, or

(*b*) having begun to take those steps fails to make such progress towards their completion as seems to the local authority reasonable.

(4) If an appeal is brought under subsection (2) of this section, the local authority shall take no further action in the matter under this section until the appeal is finally determined or withdrawn;

and on the hearing of the appeal the court may direct the local authority to take no further action or may permit the local authority to take such steps as the court may direct or may dismiss the appeal.

(5) In this section "rubbish" means rubble, waste paper, crockery and metal, and any other kind of refuse (including organic matter), but does not include any material accumulated for, or in the course of, any business[2].

[Public Health Act 1961, s 34, as amended by the Civic Amenities Act 1967, s 26.]

1. In accordance with the Public Health Act 1936, s 300, ante.

Filthy or verminous premises or articles

8–25573 **36. Power to require vacation of premises during fumigation[1].** (1) If a local authority serve a notice under section 83(3) of the Public Health Act 1936, as amended by the last foregoing section[2], on the owner and occupier of any premises requiring that they shall be allowed to employ gas for the purpose of destroying vermin on the premises—

(*a*) the notice to the occupier may also require that the premises shall, as from such date as may be specified in the notice, be vacated until the local authority give the occupier further notice that the premises can safely be reoccupied; and

(*b*) the local authority may also serve notice on the occupiers of any other premises having any floor, wall or ceiling contiguous with the first-mentioned premises, or into which there is reason to apprehend that the gas may penetrate, requiring that those other premises shall be vacated as aforesaid.

(2) No person shall be required under this section to vacate any premises used for human habitation for any period unless alternative shelter or other accommodation has been provided for him by the local authority free of charge for that period; and any notice given under this section shall specify the alternative shelter or other accommodation so provided.

(3) A person on whom a notice is served under this section may within the period of seven days from the date on which the notice was served on him appeal to a magistrates' court[3], and the requirements included in the notice in pursuance of this section shall not take effect until the expiration of that period or, where an appeal is brought within that period, before the appeal is disposed of or withdrawn.

The provisions of this subsection as to the period within which an appeal shall be brought shall have effect notwithstanding anything in section 300(2) of the Public Health Act 1936, as applied to this Part of this Act.

(4) So much of subsection (2) of the said section 83 as imposes a penalty for failure to comply with the requirements of a notice under that section shall also apply to the requirements included in the notice by virtue of this section[4].

(5) The local authority shall defray any reasonable expenses incurred in removing from and returning to any premises in compliance with a notice served under paragraph (*b*) of subsection (1) of this section, and may, if they think fit, defray any such expenses incurred in compliance with a notice under paragraph (*a*) of that subsection.

[Public Health Act 1961, s 36.]

1. This section should be considered in conjunction with s 83 of the Public Health Act 1936, ante.
2. These amendments have been carried into the text of s 83, ante.
3. In accordance with the Public Health Act 1936, s 300, ante.
4. Section 83(2) provides for a fine not exceeding **level 1** on the standard scale and a further fine not exceeding **£2** for each day on which the offence continues after conviction.

8–25574 **37. Prohibition of sale of verminous articles.** (1) No dealer shall—

(*a*) prepare for sale, or
(*b*) sell or offer or expose for sale, or
(*c*) deposit with any person for sale or preparation for sale,

any household article[1] if it is to his knowledge verminous, or if by taking reasonable precautions he could have known it to be verminous.

(2) If a household article which is verminous is on any premises—

(*a*) being prepared by a dealer for sale, or
(*b*) offered or exposed by a dealer for sale, or
(*c*) deposited by a dealer with any person for sale or preparation for sale,

the medical officer of health or public health inspector may cause the article to be disinfested or destroyed as the case may require, and if necessary for that purpose to be removed from the premises; and the local authority may recover from the dealer the expenses[2] reasonably incurred by the local authority in taking any action under this subsection.

(3) If any person contravenes the provisions of subsection (1) of this section he shall be liable to a fine not exceeding **level 1** on the standard scale[3].

(4) In this section—

(*a*) "dealer" means a person who trades or deals in any household articles;
(*b*) "household article" means an article of furniture, bedding or clothing or any similar article;
(*c*) references to preparation for sale do not include references to disinfestation.
[Public Health Act 1961, s 37, as amended by the Criminal Justice Act 1982, ss 38 and 46.]

1. Defined in sub-s (4), infra.
2. In accordance with the Public Health Act 1936, s 293, ante.
3. Prosecution will be under the Magistrates' Courts Act 1980, consolidating the Summary Jurisdiction Acts (Public Health Act 1936, s 296).

PART IV
STREETS AND PUBLIC PLACES[1]
Streets

8–25575 **45. Attachment of street lamps to buildings.** (1) Subject to the provisions of this section, a county council, local authority or parish council or parish meeting (hereafter in this section referred to as a "street lighting authority") may affix to any building such lamps, brackets, pipes, electric lines and apparatus (hereafter in this section referred to as "attachments") as may be required for the purposes of street lighting.

(2) A street lighting authority shall not under this section affix attachments to a building without the consent of the owner[2] of the building:

Providing that, where in the opinion of the street lighting authority any consent required under this subsection is unreasonably withheld, they may apply to the appropriate authority[3], who may either allow the attachments subject to such conditions, if any, as to rent or otherwise as the appropriate authority thinks fit, or disallow the attachments.

(3) Where any attachments have been affixed to a building under this section and the person who gave his consent under subsection (2) of this section, or who was the owner of the building when the attachments were allowed by the appropriate authority, ceases to be the owner of the building, the subsequent owner may give to the street lighting authority notice requiring them to remove the attachments; and subject to the provisions of this subsection, the street lighting authority shall comply with the requirements within three months after the service of the notice:

Provided that, where in the opinion of the street lighting authority any such requirement is unreasonable, they may apply to the appropriate authority[3] who may either annul the notice subject to such conditions, if any, as to rent or otherwise as the appropriate authority thinks fit or confirm the notice subject to such extension, if any, of the said period of three months as the appropriate authority thinks fit.

(4) Where any attachments have been affixed to a building under this section, the owner of the building may give the street lighting authority by whom they were affixed not less than fourteen days notice requiring them at their own expense temporarily to remove the attachments where necessary during any reconstruction or repair of the building.

(5) Where attachments are affixed to a building under this section, the street lighting authority shall have the right as against any person having an interest in the building to alter or remove them, or to repair or maintain them.

(6) (*Consequential damage to building is recoverable by owner. Disputes relating thereto are determined by Lands Tribunal.*)

(7) A street lighting authority shall not do anything under this section which would, to their knowledge, be in contravention of a building preservation order under s 29 of the Town and Country Planning Act 1947[4].

(8) In this section "appropriate authority" means a magistrates' court, except that in relation to buildings of the descriptions in the Fourth Schedule to this Act it has the meaning there given.

(9) In this section—

"building" includes a structure and a bridge or aqueduct over a street;

"owner"—

(*a*) in relation to a building occupied under a tenancy for a term of years whereof five years or more remain unexpired, means the occupier of the building, and
(*b*) in relation to any other building, has the same meaning as in the Public Health Act 1936[5], and

"owned" shall be construed accordingly;

"street lighting" includes the lighting of markets and public buildings under s 161 of the Public Health Act 1875 (which relates to the powers conferred on urban authorities within the meaning of that Act), and the lighting of public places under s 3 of the Parish Councils Act 1957,

and the definitions in this section shall apply for the purposes of the Fourth Schedule of this Act.

(10) Section 5 of the Parish Councils Act 1957 (which contains provisions as to the consents required for the exercise of the powers of street lighting conferred by that Act), shall not apply in relation to the affixing after the commencement of this Act of any attachments to a building within the meaning of this section but those powers shall not be taken to authorise anything to be done without consent for which consent is required by this section.
[Public Health Act 1961, s 45.]

1. By s 1(4) of the Act, certain provisions of Pt XII of the Public Health Act 1936, apply to this Part. These include ss 283–285, 288, 304, 305, ante, and s 343, Interpretation. Other provisions of the 1936 Act are specifically applied in the several sections contained in this Part of the Act.
2. In this section "owner" is defined by sub-s (9) thereof, infra.
3. Except in relation to buildings specified in the Sch 4, this expression means a magistrates' court (sub-s (8)).
4. See now the Planning (Listed Buildings and Conservation Areas) Act 1990, post.

PART VI
MISCELLANEOUS[1]

8–25577 73. Derelict petrol tanks. (1) Where a fixed tank or other fixed container which has been used for the storage of petroleum spirit[2], and is no longer used for that purpose, is kept on any premises, the occupier of the premises shall take all such steps as may be reasonably necessary to prevent danger from the container.

(2) An officer of the local authority[3] duly authorised by them may, on producing, if so required, some duly authenticated document showing his authority, require the occupier of premises on which there is any tank or other container to which subsection (1) of this section applies to show it to him and permit him to ascertain whether steps have been taken to comply with the provision, of this section.

(3) The local authority[3] may by notice require the occupier of the premises to take any steps reasonably necessary to prevent danger from any tank or other container to which subsection (1) of this section applies.

(4) The provisions of Part XII of the Public Health Act 1936, with respect to appeals against, and the enforcement of, notices requiring the execution of works shall apply in relation to any notice under subsection (3) of this section, and shall so apply as if this section were contained in that Act.

(5) This section shall apply in relation to premises which are unoccupied with the substitution for the references to the occupier of the premises of references to their owner (as defined in section 343(1) of the Public Health Act 1936); and this section shall not apply to premises situated within the jurisdiction of a harbour authority (as defined in section 23 of the Petroleum (Consolidation) Act 1928[4]).

(6) In this section the expression "petroleum spirit" has the same meaning as in the said Act of 1928[4].

[Public Health Act 1961, s 73.]

1. By s 1(4) of the Act, certain provisions of Pt XII of the Public Health Act 1936, apply to this Part. These include ss 283–285, 288, 304, 305, ante, and s 343, Interpretation. Other provisions of the 1936 Act are specifically applied in the several sections contained in this Part of the Act.
2. See sub-s (6), infra.
3. The functions of a local authority under s 73 of this Act shall be functions—
   (*a*) in Greater London or a metropolitan county, of the fire authority;
   (*b*) elsewhere, of the county council,

   and references in the section, and in the provisions of the Act applied by it, to a local authority shall be construed accordingly.
   (Local Government Act 1985, Sch 11, para 5).
4. See this PART: title HEALTH AND SAFETY, ante.

8–25578 Additional byelaws[1]. A local authority may make byelaws as to pleasure fairs and roller skating rinks; as to seaside pleasure boats[2]; and as to hairdressers and barbers.

[Public Health Act 1961, ss 75–77, as amended by the Local Government (Miscellaneous Provisions) Act 1976, s 22—summarised.]

1. The power to make byelaws under s 75 as to pleasure fairs replaces that under s 38 of the Public Health Acts Amendment Act 1890, without prejudice to byelaws in force thereunder. So far as penalties are concerned, the Criminal Law Act 1977, s 31(4) and the Criminal Justice Act 1982, s 46, provides that any byelaws under s 75 of the Public Health Act 1961 relating to pleasure fairs and roller skating rinks, and any byelaws under s 76 of the Public Health Act 1961 relating to seaside pleasure boats, may provide for a fine on summary conviction not exceeding **level 3** on the standard scale and in the case of a continuing offence a further fine of **£5** a day. If a byelaw in force at 17th July 1978 specifies a maximum fine of **£20** or less, it shall have effect as if it specified **level 3** on the standard scale (maximum daily fines, if any, remaining unchanged). For penalties for other byelaws, see s 237 of the Local Government Act 1972, ante, and notes thereto.
2. For extension of power to make byelaws about boating, see s 17 of the Local Government (Miscellaneous Provisions) Act 1976, post.

8–25579 81. Summary recovery of damages for negligence. Damages recoverable by a county council, local authority or parish council or parish meeting for damage caused by negligence to any lamp, lamp-post, notice board, fence, rail, post, shelter or other apparatus or equipment provided by them in a street or public place shall, if the amount thereof does not exceed **£20**, be recoverable summarily as a civil debt[1].

[Public Health Act 1961, s 81, as amended by the London Government Act 1963, Sch 11 and the Local Government Act 1985, Sch 17.]

1. Section 58 of the Magistrates' Courts Act 1980 in PART I: MAGISTRATES' COURTS, PROCEDURE, ante, will apply.

Section 45

SCHEDULE 4

ATTACHMENT OF STREET LIGHTING EQUIPMENT TO CERTAIN BUILDINGS

8–25580 As regards buildings of the descriptions in the first column of the following Table the appropriate authority for the purposes of s 45 of this Act shall be the person specified in the second column of that Table (and not a magistrates' court).

TABLE

A building which is for the time being included in a list published under section 12 of the Ancient Monuments Consolidation and Amendment Act 1913.	The Secretary of State.
A building which is included in a list compiled or approved under section 1 of the Planning (Listed Buildings and Conservation Areas) Act 1990.	The Secretary of State.
A building owned by railway, canal, dock, harbour or inland navigation undertakers.	The Secretary of State.
A building owned by electricity or gas undertakers[1] or the British Coal Corporation.*	The Secretary of State.
A building owned by statutory water undertakers.	The Secretary of State.
A building forming part of an aerodrome licensed under the Civil Aviation Act 1949, or any enactment repealed by that Act.	The Secretary of State.
A building owned by a county council, local authority or parish council or parish meeting who are not the street lighting authority concerned.	The Secretary of State.
A building owned by a development corporation established under the New Towns Act 1946, or the Commission for the New Towns established under the New Towns Act 1959.	The Secretary of State.
A building owned by a universal service provider (within the meaning of the Postal Services Act 2000) in connection with the provision of a universal postal service (within the meaning of that Act).	The Secretary of State.
A building owned by British Telecommunications.	The Secretary of State.

[Public Health Act 1961, Sch 4, as amended by the Post Office Act 1969, Sch 4, the Town and Country Planning Act 1971, Sch 23, the British Telecommunications Act 1981, Sch 3, the Planning (Consequential Provisions) Act 1990, Sch 2, the Coal Industry Act 1994, Sch 9 and SI 2001/1149.]

***Prospectively repealed by the Coal Industry Act 1994, s 67, Sch 9, para 7, Sch 11, Part IV, when in force.**

1. The reference to "gas undertakers" shall have effect as a reference to a public gas transporter (Gas Act 1995, Sch 4).

Prevention of Oil Pollution Act 1971[1]

(1971 c 60)

General provisions for preventing oil pollution

8–25590 1. Discharge of certain oils into sea outside territorial waters. (1) (*Repealed*).

(2) This section applies—

(*a*) to crude oil, fuel oil and lubricating oil; and

(*b*) to heavy diesel oil, as defined by regulations made under this section by the Secretary of State[2];

and shall also apply to any other description of oil which may be specified by regulations[3] made by the Secretary of State, having regard to the provisions of any Convention accepted by Her Majesty's Government in the United Kingdom in so far as it relates to the prevention of pollution of the sea by oil or having regard to the persistent character of oil of that description and the likelihood that it would cause pollution if discharged from a ship into any part of the sea outside the territorial waters of the United Kingdom.

(3)–(4) *Repealed.*

[Prevention of Oil Pollution Act 1971, s 1, as amended by SI 1983/1106.]

1. This Act consolidated the Oil in Navigable Waters Acts 1955 to 1971 and s 5 of the Continental Shelf Act 1964 with effect from 1 March 1973. For other statutory control see the Merchant Shipping Act 1995, in PART VII: TRANSPORT, ante.

2. See SI 1967/710 which has effect as if made hereunder by reason of s 33 (repeals and savings).

3. See the Prevention of Oil Pollution Act 1971 (Application of Section 1) Regulations 1984, SI 1984/1684, which provide that s 1 of the Act shall apply to discharges into the sea otherwise than from ships.

8–25591 **2. Discharge of oil into United Kingdom waters.** (1) If any oil or mixture containing oil is discharged as mentioned in the following paragraphs into waters to which this section applies, then, subject to the provisions of this Act, the following shall be guilty of an offence[1], that is to say—

(*a*)–(*b*) *Repealed*;

(*c*) if the discharge is from a place on land, the occupier of that place, unless he proves[2] that the discharge was caused as mentioned in paragraph (*d*) of this subsection;

(*d*) if the discharge is from a place on land and is caused by the act of a person who is in that place without the permission (express or implied) of the occupier, that person;

(*e*) if the discharge takes place otherwise than as mentioned in the preceding paragraphs and is the result of any operations for the exploration of the sea-bed and subsoil or the exploitation of their natural resources, the person carrying on the operations.

(2) This section applies to the following waters, that is to say—

(*a*) the whole of the sea within the seaward limits of the territorial waters of the United Kingdom; and

(*b*) all other waters (including inland waters) which are within those limits and are navigable by sea-going ships.

(3) In this Act "place on land" includes anything resting on the bed or shore of the sea, or of any other waters to which this section applies, and also includes anything afloat (other than a vessel) if it is anchored or attached to the bed or shore of the sea or of any such waters; and "occupier", in relation to any such thing as is mentioned in the preceding provisions of this subsection, if it has no occupier, means the owner thereof, and, in relation to a railway wagon or road vehicle, means the person in charge of the wagon or vehicle and not the occupier of the land on which the wagon or vehicle stands.

(4) A person guilty of an offence under this section shall be liable on summary conviction to a fine not exceeding **£50,000** or on conviction on indictment to a **fine**[4].

[Prevention of Oil Pollution Act 1971, s 2, as amended by SI 1983/1106, the Prevention of Oil Pollution Act 1986, s 1 and the Merchant Shipping Act 1995, Sch 12.]

---

1. See special defences in ss 5–8, post, provisions relating to the prosecution of offences in s 19, post, and enforcement and application of fines (which can be used to pay expenses and make good damage) in s 20, post.
2. On a preponderance of probabilities: *R v Carr-Briant* [1943] KB 607, [1943] 2 All ER 156, 107 JP 167.
3. The 1986 Act provides that regs 12 and 13 of the Merchant Shipping (Prevention of Oil Pollution) Regulations 1983, SI 1983/1398 as amended accordingly cease to apply to such discharges, save for the operation of regs 12(4) and 13(4) (discharge of substances in quantities or concentrations hazardous to the marine environment).
4. For procedure in respect of an offence triable either way, see the Magistrates' Courts Act 1980, ss 17A–21 in PART I: MAGISTRATES' COURTS, PROCEDURE, ante.

8–25592 **3. Discharge of certain oils from pipe-lines or as the result of exploration etc in designated areas.** (1) If any oil to which section 1 of this Act applies, or any mixture containing such oil, is discharged into any part of the sea—

(*a*) from a pipe-line; or

(*b*) (otherwise than from a ship) as the result of any operation for the exploration of the sea-bed and subsoil or the exploitation of their natural resources in a designated area,

then, subject to the following provisions of this Act, the owner of the pipe-line or, as the case may be, the person carrying on the operations shall be guilty of an offence[1] unless the discharge was from a place in his occupation and he proves[2] that it was due to the act of a person who was there without his permission (express or implied).

(2) In this section "designated area" means an area for the time being designated by an Order made under section 1 of the Continental Shelf Act 1964.

(3) A person guilty of an offence under this section shall be liable on summary conviction to a fine not exceeding **£50,000** or on conviction on indictment to a **fine**[3].

[Prevention of Oil Pollution Act 1971, s 3.]

---

1. See note 1 to s 2, ante.
2. On a preponderance of probabilities: *R v Carr-Briant* [1943] KB 607, [1943] 2 All ER 156, 107 JP 167.
3. For procedure in respect of an offence triable either way, see the Magistrates' Courts Act 1980, ss 17A–21 in PART I: MAGISTRATES' COURTS, PROCEDURE, ante.

8–25593 **4.** *Repealed.*

8–25593A **5. Defences of owner or master, charged with offence under section 1 or section 2.** (1) Where a person is charged with an offence under section 1 of this Act, or is charged with an offence under section 2 of this Act as the owner or master of a vessel, it shall be a defence to prove that the oil or mixture was discharged for the purpose of securing the safety of any vessel, or of preventing damage to any vessel or cargo, or of saving life, unless the court is satisfied that the discharge of the oil or mixture was not necessary for that purpose or was not a reasonable step to take in the circumstances.

(2) Where a person is charged as mentioned in subsection (1) of this section, it shall also be a defence to prove—

(*a*) that the oil or mixture escaped in consequence of damage to the vessel, and that as soon as practicable after the damage occurred all reasonable steps were taken for preventing, or (if it could not be prevented) for stopping or reducing, the escape of the oil or mixture, or

(*b*) that the oil or mixture escaped by reason of leakage, that neither the leakage nor any delay in discovering it was due to any want of reasonable care, and that as soon as practicable after the escape was discovered all reasonable steps were taken for stopping or reducing it.*

[Prevention of Oil Pollution Act 1971, s 5.]

***The repeal of s 5 by the Merchant Shipping Act 1995, Sch 12 does not apply so far as this section relates to s 2(1) and (3) of this Act.**

8–25594 **6. Defences of other persons charged with offences under section 2 or section 3.** (1) Where a person is charged, in respect of the escape of any oil or mixture containing oil, with an offence under section 2 or 3 of this Act—

(*a*) as the occupier of a place on land; or*

(*b*) as a person carrying on operations for the exploration of the seabed and subsoil or the exploitation of their natural resources; or

(*c*) as the owner of a pipe-line,

it shall be a defence to prove that neither the escape nor any delay in discovering it was due to any want of reasonable care and that as soon as practicable after it was discovered all reasonable steps were taken for stopping or reducing it.

(2) Where a person is charged with an offence under section 2 of this Act in respect of the discharge of a mixture containing oil from a place on land, it shall also, subject to subsection (3) of this section, be a defence to prove—

(*a*) that the oil was contained in an effluent produced by operations for the refining of oil;

(*b*) that it was not reasonably practicable to dispose of the effluent otherwise than by discharging it into waters to which that section applies; and

(*c*) that all reasonably practicable steps had been taken for eliminating oil from the effluent.

(3) If it is proved that, at a time to which the charge relates, the surface of the waters into which the mixture was discharged from the place on land, or land adjacent to those waters, was fouled by oil, subsection (2) of this section shall not apply unless the court is satisfied that the fouling was not caused, or contributed to, by oil contained in any effluent discharged at or before that time from that place.

[Prevention of Oil Pollution Act 1971, s 6, as amended by the Merchant Shipping Act 1955, Sch 12.]

***The repeal of sub-s (1)(*a*) by the Merchant Shipping Act 1995, Sch 12 does not apply so far as this subsection relates to s 2(1) and (3) of this Act.**

8–25595 **7. Protection of acts done in exercise of certain powers of harbour authorities etc.** (1) Where any oil, or mixture containing oil, is discharged in consequence of—

(*a*) the exercise of any power conferred by sections 530 to 532 of the Merchant Shipping Act 1894 (which relate to the removal of wrecks by harbour, conservancy and lighthouse authorities); or

(*b*) the exercise, for the purpose of preventing an obstruction or danger to navigation, of any power to dispose of sunk, stranded or abandoned vessels which is exercisable by a harbour authority under any local enactment;

and apart from this subsection the authority exercising the power, or a person employed by or acting on behalf of the authority, would be guilty of an offence under section 1 or section 2 of this Act in respect of that discharge, the authority or person shall not be convicted of that offence unless it is shown that they or he failed to take such steps (if any) as were reasonable in the circumstances for preventing, stopping or reducing the discharge.

(2) Subsection (1) of this section shall apply to the exercise of any power conferred by section 13 of the Dockyard Ports Regulation Act 1865 (which relates to the removal of obstructions to dockyard ports) as it applies to the exercise of any such power as is mentioned in paragraph (*a*) of that subsection, and shall, as so applying, have effect as if references to the authority exercising the power were references to the Queen's harbour master for the port in question.*

[Prevention of Oil Pollution Act 1971, s 7.]

***The repeal of s 7 by the Merchant Shipping Act 1995, Sch 12 does not apply so far as this section relates to s 2(1) and (3) of this Act.**

8–25596 **11. Duty to report discharge of oil into waters of harbours.** (1) If any oil or mixture containing oil—

(*a*) (*Repealed*).
(*b*) (*Repealed*).
(*c*) is found to be escaping or to have escaped into any such waters from a place on land;

the owner or master of the vessel, or the occupier of the place on land, as the case may be, shall forthwith report the occurrence to the harbour master, or, if the harbour has no harbour master, to the harbour authority.

(2) A report made under subsection (1) of this section by the owner or master of a vessel shall state whether the occurrence falls within paragraph (*a*) or paragraph (*b*) of that subsection.

(3) If a person fails to make a report as required by this section he shall be liable on summary conviction to a fine not exceeding **level 5** on the standard scale.

[Prevention of Oil Pollution Act 1971, s 11, as amended by the Merchant Shipping Act 1979, Sch 6, Criminal Justice Act 1982, s 46 and the Merchant Shipping Act 1995, Sch 12.]

8–25596A 11A. Certain provisions not to apply where a discharge or escape is authorised under Part I of the Environmental Protection Act 1990. (1) The provisions of sections 2(1) and 3(1) of this Act shall not apply to any discharge which is made under, and the provisions of section 11(1) of this Act shall not apply to any escape which is authorised by, an authorisation granted under Part I of the Environmental Protection Act 1990* or a permit granted under section 2 of the Pollution Prevention and Control Act 1999.

(2) This section does not extend to Northern Ireland.

[Prevention of Oil Pollution Act 1971, s 11A, as inserted by the Environment Act 1995, Sch 22 and amended by the Pollution Prevention and Control Act 1999, Sch 2.]

***Section 11A(1) is further amended by the Pollution Prevention and Control Act 1999, Sch 3, when in force.**

8–25597 18. Powers of inspection[1]. (1) The Secretary of State may appoint any person as an inspector to report to him—

(*a*) whether the prohibitions, restrictions and obligations imposed by virtue of this Act (including prohibitions so imposed by the creation of offences under any provision of this Act other than section 3) have been complied with;
(*b*) what measures (other than measures made obligatory by regulations made under section 4 of this Act) have been taken to prevent the escape of oil and mixtures containing oil;
(*c*) whether the oil reception facilities provided in harbours are adequate;

and any such inspector may be so appointed to report either in a particular case or in a class of cases specified in his appointment.

(2) Every surveyor of ships shall be taken to be a person appointed generally under the preceding subsection to report to the Secretary of State in every kind of case falling within that subsection.

(3) Sections 27 and 28(1), (3) and (4) of the Merchant Shipping Act 1979 (powers of inspectors) shall apply to persons appointed or taken to be appointed under subsection (1) of this section as it applies to the inspectors referred to in that section and shall, as so applying, have effect as if—

(*a*) any reference to a ship included any vessel, any reference to the Merchant Shipping Acts (except the second reference in sub-paragraph (iii) of section 27(1)(*h*)) were a reference to this Act and the reference in that sub-paragraph to regulations were omitted;
(*b*) any power under that section to inspect premises included power to inspect any apparatus used for transferring oil.

(4) (*Repealed*).

(5) Any power of an inspector, under section 27 as so applied, to require the production of any oil record book required to be carried or records required to be kept in pursuance of regulations made under section 17 of this Act shall include power to copy any entry therein and require the master to certify the copy as a true copy of the entry.

(6) Without prejudice to any powers exercisable by virtue of the preceding provisions of this section, in the case of a vessel which is for the time being in a harbour in the United Kingdom the harbour master, and any other person appointed by the Secretary of State under this subsection (either generally or in relation to a particular vessel), shall have power—

(*a*) to go on board and inspect the vessel or any part thereof, or any of the machinery, boats, equipment or articles on board the vessel, for the purpose of ascertaining the circumstances relating to an alleged discharge of oil or a mixture containing oil from the vessel into the waters of the harbour;
(*b*) to require the production of any oil record book required to be carried or records required to be kept in pursuance of regulations made under section 17 of this Act; and
(*c*) to copy any entry in any such book or record and require the master to certify the copy as a true copy of the entry.

(7) A person exercising any powers conferred by subsection (6) of this section shall not unnecessarily detain or delay the vessel from proceeding on any voyage.

(8) If any person fails to comply with any requirement duly made in pursuance of paragraph (*b*) or paragraph (*c*) of subsection (6) of this section, he shall be liable on summary conviction to a fine not exceeding **level 3** on the standard scale; and if any person wilfully obstructs a person acting in the exercise of any power conferred by virtue of this section and the obstruction is not punishable by virtue of the said section 28(1), he shall be liable on summary conviction to a fine not exceeding **level 4** on the standard scale.

[Prevention of Oil Pollution Act 1971, s 18, as amended by the Merchant Shipping Act 1979, s 28 and Schs 6 and 7, the Criminal Justice Act 1982, s 46 and the Merchant Shipping Act 1995, Sch 12.]

1. Section 18 is repealed by the Merchant Shipping (Registration, etc) Act 1993, Sch 5 except in its application to ss 2(1) and 3. For the purposes of the Prevention of Oil Pollution Act 1971 other than ss 2(1) and 3 see the Merchant Shipping Act 1894, s 728 as modified by the Merchant Shipping (Registration, etc) Act 1993, Sch 4. For the purposes of the Act other than ss 2(1) and 3 the powers of inspectors and harbour masters are modified by the Merchant Shipping (Registration, etc) Act 1993, Sch 4.

8–25598 19. Prosecutions. (1) Proceedings for an offence under this Act may, in England or Wales, be brought only—

(*a*) by or with the consent of the Attorney General[1], or
(*b*) if the offence is one to which subsection (2) of this section applies, by the harbour authority, or
(*c*) unless the offence is one mentioned in paragraph (*b*), (*c*) or (*d*) of subsection (2) of this section, by the Secretary of State or a person authorised by any general or special direction of the Secretary of State.

(2) This subsection applies to the following offences—

(*a*) *Repealed.*
(*b*) *Repealed.*
(*c*) any offence under section 17 of this Act relating to the keeping of records of the transfer of oil within such a harbour; and
(*d*) any offence under section 18 of this Act in respect of a failure to comply with a requirement of a harbour master, or in respect of obstruction of a harbour master acting in the exercise of any power conferred by virtue of that section.

(3) The preceding provisions of this section shall apply in relation to any part of a dockyard port within the meaning of the Dockyard Ports Regulation Act 1865 as follows, that is to say—

(*a*) if that part is comprised in a harbour in the United Kingdom, the reference to the harbour authority shall be construed as including a reference to the Queen's harbour master for the port;
(*b*) if that part is not comprised in a harbour in the United Kingdom, the references to such a harbour shall be construed as references to such a dockyard port and the reference to the harbour authority as a reference to the Queen's harbour master for the port.

(4) [2].

(4A) Any document required or authorised, by virtue of any statutory provision, to be served on a foreign company for the purposes of the institution of, or otherwise in connection with, proceedings for an offence under section 2(2A) of this Act alleged to have been committed by the company as the owner of a vessel shall be treated as duly served on that company if the document is served on the master of the vessel; and any person authorised to serve any document for the purposes of the institution of, or otherwise in connection with, proceedings for an offence under this Act (whether or not in pursuance of the foregoing provisions of this subsection) shall, for that purpose, have the right to go on board the vessel in question.

(4B) In subsection (4A) of this section a "foreign company" means a company or body which is not one to whom any of the following provisions applies—

(*a*) sections 695 and 725 of the Companies Act 1985;
(*b*) Articles 645 and 673 of the Companies (Northern Ireland) Order 1986,

so as to authorise the service of the document in question under any of those provisions.

(5) [3]

(6) If a local fisheries committee constituted by an order made, or having effect as if made, under section 1 of the Sea Fisheries Regulation Act 1966 or any of its officers is authorised in that behalf under subsection (1) of this section, the committee may institute proceedings for any offence under this Act committed within the district of the committee.

(7) The preceding provisions of this section do not apply in relation to an offence under section 3 of this Act, but proceedings for such an offence may—

(*a*) in England and Wales, be brought only by or with the consent of the Director of Public Prosecutions; and
(*b*) *Northern Ireland*;

and any such proceedings may be taken, and the offence may for all incidental purposes be treated as having been committed, in any place in the United Kingdom.

(8) Where a body corporate is guilty of an offence under section 3 of this Act and the offence is proved to have been committed with the consent or connivance of, or to be attributable to any neglect on the part of, any director, manager, secretary or other similar officer of the body corporate or any person who was purporting to act in any such capacity he, as well as the body corporate, shall be guilty of the offence and shall be liable to be proceeded against and punished accordingly.

In this subsection, "director" in relation to a body corporate established for the purpose of carrying on under national ownership any industry or part of an industry or undertaking, being a body corporate whose affairs are managed by its members, means a member of that body corporate.
[Prevention of Oil Pollution Act 1971, s 19, as amended by the Environmental Protection Act 1990, s 148 and Sch 14 and the Merchant Shipping Act 1995, Sch 12.]

1. See PART I: MAGISTRATES' COURTS, PROCEDURE, **1–380 Criminal prosecutions**, ante.

2. The time limit provisions of ss 274 and 275 of the Merchant Shipping Act 1995 apply in place of those previous contained in sub-s (4) (Merchant Shipping (Registration, etc) Act 1993, Sch 4).

3. The jurisdiction provisions of s 279 of the Merchant Shipping Act 1995 shall apply in place of those previously contained in s 19(5) (Merchant Shipping (Registration, etc) Act 1993, Sch 4).

8–25599 29. Interpretation. (1) In this Act—

"harbour authority" and "harbour in the United Kingdom," have the meanings assigned to them by section 8(2) of this Act;

"harbour master" includes a dock master or pier master, and any person specially appointed by a harbour authority for the purpose of enforcing the provisions of this Act in relation to the harbour;

"local enactment" means a local or private Act, or an order confirmed by Parliament or brought into operation in accordance with special parliamentary procedure;

"oil" means oil of any description and includes spirit produced from oil of any description, and also includes coal tar;

"oil reception facilities" has the meaning assigned to it by section 9(1) of this Act;

"oil residues" means any waste consisting of, or arising from, oil or a mixture containing oil;

"petroleum-spirit" has the same meaning as in the Petroleum (Consolidation) Act 1928;

"place on land" has the meaning assigned to it by section 2(3) of this Act;

"sea" includes any estuary or arm of the sea;

"transfer", in relation to oil, means transfer in bulk.

(2) Any reference in any provision of this Act to a mixture containing oil shall be construed as a reference to any mixture of oil (or, as the case may be, of oil of a description referred to in that provision) with water or with any other substance.*

(3) Any reference in the provisions of this Act other than section 11 to the discharge of oil or a mixture containing oil, or to its being discharged, from a vessel, place or thing, except where the reference is to its being discharged for a specified purpose, includes a reference to the escape of the oil or mixture, or (as the case may be) to its escaping, from that vessel, place or thing.

(4) *Repealed.*

(5) *Repealed.*

(6) *Repealed.*

(7) Except in so far as the context otherwise requires, any reference in this Act to an enactment shall be construed as a reference to that enactment as amended by or under any other enactment.
[Prevention of Oil Pollution Act 1971, s 29, as amended by the Merchant Shipping Act 1995, Sch 12.]

***The repeal of s 29(2) by the Merchant Shipping Act 1995, Sch 12 does not apply so far as this subsection relates to s 2(1) and (3) of this Act.**

8–25600 31. Application to hovercraft. The enactments and instruments with respect to which provision may be made by an Order[1] in Council under section 1(1)(*h*) of the Hovercraft Act 1968 shall include this Act and any instrument made under it.
[Prevention of Oil Pollution Act 1971, s 31.]

1. The Hovercraft (Application of Enactments) Order 1989, SI 1989/1350, applies ss 2(2A), (2B) and (4), 5, 7, 11, 20, 23, 24 and 30 in relation to hovercraft subject to modifications contained in art 3 of the Order.

8–25601 32. Saving for other restrictions, rights of action etc. Subject to section 33 of the Interpretation Act 1889[1] (offence under two or more laws) nothing in this Act shall affect any restriction imposed by or under any other enactment, whether contained in a public general Act or in a local or private Act, or shall derogate from any right of action or other remedy (whether civil or criminal) in proceedings instituted otherwise than under this Act.
[Prevention of Oil Pollution Act 1971, s 32.]

1. Now s 18 of the Interpretation Act 1978.

Control of Pollution Act 1974

(1974 c 40)

PART I[1]

WASTE ON LAND

Licensing of disposal of controlled waste

8–25811 **3. Prohibition of unlicensed disposal of waste[2].** (1) Except in prescribed[3] cases, a person shall not—

(*a*) deposit[4] controlled waste[5] on any land[6] or cause or knowingly permit controlled waste to be deposited on any land; or

(*b*) use any plant or equipment, or cause or knowingly permit any plant or equipment to be used, for the purpose of disposing of controlled waste[3] or of dealing in a prescribed manner with controlled waste,

unless the land[6] on which the waste[7] is deposited or, as the case may be, which forms the site of the plant or equipment is occupied by the holder of a licence issued in pursuance of section 5 of this Act (in this Part of this Act referred to as a "disposal licence") which authorises the deposit or use in question and the deposit or use is in accordance with the conditions, if any, specified in the licence[8].

(2) Except in a case falling within the following subsection, a person who contravenes any of the provisions of the preceding subsection shall, subject to subsection (4) of this section, be guilty of an offence[9] and liable on summary conviction to a fine of an amount not exceeding the statutory maximum or on conviction on indictment to imprisonment for a term not exceeding two years or a fine or both.

(3) A person who contravenes paragraph (*a*) of subsection (1) of this section in a case where—

(*a*) the waste in question is of a kind which is poisonous, noxious or polluting[10]; and

(*b*) its presence on the land is likely to give rise to an environmental hazard[10]; and

(*c*) it is deposited on the land in such circumstances or for such a period that whoever deposited it there may reasonably be assumed to have abandoned it there or to have brought it there for the purpose of its being disposed of (whether by himself or others) as waste[10],

shall, subject to the following subsection, be guilty of an offence[11] and liable on summary conviction to imprisonment for a term not exceeding six months or a fine not exceeding the statutory maximum or both or on conviction on indictment to imprisonment for a term not exceeding five years or a fine or both.

(4) It shall be a defence for a person charged with an offence under this section to prove—

(*a*) that he—

(i) took care to inform himself, from persons who were in a position to provide the information, as to whether the deposit or use to which the charge relates would be in contravention of subsection (1) of this section, and

(ii) did not know and had no reason to suppose that the information given to him was false or misleading and that the deposit or use might be in contravention of that subsection; or

(*b*) that he acted under instructions from his employer and neither knew nor had reason to suppose that the deposit or use was in contravention of the said subsection (1); or

(*c*) in the case of an offence of making, causing or permitting a deposit or use otherwise than in accordance with conditions specified in a disposal licence, that he took all such steps as were reasonably open to him to ensure that the conditions were complied with; or

(*d*) that the acts specified in the charge were done in an emergency in order to avoid danger to the public and that, as soon as reasonably practicable after they were done, particulars of them were furnished to the disposal authority in whose area the acts were done.

(5) In this section and in subsections (5) and (6) of the following section "land" includes land covered with waters where the land is above the law-water mark of ordinary spring tides and the waters are not inland waters (within the meaning of Chapter I of Part III of the Water Act 1989).★

[Control of Pollution Act 1974, s 3, as amended by the Criminal Law Act 1977, s 28 and the Water Act 1989 Sch 25.]

★. **Repealed by the Environmental Protection Act 1990, Sch 16, when in force.**

1. Part I contains ss 1–30. In Greater London or a metropolitan county, functions conferred on the local authorities by Pt I of this Act may be discharged by a single authority established by order of the Secretary of State to act on behalf of the councils where joint arrangements for waste disposal can with advantage be made (Local Government Act 1985, s 10).

2. Separate controls exist in relation to sewage sludge used in agriculture which is controlled by the Sludge (Use in Agriculture) Regulations 1989, SI 1989/1263 amended by SI 1990/880 and SI 1996/593 implementing EEC Council Directives. The Disposal of Controlled Waste (Exceptions) Regulations 1991, SI 1991/508 exempt from licensing control certain processes subject to Part I of the Environmental Protection Act 1990. There are exceptions to the regulations exemption in relation to final deposits in or on land.

3. The Collection and Disposal of Waste Regulations 1988, SI 1988/819 amended by SI 1989/1968 and SI 1994/1056 and modified by the Waste Disposal (Authorities) Order 1985, SI 1985/1884 have been made; reg 7 and Sch 5 prescribe the manner of dealing with waste for the purposes of s 3(1)(*b*).

4. "Deposit" does not mean final deposit, the fact that waste was not to remain on a site was no bar to conviction (*R v*

Metropolitan Stipendiary Magistrate, ex p London Waste Regulation Authority [1993] 3 All ER 113). A reasonable bench of magistrates was entitled on the facts to conclude that barrels containing less than 1 per cent of original volume of solid phenol waste were empty (*Durham County Council v Thomas Swan and Co Ltd* [1995] Crim LR 319).

5. Defined by s 30(1), post.

6. Special provision is made for land occupied by disposal authorities ibid, s 11.

7. Defined by s 30(3), post.

8. It is not necessary for the prosecution to prove that the defendant knowingly permitted a breach of a condition of a waste disposal licence in addition to proving that he knowingly permitted the deposit of controlled waste (*Ashcroft v Cambro Waste Products Ltd* [1981] 3 All ER 699, [1981] 1 WLR 1349).

9. For procedure in respect of offences triable either way, see the Magistrates' Courts Act 1980, ss 17A–21, PART I: MAGISTRATES' COURTS, PROCEDURE, ante.

10. See s 4(5), post (waste in containers, and "environmental hazard") and s 4(6) as to the degree of risk relevant thereunder.

11. For procedure in respect of offences triable either way, see the Magistrates' Courts Act 1980, ss 17A–21, PART I: MAGISTRATES' COURTS, PROCEDURE, ante. Civil liability following a contravention of s 3(3) is dealt with by s 88 of this Act.

8–25812 4. Provisions supplementary to section 3. (1) Where activities for which a disposal licence is required apart from this subsection have been carried on on any land during the period of six months ending with the date when subsection (1) of the preceding section comes into force[1], nothing in that subsection shall apply to the carrying on of those activities on the land during the period of one year beginning with that date and, where at the end of that period an appeal is pending in pursuance of section 10 of this Act against a rejection of an application for a disposal licence in respect of those activities on the land or against a decision to issue such a licence which specifies conditions, until the appeal is determined.

(2) Nothing in subsection (1) of the preceding section applies to household waste[2] from a private dwelling[3] which is deposited, disposed of or dealt with within the curtilage of the dwelling by or with the permission of the occupier of the dwelling.

(3) Duty of Secretary of State in prescribing exceptions.

(4) (*Repealed*).

(5) For the purposes of subsection (3) of the preceding section—

(*a*) the presence of waste on land gives rise to an environmental hazard if the waste has been deposited in such a manner or in such a quantity (whether that quantity by itself or cumulatively with other deposits of the same or different substances) as to subject persons or animals to a material risk of death, injury or impairment of health or as to threaten the pollution (whether on the surface or underground) of any water supply; and

(*b*) the fact that waste is deposited in containers shall not of itself be taken to exclude any risk which might be expected to arise if the waste were not in containers.

(6) In the case of any deposit of waste, the degree of risk relevant for the purposes of the preceding subsection shall be assessed with particular regard—

(*a*) to the measures, if any taken by the person depositing the waste, or by the owner or occupier of the land, or by others, for minimising the risk; and

(*b*) to the likelihood of the waste, or any container in which it is deposited, being tampered with by children or others.*

[Control of Pollution Act 1974, s 4, as amended by the Water Act 1989, Sch 27.]

*. **See note to s 3, ante.**

1. Section 3(1) came into force on 14th June 1976.

2. By reg 4 of the Collection and Disposal of Waste Regulations 1988, SI 1988/819 amended by SI 1989/1968 there is excluded from the definition of household waste any mineral or synthetic oil or grease, asbestos and clinical waste.

3. Defined by s 30(1), post.

8–25813 5. Licences to dispose of waste. (1)–(5) Applications for disposal licences.

(6) A person who, in an application for a disposal licence, makes any statement which he knows to be false in a material particular or recklessly makes any statement which is false in a material particular shall be guilty of an offence[1] and liable on summary conviction to a fine not exceeding the statutory maximum or on conviction on indictment to imprisonment for a term not exceeding two years or a fine or both.*

[Control of Pollution Act 1974, s 5, as amended by the Criminal Law Act 1977, s 28, the Local Government, Planning and Land Act 1980, Schs 2 and 34, the Local Government Act 1985, Sch 6, the Water Act 1989, Sch 25, the Planning (Consequential Provisions) Act 1990, Sch 2 and the Environment Act 1995, Schs 22 and 24.]

***See note to s 3, ante.**

1. For procedure in respect of an offence triable either way, see the Magistrates' Courts Act 1980, ss 17A–21, PART I: MAGISTRATES' COURTS, PROCEDURE, ante.

8–25814 6. Provisions supplementary to section 5. (1)–(2) Regulations may prescribe conditions[1] in a disposal licence.

(3) The holder of a disposal licence who without reasonable excuse contravenes a condition of the licence which in pursuance of regulations made by virtue of subsection (1) of this section is to be

disregarded for the purposes mentioned in that subsection[2] shall be guilty of an offence and liable on summary conviction to a fine not exceeding **level 5** on the standard scale; but no proceedings for such an offence shall be brought in England and Wales except by or with the consent of the Director of Public Prosecutions or by the Environment Agency.

(4)–(5) Register of licences, disposal of applications.

(6) References to land in the preceding section and this section include such water as is mentioned in section 4(4) of this Act.*

[Control of Pollution Act 1974, s 6, as amended by the Local Government, Planning and Land Act 1980, Schs 2 and 34, the Criminal Justice Act 1982, ss 38 and 46, the Environment Act 1995, Sch 22 and SI 1996/593.]

***See note to s 3, ante.**

1. Including conditions to carry out works or do something which the licence holder is not entitled as of right to do (sub-s (2)). The disposal authority does not have power to impose a condition prohibiting public nuisances of any and all kinds, whether or not they pollute water, endanger public health or constitute a serious detriment to the amenities of the locality in which the licensed activities are carried on (*A-G's Reference (No 2 of 1988)*, [1990] 1 QB 77, [1989] 3 WLR 397, 89 Cr App Rep 314, CA).

2. That is, for the purposes of s 3(1) of this Act.

8–25815 **13. Dustbins etc[1].** (1) Where a collection authority[2] has a duty by virtue of subsection (1)(*a*) of the preceding section[3] to arrange for the collection of household waste4 from any premises, the authority may, by a notice served on the occupier of the premises, require him to place the waste for collection in receptacles which are of a kind and number reasonably specified in the notice.

(1A) A person who fails to comply with any of the requirements of such a notice shall be guilty of an offence and liable on summary conviction to a fine of an amount not exceeding **level 3** on the standard scale.

(2) A notice served by an authority in pursuance of the preceding subsection may provide for the receptacles in question to be provided by the authority free of charge or—

(*a*) if the recipient of the notice agrees, by the authority on payment by the recipient of the notice of such a single payment or such periodical payments as he agrees with the authority; or

(*b*) by the recipient of the notice if he does not enter into an agreement in pursuance of the preceding paragraph within a period specified in the notice or the notice does not propose such an agreement.

(3) Where by virtue of such a notice the recipient of it is required to provide any receptacles he may within the period of twenty-one days beginning with the last day of the period specified in the notice in pursuance of paragraph (*b*) of the preceding subsection or, where no period is so specified, beginning with the day on which the notice is served on him, appeal to a magistrates' court against the notice on the ground that any requirement specified in the notice is unreasonable or on the ground that the receptacles in which household waste in the premises in question is placed for collection are adequate; and where an appeal against a notice is brought in pursuance of this subsection—

(*a*) the notice shall be of no effect pending the determination of the appeal; and

(*b*) the court shall either quash or modify the notice or dismiss the appeal; and

(*c*) no question as to whether any requirement specified in the notice is unreasonable shall be entertained in any proceedings for an offence under this section in respect of the notice.

(4) An English county disposal authority and any collection authority may at the request of any person supply him with receptacles for commercial waste or industrial waste[4] which he 1has requested the authority to arrange to collect and shall make a reasonable charge for any receptacle supplied in pursuance of this subsection unless in the case of a receptacle for commercial waste the authority considers it appropriate not to make a charge.

(5) If it appears to a collection authority that there is likely to be situated, on any premises in its area, commercial waste or industrial waste of a kind which, if the waste is not stored in receptacles of a particular kind, is likely to cause a nuisance or to be detrimental to the amenities of the locality in which the premises are situated, the authority may, by a notice served on the occupier of the premises, require him to provide at the premises receptacles for the storage of such waste which are of a kind and number reasonably specified in the notice.

(5A) A person who fails to comply with any requirement specified in a notice shall be guilty of an offence and liable on summary conviction to a fine of an amount not exceeding **level 3** on the standard scale.

(6) A person on whom a notice is served in pursuance of the preceding subsection may, within the period of twenty-one days beginning with the day on which the notice is served on him, appeal to a magistrates' court against the notice on the grounds that any requirement specified in the notice is unreasonable or that the waste is not likely to cause a nuisance or be detrimental to the amenities of the locality in which the premises are situated; and where an appeal against a notice is brought in pursuance of this subsection, paragraphs (*a*) to (*c*) of subsection (3) of this section shall apply in relation to the notice as they apply in relation to such a notice as is mentioned in that subsection.

(7) A notice under subsection (1) or (5) of this section may make provision with respect to—

(*a*) the size, construction and maintenance of receptacles for controlled waste5;

(*b*) the placing of the receptacles on premises for the purpose of facilitating the emptying of them, and access to the receptacles for that purpose;
(*c*) the placing of the receptacles for that purpose on highways;
(*d*) the substances which may and may not be put into the receptacles and the precautions to be taken where particular substances are put into them; and
(*e*) the steps to be taken by occupiers of premises for the purposes of facilitating the collection of waste from receptacles for controlled waste which are provided in connection with the premises.

(7A) A notice under subsection (1) or (5) of this section shall not require receptacles to be placed on a highway unless—

(*a*) the relevant highway authority have given their consent to their being so placed; and
(*b*) arrangements have been made as to the liability for any damage arising out of their being so placed.

(8) References to receptacles in the preceding provisions of this section include references to holders for receptacles.*

[Control of Pollution Act 1974, s 13, as amended by the Local Government, Planning and Land Act 1980, Sch 2, the Criminal Justice Act 1982, ss 38 and 46 and the Local Government Act 1985, Sch 6.]

***See note to s 3, ante**.

1. Of this section, subsections (5), (6), (7) and (8), and subsection (3) so far as it applies to an appeal under subsection (6), were brought into force on 1 August 1978 (SI 1978/954) and the remainder on 6 June 1988 (SI 1988/818).
2. Defined by s 30(1), post.
3. That is, except for waste at a place so isolated or inaccessible that the cost of collection would be unreasonably high, and as to which adequate arrangements can reasonably be expected to be made by a person who controls the waste.
4. Defined by s 30(3), post.
5. Defined by s 30(1), post.

8–25816 16. Removal of waste deposited in breach of licensing provisions. (1) If any controlled waste[1] is deposited on any land in contravention of section 3(1) of this Act, any authority to which this section applies may serve a notice on the occupier of the land requiring him—

(*a*) to remove the waste from the land within a period specified in the notice, which shall not be less than twenty-one days beginning with the date of service of the notice; or
(*b*) to take within such a period such steps as are so specified with a view to eliminating or reducing the consequences of the deposit of the waste;

or requiring him both to remove the waste as mentioned in paragraph (*a*) of this subsection and to take such steps as are mentioned in paragraph (*b*) of this subsection within such a period as aforesaid.

(2) A person served with a notice in pursuance of the preceding subsection may within the twenty-one days aforesaid appeal to a magistrates' court against the notice; and on any such appeal the court shall quash the notice if it is satisfied that—

(*a*) the appellant neither deposited nor caused nor knowingly permitted the deposit of the waste on the land; or
(*b*) service of the notice on the appellant was not authorised by the preceding subsection; or
(*c*) there is a material defect in the notice;

and in any other case shall either modify the notice or dismiss the appeal.

(3) Where a person appeals against a notice in pursuance of this section, the notice shall be of no effect pending the determination of the appeal; and where the court modifies the notice or dismisses the appeal it may extend the period specified in the notice.

(4) If a person on whom a notice if served in pursuance of subsection (1) of this section fails to comply with the notice, then—

(*a*) he shall be guilty of an offence and liable on summary conviction to a fine not exceeding **level 5** on the standard scale and a further fine not exceeding £50 for each day on which the failure continues after conviction for the offence and before the authority which served the notice has begun to exercise its powers in pursuance of the following paragraph; and
(*b*) the said authority may do what that person was required by the notice to do and may recover from him any expenses reasonably incurred by the authority in doing it.

(5)–(7) Power to remove waste and recover cost.

(8) The authorities to which this section applies are—

(*a*) the appropriate Agency;
(*b*) any collection authority in whose area the land mentioned in subsection (1) above is situated.*

[Control of Pollution Act 1974, s 16, as amended by the Criminal Justice Act 1982, ss 38 and 46 and the Environment Act 1995, Sch 22.]

***See note to s 3, ante. The repeal of s 13 has taken effect save in so far as it relates to industrial waste in England and Wales (SI 1992/266)**.

1. Defined by s 30(1), post.

8–25817 **17. Special provisions with respect to certain dangerous or intractable waste.** (1) If the Secretary of State considers that controlled waste of any kind is or may be so dangerous or difficult to dispose of that special provision in pursuance of this subsection is required for the disposal of waste of that kind by disposal authorities or other persons, it shall be his duty to make provision by regulations for the disposal of waste of that kind (hereafter in this section referred to as "special waste"); and, without prejudice to the generality of the Secretary of State's power to make regulations in pursuance of the preceding provisions of this subsection, any such regulations[1] may include provision—

(*a*)–(*d*) specific requirements;

(*e*) providing that a contravention of the regulations shall be an offence and prescribing the maximum penalty for the offence[1] (which shall not exceed, on summary conviction, a fine of the statutory maximum and, on conviction on indictment, imprisonment for a term of two years and a fine).

(2) Further specific requirements for inclusion in regulations.

(3) Provisions may also be made by regulations—

(*a*) for the giving of a direction, in respect of any place in respect of which a disposal licence or a resolution in pursuance of section 11[2] of this Act is in force, requiring the holder of the licence or the authority which passed the resolution to accept and dispose of at the place, on such terms as are specified in the direction (including terms as to the making of payments to the recipient of the direction), such special waste as is so specified;

(*b*) as to the consents to be obtained and the other steps to be taken before a direction may be given in pursuance of the regulations and as to appeals to the Secretary of State against a direction so given;

(*c*) providing that a failure to comply with such a direction shall be an offence punishable on summary conviction by a fine not exceeding **level 5** on the standard scale or such less amount

as is prescribed and that a person shall not be guilty of an offence under any prescribed enactment by reason only of anything necessarily done or omitted in order to comply with such a direction.*

[Control of Pollution Act 1974, s 17, as amended by the Criminal Law Act 1977, s 28 and the Criminal Justice Act 1982, ss 38 and 46.]

***See note to s 3, ante**.

1. For procedure in respect of an offence triable either way, see the Magistrates' Courts Act 1980, ss 17A–21, PART I: MAGISTRATES' COURTS, PROCEDURE, ante.

2. That is, a resolution specifying the conditions in accordance with which land occupied by the disposal authority itself is to be used for the deposit or disposal of controlled waste.

Waste other than controlled waste

8–25818 **18. Application of preceding provisions to other waste.** (1) The Secretary of State may, after consultation with such bodies as he considers appropriate, make regulations providing that prescribed provisions of sections 1 to 11 and 14 to 17 of this Act shall have effect in a prescribed area—

(*a*) as if references in those provisions to controlled waste or controlled waste of a kind specified in the regulations included references to such waste as is mentioned in section 30(3)(*c*)(ii) of this Act which is of a kind so specified; and

(*b*) with such other modifications as are prescribed;

and regulations made in pursuance of this subsection may make such modifications of any enactment other than the sections aforesaid as the Secretary of State considers appropriate in connection with the regulations.

(2) A person who—

(*a*) deposits on any land any waste other than controlled waste; or

(*b*) causes or knowingly permits the deposit on any land of any waste other than controlled waste,

in a case where, if the waste were controlled waste and any disposal licence relating to the land were not in force, he would be guilty of an offence under section 3(3) of this Act shall be guilty of such an offence[1] and punishable accordingly unless the act charged was done in pursuance of and in accordance with the terms of any consent, licence, approval or authority granted under any enactment (excluding any planning permission under the enactments relating to town and country planning); and in this subsection "land" includes such water as is mentioned in section 4(4) of this Act.

(3) Subsection (2) of section 12[2] and subsection (4) of section 13 of this Act shall apply to waste other than controlled waste as the subsections apply to controlled waste.*

[Control of Pollution Act 1974, s 18.]

***See note to s 3, ante**.

1. The limitation period will also be the same as for an offence under s 3(3), ie one year (s 87(3), post). Civil liability is dealt with by s 88 of this Act.

2. This enables a disposal authority or collection authority to arrange for the collection of industrial waste if so requested by the occupier of premises in its area.

8–25819 27. Interference with refuse tins and dustbins etc. (1) No person shall sort over or disturb—

(*a*) anything deposited at a place provided by a disposal authority or a collection authority for the deposit of waste or in a receptacle for waste which is provided by such an authority or a parish or community council for public use; or

(*b*) the contents of any receptacle for waste which, in accordance with a notice under section 13(1) or (5) of this Act, is placed on any highway or in any other place with a view to its being emptied;

unless he is authorised to do so by the authority or council in the case of anything deposited as mentioned in paragraph (*a*) above or, in the case of such a receptacle as is mentioned in paragraph (*b*) above, unless he is a person entitled to the custody of the receptacle or is authorised to do so by such a person or is a person having the function of emptying the receptacle.

(2) A person who contravenes any of the provisions of the preceding subsection shall be guilty of an offence and liable on summary conviction to a fine of an amount not exceeding **level 3** on the standard scale.*

[Control of Pollution Act 1974, s 27, as amended by the Local Government, Planning and Land Act 1980, Sch 2 as amended by the Criminal Justice Act 1982, ss 38 and 46.]

***See note to s 3, ante.**

8–25820 30. Interpretation etc of Part I. (1) Subject to the following subsection and to subsection (6) below, in this Part of this Act—

"the appropriate Agency" means—

(*a*) in relation to England and Wales, the Environment Agency;

(*b*) in relation to Scotland, SEPA;

"collection authority" means the council of a district or a London borough, the Common Council of the City of London, the Sub-Treasurer of the Inner Temple and the Under Treasurer of the Middle Temple and "English collection authority" means a collection authority of which the area is in the area of an English county disposal authority;

"controlled waste" means household, industrial and commercial waste or any such waste;

"disposal authority" means the council of a county or metropolitan district in England, the council of a district in Wales, the council of a London borough and the Common Council of the City of London, "English county disposal authority" means the council of a county in England and "relevant disposal authority" in relation to an English collection authority, means the English county disposal authority whose area includes that of the collection authority;

"disposal licence" has the meaning assigned to it by section 3(1) of this Act, and "holder" in relation to such a licence shall be construed in accordance with section 8(3) of this Act;

"private dwelling" means—

(*a*) a hereditament or premises used wholly for the purposes of a private dwelling or private dwellings as determined in accordance with Schedule 13 to the General Rate Act 1967[1]; and

(*b*) a caravan as defined in section 29(1) of the Caravan Sites and Control of Development Act 1960 (disregarding the amendment made by section 13(2) of the Caravan Sites Act 1968) which usually and for the time being is situated on a caravan site within the meaning of that Act;

"relevant land" means—

(*a*) in relation to a proposal to issue a disposal licence, the land on which activities may be carried on in pursuance of the licence if it is issued in accordance with the proposal; and

(*b*) in relation to a disposal licence, the land on which activities may be carried on in pursuance of the licence,

and references to land in the preceding paragraphs include such water as is mentioned in section 4(4) of this Act;

"waste"[2] includes—

(*a*) any substance which constitutes a scrap material or an effluent or other unwanted surplus substance arising from the application of any process; and

(*b*) any substance or article which requires to be disposed of as being broken, worn out, contaminated or otherwise spoiled,

but does not include a substance which is an explosive within the meaning of the Explosives Act 1875[3];*

"waste disposal provisions" means—

(*a*) sections 1 and 2 (waste disposal arrangements and plans);

(*b*) section 12 (collection of waste;

(*c*) section 13(4) (provision of receptacles for industrial or commercial waste);

(*d*) section 14 (disposal of waste);
(*e*) section 17(2)(a) and (c) (disposal of dangerous or intractable waste);
(*f*) sections 19 to 21 (powers in relation to disposal of waste which is not controlled waste, reclamation of waste and production of heat and electricity from waste); and
(*g*) section 27(1) (interference with refuse tips and dustbins etc);

"waste regulation provisions" means—

(*a*) sections 3 to 11 (disposal licences);
(*b*) section 16 (removal of waste deposited in breach of licensing provisions); and
(*c*) section 17(1)(a) and (2)(*b*) to (*d*) (directions as to disposal of dangerous or intractable waste, supervision of certain activities, recovery of expenses and charges and appeals to the Secretary of State);

and for the purposes of this Part of this Act any thing which is discarded or otherwise dealt with as if it were waste shall be presumed to be waste unless the contrary is proved.**

(2) (*Scotland*).

(3) Subject to the following subsection, or the purposes of this Part of this Act—

(*a*) household waste consists of waste from a private dwelling or residential home or from premises forming part of a university or school or other educational establishment or forming part of a hospital or nursing home;
(*b*) industrial waste[2] consists of waste from any factory within the meaning of the Factories Act 1961 and any premises occupied by a body corporate established by or under any enactment for the purpose of carrying on under national ownership any industry or part of an industry or any undertaking, excluding waste from any mine or quarry; and
(*c*) commercial waste[2] consists of waste from premises used wholly or mainly for the purposes of a trade or business or the purposes of sport, recreation or entertainment excluding—

(i) household and industrial waste, and
(ii) waste from any mine or quarry and waste from premises used for agriculture within the meaning of the Agriculture Act 1947 or, (Scotland), and
(iii) waste of any other description prescribed for the purposes of this sub-paragraph.

(4) Regulations[4] may provide that waste of a prescribed description shall be treated for the purposes of prescribed provisions of this Part of this Act as being or not being household waste or industrial waste or commercial waste; but no regulations shall be made by virtue of the preceding provisions of this subsection in respect of such waste as is mentioned in paragraph (*c*)(ii) of the preceding subsection and references in those provisions and in the preceding subsection to waste do not include sewage except so far as regulations provide otherwise. In this subsection "sewage" includes matter in or from a privy within the meaning[5] of section 12(5) of this Act.

(5) Except as provided by regulations[4] made by virtue of this subsection, nothing in this Part of this Act applies to radioactive waste within the meaning of the Radioactive Substances Act 1960; but regulations may—

(*a*) provide for prescribed provisions of this Part of this Act to have effect with such modifications as the Secretary of State considers appropriate for the purposes of dealing with such radioactive waste;
(*b*) make such modifications of the said Act of 1960 and any other Act as the Secretary of State considers appropriate in consequence of the passing of this Part of this Act or in connection with regulations made by virtue of the preceding paragraph.

(6) In the application of this Part of this Act to Wales—

"collection authority" means a county council; or county borough council; and
"disposal authority" means a county council or county borough council.**

[Control of Pollution Act 1974, s 30, as amended by the Local Government Act 1985, Sch 6, the Local Government (Wales) Act 1994, Sch 9 and the Environment Act 1995, Schs 22 and 24.]

***Definition "waste" substituted by the Environment Act 1995, Sch 22, in force in relation to Scotland, and in relation to England and Wales in force from a date to be appointed**:

""waste" has the same meaning as it has in Part II of the Environmental Protection Act 1990 by virtue of section 75(2) of that Act;".

****See note to s 3, ante.**

1. The General Rate Act 1967 has been repealed by the Local Government Finance Act 1988.

2. Material which was waste when removed from its original site is not changed by sorting or its usefulness for infill purposes (*Kent County Council v Queenborough Rolling Mill Co Ltd* (1990) 154 JP 530).

3. Until the coming into force of its repeal by the Environmental Protection Act 1990 the definition of "waste" in this section has effect as if the reference to the Explosives Act 1875 were a reference to the Manufacture and Storage of Explosives Regulations 2005, SI 2005/1082 (SI 2005/1082, Sch 5 para 15).

4. Part I of the Act divides controlled waste into three categories: household, industrial and commercial. The Collection and Disposal of Waste Regulations 1988, SI 1988/819 amended by SI 1989/1968 and SI 1994/1056 and modified by the Waste Disposal (Authorities) Order 1985, SI 1985/1884, provides that certain types of waste are to be treated as belonging to a particular category.

5. That is, a latrine which has a moveable receptacle for faecal matter.

PART III[1]
NOISE

Construction sites

8–25823 60. Control of noise on construction sites. (1) This section applies to works of the following description, that is to say—

(*a*) the erection, construction, alteration, repair or maintenance of buildings, structures or roads;
(*b*) breaking up, opening or boring under any road or adjacent land in connection with the construction, inspection, maintenance or removal of works;
(*c*) demolition or dredging work; and
(*d*) (whether or not also comprised in paragraph (*a*), (*b*) or (*c*) above) any work of engineering construction[2].

(2) Where it appears to a local authority that works to which this section applies are being, or are going to be, carried out on any premises, the local authority may serve a notice imposing requirements as to the way in which the works are to be carried out and may if it thinks fit publish notice of the requirements in such way as appears to the local authority to be appropriate.

(3) The notice may in particular—

(*a*) specify the plant or machinery which is or is not to be used;
(*b*) specify the hours during which the works may be carried out;
(*c*) specify the level of noise which may be emitted from the premises in question or at any specified point on those premises or which may be so emitted during specified hours; and
(*d*) provide for any change of circumstances.

(4) In acting under this section the local authority shall have regard—

(*a*) to the relevant provisions of any code of practice[3] issued under this Part of this Act;
(*b*) to the need for ensuring that the best practicable means[4] are employed to minimise noise;
(*c*) before specifying any particular methods or plant or machinery, to the desirability in the interests of any recipients of the notice in question of specifying other methods or plant or machinery which would be substantially as effective in minimising noise and more acceptable to them;
(*d*) to the need to protect any persons in the locality in which the premises in question are situated from the effects of noise.

(5) A notice under this section shall be served on the person who appears to the local authority to be carrying out, or going to carry out, the works, and on such other persons appearing to the local authority to be responsible for, or to have control over, the carrying out of the works as the local authority thinks fit.

(6) A notice under this section may specify the time within which the notice is to be complied with, and may require the execution of such works, and the taking of such other steps, as may be necessary for the purpose of the notice, or as may be specified in the notice.

(7) A person served with a notice under this section may appeal[5] against the notice to a magistrates' court within twenty-one days from the service of the notice.

(8) If a person on whom a notice is served under this section without reasonable excuse contravenes any requirement[6] of the notice he shall be guilty of an offence[7] against this Part of this Act.

[Control of Pollution Act 1974, s 60.]

1. Part III contains ss 57–74.
2. Defined in s 73, post.
3. Section 71 enables the Secretary of State to issue or approve codes of practice for minimising noise.
4. "Best practicable means" is defined in s 72, post.
5. For procedure on appeal, see s 70, post.
6. requirements in a notice may only apply to works under way at the date of the notice and do not apply, for example, to works undertaken under a subsequent contract in respect of the same premises (*Walter Lilly & Co Ltd v Westminster City Council* (1994) 158 JP 805).
7. For penalty, see s 74, post. Note also the defence available under s 61(8), post.

8–25824 61. Prior consent for work on construction sites. (1)–(3) *Application may be made before work begins, and consent granted.*

(5) In acting under this section a local authority shall have regard to the considerations set out in subsection (4) of the preceding section and shall have power to—

(*a*) attach any conditions to a consent; and
(*b*) limit or qualify a consent to allow for any change in circumstances; and
(*c*) limit the duration of a consent;

and any person who knowingly carries out the works, or permits the works to be carried out, in contravention of any conditions attached to a consent under this section shall be guilty of an offence[1] against this Part of this Act.

(6) The local authority shall inform the applicant of its decision on the application within twenty-

eight days from receipt of the application; and if the local authority gives its consent to the application it may if it thinks fit publish notice of the consent, and of the works to which it relates, in such way as appears to the local authority to be appropriate.

(7) If—

(*a*) the local authority does not give a consent within the said period of twenty-eight days; or

(*b*) the local authority gives its consent within the said period of twenty-eight days but attaches any condition to the consent or limits or qualifies the consent in any way;

the applicant may appeal[2] to a magistrates' court within twenty-one days from the end of that period.

(8) In any proceedings for an offence under section 60(8) of this Act it shall be a defence to prove that the alleged contravention amounted to the carrying out of the works in accordance with a consent given under this section.

(9) A consent given under this section shall contain a statement to the effect that the consent does not of itself constitute any ground of defence against any proceedings instituted under section 82 of the Environmental Protection Act 1990.

(10) Where a consent has been given under this section and the works are carried out by a person other than the applicant for the consent, it shall be the duty of the applicant to take all reasonable steps to bring the consent to the notice of that other person; and if he fails to comply with this subsection he shall be guilty of an offence[1] against this Part of this Act.

[Control of Pollution Act 1974, s 61, as amended by the Building Act 1984, Sch 7, the Environmental Protection Act 1990, Sch 15 and the Environment Act 1995, Sch 24.]

1. For penalty see s 74, post.
2. For procedure on appeal, see s 70, post.

Noise in streets

8–25825 62. Noise in streets. (1) Subject to the provisions of this section, a loudspeaker in a street[1] shall not be operated—

(*a*) between the hours of nine in the evening and eight in the following morning, for any purpose;

(*b*) at any other time, for the purpose of advertising any entertainment, trade or business;

and any person who operates or permits the operation of a loudspeaker in contravention of this subsection shall be guilty of an offence[2] against this Part of this Act.

In this subsection "street"[1] means a highway and any other road, footway, square or court which is for the time being open to the public.

(1A) Subject to subsection (1B) of this section, the Secretary of State may by order amend the times specified in subsection (1)(*a*) of this section.

(1B) An order under subsection (1A) of this section shall not amend the times so as to permit the operation of a loudspeaker in a street at any time between the hours of nine in the evening and eight in the following morning.

(2) Subsection (1) of this section shall not apply to the operation of a loudspeaker—

(*a*) for police, fire and rescue authority or ambulance purposes, by the Environment Agency, a water undertaker or a sewerage undertaker in the exercise of any of its functions, or by a local authority within its area;

(*b*) for communicating with person on a vessel for the purpose of directing the movement of that or any other vessel;

(*c*) if the loudspeaker forms part of a public telephone system;

(*d*) if the loudspeaker—

(i) is in or fixed to a vehicle, and

(ii) is operated solely for the entertainment of or for communicating with the driver or a passenger of the vehicle or, where the loudspeaker is or forms part of the horn or similar warning instrument of the vehicle, solely for giving warning to other traffic, and

(iii) is so operated as not to give reasonable cause for annoyance to persons in the vicinity;

(*e*) otherwise than on a highway, by persons employed in connection with a transport undertaking used by the public in a case where the loudspeaker is operated solely for making announcements to passengers or prospective passengers or to other persons so employed;

(*f*) by a travelling showman on land which is being used for the purposes of a pleasure fair;

(*g*) in case of emergency.

(3) Subsection (1)(*b*) of this section shall not apply to the operation of a loudspeaker between the hours of noon and seven in the evening on the same day if the loudspeaker—

(*a*) is fixed to a vehicle which is being used for the conveyance of a perishable commodity for human consumption; and

(*b*) is operated solely for informing members of the public (otherwise than by means of words) that the commodity is on sale from the vehicle; and

(*c*) is so operated as not to give reasonable cause for annoyance to persons in the vicinity.

(3A) Subsection (1) of this section shall not apply to the operation of a loudspeaker in accordance with a consent granted by a local authority under Schedule 2 to the Noise and Statutory Nuisance Act 1993.

[Control of Pollution Act 1974, s 62, as amended by the Water Act 1989, Sch 25, the Noise and Statutory Nuisance Act 1993, s 7, the Environment Act 1995, Sch 22 and the Fire and Rescue Services Act 2005.]

---

1. For a judicial consideration of the meaning of "street" within s 62(1), see *Tower Hamlets London Borough Council v Creitzman* (1984) 148 JP 630. Where equipment was attached by suckers to a street-facing window and had the effect of turning the windows into loudspeakers, this amounted to operating a loudspeaker in a street: *Westminster City Council v French Connection Ltd* [2005] EWHC Admin 933, (2005) 169 JP 312.

2. For penalty see s 74, post.

8–25826 65. Noise exceeding registered level. (1) The level of noise recorded in the noise level register[1] in respect of any premises shall not be exceeded except with the consent in writing of the local authority.

(2) The local authority's consent may be made subject to such conditions, whether as to the amount by which the level of noise may be increased, or as to the period for which, or the periods during which, the level of noise may be increased, as may be specified in the consent; and the authority shall record particulars of the consent in the noise level register.

(3) If within the period of two months beginning with the date on which a local authority receives an application for its consent under this section, or within such longer period as the authority and the applicant agree in writing, the authority has not notified the applicant of its decision on the application, the authority shall be deemed to have refused consent in pursuance of the application.

(4) An applicant for consent under this section may appeal[2] to the Secretary of State against the local authority's decision on the application within the period of three months beginning with the date on which the authority notifies him of the decision or, in a case falling within the preceding subsection, beginning with the expiration of the period or longer period there mentioned; and it shall be the duty of the local authority to act in accordance with the decision of the Secretary of State on the appeal.

(5) If noise emitted from any premises constitutes a contravention of subsection (1) of this section or of a condition attached to a consent under this section, the person responsible shall be guilty of an offence[3] against this Part of this Act.

(6) The magistrates' court convicting a person of an offence under the preceding subsection may, if satisfied that the offence is likely to continue or recur, make an order requiring the execution of any works[4] necessary to prevent it continuing or recurring; and if that person without reasonable excuse contravenes any requirement of the order he shall be guilty of an offence against this Part of this Act.

(7) The magistrates' court may, after giving the local authority in whose area the premises are situated an opportunity of being heard, direct the local authority[5] to do anything which the court has power under the preceding subsection to require the person convicted to do, either instead of, or in addition to, imposing any requirement on that person.

(8) A consent given under this section shall contain a statement to the effect that the consent does not of itself constitute any ground of defence against any proceedings instituted under section 82 of the Environmental Protection Act 1990.

[Control of Pollution Act 1974, s 65, as amended by the Environmental Protection Act 1990, Sch 15 and the Environment Act 1995, Sch 24.]

---

1. That is, a register recording all measurements of the level of noise emanating from premises within an area designated by the local authority a noise abatement zone under s 63 and Sch 1 of this Act. Provision is made by s 64 for service of a copy of the record on the owner and occupier of premises, who then have 28 days in which to appeal to the Secretary of State. The validity or accuracy of any entry in the register shall not be questioned in proceedings, except as to proper service (s 64(5)). The register is open for public inspection.

2. For procedure on appeal, see s 70, post.

3. For penalty see s 74, post.

4. For procedure where a person fails to take the steps required, see s 69, post.

5. As to recovery of expenditure, see s 69(3), post.

8–25827 66. Reduction of noise levels. (1) If it appears to the local authority—

(*a*) that the level of noise emanating from any premises to which a noise abatement order applies is not acceptable having regard to the purposes for which the order was made; and

(*b*) that a reduction in that level is practicable at reasonable cost and would afford a public benefit,

the local authority may serve a notice on the person responsible.

(2) The notice shall require that person—

(*a*) to reduce the level of noise emanating from the premises to such level as may be specified in the notice;

(*b*) to prevent any subsequent increase in the level of noise emanating from those premises without the consent of the local authority; and

(*c*) to take such steps[1] as may be specified in the notice to achieve those purposes.

(3) A notice under this section (in this Part of this Act referred to as a "noise reduction notice") shall specify a time, not being less than six months from the date of service of the notice, within which

the noise level is to be reduced to the specified level and, where the notice specifies any steps necessary to achieve that purpose, within which those steps shall be taken.

(4) A noise reduction notice may specify particular times, or particular days, during which the noise level is to be reduced, and may require the noise level to be reduced to different levels for different times or days.

(5) A notice under this section shall take effect whether or not a consent under the preceding section authorises a level of noise higher than that specified in the notice.

(6) The local authority shall record particulars of a noise reduction notice in the noise level register.

(7) A person who is served with a noise reduction notice may, within three months of the date of service, appeal[2] to a magistrates' court against the notice.

(8) A person who without reasonable excuse contravenes a noise reduction notice shall be guilty of an offence[3] against this Part of this Act.

(9) In proceedings for an offence under the preceding subsection in respect of noise caused in the course of a trade or business, it shall be a defence to prove that the best practicable means[4] had been used for preventing, or for counteracting the effect of, the noise.

[Control of Pollution Act 1974, s 66.]

1. For procedure where a person fails to take the steps required, see s 69, post.
2. For procedure on appeal, see s 70, post.
3. For penalty see s 74, post.
4. "Best practicable means" is defined in s 79, post.

8–25828 67. *New buildings, etc*[1].

1. This section makes provision for new buildings to which a noise abatement order will apply in the determination of an acceptable level of noise; if a level is not determined, then s 66 applies as if sub-ss (1)(*b*) and (9) were omitted and three months replaced six months in sub-s (3).

Noise from plant or machinery

8–25829 68. Noise from plant or machinery. (1)–(2) *Power of Secretary of State to make regulations.*

(3) Any person who contravenes or causes or permits another person to contravene regulations under this section shall be guilty of an offence[1] against this Part of this Act; but in any proceedings for a contravention of regulations made in pursuance of paragraph (*a*) of subsection (1) of this section it shall be a defence to prove that means were used for the purpose of reducing the noise in question which were not less effective for that purpose than the means required by the regulations.

(4)–(5) *Local authority to enforce; no derogation to other provisions of Act.*

[Control of Pollution Act 1974, s 68.]

1. For penalty, see s 74, post.

Supplemental

8–25840 69. Execution of works by local authority. (1) This section applies—

(*a*) (*Repealed*);
(*b*) to a noise reduction notice; and
(*c*) to an order of a magistrates' court under section 65(6) of this Act,

being a notice or order which requires any person to execute any works.

(2) If that person fails to execute all or any of the works in accordance with the notice or order, the local authority may execute those works.

(3) Where a local authority execute works in pursuance of—

(*a*) section 65(7) of this Act; or
(*b*) this section,

the local authority may recover from the person in default the expenditure incurred by the local authority in executing the works, except such of the expenditure as that person shows was unnecessary in the circumstances.

In this and the following subsection "the person in default" means—

(i) *Repealed*;
(ii) in a case under section 65(7), the person convicted of an offence under subsection (5) of that section, and
(iii) in any other case, the person to whom the notice or order applies.

(4) In proceedings to recover any amount due to a local authority under the preceding subsection in respect of works executed by the local authority in pursuance of this section, it shall not be open to

the person in default to raise any question which he could have raised on an appeal against the notice or order.
[Control of Pollution Act 1974, s 69, as amended by the Environmental Protection Act 1990, Sch 16.]

8–25841 **70. Appeals to Secretary of State and magistrates' court.** (1) Where any provision in this Part of this Act provides for an appeal to a magistrates' court, the procedure shall be by way of complaint for an order and the Magistrates' Courts Act [1980] shall apply to the proceedings.

(2)–(3) *Regulations*[1] *to be made as to appeals to the Secretary of State and to magistrates' courts.*

(4) In entertaining any appeal under this Part of this Act the Secretary of State, or as the case may be the magistrates' court, shall have regard to any duty imposed by law on the appellant which concerns the activities in the course of which the noise is emitted.
[Control of Pollution Act 1974, s 70.]

1. See the Control of Noise (Appeals) Rules 1975 and the Statutory Nuisance (Appeals) Regulations 1990, post.

8–25842 **71.** *Power to prepare and approve codes of practice for minimising noise*[1].

1. The Control of Noise (Code of Practice on Noise from Ice-Cream Van Chimes Etc) Order 1981, SI 1981/1828, the Control of Noise (Code of Practice on Noise from Audible Intruder Alarms) Order 1981, SI 1981/1829, the Control of Noise (Code of Practice on Noise from Model Aircraft) Order 1981, SI 1981/1830 , the Control of Noise (Codes of Practice for Construction and Open Sites) (England) Order 2002, SI 2002/461 and the Control of Noise (Codes of Practice for Construction and Open Sites) (Wales) Order 2002, SI 2002/1795, have been made.

8–25842A **72. "Best practicable means".** (1) This section shall apply for the construction of references in this Part of this Act to best practicable means.

(2) In that expression "practicable" means reasonably practicable having regard among other things to local conditions and circumstances, to the current state of technical knowledge and to the financial implications.

(3) The means to be employed include the design, installation, maintenance and manner and periods of operation of plant and machinery, and the design, construction and maintenance of buildings and acoustic structures.

(4) The test of best practicable means is to apply only so far as compatible with any duty imposed by law, and in particular is to apply to statutory undertakers only so far as compatible with the duties imposed on them in their capacity of statutory undertakers.

(5) The said test is to apply only so far as compatible with safety and safe working conditions, and with the exigencies of any emergency or unforeseen circumstances.

(6) Subject to the preceding provisions of this section, regard shall be had, in construing references to "best practicable means", to any relevant provision of a code of practice approved under the preceding section.
[Control of Pollution Act 1974, s 72.]

8–25843 **73. Interpretation and other supplementary provisions.** (1) Except where the context otherwise requires, in this Part of this Act—

"contravention" includes a failure to comply with the provision in question, and "contravene" shall be construed accordingly;

"local authority" means—

(*a*) in England, the council of a district or a London borough, the Common Council of the City of London, the Sub-Treasurer of the Inner Temple and the Under Treasurer of the Middle Temple;

(*aa*) in Wales, the council of a county or a county borough; and

(*b*) (*Scotland*);

"noise" includes vibration;

"noise abatement order" and "noise abatement zone" have the meanings given by section 63 of this Act;

"noise level register" has the meaning given by section 64(2) of this Act;

"noise reduction notice" has the meaning given by section 66(3) of this Act;

"person responsible", in relation to the emission of noise, means the person to whose act, default or sufferance the noise is attributable;

"statutory undertakers" means persons authorised by any enactment to carry on any railway, light railway, tramway, road transport, water transport, canal, inland navigation, dock, harbour, pier or lighthouse undertaking, or any undertaking for the supply of hydraulic power, and includes a universal service provider (within the meaning of the Postal Services Act 2000) in his capacity as a person who provides a universal service provider (within the meaning of that Act);

"work of engineering construction" means the construction, structural alteration, maintenance or repair of any railway line or siding or any dock, harbour, inland navigation, tunnel, bridge, viaduct, waterworks, reservoir, pipeline, aqueduct, sewer, sewage works or gas-holder.

(2) The area of a local authority which includes part of the seashore shall also include for the

purposes of this Part of this Act, except sections 62 to 67, the territorial sea lying seawards from that part of the shore; and—

(*a*) (*Repealed*);

(*b*) this Part of this Act (except sections 62 to 67 and this subsection) shall have effect, in relation to any area included in the area of a local authority by virtue of this subsection—

(i) as if references to premises and the occupier of premises included respectively a vessel and the master of a vessel, and

(ii) with such other modifications, if any, as are prescribed.

(3) Where more than one person is responsible for noise, this Part of this Act shall apply to each of those persons whether or not what any one of them is responsible for would by itself amount to a nuisance, or would result in a level of noise justifying action under this Part of this Act.

(4) This Part of this Act does not apply to noise caused by aircraft other than model aircraft and does not confer functions on port health authorities.

[Control of Pollution Act 1974, s 73, as amended by the Local Government, Planning and Land Act 1980, Schs 2 and 34, the Gas Act 1986, Sch 9 the Water Act 1989, Sch 25, the Electricity Act 1989, Sch 18, the Local Government (Wales) Act 1994, Sch 9 and SI 2001/1149.]

8–25844 **74. Penalties.** (1) A person guilty of an offence against this Part of this Act shall be liable on summary conviction to a fine not exceeding **level 5** on the standard scale, together, in any case, with a further fine not exceeding **£50** for each day on which the offence continues after the conviction.

(2) In determining whether an offence is a second or subsequent offence against this Part of this Act, account shall be taken of any offence—

(*a*) under section 24 of the Public Health (Scotland) Act 1897 by way of contravening a decree or interdict relating to noise; or

(*b*) under section 95 of the Public Health Act 1936 by way of contravening a nuisance order relating to noise; or

(*c*) under section 80(4) of the Environmental Protection Act 1990,

as if it were an offence against this Part of this Act.

[Control of Pollution Act 1974, s 74, as amended by the Criminal Justice Act 1982, ss 35, 38 and 46 and the Environmental Protection Act 1990, Sch 15.]

PART V[1]

SUPPLEMENTARY PROVISIONS

Legal proceedings

8–25851 **85. Appeals to Crown Court or Court of Session against decisions of magistrates' court or sheriff.** (1) An appeal against any decision of a magistrates' court in pursuance of this Act (other than a decision made in criminal proceedings) shall lie to the Crown Court at the instance of any party to the proceedings in which the decision was given if such an appeal does not lie to the Crown Court by virtue of any other enactment.

(2) *Scotland.*

(3) Where a person appeals to the Crown Court or the Court of Session against a decision of a magistrates' court or the sheriff dismissing an appeal against a notice served in pursuance of this Act which was suspended pending determination of that appeal, the notice shall again be suspended pending the determination of the appeal to the Crown Court or Court of Session.

1. Part V contains ss 85–98.

8–25852 **87. Miscellaneous provisions relating to legal proceedings.** (1) When an offence under this Act which has been committed by a body corporate is proved to have been committed with the consent or connivance of, or to be attributable to any neglect on the part of, any director, manager, secretary or other similar officer of the body corporate or any person who was purporting to act in any such capacity, he as well as the body corporate shall be guilty of that offence and be liable to be proceeded against and punished accordingly.

Where the affairs of a body corporate are managed by its members the preceding provisions of this subsection shall apply in relation to the acts and defaults of a member in connection with his functions of management as if he were a director of the body corporate.

(2) Where the commission by any person of an offence under this Act is due to the act or default of some other person, that other person shall be guilty of the offence; and a person may be charged with and convicted of an offence by virtue of this subsection whether or not proceedings for the offence are taken against any other person.

(3) *Repealed.*

(4) Where an appeal against a decision of a relevant authority lies to a magistrates' court by virtue of any provision of this Act, it shall be the duty of the authority to include in any document by which it notifies the decision to the person concerned a statement indicating that such an appeal lies as aforesaid and specifying the time within which it must be brought.

(5) Where on an appeal to any court against or arising out of a decision of a relevant authority in pursuance of this Act the court varies or reverses the decision it shall be the duty of the authority to act in accordance with the court's decision.

(6) A judge of any court and a justice of the peace shall not be disqualified from acting, in cases arising under this Act by reason of his being, as one of several ratepayers or as one of any other class of persons, liable in common with the others to contribute to or be benefited by any rate or fund out of which any expenses of a relevant authority are to be defrayed.

[Control of Pollution Act 1974, s 87, as amended by the Criminal Law Act 1977, Sch 13, the Magistrates' Courts Act 1980, Sch 7 and the Environment Act 1995, Sch 24.]

Miscellaneous

8–25853 91. Rights of entry and inspection etc. (1) Any person authorised in writing in that behalf by a relevant authority may at any reasonable time—

(*a*) enter upon any land or vessel for the purpose of—

(i) performing any function conferred on the authority or that person by virtue of this Act, or

(ii) determining whether, and if so what manner, such a function should be performed, or

(iii) determining whether any provision of this Act or of an instrument made by virtue of this Act is being complied with;

(*b*) carry out such inspections, measurements and tests on the land or vessel or of any articles on it and take away such samples of the land or articles as he considers appropriate for such a purpose.

(2) If it is shown to the satisfaction of a justice of the peace on sworn information in writing—

(*a*) that admission to any land or vessel which a person is entitled to enter in pursuance of the preceding subsection has been refused to that person or that refusal is apprehended or that the land or vessel is unoccupied or that the occupier is temporarily absent or that the case is one of emergency or that an application for admission would defeat the object of the entry; and

(*b*) that there is reasonable ground for entry upon the land or vessel for the purpose for which entry is required,

then, subject to the following subsection, the justice may by warrant under his hand authorise that person to enter the land or vessel, if need be by force.

(3) A justice of the peace shall not issue a warrant in pursuance of the preceding subsection in respect of any land or vessel unless he is satisfied—

(*a*) that admission to the land or vessel in pursuance of subsection (1) of this section was sought after not less than seven days notice of the intended entry had been served on the occupier; or

(*b*) that admission to the land or vessel in pursuance of that subsection was sought in an emergency and was refused by or on behalf of the occupier; or

(*c*) that the land or vessel is unoccupied; or

(*d*) that an application for admission to the land or vessel would defeat the object of the entry.

(4) A warrant issued in pursuance of this section shall continue in force until the purpose for which the entry is required has been satisfied.

[Control of Pollution Act 1974, s 91.]

8–25854 92. Provisions supplementary to s 91. (1) A person authorised to enter upon any land or vessel in pursuance of the preceding section shall, if so required, produce evidence of his authority before he enters upon the land or vessel.

(2) A person so authorised may take with him on to the land or vessel in question such other persons and such equipment as may be necessary.

(3) Admission to any land or vessel used for residential purposes and admission with heavy equipment to any other land or vessel shall not, except in an emergency or in a case where the land or vessel is unoccupied, be demanded as of right in pursuance of subsection (1) of the preceding section unless a notice of the intended entry has been served on the occupier not less than seven days before the demand.

(4) A person who, in the exercise of powers conferred on him by virtue of the preceding section or this section, enters upon any land or vessel which is unoccupied or of which the occupier is temporarily absent shall leave the land or vessel as effectually secured against trespassers as he found it.

(5) *Compensation.*

(6) A person who wilfully obstructs another person acting in the exercise of any powers conferred on the other person by virtue of the preceding section or this section shall be guilty of an offence and liable on summary conviction to a fine not exceeding **level 3** on the standard scale.

(7) In the preceding section and this section any reference to an emergency is a reference to a case where a person requiring entry to any land or vessel has reasonable cause to believe that circumstances exist which are likely to endanger life or health and that immediate entry to the land or vessel is necessary to verify the existence of those circumstances or to ascertain their cause or to effect a remedy.
[Control of Pollution Act 1974, s 92, as amended by the Criminal Justice Act 1982, ss 38 and 46.]

8–25855 **93. Power of authorities to obtain information.** (1) Subject to the following subsection, a relevant authority may serve on any person a notice requiring him to furnish to the authority, within a period or at times specified in the notice and in a form so specified, any information so specified which the authority reasonably considers that it needs for the purposes of any function conferred on the authority by this Act.

(2) Provision may be made by regulations for restricting the information which may be required in pursuance of the preceding subsection and for determining the form in which the information is to be so required.

(3) A person who—

(*a*) fails without reasonable excuse to comply with the requirements of a notice served on him in pursuance of this section; or

(*b*) in furnishing any information in compliance with such a notice, makes any statement which he knows to be false or misleading in a material particular or recklessly makes any statement which is false or misleading in a material particular,

shall be guilty of an offence.

(3A) A person guilty of an offence under this section shall be liable[1]

(*a*) on summary conviction, to a fine not exceeding **the statutory maximum**; or

(*b*) on conviction on indictment, to a **fine** or to imprisonment for a term not exceeding **two years**, or to **both**.

[Control of Pollution Act 1974, s 93, as amended by the Criminal Justice Act 1982, ss 38 and 46 and the Environment Act 1995, Sch 19.]

***Amended by the Environment Act 1995, Sch 19, when in force.**

1. For procedure in respect of an offence which is triable either way, see the Magistrates' Courts Act 1980 ss 17A-21, in PART I: MAGISTRATES' COURTS, PROCEDURE, ante.

8–25856 **94. Prohibition of disclosure of information.** (1) If a person discloses information relating to any trade secret used in carrying on a particular undertaking and the information has been given to him or obtained by him by virtue of this Act he shall, subject to the following subsection, be guilty of an offence and liable on summary conviction to a fine not exceeding **level 5** on the standard scale.

(2) A person shall not be guilty of an offence under the preceding subsection by virtue of the disclosure of any information if—

(*a*) the disclosure is made—

(i) in the performance of his duty, or
(ii) in pursuance of section 79(1)(*b*)[1] of this Act, or
(iii) with the consent in writing of a person having a right to disclose the information; or

(*b*) the information is of a kind prescribed for the purposes of this paragraph and, if regulations made for those purposes provide that information of that kind may only be disclosed in pursuance of the regulations to prescribed persons, the disclosure is to a prescribed person.

[Control of Pollution Act 1974, s 94, as amended by the Criminal Justice Act 1982, ss 38 and 46.]

---

1. Section 79(1)(*b*) relates to arrangements by a local authority for the publication of information on the problem of air pollution.

8–25857 **98. Interpretation of Part V.** In this Part of this Act—

"functions" includes powers and duties; and

"relevant authority" means—

(*a*) in England, the Secretary of State, a county council, a district council, a London borough council, the Common Council of the City of London, the Sub-Treasurer of the Inner Temple and Under Treasurer of the Middle Temple;

(*aa*) in Wales, the Secretary of State, a county council or a county borough council and, for the purposes of sections 91 to 93 of this Act, a sewerage undertaker; and

(*b*) (*Scotland*).

[Control of Pollution Act 1974, s 98, as amended by the Local Government Act 1985, Sch 17, the Water Act 1989, Sch 27 and the Local Government (Wales) Act 1994, Sch 9.]

PART VI[1]

MISCELLANEOUS AND GENERAL

Miscellaneous

8–25859 105. Interpretation etc—general. (1) In this Act—

"the Alkali Act" means the Alkali, &c Works Regulation Act 1906;

"county", "county borough" and "district", except in relation to Scotland, have the same meanings as in the Local Government Act 1972;

"mine" and "quarry" have the same meanings as in the Mines and Quarries Act 1954;

"modifications" includes additions, omissions and amendments and "modify" and cognate expressions shall be construed accordingly;

"notice" means notice in writing;

"owner", except in relation to Scotland, means the person for the time being receiving the rackrent of the premises in connection with which the word is used, whether on his own account or as agent or trustee for another person, or who would so receive the rackrent if the premises were let at a rackrent;

"premises" includes land;

"prescribed" means prescribed by regulations;

"regulations" means regulations made by the Secretary of State;

"trade effluent" includes any liquid (either with or without particles of matter in suspension in it) which is discharged from premises used for carrying on any trade or industry, other than surface water and domestic sewage, and for the purposes of this definition any premises wholly or mainly used (whether for profit or not) for agricultural or horticultural purposes or for scientific research or experiment shall be deemed to be premises used for carrying on a trade; and

"vessel" includes a hovercraft within the meaning of the Hovercraft Act 1968.

(2) Except so far as this Act expressly provides otherwise and subject to the provisions of section 33 of the Interpretation Act 1889[2] (which relates to offences under two or more laws), nothing in this Act—

(*a*) confers a right of action in any civil proceedings (other than proceedings for the recovery of a fine) in respect of any contravention of this Act or an instrument made in pursuance of this Act;

(*b*) affects any restriction imposed by or under any other enactment, whether public, local or private; or

(*c*) derogates from any right of action or other remedy (whether civil or criminal) in proceedings instituted otherwise than under this Act.

(3) In so far as any interest in Crown land is not an interest belonging to Her Majesty or a Crown interest or a Duchy interest, this Act shall apply to the land as if it were not Crown land; and expressions used in this subsection and subsection (1) of section 293 of the Town and Country Planning Act 1990 or, in relation to Scotland, subsection (7) of section 253 of the Town and Country Planning (Scotland) Act 1972 have the same meanings in this subsection as in that subsection.

(4) References in this Act to any enactment are references to it as amended by or under any other enactment.

[Control of Pollution Act 1974, s 105, as amended by the Planning (Consequential Provisions) Act 1990, Sch 2 and the Local Government (Wales) Act 1994, Sch 9.]

1. Part VI contains ss 99–109.
2. Now s 18 of the Interpretation Act 1978.

Refuse Disposal (Amenity) Act 1978

(1978 c 3)

Control of dumping

8–25875 1. Provision by local authorities for disposal of refuse. Duty on local authority[1] to provide places for deposit of non-business refuse.

[Refuse Disposal (Amenity) Act 1978, s 1 amended by the Local Government Act 1985, Sch 6, SI 1985/1984 and SI 1986/564—summarised.]

1. In Greater London or a metropolitan county, functions conferred on local authorities by this Act may be discharged by a single authority established by order of the Secretary of State to act on behalf of the councils where joint arrangements for waste disposal can with advantage be made (Local Government Act 1985, s 10).

8–25876 2. Penalty for unauthorised dumping. (1) Any person who, without lawful authority—

(*a*) abandons on any land in the open air, or on any other land forming part of a highway, a motor vehicle or anything which formed part of a motor vehicle and was removed from it in the course of dismantling the vehicle on the land; or (*b*) abandons on any such land any thing other than a motor vehicle, being a thing which he has brought to the land for the purpose of abandoning it there,

shall be guilty of an offence and liable on summary conviction to a fine of an amount not exceeding **level 4** on the standard scale or imprisonment for a term not exceeding **three months** or **both**.

(2) For the purposes of subsection (1) above, a person who leaves any thing on any land in such circumstances or for such a period that he may reasonably be assumed to have abandoned it or to have brought it to the land for the purpose of abandoning it there shall be deemed to have abandoned it there or, as the case may be, to have brought it to the land for the purpose unless the contrary is shown.

(3) *Scotland.*

[Refuse Disposal (Amenity) Act 1978, s 2, as amended by the Criminal Justice Act 1982, ss 35, 38 and 46.]

8–25876A 2A. Fixed penalty notices for offence of abandoning vehicles. (1) Where on any occasion it appears to an authorised officer of a local authority that a person has committed an offence under section 2(1)(a) above in the area of that authority, the officer may give that person a notice offering him the opportunity of discharging any liability to conviction for the offence by payment of a fixed penalty to the authority.

(2) Where a person is given a notice under this section in respect of an offence—

(*a*) no proceedings may be instituted for that offence before the expiration of the period of fourteen days following the date of the notice; and

(*b*) he may not be convicted of that offence if he pays the fixed penalty before the expiration of the period.

(3) A notice under this section must give such particulars of the circumstances alleged to constitute the offence as are necessary for giving reasonable information of the offence.

(4) A notice under this section must also state—

(*a*) the period during which, by virtue of subsection (2) above, proceedings will not be taken for the offence;

(*b*) the amount of the fixed penalty; and

(*c*) the person to whom and the address at which the fixed penalty may be paid.

(5) Without prejudice to payment by any other method, payment of the fixed penalty may be made by pre-paying and posting a letter containing the amount of the penalty (in cash or otherwise) to the person mentioned in subsection (4)(c) above at the address so mentioned.

(6) Where a letter is sent in accordance with subsection (5) above payment is to be regarded as having been made at the time at which that letter would be delivered in the ordinary course of post.

(7) The form of a notice under this section is to be such as the appropriate person may by order prescribe.

(8) The fixed penalty payable to a local authority under this section is, subject to subsection (9) below, £200.

(9) The appropriate person may by order substitute a different amount for the amount for the time being specified in subsection (8) above.

(10) The local authority to which a fixed penalty is payable under this section may make provision for treating it as having been paid if a lesser amount is paid before the end of a period specified by the authority.

(11) The appropriate person may by regulations restrict the extent to which, and the circumstances in which, a local authority may make provision under subsection (10) above.

(12) An order or regulations under this section may make different provision for different purposes and in relation to different areas.

(13) In any proceedings a certificate which—

(*a*) purports to be signed on behalf of the chief finance officer of the local authority, and

(*b*) states that payment of a fixed penalty was or was not received by a date specified in the certificate,

is evidence of the facts stated.

(14) In this section—

"authorised officer", in relation to a local authority, means an employee of the authority who is authorised in writing by the authority for the purposes of giving notices under this section;

"chief finance officer", in relation to a local authority, means the person having responsibility for the financial affairs of the authority.*

[Refuse Disposal (Amenity) Act 1978, s 2A, as inserted by the Clean Neighbourhoods and Environment Act 2005, s 10.]

***In force (in relation to England) 6 April 2006: see SI 2006/795. Date in force (in relation to Wales) to be appointed.**

8–25876B 2B. Fixed penalty notices: power to require name and address. (1) If an authorised officer of a local authority proposes to give a person a notice under section 2A above, the officer may require the person to give him his name and address.

(2) A person commits an offence if—

(*a*) he fails to give his name and address when required to do so under subsection (1) above, or
(*b*) he gives a false or inaccurate name or address in response to a requirement under that subsection.

(3) A person guilty of an offence under subsection (2) above is liable on summary conviction to a fine not exceeding level 3 on the standard scale.

(4) In this section "authorised officer" has the same meaning as in section 2A above.*

[Refuse Disposal (Amenity) Act 1978, s 2B, as inserted by the Clean Neighbourhoods and Environment Act 2005, s 10.]

***In force (in relation to England) 6 April 2006: see SI 2006/795. Date in force (in relation to Wales) to be appointed.**

8–25876C 2C. Use of fixed penalties under section 2A. (1) This section applies in relation to amounts paid to a local authority in pursuance of notices under section 2A above (its "fixed penalty receipts").

(2) A local authority may use its fixed penalty receipts only for the purposes of—

(*a*) its functions under this Act;
(*b*) its functions under sections 99 to 102 of the Road Traffic Regulation Act 1984;
(*c*) its functions relating to the enforcement of sections 3 and 4 of the Clean Neighbourhoods and Environment Act 2005; and
(*d*) such other of its functions as may be specified in regulations made by the appropriate person.

(3) Regulations under subsection (2)(d) above may in particular have the effect that a local authority may use its fixed penalty receipts for the purposes of any of its functions.

(4) A local authority must supply the appropriate person with such information relating to its use of its fixed penalty receipts as the appropriate person may require.

(5) The appropriate person may by regulations—

(*a*) make provision for what a local authority is to do with its fixed penalty receipts—

(i) pending their being used for the purposes of functions of the authority referred to in subsection (2) above;
(ii) if they are not so used before such time after their receipt as may be specified by the regulations;

(*b*) make provision for accounting arrangements in respect of a local authority's fixed penalty receipts.

(6) The provision that may be made under subsection (5)(a)(ii) above includes (in particular) provision for the payment of sums to a person (including the appropriate person) other than the authority.

(7) Before making regulations under this section, the appropriate person must consult—

(*a*) the authorities to which the regulations are to apply;
(*b*) such other persons as the appropriate person thinks fit.

(8) The powers to make regulations conferred by this section are, for the purposes of subsection (1) of section 100 of the Local Government Act 2003, to be regarded as included among the powers mentioned in subsection (2) of that section.*

[Refuse Disposal (Amenity) Act 1978, s 2C, as inserted by the Clean Neighbourhoods and Environment Act 2005, s 10.]

***In force (in relation to England) 6 April 2006: see SI 2006/795. Date in force (in relation to Wales) to be appointed.**

Abandoned vehicles and other refuse

8–25877 3, 4, 4A. *Removal and disposal of abandoned vehicles*[1]*, guidance.*

1. The removal of other refuse, which does not affect the courts, is dealt with by s 7. There is no provision similar to s 5(3) applying to refuse other than a motor vehicle. The Removal and Disposal of Vehicles Regulations 1986, SI 1986/183 amended by SI 1993/278 and 1708, SI 1994/1503, SI 1996/1003, SI 2004/746 and 2777 (E) and SI 2005/3252 (W) have been made.

8–25878 5. Recovery of expenses connected with removed vehicles. (1) Where a vehicle is removed in pursuance of section 3(1) above the appropriate authority shall be entitled to recover from any person responsible—

(*a*) such charges as may be prescribed[1] in respect of the removal of the vehicle; and
(*b*) charges ascertained by reference to a prescribed scale in respect of any period during which the vehicle is in the custody of the authority; and

(*c*) where the vehicle is disposed of in pursuance of section 4 above, charges determined in the prescribed manner in respect of its disposal.

(2) Any sum recoverable by virtue of this section shall be recoverable as a simple contract debt in any court of competent jurisdiction.

(3) Without prejudice to subsection (2) above, the court by which a person is convicted of an offence under section 2(1) above in respect of a motor vehicle may, on the application of the appropriate authority and in addition to any other order made by the court in relation to that person, order him to pay to the authority any sum which, in the opinion of the court, the authority are entitled to recover from him under this section in respect of the vehicles.

(4) In this section—

"the appropriate authority" means—

(*a*) in the case of a vehicle removed in pursuance of section 3(1) above by a local authority in England other than the council of a non-metropolitan district, or by a local authority in Wales, the local authority; and

(*b*) in the case of a vehicle so removed by the council of a non-metropolitan district in England, the county council; and

"person responsible", in relation to a vehicle, means—

(*a*) the owner of the vehicle at the time when it was put in the place from which it was so removed, unless he shows that he was not concerned in and did not know of its being put there;

(*b*) any person by whom it was put in the place aforesaid;

(*c*) any person convicted of an offence under section 2(1) above in consequence of the putting of the vehicle in the place aforesaid.

(5) For the purposes of subsection (1)(*b*) above—

(*a*) *Repealed*;

(*b*) a vehicle so removed by the council of a non-metropolitan district in England shall be treated as in the custody of the county council while it was in the custody of the district council by whom it was so removed.

[Refuse Disposal (Amenity) Act 1978, s 5, as amended by the Local Government Act 1985, Schs 6 and 17.]

---

1. These are contained in the Removal, Storage and Disposal of Vehicles (Prescribed Sums and Charges) Regulations 1989, SI 1989/744, amended by SI 1991/336, SI 1992/385 and SI 1993/550 and 1415.

8–25879 **11. Interpretation.** (1) In this Act, unless the contrary intention appears, the following expressions have the following meanings, that is to say—

"appropriate person" means—

(*a*) in relation to a local authority in England, the Secrtary of State;

(*b*) in relation to a local authority in Wales, the National Assembly for Wales;

"the Common Council" means the Common Council of the City of London;

"licence" means in relation to a vehicle, a licence issued for the vehicle under the Vehicle Excise and Registration Act 1994 (including a nil licence within the meaning of that Act);

"local authority" means—

(*a*) in relation to England, a district council, London borough council or the Common Council;

(*b*) *Scotland*;

(*c*) in relation to Wales, a county council or county borough council;

"motor vehicle" means a mechanically propelled vehicle intended or adapted for use on roads, whether or not it is in a fit state for such use, and includes any trailer intended or adapted for use as an attachment to such a vehicle, any chassis or body, with or without wheels, appearing to have formed part of such a vehicle or trailer and anything attached to such a vehicle or trailer;

"owner", in relation to a motor vehicle which is the subject of a hiring agreement or hire-purchase agreement, includes the person entitled to possession of the vehicle under the agreement.

[Refuse Disposal (Amenity) Act 1978, s 11, as amended by the Local Government (Wales) Act 1994, Sch 9, the Vehicle Excise and Registration Act 1994, Sch 3 and the Clean Neighbourhoods and Environment Act 2005, s 14 and the Clean Neighbourhoods and Environment Act 2005, s 12.]

Litter Act 1983

(1983 c 35)

8–25880 **5. Litter bins in England and Wales[1].** (1) A litter authority[2] in England and Wales may provide and maintain in any street or public place receptacles for refuse or litter (in this section referred to as "litter bins").

(2) It shall be the duty of a litter authority in England and Wales to make arrangements for the regular emptying and cleansing of any litter bins provided or maintained by them under this section or under section 185 of the Highways Act 1980; and such an authority shall have power to cleanse and empty litter bins provided in any street or public place by them or any other person.

(3) The regular emptying mentioned in subsection (2) above shall be sufficiently frequent to ensure that no such litter bin or its contents shall become a nuisance or give reasonable ground for complaint.

(4) In any place where a litter bin may be provided or maintained under this section or under section 185 of the Highways Act 1980, a litter authority may put up notices about the leaving of refuse and litter, and for that purpose may, subject to the provisions of this section, erect and maintain notice boards.

(5) Subject to section 13 of the City of London (Various Powers) Act 1971 (which empowers the Common Council of the City of London to affix litter bins), a litter authority shall not have power under this section to place any litter bin or any notice board—

(*a*) on any land forming part of an open space as defined in the Open Spaces Act 1906 which is provided by or under the management and control of some other litter authority or a parish meeting, without the consent of that authority or meeting, or

(*b*) on any other land not forming part of a street, without the consent of the owner and of the occupier of that land.

(6) The powers conferred by this section shall only be exercisable with the consent of the persons mentioned in the Table in paragraph 1 of Schedule 1 to this Act, and paragraphs 2 and 3 of that Schedule shall have effect in relation to those consents.

(7) A litter authority may sell refuse or litter removed by them from any litter bins.

(8) A litter authority may not, under this section, do anything that is unlawful under the law relating to ancient monuments or to town and country planning.

(9) Any person who wilfully removes or otherwise interferes with any litter bin or notice board provided or erected under this section or section 185 of the Highways Act 1980 shall be liable on summary conviction to a fine not exceeding **level 1** on the standard scale.

(10) The court by which a person is convicted under subsection (9) above may order him to pay a sum not exceeding **£20** as compensation to the litter authority concerned, and any such order shall be enforceable in the same way as an order for costs to be paid by the offender.

(11) This section applies to a receptacle provided under section 76 of the Public Health Act 1936 or section 51 of the Public Health Act 1961 as if it had been provided under this section.

[Litter Act 1983, s 5.]

---

1. Sections 283–285, 288, 304, 305, 341 and 343 of the Public Health Act 1936, title PUBLIC HEALTH, post, apply in relation to this section, s 6 and Sch 1 to this Act as if ss 5 and 6 and that Schedule were contained in the Act of 1936 (s 6(7)). In Greater London or a metropolitan county, functions conferred by ss 5 and 6 of this Act may be discharged by a single authority established by order of the Secretary of State to act on behalf of the councils where joint arrangements for waste disposal can with advantage be made (Local Government Act 1985, s 10).

2. In this section "litter authority" includes the Council of the Isles of Scilly (s 6(8)).

8–25881 6. *Provisions supplementary to section 5.*

8–25882 7–8. *Scotland.*

8–25883 9. *Orders.*

8–25884 10. Interpretation. (1) In this Act—

"joint body" means a joint body constituted solely of two or more such councils as are mentioned in paragraphs (*a*) to (*f*) of the definition of "litter authority" below;

"litter authority", in relation to England and Wales, means, except so far as is otherwise provided—

(*a*) a county council,
(*b*) a district council,
(*c*) a London borough council,
(*d*) the Common Council of the City of London,
(*e*) a parish council,
(*f*) a community council,
(*g*) a joint body,
(*h*) (*Repealed*),
(*i*) the Sub-Treasurer of the Inner Temple, or
(*j*) the Under Treasurer of the Middle Temple;

(2) In the application of this Act in relation to Wales, any reference to a county shall be read as including a reference to a county borough and any reference to a county council shall be read as including a reference to a county borough council.

[Litter Act 1983, s 10, as amended by the Statute Law (Repeals) Act 1993, Sch 1, the Local Government (Wales) Act 1994, s 6 and Sch 9 and the Environment Act 1995, Sch 24.]

8–25886 **11. Isles of Scilly.** Sections 3 and 4 above shall have effect in their application to the Isles of Scilly with such modifications, additions, omissions and amendments as the Secretary of State may by order specify.
[Litter Act 1983, s 11.]

8–25887 **12–13.** *Consequential amendments and repeals; Short title commencement and extent.*

8–25888 SCHEDULE 1
Consents required under Section 5

Public Health (Control of Disease) Act 1984
(1984 c 22)

PART I
ADMINISTRATIVE PROVISIONS

8–25910 Part I of the Act (ss 1–9) provides for local authorities to carry the Act into execution, with certain powers being assigned to port health authorities as constituted by Order of the Secretary of State. Vessels in inland and coastal waters are subject to the jurisdiction of the appropriate authority, as if they were houses, buildings or premises and the master were the occupier; this does not apply to naval and foreign government vessels, nor to certain provisions of the Act such as those applying to common lodging houses, burial and cremation, Part V (other than s 56) and Part VI.

PART II[1]
CONTROL OF DISEASE
General

8–25911 **10. Notifiable diseases.** In this Act, "notifiable disease"[2] means any of the following diseases—

(*a*) cholera;
(*b*) plague;
(*c*) relapsing fever;
(*d*) smallpox; and
(*e*) typhus.

[Public Health (Control of Disease) Act 1984, s 10.]

1. Part II comprises ss 10–45.
2. Regulations made under previous legislation and saved by Sch 1 to this Act extend the categories of disease to acute encephalitis, acute meningitis, acute poliomyelitis, anthrax, diphtheria, dysentry (amoebic or bacillary), food poisoning (all sources), infective jaundice, lassa fever, leprosy, leptospirosis, malaria, Marburg disease, measles, ophthalmia neonatorum, paratyphoid fever, rabies, scarlet fever, tetanus, tuberculosis, typhoid fever, viral haemorrhagic fever, whooping cough, yellow fever.

8–25912 **11. Cases of notifiable disease and food poisoning to be reported.** (1) If a registered medical practitioner becomes aware, or suspects, that a patient whom he is attending within the district of a local authority is suffering from a notifiable disease or from food poisoning, he shall, unless he believes, and has reasonable grounds for believing, that some other registered medical practitioner has complied with this subsection with respect to the patient, forthwith send to the proper officer of the local authority for that district a certificate stating—

(*a*) the name, age and sex of the patient and the address of the premises where the patient is,
(*b*) the disease or, as the case may be, particulars of the poisoning from which the patient is, or is suspected to be, suffering and the date, or approximate date, of its onset, and
(*c*) if the premises are a hospital, the day on which the patient was admitted, the address of the premises from which he came there and whether or not, in the opinion of the person giving the certificate, the disease or poisoning from which the patient is, or is suspected to be, suffering was contracted in the hospital.

(2), (3) *Supply of forms, onward transmission of certificates.*

(4) A person who fails to comply with an obligation imposed on him by subsection (1) above shall be liable on summary conviction to a fine not exceeding **level 1** on the standard scale.

(5) In this section, "hospital" means any institution for the reception and treatment of persons suffering from illness, any maternity home and any institution for the reception and treatment of persons during convalescence or persons requiring medical rehabilitation, and "illness" includes mental disorder within the meaning of the Mental Health Act 1983 and any injury or disability requiring medical, surgical or dental treatment or nursing.
[Public Health (Control of Disease) Act 1984, s 11, as amended by the Health Authorities Act 1995, Sch 1.]

8–25913 13. Regulations for control of certain diseases. Powers of the Secretary of State to make regulations[1].

[Public Health (Control of Disease) Act 1984, s 13 amended by the National Health Service and Community Care Act 1990, Sch 9, the Local Government (Wales) Act 1994, Sch 9, and the Health Authorities Act 1995, Sch 1 and SI 2000/90—summarised.]

---

1. The Public Health (Infectious Diseases) Regulations 1988, SI 1988/1546 amended by SI 2002/2469 apply certain sections of this Act to certain diseases. In particular s 38 is applied, with modification, to the acquired immune deficiency syndrome.

8–25914 15. Contravention of regulations under s 13. Any person who wilfully neglects or refuses to obey or carry out, or obstructs the execution of, any regulations made under section 13 above shall, in a case where no provision is made in the regulations for his punishment, be liable on summary conviction—

(*a*) to a fine not exceeding **level 5** on the standard scale, and

(*b*) in the case of a continuing offence, to a further fine not exceeding £50 for every day on which the offence continues after conviction.

[Public Health (Control of Disease) Act 1984, s 15.]

8–25915 16. Power of local authority to direct that other diseases notifiable. Local authority may make order making a disease notifiable in their area; prior approval of Secretary of State necessary except in emergency; order requires at least one week's notice in local newspaper.

[Public Health (Control of Disease) Act 1984, s 16—summarised.]

8–25916 17. Exposure of persons and articles liable to convey notifiable disease. (1) A person who—

(*a*) knowing that he is suffering from a notifiable disease, exposes other persons to the risk of infection by his presence or conduct in any street, public place, place of entertainment or assembly, club, hotel, inn or shop,

(*b*) having the care of a person whom he knows to be suffering from a notifiable disease, causes or permits that person to expose other persons to the risk of infection by his presence or conduct in any such place as aforesaid, or

(*c*) gives, lends, sells, transmits or exposes, without previous disinfection, any clothing, bedding or rags which he knows to have been exposed to infection from any such disease, or any other article which he knows to have been so exposed and which is liable to carry such infection,

shall be liable on summary conviction to a fine not exceeding **level 1** on the standard scale.

(2) A person shall not incur any liability under this section by transmitting with proper precautions any article for the purpose of having it disinfected.

[Public Health (Control of Disease) Act 1984, s 17.]

8–25917 18. Information to be furnished by occupier in case of notifiable disease or food poisoning. (1) On the application of the proper officer of the local authority for any district, the occupier of any premises in the district in which there is or has been any person suffering from a notifiable disease or food poisoning shall furnish such information within his knowledge as that officer may reasonably require for the purpose of enabling measures to be taken to prevent the spread of the disease or, as the case may be, to trace the source of food poisoning.

(2) If any person required to furnish information under this section fails to furnish it, or knowingly furnishes false information, he shall be liable on summary conviction to a fine not exceeding **level 1** on the standard scale.

(3) In this section, "occupier", in relation to any premises, includes—

(*a*) a person having the charge, management or control of the premises, or of a building of which the premises form part, and

(*b*) in the case of premises consisting of a building the whole of which is ordinarily let out in separate tenements, or of a lodging house the whole of which is ordinarily let to lodgers, the person receiving the rent payable by the tenants or by the lodgers, as the case may be, either on his own account or as the agent of another person.

[Public Health (Control of Disease) Act 1984, s 18.]

8–25918 19. Trading etc by person with notifiable disease. A person who, knowing that he is suffering from a notifiable disease, engages in or carries on any trade, business or occupation which he cannot engage in or carry on without risk of spreading the disease shall be liable on summary conviction to a fine not exceeding **level 1** on the standard scale.

[Public Health (Control of Disease) Act 1984, s 19.]

8–25919 20. Stopping of work to prevent spread of disease. (1) With a view to preventing the spread of—

(*a*) a notifiable disease, or

(*b*) a disease to which subsection (1A) below applies,

the proper officer of the local authority for any district may by notice in writing request any person to discontinue his work.

(1A) The diseases to which this subsection applies are—

(*a*) enteric fever (including typhoid and paratyphoid fevers);
(*b*) dysentery;
(*c*) diphtheria;
(*d*) scarlet fever;
(*e*) acute inflammation of the throat;
(*f*) gastro-enteritis; and
(*g*) undulant fever.

(2) The local authority shall compensate a person who has suffered any loss in complying with a request under this section, and section 57(2), (3) and (4) below shall apply to any dispute arising under this subsection.

[Public Health (Control of Disease) Act 1984, s 20, as amended by the Food Act 1984, Sch 10 and the Food Safety Act 1990, Sch 3.]

Children

8–25920 21. Exclusion from school of child liable to convey notifiable disease. (1) A person having the care of a child who—

(*a*) is or has been suffering from a notifiable disease, or
(*b*) has been exposed to infection of a notifiable disease,

shall not, after receiving notice from the proper officer of the local authority for the district that the child is not to be sent to school, permit the child to attend school until he has obtained from the proper officer a certificate that in his opinion the child may attend school without undue risk of communicating the disease to others.

(2) No charge shall be made for a certificate under this section.

(3) A person who contravenes the provisions of this section shall be liable on summary conviction to a fine not exceeding **level 1** on the standard scale.

[Public Health (Control of Disease) Act 1984, s 21.]

8–25921 22. List of day pupils at school having case of notifiable disease. (1) The principal of a school in which any pupil is suffering from a notifiable disease shall, if required by the proper officer of the local authority for the district, furnish to him within a reasonable time fixed by him a complete list of the names and addresses of the pupils, not being boarders, in or attending the school, or any specified department of the school.

(2) The local authority shall pay to the principal of a school for every list furnished by him under this section the sum of $2^1/_2$p, and, if the list contains more than 25 names, a further sum of $2^1/_2$p for every 25 names (including the first 25 names) contained in the list.

(3) If the principal of a school fails to comply with the provisions of this section, he shall be liable on summary conviction to a fine not exceeding **level 1** on the standard scale.

(4) In this section, "the principal" means the person in charge of a school, and includes, where the school is divided into departments and no one person is in charge of the whole school, the head of any department.

[Public Health (Control of Disease) Act 1984, s 22.]

8–25922 23. Exclusion of children from places of entertainment or assembly. (1) This section applies—

(*a*) to any theatre, including a cinematograph theatre, and any building used as a public hall, public concert-room or lecture room, public dance room or public gymnasium or indoor swimming baths, and
(*b*) to any sports ground, outdoor swimming baths, outdoor swimming pool, or skating or roller staking rink, to which the public are admitted, either on payment of a charge for admission or not, and
(*c*) to any circus, show, fair, fête, amusement arcade or other public place of entertainment which is not in a building.

(2) With a view to preventing the spread of a notifiable disease, a local authority may, by notice published in such manner as they think best for bringing it to the notice of persons concerned, prohibit or restrict the admission of persons under the prescribed age to any place to which this section applies for a time specified in the notice.

(3) A notice under this section may contain exemptions from the prohibitions or restrictions which it imposes, and any such exemption may be made subject to compliance with such conditions as may be specified in the notice.

(4) A notice under this section may be expressed to apply to particular premises, or parts of

premises, designated in the notice, or to part only of the district of the local authority, but, except as otherwise provided in the notice, the notice shall apply throughout the district of the local authority.

(5) If the person responsible for the management of a place to which this section applies, having been served by the local authority with a copy of a notice published under this section, admits any person under the prescribed age to that place in contravention of the notice, or fails to comply with any condition specified in the notice, he shall be liable on summary conviction to a fine not exceeding **level 1** on the standard scale.

(6) In any proceedings for an offence under subsection (5) above, it shall be a defence to prove that there were reasonable grounds for believing that the person admitted had attained the prescribed age.

(7) In this section, "prescribed age", in relation to a notice, means such age, not exceeding 16, as may be prescribed by the notice.

[Public Health (Control of Disease) Act 1984, s 23.]

Infected articles

8–25923 24. Infected articles not to be taken or sent to be washed or cleaned. (1) A person shall not send or take to any laundry or public washhouse for the purpose of being washed, or to any place for the purpose of being cleaned, any article which he knows to have been exposed to infection from a notifiable disease, unless that article—

(*a*) has been disinfected by or to the satisfaction of the proper officer of the local authority for the district or a registered medical practitioner, or

(*b*) is sent with proper precautions to a laundry for the purpose of disinfection, with notice that it has been exposed to infection.

(2) The local authority may pay the expenses of the disinfection of any such article if carried out by them or under their direction.

(3) The occupier of any building in which a person is suffering from a notifiable disease shall, if required by the local authority, furnish to them the address of any laundry, washhouse or other place to which articles from the house have been or will be sent during the continuance of the disease for the purpose of being washed or cleaned.

(4) A person who contravenes or fails to comply with any provision of this section shall be liable on summary conviction to a fine not exceeding **level 1** on the standard scale.

[Public Health (Control of Disease) Act 1984, s 24.]

8–25924 25. Library books. (1) A person who knows that he is suffering from a notifiable disease shall not take any book, or cause any book to be taken for his use, or use any book taken, from any public or circulating library.

(2) A person shall not permit any book which has been taken from a public or circulating library, and is under his control, to be used by any person whom he knows to be suffering from a notifiable disease.

(3) A person shall not return to any public or circulating library a book which he knows to have been exposed to infection from a notifiable disease, or permit any such book which is under his control to be so returned, but shall give notice to the local authority, or, in the case of a library provided by a county council, to that council, that the book has been so exposed to infection.

(4) A local authority or, as the case may be, a county council on receiving such a notice shall cause the book to be disinfected and returned to the library, or shall cause it to be destroyed.

(5) A person who contravenes any of the provisions of subsections (1) to (3) above shall be liable on summary conviction to a fine not exceeding **level 1** on the standard scale.

[Public Health (Control of Disease) Act 1984, s 25.]

8–25925 26. Infectious matter not to be placed in dustbins. (1) A person who places, or causes or permits to be placed, in a dustbin or ashpit any matter which he knows to have been exposed to infection from a notifiable disease, and which has not been disinfected, shall be liable on summary conviction to a fine not exceeding **level 1** on the standard scale.

(2) The local authority shall give notice of the provisions of this section to the occupier of any house in which they are aware that there is a person suffering from a notifiable disease.

(3) If the local authority are requested to do so by the occupier of any premises in Greater London in which there is a person suffering from a notifiable disease, they shall provide for the removal and disinfection or destruction of any rubbish that has been exposed to infection from that disease.

[Public Health (Control of Disease) Act 1984, s 26.]

8–25926 27. Provision of disinfecting stations. A local authority may provide a disinfecting station and may cause any article brought there to be disinfected free of charge.

[Public Health (Control of Disease) Act 1984, s 27.]

Infected premises

8–25927 28. Prohibition of certain work on premises where notifiable disease exists. (1) If a case of a notifiable disease occurs on any premises, then, whether the person suffering from the disease has been removed from the premises or not, the local authority for the district may make an order forbidding any work to which this section applies to be given out to any person living or working on those premises, or on such part of them as may be specified in the order; and any order so made may be served on the occupier of any factory or other place from which work is given out, or on any contractor employed by any such occupier.

(2) An order under this section may be expressed—

(*a*) to operate for a specified time or until the premises or any part of them specified in the order have been disinfected to the satisfaction of the local authority, or

(*b*) to be inoperative so long as any other reasonable precautions specified in the order are taken.

(3) If any occupier or contractor on whom an order under this section has been served contravenes the provisions of the order, he shall be liable on summary conviction to a fine not exceeding **level 1** on the standard scale.

(4) This section applies to the making, cleaning, washing, altering, ornamenting, finishing or repairing of wearing apparel and any incidental work, and to such other classes of work as may be specified by order of the Secretary of State.

(5) The power of the Secretary of State to make orders under subsection (4) above shall be exercisable by statutory instrument.

[Public Health (Control of Disease) Act 1984, s 28.]

8–25928 29. Letting of house or room after recent case of notifiable disease. (1) If a person who—

(*a*) is concerned in the letting of a house or part of a house, or in showing a house or part of a house with a view to its being let, or

(*b*) has recently ceased to occupy a house or part of a house,

is questioned by any person negotiating for the hire of the house or any part of it as to whether there is, or has been within the preceding six weeks, in any part of the house a person suffering from a notifiable disease, and knowingly makes a false answer to that question, he shall be liable on summary conviction to a fine not exceeding **level 2** on the standard scale, or to imprisonment for a term not exceeding **one month**.

(2) A person who lets any house or part of a house in which a person has to his knowledge been suffering from a notifiable disease without having the house, or the part of the house, and all articles in it liable to retain infection, properly disinfected shall be liable on summary conviction to a fine not exceeding **level 2** on the standard scale.

(3) The keeper of a hotel or inn who allows a room in it in which a person has to his knowledge been suffering from a notifiable disease to be occupied by any other person before the room and all articles in it liable to retain infection have been properly disinfected shall be liable on summary conviction to a fine not exceeding **level 2** on the standard scale.

(4) In this section and in section 30 below, "properly disinfected" means disinfected to the satisfaction of the proper officer of the local authority for the district or a registered medical practitioner, as testified by a certificate signed by him.

[Public Health (Control of Disease) Act 1984, s 29.]

8–25929 30. Duty on ceasing to occupy house after recent case of notifiable disease. (1) If a person ceases to occupy a house or part of a house in which to his knowledge a person has within six weeks previously been suffering from a notifiable disease and either—

(*a*) he fails to have the house, or the part of the house, and all articles in it liable to retain infection, properly disinfected, or

(*b*) he fails to give to the owner of the house, or the part of the house, notice of the previous existence of the disease, or

(*c*) on being questioned by the owner as to whether within the preceding six weeks there has been in it any person suffering from any notifiable disease, he makes a false answer,

he shall be liable on summary conviction—

(i) in the case of an offence under paragraph (*a*) or (*b*) above, to a fine not exceeding **level 2** on the standard scale, or

(ii) in the case of an offence under paragraph (*c*), to a fine not exceeding **level 2** on the standard scale or to imprisonment for a term not exceeding **one month**.

(2) The local authority shall give notice of the provisions of this section to the occupier and also to the owner of any house in which they are aware that there is a person suffering from a notifiable disease.

[Public Health (Control of Disease) Act 1984, s 30.]

8–25940 31. Disinfection of premises. (1) If, on a certificate of the proper officer of the local authority for a district, the local authority are satisfied that the cleansing and disinfection of any premises, and the disinfection or destruction of any articles there likely to retain infection, would tend to prevent the spread of any infectious disease, the authority shall give notice to the occupier of the premises that they will at his cost—

(*a*) cleanse and disinfect the premises, and
(*b*) disinfect or, as the case may require, destroy any such articles,

unless, within 24 hours after the receipt of the notice, he informs them that within a time to be fixed by the notice he will take such steps as are specified in it.

(2) If—

(*a*) within 24 hours after receipt of the notice the person to whom it is given does not so inform the authority, or
(*b*) having so informed the authority, he fails to take the specified steps to the satisfaction of the proper officer within the time fixed by the notice,

the authority may cause the premises to be cleansed and disinfected and the articles to be disinfected or destroyed, as the case may require, and may, if they think fit, recover from him the expenses reasonably incurred by them in doing so; and any such expenses may be so recovered as a simple contract debt in any court of the competent jurisdiction.

(3) Where the occupier of any premises is in the opinion of the local authority unable effectually to take such steps as they consider necessary, they may, without giving such notice but with his consent, take the necessary steps at their own cost.

(4) Where a local authority have under this section disinfected any premises or article or destroyed any article, they may if they think fit pay compensation to any person who has suffered damage by their action.

(5) For the purposes of this section, the owner of unoccupied premises shall be deemed to be in occupation of them.

[Public Health (Control of Disease) Act 1984, s 31.]

8–25941 **32. Removal of person from infected house.** (1) Where any infectious disease occurs in a house, or the local authority deem it necessary to disinfect any house, the authority may, on a certificate of the proper officer of the local authority for the district—

(*a*) cause any person who is not himself sick and who consents to leave the house, or whose parent or guardian, where the person is a child, consents to his leaving the house, to be removed to any temporary shelter or house accommodation provided by the authority, or
(*b*) cause any such person to be so removed without any consent, if a justice of the peace (acting, if he deems it necessary, ex parte) is satisfied, on the application of the authority, of the necessity for the removal and makes an order for the removal, subject to such conditions, if any, as may be specified in the order.

(2) The local authority shall in every case cause the removal to be effected, and the conditions of any order to be satisfied, without charge to the persons removed, or to the parent or guardian of that person.

(3) A local authority may provide temporary shelter or house accommodation for the purposes of this section.

[Public Health (Control of Disease) Act 1984, s 32.]

Public conveyances

8–25942 **33. Use of public conveyance by person with notifiable disease.** (1) No person who knows that he is suffering from a notifiable disease shall—

(*a*) enter any public conveyance used for the conveyance of persons at separate fares, or
(*b*) enter any other public conveyance without previously notifying the owner or driver that he is so suffering.

(2) No person having the care of a person whom he knows to be suffering from a notifiable disease shall permit that person to be carried—

(*a*) in any public conveyance used for the conveyance of persons at separate fares, or
(*b*) in any other public conveyance without previously informing the owner or driver that that person is so suffering.

(3) A person who contravenes any provision of this section—

(*a*) shall be liable on summary conviction to a fine not exceeding **level 1** on the standard scale, and
(*b*) in addition to any fine imposed, shall be ordered by the court to pay to any person concerned with the conveyance as owner, driver or conductor a sum sufficient to cover any loss and expense incurred by him in connection with the disinfection of the conveyance in accordance with section 34 below.

[Public Health (Control of Disease) Act 1984, s 33.]

8–25943 **34. Duty of owner, driver or conductor of public conveyance.** (1) The owner, driver or conductor of a public conveyance used for the conveyance of passengers at separate fares shall not convey in it a person whom he knows to be suffering from a notifiable disease.

(2) The owner or driver of any other public conveyance may refuse to convey in it any person suffering from a notifiable disease until he has been paid a sum sufficient to cover any loss and expense which will be incurred by reason of the provisions of subsection (3) below.

(3) If a person suffering from a notifiable disease is conveyed in a public conveyance, the person in charge of the conveyance shall—

(*a*) as soon as practicable give notice to the local authority for the district in which the conveyance is usually kept, and

(*b*) before permitting any other person to enter the conveyance, cause it to be disinfected,

and any person concerned with the conveyance as its owner, driver or conductor may recover summarily as a civil debt from the person so conveyed, or from the person causing that person to be so conveyed, a sufficient sum to cover any loss and expense incurred by him.

(4) A person who contravenes any of the foregoing provisions of this section shall be liable on summary conviction to a fine not exceeding **level 1** on the standard scale.

(5) The local authority, when so requested by the person in charge of a public conveyance in which a person suffering from a notifiable disease has been conveyed, shall provide for its disinfection, and shall make no charge for the disinfection except in a case where the owner, driver or conductor conveyed a person knowing that he was suffering from a notifiable disease.

[Public Health (Control of Disease) Act 1984, s 34.]

Infectious persons

8–25944 **35. Medical examination.** (1) If a justice of the peace (acting, if he deems it necessary, ex parte) is satisfied, on a written certificate issued by a registered medical practitioner nominated by the local authority for a district—

(*a*) that there is reason to believe that some person in the district—

(i) is or has been suffering from a notifiable disease[1], or

(ii) though not suffering from such a disease, is carrying an organism that is capable of causing it, and

(*b*) that in his own interest, or in the interest of his family, or in the public interest, it is expedient that he should be medically examined, and

(*c*) that he is not under the treatment of a registered medical practitioner or that the registered medical practitioner who is treating him consents to the making of an order under this section,

the justice may order him to be medically examined by a registered medical practitioner so nominated.

(2) An order under this section may be combined with a warrant under subsection (3) of section 61 below authorising a registered medical practitioner nominated by the local authority to enter any premises, and for the purposes of that subsection that practitioner shall, if not an officer of the local authority, be treated as one.

(3) In this section, references to a person's being medically examined shall be construed as including references to his being submitted to bacteriological and radiological tests and similar investigations.

[Public Health (Control of Disease) Act 1984, s 35.]

1. For application of this section to acquired immune deficiency syndrome and other diseases, see SI 1988/1546.

8–25945 **36. Medical examination of group of persons believed to comprise carrier of notifiable disease.** (1) If a justice of the peace (acting, if he deems it necessary, ex parte) is satisfied, on a written certificate issued by the proper officer of the local authority for a district—

(*a*) that there is reason to believe that one of a group of persons, though not suffering from a notifiable disease, is carrying an organism that is capable of causing it, and

(*b*) that in the interest of those persons or their families, or in the public interest, it is expedient that those persons should be medically examined,

the justice may order them to be medically examined by a registered medical practitioner nominated by the local authority for that district.

(2) Subsections (2) and (3) of section 35 above apply in relation to subsection (1) above as they apply in relation to subsection (1) of that section.

[Public Health (Control of Disease) Act 1984, s 36.]

8–25946 **37. Removal to hospital of person with notifiable disease.** (1) Where a justice of the peace (acting, if he deems it necessary, ex parte) is satisfied, on the application of the local authority, that a person is suffering from a notifiable disease[1] and—

(*a*) that his circumstances are such that proper precautions to prevent the spread of infection cannot be taken, or that such precautions are not being taken, and

(*b*) that serious risk of infection is thereby caused to other persons, and

(*c*) that accommodation for him is available in a suitable hospital vested in the Secretary of State, or, pursuant to arrangements made by a Health Authority or Primary Care Trust (whether under an NHS contract or otherwise) in a suitable hospital vested in a NHS trust, Primary Care Trust or other person,

the justice may, with the consent mentioned in subsection (1A) below, order him to be removed to it.

(1A) The consent referred to in subsection (1) above is that of a Primary Care Trust or Health Authority—

(*a*) any part of whose area falls within that of the local authority, and

(*b*) which appears to the local authority to be an appropriate Primary Care Trust or Health Authority from whom to obtain consent.

(2) An order under this section may be addressed to such officer of the local authority as the justice may think expedient, and that officer and any officer of the hospital may do all acts necessary for giving effect to the order.

[Public Health (Control of Disease) Act 1984, s 37, as amended by the National Health Service and Community Care Act 1990, Schs 9 and 10, the Health Authorities Act 1995, Sch 1, SI 2000/90 and SI 2002/2469.]

1. For application of this section to acquired immune deficiency syndrome and other diseases, see SI 1988/1546.

8–25947 **38. Detention in hospital of person with notifiable disease.** (1) Where a justice of the peace (acting, if he deems it necessary, ex parte) in and for the place in which a hospital for infectious diseases is situated is satisfied, on the application of any local authority, that an inmate of the hospital who is suffering from a notifiable disease[1] would not on leaving the hospital be provided with lodging or accommodation in which proper precautions could be taken to prevent the spread of the disease by him, the justice may order him to be detained in the hospital.

(2) An order made under subsection (1) above may direct detention for a period specified in the order, but any justice of the peace acting in and for the same place may extend a period so specified as often as it appears to him to be necessary to do so.

(3) Any person who leaves a hospital contrary to an order made under this section for his detention there shall be liable on summary conviction to a fine not exceeding **level 1** on the standard scale, and the court may order him to be taken back to the hospital.

(4) An order under this section may be addressed—

(*a*) in the case of an order for a person's detention, to such officer of the hospital, and

(*b*) in the case of an order made under subsection (3) above, to such officer of the local authority on whose application the order for detention was made,

as the justice may think expedient, and that officer and any officer of the hospital may do all acts necessary for giving effect to the order.

[Public Health (Control of Disease) Act 1984, s 38.]

1. In its application to acquired immune deficiency syndrome, this section is modified by SI 1988/1546 so that in addition to the circumstances specified in that section, a justice of the peace may on the application of any local authority (acting if he deems it necessary ex parte) make an order for the detention in hospital of an inmate of that hospital suffering from acquired immune deficiency syndrome if the justice is satisfied that on his leaving the hospital proper precautions to prevent the spread of the disease would not be taken by him—(*a*) in his lodging or accommodation or (*b*) in other places to which he may be expected to go if not detained in the hospital.

Common lodging-houses

8–25948 **39. Keeper of common lodging-house to notify case of infectious disease.** (1) Where a person in a common lodging-house is suffering from any infectious disease, the keeper of the lodging-house shall immediately give notice of the case to the local authority for the district.

(2) A keeper of a lodging-house who fails to comply with subsection (1) above shall be liable on summary conviction to a fine not exceeding **level 1** on the standard scale and to a further fine not exceeding £2 for each day on which the offence continues after conviction.

(3) The local authority within whose district a common lodging-house is situated shall, if possible on the day on which they receive a notice under subsection (1) above and in any case within 48 hours after the receipt of the notice, send a copy of the notice to the Health Authority within whose area that lodging-house is situated.

[Public Health (Control of Disease) Act 1984, s 39, as amended by the Health Authorities Act 1995, Sch 1.]

8–25949 **40. Medical examination of inmates of common lodging-house.** If the proper officer of a local authority has reasonable grounds for believing that there is in a common lodging-house a person who is suffering, or has recently suffered, from a notifiable disease, he may make complaint thereof upon oath to a justice of the peace, and thereupon the justice may by warrant authorise him to enter the lodging-house and examine any person found in it with a view to ascertaining whether he is suffering, or has recently suffered, from a notifiable disease.

[Public Health (Control of Disease) Act 1984, s 40.]

8–25950 **41.** *Removal to hospital of inmate of common lodging-house with notifiable disease.*

8–25951 **42. Closure of common lodging-house on account of notifiable disease.** (1) If, on the application of a local authority, a magistrates' court is satisfied that it is necessary in the interests of the public health that a common lodging-house should be closed on account of the existence, or recent occurrence, in it of a case of notifiable disease, the court may make an order directing the lodging-house to be closed until it is certified by the proper officer of the local authority for the district to be free from infection.

(2) Any person who fails to comply with an order under subsection (1) above shall be liable on summary conviction to a fine not exceeding **level 1** on the standard scale, and to a further fine not exceeding £2 for each day on which the offence continues after conviction.
[Public Health (Control of Disease) Act 1984, s 42.]

Death of person suffering from notifiable disease

8–25952 **43. Person dying in hospital with notifiable disease.** (1) If—

(*a*) a person dies in hospital while suffering from a notifiable disease[1], and
(*b*) the proper officer of the local authority for the district or a registered medical practitioner certifies that in his opinion it is desirable, in order to prevent the spread of infection, that the body should not be removed from the hospital except for the purpose of being taken direct to a mortuary or being forthwith buried or cremated,

it shall not be lawful for any person to remove the body from the hospital except for such a purpose.

(2) In any such case, when the body is removed for the purpose of burial or cremation from the hospital or any mortuary to which it has been taken, it shall forthwith be taken direct to some place of burial or crematorium and there buried or cremated.

(3) A person who contravenes any provision of this section shall be liable on summary conviction to a fine not exceeding **level 1** on the standard scale.
[Public Health (Control of Disease) Act 1984, s 43.]

1. For application of this section to acquired immune deficiency syndrome and other diseases, see SI 1988/1546.

8–25953 **44. Isolation of body of person dying with notifiable disease.** Every person having the charge or control of premises in which is lying the body of a person who has died while suffering from a notifiable disease[1] shall take such steps as may be reasonably practicable to prevent persons coming unnecessarily into contact with, or proximity to, the body, and if he fails to do so he shall be liable on summary conviction to a fine not exceeding **level 1** on the standard scale.
[Public Health (Control of Disease) Act 1984, s 44.]

1. For application of this section to acquired immune deficiency syndrome and other diseases, see SI 1988/1546.

8–25954 **45. Restriction of wakes.** It shall not be lawful to hold a wake over the body of a person who has died while suffering from a notifiable disease; and the occupier of any premises who permits or suffers any such wake to take place on them, and every person who takes part in the wake, shall be liable on summary conviction to a fine not exceeding **level 1** on the standard scale.
[Public Health (Control of Disease) Act 1984, s 45.]

PART III[1]
DISPOSAL OF DEAD BODIES

8–25955 **46.** *Burial and cremation.*

1. Part III comprises ss 46–48.

8–25956 **47.** *Regulations about dead bodies.*

8–25957 **48. Removal of body to mortuary or for immediate burial.** (1) If a justice of the peace (acting, if he deems it necessary, ex parte) is satisfied, on a certificate of the proper officer of the local authority for the district in which a dead body lies, that the retention of the body in any building would endanger the health of the inmates of that building or of any adjoining or neighbouring building, he may order—

(*a*) that the body be removed by, and at the cost of, the local authority to a mortuary, and
(*b*) that the necessary steps be taken to secure that it is buried within a time limited by the order or, if he considers immediate burial necessary, immediately.

(2) Where an order is made under subsection (1) above, relatives or friends of the deceased person shall be deemed to comply with the order if they cause the body to be cremated within the time limited by the order or, as the case may be, immediately.

(3) An order under this section shall be an authority to any officer named in it to do all acts necessary for giving effect to the order.
[Public Health (Control of Disease) Act 1984, s 48.]

PART IV[1]
CANAL BOATS

8–25958 49. Regulations as to canal boats. (1), (2) *Duty of the Secretary of State to make regulations.*

(3) If any regulation in force under this section is not complied with as respects a canal boat, the master of the boat, and also the owner, if he is himself in default, shall be liable on summary conviction to a fine not exceeding **level 1** on the standard scale, and to a further fine not exceeding £2 for each day after conviction on which the non-compliance continues.
[Public Health (Control of Disease) Act 1984, s 49.]

1. Part IV comprises ss 49–53.

8–25959 50. Power to enter and inspect canal boats. (1) An inspector appointed by the Secretary of State may, on producing, if required, evidence of his authority, enter a canal boat at any time between six o'clock in the morning and nine o'clock in the evening and examine every part of the boat and may, if need be, detain the boat for the purpose of his examination, but not for any longer period than is necessary.

(2) If an authorised officer of a local authority or port health authority has reasonable ground for believing—

(*a*) that any provision of regulations made under section 49 above is being contravened as respects a canal boat, or

(*b*) that there is on board a canal boat any person suffering from an infectious disease,

he shall, for the purpose of ascertaining whether there is any such contravention or any person on board suffering from an infectious disease, have the like rights of entering, examining and if necessary detaining the boat as an inspector appointed by the Secretary of State has under subsection (1) above.

(3) The master of a canal boat shall, if required by such an inspector or officer, furnish him with such assistance and means as he may require for the purpose of his entry on and departure from the boat and his examination of it.

(4) Any person who refuses to comply with a requisition made under subsection (3) above shall be deemed to have obstructed the person by whom the requisition was made.
[Public Health (Control of Disease) Act 1984, s 50.]

8–25970 51. *Duties of local authorities and port health authorities under Part IV.*

8–25971 52. Prosecution of offences under Part IV. Proceedings in respect of an offence under this Part of this Act may be taken before a magistrates' court acting either—

(*a*) in the place where the offence was committed, or

(*b*) in the place where the alleged offender for the time being is.

[Public Health (Control of Disease) Act 1984, s 52.]

8–25972 53. Interpretation of Part IV. In this Part of this Act—

"canal" includes any river, inland navigation or lake, and any other waters situated wholly or partly within a county or county borough, whether those waters are or are not within the ebb and flow of the tide;

"canal boat" means any vessel, however propelled, which is used for the conveyance of goods along a canal, not being—

(*a*) a sailing barge which belongs to the class generally known as "Thames sailing barge" and is registered under the Merchant Shipping Act 1995, either in the Port of London or elsewhere, or

(*b*) a sea-going ship so registered, or

(*c*) a vessel used for pleasure purposes only;

"master", in relation to a canal boat, means the person having command or charge of the boat; and

"owner", in relation to a canal boat, includes a person who, though only the hirer of the boat, appoints the master and other persons working the boat.

[Public Health (Control of Disease) Act 1984, s 53, as amended by the Local Government (Wales) Act 1994, Sch 9 and the Merchant Shipping Act 1995, Sch 13.]

PART V[1]
MISCELLANEOUS

8–25973 55. Inducements offered by dealers in rags and old clothes. (1) No person who collects or deals in rags, old clothes or similar articles, and no person assisting or acting on behalf of any such person, shall—

(*a*) in or from any shop or premises used for or in connection with the business of a dealer in any such articles, or
(*b*) while engaged in collecting any such articles,

sell or deliver, whether gratuitously or not—

(i) any article of food or drink to any person, or
(ii) any article whatsoever to a person under the age of 14 years.

(2) In subsection (1)(ii) above, "article" includes any animal, fish, bird or other living thing.

(3) A person who contravenes any of the provisions of this section shall be liable on summary conviction to a fine not exceeding **level 1** on the standard scale.
[Public Health (Control of Disease) Act 1984, s 55.]

1. Part V comprises ss 54–56.

8–25974 56. Tents, vans, sheds and similar structures. (1) Part II (other than sections 39 to 42), Part III, this Part and Part VI of this Act apply in relation to tents, vans, sheds and similar structures used for human habitation as they apply in relation to other premises, and as if a tent, van, shed or similar structure used for human habitation were a house or a building so used.

(2) A local authority may make byelaws for preventing the spread of infectious disease by the occupants or users of tents, vans, sheds and similar structures used for human habitation.

(3) The powers of a court before which proceedings are brought in respect of any contravention of byelaws made under subsection (2) above shall include power to make an order prohibiting the use for human habitation of the tent, van, shed or other structure in question at such place or within such area as may be specified in the order.
[Public Health (Control of Disease) Act 1984, s 56.]

PART VI[1]
GENERAL

8–25975 57. General provision for compensation. (1) A local authority shall make full compensation to any person who has sustained damage by reason of the exercise by the authority, in relation to a matter as to which that person has not himself been in default, of any of their powers under a relevant provision of this Act; but this subsection does not affect the discretion of a local authority under section 31(4) above in a case to which that subsection applies.

(2) Subject to subsection (3) below, any dispute arising under this section as to the fact of damage, or as to the amount of compensation, shall be determined by arbitration.

(3) If the compensation claimed does not exceed £50, all questions as to the fact of damage, liability to pay compensation and the amount of compensation may, on the application of either party, be determined by, and any compensation awarded may be recovered before, a magistrates' court.

(4) In an arbitration under this section, the reference shall be to a single arbitrator appointed by agreement between the parties or, in default of agreement, by the Secretary of State.
[Public Health (Control of Disease) Act 1984, s 57.]

1. Part VI comprises ss 57–79.

8–25976 58. Form of notices and other documents. (1) All notices, orders and other documents authorised or required by or under this Act to be given, made or issued by a local authority, and all notices and applications authorised or required by or under this Act to be given or made to or to any officer of a local authority, shall be in writing.

(2) The Secretary of State may by regulations made by statutory instrument prescribe the form of any notice, certificate or other document to be used for the purposes of this Act, and, if forms are so prescribed, those forms or forms to the like effect may be used in all cases to which those forms are applicable.
[Public Health (Control of Disease) Act 1984, s 58.]

8–25977 59. Authentication of documents. (1) Any notice, order or other document which a local authority are authorised or required by or under this Act to give, make or issue may be signed on behalf of the authority—

(*a*) by the proper officer of the authority as respects documents relating to matters within his province, or
(*b*) by any officer of the authority authorised by them in writing to sign documents of the particular kind or, as the case may be, the particular document.

(2) Any document purporting to bear the signature of an officer—

(*a*) expressed to hold an office by virtue of which he is under this section empowered to sign such a document, or (*b*) expressed to be duly authorised by the local authority to sign such a document or the particular document,

shall, for the purposes of this Act, and of any byelaws and orders made under it, be deemed, until the contrary is proved, to have been duly given, made or issued by authority of the local authority.

(3) In subsection (2) above, "signature" includes a facsimile of a signature by whatever process reproduced.

[Public Health (Control of Disease) Act 1984, s 59.]

8–25978 60. Service of notices and other documents. Any notice, order or other document which is required or authorised by or under this Act to be given to or served on any person may, in any case for which no other provision is made by this Act, be given or served either—

(*a*) by delivering it to that person, or

(*b*) in the case of a coroner or the proper officer of a local authority, by leaving it or sending it in a prepaid letter addressed to him, at either his residence or his office, and, in the case of any other officer of a local authority, by leaving it, or sending it in a prepaid letter addressed to him, at his office, or

(*c*) in the case of any other person, by leaving it, or sending it in a prepaid letter addressed to him, at his usual or last known residence, or

(*d*) in the case of an incorporated company or body, by delivering it to their secretary or clerk at their registered or principal office, or by sending it in a prepaid letter addressed to him at that office, or

(*e*) in the case of a document to be given to or served on a person as being the owner of any premises by virtue of the fact that he receives the rackrent of the premises as agent for another, or would so receive it if the premises were let at a rackrent, by leaving it, or sending it in a prepaid letter addressed to him, at his place of business, or

(*f*) in the case of a document to be given to or served on the owner or the occupier of any premises, if it is not practicable after reasonable inquiry to ascertain the name and address of the person to or on whom it should be given or served, or if the premises are unoccupied, by addressing it to the person concerned by the description of "owner" or "occupier" of the premises (naming them) to which it relates, and delivering it to some person on the premises, or, if there is no person on the premises to whom it can be delivered, by affixing it, or a copy of it, to some conspicuous part of the premises.

[Public Health (Control of Disease) Act 1984, s 60.]

8–25979 61. Power to enter premises. (1) Subject to the provisions of this section, any authorised officer of a local authority shall, on producing, if so required, some duly authenticated document showing his authority, have a right to enter any premises at all reasonable hours—

(*a*) for the purpose of ascertaining whether there is, or has been, on or in connection with the premises, any contravention of a relevant provision of this Act, or of byelaws made under this Act, which it is the duty of the local authority to enforce,

(*b*) for the purpose of ascertaining whether or not circumstances exist which would authorise or require the local authority to take any action, or execute any work, under such a provision or such byelaws,

(*c*) for the purpose of taking any action, or executing any work, authorised or required by such a provision or such byelaws, or by any order made under such a provision, to be taken, or executed, by the local authority, or

(*d*) generally, for the purpose of the performance by the local authority of their functions under such a provision or such byelaws.

(2) Admission to any premises, other than a factory or work-place, shall not be demanded as of right unless twenty-four hours' notice of the intended entry has been given to the occupier.

(3) If it is shown to the satisfaction of a justice of the peace on sworn information in writing—

(*a*) that admission to any premises has been refused, or that refusal is apprehended, or that the premises are unoccupied or the occupier is temporarily absent, or that the case is one of urgency, or that an application for admission would defeat the object of the entry, and

(*b*) that there is reasonable ground for entry into the premises for any such purpose as is mentioned in subsection (1) above,

the justice may by warrant under his hand authorise the local authority by any authorised officer to enter the premises, if need be by force.

(4) Such a warrant shall not be issued unless the justice is satisfied either that notice of the intention to apply for a warrant has been given to the occupier, or that the premises are unoccupied, or that the occupier is temporarily absent, or that the case is one of urgency, or that the giving of such notice would defeat the object of the entry.

[Public Health (Control of Disease) Act 1984, s 61.]

8–25980 62. Supplementary provisions as to entry. (1) An authorised officer entering any premises by virtue of section 61 above, or of a warrant issued under that section, may take with him such other persons as may be necessary, and on leaving any unoccupied premises which he has entered by virtue of such a warrant he shall leave them as effectively secured against trespassers as he found them.

(2) Every warrant issued under that section shall continue in force until the purpose for which the entry is necessary has been satisfied.

(3) If any person who in compliance with the provisions of that section or of a warrant issued under it is admitted into a factory or workplace discloses to any person any information obtained by him in the factory or workplace with regard to any manufacturing process or trade secret, he shall, unless the disclosure was made in the performance of his duty, be liable on summary conviction to a fine not exceeding **level 3** on the standard scale or to imprisonment for a term not exceeding 3 months.

(4) Nothing in that section or in this section limits the provisions of Parts II and IV of this Act with respect to entry into or upon, and inspection of, common lodging-houses and canal boats.
[Public Health (Control of Disease) Act 1984, s 62.]

8–25981 **63. Penalty for obstructing execution of Act.** Any person who wilfully obstructs any person acting in the execution of a relevant provision of this Act, or of any byelaw, order or warrant made or issued under this Act, shall be liable on summary conviction to a fine not exceeding **level 1** on the standard scale.
[Public Health (Control of Disease) Act 1984, s 63.]

8–25982 **64. Restriction on right to prosecute.** (1) Subject to subsection (2) below, proceedings in respect of an offence created by or under this Act shall not, without the written consent of the Attorney General, be taken by any person other than—

(*a*) a party aggrieved, or
(*b*) a local authority or a body whose function it is to enforce the provision or byelaw in question, or by whom or by whose predecessors the byelaw was made.

(2) A constable may take proceedings, without the consent of the Attorney General, in respect of an offence against a byelaw made (whether before or after the passing of this Act) by—

(*a*) a district council, Welsh County Council, county borough council or London borough council, or
(*b*) a body that was the predecessor of such a council.

[Public Health (Control of Disease) Act 1984, s 64, as amended by the Local Government (Wales) Act 1994, Sch 9.]

8–25983 **65. Daily penalties for continuing offences.** Where by or under this Act provision is made for the imposition of a daily penalty in respect of a continuing offence, the court by which a person is convicted of the original offence may fix a reasonable period from the date of conviction for compliance by the defendant with any directions given by the court; and, where the court has fixed such a period, the daily penalty shall not be recoverable in respect of any day before that period expires.
[Public Health (Control of Disease) Act 1984, s 65.]

8–25984 **66.** *Repealed.*

8–25985 **67. Applications to, and appeals from, magistrates' courts.** (1) Where this Act provides for any matter to be determined by, or for an application in respect of a matter to be made to, a magistrates' court, the procedure shall be by way of complaint for an order.

(2) Where a person aggrieved by any order, determination or other decision of a magistrates' court under a relevant provision of this Act is not by any other enactment authorised to appeal to the Crown Court, he may appeal to the Crown Court.

(3) Subsection (2) above does not confer a right of appeal from the decision of a magistrates' court in any case if each of the parties concerned might under this Act have required that the dispute should be determined by arbitration instead of by a magistrates' court.
[Public Health (Control of Disease) Act 1984, s 67.]

8–25986 **68. Judges and justices not to be disqualified by liability to rates.** A judge of any court or a justice of the peace shall not be disqualified from acting in cases arising under this Act by reason only of his being, as one of several ratepayers, or as one of any other class of persons, liable in common with the others to contribute to, or be benefited by, any rate or fund out of which any expenses of a local authority are to be defrayed.
[Public Health (Control of Disease) Act 1984, s 68.]

8–25987 **72. Cumulative effect of Act.** Powers and duties under Act are in addition to other powers and duties elsewhere.
[Public Health (Control of Disease) Act 1984, s 72—summarised.]

8–25988 73. Crown property. Act may be applied by agreement to Crown property.
[Public Health (Control of Disease) Act 1984, s 73—summarised.]

8–25989 74. Interpretation. In this Act, unless the context otherwise requires—

"authorised officer", in relation to a local authority, means—

(*a*) an officer of the authority authorised by them in writing, either generally or specially, to act in matters of a specified kind or in a specified matter, or

(*b*) by virtue of his appointment and for the purpose of matters within his province, a proper officer of the authority, appointed for purposes corresponding to any of those of the former medical officers of health, surveyors and sanitary inspectors;

"coastal waters" means waters within a distance of three nautical miles from any point on the coast measured from low-water mark of ordinary spring tides;

"common lodging-house" means a house (other than a public assistance institution) provided for the purpose of accommodating by night poor persons, not being members of the same family, who resort to it and are allowed to occupy one common room for the purpose of sleeping or eating, and, where part only of a house is so used, includes the part so used;

"district", in relation to a local authority in Greater London, means a London borough, the City of London, the Inner Temple or the Middle Temple and, in relation to a local authority in Wales, means a county or county borough;

"dustbin" means a movable receptacle for the deposit of ashes or refuse;

"factory" has the meaning given by section 175 of the Factories Act 1961;

"functions" includes powers and duties;

"hospital" includes any premises for the reception of the sick;

"house" means a dwelling-house, whether a private dwelling-house or not;

"inland waters" includes rivers, harbours and creeks;

"local Act" includes a provisional order confirmed by Parliament and the confirming Act so far as it relates to that order;

"local authority" has the meaning given by section 1(2) above;

"London port health authority" and "London port health district" have the meanings given by section 7 above;

"NHS trust" and "NHS contract" have the same meaning as in Part I of the National Health Service and Community Care Act 1990 or, as the case may require, the National Health Service (Scotland) Act 1978.

"notifiable disease" has the meaning given by section 10 above;

"officer" includes servant;

"owner" means the person for the time being receiving the rackrent of the premises in connection with which the word is used, whether on his own account or as agent or trustee for any other person, or who would so receive the rackrent if those premises were let at a rackrent;

"port" has the meaning given by section 2(1) above;

"Port of London" has the meaning given by section 6 above;

"premises" includes buildings, lands, easements and hereditaments of any tenure;

"proper officer" means, in relation to a purpose and to an authority, an officer appointed for that purpose by that authority;

"rackrent" in relation to any property means a rent which is not less than two-thirds of the rent at which the property might reasonably be expected to let from year to year, free from all usual tenant's rates and taxes, and deducting from it the probable average annual cost of the repairs, insurance and other expenses (if any) necessary to maintain the property in a state to command such a rent;

"rating district" has the meaning given by section 115(1) of the General Rate Act 1967[1];

"relevant provision of this Act" means a provision of this Act other than section 46;

"riparian authority" has the meaning given by section 2(2) above;

"school" includes a Sunday school or a Sabbath school;

"street" includes any highway, including a highway over any bridge, and any road, lane, footway, square, court, alley or passage, whether a thoroughfare or not;

"vessel" has the same meaning as "ship" in the Merchant Shipping Act 1995 except that it includes a hovercraft within the meaning of the Hovercraft Act 1968, and "master" shall be construed accordingly.

[Public Health (Control of Disease) Act 1984, s 74, as amended by the Statute Law (Repeals) Act 1993, Sch 1, the Local Government (Wales) Act 1994, Sch 9 and the Merchant Shipping Act 1995, Sch 13.]

---

1. The General Rate Act 1967 has been repealed by the Local Government Finance Act 1988 in this PART: title LOCAL GOVERNMENT, ante.

Building Act 1984[1]

(1984 c 55)

PART I[2]

BUILDING REGULATIONS

Power to make building regulations

8–26049 **1. Power to make building regulations.** (1) The Secretary of State may, for any of the purposes of—

(*a*) securing the health, safety, welfare and convenience of persons in or about buildings and of others who may be affected by buildings or matters connected with buildings,
(*b*) furthering the conservation of fuel and power,
(*c*) preventing waste, undue consumption, misuse or contamination of water,
(*d*) furthering the protection or enhancement of the environment,
(*e*) facilitating sustainable development, or
(*f*) furthering the prevention or detection of crime,

make regulations with respect to the matters mentioned in subsection (1A) below.

(1A) Those matters are—

(*a*) the design and construction of buildings;
(*b*) the demolition of buildings;
(*c*) services, fittings and equipment provided in or in connection with buildings.

(2) Regulations made under subsection (1) above are known as building regulations.

(3) Schedule 1 to this Act has effect with respect to the matters as to which building regulations may provide.

(4) The power to make building regulations is exercisable by statutory instrument, which is subject to annulment in pursuance of a resolution of either House of Parliament.

[Building Act 1984, s 1, as amended by the Sustainable and Secure Buildings Act 2004, s 1.]

---

1. This Act is to be brought into force in accordance with the provisions of s 134, post. For the purposes of this Act, the holder of a licence under s 6(1) of the Electricity Act 1989 shall be deemed to be a statutory undertaker and his undertaking a statutory undertaking (Electricity Act 1989, Sch 16, para 1).
2. Part I contains ss 1–46.
3. See the Building (Approved Inspectors etc) Regulations 2000, SI 2000/2532 amended by SI 2001/3336, SI 2002/2872. SI 2003/3133, SI 2004/1466 and 3168 and SI 2005/1541 and 2929 (W), the Building (Inner London) Regulations 1985, SI 1985/1936 amended by SI 1987/798 and SI 1991/2768, the Building Regulations 2000, SI 2000/2531 amended by SI 2001/3335, SI 2002/440 and 2871, SI 2003/2692 and 3133, SI 2004/1465, 1808 and 3210 and SI 2005/1082 and 1541 and the Building (Repeal of Provisions of Local Acts) Regulations 2003, SI 2003/3030.

8–26049A **1A. Buildings of special historical or architectural interest**

8–26050 **2.** *Continuing requirements.*

8–26050A **2A.** *Continuing requirements in relation to fuel, power and emissions.*

Exemption from building regulations

8–26051 **3. Exemption of particular classes of buildings etc.** (1) Building regulations may exempt a prescribed class of buildings, services, fittings or equipment from all or any of the provisions of building regulations[1].

(2) The Secretary of State may by direction exempt from all or any of the provisions of building regulations—

(*a*) a particular building, or
(*b*) buildings of a particular class at a particular location,

either unconditionally or subject to compliance with any conditions specified in the direction.

(3) A person who contravenes a condition specified in a direction given under subsection (2) above, or permits such a condition to be contravened, is liable on summary conviction to a fine not exceeding **level 5** on the standard scale, and to a further fine not exceeding **£50** for each day on which the offence continues after he is convicted.

[Building Act 1984, s 3.]

---

1. See the Building (Inner London) Regulations 1985, SI 1985/1936 amended by SI 1987/798 and SI 1991/2768 and the Building Regulations 2000, SI 2000/2531 amended by SI 2001/3335, SI 2002/440 and 2871, SI 2003/2692 and 3133, SI 2004/1465, 1808 and 3210 and SI 2005/1082 and 1541.

8–26052 **4*–5.** *Exemption of educational buildings and buildings of statutory undertakers; exemption of public bodies from procedural requirements of building regulations.*

***Section 4 repealed by the Sustainable and Secure Buildings Act 2004, Schedule from a date to be appointed.**

Approved documents

8–26053 6. Approval of documents for purposes of building regulations. (1) For the purpose of providing practical guidance with respect to the requirements of any provision of building regulations, the Secretary of State or a body designated by him for the purposes of this section may—

(*a*) approve and issue any document (whether or not prepared by him or by the body concerned), or

(*b*) approve any document issued or proposed to be issued otherwise than by him or by the body concerned,

if in the opinion of the Secretary of State or, as the case may be, the body concerned the document is suitable for that purpose.

(2) References in this section and section 7 below to a document include references to a part of a document; and accordingly, in relation to a document of which part only is approved, a reference in the following provisions of this section or in section 7 below to the approved document is a reference only to the part of it that is approved.

(3) An approval given under subsection (1) above takes effect in accordance with a notice that is issued by the Secretary of State or, as the case may be, the body giving the approval and that—

(*a*) identifies the approved document in question,

(*b*) states the date on which the approval of it is to take effect, and

(*c*) specifies the provisions of building regulations for the purposes of which the document is approved.

(4) The Secretary of State or, as the case may be, the body that gave the approval may—

(*a*) from time to time approve and issue a revision of the whole or any part of an approved document issued by him or it for the purposes of this section, and

(*b*) approve any revision or proposed revision of the whole or any part of an approved document,

and subsection (3) above, with the necessary modifications, applies in relation to an approval that is given under this subsection to a revision as it applies in relation to an approval that is given under subsection (1) above to a document.

(5) The Secretary of State or, as the case may be, the body that gave the approval may withdraw his or its approval of a document under this section; and such a withdrawal of approval takes effect in accordance with a notice that is issued by the Secretary of State or body concerned and that—

(*a*) identifies the approved document in question, and

(*b*) states the date on which the approval of it is to cease to have effect.

(6) References in subsections (4) and (5) above and in section 7 below to an approved document are references to that document as it has effect for the time being, regard being had to any revision of the whole or any part of it that has been approved under subsection (4) above.

(7) Where a body ceases to be a body designated by the Secretary of State for the purposes of this section, subsections (4) and (5) above have effect as if any approval given by that body had been given by the Secretary of State.

(8) The power to designate a body for the purposes of this section is exercisable by order made by statutory instrument, which is subject to annulment in pursuance of a resolution of either House of Parliament.

[Building Act 1984, s 6.]

8–26054 7. Compliance or non-compliance with approved documents. (1) A failure on the part of a person to comply with an approved document does not of itself render him liable to any civil or criminal proceedings; but if, in any proceedings whether civil or criminal, it is alleged that a person has at any time contravened a provision of building regulations—

(*a*) a failure to comply with a document that at that time was approved for the purposes of that provision may be relied upon as tending to establish liability, and

(*b*) proof of compliance with such a document may be relied on as tending to negative liability.

(2) In any proceedings, whether civil or criminal—

(*a*) a document purporting to be a notice issued as mentioned in section 6(3) above shall be taken to be such a notice unless the contrary is proved, and

(*b*) a document that appears to the court to be the approved document to which such a notice refers shall be taken to be that approved document unless the contrary is proved.

[Building Act 1984, s 7.]

Relaxation of building regulations

8–26055 8–10. *Relaxation of building regulations*[1].

1. See the Building (Inner London) Regulations 1985, SI 1985/1936 amended by SI 1987/798 and SI 1991/2768 and the Building Regulations 2000, SI 2000/2531 amended by SI 2001/3335, SI 2002/440 and 2871, SI 2003/2692 and 3133, SI 2004/1465, 1808 and 3210 and SI 2005/1082 and 1541.

8–26056 **11. Type relaxation of building regulations.** (1) If the Secretary of State considers that the operation of a requirement of building regulations would be unreasonable in relation to a particular type of building matter, he may, either on an application made to him or of his own accord, give a direction dispensing with or relaxing that requirement generally in relation to that type of building matter, either—

(*a*) unconditionally, or
(*b*) subject to compliance with any conditions specified in the direction, being conditions with respect to matters directly connected with the dispensation or relaxation.

(2) A direction under subsection (1) above—

(*a*) if it so provides, ceases to have effect at the end of such period as may be specified in the direction,
(*b*) may be varied or revoked by a subsequent direction of the Secretary of State.

(3) Building regulations may require a person making an application under subsection (1) above to pay the Secretary of State the prescribed fee, and—

(*a*) without prejudice to paragraph 10 of Schedule 1 to this Act, regulations made by virtue of this subsection may prescribe different fees for different cases, and
(*b*) the Secretary of State may in a particular case remit the whole or part of a fee payable by virtue of this subsection.

(4) Before giving a direction under subsection (1) above, the Secretary of State shall consult such bodies as appear to him to be representative of the interests concerned.

(5) Where the Secretary of State gives a direction under subsection (1) above, he shall publish notice of that fact in such manner as he thinks fit.

(6) A person who contravenes a condition specified in a direction given under subsection (1) above, or permits such a condition to be contravened, is liable on summary conviction to a fine not exceeding **level 5** on the standard scale and to a further fine not exceeding **£50** for each day on which the offence continues after he is convicted.

(7) If at any time a direction under subsection (1) above dispensing with or relaxing a requirement of building regulations ceases to have effect by virtue of subsection (2)(*a*) above, or is varied or revoked under subsection (2)(*b*) above, that fact does not affect the continued operation of the direction (with any conditions specified in it) in a case in which before that time—

(*a*) plans of the proposed work were, in accordance with building regulations, deposited with a local authority,
(*b*) *Repealed.*

(8) In this section, "building matter" means any building or other matter whatsoever to which building regulations are in any circumstances applicable.

[Building Act 1984, s 11, as amended by the Local Government Act 1985, Sch 17 and the Statute Law (Repeals) Act 2004.]

Passing of plans

8–26057 **16. Passing or rejection of plans.** (1) Where plans of any proposed work are, in accordance with building regulations, deposited with a local authority, it is the duty of the local authority, subject to any other section of this Act that expressly requires or authorises them in certain cases to reject plans, to pass the plans unless—

(*a*) they are defective, or
(*b*) they show that the proposed work would contravene any of the building regulations.

(2) If the plans—

(*a*) are defective, or
(*b*) show that the proposed work would contravene any of the building regulations,

the local authority may—

(i) reject the plans, or
(ii) subject to subsection (4) below, pass them subject to either or both of the conditions set out in subsection (3) below.

(3) The conditions mentioned in subsection (2) above are—

(*a*) that such modifications as the local authority may specify shall be made in the deposited plans, and
(*b*) that such further plans as they may specify shall be deposited.

(4) A local authority may only pass plans subject to a condition such as is specified in subsection (3) above if the person by whom or on whose behalf they were deposited—

(*a*) has requested them to do so, or
(*b*) has consented to their doing so.

(5) A request or consent under subsection (4) above shall be in writing.

(6) The authority shall within the relevant period from the deposit of the plans give notice to the person by whom or on whose behalf they were deposited whether they have been passed or rejected.

(7) A notice that plans have been rejected shall specify the defects on account of which, or the regulation or section of this Act for non-conformity with which, or under the authority of which, they have been rejected.

(8) A notice that plans have been passed shall—

(*a*) specify any condition subject to which they have been passed, and
(*b*) state that the passing of the plans operates as an approval of them only for the purposes of the requirements of—

(i) the building regulations, and
(ii) any section of this Act (other than this section) that expressly requires or authorises the local authority in certain cases to reject plans.

(9) Where the deposited plans are accompanied by—

(*a*) a certificate given by a person approved for the purposes of this subsection to the effect that the proposed work, if carried out in accordance with the deposited plans, will comply with such provisions of the regulations prescribed for the purposes of this subsection as may be specified in the certificate, and
(*b*) such evidence as may be prescribed that an approved scheme applies, or the prescribed insurance cover has been or will be provided, in relation to the certificate,

the local authority may not, except in prescribed circumstances, reject the plans on the ground that—

(i) they are defective with respect to any provisions of the building regulations that are so specified, or
(ii) they show that the proposed work would contravene any of those provisions.

(10) In any case where a question arises under this section between a local authority and a person who proposes to carry out any work—

(*a*) whether plans of the proposed work are in conformity with building regulations, or
(*b*) whether the local authority are prohibited from rejecting plans of the proposed work by virtue of subsection (9) above,

that person may refer the question to the Secretary of State for his determination; and an application for a reference under this subsection shall be accompanied by such fee as may be prescribed.

(11) Where—

(*a*) deposited plans accompanied by such a certificate and such evidence as are mentioned in subsection (9) above are passed by the local authority, or
(*b*) notice of the rejection of deposited plans so accompanied is not given within the relevant period from the deposit of the plans,

the authority may not institute proceedings under section 35 below for a contravention of building regulations that—

(i) arises out of the carrying out of the proposed work in accordance with the plans, and
(ii) is a contravention of any of the provisions of the regulations specified in the certificate.

(12) For the purposes of this Part of this Act, "the relevant period", in relation to the passing or rejection of plans, means five weeks or such extended period (expiring not later than two months from the deposit of the plans) as may before the expiration of the five weeks be agreed in writing between the person depositing the plans and the local authority.

(13) (*Repealed*).

[Building Act 1984, s 16, as amended by the Statute Law (Repeals) Act 1993, Sch 1.]

8–26058 **17. Approval of persons to give certificates etc.** (1)–(5) *Building regulations*[1] *may make provision for the approval of persons for the purposes of section 16*(*9*).

(6) Building regulations may—

(*a*) contain provision prescribing the period for which, subject to any provision made by virtue of paragraph (*b*) or (*c*) below, any such approval as is referred to in subsection (1) above continues in force,
(*b*) contain provision precluding the giving of, or requiring the withdrawal of, any such approval as is referred to in subsection (1) above in such circumstances as may be prescribed,
(*c*) contain provision authorising the withdrawal of any such approval or designation as is referred to in subsection (1) above,
(*d*) provide for the maintenance by the Secretary of State of a list of bodies that are for the time being designated by him as mentioned in subsection (1) above and for the maintenance by

the Secretary of State and by each designated body of a list of persons for the time being approved by him or them as mentioned in that subsection,

(*e*) make provision for the supply to local authorities of copies of any list of approved persons maintained by virtue of paragraph (*d*) above and for such copy lists to be made available for inspection, and

(*f*) make provision for the supply, on payment of a prescribed fee, of a certified copy of any entry in a list maintained by virtue of paragraph (*d*) above or in a copy list held by a local authority by virtue of paragraph (*e*) above.

(7) Unless the contrary is proved, in any proceedings (whether civil or criminal) a document that appears to the court to be a certified copy of an entry either in a list maintained as mentioned in subsection (6)(*d*) above or in a copy of such a list supplied as mentioned in subsection (6)(*e*) above—

(*a*) is presumed to be a true copy of an entry in the current list so maintained, and

(*b*) is evidence of the matters stated in it.

[Building Act 1984, s 17.]

---

1. See the Building (Approved Inspectors etc) Regulations 2000, SI 2000/2532 amended by SI 2001/3336, SI 2002/2872, SI 2003/3133, SI 2004/1466 and 3168 and SI 2005/1541 and 2929 (W).

8–26059 18. Building over sewer etc. *Repealed.*

8–26060 19. Use of short-lived materials. (1) Where plans of a building are, in accordance with building regulations, deposited with a local authority, and the plans show that it is proposed to construct a building of materials to which this section applies, or to place or assemble on the site a building constructed of such materials, the authority may, notwithstanding that the plans conform with the regulations—

(*a*) reject the plans, or

(*b*) in passing the plans—

(i) fix a period on the expiration of which the building must be removed, and

(ii) impose with respect to the use of the building such reasonable conditions, if any, as having regard to the nature of the materials used in its construction they deem appropriate,

but no condition shall be imposed that conflicts with any condition imposed on the grant of planning permission for that building under Part III of the Town and Country Planning Act 1990.

(2) If a building in respect of which plans ought under the building regulations to have been deposited, but have not been deposited, appears to the authority to be constructed of such materials as aforesaid, the authority, without prejudice to their right to take proceedings in respect of any contravention of the regulations, may—

(*a*) fix a period on the expiration of which the building must be removed, and

(*b*) if they think fit, impose such conditions with respect to the use of the building as might have been imposed under subsection (1) above upon the passing of plans for the building,

and where they fix such a period they shall forthwith give notice thereof, and of any conditions imposed, to the owner of the building.

(3) A local authority may from time to time extend any period fixed, or vary any conditions imposed, under this section; but, unless an application in that behalf is made to them by the owner of the building in question, they shall not exercise their power of varying conditions except when granting an extension, or further extension, of the period fixed with respect to the building.

(4) A person aggrieved by the action of a local authority under this section in rejecting plans, or in fixing or refusing to extend any period, or in imposing or refusing to vary any conditions, may appeal to a magistrates' court.

(5) The owner of a building in respect of which a period has been fixed under this section shall, on the expiration of that period, or, as the case may be, of that period as extended, remove the building, and, if he fails to do so—

(*a*) the local authority shall remove it and may recover from him the expenses reasonably incurred by them in so doing, and

(*b*) without prejudice to the right of the authority to exercise that power, he is liable on summary conviction to a fine not exceeding **level 1** on the standard scale and to a further fine not exceeding **£5** for each day during which the building is allowed to remain after he is convicted.

(6) A person who uses a building in contravention of a condition imposed under this section, or who permits a building to be so used, is liable on summary conviction to a fine not exceeding **level 1** on the standard scale and to a further fine not exceeding **£5** for each day on which the offence continues after he is convicted.

(7) Building regulations may provide that this section applies to any materials specified in the regulations as being materials that are, in the absence of special care, liable to rapid deterioration, or are otherwise unsuitable for use in the construction of permanent buildings.

(8) This section applies in relation to an extension of an existing building as it applies in relation to a new building.

(9) This section ceases to have effect upon the coming into force of section 20 below (which supersedes it).

[Building Act 1984, s 19, as amended by the Planning (Consequential Provisions) Act 1990, Sch 2.]

8–26061 **20. Use of materials unsuitable for permanent building.** (1) Where plans of any proposed work are, in accordance with building regulations, deposited with a local authority, and the plans show that the proposed work would include or consist of work to which this section applies, the authority may, notwithstanding that the plans conform with the regulations—

(*a*) reject the plans, or

(*b*) in passing the plans—

(i) fix a period on the expiration of which the work to which this section applies or the relevant building (as the authority may in passing the plans direct) must be removed, and

(ii) if they think fit, impose with respect to the use of the relevant building or with respect to the work to which this section applies such reasonable conditions, if any, as they consider appropriate,

but no condition as to the use of the relevant building shall be imposed that conflicts with any condition imposed or having effect as if imposed under Part III or VIII of the Town and Country Planning Act 1990 or under the Planning (Listed Buildings and Conservation Areas) Act 1990 or the Planning (Hazardous Substances) Act 1990.

(2) If, in the case of any work in respect of which plans ought by virtue of building regulations to have been deposited with a local authority but have not been so deposited, the work appears to the authority to include or consist of work to which this section applies, the authority, without prejudice to their right to take proceedings in respect of any contravention of the regulations, may—

(*a*) fix a period on the expiration of which the work to which this section applies or the relevant building (as the authority may in fixing the period direct) must be removed, and

(*b*) if they think fit, impose any conditions that might have been imposed under subsection (1) above in passing plans for the first-mentioned work,

and where they fix such a period they shall forthwith give notice thereof, and of any conditions imposed, to the owner of the relevant building.

(3) If, in the case of any work appearing to the local authority to fall within subsection (9)(*b*) below, plans of the work were not required by building regulations to be deposited with the authority, and were not so deposited, the authority may at any time within 12 months from the date of completion of the work—

(*a*) fix a period on the expiration of which the work must be removed, and

(*b*) if they think fit, impose any conditions that, if plans of the work had been required to be, and had been, so deposited, might have been imposed under subsection (1) above in passing the plans,

and where they fix such a period they shall forthwith give notice thereof, and of any conditions imposed, to the owner of the relevant building.

(4) A local authority may from time to time extend any period fixed, or vary any conditions imposed, under this section, but, unless an application in that behalf is made to them by the owner of the relevant building, they shall not exercise their power of varying conditions so imposed except when granting an extension or further extension of the period fixed with respect to the work or building, as the case may be.

(5) A person aggrieved by the action of a local authority under this section—

(*a*) in rejecting plans,

(*b*) in fixing or refusing to extend any period, or

(*c*) in imposing or refusing to vary any conditions,

may appeal to the Secretary of State within the prescribed time and in the prescribed manner.

(6) Where a period has been fixed under this section with respect to any work to which this section applies or with respect to the relevant building—

(*a*) the owner of that building shall on the expiration of that period, or, as the case may be, of that period as extended, remove the work or building with respect to which the period was fixed, and

(*b*) if he fails to do so, the local authority may remove that work or building, as the case may be, and may recover from him the expenses reasonably incurred by them in doing so.

(7) A person who—

(*a*) contravenes a condition imposed under this section or permits such a condition to be contravened, or

(*b*) contravenes subsection (6) above,

is liable on summary conviction to a fine not exceeding **level 5** on the standard scale and to a further fine not exceeding **£50** for each day on which the offence continues or, as the case may be, on which the work or building is allowed to remain after he is convicted; but this subsection does not prejudice a local authority's rights under subsection (6) above.

(8) In this section, "the relevant building" means, in any particular case, the building mentioned in paragraph (*a*) or, as the case may be, paragraph (*b*) of subsection (9) below.

(9) This section applies to—

(*a*) any work consisting of a part of a building, being a part in the construction of which there is used any material or component of a type that, in relation to a part of that description, is prescribed for the purposes of this paragraph under subsection (10) below, and

(*b*) any work provided in or in connection with a building, being work consisting of a service, fitting or item of equipment of a type so prescribed for the purposes of this paragraph.

(10) *Power of Secretary of State to make building regulations for the purposes of sub-section* (9)(*a*)–(*b*).

(11) Upon section 19 above ceasing to have effect—

(*a*) any building regulations made, period fixed, condition imposed or other thing done by virtue of the said section 19 shall be deemed to have been made, fixed, imposed or done by virtue of this section, and

(*b*) anything begun under the said section 19 may be continued under this Act as if begun under this section, but any appeal under section 19(4) that is pending at the time when the said section 19 ceases to have effect, and any proceedings arising out of such an appeal, shall proceed as if that section were still in force.★

[Building Act 1984, s 20, as amended by the Planning (Consequential Provisions) Act 1990, Sch 2.]

★At the date of going to press, this section had not been brought into force; see s 134(1)(*b*), post.

8–26062 21. Provision of drainage. (1)–(2) *Repealed.*

(3) Any question arising under subsection (4) below between a local authority and the person by whom, or on whose behalf, plans are deposited as to whether a proposed drain shall be required to connect with a sewer may on the application of that person be determined by a magistrates' court.

(4) Where plans of a building or of an extension of a building are, in accordance with building regulations, deposited with a local authority, the local authority, or on appeal a magistrates' court, may require a proposed drain to connect with a sewer where—

(*a*) that sewer is within one hundred feet of the site of the building or, in the case of an extension, the site either of the extension or of the original building, and is at a level that makes it reasonably practicable to construct a drain to communicate with it, and, if it is not a public sewer, is a sewer that the person constructing the drain is entitled to use, and

(*b*) the intervening land is land through which that person is entitled to construct a drain.

(5) Notwithstanding paragraph (*a*) of subsection (4) above, a drain may be required to be made to connect with a sewer that is not within the distance mentioned in that paragraph, but is otherwise such a sewer as is therein mentioned, if the authority undertake to bear so much of the expenses reasonably incurred in constructing, and in maintaining and repairing, the drain as may be attributable to the fact that the distance of the sewer exceeds the distance so mentioned.

(6) If any question arises as to the amount of a payment to be made to a person under subsection (5) above, that question may on his application be determined by a magistrates' court, or he may require it to be referred to arbitration.

[Building Act 1984, s 21, as amended by SI 2001/3335.]

8–26063 22. Drainage of buildings in combination. (1) Where—

(*a*) a local authority might under section 21 above require each of two or more buildings to be drained separately into an existing sewer, but

(*b*) it appears to the authority that those buildings may be drained more economically or advantageously in combination,

the authority may, when the drains of the buildings are first laid, require that the buildings be drained in combination into the existing sewer by means of a private sewer to be constructed either by the owners of the buildings in such manner as the authority may direct or, if the authority so elect, by the authority on behalf of the owners.

(2) A local authority shall not, except by agreement with the owners concerned, exercise the power conferred by subsection (1) above in respect of any building for whose drainage plans have been previously passed by them.

(3) A local authority who make such a requirement as aforesaid shall fix—

(*a*) the proportions in which the expenses of constructing, and of maintaining and repairing, the private sewer are to be borne by the owners concerned, or

(*b*) in a case in which the distance of the existing sewer from the site of any of the buildings in question is or exceeds one hundred feet, the proportions in which those expenses are to borne by the owners concerned and the local authority, and shall forthwith give notice of their decision to each owner affected.

(4) An owner aggrieved by the decision of a local authority under subsection (3) above may appeal to a magistrates' court.

(5) Subject to any such appeal—

(*a*) any expenses reasonably incurred in constructing, or maintaining or repairing, the private sewer shall be borne in the proportions so fixed, and

(*b*) those expenses, or, as the case may be, contributions to them, may be recovered accordingly by the persons, whether the local authority or the owners, by whom they were incurred in the first instance.

(6) A sewer constructed by a local authority under this section is not deemed a public sewer by reason of the fact that the expenses of its construction are in the first instance defrayed by the authority, or that some part of those expenses is borne by them.

[Building Act 1984, s 22.]

8–26064 23. Provision of facilities for refuse. (1) *Repealed.*

(2) *Repealed.*

(3) It is unlawful for any person except with the consent of the local authority to close or obstruct the means of access by which refuse or faecal matter is removed from a building, and the local authority in giving their consent may impose such conditions as they think fit with respect to the improvement of an alternative means of access or the substitution of other means of access.

(4) A person who contravenes subsection (3) above is liable on summary conviction to a fine not exceeding **level 4** on the standard scale.

[Building Act 1984, s 23, as amended by SI 1985/1065.]

8–26065 24. Provision of exits etc. (1) Where—

(*a*) plans of a building or of an extension of a building are, in accordance with building regulations, deposited with a local authority, and

(*b*) the building or, as the case may be, the building as extended will be a building to which this section applies,

the authority shall reject the plans unless they show that the building, or, as the case may be, the building as extended, will be provided with such means of ingress and egress and passages or gangways as the authority, after consultation with the fire and rescue authority, deem satisfactory, regard being had to the purposes for which the building is intended to be, or is, used and the number of persons likely to resort to it at any one time.

(2) Any question arising under subsection (1) above between a local authority and the person by whom, or on whose behalf, plans are deposited as to whether the means of ingress or egress or passages or gangways already existing, or proposed to be provided, ought to be accepted by the authority as satisfactory may on the application of that person be determined by a magistrates' court.

(3) Where building regulations imposing requirements as to the provision of means of escape in case of fire are applicable to a proposed building or proposed extension of a building, or would be so applicable but for a direction under section 8 above dispensing with such requirements—

(*a*) this section, and

(*b*) any provision of a local Act that has effect in place of this section,

does not apply in relation to the proposed building or extension.

(4) Subject to subsection (3) above, this section applies to—

(*a*) a theatre, and a hall or other building that is used as a place of public resort,

(*b*) a restaurant, shop, store or warehouse to which members of the public are admitted and in which more than twenty persons are employed,

(*c*) premises in respect of which a club premises certificate has effect under the Licensing Act 2003,

(*d*) a school not exempted from the operation of building regulations, and

(*e*) a church, chapel or other place of public worship,

but not—

(i) a private house to which members of the public are admitted occasionally or exceptionally,

(ii) a building that was used as a church, chapel or other place of public worship immediately before the date on which section 36 of the Public Health Acts Amendment Act 1890, or a corresponding provision in a local Act, came into operation in the district or rating district, or

(iii) a building that was so used immediately before the 1st October 1937 (the date of commencement of the Public Health Act 1936) in a district or rating district where neither the said section 36 nor such a corresponding provision ever came into operation.

[Building Act 1984, s 24, as amended by the Fire and Rescue Services Act 2004, Sch 1 and the Licensing Act 2003, Sch 6.]

8–26066 25. Provision of water supply. (1) Where plans of a house are, in accordance with building regulations, deposited with a local authority, the authority shall reject the plans unless a proposal is put before them that appears to them to be satisfactory for providing the occupants of the house with a supply of wholesome water sufficient for their domestic purposes—

(*a*) by connecting the house to a supply of water in pipes provided by water undertakers,
(*b*) if in all the circumstances it is not reasonable to require the house to be connected as aforesaid, by otherwise taking water into the house by means of a pipe, or
(*c*) if in all the circumstances neither of the preceding alternatives can reasonably be required, by providing a supply of water within a reasonable distance of the house,

and the authority are satisfied that the proposal can and will be carried into effect.

(2) Any question arising under subsection (1) above between a local authority and the person by whom, or on whose behalf, plans are deposited as to whether the local authority ought to pass the plans may on the application of that person be determined by a magistrates' court.

(3) If, after any such plans as aforesaid have been passed, it appears to the local authority that the proposal for providing a supply of water—

(*a*) has not been carried into effect, or
(*b*) has not resulted in a supply of wholesome water sufficient for the domestic purposes of the occupants,

the authority shall give notice to the owner of the house prohibiting him from occupying it, or permitting it to be occupied, until the authority, being satisfied that such a supply has been provided, have granted him a certificate to that effect.

(4) Until a certificate is granted under subsection (3) above, the owner shall not occupy the house or permit it to be occupied.

(5) A person aggrieved by the refusal of the authority to grant such a certificate may apply to a magistrates' court for an order authorising the occupation of the house, and, if the court is of opinion that a certificate ought to have been granted, the court may make an order authorising the occupation of the house, and such an order shall have the like effect as a certificate of the local authority.

(6) A person who contravenes subsection (4) above is liable on summary conviction to a fine not exceeding **level 1** on the standard scale and to a further fine not exceeding **£2** for each day on which the offence continues after he is convicted.

(7) Section 67 of the Water Industry Act 1991 (standards of wholesomeness of water) and any regulations made under that section shall apply for the purposes of subsection (1) above as they apply for the purposes of Chapter III of Part III of that Act.

[Building Act 1984, s 25, as amended by the Water Act 1989, Schs 25 and 27 and the Water Consolidation (Consequential Provisions) Act 1991, Sch 1.]

8–26067 26. Provision of closets. *Repealed.*

8–26068 27. Provision of bathrooms. *Repealed.*

8–26069 28. Provision for food storage. *Repealed.*

8–26080 29. Site containing offensive material. *Repealed.*

Determination of questions

8–26081 30. *Repealed.*

Proposed departure from plans

8–26082 31. Proposed departure from plans. (1) Where plans of any proposed work have been passed under section 16 above by a local authority, the person by or on whose behalf the plans were in accordance with building regulations deposited with the authority may, and in such cases as may be prescribed shall, for the purpose of obtaining the approval of the authority to any proposed departure or deviation from the plans as passed, deposit plans of the departure or deviation.

(2) Section 16 above applies in relation to plans deposited under subsection (1) above as it applies in relation to the plans originally deposited.*

[Building Act 1984, s 31.]

***At the date of going to press, this section had not been brought into force except in so far as it enables regulations to be made (s 134(1)(*a*), post).**

Lapse of deposit of plans

8–26083 32. Lapse of deposit of plans. (1) Where plans of any proposed work have, in accordance with building regulations, been deposited with a local authority, and—

(*a*) the plans have been passed by the authority, or
(*b*) notice of rejection of the plans has not been given within the relevant period from their deposit,

and the work to which the plans relate has not been commenced within three years from the deposit of the plans, the local authority may, at any time before the work is commenced, by notice to the person by whom or on whose behalf the plans were deposited, or other the owner for the time being of the land to which the plans relate, declare that the deposit of the plans is of no effect.

(2) Where a notice has been given under subsection (1) above, this Act and the building regulations shall, as respects the proposed work, have effect as if no plans had been deposited.
[Building Act 1984, s 32.]

Tests for conformity with building regulations

8–26084 **33. Tests for conformity with building regulations.** (1) The following subsection has effect for the purpose of enabling a local authority to ascertain, as regards any work or proposed work to which building regulations for the enforcement of which they are responsible are applicable, whether any provision of building regulations is or would be contravened by, or by anything done or proposed to be done in connection with, that work.

(2) The local authority have power for that purpose—

(*a*) to require a person by whom or on whose behalf the work was, is being or is proposed to be done to carry out such reasonable tests of or in connection with the work as may be specified in the requirement, or

(*b*) themselves to carry out any reasonable tests of or in connection with the work, and to take any samples necessary to enable them to carry out such a test.

(3) Without prejudice to the generality of subsection (2) above, the matters with respect to which tests may be required or carried out under that subsection include—

(*a*) tests of the soil or subsoil of the site of a building,

(*b*) tests of any material, component or combination of components that has been, is being or is proposed to be used in the construction of a building, and tests of any service, fitting or equipment that has been, is being or is proposed to be provided in or in connection with a building.

(4) A local authority have power, for the purpose of ascertaining whether there is or has been, in the case of a building, a contravention of a continuing requirement that applies in relation to that building—

(*a*) to require the owner or occupier of the building to carry out such reasonable tests as may be specified in the requirement under this paragraph, or

(*b*) themselves to carry out any tests that they have power to require under paragraph (*a*) above, and to take any samples necessary to enable them to carry out such a test;

and in this subsection "continuing requirement" means a continuing requirement imposed by building regulations made by virtue of section 2(1) or (2) or (2A) above.

(5) The expense of carrying out any tests that a person is required to carry out under this section shall be met by that person, except that the local authority, on an application made to them, may, if they think it reasonable to do so, direct that the expense of carrying out any such tests, or such part of that expense as may be specified in the direction, shall be met by the local authority.

(6) Any question arising under this section between a local authority and a person as to the reasonableness of—

(*a*) a test specified in a requirement imposed on him by the authority under this section,

(*b*) a refusal by the authority to give a direction under subsection (5) above on an application made by him, or

(*c*) a direction under that subsection given on such an application,

may on the application of that person be determined by a magistrates' court; and in a case falling within paragraph (*b*) or (*c*) above the court may order the expense to which the application relates to be met by the local authority to such extent as the court thinks just.*
[Building Act 1984, s 33, as amended by the Sustainable and Secure Buildings Act 2004, s 4.]

***At the date of going to press, this section had not been brought into force; see s 134(1)(*b*), post.**

Classification of buildings

8–26085 **34. Classification of buildings.** For the purposes of building regulations and of a direction given or instrument made with reference to building regulations, buildings may be classified by reference to size, description, design, purpose, location or any other characteristic whatsoever.
[Building Act 1984, s 34.]

Breach of building regulations

8–26086 **35. Penalty for contravening building regulations.** If a person contravenes any provision contained in building regulations[1], other than a provision designated in the regulations as one to which this section does not apply, he is liable on summary conviction to a fine not exceeding

level 5 on the standard scale and to a further fine not exceeding **£50** for each day on which the default continues[2] after he is convicted.
[Building Act 1984, s 35.]

1. See the Building (Inner London) Regulations 1985, SI 1985/1936 amended by SI 1987/798 and SI 1991/2768 and the Building Regulations 2000, SI 2000/2531 amended by SI 2001/3335, SI 2002/440 and 2871, SI 2003/2692 and 3133, SI 2004/1465, 1808 and 3210 and SI 2005/1082 and 1541.

2. Not every offence under the regulation is a continuing offence. Following *Hodgetts v Chiltern District Council* [1983] 2 AC 120 it is necessary to consider whether the regulation requires the doing of something; if it does the offence is not a continuing offence (*Torridge District Council v Turner* (1991) 157 JP 65).

8–26087 36. Removal or alteration of offending work. (1) If any work to which building regulations are applicable contravenes any of those regulations, the local authority, without prejudice to their right to take proceedings for a fine in respect of the contravention, may by notice require the owner—

(*a*) to pull down or remove the work, or
(*b*) if he so elects, to effect such alterations in it as may be necessary to make it comply with the regulations.

(2) If, in a case where the local authority are, by any section of this Part of this Act other than section 16, expressly required or authorised to reject plans, any work to which building regulations are applicable is executed—

(*a*) without plans having been deposited,
(*b*) notwithstanding the rejection of the plans, or
(*c*) otherwise than in accordance with any requirements subject to which the authority passed the plans,

the authority may by notice to the owner—

(i) require him to pull down or remove the work, or
(ii) require him either to pull down or remove the work or, if he so elects, to comply with any other requirements specified in the notice, being requirements that they might have made under the section in question as a condition of passing plans.

(3) If a person to whom a notice has been given under subsection (1) or (2) above fails to comply with the notice before the expiration of 28 days, or such longer period as a magistrates' court may on his application allow, the local authority may—

(*a*) pull down or remove the work in question, or
(*b*) effect such alterations in it as they deem necessary,

and may recover from him the expenses reasonably incurred by them in doing so.

(4) A notice under subsection (1) or (2) above (called a "section 36 notice") shall not be given after the expiration of 12 months from the date of the completion of the work in question.

(5) A section 36 notice shall not be given, in a case where plans were deposited and the work was shown on them, on the ground that the work contravenes any building regulations or, as the case may be, does not comply with the authority's requirements under any section of this Part of this Act other than section 16, if—

(*a*) the plans were passed by the authority, or
(*b*) notice of their rejection was not given within the relevant period from their deposit,

and if the work has been executed in accordance with the plans and of any requirement made by the local authority as a condition of passing the plans.

(6) This section does not affect the right of a local authority, the Attorney General or any other person to apply for an injunction for the removal or alteration of any work on the ground that it contravenes any regulation or any provision of this Act; but if—

(*a*) the work is one in respect of which plans were deposited,
(*b*) the plans were passed by the local authority, or notice of their rejection was not given within the relevant period from their deposit, and
(*c*) the work has been executed in accordance with the plans,

the court on granting an injunction has power to order the local authority to pay to the owner of the work such compensation as the court thinks just, but before making any such order the court shall in accordance with rules of court cause the local authority, if not a party to the proceedings, to be joined as a party to them.
[Building Act 1984, s 36.]

8–26088 37. Obtaining of report where section 36 notice given. (1) In a case where—

(*a*) a person to whom a section 36 notice has been given gives to the local authority by whom the notice was given notice of his intention to obtain from a suitably qualified person a written report concerning work to which the section 36 notice relates, and (*b*) such a report is obtained and submitted to the local authority and, as a result of their consideration of it, the local authority withdraw the section 36 notice,

the local authority may pay to the person to whom the section 36 notice was given such amount as appears to them to represent the expenses reasonably incurred by him in consequence of their having given him that notice including, in particular, his expenses in obtaining the report.

(2) Subject to subsection (3) below, if a person to whom a section 36 notice has been given gives notice under subsection (1)(*a*) above, then, so far as regards the matters to which the section 36 notice relates, the reference to 28 days in section 36(3) above shall be construed as a reference to 70 days.

(3) Notice under subsection (1)(*a*) above shall be given before the expiry of the period of 28 days referred to in section 36(3) above, or, as the case may be, within such longer period as a court allows under section 36(3); and, where such a longer period has been so allowed before notice is given under subsection (1)(*a*) above, subsection (2) above does not apply.

[Building Act 1984, s 37.]

8–26089 **38.** *Civil liability.*

Appeals in certain cases

8–26090 **39. Appeal against refusal etc to relax building regulations.** *If a local authority refuse an application to dispense with or relax a requirement in building regulations the applicant may appeal to the Secretary of State.*

8–26091 **40. Appeal against section 36 notice.** (1) A person aggrieved by the giving of a section 36 notice may appeal to a magistrates' court acting for the petty sessions area in which is situated land on which there has been carried out any work to which the notice relates.

(2) Subject to subsection (3) below, on an appeal under this section the court shall—

(*a*) if it determines that the local authority were entitled to give the notice, confirm the notice, and
(*b*) in any other case, give the local authority a direction to withdraw the notice.

(3) If, in a case where the appeal is against a notice under section 36(2) above, the court is satisfied that—

(*a*) the local authority were entitled to give the notice, but
(*b*) in all the circumstances of the case the purpose for which was enacted the section of this Act by virtue of which the notice was given has been substantially achieved,

the court may give a direction under subsection (2)(*b*) above.

(4) An appeal under this section shall be brought—

(*a*) within 28 days of the giving of the section 36 notice, or
(*b*) in a case where the person to whom the section 36 notice was given gives notice under section 37(1)(*a*) above, within 70 days of the giving of the section 36 notice.

(5) Where an appeal is brought under this section—

(*a*) the section 36 notice is of no effect pending the final determination or withdrawal of the appeal, and
(*b*) section 36(3) above has effect in relation to that notice as if after the words "28 days" there were inserted the words "(beginning, in a case where an appeal is brought under section 40 below, on the date when the appeal is finally determined or, as the case may be, withdrawn)".

(6) If, on an appeal under this section, there is produced to the court a report that has been submitted to the local authority under section 37(1) above, the court, in making an order as to costs, may treat the expenses incurred in obtaining the report as expenses incurred for the purposes of the appeal.

[Building Act 1984, s 40.]

8–26092 **41. Appeal to Crown Court.** (1) Where a person—

(*a*) is aggrieved by an order, determination or other decision of a magistrates' court under this Part of this Act, or under Part IV of this Act as it applies in relation to this Part, and
(*b*) is not by any other enactment authorised to appeal to the Crown Court,

he may appeal to the Crown Court.

(2) Subsection (1) above does not confer a right of appeal in a case in which each of the parties concerned might under this Act have required that the dispute should be determined by arbitration instead of by a magistrates' court.

[Building Act 1984, s 41.]

8–26093 **42–43.** *Appeal and statement of case to High Court in certain cases; procedure on appeal to Secretary of State on certain matters.*

Application of building regulations to Crown etc

8–26094 44–45. *Application to Crown; application to United Kingdom Atomic Energy Authority.*

Inner London

8–26095 46. Inner London. In its application to inner London, this Part of this Act has effect subject to Part I of Schedule 3 to this Act.
[Building Act 1984, s 46.]

PART II[1]

SUPERVISION OF BUILDING WORK ETC OTHERWISE THAN BY LOCAL AUTHORITIES

Supervision of plans and work by approved inspectors

8–26096 47. Giving and acceptance of initial notice. (1) If—

(*a*) a notice in the prescribed form (called an "initial notice") is given jointly to a local authority by a person intending to carry out work and a person who is an approved inspector in relation to that work,

(*b*) the initial notice is accompanied by such plans of the work as may be prescribed,

(*c*) the initial notice is accompanied by such evidence as may be prescribed that an approved scheme applies, or the prescribed insurance cover has been or will be provided, in relation to the work, and

(*d*) the initial notice is accepted by the local authority,

then, so long as the initial notice continues in force, the approved inspector by whom the notice was given shall undertake such functions as may be prescribed[2] with respect to the inspection of plans of the work to which the notice relates, the supervision of that work and the giving and receiving of certificates and other notices.

(2) A local authority to whom an initial notice is given—

(*a*) may not reject the notice except on prescribed grounds, and

(*b*) shall reject the notice if any of the prescribed grounds exists,

and, in a case where the work to which an initial notice relates is work of such a description that, if plans of it had been deposited with the local authority, the authority could, under any enactment, have imposed requirements as a condition of passing the plans, the local authority may impose the like requirements as a condition of accepting the initial notice.

(3) Unless, within the prescribed period, the local authority to whom an initial notice is given give notice of rejection, specifying the ground or grounds in question, to each of the persons by whom the initial notice was given, the authority is conclusively presumed to have accepted the initial notice and to have done so without imposing any such requirements as are referred to in subsection (2) above.

(4) An initial notice—

(*a*) comes into force when it is accepted by the local authority, either by notice given within the prescribed period to each of the persons by whom it was given or by virtue of subsection (3) above, and

(*b*) subject to section 51(3) below, continues in force until—

(i) it is cancelled by a notice under section 52 below, or

(ii) the occurrence of, or the expiry of a prescribed period of time beginning on the date of, such event as may be prescribed;

and building regulations[3] may empower a local authority to extend (whether before or after its expiry) any such period of time as is referred to in paragraph (ii) above.

(5) The form prescribed for an initial notice may be such as to require—

(*a*) either or both of the persons by whom the notice is to be given to furnish information relevant for the purposes of this Act, Part II or IV of the Public Health Act 1936 or any provision of building regulations, and

(*b*) the approved inspector by whom the notice is to be given to enter into undertakings with respect to his performance of any of the functions referred to in subsection (1) above.

(6) The Secretary of State may approve for the purposes of this section any scheme that appears to him to secure the provision of adequate insurance cover in relation to any work to which an initial notice relates and is work to which the scheme applies.

(7) Building regulations may prescribe for the purposes of this section the insurance cover that is to be provided in relation to any work to which an initial notice relates and is not work to which an approved scheme applies and may, in particular, prescribe the form and content of policies of insurance.
[Building Act 1984, s 47, as amended by SI 1996/1905 and the Sustainable and Secure Buildings Act 2004, s 8.]

1. Part II contains ss 47–58.
2. See the Building (Approved Inspectors etc) Regulations 2000, SI 2000/2532 amended by SI 2001/3336, SI 2002/2872, SI 2003/3133, SI 2004/1466 and 3168 and SI 2005/1541 and 2929 (W).

3. See the Building (Inner London) Regulations 1985, SI 1985/1936 amended by SI 1987/798 and SI 1991/2768 and the Building Regulations 2000, SI 2000/2531 amended by SI 2001/3335, SI 2002/440 and 2871, SI 2003/2692 and 3133, SI 2004/1465, 1808 and 3210 and SI 2005/1082 and 1541.

8–26097 **48. Effect of initial notice.** (1) So long as an initial notice continues in force, the function of enforcing building regulations that is conferred on a local authority by section 91(2) below is not exercisable in relation to the work to which the notice relates, and accordingly—

(*a*) a local authority may not give a notice under section 36(1) above in relation to that work, and

(*b*) a local authority may not institute proceedings under section 35 above for a contravention of building regulations that arises out of the carrying out of that work.

(2) For the purposes of the enactments specified in subsection (3) below—

(*a*) the giving of an initial notice accompanied by such plans as are referred to in section 47(1)(*b*) above shall be treated as the deposit of plans,

(*b*) the plans accompanying an initial notice shall be treated as the deposited plans,

(*c*) the acceptance or rejection of an initial notice shall be treated as the passing or, as the case may be, the rejection of plans, and

(*d*) the cancellation of an initial notice under section 52(5) below shall be treated as a declaration under section 32 above that the deposit of plans is of no effect.

(3) The enactments referred to in subsection (2) above are—

(*a*) section 36(2) above,

(*b*) section 36(5) above, in so far as it relates to a notice under section 36(2) above and to non-compliance with any such requirement as is referred to in that subsection,

(*c*) section 36(6) above, in so far as it relates to a contravention of this Act,

(*d*) section 18(2) above, and

(*e*) sections 219 to 225 of the Highways Act 1980 (the advance payments code).

(4) *Repealed.*

[Building Act 1984, s 48, as amended by the Fire Safety and Safety of Places of Sport Act 1987, s 7, SI 1996/1905, the Fire and Rescue Services Act 2004, Sch 1 and SI 2005/1541.]

8–26098 **49. Approved inspectors.** (1) In this Act, "approved inspector" means a person who, in accordance with building regulations[1], is approved for the purposes of this Part of this Act—

(*a*) by the Secretary of State, or

(*b*) by a body (corporate or unincorporated) that, in accordance with the regulations, is designated by the Secretary of State for the purpose.

(2) Any such approval as is referred to in subsection (1) above may limit the description of work in relation to which the person concerned is an approved inspector.

(3) Any such designation as is referred to in subsection (1)(*b*) above may limit the cases in which and the terms on which the body designated may approve a person and, in particular, may provide that any approval given by the body shall be limited as mentioned in subsection (2) above.

(4) There shall be paid on an application for any such approval as is referred to in subsection (1) above—

(*a*) where the application is made to the Secretary of State, such fee as may be prescribed,

(*b*) where the application is made to a body designated by him as mentioned in that subsection, such fee as that body may determine.

(5) Building regulations may—

(*a*) contain provision prescribing the period for which, subject to any provision made by virtue of paragraph (*b*) or (*c*) below, any such approval as is referred to in subsection (1) above continues in force,

(*b*) contain provision precluding the giving of, or requiring the withdrawal of, any such approval as is referred to in subsection (1) above in such circumstances as may be prescribed,

(*c*) contain provision authorising the withdrawal of any such approval or designation as is referred to in subsection (1) above,

(*d*) provide for the maintenance—

(i) by the Secretary of State of a list of bodies that are for the time being designated by him as mentioned in subsection (1) above, and

(ii) by the Secretary of State and by each designated body of a list of persons for the time being approved by him or them as mentioned in that subsection,

(*e*) make provision for the supply to local authorities of copies of any list of approved inspectors maintained by virtue of paragraph (*d*) above and for such copy lists to be made available for inspection, and

(*f*) make provision for the supply, on payment of a prescribed fee, of a certified copy of any entry in a list maintained by virtue of paragraph (*d*) above or in a copy list held by a local authority by virtue of paragraph (*e*) above.

(6) Unless the contrary is proved, in any proceedings (whether civil or criminal) a document that appears to the court to be a certified copy of an entry either in a list maintained as mentioned in subsection (5)(*d*) above or in a copy of such a list supplied as mentioned in subsection (5)(*e*) above—

(*a*) is presumed to be a true copy of an entry in the current list so maintained, and
(*b*) is evidence of the matters stated in it.

(7) An approved inspector may make such charges in respect of the carrying out of the functions referred to in section 47(1) above as may in any particular case be agreed between him and the person who intends to carry out the work in question or, as the case may be, by whom that work is being or has been carried out.

(8) Nothing in this Part of this Act prevents an approved inspector from arranging for plans or work to be inspected on his behalf by another person; but such a delegation—

(*a*) shall not extend to the giving of a certificate under section 50 or 51 below, and
(*b*) shall not affect any liability, whether civil or criminal, of the approved inspector which arises out of functions conferred on him by this Part of this Act or by building regulations,

and, without prejudice to the generality of paragraph (*b*) above, an approved inspector is liable for negligence on the part of a person carrying out an inspection on his behalf in like manner as if it were negligence by a servant of his acting in the course of his employment.
[Building Act 1984, s 49.]

---

1. See the Building (Inner London) Regulations 1985, SI 1985/1936 amended by SI 1987/798 and SI 1991/2768, the Building Regulations 2000, SI 2000/2531 amended by SI 2001/3335, SI 2002/440 and 2871, SI 2003/2692 and 3133, SI 2004/1465, 1808 and 3210 and SI 2005/1082 and 1541 and the Building (Approved Inspectors etc) Regulations 2000, SI 2000/2532 amended by SI 2001/3336, SI 2002/2872, SI 2003/3133 SI 2004/1466 and 3168 and SI 2005/1541 and 2929 (W).

8–26099 50. Plans certificates. (1) Where an approved inspector—

(*a*) has inspected plans of the work to which an initial notice given by him relates,
(*b*) is satisfied that the plans neither are defective nor show that work carried out in accordance with them would contravene any provision of building regulations[1], and
(*c*) has complied with any prescribed requirements as to consultation or otherwise,

he shall, if requested to do so by the person intending to carry out the work, give a certificate in the prescribed[2] form (called a "plans certificate") to the local authority and to that person.

(2) If any question arises under subsection (1) above between an approved inspector and a person who proposes to carry out any work whether plans of the work are in conformity with building regulations, that person may refer the question to the Secretary of State for his determination.

(3) An application for a reference under subsection (2) above shall be accompanied by such fee as may be prescribed.

(4) Building regulations may authorise the giving of an initial notice combined with a certificate under subsection (1) above, and may prescribe a single form for such a combined notice and certificate; and where such a prescribed form is used—

(*a*) a reference in this Part of this Act to an initial notice or to a plans certificate includes a reference to that form, but
(*b*) should the form cease to be in force as an initial notice by virtue of section 47(4) above, nothing in that subsection affects the continuing validity of the form as a plans certificate.

(5) A plans certificate—

(*a*) may relate either to the whole or to part only of the work to which the initial notice concerned relates, and
(*b*) does not have effect unless it is accepted by the local authority to whom it is given.

(6) A local authority to whom a plans certificate is given—

(*a*) may not reject the certificate except on prescribed grounds, and
(*b*) shall reject the certificate if any of the prescribed grounds exists.

(7) Unless, within the prescribed period, the local authority to whom a plans certificate is given give notice of rejection, specifying the ground or grounds in question, to—

(*a*) the approved inspector by whom the certificate was given, and
(*b*) the other person to whom the approved inspector gave the certificate,

the authority shall be conclusively presumed to have accepted the certificate.

(8) If it appears to a local authority by whom a plans certificate has been accepted that the work to which the certificate relates has not been commenced within the period of three years beginning on the date on which the certificate was accepted, the authority may rescind their acceptance of the certificate by notice, specifying the ground or grounds in question, given—

(*a*) to the approved inspector by whom the certificate was given, and (*b*) to the person shown in the initial notice concerned as the person intending to carry out the work.

[Building Act 1984, s 50, as amended by SI 1996/1905.]

1. See the Building (Inner London) Regulations 1985, SI 1985/1936 amended by SI 1987/798 and SI 1991/2768 and the Building Regulations 2000, SI 2000/2531 amended by SI 2001/3335, SI 2002/440 and 2871, SI 2003/2692 and 3133, SI 2004/1465, 1808 and 3210 and SI 2005/1082 and 1541.

2. See the Building (Approved Inspectors etc) Regulations 2000, SI 2000/2532 amended by SI 2001/3336, SI 2002/2872, SI 2003/3133, SI 2004/1466 and 3168 and SI 2005/1541 and 2929 (W).

8–26110 51. Final certificates. (1) Where an approved inspector is satisfied that any work to which an initial notice given by him relates has been completed, he shall give to the local authority by whom the initial notice was accepted such certificate with respect to the completion of the work and the discharge of his functions as may be prescribed (called a "final certificate").

(2) Section 50(5) to (7) above has effect in relation to a final certificate as if any reference in those subsections to a plans certificate were a reference to a final certificate.

(3) Where a final certificate—

(*a*) has been given with respect to any of the work to which an initial notice relates, and

(*b*) has been accepted by the local authority concerned,

the initial notice ceases to apply to that work, but section 48(1) above continues to apply, by virtue of this subsection, in relation to that work as if the initial notice continued in force in relation to it.

[Building Act 1984, s 51, as amended by SI 1996/1905.]

8–26110A 51A. Variation of work to which initial notice relates. (1) This section applies where it is proposed that the work to which an initial notice relates should be varied.

(2) If—

(*a*) a notice in the prescribed form (called an "amendment notice")—

(i) is given to the local authority by whom the initial notice was accepted, and

(ii) is jointly given by the approved inspector who gave the initial notice and by the person shown in the amendment notice as the person intending to carry out the relevant work,

(*b*) the amendment notice is accompanied by such plans of the proposed variation as may be prescribed,

(*c*) the amendment notice is accompanied by such evidence as may be prescribed that—

(i) a scheme approved for the purposes of section 47 above applies, or

(ii) the insurance cover prescribed for those purposes has been, or will be provided, in relation to the relevant work, and

(*d*) the amendment notice—

(i) is accepted by the local authority giving notice of acceptance within the prescribed period to each of the persons by whom the amendment notice was given, or

(ii) is deemed to have been accepted by the local authority by virtue of subsection (5) below,

the work to which the initial notice relates shall be treated as varied as proposed in the amendment notice.

(3) A local authority to whom an amendment notice is given—

(*a*) may not reject the notice except on prescribed grounds, and—

(*b*) shall reject the notice if any of the prescribed grounds exists.

(4) Where the relevant work is of such a description that, if plans of it had been deposited with the local authority, the authority could, under any enactment, have imposed requirements as a condition of passing the plans, the local authority may impose the like requirements as a condition of accepting the amendment notice.

(5) Unless, within the prescribed period, the local authority to whom an amendment notice is given give notice of rejection, specifying the ground or grounds in question, to each of the persons by whom the notice was given, the authority is conclusively presumed to have accepted it and to have done so without imposing any such requirements as are referred to in subsection (4) above.

(6) Section 47(5) shall apply in relation to the form prescribed for an amendment notice as it applies in relation to the form prescribed for an initial notice.

(7) In this section, references to the relevant work are to the work to which the initial notice, as proposed to be varied, relates.

[Building Act 1984, s 51A, as inserted by SI 1996/1905.]

8–26110B 51B. Effect of Amendment Notice. (1) For the purposes of the enactments specified in section 48(3) above—

(*a*) the giving of an amendment notice accompanied by such plans as are referred to in section 51A(2)(*b*) above shall be treated as the deposit of plans, (*b*) the acceptance or rejection of an amendment notice shall be treated as the passing, or, as the case may be, the rejection of plans,

(*c*) where an initial notice is varied by an amendment notice, the deposited plans shall be treated—

(i) as including the plans accompanying the amendment notice, and

(ii) as excluding such of the plans previously treated as the deposited plans as are superseded by the plans accompanying the amendment notice, and

(*d*) where an initial notice has been varied by an amendment notice, the cancellation of the initial notice under section 52(5) below shall be treated as a declaration under section 32 above that the deposit of plans constituted by the giving of the amendment notice is of no effect.

(2) *Repealed.*

[Building Act 1984, s 51B, as inserted by SI 1996/1905 and SI 2005/1541.]

8–26110C 51C. Change of person intending to carry out work. (1) This section applies where it is proposed that the work to which an initial notice relates should be carried out by a different person.

(2) If—

(*a*) the approved inspector who gave the initial notice, and

(*b*) the person who now proposes to carry out the work to which the initial notice relates,

jointly give written notice of the proposal to the local authority by whom the initial notice was accepted, the initial notice shall be treated as showing as the person intending to carry out the work to which it relates the person mentioned in the notice under this section.

[Building Act 1984, s 51C, as inserted by SI 1996/1905.]

8–26111 52. Cancellation of initial notice. (1) If, at a time when an initial notice is in force—

(*a*) the approved inspector becomes or expects to become unable to carry out (or to continue to carry out) his functions with respect to any of the work to which the initial notice relates,

(*b*) the approved inspector is of the opinion that any of the work is being so carried out that he is unable adequately to carry out his functions with respect to it, or

(*c*) the approved inspector is of the opinion that there is a contravention of any provision of building regulations[1] with respect to any of that work and the circumstances are as mentioned in subsection (2) below,

the approved inspector shall cancel the initial notice by notice in the prescribed[2] form given to the local authority concerned and to the person carrying out or intending to carry out the work.

(2) The circumstances referred to in subsection (1)(*c*) above are—

(*a*) that the approved inspector has, in accordance with building regulations, given notice of the contravention to the person carrying out the work or intending to carry out the work, and

(*b*) that, within the prescribed period, the prescribed steps are not taken by the person who, in accordance with building regulations, is required to take them.

(3) If, at a time when an initial notice is in force, it appears to the person carrying out or intending to carry out the work to which the initial notice relates that the approved inspector is no longer willing or able to carry out his functions with respect to any of that work, he shall cancel the initial notice by notice in the prescribed[2] form given to the local authority concerned and, if it is practicable to do so, to the approved inspector.

(4) If a person fails without reasonable excuse to give to a local authority a notice that he is required to give by subsection (3) above, he is liable on summary conviction to a fine not exceeding **level 5** on the standard scale.

(5) If, at a time when an initial notice is in force, it appears to the local authority by whom the initial notice was accepted that the work to which the initial notice relates has not been commenced within the period of three years beginning on the date on which the initial notice was accepted, the authority may cancel the initial notice by notice in the prescribed form given—

(*a*) to the approved inspector by whom the initial notice was given, and

(*b*) to the person shown in the initial notice as the person intending to carry out the work.

(6) A notice under subsection (1), (3) or (5) above has the effect of cancelling the initial notice to which it relates with effect from the day on which the notice is given.

[Building Act 1984, s 52, as amended by SI 1996/1905 and the Sustainable and Secure Buildings Act 2004, s 8.]

1. See the Building (Inner London) Regulations 1985, SI 1985/1936 amended by SI 1987/798 and SI 1991/2768 and the Building Regulations 2000, SI 2000/2531 amended by SI 2001/3335, SI 2002/440 and 2871, SI 2003/2692 and 3133, SI 2004/1465, 1808 and 3210 and SI 2005/1082 and 1541.

2. See the Building (Approved Inspectors etc) Regulations 2000, SI 2000/2532 amended by SI 2001/3336, SI 2002/2872, SI 2003/3133, SI 2004/1466 and 3168 and SI 2005/1541 and 2929 (W).

8–26112 53. Effect of initial notice ceasing to be in force. (1) This section applies where an initial notice ceases to be in force by virtue of section 47(4)(*b*)(i) or (ii) above.

(2) Building regulations[1] may provide that, if—

(*a*) a plans certificate was given before the day on which the initial notice ceased to be in force,
(*b*) that certificate was accepted by the local authority (before, on or after that day), and
(*c*) before that day, that acceptance was not rescinded by a notice under section 50(8) above,

then, with respect to the work specified in the certificate, such of the functions of a local authority referred to in section 48(1) above as may be prescribed for the purposes of this subsection either are not exercisable or are exercisable only in prescribed circumstances.

(3) If, before the day on which the initial notice ceased to be in force, a final certificate—

(*a*) was given in respect of part of the work to which the initial notice relates, and
(*b*) was accepted by the local authority (before, on or after that day),

the fact that the initial notice has ceased to be in force does not affect the continuing operation of section 51(3) above in relation to that part of the work.

(4) Notwithstanding anything in subsections (2) and (3) above, for the purpose of enabling the local authority to perform the functions referred to in section 48(1) above in relation to any part of the work not specified in a plans certificate or final certificate, as the case may be, building regulations may require the local authority to be provided with plans that relate not only to that part but also to the part to which the certificate in question relates.

(5) In any case where this section applies, the reference in subsection (4) of section 36 above to the date of the completion of the work in question has effect, in relation to a notice under subsection (1) of that section, as if it were a reference to the date on which the initial notice ceased to be in force.

(6) Subject to any provision of building regulations made by virtue of subsection (2) above, if, before the initial notice ceased to be in force, an offence under section 35 above was committed with respect to any of the work to which that notice relates, proceedings for that offence may be commenced by the local authority at any time within six months beginning with the day on which the function of the local authority referred to in section 48(1) above became exercisable with respect to the provision of building regulations to which the offence relates.

(7) The fact that an initial notice has ceased to be in force does not affect the right to give a new initial notice relating to any of the work to which the original notice related and in respect of which no final certificate has been given and accepted; but where—

(*a*) a plans certificate has been given in respect of any of that work,
(*b*) the conditions in paragraphs (*a*) to (*c*) of subsection (2) above are fulfilled with respect to that certificate, and
(*c*) such a new initial notice is given and accepted,

section 50(1) above does not apply in relation to so much of the work to which the new initial notice relates as is work specified in the plans certificate.
[Building Act 1984, s 53, as amended by SI 1996/1905.]

---

1. See the Building (Inner London) Regulations 1985, SI 1985/1936 amended by SI 1987/798 and SI 1991/2768 and the Building Regulations 2000, SI 2000/2531 amended by SI 2001/3335, SI 2002/440 and 2871, SI 2003/2692 and 3133, SI 2004/1465, 1808 and 3210 and SI 2005/1082 and 1541.

Supervision of their own work by public bodies

8–26113 54. Giving, acceptance and effect of public body's notice. (1) This section applies where a body (corporate or unincorporated) that acts under an enactment for public purposes and not for its own profit and is, or is of a description that is, approved by the Secretary of State in accordance with building regulations[1] (in this Part of this Act referred to as a "public body")—

(*a*) intends to carry out in relation to a building belonging to it work to which the substantive requirements of building regulations apply,
(*b*) considers that the work can be adequately supervised by its own servants or agents, and
(*c*) gives to the local authority in whose district the work is to be carried out notice in the prescribed[2] form (called a "public body's notice") together with such plans of the work as may be prescribed.

(2) A public body's notice is of no effect unless it is accepted by the local authority to whom it is given; and that local authority—

(*a*) may not reject the notice except on prescribed grounds, and
(*b*) shall reject the notice if any of the prescribed grounds exists,

and, in a case where the work to which the public body's notice relates is work of such a description that, if plans of it had been deposited with the local authority, the authority could, under an enactment, have imposed requirements as a condition of passing the plans, the local authority may impose the like requirements as a condition of accepting the public body's notice.

(3) Unless, within the prescribed period, the local authority to whom a public body's notice is given give notice of rejection, specifying the ground or grounds in question, the authority is conclusively presumed to have accepted the public body's notice and to have done so without imposing any such requirements as are referred to in subsection (2) above.

(4) Section 48 above has effect for the purposes of this section—

(*a*) with the substitution of a reference to a public body's notice for any reference to an initial notice, and

(*b*) with the substitution, in subsection (2)(*a*), of a reference to subsection (1)(*c*) of this section for the reference to section 47(1)(*b*).

(5) The form prescribed for a public body's notice may be such as to require the public body by whom it is to be given—

(*a*) to furnish information relevant for the purposes of this Act, Part II or IV of the Public Health Act 1936 or any provision of building regulations, and

(*b*) to enter into undertakings with respect to consultation and other matters.

(6) Where a public body's notice is given and accepted by the local authority to whom it is given, the provisions of Schedule 4 to this Act have effect, being provisions that correspond, as nearly as may be, to those made by the preceding provisions of this Part of this Act for the case where an initial notice is given and accepted.
[Building Act 1984, s 54.]

1. See the Building (Inner London) Regulations 1985, SI 1985/1936 amended by SI 1987/798 and SI 1991/2768 and the Building Regulations 2000, SI 2000/2531 amended by SI 2001/3335, SI 2002/440 and 2871, SI 2003/2692 and 3133, SI 2004/1465, 1808 and 3210 and SI 2005/1082 and 1541.

2. See the Building (Approved Inspectors etc) Regulations 2000, SI 2000/2532 amended by SI 2001/3336, SI 2002/2872, SI 2003/3133, SI 2004/1466 and 3168 and SI 2005/1541 and 2929 (W).

Supplementary

8–26114 **55. Appeals.** (1) A person aggrieved by the local authority's rejection of—

(*a*) an initial notice, amendment notice or a public body's notice, or

(*b*) a plans certificate, a final certificate, a public body's plans certificate or a public body's final certificate,

may appeal to a magistrates' court acting for the petty sessions area in which is situated land on which there will be, or there has been, carried out any work to which the notice or certificate relates.

(2) On an appeal under subsection (1) above, the court shall—

(*a*) if it determines that the notice or certificate was properly rejected, confirm the rejection, and

(*b*) in any other case, give a direction to the local authority to accept the notice or certificate.

(3) Where a person is aggrieved by a determination, confirmation, direction or other decision of a magistrates' court under this section, he may appeal to the Crown Court.
[Building Act 1984, s 55, as amended by SI 1996/1905.]

8–26115 **56. Recording and furnishing of information.** (1) Every local authority shall keep, in such manner as may be prescribed[1], a register containing such information as may be prescribed with respect to initial notices, amendment notices, notices under section 51C above, public body's notices and certificates given to them, including information (where applicable) as to whether such notices or certificates have been accepted or rejected.*

(2) The information that may be prescribed under subsection (1) above with respect to an initial notice or amendment notice includes information about the insurance cover provided with respect to the work to which the notice relates.*

(3) The reference in subsection (1) above to certificates is a reference to plans certificates, final certificates, public body's plans certificates, public body's final certificates and certificates given under section 16(9) above.*

(4) Every register kept under this section shall be available for inspection by the public at all reasonable hours.*

(5) Where an initial notice or a public body's notice has continued in force for any period, the local authority by whom it was accepted may require the approved inspector or public body by whom it was given to furnish them with any information that—

(*a*) they would have obtained themselves if during that period their function of enforcing building regulations had continued to be exercisable in relation to the work to which the notice relates, and

(*b*) they require for the purpose of performing their duty under section 230 of the Local Government Act 1972 (reports and returns),

and that section shall have effect as if during that period that function had continued to be so exercisable.
[Building Act 1984, s 56, as amended by SI 1996/1905.]

***Repealed by the Sustainable and Secure Buildings Act 2004, s 11 from a date to be appointed.**

1. See the Building (Inner London) Regulations 1985, SI 1985/1936 amended by SI 1987/798 and SI 1991/2768, the Building Regulations 2000, SI 2000/2531 amended by SI 2001/3335, SI 2002/440 and 2871, SI 2003/2692 and 3133, SI 2004/1465, 1808 and 3210 and SI 2005/1082 and 1541 and the Building (Approved Inspectors etc.) Regulations 2000,

SI 2000/2532 amended by SI 2001/3336, SI 2002/2872, SI 2003/3133, SI 2004/1466 and 3168 and SI 2005/1541 and 2929 (W).

8–26116 57. Offences. (1) If a person—

(*a*) gives a notice or certificate that—

(i) purports to comply with the requirements of this Part of this Act, section 16(9) above or building regulations falling within paragraph 4A(1)(*a*) or (*b*) of Schedule 1 to this Act, and

(ii) contains a statement that he knows to be false or misleading in a material particular, or

(*b*) recklessly gives a notice or certificate that—

(i) purports to comply with those requirements, and

(ii) contains a statement that is false or misleading in a material particular,

he is guilty of an offence.

(2) A person guilty of an offence under subsection (1) above is liable[1]—

(*a*) on summary conviction, to a fine not exceeding **the statutory maximum** or imprisonment for a term not exceeding **six months** or **both**, and

(*b*) on conviction on indictment, to a **fine** or imprisonment for a term not exceeding **two years** or **both**.

(3) Where an approved inspector or person approved for the purposes of section 16(9) above is convicted of an offence under this section, the court by or before which he is convicted shall, within one month of the date of conviction, forward a certificate of the conviction to the person by whom the approval was given.

[Building Act 1984, s 57 as amended by the Sustainable and Secure Buildings Act 2004, s 8.]

1. For procedure in respect of an offence triable either way, see the Magistrates' Courts Act 1980, ss 17A-21, in PART I: MAGISTRATES' COURTS, PROCEDURE, ante.

8–26117 58. Construction of Part II. (1) In this Part of this Act—

"amendment notice" has the meaning given by section 51A(2) above;
"final certificate" has the meaning given by section 51(1) above;
"initial notice" has the meaning given by section 47(1) above;
"plans certificate" has the meaning given by section 50(1) above;
"public body" and "public body's notice" have the meanings given by section 54(1) above;
"public body's final certificate" has the meaning given by paragraph 3 of Schedule 4 to this Act;
"public body's plans certificate" has the meaning given by paragraph 2 of Schedule 4 to this Act.

(2) A reference in this Part of this Act to the carrying out of work includes a reference to the making of a material change of use, as defined by and for the purposes of building regulations.

(3) A reference in this Part of this Act to an initial notice given by an approved inspector is a reference to a notice given by him jointly with another person as mentioned in section 47(1)(*a*) above.

[Building Act 1984, s 58, as amended by SI 1996/1905.]

PART III[1]

OTHER PROVISIONS ABOUT BUILDINGS

Drainage

8–26118 59. Drainage of building. (1) If it appears to a local authority that in the case of a building—

(*a*) satisfactory provision has not been, and ought to be, made for drainage,

(*b*) a cesspool, private sewer, drain, soil pipe, rain-water pipe, spout, sink or other necessary appliance provided for the building is insufficient or, in the case of a private sewer or drain communicating directly or indirectly with a public sewer, is so defective as to admit subsoil water,

(*c*) a cesspool or other such work or appliance as aforesaid provided for the building is in such a condition as to be prejudicial to health or a nuisance,[2] or

(*d*) a cesspool, private sewer or drain formerly used for the drainage of the building, but no longer used for it, is prejudicial to health or a nuisance,

they shall by notice require the owner of the building to make satisfactory provision for the drainage of the building, or, as the case may be, require either the owner or the occupier of the building to do such work as may be necessary for renewing, repairing or cleansing the existing cesspool, sewer, drain, pipe, spout, sink or other appliance, or for filling up, removing or otherwise rendering innocuous the disused cesspool, sewer or drain.

(2) Sections 99 and 102 below apply in relation to a notice given under subsection (1) above.

(3) Subsections (4), (5) and (6) of section 21 above apply in relation to a drain that a local authority require to be constructed under this section as they apply in relation to such a proposed drain as is mentioned in that section.

(4) Subsection (1) above, so far as it empowers a local authority to take action in the cases mentioned in paragraphs (*a*) and (*b*) of the subsection, does not apply in relation to a building belonging to statutory undertakers, the Civil Aviation Authority or a person who holds a licence under Chapter I of Part I of the Transport Act 2000 (air traffic services) and held or used by such a body or person for the purpose of that body's or that person's undertaking, unless it is—

(*a*) a house, or
(*b*) a building used as offices or showrooms, and not forming part of a railway station or in the case of the Civil Aviation Authority not being on an aerodrome owned by the Authority.*

(5) For the purposes of subsection (4) above, the undertaking of a person who holds a licence under Chapter I of Part I of the Transport Act 2000 shall be taken to be the person's undertaking as licence holder.*

(6) In subsection (1) above, "drainage" includes the conveyance, by means of a sink and any other necessary appliance, of refuse water and the conveyance of rainwater from roofs.
[Building Act 1984, s 59, as amended by the Airports Act 1986, Sch 6 and SI 2001/3335 and 4050.]

***Repealed by the Sustainable and Secure Buildings Act 2004, s 11 from a date to be appointed.**
1. Part III contains ss 59–90.
2. A notice under s 59(1)(*c*) alleging that a sewer is defective, and requiring works to be executed, must be served not only on the owner or occupier on whose premises the break has occurred, but also on all other persons whose premises are upstream of those premises (*Swansea City Council v Jenkins* (1994) 158 JP 952).

8–26119 60. Use and ventilation of soil pipes. (1) A pipe for conveying rain-water from a roof shall not be used for the purpose of conveying the soil or drainage from a sanitary convenience.

(2) The soil pipe from a water-closet shall be properly ventilated.

(3) A pipe for conveying surface water from premises shall not be permitted to act as a ventilating shaft to a drain or sewer conveying foul water.

(4) If it appears to the local authority that there is on any premises a contravention of any provision of this section, they may by notice require the owner or the occupier of those premises to execute such work as may be necessary to remedy the matter.

(5) Sections 99 and 102 below apply in relation to a notice given under subsection (4) above.
[Building Act 1984, s 60, as amended by the Water Act 1989, Sch 8.]

8–26120 61. Repair etc of drain. (1) No person shall—

(*a*) except in case of emergency, repair, reconstruct or alter the course of an underground drain that communicates with a sewer, or with a cesspool or other receptacle for drainage, or
(*b*) where in a case of emergency any such works have been executed without notice, cover over the drain or sewer,

without giving to the local authority at least 24 hours' notice of his intention to do so.

(2) While any such work as aforesaid is being executed, all persons concerned shall permit the proper officer, or any other authorised officer, of the local authority to have free access to the work.

(3) A person who fails to comply with this section is liable on summary conviction to a fine not exceeding **level 3** on the standard scale.

(4) This section does not apply to—

(*a*) so much of a drain or sewer constructed by, or belonging to, a railway company as runs under, across or along their railway, or
(*b*) so much of a drain or sewer constructed by, or belonging to, dock undertakers as is situated in or on land of the undertakers that is held or used by them for the purposes of their undertaking.

[Building Act 1984, s 61.]

8–26121 62. Disconnection of drain. (1) Where a person—

(*a*) reconstructs in the same or a new position a drain that communicates with a sewer or another drain,
(*b*) executes any works to such a drain so as permanently to discontinue its use, or
(*c*) executes any works on premises served by such a drain so as permanently to discontinue its use,

he shall cause any drains or parts of drains thereby becoming disused or unnecessary to be disconnected and sealed at such points as the local authority may reasonably require.

(2) Any question as to the reasonableness of a requirement of a local authority under this section shall be determined by a magistrates' court, and the court may vary the requirement as it thinks fit.

(3) No one shall be required under this section to carry out any work in land outside the premises served by the drain if he has no right to carry out that work, but, subject to section 101 below, the person undertaking the reconstruction of the drain or the execution of the works may break open any street for the purpose of complying with a requirement under this section.

(4) Before a person complies with a requirement under this section, he shall give at least 48 hours'

notice to the local authority, and a person who fails to comply with this subsection is liable on summary conviction to a fine not exceeding **level 1** on the standard scale.

(5) A person who knowingly fails to comply with subsection (1) above is liable on summary conviction to a fine not exceeding **level 1** on the standard scale and to a further fine not exceeding **£1** for each day on which the default continues after he is convicted.

(6) This section does not apply in relation to anything done in the course of the demolition of a building, or of part of a building, being a demolition as respects which the local authority have power under section 81 below to serve a notice on the person undertaking the demolition.

[Building Act 1984, s 62.]

8–26122 **63. Improper construction or repair of water-closet or drain.** (1) If a water-closet, drain or soil pipe is so constructed or repaired as to be prejudicial to health or a nuisance, the person who undertook or executed the construction or repair is liable on summary conviction to a fine not exceeding **level 1** on the standard scale, unless he shows that the prejudice to health or nuisance could not have been avoided by the exercise of reasonable care.

(2) A person charged with an offence under this section (hereafter in this section referred to as "the original defendant") is entitled, upon information duly laid by him and on giving to the prosecutor not less than three clear days' notice of his intention, to have any other person, being his agent or servant, to whose act or default he alleges that the offence was due brought before the court at the time appointed for the hearing of the charge; and—

(*a*) if after the commission of the offence has been proved the original defendant proves that the offence was due to the act or default of that other person, that other person may be convicted of the offence, and

(*b*) if the original defendant further proves that he used all due diligence to secure that the water-closet, drain or soil pipe in question was so constructed or repaired as not to be prejudicial to health or a nuisance, he shall be acquitted of the offence.

(3) Where the original defendant seeks to avail himself of subsection (2) above—

(*a*) the prosecutor as well as the person whom the original defendant charges with the offence has the right to cross-examine the original defendant, if he gives evidence, and any witness called by him in support of his pleas, and to call rebutting evidence, and

(*b*) the court may make such order as it thinks fit for the payment of costs by any party to the proceedings to any other party to them.

(4) In this section in its application to Greater London, a reference to a water-closet includes a reference to a urinal.

[Building Act 1984, s 63.]

Provision of sanitary conveniences

8–26123 **64. Provision of closets in building.** (1) If it appears to a local authority—

(*a*) that a building is without sufficient closet accommodation,

(*b*) that a part of a building, being a part that is occupied as a separate dwelling, is without sufficient closet accommodation, or

(*c*) that any closets provided for or in connection with a building are in such a state as to be prejudicial to health or a nuisance and cannot without reconstruction be put into a satisfactory condition,

the authority shall, by notice to the owner of the building, require him to provide the building with such closets or additional closets, or such substituted closets, being in each case either water-closets or earth-closets, as may be necessary.

(2) Unless a sufficient water supply and sewer are available, the authority shall not require the provision of a water-closet except in substitution for an existing water-closet.

(3) Sections 99 and 102 below apply in relation to a notice given under subsection (1) above.

(4) Among the grounds on which an appeal may be brought under section 102 below against such a notice is that—

(*a*) the need for the works to be executed under the notice would not, in whole or in part, arise but for the occupation of part of the building as a separate dwelling, and the occupation of that part as a separate dwelling is a matter in respect of which the appellant has a cause of action, and

(*b*) the person against whom the appellant has a cause of action ought to contribute towards the expenses of executing the works.

(5) Where the grounds on which an appeal under section 102 below is brought include the ground specified in subsection (4) above—

(*a*) the appellant shall serve a copy of his notice of appeal on the person or persons referred to in that ground of appeal, and

(*b*) on the hearing of the appeal the court may make such order as it thinks fit with respect to—

(i) the contribution to be made by any such person towards the cost of the works, or

(ii) the proportion in which any expenses that may be recoverable by the local authority are to be borne by the appellant and any such other person.

(6) This section does not apply to—

(*a*) a factory,

(*b*) a building that is used as a workplace, or

(*c*) premises to which the Offices, Shops and Railway Premises Act 1963 applies.

[Building Act 1984, s 64.]

8–26124 65. Provision of sanitary conveniences in workplace. (1) A building that is used as a workplace shall be provided with—

(*a*) sufficient and satisfactory accommodation in the way of sanitary conveniences, regard being had to the number of persons employed in, or in attendance at, the building, and

(*b*) where persons of both sexes are employed or in attendance, sufficient and satisfactory separate accommodation for persons of each sex, unless the local authority are satisfied that in the circumstances of the particular case the provision of such separate accommodation is unnecessary.

(2) If it appears to the local authority that subsection (1) above is not complied with in the case of any building, they shall by notice require the owner or the occupier of the building to make such alterations in the existing conveniences, and to provide such additional conveniences, as may be necessary.

(3) Sections 99 to 102 below apply in relation to a notice given under subsection (2) above.

(4) This section does not apply to premises to which the Offices, Shops and Railway Premises Act 1963 applies.

[Building Act 1984, s 65.]

8–26125 66. Replacement of earth-closets etc. (1) If a building has a sufficient water supply and sewer available, the local authority may, subject to this section, by notice to the owner of the building require that any closets, other than water-closets, provided for, or in connection with, the building shall be replaced by water-closets, notwithstanding that the closets are not insufficient in number and are not prejudicial to health or a nuisance.

(2) A notice under subsection (1) above shall—

(*a*) require the owner to execute the necessary works, or

(*b*) require that the authority themselves shall be allowed to execute them,

and shall state the effect of subsection (3) below.

(3) Where the local authority give a notice under subsection (1) above—

(*a*) if it requires the owner to execute the works, the owner is entitled to recover from them one-half of the expenses reasonably incurred by him in the execution of the works, and

(*b*) if it requires that they shall be allowed to execute the works, they are entitled to recover from the owner one-half of the expenses reasonably incurred by them in the execution of the works.

(4) Where the owner of a building proposes to provide it with a water-closet in substitution for a closet of any other type, the local authority may, if they think fit, agree to pay him a part, not exceeding one-half, of the expenses reasonably incurred in effecting the replacement, notwithstanding that a notice has not been given by them under subsection (1) above.

(5) Sections 99 and 102 below apply in relation to a notice given under subsection (1) above, subject to the following modifications—

(*a*) no appeal lies on the ground that the works are unnecessary, and

(*b*) any reference in the said section 99 to the expenses reasonably incurred in executing works is a reference to one-half of those expenses.

[Building Act 1984, s 66.]

8–26126 67. Loan of temporary sanitary conveniences. (1) A local authority may, at the request of the occupier of any premises connected with a cesspool, sewer or drain on which any work of maintenance, improvement or repair that necessitates the disconnection of the sanitary conveniences provided for or in connection with the premises is to be carried out—

(*a*) by a local authority, or

(*b*) by the owner or occupier of the premises in pursuance of section 59 above,

supply on loan temporary sanitary conveniences in substitution for any sanitary conveniences so disconnected.

(2) Subject to the following provisions of this section, the local authority may make reasonable charges for supplying, removing and cleansing any temporary sanitary conveniences lent under this section for more than seven days.

(3) No charge may be made under subsection (2) above—

(*a*) for the use of the temporary sanitary conveniences for the first seven days, or

(*b*) in a case where the work is made necessary by a defect in a public sewer.

(4) No charge may be made under subsection (2) above where the work is made necessary—

(*a*) (*Repealed*);

(*b*) by a defect in a cesspool, private sewer or drain in respect of which the local authority have served a notice under section 59 above,

but, if the temporary sanitary conveniences are provided for a period of more than seven days, the reasonable expenses of supplying, removing and cleansing them are recoverable from the owner of the premises (but not any charge for the use of them for the first seven days).

(5) In proceedings to recover expenses under subsection (4) above, the court may—

(*a*) inquire whether the expenses ought to be borne wholly or in part by some person other than the defendant in the proceedings, and

(*b*) make such order concerning the expenses or their apportionment as appears to the court to be just,

but the court shall not order the expenses or any part of them to be borne by any person other than the defendant in the proceedings unless the court is satisfied that that other person has had notice of the proceedings and an opportunity of being heard.

[Building Act 1984, s 67, as amended by the Water Act 1989, Sch 27.]

8–26127 68. Erection of public conveniences. (1) No person shall erect a public sanitary convenience in, or so as to be accessible from, a street without the consent of the local authority, who may give their consent upon such terms as to the use of the convenience or its removal at any time, if required by them, as they think fit.

(2) A person who contravenes subsection (1) above is liable on summary conviction to a fine not exceeding **level 1** on the standard scale, without prejudice to the right of the authority under subsection (4) below to require the convenience to be removed.

(3) A person aggrieved by the refusal of a local authority to give a consent under subsection (1) above, or by any terms imposed by them, may appeal to a magistrates' court.

(4) The local authority may by notice require—

(*a*) the owner of a sanitary convenience—

(i) that has been erected in contravention of subsection (1) above, or

(ii) that the authority are, by virtue of the terms of a consent given under that subsection, entitled to require to be removed,

to remove it, or

(*b*) the owner of a sanitary convenience that opens on a street, and is so placed or constructed as to be a nuisance or offensive to public decency, to remove it or permanently close it.

(5) Sections 99 and 102 below apply in relation to a notice given under subsection (4) above.

(6) In this section, a reference to a local authority, in relation to a street that is a highway for which the local authority are not the highway authority, is a reference to the highway authority.

(7) Subsection (1) above does not apply to a sanitary convenience erected—

(*a*) by a railway company within their railway station or its yard or approaches, or

(*b*) by dock undertakers in or on land that belongs to them and is held or used by them for the purposes of their undertaking.

(8) This section does not affect the powers of—

(*a*) a county council under section 87 of the Public Health Act 1936,

(*b*) the Secretary of State under section 112 of the Highways Act 1980, or

(*c*) a county council under section 114(1) of the Highways Act 1980.

[Building Act 1984, s 68, as amended by the Local Government Act 1985, Sch 17.]

8–26128 70. Provision of food storage accommodation in house. (1) If it appears to a local authority that a house, or part of a building that is occupied as a separate dwelling, is without sufficient and suitable accommodation for the storage of food, the local authority may by notice require the owner of the house or building to provide the house or building with sufficient and suitable accommodation for that purpose.

(2) Sections 99 and 102 below apply in relation to a notice given under subsection (1) above.

(3) Among the grounds on which an appeal may be brought under section 102 below against such a notice are—

(*a*) that it is not reasonably practicable to comply with the notice;

(*b*) that—

(i) the need for the works to be executed under the notice would not, in whole or in part, arise but for the occupation of part of the building as a separate dwelling, and that the occupation of that part as a separate dwelling is a matter in respect of which the appellant has a cause of action, and

(ii) the person against whom the appellant has a cause of action ought to contribute towards the expenses of executing the works.

(4) Where the grounds on which an appeal under section 102 below is brought include the ground specified in subsection (3)(*b*) above—

(*a*) the appellant shall serve a copy of his notice of appeal on the person or persons referred to in that ground of appeal, and

(*b*) on the hearing of the appeal the court may make such order as it thinks fit with respect to—

(i) the contribution to be made by any such person towards the cost of the works, or

(ii) the proportion in which any expenses that may be recoverable by the local authority are to be borne by the appellant and any such other person.

[Building Act 1984, s 70.]

8–26129 71. Entrances, exits etc to be required in certain cases. *Repealed.*

8–26140 72. Means of escape from fire. (1) If it appears to a local authority, after consultation with the fire and rescue authority, that—

(*a*) a building to which this section applies is not provided, or

(*b*) a proposed building that will be a building to which this section applies will not be provided,

with such means of escape in case of fire as the local authority, after such consultation, deem necessary from each storey whose floor is more than twenty feet above the surface of the street or ground on any side of the building, the authority shall by notice require the owner of the building, or, as the case may be, the person proposing to erect the building, to execute such work or make such other provision in regard to the matters aforesaid as may be necessary.

(2) Sections 99 and 102 below apply in relation to a notice given under subsection (1) above in so far as it requires a person to execute works.

(3) In so far as such a notice requires a person to make provision otherwise than by the execution of works, he is, if he fails to comply with the notice, liable on summary conviction to a fine not exceeding **level 4** on the standard scale and to a further fine not exceeding **£2** for each day on which the offence continues after he is convicted.

(4) In proceedings under subsection (3) above, it is open to the defendant to question the reasonableness of the authority's requirements.

(5) Where building regulations imposing requirements as to the provision of means of escape in case of fire are applicable to a proposed building or proposed extension of a building, or would be so applicable but for a direction under section 8 above dispensing with such requirements—

(*a*) this section, and

(*b*) any provision of a local Act that has effect in place of this section,

does not apply in relation to the proposed building or extension.

(6) This section applies to a building that exceeds two storeys in height and in which the floor of any upper storey is more than twenty feet above the surface of the street or ground on any side of the building and that—

(*a*) is let in flats or tenement dwellings,*

(b) *Repealed.*

(c) *Repealed.*

(7) *Repealed.*

[Building Act 1984, s 72, as amended by the Fire and Rescue Services Act 2004, Sch 1 and SI 2005/1541.]

***Repealed by the Housing Act 2004, Sch 16 from a date to be appointed.**

8–26141 73. Raising of chimney. (1) Where, after the 3rd October 1961 (which was the date of commencement of the relevant provisions of the Public Health Act 1961)—

(*a*) a person erects or raises a building (in this section referred to as "the taller building") to a greater height than an adjoining building, and

(*b*) any chimneys or flues of an adjoining building are in a party wall between the two buildings or are six feet or less from the nearest part of the taller building,

the local authority may by notice—

(i) require that person, within such time as may be specified in the notice, to build up those chimneys and flues, if it is reasonably practicable so to do, so that their top will be of the same height as the top of the chimneys of the taller building or the top of the taller building, whichever is the higher, and

(ii) require the owner or occupier of the adjoining building to allow the first-mentioned person to enter on that building and carry out such work as may be necessary to comply with the notice served on him,

except that, if the said owner or occupier, within fourteen days from the date of service of the notice on him, serves on the first-mentioned person and on the local authority a notice (in this section referred to as a "counter-notice") that he elects to carry out the work himself, the owner or occupier shall comply with the notice served under paragraph (i) above instead of the first-mentioned person and may recover the expenses reasonably incurred in so doing from that person.

(2) A person on whom a notice is served under paragraph (i) or paragraph (ii) of subsection (1) above may appeal to a magistrates' court.

(3) If—

(*a*) a person on whom a notice is served under paragraph (i) of subsection (1) above fails to comply with the notice, except in a case where the owner or occupier of an adjoining building has refused to allow entry on that building, or has refused to allow the carrying out of any such work as may be necessary to comply with the notice, or has served a counter-notice, or

(*b*) a person on whom a notice is served under paragraph (ii) of subsection (1) above fails to comply with the notice or, having served a counter-notice, fails to comply with the notice served under paragraph (i) of that subsection,

he is liable on summary conviction to a fine not exceeding **level 1** on the standard scale, and the local authority may themselves carry out such work as may be necessary to comply with the notice served under the said paragraph (1), and recover the expenses reasonably incurred in doing so from the person on whom that notice was served.

[Building Act 1984, s 73.]

8–26142 **74. Cellars and rooms below subsoil water level.** (1) No person shall without the consent of the local authority construct a cellar or room in, or as part of, a house, shop, inn, hotel or office if the floor level of the cellar or room is lower than the ordinary level of the subsoil water on, under or adjacent to the site of the house, shop, inn, hotel or office.

(2) Subsection (1) above does not apply to—

(*a*) *repealed*

(*b*) the construction of a cellar or room in connection with a shop, inn, hotel or office that forms part of a railway station.

(3) If a person constructs a cellar or room in contravention of subsection (1) above, or of any condition attached to a consent under this section—

(*a*) he is liable on summary conviction to a fine not exceeding **level 1** on the standard scale, and

(*b*) the local authority may by notice require him either to alter the cellar or room so that its construction will no longer contravene the said subsection or condition or, if he so elects, to fill it in or otherwise make it unusable.

(4) Sections 99 and 102 below apply in relation to a notice given under subsection (3) above, subject to the following modifications—

(*a*) section 99(1) requires the notice to indicate the nature of the works of alteration and that of the works for making the cellar or room unusable, and

(*b*) section 99(2) authorises the local authority to execute, subject to that subsection, at their election either the works of alteration or the works for making the cellar or room unusable.

(5) If the owner for the time being of the house, shop, inn, hotel or office causes or permits a cellar or room forming part of it to be used in a manner that he knows to be in contravention of a condition attached to a consent under this section, he is liable on summary conviction to a fine not exceeding **level 1** on the standard scale.

[Building Act 1984, s 74 as amended by the Licensing Act 2003, Sch 6.]

8–26143 **75. Consents under section 74.** (1) A consent under section 74 above may be given subject to such conditions as to the construction or use of the premises as may be specified in it, and conditions specified in such a consent are binding on successive owners of the house, shop, inn, hotel or office.

(2) If a local authority—

(*a*) refuse an application for such a consent, or

(*b*) attach any conditions to such a consent,

the person applying for the consent may appeal to a magistrates' court against the refusal or, as the case may be, against any of the conditions, and if a magistrates' court allows an appeal against a refusal to grant a consent it may direct the local authority to give their consent subject to such conditions, if any, as appear to the court to be appropriate.

(3) An application may be made at any time to the local authority for the variation or withdrawal of a condition attached to such a consent, and, if the local authority refuse the application, the applicant may appeal to a magistrates' court.

[Building Act 1984, s 75.]

Defective premises, demolition etc

8–26144 76. Defective premises. (1) If it appears to a local authority that—

(*a*) any premises are in such a state (in this section referred to as a "defective state") as to be prejudicial to health or a nuisance, and

(*b*) unreasonable delay in remedying the defective state would be occasioned by following the procedure prescribed by section 80 of the Environmental Protection Act 1990,

the local authority may serve on the person on whom it would have been appropriate to serve an abatement notice under the said section 93 (if the local authority had proceeded under that section) a notice stating that the local authority intend to remedy the defective state and specifying the defects that they intend to remedy.

(2) Subject to subsection (3) below, the local authority may, after the expiration of nine days after service of a notice under subsection (1) above, execute such works as may be necessary to remedy the defective state, and recover the expenses reasonably incurred in so doing from the person on whom the notice was served.

(3) If, within seven days after service of a notice under subsection (1) above, the person on whom the notice was served serves a counter-notice that he intends to remedy the defects specified in the first-mentioned notice, the local authority shall take no action in pursuance of the first-mentioned notice unless the person who served the counter-notice—

(*a*) fails within what seems to the local authority a reasonable time to begin to execute works to remedy the said defects, or

(*b*) having begun to execute such works fails to make such progress towards their completion as seems to the local authority reasonable.

(4) In proceedings to recover expenses under subsection (2) above, the court—

(*a*) shall inquire whether the local authority were justified in concluding that the premises were in a defective state, or that unreasonable delay in remedying the defective state would have been occasioned by following the procedure prescribed by sections 93 to 96 of the Public Health Act 1936, and

(*b*) if the defendant proves that he served a counter-notice under subsection (3) above, shall inquire whether the defendant failed to begin the works to remedy the defects within a reasonable time, or failed to make reasonable progress towards their completion,

and if the court determines that—

(i) the local authority were not justified in either of the conclusions mentioned in paragraph (*a*) of this subsection, or

(ii) there was no failure under paragraph (*b*) of this subsection,

the local authority shall not recover the expenses or any part of them.

(5) Subject to subsection (4) above, in proceedings to recover expenses under subsection (2) above, the court may—

(*a*) inquire whether the said expenses ought to be borne wholly or in part by some person other than the defendant in the proceedings, and

(*b*) make such order concerning the expenses or their apportionment as appears to the court to be just,

but the court shall not order the expenses or any part of them to be borne by a person other than the defendant in the proceedings unless the court is satisfied that that other person has had due notice of the proceedings and an opportunity of being heard.

(6) A local authority shall not serve a notice under subsection (1) above, or proceed with the execution of works in accordance with a notice so served, if the execution of the works would, to their knowledge, be in contravention of a building preservation order under section 29 of the Town and Country Planning Act 1947[1].

(7) The power conferred on a local authority by subsection (1) above may be exercised notwithstanding that the local authority might instead have proceeded under Part VI of the Housing Act 1985 (repair notices).

[Building Act 1984, s 76, as amended by the Housing (Consequential Provisions) Act 1985, Sch 2 and the Environmental Protection Act 1990, Sch 15.]

---

1. The issue of building preservation notices by local planning authorities and the listing of special buildings is now governed by the Planning (Listed Buildings and Conservation Areas) Act 1990, post.

8–26145 77. Dangerous building. (1) If it appears to a local authority that a building or structure, or part of a building or structure, is in such a condition, or is used to carry such loads, as to be dangerous, the authority may apply to a magistrates' court, and the court may—

(*a*) where danger arises from the condition of the building or structure, make an order requiring the owner thereof—

(i) to execute such work as may be necessary to obviate the danger or,

(ii) if he so elects, to demolish the building or structure, or any dangerous part of it, and remove any rubbish resulting from the demolition, or

(*b*) where danger arises from overloading of the building or structure, make an order restricting its use until a magistrates' court, being satisfied that any necessary works have been executed, withdraws or modifies the restriction.

(2) If the person on whom an order is made under subsection (1)(*a*) above fails to comply with the order within the time specified, the local authority may—

(*a*) execute the order in such manner as they think fit, and
(*b*) recover the expenses reasonably incurred by them in doing so from the person in default,

and, without prejudice to the right of the authority to exercise those powers, the person is liable on summary conviction to a fine not exceeding **level 1** on the standard scale.

(3) This section has effect subject to the provisions of the Planning (Listed Buildings and Conservation Areas) Act 1990 relating to listed buildings, buildings subject to building preservation notices and buildings in conservation areas.
[Building Act 1984, s 77, as amended by the Housing and Planning Act 1986, Sch 9 and the Planning (Consequential Provisions) Act 1990, Sch 2.]

8–26146 78. Dangerous building—emergency measures. (1) If it appears to a local authority that—

(*a*) a building or structure, or part of a building or structure, is in such a state, or is used to carry such loads, as to be dangerous, and
(*b*) immediate action should be taken to remove the danger,

they may take such steps as may be necessary for that purpose.

(2) Before exercising their powers under this section, the local authority shall, if it is reasonably practicable to do so, give notice of their intention to the owner and occupier of the building, or of the premises on which the structure is situated.

(3) Subject to this section, the local authority may recover from the owner the expenses reasonably incurred by them under this section.

(4) So far as expenses incurred by the local authority under this section consist of expenses of fencing off the building or structure, or arranging for it to be watched, the expenses shall not be recoverable in respect of any period—

(*a*) after the danger has been removed by other steps under this section, or
(*b*) after an order made under section 77(1) above for the purpose of its removal has been complied with or has been executed as mentioned in subsection (2) of that section.

(5) In proceedings to recover expenses under this section, the court shall inquire whether the local authority might reasonably have proceeded instead under section 77(1) above, and, if the court determines that the local authority might reasonably have proceeded instead under that subsection, the local authority shall not recover the expenses or any part of them.

(6) Subject to subsection (5) above, in proceedings to recover expenses under this section, the court may—

(*a*) inquire whether the expenses ought to be borne wholly or in part by some person other than the defendant in the proceedings, and
(*b*) make such order concerning the expenses or their apportionment as appears to the court to be just,

but the court shall not order the expenses or any part of them to be borne by any person other than the defendant in the proceedings unless it is satisfied that that other person has had due notice of the proceedings and an opportunity of being heard.

(7) Where in consequence of the exercise of the powers conferred by this section the owner or occupier of any premises sustains damage, but section 106(1) below does not apply because the owner or occupier has been in default—

(*a*) the owner or occupier may apply to a magistrates' court to determine whether the local authority were justified in exercising their powers under this section so as to occasion the damage sustained, and
(*b*) if the court determines that the local authority were not so justified, the owner or occupier is entitled to compensation, and section 106(2) and (3) below applies in relation to any dispute as regards compensation arising under this subsection.

(8) The proper officer of a local authority may, as an officer of the local authority, exercise the powers conferred on the local authority by subsection (1) above.

(9) This section does not apply to premises forming part of a mine or quarry within the meaning of the Mines and Quarries Act 1954.
[Building Act 1984, s 78.]

8–26147 79. Ruinous and dilapidated buildings and neglected sites. (1) If it appears to a local authority that a building or structure is by reason of its ruinous or dilapidated condition seriously detrimental to the amenities of the neighbourhood, the local authority may by notice require the owner thereof—

(*a*) to execute such works of repair or restoration, or
(*b*) if he so elects, to take such steps for demolishing the building or structure, or any part thereof, and removing any rubbish or other material resulting from or exposed by the demolition,

as may be necessary in the interests of amenity.

(2) If it appears to a local authority that—

(*a*) rubbish or other material resulting from, or exposed by, the demolition or collapse of a building or structure is lying on the site or on any adjoining land, and
(*b*) by reason thereof the site or land is in such a condition as to be seriously detrimental to the amenities of the neighbourhood,

the local authority may by notice require the owner of the site or land to take such steps for removing the rubbish or material as may be necessary in the interests of amenity.

(3) Sections 99 and 102 below apply in relation to a notice given under subsection (1) or (2) above, subject to the following modifications—

(*a*) section 99(1) requires the notice to indicate the nature of the works of repair or restoration and that of the works of demolition and removal of rubbish or material, and
(*b*) section 99(2) authorises the local authority to execute, subject to that subsection, at their election either the works of repair or restoration or the works of demolition and removal of rubbish or material.

(4) This section does not apply to an advertisement as defined in section 336(1) of the Town and Country Planning Act 1990.

(5) This section has effect subject to the provisions of the Planning (Listed Buildings and Conservation Areas) Act 1990 relating to listed buildings, buildings subject to building preservation notices and buildings in conservation areas.

[Building Act 1984, s 79, as amended by the Housing and Planning Act 1986, Sch 9 and the Planning (Consequential Provisions) Act 1990, Sch 2.]

8–26148 80. Notice to local authority of intended demolition. (1) This section applies to any demolition of the whole or part of a building except—

(*a*) a demolition in pursuance of a demolition order or obstructive building order made under Part IX of the Housing Act 1985, and
(*b*) a demolition—
  (i) of an internal part of a building, where the building is occupied and it is intended that it should continue to be occupied,
  (ii) of a building that has a cubic content (as ascertained by external measurement) of not more than 1,750 cubic feet, or, where a greenhouse, conservatory, shed or prefabricated garage forms part of a larger building, of that greenhouse, conservatory, shed or prefabricated garage, or
  (iii) without prejudice to sub-paragraph (ii) above, of an agricultural building (within the meaning of any paragraphs 3 to 7 of Schedule 5 to the Local Government Finance Act 1988), unless it is contiguous to another building that is not itself an agricultural building or a building of a kind mentioned in that sub-paragraph.

(2) No person shall begin a demolition to which this section applies unless—

(*a*) he has given the local authority notice of his intention to do so, and
(*b*) either—
  (i) the local authority have given a notice to him under section 81 below, or
  (ii) the relevant period (as defined in that section) has expired.

(3) A notice under subsection (2) above shall specify the building to which it relates and the works of demolition intended to be carried out, and it is the duty of a person giving such a notice to a local authority to send or give a copy of it to—

(*a*) the occupier of any building adjacent to the building,
(*b*) any public gas supplier[1] (as defined in Part I of the Gas Act 1986) in whose authorised area (as so defined) the building is situated,
(*c*) the public electricity supplier (as defined in Part I of the Electricity Act 1989) in whose authorised area (as so defined) the building is situated and any other person authorised by a licence under that Part to supply electricity to the building.

(4) A person who contravenes subsection (2) above is liable on summary conviction to a fine not exceeding **level 4** on the standard scale.

[Building Act 1984, s 80, as amended by the Housing (Consequential Provisions) Act 1985, Sch 2, the Gas Act 1986, Sch 7, the Housing and Planning Act 1986, Sch 5, the Electricity Act 1989, Sch 16 and SI 1990/1285.]

1. The reference to a "public gas supplier" shall have effect as a reference to a "public gas transporter" as defined in Pt I of the Gas Act 1986 (Gas Act 1995, Sch 4).

8–26149 81. Local authority's power to serve notice about demolition. (1) A local authority may give a notice under this section to—

(*a*) a person on whom a demolition order or obstructive building order has been served under Part IX of the Housing Act 1985,

(*b*) a person who appears to them not to be intending to comply with an order made under section 77 above or a notice given under section 79 above, and

(*c*) a person who appears to them to have begun or to be intending to begin a demolition to which section 80 above otherwise applies.

(2) Nothing contained in a notice under this section prejudices or affects the operation of any of the relevant statutory provisions, as defined in section 53(1) of the Health and Safety at Work etc Act 1974; and accordingly, if a requirement of such a notice is inconsistent with a requirement imposed by or under the said Act of 1974, the latter requirement prevails.

(3) Where—

(*a*) a person has given a notice under section 80 above, or

(*b*) the local authority have served a demolition order or obstructive building order on a person under Part IX of the Housing Act 1985,

a notice under this section may only be given to the person in question within the relevant period.

(4) In this section and section 80 above, "the relevant period" means—

(*a*) in a case such as is mentioned in subsection (3)(*a*) above, six weeks from the giving of the notice under section 80 above, or such longer period as the person who gave that notice may in writing allow, and

(*b*) in a case such as is mentioned in subsection (3)(*b*) above, seven days after the local authority served a copy of the demolition order or obstructive building order in accordance with Part IX of the Housing Act 1985, or such longer period as the person on whom the copy was served may in writing allow.

(5) It is the duty of the local authority to send or give a copy of a notice under this section to the owner and occupier of any building adjacent to the building to which the notice relates.

(6) It is also the duty of the local authority to send or give a copy of a notice under this section—

(*a*) if it contains such a requirement as is specified in section 82(1)(*h*) below, to the statutory undertakers concerned, and

(*b*) if it contains such a requirement as is specified in section 82(1)(*i*) below, to the fire and rescue authority, if they are not themselves the fire and rescue authority.

(7) *Repealed.*

[Building Act 1984, s 81, as amended by the Housing (Consequential Provisions) Act 1985, Sch 2, the Housing and Planning Act 1986, Sch 5, the Fire and Rescue Services Act 2004, Sch 1 and SI 2005/1541.]

8–26150 82. Notices under section 81. (1) A notice under section 81(1) above may require the person to whom it is given—

(*a*) to shore up any building adjacent to the building to which the notice relates,

(*b*) to weatherproof any surfaces of an adjacent building that are exposed by the demolition,

(*c*) to repair and make good any damage to an adjacent building caused by the demolition or by the negligent act or omission of any person engaged in it,

(*d*) to remove material or rubbish resulting from the demolition and clearance of the site,

(*e*) to disconnect and seal, at such points as the local authority may reasonably require, any sewer or drain in or under the building,

(*f*) to remove any such sewer or drain, and seal any sewer or drain with which the sewer or drain to be removed is connected,

(*g*) to make good to the satisfaction of the local authority the surface of the ground disturbed by anything done under paragraph (*e*) or (*f*) above,

(*h*) to make arrangements with the relevant statutory undertakers for the disconnection of the supply of gas, electricity and water to the building,

(*i*) to make such arrangements with regard to the burning of structures or materials on the site as may be reasonably required by the fire and rescue authority.

(*j*) to take such steps relating to the conditions subject to which the demolition is to be undertaken, and the condition in which the site is to be left on completion of the demolition, as the local authority may consider reasonably necessary for the protection of the public and the preservation of public amenity.

(2) No one shall be required under paragraph (*c*), (*e*) or (*f*) of subsection (1) above to carry out any work in land outside the premises on which the works of demolition are being carried out if he has no right to carry out that work, but, subject to section 101 below, the person undertaking the

demolition, or the local authority acting in his default, may break open any street for the purpose of complying with any such requirement.

(3) Before a person complies with a requirement under paragraph (*e*), (*f*) or (*g*) of subsection (1) above, he shall give to the local authority—

(*a*) at least 48 hours' notice, in the case of a requirement under paragraph (*e*) or (*f*), or
(*b*) at least 24 hours' notice, in the case of a requirement under paragraph (*g*),

and a person who fails to comply with this subsection is liable on summary conviction to a fine not exceeding **level 2** on the standard scale.

(4) This section does not authorise interference with apparatus or works of statutory undertakers authorised by an enactment to carry on an undertaking for the supply of electricity[1], or gas[2] with apparatus or works of a water undertaker or sewage undertaker.

(5) Without prejudice to the generality of subsection (4) above, this section does not exempt a person from—

(*a*) the obligation to obtain any consent required under section 174 of the Water Industry Act 1991 or section 176 of the Water Resources Act 1991 (interference with water supplies or with waterworks),
(*b*) criminal liability under any enactment relating to the supply of gas or electricity, or
(*c*) the requirements of regulations under section 31 of the Gas Act 1972 (public safety).

(6) Section 99 below applies in relation to a notice given under section 81(1) above.

[Building Act 1984, s 82, as amended by the Water Act 1989, the Water Consolidation (Consequential Provisions) Act 1991, Sch 1 and SI 2005/1541.]

---

1. The reference to a person authorised by an enactment to carry on an undertaking for the supply of electricity shall be construed as a reference to the holder of a licence under s 6 of the Electricity Act 1989, (Electricity Act 1989, Sch 16, para 1(7)).

2. The reference to a person authorised to carry on an undertaking for the supply of gas shall be construed as a reference to a public gas transporter (Gas Act 1995, Sch 4).

8–26151 **83. Appeal against notice under section 81.** (1) Section 102 below applies in relation to a notice given under section 81 above.

(2) Among the grounds on which an appeal may be brought under section 102 below against such a notice are—

(*a*) in the case of a notice requiring an adjacent building to be shored up, that the owner of the building is not entitled to the support of that building by the building that is being demolished, and ought to pay, or contribute towards, the expenses of shoring it up,
(*b*) in the case of a notice requiring any surfaces of an adjacent building to be weatherproofed, that the owner of the adjacent building ought to pay, or contribute towards, the expenses of weatherproofing those surfaces.

(3) Where the grounds on which an appeal under section 102 below is brought include a ground specified in subsection (2) above—

(*a*) the appellant shall serve a copy of his notice of appeal on the person or persons referred to in that ground of appeal, and
(*b*) on the hearing of the appeal the court may make such order as it thinks fit—
    (i) in respect of the payment of, or contribution towards, the cost of the works by any such person, or
    (ii) as to how any expenses that may be recoverable by the local authority are to be borne between the appellant and any such person.

[Building Act 1984, s 83.]

Yards and passages

8–26152 **84. Paving and drainage of yards and passages.** (1) If a court or yard appurtenant to, or a passage giving access to, buildings to which this section applies—

(*a*) is not so formed, flagged, asphalted or paved, or
(*b*) is not provided with such works on, above or below its surface,

as to allow of the satisfactory drainage of its surface or subsoil to a proper outfall, the local authority may by notice require any person who is the owner of any of the buildings to execute all such works as may be necessary to remedy the defect.

(2) Sections 99 and 102 below apply in relation to a notice given under subsection (1) above.

(3) The buildings to which this section applies are houses and industrial and commercial buildings.

(4) This section applies in relation to any court, yard or passage that is used in common by the occupiers of two or more houses, or a house and a commercial or industrial building, but is not a highway maintainable at the public expense.

[Building Act 1984, s 84.]

8–26153 85. Maintenance of entrances to courtyards. (1) Except with the consent of the local authority—

(*a*) an entrance to a court or yard on which two or more houses front or abut shall not be closed, narrowed, reduced in height or otherwise altered so as to impede the free circulation of air through the entrance, and

(*b*) no permanent structure shall be erected so as to impede the free circulation of air through such an entrance.

(2) A local authority in giving a consent under this section may impose such conditions as they think fit with respect to the provision of other openings or means of access, or other means for securing free circulation of air throughout the court or yard.

(3) A person aggrieved by the refusal of a local authority to give a consent under this section, or by a condition imposed by them, may appeal to a magistrates' court.

(4) A person who contravenes this section is liable on summary conviction to a fine not exceeding **level 1** on the standard scale and to a further fine not exceeding **£2** for each day on which the offence continues after he is convicted.

[Building Act 1984, s 85.]

Appeal to Crown Court

8–26154 86. Appeal to Crown Court. (1) Where a person—

(*a*) is aggrieved by an order, determination or other decision of a magistrates' court under this Part of this Act, or under Part IV of this Act as it applies in relation to this Part, and

(*b*) is not by any other enactment authorised to appeal to the Crown Court,

he may appeal to the Crown Court.

(2) Subsection (1) above does not confer a right of appeal in a case in which each of the parties concerned might under this Act have required that the dispute should be determined by arbitration instead of by a magistrates' court.

[Building Act 1984, s 86.]

Application of provisions to Crown property

8–26155 87. Application of provisions to Crown property. (1) This section applies to any house, building or other premises being property belonging to Her Majesty in right of the Crown or of the Duchy of Lancaster, or belonging to the Duchy of Cornwall, or belonging to a government department, or held in trust for Her Majesty for purposes of a government department.

(2) In relation to any such property, the appropriate authority may agree with—

(*a*) the council of the county, or

(*b*) the local authority of the district,

in which the property is situated that any particular provisions of this Part of this Act, and of Part IV of this Act so far as it relates to this Part, shall apply to the property; and, while the agreement is in force, those provisions shall apply to that property accordingly, subject to the terms of the agreement.

(2A) Subsection (2) above shall apply in relation to property in Wales as if—

(*a*) in paragraph (*a*) the reference to a county included a reference to a county borough; and

(*b*) paragraph (*b*) were omitted.

(3) Any such agreement may contain such consequential and incidental provisions (including, with the approval of the Treasury, provisions of a financial character) as appear to the appropriate authority to be necessary or equitable.

(4) In this section, "the appropriate authority" means—

(*a*) in the case of property belonging to Her Majesty in right of the Crown, the Crown Estate Commissioners or other government department having the management of the property,

(*b*) in the case of property belonging to Her Majesty in right of the Duchy of Lancaster, the Chancellor of the Duchy,

(*c*) in the case of property belonging to the Duchy of Cornwall, such person as the Duke of Cornwall, or the possessor for the time being of the Duchy of Cornwall, appoints, and

(*d*) in the case of property belonging to a government department or held in trust for Her Majesty for purposes of a government department, that department,

and, if a question arises as to what authority is the appropriate authority in relation to any property, that question shall be referred to the Treasury, whose decision is final.*

[Building Act 1984, s 87, as amended by the Local Government (Wales) Act 1994, Sch 9.]

Inner London

8–26156 88. Inner London. (1) In its application to inner London, this Part of this Act has effect subject to Part II of Schedule 3 to this Act.

(2) Part III of Schedule 3 to this Act has effect with respect to building and the drainage of buildings in the inner London boroughs.

(3) Part IV of Schedule 3 to this Act has effect with respect to the making of byelaws—

(*a*) for the inner London boroughs, with respect to certain matters, and

(*b*) for the inner London boroughs, the Inner Temple and the Middle Temple, with respect to certain other matters.

[Building Act 1984, s 88, as amended by the Local Government Act 1985, Sch 17.]

Miscellaneous

8–26157 **89. References in Acts to building byelaws.** (1) Subject to subsection (2) below, for any reference to—

(*a*) building byelaws as defined in section 343 of the Public Health Act 1936, or

(*b*) byelaws made under Part II of that Act with respect to buildings, works and fittings,

that occurs in an Act, or in an instrument having effect under an Act, there is substituted a reference to building regulations.

(2) *Repealed.*

[Building Act 1984, s 89, as amended by the Housing (Consequential Provisions) Act 1985, Sch 1.]

8–26158 **90. Facilities for inspecting local Acts.** (1) In an area in which there is in force a local Act containing provisions that impose an obligation or restriction as to the construction, nature or situation of buildings, the local authority shall keep a copy of those provisions at their offices for inspection by the public at all reasonable times free of charge.

(2) Any question as to what provisions of a local Act are provisions of which a copy is to be so kept shall, on the application of the local authority, be determined by the Secretary of State.

[Building Act 1984, s 90.]

PART IV[1]
GENERAL

Duties of local authorities

8–26159 **91. Duties of local authorities.** (1) It is the duty of local authorities to carry this Act into execution in their areas, subject to—

(*a*) the provisions of this Act relating to certain other authorities or persons,

(*b*) the provisions of Part I of the Public Health Act 1936 relating to united districts and joint boards,

(*c*) section 151 of the Local Government, Planning and Land Act 1980 (urban development areas), and

(*d*) section 1(3) of the Public Health (Control of Disease) Act 1984 (port health authorities).

(2) It is the function of local authorities to enforce building regulations in their areas, subject to sections 5(3), 48(1) and 53(2) above.

[Building Act 1984, s 91, as amended by the Local Government Act 1985, Sch 17.]

1. Part IV contains ss 91–131.

8–26159A **91A. Registers to be kept by local authorities**

Documents

8–26170 **92. Form of documents.** (1) All—

(*a*) notices, orders, consents, demands and other documents authorised or required by or under this Act to be given, made or issued by a local authority, and

(*b*) notices and applications authorised or required by or under this Act to be given or made to, or to any officer of, a local authority,

shall be in writing.

(2) The Secretary of State may, by regulations made by statutory instrument, prescribe the form of any notice, advertisement, certificate or other document to be used for any of the purposes of this Act, and if forms are so prescribed those forms or forms to the like effect may be used in all cases to which those forms are applicable.

[Building Act 1984, s 92.]

8–26171 **93. Authentication of documents.** (1) A notice, order, consent, demand or other document that a local authority are authorised or required by or under this Act to give, make or issue may be signed on behalf of the authority—

(*a*) by the proper officer of the authority or the district surveyor, as respects documents relating to matters within his province, or

(*b*) by an officer of the authority authorised by them in writing to sign documents of the particular kind or, as the case may be, the particular document.

(2) A document purporting to bear the signature of an officer—

(*a*) expressed to hold an office by virtue of which he is under this section empowered to sign such a document, or

(*b*) expressed to be authorised by the local authority to sign such a document or the particular document,

is deemed, for the purposes of this Act and of any building regulations and orders made under it, to have been duly given, made or issued by authority of the local authority, until the contrary is proved.

(3) In subsection (2) above, "signature" includes a facsimile of a signature by whatever process reproduced.

[Building Act 1984, s 93.]

8–26172 94. Service of documents. A notice, order, consent, demand or other document that is authorised or required by or under this Act to be given to or served on a person may, in any case for which no other provision is made by this Act, be given or served either—

(*a*) by delivering it to that person,

(*b*) in the case of an officer of a local authority, by leaving it, or sending it in a prepaid letter addressed to him, at his office,

(*c*) in the case of any other person, by leaving it, or sending it in a prepaid letter addressed to him, at his usual or last known residence,

(*d*) in the case of an incorporated company or body, by delivering it to their secretary or clerk at their registered or principal office, or by sending it in a prepaid letter addressed to him at that office,

(*e*) in the case of a document to be given to or served on a person as being the owner of any premises by virtue of the fact that he receives the rackrent thereof as agent for another, or would so receive it if the premises were let at a rackrent, by leaving it, or sending it in a prepaid letter addressed to him, at his place of business,

(*f*) in the case of a document to be given to or served on the owner or the occupier of any premises, if it is not practicable after reasonable inquiry to ascertain the name and address of the person to or on whom it should be given or served, or if the premises are unoccupied, by addressing it to the person concerned by the description of "owner" or "occupier" of the premises (naming them) to which it relates, and delivering it to some person on the premises, or, if there is no person on the premises to whom it can be delivered, by affixing it, or a copy of it, to some conspicuous part of the premises.

[Building Act 1984, s 94.]

Entry on premises

8–26173 95. Power to enter premises. (1) Subject to this section, an authorised officer of a local authority, on producing, if so required, some duly authenticated document showing his authority, has a right to enter any premises at all reasonable hours—

(*a*) for the purpose of ascertaining whether there is, or has been, on or in connection with the premises, a contravention of this Act, or of any building regulations, that it is the duty of the local authority to enforce,

(*b*) for the purpose of ascertaining whether or not circumstances exist that would authorise or require the local authority to take any action, or execute any work, under this Act or under building regulations,

(*c*) for the purpose of taking any action, or executing any work, authorised or required by this Act, or by building regulations, or by an order made under this Act, to be taken, or executed, by the local authority, or

(*d*) generally for the purpose of the performance by the local authority of their functions under this Act or under building regulations.

(2) Admission to premises, other than a factory or workplace, shall not be demanded as of right unless 24 hours' notice of the intended entry has been given to the occupier.

(3) If it is shown to the satisfaction of a justice of the peace on sworn information in writing that—

(*a*) admission to any premises has been refused, or refusal is apprehended, or the premises are unoccupied, or the occupier is temporarily absent, or the case is one of urgency, or an application for admission would defeat the object of the entry, and

(*b*) there is reasonable ground for entry into the premises for any of the purposes mentioned in subsection (1) above,

the justice may by warrant under his hand authorise the local authority by any authorised officer to enter the premises, if need be by force.

(4) A warrant shall not be issued under subsection (3) above unless the justice is satisfied that—

(*a*) notice of the intention to apply for a warrant has been given to the occupier, or

(*b*) the premises are unoccupied, or the occupier is temporarily absent, or the case is one of urgency, or the giving of the notice would defeat the object of the entry.

[Building Act 1984, s 95.]

8–26174 **96. Supplementary provisions as to entry.** (1) An authorised officer entering premises by virtue of section 95 above, or of a warrant issued under it, may take with him such other persons as may be necessary, and on leaving unoccupied premises that he has entered by virtue of such a warrant he shall leave them as effectually secured against trespassers as he found them.

(2) A warrant issued under that section shall continue in force until the purpose for which the entry is necessary has been satisfied.

(3) A person who—

(*a*) is admitted into a factory or workplace in compliance with that section or a warrant issued under it, and

(*b*) discloses to another person information obtained by him in the factory or workplace with regard to a manufacturing process or trade secret,

is liable on summary conviction to a fine not exceeding **level 3** on the standard scale or to imprisonment for a term not exceeding **three months**, unless the disclosure was made in the performance of his duty.

[Building Act 1984, s 96.]

Execution of works

8–26175 **97. Power to execute work.** A local authority may, by agreement with the owner or occupier of any premises, themselves execute at his expense—

(*a*) any work that they have under this Act required him to execute, or

(*b*) any work in connection with the construction, laying, alteration or repair of a sewer or drain that he is entitled to execute,

and for that purpose they have all the rights that he would have.

[Building Act 1984, s 97.]

8–26176 **98. Power to require occupier to permit work.** If, on a complaint made by the owner of premises, it appears to a magistrates' court that the occupier of those premises prevents the owner from executing any work that he is by or under this Act required to execute, the court may order the occupier to permit the execution of the work.

[Building Act 1984, s 98.]

8–26177 **99. Content and enforcement of notice requiring works.** (1) A notice in relation to which it is declared by any provision of this Act that this section applies shall indicate the nature of the works to be executed and state the time within which they are to be executed.

(2) Subject to any right of appeal conferred by section 102 below, if the person required by such a notice to execute works fails to execute them within the time limited by the notice—

(*a*) the local authority may themselves execute the works and recover from that person the expenses reasonably incurred by them in doing so, and

(*b*) without prejudice to that power, he is liable on summary conviction to a fine not exceeding **level 4** on the standard scale and to a further fine not exceeding **£2** for each day on which the default continues after he is convicted.

(3) This section has effect subject to any modification specified in the provision under which the notice is given.

[Building Act 1984, s 99.]

8–26178 **100. Sale of materials.** (1) A local authority may sell any materials that—

(*a*) have been removed by them from any premises, including a street, when executing works under this Act or otherwise carrying this Act into effect, and

(*b*) are not before the expiration of three days from the date of their removal claimed by the owner and taken away by him.

(2) Where a local authority sell materials under this section, they shall pay the proceeds to the person to whom the materials belonged, after deducting the amount of any expenses recoverable by them from him.

(3) This section does not apply to refuse removed by a local authority.

[Building Act 1984, s 100.]

8–26179 **101. Breaking open of streets.** (1) For the purposes of any section of this Act that confers powers on local authorities to construct, lay or maintain sewers, drains or pipes, section 158 of the Water Industry Act 1991 (street works) shall apply, with the necessary modifications, as it applies for the purpose of conferring power on a water undertaker or sewerage undertaker to lay a relevant pipe, within the meaning of that section.

(2) That section shall also so apply so far as necessary for the purposes of any power to lay or maintain a sewer or drain which is conferred by this Act on a person other than a local authority.

[Building Act 1984, s 101, as amended by the Water Act 1989, Sch 25 and the Water Consolidation (Consequential Provisions) Act 1991, Sch 1.]

Appeal against notice requiring works

8–26180 **102. Appeal against notice requiring works.** (1) Where a person is given a notice in relation to which it is declared by any provision of this Act that this section applies, he may appeal to a magistrates' court on any of the following grounds that are appropriate in the circumstances of the particular case—

(*a*) that the notice or requirement is not justified by the terms of the provision under which it purports to have been given,

(*b*) that there has been some informality, defect or error in, or in connection with, the notice,

(*c*) that the authority have refused unreasonably to approve the execution of alternative works, or that the works required by the notice to be executed are otherwise unreasonable in character or extent, or are unnecessary,

(*d*) that the time within which the works are to be executed is not reasonably sufficient for the purpose,

(*e*) that the notice might lawfully have been served on the occupier of the premises in question instead of on the owner, or on the owner instead of on the occupier, and that it would have been equitable for it to have been so served,

(*f*) where the works are works for the common benefit of the premises in question and other premises, that some other person, being the owner or occupier of premises to be benefited, ought to contribute towards the expenses of executing any works required.

(2) If and in so far as an appeal under this section is based on the ground of some informality, defect or error in or in connection with the notice, the court shall dismiss the appeal, if it is satisfied that the informality, defect or error was not a material one.

(3) The appellant—

(*a*) shall, where the grounds upon which the appeal is brought include a ground specified in subsection (1)(*e*) or (*f*) above, serve a copy of his notice of appeal on each other person referred to, and

(*b*) may, in the case of any appeal under this section, serve a copy of his notice of appeal on any other person having an estate or interest in the premises in question,

and on the hearing of the appeal the court may make such order as it thinks fit with respect to—

(i) the person by whom any works are to be executed and the contribution to be made by any other person towards the cost of the works, or

(ii) the proportions in which any expenses that may become recoverable by the local authority are to be borne by the appellant and such other person.

(4) In exercising its powers under subsection (3) above, the court shall have regard—

(*a*) as between an owner and an occupier, to the terms and conditions, whether contractual or statutory, of the tenancy and to the nature of the works required, and

(*b*) in any case, to the degree of benefit to be derived by the different persons concerned.

(5) This section has effect subject to any modification specified in the provision under which the notice is given.

[Building Act 1984, s 102.]

General provisions about appeals and applications

8–26181 **103. Procedure on appeal or application to magistrates' court.** (1) Where this Act provides—

(*a*) for an appeal to a magistrates' court against a requirement, refusal or other decision of a local authority, or

(*b*) for a matter to be determined by, or for an application in respect of a matter to be made to, a magistrates' court,

the procedure shall be by way of complaint for an order.

(2) The time within which such an appeal may be brought is 21 days from the date on which notice of the local authority's requirement, refusal or other decision was served upon the person desiring to appeal, and for the purposes of this subsection the making of the complaint is deemed to be the bringing of the appeal.

(3) In a case where such an appeal lies, the document notifying to the person concerned the local authority's decision in the matter shall state the right of appeal to a magistrates' court and the time within which such an appeal may be brought.

[Building Act 1984, s 103.]

8–26182 **104. Local authority to give effect to appeal.** Where upon an appeal under this Act a court varies or reverses a decision of a local authority, it is the duty of the local authority to give effect to the order of the court and, in particular, to grant or issue any necessary consent, certificate or other document, and to make any necessary entry in any register.

[Building Act 1984, s 104.]

8–26183 **105. Judge not disqualified by liability to rates.** A judge of a court or a justice of the peace is not disqualified from acting in cases arising under this Act by reason only of his being, as one of several ratepayers, or as one of any other class of persons, liable in common with the others to contribute to, or be benefited by, a rate or fund out of which expenses of a local authority are to be defrayed.
[Building Act 1984, s 105.]

Compensation, and recovery of sums

8–26184 **106. Compensation for damage.** (1) A local authority shall make full compensation to a person who has sustained damage by reason of the exercise by the authority, in relation to a matter as to which he has not himself been in default, of any of their powers under this Act.

(2) Subject to subsection (3) below, any dispute arising under this section as to the fact of damage, or as to the amount of compensation, shall be determined by arbitration.

(3) If the compensation claimed does not exceed £50, all questions as to the fact of damage, liability to pay compensation and the amount of compensation may on the application of either party be determined by, and any compensation awarded may be recovered before, a magistrates' court.
[Building Act 1984, s 106.]

8–26185 **107. Recovery of expenses etc.** (1) Where a local authority have incurred expenses for whose repayment the owner of the premises in respect of which the expenses were incurred is liable, either under this Act or by agreement with the authority, those expenses, together with interest from the date of service of a demand for the expenses, may be recovered by the authority—

(*a*) from the person who is the owner of the premises at the date on which the works are completed, or

(*b*) if he has ceased to be the owner of the premises before the date on which a demand for the expenses is served, either from him or from the person who is the owner at the date on which the demand is served,

and, as from the date of the completion of the works, the expenses and interest accrued due thereon are, until recovered, a charge on the premises and on all estates and interests in them.

(2) A local authority, for the purpose of enforcing a charge under subsection (1) above, have all the same powers and remedies under the Law of Property Act 1925 and otherwise as if they were mortgagees by deed having powers of sale and lease, of accepting surrenders of leases and of appointing a receiver.

(3) The rate of interest chargeable under subsection (1) above is such reasonable rate as the authority may determine.

(4) A sum that a local authority are entitled to recover under this Act, and with respect to whose recovery provision is not made by any other section of this Act, may be recovered as a simple contract debt in any court of competent jurisdiction.

(5) Where—

(*a*) a person has been given a notice in relation to which section 102 above applies, and

(*b*) the local authority take proceedings against him for the recovery of expenses that they are entitled to recover from him,

it is not open to him to raise any question that he could have raised on an appeal under that section.
[Building Act 1984, s 107.]

8–26186 **108.** *Payment by instalments.*

8–26187 **109.** *Repealed.*

Obstruction

8–26188 **112. Obstruction.** A person who wilfully obstructs a person acting in the execution of this Act, or of building regulations, or of an order or warrant made or issued under this Act, is, in a case for which no other provision is made by this Act, liable on summary conviction to a fine not exceeding **level 1** on the standard scale.
[Building Act 1984, s 112.]

Prosecutions

8–26189 **113. Prosecution of offences.** Proceedings in respect of an offence created by or under this Act shall not, without the written consent of the Attorney General, be taken by any person other than—

(*a*) a party aggrieved, or

(*b*) a local authority or a body whose function it is to enforce the provision in question.
[Building Act 1984, s 113.]

8–26200 114. Continuing offences. Where provision is made by or under this Act for the imposition of a daily penalty in respect of a continuing offence—

(*a*) the court by which a person is convicted of the original offence may fix a reasonable period from the date of conviction for the defendant to comply with any directions given by the court, and

(*b*) where the court has fixed such a period, the daily penalty is not recoverable in respect of any day before the period expires.

[Building Act 1984, s 114.]

Default powers

8–26201 116. Default powers of Secretary of State. (1) If the Secretary of State is satisfied that a local authority or joint board have failed to discharge their functions under this Act in a case in which they ought to have discharged them, he may make an order declaring them to be in default and directing them for the purpose of removing the default to discharge such of their functions, in such manner and within such time or times, as may be specified in the order.

(2) If a local authority or joint board with respect to whom an order has been made under subsection (1) above fail to comply with a requirement of the order within the time limited by the order for compliance with that requirement, the Secretary of State, in lieu of enforcing the order by mandamus or otherwise, may make an order transferring to himself such of the functions of the body in default as may be specified in his order.

[Building Act 1984, s 116.]

Orders

8–26202 120. Orders. (1) The power to make an order under section 16(13), 30(3) or (4), 42(7), 69(6) or 134(1) above, or under paragraph 5(2) of Schedule 1 to this Act, is exercisable by statutory instrument, and different days may be appointed by such an order for different provisions or for different purposes.

(2) An order under section 30(3) above or 134(1)(*a*), (*b*) or (*c*) below may contain such transitional provisions and savings as appear to the Secretary of State to be necessary or expedient in connection with the provisions thereby brought into force, including such adaptations of those provisions as appear to him necessary or expedient in consequence of the partial operation of this Act (whether before or after the day appointed by the order).

[Building Act 1984, s 120.]

Interpretation

8–26203 121. Meaning of "building". (1) The word "building", for the purposes of—

(*a*) Part I of this Act, and

(*b*) any other enactment (whether or not contained in this Act) that relates to building regulations, or that mentions "buildings" or "a building" in a context from which it appears that those expressions are there intended to have the same meaning as in Part I of this Act,

means any permanent or temporary building, and, unless the context otherwise requires, it includes any other structure or erection of whatever kind or nature (whether permanent or temporary).

(2) In subsection (1) above, "structure or erection" includes a vehicle, vessel, hovercraft, aircraft or other movable object of any kind in such circumstances as may be prescribed (being circumstances that in the opinion of the Secretary of State justify treating it for those purposes as a building).

(3) For the purposes mentioned in subsection (1) above, unless the context otherwise requires—

(*a*) a reference to a building includes a reference to part of a building, and

(*b*) a reference to the provision of services, fittings and equipment in or in connection with buildings, or to services, fittings and equipment so provided, includes a reference to the affixing of things to buildings or, as the case may be, to things so affixed.

[Building Act 1984, s 121.]

8–26204 122. Meaning of "building regulations". In this Act—

(*a*) "building regulations" means, subject to paragraph (*b*) below, regulations made under section 1 above;

(*b*) a reference to building regulations, in a particular case in relation to which a requirement of building regulations is for the time being dispensed with, waived, relaxed or modified by virtue of section 8 or 11 above or any other enactment, is a reference to building regulations as they apply in that case, unless the context otherwise requires.

[Building Act 1984, s 122.]

8–26205 123. Meaning of "construct" and "erect". (1) For the purposes of—

(*a*) Part I of this Act, and

(*b*) any other enactment (whether or not contained in this Act) that relates to building regulations, or that mentions "buildings" or "a building" in a context from which it appears that those expressions are there intended to have the same meaning as in the said Part I,

references to the construction or erection of a building include references to—

(i) the carrying out of such operations (whether for the reconstruction of a building, the roofing over of an open space between walls or buildings, or otherwise) as may be designated in building regulations as operations falling to be treated for those purposes as the construction or erection of a building, and

(ii) the conversion of a movable object into what is by virtue of section 121(1) and (2) above a building,

and "construct" and "erect" shall be construed accordingly.

(2) For the purposes of Part III of this Act, each of the following operations is deemed to be the erection of a building—

(*a*) the re-erection of a building or part of a building when an outer wall of that building or, as the case may be, that part of a building has been pulled down, or burnt down, to within 10 feet of the surface of the ground adjoining the lowest storey of the building or of that part of the building,

(*b*) the re-erection of a frame building or part of a frame building when that building or part of a building has been so far pulled down, or burnt down, as to leave only the framework of the lowest storey of the building or of that part of the building,

(*c*) the roofing over of an open space between walls or buildings,

and "erect" shall be construed accordingly.
[Building Act 1984, s 123.]

8–26206 124. Meaning of deposit of plans. In this Act, a reference to the deposit of plans in accordance with building regulations is a reference to the deposit of plans in accordance with building regulations for the purposes of section 16 above, unless the context otherwise requires.
[Building Act 1984, s 124.]

8–26207 125. Construction and availability of sewers. (1) A reference in Part I of this Act to the construction of a sewer includes a reference to the extension of an existing sewer.

(2) For the purposes of sections 64(2) and 66(1) above, a building or proposed building—

(*a*) is not deemed to have a sufficient water supply available unless—

(i) it has a sufficient supply of water laid on, or

(ii) such a supply can be laid on to it from a point within 100 feet of the site of the building or proposed building, and the intervening land is land through which the owner of the building or proposed building is, or will be, entitled to lay a communication pipe, and

(*b*) is not deemed to have a sewer available unless—

(i) there is within 100 feet of the site of the building or proposed building, and at a level that makes it reasonably practicable to construct a drain to communicate with it, a public sewer or other sewer that the owner of the building or proposed building is, or will be, entitled to use, and

(ii) the intervening land is land through which he is entitled to construct a drain.

(3) The limit of 100 feet does not apply, for the purposes of subsection (2) above, if the local authority undertake to bear so much of the expenses reasonably incurred in—

(*a*) constructing, and maintaining and repairing, a drain to communicate with a sewer, or

(*b*) laying, and maintaining and repairing, a pipe for the purpose of obtaining a supply of water,

as the case may be, as is attributable to the fact that the distance of the sewer, or of the point from which a supply of water can be laid on, exceeds 100 feet.
[Building Act 1984, s 125.]

8–26208 126. General interpretation. In this Act, unless the context otherwise requires—

"Act" includes an enactment contained in a local Act;

"approved inspector" has the meaning given by section 49(1) above;

"authorised officer", in relation to a local authority, means—

(*a*) an officer of the local authority authorised by them in writing, either generally or specially, to act in matters of a specified kind or in a specified matter, or

(*b*) by virtue of his appointment and for the purpose of matters within his province, a proper officer of the local authority;

"cesspool" includes a settlement tank or other tank for the reception or disposal of foul matter from buildings;

"closet" includes privy;

"contravention" includes failure to comply, and "contravene" has a corresponding meaning;

"drain" means a drain used for the drainage of one building or of buildings or yards appurtenant to buildings within the same curtilage, and includes any manholes, ventilating shafts, pumps or other accessories belonging to the drain;

"earth-closet" means a closet having a movable receptacle for the reception of faecal matter and its deodorisation by the use of earth, ashes or chemicals, or by other methods;

"enactment" includes an enactment contained in a local Act;

"factory" has the meaning given by section 175 of the Factories Act 1961;

"fire and rescue authority" in relation to any premises or proposed premises, means—

(*a*) where the Regulatory Reform (Fire Safety) Order 2005 applies to the premises or proposed premises, the enforcing authority within the meaning given by article 25 of that Order;

(*b*) in any other case, the fire and rescue authority under the Fire and Rescue Services Act 2004 for the area in which the premises are or are to be situated;

"functions" includes powers and duties;

"highway authority" means, in the case of a highway repairable by the inhabitants at large, the council in whom the highway is vested;

"house" means a dwelling-house, whether a private dwelling-house or not;

"inner London" means the area comprising the inner London boroughs, the City of London, the Inner Temple and the Middle Temple;

"joint board" has the meaning given by section 343(1) of the Public Health Act 1936;

"local Act" includes a provisional order confirmed by Parliament, and the confirming Act so far as it relates to that order;

"local authority" means the council of a district or London borough, the Common Council of the City of London, the Sub-Treasurer of the Inner Temple, the Under Treasurer of the Middle Temple or, for the purposes of Parts I and II above and of this Part so far as it relates to them, the Council of the Isles of Scilly but in relation to Wales, means the council of a county or a county or county borough

"modifications" includes additions, omissions and amendments, and related expressions shall be construed accordingly;

"officer" includes servant;

"owner" means the person for the time being receiving the rackrent of the premises in connection with which the word is used, whether on his own account or as agent or trustee for another person, or who would so receive it if those premises were let at a rackrent;

"plans" includes drawings of any other description, and also specifications or other information in any form;

"prejudicial to health" means injurious, or likely to cause injury, to health;

"premises" includes buildings, land, easements and hereditaments of any tenure;

"prescribed" means prescribed by building regulations;

"private sewer" means a sewer that is not a public sewer;

"proper officer", in relation to a purpose and to a local authority, means an officer appointed for that purpose by that authority;

"public sewer" has the same meaning as in the Water Industry Act 1991;

"rackrent", in relation to property, means a rent that is not less than two-thirds of the rent at which the property might reasonably be expected to let from year to year, free from all usual tenant's rates and taxes, and deducting from it the probable average annual cost of the repairs, insurance and other expenses (if any) necessary to maintain the property in a state to command such rent;

"rating district" has the meaning given by section 115(1) of the General Rate Act 1967[1];

"relevant period" has the meaning given by section 16(12) or 81(4) above, as the case may require;

"sanitary convenience" means closet or urinal;

"school" includes a Sunday school or a Sabbath school;

"sewer" does not include a drain as defined in this section, but otherwise it includes all sewers and drains used for the drainage of buildings and yards appurtenant to buildings, and any manholes, ventilating shafts, pumps or other accessories belonging to the sewer;

"statutory undertakers" means persons authorised by an enactment or statutory order to construct, work or carry on a railway, canal, inland navigation, dock harbour, tramway, or other public undertaking[2]; but does not include a universal service provider (within the meaning of the Postal Services Act 2000), the Post Office Company (within the meaning of Part IV of that Act) or any subsidiary or wholly-owned subsidiary (within the meanings given by section 736 of the Companies Act 1985) of the Post Office company;

"street" includes a highway, including a highway over a bridge, and a road, lane, footway, square, court, alley or passage, whether a thoroughfare or not;

"substantive requirements", in relation to building regulations, means the requirements of building regulations with respect to the matters mentioned in section 1(1A) above (including requirements imposed by virtue of section 2(1) or (2)(*a*) or (*b*) above and requirements that are of a kind mentioned in subsection (2)(*a*) , (*b*) or (*c*) of section 2A above and are imposed by virtue of subsection (1) of that section), as distinct from procedural requirements;

"surface water" includes water from roofs;

"water-closet" means a closet that has a separate fixed receptacle connected to a drainage system and separate provision for flushing from a supply of clean water either by the operation of mechanism or by automatic action;

"workplace" does not include a factory, but otherwise it includes any place in which persons are employed otherwise than in domestic service.

[Building Act 1984, s 126, as amended by the Local Government Act 1985, Schs 8 and 17, the Gas Act 1986, Sch 9 the Water Act 1989, Schs 25 and 27, the Electricity Act 1989, Sch 18, the Water Consolidation (Consequential Provisions) Act 1991, Sch 1, the Statute Law (Repeals) Act 1993, Sch 1, the Local Government (Wales) Act 1994, Sch 9, SI 2001/1149, the Fire and Rescue Services Act 2004, Sch 1 and SI 2005/1541.]

1. The General Rate Act 1967 has been repealed by the Local Government Finance Act 1988 in this PART: title LOCAL GOVERNMENT, ante.

8–26209 **127. Construction of certain references concerning Temples.** In relation to the Inner Temple and the Middle Temple, a reference in a provision of this Part of this Act to the proper officer or an officer or authorised officer of a local authority is a reference to an officer authorised by the Sub-Treasurer or the Under Treasurer, as the case may be, to act for the purposes of that provision.
[Building Act 1984, s 127.]

Savings

8–26210 **128. Protection for dock and railway undertakings.** Section 333 of the Public Health Act 1936 applies in relation to local authorities acting under this Act as it applies in relation to local authorities acting under that Act.
[Building Act 1984, s 128.]

8–26211 **129. Saving for Local Land Charges Act 1975.** Nothing in this Act about the recovery of expenses from owners of premises affects the Local Land Charges Act 1975.
[Building Act 1984, s 129.]

8–26212 **130. Saving for other laws.** All powers and duties conferred or imposed by this Act are in addition to, and not in derogation of, any other powers and duties conferred or imposed by Act, law or custom, and, subject to any express provision of this Act, all such other powers and duties may be exercised and shall be performed in the same manner as if this Act had not been passed.
[Building Act 1984, s 130.]

8–26213 **131. Restriction of application of Part IV to Schedule 3.** This Part has effect subject to paragraph 13 of Schedule 3 to this Act.
[Building Act 1984, s 131.]

PART V[1]

SUPPLEMENTARY

8–26214 **132. Transitional provisions.** The transitional provisions contained in Schedule 5 to this Act have effect.
[Building Act 1984, s 132.]

1. Part V contains ss 132–135.

8–26215 **133. Consequential amendments and repeals.** (1) The enactments specified in Schedule 6 to this Act have effect subject to the amendments specified in that Schedule.

(2) The enactments specified in Schedule 7 to this Act are repealed to the extent specified in the third column of that Schedule.
[Building Act 1984, s 133.]

8–26216 **134. Commencement.** (1) The following provisions of this Act—

(*a*) sections 12, 13, 31, 38, 42(4) to (6) and 43(3), except so far as they enable regulations to be made,
(*b*) sections 20, 33, 42(1) to (3), 43(1) and (2), 44 and 45,
(*c*) section 133(2) and Schedule 7 so far as they relate to the Atomic Energy Authority Act 1954, and
(*d*) section 50(2) and (3) and paragraph 9 of Schedule 1,

come into force on such day as the Secretary of State may by order[1] appoint.

(2) Subject to—

(*a*) subsection (1) above, and
(*b*) section 42(7) above,

this Act comes into force on 1st December 1984.
[Building Act 1984, s 134, as amended by the Statute Law (Repeals) Act 1993, Sch 1.]

---

1. The Building Act 1984 (Commencement No 1) Order 1985, SI 1985/1602, brought section 50(2) and (3) into force on the 11 November 1985 and the Building Act 1984 (Commencement No 2) Order 1998, SI 1998/1836, brought para 9 of Sch 1 into force on 7 August 1998.

8–26217 **135. Short title and extent.** (1) This Act may be cited as the Building Act 1984.

(2) This Act does not extend to Scotland or to Northern Ireland.
[Building Act 1984, s 135.]

8–26218

SCHEDULES

Section 1(3)

SCHEDULE 1
BUILDING REGULATIONS

8–26219

Section 9(4)

SCHEDULE 2
RELAXATION OF BUILDING REGULATIONS FOR EXISTING WORK

8–26229

Sections 46, 88 and 91(2)

SCHEDULE 3
INNER LONDON

(Amended by the Local Government Act 1985, Schs 8 and 17, SI 1985/1936 and SI 1987/798.)

PART I
APPLICATION OF PART I OF THIS ACT

1. Application to inner London. Sections 24(1), (2) and (4), 25 of this Act do not apply to inner London.

2. Application of provisions by building regulations. (1) Where, by section 91(2) above or by building regulations made under paragraph 6 of Schedule 1 to this Act or paragraph 14(1) of this Schedule, local authorities, or a prescribed person or class of persons other than local authorities, are made responsible for—

(*a*) enforcing, or
(*b*) performing prescribed functions under or in connection with,

building regulations in force in inner London, then, without prejudice to the said paragraphs 6 and 14(1), building regulations[1] may in that connection provide for any relevant provision to apply (with any prescribed modifications, and notwithstanding paragraph 1 above) in relation to any such authority, person or class of persons as that provision applies in relation to a local authority outside inner London.

(2) In sub-paragraph (1) above, "relevant provision" means any of the following provisions of this Act that may be prescribed for the purposes of sub-paragraph (1) above: sections 4, 8 to 10, 16, 18(1), (4) and (5), 21 to 23, 24(1), (2) and (4), 26 to 29, 32, 36, 37, 39 and 40.

3. Repeal and modification of Acts. Without prejudice to the generality of paragraph 11(1) of Schedule 1 to this Act, building regulations may repeal or modify—

(*a*) any provision of the London Building Acts 1930 to 1939,
(*b*) any provision of an Act passed before the 20th September 1974, in so far as that provision—
   (i) applies to or to any part of inner London, and
   (ii) relates to, or to the making of, byelaws for or for any part of inner London with respect to any matter for or in connection with which provision can be made by building regulations, or
(*c*) any provision of byelaws made or having effect under the said Acts or of any such byelaws as are mentioned in sub-paragraph (*b*)(ii) above,

if it appears to the Secretary of State that the repeal or, as the case may be, the modification of that provision is expedient—

(i) in consequence of the application of any of sections 61, 62 and 67 of the Public Health Act 1936, sections 4(2), (5), (6) and (7), 5 and 9 of the Public Health Act 1961 and sections 61 to 74 and 76 of the Health and Safety at Work etc Act 1974 to inner London by virtue of section 70(1) of the said Act of 1974 (which section is repealed by and incorporated in this Act),
(ii) in consequence of paragraph 2 or 14 of this Schedule, or
(iii) in connection with any provision contained in building regulations that apply to or to any part of inner London.

4. Consultation. Before making any building regulations that provide for the repeal or modification of any such provision the Secretary of State shall (without prejudice to the requirements as to consultation in section 14(3) of this Act) consult any local authority who appear to him to be concerned.

PART II
APPLICATION OF PART III OF THIS ACT

5. Application to inner London. Sections 71, 72(1) to (4), (6) and (7), 73 to 75, 77 to 83, 85 and 90 of this Act do not apply to inner London.

6. Application to Temples. Sections 59 to 61 of this Act do not apply to the Inner Temple or the Middle Temple.

PART III
BUILDING AND DRAINAGE OF BUILDINGS

7–9. *Repealed.*

PART IV
BYELAWS

10. Byelaws about demolition. (1) The council of an inner London borough may make byelaws in relation to the demolition of buildings in the borough—

(*a*) requiring the fixing of fans at the level of each floor of a building undergoing demolition,
(*b*) requiring the hoarding up of windows in a building from which sashes and glass have been removed,
(*c*) regulating the demolition of internal parts of buildings before any external walls are taken down,
(*d*) requiring the placing of screens or mats, the use of water or the taking of other precautions to prevent nuisances arising from dust,
(*e*) regulating the hours during which ceilings may be broken down and mortar may be shot, or be allowed to fall, into any lower floor,
(*f*) requiring any person proposing to demolish a building to give to the borough council such notice of his intention to do so as may be specified in the byelaws.

(2) Byelaws under this paragraph may make different provision for different cases, and in particular may provide that, in their application to an area specified in the byelaws, the byelaws shall have effect subject to such modifications or exceptions as may be so specified.

(3) No byelaws under this paragraph shall apply to a building (not being a dwelling-house) belonging to a board carrying on a railway undertaking and used by that board as a part of, or in connection with, that undertaking.

11. *Repealed.*

12. *Repealed.*

13. Restriction of application of Part IV of Act. Part IV of this Act does not apply in relation to this Part of this Schedule.

PART V
ENFORCEMENT OF BUILDING REGULATIONS

14. *Repealed.*

---

1. The following provisions of the Building Act 1984 are prescribed for the purposes of para 2(1) of Sch 3 to the Act and apply in relation to a local authority in inner London as they apply to a local authority outside inner London—
section 8 (relaxation of building regulations);
section 9 (application for relaxation);
section 10 (advertisement of proposal for relaxation of building regulations);
section 16 (passing or rejection of plans);
section 32 (lapse of deposit of plans);
section 36 (removal or alteration of offending work);
section 37 (obtaining of report where section 36 notice given);
section 39 (appeal against refusal etc to relax building regulations);
section 40 (appeal against section 36 notice).
(Building (Inner London) Regulations 1985 SI 1985/1936, reg 2(3), as amended by SI 1986/452).

8–26230

Section 54

SCHEDULE 4
PROVISIONS CONSEQUENTIAL UPON PUBLIC BODY'S NOTICE[1]

Duration of notice

1. (1) A public body's notice comes into force when it is accepted by the local authority, either by notice given within the prescribed period to the public body by which it was given or by virtue of section 54(3) of this Act, and, subject to paragraph 3(3) below, continues in force until the occurrence of, or the expiry of a prescribed period of time beginning on the date of such event as may be prescribed.

(2) Building regulations may empower a local authority to extend (whether before or after its expiry) any such period of time as is referred to in sub-paragraph (1) above.

Public body's plans certificates

2. (1) Where a public body—

(*a*) is satisfied that plans of the work specified in a public body's notice given by it have been inspected by a servant or agent of the body who is competent to assess the plans,
(*b*) in the light of that inspection is satisfied that the plans neither are defective nor show that work carried out in accordance with them would contravene any provision of building regulations, and

(*c*) has complied with any prescribed requirements as to consultation or otherwise,

the body may give to the local authority a certificate in the prescribed form (called a "public body's plans certificate").

(2) Building regulations may authorise the giving of a public body's notice combined with a public body's plans certificate, and may prescribe a single form for such a combined notice and certificate; and where such a prescribed form is used—

(*a*) a reference in this Schedule or in any other provision of Part II of this Act to a public body's notice or to a public body's plans certificate includes a reference to that form, but

(*b*) should the form cease to be in force as a public body's notice by virtue of paragraph 1(1) above, nothing in that paragraph affects the continuing validity of the form as a public body's plans certificate.

(3) A public body's plans certificate—

(*a*) may relate either to the whole or to part only of the work specified in the public body's notice concerned, and

(*b*) does not have effect unless it is accepted by the local authority to whom it is given.

(4) A local authority to whom a public body's plans certificate is given—

(*a*) may not reject the certificate except on prescribed grounds, and

(*b*) shall reject the certificate if any of the prescribed grounds exists.

(5) Unless, within the prescribed period, the local authority to whom a public body's plans certificate is given give notice of rejection, specifying the ground or grounds in question, to the public body by which the certificate was given, the authority are conclusively presumed to have accepted the certificate.

(6) If it appears to a local authority by whom a public body's plans certificate has been accepted that the work to which the certificate relates has not been commenced within the period of three years beginning on the date on which the certificate was accepted, the authority may rescind their acceptance of the certificate by notice, specifying the ground or grounds in question, given to the public body.

Public body's final certificates

3. (1) Where a public body is satisfied that any work specified in a public body's notice given by it has been completed, the body may give to the local authority such certificate with respect to the completion of the work and compliance with building regulations as may be prescribed (called a "public body's final certificate").

(2) Sub-paragraphs (3) to (5) of paragraph 2 above have effect in relation to a public body's final certificate as if any reference in those sub-paragraphs to a public body's plans certificate were a reference to a public body's final certificate.

(3) Where a public body's final certificate has been given with respect to any of the work specified in a public body's notice and that certificate has been accepted by the local authority concerned, the public body's notice ceases to apply to that work, but the provisions of section 48(1) of this Act, as applied by section 54(4), continue, by virtue of this sub-paragraph, to apply in relation to that work as if the public body's notice continued in force in relation to it.

Effects of public body's notice ceasing to be in force

4. (1) This paragraph applies where a public body's notice ceases to be in force by virtue of paragraph 1 above.

(2) Building regulations may provide that if—

(*a*) a public body's plans certificate was given before the day on which the public body's notice ceased to be in force, and

(*b*) that certificate was accepted by the local authority (before, on or after that day), and

(*c*) before that day, that acceptance was not rescinded by a notice under paragraph 2(6) above,

then, with respect to the work specified in the certificate, such of the functions of a local authority referred to in section 48(1) of this Act as may be prescribed for the purposes of this sub-paragraph either are not exercisable or are exercisable only in prescribed circumstances.

(3) If, before the day on which the public body's notice ceased to be in force, a public body's final certificate was given in respect of part of the work specified in the notice and that certificate was accepted by the local authority (before, on or after that day), the fact that the public body's notice has ceased to be in force does not affect the continuing operation of paragraph 3(3) above in relation to that part of the work.

(4) Notwithstanding anything in sub-paragraphs (2) and (3) above, for the purpose of enabling the local authority to perform the functions referred to in section 48(1) of this Act in relation to any part of the work not specified in a public body's plans certificate or final certificate, as the case may be, building regulations may require the local authority to be provided with plans that relate not only to that part but also to the part to which the certificate in question relates.

(5) In any case where this paragraph applies, the reference in subsection (4) of section 36 of this Act to the date of the completion of the work in question has effect, in relation to a notice under subsection (1) of that section, as if it were a reference to the date on which the public body's notice ceased to be in force.

(6) Subject to any provision of building regulations made by virtue of sub-paragraph (2) above, if, before the public body's notice ceased to be in force, an offence under section 35 of this Act was committed with respect to any of the work specified in that notice, summary proceedings for that offence may be commenced by the local authority at any time within six months beginning with the day on which the functions of the local authority referred to in section 48(1) of this Act became exercisable with respect to the provision of building regulations to which the offence relates.

(7) Any reference in the preceding provisions of this paragraph to section 48(1) of this Act is a reference to that section as applied by section 54(2) of this Act.

Consultation

5. Building regulations may make provision for requiring, in such circumstances as may be prescribed, a public body that has given a public body's notice to consult any prescribed person before taking any prescribed step in connection with any work specified in the notice.

---

1. For provisions "prescribed" by virtue of this Schedule, see the Building (Approved Inspectors etc) Regulations 2002, SI 2000/2532 amended by SI 2001/3336, SI 2002/2872, SI 2003/3133, SI 2004/1466 and 3168 and SI 2005/1541 and 2929 (W).

8–26231

Section 132

SCHEDULE 5

TRANSITIONAL PROVISIONS

(As amended by the Housing (Consequential Provisions) Act 1985 Sch 1, the Clean Air Act 1993, Sch 6 and the Statute Law (Repeals) Act 2004.)

Joint application to the Secretary of State for the determination of certain questions relating to building regulations

1. *Repealed.*

The Clean Air Act 1956 and the Housing Act 1957

2. *Repealed.*

Repeal and amendment of Acts etc

3. Any power that is exercisable by virtue of—

(*a*) section 317 of the Public Health Act 1936,
(*b*) section 82 of the Public Health Act 1961,
(*c*) section 82, 83 or 84 of the London Government Act 1963,
(*d*) section 252 or 254 of the Local Government Act 1972, or
(*e*) section 48 of the Local Government (Miscellaneous Provisions) Act 1982,

in relation to a provision that is repealed and re-enacted by this Act is exercisable in relation to that provision as so re-enacted to the extent to which it would have been exercisable immediately before such repeal.

4. *Repealed.*

5. Without prejudice to the power to make building regulations, the repeal of section 70(1) of the Health and Safety at Work etc Act 1974, and the re-enactment in this Act of that subsection down to "Wales", do not of themselves cause any building regulations to apply to inner London that were prevented by that subsection from so applying.

Control of Pollution (Amendment) Act 1989[1]

(1989 c 14)

8–26232 **1. Offence of transporting controlled waste without registering.** (1) Subject to the following provisions of this section, it shall be an offence for any person who is not a registered carrier[2] of controlled waste, in the course of any business of his or otherwise with a view to profit, to transport any controlled waste to or from any place in Great Britain.

(2) A person shall not be guilty of an offence under this section in respect of—

(*a*) the transport of controlled waste within the same premises between different places in those premises;
(*b*) the transport to a place in Great Britain of controlled waste which has been brought from a country or territory outside Great Britain and is not landed in Great Britain until it arrives at that place;
(*c*) the transport by air or sea of controlled waste from a place in Great Britain to a place outside Great Britain.

(3) The Secretary of State may by regulations provide that a person shall not be required for the purposes of this section to be a registered carrier of controlled waste if—

(*a*) he is a prescribed person or a person of such a description as may be prescribed[3]; or
(*b*) without prejudice to paragraph (*a*) above, he is a person in relation to whom the prescribed requirements under the law of any other member State are satisfied.

(4) In proceedings against any person for an offence under this section in respect of the transport of any controlled waste it shall be a defence for that person to show—

(*a*) that the waste was transported in an emergency of which notice was given, as soon as practicable after it occurred, to the regulation authority in whose area the emergency occurred;
(*b*) that he neither knew nor had reasonable grounds for suspecting that what was being transported was controlled waste and took all such steps as it was reasonable to take for ascertaining whether it was such waste; or
(*c*) that he acted under instructions from his employer.

(5) A person guilty of an offence under this section shall be liable on summary conviction to a fine not exceeding **level 5** on the standard scale.

(6) In this section "emergency", in relation to the transport of any controlled waste, means any circumstances in which, in order to avoid, remove or reduce any serious danger to the public or serious risk of damage to the environment, it is necessary for the waste to be transported from one place to another without the use of a registered carrier of such waste.

[Control of Pollution (Amendment) Act 1989, s 1, as amended by the Environmental Protection Act 1990, Sch 15 and the Clean Neighbourhoods and Environment Act 2005, s 35.]

---

1. This Act shall come into force on such day or days as the Secretary of State may by order appoint (s 11(2), post). The Control of Pollution (Amendment) Act 1989 (Commencement) Order 1991, SI 1991/1618, had brought the following provisions into force at the date of going to press: ss 1(3), 2, 3, 4, 5(3) and (6) (in part), 6 (in part), 7–11. By virtue of that Order, the remaining provisions of the Act came into force on 1 April 1992.

2. Registration under the Act is of carriers, not of vehicles; accordingly, an owner of a vehicle used by someone who has hired it to transport controlled waste does not commit an offence by virtue of not himself being registered (*Cosmick Transport v Bedfordshire County Council* [1997] RTR 132).

3. See the Controlled Waste (Registration of Carriers and Seizure of Vehicles) Regulations 1991, SI 1991/1624 amended by SI 1992/588, SI 1994/1056 and 1137, SI 1996/593 and 972 and SI 2005/894 and 1806 (W) and the Controlled Waste Regulations 1992, SI 1992/588 amended by SI 1993/566, SI 1994/1056, SI 1996/972, SI 2005/894, 1806 (W) and 1820 (W) and 2900 (E) and SI 2006/123 (W).

8–26233 2. Registration of carriers. (1) Subject to section 3 below, the Secretary of State may by regulations make provision for the registration of persons with regulation authorities[1] as carriers of controlled waste and, for that purpose, for the establishment and maintenance by such authorities, in accordance with the regulations, of such registers as may be prescribed[2].

(2)–(5) *Supplementary provisions relating to regulations.*

[Control of Pollution (Amendment) Act 1989, s 2, as amended by the Environmental Protection Act 1990, Sch 15, the Environment Act 1995, Schs 22 and 24 and the Clean Neighbourhoods and Environment Act 2005, s 36.]

---

1. For the meaning of "regulation authority", see s 9, post.

2. See the Controlled Waste (Registration of Carriers and Seizure of Vehicles) Regulations 1991, SI 1991/1624, amended by SI 1992/588, SI 1994/1056 and 1137, SI 1996/593 and 972, SI 1998/605 and SI 2005/894 and 1806 (W).

8–26234 3. Restrictions on power under section 2. *Restrictions on power of regulation authority to refuse an application for registration or to revoke any person's registration.*

8–26235 4. Appeals against refusal of registration etc. (1) Where a person has applied to a regulation authority to be registered in accordance with any regulations under section 2 above, he may appeal to the Secretary of State if—

(*a*) his application is refused; or

(*b*) the relevant period from the making of the application has expired without his having been registered;

and for the purposes of this subsection the relevant period is two months or, except in the case of an application for the renewal of his registration by a person who is already registered, such longer period as may be agreed between the applicant and the regulation authority in question.

(2) A person whose registration as a carrier of controlled waste has been revoked may appeal against the revocation to the Secretary of State.

(3) On an appeal under this section the Secretary of State may, as he thinks fit, either dismiss the appeal or give the regulation authority in question a direction to register the appellant or, as the case may be, to cancel the revocation.

(4) Where on an appeal made by virtue of subsection (1)(*b*) above the Secretary of State dismisses an appeal, he shall direct the regulation authority in question not to register the appellant.

(5) It shall be the duty of a regulation authority to comply with any direction under this section.

(6) The Secretary of State may by regulations[1] make provision as to the manner in which and time within which an appeal under this section is to be made and as to the procedure to be followed on any such appeal.

(7) Where an appeal under this section is made in accordance with regulations under this section—

(*a*) by a person whose appeal is in respect of such an application for the renewal of his registration as was made, in accordance with regulations under section 2 above, at a time when he was already registered; or

(*b*) by a person whose registration has been revoked,

that registration shall continue in force, notwithstanding the expiry of the prescribed period or the revocation, until the appeal is disposed of.

(8) For the purposes of subsection (7) above an appeal is disposed of when any of the following occurs, that is to say—

(*a*) the appeal is withdrawn;

(*b*) the appellant is notified by the Secretary of State or the regulation authority in question that his appeal has been dismissed; or

(*c*) the regulation authority comply with any direction of the Secretary of State to renew the appellant's registration or to cancel the revocation.

(9) This section is subject to section 114 of the Environment Act 1995 (delegation or reference of appeals etc).

[Control of Pollution (Amendment) Act 1989, s 4, as amended by the Environmental Protection Act 1990, Sch 15 and the Environment Act 1995, Sch 22.]

1. See the Controlled Waste (Registration of Carriers and Seizure of Vehicles) Regulations 1991, SI 1991/1624, amended by SI 1992/588, SI 1994/1056 and 1137, SI 1996/593 and 972, SI 1998/605 and SI 2005/894 and 1806 (W).

8–26236 **5. Duty to produce authority to transport controlled waste.** (1) If it reasonably appears to any duly authorised officer of a regulation authority or to a constable that any controlled waste is being or has been transported in contravention of section 1(1) above, he may—

(*a*) stop any person appearing to him to be or to have been engaged in transporting that waste and require that person to produce his authority or, as the case may be, his employer's authority for transporting that waste; and

(*b*) search any vehicle that appears to him to be a vehicle which is being or has been used for transporting that waste, carry out tests on anything found in any such vehicle and take away for testing samples of anything so found.

(2) Nothing in subsection (1) above shall authorise any person other than a constable in uniform to stop a vehicle on any road.

(3) Subject to the following provisions of this section, a person who is required by virtue of this section to produce an authority for transporting controlled waste shall do so by producing it forthwith to the person making the requirement, by producing it at the prescribed[1] place and within the prescribed[1] period or by sending it to that place within that period.

(4) A person shall be guilty of an offence under this section if he—

(*a*) intentionally obstructs any authorised officer of a regulation authority or constable in the exercise of the power conferred by subsection (1) above; or

(*b*) subject to subsection (5) below, fails without reasonable excuse to comply with a requirement imposed in exercise of that power;

and in paragraph (*b*) above the words "without reasonable excuse" shall be construed in their application to Scotland, as in their application to England and Wales, as making it a defence for a person against whom proceedings for the failure are brought to show that there was a reasonable excuse for the failure, rather than as requiring the person bringing the proceedings to show that there was no such excuse.

(5) A person shall not be guilty of an offence by virtue of subsection (4)(*b*) above unless it is shown—

(*a*) that the waste in question was controlled waste; and

(*b*) that that person did transport it to or from a place in Great Britain.

(6) For the purposes of this section a person's authority for transporting controlled waste is—

(*a*) his certificate of registration as a carrier of controlled waste or such a copy of that certificate as satisfies prescribed[1] requirements; or

(*b*) such evidence as may be prescribed[1] that he is not required to be registered as a carrier of controlled waste.

(7) A person guilty of an offence under this section shall be liable on summary conviction to a fine not exceeding **level 5** on the standard scale.*

[Control of Pollution (Amendment) Act 1989, s 5, as amended by the Environmental Protection Act 1990, Sch 15.]

***Substituted, and new ss 5A–5C inserted, in relation to England and Wales, by the Clean Neighbourhoods and Environment Act 2005, ss 37 and 38 from a date to be appointed.**

1. See the Controlled Waste (Registration of Carriers and Seizure of Vehicles) Regulations 1991, SI 1991/1624, amended by SI 1992/588, SI 1994/1056 and 1137, SI 1996/593 and 972, SI 1998/605 and SI 2005/894 and 1806 (W).

8–26237 **6. Seizure and disposal of vehicles used for illegal waste disposal.** (1) A justice of the peace or, in Scotland, a sheriff or a justice of the peace may issue a warrant to a regulation authority for the seizure of any vehicle if he is satisfied, on sworn information in writing—

(*a*) that there are reasonable grounds for believing—

(i) that an offence under section 3 of the Control of Pollution Act 1974 or section 33 of the Environmental Protection Act 1990 (prohibition on unlicensed deposit, treatment or disposal of waste) has been committed; and

(ii) that that vehicle was used in the commission of the offence;

(*b*) that proceedings for that offence have not yet been brought against any person; and

(*c*) that the authority have failed, after taking the prescribed[1] steps, to ascertain the name and address of any person who is able to provide them with the prescribed information about who was using the vehicle at the time when the offence was committed.

(2) Subject to subsections (3) and (4) below, where a warrant under this section has been issued to a regulation authority in respect of any vehicle, any duly authorised officer of the regulation authority or any constable may stop the vehicle and, on behalf of the authority, seize the vehicle and its contents.

(3) Nothing in this section shall authorise any person other than a constable in uniform to stop a vehicle on any road; and a duly authorised officer of a regulation authority shall not be entitled to seize any property under this section unless he is accompanied by a constable.

(4) A warrant under this section shall continue in force until its purpose is fulfilled; and any person seizing any property under this section shall, if required to do so, produce both the warrant and any authority in pursuance of which he is acting under the warrant.

(5) Where any property has been seized under this section on behalf of a regulation authority, the authority may, in accordance with regulations[1] made by the Secretary of state, remove it to such place as the authority consider appropriate and may retain custody of it until either—

(*a*) it is returned, in accordance with the regulations, to a person who establishes that he is entitled to it; or

(*b*) it is disposed of by the authority in exercise of a power conferred by the regulations to sell or destroy the property or to deposit it at any place.

(6)–(7) *Regulations under this section.*

(8) Subject to their powers by virtue of any regulations under this section to sell or destroy any property or to dispose of it by depositing it at any place, it shall be the duty of a regulation authority, while any property is in their custody by virtue of a warrant under this section, to take such steps as are reasonably necessary for the safe custody of that property.

(9) Any person who intentionally obstructs any authorised officer of a regulation authority or constable in the exercise of any power conferred by virtue of a warrant under this section shall be guilty of an offence and liable, on summary conviction, to a fine not exceeding **level 5** on the standard scale.*

[Control of Pollution (Amendment) Act 1989, s 6, as amended by the Environmental Protection Act 1990, Sch 15 and the Environment Act 1995, Sch 22.]

***Repealed, in relation to England and Wales, by the Clean Neighbourhoods and Environment Act 2005, s 37 from a date to be appointed.**

1. See the Controlled Waste (Registration of Carriers and Seizure of Vehicles) Regulations 1991, SI 1991/1624, amended by SI 1992/588, SI 1994/1056 and 1137, SI 1996/593 and 972, SI 1998/605 and SI 2005/894 and 1806 (W).

8–26238 **7. Further enforcement provisions.** (1) Subject to subsection (2) below, the provisions of section 71 of the Environmental Protection Act 1990 (powers of entry, of dealing with imminent pollution and to obtain information and duty not to disclose information) shall have effect as if the provisions of this Act were provisions of that Act and as if, in those sections, references to a relevant authority were references to a regulation authority.

(2) (*Repealed*).

(3) A person shall be guilty of an offence under this subsection if he—

(*a*) fails, without reasonable excuse, to comply with any requirement in pursuance of regulations under this Act to provide information to the Secretary of State or a regulation authority; or

(*b*) in complying with any such requirement, provides information which he knows to be false or misleading in a material particular or recklessly provides information which is false or misleading in a material particular;

and in paragraph (*a*) above the words "without reasonable excuse" shall be construed in their application to Scotland, as in their application to England and Wales, as making it a defence for a person against whom proceedings for the failure are brought to show that there was a reasonable excuse for the failure, rather than as requiring the person bringing the proceedings to show that there was no such excuse.

(4) A person guilty of an offence under subsection (3) above shall be liable on summary conviction to a fine not exceeding **level 5** on the standard scale.

(5) Where the commission by any person of an offence under this Act is due to the act or default of some other person, that other person shall also be guilty of the offence; and a person may be charged with and convicted of an offence by virtue of this subsection whether or not proceedings for the offence are taken against any other person.

(6) Where a body corporate is guilty of an offence under this Act (including where it is so guilty by virtue of subsection (5) above) in respect of any act or omission which is shown to have been committed with the consent or connivance of, or to be attributable to any neglect on the part of, any director, manager, secretary or other similar officer of the body corporate or any person who was purporting to act in any such capacity, he, as well as the body corporate, shall be guilty of that offence and shall be liable to be proceeded against and punished accordingly.

(7) Where the affairs of a body corporate are managed by its members, subsection (6) above shall apply in relation to the acts and defaults of a member in connection with his functions of management as if he were a director of the body corporate.

(8) (*Repealed*).

[Control of Pollution (Amendment) Act 1989, s 7, as amended by the Environmental Protection Act 1990, Schs 15 and 16 and the Environment Act 1995, Schs 19, 22 and 24.]

1. See this title, ante.

8–26239 8. *Regulations.*

8–26240 9. Interpretation. (1) In this Act—

"appropriate person" means—

(*a*) the Secretary of State, in relation to England;

(*b*) the National Assembly for Wales, in relation to Wales.

"controlled waste" has, at any time, the same meaning as for the purposes of Part II of the Environmental Protection Act 1990[1];

"prescribed" means prescribed by regulations made by the Secretary of State;

"regulation authority" means—

(*a*) in relation to England and Wales, the Environment Agency; and

(*b*) in relation to Scotland, the Scottish Environment Protection Agency;

and any reference to the area of a regulation authority shall accordingly be construed as a reference to any area in England and Wales or, as the case may be, in Scotland;

"road" has the same meaning as in the Road Traffic Act 1988;

"transport", in relation to any controlled waste, includes the transport of that waste by road or rail or by air, sea or inland waterway but does not include moving that waste from one place to another by means of any pipe or other apparatus that joins those two places.

"vehicle" means any motor vehicle or trailer within the meaning of the Road Traffic Regulation Act 1984.

(1A) In sections 5 to 7 above "regulation authority" also means a waste collection authority fallling within section 30(3)(*a*), (*b*) or (*bb*) of the Environmental Protection Act 1990.

(1B) For the purposes of any provision of this Act, "authorised officer" in relation to any authority means an officer of the authority who is authorised in writing for the purposes of that provision.

(2) *Repealed.*

[Control of Pollution (Amendment) Act 1989, s 9, as amended by the Environmental Protection Act 1990, Schs 15 and 16, the Environment Act 1995, Sch 22, the Anti-Social Behaviour Act 2003, s 55 and the Clean Neighbourhoods and Environment Act 2005, s 39.]

1. See this title, post.

8–26240A 10A. Application to Isles of Scilly

8–26241 11. Short title, commencement and extent. (1) This Act may be cited as the Control of Pollution (Amendment) Act 1989.

(2) This Act shall come into force on such day as the Secretary of State may by order[1] made by statutory instrument appoint; and different days may be so appointed for different provisions and for different purposes.

(3) *Repealed.*

(4) *Northern Ireland.*

[Control of Pollution (Amendment) Act 1989, s 11, as amended by the Environment Act 1995, s 118 and Sch 24.]

1. See note 1 to s 1, ante.

Environmental Protection Act 1990[1]

(1990 c 43)

PART I[2]

INTEGRATED POLLUTION CONTROL AND AIR POLLUTION CONTROL BY LOCAL AUTHORITIES*

Preliminary

8–26242 1. Preliminary. (1) The following provisions have effect for the interpretation of this Part.

(2) The "environment" consists of all, or any, of the following media, namely, the air, water and land; and the medium of air includes the air within buildings and the air within other natural or man-made structures above or below ground.

(3) "Pollution of the environment" means pollution of the environment due to the release (into any environmental medium) from any process of substances which are capable of causing harm to man or any other living organisms supported by the environment.

(4) "Harm" means harm to the health of living organisms or other interference with the ecological

systems of which they form part and, in the case of man, includes offence caused to any of his senses or harm to his property; and "harmless" has a corresponding meaning.

(5) "Process" means any activities carried on in Great Britain, whether on premises or by means of mobile plant, which are capable of causing pollution of the environment and "prescribed process" means a process prescribed under section 2(1) below.

(6) For the purposes of subsection (5) above—

"activities" means industrial or commercial activities or activities of any other nature whatsoever (including, with or without other activities, the keeping of a substance);

"Great Britain" includes so much of the adjacent territorial sea as is, or is treated as, relevant territorial waters for the purposes of Part III of the Water Resources Act 1991 or, as respects Scotland, Part II of the Control of Pollution Act 1974; and

"mobile plant" means plant which is designed to move or to be moved whether on roads or otherwise.

(7) The "enforcing authority", in relation to England and Wales, is the Environment Agency or the local authority by which, under section 4 below, the functions conferred or imposed by this Part otherwise than on the Secretary of State are for the time being exercisable in relation respectively to releases of substances into the environment or into the air; and "local enforcing authority" means any such local authority.

(8) (Scotland).

(9) "Authorisation" means an authorisation for a process (whether on premises or by means of mobile plant) granted under section 6 below; and a reference to the conditions of an authorisation is a reference to the conditions subject to which at any time the authorisation has effect.

(10) A substance is "released" into any environmental medium whenever it is released directly into that medium whether it is released into it within or outside Great Britain and "release" includes—

(*a*) in relation to air, any emission of the substance into the air;
(*b*) in relation to water, any entry (including any discharge) of the substance into water;
(*c*) in relation to land, any deposit, keeping or disposal of the substance in or on land;

and for this purpose "water" and "land" shall be construed in accordance with subsections (11) and (12) below.

(11) For the purpose of determining into what medium a substance is released—

(*a*) any release into—

(i) the sea or the surface of the seabed,
(ii) any river, watercourse, lake, loch or pond (whether natural or artificial or above or below ground) or reservoir or the surface of the riverbed or of other land supporting such waters, or
(iii) ground waters,

is a release into water;

(*b*) any release into—

(i) land covered by water falling outside paragraph (*a*) above or the water covering such land; or
(ii) the land beneath the surface of the seabed or of other land supporting waters falling within paragraph (*a*)(ii) above,

is a release into land; and

(*c*) any release into a sewer (within the meaning of the Water Industry Act 1991 or, in relation to Scotland, of the Sewerage (Scotland) Act 1968) shall be treated as a release into water;

but a sewer and its contents shall be disregarded in determining whether there is pollution of the environment at any time.

(12) In subsection (11) above "ground waters" means any waters contained in underground strata, or in—

(*a*) a well, borehole or similar work sunk into underground strata, including any adit or passage constructed in connection with the well, borehole or work for facilitating the collection of water in the well, borehole or work; or
(*b*) any excavation into underground strata where the level of water in the excavation depends wholly or mainly on water entering it from the strata.

(13) "Substance" shall be treated as including electricity or heat and "prescribed substance" has the meaning given by section 2(7) below.

(14) In this Part "the appropriate Agency" means—

(*a*) in relation to England and Wales, the Environment Agency; and
(*b*) in relation to Scotland, SEPA*.

[Environmental Protection Act 1990, s 1, as amended by the Water Consolidation (Consequential Provisions) Act 1991, Sch 1 and the Environment Act 1995, Sch 22.]

***Repealed by the Pollution Prevention and Control Act 1999, Sch 3, when in force.**

1. The Act is to come into force in accordance with s 164. For commencement orders made thereunder, see note 1 to s 164, post. At the date of going to press, of the provisions printed in this work, the following had not been brought fully into force—

Part II ss 33, 35–45, 57, 63 and 76;
Part VI ss 108–112, 116, 118.

2. Part I consists of ss 1–28.

8–26243 **2. Prescribed processes and prescribed substances.** (1) The Secretary of State may, by regulations[1], prescribe any description of process as a process for the carrying on of which after a prescribed date an authorisation is required under section 6 below.

(2) Regulations under subsection (1) above may frame the description of a process by reference to any characteristics of the process or the area or other circumstances in which the process is carried on or the description of person carrying it on.

(3) Regulations under subsection (1) above may prescribe or provide for the determination under the regulations of different dates for different descriptions of persons and may include such transitional provisions as the Secretary of State considers necessary or expedient as respects the making of applications for authorisations and suspending the application of section 6(1) below until the determination of applications made within the period allowed by the regulations.

(4) Regulations under subsection (1) above shall, as respects each description of process, designate it as one for central control or one for local control.

(5) The Secretary of State may, by regulations, prescribe any description of substance as a substance the release of which into the environment is subject to control under sections 6 and 7 below.

(6) Regulations under subsection (5) above may—

(*a*) prescribe separately, for each environmental medium, the substances the release of which into that medium is to be subject to control; and

(*b*) provide that a description of substance is only prescribed, for any environmental medium, so far as it is released into that medium in such amounts over such periods, in such concentrations or in such other circumstances as may be specified in the regulations;

and in relation to a substance of a description which is prescribed for releases into the air, the regulations may designate the substance as one for central control or one for local control.

(7) In this Part "prescribed substance" means any substance of a description prescribed in regulations under subsection (5) above or, in the case of a substance of a description prescribed only for releases in circumstances specified under subsection (6)(*b*) above, means any substance of that description which is released in those circumstances.*

[Environmental Protection Act 1990, s 2.]

***See note to s 1, ante.**

1. The Environmental Protection (Prescribed Processes and Substances) Regulations 1991, SI 1991/472 amended by SI 1991/836, SI 1992/614, SI 1993/1749 and 2405, SI 1994/1271 and 1329, SI 1995/3247, SI 1996/2678, SI 1998/767, SI 2000/1973 and SI 2005/894 and 1806 (W).

8–26244 **3. Emission etc limits and quality objectives.** (1) The Secretary of State may make regulations under subsection (2) or (4) below establishing standards, objectives or requirements in relation to particular prescribed processes or particular substances.

(2) Regulations under this subsection may—

(*a*) in relation to releases of any substance from prescribed processes into any environmental medium, prescribe standard limits for—

(i) the concentration, the amount or the amount in any period of that substance which may be so released; and

(ii) any other characteristic of that substance in any circumstances in which it may be so released;

(*b*) prescribe standard requirements for the measurement or analysis of, or of releases of, substances for which limits have been set under paragraph (*a*) above; and

(*c*) in relation to any prescribed process, prescribe standards or requirements as to any aspect of the process.

(3) Regulations under subsection (2) above may make different provision in relation to different cases, including different provision in relation to different processes, descriptions of person, localities or other circumstances.

(4) Regulations under this subsection may establish for any environmental medium (in all areas or in specified areas) quality objectives or quality standards in relation to any substances which may be released into that or any other medium from any process.

(5) The Secretary of State may make plans for—

(*a*) establishing limits for the total amount, or the total amount in any period, of any substance which may be released into the environment in, or in any area within, the United Kingdom;

(*b*) allocating quotas as respects the release of substances to persons carrying on processes in respect of which any such limit is established;

(*c*) establishing limits of the descriptions specified in subsection (2)(*a*) above so as progressively to reduce pollution of the environment;

(*d*) the progressive improvement in the quality objectives and quality standards established by regulations under subsection (4) above;

and the Secretary of State may, from time to time, revise any plan so made.

(6) Regulations or plans under this section may be made for any purposes of this Part or for other purposes.

(7) The Secretary of State shall give notice in the London, Edinburgh and Belfast Gazettes of the making and the revision of any plan under subsection (5) above and shall make the documents containing the plan, or the plan as so revised, available for inspection by members of the public at the places specified in the notice.

(8) Subject to any Order made after the passing of this Act by virtue of subsection (1)(*a*) of section 3 of the Northern Ireland Constitution Act 1973, the making and revision of plans under subsection (5) above shall not be a transferred matter for the purposes of that Act but shall for the purposes of subsection (2) of that section be treated as specified in Schedule 3 to that Act.*

[Environmental Protection Act 1990, s 3.]

***See note to s 1, ante.**

8–26245 **4. Discharge and scope of functions.** (1) This section determines the authority by whom the functions conferred or imposed by this Part otherwise than on the Secretary of State are exercisable and the purposes for which they are exercisable.

(2) Those functions, in their application to prescribed processes designated for central control, shall be functions of the appropriate Agency, and shall be exercisable for the purpose of preventing or minimising pollution of the environment due to the release of substances into any environmental medium.

(3) Subject to subsection (4) below, those functions, in their application to prescribed processes designated for local control, shall be functions of—

(*a*) in the case of a prescribed process carried on (or to be carried on) by means of a mobile plant, where the person carrying on the process has his principal place of business—

(i) in England and Wales, the local authority in whose area that place of business is;
(ii) in Scotland, SEPA;

(*b*) in any other cases, where the prescribed processes are (or are to be) carried on—

(i) in England and Wales, the local authority in whose area they are (or are to be) carried on;
(ii) in Scotland, SEPA;

and the functions applicable to such processes shall be exercisable for the purpose of preventing or minimising pollution of the environment due to the release of substances into the air (but not into any other environmental medium).

(4) The Secretary of State may, as respect the functions under this Part being exercised by a local authority specified in the direction, direct that those functions shall be exercised instead by the Environment Agency while the direction remains in force or during a period specified in the direction.

(4A) In England and Wales, a local authority, in exercising the functions conferred or imposed on it under this Part by virtue of subsection (3) above, shall have regard to the strategy for the time being published pursuant to section 80 of the Environment Act 1995.

(5) A transfer of functions under subsection (4) above to the Environment Agency does not make them exercisable by that Agency for the purpose of preventing or minimising pollution of the environment due to releases of substances into any other environmental medium than the air.

(6) A direction under subsection (4) above may transfer those functions as exercisable in relation to all or any description of prescribed processes carried on by all or any description of persons (a "general direction") or in relation to a prescribed process carried on by a specified person (a "specific direction").

(7) A direction under subsection (4) above may include such saving and transitional provisions as the Secretary of State considers necessary or expedient.

(8) The Secretary of State, on giving or withdrawing a direction under subsection (4) above, shall—

(*a*) in the case of a general direction—

(i) forthwith serve notice of it on the Environment Agency and on the local enforcing authorities affected by the direction; and
(ii) cause notice of it to be published as soon as practicable in the London Gazette and in at least one newspaper circulating in the area of each authority affected by the direction;

(*b*) in the case of a specific direction—

(i) forthwith serve notice of it on the chief inspector, the local enforcing authority and the person carrying on or appearing to the Secretary of State to be carrying on the process affected, and

(ii) cause notice of it to be published as soon as practicable in the London Gazette or, as the case may be, in the Edinburgh Gazette and in at least one newspaper circulating in the authority's area;

and any such notice shall specify the date at which the direction is to take (or took) effect and (where appropriate) its duration.

(8A) The requirements of sub-paragraph (ii) of paragraph (*a*) or, as the case may be, of paragraph (*b*) of subsection (8) above shall not apply in any case where, in the opinion of the Secretary of State, the publication of notice in accordance with that sub-paragraph would be contrary to the interests of national security.

(8B) Subsections (4) to (8A) above shall not apply to Scotland.

(9) It shall be the duty of local authorities to follow such developments in technology and techniques for preventing or reducing pollution of the environment due to releases of substances from prescribed processes as concern releases into the air of substances from prescribed processes designated for local control.

(10) It shall be the duty of the Environment Agency, SEPA and the local enforcing authorities to give effect to any directions given to them under any provision of this Part.

(11) In this Part "local authority" means, subject to subsection (12) below—

(*a*) in Greater London, a London borough council, the Common Council of the City of London, the Sub-Treasurer of the Inner Temple and the Under Treasurer of the Middle Temple;

(*b*) in England outside Greater London, a district council and the Council of the Isles of Scilly;

(bb) in Wales, a county council or county borough council;

(*c*) (Repealed).

(12) Where, by an order under section 2 of the Public Health (Control of Disease) Act 1984, a port health authority has been constituted for any port health district, the port health authority shall have by virtue of this subsection, as respects its district, the functions conferred or imposed by this Part and no such order shall be made assigning those functions; and "local authority" and "area" shall be construed accordingly.*

[Environmental Protection Act 1990, s 4, as amended by the Local Government (Wales) Act 1994, Sch 9 and the Environment Act 1995, Schs 22 and 24.]

***See note to s 1, ante.**

Authorisations

8–26247 **6. Authorisations: general provisions.** (1) No person shall carry on a prescribed process after the date prescribed or determined for that description of process by or under regulations under section 2(1) above (but subject to any transitional provision made by the regulations) except under an authorisation granted by the enforcing authority and in accordance with the conditions to which it is subject.

(2) An application for an authorisation shall be made to the enforcing authority in accordance with Part I of Schedule 1 to this Act and shall be accompanied by

(*a*) in a case where, by virtue of section 41 of the Environment Act 1995, a charge prescribed by a charging scheme under that section is required to be paid to the appropriate Agency in respect of the application, the charge so prescribed; or

(*b*) in any other case,

the fee prescribed under section 8(2)(*a*) below.

(3) Where an application is duly made to the enforcing authority, the authority shall either grant the authorisation subject to the conditions required or authorised to be imposed by section 7 below or refuse the application.

(4)–(8) Duties etc of Enforcing authority.*

[Environmental Protection Act 1990, s 6, as amended by the Environment Act 1995, Sch 22.]

***See note to s 1, ante.**

8–26248 **7. Conditions of authorisations.** (1) There shall be included in an authorisation—

(*a*) subject to paragraph (*b*) below, such specific conditions as the enforcing authority considers appropriate, when taken with the general condition implied by subsection (4) below, for achieving the objectives[1] specified in subsection (2) below;

(*b*) such conditions as are specified in directions given by the Secretary of State under subsection (3) below; and

(*c*) such other conditions (if any) as appear to the enforcing authority to be appropriate;

but no conditions shall be imposed for the purpose only of securing the health of persons at work (within the meaning of Part I of the Health and Safety at Work etc Act 1974).

(2) Those objectives are—

(*a*) ensuring that, in carrying on a prescribed process, the best available techniques not entailing excessive cost will be used—

(i) for preventing the release of substances prescribed for any environmental medium into that medium or, where that is not practicable by such means, for reducing the release of such substances to a minimum and for rendering harmless any such substances which are so released; and

(ii) for rendering harmless any other substances which might cause harm if released into any environmental medium;

(*b*) compliance with any directions by the Secretary of State given for the implementation of any obligations of the United Kingdom under the Community Treaties or international law relating to environmental protection;

(*c*) compliance with any limits or requirements and achievement of any quality standards or quality objectives prescribed by the Secretary of State under any of the relevant enactments;

(*d*) compliance with any requirements applicable to the grant of authorisations specified by or under a plan made by the Secretary of State under section 3(5) above.

(3) Except as respects the general condition implied by subsection (4) below, the Secretary of State may give directions to the enforcing authorities as to the conditions which are, or are not, to be included in all authorisations, in authorisations of any specified description or in any particular authorisation.

(4) Subject to subsections (5) and (6) below, there is implied in every authorisation a general condition that, in carrying on the process to which the authorisation applies, the person carrying it on must use the best available techniques not entailing excessive cost—

(*a*) for preventing the release of substances prescribed for any environmental medium into that medium or, where that is not practicable by such means, for reducing the release of such substances to a minimum and for rendering harmless any such substances which are so released; and

(*b*) for rendering harmless any other substances which might cause harm if released into any environmental medium.

(5) In the application of subsections (1) to (4) above to authorisations granted by a local enforcing authority references to the release of substances into any environmental medium are to be read as references to the release of substances into the air.

(6) The obligation implied by virtue of subsection (4) above shall not apply in relation to any aspect of the process in question which is regulated by a condition imposed under subsection (1) above.

(7) The objectives referred to in subsection (2) above shall, where the process—

(*a*) is one designated for central control; and

(*b*) is likely to involve the release of substances into more than one environmental medium;

include the objective of ensuring that the best available techniques not entailing excessive cost will be used for minimising the pollution which may be caused to the environment taken as a whole by the releases having regard to the best practicable environmental option available as respects the substances which may be released.

(8) An authorisation for carrying on a prescribed process may, without prejudice to the generality of subsection (1) above, include conditions—

(*a*) imposing limits on the amount or composition of any substance produced by or utilised in the process in any period; and

(*b*) requiring advance notification of any proposed change in the manner of carrying on the process.

(9) This section has effect subject to section 28 below.

(10) References to the best available techniques not entailing excessive cost, in relation to a process, include (in addition to references to any technical means and technology) references to the number, qualifications, training and supervision of persons employed in the process and the design, construction, lay-out and maintenance of the buildings in which it is carried on.

(11) It shall be the duty of enforcing authorities to have regard to any guidance issued to them by the Secretary of State for the purposes of the application of subsections (2) and (7) above as to the techniques and environmental options that are appropriate for any description of prescribed process.

(12) In subsection (2) above "the relevant enactments" are any enactments or instruments contained in or made for the time being under—

(*a*) section 2 of the Clean Air Act 1968;

(*b*) section 2 of the European Communities Act 1972;

(*c*) Part I of the Health and Safety at Work etc Act 1974;

(*d*) Parts II, III or IV of the Control of Pollution Act 1974;

(*e*) the Water Resources Act 1991;

(*f*) section 3 of this Act; and

(*g*) section 87 of the Environment Act 1995.*
[Environmental Protection Act 1990, s 7, as amended by the Water Consolidation (Consequential Provisions) Act 1991, Sch 1 and the Environment Act 1995, Schs 22 and 24.]

***See note to s 1, ante.**
1. The obligation under art 4 of Council Directive 75/442/EEC (states must take measures to ensure that waste is recovered/disposed of without endangering human health or using process/methods that could harm the environment) is a material consideration for competent authorities when deciding applications involving environmental issues under s 7(2) below (*R (Thornby Farms Ltd) v Daventry District Council and R (Murray) v Derbyshire County Council* [2002] EWCA Civ 31, [2003] QB 503, [2002] 3 WLR 875).

8–26249 **8.** *Fees and charges.**

***See note to s 1, ante.**

8–26250 **9. Transfer of authorisations.** (1) An authorisation for the carrying on of any prescribed process may be transferred by the holder to a person who proposes to carry on the process in the holder's place.

(2) Where an authorisation is transferred under this section, the person to whom it is transferred shall notify the enforcing authority in writing of that fact not later than the end of the period of twenty-one days beginning with the date of the transfer.

(3) An authorisation which is transferred under this section shall have effect on and after the date of the transfer as if it had been granted to that person under section 6 above, subject to the same conditions as were attached to it immediately before that date.*
[Environmental Protection Act 1990, s 9.]

***See note to s 1, ante.**

8–26251 **10. Variation of authorisations by enforcing authority.** (1) The enforcing authority may at any time, subject to the requirements of section 7 above, and, in cases to which they apply, the requirements of Part II of Schedule 1 to this Act, vary an authorisation and shall do so if it appears to the authority at that time that that section requires conditions to be included which are different from the subsisting conditions.

(2) Where the enforcing authority has decided to vary an authorisation under subsection (1) above the authority shall notify the holder of the authorisation and serve a variation notice on him.

(3) In this Part a "variation notice" is a notice served by the enforcing authority on the holder of an authorisation—

(*a*) specifying variations of the authorisation which the enforcing authority has decided to make; and

(*b*) specifying the date or dates on which the variations are to take effect;

and, unless the notice is withdrawn or is varied under subsection (3A) below, the variations specified in a variation notice shall take effect on the date or dates so specified.

(3A) An enforcing authority which has served a variation notice may vary that notice by serving on the holder of the authorisation in question a further notice—

(*a*) specifying the variations which the enforcing authority has decided to make to the variation notice; and

(*b*) specifying the date or dates on which the variations specified in the variation notice, as varied by the further notice, are to take effect;

and any reference in this Part to a variation notice, or to a variation notice served under subsection (2) above, includes a reference to such a notice as varied by a further notice served under this subsection.

(4) A variation notice served under subsection (2) above shall also—

(*a*) require the holder of the authorisation, within such period as may be specified in the notice, to notify the authority what action (if any) he proposes to take to ensure that the process is carried on in accordance with the authorisation as varied by the notice; and

(*b*) require the holder to pay, within such period as may be specified in the notice,—

(i) in a case where the enforcing authority is the Environment Agency or SEPA, the charge (if any) prescribed for the purpose by a charging scheme under section 41 of the Environment Act 1995; or

(ii) in any other case, the fee (if any) prescribed by a scheme under section 8 above.

(5) Where in the opinion of the enforcing authority any action to be taken by the holder of an authorisation in consequence of a variation notice served under subsection (2) above will involve a substantial change in the manner in which the process is being carried on, the enforcing authority shall notify the holder of its opinion.

(6) The Secretary of State may, if he thinks fit in relation to authorisations of any description or particular authorisations, direct the enforcing authorities—

(*a*) to exercise their powers under this section, or to do so in such circumstances as may be specified in the directions, in such manner as may be so specified; or

(*b*) not to exercise those powers, or not to do so in such circumstances or such manner as may be so specified;

and the Secretary of State shall have the corresponding power of direction in respect of the powers of the enforcing authorities to vary authorisations under section 11 below.

(7) In this section and section 11 below a "substantial change", in relation to a prescribed process being carried on under an authorisation, means a substantial change in the substances released from the process or in the amount or any other characteristic of any substance so released; and the Secretary of State may give directions to the enforcing authorities as to what does or does not constitute a substantial change in relation to processes generally, any description of process or any particular process.

(8) In this section and section 11 below—

"prescribed" means prescribed in regulations[1] made by the Secretary of State;

"vary",

(*a*) in relation to the subsisting conditions or other provisions of an authorisation, means adding to them or varying or rescinding any of them; and

(*b*) in relation to a variation notice, means adding to, or varying or rescinding the notice or any of its contents;

and "variation" shall be construed accordingly.*

[Environmental Protection Act 1990, s 10, as amended by the Environment Act 1995, Sch 22.]

***See note to s 1, ante.**

1. See the Environmental Protection (Applications, Appeals and Registers) Regulations 1991, SI 1991/507 amended by SI 1991/836, SI 1994/1271, SI 1996/667, 979, 2678 and SI 2000/656.

8–26252 **11. Variation of conditions etc: applications by holders of authorisations.** (1) A person carrying on a prescribed[1] process under an authorisation who wishes to make a relevant change in the process may at any time—

(*a*) notify the enforcing authority in the prescribed form of that fact, and

(*b*) request the enforcing authority to make a determination, in relation to the proposed change, of the matters mentioned in subsection (2) below;

and a person making a request under paragraph (*b*) above shall furnish the enforcing authority with such information as may be prescribed or as the authority may by notice require.

(2) On receiving a request under subsection (1) above the enforcing authority shall determine—

(*a*) whether the proposed change would involve a breach of any condition of the authorisation;

(*b*) if it would not involve such a breach, whether the authority would be likely to vary the conditions of the authorisation as a result of the change;

(*c*) if it would involve such a breach, whether the authority would consider varying the conditions of the authorisation so that the change may be made; and

(*d*) whether the change would involve a substantial change in the manner in which the process is being carried on;

and the enforcing authority shall notify the holder of the authorisation of its determination of those matters.

(3) Where the enforcing authority has determined that the proposed change would not involve a substantial change, but has also determined under paragraph (*b*) or (*c*) of subsection (2) above that the change would lead to or require the variation of the conditions of the authorisation, then—

(*a*) the enforcing authority shall (either on notifying its determination under that subsection or on a subsequent occasion) notify the holder of the authorisation of the variations which the authority is likely to consider making; and

(*b*) the holder may apply in the prescribed1 form to the enforcing authority for the variation of the conditions of the authorisation so that he may make the proposed change.

(4) Where the enforcing authority has determined that a proposed change would involve a substantial change that would lead to or require the variation of the conditions of the authorisation, then—

(*a*) the authority shall (either on notifying its determination under subsection (2) above or on a subsequent occasion) notify the holder of the authorisation of the variations which the authority is likely to consider making; and

(*b*) the holder of the authorisation shall, if he wishes to proceed with the change, apply in the prescribed form to the enforcing authority for the variation of the conditions of the authorisation.

(5) The holder of an authorisation may at any time, unless he is carrying on a prescribed process under the authorisation and wishes to make a relevant change in the process, apply to enforcing authority in the prescribed form for the variation of the conditions of the authorisation.

(6) A person carrying on a process under an authorisation who wishes to make a relevant change in the process may, where it appears to him that the change will require the variation of the conditions of the authorisation, apply to the enforcing authority in the prescribed form for the variation of the conditions of the authorisation specified in the application.

(7) A person who makes an application for the variation of the conditions of an authorisation shall furnish the authority with such information as may be prescribed1 or as the authority may by notice require.

(8) On an application for variation of the conditions of an authorisation under any provision of this section—

(*a*) the enforcing authority may, having fulfilled the requirements of Part II of Schedule 1 to this Act in cases to which they apply, as it thinks fit either refuse the application or, subject to the requirements of section 7 above, vary the conditions or, in the case of an application under subsection (6) above, treat the application as a request for a determination under subsection (2) above; and

(*b*) if the enforcing authority decides to vary the conditions, it shall serve a variation notice on the holder of the authorisation.

(9) (*Fees*).

(10) This section applies to any provision other than a condition which is contained in an authorisation as it applies to a condition with the modification that any reference to the breach of a condition shall be read as a reference to acting outside the scope of the authorisation.

(11) For the purposes of this section a relevant change in a prescribed process is a change in the manner of carrying on the process which is capable of altering the substances released from the process or of affecting the amount or any other characteristic of any substance so released.*

[Environmental Protection Act 1990, s 11, as amended by the Environment Act 1995, Sch 22.]

***See note to s 1, ante.**

1. The Environmental Protection (Applications, Appeals and Registers) Regulations 1991, SI 1991/507, amended by SI 1991/836, SI 1994/1271, SI 1996/667, 979, 2678 and SI 2000/656 have been made.

8–26253 **12. Revocation of authorisation.** (1) The enforcing authority may at any time revoke an authorisation by notice in writing to the person holding the authorisation.

(2) Without prejudice to the generality of subsection (1) above, the enforcing authority may revoke an authorisation where it has reason to believe that a prescribed process for which the authorisation is in force has not been carried on or not for a period of twelve months.

(3) The revocation of an authorisation under this section shall have effect from the date specified in the notice; and the period between the date on which the notice is served and the date so specified shall not be less than twenty-eight days.

(4) The enforcing authority may, before the date on which the revocation of an authorisation takes effect, withdraw the notice or vary the date specified in it.

(5) The Secretary of State may, if he thinks fit in relation to an authorisation, give to the enforcing authority directions as to whether the authority should revoke the authorisation under this section.*

[Environmental Protection Act 1990, s 12.]

***See note to s 1, ante.**

Enforcement

8–26254 **13. Enforcement notices.** (1) If the enforcing authority is of the opinion that the person carrying on a prescribed process under an authorisation is contravening any condition of the authorisation, or is likely to contravene any such condition, the authority may serve on him a notice ("an enforcement notice").

(2) An enforcement notice shall—

(*a*) state that the authority is of the said opinion;

(*b*) specify the matters constituting the contravention or the matters making it likely that the contravention will arise, as the case may be;

(*c*) specify the steps that must be taken to remedy the contravention or to remedy the matters making it likely that the contravention will arise, as the case may be; and

(*d*) specify the period within which those steps must be taken.

(3) The Secretary of State may, if he thinks fit in relation to the carrying on by any person of a prescribed process, give to the enforcing authority directions as to whether the authority should exercise its powers under this section and as to the steps which are to be required to be taken under this section.

(4) The enforcing authority may, as respects any enforcement notice it has issued to any person, by notice in writing served on that person, withdraw the notice.*

[Environmental Protection Act 1990, s 13, as amended by the Environment Act 1995, Sch 22.]

***See note to s 1, ante.**

8–26255 14. Prohibition notices. (1) If the enforcing authority is of the opinion, as respects the carrying on of a prescribed process under an authorisation, that the continuing to carry it on, or the continuing to carry it on in a particular manner, involves an imminent risk of serious pollution of the environment the authority shall serve a notice (a "prohibition notice") on the person carrying on the process.

(2) A prohibition notice may be served whether or not the manner of carrying on the process in question contravenes a condition of the authorisation and may relate to any aspects of the process, whether regulated by the conditions of the authorisation or not.

(3) A prohibition notice shall—

(*a*) state the authority's opinion;

(*b*) specify the risk involved in the process;

(*c*) specify the steps that must be taken to remove it and the period within which they must be taken; and

(*d*) direct that the authorisation shall, until the notice is withdrawn, wholly or to the extent specified in the notice cease to have effect to authorise the carrying on of the process;

and where the direction applies to part only of the process it may impose conditions to be observed in carrying on the part which is authorised to be carried on.

(4) The Secretary of State may, if he thinks fit in relation to the carrying on by any person of a prescribed process, give to the enforcing authority directions as to—

(*a*) whether the authority should perform its duties under this section; and

(*b*) the matters to be specified in any prohibition notice in pursuance of subsection (3) above which the authority is directed to issue.

(5) The enforcing authority shall, as respects any prohibition notice it has issued to any person, by notice in writing served on that person, withdraw the notice when it is satisfied that the steps required by the notice have been taken.*

[Environmental Protection Act 1990, s 14.]

***See note to s 1, ante.**

8–26256 15. Appeals as respects authorisations and against variation, enforcement and prohibition notices. (1)–(7) (Appeals to the Secretary of State).

(8) Where an appeal is brought under subsection (1) above against the revocation of an authorisation, the revocation shall not take effect pending the final determination or the withdrawal of the appeal.

(9) Where an appeal is brought under subsection (2) above against a notice, the bringing of the appeal shall not have the effect of suspending the operation of the notice.

(10) (*Regulations*)[1].*

[Environmental Protection Act 1990, s 15, as amended by the Environment Act 1995, Sch 22.]

***See note to s 1, ante.**

1. The Environmental Protection (Applications, Appeals and Registers) Regulations 1991, SI 1991/507, amended by SI 1991/836, SI 1994/1271, SI 1996/667, 979, 2678 and SI 2000/656 have been made.

8–26260 19. Obtaining of information from persons and authorities. (1) For the purposes of the discharge of his functions under this Part, the Secretary of State may, by notice in writing served on an enforcing authority, require the authority to furnish such information about the discharge of its functions as an enforcing authority under this Part as he may require.

(2) For the purposes of the discharge of their respective functions under this Part, the following authorities, that is to say—

(*a*) the Secretary of State,

(*b*) a local enforcing authority,

(*c*) the Environment Agency, and

(*d*) SEPA,

may, by notice in writing served on any person, require that person to furnish to the authority such information which the authority reasonably considers that it needs as is specified in the notice, in such form and within such period following service of the notice, or at such time, as is so specified.

(3) For the purposes of this section the discharge by the Secretary of State of an obligation of the United Kingdom under the Community Treaties or any international agreement relating to environmental protection shall be treated as a function of his under this Part.*

[Environmental Protection Act 1990, s 19, as amended by the Environment Act 1995, Sch 22.]

***See note to s 1, ante.**

Publicity

8–26261 20–22. *Public registers of information.**

***See note to s 1, ante.**

Provisions as to offences

8–26262 **23. Offences.** (1) It is an offence for a person—

(*a*) to contravene section 6(1) above;

(*b*) to fail to give the notice required by section 9(2) above;

(*c*) to fail to comply with or contravene any requirement or prohibition imposed by an enforcement notice or a prohibition notice;

(*d*)–(*f*) (*Repealed*);

(*g*) to fail, without reasonable excuse, to comply with any requirement imposed by a notice under section 19(2) above;

(*h*) to make a statement which he knows to be false or misleading in a material particular, or recklessly to make a statement which is false or misleading in a material particular, where the statement is made—

(i) in purported compliance with a requirement to furnish any information imposed by or under any provision of this Part; or

(ii) for the purpose of obtaining the grant of an authorisation to himself or any other person or the variation of an authorisation;

(i) intentionally to make a false entry in any record required to be kept under section 7 above;

(*j*) with intent to deceive, to forge or use a document issued or authorised to be issued under section 7 above or required for any purpose thereunder or to make or have in his possession a document so closely resembling any such document as to be likely to deceive;

(*k*) (Repealed);

(*l*) to fail to comply with an order made by a court under section 26 below.

(2) A person guilty of an offence under paragraph (*a*), (*c*) or (*l*) of subsection (1) above shall be liable[1]:

(*a*) on summary conviction, to a fine not exceeding £20,000 or to imprisonment for a term not exceeding three months, or to both;

(*b*) on conviction on indictment, to a fine or to imprisonment for a term not exceeding two years, or to both.

(3) A person guilty of an offence under paragraph (*b*), (*g*), (*h*), (i) or (*j*) of subsection (1) above shall be liable[1]—

(*a*) on summary conviction, to a fine not exceeding the statutory maximum;

(*b*) on conviction on indictment, to a fine or to imprisonment for a term not exceeding two years, or to both.

(4)–(5) (*Repealed*).*

[Environmental Protection Act 1990, s 23, as amended by the Environment Act 1995, Schs 22 and 24.]

***See note to s 1, ante.**

1. For procedure in respect of an offence triable either way; see the Magistrates' Courts Act 1980, ss 17A–21 in PART I: MAGISTRATES' COURTS, PROCEDURE, ante.

8–26263 **24.** *Enforcement by High Court.**

***See note to s 1, ante.**

8–26264 **25. Onus of proof as regards techniques and evidence.** (1) In any proceedings for an offence under section 23(1)(*a*) above consisting in a failure to comply with the general condition implied in every authorisation by section 7(4) above, it shall be for the accused to prove that there was no better available technique not entailing excessive cost than was in fact used to satisfy the condition.

(2) Where—

(*a*) an entry is required under section 7 above to be made in any record as to the observance of any condition of an authorisation; and

(*b*) the entry has not been made;

that fact shall be admissible as evidence that that condition has not been observed.*

[Environmental Protection Act 1990, s 25.]

***See note to s 1, ante.**

8–26265 **26. Power of court to order cause of offence to be remedied.** (1) Where a person is convicted of an offence under section 23(1)(*a*) or (*c*) above in respect of any matters which appear to the court to be matters which it is in his power to remedy, the court may, in addition to or instead of imposing any punishment, order him, within such time as may be fixed by the order, to take such steps as may be specified in the order for remedying those matters.

(2) The time fixed by an order under subsection (1) above may be extended or further extended by order of the court on an application made before the end of the time as originally fixed or as extended under this subsection, as the case may be.

(3) Where a person is ordered under subsection (1) above to remedy any matters, that person shall not be liable under section 23 above in respect of those matters in so far as they continue during the time fixed by the order or any further time allowed under subsection (2) above.*

[Environmental Protection Act 1990, s 26.]

***See note to s 1, ante.**

8–26266 **27. Power of appropriate Agency to remedy harm.** (1) Where the commission of an offence under section 23(1)(*a*) or (*c*) above causes any harm which it is possible to remedy, the appropriate Agency may subject to subsection (2) below—

(*a*) arrange for any reasonable steps to be taken towards remedying the harm; and

(*b*) recover the cost of taking those steps from any person convicted of that offence.

(2) The Environment Agency or SEPA, as the case may be, shall not exercise its powers under this section except with the approval in writing of the Secretary of State and, where any of the steps are to be taken on or will affect land in the occupation of any person other than the person on whose land the prescribed process is being carried on, with the permission of that person.*

[Environmental Protection Act 1990, s 27, as amended by the Environment Act 1995, Sch 22.]

***See note to s 1, ante.**

Authorisations and other statutory controls

8–26267 **28. Authorisations and other statutory controls.** (1) No condition shall at any time be attached to an authorisation so as to regulate the final disposal by deposit in or on land of controlled waste (within the meaning of Part II), nor shall any condition apply to such a disposal.

(2) Where any of the activities comprising a prescribed process are regulated both by an authorisation granted by the enforcing authority under this Part and by a registration or authorisation under the Radioactive Substances Act 1993, then, if different obligations are imposed as respects the same matter by a condition attached to the authorisation under this Part and a condition attached to the registration or authorisation under that Act, the condition imposed by the authorisation under this Part shall be treated as not binding the person carrying on the process.

(3)–(4) (*Repealed*).*

[Environmental Protection Act 1990, s 28, as amended by the Water Consolidation (Consequential Provisions) Act 1991, Sch 1, the Radioactive Substances Act 1993, Sch 4 and the Environment Act 1995, Schs 22 and 24.]

***See note to s 1, ante.**

PART II[1]
WASTE ON LAND

Preliminary

8–26268 **29. Preliminary.** (1) The following provisions have effect for the interpretation of this Part.

(2) The "environment" consists of all, or any, of the following media, namely land, water and the air.

(3) "Pollution of the environment" means pollution of the environment due to the release or escape (into any environment medium) from—

(*a*) the land on which controlled waste is treated,

(*b*) the land on which controlled waste is kept,

(*c*) the land in or on which controlled waste is deposited,

(*d*) fixed plant by means of which controlled waste is treated, kept or disposed of,

of substances or articles constituting or resulting from the waste and capable (by reason of the quantity or concentrations involved) of causing harm to man or any other living organisms supported by the environment.

(4) Subsection (3) above applies in relation to mobile plant by means of which controlled waste is treated or disposed of as it applies to plant on land by means of which controlled waste is treated or disposed of.

(5) For the purposes of subsections (3) and (4) above "harm" means harm to the health of living organisms or other interference with the ecological systems of which they form part and in the case of man includes offence to any of his senses or harm to his property; and "harmless" has a corresponding meaning.

(6) The "disposal" of waste includes its disposal by way of deposit in or on land and, subject to subsection (7) below, waste is "treated" when it is subjected to any process, including making it re-

usable or reclaiming substances from it and "recycle" (and cognate expressions) shall be construed accordingly.

(7) Regulations made by the Secretary of State may prescribe activities as activities which constitute the treatment of waste for the purposes of this Part or any provision of this Part prescribed in the regulations.

(8) "Land" includes land covered by waters where the land is above the low water mark of ordinary spring tides and references to land on which controlled waste is treated, kept or deposited are references to the surface of the land (including any structure set into the surface).

(9) "Mobile plant" means, subject to subsection (10) below, plant which is designed to move or be moved whether on roads or other land.

(10) Regulations[2] made by the Secretary of State may prescribe descriptions of plant which are to be treated as being, or as not being, mobile plant for the purposes of this Part.

(11) "Substance" means any natural or artificial substance, whether in solid or liquid form or in the form of a gas or vapour.

[Environmental Protection Act 1990, s 29.]

1. Part II consists of ss 29–78.

2. The Waste Management Licensing Regulations 1994, SI 1994/1056, amended by SI 1995/288 and 1950, SI 1996/593, 634, 972 and 1279, SI 1997/2203, SI 1998/606, 2746, SI 2000/1973, SI 2002/674, 1087 (Wales), 1559 and 2980 and SI 2003/595, 780 (W) and 2635, SI 2004/70 (W) and 3276 (E) and SI 2005/894, 1728, 1806 (W) and 2900 (E) have been made. Regulation 12 prescribes that only an incinerator exempted under the Environmental Protection (Prescribed Processes and Substances) Regulations 1991, SI 1991/472 as amended, shall be mobile plant for the purposes of Pt II of the 1990 Act.

8–26269 30. Authorities for purposes of this Part. (1) Any reference in this Part to a waste regulation authority—

(*a*) in relation to England and Wales, is a reference to the Environment Agency; and
(*b*) in relation to Scotland, is a reference to the Scottish Environment Protection Agency;

and any reference in this Part to the area of a waste regulation authority shall accordingly be taken as a reference to the area over which the Environment Agency or the Scottish Environment Protection Agency, as the case may be, exercises its functions or, in the case of any particular function, the function in question.

(2) For the purposes of this Part the following authorities are waste disposal authorities, namely—

(*a*) for any non-metropolitan county in England, the county council;
(*b*) in Greater London, the following—

(i) for the area of a London waste disposal authority, the authority constituted as the waste disposal authority for that area;
(ii) for the City of London, the Common Council;
(iii) for any other London borough, the council of the borough;

(*c*) in the metropolitan county of Greater Manchester, the following—

(i) for the metropolitan district of Wigan, the district council;
(ii) for all other areas in the county, the authority constituted as the Greater Manchester Waste Disposal Authority;

(*d*) for the metropolitan county of Merseyside, the authority constituted as the Merseyside Waste Disposal Authority;
(*e*) for any district in any other metropolitan county in England, the council of the district;
(*f*) for any county or county borough in Wales, the council of the county or county borough;
(*g*) *Scotland.*

(3) For the purposes of this Part the following authorities are waste collection authorities—

(*a*) for any district in England not within Greater London, the council of the district;
(*b*) in Greater London, the following—

(i) for any London borough, the council of the borough;
(ii) for the City of London, the Common Council;
(iii) for the Temples, the Sub-Treasurer of the Inner Temple and the Under Treasurer of the Middle Temple respectively;

(*bb*) for any county or county borough in Wales, the council of the county or county borough;
(*c*) *Scotland.*

(4) In this section references to particular authorities having been constituted as waste disposal authorities are references to their having been so constituted by the Waste Regulation and Disposal (Authorities) Order 1985 made by the Secretary of State under section 10 of the Local Government Act 1985 and the reference to London waste disposal authorities is a reference to the authorities named in Parts I, II, III, IV and V of Schedule 1 to that Order and this section has effect subject to any order made under the said section 10.

(5)–(8) *Repealed.*

[Environmental Protection Act 1990, s 30, as amended by the Local Government (Wales) Act 1994, Sch 9, the Environment Act 1995, Schs 22 and 24 and the Clean Neighbourhoods and Environment Act 2005, Sch 5.]

8–26270 32. *Repealed.*

Prohibition on unauthorised or harmful depositing, treatment or disposal of waste

8–26271 33. Prohibition on unauthorised or harmful deposit, treatment or disposal etc of waste. (1) Subject to subsection (2) and (3) below and, in relation to Scotland, to section 54 below, a person shall not—

(*a*) deposit controlled waste, or knowingly[1] cause or knowingly[1] permit controlled waste to be deposited in or on any land unless[2] a waste management licence authorising the deposit is in force and the deposit is in accordance with the licence;

(*b*) treat, keep or dispose of controlled waste, or knowingly cause or knowingly permit controlled waste to be treated, kept or disposed of—

(i) in or on any land, or

(ii) by means of any mobile plant,

except under and in accordance with a waste management licence;

(*c*) treat, keep or dispose of controlled waste in a manner likely to cause pollution of the environment or harm to human health.*

(2) Subsection (1) above does not apply in relation to household waste from a domestic property which is treated, kept or disposed of within the curtilage of the dwelling by or with the permission of the occupier of the dwelling.

(3) Subsection (1)(*a*), (*b*) or (*c*) above do not apply in cases prescribed[3] in regulations made by the Secretary of State and the regulations may make different exceptions for different areas.

(4) The Secretary of State, in exercising his power under subsection (3) above, shall have regard in particular to the expediency of excluding from the controls imposed by waste management licences—

(*a*) any deposits which are small enough or of such a temporary nature that they may be so excluded;

(*b*) any means of treatment or disposal which are innocuous enough to be so excluded;

(*c*) cases for which adequate controls are provided by another enactment than this section.

(5) Where controlled waste is carried in and deposited from a motor vehicle, the person who controls or is in a position to control the use of the vehicle shall, for the purposes of subsection (1)(*a*) above, be treated as knowingly causing the waste to be deposited whether or not he gave any instructions for this to be done[4].

(6) A person[5] who contravenes subsection (1) above or any condition of a waste management licence commits an offence.

(7) It shall be a defence for a person charged with an offence under this section to prove—

(*a*) that he took all reasonable precautions and exercised all due diligence to avoid the commission of the offence; or

(*b*) that he acted under instructions from his employer and neither knew nor had reason to suppose that the acts done by him constituted a contravention of subsection (1) above; or

(*c*) that the acts alleged to constitute the contravention were done in an emergency in order to avoid danger to human health in a case where—

(i) he took all such steps as were reasonably practicable in the circumstances for minimising pollution of the environment and harm to human health; and

(ii) particulars of the acts were furnished to the waste regulation authority as soon as reasonably practicable after they were done.

(8) Except in a case falling within subsection (9) below, a person who commits an offence under this section shall be liable[6]—

(*a*) on summary conviction, to imprisonment for a term not exceeding **six months** or a fine not exceeding **£40,000** or **both**; and

(*b*) on conviction on indictment, to imprisonment for a term not exceeding **two years** or a **fine** or **both**.

(9) A person who commits an offence under this section in relation to special waste shall be liable[5]—

(*a*) on summary conviction, to imprisonment for a term not exceeding **six months** or a fine not exceeding **£40,000** or **both**;

(*b*) on conviction on indictment, to imprisonment for a term not exceeding **five years** or a **fine** or **both**.

[Environmental Protection Act 1990, s 33, as amended by the Environment Act 1995, Sch 22 and the Antisocial Behaviour etc (Scotland) Act 2004, Sch 2.]

***Amended by the Environment Act 1995, Sch 24, post, when in force**.

1. The defendant is only required to have knowledge of the fact of the deposit and not of the breach of conditions. Therefore a company was liable where a site supervisor had wrongly discharged waste in breach of the licence conditions where it had knowledge that controlled waste was being caused or permitted to be deposited on its land. It was not necessary to prove that it had knowingly breached the conditions of the waste management licence or that it had any knowledge of the particular deposit of waste (*Shanks & McEwan (Teeside) Ltd v Environment Agency* [1997] 2 All ER 332, [1998] 2 WLR 452, [1997] Crim LR 684, DC).

2. The burden is on the prosecution to prove the type of waste deposited; as the matter does not involve reliance upon an exception or proviso the burden of proving that the waste deposited was not of the type alleged does not shift to the defendant. It will then be for the defendant to show whether the deposit comes within the terms of any licence held by him (*Environment Agency v M E Foley Contractors Ltd* [2002] EWHC 258 (Admin), [2002] 1 WLR 1754).

3. See the Controlled Waste Regulations 1992, SI 1992/588 amended by SI 1993/566, SI 1994/1056, SI 1995/288 and SI 1996/972, SI 2005/894, 1806 (W), 1820 (W) and 2900 (E) and SI 2006/123 (W).

The Waste Management Licensing Regulations 1994, SI 1994/1056 amended by SI 1995/288 and 1950, SI 1996/593, 634, 972 and 1279, SI 1997/2203, SI 1998/606 and 2746, SI 2000/1973, SI 2002/674, 1087 (Wales), 1559 and 2980, SI 2003/595, 780 (W) and 2635, SI 2004/70 (W) and 3276 (E) and SI 2005/894, 1728, 1806 (W) and 2900 (E), have been made. Regulation 16 exclude activities under other control regimes from waste management licensing whilst reg 17 provides that some other prescribed activities are exempt but do require registration under reg 18. Failure to register is an offence punishable on summary conviction by a fine not exceeding level 2.

4. Evidence that the defendant is the owner or keeper of a vehicle, such as in a response to a request for information by a notice under s 71, post, is capable, depending on the particular facts and absent evidence that the vehicle was stolen, or had been lent to another or was hired, of amounting to a prima facie case that the defendant controlled or was in a position to control the vehicle at the material time (*Environment Agency v Melland* [2002] EWHC 904 (Admin), [2002] RTR 425).

5. Any person and not only the licence holder is liable for prosecution so that where the operator is the person by whom the offence is committed, the licence holder who was not the operator, cannot be guilty of the offence (*Shanks McEwan (Midlands) Ltd v Wrexham Maelor Borough Council* (1996) Times, 10 April).

6. For procedure in respect of an offence triable either way, see the Magistrates' Courts Act 1980, ss 17A–21 in PART I: MAGISTRATES' COURTS, PROCEDURE, ante.

8–26271A 33A. Section 33 offences: investigation and enforcement costs. (1) This section applies where a person is convicted of an offence under section 33 above in respect of a contravention of subsection (1) of that section.

(2) The court by or before which the offender is convicted may make an order requiring him to pay to an enforcement authority a sum which appears to the court not to exceed the costs arising from—

(*a*) investigations of the enforcement authority which resulted in the conviction; and
(*b*) the seizure by the enforcement authority under section 34B below of a vehicle involved in the offence.

(3) The costs arising from the seizure of a vehicle as specified in subsection (2)(b) above may include the cost of disposing of the contents of the vehicle.

(4) The power of a court to make an order under this section is in addition to its power to make an order under section 18 of the Prosecution of Offences Act 1985 (award of costs against accused).

(5) In this section "enforcement authority" means the Environment Agency or a waste collection authority.

[Environmental Protection Act 1990, s 33A, as inserted by the Clean Neighbourhoods and Environment Act 2005, s 42.]

8–26271B 33B. Section 33 offences: clean-up costs. (1) This section applies where a person is convicted of an offence under section 33 above in respect of a contravention of subsection (1) of that section consisting of the deposit or disposal of controlled waste.

(2) The reference in section 130(1)(a) of the Powers of Criminal Courts (Sentencing) Act 2000 (compensation orders) to loss or damage resulting from the offence includes costs incurred or to be incurred by a relevant person in—

(*a*) removing the waste deposited or disposed of in or on the land;
(*b*) taking other steps to eliminate or reduce the consequences of the deposit or disposal; or
(*c*) both.

(3) In subsection (2) above "relevant person" means—

(*a*) the Environment Agency;
(*b*) a waste collection authority;
(*c*) the occupier of the land;
(*d*) the owner of the land (within the meaning of section 78A(9) below).

(4) The reference in subsection (2) above to costs incurred does not, in the case of the Environment Agency or a waste collection authority, include any costs which the Agency or authority has already recovered under section 59(8) below.

(5) In relation to the costs referred to in subsection (2) above, the reference in section 131(1) of the Powers of Criminal Courts (Sentencing) Act 2000 (limit on amount payable) to £5000 is instead to be construed as a reference to the amount of those costs (or, if the costs have not yet been incurred, the likely amount).

[Environmental Protection Act 1990, s 33B, as inserted by the Clean Neighbourhoods and Environment Act 2005, s 43.]

8–26271C 33C. Section 33 offences: forfeiture of vehicles. (1) This section applies where a person is convicted of an offence under section 33 above in respect of a contravention of subsection (1) of that section consisting of the deposit or disposal of controlled waste.

(2) The court by or before which the offender is convicted may make an order under this section if—

(*a*) the court is satisfied that a vehicle was used in or for the purposes of the commission of the offence; and

(*b*) at the time of his conviction the offender has rights in the vehicle.

(3) An order under this section operates to deprive the offender of his rights in the vehicle (including its fuel) at the time of his conviction and to vest those rights in the relevant enforcement authority.

(4) In a case where a vehicle has been seized under section 34B below and the offender retains rights in any of the vehicle's contents, an order under this section may, if and to the extent that it so specifies, deprive the offender of those rights and vest them in the relevant enforcement authority.

(5) Where an order under this section is made, the relevant enforcement authority may take possession of the vehicle (if it has not already done so under section 34C below).

(6) The court may make an order under this section whether or not it also deals with the offender in any other way in respect of the offence of which he is convicted.

(7) In considering whether to make an order under this section a court must in particular have regard to—

(*a*) the value of the vehicle;

(*b*) the likely financial and other effects on the offender of the making of the order (taken together with any other order that the court contemplates making);

(*c*) the offender's need to use the vehicle for lawful purposes;

(*d*) whether, in a case where it appears to the court that the offender is engaged in a business which consists wholly or partly in activities which are unlawful by virtue of section 33 above, the making of the order is likely to inhibit the offender from engaging in further such activities.

(8) Section 143 of the Powers of Criminal Courts (Sentencing) Act 2000 (power to deprive offender of property) does not apply in any case where this section applies.

(9) For the purposes of this section, where a vehicle or its contents have been seized under section 34B below in connection with the offence referred to in subsection (1) above, any transfer by the offender after the seizure and before his conviction of any of his rights in the vehicle or its contents is of no effect.

(10) In this section—

"relevant enforcement authority" means—

(*a*) the Environment Agency, where the proceedings in respect of the offence have been brought by or on behalf of the Agency, or

(*b*) in any other case, the waste collection authority in whose area the offence was committed;

"vehicle" means any motor vehicle or trailer within the meaning of the Road Traffic Regulation Act 1984 or any mobile plant.

[Environmental Protection Act 1990, s 33C, as inserted by the Clean Neighbourhoods and Environment Act 2005, s 44.]

Duty of care etc as respects waste

8–26272 34. Duty of care etc as respects waste[1]. (1) Subject to subsection (2) below, it shall be the duty of any person who imports, produces, carries, keeps, treats or disposes of controlled waste or, as a broker, has control of such waste, to take all such measures applicable to him in that capacity as are reasonable in the circumstances—

(*a*) to prevent any contravention by any other person of section 33 above;

(*aa*) to prevent any contravention by any other person of regulation 9 of the Pollution Prevention and Control (England and Wales) Regulations 2000 or of a condition of a permit granted under regulation 10 of those Regulations;

(*b*) to prevent the escape of the waste from his control or that of any other person; and

(*c*) on the transfer of the waste, to secure—

(i) that the transfer is only to an authorised person or to a person for authorised transport purposes; and

(ii) that there is transferred such a written description of the waste as will enable other persons to avoid a contravention of that section or any condition of a permit granted under regulation 10 of those Regulations and to comply with the duty under this subsection as respects the escape of waste.

(2) An occupier of domestic property—

(*a*) shall, as respects the household waste produced on the property, take reasonable steps to secure that any transfer of waste is only to an authorised person or to a person for authorised transport purposes; and (*b*) shall not otherwise be subject to the duty imposed by subsection (1) above.

(2A) It shall be the duty of the occupier of any domestic property in England or Wales to take all such measures available to him as are reasonable in the circumstances to secure that any transfer by him of household waste produced on the property is only to an authorised person or to a person for authorised transport purposes.

(3) The following are authorised persons for the purpose of subsection (1)(*c*) and (2A) above—*

(*a*) any authority which is a waste collection authority for the purposes of this Part;

(*b*) any person who is the holder of a waste management licence under section 35 below or of a disposal licence under section 5 of the Control of Pollution Act 1974**;

(*c*) any person to whom section 33(1) above does not apply by virtue of regulations under subsection (3) of that section;

(*d*) any person registered as a carrier of controlled waste under section 2 of the Control of Pollution (Amendment) Act 1989;

(*e*) any person who is not required to be so registered by virtue of regulations under section 1(3) of that Act; and

(*f*) a waste disposal authority in Scotland.

(3A) The Secretary of State may by regulations amend subsection (3) above so as to add, whether generally or in such circumstances as may be prescribed in the regulations, any person specified in the regulations, or any description of person so specified, to the persons who are authorised persons for the purposes of subsection (1)(*c*) and (2A) above.*

(4) The following are authorised transport purposes for the purposes of subsection (1)(*c*) and (2A) above—*

(*a*) the transport of controlled waste within the same premises between different places in those premises;

(*b*) the transport to a place in Great Britain of controlled waste which has been brought from a country or territory outside Great Britain not having been landed in Great Britain until it arrives at that place; and

(*c*) the transport by air or sea of controlled waste from a place in Great Britain to a place outside Great Britain;

and "transport" has the same meaning in this subsection as in the Control of Pollution (Amendment) Act 1989.

(4A) For the purposes of subsection (1)(*c*)(ii) above—

(*a*) a transfer of waste in stages shall be treated as taking place when the first stage of the transfer takes place, and

(*b*) a series of transfers between the same parties of waste of the same description shall be treated as a single transfer taking place when the first of the transfers in the series takes place[2].

(5) The Secretary of State may, by regulations[3], make provision imposing requirements on any person who is subject to the duty imposed by subsection (1) above as respects the making and retention of documents and the furnishing of documents or copies of documents.

(6) Any person who fails to comply with the duty imposed by subsection (1) or (2A) above or with any requirement imposed under subsection (5) above shall be liable[4]—

(*a*) on summary conviction, to a fine not exceeding the **statutory maximum**; and

(*b*) on conviction on indictment, to a **fine**.

(7) The Secretary of State shall, after consultation with such persons or bodies as appear to him representative of the interests concerned, prepare and issue a code of practice for the purpose of providing to persons practical guidance on how to discharge the duty imposed on them by subsection (1) above.

(8) The Secretary of State may from time to time revise a code of practice issued under subsection (7) above by revoking, amending or adding to the provisions of the code.

(9) A code of practice prepared in pursuance of subsection (7) above shall be laid before:

(*a*) both Houses of Parliament; or

(*b*) if it relates only to Scotland before the Scottish Parliament.

(10) A code of practice issued under subsection (7) above shall be admissible in evidence and if any provision of such a code appears to the court to be relevant to any question arising in the proceedings it shall be taken into account in determining that question.

(11) Different codes of practice may be prepared and issued under subsection (7) above for different areas.

[Environmental Protection Act 1990, s 34, as amended by the Deregulation and Contracting Out Act 1994, s 33, the Environment Act 1995, Sch 22, SI 1999/1820 and SI 2000/1973.]

***Reproduced as in force in England and Wales.**

****Repealed by Environmental Protection Act 1990, Sch 16 as from a day to be appointed.**

1. The duty in this section and the exceptions to it, are modified by the Controlled Waste Regulations 1992, SI 1992/588

amended by SI 1993/566, SI 1994/1056, SI 1996/972, SI 2005/894, 1806 (W), 1820 (W) and 2900 (E) and SI 2006/123 (W).

2. This provision does not apply in relation to any proceedings for failure to comply with the duty imposed by s 34(1) which were commenced before 3 November 1994 and, where any proceedings have not been disposed of before that date, it shall be a defence to show that the conduct in question would not have constituted a breach of the duty prior to that date.

3. The Environmental Protection (Duty of Care) Regulations 1991, SI 1991/2839 amended by SI 1996/972, SI 2000/2973 and SI 2005/894, 1806 (W), 1820 (W) and 2900 (E) and SI 2000/2973 have been made.

4. For procedure in respect of an offence either way, see the Magistrates' Courts Act 1980 ss 17A–21 in PART I: MAGISTRATES' COURTS, PROCEDURE, ante.

Waste Management Licences

8–26273 35. Waste management licences: general. (1) A waste management licence is a licence granted by a waste regulation authority authorising the treatment, keeping or disposal of any specified description of controlled waste in or on specified land or the treatment or disposal of any specified description of controlled waste by means of specified mobile plant.

(2) A licence shall be granted to the following person, that is to say—

(*a*) in the case of a licence relating to the treatment, keeping or disposal of waste in or on land, to the person who is in occupation of the land; and

(*b*) in the case of a licence relating to the treatment or disposal of waste by means of mobile plant, to the person who operates the plant.

(3) A licence shall be granted on such terms and subject to such conditions as appear to the waste regulation authority to be appropriate and the conditions may relate—

(*a*) to the activities which the licence authorises, and

(*b*) to the precautions to be taken and works to be carried out in connection with or in consequence of those activities;

and accordingly requirements may be imposed in the licence which are to be complied with before the activities which the licence authorises have begun or after the activities which the licence authorises have ceased.

(4) Conditions may require the holder of a licence to carry out works or do other things notwithstanding that he is not entitled to carry out the works or do the thing and any person whose consent would be required shall grant, or join in granting, the holder of the licence such rights in relation to the land as will enable the holder of the licence to comply with any requirements imposed on him by the licence.

(5) Conditions may relate, where waste other than controlled waste is to be treated, kept or disposed of, to the treatment, keeping or disposal of that other waste.

(6) The Secretary of State may, by regulations[1], make provision as to the conditions which are, or are not, to be included in a licence; and regulations under this subsection may make different provision for different circumstances.

(7) The Secretary of State may, as respects any licence for which an application is made to a waste regulation authority, give to the authority directions as to the terms and conditions which are, or are not, to be included in the licence; and it shall be the duty of the authority to give effect to the directions.

(7A) In any case where—

(*a*) an entry is required under this section to be made in any record as to the observance of any condition of a licence, and

(*b*) the entry has not been made,

that fact shall be admissible as evidence that that condition has not been observed.

(7B) Any person who—

(*a*) intentionally makes a false entry in any record required to be kept under any condition of a licence, or

(*b*) with intent to deceive, forges or uses a licence or makes or has in his possession a document so closely resembling a licence as to be likely to deceive,

shall be guilty of an offence.

(7C) A person guilty of an offence under subsection (7B) above shall be liable[2]—

(*a*) on summary conviction, to a fine not exceeding **the statutory maximum**;

(*b*) on conviction on indictment, to a fine or to imprisonment for a term not exceeding **two years**, or to **both**.

(8) It shall be the duty of waste regulation authorities to have regard to any guidance issued to them by the Secretary of State with respect to the discharge of their functions in relation to licences.

(9) A licence may not be surrendered by the holder except in accordance with section 39 below.

(10) A licence is not transferable by the holder but the waste regulation authority may transfer it to another person under section 40 below.

(11) A licence shall continue in force until it ceases to have effect under subsection (11A) below, it is revoked entirely by the waste regulation authority under section 38 below or it is surrendered or its surrender is accepted under section 39 below.

(11A) A licence shall cease to have effect if and to the extent that the treatment, keeping or disposal of waste authorised by the licence is authorised by a permit granted under regulations under section 2 of the Pollution Prevention and Control Act 1999.

(12) In this Part "licence" means a waste management licence and "site licence" and "mobile plant licence" mean, respectively, a licence authorising the treatment, keeping or disposal of waste in or on land and a licence authorising the treatment or disposal of waste by means of mobile plant.
[Environmental Protection Act 1990, s 35, as amended by the Environment Act 1995, Sch 22 and SI 2000/1973.]

---

1. The Waste Management Licensing Regulations 1994, SI 1994/1056 amended by SI 1995/288 and 1950, SI 1996/593, 634, 972 and 1279, SI 1997/2203, SI 1998/606 and 2746, SI 2000/1973, SI 2002/674, 1087 (Wales), 1559 and 2980, SI 2003/595, 780 (W) and 2635, SI 2004/70 (W) and 3276 (E) and SI 2005/894, 1728, 1806 (W) and 2900 (E) have been made.

2. For procedure in respect of an offence which is triable either way, see the Magistrates' Courts Act 1980, ss 17A–21, in PART I: MAGISTRATES' COURTS, PROCEDURE, ante.

8–26274 35A. *Compensation where rights granted pursuant to section 35(4) or 38(9A).*

8–26275 36. Grant of licences. (1) An application for a licence shall be made—

(*a*) in the case of an application for a site licence, to the waste regulation authority in whose area the land is situated; and

(*b*) in the case of an application for a mobile plant licence, to the waste regulation authority in whose area the operator of the plant has his principal place of business;

and shall be made on a form provided for the purpose by the waste regulation authority and accompanied by such information as that authority reasonably requires and the charge prescribed for the purpose by a charging scheme under section 41 of the Environment Act 1995.

(1A) Where an applicant for a licence fails to provide the waste regulation authority with any information required under subsection (1) above, the authority may refuse to proceed with the application, or refuse to proceed with it until the information is provided.

(2) A licence shall not be issued for a use of land for which planning permission is required in pursuance of the Town and County Planning Act 1990 or the Town and Country Planning (Scotland) Act 1972 unless—

(*a*) such planning permission is in force in relation to that use of the land, or

(*b*) an established use certificate is in force under section 192 of the said Act of 1990 or section 90 of the said Act of 1972 in relation to that use of the land.

(3) Subject to subsection (2) above and subsection (4) below, a waste regulation authority to which an application for a licence has been duly made shall not reject the application if it is satisfied that the applicant is a fit and proper person unless it is satisfied that its rejection is necessary for the purpose of preventing—

(*a*) pollution of the environment;

(*b*) harm to human health; or

(*c*) serious detriment to the amenities of the locality;

but paragraph (*c*) above is inapplicable where planning permission is in force in relation to the use to which the land will be put under the licence.

(4) Where the waste regulation authority proposes to issue a licence, the authority must, before it does so,—

(*a*) refer the proposal to the appropriate planning authority and the Health and Safety Executive; and

(*b*) consider any representations about the proposal which the authority or the Executive makes to it during the allowed period.

(5)–(6) *Repealed.*

(7) Where any part of the land to be used is within a site of scientific interest (within the meaning of the Wildlife and Countryside Act 1981) and the waste regulation authority proposes to issue a licence, the authority must, before it does so—

(*a*) refer the proposal to the appropriate nature conservation body; and

(*b*) consider any representations about the proposal which the body makes to it during the allowed period;

and in this section any reference to the appropriate nature conservation body is a reference to English Nature, the Nature Conservancy Council for Scotland or the Countryside Council for Wales, according as the land is situated in England, Scotland or Wales.

(8) Until the date appointed under section 131(3) below any reference in subsection (7) above to the appropriate nature conservation body is a reference to the Nature Conservancy Council.*

(9) If within the period of four months beginning with the date on which a waste regulation authority received an application for the grant of a licence, or within such longer period as the authority and the applicant may at any time agree in writing, the authority has neither granted the

licence in consequence of the application nor given notice to the applicant that the authority has rejected the application, the authority shall be deemed to have rejected the application.

(9A) Subsection (9) above—

(*a*) shall not have effect in any case where, by virtue of subsection (1A) above, the waste regulation authority refuses to proceed with the application in question, and

(*b*) shall have effect in any case where, by virtue of subsection (1A) above, the waste regulation authority refuses to proceed with it until the required information is provided, with the substitution for the period of four months there mentioned of the period of four months beginning with the date on which the authority received the information.

(10) The period allowed to the appropriate planning authority, the Health and Safety Executive or the appropriate nature conservancy body for the making of representations under subsection (4) or (7) above about a proposal is the period of twenty-eight days beginning with the day on which the proposal is received by the waste regulation authority or such longer period as the waste regulation authority, the appropriate planning authority, the Executive or the body, as the case may be, agree in writing.

(11) In this section—

"the appropriate planning authority" means—

(*a*) where the relevant land is situated in the area of a London borough council, that London borough council;

(*b*) where the relevant land is situated in the City of London, the Common Council of the City of London;

(*c*) where the relevant land is situated in a non-metropolitan county in England, the council of that county;

(*d*) where the relevant land is situated in a National Park or the Broads, the National Park authority for that National Park or, as the case may be, the Broads Authority;

(*e*) where the relevant land is situated elsewhere in England or Wales, the council of the district or, in Wales, the county or county borough, in which the land is situated;

(*f*) where the relevant land is situated in Scotland, the council constituted under section 2 of the Local Government etc. (Scotland) Act 1994 for the area in which the land is situated;

"the Broads" has the same meaning as in the Norfolk and Suffolk Broads Act 1988;

"National Park authority" means a National Park authority established under section 63 of the Environment Act 1995 which has become the local planning authority for the National Park in question;

"the relevant land" means—

(*a*) in relation to a site licence, the land to which the licence relates; and

(*b*) in relation to a mobile plant licence, the principal place of business of the operator of the plant to which the licence relates.

(12) *Repealed.*

(13) The Secretary of State may by regulations amend the definition of "appropriate planning authority" in subsection (11) above.

(14) This section shall have effect subject to section 36A below.

[Environmental Protection Act 1990, s 36, as amended by the Environment Act 1995, Sch 22 and Sch 24 and the Countryside and Rights of Way Act 2000, Sch 10.]

***Repealed by the Environment Protection Act 1990, Sch 16, from a date to be appointed.**

1. See the Waste Management Licensing Regulations 1994, SI 1994/1056 amended by SI 1995/288 and 1950, SI 1996/593, 634, 972 and 1279, SI 1997/2203, SI 1998/606 and 2746, SI 2000/1973, SI 2002/674, 1087 (Wales), 1559 and 2980 and SI 2003/595, 780 (W) and 2635, SI 2004/70 (W) and 3276 (E) and SI 2005/894, 1728, 1806 (W) and 2900 (E).

8–26276 36A. *Consultation before the grant of certain licences.*

8–26277 37. Variation of licences. (1) While a licence issued by a waste regulation authority is in force, the authority may, subject to regulations under section 35(6) above and to subsection (3) below—

(*a*) on its own initiative, modify the conditions of the licence to any extent which, in the opinion of the authority, is desirable and is unlikely to require unreasonable expense on the part of the holder; and

(*b*) on the application of the licence holder accompanied by the charge prescribed for the purpose by a charging scheme under section 41 of the Environment Act 1995, modify the conditions of his licence to the extent requested in the application.

(2) While a licence issued by a waste regulation authority is in force the authority shall, except where it revokes the licence entirely under section 38 below, modify the conditions of the licence—

(*a*) to the extent which in the opinion of the authority is required for the purpose of ensuring that the activities authorised by the licence do not cause pollution of the environment or harm to human health or become seriously detrimental to the amenities of the locality affected by the activities; and

(*b*) to the extent required by any regulations in force under section 35(6) above.

(3) The Secretary of State may, as respects any licence issued by a waste regulation authority, give to the authority directions as to the modifications which are to be made in the conditions of the licence under subsection (1)(*a*) or (2)(*a*) above; and it shall be the duty of the authority to give effect to the directions.

(4) Any modification of a licence under this section shall be effected by notice served on the holder of the licence and the notice shall state the time at which the modification is to take effect.

(5) Section 36(4), (7) and (10) above shall with the necessary modifications apply to a proposal by a waste regulation authority to modify a licence under subsection (1) or (2)(*a*) above as they apply to a proposal to issue a licence, except that—

(*a*) the authority may postpone the reference so far as the authority considers that by reason of an emergency it is appropriate to do so; and

(*b*) the authority need not consider any representations as respects a modification which, in the opinion of the waste regulation authority, will not affect any authority mentioned in the subsections so applied.

(6) If within the period of two months beginning with the date on which a waste regulation authority received an application by the holder of a licence for a modification of it, or within such longer period as the authority and the applicant may at any time agree in writing, the authority has neither granted a modification of the licence in consequence of the application nor given notice to the applicant that the authority has rejected the application, the authority shall be deemed to have rejected the application.

(7) This section shall have effect subject to section 37A below.

[Environmental Protection Act 1990, s 37, as amended by the Environment Act 1995, Schs 22 and 24.]

8–26277A 37A. *Consultation before certain variations.*

8–26278 38. Revocation and suspension of licences. (1) Where a licence granted by a waste regulation authority is in force and it appears to the authority—

(*a*) that the holder of the licence has ceased to be a fit and proper person by reason of his having been convicted of a relevant offence; or

(*b*) that the continuation of the activities authorised by the licence would cause pollution of the environment or harm to human health or would be seriously detrimental to the amenities of the locality affected; and

(*c*) that the pollution, harm or detriment cannot be avoided by modifying the conditions of the licence;

the authority may exercise, as it thinks fit, either of the powers conferred by subsections (3) and (4) below.

(2) Where a licence granted by a waste regulation authority is in force and it appears to the authority that the holder of the licence has ceased to be a fit and proper person by reason of the management of the activities authorised by the licence having ceased to be in the hands of a technically competent person, the authority may exercise the power conferred by subsection (3) below.

(3) The authority may, under this subsection, revoke the licence so far as it authorises the carrying on of the activities specified in the licence or such of them as the authority specifies in revoking the licence.

(4) The authority may, under this subsection, revoke the licence entirely.

(5) A licence revoked under subsection (3) above shall cease to have effect to authorise the carrying on of the activities specified in the licence or, as the case may be, the activities specified by the authority in revoking the licence but shall not affect the requirements imposed by the licence which the authority, in revoking the licence, specify as requirements which are to continue to bind the licence holder.

(6) Where a licence granted by a waste regulation authority is in force and it appears to the authority—

(*a*) that the holder of the licence has ceased to be a fit and proper person by reason of the management of the activities authorised by the licence having ceased to be in the hands of a technically competent person; or

(*b*) that serious pollution of the environment or serious harm to human health has resulted from, or is about to be caused by, the activities to which the licence relates or the happening or threatened happening of an event affecting those activities; and

(*c*) that the continuing to carry on those activities, or any of those activities, in the circumstances will continue or, as the case may be, cause serious pollution of the environment or serious harm to human health;

the authority may suspend the licence so far as it authorises the carrying on of the activities specified in the licence or such of them as the authority specifies in suspending the licence.

(7) The Secretary of State may, if he thinks fit in relation to a licence granted by a waste regulation authority, give to the authority directions as to whether and in what manner the authority should exercise its powers under this section; and it shall be the duty of the authority to give effect to the directions.

(8) A licence suspended under subsection (6) above shall, while the suspension has effect, be of no effect to authorise the carrying on of the activities specified in the licence or, as the case may be, the activities specified by the authority in suspending the licence.

(9) Where a licence is suspended under subsection (6) above, the authority, in suspending it or at any time while it is suspended, may require the holder of the licence to take such measures to deal with or avert the pollution or harm as the authority considers necessary.

(9A) A requirement imposed under subsection (9) above may require the holder of a licence to carry out works or do other things notwithstanding that he is not entitled to carry out the works or do the thing and any person whose consent would be required shall grant, or join in granting, the holder of the licence such rights in relation to the land as will enable the holder of the licence to comply with any requirements imposed on him under that subsection.

(9B) Subsections (2) to (8) of section 36A above shall, with the necessary modifications, apply where the authority proposes to impose a requirement under subsection (9) above which may require the holder of a licence to carry out any such works or do any such thing as is mentioned in subsection (9A) above as they apply where the authority proposes to issue a licence subject to any such condition as is mentioned in subsection (1) of that section, but as if—

(*a*) the reference in subsection (3) of that section to section 35(4) above were a reference to subsection (9A) above; and

(*b*) any reference in those subsections—

(i) to the condition, or the condition in question, were a reference to the requirement; and

(ii) to issuing a licence were a reference to serving a notice, under subsection (12) below, effecting the requirement.

(9C) The authority may postpone the service of any notice or the consideration of any representations required under section 36A above, as applied by subsection (9B) above, so far as the authority considers that by reason of an emergency it is appropriate to do so.

(10) A person who, without reasonable excuse, fails to comply with any requirement imposed under subsection (9) above otherwise than in relation to special waste shall be liable[1]—

(*a*) on summary conviction, to a fine of an amount not exceeding the **statutory maximum**; and

(*b*) on conviction on indictment, to imprisonment for a term not exceeding **two years** or a **fine** or **both**.

(11) A person who, without reasonable excuse, fails to comply with any requirement imposed under subsection (9) above in relation to special waste shall be liable[1]—

(*a*) on summary conviction, to imprisonment for a term not exceeding six months or a fine not exceeding the **statutory maximum** or **both**; and

(*b*) on conviction on indictment, to imprisonment for a term not exceeding **five years** or a **fine** or **both**.

(12) Any revocation or suspension of a licence or requirement imposed during the suspension of a licence under this section shall be effected by notice served on the holder of the licence and the notice shall state the time at which the revocation or suspension or the requirement is to take effect and, in the case of suspension, the period at the end of which, or the event on the occurrence of which, the suspension is to cease.

(13) If a waste regulation authority is of the opinion that proceedings for an offence under subsection (10) or (11) above would afford an ineffectual remedy against a person who has failed to comply with any requirement imposed under subsection (9) above, the authority may take proceedings in the High Court or, in Scotland, in any court of competent jurisdiction for the purpose of securing compliance with the requirement.

[Environmental Protection Act 1990, s 38, as amended by the Environment Act 1995, Sch 22.]

1. For procedure in respect of an offence triable either way, see the Magistrates' Courts Act 1980, ss 17A–21 in PART I: MAGISTRATES' COURTS, PROCEDURE, ante.

8–26279 **39. Surrender of licences.** (1) A licence may be surrendered by its holder to the authority which granted it but, in the case of a site licence, only if the authority accepts the surrender.

(2) The following provisions apply to the surrender and acceptance of the surrender of a site licence.

(3) The holder of a site licence who desires to surrender it shall make an application for that purpose to the authority on a form provided by the authority for the purpose, giving such information and accompanied by such evidence as the authority reasonably requires and accompanied by the charge prescribed for the purpose by a charging scheme under section 41 of the Environment Act 1995.

(4) An authority which receives an application for the surrender of a site licence—

(*a*) shall inspect the land to which the licence relates, and

(*b*) may require the holder of the licence to furnish to it further information or further evidence.

(5) The authority shall determine whether it is likely or unlikely that the condition of the land, so far as that condition is the result of the use of the land for the treatment, keeping or disposal of waste (whether or not in pursuance of the licence), will cause pollution of the environment or harm to human health.

(6) If the authority is satisfied that the condition of the land is unlikely to cause the pollution or harm mentioned in subsection (5) above, the authority shall, subject to subsection (7) below, accept the surrender of the licence; but otherwise the authority shall refuse to accept it.

(7) Where the authority proposes to accept the surrender of a site licence, the authority must, before it does so,—

(*a*) refer the proposal to the appropriate planning authority; and

(*b*) consider any representations about the proposal which the appropriate planning authority makes to it during the allowed period;

(8) (*Repealed*).

(9) Where the surrender of a licence is accepted under this section the authority shall issue to the applicant, with the notice of its determination, a certificate (a "certificate of completion") stating that it is satisfied as mentioned in subsection (6) above and, on the issue of that certificate, the licence shall cease to have effect.

(10) If within the period of three months beginning with the date on which an authority receives an application to surrender a licence, or within such longer period as the authority and the applicant may at any time agree in writing, the authority has neither issued a certificate of completion nor given notice to the applicant that the authority has rejected the application, the authority shall be deemed to have rejected the application.

(11) Section 36(10) above applies for the interpretation of the "allowed period" in subsection (7) above.

(12) In this section—

"the appropriate planning authority" means—

(*a*) where the relevant land is situated in the area of a London borough council, that London borough council;

(*b*) where the relevant land is situated in the City of London, the Common Council of the City of London;

(*c*) where the relevant land is situated in a non-metropolitan county in England, the council of that county;

(*d*) where the relevant land is situated in a National Park or the Broads, the National Park authority for that National Park or, as the case may be, the Broads Authority;

(*e*) where the relevant land is situated elsewhere in England or Wales, the council of the district or, in Wales, the county or county borough, in which the land is situated;

(*f*) where the relevant land is situated in Scotland, the council constituted under section 2 of the Local Government etc. (Scotland) Act 1994 for the area in which the land is situated;

"the Broads" has the same meaning as in the Norfolk and Suffolk Broads Act 1988;

"National Park authority" means a National Park authority established under section 63 of the Environment Act 1995 which has become the local planning authority for the National Park in question;

"the relevant land", in the case of any site licence, means the land to which the licence relates.

(13) (*Repealed*).

(14) The Secretary of State may by regulations amend the definition of "appropriate planning authority" in subsection (12) above.

[Environmental Protection Act 1990, s 39, as amended by the Environment Act 1995, Schs 22 and 24.]

---

1. See the Waste Management Licensing Regulations 1994, SI 1994/1056 amended by SI 1995/288 and 1950, SI 1996/593, 634, 972 and 1279, SI 1997/2203, SI 1998/606 and 2746, SI 2000/1973, SI 2002/674, 1087 (Wales), 1559 and 2980 and SI 2003/595, 780 (W) and 2635, SI 2004/70 (W) and 3276 (E) and SI 2005/894, 1728, 1806 (W) and 2900 (E).

8–26280 **40.** *Transfer of licences.*

8–26281 **42. Supervision of licensed activities.** (1) While a licence is in force it shall be the duty of the waste regulation authority which granted the licence to take the steps needed—

(*a*) for the purpose of ensuring that the activities authorised by the licence do not cause pollution of the environment or harm to human health or become seriously detrimental to the amenities of the locality affected by the activities; and

(*b*) for the purpose of ensuring that the conditions of the licence are complied with.

(2) (*Repealed*).

(3) For the purpose of performing the duty imposed on it by subsection (1) above, any officer of

the authority authorised in writing for the purpose by the authority may, if it appears to him that by reason of an emergency it is necessary to do so, carry out work on the land or in relation to plant or equipment on the land to which the licence relates or, as the case may be, in relation to the mobile plant to which the licence relates.

(4) Where a waste regulation authority incurs any expenditure by virtue of subsection (3) above, the authority may recover the amount of the expenditure from the holder, or (as the case may be) the former holder, of the licence, except where the holder or former holder of the licence shows that there was no emergency requiring any work or except such of the expenditure as he shows was unnecessary.

(5) Where it appears to a waste regulation authority that a condition of a licence granted by it is not being complied with, or is likely not to be complied with, then, without prejudice to any proceedings under section 33(6) above, the authority may—

(*a*) serve on the holder of the licence a notice—

(i) stating that the authority is of the opinion that a condition of the licence is not being complied with or, as the case may be, is likely not to be complied with;

(ii) specifying the matters which constitute the non-compliance or, as the case may be, which make the anticipated non-compliance likely;

(iii) specifying the steps which must be taken to remedy the non-compliance or, as the case may be, to prevent the anticipated non-compliance from occurring; and

(iv) specifying the period within which those steps must be taken; and

(*b*) if in the opinion of the authority the licence holder has not taken the steps specified in the notice within the period so specified, exercise any of the powers specified in subsection (6) below.

(6) The powers which become exercisable in the event mentioned in subsection (5)(*b*) above are the following—

(*a*) to revoke the licence so far as it authorises the carrying on of the activities specified in the licence or such of them as the authority specifies in revoking the licence;

(*b*) to revoke the licence entirely; and

(*c*) to suspend the licence so far as it authorises the carrying on of the activities specified in the licence or, as the case may be, the activities specified by the authority in suspending the licence.

(6A) If a waste regulation authority is of the opinion that revocation or suspension of the licence, whether entirely or to any extent, under subsection (6) above would afford an ineffectual remedy against a person who has failed to comply with any requirement imposed under subsection (5)(*a*) above, the authority may take proceedings in the High Court or, in Scotland, in any court of competent jurisdiction for the purpose of securing compliance with the requirement.

(7) Where a licence is revoked or suspended under subsection (6) above, subsections (5) and (12) or, as the case may be, subsections (8) to (12) of section 38 above shall apply with the necessary modifications as they respectively apply to revocations or suspensions of licences under that section.

(8) The Secretary of State may, if he thinks fit in relation to a licence granted by a waste regulation authority, give to the authority directions as to whether and in what manner the authority should exercise its powers under this section; and it shall be the duty of the authority to give effect to the directions.

[Environmental Protection Act 1990, s 42, as amended by the Environment Act 1995, Sch 22 and Sch 24.]

8–26282 **43.** *Appeals to Secretary of State from decisions with respect to licences.*

8–26283 **44. Offences of making false or misleading statements or false entries.** (1) A person who—

(*a*) in purported compliance with a requirement to furnish any information imposed by or under any provision of this Part, or

(*b*) for the purpose of obtaining for himself or another any grant of a licence, any modification of the conditions of a licence, any acceptance of the surrender of a licence or any transfer of a licence,

makes a statement which he knows to be false or misleading in a material particular, or recklessly makes any statement which is false or misleading in a material particular, commits an offence.

(2) A person who intentionally makes a false entry in any record required to be kept by virtue of a licence commits an offence.

(3) A person who commits an offence under this section shall be liable[1]—

(*a*) on summary conviction, to a fine not exceeding **the statutory maximum**;

(*b*) on conviction on indictment, to a fine or to imprisonment for a term not exceeding **two years**, or to **both**.

[Environmental Protection Act 1990, s 44 as substituted by the Environment Act 1995, Sch 19.]

1. For procedure in respect of an offence which is triable either way, see the Magistrates' Courts Act 1980, ss 17A–21, in PART I: MAGISTRATES' COURTS, PROCEDURE, ante.

8–26283A **44A. National waste strategy: England and Wales.** Secretary of State to prepare a statement—"the strategy"—containing policies in relation to the recovery and disposal of waste in England and Wales.*
[Environmental Protection Act 1990, s 44A as inserted by the Environment Act 1995, Sch 19.]

* **Sections 44ZA–D about integrated waste management plans inserted in relation to Scotland by the Local Government in Scotland Act 2003, s 34.**

Collection, disposal or treatment of controlled waste

8–26284 **45. Collection of controlled waste.** (1) It shall be the duty of each waste collection authority—

(*a*) to arrange for the collection of household waste in its area except waste—

(i) which is situated at a place which in the opinion of the authority is so isolated or inaccessible that the cost of collecting it would be unreasonably high, and

(ii) as to which the authority is satisfied that adequate arrangements for its disposal have been or can reasonably be expected to be made by a person who controls the waste; and

(*b*) if requested by the occupier of premises in its area to collect any commercial waste from the premises, to arrange for the collection of the waste.

(2) Each waste collection authority may, if requested by the occupier of premises in its area to collect any industrial waste from the premises, arrange for the collection of the waste; but a collection authority in England and Wales shall not exercise the power except with the consent of the waste disposal authority whose area includes the area of the waste collection authority.

(3) *No charge shall be made for the collection of household waste except in cases prescribed in regulations*[1] *made by the Secretary of State.*

(4) *Charges for the collection and disposal of waste other than household waste.*

(5)–(7) *Duty of each waste collection authority to make arrangements for the emptying of privies, and on request, cesspools.*

(8) A waste collection authority may contribute towards the cost incurred by another person in providing or maintaining plant or equipment intended to deal with commercial or industrial waste before it is collected under arrangements made by the authority under subsection (1)(*b*) or (2) above.

(9) Subject to section 48(1) below, anything collected under arrangements made by a waste collection authority under this section shall belong to the authority and may be dealt with accordingly.

(10)–(11) *Scotland.*

(12) *Meaning of "privy" and "cesspool".*

[Environmental Protection Act 1990, s 45.]

1. See the Waste Management Licensing Regulations 1994, SI 1994/1056 amended by SI 1995/288 and 1950, SI 1996/593, 634, 972 and 1279, SI 1997/2203, SI 1998/606 and 2746, SI 2000/1973, SI 2002/674, 1087 (Wales), 1559 and 2980 and SI 2003/595, 780 (W) and 2635, SI 2004/70 (W) and 3276 (E) and SI 2005/894, 1728, 1806 (W) and 2900 (E).

8–26284A **45A. Arrangements for separate collection of recyclable waste.** (1) This section applies to any waste collection authority whose area is in England (an "English waste collection authority").

(2) Where an English waste collection authority has a duty by virtue of section 45(1)(a) above to arrange for the collection of household waste from any premises, the authority shall ensure that the arrangements it makes in relation to those premises include the arrangements mentioned in subsection (3) below, unless it is satisfied that (in that case)—

(*a*) the cost of doing so would be unreasonably high; or

(*b*) comparable alternative arrangements are available.

(3) The arrangements are arrangements for the collection of at least two types of recyclable waste together or individually separated from the rest of the household waste.

(4) The requirement in subsection (2) above shall apply from 31st December 2010.

(5) The Secretary of State may, if requested to do so by an English waste collection authority, direct the authority that subsection (4) above shall have effect in relation to that authority as if the date mentioned there were such later date as may be specified in the direction (being a date no later than 31st December 2015).

(6) In this section, "recyclable waste" means household waste which is capable of being recycled or composted.

[Environmental Protection Act 1990, s 45A, inserted by the Household Waste Recycling Act 2003, s 3.]

8–26284B **45B. Power to apply section 45A to Welsh waste collection authorities.** (1) The National Assembly for Wales may by order made by statutory instrument provide that section 45A above shall apply, subject to subsection (2) below, to all waste collection authorities whose areas are in Wales, as it applies to English waste collection authorities.

(2) Where the Assembly provides as mentioned in subsection (1) above, the reference to the

Secretary of State in section 45A(5) above shall be read for these purposes as a reference to the National Assembly for Wales.

Section 161(3) below (which relates to order-making powers) shall not apply to the making of an order under this section.

[Environmental Protection Act 1990, s 45B, inserted by the Household Waste Recycling Act 2003, s 3.]

8–26285 **46. Receptacles for household waste.** (1) Where a waste collection authority has a duty by virtue of section 45(1)(*a*) above to arrange for the collection of household waste from any premises, the authority may, by notice served on him, require the occupier to place the waste for collection in receptacles of a kind and number specified.

(2) The kind and number of the receptacles required under subsection (1) above to be used shall be such only as are reasonable but, subject to that, separate receptacles or compartments of receptacles may be required to be used for waste which is to be recycled and waste which is not.

(3) In making requirements under subsection (1) above the authority may, as respects the provision of the receptacles—

(*a*) determine that they be provided by the authority free of charge;
(*b*) propose that they be provided, if the occupier agrees, by the authority on payment by him of such a single payment or such periodical payments as he agrees with the authority;
(*c*) require the occupier to provide them if he does not enter into an agreement under paragraph (*b*) above within a specified period; or
(*d*) require the occupier to provide them.

(4) In making requirements as respects receptacles under subsection (1) above, the authority may, by the notice under that subsection, make provision with respect to—

(*a*) the size, construction and maintenance of the receptacles;
(*b*) the placing of the receptacles for the purpose of facilitating the emptying of them, and access to the receptacles for that purpose;
(*c*) the placing of the receptacles for that purpose on highways or, in Scotland, roads;
(*d*) the substances or articles which may or may not be put into the receptacles or compartments of receptacles of any description and the precautions to be taken where particular substances or articles are put into them; and
(*e*) the steps to be taken by occupiers of premises to facilitate the collection of waste from the receptacles.

(5) No requirement shall be made under subsection (1) above for receptacles to be placed on a highway or, as the case may be, road, unless—

(*a*) the relevant highway authority or roads authority have given their consent to their being so placed; and
(*b*) arrangements have been made as to the liability for any damage arising out of their being so placed.

(6) A person who fails, without reasonable excuse, to comply with any requirements imposed under subsection (1), (3)(*c*) or (*d*) or (4) above shall be liable on summary conviction to a fine not exceeding **level 3** on the standard scale.

(7) Where an occupier is required under subsection (1) above to provide any receptacles he may, within the period allowed by subsection (8) below, appeal to a magistrates' court or, in Scotland, to the sheriff by way of summary application against any requirement imposed under subsection (1), subsection (3)(*c*) or (*d*) or (4) above on the ground that—

(*a*) the requirement is unreasonable; or
(*b*) the receptacles in which household waste is placed for collection from the premises are adequate.

(8) The period allowed to the occupier of premises for appealing against such a requirement is the period of twenty-one days beginning—

(*a*) in a case where a period was specified under subsection (3)(*c*) above, with the end of that period; and
(*b*) where no period was specified, with the day on which the notice making the requirement was served on him.

(9) Where an appeal against a requirement is brought under subsection (7) above—

(*a*) the requirement shall be of no effect pending the determination of the appeal;
(*b*) the court shall either quash or modify the requirement or dismiss the appeal; and
(*c*) no question as to whether the requirement is, in any respect, unreasonable shall be entertained in any proceedings for an offence under subsection (6) above.

(10) In this section—

"receptacle" includes a holder for receptacles; and
"specified" means specified in a notice under subsection (1) above.

[Environmental Protection Act 1990, s 46.]

8–26286 47. Receptacles for commercial or industrial waste. (1) A waste collection authority may, at the request of any person, supply him with receptacles for commercial or industrial waste which he has requested the authority to arrange to collect and shall make a reasonable charge for any receptacle supplied unless in the case of a receptacle for commercial waste the authority considers it appropriate not to make a charge.

(2) If it appears to a waste collection authority that there is likely to be situated, on any premises in its area, commercial waste or industrial waste of a kind which, if the waste is not stored in receptacles of a particular kind, is likely to cause a nuisance or to be detrimental to the amenities of the locality, the authority may, by notice served on him, require the occupier of the premises to provide at the premises receptacles for the storage of such waste of a kind and number specified.

(3) The kind and number of the receptacles required under subsection (2) above to be used shall be such only as are reasonable.

(4) In making requirements as respects receptacles under subsection (2) above, the authority may, by the notice under that subsection, make provision with respect to—

(*a*) the size, construction and maintenance of the receptacles;

(*b*) the placing of the receptacles for the purpose of facilitating the emptying of them, and access to the receptacles for that purpose;

(*c*) the placing of the receptacles for that purpose on highways or, in Scotland, roads;

(*d*) the substances or articles which may or may not be put into the receptacles and the precautions to be taken where particular substances or articles are put into them; and

(*e*) the steps to be taken by occupiers of premises to facilitate the collection of waste from the receptacles.

(5) No requirement shall be made under subsection (2) above for receptacles to be placed on a highway or, as the case may be, road unless—

(*a*) the relevant highway authority or roads authority have given their consent to their being so placed; and

(*b*) arrangements have been made as to the liability for any damage arising out of their being so placed.

(6) A person who fails, without reasonable excuse, to comply with any requirements imposed under subsection (2) or (4) above shall be liable on summary conviction to a fine not exceeding **level 3** on the standard scale.

(7) Where an occupier is required under subsection (2) above to provide any receptacles he may, within the period allowed by subsection (8) below, appeal to a magistrates' court or, in Scotland, to the sheriff by way of summary application against any requirement imposed under subsection (2) or (4) above on the ground that—

(*a*) the requirement is unreasonable; or

(*b*) the waste is not likely to cause a nuisance or be detrimental to the amenities of the locality.

(8) The period allowed to the occupier of premises for appealing against such a requirement is the period of twenty-one days beginning with the day on which the notice making the requirement was served on him.

(9) Where an appeal against a requirement is brought under subsection (7) above—

(*a*) the requirement shall be of no effect pending the determination of the appeal;

(*b*) the court shall either quash or modify the requirement or dismiss the appeal; and

(*c*) no question as to whether the requirement is, in any respect, unreasonable shall be entertained in any proceedings for an offence under subsection (6) above.

(10) In this section—

"receptacle" includes a holder for receptacles; and

"specific" means specified in a notice under subsection (2) above.

[Environmental Protection Act 1990, s 47.]

8–26286A 47A. Recycling and composting: duty to report to Parliament. (1) Not later than 31st October 2004, the Secretary of State shall lay before each House of Parliament a report of the performance—

(*a*) of each English waste authority in meeting its recycling and composting standards (if any); and

(*b*) of each English waste collection authority towards meeting the requirement imposed by section 45A(2) above.

(2) In this section—

"English waste authority" means a waste collection authority or a waste disposal authority whose area is in England;

"English waste collection authority" means a waste collection authority whose area is in England; and "recycling and composting standards" means, in relation to an English waste authority, such performance standards and performance indicators (if any) as may be specified for that authority in an order made under section 4 of the Local Government Act 1999 in connection with the recycling and composting of household waste.

[Environmental Protection Act 1990, s 47A, inserted by the Household Waste Recycing Act 2003, s 3.]

8–26287 48–56. *Duties of waste collection authorities as respects disposal of waste collected (s 48). Waste recycling plans by collection authorities (s 49). Functions of waste disposal authorities (s 51). Payments for recycling and disposal etc of waste (s 52). Payments for delivering waste pre-separated (s 52A). Scotland (s 53). Powers for recycling waste (s 55). Scotland (s 56).*

8–26288 57. Power of Secretary of State to require waste to be accepted, treated, disposed of or delivered. (1) The Secretary of State may, by notice in writing, direct the holder of any waste management licence or waste permit to accept and keep, or accept and treat or dispose of, waste at specified places on specified terms.

(2) The Secretary of State may, by notice in writing, direct any person who is keeping waste on any land to deliver the waste to a specified person on specified terms with a view to its being treated or disposed of by that other person.

(3) A direction under this section may impose a requirement as respects waste of any specified kind or as respects any specified consignment of waste.

(4) A direction under subsection (2) above may require the person who is directed to deliver the waste to pay to the specified person his reasonable costs of treating or disposing of the waste.

(5) A person who fails, without reasonable excuse, to comply with a direction under this section shall be liable on summary conviction to a fine not exceeding **level 5** on the standard scale.

(6) A person shall not be guilty of an offence under any other enactment prescribed by the Secretary of State by regulations[1] made for the purposes of this subsection by reason only of anything necessarily done or omitted in order to comply with a direction under this section.

(7) The Secretary of State may, where the costs of the treatment or disposal of waste are not paid or not fully paid in pursuance of subsection (4) above to the person treating or disposing of the waste, pay the costs or the unpaid costs, as the case may be, to that person.

(7A) In subsection (1) "waste permit" means a permit under the Pollution Prevention and Control (England and Wales) Regulations 2000 which authorises the disposal or recovery of waste; and for this purpose "disposal or recovery" means an operation listed in Annex IIA or Annex IIB of Council Directive 75/442/EEC on waste (as amended by Commission Decision 96/350/EEC).

(8) In this section—

"specified" means specified in a direction under this section; and

"waste" means anything which is waste as defined in Article 1 of, and Annex 1 to, Directive 75/442/EEC (as amended by Directive 91/156/EEC) including anything which is excluded from the scope of that Directive by Article 2(1)(b)(iii) of that Directive, but not including anything excluded by the remainder of that Article.

[Environmental Protection Act 1990, s 57 as amended by SI 2005/3026.]

1. The Waste (Foot-and-Mouth Disease) (England) Regulations 2001, SI 2001/1478 amended by SI 2001/3189 (England) have been made.

8–26289 58. *Scotland.*

8–26290 59. Powers to require removal of waste unlawfully deposited. (1) If any controlled waste is deposited in or on any land in the area of a waste regulation authority or waste collection authority in contravention of section 33(1) above, the authority may, by notice served on him, require the occupier to do either or both of the following, that is—

(*a*) to remove the waste from the land within a specified period not less than a period of twenty-one days beginning with the service of the notice;

(*b*) to take within such a period specified steps with a view to eliminating or reducing the consequences of the deposit of the waste.

(2) A person on whom any requirements are imposed under subsection (1) above may, within the period of twenty-one days mentioned in that subsection, appeal against the requirement to a magistrates' court or, in Scotland, to the sheriff by way of summary application.

(3) On any appeal under subsection (2) above the court shall quash the requirement if it is satisfied that—

(*a*) the appellant neither deposited nor knowingly caused nor knowingly permitted the deposit of the waste; or

(*b*) there is a material defect in the notice;

and in any other case shall either modify the requirement or dismiss the appeal.

(4) Where a person appeals against any requirement imposed under subsection (1) above, the

requirement shall be of no effect pending the determination of the appeal; and where the court modifies the requirement or dismisses the appeal it may extend the period specified in the notice.

(5) If a person on whom a requirement imposed under subsection (1) above fails, without reasonable excuse, to comply with the requirement he shall be liable, on summary conviction, to a fine not exceeding **level 5** on the standard scale and to a further fine of an amount equal to **one-tenth of level 5** on the standard scale for each day on which the failure continues after conviction of the offence and before the authority has begun to exercise its powers under subsection (6) below.

(6) Where a person on whom a requirement has been imposed under subsection (1) above by an authority fails to comply with the requirement the authority may do what that person was required to do and may recover from him any expenses reasonably incurred by the authority in doing it.

(7) If it appears to a waste regulation authority or waste collection authority that waste has been deposited in or on any land in contravention of section 33(1) above and that—

(*a*) in order to remove or prevent pollution of land, water or air or harm to human health it is necessary that the waste be forthwith removed or other steps taken to eliminate or reduce the consequences of the deposit or both; or

(*b*) there is no occupier of the land; or

(*c*) the occupier neither made nor knowingly permitted the deposit of the waste;

the authority may remove the waste from the land or take other steps to eliminate or reduce the consequences of the deposit or, as the case may require, to remove the waste and take those steps.

(8) Where an authority exercises any of the powers conferred on it by subsection (7) above it shall be entitled to recover the cost incurred by it in removing the waste or taking the steps or both and in disposing of the waste—

(*a*) in a case falling within subsection (7)(*a*) above, from the occupier of the land unless he proves that he neither made nor knowingly caused nor knowingly permitted the deposit of the waste;

(*b*) in any case, from any person who deposited or knowingly caused or knowingly permitted the deposit of any of the waste;

except such of the cost as the occupier or that person shows was incurred unnecessarily.

(8A) An authority may not recover costs under subsection (8) above if a compensation order has been made under section 130 of the Powers of Criminal Courts (Sentencing) Act 2000 in favour of the authority in respect of any part of those costs.*

(8B) Subsection (8A) does not apply if the order is set aside on appeal.*

(9) Any waste removed by an authority under subsection (7) above shall belong to that authority and may be dealt with accordingly.

[Environmental Protection Act 1990, s 59 as amended by the Clean Neighbourhoods and Environment Act 2005, s 43.]

***Inserted in relation to England and Wales only.**

8–26291 **60. Interference with waste sites and receptacles for waste.** (1) No person shall sort over or disturb—

(*a*) anything deposited at a place for the deposit of waste provided by a waste collection authority, by a waste disposal contractor under arrangements made with a waste disposal authority or by any other local authority or person or, in Scotland, by a waste disposal authority;

(*b*) anything deposited in a receptacle for waste, whether for public or private use, provided by a waste collection authority, by a waste disposal contractor under arrangements made with a waste disposal authority, by a parish or community council or by a holder of a waste management licence or, in Scotland, by a waste disposal authority or a roads authority; or

(*c*) the contents of any receptacle for waste which, in accordance with a requirement under section 46 or 47 above, is placed on any highway or, in Scotland, road or in any other place with a view to its being emptied;

unless he has the relevant consent or right to do so specified in subsection (2) below.

(2) The consent or right that is relevant for the purposes of subsection (1)(*a*), (*b*) or (*c*) above is—

(*a*) in the case of paragraph (*a*), the consent of the authority, contractor or other person who provides the place for the deposit of the waste;

(*b*) in the case of paragraph (*b*), the consent of the authority, contractor or other person who provides the receptacle for the deposit of the waste;

(*c*) in the case of paragraph (*c*), the right to the custody of the receptacle, the consent of the person having the right to the custody of the receptacle or the right conferred by the function by or under this Part of emptying such receptacles.

(3) A person who contravenes subsection (1) above shall be liable on summary conviction to a fine of an amount not exceeding **level 3** on the standard scale.

[Environmental Protection Act 1990, s 60.]

Special waste and non-controlled waste

8–26293 **62. Special provision with respect to certain dangerous or intractable waste.** (1) If the Secretary of State considers that controlled waste of any kind is or may be so dangerous or difficult to treat, keep or dispose of that special provision is required for dealing with it he shall make provision by regulations for the treatment, keeping or disposal of waste of that kind ("special waste").

(2) Without prejudice to the generality of subsection (1) above, the regulations may include provision—

(*a*) for the giving of directions by waste regulation authorities with respect to matters connected with the treatment, keeping or disposal of special waste;

(*b*) for securing that special waste is not, while awaiting treatment or disposal in pursuance of the regulations, kept at any one place in quantities greater than those which are prescribed and in circumstances which differ from those which are prescribed;

(*c*) in connection with requirements imposed on consignors or consignees of special waste, imposing, in the event of non-compliance, requirements on any person carrying the consignment to re-deliver it as directed;

(*d*) for requiring the occupier of premises on which special waste is situated to give notice of that fact and other prescribed information to a prescribed authority;

(*e*) for the keeping of records by waste regulation authorities and by persons who import, export, produce, keep, treat or dispose of special waste or deliver it to another person for treatment or disposal, for the inspection of the records and for the furnishing by such persons to waste regulation authorities of copies of or information derived from the records;

(*f*) for the keeping in the register under section 64(1) below of copies of such of those records, or such information derived from those records, as may be prescribed;

(*g*) providing that a contravention of the regulations shall be an offence and prescribing the maximum penalty for the offence, which shall not exceed, on summary conviction, a fine at level 5 on the standard scale and, on conviction on indictment, imprisonment for a term of two years or a fine or both.

(3) Without prejudice to the generality of subsection (1) above, the regulations may include provision—

(*a*) for the supervision by waste regulation authorities—

(i) of activities authorised by virtue of the regulations or of activities by virtue of carrying on which persons are subject to provisions of the regulations, or

(ii) of persons who carry on activities authorised by virtue of the regulations or who are subject to provisions of the regulations,

and for the recovery from persons falling within sub-paragraph (ii) above of the costs incurred by waste regulation authorities in performing functions conferred upon those authorities by the regulations;

(*b*) as to the recovery of expenses or other charges for the treatment, keeping or disposal or the re-delivery of special waste in pursuance of the regulations;

(*c*) as to appeals to the Secretary of State from decisions of waste regulation authorities under the regulations.

(3A) This section is subject to section 114 of the Environment Act 1995 (delegation or reference of appeals etc.)

(4) *Northern Ireland.*

[Environmental Protection Act 1990, s 62, as amended by the Environment Act 1995, Sch 22.]

8–26294 63. Waste other than controlled waste. (1) The Secretary of State may, after consultation with such bodies as he considers appropriate, make regulations[1] providing that prescribed provisions of this Part shall have effect in a prescribed area—

(*a*) as if references in those provisions to controlled waste or controlled waste of a kind specified in the regulations included references to such waste as is mentioned in section 75(7)(*c*) below which is of a kind so specified; and

(*b*) with such modifications as may be prescribed;

and the regulations may make such modifications of other enactments as the Secretary of State considers appropriate.

(2) *Repealed.**

(3) *Repealed.**

(4) Section 45(2) and section 47(1) above shall apply to waste other than controlled waste as they apply to controlled waste.

[Environmental Protection Act 1990, s 63 as amended by SI 2005/894.]

***Repealed in relation to England and Wales by SI 2005/894.**

1. The Waste (Foot-and-Mouth Disease) (England) Regulations 2001, SI 2001/1478 amended by SI 2001/3189 (England) have been made.

8–26294A 63A. Power to take steps to minimise generation of controlled waste.

8–26295 64–66. *Public registers.*

Supervision and enforcement

8–26299 **71. Obtaining of information from persons and authorities.** (1) *Repealed.*

(2) For the purpose of the discharge of their respective functions under this Part—

(*a*) the Secretary of State, and
(*b*) a waste regulation authority,

may, by notice in writing served on him, require any person to furnish such information specified in the notice as the Secretary of State or the authority, as the case may be, reasonably considers he or it needs, in such form and within such period following service of the notice, or at such time as is so specified[1].

(3) A person who—

(*a*) fails, without reasonable excuse, to comply with a requirement imposed under subsection (2) above;
(*b*) *Repealed.*

shall be liable[2]—

(i) on summary conviction, to a fine not exceeding the **statutory maximum**;
(ii) on conviction on indictment, to a **fine** or to imprisonment for a term not exceeding **two years**, or to **both**.

(4) The Secretary of State may, by notice in writing, require a waste regulation authority or waste collection authority in England and Wales to supply to him, or to such other person as may be specified in the notice, such information as may be so specified in respect of—

(*a*) cases where the authority has exercised any powers under section 59 above, and
(*b*) cases where the authority has taken action under any other enactment in respect of any deposit or other disposal of controlled waste in contravention of section 33(1) above.*

[Environmental Protection Act 1990, s 71, as amended by the Environment Act 1995, Schs 19, 22 and 24 and the Anti-social Behaviour Act 2003, s 55.]

***Subsection (4) reproduced as inserted in relation to England and Wales.**

1. The power given by s 71(2) has been conferred not merely for the purpose of obtaining evidence against offenders but also for the broad public purpose of protecting public health and the environment. Accordingly, persons who are required under s 71(2) to provide information cannot rely on the privilege against self-incrimination under English law or the principles under the European Convention on Human Rights for refusing to do so, although the question of exclusion on the ground of prejudice of any potentially incriminating answers may arise in any subsequent criminal proceedings (*R v Hertfordshire County Council, ex p Green Environmental Industries Ltd* [2000] 2 AC 412, [2000] 1 All ER 773, [2000] 2 WLR 373, HL).

2. For procedure in respect of an offence triable either way, see the Magistrates' Courts Act 1980, ss 17A–21 in PART I: MAGISTRATES' COURTS, PROCEDURE, ante.

Supplemental

8–26301 **73. Appeals and other provisions relating to legal proceedings and civil liability.** (1) An appeal against any decision of a magistrates' court under this Part (other than a decision made in criminal proceedings) shall lie to the Crown Court at the instance of any party to the proceedings in which the decision was given if such an appeal does not lie to the Crown Court by virtue of any other enactment.

(2) *Scotland.*

(3) Where a person appeals to the Crown Court or the Court of Session against a decision of a magistrates' court or the sheriff dismissing an appeal against any requirement imposed under this Part which was suspended pending determination of that appeal, the requirement shall again be suspended pending the determination of the appeal to the Crown Court or Court of Session.

(4) Where an appeal against a decision of any authority lies to a magistrates' court or to the sheriff by virtue of any provision of this Part, it shall be the duty of the authority to include in any document by which it notifies the decision to the person concerned a statement indicating that such an appeal lies and specifying the time within which it must be brought.

(5) Where on an appeal to any court against or arising out of a decision of any authority under this Part the court varies or reverses the decision it shall be the duty of the authority to act in accordance with the court's decision.

(6)–(9) *Civil liability.*

[Environmental Protection Act 1990, s 73.]

8–26302 **74. Meaning of "fit and proper person".** (1) The following provisions apply for the purposes of the discharge by a waste regulation authority of any function under this Part which requires the authority to determine whether a person is or is not a fit and proper person to hold a waste management licence.

(2) Whether a person is or is not a fit and proper person to hold a licence is to be determined by reference to the carrying on by him of the activities which are or are to be authorised by the licence and the fulfilment of the requirements of the licence.

(3) Subject to subsection (4) below, a person shall be treated as not being a fit and proper person if it appears to the authority—

(*a*) that he or another relevant person has been convicted of a relevant offence;

(*b*) that the management of the activities which are or are to be authorised by the licence are not or will not be in the hands of a technically competent person; or

(*c*) that the person who holds or is to hold the licence has not made and either has no intention of making or is in no position to make financial provision adequate to discharge the obligations arising from the licence.

(4) The authority may, if it considers it proper to do so in any particular case, treat a person as a fit and proper person notwithstanding that subsection (3)(*a*) above applies in his case.

(5) It shall be the duty of waste regulation authorities to have regard to any guidance issued to them by the Secretary of State with respect to the discharge of their functions of making the determinations to which this section applies.

(6) The Secretary of State may, by regulations[1], prescribe the offences that are relevant for the purposes of subsection (3)(*a*) above and the qualifications and experience required of a person for the purposes of subsection (3)(*b*) above.

(7) For the purposes of subsection (3)(*a*) above, another relevant person shall be treated, in relation to the licence holder or proposed licence holder, as the case may be, as having been convicted of a relevant offence if—

(*a*) any person has been convicted of a relevant offence committed by him in the course of his employment by the holder or, as the case may be, the proposed holder of the licence or in the course of the carrying on of any business by a partnership one of the members of which was the holder or, as the case may be, the proposed holder of the licence;

(*b*) a body corporate has been convicted of a relevant offence committed when the holder or, as the case may be, the proposed holder of the licence was a director, manager, secretary or other similar officer of that body corporate; or

(*c*) where the holder or, as the case may be, the proposed holder of the licence is a body corporate, a person who is a director, manager, secretary or other similar officer of that body corporate—

(i) has been convicted of a relevant offence; or

(ii) was a director, manager, secretary or other similar officer of another body corporate at a time when a relevant offence for which that other body corporate has been convicted was committed.

[Environmental Protection Act 1990, s 74.]

1. See the Environmental Protection (Waste Recycling Payments) Regulations 1992, SI 1992/462 amended by SI 1994/522, SI 1996/634 and SI 1997/351, the Waste Management Licensing Regulations 1994, SI 1994/1056 amended by SI 1995/288 and 1950, SI 1996/593, 634, 972 and 1279, SI 1997/2203, SI 1998/606 and 2746, SI 2000/1973, SI 2002/674, 1087 (Wales), 1559 and 2980 and SI 2003/595, 780 (W) and 2635, SI 2004/70 (W) and 3276 (E) and SI 2005/894, 1728, 1806 (W) and 2900 (E).

8–26303 **75. Meaning of "waste" and household, commercial and industrial waste and special waste.** (1) The following provisions apply for the interpretation of this Part.

(2) "Waste" includes—

(*a*) any substance which constitutes a scrap material or any effluent or other unwanted surplus substance arising from the application of any process[1]; and

(*b*) any substance or article which requires to be disposed of as being broken, worn out, contaminated or otherwise spoiled;

but does not include a substance which is an explosive within the meaning of the Explosives Act 1875.*

(3) Any thing which is discarded or otherwise dealt with as if it were waste shall be presumed to be waste unless the contrary is proved.**

(4) "Controlled waste"[2] means household, industrial and commercial waste or any such waste.

(5) Subject to subsection (8) below, "household waste" means waste from—

(*a*) domestic property, that is to say, a building or self-contained part of a building which is used wholly for the purposes of living accommodation;

(*b*) a caravan (as defined in section 29(1) of the Caravan Sites and Control of Development Act 1960) which usually and for the time being is situated on a caravan site (within the meaning of that Act);

(*c*) a residential home;

(*d*) premises forming part of a university or school or other educational establishment;

(*e*) premises forming part of a hospital or nursing home.***

(6) Subject to subsection (8) below, "industrial waste" means waste from any of the following premises—

(*a*) any factory (within the meaning of the Factories Act 1961);

(*b*) any premises used for the purposes of, or in connection with, the provision to the public of transport services by land, water or air;

(*c*) any premises used for the purposes of, or in connection with, the supply to the public of gas, water or electricity or the provision of sewerage services; or

(*d*) any premises used for the purposes of, or in connection with, the provision to the public of postal or telecommunications services.

(7) Subject to subsection (8) below, "commercial waste" means waste from premises used wholly or mainly for the purposes of a trade or business or the purposes of sport, recreation or entertainment excluding—

(*a*) household waste;

(*b*) industrial waste;

(*c*) waste from any mine or quarry and waste from premises used for agriculture within the meaning of the Agriculture Act 1947 or, in Scotland, the Agriculture (Scotland) Act 1948; and

(*d*) waste of any other description prescribed[3] by regulations made by the Secretary of State for the purposes of this paragraph.

(8) Regulations[3] made by the Secretary of State may provide that waste of a description prescribed in the regulations shall be treated for the purposes of provisions of this Part prescribed in the regulations as being or not being household waste or industrial waste or commercial waste; but no regulations shall be made in respect of such waste as is mentioned in subsection (7)(*c*) above and references to waste in subsection (7) above and this subsection do not include sewage (including matter in or from a privy) except so far as the regulations provide otherwise.

(9) "Special waste" means controlled waste as respects which regulations are in force under section 62 above.

(10) Schedule 2B to this Act (which reproduces Annex I to the Waste Directive) shall have effect.

(11) Subsection (2) above is substituted, and Schedule 2B to this Act is inserted, for the purpose of assigning to "waste" in this Part the meaning which it has in the Waste Directive by virtue of paragraphs (*a*) to (*c*) of Article 1 of, and Annex I to, that Directive, and those provisions shall be construed accordingly.

(12) In this section "the Waste Directive" means the directive of the Council of the European Communities, dated 15th July 1975, on waste, as amended by—

(*a*) the directive of that Council, dated 18th March 1991, amending directive 75/442/EEC on waste; and

(*b*) the directive of that Council, dated 23rd December 1991, standardising and rationalising reports on the implementation of certain Directives relating to the environment.

[Environmental Protection Act 1990, s 75 as amended by the Environment Act 1985, Sch 22,.]

***Section 75(2) is substituted by the Environment Act 1995, Sch 22, from a date to be appointed.**

****Section 75(3) is repealed by the Environment Act 1995, Sch 22, from a date to be appointed.**

*****Paragraph (*e*) text differs in relation to Scotland by virtue of the Regulations of Care (Scotland) Act 2002, s 79.**

1. The European Court on a preliminary reference has held that 'waste' within the meaning of Council Directive 75/442/ EEC, art 1(a) includes stone left over after quarrying even though the residue stone could be put to use directly, without further processing (*Application by Palin Granit Oy* (Case C-9/00) [2002] 1 WLR 2644).

2. It was decided under the Control of Pollution Act 1974 that seaweed was not controlled waste for the purpose of the predecessor legislation (*Thanet District Council v Kent County Council* [1993] Crim LR 703.

3. See the Controlled Waste Regulations 1992, SI 1992/588 amended by SI 1993/566, SI 1994/1056, SI 1996/972, SI 2005/894, 1806 (W) and 1820 (W) and 2900 (E) and SI 2006/123 (W).

4. The Waste Management Licensing Regulations 1994, SI 1994/1056 amended by SI 1995/288 and 1950, SI 1996/593, 634, 972 and 1279, SI 1997/2203, SI 1998/606 and 2746, SI 2000/1973, SI 2002/674, 1087 (Wales), 1559 and 2980 and SI 2003/595, 780 (W) and 2635, SI 2004/70 (W) and 3276 (E) and SI 2005/894, 1728, 1806 (W) and 2900 (E) have been made.

8–26304 **76.** *Application to the Isles of Scilly.*

8–26305 **77. Transition from Control of Pollution Act 1974 to this Part.** (1) This section has effect for the purposes of the transition from the provisions of Part I of the Control of Pollution Act 1974 ("the 1974 Act") to the corresponding provisions of this Part of this Act and in this section—

"existing disposal authority" has the same meaning as in section 32 above;

"existing disposal licence" means a disposal licence under section 5 of the 1974 Act subsisting on the day appointed under section 164(3) below for the repeal of sections 3 to 10 of the 1974 Act and "relevant appointed day for licences" shall be construed accordingly;

"existing disposal plan" means a plan under section 2 of the 1974 Act subsisting on the day appointed under section 164(3) below for the repeal of that section and "relevant appointed day for plans" shall be construed accordingly;

"relevant part of its undertaking", in relation to an existing disposal authority, has the same meaning as in section 32 above; and "the vesting date", in relation to an existing disposal authority and its waste disposal contractors, means the vesting date under Schedule 2 to this Act.

(2) Subject to section 4 of the Pollution Prevention and Control Act 1999, an existing disposal licence shall, on and after the relevant appointed day for licences, be treated as a site licence until it expires or otherwise ceases to have effect; and accordingly it shall be variable and subject to revocation or suspension under this Part of this Act and may not be surrendered or transferred except under this Part of this Act.

(3) *Repealed.*

(4) Any existing disposal plan of an existing disposal authority shall, on and after the relevant appointed day for plans, be treated as the plan of that authority under section 50 above and that section shall accordingly have effect as if references in it to "the plan" included the existing disposal plan of that authority.

(5) *Scotland.*

(6) Subject to subsection (7) below, as respects any existing disposal authority—

(*a*) the restriction imposed by section 51(1) of this Act on the means whereby the authority arranges for the disposal of controlled waste shall not apply to the authority—

(i) in the case of an authority which transfers the relevant part of its undertaking in accordance with a scheme under Schedule 2 to this Act, until the date which is the vesting date for that authority; and

(ii) in any other case, until the date on which the authority transfers, or ceases itself to carry on, the relevant part of its undertaking or ceases to provide places at which and plant and equipment by means of which controlled waste can be disposed of or deposited for the purposes of disposal; and

(*b*) on and after that date, section 14(4) of the 1974 Act shall not authorise the authority to arrange for the disposal of controlled waste except by means of arrangements made (in accordance with Part II of Schedule 2 to this Act) with waste disposal contractors.

(7) The Secretary of State may, as respects any existing disposal authority, direct that the restriction imposed by section 51(1) above shall not apply in the case of that authority until such date as he specifies in the direction and where he does so paragraph (*a*) of subsection (6) above shall not apply and paragraph (*b*) shall be read as referring to the date so specified.

(8) *Repealed.*

(9) As respects any existing disposal authority, until the date which is, under subsection (6)(*a*) above, the date until which the restriction imposed by section 51(1) of this Act is disapplied,—

(*a*) the powers conferred on a waste disposal authority by section 55(2)(*a*) and (*b*) of this Act as respects the recycling of waste and the use of waste to produce heat or electricity shall be treated as powers which the authority may exercise itself; and

(*b*) the power conferred on a waste disposal authority by section 48(4) of this Act to object to a waste collection authority having waste recycled where the disposal authority has made arrangements with a waste disposal contractor for the contractor to recycle the waste shall be available to the waste disposal authority where it itself has the waste recycled.

[Environmental Protection Act 1990, s 77, as amended by the Pollution Prevention and Control Act 1999, Sch 2 and the Statute Law (Repeals) Act 2004.]

8–26306 **78. This Part and radioactive substances.** Except as provided by regulations made by the Secretary of State under this section, nothing in this Part applies to radioactive waste within the meaning of the Radioactive Substances Act 1993; but regulations[1] may—

(*a*) provide for prescribed provisions of this Part to have effect with such modifications as the Secretary of State considers appropriate for the purposes of dealing with such radioactive waste;

(*b*) make such modifications of the Radioactive Substances Act 1993 and any other Act as the Secretary of State considers appropriate.

[Environmental Protection Act 1990, s 78, as amended by the Radioactive Substances Act 1993, Sch 4.]

PART IIA[1]
CONTAMINATED LAND

8–26306A **78A. Preliminary[1].** (1) The following provisions have effect for the interpretation of this Part.

(2) "Contaminated land" is any land which appears to the local authority in whose area it is situated to be in such a condition, by reason of substances in, on or under the land, that—

(*a*) significant harm is being caused or there is a significant possibility of such harm being caused; or

(*b*) pollution of controlled waters is being, or is likely to be, caused;*

and, in determining whether any land appears to be such land, a local authority shall, subject to subsection (5) below, act in accordance with guidance issued by the Secretary of State in accordance with section 78YA below with respect to the manner in which that determination is to be made.

(3) A "special site" is any contaminated land—

(*a*) which has been designated as such a site by virtue of section 78C(7) or 78D(6) below; and

(*b*) whose designation as such has not been terminated by the appropriate Agency under section 78Q(4) below.

(4) "Harm" means harm to the health of living organisms or other interference with the ecological systems of which they form part and, in the case of man, includes harm to his property.

(5) The questions—

(*a*) what harm is to be regarded as "significant",

(*b*) whether the possibility of significant harm being caused is "significant",

(*c*) whether pollution of controlled waters is being, or is likely to be caused,*

shall be determined in accordance with guidance issued for the purpose by the Secretary of State in accordance with section 78YA below.*

(6) Without prejudice to the guidance that may be issued under subsection (5) above, guidance under paragraph (*a*) of that subsection may make provision for different degrees of importance to be assigned to, or for the disregard of,—

(*a*) different descriptions of living organisms or ecological systems;

(*b*) different descriptions of places; or

(*c*) different descriptions of harm to health or property, or other interference;

and guidance under paragraph (*b*) of that subsection may make provision for different degrees of possibility to be regarded as "significant" (or as not being "significant") in relation to different descriptions of significant harm.*

(7) "Remediation" means—

(*a*) the doing of anything for the purpose of assessing the condition of—

(i) the contaminated land in question;

(ii) any controlled waters affected by that land; or

(iii) any land adjoining or adjacent to that land;

(*b*) the doing of any works, the carrying out of any operations or the taking of any steps in relation to any such land or waters for the purpose—

(i) of preventing or minimising, or remedying or mitigating the effects of, any significant harm, or any pollution of controlled waters, by reason of which the contaminated land is such land; or

(ii) of restoring the land or waters to their former state; or

(*c*) the making of subsequent inspections from time to time for the purpose of keeping under review the condition of the land or waters;

and cognate expressions shall be construed accordingly.*

(8) Controlled waters are "affected by" contaminated land if (and only if) it appears to the enforcing authority that the contaminated land in question is, for the purposes of subsection (2) above, in such a condition, by reason of substances in, on or under the land, that pollution of those waters is being, or is likely to be caused.*

(9) The following expressions have the meaning respectively assigned to them—

"the appropriate Agency" means—

(*a*) in relation to England and Wales, the Environment Agency;

(*b*) in relation to Scotland, the Scottish Environment Protection Agency;

"appropriate person" means any person who is an appropriate person, determined in accordance with section 78F below, to bear responsibility for anything which is to be done by way of remediation in any particular case;

"charging notice" has the meaning given by section 78P(3)(*b*) below;

"controlled waters"—

(*a*) in relation to England and Wales, has the same meaning as in Part III of the Water Resources Act 1991 except that "ground waters" does not include waters contained in underground strata but above the saturation zone; and

(*b*) in relation to Scotland, has the same meaning as in section 30A of the Control of Pollution Act 1974;

"creditor" has the same meaning as in the Conveyancing and Feudal Reform (Scotland) Act 1970;

"enforcing authority" means—

(*a*) in relation to a special site, the appropriate Agency;

(*b*) in relation to contaminated land other than a special site, the local authority in whose area the land is situated;

"heritable security" has the same meaning as in the Conveyancing and Feudal Reform (Scotland) Act 1970;

"local authority" in relation to England and Wales means—

(*a*) any unitary authority;
(*b*) any district council, so far as it is not a unitary authority;
(*c*) the Common Council of the City of London and, as respects the Temples, the Sub-Treasurer of the Inner Temple and the Under-Treasurer of the Middle Temple respectively;

and in relation to Scotland means a council for an area constituted under section 2 of the Local Government etc. (Scotland) Act 1994;

"notice" means notice in writing;
"notification" means notification in writing;
"owner", in relation to any land in England and Wales, means a person (other than a mortgagee not in possession) who, whether in his own right or as trustee for any other person, is entitled to receive the rack rent of the land, or, where the land is not let at a rack rent, would be so entitled if it were so let;
"owner", in relation to any land in Scotland, means a person (other than a creditor in a heritable security not in possession of the security subjects) for the time being entitled to receive or who would, if the land were let, be entitled to receive, the rents of the land in connection with which the word is used and includes a trustee, factor, guardian or curator and in the case of public or municipal land includes the persons to whom the management of the land is entrusted;
"pollution of controlled waters" means the entry into controlled waters of any poisonous, noxious or polluting matter or any solid waste matter;
"prescribed" means prescribed by regulations;
"regulations" means regulations[2] made by the Secretary of State;
"remediation declaration" has the meaning given by section 78H(6) below;
"remediation notice" has the meaning given by section 78E(1) below;
"remediation statement" has the meaning given by section 78H(7) below;
"required to be designated as a special site" shall be construed in accordance with section 78C(8) below;
"substance" means any natural or artificial substance, whether in solid or liquid form or in the form of a gas or vapour;
"unitary authority" means—

(*a*) the council of a county, so far as it is the council of an area for which there are no district councils;
(*b*) the council of any district comprised in an area for which there is no county council;
(*c*) the council of a London borough;
(*d*) the council of a county borough in Wales

[Environmental Protection Act, 1990, s 78A, as inserted by the Environment Act 1995, s 57 and the Water Act 2003, s 86.]

***In relation to England and Wales, sub-s (2)(*b*) substituted, sub-s (5)(*c*) repealed and other sub-ss amended by the Water Act 2003, s 86, from a date to be appointed.**

1. Part IIA contains ss 78A–78YC.
2. The Radio-active Contaminated Land (Enabling Powers) (England) Regulations 2005, SI 2005/3467 have been made.

8–26306B 78B. Identification of contaminated land. (1) Every local authority shall cause its area to be inspected from time to time for the purpose—

(*a*) of identifying contaminated land; and
(*b*) of enabling the authority to decide whether any such land is land which is required to be designated as a special site.

(2) In performing its functions under subsection (1) above a local authority shall act in accordance with any guidance issued for the purpose by the Secretary of State in accordance with section 78YA below.

(3) If a local authority identifies any contaminated land in its area, it shall give notice of that fact to—

(*a*) the appropriate Agency;
(*b*) the owner of the land;
(*c*) any person who appears to the authority to be in occupation of the whole or any part of the land; and
(*d*) each person who appears to the authority to be an appropriate person;

and any notice given under this subsection shall state by virtue of which of paragraphs (*a*) to (*d*) above it is given.

(4) If, at any time after a local authority has given any person a notice pursuant to subsection (3)(*d*) above in respect of any land, it appears to the enforcing authority that another person is an appropriate person, the enforcing authority shall give notice to that other person—

(*a*) of the fact that the local authority has identified the land in question as contaminated land; and

(*b*) that he appears to the enforcing authority to be an appropriate person.

[Environmental Protection Act 1990, s 78B, as inserted by the Environment Act 1995, s 57.]

8–26306C 78C. Identification and designation of special sites. (1) If at any time it appears to a local authority that any contaminated land in its area might be land which is required to be designated as a special site, the authority—

(*a*) shall decide whether or not the land is land which is required to be so designated; and

(*b*) if the authority decides that the land is land which is required to be so designated, shall give notice of that decision to the relevant persons.

(2) For the purposes of this section, "the relevant persons" at any time in the case of any land are the persons who at that time fall within paragraphs (*a*) to (*d*) below, that is to say—

(*a*) the appropriate Agency;

(*b*) the owner of the land;

(*c*) any person who appears to the local authority concerned to be in occupation of the whole or any part of the land; and

(*d*) each person who appears to that authority to be an appropriate person.

(3) Before making a decision under paragraph (*a*) of subsection (1) above in any particular case, a local authority shall request the advice of the appropriate Agency, and in making its decision shall have regard to any advice given by that Agency in response to the request.

(4) If at any time the appropriate Agency considers that any contaminated land is land which is required to be designated as a special site, that Agency may give notice of the fact to the local authority in whose area the land is situated.

(5) Where notice under subsection (4) above is given to a local authority, the authority shall decide whether the land in question—

(*a*) is land which is required to be designated as a special site, or

(*b*) is not land which is required to be so designated,

and shall give notice of that decision to the relevant persons.

(6) Where a local authority makes a decision falling within subsection (1)(*b*) or (5)(*a*) above, the decision shall, subject to section 78D below, take effect on the day after whichever of the following events first occurs, that is to say—

(*a*) the expiration of the period of twenty-one days beginning with the day on which the notice required by virtue of subsection (1)(*b*) or, as the case may be, (5)(*a*) above is given to the appropriate Agency; or

(*b*) if the appropriate agency gives notification to the local authority in question that it agrees with the decision, the giving of that notification;

and where a decision takes effect by virtue of this subsection, the local authority shall give notice of that fact to the relevant persons.

(7) Where a decision that any land is land which is required to be designated as a special site takes effect in accordance with subsection (6) above, the notice given under subsection (1)(*b*) or, as the case may be, (5)(*a*) above shall have effect, as from the time when the decision takes effect, as the designation of that land as such a site.

(8) For the purposes of this Part, land is required to be designated as a special site if, and only if, it is land of a description prescribed[1] for the purposes of this subsection.

(9) Regulations under subsection (8) above may make different provision for different cases or circumstances or different areas or localities and may, in particular, describe land by reference to the area or locality in which it is situated.

(10) Without prejudice to the generality of his power to prescribe any description of land for the purposes of subsection (8) above, the Secretary of State, in deciding whether to prescribe a particular description of contaminated land for those purposes, may, in particular, have regard to—

(*a*) whether land of the description in question appears to him to be land which is likely to be in such a condition, by reason of substances in, on or under the land that—

(i) serious harm would or might be caused, or

(ii) serious pollution of controlled waters would be, or would be likely to be, caused; or*

(*b*) whether the appropriate Agency is likely to have expertise in dealing with the kind of significant harm, or pollution of controlled waters, by reason of which land of the description in question is contaminated land.*

[Environmental Protection Act 1990, s 78C, as inserted by the Environment Act 1995, s 57.]

***Amended in relation to England and Wales by the Water Act 2003, s 86, from a date to be appointed.**

1. See the Contaminated Land Regulations 2000, SI 2000/227 amended by SI 2000/1973 and SI 2001/663 (England) and the Contaminated Land (Wales) Regulations 2001, SI 2001/2197.

8–26306D 78D. Referral of special site decisions to the Secretary of State. (1) In any case where—

(*a*) a local authority gives notice of a decision to the appropriate Agency pursuant to subsection (1)(*b*) or (5)(*b*) of section 78C above, but

(*b*) before the expiration of the period of twenty-one days beginning with the day on which that notice is so given, that Agency gives the local authority notice that it disagrees with the decision, together with a statement of its reasons for disagreeing

the authority shall refer the decision to the Secretary of State and shall send to him a statement of its reasons for reaching the decision.

(2) Where the appropriate Agency gives notice to a local authority under paragraph (*b*) of subsection (1) above, it shall also send to the Secretary of State a copy of the notice and of the statement given under that paragraph.

(3) Where a local authority refers a decision to the Secretary of State under subsection (1) above, it shall give notice of that fact to the relevant persons.

(4) Where a decision of a local authority is referred to the Secretary of State under subsection (1) above, he—

(*a*) may confirm or reverse the decision with respect to the whole or any part of the land to which it relates; and

(*b*) shall give notice of his decision on the referral—

(i) to the relevant persons; and

(ii) to the local authority.

(5) Where a decision of a local authority is referred to the Secretary of State under subsection (1) above, the decision shall not take effect until the day after that on which the Secretary of State gives the notice required by subsection (4) above to the persons there mentioned and shall then take effect as confirmed or reversed by him.

(6) Where a decision which takes effect in accordance with subsection (5) above is to the effect that at least some land is land which is required to be designated as a special site, the notice given under subsection (4)(*b*) above shall have effect, as from the time when the decision takes effect, as the designation of that land as such a site.

(7) In this section "the relevant persons" has the same meaning as in section 78C above.

[Environmental Protection Act 1990, s 78D, as inserted by the Environment Act 1995, s 57.]

8–26306E 78E. Duty of enforcing authority to require remediation of contaminated land etc. (1) In any case where—

(*a*) any land has been designated as a special site by virtue of section 78C(7) or 78D(6) above, or

(*b*) a local authority has identified any contaminated land (other than a special site) in its area,

the enforcing authority shall, in accordance with such procedure as may be prescribed and subject to the following provisions of this Part, serve on each person who is an appropriate person a notice (in this Part referred to as a "remediation notice") specifying what that person is to do by way of remediation and the periods within which he is required to do each of the things so specified.

(2) Different remediation notices requiring the doing of different things by way of remediation may be served on different persons in consequence of the presence of different substances in, on or under any land or waters.

(3) Where two or more persons are appropriate persons in relation to any particular thing which is to be done by way of remediation, the remediation notice served on each of them shall state the proportion, determined under section 78F(7) below, of the cost of doing that thing which each of them respectively is liable to bear.

(4) The only things by way of remediation which the enforcing authority may do, or require to be done, under or by virtue of this Part are things which it considers reasonable, having regard to—

(*a*) the cost which is likely to be involved; and

(*b*) the seriousness of the harm, or pollution of controlled waters, in question.*

(5) In determining for any purpose of this Part—

(*a*) what is to be done (whether by an appropriate person, the enforcing authority or any other person) by way of remediation in any particular case,

(*b*) the standard to which any land is, or waters are, to be remediated pursuant to the notice, or

(*c*) what is, or is not, to be regarded as reasonable for the purposes of subsection (4) above,

the enforcing authority shall have regard to any guidance issued for the purpose by the Secretary of State.

(6) Regulations[1] may make provision for or in connection with—

(*a*) the form or content of remediation notices; or

(*b*) any steps of a procedural nature which are to be taken in connection with, or in consequence of, the service of a remediation notice.

[Environmental Protection Act 1990, s 78E, as inserted by the Environment Act 1995, s 57.]

***Amended in relation to England and Wales by the Water Act 2003, s 86, from a date to be appointed.**

1. See the Contaminated Land Regulations 2000, SI 2000/227 amended by SI 2000/1973 and SI 2001/663 (England) and the Contaminated Land (Wales) Regulations 2001, SI 2001/2197.

8–26306F 78F. Determination of the appropriate person to bear responsibility for remediation. (1) This section has effect for the purpose of determining who is the appropriate person to bear responsibility for any particular thing which the enforcing authority determines is to be done by way of remediation in any particular case.

(2) subject to the following provisions of this section, any person, or any of the persons, who caused or knowingly permitted the substances, or any of the substances, by reason of which the contaminated land in question is such land to be in, on or under that land is an appropriate person.

(3) A person shall only be an appropriate person by virtue of subsection (2) above in relation to things which are to be done by way of remediation which are to any extent referable to substances which he caused or knowingly permitted to be present in, on or under the contaminated land in question.

(4) If no person has, after reasonable inquiry, been found who is by virtue of subsection (2) above an appropriate person to bear responsibility for the things which are to be done by way of remediation, the owner or occupier for the time being of the contaminated land in question is an appropriate person.

(5) If, in consequence of subsection (3) above, there are things which are to be done by way of remediation in relation to which no person has, after reasonable inquiry, been found who is an appropriate person by virtue of subsection (2) above, the owner or occupier for the time being of the contaminated land in question is an appropriate person in relation to those things.

(6) Where two or more persons would, apart from this subsection, be appropriate persons in relation to any particular thing which is to be done by way of remediation, the enforcing authority shall determine in accordance with guidance issued for the purpose by the Secretary of State whether any, and if so which, of them is to be treated as not being an appropriate person in relation to that thing,

(7) Where two or more persons are appropriate persons in relation to any particular thing which is to be done by way of remediation, they shall be liable to bear the cost of doing that thing in proportions determined by the enforcing authority in accordance with guidance issued for the purpose by the Secretary of State.

(8) Any guidance issued for the purposes of subsection (6) or (7) above shall be issued in accordance with section 78YA below.

(9) A person who has caused or knowingly permitted any substance ("substance A") to be in, on or under any land shall also be taken for the purposes of this section to have caused or knowingly permitted there to be in, on or under that land any substance which is there as a result of a chemical reaction or biological process affecting substance A.

(10) A thing which is to be done by way of remediation may be regarded for the purposes of this Part as referable to the presence of any substance notwithstanding that the thing in question would not have to be done—

(*a*) in consequence only of the presence of that substance in any quantity; or

(*b*) in consequence only of the quantity of that substance which any particular person caused or knowingly permitted to be present.

[Environmental Protection Act 1990, s 78F, as inserted by the Environment Act 1995, s 57.]

8–26306G 78G. Grant of, and compensation for, rights of entry etc. (1) A remediation notice may require an appropriate person to do things by way of remediation, notwithstanding that he is not entitled to do those things.

(2) Any person whose consent is required before any thing required by a remediation notice may be done shall grant, or join in granting, such rights in relation to any of the relevant land or waters as will enable the appropriate person to comply with any requirements imposed by the remediation notice.

(3) Before serving a remediation notice, the enforcing authority shall reasonably endeavour to consult every person who appears to the authority—

(*a*) to be the owner or occupier of any of the relevant land or waters, and

(*b*) to be a person who might be required by subsection (2) above to grant, or join in granting, any rights,

concerning the rights which that person may be so required to grant.

(4) Subsection (3) above shall not preclude the service of a remediation notice in any case where it appears to the enforcing authority that the contaminated land in question is in such a condition, by reason of substances in, on or under the land, that there is imminent danger of serious harm, or serious pollution of controlled waters, being caused.

(5) A person who grants, or joins in granting, any rights pursuant to subsection (2) above shall be entitled, on making an application within such period as may be prescribed[1] and in such manner as may be prescribed[1] to such person as may be prescribed, to be paid by the appropriate person compensation of such amount as may be determined in such manner as may be prescribed.

(6) Without prejudice to the generality of the regulations[1] that may be made by virtue of subsection (5) above, regulations by virtue of that subsection may make such provision in relation to compensation under this section as may be made by regulations by virtue of subsection (4) of section 35A above in relation to compensation under that section.

(7) In this section, "relevant land or waters" means—

(*a*) the contaminated land in question;

(*b*) any controlled waters affected by that land; or

(*c*) any land adjoining or adjacent to that land or those waters.

[Environmental Protection Act 1990, s 78G, as inserted by the Environment Act 1995, s 57.]

---

1. See the Contaminated Land Regulations 2000, SI 2000/227 amended by SI 2000/1973 and SI 2001/663 (England) and the Contaminated Land (Wales) Regulations 2001, SI 2001/2197.

8–26306H 78H. Restrictions and prohibitions on serving remediation notices. (1) Before serving a remediation notice, the enforcing authority shall reasonably endeavour to consult—

(*a*) the person on whom the notice is to be served,

(*b*) the owner of any land to which the notice relates,

(*c*) any person who appears to that authority to be in occupation of the whole or any part of the land, and

(*d*) any person of such other description as may be prescribed,

concerning what is to be done by way of remediation.

(2) Regulations may make provision for, or in connection with, steps to be taken for the purposes of subsection (1) above.

(3) No remediation notice shall be served on any person by reference to any contaminated land during any of the following periods, that is to say—

(*a*) the period—

(i) beginning with the identification of the contaminated land in question pursuant to section 78B(1) above, and

(ii) ending with the expiration of the period of three months beginning with the day on which the notice required by subsection (3)(*d*) or, as the case may be, (4) of section 78B above is given to that person in respect of that land;

(*b*) if a decision falling within paragraph (*b*) of section 78C(1) above is made in relation to the contaminated land in question, the period beginning with the making of the decision and ending with the expiration of the period of three months beginning with—

(i) in a case where the decision is not referred to the Secretary of State under section 78D above, the day on which the notice required by section 78C(6) above is given, or

(ii) in a case where the decision is referred to the Secretary of State under section 78D above, the day on which he gives the notice required by subsection (4)(*b*) of that section;

(*c*) if the appropriate Agency gives a notice under subsection (4) of section 78C above to a local authority in relation to the contaminated land in question, the period beginning with the day on which that notice is given and ending with the expiration of the period of three months beginning with—

(i) in a case where notice is given under subsection (6) of that section, the day on which that notice is given;

(ii) in a case where the authority makes a decision falling within subsection (5)(*b*) of that section and the appropriate Agency fails to give notice under paragraph (*b*) of section 78D(1) above, the day following the expiration of the period of twenty-one days mentioned in that paragraph; or

(iii) in a case where the authority makes a decision falling within section 78C(5)(*b*) above which is referred to the Secretary of State under section 78D above, the day on which the Secretary of State gives the notice required by subsection (4)(*b*) of that section.

(4) Neither subsection (1) nor subsection (3) above shall preclude the service of a remediation notice in any case where it appears to the enforcing authority that the land in question is in such a condition, by reason of substances in, on or under the land, that there is imminent danger of serious harm, or serious pollution of controlled waters, being caused.

(5) The enforcing authority shall not serve a remediation notice on a person if and so long as any one or more of the following conditions is for the time being satisfied in the particular case, that is to say—

(*a*) the authority is satisfied, in consequence of section 78E(4) and (5) above, that there is nothing by way of remediation which could be specified in a remediation notice served on that person;

(*b*) the authority is satisfied that appropriate things are being, or will be, done by way of remediation without the service of a remediation notice on that person;

(*c*) it appears to the authority that the person on whom the notice would be served is the authority itself; or (*d*) the authority is satisfied that the powers conferred on it by section 78N below to do what is appropriate by way of remediation are exercisable.

(6) Where the enforcing authority is precluded by virtue of section 78E(4) or (5) above from specifying in a remediation notice any particular thing by way of remediation which it would otherwise have specified in such a notice, the authority shall prepare and publish a document (in this Part referred to as a "remediation declaration") which shall record—

(*a*) the reasons why the authority would have specified that thing; and
(*b*) the grounds on which the authority is satisfied that it is precluded from specifying that thing in such a notice.

(7) In any case where the enforcing authority is precluded, by virtue of paragraph (*b*), (*c*) or (*d*) of subsection (5) above, from serving a remediation notice, the responsible person shall prepare and publish a document (in this Part referred to as a "remediation statement") which shall record—

(*a*) the things which are being, have been, or are expected to be, done by way of remediation in the particular case;
(*b*) the name and address of the person who is doing, has done, or is expected to do, each of those things; and
(*c*) the periods within which each of those things is being, or is expected to be, done.

(8) For the purposes of subsection (7) above, the "responsible person" is—

(*a*) in a case where the condition in paragraph (*b*) of subsection (5) above is satisfied, the person who is doing or has done, or who the enforcing authority is satisfied will do, the things there mentioned; or
(*b*) in a case where the condition in paragraph (*c*) or (*d*) of that subsection is satisfied, the enforcing authority.

(9) If a person who is required by virtue of subsection (8)(*a*) above to prepare and publish a remediation statement fails to do so within a reasonable time after the date on which a remediation notice specifying the things there mentioned could, apart from subsection (5) above, have been served, the enforcing authority may itself prepare and publish the statement and may recover its reasonable costs of doing so from that person.

(10) Where the enforcing authority has been precluded by virtue only of subsection (5) above from serving a remediation notice on an appropriate person but—

(*a*) none of the conditions in that subsection is for the time being satisfied in the particular case, and
(*b*) the authority is not precluded by any other provision of this Part from serving a remediation notice on that appropriate person,

the authority shall serve a remediation notice on that person; and any such notice may be so served without any further endeavours by the authority to consult persons pursuant to subsection (1) above, if and to the extent that that person has been consulted pursuant to that subsection concerning the things which will be specified in the notice.

[Environmental Protection Act 1990, s 78H, as inserted by the Environment Act 1995, s 57.]

8–26306J 78J. Restrictions on liability relating to the pollution of controlled waters. (1) This section applies where any land is contaminated land by virtue of paragraph (*b*) of subsection (2) of section 78A above (whether or not the land is also contaminated land by virtue of paragraph (*a*) of that subsection).

(2) Where this section applies, no remediation notice given in consequence of the land in question being contaminated land shall require a person who is an appropriate person by virtue of section 78F(4) or (5) above to do anything by way of remediation to that or any other land, or any waters, which he could not have been required to do by such a notice had paragraph (*b*) of section 78A(2) above (and all other references to pollution of controlled waters) been omitted from this Part.

(3) If, in a case where this section applies a person permits, has permitted, or might permit, water from an abandoned mine or part of a mine—

(*a*) to enter any controlled waters, or
(*b*) to reach a place from which it is or, as the case may be, was likely, in the opinion of the enforcing authority, to enter such waters,

no remediation notice shall require him in consequence to do anything by way of remediation (whether to the contaminated land in question or to any other land or waters) which he could not have been required to do by such a notice had paragraph (*b*) of section 78A(2) above (and all other references to pollution of controlled waters) been omitted from this Part.

(4) Subsection (3) above shall not apply to the owner or former operator of any mine or part of a mine if the mine or part in question became abandoned after 31st December 1999.

(5) In determining for the purposes of subsection (4) above whether a mine or part of a mine became abandoned before, on or after 31st December 1999 in a case where the mine or part has become abandoned on two or more occasions, of which—

(*a*) at least one falls on or before that date, and
(*b*) at least one falls after that date,

the mine or part shall be regarded as becoming abandoned after that date (but without prejudice to the operation of subsection (3) above in relation to that mine or part at, or in relation to, any time before the first of those occasions which falls after that date).

(6) Where, immediately before a part of a mine becomes abandoned, that part is the only part of the mine not falling to be regarded as abandoned for the time being, the abandonment of that part shall not be regarded for the purposes of subsection (4) or (5) above as constituting the abandonment of the mine, but only of that part of it.

(7) Nothing in subsection (2) or (3) above prevents the enforcing authority from doing anything by way of remediation under section 78N below which it could have done apart from that subsection, but the authority shall not be entitled under section 78P below to recover from any person any part of the cost incurred by the authority in doing by way of remediation anything which it is precluded by subsection (2) or (3) above from requiring that person to do.

(8) In this section "mine" has the same meaning as in the Mines and Quarries Act 1954.
[Environmental Protection Act 1990, s 78J, as inserted by the Environment Act 1995, s 57.]

8–26306K 78K. Liability in respect of contaminating substances which escape to other land. (1) A person who has caused or knowingly permitted any substances to be in, on or under any land shall also be taken for the purposes of this Part to have caused or, as the case may be, knowingly permitted those substances to be in, on or under any other land to which they appear to have escaped.

(2) Subsections (3) and (4) below apply in any case where it appears that any substances are or have been in, on or under any land (in this section referred to as "land A") as a result of their escape, whether directly or indirectly, from other land in, on or under which a person caused or knowingly permitted them to be.

(3) Where this subsection applies, no remediation notice shall require a person—

(*a*) who is the owner or occupier of land A, and
(*b*) who has not caused or knowingly permitted the substances in question to be in, on or under that land,

to do anything by way of remediation to any land or waters (other than land or waters of which he is the owner or occupier) in consequence of land A appearing to be in such a condition, by reason of the presence of those substances in, on or under it, that significant harm is being caused, or there is a significant possibility of such harm being caused, or that pollution of controlled waters is being, or is likely to be caused*.

(4) Where this subsection applies, no remediation notice shall require a person—

(*a*) who is the owner or occupier of land A, and
(*b*) who has not caused or knowingly permitted the substances in question to be in, on or under that land,

to do anything by way of remediation in consequence of any further land in, on or under which those substances or any of them appear to be or to have been present as a result of their escape from land A ("land B") appearing to be in such a condition, by reason of the presence of those substances in, on or under it, that significant harm is being caused, or there is a significant possibility of such harm being caused, or that pollution of controlled waters is being, or is likely to be caused*, unless he is also the owner or occupier of land B.

(5) In any case where—

(*a*) a person ("person A") has caused or knowingly permitted any substances to be in, on, or under any land,
(*b*) another person ("person B") who has not caused or knowingly permitted those substances to be in, on or under that land becomes the owner or occupier of that land, and
(*c*) the substances, or any of the substances, mentioned in paragraph (*a*) above appear to have escaped to other land,

no remediation notice shall require person B to do anything by way of remediation to that other land in consequence of the apparent acts or omissions of person A, except to the extent that person B caused or knowingly permitted the escape.

(6) Nothing in subsection (3), (4) or (5) above prevents the enforcing authority from doing anything by way of remediation under section 78N below which it could have done apart from that subsection, but the authority shall not be entitled under section 78P below to recover from any person any part of the cost incurred by the authority in doing by way of remediation anything which it is precluded by subsection (3), (4) or (5) above from requiring that person to do.

(7) In this section, "appear" means appear to the enforcing authority, and cognate expressions shall be construed accordingly.
[Environmental Protection Act 1990, s 78K, as inserted by the Environment Act 1995, s 57.]

***Substituted in relation to England and Wales by the Water Act 2003, s 86, from a date to be appointed.**

8–26306L **78L. Appeals against remediation notices.** (1) A person on whom a remediation notice is served may, within the period of twenty-one days beginning with the day on which the notice is served, appeal against the notice—

(*a*) if it was served by a local authority, to a magistrates court or, in Scotland, to the sheriff by way of summary application; or

(*b*) if it was served by the appropriate Agency, to the Secretary of State;

and in the following provisions of this section "the appellate authority" means the magistrates' court, the sheriff or the Secretary of State, as the case may be.

(2) On any appeal under subsection (1) above the appellate authority—

(*a*) shall quash the notice, if it is satisfied that there is a material defect in the notice; but

(*b*) subject to that, may confirm the remediation notice, with or without modification, or quash it.

(3) Where an appellate authority confirms a remediation notice, with or without modification it may extend the period specified in the notice for doing what the notice requires to be done.

(4) Regulations[1] may make provision with respect to—

(*a*) the grounds on which, appeals under subsection (1) above may be made;

(*b*) the cases in which, grounds on which, court or tribunal to which, or person at whose instance, an appeal against a decision of a magistrates' court or sheriff court in pursuance of an appeal under subsection (1) above shall lie; or

(*c*) the procedure on an appeal under subsection (1) above or on an appeal by virtue of paragraph (*b*) above.

(5) Regulations[1] under subsection (4) above may (among other things)—

(*a*) include provisions comparable to those in section 290 of the Public Health Act 1936 (appeals against notices requiring the execution of works);

(*b*) prescribe the cases in which a remediation notice is, or is not, to be suspended until the appeal is decided, or until some other stage in the proceedings;

(*c*) prescribe the cases in which the decision on an appeal may in some respects be less favourable to the appellant than the remediation notice against which he is appealing;

(*d*) prescribe the cases in which the appellant may claim that a remediation notice should have been served on some other person and prescribe the procedure to be followed in those cases;

(*e*) make provision as respects—

(i) the particulars to be included in the notice of appeal;

(ii) the persons on whom notice of appeal is to be served and the particulars, if any, which are to accompany the notice; and

(iii) the abandonment of an appeal;

(*f*) make different provision for different cases or classes of case.

(6) This section, so far as relating to appeals to the Secretary of State, is subject to section 114 of the Environment Act 1995 (delegation or reference of appeals etc).

[Environmental Protection Act 1990, s 78L, as inserted by the Environment Act 1995, s 57.]

---

1. See the Contaminated Land Regulations 2000, SI 2000/227 amended by SI 2000/1973 and SI 2001/663 (England) and the Contaminated Land (Wales) Regulations 2001, SI 2001/2197.

8–26306M **78M. Offences of not complying with a remediation notice.** (1) If a person on whom an enforcing authority serves a remediation notice fails, without reasonable excuse, to comply with any of the requirements of the notice, he shall be guilty of an offence.

(2) Where the remediation notice in question is one which was required by section 78E(3) above to state, in relation to the requirement which has not been complied with, the proportion of the cost involved which the person charged with the offence is liable to bear, it shall be a defence for that person to prove that the only reason why he has not complied with the requirement is that one or more of the other persons who are liable to bear a proportion of that cost refused, or was not able, to comply with the requirement.

(3) Except in a case falling within subsection (4) below, a person who commits an offence under subsection (1) above shall be liable, on summary conviction, to a fine not exceeding **level 5** on the standard scale and to a further fine of an amount equal to **one-tenth of level 5** on the standard scale for each day on which the failure continues after conviction of the offence and before the enforcing authority has begun to exercise its powers by virtue of section 78N(3)(*c*) below.

(4) A person who commits an offence under subsection (1) above in a case where the contaminated land to which the remediation notice relates is industrial, trade or business premises shall be liable on summary conviction to a fine not exceeding **£20,000** or such greater sum as the Secretary of State may from time to time by order substitute and to a further fine of an amount equal to **one-tenth of that sum** for each day on which the failure continues after conviction of the offence and before the enforcing authority has begun to exercise its powers by virtue of section 78N(3)(*c*) below.

(5) If the enforcing authority is of the opinion that proceedings for an offence under this section would afford an ineffectual remedy against a person who has failed to comply with any of the

requirements of a remediation notice which that authority has served on him, that authority may take proceedings in the High Court or, in Scotland, in any court of competent jurisdiction, for the purpose of securing compliance with the remediation notice.

(6) In this section, "industrial, trade or business premises" means premises used for any industrial, trade or business purposes or premises not so used on which matter is burnt in connection with any industrial, trade or business process, and premises are used for industrial purposes where they are used for the purposes of any treatment or process as well as where they are used for the purpose of manufacturing.

(7) No order shall be made under subsection (4) above unless a draft of the order has been laid before, and approved by a resolution of, each House of Parliament.

[Environmental Protection Act 1990, s 78M, as inserted by the Environment Act 1995, s 57.]

8–26306N 78N. Powers of the enforcing authority to carry out remediation. (1) Where this section applies, the enforcing authority shall itself have power, in a case falling within paragraph (*a*) or (*b*) of section 78E(1) above, to do what is appropriate by way of remediation to the relevant land or waters.

(2) Subsection (1) above shall not confer power on the enforcing authority to do anything by way of remediation if the authority would, in the particular case, be precluded by section 78YB below from serving a remediation notice requiring that thing to be done.

(3) This section applies in each of the following cases, that is to say—

(*a*) where the enforcing authority considers it necessary to do anything itself by way of remediation for the purpose of preventing the occurrence of any serious harm, or serious pollution of controlled waters, of which there is imminent danger;

(*b*) where an appropriate person has entered into a written agreement with the enforcing authority for that authority to do, at the cost of that person, that which he would otherwise be required to do under this Part by way of remediation;

(*c*) where a person on whom the enforcing authority serves a remediation notice fails to comply with any of the requirements of the notice;

(*d*) where the enforcing authority is precluded by section 78J or 78K above from including something by way of remediation in a remediation notice;

(*e*) where the enforcing authority considers that, were it to do some particular thing by way of remediation, it would decide, by virtue of subsection (2) of section 78P below or any guidance issued under that subsection,—

(i) not to seek to recover under subsection (1) of that section any of the reasonable cost incurred by it in doing that thing; or

(ii) to seek so to recover only a portion of that cost;

(*f*) where no person has, after reasonable inquiry, been found who is an appropriate person in relation to any particular thing.

(4) Subject to section 78E(4) and (5) above, for the purposes of this section, the things which it is appropriate for the enforcing authority to do by way of remediation are—

(*a*) in a case falling within paragraph (*a*) of subsection (3) above, anything by way of remediation which the enforcing authority considers necessary for the purpose mentioned in that paragraph;

(*b*) in a case falling within paragraph (*b*) of that subsection, anything specified in, or determined under, the agreement mentioned in that paragraph;

(*c*) in a case falling within paragraph (*c*) of that subsection, anything which the person mentioned in that paragraph was required to do by virtue of the remediation notice;

(*d*) in a case falling within paragraph (*d*) of that subsection, anything by way of remediation which the enforcing authority is precluded by section 78J or 78K above from including in a remediation notice;

(*e*) in a case falling within paragraph (*e*) or (*f*) of that subsection, the particular thing mentioned in the paragraph in question.

(5) In this section "the relevant land or waters" means—

(*a*) the contaminated land in question;

(*b*) any controlled waters affected by that land; or

(*c*) any land adjoining or adjacent to that land or those waters.

[Environmental Protection Act 1990, s 78N, as inserted by the Environment Act 1995, s 57.]

8–26306P 78P. *Recovery of, and security for, the cost of remediation by the enforcing authority.*

8–26306Q 78Q. Special sites. (1) If, in a case where a local authority has served a remediation notice, the contaminated land in question becomes a special site, the appropriate Agency may adopt the remediation notice and, if it does so,—

(*a*) it shall give notice of its decision to adopt the remediation notice to the appropriate person and to the local authority;

(*b*) the remediation notice shall have effect, as from the time at which the appropriate Agency decides to adopt it, as a remediation notice given by that Agency; and

(*c*) the validity of the remediation notice shall not be affected by—

(i) the contaminated land having become a special site;

(ii) the adoption of the remediation notice by the appropriate Agency; or

(iii) anything in paragraph (*b*) above.

(2) Where a local authority has, by virtue of section 78N above, begun to do anything, or any series of things, by way of remediation—

(*a*) the authority may continue doing that thing, or that series of things, by virtue of that section, notwithstanding that the contaminated land in question becomes a special site; and

(*b*) section 78P above shall apply in relation to the reasonable cost incurred by the authority in doing that thing or those things as if that authority were the enforcing authority.

(3) If and so long as any land is a special site, the appropriate Agency may from time to time inspect that land for the purpose of keeping its condition under review.

(4) If it appears to the appropriate Agency that a special site is no longer land which is required to be designated as such a site, the appropriate Agency may give notice—

(*a*) to the Secretary of State, and

(*b*) to the local authority in whose area the site is situated,

terminating the designation of the land in question as a special site as from such date as may be specified in the notice.

(5) A notice under subsection (4) above shall not prevent the land, or any of the land, to which the notice relates being designated as a special site on a subsequent occasion.

(6) In exercising its functions under subsection (3) or (4) above; the appropriate Agency shall act in accordance with any guidance given for the purpose by the Secretary of State.

[Environmental Protection Act 1990, s 78Q, as inserted by the Environment Act 1995, s 57.]

8–26306R 78R. Registers. (1) Every enforcing authority shall maintain a register containing prescribed particulars of or relating to—

(*a*) remediation notices served by that authority;

(*b*) appeals against any such remediation notices;

(*c*) remediation statements or remediation declarations prepared and published under section 78H above;

(*d*) in relation to an enforcing authority in England and Wales, appeals against charging notices served by that authority;

(*e*) notices under subsection (1)(*b*) or (5)(*a*) of section 78C above which have effect by virtue of subsection (7) of that section as the designation of any land as a special site;

(*f*) notices under subsection (4)(*b*) of section 78D above which have effect by virtue of subsection (6) of that section as the designation of any land as a special site;

(*g*) notices given by or to the enforcing authority under section 78Q(4) above terminating the designation of any land as a special site;

(*h*) notifications given to that authority by persons—

(i) on whom a remediation notice has been served, or

(ii) who are or were required by virtue of section 78H(8)(*a*) above to prepare and publish a remediation statement,

of what they claim has been done by them by way of remediation;

(*j*) notifications given to that authority by owners or occupiers of land—

(i) in respect of which a remediation notice has been served, or

(ii) in respect of which a remediation statement has been prepared and published.

of what they claim has been done on the land in question by way of remediation;

(*k*) convictions for such offences under section 78M above as may be prescribed;

(*l*) such other matters relating to contaminated land as may be prescribed;

but that duty is subject to section 78S and 78T below.

(2) The form of, and the descriptions of information to be contained in, notifications for the purposes of subsection (1)(*h*) or (*j*) above may be prescribed by the Secretary of State.

(3) No entry made in a register by virtue of subsection (1)(*h*) or (*j*) above constitutes a representation by the body maintaining the register or, in a case where the entry is made by virtue of subsection (6) below, the authority which sent the copy of the particulars in question pursuant to subsection (4) or (5) below—

(*a*) that what is stated in the entry to have been done has in fact been done; or

(*b*) as to the manner in which it has been done.

(4) Where any particulars are entered on a register maintained under this section by the

appropriate Agency, the appropriate Agency shall send a copy of those particulars to the local authority in whose area is situated the land to which the particulars relate.

(5) In any case where—

(*a*) any land is treated by virtue of section 78X(2) below as situated in the area of a local authority other than the local authority in whose area it is in fact situated, and

(*b*) any particulars relating to that land are entered on the register maintained under this section by the local authority in whose area the land is so treated as situated,

that authority shall send a copy of those particulars to the local authority in whose area the land is in fact situated.

(6) Where a local authority receives a copy of any particulars sent to it pursuant to subsection (4) or (5) above, it shall enter those particulars on the register maintained by it under this section.

(7) Where information of any description is excluded by virtue of section 78T below from any register maintained under this section, a statement shall be entered in the register indicating the existence of information of that description.

(8) It shall be the duty of each enforcing authority—

(*a*) to secure that the registers maintained by it under this section are available, at all reasonable times, for inspection by the public free of charge; and

(*b*) to afford to members of the public facilities for obtaining copies of entries, on payment of reasonable charges;

and, for the purposes of this subsection, places may be prescribed by the Secretary of State at which any such registers or facilities as are mentioned in paragraph (*a*) or (*b*) above are to be available or afforded to the public in pursuance of the paragraph in question.

(9) Registers under this section may be kept in any form.

[Environmental Protection Act 1990, s 78R, as inserted by the Environment Act 1995, s 57.]

8–26306S 78S. *Exclusion from registers of information affecting national security.*

8–26306T 78T. *Exclusion from registers of certain confidential information.*

8–26306TA 78U. *Reports by the appropriate Agency on the state of contaminated land*

8–26306TB 78V. *Site-specific guidance by the appropriate Agency concerning contaminated land*

8–26306TC 78W. *The appropriate Agency to have regard to guidance given by the Secretary of State*

8–26306U 78X. Supplementary provisions. (1) Where it appears to a local authority that two or more different sites, when considered together, are in such a condition, by reason of substances in, on or under the land, that—

(*a*) significant harm is being caused or there is a significant possibility of such harm being caused, or

(*b*) pollution of controlled waters is being, or is likely to be, caused,*

this Part shall apply in relation to each of those sites, whether or not the condition of the land at any of them, when considered alone, appears to the authority to be such that significant harm is being caused, or there is a significant possibility of such harm being caused, or that pollution of controlled waters is being or is likely to be caused*.

(2) Where it appears to a local authority that any land outside, but adjoining or adjacent to, its area is in such a condition, by reason of substances in, on or under the land, that significant harm is being caused, or that pollution of controlled waters is being, or is likely to be, caused* within its area—

(*a*) the authority may, in exercising its functions under this Part, treat that land as if it were land situated within its area; and

(*b*) except in this subsection, any reference—

(i) to land within the area of a local authority, or

(ii) to the local authority in whose area any land is situated,

shall be construed accordingly;

but this subsection is without prejudice to the functions of the local authority in whose area the land is in fact situated.

(3) A person acting in a relevant capacity—

(*a*) shall not thereby be personally liable, under this Part, to bear the whole or any part of the cost of doing any thing by way of remediation, unless that thing is to any extent referable to substances whose presence in, on or under the contaminated land in question is a result of any act done or omission made by him which it was unreasonable for a person acting in that capacity to do or make; and (*b*) shall not thereby be guilty of an offence under or by virtue of section 78M above unless the requirement which has not been complied with is a requirement to do some particular thing for which he is personally liable to bear the whole or any part of the cost.

(4) In subsection (3) above, "person acting in a relevant capacity" means—

(*a*) a person acting as an insolvency practitioner, within the meaning of section 388 of the Insolvency Act 1986 (including that section as it applies in relation to an insolvent partnership by virtue of any order made under section 421 of that Act);

(*b*) the official receiver acting in a capacity in which he would be regarded as acting as an insolvency practitioner within the meaning of section 388 of the Insolvency Act 1986 if subsection (5) of that section were disregarded;

(*c*) the official receiver acting as receiver or manager;

(*d*) a person acting as a special manager under section 177 or 370 of the Insolvency Act 1986;

(*e*) the Accountant in Bankruptcy acting as permanent or interim trustee in a sequestration (within the meaning of the Bankruptcy (Scotland) Act 1985);

(*f*) a person acting as a receiver or receiver and manager—

(i) under or by virtue of any enactment; or

(ii) by virtue of his appointment as such by an order of a court or by any other instrument.

(5) Regulations may make different provision for different cases or circumstances.

[Environmental Protection Act 1990, s 78X, as inserted by the Environment Act 1995, s 57.]

***Substituted in relation to England and Wales by the Water Act 2003, s 86, from a date to be appointed.**

8–26306V 78Y. Application to the Isles of Scilly. (1) Subject to the provisions of any order under this section, this Part shall not apply in relation to the Isles of Scilly.

(2) The Secretary of State may, after consultation with the Council of the Isles of Scilly, by order provide for the application of any provisions of this Part to the Isles of Scilly; and any such order may provide for the application of those provisions to those Isles with such modifications as may be specified in the order.

(3) An order under this section may—

(*a*) make different provision for different cases, including different provision in relation to different persons, circumstances or localities; and

(*b*) contain such supplemental, consequential and transitional provision as the Secretary of State considers appropriate, including provision saving provision repealed by or under any enactment.

[Environmental Protection Act 1990, s 78Y, as inserted by the Environment Act 1995, s 57.]

8–26306W 78YA. *Supplementary provisions with respect to guidance by the Secretary of State.*

8–26306X 78YB. Interaction of this Part with other enactments. (1) A remediation notice shall not be served if and to the extent that it appears to the enforcing authority that the powers of the appropriate Agency under section 27 above may be exercised in relation to—

(*a*) the significant harm (if any), and

(*b*) the *pollution of controlled waters (if any),

by reason of which the contaminated land in question is such land.

(2) Nothing in this Part shall apply in relation to any land in respect of which there is for the time being in force a site licence under Part II above, except to the extent that any significant harm, or *pollution of controlled waters, by reason of which that land would otherwise fall to be regarded as contaminated land is attributable to causes other than—

(*a*) breach of the conditions of the licence; or

(*b*) the carrying on in accordance with the conditions of the licence, of any activity authorised by the licence.

(2A) This Part shall not apply if and to the extent that—

(*a*) any significant harm, or pollution of controlled waters, by reason of which the land would otherwise fall to be regarded as contaminated, is attributable to the final disposal by deposit in or on land of controlled waste, and

(*b*) enforcement action may be taken in relation to that disposal.

(2B) A remediation notice shall not be served in respect of contaminated land if and to the extent that—

(*a*) the significant harm, or pollution of controlled waters, by reason of which the contaminated land is such land is attributable to an activity other than the final disposal by deposit in or on land of controlled waste, and

(*b*) enforcement action may be taken in relation to that activity.

(2C) In subsections (2A) and (2B) above—

"controlled waste" has the meaning given in section 75(4) of this Act; and

"enforcement action" means action under regulation 24 (enforcement notices) or regulation 26(2)(power of regulator to remedy pollution) of the Pollution Prevention and Control (England and Wales) Regulations 2000.

(3) If, in a case falling within subsection (1) or (7) of section 59 above, the land in question is contaminated land, or becomes such land by reason of the deposit of the controlled waste in question, a remediation notice shall not be served in respect of that land by reason of that waste or any consequences of its deposit, if and to the extent that it appears to the enforcing authority that the powers of a waste regulation authority or waste collection authority under that section may be exercised in relation to that waste or the consequences of its deposit.

(4) No remediation notice shall require a person to do anything the effect of which would be to impede or prevent the making of a discharge in pursuance of a consent given under Chapter II of Part III of the Water Resources Act 1991 (pollution offences) or, in relation to Scotland, in pursuance of a consent given under Part II of the Control of Pollution Act 1974.

[Environmental Protection Act 1990, s 78YB, as inserted by the Environment Act 1995, s 57 and amended by SI 2000/1973.]

***"Significant" inserted (twice) in relation to England and Wales by the Water Act 2003, s 86, from a date to be appointed.**

8–26306Y 78YC. This Part and radioactivity. Except as provided by regulations, nothing in this Part applies in relation to harm, or pollution of controlled waters, so far as attributable to any radioactivity possessed by any substance; but regulations[1] may—

(*a*) provide for prescribed provisions of this Part to have effect with such modifications as the Secretary of State considers appropriate for the purpose of dealing with harm, or pollution of controlled waters, so far as attributable to any radioactivity possessed by any substances; or

(*b*) make such modifications of the Radioactive Substances Act 1993 or any other Act as the Secretary of State considers appropriate.

[Environmental Protection Act 1990, s 78YC, as inserted by the Environment Act 1995, s 57.]

---

1. The Radio-active Contaminated Land (Enabling Powers) (England) Regulations 2005, SI 2005/3467 have been made.

PART III
STATUTORY NUISANCES AND CLEAN AIR
Statutory nuisances

8–26307 79. Statutory nuisances and inspection therefor[2]. (1) Subject to subsections (1A) to (6A) below, the following matters constitute "statutory nuisances" for the purposes of this Part, that is to say—

(*a*) any premises in such a state as to be prejudicial to health[3] or a nuisance;

(*b*) smoke emitted from premises so as to be prejudicial to health or a nuisance;

(*c*) fumes or gases emitted from premises so as to be prejudicial to health or a nuisance;

(*d*) any dust, steam, smell or other effluvia arising on industrial, trade or business premises and being prejudicial to health or a nuisance;

(*e*) any accumulation or deposit which is prejudicial to health or a nuisance;

(*f*) any animal kept in such a place or manner as to be prejudicial to health or a nuisance;

(*g*) noise[4] emitted from premises so as to be prejudicial to health or a nuisance;

(*ga*) noise that is prejudicial to health or a nuisance and is emitted from or caused by a vehicle, machinery or equipment in a street or in Scotland, road;

(*h*) any other matter declared by any enactment to be a statutory nuisance;

and it shall be the duty of every local authority to cause its area to be inspected from time to time to detect any statutory nuisances which ought to be dealt with under section 80 below or sections 80 and 80A below and, where a complaint of a statutory nuisance is made to it by a person living within its area, to take such steps as are reasonably practicable to investigate the complaint.

(1A) No matter shall constitute a statutory nuisance to the extent that it consists of, or is caused by, any land being in a contaminated state.

(1B) Land is in a "contaminated state" for the purposes of subsection (1A) above if, and only if, it is in such a condition, by reason of substances in, on or under the land, that—

(*a*) harm is being caused or there is a possibility of harm being caused; or

(*b*) pollution of controlled waters is being, or is likely to be, caused;

and in this subsection "harm", "pollution of controlled waters" and "substance" have the same meaning as in Part IIA of this Act.

(2) Subsection (1)(*b*) and (*g*) above do not apply in relation to premises—

(*a*) occupied on behalf of the Crown for naval, military or air force purposes or for the purposes of the department of the Secretary of State having responsibility for defence, or
(*b*) occupied by or for the purposes of a visiting force;

and "visiting force" means any such body, contingent or detachment of the forces of any country as is a visiting force for the purposes of any of the provisions of the Visiting Forces Act 1952.

(3) Subsection (1)(*b*) above does not apply to—

(i) smoke emitted from a chimney of a private dwelling within a smoke control area,
(ii) dark smoke emitted from a chimney of a building or a chimney serving the furnace of a boiler or industrial plant attached to a building or for the time being fixed to or installed on any land,
(iii) smoke emitted from a railway locomotive steam engine, or
(iv) dark smoke emitted otherwise than as mentioned above from industrial or trade premises.

(4) Subsection (1)(*c*) above does not apply in relation to premises other than private dwellings.
(5) Subsection (1)(*d*) above does not apply to steam emitted from a railway locomotive engine.
(6) Subsection (1)(*g*) above does not apply to noise caused by aircraft other than model aircraft.
(6A) Subsection (1)(*ga*) above does not apply to noise made—

(*a*) by traffic,
(*b*) by any naval, military or air force of the Crown or by a visiting force (as defined in subsection (2) above), or
(*c*) by a political demonstration or a demonstration supporting or opposing a cause or campaign.

(7) In this Part—

"chimney" includes structures and openings of any kind from or through which smoke may be emitted;
"dust" does not include dust emitted from a chimney as an ingredient of smoke;
"equipment" includes a musical instrument;
"fumes" means any airborne solid matter smaller than dust;
"gas" includes vapour and moisture precipitated from vapour;
"industrial, trade or business premises" means premises used for any industrial, trade or business purposes or premises not so used on which matter is burnt in connection with any industrial, trade or business process, and premises are used for industrial purposes where they are used for the purposes of any treatment or process as well as where they are used for the purposes of manufacturing[5];
"local authority" means, subject to subsection (8) below,—

(*a*) in Greater London, a London borough council, the Common Council of the City of London and, as respects the Temples, the Sub-Treasurer of the Inner Temple and the Under-Treasurer of the Middle Temple respectively;
(*b*) in England and Wales outside Greater London, a district council in England;
(*bb*) in Wales, a county council or county borough council;
(*c*) the Council of the Isles of Scilly; and
(*d*) in Scotland, a district or islands council or a council constituted under section 2 of the Local Government etc (Scotland) Act 1994;

"noise" includes vibration;
"person responsible—

(*a*) in relation to a statutory nuisance, means the person to whose act, default or sufferance the nuisance is attributable;
(*b*) in relation to a vehicle, includes the person in whose name the vehicle is for the time being registered under the Vehicles Excise and Registration Act 1994 and any other person who is for the time being the driver of the vehicle;
(*c*) in relation to machinery or equipment, includes any person who is for the time being the operator of the machinery or equipment;

"prejudicial to health" means injurious, or likely to cause injury, to health[6];
"premises" includes land and, in relation to England and Wales, subject to subsection (12) and section 81A(9) below, any vessel;
"private dwelling" means any building, or part of a building, used or intended to be used, as a dwelling;
"road" has the same meaning as in Part IV of the New Roads and Street Works Act 1991;
"smoke" includes soot, ash, grit and gritty particles emitted in smoke[7];
"street" means a highway and any other road, footway, square or court that is for the time being open to the public;

and any expression used in this section and in the Clean Air Act 1993 have the same meaning in this section as in that Act and section 3 of the Clean Air Act 1993 shall apply for the interpretation of the expression "dark smoke" and the operation of this Part in relation to it.

(8) Where, by an order under section 2 of the Public Health (Control of Disease) Act 1984, a port health authority has been constituted for any port health district or in Scotland where by an order under section 172 of the Public Health (Scotland) Act 1897 a port local authority or a joint

port local authority has been constituted for the whole or part of a port, the port health authority, port local authority or joint port local authority, as the case may be shall have by virtue of this subsection, as respects its district, the functions conferred or imposed by this Part in relation to statutory nuisance other than a nuisance falling within paragraph (*g*) or (*ga*) of subsection (1) above and no such order shall be made assigning those functions; and "local authority" and "area" shall be construed accordingly.

(9) In this Part "best practicable means" is to be interpreted by reference to the following provisions—

(*a*) "practicable" means reasonably practicable having regard among other things to local conditions and circumstances, to the current state of technical knowledge and to the financial implications;

(*b*) the means to be employed include the design, installation, maintenance and manner and periods of operation of plant and machinery, and the design, construction and maintenance of buildings and structures;

(*c*) the test is to apply only so far as compatible with any duty imposed by law;

(*d*) the test is to apply only so far as compatible with safety and safe working conditions, and with the exigencies of any emergency or unforseeable circumstances;

and, in circumstances where a code of practice under section 71 of the Control of Pollution Act 1974 (noise minimisation) is applicable, regard shall also be had to guidance given in it.

(10) A local authority shall not without the consent of the Secretary of State institute summary proceedings under this Part in respect of a nuisance falling within paragraph (*b*), (*d*), (*e*) or (*g*) and, in relation to Scotland, paragraph (*ga*), of subsection (1) above if proceedings in respect thereof might be instituted under Part I or under regulations under section 2 of the Pollution Prevention and Control Act 1999.

(11) The area of a local authority which includes part of the seashore shall also include for the purposes of this Part the territorial sea lying seawards from that part of the shore; and subject to subsection (12) and, in relation to England and Wales section 81A(9) below, this Part shall have effect, in relation to any area included in the area of a local authority by virtue of this subsection—

(*a*) as if references to premises and the occupier of premises included respectively a vessel and the master of a vessel; and

(*b*) with such other modifications, if any, as are prescribed in regulations made by the Secretary of State.

(12) A vessel powered by steam reciprocating machinery is not a vessel to which this Part of this Act applies.

[Environmental Protection Act 1990, s 79, as amended by Sch 16 to that Act, the Clean Air Act 1993, Sch 4, the Noise and Statutory Nuisance Act 1993, ss 2 and 10, the Local Government (Wales) Act 1994, Sch 9, the Vehicle Excise and Registration Act 1994, Sch 3, the Environment Act 1995, Sch 17, the Pollution Prevention and Control Act 1999, Schs 2 and 3 and SI 2000/1973.]

---

1. Part III consists of ss 79–85.

2. The application of this section to London Boroughs is modified by the London Local Authorities Act 1996, s 24 in this PART: title LONDON, ante.

3. The expressions "prejudicial to health" and "injurious or likely to cause injury to health" are aimed at the effect on people's health of filthy or unwholesome premises and the like: in particular, the risk of disease or illness. There is nothing in s 79 to suggest that the powers were intended to protect against the danger of accidental physical injury; accordingly, premises that are in such a state as to create the likelihood of accident causing personal injury are not as a matter of law capable of giving rise to a statutory nuisance within s 79 (1)(*a*) (*R v Bristol City Council, ex p Everett* [1999] 2 All ER 193, [1999] 1 WLR 1170, CA). The powers in this provision do not extend to a lack of adequate sound insulation for which there is a separate statutory code under which local authorities have express powers and, in serious cases, duties to deal with sound insulation (*R (Vella) v Lambeth Borough Council* [2005] TLR 533, QBD).

The powers in this section are directed to the presence of some feature which in itself is prejudicial to health in that it is the source of possible infection or disease or illness such as dampness, mould, dirt or evil-smelling accumulations or the presence of rats. They do not extend to the arrangement of rooms otherwise not in themselves insanitary so as to be prejudicial to health, such as where the nearest facility for washing hands after use of a lavatory required access through kitchen or use of the kitchen sink (*Birmingham City Council v Oakley* [2001] 1 All ER 385, [2000] 3 WLR 1936, HL).

Evidence given by experts about the condition of premises is sufficient by itself, in the absence of evidence relating to the health and medical condition of the tenant, to establish a prima facie case that premises were prejudicial to health and a statutory nuisance (*O'Toole v Knowsley Metropolitan Borough Council* [1999] LS Gaz R 36).

Traffic noise from vehicles, machinery or equipment in the street which renders premises to be in such a state as to be prejudicial to health or a nuisance does not constitute a statutory nuisance within the meaning of s 79(1)(*a*) because s 79(1)(*ga*) subject to the limitations in s 79(6A), deals directly with vehicle noise (*Haringey London Borough Council v Jowett* (1999) 78 P & CR D24, [1999] EGCS 64).

4. It is wrong for justices to refuse to convict of an offence under s 80(4) and (5) merely on the basis that no reliable acoustic measurement evidence has been adduced; however, where the evidence of the environmental enforcement officer is that the nuisance was "marginal" justices are perfectly entitled to say that they are not sure and to acquit (*Lewisham Borough Council v Hall* [2002] EWHC 960 (Admin), [2002] All ER (D) 83 (May), [2002] JPN 378.

5. This definition includes a sewage treatment works (*Hounslow London Borough Council v Thames Water Utilities Ltd* [2003] EWHC 1197 (Admin), [2004] QB 212, [2003] 3 WLR 1243.

6. See note 3 ante.

7. Whilst "smoke" has a primary meaning of 'the visible volatile product given off by burning or smouldering substance' the term can also be applied to the smell of smoke (*Griffiths v Pembrokeshire County Council* [2000] 18 LS Gaz R 36, DC).

8–26308 **80. Summary proceedings for statutory nuisances.** (1) Where a local authority is satisfied that a statutory nuisance exists, or is likely to occur or recur, in the area of the authority, the local authority shall serve a notice[1] ("an abatement notice") imposing all or any of the following requirements—

(*a*) requiring the abatement of the nuisance of prohibiting or restricting its occurrence or recurrence;

(*b*) requiring the execution of such works, and the taking of such other steps, as may be necessary for any of those purposes,

and the notice shall specify the time or times within[2] which the requirements of the notice are to be complied with.

(2) Subject to section 80A(1) below, the abatement notice shall be served[3]—

(*a*) except in a case falling within paragraph (*b*) or (*c*) below, on the person responsible for the nuisance;

(*b*) where the nuisance arises from any defect of a structural character, on the owner[4] of the premises;

(*c*) where the person responsible for the nuisance cannot be found or the nuisance has not yet occurred, on the owner or occupier of the premises.

(3) A person served with an abatement notice may appeal[5] against the notice to a magistrates' court or in Scotland, the sheriff within the period of twenty-one days beginning with the date on which he was served with the notice.

(4) If a person on whom an abatement notice[6] is served, without reasonable excuse[7], contravenes[8] or fails to comply with any requirement or prohibition imposed by the notice, he shall be guilty of an offence[9].

(5) Except in a case falling within subsection (6) below, a person who commits an offence under subsection (4) above shall be liable on summary conviction to a fine not exceeding **level 5** on the standard scale together with a further fine of an amount equal to **one-tenth of that level** for each day on which the offence continues after the conviction.

(6) A person who commits an offence under subsection (4) above on industrial, trade or business premises shall be liable on summary conviction to a fine not exceeding **£20,000**.

(7) Subject to subsection (8) below, in any proceedings for an offence under subsection (4) above in respect of a statutory nuisance it shall be a defence to prove that the best practicable means[10] were used to prevent, or to counteract the effects of, the nuisance.

(8) The defence under subsection (7) above is not available—

(*a*) in the case of a nuisance falling within paragraph (*a*), (*d*), (*e*), (*f*) or (*g*) of section 79(1) above except where the nuisance arises on industrial, trade or business premises;

(*aa*) in the case of a nuisance falling within paragraph (*ga*) of section 79(1) above except where the noise is emitted from or caused by a vehicle, machinery or equipment being used for industrial, trade or business purposes;

(*b*) in the case of a nuisance falling within paragraph (*b*) of section 79(1) above except where the smoke is emitted from a chimney; and

(*c*) in the case of a nuisance falling within paragraph (*c*) or (*h*) of section 79(1) above.

(9) In proceedings for an offence under subsection (4) above in respect of a statutory nuisance falling within paragraph (*g*) or (*ga*) of section 79(1) above where the offence consists in contravening requirements imposed by virtue of subsection (1)(*a*) above it shall be a defence to prove—

(*a*) that the alleged offence was covered by a notice served under section 60 or a consent given under section 61 or 65 of the Control of Pollution Act 1974 (construction sites, etc); or

(*b*) where the alleged offence was committed at a time when the premises were subject to a notice under section 66 of that Act (noise reduction notice), that the level of noise emitted from the premises at that time was not such as to constitute a contravention of the notice under that section; or

(*c*) where the alleged offence was committed at a time when the premises were not subject to a notice under section 66 of that Act, and when a level fixed under section 67 of that Act (new buildings liable to abatement order) applied to the premises, that the level of noise emitted from the premises at that time did not exceed that level.

(10) Paragraphs (*b*) and (*c*) of subsection (9) above apply whether or not the relevant notice was subject to appeal at the time when the offence was alleged to have been committed.

[Environmental Protection Act 1990, s 80, as amended by the Noise and Statutory Nuisance Act 1993, s 3 and the Environment Act 1995, Sch 17.]

---

1. An abatement notice must inform the person on whom it is served the nature of the nuisance complained of, but it need not specify the works or other steps to be taken to abate the nuisance. In all cases the local authority has a discretion to leave the choice of means of abatement to the perpetrator of the nuisance. If, however, the means of abatement are required by the local authority, then they must be specified in the notice (*R v Falmouth and Truro Port Health Authority, ex p South West Water Ltd* [2001] QB 445, [2000] 3 All ER 306, [2000] 3 WLR 1464, CA).

The local authority has an implied power to withdraw an abatement notice after it has been served (*R v Bristol City Council, ex p Everett* [1999] 2 All ER 193, [1999] 1 WLR 1170, CA). However, a local authority is entitled to serve a notice simply requiring the recipient to abate a nuisance created by barking dogs without specifying the manner of abatement or the level of barking, either which constituted the nuisance or the level of barking which would be acceptable (*Budd v Colchester Borough Council* (1999) 97 LGR 601).

2. In relation to a similarly worded provision in the predecessor to this section, namely s 58(1) of the Control of Pollution Act 1974, it was held that the notice must specify a period within which a nuisance is to be abated or within which works are to be executed or other steps taken, but the notice does not have to state a period within which a prohibition on recurrence has to be complied with (*R v Birmingham City Justices, ex p Guppy* (1987) 86 LGR 264, 152 JP 159) and see *R v Tunbridge Wells Justices, ex p Tunbridge Wells Borough Council* (1995) 160 JP 574, DC.

3. For service of notices, see s 160, post.

4. The word "owner" includes a managing agent who receives rack rent for the premises (*Camden London Borough Council v Gunby* [1999] 4 All ER 602, [2000] 1 WLR 465, DC).

5. For further provisions with respect to such an appeal, see s 81 and Sch 3, post, and the Statutory Nuisance (Appeals) Regulations 1995, this title, post.

In considering the validity of a noise abatement notice served by a local authority under s 80, a magistrates' court or the Crown Court on appeal are required to consider the facts at the time the notice was served and not at the time of the appeal (*SFI Group plc (formerly Surrey Free Inns plc) v Gosport Borough Council* [1999] EGCS 51, CA).

6. The effectiveness of a notice served under the repealed Control of Pollution Act 1974, s 58(1) is preserved by the Interpretation Act 1978, s 16(1) and may be enforced under s 58(4) of the 1974 Act (*Aitken v South Hams District Council* [1995] 1 AC 262, [1994] 3 All ER 400, 159 JP 25).

7. "Reasonable excuse" does not include matters that should have been raised on an appeal under sub-s (3) challenging the validity of the notice, unless there has been some special reason for not entering an appeal (*A Lambert Flat Management Ltd v Lomas* [1981] 2 All ER 280, [1981] 1 WLR 898). Mitigating factors, such as loud reggae music playing to celebrate a birthday, do not amount to a reasonable excuse if other ingredients of a nuisance are established (*Wellingborough Borough Council v Gordon* (1990) 155 JP 494). The burden is on the prosecution to disprove reasonable excuse once raised by the defendant (as distinct from the defences in sub-sections (7) and (9)) (*Polychronakis v Richards and Jerrom* [1998] JPL B35, [1998] Env LR 346, DC).

8. When proving that noise amounting to a nuisance has occurred or recurred in contravention of a notice served under s 80, the prosecution need not necessarily prove that a particular occupier of property has actually suffered interference with his reasonable enjoyment of his property, but, depending on the circumstances of a particular case, may seek to rely on other evidence including expert evidence (*Cooke v Adatia* (1988) 153 JP 129).

9. Whether or not the defendant is dealt with in any other way, in the case of a noise offence, the court may make a forfeiture order in respect of any seized equipment used or alleged to have been used in the commission of the offence (Noise Act 1996, Schedule, this title, post).

A person guilty of an offence under s 80(4) is not also liable in a civil action for damages at the suit of any person who thereby suffers loss or damage (*Issa v Hackney London Borough Council* [1997] 1 WLR 956).

10. "Best practicable means" is defined in s 79(9), ante.

8–26308A 80A. Abatement notice in respect of noise in street[1]**.** (1) In the case of a statutory nuisance within section 79(1)(*ga*) above that—

(*a*) has not yet occurred, or
(*b*) arises from noise emitted from or caused by an unattended vehicle or unattended machinery or equipment,

the abatement notice shall be served in accordance with subsection (2) below,

(2) The notice shall be served—

(*a*) where the person responsible for the vehicle, machinery or equipment can be found, on that person;
(*b*) where that person cannot be found or where the local authority determines that this paragraph should apply, by fixing the notice to the vehicle, machinery or equipment.

(3) Where—

(*a*) an abatement notice is served in accordance with subsection (2)(*b*) above by virtue of a determination of the local authority, and
(*b*) the person responsible for the vehicle, machinery or equipment can be found and served with a copy of the notice within an hour of the notice being fixed to the vehicle, machinery or equipment,

a copy of the notice shall be served on that person accordingly.

(4) Where an abatement notice is served in accordance with subsection (2)(*b*) above by virtue of a determination of the local authority, the notice shall state that, if a copy of the notice is subsequently served under subsection (3) above, the time specified in the notice as the time within which its requirements are to be complied with is extended by such further period as is specified in the notice.

(5) Where an abatement notice is served in accordance with subsection (2)(*b*) above, the person responsible for the vehicle, machinery or equipment may appeal against the notice under section 80(3) above as if he had been served with the notice on the date on which it was fixed to the vehicle, machinery or equipment.

(6) Section 80(4) above shall apply in relation to a person on whom a copy of an abatement notice is served under subsection (3) above as if the copy were the notice itself.

(7) A person who removes or interferes with a notice fixed to a vehicle, machinery or equipment in accordance with subsection (2)(*b*) above shall be guilty of an offence, unless he is the person responsible for the vehicle, machinery or equipment or he does so with the authority of that person.

(8) A person who commits an offence under subsection (7) above shall be liable on summary conviction to a fine not exceeding **level 3** on the standard scale.

[Environmental Protection Act 1990, s 80A, inserted by the Noise and Statutory Nuisance Act 1993, s 3.]

1. The application of this section to London Boroughs is modified by the London Local Authorities Act 1996, s 24 in this PART: title LONDON, ante.

8–26309 **81. Supplementary provisions.** (1) Subject to subsection (1A) below, where more than one person is responsible for a statutory nuisance section 80 above shall apply to each of those persons whether or not what any one of them is responsible for would by itself amount to a nuisance.

(1A) In relation to a statutory nuisance within section 79(1)(*ga*) above for which more than one person is responsible (whether or not what any one of those persons is responsible for would by itself amount to such a nuisance), section 80(2)(*a*) above shall apply with the substitution of "any one of the persons" for "the person".

(1B) In relation to a statutory nuisance within section 79(1)(*ga*) above caused by noise emitted from or caused by an unattended vehicle or unattended machinery or equipment for which more than one person is responsible, section 80A above shall apply with the substitution—

(*a*) in subsection (2)(*a*), of "any of the persons" for "the person" and of "one such person" for "that person",
(*b*) in subsection (2)(*b*), of "such a person" for "that person",
(*c*) in subsection (3), of "any of the persons" for "the person" and of "one such person" for "that person",
(*d*) in subsection (5), of "any person" for "the person", and
(*e*) in subsection (7), of "a person;" for "the person", and of "such a person" for "that person".

(2) Where a statutory nuisance which exists or has occurred within the area of a local authority, or which has affected any part of that area, appears to the local authority to be wholly or partly caused by some act or default committed or taking place outside the area, the local authority may act under section 80 above as if the act or default were wholly within that area, except that any appeal shall be heard by a magistrates' court or in Scotland, the sheriff having jurisdiction where the act or default is alleged to have taken place.

(3) Where an abatement notice has not been complied with the local authority may, whether or not they take proceedings for an offence or, in Scotland, whether or not proceedings have been taken for an offence, under section 80(4) above, abate the nuisance and do whatever may be necessary[1] in execution of the notice.

(4) Any expenses reasonably incurred by a local authority in abating, or preventing the recurrence of, a statutory nuisance under subsection (3) above may be recovered by them from the person by whose act or default the nuisance was caused and, if that person is the owner of the premises, from any person who is for the time being the owner thereof; and the court or sheriff may apportion the expenses between persons by whose acts or defaults the nuisance is caused in such manner as the court consider or sheriff considers fair and reasonable.

(5) If a local authority is of opinion that proceedings for an offence under section 80(4) above would afford an inadequate remedy in the case of any statutory nuisance, they may, subject to subsection (6) below, take proceedings[2] in the High Court or, in Scotland, in any court of competent jurisdiction, for the purpose of securing the abatement, prohibition or restriction of the nuisance, and the proceedings shall be maintainable notwithstanding the local authority have suffered no damage from the nuisance.

(6) In any proceedings under subsection (5) above in respect of a nuisance falling within paragraph (*g*) or (*ga*) of section 79(1) above, it shall be a defence to prove that the noise was authorised by a notice under section 60 or a consent under section 61 (construction sites) of the Control of Pollution Act 1974.

(7) The further supplementary provisions in Schedule 3 to this Act shall have effect.

[Environmental Protection Act 1990, s 81, as amended by the Noise and Statutory Nuisance Act 1993, s 4 and the Environment Act 1995, Sch 17.]

1. In the case of nuisance by noise, the local authority has the power to seize and remove any equipment which appears to the authority as being or has been used in the emission of the noise in question (Noise Act 1996, s 10(7), this title, post).

2. This remedy is additional to those available summarily, and a local authority may seek an injunction notwithstanding that the statutory procedure for appealing to a magistrates' court has not been exhausted (*Hammersmith London Borough Council v Magnum Automated Forecourts Ltd* [1978] 1 All ER 401, 142 JP 130).

8–26309A **81A, 81B.** *Recovery and payment of expenses.*

8–26310 **82. Summary proceedings by persons aggrieved by statutory nuisances.** (1) A magistrates' court may act under this section on a complaint[1] or, in Scotland, the sheriff may act under this section on a summary application made by any person on the ground that he is aggrieved by the existence of a statutory nuisance.

(2) If the magistrates' court or, in Scotland, the sheriff is satisfied that the alleged nuisance exists, or that although abated it is likely to recur on the same premises or, in the case of a nuisance within section 79(1)(*ga*) above, in the same street or, in Scotland, road, the court or the sheriff shall make an order for either or both of the following purposes—

(*a*) requiring the defendant[2] or, in Scotland, defender to abate the nuisance, within a time specified in the order, and to execute any works necessary for that purpose;

(*b*) prohibiting a recurrence of the nuisance, and requiring the defendant or defender, within a time specified in the order, to execute any works necessary to prevent the recurrence;

and, in England and Wales may also impose on the defendant a fine not exceeding **level 5** on the standard scale.

(3) If the magistrates' court, or the sheriff is satisfied that the alleged nuisance exists and is such as, in the opinion of the court, or of the sheriff to render premises unfit for human habitation, an order under subsection (2) above may prohibit the use of the premises for human habitation until the premises are, to the satisfaction of the court or of the sheriff, rendered fit for that purpose.

(4) Proceedings for an order under subsection (2) above shall be brought—

(*a*) except in a case falling within paragraph (*b*), (*c*) or (*d*) below, against the person responsible for the nuisance;

(*b*) where the nuisance arises from any defect of a structural character, against the owner of the premises;

(*c*) where the person responsible for the nuisance cannot be found, against the owner or occupier of the premises;

(*d*) in the case of a statutory nuisance within section 79(1)(*ga*) above caused by noise emitted from or caused by an unattended vehicle or unattended machinery or equipment, against the person responsible for the vehicle, machinery or equipment.

(5) Subject to subsection (5A) below, where more than one person is responsible for a statutory nuisance, subsections (1) to (4) above shall apply to each of those persons whether or not what any one of them is responsible for would by itself amount to a nuisance.

(5A) In relation to a statutory nuisance within section 79(1)(*ga*) above for which more than one person is responsible (whether or not what any one of those persons is responsible for would by itself amount to such a nuisance), subsection (4)(*a*) above shall apply with the substitution of "each person responsible for the nuisance who can be found" for "the person responsible for the nuisance".

(5B) In relation to a statutory nuisance within section 79(1)(*ga*) above caused by noise emitted from or caused by an unattended vehicle or unattended machinery or equipment for which more than one person is responsible, subsection (4)(*d*) above shall apply with the substitution of "any person" for "the person".

(6) Before instituting proceedings for an order under subsection (2) above against any person, the person aggrieved by the nuisance shall give to that person such notice[3] in writing of his intention to bring the proceedings as is applicable to proceedings in respect of a nuisance of that description and the notice shall specify the matter complained of.

(7) The notice of the bringing of proceedings in respect of a statutory nuisance required by subsection (6) above which is applicable is—

(*a*) in the case of a nuisance falling within paragraph (*g*) or (*ga*) of section 79(1) above, not less than three days' notice; and

(*b*) in the case of a nuisance of any other description, not less than twenty-one days' notice;

but the Secretary of State may, by order, provide that this subsection shall have effect as if such period as is specified in the order were the minimum period of notice applicable to any description of statutory nuisance specified in the order.

(8) A person who, without reasonable excuse, contravenes any requirement or prohibition imposed by an order under subsection (2) above shall be guilty of an offence and liable on summary conviction to a fine not exceeding **level 5** on the standard scale together with a further fine of an amount equal to **one-tenth of that level** for each day on which the offence continues after the conviction.

(9) Subject to subsection (10) below, in any proceedings for an offence under subsection (8) above in respect of a statutory nuisance it shall be a defence to prove that the best practicable means were used to prevent, or to counteract the effects of, the nuisance.

(10) The defence under subsection (9) above is not available—

(*a*) in the case of a nuisance falling within paragraph (*a*), (*d*), (*e*), (*f*) or (*g*) of section 79(1) above except where the nuisance arises on industrial, trade or business premises;

(*aa*) in the case of a nuisance falling within paragraph (*ga*) of section 79(1) above except where the noise is emitted from or caused by a vehicle, machinery or equipment being used for industrial, trade or business purposes;

(*b*) in the case of a nuisance falling within paragraph (*b*) of section 79(1) above except where the smoke is emitted from a chimney;

(*c*) in the case of a nuisance falling within paragraph (*c*) or (*h*) of section 79(1) above; and

(*d*) in the case of a nuisance which is such as to render the premises unfit for human habitation.

(11) If a person is convicted of an offence under subsection (8) above, a magistrates' court or the sheriff may, after giving the local authority in whose area the nuisance has occurred an opportunity of being heard, direct the authority to do anything which the person convicted was required to do by the order to which the conviction relates.

(12) Where on the hearing of proceedings for an order under subsection (2) above it is proved that the alleged nuisance existed at the date of the making of the complaint or summary application, then, whether or not at the date of the hearing it still exists or is likely to recur, the court or the sheriff shall[4] order the defendant or defender (or defendants or defenders in such proportions as appears fair and reasonable) to pay to the person bringing the proceedings such amount as the court or the sheriff considers reasonably sufficient to compensate him for any expenses properly incurred[5] by him in the proceedings.

(13) If it appears to the magistrates' court or to the sheriff that neither the person responsible for the nuisance nor the owner or occupier of the premises or (as the case may be) the person responsible for the vehicle, machinery or equipment can be found the court or the sheriff may, after giving the local authority in whose area the nuisance has occurred an opportunity of being heard, direct the authority to do anything which the court or the sheriff would have ordered that person to do.

[Environmental Protection Act 1990, s 82, as amended by the Noise and Statutory Nuisance Act 1993, s 5 and the Environment Act 1995, Sch 17.]

1. Where an order may require work to be done which cannot be required of a landlord under a contractual or other statutory duty, there is no ground for refusal to issue a summons. It would be otherwise if the two sets of proceedings were co-extensive and it is clear that no bench of magistrates could or would impose a fine (*R v Highbury Corner Magistrates' Court, ex p Edwards* [1995] Crim LR 65).

Notwithstanding that proceedings are commenced by way of complaint, they are criminal in nature and the court has power to make a compensation order under s 35 of the Powers of Criminal Courts Act 1973 (*Botross v Hammersmith and Fulham London Borough Council* (1994) 27 HLR 179). The justices have no power to adjourn the hearing without taking a plea when to do so would avoid the consequence of a conviction under s 82(2) and the right to compensation under s 35 of the Powers of Criminal Courts Act 1973 (*R v Dudley Magistrates' Court, ex p Hollis* [1998] 1 All ER 759).

2. It is open to the defendant to avoid liability by showing that he was not a person by whose act, default or sufferance the nuisance arose or continued (*Carr v Hackney London Borough Council* (1995) 160 JP 402).

3. It is important that ordinary members of the public who might not have any legal expertise, such as tenants, are not deterred from pursuing complaints which are well founded on the merits over technical requirements. Accordingly, it is not necessary for a s 82(6) notice to specify the works required to remedy the complaint, nor does it need to identify the capacity in which the proposed defendant is to be proceeded against (*East Staffordshire Borough Council v Fairless* [1998] 41 LS Gaz R 46).

When assessing compensation pursuant to s 35 of the Powers of Criminal Courts Act 1973, in **PART III: SENTENCING**, ante, in respect of an offence of statutory nuisance by a landlord under s 82 of this Act, the court should take into account only the injury, loss or damage caused by the continuation of the nuisance from the date when the period stated in the complainant's s 82(6) notice expired to the date of the hearing. However, if the complainant should delay for more than six months after the expiry of the s 82(6) notice before making complaint to the magistrates, then the offence which could form the basis for compensation would not commence earlier than a date six months before the complaint was made (*R v Crown Court at Liverpool, ex p Cooke* [1996] 4 All ER 589). For service of notices see s 160, post.

4. The court is bound to order costs provided that it is satisfied that the statutory nuisance existed at the time of the complaint. The court is not entitled to refuse costs on the grounds that it considers it was unnecessary for the complainant to institute proceedings or because the nuisance has since been abated. The courts consideration is limited to questions as to whether a particular items of expenditure were unnecessary and as to whether the amounts claimed are more than those warranted by the particular proceedings before the court, such as the engagement of unduly expensive solicitors or counsel or a excessive number of experts (*R v Dudley Magistrates' Court, ex p Hollis* [1998] 1 All ER 759, [1999] 1 WLR 642, DC).

5. See note 4 ante.

Termination of existing controls over offensive trades and businesses

8–26312 **84. Termination of Public Health Act controls over offensive trades etc.** (1) Where a person carries on, in the area or part of the area of any local authority—

(*a*) in England or Wales, a trade which—

(i) is an offensive trade within the meaning of section 107 of the Public Health Act 1936 in that area or part of that area, and

(ii) constitutes a prescribed process designated for local control for the carrying on of which an authorisation is required under section 6 of this Act; or

(*b*) in Scotland, a business which—

(i) is mentioned in section 32(1) of the Public Health (Scotland) Act 1897 (or is an offensive business by virtue of that section) in that area or part of that area; and

(ii) constitutes a prescribed process designated for local control for the carrying on of which an authorisation is required under the said section 6,

subsection (2) below shall have effect in relation to that trade or business as from the date on which an authorisation is granted under section 6 of this Act or, if that person has not applied for such an authorisation within the period allowed under section 2(1) above for making applications under that section, as from the end of that period.

(2) Where this subsection applies in relation to the trade or business carried on by any person—

(*a*) nothing in section 107 of the Public Health Act 1936 or in section 32 of the Public Health (Scotland) Act 1897 shall apply in relation to it, and

(*b*) no byelaws or further byelaws made under section 108(2) of the said Act of 1936, or under subsection (2) of the said section 32, with respect to a trade or business of that description shall apply in relation to it;

but without prejudice to the continuance of, and imposition of any penalty in, any proceedings under the said section 107 or the said section 32 which were instituted before the date as from which this subsection has effect in relation to the trade or business.

(3) Subsection (2)(*b*) above shall apply in relation to the trade of fish frying as it applies in relation to an offensive trade.

(4) When the Secretary of State considers it expedient to do so, having regard to the operation of Part I and the preceding provisions of this Part of this Act in relation to offensive trades or businesses, he may by order[1] repeal—

(*a*) sections 107 and 108 of the Public Health Act 1936; and
(*b*) section 32 of the Public Health (Scotland) Act 1897;

and different days may be so appointed in relation to trades or businesses which constitute prescribed processes and those which do not.

(5) In this section—

"prescribed process" has the same meaning as in Part I of this Act; and

"offensive trade" or "trade" has the same meaning as in section 107 of the Public Health Act 1936.

[Environmental Protection Act 1990, s 84.]

---

1. The Repeal of Offensive Trades or Business Provisions Order 1995, SI 1995/205, which repeals ss 107 and 108 of the Public Health Act 1936 has been made.

PART IV[1]
LITTER ETC

Provisions relating to litter

8–26314 **86. Preliminary.** (1) The following provisions have effect for the purposes of this Part.

(2) In England and Wales the following are "principal litter authorities"—

(*a*) a county council,
(*aa*) a county borough council,
(*b*) a district council,
(*c*) a London borough council,
(*d*) the Common Council of the City of London, and
(*e*) the Council of the Isles of Scilly;

but the Secretary of State may, by order, designate other descriptions of local authorities as litter authorities for the purposes of this Part; and any such authority shall also be a principal litter authority.

(3) *Scotland.*

(4) Subject to subsection (8) below, land is "relevant land" of a principal litter authority if, not being relevant land falling within subsection (7) below, it is open to the air and is land (but not a highway or in Scotland a public road) which is under the direct control of such an authority to which the public are entitled or permitted to have access with or without payment.

(5) Land is "Crown land" if it is land—

(*a*) occupied by the Crown Estate Commissioners as part of the Crown Estate,
(*b*) occupied by or for the purposes of a government department or for naval, military or air force purposes, or
(*c*) occupied or managed by any body acting on behalf of the Crown;

is "relevant Crown land" if it is Crown land which is open to the air and is land (but not a highway or in Scotland a public road) to which the public are entitled or permitted to have access with or without payment; and "the appropriate Crown authority" for any Crown land is the Crown Estate Commissioners, the Minister in charge of the government department or the body which occupies or manages the land on the Crown's behalf, as the case may be.

(6) Subject to subsection (8) below, land is "relevant land" of a designated statutory undertaker if it is land which is under the direct control of any statutory undertaker or statutory undertaker of any description which may be designated by the Secretary of State, by order[2], for the purposes of this Part, being land to which the public are entitled or permitted to have access with or without payment or, in such cases as may be prescribed in the designation order, land in relation to which the public have no such right or permission.

(7) Subject to subsection (8) below, land is "relevant land" of a designated[3] educational institution if it is open to the air and is land which is under the direct control of the governing body of or, in Scotland, of such body or of the education authority responsible for the management of, any educational institution or educational institution of any description which may be designated by the Secretary of State, by order, for the purposes of this Part.

(8) The Secretary of State may, by order[4], designate descriptions of land which are not to be treated as relevant Crown land or as relevant land of principal litter authorities, of designated statutory undertakers or of designated educational institutions or of any description of any of them.

(9) Every highway maintainable at the public expense other than a trunk road which is a special road is a "relevant highway" and the local authority which is, for the purposes of this Part, "responsible" for so much of it as lies within its area is, subject to any order under subsection (11) below—

(*a*) in Greater London, the council of the London borough or the Common Council of the City of London;
(*b*) in England outside Greater London, the council of the district;
(*bb*) in Wales, the council of the county or county borough;
(*c*) the Council of the Isles of Scilly.

(10) *Scotland.*

(11) The Secretary of State may, by order[5], as respects relevant highways or relevant roads, relevant highways or relevant roads of any class or any part of a relevant highway or relevant road specified in the order, transfer the responsibility for the discharge of the duties imposed by section 89 below from the local authority to the highway or roads authority; but he shall not make an order under this subsection unless—

(*a*) (except where he is the highway or roads authority) he is requested to do so by the highway or roads authority;
(*b*) he consults the local authority; and
(*c*) it appears to him to be necessary or expedient to do so in order to prevent or minimise interference with the passage or with the safety of traffic along the highway or, in Scotland, road in question;

and where, by an order under this subsection, responsibility for the discharge of those duties is transferred, the authority to which the transfer is made is, for the purposes of this Part, "responsible" for the highway, road or part specified in the order.

(12) Land is "relevant land within a litter control area of a local authority" if it is land included in an area designated by the local authority under section 90 below to which the public are entitled or permitted to have access with or without payment.*

(13) A place on land shall be treated as "open to the air" notwithstanding that it is covered if it is open to the air on at least one side.

(14) The Secretary of State may, by order[6], apply the provisions of this Part which apply to refuse to any description of animal droppings in all or any prescribed circumstances subject to such modifications as appear to him to be necessary.

(15) Any power under this section may be exercised differently as respects different areas, different descriptions of land or for different circumstances.

[Environmental Protection Act 1990, s 86, as amended by the Local Government (Wales) Act 1994, Sch 9.]

***Subsection (12) repealed by the Clean Neighbourhoods and Environment Act 2005, Sch 5 from a date to be appointed.**

1. Part IV consists of ss 86–99.
2. See the Litter (Statutory Undertakers) (Designation and Relevant Land) Order 1991 in this PART, post.
3. See the Litter (Designated Educational Institutions) Order 1991, SI 1991/561.
4. The Litter (Relevant Land of Principal Litter Authorities and Relevant Crown Land) Order 1991, SI 1991/476 has been made.
5. Certain highways and lengths of highway are the subject of the Highway Litter Clearance and Cleaning (Transfer of Duties) Order transferring duties under s 89(1)(*a*) and (2)(*a*) to the Secretary of State. See SI 1991/337, SI 1997/2960, SI 1998/467, SI 1999/1007.
6. The Litter (Animal Droppings) Order 1991, SI 1991/961, provides that Pt IV of the Act will apply to dog faeces on the kinds of land prescribed in the Order.

8–26315 **87. Offence of leaving litter.** (1) A person is guilty of an offence if he throws down, drops or otherwise deposits any litter in[1] any place to which this section applies and leaves it.

(2) This section applies to any place in the area of a principal litter authority which is open to the air, subject to subsection (3) below.

(3) This section does not apply to a place which is "open to the air"[2] for the purposes of this Part by virtue of section 86(13) above if the public does not have access to it, with or without payment.

(4) It is immaterial for the purposes of this section whether the litter is deposited on land or in water.

(4A) No offence is committed under subsection (1) above where the depositing of the litter is—

(*a*) authorised by law; or
(*b*) done by or with the consent of the owner, occupier or other person having control of the place where it is deposited.

(4B) A person may only give consent under subsection (4A)(*b*) above in relation to the depositing of litter in a lake or pond or watercourse if he is the owner, occupier or other person having control of—

(*a*) all the land adjoining that lake or pond or watercourse; and
(*b*) all the land through or into which water in that lake or pond or watercourse directly or indirectly discharges, otherwise than by means of a public sewer.

(4C) In subsection (4B) above, "lake or pond", "watercourse" and "public sewer" have the same meanings as in section 104 of the Water Resources Act 1991.

(5) A person who is guilty of an offence under this section shall be liable on summary conviction to a fine not exceeding **level 4** on the standard scale.

(6) A local authority, with a view to promoting the abatement of litter, may take such steps as the authority think appropriate for making the effect of subsection (5) above known to the public in their area.

(7) (*Scotland.*)

[Environmental Protection Act 1990, s 87 as amended by the Clean Neighbourhoods and Environment Act 2005, s 18.]

1. The words "otherwise deposits in" are extremely wide and "deposits" means no more than places or puts; see *Felix v DPP* [1998] Crim LR 657.

2. A telephone kiosk which was enclosed on three sides, had a roof and a door which was normally closed was held not to be a "place in the open air"; see *Felix v DPP* [1998] Crim LR 657.

3. Subsections (1)–(4), (4A)–(4C) reproduced as substituted in relation to England and Wales by the Clean Neighbourhoods and Environment Act 2005, s 18.

8–26316 **88. Fixed penalty notices for leaving litter.** (1) Where on any occasion—

(*a*) an authorised officer of a litter authority finds a person who he has reason to believe has on that occasion committed an offence under section 87 above in the area of that authority; or*

(*b*) a constable has reason to believe that a person has committed an offence under that section,

he may give that person a notice offering him the opportunity of discharging any liability to conviction for that offence by payment of a fixed penalty.

(1A) Where a constable gives a notice under this section to a person, he shall, no later than 24 hours after the giving of the notice, send a copy of it to the litter authority in whose area the offence was committed.

(2) Where a person is given a notice under this section in respect of an offence—

(*a*) no proceedings shall be instituted for that offence before the expiration of fourteen days following the date of the notice; and

(*b*) he shall not be convicted of that offence if he pays the fixed penalty before the expiration of that period.

(3) A notice under this section shall give such particulars of the circumstances alleged to constitute the offence as are necessary for giving reasonable information of the offence and shall state—

(*a*) the period during which, by virtue of subsection (2) above, proceedings will not be taken for the offence;

(*b*) the amount of the fixed penalty; and

(*c*) the person to whom and the address at which the fixed penalty may be paid;

and, without prejudice to payment by any other method, payment of the fixed penalty may be made by pre-paying and posting to that person at that address a letter containing the amount of the penalty (in cash or otherwise).

(4) Where a letter is sent in accordance with subsection (3) above payment shall be regarded as having been made at the time at which that letter would be delivered in the ordinary course of post.

(5) The form of notices under this section shall be such as the Secretary of State may by order[1] prescribe.

(6) The fixed penalty payable to a litter authority in pursuance of a notice under this section shall, subject to subsection (7) below, be £50 or , in Wales, £75 and as respects the sums received by the authority, those sums—

(*a*) *repealed*

(*b*) if received by an authority in Scotland, shall be treated as if the penalty were a fine imposed by a district court.*

(7) The Secretary of State may by order substitute a different amount for the amount for the time being specified as the amount of the fixed penalty in subsection (6) above.*

(8) In any proceedings a certificate which—

(*a*) purports to be signed by or on behalf of—

(i) in England and Wales, the chief finance officer of the litter authority; or

(ii) in Scotland, the proper officer; and

(*b*) states that payment of a fixed penalty was or was not received by a date specified in the certificate,

shall be evidence of the facts stated.*

(9) For the purposes of this section the following are "litter authorities"—

(*a*) any principal litter authority, other than an English county council or a joint board;

(*b*) any English county council or joint board designated by the Secretary of State, by order, in relation to such area as is specified in the order (not being an area in a National Park);

(*c*), (*d*) *Repealed*;
(*e*) the Broads Authority.*

(10) In this section—

"authorised officer" means an officer of, a litter authority who is authorised in writing by the authority for the purpose of issuing notices under this section;*

"chief finance officer", in relation to a litter authority, means the person having responsibility for the financial affairs of the authority;

"proper officer" means the officer who has, as respects the authority, the responsibility mentioned in section 95 of the Local Government (Scotland) Act 1973 (financial administration).*

[Environmental Protection Act 1990, s 88, as amended by the Local Government (Wales) Act 1994, Schs 6 and 16; the Environment Act 1995, Sch 24, SI 1996/3055, SI 2002/424, SI 2004/909 and the Local Government Act 2003, Sch 8.]

***Subsections (6) and (7) and definition in sub-s (10) substituted, and subs-ss (8A)–(8C) and para (9)(*f*) inserted, in relation to England and Wales, by the Clean Neighbourhoods and Environment Act 2005, s 19 from a date to be appointed.**

1. The Litter (Fixed Penalty Notices) Order 1991, SI 1991/111 revoked in relation to England by the Litter (Fixed Penalty Notices) Order 1991 and the Dog Fouling (Fixed Penalties) Order 1996 (Revocation) (England) Order 2005, SI 2005/3223, prescribes the form of notice which may be given by an authorised officer of a litter authority. The Dogs Fouling (Fixed Penalties) Order 1996, SI 1996/2763 amended by SI 2002/425 and SI 2004/909 (W) revoked in relation to England by the Litter (Fixed Penalty Notices) Order 1991 and the Dog Fouling (Fixed Penalties) Order 1996 (Revocation) (England) Order 2005, SI 2005/3223 has also been made.

8–26317 **89. Duty to keep land and highways clear of litter etc.** (1) It shall be the duty of—

(*a*) each local authority, as respects any relevant highway or, in Scotland, relevant road for which it is responsible,
(*b*) the Secretary of State, as respects any trunk road which is a special road and any relevant highway or relevant road for which he is responsible,
(*c*) each principal litter authority, as respects its relevant land,
(*d*) the appropriate Crown authority, as respects its relevant Crown land,
(*e*) each designated statutory undertaker, as respects its relevant land,*
(*f*) the governing body of each designated educational institution or in Scotland such body or, as the case may be, the education authority responsible for the management of the institution, as respects its relevant land, and
(*g*) the occupier of any relevant land within a litter control area of a local authority,*

to ensure that the land is, so far as is practicable, kept clear of litter and refuse.

(2) Subject to subsection (6) below, it shall also be the duty of—

(*a*) each local authority, as respects any relevant highway or relevant road for which it is responsible,
(*b*) the Secretary of State, as respects any trunk road which is a special road and any relevant highway or relevant road for which he is responsible,

to ensure that the highway or road is, so far as is practicable, kept clean.

(3) In determining what standard is required, as respects any description of land, highway or road, for compliance with subsections (1) and (2) above, regard shall be had to the character and use of the land, highway or road as well as the measures which are practicable in the circumstances.

(4) Matter of any description prescribed by regulations made by the Secretary of State for the purposes of subsections (1)(*a*) and (2) above shall be litter or refuse to which the duties imposed by those subsections apply as respects relevant highways or relevant roads whether or not it would be litter or refuse apart from this subsection.

(5) It shall be the duty of a local authority, when discharging its duty under subsection (1)(*a*) or (2) above as respects any relevant highway or relevant road, to place and maintain on the highway or road such traffic signs and barriers as may be necessary for giving warning and preventing danger to traffic or for regulating it and afterwards to remove them as soon as they cease to be necessary for those purposes; but this subsection has effect subject to any directions given under subsection (6) below.

(6) In discharging its duty under subsection (1)(*a*) or (2) above to keep clear of litter and refuse or to clean any relevant highway or relevant road for which it is responsible, the local authority shall comply with any directions given to it by the highway or roads authority with respect to—

(*a*) the placing and maintenance of any traffic signs or barriers;
(*b*) the days or periods during which clearing or cleaning shall not be undertaken or undertaken to any extent specified in the direction;

and for the purpose of enabling it to discharge its duty under subsection (1)(*a*) or (2) above as respects any relevant highway or relevant road the local authority may apply to the highway authority or roads authority for that authority to exercise its powers under section 14(1) or (3) of the Road Traffic Regulation Act 1984 (temporary prohibition or restriction of traffic).

(7) The Secretary of State shall prepare and issue a code of practice for the purpose of providing practical guidance on the discharge of the duties imposed by subsections (1) and (2) above.

(8) Different codes of practice may be prepared and issued under subsection (7) above for different areas.

(9) The Secretary of State may issue modifications of, or withdraw, a code issued under subsection (7) above; but where a code is withdrawn, he shall prepare and issue a new code under that subsection in substitution for it.

(10) Any person subject to any duty imposed by subsection (1) or (2) above shall have regard to the code of practice in force under subsection (7) above in discharging that duty.

(11) A draft code prepared under subsection (7) above shall be laid before both Houses of Parliament and shall not be issued until after the end of the period of 40 days beginning with the day on which the code was so laid, or if the draft is laid on different days, the later of the two days.

(12) If, within the period mentioned in subsection (11) above, either House resolves that the code the draft of which was laid before it should not be issued, the Secretary of State shall not issue that code.

(13) No account shall be taken in reckoning any period of 40 days for the purposes of subsection (11) above of any time during which Parliament is dissolved or prorogued or during which both Houses are adjourned for more than four days.

(13A) Subsections (11) to (13) shall not apply in respect of a draft code prepared under subsection (7) above which relates only to Scotland and such a code shall be laid before the Scottish Parliament and shall not be issued until after the end of the period of 40 days beginning with the day on which the code was so laid.

(13B) If within the period mentioned in subsection (13A) above the Scottish Parliament resolves that the code, the draft of which was laid before it, should not be issued the Scottish Ministers shall not issue that code.

(13C) No account shall be taken in reckoning any period of 40 days for the purposes of subsection (13A) above of any time during which the Scottish Parliament is dissolved or is in recess for more than 4 days.

(14) In this section "traffic sign" has the meaning given in section 64(1) of the Road Traffic Regulation Act 1984.

[Environmental Protection Act 1990, s 89, as amended by SI 1999/1820.]

***Paragraph (1) amended, in relation to England and Wales, by the Clean Neighbourhoods and Environment Act 2005, s 106 from a date to be appointed.**

8–26318 90. Litter control areas. (1) The Secretary of State may, by order[1], prescribe descriptions of land which may be designated under subsection (3) below as, or as part of, a litter control area.

(2) The power of the Secretary of State to prescribe descriptions of land under subsection (1) above includes power to describe land by reference to the ownership or occupation of the land or the activities carried on on it.

(3) any principal litter authority other than an English county council, a regional council or a joint board may, in accordance with the following provisions of this section, by order designate any land in their area as, or as part of, a litter control area.

(4) No order under subsection (3) above designating any land shall be made unless the authority is of the opinion that, by reason of the presence of litter or refuse, the condition of the land is, and unless they make a designation order is likely to continue to be, such as to be detrimental to the amenities of the locality.

(5) The power to make a designation order under subsection (3) above shall be excluded from the functions to which section 101 of the Local Government Act 1972 (functions capable of delegation) applies.

(6) An authority proposing to make a designation order in relation to any land shall—

(*a*) notify persons who appear to the authority to be persons who will be affected by the proposed order;

(*b*) give them an opportunity to make representations about it within the period of twenty-one days beginning with the service of the notice; and

(*c*) take any representations so made into account in making their decision.

(7) A designation order under subsection (3) above shall identify the land to which it applies and shall be in such form as the Secretary of State may by order prescribe.*

[Environmental Protection Act 1990, s 90, as amended by the Local Government (Wales) Act 1994, Sch 9.]

***Repealed, in relation to England and Wales, by the Clean Neighbourhoods and Environment Act 2005, s 107 from a date to be appointed.**

1. See the Litter Control Areas Order 1991, SI 1991/1325 amended by SI 1997/633.

8–26319 91. Summary proceedings by persons aggrieved by litter. (1) A magistrates' court may act under this section on a complaint made by any person on the ground that he is aggrieved by the defacement, by litter or refuse, of—

(*a*) any relevant highway;
(*b*) any trunk road which is a special road;
(*c*) any relevant land of a principal litter authority;
(*d*) any relevant Crown land;
(*e*) any relevant land of a designated statutory undertaker;*
(*f*) any relevant land of a designated educational institution; or
(*g*) any relevant land within a litter control area of a local authority.*

(2) A magistrates' court may also act under this section on a complaint made by any person on the ground that he is aggrieved by the want of cleanliness of any relevant highway or any trunk road which is a special road.

(3) A principal litter authority shall not be treated as a person aggrieved for the purposes of proceedings under this section.

(4) Proceedings under this section shall be brought against the person who has the duty to keep the land clear under section 89(1) above or to keep the highway clean under section 89(2) above, as the case may be.

(5) Before instituting proceedings under this section against any person, the complainant shall give to the person not less than five days written notice of his intention to make the complaint and the notice shall specify the matter complained of.

(6) If the magistrates' court is satisfied that the highway or land in question is defaced by litter or refuse or, in the case of a highway, is wanting in cleanliness, the court may, subject to subsections (7) and (8) below, make an order ("a litter abatement order") requiring the defendant to clear the litter or refuse away or, as the case may be, clean the highway within a time specified in the order.

(7) The magistrates' court shall not make a litter abatement order if the defendant proves that he has complied, as respects the highway or land in question, with his duty under section 89(1) and (2) above.

(8) The magistrates' court shall not make a litter abatement order where it appears that the matter complained of is the result of directions given to the local authority under section 89(6) above by the highway authority.

(9) A person who, without reasonable excuse, fails to comply with a litter abatement order shall be guilty of an offence and liable on summary conviction to a fine not exceeding **level 4** on the standard scale together with a further fine of an amount equal to **one-twentieth of that level** for each day on which the offence continues after the conviction.

(10) In any proceedings for an offence under subsection (9) above it shall be a defence for the defendant to prove that he has complied, as respects the highway or land in question, with his duty under section 89(1) and (2) above.

(11) A code of practice under section 89(7) shall be admissible in evidence in any proceedings under this section and if any provision of such a code appears to the court to be relevant to any question in the proceedings it shall be taken into account in determining that question.

(12) Where a magistrates' court is satisfied on the hearing of a complaint under this section—

(*a*) that, when the complaint was made to it, the highway or land in question was defaced by litter or refuse or, as the case may be, was wanting in cleanliness, and
(*b*) that there were reasonable grounds for bringing the complaint,

the court shall order the defendant to pay such reasonable sum to the complainant as the court may determine in respect of the expenses incurred by the complainant in bringing the complaint and the proceedings before the court.

(13) (*Scotland.*)

[Environmental Protection Act 1990, s 91.]

***Paragraph (1) amended, in relation to England and Wales, by the Clean Neighbourhoods and Environment Act 2005, s 106 from a date to be appointed.**

8–26320 **92. Summary proceedings by litter authorities.** (1) Where a principal litter authority other than an English county council or a joint board are satisfied as respects—

(*a*) any relevant Crown land,
(*b*) any relevant land of a designated statutory undertaker,*
(*c*) any relevant land of a designated educational institution, or
(*d*) any relevant land within a litter control area of a local authority,*

that it is defaced by litter or refuse or that defacement of it by litter or refuse is likely to recur, the authority shall serve a notice (a "litter abatement notice") imposing either the requirement or the prohibition or both the requirement and the prohibition specified in subsection (2) below.

(2) The requirement and prohibition referred to in subsection (1) above are as follows, namely—

(*a*) a requirement that the litter or refuse be cleared within a time specified in the notice;
(*b*) a prohibition on permitting the land to become defaced by litter or refuse.

(3) The litter abatement notice shall be served—

(*a*) as respects relevant Crown land, on the appropriate Crown authority;

(*b*) as respects relevant land of a designated statutory undertaker, on the undertaker;
(*c*) as respects relevant land of a designated educational institution, on the governing body of the institution or in Scotland on such body or, as the case may be, on the education authority responsible for the management of the institution;
(*d*) in any other case, on the occupier of the land or, if it is unoccupied, on the owner of the land.*

(4) The person served with the notice may appeal against the notice to a magistrates' court or, in Scotland, to the sheriff by way of summary application within the period of twenty-one days beginning with the date on which the notice was served.

(5) If, on any appeal under subsection (4) above, the appellant proves that, as respects the land in question, he has complied with his duty under section 89(1) above, the court shall allow the appeal.

(6) If a person on whom a litter abatement notice is served, without reasonable excuse, fails to comply with or contravenes the requirement or prohibition imposed by the notice, he shall be guilty of an offence and liable on summary conviction to a fine not exceeding **level 4** on the standard scale together with a further fine of an amount equal to **one-twentieth of that level** for each day on which the offence continues after the conviction.

(7) In any proceedings for an offence under subsection (6) above it shall be a defence for the person charged to prove that he has complied, as respects the land in question, with his duty under section 89(1) above.

(8) A code of practice under section 89(7) above shall be admissible in evidence in any proceedings under this section and if any provision of such a code appears to the court to be relevant to any question in the proceedings it shall be taken into account in determining that question.

(9) If a person on whom a litter abatement notice is served fails to comply with the requirement imposed by the notice in respect of any land, the authority may, subject to subsection (10) below—

(*a*) enter on the land and clear the litter or refuse; and
(*b*) recover from that person the expenditure attributable to their having done so, except such of the expenditure as that person shows was unnecessary in the circumstances.

(10) Subsection (9) above does not apply in relation to any land to which subsection (11) or (12) below applies.

(11) This subsection applies to any relevant Crown land which is occupied for naval, military or air force purposes.

(12) This subsection applies to any relevant land of a statutory undertaker in relation to which the Secretary of State has specified, by order, that it is requisite or expedient that, in the national interest, subsection (9) above should not apply.** [1]

[Environmental Protection Act 1990, s 92, as amended by the Local Government (Wales) Act 1994, Sch 9 and the Anti-social Behaviour Act 2003, s 56.]

***Paragraphs (1) and (3) amended, in relation to England and Wales, by the Clean Neighbourhoods and Environment Act 2005, s 107 from a date to be appointed.**

****New sections 92A–92C inserted, in relation to England and Wales, by the Clean Neighbourhoods and Environment Act 2005, s 20 from a date to be appointed.**

1. Subsections (10)–(12) reproduced as substituted, in relation to England and Wales, by the Anti-Social Behaviour Act 2003, s 56.

8–26321 **93. Street litter control notices.** (1) A principal litter authority other than an English county council or a joint board may, with a view to the prevention of accumulations of litter or refuse in and around any street or open land adjacent to any street, issue notices ("street litter control notices") imposing requirements on occupiers of premises in relation to such litter or refuse, in accordance with this section and section 94 below.

(2) If the authority is satisfied, in respect of any premises which are of a description prescribed under section 94(1)(*a*) below and have a frontage on a street in their area, that—

(*a*) there is recurrent defacement by litter or refuse of any land, being part of the street or open land adjacent to the street, which is in the vicinity of the premises, or
(*b*) the condition of any part of the premises which is open land in the vicinity of the frontage is, and if no notice is served is likely to continue to be, detrimental to the amenities of the locality by reason of the presence of litter or refuse, or
(*c*) there is produced, as a result of the activities carried on on the premises, quantities of litter or refuse of such nature and in such amounts as are likely to cause the defacement of any part of the street, or of open land adjacent to the street, which is in the vicinity of the premises,

the authority may serve a street litter control notice on the occupier or, if the premises are unoccupied, on the owner of the premises.

(3) A notice shall, subject to section 94(2), (3) and (4) below—

(*a*) identify the premises and state the grounds under subsection (2) above on which it is issued;
(*b*) specify an area of open land which adjoins or is in the vicinity of the frontage of the premises on the street;
(*c*) specify, in relation to that area or any part of it, such reasonable requirements as the authority considers appropriate in the circumstances;

and, for the purposes of paragraph (*b*) above, an area which includes land on both sides of the frontage of the premises shall be treated as an area adjoining that frontage.*

(4) In this section and section 94 below—

"notice" means a street litter control notice;
"open land" means land in the open air;
"the premises", in relation to a notice, means the premises in respect of which the notice is issued;
"specified area" means the area specified in a notice under subsection (3)(*b*) above; and
"street" means a relevant highway, a relevant road or any other highway or road over which there is a right of way on foot.

[Environmental Protection Act 1990, s 93, as amended by the Local Government (Wales) Act 1994, Sch 9.]

***New subsections (3A) and (3B) inserted, in relation to England and Wales, by the Clean Neighbourhoods and Environment Act 2005, s 107 from a date to be appointed.**

8–26322 **94. Street litter: supplementary provisions.** (1) The Secretary of State may by order[1] prescribe—

(*a*) the descriptions of commercial or retail premises in respect of which a street litter control notice may be issued;
(*b*) the descriptions of land which may be included in a specified area; and
(*c*) the maximum area of land which may be included in a specified area;

and different descriptions or maximum dimensions may be prescribed under paragraph (*b*) or (*c*) above for different cases or circumstances.

(2) The power to describe premises or land under subsection (1)(*a*) or (*b*) above includes power to describe the premises or land by reference to occupation or ownership or to the activities carried on there.

(3) The land comprised in a specified area—

(*a*) shall include only land of one or more of the descriptions prescribed under subsection (1)(*b*) above;
(*b*) shall not include any land which is not—

(i) part of the premises,
(ii) part of a street,
(iii) relevant land of a principal litter authority, or
(iv) land under the direct control of any other local authority; and

(*c*) shall not exceed any applicable maximum area prescribed under subsection (1)(*c*) above;

but a specified area shall not include any part of the premises which is or is part of a litter control area.*

(4) The requirements which may be imposed by a notice shall relate to the clearing of litter or refuse from the specified area and may in particular require—

(*a*) the provision or emptying of receptacles for litter or refuse;
(*b*) the doing within a period specified in the notice of any such thing as may be so specified; or*
(*c*) the doing (while the notice remains in force) at such times or intervals, or within such periods, of any such thing as may be so specified;

but a notice may not require the clearing of litter or refuse from any carriageway, except at a time when the carriageway is closed to all vehicular traffic.

(5) In relation to so much of the specified area as is not part of the premises the authority shall take account, in determining what requirements to impose, of their own duties under this Part or otherwise, and of any similar duties of any other local authority, in relation to that land.

(6) An authority proposing to serve a notice shall—

(*a*) inform the person on whom the notice is to be served;
(*b*) give him the opportunity to make representations about the notice within the period of twenty-one days beginning with the day on which he is so informed; and
(*c*) take any representations so made into account in making their decision.

(7) A person on whom a notice is served may appeal against the notice to a magistrate's court or, in Scotland, to the sheriff by way of summary application; and the court may quash the notice or may quash, vary or add to any requirement imposed by the notice.

(8) If it appears to the authority that a person has failed or is failing to comply with any requirement imposed by a notice the authority may apply to a magistrate's court or, in Scotland, to the sheriff by way of summary application for an order requiring the person to comply with the requirement within such time as may be specified in the order.

(9) A person who, without reasonable excuse, fails to comply with an order under subsection (8) above shall be guilty of an offence and liable on summary conviction to a fine not exceeding **level 4** on the standard scale.*

[Environmental Protection Act 1990, s 94.]

***Paragraphs (3) and (4) amended, and sub-ss(8) and (9) substituted and new ss 94A and 94B inserted in relation to England and Wales, by the Clean Neighbourhoods and Environment Act 2005, ss 21, 23 and 107 from a date to be appointed.**

1. See the Street Litter Control Notices Order 1991, SI 1991/1324 amended by SI 1997/632.

8–26323 95. *Public registers.*

8–26324 96. Application of Part II. (1) This section applies to litter and refuse collected—

(*a*) by any authority or person in pursuance of section 89(1) above;

(*b*) by a principal litter authority in pursuance of section 92(9) above; or*

(*c*) by any person in pursuance of section 93 above.

(2) The Secretary of State may make regulations providing that prescribed provisions of Part II shall have effect, with such modifications (if any) as may be prescribed—

(*a*) as if references to controlled waste or controlled waste of a prescribed description included references to litter and refuse to which this section applies or any description of such litter and refuse;

(*b*) as if references to controlled waste or controlled waste of a prescribed description collected under section 45 above included references to litter and refuse collected as mentioned in subsection (1) above or any description of such litter and refuse.

(3) The powers conferred by this section are exercisable in relation to litter and refuse to which it applies whether or not the circumstances are such that the litter or refuse would be treated as controlled waste apart from this section and this section is not to affect the interpretation of the expressions defined in section 75 above.

[Environmental Protection Act 1990, s 96.]

***Paragraph (1) amended, in relation to England and Wales, by the Clean Neighbourhoods and Environment Act 2005, s 106 from a date to be appointed.**

8–26325 97. Transitional provision relating to section 89. (1) The Secretary of State may, for the purposes of the transition to the duties imposed by section 89 above on local authorities and educational bodies, by regulations[1], make provision—

(*a*) modifying that section, or

(*b*) modifying Part I of the Local Government Act 1988 (competition rules for functional work or works contracts).

(2) Regulations under this section may make different provision for different descriptions of authorities, different areas or other different circumstances or cases.

(3) In this section—

"educational bodies" means the governing bodies and education authorities mentioned in section 89(1)(*f*) above; and

"local authorities" means the local authorities mentioned in section 89(1)(*a*) and (*c*) and (2)(*a*) above.*

[Environmental Protection Act 1990, s 97.]

***New ss 97A and 97B inserted in relation to England and Wales, by the Clean Neighbourhoods and Environment Act 2005, ss 24 and 25 from a date to be appointed.**

1. The Litter Etc (Transitional Provisions) Regulations 1991, SI 1991/719, have been made.

8–26326 98. Definitions. (1) The following definitions apply for the interpretation of this Part.

(1A) "Appropriate person" means—

(*a*) in relation to England, the Secretary of State;

(*b*) in relation to Wales, the National Assembly for Wales.

(2) "Educational institution", in relation to England and Wales, means—

(*a*) *repealed*;

(*b*) the Open University;

(*c*) any institution which provides higher education or further education (or both) which is full-time education being an institution which—

(i) is maintained by grants made by the Secretary of State under section 485 of the Education Act 1996;

(ii) is designated by or under regulations under section 218 of the Education Reform Act 1988 as an institution dependent for its maintenance on assistance from local education authorities; or*

(iii) is maintained by a local education authority;

(*d*) any institution within the higher education sector within the meaning of section 91(5) of the Further and Higher Education Act 1992;

(*da*) any institution within the further education sector within the meaning of section 91(3) of the Further and Higher Education Act 1992;
(*e*) any city technology college, city college for the technology of the arts or Academy;
(*f*) any community, foundation or voluntary school;
(*g*) any community or foundation special school.

(3)–(4) (*Scotland*).
(5) "Highway" (and "highway maintainable at the public expense"), "special road" and "trunk road", in relation to England and Wales, have the same meaning as in the Highways Act 1980 and "public road", "special road" and "trunk road", in relation to Scotland, have the same meaning as in the Roads (Scotland) Act 1984.
(5A) "Litter" includes—

(*a*) the discarded ends of cigarettes, cigars and like products, and
(*b*) discarded chewing-gum and the discarded remains of other products designed for chewing.

(6) "Statutory undertaker" means—

(*a*) any person authorised by any enactment to carry on any railway, light railway, tramway or road transport undertaking;
(*aa*) any operator of a relevant railway asset;
(*b*) any person authorised by any enactment to carry on any canal, inland navigation, dock, harbour or pier undertaking; or
(*c*) any relevant airport operator (within the meaning of Part V of the Airports Act 1986).

(7) Subject to subsection (8) below, "relevant railway asset" means—

(*a*) a transferred network, that is to say a network which was transferred by virtue of a transfer scheme made under section 85 of the Railways Act 1993 from the British Railways Board and vested in the company formed and registered under the Companies Act 1985 and known, at the date of the vesting, as Railtrack PLC,
(*b*) a station which is used in connection with the provision of services for the carriage of passengers on a transferred network and is operated by a provider of such services or by the operator of such a network, or
(*c*) a light maintenance depot which is used to provide light maintenance services for rolling stock which is used on a transferred network.

(8) A transferred network shall not cease to be such a network where it is modified by virtue of having any network or part of a network added to or removed from it.
(9) Expressions used in subsections (6)(*aa*), (7) and (8) above and in Part I of the Railways Act 1993 have the same meaning in those subsections as they have in that Part.
[Environmental Protection Act 1990, s 98, as amended by the Further and Higher Education Act 1992, Sch 8, the Education Act 1996, Sch 37, the School Standards and Framework Act 1998, Sch 30, SI 1999/1443, the Learning and Skills Act 2000, Sch 9, SI 2002/2002 and the Clean Neighbourhoods and Environment Act 2005, ss 26 and 27.]

***Sub-section (2), para (*c*)(ii) repealed by the Education Act 2002, s 215, from a date to be appointed.**

Abandoned trolleys

8–26327 **99.** *Powers in relation to abandoned shopping and luggage trolleys.*

PART VI[1]
GENETICALLY MODIFIED ORGANISMS

Preliminary

8–26328 **106. Purpose of Part VI and meaning of "genetically modified organisms" and related expressions.** (1) This Part has effect for the purpose of ensuring that all appropriate measures are taken to avoid damage to the environment which may arise from the escape or release from human control of genetically modified organisms.*
(2) In this Part the term "organism" means any acellular, unicellular or multicellular entity (in any form), other than humans or human embryos; and, unless the context otherwise requires, the term also includes any article or substance consisting of or including biological matter.
(3) For the purpose of subsection (2) above "biological matter" means anything (other than an entity mentioned in that subsection) which consists of or includes—

(*a*) tissue or cells (including gametes or propagules) or subcellular entities, of any kind, capable of replication or of transferring genetic material, or
(*b*) genes or other genetic material, in any form, which are so capable,

and it is immaterial, in determining if something is or is not an organism or biological matter, whether it is the product of natural or artificial processes of reproduction and, in the case of biological matter, whether it has ever been part of a whole organism.

(4) For the purposes of this Part an organism is "genetically modified" if any of the genes or other genetic material in the organism—

(*a*) have been artificially modified; or*

(*b*) are inherited or otherwise derived, through any number of replications, from genes or other genetic material (from any source) which were so modified.

(4A) Genes or other genetic material in an organism are "artificially modified" for the purposes of subsection (4) above if they are altered otherwise than by a process which occurs naturally in mating or natural recombination.

This subsection is subject to subsections (4B) and (4C) below.**

(4B) For the purposes of subsection (4) above—

(*a*) genes or other genetic material shall be taken to be artificially modified if they are altered using such techniques as may be prescribed for the purposes of this paragraph;

(*b*) genes or other genetic material shall not be regarded as artificially modified by reason only of being altered by the use of such techniques as may be prescribed for the purposes of this paragraph.**

(4C) An organism shall be taken not to be a genetically modified organism for the purposes of this Part if it is an organism of a prescribed description.**

(4D) In subsections (4B) and (4C) above "prescribed" means prescribed by regulations made by the Secretary of State.**

(5) The techniques which may be prescribed for the purposes of subsection (4) above include—

(*a*) any technique for the modification of any genes or other genetic material by the recombination, insertion or deletion of, or of any component parts of, that material from its previously occurring state, and

(*b*) any other technique for modifying genes or other genetic material which in the opinion of the Secretary of State would produce organisms which should for the purposes of this Part be treated as having been genetically modified,

but do not include techniques which involve no more than, or no more than the assistance of, naturally occurring processes of reproduction (including selective breeding techniques or *in vitro* fertilisation).***

(6) It is immaterial for the purposes of subsections (4) and (5) above whether the modifications of genes or other genetic material effected by a prescribed technique are produced by direct operations on that genetic material or are induced by indirect means (including in particular the use of viruses, microbial plasmids or other vector systems or of mutation inducing agents).***

(7) In this Part, where the context permits, a reference to "reproduction", in relation to an organism, includes a reference to its replication or its transferring genetic material.

[Environmental Protection Act 1990, s 106.]

***Sub-sections (1), (4)(*a*) printed as substituted by SI 2002/2443, in force in relation to England from 17 October 2002.**

****Sub-sections (4A)–(4D) printed as inserted by SI 2002/2443, in force in relation to England from 17 October 2002.**

*****Sub-sections (5) and (6) repealed by SI 2002/2443, in force in relation to England from 17 October 2002.**

1. Part VI consists of ss 106–127.

8–26329 107. Meaning of "damage to the environment", "control" and related expressions in Part VI. (1) The following provisions have effect for the interpretation of this Part.

(2) The "environment" includes land, air and water and living organisms supported by any of those media.*

(3) "Damage to the environment" is caused by the presence in the environment of genetically modified organisms which have (or of a single such organism which has) escaped or been released from a person's control and are (or is) capable of causing harm to the living organisms supported by the environment.**

(4) An organism shall be regarded as present in the environment notwithstanding that it is present in or on any human or other organism, or any other thing, which is itself present in the environment.

(5) Genetically modified organisms present in the environment are capable of causing harm if—

(*a*) they are individually capable, or are present in numbers such that together they are capable, of causing harm; or

(*b*) they are able to produce descendants which will be capable, or which will be present in numbers such that together they will be capable, of causing harm;

and a single organism is capable of causing harm either if it is itself capable of causing harm or if it is able to produce descendants which will be so capable.

(6) "Harm" means adverse effects as regards the health of humans or the environment.

(7) "Harmful" and "harmless" mean respectively, in relation to genetically modified organisms, their being capable or their being incapable of causing harm.

(8) The Secretary of State[1] may by regulations[2] provide, in relation to genetically modified organisms of any description specified in the regulations, that—

(*a*) the capacity of those organisms for causing harm of any description so specified, or
(*b*) harm of any description so specified,

shall be disregarded for such purposes of this Part as may be so specified.

(9) Organisms of any description are under the "control" of a person where he keeps them contained measures designed to limit their contact with humans and the environment and to prevent or minimise the risk of harm.***

(10) An organism under a person's control is "released" if he deliberately causes or permits it to cease to be under his control or the control of any other person and to enter the environment; and such an organism "escapes" if, otherwise than by being released, it ceases to be under his control or that of any other person and enters the environment.

(11) Genetically modified organisms of any description are "marketed" by a person when products consisting of or including such organisms are placed on the market by being made available to other persons, whether or not for consideration.***

[Environmental Protection Act 1990, s 107.]

***Sub-section (2) printed as substituted by SI 2002/2443. In force in relation to England from 17 October 2002.**

****Sub-section (3) words repealed by SI 2002/2443. In force in relation to England from 17 October 2002.**

*****Sub-sections (6), (9) and (11) printed as substituted by SI 2002/2443. In force in relation to England from 17 October 2002.**

1. The functions of the Secretary of State under Part VI of this Act, so far as exercisable in relation to Wales, have been transferred to the National Assembly for Wales (Transfer of Functions) Order 2000, SI 2000/253, art 2, Sch 1.

General controls

8–26330 **108. Risk assessment and notification requirements.** (1) Subject to subsections (2) and (7) below, no person shall import or acquire, release or market any genetically modified organisms unless, before doing that act—

(*a*) he has carried out an assessment of any risks there are (by reference to the nature of the organisms and the manner in which he intends to keep them after their importation or acquisition or, as the case may be, to release or market them) of damage to the environment being caused as a result of doing that act; and
(*b*) in such cases and circumstances as may be prescribed, he has given the Secretary of State such notice of his intention of doing that act and such information as may be prescribed.

(2) Subsection (1) above does not apply to a person proposing to do an act mentioned in that subsection who is required under section 111(1)(*a*) below to have a consent before doing that act.

(3) Subject to subsections (4) and (7) below, a person who is keeping genetically modified organisms shall, in such cases or circumstances and at such times or intervals as may be prescribed—

(*a*) carry out an assessment of any risks there are of damage to the environment being caused as a result of his continuing to keep them;
(*b*) give the Secretary of State notice of the fact that he is keeping the organisms and such information as may be prescribed.

(4) Subsection (3) above does not apply to a person who is keeping genetically modified organisms and is required under section 111(2) below to have a consent authorising him to continue to keep the organisms.

(5) It shall be the duty of a person who carries out an assessment under subsection (1)(*a*) or (3)(*a*) above to keep, for the prescribed period, such a record of the assessment as may be prescribed.

(6) A person required by subsection (1)(*b*) or (3)(*b*) above to give notice to the Secretary of State shall give the Secretary of State[1] such further information as the Secretary of State may by notice in writing require.

(7) Regulations under this section may provide for exemptions, or for the granting by the Secretary of State, or by the Secretary of State and the Food Standards Agency acting jointly, of exemptions to particular persons or classes of person, from the requirements of subsection (1) or (3) above in such cases or circumstances, and to such extent, as may be prescribed.

(8) The Secretary of State may at any time—

(*a*) give directions to a person falling within subsection (1) above requiring that person to apply for a consent before doing the act in question; or
(*b*) give directions to a person falling within subsection (3) above requiring that person, before such date as may be specified in the direction, to apply for a consent authorising him to continue keeping the organisms in question;

and a person given directions under paragraph (*a*) above shall then, and a person given directions under paragraph (*b*) above shall from the specified date, be subject to section 111 below in place of the requirements of this section.

(9) Regulations[2] under this section may—

(*a*) prescribe the manner in which assessments under subsection (1) or (3) above are to be carried out and the matters which must be investigated and assessed;

(*b*) prescribe minimum periods of notice between the giving of a notice under subsection (1)(*b*) above and the doing of the act in question;

(*c*) make provision allowing the Secretary of State to shorten or to extend any such period;

(*d*) prescribe maximum intervals at which assessments under subsection (3)(*a*) above must be carried out;

and the regulations may make different provision for different cases and different circumstances.

(10) In this section "prescribed" means prescribed by the Secretary of State in regulations under this section.

[Environmental Protection Act 1990, s 108, as amended by the Food Standards Act 1999, Sch 3.]

---

1. The functions of the Secretary of State under Part VI of this Act, so far as exercisable in relation to Wales, have been transferred to the National Assembly for Wales (Transfer of Functions) Order 2000, SI 2000/253 art 2, Sch 1.

2. The Genetically Modified Organisms (Risk Assessment) (Records and Exemptions) Regulations 1996, SI 1996/1106, amended by SI 1997/1900, SI 2000/2831 and SI 2005/2759, have been made.

8–26331 109. General duties relating to importation, acquisition, keeping, release or marketing of organisms. (1) A person who—

(*a*) is proposing to import or acquire any genetically modified organisms, or

(*b*) is keeping any such organisms, or

(*c*) is proposing to release or market any such organisms,

shall, subject to subsection (5) below, be subject to the duties specified in subsection (2), (3) or (4) below, as the case may be.

(2) A person who proposes to import or acquire genetically modified organisms—

(*a*) shall take all reasonable steps to identify, by reference to the nature of the organisms and the manner in which he intends to keep them (including any precautions to be taken against their escaping or causing damage to the environment), what risks there are of damage to the environment being caused as a result of their importation or acquisition; and

(*b*) shall not import or acquire the organisms if it appears that, despite any precautions which can be taken, there is a risk of damage to the environment being caused as a result of their importation or acquisition.

(3) A person who is keeping genetically modified organisms—

(*a*) shall take all reasonable steps to keep himself informed of any damage to the environment which may have been caused as a result of his keeping the organisms and to identify what risks there are of damage to the environment being caused as a result of his continuing to keep them;

(*b*) shall cease keeping the organisms if, despite any additional precautions which can be taken, it appears, at any time, that there is a risk of damage to the environment being caused as a result of his continuing to keep them; and

(*c*) shall use the best available techniques not entailing excessive cost for keeping the organisms under this control and for preventing any damage to the environment being caused as a result of his continuing to keep the organisms;

and where a person is required by paragraph (*b*) above to cease keeping the organisms he shall dispose of them as safely and as quickly as practicable and paragraph (*c*) above shall continue to apply until he has done so.

(4) A person who proposes to release genetically modified organisms—

(*a*) shall take all reasonable steps to keep himself informed, by reference to the nature of the organisms and the extent and manner of the release (including any precautions to be taken against their causing damage to the environment), what risks there are of damage to the environment being caused as a result of their being released;

(*b*) shall not release the organisms if it appears that, despite the precautions which can be taken, there is a risk of damage to the environment being caused as a result of their being released; and

(*c*) subject to paragraph (*b*) above, shall use the best available techniques not entailing excessive cost for preventing any damage to the environment being caused as a result of their being released;

and this subsection applies, with the necessary modifications, to a person proposing to market organisms as it applies to a person proposing to release organisms.

(5) This section does not apply—

(*a*) to persons proposing to import or acquire, to release or to market any genetically modified organisms, in cases or circumstances where, under section 108 above, they are not required to carry out a risk assessment before doing that act;

(*b*) to persons who are keeping any genetically modified organisms and who—

(i) were not required under section 108 above to carry out a risk assessment before importing or acquiring them;

(ii) have not been required under that section to carry out a risk assessment in respect of the keeping of those organisms since importing or acquiring them; or

(*c*) to holders of consents, in the case of acts authorised by those consents.

[Environmental Protection Act 1990, s 109.]

8–26332 **110. Prohibition notices.** (1) The Secretary of State[1] may serve a notice under this section (a "prohibition notice") on any person he has reason to believe—

(*a*) is proposing to import or acquire, release or market any genetically modified organisms; or

(*b*) is keeping any such organisms;

if he is of the opinion that doing any such act in relation to those organisms or continuing to keep them, as the case may be, would involve a risk of causing damage[2] to the environment.

(2) A prohibition notice may prohibit a person from doing an act mentioned in subsection (1)(*a*) above in relation to any genetically modified organisms or from continuing to keep them; and the prohibition may apply in all cases or circumstances or in such cases or circumstances as may be specified in the notice.

(3) A prohibition notice shall—

(*a*) state that the Secretary of State is, in relation to the person on whom it is served, of the opinion mentioned in subsection (1) above;

(*b*) specify what is, or is to be, prohibited by the notice; and

(*c*) if the prohibition is not to be effective on being served, specify the date on which the prohibition is to take effect;

and a notice may be served on a person notwithstanding that he may have a consent authorising any act which is, or is to be, prohibited by the notice.

(4) Where a person is prohibited by a prohibited notice from continuing to keep any genetically modified organisms, he shall dispose of them as quickly and safely as practicable or, if the notice so provides, as may be specified in the notice.

(5) The Secretary of State may at any time withdraw a prohibition notice served on any person by notice given to that person.

[Environmental Protection Act 1990, s 110.]

---

1. The functions of the Secretary of State under Part VI of this Act, so far as exercisable in relation to Wales, have been transferred to the National Assembly for Wales (Transfer of Functions) Order 2000, SI 2000/253 art 2, Sch 1.

2. For the circumstances in which the capacity of organisms for causing harm is to be disregarded see the Genetically Modified Organisms (Deliberate Release) Regulations 2002, SI 2002/2443 amended by SI 2004/2411 and SI 2005/2759 and the Genetically Modified Organisms (Deliberate Release) (Wales) Regulations 2002, SI 2002/3188 amended by SI 2005/1913 and 2759.

Consents

8–26333 **111. Consents required by certain persons.** (1) Subject to subsection (7) below, no person shall import or acquire, release or market any genetically modified organisms—

(*a*) in such cases or circumstances as may be prescribed[1] in relation to that act, or

(*b*) in any case where he has been given directions under section 108(8)(*a*) above,

except in pursuance of a consent[2] granted by the Secretary of State and in accordance with any limitations and conditions to which the consent is subject.

(2) Subject to subsection (7) below, no person who has imported or acquired any genetically modified organisms (whether under a consent or not) shall continue to keep the organisms—

(*a*) in such cases or circumstances as may be prescribed, after the end of the prescribed period, or

(*b*) if he has been given directions under section 108(8)(*b*) above, after the date specified in the directions,

except in pursuance of a consent granted by the Secretary of State[3] and in accordance with any limitations or conditions to which the consent is subject.

(3) A person who is required under subsection (2) above to cease keeping any genetically modified organisms shall dispose of them as quickly and safely as practicable.

(4) An application for a consent must contain such information and be made and advertised in such manner as may be prescribed and shall be accompanied by the fee required under section 113 below.

(5) The applicant shall, in prescribed circumstances, give such notice of his application to such persons as may be prescribed.

(6) The Secretary of State may by notice to the applicant require him to furnish such further information specified in the notice, within such period as may be so specified, as he may require for

the purpose of determining the application; and if the applicant fails to furnish the information within the specified period the Secretary of State may refuse to proceed with the application.*

A notice under this subsection must state the reasons for requiring the further information specified in the notice.

(6A) Where an applicant for consent for releasing or marketing genetically modified organisms becomes aware, before his application is either granted or rejected, of any new information with regard to any risks there are of damage to the environment being caused as a result of the organisms being released or marketed, he shall notify the Secretary of State of that new information forthwith.

(7) Regulations under this section may provide for exemptions, or for the granting by the Secretary of State, or by the Secretary of State and the Food Standards Agency acting jointly, of exemptions to particular persons or classes of person, from—

(*a*) any requirement under subsection (1) or (2) above to have a consent, or
(*b*) any of the requirements to be fulfilled under the regulations by an applicant for a consent,

in such cases or circumstances as may be prescribed.

(8) Where an application for a consent is duly made to him, the Secretary of State may grant the consent subject to such limitations and conditions as may be imposed under section 112 below or he may refuse the application.

(9) The conditions attached to a consent may include conditions which are to continue to have effect notwithstanding that the holder has completed or ceased the act or acts authorised by the consent.

(10) The Secretary of State may at any time, by notice given to the holder of a consent, revoke the consent or vary the consent (whether by attaching new limitations and conditions or by revoking or varying any limitations and conditions to which it is at that time subject).

(11) Regulations under this section may make different provision for different cases and different circumstances; and in this section "prescribed" means prescribed in regulations under this section.

[Environmental Protection Act 1990, s 111, as amended by SI 1992/3280 amended by SI 1993/152, the Food Standards Act 1999, Sch 3, SI 2002/2443 (E) and SI 2002/3188 (W).]

***The wording of this subsection differs in relation to Scotland by virtue of SSI 2002/541, reg 19.**

1. The Genetically Modified Organisms (Deliberate Release) Regulations 2002, SI 2002/2443 amended by SI 2004/2411 and SI 2005/2759 and the Genetically Modified Organisms (Deliberate Release) (Wales) Regulations 2002, SI 2002/3188 amended by SI 2005/1913 and 2759 prescribe any cases or circumstances other than the release of an approved product in accordance with the conditions and limitations to which the use of the product is subject.

2. For applications for consent and the conditions on which consents are held see s 112 below and the Genetically Modified Organisms (Deliberate Release) Regulations 2002, SI 2002/2443 amended by SI 2004/2411 and SI 2005/2759 and the Genetically Modified Organisms (Deliberate Release) (Wales) Regulations 2002, SI 2002/3188 amended by SI 2005/1913 and 2759.

3. The functions of the Secretary of State under Part VI of this Act, so far as exercisable in relation to Wales, have been transferred to the National Assembly for Wales (Transfer of Functions) Order 2000, SI 2000/253 art 2, Sch 1.

8–26334 112. Consents: limitations and conditions. (1) The Secretary of State[1] may include in a consent such limitations and conditions as he may think fit for the purpose of ensuring that all appropriate measures are taken to avoid damage to the environment which may arise from the activity permitted by the consent.

(2) Without prejudice to the generality of subsection (1) above, the conditions included in a consent may—

(*a*) require the giving of notice of any fact to the Secretary of State; or
(*b*) prohibit or restrict the keeping, releasing or marketing of genetically modified organisms under the consent in specified cases or circumstances;

and where, under any condition, the holder of a consent is required to cease keeping any genetically modified organisms, he shall dispose of them, if no manner is specified in the conditions, as quickly and safely as practicable.

(3) Subject to subsection (6) below, there is implied in every consent for the importation or acquisition of genetically modified organisms a general condition that the holder of the consent shall—

(*a*) take all reasonable steps to keep himself informed (by reference to the nature of the organisms and the manner in which he intends to keep them after their importation or acquisition) of any risks there are of damage to the environment being caused as a result of their importation or acquisition; and
(*b*) if at any time it appears that any such risks are more serious than were apparent when the consent was granted, notify the Secretary of State forthwith.

(4) Subject to subsection (6) below, there is implied in every consent for keeping genetically modified organisms a general condition that the holder of the consent shall—

(*a*) take all reasonable steps to keep himself informed of any damage to the environment which may have been caused as a result of his keeping the organisms and of any risks there are of such damage being caused as a result of his continuing to keep them;
(*b*) if at any time it appears that any such risks are more serious than were apparent when the consent was granted, notify the Secretary of State forthwith; and

(*c*) use the best available techniques not entailing excessive cost for keeping the organisms under his control and for preventing any damage to the environment being caused as a result of his continuing to keep them.

(5) Subject to subsection (6) below, there is implied in every consent for releasing or marketing genetically modified organisms a general condition that the holder of the consent shall—

(*a*) take all reasonable steps to keep himself informed (by reference to the nature of the organisms and the extent and manner of the release or marketing) of any risks there are of damage[2] to the environment being caused as a result of their being released or, as the case may be, marketed;

(*b*) notify the Secretary of State forthwith of—

(i) any new information which becomes available with regard to any risks there are of damage[1] to the environment being so caused, and

(ii) *repealed*,

(iii) any unforeseen event, occurring in connection with a release by him, which might affect the risks there are of damage to the environment being caused as a result of their being released.

(*c*) take such measures as are necessary to prevent damage[2] to the environment being caused as a result of the release or, as the case may be, the marketing of the organisms;

(*d*) notify the Secretary of State of the measures (if any) taken as a result of new information becoming available or an unforeseen event occurring as described in paragraph (*b*)(ii) above; and

(*e*) in a case where new information becomes available or an unforeseen event so occurs, revise the information contained in his application for a consent accordingly and supply the revised information to the Secretary of State.

(6) The general condition implied into a consent under subsection (3), (4) or (5) above has effect subject to any conditions imposed under subsection (1) above; and the obligations imposed by virtue of subsection (4)(*c*) or (5)(*c*) above shall not apply to any aspect of an act authorised by a consent which is regulated by such a condition.

(7) There shall be implied in every consent for keeping, releasing or marketing genetically modified organisms of any description a general condition that the holder of the consent—

(*a*) shall take all reasonable steps to keep himself informed of developments in the techniques which may be available in his case for preventing damage[2] to the environment being caused as a result of the doing of the act authorised by the consent in relation to organisms of that description; and

(*b*) if it appears at any time that any better techniques are available to him than is required by any condition included in the consent under subsection (1) above, shall notify the Secretary of State of that fact forthwith.

But this general condition shall have effect subject to any conditions imposed under subsection (1) above.

[Environmental Protection Act 1990, s 112, as amended by SI 1992/2617 and 3280, SI 1993/152, SI 2002/2443 (E) and 3188(W).]

---

1. The functions of the Secretary of State under Part VI of this Act, so far as exercisable in relation to Wales, have been transferred to the National Assembly for Wales (Transfer of Functions) Order 2000, SI 2000/253, art 2, Sch 1.

2. For the circumstances in which the capacity of organisms for causing harm is to be disregarded see the Genetically Modified Organisms (Deliberate Release) Regulations 2002, SI 2002/2443 amended by SI 2004/2411 and SI 2005/2759 and the Genetically Modified Organisms (Deliberate Release) (Wales) Regulations 2002, SI 2002/3188 amended by SI 2005/1913 and 2759.

8–26335 113. *Fees and charges.*

Inspectors

8–26336 114. Appointment etc of inspectors. (1) The Secretary of State[1] may appoint as inspectors, for carrying this Part into effect, such number of persons appearing to him to be qualified for the purpose as he may consider necessary.

(2) The Secretary of State may make to or in respect of any person so appointed such payments by way of remuneration, allowances or otherwise as he may with the approval of the Treasury determine.

(3) An inspector shall not be personally liable in any civil or criminal proceedings for anything done in the purported exercise of any power under section 115 or 117 below if the court is satisfied that the act was done in good faith and that there were reasonable grounds for doing it.

(4) In England and Wales an inspector, if authorised to do so by the Secretary of State, may, although not of counsel or a solicitor, prosecute before a magistrates' court proceedings for an offence under section 118(1) below.

(5) In this Part "inspector" means, subject to section 125 below, a person appointed as an inspector under subsection (1) above.
[Environmental Protection Act 1990, s 114.]

1. The functions of the Secretary of State under Part VI of this Act, so far as exercisable in relation to Wales, have been transferred to the National Assembly for Wales (Transfer of Functions) Order 2000, SI 2000/253, art 2, Sch 1.

8–26337 115. Rights of entry and inspection. (1) An inspector may, on production (if so required) of his authority, exercise any of the powers specified in subsection (3) below for the purposes of the discharge of the functions of the Secretary of State[1] under this Part.

(2) Those powers are exercisable—

(*a*) in relation to premises—

(i) on which the inspector has reason to believe a person is keeping or has kept any genetically modified organisms, or

(ii) from which he has reason to believe any such organisms have been released or have escaped; and

(*b*) in relation to premises on which the inspector has reason to believe there may be harmful genetically modified organisms or evidence of damage to the environment caused by genetically modified organisms;

but they are not exercisable in relation to premises used wholly or mainly for domestic purposes.

(3) The powers of an inspector are—

(*a*) at any reasonable time (or, in a situation in which in his opinion there is an immediate risk of damage to the environment, at any time)—

(i) to enter premises which he has reason to believe it is necessary for him to enter and to take with him any person duly authorised by the Secretary of State and, if the inspector has reasonable cause to apprehend any serious obstruction in the execution of his duty, a constable; and

(ii) to take with him any equipment or materials required for any purpose for which the power of entry is being exercised;

(*b*) to carry out such tests and inspections (and to make such recordings), as may in any circumstances be necessary;

(*c*) to direct that any, or any part of, premises which he has power to enter, or anything in or on such premises, shall be left undisturbed (whether generally or in particular respects) for so long as is reasonably necessary for the purpose of any test or inspection;

(*d*) to take samples of any organisms, articles or substances found in or on any premises which he has power to enter, and of the air, water or land in, on, or in the vicinity of, the premises;

(*e*) in the case of anything found in or on any premises which he has power to enter, which appears to him to contain or to have contained genetically modified organisms which have caused or are likely to cause damage to the environment, to cause it to be dismantled or subjected to any process or test (but not so as to damage or destroy it unless this is necessary);

(*f*) in the case of anything mentioned in paragraph (*e*) above or anything found on premises which he has power to enter which appears to be a genetically modified organism or to consist of or include genetically modified organisms, to take possession of it and detain it for so long as is necessary for all or any of the following purposes, namely—

(i) to examine it and do to it anything which he has power to do under that paragraph;

(ii) to ensure that it is not tampered with before his examination of it is completed; and

(iii) to ensure that it is available for use as evidence in any proceedings for an offence under section 118 below;

(*g*) to require any person whom he has reasonable cause to believe to be able to give any information relevant to any test or inspection under this subsection to answer (in the absence of persons other than a person nominated to be present and any persons whom the inspector may allow to be present) such questions as the inspector thinks fit to ask and to sign a declaration of the truth of his answers;

(*h*) to require the production of, or where the information is recorded in computerised form, the furnishing of extracts from, any records which are required to be kept under this Part or it is necessary for him to see for the purposes of any test or inspection under this subsection and to inspect, and take copies of, or of any entry in, the records;

(*i*) to require any person to afford him such facilities and assistance with respect to any matters or things within that person's control or in relation to which that person has responsibilities as are necessary to enable the inspector to exercise any of the powers conferred on him by this section;

(*j*) any other power for the purpose mentioned in subsection (1) above which is conferred by regulations made by the Secretary of State.

(4) The Secretary of State may by regulations make provision as to the procedure to be followed in connection with the taking of, and the dealing with, samples under subsection (3)(*d*) above.

(5) Where an inspector proposes to exercise the power conferred by subsection (3)(*e*) above, he shall, if so requested by a person who at the time is present on and has responsibilities in relation to those premises, cause anything which is to be done by virtue of that power to be done in the presence of that person.

(6) Before exercising the power conferred by subsection (3)(*e*) above, an inspector shall consult such persons as appear to him appropriate for the purpose of ascertaining what dangers, if any, there may be in doing anything which he proposes to do under the power.

(7) Where under the power conferred by subsection (3)(*f*) above an inspector takes possession of anything found on any premises, he shall leave there, either with a responsible person or, if that is impracticable, fixed in a conspicuous position, a notice giving particulars sufficient to identify what he has seized and stating that he has taken possession of it under that power; and before taking possession under that power of—

(*a*) any thing that forms part of a batch of similar things, or
(*b*) any substance,

an inspector shall, if it is practical and safe for him to do so, take a sample of it and give to a responsible person at the premises a portion of the sample marked in a manner sufficient to identify it.

(8) No answer given by a person in pursuance of a requirement imposed under subsection (3)(*g*) above shall be admissible in evidence—

(*a*) in any proceedings in England and Wales against that person; or
(*b*) in any criminal proceedings in Scotland against that person.

(9) The powers conferred by subsection (3)(*a*), (*b*), (*c*), (*d*), (*e*) and (*h*) above shall also be exercisable (subject to subsections (4), (5) and (6) above) by any person authorised for the purpose in writing by the Secretary of State.

(10) Nothing in this section shall be taken to compel the production by any person of a document of which he would on grounds of legal professional privilege be entitled to withhold production on an order for discovery in an action in the High Court or, in relation to Scotland, on an order for the production of documents in an action in the Court of Session.
[Environmental Protection Act 1990, s 115.]

1. The functions of the Secretary of State under Part VI of this Act, so far as exercisable in relation to Wales, have been transferred to the National Assembly for Wales (Transfer of Functions) Order 2000, SI 2000/253, art 2, Sch 1.

Enforcement powers and offences

8–26338 **116. Obtaining of information from persons.** (1) For the purposes of the discharge of his functions under this Part, the Secretary of State[1] may, by notice in writing served on any person who appears to him—

(*a*) to be involved in the importation, acquisition, keeping, release or marketing of genetically modified organisms; or
(*b*) to be about to become, or to have been, involved in any of those activities;

require that person to furnish such relevant information available to him as is specified in the notice, in such form and within such period following service of the notice as is so specified.

(2) For the purposes of this section "relevant information" means information concerning any aspects of the activities in question, including any damage to the environment which may be or have been caused thereby; and the discharge by the Secretary of State of an obligation of the United Kingdom under the Community Treaties or any international agreement concerning the protection of the environment from harm caused by genetically modified organisms shall be treated as a function of his under this Part.
[Environmental Protection Act 1990, s 116.]

1. The functions of the Secretary of State under Part VI of this Act, so far as exercisable in relation to Wales, have been transferred to the National Assembly for Wales (Transfer of Functions) Order 2000, SI 2000/253, art 2, Sch 1.

8–26339 **117. Power to deal with cause of imminent danger of damage to the environment.** (1) Where, in the case of anything found by him on any premises which he has power to enter, an inspector has reason to believe that it is a genetically modified organism or that it consists of or includes genetically modified organisms and that, in the circumstances in which he finds it, it is a cause of imminent danger of damage[1] to the environment, he may seize it and cause it to be rendered harmless (whether by destruction, by bringing it under proper control or otherwise).

(2) Before there is rendered harmless under this section—

(*a*) any thing that forms part of a batch of similar things, or
(*b*) any substance,

the inspector shall, if it is practicable and safe for him to do so, take a sample of it and give to a responsible person at the premises a portion of the sample marked in a manner sufficient to identify it.

(3) As soon as may be after anything has been seized and rendered harmless under this section, the inspector shall prepare and sign a written report giving particulars of the circumstances in which it was seized and so dealt with by him, and shall—

(*a*) give a signed copy of the report to a responsible person at the premises where it was found by him; and

(*b*) unless that person is the owner of it, also serve a signed copy of the report on the owner;

and if, where paragraph (*b*) above applies, the inspector cannot after reasonable inquiry ascertain the name or address of the owner, the copy may be served on him by giving it to the person to whom a copy was given under paragraph (*a*) above.

[Environmental Protection Act 1990, s 117.]

---

1. For the circumstances in which the capacity of organisms for causing harm is to be disregarded see the Genetically Modified Organisms (Deliberate Release) Regulations 2002, SI 2002/2443 amended by SI 2004/2411 and SI 2005/2759 and the Genetically Modified Organisms (Deliberate Release) (Wales) Regulations 2002, SI 2002/3188 amended by SI 2005/1913 and 2759.

8–26340 **118. Offences.** (1) It is an offence for a person—

(*a*) to do anything in contravention of section 108(1) above in relation to something which is, and which he knows or has reason to believe is, a genetically modified organism;

(*b*) to fail to comply with section 108(3) above when keeping something which is, and which he knows or has reason to believe is, genetically modified organism;

(*c*) to do anything in contravention of section 111(1) or (2) above in relation to something which is, and which he knows or has reason to believe is, a genetically modified organism;

(*d*) to fail to comply with any requirement of subsection (2), (3)(*a*), (*b*) or (*c*) or (4) of section 109 above in relation to something which is, and which he knows or has reason to believe is, a genetically modified organism;

(*e*) to fail, without reasonable excuse, to comply with section 108(5) or (6) or section 111(6A) above;

(*f*) to contravene any prohibition imposed on him by a prohibition notice;

(*g*) without reasonable excuse, to fail to comply with any requirement imposed under section 115 above;

(*h*) to prevent any other person from appearing before or from answering any question to which an inspector may, by virtue of section 115(3) above, require an answer;

(*i*) intentionally to obstruct an inspector in the exercise or performance of his powers or duties, other than his powers or duties under section 117 above;

(*j*) intentionally to obstruct an inspector in the exercise of his powers or duties under section 117 above;

(*k*) to fail, without reasonable excuse, to comply with any requirement imposed by a notice under section 116 above;

(*l*) to make a statement which he knows to be false or misleading in a material particular, or recklessly to make a statement which is false or misleading in a material particular, where the statement is made—

(i) in purported compliance with a requirement to furnish any information imposed by or under any provision of this Part; or

(ii) for the purpose of obtaining the grant of a consent to himself or any other person or the variation of a consent;

(*m*) intentionally to make a false entry in any record required to be kept under section 108 or 111 above;

(*n*) with intent to deceive, to forge or use a document purporting to be issued under section 111 above or required for any purpose thereunder or to make or have in his possession a document so closely resembling any such document as to be likely to deceive;

(*o*) falsely to pretend to be an inspector.

(2) It shall be a defence for a person charged with an offence under paragraph (*a*), (*b*), (*c*), (*d*) or (*f*) of subsection (1) above to prove that he took all reasonable precautions and exercised all due diligence to avoid the commission of the offence.

(3) A person guilty of an offence under paragraph (*c*) or (*d*) of subsection (1) above shall be liable[1]—

(*a*) on summary conviction, to a fine not exceeding **£20,000** or to imprisonment for a term not exceeding **six months**, or to **both**;

(*b*) on conviction on indictment, to a **fine** or to imprisonment for a term not exceeding **five years**, or to **both**.

(4) A person guilty of an offence under paragraph (*f*) of subsection (1) above shall be liable[1]—

(*a*) on summary conviction, to a fine not exceeding **£20,000** or to imprisonment for a term not exceeding **six months**, or to **both**;

(*b*) on conviction on indictment, to a **fine** or to imprisonment for a term not exceeding **two years**, or to **both**.

(5) A person guilty of an offence under paragraph (*a*) or (*b*) of subsection (1) above shall be liable[1]—

(*a*) on summary conviction, to a fine not exceeding the **statutory maximum** or to imprisonment for a term not exceeding **six months**, or to **both**;

(*b*) on conviction on indictment, to a **fine** or to imprisonment for a term not exceeding **five years**, or to **both**.

(6) A person guilty of an offence under paragraph (*e*), (*j*), (*k*), (*l*), (*m*) or (*n*) of subsection (1) above shall be liable[1]—

(*a*) on summary conviction, to a fine not exceeding the **statutory maximum** or to imprisonment for a term not exceeding **six months**, or to **both**;

(*b*) on conviction on indictment, to a **fine** or to imprisonment for a term not exceeding **two years**, or to **both**.

(7) A person guilty of an offence under paragraph (*g*), (*h*) or (*i*) of subsection (1) above shall be liable on summary conviction to a fine not exceeding the **statutory maximum** or to imprisonment for a term not exceeding **three months**, or to **both**.

(8) A person guilty of an offence under paragraph (*o*) of subsection (1) above shall be liable on summary conviction to a fine not exceeding **level 5** on the standard scale.

(9) Where a person is convicted of an offence under paragraph (*b*) of subsection (1) above in respect of his keeping any genetically modified organism, then, if the contravention in respect of which he was convicted is continued after he was convicted he shall be guilty of a further offence and liable on summary conviction to a fine of **one-fifth of level 5** on the standard scale for each day on which the contravention is so continued.

(10) Proceedings in respect of an offence under this section shall not be instituted in England and Wales except by the Secretary of State or with the consent of the Director of Public Prosecutions or in Northern Ireland except with the consent of the Director of Public Prosecutions for Northern Ireland.

[Environmental Protection Act 1990, s 118, as amended by SI 1992/3280 and SI 1993/152.]

---

1. For procedure in respect of an offence triable either way, see the Magistrates' Courts Act 1980, ss 17A–21 in PART I: MAGISTRATES' COURTS, PROCEDURE, ante.

8–26341 **119. Onus of proof as regards techniques and evidence.** (1) In any proceedings for either of the following offences, that is to say—

(*a*) an offence under section 118(1)(*c*) above consisting in a failure to comply with the general condition implied by section 112(4)(*c*) or (5)(*c*) above; or

(*b*) an offence under section 118(1)(*d*) above consisting in a failure to comply with section 109(3)(*c*) or (4)(*c*) above;

it shall be for the accused to prove the matters described in subsection (1A) below.*

(1A) The matters referred to in subsection (1) above are—

(*a*) in the case of an offence under section 118(1)(*c*) above consisting in a failure to comply with the general condition implied by section 112(5)(*c*) above—

(i) that no measures, other than the measures taken by him, were necessary to prevent damage being caused to the environment from the release or, as the case may be, marketing of the organisms, or

(ii) in a case where he took no measures, that no measures were necessary; and

(*b*) in any other case.*

(2) Where an entry is required by a condition in a consent to be made in any record as to the observance of any other condition and the entry has not been made, that fact shall be admissible as evidence that that other condition has not been observed.

[Environmental Protection Act 1990, s 119 as amended by SI 2002/2443 (E) and 3188 (W).]

8–26342 **120. Power of court to order cause of offence to be remedied.** (1) Where a person is convicted of an offence under section 118(1)(*a*), (*b*), (*c*), (*d*), (*e*) or (*f*) above in respect of any matters which appear to the court to be matters which it is in his power to remedy, the court may, in addition to or instead of imposing any punishment, order him, within such time as may be fixed by the order, to take such steps as may be specified in the order for remedying those matters.

(2) The time fixed by an order under subsection (1) above may be extended or further extended by order of the court on an application made before the end of the time as originally fixed or as extended under this subsection, as the case may be.

(3) Where a person is ordered under subsection (1) above to remedy any matters, that person

shall not be liable under section 118 above in respect of those matters, in so far as they continue during the time fixed by the order or any further time allowed under subsection (2) above.
[Environmental Protection Act 1990, s 120.]

8–26343 **121.** *Power of Secretary of State to remedy harm.*

Publicity

8–26344 **122–123.** *Public register of information.*

Supplementary

8–26344A **124.** *Advisory committee for purposes of Part VI.*

8–26345 **125. Delegation of enforcement functions.** (1) The Secretary of State[1] may, by an agreement made with any public authority, delegate to that authority or to any officer appointed by an authority exercising functions on behalf of that authority any of his enforcement functions under this Part, subject to such restrictions and conditions as may be specified in the agreement.

(2) For the purposes of this section the following are "enforcement functions" of the Secretary of State, that is to say, his functions under—

section 110;
section 114(1) and (4);
section 116;
section 118(10); and
section 121;

and "inspector" in sections 115 and 117 includes, to the extent of the delegation, any inspector appointed by an authority other than the Secretary of State by virtue of an agreement under this section.

(3) The Secretary of State shall, if and so far as an agreement under this section so provides, make payments to the authority to reimburse the authority the expenses incurred in the performance of functions delegated under this section; but no such agreement shall be made without the approval of the Treasury.
[Environmental Protection Act 1990, s 125.]

1. The functions of the Secretary of State under Part VI of this Act, so far as exercisable in relation to Wales, have been transferred to the National Assembly for Wales (Transfer of Functions) Order 2000, SI 2000/253, art 2, Sch 1.

8–26346 **126.** *Exercise of certain functions jointly by Secretary of State and Minister of Agriculture, Fisheries and Food.*

8–26347 **127. Definitions.** (1) In this Part—

"acquire", in relation to genetically modified organisms, includes any method by which such organisms may come to be in a person's possession, other than by their being imported;

"consent" means a consent granted under section 111 above, and a reference to the limitations or conditions to which a consent is subject is a reference to the limitations or conditions subject to which the consent for the time being has effect;

"descendant", in relation to a genetically modified organism, means any other organism whose genes or other genetic material is derived, through any number of generations, from that organism by any process of reproduction;

"import" means import into the United Kingdom;

"premises" includes any land;

"prohibition notice" means a notice under section 110 above.

(2) This Part, except in so far as it relates to importations of genetically modified organisms, applies to the territorial sea adjacent to England as it applies in England, and applies to any area for the time being designated under section 1(7) of the Continental Shelf Act 1964, as it applies in England.*
[Environmental Protection Act 1990, s 127 as amended by SI 2002/2443.]

***Sub-section (2) printed as amended by SI 2002/2443. In force as regards England from 17 October 2002.**

8–26348

PART VII[1]

NATURE CONSERVATION IN GREAT BRITAIN AND COUNTRYSIDE MATTERS IN WALES

1. Part VII consists of ss 128–139.

PART VIII[1]
MISCELLANEOUS

Other controls on substances, articles or waste

8–26349 **140. Power to prohibit or restrict the importation, use, supply or storage of injurious substances or articles**[2]. (1) The Secretary of State may by regulations[3] prohibit or restrict—

(*a*) the importation into and the landing and unloading in the United Kingdom,
(*b*) the use for any purpose,
(*c*) the supply for any purpose, and
(*d*) the storage,

of any specified substance or article if he considers it appropriate to do so for the purpose of preventing the substance or article from causing pollution of the environment or harm to human health or to the health of animals or plants.

(2) Any such prohibition or restriction may apply—

(*a*) in all, or only in specified, areas;
(*b*) in all, or only in specified, circumstances or if conditions imposed by the regulations are not complied with; and
(*c*) to all, or only to specified descriptions of, persons.

(3) Regulations under this section may—

(*a*) confer on the Secretary of State power to direct that any substance or article whose use, supply or storage is prohibited or restricted is to be treated as waste or controlled waste of any description and in relation to any such substance or article—
   (i) to apply, with or without modification, specified provisions of Part II; or
   (ii) to direct that it be disposed of or treated in accordance with the direction;
(*b*) confer on the Secretary of State power, where a substance or article has been imported, landed or unloaded in contravention of a prohibition or restriction imposed under subsection (1)(*a*) above, to require that the substance or article be disposed of or treated in or removed from the United Kingdom;
(*c*) confer powers corresponding to those conferred by section 108 of the Environment Act 1995 on persons authorised for any purpose of the regulations by the Secretary of State or any local or other authority; and
(*d*) include such other incidental and supplemental, and such transitional provisions, as the Secretary of State considers appropriate.

(4) The Secretary of State may, by regulations under this section, direct that, for the purposes of any power conferred on him under subsection (3)(*b*) above, any prohibition or restriction on the importation into or the landing and unloading in the United Kingdom imposed—

(*a*) by or under any Community instrument, or
(*b*) by or under any enactment,

shall be treated as imposed under subsection (1)(*a*) above and any power conferred on him under subsection (3)(*b*) above shall be exercisable accordingly.

(5) The Secretary of State may by order establish a committee to give him advice in relation to the exercise of the power to make regulations under this section and Schedule 12 to this Act shall have effect in relation to it.

(6) Subject to subsection (7) below, it shall be the duty of the Secretary of State before he makes any regulations under this section other than regulations under subsection (4) above—

(*a*) to consult the committee constituted under subsection (5) above about the proposed regulations;
(*b*) having consulted the committee, to publish in the London Gazette and, if the regulations apply in Scotland or Northern Ireland, the Edinburgh Gazette or, as the case may be, Belfast Gazette and in any other publication which he considers appropriate, a notice indicating the effect of the proposed regulations and specifying—
   (i) the date on which it is proposed that the regulations will come into force;
   (ii) a place where a draft of the proposed regulations may be inspected free of charge by members of the public during office hours; and
   (iii) a period of not less than fourteen days, beginning with the date on which the notice is first published, during which representations in writing may be made to the Secretary of State about the proposed regulations; and
(*c*) to consider any representations which are made to him in accordance with the notice.

(7) The Secretary of State may make regulations under this section in relation to any substance or article without observing the requirements of subsection (6) above where it appears to him that there is an imminent risk, if those requirements are observed, that serious pollution of the environment will be caused.

(8) The Secretary of State may, after performing the duty imposed on him by subsection (6) above with respect of any proposed regulations, make the regulations either—

(*a*) in the form of the draft mentioned in subsection (6)(*b*) above, or
(*b*) in that form with such modifications as he considers appropriate;

but the Secretary of State shall not make any regulations incorporating modifications unless he is of opinion that it is appropriate for the requirements of subsection (6) above to be disregarded.

(9) Regulations under this section may provide that a person who contravenes or fails to comply with a specified provision of the regulations or causes or permits another person to contravene or fail to comply with a specified provision of the regulations commits an offence and may prescribe the maximum penalty for the offence.

(10) No offence under the regulations shall be made punishable with imprisonment for more than two years or punishable on summary conviction with a fine exceeding level 5 on the standard scale (if not calculated on a daily basis) or, in the case of a continuing offence, exceeding one-tenth of the level on the standard scale specified as the maximum penalty for the original offence.

(11) In this section—

"the environment" means the air, water and land, or any of those media, and the medium of air includes the air within buildings and the air within other natural or man-made structures above or below ground;

"specified" means specified in the regulations; and

"substance" means any natural or artificial substance, whether in solid or liquid form or in the form of a gas or vapour and it includes mixtures of substances.

[Environmental Protection Act 1990, s 140, as amended by SI 1999/1108.]

---

1. Part VIII consists of ss 140–155.
2. For the power of the Secretary of State to extend the provisions of this section to give effect to community and other obligations, see s 156, post.
3. The Environmental Protection (Control of Injurious Substances) Regulations 1992, SI 1992/31 amended by SI 1992/1583, SI 1993/1 and SI 2003/3274, the Environmental Protection (Controls on Injurious Substances) Regulations 1993, SI 1993/1 amended by SI 2001/3141, the Environmental Protection (Restrictions on Use of Lead Shot) (England) Regulations 1999, SI 1999/2170 amended by SI 2002/2102 and SI 2003/2512, the Environmental Protection (Controls on Ozone-depleting Substances) Regulations 2002, SI 2002/528 and the Environmental Protection (Restriction on Use of Lead Shot) (Wales) Regulations 2002, SI 2002/1730, have been made.

8–26350 **141. Power to prohibit or restrict the importation or exportation of waste.** (1) The Secretary of State may, for the purpose of preventing any risk of pollution of the environment or of harm to human health arising from waste being imported or exported or of conserving the facilities or resources for dealing with waste, make regulations prohibiting or restricting, or providing for the prohibition or restriction of—

(*a*) the importation into and the landing and unloading in the United Kingdom, or
(*b*) the exportation, or the loading for exportation, from the United Kingdom,

of waste of any description.

(2) Regulations under this section may make different provision for different descriptions of waste or waste of any description in different circumstances.

(3) Regulations under this section may, as respects any description of waste, confer or impose on waste regulation authorities or any of them such functions in relation to the importation of waste as appear to be appropriate to the Secretary of State, subject to such limitations and conditions as are specified in the regulations.

(4) Regulations under this section may confer or impose on waste regulation authorities or any of them functions of enforcing any of the regulations on behalf of the Secretary of State whether or not the functions fall within subsection (3) above.

(5) Regulations under this section may—

(*a*) as respects functions conferred or imposed on waste regulation authorities—
  (i) make them exercisable in relation to individual consignments or consignments in a series by the same person but not in relation to consignments or descriptions of consignments generally;
  (ii) (*Repealed*);
(*b*) impose or provide for the imposition of prohibitions either absolutely or only if conditions or procedures prescribed in or under the regulations are not complied with;
(*c*) impose duties to be complied with before, on or after any importation or exportation of waste by persons who are, or are to be, consignors, consignees, carriers or holders of the waste or any waste derived from it.
(*d*) confer powers corresponding to those conferred by section 69(3) above;
(*e*) provide for appeals to the Secretary of State from determinations made by authorities under the regulations;
(*f*) provide for the keeping by the Secretary of State, waste regulation authorities and waste collection authorities of public registers of information relating to the importation and

exportation of waste and for the transmission of such information between any of those persons;

(*g*) create offences, subject to the limitation that no offence shall be punishable with imprisonment for more than two years or punishable on summary conviction with imprisonment for more than six months* or a fine exceeding level 5 on the standard scale (if not calculated on a daily basis) or, in the case of a continuing offence, exceeding one-tenth of the level on the standard scale specified as the maximum penalty for the original offence.*

(6) In this section—

"the environment" means land, water and air or any of them;

"harm" includes offence to any of man's senses;

"waste", "waste collection authority", and "waste regulation authority" have the same meaning as in Part II; and

"the United Kingdom" includes its territorial sea.

(7) (*Northern Ireland*)

[Environmental Protection Act 1990, s 141, as amended by the Environment Act 1995, Schs 22 and 24.]

***Words substituted and new sub-s (5A) inserted by the Criminal Justice Act 2003, Sch 27, from a date to be appointed.**

8–26351 **142. Powers to obtain information about potentially hazardous substances.** (1) The Secretary of State may, for the purpose of assessing their potential for causing pollution of the environment or harm to human health, by regulations make provision for and in connection with the obtaining of relevant information relating to substances which may be specified by him by order for the purposes of this section.

(2) The Secretary of State shall not make an order under subsection (1) above specifying any substance—

(*a*) which was first supplied in any member State on or after 18th September 1981; or

(*b*) in so far as it is a regulated substance for the purposes of any relevant enactment.

(3) The Secretary of State shall not make an order under subsection (1) above specifying any substance without consulting the committee established under section 140(5) except where it appears to him that information about the substance needs to be obtained urgently under this section.

(4) Regulations under this section may—

(*a*) prescribe the descriptions of relevant information which are to be furnished under this section in relation to specified substances;

(*b*) impose requirements on manufacturers, importers or suppliers generally to furnish information prescribed under paragraph (*a*) above;

(*c*) provide for the imposition of requirements on manufacturers, importers or suppliers generally to furnish relevant information relating to products or articles containing specified substances in relation to which information has been furnished in pursuance of paragraph (*b*) above;

(*d*) provide for the imposition of requirements on particular manufacturers, importers or suppliers to furnish further information relating to specified substances in relation to which information has been furnished in pursuance of paragraph (*b*) above;

(*e*) provide for the imposition of requirements on particular manufacturers or importers to carry out tests of specified substances and to furnish information of the results of the tests;

(*f*) authorise persons to comply with requirements to furnish information imposed on them by or under the regulations by means of representative persons or bodies;

(*g*) impose restrictions on the disclosure of information obtained under this section and provide for determining what information is, and what information is not, to be treated as furnished in confidence;

(*h*) create offences, subject to the limitation that no offence shall be punishable with imprisonment or punishable on summary conviction with a fine exceeding level 5 on the standard scale;

(*i*) make any public authority designated by the regulations responsible for the enforcement of the regulations to such extent as may be specified in the regulations;

(*j*) include such other incidental and supplemental, and such transitional, provisions as the Secretary of State considers appropriate.

(5) The Secretary of State shall have regard, in imposing or providing for the imposition of any requirement under subsection (4)(*b*), (*c*), (*d*) or (*e*) above, to the cost likely to be involved in complying with the requirement.

(6) In this section—

"the environment" means the air, water and land or any of them;

"relevant information", in relation to substances, produces or articles, means information relating to their properties, production, distribution, importation or use or intended use and, in relation to products or articles, to their disposal as waste;

"substance" means any natural or artificial substance, whether in solid or liquid form or in the form of a gas or vapour and it includes mixtures of substances.

(7) The enactments which are relevant for the purposes of subsection (2)(*b*) above are the following—

the Manufacture and Storage of Explosives Regulations 2005;
the Radioactive Substsnces act 1993;
Parts II, III and VIII of the Medicines Act 1968;
Part IV of the Agriculture Act 1970;
the Misuse of Drugs Act 1971;
Part III of the Food and Environment Protection Act 1985; and
the Food Safety Act 1990;

and a substance is a regulated substance for the purposes of any such enactment in so far as any prohibition, restriction or requirement is imposed in relation to it by or under the enactment for the purposes of that enactment.
[Environmental Protection Act 1990, s 142, as amended by the Radioactive Substances Act 1993, Sch 4 and SI 2005/1082, Sch 5.]

8–26352 **143.** *Repealed.*

8–26353 **144.** *Amendments of hazardous substances legislation.*

8–26354 **145.** *Penalties for offences of polluting controlled waters etc.*

8–26355 **146–147.** *Pollution at sea.*

Control of Dogs

8–26356 **149. Seizure of stray dogs.** (1) Every local authority shall appoint an officer (under whatever title the authority may determine) for the purpose of discharging the functions imposed or conferred by this section for dealing with stray dogs found in the area of the authority.

(2) The officer may delegate the discharge of his functions to another person but he shall remain responsible for securing that the functions are properly discharged.

(3) Where the officer has reason to believe that any dog found in a public place or on any other land or premises is a stray dog, he shall (if practicable) seize the dog and detain it, but, where he finds it on land or premises which is not a public place, only with the consent of the owner or occupier of the land or premises.

(4) Where any dog seized under this section wears a collar having inscribed thereon or attached thereto the address of any person, or the owner of the dog is known, the officer shall serve on the person whose address is given on the collar, or on the owner, a notice in writing stating that the dog has been seized and where it is being kept and stating that the dog will be liable to be disposed of if it is not claimed within seven clear days after the service of the notice and the amounts for which he would be liable under subsection (5) below are not paid.

(5) A person claiming to be the owner of a dog seized under this section shall not be entitled to have the dog returned to him unless he pays all the expenses incurred by reason of its detention and such further amount as is for the time being prescribed[1].

(6) Where any dog seized under this section has been detained for seven clear days after the seizure or, where a notice has been served under subsection (4) above, the service of the notice and the owner has not claimed the dog and paid the amounts due under subsection (5) above the officer may dispose of the dog—

(*a*) by selling it or giving it to a person who will, in his opinion, care properly for the dog;
(*b*) by selling it or giving it to an establishment for the reception of stray dogs; or
(*c*) by destroying it in a manner to cause as little pain as possible;

but no dog seized under this section shall be sold or given for the purposes of vivisection.

(7) Where a dog is disposed of under subsection (6)(*a*) or (*b*) above to a person acting in good faith, the ownership of the dog shall be vested in the recipient.

(8) The officer shall keep a register containing the prescribed particulars of or relating to dogs seized under this section and the register shall be available, at all reasonable times, for inspection by the public free of charge.

(9) The officer shall cause any dog detained under this section to be properly fed and maintained.

(10) Notwithstanding anything in this section, the officer may cause a dog detained under this section to be destroyed before the expiration of the period mentioned in subsection (6) above where he is of the opinion that this should be done to avoid suffering.

(11) In this section—

"local authority", in relation to England, means a district council, a London borough council, the Common Council of the City of London or the Council of the Isles of Scilly, in relation to Wales, means a county council or a county borough council and, in relation to Scotland, means an islands or district council;

"officer" means an officer appointed under subsection (1) above;

"prescribed" means prescribed in regulations[1] made by the Secretary of State; and
"public place" means—

(i) as respects England and Wales, any highway and any other place to which the public are entitled or permitted to have access;
(ii) (*Scotland*);

and, for the purposes of section 160 below in its application to this section, the proper address of the owner of a dog which wears a collar includes the address given on the collar.
[Environmental Protection Act 1990, s 149, as amended by the Local Government (Wales) Act 1994, Sch 9.]

1. See the Environmental Protection (Stray Dogs) Regulations 1992, SI 1992/288.

8–26357 150. Delivery of stray dogs to police or local authority officer*. (1) Any person (in this section referred to as "the finder") who takes possession of a stray dog shall forthwith either—

(*a*) return the dog to its owner; or
(*b*) take the dog—

(i) to the officer of the local authority for the area in which the dog was found; or
(ii) to the police station which is nearest to the place where the dog was found;*

and shall inform the officer of the local authority or the police officer in charge of the police station, as the case may be, where the dog was found.

(2) Where a dog has been taken under subsection (1) above to the officer of a local authority, then—

(*a*) if the finder desires to keep the dog, he shall inform the officer of this fact and shall furnish his name and address and the officer shall, having complied with the procedure (if any) prescribed under subsection (6) below, allow the finder to remove the dog;
(*b*) if the finder does not desire to keep the dog, the officer shall, unless he has reason to believe it is not a stray, treat it as if it had been seized by him under section 149 above.

(3) Where the finder of a dog keeps the dog by virtue of this section he must keep it for not less than one month.

(4) *Scotland.*

(5) If the finder of a dog fails to comply with the requirements of subsection (1) or (3) above he shall be liable on summary conviction to a fine not exceeding **level 2** on the standards scale.

(6) The Secretary of State may, by regulations, prescribe the procedure to be followed under subsection (2)(*a*) above.

(7) In this section "local authority" and "officer" have the same meaning as in section 149 above.
[Environmental Protection Act 1990, s 150.]

***Section heading amended and para (1)(*b*)(ii) repealed, in relation to England and Wales, by the Clean Neighbourhoods and Environment Act 2005, Sch 5 from a date to be appointed.**

8–26358 151. *Enforcement of orders about collars and tags for dogs—Amendment of the Animal Health Act 1981.*

Straw and stubble burning

8–26359 152. Burning of straw and stubble etc. (1) The appropriate Minister may by regulations[1] prohibit or restrict the burning of crop residues on agricultural land by persons engaged in agriculture and he may (by the same or other regulations) provide exemptions from any prohibition or restriction so imposed.

(2) Regulations providing an exemption from any prohibition or restriction may make the exemption applicable—

(*a*) in all, or only in specified, areas;
(*b*) to all, or only to specified, crop residues; or
(*c*) in all, or only in specified, circumstances.

(3) Any power to make regulations under this section includes power—

(*a*) to make different provision for different areas or circumstances;
(*b*) where burning of a crop residue is restricted, to impose requirements to be complied with before or after the burning;
(*c*) to create offences subject to the limitation that no offence shall be made punishable otherwise than on summary conviction and the fine prescribed for the offence shall not exceed level 5 on the standard scale; and
(*d*) to make such incidental, supplemental and transitional provision as the appropriate Minister considers appropriate.

(4) Where it appears to the appropriate Minister appropriate to do so in consequence of any regulations made under the foregoing provisions of this section, the appropriate Minister may, by

order, repeal any byelaws of local authorities dealing with the burning of crop residues on agricultural land.

(5) In this section—

"agriculture" and "agricultural land" have, as respects England or as respects Wales, the same meaning as in the Agriculture Act 1947 and, as respects Scotland, the same meaning as in the Agriculture (Scotland) Act 1948;

"crop residue" means straw or stubble or any other crop residue;

"the appropriate Minister" means the Minister of Agriculture, Fisheries and Food or the Secretary of State or both of them.

[Environmental Protection Act 1990, s 152.]

---

1. The Crop Residues (Restrictions on Burning) Regulations 1993, SI 1993/1366 have been made.

PART IX[1]
GENERAL

8–26360 **156. Power to give effect to Community and other international obligations etc.** (1) The Secretary of State may by regulations[2] provide that the provisions to which this section applies shall have effect with such modifications as may be prescribed for the purpose of enabling Her Majesty's Government in the United Kingdom—

(*a*) to give effect to any Community obligation or exercise any related right; or

(*b*) to give effect to any obligation or exercise any related right under any international agreement to which the United Kingdom is for the time being a party.

(2) This section applies to the following provisions of this Act—

(*a*) Part I;

(*b*) Part II;

(*c*) Part VI; and

(*d*) in Part VIII, sections 140, 141 or 142;

and the provisions of the Radioactive Substances Act 1993.

(3) In this section—

"modifications" includes additions, alterations and omissions;

"prescribed" means prescribed in regulations under this section; and

"related right", in relation to an obligation, includes any derogation or other right to make more onerous provisions available in respect of that obligation.

(4) *Northern Ireland.*

[Environmental Protection Act 1990, s 156, as amended by the Radioactive Substances Act 1993, Sch 4.]

---

1. Part IX consists of ss 156–164.

2. The Environmental Protection Act 1990 (Extension of s 140) Regulations 1999, SI 1999/396 have been made for the purpose of implementing Council Directive 96/56/EC, on the disposal of polychlorinated biphenyls and polychlorinated terphenyls (PCB/PCT) and under PARCOM Decision 92/3 on the phasing out of PCBs and Hazardous PCB substitutes.

8–26361 **157. Offences by bodies corporate.** (1) Where an offence under any provision of this Act committed by a body corporate is proved to have been committed with the consent or connivance of, or to have been attributable to any neglect on the part of, any director, manager, secretary or other similar officer of the body corporate or a person who was purporting to act in any such capacity, he as well as the body corporate shall be guilty of that offence and shall be liable to be proceeded against and punished accordingly.

(2) Where the affairs of a body corporate are managed by its members, subsection (1) above shall apply in relation to the acts or defaults of a member in connection with his functions of management as if he were a director of the body corporate.

[Environmental Protection Act 1990, s 157.]

8–26362 **158. Offences under Parts I, II, IV, VI, etc due to fault of others.** Where the commission by any person of an offence under Part I, II, IV, or VI, or section 140, 141 or 142 above is due to the act or default of some other person, that other person may be charged with and convicted of the offence by virtue of this section whether or not proceedings for the offence are taken against the first-mentioned person.

[Environmental Protection Act 1990, s 158.]

8–26363 **159. Application to Crown.** (1) Subject to the provisions of this section, the provisions of this Act and of regulations and orders made under it shall bind the Crown.

(2) No contravention by the Crown of any provision of this Act or of any regulations or order made under it shall make the Crown criminally liable; but the High Court or, in Scotland, the Court of Session may, on the application of any public or local authority charged with enforcing that provision, declare unlawful any act or omission of the Crown which constitutes such a contravention.

(3) Notwithstanding anything in subsection (2) above, the provisions of this Act and of regulations and orders made under it shall apply to persons in the public service of the Crown as they apply to other persons.

(4) If the Secretary of State certifies that it appears to him, as respects any Crown premises and any powers of entry exercisable in relation to them specified in the certificate that it is requisite or expedient that, in the interests of national security, the powers should not be exercisable in relation to the premises, those powers shall not be exercisable in relation to those premises; and in this subsection "Crown premises" means premises held or used by or on behalf of the Crown.

(5) Nothing in this section shall be taken as in any way affecting Her Majesty in her private capacity; and this subsection shall be construed as if section 38(3) of the Crown Proceedings Act 1947 (interpretation of references in that Act to Her Majesty in her private capacity) were contained in this Act.

(6) References in this section to regulations or orders are references to regulations or orders made by statutory instrument.

(7) For the purposes of this section in its application to Part II and Part IV the authority charged with enforcing the provisions of those parts in its area is—

(*a*) in the case of Part II, any waste regulation authority, and
(*b*) in the case of Part IV, any principal litter authority.

[Environmental Protection Act 1990, s 159.]

8–26364 **160. Service of notices.** (1) Any notice required or authorised by or under this Act to be served on or given to an inspector may be served or given by delivering it to him or by leaving it at, or sending it by post to, his office.

(2) Any such notice required or authorised to be served on or given to a person other than an inspector may be served or given by delivering it to him, or by leaving it at his proper address, or by sending it by post to him at that address.

(3) Any such notice may—

(*a*) in the case of a body corporate, be served on or given to the secretary or clerk of that body;
(*b*) in the case of a partnership, be served on or given to a partner or a person having the control of management of the partnership business.

(4) For the purposes of this section and of section 7 of the Interpretation Act 1978 (service of documents by post) in its application to this section, the proper address of any person on or to whom any such notice is to be served or given shall be his last known address, except that—

(*a*) in the case of a body corporate or their secretary or clerk, it shall be the address of the registered or principal office of that body;
(*b*) in the case of a partnership or person having the control or the management of the partnership business, it shall be the principal office of the partnership;

and for the purposes of this subsection the principal office of a company registered outside the United Kingdom or of a partnership carrying on business outside the United Kingdom shall be their principal office within the United Kingdom.

(5) If the person[1] to be served with or given any such notice has specified an address in the United Kingdom other than his proper address within the meaning of subsection (4) above as the one at which he or someone on his behalf will accept notices of the same description as that notice, that address shall also be treated for the purposes of this section and section 7 of the Interpretation Act 1978 as his proper address.

(6) The preceding provisions of this section shall apply to the sending or giving of a document as they apply to the giving of a notice.

[Environmental Protection Act 1990, s 160.]

1. Where the landlord is a body corporate, such as a local authority, although notice may be served on the secretary or clerk of the local authority, the persons through whom a local authority could specify an alternative address are not confined to the secretary or clerk, so that a letter emanating from some other appropriate source will be effective, *Hall v Kingston upon Hull City Council* [1999] 2 All ER 609, 164 JP 9, QBD. The provisions as to notice in this section are permissive rather than mandatory and are not to put technical obstacles in the way of ordinary citizens using a summary procedure to gain relief from statutory nuisances. Accordingly where a company knew full well what was being alleged against it, there was effective service of a notice where the complainant wrote to a company's director and general manager at the principal office identified on the company notepaper although that office was not at the company's registered office as specified in sub-s (4) (*Hewlings v McLean Homes East Anglia Ltd* ([2001] 2 All ER 281, DC).

8–26365 **161. Regulations, orders and directions.** (1) Any power of the Secretary of State, National Assembly for Wales or the Minister of Agriculture, Fisheries and Food under this Act to make regulations or orders shall be exercisable by statutory instrument; but this subsection does not apply to a statutory instrument—

(*a*) which contains an order under section 78M(4) above, or
(*b*) by reason only that it contains to orders under section 72 above or paragraph 4 of Schedule 3.

(2) A statutory instrument containing regulations under this Act shall be subject to annulment in pursuance of a resolution of either House of Parliament.

(2A) Subsection (2) does not apply to a statutory instrument made solely by the National Assembly for Wales.

(3) Except in the cases specified in subsection (4) below, a statutory instrument containing an order under this Act shall be subject to annulment in pursuance of a resolution of either House of Parliament.

(4) Subsection (3) above does not apply to a statutory instrument—

(*a*) which contains an order under s 78M above, or

(*b*) by reason only that it contains an order under section 130(4), 131(3) or 138(2) above or section 164 (3) below, or

(*c*) which is made solely by the National Assembly for Wales.

(5) Any power conferred by this Act to give a direction shall include power to vary or revoke the direction.

(6) Any direction given under this Act shall be in writing.

[Environmental Protection Act 1990, s 161, as amended by the Environment Act 1995, Sch 22 and the Clean Neighbourhoods and Environment Act 2005, Sch 4.]

8–26366 **162. Consequential and minor amendments and repeals.** (1) The enactments specified in Schedule 15 to this Act shall have effect subject to the amendments specified in that Schedule.

(2) The enactments specified in Schedule 16 to this Act are hereby repealed subject to section 77 above, Schedule 11 to this Act and any provision made by way of a note in Schedule 16.

(3) *Scotland.*

(4) The Secretary of State may by order repeal or amend any provision of any local Act passed before this Act (including an Act confirming a provisional order) or of any order or other instrument made under an Act so passed if it appears to him that the provision is inconsistent with, or has become unnecessary or requires alteration in consequence of, any provision of this Act or corresponds to any provision repealed by this Act.

(5) Any regulations made under section 100 of the Control of Pollution Act 1974 shall have effect after the repeal of that section by subsection (2) above as if made under section 140 of this Act.

[Environmental Protection Act 1990, s 162.]

8–26366A **163A. Application of Part VI: England and Wales.** (1) The amendments made to the provisions of Part VI by the 2002 Regulations, other than the amendment of section 127(2) as it relates to the continental shelf, have effect in relation to England only, and accordingly, in the application of that Part in relation to Wales, the provisions listed in subsection (2) below continue to have effect without the amendments made by the 2002 Regulations.

(2) The provisions referred to in subsection (1) above are—

(a) section 106(1) and (4) to (6);
(b) section 107(2), (3), (6), (9) and (11);
(c) section 111(6);
(d) section 112(1) and (5);
(e) section 119(1);
(f) section 123(7);
(g) section 127(2) in so far as it relates to the territorial sea.

(3) In this section "the 2002 Regulations" means the Genetically Modified Organisms (Deliberate Release) Regulations 2002.

[Environmental Protection Act 1990, s 163A, as inserted by SI 2002/2443.]

8–26367 **164. Short title, commencement and extent.** (1) This Act may be cited as the Environmental Protection Act 1990.

(2) The following provisions of the Act shall come into force at the end of the period of two months beginning with the day on which it is passed, namely—

sections 79 to 85;
section 97;
section 99;
section 105 in so far as it relates to paragraphs 7, 13, 14 and 15 of Schedule 5;
section 140;
section 141;
section 142;
section 145;
section 146;
section 148;
section 153;
section 154;

section 155;
section 157;
section 160;
section 161;
section 162(1) in so far as it relates to paragraphs 4, 5, 7, 8, 9, 18, 22, 24 and 31(4)(*b*) of Schedule 15; but, in the case of paragraph 22, in so far only as that paragraph inserts a paragraph (*m*) into section 7(4) of the Act of 1984;
section 162(2) in so far as it relates to Part III of Schedule 16 and, in Part IX of that Schedule, the repeal of section 100 of the Control of Pollution Act 1974;
section 162(5);
section 163.

(3) The remainder of this Act (except this section) shall come into force on such day as the Secretary of State may by order[1] appoint and different days may be appointed for different provisions or different purposes.

(4) *Northern Ireland.*

(4A) Sections 45A, 45B and 47A do not extend to Scotland.

(5) Where any enactment amended or repealed by this Act extends to any part of the United Kingdom, the amendment or repeal extends to that part, subject, however, to any express provision in Schedule 15 or 16.

[Environmental Protection Act 1990, s 164 as amended by the Household Waste Recycling Act 2003, s 4.]

---

1. The following commencement orders had been made at the date of going to press: Environmental Protection Act 1990 (Commencement No 1) Order 1990, SI 1990/2226; (No 2) Order 1990, SI 1990/2243; (No 3) Order 1990, SI 1990/2565 (amended by SI 1990/2635); (No 4) Order 1990, SI 1990/2635; (No 5) Order 1991, SI 1991/96; (No 6) Order 1991, SI 1991/685; (No 7) Order 1991, SI 1991/1042; (No 8) Order 1991, SI 1991/1319; (No 9) Order 1991, SI 1991/1577; (No 10) Order 1991, SI 1991/2829; (No 11) Order 1992, SI 1992/266; (No 12) Order 1992, SI 1992/3253; (No 13) Order 1993, SI 1993/274; (No 14) Order 1994, SI 1994/780; (No 15) Order 1994, SI 1994/1096, amended by SI 1994/2487 and 3234; (No 16) Order 1994, SI 1994/2854; (No 17) Order 1995, SI 1995/2152.

Section 81

SCHEDULE 3

STATUTORY NUISANCES: SUPPLEMENTARY PROVISIONS

(Amended by the Noise and Statutory Nuisance Act 1993, s 4, the Environment Act 1995, Sch 17 and the Audit Commission Act 1998, Sch 3.)

Appeals to magistrates' court

8–26368 **1.** (1) This paragraph applies in relation to appeals under section 80(3) against an abatement notice to a magistrates' court.

(2) An appeal to which this paragraph applies shall be by way of complaint for an order and the Magistrates' Courts Act 1980 shall apply to the proceedings.

(3) An appeal against any decision of a magistrates' court in pursuance of an appeal to which this paragraph applies shall lie to the Crown Court at the instance of any party to the proceedings in which the decision was given.

(4) The Secretary of State may make regulations[1] as to appeals to which this paragraph applies and the regulations may in particular—

(*a*) include provisions comparable to those in section 290 of the Public Health Act 1936 (appeals against notices requiring the execution of works);
(*b*) prescribe the cases in which an abatement notice is, or is not, to be suspended until the appeal is decided, or until some other stage in the proceedings;
(*c*) prescribe the cases in which the decision on appeal may in some respects be less favourable to the appellant than the decision from which he is appealing;
(*d*) prescribe the cases in which the appellant may claim that an abatement notice should have been served on some other person and prescribe the procedure to be followed in those cases.

---

1. The Statutory Nuisance (Appeals) Regulations 1990 are contained in this title, post.

8–26368A **1A.** *Appeals to sheriff.*

Powers of entry etc

8–26369 **2.** (1) Subject to sub-paragraph (2) below, any person authorised by a local authority may, on production (if so required) of his authority, enter any premises at any reasonable time—

(*a*) for the purpose of ascertaining whether or not a statutory nuisance exists; or
(*b*) for the purpose of taking any action, or executing any work, authorised or required by Part III.

(2) Admission by virtue of sub-paragraph (1) above to any premises used wholly or mainly for residential purposes shall not except in an emergency be demanded as of right unless twenty-four hours notice of the intended entry has been given to the occupier.

(3) If it is shown to the satisfaction of a justice of the peace on sworn information in writing—

(*a*) that admission to any premises has been refused, or that refusal is apprehended, or that the premises are unoccupied or the occupier is temporarily absent, or that the case is one of emergency, or that an application for admission would defeat the object of the entry; and (*b*) that there is reasonable ground for entry into the premises for the purpose for which entry is required,

the justice may by warrant under his hand authorise the local authority by any authorised person to enter the premises, if need be by force.

(4) An authorised person entering any premises by virtue of sub-paragraph (1) or a warrant under sub-paragraph (3) above may—

(*a*) take with him such other persons and such equipment as may be necessary;
(*b*) carry out such inspections, measurements and tests as he considers necessary for the discharge of any of the local authority's functions under Part III; and
(*c*) take away such samples or articles as he considers necessary for that purpose.

(5) On leaving any unoccupied premises which he has entered by virtue of sub-paragraph (1) above or a warrant under sub-paragraph (3) above the authorised person shall leave them as effectually secured against trespassers as he found them.

(6) A warrant issued in pursuance of sub-paragraph (3) above shall continue in force until the purpose for which the entry is required has been satisfied.

(7) Any reference in this paragraph to an emergency is a reference to a case where the person requiring entry has reasonable cause to believe that circumstances exist which are likely to endanger life or health and that immediate entry is necessary to verify the existence of those circumstances or to ascertain their cause and to effect a remedy.

(8) *Scotland.*

8–26369A **2A.** (1) Any person authorised by a local authority may on production (if so required) of his authority—

(*a*) enter or open a vehicle, machinery or equipment, if necessary by force, or
(*b*) remove a vehicle, machinery or equipment from a street or, in Scotland, road to a secure place,

for the purpose of taking any action, or executing any work, authorised by or required under Part III in relation to a statutory nuisance within section 79(1)(*ga*) above caused by noise emitted from or caused by the vehicle, machinery or equipment.

(2) On leaving any unattended vehicle, machinery or equipment that he has entered or opened under sub-paragraph (1) above, the authorised person shall (subject to sub-paragraph (3) below) leave it secured against interference or theft in such manner and as effectually as he found it.

(3) If the authorised person is unable to comply with sub-paragraph (2) above, he shall for the purpose of securing the unattended vehicle, machinery or equipment either—

(*a*) immobilise it by such means as he considers expedient, or
(*b*) remove it from the street to a secure place.

(4) In carrying out any function under sub-paragraph (1), (2) or (3) above, the authorised person shall not cause more damage than is necessary.

(5) Before a vehicle, machinery or equipment is entered, opened or removed under sub-paragraph (1) above, the local authority shall notify the police of the intention to take action under that sub-paragraph.

(6) After a vehicle, machinery or equipment has been removed under sub-paragraph (1) or (3) above, the local authority shall notify the police of its removal and current location.

(7) Notification under sub-paragraph (5) or (6) above may be given to the police at any police station in the local authority's area or, in the case of the Temples, at any police station of the City of London Police.

(8) For the purposes of section 81(4) above, any expenses reasonably incurred by a local authority under sub-paragraph (2) or (3) above shall be treated as incurred by the authority under section 81(3) above in abating or preventing the recurrence of the statutory nuisance in question.

Offences relating to entry

8–26370 **3.** (1) A person who wilfully obstructs any person acting in the exercise of any powers conferred by paragraph 2 or 2A above shall be liable, on summary conviction, to a fine not exceeding **level 3** on the standard scale.

(2) If a person discloses any information relating to any trade secret obtained in the exercise of any powers conferred by paragraph 2 above he shall, unless the disclosure was made in the performance of his duty or with the consent of the person having the right to disclose the information, be liable, on summary conviction, to a fine not exceeding **level 5** on the standard scale.

Default powers

8–26371 **4.** (1) This paragraph applies to the following functions of a local authority, that is to say its duty under section 79 to cause its area to be inspected to detect any statutory nuisance which ought to be dealt with under section 80 or sections 80 and 80A and its powers under paragraph 2 or 2A above.

(2) If the Secretary of State is satisfied that any local authority has failed, in any respect, to discharge the function to which this paragraph applies which it ought to have discharged, he may make an order declaring the authority to be in default.

(3) An order made under sub-paragraph (2) above which declares an authority to be in default may, for the purpose of remedying the default, direct the authority ("the defaulting authority") to perform the function specified in the order and may specify the manner in which and the time or times within which the function is to be performed by the authority.

(4) If the defaulting authority fails to comply with any direction contained in such an order the Secretary of State may, instead of enforcing the order by mandamus, make an order transferring to himself the function of the authority specified in the order.

(5) Where the function of a defaulting authority is transferred under sub-paragraph (4) above, the amount of any expenses which the Secretary of State certifies were incurred by him in performing the function shall on demand be paid to him by the defaulting authority.

(6) Any expenses required to be paid by a defaulting authority under sub-paragraph (5) above shall be defrayed

by the authority in like manner, and shall be debited to the like account, as if the function had not been transferred and the expenses had been incurred by the authority in performing them.

(7) The Secretary of State may by order vary or revoke any order previously made by him under this paragraph.

(8) Any order under this paragraph may include such incidental, supplemental and transitional provisions as the Secretary of State considers appropriate.

(9) This paragraph does not apply to Scotland.

Protection from personal liability

8–26372 **5.** Nothing done by, or by a member of, a local authority or by any officer of or other person authorised by a local authority shall, if done in good faith for the purpose of executing Part III, subject them or any of them personally to any action, liability, claim or demand whatsoever (other than any liability under section 17 or 18 of the Audit Commission Act 1998 (powers of district auditor and court)).

Statement of right of appeal in notices

8–26373 **6.** Where an appeal against a notice served by a local authority lies to a magistrates' court or, in Scotland, the sheriff by virtue of section 80, it shall be the duty of the authority to include in such a notice a statement indicating that such an appeal lies as aforesaid and specifying the time within which it must be brought.

Clean Air Act 1993[1]

(1993 c 11)

PART I[2]

DARK SMOKE

8–26580 **1. Prohibition of dark smoke from chimneys.** (1) Dark smoke shall not be emitted from a chimney of any building, and if, on any day, dark smoke is so emitted, the occupier of the building shall be guilty of an offence.

(2) Dark smoke shall not be emitted from a chimney (not being a chimney of a building) which serves the furnace of any fixed boiler or industrial plant, and if, on any day, dark smoke is so emitted, the person having possession of the boiler or plant shall be guilty of an offence.

(3) This section does not apply to emissions of smoke from any chimney, in such classes of case and subject to such limitations as may be prescribed in regulations[3] made by the Secretary of State, lasting for not longer than such periods as may be so prescribed.

(4) In any proceedings for an offence under this section, it shall be a defence to prove—

(*a*) that the alleged emission was solely due to the lighting up of a furnace which was cold and that all practicable steps had been taken to prevent or minimise the emission of dark smoke;

(*b*) that the alleged emission was solely due to some failure of a furnace, or of apparatus used in connection with a furnace, and that—

(i) the failure could not reasonably have been foreseen, or, if foreseen, could not reasonably have been provided against; and

(ii) the alleged emission could not reasonably have been prevented by action taken after the failure occurred; or

(*c*) that the alleged emission was solely due to the use of unsuitable fuel and that—

(i) suitable fuel was unobtainable and the least unsuitable fuel which was available was used; and

(ii) all practicable steps had been taken to prevent or minimise the emission of dark smoke as the result of the use of that fuel;

or that the alleged emission was due to the combination of two or more of the causes specified in paragraphs (*a*) to (*c*) and that the other conditions specified in those paragraphs are satisfied in relation to those causes respectively.

(5) A person guilty of an offence under this section shall be liable on summary conviction—

(*a*) in the case of a contravention of subsection (1) as respects a chimney of a private dwelling, to a fine not exceeding **level 3** on the standard scale; and

(*b*) in any other case, to a fine not exceeding **level 5** on the standard scale.

(6) This section has effect subject to section 51 (duty to notify offences to occupier or other person liable).

[Clean Air Act 1993, s 14.]

---

1. This Act consolidates the Clean Air Acts 1956 and 1968 and certain related enactments, with amendments to give effect to recommendations of the Law Commission. Until the coming into force of the repeal by the Environmental Protection Act 1990 of the Alkali, etc Works Regulation Act 1906, the application of this Act to any work subject or potentially subject to the Alkali Act is modified by s 66 and Sch 3, post.

2. Part I contains ss 1–3.

3. See the Dark Smoke (Permitted Periods) Regulations and Dark Smoke (Vessels) Regulations 1958, SI 1958/498 and 878.

4. For the application of this section to railway locomotive engines, see s 43, post, and to vessels, see s 44, post.

8–26581 **2. Prohibition of dark smoke from industrial or trade premises.** (1) Dark smoke shall not be emitted[1] from any industrial or trade premises and if, on any day, dark smoke is so emitted the occupier of the premises and any person who causes or permits the emission shall be guilty of an offence.

(2) This section does not apply—

(*a*) to the emission of dark smoke from any chimney to which section 1 above applies; or
(*b*) to the emission of dark smoke caused by the burning of any matter prescribed in regulations[2] made by the Secretary of State, subject to compliance with such conditions (if any) as may be so prescribed.

(3) In proceedings for an offence under this section, there shall be taken to have been an emission of dark smoke from industrial or trade premises in any case where—

(*a*) material is burned on those premises; and
(*b*) the circumstances are such that the burning would be likely to give rise to the emission of dark smoke,

unless the occupier or any person who caused or permitted the burning shows that no dark smoke was emitted.

(4) In proceedings for an offence under this section, it shall be a defence to prove—

(*a*) that the alleged emission was inadvertent; and
(*b*) that all practicable steps had been taken to prevent or minimise the emission of dark smoke.

(5) A person guilty of an offence under this section shall be liable on summary conviction to a fine not exceeding **£20,000**.

(6) In this section "industrial or trade premises" means—

(*a*) premises used for any industrial or trade purposes; or
(*b*) premises not so used on which matter is burnt in connection with any industrial or trade process[3].

(7) This section has effect subject to section 51 (duty to notify offences to occupier or other person liable).

[Clean Air Act 1993, s 2, as amended by the Environment Act 1995, Sch 22.]

1. Where the premises consist of land (read with s 64, post), it is unnecessary for the prosecutor to prove that dark smoke was emitted over and beyond the territorial boundary of the land. Therefore, if the fire was on open ground not served by a chimney, to establish the offence it is sufficient for the prosecutor to prove that dark smoke was emitted from the fire on land into the air occupying the space above the land (*O'Fee v Copeland Borough Council* (1995) 160 JP 20).
2. See the Clean Air (Emission of Dark Smoke) (Exemption) Regulations 1969, SI 1969/1263.
3. A vacant site is capable of being "premises" within the meaning of this subsection, and the burning of rubble as part of a demolition scheme has been held to be a trade process within the subsection (*Sheffield City Council v ADH Demolition Ltd* [1983] LS Gaz R 1919).

8–26582 **3. Meaning of "dark smoke".** (1) In this Act "dark smoke" means smoke which, if compared in the appropriate manner with a chart of the type known on 5th July 1956 (the date of the passing of the Clean Air Act 1956) as the Ringelmann Chart, would appear to be as dark as or darker than shade 2 on the chart.

(2) For the avoidance of doubt it is hereby declared that in proceedings—

(*a*) for an offence under section 1 or 2 (prohibition of emissions of dark smoke);
(*b*) *Repealed*,

the court may be satisfied that smoke is or is not dark smoke as defined in subsection (1) notwithstanding that there has been no actual comparison of the smoke with a chart of the type mentioned in that subsection.

(3) Without prejudice to the generality of subsections (1) and (2), if the Secretary of State by regulations prescribes any method of ascertaining whether smoke is dark smoke as defined in subsection (1), proof in any such proceedings as are mentioned in subsection (2)—

(*a*) that that method was properly applied, and
(*b*) that the smoke was thereby ascertained to be or not to be dark smoke as so defined,

shall be accepted as sufficient.

[Clean Air Act 1993, s 3, as amended by the Environment Act 1995, Sch 24.]

PART II[1]

SMOKE, GRIT, DUST AND FUMES

Installation of furnaces

8–26583 **4. Requirement that new furnaces shall be so far as practicable smokeless.** (1) No furnace shall be installed in a building or in any fixed boiler or industrial plant unless notice of the proposal to install it has been given to the local authority.

(2) No furnace shall be installed in a building or in any fixed boiler or industrial plant unless the

furnace is so far as practicable capable of being operated continuously without emitting smoke when burning fuel of a type for which the furnace was designed.

(3) Any furnace installed in accordance with plans and specifications submitted to, and approved for the purposes of this section by, the local authority shall be treated as complying with the provisions of subsection (2).

(4) Any person who installs a furnace in contravention of subsection (1) or (2) or on whose instructions a furnace is so installed shall be guilty of an offence and liable on summary conviction—

(*a*) in the case of a contravention of subsection (1), to a fine not exceeding **level 3** on the standard scale; and

(*b*) in the case of a contravention of subsection (2), to a fine not exceeding **level 5** on that scale.

(5) This section does not apply to the installation of domestic furnaces.

(6) This section applies in relation to—

(*a*) the attachment to a building of a boiler or industrial plant which already contains a furnace; or

(*b*) the fixing to or installation on any land of any such boiler or plant;

as it applies in relation to the installation of a furnace in any fixed boiler or industrial plant.

[Clean Air Act 1993, s 4.]

1. Part II contains ss 4–17.

Limits on rate of emission of grit and dust

8–26584 **5. Emission of grit and dust from furnaces.** (1) This section applies to any furnace other than a domestic furnace.

(2) The Secretary of State may by regulations[1] prescribe limits on the rates of emission of grit and dust from the chimneys of furnaces to which this section applies.

(3) If on any day grit or dust is emitted from a chimney serving a furnace to which this section applies at a rate exceeding the relevant limit prescribed under subsection (2), the occupier of any building in which the furnace is situated shall be guilty of an offence.

(4) In proceedings for an offence under subsection (3) it shall be a defence to prove that the best practicable means had been used for minimising the alleged emission.

(5) If, in the case of a building containing a furnace to which this section applies and which is served by a chimney to which there is no limit applicable under subsection (2), the occupier fails to use any practicable means there may be for minimising the emission of grit or dust from the chimney, he shall be guilty of an offence.

(6) A person guilty of an offence under this section shall be liable on summary conviction to a fine not exceeding **level 5** on the standard scale.

[Clean Air Act 1993, s 5.]

1. See the Clean Air (Emission of Grit and Dust from Furnaces) Regulations 1971, SI 1971/162.

Arrestment plant for furnaces

8–26585 **6. Arrestment plant for new non-domestic furnaces.** (1) A furnace other than a domestic furnace shall not be used in a building—

(*a*) to burn pulverised fuel; or

(*b*) to burn, at a rate of 45.4 kilograms or more an hour, any other solid matter; or

(*c*) to burn, at a rate equivalent to 366.4 kilowatts or more, any liquid or gaseous matter,

unless the furnace is provided with plant for arresting grit and dust which has been approved by the local authority or which has been installed in accordance with plans and specifications submitted to and approved by the local authority, and that plant is properly maintained and used.

(2) Subsection (1) has effect subject to any exemptions prescribed or granted under section 7.

(3) The Secretary of State may by regulations substitute for any rate mentioned in subsection (1)(*b*) or (*c*) such other rate as he thinks fit: but no regulations shall be made so as to reduce any rate unless a draft of the regulations has been laid before and approved by each House of Parliament.

(4) Regulations under subsection (3) reducing any rate shall not apply to a furnace which has been installed, the installation of which has been begun, or an agreement for the purchase or installation of which has been entered into, before the date on which the regulations come into force.

(5) If on any day a furnace is used in contravention of subsection (1), the occupier of the building shall be guilty of an offence and liable on summary conviction to a fine not exceeding **level 5** on the standard scale.

[Clean Air Act 1993, s 6.]

8–26586 **7. Exemptions from section 6.** (1) The Secretary of State may by regulations[1] provide that furnaces of any class prescribed in the regulations shall, while used for a purpose so prescribed, be exempted from the operation of section 6(1).

(2) If on the application of the occupier of a building a local authority are satisfied that the

emission of grit and dust from any chimney serving a furnace in the building will not be prejudicial to health or a nuisance if the furnace is used for a particular purpose without compliance with section 6(1), they may exempt the furnace from the operation of that subsection while used for that purpose.

(3) If a local authority to whom an application is duly made for an exemption under subsection (2) fail to determine the application and to give a written notice of their decision to the applicant within—

(*a*) eight weeks of receiving the application; or
(*b*) such longer period as may be agreed in writing between the applicant and the authority,

the furnace shall be treated as having been granted an exemption from the operation of section 6(1) while used for the purpose specified in the application.

(4) If a local authority decide not to grant an exemption under subsection (2), they shall give the applicant a written notification of their decision stating their reasons, and the applicant may within twenty-eight days of receiving the notification appeal against the decision to the Secretary of State.

(5) On an appeal under this section the Secretary of State—

(*a*) may confirm the decision appealed against; or
(*b*) may grant the exemption applied for or vary the purpose for which the furnace to which the application relates may be used without compliance with section 6(1);

and shall give the appellant a written notification of his decision, stating his reasons for it.

(6) If on any day a furnace which is exempt from the operation of section 6(1) is used for a purpose other than a prescribed purpose or, as the case may be, a purpose for which the furnace may be used by virtue of subsection (2), (3) or (5), the occupier of the building shall be guilty of an offence and liable on summary conviction to a fine not exceeding **level 5** on the standard scale.
[Clean Air Act 1993, s 7.]

---

1. See the Clean Air Act (Arrestment Plant) (Exemption) Regulations 1969, SI 1969/1262.

8–26587 **8. Requirement to fit arrestment plant for burning solid fuel in other cases.** (1) A domestic furnace shall not be used in a building—

(*a*) to burn pulverised fuel; or
(*b*) to burn, at a rate of 1.02 tonnes an hour or more, solid fuel in any other form or solid waste;

unless the furnace is provided with plant for arresting grit and dust which has been approved by the local authority or which has been installed in accordance with plans and specifications submitted to and approved by the local authority, and that plant is properly maintained and used.

(2) If a furnace is used in a building in contravention of subsection (1), the occupier of the building shall be guilty of an offence and liable on summary conviction to a fine not exceeding **level 5** on the standard scale.
[Clean Air Act 1993, s 8.]

8–26588 **9. Appeal to Secretary of State against refusal of approval.** (1) Where a local authority determine an application for approval under section 6 or 8, they shall give the applicant a written notification of their decision and, in the case of a decision not to grant approval, shall state their reasons for not doing so.

(2) A person who—

(*a*) has made such an application to a local authority; or
(*b*) is interested in a building with respect to which such an application has been made,

may, if he is dissatisfied with the decision of the authority on the application, appeal within twenty-eight days after he is notified of the decision to the Secretary of State; and the Secretary of State may give any approval which the local authority might have given.

(3) An approval given by the Secretary of State under this section shall have the like effect as an approval of the local authority.
[Clean Air Act 1993, s 9.]

Measurement of grit, dust and fumes

8–26589 **10. Measurement of grit, dust and fumes by occupiers.** (1) If a furnace in a building is used—

(*a*) to burn pulverised fuel;
(*b*) to burn, at a rate of 45.4 kilograms or more an hour, any other solid matter; or
(*c*) to burn, at a rate equivalent to 366.4 kilowatts or more, any liquid or gaseous matter,

the local authority may, by notice in writing served on the occupier of the building, direct that the provisions of subsection (2) below shall apply to the furnace, and those provisions shall apply accordingly.

(2) In the case of a furnace to which this subsection for the time being applies, the occupier of the building shall comply with such requirements as may be prescribed as to—

(*a*) making and recording measurements from time to time of the grit, dust and fumes emitted from the furnace;
(*b*) making adaptations for that purpose to the chimney serving the furnace;
(*c*) providing and maintaining apparatus for making and recording the measurements; and
(*d*) informing the local authority of the results obtained from the measurements or otherwise making those results available to them;

and in this subsection "prescribed" means prescribed (whether generally or for any class of furnace) by regulations[1] made by the Secretary of State.

(3) If the occupier of the building fails to comply with those requirements, he shall be guilty of an offence and liable on summary conviction—

(*a*) to a fine not exceeding **level 5** on the standard scale; or
(*b*) to cumulative penalties on continuance in accordance with section 50.

(4) The occupier of a building who by virtue of subsection (2) is under a duty to make and record measurements of grit, dust and fumes emitted from a furnace in the building shall permit the local authority to be represented during the making and recording of those measurements.

(5) The Secretary of State may by regulations substitute for any rate mentioned in subsection (1)(*b*) or (*c*) such other rate as he thinks fit; but regulations shall not be made under this subsection so as to reduce any rate unless a draft of the regulations has been laid before and approved by each House of Parliament.

(6) Any direction given by a local authority under subsection (1) with respect to a furnace in a building may be revoked by the local authority by a subsequent notice in writing served on the occupier of the building, without prejudice, however, to their power to give another direction under that subsection.
[Clean Air Act 1993, s 10.]

1. See the Clean Air (Measurement of Dust and Grit from Furnaces) Regulations 1971, SI 1971/161.

8–26590 **11. Measurement of grit, dust and fumes by local authorities.** (1) This section applies to any furnace to which section 10(2) (duty to comply with prescribed requirements) for the time being applies and which is used—

(*a*) to burn, at a rate less than 1.02 tonnes an hour, solid matter other than pulverised fuel; or
(*b*) to burn, at a rate of less than 8.21 Megawatts, any liquid or gaseous matter.

(2) The occupier of the building in which the furnace is situated may, by notice in writing given to the local authority, request that authority to make and record measurements of the grit, dust and fumes emitted from the furnace.

(3) While a notice is in force under subsection (2)—

(*a*) the local authority shall from time to time make and record measurements of the grit, dust and fumes emitted from the furnace; and
(*b*) the occupier shall not be under a duty to comply with any requirements of regulations under subsection (2) of section 10 in relation to the furnace, except those imposed by virtue of paragraph (*b*) of that subsection;

and any such notice given by the occupier of a building may be withdrawn by a subsequent notice in writing given to the local authority by him or any subsequent occupier of that building.

(4) A direction under section 10(1) applying section 10(2) to a furnace which is used as mentioned in subsection (1)(*a*) or (*b*) of this section shall contain a statement of the effect of subsections (1) to (3) of this section.
[Clean Air Act 1993, s 11.]

8–26591 **12. Information about furnaces and fuel consumed.** (1) For the purpose of enabling the local authority properly to perform their functions under and in connection with sections 5 to 11, the local authority may, by notice in writing served on the occupier of any building, require the occupier to furnish to them, within fourteen days or such longer time as may be limited by the notice, such information as to the furnaces in the building and the fuel or waste burned in those furnaces as they may reasonably require for that purpose.

(2) Any person who, having been duly served with a notice under subsection (1)—

(*a*) fails to comply with the requirements of the notice within the time limited, or
(*b*) furnishes any information in reply to the notice which he knows to be false in a material particular,

shall be guilty of an offence and liable on summary conviction to a fine not exceeding **level 5** on the standard scale.
[Clean Air Act 1993, s 12.]

Outdoor furnaces

8–26592 **13. Grit and dust from outdoor furnaces, etc.** (1) Sections 5 to 12 shall apply in relation to the furnace of any fixed boiler or industrial plant as they apply in relation to a furnace in a building.

(2) References in those sections to the occupier of the building shall, in relation to a furnace falling within subsection (1), be read as references to the person having possession of the boiler or plant.

(3) The reference in section 6(4) (and the reference in paragraph 6(1) and (3) of Schedule 5) to the installation and to the purchase of a furnace shall, in relation to a furnace which is already contained in any fixed boiler or industrial plant, be read as a reference to attaching the boiler or plant to the building or fixing it to or installing it on any land and to purchasing it respectively.
[Clean Air Act 1993, s 13.]

Height of chimneys

8–26593 **14. Height of chimneys for furnaces.** (1) This section applies to any furnace served by a chimney.

(2) An occupier of a building shall not knowingly cause or permit a furnace to be used in the building—

(*a*) to burn pulverised fuel;
(*b*) to burn, at a rate of 45.4 kilograms or more an hour, any other solid matter; or
(*c*) to burn, at a rate equivalent to 366.4 kilowatts or more, any liquid or gaseous matter,

unless the height of the chimney serving the furnace has been approved for the purposes of this section and any conditions subject to which the approval was granted are complied with.

(3) If on any day the occupier of a building contravenes subsection (2), he shall be guilty of an offence.

(4) A person having possession of any fixed boiler or industrial plant, other than an exempted boiler or plant, shall not knowingly cause or permit a furnace of that boiler or plant to be used as mentioned in subsection (2), unless the height of the chimney serving the furnace has been approved for the purposes of this section and any conditions subject to which the approval was granted are complied with.

(5) If on any day a person having possession of any boiler or plant contravenes subsection (4), he shall be guilty of an offence.

(6) A person guilty of an offence under this section shall be liable on summary conviction to a fine not exceeding **level 5** on the standard scale.

(7) In this section "exempted boiler or plant" means a boiler or plant which is used or to be used wholly for any purpose prescribed in regulations made by the Secretary of State; and the height of a chimney is approved for the purposes of this section if approval is granted by the local authority or the Secretary of State under section 15.
[Clean Air Act 1993, s 14.]

8–26594 **15.** *Applications for approval of height of chimneys of furnaces.*

PART III[1]

SMOKE CONTROL AREAS

Creation of smoke control areas

8–26595 **18. Declaration of smoke control area by local authority.** (1) A local authority may by order declare the whole or any part of the district of the authority to be a smoke control area; and any order made under this section is referred to in this Act as a "smoke control order".

(2) A smoke control order—

(*a*) may make different provision for different parts of the smoke control area;
(*b*) may limit the operation of section 20 (prohibition of emissions of smoke) to specified classes of building in the area; and
(*c*) may exempt specified buildings or classes of building or specified fireplaces or classes of fireplace in the area from the operation of that section, upon such conditions as may be specified in the order;

and the reference in paragraph (*c*) to specified buildings or classes of building include a reference to any specified, or to any specified classes of, fixed boiler or industrial plant.

(3) A smoke control order may be revoked or varied by a subsequent order.

(4) The provisions of Schedule 1 apply to the coming into operation of smoke control orders.
[Clean Air Act 1993, s 18.]

1. Part III contains ss 18–29.

8–26596 **19.** *Power of Secretary of State to require creation of smoke control areas.*

Prohibition on emission of smoke in smoke control area

8–26597 **20. Prohibition on emission of smoke in smoke control area.** (1) If, on any day, smoke is emitted from a chimney of any building within a smoke control area, the occupier of the building shall be guilty of an offence.

(2) If, on any day, smoke is emitted from a chimney (not being a chimney of a building) which serves the furnace of any fixed boiler or industrial plant within a smoke control area, the person having possession of the boiler or plant shall be guilty of an offence.

(3) Subsections (1) and (2) have effect—

(*a*) subject to any exemptions for the time being in force under section 18, 21 or 22;
(*b*) subject to section 51 (duty to notify offences to occupier or other person liable).

(4) In proceedings for an offence under this section it shall be a defence to prove that the alleged emission was not caused by the use of any fuel other than an authorised fuel.

(5) A person guilty of an offence under this section shall be liable on summary conviction to a fine not exceeding **level 3** on the standard scale.

(6) In this Part "authorised fuel" means a fuel declared by regulations[1] of the Secretary of State to be an authorised fuel for the purposes of this Part.
[Clean Air Act 1993, s 20.]

1. The Smoke Control Areas (Authorised Fuels) (England) Regulations 2001, SI 2001/3745 amended by SI 2002/3046 and SI 2005/2895 and the Smoke Control Areas (Authorised Fuels) (Wales) Regulations 2001, SI 2001/3762 amended by SI 2001/3996 and SI 2002/3160 have been made.

8–26598 **21. Power by order to exempt certain fireplaces.** The Secretary of State may by order[1] exempt any class of fireplace, upon such conditions as may be specified in the order, from the provisions of section 20 (prohibition of smoke emissions in smoke control area), if he is satisfied that such fireplaces can be used for burning fuel other than authorised fuels without producing any smoke or a substantial quantity of smoke.
[Clean Air Act 1993, s 21.]

1. Numerous Smoke Control (Exempted Fireplaces) Orders have been made which exempt such fireplaces as can be used for burning fuel other than authorised fuels without producing smoke or a substantial quantity of smoke.

8–26599 **22. Exemptions relating to particular areas.** (1) The Secretary of State may, if it appears to him to be necessary or expedient so to do, by order suspend or relax the operation of section 20 (prohibition of smoke emissions in smoke control area) in relation to the whole or any part of a smoke control area.

(2) Before making an order under subsection (1) the Secretary of State shall consult with the local authority unless he is satisfied that, on account of urgency, such consultation is impracticable.

(3) As soon as practicable after the making of such an order the local authority shall take such steps as appear to them suitable for bringing the effect of the order to the notice of persons affected.
[Clean Air Act 1993, s 22.]

Dealings with unauthorised fuel

8–26600 **23. Acquisition and sale of unauthorised fuel in a smoke control area.** (1) Any person who—

(*a*) acquires any solid fuel for use in a building in a smoke control area otherwise than in a building or fireplace exempted from the operation of section 20 (prohibition of smoke emissions in smoke control area);
(*b*) acquires any solid fuel for use in any fixed boiler or industrial plant in a smoke control area, not being a boiler or plant so exempted; or
(*c*) sells by retail any solid fuel for delivery by him or on his behalf to—
  (i) a building in a smoke control area; or
  (ii) premises in such an area in which there is any fixed boiler or industrial plant,

shall be guilty of an offence and liable on summary conviction to a fine not exceeding **level 3** on the standard scale.

(2) In subsection (1), "solid fuel" means any solid fuel other than an authorised fuel.

(3) Subsection (1) shall, in its application to a smoke control area in which the operation of section 20 is limited by a smoke control order to specified classes of buildings, boilers or plant, have effect as if references to a building, boiler or plant were references to a building, boiler or plant of a class specified in the order.

(4) The power of the Secretary of State under section 22 (exemptions relating to particular areas) to suspend or relax the operation of section 20 in relation to the whole or any part of a smoke control area includes power to suspend or relax the operation of subsection (1) in relation to the whole or any part of such an area.

(5) In proceedings for an offence under this section consisting of the sale of fuel for delivery to a building or premises, it shall be a defence for the person accused to prove that he believed and had reasonable grounds for believing—

(*a*) that the building was exempted from the operation of section 20 or, in a case where the operation of that section is limited to specified classes of building, was not of a specified class; or

(*b*) that the fuel was acquired for use in a fireplace, boiler or plant so exempted or, in a case where the operation of that section is limited to specified classes of boilers or plant, in a boiler or plant not of a specified class.

[Clean Air Act 1993, s 23.]

Adaptation of fireplaces

8–26601 24. Power of local authority to require adaptation of fireplaces in private dwellings. (1) The local authority may, by notice in writing served on the occupier or owner of a private dwelling which is, or when a smoke control order comes into operation will be, within a smoke control area, require the carrying out of adaptations in or in connection with the dwelling to avoid contraventions of section 20 (prohibition of smoke emissions in smoke control area).

(2) The provisions of Part XII of the Public Health Act 1936 with respect to appeals against, and the enforcement of, notices requiring the execution of works shall apply in relation to any notice under subsection (1).

(3) Any reference in those provisions to the expenses reasonably incurred in executing the works shall, in relation to a notice under subsection (1), be read as a reference to three-tenths of those expenses or such smaller fraction of those expenses as the local authority may in any particular case determine.

(4) *Scotland.*

[Clean Air Act 1993, s 24.]

8–26602 25. Expenditure incurred in relation to adaptations in private dwellings. Schedule 2 to this Act shall have effect with respect to certain expenditure incurred in adapting old private dwellings in smoke control areas.

[Clean Air Act 1993, s 25—summarised.]

Supplementary provisions

8–26603 27. References to adaptations for avoiding contraventions of section 20. (1) References in this Part to adaptations in or in connection with a dwelling to avoid contraventions of section 20 (prohibition of smoke emissions from smoke control area) shall be read as references to the execution of any of the following works (whether in or outside the dwelling), that is to say—

(*a*) adapting or converting any fireplace;

(*b*) replacing any fireplace by another fireplace or by some other means of heating or cooking;

(*c*) altering any chimney which serves any fireplace;

(*d*) providing gas ignition, electric ignition or any other special means of ignition; or

(*e*) carrying out any operation incidental to any of the operations mentioned in paragraphs (*a*) to (*d*);

being works which are reasonably necessary in order to make what is in all the circumstances suitable provision for heating and cooking without contraventions of section 20.

(2) For the purposes of this section the provision of any igniting apparatus or appliance (whether fixed or not) operating by means of gas, electricity or other special means shall be treated as the execution of works.

(3) Except for the purposes of section 24 (power of local authority to require certain adaptations), works which make such suitable provision as is mentioned in subsection (1) shall not be treated as not being adaptations to avoid contraventions of section 20 of this Act by reason that they go beyond what is reasonably necessary for that purpose, but any expenditure incurred in executing them in excess of the expenditure which would have been reasonably incurred in doing what was reasonably necessary shall be left out of account.

(4) References in this section to a dwelling include references to any premises or part of any premises to which section 26 (grants towards certain adaptations in churches and other buildings) applies.

[Clean Air Act 1993, s 27.]

8–26604 29. Interpretation of Part III. In this Part, except so far as the context otherwise requires—

"authorised fuel" has the meaning given in section 20(6);

"conditional sale agreement" means an agreement for the sale of goods under which—

(*a*) the purchase price or part of it is payable by instalments; and

(*b*) the property in the goods is to remain in the seller (notwithstanding that the buyer is to be in possession of the goods) until such conditions as to the payment of instalments or otherwise as may be specified in the agreement are fulfilled;

"heating", in relation to a dwelling, includes the heating of water;

"hire-purchase agreement" means an agreement, other than a conditional sale agreement, under which—

(*a*) goods are bailed or (in Scotland) hired in return for periodical payments by the person to whom they are bailed or hired; and

(*b*) the property in the goods will pass to that person if the terms of the agreement are complied with and one or more of the following occurs—

(i) the exercise of an option to purchase by that person;

(ii) the doing of any other specified act by any party to the agreement; and

(iii) the happening of any other specified event;

"old private dwelling" has the meaning given in section 25; and

"smoke control order" means an order made by a local authority under section 18.

[Clean Air Act 1993, s 29.]

PART IV[1]

CONTROL OF CERTAIN FORMS OF AIR POLLUTION

8–26605 30. Regulations about motor fuel. (1) For the purpose of limiting or reducing air pollution, the Secretary of State may by regulations[2]—

(*a*) impose requirements as to the composition and contents of any fuel of a kind used in motor vehicles; and

(*b*) where such requirements are in force, prevent or restrict the production, treatment, distribution, import, sale or use of any fuel which in any respect fails to comply with the requirements, and which is for use in the United Kingdom.

(2)–(3) *Supplementary provisions as to regulations.*

(4) It shall be duty of every local weights and measures authority to enforce the provisions of regulations under this section within its area; and subsection (2) of section 26 of the Trade Descriptions Act 1968 (reports and inquiries) shall apply as respects those authorities' functions under this subsection as it applies to their functions under that Act.

(5) The following provisions of the Trade Descriptions Act 1968[3] shall apply in relation to the enforcement of regulations under this section as they apply to the enforcement of that Act, that is to say—

section 27 (power to make test purchases);

section 28 (power to enter premises and inspect and seize goods and documents);

section 29 (obstruction of authorised officers);

section 30 (notice of test);

and section 33 of that Act shall apply to the exercise of powers under section 28 as applied by this subsection.

References to an offence under that Act in those provisions as applied by this subsection, except the reference in section 30(2) to an offence under section 28(5) or 29 of that Act, shall be construed as references to an offence under section 32 of this Act (provisions supplementary to this section) relating to regulations under this section.

(6) *Scotland.*

(7)–(9) *Northern Ireland.*

[Clean Air Act 1993, s 30, as amended by the Statute Law (Repeals) Act 1998, Sch 2.]

---

1. Part IV contains ss 30–33.
2. See the Motor Fuel (Composition and Content) Regulations 1999, SI 1999/3107 amended by SI 2001/3896 and SI 2003/3078.
3. See this PART: title CONSUMER PROTECTION, ante.

8–26606 31. Regulations about sulphur content of oil fuel for furnaces or engines. (1) For the purpose of limiting or reducing air pollution, the Secretary of State may by regulations[1] impose limits on the sulphur content of oil fuel which is used in furnaces or engines.

(2)–(3) *Supplementary provisions with respect to regulations.*

(4) It shall be the duty—

(*a*) of every local authority to enforce the provisions of regulations under this section within its area, except in relation to a furnace which is—

(i) part of a process subject to Part I of the Environmental Protection Act 1990, or

(ii) part of an installation subject to regulation by the Environmental Agency under regulations made under section 2 of the Pollution Prevention and Control Act 1999; and

(*b*) of the inspectors appointed under that Part to enforce those provisions in relation to furnaces within sub-paragraph (1) of paragraph (*a*) above and of the Environment Agency to enforce those provision in relation to furnaces within sub-paragraph (ii) of that paragraph;

but nothing in this section shall be taken to authorise a local authority in Scotland to institute proceedings for any offence.

(5) In this section "oil fuel" means any liquid petroleum product produced in a refinery.
[Clean Air Act 1993, s 31, as amended by SI 2000/1973.]

1. See the Oil Fuel (Sulphur Content of Gas Oil) Regulations 1990, SI 1990/1096.

8–26607 **32. Provisions supplementary to sections 30 and 31.** (1) Regulations[1] under section 30 or 31 (regulation of content of motor fuel and fuel oil) may authorise the Secretary of State to confer exemptions from any provision of the regulations.

(2) A person who contravenes or fails to comply with any provision of regulations under section 30 or 31 shall be guilty of an offence and liable[2]—

(*a*) on conviction on indictment, to a **fine**; and
(*b*) on summary conviction, to a fine not exceeding **the statutory maximum**;

but the regulations may in any case exclude liability to conviction on indictment or reduce the maximum fine on summary conviction.

(3) Regulations under section 30 or 31 shall, subject to any provision to the contrary in the regulations, apply to fuel used for, and to persons in, the public service of the Crown as they apply to fuel used for other purposes and to other persons.

(4) A local authority shall not be entitled by virtue of subsection (3) to exercise, in relation to fuel used for and persons in that service, any power conferred on the authority by virtue of sections 56 to 58 (rights of entry and inspection and other local authority powers).
[Clean Air Act 1993, s 32.]

1. See the Motor Fuel (Lead Content of Petrol) Regulations 1981, SI 1981/1523, amended by SI 1985/1728 and SI 1989/547. See also the Motor Fuel (Sulphur Content of Gas Oil) Regulations 1976, SI 1976/1989, amended by SI 1990/1097 under which a contravention of reg 5(*b*) is punishable only on summary conviction by a fine not exceeding level 2 on the standard scale (reg 8) and the Oil Fuel (Sulphur Content of Gas Oil) Regulations 1990, SI 1990/1096 under which a contravention of reg 4 is punishable only on summary conviction by a fine not exceeding level 2 on the standard scale (reg 7).

2. For procedure in respect of an offence which is triable either way, see the Magistrates' Courts Act 1980, ss 17A–21, in PART I: MAGISTRATES' COURTS, PROCEDURE ante.

8–26608 **33. Cable burning.** (1) A person who burns insulation from a cable with a view to recovering metal from the cable shall be guilty of an offence unless the burning is part of a process subject to Part I of the Environmental Protection Act 1990 or an activity subject to regulations under section 2 of the Pollution Prevention and Control Act 1999.

(2) A person guilty of an offence under this section shall be liable on summary conviction to a fine not exceeding **level 5** on the standard scale.
[Clean Air Act 1993, s 33, as amended by the Pollution Prevention and Control Act 1999, Sch 2.]

PART V[1]
INFORMATION ABOUT AIR POLLUTION

8–26609 **34. Research and publicity.** (1) A local authority may—

(*a*) undertake, or contribute towards the cost of, investigation and research relevant to the problem of air pollution;
(*b*) arrange for the publication of information on that problem;
(*c*) arrange for the delivery of lectures and addresses, and the holding of discussions, on that problem;
(*d*) arrange for the display of pictures, cinematograph films or models, or the holding of exhibitions, relating to that problem; and
(*e*) prepare, or join in or contribute to the cost of the preparation of, pictures, films, models or exhibitions to be displayed or held as mentioned in paragraph (*d*).

(2) In acting under subsection (1)(*b*), a local authority shall ensure that the material published is presented in such a way that no information relating to a trade secret is disclosed, except with the consent in writing of a person authorised to disclose it.

(3) Breach of a duty imposed by subsection (2) shall be actionable.

(4) In any civil or criminal proceedings (whether or not arising under this Act) brought against a local authority, or any member or officer of a local authority, on the grounds that any information has been published, it shall be a defence to show that it was published in compliance with subsections (1) and (2).
[Clean Air Act 1993, s 34.]

1. Part V contains ss 34–40.

8–26610 **35. Obtaining information.** (1) Without prejudice to the generality of section 34 (research, etc. by local authorities), local authorities may obtain information about the emission of pollutants and other substances into the air—

(*a*) by issuing notices under section 36 (information about emissions from premises);
(*b*) by measuring and recording the emissions, and for that purpose entering on any premises, whether by agreement or in exercise of the power conferred by section 56 (rights of entry and inspection); and
(*c*) by entering into arrangements with occupiers of premises under which they measure and record emissions on behalf of the local authority;

but references to premises in paragraphs (*b*) and (*c*) do not include private dwellings or caravans.

(2) A local authority shall not be entitled to exercise the power of entry mentioned in subsection (1)(*b*) for the purpose of measuring and recording such emissions on any premises unless—

(*a*) the authority has given to the occupier of the premises a notice in writing—
  (i) specifying the kind of emissions in question and the steps it proposes to take on the premises for the purpose of measuring and recording emissions of that kind; and
  (ii) stating that it proposes to exercise that power for that purpose unless the occupier requests the authority to serve on him a notice under section 36 (information about emissions from premises) with respect to the emissions; and
(*b*) the period of twenty-one days beginning with the day on which the notice was given has expired;

and the authority shall not be entitled to exercise that power if, during that period, the occupier gives a notice to the authority requesting it to serve on him a notice under section 36.

(3) Nothing in this section shall authorise a local authority to investigate emissions from any process subject to Part I of the Environmental Protection Act 1990 or activity subject to regulations under section 2 of the Pollution Prevention and Control Act 1999 otherwise than—

(*a*) by issuing notices under section 36; or
(*b*) by exercising the powers conferred on the authority by section 34(1)(*a*) (investigation and research etc.) without entering the premises concerned.*

(4) So long as a local authority exercises any of its powers under subsection (1), it shall from time to time consult the persons mentioned in subsection (5)—

(*a*) about the way in which the local authority exercises those powers (under this section and section 36); and
(*b*) about the extent to which, and the manner in which, any information collected under those powers should be made available to the public.

(5) The consultations required by subsection (4) shall be with—

(*a*) such persons carrying on any trade or business in the authority's area or such organisations appearing to the authority to be representative of those persons; and
(*b*) such persons appearing to the authority to be conversant with problems of air pollution or to have an interest in local amenity;

as appear to the authority to be appropriate.

(6) The consultations shall take place as the authority think necessary, but not less than twice in each financial year.

[Clean Air Act 1993, s 35, as amended by the Pollution Prevention and Control Act 1999, Sch 2.]

8–26611 36. Notices requiring information about air pollution. (1) A local authority may by notice in writing require the occupier of any premises in its area to furnish, whether by periodical returns or by other means, such estimates or other information as may be specified or described in the notice concerning the emission of pollutants and other substances into the air from the premises.

(2) This section does not apply to premises in so far as they consist of a private dwelling or a caravan.

(2A) If the notice relates to an installation subject to regulation by the Environment Agency under regulations made under section 2 of the Pollution Prevention and Control Act 1999, the person on whom the notice is served shall not be obliged to supply any information which, as certified by the Environment Agency, is not of a kind which is being supplied to the Environment Agency for the purposes of those regulations.

(3) If the notice relates to a process subject to Part I of the Environmental Protection Act 1990, the person on whom the notice is served shall not be obliged to supply any information which, as certified by an inspector appointed under that Part, is not of a kind which is being supplied to the inspector for the purposes of that Part.*

(4) The person on whom a notice is served under this section shall comply with the notice within six weeks of the date of service, or within such longer period as the local authority may by notice allow.

(5) A notice under this section shall not require returns at intervals of less than three months, and no one notice (whether or not requiring periodical returns) shall call for information covering a period of more than twelve months.

(6) Except so far as regulations[1] made by the Secretary of State provide otherwise, this section

applies to premises used for, and to persons in, the public service of the Crown as it applies to other premises and persons.

(7) A local authority shall not be entitled by virtue of subsection (6) to exercise, in relation to premises used for and persons in the public service of the Crown, any power conferred on the authority by virtue of sections 56 to 58 (rights of entry and other local authority powers).

(8) A person who—

(*a*) fails without reasonable excuse to comply with the requirements of a notice served on him in pursuance of this section; or

(*b*) in furnishing any estimate or other information in compliance with a notice under this section, makes any statement which he knows to be false in a material particular or recklessly makes any statement which is false in a material particular,

shall be guilty of an offence and liable on summary conviction to a fine not exceeding **level 5** on the standard scale.

(9) Where a person is convicted of an offence under subsection (8) in respect of any premises and information of any kind, nothing in section 35(2) (limits on exercise of power of entry) shall prevent a local authority from exercising the power of entry there mentioned for the purpose of obtaining information of that kind in respect of the premises.

[Clean Air Act 1993, s 36, as amended by the Pollution Prevention and Control Act 1999, Sch 2.]

***Section 36(3) is repealed by the Pollution Prevention and Control Act 1999, Sch 3, when in force.**

1. See the Control of Atmospheric Pollution (Exempted Premises) Regulations 1977, SI 1977/18.

8–26612 37. Appeals against notices under section 36. *A person served with a notice under section 36 (information about air pollution), or any other person having an interest in the premises to which the notice relates, may appeal to the Secretary of State.*

8–26613 38. Regulations about local authority functions under sections 34, 35 and 36. *Power of the Secretary of State by regulations to prescribe the manner in which, and the methods by which, local authorities are to perform their functions under sections 34(1)(a) and (b), 35 and 36 (investigation and research etc into, and the obtaining of information about, air pollution).*

8–26614 40. Interpretation of Part V. In this Part—

(*a*) references to the emission of substances into the atmosphere are to be construed as applying to substances in a gaseous or liquid or solid state, or any combination of those states; and

(*b*) any reference to measurement includes a reference to the taking of samples.

[Clean Air Act 1993, s 40.]

PART VI[1]

SPECIAL CASES

8–26615 41. Relation to Environmental Protection Act 1990. (1) Parts I to III shall not apply to any process which is a prescribed process as from the date which is the determination date for that process.

(2) The "determination date" for a prescribed process is—

(*a*) in the case of a process for which an authorisation is granted, the date on which the enforcing authority grants it, whether in pursuance of the application or, on an appeal, of a direction to grant it, and

(*b*) in the case of a process for which an authorisation is refused, the date of the refusal or, on an appeal, of the affirmation of the refusal.

(3) In this section "authorisation", "enforcing authority" and "prescribed process" have the meaning given in section 1 of the Environmental Protection Act 1990 and the reference to an appeal is a reference to an appeal under section 15 of that Act.*

[Clean Air Act 1993, s 41.]

***Section 41 is repealed by the Pollution Prevention and Control Act 1999, Sch 3, when in force.**

1. Part VI contains ss 41–46.

8–26615A 41A. Relation to the Pollution Prevention and Control Act 1999. (1) Where an activity is subject to regulations under section 2 of the Pollution Prevention and Control Act 1999 (regulation of polluting activities), Parts I to III of this Act shall not apply as from the determination date for the activity in question.

(2) The "determination date", for an activity, is—

(*a*) in the case of an activity for which a permit is granted, the date on which it is granted, whether in pursuance of the application, or on an appeal, of a direction to grant it;

(*b*) in the case of an activity for which a permit is refused, the date of refusal or, on appeal, of the affirmation of the refusal.

(3) In subsection (2) "permit" means a permit under regulations under section 2 of the Pollution Prevention and Control Act 1999 and the reference to an appeal is a reference to an appeal under those regulations.
[Clean Air Act 1993, s 41A, as inserted by SI 2001/1973.]

8–26616 **42. Colliery spoilbanks.** (1) This section applies to any mine or quarry from which coal or shale has been, is being or is to be got.

(2) The owner of a mine or quarry to which this section applies shall employ all practicable means—

(*a*) for preventing combustion of refuse deposited from the mine or quarry; and
(*b*) for preventing or minimising the emission of smoke and fumes from such refuse;

and, if he fails to do so, he shall be guilty of an offence.

(3) A person guilty of an offence under subsection (2) shall be liable on summary conviction—

(*a*) to a fine not exceeding **level 5** on the standard scale; or
(*b*) to cumulative penalties on continuance in accordance with section 50.

(4) Neither the provisions of Part III of the Environmental Protection Act 1990 nor any provision of Parts I to III of this Act shall apply in relation to smoke, grit or dust from the combustion of refuse deposited from any mine or quarry to which this section applies.

(5) *Repealed.*

(6) In this section, "mine", "quarry" and "owner" have the same meaning as in the Mines and Quarries Act 1954.
[Clean Air Act 1993, s 42, as amended by the Environment Act 1995, Sch 24.]

8–26617 **43. Railway engines.** (1) Section 1 (prohibition of emissions of dark smoke) shall apply in relation to railway locomotive engines as it applies in relation to buildings.

(2) In the application of section 1 to such engines, for the reference in subsection (1) of that section to the occupier of the building there shall be substituted a reference to the owner of the engine.

(3) The owner of any railway locomotive engine shall use any practicable means there may be for minimising the emission of smoke from the chimney on the engine and, if he fails to do so, he shall, if smoke is emitted from that chimney, be guilty of an offence.

(4) A person guilty of an offence under subsection (3) shall be liable on summary conviction—

(*a*) to a fine not exceeding **level 5** on the standard scale; or
(*b*) to cumulative penalties on continuance in accordance with section 50.

(5) Except as provided in this section, nothing in Parts I to III applies to smoke, grit or dust from any railway locomotive engine.
[Clean Air Act 1993, s 43.]

8–26618 **44. Vessels.** (1) Section 1 (prohibition of emissions of dark smoke) shall apply in relation to vessels in waters to which this section applies as it applies in relation to buildings.

(2) In the application of section 1 to a vessel—

(*a*) for the reference in subsection (1) of that section to the occupier of the building there shall be substituted a reference to the owner of, and to the master or other officer or person in charge of, the vessel;
(*b*) references to a furnace shall be read as including references to an engine of the vessel; and
(*c*) subsection (5) of that section shall be omitted;

and a person guilty of an offence under that section in relation to a vessel shall be liable on summary conviction to a fine not exceeding **level 5** on the standard scale.

(3) For the purposes of this Act a vessel in any waters to which this section applies which are not within the district of any local authority shall be deemed to be within the district of the local authority whose district includes that point on land which is nearest to the spot where the vessel is.

(4) The waters to which this section applies are—

(*a*) all waters not navigable by sea-going ships; and
(*b*) all waters navigable by sea-going ships which are within the seaward limits of the territorial waters of the United Kingdom and are contained within any port, harbour, river, estuary, haven, dock, canal or other place so long as a person or body of persons is empowered by or under any Act to make charges in respect of vessels entering it or using facilities in it.

(5) In subsection (4) "charges" means any charges with the exception of light dues, local light dues and any other charges payable in respect of lighthouses, buoys or beacons and of charges in respect of pilotage.

(6) Except as provided in this section, nothing in Parts I to III applies to smoke, grit or dust from any vessel.
[Clean Air Act 1993, s 44.]

8–26619 **45. Exemption for purposes of investigations and research.** (1) If the local authority are satisfied, on the application of any person interested, that it is expedient to do so for the purpose of enabling investigations or research relevant to the problem of the pollution of the air to be carried out without rendering the applicant liable to proceedings brought under or by virtue of any of the provisions of this Act or the Environmental Protection Act 1990 mentioned below, the local authority may by notice in writing given to the applicant exempt, wholly or to a limited extent,—

(*a*) any chimney from the operation of sections 1 (dark smoke), 5 (grit and dust), 20 (smoke in smoke control area) and 43 (railway engines) of this Act and Part III of the Environmental Protection Act 1990 (statutory nuisances);
(*b*) any furnace, boiler or industrial plant from the operation of section 4(2) (new furnaces to be as far as practicable smokeless);
(*c*) any premises from the operation of section 2 (emissions of dark smoke);
(*d*) any furnace from the operation of sections 6 or 8 (arrestment plant) and 10 (measurement of grit, dust and fumes by occupier), and
(*e*) the acquisition or sale of any fuel specified in the notice from the operation of section 23 (acquisition and sale of unauthorised fuel in smoke control area),

in each case subject to such conditions, if any, and for such period as may be specified in the notice.

(2) Any person who has applied to the local authority for an exemption under this section may, if he is dissatisfied with the decision of the authority on the application, appeal to the Secretary of State; and the Secretary of State may, if he thinks fit, by notice in writing given to the applicant and the local authority, give any exemption which the authority might have given or vary the terms of any exemption which they have given.
[Clean Air Act 1993, s 45.]

8–26620 **46. Crown premises, etc.** (1) It shall be part of the functions of the local authority, in cases where it seems to them proper to do so, to report to the responsible Minister any cases of—

(*a*) emissions of dark smoke, or of grit or dust, from any premises which are under the control of any Government department and are occupied for the public service of the Crown or for any of the purposes of any Government department;
(*b*) emissions of smoke, whether dark smoke or not, from any such premises which are within a smoke control area;
(*c*) emissions of smoke, whether dark smoke or not, from any such premises which appear to them to constitute a nuisance to the inhabitants of the neighbourhood; or
(*d*) emissions of dark smoke from any vessel of Her Majesty's navy, or any Government ship in the service of the Secretary of State while employed for the purposes of Her Majesty's navy, which appear to them to constitute a nuisance to the inhabitants of the neighbourhood,

and on receiving any such report the responsible Minister shall inquire into the circumstances and, if his inquiry reveals that there is cause for complaint, shall employ all practicable means for preventing or minimising the emission of the smoke, grit or dust or for abating the nuisance and preventing a recurrence of it, as the case may be.

(2) Subsection (1) shall apply to premises occupied for the purposes of the Duchy of Lancaster or the Duchy of Cornwall as it applies to premises occupied for the public service of the Crown which are under the control of a Government department, with the substitution, in the case of the Duchy of Cornwall, for references to the responsible Minister of references to such person as the Duke of Cornwall or the possessor for the time being of the Duchy of Cornwall appoints.

(3) The fact that there subsists in any premises an interest belonging to Her Majesty in right of the Crown or of the Duchy of Lancaster, or to the Duchy of Cornwall, or belonging to a Government department or held in trust for Her Majesty for the purposes of a Government department, shall not affect the application of this Act to those premises so long as that interest is not the interest of the occupier of the premises, and this Act shall have effect accordingly in relation to the premises and that and all other interests in the premises.

(4) Section 44 (vessels) shall, with the omission of the reference in subsection (2) of that section to the owner, apply to vessels owned by the Crown, except that it shall not apply to vessels of Her Majesty's navy or to Government ships in the service of the Secretary of State while employed for the purposes of Her Majesty's navy.

(5) This Act (except Parts IV and V) shall have effect in relation to premises occupied for the service of a visiting force as if the premises were occupied for the public service of the Crown and were under the control of the Government department by arrangement with whom the premises are occupied.

(6) In this section—

"Government ship" has the same meaning as in the Merchant Shipping Act 1995; and
"visiting force" means any such body, contingent or detachment of the forces of any country as is a visiting force for the purposes of any of the provisions of the Visiting Forces Act 1952.
[Clean Air Act 1993, s 46, as amended by the Merchant Shipping Act 1995, Sch 13.]

PART VII[1]

MISCELLANEOUS AND GENERAL

Power to apply certain provisions to fumes and gases

8–26621 **47. Application to fumes and gases of certain provisions as to grit, dust and smoke.** (1) The Secretary of State may by regulations—

(*a*) apply all or any of the provisions of sections 5, 6, 7, 42(4) 43(5), 44(6) and 46(1) to fumes or prescribed gases or both as they apply to grit and dust;

(*b*) apply all or any of the provisions of section 4 to fumes or prescribed gases or both as they apply to smoke; and

(*c*) apply all or any of the provisions of section 11 to prescribed gases as they apply to grit and dust,

subject, in each case, to such exceptions and modifications as he thinks expedient.

(2) No regulations shall be made under this section unless a draft of the regulations has been laid before and approved by each House of Parliament.

(3) In the application of any provision of this Act to prescribed gases by virtue of regulations under this section, any reference to the rate of emission of any substance shall be construed as a reference to the percentage by volume or by mass of the gas which may be emitted during a period specified in the regulations.

(4) In this section—

"gas" includes vapour and moisture precipitated from vapour; and

"prescribed" means prescribed in regulations under this section.

[Clean Air Act 1993, s 47.]

1. Part VII contains ss 47–68.

Power to give effect to international agreements

8–26622 **48. Power to give effect to international agreements.** The Secretary of State may by regulations provide that any provision of Parts IV and V, or of this Part (apart from this section) so far as relating to those Parts, shall have effect with such modifications as are prescribed in the regulations with a view to enabling the Government of the United Kingdom to give effect to any provision made by or under any international agreement to which the Government is for the time being a party.

[Clean Air Act 1993, s 48.]

Administration and enforcement

8–26623 **49. Unjustified disclosures of information.** (1) If a person discloses any information relating to any trade secret used in carrying on any particular undertaking which has been given to him or obtained by him by virtue of this Act, he shall, subject to subsection (2), be guilty of an offence and liable on summary conviction to a fine not exceeding **level 5** on the standard scale.

(2) A person shall not be guilty of an offence under subsection (1) by reason of the disclosure of any information if the disclosure is made—

(*a*) in the performance of his duty;

(*b*) in pursuance of section 34(1)(*b*); or

(*c*) with the consent of a person having a right to disclose the information.

[Clean Air Act 1993, s 49.]

8–26624 **50. Cumulative penalties on continuance of certain offences.** (1) Where—

(*a*) a person is convicted of an offence which is subject to cumulative penalties on continuance in accordance with this section; and

(*b*) it is shown to the satisfaction of the court that the offence was substantially a repetition or continuation of an earlier offence by him after he had been convicted of the earlier offence,

the penalty provided by subsection (2) shall apply instead of the penalty otherwise specified for the offence.

(2) Where this subsection applies the person convicted shall be liable on summary conviction to a fine not exceeding—

(*a*) **level 5** on the standard scale; or

(*b*) **£50** for every day on which the earlier offence has been so repeated or continued by him within the three months next following his conviction of that offence,

whichever is the greater.

(3) Where an offence is subject to cumulative penalties in accordance with this section—

(*a*) the court by which a person is convicted of the original offence may fix a reasonable period from the date of conviction for compliance by the defendant with any directions given by the court; and (*b*) where a court has fixed such a period, the daily penalty referred to in subsection (2) is not recoverable in respect of any day before the end of that period.

[Clean Air Act 1993, s 50.]

8–26625 51. Duty to notify occupiers of offences. (1) If, in the opinion of an authorised officer of the local authority—

(*a*) an offence is being or has been committed under section 1, 2 or 20 (prohibition of certain emissions of smoke);

(*b*) (*Repealed*),

he shall, unless he has reason to believe that notice of it has already been given by or on behalf of the local authority, as soon as may be notify the appropriate person, and, if his notification is not in writing, shall before the end of the four days next following the day on which he became aware of the offence, confirm the notification in writing.

(2) For the purposes of subsection (1), the appropriate person to notify is the occupier of the premises, the person having possession of the boiler or plant, the owner of the railway locomotive engine or the owner or master or other officer or person in charge of the vessel concerned, as the case may be.

(3) In any proceedings for an offence under section 1, 2 or 20 it shall be a defence to prove that the provisions of subsection (1) have not been complied with in the case of the offence; and if no such notification as is required by that subsection has been given before the end of the four days next following the day of the offence, that subsection shall be taken not to have been complied with unless the contrary is proved.

[Clean Air Act 1993, s 51, as amended by the Environment Act 1995, Sch 24.]

8–26626 52. Offences committed by bodies corporate. (1) Where an offence under this Act which has been committed by a body corporate is proved to have been committed with the consent or connivance of, or to be attributable to any neglect on the part of, any director, manager, secretary or other similar officer of the body corporate or any person who was purporting to act in any such capacity, he as well as the body corporate shall be guilty of that offence and be liable to be proceeded against and punished accordingly.

(2) Where the affairs of a body corporate are managed by its members this section shall apply in relation to the acts and defaults of a member in connection with his functions of management as if he were a director of the body corporate.

[Clean Air Act 1993, s 52.]

8–26627 53. Offence due to act or default of another. (1) Where the commission by any person of an offence under this Act is due to the act or default of some other person, that other person shall be guilty of the offence.

(2) A person may be charged with and convicted of an offence by virtue of this section whether or not proceedings for the offence are taken against any other person.

[Clean Air Act 1993, s 53.]

8–26628 55. General provisions as to enforcement. (1) It shall be the duty of the local authority to enforce—

(*a*) the provisions of Parts I to III, section 33 and Part VI; and

(*b*) the provisions of this Part so far as relating to those provisions;

but nothing in this section shall be taken as extending to the enforcement of any building regulations.

(2) A local authority in England and Wales may institute proceedings for an offence under section 1 or 2 (prohibition of emissions of dark smoke) in the case of any smoke which affects any part of their district notwithstanding, in the case of an offence under section 1, that the smoke is emitted from a chimney outside their district and, in the case of an offence under section 2, that the smoke is emitted from premises outside their district.

(3) Nothing in this section shall be taken as authorising a local authority in Scotland to institute proceedings for an offence against this Act.

[Clean Air Act 1993, s 55.]

8–26629 56. Rights of entry and inspection etc. (1) Any person authorised in that behalf by a local authority may at any reasonable time—

(*a*) enter upon any land or vessel for the purpose of—

(i) performing any function conferred on the authority or that person by virtue of this Act,

(ii) determining whether, and if so in what manner, such a function should be performed, or

(iii) determining whether any provision of this Act or of an instrument made under this Act is being complied with; and (*b*) carry out such inspections, measurements and tests on the land or vessel or of any articles on it and take away such samples of the land or articles as he considers appropriate for such a purpose.

(2) Subsection (1) above does not, except in relation to work under section 24(1) (adaptations to dwellings in smoke control area), apply in relation to a private dwelling.

(3) If it is shown to the satisfaction of a justice of the peace on sworn information in writing—

(*a*) that admission to any land or vessel which a person is entitled to enter in pursuance of subsection (1) has been refused to that person or that refusal is apprehended or that the land or vessel is unoccupied or that the occupier is temporarily absent or that the case is one of emergency or that an application for admission would defeat the object of the entry; and
(*b*) that there is reasonable ground for entry upon the land or vessel for the purpose for which entry is required,

then, subject to subsection (4), the justice may by warrant under his hand authorise that person to enter the land or vessel, if need be by force.

(4) A justice of the peace shall not issue a warrant in pursuance of subsection (3) in respect of any land or vessel unless he is satisfied—

(*a*) that admission to the land or vessel in pursuance of subsection (1) was sought after not less than seven days notice of the intended entry had been served on the occupier; or
(*b*) that admission to the land or vessel in pursuance of that subsection was sought in an emergency and was refused by or on behalf of the occupier; or
(*c*) that the land or vessel is unoccupied; or
(*d*) that an application for admission to the land or vessel would defeat the object of the entry.

(5) A warrant issued in pursuance of this section shall continue in force until the purpose for which the entry is required has been satisfied.

(6) *Scotland.*

[Clean Air Act 1993, s 56.]

8–26630 **57. Provisions supplementary to section 56.** (1) A person authorised to enter upon any land or vessel in pursuance of section 56 shall, if so required, produce evidence of his authority before he enters upon the land or vessel.

(2) A person so authorised may take with him on to the land or vessel in question such other persons and such equipment as may be necessary.

(3) Admission to any land or vessel used for residential purposes and admission with heavy equipment to any other land or vessel shall not, except in an emergency or in a case where the land or vessel is unoccupied, be demanded as of right in pursuance of section 56(1) unless notice of the intended entry has been served on the occupier not less than seven days before the demand.

(4) A person who, in the exercise of powers conferred on him by virtue of section 56 or this section, enters upon any land or vessel which is unoccupied or of which the occupier is temporarily absent shall leave the land or vessel as effectually secured against unauthorised entry as he found it.

(5) It shall be the duty of a local authority to make full compensation to any person who has sustained damage by reason of—

(*a*) the exercise by a person authorised by the authority of any of the powers conferred on the person so authorised by virtue of section 56 or this section; or
(*b*) the failure of a person so authorised to perform the duty imposed on him by subsection (4),

except where the damage is attributable to the default of the person who sustained it; and any dispute as to a person's entitlement to compensation in pursuance of this subsection or as to the amount of the compensation shall be determined by arbitration.

(6) A person who wilfully obstructs another person acting in the exercise of any powers conferred on the other person by virtue of section 56 or this section shall be guilty of an offence and liable on summary conviction to a fine not exceeding **level 3** on the standard scale.

(7) In section 56 and this section any reference to an emergency is a reference to a case where a person requiring entry to any land or vessel has reasonable cause to believe that circumstances exist which are likely to endanger life or health and that immediate entry to the land or vessel is necessary to verify the existence of those circumstances or to ascertain their cause or to effect a remedy.

[Clean Air Act 1993, s 57.]

8–26631 **58. Power of local authorities to obtain information.** (1) A local authority may serve on any person a notice requiring him to furnish to the authority, within a period or at times specified in the notice and in a form so specified, any information so specified which the authority reasonably considers that it needs for the purposes of any function conferred on the authority by Part IV or V of this Act (or by this Part of this Act so far as relating to those Parts).

(2) The Secretary of State may by regulations provide for restricting the information which may be required in pursuance of subsection (1) and for determining the form in which the information is to be so required.

(3) Any person who—

(*a*) fails without reasonable excuse to comply with the requirements of a notice served on him in pursuance of this section; or
(*b*) in furnishing any information in compliance with such a notice, makes any statement which he knows to be false in a material particular or recklessly makes any statement which is false in a material particular,

shall be guilty of an offence and liable on summary conviction to a fine not exceeding **level 5** on the standard scale.
[Clean Air Act 1993, s 58.]

8–26632 61. Joint exercise of local authority functions. (1) Sections 6, 7, 9 and 10 of the Public Health Act 1936 (provisions relating to joint boards) shall, so far as applicable, have effect in relation to this Act as if the provisions of this Act were provisions of that Act.

(2) Section 172 of the Public Health (Scotland) Act 1897 (constitution of port health authorities) shall have effect as if the provisions of this Act were provisions of that Act.

(3) Without prejudice to subsections (1) and (2), any two or more local authorities may combine for the purpose of declaring an area to be a smoke control area and in that event—

(*a*) the smoke control area may be the whole of the districts of those authorities or any part of those districts;
(*b*) the references in section 18, Schedule 1 and paragraph 1 of Schedule 2 to the local authority shall be read as references to the local authorities acting jointly;
(*c*) the reference in paragraph 1 of Schedule 1 to a place in the district of the local authority shall be construed as a reference to a place in each of the districts of the local authorities;

but, except as provided in this subsection, references in this Act to the local authority shall, in relation to a building or dwelling, or to a boiler or industrial plant, in the smoke control area, be read as references to that one of the local authorities within whose district the building, dwelling, boiler or plant is situated.

(4) For the avoidance of doubt it is hereby declared that where a port health authority or joint board has functions, rights or liabilities under this Act—

(*a*) any reference in this Act to a local authority or its district includes, in relation to those functions, rights or liabilities, a reference to the port health authority or board or its district;
(*b*) for the purposes of this Act, no part of the district of any such port health authority or board is to be treated, in relation to any matter falling within the competence of the authority or board, as forming part of the district of any other authority.

(5) Any premises which extend into the districts of two or more authorities shall be treated for the purposes of this Act as being wholly within such one of those districts—

(*a*) in England and Wales, as may from time to time be agreed by those authorities; or
(*b*) in Scotland, as may from time to time be so agreed or, in default of agreement, determined by the Secretary of State.

[Clean Air Act 1993, s 61.]

8–26633 62. Application of certain provisions of Part XII of Public Health Act 1936 and corresponding Scottish legislation. (1) In the application of this Act to England and Wales, the following provisions of Part XII of the Public Health Act 1936 shall have effect in relation to the provisions of this Act (apart from Parts IV and V) as if those provisions were provisions of that Act—

section 275 (power of local authority to execute works);
section 276 (power of local authority to sell materials);
section 278 (compensation to individuals for damage resulting from exercise of powers under Act);
section 283 (form of notices);
section 284 (authentication of documents);
section 285 (service of notices);
section 289 (power to require occupier to permit works to be executed by owner);
section 291 (expenses to be a charge on the premises);
section 293 (recovery of expenses);
section 294 (limitation of liability of certain owners);
section 305 (protection of members and officers of local authorities from personal liability).

(2) *Scotland.*
[Clean Air Act 1993, s 62.]

General

8–26634 63. *Regulations and orders.*

8–26635 **64. General provisions as to interpretation.** (1) In this Act, except so far as the context otherwise requires,—

"authorised officer" means any officer of a local authority authorised by them in writing, either generally or specially, to act in matters of any specified kind or in any specified matter;

"building regulations" means as respects Scotland, any statutory enactments, byelaws, rules and regulations or other provisions under whatever authority made, relating to the construction, alteration or extension of buildings;

"caravan" means a caravan within the meaning of Part I of the Caravan Sites and Control of Development Act 1960, disregarding the amendment made by section 13(2) of the Caravan Sites Act 1968, which usually and for the time being is situated on a caravan site within the meaning of that Act;

"chimney" includes structures and openings of any kind from or through which smoke, grit, dust or fumes may be emitted, and, in particular, includes flues, and references to a chimney of a building include references to a chimney which serves the whole or a part of a building but is structurally separate from the building;

"dark smoke" has the meaning given by section 3(1);

"day" means a period of twenty-four hours beginning at midnight;

"domestic furnace" means any furnace which is—

(*a*) designed solely or mainly for domestic purposes, and

(*b*) used for heating a boiler with a maximum heating capacity of less than 16.12 kilowatts;

"fireplace" includes any furnace, grate or stove, whether open or closed;

"fixed boiler or industrial plant" means any boiler or industrial plant which is attached to a building or is for the time being fixed to or installed on any land;

"fumes" means any airborne solid matter smaller than dust;

"industrial plant" includes any still, melting pot or other plant used for any industrial or trade purposes, and also any incinerator used for or in connection with any such purposes;

"local authority" means—

(*a*) in England, the council of a district or a London borough, the Common Council of the City of London, the Sub-Treasurer of the Inner Temple and the Under Treasurer of the Middle Temple;

(*aa*) in Wales, the council of a county or county borough; and

(*b*) *Scotland*;

"owner", in relation to premises—

(*a*) as respects England and Wales, means the person for the time being receiving the rackrent of the premises, whether on his own account or as agent or trustee for another person, or who would so receive the rackrent if the premises were let at a rackrent; and

(*b*) as respects Scotland, means the person for the time being entitled to receive or who would, if the premises were let, be entitled to receive, the rents of the premises and includes a trustee, factor, or person entitled to act as a legal representative of a person under disability by reason of nonage or mental or other incapacity and, in the case of public or municipal property, includes the persons to whom the management of the property is entrusted;

"port health authority" means, as respects Scotland, a port local authority constituted under Part X of the Public Health (Scotland) Act 1897 and includes a reference to a joint port health authority constituted under that Part;

"practicable" means reasonably practicable having regard, amongst other things, to local conditions and circumstances, to the financial implications and to the current state of technical knowledge, and "practicable means" includes the provision and maintenance of plant and its proper use;

"premises" includes land;

"smoke", includes soot, ash, grit and gritty particles emitted in smoke; and

"vessel" has the same meaning as "ship" in the Merchant Shipping Act 1995.

(2) Any reference in this Act to the occupier of a building shall, in relation to any building different parts of which are occupied by different persons, be read as a reference to the occupier or other person in control of the part of the building in which the relevant fireplace is situated.

(3) In this Act any reference to the rate of emission of any substance or any reference which is to be understood as such a reference shall, in relation to any regulations or conditions, be construed as a reference to the quantities of that substance which may be emitted during a period specified in the regulations or conditions.

(4) In this Act, except so far as the context otherwise requires, "private dwelling" means any building or part of a building used or intended to be used as such, and a building or part of a building is not to be taken for the purposes of this Act to be used or intended to be used otherwise than as a private dwelling by reason that a person who resides or is to reside in it is or is to be required or permitted to reside in it in consequence of his employment or of holding an office.

(5) In considering for the purposes of this Act whether any and, if so, what works are reasonably necessary in order to make suitable provision for heating and cooking in the case of a dwelling or are

reasonably necessary in order to enable a building to be used for a purpose without contravention of any of the provisions of this Act, regard shall be had to any difficulty there may be in obtaining, or in obtaining otherwise than at a high price, any fuels which would have to be used but for the execution of the works.

(6) Any furnaces which are in the occupation of the same person and are served by a single chimney shall, for the purposes of sections 5 to 12, 14 and 15, be taken to be one furnace.
[Clean Air Act 1993, s 64, as amended by the Local Government (Wales) Act 1994, Sch 9, the Merchant Shipping Act 1995, Sch 13 and the Adults with Incapacity (Scotland) Act 2000, Sch 5.]

8–26636 65. Application to Isles of Scilly. Parts IV and V, and this Part so far as relating to those Parts, shall have effect in their application to the Isles of Scilly with such modifications as the Secretary of State may by order specify.
[Clean Air Act 1993, s 65.]

8–26637 66. Transitory provisions relating to Alkali, &c. Works Regulation Act 1906. (1) Until the coming into force of the repeal by the Environmental Protection Act 1990 of the Alkali, &c. Works Regulation Act 1906—

(*a*) Part I of Schedule 3 shall have effect;
(*b*) this Act shall have effect subject to the modifications in Part II of that Schedule; and
(*c*) the Alkali, &c. Works Regulation Act 1906 shall continue to have effect as amended by Schedule 2 to the Clean Air Act 1956 notwithstanding the repeal by this Act of the last-mentioned Act.

(2) On the coming into force of the repeal by the Environmental Protection Act 1990 of the Alkali, &c. Works Regulation Act 1906, this section and Schedule 3 shall cease to have effect.
[Clean Air Act 1993, s 66.]

8–26638 67. *Consequential amendments, transitional provisions and repeals.*

8–26639 68. *Short title, commencement and extent.*

8–26640

SCHEDULES

Section 66(1)

SCHEDULE 3
PROVISIONS HAVING EFFECT UNTIL REPEAL OF ALKALI, &C WORKS REGULATION ACT 1906

(As amended by the Environment Act 1995, Sch 24.)

PART I
RELATION OF THIS ACT TO ALKALI, &C. WORKS REGULATION ACT 1906

1. (1) In this Part of this Schedule—

"the Alkali Act" means the Alkali, &c. Works Regulation Act 1906; and
"work subject or potentially subject to the Alkali Act" means—

(*a*) so much of any work registered under section 9 of that Act as is directly concerned in the processes which necessitate its registration under that section; and
(*b*) so much of any work in the course of erection or alteration as will on completion of the erection or alteration be directly concerned in such processes.

(2) The Secretary of State may from time to time determine how much of any work mentioned in sub-paragraph (1) is or will be directly concerned as there mentioned and his determination shall, until revoked or varied by him, be conclusive.

2. Subject to paragraphs 3 and 4, Parts I to III of this Act shall not apply to any work subject or potentially subject to the Alkali Act.

3. If, on the application of the local authority, the Secretary of State is satisfied that in all the circumstances it is expedient to do so, he may by order exclude the application of paragraph 2 to the whole or any specified part of any work subject or potentially subject to the Alkali Act.

4. While, by virtue of an order under paragraph 3 above, paragraph 2 is excluded from applying to any work or to any specified part of any work—

(*a*) in any proceedings brought under section 1, 2 or 20 in respect of the emission of smoke from the work or (as the case may be) from the specified part of the work it shall be a defence to prove that the best practicable means had been employed to prevent or minimise the alleged emission;
(*b*) *Repealed.*

5. Any order made under paragraph 3 may be varied or revoked by a subsequent order of the Secretary of State.

6. Nothing in section 55 shall be taken as extending to the enforcement of any of the provisions of the Alkali Act.

PART II
MODIFICATIONS OF THIS ACT

7. In section 31(4)—

(*a*) in paragraph (*a*), after "1990" there is inserted "or a work subject to the Alkali Act"; and

(*b*) for paragraph (*b*) there is substituted—

"(*b*) of the inspectors appointed under Part I of the Environmental Protection Act 1990 or, as the case may be, under the Alkali Act, to enforce those provisions in relation to such furnaces;".

8. In section 33(1), after "1990" there is inserted "or the place at which he does so is a work registered in pursuance of section 9 of the Alkali, &c. Works Regulation Act 1906".

9. In section 35(3), after "1990" there is inserted "or any work subject to the Alkali Act".

10. In section 36, after subsection (3) there is inserted—

"(3A) If the notice relates to a work subject to the Alkali Act, the person on whom the notice is served shall not be obliged to supply any information which, as certified by an inspector appointed under that Act, is not of a kind which is being supplied to the inspector for the purposes of that Act."

11. At the end of section 40 there is inserted—

"and 'the Alkali Act' means the Alkali, &c. Works Regulation Act 1906 and 'a work subject to the Alkali Act' means a work registered under section 9 of the Alkali Act, excluding the whole or part of such a work while the work or part is the subject of an order made or treated as made under paragraph 3 of Schedule 3 to this Act."

Noise and Statutory Nuisance Act 1993

(1993 c 40)

Loudspeakers

8–26650 8. Consent of local authorities to the operation of loudspeakers in streets or roads.

(1) A local authority may resolve that Schedule 2 is to apply to its area.

(2) If a local authority does so resolve, Schedule 2 shall come into force in its area on such date as may be specified for that purpose in the resolution, being a date at least one month after the date on which the resolution is passed.

(3) Where a local authority has passed a resolution under this section, the authority shall cause a notice to be published, in two consecutive weeks before the Schedule comes into force in its area, in a local newspaper circulating in the area.

(4) The notice shall—

(*a*) state that the resolution has been passed, and

(*b*) set out the general effect of Schedule 2 and, in particular, the procedure for applying for a consent under that Schedule.

(5) In this section "local authority" means—

(*a*) in relation to England and Wales—

(i) the council of a district,

(ii) the council of a London borough,

(iii) the Common Council of the City of London,

(iv) the Sub-Treasurer of the Inner Temple, or

(v) the Under Treasurer of the Middle Temple, and

(*b*) in relation to Scotland, a district or islands council.

[Noise and Statutory Nuisance Act 1993, s 8.]

Audible intruder alarms

8–26651 9. Audible intruder alarms[1]. (1) A local authority may, after consulting the chief officer of police, resolve that Schedule 3 is to apply to its area.

(2) If a local authority does so resolve—

(*a*) Schedule 3 (other than paragraph 4) shall come into force in its area on such date as may be specified for that purpose in the resolution ("the first appointed day"), and

(*b*) paragraph 4 of Schedule 3 shall come into force in its area, and accordingly paragraphs 2 and 3 of that Schedule shall cease to have effect in its area, on such later date as may be so specified ("the second appointed day").

(3) The first appointed day shall be at least four months after the date on which the resolution is passed.

(4) The second appointed day shall be at least nine months after the first appointed day.

(5) Where a local authority has passed a resolution under this section, the authority shall cause a notice to be published, in two consecutive weeks ending at least three months before the first appointed day, in a local newspaper circulating in its area.

(6) The notice shall—

(*a*) state that the resolution has been passed,

(*b*) state the first and second appointed days, and

(*c*) set out the general effect of Schedule 3 as it will apply from each of those days.

(7) In this section—

"chief officer of police", in relation to a local authority, means—

(*a*) the chief officer of police for the police area in which the area of the local authority is situated, or

(*b*) where part of the local authority's area is situated in one police area and part in another, the chief officer of police for each police area in which a part of the local authority's area is situated;

"local authority" means—

(*a*) in relation to England and Wales, the council of a district, and

(*b*) in relation to Scotland, a district or islands council.*

[Noise and Statutory Nuisance Act 1993, s 9.]

***Repealed, in relation to England and Wales, by the Clean Neighbourhoods and Environment Act 2005, Sch 1 from a date to be appointed.**

1. At the date of going to press no order had been made under s 12(2) of the Act to bring s 9 and Sch 3 into force.

8–26652

Section 8

SCHEDULE 2

CONSENT TO THE OPERATION OF LOUDSPEAKERS IN STREETS OR ROADS

(*Amended by the Serious Organised Crime and Police Act 2005, s 137.*)

Local authority consent

1. (1) Subject to sub-paragraph (2), on an application made by any person, the local authority may consent to the operation in its area of a loudspeaker in contravention of section 62(1) of the 1974 Act or of section 137(1) of the Serious Organised Crime and Police Act 2005.

(2) A consent shall not be given to the operation of a loudspeaker in connection with any election or for the purpose of advertising any entertainment, trade or business.

2. A consent may be granted subject to such conditions as the local authority considers appropriate.

Procedure

3. An application for a consent shall be made in writing and shall contain such information as the local authority may reasonably require.

4. (1) Where an application is duly made to the local authority for a consent, the authority shall determine the application and notify the applicant in writing of its decision within the period of twenty-one days beginning with the day on which the application is received by the authority.

(2) In a case where a consent is granted, the notification under sub-paragraph (1) shall specify the conditions, if any, subject to which the consent is granted.

5. An applicant for a consent shall pay such reasonable fee in respect of his application as the local authority may determine.

Publication of consent

6. Where the local authority grants a consent, the authority may cause a notice giving details of that consent to be published in a local newspaper circulating in its area.

Interpretation

7. In this Schedule "a consent" means a consent under paragraph 1.

8–26653

Section 9

SCHEDULE 3

AUDIBLE INTRUDER ALARMS

(*Amended by the Audit Commission Act 1998.*)

Installation of new alarms

1. (1) A person who installs an audible intruder alarm on or in any premises shall ensure—

(*a*) that the alarm complies with any prescribed requirements, and

(*b*) that the local authority is notified within 48 hours of the installation.

(2) A person who without reasonable excuse contravenes sub-paragraph (1) shall be guilty of an offence and liable on summary conviction—

(*a*) where the alarm does not comply with any prescribed requirements, to a fine not exceeding **level 5** on the standard scale, and

(*b*) in any other case, to a fine not exceeding **level 2** on the standard scale.

Operation of alarms before second appointed day

2. (1) A person who is the occupier of any premises when (on or after the first appointed day) an audible intruder alarm is installed on or in the premises shall not permit the alarm to be operated unless paragraph 5 is satisfied.

(2) A person who without reasonable excuse contravenes sub-paragraph (1) shall be guilty of an offence and liable on summary conviction—

(*a*) where the alarm does not comply with any prescribed requirements, to a fine not exceeding **level 5** on the standard scale, and

(*b*) in any other case, to a fine not exceeding **level 2** on the standard scale.

3. (1) A person who (on or after the first appointed day) becomes the occupier of any premises on or in which an audible intruder alarm has been installed, shall not permit the alarm to be operated unless paragraph 5 is satisfied.

(2) A person who without reasonable excuse contravenes sub-paragraph (1) shall be guilty of an offence and liable on summary conviction—

(*a*) where the alarm does not comply with any prescribed requirements, to a fine not exceeding **level 4** on the standard scale, and

(*b*) in any other case, to a fine not exceeding **level 2** on the standard scale.

Operation of alarms on or after second appointed day

4. (1) The occupier of any premises shall not permit any audible intruder alarm installed on or in those premises to be operated unless paragraph 5 is satisfied.

(2) A person who without reasonable excuse contravenes sub-paragraph (1) shall be guilty of an offence and liable on summary conviction—

(*a*) where the alarm does not comply with any prescribed requirements, to a fine not exceeding **level 5** on the standard scale, and

(*b*) in any other case, to a fine not exceeding **level 2** on the standard scale.

Requirements for operation of alarms

5. (1) This paragraph is satisfied if—

(*a*) the alarm complies with any prescribed requirements,

(*b*) the police have been notified in writing of the names, addresses and telephone numbers of the current key-holders, and

(*c*) the local authority has been informed of the address of the police station to which notification has been given under paragraph (*b*).

(2) Notification under sub-paragraph (1)(*b*) may be given to the police at any police station in the local authority's area.

Entry to premises

6. (1) Where—

(*a*) an intruder alarm installed on or in any premises is operating audibly more than one hour after it was activated, and

(*b*) the audible operation of the alarm is such as to give persons living or working in the vicinity of the premises reasonable cause for annoyance,

an officer of the local authority who has been authorised (whether generally or specially) for that purpose may, on production (if so required) of his authority, enter the premises to turn off the alarm.

(2) An officer may not enter premises by force under this paragraph.

7. (1) If, on an application made by an officer of the local authority who has been authorised (whether generally or specially) for that purpose, a justice of the peace is satisfied—

(*a*) that an intruder alarm installed on or in any premises is operating audibly more than one hour after it was activated,

(*b*) that the audible operation of the alarm is such as to give persons living or working in the vicinity of the premises reasonable cause for annoyance,

(*c*) where notification of any current key-holders has been given in accordance with paragraph 5(1)(*b*), that the officer has taken steps to obtain access to the premises with their assistance, and

(*d*) that the officer has been unable to obtain access to the premises without the use of force,

the justice may issue a warrant authorising the officer to enter the premises, if need be by force.

(2) Before applying for such a warrant, an officer shall leave a notice at the premises stating—

(*a*) that the audible operation of the alarm is such as to give persons living or working in the vicinity reasonable cause for annoyance, and

(*b*) that an application is to be made to a justice of the peace for a warrant authorising the officer to enter the premises and turn off the alarm.

(3) An officer shall not enter premises by virtue of this paragraph unless he is accompanied by a constable.

(4) A warrant under this paragraph shall continue in force until the alarm has been turned off and the officer has complied with paragraph 10.

8. An officer who enters premises by virtue of paragraph 6 or 7 may take with him such other persons and such equipment as may be necessary to turn off the alarm.

9. A person who enters premises by virtue of paragraph 6, 7 or 8 shall not cause more damage or disturbance than is necessary.

10. An officer who has entered premises by virtue of paragraph 6 or 7 which are unoccupied or from which the occupier is temporarily absent shall—

(*a*) after the alarm has been turned off, re-set it if reasonably practicable,

(*b*) leave a notice at the premises stating what action has been taken on the premises under this Schedule, and

(*c*) leave the premises, so far as reasonably practicable, as effectually secured against trespassers as he found them.

11. *Recovery of expenses.*

12. *Protection from personal liability.*

Interpretation

13. (1) In this Schedule references to the first appointed day or the second appointed day are to be read in accordance with section 9(2).

(2) In this Schedule—

"justice of the peace", in relation to Scotland, includes a sheriff;

"key-holders", in relation to an alarm, means—

(*a*) two persons, other than the occupier of the premises on or in which the alarm is installed, each of whom holds keys sufficient to obtain access to those premises, or

(*b*) a company which holds keys sufficient to obtain access to those premises, from which those keys can be obtained at any time and the business of which consists of or includes the service of holding keys for occupiers of premises;

"occupier"—

(*a*) in relation to premises that are unoccupied, means any person entitled to occupy the premises, and

(*b*) in relation to premises comprising a building that is being erected, constructed, altered, improved, maintained, cleaned or repaired, does not include a person whose occupancy—

(i) is connected with the erection, construction, alteration, improvement, maintenance, cleaning or repair, and

(ii) is by virtue of a licence granted for less than four weeks;

"prescribed" means prescribed in regulations made by the Secretary of State for the purposes of this Schedule.

(3) The Secretary of State's power to make such regulations shall be exercisable by statutory instrument, and an instrument containing such regulations shall be subject to annulment in pursuance of a resolution of either House of Parliament.

(4) Such regulations may make different provision for different cases, circumstances or areas.

(5) Nothing in this Schedule applies to an audible intruder alarm installed on or in a vehicle.*

***Repealed, in relation to England and Wales, by the Clean Neighbourhoods and Environment Act 2005, Sch 5 from a date to be appointed.**

Environment Act 1995[1]

(1995 c 25)

PART I[2]

THE ENVIRONMENT AGENCY AND THE SCOTTISH ENVIRONMENT PROTECTION AGENCY

CHAPTER I[3]

THE ENVIRONMENT AGENCY

Establishment of the Agency

8–26660 **1. The Environment Agency.** (1) There shall be a body corporate to be known as the Environment Agency or, in Welsh, Asiantaeth yr Amgylchedd (in this Act referred to as "the Agency"), for the purpose of carrying out the functions transferred or assigned to it by or under this Act.

(2)–(4) *Appointment of members of the Agency.*

(5) Subject to the provisions of section 38[4] below, the Agency shall not be regarded—

(*a*) as the servant or agent of the Crown, or as enjoying any status, immunity or privilege of the Crown; or

(*b*) by virtue of any connection with the Crown, as exempt from any tax, duty, rate, levy or other charge whatsoever, whether general or local;

and the Agency's property shall not be regarded as property of, or property held on behalf of, the Crown.

(6) The provisions of Schedule 1[5] to this Act shall have effect with respect to the Agency.
[Environment Act 1995, s 1.]

1. The Environment Act 1995 establishes a body corporate to be known as the Environment Agency and abolishes the National Rivers Authority and the London Waste Regulation Authority. With effect from the transfer date the property, right or liabilities of those Authorities are transferred to and vested in the Agency. The Act also makes provision with respect to contaminated land and abandoned mines, and makes further provision for the control of pollution, the conservation of natural resources and the conservation or enhancement of the environment.

The Act is to be brought into force in accordance with s 125, post. Of the provisions set out below, at the date of going to press, certain provisions in the following Schedules had not been brought fully into force: Schs 15, 22 and 24.

Only those provisions of the Environment Act 1995 which are relevant to proceedings in magistrates' courts are contained in this work.

2. Part I contains Ch 1, ss 1–19, Ch II, ss 20–36, and Ch III, ss 37–56.

3. Chapter I contains ss 1–19.

4. Section 38—delegation of functions by Ministers etc. to the new Agencies—is concerned with agreements made between a Minister of the Crown and a new Agency; s 38 is not printed in this work.

5. Schedule 1 is printed in an abridged form, post.

Transfer of functions, property etc to the Agency

8–26661 **2. Transfer of functions to the Agency.** (1) On the transfer date there shall by virtue of this section be transferred to the Agency—

(*a*) the functions of the National Rivers Authority, that is to say

(i) its functions under or by virtue of Part II (water resources management) of the Water Resources Act 1991 (in this Part referred to as "the 1991 Act");
(ii) its functions under or by virtue of Part III of that Act (control of pollution of water resources);
(iii) its functions under or by virtue of Part IV of that Act (flood defence) and the Land Drainage Act 1991 and the functions transferred to the Authority by virtue of section 136(8) of the Water Act 1989 and paragraph 1(3) of Schedule 15 to that Act (transfer of land drainage functions under local statutory provisions and subordinate legislation);
(iv) its functions under or by virtue of Part VII of the 1991 Act (land and works powers);
(v) its functions under or by virtue of the Diseases of Fish Act 1937, the Sea Fisheries Regulation Act 1966, the Salmon and Freshwater Fisheries Act 1975, Part V of the 1991 Act or any other enactment relating to fisheries;
(vi) the functions as a navigation authority, harbour authority or conservancy authority which were transferred to the Authority by virtue of Chapter V of Part III of the Water Act 1989 or paragraph 23(3) of Schedule 13 to that Act or which have been transferred to the Authority by any order or agreement under Schedule 2 to the 1991 Act;
(vii) its functions under Schedule 2 to the 1991 Act;
(viii) the functions assigned to the Authority by or under any other enactment, apart from this Act;

(*b*) the functions of waste regulation authorities, that is to say, the functions conferred or imposed on them by or under

(i) the Control of Pollution (Amendment) Act 1989, or
(ii) Part II of the Environmental Protection Act 1990 (in this Part referred to as "the 1990 Act"),

or assigned to them by or under any other enactment, apart from this Act;

(*c*) the functions of disposal authorities under or by virtue of the waste regulation provisions of the Control of Pollution Act 1974;
(*d*) the functions of the chief inspector for England and Wales constituted under section 16(3) of the 1990 Act, that is to say, the functions conferred or imposed on him by or under Part I of that Act or assigned to him by or under any other enactment, apart from this Act;
(*e*) the functions of the chief inspector for England and Wales appointed under section 4(2)(*a*) of the Radioactive Substances Act 1993, that is to say, the functions conferred or imposed on him by or under that Act or assigned to him by or under any other enactment, apart from this Act;
(*f*) the functions conferred or imposed by or under the Alkali, &c, Works Regulation Act 1906 (in this section referred to as "the 1906 Act") on the chief, or any other, inspector (within the meaning of that Act), so far as exercisable in relation to England and Wales;
(*g*) so far as exercisable in relation to England and Wales, the functions in relation to improvement notices and prohibition notices under Part I of the Health and Safety at Work etc. Act 1974 (in this section referred to as "the 1974 Act") of inspectors appointed under section 19 of that Act by the Secretary of State in his capacity as the enforcing authority responsible in relation to England and Wales for the Enforcement of the 1906 Act and section 5 of the 1974 Act; and
(*h*) the functions of the Secretary of State specified in subsection (2) below.

(2) The functions of the Secretary of State mentioned in subsection (1)(*h*) above are the following, that is to say—

(*a*) so far as exercisable in relation to England and Wales, his functions under section 30(1) of the Radioactive Substances Act 1993 (power to dispose of radioactive waste);

(*b*) his functions under Chapter III of Part IV of the Water Industry Act 1991 in relation to special category effluent, within the meaning of that Chapter, other than any function of making regulations or of making orders under section 139 of that Act;

(*c*) so far as exercisable in relation to England and Wales, the functions conferred or imposed on him by virtue of his being, for the purposes of Part I of the 1974 Act, the authority which is by any of the relevant statutory provisions made responsible for the enforcement of the 1906 Act and section 5 of the 1974 Act;

(*d*) so far as exercisable in relation to England and Wales, his functions under, or under regulations made by virtue of, section 9 of the 1906 Act (registration of works), other than any functions of his as an appellate authority or any function of making regulations;

(*e*) so far as exercisable in relation to England and Wales, his functions under regulations 7(1) and 8(2) of, and paragraph 2(2)(*c*) of Schedule 2 to, the Sludge (Use in Agriculture) Regulations 1989 (which relate to the provision of information and the testing of soil).

(3) *Repealed.*

[Environment Act 1995, s 2, as amended by the Statute Law (Repeals) Act 2004.]

8–26662 **3.** *Transfer of property, rights and liabilities to the Agency.*

8–26663 **4.** *Principal aim and objectives of the Agency.*

8–26664 **5. General functions with respect to pollution control.** (1) The Agency's pollution control powers shall be exercisable for the purpose of preventing or minimising, or remedying or mitigating the effects of, pollution of the environment.

(2) The Agency shall, for the purpose—

(*a*) of facilitating the carrying out of its pollution control functions, or

(*b*) of enabling it to form an opinion of the general state of pollution of the environment,

compile information relating to such pollution (whether the information is acquired by the Agency carrying out observations or is obtained in any other way).

(3) If required by either of the Ministers to do so, the Agency shall—

(*a*) carry out assessments (whether generally or for such particular purpose as may be specified in the requirement) of the effect, or likely effect, on the environment of existing or potential levels of pollution of the environment and report its findings to that Minister; or

(*b*) prepare and send to that Minister a report identifying—

(i) the options which the Agency considers to be available for preventing or minimising, or remedying or mitigating the effects of, pollution of the environment, whether generally or in cases or circumstances specified in the requirement; and

(ii) the costs and benefits of such options as are identified by the Agency pursuant to sub-paragraph (i) above.

(4) The Agency shall follow developments in technology and techniques for preventing or minimising, or remedying or mitigating the effects of, pollution of the environment.

(5) In this section, "pollution control powers" and "pollution control functions", in relation to the Agency, mean respectively its powers or its functions under or by virtue of the following enactments, that is to say—

(*a*) the Alkali, &c, Works Regulation Act 1906;

(*b*) Part I of the Health and Safety at Work etc. Act 1974;

(*c*) Part I of the Control of Pollution Act 1974;

(*d*) the Control of Pollution (Amendment) Act 1989;

(*e*) parts I, II and IIA of the 1990 Act (integrated pollution control etc, waste on land and contaminated land);

(*f*) Chapter III of Part IV of the Water Industry Act 1991 (special category effluent);

(*g*) Part III and sections 161 to 161D of the 1991 Act (control of pollution of water resources);

(*h*) the Radioactive Substances Act 1993;

(*i*) regulations under section 2 of the Pollution Prevention and Control Act 1999;

(*j*) regulations made by virtue of section 2(2) of the European Communities Act 1972, to the extent that the regulations relate to pollution.

[Environment Act 1995, s 5, as amended by the Pollution Prevention and Control Act 1999, Sch 2.]

8–26665 **6. General provisions with respect to water.** (1) It shall be the duty of the Agency, to such extent as it considers desirable, generally to promote—

(*a*) the conservation and enhancement of the natural beauty and amenity of inland and coastal waters and of land associated with such waters;
(*b*) the conservation of flora and fauna which are dependent on an aquatic environment; and
(*c*) the use of such waters and land for recreational purposes;

and it shall be the duty of the Agency, in determining what steps to take in performance of the duty imposed by virtue of paragraph (*c*) above, to take into account the needs of persons who are chronically sick or disabled.

This subsection is without prejudice to the duties of the Agency under section 7 below.

(2) It shall be the duty of the Agency to take all such action as it may from time to time consider, in accordance with any directions given under section 40 below, to be necessary or expedient for the purpose—

(*a*) of conserving, redistributing or otherwise augmenting water resources in England and Wales; and
(*b*) of securing the proper use of water resources in England and Wales;*

but nothing in this subsection shall be construed as relieving any water undertaker of the obligation to develop water resources for the purpose of performing any duty imposed on it by virtue of section 37 of the Water Industry Act 1991 (general duty to maintain water supply system).

(3) The provisions of the 1991 Act relating to the functions of the Agency under Chapter II of Part II of that Act and the related water resources provisions so far as they relate to other functions of the Agency shall not apply to so much of any inland waters as—

(*a*) are part of the River Tweed;
(*b*) are part of the River Esk or River Sark at a point where either of the banks of the river is in Scotland; or
(*c*) are part of any tributary stream of the River Esk or the River Sark at a point where either of the banks of the tributary stream is in Scotland.*

(4) Subject to section 106 of the 1991 Act (obligation to carry out flood defence functions through committees), the Agency shall in relation to England and Wales exercise a general supervision over all matters relating to flood defence.

(5) The Agency's flood defence functions shall extend to the territorial sea adjacent to England and Wales in so far as—

(*a*) the area of any regional flood defence committee includes any area of that territorial sea; or
(*b*) section 165(2) or (3) of the 1991 Act (drainage works for the purpose of defence against sea water or tidal water, and works etc to secure an adequate outfall for a main river) provides for the exercise of any power in the territorial sea.

(6) It shall be the duty of the Agency to maintain, improve and develop salmon fisheries, trout fisheries, freshwater fisheries and eel fisheries.

(7) The area in respect of which the Agency shall carry out its functions relating to fisheries shall be the whole of England and Wales, together with—

(*a*) such part of the territorial sea adjacent to England and Wales as extends for six miles from the baselines from which the breadth of that sea is measured,
(*b*) in the case of—
    (i) the Diseases of Fish Act 1937
    (ii) the Salmon and Freshwater Fisheries Act 1975,
    (iii) Part V of the 1991 Act (general control of fisheries), and
    (iv) subsection (6) above,

so much of the River Esk, with its banks and tributary streams up to their source, as is situated in Scotland, and

(*c*) in the case of sections 31 to 34 and 36(2) of the Salmon and Freshwater Fisheries Act 1975 as applied by section 39(1B) of that Act, so much of the catchment area of the River Esk as is situated in Scotland,

but, in the case of the enactments specified in paragraph (*b*) above, excluding the River Tweed.

(8) In this section—

"miles" means international nautical miles of 1,852 metres;
"the related water resources provisions" has the same meaning as it has in the 1991 Act;
"the River Tweed" means "the river" within the meaning of the Tweed Fisheries Amendment Act 1859 as amended by byelaws.

[Environment Act 1995, s 6.]

***Amended by the Water Act 2003, s 105, from a date to be appointed.**

CHAPTER III[1]

MISCELLANEOUS, GENERAL AND SUPPLEMENTAL PROVISIONS RELATING TO THE NEW AGENCIES

Supplemental provisions

8–26666 54. Appearance in legal proceedings. In England and Wales, a person who is authorised by the Agency to prosecute on its behalf in proceedings before a magistrates' court shall be entitled to prosecute in any such proceedings although not of counsel or a solicitor.
[Environment Act 1995, s 54.]

1. Chapter III contains ss 37–56.

8–26667 55. Continuity of exercise of functions: the new Agencies. (1) The abolition of—

(*a*) the National Rivers Authority
(*b*) the London Waste Regulation Authority, or
(*c*) a river purification board, shall not affect the validity of anything done by that Authority or board before the transfer date.

(2) Anything which, at the transfer date, is in the process of being done by or in relation to a transferor in the exercise of, or in connection with, any of the transferred functions may be continued by or in relation to the transferee.

(3) Anything done by or in relation to a transferor before the transfer date in the exercise of, or otherwise in connection with, any of the transferred functions, shall, so far as is required for continuing its effect on and after that date, have effect as if done by or in relation to the transferee.

(4) Subsection (3) above applies in particular to—

(*a*) any decision, determination, declaration, designation, agreement or instrument made by a transferor;
(*b*) any regulations or byelaws made by a transferor;
(*c*) any licence, permission, consent, approval, authorisation, exemption, dispensation or relaxation granted by or to a transferor;
(*d*) any notice, direction or certificate given by or to a transferor;
(*e*) any application, request, proposal or objection made by or to a transferor;
(*f*) any condition or requirement imposed by or on a transferor;
(*g*) any fee or charge paid by or to a transferor;
(*h*) any appeal allowed by or in favour of or against a transferor;
(*j*) any proceedings instituted by or against a transferor.

(5) Any reference in the foregoing provisions of this section to anything done by or in relation to a transferor includes a reference to anything which, by virtue of any enactment, is treated as having been done by or in relation to that transferor.

(6) Any reference to a transferor in any document constituting or relating to anything to which the foregoing provisions of this section apply shall, so far as is required for giving effect to those provisions, be construed as a reference to the transferee.

(7) The foregoing provisions of this section—

(*a*) are without prejudice to any provision made by this Act in relation to any particular functions; and
(*b*) shall not be construed as continuing in force any contract of employment made by a transferor;

and the Secretary of State may, in relation to any particular functions, by order exclude, modify or supplement any of the foregoing provisions of this section or make such other transitional provisions as he thinks necessary or expedient.

(8) Where, by virtue of any provision of Schedule 15 to this Act, the Minister is the transferor in the case of any functions, he shall have the same powers under subsection (7) above in relation to those functions as the Secretary of State.

(9) The power to make an order under subsection (7) above shall be exercisable by statutory instrument; and any statutory instrument containing such an order shall be subject to annulment pursuant to a resolution of either House of Parliament.

(10) In this section—

"the transferee", in the case of any transferred functions, means the new Agency whose functions they become by virtue of any provision made by or under this Act;

"transferred functions" means any functions which, by virtue of any provision made by or under this Act, become functions of a new Agency; and

"transferor" means any body or person any or all of whose functions become, by virtue of any provision made by or under this Act, functions of a new Agency.
[Environment Act 1995, s 55.]

8–26668 56. Interpretation of Part I. (1) In this Part of this Act, except where the context otherwise requires—

"the 1951 Act" means the Rivers (Prevention of Pollution) (Scotland) Act 1951;
"the 1990 Act" means the Environmental Protection Act 1990;
"the 1991 Act" means the Water Resources Act 1991;
"the appropriate Minister"—

(*a*) in the case of the Agency, means the Secretary of State or the Minister; and
(*b*) in the case of SEPA, means the Secretary of State;

"the appropriate Ministers"—

(*a*) in the case of the Agency, means the Secretary of State and the Minister; and
(*b*) in the case of SEPA, means the Secretary of State;

"conservancy authority" has the meaning given by section 221(1) of the 1991 Act;
"costs" includes—

(*a*) costs to any person; and
(*b*) costs to the environment;

"disposal authority"—

(*a*) in the application of this Part in relation to the Agency, has the same meaning as it has in Part I of the Control of Pollution Act 1974 by virtue of section 30(1) of that Act; and
(*b*) in the application of this Part in relation to SEPA, has the meaning assigned to it by section 30(2) of that Act;

"the environment" means all, or any, of the following media, namely, the air, water and land (and the medium of air includes the air within buildings and the air within other natural or man-made structures above or below ground);

"environmental licence", in the application of this Part in relation to the Agency, means any of the following—

(*a*) registration of a person as a carrier of controlled waste under section 2 of the Control of Pollution (Amendment) Act 1989.
(*aa*) a permit granted by the Agency under regulations under section 2 of the Pollution Prevention and Control Act 1999,
(*b*) an authorisation under Part I of the 1990 Act, other than any such authorisation granted by a local enforcing authority,*
(*c*) a waste management licence under Part II of that Act,
(*d*) a licence under Chapter II of Part II of the 1991 Act,
(*e*) a consent for the purposes of section 88(1)(*a*), 89(4)(*a*) or 90 of that Act,
(*f*) registration under the Radioactive Substances Act 1993,
(*g*) an authorisation under that Act,
(*h*) registration of a person as a broker of controlled waste under the Waste Management Licensing Regulations 1994,
(*j*) registration in respect of an activity which requires notification under regulation 18AA of those Regulations or an activity falling within paragraph 45(1) or (2) of Schedule 3 to those Regulations,
(*k*) a greenhouse gas emissions permit granted under the Greenhouse Gas Emissions Trading Scheme Regulations 2005.

so far as having effect in relation to England and Wales;

"environmental licence", in the application of this Part in relation to SEPA, means any of the following—

(*a*) a consent under Part II of the Control of Pollution Act 1974,
(*b*) registration of a person as a carrier of controlled waste under section 2 of the Control of Pollution (Amendment) Act 1989,
(*c*) an authorisation under Part I of the 1990 Act,*
(*d*) a waste management licence under Part II of that Act,
(*e*) a licence under section 17 of the Natural Heritage (Scotland) Act 1991,
(*f*) registration under the Radioactive Substances Act 1993,
(*g*) an authorisation under that Act,
(*h*) registration of a person as a broker of controlled waste under the Waste Management Licensing Regulations 1994,
(*j*) registration in respect of an activity falling within paragraphs 7, 8(2), 9, 10, 12, 12A, 19, 45(1) or (2) or 46 of Schedule 3 to those Regulations, except where the waste which is the subject of the activity consists of agricultural waste within the meaning of those Regulations,
(*k*) a greenhouse gas emissions permit granted under the Greenhouse Gas Emissions Trading Scheme Regulations 2005.

so far as having effect in relation to Scotland;

"flood defence functions", in relation to the Agency, has the same meaning as in the 1991 Act;
"harbour authority" has the meaning given by section 221(1) of the 1991 Act;

"local authority", in the application of this Part in relation to SEPA, means a district or islands council in Scotland;

"the Minister" means the Minister of Agriculture, Fisheries and Food;

"the Ministers" means the Secretary of State and the Minister;

"navigation authority" has the meaning given by section 221(1) of the 1991 Act;

"new Agency" means the Agency or SEPA;

"river purification authority" means a river purification authority within the meaning of the 1951 Act;

"river purification board" means a river purification board established by virtue of section 135 of the Local Government (Scotland) Act 1973;

"the transfer date" means such date as the Secretary of State may by order[1] made by statutory instrument appoint as the transfer date for the purposes of this Part; and different dates may be appointed for the purposes of this Part—

(i) as it applies for or in connection with transfers under or by virtue of Chapter I above, and
(ii) as it applies for or in connection with transfers under or by virtue of Chapter II above;

"waste regulation authority"—

(*a*) in the application of this Part in relation to the Agency, means any authority in England or Wales which, by virtue of section 30(1) of the 1990 Act, is a waste regulation authority for the purposes of Part II of that Act; and

(*b*) in the application of this Part in relation to SEPA, means any council which, by virtue of section 30(1)(*g*) of the 1990 Act, is a waste regulation authority for the purposes of Part II of that Act.

(2) *Scotland.*

(3) Where by virtue of any provision of this Part any function of a Minister of the Crown is exercisable concurrently by different Ministers, that function shall also be exercisable jointly by any two or more of those Ministers.

[Environment Act 1995, s 56, as amended by the Pollution Prevention and Control Act 1999, Sch 2, SI 2000/1973, SI 2005/925, SI 2005/1728 and SSI 2004/275.]

***Prospectively repealed by the Pollution Prevention and Control Act 1999, Sch 3 from a date to be appointed.**

1. The Environment Agency (Transfer Date) Order 1996, SI 1996/234, set 1 April 1996 as the transfer date for the purposes of transfers under or by virtue of CHAPTER I of PART I of this Act.

PART IV[1]
AIR QUALITY

8–26672 **80. National air quality strategy.** (1) The Secretary of State shall as soon as possible prepare and publish a statement (in this Part referred to as "the strategy") containing policies with respect to the assessment or management of the quality of air.

(2) The strategy may also contain policies for implementing—

(*a*) obligations of the United Kingdom under the Community Treaties, or
(*b*) international agreements to which the United Kingdom is for the time being a party,

so far as relating to the quality of air.

(3) The strategy shall consist of or include—

(*a*) a statement which relates to the whole of Great Britain; or
(*b*) two or more statements which between them relate to every part of Great Britain.

(4) The Secretary of State—

(*a*) shall keep under review his policies with respect to the quality of air; and
(*b*) may from time to time modify the strategy.

(5) Without prejudice to the generality of what may be included in the strategy, the strategy must include statements with respect to—

(*a*) standards relating to the quality of air;
(*b*) objectives for the restriction of the levels at which particular substances are present in the air; and
(*c*) measures which are to be taken by local authorities and other persons for the purpose of achieving those objectives.

(6)–(7) *Supplementary provisions with respect to strategy.*

[Environment Act 1995, s 80.]

---

1. Part IV contains ss 80–91.

8–26673 **87. Regulations for the purposes of Part IV.** (1) Regulations[1] may make provision—

(*a*) for, or in connection with, implementing the strategy;

(*b*) for, or in connection with, implementing—

(i) obligations of the United Kingdom under the Community Treaties, or

(ii) international agreements to which the United Kingdom is for the time being a party,

so far as relating to the quality of air; or

(*c*) otherwise with respect to the assessment or management of the quality of air.

(2) Without prejudice to the generality of subsection (1) above, regulations under that subsection may make provision—

(*a*) prescribing standards relating to the quality of air;

(*b*) prescribing objectives for the restriction of the levels at which particular substances are present in the air;

(*c*) conferring powers or imposing duties on local authorities;

(*d*) for or in connection with—

(i) authorising local authorities (whether by agreements or otherwise) to exercise any functions of a Minister of the Crown on his behalf;

(ii) directing that functions of a Minister of the Crown shall be exercisable concurrently with local authorities; or

(iii) transferring functions of a Minister of the Crown to local authorities;

(*e*) prohibiting or restricting, or for or in connection with prohibiting or restricting,—

(i) the carrying on of prescribed activities, or

(ii) the access of prescribed vehicles or mobile equipment to prescribed areas,

whether generally or in prescribed circumstances;

(*f*) for or in connection with the designation of air quality management areas by orders made by local authorities in such cases or circumstances not falling within section 83 above as may be prescribed;

(*g*) for the application, with or without modifications, of any provisions of this Part in relation to areas designated by virtue of paragraph (*f*) above or in relation to orders made by virtue of that paragraph;

(*h*) with respect to—

(i) air quality reviews;

(ii) assessments under this Part;

(iii) orders designating air quality management areas; or

(iv) action plans;

(*j*) prescribing measures which are to be adopted by local authorities (whether in action plans or otherwise) or other persons in pursuance of the achievement of air quality standards or objectives;

(*k*) for or in connection with the communication to the public of information relating to quality for the time being, or likely future quality, of the air;

(*l*) for or in connection with the obtaining by local authorities from any person of information which is reasonably necessary for the discharge of functions conferred or imposed on them under or by virtue of this Part;

(*m*) for or in connection with the recovery by a local authority from prescribed persons in prescribed circumstances, and in such manner as may be prescribed, of costs incurred by the authority in discharging functions conferred or imposed on the authority under or by virtue of this Part;

(*n*) for a person who contravenes, or fails to comply with, any prescribed provision of the regulations to be guilty of an offence and liable on summary conviction to a fine not exceeding level 5 on the standard scale or such lower level on that scale as may be prescribed in relation to the offence;

(*o*) for or in connection with arrangements under which a person may discharge any liability to conviction for a prescribed offence by payment of a penalty of a prescribed amount;

(*p*) for or in connection with appeals against determinations or decisions made, notices given or served, or other things done under or by virtue of the regulations.

(3)–(4) *Supplementary provisions with regard to regulations.*

(5) The provisions of any regulations under this Part may include—

(*a*) provision for anything that may be prescribed by the regulations to be determined under the regulations and for anything falling to be so determined to be determined by such persons, in accordance with such procedure and by reference to such matters, and to the opinion of such persons, as may be prescribed;

(*b*) different provision for different cases, including different provision in relation to different persons, circumstances, areas or localities; and

(*c*) such supplemental, consequential, incidental or transitional provision (including provision amending any enactment or any instrument made under any enactment) as the Secretary of State considers appropriate.

(6) Nothing in regulations under this Part shall authorise any person other than a constable in uniform to stop a vehicle on any road.

(7) *Consultation before the making of regulations under this Part.*

(8) Any power conferred by this Part to make regulations shall be exercisable by statutory instrument; and no statutory instrument containing regulations under this Part shall be made unless a draft of the instrument has been laid before, and approved by a resolution of, each House of Parliament.

(9) If, apart from this subsection, the draft of an instrument containing regulations under this Part would be treated for the purposes of the Standing Orders of either House of Parliament as a hybrid instrument, it shall proceed in that House as if it were not such an instrument.
[Environment Act 1995, s 87.]

1. The following regulations have been made: Air Quality (England) Regulations 2000, SI 2000/928 amended by SI 2002/3043, Air Quality (Wales) Regulations 2000, SI 2000/1940; the Road Traffic (Vehicle Emissions) (Fixed Penalty) (England) Regulations 2002, SI 2002/1808; the Road Traffic (Vehicle Emissions) (Fixed Penalty) (Wales) Regulations 2003, SI 2003/300.

8–26674 **89.** *Application of Part IV to the Isles of Scilly.*

8–26675 **90. Supplemental provisions.** Schedule 11 to this Act shall have effect.
[Environment Act 1995, s 90.]

8–26676 **91. Interpretation of Part IV.** (1) In this Part—

"action plan" shall be construed in accordance with section 84(2)(*b*) above;

"air quality objectives" means objectives prescribed by virtue of section 87(2)(*b*) above;

"air quality review" means a review under section 82 or 85 above;

"air quality standards" means standards prescribed by virtue of section 87(2)(*a*) above;

"the appropriate new Agency" means—

(*a*) in relation to England and Wales, the Agency;
(*b*) in relation to Scotland, SEPA;

"designated area" has the meaning given by section 83(1) above;

"local authority", in relation to England and Wales, means—

(*a*) any unitary authority,
(*b*) any district council, so far as it is not a unitary authority;
(*c*) the Common Council of the City of London and, as respects the Temples, the Sub-Treasurer of the Inner Temple and the Under-Treasurer of the Middle Temple respectively,

and, in relation to Scotland, means a council for an area constituted under section 2 of the Local Government etc. (Scotland) Act 1994;

"new Agency" means the Agency or SEPA;

"prescribed" means prescribed, or of a description prescribed, by or under regulations;

"regulations" means regulations made by the Secretary of State;

"the relevant period", in the case of any provision of this Part, means such period as may be prescribed for the purposes of that provision;

"the strategy" has the meaning given by section 80(1) above;

"unitary authority" means—

(*a*) the council of a county, so far as it is the council of an area for which there are no district councils;
(*b*) the council of any district comprised in an area for which there is no county council;
(*c*) the council of a London borough;
(*d*) the council of a county borough in Wales.

(2) Any reference in this Part to it appearing that any air quality standards or objectives are not likely within the relevant period to be achieved includes a reference to it appearing that those standards or objectives are likely within that period not to be achieved.
[Environment Act 1995, s 91.]

PART V[1]

MISCELLANEOUS, GENERAL AND SUPPLEMENTAL PROVISIONS

Waste

8–26677 **93. Producer responsibility: general.** (1) For the purpose of promoting or securing an increase in the re-use, recovery or recycling of products or materials, the Secretary of State may by regulations[2] make provision for imposing producer responsibility obligations on such persons, and in respect of such products or materials, as may be prescribed.

(2) The power of the Secretary of State to make regulations shall be exercisable only after consultation with bodies or persons appearing to him to be representative of bodies or persons whose interests are, or are likely to be, substantially affected by the regulations which he proposes to make.

(3) Except in the case of regulations for the implementation of—

(*a*) any obligations of the United Kingdom under the Community Treaties, or

(*b*) any international agreement to which the United Kingdom is for the time being a party,

the power to make regulations shall be exercisable only where the Secretary of State, after such consultation as is required by subsection (2) above, is satisfied as to the matters specified in subsection (6) below.

(4) The powers conferred by subsection (1) above shall also be exercisable, in a case falling within paragraph (*a*) or (*b*) of subsection (3) above, for the purpose of sustaining at least a minimum level of (rather than promoting or securing an increase in) re-use, recovery or recycling of products or materials.

(5)–(6) *Matters to which the Secretary of State shall have regard in making regulations.*

(7) The Secretary of State shall have a duty to exercise the power to make regulations in the manner which he considers best calculated to secure that the exercise does not have the effect of restricting, distorting or preventing competition or, if it is likely to have any such effect, that the effect is no greater than is necessary for achieving the environmental or economic benefits mentioned in subsection (6) above.

(8) In this section—

"prescribed" means prescribed in regulations;

"product" and "material" include a reference to any product or material (as the case may be) at a time when it becomes, or has become, waste;

"producer responsibility obligation" means the steps which are required to be taken by relevant persons of the classes or descriptions to which the regulations in question apply in order to secure attainment of the targets specified or described in the regulations;

"recovery", in relation to products or materials, includes—

(*a*) composting, or any other form of transformation by biological processes, of products or materials; or

(*b*) the obtaining, by any means, of energy from products or materials;

"regulations" means regulations under this section;

"relevant persons", in the case of any regulations or any producer responsibility obligation, means persons of the class or description to which the producer responsibility obligation imposed by the regulations applies;

"relevant targets" means the targets specified or described in the regulations imposing the producer responsibility obligation in question;

and regulations may prescribe, in relation to prescribed products or materials, activities, or the activities, which are to be regarded for the purposes of this section and sections 94 and 95 below or any regulations as re-use, recovery or recycling of those products or materials.

(9) The power to make regulations shall be exercisable by statutory instrument.

(10) Subject to the following provisions of this section, a statutory instrument containing regulations shall not be made unless a draft of the instrument has been laid before and approved by a resolution of each House of Parliament.

(11) Subsection (10) above shall not apply to a statutory instrument by reason only that it contains regulations varying any relevant targets.

(12) A statutory instrument which, by virtue of subsection (11) above, is not subject to any requirement that a draft of the instrument be laid before and approved by a resolution of each House of Parliament shall be subject to annulment in pursuance of a resolution of either House of Parliament.
[Environment Act 1995, s 93.]

1. Part V contains ss 92–125.
2. The Producer Responsibility Obligations (Packaging Waste) Regulations 2005, SI 2005/3468 have been made.

8–26678 94–94A. *Producer responsibility: supplementary provisions and competition matters*

8–26679 95. Producer responsibility: offences. (1) Regulations[1] may make provision for a person who contravenes a prescribed requirement of the regulations to be guilty of an offence and liable—

(*a*) on summary conviction, to a fine not exceeding the statutory maximum;

(*b*) on conviction on indictment, to a fine.

(2) Where an offence under any provision of the regulations committed by a body corporate is proved to have been committed with the consent or connivance of, or to have been attributable to any neglect on the part of, any director, manager, secretary or other similar officer of the body corporate or a person who was purporting to act in any such capacity, he as well as the body corporate shall be guilty of that offence and shall be liable to be proceeded against and punished accordingly.

(3) Where the affairs of a body corporate are managed by its members, subsection (2) above shall apply in relation to the acts or defaults of a member in connection with his functions of management as if he were a director of the body corporate.

(4) Where the commission by any person of an offence under the regulations is due to the act or default of some other person, that other person may be charged with and convicted of the offence by virtue of this section whether or not proceedings for the offence are taken against the first-mentioned person.

(5) Expressions used in this section and in section 93 or 94 above have the same meaning in this section as they have in that section.
[Environment Act 1995, s 95.]

---

1. The Producer Responsibility Obligations (Packaging Waste) Regulations 2005, SI 2005/3468 have been made.

Hedgerows etc

8–26680 **97. Hedgerows.** (1) The appropriate Ministers may by regulations[1] make provision for, or in connection with, the protection of important hedgerows in England or Wales.

(2) The question whether a hedgerow is or is not "important" for the purposes of this section shall be determined in accordance with prescribed criteria.

(3) For the purpose of facilitating the protection of important hedgerows, regulations under subsection (1) above may also make provision in relation to other hedgerows in England or Wales.

(4) Without prejudice to the generality of subsections (1) to (3) above, regulations under subsection (1) above may provide for the application (with or without modifications) of, or include provision comparable to, any provision contained in the planning Acts and may, in particular, make provision—

(*a*) prohibiting, or for prohibiting, the removal of, or the carrying out of prescribed acts in relation to, a hedgerow except in prescribed cases;

(*b*) for or with respect to appeals against determinations or decisions made, or notices given or served, under or by virtue of the regulations, including provision authorising or requiring any body or person to whom an appeal lies to consult prescribed persons with respect to the appeal in prescribed cases;

(*c*) for a person who contravenes, or fails to comply with, any prescribed provision of the regulations to be guilty of an offence;

(*d*) for a person guilty of an offence by virtue of paragraph (*c*) above which consists of the removal, in contravention of the regulations, of a hedgerow of a description prescribed for the purposes of this paragraph to be liable—

(i) on summary conviction, to a fine not exceeding the statutory maximum, or

(ii) on conviction on indictment, to a fine;

(*e*) for a person guilty of any other offence by virtue of paragraph (*c*) above to be liable on summary conviction to a fine not exceeding such level on the standard scale as may be prescribed.

(5) Regulations under this section may make different provision for different cases, including different provision in relation to different descriptions of hedgerow, different descriptions of person, different areas or localities or different circumstances.

(6) *Consultation before making any regulations.*

(7) No statutory instrument containing regulations under this section shall be made unless a draft of the instrument has been laid before, and approved by a resolution of, each House of Parliament.

(8) In this section—

"the appropriate Ministers" means—

(*a*) as respects England, the Secretary of State and the Minister of Agriculture, Fisheries and Food;

(*b*) as respects Wales, the Secretary of State;

"environmental conservation" means conservation—

(*a*) of the natural beauty or amenity, or flora or fauna, of England or Wales; or

(*b*) of features of archaeological or historic interest in England or Wales;

"hedgerow" includes any stretch of hedgerow;

"local authority" means—

(*a*) the council of a county, county borough, district, London borough, parish or community;

(*b*) the Common Council of the City of London;

(*c*) the Council of the Isles of Scilly;

"the planning Acts" has the same meaning as it has in the Town and Country Planning Act 1990 by virtue of section 336(1) of that Act;

"prescribed" means specified, or of a description specified, in regulations;

"regulations" means regulations made by statutory instrument;

"remove", in relation to a hedgerow, means uproot or otherwise destroy, and cognate expressions shall be construed accordingly;

"statutory functions" means functions conferred or imposed by or under any enactment.

(9) Any reference in this section to removing, or carrying out an act in relation to, a hedgerow

includes a reference to causing or permitting another to remove, or (as the case may be) carry out an act in relation to, a hedgerow.
[Environment Act 1995, s 97.]

1. The Hedgerows Regulations 1997, SI 1997/1160 amended by SI 2003/2155 have been made. Regulation 6(1)(j) of the 1997 regulations permits the removal of any hedgerow to which the regulations apply if it is required for the proper management of the hedgerow and this includes removal of the whole hedgerow if this is required although the regulations are silent as to whether there is a persuasive or evidential burden on the defendant to prove this: *Conway County Borough Council v Lloyd* [2003] EWHC 264 (Admin), 167 JP 223.

8–26681 98. Grants for purposes conducive to conservation[1]

1. The Countryside Stewardship Regulations 2000, SI 2000/3048 amended by SI 2001/3991 and SI 2004/114 and the Entry Level Agri-Environmental Scheme (Pilot) (England) Regulations 2003, SI 2003/838 have been made under this section.

Fisheries

8–26682 105. Minor and consequential amendments relating to fisheries. Schedule 15 to this Act (which makes minor and consequential amendments relating to fisheries) shall have effect.
[Environment Act 1995, s 105.]

Powers of entry

8–26683 108. Powers of enforcing authorities and persons authorised by them. (1) A person who appears suitable to an enforcing authority may be authorised in writing by that authority to exercise, in accordance with the terms of the authorisation, any of the powers specified in subsection (4) below for the purpose—

(*a*) of determining whether any provision of the pollution control enactments in the case of that authority is being, or has been, complied with;
(*b*) of exercising or performing one or more of the pollution control functions of that authority; or
(*c*) of determining whether and, if so, how such a function should be exercised or performed.

(2) A person who appears suitable to the Agency or SEPA may be authorised in writing by the Agency or, as the case may be, SEPA to exercise, in accordance with the terms of the authorisation, any of the powers specified in subsection (4) below for the purpose of enabling the Agency or, as the case may be, SEPA to carry out any assessment or prepare any report which the Agency or, as the case may be, SEPA is required to carry out or prepare under section 5(3) or 33(3) above.

(3) Subsection (2) above only applies where the Minister who required the assessment to be carried out, or the report to be prepared, has, whether at the time of making the requirement or at any later time, notified the Agency or, as the case may be, SEPA that the assessment or report appears to him to relate to an incident or possible incident involving or having the potential to involve—

(*a*) serious pollution of the environment,
(*b*) serious harm to human health, or
(*c*) danger to life or health.

(4) The powers which a person may be authorised to exercise under subsection (1) or (2) above are—

(*a*) to enter at any reasonable time (or, in an emergency, at any time and, if need be, by force) any premises which he has reason to believe it is necessary for him to enter;
(*b*) on entering any premises by virtue of paragraph (*a*) above, to take with him—
  (i) any other person duly authorised by the enforcing authority and, if the authorised person has reasonable cause to apprehend any serious obstruction in the execution of his duty, a constable; and
  (ii) any equipment or materials required for any purpose for which the power of entry is being exercised;
(*c*) to make such examination and investigation as may in any circumstances be necessary;
(*d*) as regards any premises which he has power to enter, to direct that those premises or any part of them, or anything in them, shall be left undisturbed (whether generally or in particular respects) for so long as is reasonably necessary for the purpose of any examination or investigation under paragraph (*c*) above;
(*e*) to take such measurements and photographs and make such recordings as he considers necessary for the purpose of any examination or investigation under paragraph (*c*) above;
(*f*) to take samples, or cause samples to be taken, of any articles or substances found in or on any premises which he has power to enter, and of the air, water or land in, on, or in the vicinity of, the premises;

(*g*) in the case of any article or substance found in or on any premises which he has power to enter, being an article or substance which appears to him to have caused or to be likely to cause pollution of the environment or harm to human health, to cause it to be dismantled or subjected to any process or test (but not so as to damage or destroy it, unless that is necessary);

(*h*) in the case of any such article or substance as is mentioned in paragraph (*g*) above, to take possession of it and detain it for so long as is necessary for all or any of the following purposes, namely—

(i) to examine it, or cause it to be examined, and to do, or cause to be done, to it anything which he has power to do under that paragraph;

(ii) to ensure that it is not tampered with before examination of it is completed;

(iii) to ensure that it is available for use as evidence in any proceedings for an offence under the pollution control enactments in the case of the enforcing authority under whose authorisation he acts or in any other proceedings relating to a variation notice, enforcement notice or prohibition notice under those enactments;

(*j*) to require any person whom he has reasonable cause to believe to be able to give any information relevant to any examination or investigation under paragraph (*c*) above to answer (in the absence of persons other than a person nominated by that person to be present and any persons whom the authorised person may allow to be present) such questions as the authorised person thinks fit to ask and to sign a declaration of the truth of his answers;

(*k*) to require the production of, or where the information is recorded in computerised form, the furnishing of extracts from, any records—

(i) which are required to be kept under the pollution control enactments for the enforcing authority under whose authorisation he acts, or

(ii) which it is necessary for him to see for the purposes of an examination or investigation under paragraph (*c*) above,

and to inspect and take copies of, or of any entry in, the records;

(*l*) to require any person to afford him such facilities and assistance with respect to any matters or things within that person's control or in relation to which that person has responsibilities as are necessary to enable the authorised person to exercise any of the powers conferred on him by this section;

(*m*) any other power for—

(i) a purpose falling within any paragraph of subsection (1) above, or

(ii) any such purpose as is mentioned in subsection (2) above,

which is conferred by regulations made by the Secretary of State.

(5) The powers which by virtue of subsections (1) and (4) above are conferred in relation to any premises for the purpose of enabling an enforcing authority to determine whether any provision of the pollution control enactments in the case of that authority is being, or has been, complied with shall include power, in order to obtain the information on which that determination may be made,—

(*a*) to carry out experimental borings or other works on those premises; and

(*b*) to install, keep or maintain monitoring and other apparatus there.

(6) Except in an emergency, in any case where it is proposed to enter any premises used for residential purposes, or to take heavy equipment on to any premises which are to be entered, any entry by virtue of this section shall only be effected—

(*a*) after the expiration of at least seven days' notice of the proposed entry given to a person who appears to the authorised person in question to be in occupation of the premises in question, and

(*b*) either—

(i) with the consent of a person who is in occupation of those premises; or

(ii) under the authority of a warrant by virtue of Schedule 18 to this Act.

(7) Except in an emergency, where an authorised person proposes to enter any premises and—

(*a*) entry has been refused and he apprehends on reasonable grounds that the use of force may be necessary to effect entry, or

(*b*) he apprehends on reasonable grounds that entry is likely to be refused and that the use of force may be necessary to effect entry,

any entry on to those premises by virtue of this section shall only be effected under the authority of a warrant by virtue of Schedule 18 to this Act.

(8) In relation to any premises belonging to or used for the purposes of the United Kingdom Atomic Energy Authority, subsections (1) to (4) above shall have effect subject to section 6(3) of the Atomic Energy Authority Act 1954 (which restricts entry to such premises where they have been declared to be prohibited places for the purposes of the Official Secrets Act 1911).

(9) The Secretary of State may by regulations make provision as to the procedure to be followed in connection with the taking of, and the dealing with, samples under subsection (4)(*f*) above.

(10) Where an authorised person proposes to exercise the power conferred by subsection (4)(*g*)

above in the case of an article or substance found on any premises, he shall, if so requested by a person who at the time is present on and has responsibilities in relation to those premises, cause anything which is to be done by virtue of that power to be done in the presence of that person.

(11) Before exercising the power conferred by subsection (4)(*g*) above in the case of any article or substance, an authorised person shall consult—

(*a*) such persons having duties on the premises where the article or substance is to be dismantled or subjected to the process or test, and

(*b*) such other persons,

as appear to him appropriate for the purpose of ascertaining what dangers, if any, there may be in doing anything which he proposes to do or cause to be done under the power.

(12) No answer given by a person in pursuance of a requirement imposed under subsection (4)(*j*) above shall be admissible in evidence in England and Wales against that person in any proceedings, or in Scotland against that person in any criminal proceedings.

(13) Nothing in this section shall be taken to compel the production by any person of a document of which he would on grounds of legal professional privilege be entitled to withhold production on an order for discovery in an action in the High Court or, in relation to Scotland, on an order for the production of documents in an action in the Court of Session.

(14) Schedule 18 to this Act shall have effect with respect to the powers of entry and related powers which are conferred by this section.

(15) In this section—

"authorised person" means a person authorised under subsection (1) or (2) above;

"emergency" means a case in which it appears to the authorised person in question—

(*a*) that there is an immediate risk of serious pollution of the environment or serious harm to human health, or

(*b*) that circumstances exist which are likely to endanger life or health,

and that immediate entry to any premises is necessary to verify the existence of that risk or those circumstances or to ascertain the cause of that risk or those circumstances or to effect a remedy;

"enforcing authority" means—

(*a*) the Secretary of State;

(*b*) the Agency;

(*ba*) a waste collection authority;

(*c*) SEPA; or

(*d*) a local enforcing authority;

"local enforcing authority" means—

(*a*) a local enforcing authority, within the meaning of Part I of the Environmental Protection Act 1990;*

(*b*) a local authority, within the meaning of Part IIA of that Act, in its capacity as an enforcing authority for the purposes of that Part;

(*c*) a local authority for the purposes of Part IV of this Act or regulations under that Part;

(*d*) a local authority for the purposes of regulations under section 2 of the Pollution Prevention and Control Act 1999 extending to England and Wales;

"mobile plant" means plant which is designed to move or to be moved whether on roads or otherwise;

"pollution control enactments", in relation to an enforcing authority, means the enactments and instruments relating to the pollution control functions of that authority;*

"pollution control functions", in relation to the Agency or SEPA, means the functions conferred or imposed on it by or under—

(*a*) the Alkali, &c, Works Regulations Act 1906;

(*b*) Part III of the Rivers (Prevention of Pollution) (Scotland) Act 1951;

(*c*) the Rivers (Prevention of Pollution) (Scotland) Act 1965;

(*d*) Part I of the Health and Safety at Work etc. Act 1974;

(*e*) Parts I, IA and II of the Control of Pollution Act 1974;

(*f*) the Control of Pollution (Amendment) Act 1989;

(*g*) Parts I*, II and IIA of the Environmental Protection Act 1990 (integrated pollution control, waste on land and contaminated land);

(*h*) Chapter III of Part IV of the Water Industry Act 1991 (special category effluent);

(*j*) Part III and section 161 to 161D of the Water Resources Act 1991;

(*k*) section 19 of the Clean Air Act 1993

(*l*) the Radioactive Substances Act 1993;

(*m*) regulations made by virtue of section 2(2) of the European Communities act 1972, to the extent that the regulations relate to pollution;

and, in relation to the Agency, includes the functions conferred or imposed on, or transferred to, it under section 2 of the Pollution Prevention and Control Act 1999;

"pollution control functions", in relation to a waste collection authority, means the functions conferred or imposed on it by or under Part 2 of the Environment Protection Act 1990;*

"pollution control functions", in relation to a local enforcing authority, means the functions conferred or imposed on, or transferred to, that authority—

(*a*) by or under Part I or IIA of the Environmental Protection Act 1990;
(*b*) by or under regulations made by virtue of Part IV of this Act; or
(*c*) by or under regulations made by virtue of section 2(2) of the European Communities Act 1972, to the extent that the regulations relate to pollution;

and, in relation to an authority in England or Wales, includes the functions conferred or imposed on, or transferred to, that authority under section 2of the Pollution Prevention and Control Act 1999;

"pollution control functions", in relation to the Secretary of State, means any functions which are conferred or imposed upon him by or under any enactment or instrument and which relate to the control of pollution;

"premises" includes any land, vehicle, vessel or mobile plant.

"waste collection authority" shall be construed in accordance with section 30(3)(*a*), (*b*) and (*bb*) of the Environmental Protection Act 1990.**

(16) Any power to make regulations under this section shall be exercisable by statutory instrument; and a statutory instrument containing any such regulations shall be subject to annulment pursuant to a resolution of either House of Parliament.

[Environment Act 1995, s 108, as amended by SI 2000/1973, the Anti-social Behaviour Act 2003, s 55 and the Clean Neighbourhoods and Environment Act 2005, s 53.]

***Reproduced as in force in England.**
****Section 108(15) is prospectively repealed by the Pollution Prevention and Control Act 1999, Sch 3**

8–26684 **109. Power to deal with cause of imminent danger of serious pollution etc.** (1) Where, in the case of any article or substance found by him on any premises which he has power to enter, an authorised person has reasonable cause to believe that, in the circumstances in which he finds it, the article or substance is a cause of imminent danger of serious pollution of the environment or serious harm to human health, he may seize it and cause it to be rendered harmless (whether by destruction or otherwise).

(2) As soon as may be after any article or substance has been seized and rendered harmless under this section, the authorised person shall prepare and sign a written report giving particulars of the circumstances in which the article or substance was seized and so dealt with by him, and shall—

(*a*) give a signed copy of the report to a responsible person at the premises where the article or substance was found by him; and
(*b*) unless that person is the owner of the article or substance, also serve a signed copy of the report on the owner;

and if, where paragraph (*b*) above applies, the authorised person cannot after reasonable inquiry ascertain the name or address of the owner, the copy may be served on him by giving it to the person to whom a copy was given under paragraph (*a*) above.

(3) In this section, "authorised person" has the same meaning as in section 108 above.

[Environment Act 1995, s 109.]

8–26685 **110. Offences.** (1) It is an offence for a person intentionally to obstruct an authorised person in the exercise or performance of his powers or duties.

(2) It is an offence for a person, without reasonable excuse,—

(*a*) to fail to comply with any requirement imposed under section 108 above;
(*b*) to fail or refuse to provide facilities or assistance or any information or to permit any inspection reasonably required by an authorised person in the execution of his powers or duties under or by virtue of that section; or
(*c*) to prevent any other person from appearing before an authorised person, or answering any question to which an authorised person may require an answer, pursuant to subsection (4) of that section.

(3) It is an offence for a person falsely to pretend to be an authorised person.

(4) A person guilty of an offence under subsection (1) above shall be liable—

(*a*) in the case of an offence of obstructing an authorised person in the execution of his powers under section 109 above[1]—
  (i) on summary conviction, to a fine not exceeding **the statutory maximum**;
  (ii) on conviction on indictment, to a **fine** or to imprisonment for a term not exceeding **two years**, or to **both**;
(*b*) in any other case, on summary conviction, to a fine not exceeding **level 5** on the standard scale.

(5) A person guilty of an offence under subsection (2) or (3) above shall be liable on summary conviction to a fine not exceeding **level 5** on the standard scale.

(6) In this section—

"authorised person" means a person authorised under section 108 above and includes a person designated under paragraph 2 of Schedule 18 to this Act;

"powers and duties" includes powers or duties exercisable by virtue of a warrant under Schedule 18 to this Act.

[Environment Act 1995, s 110.]

---

1. For procedure in respect of this offence which is triable either way, see the Magistrates' Courts Act 1980, ss 17A–21, in PART I: MAGISTRATES' COURTS, PROCEDURE, ante.

Evidence

8–26686 **111. Evidence in connection with certain pollution offences.** (1) *Repealed.*

(2) Information provided or obtained pursuant to or by virtue of a condition of a relevant licence (including information so provided or obtained, or recorded, by means of any apparatus) shall be admissible in evidence in any proceedings, whether against the person subject to the condition or any other person.

(3) For the purposes of subsection (2) above, apparatus shall be presumed in any proceedings to register or record accurately, unless the contrary is shown or the relevant licence otherwise provides.

(4) Where—

(*a*) by virtue of a condition of a relevant licence, an entry is required to be made in any record as to the observance of any condition of the relevant licence, and

(*b*) the entry has not been made,

that fact shall be admissible in any proceedings as evidence that that condition has not been observed.

(5) In this section—

"apparatus" includes any meter or other device for measuring, assessing, determining, recording or enabling to be recorded, the volume, temperature, radioactivity, rate, nature, origin, composition or effect of any substance, flow, discharge, emission, deposit or abstraction;

"condition of a relevant licence" includes any requirement to which a person is subject under, by virtue of or in consequence of a relevant licence;

"environmental licence" has the same meaning as it has in Part I above as it applies in relation to the Agency or SEPA, as the case may be;

"relevant licence" means—

(*a*) any environmental licence;

(*b*) any consent under Part II of the Sewerage (Scotland) Act 1968 to make discharges of trade effluent;

(*c*) any agreement under section 37 of that Act with respect to, or to any matter connected with, the reception, treatment or disposal of such effluent;

(6) In section 25 of the Environmental Protection Act, after subsection (2) (which makes similar provision to subsection (4) above) there shall be inserted—

"(3) Subsection (2) above shall not have effect in relation to any entry required to be made in any record by virtue of a condition of a relevant licence, within the meaning of section 111 of the Environment Act 1995 (which makes corresponding provision in relation to such licences)."*

[Environment Act 1995, s 111, as amended by the Statute Law (Repeals) Act 2004.]

***Section 111(6) is repealed by the Pollution Prevention and Control Act 1999, Sch 3, when in force.**

Information

8–26688 **113. Disclosure of information.** (1) Notwithstanding any prohibition or restriction imposed by or under any enactment or rule of law, information of any description may be disclosed—

(*a*) by a new Agency to a Minister of the Crown, the other new Agency or local enforcing authority,

(*b*) by a Minister of the Crown to a new Agency, another Minister of the Crown or a local enforcing authority, or

(*c*) by a local enforcing authority to a Minister of the Crown, a new Agency or another local enforcing authority,

for the purpose of facilitating the carrying out by either of the new Agencies of any of its functions, by any such Minister of any of his environmental functions or by any local enforcing authority of any of its relevant functions; and no person shall be subject to any civil or criminal liability in consequence of any disclosure made by virtue of this subsection.

(2) Nothing in this section shall authorise the disclosure to a local enforcing authority by a new Agency or another local enforcing authority of information—

(*a*) disclosure of which would, in the opinion of a Minister of the Crown, be contrary to the interests of national security; or

(*b*) which was obtained under or by virtue of the Statistics of Trade Act 1947 and which was disclosed to a new Agency or any of its officers by the Secretary of State.

(3) No information disclosed to any person under or by virtue of this section shall be disclosed by that person to any other person otherwise than in accordance with the provisions of this section, or any provision of any other enactment which authorises or requires the disclosure, if that information is information—

(*a*) which relates to a trade secret of any person or which otherwise is or might be commercially confidential in relation to any person; or

(*b*) whose disclosure otherwise than under or by virtue of this section would, in the opinion of a Minister of the Crown, be contrary to the interests of national security.

(4) Any authorisation by or under this section of the disclosure of information by or to any person shall also be taken to authorise the disclosure of that information by or, as the case may be, to any officer of his who is authorised by him to make the disclosure or, as the case may be, to receive the information.

(5) In this section—

"new Agency" means the Agency or SEPA;

"the environment" means all, or any, of the following media, namely, the air, water and land (and the medium of air includes the air within buildings and the air within other natural or man-made structures above or below ground);

"environmental functions", in relation to a Minister of the Crown, means any function of that Minister, whether conferred or imposed under or by virtue of any enactment or otherwise, relating to the environment; and

"local enforcing authority" means—

(*a*) any local authority within the meaning of Part IIA of the Environmental Protection Act 1990, and the "relevant functions" of such an authority are its functions under or by virtue of that Part;

(*aa*) in relation to England and Wales, any local authority within the meaning of the regulations under section 2 of the Pollution Prevention and Control Act 1999;

(*b*) any local authority within the meaning of Part IV of this Act, and the "relevant functions" of such an authority are its functions under or by virtue of that Part; or

(*c*) in relation to England, any county council for an area for which there are district councils, and the "relevant functions" of such a county council are its functions under or by virtue of Part IV of this Act; or

(*d*) in relation to England and Wales, any local enforcing authority within the meaning of section 1(7) of the Environmental Protection Act 1990, and the "relevant functions" of such an authority are its functions under or by virtue of Part I of that Act.*

[Environment Act 1995, s 113, as amended by the Pollution Prevention and Control Act 1999, Sch 2 and SI 2000/1973.]

***Section 113(5) is further amended by the Pollution Prevention and Control Act 1999, Sch 3, when in force.**

Crown application

8–26689 115. Application of this Act to the Crown. (1) Subject to the provisions of this section, this Act shall bind the Crown.

(2) Part III of this Act and any amendments, repeals and revocations made by other provisions of this Act (other than those made by Schedule 21, which shall bind the Crown) bind the Crown to the extent that the enactments to which they relate bind the Crown.

(3) No contravention by the Crown of any provision made by or under this Act shall make the Crown criminally liable; but the High Court or, in Scotland, the Court of Session may, on the application of the Agency or, in Scotland, SEPA, declare unlawful any act or omission of the Crown which constitutes such a contravention.

(4) Notwithstanding anything in subsection (3) above, any provision made by or under this Act shall apply to persons in the public service of the Crown as it applies to other persons.

(5) If the Secretary of State certifies that it appears to him, as respects any Crown premises and any powers of entry exercisable in relation to them specified in the certificate, that it is requisite or expedient that, in the interests of national security, the powers should not be exercisable in relation to those premises, those powers shall not be exercisable in relation to those premises; and in this subsection "Crown premises" means premises held or used by or on behalf of the Crown.

(6) Nothing in this section shall be taken as in any way affecting Her Majesty in her private capacity; and this subsection shall be construed as if section 38(3) of the Crown Proceedings Act 1947 (interpretation of references to Her Majesty in her private capacity) were contained in this Act.

[Environment Act 1995, s 115.]

Isles of Scilly

8–26691 **117.** *Application of this Act to the Isles of Scilly.*[1]

1. The Environment Act 1995 (Isles of Scilly) Order 1996, SI 1996/1030, which is made under s 117, gives the Environment Agency certain functions in the Isles of Scilly which it has in other parts of England and Wales.

8–26692 **118.** *Application of certain other enactments to the Isles of Scilly.*

Miscellaneous and supplemental

8–26693 **120. Minor and consequential amendments, transitional and transitory provisions, savings and repeals.** (1) The enactments mentioned in Schedule 22 to this Act shall have effect with the amendments there specified (being minor amendments and amendments consequential on provisions of this Act); and, without prejudice to any power conferred by any other provision of this Act, the Secretary of State and the Minister shall each have power by regulations to make such additional consequential amendments—

(*a*) of public general enactments passed before, or in the same Session as, this Act, and
(*b*) of subordinate legislation made before the passing of this Act,

as he considers necessary or expedient by reason of the coming into force of any provision of this Act.

(2) The transitional provisions, transitory provisions and savings contained in Schedule 23 to this Act shall have effect; but those provisions are without prejudice to sections 16 and 17 of the Interpretation Act 1978 (effect of repeals).

(3) The enactments mentioned in Schedule 24 to this Act (which include some that are spent or no longer of practical utility) are hereby repealed to the extent specified in the third column of that Schedule.

(4) The power to make regulations under subsection (1) above shall be exercisable by statutory instrument; and a statutory instrument containing any such regulations shall be subject to annulment in pursuance of a resolution of either House of Parliament.

(5) The power to make regulations under subsection (1) above includes power to make such incidental, supplemental, consequential and transitional provision as the Secretary of State or the Minister thinks necessary or expedient.

(6) In this section—

"the Minister" means the Minister of Agriculture, Fisheries and Food;
"subordinate legislation" has the same meaning as in the Interpretation Act 1978.
[Environment Act 1995, s 120.]

8–26694 **121. Local statutory provisions; consequential amendments etc.** (1) If it appears to the Secretary of State or the Minister to be appropriate to do so—

(*a*) for the purposes of, or in consequence of, the coming into force of any enactment contained in this Act; or
(*b*) in consequence of the effect or operation at any time after the transfer date of any such enactment or of anything done under any such enactment,

he may by order repeal, amend or re-enact (with or without modifications) any local statutory provision, including, in the case of an order by virtue of paragraph (*b*) above, a provision amended by virtue of paragraph (*a*) above.

(2) An order made by the Secretary of State or the Minister under subsection (1) above may—

(*a*) make provision applying generally in relation to local statutory provisions of a description specified in the order;
(*b*) make different provision for different cases, including different provision in relation to different persons, circumstances or localities;
(*c*) contain such supplemental, consequential and transitional provision as the Secretary of State or, as the case may be, the Minister considers appropriate; and
(*d*) in the case of an order made after the transfer date, require provision contained in the order to be treated as if it came into force on that date.

(3) The power under this section to repeal or amend a local statutory provision shall include power to modify the effect in relation to any local statutory provision of any provision of Schedule 23 to this Act.

(4) Nothing in any order under this section may abrogate or curtail the effect of so much of any local statutory provision as confers any right of way or confers on or preserves for the public—

(*a*) any right of enjoyment of air, exercise or recreation on land; or
(*b*) any right of access to land for the purposes of exercise or recreation.

(5) The power to make an order under subsection (1) above shall be exercisable by statutory instrument subject to annulment in pursuance of a resolution of either House of Parliament.

(6) The power to make an order under subsection (1) above shall be without prejudice to any power conferred by any other provision of this Act.

(7) In this section—

"local statutory provision" means—

(*a*) a provision of a local Act (including an Act confirming a provisional order);

(*b*) a provision of so much of any public general Act as has effect with respect to a particular area, with respect to particular persons or works or with respect to particular provisions falling within any paragraph of this definition;

(*c*) a provision of an instrument made under any provision falling within paragraph (*a*) or (*b*) above; or

(*d*) a provision of any other instrument which is in the nature of a local enactment;

"the Minister" means the Minister of Agriculture, Fisheries and Food;

"the transfer date" has the same meaning as in Part I of this Act.

[Environment Act 1995, s 121.]

8–26695 122. Directions. (1) Any direction given under this Act shall be in writing.

(2) Any power conferred by this Act to give a direction shall include power to vary or revoke the direction.

(3) Subsection (4) and (5) below apply to any direction given—

(*a*) to the Agency or SEPA under any provision of this Act or any other enactment, or

(*b*) to any other body or person under any provision of this Act,

being a direction to any extent so given for the purpose of implementing any obligations of the United Kingdom under the Community Treaties.

(4) A direction to which this subsection applies shall not be varied or revoked unless, notwithstanding the variation or revocation, the obligations mentioned in subsection (3) above, as they have effect for the time being, continue to be implemented, whether by directions or any other instrument or by any enactment.

(5) Any variation or revocation of a direction to which this subsection applies shall be published in such manner as the Minister giving it considers appropriate for the purpose of bring the matters to which it relates to the attention of persons likely to be affected by them; and—

(*a*) copies of the variation or revocation shall be made available to the public; and

(*b*) notice of the variation or revocation, and of where a copy of the variation or revocation may be obtained, shall be given—

(i) if the direction has effect in England and Wales, in the London Gazette;

(ii) if the direction has effect in Scotland, in the Edinburgh Gazette.

[Environment Act 1995, s 122.]

8–26696 123. Service of documents. (1) Without prejudice to paragraph 17(2)(*d*) of Schedule 7 to this Act, any notice required or authorised by or under this Act to be served (whether the expression "serve" or the expression "give" or "send" or any other expression is used) on any person may be served by delivering it to him, or by leaving it at his proper address, or by sending it by post to him at that address.

(2) Any such notice may—

(*a*) in the case of a body corporate, be served on the secretary or clerk of that body;

(*b*) in the case of a partnership, be served on a partner or a person having the control or management of the partnership business.

(3) For the purposes of this section and of section 7 of the Interpretation Act 1978 (service of documents by post) in its application to this section, the proper address of any person on whom any such notice is to be served shall be his last known address, except that—

(*a*) in the case of a body corporate or their secretary or clerk, it shall be the address of the registered or principal office of that body;

(*b*) in the case of a partnership or person having the control or the management of the partnership business, it shall be the principal office of the partnership;

and for the purposes of this subsection the principal office of a company registered outside the United Kingdom or of a partnership carrying on business outside the United Kingdom shall be their principal office within the United Kingdom.

(4) If the person to be served with any such notice has specified an address in the United Kingdom other than his proper address within the meaning of subsection (3) above as the one at which he or someone on his behalf will accept notices of the same description as that notice, that address shall also be treated for the purposes of this section and section 7 of the Interpretation Act 1978 as his proper address.

(5) Where under any provision of this Act any notice is required to be served on a person who is, or appears to be, in occupation of any premises then—

(*a*) if the name or address of such a person cannot after reasonable inquiry be ascertained, or (*b*) if the premises appear to be or are unoccupied,

that notice may be served either by leaving it in the hands of a person who is or appears to be resident or employed on the premises or by leaving it conspicuously affixed to some building or object on the premises.

(6) This section shall not apply to any notice in relation to the service of which provision is made by rules of court.

(7) The preceding provisions of this section shall apply to the service of a document as they apply to the service of a notice.

(8) In this section—

"premises" includes any land, vehicle, vessel or mobile plant;

"serve" shall be construed in accordance with subsection (1) above.

[Environment Act 1995, s 123.]

8–26697 **124. General interpretation.** (1) In this Act, except in so far as the context otherwise requires—

"the Agency" means the Environment Agency;

"financial year" means a period of twelve months ending with 31st March;

"functions" includes powers and duties;

"modifications" includes additions, alterations and omissions and cognate expressions shall be construed accordingly;

"notice" means notice in writing;

"records", without prejudice to the generality of the expression, includes computer records and any other records kept otherwise than in a document;

"SEPA" means the Scottish Environment Protection Agency.

(2) The amendment by this Act of any provision contained in subordinate legislation shall not be taken to have prejudiced any power to make further subordinate legislation amending or revoking that provision.

(3) In subsection (2) above, "subordinate legislation" has the same meaning as in the Interpretation Act 1978.

[Environment Act 1995, s 124.]

8–26698 **125. Short title, commencement, extent, etc.** (1) This Act may be cited as the Environment Act 1995.

(2) Part III of this Act, except for section 78, paragraph 7(2) of Schedule 7 and Schedule 10, shall come into force at the end of the period of two months beginning with the day on which this Act is passed.

(3) Except as provided in subsection (2) above and except for this section, section 74 above and paragraphs 76(8)(*a*) and 135 of Schedule 22 to this Act (which come into force on the passing of this Act) and the repeal of sub-paragraph (1) of paragraph 22 of Schedule 10 to this Act (which comes into force in accordance with sub-paragraph (7) of that paragraph) this Act shall come into force on such day as the Secretary of State may specify by order[1] made by statutory instrument; and different days may be so specified for different provisions or for different purposes of the same provision.

(4) Without prejudice to the provisions of Schedule 23 to this Act, an order under subsection (3) above may make such transitional provisions and savings as appear to the Secretary of State necessary or expedient in connection with any provision brought into force by the order.

(5) The power conferred by subsection (4) above includes power to modify any enactment contained in this or any other Act.

(6) An Order in Council under paragraph 1(1)(*b*) of Schedule 1 to the Northern Ireland Act 1974 (legislation for Northern Ireland in the interim period) which states that it is made only for purposes corresponding to those of section 98 of this Act—

(*a*) shall not be subject to paragraph 1(4) and (5) of that Schedule (affirmative resolution of both Houses of Parliament); but

(*b*) shall be subject to annulment in pursuance of a resolution of either House of Parliament.

(7) Except for this section and any amendment or repeal by this Act of any provision contained in—

(*a*) the Parliamentary Commissioner Act 1967,

(*b*) the Sea Fish (Conservation) Act 1967,

(*c*) the House of Commons Disqualification Act 1975, or

(*d*) the Northern Ireland Assembly Disqualification Act 1975,

this Act shall not extend to Northern Ireland.

(8) Part III of this Act, and Schedule 24 to this Act so far as relating to that Part, extends to England and Wales only.

(9) Section 106 of, and Schedule 16 to, this Act extend to Scotland only.

(10) Subject to the foregoing provisions of this section and to any express provision made by this

Act to the contrary, any amendment, repeal or revocation made by this Act shall have the same extent as the enactment or instrument to which it relates.
[Environment Act 1995, s 125.]

1. At the date of going to press the following commencement orders had been made: Environment Act 1995 (Commencement No 1) Order 1995, SI 1995/1983; Environment Act 1995 (Commencement No 2) Order 1995, SI 1995/2649; the Environment Act 1995 (Commencement No 3) Order 1995, SI 1995/2765, the Environment Act 1995 (Commencement No 4 and Saving Provisions) Order 1995, SI 1995/2950, the Environment Act 1995 (Commencement No 5) Order 1996, SI 1996/186, the Environment Act (Commencement No 6 and Repeal Provisions) Order 1996, SI 1996/2560, the Environment Act 1995 (Commencement No 7) (Scotland) Order 1996, SI 1996/2857, the Environment Act 1995 (Commencement No 8 and Saving Provisions) Order 1996, SI 1996/2909, the Environment Act 1995 (Commencement No 9 and Transitional Provisions) Order 1997, SI 1997/1626, the Environment Act 1995 (Commencement No 10) Order 1997, SI 1997/3044, the Environment Act 1995 (Commencement No 11) Order 1998, SI 1998/604, the Environment Act 1995 (Commencement No 12 and Transitional Provisions) (Scotland) Order 1998, SI 1998/781, the Environment Act 1995 (Commencement No 13) (Scotland) Order 1998, SI 1998/3272, the Environment Act 1995 (Commencement No 14) Order, SI 1999/803, the Environment Act 1995 (Commencement No 15) Order 1999, SI 1999/1301 the Environment Act 1995 (Commencement No 16 and Saving Provision) (England) Order 2000, SI 2000/340, the Environment Act 1995 (Commencement No 17) (Scotland) Order 2000, SSI 2000/180, the Environment Act 1995 (Commencement No 18) (England and Wales) Order 2000, SI 2000/3033, the Environment Act 1995 (Commencement No 16 and Saving Provision) (England) Order 2000, SI 2000/340; the Environment Act 1995 (Commencement No 17 and Savings Provision) (Scotland) Order 2000, SSI 2000/180, and the Environment Act 1995 (Commencement No 18) (England and Wales) Order 2000, SI 2000/3033;.

8–26698A 126. *Modes of exercise of certain functions*

SCHEDULES

Section 1

SCHEDULE 1
THE ENVIRONMENT AGENCY

8–26699 1–9. *Membership; staff; delegation of powers; members' interests and minutes.*

Application of seal and proof of instruments

8–26700 10. (1) The application of the seal of the Agency shall be authenticated by the signature of any member, officer or employee of the Agency who has been authorised for the purpose, whether generally or specially, by the Agency.

(2) In this paragraph the reference to the signature of a person includes a reference to a facsimile of a signature by whatever process reproduced; and, in paragraph 11 below, the word "signed" shall be construed accordingly.

Documents served etc by or on the Agency

8–26700A 11. (1) Any document which the Agency is authorised or required by or under any enactment to serve, make or issue may be signed on behalf of the Agency by any member, officer or employee of the Agency who has been authorised for the purpose, whether generally or specially, by the Agency.

(2) Every document purporting to be an instrument made or issued by or on behalf of the Agency and to be duly executed under the seal of the Agency, or to be signed or executed by a person authorised by the Agency for the purpose, shall be received in evidence and be treated, without further proof, as being so made or issued unless the contrary is shown.

(3) Any notice which is required or authorised, by or under any provision of any other Act, to be given, served or issued by, to or on the Agency shall be in writing.

Interpretation

8–26701 12. In this Schedule—

"the appropriate Minister", in relation to any person who is or has been a member, means the Minister or the Secretary of State, according to whether that person was appointed as a member by the Minister or by the Secretary of State; and

"member", except where the context otherwise requires, means any member of the Agency (including the chairman and deputy chairman).

Section 90

SCHEDULE 11
AIR QUALITY: SUPPLEMENTAL PROVISIONS

8–26711 1–4. *Consultation requirements; exchange of information with county councils in England; joint exercise of local authority functions; public access to information about air quality.*

Fixed penalty offences

8–26712 5. (1) Without prejudice to the generality of paragraph (*o*) of subsection (2) of section 87 of this Act, regulations may, in particular, make provision—

(*a*) for the qualifications, appointment or authorisation of persons who are to issue fixed penalty notices;

(*b*) for the offences in connection with which, the cases or circumstances in which, the time or period at or within which, or the manner in which fixed penalty notices may be issued;

(*c*) prohibiting the institution, before the expiration of the period for paying the fixed penalty, of proceedings against a person for an offence in connection with which a fixed penalty notice has been issued;

(*d*) prohibiting the conviction of a person for an offence in connection with which a fixed penalty notice has been issued if the fixed penalty is paid before the expiration of the period for paying it;

(*e*) entitling, in prescribed cases, a person to whom a fixed penalty notice is issued to give, within a prescribed period, notice requesting a hearing in respect of the offence to which the fixed penalty notice relates;

(*f*) for the amount of the fixed penalty to be increased by a prescribed amount in any case where the person liable to pay the fixed penalty fails to pay it before the expiration of the period for paying it, without having given notice requesting a hearing in respect of the offence to which the fixed penalty notice relates;

(*g*) for or in connection with the recovery of an unpaid fixed penalty as a fine or as a civil debt or as if it were a sum payable under a county court order;

(*h*) for or in connection with execution or other enforcement in respect of an unpaid fixed penalty by prescribed persons;

(*j*) for a fixed penalty notice, and any prescribed proceedings or other prescribed steps taken by reference to the notice, to be rendered void in prescribed cases where a person makes a prescribed statutory declaration, and for the consequences of any notice, proceedings or other steps being so rendered void (including extension of any time limit for instituting criminal proceedings);

(*k*) for or in connection with the extension, in prescribed cases or circumstances, by a prescribed person of the period for paying a fixed penalty;

(*l*) for or in connection with the withdrawal, in prescribed circumstances, of a fixed penalty notice, including—

(i) repayment of any amount paid by way of fixed penalty in pursuance of a fixed penalty notice which is withdrawn; and

(ii) prohibition of the institution or continuation of proceedings for the offence in connection with which the withdrawn notice was issued;

(*m*) for or in connection with the disposition of sums received by way of fixed penalty;

(*n*) for a certificate purporting to be signed by or on behalf of a prescribed person and stating either—

(i) that payment of a fixed penalty was, or (as the case may be) was not, received on or before a date specified in the certificate, or

(ii) that an envelope containing an amount sent by post in payment of a fixed penalty was marked as posted on a date specified in the certificate,

to be received as evidence of the matters so stated and to be treated, without further proof, as being so signed unless the contrary is shown;

(*o*) requiring a fixed penalty notice to give such reasonable particulars of the circumstances alleged to constitute the fixed penalty offence to which the notice relates as are necessary for giving reasonable information of the offence and to state—

(i) the monetary amount of the fixed penalty which may be paid;

(ii) the person to whom, and the address at which, the fixed penalty may be paid and any correspondence relating to the fixed penalty notice may be sent;

(iii) the method of methods by which payment of the fixed penalty may be made;

(iv) the period for paying the fixed penalty;

(v) the consequences of the fixed penalty not being paid before the expiration of that period;

(*p*) similar to any provision made by section 79 of the Road Traffic Offenders Act 1988 (statements by constables in fixed penalty cases);

(*q*) for presuming, in any proceedings, that any document of a prescribed description purporting to have been signed by a person to whom a fixed penalty notice has been issued has been signed by that person;

(*r*) requiring or authorising a fixed penalty notice to contain prescribed information relating to, or for the purpose of facilitating, the administration of the fixed penalty system;

(*s*) with respect to the giving of fixed penalty notices, including, in particular, provision with respect to—

(i) the methods by which,

(ii) the officers, servants or agents by, to or on whom, and

(iii) the places at which,

fixed penalty notices may be given by, or served on behalf of, a prescribed person;

(*t*) prescribing the method or methods by which fixed penalties may be paid;

(*u*) for or with respect to the issue of prescribed documents to persons to whom fixed penalty notices are or have been given;

(*w*) for a fixed penalty notice to be treated for prescribed purposes as if it were an information or summons or any other document of a prescribed description.

(2) The provision that may be made by regulations prescribing fixed penalty offences includes provision for an offence to be a fixed penalty offence—

(*a*) only if it is committed in such circumstances or manner as may be prescribed; or

(*b*) except if it is committed in such circumstances or manner as may be prescribed.

(3) Regulations may provide for any offence which is a fixed penalty offence to cease to be such an offence.

(4) An offence which, in consequence of regulations made by virtue of sub-paragraph (3) above, has ceased to be a fixed penalty offence shall be eligible to be prescribed as such an offence again.

(5) Regulations may make provision for such exceptions, limitations and conditions as the Secretary of State considers necessary or expedient.

(6) In this paragraph—

"fixed penalty" means a penalty of such amount as may be prescribed (whether by being specified in, or made calculable under, regulations);

"fixed penalty notice" means a notice offering a person an opportunity to discharge any liability to conviction for a fixed penalty offence by payment of a penalty of a prescribed amount;

"fixed penalty offence" means, subject to sub-paragraph (2) above, any offence (whether under or by virtue of this Part or any other enactment) which is for the time being prescribed as a fixed penalty offence;

"the fixed penalty system" means the system implementing regulations made under or by virtue of paragraph (*o*) of subsection (2) of section 87 of this Act;

"the period for paying", in relation to any fixed penalty, means such period as may be prescribed for the purpose;

"regulations" means regulations under or by virtue of paragraph (*o*) of subsection (2) of section 87 of this Act.

Section 105

SCHEDULE 15

MINOR AND CONSEQUENTIAL AMENDMENTS RELATING TO FISHERIES[1]

Interpretation

8–26713 **1.** In this Schedule—

"local statutory provision" means—

(*a*) a provision of a local Act (including an Act confirming a provisional order);

(*b*) a provision of so much of any public general Act as has effect with respect to particular persons or works or with respect to particular provisions falling within any paragraph of this definition;

(*c*) a provision of an instrument made under any provision falling within paragraph (*a*) or (*b*) above;

(*d*) a provision of any other instrument which is in the nature of a local enactment;

"the Minister" means the Minister of Agriculture, Fisheries and Food;

"subordinate legislation" has the same meaning as in the Interpretation Act 1978;

"the transfer date" has the same meaning as in Part I of this Act.

General modifications of references to the National Rivers Authority

8–26714 **2.** (1) Subject to—

(*a*) the following provisions of this Schedule,

(*b*) the provisions of sections 102 to 104 of this Act, and

(*c*) any repeal made by this Act,

any provision to which this paragraph applies which contains, or falls to be construed as containing, a reference (however framed and whether or not in relation to an area) to the National Rivers Authority shall have effect on and after the transfer date as if that reference were a reference to the Agency.

(2) Sub-paragraph (1) above is subject to paragraph 1(2)(*a*) of Schedule 17 to the Water Act 1989 (references in certain local statutory provisions or subordinate legislation to the area of a particular water authority to have effect as references to the area which, immediately before the transfer date within the meaning of that Act, was the area of that authority for the purposes of their functions relating to fisheries).

(3) Subject as mentioned in sub-paragraph (1) above, any provision to which this paragraph applies which contains, or falls to be construed as containing, a reference (however framed) to the whole area in relation to which the National Rivers Authority carries out its functions in relation to fisheries shall have effect on and after the transfer date as if that reference were a reference to the whole area in relation to which the Agency carries out its functions relating to fisheries.

(4) The provisions to which this paragraph applies are the provisions of—

(*a*) the Sea Fisheries Regulation Act 1966;

(*b*) the Salmon and Freshwater Fisheries Act 1975; and

(*c*) any local statutory provision or subordinate legislation which is in force immediately before the transfer date and—

(i) relates to the carrying out by the National Rivers Authority of any function relating to fisheries; or

(ii) in the case of subordinate legislation, was made by virtue of any provision to which this paragraph applies or under the Diseases of Fish Act 1937.

(5) The modifications made by this paragraph shall be subject to any power by subordinate legislation to revoke or amend any provision to which this paragraph applies; and, accordingly, any such power, including the powers conferred by section 121 of this Act and paragraph 3 below, shall be exercisable so as to exclude the operation of this paragraph in relation to the provisions in relation to which the power is conferred.

Power to amend subordinate legislation etc

8–26715 **3.** (1) If it appears to the Minister or the Secretary of State to be appropriate to do so for the purposes of, or in consequence of, the coming into force of any provision of this Schedule, he may by order revoke or amend any subordinate legislation.

(2) An order under this paragraph may—

(*a*) make different provision for different cases, including different provision in relation to different persons, circumstances or localities; and

(*b*) contain such supplemental, consequential and transitional provision as the Minister or the Secretary of State considers appropriate.

(3) The power conferred by virtue of this paragraph in relation to subordinate legislation made under any enactment shall be without prejudice to any other power to revoke or amend subordinate legislation made under that enactment, but—

(*a*) no requirement imposed with respect to the exercise of any such other power shall apply in relation to any revocation or amendment of that legislation by an order under this paragraph; and

(*b*) the power to make an order under this paragraph shall be exercisable (instead of in accordance with any such requirement) by statutory instrument subject to annulment in pursuance of a resolution of either House of Parliament.

Section 108

SCHEDULE 18

SUPPLEMENTAL PROVISIONS WITH RESPECT TO POWERS OF ENTRY

Interpretation

8–26717 **1.** (1) In this Schedule—

"designated person" means an authorised person, within the meaning of section 108 of this Act and includes a person designated by virtue of paragraph 2 below;

"relevant power" means a power conferred by section 108 of this Act, including a power exercisable by virtue of a warrant under this Schedule.

(2) Expressions used in this Schedule and in section 108 of this Act have the same meaning in this Schedule as they have in that section.

Issue of warrants

8–26718 **2.** (1) If it is shown to the satisfaction of a justice of the peace or, in Scotland, the sheriff or a justice of the peace, on sworn information in writing—

(*a*) that there are reasonable grounds for the exercise in relation to any premises of a relevant power; and

(*b*) that one or more of the conditions specified in sub-paragraph (2) below is fulfilled in relation to those premises,

the justice or sheriff may by warrant authorise an enforcing authority to designate a person who shall be authorised to exercise the power in relation to those premises, in accordance with the warrant and, if need be, by force.

(2) The conditions mentioned in sub-paragraph (1)(*b*) above are—

(*a*) that the exercise of the power in relation to the premises has been refused;

(*b*) that such a refusal is reasonably apprehended;

(*c*) that the premises are unoccupied;

(*d*) that the occupier is temporarily absent from the premises and the case is one of urgency; or

(*e*) that an application for admission to the premises would defeat the object of the proposed entry.

(3) In a case where subsection (6) of section 108 of this Act applies, a justice of the peace or sheriff shall not issue a warrant under this Schedule by virtue only of being satisfied that the exercise of a power in relation to any premises has been refused, or that a refusal is reasonably apprehended, unless he is also satisfied that the notice required by that subsection has been given and that the period of that notice has expired.

(4) Every warrant under this Schedule shall continue in force until the purposes for which the warrant was issued have been fulfilled.

Manner of exercise of powers

8–26719 **3.** A person designated as the person who may exercise a relevant power shall produce evidence of his designation and other authority before he exercises the power.

Information obtained to be admissible in evidence

8–26720 **4.** (1) Subject to section 108(12) of this Act, information obtained in consequence of the exercise of a relevant power, with or without the consent of any person, shall be admissible in evidence against that or any other person.

(2) Without prejudice to the generality of sub-paragraph (1) above, information obtained by means of monitoring or other apparatus installed on any premises in the exercise of a relevant power, with or without the consent of any person in occupation of the premises, shall be admissible in evidence in any proceedings against that or any other person.

Duty to secure premises

8–26721 **5.** A person who, in the exercise of a relevant power enters on any premises which are unoccupied or whose occupier is temporarily absent shall leave the premises as effectually secured against trespassers as he found them.

Compensation

8–26722 **6.** (1) Where any person exercises any power conferred by section 108(4)(*a*) or (*b*) or (5) of this Act, it shall be the duty of the enforcing authority under whose authorisation he acts to make full compensation to any person who has sustained loss or damage by reason of—

(*a*) the exercise by the designated person of that power; or

(*b*) the performance of, or failure of the designated person to perform, the duty imposed by paragraph 5 above.

(2) Compensation shall not be payable by virtue of sub-paragraph (1) above in respect of any loss or damage if the loss or damage—

(*a*) is attributable to the default of the person who sustained it; or

(*b*) is loss or damage in respect of which compensation is payable by virtue of any other provision of the pollution control enactments.

(3) Any dispute as to a person's entitlement to compensation under this paragraph, or as to the amount of any such compensation, shall be referred to the arbitration of a single arbitrator or, in Scotland, arbiter appointed by agreement between the enforcing authority in question and the person who claims to have sustained the loss or damage or, in default of agreement, by the Secretary of State.

(4) A designated person shall not be liable in any civil or criminal proceedings for anything done in the

purported exercise of any relevant power if the court is satisfied that the act was done in good faith and that there were reasonable grounds for doing it.

Section 120

SCHEDULE 22
Minor and Consequential Amendments

This Schedule is reproduced in an abridged form and contains only those enactments relevant to this work; only those consequential amendments which, at the date of going to press, had not been brought fully into force are reproduced here.

The Control of Pollution Act 1974

8–26723 **27.** In section 30 of that Act (interpretation of Part I) in subsection (1)—

(*a*) the following definition shall be inserted at the appropriate place—

""the appropriate Agency" means—

(*a*) in relation to England and Wales, the Environment Agency;
(*b*) in relation to Scotland, SEPA;";

(*b*) for the definition of "waste" there shall be substituted—

""waste" has the same meaning as it has in Part II of the Environmental Protection Act 1990 by virtue of section 75(2) of that Act;"; and

(*c*) the words from "and for the purposes" to the end (which provide a presumption that anything discarded is waste unless the contrary is proved) shall cease to have effect.

The Health and Safety at Work etc Act 1974

8–26724 **30.** (1) The Health and Safety at Work etc Act 1974 (in this paragraph referred to as "the 1974 Act") shall have effect in accordance with the following provisions of this paragraph.

(2) The appropriate new Agency shall, in consequence of the transfer effected by virtue of section 2(2)(*c*) or, as the case may be, 21(2)(*a*) of this Act, be regarded for the purposes of Part I of the 1974 Act as the authority which is, by any of the relevant statutory provisions, made responsible in relation to England and Wales or, as the case may be, Scotland for the enforcement of the relevant enactments (and accordingly, as the enforcing authority in relation to those enactments).

(3) Neither the Agency nor SEPA shall have power to appoint inspectors under section 19 of the 1974 Act.

(4) Sections 21 to 23 (improvement notices and prohibition notices) shall have effect in any case where the relevant statutory provision in question is any of the relevant enactments as if references in those sections to an inspector were references to the appropriate new Agency.

(5) Section 27 (obtaining of information by the Commission etc) shall have effect in relation to the appropriate new Agency, in its relevant capacity, as it has effect in relation to the Health and Safety Commission (and not as it has effect in relation to an enforcing authority), except that the consent of the Secretary of State shall not be required to the service by the appropriate new Agency of a notice under subsection (1) of that section; and, accordingly, where that section has effect by virtue of this sub-paragraph—

(*a*) any reference in that section to the Commission shall be construed as a reference to the appropriate new Agency;
(*b*) any reference to an enforcing authority shall be disregarded; and
(*c*) in subsection (3) of that section, the words from "and also" onwards shall be disregarded.

(6)–(7) *Amendment of sections 28 and 38 of the 1974 Act.*

(8) In this paragraph—

"the appropriate new Agency" means—

(*a*) in relation to England and Wales, the Agency; and
(*b*) in relation to Scotland, SEPA;

"relevant capacity", in relation to the appropriate new Agency, means its capacity as the enforcing authority, for the purposes of Part I of the 1974 Act, which is responsible in relation to England and Wales or, as the case may be, Scotland for the enforcement of the relevant enactments;

"the relevant enactments" means the Alkali, etc, Works Regulation Act 1906 and section 5 of the 1974 Act;

"the relevant statutory provisions" has the same meaning as in Part I of the 1974 Act.

The Environment Protection Act 1990

8–26725 **79.** Section 61 of that Act (duty of waste regulation authorities as respects closed landfills) shall cease to have effect.

81. In section 63 of that Act (waste other than controlled waste) for subsection (2) (offences relating to the deposit of waste which is not controlled waste but which, if it were such waste, would be special waste) there shall be substituted—

"(2) A person who deposits, or knowingly causes or knowingly permits the deposit of, any waste—

(*a*) which is not controlled waste, but
(*b*) which, if it were controlled waste, would be special waste,

in a case where he would be guilty of an offence under section 33 above if the waste were special waste and any waste management licence were not in force, shall, subject to subsection (3) below, be guilty of that offence and punishable as if the waste were special waste."

88. (1) Section 75 of that Act (meaning of "waste" etc.) shall be amended in accordance with the following provisions of this paragraph.

(2) For subsection (2) (definition of "waste") there shall be substituted—

"(2) "Waste" means any substance or object in the categories set out in Schedule 2B to this Act which the holder discards or intends or is required to discard; and for the purposes of this definition—

"holder" means the producer of the waste or the person who is in possession of it; and

"producer" means any person whose activities produce waste or any person who carries out pre-processing, mixing or other operations resulting in a change in the nature or composition of this waste."

(3) Subsection (3) (presumption that anything discarded is waste unless the contrary is proved) shall cease to have effect.

(4) After subsection (9) there shall be added—

"(10) Schedule 2B to this Act (which reproduces Annex I to the Waste Directive) shall have effect.

(11) Subsection (2) above is substituted, and Schedule 2B to this Act is inserted, for the purpose of assigning to "waste" in this Part the meaning which it has in the Waste Directive by virtue of paragraphs (*a*) to (*c*) of Article 1 of, and Annex I to, that Directive, and those provisions shall be construed accordingly.

(12) In this section "the Waste Directive" means the directive of the Council of the European Communities, dated 15th July 1975, on waste, as amended by—

(*a*) the directive of that Council, dated 18th March 1991, amending directive 75/442/EEC on waste; and

(*b*) the directive of that Council, dated 23rd December 1991, standardising and rationalising reports on the implementation of certain Directives relating to the environment."

89. (1) Section 79 of that Act (statutory nuisances) shall be amended in accordance with the following provisions of this paragraph.

(2) In subsection (1) (the paragraphs of which specify, subject to subsections (2) to (6A), the matters which constitute statutory nuisances) for the words "Subject to subsections (2) to (6A) below" there shall be substituted the words "Subject to subsections (1A) to (6A) below".

(3) After that subsection there shall be inserted—

"(1A) No matter shall constitute a statutory nuisance to the extent that it consists of, or is caused by, any land being in a contaminated state.

(1B) Land is in a "contaminated state" for the purposes of subsection (1A) above if, and only if, it is in such a condition, by reason of substances in, on or under the land, that—

(*a*) harm is being caused or there is a possibility of harm being caused; or

(*b*) pollution of controlled waters is being, or is likely to be, caused;

and in this subsection "harm", "pollution of controlled waters" and "substance" have the same meaning as in Part IIA of this Act.".

91. Section 143 of that Act (public registers of land which may be contaminated) shall cease to have effect.

92. In section 161 of that Act (regulations and orders) in subsection (4) (which specifies the orders under that Act which are not subject to negative resolution procedure under subsection (3)) after the words "does not apply to" there shall be inserted the words "a statutory instrument—

(*a*) which contains an order under section 78M(4) above, or

(*b*) by reason only that it contains".

95. After Schedule 2A to that Act there shall be inserted—

Section 75

"SCHEDULE 2B

CATEGORIES OF WASTE

1. Production or consumption residues not otherwise specified below.

2. Off-specification products.

3. Products whose date for appropriate use has expired.

4. Materials spilled, lost or having undergone other mishap, including any materials, equipment, etc, contaminated as a result of the mishap.

5. Materials contaminated or soiled as a result of planned actions (eg residues from cleaning operations, packing materials, containers, etc).

6. Unusable parts (e.g. reject batteries, exhausted catalysts, etc).

7. Substances which no longer perform satisfactorily (eg contaminated acids, contaminated solvents, exhausted tempering salts, etc).

8. Residues of industrial processes (eg slags, still bottoms, etc).

9. Residues from pollution abatement processes (e.g. scrubber sludges, baghouse dusts, spent filters, etc).

10. Machining or finishing residues (eg lathe turnings, mill scales, etc).

11. Residues from raw materials extraction and processing (e.g. mining residues, oil field slops, etc).

12. Adulterated materials (eg oils contaminated with PCBs, etc).

13. Any material, substances or products whose use has been banned by law.

14. Products for which the holder has no further use (eg agricultural, household, office, commercial and shop discards, etc).

15. Contaminated materials, substances or products resulting from remedial action with respect to land.

16. Any materials, substances or products which are not contained in the above categories."

Subordinate legislation and local statutory provisions

8–26726 **233.** (1) In any subordinate legislation or local statutory provisions, for any reference (however framed) to the National Rivers Authority, and for any reference which falls to be construed as such a reference, there shall be substituted a reference to the Agency.

(2) In any subordinate legislation, for any reference (however framed) to a relevant inspector, and for any reference which falls to be construed as such a reference, there shall be substituted a reference to the appropriate Agency.

(3) The provisions of this paragraph are subject to the other provisions of this Act and to any provision made under or by virtue of this Act.

(4) In this paragraph—

"the appropriate Agency" means—

(*a*) in relation to England and Wales, the Agency;
(*b*) in relation to Scotland, SEPA;

"local statutory provision" means—

(*a*) a provision of a local Act (including an Act confirming a provisional order);
(*b*) a provision of so much of any public general Act as has effect with respect to particular persons or works or with respect to particular provisions falling within any paragraph of this definition;
(*c*) a provision of an instrument made under any provision falling within paragraph (*a*) or (*b*) above;
(*d*) a provision of any other instrument which is in the nature of a local enactment;

"relevant inspector" means—

(i) the chief inspector for England and Wales constituted under section 16(3) of the Environmental Protection Act 1990;
(ii) the chief inspector for Scotland constituted under section 16(3) of that Act;
(iii) the chief inspector for England and Wales appointed under section 4(2)(*a*) of the Radioactive Substances Act 1993;
(iv) the chief inspector for Scotland appointed under section 4(2)(*b*) of that Act;
(v) the chief, or any other, inspector, within the meaning of the Alkali, &c, Works Regulation Act 1906;
(vi) an inspector appointed under section 19 of the Health and Safety at Work etc. Act 1974 by the Secretary of State in his capacity as the enforcing authority responsible for the enforcement of the Alkali, &c, Works Regulation Act 1906 or section 5 of the said Act of 1974;

"subordinate legislation" has the same meaning as in the Interpretation Act 1978.

8–26727

SCHEDULE 23

TRANSITIONAL AND TRANSITORY PROVISIONS AND SAVINGS

8–26728

Section 120

SCHEDULE 24

REPEALS AND REVOCATIONS

This Schedule is reproduced in an abridged form and contains only those repeals which are relevant to this work and which had not been brought into force at the date of going to press.

Reference	Short title or title	Extent of repeal or revocation
1974 c 40	The Control of Pollution Act 1974	In section 30(1), the words from "and for the purposes" to the end.
1975 c 51	The Salmon and Freshwater Fisheries Act 1975	In section 30, the paragraph defining "fish farm". In section 41(1), the definition of "grating".
1982 c 30	The Local Government (Miscellaneous Provisions) Act 1982	In section 33(9), in paragraph (*a*), the words from "or reconstituted" to "1972" and, in paragraph (*b*), the words "or reconstituted".
1983 c 35	The Litter Act 1983	In section 10, paragraph (*h*) of the definition of "litter authority" and the definitions of "National Park Committee" and "Park board".
1990 c 43	The Environmental Protection Act 1990	Section 61. In section 88, in subsection (9), paragraphs (*c*) and (*d*), and, in subsection (10), in the definition of "authorised officer", the words from "or in the case" to "on behalf of" and the definitions of "National Park Committee" and "Park board".

Dogs (Fouling of Land) Act 1996

(1996 c 20)

8–26729 **1. Land to which Act applies.** (1) Subject to subsections (2) to (4) below, this Act applies to any land which is open to the air and to which the public are entitled or permitted to have access (with or without payment).

(2) This Act does not apply to land comprised in or running alongside a highway which comprises a carriageway unless the driving of motor vehicles on the carriageway is subject, otherwise than temporarily, to a speed limit of 40 miles per hour or less.

(3) This Act does not apply to land of any of the following descriptions, namely—

(*a*) land used for agriculture or for woodlands;
(*b*) land which is predominantly marshland, moor or heath; and
(*c*) common land to which the public are entitled or permitted to have access otherwise than by virtue of section 193(1) of the Law of Property Act 1925 (right to access to urban common land).

(4) Where a private Act confers powers for the regulation of any land, the person entitled to

exercise those powers may, by notice in writing given to the local authority in whose area the land is situated, exclude the application of this Act to that land.

(5) For the purposes of this section, any land which is covered shall be treated as land which is "open to the air" if it is open to the air on at least one side.

(6) In this section—

"agriculture" includes horticulture, fruit growing, seed growing, dairy farming and livestock breeding and keeping, and the use of land as grazing land, meadow land, osier land, market gardens and nursery grounds;

"carriageway" has the same meaning as in the Highways Act 1980;

"common land" has the same meaning as in the Commons Registration Act 1965;

"speed limit" means a speed limit imposed or having effect as if imposed under the Road Traffic Regulation Act 1984[1].★

[Dogs (Fouling of Land) Act 1996, s 1.]

★Repealed by the Clean Neighbourhoods and Environment Act 2005, Sch 5 from a date to be appointed.

1. See PART VII: TRANSPORT, ante.

8–26730 **2. Designation of such land.** (1) A local authority may by order designate for the purposes of this Act any land in their area which is land to which this Act applies; and in this Act "designated land" means land to which this Act applies which is for the time being so designated.

(2) The power conferred by subsection (1) above includes power to designate land either specifically or by description, and to revoke or amend orders previously made.

(3) The Secretary of State shall by regulations[1] prescribe the form of orders under subsection (1) above, and the procedure to be followed in the making of such orders.

(4) Such regulations shall in particular include provision requiring local authorities to publicise the making and effect of such orders.★

[Dogs (Fouling of Land) Act 1996, s 2.]

★Repealed by the Clean Neighbourhoods and Environment Act 2005, Sch 5 from a date to be appointed.

1. The Dogs (Fouling of Land) Regulations 1996, SI 1996/2762, have been made.

8–26731 **3. Offence.** (1) If a dog defecates at any time on designated land and a person who is in charge of the dog at that time fails to remove the faeces from the land forthwith, that person shall be guilty of an offence unless—

(*a*) he has a reasonable excuse for failing to do so; or

(*b*) the owner, occupier or other person or authority having control of the land has consented (generally or specifically) to his failing to do so.

(2) A person who is guilty of an offence under this section shall be liable on summary conviction to a fine not exceeding **level 3** on the standard scale.

(3) Nothing in this section applies to a person registered as a blind person in a register compiled under section 29 of the National Assistance Act 1948.

(4) For the purposes of this section—

(*a*) a person who habitually has a dog in his possession shall be taken to be in charge of the dog at any time unless at that time some other person is in charge of the dog;

(*b*) placing the faeces in a receptacle on the land which is provided for the purpose, or for the disposal of waste, shall be a sufficient removal from the land; and

(*c*) being unaware of the defecation (whether by reason of not being in the vicinity or otherwise), or not having a device for or other suitable means of removing the faeces, shall not be a reasonable excuse for failing to remove the faeces.★

[Dogs (Fouling of Land) Act 1996, s 3.]

★Repealed by the Clean Neighbourhoods and Environment Act 2005, Sch 5 from a date to be appointed.

8–26732 **4. Fixed penalty notices.** (1) Where on any occasion an authorised officer of a local authority finds a person who he has reason to believe has on that occasion committed an offence under section 3 above in the area of that authority, he may give that person a notice offering him the opportunity of discharging any liability to conviction for that offence by payment of a fixed penalty.

(2) Subsections (2) to (8) of section 88 of the Environmental Protection Act 1990[1] shall apply for the purposes of this section as they apply for the purposes of that section but as if references to a litter authority were references to a local authority.

(3) In subsection (8) of that section as it applies for the purposes of this section "chief finance officer", in relation to a local authority, means the person having responsibility for the financial affairs of the authority.

(4) In this section "authorised officer", in relation to a local authority, means any employee of the authority who is authorised in writing by the authority for the purpose of issuing notices under this section.

(5) In subsection (4) above, the reference to any employee of the authority includes references to—

(*a*) any person by whom, in pursuance of arrangements made with the authority, any functions relating to the enforcement of this Act fall to be discharged; and

(*b*) any employee of any such person.*

[Dogs (Fouling of Land) Act 1996, s 4.]

***Repealed by the Clean Neighbourhoods and Environment Act 2005, Sch 5 from a date to be appointed.**

1. See this title ante. For the purposes of s 4 of the Dogs (Fouling of Land) Act 1996 (fixed penalty notices), for the amount of £25 specified as the amount of the fixed penalty in s 88(6) of the Environmental Protection Act 1990, the amount of amount of £50 is substituted by the Dog Fouling (Fixed Penalty) (England) Order 2002, SI 2002/425.

8–26733 **5. Orders and regulations by Secretary of State.** (1) Any power of the Secretary of State to make an order or regulations under this Act shall be exercisable by statutory instrument.

(2) A statutory instrument containing an order or regulations under this Act shall be subject to annulment in pursuance of a resolution of either House of Parliament.*

[Dogs (Fouling of Land) Act 1996, s 5.]

***Repealed by the Clean Neighbourhoods and Environment Act 2005, Sch 5 from a date to be appointed.**

8–26734 **6. Effect of Act on byelaws.** (1) Subsections (2) and (3) below apply to any byelaw made by a local authority which has the effect of making any person in charge of a dog guilty of an offence if—

(*a*) he permits the dog to defecate on any land; or

(*b*) in a case where the dog defecates on any land, he fails to remove the faeces from the land.

(2) In so far as any byelaw to which this subsection applies would, apart from this subsection, have effect in relation to any designated land, the byelaw—

(*a*) shall cease to have effect in relation to the land; or

(*b*) where it is made after the order under section 2(1) above, shall not have effect in relation to the land.

(3) In so far as any byelaw to which this subsection applies still has effect at the end of the period of 10 years beginning with the day on which this Act comes into force, it shall cease to have effect at the end of that period in relation to any land to which this Act applies.

(4) Where any omission would, apart from this subsection, constitute an offence both under section 3 above and under any byelaw other than one to which subsections (2) and (3) above apply, the omission shall not constitute an offence under the byelaw.*

[Dogs (Fouling of Land) Act 1996, s 6.]

***Repealed by the Clean Neighbourhoods and Environment Act 2005, Sch 5 from a date to be appointed.**

8–26735 **7. Interpretation.** (1) In this Act "local authority"—

(*a*) in relation to England, means any unitary authority or any district council so far as they are not a unitary authority; and

(*b*) in relation to Wales, means the council of any county or county borough.

(2) The following are unitary authorities for the purposes of subsection (1)(*a*) above, namely—

(*a*) any county council so far as they are the council for an area for which there are no district councils;

(*b*) the council of any district comprised in an area for which there is no county council;

(*c*) any London borough council;

(*d*) the Common Council of the City of London; and

(*e*) the Council of the Isles of Scilly.*

[Dogs (Fouling of Land) Act 1996, s 7.]

***Repealed by the Clean Neighbourhoods and Environment Act 2005, Sch 5 from a date to be appointed.**

8–26736 **8. Short title, commencement and extent.** (1) This Act may be cited as the Dogs (Fouling of Land) Act 1996.

(2) This Act shall come into force at the end of the period of two months beginning with the day on which it is passed[1].

(3) This Act extends to England and Wales only.*

[Dogs (Fouling of Land) Act 1996, s 8.]

***Repealed by the Clean Neighbourhoods and Environment Act 2005, Sch 5 from a date to be appointed.**

1. This Act was passed on 17 June 1996.

Noise Act 1996

(1996 c 37)

Summary procedure for dealing with noise at night

8–26737 **1. Application of sections 2 to 9.** Sections 2 to 9 apply to the area of every local authority in England and Wales.
[Noise Act 1996, s 1 as substituted by the Anti-social Behaviour Act 2003, s 42.]

8–26738 **2. Investigation of complaints of noise from a dwelling at night.** (1) A local authority may, if they receive a complaint of the kind mentioned in subsection (2), arrange for an officer of the authority to take reasonable steps to investigate the complaint.

(2) The kind of complaint referred to is one made by any individual present in a dwelling during night hours (referred to in this Act as "the complainant's dwelling" that excessive noise is being emitted from another dwelling (referred to in this group of sections as "the offending dwelling").*

(3) A complaint under subsection (2) may be made by any means.

(4) If an officer of the authority is satisfied, in consequence of an investigation under subsection (1), that—

(*a*) noise is being emitted from the offending dwelling during night hours, and*

(*b*) the noise, if it were measured from within the complainant's dwelling, would or might exceed the permitted level,

he may serve a notice about the noise under section 3.

(5) For the purposes of subsection (4), it is for the officer of the authority dealing with the particular case—

(*a*) to decide whether any noise, if it were measured from within the complainant's dwelling, would or might exceed the permitted level, and

(*b*) for the purposes of that decision, to decide whether to assess the noise from within or outside the complainant's dwelling and whether or not to use any device for measuring the noise.

(6) In this group of sections, "night hours" means the period beginning with 11 p.m. and ending with the following 7 a.m.

(7) Where a local authority receive a complaint under subsection (2) and the offending dwelling is within the area of another local authority, the first local authority may act under this group of sections as if the offending dwelling were within their area.*

(8) In this section and sections 3 to 9, "this group of sections" means this and those sections.
[Noise Act 1996, s 2 as amended by the Anti-social Behaviour Act 2003, s 42.]

***Subsections (2), (4) and (7) amended and new sub-s (7A) inserted by the Clean Neighbourhoods and Environment Act 2005, Sch 1, from a date to be appointed.**

8–26739 **3. Warning notices.** (1) A notice under this section (referred to in this Act as "a warning notice") must—

(*a*) state that an officer of the authority considers—

(i) that noise is being emitted from the offending dwelling during night hours, and*

(ii) that the noise exceeds, or may exceed, the permitted level, as measured from within the complainant's dwelling, and

(*b*) give warning that any person who is responsible for noise which is emitted from the dwelling, in the period specified in the notice, and exceeds the permitted level, as measured from within the complainant's dwelling, may be guilty of an offence.*

(2) The period specified in a warning notice must be a period—

(*a*) beginning not earlier than ten minutes after the time when the notice is served, and

(*b*) ending with the following 7 a.m.

(3) A warning notice must be served—

(*a*) by delivering it to any person present at or near the offending dwelling and appearing to the officer of the authority to be responsible for the noise, or

(*b*) if it is not reasonably practicable to identify any person present at or near the dwelling as being a person responsible for the noise on whom the notice may reasonably be served, by leaving it at the offending dwelling.*

(4) A warning notice must state the time at which it is served.

(5) For the purposes of this group of sections, a person is responsible for noise emitted from a dwelling if he is a person to whose act, default or sufferance the emission of the noise is wholly or partly attributable.*
[Noise Act 1996, s 3.]

***Subsections (1) and (3) amended and new sub-ss (3A) and (6) inserted by the Clean Neighbourhoods and Environment Act 2005, Sch 1, from a date to be appointed.**

8–26740 4. Offence where noise exceeds permitted level after service of notice*. (1) If a warning notice has been served in respect of noise emitted from a dwelling, any person who is responsible for noise which—

(*a*) is emitted from the dwelling in the period specified in the notice, and
(*b*) exceeds the permitted level, as measured from within the complainant's dwelling,

is guilty of an offence.

(2) It is a defence for a person charged with an offence under this section to show that there was a reasonable excuse for the act, default or sufferance in question.

(3) A person guilty of an offence under this section is liable on summary conviction to a fine not exceeding **level 3** on the standard scale[1].*

[Noise Act 1996, s 4.]

***Section heading amended and new s 4A inserted by the Clean Neighbourhoods and Environment Act 2005, Sch 1, from a date to be appointed.**

1. For power of the court to order forfeiture of any seized equipment used in the commission of the offence, see the Schedule to the Act, post.

8–26741 5. Permitted level of noise. (1)–(4) *Secretary of State may give directions as to permitted level of noise.*

[Noise Act 1996, s 5.]

8–26741A 6. *Approval of measuring devices.*

8–26742 7. Evidence. (1) In proceedings for an offence under section 4, evidence—*

(*a*) of a measurement of noise made by a device, or of the circumstances in which it was made, or
(*b*) that a device was of a type approved for the purposes of section 6, or that any conditions subject to which the approval was given were satisfied,

may be given by the production of a document mentioned in subsection (2).

(2) The document referred to is one which is signed by an officer of the local authority and which (as the case may be)—

(*a*) gives particulars of the measurement or of the circumstances in which it was made, or
(*b*) states that the device was of such a type or that, to the best of the knowledge and belief of the person making the statement, all such conditions were satisfied;

and if the document contains evidence of a measurement of noise it may consist partly of a record of the measurement produced automatically by a device.

(3) In proceedings for an offence under section 4, evidence that noise, or noise of any kind, measured by a device at any time was noise emitted from a dwelling may be given by the production of a document—

(*a*) signed by an officer of the local authority, and
(*b*) stating that he had identified that dwelling as the source at that time of the noise or, as the case may be, the noise of that kind.*

(4) For the purposes of this section, a document purporting to be signed as mentioned in subsection (2) or (3)(*a*) is to be treated as being so signed unless the contrary is proved.*

(5) This section does not make a document admissible as evidence in proceedings for an offence unless a copy of it has, not less than seven days before the hearing or trial, been served on the person charged with the offence.

(6) This section does not make a document admissible as evidence of anything other than the matters shown on a record produced automatically by a device if, not less than three days before the hearing or trial or within such further time as the court may in special circumstances allow, the person charged with the offence serves a notice on the prosecutor requiring attendance at the hearing or trial of the person who signed the document.

[Noise Act 1996, s 7.]

***Subsections (1) and (4) amended and new sub-s (3A) inserted by the Clean Neighbourhoods and Environment Act 2005, Sch 1, from a date to be appointed.**

8–26743 8. Fixed penalty notices. (1) Where an officer of a local authority who is authorised for the purposes of this section has reason to believe that a person is committing or has just committed an offence under section 4, he may give that person a notice (referred to in this Act as a "fixed penalty notice") offering him the opportunity of discharging any liability to conviction for that offence by payment of a fixed penalty.*

(2) A fixed penalty notice may be given to a person—

(*a*) by delivering the notice to him, or
(*b*) if it is not reasonably practicable to deliver it to him, by leaving the notice, addressed to him, at the offending dwelling.*

(3) Where a person is given a fixed penalty notice in respect of such an offence—
(*a*) proceedings for that offence must not be instituted before the end of the period of fourteen days following the date of the notice, and
(*b*) he cannot be convicted of that offence if he pays the fixed penalty before the end of that period.

(4) A fixed penalty notice must give such particulars of the circumstances alleged to constitute the offence as are necessary for giving reasonable information of the offence.

(5) A fixed penalty notice must state—
(*a*) the period during which, because of subsection (3)(*a*), proceedings will not be taken for the offence,
(*b*) the amount of the fixed penalty, and
(*c*) the person to whom and the address at which the fixed penalty may be paid.

(6) Payment of the fixed penalty may (among other methods) be made by pre-paying and posting to that person at that address a letter containing the amount of the penalty (in cash or otherwise).

(7) Where a letter containing the amount of the penalty is sent in accordance with subsection (6), payment is to be regarded as having been made at the time at which that letter would be delivered in the ordinary course of post.

(8) The fixed penalty payable under this section is £100.*
[Noise Act 1996, s 8.]

***Subsections (1) and (2) amended, sub-s (8) repealed and new ss 8A and 8B inserted by the Clean Neighbourhoods and Environment Act 2005, Sch 1, from a date to be appointed.**

8–26744 **9. Section 8: supplementary.** (1) If a form for a fixed penalty notice is specified in an order made by the Secretary of State, a fixed penalty notice must be in that form.*

(2) If a fixed penalty notice is given to a person in respect of noise emitted from a dwelling in any period specified in a warning notice—
(*a*) no further fixed penalty notice may be given to that person in respect of noise emitted from the dwelling during that period, but
(*b*) that person may be convicted of a further offence under section 4 in respect of noise emitted from the dwelling after the fixed penalty notice is given and before the end of that period.*

(3) The Secretary of State may from time to time by order amend section 8(8) so as to change the amount of the fixed penalty payable under that section.**

(4) A local authority may use any sums it receives under section 8 (its "penalty receipts") only for the purposes of functions of its that are qualifying functions.

(4A) The following are qualifying functions for the purposes of this section—
(*a*) functions under this Act, . . .
(*aa*) functions under Chapter 1 of Part 7 of the Clean Neighbourhoods and Environment Act 2005;
(*ab*) functions under sections 79 to 82 of the Environmental Protection Act 1990 (statutory nuisances) in connection with statutory nuisances falling with section 79(1)(*g*) or (*ga*) (noise) of that Act;
(*b*) functions of a description specified in regulations made by the Secretary of State.*

(4B) Regulations under subsection (4A)(*b*) may (in particular) have the effect that a local authority may use its penalty receipts for the purposes of any of its functions.

(4C) A local authority must supply the Secretary of State with such information relating to the use of its penalty receipts as the Secretary of State may require.*

(4D) The Secretary of State may by regulations—*
(*a*) make provision for what a local authority is to do with its penalty receipts—
(i) pending their being used for the purposes of qualifying functions of the authority;
(ii) if they are not so used before such time after their receipt as may be specified by the regulations;
(*b*) make provision for accounting arrangements in respect of a local authority's penalty receipts.

(4E) The provision that may be made under subsection (4D)(*a*)(ii) includes (in particular) provision for the payment of sums to a person (including the Secretary of State) other than the local authority.*

(4F) Before making regulations under this section, the Secretary of State must consult—
(a) the local authorities to which the regulations are to apply, and
(b) such other persons as the Secretary of State considers appropriate.*

(5) In proceedings for an offence under section 4, evidence that payment of a fixed penalty was or was not made before the end of any period may be given by the production of a certificate which—

(*a*) purports to be signed by or on behalf of the person having responsibility for the financial affairs of the local authority, and

(*b*) states that payment of a fixed penalty was made on any date or, as the case may be, was not received before the end of that period.*

[Noise Act 1996, s 9 as amended by the Anti-social Behaviour Act 2003, s 42 and the Clean Neighbourhoods and Environment Act 2005, Sch 5.]

***Subsections amended and new sub-ss (4G) and (4H) inserted by the Clean Neighbourhoods and Environment Act 2005, Sch 1 from a date to be appointed.**

Seizure, etc of equipment used to make noise unlawfully

8–26745 **10. Powers of entry and seizure etc.** (1) The power conferred by subsection (2) may be exercised where an officer of a local authority has reason to believe that—

(*a*) a warning notice has been served in respect of noise emitted from a dwelling, and

(*b*) at any time in the period specified in the notice, noise emitted from the dwelling has exceeded the permitted level, as measured from within the complainant's dwelling.*

(2) An officer of the local authority, or a person authorised by the authority for the purpose, may enter the dwelling from which the noise in question is being or has been emitted and may seize and remove any equipment which it appears to him is being or has been used in the emission of the noise.*

(3) A person exercising the power conferred by subsection (2) must produce his authority, if he is required to do so.

(4) If it is shown to a justice of the peace on sworn information in writing that—

(*a*) a warning notice has been served in respect of noise emitted from a dwelling,

(*b*) at any time in the period specified in the notice, noise emitted from the dwelling has exceeded the permitted level, as measured from within the complainant's dwelling, and

(*c*) entry of an officer of the local authority, or of a person authorised by the authority for the purpose, to the dwelling has been refused, or such a refusal is apprehended, or a request by an officer of the authority, or of such a person, for admission would defeat the object of the entry,

the justice may by warrant under his hand authorise the local authority, by any of their officers or any person authorised by them for the purpose, to enter the premises, if need be by force.*

(5) A person who enters any premises under subsection (2), or by virtue of a warrant issued under subsection (4), may take with him such other persons and such equipment as may be necessary; and if, when he leaves, the premises are unoccupied, must leave them as effectively secured against trespassers as he found them.*

(6) A warrant issued under subsection (4) continues in force until the purpose for which the entry is required has been satisfied.

(7) The power of a local authority under section 81(3) of the Environmental Protection Act 1990[1] to abate any matter, where that matter is a statutory nuisance by virtue of section 79(1)(*g*) of that Act (noise emitted from premises so as to be prejudicial to health or a nuisance), includes power to seize and remove any equipment which it appears to the authority is being or has been used in the emission of the noise in question.

(8) A person who wilfully obstructs any person exercising any powers conferred under subsection (2) or by virtue of subsection (7) is liable, on summary conviction, to a fine not exceeding **level 3** on the standard scale.

(9) The Schedule to this Act (which makes further provision in relation to anything seized and removed by virtue of this section) has effect.

[Noise Act 1996, s 10.]

***Subsections (1). (2), (4) and (5) amended by the Clean Neighbourhoods and Environment Act 2005, Sch 1 from a date to be appointed.**

1. In this title, ante.

General

8–26746 **11. Interpretation and subordinate legislation.** (1) In this Act, "local authority" means—

(*a*) in Greater London, a London borough council, the Common Council of the City of London and, as respects the Temples, the Sub-Treasurer of the Inner Temple and the Under-Treasurer of the Middle Temple respectively,

(*b*) outside Greater London—

(i) any district council,

(ii) the council of any county so far as they are the council for any area for which there are no district councils,

(iii) in Wales, the council of a county borough, and

(*c*) the Council of the Isles of Scilly.

(2) In this Act—

(*a*) "dwelling" means any building, or part of a building, used or intended to be used as a dwelling,

(*b*) references to noise emitted from a dwelling include noise emitted from any garden, yard, outhouse or other appurtenance belonging to or enjoyed with the dwelling.

(2A) In this Act "appropriate person" means—

(a) the Secreatry of State, in relation to England;

(*b*) the National Assembly for Wales, in relation to Wales.

(3) The power to make an order or regulations under this Act is exercisable by statutory instrument which (except in the case of an order under section 14 or an order or regulations made solely by the National Assembly for Wales) shall be subject to annulment in pursuance of a resolution of either House of Parliament.*

[Noise Act 1996, s 11 as amended by the Anti-social Behaviour Act 2003, s 42 and the Clean Neighbourhoods and Environment Act 2005, s 85.]

8–26747 12. *Protection from personal liability.*

8–26748 13. *Expenses.*

8–26749 14. Short title, commencement and extent. (1) This Act may be cited as the Noise Act 1996.

(2) This Act is to come into force on such day as the Secretary of State may by order appoint, and different days may be appointed for different purposes[1].

(3) This Act does not extend to Scotland.

(4) *Northern Ireland.*

---

1. This Act was brought into force by the following commencement orders: Commencement (No 1) Order 1996, SI 1996/2219 and Commencement (No 2) Order 1997, SI 1997/1695.

SCHEDULE
POWERS IN RELATION TO SEIZED EQUIPMENT

Introductory

8–26750 1. In this Schedule—

(*a*) a "noise offence" means—

(i) in relation to equipment seized under section 10(2) of this Act, an offence under section 4 of this Act, and*

(ii) in relation to equipment seized under section 81(3) of the Environmental Protection Act 1990 (as extended by section 10(7) of this Act), an offence under section 80(4) of that Act in respect of a statutory nuisance falling within section 79(1)(*g*) of that Act,

(*b*) "seized equipment" means equipment seized in the exercise of the power of seizure and removal conferred by section 10(2) of this Act or section 81(3) of the Environmental Protection Act 1990 (as so extended),

(*c*) "related equipment", in relation to any conviction of or proceedings for a noise offence, means seized equipment used or alleged to have been used in the commission of the offence,

(*d*) "responsible local authority", in relation to seized equipment, means the local authority by or on whose behalf the equipment was seized.

***Amended by the Clean Neighbourhoods and Environment Act 2005, Sch 1 from a date to be appointed.**

Retention

8–26751 2. (1) Any seized equipment may be retained—

(*a*) during the period of twenty-eight days beginning with the seizure, or

(*b*) if it is related equipment in proceedings for a noise offence instituted within that period against any person, until—

(i) he is sentenced or otherwise dealt with for the offence or acquitted of the offence, or

(ii) the proceedings are discontinued.

(2) Sub-paragraph (1) does not authorise the retention of seized equipment if—

(*a*) a person has been given a fixed penalty notice under section 8 of this Act in respect of any noise, (*b*) the equipment was seized because of its use in the emission of the noise in respect of which the fixed penalty notice was given, and

(*c*) that person has paid the fixed penalty before the end of the period allowed for its payment.

Forfeiture

8-26752 **3.** (1) Where a person is convicted of a noise offence the court may make an order ("a forfeiture order") for forfeiture of any related equipment.

(2) The court may make a forfeiture order whether or not it also deals with the offender in respect of the offence in any other way and without regard to any restrictions on forfeiture in any enactment.

(3) In considering whether to make a forfeiture order in respect of any equipment a court must have regard—

(*a*) to the value of the equipment, and

(*b*) to the likely financial and other effects on the offender of the making of the order (taken together with any other order that the court contemplates making).

(4) A forfeiture order operates to deprive the offender of any rights in the equipment to which it relates.

Consequences of forfeiture

8-26753 **4.** (1) Where any equipment has been forfeited under paragraph 3, a magistrates' court may, on application by a claimant of the equipment (other than the person in whose case the forfeiture order was made) make an order for delivery of the equipment to the applicant if it appears to the court that he is the owner of the equipment.

(2) No application may be made under sub-paragraph (1) by any claimant of the equipment after the expiry of the period of six months beginning with the date on which a forfeiture order was made in respect of the equipment.

(3) Such an application cannot succeed unless the claimant satisfies the court—

(*a*) that he had not consented to the offender having possession of the equipment, or

(*b*) that he did not know, and had no reason to suspect, that the equipment was likely to be used in the commission of a noise offence.

(4) Where the responsible local authority is of the opinion that the person in whose case the forfeiture order was made is not the owner of the equipment, it must take reasonable steps to bring to the attention of persons who may be entitled to do so their right to make an application under sub-paragraph (1).

(5) An order under sub-paragraph (1) does not affect the right of any person to take, within the period of six months beginning with the date of the order, proceedings for the recovery of the equipment from the person in possession of it in pursuance of the order, but the right ceases on the expiry of that period.

(6) If on the expiry of the period of six months beginning with the date on which a forfeiture order was made in respect of the equipment no order has been made under sub-paragraph (1), the responsible local authority may dispose of the equipment.

Return etc of seized equipment

8-26754 **5.** If in proceedings for a noise offence no order for forfeiture of related equipment is made, the court (whether or not a person is convicted of the offence) may give such directions as to the return, retention or disposal of the equipment by the responsible local authority as it thinks fit.

6. (1) Where in the case of any seized equipment no proceedings in which it is related equipment are begun within the period mentioned in paragraph 2(1)(*a*)—

(*a*) the responsible local authority must return the equipment to any person who—

(i) appears to them to be the owner of the equipment, and

(ii) makes a claim for the return of the equipment within the period mentioned in sub-paragraph (2), and

(*b*) if no such person makes such a claim within that period, the responsible local authority may dispose of the equipment.

(2) The period referred to in sub-paragraph (1)(*a*)(ii) is the period of six months beginning with the expiry of the period mentioned in paragraph 2(1)(*a*).

(3) The responsible local authority must take reasonable steps to bring to the attention of persons who may be entitled to do so their right to make such a claim.

(4) Subject to sub-paragraph (6), the responsible local authority is not required to return any seized equipment under sub-paragraph (1)(*a*) until the person making the claim has paid any such reasonable charges for the seizure, removal and retention of the equipment as the authority may demand.

(5) If—

(*a*) equipment is sold in pursuance of—

(i) paragraph 4(6),

(ii) directions under paragraph 5, or

(iii) this paragraph, and

(*b*) before the expiration of the period of one year beginning with the date on which the equipment is sold any person satisfies the responsible local authority that at the time of its sale he was the owner of the equipment,

the authority is to pay him any sum by which any proceeds of sale exceed any such reasonable charges for the seizure, removal or retention of the equipment as the authority may demand.

(6) The responsible local authority cannot demand charges from any person under sub-paragraph (4) or (5) who they are satisfied did not know, and had no reason to suspect, that the equipment was likely to be used in the emission of noise exceeding the level determined under section 5.

Party Wall etc Act 1996[1]

(1996 c 40)

Rights etc

8–26755 **8. Rights of entry.** (1) A building owner[2], his servants, agents and workmen may during usual working hours enter and remain on any land or premises for the purpose of executing any work in pursuance of this Act and may remove any furniture or fittings or take any other action necessary for that purpose.

(2) If the premises are closed, the building owner, his agents and workmen may, if accompanied by a constable or other police officer, break open any fences or doors in order to enter the premises.

(3) No land or premises may be entered by any person under subsection (1) unless the building owner serves on the owner and the occupier of the land or premises—

(*a*) in case of emergency, such notice[3] of the intention to enter as may be reasonably practicable;
(*b*) in any other case, such notice[3] of the intention to enter as complies with subsection (4).

(4) Notice complies with this subsection if it is served in a period of not less than fourteen days ending with the day of the proposed entry.

(5) A surveyor appointed or selected under section 10[4] may during usual working hours enter and remain on any land or premises for the purpose of carrying out the object for which he is appointed or selected.

(6) No land or premises may be entered by a surveyor under subsection (5) unless the building owner who is a party to the dispute concerned serves on the owner and the occupier of the land or premises—

(*a*) in case of emergency, such notice of the intention to enter as may be reasonably practicable;
(*b*) in any other case, such notice of the intention to enter as complies with subsection (4).

[Party Wall etc Act 1996, s 8.]

1. This Act makes provision for the construction and repair of walls on the line of the junction of lands of different owners (ss 1-2). Before construction or repair, notices must be served and provision is made for adjacent excavation and construction and compensation (ss 3-7).
2. "Building owner" means an owner of land who is desirous of exercising rights under this Act (s 20).
   "Owner" includes—
   (*a*) a person in receipt of, or entitled to receive, the whole or part of the rents or profits of land;
   (*b*) a person in possession of land, otherwise than as a mortgagee or as a tenant from year to year or for a lesser term or as a tenant at will;
   (*c*) a purchaser of an interest in land under a contract for purchase or under an agreement for a lease, otherwise than under an agreement for a tenancy from year to year or for a lesser term (s 20).
3. As to service of notice see s 15, post.
4. Section 10 relates to the appointment of surveyors to resolve disputes under the Act.

Miscellaneous

8–26756 **15. Service of notices etc.** (1) A notice or other document required or authorised to be served under this Act may be served on a person—

(*a*) by delivering it to him in person;
(*b*) by sending it by post to him at his usual or last-known residence or place of business in the United Kingdom; or
(*c*) in the case of a body corporate, by delivering it to the secretary or clerk of the body corporate at its registered or principal office or sending it by post to the secretary or clerk of that body corporate at that office.

(2) In the case of a notice or other document required or authorised to be served under this Act on a person as owner of premises, it may alternatively be served by—

(*a*) addressing it "the owner" of the premises (naming them), and
(*b*) delivering it to a person on the premises or, if no person to whom it can be delivered is found there, fixing it to a conspicuous part of the premises.

[Party Wall etc Act 1996, s 15.]

8–26757 **16. Offences.** (1) If—

(*a*) an occupier of land or premises refuses to permit a person to do anything which he is entitled to do with regard to the land or premises under section 8(1) or (5); and
(*b*) the occupier knows or has reasonable cause to believe that the person is so entitled,

the occupier is guilty of an offence.

(2) If—

(*a*) a person hinders or obstructs a person in attempting to do anything which he is entitled to do with regard to land or premises under section 8(1) or (5); and
(*b*) the first-mentioned person knows or has reasonable cause to believe that the other person is so entitled,

the first-mentioned person is guilty of an offence.

(3) A person guilty of an offence under subsection (1) or (2) is liable on summary conviction to a fine of an amount not exceeding **level 3** on the standard scale.
[Party Wall etc Act 1996, s 16.]

8–26758 18. Exception in case of Temples etc. (1) This Act shall not apply to land which is situated in inner London and in which there is an interest belonging to—

(*a*) the Honourable Society of the Inner Temple,
(*b*) the Honourable Society of the Middle Temple,
(*c*) the Honourable Society of Lincoln's Inn, or
(*d*) the Honourable Society of Gray's Inn.

(2) The reference in subsection (1) to inner London is to Greater London other than the outer London boroughs.
[Party Wall etc Act 1996, s 18.]

8–26759 19. The Crown. (1) This Act shall apply to land in which there is—

(*a*) an interest belonging to Her Majesty in right of the Crown,
(*b*) an interest belonging to a government department, or
(*c*) an interest held in trust for Her Majesty for the purposes of any such department.

(2) This Act shall apply to—

(*a*) land which is vested in, but not occupied by, Her Majesty in right of the Duchy of Lancaster;
(*b*) land which is vested in, but not occupied by, the possessor for the time being of the Duchy of Cornwall.

[Party Wall etc Act 1996, s 19.]

8–26760 20. *Interpretation.*

8–26761 21. *Other statutory provisions.*

General

8–26762 22. Short title, commencement and extent. (1) This Act may be cited as the Party Wall etc Act 1996.

(2) This Act shall come into force in accordance with provision made by the Secretary of State by order[1] made by statutory instrument.

(3) An order under subsection (2) may—

(*a*) contain such savings or transitional provisions as the Secretary of State thinks fit;
(*b*) make different provision for different purposes.

(4) This Act extends to England and Wales only.
[Party Wall etc Act 1996, s 22.]

1. The Party Wall etc Act 1996 (Commencement) Order 1997, SI 1997/670 has been made.

Pollution Prevention and Control Act 1999[1]

(1999 c 24)

8–26763 1. General purpose of section 2 and definitions. (1) The purpose of section 2 is to enable provision to be made for or in connection with—

(*a*) implementing Council Directive 96/61/EC concerning integrated pollution prevention and control;
(*b*) regulating, otherwise than in pursuance of that Directive, activities which are capable of causing any environmental pollution;
(*c*) otherwise preventing or controlling emissions capable of causing any such pollution.

(2) In this Act—

"activities" means activities of any nature, whether—

(*a*) industrial or commercial or other activities, or
(*b*) carried on on particular premises or otherwise,

and includes (with or without other activities) the depositing, keeping or disposal of any substance;

"environmental pollution" means pollution of the air, water or land which may give rise to any harm; and for the purposes of this definition (but without prejudice to its generality)—

(*a*) "pollution" includes pollution caused by noise, heat or vibrations or any other kind of release of energy, and

(*b*) "air" includes air within buildings and air within other natural or man-made structures above or below ground.

(3) In the definition of "environmental pollution" in subsection (2), "harm" means—

(*a*) harm to the health of human beings or other living organisms;

(*b*) harm to the quality of the environment, including—

(i) harm to the quality of the environment taken as a whole,

(ii) harm to the quality of the air, water or land, and

(iii) other impairment of, or interference with, the ecological systems of which any living organisms form part;

(*c*) offence to the senses of human beings;

(*d*) damage to property; or

(*e*) impairment of, or interference with, amenities or other legitimate uses of the environment (expressions used in this paragraph having the same meaning as in Council Directive 96/61/ EC).

[Pollution Prevention and Control Act 1999, s 1.]

---

1. This Act came into force on 27 July 1999 except for s 6 and Schs 2 and 3 (Consequential and minor amendments and repeals) which are to come into force no such day as may be appointed by the Secretary of State. At the date of going to press the following commencement order had been made: Commencement No 1, SI 2000/800 bringing into effect s 6(1) and Sch 2.

8–26764 2. *Regulation of polluting activities*[1]

---

1. See the Pollution Prevention and Control (England and Wales) Regulations 2000, in this title, post. The following Pollution Prevention and Control Regulations have been made:

Combustion Installations (Prevention and Control of Pollution) Regulations 2001, SI 2001/1091;
Offshore Chemicals Regulations 2002, SI 2002/1355;
Landfill (England and Wales) Regulations 2002, SI 2002/1559 amended by SI 2004/1375 and SI 2005/894, 895, 1640, 1806 (W) and 1820 (W);
Foot-and-Mouth Disease (Air Curtain Incinerators) (England and Wales) Regulations 2001, SI 2001/1623;
Offshore Installations (Emergency Pollution Control) Regulations 2002, SI 2002/1861;
Large Combustion Plants (England and Wales) Regulations 2002, SI 2002/2688;
Waste Incineration (England and Wales) Regulations 2002, SI 2002/2980;
Solvent Emissions (England and Wales) Regulations 2004, SI 2004/107;
Offshore Petroleum Activities (Oil Pollution Prevention and Control) Regulations 2005, SI 2005/2055.

8–26765 3. *Prevention etc of pollution after accidents involving offshore installations*

8–26766 4. Time-limited disposal or waste management licences. (1) Where—

(*a*) a disposal licence under section 5 of the 1974 Act became a site licence by virtue of section 77(2) of the 1990 Act (conversion, on the appointed day, of existing disposal licence under section 5 of the 1974 Act into a site licence),

(*b*) the licence has expired at a time ("the time of expiry") falling before the day on which this Act is passed but not earlier than the appointed day,

(*c*) the licence authorised the carrying on of activities in or on land in England or Wales, and

(*d*) relevant activities have taken place at a time falling not more than one year before the day on which this Act is passed,

the licence shall (subject to subsection (7)) for all purposes be deemed not to have expired but to have become, at the time of expiry, a site licence continuing in force in accordance with section 35(11) of the 1990 Act.

(2) Subsection (3) applies where—

(*a*) a disposal licence under section 5 of the 1974 Act expired at a time ("the time of expiry") falling before the appointed day (so that it was not converted into a site licence by section 77(2) of the 1990 Act),

(*b*) the licence authorised the carrying on of activities in or on land in England or Wales, and

(*c*) relevant activities have taken place at a time falling not more than one year before the day on which this Act is passed.

(3) The licence shall (subject to subsection (7)) for all purposes be deemed—

(*a*) not to have expired, and

(*b*) to have been subsisting on the appointed day and (accordingly) to have become on that day a site licence by virtue of section 77(2) of the 1990 Act,

and the site licence which the licence is deemed to have become on that day shall for all purposes be deemed to have been one that continues in force in accordance with section 35(11) of the 1990 Act.

(4) Where—

(*a*) a site licence in force immediately before the day on which this Act is passed—

(i) became a site licence by virtue of section 77(2) of the 1990 Act, and

(ii) will expire on or after the day on which this Act is passed (if it has not previously been revoked entirely, or had its surrender accepted, under Part II of the 1990 Act), and

(*b*) relevant activities have taken place at a time falling not more than one year before that day,

the licence shall for all purposes be deemed to have become at the beginning of that day a site licence continuing in force in accordance with section 35(11) of the 1990 Act.

(5) Where subsection (1), (3) or (4) has effect in relation to a licence, the terms and conditions of the licence as continued in force by that subsection shall, except so far as providing for the expiry of the licence and subject to subsection (6)(*b*) and (*c*), be such as were in force immediately before the relevant time (unless and until varied under Part II of the 1990 Act); and "the relevant time" means—

(*a*) where subsection (1) or (3) has effect in relation to a licence, the time of expiry;

(*b*) where subsection (4) has effect in relation to a licence, the beginning of the day on which this Act is passed.

(6) Where subsection (1) or (3) has effect in relation to a licence (but without prejudice to the generality of that subsection)—

(*a*) activities carried out during the interim period which (by virtue of subsection (1) or (3)) become authorised by the licence shall be treated as authorised at the time they were carried out (even though at that time their being carried out amounted to a contravention of section 33(1)(*a*) or (*b*) of the 1990 Act or section 3(1) of the 1974 Act);

(*b*) anything done in relation to the licence before the time of expiry but purporting to take effect after that time (such as the serving of a notice under section 37(4) or 38(12) of the 1990 Act, or in pursuance of section 7 of the 1974 Act, specifying a time falling during or after the interim period) shall be treated as having had (or having) effect as if the licence had not in fact expired;

(*c*) anything which during the interim period purported to be done in relation to the licence (such as a modification of the licence or the revocation, suspension, transfer or acceptance of the surrender of the licence or the carrying out of consultation, exercise of functions under section 9 of the 1974 Act or section 42 of the 1990 Act, imposition of requirements during a suspension or bringing or determination of an appeal) shall be treated as having had effect as if the licence had then been in force;

(*d*) any fees which (by virtue of subsection (1) or (3)) are treated as having become payable before the passing of this Act shall be taken to have become payable at the time they would have become payable had the licence not in fact expired; and

(*e*) the holder of the licence shall be treated as having been, during the interim period, an authorised person for the purposes of section 34(1)(*c*) of the 1990 Act.

(7) Where subsection (1) or (3) has effect in relation to a licence, a person shall not be guilty of an offence under section 33(6) or 38(10) or (11) of the 1990 Act as a result of anything done or omitted to be done during the interim period becoming (by virtue of subsection (1) or (3)) a contravention of any condition of the licence or (as the case may be) a failure to comply with any requirement imposed under section 38(9) of the 1990 Act.

(8) Nothing in this section affects any criminal proceedings which have been concluded before the passing of this Act.

(9) The waste regulation authority (within the meaning given by section 30(1) of the 1990 Act) shall notify the holder of a licence affected by this section of the fact that the licence is so affected and of how it is so affected.

(10) For the purposes of this section "relevant activities", in relation to a licence, are—

(*a*) any activities authorised by the licence or, in the case of an expired licence, any which would have been authorised by it had it not expired, and

(*b*) any precautions or works required by the licence to be taken or carried out in connection with or in consequence of those activities or, in the case of an expired licence, any which would have been so required had the licence not expired.

(11) In this section—

"the 1974 Act" means the Control of Pollution Act 1974;

"the 1990 Act" means the Environmental Protection Act 1990;

"the appointed day", in relation to a licence, means the day which in relation to that licence is (or would have been if the licence had not previously expired) the relevant appointed day for licences (within the meaning of section 77 of the 1990 Act);

"the interim period", in connection with a licence in relation to which subsection (1) or (3) has effect, means the period beginning with the time of expiry and ending immediately before the day on which this Act is passed;

"site licence" has the same meaning as it has in Part II of the 1990 Act by virtue of section 35(12) of that Act.

[Pollution Prevention and Control Act 1999, s 4.]

8–26767 **5.** *Application to Wales and Scotland*

8–26768 **6.** *Consequential and minor amendments and repeals*

8–26769 **7.** *Short title, interpretation, commencement and extent*

8–26770 SCHEDULE 1
PARTICULAR PURPOSES FOR WHICH PROVISION MAY BE MADE UNDER SECTION 2

SCHEDULE 2
CONSEQUENTIAL AND MINOR AMENDMENTS

SCHEDULE 3
REPEALS

Waste and Emissions Trading Act 2003[1]

(2003 c 33)

PART 1
WASTE

CHAPTER 1
WASTE SENT TO LANDFILLS

8–26780 Part 1 provides for the Secretary of State by regulations to specify the maximum amounts of biodegradable material waste in the United Kingdom allowed to be sent to landfills in specified "target" years (s 1) and "non target" years (ss 2–4). The Secretary of State (or in Wales, the National Assembly) is the 'Allocating Authority' which allocates landfill allowances (ss 4–5) and may make provision by regulations for the "banking" or "borrowing" of allowances from year to year (s 6) and for trading of allowances with other authorities (s 7). Supplementary provision for the creating of offences in regulations is made by s 8. Waste disposal authorities which exceed their allowances are subject to a civil penalty to the allocating authority (s 9).

An allocating authority must appoint a person to monitor the operation of the landfill allowances scheme and audit the performance of the waste disposal authorities. Regulations may make further provision for the purposes of landfill allowances (s 11) and record-keeping by waste disposal authorities (s 12).

1. This Act is to be brought into force in accordance with orders made under s 40. At the date of going to press the following orders had been made: (No 1) SI 2004/1163; (No 2) SI 2004/1874; (Wales) SI 2004/1488 ; (No 1) (England) SI 2004/3181; (No 3) SI 2004/3192; (No 1) (England and Wales) SI 2004/3319; (No 1) (Great Britain) SI 2004/3320; (No 2) (England) SI 2004/3321).

8–26781 **13. Powers in relation to landfill operators.** (1) An allocating authority may, for purposes connected with the sending of biodegradable municipal waste to landfills, by regulations[1] make provision for requiring a person concerned in the operation of a landfill to—

(*a*) maintain prescribed records;
(*b*) gather prescribed information by carrying out prescribed operations on prescribed waste;
(*c*) make prescribed returns, or provide prescribed information or prescribed evidence, to prescribed persons.

(2) A person commits an offence if he fails to comply with a requirement imposed on him under subsection (1).

(3) An allocating authority may by regulations[1] make provision enabling the monitoring authority for its area, or persons authorised by the monitoring authority—

(*a*) to require persons concerned in the operation of a landfill to produce records related to the operation of the landfill for inspection or for removal for inspection elsewhere;
(*b*) to specify the form in which, the place at which and the time at or by which records are to be produced;
(*c*) to copy records that are produced;
(*d*) to enter premises (with or without a constable, with any necessary equipment or material and, if need be, by force) for the purposes of—
 (i) finding records relating to the operation of a landfill,
 (ii) inspecting them or removing them for inspection elsewhere, and
 (iii) copying them;
(*e*) to require persons to afford, to a person exercising any power conferred under paragraphs (*a*) to (*d*), such facilities and assistance within their control or in relation to which they have responsibilities as are necessary to enable the person to exercise the power.

(4) A person commits an offence if—

(*a*) he intentionally obstructs a person exercising a power conferred under subsection (3), or
(*b*) he fails to comply with a requirement imposed on him under that subsection.

(5) A person guilty of an offence under subsection (2) or (4)(*a*) is liable—

(*a*) on summary conviction, to a fine not exceeding the statutory maximum;
(*b*) on conviction on indictment, to imprisonment for a term not exceeding 2 years or to a fine, or to both.

(6) A person guilty of an offence under subsection (4)(*b*) is liable on summary conviction to a fine not exceeding level 5 on the standard scale.

(7) In subsection (1) "prescribed" means prescribed by or under regulations under that subsection.
[Waste and Emissions Trading Act 2003, s 13.]

1. The Landfill Allowances Scheme (Wales) Regulations 2004, SI 2004/1490 amended by SI 2005/1820 and the Landfill Allowances and Trading Scheme (England) Regulations 2004, SI 2004/3212 amended by SI 2005/880 and 895 have been made.

8–26782 14–15. *Disclosure of information by monitoring and allocating authorities and registers.*

Scheme operation and monitoring etc

8–26783 16. Registers: public access. An allocating authority may, in relation to a register that a person is required to maintain by regulations under this Chapter made by the authority, by regulations[1]—

(*a*) make provision for public inspection of such of the information contained in the register as is of a description specified by the regulations;
(*b*) make provision for members of the public to obtain copies of information in the register that is open to public inspection under paragraph (a), including provision for the payment of reasonable charges.

[Waste and Emissions Trading Act 2003, s 16.]

1. The Landfill Allowances Scheme (Wales) Regulations 2004, SI 2004/1490 amended by SI 2005/1820 and the Landfill Allowances and Trading Scheme (England) Regulations 2004, SI 2004/3212 amended by SI 2005/880 and 895 have been made.

8–26784 17–20. *Strategies for reducing landfilling of biodegradable waste.*

Interpretation of Chapter 1

8–26785 21. "Biodegradable waste" and "municipal waste". (1) In this Chapter "biodegradable waste" means any waste that is capable of undergoing anaerobic or aerobic decomposition, such as—

food and garden waste, and
paper and paperboard.

(2) In this Chapter "biodegradable municipal waste" means waste that is both biodegradable waste and municipal waste.

(3) In subsection (2) "municipal waste" means—

(*a*) waste from households, and
(*b*) other waste that, because of its nature or composition, is similar to waste from households.

[Waste and Emissions Trading Act 2003, s 21.]

8–26786 22. "Landfill". (1) In this Chapter "landfill" means a site for the deposit of waste onto or into land where the site is—

(*a*) a waste disposal site, or
(*b*) used for the storage of waste.

(2) In determining whether a site is a landfill for the purposes of this Chapter, the following activities at the site are to be ignored—

(*a*) the temporary storage of waste if the site is used for such storage for less than one year;
(*b*) the unloading of waste in order to permit the waste to be prepared for further transport for recovery, treatment or disposal elsewhere;
(*c*) the storage of waste, prior to recovery or treatment, for a period of less than three years as a general rule;
(*d*) the storage of waste, prior to disposal, for a period of less than one year.

(3) The fact that a site for the deposit of waste is at the place of production of the waste does not prevent the site from being a landfill for the purposes of this Chapter.

(4) In subsection (2) "treatment" means the physical, thermal, chemical or biological processes, including sorting, that change the characteristics of waste in order to—

(*a*) reduce its volume,
(*b*) reduce its hazardous nature,
(*c*) facilitate its handling, or
(*d*) enhance its recoverability.

[Waste and Emissions Trading Act 2003, s 22.]

8–26787 23. "Scheme year" and "target year"[1]

---

1. See the Landfill (Scheme Year and Maximum Landfill Amount) Regulations 2004, SI 2004/1936.

8–26788 24. Other definitions. (1) For the purposes of this Chapter, the "allocating authority"—

(*a*) for England is the Secretary of State,
(*b*) for Scotland is the Scottish Ministers,
(*c*) for Wales is the National Assembly for Wales, and
(*d*) for Northern Ireland is the Department of the Environment.

(2) In this Chapter, any reference to an allocating authority's "area" is to the area for which it is the allocating authority for the purposes of this Chapter.

(3) In this Chapter "landfill allowances" means allowances allocated under section 4(1).

(4) References in this Chapter to the monitoring authority for an area are to the monitoring authority designated for the area by regulations under section 10(1).

(5) In this Chapter "waste disposal authority"—

(*a*) in relation to England, Wales and Scotland has the same meaning as in Part 2 of the Environmental Protection Act 1990 (c 43);
(*b*) in relation to Northern Ireland means a district council.

[Waste and Emissions Trading Act 2003, s 24.]

Supplementary

8–26789 25. Activities to which Chapter 1 does not apply. (1) References in this Chapter to sending biodegradable waste, or biodegradable municipal waste, to landfills do not include—

(*a*) the spreading of sludges (including sewage sludges and sludges resulting from dredging operations), or similar matter, on the soil for the purposes of fertilisation or improvement,
(*b*) the deposit of non-hazardous dredging sludges alongside small waterways from out of which they have been dredged,
(*c*) the deposit of non-hazardous sludges in surface water or in the bed or subsoil of surface water, or
(*d*) the deposit of unpolluted soil resulting from—
 (i) prospecting for, or the extraction, treatment or storage of, mineral resources, or
 (ii) the operation of quarries.

(2) For the purposes of this section, sludge is "non-hazardous" if it is not hazardous waste within the meaning of regulation 6 of the Hazardous Waste (England and Wales) Regultions 2005[1].

[Waste and Emissions Trading Act 2003, s 25 as amended by SI 2005/894.]

---

1. Reproduced as in force in England and Wales.

8–26790 26–28. *Penalties and regulations.*

PART 3
GENERAL

8–26791 40. Commencement

41. Extent

42. Short title

Clean Neighbourhoods and Environment Act 2005[1]

(2005 c 16)

8–26801

PART 1[2]

CRIME AND DISORDER

1. This Act received the Royal Assent on 7 April 2005. It was enacted following a review of the legislative framework for providing and maintaining a clean and safe local environment. The Act tackles various kinds of nuisance and anti-social behaviour, primarily by adding provisions to existing legislation.

The Act contains 10 Parts and 5 Schedules:

Part 1 amends the law relating to crime and disorder reduction partnerships; it also makes provision for the gating of minor highways (the latter is not reproduced).

Part 2 introduces two new offences relating to nuisance parking and amends the law relating to abandoned and illegally parked vehicles.

Part 3 extends the statutory offence of dropping litter and amends the powers and duties of local authorities in relation to litter.

Part 4 amends the law relating to graffiti, fly-posting and the illegal display of advertisements.

Part 5 makes miscellaneous provision about waste.

Part 6 allows local authorities and parish and community councils to create offences relating to the control of dogs; the new system replaces the Dogs (Fouling of Land) Act 1996.

Part 7 addresses various issues relating to nuisance by noise; it also allows local authorities to employ alternative means to resolve complaints prior to issuing an abatement notice.

Part 8 (not reproduced in this work) creates the Commission for Architecture and Built Environment.

Parts 9 and 10 contain miscellaneous and supplementary provisions.

The Act will be brought into force in accordance with commencement orders made under s 108.

At the time of going to press the following orders had been made: Clean Neighbourhoods and Environment Act 2005 (Commencement No 1) Order 2005, SI 2005/1675; and Clean Neighbourhoods and Environment Act 2005 (Commencement No 2, Transitional Provisions and Savings) (England and Wales) Order 2005, SI 2005/2896. The former brought s 32 into force in relation to both England and Wales. The latter brought into force ss 42–44 in relation to England and Wales; and ss 11–17, 47, 53, and some provisions of Parts 1 and 4 of Sch 4, in relation to England only. The amendments made by ss 11-13 to the Refuse Disposal (Amenity) Act 1978 are subject to the transitional provisions set out in art 4 of the latter order. The amendments made by ss 15-17 to the Road Traffic Regulation Act 1984 are subject to the transitional arrangements set out in art 5 of the latter order. The repeals made by s 47 are subject to the savings set out in art 6 of the latter order.

2. Part 1 contains ss 1–2.

PART 2[1]

VEHICLES

Nuisance parking offences

8–26802 3. Exposing vehicles for sale on a road. (1) A person is guilty of an offence if at any time—

(a) he leaves two or more motor vehicles parked within 500 metres of each other on a road or roads where they are exposed or advertised for sale, or

(b) he causes two or more motor vehicles to be so left.

(2) A person is not to be convicted of an offence under subsection (1) if he proves to the satisfaction of the court that he was not acting for the purposes of a business of selling motor vehicles.

(3) A person guilty of an offence under subsection (1) is liable on summary conviction to a fine not exceeding level 4 on the standard scale.

(4) In this section—

"motor vehicle" has the same meaning as in the Refuse Disposal (Amenity) Act 1978 (c 3);

"road" has the same meaning as in the Road Traffic Regulation Act 1984 (c 27).

[Clean Neighbourhoods and Environment Act 2005, s 3.]

1. Part 2 contains ss 3–17. Sections 11–17 are in force, but only in relation to England: see the Clean Neighbourhoods and Environment Act 2005 (Commencement No 2, Transitional Provisions and Savings) (England and Wales) Order 2005, SI 2005/2896. The amendments made by ss 11–13 to the Refuse Disposal (Amenity) Act 1978 are subject to the transitional provisions set out in art 4 of the order. The amendments made by ss 15–17 to the Road Traffic Regulation Act 1984 are subject to the transitional arrangements set out in art 5 of the order.

8–26803 4. Repairing vehicles on a road. (1) A person who carries out restricted works on a motor vehicle on a road is guilty of an offence, subject as follows.

(2) For the purposes of this section "restricted works" means—

(a) works for the repair, maintenance, servicing, improvement or dismantling of a motor vehicle or of any part of or accessory to a motor vehicle;

(b) works for the installation, replacement or renewal of any such part or accessory.

(3) A person is not to be convicted of an offence under this section in relation to any works if he proves to the satisfaction of the court that the works were not carried out—

(a) in the course of, or for the purposes of, a business of carrying out restricted works; or
(b) for gain or reward.

(4) Subsection (3) does not apply where the carrying out of the works gave reasonable cause for annoyance to persons in the vicinity.

(5) A person is also not to be convicted of an offence under this section in relation to any works if he proves to the satisfaction of the court that the works carried out were works of repair which—

(a) arose from an accident or breakdown in circumstances where repairs on the spot or elsewhere on the road were necessary; and
(b) were carried out within 72 hours of the accident or breakdown or were within that period authorised to be carried out at a later time by the local authority for the area.

(6) A person guilty of an offence under this section is liable on summary conviction to a fine not exceeding level 4 on the standard scale.

(7) In this section—

"motor vehicle" has the same meaning as in the Refuse Disposal (Amenity) Act 1978;
"road" has the same meaning as in the Road Traffic Regulation Act 1984;
"local authority" has the meaning given in section 9.

[Clean Neighbourhoods and Environment Act 2005, s 4.]

8–26804 **5. Liability of directors etc.** (1) Where an offence under section 3 or 4 committed by a body corporate is proved to have been committed with the consent or connivance of, or to have been attributable to any neglect on the part of—

(a) any director, manager, secretary or other similar officer of the body corporate, or
(b) a person who was purporting to act in any such capacity,

he as well as the body corporate is guilty of the offence and liable to be proceeded against and punished accordingly.

(2) Where the affairs of a body corporate are managed by its members, subsection (1) applies in relation to the acts or defaults of a member in connection with his functions of management as if he were a director of the body.

[Clean Neighbourhoods and Environment Act 2005, s 5.]

Nuisance parking offences: fixed penalty notices

8–26805 **6. Power to give fixed penalty notices.** (1) Where on any occasion an authorised officer of a local authority has reason to believe that a person has committed an offence under section 3 or 4 in the area of that authority, the officer may give that person a notice offering him the opportunity of discharging any liability to conviction for that offence by payment of a fixed penalty to the local authority.

(2) Where a person is given a notice under this section in respect of an offence—

(a) no proceedings may be instituted for that offence before the expiration of the period of fourteen days following the date of the notice; and
(b) he may not be convicted of that offence if he pays the fixed penalty before the expiration of that period.

(3) A notice under this section must give such particulars of the circumstances alleged to constitute the offence as are necessary for giving reasonable information of the offence.

(4) A notice under this section must also state—

(a) the period during which, by virtue of subsection (2), proceedings will not be taken for the offence;
(b) the amount of the fixed penalty; and
(c) the person to whom and the address at which the fixed penalty may be paid.

(5) Without prejudice to payment by any other method, payment of the fixed penalty may be made by pre-paying and posting a letter containing the amount of the penalty (in cash or otherwise) to the person mentioned in subsection (4)(c) at the address so mentioned.

(6) Where a letter is sent in accordance with subsection (5) payment is to be regarded as having been made at the time at which that letter would be delivered in the ordinary course of post.

(7) The form of a notice under this section is to be such as the appropriate person may by order prescribe.

(8) The fixed penalty payable to a local authority under this section is, subject to subsection (9), £100.

(9) The appropriate person may by order substitute a different amount for the amount for the time being specified in subsection (8).

(10) The local authority to which a fixed penalty is payable under this section may make provision

for treating it as having been paid if a lesser amount is paid before the end of a period specified by the authority.

(11) The appropriate person may by regulations restrict the extent to which, and the circumstances in which, a local authority may make provision under subsection (10).

(12) In any proceedings a certificate which—

(a) purports to be signed on behalf of the chief finance officer of the local authority, and

(b) states that payment of a fixed penalty was or was not received by a date specified in the certificate,

is evidence of the facts stated.

(13) In this section "chief finance officer", in relation to a local authority, means the person having responsibility for the financial affairs of the authority.

[Clean Neighbourhoods and Environment Act 2005, s 6.]

8–26806 7. Power to require name and address. (1) If an authorised officer of a local authority proposes to give a person a notice under section 6, the officer may require the person to give him his name and address.

(2) A person commits an offence if—

(a) he fails to give his name and address when required to do so under subsection (1), or

(b) he gives a false or inaccurate name or address in response to a requirement under that subsection.

(3) A person guilty of an offence under subsection (2) is liable on summary conviction to a fine not exceeding level 3 on the standard scale.

[Clean Neighbourhoods and Environment Act 2005, s 7.]

8. Use of fixed penalty receipts

8–26807 9. Fixed penalty notices: supplementary. (1) For the purposes of this section, "this group of sections" means sections 6 to 8 and this section.

(2) In this group of sections—

"local authority" means—

(a) a district council in England;
(b) a county council in England for an area for which there is no district council;
(c) a London borough council;
(d) the Common Council of the City of London;
(e) the Council of the Isles of Scilly;
(f) a county or county borough council in Wales;

"appropriate person" means—

(a) in relation to England, the Secretary of State;
(b) in relation to Wales, the National Assembly for Wales;

"authorised officer", in relation to a local authority, means an employee of the authority who is authorised in writing by the authority for the purposes of giving notices under section 6.

(3) Any order or regulations under this group of sections must be made by statutory instrument.

(4) Any such order or regulations may make different provision for different purposes (including different provision in relation to different authorities or different descriptions of authority).

(5) A statutory instrument containing an order or regulations made by the Secretary of State under this group of sections is subject to annulment in pursuance of a resolution of either House of Parliament.

[Clean Neighbourhoods and Environment Act 2005, s 9.]

Abandoned vehicles

8–26808 10. Offence of abandoning a vehicle: fixed penalty notices. *Inserts new ss 2A–2C into the Refuse Disposal (Amenity) Act 1978 (c 3).*

8–26809 11. Notice of removal. (1) Section 3 of the Refuse Disposal (Amenity) Act 1978 (c 3) (removal of abandoned vehicles) is amended as follows.

(2) After subsection (2) (requirement to give notice to occupier) insert—

"(2A) Subsection (2) does not apply where the vehicle is abandoned on a road (within the meaning of the Road Traffic Regulation Act 1984)."

(3) Omit subsection (5) (requirement to give notice of removal of vehicle which ought to be destroyed).

[Clean Neighbourhoods and Environment Act 2005, s 11.]

8–26810 12. Disposal. (1) Section 4(1) of the Refuse Disposal (Amenity) Act 1978 (disposal of abandoned vehicles) is amended as follows.

(2) For paragraphs (a) and (b) substitute—

"(a) in the case of a vehicle which in the opinion of the authority is in such a condition that it ought to be destroyed, at any time after its removal;

(b) in the case of a vehicle, not falling within paragraph (a), which—

(i) does not display a licence (whether current or otherwise and whether or not the vehicle is required to display a licence), and

(ii) does not display any registration mark (whether indicating registration within or outside the United Kingdom),

at any time after its removal;".

(3) Omit the words from "but not earlier" to the end.

(4) In section 11(1) of that Act (interpretation), in the definition of "licence", at the end insert "(including a nil licence within the meaning of that Act)".

[Clean Neighbourhoods and Environment Act 2005, s 12.]

8–26811 13. Guidance. In the Refuse Disposal (Amenity) Act 1978 (c 3), after section 4 insert—

"**4A. Guidance.** Any authority on whom functions are conferred under section 3 or 4 above must, in exercising those functions, have regard to any guidance given to the authority for the purpose by the appropriate person."

[Clean Neighbourhoods and Environment Act 2005, s 13.]

8–26812 14. Abandoned vehicles: supplementary. (1) The Refuse Disposal (Amenity) Act 1978 is amended as follows.

(2) In section 10(5), after "except" insert—

"(za) an order or regulations under section 2A above, or regulations under section 2C above, made by the National Assembly for Wales; or".

(3) In section 11(1), after "that is to say—" insert—

""appropriate person" means—

(a) in relation to a local authority in England, the Secretary of State;

(b) in relation to a local authority in Wales, the National Assembly for Wales;".

[Clean Neighbourhoods and Environment Act 2005, s 14.]

Illegally parked vehicles etc

8–26813 15. Notice of removal. (1) Section 99 of the Road Traffic Regulation Act 1984 (c 27) (removal of vehicles) is amended as follows.

(2) In subsection (3) (requirement to give notice of removal to occupier), after "land" insert "other than a road".

(3) Omit subsection (4) (requirement to give notice of removal of vehicle which ought to be destroyed).

[Clean Neighbourhoods and Environment Act 2005, s 15.]

8–26814 16. Disposal. (1) Section 101 of the Road Traffic Regulation Act 1984 (c 27) (ultimate disposal of removed vehicles) is amended as follows.

(2) In subsection (3), in paragraph (a), omit the words from "and on which" to "at the time of its removal".

(3) In that subsection, for paragraph (b) substitute—

"(b) in the case of a vehicle, not falling within paragraph (a), which—

(i) does not display a licence (whether current or otherwise and whether or not the vehicle is required to display a licence), and

(ii) does not display any registration mark (whether indicating registration within or outside the United Kingdom),

at any time after its removal;".

(4) In that subsection, omit the words from "but, in a case" to the end.

(5) In subsection (8), in the definition of "licence", at the end insert "(including a nil licence within the meaning of that Act)".

[Clean Neighbourhoods and Environment Act 2005, s 16.]

8–26815 17. Guidance. In section 103 of the Road Traffic Regulation Act 1984 (supplementary provision as to removal of vehicles), at the end insert—

"(4) A local authority must in exercising any of their functions under sections 99 to 102 have regard to any guidance given to the authority for the purpose by—

(a) the Secretary of State, in the case of a local authority in England;

(b) the National Assembly for Wales, in the case of a local authority in Wales.

(5) In subsection (4) "local authority" has the meaning given by section 100(5)(a) and (b)."
[Clean Neighbourhoods and Environment Act 2005, s 17.]

PART 3[1]
LITTER AND REFUSE
Offence of dropping litter

8–26816 **18. Extension of litter offence to all open places.** In section 87 of the Environmental Protection Act 1990 (c 43) (offence of leaving litter), for subsections (1) to (4) substitute—

"(1) A person is guilty of an offence if he throws down, drops or otherwise deposits any litter in any place to which this section applies and leaves it.

(2) This section applies to any place in the area of a principal litter authority which is open to the air, subject to subsection (3) below.

(3) This section does not apply to a place which is "open to the air" for the purposes of this Part by virtue of section 86(13) above if the public does not have access to it, with or without payment.

(4) It is immaterial for the purposes of this section whether the litter is deposited on land or in water.

(4A) No offence is committed under subsection (1) above where the depositing of the litter is—

(a) authorised by law; or
(b) done by or with the consent of the owner, occupier or other person having control of the place where it is deposited.

(4B) A person may only give consent under subsection (4A)(b) above in relation to the depositing of litter in a lake or pond or watercourse if he is the owner, occupier or other person having control of—

(a) all the land adjoining that lake or pond or watercourse; and
(b) all the land through or into which water in that lake or pond or watercourse directly or indirectly discharges, otherwise than by means of a public sewer.

(4C) In subsection (4B) above, "lake or pond", "watercourse" and "public sewer" have the same meanings as in section 104 of the Water Resources Act 1991."
[Clean Neighbourhoods and Environment Act 2005, s 18.]

1. Part 3 contains ss 18–27.

8–26817 **19. Litter offence: fixed penalty notices.** (1) Section 88 of the Environmental Protection Act 1990 (c 43) (fixed penalty notices for leaving litter) is amended as follows.

(2) For subsections (6) and (7) (amount of fixed penalty) substitute—

"(6) The fixed penalty payable in pursuance of a notice under this section is payable to the litter authority whose authorised officer gave the notice.

(6A) The amount of a fixed penalty payable in pursuance of a notice under this section—

(a) is the amount specified by a principal litter authority in relation to its area (whether the penalty is payable to that or another authority), or
(b) if no amount is so specified, is £75.

(6B) The reference in subsection (6A) above to a principal litter authority does not include an English county council for an area for which there is also a district council.

(7) The litter authority to which a fixed penalty is payable under this section may make provision for treating it as having been paid if a lesser amount is paid before the end of a period specified by the authority."

(3) After subsection (8) insert—

"(8A) If an authorised officer of a litter authority proposes to give a person a notice under this section, the officer may require the person to give him his name and address.

(8B) A person commits an offence if—

(a) he fails to give his name and address when required to do so under subsection (8A) above, or
(b) he gives a false or inaccurate name or address in response to a requirement under that subsection.

(8C) A person guilty of an offence under subsection (8B) above is liable on summary conviction to a fine not exceeding level 3 on the standard scale."

(4) In subsection (9), at the end insert—

"(f) a parish or community council."

(5) In subsection (10), for the definition of "authorised officer" substitute—

""authorised officer", in relation to a litter authority, means—

(a) an employee of the authority who is authorised in writing by the authority for the purpose of giving notices under this section;
(b) any person who, in pursuance of arrangements made with the authority, has the function of giving such notices and is authorised in writing by the authority to perform that function; and
(c) any employee of such a person who is authorised in writing by the authority for the purpose of giving such notices;".

(6) After that subsection insert—

"(11) The appropriate person may by regulations prescribe conditions to be satisfied by a person before a parish or community council may authorise him in writing for the purpose of giving notices under this section."

[Clean Neighbourhoods and Environment Act 2005, s 19.]

Local authority notices

8–26818 **20. Litter clearing notices.** (1) Section 90 of the Environmental Protection Act 1990 (c 43) (litter control areas) shall cease to have effect.

(2) After section 92 of that Act insert—

"**92A. Litter clearing notices.** (1) A principal litter authority may in accordance with this section serve a notice (a "litter clearing notice") in relation to any land in its area which is open to the air.

(2) Before serving a litter clearing notice in relation to any land a principal litter authority must be satisfied that the land is defaced by litter or refuse so as to be detrimental to the amenity of the locality.

(3) A litter clearing notice is to require the person on whom it is served—

(a) to clear the land of the litter or refuse; and
(b) if the principal litter authority is satisfied that the land is likely to become defaced by litter or refuse again, to take reasonable steps to prevent it from becoming so defaced.

(4) A litter clearing notice must be served on—

(a) the occupier of the land to which it relates; or
(b) if the land is not occupied, the owner.

(5) A litter clearing notice imposing a requirement under subsection (3)(a) above may specify—

(a) a period within which the requirement must be complied with;
(b) standards of compliance.

(6) A period specified under subsection (5)(a) above may not be less than 28 days beginning with the day on which the notice is served.

(7) A principal litter authority must, in discharging its functions under this section, have regard to any guidance given to the authority by the appropriate person.

(8) The form and content of a litter clearing notice is to be such as the appropriate person may by order specify.

(9) Where a principal litter authority proposes to serve a litter clearing notice in respect of any land but is unable after reasonable enquiry to ascertain the name or proper address of the occupier of the land (or, if the land is unoccupied, the owner)—

(a) the authority may post the notice on the land (and may enter any land to the extent reasonably necessary for that purpose), and
(b) the notice is to be treated as having been served upon the occupier (or, if the land is unoccupied, the owner) at the time the notice is posted.

(10) Subsection (1) above does not apply to an English county council for an area for which there is a district council.

(11) A litter clearing notice may not be served in relation to land of any of the following descriptions—

(a) a highway maintainable at the public expense;
(b) land under the direct control of a principal litter authority;
(c) Crown land;
(d) relevant land of a designated statutory undertaker;
(e) relevant land of a designated educational institution;
(f) land which is covered (but "open to the air" for the purposes of this Part by virtue of section 86(13) above) and to which the public are not entitled or permitted to have access, with or without payment.

92B. Appeals against litter clearing notices. (1) A person on whom a litter clearing notice is served under section 92A above may appeal against it to a magistrates' court in accordance with the provisions of this section.

(2) An appeal under this section must be made within a period of 21 days beginning with the day on which the notice is served.

(3) The grounds on which an appeal under this section may be made are that—

(a) there is a material defect or error in, or in connection with, the notice;
(b) the notice should have been served on another person;
(c) the land is not defaced by litter or refuse so as to be detrimental to the amenity of the locality;
(d) the action required is unfair or unduly onerous.

(4) A notice against which an appeal under this section is made is of no effect pending the final determination or withdrawal of the appeal.

(5) On the determination of an appeal under this section, the magistrates' court must—

(a) quash the notice;
(b) modify the notice (including modifying it by extending the period specified in it); or
(c) dismiss the appeal.

92C. Failure to comply with litter clearing notice. (1) This section applies where the person on whom a litter clearing notice is served under section 92A above fails without reasonable excuse to comply with any requirement imposed by the notice.

(2) The person is guilty of an offence and liable on summary conviction to a fine not exceeding level 4 on the standard scale.

(3) The principal litter authority which served the notice or any person authorised by the authority may enter the land to which the notice relates and clear it of litter and refuse.

(4) Where a principal litter authority exercises the power in subsection (3) above, it may require the person on whom the notice was served to pay a reasonable charge in respect of the exercise of the power.

(5) A principal litter authority may for the purposes of subsection (4) above impose charges by reference to land of particular descriptions or categories (including categories determined by reference to surface area)."

[Clean Neighbourhoods and Environment Act 2005, s 20.]

8–26819 21. Street litter control notices. (1) In section 93 of the Environmental Protection Act 1990 (c 43) (street litter control notices), after subsection (3) insert—

"(3A) A vehicle or stall or other moveable structure which is used for one or more commercial or retail activities while parked or set at a particular place on or verging a street is to be treated for the purposes of this section and section 94 below as if it were premises situated at that place having a frontage on that street in the place where it is parked or set.

(3B) In subsection (3A) above, "vehicle" means any vehicle intended or adapted for use on roads."

(2) In section 94 of that Act (supplementary provisions in relation to street litter control notices), in subsection (4)(b) after "so specified" insert "(including the standards to which any such thing must be done)".

(3) In that section, for subsections (8) and (9) substitute—

"(8) A person commits an offence if, without reasonable excuse, he fails to comply with a requirement imposed on him by a notice.

(9) A person guilty of an offence under subsection (8) above is liable on summary conviction to a fine not exceeding level 4 on the standard scale."

[Clean Neighbourhoods and Environment Act 2005, s 21.]

8–26820 22. Failure to comply with notice: fixed penalty notices. After section 94 of the Environmental Protection Act 1990 (c 43) insert—

"94A. Fixed penalty notices relating to sections 92C and 94. (1) This section applies where on any occasion it appears to an authorised officer of a principal litter authority that a person has committed an offence under section 92C(2) or 94(8) above in relation to a notice served by that authority.

(2) The authorised officer may give that person a notice offering him the opportunity of discharging any liability to conviction for the offence by payment of a fixed penalty to the principal litter authority.

(3) Subsections (2) to (5) of section 88 above (fixed penalty notices for leaving litter) apply in relation to notices given under this section as they apply in relation to notices given under that section.

(4) The amount of a fixed penalty payable to a principal litter authority under this section is—

(a) the amount specified by the authority in relation to its area (and an authority may specify different amounts for the two different offences referred to in subsection (1) above); or

(b) if no amount is so specified, £100.

(5) The principal litter authority to which a fixed penalty is payable under this section may make provision for treating it as having been paid if a lesser amount is paid before the end of a period specified by the authority.

(6) In any proceedings a certificate which—

(a) purports to be signed by or on behalf of the chief finance officer of a principal litter authority; and

(b) states that payment of a fixed penalty was or was not received by the date specified in the certificate,

is evidence of the facts stated.

(7) In this section—

"authorised officer", in relation to a principal litter authority, means an officer of the authority who is authorised in writing by the authority for the purposes of giving notices under this section;

"chief finance officer", in relation to a principal litter authority, means the person having responsibility for the financial affairs of that authority."

[Clean Neighbourhoods and Environment Act 2005, s 22.]

Free distribution of printed matter

8–26821 **23. Controls on free distribution of printed matter.** (1) In the Environmental Protection Act 1990 (c 43), after section 94A (as inserted by section 22 above) insert—

"94B. Free distribution of printed matter. Schedule 3A (distribution of printed matter on designated land) has effect."

(2) In that Act, after Schedule 3 insert—

"SCHEDULE 3A

FREE DISTRIBUTION OF PRINTED MATTER ON DESIGNATED LAND

Offence of unauthorised distribution

1. (1) A person commits an offence if he distributes any free printed matter without the consent of a principal litter authority on any land which is designated by the authority under this Schedule, where the person knows that the land is so designated.

(2) A person commits an offence if he causes another person to distribute any free printed matter without the consent of a principal litter authority on any land designated by the authority under this Schedule.

(3) A person is not guilty of an offence under sub-paragraph (2) if he took reasonable steps to ensure that the distribution did not occur on any land designated under this Schedule.

(4) Nothing in this paragraph applies to the distribution of printed matter—

(a) by or on behalf of a charity within the meaning of the Charities Act 1993, where the printed matter relates to or is intended for the benefit of the charity;

(b) where the distribution is for political purposes or for the purposes of a religion or belief.

(5) A person guilty of an offence under this paragraph is liable on summary conviction to a fine not exceeding level 4 on the standard scale.

(6) For the purposes of this Schedule—

(a) to "distribute" printed matter means to give it out to, or offer or make it available to, members of the public and includes placing it on or affixing it to vehicles, but does not include putting it inside a building or letter-box;

(b) printed matter is "free" if it is distributed without charge to the persons to whom it is distributed.

(7) For the purposes of this Schedule a person does not distribute printed matter if the distribution takes place inside a public service vehicle (within the meaning of the Public Passenger Vehicles Act 1981).

Designation

2. (1) A principal litter authority may by order in accordance with this paragraph designate land in its area for the purposes of this Schedule.

(2) The land designated must consist of—

(a) relevant land of the authority;

(b) all or part of any relevant highway for which the authority is responsible; or

(c) both.

(3) A principal litter authority may only designate land where it is satisfied that the land is being defaced by the discarding of free printed matter which has been distributed there.

(4) Where a principal litter authority proposes to make an order under sub-paragraph (1) above in respect of any land, it must—

(a) publish a notice of its proposal in at least one newspaper circulating in an area which includes the land; and

(b) post such a notice on the land.

(5) A notice under sub-paragraph (4) above must specify—

(a) the land proposed to be designated;

(b) the date on which it is proposed that the order is to come into force (which may not be earlier than the end of a period of 28 days beginning with the day on which the notice is given);

(c) the fact that objections may be made to the proposal, how they may be made and the period within which they may be made (being a period of at least 14 days beginning with the day on which the notice is given).

(6) Where after giving notice under sub-paragraph (4) above and taking into account any objections duly made pursuant to sub-paragraph (5)(c) above an authority decides to make an order under sub-paragraph (1) above in respect of any or all of the land in respect of which the notice was given, the authority must—

(a) publish a notice of its decision in at least one newspaper circulating in an area which includes the land; and

(b) post such a notice on the land.

(7) A notice under sub-paragraph (6) above must specify the date on which the order is to come into force, being a date not earlier than—

(a) the end of the period of 14 days beginning with the day on which the notice is given; and

(b) the date referred to in sub-paragraph (5)(b) above.

(8) A principal litter authority may at any time revoke an order under sub-paragraph (1) above in respect of any land to which the order relates.

(9) A principal litter authority must—

(a) publish a notice of any revocation under sub-paragraph (8) above in at least one newspaper circulating in an area which includes the land in question; and

(b) post such a notice on the land.

(10) Sub-paragraph (1) above does not apply to an English county council for an area for which there is a district council.

Consent and conditions

3. (1) A principal litter authority may on the application of any person consent to that person or any other person (identified specifically or by description) distributing free printed matter on any land designated by the authority under this Schedule.

(2) Consent under this paragraph may be given without limitation or may be limited—

(a) by reference to the material to be distributed;

(b) by reference to a particular period, or particular times or dates;

(c) by reference to any part of the designated land;

(d) to a particular distribution.

(3) A principal litter authority need not give consent under this paragraph to any applicant where it considers that the proposed distribution would in all the circumstances be likely to lead to defacement of the designated land.

(4) Consent need not be given to any applicant if within the period of five years ending on the date of his application—

(a) he has been convicted of an offence under paragraph 1 above; or

(b) he has paid a fixed penalty under paragraph 7 below.

(5) Consent may be given under this paragraph subject to such conditions as the authority consider necessary or desirable for—

(a) protecting the designated land from defacement; or

(b) the effective operation and enforcement of this Schedule.

(6) The conditions which may be imposed by a principal litter authority under this paragraph include conditions requiring any person distributing printed matter pursuant to consent given under this paragraph to produce on demand written evidence of the consent to an authorised officer of the authority.

(7) Consent given by a principal litter authority under this paragraph may at any time be revoked (entirely or to any extent) by notice to the person to whom it was given, where—

(a) he has failed to comply with any condition subject to which it was given; or

(b) he is convicted of an offence under paragraph 1 above or pays a fixed penalty under paragraph 7 below.

(8) Any condition imposed under this paragraph in relation to any consent may be varied or revoked by notice given to the person to whom the consent was given.

Fees

4. (1) A principal litter authority may require the payment of a fee before giving consent under paragraph 3 above.

(2) The amount of a fee under this paragraph is to be such as the authority may determine, but may not be more than, when taken together with all other fees charged by the authority under this paragraph, is reasonable to cover the costs of operating and enforcing this Schedule.

Appeals

5. (1) Any person aggrieved by a decision of a principal litter authority under paragraph 3 above—

(a) to refuse consent,
(b) to impose any limitation or condition subject to which consent is given,
(c) to revoke consent (or to revoke it to any extent),

may appeal against the decision to a magistrates' court.

(2) A magistrates' court may on an appeal under this paragraph—

(a) uphold any refusal of consent or require the authority to grant consent (without limitation or condition or subject to any limitation or condition);
(b) require the authority to revoke or vary any condition;
(c) uphold or quash revocation of consent (or uphold or quash revocation to any extent).

Seizure of material

6. (1) Where it appears to an authorised officer of a principal litter authority that a person distributing any printed matter is committing an offence under paragraph 1 above, he may seize all or any of it.

(2) Any person claiming to own any printed matter seized under this paragraph may apply to a magistrates' court for an order that the printed matter be released to him.

(3) On an application under sub-paragraph (2) above, if the magistrates' court considers that the applicant does own the printed matter, the court shall order the principal litter authority to release it to him, except to the extent that the court considers that the authority needs to retain it for the purposes of proceedings relating to an offence under paragraph 1 above.

(4) Any printed matter seized under this paragraph (and not released under sub-paragraph (3) above) must be returned to the person from whom it is seized—

(a) at the conclusion of proceedings for the offence (unless the court orders otherwise);
(b) at the end of the period in which proceedings for the offence may be instituted, if no such proceedings have been instituted in that period (or have been instituted but discontinued).

(5) Where it is not possible to return any printed matter under sub-paragraph (4) above because the name and address of the person from whom it was seized are not known, a principal litter authority may dispose of or destroy it.

Fixed penalty notices

7. (1) This paragraph applies where on any occasion it appears to an authorised officer of a principal litter authority that a person has committed an offence under paragraph 1 above on any land designated by the authority under this Schedule.

(2) The authorised officer may give that person a notice offering him the opportunity of discharging any liability to conviction for the offence by payment of a fixed penalty to the principal litter authority.

(3) Subsections (2) to (5) of section 88 above apply in relation to notices given under this paragraph as they apply to notices under that section.

(4) The amount of the fixed penalty payable to a principal litter authority under this paragraph—

(a) is the amount specified by the authority in relation to its area; or
(b) if no amount is so specified, is £75.

(5) The principal litter authority to which a fixed penalty is payable under this paragraph may make provision for treating it as having been paid if a lesser amount is paid before the end of a period specified by the authority.

(6) In any proceedings a certificate which—

(a) purports to be signed on behalf of the chief finance officer of a principal litter authority, and

(b) states that payment of a fixed penalty was or was not received by a date specified in the certificate,

is evidence of the facts stated.

(7) If an authorised officer of a principal litter authority proposes to give a person a notice under this paragraph, the officer may require the person to give him his name and address.

(8) A person commits an offence if—

(a) he fails to give his name and address when required to do so under sub-paragraph (7) above; or

(b) he gives a false or inaccurate name or address in response to a requirement under that sub-paragraph.

(9) A person guilty of an offence under sub-paragraph (8) above is liable on summary conviction to a fine not exceeding level 3 on the standard scale.

(10) In this paragraph, "chief finance officer", in relation to a principal litter authority, means the person having responsibility for the financial affairs of that authority.

Supplementary

8. In this Schedule "authorised officer", in relation to a principal litter authority, means—

(a) an employee of the authority who is authorised in writing by the authority for the purpose of giving notices under paragraph 7 above;

(b) any person who, in pursuance of arrangements made with the authority, has the function of giving such notices and is authorised in writing by the authority to perform that function; and

(c) any employee of such a person who is authorised in writing by the authority for the purpose of giving such notices."

[Clean Neighbourhoods and Environment Act 2005, s 23.]

General

8–26822 **24. Fixed penalty notices: common provision.** After section 97 of the Environmental Protection Act 1990 (c 43) insert—

"97A. Fixed penalty notices: supplementary. (1) The appropriate person may by regulations make provision in connection with the powers conferred under—

(a) section 88(6A)(a) and (7) above;

(b) section 94A(4)(a) and (5) above;

(c) paragraph 7(4)(a) and (5) of Schedule 3A.

(2) Regulations under subsection (1) may (in particular)—

(a) require an amount specified under section 88(6A)(a), 94A(4)(a) or paragraph 7(4)(a) of Schedule 3A to fall within a range prescribed in the regulations;

(b) restrict the extent to which, and the circumstances in which, an authority can make provision under section 88(7), 94A(5) or paragraph 7(5) of Schedule 3A.

(3) The appropriate person may by order substitute a different amount for the amount for the time being specified in section 88(6A)(b), 94A(4)(b) or paragraph 7(4)(b) of Schedule 3A.

(4) Regulations or an order under this section may make different provision for different purposes."

[Clean Neighbourhoods and Environment Act 2005, s 24.]

8–26823 **25. Exclusion of liability.** In the Environmental Protection Act 1990 (c 43), after section 97A (as inserted by section 24 above) insert—

"97B. Exclusion of liability. (1) None of the persons mentioned in subsection (2) below is to have any liability to an occupier or owner of land for damages or otherwise (whether at common law or otherwise) arising out of anything done or omitted to be done in the exercise or purported exercise of the power in section 92(9), 92A(9) or 92C(3) above.

(2) Those persons are—

(a) the principal litter authority and any employee of the authority; and

(b) in the case of the power in section 92C(3) above, any person authorised by the authority under that provision and the employer or any employee of that person.

(3) Subsection (1) above does not apply—

(a) if the act or omission is shown to be in bad faith;

(b) to liability arising out of a failure to exercise due care and attention;

(c) so as to prevent an award of damages in respect of an act or omission on the ground that the act or omission was unlawful by virtue of section 6(1) of the Human Rights Act 1998.

(4) This section does not affect any other exemption from liability (whether at common law or otherwise)."

[Clean Neighbourhoods and Environment Act 2005, s 25.]

8–26824 **26. "Appropriate person".** In section 98 of the Environmental Protection Act 1990 (definitions), after subsection (1) insert—

"(1A) "Appropriate person" means—

(a) in relation to England, the Secretary of State;
(b) in relation to Wales, the National Assembly for Wales."

[Clean Neighbourhoods and Environment Act 2005, s 26.]

8–26825 **27. "Litter".** In section 98 of the Environmental Protection Act 1990 (definitions), after subsection (5) insert—

"(5A) "Litter" includes—

(a) the discarded ends of cigarettes, cigars and like products, and
(b) discarded chewing-gum and the discarded remains of other products designed for chewing."

[Clean Neighbourhoods and Environment Act 2005, s 27.]

PART 4[1]

GRAFFITI AND OTHER DEFACEMENT

Graffiti and fly-posting

8–26826 **28. Fixed penalty notices: amount of fixed penalty.** (1) In section 43 of the Anti-social Behaviour Act 2003 (c 38) (penalty notices for graffiti and fly-posting) omit subsections (10) and (11).

(2) After that section insert—

"43A. Amount of penalty. (1) The amount of a penalty payable in pursuance of a notice under section 43(1)—

(a) is the amount specified by a relevant local authority in relation to its area (whether or not the penalty is payable to that or another authority), or
(b) if no amount is so specified, is £75.

(2) In subsection (1)(a), "relevant local authority" means—

(a) a district council in England;
(b) a county council in England for an area for which there is no district council;
(c) a London borough council;
(d) the Common Council of the City of London;
(e) the Council of the Isles of Scilly;
(f) a county or county borough council in Wales.

(3) The local authority to which a penalty is payable in pursuance of a notice under section 43(1) may make provision for treating it as having been paid if a lesser amount is paid before the end of a period specified by the authority.

(4) The appropriate person may by regulations make provision in connection with the powers conferred under subsections (1)(a) and (3).

(5) Regulations under subsection (4) may (in particular)—

(a) require an amount specified under subsection (1)(a) to fall within a range prescribed in the regulations;
(b) restrict the extent to which, and the circumstances in which, a local authority can make provision under subsection (3).

(6) The appropriate person may by order substitute a different amount for the amount for the time being specified in subsection (1)(b)."

[Clean Neighbourhoods and Environment Act 2005, s 28.]

1. Part 4 contains ss 28–34.

8–26827 **29. Fixed penalty notices: power to require name and address.** After section 43A of the Anti-social Behaviour Act 2003 (c 38) (as inserted by section 28 above) insert—

"43B. Penalty notices: power to require name and address. (1) If an authorised officer of a local authority proposes to give a person a notice under section 43(1), the officer may require the person to give him his name and address.

(2) A person commits an offence if—

(a) he fails to give his name and address when required to do so under subsection (1), or

(b) he gives a false or inaccurate name or address in response to a requirement under that subsection.

(3) A person guilty of an offence under subsection (2) is liable on summary conviction to a fine not exceeding level 3 on the standard scale."

[Clean Neighbourhoods and Environment Act 2005, s 29.]

8–26828 30. Fixed penalty notices: authorised officers. (1) In section 47 of the Anti-social Behaviour Act 2003 (c 38) (interpretation etc), in subsection (1), for the definition of "authorised officer" substitute—

""authorised officer", in relation to a local authority, means—

(a) an employee of the authority who is authorised in writing by the authority for the purpose of giving notices under section 43(1);

(b) any person who, in pursuance of arrangements made with the authority, has the function of giving such notices and is authorised in writing by the authority to perform that function; and

(c) any employee of such a person who is authorised in writing by the authority for the purpose of giving such notices,".

(2) In that section, at the end insert—

"(4) The appropriate person may by regulations prescribe conditions to be satisfied by a person before a parish or community council may authorise him in writing for the purpose of giving notices under section 43(1)."

[Clean Neighbourhoods and Environment Act 2005, s 30.]

8–26829 31. Extension of graffiti removal notices to fly-posting. (1) Section 48 of the Anti-social Behaviour Act 2003 (c 38) (graffiti removal notices) is amended as follows.

(2) In subsection (1)(a) (section to apply where a relevant surface has been defaced by graffiti), after "graffiti" insert "or any poster or flyer the display of which contravenes regulations under section 220 of the Town and Country Planning Act 1990".

[Clean Neighbourhoods and Environment Act 2005, s 31.]

32. Sale of aerosol paint to children. *Inserted new s 54A into the Anti-social Behaviour Act 2003.*

Advertisements

8–26830 33. Unlawful display of advertisements: defences. (1) Section 224 of the Town and Country Planning Act 1990 (c 8) (enforcement of control as to advertisements) is amended as follows.

(2) In subsection (5) (person not guilty of offence of displaying advertisement in contravention of regulations if he proves it was displayed without his knowledge or consent), for "that it was displayed without his knowledge or consent" substitute "either of the matters specified in subsection (6)".

(3) After that subsection insert—

"(6) The matters are that—

(a) the advertisement was displayed without his knowledge; or

(b) he took all reasonable steps to prevent the display or, after the advertisement had been displayed, to secure its removal."

(4) This section does not have effect in relation to an offence committed, or alleged to have been committed, before the commencement of this section.

[Clean Neighbourhoods and Environment Act 2005, s 33.]

8–26831 34. Removal of placards and posters. (1) Section 225 of the Town and Country Planning Act 1990 (power to remove or obliterate placards and posters) is amended as follows.

(2) In subsection (3)(b) after "notice" insert "and recover from him the costs they may reasonably incur in doing so".

(3) After subsection (5) insert—

"(6) Where—

(a) a local planning authority serve a notice on a person under subsection (3) in relation to a placard or poster, and

(b) the person fails to remove or obliterate it within the period specified in the notice,

the authority may recover from that person the costs they may reasonably incur in exercising their power under subsection (1)."

(4) After subsection (6) (as inserted by subsection (3) above) insert—

"(7) This subsection applies in relation to a placard or poster where—

(a) the placard or poster does not identify the person who displayed it or caused it to be displayed, or

(b) it does do so, but subsection (3) does not apply by reason of subsection (4), and

the placard or poster publicises the goods, services or concerns of an identifiable person.

(8) Where subsection (7) applies, subsections (3) to (6) have effect as if the reference in subsection (3) to the person who displayed the placard or poster or caused it to be displayed were a reference to the person whose goods, services or concerns are publicised."

(5) After subsection (8) (as inserted by subsection (4) above) insert—

"(9) Where any damage is caused to land or chattels in the exercise of the power under subsection (1) in relation to a placard or poster, compensation may be recovered by any person suffering the damage from the local planning authority exercising the power.

(10) Subsection (9) does not permit the recovery of compensation by the person who displayed the placard or poster or caused it to be displayed.

(11) The provisions of section 118 apply in relation to compensation under subsection (9) as they apply in relation to compensation under Part 4."

(6) In section 324 of that Act (rights of entry), omit subsection (3)(a).

[Clean Neighbourhoods and Environment Act 2005, s 34.]

PART 5[1]
WASTE

CHAPTER 1[2]
Transport of Waste

8–26832 **35. Unregistered transport: defence of acting under employer's instructions.** (1) In section 1 of the Control of Pollution (Amendment) Act 1989 (c 14) (offence of transporting controlled waste without registering), in subsection (4)—

(a) at the end of paragraph (a), insert "or";
(b) omit paragraph (c) (defence of acting under employer's instructions) and the preceding "or".

(2) This section does not have effect in relation to an offence committed, or alleged to have been committed, before the commencement of this section.

[Clean Neighbourhoods and Environment Act 2005, s 35.]

1. Part 5 contains ss 35–54.
2. Chapter 1 contains ss 35–39.

8–26833 **36. Registration requirements and conditions.** (1) Section 2 of the Control of Pollution (Amendment) Act 1989 (c 14) (power to make regulations about registration of carriers) is amended as follows.

(2) In subsection (2)—

(a) in paragraph (c), omit "free of charge";
(b) omit paragraph (d);
(c) in paragraph (e), omit "free of charge".

(3) In subsection (3), omit paragraph (b) (provision as to form of applications).

(4) In subsection (3A)—

(a) for "paragraphs (b) and (d)" substitute "paragraph (d)"; and
(b) omit paragraph (a) (further provision as to form of application).

(5) After subsection (4) insert—

"(4A) Regulations under this section may include provision for—

(a) the registration of a person as a carrier of controlled waste to be subject to conditions relating to the vehicles used by him in transporting such waste; or
(b) the revocation by a regulation authority of the registration of a carrier of controlled waste who has breached a condition imposed on him under paragraph (a) above.

(4B) Provision contained in any regulations under this section by virtue of subsection (4A) above may, in particular, include provision—

(a) for inspection by a regulation authority of the vehicles of registered carriers of controlled waste for the purpose of ensuring compliance with conditions imposed under subsection (4A)(a) above;
(b) for a regulation authority to impose charges on registered carriers of controlled waste in respect of such inspections."

(6) In subsection (5), for "to (4)" substitute "to (4B)".

(7) In section 3 of that Act (restrictions on power under section 2), in subsection (2), after "except" insert "in accordance with regulations under subsection (4A) of that section or".

[Clean Neighbourhoods and Environment Act 2005, s 36.]

8-26834 37. Enforcement powers. For section 5 of the Control of Pollution (Amendment) Act 1989 substitute—

"5. Power to require production of authority, stop and search etc. (1) This section applies where an authorised officer of a regulation authority or a constable reasonably believes that controlled waste has been, is being or is about to be transported in contravention of section 1(1) above.

(2) The authorised officer or constable may—

(a) require any person appearing to him to be or to have been engaged in transporting that waste to produce his (or, as the case may be, his employer's) authority to do so;
(b) search any vehicle that appears to him to be a vehicle that has been, is being or is about to be used for transporting that waste;
(c) carry out tests on anything found in any such vehicle (including by taking away samples for testing of anything so found);
(d) seize any such vehicle and any of its contents.

(3) For the purposes of subsection (2)(a) above, a person's authority for transporting controlled waste is—

(a) his certificate of registration as a carrier of controlled waste;
(b) such copy of that certificate as satisfies requirements specified in regulations made by the appropriate person; or
(c) such evidence as may be so specified that he is not required to be registered as a carrier of controlled waste.

(4) Where an authorised officer or constable has required a person to produce an authority under subsection (2)(a) above, the person must do so—

(a) by producing it forthwith to the authorised officer or constable;
(b) by producing it at a place and within a period specified in regulations made by the appropriate person; or
(c) by sending it to that place and within that period.

(5) In acting under subsection (2) above an authorised officer or constable may—

(a) stop any vehicle as referred to in paragraph (b) of that subsection (but only a constable in uniform may stop a vehicle on any road);
(b) enter any premises for the purpose specified in paragraph (b) or (d) of that subsection.

(6) A vehicle or its contents seized under subsection (2)(d) above—

(a) by an authorised officer of a regulation authority, are seized on behalf of that authority;
(b) by a constable in the presence of an authorised officer of a regulation authority, are seized on behalf of that authority;
(c) by a constable without such an officer present, are seized on behalf of the waste collection authority in whose area the seizure takes place.

(7) A person commits an offence if—

(a) he fails without reasonable excuse to comply with a requirement imposed under paragraph (a) of subsection (2) above;
(b) he fails without reasonable excuse to give any assistance that an authorised officer or constable may reasonably request in the exercise of a power under that subsection;
(c) he otherwise intentionally obstructs an authorised officer or constable in the exercise of a power under that subsection.

(8) A person is not guilty of an offence by virtue of subsection (7)(a) above unless it is shown—

(a) that the waste in question was controlled waste; and
(b) that the waste was or was being transported to or from a place in Great Britain.

(9) Where an authorised officer or constable has stopped a vehicle under subsection (5) above, he may (in addition to any requirement that may be imposed under paragraph (a) of subsection (2) above) require any occupant of the vehicle to give him—

(a) the occupant's name and address;
(b) the name and address of the registered owner of the vehicle;
(c) any other information he may reasonably request.

(10) A person commits an offence if—

(a) he fails without reasonable excuse to comply with a requirement under subsection (9) above;
(b) he gives information required under that subsection that is—

(i) to his knowledge false or misleading in a material way, or
(ii) given recklessly and is false or misleading in a material way.

(11) A person guilty of an offence under this section is liable on summary conviction to a fine not exceeding level 5 on the standard scale.

5A. Seizure of vehicles etc: supplementary. (1) Where under section 5 above an authorised officer of a regulation authority or a constable seizes a vehicle or its contents ("seized property") on behalf of a regulation authority, the authority may remove the seized property to such a place as the authority consider appropriate.

(2) A regulation authority must deal with any seized property in accordance with regulations made by the appropriate person.

(3) Regulations under subsection (2) above may in particular include provision as to—

(a) the duties of a regulation authority in relation to the safe custody of seized property;

(b) the circumstances in which the authority must return any such property to a person claiming entitlement to it;

(c) the manner in which such persons, and the seized property to which they are entitled, may be determined;

(d) the circumstances in which the authority may sell, destroy or otherwise dispose of seized property;

(e) the uses to which the proceeds of any such sale may be put.

(4) Regulations making provision under subsection (3)(d) above—

(a) must (subject to paragraph (c) below) require the regulation authority to publish a notice in such form, and to take any other steps, as may be specified in the regulations for informing persons who may be entitled to the seized property that it has been seized and is available to be claimed;

(b) must (subject to paragraph (c) below) prohibit the authority from selling, destroying or otherwise disposing of any seized property unless a period specified in the regulations has expired without any obligation arising under the regulations for the authority to return the property to any person;

(c) may allow for the requirements in paragraphs (a) and (b) above to be dispensed with if the condition of the seized property requires its disposal without delay.

(5) The appropriate person may issue guidance to regulation authorities in relation to the performance of their functions under regulations under subsection (2) above."

[Clean Neighbourhoods and Environment Act 2005, s 37.]

8–26835 **38. Failure to produce authority: fixed penalty notices.** (1) In the Control of Pollution (Amendment) Act 1989 (c 14), after section 5A (as inserted by section 37 above) insert—

"5B. Fixed penalty notices for offences under section 5. (1) This section applies where it appears to a regulation authority that a person has failed without reasonable excuse to comply with a requirement under section 5(2)(a) above (requirement to produce authority to transport waste).

(2) The regulation authority may give that person a notice offering him the opportunity of discharging any liability to conviction for an offence under section 5(7)(a) above by payment of a fixed penalty.

(3) Where a person is given a notice under this section in respect of an offence—

(a) no proceedings may be instituted for that offence before expiration of the period of fourteen days following the date of the notice; and

(b) he may not be convicted of that offence if he pays the fixed penalty before the expiration of the period.

(4) A notice under this section must give such particulars of the circumstances alleged to constitute the offence as are necessary for giving reasonable information of the offence.

(5) A notice under this section must also state—

(a) the period during which, by virtue of subsection (3) above, proceedings will not be taken for the offence;

(b) the amount of the fixed penalty; and

(c) the person to whom and the address at which the fixed penalty may be paid.

(6) Without prejudice to payment by any other method, payment of the fixed penalty may be made by pre-paying and posting a letter containing the amount of the penalty (in cash or otherwise) to the person mentioned in subsection (5)(c) above at the address so mentioned.

(7) Where a letter is sent in accordance with subsection (6) above payment is to be regarded as having been made at the time at which that letter would be delivered in the ordinary course of post.

(8) The form of a notice under this section must be such as the appropriate person may by order prescribe.

(9) The fixed penalty payable to a regulation authority under this section is, subject to subsection (10) below, £300.

(10) The appropriate person may by order substitute a different amount for the amount for the time being specified in subsection (9) above.

(11) The regulation authority to which a fixed penalty is payable under this section may make provision for treating it as having been paid if a lesser amount is paid before the end of a period specified by the authority.

(12) The appropriate person may by regulations restrict the extent to which, and the circumstances in which, a regulation authority may make provision under subsection (11) above.

(13) In any proceedings a certificate which—

(a) purports to be signed on behalf of the chief finance officer of the regulation authority, and
(b) states that payment of a fixed penalty was or was not received by a date specified in the certificate,

is evidence of the facts stated.

(14) In this section "chief finance officer", in relation to a regulation authority, means the person having responsibility for the financial affairs of the authority.

5C. Use of fixed penalties under section 5B. (1) This section applies in relation to amounts paid to a regulation authority in pursuance of notices under section 5B above (its "fixed penalty receipts").

(2) Fixed penalty receipts—

(a) where received by the Environment Agency, must be paid to the Secretary of State;
(b) where received by a waste collection authority, must be used in accordance with the following provisions of this section.

(3) A waste collection authority may use its fixed penalty receipts only for the purposes of—

(a) its functions under section 5 above (including functions relating to the enforcement of offences under that section);
(b) such other of its functions as may be specified in regulations made by the appropriate person.

(4) Regulations under subsection (3)(b) above may in particular have the effect that an authority may use its fixed penalty receipts for the purposes of any of its functions.

(5) A waste collection authority must supply the appropriate person with such information relating to its use of its fixed penalty receipts as the appropriate person may require.

(6) The appropriate person may by regulations—

(a) make provision for what a waste collection authority is to do with its fixed penalty receipts—
   (i) pending their being used for the purposes of functions of the authority referred to in subsection (3) above;
   (ii) if they are not so used before such time after their receipt as may be specified by the order;
(b) make provision for accounting arrangements in respect of a waste collection authority's fixed penalty receipts.

(7) The provision that may be made under subsection (6)(a)(ii) above includes (in particular) provision for the payment of sums to a person (including the appropriate person) other than the authority.

(8) Before making regulations under this section, the appropriate person must consult—

(a) the authorities to which the regulations are to apply;
(b) such other persons as the appropriate person thinks fit.

(9) The powers to make regulations conferred by this section are, for the purposes of subsection (1) of section 100 of the Local Government Act 2003, to be regarded as included among the powers mentioned in subsection (2) of that section."

[Clean Neighbourhoods and Environment Act 2005, s 38.]

8–26836 39. Interpretation. (1) Section 9 of the Control of Pollution (Amendment) Act 1989 (c 14) (interpretation) is amended as follows.

(2) In subsection (1), at the appropriate place insert—

""""appropriate person" means—

(a) the Secretary of State, in relation to England;
(b) the National Assembly for Wales, in relation to Wales."

(3) After subsection (1A) insert—

"(1B) For the purposes of any provision of this Act, "authorised officer" in relation to any authority means an officer of the authority who is authorised in writing by the authority for the purposes of that provision."

[Clean Neighbourhoods and Environment Act 2005, s 39.]

CHAPTER 2[1]

Deposit and Disposal of Waste

Offence of unlawful deposit of waste etc

8–26837 **40. Defence of acting under employer's instructions.** (1) In section 33 of the Environmental Protection Act 1990 (c 43) (offence of unauthorised or harmful deposit etc of controlled waste), omit subsection (7)(b) (defence of acting on employer's instructions).

(2) This section does not have effect in relation to an offence committed, or alleged to have been committed, before the commencement of this section.

[Clean Neighbourhoods and Environment Act 2005, s 40.]

1. Chapter 2 contains ss 40–53.

8–26838 **41. Penalties on conviction.** (1) In section 33 of the Environmental Protection Act 1990 (offence of unauthorised or harmful deposit etc of waste), for subsections (8) and (9) (penalties) substitute—

"(8) A person who commits an offence under this section is liable—

(a) on summary conviction, to imprisonment for a term not exceeding 12 months or a fine not exceeding £50,000 or both;

(b) on conviction on indictment, to imprisonment for a term not exceeding five years or a fine or both."

(2) Subsection (1) does not have effect in relation to offences committed before the commencement of this section.

(3) In relation to offences committed after the commencement of this section but before the commencement of section 154(1) of the Criminal Justice Act 2003 (c 44), the amendment made by this section has effect as if for "12 months" there were substituted "6 months".

[Clean Neighbourhoods and Environment Act 2005, s 41.]

42–44. *These sections inserted new ss 33A–33C in the Environmental Protection Act 1990.*

Offences relating to documentation

8–26839 **45. Failure to furnish documentation: fixed penalty notices.** In the Environmental Protection Act 1990 (c 43), after section 34 (duty of care etc as respects waste) insert—

"34A. Fixed penalty notices for certain offences under section 34. (1) This section applies where it appears to an enforcement authority that a person has failed to comply with a duty to furnish documents to that authority imposed under regulations made at any time under section 34(5) above.

(2) The authority may serve on that person a notice offering him the opportunity of discharging any liability to conviction for an offence under section 34(6) above by payment of a fixed penalty.

(3) Where a person is given a notice under this section in respect of an offence—

(a) no proceedings may be instituted for that offence before expiration of the period of fourteen days following the date of the notice; and

(b) he may not be convicted of that offence if he pays the fixed penalty before the expiration of the period.

(4) A notice under this section must give such particulars of the circumstances alleged to constitute the offence as are necessary for giving reasonable information of the offence.

(5) A notice under this section must also state—

(a) the period during which, by virtue of subsection (3) above, proceedings will not be taken for the offence;

(b) the amount of the fixed penalty; and

(c) the person to whom and the address at which the fixed penalty may be paid.

(6) Without prejudice to payment by any other method, payment of the fixed penalty may be made by pre-paying and posting a letter containing the amount of the penalty (in cash or otherwise) to the person mentioned in subsection (5)(c) above at the address so mentioned.

(7) Where a letter is sent in accordance with subsection (6) above payment is to be regarded as having been made at the time at which that letter would be delivered in the ordinary course of post.

(8) The form of a notice under this section is to be such as the appropriate person may by order prescribe.

(9) The fixed penalty payable to an enforcement authority under this section is, subject to subsection (10) below, £300.

(10) The appropriate person may by order substitute a different amount for the amount for the time being specified in subsection (9) above.

(11) The enforcement authority to which a fixed penalty is payable under this section may make provision for treating it as having been paid if a lesser amount is paid before the end of a period specified by the authority.

(12) The appropriate person may by regulations restrict the extent to which, and the circumstances in which, an enforcement authority may make provision under subsection (11) above.

(13) In any proceedings a certificate which—

(a) purports to be signed on behalf of the chief finance officer of the enforcement authority, and

(b) states that payment of a fixed penalty was or was not received by a date specified in the certificate,

is evidence of the facts stated.

(14) In this section—

"chief finance officer", in relation to an enforcement authority, means the person having responsibility for the financial affairs of the authority;

"enforcement authority" means the Environment Agency or a waste collection authority."

[Clean Neighbourhoods and Environment Act 2005, s 45.]

Offences: powers of seizure

8–26840 **46. Power to search and seize vehicles.** (1) After section 34A of the Environmental Protection Act 1990 (c 43) (as inserted by section 45 above), insert—

"Offences under sections 33 and 34: powers of seizure etc

34B. Power to search and seize vehicles etc. (1) This section applies where an authorised officer of an enforcement authority or a constable reasonably believes that the grounds in subsection (2) or (3) below exist.

(2) The grounds in this subsection are that—

(a) a relevant offence has been committed,
(b) a vehicle was used in the commission of the offence, and
(c) proceedings for the offence have not yet been brought against any person.

(3) The grounds in this subsection are that—

(a) a relevant offence is being or is about to be committed, and
(b) a vehicle is being or is about to be used in the commission of the offence.

(4) The authorised officer or constable may—

(a) search the vehicle;
(b) seize the vehicle and any of its contents.

(5) In acting under subsection (4) above the authorised officer or constable may—

(a) stop the vehicle (but only a constable in uniform may stop a vehicle on any road);
(b) enter any premises for the purpose of searching or seizing the vehicle.

(6) A vehicle or its contents seized under subsection (4) above—

(a) by an authorised officer of an enforcement authority, are seized on behalf of that authority;
(b) by a constable in the presence of an authorised officer of an enforcement authority, are seized on behalf of that authority;
(c) by a constable without such an officer present, are seized on behalf of the waste collection authority in whose area the seizure takes place.

(7) A person commits an offence if—

(a) he fails without reasonable excuse to give any assistance that an authorised officer or constable may reasonably request in the exercise of a power under subsection (4) or (5) above;
(b) he otherwise intentionally obstructs an authorised officer or constable in exercising that power.

(8) Where an authorised officer or constable has stopped a vehicle under subsection (5)(a) above, he may require any occupant of the vehicle to give him—

(a) the occupant's name and address;
(b) the name and address of the registered owner of the vehicle;
(c) any other information he may reasonably request.

(9) A person commits an offence if—

(a) he fails without reasonable excuse to comply with a requirement under subsection (8) above;

(b) he gives information required under that subsection that is—

(i) to his knowledge false or misleading in a material way, or

(ii) given recklessly and is false or misleading in a material way.

(10) A person guilty of an offence under this section is liable on summary conviction to a fine not exceeding level 5 on the standard scale.

(11) In this section and section 34C below—

"authorised officer" means an officer of an enforcement authority who is authorised in writing by the authority for the purposes of this section;

"enforcement authority" means—

(a) the Environment Agency, or

(b) a waste collection authority;

"relevant offence" means—

(a) an offence under section 33 above, or

(b) an offence under section 34 above consisting of a failure to comply with the duty imposed by subsection (1) of that section;

"road" has the same meaning as in the Road Traffic Regulation Act 1984;

"vehicle" means any motor vehicle or trailer within the meaning of that Act or any mobile plant.

34C. Seizure of vehicles etc: supplementary. (1) Where under section 34B above an authorised officer or constable seizes a vehicle or its contents ("seized property") on behalf of an enforcement authority, the authority may remove the seized property to such a place as it considers appropriate.

(2) An enforcement authority must deal with any seized property in accordance with regulations made by the appropriate person.

(3) Regulations under subsection (2) above may in particular include provision as to—

(a) the duties of enforcement authorities in relation to the safe custody of seized property;

(b) the circumstances in which they must return any such property to a person claiming entitlement to it;

(c) the manner in which such persons, and the seized property to which they are entitled, may be determined;

(d) the circumstances in which an enforcement authority may sell, destroy or otherwise dispose of seized property;

(e) the uses to which the proceeds of any such sale may be put.

(4) Regulations making provision under subsection (3)(d) above—

(a) must (subject to paragraph (c) below) require the enforcement authority to publish a notice in such form, and to take any other steps, as may be specified in the regulations for informing persons who may be entitled to the seized property that it has been seized and is available to be claimed;

(b) must (subject to paragraph (c) below) prohibit the authority from selling, destroying or otherwise disposing of any seized property unless a period specified in the regulations has expired without any obligation arising under the regulations for the authority to return the property to any person;

(c) may allow for the requirements in paragraphs (a) and (b) above to be dispensed with if the condition of the seized property requires its disposal without delay.

(5) The appropriate person may issue guidance to enforcement authorities in relation to the performance of their functions under regulations under subsection (2) above."

(2) In section 71 of that Act (obtaining information from persons and authorities)—

(a) after subsection (2) insert—

"(2A) A waste collection authority has the power referred to in subsection (2) for the purpose of the discharge of its functions under sections 34B and 34C above.";

(b) in subsection (3) after "subsection (2)" insert "or (2A)".

[Clean Neighbourhoods and Environment Act 2005, s 46 as amended by SI 2005/2900.]

Local authority waste collection and disposal

8–26841 **47. Abolition of requirement to contract out waste disposal functions[1].** Section 32 of and Schedule 2 to the Environmental Protection Act 1990 (c 43) (power to require local authorities to transfer waste disposal functions etc to specially formed companies) shall cease to have effect.

[Clean Neighbourhoods and Environment Act 2005, s 47.]

1. Section 47 is in force in relation to England only and subject to savings. See Note 1 to the title of this Act, ante.

8–26842 48. Offences relating to waste receptacles: fixed penalty notices. In the Environmental Protection Act 1990, after section 47 (receptacles for commercial or industrial waste) insert—

"47ZA. Fixed penalty notices for offences under sections 46 and 47. (1) This section applies where on any occasion an authorised officer of a waste collection authority has reason to believe that a person has committed an offence under section 46 or 47 above in the area of that authority.

(2) The authorised officer may give that person a notice offering him the opportunity of discharging any liability to conviction for the offence by payment of a fixed penalty to the waste collection authority.

(3) Where a person is given a notice under this section in respect of an offence—

(a) no proceedings may be instituted for that offence before the expiration of the period of fourteen days following the date of the notice; and

(b) he may not be convicted of that offence if he pays the fixed penalty before the expiration of that period.

(4) A notice under this section must give such particulars of the circumstances alleged to constitute the offence as are necessary for giving reasonable information of the offence.

(5) A notice under this section must also state—

(a) the period during which, by virtue of subsection (3) above, proceedings will not be taken for the offence;

(b) the amount of the fixed penalty; and

(c) the person to whom and the address at which the fixed penalty may be paid.

(6) Without prejudice to payment by any other method, payment of the fixed penalty may be made by pre-paying and posting a letter containing the amount of the penalty (in cash or otherwise) to the person mentioned in subsection (5)(c) above at the address so mentioned.

(7) Where a letter is sent in accordance with subsection (6) above payment is to be regarded as having been made at the time at which that letter would be delivered in the ordinary course of post.

(8) The form of a notice under this section is to be such as the appropriate person may by order prescribe.

(9) In any proceedings a certificate which—

(a) purports to be signed on behalf of the chief finance officer of the waste collection authority, and

(b) states that payment of a fixed penalty was or was not received by a date specified in the certificate,

is evidence of the facts stated.

(10) In this section—

"authorised officer", in relation to a waste collection authority, means—

(a) an employee of the authority who is authorised in writing by the authority for the purposes of giving notices under this section;

(b) any person who, in pursuance of arrangements made with the authority, has the function of giving such notices and is authorised in writing by the authority to perform that function;

(c) any employee of such a person who is authorised in writing by the authority for the purpose of giving such notices;

"chief finance officer", in relation to a waste collection authority, means the person having responsibility for the financial affairs of the authority.

47ZB. Amount of fixed penalty under section 47ZA. (1) This section applies in relation to a fixed penalty payable to a waste collection authority in pursuance of a notice under section 47ZA above.

(2) The amount of the fixed penalty—

(a) is the amount specified by the waste collection authority in relation to the authority's area, or

(b) if no amount is so specified, is £100.

(3) The waste collection authority may make provision for treating the fixed penalty as having been paid if a lesser amount is paid before the end of a period specified by the authority.

(4) The appropriate person may by regulations make provision in connection with the powers conferred on waste collection authorities under subsections (2)(a) and (3) above.

(5) Regulations under subsection (4) may (in particular)—

(a) require an amount specified under subsection (2)(a) above to fall within a range prescribed in the regulations;

(b) restrict the extent to which, and the circumstances in which, a waste collection authority can make provision under subsection (3) above.

(6) The appropriate person may by order substitute a different amount for the amount for the time being specified in subsection (2)(b) above."

[Clean Neighbourhoods and Environment Act 2005, s 48.]

8–26843 **49. Payments for waste recycling and disposal.** (1) Section 52 of the Environmental Protection Act 1990 (c 43) (payments for recycling and disposal etc of waste) is amended as follows.

(2) In subsection (1) after "so retained" insert—

"(a) in the case of a waste disposal authority in England, of such amounts as may be determined in accordance with regulations made by the Secretary of State; and

(b) in the case of a waste disposal authority in Wales".

(3) After subsection (1) insert—

"(1A) The Secretary of State may by order disapply subsection (1) above in relation to any waste disposal authority constituted under section 10 of the Local Government Act 1985 (joint arrangements for waste disposal in London and metropolitan counties)."

(4) After subsection (1A) (as inserted by subsection (3) above) insert—

"(1B) A waste disposal authority is not required to make payments to a waste collection authority under subsection (1) above where, on the basis of arrangements involving the two authorities, the waste collection authority has agreed that such payments need not be made."

(5) In subsection (2) after "so collected" insert—

"(a) in the case of a waste collection authority in England, of such amounts as may be determined in accordance with regulations made by the Secretary of State; and

(b) in the case of a waste collection authority in Wales".

(6) In subsection (3) after "so collected" insert—

"(a) in the case of a waste disposal authority in England, of such amounts as may be determined in accordance with regulations made by the Secretary of State; and

(b) in the case of a waste disposal authority in Wales".

(7) In subsection (4) after "so collected" insert—

"(a) in the case of a waste collection authority in England, of such amounts as may be determined in accordance with regulations made by the Secretary of State; and

(b) in the case of a waste collection authority in Wales".

(8) After subsection (8) insert—

"(8A) The Secretary of State may give guidance—

(a) to a waste disposal authority in England, for the purposes of determining whether to exercise the power in subsection (3) above;

(b) to a waste collection authority in England, for the purposes of determining whether to exercise the power in subsection (4) above."

(9) At the end insert—

"(12) In this section, references to recycling waste include re-using it (whether or not the waste is subjected to any process)."

[Clean Neighbourhoods and Environment Act 2005, s 49.]

8–26844 **50. Power to require owner of land to remove waste.** (1) In section 59 of the Environmental Protection Act 1990 (c 43) (power to require removal of waste unlawfully deposited), in subsection (7)(b) after "occupier of the land" insert "or the occupier cannot be found without the authority incurring unreasonable expense".

(2) After that section insert—

"59ZA. Section 59: supplementary power in relation to owner of land. (1) Where the grounds in subsection (2), (3) or (4) below are met, a waste regulation authority or waste collection authority may, by notice served on him, require the owner of any land in its area to comply with either or both of the requirements mentioned in subsection (1)(a) and (b) of section 59 above.

(2) The grounds in this subsection are that it appears to the authority that waste has been deposited in or on the land in contravention of section 33(1) above and—

(a) there is no occupier of the land, or

(b) the occupier cannot be found without the authority incurring unreasonable expense.

(3) The grounds in this subsection are that—

(a) the authority has served a notice under subsection (1) of section 59 above imposing a requirement on the occupier of the land,
(b) the occupier of the land is not the same person as the owner of the land, and
(c) the occupier has failed to comply with the requirement mentioned in paragraph (a) above within the period specified in the notice.

(4) The grounds in this subsection are that—

(a) the authority has served a notice under subsection (1) of section 59 above imposing a requirement on the occupier of the land,
(b) the occupier of the land is not the same person as the owner of the land, and
(c) the requirement mentioned in paragraph (a) above has been quashed on the ground specified in subsection (3)(a) of that section.

(5) Subsections (2) to (6) of section 59 above apply in relation to requirements imposed under this section on the owner of the land as they apply in relation to requirements imposed under that section on the occupier of the land but as if in subsection (3) there were inserted after paragraph (a)—

"(aa) in order to comply with the requirement the appellant would be required to enter the land unlawfully; or"

(6) In this section "owner" has the meaning given to it in section 78A(9) below."
[Clean Neighbourhoods and Environment Act 2005, s 50.]

Supplementary

8–26845 **51. "Appropriate person".** In section 29 of the Environmental Protection Act 1990 (c 43), after subsection (1) insert—

"(1A) "Appropriate person" means—

(a) in relation to England, the Secretary of State;
(b) in relation to Wales, the National Assembly for Wales."
[Clean Neighbourhoods and Environment Act 2005, s 51.]

52. Use of fixed penalty receipts. *Inserts new s 73A in the Environmental Protection Act 1990.*

8–26846 **53. Supplementary enforcement powers.** In section 108 of the Environment Act 1995 (c 25) (powers of enforcing authorities etc), in subsection (15), in the definition of "pollution control functions" in relation to a waste collection authority, for "conferred on it by section 59" substitute "conferred or imposed on it by or under Part 2".
[Clean Neighbourhoods and Environment Act 2005, s 53.]

CHAPTER 3[1]
Site Waste

8–26847 **54. Site waste management plans.** (1) The appropriate person may by regulations make provision requiring persons of a specified description—

(a) to prepare plans for the management and disposal of waste created in the course of specified descriptions of works involving construction or demolition;
(b) to comply with such plans.

(2) Descriptions of works that may be specified under subsection (1)(a) include in particular description by reference to the cost or likely cost of such works.

(3) Regulations under this section may make supplementary and incidental provision, including in particular provision as to—

(a) the circumstances in which plans must be prepared;
(b) the contents of plans;
(c) enforcement authorities in relation to plans and the powers of such authorities;
(d) the keeping of plans and their production to enforcement authorities;
(e) offences in relation to a failure to comply with a requirement under the regulations;
(f) penalties for those offences;
(g) the discharging of liability for an offence under the regulations by the payment of a fixed penalty to an enforcement authority;
(h) the uses to which such payments may be put by enforcement authorities.

(4) Regulations under this section may make different provision for different purposes.

(5) Regulations under this section making provision under subsection (3)(h) may in particular make different provision relating to different enforcement authorities or different descriptions of enforcement authority (including provision framed by reference to performance categories under section 99(4) of the Local Government Act 2003 (c 26)).

(6) Regulations under this section are to be made by statutory instrument.

(7) A statutory instrument containing regulations made by the Secretary of State under this section is subject to annulment in pursuance of a resolution of either House of Parliament.

(8) The appropriate person may give guidance to persons who are enforcement authorities under subsection (3)(c) in relation to the powers conferred on them under that provision.

(9) In this section—

"appropriate person" means—

(a) in relation to works in England, the Secretary of State;
(b) in relation to works in Wales, the National Assembly for Wales;

"specified" means specified in regulations under this section.
[Clean Neighbourhoods and Environment Act 2005, s 54.]

---

1. Chapter 3 contains s 54.

PART 6[1]
DOGS
CHAPTER 1[2]
Controls on Dogs
Dog control orders

8–26848 **55. Power to make dog control orders.** (1) A primary or secondary authority may in accordance with this Chapter make an order providing for an offence or offences relating to the control of dogs in respect of any land in its area to which this Chapter applies.

(2) An order under subsection (1) is to be known as a "dog control order".

(3) For the purposes of this Chapter an offence relates to the control of dogs if it relates to one of the following matters—

(a) fouling of land by dogs and the removal of dog faeces;
(b) the keeping of dogs on leads;
(c) the exclusion of dogs from land;
(d) the number of dogs which a person may take on to any land.

(4) An offence provided for in a dog control order must be an offence which is prescribed for the purposes of this section by regulations made by the appropriate person.

(5) Regulations under subsection (4) may in particular—

(a) specify all or part of the wording to be used in a dog control order for the purpose of providing for any offence;
(b) permit a dog control order to specify the times at which, or periods during which, an offence is to apply;
(c) provide for an offence to be defined by reference to failure to comply with the directions of a person of a description specified in the regulations.

(6) A dog control order may specify the land in respect of which it applies specifically or by description.

(7) A dog control order may be revoked or amended by the authority which made it; but this Chapter applies in relation to any amendment of a dog control order as if it were the making of a new order.
[Clean Neighbourhoods and Environment Act 2005, s 55.]

---

1. Part 1 contains ss 55–68.
2. Chapter 1 contains ss 55–67.

8–26849 **56. Dog control orders: supplementary.** (1) The appropriate person must by regulations prescribe the penalties, or maximum penalties, which may be provided for in a dog control order in relation to any offence.

(2) Regulations under subsection (1) may not in any case permit a dog control order to provide for a penalty other than a fine not exceeding level 3 on the standard scale in relation to any offence.

(3) The appropriate person must by regulations prescribe such other requirements relating to the content and form of a dog control order as the appropriate person thinks fit.

(4) The appropriate person must by regulations prescribe the procedure to be followed by a primary or secondary authority before and after making a dog control order.

(5) Regulations under subsection (4) must in particular include provision as to—

(a) consultation to be undertaken before a dog control order is made;
(b) the publicising of a dog control order after it has been made.

[Clean Neighbourhoods and Environment Act 2005, s 56.]

8–26850 57. Land to which Chapter 1 applies. (1) Subject to this section, this Chapter applies to any land which is open to the air and to which the public are entitled or permitted to have access (with or without payment).

(2) For the purposes of this section, any land which is covered is to be treated as land which is "open to the air" if it is open to the air on at least one side.

(3) The appropriate person may by order designate land as land to which this Chapter does not apply (generally or for such purposes as may be specified in the order).

(4) Land may be designated under subsection (3) specifically or by description.

(5) Where a private Act confers powers on a person other than a primary or secondary authority for the regulation of any land, that person may, by notice in writing given to the primary and secondary authorities in whose area the land is situated, exclude the application of this Chapter to that land.

[Clean Neighbourhoods and Environment Act 2005, s 57.]

8–26851 58. Primary and secondary authorities. (1) Each of the following is a "primary authority" for the purposes of this Chapter—

(a) a district council in England;
(b) a county council in England for an area for which there is no district council;
(c) a London borough council;
(d) the Common Council of the City of London;
(e) the Council of the Isles of Scilly;
(f) a county or county borough council in Wales.

(2) Each of the following is a "secondary authority" for the purposes of this Chapter—

(a) a parish council in England;
(b) a community council in Wales.

(3) The appropriate person may by order designate any person or body exercising functions under an enactment as a secondary authority for the purposes of this Chapter in respect of an area specified in the order.

[Clean Neighbourhoods and Environment Act 2005, s 58.]

Fixed penalty notices

8–26852 59. Fixed penalty notices. (1) This section applies where on any occasion—

(a) an authorised officer of a primary or secondary authority has reason to believe that a person has committed an offence under a dog control order made by that authority; or
(b) an authorised officer of a secondary authority has reason to believe that a person has in its area committed an offence under a dog control order made by a primary authority.

(2) The authorised officer may give that person a notice offering him the opportunity of discharging any liability to conviction for the offence by payment of a fixed penalty.

(3) A fixed penalty payable under this section is payable to the primary or secondary authority whose officer gave the notice.

(4) Where a person is given a notice under this section in respect of an offence—

(a) no proceedings may be instituted for that offence before the expiration of the period of fourteen days following the date of the notice; and
(b) he may not be convicted of that offence if he pays the fixed penalty before the expiration of that period.

(5) A notice under this section must give such particulars of the circumstances alleged to constitute the offence as are necessary for giving reasonable information of the offence.

(6) A notice under this section must also state—

(a) the period during which, by virtue of subsection (4), proceedings will not be taken for the offence;
(b) the amount of the fixed penalty; and
(c) the person to whom and the address at which the fixed penalty may be paid.

(7) Without prejudice to payment by any other method, payment of the fixed penalty may be made by pre-paying and posting a letter containing the amount of the penalty (in cash or otherwise) to the person mentioned in subsection (6)(c) at the address so mentioned.

(8) Where a letter is sent in accordance with subsection (7) payment is to be regarded as having been made at the time at which that letter would be delivered in the ordinary course of post.

(9) The form of a notice under this section is to be such as the appropriate person may by order prescribe.

(10) In any proceedings a certificate which—

(a) purports to be signed on behalf of the chief finance officer of a primary or secondary authority, and

(b) states that payment of a fixed penalty was or was not received by a date specified in the certificate,

is evidence of the facts stated.

(11) In this section—

"authorised officer", in relation to a primary or secondary authority, means—

(a) an employee of the authority who is authorised in writing by the authority for the purpose of giving notices under this section;

(b) any person who, in pursuance of arrangements made with the authority, has the function of giving such notices and is authorised in writing by the authority to perform that function; and

(c) any employee of such a person who is authorised in writing by the authority for the purpose of giving such notices;

"chief finance officer", in relation to a primary or secondary authority, means the person having responsibility for the financial affairs of the authority.

(12) The appropriate person may by regulations prescribe conditions to be satisfied by a person before a secondary authority may authorise him in writing for the purpose of giving notices under this section.

[Clean Neighbourhoods and Environment Act 2005, s 59.]

8–26853 **60. Amount of fixed penalties.** (1) The amount of a fixed penalty payable to a primary or secondary authority in pursuance of a notice under section 59 in respect of an offence under a dog control order—

(a) is the amount specified by the authority which made the order;

(b) if no amount is so specified, is £75.

(2) A primary or secondary authority may under subsection (1)(a) specify different amounts in relation to different offences.

(3) A primary or secondary authority may make provision for treating a fixed penalty payable to that authority in pursuance of a notice under section 59 as having been paid if a lesser amount is paid before the end of a period specified by the authority.

(4) The appropriate person may by regulations make provision in connection with the powers conferred on primary and secondary authorities under subsections (1)(a) and (3).

(5) Regulations under subsection (4) may (in particular)—

(a) require an amount specified under subsection (1)(a) to fall within a range prescribed in the regulations;

(b) restrict the extent to which, and the circumstances in which, a primary or secondary authority can make provision under subsection (3).

(6) The appropriate person may by order substitute a different amount for the amount for the time being specified in subsection (1)(b).

[Clean Neighbourhoods and Environment Act 2005, s 60.]

8–26854 **61. Power to require name and address.** (1) If an authorised officer of a primary or secondary authority proposes to give a person a notice under section 59, the officer may require the person to give him his name and address.

(2) A person commits an offence if—

(a) he fails to give his name and address when required to do so under subsection (1), or

(b) he gives a false or inaccurate name or address in response to a requirement under that subsection.

(3) A person guilty of an offence under subsection (2) is liable on summary conviction to a fine not exceeding level 3 on the standard scale.

(4) In this section "authorised officer" has the same meaning as in section 59.

[Clean Neighbourhoods and Environment Act 2005, s 61.]

8–26855 **62. Community support officers etc.** (1) The Police Reform Act 2002 (c 30) is amended as follows.

(2) In Schedule 4 (community support officers), in paragraph 1(2), after paragraph (d) insert

"and

(e) the power of an authorised officer of a primary or secondary authority, within the meaning of section 59 of the Clean Neighbourhoods and Environment Act 2005, to give a notice under that section (fixed penalty notices in respect of offences under dog control orders)."

(3) In Schedule 5 (accredited persons), in paragraph 1(2), after paragraph (c) insert

"and

(d) the power of an authorised officer of a primary or secondary authority, within the meaning of section 59 of the Clean Neighbourhoods and Environment Act 2005, to give a notice under that section (fixed penalty notices in respect of offences under dog control orders)."

[Clean Neighbourhoods and Environment Act 2005, s 62.]

Supplementary

8–26856 **63. Overlapping powers.** (1) Where a primary authority makes a dog control order providing for an offence relating to a matter specified in any of paragraphs (a) to (d) of section 55(3) as respects any land—

(a) a secondary authority may not make a dog control order providing for any offence which relates to the matter specified in that paragraph as respects that land;

(b) any dog control order previously made by a secondary authority providing for any offence which relates to the matter specified in that paragraph shall, to the extent that it so provides, cease to have effect.

(2) Where the area of an authority designated as a secondary authority under section 58(3) is to any extent the same as that of a parish or community council, subsection (1) applies in relation to orders made by the designated authority and that council as if the council were a primary authority.

[Clean Neighbourhoods and Environment Act 2005, s 63.]

8–26857 **64. Byelaws.** (1) Where, apart from this subsection, a primary or secondary authority has at any time power to make a byelaw in relation to any matter specified in any of paragraphs (a) to (d) of section 55(3) as respects any land, it may not make such a byelaw if at that time it has power under this Chapter to make a dog control order as respects that land in relation to the matter specified in that paragraph.

(2) Subsection (1) does not affect any byelaw which the authority had power to make at the time it was made.

(3) Where a dog control order is made in relation to any matter specified in any of paragraphs (a) to (d) of section 55(3) as respects any land, any byelaw previously made by a primary or secondary authority which has the effect of making a person guilty of any offence in relation to the matter specified in that paragraph as respects that land shall cease to have that effect.

(4) Where any act or omission would, apart from this subsection, constitute an offence under a dog control order and any byelaw, the act or omission shall not constitute an offence under the byelaw.

[Clean Neighbourhoods and Environment Act 2005, s 64.]

8–26858 **65. Dogs (Fouling of Land) Act 1996.** The Dogs (Fouling of Land) Act 1996 (c 20) shall cease to have effect.

[Clean Neighbourhoods and Environment Act 2005, s 65.]

General

8–26859 **66. "Appropriate person".** In this Chapter, "appropriate person" means—

(a) the Secretary of State, in relation to England;

(b) the National Assembly for Wales, in relation to Wales.

[Clean Neighbourhoods and Environment Act 2005, s 66.]

8–26860 **67. Regulations and orders.** (1) Any power conferred by this Chapter on the Secretary of State or National Assembly for Wales to make regulations or an order includes—

(a) power to make different provision for different purposes (including different provision for different authorities or different descriptions of authority);

(b) power to make consequential, supplementary, incidental and transitional provision and savings.

(2) Any power conferred by this Chapter on the Secretary of State or National Assembly for Wales to make regulations or an order is exercisable by statutory instrument.

(3) The Secretary of State may not make a statutory instrument containing regulations under section 55(4) or 56(1) unless a draft of the instrument has been laid before, and approved by a resolution of, each House of Parliament.

(4) A statutory instrument containing—

(a) regulations made by the Secretary of State under this Chapter to which subsection (3) does not apply, or

(b) an order made by the Secretary of State under this Chapter,

is subject to annulment in pursuance of a resolution of either House of Parliament.

[Clean Neighbourhoods and Environment Act 2005, s 67.]

CHAPTER 2[1]
Stray Dogs

8–26861 **68. Termination of police responsibility for stray dogs.** (1) Section 3 of the Dogs Act 1906 (c 32) (seizure of stray dogs by police) shall, subject to subsection (2), cease to have effect.

(2) The repeal in subsection (1) does not apply for the purposes of section 2(2) and (3) of the Dogs (Protection of Livestock) Act 1953 (c 28).

(3) In section 150 of the Environmental Protection Act 1990 (c 43) (delivery of stray dogs to police or local authority officer), in subsection (1)—

(a) in paragraph (b), omit sub-paragraph (ii) and the preceding "or";
(b) omit the words from "or the police officer" to "as the case may be,".

(4) In the heading to that section, omit "police or".

[Clean Neighbourhoods and Environment Act 2005, s 68.]

1. Chapter 2 contains s 68.

PART 7[1]
NOISE

CHAPTER 1[2]
Audible Intruder Alarms

Alarm notification areas

8–26862 **69. Designation of alarm notification areas.** (1) A local authority may designate all or any part of its area as an alarm notification area.

(2) If a local authority proposes to designate an area as an alarm notification area it must arrange for notice of the proposal to be published in a newspaper circulating in the area.

(3) The notice must state—

(a) that representations may be made to the authority about the proposal;
(b) that any such representations must be made before a specified date.

(4) The specified date must be at least 28 days after the date on which the notice is published in accordance with subsection (2).

(5) The local authority must consider any representations about the proposal which it receives before the specified date.

(6) If a local authority decides to designate an area as an alarm notification area it must—

(a) arrange for notice of the decision to be published in a newspaper circulating in the area, and
(b) send a copy of the notice to the address of all premises in the area.

(7) The notice must specify the date on which the designation is to have effect.

(8) The date specified must be at least 28 days after the date on which the notice is published in accordance with subsection (6)(a).

(9) If a local authority decides not to designate an area as an alarm notification area it must arrange for notice of the decision to be published in a newspaper circulating in the area.

[Clean Neighbourhoods and Environment Act 2005, s 69.]

1. Part 7 contains ss 69–86.
2. Chapter 1 contains ss 69–81.

8–26863 **70. Withdrawal of designation.** (1) A local authority which has designated an area as an alarm notification area may withdraw the designation.

(2) If a local authority decides to withdraw a designation of an area as an alarm notification area, it must—

(a) arrange for notice of the decision to be published in a newspaper circulating in the area, and
(b) send a copy of the notice to the address of all premises in the area.

(3) The notice must specify the date on which the withdrawal of the designation is to have effect.

[Clean Neighbourhoods and Environment Act 2005, s 70.]

8–26864 **71. Notification of nominated key-holders.** (1) This section and section 72 apply in relation to premises if—

(a) the premises are in an area designated by a local authority as an alarm notification area, and
(b) an audible intruder alarm has been installed in or on the premises.

(2) The responsible person must—

(a) nominate a key-holder in respect of the premises in accordance with section 72;
(b) notify the local authority in writing before the end of the required period of the name, address and telephone number of the key-holder nominated in respect of the premises in accordance with that section.

(3) The required period for the purposes of subsection (2)(b) is the period before the end of which the key-holder is required to be nominated in accordance with section 72.

(4) A person commits an offence if he fails to comply with a requirement of subsection (2).

(5) A person guilty of an offence under subsection (4) is liable on summary conviction to a fine not exceeding level 3 on the standard scale.

[Clean Neighbourhoods and Environment Act 2005, s 71.]

8–26865 72. Nomination of key-holders. (1) The responsible person must before the end of the required period nominate a person as a key-holder in respect of the premises.

(2) The required period for the purposes of subsection (1) is—

(a) if the alarm was installed before the date on which the designation of the area had effect, the period of 28 days starting with that date;

(b) if the alarm was installed on or after that date, the period of 28 days starting with the date on which the installation was completed.

(3) A person may be nominated as a key-holder in respect of premises under this section only if—

(a) he holds keys sufficient to enable him to gain access to the part of the premises in which the controls for the alarm are situated;

(b) he normally resides or is situated in the vicinity of the premises;

(c) he has information sufficient to enable him to silence the alarm;

(d) he agrees to be a nominated key-holder in respect of the premises;

(e) where the premises are residential premises, he falls within subsection (4);

(f) where the premises are non-residential premises, he falls within subsection (5).

(4) A person falls within this subsection if he is—

(a) an individual who is not the occupier of the premises, or

(b) a key-holding company.

(5) A person falls within this subsection if he is—

(a) an individual who—

(i) is the responsible person, or

(ii) is acting on behalf of the responsible person, if the responsible person is not an individual, or

(b) a key-holding company.

(6) If the responsible person becomes aware that a person who has been nominated as a key-holder in respect of premises under this section no longer satisfies one or more of the requirements in subsection (3), the responsible person must before the end of the required period nominate another person as a key-holder in respect of the premises.

(7) The required period for the purposes of subsection (6) is the period of 28 days starting with the date on which the responsible person becomes aware of that fact.

(8) In this section—

"key-holding company" means a body corporate or an unincorporated association—

(a) the business of which consists of or includes holding keys, and

(b) which is capable of being contacted at any hour of the day;

"non-residential premises" means premises which are not residential premises;

"residential premises" means premises all or part of which comprise a dwelling.

[Clean Neighbourhoods and Environment Act 2005, s 72.]

8–26866 73. Offences under section 71: fixed penalty notices. (1) This section applies if it appears to an authorised officer of a local authority that a person has committed an offence under section 71(4) in the area of the local authority.

(2) The officer may give the person a notice offering him the opportunity of discharging any liability to conviction for the offence by payment of a fixed penalty.

(3) If a person is given a notice under this section in respect of an offence—

(a) no proceedings may be instituted for the offence before the end of the period of 14 days starting with the day after that on which the notice is given, and

(b) he may not be convicted of the offence if he pays the fixed penalty before the end of that period.

(4) A notice under this section must give such particulars of the circumstances alleged to constitute the offence as are necessary for giving reasonable information of the offence.

(5) A notice under this section must also state—

(a) the period during which, by virtue of subsection (3), proceedings will not be taken for the offence,

(b) the amount of the fixed penalty, and

(c) the person to whom and the address at which the fixed penalty may be paid.

(6) Payment of the fixed penalty may be made by pre-paying and posting a letter containing the amount of the penalty (in cash or otherwise) to the person mentioned in subsection (5)(c) at the address so mentioned.

(7) If a letter is sent in accordance with subsection (6) payment is to be regarded as having been made at the time at which the letter would be delivered in the ordinary course of post.

(8) Subsection (6) does not prevent payment of the fixed penalty being made by another method.

(9) In any proceedings a certificate which—

(a) purports to be signed by or on behalf of the chief finance officer of a local authority, and
(b) states that payment of a fixed penalty was or was not received by a date specified in the certificate,

is evidence of the facts stated.

(10) The form of a notice under this section is to be such as the appropriate person may by order prescribe.

(11) In this section—

"authorised officer", in relation to a local authority, means—

(a) an employee of the authority who is authorised in writing by the authority for the purpose of giving notices under this section;
(b) any person who, in pursuance of arrangements made with the authority, has the function of giving such notices and is authorised in writing by the authority to perform that function;
(c) any employee of such a person who is authorised in writing by the authority for the purpose of giving such notices;

"chief finance officer", in relation to a local authority, is the person having responsibility for the financial affairs of the authority.

[Clean Neighbourhoods and Environment Act 2005, s 73.]

8–26867 **74. Amount of fixed penalty.** (1) This section applies in relation to a penalty payable to a local authority in pursuance of a notice under section 73.

(2) The amount of the penalty is—

(a) the amount specified by the local authority in relation to its area, or
(b) if no amount is so specified, £75.

(3) The local authority may make provision for treating the penalty as having been paid if a lesser amount is paid before the end of a period specified by the authority.

(4) The appropriate person may by regulations make provision in connection with the powers conferred on local authorities under subsections (2)(a) and (3).

(5) Regulations under subsection (4) may (in particular)—

(a) require an amount specified under subsection (2)(a) to fall within a range prescribed in the regulations;
(b) restrict the extent to which, and the circumstances in which, an authority can make provision under subsection (3).

(6) The appropriate person may by order substitute a different amount for the amount for the time being specified in subsection (2)(b).

[Clean Neighbourhoods and Environment Act 2005, s 74.]

8–26868 **75. Use of fixed penalty receipts.** (1) A local authority may use any sums it receives in respect of fixed penalties payable in pursuance of notices given under section 73 (its "penalty receipts") only for the purposes of functions of its that are qualifying functions.

(2) The following are qualifying functions for the purposes of this section—

(a) functions under this Chapter;
(b) functions under the Noise Act 1996 (c 37);
(c) functions under sections 79 to 82 of the Environmental Protection Act 1990 (c 43) (statutory nuisances) in connection with statutory nuisances falling with section 79(1)(g) or (ga) (noise) of that Act;
(d) functions of a description specified in regulations made by the appropriate person.

(3) Regulations under subsection (2)(d) may (in particular) have the effect that a local authority may use its penalty receipts for the purposes of any of its functions.

(4) A local authority must supply the appropriate person with such information relating to the use of its penalty receipts as the appropriate person may require.

(5) The appropriate person may by regulations—

(a) make provision for what a local authority is to do with its penalty receipts—
    (i) pending their being used for the purposes of qualifying functions of the authority;
    (ii) if they are not so used before such time after their receipt as may be specified by the regulations;

(b) make provision for accounting arrangements in respect of a local authority's penalty receipts.

(6) The provision that may be made under subsection (5)(a)(ii) includes (in particular) provision for the payment of sums to a person (including the appropriate person) other than the local authority.

(7) Before making regulations under this section the appropriate person must consult—

(a) the local authorities to which the regulations are to apply, and
(b) such other persons as the appropriate person thinks fit.

(8) The powers to make regulations conferred by this section are, for the purposes of subsection (1) of section 100 of the Local Government Act 2003 (c 26), to be regarded as included among the powers mentioned in subsection (2) of that section.
[Clean Neighbourhoods and Environment Act 2005, s 75.]

8–26869 **76. Fixed penalty notices: power to require name and address.** (1) If an authorised officer of a local authority proposes to give a person a notice under section 73, the officer may require the person to give him his name and address.

(2) A person commits an offence if—

(a) he fails to give his name and address when required to do so under subsection (1), or
(b) he gives a false or inaccurate name or address in response to a requirement under that subsection.

(3) A person guilty of an offence under subsection (2) is liable on summary conviction to a fine not exceeding level 3 on the standard scale.

(4) "Authorised officer" has the meaning given in section 73.
[Clean Neighbourhoods and Environment Act 2005, s 76.]

Powers in relation to alarms

8–26870 **77. Power of entry.** (1) This section applies if an authorised officer of a local authority is satisfied that the conditions in subsection (2) are met in relation to an audible intruder alarm installed in or on premises in the area of the local authority.

(2) The conditions are—

(a) that the alarm has been sounding continuously for more than twenty minutes or intermittently for more than one hour;
(b) that the sounding of the alarm is likely to give persons living or working in the vicinity of the premises reasonable cause for annoyance;
(c) if the premises are in an alarm notification area, that reasonable steps have been taken to get the nominated key-holder to silence the alarm.

(3) The officer may enter the premises for the purpose of silencing the alarm.

(4) The officer may not enter premises by force under this section.

(5) The officer must, if required, show evidence of his authority to act under this section.

(6) In this section—

"authorised officer" means an officer of a local authority who is authorised by the authority (generally or specifically) for the purposes of this section;

"nominated key-holder", in respect of premises in the area of a local authority, means a person in respect of whom the authority has received notification in accordance with section 71(2)(b).
[Clean Neighbourhoods and Environment Act 2005, s 77.]

8–26871 **78. Warrant to enter premises by force.** (1) This section applies if, on an application made by an authorised officer of a local authority, a justice of the peace is satisfied—

(a) that the conditions in section 77(2)(a) and (b) are met in relation to an audible intruder alarm installed in or on premises in the area of the local authority,
(b) if the premises are in an alarm notification area, that the condition in section 77(2)(c) is met, and
(c) that the officer is unable to gain entry to the premises without the use of force.

(2) The justice of the peace may issue a warrant authorising the officer to enter the premises, using reasonable force if necessary, for the purpose of silencing the alarm.

(3) Before applying for a warrant under this section, the officer must leave a notice at the premises stating—

(a) that the officer is satisfied that the sounding of the alarm is likely to give persons living or working in the vicinity of the premises reasonable cause for annoyance, and
(b) that an application is to be made for a warrant authorising the officer to enter the premises, using reasonable force if necessary, for the purpose of silencing the alarm.

(4) The officer must, if required, show evidence of a warrant issued under this section.

(5) "Authorised officer" has the meaning given in section 77.
[Clean Neighbourhoods and Environment Act 2005, s 78.]

8–26872 **79. Powers of entry: supplementary.** (1) This section applies where an officer of a local authority enters any premises under section 77 or under a warrant issued under section 78.

(2) The officer may take any steps he thinks necessary for the purpose of silencing the alarm.

(3) The officer may take with him—

(a) such other persons, and
(b) such equipment,

as he thinks necessary for the purpose of silencing the alarm.

(4) The officer and any person who enters the premises with him by virtue of subsection (3) must not cause more damage to or disturbance at the premises than is necessary for the purpose of silencing the alarm.

(5) If the premises are unoccupied or (where the premises are occupied) the occupier of the premises is temporarily absent the officer must—

(a) leave a notice at the premises stating what action has been taken on the premises under this section and section 77 or 78;
(b) leave the premises (so far as is reasonably practicable) as effectively secured against entry as he found them.

(6) But the officer is not required by virtue of subsection (5)(b) to re-set the alarm.

(7) Any expenses reasonably incurred by the local authority in connection with entering the premises, silencing the alarm and complying with subsection (5) may be recovered by the authority from the responsible person.

(8) A warrant under section 78 continues in force until—

(a) the alarm has been silenced, and
(b) the officer has complied with subsection (5) (if that subsection applies).

(9) Nothing done by, or by a member of, a local authority or by an officer of or another person authorised by a local authority, if done in good faith for the purposes of section 77, 78 or this section, is to subject the authority or any of those persons personally to any action, liability, claim or demand.
[Clean Neighbourhoods and Environment Act 2005, s 79.]

Supplementary

8–26873 **80. Orders and regulations.** (1) This section applies to a power conferred on the appropriate person under any provision of this Chapter to make an order or regulations.

(2) The power includes—

(a) power to make different provision for different purposes (including different provision for different local authorities and descriptions of local authority);
(b) power to make consequential, supplementary, incidental, transitional and saving provision.

(3) The power is exercisable by statutory instrument.

(4) A statutory instrument containing an order or regulations made by the Secretary of State under any provision of this Chapter is subject to annulment in pursuance of a resolution of either House of Parliament.
[Clean Neighbourhoods and Environment Act 2005, s 80.]

8–26874 **81. Interpretation.** (1) In this Chapter—

"alarm notification area" means an area in respect of which a designation under section 69 has effect;

"the appropriate person" is—

(a) in relation to a local authority in England, the Secretary of State;
(b) in relation to a local authority in Wales, the National Assembly for Wales;

"local authority" means—

(a) a district council in England;
(b) a county council in England for an area for which there is no district council;
(c) a London borough council;
(d) the Common Council of the City of London;
(e) the Council of the Isles of Scilly;
(f) a county or county borough council in Wales;

"the occupier" in respect of premises means (subject to subsection (2))—

(a) a person occupying the premises, or
(b) if the premises are unoccupied, a person entitled to occupy the premises (other than the owner);

"premises" does not include a vehicle;

"the responsible person" in respect of premises means—

(a) the occupier, or
(b) if there is no occupier, the owner.

(2) The fact that a person is occupying premises is to be disregarded for the purposes of this Chapter if—

(a) the premises comprise a building that is being erected, constructed, altered, improved, maintained, cleaned or repaired,

(b) the person is occupying the premises in connection with the erection, construction, alteration, improvement, maintenance, cleaning or repair, and

(c) the person is doing so by virtue of a licence granted for less than four weeks.

[Clean Neighbourhoods and Environment Act 2005, s 81.]

CHAPTER 2[1]

General

Noise from premises

8–26875 82. Noise offences: fixed penalty notices. (1) In section 8 of the Noise Act 1996 (c 37) (fixed penalty notices), omit subsection (8) (amount of fixed penalty).

(2) After that section insert—

"8A. Amount of fixed penalty. (1) This section applies in relation to a fixed penalty payable to a local authority in pursuance of a notice under section 8.

(2) The amount of the fixed penalty—

(a) is the amount specified by the local authority in relation to the authority's area, or

(b) if no amount is so specified, is £100.

(3) The local authority may make provision for treating the fixed penalty as having been paid if a lesser amount is paid before the end of a period specified by the authority.

(4) The appropriate person may by regulations make provision in connection with the powers conferred on local authorities under subsections (2)(a) and (3).

(5) Regulations under subsection (4) may (in particular)—

(a) require an amount specified under subsection (2)(a) to fall within a range prescribed in the regulations;

(b) restrict the extent to which, and the circumstances in which, a local authority can make provision under subsection (3).

(6) The appropriate person may by order substitute a different amount for the amount for the time being specified in subsection (2)(b).

8B. Fixed penalty notices: power to require name and address. (1) If an officer of a local authority who is authorised for the purposes of section 8 proposes to give a person a fixed penalty notice, the officer may require the person to give him his name and address.

(2) A person commits an offence if—

(a) he fails to give his name and address when required to do so under subsection (1), or

(b) he gives a false or inaccurate name or address in response to a requirement under that subsection.

(3) A person guilty of an offence under subsection (2) is liable on summary conviction to a fine not exceeding level 3 on the standard scale."

[Clean Neighbourhoods and Environment Act 2005, s 82.]

1. Chapter 2 contains ss 82–86.

8–26876 83. Noise offences: use of fixed penalty receipts. (1) Section 9 of the Noise Act 1996 (c 37) (fixed penalty notices: supplementary) is amended as follows.

(2) In subsection (4A) (qualifying functions for the use of penalty receipts), omit "and" at the end of paragraph (a) and after that paragraph insert—

"(aa) functions under Chapter 1 of Part 7 of the Clean Neighbourhoods and Environment Act 2005;

(ab) functions under sections 79 to 82 of the Environmental Protection Act 1990 (statutory nuisances) in connection with statutory nuisances falling with section 79(1)(g) or (ga) (noise) of that Act;".

(3) After subsection (4F) insert—

"(4G) The powers to make regulations conferred by this section are, for the purposes of subsection (1) of section 100 of the Local Government Act 2003, to be regarded as included among the powers mentioned in subsection (2) of that section.

(4H) Regulations under this section relating to local authorities in England may—

(a) make provision in relation to—

(i) all local authorities,

(ii) particular local authorities, or
(iii) particular descriptions of local authority;

(b) make different provision in relation to different local authorities or descriptions of local authority."

[Clean Neighbourhoods and Environment Act 2005, s 83.]

8–26877 **84. Extension of Noise Act 1996 to licensed premises etc.** Schedule 1 (which makes provision amending the Noise Act 1996 (c 37) so that it applies to licensed premises etc) has effect.

[Clean Neighbourhoods and Environment Act 2005, s 84.]

8–26878 **85. Noise Act 1996: supplementary.** (1) Section 11 of the Noise Act 1996 (interpretation and subordinate legislation) is amended as follows.

(2) After subsection (2) insert—

"(2A) In this Act "appropriate person" means—

(a) the Secretary of State, in relation to England;
(b) the National Assembly for Wales, in relation to Wales."

(3) In subsection (3), after "section 14" insert "or an order or regulations made solely by the National Assembly for Wales".

[Clean Neighbourhoods and Environment Act 2005, s 85.]

Statutory noise nuisances

8–26879 **86. Deferral of duty to serve abatement notice.** In section 80 of the Environmental Protection Act 1990 (c 43) (summary proceedings for statutory nuisances), at the beginning of subsection (1) insert "Subject to subsection (2A)" and after subsection (2) insert—

"(2A) Where a local authority is satisfied that a statutory nuisance falling within paragraph (g) of section 79(1) above exists, or is likely to occur or recur, in the area of the authority, the authority shall—

(a) serve an abatement notice in respect of the nuisance in accordance with subsections (1) and (2) above; or
(b) take such other steps as it thinks appropriate for the purpose of persuading the appropriate person to abate the nuisance or prohibit or restrict its occurrence or recurrence.

(2B) If a local authority has taken steps under subsection (2A)(b) above and either of the conditions in subsection (2C) below is satisfied, the authority shall serve an abatement notice in respect of the nuisance.

(2C) The conditions are—

(a) that the authority is satisfied at any time before the end of the relevant period that the steps taken will not be successful in persuading the appropriate person to abate the nuisance or prohibit or restrict its occurrence or recurrence;
(b) that the authority is satisfied at the end of the relevant period that the nuisance continues to exist, or continues to be likely to occur or recur, in the area of the authority.

(2D) The relevant period is the period of seven days starting with the day on which the authority was first satisfied that the nuisance existed, or was likely to occur or recur.

(2E) The appropriate person is the person on whom the authority would otherwise be required under subsection (2A)(a) above to serve an abatement notice in respect of the nuisance."

[Clean Neighbourhoods and Environment Act 2005, s 86.]

PART 9[1]
MISCELLANEOUS

96–98. *Use of fixed penalty receipts.*

99. *Abandoned shopping and luggage trolleys.*

1. Part 9 contains ss 96–105.

8–26880 **100. Section 99: transitional provision.** (1) This section applies if, before the commencement date, a local authority in England and Wales has resolved under section 99 of the Environmental Protection Act 1990 that Schedule 4 to that Act is to apply in its area.

(2) If the day specified in the resolution for the coming into force of Schedule 4 in the authority's area falls on or after the commencement date, the resolution is to be of no effect.

(3) If Schedule 4 applies in the authority's area immediately before the commencement date, the Schedule is to continue to apply in the authority's area on and after the commencement date as it applied before that date.

(4) But Schedule 4 shall not so apply in relation to any shopping or luggage trolley seized by the authority on or after the relevant day.

(5) For the purposes of subsection (4) the relevant day is the earlier of—

(a) the third anniversary of the commencement date;

(b) if the authority resolves under section 99 of the Environmental Protection Act 1990 (c 43) that Schedule 4 (as amended by section 99 of this Act) is to apply in its area, the day specified in the resolution as the day on which the Schedule (as so amended) comes into force in its area.

(6) So long as Schedule 4 continues to apply as described in subsection (3), the reference in section 99(4) of the Environmental Protection Act 1990 to Schedule 4 is to be treated as including a reference to Schedule 4 as it so applies.

(7) If the authority resolves under section 99 that Schedule 4 (as amended by section 99 of this Act) is to apply in its area, the authority may not in giving effect to paragraph 4(1) of Schedule 4 (as so amended) take into account charges payable in relation to shopping or luggage trolleys seized before the Schedule (as so amended) comes into force in its area.

(8) Nothing in this section prevents the authority from bringing to an end the application of Schedule 4 in its area.

(9) In this section—

"the commencement date" is the day on which section 99 of this Act comes into force;

"local authority" has the same meaning as in section 99 of the Environmental Protection Act 1990;

"luggage trolley" and "shopping trolley" have the same meaning as in Schedule 4 to that Act.

[Clean Neighbourhoods and Environment Act 2005, s 100.]

Statutory nuisances

8–26881 101. Statutory nuisance: insects. (1) Section 79 of the Environmental Protection Act 1990 (statutory nuisances and inspections) is amended as follows.

(2) In subsection (1) (matters constituting statutory nuisances) after paragraph (f) insert—

"(fa)any insects emanating from relevant industrial, trade or business premises and being prejudicial to health or a nuisance;".

(3) After subsection (5) insert—

"(5A) Subsection (1)(fa) does not apply to insects that are wild animals included in Schedule 5 to the Wildlife and Countryside Act 1981 (animals which are protected), unless they are included in respect of section 9(5) of that Act only."

(4) In subsection (7) at the appropriate place insert—

""appropriate person" means—

(a) in relation to England, the Secretary of State;

(b) in relation to Wales, the National Assembly for Wales;".

(5) After subsection (7B) (as inserted by section 102(6)) insert—

"(7C) In this Part "relevant industrial, trade or business premises" means premises that are industrial, trade or business premises as defined in subsection (7), but excluding—

(a) land used as arable, grazing, meadow or pasture land,

(b) land used as osier land, reed beds or woodland,

(c) land used for market gardens, nursery grounds or orchards,

(d) land forming part of an agricultural unit, not being land falling within any of paragraphs (a) to (c), where the land is of a description prescribed by regulations made by the appropriate person, and

(e) land included in a site of special scientific interest (as defined in section 52(1) of the Wildlife and Countryside Act 1981),

and excluding land covered by, and the waters of, any river or watercourse, that is neither a sewer nor a drain, or any lake or pond.

(7D) For the purposes of subsection (7C)—

"agricultural" has the same meaning as in section 109 of the Agriculture Act 1947;

"agricultural unit" means land which is occupied as a unit for agricultural purposes;

"drain" has the same meaning as in the Water Resources Act 1991;

"lake or pond" has the same meaning as in section 104 of that Act;

"sewer" has the same meaning as in that Act."

[Clean Neighbourhoods and Environment Act 2005, s 101.]

8–26882 102. Statutory nuisance: lighting. (1) Section 79 of the Environmental Protection Act 1990 (c 43) is amended as follows.

(2) In subsection (1) (matters constituting statutory nuisances) after paragraph (fa) (as inserted by section 101 (2)) insert—

"(fb)artificial light emitted from premises so as to be prejudicial to health or a nuisance;".

(3) In subsection (2) (exception from subsection (1)(b) and (g) for premises occupied for defence purposes) after "Subsection (1)(b)" insert ", (fb)".

(4) After subsection (5A) (as inserted by section 101 (3)) insert—

"(5B) Subsection (1)(fb) does not apply to artificial light emitted from—

(a) an airport;
(b) harbour premises;
(c) railway premises, not being relevant separate railway premises;
(d) tramway premises;
(e) a bus station and any associated facilities;
(f) a public service vehicle operating centre;
(g) a goods vehicle operating centre;
(h) a lighthouse;
(i) a prison."

(5) In subsection (7) (definitions) at the appropriate place insert—

"“airport" has the meaning given by section 95 of the Transport Act 2000;";

"“associated facilities", in relation to a bus station, has the meaning given by section 83 of the Transport Act 1985;";

"“bus station" has the meaning given by section 83 of the Transport Act 1985;";

"“goods vehicle operating centre", in relation to vehicles used under an operator's licence, means a place which is specified in the licence as an operating centre for those vehicles, and for the purposes of this definition "operating centre" and "operator's licence" have the same meaning as in the Goods Vehicles (Licensing of Operators) Act 1995;";

"“harbour premises" means premises which form part of a harbour area and which are occupied wholly or mainly for the purposes of harbour operations, and for the purposes of this definition "harbour area" and "harbour operations" have the same meaning as in Part 3 of the Aviation and Maritime Security Act 1990;";

"“lighthouse" has the same meaning as in Part 8 of the Merchant Shipping Act 1995;";

"“prison" includes a young offender institution;";

"“public service vehicle operating centre", in relation to public service vehicles used under a PSV operator's licence, means a place which is an operating centre of those vehicles, and for the purposes of this definition "operating centre", "PSV operator's licence" and "public service vehicle" have the same meaning as in the Public Passenger Vehicles Act 1981;";

"“railway premises" means any premises which fall within the definition of "light maintenance depot", "network", "station" or "track" in section 83 of the Railways Act 1993;";

"“relevant separate railway premises" has the meaning given by subsection (7A);";

"“tramway premises" means any premises which, in relation to a tramway, are the equivalent of the premises which, in relation to a railway, fall within the definition of "light maintenance depot", "network", "station" or "track" in section 83 of the Railways Act 1993;".

(6) After subsection (7) insert—

"(7A) Railway premises are relevant separate railway premises if—

(a) they are situated within—
   (i) premises used as a museum or other place of cultural, scientific or historical interest, or
   (ii) premises used for the purposes of a funfair or other entertainment, recreation or amusement, and
(b) they are not associated with any other railway premises.

(7B) For the purposes of subsection (7A)—

(a) a network situated as described in subsection (7A)(a) is associated with other railway premises if it is connected to another network (not being a network situated as described in subsection (7A)(a));
(b) track that is situated as described in subsection (7A)(a) but is not part of a network is associated with other railway premises if it is connected to track that forms part of a network (not being a network situated as described in subsection (7A)(a));
(c) a station or light maintenance depot situated as described in subsection (7A)(a) is associated with other railway premises if it is used in connection with the provision of railway services other than services provided wholly within the premises where it is situated.

In this subsection "light maintenance depot", "network", "railway services", "station" and "track" have the same meaning as in Part 1 of the Railways Act 1993."

(7) In subsection (8) (port health authority to have functions of local authority under Part 3 of

that Act, except those relating to statutory nuisance within section 79(1)(g) or (ga)) after "paragraph" insert "(fb),".

(8) In subsection (10) (consent of Secretary of State or National Assembly for Wales required before taking proceedings for certain statutory nuisances) after "paragraph (b), (d), (e)" insert ", (fb)".

[Clean Neighbourhoods and Environment Act 2005, s 102.]

8–26883 103. Sections 101 and 102: supplementary. (1) The Environmental Protection Act 1990 (c 43) is amended as follows.

(2) In section 80(8) (summary proceedings for statutory nuisances: defence of best practicable means not available in certain cases)—

(a) in paragraph (a) after "paragraph (a), (d), (e), (f)" insert ", (fa)", and
(b) after paragraph (a) insert—

"(aza) in the case of a nuisance falling within paragraph (fb) of section 79(1) above except where—

(i) the artificial light is emitted from industrial, trade or business premises, or
(ii) the artificial light (not being light to which sub-paragraph (i) applies) is emitted by lights used for the purpose only of illuminating an outdoor relevant sports facility;".

(3) After section 80(8) insert—

"(8A) For the purposes of subsection (8)(aza) a relevant sports facility is an area, with or without structures, that is used when participating in a relevant sport, but does not include such an area comprised in domestic premises.

(8B) For the purposes of subsection (8A) "relevant sport" means a sport that is designated for those purposes by order made by the Secretary of State, in relation to England, or the National Assembly for Wales, in relation to Wales.

A sport may be so designated by reference to its appearing in a list maintained by a body specified in the order.

(8C) In subsection (8A) "domestic premises" means—

(a) premises used wholly or mainly as a private dwelling, or
(b) land or other premises belonging to, or enjoyed with, premises so used."

(4) In section 82(10) (summary proceedings by aggrieved person: defence of best practicable means not available in certain cases)—

(a) in paragraph (a) after "paragraph (a), (d), (e), (f)" insert ", (fa)", and
(b) after paragraph (a) insert—

"(aza) in the case of a nuisance falling within paragraph (fb) of section 79(1) above except where—

(i) the artificial light is emitted from industrial, trade or business premises, or
(ii) the artificial light (not being light to which sub-paragraph (i) applies) is emitted by lights used for the purpose only of illuminating an outdoor relevant sports facility;".

(5) After section 82(10) insert—

"(10A) For the purposes of subsection (10)(aza) "relevant sports facility" has the same meaning as it has for the purposes of section 80(8)(aza)."

[Clean Neighbourhoods and Environment Act 2005, s 103.]

Pollution

8–26884 104. Contaminated land: appeals against remediation notices. (1) Section 78L of the Environmental Protection Act 1990 (c 43) (appeals against remediation notices) is amended as follows.

(2) In subsection (1), for paragraphs (a) and (b) substitute—

"(a) if it was served by a local authority in England, or served by the Environment Agency in relation to land in England, to the Secretary of State;
(b) if it was served by a local authority in Wales, or served by the Environment Agency in relation to land in Wales, to the National Assembly for Wales;".

(3) In that subsection, for the words from "means" to the end substitute "the Secretary of State or the National Assembly for Wales, as the case may be".

(4) In subsection (4)—

(a) omit paragraph (b);
(b) in paragraph (c), omit the words from "or on" to the end.

(5) In subsection (6), omit the words "so far as relating to appeals to the Secretary of State".

(6) This section does not have effect in relation to a remediation notice served under Part 2A of the Environmental Protection Act 1990 before the commencement of this section.

(7) The power of the Secretary of State and National Assembly for Wales under section 114 of the Environment Act 1995 (c 25) in relation to appeals under section 78L of the Environmental Protection Act 1990 extends to appeals under that section as amended by this section.
[Clean Neighbourhoods and Environment Act 2005, s 104.]

8–26885 **105. Offences relating to pollution etc: penalties on conviction.** (1) In paragraph 25 of Schedule 1 to the Pollution Prevention and Control Act 1999 (c 24) (purposes for which regulations may be made under section 2: offences), in sub-paragraph (2)(a)—

(a) in paragraph (i) for "six months" substitute "12 months";
(b) in paragraph (ii) for "£20,000" substitute "£50,000".

(2) Subsection (1) does not have effect in relation to regulations under section 2 of the Pollution Prevention and Control Act 1999 so far as relating to offences committed before the commencement of section 154(1) of the Criminal Justice Act 2003 (c 44).
[Clean Neighbourhoods and Environment Act 2005, s 105.]

PART 10[1]
GENERAL

8–26886 **106. Minor and consequential amendments.** Schedule 4 (minor and consequential amendments) has effect.
[Clean Neighbourhoods and Environment Act 2005, s 106.]

1. Part 10 contains ss 106–111. Section 107 introduces Sch 5 (repeals).

8–26887 **107. Repeals.** Schedule 5 (repeals) has effect.
[Clean Neighbourhoods and Environment Act 2005, s 107.]

8–26888 **108. Commencement.** (1) The provisions specified in subsection (2) come into force—

(a) in relation to England, in accordance with provision made by order[1] by the Secretary of State; and
(b) in relation to Wales, in accordance with provision so made by the National Assembly for Wales.

(2) The provisions referred to in subsection (1) are—

(a) section 2;
(b) sections 6 to 13 and 15 to 17 and, in Part 1 of Schedule 5, the repeals to the Refuse Disposal (Amenity) Act 1978 (c 3) and the Road Traffic Regulation Act 1984 (c 27);
(c) sections 19 to 25, paragraphs 5 to 9 of Schedule 4 and, in Part 2 of Schedule 5, the repeals to the Environmental Protection Act 1990 (c 43);
(d) sections 28 to 31, paragraphs 14 to 19 of Schedule 4 and, in Part 3 of Schedule 5, the repeals to the Anti-Social Behaviour Act 2003 (c 38);
(e) section 34 and, in Part 3 of Schedule 5, the repeal to the Town and Country Planning Act 1990 (c 8);
(f) sections 37 and 38 and, in Part 4 of Schedule 5, the repeal of section 6 of the Control of Pollution (Amendment) Act 1989 (c 14);
(g) sections 45 and 46;
(h) section 47, paragraph 4 of Schedule 4 and, in Part 4 of Schedule 5, the repeals to the Environmental Protection Act 1990, other than the repeal to section 33 of that Act;
(i) section 48;
(j) section 50;
(k) section 52;
(l) section 53;
(m) Chapter 1 of Part 6 above and Part 5 of Schedule 5;
(n) Part 7 above except sections 83(2) and 85, and in Part 7 of Schedule 5, the repeals to the Noise and Statutory Nuisance Act 1993 (c 40) and the Noise Act 1996 (c 37);
(o) sections 96 to 98 and Part 9 of Schedule 5;
(p) sections 99 and 100;
(q) sections 101 to 103;
(r) section 104 and Part 10 of Schedule 5.

(3) These provisions come into force in accordance with provision made by order by the Secretary of State—

(a) section 1;
(b) section 32;
(c) sections 42 to 44;
(d) section 49 and paragraph 3 of Schedule 4;
(e) section 68 and Part 6 of Schedule 5;
(f) Part 8 above and Part 8 of Schedule 5;

(g) in Part 1 of Schedule 5, the repeal to section 3 of the London Local Authorities Act 2004 (c i).
(h) in Part 2 of Schedule 5, the repeals to the London Local Authorities Act 1994 (c xii) and the City of Newcastle upon Tyne Act 2000 (c viii);
(i) in Part 3 of Schedule 5, the repeal to the London Local Authorities Act 1995 (c x);
(j) in Part 7 of Schedule 5, the repeal to the London Local Authorities Act 1991 (c xiii).

(4) These provisions come into force at the end of the period of two months beginning with the day on which this Act is passed—

(a) sections 3 to 5 and, in Part 1 of Schedule 5, the repeals to the Greater London Council (General Powers) Act 1982 (c i) and section 11 of the London Local Authorities Act 2004 (c i);
(b) section 18;
(c) section 27;
(d) section 33 and, in Part 3 of Schedule 5, the repeal to the London Local Authorities Act 2004 (c i);
(e) sections 35 and 36, and in Part 4 of Schedule 5, the repeals to sections 1 and 2 of the Control of Pollution (Amendment) Act 1989 (c 14);
(f) section 40 and, in Part 4 of Schedule 5, the repeal to section 33 of the Environmental Protection Act 1990 (c 43);
(g) section 41;
(h) section 54;
(i) section 83(2);
(j) section 105.

(5) An order under subsection (1) or (3) may make—

(a) transitional, consequential, incidental and supplemental provision, or savings;
(b) different provision for different purposes.

(6) Where a provision of this Act comes into force otherwise than under subsection (1) or (3), the Secretary of State may by order make any transitional, consequential, incidental or supplemental provision, or savings, that he considers necessary or expedient in relation to the coming into force of that provision.

(7) An order under subsection (6) may make different provision for different purposes.

(8) An order under this section is to be made by statutory instrument.

[Clean Neighbourhoods and Environment Act 2005, s 108.]

1. At the time of going to press the Clean Neighbourhoods and Environment Act 2005 (Commencement No 1) Order 2005, SI 2005/1675; and Clean Neighbourhoods and Environment Act 2005 (Commencement No 2, Transitional Provisions and Savings) (England and Wales) Order 2005, SI 2005/2896 had been made. See the note to the title of the Act for the provisions brought into force and transitional provisions and savings.

8–26889 **109. Money.** There shall be paid out of money provided by Parliament—

(a) any expenditure incurred by the Secretary of State under this Act;
(b) any increase attributable to this Act in the sums payable out of money so provided under any other Act.

[Clean Neighbourhoods and Environment Act 2005, s 109.]

8–26890 **110. Extent.** (1) This Act extends to England and Wales only, subject as follows.

(2) An amendment in Schedule 2 has the same extent as the provision amended.

(3) The repeal in Part 8 of Schedule 5 has the same extent as the provision repealed.

[Clean Neighbourhoods and Environment Act 2005, s 110.]

8–26891 **111. Short title.** This Act may be cited as the Clean Neighbourhoods and Environment Act 2005.

[Clean Neighbourhoods and Environment Act 2005, s 111.]

8–26892

Section 84

SCHEDULE 1

Application of the Noise Act 1996 to Licensed Premises etc

1. The Noise Act 1996 (c 37) is amended as follows.

2. In the heading to section 2, omit "from a dwelling".

3. (1) Section 2 (investigations of complaints of noise) is amended as follows.

(2) In subsection (2), after "emitted from" insert "(a)" and at the end insert

", or

(b) any premises in respect of which a premises licence or a temporary event notice has effect (referred to in this group of sections as "the offending premises")".

(3) In subsection (4)(a), after "the offending dwelling" insert "or the offending premises".

(4) In subsection (7)—

(a) after "the offending dwelling is" insert ", or the offending premises are,";
(b) after "if the offending dwelling" insert "or the offending premises".

(5) After subsection (7) insert—

"(7A) In this group of sections—

"premises licence" has the same meaning as in the Licensing Act 2003 (c 17);

"temporary event notice" has the same meaning as in the Licensing Act 2003 (and is to be treated as having effect in accordance with section 171(6) of that Act)."

4. (1) Section 3 (warning notices) is amended as follows.

(2) In subsection (1)—

(a) in paragraph (a)(i), after "offending dwelling" insert "or the offending premises";
(b) for paragraph (b) substitute—

"(b) give warning—

(i) in a case where the complaint is in respect of a dwelling, that any person who is responsible for noise which is emitted from the offending dwelling in the period specified in the notice and which exceeds the permitted level, as measured from within the complainant's dwelling, may be guilty of an offence;
(ii) in a case where the complaint is in respect of other premises, that the responsible person in relation to the offending premises may be guilty of an offence if noise which exceeds the permitted level, as measured from within the complainant's dwelling, is emitted from the premises in the period specified in the notice."

(3) In subsection (3), at the beginning insert "In a case where the complaint is in respect of a dwelling,".

(4) After subsection (3) insert—

"(3A) In a case where the complaint is in respect of other premises, a warning notice must be served by delivering it to the person who appears to the officer of the authority to be the responsible person in relation to the offending premises at the time the notice is delivered."

(5) After subsection (5) insert—

"(6) For the purposes of this group of sections, the responsible person in relation to premises at a particular time is—

(a) where a premises licence has effect in respect of the premises—

(i) the person who holds the premises licence if he is present at the premises at that time,
(ii) where that person is not present at the premises at that time, the designated premises supervisor under the licence if he is present at the premises at that time, or
(iii) where neither of the persons mentioned in sub-paragraphs (i) and (ii) is present at the premises at that time, any other person present at the premises at that time who is in charge of the premises;

(b) where a temporary event notice has effect in respect of the premises—

(i) the premises user in relation to that notice if he is present at the premises at that time, or
(ii) where the premises user is not present at the premises at that time, any other person present at the premises at that time who is in charge of the premises."

5. In the heading to section 4, after "where noise" insert "from a dwelling".

6. After section 4 insert—

"4A. Offence where noise from other premises exceeds permitted level after service of notice.

(1) If—

(a) a warning notice has been served under section 3 in respect of noise emitted from premises,
(b) noise is emitted from the premises in the period specified in the notice, and
(c) the noise exceeds the permitted level, as measured from within the complainant's dwelling,

the responsible person in relation to the offending premises at the time at which the noise referred to in paragraph (c) is emitted is guilty of an offence.

(2) A person guilty of an offence under this section is liable on summary conviction to a fine not exceeding level 5 on the standard scale."

7. (1) Section 5 (permitted level of noise) is amended as follows.

(2) In subsection (1)—

(a) for "the Secretary of State" substitute "the appropriate person";
(b) after "from any dwelling" insert "or other premises".

(3) In subsection (4), for "The Secretary of State" substitute "The appropriate person".

8. (1) Section 6 (approval of measuring devices) is amended as follows.

(2) In subsection (1), for "the Secretary of State" substitute "the appropriate person".

(3) In subsection (3), after "section 4" insert "or 4A".

9. (1) Section 7 (evidence) is amended as follows.

(2) In subsection (1), after "section 4" insert "or 4A".

(3) After subsection (3) insert—

"(3A) In proceedings for an offence under section 4A, evidence that noise, or noise of any kind, measured by a device at any time was noise emitted from any other premises may be given by the production of a document—

(a) signed by an officer of the local authority, and
(b) stating that he had identified those premises as the source at that time of the noise or, as the case may be, noise of that kind."

(4) In subsection (4), for "or (3)(a)" substitute ", (3)(a) or (3A)(a)".

10. (1) Section 8 (fixed penalty notices) is amended as follows.

(2) In subsection (1), after "section 4" insert "or 4A".
(3) In subsection (2)(b), after "the offending dwelling" insert "or the offending premises (as the case may be)".
11. (1) Section 8A (amount of fixed penalty), as inserted by section 82 of this Act, is amended as follows.
(2) In subsection (2), at the beginning insert "In the case of an offence under section 4".
(3) After subsection (2) insert—

"(2A) In the case of an offence under section 4A the amount of the fixed penalty is £500."
(4) In subsection (3), after "the fixed penalty" insert "payable in the case of an offence under section 4".
(5) In subsection (6), after "(2)(b)" insert "or (2A)".
12. (1) Section 9 (section 8: supplementary) is amended as follows.
(2) In subsection (1), for "the Secretary of State" substitute "the appropriate person".
(3) After subsection (2) insert—

"(2A) If a fixed penalty notice is given to a person in respect of noise emitted from other premises in any period in a warning notice—

(a) no further fixed penalty notice may be given to that person in respect of noise emitted from the premises during that period, but
(b) that person may be convicted of a further offence under section 4A in respect of noise emitted from the premises after the fixed penalty notice is given and before the end of that period."

(4) In subsections (4A)(b) and (4C), for each occurrence of "the Secretary of State" substitute "the appropriate person".
(5) In subsection (4D), for "The Secretary of State" substitute "The appropriate person".
(6) In subsections (4E) and (4F), for each occurrence of "the Secretary of State" substitute "the appropriate person".
(7) In subsection (5), after "section 4" insert "or 4A".
13. (1) Section 10 (powers of entry and seizure etc) is amended as follows.
(2) In subsection (1)—

(a) in paragraph (a), after "a dwelling" insert "or other premises";
(b) in paragraph (b), after "the dwelling" insert "or other premises".

(3) In subsection (2), after "the dwelling" insert "or other premises".
(4) In subsection (4)—

(a) in paragraph (a), after "a dwelling" insert "or other premises";
(b) in paragraph (b), after "the dwelling" insert "or other premises";
(c) in paragraph (c), after "the dwelling" insert "or other premises";
(d) after "to enter the" insert "dwelling or other".

(5) In subsection (5)—

(a) after "enters any" insert "dwelling or other";
(b) for the words from "the premises are unoccupied" to the end substitute "the dwelling is, or the other premises are, unoccupied, must leave it or them as effectively secured against trespassers as he found it or them."

14. In the Schedule (powers in relation to seized equipment) in paragraph 1(a)(i), after "section 4" insert "or 4A".

8–26893
Section 106

SCHEDULE 4
Minor and Consequential Amendments

Highways Act 1980 (c 66)

1. In section 325 of the Highways Act 1980, in subsection (2)(a), after "subsection (2A) below" insert "or regulations made by the National Assembly for Wales under Part 8A".

Environmental Protection Act 1990 (c 43)

2. The Environmental Protection Act 1990 is amended as follows.
3. (1) Section 52 is amended as follows.
(2) After subsection (4) insert—

"(4A) The Secretary of State may by regulations impose on waste disposal authorities in England a duty to make payments corresponding to the payments which are authorised by subsection (3)(a) above to such persons in such circumstances and in respect of such descriptions or quantities of waste as are specified in the regulations."
(3) In subsection (5)—

(a) after "authorities" insert "in Wales"; and
(b) for "subsection (3)" substitute "subsection (3)(b)".

(4) In subsection (6), for "subsections (1), (3)" substitute "subsections (1)(b), (3)(b)".
(5) In subsection (7), for "subsections (2) and (4)" substitute "subsections (2)(b) and (4)(b)".
(6) In subsection (8), for "subsections (1), (2), (3), (4)" substitute "subsections (1)(b), (2)(b), (3)(b), (4)(b)".
4. In section 60(1)—

(a) in paragraph (a), for the words from "a waste disposal contractor" to the end substitute "or under arrangements made with a waste disposal authority or by any other local authority or person";
(b) in paragraph (b), for the words from "a waste disposal contractor" to the end substitute "or under arrangements made with a waste disposal authority, by a parish or community council or by a holder of a waste management licence; or".

5. In section 89(1), at the end of paragraph (e) insert "and".
6. In section 91(1), at the end of paragraph (e) insert "or".
7. In section 92(1), at the end of paragraph (b) insert "or".
8. In section 95(1), after paragraph (b) insert
"and
(c) all orders made by the authority under paragraph 2(1) of Schedule 3A."
9. In section 96(1)(b), after "section 92(9)" insert "or 92C(3)".
10. (1) Section 161 is amended as follows.
(2) In subsection (1) after "Secretary of State" insert ", National Assembly for Wales".
(3) After subsection (2), insert—

"(2A) Subsection (2) does not apply to a statutory instrument made solely by the National Assembly for Wales."

(4) In subsection (4), at the end insert
"or
(c) which is made solely by the National Assembly for Wales."

Control of Pollution (Amendment) Act 1989 (c 14)

11. (1) Section 8 of the Control of Pollution (Amendment) Act 1989 is amended as follows.
(2) In subsection (1), after "regulations" insert "or orders".
(3) After that subsection insert—

"(1A) The powers of the National Assembly for Wales to make regulations or orders under sections 5 to 5C above are exercisable by statutory instrument."

(4) In subsection (2)—
(a) after "Regulations" insert "or orders";
(b) in paragraph (a) for "Secretary of State" substitute "person making the regulations or order".

Anti-social Behaviour Act 2003 (c 38)

12. The Anti-social Behaviour Act 2003 is amended as follows.
13. In section 41(3), in the definition of "temporary event notice" for "section 170(6)" substitute "section 171(6)".
14. In section 45, for subsection (1) substitute—

"(1) The fixed penalty payable in pursuance of a notice under section 43(1) is payable to the local authority whose authorised officer gave the notice."

15. In section 47(1), after "sections 43" insert "to 43B".
16. In the cross-heading preceding section 48, after "graffiti" insert "and fly-posting".
17. (1) Section 48 is amended as follows.
(2) In the heading, for "Graffiti removal notices" substitute "Defacement removal notices".
(3) In subsections (2) and (6), for "graffiti removal notice" substitute "defacement removal notice".
(4) In subsection (7), for "graffiti removal notices" substitute "defacement removal notices".
(5) In subsection (8)(a), for "graffiti removal notice" substitute "defacement removal notice".
(6) In subsection (12), for ""graffiti removal notice"" substitute ""defacement removal notice"".
(7) In that subsection, in the definition of "local authority", at the end insert "but not a parish or community council".
18. In sections 49(1) and 51(1) and (3), for "graffiti removal notice" substitute "defacement removal notice".
19. In the heading to section 52, for "graffiti removal notices" substitute "defacement removal notices".

8–26894

Section 107

SCHEDULE 5
REPEALS

PART 1
VEHICLES

Short title and chapter	*Extent of repeal*
Refuse Disposal (Amenity) Act 1978 (c 3)	In section 3— (*a*) subsection (5); (*b*) in subsection (8), the words from ", other than" to "subsection (5) above,". In section 4— (*a*) in subsection (1), the words from "but not earlier" to the end; (*b*) subsection (2).
Greater London Council (General Powers) Act 1982 (c i)	Section 5.
Road Traffic Regulation Act 1984 (c 27)	Section 99(4). In section 101(3)— (*a*) in paragraph (a), the words from "and on which" to "at the time of its removal"; (*b*) the words from "but, in a case" to the end.
London Local Authorities Act 2004 (c i)	Section 3. Section 11.

PART 2
LITTER AND REFUSE

Short title and chapter	*Extent of repeal*
Environmental Protection Act 1990 (c 43)	Section 86(12). Section 89(1)(g) and the preceding "and". Section 90. Section 91(1)(g) and the preceding "or". In section 92— (*a*) subsection (1)(d) and the preceding "or"; (*b*) subsection (3)(d). In section 94(3), the words from "but a specified area" to the end. Section 95(1)(a).
London Local Authorities Act 1994 (c xii)	Section 4.
City of Newcastle upon Tyne Act 2000 (c viii)	Sections 21 and 22.

PART 3
GRAFFITI AND OTHER DEFACEMENT

Short title and chapter	*Extent of repeal*
Town and Country Planning Act 1990 (c 8)	Section 324(3)(a).
London Local Authorities Act 1995 (c x)	Section 10.
Anti-social Behaviour Act 2003 (c 38)	Section 43(10) and (11).
London Local Authorities Act 2004 (c i)	Section 25.

PART 4
WASTE

Short title and chapter	*Extent of repeal*
Control of Pollution (Amendment) Act 1989 (c 14)	Section 1(4)(c) and the preceding "or". In section 2— (*a*) in subsection (2)(c), the words "free of charge"; (*b*) subsection (2)(d); (*c*) in subsection (2)(e), the words "free of charge"; (*d*) subsection (3)(b); (*e*) subsection (3A)(a). Section 6.
Environmental Protection Act 1990 (c 43)	Section 30(5). Section 32. Section 33(7)(b). In section 48— (*a*) in subsection (4), the words "with a waste disposal contractor" and "for the contractor"; (*b*) in subsection (6), the words ", subject to subsection (7) below,"; (*c*) subsection (7). In section 51— (*a*) in subsection (1), the words from "in either case" to the end; (*b*) subsection (4)(b) to (d); (*c*) subsections (5) and (6). In section 55(2)(a) and (b), the words "with waste disposal contractors for them". In section 60(2)(a) and (b), the word ", contractor". In section 77— (*a*) subsection (1), the definitions of "existing disposal authority", "existing disposal plan", "relevant part of its undertaking" and "the vesting date"; (*b*) subsection (4); (*c*) subsections (6) to (9). Schedule 2.

PART 5
DOG CONTROLS

Short title and chapter	*Extent of repeal*
Dogs (Fouling of Land) Act 1996 (c 20)	The whole Act.
Police Reform Act 2002 (c 30)	In Schedule 4, paragraph 1(2)(c). In Schedule 5, paragraph 1(2)(b).

PART 6
STRAY DOGS

Short title and chapter	*Extent of repeal*
Dogs Act 1906 (c 32)	Sections 3 and 4.
Dogs (Amendment) Act 1928 (c 21)	Section 2.
Local Government Act 1988 (c 9)	Section 39.
Environmental Protection Act 1990 (c 43)	In the heading to section 150, the words "police or". In section 150— (*a*) in subsection (1), in paragraph (b), sub-paragraph (ii) and the preceding "or"; (*b*) in that subsection, the words from "or the police officer" to "as the case may be,". In Schedule 15, paragraph 3.

PART 7
NOISE

Short title and chapter	*Extent of repeal*
London Local Authorities Act 1991 (c xiii)	Section 23.
Noise and Statutory Nuisance Act 1993 (c 40)	Section 9. Schedule 3.
Noise Act 1996 (c 37)	In the heading to section 2, the words "from a dwelling". Section 8(8). Section 9(3). In section 9(4A), the word "and" at the end of paragraph (a).

PART 8
ARCHITECTURE AND THE BUILT ENVIRONMENT

Short title and chapter	*Extent of repeal*
Environmental Protection Act 1990	In section 153(1), the paragraph (rr) inserted by article 2 of the Financial Assistance for Environmental Purposes (England) Order 2003 (SI 2003/714).

PART 9
USE OF FIXED PENALTY RECEIPTS

Short title and chapter	*Extent of repeal*
Local Government Act 2003 (c 26)	Section 100(2)(f). Section 119.
Anti-social Behaviour Act 2003 (c 38)	Section 45(3) to (9).

PART 10
CONTAMINATED LAND

Short title and chapter	*Extent of repeal*
Environmental Protection Act 1990 (c 43)	In section 78L— (*a*) in subsection (4), paragraph (b) and, in paragraph (c), the words from "or on" to the end; (*b*) in subsection (6), the words ", so far as relating to appeals to the Secretary of State,".

Control of Noise (Appeals) Rules 1975[1]

(SI 1975/2116 amended by SI 1990/2276)

Interpretation

8–27160 **2.** (1) The Interpretation Act [1978] shall apply for the interpretation of these regulations, as it applies for the interpretation of an Act of Parliament.

(2) In these regulations, unless the context otherwise requires—

"the Act" means the Control of Pollution Act 1974, and any reference in these regulations to a numbered section shall be construed as a reference to the section bearing that number in the Act;

"best practicable means" shall be construed in accordance with section 72;

"person responsible" has the meaning given to it by section 73(1).

(3) Any reference in these regulations to a numbered regulation shall be construed as a reference to the regulation bearing that number in these regulations.

---

1. Made under the Control of Pollution Act 1974, ss 70(2) and (3) and 104(1).

PART II

APPEALS TO MAGISTRATES' COURTS

Interpretation of Part II

8–27161 **3.** This part of these regulations relates only to appeals brought to magistrates' courts under Part III of the Act, and any reference in this part to an appeal or an appellant shall be construed accordingly.

Appeals under section 60(7)

8–27163 **5.** (1) The provisions of this regulation shall apply to an appeal brought by any person under subsection (7) of section 60 (control of noise on construction sites) against a notice served upon him by a local authority under that section.

(2) The grounds on which a person served with such a notice may appeal under the said subsection (7) may include any of the following grounds which are appropriate in the circumstances of the particular case:—

(*a*) that the notice is not justified by the terms of section 60;

(*b*) that there has been some informality, defect or error in, or in connection with, the notice;

(*c*) that the authority have refused unreasonably to accept compliance with alternative requirements, or that the requirements of the notice are otherwise unreasonable in character or extent, or are unnecessary;

(*d*) that the time, or, where more than one time is specified, any of the times, within which the requirements of the notice are to be complied with is not reasonably sufficient for the purpose;

(*e*) that the notice should have been served on some person instead of the appellant, being a person who is carrying out, or going to carry out, the works, or is responsible for, or has control over, the carrying out of the works;

(*f*) that the notice might lawfully have been served on some person in addition to the appellant, being a person who is carrying out, or going to carry out, the works, or is responsible for, or has control over, the carrying out of the works, and that it would have been equitable for it to have been so served;

(*g*) that the authority have not had regard to some or all of the provisions of section 60(4).

(3) If and so far as an appeal is based on the ground of some informality, defect or error in, or in connection with, the notice, the court shall dismiss the appeal, if it is satisfied that the informality, defect or error was not a material one.

(4) Where the grounds upon which an appeal is brought include a ground specified in paragraph (2)(*e*) or (*f*) above, the appellant shall serve a copy of his notice of appeal on any other person referred to, and in the case of any appeal to which this regulation applies he may serve a copy of his notice of appeal on any other person having an estate or interest in the premises in question.

(5) On the hearing of the appeal the court may—

(*a*) quash the notice to which the appeal relates, or

(*b*) vary the notice in favour of the appellant in such manner as it thinks fit, or

(*c*) dismiss the appeal;

and a notice which is varied under sub-paragraph (*b*) above shall be final and shall otherwise have effect, as so varied, as if it had been so made by the local authority.

Appeals under section 61(7)

8–27164 **6.** (1) The provisions of this regulation shall apply to an appeal brought by any person under subsection (7) of section 61 (prior consent for work on construction sites) in relation to a conditional consent given by a local authority under that section or in relation to an authority's refusal or failure to give a consent within the period specified in subsection (6) of that section.

(2) In this regulation, "conditional consent" means a consent given by a local authority under section 61 in respect of which the authority have attached any condition or imposed any limitation or qualification in pursuance of section 61(5)(*a*), (*b*) or (*c*); and "conditions" includes any limitation or qualification so imposed.

(3) The grounds on which a person to whom a local authority give a conditional consent may appeal under the said subsection (7) may include any of the following grounds which are appropriate in the circumstances of the particular case:—

(*a*) that any condition attached or imposed in relation to the consent (in this regulation referred to as "a relevant condition") is not justified by the terms of section 61;

(*b*) that there has been some informality, defect or error in, or in connection with, the consent;

(*c*) that the requirements of any relevant condition are unreasonable in character or extent, or are unnecessary;

(*d*) that the time, or where more than one time is specified, any of the times, within which the requirements of any relevant condition are to be complied with is not reasonably sufficient for the purpose.

(4) If and so far as an appeal is based on the ground of some informality, defect or error in, or in connection with, the consent, the court shall dismiss the appeal, if it is satisfied that the informality, defect or error was not a material one.

(5) Where the appeal relates to a conditional consent given by a local authority, on the hearing of the appeal the court may—

(*a*) vary the consent or any relevant condition in favour of the appellant in such manner as it thinks fit, or

(*b*) quash any relevant condition, or

(*c*) dismiss the appeal;

and a consent or condition which is varied under sub-paragraph (*a*) above shall be final and shall otherwise have effect, as so varied, as if it had been given, attached or imposed in that form by the authority.

(6) Where the appeal relates to a local authority's refusal or failure to give a consent within the period specified in section 61(6), on the hearing of the appeal the court shall afford to the appellant and to the authority an opportunity of making representations to it concerning the application under section 61(1) to which the appeal relates and concerning the terms and conditions of any consent which they consider to be appropriate thereto, and thereafter the court shall either—

(*a*) adjourn the appeal to enable the appellant to submit to the authority a new application under section 61(1) relating to the matters which are the subject of the appeal, or

(*b*) make an order giving consent to the application either unconditionally or subject to such conditions as it thinks fit, having regard to the provisions of section 61(4), (5) and (9), and any other matters which appear to it to be relevant,

and any consent given by an order made under sub-paragraph (*b*) above shall be final and shall otherwise have effect for the purpose of Part III of the Act as if it were a consent given by the local authority under section 61.

Appeals under section 66(7)

8–27165 **7.** (1) The provisions of this regulation shall apply to an appeal brought by any person under subsection (7) of section 66 (reduction of noise levels) against a noise reduction notice served upon him by a local authority under that section.

(2) The grounds on which a person served with such a notice may appeal under the said subsection (7) may include any of the following grounds which are appropriate in the circumstances of the particular case:—

(*a*) that the notice is not justified by the terms of section 66;

(*b*) that there has been some informality, defect or error in, or in connection with, the notice;

(*c*) that the authority have refused unreasonably to accept compliance with alternative requirements, or that the requirements of the notice are otherwise unreasonable in character or extent, or are unnecessary;

(*d*) that the time, or, where more than one time is specified, any of the times, within which the requirements of the notice are to be complied with is not reasonably sufficient for the purpose;

(*e*) where the noise to which the notice relates is noise caused in the course of a trade or business, that the best practicable means have been used for preventing, or for counteracting the effect of, the noise;

(*f*) that the notice should have been served on some person instead of the appellant, being the person responsible for the noise;

(*g*) that the notice might lawfully have been served on some person in addition to the appellant, being a person also responsible for the noise and that it would have been equitable for it to have been so served.

(3) If and so far as an appeal is based on the ground of some informality, defect or error in, or

in connection with, the notice, the court shall dismiss the appeal, if it is satisfied that the informality, defect or error was not a material one.

(4) Where the grounds upon which an appeal is brought include a ground specified in paragraph (2)(*g*) above, the appellant shall serve a copy of his notice of appeal on any other person referred to, and in the case of any appeal to which this regulation applies he may serve a copy of his notice of appeal on any other person having an estate or interest in the premises in question.

(5) On the hearing of the appeal the court may—

(*a*) quash the notice to which the appeal relates, or

(*b*) vary the notice in favour of the appellant in such manner as it thinks fit, or

(*c*) dismiss the appeal;

and a notice which is varied under sub-paragraph (*b*) above shall be final and shall otherwise have effect as so varied as if it had been so made by the local authority.

(6) Subject to paragraph (7) below, on the hearing of the appeal the court may make such order as it thinks fit—

(*a*) with respect to the person by whom any work is to be executed and the contribution to be made by any person towards the cost of the work, or

(*b*) as to the proportions in which any expenses which may become recoverable by the local authority under Part III of the Act are to be borne by the appellant and any other person.

(7) In exercising its powers under paragraph (6) above, the court shall be satisfied, before it imposes any requirements thereunder on any person other than the appellant, that the person has received a copy of the notice of appeal in pursuance of paragraph (4) above.

PART III
APPEALS TO THE SECRETARY OF STATE

PART IV
SUSPENSION OF NOTICES

8–27166 **10.** (1) Subject to paragraph (2) of this regulation, where an appeal is brought against a notice served under section 60, or 66 and—

(*a*) the noise to which the notice relates is noise caused in the course of the performance of some duty imposed by law on the appellant, or

(*b*) compliance with the notice would involve any person in expenditure on the carrying out of works before the hearing of the appeal,

the notice shall be suspended until the appeal has been abandoned or decided by the court.

(2) A notice to which this regulation applies shall not be suspended if in the opinion of the local authority—

(*a*) the noise to which the notice relates—

(i) is injurious to health, or

(ii) is likely to be of a limited duration such that suspension of the notice would render the notice of no practical effect, or

(*b*) the expenditure which would be incurred by any person in the carrying out of works in compliance with the notice before any appeal has been decided would not be disproportionate to the public benefit to be expected in that period from such compliance,

and the notice includes a statement that it shall have effect notwithstanding any appeal to a magistrates' court which has not been decided by the court.

(3) Save as provided in this regulation a notice under Part III of the Act shall not be suspended by reason only of the bringing of an appeal to a magistrates' court or the Secretary of State.

Litter (Statutory Undertakers) (Designation and Relevant Land) Order 1991[1]

(SI 1991/1043 amended by SI 1992/406, SI 1999/1443 and SI 2003/1615)

Citation, commencement and interpretation

8–27171 **1.** (1) This Order may be cited as the Litter (Statutory Undertakers) (Designation and Relevant Land) Order 1991 and shall come into force on 13th May 1991.

(2) In this Order—

"the Act" means the Environmental Protection Act 1990;

"operational land" means—

(*a*) in relation to any person authorised by any enactment to carry on any railway or light railway undertaking, land required or used for the operation of rail or light rail services,

(*aa*) in relation to any operator of a relevant railway asset, land required or used for the operation of that asset,

(*b*) in relation to any other designated statutory undertaker—

(i) land which is used for the purpose of carrying on their undertaking; and
(ii) land in which an interest is held for that purpose;

but does not include land which, in respect of its nature and situation, is comparable rather with land in general than with land which is used, or in which interests are held, for the purpose of the carrying on of statutory undertakings.

(3) For the purposes of article 3 of this Order, land is in an urban area if it is surrounded by, or adjoins for a continuous distance of not less than one kilometre, built-up sites (other than sites used for horticultural or agricultural purposes) on which there are permanent structures, and—

(*a*) for the purpose of determining whether any distance is continuous, any gap between built-up sites of 50 metres or less shall be disregarded,
(*b*) highways, navigable rivers and operational land which is not relevant land—
(i) shall not be treated as built-up sites for the purposes of determining whether or not land is in an urban area,
(ii) shall be ignored for the purposes of determining whether or not land adjoins built-up sites.

---

1. Made by the Secretary of State for the Environment, as respects England, the Secretary of State for Wales, as respects Wales, and the Secretary of State for Scotland, as respects Scotland, in exercise of the powers conferred on them by section 86(6), (8) and (15) of the Environmental Protection Act 1990.

Designation of statutory undertakers

8–27172 **2.** The statutory undertakers described below, and statutory undertakers of the descriptions described below, are designated for the purposes of Part IV of the Act—

the British Railways Board and Transport for London, or any of its subsidiaries (within the meaning of the Greater London Authority 1999) or company as respects which Transport for London has, or at any time has had, a beneficial interest (either directly or through nominees or subsidiaries) in not less than 20 per cent of its issued ordinary share capital,
any operator of a relevant railway asset,
any Passenger Transport Executive established pursuant to section 9(1) of the Transport Act 1968, in so far as it is authorised by any enactment to carry on any railway undertaking,
any person authorised by any enactment to carry on any light railway undertaking other than an independent railway undertaking within the meaning of section 83(7) of the Transport Act 1962,
any person authorised by any enactment to carry on any tramway undertaking,
any person authorised by any enactment to carry on any road transport undertaking, other than the operator of a licensed taxi or licensed hire car as defined in section 13(3) of the Transport Act 1985.
any person authorised by any enactment to carry on any canal, inland navigation, dock, harbour or pier undertaking,
any relevant airport operator (within the meaning of Part V of the Airports Act 1986).

Prescribed land of statutory undertakers

8–27173 **3.** (1) For the purposes of Part IV of the Act, land—

(*a*) which is under the direct control of a designated statutory undertaker,
(*b*) in relation to which the public have no right or permission to have access with or without payment, and
(*c*) which is within the description in paragraph (2) below but not within the description in paragraph (3) below;

is prescribed as relevant land of the designated statutory undertaker under whose control it is.

(2) The land described in this paragraph is operational land which is within 100 metres of a railway station platform to which the public is entitled or permitted to have access with or without payment and any other land which is not so situated but is land in an urban area, being in either case land which—

(*a*) forms an embankment, cutting, siding, level or junction, but is not part of a depot, goods yard, or enclosed area where plant and machinery is kept, or
(*b*) is within the rails or on the tracksides, but is not within a tunnel, or
(*c*) is on a viaduct or bridge.

(3) The land described in this paragraph is land below the place to which the tide flows at mean high water springs.

Land not to be treated as relevant land

8–27174 **4.** For the purposes of Part IV of the Act, land to which the public are entitled or permitted to have access with or without payment which is—

land other than operational land,
land used solely for the provision of freight services,

land adjacent to an unpaved towing path or adjacent to a paved towing path where the paving extends for a length of less than 1 kilometre, or

land below the place to which the tide flows at mean high water springs,

is not to be treated as relevant land of any designated statutory undertaker.

Statutory Nuisance (Appeals) Regulations 1995

(SI 1995/2644)

Citation, commencement and interpretation

8–27180 **1.** (1) These Regulations may be cited as the Statutory Nuisance (Appeals) Regulations 1995 and shall come into force on 8th November 1995.

(2) In these Regulations—

"the 1974 Act" means the Control of Pollution Act 1974;
"the 1990 Act" means the Environmental Protection Act 1990; and
"the 1993 Act" means the Noise and Statutory Nuisance Act 1993.

Appeals under section 80(3) of the 1990 Act

8–27181 **2.** (1) The provisions of this regulation apply in relation to an appeal brought by any person under section 80(3) of the 1990 Act (appeals to magistrates) against an abatement notice served upon him by a local authority.

(2) The grounds on which a person served with such a notice may appeal under section 80(3) are any one or more of the following grounds that are appropriate in the circumstances of the particular case—

(*a*) that the abatement notice is not justified by section 80 of the 1990 Act (summary proceedings for statutory nuisances);

(*b*) that there has been some informality, defect or error in, or in connection with, the abatement notice, or in, or in connection with, any copy of the abatement notice served under section 80A(3) (certain notices in respect of vehicles, machinery or equipment);

(*c*) that the authority have refused unreasonably to accept compliance with alternative requirements, or that the requirements of the abatement notice are otherwise unreasonable in character or extent, or are unnecessary;

(*d*) that the time, or where more than one time is specified, any of the times, within which the requirements of the abatement notice are to be complied with is not reasonably sufficient for the purpose;

(*e*) where the nuisance to which the notice relates—

(i) is a nuisance falling within section 79(1)(*a*), (*d*), (*e*), (*f*) or (*g*) of the 1990 Act and arises on industrial, trade, or business premises, or

(ii) is a nuisance falling within section 79(1)(*b*) of the 1990 Act and the smoke is emitted from a chimney, or

(iii) is a nuisance falling within section 79(1)(*ga*) of the 1990 Act and is noise emitted from or caused by a vehicle, machinery or equipment being used for industrial, trade or business purposes,

that the best practicable means were used to prevent, or to counteract the effects of, the nuisance;

(*f*) that, in the case of a nuisance under section 79(1)(*g*) or (*ga*) of the 1990 Act (noise emitted from premises), the requirements imposed by the abatement notice by virtue of section 80(1)(*a*) of that Act are more onerous than the requirements for the time being in force, in relation to the noise to which the notice relates, of—

(i) any notice served under section 60 or 66 of the 1974 Act (control of noise on construction sites and from certain premises), or

(ii) any consent given under section 61 or 65 of the 1974 Act (consent for work on construction sites and consent for noise to exceed registered level in a noise abatement zone), or

(iii) any determination made under section 67 of the 1974 Act (noise control of new buildings);

(*g*) that, in the case of a nuisance under section 79(1)(*ga*) of the 1990 Act (noise emitted from or caused by vehicles, machinery or equipment), the requirements imposed by the abatement notice by virtue of section 80(1)(*a*) of the Act are more onerous than the requirements for the time being in force, in relation to the noise to which the notice relates, of any condition of a consent given under paragraph 1 of Schedule 2 to the 1993 Act (loudspeakers in streets or roads);

(*h*) that the abatement notice should have been served on some person instead of the appellant, being—

(i) the person responsible for the nuisance, or

(ii) the person responsible for the vehicle, machinery or equipment, or

(iii) in the case of a nuisance arising from any defect of a structural character, the owner of the premises, or
(iv) in the case where the person responsible for the nuisance cannot be found or the nuisance has not yet occurred, the owner or occupier of the premises;

(*i*) that the abatement notice might lawfully have been served on some person instead of the appellant being—

(i) in the case where the appellant is the owner of the premises, the occupier of the premises, or,
(ii) in the case where the appellant is the occupier of the premises, the owner of the premises,

and that it would have been equitable for it to have been so served;

(*j*) that the abatement notice might lawfully have been served on some person in addition to the appellant, being—

(i) a person also responsible for the nuisance, or
(ii) a person who is also owner of the premises, or
(iii) a person who is also an occupier of the premises, or
(iv) a person who is also the person responsible for the vehicle, machinery or equipment,

and that it would have been equitable for it to have been so served.

(3) If and so far as an appeal is based on the ground of some informality, defect or error in, or in connection with, the abatement notice, or in, or in connection with, any copy of the notice served under section 80A(3), the court shall dismiss the appeal if it is satisfied that the informality, defect or error was not a material one.

(4) Where the grounds upon which an appeal is brought include a ground specified in paragraph 2(*i*) or (*j*) above, the appellant shall serve a copy of his notice of appeal on any other person referred to, and in the case of any appeal to which these regulations apply he may serve a copy of his notice of appeal on any other person having an estate or interest in the premises, vehicle, machinery or equipment in question.

(5) On the hearing of the appeal the court may—

(*a*) quash the abatement notice to which the appeal relates, or
(*b*) vary the abatement notice in favour of the appellant in such manner as it thinks fit, or
(*c*) dismiss the appeal;

and an abatement notice that is varied under sub-paragraph (*b*) above shall be final and shall otherwise have effect, as so varied, as if it had been so made by the local authority.

(6) Subject to paragraph (7) below, on the hearing of an appeal the court may make such order as it thinks fit—

(*a*) with respect to the person by whom any work is to be executed and the contribution to be made by any person towards the cost of the work, or
(*b*) as to the proportions in which any expenses which may become recoverable by the authority under Part III of the 1990 Act are to be borne by the appellant and by any other person.

(7) In exercising its powers under paragraph (6) above the court—

(*a*) shall have regard, as between an owner and an occupier, to the terms and conditions, whether contractual or statutory, of any relevant tenancy and to the nature of the works required, and
(*b*) shall be satisfied before it imposes any requirement thereunder on any person other than the appellant, that that person has received a copy of the notice of appeal in pursuance of paragraph (4) above.

Suspension of notice

8–27182 **3.** (1) Where—

(*a*) an appeal is brought against an abatement notice served under section 80 or section 80A of the 1990 Act, and—
(*b*) either—

(i) compliance with the abatement notice would involve any person in expenditure on the carrying out of works before the hearing of the appeal, or
(ii) in the case of a nuisance under section 79(1)(*g*) or (*ga*) of the 1990 Act, the noise to which the abatement notice relates is noise necessarily caused in the course of the performance of some duty imposed by law on the appellant, and

(*c*) either paragraph (2) does not apply, or it does apply but the requirements of paragraph (3) have not been met,

the abatement notice shall be suspended until the appeal has been abandoned or decided by the court.

(2) This paragraph applies where—

(*a*) the nuisance to which the abatement notice relates—

(i) is injurious to health, or

(ii) is likely to be of a limited duration such that suspension of the notice would render it of no practical effect, or

(*b*) the expenditure which would be incurred by any person in the carrying out of works in compliance with the abatement notice before any appeal has been decided would not be disproportionate to the public benefit to be expected in that period from such compliance.

(3) Where paragraph (2) applies the abatement notice—

(*a*) shall include a statement that paragraph (2) applies, and that as a consequence it shall have effect notwithstanding any appeal to a magistrates' court which has not been decided by the court, and

(*b*) shall include a statement as to which of the grounds set out in paragraph (2) apply.

Revocations

8–27183 4. The Statutory Nuisance (Appeals) Regulations 1990 and the Statutory Nuisance (Appeals) (Amendment) Regulations 1990 are hereby revoked.

Pollution Prevention and Control (England and Wales) Regs 2000[1]

(SI 2000/1973 amended by SI 2001/503, SI 2002/275, 1559, 1702, 2469, 2688 and 2980, SI 2003/1699 and 3296, SI 2004/107, 1375 and 3276 and SI 2005/894, 1448, 1806 (W) and 2773)

PART I
GENERAL

8–27184 **1. Citation, commencement and extent.** (1) These Regulations may be cited as the Pollution Prevention and Control (England and Wales) Regulations 2000 and shall come into force on the 1st August 2000.

(2) These Regulations extend to England and Wales only.

(3) For the purpose of paragraph (2), "England and Wales" includes the territorial waters adjacent to England and Wales.

1. Made by the Secretary of State, in exercise of the powers conferred on him by s 2 of the Pollution Prevention and Control Act 1999, having, in accordance with s 2(4) of the 1999 Act, consulted the Environment Agency, such bodies or persons appearing to him to be representative of the interests of local government, industry, agriculture and small businesses respectively as he considers appropriate and such other bodies and persons as he considers appropriate.

8–27185 **2. Interpretation: general.** (1) In these Regulations, except in so far as the context otherwise requires—

"the 2002 Regulations" means the Landfill (England and Wales) Regulations 2002;

"change in operation" means, in relation to an installation or mobile plant, a change in the nature or functioning or an extension of the installation or mobile plant which may have consequences for the environment; and "substantial change in operation" means, in relation to an installation or mobile plant, a change in operation which, in the opinion of the regulator, may have significant negative effects on human beings or the environment and shall include (except in relation to Part 1 of Schedule 3)—

(i) in relation to a small SED installation which does not fall wholly within the scope of the IPPC Directive, a change of the nominal capacity leading to an increase of emissions of volatile organic compounds of more than 25 per cent;

(ii) in relation to all other SED installations which do not fall wholly within the scope of the IPPC Directive, a change of the nominal capacity leading to an increase of emissions of volatile organic compounds of more than 10 per cent;

"directly associated activity" means—

(i) in relation to an activity carried out in a stationary technical unit and falling within any description in sections 1.1 to 6.9 of Part 1 of Schedule 1, any directly associated activity which has a technical connection with the activity carried out in the stationary technical unit and which could have an effect on pollution; and

(ii) in relation to an SED activity, any directly associated activity which has a technical connection with the SED activity carried out on the same site and which could have an effect on any discharge of volatile organic compounds into the environment;

"emission" means—

(i) in relation to Part A installations, the direct or indirect release of substances, vibrations, heat or noise from individual or diffuse sources in an installation into the air, water or land;

(ii) in relation to Part B installations, the direct release of substances or heat from individual or diffuse sources in an installation into the air;

(iii) in relation to Part A mobile plant, the direct or indirect release of substances, vibrations, heat or noise from the mobile plant into the air, water or land;

(iv) in relation to Part B mobile plant, the direct release of substances or heat from the mobile plant into the air;

"emission limit value" means the mass, expressed in terms of specific parameters, concentration or level of an emission, which may not be exceeded during one or more periods of time;

"enforcement notice" has the meaning given by regulation 24(1);

"general binding rules" has the meaning given by regulation 14(1);

"installation" means (except where used in the term SED installation)—

(i) a stationary technical unit where one or more activities listed in Part 1 of Schedule 1 are carried out;

(ii) any other location on the same site where any other directly associated activities are carried out,

and, other than in Schedule 3, references to an installation include references to part of an installation;

"the IPPC Directive" means Council Directive 96/61/EC concerning integrated pollution prevention and control;

"landfill" means a landfill to which the 2002 Regulations apply;

"mobile plant" means plant which is designed to move or to be moved whether on roads or otherwise and which is used to carry out one or more activities listed sections 1.1 to 6.9 of Part 1 of Schedule 1;

"new SED installation" and "existing SED installation" shall be interpreted in accordance with Schedule 3;

"off-site condition" has the meaning given by regulation 12(12);

"operator", subject to paragraph (2), means, in relation to an installation or mobile plant, the person who has control over its operation;

"Part A installation", "Part A(1) installation", "Part A(2) installation" and "Part B installation" shall be interpreted in accordance with Part 3 of Schedule 1;

"Part A mobile plant", "Part A(1) mobile plant", "Part A(2) mobile plant" and "Part B mobile plant" shall be interpreted in accordance with Part 3 of Schedule 1;

"permit" means a permit granted under regulation 10;

"pollution" means emissions as a result of human activity which may be harmful to human health or the quality of the environment, cause offence to any human senses, result in damage to material property, or impair or interfere with amenities and other legitimate uses of the environment; and "pollutant" means any substance, vibration, heat or noise released as a result of such an emission which may have such an effect;

"reduction scheme" means a reduction scheme which complies with Annex IIB of the Solvent Emissions Directive;

"regulator" means, in relation to the exercise of functions under these Regulations, the authority by whom, under regulation 8, the functions are exercisable; and "local authority regulator" means a regulator which is a local authority as defined in regulation 8(15) and (16);

"revocation notice" has the meaning given by regulation 21(1);

"SED activity" means any activity falling within section 7 of Part 1 of Schedule 1;]

"SED installation" means—

(i) a stationary technical unit where one or more SED activities are carried out; and

(ii) any other location on the same site where any other directly associated activities are carried out;

"small SED installation" means an SED installation which falls within the lower threshold band of items 1, 3, 4, 5, 8, 10, 13, 16 or 17 of Annex IIA to the Solvent Emissions Directive or, for the other activities of Annex IIA, which have a solvent consumption of less than 10 tonnes/year;]

"the Solvent Emissions Directive" means Council Directive 1999/13/EC on the limitation of emissions of volatile organic compounds due to the use of solvents in certain activities and installations;

"specified waste management activity" means any one of the following activities—

(*a*) the disposal of waste in a landfill falling within Section 5.2 of Part 1 of Schedule 1;

(*b*) the disposal of waste falling within Section 5.3 of that Part of that Schedule;

(*c*) the recovery of waste falling within paragraphs (i), (ii), (v) or (vii) of paragraph (*c*) of Part A(1) of Section 5.4 of that Part of that Schedule,

but does not include any activity specified in sub-paragraphs (*b*) or (*c*) above where that activity—

(i) is carried on at the same installation as any activity falling within Part A(1) of any Section in Part 1 of that Schedule, which is not an activity specified in sub-paragraphs (*a*) to (*c*) above; and

(ii) is not the primary activity of that installation,

and, for the purpose of this definition the primary activity of an installation is the activity the carrying out of which constitutes the primary purpose for operating the installation.

"substance" includes any chemical element and its compounds and any biological entity or micro-organism, with the exception of radioactive substances within the meaning of Council Directive 80/836/Euratom, genetically modified micro-organisms within the meaning of Council Directive 90/219/EEC and genetically modified organisms within the meaning of Council Directive 90/220/EEC;

"suspension notice" has the meaning given by regulation 25(1);

"variation notice" has the meaning given by regulation 17(5).

"waste incineration installation" means that part of an installation or mobile plant in which any of the following activities is carried out—

(*a*) the incineration of waste falling within Section 5.1A(1)(*a*), (*b*) or (*c*) or A(2) of Part 1 of Schedule 1; or

(*b*) any activity falling within any Section of that Part of that Schedule which is carried out in a co-incineration plant as defined in Section 5.1 of that Part of that Schedule.

(2) For the purposes of these Regulations—

(*a*) where an installation or mobile plant has not been put into operation, the person who will have control over the operation of the installation or mobile plant when it is put into operation shall be treated as the operator of the installation or mobile plant;

(*b*) where an installation or mobile plant has ceased to be in operation, the person who holds the permit which applies to the installation or mobile plant shall be treated as the operator of the installation or mobile plant.

(2A) For the purposes of these Regulations where—

(*a*) an installation includes a combustion plant as defined in Article 2(7) of Council Directive 2001/80/EC on the limitation of emissions of certain pollutants into the air from large combustion plants and to which that Directive applies; and

(*b*) the rated thermal input of the combustion plant is extended by 50 megawatts or more,

the extension shall be treated as a substantial change in operation.

(2B) For the purposes of these Regulations a change in the operation of a waste incineration installation which involves incineration or co-incineration for the first time of hazardous waste shall be treated as a substantial change in operation, and for the purposes of this paragraph "co-incineration" and "hazardous waste" shall have the meanings given in Section 5.1 of Part I of Schedule 1.

(2C) For the purposes of these Regulations any change in operation of an installation which in itself meets any of the thresholds specified for a Part A activity under any Section in Part 1 of Schedule 1 shall be treated as a substantial change in operation.

(3) In these Regulations—

(*a*) a reference to a release into water includes a release into a sewer (within the meaning of section 219(1) of the Water Industry Act 1991);

(*b*) a reference to a Council Directive is a reference to that Directive together with any amendment made before the date on which these Regulations are made.

(4) Part 1 of Schedule 1 shall be interpreted in accordance with the provisions as to interpretation in Part 1 and 2 of that Schedule.

(5) Parts 1 and 2 of Schedule 3 shall be interpreted in accordance with Part 3 of that Schedule.

8–27186 3. Interpretation: "best available techniques". (1) For the purpose of these Regulations, "best available techniques" means the most effective and advanced stage in the development of activities and their methods of operation which indicates the practical suitability of particular techniques for providing in principle the basis for emission limit values designed to prevent and, where that is not practicable, generally to reduce emissions and the impact on the environment as a whole; and for the purpose of this definition—

(*a*) "available techniques" means those techniques which have been developed on a scale which allows implementation in the relevant industrial sector, under economically and technically viable conditions, taking into consideration the cost and advantages, whether or not the techniques are used or produced inside the United Kingdom, as long as they are reasonably accessible to the operator;

(*b*) "best" means, in relation to techniques, the most effective in achieving a high general level of protection of the environment as a whole;

(*c*) "techniques" includes both the technology used and the way in which the installation is designed, built, maintained, operated and decommissioned.

(2) Schedule 2 shall have effect in relation to the determination of best available techniques.

8–27187 4. Fit and proper person. (1) This regulation applies for the purpose of the discharge of any function under these Regulations which requires the regulator to determine whether a person is or is not a fit and proper person to carry out a specified waste management activity.

(2) Whether a person is or is not a fit and proper person to carry out a specified waste management activity shall be determined by reference to the fulfilment of the conditions of the permit which apply or will apply to the carrying out of that activity.

(3) Subject to paragraph (4), a person shall be treated as not being a fit and proper person if it appears to the regulator that—

(*a*) he or another relevant person has been convicted of a relevant offence;
(*b*) the management of the specified waste management activity which is to be carried out will not be in the hands of a technically competent person;
(*c*) he has not made, or will not before commencement of any specified waste management activity consisting of the disposal of waste in a landfill falling within Section 5.2 of Part 1 of Schedule 1 make, adequate financial provision (either by way of financial security or its equivalent) to ensure that—

(i) the obligations (including after-care provisions) arising from the permit in relation to that activity are discharged; and
(ii) any closure procedures required by the permit in relation to that activity are followed;

(*d*) he and all staff engaged in carrying out any specified waste management activity falling within sub-paragraph (c) will not be provided with adequate professional technical development and training; or

(*e*) for specified waste management activities not falling within sub-paragraph (c), the person who holds or is to hold the permit has not made and either has no intention of making or is in no position to make financial provision adequate to discharge the obligations arising from the permit in relation to the specified waste management activity.(4)The regulator may, if it considers it proper to do so in any particular case, treat a person as a fit and proper person notwithstanding that paragraph (3)(*a*) applies in his case.

(5) For the purposes of paragraph (3)—

(*a*) "relevant offence" means an offence prescribed under section 74(6) of the Environmental Protection Act 1990 for the purposes of section 74(3)(*a*) of that Act; and
(*b*) the qualifications and experience required of a person for the purposes of section 74(3)(*b*) of that Act which are prescribed under section 74(6) of that Act shall be treated as the qualifications and experience required of a person for the purposes of paragraph (3)(*b*).

(6) In paragraph (3)(*a*), "another relevant person" means, in relation to the holder or proposed holder of a permit—

(*a*) any person who has been convicted of a relevant offence committed by him in the course of his employment by the holder or proposed holder of the permit or in the course of the carrying on of any business by a partnership one of the members of which was the holder or proposed holder of the permit;
(*b*) a body corporate which has been convicted of a relevant offence committed when the holder or proposed holder of the permit was a director, manager, secretary or other similar officer of that body corporate; or
(*c*) where the holder or proposed holder of the permit is a body corporate, a person who is a director, manager, secretary or other similar officer of that body corporate and who—

(i) has been convicted of a relevant offence; or
(ii) was a director, manager, secretary or other similar officer of another body corporate at a time when a relevant offence for which that other body corporate has been convicted was committed.

8–27188 5. *Application to the Crown*

8–27189 6. Notices. (1) Any notice served or given under these Regulations or the 2002 Regulations by the Secretary of State or a regulator shall be in writing.

(2) Any such notice may be served on or given to a person by leaving it at his proper address or by sending it by post to him at that address.

(3) Any such notice may—

(*a*) in the case of a body corporate, be served on the secretary or clerk of that body;
(*b*) in the case of a partnership, be served on or given to a partner or person having the control or management of the partnership business.

(4) For the purpose of this regulation and of section 7 of the Interpretation Act 1978 (service of documents by post) in its application to this regulation, the proper address of any person on or to whom any such notice is to be served or given shall be his last known address, except that—

(*a*) in the case of a body corporate or their secretary or clerk, it shall be the address of the registered or principal office of that body;
(*b*) in the case of a partnership or person having the control or management of the partnership business, it shall be the principal office of the partnership,

and for the purposes of this paragraph the principal office of a company registered outside the United Kingdom or of a partnership carrying on business outside the United Kingdom shall be their principal office within the United Kingdom.

(5) If the person to be served with or given any such notice has specified an address in the United Kingdom other than his proper address within the meaning of paragraph (4) as the one at which he or someone on his behalf will accept notices of the same description as that notice, that address shall also be treated for the purposes of this regulation and section 7 of the Interpretation Act 1978 as his proper address.

8–27190 7. *Applications*

8–27191 8. *Authority by whom the functions conferred or imposed by these Regulations on a regulator are exercisable and the purposes for which they are exercisable*

PART II
PERMITS

8–27192 **9. Requirement for permit to operate installation and mobile plant.** (1) No person shall operate an installation or mobile plant after the prescribed date for that installation or mobile plant except under and to the extent authorised by a permit granted by the regulator.

(2) In paragraph (1), the "prescribed date" means the appropriate date set out in or determined in accordance with Schedule 3.

8–27193 10. *Permits: general provisions*

8–27194 **13. Conditions of permits: Environment Agency notice in relation to emissions into water.** (1) In the case of a Part A installation or Part A mobile plant in relation to which a local authority regulator exercises functions under these Regulations, the Environment Agency may, at any time, give notice to the local authority regulator specifying the emission limit values or conditions (not containing emission limit values) which it considers are appropriate in relation to preventing or reducing emissions into water.

(2) Where a notice under paragraph (1) specifies emission limit values, the emission limit values required by paragraph (2) of regulation 12 in relation to emissions into water from the installation or mobile plant concerned shall be those specified in that notice or such stricter emission limit values as may be determined by the local authority regulator in accordance with paragraph (6) of that regulation or required by paragraph (7) of that regulation.

(3) Where a notice under paragraph (1) specifies conditions in relation to emissions into water from an installation or mobile plant, the permit authorising the operation of that installation or mobile plant shall include those conditions or any more onerous conditions dealing with the same matters as the local authority regulator considers to be appropriate.

8–27195 14. *Secretary of State may make general binding rules*

8–27196 15. *Review of conditions of permits*

8–27197 **16. Proposed change in the operation of an installation.** (1) Subject to paragraph (4), where an operator of an installation which is permitted under these Regulations proposes to make a change in the operation of that installation he shall, at least 14 days before making the change, notify the regulator.

(2) A notification under paragraph (1) shall be in writing and shall contain a description of the proposed change in the operation of the installation.

(3) A regulator shall, by notice served on the operator, acknowledge receipt of any notification received under paragraph (1).

(4) Paragraph (1) shall not apply where the operator applies under regulation 17(2) for the variation of the conditions of his permit before making the proposed change and the application contains a description of the change.

8–27198 17. *Variation of conditions of permits*

8–27199 18. *Transfer of permits*

8–27200 19. *Application to surrender a permit for a Part A installation or Part A mobile plant*

8–27201 20. *Notification of surrender of a permit for a Part B installation or Part B mobile plant*

8–27202 **21. Revocation of permits.** (1) The regulator may at any time revoke a permit, in whole or in part, by serving a notice ("a revocation notice") on the operator.

(2) Without prejudice to the generality of paragraph (1), the regulator may serve a notice under this regulation in relation to a permit where—

(*a*) the permit authorises the carrying out of a specified waste management activity and it appears to the regulator that the operator of the installation or mobile plant concerned has ceased to be a fit and proper person to carry out that activity by reason of his having been convicted of a relevant offence within the meaning of regulation 4(5)(*a*) or by reason of the management of that activity having ceased to be in the hands of a technically competent person;

(*b*) the holder of the permit has ceased to be the operator of the installation or mobile plant covered by the permit.

(3) A revocation notice may—

(*a*) revoke a permit entirely;

(*b*) revoke a permit only in so far as it authorises the operation of some of the installations or mobile plant to which it applies;

(*c*) revoke a permit only in so far as it authorises the carrying out of some of the activities which may be carried out in an installation or by means of mobile plant to which it applies.

(4) A revocation notice shall specify—

(*a*) in the case of a revocation mentioned in sub-paragraph (*b*) or (*c*) of paragraph (3) (a "partial revocation"), the extent to which the permit is being revoked;

(*b*) in all cases, the date on which the revocation shall take effect, which shall be at least 28 days after the date on which the notice is served.

(5) If, in the case of a revocation mentioned in sub-paragraph (*a*) or (*b*) of paragraph (3) applying to a Part A installation or Part A mobile plant, the regulator considers that it is appropriate to require the operator to take steps, once the installation or mobile plant is no longer in operation, to—

(*a*) avoid any pollution risk resulting from the operation of the installation or mobile plant on the site or, in the case of a partial revocation, that part of the site used for the operation of that installation or mobile plant, or

(*b*) return the site, or that part of the site, to a satisfactory state,

the revocation notice shall specify that this is the case and, in so far as those steps are not already required to be taken by the conditions of the permit, the steps to be taken.

(6) Subject to paragraph (7) and regulation 27(6), a permit shall cease to have effect, or, in the case of a partial revocation, shall cease to have effect to the extent specified in the revocation notice, from the date specified in the notice.

(7) Where paragraph (5) applies the permit shall cease to have effect to authorise the operation of the Part A installation or Part A mobile plant from the date specified in the revocation notice but shall continue to have effect in so far as the permit requires steps to be taken once it is no longer in operation until the regulator issues a certificate stating that it is satisfied that all such steps have been taken.

(8) Where a permit continues to have effect as mentioned in paragraph (7), any steps specified in a revocation notice pursuant to paragraph (5) shall be treated as if they were required to be taken by a condition of the permit and regulations 17, 23, 24, and 32(1)(*b*) shall apply in relation to the requirement to take such steps, and to any other conditions in the permit which require steps to be taken once the installation is no longer in operation, until the regulator issues a certificate as mentioned in paragraph (7).

(9) A regulator which has served a revocation notice may, before the date on which the revocation takes effect, withdraw the notice.

(10) Regulation 19(11) shall apply for the purpose of deciding whether a pollution risk results from the operation of a Part A installation or Part A mobile plant for the purpose of this regulation as it applies for the purpose of regulation 19.

8–27203 **22.** *Fees and charges in relation to local authority permits*

PART III
ENFORCEMENT

8–27204 **23–26.** *Duty of regulator to ensure compliance with conditions etc*

PART IV
APPEALS

8–27205 **27.** *Appeals to the Secretary of State*

PART V
INFORMATION AND PUBLICITY

8–27206 **28.** *Information*

8–27207 **29. Public registers of information.** (1) Subject to regulations 30 and 31 and to paragraphs 2 to 5 of Schedule 9, it shall be the duty of each regulator, as respects installations or mobile plant for which it is the regulator, to maintain a register containing the particulars described in paragraph 1 of that Schedule.

(2) Subject to paragraph (3), the register maintained by a local authority regulator shall also contain any particulars contained in any register maintained by the Environment Agency relating to the operation of an installation or Part A mobile plant in the area of the local authority regulator in relation to which the Environment Agency has functions under these Regulations.

(3) Paragraph (2) does not apply to port health authorities but each local authority regulator whose area adjoins that of a port health authority shall include in its register the information that it would have had to include under paragraph (2) in relation to the operation of installations and Part A mobile plant in the area of the port health authority if the port health authority had not been constituted.

(4) The Environment Agency shall furnish each local authority regulator with the particulars which are necessary to enable it to discharge its duty under paragraphs (2) and (3).

(5) Where information of any description is excluded from any register by virtue of regulation 31, a statement shall be entered in the register indicating the existence of information of that description.

(6) It shall be the duty of each regulator—

(*a*) to secure that the registers maintained by them under this regulation are available, at all reasonable times, for inspection by the public free of charge; and

(*b*) to afford to members of the public facilities for obtaining copies of entries, on payment of reasonable charges.

(7) Registers under this regulation may be kept in any form.

8–27208 **30.** *Exclusion from registers of information affection National security*

8–27209 **31.** *Exclusion from registers of certain confidential information*

PART VI
PROVISION AS TO OFFENCES

8–27210 **32. Offences.** (1) It is an offence for a person—

(*a*) to contravene regulation 9(1);

(*b*) to fail to comply with or to contravene a condition of a permit;

(*c*) to fail to comply with regulation 16(1);

(*d*) to fail to comply with the requirements of an enforcement notice or a suspension notice, a suspension notice or a closure notice under regulation 16 of the 2002 Regulations;

(*e*) to fail, without reasonable excuse, to comply with any requirement imposed by a notice under regulation 28(2);

(*f*) to make a statement which he knows to be false or misleading in a material particular, or recklessly to make a statement which is false or misleading in a material particular, where the statement is made—

(i) in purported compliance with a requirement to furnish any information imposed by or under any provision of these Regulations or the 2002 Regulations; or

(ii) for the purpose of obtaining the grant of a permit to himself or any other person, or the variation, transfer or surrender of a permit;

(*g*) intentionally to make a false entry in any record required to be kept under the condition of a permit;

(h) with intent to deceive, to forge or use a document issued or authorised to be issued under a condition of a permit or required for any purpose under a condition of a permit or to make or have in his possession a document so closely resembling any such document as to be likely to deceive;

(i) to fail to comply with an order made by a court under regulation 35.

(2) A person guilty of an offence under sub-paragraph (*a*), (*b*), (*d*) or (i) of paragraph (1) shall be liable—

(*a*) on summary conviction, to a fine not exceeding £20,000 or to imprisonment for a term not exceeding six months or to both;

(*b*) on conviction on indictment, to a fine or to imprisonment for a term not exceeding five years or to both.

(3) A person guilty of an offence under sub-paragraph (*c*), (*e*) and (*f*) to (h) of paragraph (1) shall be liable—

(*a*) on summary conviction, to a fine not exceeding the statutory maximum;

(*b*) on conviction on indictment, to a fine or to imprisonment for a term not exceeding two years or to both.

(4) Where an offence under this regulation committed by a body corporate is proved to have been committed with the consent or connivance of, or to have been attributable to any neglect on the part of, any director, manager, secretary or other similar officer of the body corporate or a person who was purporting to act in any such capacity, he as well as the body corporate shall be guilty of that offence and shall be liable to be proceeded against and punished accordingly.

(5) Where the affairs of a body corporate are managed by its members, paragraph (4) shall apply in relation to the acts or defaults of a member in connection with his functions of management as if he were a director of the body corporate.

(6) Where the commission by any person of an offence under this regulation is due to the act or default of some other person, that other person may be charged with and convicted of the offence by virtue of this paragraph whether or not proceedings for the offence are taken against the first-mentioned person.

8–27211 **33. Enforcement by High Court.** If the regulator is of the opinion that proceedings for an offence under regulation 32(1)(*d*) would afford an ineffectual remedy against a person who has failed to comply with the requirements of an enforcement notice or a suspension notice, the regulator may take proceedings in the High Court for the purpose of securing compliance with the notice.

8–27212 **34. Admissibility of evidence.** Where—

(*a*) by virtue of a condition of a permit granted by a local authority regulator an entry is required to be made in any record as to the observance of any condition of the permit; and
(*b*) the entry has not been made,

that fact shall be admissible as evidence that that condition has not been observed.

8–27213 **35. Power of court to order cause of offence to be remedied.** (1) Where a person is convicted of an offence under regulation 32(1)(*a*), (*b*) or (*d*) in respect of any matters which appear to the court to be matters which it is in his power to remedy, the court may, in addition to or instead of imposing any punishment, order him, within such time as may be fixed by the order, to take such steps as may be specified in the order for remedying those matters.

(2) The time fixed by an order under paragraph (1) may be extended or further extended by order of the court on an application made before the end of the time as originally fixed or extended under this paragraph, as the case may be.

(3) Where a person is ordered under paragraph (1) to remedy any matters, that person shall not be liable under regulation 32 in respect of those matters in so far as they continue during the time fixed by the order or any further time allowed under paragraph (2).

8–27214

PART VII
SECRETARY OF STATE'S POWERS

PART VIII
CONSEQUENTIAL AMENDMENTS

PUBLIC MEETING AND PUBLIC ORDER

8–27670 This title contains the following statutes—

8–27672 LICENSING ACT 1872
8–27673 INEBRIATES ACT 1898
8–27674 LICENSING ACT 1902
8–27680 PUBLIC MEETING ACT 1908
8–27690 PUBLIC ORDER ACT 1936
8–27700 CRIMINAL JUSTICE ACT 1967
8–27710 RACE RELATIONS ACT 1976
8–27715 SPORTING EVENTS (CONTROL OF ALCOHOL ETC) ACT 1985
8–27720 PUBLIC ORDER ACT 1986
8–27781 FOOTBALL SPECTATORS ACT 1989
8–27822 FOOTBALL (OFFENCES) ACT 1991
8–27830 CONFISCATION OF ALCOHOL (YOUNG PERSONS) ACT 1997
8–27835 SERIOUS ORGANISED CRIME AND POLICE ACT 2005
8–27849D RACIAL AND RELIGIOUS HATRED ACT 2006

and the following statutory instrument—

8–27850 Sports Grounds and Sporting Events (Designation) Order 2005

Licensing Act 1872

(35 & 36 Vict c 94)

Offences against Public Order

8–27672 **12. Penalty on persons found drunk**[1]**.** Every person[2] found drunk in any highway[3] or other public place[4], whether a building or not, or on any licensed premises[5], shall be liable to a penalty not exceeding **level 1** on the standard scale[6].

Every person who is drunk[7] while in charge on any highway or other public place[4] of any carriage[8], horse, cattle[9], or steam engine, or who is drunk when in possession of any loaded firearms[10], may be apprehended[11], and shall be liable to a penalty not exceeding **level 1** on the standard scale or in the discretion of the court to imprisonment . . . for any term not exceeding **one month**.

[Licensing Act 1872, s 12, as amended by the Statute Law Revision Act 1953, the Penalties for Drunkenness Act

1962, s 1, the Criminal Justice Act 1967, Sch 7, the Criminal Law Act 1977, Sch 6 and the Criminal Justice Act 1982, ss 38 and 46.]

---

1. The Criminal Justice Act 1967, s 91, this title, post, has effect in place of this section where a person is guilty whilst drunk of disorderly behaviour (The Criminal Justice Act 1967, s 91(2)). Note also the power of a constable on arresting a drunken offender to take him to a treatment centre (Criminal Justice Act 1972, s 34 in PART III: SENTENCING, ante).

2. One justice may deal with the offence (Criminal Justice Administration Act 1914, s 38), but may not in any case impose a greater penalty than £1 (Magistrates' Courts Act 1980, s 121, in PART I: MAGISTRATES' COURTS PROCEDURE, ante). As it is not strictly necessary for the exact language of the statute to be used in the charge sheet if the words used are sufficient to embody the elements of the offence, a person may be rightly convicted under this section though the word "found" be omitted from the charge sheet. "Found" means ascertained to be (*Thomas v Powell* (1893) 57 JP 329; *Moran v Jones* (1911) 75 JP 411; *Martin v McIntyre* 1910 47 SLR 645, 74 JP Jo 482; *Davis v Sly* (1910) 26 TLR 460; *R v Judge Radcliffe, ex p Oxfordshire County Council* [1915] 3 KB 418, 79 JP 540; *R v Goodwin* [1944] KB 518, [1944] 1 All ER 506, 108 JP 159). A person is to be regarded as drunk if he had consumed intoxicating liquor to the extent that he had lost the power of self-control; if he had taken drugs as well, the justices must be satisfied that he would in any event have been deprived of his self-control as a result of having consumed the intoxicating liquor, before convicting under this provision (*Lanham v Rickwood* (1984) 148 JP 737).

3. An offence is committed if a person is in a highway and, while there, is ascertained or perceived to be drunk; the fact that his presence there was momentary or involuntary is immaterial (*Winzar v Chief Constable of Kent* [1983] LS Gaz R 1205).

4. "Public place" includes any place to which the public have access whether on payment or otherwise (Licensing Act 1902, s 8, post). A man in a tramcar was held to be in the street (*Martin v McIntyre* 1910 47 SLR 645, 74 JP Jo 482). A hackney carriage in the street was held a "public place" under a repealed statute (*R v Weller* (1894) 58 JP 286).

5. The expression "licensed premises" means premises in respect of which a premises licence has effect (Licensing Act 2003, s 193).

It was held that a publican could not be convicted of being found drunk on his own licensed premises after the house was closed, it being then his private place (*Lester v Torrens* (1877) 2 QBD 403, 41 JP 821). And the same applies to a lodger (*Young v Gentle* [1915] 2 KB 661, 79 JP 347). But a person who enters the house to use it as licensed premises, and not as a lodger or inmate, found drunk in the house after that time may be convicted (*R v Pelly* [1897] 2 QB 33, 61 JP 373). A resident on licensed premises who was found drunk on the premises at an hour when they were lawfully open for the sale of non-intoxicants and might have been open for the sale of intoxicants but for the restrictions imposed by the Regulations of the Central Control Board (Liquor Traffic), was held liable to conviction (*Lewis v Dodd* [1919] 1 KB 1, 83 JP 25). And where the front door was wide open, and a non-resident found therein, a conviction was ordered (*Evans v Fletcher* (1926) 90 JP 157). We think that residents in licensed premises cannot be convicted of being drunk thereon during the period when intoxicants cannot legally be sold if the licensed premises are actually closed to the public. Whether actually closed or not, the licensee's liability to be convicted for permitting drunkenness is the same (*Thompson v McKenzie* [1908] 1 KB 905, 72 JP 150). A part of the premises which has been let for a private party does not thereby cease to be "licensed premises" (*Stevens v Dickson* [1952] 2 All ER 246, 116 JP 439).

6. A person found drunk in a highway or public place is liable to arrest if he appears to be incapable of taking care of himself (Licensing Act 1902, s 1, post).

7. There is no varying standard of drunkenness depending on the occupation carried on by the accused (*R v Presdee* (1927) 20 Cr App Rep 95).

8. A motor vehicle or trailer is a carriage (Road Traffic Act 1988, s 191, in PART IV: ROAD TRAFFIC, ante). A person liable to be charged with an offence of driving or being in charge of a motor vehicle when under the influence of drink or drugs, shall not be liable to be charged under this section (Road Traffic Act 1988, s 5, in PART VII, title ROAD TRAFFIC, post). A bicycle, whether ridden or pushed, is a carriage within the meaning of this section (*Corkery v Carpenter* [1951] 1 KB 102, [1950] 2 All ER 745, 114 JP 481).

9. Including pigs and sheep (*Child v Hearn* (1874) LR 9 Exch 176).

10. The Act does not define "firearms"; adopting the ordinary modern meaning, the term would include an airgun (*Seamark v Prouse* [1980] 3 All ER 26, 70 Cr App Rep 236).

11. For powers of arrest see the Police and Criminal Evidence Act 1984, s 25 in PART I: MAGISTRATES' COURTS, PROCEDURE, ante.

Inebriates Act 1898[1]

(61 & 62 Vict c 60)

8–27673

Sections 2, 24

FIRST SCHEDULE

(*As amended by the Licensing Act 1902, s 2, the Criminal Justice Act 1967, Sch 7, and the Statute Law (Repeals) Act 1976, Sch 1.*)

Description of Offence	**Statute enacting Offence**
Being found drunk in a highway or other public place, whether a building or not, or on licensed premises.	Licensing Act 1872 (35 & 36 Vict c 94), s 12
Being drunk while in charge, on any highway or other public place, of any carriage, horse, cattle, or steam-engine.	
Being drunk when in possession of any loaded firearms.	
Refusing or failing when drunk to quit licensed premises when requested	Licensing Act 1872 (35 & 36 Vict c 94), s 18

Description of Offence	Statute enacting Offence
Refusing or failing when drunk to quit any premises or place licensed under the Refreshment Houses Act 1860 when requested.	Refreshment Houses Act 1860 (23 & 24 Vict c 27), s 41.
Being intoxicated while driving a hackney carriage.	Town Police Clauses Act 1847 (10 & 11 Vict c 89), s 61.
Being drunk during employment as a driver of a hackney carriage, or as a driver or conductor of a stage carriage in the Metropolitan Police District.	London Hackney Carriages Act 1843 (6 & 7 Vict c 86), s 28.
Being drunk and persisting, after being refused admission on that account, in attempting to enter a passenger steamer.	Merchant Shipping Act 1894 (57 & 58 Vict c 60), s 287.
Being drunk on board a passenger steamer, and refusing to leave such steamer when requested.	

1. With the exception of s 30 (Short title) and the First Schedule, the whole of this Act has been repealed. Section 30, as amended by the Statute Law (Repeals) Act 1976, Sch 2, provides that the First Schedule shall have effect for the purposes of the Licensing Act 1902, s 6, post.

Licensing Act 1902

(2 Edw 7 c 28)

PART I

Amendment of Law as to Drunkenness

8–27674 **1. Apprehension of person found drunk and incapable in public place**[1]. If a person is found drunk in any highway or other public place[2], whether a building or not, or on any licensed premises, and appears to be incapable of taking care of himself, he may be apprehended and dealt with according to law.
[Licensing Act 1902, s 1.]

1. This section is complementary to s 12 of the Licensing Act 1872, ante. Where a constable has power to arrest a person under this section, the constable may take him to a treatment centre for alcoholics; see the Criminal Justice Act 1972, s 34, in PART III: SENTENCING, ante.
2. For meaning of "public place", see s 8, post.

8–27675 **2. Penalty for being drunk while in charge of child.** (1) If any person is found drunk in any highway or other public place[1], whether a building or not, or on any licensed premises, while having the charge of a child apparently under the age of seven years, he may be apprehended, and shall, if the child is under that age, be liable, on summary conviction, to a fine not exceeding **level 2** on the standard scale, or to imprisonment, for any period not exceeding **one month***.

(2) If the child appears to the court to be under the age of seven, the child shall, for the purposes of this section, be deemed to be under that age unless the contrary is proved.

(3) The offence under this section shall be included in the list of offences mentioned in the First Schedule to the Inebriates Act, 1898[2].
[Licensing Act 1902, s 2, as amended by the Penalties for Drunkenness Act 1962, s 1, the Statute Law (Repeals) Act 1976, Sch 1, the Criminal Law Act 1977, Sch 6 and the Criminal Justice Act 1982, s 46.]

***Words repealed and substituted with "51 weeks" by the Criminal Justice Act 2003, Sch 26, from a date to be appointed.**
1. For meaning of "public place", see s 8, post.
2. See this title, ante.

8–27676 **6. Prohibition of sale of liquor to persons declared to be habitual drunkards.** (1) Where a person is convicted of an offence mentioned in the First Schedule to the Inebriates Act 1898[1] and such person has during the period of twelve months immediately preceding the date of the offence, been convicted on three occasions of an offence mentioned in the said Schedule, the court may order that notice of the conviction, with such particulars as may be prescribed[2] by the Secretary of State, be sent to the police authority for the police area in which the court is situate.

(2) Subsections (2A) to (2C) apply where a court, in pursuance of this Act, orders notice of a conviction to be sent to a police authority.

(2A) The court shall inform[3] the convicted person that the notice is to be sent to a police authority.

(2B) The convicted person commits an offence if, within the three year period, he buys[4] or obtains, or attempts to buy or obtain, alcohol on relevant premises.

(2C) A person to whom subsection (2D) applies commits an offence if, within the three year period, he knowingly[5]—

(*a*) sells, supplies or distributes alcohol on relevant premises, or
(*b*) allows the sale, supply or distribution of alcohol on relevant premises,

to, or for consumption by, the convicted person.

(2D) This subsection applies—

(*a*) to any person who works at the premises in a capacity, whether paid or unpaid, which gives him authority to sell, supply or distribute the alcohol concerned,
(*b*) in the case of licensed premises, to—

(i) the holder of a premises licence which authorises the sale or supply of alcohol, and
(ii) the designated premises supervisor (if any) under such a licence,

(*c*) in the case of premises in respect of which a club premises certificate authorising the sale or supply of alcohol has effect, to any member or officer of the club which holds the certificate who at the time the sale, supply or distribution takes place is present on the premises in a capacity which enables him to prevent it, and
(*d*) in the case of premises which may be used for a permitted temporary activity by virtue of Part 5 of the Licensing Act 2003, the premises user in respect of a temporary event notice authorising the sale or supply of alcohol.

(2E) A person guilty of an offence under this section is liable on summary conviction—

(*a*) in the case of an offence under subsection (2B), to a fine not exceeding level 1 on the standard scale, and
(*b*) in the case of an offence under subsection (2C), to a fine not exceeding level 2 on the standard scale.

(3) Regulations shall be made by the police authority for the purpose of securing the giving of information to persons to whom subsection (4) applies, of orders made under this section, and for assisting in the identification of the convicted persons.

(4) This subsection applies to—

(*a*) the holder of a premises licence which authorises the sale or supply of alcohol,
(*b*) the designated premises supervisor (if any) under such a licence,
(*c*) the holder of a club premises certificate authorising the sale or supply of alcohol, and
(*d*) the premises user in relation to a temporary event notice authorising the sale or supply or alcohol.

(5) In this section—

"alcohol", "club premises certificate", "designated premises supervisor", "licensed premises", "permitted temporary activity", "premises licence", "premises user" and "temporary event notice" have the same meaning as in the Licensing Act 2003,

"relevant premises" means premises which are relevant premises within the meaning of section 159 of that Act and on which alcohol may be lawfully sold or supplied, and

"the three year period", in relation to the convicted person, means the period of three years beginning with the day of the conviction."

[Licensing Act 1902, s 6, as amended by the Statute Law (Repeals) Act 1976, Sch 2, the Criminal Law Act 1977, s 31, the Criminal Justice Act 1982, ss 35 and 46, the Police and Magistrates' Courts Act 1994, Sch 9 and the Licensing Act 2003, Sch 6.]

---

1. See this title, ante.
2. These have been prescribed by SR & O 1902/831 amended by SI 2001/1098 and are as follows: date of conviction, date of order directing notice to police authority, name of person convicted, age, address of person convicted, place of business or where employed, offence of which convicted, sentence, licensed premises or clubs usually frequented (if known).
3. If the defendant is not present then presumably he should be sent a notice by registered post. The order of the court should be recorded in the court register.
4. Under this section prior to its amendment by the Licensing Act 2003, it has was held that a habitual drunkard placed on the "black list" who sends another person to purchase intoxicating liquor for him is liable to be convicted under this section (*Darbyshire v Downes* (1905) 40 L Jo 299).
5. These provisions are now contained in Pt II of the Licensing Act 1964, post.
6. The licence-holder will be responsible for the acts of his servants within the scope of their authority.
7. These words are very comprehensive, and will include anyone from the manager down to the club waiter.
8. The onus of proving "knowledge" will be on the prosecution.

8–27677 **8. Interpretation of "public place".** For the purposes of section twelve of the Licensing Act, 1872, and of sections one and two of this Act, the expression "public place" shall include any place to which the public have access, whether on payment or otherwise[1].

[Licensing Act 1902, s 8.]

---

1. A man in a tramcar was held to be in the street (*Martin v McIntyre* 1910 47 SLR 645, 74 JP Jo 482). A hackney carriage in the street was held a "public place" under a repealed statute (*R v Weller* (1894) 58 JP 286).

8–27677A 8A Interpretation of "licensed premises. For those purposes, "licensed premises" includes—

(*a*) any licensed premises within the meaning of section 193 of the Licensing Act 2003, and
(*b*) any premises which may be used for a permitted temporary activity by virtue of Part 5 of that Act.

[Licensing Act 1902, s 8A as inserted by the Licensing Act 2003, Sch 6.]

8–27678 34. Short title, construction and extent. (1) This Act may be cited as the Licensing Act, 1902, and may be cited, and shall be construed, as one with the Licensing Acts, 1828 to 1886.

(2) This Act shall not extend to Scotland or Ireland.

(3) *Repealed.*

[Licensing Act 1902, s 34, as amended by the Statute Law Revision Act, 1927.]

Public Meeting Act 1908

(8 Edw 7 c 66)

8–27680 1. Breaking up public meeting. (1) Any person who at a lawful[1] public meeting acts in a disorderly manner for the purpose of preventing the transaction of the business for which the meeting was called together shall be guilty of an offence[2].

(2) Any person who incites others to commit an offence under this section shall be guilty of a like offence[2].

(3) If any constable reasonably suspects any person of committing an offence under the foregoing provisions of this section, he may, if requested so to do by the chairman of the meeting, require that person to declare to him immediately his name and address, and if that person refuses or fails so to declare his name and address or gives a false name and address he shall be guilty of an offence[3] under this subsection and liable on summary conviction thereof to a fine not exceeding **level 1** on the standard scale.

(4) This section does not apply as respects meetings to which section 97 of the Representation of the People Act 1983 applies.

[Public Meeting Act 1908 as amended by the Public Order Act 1936, s 6, the Representation of the People Act 1949, the Public Order Act 1963, s 1(2), the Criminal Law Act 1977, s 31, the Criminal Justice Act 1982, s 46, the Representation of the People Act 1983, Sch 8 and the Police and Criminal Evidence Act 1984, Sch 7.]

---

1. If they reasonably apprehend a breach of the peace, the police have a right to enter private premises at which the public have been invited to attend (*Thomas v Sawkins* [1935] 2 KB 249, [1935] All ER Rep 655, 99 JP 295). As to removal of a disorderly person (cf *Marshall v Tinnelly* (1937) 81 Sol Jo 902). A public meeting on the highway is not necessarily unlawful (*Burden v Rigler* [1911] 1 KB 337, 75 JP 36). The test is whether there will be a nuisance or danger of breach of the peace (*R v Prebble* (1858) 1 F & F 325). In *Beatty v Gillbanks* (1882) 9 QBD 308, 46 JP 789), where the defendant was charged with an unlawful assembly, FIELD, J, said there was no authority for the proposition that a man may be punished for acting lawfully if he knows that his so doing may induce another man to act unlawfully. In *Duncan v Jones* [1936] 1 KB 218, 99 JP 399, it was held that it is the duty of the police to prevent any action likely to result in a breach of the peace by any one, and that refusing to desist was obstructing the police in the execution of their duty. Cf *Great Central Rly Co v Bates* [1921] 3 KB 578, and *Davis v Lisle* [1936] 2 KB 434, [1936] 2 All ER 213, 100 JP 280.
2. Triable summarily and punishable by **six months** imprisonment or a fine not exceeding **level 5** on the standard scale (Criminal Law Act 1977, Sch 1).
3. See the Police and Criminal Evidence Act 1984, s 25, ante in PART I: MAGISTRATES' COURTS, PROCEDURE, for power of arrest.

Public Order Act 1936

(1 Edw 8 & 1 Geo 6 c 6)

8–27690 1. Prohibition of uniforms in connection with political objects. (1) Subject as hereinafter provided, any person who in any public place, or at any public meeting[1] wears uniform[2] signifying his association with any political organisation or with the promotion of any political object shall be guilty of an offence[3]:

Provided that if the chief officer of police[4] is satisfied that the wearing of any such uniform as aforesaid on any ceremonial, anniversary or other special occasion will not be likely to involve risk of public disorder, he may, with the consent of a Secretary of State by order[5], permit the wearing of such uniform on that occasion either absolutely or subject to such conditions as may be specified in the order.

(2) Where any person is charged before any court with an offence under this section, no further proceedings in respect thereof shall be taken against him without the consent of the Attorney-General except such as are authorised by section 6 of the Prosecution of Offences Act 1979[6], so, however, that if that person is remanded in custody he shall, after the expiration of a period of eight days from the date on which he was so remanded, be entitled to be released on bail without sureties unless within that period the Attorney-General has consented to such further proceedings as aforesaid.

[Public Order Act 1936, s 1, as amended by the Bail Act 1976, Sch 2, and the Prosecution of Offences Act 1979, Sch 1.]

---

1. "Meeting" means a meeting held for the purpose of the discussion of matters of public interest or for the purpose of the expression of views on such matters; "Public meeting" includes any meeting in a public place and any meeting which the public or any section thereof are permitted to attend, whether on payment or otherwise; "Public place" includes any highway and any other premises or place to which at the material time the public have or are permitted to have access, whether on payment or otherwise (s 9(1), as amended by the Criminal Justice Act 1972, s 33). Where an establishment such as a football ground is involved, it should be treated as a public place in its entirety. Accordingly a speedway track surrounding a football pitch was held to be part of premises constituting a public place (*Cawley v Frost* [1978] 3 All ER 743, 141 JP 30). The front garden of a house in which an altercation occurred was held not to be a public place (*R v Roberts* (1978) 67 Cr App Rep 228). A public house with open doors inviting the public to enter is a public place (*Lawrenson v Oxford* [1982] Crim LR 185).

2. See *O'Moran v DPP* [1975] QB 864, [1975] 1 All ER 473, 139 JP 245, for circumstances where a black beret, dark glasses, black pullover and other dark clothing was held to be a uniform.

3. For penalty and power of arrest on reasonable suspicion, see s 7(2), (3), post.

4. "Chief officer of police" is now defined by the Police Act 1964, Sch 8 in this PART: title POLICE, ante. In the event of a vacancy in the office or in the event of the chief officer being unable to act owing to illness or absence, these powers may be exercised by the person duly appointed to act as his deputy authorised in accordance with directions given by a Secretary of State to exercise those powers on behalf of the chief officer of police (s 9(4)).

5. This order should be in writing. It may be revoked or varied by a subsequent order, made in like manner (s 9(3)).

6. Now replaced by the Prosecution of Offences Act 1985, s 25(2) in PART I: MAGISTRATES' COURTS, PROCEDURE, ante.

8–27691 2. Prohibition of quasi-military organisations, evidence and search warrant. (1) If the members or adherents of any association of persons, whether incorporated or not, are—

(*a*) organised or trained or equipped for the purpose of enabling them to be employed in usurping the functions of the police or of the armed forces of the Crown; or

(*b*) organised and trained or organised and equipped either for the purpose of enabling them to be employed for the use or display of physical force in promoting any political object, or in such manner as to arouse reasonable apprehension that they are organised and either trained or equipped for that purpose;

then any person who takes part in the control or management of the association, or in so organising or training as aforesaid any members or adherents thereof, shall be guilty of an offence[1] under this section:

Provided that in any proceedings against a person charged with the offence of taking part in the control or management of such an association as aforesaid it shall be a defence to that charge to prove that he neither consented to nor connived at the organisation, training, or equipment of members or adherents of his association in contravention of the provisions of this section.

(2) No prosecution shall be instituted under this section without the consent of the Attorney-General.

(3) *Disposal of property belonging to any association within subsection (2) by order of the High Court upon the application of the Attorney-General.*

(4) In any criminal or civil proceedings under this section proof of things done or of words written, spoken or published (whether or not in the presence of any party to the proceedings) by any person taking part in the control or management of an association or in organising, training or equipping members or adherents of an association shall be admissible as evidence of the purposes for which, or the manner in which members or adherents of the association (whether those persons or others) were organised, or trained or equipped.

(5) If a judge of the High Court is satisfied by information on oath that there is reasonable ground for suspecting that an offence under this section has been committed, and that evidence of the commission thereof is to be found at any premises or place specified in the information, he may, on an application made by an officer of police of a rank not lower than that of inspector, grant a search warrant authorising any such officer as aforesaid named in the warrant together with any other persons named in the warrant and any other officers of police to enter the premises or place at any time within three months from the date of the warrant, if necessary by force, and to search the premises or place and every person found therein, and to seize[2] anything found on the premises or place or on any such person which the officer has reasonable ground for suspecting to be evidence of the commission of such an offence as aforesaid:

Provided that no woman shall, in pursuance of a warrant issued under this subsection, be searched except by a woman.

(6) Nothing in this section shall be construed as prohibiting the employment of a reasonable number of persons as stewards to assist in the preservation of order at any public meeting held upon private premises[3], or the making of arrangements for that purpose or the instruction of the persons to be so employed in their lawful duties as such stewards, or their being furnished with badges or other distinguishing signs.

[Public Order Act 1936, s 2 as amended by the Serious Organised Crime and Police Act 2005, Sch 16.]

---

1. For penalty, see s 7(1), post.

2. As to the common law powers of seizure under a search warrant, see *Elias v Pasmore* [1934] 2 KB 164, 98 JP 92.

3. "Private premises" means premises to which the public have access (whether on payment or otherwise) only by permission of the owner, occupier or lessee of the premises (s 9(1)).

8–27692 7. Enforcement and power of arrest. (1) Any person who commits an offence under section 2 of this Act shall be liable on summary conviction to imprisonment for a term not exceeding **six months**[1], or to a fine not exceeding **the statutory maximum**, or to **both** such imprisonment and fine, or, on conviction on indictment, to imprisonment for a term not exceeding **two years** or to a **fine**, or to **both** such imprisonment and fine.

(2) Any person guilty of any offence under this Act other than an offence under s 2 shall be liable on summary conviction to imprisonment for a term not exceeding **three months** or to a fine not exceeding **level 4** on the standard scale or to **both** such imprisonment and fine.

(3) *Repealed.*

[Public Order Act 1936, s 7, as amended by the Public Order Act 1963, s 1(2), the Race Relations Act 1976, s 70, the Criminal Law Act 1977, s 28, Sch 6, the Criminal Justice Act 1982, s 46, the Public Order Act 1986 Sch 3 and the Serious Organised Crime and Police Act 2005, s 125.]

1. For procedure in respect of an offence triable either way, see the Magistrates' Courts Act 1980, ss 17A–21, in PART I: MAGISTRATES' COURTS, PROCEDURE, ante.
2. This power of arrest is preserved by the Police and Criminal Evidence Act 1984, s 26 and Sch 2.

Criminal Justice Act 1967[1]

(1967 c 80)

PART VI

MISCELLANEOUS AND GENERAL

Offences

8–27700 91. Drunkenness in a public place. (1) Any person who in any public place[2] is guilty, while drunk[3], of disorderly behaviour shall be liable on summary conviction to a fine not exceeding **level 3** on the standard scale.

(2) The foregoing subsection shall have effect instead of any corresponding provision contained in s 12 of the Licensing Act 1872, s 58 of the Metropolitan Police Act 1839, s 37 of the City of London Police Act 1839, and 29 of the Town Police Clauses Act 1847 (being enactments which authorise the imposition of a short term of imprisonment or of a fine not exceeding [**£10** or **£25**] or both for the corresponding offence) and instead of any corresponding provisions contained in any local Act.

(3) The Secretary of State may by order repeal any provision of a local Act which appears to him to be a provision corresponding to subsection (1) of this section or to impose a liability to imprisonment for an offence of drunkenness or of being incapable while drunk.

(4) In this section "public place" includes any highway and any other premises or place to which at the material time the public have or are permitted to have access, whether on payment or otherwise.

(5) *Repealed.*

[Criminal Justice Act 1967, s 91, as amended by the Criminal Law Act 1977, Sch 13, the Criminal Justice Act 1982, ss 38 and 46 and the Serious Organised Crime and Police Act 2005, Sch 7.]

1. For other provisions of this Act, see PART I: MAGISTRATES' COURTS, PROCEDURE, ante.
2. A landing in a block of flats, to which access was gained by way of key, security code, tenants' intercom or caretaker, was held not to be a public place because only those admitted by or with the implied consent of the occupiers had access (*Williams (Richard) v DPP* (1992) 156 JP 804, [1992] Crim LR 503).
3. "Drunk" refers to a person who has taken intoxicating liquor to excess so that he has lost the power of self-control; it does not apply to a person who is disorderly as a result of sniffing glue *(Neale v E (a minor)* (1983) 80 Cr App Rep 20, [1984] Crim LR 485).
4. Where a constable has power to arrest a person under this section, the constable may take him to a treatment centre for alcoholics; see the Criminal Justice Act 1972, s. 34, in PART III: SENTENCING, ante. This statutory power of arrest was not repealed by the Police and Criminal Evidence Act 1984 (*DPP v Kitching* (1989) 154 JP 293).

Race Relations Act 1976

(1976 c 74)

8–27710 This Act prohibits discrimination on racial grounds, and is enforceable by civil proceedings. The only parts of concern to magistrates' courts are several offences of knowingly or recklessly making a statement which in a material particular is false or misleading, or suppressing a document required to be produced, punishable on summary conviction by a fine not exceeding **level 5** on the standard scale (as amended by the Criminal Justice Act 1982, ss 38 and 46). Criminal proceedings relating to incitement to racial hatred are now brought under the Public Order Act 1986.

Sporting Events (Control of Alcohol etc) Act 1985

(1985 c 57)

8–27715 1. Offences in connection with alcohol on coaches and trains. (1) This section applies to a vehicle which—

(*a*) is a public service vehicle or railway passenger vehicle, and

(*b*) is being used for the principal purpose of carrying passengers for the whole or part of a journey to or from a designated sporting event.

(2) A person who knowingly causes or permits alcohol to be carried on a vehicle to which this section applies is guilty of an offence—

(*a*) if the vehicle is a public service vehicle and he is the operator of the vehicle or the servant or agent of the operator, or

(*b*) if the vehicle is a hired vehicle and he is the person to whom it is hired or the servant or agent of that person.

(3) A person who has alcohol in his possession while on a vehicle to which this section applies is guilty of an offence.

(4) A person who is drunk on a vehicle to which this section applies is guilty of an offence.

(5) In this section "public service vehicle" and "operator" have the same meaning as in the Public Passenger Vehicles Act 1981.

[Sporting Events (Control of Alcohol etc) Act 1985, s 1 as amended by the Licensing Act 2003, Sch 6.]

8–27715A 1A. Alcohol on certain other vehicles. (1) This section applies to a motor vehicle which—

(*a*) is not a public service vehicle but is adapted to carry more than 8 passengers, and

(*b*) is being used for the principal purpose of carrying two or more passengers for the whole or part of a journey to or from a designated sporting event.

(2) A person who knowingly causes or permits alcohol to be carried on a motor vehicle to which this section applies is guilty of an offence—

(*a*) if he is its driver, or

(*b*) if he is not its driver but is its keeper, the servant or agent of its keeper, a person to whom it is made available (by hire, loan or otherwise) by its keeper or the keeper's servant or agent, or the servant or agent of a person to whom it is so made available.

(3) A person who has alcohol in his possession while on a motor vehicle to which this section applies is guilty of an offence.

(4) A person who is drunk on a motor vehicle to which this section applies is guilty of an offence.

(5) In this section—

"keeper", in relation to a vehicle, means the person having the duty to take out a licence for it under the Vehicle Excise and Registration Act 1994,

"motor vehicle" means a mechanically propelled vehicle intended or adapted for use on roads, and

"public service vehicle" has the same meaning as in the Public Passenger Vehicles Act 1981.

[Sporting Events (Control of Alcohol etc) Act 1985, s 1A added by the Public Order Act 1986, Sch 1 and amended by the Vehicle Excise and Registration Act 1994, Sch 3 and the Licensing Act 2003, Sch 6.]

8–27715B 2. Offences in connection with alcohol, containers etc at sports grounds. (1) A person who has alcohol or an article to which this section applies in his possession—

(*a*) at any time during the period of a designated sporting event when he is in any area of a designated sports ground from which the event may be directly viewed, or

(*b*) while entering or trying to enter a designated sports ground at any time during the period of a designated sporting event at that ground,

is guilty of an offence.

(1A) *Repealed.*

(2) A person who is drunk in a designated sports ground at any time during the period of a designated sporting event at that ground or is drunk while entering or trying to enter such a ground at any time during the period of a designated sporting event at that ground is guilty of an offence.

(3) This section applies to any article capable of causing injury to a person struck by it, being—

(*a*) a bottle, can or other portable container (including such an article when crushed or broken) which—

(i) is for holding any drink, and

(ii) is of a kind which, when empty, is normally discarded or returned to, or left to be recovered by, the supplier, or

(*b*) part of an article falling within paragraph (*a*) above;

but does not apply to anything that is for holding any medicinal product (within the meaning of the Medicines Act 1968).
[Sporting Events (Control of Alcohol etc) Act 1985, s 2 as amended by the Public Order Act 1986, Sch 1 and the Licensing Act 2003, Sch 6.]

8–27715C 2A. Fireworks etc. (1) A person is guilty of an offence if he has an article or substance to which this section applies in his possession—

(*a*) at any time during the period of a designated sporting event when he is in any area of a designated sports ground from which the event may be directly viewed, or
(*b*) while entering or trying to enter a designated sports ground at any time during the period of a designated sporting event at the ground.

(2) It is a defence for the accused to prove that he had possession with lawful authority.

(3) This section applies to any article or substance whose main purpose is the emission of a flare for purposes of illuminating or signalling (as opposed to igniting or heating) or the emission of smoke or a visible gas; and in particular its applies to distress flares, fog signals, and pellets and capsules intended to be used as fumigators or for testing pipes, but not to matches, cigarette lighters or heaters.

(4) This section also applies to any article which is a firework.
[Sporting Events (Control of Alcohol etc) Act 1985, s 2A as inserted by the Public Order Act 1986, Sch 1.]

8–27715D 7. Powers of enforcement. (1) A constable may, at any time during the period of a designated sporting event at any designated sports ground, enter any part of the ground for the purpose of enforcing the provisions of this Act.

(2) A constable may search a person he has reasonable grounds to suspect is committing or has committed an offence under this Act, and may arrest such a person.

(3) A constable may stop a public service vehicle (within the meaning of section 1 of this Act) or a motor vehicle to which section 1A of this Act applies and may search such a vehicle or a railway passenger vehicle if he has reasonable grounds to suspect that an offence under that section is being or has been committed in respect of the vehicle.
[Sporting Events (Control of Alcohol etc) Act 1985, s 7 as amended by the Public Order Act 1986, Sch 1.]

8–27715E 8. Penalties for offences. A person guilty of an offence under this Act shall be liable on summary conviction—

(*a*) in the case of an offence under section 1(2) or 1A(2), to a fine not exceeding **level 4** on the standard scale,
(*b*) in the case of an offence under section 1(3), 1A(3), 2(1) or 2A(1), to a fine not exceeding **level 3** on the standard scale or to imprisonment for a term not exceeding **three months or both**, and
(*c*) in the case of an offence under section 1(4), 1A(4) or 2(2), to a fine not exceeding **level 2** on the standard scale.
(*d*) *repealed,*
(*e*) *repealed.*

[Sporting Events (Control of Alcohol etc) Act 1985, s 8 as amended by the Public Order Act 1986, Schs 1 and 3 and the Licensing Act 2003, Sch 6.]

8–27715F 9. Interpretation. (1) The following provisions shall have effect for the interpretation of this Act.

(2) "Designated sports ground" means any place—

(*a*) used (wholly or partly) for sporting events where accommodation is provided for spectators, and
(*b*) for the time being designated, or of a class designated, by order[1] made by the Secretary of State;

and an order under this subsection may include provision for determining for the purposes of this Act the outer limit of any designated sports ground.

(3) "Designated sporting event"—

(*a*) means a sporting event or proposed sporting event for the time being designated, or of a class designated, by order[1] made by the Secretary of State, and
(*b*) includes a designated sporting event within the meaning of Part V of the Criminal Justice (Scotland) Act 1980;

and an order under this subsection may apply to events or proposed events outside Great Britain as well as those in England and Wales.

(4) The period of a designated sporting event is the period beginning two hours before the start of the event or (if earlier) two hours before the time at which it is advertised to start and ending one hour after the end of the event, but—

(*a*) where an event advertised to start at a particular time on a particular day is postponed to a later day, the period includes the period in the day on which it is advertised to take place beginning two hours before and ending one hour after that time, and

(*b*) where an event advertised to start at a particular time on a particular day does not take place, the period is the period referred to in paragraph (*a*) above.

(5) *Revoked.*

(6) This Act does not apply to any sporting event or proposed sporting event—

(*a*) where all competitors are to take part otherwise than for reward, and

(*b*) to which all spectators are to be admitted free of charge.

(7) An expression used in this Act and in the Licensing Act 2003 has the same meaning in this Act as in that Act.

(8) Any power to make an order under this section shall be exercisable by statutory instrument subject to annulment in pursuance of a resolution of either House of Parliament.

[Sporting Events (Control of Alcohol etc) Act 1985, s 9 and the Licensing Act 2003, Sch 6.]

1. The Sports Grounds and Sporting Events (Designation) Order 2005, SI 2005/3204 has been made.

SCHEDULE

PROCEDURE

8–27715G *Repealed.*

Public Order Act 1986

(1986 c 64)

PART I[2]

NEW OFFENCES

8–27720 1. Riot. (1) Where 12 or more persons who are present together use or threaten unlawful violence[3] for a common purpose and the conduct of them (taken together) is such as would cause a person of reasonable firmness present at the scene to fear for his personal safety, each of the persons using unlawful violence for the common purpose is guilty of riot[4].

(2) It is immaterial whether or not the 12 or more use or threaten unlawful violence simultaneously.

(3) The common purpose may be inferred from conduct.

(4) No person of reasonable firmness need actually be, or be likely to be, present at the scene.

(5) Riot may be committed in private as well as in public places.

(6) A person guilty of riot is liable on conviction on indictment to imprisonment for a term not exceeding ten years or a fine or both.

[Public Order Act 1986, s 1.]

2. Part I contains ss 1–10.

3. As to the mental element, see s 6, post.

4. See s 7 post as to the consent necessary for instituting prosecutions.

An indictment charging an offence of riot should reflect the two parts of s 1(1) of the Act, first stating the statutory context and second the commission, within that context, of the offence as defined (*R v Jefferson* [1994] 1 All ER 270, 158 JP 76, 99 Cr App Rep 13).

By the Riot (Damages) Act 1886 (as amended by the Police Act 1964) claims for compensation for damage due to riot may be made against a police authority. The Riot (Damages) Regulations 1921, SR & O 1921/1536 as amended by SI 1986/76 have been made, prescribing the procedure to be followed for a claim. See *J W Dwyer Ltd v Metropolitan Police District Receiver* [1967] 2 QB 970, [1967] 2 All ER 1051, 131 JP 416, for an analysis of the basis for such a claim. By the Merchant Shipping Act 1894, s 515, similar claims may be made in respect of the riotous plundering of wrecked vessels.

The Queen's Regulations for the Army provide that should the assistance of the Armed Forces be called for to maintain peace and public order, the officer to whom the application is made is at once to inform the Ministry of Defence and his immediate superior authority. Assistance will normally be requested by the Chief Officer of Police and is to be confirmed in writing. Where a request is received from a source other than the Chief Officer of Police, the Service Commander on the spot is to refer the request to the Chief Officer of Police and report it to his superiors. It is possible, however, in very exceptional circumstances for grave and sudden emergencies to arise which in the opinion of the commander demand his immediate intervention to protect life and property. In such emergencies he is to act on his own responsibility and is to report as early as possible the matter and the action he has taken to the Service authorities mentioned above and to the Chief Officer of Police.

The "Chief Officer of Police" means in England and Wales, the Commissioner of Police for the City of London, the Commissioner of Police of the Metropolis or the Chief Constable of a county or a combined area (Police Act 1964, s 62).

See also Reserve Forces Act 1980, s 23, Army and air force reserves in aid of civil power.

8–27721 2. Violent disorder. (1) Where 3 or more persons[1] who are present together use or threaten unlawful[2] violence[3] and the conduct of them (taken together) is such as would cause a person of reasonable firmness present at the scene to fear for his personal safety, each of the persons using or threatening unlawful violence is guilty of violent disorder.

(2) It is immaterial whether or not the 3 or more use or threaten unlawful violence simultaneously.

(3) No person of reasonable firmness need actually be, or be likely to be, present at the scene.

(4) Violent disorder may be committed in private as well as in public places.

(5) A person guilty of violent disorder is liable on conviction on indictment to imprisonment for a term not exceeding 5 years or a fine or both, or on summary conviction to imprisonment for a term not exceeding **6 months** or a fine not exceeding the **statutory maximum** or **both**[4].

[Public Order Act 1986, s 2.]

---

1. Where the allegation involves only three named defendants, acquittal of one or two would seem to necessitate acquittal of the remainder; see *R v Mahroof* (1988) 88 Cr App Rep 317, and commentary thereon in [1989] Crim LR 72, CA. See also *R v Fleming and Robinson* (1989) 153 JP 517, [1989] Crim LR 658, CA and *R v McGuigan and Cameron* [1991] Crim LR 719.

2. Self defence, reasonable defence of another and actions which were no more than necessary to restore the peace are three examples of lawful action which could amount to defences (*R v Rothwell and Barton* [1993] Crim LR 626).

3. As to the mental element see s 6, post.

4. For procedure in respect of an offence triable either way, see the Magistrates' Courts Act 1980, ss 17A–21, ante in PART I: MAGISTRATES' COURTS PROCEDURE, ante.

8–27722 **3. Affray.** (1) A person is guilty of affray[1] if he uses or threatens[2] unlawful violence[3] towards another[4] and his conduct is such as would cause a person[5] of reasonable firmness present at the scene[6] to fear for his personal safety[7].

(2) Where 2 or more persons use or threaten the unlawful violence, it is the conduct of them taken together that must be considered for the purposes of subsection (1).

(3) For the purposes of this section a threat cannot be made by the use of words[8] alone.

(4) No person of reasonable firmness need actually be, or be likely to be, present at the scene.

(5) Affray may be committed in private as well as in public places.

(6) *Repealed.*

(7) A person guilty of affray is liable on conviction on indictment to imprisonment for a term not exceeding 3 years or a fine or both, or on summary conviction to imprisonment for a term not exceeding **6 months** or a fine not exceeding the **statutory maximum** or **both**[9].

[Public Order Act 1986, s 3 as amended by the Serious Organised Crime and Police Act 2005, Sch 7.]

---

1. Affray typically involves a continuous course of conduct, the criminal character of which depends on the general nature and effect of the conduct as a whole. In such cases the prosecution does not have to identify and prove particular incidents. However where the conduct is not continuous but falls into separate sequences, before there can be a conviction based on any one sequence the court must be satisfied on that sequence and it does not suffice that some members of the court are satisfied on one sequence and others on another sequence, *R v Smith* [1997] 1 Cr App Rep 14, CA. For the purposes of s 3(1), the carrying of dangerous weapons by a group of persons can in some circumstances constitute a threat of violence without those weapons being waved or brandished, but the mere possession of a weapon, without threatening circumstances, is insufficient to constitute such a threat. Nor can carrying a concealed weapon itself be such a threat. However, the visible carrying in public of primed petrol bombs by a large number of what is obvious a gang out for no good is clearly capable of constituting a threat of unlawful violence: *I v DPP, M v DPP, H v DPP* [2001] UKHL 10, [2002] AC 285, [2001] 2 All ER 583, [2001] 2 WLR 765.

2. What amounts to a threat is essentially a question of fact in each case. Where a threat of violence takes the form of a gathering of armed persons in a public place, it is not necessary to prove that a person or persons present actually felt threatened, but it must be shown that there was someone at or in the vicinity towards whom the threat of violence could be said to have been directed (*I v DPP* [2001] UKHL 10, [2002] AC 285, [2001] 2 All ER 583, [2001] 2 WLR 765 – the visible carrying in public of primed petrol bombs by a large number of youths held to be capable of constituting a threat of unlawful violence).

3. As to the mental element, see s 6, post.

4. The threat of unlawful violence must be directed towards a person or persons present at the scene, and it does not necessarily follow that because a person is present at a location where a gang are carrying petrol bombs there is a threat of violence towards that person; whether the latter is the case will depend on the facts of the actual case: *I v DPP, M v DPP, H v DPP* (supra).

5. The court must consider the reaction of the hypothetical reasonable bystander, not that of the victim of any violent conduct (*R v Sanchez* (1996) 160 JP 321, [1996] Crim LR 572, CA).

6. The concept of presence at the scene suggests that the notional bystander would be in the presence of both the offender and the victim: *I v DPP, M v DPP, H v DPP* (supra).

7. Where an information charging affray includes specific allegations such as causing damage or assault, it is not necessary for the prosecution to prove these allegations since they are not essential elements of the offence (*Cobb v DPP* (1992) 156 JP 746).

8. As to the application of sub-s (3) see *R v Robinson* [1993] Crim LR 581.

9. For procedure in respect of an offence triable either way, see the Magistrates' Courts Act 1980, ss 17A–21 in PART I: MAGISTRATES' COURTS PROCEDURE, ante.

8–27723 **4. Fear or provocation of violence.** (1) A person is guilty of an offence[1] if he—

(*a*) uses towards another person[2] threatening, abusive or insulting words or behaviour[3], or

(*b*) distributes or displays to another person any writing, sign or other visible representation[3] which is threatening, abusive or insulting,

with intent to cause that person to believe[4] that immediate[5] unlawful violence will be used against him or another by any person, or to provoke the immediate use of unlawful violence by that person or another, or whereby that person is likely to believe that such violence[6] will be used or it is likely that such violence will be provoked[7].

(2) An offence under this section may be committed in a public or a private place, except that no offence is committed where the words or behaviour are used, or the writing, sign or other visible

representation is distributed or displayed, by a person inside a dwelling[8] and the other person is also inside that or another dwelling.

(3) *Repealed.*

(4) A person guilty of an offence under this section is liable on summary conviction to imprisonment for a term not exceeding **6 months** or a fine not exceeding **level 5** on the standard scale or **both**.

[Public Order Act 1986, s 4 as amended by the Serious Organised Crime and Police Act 2005, Sch 7.]

---

1. Although s 4(1) creates only one offence, that offence may be committed in four different ways. Common to all four is the requirement that the accused must intend or be aware that his words or behaviour are or may be threatening, abusive or insulting, and must be directed to another person; see *Winn v DPP* (1992) 156 JP 881.

2. The words "uses towards another person" mean that threatening words must be addressed directly to another person who is present and either in earshot or aimed at as being putatively in earshot (*Atkin v DPP* (1989) 153 JP 383, [1989] Crim LR 581, DC). It is inappropriate to use the words "another person" in an information charging an offence under section 4 because the person in whom the belief that unlawful violence would be used has to be the same person as the person threatened, abused or insulted; see *Loade v DPP* (1990) 90 Cr App Rep 162.

3. As to the mental element, see s 6, post.

4. To establish the offence it does not have to be shown what the other person believed; it has to be shown that the defendant had the intention to cause that person to believe. This can be proved by any admissible evidence and it is not necessary for the person to whom the threats or insulting behaviour were directed to give evidence (*Swanston v DPP* (1996) 161 JP 203).

5. Provided the victim believes and is likely to believe that something will happen at any time, there is a case to answer (*DPP v Ramos* [2000] Crim LR 768, DC (letters sent threatening a bombing hate campaign and that the recipient, if seen, would be killed).

6. "Such violence" must be "immediate", and the phrase refers back to the words "immediate unlawful violence" (*R v Horseferry Road Metropolitan Stipendiary Magistrate, ex p Siadatan* [1991] 1 QB 260, [1991] 1 All ER 324).

7. For the position under the European Convention on Human Rights see para **8–27724**, footnote (1), post.

8. A communal landing in a block of flats has been held not to be a dwelling for this purpose, since the common parts were not part of the structure occupied as a person's home (*Rukwira v DPP* (1993) 158 JP 65, [1993] Crim LR 882.

8–27723A 4A. Intentional harassment, alarm or distress. (1) A person is guilty of an offence if, with intent to cause a person harassment, alarm or distress, he—

(*a*) uses threatening, abusive or insulting words or behaviour, or disorderly behaviour, or

(*b*) displays any writing, sign or other visible representation which is threatening, abusive or insulting,

thereby causing that or another person harassment, alarm or distress[1].

(2) An offence under this section may be committed in a public or a private place, except that no offence is committed where the words or behaviour are used, or the writing, sign or other visible representation is displayed, by a person inside a dwelling and the person who is harassed, alarmed or distressed is also inside that or another dwelling.

(3) It is a defence for the accused to prove—

(*a*) that he was inside a dwelling and had no reason to believe that the words or behaviour used, or the writing, sign or other visible representation displayed, would be heard or seen by a person outside that or any other dwelling, or

(*b*) that his conduct was reasonable.

(4) *Repealed.*

(5) A person guilty of an offence under this section is liable on summary conviction to imprisonment for a term not exceeding **6 months** or a fine not exceeding **level 5** on the standard scale or **both**.

[Public Order Act 1986, s 4A, as inserted by the Criminal Justice and Public Order Act 1994, s 154 and amended by the Serious Organised Crime and Police Act 2005, Sch 7.]

---

1. For the position under the European Convention on Human Rights see para **8–27724**, footnote 1, post.

8–27724 5. Harassment, alarm or distress. (1) A person is guilty of an offence if he—

(*a*) uses threatening, abusive or insulting[1] words or behaviour[2], or disorderly behaviour, or

(*b*) displays any writing, sign or other visible representation which is threatening, abusive or insulting[3],

within the hearing or sight[4] of a person likely to be caused harassment[5], alarm[6] or distress[7] thereby[8].

(2) An offence under this section may be committed in a public or a private place, except that no offence is committed where the words or behaviour are used, or the writing, sign or other visible representation is displayed, by a person inside a dwelling and the other person is also inside that or another dwelling.

(3) It is a defence for the accused to prove[9]—

(*a*) that he had no reason to believe that there was any person within hearing or sight who was likely to be caused harassment, alarm or distress, or (*b*) that he was inside a dwelling and had no reason to believe that the words or behaviour used, or the writing, sign or other visible representation displayed, would be heard or seen by a person outside that or any other dwelling, or

(*c*) that his conduct was reasonable[10].

(4) *Repealed.*

(5) *Repealed.*

(6) A person guilty of an offence under this section is liable on summary conviction to a fine not exceeding **level 3** on the standard scale.

[Public Order Act 1986, s 5 as amended by the Public Order (Amendment) Act 1996, s 1 and the Serious Organised Crime and Police Act 2005, Sch 7.]

---

1. It was appropriate to have in mind art 10 of the ECHR when considering whether a sign bearing the words "stop immorality", "stop homosexuality" and "stop lesbianism", that caused a group of 30–40 people to gather round the bearer (an evangelical church minister) was insulting (cf the view expressed in para 55 of the judgement of Auld LJ in *Norwood v DPP* in the note to s 5(3), post); such words were, however, capable of being found to be insulting as they were directed towards the homosexual and lesbian community, implying that they were immoral (though the court did not find it easy to determine that the justices' finding was not "Wednesbury" unreasonable) (*Hammond v DPP* [2004] EWHC Admin 69, (2004) 168 JP 601, [2004] Crim LR 851).

In *Dehal v CPS* [2005] EWHC Admin 2154, (2005) 169 JP 581, the defendant faced a charged under s 4A, above, on facts that he had entered a Sikh temple and affixed a notice to a notice board that stated, inter alia, that the president of the temple was a hypocrite. It was held that to justify such an interference with art 10 the prosecution had to demonstrate that the criminal proceedings were being brought in pursuance of a legitimate aim and were the minimum necessary to achieve that aim. Since no such reasoning had been given in the case stated it had not been open to the court to find that the prosecution had been a proportionate response to the defendant's conduct.

2. As to the mental element, see s 6, post. Section 5 is not limited to rowdy or obscene behaviour in a public context, but will cover the behaviour of a person who peeps between the curtain of a changing room and watches his customers undressing, or who installs a video camera to film customers in a state of undress (*Vigon v DPP* (1997) 162 JP 115, [1998] Crim LR 289).

3. Only those elements of the offence in either paragraph (*a*) or (*b*) of s 5(1) are reflected in s 6(4), post; see *DPP v Clarke* (1991) 156 JP 267. The structure of the s 5(1)(*b*) limb of the offence was considered by the Divisional Court in *Norwood v DPP* [2002] EWHC 1564 (Admin), [2002] Crim LR 888, 167 JPN 522. It requires proof by the prosecution of the following four elements: (1) a fact – display by a defendant of a visible representation; (2) a value judgment that the representation is threatening, abusive or insulting; (3) a fact – that the defendant either intended, or was aware that it might be, threatening, abusive or insulting; and (4) a mixed fact and value judgment – that the display was within sight of a person likely to be caused, harassment, alarm or distress by it.

4. The prosecution must show that some person actually saw the abusive or insulting words or behaviour (*Holloway v DPP* [2004] EWHC Admin 2621, (2005) 169 JP 14), though it is not necessary for the prosecution to call that person, provided the court can draw the inference to the criminal standard that what the defendant was doing was visible or audible to a person who was in the vicinity at the relevant time (per Collins LJ at para 32).

It was held that an offence under s 5(1)(*a*) was not committed merely by causing some "writing, sign or other visible representation" to be delivered through the letter box of an intended recipient, because the sender was not a person who "uses . . . words or behaviour . . . within the hearing or sight of a person" who received it (*Chappell v DPP* (1988) 89 Cr App Rep 82).

5. No element of apprehension about one's personal safety is necessary for there to be harassment (*Chambers and Edwards v DPP* [1995] Crim LR 896).

6. It is not necessary that the person alarmed should be concerned at physical danger to himself; it may be alarm about the safety of an unconnected third party (*Lodge v DPP* (1988) Times, 26 October).

7. A police officer might be the person caused harassment, alarm or distress, although on the facts the magistrates might equally well decide that the words and behaviour did not have this effect (*DPP v Orum* [1988] 3 All ER 449, [1989] 1 WLR 88, 153, JP 85).

8. Under the Human Rights Act 1998, this provision, so far as it is possible to do so, must be read and given effect in a way which is compatible with the Convention rights. Article 10(1) of the European Convention on Human Rights applies 'not only to ideas that are favourably received, or regarded as inoffensive or as a matter of indifference, but also to those that offend, shock or disturb the State or any sector of the population': *Handyside v United Kingdom* (1976) 1 EHRR 737.

9. The burden of proof rests on the defence on the balance of probabilities (*DPP v Clarke* (1991) 156 JP 267). This would seem to remain the case after commencement of the Human Rights Act 1998 (*Norwood v DPP*, supra, where the court indicated a predilection for a legal burden, but did not come to a firm conclusion on the point).

In *Norwood* Auld LJ stated, in relation to the defence under s 5(3):

> "[20] However, in this statutory context, whatever the nature of the burden cast on the defence, it is, in any event, hard to find much of a role for any of the s 5(3) defences, directed, as they are, to an objective assessment by the court of the reasonableness of the accused's conduct. That is because the essentials of the basic s 5 offence require the court to be satisfied as to the accused's subjective state of mind, namely that he intended that the representation should be, or was aware that it might be, threatening, abusive or insulting. See eg *DPP v Clarke* (1991) 94 Cr App Rep 359, per Nolan LJ. If the s 5(3) burden on the defence is to be "read down" to an evidential burden so as to make it Convention compliant, with the result of casting upon the prosecution the burden of disproving it, it would be harder to find any sensible role for s 5(3) . . .
>
> [*Norwood* concerned a racially aggravated s 5 offence]
>
> [21] Add now the fifth element that the prosecution must prove on this religiously aggravated charge, that the appellant, in displaying the poster within the hearing or sight of a person to whom it was likely to cause harassment, harm or distress, was motivated by hostility towards a religious group, and it is even harder to see much of a role for s 5(3) once the prosecution has proved its case under s 5(1) and 6 (4)."

As for the impact of art 10 (freedom of expression) his lordship stated:

> "[35] . . . often, and certainly in the circumstances of this case, the question whether a defendant's conduct is objectively reasonable necessarily includes consideration of his right to freedom of expression under art 10 . . . [37] As this Court said in *Percy*, a prosecution under s 5 does not per se engage art 10. It depends on the facts and the drawing of an appropriate balance of competing interests under art 10.1 and 10.2, bearing always in mind that the restrictions in art 10.2 should be narrowly construed and convincingly established. As I have indicated earlier in this judgment, in the absence of a challenge to the compatibility of s 5 with the Convention, the mechanics of the Article's operation on a

prosecution under it seem to me to be confined to the objective defence of reasonableness in s 5(3). It cannot bear in any reasoned way on whether the prosecution have proved the two limbs under s 5(1), first, intentional or foreseen insulting conduct and, second, an objective likelihood of harassment, alarm or distress. Putting aside for the moment, questions as to the nature of the reverse burden of proof provided by s 5(3), the way in which art 10 intrudes on the operation of a s 5 prosecution is whether the defendant's conduct was objectively reasonable, having regard to all the circumstances, including importantly those for which the art 10.2 itself provides. These will include consideration whether to mark as criminal the accused's conduct in displaying the poster as a necessary restriction of his freedom of expression for the prevention of disorder or crime and/or for the protection of the rights of others. Hallett J, who gave the leading judgment in *Percy*, identified, at para 11 of her judgment, two of a number of relevant factors in that case, which seem to me to be of general application in this context: namely: whether the accused's conduct went beyond legitimate protest and whether the behaviour had not formed part of an open expression of opinion on a matter of public interest, but had become disproportionate and unreasonable.'

See further Note 9, infra.

10. The defence of reasonable conduct is to be viewed objectively (*DPP v Clarke* (1991) 156 JP 267). In a case involving the defacement of the American flag (the defendant's own property) near the gate of an RAF base, in the course of a protest against the use of weapons of mass destruction and American military policy including the national missile defence system, it was held that the court had to presume that the defendant's conduct was protected by art 10 unless and until is was established that a restriction on her freedom was strictly necessary. While the district judge had been entitled to find that there was a pressing social need in a multicultural society to prevent the denigration of objects veneration and symbolic importance for one social group, the next stage was to assess whether or not interference, by means of prosecution, with the defendant's right to free expression by using her own property to convey a lawful message, was a proportionate response to that aim, and the fact that the defendant could have demonstrated in other ways was only one factor to be taken into account when determining the overall reasonableness of the defendant's behaviour and the state's response to it: *Percy v DPP* [2001] EWHC Admin 1125, (2001) 166 JP 93, [2002] Crim LR 835.

11. The warning does not have to be in any particular words, but the instruction to stop offensive conduct should, of necessity, convey that should the conduct be repeated or continued the person concerned would be breaking the law; see *Groom v DPP* [1991] Crim LR 713.

8–27725 6. Mental element: miscellaneous[1].. (1) A person is guilty of riot only if he intends to use violence or is aware that his conduct may be violent.

(2) A person is guilty of violent disorder or affray only if he intends to use or threaten violence or is aware that his conduct may be violent or threaten violence.

(3) A person is guilty of an offence under section 4 only if he intends his words or behaviour, or the writing, sign or other visible representation, to be threatening, abusive or insulting, or is aware that it may be threatening, abusive or insulting.

(4) A person is guilty of an offence under section 5 only if he intends his words or behaviour, or the writing, sign or other visible representation, to be threatening, abusive or insulting, or is aware that it may be threatening, abusive or insulting or (as the case may be) he intends his behaviour to be or is aware that it may be disorderly[2].

(5) For the purposes of this section a person whose awareness is impaired by intoxication shall be taken to be aware of that of which he would be aware if not intoxicated, unless he shows either that his intoxication was not self-induced or that it was caused solely by the taking or administration of a substance in the course of medical treatment.

(6) In subsection (5) "intoxication" means any intoxication, whether caused by drink, drugs or other means, or by a combination of means.

(7) Subsections (1) and (2) do not affect the determination for the purposes of riot or violent disorder of the number of persons who use or threaten violence.

[Public Order Act 1986, s 6.]

1. The offences created by the Public Order Act 1986 may be committed by aiders and abettors as well as by principals. Section 6 of the Act is concerned only with identifying the requisite *mens rea* for each of the offences under ss 1–5, and it does not exclude in relation to any of those offences the liability of an aider and abettor who is aware of and party to the requisite intent of the principal offender (*R v Jefferson* [1994] 1 All ER 270, 158 JP 76, 99 Cr App Rep 13).

2. The burden of proof in relation to the mental element in s 6(4) rests on the prosecution the standard of proof being beyond reasonable doubt (*DPP v Clarke* (1991) 156 JP 267). The words "is aware that it may be threatening, abusive or insulting" impute a subjective awareness on the part of the defendant (*DPP v Clarke*, supra). See also the note to s 5(3)(*c*), supra.

8–27726 7. Procedure: miscellaneous. (1) No prosecution for an offence of riot or incitement to riot may be instituted except by or with the consent of the Director of Public Prosecutions.

(2) For the purposes of the rules against charging more than one offence in the same count or information, each of sections 1 to 5 creates one offence.

(3) If on the trial on indictment of a person charged with violent disorder or affray the jury find him not guilty of the offence charged, they may (without prejudice to section 6(3) of the Criminal Law Act 1967) find him guilty of an offence under section 4.

(4) The Crown Court has the same powers and duties in relation to a person who is by virtue of subsection (3) convicted before it of an offence under section 4 as a magistrates' court would have on convicting him of the offence.

[Public Order Act 1986, s 7.]

8–27727 8. Interpretation. In this Part—

"dwelling" means any structure or part of a structure occupied as a person's home or as other living accommodation (whether the occupation is separate or shared with others) but does not include any part not so occupied, and for this purpose "structure" includes a tent, caravan, vehicle, vessel or other temporary or movable structure;

"violence" means any violent conduct, so that—

(*a*) except in the context of affray, it includes violent conduct towards property as well as violent conduct towards persons, and

(*b*) it is not restricted to conduct causing or intended to cause injury or damage but includes any other violent conduct (for example, throwing at or towards a person a missile of a kind capable of causing injury which does not hit or falls short).

[Public Order Act 1986, s 8.]

8–27728 **9. Offences abolished.** (1) The common law offences of riot, rout, unlawful assembly and affray are abolished.

(2) The offences under the following enactments are abolished—

(*a*) section 1 of the Tumultuous Petitioning Act 1661 (presentation of petition to monarch or Parliament accompanied by excessive number of persons),

(*b*) section 1 of the Shipping Offences Act 1793 (interference with operation of vessel by persons riotously assembled),

(*c*) section 23 of the Seditious Meetings Act 1817 (prohibition of certain meetings within one mile of Westminster Hall when Parliament sitting), and

(*d*) section 5 of the Public Order Act 1936 (conduct conducive to breach of the peace).

[Public Order Act 1986, s 9.]

8–27729 **10. Construction of other instruments.** (1) In the Riot (Damages) Act 1886 (compensation for riot damage) "riotous" and "riotously" shall be construed in accordance with section 1 above.

(2) In Schedule 1 to the Marine Insurance Act 1906 (form and rules for the construction of certain insurance policies) "rioters" in rule 8 and "riot" in rule 10 shall, in the application of the rules to any policy taking effect on or after the coming into force of this section, be construed in accordance with section 1 above unless a different intention appears.

(3) "Riot" and cognate expressions in any enactment in force before the coming into force of this section (other than the enactments mentioned in subsections (1) and (2) above) shall be construed in accordance with section 1 above if they would have been construed in accordance with the common law offence of riot apart from this Part.

(4) Subject to subsections (1) to (3) above and unless a different intention appears, nothing in this Part affects the meaning of "riot" or any cognate expression in any enactment in force, or other instrument taking effect, before the coming into force of this section.

[Public Order Act 1986, s 10 as amended by the Merchant Shipping Act 1995, Sch 12.]

PART II[1]

PROCESSIONS AND ASSEMBLIES

8–27730 **11. Advance notice of public processions[2].** (1) Written notice shall be given in accordance with this section of any proposal to hold a public procession intended—

(*a*) to demonstrate support for or opposition to the views or actions of any person or body of persons,

(*b*) to publicise a cause or campaign, or

(*c*) to mark or commemorate an event,

unless it is not reasonably practicable to give any advance notice of the procession.

(2) Subsection (1) does not apply where the procession is one commonly or customarily held in the police area (or areas) in which it is proposed to be held or is a funeral procession organised by a funeral director acting in the normal course of his business.

(3) The notice must specify the date when it is intended to hold the procession, the time when it is intended to start it, its proposed route, and the name and address of the person (or of one of the persons) proposing to organise it.

(4) Notice must be delivered to a police station—

(*a*) in the police area in which it is proposed the procession will start, or

(*b*) where it is proposed the procession will start in Scotland and cross into England, in the first police area in England on the proposed route.

(5) If delivered not less than 6 clear days before the date when the procession is intended to be held, the notice may be delivered by post by the recorded delivery service; but section 7 of the Interpretation Act 1978 (under which a document sent by post is deemed to have been served when posted and to have been delivered in the ordinary course of post) does not apply.

(6) If not delivered in accordance with subsection (5), the notice must be delivered by hand not less than 6 clear days before the date when the procession is intended to be held or, if that is not reasonably practicable, as soon as delivery is reasonably practicable.

(7) Where a public procession is held, each of the persons organising it is guilty of an offence if—

(*a*) the requirements of this section as to notice have not been satisfied, or

(*b*) the date when it is held, the time when it starts, or its route, differs from the date, time or route specified in the notice.

(8) It is a defence for the accused to prove that he did not know of, and neither suspected nor had reason to suspect, the failure to satisfy the requirements or (as the case may be) the difference of date, time or route.

(9) To the extent that an alleged offence turns on a difference of date, time or route, it is a defence for the accused to prove that the difference arose from circumstances beyond his control or from something done with the agreement of a police officer or by his direction.

(10) A person guilty of an offence under subsection (7) is liable on summary conviction to a fine not exceeding **level 3** on the standard scale.

[Public Order Act 1986, s 11.]

1. Part II contains ss 11–16.

2. An obligation to notify the police or to seek authorisation in relation to marches and assemblies will not necessarily infringe art 10 (freedom of expression) or art 11 (the right to peaceful assembly) of the European Convention on Human Rights: *Rassemblement Jurassien and Unite Jurassienne v Switzerland* (1979) 17 DR 93.

8–27731 **12. Imposing conditions on public processions.** (1) If the senior police officer, having regard to the time or place at which and the circumstances in which any public procession is being held or is intended to be held and to its route or proposed route, reasonably believes that—

(*a*) it may result in serious public disorder, serious damage to property or serious disruption to the life of the community, or

(*b*) the purpose of the persons organising it is the intimidation of others with a view to compelling them not to do an act they have a right to do, or to do an act they have a right not to do,

he may give directions imposing on the persons organising or taking part in the procession such conditions as appear to him necessary to prevent such disorder, damage, disruption or intimidation, including conditions as to the route of the procession or prohibiting it from entering any public place specified in the directions.

(2) In subsection (1) "the senior police officer" means—

(*a*) in relation to a procession being held, or to a procession intended to be held in a case where persons are assembling with a view to taking part in it, the most senior in rank of the police officers present at the scene, and

(*b*) in relation to a procession intended to be held in a case where paragraph (*a*) does not apply, the chief officer of police.

(3) A direction given by a chief officer of police by virtue of subsection (2)(*b*) shall be given in writing.

(4) A person who organises a public procession and knowingly fails to comply with a condition imposed under this section is guilty of an offence, but it is a defence for him to prove that the failure arose from circumstances beyond his control.

(5) A person who takes part in a public procession and knowingly fails to comply with a condition imposed under this section is guilty of an offence, but it is a defence for him to prove that the failure arose from circumstances beyond his control.

(6) A person who incites another to commit an offence under subsection (5) is guilty of an offence.

(7) *Repealed.*

(8) A person guilty of an offence under subsection (4) is liable on summary conviction to imprisonment for a term not exceeding **3 months*** or a fine not exceeding **level 4** on the standard scale or both.

(9) A person guilty of an offence under subsection (5) is liable on summary conviction to a fine not exceeding **level 3** on the standard scale.

(10) A person guilty of an offence under subsection (6) is liable on summary conviction to imprisonment for a term not exceeding **3 months*** or a fine not exceeding **level 4** on the standard scale or **both**, notwithstanding section 45(3) of the Magistrates' Courts Act 1980 (inciter liable to same penalty as incited).

(11) *Scotland.*

[Public Order Act 1986, s 12.]

***"51 weeks" substituted by the Criminal Justice Act 2003, Sch 26 from a date to be appointed.**

8–27732 **13. Prohibiting public processions.** (1) If at any time the chief officer of police reasonably believes that, because of particular circumstances existing in any district or part of a district, the powers under section 12 will not be sufficient to prevent the holding of public processions in that district or part from resulting in serious public disorder, he shall apply to the council of the district for an order prohibiting for such period not exceeding 3 months as may be specified in the application the holding of all public processions (or of any class of public procession so specified) in the district or part concerned.

(2) On receiving such an application, a council may with the consent of the Secretary of State make an order either in the terms of the application or with such modifications as may be approved by the Secretary of State.

(3) Subsection (1) does not apply in the City of London or the metropolitan police district.

(4) If at any time the Commissioner of Police for the City of London or the Commissioner of Police of the Metropolis reasonably believes that, because of particular circumstances existing in his police area or part of it, the powers under section 12 will not be sufficient to prevent the holding of public processions in that area or part from resulting in serious public disorder, he may with the consent of the Secretary of State make an order prohibiting for such period not exceeding 3 months as may be specified in the order the holding of all public processions (or of any class of public procession so specified) in the area or part concerned.

(5) An order made under this section may be revoked or varied by a subsequent order made in the same way, that is, in accordance with subsections (1) and (2) or subsection (4), as the case may be.

(6) Any order under this section shall, if not made in writing, be recorded in writing as soon as practicable after being made.

(7) A person who organises a public procession the holding of which he knows is prohibited by virtue of an order under this section is guilty of an offence.

(8) A person who takes part in a public procession the holding of which he knows is prohibited by virtue of an order under this section is guilty of an offence.

(9) A person who incites another to commit an offence under subsection (8) is guilty of an offence.

(10) *Repealed.*

(11) A person guilty of an offence under subsection (7) is liable on summary conviction to imprisonment for a term not exceeding **3 months*** or a fine not exceeding **level 4** on the standard scale or **both**.

(12) A person guilty of an offence under subsection (8) is liable on summary conviction to a fine not exceeding **level 3** on the standard scale.

(13) A person guilty of an offence under subsection (9) is liable on summary conviction to imprisonment for a term not exceeding **3 months*** or a fine not exceeding **level 4** on the standard scale or **both**, notwithstanding section 45(3) of the Magistrates' Courts Act 1980.

[Public Order Act 1986, s 13 as amended by the Serious Organised Crime and Police Act 2005, Sch 7.]

***"51 weeks" substituted by the Criminal Justice Act 2003, Sch 26 from a date to be appointed.**

8–27733 **14. Imposing conditions on public assemblies.** (1) If the senior police officer, having regard to the time or place at which and the circumstances in which any public assembly is being held or is intended to be held, reasonably believes that—

(*a*) it may result in serious public disorder, serious damage to property or serious disruption to the life of the community, or

(*b*) the purpose of the persons organising it is the intimidation of others with a view to compelling them not to do an act they have a right to do, or to do an act they have a right not to do,

he may give directions imposing on the persons organising or taking part in the assembly such conditions[1] as to the place at which the assembly may be (or continue to be) held, its maximum duration, or the maximum number of persons who may constitute it, as appear to him necessary to prevent such disorder, damage, disruption or intimidation.

(2) In subsection (1) "the senior police officer" means—

(*a*) in relation to an assembly being held, the most senior in rank of the police officers present at the scene, and

(*b*) in relation to an assembly intended to be held, the chief officer of police.

(3) A direction given by a chief officer of police by virtue of subsection (2)(*b*) shall be given in writing.

(4) A person who organises a public assembly and knowingly fails to comply with a condition imposed under this section is guilty of an offence, but it is a defence for him to prove that the failure arose from circumstances beyond his control.

(5) A person who takes part in a public assembly and knowingly fails to comply with a condition imposed under this section is guilty of an offence, but it is a defence for him to prove that the failure arose from circumstances beyond his control.

(6) A person who incites another to commit an offence under subsection (5) is guilty of an offence.

(7) *Repealed.*

(8) A person guilty of an offence under subsection (4) is liable on summary conviction to imprisonment for a term not exceeding **3 months*** or a fine not exceeding **level 4** on the standard scale or **both**.

(9) A person guilty of an offence under subsection (5) is liable on summary conviction to a fine not exceeding **level 3** on the standard scale.

(10) A person guilty of an offence under subsection (6) is liable on summary conviction to imprisonment for a term not exceeding **3 months*** or a fine not exceeding **level 4** on the standard scale or **both**, notwithstanding section 45(3) of the Magistrates' Courts Act 1980.
[Public Order Act 1986, s 14.]

***"51 weeks" substituted by the Criminal Justice Act 2003, Sch 26 from a date to be appointed.**

1. The designation of entrance and exit points that are not within the assembly area falls outside the power contained in s 14; however, such conditions can be severed from other conditions in the notice that envisage a different activity, the test of severance being that which applies to legislation and legislative instruments (*DPP v Jones* [2002] All ER (D) 157 (Jan), [2002] JPN 78).

8–27733A 14A. Prohibiting trespassory assemblies. (1) If at any time the chief officer of police reasonably believes that an assembly is intended to be held in any district at a place on land to which the public has no right of access or only a limited right of access and that the assembly—

(*a*) is likely to be held without the permission of the occupier of the land or to conduct itself in such a way as to exceed the limits of any permission of his or the limits of the public's right of access, and

(*b*) may result—

(i) in serious disruption to the life of the community, or

(ii) where the land, or a building or monument on it, is of historical, architectural, archaeological or scientific importance, in significant damage to the land, building or monument,

he may apply to the council of the district for an order prohibiting for a specified period the holding of all trespassory assemblies in the district or a part of it, as specified.

(2) On receiving such an application, a council may—

(*a*) in England and Wales, with the consent of the Secretary of State make an order[1] either in the terms of the application or with such modifications as may be approved by the Secretary of State; or

(*b*) in Scotland, make an order in the terms of the application.

(3) Subsection (1) does not apply in the City of London or the metropolitan police district.

(4) If at any time the Commissioner of Police for the City of London or the Commissioner of Police of the Metropolis reasonably believes that an assembly is intended to be held at a place on land to which the public has no right of access or only a limited right of access in his police area and that the assembly—

(*a*) is likely to be held without the permission of the occupier of the land or to conduct itself in such a way as to exceed the limits of any permission of his or the limits of the public's right of access, and

(*b*) may result—

(i) in serious disruption to the life of the community, or

(ii) where the land, or a building or monument on it, is of historical, architectural, archaeological or scientific importance, in significant damage to the land, building or monument,

he may with the consent of the Secretary of State make an order prohibiting for a specified period the holding of all trespassory assemblies in the area or a part of it, as specified.

(5) An order[1] prohibiting the holding of trespassory assemblies operates to prohibit any assembly which—

(*a*) is held on land to which the public has no right of access or only a limited right of access, and

(*b*) takes place in the prohibited circumstances, that is to say, without the permission of the occupier of the land or so as to exceed the limits of any permission of his or the limits of the public's right of access.

(6) No order under this section shall prohibit the holding of assemblies for a period exceeding 4 days or in an area exceeding an area represented by a circle with a radius of 5 miles from a specified centre.

(7) An order made under this section may be revoked or varied by a subsequent order made in the same way, that is, in accordance with subsection (1) and (2) or subsection (4), as the case may be.

(8) Any order under this section shall, if not made in writing, be recorded in writing as soon as practicable after being made.

(9) In this section and sections 14B and 14C—

"assembly" means an assembly of 20 or more persons;

"land" means land in the open air;

"limited", in relation to a right of access by the public to land, means that their use of it is restricted to use for a particular purpose (as in the case of a highway or road) or is subject to other restrictions;

"occupier" means—

(*a*) in England and Wales, the person entitled to possession of the land by virtue of an estate or interest held by him; or

(*b*) in Scotland, the person lawfully entitled to natural possession of the land,

and in subsections (1) and (4) includes the person reasonably believed by the authority applying for or making the order to be the occupier;

"public" includes a section of the public; and

"specified" means specified in an order under this section.

(9A) *Scotland.*

(10) In relation to Scotland, the references in subsection (1) above to a district and to the council of the district shall be construed—

(*a*) as respects applications before 1st April 1996, as references to the area of a regional or islands authority and to the authority in question; and

(*b*) as respects applications on and after that date, as references to a local government area and to the council for that area.

(11) In relation to Wales, the references in subsection (1) above to a district and to the council of the district shall be construed, as respects applications on and after 1st April 1996, as references to a county or county borough and to the council for that county or county borough.

[Public Order Act 1986, s 14A, as inserted by the Criminal Justice and Public Order Act 1994, s 70 and the Land Reform (Scotland) Act 2003, s 70.]

1. The public highway is a public place which the public may enjoy for any reasonable purpose, provided the activity in question does not amount to a public or private nuisance, and does not obstruct the highway by unreasonably impeding the primary right of the public to pass and re-pass. Within these qualifications, a peaceful and non-obstructive assembly does not necessarily exceed the limits of the public's right of access to the highway; however, it is for the justices in each case to decide whether the user of the highway under consideration is reasonable and, therefore, not a trespass (*DPP v Jones* [1999] 2 All ER 257, [1999] 2 WLR 625, 163 JP 285, HL).

8–27733B 14B. Offences in connection with trespassory assemblies and arrest therefor. (1) A person who organises an assembly the holding of which he knows is prohibited by an order under section 14A is guilty of an offence.

(2) A person who takes part in an assembly which he knows is prohibited by an order under section 14A is guilty of an offence.

(3) In England and Wales, a person who incites another to commit an offence under subsection (2) is guilty of an offence.

(4) *Repealed.*

(5) A person guilty of an offence under subsection (1) is liable on summary conviction to imprisonment for a term not exceeding **3 months*** or a fine not exceeding **level 4** on the standard scale or both.

(6) A person guilty of an offence under subsection (2) is liable on summary conviction to a fine not exceeding **level 3** on the standard scale.

(7) A person guilty of an offence under subsection (3) is liable on summary conviction to imprisonment for a term not exceeding **3 months*** or a fine not exceeding **level 4** on the standard scale or **both**, notwithstanding section 45(3) of the Magistrates' Courts Act 1980.

(8) Subsection (3) above is without prejudice to the application of any principle of Scots Law as respects art and part guilt to such incitement as is mentioned in that subsection.

[Public Order Act 1986, s 14B, as inserted by the Criminal Justice and Public Order Act 1994, s 70.]

***"51 weeks" substituted by the Criminal Justice Act 2003, Sch 26 from a date to be appointed.**

8–27733C 14C. Stopping persons from proceeding to trespassory assemblies. (1) If a constable in uniform reasonably believes that a person is on his way to an assembly within the area to which an order under section 14A applies which the constable reasonably believes is likely to be an assembly which is prohibited by that order, he may, subject to subsection (2) below—

(*a*) stop that person, and

(*b*) direct him not to proceed in the direction of the assembly.

(2) The power conferred by subsection (1) may only be exercised within the area to which the order applies.

(3) A person who fails to comply with a direction under subsection (1) which he knows has been given to him is guilty of an offence.

(4) *Repealed.*

(5) A person guilty of an offence under subsection (3) is liable on summary conviction to a fine not exceeding **level 3** on the standard scale.
[Public Order Act 1986, s 14C, as inserted by the Criminal Justice and Public Order Act 1994, s 71.]

8–27734 **15. Delegation.** (1) The chief officer of police may delegate, to such extent and subject to such conditions as he may specify, any of his functions under sections 12 to 14A to an assistant chief constable; and references in those sections to the person delegating shall be construed accordingly.

(2) Subsection (1) shall have effect in the City of London and the metropolitan police district as if "an assistant chief constable" read "an assistant commissioner of police".
[Public Order Act 1986, s 15 as amended by the Police and Magistrates' Courts Act 1994, Sch 5 and the Criminal Justice and Public Order Act 1994, Sch 10.]

8–27735 **16. Interpretation.** In this Part—

"the City of London" means the City as defined for the purposes of the Acts relating to the City of London police;

"the metropolitan police district" means that district as defined in section 76 of the London Government Act 1963;

"public assembly" means an assembly of 2[1] or more persons in a public place which is wholly or partly open to the air;

"public place" means—

(*a*) any highway, or in Scotland any road within the meaning of the Roads (Scotland) Act 1984, and

(*b*) any place to which at the material time the public or any section of the public has access, on payment or otherwise, as of right or by virtue of express or implied permission;

"public procession" means a procession in a public place.
[Public Order Act 1986, s 16 as amended by the Anti-Social Behaviour Act 2003, s 57.]

1. Reference to "2" substituted for "20", in relation to England and Wales.

PART III[1]

RACIAL HATRED

Meaning of "racial hatred"

8–27736 **17. Meaning of "racial hatred".** In this Part "racial hatred" means hatred against a group of persons defined by reference to colour, race, nationality (including citizenship) or ethnic or national origins.
[Public Order Act 1986, s 17, as amended by the Anti-terrorism, Crime and Security Act 2001, Sch 8.]

1. Part III contains ss 17–29.

Acts intended or likely to stir up racial hatred

8–27737 **18. Use of words or behaviour or display of written material[1].** (1) A person who uses threatening, abusive or insulting words or behaviour, or displays any written material which is threatening, abusive or insulting, is guilty of an offence if—

(*a*) he intends thereby to stir up racial hatred, or

(*b*) having regard to all the circumstances racial hatred is likely to be stirred up thereby.

(2) An offence under this section may be committed in a public or a private place, except that no offence is committed where the words or behaviour are used, or the written material is displayed, by a person inside a dwelling and are not heard or seen except by other persons in that or another dwelling.

(3) *Repealed.*

(4) In proceedings for an offence under this section it is a defence for the accused to prove that he was inside a dwelling and had no reason to believe that the words or behaviour used, or the written material displayed, would be heard or seen by a person outside that or any other dwelling.

(5) A person who is not shown to have intended to stir up racial hatred is not guilty of an offence under this section if he did not intend his words or behaviour, or the written material, to be, and was not aware that it might be, threatening, abusive or insulting.

(6) This section does not apply to words or behaviour used, or written material displayed, solely for the purpose of being included in a programme included in a programme service.
[Public Order Act 1986, s 18 as amended by the Broadcasting Act 1990, s 164 and the Serious Organised Crime and Police Act 2005, Sch 7.]

1. Restrictions on the expression of racist ideas are legitimate under art 10(2) of the European Convention on Human Rights as being for the protection of the rights of others. They are also specifically provided for in art 17 of the Convention. See further *Glimmerveen and Hagenbeek v Netherlands* (1979) 18 DR 187, *Kuhnen v Germany* (1988) 56 DR 205 and *Jersild v Denmark* (1994) 19 EHRR 1.

8–27738 **19. Publishing or distributing written material**[1]**.** (1) A person who publishes or distributes written material which is threatening, abusive or insulting is guilty of an offence if—

(*a*) he intends thereby to stir up racial hatred, or
(*b*) having regard to all the circumstances racial hatred is likely to be stirred up thereby.

(2) In proceedings for an offence under this section it is a defence for an accused who is not shown to have intended to stir up racial hatred to prove that he was not aware of the content of the material and did not suspect, and had no reason to suspect, that it was threatening, abusive or insulting.

(3) References in this Part to the publication or distribution of written material are to its publication or distribution to the public or a section of the public.
[Public Order Act 1986, s 19.]

1. For the position under the European Convention on Human Rights see para **8–27737**, footnote (1), ante.

8–27739 **20. Public performance of play**[1]**.** (1) If a public performance of a play is given which involves the use of threatening, abusive or insulting words or behaviour, any person who presents or directs the performance is guilty of an offence if—

(*a*) he intends thereby to stir up racial hatred, or
(*b*) having regard to all the circumstances (and, in particular, taking the performance as a whole) racial hatred is likely to be stirred up thereby.

(2) If a person presenting or directing the performance is not shown to have intended to stir up racial hatred, it is a defence for him to prove—

(*a*) that he did not know and had no reason to suspect that the performance would involve the use of the offending words or behaviour, or
(*b*) that he did not know and had no reason to suspect that the offending words or behaviour were threatening, abusive or insulting, or
(*c*) that he did not know and had no reason to suspect that the circumstances in which the performance would be given would be such that racial hatred would be likely to be stirred up.

(3) This section does not apply to a performance given solely or primarily for one or more of the following purposes—

(*a*) rehearsal,
(*b*) making a recording of the performance, or
(*c*) enabling the performance to be included in a programme service;

but if it is proved that the performance was attended by persons other than those directly connected with the giving of the performance or the doing in relation to it of the things mentioned in paragraph (*b*) or (*c*), the performance shall, unless the contrary is shown, be taken not to have been given solely or primarily for the purposes mentioned above.

(4) For the purposes of this section—

(*a*) a person shall not be treated as presenting a performance of a play by reason only of his taking part in it as a performer,
(*b*) a person taking part as a performer in a performance directed by another shall be treated as a person who directed the performance if without reasonable excuse he performs otherwise than in accordance with that person's direction, and
(*c*) a person shall be taken to have directed a performance of a play given under his direction notwithstanding that he was not present during the performance;

and a person shall not be treated as aiding or abetting the commission of an offence under this section by reason only of his taking part in a performance as a performer.

(5) In this section "play" and "public performance" have the same meaning as in the Theatres Act 1968.

(6) The following provisions of the Theatres Act 1968 apply in relation to an offence under this section as they apply to an offence under section 2 of that Act—

section 9 (script as evidence of what was performed),
section 10 (power to make copies of script),
section 15 (powers of entry and inspection).

[Public Order Act 1986, s 20 as amended by the Broadcasting Act 1990, s 164.]

1. For the position under the European Convention on Human Rights see para **8–27737**, footnote (1), ante.

8–27750 **21. Distributing, showing or playing a recording**[1]**.** (1) A person who distributes, or shows or plays, a recording of visual images or sounds which are threatening, abusive or insulting is guilty of an offence if—

(*a*) he intends thereby to stir up racial hatred, or
(*b*) having regard to all the circumstances racial hatred is likely to be stirred up thereby.

(2) In this Part "recording" means any record from which visual images or sounds may, by any

means, be reproduced; and references to the distribution, showing or playing of a recording are to its distribution, showing or playing to the public or a section of the public.

(3) In proceedings for an offence under this section it is a defence for an accused who is not shown to have intended to stir up racial hatred to prove that he was not aware of the content of the recording and did not suspect, and had no reason to suspect, that it was threatening, abusive or insulting.

(4) This section does not apply to the showing or playing of a recording solely for the purpose of enabling the recording to be included in a programme service.

[Public Order Act 1986, s 21 as amended by the Broadcasting Act 1990, s 164.]

1. For the position under the European Convention on Human Rights see para **8–27737**, footnote (1), ante.

8–27751 **22. Broadcasting or including programme in programme service**[1]**.** (1) If a programme involving threatening, abusive or insulting visual images or sounds is included in a programme service, each of the persons mentioned in subsection (2) is guilty of an offence if—

(*a*) he intends thereby to stir up racial hatred, or

(*b*) having regard to all the circumstances racial hatred is likely to be stirred up thereby.

(2) The persons are—

(*a*) the person providing the programme service,

(*b*) any person by whom the programme is produced or directed, and

(*c*) any person by whom offending words or behaviour are used.

(3) If the person providing the service, or a person by whom the programme was produced or directed, is not shown to have intended to stir up racial hatred, it is a defence for him to prove that—

(*a*) he did not know and had no reason to suspect that the programme would involve the offending material, and

(*b*) having regard to the circumstances in which the programme was included in a programme service, it was not reasonably practicable for him to secure the removal of the material.

(4) It is a defence for a person by whom the programme was produced or directed who is not shown to have intended to stir up racial hatred to prove that he did not know and had no reason to suspect—

(*a*) that the programme would be included in a programme service, or

(*b*) that the circumstances in which the programme would be so included would be such that racial hatred would be likely to be stirred up.

(5) It is a defence for a person by whom offending words or behaviour were used and who is not shown to have intended to stir up racial hatred to prove that he did not know and had no reason to suspect—

(*a*) that a programme involving the use of the offending material would be included in a programme service, or

(*b*) that the circumstances in which a programme involving the use of the offending material would be so included, or in which a programme so included would involve the use of the offending material, would be such that racial hatred would be likely to be stirred up.

(6) A person who is not shown to have intended to stir up racial hatred is not guilty of an offence under this section if he did not know, and had no reason to suspect, that the offending material was threatening, abusive or insulting.

(7)–(8) (*Repealed*).

[Public Order Act 1986, s 22 as amended by the Broadcasting Act 1990, s 164 and Sch 21.]

1. For the position under the European Convention on Human Rights see para **8–27737**, footnote (1), ante.

Racially inflammatory material

8–27752 **23. Possession of racially inflammatory material**[1]**.** (1) A person who has in his possession written material which is threatening, abusive or insulting, or a recording of visual images or sounds which are threatening, abusive or insulting, with a view to—

(*a*) in the case of written material, its being displayed, published, distributed, or included in a programme service whether by himself or another, or

(*b*) in the case of a recording, its being distributed, shown, played, or included in a programme service whether by himself or another,

is guilty of an offence if he intends racial hatred to be stirred up thereby or, having regard to all the circumstances, racial hatred is likely to be stirred up thereby.

(2) For this purpose regard shall be had to such display, publication, distribution, showing, playing, or inclusion in a programme service as he has, or it may reasonably be inferred that he has, in view.

(3) In proceedings for an offence under this section it is a defence for an accused who is not shown to have intended to stir up racial hatred to prove that he was not aware of the content of the written

material or recording and did not suspect, and had no reason to suspect, that it was threatening, abusive or insulting.

(4) (*Repealed*).

[Public Order Act 1986, s 23 as amended by the Broadcasting Act 1990, s 164 and Sch 21.]

1. For the position under the European Convention on Human Rights see para **8–27737**, footnote (1), ante.

8–27753 **24. Powers of entry and search.** (1) If in England and Wales a justice of the peace is satisfied by information on oath laid by a constable that there are reasonable grounds for suspecting that a person has possession of written material or a recording in contravention of section 23, the justice may issue a warrant under his hand authorising any constable to enter and search the premises where it is suspected the material or recording is situated.

(2) *Scotland.*

(3) A constable entering or searching premises in pursuance of a warrant issued under this section may use reasonable force if necessary.

(4) In this section "premises" means any place and, in particular, includes—

(*a*) any vehicle, vessel, aircraft or hovercraft,

(*b*) any offshore installation as defined in section 1(3)(*b*) of the Mineral Workings (Offshore Installations) Act 1971, and

(*c*) any tent or movable structure.

[Public Order Act 1986, s 24.]

8–27754 **25. Power to order forfeiture.** (1) A court by or before which a person is convicted of—

(*a*) an offence under section 18 relating to the display of written material, or

(*b*) an offence under section 19, 21 or 23,

shall order to be forfeited any written material or recording produced to the court and shown to its satisfaction to be written material or a recording to which the offence relates.

(2) An order made under this section shall not take effect—

(*a*) in the case of an order made in proceedings in England and Wales, until the expiry of the ordinary time within which an appeal may be instituted or, where an appeal is duly instituted, until it is finally decided or abandoned;

(*b*) in the case of an order made in proceedings in Scotland, until the expiration of the time within which, by virtue of any statute, an appeal may be instituted or, where such an appeal is duly instituted, until the appeal is finally decided or abandoned.

(3) For the purposes of subsection (2)(*a*)—

(*a*) an application for a case stated or for leave to appeal shall be treated as the institution of an appeal, and

(*b*) where a decision on appeal is subject to a further appeal, the appeal is not finally determined until the expiry of the ordinary time within which a further appeal may be instituted or, where a further appeal is duly instituted, until the further appeal is finally decided or abandoned.

(4) For the purposes of subsection (2)(*b*) the lodging of an application for a stated case or note of appeal against sentence shall be treated as the institution of an appeal.

[Public Order Act 1986, s 25.]

Supplementary provisions

8–27755 **26. Savings for reports of parliamentary or judicial proceedings.** (1) Nothing in this Part applies to a fair and accurate report of proceedings in Parliament or in the Scottish Parliament.

(2) Nothing in this Part applies to a fair and accurate report of proceedings publicly heard before a court or tribunal exercising judicial authority where the report is published contemporaneously with the proceedings or, if it is not reasonably practicable or would be unlawful to publish a report of them contemporaneously, as soon as publication is reasonably practicable and lawful.

[Public Order Act 1986, s 24, as amended by the Scotland Act 1998, Sch 8.]

8–27756 **27. Procedure and punishment.** (1) No proceedings for an offence under this Part may be instituted in England and Wales except by or with the consent of the Attorney General.

(2) For the purposes of the rules in England and Wales against charging more than one offence in the same count or information, each of sections 18 to 23 creates one offence.

(3) A person guilty of an offence under this Part is liable[1]—

(*a*) on conviction on indictment to imprisonment for a term not exceeding **seven years** or a **fine** or **both**;

(*b*) on summary conviction to imprisonment for a term not exceeding **six months** or a fine not exceeding the **statutory maximum** or **both**.

[Public Order Act 1986, s 27, as amened by the Anti-terrorism, Crime and Security Act 2001, s 40.]

1. For procedure in respect of an offence triable either way, see the Magistrates' Courts Act 1980, ss 17A–21 in PART I: MAGISTRATES' COURTS PROCEDURE, ante.

8–27757 28. Offences by corporations. (1) Where a body corporate is guilty of an offence under this Part and it is shown that the offence was committed with the consent or connivance of a director, manager, secretary or other similar officer of the body, or a person purporting to act in any such capacity, he as well as the body corporate is guilty of the offence and liable to be proceeded against and punished accordingly.

(2) Where the affairs of a body corporate are managed by its members, subsection (1) applies in relation to the acts and defaults of a member in connection with his functions of management as it applies to a director.
[Public Order Act 1986, s 28.]

8–27758 29. Interpretation. In this Part—

"distribute", and related expressions, shall be construed in accordance with section 19(3) (written material) and section 21(2) (recordings);

"dwelling" means any structure or part of a structure occupied as a person's home or other living accommodation (whether the occupation is separate or shared with others) but does not include any part not so occupied, and for this purpose "structure" includes a tent, caravan, vehicle, vessel or other temporary or movable structure;

"programme" means any item which is included in a programme service;

"programme service" has the same meaning as in the Broadcasting Act 1990;

"publish", and related expressions, in relation to written material, shall be construed in accordance with section 19(3);

"racial hatred" has the meaning given by section 17;

"recording" has the meaning given by section 21(2), and "play" and "show", and related expressions, in relation to a recording, shall be construed in accordance with that provision;

"written material" includes any sign or other visible representation.

[Public Order Act 1986, s 29 as amended by the Broadcasting Act 1990, s 164 and Sch 21.]

PART IV[1]
EXCLUSION ORDERS

8–27764 35. Photographs. (1) The court by which a banning order is made may make an order which—

(*a*) requires a constable to take a photograph of the person to whom the banning order relates or to cause such a photograph to be taken, and

(*b*) requires that person to go to a specified police station not later than 7 clear days after the day on which the order under this section is made, and at a specified time of day or between specified times of day, in order to have his photograph taken.

(2) In subsection (1) "specified" means specified in the order made under this section and "banning order" has the same meaning as in Part II of the Football Spectators Act 1989.

(3) No order may be made under this section unless an application to make it is made to the court by or on behalf of the person who is the prosecutor in respect of the offence leading to the banning order or (in the case of a banning order made under section 14B of the Football Spectators Act 1989) the complainant.

(4) If the person to whom the banning order relates fails to comply with an order under this section a constable may arrest him without warrant in order that his photograph may be taken.
[Public Order Act 1986, s 35, as amended by the Football (Disorder) Act 2000, Sch 2.]

1. Part IV comprises ss 30–37 of which ss 30–34 and 36 have been repealed. For Banning Orders, see the Football Spectators Act 1989, Pt II, in this PART, post.

8–27766 37. Extension to other sporting events. (1) The Secretary of State may by order provide for section 35 of this Act and Part II of the Football Spectators Act 1989 to apply as if—

(*a*) any reference to an association football match included a reference to a sporting event of a kind specified in the order, and

(*b*) any reference to a prescribed football match included a reference to such a sporting event of a description specified in the order.

(2) An order under subsection (1) may make such modifications of that section and that Part, as they apply by virtue of the order, as the Secretary of State thinks fit.

(3) The power to make an order under this section shall be exercisable by statutory instrument, and no such order shall be made unless a draft of the order has been laid before and approved by resolution of each House of Parliament.
[Public Order Act 1986, s 37, as amended by the Football (Disorder) Act 2000, Sch 2.]

PART V[1]
MISCELLANEOUS AND GENERAL

8–27767 **38. Contamination of or interference with goods with intention of causing public alarm or anxiety, etc.** (1) It is an offence for a person, with the intention—

(*a*) of causing public alarm or anxiety, or
(*b*) of causing injury to members of the public consuming or using the goods, or
(*c*) of causing economic loss to any person by reason of the goods being shunned by members of the public, or
(*d*) of causing economic loss to any person by reason of steps taken to avoid any such alarm or anxiety, injury or loss,

to contaminate or interfere with goods, or make it appear that goods have been contaminated or interfered with, or to place goods which have been contaminated or interfered with, or which appear to have been contaminated or interfered with, in a place where goods of that description are consumed, used, sold or otherwise supplied.

(2) It is also an offence for a person, with any such intention as is mentioned in paragraph (*a*), (*c*) or (*d*) of subsection (1), to threaten that he or another will do, or to claim that he or another has done, any of the acts mentioned in that subsection.

(3) It is an offence for a person to be in possession of any of the following articles with a view to the commission of an offence under subsection (1)—

(*a*) materials to be used for contaminating or interfering with goods or making it appear that goods have been contaminated or interfered with, or
(*b*) goods which have been contaminated or interfered with, or which appear to have been contaminated or interfered with.

(4) A person guilty of an offence under this section is liable[2]—

(*a*) on conviction on indictment to imprisonment for a term not exceeding **10 years** or a **fine** or **both**, or
(*b*) on summary conviction to imprisonment for a term not exceeding **six months** or a fine not exceeding the **statutory maximum** or **both**.

(5) In this section "goods" includes substances whether natural or manufactured and whether or not incorporated in or mixed with other goods.

(6) The reference in subsection (2) to a person claiming that certain acts have been committed does not include a person who in good faith reports or warns that such acts have been, or appear to have been, committed.
[Public Order Act 1986, s 38.]

1. Part V contains ss 38–43.
2. For procedure in respect of an offence triable either way, see the Magistrates' Courts Act 1980, ss 17A–21 in PART I: MAGISTRATES' COURTS PROCEDURE, ante.

8–27769 **40. Amendments, repeals and savings.** (1)–(3) *Amendments and repeals incorporated in text.*

(4) Nothing in this Act affects the common law powers in England and Wales to deal with or prevent a breach of the peace.

(5) *Scotland.*
[Public Order Act 1986, s 40.]

8–27780 **41. Commencement.** (1) This Act shall come into force on such day as the Secretary of State may appoint by order made by statutory instrument, and different days may be appointed for different provisions or different purposes.

(2) Nothing in a provision of this Act applies in relation to an offence committed or act done before the provision comes into force.

(3) Where a provision of this Act comes into force for certain purposes only, the references in subsection (2) to the provision are references to it so far as it relates to those purposes.
[Public Order Act 1986, s 41.]

Football Spectators Act 1989[1]

(1989 c 37)

PART I[2]
FOOTBALL MATCHES IN ENGLAND AND WALES

Preliminary

8–27781 **1. Scope and interpretation of this Part.** (1) This Part of this Act applies in relation to association football matches played in England and Wales which are regulated football matches and the following provisions have effect for its interpretation.

(2) "Regulated football match" means any such match of a description for the time being designated for the purposes of this Part by order[3] made by the Secretary of State or a particular such match so designated.

(3) The Secretary of State shall not make a designation under subsection (2) above without giving the Football Membership Authority an opportunity to make representations about the proposed designation, and taking any representations he receives into account.

(4) An order under subsection (2) above—

(*a*) may designate descriptions of football matches wherever played or when played at descriptions of ground or in any area specified in the order; and

(*b*) may provide, in relation to the match or description of match designated by the order or any description of match falling within the designation, that spectators admitted to the ground shall be authorised spectators to the extent, and subject to any restrictions or conditions, determined in pursuance of the order by the licensing authority under this Part of this Act.

(5) The "national football membership scheme" (or "the scheme") means the scheme made and approved and for the time being in force under section 4 below for the purpose of restricting the generality of spectators attending regulated football matches to persons who are members of the scheme.

(6) A person is, in relation to any regulated football match, an "authorised spectator" if—

(*a*) he is a member of the national football membership scheme or is otherwise authorised by the scheme to attend the match; or

(*b*) he is an authorised spectator by virtue of subsection 4(*b*) above,

and a person is not to be treated as a "spectator" in relation to such a match if the principal purpose of his being on the premises is to provide services in connection with the match or to report on it.

(7) A "licence to admit spectators" is a licence granted in respect of any premises by the licensing authority under this Part of this Act authorising the admission to the premises of spectators for the purpose of watching any regulated football match played at those premises.

(8) Each of the following periods is "relevant to" a regulated football match, that is to say—

(*a*) the period beginning—

(i) two hours before the start of the match, or

(ii) two hours before the time at which it is advertised to start, or

(iii) with the time at which spectators are first admitted to the premises,

whichever is the earliest, and ending one hour after the end of the match;

(*b*) where a match advertised to start at a particular time on a particular day is postponed to a later day, or does not take place, the period in the advertised day beginning two hours before and ending one hour after that time.

(8A) In its application to an offence specified in paragraph 1(*q*), (*r*), (*s*) or (*t*) of Schedule 1 to this Act, subsection (8) above shall have effect as if—

(*a*) the reference to a regulated football match included a reference to a regulated football matches (within the meaning of Part II of this Act,

(*b*) for "two hours", wherever occurring, there were substituted "24 hours",

(*c*) for "one hour", wherever occurring, there were substituted "24 hours", and

(*d*) paragraph (*a*)(iii) were omitted;

(9) *Repealed.*

(10) The power to make an order under subsection (2) above is exercisable by statutory instrument which shall be subject to annulment in pursuance of a resolution of either House of Parliament.

(11) The imposition under this Part of this Act of restrictions on the persons who may attend as spectators at any regulated football match does not affect any other right of any person to exclude persons from admission to the premises at which the match is played.

[Football Spectators Act 1989, s 1 as amended by the Football (Offences and Disorder) Act 1999, s 2, the Football (Disorder) Act 2000, Sch 2 and the Criminal Justice Act 2003, Sch 32.]

1. This Act, other than s 27, shall come into force on such day or days as may be appointed by order made by the Secretary of State (s 27, post). At the date of going to press all provisions of the Act had been brought into force by SI 1990/690 and 926, and SI 1991/107 and SI 1993/1690 except: ss 1(3), (4)(*b*), (5), (6), 2, 3, 4, 5, 6, 7, 10(6), (7), (8)(*c*), (12)(*a*)–(*b*). Guidance on Football Related Legislation is contained in Home Office Circular 34/2000.

2. Part I contains ss 1–13.

3. The Football Spectators (Designation of Football Matches in England and Wales) Order 2000, SI 2000/3331 designates the following matches:

"any association football match which is played at Wembley Stadium, at the Millennium Stadium in Cardiff or at a sports ground in England and Wales which is registered with the Football League or the Football Association Premier League as the home ground of a club which is a member of the Football League or the Football Association Premier League at the time the match is played."

National Membership Scheme

8–27782 2. Offences relating to unauthorised attendance at regulated football matches. (1) If a person who is not, in relation to the match, an authorised spectator enters or remains on premises as a spectator during a period relevant to a regulated football match that person commits an offence and so does a person who attempts to commit an offence under this subsection of entering premises.

(2) Where a person is charged under subsection (1) above with an offence of entering or remaining on premises, and was at the time of the alleged offence not disqualified from being a member of the national football membership scheme, it shall be a defence to prove that he was allowed to enter the premises as a spectator by a person reasonably appearing to him to have lawful authority to do so.

(3) A person guilty of an offence under subsection (1) above shall be liable on summary conviction to imprisonment for a term not exceeding **one month*** or a fine not exceeding **level 3** on the standard scale or to both.

(4) *Repealed.*

[Football Spectators Act 1989, s 2 and the Football (Disorder) Act 2000, Sch 1 and the Serious Organised Crime and Police Act 2005, Sch 7.]

***"51 weeks" substituted by the Criminal Justice Act 2003, Sch 26, from a date to be appointed.**

8–27783 3. The Football Membership Authority. (1) There shall be a body responsible for the administration of the national football membership scheme which shall be designated for the purpose by the Secretary of State under the name (and herein referred to as) "the Football Membership Authority".

(2) Subject to subsection (4) below, the Secretary of State may designate as the Football Membership Authority any body corporate formed for the purpose by the Football Association and the Football League or any body corporate formed by any other persons or, for the purpose, on his behalf.

(3)–(12) *Supplementary provisions as to designation of a body corporate as the Football Membership Authority and function of such authority.*

[Football Spectators Act 1989, s 3.]

8–27784 4. National membership scheme: making, approval, modification etc. (1) The Football Membership Authority shall, as soon as reasonably practicable after its designation takes effect, prepare a draft scheme which fulfils the requirements of section 5 below.

(2)–(8) *Duty of the Authority to consult over draft scheme; submission to and approval of scheme by the Secretary of State.*

[Football Spectators Act 1989, s 4.]

8–27785 5. National membership scheme: contents and penalties. (1) The requirements for a national football membership scheme referred to in section 4(1) and (5) above are those specified in subsection (2) below.

(2) The scheme must include provision—

(*a*) securing that the only spectators permitted to attend at regulated football matches are authorised spectators;

(*b*) providing for temporary membership of the scheme, including (in particular) the temporary membership of football club guests;

(*c*) providing for the admission as spectators at regulated football matches, without their being members of the scheme, of—

(i) disabled persons, and
(ii) accompanied children,

in such circumstances and subject to such conditions as are specified in the scheme;

(*d*) securing that persons who are disqualified under section 7 below are excluded from membership while so disqualified;

(*e*) providing for the exclusion from membership, for an appropriate period not exceeding two years determined under the scheme, of persons who are, by reference to circumstances specified in the scheme, determined under the scheme to be unfit for membership and for notifying persons who are excluded from membership of the grounds for the exclusion;

(*f*) imposing pecuniary penalties on any persons having functions under the scheme for failure to discharge those functions;

(*g*) imposing requirements as respects the procedure to be followed in dealing with applications for membership of the scheme and requiring that in Wales any application form for membership of the scheme shall also be available in Welsh;

(*h*) imposing requirements on responsible persons as respects the procedure to be followed and equipment to be used in relation to any regulated football match to secure that, except in an emergency, the only spectators admitted to and permitted to remain on the premises are authorised spectators;

(*i*) to such effect, in relation to the admission of spectators to the premises, as the Secretary of State may specify in writing;

(*j*) establishing and maintaining a central register of members of the scheme;

(*k*) regulating the form and contents of membership cards; and

(*l*) establishing procedures for the making and consideration of representations against decisions made under the scheme refusing or withdrawing membership of it and for the independent review of the decisions in the light of the representations;

and in this subsection "accompanied children" means persons under the age of 10 years in the charge of an authorised spectator.

(3) The scheme may make provision—

(*a*) for the discharge of functions under the scheme by persons specified in the scheme on such terms as may be agreed with the Football Membership Authority and approved by the Secretary of State;

(*b*) for the imposition of charges under the scheme (including different charges for different cases) in connection with the issue of membership cards to persons becoming members of the scheme; and

(*c*) providing for the admission as spectators at regulated football matches, without their being members of the scheme, of descriptions of person specified in the scheme in such circumstances and subject to such conditions as are so specified.

(4) The scheme may make different provision for different circumstances.

(5) Information obtained from persons under the national football membership scheme shall be treated as not obtained under an enactment for the purposes of paragraph 1(2) of Part II of Schedule 1 to the Data Protection Act 1998 (which treats information obtained under enactments as fairly obtained).

(6) Nothing in section 29(1) and (2) of the Data Protection Act 1998 (which exempt personal data relating to crime from the subject access provisions in certain cases) shall apply to personal data held by the Football Membership Authority for the purposes of the national football membership scheme.

(7) Any person commits an offence who, for the purpose of being admitted to membership of the national football membership scheme—

(*a*) makes a statement which he knows to be false or misleading in a material particular or recklessly makes a statement which is false or misleading in a material particular, or

(*b*) produces, furnishes, signs or otherwise makes use of a document which he knows to be false or misleading in a material particular or recklessly produces, furnishes, signs or otherwise makes use of a document which is false or misleading in a material particular.

(8) A person guilty of an offence under subsection (7) above shall be liable on summary conviction to a fine not exceeding **level 3** on the standard scale.

[Football Spectators Act 1989, s 5 as amended by the Data Protection Act 1998, Sch 15.]

8–27786 **6. Phased application of scheme.** (1) The Secretary of State, in exercising his function of designating football matches under section 1(2) above as matches in relation to which the national football membership scheme applies, shall have regard to whether it is desirable to achieve a phased application of the scheme.

(2) For this purpose—

(*a*) the Football Membership Authority shall consider the possibility of a phased application of the scheme and may make recommendations to the Secretary of State; and

(*b*) the Secretary of State shall have regard to any recommendations so made.

[Football Spectators Act 1989, s 6.]

8–27787 **7. Disqualification for membership of scheme.** (1) Any person who is subject to a domestic football banning order under section 30 of the Public Order Act 1986 (exclusion from prescribed football matches) or a banning order under Part II of this Act whenever made is disqualified from becoming or continuing to be a member of the national football membership scheme and while he is so subject he shall not be admitted as a member of the scheme or, if he is a member, his membership shall be withdrawn.

(2) Any person convicted of a relevant offence is disqualified from becoming or continuing to be a member of the national football membership scheme, and the following provisions of this section have effect in relation to such a person.

(3) The period during which a person's disqualification under subsection (2) above continues shall be—

(*a*) in a case where he was sentenced to a period of imprisonment taking immediate effect, five years, and

(*b*) in any other case, two years,

beginning with the date of the conviction.

(4) During the period for which a person is disqualified he shall not be admitted as a member of the scheme or, if he is a member, his membership shall cease on the date of the conviction.

(5) The offences relevant for the purposes of subsection (2) above are those to which Schedule 1 to this Act applies.

(6) *Repealed.*

(7) Where a court convicts a person of a relevant offence, then—

(*a*) the court—

(i) shall, except in the case of an offence under section 2(1) or 5(7) above, certify that the offence is a relevant offence, and

(ii) shall explain to him in ordinary language the effect of the conviction on his membership of the national football membership scheme; and

(*b*) designated officer for the court (in the case of a magistrates' court) or the appropriate officer (in the case of the Crown Court)—

(i) shall (as soon as reasonably practicable) send to the Football Membership Authority and to the chief officer of police for the police area in which the offence was committed notice of the conviction and sentence and of the giving of any certificate that the offence is a relevant offence, and

(ii) shall give a copy of the notices to the person who was convicted of the offence.

(8) Where, on an appeal against a person's conviction of the relevant offence or against a sentence of imprisonment imposed on him in dealing with him for the offence, his conviction is quashed or the sentence is reduced to one which is not a sentence of imprisonment taking immediate effect, the court which determines the appeal or, as the case may be, the court to which the case is remitted, shall cause notice of the quashing of the conviction or of the sentence imposed to be sent to the persons specified in subsection (7)(*b*)(i) and (ii) above and, where his conviction is quashed, the Authority shall re-admit him to membership of the scheme, but without prejudice to any proceedings under the scheme to exclude him from membership.

(9) *Repealed.*

(10) In this section and Schedule 1 to this Act—

(*a*) "declaration of relevance" means a declaration by the court that the offence related to football matches;

(*b*) "imprisonment" includes any form of detention (or, in the case of a person under twenty-one years of age sentenced to custody for life, custody); and

(*c*) the reference to a clerk of a magistrates' court is to be construed in accordance with section 141 of the Magistrates' Courts Act 1980, reading references to that Act as references to this section.

[Football Spectators Act 1989, s 7, as amended by the Football (Offences and Disorder) Act 1999, ss 2 and 6, the Football (Disorder) Act 2000, Sch 2, the Access to Justice Act 1999, Sch 13 and the Criminal Justice Act 2003, Sch 32.]

***"51 weeks" substituted by the Criminal Justice Act 2003, Sch 32, from a date to be appointed.**

Licences to admit spectators

8–27788 **8. The Football Licensing Authority.** (1) There shall be a body called the Football Licensing Authority (in this Part of this Act referred to as "the licensing authority") which shall perform the functions assigned to it by this Part of this Act.

(2)–(3) *Constitution and appointment of the licensing authority.*

(4) Schedule 2[1] to this Act shall have effect with respect to the licensing authority.

(5) *Expenses.*

[Football Spectators Act 1989, s 8.]

---

1. See post, for those provisions of Sch 2 which may be relevant to proceedings in magistrates' courts.

8–27789 **9. Offence of admitting spectators to unlicensed premises.** (1) Subject to subsection (2) below, if persons are admitted as spectators to, or permitted to remain as spectators on, any premises during a period relevant to a regulated football match without a licence to admit spectators being in force, any responsible person commits an offence.

(2) Where a person is charged with an offence under this section it shall be a defence to prove either that the spectators were admitted in an emergency or—

(*a*) that the spectators were admitted without his consent; and

(*b*) that he took all reasonable precautions and exercised all due diligence to avoid the commission of such an offence.

(3) A person guilty of an offence under this section shall be liable[1]—

(*a*) on summary conviction, to a fine not exceeding **the statutory maximum**; or

(*b*) on conviction on indictment, to a **fine** or to imprisonment for a term not exceeding **two years**, or to both.

[Football Spectators Act 1989, s 9 as amended by the Football (Disorder) Act 2000, Sch 1.]

1. For procedure in respect of this offence which is triable either way, see the Magistrates' Courts Act 1980, ss 17A–21, in PART I: MAGISTRATES' COURTS, PROCEDURE, ante.

8-27790 10. Licences to admit spectators: general. (1) The licensing authority may, on an application duly made by a responsible person, grant a licence to admit spectators to any premises for the purpose of watching any regulated football match played at those premises.

(2) An application for a licence in respect of any premises shall be made in such manner, in such form and accompanied by such fee as may be determined by the Secretary of State.

(3) The licensing authority shall not refuse to grant a licence without—

(*a*) notifying the applicant in writing of the proposed refusal and of the grounds for it;

(*b*) giving him an opportunity to make representations about them within the period of twenty-eight days beginning with the service of the notice; and

(*c*) taking any representations so made into account in making its decision.

(4) A licence to admit spectators to any premises may authorise the admission of spectators to watch all regulated football matches or specified descriptions of regulated football matches or a particular such match.

(5) A licence to admit spectators shall be in writing and shall be granted on such terms and conditions as the licensing authority considers appropriate and, if the Secretary of State gives to the licensing authority a direction under section 11 below, the conditions may include conditions imposing requirements as respects the seating of spectators.

(6) A licence to admit spectators may also include conditions requiring specified descriptions of spectators to be refused admittance to the premises to watch regulated football matches or specified descriptions of regulated football matches or a particular such match.

(7) Where a designation order includes the provision authorised by section 1(4)(*b*) above as respects the admission of spectators to any ground as authorised spectators, the licensing authority may, by notice in writing to the licence holder, direct that, for the purposes of any match or description of match specified in the direction, the licence shall be treated as including such specified terms and conditions as respects the admission of spectators as authorised spectators as the licensing authority considers appropriate; and the licence shall have effect, for that purpose, subject to those terms and conditions.

(8) It shall be a condition of every licence that any authorised person shall be entitled, on production, if so required, of his authority—

(*a*) to enter at any reasonable time any premises on which a regulated football match is being or is to be played;

(*b*) to make such inspection of the premises and such inquiries relating to them as he considers necessary for the purposes of this Part of this Act; or

(*c*) to examine any records relating to the operation of the national football membership scheme on the premises, and take copies of such records.

(9) A licence to admit spectators shall, unless revoked or suspended under section 12 below or surrendered, remain in force for a specified period.

(10) Subject to subsection (11) below, the licensing authority may at any time, by notice in writing to the licence holder, vary the terms and conditions of the licence.

(11) The licensing authority shall not vary the terms or conditions of a licence without—

(*a*) notifying the licence holder in writing of the proposed alterations or additions;

(*b*) giving him an opportunity to make representations about them within the period of twenty-one days beginning with the service of the notice; and

(*c*) taking any representations so made into account in making the decision.

(12) In taking any decision under this section the licensing authority shall have regard, among the other relevant circumstances, to the following matters or to such of them as are applicable to the decision, that is to say—

(*a*) whether the premises and the equipment provided and procedures used at the premises are such as to secure that, except (in the case of the procedures) in an emergency, only authorised spectators are admitted to regulated football matches;

(*b*) whether and to what extent the requirements imposed for that purpose by the national football membership scheme on responsible persons have been complied with;

(*c*) whether the equipment provided, procedures used and other arrangements in force at the premises are such as are reasonably required to prevent the commission or minimise the effects of offences at regulated football matches; and

(*d*) such other considerations as the Secretary of State determines from time to time and notifies to the licensing authority.

(13) Subject to subsection (14) below, if any term or condition of a licence is contravened any responsible person commits an offence.

(14) Where a person is charged with an offence under subsection (13) above it shall be a defence to prove—

(*a*) that the contravention took place without his consent; and
(*b*) that he took all reasonable precautions and exercised all due diligence to avoid the commission of such an offence.

(15) A person guilty of an offence under subsection (13) above shall be liable, on summary conviction, to a fine not exceeding **level 5** on the standard scale.

(16) The fees charged on the issue of licences—

(*a*) may be fixed so as to reimburse the licensing authority their expenses under this Part of this Act; and
(*b*) shall be paid by the licensing authority to the Secretary of State.

(17) In this section—

"authorised person" means any person authorised by the Secretary of State, the licensing authority or the Football Membership Authority;

"specified" means specified in the licence or in the case of subsection (7) in the direction; and

"vary", in relation to a licence, includes the addition of further terms or conditions.

[Football Spectators Act 1989, s 10 as amended by the Football (Disorder) Act 2000, Sch 1.]

8–27791 **11. Power of Secretary of State to require conditions in licences relating to seating.** (1) The Secretary of State may, by order[1], direct the licensing authority to include in any licence to admit spectators to any specified premises a condition imposing requirements as respects the seating of spectators at regulated football matches at the premises; and it shall be the duty of the authority to comply with the direction.

(2) The requirements imposed by a condition in pursuance of this section may relate to the accommodation to be provided at, or the arrangements to be made as respects the spectators admitted to, the premises.

(3) A direction may require the licensing authority to include the condition in the licence when granting it or by way of varying the conditions of a licence.

(4) Before giving a direction under this section in relation to any premises the Secretary of State shall consult the licensing authority which may, if it thinks fit, make recommendations to him.

(5) The licensing authority shall not make any recommendations under subsection (4) above without consulting the local authority in whose area the premises are situated.

(6) The power to make an order containing a direction under this section is exercisable by statutory instrument which shall be subject to annulment in pursuance of a resolution of either House of Parliament.

(7) In this section "local authority" has the same meaning as in the Safety of Sports Grounds Act 1975[2].

[Football Spectators Act 1989, s 11 as amended by the Football (Disorder) Act 2000, Sch 1.]

1. The Football Spectators (Seating) Orders, SI 1994/1666, SI 1995/1706, SI 1996/1706, SI 1997/1677, SI 1998/1599, SI 1999/1926, SI 2000/1739, SI 2001/2373, SI 2002/1755, SI 2004/1737 and SI 2005/1751 have been made.
2. In this PART, title HEALTH AND SAFETY, ante.

8–27792 **12. Licences to admit spectators: revocation and suspension.** (1) The licensing authority may, subject to subsections (2), (3) and (4) below, at any time, by notice in writing to the holder of a licence to admit spectators, revoke the licence or suspend the licence indefinitely or for such period as the authority considers appropriate.

(2) The licensing authority shall not suspend or revoke a licence under this section unless satisfied that it is necessary to do so having regard to the matters which are relevant for the purposes of this section.

(3) The matters which are relevant for the purposes of this section are—

(*a*) the matters specified in paragraphs (*a*), (*b*) and (*c*) of section 10(12) above; and
(*b*) such other considerations as the Secretary of State determines from time to time and notifies to the licensing authority.

(4) The licensing authority shall not revoke or suspend a licence to admit spectators without—

(*a*) notifying the licence holder of the proposed revocation or suspension and of the grounds for it;
(*b*) giving him an opportunity to make representations about the matter within the period of twenty-one days beginning with the date of the service of the notice; and
(*c*) taking any representations so made into account in making the decision.

(5) The licensing authority may, if satisfied that the urgency of the case so requires, suspend a licence under this section without observing the requirements of subsection (4) above but the authority shall, as soon as is practicable, notify the person to whom the licence was granted of the grounds for the suspension.

(6) A licence suspended under this section shall during the time of suspension be of no effect.

(7) Where a licence has been suspended under this section the person to whom the licence was granted may at any time apply to the licensing authority to terminate the suspension and the licensing

authority may terminate the suspension if it appears to be appropriate to do so having regard to the relevant matters and after taking into account any representations made by the applicant.
[Football Spectators Act 1989, s 12.]

8–27793 **13. Licensing authority's powers in relation to safety at football grounds.** (1) The licensing authority shall have the function of keeping under review the discharge by local authorities of their functions under the Safety of Sports Grounds Act 1975[1] in relation to sports grounds at which regulated football matches are played and shall have the powers conferred in relation to those functions by the following provisions of this section.

(2) The licensing authority may, by notice in writing to the local authority concerned, require the local authority to include in any safety certificate such terms and conditions as are specified in the notice; and it shall be the duty of the local authority to comply with the requirement.

(3) Before exercising its powers under subsection (2) above to require the inclusion of specified terms and conditions in any safety certificate, the licensing authority shall consult the local authority, the chief officer of police and either the fire authority (where the local authority is in Wales, Greater London or a metropolitan county) or the building authority (in any other case).

(4) As respects those terms and conditions, the local authority need not consult the chief officer of police, the fire authority or the building authority under section 3(3) or 4(8) of the Safety of Sports Grounds Act 1975[1] before issuing a safety certificate or about any proposal to amend or replace one.

(5) A notice under subsection (2) above may require the issue under that Act of a safety certificate incorporating the specified terms or conditions or the amendment under that Act of a safety certificate so that it incorporates the specified terms or conditions.

(6) Any inspector appointed by the licensing authority may, for the purposes of the discharge by the licensing authority of its function under subsection (1) above, on production, if so required, of his authority—

(*a*) enter at any reasonable time any sports ground at which regulated football matches are played;
(*b*) make such inspection of the ground and such inquiries relating to the ground as he considers necessary; or
(*c*) examine the safety certificate and any records kept under the Safety of Sports Grounds Act 1975 or this Part of this Act, and take copies of such records.

(7) The licensing authority may, by notice in writing to any local authority, require the local authority to furnish to the licensing authority such information relating to the discharge by the local authority of its functions under the Safety of Sports Grounds Act 1975 as is specified in the notice; and it shall be the duty of the local authority to comply with the requirement.

(8) Section 5(3) of the Safety of Sports Grounds Act 1975[1] (appeals against terms and conditions of safety certificates) shall have effect with the insertion, after paragraph (ii), of the words "but not against the inclusion in a safety certificate of anything required to be included in it by the Football Licensing Authority under section 13(2) of the Football Spectators Act 1989".

(9) Any expression used in this section and in the Safety of Sports Grounds Act 1975[1] has the same meaning in this section as in that Act.
[Football Spectators Act 1989, s 13 amended by the Local Government (Wales) Act 1994, Sch 16 and the Football (Disorder) Act 2000, Sch 1.]

1. In this PART, title HEALTH AND SAFETY, ante.

PART II[1]
FOOTBALL MATCHES OUTSIDE ENGLAND AND WALES

Preliminary

8–27794 **14. Main definitions.** (1) This section applies for the purposes of this Part.

(2) "Regulated football match" means an association football match (whether in England and Wales or elsewhere) which is a prescribed[2] match or a match of a prescribed[2] description.

(3) "External tournament" means a football competition which includes regulated football matches outside England and Wales.

(4) "Banning order" means an order made by the court under this Part which—

(*a*) in relation to regulated football matches in England and Wales, prohibits the person who is subject to the order from entering any premises for the purpose of attending such matches, and
(*b*) in relation to regulated football matches outside England and Wales, requires that person to report at a police station in accordance with this Part.

(5) "Control period", in relation to a regulated football match outside England and Wales, means the period—

(*a*) beginning five days before the day of the match, and
(*b*) ending when the match is finished or cancelled.

(6) "Control period", in relation to an external tournament, means any period described in an order made by the Secretary of State—

(*a*) beginning five days before the day of the first football match outside England and Wales which is included in the tournament, and

(*b*) ending when the last football match outside England and Wales which is included in the tournament is finished or cancelled,

but, for the purposes of paragraph (*a*), any football match included in the qualifying or pre-qualifying stages of the tournament is to be left out of account.

(7) References to football matches are to football matches played or intended to be played.

(8) "Relevant offence" means an offence to which Schedule 1 to this Act applies.

[Football Spectators Act 1989, s 14 as amended by the Football (Disorder) Act 2000, Sch 1.]

---

1. Part II contains ss 14–22. For legal advice and assistance in respect of proceedings under this Part, see the Football (Disorder) (Legal Advice and Assistance) Order 2000, in PART I: MAGISTRATES' COURTS, PROCEDURE, ante.

2. The Football Spectators (Prescription) Order 2004, SI 2004/2409 has been made which provides that for the purposes of Part 2 of this Act the following matches are regulated football matches:

- an association football match in England and Wales in which one or both of the participating teams represents a club which is for the time being a member (whether a full or associate member) of the Football League, the Football Association Premier League, the Football Conference or the League of Wales, or represents a country or territory.
- an association football match outside England and Wales involving—

(*a*) a national team appointed by the Football Association to represent England or the Football Association of Wales to represent Wales; or

(*b*) a team representing a club which is, at the time the match is played, a member (whether a full or associate member) of the Football League, the Football Association Premier League, the Football Conference or the League of Wales.

Banning orders

8–27795 **14A. Banning orders made on conviction of an offence**[1]. (1) This section applies where a person (the "offender") is convicted of a relevant offence.

(2) If the court is satisfied that there are reasonable grounds to believe that making a banning order would help to prevent violence or disorder at or in connection with any regulated football matches, it must make such an order in respect of the offender.

(3) If the court is not so satisfied, it must in open court state that fact and give its reasons.

(3A) For the purpose of deciding whether to make an order under this section the court may consider evidence led by the prosecution and the defence.

(3B) It is immaterial whether evidence led in pursuance of subsection (3A) would have been admissible in the proceedings in which the offender was convicted.

(4) A banning order may only be made under this section—

(*a*) in addition to a sentence imposed in respect of the relevant offence, or

(*b*) in addition to an order discharging him conditionally.

(4A) The court may adjourn any proceedings in relation to an order under this section even after sentencing the offender.

(4B) If the offender does not appear for any adjourned proceedings, the court may further adjourn the proceedings or may issue a warrant for his arrest.

(4C) But the court may not issue a warrant for the offender's arrest unless it is satisfied that he has had adequate notice of the time and place of the adjourned proceedings.

(5) A banning order may be made as mentioned in subsection (4)(b) above in spite of anything in sections 12 and 14 of the Powers of the Criminal Courts (Sentencing) Act 2000 (which relate to orders discharging a person absolutely or conditionally and their effect).

(6) In this section, "the court" in relation to an offender means—

(*a*) the court by or before which he is convicted of the relevant offence, or

(*b*) if he is committed to the Crown Court to be dealt with for that offence, the Crown Court.

[Football Spectators Act 1989, s 14A as inserted by the Football (Disorder) Act 2000, Sch 1 and amended by the Anti-social Behaviour Act 2003, s 86 and the Serious Organised Crime and Police Act 2005, s 139.]

---

1. In *Gough v Chief Constable of the Derbyshire Constabulary, R (on the application of Miller) v Leeds Magistrates' Court, Lilley v DPP* [2001] EWHC Admin 554, [2001] 4 All ER 289, [2001] 3 WLR 1392 the Court of Appeal held as follows in relation to the legislative regime on banning orders. The objective of these provisions was sufficiently important to justify their limits on the right of freedom of movement and they did not, therefore, contravene EC law. However, those that have to apply them are under a duty to interpret them in a manner that is compatible with EC law and the ECHR. While banning orders are not "penalties", and proceedings under s 14B below are not "criminal", banning orders fall into the same category as anti-social behaviour orders and sex offender orders. Therefore, magistrates should apply an exacting standard of proof that will, in practice, be hard to distinguish from the criminal standard. This applies to both of the conditions in s 14B. In practice, the second "reasonable grounds" condition will almost inevitably consist of evidence of past conduct, and this may or may not consist of or include the matters that have to be proved under the first condition, but it must be proved to the same strict standard of proof. Furthermore, it must be conduct that gives rise to the likelihood that, if the respondent is not banned from attending prescribed football matches, he will attend them, or the environs of them, and take part in violence or disorder.

The requirement of a "special circumstances" as a precondition to granting an applicant permission to go abroad during a prescribed period (see s 20) must not be interpreted as meaning "extraordinary circumstances". When considering whether or not there are "special circumstances" the FBOA or, on appeal, a magistrates' court should do not more than satisfy itself on a balance of probabilities that the reason for going abroad is not to attend a prescribed match. This should not be something that is difficult to prove (eg a bona fide traveller is likely to be in a position to produce some evidence of the proposed trip).

If a banning order, properly made, interferes with the right to respect for private or family life under art 8, the interference is likely to prove justified under art 8(2) on the grounds that it is necessary for the prevention of disorder.

8–27796 14B. Banning orders made on a complaint[1]. (1) An application[2] for a banning order in respect of any person may be made by the chief officer of police for the area in which the person resides or appears to reside, if it appears to the officer that the condition in subsection (2) below is met.

(2) That condition is that the respondent has at any time caused or contributed to any violence or disorder in the United Kingdom or elsewhere.

(3) The application is to be made by complaint to a magistrates' court.

(4) If—

(*a*) it is proved on the application that the condition in subsection (2) above is met, and

(*b*) the court is satisfied that there are reasonable grounds to believe that making a banning order would help to prevent violence or disorder at or in connection with any regulated football matches,

the court must make a banning order in respect of the respondent.

[Football Spectators Act 1989, s 14B as inserted by the Football (Disorder) Act 2000, Sch 1.]

---

1. See note 1 to s 14A, above. Proceedings under s 14B of this Act are "criminal proceedings" for the purposes of s 12(2)(*g*) of the Access to Justice Act 1999 by virtue of reg 3 of the Criminal Defence Service (General) (No 2) Regulations 2001 (eligibility for criminal legal aid).

2. An application under this section might originally be made during the period of one year from 28 August 2001: Football (Disorder) (Duration of Powers) Order 2001, SI 2001/2646 made under s 5(4) of the Football (Disorder) Act 2000. Section 1 of the Football (Disorder) (Amendment) Act 2002 amended s 5 of the Football (Disorder) Act 2000 to enable the making of applications under s 14B (and the exercise of powers under ss 21A and 21B) of the Football Spectators Act 1989 within the period of 5 years beginning with the day on which s 1 of the 2002 Act came into force. Section 1 of the 2002 Act was brought into force on 28 August 2002 by the Football (Disorder) (Amendment) Act 2002 (Commencement) Order 2002, SI 2002/2200.

8–27797 14C. Banning orders: supplementary. (1) In this Part, "violence" means violence against persons or property and includes threatening violence and doing anything which endangers the life of any person.

(2) In this Part, "disorder" includes—

(*a*) stirring up hatred against a group of persons defined by reference to colour, race, nationality (including citizenship) or ethnic or national origins, or against an individual as a member of such a group,

(*b*) using threatening, abusive or insulting words or behaviour or disorderly behaviour,

(*c*) displaying any writing or other thing which is threatening, abusive or insulting.

(3) In this Part, "violence" and "disorder" are not limited to violence or disorder in connection with football.

(4) The magistrates' court may take into account the following matters (among others), so far as they consider it appropriate to do so, in determining whether to make an order under section 14B above—

(*a*) any decision of a court or tribunal outside the United Kingdom,

(*b*) deportation or exclusion from a country outside the United Kingdom,

(*c*) removal or exclusion from premises used for playing football matches, whether in the United Kingdom or elsewhere,

(*d*) conduct recorded on video or by any other means.

(5) In determining whether to make such an order—

(*a*) the magistrates' court may not take into account anything done by the respondent before the beginning of the period of ten years ending with the application under section 14B(1) above, except circumstances ancillary to a conviction,

(*b*) before taking into account any conviction for a relevant offence, where a court made a statement under section 14A(3) above (or section 15(2A) below or section 30(3) of the Public Order Act 1986), the magistrates' court must consider the reasons given in the statement,

and in this subsection "circumstances ancillary to a conviction" has the same meaning as it has for the purposes of section 4 of the Rehabilitation of Offenders Act 1974 (effect of rehabilitation).

(6) Subsection (5) does not prejudice anything in the Rehabilitation of Offenders Act 1974.

[Football Spectators Act 1989, s 14C as inserted by the Football (Disorder) Act 2000, Sch 1.]

8–27798 14D. Banning orders made on a complaint: appeals[1]. (1) An appeal lies to the Crown Court against the making by a magistrates' court of a banning order under section 14B above.

(2) On the appeal the Crown Court—

(*a*) may make any orders necessary to give effect to its determination of the appeal, and

(*b*) may also make any incidental or consequential orders which appear to it to be just.

(3) An order of the Crown Court made on an appeal under this section (other than one directing that an application be re-heard by a magistrates' court) is to be treated for the purposes of this Part as if it were an order of the magistrates' court from which the appeal was brought.

[Football Spectators Act 1989, s 14D as inserted by the Football (Disorder) Act 2000, Sch 1.]

1. Proceedings under s 14D of this Act are "criminal proceedings" for the purposes of s 12(2)(*g*) of the Access to Justice Act 1999 by virtue of reg 3 of the Criminal Defence Service (General) (No 2) Regulations 2001 (eligibility for criminal legal aid).

8–27799 14E. Banning orders: general. (1) On making a banning order, a court must in ordinary language explain its effect to the person subject to the order.

(2) A banning order must require the person subject to the order to report initially at a police station in England and Wales specified in the order within the period of five days beginning with the day on which the order is made.

(3) A banning order must, unless it appears to the court that there are exceptional circumstances, impose a requirement as to the surrender in accordance with this Part, in connection with regulated football matches outside the United Kingdom, of the passport of the person subject to the order.

(4) If it appears to the court that there are such circumstances, it must in open court state what they are.

(5) In the case of a person detained in legal custody—

(*a*) the requirement under this section to report at a police station, and

(*b*) any requirement imposed under section 19 below,

is suspended until his release from custody.

(6) If—

(a) he is released from custody more than five days before the expiry of the period for which the order has effect, and

(*b*) he was precluded by his being in custody from reporting initially,

the order is to have effect as if it required him to report initially at the police station specified in the order within the period of five days beginning with the date of his release.*

[Football Spectators Act 1989, s 14E as inserted by the Football (Disorder) Act 2000, Sch 1.]

***New sub-s (7) inserted by the Criminal Justice Act 2003, Sch 32, from a date to be appointed.**

8–27800 14F. Period of banning orders. (1) Subject to the following provisions of this Part, a banning order has effect for a period beginning with the day on which the order is made.

(2) The period must not be longer than the maximum or shorter than the minimum.

(3) Where the order is made under section 14A above in addition to a sentence of imprisonment taking immediate effect, the maximum is ten years and the minimum is six years; and in this subsection "imprisonment" includes any form of detention.

(4) In any other case where the order is made under section 14A above, the maximum is five years and the minimum is three years.

(5) Where the order is made under section 14B above, the maximum is three years and the minimum is two years.

[Football Spectators Act 1989, s 14F as inserted by the Football (Disorder) Act 2000, Sch 1.]

8–27801 14G. Additional requirements of orders[1]. (1) A banning order may, if the court making the order thinks fit, impose additional requirements on the person subject to the order in relation to any regulated football matches.

(2) The court by which a banning order was made may, on an application made by—

(*a*) the person subject to the order, or

(*b*) the person who applied for the order or who was the prosecutor in relation to the order,

vary the order so as to impose, replace or omit any such requirements.

(3) In the case of a banning order made by a magistrates' court, the reference in subsection (2) above to the court by which it was made includes a reference to any magistrates' court acting for the same petty sessions area as that court.

[Football Spectators Act 1989, s 14G as inserted by the Football (Disorder) Act 2000, Sch 1.]

1. Proceedings under s 14G of this Act are "criminal proceedings" for the purposes of s 12(2)(*g*) of the Access to Justice Act 1999 by virtue of reg 3 of the Criminal Defence Service (General) (No 2) Regulations 2001 (eligibility for criminal legal aid).

8–27803 14H. Termination of orders. (1) If a banning order has had effect for at least two-thirds of the period determined under section 14F above, the person subject to the order may apply to the court by which it was made to terminate it.

(2) On the application, the court may by order terminate the banning order as from a specified date or refuse the application.

(3) In exercising its powers under subsection (2) above, the court must have regard to the person's character, his conduct since the banning order was made, the nature of the offence or conduct which led to it and any other circumstances which appear to it to be relevant.

(4) Where an application under subsection (1) above in respect of a banning order is refused, no further application in respect of the order may be made within the period of six months beginning with the day of the refusal.

(5) The court may order the applicant to pay all or any part of the costs of an application under this section.

(6) In the case of a banning order made by a magistrates' court, the reference in subsection (1) above to the court by which it was made includes a reference to any magistrates' court acting for the same petty sessions area as that court.

[Football Spectators Act 1989, s 14H as inserted by the Football (Disorder) Act 2000, Sch 1.]

---

1. Proceedings under s 14H of this Act are "criminal proceedings" for the purposes of s 12(2)(*g*) of the Access to Justice Act 1999 by virtue of reg 3 of the Criminal Defence Service (General) (No 2) Regulations 2001 (eligibility for criminal legal aid).

8–27804 14J. Offences. (1) A person subject to a banning order who fails to comply with—

(*a*) any requirement imposed by the order, or

(*b*) any requirement imposed under section 19(2B) or (2C) below,

is guilty of an offence.

(2) A person guilty of an offence under this section is liable on summary conviction to imprisonment for a term not exceeding six months, or a fine not exceeding **level 5** on the standard scale, or both.

[Football Spectators Act 1989, s 14J as inserted by the Football (Disorder) Act 2000, Sch 1.]

Banning orders

8–27805 18. Information. (1) Where a court makes a banning order, the justices' chief executive for the court (in the case of a magistrates' court) or the appropriate officer (in the case of the Crown Court)—

(*a*) shall give a copy of it to the person to whom it relates;

(*b*) shall (as soon as reasonably practicable) send a copy of it to the enforcing authority[1] and to any prescribed[1] person;

(*c*) shall (as soon as reasonably practicable) send a copy of it to the police station (addressed to the officer responsible for the police station) at which the person subject to the order is to report initially; and

(*d*) in a case where the person subject to the order detained in legal custody, shall (as soon as reasonably practicable) send a copy of it to the person in whose custody he is detained.

(2) Where a court terminates a banning order under section 14H above, the clerk of the court (in the case of a magistrates' court) or the appropriate officer (in the case of the Crown Court)—

(*a*) shall give a copy of the terminating order to the person to whom the banning order;

(*b*) shall (as soon as reasonably practicable) send a copy of it to the enforcing authority[1] and to any prescribed person[1]; and

(*c*) in a case where the person subject to the banning order detained in legal custody, shall (as soon as reasonably practicable) send a copy of the terminating order to the person in whose custody he is detained.

(3) Where a person subject to a banning order is released from custody and, in the case of a person who has not reported initially to a police station, is released more than five days before the expiry of the banning order, the person in whose custody he is shall (as soon as reasonably practicable) give notice of his release to the enforcing authority[2].

(4) References in this section to the clerk of a magistrates' court shall be construed in accordance with section 141 of the Magistrates' Courts Act 1980, reading references to that Act as references to this section.

(5) In relation to a person serving a sentence of imprisonment to which an intermittent custody order under section 183 of the Criminal Justice Act 2003 relates, any reference in this section to his detention or to his release shall be construed in accordance with section 14E(7).

[Football Spectators Act 1989, s 18 as amended by the Football Spectators Act 1989, s 1 and the Access to Justice Act 1999, Sch 13, the Football (Disorder) Act 2000, Sch 2, the Access to Justice Act 1999, Sch 13 and the Criminal Justice Act 2003, Sch 32.]

1. See the Football Spectators (Prescription) Order 2004, SI 2004/2409 which prescribes for these purposes the Football Banning Orders Authority and the Chief Executive of the Football Association Limited.

2. The Football Banning Orders Authority is prescribed as the enforcing authority for the purposes of Part II of this Act by the Football Spectators (Prescription) Order 2004, SI 2004/2409 which prescribes for these purposes the Football Banning Orders Authority.

Reporting

8–27806 **19. Functions of enforcing authority and local police.** (1) The enforcing authority[1] and the officer responsible for the police station at which he reports initially shall have the following functions as respects any person subject to a banning order.

(2) On a person reporting initially at the police station, the officer responsible for the station may make such requirements of that person as are determined by the enforcing authority[1] to be necessary or expedient for giving effect to the banning order, so far as relating to regulated football matches outside England and Wales.

(2A) If, in connection with any regulated football match outside England and Wales, the enforcing authority[1] is of the opinion that requiring any person subject to a banning order to report is necessary or expedient in order to reduce the likelihood of violence or disorder at or in connection with the match, the authority must give him a notice in writing under subsection (2B) below.

(2B) The notice must require that person—

(*a*) to report at a police station specified in the notice at the time, or between the times, specified in the notice,

(*b*) if the match is outside the United Kingdom and the order imposes a requirement as to the surrender by him of his passport, to surrender his passport at a police station specified in the notice at the time, or between the times, specified in the notice,

and may require him to comply with any additional requirements of the order in the manner specified in the notice.

(2C) In the case of any regulated football match, the enforcing authority[1] may by notice in writing require any person subject to a banning order to comply with any additional requirements of the order in the manner specified in the notice.

(2D) The enforcing authority[1] may establish criteria for determining whether any requirement under subsection (2B) or (2C) above ought to be imposed on any person or any class of person.

(2E) A notice under this section—

(*a*) may not require the person subject to the order to report except in the control period in relation to a regulated football match outside England and Wales or an external tournament,

(*b*) may not require him to surrender his passport except in the control period in relation to a regulated football match outside the United Kingdom or an external tournament which includes such matches.

(2F) Where a notice under this section requires the person subject to the order to surrender his passport, the passport must be returned to him as soon as reasonably practicable after the end of the control period in question.

(3) During the currency of a banning order in force in relation to any person the enforcing authority shall perform the following functions on the occasion of any regulated football match, that is to say—

(*a*) where the match is one for which reporting is obligatory for all persons subject to banning orders, the authority shall, by notice in writing to that person,

(i) require him to report to the police station specified in the notice at the time or between the times specified in the notice; and

(ii) require him to comply with the conditions (if any) imposed by the order;

(*b*) where the match is one for which reporting is obligatory for such persons only as are required to report under this paragraph, the authority shall, if that person is one as respects whom subsection (4) below is satisfied, by notice in writing to that person,

(i) require him to report to the police station specified in the notice at the time or between the times specified in the notice; and

(ii) require him to comply with the conditions (if any) imposed by the order;

(4) No requirements under subsection (3)(*b*) above shall be imposed by the enforcing authority on any person unless imposing them is, in their opinion, necessary or expedient in order to reduce the likelihood of violence or disorder at, or in connection with, the regulated football match; and the authority may establish criteria for determining whether requirements under that paragraph ought to be imposed on any person or class of person.

(5) The enforcing authority[1], in exercising their functions under this section shall have regard to any guidance issued by the Secretary of State under section 21 below.

(6) A person who, without reasonable excuse, fails to comply with any requirement imposed on him under subsection (2) above shall be guilty of an offence.

(7) A person guilty of an offence under subsection (6) above shall be liable on summary conviction to a fine not exceeding **level 2** on the standard scale.

[Football Spectators Act 1989, s 19, as amended by the Football (Offences and Disorder) Act 1999, ss 1 and 3 and the Football (Disorder) Act 2000, Schs 1 and 2.]

1. The Football Banning Orders Authority is prescribed as the enforcing authority for the purposes of Part II of this Act by the Football Spectators (Prescription) Order 2004, SI 2004/2409.

8–27807 20. Exemptions from requirement to report as respects a match[1]**.** (1) A person who is subject to a banning order may—

(*a*) as respects a particular regulated football match, or
(*b*) as respects regulated football matches played during a period,

apply to the authority empowered to grant exemptions under this section ("the exempting authority") to be exempt from the requirements imposed by or under this Part, or any of them as respects that match or matches played during that period.

(2) The enforcing authority[2] may grant exemptions under this section in all cases; but where the application is made during the control period in relation to any match to which the application applies, the officer responsible for a police station may grant the exemption as respects that match, subject to subsection (3) below.

(3) The officer responsible for a police station shall not grant an exemption without referring the question of exemption to the enforcing authority, unless he considers that it is not reasonably practicable to do so.

(4) The exempting authority shall exempt the applicant from the requirements imposed by or under this Part, or any of them, as respects any match or matches to which the application relates if he shows to the authority's satisfaction—

(*a*) that there are special circumstances which justify his being so exempted; and
(*b*) that, because of those circumstances, he would not attend the match or matches if he were so exempted.

(5) The exempting authority shall, in taking any decision under subsection (4) above, have regard to any guidance issued by the Secretary of State under section 21 below.

(6) Where an exemption is granted by the exempting authority to a person under subsection (4) above the banning order is to have effect subject to the exemption and, accordingly, no requirement is to be imposed under section 19 which is inconsistent with the exemption.

(7) A person who is aggrieved by the refusal of the exempting authority to grant him an exemption under subsection (4) above may, after giving the authority notice in writing of his intention to do so, appeal to a magistrates' court acting for the petty sessions area in which he resides.

(8) On any appeal under subsection (7) above the court may make such order as it thinks fit.

(9) The court may order the appellant to pay all or any part of the costs of an appeal under subsection (7) above.

(10) Any person commits an offence who, in connection with an application under this section to be exempted from the requirements imposed by or under this Part, or any of them—

(*a*) makes a statement which he knows to be false or misleading in a material particular or recklessly makes a statement which is false or misleading in a material particular, or
(*b*) produces, furnishes, signs or otherwise makes use of a document which he knows to be false or misleading in a material particular or recklessly produces, furnishes, signs or otherwise makes use of a document which is false or misleading in a material particular.

(11) A person guilty of an offence under subsection (10) above shall be liable on summary conviction to a fine not exceeding **level 3** on the standard scale.

[Football Spectators Act 1989, s 20, as amended by the Football (offences and Disorder) Act 1999. ss 1 and 3 and the Football (Disorder) Act 2000, Sch 2.]

1. See note 1 to s 14A above.
2. The Football Banning Orders Authority is prescribed as the enforcing authority for the purposes of Part II of this Act by the Football Spectators (Prescription) Order 2004, SI 2004/2409.

8–27808 21. Functions of enforcing authority: supplementary provisions. (1) The Secretary of State may issue to the enforcing authority[1] such guidance as he considers appropriate for the purposes of the exercise of their functions under sections 19 and 20 above.

(2) The Secretary of State shall make such arrangements as he considers appropriate for publishing the guidance issued from time to time under subsection (1) above.

(3) The Secretary of State may make regulations regulating the giving by the enforcing authority[1] to persons subject to banning orders of notices under section 19 above; and it shall be the duty of the enforcing authority to comply with the regulations.

(4) Regulations under subsection (3) above may exclude the operation of section 25 below.

(5) The power to make regulations under subsection (3) above is exercisable by statutory

instrument which shall be subject to annulment in pursuance of a resolution of either House of Parliament.

(6) Where any notice is given under section 19 above by the enforcing authority[1] in accordance with regulations under subsection (3) above, the notice shall be taken to have been received by the person to whom it was addressed unless he proves that he did not receive the notice and did not know and had no reasonable cause to believe requirements had been imposed on him under section 19 above.

(7) Where any notice is given under section 19 above by the enforcing authority[1] in accordance with section 25 below, subsection (6) above shall apply as it applies to such a notice given in accordance with regulations under subsection (3) above.

(8) The Secretary of State may pay to the enforcing authority[1] any expenses incurred by them in exercising their functions under sections 19 and 20 above.

[Football Spectators Act 1989, s 21, as amended by the Football (offences and Disorder) Act 1999, ss 1 and 3 and the Football (Disorder) Act 2000, Sch 1.]

1. The Football Banning Orders Authority is prescribed as the enforcing authority for the purposes of Part II of this Act by the Football Spectators (Prescription) Order 2000, SI 2000/2126.

8–27809 21A. Summary measures: detention[1]. (1) This section and section 21B below apply during any control period in relation to a regulated football match outside England and Wales or an external tournament if a constable in uniform—

(*a*) has reasonable grounds for suspecting that the condition in section 14B(2) above is met in the case of a person present before him, and

(*b*) has reasonable grounds to believe that making a banning order in his case would help to prevent violence or disorder at or in connection with any regulated football matches.

(2) The constable may detain the person in his custody (whether there or elsewhere) until he has decided whether or not to issue a notice under section 21B below, and shall give the person his reasons for detaining him in writing.

This is without prejudice to any power of the constable apart from this section to arrest the person.

(3) A person may not be detained under subsection (2) above for more than four hours or, with the authority of an officer of at least the rank of inspector, six hours.

(4) A person who has been detained under subsection (2) above may only be further detained under that subsection in the same control period in reliance on information which was not available to the constable who previously detained him; and a person on whom a notice has been served under section 21B(2) below may not be detained under subsection (2) above in the same control period.

[Football Spectators Act 1989, s 21A, as inserted by the Football (Disorder) Act 2000, Sch 1.]

1. Section 1 of the Football (Disorder) (Amendment) Act 2002 amended s 5 of the Amendment of Football (Disorder) Act 2000 to enable the exercise of powers under ss 21A and 21B (and the making of applications under s 14B) of the Football Spectators Act 1989 within the period of 5 years beginning with the day on which s 1 of the 2002 Act came into force. Section 1 came into force on August 28, 2002 (see Football (Disorder) (Amendment) Act 2002 (Commencement) Order 2002 (SI 2002/2200).

8–27810 21B. Summary measures: reference to a court[1]. (1) A constable in uniform may exercise the power in subsection (2) below if authorised to do so by an officer of at least the rank of inspector.

(2) The constable may give the person a notice in writing requiring him—

(*a*) to appear before a magistrates' court at a time, or between the times, specified in the notice,

(*b*) not to leave England and Wales before that time (or the later of those times), and

(*c*) if the control period relates to a regulated football match outside the United Kingdom or to an external tournament which includes such matches, to surrender his passport to the constable,

and stating the grounds referred to in section 21A(1) above.

(3) The times for appearance before the magistrates' court must be within the period of 24 hours beginning with—

(*a*) the giving of the notice, or

(*b*) the person's detention under section 21A(2) above,

whichever is the earlier.

(4) For the purposes of section 14B above, the notice is to be treated as an application[2] for a banning order made by complaint by the constable to the court in question and subsection (1) of that section is to have effect as if the references to the chief officer of police for the area in which the person resides or appears to reside were references to that constable.

(5) A constable may arrest a person to whom he is giving such a notice if he has reasonable grounds to believe that it is necessary to do so in order to secure that the person complies with the notice.

(6) Any passport surrendered by a person under this section must be returned to him in accordance with directions given by the court.

[Football Spectators Act 1989, s 21B, as inserted by the Football (Disorder) Act 2000, Sch 1.]

---

1. Section 1 of the Football (Disorder) (Amendment) Act 2002 amended s 5 of the Amendment of Football (Disorder) Act 2000 to enable the exercise of powers under ss 21A and 21B (and the making of applications under s 14B) of the Football Spectators Act 1989 within the period of 5 years beginning with the day on which s 1 of the 2002 Act came into force. Section 1 came into force on August 28, 2002 (see Football (Disorder) (Amendment) Act 2002 (Commencement) Order 2002 (SI 2002/2200).

2. Proceedings under s 21B of this Act are "criminal proceedings" for the purposes of s 12(2)(*g*) of the Access to Justice Act 1999 by virtue of reg 3 of the Criminal Defence Service (General) (No 2) Regulations 2001 (eligibility for criminal legal aid).

8–27811 **21C. Summary measures: supplementary.** (1) The powers conferred by sections 21A and 21B above may only be exercised in relation to a person who is a British citizen.

(2) A person who fails to comply with a notice given to him under section 21B above is guilty of an offence and liable on summary conviction to imprisonment for a term not exceeding six months, or a fine not exceeding level 5 on the standard scale, or both.

(3) Where a person to whom a notice has been given under section 21B above appears before a magistrates' court as required by the notice (whether under arrest or not), the court may remand him.

(4) A person who, by virtue of subsection (3) above, is remanded on bail under section 128 of the Magistrates' Courts Act 1980 may be required by the conditions of his bail—

(*a*) not to leave England and Wales before his appearance before the court, and

(*b*) if the control period relates to a regulated football match outside the United Kingdom or to an external tournament which includes such matches, to surrender his passport to a police constable, if he has not already done so.

[Football Spectators Act 1989, s 21C, as inserted by the Football (Disorder) Act 2000, Sch 1.]

8–27812 **21D. Summary measures: compensation.** (1) Where a person to whom a notice has been given under section 21B above appears before a magistrates' court and the court refuses the application for a banning order in respect of him, it may order compensation to be paid to him out of central funds if it is satisfied—

(*a*) that the notice should not have been given,

(*b*) that he has suffered loss as a result of the giving of the notice, and

(*c*) that, having regard to all the circumstances, it is appropriate to order the payment of compensation in respect of that loss.

(2) An appeal lies to the Crown Court against any refusal by a magistrates' court to order the payment of compensation under subsection (1) above.

(3) The compensation to be paid by order of the magistrates' court under subsection (1) above or by order of the Crown Court on an appeal under subsection (2) above shall not exceed £5,000 (but no appeal may be made under subsection (2) in respect of the amount of compensation awarded).

(4) If it appears to the Secretary of State that there has been a change in the value of money since the coming into force of this section or, as the case may be, the last occasion when the power conferred by this subsection was exercised, he may by order substitute for the amount specified in subsection (3) above such other amount as appears to him to be justified by the change.

(5) In this section, "central funds" has the same meaning as in enactments providing for the payment of costs[1].

[Football Spectators Act 1989, s 21C, as inserted by the Football (Disorder) Act 2000, Sch 1.]

---

1. Proceedings under s 21D of this Act are "criminal proceedings" for the purposes of s 12(2)(*g*) of the Access to Justice Act 1999 by virtue of reg 3 of the Criminal Defence Service (General) (No 2) Regulations 2001 (eligibility for criminal legal aid).

Relevant offences outside England and Wales

8–27813 **22. Banning orders arising out of offences outside England and Wales.** (1) Her Majesty may, by Order[1] in Council, specify offences ("corresponding offences") under the law of any country outside England and Wales which appear to Her to correspond to any offence to which Schedule 1 to this Act applies.

(1A) For the purposes of subsection (1) above, an offence specified in an Order in Council under that subsection shall be regarded as corresponding to an offence to which Schedule 1 to this Act applies notwithstanding that any period specified in the Order is longer than any corresponding period specified in that Schedule.

(2) Upon an information being laid before a justice of the peace for any area that a person who resides or is believed to reside in that area has been convicted of a corresponding offence in a country outside England and Wales, the justice may—

(*a*) issue a summons directed to that person requiring him to appear before a magistrates' court for that area to answer to the information; or

(*b*) subject to subsection (3) below, issue a warrant to arrest that person and bring him before a magistrates' court for that area.

(3) No warrant shall be issued under subsection (2) above unless the information is in writing and substantiated on oath.

(4) Where a person appears or is brought before a magistrates' court in pursuance of subsection (2) above, the court, if satisfied that—

(*a*) he is ordinarily resident in England and Wales, and

(*b*) has been convicted in the country outside England and Wales of the corresponding offence,

may, unless it appears that the conviction is the subject of proceedings in a court of law in that country questioning the conviction, make a banning order in relation to him.

(5) A magistrates' court which has power to make a banning order in relation to a person shall be under a duty to make the order in relation to him if it is satisfied that there are reasonable grounds to believe that making the order would help to prevent violence or disorder at or in connection with regulated football matches.

(5A) Where a magistrates' court has power to make a banning order in relation to a person but does not do so, it shall state in open court that it is not satisfied that there are such reasonable grounds as are mentioned in subsection (5) above and give reasons why it is not satisfied.

(6) In proceedings under subsection (4) above, the court shall have the like powers, including power to adjourn the proceedings and meanwhile to remand the defendant on bail (but not in custody), and the proceedings shall be conducted as nearly as may be in the like manner, as if the proceedings were the trial of an information for a summary offence.

(7) Any person aggrieved by the decision of a magistrates' court making a banning order under this section may appeal to the Crown Court against the decision.

(8) Sections 14E to 14J and 18 to 21 shall apply in relation to a person subject to a banning order under this section as they apply in relation to a person subject to a banning order made by a magistrates' court under section 14A.

(9) An Order in Council under subsection (1) above relating to any country may include provision specifying the documentary form in which details are to be given of—

(*a*) the conviction of a person in that country of a corresponding offence,

(*b*) the nature and circumstances of the offence, and

(*c*) whether or not the conviction is the subject of proceedings in that country questioning it.

(10) A document in the form so specified—

(*a*) shall be admissible in any proceedings under this Part of this Act as evidence of the facts stated in it unless the contrary is proved, and

(*b*) shall be taken as such a document unless the contrary is proved.

(11) In proceedings against a person under this section, the facts stated in a document in the form so specified shall, on production of the document and proof that that person is the person whose conviction is set out in the document, be taken to be proved unless the contrary is proved.

(12) Any statutory instrument containing an Order under subsection (1) above shall be subject to annulment in pursuance of a resolution of either House of Parliament.

[Football Spectators Act 1989, s 22, as amended by the Football (Offences and Disorder) Act 1999, ss 1, 3.and 5 and the Football (Disorder) Act 2000, Sch 2.]

1. Orders have been made in respect of Italy (SI 1990/992 amended by SI 1992/1724, Scotland (see post)), Sweden (SI 1992/708 amended by SI 1992/1724), Norway (SI 1996/1634), Republic of Ireland (SI 1996/1635), France (SI 1998/1266), Belgium (SI 2000/1108) and the Netherlands (SI 2000/1109).

8–27814 22A. Other interpretation, etc. (1) In this Part—

"British citizen" has the same meaning as in the British Nationality Act 1981,

"country" includes territory,

"declaration of relevance" has the same meaning as in section 7,

"enforcing authority" means a prescribed organisation established by the Secretary of State under section 57 of the Police Act 1996 (central police organisations),

"passport" means a United Kingdom passport within the meaning of the Immigration Act 1971,

"prescribed" means prescribed by an order made by the Secretary of State.

(2) The Secretary of State may, if he considers it necessary or expedient to do so in order to secure the effective enforcement of this Part, by order provide for section 14(5) and (6) above to have effect in relation to any, or any description of, regulated football match or external tournament as if, for any reference to five days, there were substituted a reference to the number of days (not exceeding ten) specified in the order.

(3) Any power of the Secretary of State to make an order under this Part is exercisable by statutory instrument.

(4) An instrument containing an order made by the Secretary of State under this Part shall be subject to annulment in pursuance of a resolution of either House of Parliament.
[Football Spectators Act 1989, s 22A, as inserted by the Football (Disorder) Act 2000, Sch 2.]

Part III[1]
General

8–27815 23. Further provision about, and appeals against, declarations of relevance. (1) Subject to subsection (2) below, a court may not make a declaration of relevance as respects any offence unless it is satisfied that the prosecutor gave notice to the defendant, at least five days before the first day of the trial, that it was proposed to show that the offence related to football matches, to a particular football match or to particular football matches (as the case may be).

(2) A court may, in any particular case, make a declaration of relevance notwithstanding that notice to the defendant as required by subsection (1) above has not been given if he consents to waive the giving of full notice or the court is satisfied that the interests of justice do not require more notice to be given.

(3) A person convicted of an offence as respects which the court makes a declaration of relevance may appeal against the making of the declaration of relevance as if the declaration were included in any sentence passed on him for the offence, and accordingly—

(*a*)–(*c*) *amendments*.

(4) A banning order made upon a person's conviction of a relevant offence shall be quashed if the making of a declaration of relevance as respects that offence is reversed on appeal.
[Football Spectators Act 1989, s 23, as amended by the Football (Offences and Disorder) Act 1999, ss 1 and 2 and the Football (Disorder) Act 2000, Sch 2.]

1. Part III contains ss 23–27.

8–27816 24. Offences by bodies corporate. (1) Where an offence under this Act which has been committed by a body corporate is proved to have been committed with the consent or connivance of, or to be attributable to any neglect on the part of, a director, manager, secretary or similar officer of the body corporate, or any person purporting to act in that capacity, he, as well as the body corporate, shall be guilty of that offence and be liable to be proceeded against and punished accordingly.

(2) Where the affairs of a body corporate are managed by its members, subsection (1) above shall apply to the acts and defaults of a member in connection with his functions of management as if he were a director of the body corporate.
[Football Spectators Act 1989, s 24.]

8–27817 25. Service of documents. (1) Any notice or other document required or authorised by or by virtue of this Act to be served on any person may be served on him either by delivering it to him or by leaving it at his proper address or by sending it by post.

(2) Any notice or other document so required or authorised to be served on a body corporate or a firm shall be duly served if it is served on the secretary or clerk of that body or a partner of that firm.

(3) For the purposes of this section, and of section 7 of the Interpretation Act 1978 in its application to this section, the proper address of a person, in the case of a secretary or clerk of a body corporate, shall be that of the registered office or principal office of that body, in the case of a partner of a firm shall be that of the principal office of the firm, and in any other case shall be the last known address of the person to be served.

(4) This section, and the said section 7 in its application to this section, is subject to section 21(4) and (7) above.
[Football Spectators Act 1989, s 25.]

8–27818 26. *Financial provision.*

8–27819 27. Citation, commencement, consequential repeal and extent. (1) This Act may be cited as the Football Spectators Act 1989.

(2) The provisions of this Act (other than this section) shall not come into operation until such day as the Secretary of State may appoint by order[1] made by statutory instrument.

(3) Different days may be appointed under subsection (2) above for different provisions of this Act.

(4) A statutory instrument appointing a commencement date for section 3 or section 13 above shall be subject to annulment in pursuance of a resolution of either House of Parliament.

(4A) Any power of Her Majesty to make an Order in Council under this Act, and any power of the Secretary of State to make regulations or an order under this Act, may be exercised so as to make different provision for different purposes

(5) Sections 35 and 37 of the Public Order Act 1986 (which provide for exclusion orders) shall cease to have effect on the date appointed under subsection (2) above for the commencement of section 2 of this Act.

(6) This Act, except paragraph 14 of Schedule 2, extends to England and Wales only.

[Football Spectators Act 1989, s 27, as amended by the Football (Offences and Disorder) Act 1999, s 6 and the Football (Disorder) Act 2000, Sch 2.]

---

1. The Football Spectators Act 1989 (Commencement No 1) Order 1990/690, the Football Spectators Act 1989 (Commencement No 2) Order 1990, SI 1990/926, the Football Spectators Act 1989 (Commencement No 3) Order 1991, SI 1991/1071 and the Football Spectators Act 1989 (Commencement No 4) Order 1993, SI 1993/1690 have been made.

SCHEDULES

8–27820

Sections 7(5), 14(5) and 22(1)

SCHEDULE 1
RELEVANT OFFENCES

(*As substituted by the Football (Disorder) Act 2000, Sch 1.*)

1. This Schedule applies to the following offences:

(*a*) any offence under section 2(1), 5(7), 14J(1) or 21C(2) of this Act,

(*b*) any offence under section 2 or 2A of the Sporting Events (Control of Alcohol etc) Act 1985[1] (alcohol, containers and fireworks) committed by the accused at any football match to which this Schedule applies or while entering or trying to enter the ground,

(*c*) any offence under section 5 of the Public Order Act 1986[2] (harassment, alarm or distress) or any provision of Part III of that Act (racial hatred) committed during a period relevant to a football match to which this Schedule applies at any premises while the accused was at, or was entering or leaving or trying to enter or leave, the premises,

(*d*) any offence involving the use or threat of violence by the accused towards another person committed during a period relevant to a football match to which this Schedule applies at any premises while the accused was at, or was entering or leaving or trying to enter or leave, the premises,

(*e*) any offence involving the use or threat of violence towards property committed during a period relevant to a football match to which this Schedule applies at any premises while the accused was at, or was entering or leaving or trying to enter or leave, the premises,

(*f*) any offence involving the use, carrying or possession of an offensive weapon or a firearm committed during a period relevant to a football match to which this Schedule applies at any premises while the accused was at, or was entering or leaving or trying to enter or leave, the premises,

(*g*) any offence under section 12 of the Licensing Act 1872[1] (persons found drunk in public places, etc) of being found drunk in a highway or other public place committed while the accused was on a journey to or from a football match to which this Schedule applies being an offence as respects which the court makes a declaration that the offence related to football matches,

(*h*) any offence under section 91(1) of the Criminal Justice Act 1967[1] (disorderly behaviour while drunk in a public place) committed in a highway or other public place while the accused was on a journey to or from a football match to which this Schedule applies being an offence as respects which the court makes a declaration that the offence related to football matches,

(*j*) any offence under section 1 of the Sporting Events (Control of Alcohol etc) Act 1985[1] (alcohol on coaches or trains to or from sporting events) committed while the accused was on a journey to or from a football match to which this Schedule applies being an offence as respects which the court makes a declaration that the offence related to football matches,

(*k*) any offence under section 5 of the Public Order Act 1986[2] (harassment, alarm or distress) or any provision of Part III of that Act (racial hatred) committed while the accused was on a journey to or from a football match to which this Schedule applies being an offence as respects which the court makes a declaration that the offence related to football matches,

(*l*) any offence under section 4 or 5 of the Road Traffic Act 1988[3] (driving etc when under the influence of drink or drugs or with an alcohol concentration above the prescribed limit) committed while the accused was on a journey to or from a football match to which this Schedule applies being an offence as respects which the court makes a declaration that the offence related to football matches,

(*m*) any offence involving the use or threat of violence by the accused towards another person committed while one or each of them was on a journey to or from a football match to which this Schedule applies being an offence as respects which the court makes a declaration that the offence related to football matches,

(*n*) any offence involving the use or threat of violence towards property committed while the accused was on a journey to or from a football match to which this Schedule applies being an offence as respects which the court makes a declaration that the offence related to football matches,

(*o*) any offence involving the use, carrying or possession of an offensive weapon or a firearm committed while the accused was on a journey to or from a football match to which this Schedule applies being an offence as respects which the court makes a declaration that the offence related to football matches,

(*p*) any offence under the Football (Offences) Act 1991,

(*q*) any offence under section 5 of the Public Order Act 1986 (harassment, alarm or distress) or any provision of Part III of that Act (racial hatred)—

(i) which does not fall within paragraph (*c*) or (*k*) above,

(ii) which was committed during a period relevant to a football match to which this Schedule applies, and

(iii) as respects which the court makes a declaration that the offence related to that match or to that match and any other football match which took place during that period,

(*r*) any offence involving the use or threat of violence by the accused towards another person—

(i) which does not fall within paragraph (*d*) or (*m*) above,

(ii) which was committed during a period relevant to a football match to which this Schedule applies, and

(iii) as respects which the court makes a declaration that the offence related to that match or to that match and any other football match which took place during that period, (*s*) any offence involving the use or threat of violence towards property—

(i) which does not fall within paragraph (e) or (n) above,
(ii) which was committed during a period relevant to a football match to which this Schedule applies, and
(iii) as respects which the court makes a declaration that the offence related to that match or to that match and any other football match which took place during that period,

(*t*) any offence involving the use, carrying or possession of an offensive weapon or a firearm—

(i) which does not fall within paragraph (*f*) or (*o*) above,
(ii) which was committed during a period relevant to a football match to which this Schedule applies, and
(iii) as respects which the court makes a declaration that the offence related to that match or to that match and any other football match which took place during that period.

(*u*) any offence under section 166 of the Criminal Justice and Public Order Act 1994 (sale of tickets by unauthorised persons) which relates to tickets for a football match.

2. Any reference to an offence in paragraph 1 above includes—

(*a*) a reference to any attempt, conspiracy or incitement to commit that offence, and
(*b*) a reference to aiding and abetting, counselling or procuring the commission of that offence.

3. For the purposes of paragraphs 1(*g*) to (*o*) above—

(*a*) a person may be regarded as having been on a journey to or from a football match to which this Schedule applies whether or not he attended or intended to attend the match, and
(*b*) a person's journey includes breaks (including overnight breaks).

4. In this Schedule, "football match" means a match which is a regulated football match for the purposes of Part II of this Act.

(2) Section 1(8) and (8A) above apply for the interpretation of references to periods relevant to football matches.

---

1. See PART VI: LICENSING, ante.
2. See title PUBLIC MEETING AND PUBLIC ORDER, in this PART, post.
3. See PART VII: title ROAD TRAFFIC, ante.

8–27821

Section 8

SCHEDULE 2
THE FOOTBALL LICENSING AUTHORITY: SUPPLEMENTARY PROVISIONS

1–28. *Supplementary provisions relating to status of the licensing authority, appointment of members, proceedings of the authority, officers, and accounts and audit.*

Authentication of licensing authority's seal

29. The application of the seal of the licensing authority shall be authenticated by the signature of the chairman of the authority or some other person authorised by the authority to act for that purpose and that of one other member.

Presumption of authenticity of documents issued by licensing authority

30. Any document purporting to be an instrument issued by the licensing authority and to be sealed in accordance with paragraph 29 above, or to be signed on behalf of the authority, shall be received in evidence and shall be deemed to be such an instrument without further proof unless the contrary is shown.

Football (Offences) Act 1991
(1991 c 19)

8–27822 1. Regulated football matches. (1) In this Act a "regulated football match" means an association football match designated, or of a description designated[1], for the purposes of this Act by order of the Secretary of State.

Any such order shall be made by statutory instrument which shall be subject to annulment in pursuance of a resolution of either House of Parliament.

(2) References in this Act to things done at a regulated football match include anything done at the ground—

(*a*) within the period beginning two hours before the start of the match or (if earlier) two hours before the time at which it is advertised to start and ending one hour after the end of the match; or
(*b*) where the match is advertised to start at a particular time on a particular day but does not take place on that day, within the period beginning two hours before and ending one hour after the advertised starting time.

[Football (Offences) Act 1991, s 1.]

---

1. The Football (Offences) (Designation of Football Matches) Order 2004, SI 2004/2410 designates football matches for the purpose of this Act. A designated football match is an association football match in which one or both of the participating teams represents a club which is for the time being a member (whether a full or associate member) of the

Football League, the Football Association Premier League, the Football Conference or the League of Wales, or represents a country or territory.

8–27823 **2. Throwing of missiles.** It is an offence for a person at a regulated football match to throw anything at or towards—

(*a*) the playing area, or any area adjacent to the playing area to which spectators are not generally admitted, or

(*b*) any area in which spectators or other persons are or may be present,

without lawful authority or lawful excuse (which shall be for him to prove).
[Football (Offences) Act 1991, s 2.]

8–27824 **3. Indecent or racialist chanting.** (1) It is an offence to engage or take part in chanting of an indecent or racialist nature at a regulated football match.

(2) For this purpose—

(*a*) "chanting" means the repeated uttering of any words or sounds (whether alone or in concert with one or more others); and

(*b*) "of a racialist nature" means consisting of or including matter which is threatening, abusive or insulting to a person by reason of his colour, race, nationality (including citizenship) or ethnic or national origins[1].

[Football (Offences) Act 1991, s 3 as amended by the Football (Offences and Disorder Act 1999 s 9.]

---

1. Although the use of the word "Paki" must, be considered on a case-by-case basis in the context in which it is used, as a slang expression the modern common understanding of the term is that it is racially offensive. Furthermore, it is immaterial whether persons of the racial group referred to in the offending words are present or, if present, are offended or affected in any way by them. Therefore the chanting by the accused of the words "You're just a town full of Pakis" at supporters of Oldham Athletic was of a racialist nature (*DPP v Stoke on Trent Magistrates' Court* [2003] EWHC 1593 (Admin), [2003] 3 All ER 1086, 167 JP 436, [2003] Crim LR 804).

8–27825 **4. Going onto the playing area.** It is an offence for a person at a regulated football match to go onto the playing area, or any area adjacent to the playing area to which spectators are not generally admitted, without lawful authority or lawful excuse (which shall be for him to prove).
[Football (Offences) Act 1991, s 4.]

8–27826 **5. Supplementary provisions.** (1) *Repealed.*

(2) A person guilty of an offence under this Act is liable on summary conviction to a fine not exceeding **level 3** on the standard scale.

(3) *Repealed.*

[Football (Offences) Act 1991, s 5 as amended by the Football (Disorder) Act 2000, Sch 3 and the Serious Organised Crime and Police Act 2005, Sch 17.]

8–27827 **6.** Short title, commencement and extent.

Confiscation of Alcohol (Young Persons) Act 1997

(1997 c 33)

8–27830 **1. Confiscation of intoxicating liquor.** (1) Where a constable reasonably suspects that a person in a relevant place is in possession of alcohol and that either—

(*a*) he is under the age of 18; or

(*b*) he intends that any of the alcohol should be consumed by a person under the age of 18 in that or any other relevant place; or

(*c*) a person under the age of 18 who is, or has recently been, with him has recently consumed alcohol in that or any other relevant place,

the constable may require him to surrender anything in his possession which is, or which the constable reasonably believes to be, alcohol or a container for alcohol (other than a sealed container) and to state his name and address.

(1A) But a constable may not under subsection (1) require a person to surrender any sealed container unless the constable reasonably believes that the person is, or has been, consuming, or intends to consume, alcohol in any relevant place.

(2) A constable may dispose of anything surrendered to him under subsection (1) in such manner as he considers appropriate.

(3) A person who fails without reasonable excuse to comply with a requirement imposed on him under subsection (1) commits an offence and is liable on summary conviction to a fine not exceeding **level 2** on the standard scale.

(4) A constable who imposes a requirement on a person under subsection (1) shall inform him of his suspicion and that failing without reasonable excuse to comply with a requirement imposed under that subsection is an offence.

(5) A constable may arrest without warrant a person who fails to comply with a requirement imposed on him under subsection (1).

(6) In subsection (1) and (1A) "relevant place", in relation to a person, means—

(*a*) any public place, other than licensed premises; or
(*b*) any place, other than a public place, to which the person has unlawfully gained access;

and for this purpose a place is a public place if at the material time the public or any section of the public has access to it, on payment or otherwise, as of right or by virtue of express or implied permission.

(7) In this section—

"alcohol"—

(*a*) in relation to England and Wales, has the same meaning as in the Licensing Act 2003;
(*b*) in relation to Northern Ireland, has the same meaning as "intoxicating liquor" in the Licensing (Northern Ireland) Order 1996; and

"licensed premises"—

(*a*) in relation to England and Wales, means premises which may by virtue of Part 3 or Part 5 of the Licensing Act 2003 (premises licence; permitted temporary activity) be used for the supply of alcohol within the meaning of section 14 of that Act;
(*b*) in relation to Northern Ireland, has the same meaning as in the Licensing (Northern Ireland) Order 1996.

[Confiscation of Alcohol (Young Persons) Act 1997, s 1 as amended by the Criminal Justice and Police Act 2001, s 29 and the Licensing Act 2003, Sch 6.]

8–27831 **2. Short title, commencement and extent.** (1) This Act may be cited as the Confiscation of Alcohol (Young Persons) Act 1997.

(2) Section 1 shall not come into force until such day as the Secretary of State may by order[1] made by statutory instrument appoint.

(3) This Act extends to England and Wales and Northern Ireland.

[Confiscation of Alcohol (Young Persons) Act 1997, s 2.]

---

1. Section 1 came into force on 1 August 1997 (SI 1997/1725).

Serious Organised Crime and Police Act 2005

(2005 c 15)

PART 4[1]

PUBLIC ORDER AND CONDUCT IN PUBLIC PLACES ETC

Harassment

8–27835 **125. Harassment intended to deter lawful activities.** *Amends the Protection from Harassment Act 1997.*

---

1. Part 4 comprises ss 125–144 and Sch 10. Other provisions of this Act are reproduced in PART I: MAGISTRATES' COURTS, PROCEDURE, ante. Of the provisions referred to here, all were brought into force on 1 July 2005 (s 132(1)–(6) 1 August 2005). The following were not in force: 135–137, 144 and Sch 10.

126. Harassment etc of a person in his home. *Inserts s 42A into the Criminal Justice and Police Act 2001.*

127. Harassment etc: police direction to stay away from person's home. *Amends s 42 of the Criminal Justice and Police Act 2001.*

Trespass on designated site

8–27836 **128. Offence of trespassing on designated site.** (1) A person commits an offence if he enters, or is on, any designated site in England and Wales or Northern Ireland as a trespasser.

(2) A "designated site" means a site—

(a) specified or described (in any way) in an order[1] made by the Secretary of State, and
(b) designated for the purposes of this section by the order[1].

(3) The Secretary of State may only designate a site for the purposes of this section if—

(a) it is comprised in Crown land; or
(b) it is comprised in land belonging to Her Majesty in Her private capacity or to the immediate heir to the Throne in his private capacity; or
(c) it appears to the Secretary of State that it is appropriate to designate the site in the interests of national security.

(4) It is a defence for a person charged with an offence under this section to prove that he did not know, and had no reasonable cause to suspect, that the site in relation to which the offence is alleged to have been committed was a designated site.

(5) A person guilty of an offence under this section is liable on summary conviction—

(a) to imprisonment for a term not exceeding 51 weeks[2], or
(b) to a fine not exceeding level 5 on the standard scale,

or to both.

(6) No proceedings for an offence under this section may be instituted against any person—

(a) in England and Wales, except by or with the consent of the Attorney General, or
(b) in Northern Ireland, except by or with the consent of the Attorney General for Northern Ireland.

(7) For the purposes of this section a person who is on any designated site as a trespasser does not cease to be a trespasser by virtue of being allowed time to leave the site.

(8) In this section—

(a) "site" means the whole or part of any building or buildings, or any land, or both;
(b) "Crown land" means land in which there is a Crown interest or a Duchy interest.

(9) For this purpose—

"Crown interest" means an interest belonging to Her Majesty in right of the Crown, and
"Duchy interest" means an interest belonging to Her Majesty in right of the Duchy of Lancaster or belonging to the Duchy of Cornwall.

(10) In the application of this section to Northern Ireland, the reference to 51 weeks in subsection (5)(a) is to be read as a reference to 6 months.
[Serious Organised Crime and Police Act 2005, s 128.]

1. The Serious Organised Crime and Police Act 2005 (Designated Sites) Order 2005, SI 2005/3447 has been made.
2. In relation to an offence committed before the commencement of s 281(5) of the Criminal Justice Act 2003 this is to be read as a reference to "6 months", s 175(3), post.

129. Corresponding Scottish offence

8–27837 **130. Designated sites: powers of arrest.** *(Spent in so far as this section applies to England and Wales).*

8–27838 **131. Designated sites: access.** (1) The following provisions do not apply to land in respect of which a designation order is in force—

(a) section 2(1) of the Countryside and Rights of Way Act 2000 (c 37) (rights of public in relation to access land),
(b) Part III of the Countryside (Northern Ireland) Order 1983 (SI 1983/1895 (NI 18)) (access to open country), and
(c) section 1 of the Land Reform (Scotland) Act 2003 (asp 2) (access rights).

(2) The Secretary of State may take such steps as he considers appropriate to inform the public of the effect of any designation order, including, in particular, displaying notices on or near the site to which the order relates.

(3) But the Secretary of State may only—

(a) display any such notice, or
(b) take any other steps under subsection (2),

in or on any building or land, if the appropriate person consents.

(4) The "appropriate person" is—

(a) a person appearing to the Secretary of State to have a sufficient interest in the building or land to consent to the notice being displayed or the steps being taken, or
(b) a person acting on behalf of such a person.

(5) In this section a "designation order" means—

(a) in relation to England and Wales or Northern Ireland, an order under section 128, or
(b) in relation to Scotland, an order under section 129.

[Serious Organised Crime and Police Act 2005, s 131.]

Demonstrations in vicinity of Parliament[1]

8–27839 **132. Demonstrating without authorisation in designated area.** (1) Any person who—

(a) organises a demonstration in a public place in the designated area, or
(b) takes part in a demonstration in a public place in the designated area, or

(c) carries on a demonstration by himself in a public place in the designated area,

is guilty of an offence if, when the demonstration starts, authorisation for the demonstration has not been given under section 134(2).

(2) It is a defence for a person accused of an offence under subsection (1) to show that he reasonably believed that authorisation had been given.

(3) Subsection (1) does not apply if the demonstration is—

(a) a public procession of which notice is required to be given under subsection (1) of section 11 of the Public Order Act 1986 (c 64), or of which (by virtue of subsection (2) of that section) notice is not required to be given, or

(b) a public procession for the purposes of section 12 or 13 of that Act.

(4) Subsection (1) also does not apply in relation to any conduct which is lawful under section 220 of the Trade Union and Labour Relations (Consolidation) Act 1992 (c 52).

(5) If subsection (1) does not apply by virtue of subsection (3) or (4), nothing in sections 133 to 136 applies either.

(6) Section 14 of the Public Order Act 1986 (imposition of conditions on public assemblies) does not apply in relation to a public assembly which is also a demonstration in a public place in the designated area.

(7) In this section and in sections 133 to 136—

(a) "the designated area" means the area specified in an order under section 138,

(b) "public place" means any highway or any place to which at the material time the public or any section of the public has access, on payment or otherwise, as of right or by virtue of express or implied permission,

(c) references to any person organising a demonstration include a person participating in its organisation,

(d) references to any person organising a demonstration do not include a person carrying on a demonstration by himself,

(e) references to any person or persons taking part in a demonstration (except in subsection (1) of this section) include a person carrying on a demonstration by himself.

[Serious Organised Crime and Police Act 2005, s 132.]

1. The provisions of ss 132–138 do not apply to demonstrations continuing at the date of implementation of these provisions as articles 3(5) and 4(2) of the Serious Organized Crime and Police Act 2005 (Commencement No 1, Transitional and Transitory Provisions) Order 2005, SI 2005/1521 purporting to apply to "continuing" demonstrations were ultra vires (*R (Haw) v Secretary of State for the Home Department* [2005] EWHC 2061 (Admin), [2006] 2 WLR 50).

8–27840 **133. Notice of demonstrations in designated area.** (1) A person seeking authorisation for a demonstration in the designated area must give written notice to that effect to the Commissioner of Police of the Metropolis (referred to in this section and section 134 as "the Commissioner").

(2) The notice must be given—

(a) if reasonably practicable, not less than 6 clear days before the day on which the demonstration is to start, or

(b) if that is not reasonably practicable, then as soon as it is, and in any event not less than 24 hours before the time the demonstration is to start.

(3) The notice must be given—

(a) if the demonstration is to be carried on by more than one person, by any of the persons organising it,

(b) if it is to be carried on by a person by himself, by that person.

(4) The notice must state—

(a) the date and time when the demonstration is to start,

(b) the place where it is to be carried on,

(c) how long it is to last,

(d) whether it is to be carried on by a person by himself or not,

(e) the name and address of the person giving the notice.

(5) A notice under this section must be given by—

(a) delivering it to a police station in the metropolitan police district, or

(b) sending it by post by recorded delivery to such a police station.

(6) Section 7 of the Interpretation Act 1978 (c 30) (under which service of a document is deemed to have been effected at the time it would be delivered in the ordinary course of post) does not apply to a notice under this section.

[Serious Organised Crime and Police Act 2005, s 133.]

8–27841 **134. Authorisation of demonstrations in designated area.** (1) This section applies if a notice complying with the requirements of section 133 is received at a police station in the metropolitan police district by the time specified in section 133(2).

(2) The Commissioner must give authorisation for the demonstration to which the notice relates.

(3) In giving authorisation, the Commissioner may impose on the persons organising or taking part in the demonstration such conditions specified in the authorisation and relating to the demonstration as in the Commissioner's reasonable opinion are necessary for the purpose of preventing any of the following—

(a) hindrance to any person wishing to enter or leave the Palace of Westminster,
(b) hindrance to the proper operation of Parliament,
(c) serious public disorder,
(d) serious damage to property,
(e) disruption to the life of the community,
(f) a security risk in any part of the designated area,
(g) risk to the safety of members of the public (including any taking part in the demonstration).

(4) The conditions may, in particular, impose requirements as to—

(a) the place where the demonstration may, or may not, be carried on,
(b) the times at which it may be carried on,
(c) the period during which it may be carried on,
(d) the number of persons who may take part in it,
(e) the number and size of banners or placards used,
(f) maximum permissible noise levels.

(5) The authorisation must specify the particulars of the demonstration given in the notice under section 133 pursuant to subsection (4) of that section, with any modifications made necessary by any condition imposed under subsection (3) of this section.

(6) The Commissioner must give notice in writing of—

(a) the authorisation,
(b) any conditions imposed under subsection (3), and
(c) the particulars mentioned in subsection (5),

to the person who gave the notice under section 133.

(7) Each person who takes part in or organises a demonstration in the designated area is guilty of an offence if—

(a) he knowingly fails to comply with a condition imposed under subsection (3) which is applicable to him (except where it is varied under section 135), or
(b) he knows or should have known that the demonstration is carried on otherwise than in accordance with the particulars set out in the authorisation by virtue of subsection (5).

(8) It is a defence for a person accused of an offence under subsection (7) to show—

(a) (in a paragraph (a) case) that the failure to comply, or
(b) (in a paragraph (b) case) that the divergence from the particulars,

arose from circumstances beyond his control, or from something done with the agreement, or by the direction, of a police officer.

(9) The notice required by subsection (6) may be sent by post to the person who gave the notice under section 133 at the address stated in that notice pursuant to subsection (4)(e) of that section.

(10) If the person to whom the notice required by subsection (6) is to be given has agreed, it may be sent to him by email or by facsimile transmission at the address or number notified by him for the purpose to the Commissioner (and a notice so sent is "in writing" for the purposes of that subsection).
[Serious Organised Crime and Police Act 2005, s 134.]

8–27842 **135. Supplementary directions.** (1) This section applies if the senior police officer reasonably believes that it is necessary, in order to prevent any of the things mentioned in paragraphs (a) to (g) of subsection (3) of section 134—

(a) to impose additional conditions on those taking part in or organising a demonstration authorised under that section, or
(b) to vary any condition imposed under that subsection or under paragraph (a) (including such a condition as varied under subsection (2)).

(2) The senior police office may give directions to those taking part in or organising the demonstration imposing such additional conditions or varying any such condition already imposed.

(3) A person taking part in or organising the demonstration who knowingly fails to comply with a condition which is applicable to him and which is imposed or varied by a direction under this section is guilty of an offence.

(4) It is a defence for him to show that the failure to comply arose from circumstances beyond his control.

(5) In this section, "the senior police officer" means the most senior in rank of the police officers present at the scene (or any one of them if there are more than one of the same rank).
[Serious Organised Crime and Police Act 2005, s 135.]

8–27843 **136. Offences under sections 132 to 135: penalties.** (1) A person guilty of an offence under section 132(1)(a) is liable on summary conviction to imprisonment for a term not exceeding 51 weeks[1], to a fine not exceeding level 4 on the standard scale, or to both.

(2) A person guilty of an offence under section 132(1)(b) or (c) is liable on summary conviction to a fine not exceeding level 3 on the standard scale.

(3) A person guilty of an offence under section 134(7) or 135(3) is liable on summary conviction—

(a) if the offence was in relation to his capacity as organiser of the demonstration, to imprisonment for a term not exceeding 51 weeks[1], to a fine not exceeding level 4 on the standard scale, or to both,

(b) otherwise, to a fine not exceeding level 3 on the standard scale.

(4) A person who is guilty of the offence of inciting another to—

(a) do anything which would constitute an offence mentioned in subsection (1), (2) or (3), or

(b) fail to do anything where the failure would constitute such an offence,

is liable on summary conviction to imprisonment for a term not exceeding 51 weeks[1], to a fine not exceeding level 4 on the standard scale, or to both, notwithstanding section 45(3) of the Magistrates' Courts Act 1980 (c 43).

(5) *A constable in uniform may arrest without warrant anyone he reasonably believes is committing an offence mentioned in subsections (1) to (4).*

This subsection ceases to have effect on the coming into force of section 110.

[Serious Organised Crime and Police Act 2005, s 136.]

---

1. In relation to an offence committed before the commencement of s 281(5) of the Criminal Justice Act 2003 this is to be read as a reference to "3 months", s 175(3), post.

8–27844 **137. Loudspeakers in designated area.** (1) Subject to subsection (2), a loudspeaker shall not be operated, at any time or for any purpose, in a street in the designated area.

(2) Subsection (1) does not apply to the operation of a loudspeaker—

(a) in case of emergency,

(b) for police, fire and rescue authority or ambulance purposes,

(c) by the Environment Agency, a water undertaker or a sewerage undertaker in the exercise of any of its functions,

(d) by a local authority within its area,

(e) for communicating with persons on a vessel for the purpose of directing the movement of that or any other vessel,

(f) if the loudspeaker forms part of a public telephone system,

(g) if the loudspeaker is in or fixed to a vehicle and subsection (3) applies,

(h) otherwise than on a highway, by persons employed in connection with a transport undertaking used by the public, but only if the loudspeaker is operated solely for making announcements to passengers or prospective passengers or to other persons so employed,

(i) in accordance with a consent granted by a local authority under Schedule 2 to the Noise and Statutory Nuisance Act 1993 (c 40).

(3) This subsection applies if the loudspeaker referred to in subsection (2)(g)—

(a) is operated solely for the entertainment of or for communicating with the driver or a passenger of the vehicle (or, if the loudspeaker is or forms part of the horn or similar warning instrument of the vehicle, solely for giving warning to other traffic), and

(b) is so operated as not to give reasonable cause for annoyance to persons in the vicinity.

(4) A person who operates or permits the operation of a loudspeaker in contravention of subsection (1) is guilty of an offence and is liable on summary conviction to—

(a) a fine not exceeding level 5 on the standard scale, together with

(b) a further fine not exceeding £50 for each day on which the offence continues after the conviction.

(5) In this section—

"local authority" means a London borough council (and, in subsection (2)(d), the Greater London Authority),

"street" means a street within the meaning of section 48(1) of the New Roads and Street Works Act 1991 (c 22) which is for the time being open to the public,

"the designated area" means the area specified in an order under section 138,

"vessel" includes a hovercraft within the meaning of the Hovercraft Act 1968 (c 59).

(6) In Schedule 2 to the Noise and Statutory Nuisance Act 1993 (consent to the operation of loudspeakers in streets or roads), in paragraph 1(1), at the end add "or of section 137(1) of the Serious Organised Crime and Police Act 2005".

[Serious Organised Crime and Police Act 2005, s 137.]

8–27845 138. The designated area. (1) The Secretary of State may by order specify an area as the designated area for the purposes of sections 132 to 137.

(2) The area may be specified by description, by reference to a map or in any other way.

(3) No point in the area so specified may be more than one kilometre in a straight line from the point nearest to it in Parliament Square.

[Serious Organised Crime and Police Act 2005, s 138.]

Anti-social behaviour

8–27846 139–143. *Amends the Prosecution of Offences Act 1985, the Football Spectators Act 1989 and the Crime and Disorder Act 1998.*

Parental compensation orders

8–27847 144. Parental compensation orders. Schedule 10 is to have effect.

[Serious Organised Crime and Police Act 2005, s 144.]

PART 5[1]

MISCELLANEOUS

Protection of activities of certain organisations

8–27848 145. Interference with contractual relationships so as to harm animal research organisation. (1) A person (A) commits an offence if, with the intention of harming an animal research organisation, he—

(a) does a relevant act, or
(b) threatens that he or somebody else will do a relevant act,

in circumstances in which that act or threat is intended or likely to cause a second person (B) to take any of the steps in subsection (2).

(2) The steps are—

(a) not to perform any contractual obligation owed by B to a third person (C) (whether or not such non-performance amounts to a breach of contract);
(b) to terminate any contract B has with C;
(c) not to enter into a contract with C

(3) For the purposes of this section, a "relevant act" is—

(a) an act amounting to a criminal offence, or
(b) a tortious act causing B to suffer loss or damage of any description;

but paragraph (b) does not include an act which is actionable on the ground only that it induces another person to break a contract with B.

(4) For the purposes of this section, "contract" includes any other arrangement (and "contractual" is to be read accordingly).

(5) For the purposes of this section, to "harm" an animal research organisation means—

(a) to cause the organisation to suffer loss or damage of any description, or
(b) to prevent or hinder the carrying out by the organisation of any of its activities.

(6) This section does not apply to any act done wholly or mainly in contemplation or furtherance of a trade dispute.

(7) In subsection (6) "trade dispute" has the same meaning as in Part 4 of the Trade Union and Labour Relations (Consolidation) Act 1992 (c 52), except that section 218 of that Act shall be read as if—

(a) it made provision corresponding to section 244(4) of that Act, and
(b) in subsection (5), the definition of "worker" included any person falling within paragraph (b) of the definition of "worker" in section 244(5).

[Serious Organised Crime and Police Act 2005, s 145.]

1. Part 5 comprises ss 145–171 and Schs 11–15.

8–27849 146. Intimidation of persons connected with animal research organisation. (1) A person (A) commits an offence if, with the intention of causing a second person (B) to abstain from doing something which B is entitled to do (or to do something which B is entitled to abstain from doing)—

(a) A threatens B that A or somebody else will do a relevant act, and
(b) A does so wholly or mainly because B is a person falling within subsection (2).

(2) A person falls within this subsection if he is—

(a) an employee or officer of an animal research organisation;
(b) a student at an educational establishment that is an animal research organisation;
(c) a lessor or licensor of any premises occupied by an animal research organisation;

(d) a person with a financial interest in, or who provides financial assistance to, an animal research organisation;
(e) a customer or supplier of an animal research organisation;
(f) a person who is contemplating becoming someone within paragraph (c), (d) or (e);
(g) a person who is, or is contemplating becoming, a customer or supplier of someone within paragraph (c), (d), (e) or (f);
(h) an employee or officer of someone within paragraph (c), (d), (e), (f) or (g);
(i) a person with a financial interest in, or who provides financial assistance to, someone within paragraph (c), (d), (e), (f) or (g);
(j) a spouse, civil partner, friend or relative of, or a person who is known personally to, someone within any of paragraphs (a) to (i);
(k) a person who is, or is contemplating becoming, a customer or supplier of someone within paragraph (a), (b), (h), (i) or (j); or
(l) an employer of someone within paragraph (j).

(3) For the purposes of this section, an "officer" of an animal research organisation or a person includes—

(a) where the organisation or person is a body corporate, a director, manager or secretary;
(b) where the organisation or person is a charity, a charity trustee (within the meaning of the Charities Act 1993 (c 10));
(c) where the organisation or person is a partnership, a partner.

(4) For the purposes of this section—

(a) a person is a customer or supplier of another person if he purchases goods, services or facilities from, or (as the case may be) supplies goods, services or facilities to, that other; and
(b) "supplier" includes a person who supplies services in pursuance of any enactment that requires or authorises such services to be provided.

(5) For the purposes of this section, a "relevant act" is—

(a) an act amounting to a criminal offence, or
(b) a tortious act causing B or another person to suffer loss or damage of any description.

(6) The Secretary of State may by order amend this section so as to include within subsection (2) any description of persons framed by reference to their connection with—

(a) an animal research organisation, or
(b) any description of persons for the time being mentioned in that subsection.

(7) This section does not apply to any act done wholly or mainly in contemplation or furtherance of a trade dispute.

(8) In subsection (7) "trade dispute" has the meaning given by section 145(7).
[Serious Organised Crime and Police Act 2005, s 146.]

8–27849A 147. Penalty for offences under sections 145 and 146. (1) A person guilty of an offence under section 145 or 146 is liable[1]—

(a) on summary conviction, to imprisonment for a term not exceeding 12 months[2] or to a fine not exceeding the statutory maximum, or to both;
(b) on conviction on indictment, to imprisonment for a term not exceeding five years or to a fine, or to both.

(2) No proceedings for an offence under either of those sections may be instituted except by or with the consent of the Director of Public Prosecutions.
[Serious Organised Crime and Police Act 2005, s 147.]

1. For procedure in respect of an offence triable either way, see the Magistrates' Courts Act 1980, ss 17A–21, in PART I: MAGISTRATES' COURTS, PROCEDURE, ante.

2. In relation to an offence committed before the commencement of s 154(1) of the Criminal Justice Act 2003 this is to be read as a reference to "6 months", s 175(2), post.

8–27849B 148. Animal research organisations. (1) For the purposes of sections 145 and 146 "animal research organisation" means any person or organisation falling within subsection (2) or (3).

(2) A person or organisation falls within this subsection if he or it is the owner, lessee or licensee of premises constituting or including—

(a) a place specified in a licence granted under section 4 or 5 of the 1986 Act,
(b) a scientific procedure establishment designated under section 6 of that Act, or
(c) a breeding or supplying establishment designated under section 7 of that Act.

(3) A person or organisation falls within this subsection if he or it employs, or engages under a contract for services, any of the following in his capacity as such—

(a) the holder of a personal licence granted under section 4 of the 1986 Act,

(b) the holder of a project licence granted under section 5 of that Act,
(c) a person specified under section 6(5) of that Act, or
(d) a person specified under section 7(5) of that Act.

(4) The Secretary of State may by order amend this section so as to include a reference to any description of persons whom he considers to be involved in, or to have a direct connection with persons who are involved in, the application of regulated procedures.

(5) In this section—

"the 1986 Act" means the Animals (Scientific Procedures) Act 1986 (c 14);
"organisation" includes any institution, trust, undertaking or association of persons;
"premises" includes any place within the meaning of the 1986 Act;
"regulated procedures" has the meaning given by section 2 of the 1986 Act.

[Serious Organised Crime and Police Act 2005, s 148.]

8–27849C 149. Extension of sections 145 to 147. (1) The Secretary of State may by order provide for sections 145, 146 and 147 to apply in relation to persons or organisations of a description specified in the order as they apply in relation to animal research organisations.

(2) The Secretary of State may, however, only make an order under this section if satisfied that a series of acts has taken place and—

(a) that those acts were directed at persons or organisations of the description specified in the order or at persons having a connection with them, and
(b) that, if those persons or organisations had been animal research organisations, those acts would have constituted offences under section 145 or 146.

(3) In this section "organisation" and "animal research organisation" have the meanings given by section 148.

[Serious Organised Crime and Police Act 2005, s 149.]

Racial and Religious Hatred Act 2006[1]

(2006 c 1)

8–27849D 1. Hatred against persons on religious grounds. The Public Order Act 1986 (c 64) is amended in accordance with the Schedule to this Act, which creates offences involving stirring up hatred against persons on religious grounds.

1. This Act is to be brought into force in accordance with an order made under s 3. At the date of going to press, no such order had been made.

8–27849E 2. Racial and religious hatred offences: powers of arrest. In section 24A of the Police and Criminal Evidence Act 1984 (c 60) (arrest without warrant by persons other than constables) after subsection (4) add—

"(5) This section does not apply in relation to an offence under Part 3 or 3A of the Public Order Act 1986."

3. Short title, commencement and extent

8–27849F

Section 1

SCHEDULE

HATRED AGAINST PERSONS ON RELIGIOUS GROUNDS

In the Public Order Act 1986 (c 64), after Part 3 insert—

"PART 3A

HATRED AGAINST PERSONS ON RELIGIOUS GROUNDS

Meaning of "religious hatred"

29A. Meaning of "religious hatred". In this Part "religious hatred" means hatred against a group of persons defined by reference to religious belief or lack of religious belief.

Acts intended to stir up religious hatred

29B. Use of words or behaviour or display of written material. (1) A person who uses threatening words or behaviour, or displays any written material which is threatening, is guilty of an offence if he intends thereby to stir up religious hatred.

(2) An offence under this section may be committed in a public or a private place, except that no offence is committed where the words or behaviour are used, or the written material is displayed, by a person inside a dwelling and are not heard or seen except by other persons in that or another dwelling.

(3) A constable may arrest without warrant anyone he reasonably suspects is committing an offence under this section.

(4) In proceedings for an offence under this section it is a defence for the accused to prove that he was inside a dwelling and had no reason to believe that the words or behaviour used, or the written material displayed, would be heard or seen by a person outside that or any other dwelling.

(5) This section does not apply to words or behaviour used, or written material displayed, solely for the purpose of being included in a programme service.

29C. Publishing or distributing written material. (1) A person who publishes or distributes written material which is threatening is guilty of an offence if he intends thereby to stir up religious hatred.

(2) References in this Part to the publication or distribution of written material are to its publication or distribution to the public or a section of the public.

29D. Public performance of play. (1) If a public performance of a play is given which involves the use of threatening words or behaviour, any person who presents or directs the performance is guilty of an offence if he intends thereby to stir up religious hatred.

(2) This section does not apply to a performance given solely or primarily for one or more of the following purposes—

(a) rehearsal,
(b) making a recording of the performance, or
(c) enabling the performance to be included in a programme service;

but if it is proved that the performance was attended by persons other than those directly connected with the giving of the performance or the doing in relation to it of the things mentioned in paragraph (b) or (c), the performance shall, unless the contrary is shown, be taken not to have been given solely or primarily for the purpose mentioned above.

(3) For the purposes of this section—

(a) a person shall not be treated as presenting a performance of a play by reason only of his taking part in it as a performer,
(b) a person taking part as a performer in a performance directed by another shall be treated as a person who directed the performance if without reasonable excuse he performs otherwise than in accordance with that person's direction, and
(c) a person shall be taken to have directed a performance of a play given under his direction notwithstanding that he was not present during the performance;

and a person shall not be treated as aiding or abetting the commission of an offence under this section by reason only of his taking part in a performance as a performer.

(4) In this section "play" and "public performance" have the same meaning as in the Theatres Act 1968.

(5) The following provisions of the Theatres Act 1968 apply in relation to an offence under this section as they apply to an offence under section 2 of that Act—

section 9 (script as evidence of what was performed),
section 10 (power to make copies of script),
section 15 (powers of entry and inspection).

29E. Distributing, showing or playing a recording. (1) A person who distributes, or shows or plays, a recording of visual images or sounds which are threatening is guilty of an offence if he intends thereby to stir up religious hatred.

(2) In this Part "recording" means any record from which visual images or sounds may, by any means, be reproduced; and references to the distribution, showing or playing of a recording are to its distribution, showing or playing to the public or a section of the public.

(3) This section does not apply to the showing or playing of a recording solely for the purpose of enabling the recording to be included in a programme service.

29F. Broadcasting or including programme in programme service. (1) If a programme involving threatening visual images or sounds is included in a programme service, each of the persons mentioned in subsection (2) is guilty of an offence if he intends thereby to stir up religious hatred.

(2) The persons are—

(a) the person providing the programme service,
(b) any person by whom the programme is produced or directed, and
(c) any person by whom offending words or behaviour are used.

Inflammatory material

29G. Possession of inflammatory material. (1) A person who has in his possession written material which is threatening, or a recording of visual images or sounds which are threatening, with a view to—

(a) in the case of written material, its being displayed, published, distributed, or included in a programme service whether by himself or another, or
(b) in the case of a recording, its being distributed, shown, played, or included in a programme service, whether by himself or another,

is guilty of an offence if he intends religious hatred to be stirred up thereby.

(2) For this purpose regard shall be had to such display, publication, distribution, showing, playing, or inclusion in a programme service as he has, or it may be reasonably be inferred that he has, in view.

29H. Powers of entry and search. (1) If in England and Wales a justice of the peace is satisfied by information on oath laid by a constable that there are reasonable grounds for suspecting that a person has possession of written material or a recording in contravention of section 29G, the justice may issue a warrant under his hand authorising any constable to enter and search the premises where it is suspected the material or recording is situated.

(2) If in Scotland a sheriff or justice of the peace is satisfied by evidence on oath that there are reasonable grounds for suspecting that a person has possession of written material or a recording in contravention of section 29G, the sheriff or justice may issue a warrant authorising any constable to enter and search the premises where it is suspected the material or recording is situated.

(3) A constable entering or searching premises in pursuance of a warrant issued under this section may use reasonable force if necessary.

(4) In this section "premises" means any place and, in particular, includes—

(a) any vehicle, vessel, aircraft or hovercraft,
(b) any offshore installation as defined in section 12 of the Mineral Workings (Offshore Installations) Act 1971, and
(c) any tent or movable structure.

29I. Power to order forfeiture. (1) A court by or before which a person is convicted of—

(a) an offence under section 29B relating to the display of written material, or
(b) an offence under section 29C, 29E or 29G,

shall order to be forfeited any written material or recording produced to the court and shown to its satisfaction to be written material or a recording to which the offence relates.

(2) An order made under this section shall not take effect—

(a) in the case of an order made in proceedings in England and Wales, until the expiry of the ordinary time within which an appeal may be instituted or, where an appeal is duly instituted, until it is finally decided or abandoned;
(b) in the case of an order made in proceedings in Scotland, until the expiration of the time within which, by virtue of any statute, an appeal may be instituted or, where such an appeal is duly instituted, until the appeal is finally decided or abandoned.

(3) For the purposes of subsection (2)(a)—

(a) an application for a case stated or for leave to appeal shall be treated as the institution of an appeal, and
(b) where a decision on appeal is subject to a further appeal, the appeal is not finally determined until the expiry of the ordinary time within which a further appeal may be instituted or, where a further appeal is duly instituted, until the further appeal is finally decided or abandoned.

(4) For the purposes of subsection (2)(b) the lodging of an application for a stated case or note of appeal against sentence shall be treated as the institution of an appeal.

29J. Protection of freedom of expression. Nothing in this Part shall be read or given effect in a way which prohibits or restricts discussion, criticism or expressions of antipathy, dislike, ridicule, insult or abuse of particular religions or the beliefs or practices of their adherents, or of any other belief system or the beliefs or practices of its adherents, or proselytising or urging adherents of a different religion or belief system to cease practising their religion or belief system.

Supplementary provisions

29K. Savings for reports of parliamentary or judicial proceedings. (1) Nothing in this Part applies to a fair and accurate report of proceedings in Parliament or in the Scottish Parliament.

(2) Nothing in this Part applies to a fair and accurate report of proceedings publicly heard before a court or tribunal exercising judicial authority where the report is published contemporaneously with the proceedings or, if it is not reasonably practicable or would be unlawful to publish a report of them contemporaneously, as soon as publication is reasonably practicable and lawful.

29L. Procedure and punishment. (1) No proceedings for an offence under this Part may be instituted in England and Wales except by or with the consent of the Attorney General.

(2) For the purposes of the rules in England and Wales against charging more than one offence in the same count or information, each of sections 29B to 29G creates one offence.

(3) A person guilty of an offence under this Part is liable—

(a) on conviction on indictment to imprisonment for a term not exceeding seven years or a fine or both;
(b) on summary conviction to imprisonment for a term not exceeding six months or a fine not exceeding the statutory maximum or both.

29M. Offences by corporations. (1) Where a body corporate is guilty of an offence under this Part and it is shown that the offence was committed with the consent or connivance of a director, manager, secretary or other similar officer of the body, or a person purporting to act in any such capacity, he as well as the body corporate is guilty of the offence and liable to be proceeded against and punished accordingly.

(2) Where the affairs of a body corporate are managed by its members, subsection (1) applies in relation to the acts and defaults of a member in connection with his functions of management as it applies to a director.

29N. Interpretation. In this Part—

"distribute", and related expressions, shall be construed in accordance with section 29C(2) (written material) and section 29E(2) (recordings);

"dwelling" means any structure or part of a structure occupied as a person's home or other living accommodation (whether the occupation is separate or shared with others) but does not include any part not so occupied, and for this purpose "structure" includes a tent, caravan, vehicle, vessel or other temporary or movable structure;

"programme" means any item which is included in a programme service;

"programme service" has the same meaning as in the Broadcasting Act 1990;

"publish", and related expressions, in relation to written material, shall be construed in accordance with section 29C(2);

"religious hatred" has the meaning given by section 29A;

"recording" has the meaning given by section 29E(2), and "play" and "show", and related expressions, in relation to a recording, shall be construed in accordance with that provision;

"written material" includes any sign or other visible representation."

Sports Grounds and Sporting Events (Designation) Order 2005

(SI 2005/3204)

8–27850 1. This Order may be cited as the Sports Grounds and Sporting Events (Designation) Order 2005 and shall come into force on 14th December 2005.

8–27851 2. For the purposes of the Sporting Events (Control of Alcohol etc) Act 1985, there are hereby designated—

(1) the classes of sports ground specified in Schedule 1 to this Order;
(2) the classes of sporting events specified in Part 1 of Schedule 2 to this Order at any sports ground specified in Schedule 1; and
(3) the classes of sporting events specified in Part 2 of Schedule 2.

8–27852 3. The Sports Grounds and Sporting Events (Designation) Order 1985, the Sports Grounds and Sporting Events (Designation) (Amendment) Order 1987, and article 2(2)(a) of the Sports Grounds and Football (Amendment of Various Orders) Order 1992 are hereby revoked.

8–27853

Article 2(1)

SCHEDULE 1
SPORTS GROUNDS

Any sports ground in England or Wales.

8–27854

SCHEDULE 2
CLASSES OF SPORTING EVENTS

PART I

Article 2(1), 2(2)

1. Association football matches in which one or both of the participating teams represents a club which is for the time being a member (whether a full or associate member) of the Football League, the Football Association Premier League, the Football Conference National Division, the Scottish Football League or Welsh Premier League, or represents a country or territory.

2. Association football matches in competition for the Football Association Cup (other than in a preliminary or qualifying round).

PART 2

Article 2(3)

Association football matches at a sports ground outside England and Wales in which one or both of the participating teams represents a club which is for the time being a member (whether a full or associate member) of the Football League, the Football Association Premier League, the Football Conference National division, the Scottish Football League or Welsh Premier League, or represents the Football Association or the Football Association of Wales.

PUBLIC OFFICE

8–27900 Misconduct in a public office. A public officer who wilfully and without reasonable excuse or justification neglects to perform any duty he is bound to perform by common law or statute is guilty of the common law offence of misconduct in a public office. "Public officer" embraces everyone who is appointed to discharge a public duty, and receives compensation in whatever shape whether from the Crown or otherwise[1]. The element of culpability required is not restricted to corruption or dishonesty, although it has to be such that the conduct impugned was calculated to injure the public interest and calls for condemnation and punishment. Whether there is such conduct is a matter for the jury on the evidence[2]. Triable on indictment.

The elements of this offence, particularly whether recklessness as to a duty to act is sufficient and whether the concept of "bad faith" has any relevance, were considered in *A-G's Reference (No 3 of 2003)*[3]. The offence may be charged in a great variety of circumstances. However, it consists essentially of a public officer, acting as such, wilfully neglecting to perform his duty and/or wilfully misconducting himself in a way which amounts to an abuse of the public's trust in the office holder, without reasonable excuse or justification. Whether the misconduct is of a sufficiently serious nature depends upon the responsibilities of the office and the office holder, the importance of the public objects which they serve, the nature and extent of the departure from those responsibilities and the seriousness of the consequences which may follow from the misconduct. The relevant mental element is that the office holder is aware of the duty to act or is subjectively reckless as to the existence of the duty. The test of recklessness applies both to the question whether in particular circumstances a duty arises at all and to the conduct of the defendant if it does arise; and that the subjective test applies both to reckless indifference to the legality of the act or omission and in relation to the consequences of the act or omission. The expression "bad faith" should not routinely be introduced into a criminal trial because of the confusion it is liable to cause and the risk it might confuse the jury and deflect them from their task of deciding whether the public office had been abused by the conduct of the office holder, although there may be cases in which the concept of bad faith may be relevant to an assessment of the standard of the defendant's conduct.

---

1. *R v Bowden* [1995] 4 All ER 505, [1996] 1 WLR 98, [1996] 1 Cr App Rep 104 (maintenance manager in a local authority's direct labour organisation held to be a public officer).
2. *R v Dytham* [1979] QB 722, [1979] 3 All ER 641 where the deliberate and wilful neglect of a police officer to perform his duty amounted to an offence of misconduct in a public office. See also *R v Wyat* (1705) 1 Salk 380; *R v Bembridge* (1783) 3 Doug KB 327 and *R v Llewellyn-Jones and Lougher* (1966) 51 Cr App Rep 4.
3. [2005] 1 QB 73, [2004] EWCA Crim 868, [2004] 3 WLR 451, [2004] 2 Cr App R 23.

RELIGION

Blasphemy

8–27905 **General rules.** "Serious arguments" (observes Paley) "are fair on all sides. Christianity is but ill defended by refusing audience or toleration to the objection of unbelievers. But whilst we would have freedom of inquiry restrained by no laws but those of decency, we are entitled to demand on behalf of a religion which holds forth to mankind assurances of immortality, that its credit be assailed by no other weapons than those of sober discussion and legitimate reasoning." Our law has adopted this as the rule; sober argument you may answer, but indecent reviling you cannot, and therefore the law steps in and punishes it (*per* Lord ERSKINE). Assuming the correctness of this proposition, it may be laid down that no prosecution could be sustained at the present day for calmly and dispassionately discussing, or even calling in question, the truth of Christianity; and that the offence of blasphemy consists in attacking it by ribaldry, profanity, or indecency, and not in endeavouring by legitimate argument to prove its falsity. On 5th March 1883, in a prosecution against the *Freethinker*, NORTH J, defined the legal meaning of blasphemy as being a contumelious reproach or profane scoffing against the Christian religion or the Holy Scriptures, and any act exposing the Holy Scriptures and the Christian religion to ridicule, contempt, or derision (*R v Foote* (1883) 10 QBD 378, Central Criminal Court). In the case of *R v Ramsay and Foote* (1883) 48 LT 733, Lord COLERIDGE directed the jury that the mere denial of the truths of Christianity does not amount to blasphemy; but a wilful intention to pervert, insult, and mislead others by means of licentious and contumelious abuse applied to sacred subjects, or by wilful misrepresentations or artful sophistry calculated to mislead the ignorant and unwary, is the criterion and test of guilt; and supposing that the decencies of controversy were observed, even the fundamentals of religion might be attacked; this was approved by PHILLIMORE J, in *R v Boulter* (1908) 72 JP 188. The offence may be committed by written matter as well as by spoken words (*R v Gott* (1922) 16 Cr App Rep 87). In *R v Lemon* [1979] 1 All ER 898, 143 JP 315, the House of Lords, after reviewing earlier authorities on the law of blasphemy, held (1) that blasphemous libel was the publication of any matter that insulted, offended or vilified the Deity or Christ or the Christian religion; that it was the publication of an offensive nature, or in offensive terms, to the Christian religon that constituted the offence; and (2) that provided there was an intention to publish the material the absence of an intention to be blasphemous was irrelevant.

The law of blasphemy does not extend to religions other than Christianity (*R v Chief Metropolitan Stipendiary Magistrate, ex p Choudhury* [1991] 1 QB 429, [1991] 1 All ER 306, 91 Cr App Rep 363, DC).

The crime of blasphemy is triable on indictment. It is punishable by fine or imprisonment, or both.

Under the European Convention of Human Rights there is a tension between the protection of religion under Article 9 and freedom of expression under Article 10. Blasphemy laws can be justified[1], but only if-

1. restrictions apply only to the *manner* in which information or ideas are conveyed
2. a high profanity threshold is applied and
3. there are effective safeguards against the over-broad application of any such restrictions[2].

---

1. *Otto-Preminger Institute v Austria* (1994) 19 EHRR 34 and *Wingrove v United Kingdom* (1996) 24 EHRR 1.
2. *Wingrove v United Kingdom* (1997) 24 EHRR 1.

Ecclesiastical Courts Jurisdiction Act 1860

(1860 c 32)

8–27910 2. Penalty for making a disturbance in churches, chapels, churchyards etc. Any[1] person who shall be guilty[2] of riotous, violent, or indecent[3] behaviour in England in any cathedral church, parish or district church, or chapel of the Church of England, or in any chapel of any religious denomination, or in England in any place[4] of religious worship duly certified[5] under the Places of Worship Registration Act 1855, 18 & 19 Vict c 81, whether during the celebration of[6] Divine service, or at any other time, or in any churchyard, or burial-ground, or who shall molest, let[7], disturb, vex, or trouble, or by any other unlawful means disquiet or misuse any preacher duly authorised to preach therein, or any clergyman in Holy Orders[8] ministering or celebrating any sacrament or any Divine service, rite, or office in any cathedral church or chapel, churchyard, or burial ground shall on conviction thereof before two justices of the peace★, be liable to a penalty of not more than★ **level 1** on the standard scale for every such offence, or may, if the justices before whom he shall be convicted think fit, instead of being subjected to any pecuniary penalty be committed to prison for any time★ not exceeding **two months**.

[Ecclesiastical Courts Jurisdiction Act 1860 s 2, as amended by Criminal Justice Act 1967, Sch 3 and the Criminal Justice Act 1982, ss 38 and 46.]

★Words susbstituted in relation to England and Wales by the Courts Act 2003, Sch 8 from a date to be appointed.

1. In an appeal from a conviction by justices of a clergyman for violent and indecent behaviour in the churchyard of his own church, the Queen's Bench Division held without hesitation that the Act applies to persons in holy orders just as much as to laymen, and confirmed the view of the justices that violent and indecent conduct could not be justified by a claim of right (*Vallancey v Fletcher* [1897] 1 QB 265, 61 JP 183).

2. The offender may be apprehended by a churchwarden (Ecclesiastical Courts Jurisdiction Act 1860, s 3), note also the powers of a constable under s 25 of the Police and Criminal Evidence Act 1984, ante, and the common law powers generally to arrest for a breach of the peace, see para **1–183** in Part I: Magistrates Courts, Procedure ante.

3. Interrupting and shouting and creating disturbance is "indecent behaviour" in the context of this section (*Abrahams v Cavey* [1968] 1 QB 479, [1967] 3 All ER 179). A churchwarden has no right forcibly to exclude an inhabitant from entering a church to attend Divine service, although in his opinion the person cannot be conveniently accommodated (*Taylor v Timson* (1888) 20 QBD 671, 52 JP 135). Churchwardens have authority, for preserving order and decorum, to direct where any member of the congregation shall sit who wishes to occupy a free seat (*Asher v Calcraft* (1887) 18 QBD 607, 51 JP 598).

4. Any place actually used as the "chapel of any religious deonomination", whether certified or not, will be within the protection of the statute (34 JP 12). The law officers of the Crown (Sir R E WEBSTER and SIR EDWARD CLARKE, 28 January 1892) gave an opinion that if the place of meeting is a defined and enclosed area, which can be defined by metes and bounds, and does not form part of an open space to which the public have access, it is a place of meeting to which a certificate may be granted, although there may be no building thereon (56 JP 154).

5. The certificate contains the words "at the date hereof the certificate of registration remained uncancelled," and is not evidence that the place was certified after the date of the certificate.

6. The celebration of a sacrament is a "divine service". The question whether the clergyman or celebrant complied with the ceremonial law of the Church of England is immaterial (*Matthews v King* [1934] 1 KB 505, 97 JP 345). The London Quarter Sessions held that questions as to the nature of the services used were immaterial, and should not be allowed (*Kensit v Rose* (1898) 62 JP 489).

7. See *Kensit v St Paul's (Dean and Chapter)* [1905] 2 KB 249, 69 JP 250.

8. Molesting a clergyman while engaged in collecting alms after a sermon is not an offence under these words, the Rubric not contemplating the collecting of alms is to be done by him (*Cope v Barber* (1872) LR 7 CP 393, 36 JP 439).

RESCUE

8–27920 Rescue of persons. Rescue is the forcible liberation of another from legal custody. To constitute this offence, the party must be in actual custody, though whether in that of a constable or private individual is not material, but in the latter case the party should know that the prisoner is in lawful custody, while in the former he is bound to take notice at his peril (1 *Hale* 606). Punishable on indictment by a fine and imprisonment. See s 39 of the Prison Act 1952—assisting prisoner to escape in this PART: title PRISONS, ante.

8–27930 Rescue of goods. The forcible rescue of goods distrained, and the rescuing of cattle by the breach of the pound in which they have been placed, are offences at common law, and have been made the subject of indictment. An indictment will lie for taking goods forcibly if such taking be proved to be a breach of the peace, but if a mere trespass, without circumstances of violence, it is not indictable. See this PART: title POUND BREACH, ante.

ROYAL PARKS AND GARDENS

8–27931 This title contains the following statute—

8–27940 The **Parks Regulation Acts 1872 to 1974** have for their object the protection from injury of the parks under the management of the Secretary of State for Culture, Media and Sport, and securing the public from molestation and annoyance while enjoying the same. The 1872 Act provides for the powers under the Act to be exercised by a duly attested park constable or a police constable and creates an offence of assaulting such a park constable. The 1872 Act does not apply to those parks specified by order made under s 162 of the Serious Organised Crime and Police Act 2005 for which there are no park constables and which are policed by the Metropolitan Police (and community support officers).

Regulations are made under s 2 of the Parks Regulation (Amendment) Act 1926 which apply to parks to which the 1872 Act applies and to specified parks and which create offences punishable by a fine not exceeding **level 1** on the standard scale (**level 3** in the case of park trading offences).

Parks Regulation Act 1872[1]

(35 & 36 Vict c 15)

8–27940A 1. Short title. This Act may be cited for all purposes as "The Parks Regulation Act 1872".

[Parks Regulation Act 1872, s 1.]

1. This Act came into force on Royal Assent (27 June 1872).

8–27940B 3. Definition of park constable. "Park constable" shall mean any person who, previously to the passing of this Act, has been or may hereafter be appointed park constable of a park as defined by this Act.

[Parks Regulation Act 1872, s 3 as amended by the Parks Regulation (Amendment) Act 1974, Schedule.]

8–27940C 3A. Attestation of park constables. Every park constable shall on appointment be attested as a constable by making a declaration before a justice of the peace that he will duly execute the office of constable.

[Parks Regulation Act 1872, s 3A as inserted by the Parks Regulation (Amendment) Act 1974, Schedule.]

8–27940D 5. Park constable may apprehend any offender whose name or residence is not known. Any person who—

(*a*) within the view of a park constable acts in contravention of any of the said regulations in the park where the park constable has jurisdiction; and

(*b*) when required by any park constable or by any police constable to give his name and address gives a false name or false address,

shall be liable on summary conviction to a penalty of an amount not exceeding level 1 on the standard scale.

[Parks Regulation Act 1872, s 5 as substituted by the Police and Criminal Evidence Act 1984, Sch 6 and amended by the Statute Law (Repeals) Act 1993.]

8–27940E 6. Penalty on assaults on park constable. Where any person is convicted of an assault on any park constable when in the execution of his duty, such person shall, on conviction by a court of summary jurisdiction, in the discretion of the court, be liable either to pay a penalty not exceeding level 2 on the standard scale, or to be imprisoned for any term not exceeding six months with or without hard labour.

[Parks Regulation Act 1872, s 6 as amended by the Parks Regulation (Amendment) Act 1974, Schedule, the Criminal Law Act 1977, s 31(6), the Criminal Justice Act 1982, ss 37, 46 and the Statute Law (Repeals) Act 1993.]

8–27940F 7. Powers, duties, and privileges of park constable. Every park constable in addition to any powers and immunities specially conferred on him by this Act, shall, within the limits of the park of which he is park constable, have all such powers, privileges, and immunities, and be liable to all such duties and responsibilities, as any police constable has within the police area in which such park is situated; and any person so appointed a park constable as aforesaid shall obey such lawful commands as he may from time to time receive from the Commissioners in respect of his conduct in the execution of his office.

[Parks Regulation Act 1872, s 7 as amended by the Parks Regulation (Amendment) Act 1974, Schedule and the Police Act 1996, s 103, Sch 7, para 7.]

8–27940G 8. Police constables to have the same powers, etc, as park constables. Every police constable belonging to the police force for the police area in which any park to which this Act applies is situate shall have the powers, privileges, and immunities of a park constable within such park.

[Parks Regulation Act 1872, s 8 as amended by the Police Act 1996, Sch 7, the Parks Regulation (Amendment) Act 1926, Schedule and the Parks Regulation (Amendment) Act 1974, Schedule.]

8–27940H 10. Publication of regulations. Copies of regulations to be observed in pursuance of this Act by persons using a park to which this Act applies shall be put up in such park in such conspicuous manner as the Commissioners may deem best calculated to give information to the persons using the park.

[Parks Regulation Act 1872, s 10 as amended by the Parks Regulation (Amendment) Act 1926, Schedule.]

8–27940I 11. Saving of certain rights. Nothing in this Act shall authorise any interference with any rights of way or any right whatever to which any person or persons may be by law entitled.

[Parks Regulation Act 1872, s 11.]

8–27940J 12. Act to be cumulative. All powers conferred by this Act shall be deemed to be in addition to and not in derogation of any powers conferred by any other Act of Parliament, and any such powers may be exercised as if this Act had not been passed.

[Parks Regulation Act 1872, s 12.]

8–27940K 13. Saving of the rights of the Crown. Nothing in this Act contained shall be deemed to prejudice or affect any prerogative or right of Her Majesty, or any power, right, or duty of the Commissioners, or any powers or duties of any officers, clerks, or servants, appointed by Her Majesty or by the Commissioners.

[Parks Regulation Act 1872, s 13.]

8–27940L 14. Saving of 30 & 31 Vict c 134. Nothing in this Act contained shall affect the Metropolitan Streets Act 1867, or the application thereof to any park to which it is by law applicable.

[Parks Regulation Act 1872, s 14.]

Parks (Amendment) Act 1926[1]

(16 & 17 Geo 5 c 36)

8–27940M 1. Application. The Parks Regulation Act 1872 (hereinafter referred to as the principal Act), shall apply to all parks, gardens, recreation grounds, open spaces and other land for the time being vested in, or under the control or management of, the Commissioners of Works, and accordingly in that Act the expression "park" shall include all such parks, gardens, recreation grounds, open spaces and land as aforesaid.

[Parks (Amendment) Act 1926, s 1 as amended by the Statute Law (Repeals) Act 1989.]

---

1. This Act came into force on Royal Assent (15 December 1926).

8–27940N 2. Power to make regulations. (1) Subject to the provisions of this Act, the Commissioners of Works may make such regulations to be observed by persons using any park to which the principal Act applies, as they consider necessary for securing the proper management of the park, and the preservation of order and prevention of abuses therein, and if any person fails to comply with, or acts in contravention of, any regulations so made, he shall be guilty of an offence against the principal Act and shall be liable on conviction thereof by a court of summary jurisdiction to a penalty not exceeding level 1 on the standard scale.

(2) Before any regulation made under this Act comes into operation, a draft thereof shall be laid before each House of Parliament for a period of not less than twenty-one days on which that House has sat, and if either House before the expiration of that period presents an Address to His Majesty against the draft or any part thereof, no further proceedings shall be taken thereon, but without prejudice to the making of any new draft regulation.

(3) As from and after the date upon which regulations made under this Act come into operation as respects any park, all references in the principal Act to regulations shall, as respects that park, be construed as references to regulations made under this Act.

(4) The Documentary Evidence Act 1868, as amended by the Documentary Evidence Act 1882, shall apply to the Commissioners of Works as though the Commissioners were included in the first column of the Schedule to the first- mentioned Act, and any Commissioner or the Secretary, or any person authorised to act on behalf of the Secretary, were mentioned in the second column of that Schedule, and as if the regulations referred to in those Acts included any regulations made under this Act.

[Parks (Amendment) Act 1926, s 2 as amended by the Criminal Justice Act 1982, ss 37, 38, 46.]

1. The following regulations have been made:

Hyde Park and The Regents Park (Vehicle Parking) (Amendment) Regulations 1999, SI 1999/392;
Osborne Regulations 1952, SI 1952/1468;
Hampton Court and Bushy Park (Outer Areas) Regulations 1973, SI 1973/214;
Royal Parks and Other Open Spaces Regulations 1997, SI 1997/1639;
Royal Parks and Other Open Spaces (Park Trading) Regulations 2000, SI 2000/2949;
Royal Parks and Other Open Spaces (Amendment) Regulations 2004, SI 2004/1308.

Royal Parks (Trading) Act 2000[1]

(2000 c 13)

8–27941 **1. Park trading offence.** (1) Regulations under section 2 of the Parks Regulation (Amendment) Act 1926 may designate specified provisions of the regulations as park trading regulations.

(2) An offence under that section which is committed by failing to comply with or acting in contravention of a park trading regulation is a park trading offence[2] for the purposes of this Act.

[Royal Parks (Trading) Act 2000, s 1.]

1. This Act came into force on Royal Assent (20 July 2000).
2. The maximum penalty for an offence under park trading regulations is a fine not exceeding **level 3** on the standard scale (s 2).

8–27942 **3. Offence by body corporate.** (1) Where a park trading offence committed by a body corporate is proved—

(*a*) to have been committed with the consent or connivance of an officer, or
(*b*) to be attributable to any neglect on the part of an officer,

he as well as the body corporate is guilty of the offence and liable to be proceeded against and punished accordingly.

(2) For the purposes of this section the following are officers of a body corporate—

(*a*) a director,
(*b*) a manager,
(*c*) a secretary,
(*d*) another similar officer,
(*e*) a person purporting to act in any of the capacities listed in paragraphs (*a*) to (*d*).

[Royal Parks (Trading) Act 2000, s 3.]

8–27943 **4. Seizure of property.** (1) A park constable who reasonably suspects that a person has committed a park trading offence may, subject to subsection (2), seize anything of a non-perishable nature which—

(*a*) the person has in his possession or under his control, and
(*b*) the constable reasonably believes to have been used in the commission of the offence.

(2) A park constable may exercise the power conferred by subsection (1) only in the park where he has jurisdiction.

(3) In this section "park constable" has the meaning given by section 3 of the Parks Regulation Act 1872.*

[Royal Parks (Trading) Act 2000, s 4.]

***New sub-ss (4) and (5) inserted by the Serious Organised Crime and Police Act 2005 from a date to be appointed.**

8–27944 **5. Retention and disposal.** (1) The Secretary of State may retain anything which has been seized under section 4 until the end of the period of 28 days beginning with the date of the seizure.

(2) Subsection (3) applies where before the end of that period an information for a park trading offence is laid—

(*a*) against the person from whom the thing was seized, and
(*b*) in respect of his activities at the time of the seizure.

(3) Where this subsection applies—

(*a*) the Secretary of State may retain the thing seized until the conclusion of proceedings relating to the offence (including any appeal), and
(*b*) if an award is made of costs to be paid by the accused to the Secretary of State, the Secretary of State may retain the thing seized until the costs have been paid.

(4) Subsection (3) has effect subject to any order for forfeiture under section 6.
(5) If the Secretary of State has retained a thing in reliance on subsection (3)(*b*) for the period of 28 days beginning with the date of the conclusion of proceedings relating to the offence (including any appeal)—

(*a*) he may sell it for the best price which he can reasonably obtain and apply the proceeds in discharge of the award of costs, and
(*b*) if he does so, he shall pay any balance to the person whom he believes to have owned the thing immediately before the sale.

(6) Where the Secretary of State ceases to be entitled to retain a thing under this section he shall, subject to any order for forfeiture under section 6, return it to the person whom he believes to be its owner.
(7) If the Secretary of State cannot after reasonable inquiry identify a person for the purposes of subsection (5)(*b*) or (6)—

(*a*) he shall apply to a magistrates' court for directions, and
(*b*) the court shall make an order about the treatment of the thing or the balance of its price.
[Royal Parks (Trading) Act 2000, s 5.]

8–27945 6. Forfeiture. (1) A court which convicts a person of a park trading offence may order anything to which subsection (2) applies to be forfeited and dealt with in a manner specified in the order.
(2) This subsection applies to anything which—

(*a*) was seized under section 4,
(*b*) is retained by the Secretary of State under section 5, and
(*c*) the court believes to have been used in the commission of the offence.

(3) Before making an order for the forfeiture of a thing a court shall—

(*a*) permit anyone who claims to be its owner or to have an interest in it to make representations, and
(*b*) consider its value and the likely consequences of forfeiture.
[Royal Parks (Trading) Act 2000, s 6.]

Serious Organised Crime and Police Act 2005[1]

(2000 c 15)

8–27946 162. Regulation of specified parks. (1) From the appointed day[1] the Parks Regulation Act 1872 (c 15) does not apply to the specified parks.
(2) But from the appointed day[1] section 2 of the Parks Regulation (Amendment) Act 1926 (c 36) applies in relation to the specified parks in the same way as it applies in relation to parks to which the Parks Regulation Act 1872 applies.
(3) The Secretary of State must ensure that copies of any regulations made under section 2 of the Parks Regulation (Amendment) Act 1926 (c 36) which are in force in relation to a specified park are displayed in a suitable position in that park.
(4) In this section "specified park" means a park, garden, recreation ground, open space or other land in the metropolitan police district—

(*a*) which is specified in an order[2] made by the Secretary of State before the appointed day[1], and
(*b*) to which the Parks Regulation Act 1872 (c 15) then applied by virtue of section 1 of the Parks Regulation (Amendment) Act 1926.
[Serious Organised Crime and Police Act 2005, s 162.]

1. 1st July 2005 was appointed by SI 2005/1521.
2. The Royal Parks (Regulation of Specified Parks) Order 2005, SI 2005/1522 has been made.

SEXUAL OFFENCES

8–27950 This title comprises the parts of the following statutes relevant to proceedings in magistrates' courts—

and the following statutory instrument—

Sexual Offences Act 1956

(4 & 5 Eliz 2 c 69)

PART I

OFFENCES, AND THE PROSECUTION AND PUNISHMENTS OF OFFENCES

Intercourse by force, intimidation, etc

8–27969 1–32. *Repealed.*

Suppression of brothels

8–28009 33. Keeping a brothel. It is an offence[1] for a person to keep a brothel[2], or to manage or act or assist in the management[3] of, a brothel.
[Sexual Offences Act 1956, s 33.]

---

1. For mode of prosecution and penalty, see Sch 2, post. The evidence of a police officer that he knew women who visited a house to be prostitutes is admissible (*R v Korie* [1966] 1 All ER 50). If the information charges a single transaction, taking place over a period of time within the preceding 6 months, it will not be bad for duplicity (*Anderton v Cooper* (1981) 145 JP 128, [1981] Crim LR 177).

2. A brothel is a place where people of opposite sexes are allowed to resort for illicit intercourse, whether the women are common prostitutes or not (*Winter v Woolfe* [1931] 1 KB 549, 95 JP 20). A house occupied by one woman and used by her for prostitution but not allowed by her to be used by other women for a like purpose, is not a brothel (*Singleton v Ellison* [1895] 1 QB 607, 59 JP 119). This was followed in *Caldwell v Leech* (1913) 77 JP 254, where the defendant, the wife of the occupier of the premises, was charged with managing a brothel: she allowed her sister, a prostitute, to use the premises for prostitution with different men, no other woman so using the premises; but the facts justified a finding that premises were used as a brothel where two women, one being the tenant and occupier both used the premises for prostitution (*Gorman v Standen, Palace-Clark v Standen* [1964] 1 QB 294, [1963] 3 All ER 627, 128 JP 28). On other facts it has been held that two flats in one building, separately let to prostitutes, did not justify a finding that the building was used as a brothel (*Strath v Foxon* [1956] 1 QB 67, [1955] 3 All ER 398, 119 JP 581); but a block of flats, inhabited by different women and used by them for prostitution was held, on the facts, to be a brothel (*Durose v Wilson* (1907) 71 JP 263); and where there was use by three prostitutes in separate rooms, separately let to them, in such proximity as to constitute a "nest" of prostitutes, it was held that the premises were a brothel (*Donovan v Gavin* [1965] 2 QB 648, [1965] 2 All ER 611, 129 JP 404, approving *Abbott v Smith* [1965] 2 QB 662n, [1964] 3 All ER 762, 129 JP 3). Similarly where premises were used by a team of different prostitutes, but no more than one used the premises each day, the premises were held to constitute a brothel (*Stevens v Christy* (1987) 151 JP 366, [1987] Crim LR 503).

Premises which are resorted to for the purposes of lewd homosexual practices shall be treated as a brothel for the purposes of ss 33–35 of this Act. See Sexual Offences Act 1967, s 6, post.

3. Evidence of normal sexual intercourse provided on the premises is not essential to prove a charge of assisting in the management of a brothel: it is sufficient to prove that more than one woman offered herself as a participant in physical acts of indecency for the sexual gratification of men (*Kelly v Purvis* [1983] QB 663, [1983] 1 All ER 525, 76 Cr App Rep 165). Women in a massage parlour, who not only performed lewd acts, but also discussed the nature of the acts to be performed and negotiated the terms of payment for their services, were held to be assisting in the management of a brothel (*Elliott v DPP* (1989) Times, 19 January, DC). To establish the offence of assisting in the management it is not necessary to show that the defendant exercised some sort of control over the management, nor is it necessary to show there was a specific act of management for that would be acting in the management (*Jones and Wood v DPP* (1992) 156 JP 866).

4. The wife or husband of the accused may be called as a witness by the defence or the prosecution, see Police and Criminal Evidence Act 1984, s 80 in PART II: EVIDENCE, ante.

8–28009A 33A. Keeping a brothel used for prostitution. (1) It is an offence for a person to keep, or to manage, or act or assist in the management of, a brothel to which people resort for practices involving prostitution (whether or not also for other practices).

(2) In this section "prostitution" has the meaning given by section 51(2) of the Sexual Offences Act 2003.
[Sexual Offences Act 1956, s 33A.]

8–28010 34. Landlord letting premises for use as brothel. It is an offence[1] for the lessor or landlord of any premises or his agent to let the whole or part of the premises with the knowledge[2] that it is to be used, in whole or in part, as a brothel, or, where the whole or part of the premises is used as a brothel, to be wilfully a party[3] to that use continuing.
[Sexual Offences Act 1956, s 34.]

---

1. For mode of prosecution and penalty, see Sch 2, post.
2. The use of the premises as a brothel is a finding of fact: the whole or part of a house may be so used where there is use by more than one prostitute; see *Donovan v Gavin* [1965] 2 QB 648, [1965] 2 All ER 611, 129 JP 404, supra, approving *Abbott v Smith* [1965] 2 QB 662n, [1964] 3 All ER 762, 129 JP 3, supra.
3. It is our view that to be wilfully a party requires something in the nature of a positive act, and more than mere negative acquiescence; cf *Bell v Alfred Franks & Barlett Co Ltd* [1980] 1 All ER 356, [1980] 1 WLR 340.
4. The wife or husband of the accused may be called as a witness by the defence or the prosecution, see Police and Criminal Evidence Act 1984, s 80 in PART II: EVIDENCE, ante.

8–28011 35. Tenant permitting premises to be used as brothel. (1) It is an offence[1] for the tenant or occupier, or person in charge, of any premises knowingly to permit the whole or part of the premises to be used as a brothel.

(2) Where the tenant or occupier of any premises is convicted (whether under this section or, for an offence committed before the commencement of this Act, under section thirteen of the Criminal Law Amendment Act 1885) of knowingly permitting the whole or part of the premises to be used as a brothel, the First Schedule to this Act shall apply to enlarge the rights of the lessor or landlord with respect to the assignment or determination of the lease or other contract under which the premises are held by the person convicted.

(3) Where the tenant or occupier of any premises is so convicted, or was so convicted under the said section thirteen before the commencement of this Act, and either—

(*a*) the lessor or landlord, after having the conviction brought to his notice, fails or failed to exercise his statutory rights in relation to the lease or contract under which the premises are or were held by the person convicted; or

(*b*) the lessor or landlord, after exercising his statutory rights so as to determine that lease or contract, grants or granted a new lease or enters or entered into a new contract of tenancy of the premises to, with or for the benefit of the same person, without having all reasonable provisions to prevent the recurrence of the offence inserted in the new lease or contract;

then, if subsequently an offence under this section is committed in respect of the premises during the subsistence of the lease or contract referred to in paragraph (*a*) of this subsection or (where paragraph (*b*) applies) during the subsistence of the new lease or contract, the lessor or landlord shall be deemed to be a party to that offence unless he shows that he took all reasonable steps to prevent the recurrence of the offence.

References in this subsection to the statutory rights of a lessor or landlord refer to his rights under the First Schedule to this Act or under subsection (1) of section five of the Criminal Law Amendment Act 1912 (the provisions replaced for England and Wales by that Schedule).
[Sexual Offences Act 1956, s 35.]

---

1. For mode of prosecution and penalty, see Sch 2, post.
2. The wife or husband of the accused may be called as a witness by the defence or the prosecution, see Police and Criminal Evidence Act 1984, s 80 in PART II: EVIDENCE, ante.

8–28012 36. Tenant permitting premises to be used for prostitution. It is an offence[1] for the tenant or occupier of any premises knowingly to permit[2] the whole or part of the premises to be used for the purposes of habitual prostitution*.
[Sexual Offences Act 1956, s 36(1).]

***Words inserted by the Sexual Offences Act 2003, s 56, from a date to be appointed.**

1. For mode of prosecution and penalty, see Sch 2, post. The wife or husband of the accused may be called as a witness for the prosecution or the defence, see Police and Criminal Evidence Act 1984, s 80 in PART II: EVIDENCE, ante.
2. This implies a permission by the tenant or occupier given to some other woman or women: a woman who is the sole occupier, using the premises for her own habitual prostitution, cannot be convicted of "permitting" the premises to be so used (*Mattison v Johnson* (1916) 80 JP 243).

Powers and procedure for dealing with offenders

8–28013 37. Prosecution and punishment of offences.—*Sub-ss* (1) *to* (6) *refer to the Second Schedule in which is tabulated all offences under the Act.*

(7) Nothing in this section or in the Second Schedule to this Act shall exclude the application to any of the offences referred to in the first column of the Schedule—

(*a*) of s 24 of the Magistrates' Courts Act 1980 (which relates to the summary trial of young offenders for indictable offences); or

(*b*) of subsection (5) of s 121 of the Magistrates' Courts Act 1980 (which limits the punishment which may be imposed by a magistrates' court sitting in an occasional courthouse); or

(*c*) of any enactments[1] or rule of law restricting a court's power to imprison; or

(*d*) of any enactment[2] or rule of law authorising an offender to be dealt with in a way not authorised by the enactments specially relating to his offence; or

(*e*) of any enactment or rule of law[3] authorising a jury to find a person guilty of an offence other than that with which he is charged.

[Sexual Offences Act 1956, s 37, as amended by the Children and Young Persons Act 1969, Sch 5.]

---

1. See, for example, s 1 of the Criminal Justice Act 1991 in PART III: SENTENCING, ante.
2. Examples of this occur in a court's power to impose a fine, or to make a probation order or an order of absolute or conditional discharge.
3. See, eg, *R v Simmonite* [1916] 2 KB 821, 31 JP 80.

Powers of arrest and search

8–28015 41–47. *Repealed.*

FIRST SCHEDULE

RIGHTS OF LANDLORD WHERE TENANT CONVICTED OF PERMITTING USE OF PREMISES AS BROTHEL

(*As amended by the Local Government and Housing Act 1989, Sch 11.*)

8–28047 1. Upon the conviction[1] of the tenant or occupier (in this Schedule referred to as "the tenant"), the lessor or landlord may require the tenant to assign the lease or other contract under which the premises are held by him to some person approved by the lessor or landlord.

2. If the tenant fails to do so within three months, the lessor or landlord may determine the lease or contract (but without prejudice to the rights or remedies of any party thereto accrued before the date of the determination).

3. Where the lease or contract is determined under this Schedule, the court by which the tenant was convicted may make a summary order for delivery of possession of the premises to the lessor or landlord.

4. The approval of the lessor or landlord for the purposes of paragraph 1 of this Schedule shall not be unreasonably withheld.

5. This Schedule shall have effect subject to the Rent and Mortgage Interest Restrictions Acts 1920 to 1939, the Furnished Houses (Rent Control) Act 1946, Part II of the Reserve and Auxiliary Forces (Protection of Civil Interests) Act 1951, Part I of the Landlord and Tenant Act 1954, Part I of the Housing Act 1988 and Sch 10 to the Local Government and Housing Act 1989.

---

1. Convicted under s 35 of the Act, ante.

8–28048

Section 37

SECOND SCHEDULE

TABLE OF OFFENCES, MODE OF PROSECUTION, PUNISHMENTS, ETC

(*As amended by Mental Health Act 1959, Schs 7 and 8, Street Offences Act 1959, s 4, Indecency with Children Act 1960, s 2(3), Criminal Justice Administration Act 1962, Sch 4, Sexual Offences Act 1967, ss 3 and 9, Criminal Law Act 1967, Schs 2 and 3, Family Law Reform Act 1969, s 11, Courts Act 1971, Sch 11, Criminal Jurisdiction Act 1975, Sch 6, Criminal Law Act 1977, Schs 3, 12 and 13, the Magistrates' Courts Act 1980, Sch 7, the Criminal Justice Act 1982, ss 38 and 46, the Sexual Offences Act 1985, s 3, the Criminal Justice and Public Order Act 1994, s 144, the Sexual Offences (Amendment) Act 2000 s 1(1)(b) and the Sexual Offences Act 2003, s 55.*)

PART I

Repealed.

8–28059

PART II

Offence	Mode of prosecution	Punishment
1.–32. *Repealed.*		
33. Keeping a brothel (section 33).	Summarily.	For an offence committed after a previous conviction[2], **6 months or level 4** on the standard scale **or both**; otherwise **three months or level 3** on the standard scale **or both**.
33A. Keeping a brothel used for prostitution (section 33A).	(i) on indictment (ii) summarily	Seven years Six months, or the statutory maximum, or both.

Offence	Mode of prosecution	Punishment
34. Letting premises for use as brothel (section 34).	Summarily.	For an offence committed after a previous conviction[2], **6 months or level 4** on the standard scale **or both**; otherwise **three months or level 3** on the standard scale **or both**.
35. Tenant permitting premises to be used as brothel (section 35).	Summarily.	For an offence committed after a previous conviction[2], **6 months or level 4** on the standard scale **or both**; otherwise **three months or level 3** on the standard scale **or both**.
36. Tenant permitting premises to be used for prostitution (section 36).	Summarily.	For an offence committed after a previous conviction[2], **6 months or level 4** on the standard scale **or both**; otherwise **three months or level 3** on the standard scale **or both**.

1. For procedure in respect of an offence triable either way, see Magistrates' Courts Act 1980, ss 17A–21, In PART I: MAGISTRATES' COURTS, PROCEDURE, ante.
2. For prosecutions under ss 33–36 of this Act, previous convictions under any of the said four sections count for the purposes of rendering the accused liable to the heavier penalty.

Street Offences Act 1959

(7 & 8 Eliz 2 c 57)

8–28160 1. Loitering or soliciting for purposes of prostitution. (1) It shall be an offence for a common prostitute*[1] to loiter or solicit[2] in a street[3] or public place[4] for the purpose of prostitution[5].

(2) A person guilty of an offence under this section shall be liable on summary conviction to a fine of an amount not exceeding **level 2** on the standard scale or, for an offence committed after a previous[6] conviction, to a fine of an amount not exceeding **level 3** on that scale.

(3) *Repealed.*

(4) For the purposes of this section "street" includes any bridge, road, lane, footway, subway, square, court, alley or passage, whether a thoroughfare or not, which is for the time being open to the public; and the doorways and entrances of premises abutting on a street (as hereinbefore defined), and any ground adjoining and open to a street, shall be treated as forming part of the street.

(5) *Repealed.*

[Street Offences Act 1959, s 1, as amended by the Criminal Law Act 1977, Sch 6, the Criminal Justice Act 1982, ss 46 and 71, the Statute Law (Repeals) Act 1989, Sch 1 and the Statute Law (Repeals) Act 1993, Sch 1 and the Serious Organised Crime and Police Act 2005, Sch 7.]

1. This may be proved by showing that the woman has persisted in conduct for which she had previously been cautioned by a constable (see s 2, infra). The term "common prostitute" is limited to female prostitutes and does not extend to encompass male prostitutes (*DPP v Bull* [1994] 4 All ER 411, [1994] 3 WLR 1196, 158 JP 1005).
2. A prostitute who does not make any active approach by gesture, word or signal may solicit in the sense of tempting or alluring prospective customers to come in for the purposes of prostitution and project her solicitation to passers by (*Behrendt v Burridge* [1976] 3 All ER 285, 140 JP 613).
3. An offence is committed if the person solicited is in a street or public place, although the prostitute may be on a balcony or at a window of a house adjoining the street or public place (*Smith v Hughes* [1960] 2 All ER 859, 124 JP 430); but not where a prostitute offers her services by displaying a notice board, she not being present and importuning prospective customers (*Weiss v Monahan* [1962] 1 All ER 664, 126 JP 184; *Burge v DPP* [1962] 1 All ER 666n).
4. "Public place" is not defined, but it must be construed *ejusdem generis* with the extended definition of "street" set out in sub-s (4); cf *R v Collinson* (1931) 23 Cr App Rep 49, in which a field to which the public were admitted (for one day) was held to be a public place; *Elkins v Cartlidge* [1947] 1 All ER 829, where an enclosure at the rear of an inn, entered through an open gateway, and in which cars were parked, was held to be a public place; *Glynn v Simmonds* [1952] 2 All ER 47, 116 JP 389, in which it was held that Tattersall's enclosure at a racecourse was a "place of public resort" notwithstanding a charge for admission and a right to exclude any person.
5. Kerb-crawling and persistent soliciting by a man is an offence under the Sexual Offences Act 1985, post.
6. The previous conviction may have been under a statute repealed by the Act (sub-s (5), infra).
7. This power of arrest is preserved by the Police and Criminal Evidence Act 1984, s 26 and Sch 2.

8–28161 2. Application to court by woman cautioned for loitering or soliciting. (1) Where a woman is cautioned[1] by a constable[2], in respect of her conduct in a street or public place, that if she persists in such conduct it may result in her being charged with an offence under section one of this Act, she may not later than fourteen clear days[3] afterwards apply to a magistrates' court for an order directing that there is to be no entry made in respect of that caution in any record maintained by the police of those so cautioned and that any such entry already made is to be expunged; and the court shall make the order unless satisfied that on the occasion when she was cautioned she was loitering or soliciting in a street or public place for the purpose of prostitution.*

(2) An application under this section shall be by way of complaint against the chief officer of police for the area in which the woman is cautioned or against such officer of police as he may designate for the purpose in relation to that area or any part of it; and, subject to any provision to the contrary in rules made under s 144 of the Magistrates' Courts Act 1980, on the hearing of any such complaint the procedure shall be the same as if it were a complaint by the police officer[4] against the woman, except that this shall not affect the operation of sections 55 to 57 of that Act (which relate to the non-attendance of the parties to a complaint).*

(3) Unless the woman desires[5] that the proceedings shall be conducted in public, an application under this section shall be heard and determined in camera.*

(4) In this section references to a street shall be construed in accordance with subsection (4) of section one of this Act.

[Street Offences Act 1959, s 2 amended by the Magistrates' Courts Act 1980, Sch 7.]

***Amended by the Sexual Offences Act 2003, Sch 1, from a date to be appointed.**

1. This relates to a system of cautioning introduced by the Commissioner of Police of the Metropolis whereby a woman who has not been previously convicted of loitering or soliciting for the purpose of prostitution will not be charged with an offence under s 1(1) of this Act unless she has been cautioned by the police on at least two occasions and such cautions have been formally recorded. See Home Office Circular No 109/1959: August 13th 1959. The practice of cautioning does not imply that police officers have the power to stop and detain women for this purpose: the system requires the co-operation of women; see *Collins v Wilcock* [1984] 3 All ER 374, [1984] 1 WLR 1172.

2. This refers to the offence ultimately charged. Accordingly, where sexual intercourse was taking place on a fortnightly basis and the original charge of an offence between 1 and 14 September was amended outside the time limit to an allegation of an offence between 31 May and 14 September, the defendant may have been found guilty in respect of an act other than one in the original period specified so that the time limits were not complied with (*R v Richards* [1995] Crim LR 894).

3. This means fourteen complete intervening days; ie, a woman cautioned on the 1st day of a month might apply on any day thereafter until and including the 16th day of that month.

4. Therefore, although the woman is complainant the proceedings are accusatorial requiring that the police officer must establish his case before the woman is called upon to reply.

5. It will be good practice to inform the woman of her rights under this subsection.

Protection of Children Act 1978[1]

(1978 c 37)

8–28240 **1. Indecent photographs of children.** (1) Subject to sections 1A and 1B, it is an offence for a person—

(*a*) to take, or permit to be taken or to make[2], any indecent[3] photograph or pseudo-photograph of a child; or

(*b*) to distribute[4] or show such indecent photographs or pseudo-photographs; or

(*c*) to have in his possession[5] such indecent photographs or pseudo-photographs, with a view to their being distributed or shown[6] by himself or others; or

(*d*) to publish or cause to be published any advertisement likely to be understood as conveying that the advertiser distributes or shows such indecent photographs or pseudo-photographs, or intends to do so.

(2) For the purposes of this Act, a person is to be regarded as distributing an indecent photograph or pseudo-photographs if he parts with possession of it to, or exposes or offers it for acquisition by, another person.

(3) Proceedings for an offence under this Act shall not be instituted except by or with the consent of the Director of Public Prosecutions.

(4) Where a person is charged with an offence under subsection (1) (*b*) or (*c*), it shall be a defence[7] for him to prove—

(*a*) that he had a legitimate reason for distributing or showing the photographs or pseudo-photographs or (as the case may be) having them in his possession; or

(*b*) that he had not himself seen the photographs or pseudo-photographs and did not know, nor had any cause to suspect, them to be indecent.

(5)–(7) *References to Children and Young Persons Act* 1933; *Visiting Forces Act* 1952.

[Protection of Children Act 1978, s 1, amended by the Criminal Justice Act 1988, Sch 16, the Extradition Act 1989, Sch 2, the Criminal Justice and Public Order Act 1994, s 84 and Sch 11 and the Sexual Offences Act 2003, s 141.]

---

1. For a summary offence of possession of an indecent photograph of a child, see the Criminal Justice Act 1988, s 160, this title post, to which specified provisions of this Act are applied.

2. Section 1(1)(a) renders unlawful the making of not only a photograph or pseudo-photograph but also, by virtue of section 7 post, negatives, copies of photographs and data stored on computer disk. Accordingly, a person who downloads indecent images from the Internet on to a disk or prints them off is "making an indecent photograph" within the meaning of s 1(1)(*a*), even where he was doing so only for his own use (*R v Bowden* [2000] 2 All ER 418, [2000] 2 WLR 1083, [2000] 1 Cr App Rep 438, CA). See also *Atkins v DPP* [2000] 2 All ER 425, [2000] 1 WLR 1427, [2000] 2 Cr App Rep 248, DC. However, s 1(1)(*a*) does not create an absolute offence. Therefore a person who opens an attachment to an unsolicited e-mail not knowing that the e-mail or attachment contained or was likely to contain indecent photographs of a

child is not guilty of the offence of making those photographs. But the act of voluntarily down loading an indecent image from a Web page on to a computer screen is an act of making a photograph or pseudo-photograph; there is no need for an intention to store the images with a view to future retrieval (*R v Smith, R v Jayson* [2002] Crim LR 659, [2002] EWCA Crim 683, [2003] 1 Cr App R 13).

3. The age of the child is a material consideration for the court in determining whether the photograph of the child was in fact indecent (*R v Owen* [1988] 1 WLR 134, 86 Cr App Rep 291, CA). In order to convict a person of taking an indecent photograph, it must be proved that the defendant took the photograph deliberately and intentionally. If so satisfied, the court must then decide whether the photograph was indecent by applying the recognised standards of propriety, but for this purpose the circumstances in which the photograph was taken and the motivation of the taker are irrelevant (*R v Graham-Kerr* [1988] 1 WLR 1098, 153 JP 171, CA). Articles 8 and 10 of the European Convention on Human Rights do not require a reconsideration of the interpretation of s 1 of the 1978 Act as the exceptions in art 8(2) and 10(2) apply as the Act is there for the prevention of crime, for the protection of morals, and in particular for the protection of children from being exploited, which is a matter necessary in a democratic society (*R v Smethurst* [2001] EWCA 772, 165 JP 377, [2001] Crim LR 657, [2002] 1 Cr App Rep 50).

4. Where a defendant responded to an advertisement for the sale of pornographic videos by writing to request a compilation tape showing very young girls (aged 7–13) he could be guilty in law of inciting or attempting to incite the distribution of indecent photographs of children, contrary to s 1(1) of the Criminal Attempts Act 1981; the fact that the advertiser was willing to supply its wares was nothing to the point: *R v Goldman* [2001] Crim LR 822, CA.

5. The concept of "possession" varies according to its statutory context and in this legislation an employee in a shop who knowingly has custody or control of a video, has possession of it. If he maintains that he is unaware of its obscene nature, it is open to him to rely on the defence in s 1(4)(*b*) (*R v Matrix* [1997] Crim LR 901, CA).

6. To be guilty of the offence the defendant must have had possession of the indecent photograph with a view either to its being distributed to third parties or to its being shown to persons other than himself (*R v ET* (1999) 163 JP 349, [1999] Crim LR 749).

7. The statutory defences under s 1(4) are limited to persons who distribute or are in possession of such material for a legitimate reason (eg the police) or an individual who was ignorant of and had no reason to believe that he was in possession of or distributing indecent material or in the case of simple possession, who received it unsolicited and gets rid of it with reasonable promptness. No statutory defence is available for the person who creates the material or advertises its availability. It is also not a defence that a person did not know nor had any cause to suspect that the photograph depicted persons who were 16 years or older (*R v Land* [1998]) 1 All ER 403, [1998] 3 WLR 322, [1998] 1 Cr App Rep 301.

8–28240A 1A. Marriage and other relationships. (1) This section applies where, in proceedings for an offence under section 1(1)(*a*) of taking or making an indecent photograph of a child, or for an offence under section 1(1)(*b*) or (*c*) relating to an indecent photograph of a child, the defendant proves that the photograph was of the child aged 16 or over, and that at the time of the offence charged the child and he—

(*a*) were married or civil partners of each other, or
(*b*) lived together as partners in an enduring family relationship.

(2) Subsections (5) and (6) also apply where, in proceedings for an offence under section 1(1)(*b*) or (*c*) relating to an indecent photograph of a child, the defendant proves that the photograph was of the child aged 16 or over, and that at the time when he obtained it the child and he—

(*a*) were married or civil partners of each other, or
(*b*) lived together as partners in an enduring family relationship.

(3) This section applies whether the photograph showed the child alone or with the defendant, but not if it showed any other person.

(4) In the case of an offence under section 1(1)(*a*), if sufficient evidence is adduced to raise an issue as to whether the child consented to the photograph being taken or made, or as to whether the defendant reasonably believed that the child so consented, the defendant is not guilty of the offence unless it is proved that the child did not so consent and that the defendant did not reasonably believe that the child so consented.

(5) In the case of an offence under section 1(1)(*b*), the defendant is not guilty of the offence unless it is proved that the showing or distributing was to a person other than the child.

(6) In the case of an offence under section 1(1)(*c*), if sufficient evidence is adduced to raise an issue both—

(*a*) as to whether the child consented to the photograph being in the defendant's possession, or as to whether the defendant reasonably believed that the child so consented, and
(*b*) as to whether the defendant had the photograph in his possession with a view to its being distributed or shown to anyone other than the child,

the defendant is not guilty of the offence unless it is proved either that the child did not so consent and that the defendant did not reasonably believe that the child so consented, or that the defendant had the photograph in his possession with a view to its being distributed or shown to a person other than the child.

[Protection of Children Act 1978, s 1A, as inserted by the Sexual Offences Act 2003, s 45 and the Civil Partnership Act 2004, Sch 27.]

8–28240B 1B. Exception for criminal proceedings, investigations etc. (1) In proceedings for an offence under section 1(1)(*a*) of making an indecent photograph or pseudo-photograph of a child, the defendant is not guilty of the offence if he proves that—

(*a*) it was necessary for him to make the photograph or pseudo-photograph for the purposes of the prevention, detection or investigation of crime, or for the purposes of criminal proceedings, in any part of the world, (*b*) at the time of the offence charged he was a member of the Security Service, and it was necessary for him to make the photograph or pseudo-photograph for the exercise of any of the functions of the Service, or

(*c*) at the time of the offence charged he was a member of GCHQ, and it was necessary for him to make the photograph or pseudo-photograph for the exercise of any of the functions of GCHQ.

(2) In this section "GCHQ" has the same meaning as in the Intelligence Services Act 1994.
[Protection of Children Act 1978, s 1B, as inserted by the Sexual Offences Act 2003, s 46.]

8–28241 **2. Evidence.** (1), (2) *Repealed.*

(3) In proceedings under this Act relating to indecent photographs of children a person is to be taken as having been a child at any material time if it appears from the evidence as a whole that he was then under the age of 18[1].
[Protection of Children Act 1978, s 2, as amended by the Magistrates' Courts Act 1980, Sch 9, the Police and Criminal Evidence Act 1984, Sch 7, the Criminal Justice and Public Order Act 1994, Sch 10 and the Sexual Offences Act 2003, s 45.]

---

1. It is a matter for the court to decide whether an unknown person depicted in a photograph is under the age of 16 years. There is no requirement for paediatric or other expert evidence which in any event will be inadmissible (*R v Land* [1998]) 1 All ER 403, [1998] 3 WLR 322, [1998] 1 Cr App Rep 301).

8–28242 **3. Offences by corporations.** (1) Where a body corporate is guilty of an offence under this Act and it is proved that the offence occurred with the consent or connivance of, or was attributable to any neglect on the part of, any director, manager, secretary or other officer of the body, or any person who was purporting to act in any such capacity he, as well as the body corporate, shall be deemed to be guilty of that offence and shall be liable to be proceeded against and punished accordingly.

(2) Where the affairs of a body corporate are managed by its members, subsection (1) shall apply in relation to the acts and defaults of a member in connection with his functions of management as if he were a director of the body corporate.
[Protection of Children Act 1978, s 3.]

8–28243 **4. Entry, search and seizure.** (1) The following applies where a justice of the peace is satisfied by information on oath, laid by or on behalf of the Director of Public Prosecutions or by a constable, that there is reasonable ground for suspecting that, in any premises in the petty sessions area for which he acts, there is an indecent photograph or pseudo-photograph of a child.

(2) The justice may issue a warrant under his hand authorising any constable to enter (if need be by force) and search the premises, and to seize and remove any articles which he believes (with reasonable cause) to be or include indecent photographs or pseudo-photographs of children.

(3) Articles seized under the authority of the warrant, and not returned to the occupier of the premises, shall be brought before a justice of the peace acting for the same petty sessions area as the justice who issued the warrant.

(4) This section and section 5 below apply in relation to any stall or vehicle, as they apply in relation to premises, with the necessary modifications of references to premises and the substitution of references to use for references to occupation.
[Protection of Children Act 1978, s 4, as amended by the Criminal Justice Act 1988, Schs 15 and 16 and the Criminal Justice and Public Order Act 1994, Schs 9, 10 and 11.]

8–28244 **5. Forfeiture.** (1) The justice before whom any articles are brought in pursuance of section 4 above may issue a summons to the occupier of the premises to appear on a day specified in the summons before a magistrates' court for that petty sessions area to show cause why they should not be forfeited.

(2) If the court is satisfied that the articles are in fact indecent photographs or pseudo-photographs of children, the court shall order them to be forfeited; but if the person summoned does not appear, the court shall not make an order unless service of the summons is proved.

(3) In addition to the persons summoned, any other person being the owner of the articles brought before the court, or the persons who made them, or any other person through whose hands they had passed before being seized, shall be entitled to appear before the court on the day specified in the summons to show cause why they should not be forfeited.

(4) Where any of the articles are ordered to be forfeited under subsection (2), any person who appears, or was entitled to appear, to show cause against the making of the order may appeal to the Crown Court.

(5) If as respects any articles brought before it the court does not order forfeiture, the court may if it thinks fit order the person on whose information the warrant for their seizure was issued to pay such costs as the court thinks reasonable to any person who has appeared before it to show cause why the photographs or pseudo-photographs should not be forfeited; and costs ordered to be paid under this subsection shall be recoverable as a civil debt.

(6) Where indecent photographs or pseudo-photographs of children are seized under section 4

above, and a person is convicted under section 1(1) or section 160 of the Criminal Justice Act 1988[1] of offences in respect of those photographs, the court shall order them to be forfeited.

(7) An order made under subsection (2) or (6) above (including an order made on appeal) shall not take effect until the expiration of the ordinary time within which an appeal may be instituted or, where such an appeal is duly instituted, until the appeal is finally decided or abandoned; and for this purpose—

(*a*) an application for a case to be stated or for leave to appeal shall be treated as the institution of an appeal; and

(*b*) where a decision on appeal is subject to a further appeal, the appeal is not finally decided until the expiration of the ordinary time within which a further appeal may be instituted or, where a further appeal is duly instituted, until the further appeal is finally decided or abandoned.

[Protection of Children Act 1978, s 5, as amended by the Criminal Justice Act 1988, Schs 15 and 16 and the Criminal Justice and Public Order Act 1994, Sch 10.]

1. See this title, post.

8–28245 **6. Punishments.** (1) Offences under this Act shall be punishable either on conviction on indictment or on summary conviction.

(2) A person convicted on indictment of any offence under this Act shall be liable to imprisonment for a term of not more than **ten years**, or to a **fine** or to **both**.

(3) A person convicted summarily of any offence under this Act shall be liable[1]—

(*a*) to imprisonment for a term not exceeding **six months**; or

(*b*) to a fine not exceeding **the prescribed sum** for the purposes of section 32 of the Magistrates' Courts Act 1980 (punishment on summary conviction of offences triable either way: **£1,000** or other sum substituted by order under that Act), or to **both**.

[Protection of Children Act 1978, s 6, as amended by the Magistrates' Courts Act 1980, Sch 7 and the Criminal Justice and Court Services Act 2000, s 41.]

1. For procedure with respect to an offence triable either way, see the Magistrates' Courts Act 1980, ss 17A–21, in PART I, MAGISTRATES' COURTS, PROCEDURE, ante.

8–28246 **7. Interpretation.** (1) The following subsections apply for the interpretation of the Act.

(2) References to an indecent photograph include an indecent film, a copy of an indecent photograph or film, and an indecent photograph comprised in a film.

(3) Photographs (including those comprised in a film) shall, if they show children and are indecent, be treated for all purposes of this Act as indecent photographs of children and so as respects pseudo-photographs.

(4) References to a photograph include—

(*a*) the negative as well as the positive version; and

(*b*) data stored on a computer disc or by other electronic means which is capable of conversion into a photograph.

(5) "Film" includes any form of video-recording.

(6) "Child", subject to subsection (8), means a person under the age of 16*.

(7) "Pseudo-photograph" means an image, whether made by computer-graphics or otherwise howsoever, which appears to be a photograph.

(8) If the impression conveyed by a pseudo-photograph is that the person shown is a child, the pseudo-photograph shall be treated for all purposes of this Act as showing a child and so shall a pseudo-photograph where the predominant impression conveyed is that the person shown is a child notwithstanding that some of the physical characteristics shown are those of an adult.

(9) References to an indecent pseudo-photograph include—

(*a*) a copy of an indecent pseudo-photograph; and

(*b*) data stored on a computer disc or by other electronic means which is capable of conversion into a pseudo-photograph.

[Protection of Children Act 1978, s 7, as amended by the Criminal Justice and Public Order Act 1994, s 84.]

***Reference "18" substituted by Sexual Offences Act 2003, s 45, from a date to be appointed.**

Sexual Offences Act 1985

(1985 c 44)

Soliciting of women by men

8–28260 **1. Kerb-crawling.** (1) A person commits an offence if he solicits another person (or different persons) for the purpose of prostitution—

(*a*) from a motor vehicle while it is in a street or public place; or (*b*) in a street or public place while in the immediate vicinity of a motor vehicle that he has just got out of or off,

persistently or in such manner or in such circumstances as to be likely[1] to cause annoyance to the person (or any of the persons) solicited, or nuisance to other persons in the neighbourhood.

(2) A person guilty of an offence under this section shall be liable on summary conviction to a fine not exceeding **level 3** on the standard scale.

(3) In this section "motor vehicle" has the same meaning as in the Road Traffic Act 1988.

[Sexual Offences Act 1985, s 1 amended by the Road Traffic (Consequential Provisions) Act 1988, Sch 3 and the Statute Law (Repeals) Act 1993, Sch 1 and the Sexual Offences Act 2003, Sch 1.]

1. It is sufficient for the prosecution to prove there was a likelihood of nuisance to other persons in the neighbourhood, and it is not necessary to call evidence that a specific individual was in fact caused nuisance or annoyance. Moreover, justices are entitled to take account of their local knowledge of the regular presence of prostitutes in a particular neighbourhood and of the fact that an area is heavily populated and residential (*Paul v DPP* (1989) 90 Cr App Rep 173, 153 JP 512, DC).

8–28261 **2. Persistent soliciting of women for the purpose of prostitution.** (1) A man commits an offence if in a street or public place he persistently solicits[1] a woman (or different women) for the purpose of prostitution.

(2) A person guilty of an offence under this section shall be liable on summary conviction to a fine not exceeding **level 3** on the standard scale.★

[Sexual Offences Act 1985, s 2 and the Statute Law (Repeals) Act 1993, Sch 1.]

★Section amended by the Sexual Offences Act 2003, Sch 1, from a date to be appointed.

1. The prosecution must prove that the defendant gave some positive indication by physical act or words to a prostitute that he required her services; the act of driving a car again and again late at night down a street known to be frequented by prostitutes was held not to constitute soliciting (*Darroch v DPP* (1990) 154 JP 844, [1990] Crim LR 814).

Supplementary

8–28262 **4. Interpretation.** (1) References in this Act to a man soliciting a woman for the purpose of prostitution are references to his soliciting her for the purpose of obtaining her services as a prostitute.★

(2) The use in any provision of this Act of the word "man" without the addition of the word "boy" shall not prevent the provision applying to any person to whom it would have applied if both words had been used, and similarly with the words "woman" and "girl".★

(3) Paragraphs (*a*) and (*b*) of section 6 of the Interpretation Act 1978 (words importing the masculine gender to include the feminine, and vice versa) do not apply to this Act.★

(4) For the purposes of this Act "street" includes any bridge, road, lane, footway, subway, square, court, alley or passage, whether a thoroughfare or not, which is for the time being open to the public; and the doorways and entrances of premises abutting on a street (as hereinbefore defined), and any ground adjoining and open to a street, shall be treated as forming part of the street.

[Sexual Offences Act 1985, s 4.]

★Subsection (1) amended and sub-ss (2) and (3) repealed by the Sexual Offences Act 2003, Sch 1, from a date to be appointed.

Criminal Justice Act 1988[1]

(1988 c 33)

PART XI[2]

MISCELLANEOUS

Possession of indecent photograph of child

8–28270 **160. Summary offence of possession of indecent photograph of child.** (1) It is an offence[3] for a person to have any indecent photograph or pseudo-photograph of a child in his possession.★

(2) Where a person is charged with an offence under subsection (1) above, it shall be a defence for him to prove—

(*a*) that he had a legitimate reason for having the photograph or pseudo-photograph in his possession; or

(*b*) that he had not himself seen the photograph or pseudo-photograph and did not know, nor had any cause to suspect, it[4] to be indecent; or

(*c*) that the photograph or pseudo-photograph was sent to him without any prior request made by him or on his behalf and that he did not keep it for an unreasonable time.

(2A) A person shall be liable onconviction on indictment of an offence under this section to imprisonment for a term not exceeding **five years** or a fine, or **both**.

(3) A person shall be liable[5] on summary conviction of an offence under this section to imprisonment for a term not exceeding **six months** or a fine not exceeding **level 5** on the standard scale, or **both**.

(4) Sections 1(3), 2(3), 3 and 7 of the Protection of Children Act 1978[6] shall have effect as if any reference in them to that Act included a reference to this section.

(5) (*Repealed*)[7].*

[Criminal Justice Act 1988, s 160, as amended by the Criminal Justice and Public Order Act 1994, ss 84 and 86 and Sch 11 and the Criminal Justice and Court Services Act 2000, s 41(3).]

***Subsection (1) amended and new s 160A inserted by the Sexual Offences Act 2003, s 45 and Sch 6, from a date to be appointed.**

1. For other provisions of the Criminal Justice Act 1988, see in particular PART I: MAGISTRATES' COURTS, PROCEDURE, ante.
2. Part XI contains ss 133–167.
3. In *R v Richard Thompson* [2004] EWCA Crim 669, [2005] 1 Cr App R (S) 1, the Court of Appeal gave the following guidance on the drafting of indictments and informations: (1) in cases where there are significant numbers of photographs, in addition to the specific counts there should be a comprehensive count dealing with the remainder; (2) the specific counts should reflect the range of images in the comprehensive count; (3) where it is impractical to present the court with specific counts that are agreed to be representative of the comprehensive count, there needs to be an approximate breakdown, best achieved by means of a prosecution schedule, of the number of images at each level; (4) each of the counts should make clear whether the image is a real image or a pseudo image; (5) each image charged in a specific count should be identified by a reference; and (6) the estimated age range of the child shown in each of the images should where possible be provided.
The offence of possession under s 160(1) is not committed unless the defendant knows that he has the photographs in his possession (*Atkins v DPP* [2000] 2 All ER 425, [2000] 1 WLR 1427, [2000] 2 Cr App Rep 248, DC).
4. The "it" in s 160(2)(*b*) refers to an indecent image of a child and not an indecent image alone; thus, the defence is available where the defendant had reason to suspect that the image was indecent but not that it was an indecent image of a child: *R v Collier* [2004] EWCA Crim 1411, [2005] 1 WLR 843, [2004] Crim LR 1039, [2005] 1 Cr App R 9.
5. For procedure in respect of an offence triable either way, see the Magistrates' Courts Act 1980, ss 17A–21 in PART I: MAGISTRATES' COURTS, PROCEDURE, ante.
6. See this title, ante.
7. The reference to the coming into force of s 160 is to be construed, for the purpose of the amendments made by s 84(4) of the Criminal Justice and Public Order Act 1994, as a reference to the coming into force of s 84(4) (Criminal Justice and Public Order Act 1994, s 84(4)).

8–28270A **160A. Marriage and other relationships.** (1) This section applies where, in proceedings for an offence under section 160 relating to an indecent photograph of a child, the defendant proves that the photograph was of the child aged 16 or over, and that at the time of the offence charged the child and he—

(*a*) were married*, or
(*b*) lived together as partners in an enduring family relationship.

(2) This section also applies where, in proceedings for an offence under section 160 relating to an indecent photograph of a child, the defendant proves that the photograph was of the child aged 16 or over, and that at the time when he obtained it the child and he—

(*a*) were married or were civil partners of each other, or
(*b*) lived together as partners in an enduring family relationship.

(3) This section applies whether the photograph showed the child alone or with the defendant, but not if it showed any other person.

(4) If sufficient evidence is adduced to raise an issue as to whether the child consented to the photograph being in the defendant's possession, or as to whether the defendant reasonably believed that the child so consented, the defendant is not guilty of the offence unless it is proved that the child did not so consent and that the defendant did not reasonably believe that the child so consented.

[Criminal Justice Act 1988, s 160A, as inserted by the Sexual Offences Act 2003, s 45 and the Civil Partnership Act 2004, Sch 27.]

Sexual Offences (Amendment) Act 1992

(1992 c 34)

8–28271 **1. Anonymity of victims of certain offences.** (1) Where an allegation has been made that an offence to which this Act applies has been committed against a person, No matter relating to that person shall during that person's lifetime be included in any publication,if it is likely to lead members of the public to identify that person as the person against whom the offence is alleged to have been committed.

(2) Where a person is accused of an offence to which this Act applies, no matter likely to lead members of the public to identify a person as the person against whom the offence is alleged to have been committed ("the complainant") shall during the complainant's lifetime be included in any publication.

(3) This section—

(*a*) does not apply in relation to a person by virtue of subsection (1) at any time after a person has been accused of the offence, and

(*b*) in its application in relation to a person by virtue of subsection (2), has effect subject to any direction given under section 3.

(3A) The matters relating to a person in relation to which the restrictions imposed by subsection (1) or (2) apply (if their inclusion in any publication is likely to have the result mentioned in that subsection) include in particular—

(*a*) the person's name,
(*b*) the person's address,
(*c*) the identity of any school or other educational establishment attended by the person,
(*d*) the identity of any place of work, and
(*e*) any still or moving picture of the person.

(4) Nothing in this section prohibits the publication or inclusion in a relevant programme of matter consisting only of a report of criminal proceedings other than proceedings at, or intended to lead to, or on an appeal arising out of, a trial at which the accused is charged with the offence.*
[Sexual Offences (Amendment) Act 1992, s 1, as amended by the Youth Justice and Criminal Evidence Act 1999, Sch 2.]

***Section reproduced as amended by the Youth Justice and Criminal Evidence Act 1999, in force 7 October 2004 in England and Wales. In force in relation to Scotland for the purposes of a making a prosecution under s 5; date to be appointed for remaining purposes.**

8–28272 **2. Offences to which this Act applies.** (1) This Act applies to the following offences against the law of England and Wales—

(*aa*) rape;
(*ab*) burglary with intent to rape;
(*a*) any offence under any of the provisions of the Sexual Offences Act 1956 mentioned in subsection (2);
(*b*) any offence under section 128 of the Mental Health Act 1959 (intercourse with mentally handicapped person by hospital staff etc);
(*c*) any offence under section 1 of the Indecency with Children Act 1960 (indecent conduct towards young child);
(*d*) any offence under section 54 of the Criminal Law Act 1977 (incitement by man of his grand-daughter, daughter or sister under the age of 16 to commit incest with him);
(*da*) any offence under any of the provisions of Part 1 of the Sexual Offences Act 2003 except section 64, 65, 69 or 71;
(*e*) any attempt to commit any of the offences mentioned in paragraphs (*aa*) to (*da*).
(*f*) any conspiracy to commit any of those offences;
(*g*) any incitement of another to commit any of those offences;
(*h*) aiding, abetting, counselling or procuring the commission of any of the offences mentioned in paragraphs (*aa*) to (*e*) and (*g*);

(2) The provisions of the Act of 1956 are—

(*a*) section 2 (procurement of a woman by threats);
(*b*) section 3 (procurement of a woman by false pretences);
(*c*) section 4 (administering drugs to obtain intercourse with a woman);
(*d*) section 5 (intercourse with a girl under the age of 13);
(*e*) section 6 (intercourse with a girl between the ages of 13 and 16);
(*f*) section 7 (intercourse with a mentally handicapped person);
(*g*) section 9 (procurement of a mentally handicapped person);
(*h*) section 10 (incest by a man);
(*i*) section 11 (incest by a woman);
(*j*) section 12 (buggery);
(*k*) section 14 (indecent assault on a woman);
(*l*) section 15 (indecent assault on a man);
(*m*) section 16 (assault with intent to commit buggery).
(*n*) section 17 (abduction of woman by force).

(3) This Act applies to the following offences against the law of Northern Ireland—

(*a*) rape;
(*b*) burglary with intent to rape;
(*c*) any offence under any of the following provisions of the Offences against the Person Act 1861—

(i) section 52 (indecent assault on a female);
(ii) section 53 so far as it relates to abduction of a woman against her will;
(iii) section 61 (buggery);

(iv) section 62 (attempt to commit buggery, assault with intent to commit buggery or indecent assault on a male);

(*d*) any offence under any of the following provisions of the Criminal Law Amendment Act 1885—

(i) section 3 (procuring unlawful carnal knowledge of woman by threats, false pretences or administering drugs);

(ii) section 4 (unlawful carnal knowledge, or attempted unlawful carnal knowledge, of a girl under 14);

(iii) section 5 (unlawful carnal knowledge of a girl under 17);

(*e*) any offence under any of the following provisions of the Punishment of Incest Act 1908—

(i) section 1 (incest, attempted incest by males);

(ii) section 2 (incest by females over 16);

(*f*) any offence under section 22 of the Children and Young Persons Act (Northern Ireland) 1968 (indecent conduct towards child);

(*g*) any offence under Article 9 of the Criminal Justice (Northern Ireland) Order 1980 (inciting girl under 16 to have incestuous sexual intercourse);

(*h*) any offence under any of the following provisions of the Mental Health (Northern Ireland) Order 1986—

(i) Article 122(1)(*a*) (unlawful sexual intercourse with a woman suffering from severe mental handicap);

(ii) Article 122(1)(*b*) (procuring a woman suffering from severe mental handicap to have unlawful sexual intercourse);

(iii) Article 123 (unlawful sexual intercourse by hospital staff, etc with a person receiving treatment for mental disorder);*

(*i*) any attempt to commit any of the offences mentioned in paragraphs (*a*) to (*ha*);

(*j*) any conspiracy to commit any of those offences;

(*k*) any incitement of another to commit any of those offences;

(*l*) aiding, abetting, counselling or procuring the commission of any of the offences mentioned in paragraphs (*a*) to (*i*) and (*k*).

(4) *Application to a service offence.*

[Sexual Offences (Amendment) Act 1992, s 2, as amended by the Criminal Justice and Public Order Act 1994, Sch 9, the Armed Forces Act 2001, Sch 6, the Youth Justice and Criminal Evidence Act 1999, s 48 and Sch 2, the Sexual Offences Act 2003, Sch 6.]

***New para (*hh*) inserted by SI 2003/1247, Sch 1 from a date to be appointed.**

8–28273 3. Power to displace section 1. (1) If, before the commencement of a trial at which a person is charged with an offence to which this Act applies, he or another person against whom the complainant may be expected to give evidence at the trial, applies to the judge for a direction under this subsection and satisfies the judge—

(*a*) that the direction is required for the purpose of inducing persons who are likely to be needed as witnesses at the trial to come forward; and

(*b*) that the conduct of the applicant's defence at the trial is likely to be substantially prejudiced if the direction is not given,

the judge shall direct that section 1 shall not, by virtue of the accusation alleging the offence in question, apply in relation to the complainant.

(2) If at a trial the judge is satisfied—

(*a*) that the effect of section 1 is to impose a substantial and unreasonable restriction upon the reporting of proceedings at the trial, and

(*b*) that it is in the public interest to remove or relax the restriction,

he shall direct that that section shall not apply to such matter as is specified in the direction.

(3) A direction shall not be given under subsection (2) by reason only of the outcome of the trial.

(4) If a person who has been convicted of an offence and has given notice of appeal against the conviction, or notice of an application for leave so to appeal, applies to the appellate court for a direction under this subsection and satisfies the court—

(*a*) that the direction is required for the purpose of obtaining evidence in support of the appeal; and

(*b*) that the applicant is likely to suffer substantial injustice if the direction is not given,

the court shall direct that section 1 shall not, by virtue of an accusation which alleges an offence to which this Act applies and is specified in the direction, apply in relation to a complainant so specified.

(5) A direction given under any provision of this section does not affect the operation of section 1 at any time before the direction is given.

(6) In subsections (1) and (2), "judge" means—

(*a*) in the case of an offence which is to be tried summarily or for which the mode of trial has not been determined, any justice of the peace; and

(*b*) in any other case, any judge of the Crown Court in England and Wales.

(6A) In its application to Northern Ireland, this section has effect as if—

(*a*) in subsections (1) and (2) for any reference to the judge there were substituted a reference to the court; and

(*b*) subsection (6) were omitted.

(7) If, after the commencement of a trial at which a person is charged with an offence to which this Act applies, a new trial of the person for that offence is ordered, the commencement of any previous trial shall be disregarded for the purposes of subsection (1).

[Sexual Offences (Amendment) Act 1992, s 3, as amended by the Youth Justice and Criminal Evidence Act 1999, s 48, Sch 2 and SI 2005/886.]

8–28274 **4. Special rules for cases of incest or buggery.** (1) In this section—

"section 10 offence" means an offence under section 10 of the Sexual Offences Act 1956 (incest by a man) or an attempt to commit that offence;

"section 11 offence" means an offence under section 11 of that Act (incest by a woman) or an attempt to commit that offence;

"section 12 offence" means an offence under section 12 of that Act (buggery) or an attempt to commit that offence.

(2) Section 1 does not apply to a woman against whom a section 10 offence is alleged to have been committed if she is accused of having committed a section 11 offence against the man who is alleged to have committed the section 10 offence against her.

(3) Section 1 does not apply to a man against whom a section 11 offence is alleged to have been committed if he is accused of having committed a section 10 offence against the woman who is alleged to have committed the section 11 offence against him.

(4) Section 1 does not apply to a person against whom a section 12 offence is alleged to have been committed if that person is accused of having committed a section 12 offence against the person who is alleged to have committed the section 12 offence against him.

(5) Subsection (2) does not affect the operation of this Act in relation to anything done at any time before the woman is accused.

(6) Subsection (3) does not affect the operation of this Act in relation to anything done at any time before the man is accused.

(7) Subsection (4) does not affect the operation of this Act in relation to anything done at any time before the person mentioned first in that subsection is accused.

(8) In its application to Northern Ireland, this section has effect as if—

(*a*) subsection (1) were omitted;

(*b*) for references to a section 10 offence there were substituted references to an offence under section 1 of the Punishment of Incest Act 1908 (incest by a man) or an attempt to commit that offence;

(*c*) for references to a section 11 offence there were substituted references to an offence under section 2 of that Act (incest by a woman) or an attempt to commit that offence; and

(*d*) for references to a section 12 offence there were substituted references to an offence under section 61 of the Offences against the Person Act 1861* (buggery) or an attempt to commit that offence.

(9) *Application to a service offence.*

[Sexual Offences (Amendment) Act 1992, s 4, as amended by the Armed Forces Act 2001, Sch 6 and the Youth Justice and Criminal Evidence Act 1999, Sch 2.]

***Words substituted by SI 2003/1247 from a date to be appointed.**

8–28275 **5. Offences.** (1) If any matter is included in a publication in contravention of section 1, the following persons shall be guilty of an offence and liable on summary conviction to a fine not exceeding **level 5** on the standard scale—

(*a*) where the publication is a newspaper or periodical, any proprietor, any editor and any publisher of the newspaper or periodical;

(*b*) where the publication is a relevant programme—

(i) any body corporate or Scottish partnership engaged in providing the programme service in which the programme is included; and

(ii) any person having functions in relation to the programme corresponding to those of an editor of a newspaper;

(*c*) in the case of any other publication, any person publishing it.

(2) Where a person is charged with an offence under this section in respect of theinclusion of any matter in a publication, it shall be a defence, subject to subsection (3), to prove that the publication

in which the matter appeared was one in respect of which the person against whom the offence mentioned in section 1 is alleged to have been committed had given written consent to the appearance of matter of that description.

(3) Written consent is not a defence if it is proved that any person interfered unreasonably with the peace or comfort of the person giving the consent, with intent to obtain it, or that person was under the age of 16 at the time when it was given.

(4) Proceedings for an offence under this section shall not be instituted except by or with the consent of the Attorney General if the offence is alleged to have been committed in England and Wales or of the Attorney General for Northern Ireland if the offence is alleged to have been committed in Northern Ireland.

(5) Where a person is charged with an offence under this section it shall be a defence to prove that at the time of the alleged offence he was not aware, and neither suspected nor had reason to suspect, that the publication included the matter in question.

(5A) Where—

(*a*) a person is charged with an offence under this section, and

(*b*) the offence relates to the inclusion of any matter in a publication in contravention of section 1(1),

it shall be a defence to prove that at the time of the alleged offence he was not aware, and neither suspected nor had reason to suspect, that the allegation in question had been made.

(6) Where an offence under this section committed by a body corporate is proved to have been committed with the consent or connivance of, or to be attributable to any neglect on the part of—

(*a*) a director, manager, secretary or other similar officer of the body corporate, or

(*b*) a person purporting to act in any such capacity,

he as well as the body corporate shall be guilty of the offence and liable to be proceeded against and punished accordingly.

(7) In relation to a body corporate whose affairs are managed by its members "director", in subsection (6), means a member of the body corporate.

(8) Where an offence under this section is committed by a Scottish partnership and is proved to have been committed with the consent or connivance of a partner, he as well as the partnership shall be guilty of the offence and shall be liable to be proceeded against and punished accordingly.★

[Sexual Offences (Amendment) Act 1992, s 5, as amended by the the Youth Justice and Criminal Evidence Act 1999, Sch 2.]

★Section reproduced as amended by the Youth Justice and Criminal Evidence Act 1999, in force 7 October 2004 in England and Wales. In force in relation to Scotland for the purposes of a making a prosecution under s 5; date to be appointed for remaining purposes.

8–28276 6. Interpretation etc. (1) In this Act—

"complainant" has the meaning given in section 1(2)[1];

"corresponding civil offence", in relation to a service offence, means the civil offence (within the meaning of the Army Act 1955, the Air Force Act 1955 or the Naval Discipline Act 1957) the commission of which constitutes the service offence;

"picture" includes a likeness however produced;

"publication" includes any speech, writing, relevant programme or other communication in whatever form, which is addressed to the public at large or any section of the public (and for this purpose every relevant programme shall be taken to be so addressed), but does not include an indictment or other document prepared for use in particular legal proceedings;

"relevant programme" means a programme included in a programme service, within the meaning of the Broadcasting Act 1990[1]; and

"service offence" means an offence against section 70 of the Army Act 1955, section 70 of the Air Force Act 1955 or section 42 of the Naval Discipline Act 1957.

(2) For the purposes of this Act, where it is alleged or there is an accusation—

(*a*) that an offence of conspiracy or incitement of another to commit an offence mentioned in section 2(1)(*aa*) to (*d*) or (3)(*a*) to (*h*)★ has been committed, or

(*b*) that an offence of aiding, abetting, counselling or procuring the commission of an offence of incitement of another to commit an offence mentioned in section 2(1)(*aa*) to (*d*) or (3)(*a*) to (*h*)★ has been committed,

the person against whom the substantive offence is alleged to have been intended to be committed shall be regarded as the person against whom the conspiracy or incitement is alleged to have been committed.

In this subsection, "the substantive offence" means the offence to which the alleged conspiracy or incitement related.

(3) For the purposes of this Act, a person is accused of an offence[1], other than a service offence, if—

(*a*) an information is laid, or, (in Northern Ireland) a complaint is made, alleging that he has committed the offence,
(*b*) he appears before a court charged with the offence,
(*c*) a court before which he is appearing commits him** for trial on a new charge alleging the offence, or
(*d*) a bill of indictment charging him with the offence is preferred before a court in which he may lawfully be indicted for the offence,

and references in subsection (2A) and in section 3 to an accusation alleging an offence shall be construed accordingly.*

(3A) *Application to a service offence.*

(4) Nothing in this Act affects any prohibition or restriction imposed by virtue of any other enactment upon a publication or upon matter included in a relevant programme.
[Sexual Offences (Amendment) Act 1992, s 6, as amended by the Criminal Justice and Public Order Act 1994, Sch 9, the Youth Justice and Criminal Evidence Act 1999, Sch 2, the Armed Forces Act 2001, Sch 6 and the Youth Justice and Criminal Evidence Act 1999, s 48.]

***References substituted by SI 2003/1247 from a date to be appointed.**
****Words substituted by the Criminal Justice Act 2003, Sch 3 from a date to be appointed.**
1. Text (not reproduced) is inserted here by the Armed Forces Act 2001, Sch 6, Part I in relation to service offences.

8–28276A 7. Courts-martial. *Application to courts-martial.*

Sexual Offences Act 1993

(1993 c 30)

8–28277 1. Abolition of presumption of sexual incapacity. The presumption of criminal law that a boy under the age of fourteen is incapable of sexual intercourse (whether natural or unnatural) is hereby abolished.
[Sexual Offences Act 1993, s 1.]

8–28278 2. Short title, commencement and extent. (1) This Act may be cited as the Sexual Offences Act 1993.

(2) This Act shall come into force at the end of the period of two months beginning with the day on which it is passed.

(3) This Act does not apply to acts done before its commencement.

(4) This Act extends to England and Wales only.
[Sexual Offences Act 1993, s 2.]

Sexual Offences (Conspiracy and Incitement) Act 1996[1]

(1996 c 29)

England and Wales and Northern Ireland

8–28279 1 Conspiracy to commit certain sexual acts outside the United Kingdom. *Repealed.*

1. The Sexual Offences (Conspiracy and Incitement (Act 1996 was brought into force on 1 October 1996 by the Sexual Offences (Conspiracy and Incitement) Act 1996 (Commencement) Order 1996, SI 1996/2262.

8–28280 2. Incitement to commit certain sexual acts outside the United Kingdom. (1) This section applies where—

(*a*) any act done by a person in England and Wales would amount to the offence of incitement to commit a listed sexual offence but for the fact that what he had in view would not be an offence triable in England and Wales,
(*b*) the whole or part of what he had in view was intended to take place in a country or territory outside the United Kingdom, and
(*c*) what he had in view would involve the commission of an offence under the law in force in that country or territory.

(2) Where this section applies—

(*a*) what he had in view is to be treated as that listed sexual offence for the purposes of any charge of incitement brought in respect of that act, and
(*b*) any such charge is accordingly triable in England and Wales.

(3) Any act of incitement by means of a message (however communicated) is to be treated as done in England and Wales if the message is sent or received in England and Wales.
[Sexual Offences (Conspiracy and Incitement) Act 1996, s 2.]

8–28281 3. Sections 1 and 2: supplementary. (1) Conduct punishable under the law in force in any country or territory is an offence under the law for the purposes of section 2, however it is described in that law.

(2) Subject to subsection (3), a condition in section 2(1)(*c*) is to be taken to be satisfied unless, not later than rules of court may provide, the defence serve on the prosecution a notice—

(*a*) stating that, on the facts as alleged with respect to what the accused had in view, the condition is not in their opinion satisfied,
(*b*) showing their grounds for that opinion, and
(*c*) requiring the prosecution to show that it is satisfied.

(3) *Repealed.*

(4) The court, if it thinks fit, may permit the defence to require the prosecution to show that the condition is satisfied without the prior service of a notice under subsection (2).

(5) In the Crown Court the question whether the condition is satisfied is to be decided by the judge alone.

(6) In any proceedings in respect of any offence triable by virtue of section 2, it is immaterial to guilt whether or not the accused was a British citizen at the time of any act or other event proof of which is required for conviction of the offence.

(7) *Repealed.*

(8) References to an offence of incitement to commit a listed sexual offence include an offence triable in England and Wales as such an incitement by virtue of section 2 (without prejudice to subsection (2) of that section).

(9) Subsection (8) applies to references in any enactment, instrument or document (except those in section 2 of this Act and in Part I of the Criminal Law Act 1977).

[Sexual Offences (Conspiracy and Incitement) Act 1996, s 3, as amended by the Criminal Justice (Terrorism and Conspiracy) Act 1998, Schs 1 and 2.]

8–28282 4. *Northern Ireland.*

8–28283 5. Interpretation. In this Act "listed sexual offence" has the meaning given by the Schedule.

[Sexual Offences (Conspiracy and Incitement) Act 1996, s 5.]

Scotland

8–28284 6. *Scottish provision.*

General

8–28285 7. Short title, commencement and extent. (1) This Act may be cited as the Sexual Offences (Conspiracy and Incitement) Act 1996.

(2) This Act is to come into force on such day as the Secretary of State may by order made by statutory instrument appoint[1], and different days may be appointed for different purposes and for different areas.

(3) Nothing in section 2 or 6 applies to any act or other event occurring before the coming into force of that section.

(4) This Act, except sections 4 and 6, extends to England and Wales.

(5) Section 6 and this section extend to Scotland.

(6) This Act, except section 6, extends to Northern Ireland.

[Sexual Offences (Conspiracy and Incitement) Act 1996, s 7, as amended by the Criminal Justice (Terrorism and Conspiracy) Act 1998, Schs 1 and 2 .]

1. As to commencement, see note 1 to the short title of this Act, ante.

Section 5

SCHEDULE

LISTED SEXUAL OFFENCES

(Amended by the Sexual Offences Act 2003, Sch 6.)

England and Wales

8–28286s a 1. (1) In relation to England and Wales, the following are listed sexual offences:

(*a*) *repealed*
(*b*) an offence under any of sections 1 to 12, 14 and 15 to 26 of the Sexual Offences Act 2003.

(2) Sub-paragraph (1)(*b*) does not apply where the victim of the offence has attained the age of sixteen years.

Northern Ireland

8–28287 2. *Northern Ireland.*

Sexual Offences (Protected Material) Act 1997[1]

(1997 c 39)

Introductory

8–28301 1. Meaning of "protected material". (1) In this Act "protected material", in relation to proceedings for a sexual offence, means a copy (in whatever form) of any of the following material, namely—

(*a*) a statement relating to that or any other sexual offence made by any victim of the offence (whether the statement is recorded in writing or in any other form),
(*b*) a photograph or pseudo-photograph of any such victim, or
(*c*) a report of a medical examination of the physical condition of any such victim,

which is a copy given by the prosecutor to any person under this Act.

(2) For the purposes of subsection (1) a person is, in relation to any proceedings for a sexual offence, a victim of that offence if—

(*a*) the charge, summons or indictment by which the proceedings are instituted names that person as a person in relation to whom that offence was committed; or
(*b*) that offence can, in the prosecutor's opinion, be reasonably regarded as having been committed in relation to that person;

and a person is, in relation to any such proceedings, a victim of any other sexual offence if that offence can, in the prosecutor's opinion, be reasonably regarded as having been committed in relation to that person.

(3) In this Act, where the context so permits (and subject to subsection (4))—

(*a*) references to any protected material include references to any part of any such material; and
(*b*) references to a copy of any such material include references to any part of any such copy.

(4) Nothing in this Act—

(*a*) so far as it refers to a defendant making any copy of—
  (i) any protected material, or
  (ii) a copy of any such material,

  applies to a manuscript copy which is not a verbatim copy of the whole of that material or copy; or

(*b*) so far as it refers to a defendant having in his possession any copy of any protected material, applies to a manuscript copy made by him which is not a verbatim copy of the whole of that material.

[Sexual Offences (Protected Material) Act 1997, s 1.]

1. This Act is to be brought into force in accordance with orders made under s 11. At the date of going to press no commencement order has been made.

8–28302 2. Meaning of other expressions. (1) In this Act

"contracted out prison" means a contracted out prison within the meaning of Part IV of the Criminal Justice Act 1991;
"defendant", in relation to any proceedings for a sexual offence, means any person charged with that offence (whether or not he has been convicted);
"governor", in relation to a contracted out prison, means the director of the prison;
"inform" means inform in writing;
"legal representative", in relation to a defendant, means any authorised advocate or authorised litigator (as defined by section 119(1) of the Courts and Legal Services Act 1990) acting for the defendant in connection with any proceedings for the sexual offence in question;
"photograph" and "pseudo-photograph" shall be construed in accordance with section 7(4) and (7) of the Protection of Children Act 1978;
"prison" means any prison, young offender institution or remand centre which is under the general superintendence of, or is provided by, the Secretary of State under the Prison Act 1952, including a contracted out prison;
"proceedings" means (subject to subsection (2)) criminal proceedings;
"the prosecutor", in relation to any proceedings for a sexual offence, means any person acting as prosecutor (whether an individual or a body);
"relevant proceedings", in relation to any material which has been disclosed by the prosecutor under this Act, means any proceedings for the purposes of which it has been so disclosed or any further proceedings for the sexual offence in question;
"sexual offence" means one of the offences listed in the Schedule to this Act.

(2) For the purposes of this Act references to proceedings for a sexual offence include references to—

(*a*) any appeal or application for leave to appeal brought or made by or in relation to a defendant in such proceedings;

(*b*) any application made to the Criminal Cases Review Commission for the reference under section 9 or 11 of the Criminal Appeal Act 1995 of any conviction, verdict, finding or sentence recorded or imposed in relation to any such defendant; and

(*c*) any petition to the Secretary of State requesting him to recommend the exercise of Her Majesty's prerogative of mercy in relation to any such defendant.

(3) In this Act, in the context of the prosecutor giving a copy of any material to any person—

(*a*) references to the prosecutor include references to a person acting on behalf of the prosecutor; and

(*b*) where any such copy falls to be given to the defendant's legal representative, references to the defendant's legal representative include references to a person acting on behalf of the defendant's legal representative.

[Sexual Offences (Protected Material) Act 1997, s 2.]

Regulation of disclosures to defendant

8–28303 **3. Regulation of disclosures by prosecutor.** (1) Where, in connection with any proceedings for a sexual offence, any statement or other material falling within any of paragraphs (*a*) to (*c*) of section 1(1) would (apart from this section) fall to be disclosed by the prosecutor to the defendant—

(*a*) the prosecutor shall not disclose that material to the defendant; and

(*b*) it shall instead be disclosed under this Act in accordance with whichever of subsection (2) and (3) below is applicable.

(2) If—

(*a*) the defendant has a legal representative, and

(*b*) the defendant's legal representative gives the prosecutor the undertaking required by section 4 (disclosure to defendant's legal representative),

the prosecutor shall disclose the material in question by giving a copy of it to the defendant's legal representative.

(3) If subsection (2) is not applicable, the prosecutor shall disclose the material in question by giving a copy of it to the appropriate person for the purposes of section 5 (disclosure to unrepresented defendant) in order for that person to show that copy to the defendant under that section.

(4) Where under this Act a copy of any material falls to be given to any person by the prosecutor, any such copy—

(*a*) may be in such form as the prosecutor thinks fit, and

(*b*) where the material consists of information which has been recorded in any form, need not be in the same form as that in which the information has already been recorded.

(5) Once a copy of any material is given to any person under this Act by the prosecutor, the copy shall (in accordance with section 1(1)) be protected material for the purposes of this Act.

[Sexual Offences (Protected Material) Act 1997, s 3.]

8–28304 **4. Disclosure to defendant's legal representative.** (1) For the purposes of this Act the undertaking which a defendant's legal representative is required to give in relation to any protected material given to him under this Act is an undertaking by him to discharge the obligations set out in subsections (2) to (7).

(2) He must take reasonable steps to ensure—

(*a*) that the protected material, or any copy of it, is only shown to the defendant in circumstances where it is possible to exercise adequate supervision to prevent the defendant retaining possession of the material or copy or making a copy of it, and

(*b*) that the protected material is not shown and no copy of it is given, and its contents are not otherwise revealed, to any person other than the defendant, except so far as it appears to him necessary to show the material or give a copy of it to any such person—

(i) in connection with any relevant proceedings, or

(ii) for the purposes of any assessment or treatment of the defendant (whether before or after conviction).

(3) He must inform the defendant—

(*a*) that the protected material is such material for the purposes of this Act,

(*b*) that the defendant can only inspect that material, or any copy of it, in circumstances such as are described in subsection (2)(*a*), and

(*c*) that it would be an offence for the defendant—

(i) to have material, or any copy of it, in his possession otherwise than while inspecting it or the copy in such circumstances, or

(ii) to give that material or any copy of it, or otherwise reveal its contents, to any other person.

(4) He must, where the protected material or a copy of it has been shown or given in accordance with subsection (2)(*b*)(i) or (ii) to a person other than the defendant, inform that person—

(*a*) that that person must not give any copy of that material, or otherwise reveal its contents—

(i) to any other person other than the defendant, or
(ii) to the defendant otherwise than in circumstances such as are described in subsection (2)(*a*); and

(*b*) that it would be an offence for that person to do so.

(5) He must, where he ceases to act as the defendant's legal representative at a time when any relevant proceedings are current or in contemplation—

(*a*) inform the prosecutor of that fact, and
(*b*) if he is informed by the prosecutor that the defendant has a new legal representative who has given the prosecutor the undertaking required by this section, give the protected material, and any copies of it in his possession, to the defendant's new legal representative.

(6) He must, at the time of giving the protected material to the new legal representative under subsection (5), inform that person—

(*a*) that that material is protected material for the purposes of this Act, and
(*b*) of the extent to which—

(i) that material has been shown by him, and
(ii) any copies of it have been given by him,

to any other person (including the defendant).

(7) He must keep a record of every occasion on which the protected material was shown, or a copy of it was given, as mentioned in subsection (6)(*b*).
[Sexual Offences (Protected Material) Act 1997, s 4.]

8–28305 **5. Disclosure to unrepresented defendant.** (1) This section applies where, in accordance with section 3(3), a copy of any material falls to be given by the prosecutor to the appropriate person for the purposes of this section in order for that person to show that copy to the defendant under this section.

(2) Subject to subsection (3), the appropriate person in such a case is—

(*a*) if the defendant is detained in a prison, the governor of the prison or any person nominated by the governor for the purposes of this section; and
(*b*) otherwise the officer in charge of such police station as appears to the prosecutor to be suitable for enabling the defendant to have access to the material in accordance with this section or any person nominated by that officer for the purposes of this section.

(3) The Secretary of State may by regulations provide that, in such circumstances as are specified in the regulations, the appropriate person for the purposes of this section shall be a person of any description so specified.

(4) The appropriate person shall take reasonable steps to ensure—

(*a*) that the protected material, or any copy of it, is only shown to the defendant in circumstances where it is possible to exercise adequate supervision to prevent the defendant retaining possession of the material or copy or making a copy of it,
(*b*) that, subject to paragraph (*a*), the defendant is given such access to that material, or a copy of it, as he reasonably requires in connection with any relevant proceedings, and
(*c*) that that material is not shown and no copy of it is given, and its contents are not otherwise revealed, to any person other than the defendant.

(5) The prosecutor shall, at the time of giving the protected material to the appropriate person, inform him—

(*a*) that that material is protected material for the purposes of this Act, and
(*b*) that he is required to discharge the obligations set out in subsection (4) in relation to that material.

(6) The prosecutor shall at that time also inform the defendant—

(*a*) that that material is protected material for the purposes of this Act,
(*b*) that the defendant can only inspect that material, or any copy of it, in circumstances such as are described in subsection (4)(*a*), and
(*c*) that it would be an offence for the defendant—

(i) to have that material, or any copy of it, in his possession otherwise than while inspecting it or the copy in such circumstances, or
(ii) to give that material or any copy of it, or otherwise reveal its contents, to any other person,

as well as inform him of the effect of subsection (7).

(7) If—

(*a*) the defendant requests the prosecutor in writing to give a further copy of the material mentioned in subsection (1) to some other person, and

(*b*) it appears to the prosecutor to be necessary to do so—

(i) in connection with any relevant proceedings, or

(ii) for the purposes of any assessment or treatment of the defendant (whether before or after conviction),

the prosecutor shall give such a copy to that other person.

(8) The prosecutor may give such a copy to some other person where no request has been made under subsection (7) but it appears to him that in the interests of the defendant it is necessary to do so as mentioned in paragraph (*b*) of that subsection.

(9) The prosecutor shall, at the time of giving such a copy to a person under subsection (7) or (8), inform that person—

(*a*) that the copy is protected material for the purposes of this Act,

(*b*) that he must not give any copy of the protected material or otherwise reveal its contents—

(i) to any person other than the defendant, or

(ii) to the defendant otherwise than in circumstances such as are described in subsection (4)(*a*); and

(*c*) that it would be an offence for him to do so.

(10) If the prosecutor—

(*a*) receives a request from the defendant under subsection (7) to give a further copy of the material in question to another person, but

(*b*) does not consider it to be necessary to do so as mentioned in paragraph (*b*) of that subsection and accordingly refuses the request,

he shall inform the defendant of his refusal.

(11) Any regulations under subsection (3) shall be made by statutory instrument subject to annulment in pursuance of a resolution of either House of Parliament.

[Sexual Offences (Protected Material) Act 1997, s 5.]

8–28306 6. Further disclosures by prosecutor. (1) Where—

(*a*) any material has been disclosed in accordance with section 3(2) to the defendant's legal representative, and

(*b*) at a time when any relevant proceedings are current or in contemplation the legal representative either—

(i) ceases to act as the defendant's legal representative in circumstances where section 4(5)(*b*) does not apply, or

(ii) dies or becomes incapacitated,

that material shall be further disclosed under this Act in accordance with whichever of section 3(2) or (3) is for the time being applicable.

(2) Where—

(*a*) any material has been disclosed in accordance with section 3(3), and

(*b*) at a time when any relevant proceedings are current or in contemplation the defendant acquires a legal representative who gives the prosecutor the undertaking required by section 4,

that material shall be further disclosed under this Act, in accordance with section 3(2), to the defendant's legal representative.

[Sexual Offences (Protected Material) Act 1997, s 6.]

8–28307 7. *Regulation of disclosures by Criminal Cases Review Commission.*

Supplementary

8–28308 8. Offences. (1) Where any material has been disclosed under this Act in connection with any proceedings for a sexual offence, it is an offence for the defendant—

(*a*) to have the protected material, or any copy of it, in his possession otherwise than while inspecting it or the copy in circumstances such as are described in section 4(2)(*a*) or 5(4)(*a*), or

(*b*) to give that material or any copy of it, or otherwise reveal its contents, to any other person.

(2) Where any protected material, or any copy of any such material, has been shown or given to any person in accordance with section 4(2)(*b*)(i) or (ii) or section 5(7) or (8), it is an offence for that person to give any copy of that material or otherwise reveal its contents—

(*a*) to any person other than the defendant, or

(*b*) to the defendant otherwise than in circumstances such as are described in section 4(2)(*a*) or 5(4)(*a*).

(3) Subsections (1) and (2) apply whether or not any relevant proceedings are current or in contemplation (and references to the defendant shall be construed accordingly).

(4) A person guilty of an offence under this section is liable[1]—

(*a*) on summary conviction, to imprisonment for a term not exceeding **six months** or a fine not exceeding the **statutory maximum** or **both**;

(*b*) on conviction on indictment, to imprisonment for a term not exceeding **two years** or a **fine** or **both**.

(5) Where a person is charged with an offence under this section relating to any protected material or copy of any such material, it is a defence to prove that, at the time of the alleged offence, he was not aware, and neither suspected nor had reason to suspect, that the material or copy in question was protected material or (as the case may be) a copy of any such material.

(6) The court before which a person is tried for an offence under this section may (whether or not he is convicted of that offence) make an order requiring him to return any protected material, or any copy of any such material, in his possession to the prosecutor.

(7) Nothing in subsection (1) or (2) shall be taken to apply to—

(*a*) any disclosure made in the course of any proceedings before a court or in any report of any such proceedings, or

(*b*) any disclosure made or copy given by a person when returning any protected material, or a copy of any such material, to the prosecutor or the defendant's legal representative;

and accordingly nothing in section 4 or 5 shall be read as precluding the making of any disclosure or the giving of any copy in circumstances falling within paragraph (*a*) or (as the case may be) paragraph (*b*) above.

[Sexual Offences (Protected Material) Act 1997, s 8.]

---

1. For procedure in respect of this offence which is triable either way, see the Magistrates' Courts Act 1980, ss 17A–21, in PART I: MAGISTRATES' COURTS, PROCEDURE, ante.

8–28309 9. *Modification and amendment of other enactments.*

8–28310 10. *Financial provision.*

8–28311 11. Short title, commencement and extent. (1) *Short title.*

(2) This Act shall come into force on such day as the Secretary of State may appoint by order[1] made by statutory instrument.

(3) Nothing in this Act applies to any proceedings for a sexual offence where the defendant was charged with the offence before the commencement of this Act.

(4) This Act extends to England and Wales only.

[Sexual Offences (Protected Material) Act 1997, s 11.]

---

1. As to commencement, see note 1 to the short title of this Act, ante.

Section 2(1)

SCHEDULE

SEXUAL OFFENCES FOR PURPOSES OF THIS ACT

(As amended by the Sexual Offences Act 2003, Sch 7.)

8–28312 1. *Repealed.*

8–28313 2. *Repealed.*

8–28314 3. *Repealed.*

8–28315 4. *Repealed.*

8–28316 5. Any offence under section 1 of the Protection of Children Act 1978 or section 160 of the Criminal Justice Act 1988 (indecent photographs of children).

8–28316A 5A. Any offence under any provision of Part 1 of the Sexual Offences Act 2003 except section 64, 65, 69 or 71.

8–28317 6. Any offence under section 1 of the Criminal Law Act 1977 of conspiracy to commit any of the offences mentioned in paragraphs 5 and 5A.

8–28318 7. Any offence under section 1 of the Criminal Attempts Act 1981 of attempting to commit any of those offences.

8–28319 8. Any offence of inciting another to commit any of those offences.

Sexual Offences Act 2003[1]

(2003 c 42)

PART 1[2]
SEXUAL OFFENCES

Rape

8–28421A 1. Rape. (1) A person (A) commits an offence if—

(*a*) he intentionally penetrates[3] the vagina[3], anus or mouth of another person (B) with his penis,
(*b*) B does not consent[4] to the penetration, and
(*c*) A does not reasonably believe that B consents.

(2) Whether a belief is reasonable is to be determined having regard to all the circumstances, including any steps A has taken to ascertain whether B consents.

(3) Sections 75[5] and 76[6] apply to an offence under this section.

(4) A person guilty of an offence under this section is liable, on conviction on indictment, to imprisonment for life.

[Sexual Offences Act 2003, s 1.]

---

1. This Act, with the exception of ss 138, 141, 142 and 143 which came into force on Royal Assent (20 November 2003), is to be brought into force in accordance with commencement orders made under s 141, post. At the date of going to press no such orders had been made.
2. Part 1 comprises ss 1–79 and Schs 1 and 2.
3. For "penetration" and "vagina", see s 79, post.
4. For "consent", see s 74, post.
5. Evidential presumptions about consent, post.
6. Conclusive presumptions about consent, post.

Assault

8–28421B 2. Assault by penetration. (1) A person (A) commits an offence if—

(*a*) he intentionally penetrates[1] the vagina[1] or anus of another person (B) with a part of his body[1] or anything else,
(*b*) the penetration is sexual[2],
(*c*) B does not consent[3] to the penetration, and
(*d*) A does not reasonably believe that B consents.

(2) Whether a belief is reasonable is to be determined having regard to all the circumstances, including any steps A has taken to ascertain whether B consents.

(3) Sections 75[4] and 76[5] apply to an offence under this section.

(4) A person guilty of an offence under this section is liable, on conviction on indictment, to imprisonment for life.

[Sexual Offences Act 2003, s 2.]

---

1. For "penetration", "vagina" and "part of his body" see s 79, post.
2. For "sexual", see s 78, post.
3. For "consent", see s 74, post.
4. Evidential presumptions about consent, post.
5. Conclusive presumptions about consent, post.

8–28421C 3. Sexual assault. (1) A person (A) commits an offence if—

(*a*) he intentionally touches[1] another person (B),
(*b*) the touching is sexual[2],
(*c*) B does not consent[3] to the touching, and
(*d*) A does not reasonably believe that B consents.

(2) Whether a belief is reasonable is to be determined having regard to all the circumstances, including any steps A has taken to ascertain whether B consents.

(3) Sections 75[4] and 76[5] apply to an offence under this section.

(4) A person guilty of an offence under this section is liable[6]—

(*a*) on summary conviction, to imprisonment for a term not exceeding 6 months or a fine not exceeding the statutory maximum or both;
(*b*) on conviction on indictment, to imprisonment for a term not exceeding 10 years.

[Sexual Offences Act 2003, s 3.]

---

1. For "touching", see s 79, post.
2. For "sexual", see s 78, post.
3. For "consent", see s 74, post.
4. Evidential presumptions about consent, post.
5. Conclusive presumptions about consent, post.

6. For procedure in respect of this offence which is triable either way, see the Magistrates' Courts Act 1980, ss 17A–21 in PART I: MAGISTRATES' COURTS, PROCEDURE, ante.

Causing sexual activity without consent

8–28421D 4. Causing a person to engage in sexual activity without consent. (1) A person (A) commits an offence if—

(*a*) he intentionally causes another person (B) to engage in an activity,
(*b*) the activity is sexual[1],
(*c*) B does not consent[2] to engaging in the activity, and
(*d*) A does not reasonably believe that B consents.

(2) Whether a belief is reasonable is to be determined having regard to all the circumstances, including any steps A has taken to ascertain whether B consents.

(3) Sections 75[3] and 76[4] apply to an offence under this section.

(4) A person guilty of an offence under this section, if the activity caused involved—

(*a*) penetration[6] of B's anus or vagina[5],
(*b*) penetration of B's mouth with a person's penis,
(*c*) penetration of a person's anus or vagina with a part of B's body or by B with anything else, or
(*d*) penetration of a person's mouth with B's penis,

is liable, on conviction on indictment, to imprisonment for life.

(5) Unless subsection (4) applies, a person guilty of an offence under this section is liable[6]—

(*a*) on summary conviction, to imprisonment for a term not exceeding 6 months or to a fine not exceeding the statutory maximum or both;
(*b*) on conviction on indictment, to imprisonment for a term not exceeding 10 years.

[Sexual Offences Act 2003, s 4.]

1. For "sexual", see s 78, post.
2. For "consent", see s 74, post.
3. Evidential presumptions about consent, post.
4. Conclusive presumptions about consent, post.
5. For "penetration" and "vagina", see s 79, post.
6. For procedure in respect of this offence which is triable either way, see the Magistrates' Courts Act 1980, ss 17A–21 in PART I: MAGISTRATES' COURTS, PROCEDURE, ante.

Rape and other offences against children under 13

8–28421E 5. Rape of a child under 13. (1) A person commits an offence if—

(*a*) he intentionally penetrates[1] the vagina[1], anus or mouth of another person with his penis, and
(*b*) the other person is under 13.

(2) A person guilty of an offence under this section is liable, on conviction on indictment, to imprisonment for life.

[Sexual Offences Act 2003, s 5.]

1. For "penetration" and "vagina", see s 79, post.

8–28421F 6. Assault of a child under 13 by penetration. (1) A person commits an offence if—

(*a*) he intentionally penetrates[1] the vagina[1] or anus of another person with a part of his body[1] or anything else,
(*b*) the penetration is sexual[2], and
(*c*) the other person is under 13.

(2) A person guilty of an offence under this section is liable, on conviction on indictment, to imprisonment for life.

[Sexual Offences Act 2003, s 6.]

1. For "penetration", "vagina" and "part of his body", see s 79, post.
2. For "sexual", see s 78, post.

8–28421G 7. Sexual assault of a child under 13. (1) A person commits an offence if—

(*a*) he intentionally touches another person,
(*b*) the touching[1] is sexual[2], and
(*c*) the other person is under 13.

(2) A person guilty of an offence under this section is liable[3]—

(*a*) on summary conviction, to imprisonment for a term not exceeding 6 months or a fine not exceeding the statutory maximum or both;
(*b*) on conviction on indictment, to imprisonment for a term not exceeding 14 years.

[Sexual Offences Act 2003, s 7.]

1. For "touching", see s 79, post.
2. For "sexual", see s 78, post.
3. For procedure in respect of this offence which is triable either way, see the Magistrates' Courts Act 1980, ss 17A–21 in PART I: MAGISTRATES' COURTS, PROCEDURE, ante.

8–28421H 8. Causing or inciting a child under 13 to engage in sexual activity. (1) A person commits an offence if—

(*a*) he intentionally causes or incites another person (B) to engage in an activity,
(*b*) the activity is sexual[1], and
(*c*) B is under 13.

(2) A person guilty of an offence under this section, if the activity caused or incited involved—

(*a*) penetration[2] of B's anus or vagina,
(*b*) penetration of B's mouth with a person's penis,
(*c*) penetration of a person's anus or vagina[2] with a part of B's body[2] or by B with anything else, or
(*d*) penetration of a person's mouth with B's penis,

is liable, on conviction on indictment, to imprisonment for life.

(3) Unless subsection (2) applies, a person guilty of an offence under this section is liable[3]—

(*a*) on summary conviction, to imprisonment for a term not exceeding 6 months or to a fine not exceeding the statutory maximum or both;
(*b*) on conviction on indictment, to imprisonment for a term not exceeding 14 years.

[Sexual Offences Act 2003, s 8.]

1. For "sexual", see s 78, post.
2. For "penetration", "vagina" and "part of his body", see s 79, post.
3. For procedure in respect of this offence which is triable either way, see the Magistrates' Courts Act 1980, ss 17A–21 in PART I: MAGISTRATES' COURTS, PROCEDURE, ante.

Child sex offences

8–28421I 9. Sexual activity with a child. (1) A person aged 18 or over (A) commits an offence if—

(*a*) he intentionally touches[1] another person (B),
(*b*) the touching is sexual[2], and
(*c*) either—
(i) B is under 16 and A does not reasonably believe that B is 16 or over, or
(ii) B is under 13.

(2) A person guilty of an offence under this section, if the touching involved—

(*a*) penetration[3] of B's anus or vagina[3] with a part of A's body[3] or anything else,
(*b*) penetration of B's mouth with A's penis,
(*c*) penetration of A's anus or vagina with a part of B's body, or
(*d*) penetration of A's mouth with B's penis,

is liable, on conviction on indictment, to imprisonment for a term not exceeding 14 years.

(3) Unless subsection (2) applies, a person guilty of an offence under this section is liable[4]—

(*a*) on summary conviction, to imprisonment for a term not exceeding 6 months or to a fine not exceeding the statutory maximum or both;
(*b*) on conviction on indictment, to imprisonment for a term not exceeding 14 years.

[Sexual Offences Act 2003, s 9.]

1. For "touching", see s 79, post.
2. For "sexual", see s 78, post.
3. For "penetration", "vagina" and "part of his body", see s 79, post.
4. For procedure in respect of this offence which is triable either way, see the Magistrates' Courts Act 1980, ss 17A–21 in PART I: MAGISTRATES' COURTS, PROCEDURE, ante.

8–28421J 10. Causing or inciting a child to engage in sexual activity. (1) A person aged 18 or over (A) commits an offence if—

(*a*) he intentionally causes or incites another person (B) to engage in an activity,
(*b*) the activity is sexual[1], and
(*c*) either—
(i) B is under 16 and A does not reasonably believe that B is 16 or over, or
(ii) B is under 13.

(2) A person guilty of an offence under this section, if the activity caused or incited involved—

(*a*) penetration[3] of B's anus or vagina[2],

(*b*) penetration of B's mouth with a person's penis,
(*c*) penetration of a person's anus or vagina with a part of B's body[2] or by B with anything else, or
(*d*) penetration of a person's mouth with B's penis,

is liable, on conviction on indictment, to imprisonment for a term not exceeding 14 years.

(3) Unless subsection (2) applies, a person guilty of an offence under this section is liable[3]—

(*a*) on summary conviction, to imprisonment for a term not exceeding 6 months or to a fine not exceeding the statutory maximum or both;
(*b*) on conviction on indictment, to imprisonment for a term not exceeding 14 years.

[Sexual Offences Act 2003, s 10.]

---

1. For "sexual", see s 78, post.
2. For "penetration", "vagina" and "part of his body", see s 79, post.
3. For procedure in respect of this offence which is triable either way, see the Magistrates' Courts Act 1980, ss 17A–21 in PART I: MAGISTRATES' COURTS, PROCEDURE, ante.

8–28421K 11. Engaging in sexual activity in the presence of a child. (1) A person aged 18 or over (A) commits an offence if—

(*a*) he intentionally engages in an activity,
(*b*) the activity is sexual[1],
(*c*) for the purpose of obtaining sexual gratification, he engages in it—
  (i) when another person (B) is present or is in a place from which A can be observed, and
  (ii) knowing or believing that B is aware, or intending that B should be aware, that he is engaging in it, and
(*d*) either—
  (i) B is under 16 and A does not reasonably believe that B is 16 or over, or
  (ii) B is under 13.

(2) A person guilty of an offence under this section is liable[2]—

(*a*) on summary conviction, to imprisonment for a term not exceeding 6 months or a fine not exceeding the statutory maximum or both;
(*b*) on conviction on indictment, to imprisonment for a term not exceeding 10 years.

[Sexual Offences Act 2003, s 11.]

---

1. For "sexual", see s 78, post.
2. For procedure in respect of this offence which is triable either way, see the Magistrates' Courts Act 1980, ss 17A–21 in PART I: MAGISTRATES' COURTS, PROCEDURE, ante.

8–28421L 12. Causing a child to watch a sexual act. (1) A person aged 18 or over (A) commits an offence if—

(*a*) for the purpose of obtaining sexual gratification, he intentionally causes another person (B) to watch a third person engaging in an activity, or to look at an image[1] of any person engaging in an activity,
(*b*) the activity is sexual[2], and
(*c*) either—
  (i) B is under 16 and A does not reasonably believe that B is 16 or over, or
  (ii) B is under 13.

(2) A person guilty of an offence under this section is liable[3]—

(*a*) on summary conviction, to imprisonment for a term not exceeding 6 months or a fine not exceeding the statutory maximum or both;
(*b*) on conviction on indictment, to imprisonment for a term not exceeding 10 years.

[Sexual Offences Act 2003, s 12.]

---

1. For "image", see s 79, post.
2. For "sexual", see s 78, post.
3. For procedure in respect of this offence which is triable either way, see the Magistrates' Courts Act 1980, ss 17A–21 in PART I: MAGISTRATES' COURTS, PROCEDURE, ante.

8–28421M 13. Child sex offences committed by children or young persons. (1) A person under 18 commits an offence if he does anything which would be an offence under any of sections 9 to 12 if he were aged 18.

(2) A person guilty of an offence under this section is liable[1]—

(*a*) on summary conviction, to imprisonment for a term not exceeding 6 months or a fine not exceeding the statutory maximum or both;
(*b*) on conviction on indictment, to imprisonment for a term not exceeding 5 years.

[Sexual Offences Act 2003, s 13.]

1. For procedure in respect of this offence which is triable either way, see the Magistrates' Courts Act 1980, ss 17A–21 in PART I: MAGISTRATES' COURTS, PROCEDURE, ante. For mode of trial where the defendant is under 18 years, see the Magistrates' Courts Act 1980, s 24, ante and para **5–11 ff Jurisdiction of the magistrates' and Crown Courts** in PART V: YOUTH COURTS, ante.

8–28421N 14. Arranging or facilitating commission of a child sex offence. (1) A person commits an offence if—

(*a*) he intentionally arranges or facilitates something that he intends to do, intends another person to do, or believes that another person will do, in any part of the world, and
(*b*) doing it will involve the commission of an offence under any of sections 9 to 13.

(2) A person does not commit an offence under this section if—

(*a*) he arranges or facilitates something that he believes another person will do, but that he does not intend to do or intend another person to do, and
(*b*) any offence within subsection (1)(*b*) would be an offence against a child for whose protection he acts.

(3) For the purposes of subsection (2), a person acts for the protection of a child if he acts for the purpose of—

(*a*) protecting the child from sexually transmitted infection,
(*b*) protecting the physical safety of the child,
(*c*) preventing the child from becoming pregnant, or
(*d*) promoting the child's emotional well-being by the giving of advice,

and not for the purpose of obtaining sexual gratification or for the purpose of causing or encouraging the activity constituting the offence within subsection (1)(*b*) or the child's participation in it.

(4) A person guilty of an offence under this section is liable[1]—

(*a*) on summary conviction, to imprisonment for a term not exceeding 6 months or a fine not exceeding the statutory maximum or both;
(*b*) on conviction on indictment, to imprisonment for a term not exceeding 14 years.

[Sexual Offences Act 2003, s 14.]

1. For procedure in respect of this offence which is triable either way, see the Magistrates' Courts Act 1980, ss 17A–21 in PART I: MAGISTRATES' COURTS, PROCEDURE, ante.

8–28421O 15. Meeting a child following sexual grooming etc. (1) A person aged 18 or over (A) commits an offence if—

(*a*) having met or communicated with another person (B) on at least two earlier occasions, he—
   (i) intentionally meets B, or
   (ii) travels with the intention of meeting B in any part of the world,
(*b*) at the time, he intends to do anything to or in respect of B, during or after the meeting and in any part of the world, which if done will involve the commission by A of a relevant offence,
(*c*) B is under 16, and
(*d*) A does not reasonably believe that B is 16 or over.

(2) In subsection (1)—

(*a*) the reference to A having met or communicated with B is a reference to A having met B in any part of the world or having communicated with B by any means from, to or in any part of the world;
(*b*) "relevant offence" means—
   (i) an offence under this Part[1],
   (ii) an offence within any of paragraphs 61 to 92 of Schedule 3, or
   (iii) anything done outside England and Wales and Northern Ireland which is not an offence within sub-paragraph (i) or (ii) but would be an offence within sub-paragraph (i) if done in England and Wales.

(3) In this section as it applies to Northern Ireland—

(*a*) subsection (1) has effect with the substitution of "17" for "16" in both places;
(*b*) subsection (2)(b)(iii) has effect with the substitution of "sub-paragraph (ii) if done in Northern Ireland" for "sub-paragraph (i) if done in England and Wales".

(4) A person guilty of an offence under this section is liable[2]—

(*a*) on summary conviction, to imprisonment for a term not exceeding 6 months or a fine not exceeding the statutory maximum or both;
(*b*) on conviction on indictment, to imprisonment for a term not exceeding 10 years.

[Sexual Offences Act 2003, s 15.]

1. "This Part" i.e. ss 1–79 and Schs 1 and 2.
2. For procedure in respect of this offence which is triable either way, see the Magistrates' Courts Act 1980, ss 17A–21 in PART I: MAGISTRATES' COURTS, PROCEDURE, ante.

Abuse of position of trust

8–28421P 16. Abuse of position of trust: sexual activity with a child. (1) A person aged 18 or over (A) commits an offence[1] if—

(*a*) he intentionally touches[2] another person (B),
(*b*) the touching is sexual[3],
(*c*) A is in a position of trust[4] in relation to B,
(*d*) where subsection (2) applies, A knows or could reasonably be expected to know of the circumstances by virtue of which he is in a position of trust in relation to B, and
(*e*) either—

(i) B is under 18 and A does not reasonably believe that B is 18 or over, or
(ii) B is under 13.

(2) This subsection applies where A—

(*a*) is in a position of trust in relation to B by virtue of circumstances within section 21(2), (3), (4) or (5), and
(*b*) is not in such a position of trust by virtue of other circumstances.

(3) Where in proceedings for an offence under this section it is proved that the other person was under 18, the defendant is to be taken not to have reasonably believed that that person was 18 or over unless sufficient evidence is adduced to raise an issue as to whether he reasonably believed it.

(4) Where in proceedings for an offence under this section—

(*a*) it is proved that the defendant was in a position of trust in relation to the other person by virtue of circumstances within section 21(2), (3), (4) or (5), and
(*b*) it is not proved that he was in such a position of trust by virtue of other circumstances,

it is to be taken that the defendant knew or could reasonably have been expected to know of the circumstances by virtue of which he was in such a position of trust unless sufficient evidence is adduced to raise an issue as to whether he knew or could reasonably have been expected to know of those circumstances.

(5) A person guilty of an offence under this section is liable[5]—

(*a*) on summary conviction, to imprisonment for a term not exceeding 6 months or a fine not exceeding the statutory maximum or both;
(*b*) on conviction on indictment, to imprisonment for a term not exceeding 5 years.

[Sexual Offences Act 2003, s 16.]

1. For marriage exception, see s 23, post.
2. For "touching", see s 79, post.
3. For "sexual", see s 78, post.
4. For "position of trust", see ss 21 and 22 and for sexual relationships which pre-date position of trust, see s 24, post.
5. For procedure in respect of this offence which is triable either way, see the Magistrates' Courts Act 1980, ss 17A–21 in PART I: MAGISTRATES' COURTS, PROCEDURE, ante.

8–28421Q 17. Abuse of position of trust: causing or inciting a child to engage in sexual activity. (1) A person aged 18 or over (A) commits an offence if—

(*a*) he intentionally causes or incites another person (B) to engage in an activity,
(*b*) the activity is sexual[1],
(*c*) A is in a position of trust[2] in relation to B,
(*d*) where subsection (2) applies, A knows or could reasonably be expected to know of the circumstances by virtue of which he is in a position of trust in relation to B, and
(*e*) either—

(i) B is under 18 and A does not reasonably believe that B is 18 or over, or
(ii) B is under 13.

(2) This subsection applies where A—

(*a*) is in a position of trust in relation to B by virtue of circumstances within section 21(2), (3), (4) or (5), and
(*b*) is not in such a position of trust by virtue of other circumstances.

(3) Where in proceedings for an offence under this section it is proved that the other person was under 18, the defendant is to be taken not to have reasonably believed that that person was 18 or over unless sufficient evidence is adduced to raise an issue as to whether he reasonably believed it.

(4) Where in proceedings for an offence under this section—

(*a*) it is proved that the defendant was in a position of trust in relation to the other person by virtue of circumstances within section 21(2), (3), (4) or (5), and (*b*) it is not proved that he was in such a position of trust by virtue of other circumstances,

it is to be taken that the defendant knew or could reasonably have been expected to know of the circumstances by virtue of which he was in such a position of trust unless sufficient evidence is adduced to raise an issue as to whether he knew or could reasonably have been expected to know of those circumstances.

(5) A person guilty of an offence under this section is liable[3]—

(*a*) on summary conviction, to imprisonment for a term not exceeding 6 months or a fine not exceeding the statutory maximum or both;

(*b*) on conviction on indictment, to imprisonment for a term not exceeding 5 years.

[Sexual Offences Act 2003, s 17.]

1. For "sexual", see s 78, post.
2. For "position of trust", see ss 21 and 22 and for sexual relationships which pre-date position of trust, see s 24, post.
3. For procedure in respect of this offence which is triable either way, see the Magistrates' Courts Act 1980, ss 17A–21 in PART I: MAGISTRATES' COURTS, PROCEDURE, ante.

8–28421R 18. Abuse of position of trust: sexual activity in the presence of a child. (1) A person aged 18 or over (A) commits an offence if—

(*a*) he intentionally engages in an activity,
(*b*) the activity is sexual[1],
(*c*) for the purpose of obtaining sexual gratification, he engages in it—

(i) when another person (B) is present or is in a place from which A can be observed, and
(ii) knowing or believing that B is aware, or intending that B should be aware, that he is engaging in it,

(*d*) A is in a position of trust[2] in relation to B,
(*e*) where subsection (2) applies, A knows or could reasonably be expected to know of the circumstances by virtue of which he is in a position of trust in relation to B, and
(*f*) either—

(i) B is under 18 and A does not reasonably believe that B is 18 or over, or
(ii) B is under 13.

(2) This subsection applies where A—

(*a*) is in a position of trust in relation to B by virtue of circumstances within section 21(2), (3), (4) or (5), and
(*b*) is not in such a position of trust by virtue of other circumstances.

(3) Where in proceedings for an offence under this section it is proved that the other person was under 18, the defendant is to be taken not to have reasonably believed that that person was 18 or over unless sufficient evidence is adduced to raise an issue as to whether he reasonably believed it.

(4) Where in proceedings for an offence under this section—

(*a*) it is proved that the defendant was in a position of trust in relation to the other person by virtue of circumstances within section 21(2), (3), (4) or (5), and
(*b*) it is not proved that he was in such a position of trust by virtue of other circumstances,

it is to be taken that the defendant knew or could reasonably have been expected to know of the circumstances by virtue of which he was in such a position of trust unless sufficient evidence is adduced to raise an issue as to whether he knew or could reasonably have been expected to know of those circumstances.

(5) A person guilty of an offence under this section is liable[3]—

(*a*) on summary conviction, to imprisonment for a term not exceeding 6 months or a fine not exceeding the statutory maximum or both;
(*b*) on conviction on indictment, to imprisonment for a term not exceeding 5 years.

[Sexual Offences Act 2003, s 18.]

1. For "sexual", see s 78, post.
2. For "position of trust", see ss 21 and 22 and for sexual relationships which pre-date position of trust, see s 24, post.
3. For procedure in respect of this offence which is triable either way, see the Magistrates' Courts Act 1980, ss 17A–21 in PART I: MAGISTRATES' COURTS, PROCEDURE, ante.

8–28421S 19. Abuse of position of trust: causing a child to watch a sexual act. (1) A person aged 18 or over (A) commits an offence if—

(*a*) for the purpose of obtaining sexual gratification, he intentionally causes another person (B) to watch a third person engaging in an activity, or to look at an image of any person engaging in an activity,
(*b*) the activity is sexual[1],
(*c*) A is in a position of trust[2] in relation to B,

(*d*) where subsection (2) applies, A knows or could reasonably be expected to know of the circumstances by virtue of which he is in a position of trust in relation to B, and

(*e*) either—

(i) B is under 18 and A does not reasonably believe that B is 18 or over, or

(ii) B is under 13.

(2) This subsection applies where A—

(*a*) is in a position of trust in relation to B by virtue of circumstances within section 21(2), (3), (4) or (5), and

(*b*) is not in such a position of trust by virtue of other circumstances.

(3) Where in proceedings for an offence under this section it is proved that the other person was under 18, the defendant is to be taken not to have reasonably believed that that person was 18 or over unless sufficient evidence is adduced to raise an issue as to whether he reasonably believed it.

(4) Where in proceedings for an offence under this section—

(*a*) it is proved that the defendant was in a position of trust in relation to the other person by virtue of circumstances within section 21(2), (3), (4) or (5), and

(*b*) it is not proved that he was in such a position of trust by virtue of other circumstances,

it is to be taken that the defendant knew or could reasonably have been expected to know of the circumstances by virtue of which he was in such a position of trust unless sufficient evidence is adduced to raise an issue as to whether he knew or could reasonably have been expected to know of those circumstances.

(5) A person guilty of an offence under this section is liable[3]—

(*a*) on summary conviction, to imprisonment for a term not exceeding 6 months or a fine not exceeding the statutory maximum or both;

(*b*) on conviction on indictment, to imprisonment for a term not exceeding 5 years.

[Sexual Offences Act 2003, s 19.]

---

1. For "sexual", see s 78, post.
2. For "position of trust", see ss 21 and 22 and for sexual relationships which pre-date position of trust, see s 24, post.
3. For procedure in respect of this offence which is triable either way, see the Magistrates' Courts Act 1980, ss 17A–21 in PART I: MAGISTRATES' COURTS, PROCEDURE, ante.

8–28421T 20. Abuse of position of trust: acts done in Scotland. Anything which, if done in England and Wales or Northern Ireland, would constitute an offence under any of sections 16 to 19 also constitutes that offence if done in Scotland.

[Sexual Offences Act 2003, s 20.]

8–28421U 21. Positions of trust. (1) For the purposes of sections 16 to 19, a person (A) is in a position of trust in relation to another person (B) if—

(*a*) any of the following subsections applies, or

(*b*) any condition specified in an order made by the Secretary of State is met.

(2) This subsection applies if A looks after persons under 18 who are detained in an institution by virtue of a court order or under an enactment, and B is so detained in that institution.

(3) This subsection applies if A looks after persons under 18 who are resident in a home or other place in which—

(*a*) accommodation and maintenance are provided by an authority under section 23(2) of the Children Act 1989 (c 41) or Article 27(2) of the Children (Northern Ireland) Order 1995 (SI 1995/755 (NI 2)), or

(*b*) accommodation is provided by a voluntary organisation under section 59(1) of that Act or Article 75(1) of that Order,

and B is resident, and is so provided with accommodation and maintenance or accommodation, in that place.

(4) This subsection applies if A looks after persons under 18 who are accommodated and cared for in one of the following institutions—

(*a*) a hospital,

(*b*) an independent clinic,

(*c*) a care home, residential care home or private hospital,

(*d*) a community home, voluntary home or children's home,

(*e*) a home provided under section 82(5) of the Children Act 1989, or

(*f*) a residential family centre,

and B is accommodated and cared for in that institution.

(5) This subsection applies if A looks after persons under 18 who are receiving education at an educational institution and B is receiving, and A is not receiving, education at that institution.

(6) This subsection applies if A is appointed to be the guardian of B under Article 159 or 160 of the Children (Northern Ireland) Order 1995 (SI 1995/755 (NI 2)).

(7) This subsection applies if A is engaged in the provision of services under, or pursuant to anything done under—

(*a*) sections 8 to 10 of the Employment and Training Act 1973 (c 50), or
(*b*) section 114 of the Learning and Skills Act 2000 (c 21),

and, in that capacity, looks after B on an individual basis.

(8) This subsection applies if A regularly has unsupervised contact with B (whether face to face or by any other means)—

(*a*) in the exercise of functions of a local authority under section 20 or 21 of the Children Act 1989 (c 41), or
(*b*) in the exercise of functions of an authority under Article 21 or 23 of the Children (Northern Ireland) Order 1995.

(9) This subsection applies if A, as a person who is to report to the court under section 7 of the Children Act 1989 or Article 4 of the Children (Northern Ireland) Order 1995 on matters relating to the welfare of B, regularly has unsupervised contact with B (whether face to face or by any other means).

(10) This subsection applies if A is a personal adviser appointed for B under—

(*a*) section 23B(2) of, or paragraph 19C of Schedule 2 to, the Children Act 1989, or
(*b*) Article 34A(10) or 34C(2) of the Children (Northern Ireland) Order 1995,

and, in that capacity, looks after B on an individual basis.

(11) This subsection applies if—

(*a*) B is subject to a care order, a supervision order or an education supervision order, and
(*b*) in the exercise of functions conferred by virtue of the order on an authorised person or the authority designated by the order, A looks after B on an individual basis.

(12) This subsection applies if A—

(*a*) is an officer of the Service or Welsh family proceedings officer (within the meaning given by section 35 of the Children Act 2004) appointed for B under section 41(1) of the Children Act 1989,
(*b*) is appointed a children's guardian of B under rule 6 or rule 18 of the Adoption Rules 1984 (SI 1984/265), or
(*c*) is appointed to be the guardian ad litem of B under rule 9.5 of the Family Proceedings Rules 1991 (S. I. 1991/1247) or under Article 60(1) of the Children (Northern Ireland) Order 1995,

and, in that capacity, regularly has unsupervised contact with B (whether face to face or by any other means).

(13) This subsection applies if—

(*a*) B is subject to requirements imposed by or under an enactment on his release from detention for a criminal offence, or is subject to requirements imposed by a court order made in criminal proceedings, and
(*b*) A looks after B on an individual basis in pursuance of the requirements.

[Sexual Offences Act 2003, s 21 as amended by the Children Act 2004, Sch 3.]

8–28421V 22. Positions of trust: interpretation. (1) The following provisions apply for the purposes of section 21.

(2) Subject to subsection (3), a person looks after persons under 18 if he is regularly involved in caring for, training, supervising or being in sole charge of such persons.

(3) A person (A) looks after another person (B) on an individual basis if—

(*a*) A is regularly involved in caring for, training or supervising B, and
(*b*) in the course of his involvement, A regularly has unsupervised contact with B (whether face to face or by any other means).

(4) A person receives education at an educational institution if—

(*a*) he is registered or otherwise enrolled as a pupil or student at the institution, or
(*b*) he receives education at the institution under arrangements with another educational institution at which he is so registered or otherwise enrolled.

(5) In section 21—

"authority"—

(*a*) in relation to England and Wales, means a local authority;
(*b*) in relation to Northern Ireland, has the meaning given by Article 2(2) of the Children (Northern Ireland) Order 1995 (SI 1995/755 (NI 2));

"care home" means an establishment which is a care home for the purposes of the Care Standards Act 2000 (c 14);

"care order" has—

(*a*) in relation to England and Wales, the same meaning as in the Children Act 1989 (c 41), and
(*b*) in relation to Northern Ireland, the same meaning as in the Children (Northern Ireland) Order 1995;

"children's home" has—

(*a*) in relation to England and Wales, the meaning given by section 1 of the Care Standards Act 2000, and
(*b*) in relation to Northern Ireland, the meaning that would be given by Article 9 of the Health and Personal Social Services (Quality, Improvement and Regulation) (Northern Ireland) Order 2003 (SI 2003/431 (NI 9)) ("the 2003 Order") if in paragraph (4) of that Article sub-paragraphs (d), (f) and (g) were omitted;

"community home" has the meaning given by section 53 of the Children Act 1989;
"education supervision order" has—

(*a*) in relation to England and Wales, the meaning given by section 36 of the Children Act 1989, and
(*b*) in relation to Northern Ireland, the meaning given by Article 49(1) of the Children (Northern Ireland) Order 1995;

"hospital"—

(*a*) in relation to England and Wales, means a hospital within the meaning given by section 128(1) of the National Health Service Act 1977 (c 49), or any other establishment which is a hospital within the meaning given by section 2(3) of the Care Standards Act 2000 (c 14);
(*b*) in relation to Northern Ireland, means a hospital within the meaning given by Article 2(2) of the Health and Personal Social Services (Northern Ireland) Order 1972 (SI 1972/1265 (NI 14)), or any other establishment which is a hospital within the meaning given by Article 2(2) of the 2003 Order;

"independent clinic" has—

(*a*) in relation to England and Wales, the meaning given by section 2 of the Care Standards Act 2000;
(*b*) in relation to Northern Ireland, the meaning given by Article 2(2) of the 2003 Order;

"private hospital" has the meaning given by Article 90(2) of the Mental Health (Northern Ireland) Order 1986 (SI 1986/595 (NI 4));
"residential care home" means an establishment which is a residential care home for the purposes of the 2003 Order;
"residential family centre" has the meaning given by section 22 of the Health and Personal Social Services Act (Northern Ireland) 2001 (c 3);
"supervision order" has—

(*a*) in relation to England and Wales, the meaning given by section 31(11) of the Children Act 1989 (c 41), and
(*b*) in relation to Northern Ireland, the meaning given by Article 49(1) of the Children (Northern Ireland) Order 1995 (SI 1995/ 755 (NI 2));

"voluntary home" has—

(*a*) in relation to England and Wales, the meaning given by section 60(3) of the Children Act 1989, and
(*b*) in relation to Northern Ireland, the meaning given by Article 74(1) of the Children (Northern Ireland) Order 1995.

[Sexual Offences Act 2003, s 22.]

8–28421W 23. Sections 16 to 19: marriage exception★. (1) Conduct by a person (A) which would otherwise be an offence under any of sections 16 to 19 against another person (B) is not an offence under that section if at the time—

(*a*) B is 16 or over, and
(*b*) A and B are lawfully married★.

(2) In proceedings for such an offence it is for the defendant to prove that A and B were lawfully married at the time★.
[Sexual Offences Act 2003, s 23.]

★Words substituted and sub-s (1)(*b*) amended by the Civil Partnership Act 2004, Sch 27 from a date to be appointed.

8–28421X 24. Sections 16 to 19: sexual relationships which pre-date position of trust. (1) Conduct by a person (A) which would otherwise be an offence under any of sections 16 to 19 against another person (B) is not an offence under that section if, immediately before the position of trust arose, a sexual relationship existed between A and B.

(2) Subsection (1) does not apply if at that time sexual intercourse between A and B would have been unlawful.

(3) In proceedings for an offence under any of sections 16 to 19 it is for the defendant to prove that such a relationship existed at that time.

[Sexual Offences Act 2003, s 24.]

Familial child sex offences

8–28421Y 25. Sexual activity with a child family member. (1) A person (A) commits an offence[1] if—

(*a*) he intentionally touches another person (B),

(*b*) the touching[2] is sexual[3],

(*c*) the relation of A to B is within section 27,

(*d*) A knows or could reasonably be expected to know that his relation to B is of a description falling within that section, and

(*e*) either—

(i) B is under 18 and A does not reasonably believe that B is 18 or over, or

(ii) B is under 13.

(2) Where in proceedings for an offence under this section it is proved that the other person was under 18, the defendant is to be taken not to have reasonably believed that that person was 18 or over unless sufficient evidence is adduced to raise an issue as to whether he reasonably believed it.

(3) Where in proceedings for an offence under this section it is proved that the relation of the defendant to the other person was of a description falling within section 27, it is to be taken that the defendant knew or could reasonably have been expected to know that his relation to the other person was of that description unless sufficient evidence is adduced to raise an issue as to whether he knew or could reasonably have been expected to know that it was.

(4) A person guilty of an offence under this section, if aged 18 or over at the time of the offence, is liable—

(*a*) where subsection (6) applies, on conviction on indictment to imprisonment for a term not exceeding 14 years;

(*b*) in any other case[4]—

(i) on summary conviction, to imprisonment for a term not exceeding 6 months or a fine not exceeding the statutory maximum or both;

(ii) on conviction on indictment, to imprisonment for a term not exceeding 14 years.

(5) Unless subsection (4) applies, a person guilty of an offence under this section is liable[4]—

(*a*) on summary conviction, to imprisonment for a term not exceeding 6 months or a fine not exceeding the statutory maximum or both;

(*b*) on conviction on indictment, to imprisonment for a term not exceeding 5 years.

(6) This subsection applies where the touching involved—

(*a*) penetration[2] of B's anus or vagina[2] with a part of A's body[2] or anything else,

(*b*) penetration of B's mouth with A's penis,

(*c*) penetration of A's anus or vagina with a part of B's body, or

(*d*) penetration of A's mouth with B's penis.

[Sexual Offences Act 2003, s 25.]

---

1. For marriage exception and sexual relationships which pre-date family relationships, see ss 28 and 29, post.
2. For "touching", "penetration", "vagina" and "part of his body", see s 79, post.
3. For "sexual", see s 78, post.
4. For procedure in respect of this offence which is triable either way, see the Magistrates' Courts Act 1980, ss 17A–21 in PART I: MAGISTRATES' COURTS, PROCEDURE, ante.

8–28421Z 26. Inciting a child family member to engage in sexual activity. (1) A person (A) commits an offence[1] if—

(*a*) he intentionally incites another person (B) to touch[2], or allow himself to be touched by, A,

(*b*) the touching is sexual[3],

(*c*) the relation of A to B is within section 27,

(*d*) A knows or could reasonably be expected to know that his relation to B is of a description falling within that section, and

(*e*) either—

(i) B is under 18 and A does not reasonably believe that B is 18 or over, or

(ii) B is under 13.

(2) Where in proceedings for an offence under this section it is proved that the other person was

under 18, the defendant is to be taken not to have reasonably believed that that person was 18 or over unless sufficient evidence is adduced to raise an issue as to whether he reasonably believed it.

(3) Where in proceedings for an offence under this section it is proved that the relation of the defendant to the other person was of a description falling within section 27, it is to be taken that the defendant knew or could reasonably have been expected to know that his relation to the other person was of that description unless sufficient evidence is adduced to raise an issue as to whether he knew or could reasonably have been expected to know that it was.

(4) A person guilty of an offence under this section, if he was aged 18 or over at the time of the offence, is liable—

(*a*) where subsection (6) applies, on conviction on indictment to imprisonment for a term not exceeding 14 years;

(*b*) in any other case[4]—

(i) on summary conviction, to imprisonment for a term not exceeding 6 months or a fine not exceeding the statutory maximum or both;

(ii) on conviction on indictment, to imprisonment for a term not exceeding 14 years.

(5) Unless subsection (4) applies, a person guilty of an offence under this section is liable[4]—

(*a*) on summary conviction, to imprisonment for a term not exceeding 6 months or a fine not exceeding the statutory maximum or both;

(*b*) on conviction on indictment, to imprisonment for a term not exceeding 5 years.

(6) This subsection applies where the touching to which the incitement related involved—

(*a*) penetration[2] of B's anus or vagina[2] with a part of A's body[2] or anything else,

(*b*) penetration of B's mouth with A's penis,

(*c*) penetration of A's anus or vagina with a part of B's body, or

(*d*) penetration of A's mouth with B's penis.

[Sexual Offences Act 2003, s 26.]

---

1. For marriage exception and sexual relationships which pre-date family relationships, see ss 28 and 29, post.
2. For "touching", "penetration", "vagina" and "part of his body", see s 79, post.
3. For "sexual", see s 78, post.
4. For procedure in respect of this offence which is triable either way, see the Magistrates' Courts Act 1980, ss 17A–21 in PART I: MAGISTRATES' COURTS, PROCEDURE, ante.

8–28422 **27. Family relationships.** (1) The relation of one person (A) to another (B) is within this section if—

(*a*) it is within any of subsections (2) to (4), or

(*b*) it would be within one of those subsections but for section 67 of the Adoption and Children Act 2002 (c 38) (status conferred by adoption).

(2) The relation of A to B is within this subsection if—

(*a*) one of them is the other's parent, grandparent, brother, sister, half-brother, half-sister, aunt or uncle, or

(*b*) A is or has been B's foster parent.

(3) The relation of A to B is within this subsection if A and B live or have lived in the same household, or A is or has been regularly involved in caring for, training, supervising or being in sole charge of B, and—

(*a*) one of them is or has been the other's step-parent,

(*b*) A and B are cousins,

(*c*) one of them is or has been the other's stepbrother or stepsister, or

(*d*) the parent or present or former foster parent of one of them is or has been the other's foster parent.

(4) The relation of A to B is within this subsection if—

(*a*) A and B live in the same household, and

(*b*) A is regularly involved in caring for, training, supervising or being in sole charge of B.

(5) For the purposes of this section—

(*a*) "aunt" means the sister or half-sister of a person's parent, and "uncle" has a corresponding meaning;

(*b*) "cousin" means the child of an aunt or uncle;

(*c*) a person is a child's foster parent if—

(i) he is a person with whom the child has been placed under section 23(2)(a) or 59(1)(a) of the Children Act 1989 (c 41) (fostering for local authority or voluntary organisation), or

(ii) he fosters the child privately, within the meaning given by section 66(1)(b) of that Act;

(*d*) a person is another's partner (whether they are of different sexes or the same sex) if they live together as partners in an enduring family relationship;
(*e*) "step-parent" includes a parent's partner and "stepbrother" and "stepsister" include the child of a parent's partner.
[Sexual Offences Act 2003, s 27.]

8–28422A 28. Sections 25 and 26: marriage exception*. (1) Conduct by a person (A) which would otherwise be an offence under section 25 or 26 against another person (B) is not an offence under that section if at the time—

(*a*) B is 16 or over, and
(*b*) A and B are lawfully married*.

(2) In proceedings for such an offence it is for the defendant to prove that A and B were lawfully married at the time*.
[Sexual Offences Act 2003, s 28.]

***Words substituted and sub-s (1)(*b*) amended by the Civil Partnership Act 2004, Sch 27 from a date to be appointed.**

8–28422B 29. Sections 25 and 26: sexual relationships which pre-date family relationships. (1) Conduct by a person (A) which would otherwise be an offence under section 25 or 26 against another person (B) is not an offence under that section if—

(*a*) the relation of A to B is not within subsection (2) of section 27,
(*b*) it would not be within that subsection if section 67 of the Adoption and Children Act 2002 (c 38) did not apply, and
(*c*) immediately before the relation of A to B first became such as to fall within section 27, a sexual relationship existed between A and B.

(2) Subsection (1) does not apply if at the time referred to in subsection (1)(c) sexual intercourse between A and B would have been unlawful.

(3) In proceedings for an offence under section 25 or 26 it is for the defendant to prove the matters mentioned in subsection (1)(a) to (c).
[Sexual Offences Act 2003, s 29.]

Offences against persons with a mental disorder impeding choice

8–28422C 30. Sexual activity with a person with a mental disorder impeding choice. (1) A person (A) commits an offence if—

(*a*) he intentionally touches[1] another person (B),
(*b*) the touching is sexual[2],
(*c*) B is unable to refuse because of or for a reason related to a mental disorder[1], and
(*d*) A knows or could reasonably be expected to know that B has a mental disorder and that because of it or for a reason related to it B is likely to be unable to refuse.

(2) B is unable to refuse if—

(*a*) he lacks the capacity to choose whether to agree to the touching (whether because he lacks sufficient understanding of the nature or reasonably foreseeable consequences of what is being done, or for any other reason), or
(*b*) he is unable to communicate such a choice to A.

(3) A person guilty of an offence under this section, if the touching involved—

(*a*) penetration[1] of B's anus or vagina[1] with a part of A's body or anything else,
(*b*) penetration of B's mouth with A's penis,
(*c*) penetration of A's anus or vagina with a part of B's body[1], or
(*d*) penetration of A's mouth with B's penis,

is liable, on conviction on indictment, to imprisonment for life.

(4) Unless subsection (3) applies, a person guilty of an offence under this section is liable[3]—

(*a*) on summary conviction, to imprisonment for a term not exceeding 6 months or to a fine not exceeding the statutory maximum or both;
(*b*) on conviction on indictment, to imprisonment for a term not exceeding 14 years.
[Sexual Offences Act 2003, s 30.]

1. For "touching", "mental disorder", "penetration", "vagina" and "part of his body", see s 79, post.
2. For "sexual", see s 78, post.
3. For procedure in respect of this offence which is triable either way, see the Magistrates' Courts Act 1980, ss 17A–21 in PART I: MAGISTRATES' COURTS, PROCEDURE, ante.

8–28422D 31. Causing or inciting a person, with a mental disorder impeding choice, to engage in sexual activity. (1) A person (A) commits an offence if—

(*a*) he intentionally causes or incites another person (B) to engage in an activity,
(*b*) the activity is sexual[1],
(*c*) B is unable to refuse because of or for a reason related to a mental disorder[2], and
(*d*) A knows or could reasonably be expected to know that B has a mental disorder and that because of it or for a reason related to it B is likely to be unable to refuse.

(2) B is unable to refuse if—

(*a*) he lacks the capacity to choose whether to agree to engaging in the activity caused or incited (whether because he lacks sufficient understanding of the nature or reasonably foreseeable consequences of the activity, or for any other reason), or
(*b*) he is unable to communicate such a choice to A.

(3) A person guilty of an offence under this section, if the activity caused or incited involved—

(*a*) penetration[2] of B's anus or vagina[2],
(*b*) penetration of B's mouth with a person's penis,
(*c*) penetration of a person's anus or vagina with a part of B's body[2] or by B with anything else, or
(*d*) penetration of a person's mouth with B's penis,

is liable, on conviction on indictment, to imprisonment for life.

(4) Unless subsection (3) applies, a person guilty of an offence under this section is liable[3]—

(*a*) on summary conviction, to imprisonment for a term not exceeding 6 months or to a fine not exceeding the statutory maximum or both;
(*b*) on conviction on indictment, to imprisonment for a term not exceeding 14 years.

[Sexual Offences Act 2003, s 31.]

---

1. For "sexual", see s 78, post.
2. For "mental disorder", "penetration", "vagina" and "part of his body", see s 79, post.
3. For procedure in respect of this offence which is triable either way, see the Magistrates' Courts Act 1980, ss 17A–21 in PART I: MAGISTRATES' COURTS, PROCEDURE, ante.

8–28422E 32. Engaging in sexual activity in the presence of a person with a mental disorder impeding choice. (1) A person (A) commits an offence if—

(*a*) he intentionally engages in an activity,
(*b*) the activity is sexual[1],
(*c*) for the purpose of obtaining sexual gratification, he engages in it—
  (i) when another person (B) is present or is in a place from which A can be observed, and
  (ii) knowing or believing that B is aware, or intending that B should be aware, that he is engaging in it,
(*d*) B is unable to refuse because of or for a reason related to a mental disorder[2], and
(*e*) A knows or could reasonably be expected to know that B has a mental disorder and that because of it or for a reason related to it B is likely to be unable to refuse.

(2) B is unable to refuse if—

(*a*) he lacks the capacity to choose whether to agree to being present (whether because he lacks sufficient understanding of the nature of the activity, or for any other reason), or
(*b*) he is unable to communicate such a choice to A.

(3) A person guilty of an offence under this section is liable[3]—

(*a*) on summary conviction, to imprisonment for a term not exceeding 6 months or a fine not exceeding the statutory maximum or both;
(*b*) on conviction on indictment, to imprisonment for a term not exceeding 10 years.

[Sexual Offences Act 2003, s 32.]

---

1. For "sexual", see s 78, post.
2. For "mental disorder", see s 79, post.
3. For procedure in respect of this offence which is triable either way, see the Magistrates' Courts Act 1980, ss 17A–21 in PART I: MAGISTRATES' COURTS, PROCEDURE, ante.

8–28422F 33. Causing a person, with a mental disorder impeding choice, to watch a sexual act. (1) A person (A) commits an offence if—

(*a*) for the purpose of obtaining sexual gratification, he intentionally causes another person (B) to watch a third person engaging in an activity, or to look at an image of any person engaging in an activity,
(*b*) the activity is sexual[1],
(*c*) B is unable to refuse because of or for a reason related to a mental disorder[2], and

(*d*) A knows or could reasonably be expected to know that B has a mental disorder and that because of it or for a reason related to it B is likely to be unable to refuse.

(2) B is unable to refuse if—

(*a*) he lacks the capacity to choose whether to agree to watching or looking (whether because he lacks sufficient understanding of the nature of the activity, or for any other reason), or

(*b*) he is unable to communicate such a choice to A.

(3) A person guilty of an offence under this section is liable[3]—

(*a*) on summary conviction, to imprisonment for a term not exceeding 6 months or a fine not exceeding the statutory maximum or both;

(*b*) on conviction on indictment, to imprisonment for a term not exceeding 10 years.

[Sexual Offences Act 2003, s 33.]

1. For "sexual", see s 78, post.
2. For "mental disorder", see s 79, post.
3. For procedure in respect of this offence which is triable either way, see the Magistrates' Courts Act 1980, ss 17A–21 in PART I: MAGISTRATES' COURTS, PROCEDURE, ante.

Inducements etc to persons with a mental disorder

8–28422G **34. Inducement, threat or deception to procure sexual activity with a person with a mental disorder.** (1) A person (A) commits an offence if—

(*a*) with the agreement of another person (B) he intentionally touches[1] that person,

(*b*) the touching is sexual[2],

(*c*) A obtains B's agreement by means of an inducement offered or given, a threat made or a deception practised by A for that purpose,

(*d*) B has a mental disorder[1], and

(*e*) A knows or could reasonably be expected to know that B has a mental disorder.

(2) A person guilty of an offence under this section, if the touching involved—

(*a*) penetration[1] of B's anus or vagina[1] with a part of A's body[1] or anything else,

(*b*) penetration of B's mouth with A's penis,

(*c*) penetration of A's anus or vagina with a part of B's body, or

(*d*) penetration of A's mouth with B's penis,

is liable, on conviction on indictment, to imprisonment for life.

(3) Unless subsection (2) applies, a person guilty of an offence under this section is liable[3]—

(*a*) on summary conviction, to imprisonment for a term not exceeding 6 months or a fine not exceeding the statutory maximum or both;

(*b*) on conviction on indictment, to imprisonment for a term not exceeding 14 years.

[Sexual Offences Act 2003, s 34.]

1. For "touching", "mental disorder", "penetration", "vagina" and "part of his body", see s 79, post.
2. For "sexual", see s 78, post.
3. For procedure in respect of this offence which is triable either way, see the Magistrates' Courts Act 1980, ss 17A–21 in PART I: MAGISTRATES' COURTS, PROCEDURE, ante.

8–28422H **35. Causing a person with a mental disorder to engage in or agree to engage in sexual activity by inducement, threat or deception.** (1) A person (A) commits an offence if—

(*a*) by means of an inducement offered or given, a threat made or a deception practised by him for this purpose, he intentionally causes another person (B) to engage in, or to agree to engage in, an activity,

(*b*) the activity is sexual[1],

(*c*) B has a mental disorder, and

(*d*) A knows or could reasonably be expected to know that B has a mental disorder.

(2) A person guilty of an offence under this section, if the activity caused or agreed to involved—

(*a*) penetration[2] of B's anus or vagina[2],

(*b*) penetration of B's mouth with a person's penis,

(*c*) penetration of a person's anus or vagina with a part of B's body[2] or by B with anything else, or

(*d*) penetration of a person's mouth with B's penis,

is liable, on conviction on indictment, to imprisonment for life.

(3) Unless subsection (2) applies, a person guilty of an offence under this section is liable[3]—

(*a*) on summary conviction, to imprisonment for a term not exceeding 6 months or a fine not exceeding the statutory maximum or both;

(*b*) on conviction on indictment, to imprisonment for a term not exceeding 14 years.

[Sexual Offences Act 2003, s 35.]

1. For "sexual", see s 78, post.
2. For "mental disorder", "penetration", "vagina" and "part of his body", see s 79, post.
3. For procedure in respect of this offence which is triable either way, see the Magistrates' Courts Act 1980, ss 17A–21 in PART I: MAGISTRATES' COURTS, PROCEDURE, ante.

8–28422I 36. Engaging in sexual activity in the presence, procured by inducement, threat or deception, of a person with a mental disorder. (1) A person (A) commits an offence if—

(*a*) he intentionally engages in an activity,
(*b*) the activity is sexual[1],
(*c*) for the purpose of obtaining sexual gratification, he engages in it—
 (i) when another person (B) is present or is in a place from which A can be observed, and
 (ii) knowing or believing that B is aware, or intending that B should be aware, that he is engaging in it,
(*d*) B agrees to be present or in the place referred to in paragraph (c)(i) because of an inducement offered or given, a threat made or a deception practised by A for the purpose of obtaining that agreement,
(*e*) B has a mental disorder[2], and
(*f*) A knows or could reasonably be expected to know that B has a mental disorder.

(2) A person guilty of an offence under this section is liable[3]—

(*a*) on summary conviction, to imprisonment for a term not exceeding 6 months or a fine not exceeding the statutory maximum or both;
(*b*) on conviction on indictment, to imprisonment for a term not exceeding 10 years.

[Sexual Offences Act 2003, s 36.]

1. For "sexual", see s 78, post.
2. For "mental disorder", see s 79, post.
3. For procedure in respect of this offence which is triable either way, see the Magistrates' Courts Act 1980, ss 17A–21 in PART I: MAGISTRATES' COURTS, PROCEDURE, ante.

8–28422J 37. Causing a person with a mental disorder to watch a sexual act by inducement, threat or deception. (1) A person (A) commits an offence if—

(*a*) for the purpose of obtaining sexual gratification, he intentionally causes another person (B) to watch a third person engaging in an activity, or to look at an image of any person engaging in an activity,
(*b*) the activity is sexual[1],
(*c*) B agrees to watch or look because of an inducement offered or given, a threat made or a deception practised by A for the purpose of obtaining that agreement,
(*d*) B has a mental disorder[2], and
(*e*) A knows or could reasonably be expected to know that B has a mental disorder.

(2) A person guilty of an offence under this section is liable[3]—

(*a*) on summary conviction, to imprisonment for a term not exceeding 6 months or a fine not exceeding the statutory maximum or both;
(*b*) on conviction on indictment, to imprisonment for a term not exceeding 10 years.

[Sexual Offences Act 2003, s 37.]

1. For "sexual", see s 78, post.
2. For "mental disorder", see s 79, post.
3. For procedure in respect of this offence which is triable either way, see the Magistrates' Courts Act 1980, ss 17A–21 in PART I: MAGISTRATES' COURTS, PROCEDURE, ante.

Care workers for persons with a mental disorder

8–28422K 38. Care workers: sexual activity with a person with a mental disorder. (1) A person (A) commits an offence[1] if—

(*a*) he intentionally touches another person (B),
(*b*) the touching[2] is sexual[3],
(*c*) B has a mental disorder[2],
(*d*) A knows or could reasonably be expected to know that B has a mental disorder, and
(*e*) A is involved in B's care in a way that falls within section 42.

(2) Where in proceedings for an offence under this section it is proved that the other person had a mental disorder, it is to be taken that the defendant knew or could reasonably have been expected to know that that person had a mental disorder unless sufficient evidence is adduced to raise an issue as to whether he knew or could reasonably have been expected to know it.

(3) A person guilty of an offence under this section, if the touching involved—

(*a*) penetration[2] of B's anus or vagina[2] with a part of A's body[2] or anything else,

(*b*) penetration of B's mouth with A's penis,
(*c*) penetration of A's anus or vagina with a part of B's body, or
(*d*) penetration of A's mouth with B's penis,

is liable, on conviction on indictment, to imprisonment for a term not exceeding 14 years.

(4) Unless subsection (3) applies, a person guilty of an offence under this section is liable[4]—

(*a*) on summary conviction, to imprisonment for a term not exceeding 6 months or a fine not exceeding the statutory maximum or both;

(*b*) on conviction on indictment, to imprisonment for a term not exceeding 10 years.

[Sexual Offences Act 2003, s 38.]

---

1. For marriage exception and sexual relationships which pre-date care relationships, see ss 43 and 44, post.
2. For "touching", "mental disorder", "penetration", "vagina" and "part of his body", see s 79, post.
3. For "sexual", see s 78, post.
45. For procedure in respect of this offence which is triable either way, see the Magistrates' Courts Act 1980, ss 17A–21 in PART I: MAGISTRATES' COURTS, PROCEDURE, ante.

8–28422L 39. Care workers: causing or inciting sexual activity. (1) A person (A) commits an offence[1] if—

(*a*) he intentionally causes or incites another person (B) to engage in an activity,
(*b*) the activity is sexual[2],
(*c*) B has a mental disorder[3],
(*d*) A knows or could reasonably be expected to know that B has a mental disorder, and
(*e*) A is involved in B's care in a way that falls within section 42.

(2) Where in proceedings for an offence under this section it is proved that the other person had a mental disorder, it is to be taken that the defendant knew or could reasonably have been expected to know that that person had a mental disorder unless sufficient evidence is adduced to raise an issue as to whether he knew or could reasonably have been expected to know it.

(3) A person guilty of an offence under this section, if the activity caused or incited involved—

(*a*) penetration[3] of B's anus or vagina[3],
(*b*) penetration of B's mouth with a person's penis,
(*c*) penetration of a person's anus or vagina with a part of B's body[3] or by B with anything else, or
(*d*) penetration of a person's mouth with B's penis,

is liable, on conviction on indictment, to imprisonment for a term not exceeding 14 years.

(4) Unless subsection (3) applies, a person guilty of an offence under this section is liable[4]—

(*a*) on summary conviction, to imprisonment for a term not exceeding 6 months or a fine not exceeding the statutory maximum or both;

(*b*) on conviction on indictment, to imprisonment for a term not exceeding 10 years.

[Sexual Offences Act 2003, s 39.]

---

1. For marriage exception and sexual relationships which pre-date care relationships, see ss 43 and 44, post.
2. For "sexual", see s 78, post.
3. For "mental disorder", "penetration", "vagina" and "part of his body", see s 79, post.
4. For procedure in respect of this offence which is triable either way, see the Magistrates' Courts Act 1980, ss 17A–21 in PART I: MAGISTRATES' COURTS, PROCEDURE, ante.

8–28422M 40. Care workers: sexual activity in the presence of a person with a mental disorder. (1) A person (A) commits an offence[1] if—

(*a*) he intentionally engages in an activity,
(*b*) the activity is sexual[2],
(*c*) for the purpose of obtaining sexual gratification, he engages in it—

(i) when another person (B) is present or is in a place from which A can be observed, and
(ii) knowing or believing that B is aware, or intending that B should be aware, that he is engaging in it,

(*d*) B has a mental disorder[3],
(*e*) A knows or could reasonably be expected to know that B has a mental disorder, and
(*f*) A is involved in B's care in a way that falls within section 42.

(2) Where in proceedings for an offence under this section it is proved that the other person had a mental disorder, it is to be taken that the defendant knew or could reasonably have been expected to know that that person had a mental disorder unless sufficient evidence is adduced to raise an issue as to whether he knew or could reasonably have been expected to know it.

(3) A person guilty of an offence under this section is liable[4]—

(*a*) on summary conviction, to imprisonment for a term not exceeding 6 months or a fine not exceeding the statutory maximum or both;

(*b*) on conviction on indictment, to imprisonment for a term not exceeding 7 years.

[Sexual Offences Act 2003, s 40.]

1. For marriage exception and sexual relationships which pre-date care relationships, see ss 43 and 44, post.
2. For "sexual", see s 78, post.
3. For "mental disorder", see s 79, post.
4. For procedure in respect of this offence which is triable either way, see the Magistrates' Courts Act 1980, ss 17A–21 in PART I: MAGISTRATES' COURTS, PROCEDURE, ante.

8–28422N 41. Care workers: causing a person with a mental disorder to watch a sexual act. (1) A person (A) commits an offence[1] if—

(*a*) for the purpose of obtaining sexual gratification, he intentionally causes another person (B) to watch a third person engaging in an activity, or to look at an image of any person engaging in an activity,
(*b*) the activity is sexual[2],
(*c*) B has a mental disorder,
(*d*) A knows or could reasonably be expected to know that B has a mental disorder[3], and
(*e*) A is involved in B's care in a way that falls within section 42.

(2) Where in proceedings for an offence under this section it is proved that the other person had a mental disorder, it is to be taken that the defendant knew or could reasonably have been expected to know that that person had a mental disorder unless sufficient evidence is adduced to raise an issue as to whether he knew or could reasonably have been expected to know it.

(3) A person guilty of an offence under this section is liable[4]—

(*a*) on summary conviction, to imprisonment for a term not exceeding 6 months or a fine not exceeding the statutory maximum or both;
(*b*) on conviction on indictment, to imprisonment for a term not exceeding 7 years.

[Sexual Offences Act 2003, s 41.]

1. For marriage exception and sexual relationships which pre-date care relationships, see ss 43 and 44, post.
2. For "sexual", see s 78, post.
3. For "mental disorder", see s 79, post.
4. For procedure in respect of this offence which is triable either way, see the Magistrates' Courts Act 1980, ss 17A–21 in PART I: MAGISTRATES' COURTS, PROCEDURE, ante.

8–28422O 42. Care workers: interpretation. (1) For the purposes of sections 38 to 41, a person (A) is involved in the care of another person (B) in a way that falls within this section if any of subsections (2) to (4) applies.

(2) This subsection applies if—

(*a*) B is accommodated and cared for in a care home, community home, voluntary home or children's home, and
(*b*) A has functions to perform in the home in the course of employment which have brought him or are likely to bring him into regular face to face contact with B.

(3) This subsection applies if B is a patient for whom services are provided—

(*a*) by a National Health Service body or an independent medical agency, or
(*b*) in an independent clinic or an independent hospital,

and A has functions to perform for the body or agency or in the clinic or hospital in the course of employment which have brought him or are likely to bring him into regular face to face contact with B.

(4) This subsection applies if A—

(*a*) is, whether or not in the course of employment, a provider of care, assistance or services to B in connection with B's mental disorder, and
(*b*) as such, has had or is likely to have regular face to face contact with B.

(5) In this section—

"care home" means an establishment which is a care home for the purposes of the Care Standards Act 2000 (c 14);
"children's home" has the meaning given by section 1 of that Act;
"community home" has the meaning given by section 53 of the Children Act 1989 (c 41);
"employment" means any employment, whether paid or unpaid and whether under a contract of service or apprenticeship, under a contract for services, or otherwise than under a contract;
"independent clinic", "independent hospital" and "independent medical agency" have the meaning given by section 2 of the Care Standards Act 2000;
"National Health Service body" means—

(*a*) a Health Authority,
(*b*) a National Health Service trust,
(*c*) a Primary Care Trust, or
(*d*) a Special Health Authority;

"voluntary home" has the meaning given by section 60(3) of the Children Act 1989.
[Sexual Offences Act 2003, s 42.]

8–28422P 43. Sections 38 to 41: exception for spouses and civil partners. (1) Conduct by a person (A) which would otherwise be an offence under any of sections 38 to 41 against another person (B) is not an offence under that section if at the time—

(*a*) B is 16 or over, and
(*b*) A and B are lawfully marriedor civil partners of each other.

(2) In proceedings for such an offence it is for the defendant to prove that A and B were at the time lawfully married or civil partners of each other.
[Sexual Offences Act 2003, s 43 as amended by the Civil Partnership Act 2004, Sch 27.]

8–28422Q 44. Sections 38 to 41: sexual relationships which pre-date care relationships. (1) Conduct by a person (A) which would otherwise be an offence under any of sections 38 to 41 against another person (B) is not an offence under that section if, immediately before A became involved in B's care in a way that falls within section 42, a sexual relationship existed between A and B.

(2) Subsection (1) does not apply if at that time sexual intercourse between A and B would have been unlawful.

(3) In proceedings for an offence under any of sections 38 to 41 it is for the defendant to prove that such a relationship existed at that time.
[Sexual Offences Act 2003, s 44.]

Indecent photographs of children

8–28422R 45. Indecent photographs of persons aged 16 or 17. *Amends ss 2(3) and 7(6) of and inserts s 1A into the Protection of Children Act 1978 and inserts s 160A into the Criminal Justice Act 1988.*

8–28422S 46. Criminal proceedings, investigations etc. *Inserts s 1B into the Protection of Children Act 1978.*

Abuse of children through prostitution and pornography

8–28422T 47. Paying for sexual services of a child. (1) A person (A) commits an offence if—

(*a*) he intentionally obtains for himself the sexual[1] services of another person (B),
(*b*) before obtaining those services, he has made or promised payment for those services to B or a third person, or knows that another person has made or promised such a payment, and
(*c*) either—

(i) B is under 18, and A does not reasonably believe that B is 18 or over, or
(ii) B is under 13.

(2) In this section, "payment" means any financial advantage, including the discharge of an obligation to pay or the provision of goods or services (including sexual services) gratuitously or at a discount.

(3) A person guilty of an offence under this section against a person under 13, where subsection (6) applies, is liable on conviction on indictment to imprisonment for life.

(4) Unless subsection (3) applies, a person guilty of an offence under this section against a person under 16 is liable—

(*a*) where subsection (6) applies, on conviction on indictment, to imprisonment for a term not exceeding 14 years;
(*b*) in any other case[2]—

(i) on summary conviction, to imprisonment for a term not exceeding 6 months or a fine not exceeding the statutory maximum or both;
(ii) on conviction on indictment, to imprisonment for a term not exceeding 14 years.

(5) Unless subsection (3) or (4) applies, a person guilty of an offence under this section is liable[2]—

(*a*) on summary conviction, to imprisonment for a term not exceeding 6 months or a fine not exceeding the statutory maximum or both;
(*b*) on conviction on indictment, to imprisonment for a term not exceeding 7 years.

(6) This subsection applies where the offence involved—

(*a*) penetration[3] of B's anus or vagina[3] with a part of A's body or anything else,
(*b*) penetration of B's mouth with A's penis,
(*c*) penetration of A's anus or vagina with a part of B's body or by B with anything else, or
(*d*) penetration of A's mouth with B's penis.

(7) *Northern Ireland.*
[Sexual Offences Act 2003, s 47.]

1. For "sexual", see s 78, post.
2. For procedure in respect of this offence which is triable either way, see the Magistrates' Courts Act 1980, ss 17A–21 in PART I: MAGISTRATES' COURTS, PROCEDURE, ante.
3. For "penetration" and "vagina", see s 79, post.

8–28422U 48. Causing or inciting child prostitution or pornography. (1) A person (A) commits an offence if—

(*a*) he intentionally causes or incites another person (B) to become a prostitute[1], or to be involved in pornography[1], in any part of the world, and
(*b*) either—

(i) B is under 18, and A does not reasonably believe that B is 18 or over, or
(ii) B is under 13.

(2) A person guilty of an offence under this section is liable[2]—

(*a*) on summary conviction, to imprisonment for a term not exceeding 6 months or a fine not exceeding the statutory maximum or both;
(*b*) on conviction on indictment, to imprisonment for a term not exceeding 14 years.

[Sexual Offences Act 2003, s 48.]

1. For "prostitute" and "pornography", see s 51, post.
2. For procedure in respect of this offence which is triable either way, see the Magistrates' Courts Act 1980, ss 17A–21 in PART I: MAGISTRATES' COURTS, PROCEDURE, ante.

8–28422V 49. Controlling a child prostitute or a child involved in pornography. (1) A person (A) commits an offence if—

(*a*) he intentionally controls any of the activities of another person (B) relating to B's prostitution[1] or involvement in pornography[1] in any part of the world, and
(*b*) either—

(i) B is under 18, and A does not reasonably believe that B is 18 or over, or
(ii) B is under 13.

(2) A person guilty of an offence under this section is liable[2]—

(*a*) on summary conviction, to imprisonment for a term not exceeding 6 months or a fine not exceeding the statutory maximum or both;
(*b*) on conviction on indictment, to imprisonment for a term not exceeding 14 years.

[Sexual Offences Act 2003, s 49.]

1. For "prostitute" and "pornography", see s 51, post.
2. For procedure in respect of this offence which is triable either way, see the Magistrates' Courts Act 1980, ss 17A–21 in PART I: MAGISTRATES' COURTS, PROCEDURE, ante.

8–28422W 50. Arranging or facilitating child prostitution or pornography. (1) A person (A) commits an offence if—

(*a*) he intentionally arranges or facilitates the prostitution[1] or involvement in pornography[1] in any part of the world of another person (B), and
(*b*) either—

(i) B is under 18, and A does not reasonably believe that B is 18 or over, or
(ii) B is under 13.

(2) A person guilty of an offence under this section is liable[2]—

(*a*) on summary conviction, to imprisonment for a term not exceeding 6 months or a fine not exceeding the statutory maximum or both;
(*b*) on conviction on indictment, to imprisonment for a term not exceeding 14 years.

[Sexual Offences Act 2003, s 50.]

1. For "prostitute" and "pornography", see s 51, post.
2. For procedure in respect of this offence which is triable either way, see the Magistrates' Courts Act 1980, ss 17A–21 in PART I: MAGISTRATES' COURTS, PROCEDURE, ante.

8–28422X 51. Sections 48 to 50: interpretation. (1) For the purposes of sections 48 to 50, a person is involved in pornography if an indecent image of that person is recorded; and similar expressions, and "pornography", are to be interpreted accordingly.

(2) In those sections "prostitute" means a person (A) who, on at least one occasion and whether or not compelled to do so, offers or provides sexual services to another person in return for payment or a promise of payment to A or a third person; and "prostitution" is to be interpreted accordingly.

(3) In subsection (2), "payment" means any financial advantage, including the discharge of an

obligation to pay or the provision of goods or services (including sexual services) gratuitously or at a discount.
[Sexual Offences Act 2003, s 51.]

Exploitation of prostitution

8–28422Y 52. Causing or inciting prostitution for gain. (1) A person commits an offence if—

(*a*) he intentionally causes or incites another person to become a prostitute[1] in any part of the world, and

(*b*) he does so for or in the expectation of gain[2] for himself or a third person.

(2) A person guilty of an offence under this section is liable[3]—

(*a*) on summary conviction, to imprisonment for a term not exceeding 6 months or a fine not exceeding the statutory maximum or both;

(*b*) on conviction on indictment, to imprisonment for a term not exceeding 7 years.

[Sexual Offences Act 2003, s 52.]

---

1. For "prostitute", see s 54(2), post.
2. For "gain", see s 54(1), post.
3. For procedure in respect of this offence which is triable either way, see the Magistrates' Courts Act 1980, ss 17A–21 in PART I: MAGISTRATES' COURTS, PROCEDURE, ante.

8–28422Z 53. Controlling prostitution for gain. (1) A person commits an offence if—

(*a*) he intentionally controls any of the activities of another person relating to that person's prostitution[1] in any part of the world, and

(*b*) he does so for or in the expectation of gain[2] for himself or a third person.

(2) A person guilty of an offence under this section is liable[3]—

(*a*) on summary conviction, to imprisonment for a term not exceeding 6 months or a fine not exceeding the statutory maximum or both;

(*b*) on conviction on indictment, to imprisonment for a term not exceeding 7 years.

[Sexual Offences Act 2003, s 53.]

---

1. For "prostitute", see s 54(2), post.
2. For "gain", see s 54(1), post.
3. For procedure in respect of this offence which is triable either way, see the Magistrates' Courts Act 1980, ss 17A–21 in PART I: MAGISTRATES' COURTS, PROCEDURE, ante.

8–28423 54. Sections 52 and 53: interpretation. (1) In sections 52 and 53, "gain" means—

(*a*) any financial advantage, including the discharge of an obligation to pay or the provision of goods or services (including sexual services) gratuitously or at a discount; or

(*b*) the goodwill of any person which is or appears likely, in time, to bring financial advantage.

(2) In those sections "prostitute" and "prostitution" have the meaning given by section 51(2).

[Sexual Offences Act 2003, s 54.]

Amendments relating to prostitution

8–28423A 55. Penalties for keeping a brothel used for prostitution. *Inserts s 33A into and amends Sch 2 to the Sexual Offences Act 1956.*

8–28423B 56. Extension of gender-specific prostitution offences. *Amends the Sexual Offences Act 1956, the Street Offences Act 1959 and the Sexual Offences Act 1985 to extend prostitution offences including soliciting for the purposes of prostitution to male prostitution.*

Trafficking

8–28423C 57. Trafficking into the UK for sexual exploitation. (1) A person commits an offence if he intentionally arranges or facilitates the arrival in the United Kingdom of another person (B) and either—

(*a*) he intends to do anything to or in respect of B, after B's arrival but in any part of the world, which if done will involve the commission of a relevant offence[1], or

(*b*) he believes that another person is likely to do something to or in respect of B, after B's arrival but in any part of the world, which if done will involve the commission of a relevant offence.

(2) A person guilty of an offence under this section is liable[2]—

(*a*) on summary conviction, to imprisonment for a term not exceeding 6 months or a fine not exceeding the statutory maximum or both;

(*b*) on conviction on indictment, to imprisonment for a term not exceeding 14 years.

[Sexual Offences Act 2003, s 57.]

1. For "relevant offence", see s 60(1), post.
2. For procedure in respect of this offence which is triable either way, see the Magistrates' Courts Act 1980, ss 17A–21 in PART I: MAGISTRATES' COURTS, PROCEDURE, ante.

8–28423D 58. Trafficking within the UK for sexual exploitation. (1) A person commits an offence if he intentionally arranges or facilitates travel within the United Kingdom by another person (B) and either—

(*a*) he intends to do anything to or in respect of B, during or after the journey and in any part of the world, which if done will involve the commission of a relevant offence, or
(*b*) he believes that another person is likely to do something to or in respect of B, during or after the journey and in any part of the world, which if done will involve the commission of a relevant offence[1].

(2) A person guilty of an offence under this section is liable[2]—

(*a*) on summary conviction, to imprisonment for a term not exceeding 6 months or a fine not exceeding the statutory maximum or both;
(*b*) on conviction on indictment, to imprisonment for a term not exceeding 14 years.

[Sexual Offences Act 2003, s 58.]

1. For "relevant offence", see s 60(1), post.
2. For procedure in respect of this offence which is triable either way, see the Magistrates' Courts Act 1980, ss 17A–21 in PART I: MAGISTRATES' COURTS, PROCEDURE, ante.

8–28423E 59. Trafficking out of the UK for sexual exploitation. (1) A person commits an offence if he intentionally arranges or facilitates the departure from the United Kingdom of another person (B) and either—

(*a*) he intends to do anything to or in respect of B, after B's departure but in any part of the world, which if done will involve the commission of a relevant offence[1], or
(*b*) he believes that another person is likely to do something to or in respect of B, after B's departure but in any part of the world, which if done will involve the commission of a relevant offence.

(2) A person guilty of an offence under this section is liable[2]—

(*a*) on summary conviction, to imprisonment for a term not exceeding 6 months or a fine not exceeding the statutory maximum or both;
(*b*) on conviction on indictment, to imprisonment for a term not exceeding 14 years.

[Sexual Offences Act 2003, s 59.]

1. For "relevant offence", see s 60(1), post.
2. For procedure in respect of this offence which is triable either way, see the Magistrates' Courts Act 1980, ss 17A–21 in PART I: MAGISTRATES' COURTS, PROCEDURE, ante.

8–28423F 60. Sections 57 to 59: interpretation and jurisdiction. (1) In sections 57 to 59, "relevant offence" means—

(*a*) an offence under this Part,
(*b*) an offence under section 1(1)(a) of the Protection of Children Act 1978 (c 37),
(*c*) an offence listed in Schedule 1 to the Criminal Justice (Children) (Northern Ireland) Order 1998 (SI 1998/1504 (NI 9)),
(*d*) an offence under Article 3(1)(a) of the Protection of Children (Northern Ireland) Order 1978 (SI 1978/1047 (NI 17)), or
(*e*) anything done outside England and Wales and Northern Ireland which is not an offence within any of paragraphs (*a*) to (*d*) but would be if done in England and Wales or Northern Ireland.

(2) Sections 57 to 59 apply to anything done—

(*a*) in the United Kingdom, or
(*b*) outside the United Kingdom, by a body incorporated under the law of a part of the United Kingdom or by an individual to whom subsection (3) applies.

(3) This subsection applies to—

(*a*) a British citizen,
(*b*) a British overseas territories citizen,
(*c*) a British National (Overseas),
(*d*) a British Overseas citizen,
(*e*) a person who is a British subject under the British Nationality Act 1981 (c 61),
(*f*) a British protected person within the meaning given by section 50(1) of that Act.

[Sexual Offences Act 2003, s 60.]

Preparatory offences

8–28423G 61. Administering a substance with intent. (1) A person commits an offence if he intentionally administers a substance to, or causes a substance to be taken by, another person (B)—

(*a*) knowing that B does not consent[1], and

(*b*) with the intention of stupefying or overpowering B, so as to enable any person to engage in a sexual activity that involves B.

(2) A person guilty of an offence under this section is liable[2]—

(*a*) on summary conviction, to imprisonment for a term not exceeding 6 months or a fine not exceeding the statutory maximum or both;

(*b*) on conviction on indictment, to imprisonment for a term not exceeding 10 years.

[Sexual Offences Act 2003, s 61.]

---

1. For "consent", see s 74, post.
2. For procedure in respect of this offence which is triable either way, see the Magistrates' Courts Act 1980, ss 17A–21 in PART I: MAGISTRATES' COURTS, PROCEDURE, ante

8–28423H 62. Committing an offence with intent to commit a sexual offence. (1) A person commits an offence under this section if he commits any offence with the intention of committing a relevant sexual offence.

(2) In this section, "relevant sexual offence" means any offence under this Part (including an offence of aiding, abetting, counselling or procuring such an offence).

(3) A person guilty of an offence under this section is liable on conviction on indictment, where the offence is committed by kidnapping or false imprisonment, to imprisonment for life.

(4) Unless subsection (3) applies, a person guilty of an offence under this section is liable[1]—

(*a*) on summary conviction, to imprisonment for a term not exceeding 6 months or a fine not exceeding the statutory maximum or both;

(*b*) on conviction on indictment, to imprisonment for a term not exceeding 10 years.

[Sexual Offences Act 2003, s 62.]

---

1. For procedure in respect of this offence which is triable either way, see the Magistrates' Courts Act 1980, ss 17A–21 in PART I: MAGISTRATES' COURTS, PROCEDURE, ante.

8–28423I 63. Trespass with intent to commit a sexual offence. (1) A person commits an offence if—

(*a*) he is a trespasser on any premises,

(*b*) he intends to commit a relevant sexual offence on the premises, and

(*c*) he knows that, or is reckless as to whether, he is a trespasser.

(2) In this section—

"premises" includes a structure or part of a structure;

"relevant sexual offence" has the same meaning as in section 62;

"structure" includes a tent, vehicle or vessel or other temporary or movable structure.

(3) A person guilty of an offence under this section is liable[1]—

(*a*) on summary conviction, to imprisonment for a term not exceeding 6 months or a fine not exceeding the statutory maximum or both;

(*b*) on conviction on indictment, to imprisonment for a term not exceeding 10 years.

[Sexual Offences Act 2003, s 63.]

---

1. For procedure in respect of this offence which is triable either way, see the Magistrates' Courts Act 1980, ss 17A–21 in PART I: MAGISTRATES' COURTS, PROCEDURE, ante.

Sex with an adult relative

8–28423J 64. Sex with an adult relative: penetration. (1) A person aged 16 or over (A) commits an offence if—

(*a*) he intentionally penetrates[1] another person's vagina[1] or anus with a part of his body[1] or anything else, or penetrates another person's mouth with his penis,

(*b*) the penetration is sexual[2],

(*c*) the other person (B) is aged 18 or over,

(*d*) A is related to B in a way mentioned in subsection (2), and

(*e*) A knows or could reasonably be expected to know that he is related to B in that way.

(2) The ways that A may be related to B are as parent, grandparent, child, grandchild, brother, sister, half-brother, half-sister, uncle, aunt, nephew or niece.

(3) In subsection (2)—

(*a*) "uncle" means the brother of a person's parent, and "aunt" has a corresponding meaning;

(*b*) "nephew" means the child of a person's brother or sister, and "niece" has a corresponding meaning.

(4) Where in proceedings for an offence under this section it is proved that the defendant was related to the other person in any of those ways, it is to be taken that the defendant knew or could reasonably have been expected to know that he was related in that way unless sufficient evidence is adduced to raise an issue as to whether he knew or could reasonably have been expected to know that he was.

(5) A person guilty of an offence under this section is liable[3]—

(*a*) on summary conviction, to imprisonment for a term not exceeding 6 months or a fine not exceeding the statutory maximum or both;

(*b*) on conviction on indictment, to imprisonment for a term not exceeding 2 years.

[Sexual Offences Act 2003, s 64.]

1. For "penetration", "vagina" and "part of his body", see s 79, post.
2. For "sexual", see s 78, post.
3. For procedure in respect of this offence which is triable either way, see the Magistrates' Courts Act 1980, ss 17A–21 in PART I: MAGISTRATES' COURTS, PROCEDURE, ante.

8–28423K 65. Sex with an adult relative: consenting to penetration. (1) A person aged 16 or over (A) commits an offence if—

(*a*) another person (B) penetrates[1] A's vagina[1] or anus with a part of B's body[1] or anything else, or penetrates A's mouth with B's penis,
(*b*) A consents[2] to the penetration,
(*c*) the penetration is sexual[3],
(*d*) B is aged 18 or over,
(*e*) A is related to B in a way mentioned in subsection (2), and
(*f*) A knows or could reasonably be expected to know that he is related to B in that way.

(2) The ways that A may be related to B are as parent, grandparent, child, grandchild, brother, sister, half-brother, half-sister, uncle, aunt, nephew or niece.

(3) In subsection (2)—

(*a*) "uncle" means the brother of a person's parent, and "aunt" has a corresponding meaning;
(*b*) "nephew" means the child of a person's brother or sister, and "niece" has a corresponding meaning.

(4) Where in proceedings for an offence under this section it is proved that the defendant was related to the other person in any of those ways, it is to be taken that the defendant knew or could reasonably have been expected to know that he was related in that way unless sufficient evidence is adduced to raise an issue as to whether he knew or could reasonably have been expected to know that he was.

(5) A person guilty of an offence under this section is liable[4]—

(*a*) on summary conviction, to imprisonment for a term not exceeding 6 months or a fine not exceeding the statutory maximum or both;

(*b*) on conviction on indictment, to imprisonment for a term not exceeding 2 years.

[Sexual Offences Act 2003, s 65.]

1. For "penetration", "vagina" and "part of his body", see s 79, post.
2. For "consent", see s 74, post.
3. For "sexual", see s 78, post.
4. For procedure in respect of this offence which is triable either way, see the Magistrates' Courts Act 1980, ss 17A–21 in PART I: MAGISTRATES' COURTS, PROCEDURE, ante.

Other offences

8–28423L 66. Exposure. (1) A person commits an offence if—

(*a*) he intentionally exposes his genitals, and
(*b*) he intends that someone will see them and be caused alarm or distress.

(2) A person guilty of an offence under this section is liable[1]—

(*a*) on summary conviction, to imprisonment for a term not exceeding 6 months or a fine not exceeding the statutory maximum or both;

(*b*) on conviction on indictment, to imprisonment for a term not exceeding 2 years.

[Sexual Offences Act 2003, s 66.]

1. For procedure in respect of this offence which is triable either way, see the Magistrates' Courts Act 1980, ss 17A–21 in PART I: MAGISTRATES' COURTS, PROCEDURE, ante.

8–28423M 67. Voyeurism. (1) A person commits an offence if—

(*a*) for the purpose of obtaining sexual gratification, he observes another person doing a private act[1], and
(*b*) he knows that the other person does not consent[3] to being observed for his sexual gratification.

(2) A person commits an offence if—

(*a*) he operates equipment with the intention of enabling another person to observe[2], for the purpose of obtaining sexual gratification, a third person (B) doing a private act, and
(*b*) he knows that B does not consent[3] to his operating equipment with that intention.

(3) A person commits an offence if—

(*a*) he records another person (B) doing a private act,
(*b*) he does so with the intention that he or a third person will, for the purpose of obtaining sexual gratification, look at an image[2] of B doing the act, and
(*c*) he knows that B does not consent[3] to his recording the act with that intention.

(4) A person commits an offence if he instals equipment, or constructs or adapts a structure[4] or part of a structure, with the intention of enabling himself or another person to commit an offence under subsection (1).

(5) A person guilty of an offence under this section is liable[5]—

(*a*) on summary conviction, to imprisonment for a term not exceeding 6 months or a fine not exceeding the statutory maximum or both;
(*b*) on conviction on indictment, to imprisonment for a term not exceeding 2 years.

[Sexual Offences Act 2003, s 67.]

1. For "private act", see s 68(1), post.
2. For "observes" and "image", see s 79, post.
3. For "consent", see s 74, post.
4. For "structure", see s 68(2), post.
5. For procedure in respect of this offence which is triable either way, see the Magistrates' Courts Act 1980, ss 17A–21 in PART I: MAGISTRATES' COURTS, PROCEDURE, ante.

8–28423N 68. Voyeurism: interpretation. (1) For the purposes of section 67, a person is doing a private act if the person is in a place which, in the circumstances, would reasonably be expected to provide privacy, and—

(*a*) the person's genitals, buttocks or breasts are exposed or covered only with underwear,
(*b*) the person is using a lavatory, or
(*c*) the person is doing a sexual act that is not of a kind ordinarily done in public.

(2) In section 67, "structure" includes a tent, vehicle or vessel or other temporary or movable structure.

[Sexual Offences Act 2003, s 68.]

8–28423O 69. Intercourse with an animal. (1) A person commits an offence if—

(*a*) he intentionally performs an act of penetration with his penis,
(*b*) what is penetrated is the vagina or anus[1] of a living animal, and
(*c*) he knows that, or is reckless as to whether, that is what is penetrated.

(2) A person (A) commits an offence if—

(*a*) A intentionally causes, or allows, A's vagina or anus to be penetrated,
(*b*) the penetration is by the penis of a living animal, and
(*c*) A knows that, or is reckless as to whether, that is what A is being penetrated by.

(3) A person guilty of an offence under this section is liable[2]—

(*a*) on summary conviction, to imprisonment for a term not exceeding 6 months or a fine not exceeding the statutory maximum or both;
(*b*) on conviction on indictment, to imprisonment for a term not exceeding 2 years.

[Sexual Offences Act 2003, s 69.]

1. In relation to an animal, references to the vagina or anus include references to any similar part (s 79(10), post).
2. For procedure in respect of this offence which is triable either way, see the Magistrates' Courts Act 1980, ss 17A–21 in PART I: MAGISTRATES' COURTS, PROCEDURE, ante.

8–28423P 70. Sexual penetration of a corpse. (1) A person commits an offence if—

(*a*) he intentionally performs an act of penetration[1] with a part of his body or anything else,
(*b*) what is penetrated is a part of the body of a dead person,
(*c*) he knows that, or is reckless as to whether, that is what is penetrated, and
(*d*) the penetration is sexual[2].

(2) A person guilty of an offence under this section is liable[3]—

(*a*) on summary conviction, to imprisonment for a term not exceeding 6 months or a fine not exceeding the statutory maximum or both;
(*b*) on conviction on indictment, to imprisonment for a term not exceeding 2 years.
[Sexual Offences Act 2003, s 70.]

1. For "penetration", see s 79, post.
2. For "sexual", see s 78, post.
3. For procedure in respect of this offence which is triable either way, see the Magistrates' Courts Act 1980, ss 17A–21 in PART I: MAGISTRATES' COURTS, PROCEDURE, ante.

8–28423Q 71. Sexual activity in a public lavatory. (1) A person commits an offence if—
(*a*) he is in a lavatory to which the public or a section of the public has or is permitted to have access, whether on payment or otherwise,
(*b*) he intentionally engages in an activity, and,
(*c*) the activity is sexual.

(2) For the purposes of this section, an activity is sexual if a reasonable person would, in all the circumstances but regardless of any person's purpose, consider it to be sexual.

(3) A person guilty of an offence under this section is liable on summary conviction, to imprisonment for a term not exceeding 6 months or a fine not exceeding level 5 on the standard scale or both.
[Sexual Offences Act 2003, s 71.]

Offences outside the United Kingdom

8–28423R 72. Offences outside the United Kingdom. (1) Subject to subsection (2), any act done by a person in a country or territory outside the United Kingdom which—
(*a*) constituted an offence under the law in force in that country or territory, and
(*b*) would constitute a sexual offence to which this section applies if it had been done in England and Wales or in Northern Ireland,

constitutes that sexual offence under the law of that part of the United Kingdom.

(2) Proceedings by virtue of this section may be brought only against a person who was on 1st September 1997, or has since become, a British citizen or resident in the United Kingdom.

(3) An act punishable under the law in force in any country or territory constitutes an offence under that law for the purposes of this section, however it is described in that law.

(4) Subject to subsection (5), the condition in subsection (1)(*a*) is to be taken to be met unless, not later than rules of court may provide, the defendant serves on the prosecution a notice—
(*a*) stating that, on the facts as alleged with respect to the act in question, the condition is not in his opinion met,
(*b*) showing his grounds for that opinion, and
(*c*) requiring the prosecution to prove that it is met.

(5) The court, if it thinks fit, may permit the defendant to require the prosecution to prove that the condition is met without service of a notice under subsection (4).

(6) In the Crown Court the question whether the condition is met is to be decided by the judge alone.

(7) Schedule 2 lists the sexual offences to which this section applies.
[Sexual Offences Act 2003, s 72.]

Supplementary and general

8–28423S 73. Exceptions to aiding, abetting and counselling. (1) A person is not guilty of aiding, abetting or counselling the commission against a child of an offence to which this section applies if he acts for the purpose of—
(*a*) protecting the child from sexually transmitted infection,
(*b*) protecting the physical safety of the child,
(*c*) preventing the child from becoming pregnant, or
(*d*) promoting the child's emotional well-being by the giving of advice,

and not for the purpose of obtaining sexual gratification or for the purpose of causing or encouraging the activity constituting the offence or the child's participation in it.

(2) This section applies to—
(*a*) an offence under any of sections 5 to 7 (offences against children under 13);
(*b*) an offence under section 9 (sexual activity with a child);
(*c*) an offence under section 13 which would be an offence under section 9 if the offender were aged 18;
(*d*) an offence under any of sections 16, 25, 30, 34 and 38 (sexual activity) against a person under 16.

(3) This section does not affect any other enactment or any rule of law restricting the circumstances in which a person is guilty of aiding, abetting or counselling an offence under this Part.
[Sexual Offences Act 2003, s 73.]

8–28423T 74. "Consent". For the purposes of this Part, a person consents if he agrees by choice, and has the freedom and capacity to make that choice.
[Sexual Offences Act 2003, s 74.]

8–28423U 75. Evidential presumptions about consent. (1) If in proceedings for an offence to which this section applies it is proved—

(*a*) that the defendant did the relevant act,
(*b*) that any of the circumstances specified in subsection (2) existed, and
(*c*) that the defendant knew that those circumstances existed,

the complainant is to be taken not to have consented to the relevant act unless sufficient evidence is adduced to raise an issue as to whether he consented, and the defendant is to be taken not to have reasonably believed that the complainant consented unless sufficient evidence is adduced to raise an issue as to whether he reasonably believed it.

(2) The circumstances are that—

(*a*) any person was, at the time of the relevant act or immediately before it began, using violence against the complainant or causing the complainant to fear that immediate violence would be used against him;
(*b*) any person was, at the time of the relevant act or immediately before it began, causing the complainant to fear that violence was being used, or that immediate violence would be used, against another person;
(*c*) the complainant was, and the defendant was not, unlawfully detained at the time of the relevant act;
(*d*) the complainant was asleep or otherwise unconscious at the time of the relevant act;
(*e*) because of the complainant's physical disability, the complainant would not have been able at the time of the relevant act to communicate to the defendant whether the complainant consented;
(*f*) any person had administered to or caused to be taken by the complainant, without the complainant's consent, a substance which, having regard to when it was administered or taken, was capable of causing or enabling the complainant to be stupefied or overpowered at the time of the relevant act.

(3) In subsection (2)(*a*) and (*b*), the reference to the time immediately before the relevant act began is, in the case of an act which is one of a continuous series of sexual activities, a reference to the time immediately before the first sexual activity began.
[Sexual Offences Act 2003, s 75.]

8–28423V 76. Conclusive presumptions about consent. (1) If in proceedings for an offence to which this section applies it is proved that the defendant did the relevant act and that any of the circumstances specified in subsection (2) existed, it is to be conclusively presumed—

(*a*) that the complainant did not consent to the relevant act, and
(*b*) that the defendant did not believe that the complainant consented to the relevant act.

(2) The circumstances are that—

(*a*) the defendant intentionally deceived the complainant as to the nature or purpose of the relevant act;
(*b*) the defendant intentionally induced the complainant to consent to the relevant act by impersonating a person known personally to the complainant.

[Sexual Offences Act 2003, s 76.]

8–28423W 77. Sections 75 and 76: relevant acts. In relation to an offence to which sections 75 and 76 apply, references in those sections to the relevant act and to the complainant are to be read as follows—

Offence	*Relevant Act*
An offence under section 1 (rape).	The defendant intentionally penetrating, with his penis, the vagina, anus or mouth of another person ("the complainant").
An offence under section 2 (assault by penetration).	The defendant intentionally penetrating, with a part of his body or anything else, the vagina or anus of another person ("the complainant"), where the penetration is sexual.
An offence under section 3 (sexual assault).	The defendant intentionally touching another person ("the complainant"), where the touching is sexual.
An offence under section 4 (causing a person to engage in sexual activity without consent).	The defendant intentionally causing another person ("the complainant") to engage in an activity, where the activity is sexual.

[Sexual Offences Act 2003, s 77.]

8–28423X 78. "Sexual". For the purposes of this Part (except section 71), penetration, touching or any other activity is sexual if a reasonable person would consider that—

(*a*) whatever its circumstances or any person's purpose in relation to it, it is because of its nature sexual, or

(*b*) because of its nature it may be sexual and because of its circumstances or the purpose of any person in relation to it (or both) it is sexual.

[Sexual Offences Act 2003, s 78.]

8–28423Y 79. Part 1: general interpretation. (1) The following apply for the purposes of this Part.

(2) Penetration is a continuing act from entry to withdrawal.

(3) References to a part of the body include references to a part surgically constructed (in particular, through gender reassignment surgery).

(4) "Image" means a moving or still image and includes an image produced by any means and, where the context permits, a three-dimensional image.

(5) References to an image of a person include references to an image of an imaginary person.

(6) "Mental disorder" has the meaning given by section 1 of the Mental Health Act 1983 (c 20).

(7) References to observation (however expressed) are to observation whether direct or by looking at an image.

(8) Touching[1] includes touching—

(*a*) with any part of the body,

(*b*) with anything else,

(*c*) through anything,

and in particular includes touching amounting to penetration.

(9) "Vagina" includes vulva.

(10) In relation to an animal, references to the vagina or anus include references to any similar part.

[Sexual Offences Act 2003, s 79.]

1. The matters referred to in s 79(8) are not exhaustive and s 78 is not a definition section; where a person is wearing clothing, touching of that clothing constitutes "touching" for the purposes of the offence contrary to s 3 of the Act: *R v H* [2005] EWCA Crim 732, [2005] 2 ALL ER 859, [2005] 2 Cr App R 9, [2005] Crim LR 735. Where touching is not inevitably sexual because of its nature, s 78(*b*) of the Act applies and in such a case, two distinct questions should be identified for the court/jury (both of which must be answered in the affirmative to find the defendant guilty), namely: (i) whether they, as reasonable people, consider that the touching, in the particular circumstances before them, because of its nature, may be sexual; and (ii) whether they, as 12 reasonable people, consider that the touching, in view of its circumstances, or the purpose of any person in relation to it, or both, was in fact sexual. In relation to the first question, evidence as to the circumstances before and after the touching, and evidence of the purpose of any person in relation to that touching is irrelevant. However, in most cases, the answer will be same whether the two-stage approach is adopted or whether the matter is looked at as a whole: *R v H*, supra.

PART 2[1]

NOTIFICATION AND ORDERS

Notification requirements

8–28423Z 80. Persons becoming subject to notification requirements. (1) A person is subject to the notification requirements of this Part for the period set out in section 82 ("the notification period") if—

(*a*) he is convicted[2] of an offence listed in Schedule 3;

(*b*) he is found not guilty of such an offence by reason of insanity;

(*c*) he is found to be under a disability and to have done the act charged against him in respect of such an offence; or

(*d*) in England and Wales or Northern Ireland, he is cautioned in respect of such an offence.

(2) A person for the time being subject to the notification requirements of this Part is referred to in this Part as a "relevant offender".

[Sexual Offences Act 2003, s 80.]

1. Part 2 comprises ss 80–136 and Schs 3–5.

2. The notification requirement arises on the date of conviction, and not the date of sentence if this occurs later; but in the case of an offender sentenced to an absolute discharge the notification requirement does not arise if sentencing occurs on the date of conviction, or survive if sentence is passed on a later date: *R v Longworth* [2006] UKHL 1, [2006] 1 ALL ER 887, [2006] 1 WLR 313.

8–28424 81. Persons formerly subject to Part 1 of the Sex Offenders Act 1997. (1) A person is, from the commencement of this Part until the end of the notification period, subject to the notification requirements of this Part if, before the commencement of this Part—

(*a*) he was convicted[1] of an offence listed in Schedule 3;
(*b*) he was found not guilty of such an offence by reason of insanity;
(*c*) he was found to be under a disability and to have done the act charged against him in respect of such an offence; or
(*d*) in England and Wales or Northern Ireland, he was cautioned in respect of such an offence.

(2) Subsection (1) does not apply if the notification period ended before the commencement of this Part.

(3) Subsection (1)(*a*) does not apply to a conviction before 1st September 1997 unless, at the beginning of that day, the person—

(*a*) had not been dealt with in respect of the offence;
(*b*) was serving a sentence of imprisonment or a term of service detention, or was subject to a community order, in respect of the offence;
(*c*) was subject to supervision, having been released from prison after serving the whole or part of a sentence of imprisonment in respect of the offence; or
(*d*) was detained in a hospital or was subject to a guardianship order, following the conviction.

(4) Paragraphs (*b*) and (*c*) of subsection (1) do not apply to a finding made before 1st September 1997 unless, at the beginning of that day, the person—

(*a*) had not been dealt with in respect of the finding; or
(*b*) was detained in a hospital, following the finding.

(5) Subsection (1)(*d*) does not apply to a caution given before 1st September 1997.

(6) A person who would have been within subsection (3)(*b*) or (*d*) or (4)(*b*) but for the fact that at the beginning of 1st September 1997 he was unlawfully at large or absent without leave, on temporary release or leave of absence, or on bail pending an appeal, is to be treated as being within that provision.

(7) Where, immediately before the commencement of this Part, an order under a provision within subsection (8) was in force in respect of a person, the person is subject to the notification requirements of this Part from that commencement until the order is discharged or otherwise ceases to have effect.

(8) The provisions are—

(*a*) section 5A of the Sex Offenders Act 1997 (c 51) (restraining orders);
(*b*) section 2 of the Crime and Disorder Act 1998 (c 37) (sex offender orders made in England and Wales);
(*c*) section 2A of the Crime and Disorder Act 1998 (interim orders made in England and Wales);
(*d*) section 20 of the Crime and Disorder Act 1998 (sex offender orders and interim orders made in Scotland);
(*e*) Article 6 of the Criminal Justice (Northern Ireland) Order 1998 (SI 1998/2839 (NI 20)) (sex offender orders made in Northern Ireland);
(*f*) Article 6A of the Criminal Justice (Northern Ireland) Order 1998 (interim orders made in Northern Ireland).

[Sexual Offences Act 2003, s 81.]

---

1. A person sentenced to an absolute or conditional discharge for a pre-commencement offence is not subject to the notification requirements of the 1997 Act and, consequently, is not subject to the notification requirements of the 2003 Act: *R v Longworth* [2006] UKHL 1, [2006] 1 All ER 887, [2006] 1 WLR 313.

8–28424A 82. The notification period. (1) The notification period for a person within section 80(1) or 81(1) is the period in the second column of the following Table opposite the description that applies to him.

TABLE

Description of relevant offender	Notification period
A person who, in respect of the offence, is or has been sentenced to imprisonment for life or for a term of 30 months or more	An indefinite period beginning with the relevant date
A person who, in respect of the offence, has been made the subject of an order under section 210F(1) of the Criminal Procedure (Scotland) Act 1995 (order for lifelong restriction)	An indefinite period beginning with that date
A person who, in respect of the offence or finding, is or has been admitted to a hospital subject to a restriction order	An indefinite period beginning with that date

Description of relevant offender	Notification period
A person who, in respect of the offence, is or has been sentenced to imprisonment for a term of more than 6 months but less than 30 months	10 years beginning with that date
A person who, in respect of the offence, is or has been sentenced to imprisonment for a term of 6 months or less	7 years beginning with that date
A person who, in respect of the offence or finding, is or has been admitted to a hospital without being subject to a restriction order	7 years beginning with that date
A person within section 80(1)(d)	2 years beginning with that date
A person in whose case an order for conditional discharge or, in Scotland, a probation order, is made in respect of the offence	The period of conditional discharge or, in Scotland, the probation period
A person of any other description	5 years beginning with the relevant date

(2) Where a person is under 18 on the relevant date, subsection (1) has effect as if for any reference to a period of 10 years, 7 years, 5 years or 2 years there were substituted a reference to one-half of that period.

(3) Subsection (4) applies where a relevant offender within section 80(1)(*a*) or 81(1)(*a*) is or has been sentenced, in respect of two or more offences listed in Schedule 3—

(*a*) to consecutive terms of imprisonment; or

(*b*) to terms of imprisonment which are partly concurrent.

(4) Where this subsection applies, subsection (1) has effect as if the relevant offender were or had been sentenced, in respect of each of the offences, to a term of imprisonment which—

(*a*) in the case of consecutive terms, is equal to the aggregate of those terms;

(*b*) in the case of partly concurrent terms (X and Y, which overlap for a period Z), is equal to X plus Y minus Z.

(5) Where a relevant offender the subject of a finding within section 80(1)(*c*) or 81(1)(*c*) is subsequently tried for the offence, the notification period relating to the finding ends at the conclusion of the trial.

(6) In this Part, "relevant date" means—

(*a*) in the case of a person within section 80(1)(*a*) or 81(1)(*a*), the date of the conviction;

(*b*) in the case of a person within section 80(1)(*b*) or (*c*) or 81(1)(*b*) or (*c*), the date of the finding;

(*c*) in the case of a person within section 80(1)(*d*) or 81(1)(*d*), the date of the caution;

(*d*) in the case of a person within section 81(7), the date which, for the purposes of Part 1 of the Sex Offenders Act 1997 (c 51), was the relevant date in relation to that person.

[Sexual Offences Act 2003, s 82.]

8–28424B 83. Notification requirements: initial notification. (1) A relevant offender must, within the period of 3 days beginning with the relevant date (or, if later, the commencement of this Part), notify to the police the information set out in subsection (5).

(2) Subsection (1) does not apply to a relevant offender in respect of a conviction, finding or caution within section 80(1) if—

(*a*) immediately before the conviction, finding or caution, he was subject to the notification requirements of this Part as a result of another conviction, finding or caution or an order of a court ("the earlier event"),

(*b*) at that time, he had made a notification under subsection (1) in respect of the earlier event, and

(*c*) throughout the period referred to in subsection (1), he remains subject to the notification requirements as a result of the earlier event.

(3) Subsection (1) does not apply to a relevant offender in respect of a conviction, finding or caution within section 81(1) or an order within section 81(7) if the offender complied with section 2(1) of the Sex Offenders Act 1997 in respect of the conviction, finding, caution or order.

(4) Where a notification order is made in respect of a conviction, finding or caution, subsection (1) does not apply to the relevant offender in respect of the conviction, finding or caution if—

(*a*) immediately before the order was made, he was subject to the notification requirements of this Part as a result of another conviction, finding or caution or an order of a court ("the earlier event"),

(*b*) at that time, he had made a notification under subsection (1) in respect of the earlier event, and (*c*) throughout the period referred to in subsection (1), he remains subject to the notification requirements as a result of the earlier event.

(5) The information is—

(*a*) the relevant offender's date of birth;
(*b*) his national insurance number;
(*c*) his name on the relevant date and, where he used one or more other names on that date, each of those names;
(*d*) his home address on the relevant date;
(*e*) his name on the date on which notification is given and, where he uses one or more other names on that date, each of those names;
(*f*) his home address on the date on which notification is given;
(*g*) the address of any other premises in the United Kingdom at which, at the time the notification is given, he regularly resides or stays.

(6) When determining the period for the purpose of subsection (1), there is to be disregarded any time when the relevant offender is—

(*a*) remanded in or committed to custody by an order of a court;
(*b*) serving a sentence of imprisonment or a term of service detention;
(*c*) detained in a hospital; or
(*d*) outside the United Kingdom.

(7) In this Part, "home address" means, in relation to any person—

(*a*) the address of his sole or main residence in the United Kingdom, or
(*b*) where he has no such residence, the address or location of a place in the United Kingdom where he can regularly be found and, if there is more than one such place, such one of those places as the person may select.

[Sexual Offences Act 2003, s 83.]

8–28424C 84. Notification requirements: changes. (1) A relevant offender must, within the period of 3 days beginning with—

(*a*) his using a name which has not been notified to the police under section 83(1), this subsection, or section 2 of the Sex Offenders Act 1997 (c 51),
(*b*) any change of his home address,
(*c*) his having resided or stayed, for a qualifying period, at any premises in the United Kingdom the address of which has not been notified to the police under section 83(1), this subsection, or section 2 of the Sex Offenders Act 1997, or
(*d*) his release from custody pursuant to an order of a court or from imprisonment, service detention or detention in a hospital,

notify to the police that name, the new home address, the address of those premises or (as the case may be) the fact that he has been released, and (in addition) the information set out in section 83(5).

(2) A notification under subsection (1) may be given before the name is used, the change of home address occurs or the qualifying period ends, but in that case the relevant offender must also specify the date when the event is expected to occur.

(3) If a notification is given in accordance with subsection (2) and the event to which it relates occurs more than 2 days before the date specified, the notification does not affect the duty imposed by subsection (1).

(4) If a notification is given in accordance with subsection (2) and the event to which it relates has not occurred by the end of the period of 3 days beginning with the date specified—

(*a*) the notification does not affect the duty imposed by subsection (1), and
(*b*) the relevant offender must, within the period of 6 days beginning with the date specified, notify to the police the fact that the event did not occur within the period of 3 days beginning with the date specified.

(5) Section 83(6) applies to the determination of the period of 3 days mentioned in subsection (1) and the period of 6 days mentioned in subsection (4)(b), as it applies to the determination of the period mentioned in section 83(1).

(6) In this section, "qualifying period" means—

(*a*) a period of 7 days, or
(*b*) two or more periods, in any period of 12 months, which taken together amount to 7 days.

[Sexual Offences Act 2003, s 84.]

8–28424D 85. Notification requirements: periodic notification. (1) A relevant offender must, within the period of one year after each event within subsection (2), notify to the police the information set out in section 83(5), unless within that period he has given a notification under section 84(1).

(2) The events are—

(*a*) the commencement of this Part (but only in the case of a person who is a relevant offender from that commencement);
(*b*) any notification given by the relevant offender under section 83(1) or 84(1); and
(*c*) any notification given by him under subsection (1).

(3) Where the period referred to in subsection (1) would (apart from this subsection) end whilst subsection (4) applies to the relevant offender, that period is to be treated as continuing until the end of the period of 3 days beginning when subsection (4) first ceases to apply to him.

(4) This subsection applies to the relevant offender if he is—

(*a*) remanded in or committed to custody by an order of a court,
(*b*) serving a sentence of imprisonment or a term of service detention,
(*c*) detained in a hospital, or
(*d*) outside the United Kingdom.

[Sexual Offences Act 2003, s 85.]

8–28424E 86. Notification requirements: travel outside the United Kingdom. (1) The Secretary of State may by regulations[1] make provision requiring relevant offenders who leave the United Kingdom, or any description of such offenders—

(*a*) to give in accordance with the regulations, before they leave, a notification under subsection (2);
(*b*) if they subsequently return to the United Kingdom, to give in accordance with the regulations a notification under subsection (3).

(2) A notification under this subsection must disclose—

(*a*) the date on which the offender will leave the United Kingdom;
(*b*) the country (or, if there is more than one, the first country) to which he will travel and his point of arrival (determined in accordance with the regulations) in that country;
(*c*) any other information prescribed by the regulations which the offender holds about his departure from or return to the United Kingdom or his movements while outside the United Kingdom.

(3) A notification under this subsection must disclose any information prescribed by the regulations about the offender's return to the United Kingdom.

(4) Regulations under subsection (1) may make different provision for different categories of person.

[Sexual Offences Act 2003, s 86.]

1. See the Sexual Offences Act 2003 (Travel Notification Requirements) Regulations 2004, in this title, post.

8–28424F 87. Method of notification and related matters. (1) A person gives a notification under section 83(1), 84(1) or 85(1) by—

(*a*) attending at such police station in his local police area as the Secretary of State may by regulations[1] prescribe or, if there is more than one, at any of them, and
(*b*) giving an oral notification to any police officer, or to any person authorised for the purpose by the officer in charge of the station.

(2) A person giving a notification under section 84(1)—

(*a*) in relation to a prospective change of home address, or
(*b*) in relation to premises referred to in subsection (1)(*c*) of that section,

may give the notification at a police station that would fall within subsection (1) above if the change in home address had already occurred or (as the case may be) if the address of those premises were his home address.

(3) Any notification under this section must be acknowledged; and an acknowledgement under this subsection must be in writing, and in such form as the Secretary of State may direct.

(4) Where a notification is given under section 83(1), 84(1) or 85(1), the relevant offender must, if requested to do so by the police officer or person referred to in subsection (1)(*b*), allow the officer or person to—

(*a*) take his fingerprints,
(*b*) photograph any part of him, or
(*c*) do both these things.

(5) The power in subsection (4) is exercisable for the purpose of verifying the identity of the relevant offender.

(6) Regulations under subsection (1) may make different provision for different categories of person.

[Sexual Offences Act 2003, s 87.]

1. See the Sexual Offences Act 2003 (Prescribed Police Stations) Regulations 2005, SI 2005/210.

8–28424G 88. Section 87: interpretation. (1) Subsections (2) to (4) apply for the purposes of section 87.

(2) "Photograph" includes any process by means of which an image may be produced.

(3) "Local police area" means, in relation to a person—

(*a*) the police area in which his home address is situated;

(*b*) in the absence of a home address, the police area in which the home address last notified is situated;

(*c*) in the absence of a home address and of any such notification, the police area in which the court which last dealt with the person in a way mentioned in subsection (4) is situated.

(4) The ways are—

(*a*) dealing with a person in respect of an offence listed in Schedule 3 or a finding in relation to such an offence;

(*b*) dealing with a person in respect of an offence under section 128 or a finding in relation to such an offence;

(*c*) making, in respect of a person, a notification order, interim notification order, sexual offences prevention order or interim sexual offences prevention order;

(*d*) making, in respect of a person, an order under section 2, 2A or 20 of the Crime and Disorder Act 1998 (c 37) (sex offender orders and interim orders made in England and Wales or Scotland) or Article 6 or 6A of the Criminal Justice (Northern Ireland) Order 1998 (SI 1998/2839 (NI 20)) (sex offender orders and interim orders made in Northern Ireland);

and in paragraphs (*a*) and (*b*), "finding" in relation to an offence means a finding of not guilty of the offence by reason of insanity or a finding that the person was under a disability and did the act or omission charged against him in respect of the offence.

(5) Subsection (3) applies as if Northern Ireland were a police area.

[Sexual Offences Act 2003, s 88.]

8–28424H 89. Young offenders: parental directions. (1) Where a person within the first column of the following Table ("the young offender") is under 18 (or, in Scotland, 16) when he is before the court referred to in the second column of the Table opposite the description that applies to him, that court may direct that subsection (2) applies in respect of an individual ("the parent") having parental responsibility for (or, in Scotland, parental responsibilities in relation to) the young offender.

TABLE

Description of person	Court which may make the direction
A relevant offender within section 80(1)(*a*) to (*c*) or 81(1)(*a*) to (*c*)	The court which deals with the offender in respect of the offence or finding
A relevant offender within section 129(1)(*a*) to (*c*)	The court which deals with the offender in respect of the offence or finding
A person who is the subject of a notification order, interim notification order, sexual offences prevention order or interim sexual offences prevention order	The court which makes the order
A relevant offender who is the defendant to an application under subsection (4) (or, in Scotland, the subject of an application under subsection (5))	The court which hears the application

(2) Where this subsection applies—

(*a*) the obligations that would (apart from this subsection) be imposed by or under sections 83 to 86 on the young offender are to be treated instead as obligations on the parent, and

(*b*) the parent must ensure that the young offender attends at the police station with him, when a notification is being given.

(3) A direction under subsection (1) takes immediate effect and applies—

(*a*) until the young offender attains the age of 18 (or, where a court in Scotland gives the direction, 16); or

(*b*) for such shorter period as the court may, at the time the direction is given, direct.

(4) A chief officer of police may, by complaint to any magistrates' court whose commission area includes any part of his police area, apply for a direction under subsection (1) in respect of a relevant offender ("the defendant")—

(*a*) who resides in his police area, or who the chief officer believes is in or is intending to come to his police area, and (*b*) who the chief officer believes is under 18.

(5) In Scotland, a chief constable may, by summary application to any sheriff within whose sheriffdom lies any part of the area of his police force, apply for a direction under subsection (1) in respect of a relevant offender ("the subject")—

(*a*) who resides in that area, or who the chief constable believes is in or is intending to come to that area, and

(*b*) who the chief constable believes is under 16.

[Sexual Offences Act 2003, s 89.]

8–28424I 90. Parental directions: variations, renewals and discharges. (1) A person within subsection (2) may apply to the appropriate court for an order varying, renewing or discharging a direction under section 89(1).

(2) The persons are—

(*a*) the young offender;

(*b*) the parent;

(*c*) the chief officer of police for the area in which the young offender resides;

(*d*) a chief officer of police who believes that the young offender is in, or is intending to come to, his police area;

(*e*) in Scotland, where the appropriate court is a civil court—

(i) the chief constable of the police force within the area of which the young offender resides;

(ii) a chief constable who believes that the young offender is in, or is intending to come to, the area of his police force,

and in any other case, the prosecutor;

(*f*) where the direction was made on an application under section 89(4), the chief officer of police who made the application;

(*g*) where the direction was made on an application under section 89(5), the chief constable who made the application.

(3) An application under subsection (1) may be made—

(*a*) where the appropriate court is the Crown Court (or in Scotland a criminal court), in accordance with rules of court;

(*b*) in any other case, by complaint (or, in Scotland, by summary application).

(4) On the application the court, after hearing the person making the application and (if they wish to be heard) the other persons mentioned in subsection (2), may make any order, varying, renewing or discharging the direction, that the court considers appropriate.

(5) In this section, the "appropriate court" means—

(*a*) where the Court of Appeal made the order, the Crown Court;

(*b*) in any other case, the court that made the direction under section 89(1).

[Sexual Offences Act 2003, s 90.]

8–28424J 91. Offences relating to notification. (1) A person commits an offence if he—

(*a*) fails, without reasonable excuse, to comply with section 83(1), 84(1), 84(4)(b), 85(1), 87(4) or 89(2)(*b*) or any requirement imposed by regulations made under section 86(1); or

(*b*) notifies to the police, in purported compliance with section 83(1), 84(1) or 85(1) or any requirement imposed by regulations made under section 86(1), any information which he knows to be false.

(2) A person guilty of an offence under this section is liable[1]—

(*a*) on summary conviction, to imprisonment for a term not exceeding 6 months or a fine not exceeding the statutory maximum or both;

(*b*) on conviction on indictment, to imprisonment for a term not exceeding 5 years.

(3) A person commits an offence under paragraph (*a*) of subsection (1) on the day on which he first fails, without reasonable excuse, to comply with section 83(1), 84(1) or 85(1) or a requirement imposed by regulations made under section 86(1), and continues to commit it throughout any period during which the failure continues; but a person must not be prosecuted under subsection (1) more than once in respect of the same failure.

(4) Proceedings for an offence under this section may be commenced in any court having jurisdiction in any place where the person charged with the offence resides or is found.

[Sexual Offences Act 2003, s 91.]

---

1. For procedure in respect of this offence which is triable either way, see the Magistrates' Courts Act 1980, ss 17A–21 in PART I: MAGISTRATES' COURTS, PROCEDURE, ante.

8–28424K 92. Certificates for purposes of Part 2. (1) Subsection (2) applies where on any date a person is—

(*a*) convicted of an offence listed in Schedule 3;
(*b*) found not guilty of such an offence by reason of insanity; or
(*c*) found to be under a disability and to have done the act charged against him in respect of such an offence.

(2) If the court by or before which the person is so convicted or found—

(*a*) states in open court—

(i) that on that date he has been convicted, found not guilty by reason of insanity or found to be under a disability and to have done the act charged against him, and
(ii) that the offence in question is an offence listed in Schedule 3, and

(*b*) certifies those facts, whether at the time or subsequently,

the certificate is, for the purposes of this Part, evidence (or, in Scotland, sufficient evidence) of those facts.

(3) Subsection (4) applies where on any date a person is, in England and Wales or Northern Ireland, cautioned in respect of an offence listed in Schedule 3.

(4) If the constable—

(*a*) informs the person that he has been cautioned on that date and that the offence in question is an offence listed in Schedule 3, and
(*b*) certifies those facts, whether at the time or subsequently, in such form as the Secretary of State may by order prescribe,

the certificate is, for the purposes of this Part, evidence (or, in Scotland, sufficient evidence) of those facts.

[Sexual Offences Act 2003, s 92.]

8–28424L 93. Abolished homosexual offences. Schedule 4 (procedure for ending notification requirements for abolished homosexual offences) has effect.

[Sexual Offences Act 2003, s 93.]

Information for verification

8–28424M 94. Part 2: supply of information to Secretary of State etc for verification. (1) This section applies to information notified to the police under—

(*a*) section 83, 84 or 85, or
(*b*) section 2(1) to (3) of the Sex Offenders Act 1997 (c 51).

(2) A person within subsection (3) may, for the purposes of the prevention, detection, investigation or prosecution of offences under this Part, supply information to which this section applies to—

(*a*) the Secretary of State,
(*b*) a Northern Ireland Department, or
(*c*) a person providing services to the Secretary of State or a Northern Ireland Department in connection with a relevant function,

for use for the purpose of verifying the information.

(3) The persons are—

(*a*) a chief officer of police (in Scotland, a chief constable),
(*b*) the Police Information Technology Organisation,
(*c*) the Director General of the National Criminal Intelligence Service,*
(*d*) the Director General of the National Crime Squad.*

(4) In relation to information supplied under subsection (2) to any person, the reference to verifying the information is a reference to—

(*a*) checking its accuracy by comparing it with information held—

(i) where the person is the Secretary of State or a Northern Ireland Department, by him or it in connection with the exercise of a relevant function, or
(ii) where the person is within subsection (2)(*c*), by that person in connection with the provision of services referred to there, and

(*b*) compiling a report of that comparison.

(5) Subject to subsection (6), the supply of information under this section is to be taken not to breach any restriction on the disclosure of information (however arising or imposed).

(6) This section does not authorise the doing of anything that contravenes the Data Protection Act 1998 (c 29).

(7) This section does not affect any power existing apart from this section to supply information.

(8) In this section—

"Northern Ireland Department" means the Department for Employment and Learning, the Department of the Environment or the Department for Social Development;

"relevant function" means—

(*a*) a function relating to social security, child support, employment or training,

(*b*) a function relating to passports,

(*c*) a function under Part 3 of the Road Traffic Act 1988 (c 52) or Part 2 of the Road Traffic (Northern Ireland) Order 1981 (SI 1981/154 (NI 1)).

[Sexual Offences Act 2003, s 94.]

***Substituted by the Serious Organised Crime and Police Act 2005, Sch 4 from a date to be appointed.**

8–28424N 95. Part 2: supply of information by Secretary of State etc. (1) A report compiled under section 94 may be supplied by—

(*a*) the Secretary of State,

(*b*) a Northern Ireland Department, or

(*c*) a person within section 94(2)(*c*),

to a person within subsection (2).

(2) The persons are—

(*a*) a chief officer of police (in Scotland, a chief constable),

(*b*) the Director General of the National Criminal Intelligence Service,*

(*c*) the Director General of the National Crime Squad.*

(3) Such a report may contain any information held—

(*a*) by the Secretary of State or a Northern Ireland Department in connection with the exercise of a relevant function, or

(*b*) by a person within section 94(2)(*c*) in connection with the provision of services referred to there.

(4) Where such a report contains information within subsection (3), the person within subsection (2) to whom it is supplied—

(*a*) may retain the information, whether or not used for the purposes of the prevention, detection, investigation or prosecution of an offence under this Part, and

(*b*) may use the information for any purpose related to the prevention, detection, investigation or prosecution of offences (whether or not under this Part), but for no other purpose.

(5) Subsections (5) to (8) of section 94 apply in relation to this section as they apply in relation to section 94.

[Sexual Offences Act 2003, s 95.]

***Substituted by the Serious Organised Crime and Police Act 2005, Sch 4 from a date to be appointed.**

Information about release or transfer

8–28424O 96. Information about release or transfer. (1) This section applies to a relevant offender who is serving a sentence of imprisonment or a term of service detention, or is detained in a hospital.

(2) The Secretary of State may by regulations make provision requiring notice to be given by the person who is responsible for that offender to persons prescribed by the regulations, of any occasion when the offender is released or a different person becomes responsible for him.

(3) The regulations may make provision for determining who is to be treated for the purposes of this section as responsible for an offender.

[Sexual Offences Act 2003, s 96.]

Notification orders

8–28424P 97. Notification orders: applications and grounds. (1) A chief officer of police may, by complaint to any magistrates' court whose commission area includes any part of his police area, apply[1] for an order under this section (a "notification order") in respect of a person ("the defendant") if—

(*a*) it appears to him that the following three conditions are met with respect to the defendant, and

(*b*) the defendant resides in his police area or the chief officer believes that the defendant is in, or is intending to come to, his police area.

(2) The first condition is that under the law in force in a country outside the United Kingdom—

(*a*) he has been convicted of a relevant offence (whether or not he has been punished for it),

(*b*) a court exercising jurisdiction under that law has made in respect of a relevant offence a finding equivalent to a finding that he is not guilty by reason of insanity,
(*c*) such a court has made in respect of a relevant offence a finding equivalent to a finding that he is under a disability and did the act charged against him in respect of the offence, or
(*d*) he has been cautioned in respect of a relevant offence.

(3) The second condition is that—

(*a*) the first condition is met because of a conviction, finding or caution which occurred on or after 1st September 1997,
(*b*) the first condition is met because of a conviction or finding which occurred before that date, but the person was dealt with in respect of the offence or finding on or after that date, or has yet to be dealt with in respect of it, or
(*c*) the first condition is met because of a conviction or finding which occurred before that date, but on that date the person was, in respect of the offence or finding, subject under the law in force in the country concerned to detention, supervision or any other disposal equivalent to any of those mentioned in section 81(3) (read with sections 81(6) and 131).

(4) The third condition is that the period set out in section 82 (as modified by subsections (2) and (3) of section 98) in respect of the relevant offence has not expired.

(5) If on the application it is proved that the conditions in subsections (2) to (4) are met, the court must make a notification order.

(6) In this section and section 98, "relevant offence" has the meaning given by section 99.
[Sexual Offences Act 2003, s 97.]

---

1. For form of application and procedure, see the Magistrates' Courts (Notification Orders) Rules 2004, in PART I: MAGISTRATES' COURTS, PROCEDURE, ante.

8–28424Q 98. Notification orders: effect. (1) Where a notification order is made—

(*a*) the application of this Part to the defendant in respect of the conviction, finding or caution to which the order relates is subject to the modifications set out below, and
(*b*) subject to those modifications, the defendant becomes or (as the case may be) remains subject to the notification requirements of this Part for the notification period set out in section 82.

(2) The "relevant date" means—

(*a*) in the case of a person within section 97(2)(*a*), the date of the conviction;
(*b*) in the case of a person within section 97(2)(*b*) or (*c*), the date of the finding;
(*c*) in the case of a person within section 97(2)(*d*), the date of the caution.

(3) In section 82—

(*a*) references, except in the Table, to a person (or relevant offender) within any provision of section 80 are to be read as references to the defendant;
(*b*) the reference in the Table to section 80(1)(*d*) is to be read as a reference to section 97(2)(*d*);
(*c*) references to an order of any description are to be read as references to any corresponding disposal made in relation to the defendant in respect of an offence or finding by reference to which the notification order was made;
(*d*) the reference to offences listed in Schedule 3 is to be read as a reference to relevant offences.

(4) In sections 83 and 85, references to the commencement of this Part are to be read as references to the date of service of the notification order.
[Sexual Offences Act 2003, s 98.]

8–28424R 99. Sections 97 and 98: relevant offences. (1) "Relevant offence" in sections 97 and 98 means an act which—

(*a*) constituted an offence under the law in force in the country concerned, and
(*b*) would have constituted an offence listed in Schedule 3 (other than at paragraph 60) if it had been done in any part of the United Kingdom.

(2) An act punishable under the law in force in a country outside the United Kingdom constitutes an offence under that law for the purposes of subsection (1) however it is described in that law.

(3) Subject to subsection (4), on an application for a notification order the condition in subsection (1)(*b*) is to be taken as met unless, not later than rules of court[1] may provide, the defendant serves on the applicant a notice—

(*a*) stating that, on the facts as alleged with respect to the act concerned, the condition is not in his opinion met,
(*b*) showing his grounds for that opinion, and
(*c*) requiring the applicant to prove that the condition is met.

(4) The court, if it thinks fit, may permit the defendant to require the applicant to prove that the condition is met without service of a notice under subsection (3).
[Sexual Offences Act 2003, s 99.]

1. See the Magistrates' Courts (Notification Orders) Rules 2004, in PART I: MAGISTRATES' COURTS, PROCEDURE, ante.

8–28424S 100. Interim notification orders. (1) This section applies where an application for a notification order ("the main application") has not been determined.

(2) An application[1] for an order under this section ("an interim notification order")—

(*a*) may be made in the complaint containing the main application, or

(*b*) if the main application has been made, may be made by the person who has made that application, by complaint to the court to which that application has been made.

(3) The court may, if it considers it just to do so, make an interim notification order.

(4) Such an order—

(*a*) has effect only for a fixed period, specified in the order;

(*b*) ceases to have effect, if it has not already done so, on the determination of the main application.

(5) While such an order has effect—

(*a*) the defendant is subject to the notification requirements of this Part;

(*b*) this Part applies to the defendant, subject to the modification set out in subsection (6).

(6) The "relevant date" means the date of service of the order.

(7) The applicant or the defendant may by complaint apply to the court that made the interim notification order for the order to be varied, renewed or discharged.

[Sexual Offences Act 2003, s 100.]

1. For form of application and procedure, see the Magistrates' Courts (Notification Orders) Rules 2004, in PART I: MAGISTRATES' COURTS, PROCEDURE, ante.

8–28424T 101. Notification orders and interim notification orders: appeals. A defendant may appeal to the Crown Court against the making of a notification order or interim notification order.

[Sexual Offences Act 2003, s 101.]

8–28424U 102. Appeals in relation to notification orders and interim notification orders: Scotland

8–28424V 103. Sections 97 to 100: Scotland

Sexual offences prevention orders

8–28424W 104. Sexual offences prevention orders: applications and grounds. (1) A court may make an order under this section in respect of a person ("the defendant") where any of subsections (2) to (4) applies to the defendant and—

(*a*) where subsection (4) applies, it is satisfied that the defendant's behaviour since the appropriate date makes it necessary to make such an order, for the purpose of protecting the public or any particular members of the public from serious sexual harm from the defendant;

(*b*) in any other case, it is satisfied that it is necessary to make such an order, for the purpose of protecting the public or any particular members of the public from serious sexual harm from the defendant.

(2) This subsection applies to the defendant where the court deals with him in respect of an offence listed in Schedule 3 or 5.

(3) This subsection applies to the defendant where the court deals with him in respect of a finding—

(*a*) that he is not guilty of an offence listed in Schedule 3 or 5 by reason of insanity, or

(*b*) that he is under a disability and has done the act charged against him in respect of such an offence.

(4) This subsection applies to the defendant where—

(*a*) an application under subsection (5) has been made to the court in respect of him, and

(*b*) on the application, it is proved that he is a qualifying offender.

(5) A chief officer of police may by complaint to a magistrates' court apply[1] for an order under this section in respect of a person who resides in his police area or who the chief officer believes is in, or is intending to come to, his police area if it appears to the chief officer that—

(*a*) the person is a qualifying offender, and

(*b*) the person has since the appropriate date acted in such a way as to give reasonable cause to believe that it is necessary for such an order to be made.

(6) An application under subsection (5) may be made to any magistrates' court whose commission area includes—

(*a*) any part of the applicant's police area, or

(*b*) any place where it is alleged that the person acted in a way mentioned in subsection (5)(*b*).

[Sexual Offences Act 2003, s 104.]

---

1. For form of application and procedure, see the Magistrates' Courts (Sexual Offences Prevention Orders) Rules 2004 and the Criminal Procedure Rules 2005, Part 50, in PART I: MAGISTRATES' COURTS, PROCEDURE, ante.

8–28424X 105. SOPOs: further provision as respects Scotland. (1) A chief constable may apply for an order under this section in respect of a person who he believes is in, or is intending to come to, the area of his police force if it appears to the chief constable that—

(*a*) the person has been convicted of, found not guilty by reason of insanity of or found to be under a disability and to have done the act charged against him in respect of—

(i) an offence listed in paragraph 60 of Schedule 3; or

(ii) before the commencement of this Part, an offence in Scotland other than is mentioned in paragraphs 36 to 59 of that Schedule if the chief constable considers that had the conviction or finding been after such commencement it is likely that a determination such as is mentioned in paragraph 60 would have been made in relation to the offence; and

(*b*) the person has since the conviction or finding acted in such a way as to give reasonable cause to believe that it is necessary for such an order to be made.

(2) An application under subsection (1) may be made by summary application to a sheriff within whose sheriffdom lies—

(*a*) any part of the area of the applicant's police force; or

(*b*) any place where it is alleged that the person acted in a way mentioned in subsection (1)(*b*).*

(3) The sheriff may make the order where satisfied—

(*a*) that the person's behaviour since the conviction or finding makes it necessary to make such an order, for the purposes of protecting the public or any particular members of the public from serious sexual harm from the person; and

(*b*) where the application is by virtue of subsection (1)(*a*)(ii), that there was a significant sexual aspect to the person's behaviour in committing the offence.

(4) Subsection (3) of section 106 applies for the purposes of this section as it applies for the purposes of section 104 and subsections (2) and (3) of section 112 apply in relation to a summary application made by virtue of subsection (1) as they apply in relation to one made by virtue of subsection (1)(g) of that section.

[Sexual Offences Act 2003, s 105.]

***Amended by the Protection of Children and Prevention of Sexual Offences (Scotland) Act 2005, ss 17 and 20 from a date to be appointed.**

8–28424Y 106. Section 104: supplemental. (1) In this Part, "sexual offences prevention order" means an order under section 104 or 105.

(2) Subsections (3) to (8) apply for the purposes of section 104.

(3) "Protecting the public or any particular members of the public from serious sexual harm from the defendant" means protecting the public in the United Kingdom or any particular members of that public from serious physical or psychological harm, caused by the defendant committing one or more offences listed in Schedule 3.

(4) Acts, behaviour, convictions and findings include those occurring before the commencement of this Part.

(5) "Qualifying offender" means a person within subsection (6) or (7).

(6) A person is within this subsection if, whether before or after the commencement of this Part, he—

(*a*) has been convicted of an offence listed in Schedule 3 (other than at paragraph 60) or in Schedule 5,

(*b*) has been found not guilty of such an offence by reason of insanity,

(*c*) has been found to be under a disability and to have done the act charged against him in respect of such an offence, or

(*d*) in England and Wales or Northern Ireland, has been cautioned in respect of such an offence.

(7) A person is within this subsection if, under the law in force in a country outside the United Kingdom and whether before or after the commencement of this Part—

(*a*) he has been convicted of a relevant offence (whether or not he has been punished for it),

(*b*) a court exercising jurisdiction under that law has made in respect of a relevant offence a finding equivalent to a finding that he is not guilty by reason of insanity,

(*c*) such a court has made in respect of a relevant offence a finding equivalent to a finding that he is under a disability and did the act charged against him in respect of the offence, or

(*d*) he has been cautioned in respect of a relevant offence.

(8) "Appropriate date", in relation to a qualifying offender, means the date or (as the case may be) the first date on which he was convicted, found or cautioned as mentioned in subsection (6) or (7).

(9) In subsection (7), "relevant offence" means an act which—

(*a*) constituted an offence under the law in force in the country concerned, and

(*b*) would have constituted an offence listed in Schedule 3 (other than at paragraph 60) or in Schedule 5 if it had been done in any part of the United Kingdom.

(10) An act punishable under the law in force in a country outside the United Kingdom constitutes an offence under that law for the purposes of subsection (9), however it is described in that law.

(11) Subject to subsection (12), on an application under section 104(5) the condition in subsection (9)(b) (where relevant) is to be taken as met unless, not later than rules of court may provide, the defendant serves on the applicant a notice—

(*a*) stating that, on the facts as alleged with respect to the act concerned, the condition is not in his opinion met,

(*b*) showing his grounds for that opinion, and

(*c*) requiring the applicant to prove that the condition is met.

(12) The court, if it thinks fit, may permit the defendant to require the applicant to prove that the condition is met without service of a notice under subsection (11).

[Sexual Offences Act 2003, s 106.]

8–28424Z 107. SOPOs: effect. (1) A sexual offences prevention order—

(*a*) prohibits the defendant from doing anything described in the order, and

(*b*) has effect for a fixed period (not less than 5 years) specified in the order or until further order.

(2) The only prohibitions that may be included in the order are those necessary for the purpose of protecting the public or any particular members of the public from serious sexual harm from the defendant.

(3) Where—

(*a*) an order is made in respect of a defendant who was a relevant offender immediately before the making of the order, and

(*b*) the defendant would (apart from this subsection) cease to be subject to the notification requirements of this Part while the order (as renewed from time to time) has effect,

the defendant remains subject to the notification requirements.

(4) Where an order is made in respect of a defendant who was not a relevant offender immediately before the making of the order—

(*a*) the order causes the defendant to become subject to the notification requirements of this Part from the making of the order until the order (as renewed from time to time) ceases to have effect, and

(*b*) this Part applies to the defendant, subject to the modification set out in subsection (5).

(5) The "relevant date" is the date of service of the order.

(6) Where a court makes a sexual offences prevention order in relation to a person already subject to such an order (whether made by that court or another), the earlier order ceases to have effect.

(7) Section 106(3) applies for the purposes of this section and section 108.

[Sexual Offences Act 2003, s 107.]

8–28425 108. SOPOs: variations, renewals and discharges. (1) A person within subsection (2) may apply to the appropriate court for an order varying, renewing or discharging a sexual offences prevention order.

(2) The persons are—

(*a*) the defendant;

(*b*) the chief officer of police for the area in which the defendant resides;

(*c*) a chief officer of police who believes that the defendant is in, or is intending to come to, his police area;

(*d*) where the order was made on an application under section 104(5), the chief officer of police who made the application.

(3) An application under subsection (1) may be made—

(*a*) where the appropriate court is the Crown Court, in accordance with rules of court;

(*b*) in any other case, by complaint.

(4) Subject to subsections (5) and (6), on the application the court, after hearing the person making the application and (if they wish to be heard) the other persons mentioned in subsection (2), may make any order, varying, renewing or discharging the sexual offences prevention order, that the court considers appropriate.

(5) An order may be renewed, or varied so as to impose additional prohibitions on the defendant, only if it is necessary to do so for the purpose of protecting the public or any particular members of

the public from serious sexual harm from the defendant (and any renewed or varied order may contain only such prohibitions as are necessary for this purpose).

(6) The court must not discharge an order before the end of 5 years beginning with the day on which the order was made, without the consent of the defendant and—

(*a*) where the application is made by a chief officer of police, that chief officer, or

(*b*) in any other case, the chief officer of police for the area in which the defendant resides.

(7) In this section "the appropriate court" means—

(*a*) where the Crown Court or the Court of Appeal made the sexual offences prevention order, the Crown Court;

(*b*) where a magistrates' court made the order, that court, a magistrates' court for the area in which the defendant resides or, where the application is made by a chief officer of police, any magistrates' court whose commission area includes any part of the chief officer's police area;

(*c*) where a youth court made the order, that court, a youth court for the area in which the defendant resides or, where the application is made by a chief officer of police, any youth court whose commission area includes any part of the chief officer's police area.

(8) This section applies to orders under—

(*a*) section 5A of the Sex Offenders Act 1997 (c 51) (restraining orders),

(*b*) section 2 or 20 of the Crime and Disorder Act 1998 (c 37) (sex offender orders made in England and Wales or Scotland), and

(*c*) Article 6 of the Criminal Justice (Northern Ireland) Order 1998 (SI 1998/2839 (NI 20)) (sex offender orders made in Northern Ireland),

as it applies to sexual offences prevention orders.

[Sexual Offences Act 2003, s 108.]

8–28425A 109. Interim SOPOs. (1) This section applies where an application under section 104(5) or 105(1) ("the main application") has not been determined.

(2) An application[1] for an order under this section ("an interim sexual offences prevention order")—

(*a*) may be made by the complaint by which the main application is made, or

(*b*) if the main application has been made, may be made by the person who has made that application, by complaint to the court to which that application has been made.

(3) The court may, if it considers it just to do so, make an interim sexual offences prevention order, prohibiting the defendant from doing anything described in the order.

(4) Such an order—

(*a*) has effect only for a fixed period, specified in the order;

(*b*) ceases to have effect, if it has not already done so, on the determination of the main application.

(5) Section 107(3) to (5) apply to an interim sexual offences prevention order as if references to an order were references to such an order, and with the omission of "as renewed from time to time" in both places.

(6) The applicant or the defendant may by complaint apply to the court that made the interim sexual offences prevention order for the order to be varied, renewed or discharged.

(7) Subsection (6) applies to orders under—

(*a*) section 2A or 20(4)(a) of the Crime and Disorder Act 1998 (c 37) (interim orders made in England and Wales or Scotland), and

(*b*) Article 6A of the Criminal Justice (Northern Ireland) Order 1998 (SI 1998/2839 (NI 20)) (interim orders made in Northern Ireland),

as it applies to interim sexual offences prevention orders.

[Sexual Offences Act 2003, s 109.]

1. For form of application and procedure, see the Magistrates' Courts (Sexual Offences Prevention Orders) Rules 2004 and the Criminal Procedure Rules 2005, Part 50, in PART I: MAGISTRATES' COURTS, PROCEDURE, ante.

8–28425B 110. SOPOs and interim SOPOs: appeals. (1) A defendant may appeal against the making of a sexual offences prevention order—

(*a*) where section 104(2) applied to him, as if the order were a sentence passed on him for the offence;

(*b*) where section 104(3) (but not section 104(2)) applied to him, as if he had been convicted of the offence and the order were a sentence passed on him for that offence;

(*c*) where the order was made on an application under section 104(5), to the Crown Court.

(2) A defendant may appeal to the Crown Court against the making of an interim sexual offences prevention order.

(3) A defendant may appeal against the making of an order under section 108, or the refusal to make such an order—

(*a*) where the application for such an order was made to the Crown Court, to the Court of Appeal;
(*b*) in any other case, to the Crown Court.

(4) On an appeal under subsection (1)(*c*), (2) or (3)(*b*), the Crown Court may make such orders as may be necessary to give effect to its determination of the appeal, and may also make such incidental or consequential orders as appear to it to be just.

(5) Any order made by the Crown Court on an appeal under subsection (1)(*c*) or (2) (other than an order directing that an application be re-heard by a magistrates' court) is for the purpose of section 108(7) or 109(7) (respectively) to be treated as if it were an order of the court from which the appeal was brought (and not an order of the Crown Court).
[Sexual Offences Act 2003, s 110.]

8–28425C 111. Appeals in relation to SOPOs and interim SOPOs: Scotland

8–28425D 112. Sections 104 and 106 to 109: Scotland

8–28425E 113. Offence: breach of SOPO or interim SOPO. (1) A person commits an offence if, without reasonable excuse, he does anything which he is prohibited from doing by—

(*a*) a sexual offences prevention order;
(*b*) an interim sexual offences prevention order;
(*c*) an order under section 5A of the Sex Offenders Act 1997 (c 51) (restraining orders);
(*d*) an order under section 2, 2A or 20 of the Crime and Disorder Act 1998 (c 37) (sex offender orders and interim orders made in England and Wales and in Scotland);
(*e*) an order under Article 6 or 6A of the Criminal Justice (Northern Ireland) Order 1998 (SI 1998/2839 (NI 20)) (sex offender orders and interim orders made in Northern Ireland).

(2) A person guilty of an offence under this section is liable[1]—

(*a*) on summary conviction, to imprisonment for a term not exceeding 6 months or a fine not exceeding the statutory maximum or both;
(*b*) on conviction on indictment, to imprisonment for a term not exceeding 5 years.

(3) Where a person is convicted of an offence under this section, it is not open to the court by or before which he is convicted to make, in respect of the offence, an order for conditional discharge or, in Scotland, a probation order.
[Sexual Offences Act 2003, s 113.]

1. For procedure in respect of this offence which is triable either way, see the Magistrates' Courts Act 1980, ss 17A–21 in PART I: MAGISTRATES' COURTS, PROCEDURE, ante.

Foreign travel orders

8–28425F 114. Foreign travel orders: applications and grounds. (1) A chief officer of police may by complaint to a magistrates' court apply[1] for an order under this section (a "foreign travel order") in respect of a person ("the defendant") who resides in his police area or who the chief officer believes is in or is intending to come to his police area if it appears to the chief officer that—

(*a*) the defendant is a qualifying offender, and
(*b*) the defendant has since the appropriate date acted in such a way as to give reasonable cause to believe that it is necessary for such an order to be made.

(2) An application under subsection (1) may be made to any magistrates' court whose commission area includes any part of the applicant's police area.

(3) On the application, the court may make a foreign travel order if it is satisfied that—

(*a*) the defendant is a qualifying offender, and
(*b*) the defendant's behaviour since the appropriate date makes it necessary to make such an order, for the purpose of protecting children generally or any child from serious sexual harm from the defendant outside the United Kingdom.

[Sexual Offences Act 2003, s 114.]

1. For form of application and procedure, see the Magistrates' Courts (Foreign Travel Orders) Rules 2004, in PART I: MAGISTRATES' COURTS, PROCEDURE, ante.

8–28425G 115. Section 114: interpretation. (1) Subsections (2) to (5) apply for the purposes of section 114.

(2) "Protecting children generally or any child from serious sexual harm from the defendant outside the United Kingdom" means protecting persons under 16 generally or any particular person under 16 from serious physical or psychological harm caused by the defendant doing, outside the United Kingdom, anything which would constitute an offence listed in Schedule 3 if done in any part of the United Kingdom.

(3) Acts and behaviour include those occurring before the commencement of this Part.

(4) "Qualifying offender" has the meaning given by section 116.

(5) "Appropriate date", in relation to a qualifying offender, means the date or (as the case may be) the first date on which he was convicted, found or cautioned as mentioned in subsection (1) or (3) of section 116.

(6) In this section and section 116 as they apply to Northern Ireland, references to persons, or to a person, under 16 are to be read as references to persons, or to a person, under 17.
[Sexual Offences Act 2003, s 115.]

8–28425H 116. Section 114: qualifying offenders. (1) A person is a qualifying offender for the purposes of section 114 if, whether before or after the commencement of this Part, he—

(*a*) has been convicted of an offence within subsection (2),
(*b*) has been found not guilty of such an offence by reason of insanity,
(*c*) has been found to be under a disability and to have done the act charged against him in respect of such an offence, or
(*d*) in England and Wales or Northern Ireland, has been cautioned in respect of such an offence.

(2) The offences are—

(*a*) an offence within any of paragraphs 13 to 15, 44 to 46, 77, 78 and 82 of Schedule 3;
(*b*) an offence within paragraph 31 of that Schedule, if the intended offence was an offence against a person under 16;
(*c*) an offence within paragraph 93 of that Schedule, if—
    (i) the corresponding civil offence is an offence within any of paragraphs 13 to 15 of that Schedule;
    (ii) the corresponding civil offence is an offence within paragraph 31 of that Schedule, and the intended offence was an offence against a person under 16; or
    (iii) the corresponding civil offence is an offence within any of paragraphs 1 to 12, 16 to 30 and 32 to 35 of that Schedule, and the victim of the offence was under 16 at the time of the offence.
(*d*) an offence within any other paragraph of that Schedule, if the victim of the offence was under 16 at the time of the offence.

(3) A person is also a qualifying offender for the purposes of section 114 if, under the law in force in a country outside the United Kingdom and whether before or after the commencement of this Part—

(*a*) he has been convicted of a relevant offence (whether or not he has been punished for it),
(*b*) a court exercising jurisdiction under that law has made in respect of a relevant offence a finding equivalent to a finding that he is not guilty by reason of insanity,
(*c*) such a court has made in respect of a relevant offence a finding equivalent to a finding that he is under a disability and did the act charged against him in respect of the offence, or
(*d*) he has been cautioned in respect of a relevant offence.

(4) In subsection (3), "relevant offence" means an act which—

(*a*) constituted an offence under the law in force in the country concerned, and
(*b*) would have constituted an offence within subsection (2) if it had been done in any part of the United Kingdom.

(5) An act punishable under the law in force in a country outside the United Kingdom constitutes an offence under that law for the purposes of subsection (4), however it is described in that law.

(6) Subject to subsection (7), on an application under section 114 the condition in subsection (4)(b) above (where relevant) is to be taken as met unless, not later than rules of court[1] may provide, the defendant serves on the applicant a notice—

(*a*) stating that, on the facts as alleged with respect to the act concerned, the condition is not in his opinion met,
(*b*) showing his grounds for that opinion, and
(*c*) requiring the applicant to prove that the condition is met.

(7) The court, if it thinks fit, may permit the defendant to require the applicant to prove that the condition is met without service of a notice under subsection (6).
[Sexual Offences Act 2003, s 116.]

---

1. See the Magistrates' Courts (Foreign Travel Orders) Rules 2004, in PART I: MAGISTRATES' COURTS, PROCEDURE, ante.

8–28425I 117. Foreign travel orders: effect. (1) A foreign travel order has effect for a fixed period of not more than 6 months, specified in the order.

(2) The order prohibits the defendant from doing whichever of the following is specified in the order—

(*a*) travelling to any country outside the United Kingdom named or described in the order, (*b*) travelling to any country outside the United Kingdom other than a country named or described in the order, or

(*c*) travelling to any country outside the United Kingdom.

(3) The only prohibitions that may be included in the order are those necessary for the purpose of protecting children generally or any child from serious sexual harm from the defendant outside the United Kingdom.

(4) If at any time while an order (as renewed from time to time) has effect a defendant is not a relevant offender, the order causes him to be subject to the requirements imposed by regulations made under section 86(1) (and for these purposes the defendant is to be treated as if he were a relevant offender).

(5) Where a court makes a foreign travel order in relation to a person already subject to such an order (whether made by that court or another), the earlier order ceases to have effect.

(6) Section 115(2) applies for the purposes of this section and section 118.

[Sexual Offences Act 2003, s 117.]

8–28425J 118. Foreign travel orders: variations, renewals and discharges. (1) A person within subsection (2) may by complaint to the appropriate court apply for an order varying, renewing or discharging a foreign travel order.

(2) The persons are—

(*a*) the defendant;

(*b*) the chief officer of police on whose application the foreign travel order was made;

(*c*) the chief officer of police for the area in which the defendant resides;

(*d*) a chief officer of police who believes that the defendant is in, or is intending to come to, his police area.

(3) Subject to subsection (4), on the application the court, after hearing the person making the application and (if they wish to be heard) the other persons mentioned in subsection (2), may make any order, varying, renewing or discharging the foreign travel order, that the court considers appropriate.

(4) An order may be renewed, or varied so as to impose additional prohibitions on the defendant, only if it is necessary to do so for the purpose of protecting children generally or any child from serious sexual harm from the defendant outside the United Kingdom (and any renewed or varied order may contain only such prohibitions as are necessary for this purpose).

(5) In this section "the appropriate court" means—

(*a*) the court which made the foreign travel order;

(*b*) a magistrates' court for the area in which the defendant resides; or

(*c*) where the application is made by a chief officer of police, any magistrates' court whose commission area includes any part of his police area.

[Sexual Offences Act 2003, s 118.]

8–28425K 119. Foreign travel orders: appeals. (1) A defendant may appeal to the Crown Court—

(*a*) against the making of a foreign travel order;

(*b*) against the making of an order under section 118, or the refusal to make such an order.

(2) On any such appeal, the Crown Court may make such orders as may be necessary to give effect to its determination of the appeal, and may also make such incidental or consequential orders as appear to it to be just.

(3) Any order made by the Crown Court on an appeal under subsection (1)(*a*) (other than an order directing that an application be re-heard by a magistrates' court) is for the purposes of section 118(5) to be treated as if it were an order of the court from which the appeal was brought (and not an order of the Crown Court).

[Sexual Offences Act 2003, s 119.]

8–28425L 120. Appeals in relation to foreign travel orders: Scotland

8–28425M 121. Sections 114 to 118: Scotland

8–28425N 122. Offence: breach of foreign travel order. (1) A person commits an offence if, without reasonable excuse, he does anything which he is prohibited from doing by a foreign travel order.

(2) A person guilty of an offence under this section is liable[1]—

(*a*) on summary conviction, to imprisonment for a term not exceeding 6 months or a fine not exceeding the statutory maximum or both;

(*b*) on conviction on indictment, to imprisonment for a term not exceeding 5 years.

(3) Where a person is convicted of an offence under this section, it is not open to the court by or

before which he is convicted to make, in respect of the offence, an order for conditional discharge (or, in Scotland, a probation order).
[Sexual Offences Act 2003, s 122.]

1. For procedure in respect of this offence which is triable either way, see the Magistrates' Courts Act 1980, ss 17A–21 in PART I: MAGISTRATES' COURTS, PROCEDURE, ante.

Risk of sexual harm orders

8–28425O **123. Risk of sexual harm orders: applications, grounds and effect.** (1) A chief officer of police may by complaint to a magistrates' court apply[1] for an order under this section (a "risk of sexual harm order") in respect of a person aged 18 or over ("the defendant") who resides in his police area or who the chief officer believes is in, or is intending to come to, his police area if it appears to the chief officer that—

(*a*) the defendant has on at least two occasions, whether before or after the commencement of this Part, done an act within subsection (3), and
(*b*) as a result of those acts, there is reasonable cause to believe that it is necessary for such an order to be made.

(2) An application under subsection (1) may be made to any magistrates' court whose commission area includes—

(*a*) any part of the applicant's police area, or
(*b*) any place where it is alleged that the defendant acted in a way mentioned in subsection (1)(a).

(3) The acts are—

(*a*) engaging in sexual activity involving a child or in the presence of a child;
(*b*) causing or inciting a child to watch a person engaging in sexual activity or to look at a moving or still image that is sexual;
(*c*) giving a child anything that relates to sexual activity or contains a reference to such activity;
(*d*) communicating with a child, where any part of the communication is sexual.

(4) On the application, the court may make a risk of sexual harm order if it is satisfied that—

(*a*) the defendant has on at least two occasions, whether before or after the commencement of this section, done an act within subsection (3); and
(*b*) it is necessary to make such an order, for the purpose of protecting children generally or any child from harm from the defendant.

(5) Such an order—

(*a*) prohibits the defendant from doing anything described in the order;
(*b*) has effect for a fixed period (not less than 2 years) specified in the order or until further order.

(6) The only prohibitions that may be imposed are those necessary for the purpose of protecting children generally or any child from harm from the defendant.

(7) Where a court makes a risk of sexual harm order in relation to a person already subject to such an order (whether made by that court or another), the earlier order ceases to have effect.
[Sexual Offences Act 2003, s 123.]

1. For form of application and procedure, see the Magistrates' Courts (Risk of Sexual Harm Orders) Rules 2004, in PART I: MAGISTRATES' COURTS, PROCEDURE, ante.

8–28425P **124. Section 123: interpretation.** (1) Subsections (2) to (7) apply for the purposes of section 123.

(2) "Protecting children generally or any child from harm from the defendant" means protecting children generally or any child from physical or psychological harm, caused by the defendant doing acts within section 123(3).

(3) "Child" means a person under 16.

(4) "Image" means an image produced by any means, whether of a real or imaginary subject.

(5) "Sexual activity" means an activity that a reasonable person would, in all the circumstances but regardless of any person's purpose, consider to be sexual.

(6) A communication is sexual if—

(*a*) any part of it relates to sexual activity, or
(*b*) a reasonable person would, in all the circumstances but regardless of any person's purpose, consider that any part of the communication is sexual.

(7) An image is sexual if—

(*a*) any part of it relates to sexual activity, or
(*b*) a reasonable person would, in all the circumstances but regardless of any person's purpose, consider that any part of the image is sexual.

(8) In this section, as it applies to Northern Ireland, subsection (3) has effect with the substitution of "17" for "16".
[Sexual Offences Act 2003, s 124.]

8–28425Q 125. RSHOs: variations, renewals and discharges. (1) A person within subsection (2) may by complaint to the appropriate court apply for an order varying, renewing or discharging a risk of sexual harm order.

(2) The persons are—

(*a*) the defendant;
(*b*) the chief officer of police on whose application the risk of sexual harm order was made;
(*c*) the chief officer of police for the area in which the defendant resides;
(*d*) a chief officer of police who believes that the defendant is in, or is intending to come to, his police area.

(3) Subject to subsections (4) and (5), on the application the court, after hearing the person making the application and (if they wish to be heard) the other persons mentioned in subsection (2), may make any order, varying, renewing or discharging the risk of sexual harm order, that the court considers appropriate.

(4) An order may be renewed, or varied so as to impose additional prohibitions on the defendant, only if it is necessary to do so for the purpose of protecting children generally or any child from harm from the defendant (and any renewed or varied order may contain only such prohibitions as are necessary for this purpose).

(5) The court must not discharge an order before the end of 2 years beginning with the day on which the order was made, without the consent of the defendant and—

(*a*) where the application is made by a chief officer of police, that chief officer, or
(*b*) in any other case, the chief officer of police for the area in which the defendant resides.

(6) Section 124(2) applies for the purposes of this section.

(7) In this section "the appropriate court" means—

(*a*) the court which made the risk of sexual harm order;
(*b*) a magistrates' court for the area in which the defendant resides; or
(*c*) where the application is made by a chief officer of police, any magistrates' court whose commission area includes any part of his police area.

[Sexual Offences Act 2003, s 125.]

8–28425R 126. Interim RSHOs. (1) This section applies where an application for a risk of sexual harm order ("the main application") has not been determined.

(2) An application[1] for an order under this section ("an interim risk of sexual harm order")—

(*a*) may be made by the complaint by which the main application is made, or
(*b*) if the main application has been made, may be made by the person who has made that application, by complaint to the court to which that application has been made.

(3) The court may, if it considers it just to do so, make an interim risk of sexual harm order, prohibiting the defendant from doing anything described in the order.

(4) Such an order—

(*a*) has effect only for a fixed period, specified in the order;
(*b*) ceases to have effect, if it has not already done so, on the determination of the main application.

(5) The applicant or the defendant may by complaint apply to the court that made the interim risk of sexual harm order for the order to be varied, renewed or discharged.
[Sexual Offences Act 2003, s 126.]

---

1. For form of application and procedure, see the Magistrates' Courts (Risk of Sexual Harm Orders) Rules 2004, in PART I: MAGISTRATES' COURTS, PROCEDURE, ante.

8–28425S 127. RSHOs and interim RSHOs: appeals. (1) A defendant may appeal to the Crown Court—

(*a*) against the making of a risk of sexual harm order;
(*b*) against the making of an interim risk of sexual harm order; or
(*c*) against the making of an order under section 125, or the refusal to make such an order.

(2) On any such appeal, the Crown Court may make such orders as may be necessary to give effect to its determination of the appeal, and may also make such incidental or consequential orders as appear to it to be just.

(3) Any order made by the Crown Court on an appeal under subsection (1)(*a*) or (*b*) (other than an order directing that an application be re-heard by a magistrates' court) is for the purpose of section 125(7) or 126(5) (respectively) to be treated as if it were an order of the court from which the appeal was brought (and not an order of the Crown Court).
[Sexual Offences Act 2003, s 127.]

8–28425T 128. Offence: breach of RSHO or interim RSHO. (1) A person commits an offence if, without reasonable excuse, he does anything which he is prohibited from doing by—

(*a*) a risk of sexual harm order; or

(*b*) an interim risk of sexual harm order.

(2) A person guilty of an offence under this section is liable[1]—

(*a*) on summary conviction, to imprisonment for a term not exceeding 6 months or a fine not exceeding the statutory maximum or both;

(*b*) on conviction on indictment, to imprisonment for a term not exceeding 5 years.

(3) Where a person is convicted of an offence under this section, it is not open to the court by or before which he is convicted to make, in respect of the offence, an order for conditional discharge.
[Sexual Offences Act 2003, s 128.]

1. For procedure in respect of this offence which is triable either way, see the Magistrates' Courts Act 1980, ss 17A–21 in PART I: MAGISTRATES' COURTS, PROCEDURE, ante.

Power to amend Schedules 3 and 5

8–28425U 130. Power to amend Schedules 3 and 5. *Secretary of State may by order amend Schedules 3 and 5.*

General

8–28425V 131. Young offenders: application. This Part applies to—

(*a*) a period of detention which a person is liable to serve[1] under a detention and training order, or a secure training order,

(*b*) a period for which a person is ordered to be detained in residential accommodation under section 44(1) of the Criminal Procedure (Scotland) Act 1995 (c 46),

(*c*) a period of training in a training school, or of custody in a remand centre, which a person is liable to undergo or serve by virtue of an order under section 74(1)(*a*) or (*e*) of the Children and Young Persons Act (Northern Ireland) 1968 (c 34 (NI)),

(*d*) a period for which a person is ordered to be detained in a juvenile justice centre under Article 39 of the Criminal Justice (Children) (Northern Ireland) Order 1998 (SI 1998/1504 (NI 9)),

(*e*) a period for which a person is ordered to be kept in secure accommodation under Article 44A of the Order referred to in paragraph (*d*),

(*f*) a sentence of detention in a young offender institution, a young offenders institution or a young offenders centre,

(*g*) a sentence under a custodial order within the meaning of section 71AA of, or paragraph 10(1) of Schedule 5A to, the Army Act 1955 (3 & 4 Eliz 2 c 18) or the Air Force Act 1955 (3 & 4 Eliz 2 c 19) or section 43AA of, or paragraph 10(1) of Schedule 4A to, the Naval Discipline Act 1957 (c 53),

(*h*) a sentence of detention under section 90 or 91 of the Powers of Criminal Courts (Sentencing) Act 2000 (c 6), section 208 of the Criminal Procedure (Scotland) Act 1995 or Article 45 of the Criminal Justice (Children) (Northern Ireland) Order 1998,

(*i*) a sentence of custody for life under section 93 or 94 of the Powers of Criminal Courts (Sentencing) Act 2000 (c 6),

(*j*) a sentence of detention, or custody for life, under section 71A of the Army Act 1955 (3 & 4 Eliz 2 c 18) or the Air Force Act 1955 (3 & 4 Eliz 2 c 19) or section 43A of the Naval Discipline Act 1957 (c 53),

(*k*) a sentence of detention for public protection under section 226 of the Criminal Justice Act 2003'

(*l*) an extended sentence under section 228 of that Act,

as it applies to an equivalent sentence of imprisonment; and references in this Part to prison or imprisonment are to be interpreted accordingly.
[Sexual Offences Act 2003, s 131 as amended by the Criminal Justice Act 2003, Sch 32.]

1. This refers to the period of detention and training and not to the entire term of the detention and training: *R v Slocombe* [2005] EWCA Crim 2297, [2006] 1 All ER 670, [2006] 1 WLR 313.

8–28425W 132. Offences with thresholds. (1) This section applies to an offence which in Schedule 3 is listed subject to a condition relating to the way in which the defendant is dealt with in respect of the offence or (where a relevant finding has been made in respect of him) in respect of the finding (a "sentencing condition").

(2) Where an offence is listed if either a sentencing condition or a condition of another description is met, this section applies only to the offence as listed subject to the sentencing condition.

(3) For the purposes of this Part (including in particular section 82(6))—

(*a*) a person is to be regarded as convicted of an offence to which this section applies, or (*b*) (as the case may be) a relevant finding in relation to such an offence is to be regarded as made,

at the time when the sentencing condition is met.

(4) In the following subsections, references to a foreign offence are references to an act which—

(*a*) constituted an offence under the law in force in a country outside the United Kingdom ("the relevant foreign law"), and

(*b*) would have constituted an offence to which this section applies (but not an offence, listed in Schedule 3, to which this section does not apply) if it had been done in any part of the United Kingdom.

(5) In relation to a foreign offence, references to the corresponding UK offence are references to the offence (or any offence) to which subsection (3)(b) applies in the case of that foreign offence.

(6) For the purposes of this Part, a person is to be regarded as convicted under the relevant foreign law of a foreign offence at the time when he is, in respect of the offence, dealt with under that law in a way equivalent to that mentioned in Schedule 3 as it applies to the corresponding UK offence.

(7) Where in the case of any person a court exercising jurisdiction under the relevant foreign law makes in respect of a foreign offence a finding equivalent to a relevant finding, the court's finding is, for the purposes of this Part, to be regarded as made at the time when the person is, in respect of the finding, dealt with under that law in a way equivalent to that mentioned in Schedule 3 as it applies to the corresponding UK offence.

(8) Where (by virtue of an order under section 130 or otherwise) an offence is listed in Schedule 5 subject to a sentencing condition, this section applies to that offence as if references to Schedule 3 were references to Schedule 5.

(9) In this section, "relevant finding", in relation to an offence, means—

(*a*) a finding that a person is not guilty of the offence by reason of insanity, or

(*b*) a finding that a person is under a disability and did the act charged against him in respect of the offence.

[Sexual Offences Act 2003, s 132.]

8–28425X 133. Part 2: general interpretation. (1) In this Part—

"admitted to a hospital" means admitted to a hospital under—

(*a*) section 37 of the Mental Health Act 1983 (c 20), section 57(2)(*a*) or 58 of the Criminal Procedure (Scotland) Act 1995 (c 46) or Article 44 or 50A(2) of the Mental Health (Northern Ireland) Order 1986 (SI 1986/595 (NI 4));

(*b*) Schedule 1 to the Criminal Procedure (Insanity and Unfitness to Plead) Act 1991 (c 25); or

(*c*) section 46 of the Mental Health Act 1983, section 69 of the Mental Health (Scotland) Act 1984 or Article 52 of the Mental Health (Northern Ireland) Order 1986;

"cautioned" means—

(*a*) cautioned by a police officer after the person concerned has admitted the offence, or

(*b*) reprimanded or warned within the meaning given by section 65 of the Crime and Disorder Act 1998 (c 37),

and "caution" is to be interpreted accordingly;

"community order" means—

(*a*) a community order within the meaning of the Powers of Criminal Courts (Sentencing) Act 2000 (c 6) as that Act had effect before the passing of the Criminal Justice Act 2003);

(*b*) a probation order or community service order under the Criminal Procedure (Scotland) Act 1995 or a supervised attendance order made in pursuance of section 235 of that Act;

(*c*) a community order within the meaning of the Criminal Justice (Northern Ireland) Order 1996 (SI 1996/3160 (NI 24)), a probation order under section 1 of the Probation Act (Northern Ireland) 1950 (c 7 (NI)) or a community service order under Article 7 of the Treatment of Offenders (Northern Ireland) Order 1976 (SI 1976/226 (NI 40)); or

(*d*) a community supervision order;

"community supervision order" means an order under paragraph 4 of Schedule 5A to the Army Act 1955 or the Air Force Act 1955 or Schedule 4A to the Naval Discipline Act 1957;

"country" includes territory;

"detained in a hospital" means detained in a hospital under—

(*a*) Part 3 of the Mental Health Act 1983, section 71 of the Mental Health (Scotland) Act 1984 (c 36), Part 6 of the Criminal Procedure (Scotland) Act 1995 or Part III of the Mental Health (Northern Ireland) Order 1986;

(*b*) Schedule 1 to the Criminal Procedure (Insanity and Unfitness to Plead) Act 1991; or

(*c*) section 46 of the Mental Health Act 1983, section 69 of the Mental Health (Scotland) Act 1984 or Article 52 of the Mental Health (Northern Ireland) Order 1986;

"guardianship order" means a guardianship order under section 37 of the Mental Health Act 1983 (c 20), section 58 of the Criminal Procedure (Scotland) Act 1995 (c 46) or Article 44 of the Mental Health (Northern Ireland) Order 1986 (SI 1986/595 (NI 4));
"home address" has the meaning given by section 83(7);
"interim notification order" has the meaning given by section 100(2);
"interim risk of sexual harm order" has the meaning given by section 126(2);
"interim sexual offences prevention order" has the meaning given by section 109(2);
"local police area" has the meaning given by section 88(3);
"local probation board" has the same meaning as in the Criminal Justice and Court Services Act 2000 (c 43);
"notification order" has the meaning given by section 97(1);
"notification period" has the meaning given by section 80(1);
"order for conditional discharge" has the meaning given by each of the following—

(*a*) section 12(3) of the Powers of Criminal Courts (Sentencing) Act 2000 (c 6);
(*b*) Article 2(2) of the Criminal Justice (Northern Ireland) Order 1996 (SI 1996/3160 (NI 24));
(*c*) paragraph 2(1) of Schedule 5A to the Army Act 1955 (3 & 4 Eliz 2 c 18);
(*d*) paragraph 2(1) of Schedule 5A to the Air Force Act 1955 (3 & 4 Eliz 2 c 19);
(*e*) paragraph 2(1) of Schedule 4A to the Naval Discipline Act 1957 (c 53);

"parental responsibility" has the same meaning as in the Children Act 1989 (c 41) or the Children (Northern Ireland) Order 1995 (SI 1995/ 755 (NI 2)), and "parental responsibilities" has the same meaning as in Part 1 of the Children (Scotland) Act 1995 (c 36);
"the period of conditional discharge" has the meaning given by each of the following—
(*a*) section 12(3) of the Powers of Criminal Courts (Sentencing) Act 2000;
(*b*) Article 2(2) of the Criminal Justice (Northern Ireland) Order 1996;
(*c*) paragraph 2(1) of Schedule 5A to the Army Act 1955;
(*d*) paragraph 2(1) of Schedule 5A to the Air Force Act 1955;
(*e*) paragraph 2(1) of Schedule 4A to the Naval Discipline Act 1957;

"probation order" has the meaning given by section 228(1) of the Criminal Procedure (Scotland) Act 1995;
"probation period" has the meaning given by section 307(1) of the Criminal Procedure (Scotland) Act 1995;
"relevant date" has the meaning given by section 82(6) (save in the circumstances mentioned in sections 98, 100, 107, 109 and 129);
"relevant offender" has the meaning given by section 80(2);
"restriction order" means—
(*a*) an order under section 41 of the Mental Health Act 1983, section 57(2)(*b*) or 59 of the Criminal Procedure (Scotland) Act 1995 or Article 47(1) of the Mental Health (Northern Ireland) Order 1986;
(*b*) a direction under paragraph 2(1)(*b*) of Schedule 1 to the Criminal Procedure (Insanity and Unfitness to Plead) Act 1991 (c 25) or Article 50A(3)(*b*) of the Mental Health (Northern Ireland) Order 1986 (SI 1986/595 (NI 4)); or
(*c*) a direction under section 46 of the Mental Health Act 1983, section 69 of the Mental Health (Scotland) Act 1984 or Article 52 of the Mental Health (Northern Ireland) Order 1986;

"risk of sexual harm order" has the meaning given by section 123(1);
"sexual offences prevention order" has the meaning given by section 106(1);
"supervision" means supervision in pursuance of an order made for the purpose or, in the case of a person released from prison on licence, in pursuance of a condition contained in his licence;
"term of service detention" means a term of detention awarded under section 71(1)(*e*) of the Army Act 1955 or the Air Force Act 1955 or section 43(1)(*e*) of the Naval Discipline Act 1957.*

(1A) A reference to a provision specified in paragraph (a) of the definition of "admitted to a hospital", "detained in a hospital" or "restriction order" includes a reference to the provision as it applies by virtue of—

(*a*) section 5 of the Criminal Procedure (Insanity) Act 1964,
(*b*) section 6 or 14 of the Criminal Appeal Act 1968,
(*c*) section 116A of the Army Act 1955 or the Air Force Act 1955 or section 63A of the Naval Discipline Act 1957, or
(*d*) section 16 or 23 of the Courts-Martial (Appeals) Act 1968.

(2) Where under section 141 different days are appointed for the commencement of different provisions of this Part, a reference in any such provision to the commencement of this Part is to be read (subject to section 98(4)) as a reference to the commencement of that provision.
[Sexual Offences Act 2003, s 133 as amended by the Domestic Violence, Crime and Victims Act 2004, Sch 10.]

8–28425Y 134. Conditional discharges and probation orders[1]. (1) The following provisions do not apply for the purposes of this Part to a conviction for an offence in respect of which an order for conditional discharge or, in Scotland, a probation order is made—

(*a*) section 14(1) of the Powers of Criminal Courts (Sentencing) Act 2000 (c 6) (conviction with absolute or conditional discharge deemed not to be a conviction);
(*b*) Article 6(1) of the Criminal Justice (Northern Ireland) Order 1996 (SI 1996/3160 (NI 24)) (conviction with absolute or conditional discharge deemed not to be a conviction);
(*c*) section 247(1) of the Criminal Procedure (Scotland) Act 1995 (c 46) (conviction with probation order or absolute discharge deemed not to be a conviction);
(*d*) paragraph 5(1) of Schedule 5A to the Army Act 1955 (3 & 4 Eliz 2 c 18) or the Air Force Act 1955 (3 & 4 Eliz 2 c 19) or Schedule 4A to the Naval Discipline Act 1957 (c 53) (conviction with absolute or conditional discharge or community supervision order deemed not to be a conviction).

(2) Subsection (1) applies only to convictions after the commencement of this Part.

(3) The provisions listed in subsection (1)(*d*) do not apply for the purposes of this Part to a conviction for an offence in respect of which a community supervision order is or has (before or after the commencement of this Part) been made.

[Sexual Offences Act 2003, s 134.]

1. Section 134 does not refer to absolute discharges; consequently, the notification does not arise, or survive is sentence is passed on a later date than the date of conviction, if the offender is so sentenced: *R v Longworth* [2006] UKHL 1, [2006] 1 All ER 887, [2006] 1 WLR 313.

8–28425Z 135. Interpretation: mentally disordered offenders. (1) In this Part, a reference to a conviction includes a reference to a finding of a court in summary proceedings, where the court makes an order under an enactment within subsection (2), that the accused did the act charged; and similar references are to be interpreted accordingly.

(2) The enactments are—

(*a*) section 37(3) of the Mental Health Act 1983 (c 20);
(*b*) section 58(3) of the Criminal Procedure (Scotland) Act 1995 (c 46);
(*c*) Article 44(4) of the Mental Health (Northern Ireland) Order 1986 (SI 1986/595 (NI 4)).

(3) In this Part, a reference to a person being or having been found to be under a disability and to have done the act charged against him in respect of an offence includes a reference to his being or having been found—

(*a*) unfit to be tried for the offence;
(*b*) to be insane so that his trial for the offence cannot or could not proceed; or
(*c*) unfit to be tried and to have done the act charged against him in respect of the offence.

(4) In section 133—

(*a*) a reference to admission or detention under Schedule 1 to the Criminal Procedure (Insanity and Unfitness to Plead) Act 1991 (c 25), and the reference to a direction under paragraph 2(1)(b) of that Schedule, include respectively—

 (i) a reference to admission or detention under Schedule 1 to the Criminal Procedure (Insanity) Act 1964 (c 84); and
 (ii) a reference to a restriction order treated as made by paragraph 2(1) of that Schedule;

(*b*) a reference to admission or detention under any provision of Part 6 of the Criminal Procedure (Scotland) Act 1995, and the reference to an order under section 57(2)(b) or 59 of that Act, include respectively—

 (i) a reference to admission or detention under section 174(3) or 376(2) of the Criminal Procedure (Scotland) Act 1975 (c 21); and
 (ii) a reference to a restriction order made under section 178(1) or 379(1) of that Act;

(*c*) *Repealed.*

[Sexual Offences Act 2003, s 135 as amended by the Domestic Violence, Crime and Victims Act 2004, Sch 10.]

8–28426 136. Part 2: Northern Ireland

PART 3
GENERAL

8–28426A 137. Service courts. (1) In this Act—

(*a*) a reference to a court order or a conviction or finding includes a reference to an order of or a conviction or finding by a service court,
(*b*) a reference to an offence includes a reference to an offence triable by a service court,
(*c*) "proceedings" includes proceedings before a service court, and

(*d*) a reference to proceedings for an offence under this Act includes a reference to proceedings for the offence under section 70 of the Army Act 1955 (3 & 4 Eliz 2 c 18) or the Air Force Act 1955 (3 & 4 Eliz 2 c 19) or section 42 of the Naval Discipline Act 1957 (c 53) for which the offence under this Act is the corresponding civil offence.

(2) In sections 92 and 104(1), "court" includes a service court.

(3) Where the court making a sexual offences prevention order is a service court—

(*a*) sections 104(1)(a) and (4) to (6), 105, 109, 111 and 112 do not apply,

(*b*) in section 108, "the appropriate court" means the Crown Court in England and Wales, and

(*c*) in section 110(3)(*a*), the references to the Crown Court and Court of Appeal are references to the Crown Court and Court of Appeal in England and Wales.

(4) In this section "service court" means a court-martial or Standing Civilian Court.

[Sexual Offences Act 2003, s 137.]

8–28426B 138. Orders and regulations

8–28426C 139. Minor and consequential amendments

8–28426D 140. Repeals and revocations

8–28426E 141. Commencement. (1) This Act, except this section and sections 138, 142 and 143, comes into force in accordance with provision made by the Secretary of State by order[1].

(2) An order under subsection (1) may—

(*a*) make different provision for different purposes;

(*b*) include supplementary, incidental, saving or transitional provisions.

[Sexual Offences Act 2003, s 141.]

1. For orders made under this provision, see the note to the title of this Act, ante.

8–28426F 142. Extent, saving etc

8–28426G 143. Short title

8–28426H

SCHEDULE 1

EXTENSION OF GENDER-SPECIFIC PROSTITUTION OFFENCES

Amends the Sexual Offences Act 1956, the Street Offences Act 1959 and the Sexual Offences Act 1985 to extend prostitution offences including soliciting for the purposes of prostitution to male prostitution.

8–28426I

Section 72(7)

SCHEDULE 2

SEXUAL OFFENCES TO WHICH SECTION 72 APPLIES

England and Wales

1. In relation to England and Wales, the following are sexual offences to which section 72 applies—

(*a*) an offence under any of sections 5 to 15 (offences against children under 13 or under 16);

(*b*) an offence under any of sections 1 to 4, 16 to 41, 47 to 50 and 61 where the victim of the offence was under 16 at the time of the offence;

(*c*) an offence under section 62 or 63 where the intended offence was an offence against a person under 16;

(*d*) an offence under—

(i) section 1 of the Protection of Children Act 1978 (c 37) (indecent photographs of children), or

(ii) section 160 of the Criminal Justice Act 1988 (c 33) (possession of indecent photograph of child),

in relation to a photograph or pseudo-photograph showing a child under 16.

Northern Ireland

2. (1) In relation to Northern Ireland, the following are sexual offences to which section 72 applies—

(*a*) rape;

(*b*) an offence under—

(i) section 52 of the Offences against the Person Act 1861 (c 100) (indecent assault upon a female person), or

(ii) section 53 or 54 of that Act (abduction of woman);

(*c*) an offence under—

(i) section 2 of the Criminal Law Amendment Act 1885 (c 69) (procuration of girl under 21),

(ii) section 3 of that Act (procuring defilement of woman using threats, etc),

(iii) section 4 of that Act of unlawful carnal knowledge of a girl under 14,

(iv) section 5 of that Act of unlawful carnal knowledge of a girl under 17, or

(v) section 7 of that Act (abduction of girl under 18);

(*d*) an offence under—

(i) section 1 of the Punishment of Incest Act 1908 (c 45) (incest by males), or

(ii) section 2 of that Act (incest by females);

(*e*) an offence under—

(i) section 21 of the Children and Young Persons Act (Northern Ireland) 1968 (c 34 (NI)) (causing or encouraging seduction, etc of girl under 17), or

(ii) section 22 of that Act (indecent conduct towards a child);

(*f*) an offence under Article 3 of the Protection of Children (Northern Ireland) Order 1978 (SI 1978/1047 (NI 17)) (indecent photographs of children);

(*g*) an offence under Article 9 of the Criminal Justice (Northern Ireland) Order 1980 (SI 1980/704 (NI 6)) (inciting girl under 16 to have incestuous sexual intercourse);

(*h*) an offence under Article 15 of the Criminal Justice (Evidence, Etc) (Northern Ireland) Order 1988 (SI 1988/1847 (NI 17)) (indecent photographs of children);

(*i*) an offence under—

(i) Article 19 of the Criminal Justice (Northern Ireland) Order 2003 (SI 2003/1247 (NI 13)) (buggery),
(ii) Article 20 of that Order (assault with intent to commit buggery), or
(iii) Article 21 of that Order (indecent assault on a male);

(*j*) an offence under—

(i) section 15 of this Act (meeting a child following sexual grooming etc), or
(ii) any of sections 16 to 19 or 47 to 50 of this Act (abuse of trust, prostitution, child pornography).

(2) Sub-paragraph (1), apart from paragraphs (*f*) and (*h*), does not apply where the victim of the offence was 17 or over at the time of the offence.

General

3. A reference in paragraph 1 or 2(1) to an offence includes—

(*a*) a reference to an attempt, conspiracy or incitement to commit that offence; and
(*b*) a reference to aiding and abetting, counselling or procuring the commission of that offence.

8–28426J

Section 80

SCHEDULE 3
SEXUAL OFFENCES FOR PURPOSES OF PART 2

(Amended by the Protection of Children and Prevention of Sexual Offences (Scotland) Act 2004, Schedule.)

England and Wales

1. An offence under section 1 of the Sexual Offences Act 1956 (c 69) (rape).

2. An offence under section 5 of that Act (intercourse with girl under 13).

3. An offence under section 6 of that Act (intercourse with girl under 16), if the offender was 20 or over.

4. An offence under section 10 of that Act (incest by a man), if the victim or (as the case may be) other party was under 18.

5. An offence under section 12 of that Act (buggery) if—

(*a*) the offender was 20 or over, and
(*b*) the victim or (as the case may be) other party was under 18.

6. An offence under section 13 of that Act (indecency between men) if—

(*a*) the offender was 20 or over, and
(*b*) the victim or (as the case may be) other party was under 18.

7. An offence under section 14 of that Act (indecent assault on a woman) if—

(*a*) the victim or (as the case may be) other party was under 18, or
(*b*) the offender, in respect of the offence or finding, is or has been—

(i) sentenced to imprisonment for a term of at least 30 months; or
(ii) admitted to a hospital subject to a restriction order.

8. An offence under section 15 of that Act (indecent assault on a man) if—

(*a*) the victim or (as the case may be) other party was under 18, or
(*b*) the offender, in respect of the offence or finding, is or has been—

(i) sentenced to imprisonment for a term of at least 30 months; or
(ii) admitted to a hospital subject to a restriction order.

9. An offence under section 16 of that Act (assault with intent to commit buggery), if the victim or (as the case may be) other party was under 18.

10. An offence under section 28 of that Act (causing or encouraging the prostitution of, intercourse with or indecent assault on girl under 16).

11. An offence under section 1 of the Indecency with Children Act 1960 (c 33) (indecent conduct towards young child).

12. An offence under section 54 of the Criminal Law Act 1977 (c 45) (inciting girl under 16 to have incestuous sexual intercourse).

13. An offence under section 1 of the Protection of Children Act 1978 (c 37) (indecent photographs of children), if the indecent photographs or pseudo-photographs showed persons under 16 and—

(*a*) the conviction, finding or caution was before the commencement of this Part, or
(*b*) the offender—

(i) was 18 or over, or
(ii) is sentenced in respect of the offence to imprisonment for a term of at least 12 months.

14. An offence under section 170 of the Customs and Excise Management Act 1979 (c 2) (penalty for fraudulent evasion of duty etc) in relation to goods prohibited to be imported under section 42 of the Customs Consolidation Act 1876 (c 36) (indecent or obscene articles), if the prohibited goods included indecent photographs of persons under 16 and—

(*a*) the conviction, finding or caution was before the commencement of this Part, or
(*b*) the offender—
 (i) was 18 or over, or
 (ii) is sentenced in respect of the offence to imprisonment for a term of at least 12 months.

15. An offence under section 160 of the Criminal Justice Act 1988 (c 33) (possession of indecent photograph of a child), if the indecent photographs or pseudo-photographs showed persons under 16 and—

(*a*) the conviction, finding or caution was before the commencement of this Part, or
(*b*) the offender—
 (i) was 18 or over, or
 (ii) is sentenced in respect of the offence to imprisonment for a term of at least 12 months.

16. An offence under section 3 of the Sexual Offences (Amendment) Act 2000 (c 44) (abuse of position of trust), if the offender was 20 or over.

17. An offence under section 1 or 2 of this Act (rape, assault by penetration).

18. An offence under section 3 of this Act (sexual assault) if—

(*a*) where the offender was under 18, he is or has been sentenced, in respect of the offence, to imprisonment for a term of at least 12 months;
(*b*) in any other case—
 (i) the victim was under 18, or
 (ii) the offender, in respect of the offence or finding, is or has been—
  (a) sentenced to a term of imprisonment,
  (b) detained in a hospital, or
  (c) made the subject of a community sentence of at least 12 months.

19. An offence under any of sections 4 to 6 of this Act (causing sexual activity without consent, rape of a child under 13, assault of a child under 13 by penetration).

20. An offence under section 7 of this Act (sexual assault of a child under 13) if the offender—

(*a*) was 18 or over, or
(*b*) is or has been sentenced in respect of the offence to imprisonment for a term of at least 12 months.

21. An offence under any of sections 8 to 12 of this Act (causing or inciting a child under 13 to engage in sexual activity, child sex offences committed by adults).

22. An offence under section 13 of this Act (child sex offences committed by children or young persons), if the offender is or has been sentenced, in respect of the offence, to imprisonment for a term of at least 12 months.

23. An offence under section 14 of this Act (arranging or facilitating the commission of a child sex offence) if the offender—

(*a*) was 18 or over, or
(*b*) is or has been sentenced, in respect of the offence, to imprisonment for a term of at least 12 months.

24. An offence under section 15 of this Act (meeting a child following sexual grooming etc).

25. An offence under any of sections 16 to 19 of this Act (abuse of a position of trust) if the offender, in respect of the offence, is or has been—

(*a*) sentenced to a term of imprisonment,
(*b*) detained in a hospital, or
(*c*) made the subject of a community sentence of at least 12 months.

26. An offence under section 25 or 26 of this Act (familial child sex offences) if the offender—

(*a*) was 18 or over, or
(*b*) is or has been sentenced in respect of the offence to imprisonment for a term of at least 12 months.

27. An offence under any of sections 30 to 37 of this Act (offences against persons with a mental disorder impeding choice, inducements etc to persons with mental disorder).

28. An offence under any of sections 38 to 41 of this Act (care workers for persons with mental disorder) if—

(*a*) where the offender was under 18, he is or has been sentenced in respect of the offence to imprisonment for a term of at least 12 months;
(*b*) in any other case, the offender, in respect of the offence or finding, is or has been—
 (i) sentenced to a term of imprisonment,
 (ii) detained in a hospital, or
 (iii) made the subject of a community sentence of at least 12 months.

29. An offence under section 47 of this Act (paying for sexual services of a child) if the victim or (as the case may be) other party was under 16, and the offender—

(*a*) was 18 or over, or
(*b*) is or has been sentenced in respect of the offence to imprisonment for a term of at least 12 months.

30. An offence under section 61 of this Act (administering a substance with intent).

31. An offence under section 62 or 63 of this Act (committing an offence or trespassing, with intent to commit a sexual offence) if—

(*a*) where the offender was under 18, he is or has been sentenced in respect of the offence to imprisonment for a term of at least 12 months;
(*b*) in any other case—
 (i) the intended offence was an offence against a person under 18, or
 (ii) the offender, in respect of the offence or finding, is or has been—
  (a) sentenced to a term of imprisonment,
  (b) detained in a hospital, or
  (c) made the subject of a community sentence of at least 12 months.

32. An offence under section 64 or 65 of this Act (sex with an adult relative) if—

(*a*) where the offender was under 18, he is or has been sentenced in respect of the offence to imprisonment for a term of at least 12 months;

(*b*) in any other case, the offender, in respect of the offence or finding, is or has been—

(i) sentenced to a term of imprisonment, or
(ii) detained in a hospital.

33. An offence under section 66 of this Act (exposure) if—

(*a*) where the offender was under 18, he is or has been sentenced in respect of the offence to imprisonment for a term of at least 12 months;

(*b*) in any other case—

(i) the victim was under 18, or
(ii) the offender, in respect of the offence or finding, is or has been—

(a) sentenced to a term of imprisonment,
(b) detained in a hospital, or
(c) made the subject of a community sentence of at least 12 months.

34. An offence under section 67 of this Act (voyeurism) if—

(*a*) where the offender was under 18, he is or has been sentenced in respect of the offence to imprisonment for a term of at least 12 months;

(*b*) in any other case—

(i) the victim was under 18, or
(ii) the offender, in respect of the offence or finding, is or has been—

(a) sentenced to a term of imprisonment,
(b) detained in a hospital, or
(c) made the subject of a community sentence of at least 12 months.

35. An offence under section 69 or 70 of this Act (intercourse with an animal, sexual penetration of a corpse) if—

(*a*) where the offender was under 18, he is or has been sentenced in respect of the offence to imprisonment for a term of at least 12 months;

(*b*) in any other case, the offender, in respect of the offence or finding, is or has been—

(i) sentenced to a term of imprisonment, or
(ii) detained in a hospital.

Scotland

36. Rape.
37. Clandestine injury to women.
38. Abduction of woman or girl with intent to rape.
39. Assault with intent to rape or ravish.
40. Indecent assault.
41. Lewd, indecent or libidinous behaviour or practices.
42. Shameless indecency, if a person (other than the offender) involved in the offence was under 18.
43. Sodomy, unless every person involved in the offence was 16 or over and was a willing participant.

44. An offence under section 170 of the Customs and Excise Management Act 1979 (c 2) (penalty for fraudulent evasion of duty etc) in relation to goods prohibited to be imported under section 42 of the Customs Consolidation Act 1876 (c 36) (indecent or obscene articles), if the prohibited goods included indecent photographs of persons under 16.

45. An offence under section 52 of the Civic Government (Scotland) Act 1982 (c 45) (taking and distribution of indecent images of children).*

46. An offence under section 52A of that Act (possession of indecent images of children).*

47. An offence under section 106 of the Mental Health (Scotland) Act 1984 (c 36) (protection of mentally handicapped females).

48. An offence under section 107 of that Act (protection of patients).

49. An offence under section 1 of the Criminal Law (Consolidation) (Scotland) Act 1995 (c 39) (incest), if a person (other than the offender) involved in the offence was under 18.

50. An offence under section 2 of that Act (intercourse with a stepchild), if a person (other than the offender) involved in the offence was under 18.

51. An offence under section 3 of that Act (intercourse with child under 16 by person in position of trust).

52. An offence under section 5 of that Act (unlawful intercourse with girl under 16), save in the case of an offence in contravention of subsection (3) of that section where the offender was under 20.

53. An offence under section 6 of that Act (indecent behaviour towards girl between 12 and 16).

54. An offence under section 8 of that Act (abduction of girl under 18 for purposes of unlawful intercourse).

55. An offence under section 10 of that Act (person having parental responsibilities causing or encouraging sexual activity in relation to a girl under 16).

56. An offence under section 13(5) of that Act (homosexual offences) unless every person involved (whether in the offence or in the homosexual act) was 16 or over and was a willing participant.

57. An offence under section 3 of the Sexual Offences (Amendment) Act 2000 (c 44) (abuse of position of trust), where the offender was 20 or over.

58. An offence under section 311(1) of the Mental Health (Care and Treatment) (Scotland) Act 2003 (asp 13) (non-consensual sexual acts).

59. An offence under section 313(1) of that Act (persons providing care services: sexual offences).*

59A. An offence under section 1 of the Protection of Children and Prevention of Sexual Offences (Scotland) Act 2005 (asp 9) (meeting a child following certain preliminary contact) if—

(*a*) the offender—

(i) was 18 or over, or

(ii) is or has been sentenced in respect of the offence to imprisonment for a term of at least 12 months, or

(*b*) in imposing sentence or otherwise disposing of the case, the court determines that it is appropriate that the offender be regarded, for the purposes of Part 2 of this Act, as a person who has committed an offence under this paragraph.

59B . An offence under section 9 of that Act (paying for sexual services of a child), if—

(*a*) the victim or (as the case may be) other party was under 16 and the offender—

(i) was 18 or over, or

(ii) is or has been sentenced in respect of the offence to imprisonment for a term of at least 12 months, or

(*b*) in imposing sentence or otherwise disposing of the case, the court determines that it is appropriate that the offender be regarded, for the purposes of Part 2 of this Act, as a person who has committed an offence under this paragraph.

59C. An offence under any of sections 10 to 12 of that Act, if—

(*a*) the provider of sexual services or (as the case may be) person involved in pornography was under 16 and the offender—

(i) was 18 or over, or

(ii) is or has been sentenced in respect of the offence to imprisonment for a term of at least 12 months, or

(*b*) in imposing sentence or otherwise disposing of the case, the court determines that it is appropriate that the offender be regarded, for the purposes of Part 2 of this Act, as a person who has committed an offence under this paragraph.

60. An offence in Scotland other than is mentioned in paragraphs 36 to 59 if the court, in imposing sentence or otherwise disposing of the case, determines for the purposes of this paragraph that there was a significant sexual aspect to the offender's behaviour in committing the offence.

Northern Ireland

61. Rape.

62. An offence under section 52 of the Offences against the Person Act 1861 (c 100) (indecent assault upon a female) if—

(*a*) where the offender was under 18, he is or has been sentenced, in respect of the offence, to imprisonment for a term of at least 12 months;

(*b*) in any other case—

(i) the victim was under 18, or

(ii) the offender, in respect of the offence or finding, is or has been—

(a) sentenced to a term of imprisonment,

(b) detained in a hospital, or

(c) made the subject of a community sentence of at least 12 months.

63. An offence under section 53 or 54 of that Act (abduction of woman by force for unlawful sexual intercourse) if the offender—

(*a*) was 18 or over, or

(*b*) is or has been sentenced in respect of the offence to imprisonment for a term of at least 12 months.

64. An offence under section 61 of that Act (buggery) if—

(*a*) the offender was 20 or over, and

(*b*) the victim or (as the case may be) other party was under 18.

65. An offence under section 62 of that Act of assault with intent to commit buggery if the victim or (as the case may be) other party was under 18, and the offender—

(*a*) was 18 or over, or

(*b*) is or has been sentenced in respect of the offence to imprisonment for a term of at least 12 months.

66. An offence under section 62 of that Act of indecent assault upon a male person if—

(*a*) where the offender was under 18, he is or has been sentenced, in respect of the offence, to imprisonment for a term of at least 12 months;

(*b*) in any other case—

(i) the victim was under 18, or

(ii) the offender, in respect of the offence or finding, is or has been—

(a) sentenced to a term of imprisonment,

(b) detained in a hospital, or

(c) made the subject of a community sentence of at least 12 months.

67. An offence under section 2 of the Criminal Law Amendment Act 1885 (c 69) (procuration) if the offender—

(*a*) was 18 or over, or

(*b*) is or has been sentenced in respect of the offence to imprisonment for a term of at least 12 months.

68. An offence under section 3 of that Act (procuring defilement of woman by threats or fraud, etc) if the offender—

(*a*) was 18 or over, or
(*b*) is or has been sentenced in respect of the offence to imprisonment for a term of at least 12 months.

69. An offence under section 4 of that Act of unlawful carnal knowledge of a girl under 14 if the offender—

(*a*) was 18 or over, or
(*b*) is or has been sentenced in respect of the offence to imprisonment for a term of at least 12 months.

70. An offence under section 5 of that Act of unlawful carnal knowledge of a girl under 17, if the offender was 20 or over.

71. An offence under section 7 of that Act (abduction of girl under 18) if the offender—

(*a*) was 18 or over, or
(*b*) is or has been sentenced in respect of the offence to imprisonment for a term of at least 12 months.

72. An offence under section 11 of that Act (homosexual offences) if—

(*a*) the offender was 20 or over, and
(*b*) the victim or (as the case may be) other party was under 18.

73. An offence under section 1 of the Punishment of Incest Act 1908 (c 45) (incest by males), if—

(*a*) where the offender was under 18, he is or has been sentenced in respect of the offence to imprisonment for a term of at least 12 months;
(*b*) in any other case—
   (i) the victim or (as the case may be) other party was under 18, or
   (ii) the offender, in respect of the offence or finding, is or has been—
      (a) sentenced to a term of imprisonment, or
      (b) detained in a hospital.

74. An offence under section 2 of that Act (incest by females), if—

(*a*) where the offender was under 18, he is or has been sentenced in respect of the offence to imprisonment for a term of at least 12 months;
(*b*) in any other case—
   (i) the victim or (as the case may be) other party was under 18, or
   (ii) the offender, in respect of the offence or finding, is or has been—
      (a) sentenced to a term of imprisonment, or
      (b) detained in a hospital.

75. An offence under section 21 of the Children and Young Persons Act (Northern Ireland) 1968 (c 34) (causing or encouraging seduction or prostitution of a girl under 17) if the offender—

(*a*) was 18 or over, or
(*b*) is or has been sentenced in respect of the offence to imprisonment for a term of at least 12 months.

76. An offence under section 22 of that Act (indecent conduct towards a child) if the offender—

(*a*) was 18 or over, or
(*b*) is or has been sentenced in respect of the offence to imprisonment for a term of at least 12 months.

77. An offence under Article 3 of the Protection of Children (Northern Ireland) Order 1978 (SI 1978/1047 (NI 17)) (indecent photographs of children) if the offender—

(*a*) was 18 or over, or
(*b*) is or has been sentenced in respect of the offence to imprisonment for a term of at least 12 months.

78. An offence under section 170 of the Customs and Excise Management Act 1979 (c 2) (penalty for fraudulent evasion of duty etc) in relation to goods prohibited to be imported under section 42 of the Customs Consolidation Act 1876 (c 36) (indecent or obscene articles), if the prohibited goods included indecent photographs of persons under 16, and the offender—

(*a*) was 18 or over, or
(*b*) is or has been sentenced in respect of the offence to imprisonment for a term of at least 12 months.

79. An offence under Article 9 of the Criminal Justice (Northern Ireland) Order 1980 (SI 1980/704 (NI 6)) (inciting girl under 16 to have incestuous sexual intercourse) if the offender—

(*a*) was 18 or over, or
(*b*) is or has been sentenced in respect of the offence to imprisonment for a term of at least 12 months.

80. An offence under Article 122 of the Mental Health (Northern Ireland) Order 1986 (SI 1986/595 (NI 4)) (offences against women suffering from severe mental handicap).

81. An offence under Article 123 of that Order (offences against patients) if—

(*a*) where the offender was under 18, he is or has been sentenced in respect of the offence to imprisonment for a term of at least 12 months;
(*b*) in any other case, the offender, in respect of the offence or finding, is or has been—
   (i) sentenced to a term of imprisonment,
   (ii) detained in a hospital, or
   (iii) made the subject of a community sentence of at least 12 months.

82. An offence under Article 15 of the Criminal Justice (Evidence, etc) (Northern Ireland) Order 1988 (SI 1988/1847 (NI 17) (possession of indecent photographs of children) if the offender—

(*a*) was 18 or over, or
(*b*) is or has been sentenced in respect of the offence to imprisonment for a term of at least 12 months.

83. An offence under section 3 of the Sexual Offences (Amendment) Act 2000 (c 44) (abuse of position of trust), if the offender, in respect of the offence or finding, is or has been—

(*a*) sentenced to a term of imprisonment,
(*b*) detained in a hospital, or
(*c*) made the subject of a community sentence of at least 12 months.

84. An offence under Article 19 of the Criminal Justice (Northern Ireland) Order 2003 (SI 2003/1247 (NI 13)) (buggery) if—

(*a*) the offender was 20 or over, and
(*b*) the victim or (as the case may be) other party was under 17.

85. An offence under Article 20 of that Order (assault with intent to commit buggery) if the victim was under 18 and the offender—

(*a*) was 18 or over, or
(*b*) is or has been sentenced in respect of the offence to imprisonment for a term of at least 12 months.

86. An offence under Article 21 of that Order (indecent assault upon a male) if—

(*a*) where the offender was under 18, he is or has been sentenced, in respect of the offence, to imprisonment for a term of at least 12 months;
(*b*) in any other case—

(i) the victim was under 18, or
(ii) the offender, in respect of the offence or finding, is or has been—

(a) sentenced to a term of imprisonment,
(b) detained in a hospital, or
(c) made the subject of a community sentence of at least 12 months.

87. An offence under section 15 of this Act (meeting a child following sexual grooming etc).

88. An offence under any of sections 16 to 19 of this Act (abuse of trust) if the offender, in respect of the offence or finding, is or has been—

(*a*) sentenced to a term of imprisonment,
(*b*) detained in a hospital, or
(*c*) made the subject of a community sentence of at least 12 months.

89. An offence under section 47 of this Act (paying for sexual services of a child) if the victim or (as the case may be) other party was under 17 and the offender—

(*a*) was 18 or over, or
(*b*) is or has been sentenced in respect of the offence to a term of imprisonment of at least 12 months.

90. An offence under section 66 of this Act (exposure) if—

(*a*) where the offender was under 18, he is or has been sentenced in respect of the offence to imprisonment for a term of at least 12 months;
(*b*) in any other case—

(i) the victim was under 18, or
(ii) the offender, in respect of the offence or finding, is or has been—

(a) sentenced to a term of imprisonment,
(b) detained in a hospital, or
(c) made the subject of a community sentence of at least 12 months.

91. An offence under section 67 of this Act (voyeurism) if—

(*a*) where the offender was under 18, he is or has been sentenced in respect of the offence to imprisonment for a term of at least 12 months;
(*b*) in any other case—

(i) the victim was under 18, or
(ii) the offender, in respect of the offence or finding, is or has been—

(a) sentenced to a term of imprisonment,
(b) detained in a hospital, or
(c) made the subject of a community sentence of at least 12 months.

92. An offence under section 69 or 70 of this Act (intercourse with an animal, sexual penetration of a corpse) if—

(*a*) where the offender was under 18, he is or has been sentenced in respect of the offence to imprisonment for a term of at least 12 months;
(*b*) in any other case, the offender, in respect of the offence or finding, is or has been—

(i) sentenced to a term of imprisonment, or
(ii) detained in a hospital.

Service offences

93. (1) An offence under—

(*a*) section 70 of the Army Act 1955 (3 & 4 Eliz 2 c 18),
(*b*) section 70 of the Air Force Act 1955 (3 & 4 Eliz 2 c 19), or
(*c*) section 42 of the Naval Discipline Act 1957 (c 53),

of which the corresponding civil offence (within the meaning of that Act) is an offence listed in any of paragraphs 1 to 35.

(2) A reference in any of those paragraphs to being made the subject of a community sentence of at least 12 months is to be read, in relation to an offence under an enactment referred to in sub-paragraph (1), as a reference to being sentenced to a term of service detention of at least 112 days.

General

94. A reference in a preceding paragraph to an offence includes—

(*a*) a reference to an attempt, conspiracy or incitement to commit that offence, and
(*b*) except in paragraphs 36 to 43, a reference to aiding, abetting, counselling or procuring the commission of that offence.

95. A reference in a preceding paragraph to a person's age is—

(*a*) in the case of an indecent photograph, a reference to the person's age when the photograph was taken;
(*b*) in any other case, a reference to his age at the time of the offence.

96. In this Schedule "community sentence" has—

(*a*) in relation to England and Wales, the same meaning as in the Powers of Criminal Courts (Sentencing) Act 2000 (c 6), and
(*b*) in relation to Northern Ireland, the same meaning as in the Criminal Justice (Northern Ireland) Order 1996 (SI 1996/3160 (NI 24)).

97. For the purposes of paragraphs 14, 44 and 78—

(*a*) a person is to be taken to have been under 16 at any time if it appears from the evidence as a whole that he was under that age at that time;
(*b*) section 7 of the Protection of Children Act 1978 (c 37) (interpretation), subsections (2) to (2C) and (8) of section 52 of the Civic Government (Scotland) Act 1982 (c 45), and Article 2(2) and (3) of the Protection of Children (Northern Ireland) Order 1978 (SI 1978/1047 (NI 17)) (interpretation) (respectively) apply as each provision applies for the purposes of the Act or Order of which it forms part.

98. A determination under paragraph 60 constitutes part of a person's sentence, within the meaning of the Criminal Procedure (Scotland) Act 1995 (c 46), for the purposes of any appeal or review.

8–28426K

Section 93

SCHEDULE 4

PROCEDURE FOR ENDING NOTIFICATION REQUIREMENTS FOR ABOLISHED HOMOSEXUAL OFFENCES

Scope of Schedule

1. This Schedule applies where a relevant offender is subject to the notification requirements of this Part as a result of a conviction, finding or caution in respect of an offence under—

(*a*) section 12 or 13 of the Sexual Offences Act 1956 (c 69) (buggery or indecency between men), or
(*b*) section 61 of the Offences against the Person Act 1861 (c 100) or section 11 of the Criminal Law Amendment Act 1885 (c 69) (corresponding Northern Ireland offences).

Application for decision

2. (1) The relevant offender may apply to the Secretary of State for a decision as to whether it appears that, at the time of the offence, the other party to the act of buggery or gross indecency—

(*a*) where paragraph 1(a) applies, was aged 16 or over,
(*b*) where paragraph 1(b) applies, was aged 17 or over,

and consented to the act.

(2) An application must be in writing and state—

(*a*) the name, address and date of birth of the relevant offender,
(*b*) his name and address at the time of the conviction, finding or caution,
(*c*) so far as known to him, the time when and the place where the conviction or finding was made or the caution given and, for a conviction or finding, the case number,
(*d*) such other information as the Secretary of State may require.

(3) An application may include representations by the relevant offender about the matters mentioned in sub-paragraph (1).

Decision by Secretary of State

3. (1) In making the decision applied for, the Secretary of State must consider—

(*a*) any representations included in the application, and
(*b*) any available record of the investigation of the offence and of any proceedings relating to it that appears to him to be relevant,

but is not to seek evidence from any witness.

(2) On making the decision the Secretary of State must—

(*a*) record it in writing, and
(*b*) give notice in writing to the relevant offender.

Effect of decision

4. (1) If the Secretary of State decides that it appears as mentioned in paragraph 2(1), the relevant offender ceases, from the beginning of the day on which the decision is recorded under paragraph 3(2)(*a*), to be subject to the notification requirements of this Part as a result of the conviction, finding or caution in respect of the offence.

(2) Sub-paragraph (1) does not affect the operation of this Part as a result of any other conviction, finding or caution or any court order.

Right of appeal

5. (1) If the Secretary of State decides that it does not appear as mentioned in paragraph 2(1), and if the High Court gives permission, the relevant offender may appeal to that court.

(2) On an appeal the court may not receive oral evidence.

(3) The court—

(*a*) if it decides that it appears as mentioned in paragraph 2(1), must make an order to that effect,
(*b*) otherwise, must dismiss the appeal.

(4) An order under sub-paragraph (3)(*a*) has the same effect as a decision of the Secretary of State recorded under paragraph 3(2)(*a*) has under paragraph 4.

(5) There is no appeal from the decision of the High Court.

Interpretation

6. (1) In this Schedule a reference to an offence includes—

(*a*) a reference to an attempt, conspiracy or incitement to commit that offence, and
(*b*) a reference to aiding, abetting, counselling or procuring the commission of that offence.

(2) In the case of an attempt, conspiracy or incitement, references in paragraph 2 to the act of buggery or gross indecency are references to the act of buggery or gross indecency to which the attempt, conspiracy or incitement related (whether or not that act occurred).

Transitional provision

7. Until the coming into force of the repeal by this Act of Part 1 of the Sex Offenders Act 1997 (c 51), this Schedule has effect as if references to this Part of this Act were references to Part 1 of that Act.

8–28426L

Section 104

SCHEDULE 5
OTHER OFFENCES FOR PURPOSES OF PART 2

(*Amended by the Domestic Violence, Crime and Victims Act 2004, Sch 10 amd SI 2004/702.*)

England and Wales

1. Murder.
2. Manslaughter.
3. Kidnapping.
4. False imprisonment.
5. An offence under section 4 of the Offences against the Person Act 1861 (c 100) (soliciting murder).
6. An offence under section 16 of that Act (threats to kill).
7. An offence under section 18 of that Act (wounding with intent to cause grievous bodily harm).
8. An offence under section 20 of that Act (malicious wounding).
9. An offence under section 21 of that Act (attempting to choke, suffocate or strangle in order to commit or assist in committing an indictable offence).
10. An offence under section 22 of that Act (using chloroform etc to commit or assist in the committing of any indictable offence).
11. An offence under section 23 of that Act (maliciously administering poison etc so as to endanger life or inflict grievous bodily harm).
12. An offence under section 27 of that Act (abandoning children).
13. An offence under section 28 of that Act (causing bodily injury by explosives).
14. An offence under section 29 of that Act (using explosives etc with intent to do grievous bodily harm).
15. An offence under section 30 of that Act (placing explosives with intent to do bodily injury).
16. An offence under section 31 of that Act (setting spring guns etc with intent to do grievous bodily harm).
17. An offence under section 32 of that Act (endangering the safety of railway passengers).
18. An offence under section 35 of that Act (injuring persons by furious driving).
19. An offence under section 37 of that Act (assaulting officer preserving wreck).
20. An offence under section 38 of that Act (assault with intent to resist arrest).
21. An offence under section 47 of that Act (assault occasioning actual bodily harm).
22. An offence under section 2 of the Explosive Substances Act 1883 (c 3) (causing explosion likely to endanger life or property).
23. An offence under section 3 of that Act (attempt to cause explosion, or making or keeping explosive with intent to endanger life or property).
24. An offence under section 1 of the Infant Life (Preservation) Act 1929 (c 34) (child destruction).
25. An offence under section 1 of the Children and Young Persons Act 1933 (c 12) (cruelty to children).
26. An offence under section 1 of the Infanticide Act 1938 (c 36) (infanticide).
27. An offence under section 16 of the Firearms Act 1968 (c 27) (possession of firearm with intent to endanger life).
28. An offence under section 16A of that Act (possession of firearm with intent to cause fear of violence).
29. An offence under section 17(1) of that Act (use of firearm to resist arrest).
30. An offence under section 17(2) of that Act (possession of firearm at time of committing or being arrested for offence specified in Schedule 1 to that Act).
31. An offence under section 18 of that Act (carrying a firearm with criminal intent).
32. An offence under section 8 of the Theft Act 1968 (c 60) (robbery or assault with intent to rob).
33. An offence under section 9 of that Act of burglary with intent to—

(*a*) inflict grievous bodily harm on a person, or

(*b*) do unlawful damage to a building or anything in it.

34. An offence under section 10 of that Act (aggravated burglary).

35. An offence under section 12A of that Act (aggravated vehicle-taking) involving an accident which caused the death of any person.

36. An offence of arson under section 1 of the Criminal Damage Act 1971 (c 48).

37. An offence under section 1(2) of that Act (destroying or damaging property) other than an offence of arson.

38. An offence under section 1 of the Taking of Hostages Act 1982 (c 28) (hostage-taking).

39. An offence under section 1 of the Aviation Security Act 1982 (c 36) (hijacking).

40. An offence under section 2 of that Act (destroying, damaging or endangering safety of aircraft).

41. An offence under section 3 of that Act (other acts endangering or likely to endanger safety of aircraft).

42. An offence under section 4 of that Act (offences in relation to certain dangerous articles).

43. An offence under section 127 of the Mental Health Act 1983 (c 20) (ill-treatment of patients).

44. An offence under section 1 of the Prohibition of Female Circumcision Act 1985 (c 38) (prohibition of female circumcision).

45. An offence under section 1 of the Public Order Act 1986 (c 64) (riot).

46. An offence under section 2 of that Act (violent disorder).

47. An offence under section 3 of that Act (affray).

48. An offence under section 134 of the Criminal Justice Act 1988 (c 33) (torture).

49. An offence under section 1 of the Road Traffic Act 1988 (c 52) (causing death by dangerous driving).

50. An offence under section 3A of that Act (causing death by careless driving when under influence of drink or drugs).

51. An offence under section 1 of the Aviation and Maritime Security Act 1990 (c 31) (endangering safety at aerodromes).

52. An offence under section 9 of that Act (hijacking of ships).

53. An offence under section 10 of that Act (seizing or exercising control of fixed platforms).

54. An offence under section 11 of that Act (destroying fixed platforms or endangering their safety).

55. An offence under section 12 of that Act (other acts endangering or likely to endanger safe navigation).

56. An offence under section 13 of that Act (offences involving threats).

57. An offence under section 4 of the Protection from Harassment Act 1997 (c 40) (putting people in fear of violence).

58. An offence under section 29 of the Crime and Disorder Act 1998 (c 37) (racially or religiously aggravated assaults).

59. An offence falling within section 31(1)(a) or (b) of that Act (racially or religiously aggravated offences under section 4 or 4A of the Public Order Act 1986 (c 64)).

60. An offence under Part II of the Channel Tunnel (Security) Order 1994 (SI 1994/570) (offences relating to Channel Tunnel trains and the tunnel system).

61. An offence under section 51 or 52 of the International Criminal Court Act 2001 (c 17) (genocide, crimes against humanity, war crimes and related offences), other than one involving murder.

62. An offence under section 47 of this Act, where the victim or (as the case may be) other party was 16 or over.

63. An offence under any of sections 48 to 53 or 57 to 59 of this Act.

63A. An offence under section 5 of the Domestic Violence, Crime and Victims Act 2004 (causing or allowing the death of a child or vulnerable adult).Scotland

64. Murder.

65. Culpable homicide.

66. Assault.

67. Assault and robbery.

68. Abduction.

69. Plagium.

70. Wrongful imprisonment.

71. Threatening personal violence.

72. Breach of the peace inferring personal violence.

73. Wilful fireraising.

74. Culpable and reckless fireraising.

75. Mobbing and rioting.

76. An offence under section 2 of the Explosive Substances Act 1883 (c 3) (causing explosion likely to endanger life or property).

77. An offence under section 3 of that Act (attempt to cause explosion, or making or keeping explosives with intent to endanger life or property).

78. An offence under section 12 of the Children and Young Persons (Scotland) Act 1937 (c 37) (cruelty to persons under 16).

79. An offence under section 16 of the Firearms Act 1968 (c 27) (possession of firearm with intent to endanger life).

80. An offence under section 16A of that Act (possession of firearm with intent to cause fear of violence).

81. An offence under section 17(1) of that Act (use of firearm to resist arrest).

82. An offence under section 17(2) of that Act (possession of firearm at time of committing or being arrested for offence specified in Schedule 1 to that Act).

83. An offence under section 18 of that Act (carrying a firearm with criminal intent).

84. An offence under section 1 of the Taking of Hostages Act 1982 (c 28) (hostage-taking).

85. An offence under section 1 of the Aviation Security Act 1982 (c 36) (hijacking).

86. An offence under section 2 of that Act (destroying, damaging or endangering safety of aircraft).

87. An offence under section 3 of that Act (other acts endangering or likely to endanger safety of aircraft).

88. An offence under section 4 of that Act (offences in relation to certain dangerous articles).

89. An offence under section 105 of the Mental Health (Scotland) Act 1984 (c 36) (ill-treatment of patients).

90. An offence under section 1 of the Prohibition of Female Circumcision Act 1985 (c 38) (prohibition of female circumcision).

91. An offence under section 134 of the Criminal Justice Act 1988 (c 33) (torture).

92. An offence under section 1 of the Road Traffic Act 1988 (c 52) (causing death by dangerous driving).

93. An offence under section 3A of that Act (causing death by careless driving when under influence of drink or drugs).

94. An offence under section 1 of the Aviation and Maritime Security Act 1990 (c 31) (endangering safety at aerodromes).

95. An offence under section 9 of that Act (hijacking of ships).

96. An offence under section 10 of that Act (seizing or exercising control of fixed platforms).

97. An offence under section 11 of that Act (destroying fixed platforms or endangering their safety).

98. An offence under section 12 of that Act (other acts endangering or likely to endanger safe navigation).

99. An offence under section 13 of that Act (offences involving threats).

100. An offence under Part II of the Channel Tunnel (Security) Order 1994 (SI 1994/570) (offences relating to Channel Tunnel trains and the tunnel system).

101. An offence under section 7 of the Criminal Law (Consolidation) (Scotland) Act 1995 (c 39) (procuring).

102. An offence under section 9 of that Act (permitting girl to use premises for intercourse).

103. An offence under section 11 of that Act (trading in prostitution and brothel-keeping).

104. An offence under section 12 of that Act (allowing child to be in brothel).

105. An offence under section 13(9) of that Act (living on earnings of male prostitution etc).

106. An offence under section 50A of that Act (racially-aggravated harassment).

107. An offence under section 51 or 52 of the International Criminal Court Act 2001 (c 17) (genocide, crimes against humanity, war crimes and related offences), other than one involving murder.

108. An offence under section 1 of the International Criminal Court (Scotland) Act 2001 (asp 13) (genocide, crimes against humanity, war crimes and related offences as specified in Schedule 1 to that Act).

109. An offence under section 22 of the Criminal Justice (Scotland) Act 2003 (asp 7) (traffic in prostitution etc).

110. An offence to which section 74 of that Act applies (offences aggravated by religious prejudice).

111. An offence under section 315 of the Mental Health (Care and Treatment) (Scotland) Act 2003 (asp 13) (ill-treatment and wilful neglect of mentally disordered person).

Northern Ireland

112. Murder.

113. Manslaughter.

114. Kidnapping.

115. Riot.

116. Affray.

117. False imprisonment.

118. An offence under section 4 of the Offences against the Person Act 1861 (c 100) (soliciting murder).

119. An offence under section 16 of that Act (threats to kill).

120. An offence under section 18 of that Act (wounding with intent to cause grievous bodily harm).

121. An offence under section 20 of that Act (malicious wounding).

122. An offence under section 21 of that Act (attempting to choke, suffocate or strangle in order to commit or assist in committing an indictable offence).

123. An offence under section 22 of that Act (using chloroform etc to commit or assist in the committing of any indictable offence).

124. An offence under section 23 of that Act (maliciously administering poison etc so as to endanger life or inflict grievous bodily harm).

125. An offence under section 27 of that Act (abandoning children).

126. An offence under section 28 of that Act (causing bodily injury by explosives).

127. An offence under section 29 of that Act (using explosives etc with intent to do grievous bodily harm).

128. An offence under section 30 of that Act (placing explosives with intent to do bodily injury).

129. An offence under section 31 of that Act (setting spring guns etc with intent to do grievous bodily harm).

130. An offence under section 32 of that Act (endangering the safety of railway passengers).

131. An offence under section 35 of that Act (injuring persons by furious driving).

132. An offence under section 37 of that Act (assaulting officer preserving wreck).

133. An offence under section 47 of that Act of assault occasioning actual bodily harm.

134. An offence under section 2 of the Explosive Substances Act 1883 (c 3) (causing explosion likely to endanger life or property).

135. An offence under section 3 of that Act (attempt to cause explosion, or making or keeping explosive with intent to endanger life or property).

136. An offence under section 25 of the Criminal Justice (Northern Ireland) Act 1945 (c 15) (child destruction).

137. An offence under section 1 of the Infanticide Act (Northern Ireland) 1939 (c 5) (infanticide).

138. An offence under section 7(1)(b) of the Criminal Justice (Miscellaneous Provisions) Act (Northern Ireland) 1968 (c 28) (assault with intent to resist arrest).

139. An offence under section 20 of the Children and Young Persons Act (Northern Ireland) 1968 (c 34) (cruelty to children).

140. An offence under section 8 of the Theft Act (Northern Ireland) 1969 (c 16) (robbery or assault with intent to rob).

141. An offence under section 9 of that Act of burglary with intent to—

(*a*) inflict grievous bodily harm on a person, or
(*b*) do unlawful damage to a building or anything in it.

142. An offence under section 10 of that Act (aggravated burglary).

143. An offence of arson under Article 3 of the Criminal Damage Northern Ireland) Order 1977 (SI 1977/426 (NI 4)).

144. An offence under Article 3(2) of that Order (destroying or damaging property) other than an offence of arson.

145. An offence under Article 58(1) of the Firearms (Northern Ireland) Order 2004 (SI 2004/702 (NI 3)) (possession of firearm with intent to endanger life).

146. An offence under Article 58(2) of that Order (possession of firearm with intent to cause fear of violence).

147. An offence under Article 59(1) of that Order (use of firearm to resist arrest).

148. An offence under Article 59(2) of that Order (possession of firearm at time of committing or being arrested for an offence specified in Schedule 1 to that Order).

149. An offence under Article 60 of that Order (carrying a firearm with criminal intent).

150. An offence under section 1 of the Taking of Hostages Act 1982 (c 28) (hostage-taking).

151. An offence under section 1 of the Aviation Security Act 1982 (c 36) (hijacking).

152. An offence under section 2 of that Act (destroying, damaging or endangering safety of aircraft).

153. An offence under section 3 of that Act (other acts endangering or likely to endanger safety of aircraft).

154. An offence under section 4 of that Act (offences in relation to certain dangerous articles).

155. An offence under section 1 of the Prohibition of Female Circumcision Act 1985 (c 38) (prohibition of female circumcision).

156. An offence under Article 121 of the Mental Health (Northern Ireland) Order 1986 (SI 1986/595 (NI 4) (ill-treatment of patients).

157. An offence under section 134 of the Criminal Justice Act 1988 (c 33) (torture).

158. An offence under section 1 of the Aviation and Maritime Security Act 1990 (c 31) (endangering safety at aerodromes).

159. An offence under section 9 of that Act (hijacking of ships).

160. An offence under section 10 of that Act (seizing or exercising control of fixed platforms).

161. An offence under section 11 of that Act (destroying fixed platforms or endangering their safety).

162. An offence under section 12 of that Act (other acts endangering or likely to endanger safe navigation).

163. An offence under section 13 of that Act (offences involving threats).

164. An offence under Article 9 of the Road Traffic (Northern Ireland) Order 1995 (SI 1995/2994 (NI 18)) (causing death or grievous bodily injury by dangerous driving).

165. An offence under Article 14 of that Order (causing death or grievous bodily injury by careless driving when under the influence of drink or drugs).

166. An offence under Article 6 of the Protection from Harassment (Northern Ireland) Order 1997 (SI 1997/1180 (NI 9) (putting people in fear of violence).

167. An offence under section 66 of the Police (Northern Ireland) Act 1998 (c 32) (assaulting or obstructing a constable etc).

168. An offence under Part II of the Channel Tunnel (Security) Order 1994 (SI 1994/570) (offences relating to Channel Tunnel trains and the tunnel system).

169. An offence under section 51 or 52 of the International Criminal Court Act 2001 (c 17) (genocide, crimes against humanity, war crimes and related offences), other than one involving murder.

170. An offence under section 47 of this Act, where the victim or (as the case may be) other party was 17 or over.

171. An offence under any of sections 48 to 53 or 57 to 59 of this Act.

171A. An offence under section 5 of the Domestic Violence, Crime and Victims Act 2004 (causing or allowing the death of a child or vulnerable adult).

Service offences

172. An offence under—

(*a*) section 70 of the Army Act 1955 (3 & 4 Eliz 2 c 18),
(*b*) section 70 of the Air Force Act 1955 (3 & 4 Eliz 2 c 19), or
(*c*) section 42 of the Naval Discipline Act 1957 (c 53),

of which the corresponding civil offence (within the meaning of that Act) is an offence under a provision listed in any of paragraphs 1 to 63A.

General

173. A reference in a preceding paragraph to an offence includes—

(*a*) a reference to an attempt, conspiracy or incitement to commit that offence, and
(*b*) a reference to aiding, abetting, counselling or procuring the commission of that offence.

174. A reference in a preceding paragraph to a person's age is a reference to his age at the time of the offence.

8–28426M SCHEDULE 6

MINOR AND CONSEQUENTIAL AMENDMENTS

8–28426N SCHEDULE 7

REPEALS AND REVOCATIONS

Sexual Offences Act 2003 (Travel Notification Requirements) Regulations 2004[1]

(SI 2004/1220)

8–28426N 1. Citation and extent. (1) These Regulations may be cited as the Sexual Offences Act 2003 (Travel Notification Requirements) Regulations 2004.

(2) These Regulations do not extend to Scotland.

1. Made by the Secretary of State, in exercise of the powers conferred upon him by section 86 of the Sexual Offences Act 2003.

8–28426O 2. Interpretation. In these Regulations:

(*a*) a reference to a numbered section is to the section of that number in the Sexual Offences Act 2003, and

(*b*) a reference to the "2001 Regulations" is to the Sex Offenders (Notice Requirements) (Foreign Travel) Regulations 2001.

8–28426P 3. Commencement, revocation and transitional provision. (1) Subject to paragraph (2), these Regulations shall come into force on 1st May 2004.

(2) A relevant offender who intends to leave the United Kingdom for a period of less than eight days is not required to give a notification pursuant to regulation 5(1) if his intended date of departure is on or before 9th May 2004.

(3) Subject to paragraphs (4) and (5), the 2001 Regulations are hereby revoked.

(4) Where a relevant offender has given notice in accordance with section 2(6E) of the Sex Offenders Act 1997 before the coming into force of these Regulations, the requirements of the 2001 Regulations shall apply to the departure and return so notified as if these Regulations had not been made.

(5) Where a relevant offender subject to the notice requirements of the 2001 Regulations whose intended date of departure is on or before 9th May 2004 has not given notice in accordance with section 2(6E) of the Sex Offenders Act 1997 before the coming into force of these Regulations, the requirements of the 2001 Regulations shall apply to the departure and return as if these Regulations had not been made.

8–28426Q 4. Determination of point of arrival. (1) For the purposes of section 86(2)(*b*) and of these Regulations, a relevant offender's point of arrival in a country is to be determined in accordance with this regulation.

(2) In a case in which a relevant offender will arrive in a country by rail, sea or air, his point of arrival is the station, port or airport at which he will first disembark.

(3) In a case in which a relevant offender will arrive in a country by any means other than those mentioned in paragraph (2) above, his point of arrival is the place at which he will first enter the country.

8–28426R 5. Notification to be given before leaving the United Kingdom. (1) A relevant offender who intends to leave the United Kingdom for a period of three days or longer must give a notification under section 86(2) in accordance with these Regulations.

(2) Where a relevant offender to whom these Regulations apply knows the information required to be disclosed by section 86(2)(*a*) and (*b*) more than seven days before the date of his intended departure, he shall give a notification which sets out that information and as much of the information required by regulation 6 as he holds—

(*a*) not less than seven days before that date (the seven day notification requirement); or

(*b*) as soon as reasonably practicable but not less than 24 hours before that date, if and only if the relevant offender has a reasonable excuse for not complying with the seven day notification requirement.

(3) Where the relevant offender does not know the information required to be disclosed by section 86(2)(*a*) and (*b*) more than seven days before the date of his intended departure, he shall give not less than 24 hours before that date, a notification which sets out that information and as much of the information required by regulation 6 as he holds.

8–28426S 6. Information to be disclosed in a notification under section 86(2). In addition to the information required by section 86(2)(*a*) and (*b*), a relevant offender to whom these Regulations apply must disclose, where he holds such information—

(*a*) where he intends to travel to more than one country outside the United Kingdom, his intended point of arrival in each such additional country,

(*b*) the identity of any carrier or carriers he intends to use for the purposes of his departure from and return to the United Kingdom, and of travelling to any other point of arrival,

(*c*) details of his accommodation arrangements for his first night outside the United Kingdom,

(*d*) in a case in which he intends to return to the United Kingdom on a particular date, that date, and

(*e*) in a case in which he intends to return to the United Kingdom at a particular point of arrival, that point of arrival.

8–28426T 7. Change to information disclosed in a notification under section 86(2). (1) Where—

(*a*) a relevant offender has given a notification under section 86(2), and

(*b*) at any time prior to his intended departure from the United Kingdom, the information disclosed in that notification becomes inaccurate or incomplete as a statement of all the information mentioned in section 86(2)(*a*) and (*b*) and regulation 6 which he currently holds, he must give a further notification under section 86(2).

(2) A further notification under paragraph (1) above must be given not less than 24 hours before the relevant offender's intended departure from the United Kingdom.

8–28426U **8. Notification to be given on return to the United Kingdom.** (1) This regulation applies to a relevant offender who—

(*a*) is required to give a notification under section 86(2),
(*b*) has left the United Kingdom, and
(*c*) subsequently returns to the United Kingdom.

(2) Except as provided by paragraph (3) below, every relevant offender to whom this regulation applies must give a notification under section 86(3) within three days of his return to the United Kingdom.

(3) A relevant offender to whom this regulation applies need not give a notification under section 86(3) in any case in which he gave a relevant notification under 86(2) which—

(*a*) disclosed a date under the provisions of regulation 6(d) above, and
(*b*) disclosed a point of arrival under the provisions of regulation 6(e) above,

provided his return to the United Kingdom was on that date and at that point of arrival.

8–28426V **9. Information to be disclosed in a notification under section 86(3).** A notification under section 86(3) must disclose the date of the relevant offender's return to the United Kingdom and his point of arrival in the United Kingdom.

8–28426W **10. Giving a notification.** (1) Subject to paragraph (2) below, for the purpose of giving a notification under section 86(2) or 86(3), a relevant offender must attend at a police station—

(*a*) which is in his local police area within the meaning of section 88(3), and
(*b*) at which, pursuant to the provisions of section 87, notifications under section 83, 84 or 85 may be made.

(2) For the purpose of giving a notification under section 86(2) as required by regulation 5(3) or 7 above, a relevant offender must attend at a police station prescribed under section 87, but such a police station need not be in his local police area.

(3) A notification under section 86(2) or 86(3) must be given to a police officer, or to a person authorised by the officer in charge of the station under section 87(1)(b) for the purpose of receiving a notification under that section.

(4) A relevant offender giving a notification under section 86(2) or 86(3) must inform the person to whom he gives the notice of—

(*a*) his name and other names he is using,
(*b*) his home address, and
(*c*) his date of birth,

as currently notified under Part 2 of the Act.

(5) A relevant offender giving a further notification under section 86(2) as required by regulation 7 above must inform the person to whom he gives the notification of the police station at which he first gave a notification in respect of the journey in question under section 86(2).

SHOPS

8–28439 This title contains the following statute—

Sunday Trading Act 1994

(1994 c 20)

8–28540 2. Loading and unloading at large shops on Sunday morning. (1) A local authority may by resolution designate their area as a loading control area for the purposes of this section with effect from a date specified in the resolution, which must be a date at least one month after the date on which the resolution is passed.

(2) A local authority may by resolution revoke any designation made by them under subsection (1) above.

(3) It shall be the duty of a local authority, before making or revoking any designation under subsection (1) above, to consult persons appearing to the local authority to be likely to be affected by the proposed designation or revocation (whether as the occupiers of shops or as local residents) or persons appearing to the local authority to represent such persons.

(4) Where a local authority make or revoke a designation under this section, they shall publish notice of the designation or revocation in such manner as they consider appropriate.

(5) Schedule 3 to this Act (which imposes restrictions on loading and unloading on Sunday before 9 am at large shops in loading control areas) shall have effect.
[Sunday Trading Act 1994, s 2.]

8–28541 8. Meaning of "local authority". (1) In this Act "local authority" means any unitary authority or any district council so far as they are not a unitary authority.

(2) In subsection (1) above "unitary authority" means—

(*a*) the council of any county so far as they are the council for an area for which there are no district councils,
(*b*) the council of any district comprised in an area for which there is no county council.
(*c*) a county borough council,
(*d*) a London borough council,
(*e*) the Common Council of the City of London, or
(*f*) the Council of the Isles of Scilly.

(3) Until 1st April 1996, the definition of "unitary authority" in subsection (2) above shall have effect with the omission of paragraph (*c*).
[Sunday Trading Act 1994, s 8.]

8–28542

SCHEDULES

Section 1(1)

SCHEDULE 1
Restrictions on Sunday opening of Large Shops[1]

(Amended by the Regulatory Reform (Sunday Trading) Order 2004, SI 2004/470, the Christmas Day (Trading) Act 2004, s 4, SI 2004/470 and the Licensing Act 2003, Sch 6.)

Interpretation

1. In this Schedule—

"alcohol" has the same meaning as in the Licensing Act 2003,
"large shop" means a shop which has a relevant floor area exceeding 280 square metres,
"medicinal product" and "registered pharmacy" have the same meaning as in the Medicines Act 1968,
"relevant floor area", in relation to a shop, means the internal floor area of so much of the shop as consists of or is comprised in a building, but excluding any part of the shop which, throughout the week ending with the Sunday in question, is used neither for the serving of customers in connection with the sale of goods nor for the display of goods,
"retail customer" means a person who purchases goods retail,
"retail sale" means any sale other than a sale for use or resale in the course of a trade or business, and references to retail purchase shall be construed accordingly,
"sale of goods" does not include—

(*a*) the sale of meals, refreshments or alcohol for consumption on the premises on which they are sold, or
(*b*) the sale of meals or refreshments prepared to order for immediate consumption off those premises,

"shop" means any premises where there is carried on a trade or business consisting wholly or mainly of the sale of goods, and
"stand", in relation to an exhibition, means any platform, structure, space or other area provided for exhibition purposes.

Restrictions on Sunday opening hours of large shops

2. (1) Subject to sub-paragraphs (2) and (3) below, a large shop[2] shall not be open on Sunday for the serving of retail customers[3].

(2) Sub-paragraph (1) above does not apply in relation to–

(*a*) any of the shops mentioned in paragraph 3(1) below, or
(*b*) any shop in respect of which a notice under paragraph 8(1) of Schedule 2 to this Act (shops occupied by persons observing the Jewish Sabbath) has effect

(3) Sub-paragraph (1) above does not apply in relation to the opening of a large shop during any continuous period of six hours on a Sunday beginning no earlier than 10 am and ending no later than 6 pm, but this sub-paragraph has effect subject to sub-paragraph (4) below.

(4) The exemption conferred by sub-paragraph (3) above does not apply where the Sunday is Easter Day.

(5) Nothing in this paragraph applies where the Sunday is Christmas Day (the opening of large shops on Christmas Day being prohibited by section 1 of the Christmas Day (Trading) Act 2004).

Exemptions

3. (1) The shops referred to in paragraph 2(2)(*a*) above are—

(*a*) any shop which is at a farm and where the trade or business carried on consists wholly or mainly of the sale of produce from that farm,
(*b*) any shop where the trade or business carried on consists wholly or mainly of the sale of alcohol,
(*c*) any shop where the trade or business carried on consists wholly or mainly of the sale of any one or more of the following—

(i) motor supplies and accessories[4], and
(ii) cycle supplies and accessories,

(*d*) any shop which—

(i) is a registered pharmacy, and
(ii) is not open for the retail sale of any goods other than medicinal products and medical and surgical appliances,

(*e*) any shop at a designated airport which is situated in a part of the airport to which sub-paragraph (3) below applies,
(*f*) any shop in a railway station,
(*g*) any shop at a service area within the meaning of the Highways Act 1980,
(*h*) any petrol filling station,
(*j*) any shop which is not open for the retail sale of any goods other than food, stores or other necessaries required by any person for a vessel or aircraft on its arrival at, or immediately before its departure from, a port, harbour or airport, and
(*k*) any stand used for the retail sale of goods during the course of an exhibition.

(2) In determining whether a shop falls within sub-paragraph (1)(*a*), (*b*) or (*c*) above, regard shall be had to the nature of the trade or business carried on there on weekdays as well as to the nature of the trade or business carried on there on Sunday.

(3) This sub-paragraph applies to every part of a designated airport, except any part which is not ordinarily used by persons travelling by air to or from the airport.

(4) In this paragraph "designated airport" means an airport designated for the purposes of this paragraph by an order made by the Secretary of State, as being an airport at which there appears to him to be a substantial amount of international passenger traffic.

(5) The power to make an order under sub-paragraph (4) above shall be exercisable by statutory instrument.

(6) Any order made under section 1(2) of the Shops (Airports) Act 1962[5] and in force at the commencement of this Schedule shall, so far as it relates to England and Wales, have effect as if made also under sub-paragraph (4) above, and may be amended or revoked as it has effect for the purposes of this paragraph by an order under sub-paragraph (4) above.

4–5. *Repealed.*

Duty to display notice

6. At any time when—

(*a*) a large shop is open on Sunday for the serving of retail customers, and
(*b*) the prohibition in sub-paragraph (1) of paragraph 2 above is excluded only by sub-paragraph (3) of that paragraph,

a notice specifying the Sunday opening hours shall be displayed in a conspicuous position inside and outside the shop[3].

Offences

7. (1) If paragraph 2(1)[6] above is contravened in relation to a shop, the occupier of the shop shall be liable on summary conviction to a **fine not exceeding £50,000**[7].

(2) If paragraph 6 above is contravened in relation to a shop, the occupier of the shop shall be liable on summary conviction to a fine not exceeding **level 2** on the standard scale[7].

8. Where a person is charged with having contravened paragraph 2(1) above, in relation to a large shop which was permitted to be open for the serving of retail customers on the Sunday in questionby reason of his having served a retail customer after the end of the period during which the shop is permitted to be open by virtue of paragraph 2(3) above, it shall be a defence to prove that the customer was in the shop before the end of that period and left not later than half an hour after the end of that period.

9. *Repealed.*

---

1. It has been held that the prohibition in Art 30 of the EEC Treaty on quantitative restrictions on imports does not apply to national legislation, prohibiting retailers from opening their premises on Sundays (*Stoke on Trent City Council v B & Q plc* [1993] 2 All ER 297n).

2. Whether a shop is a "large shop", must be determined in the light of the situation which continues for a period of time. Accordingly, a shop in which only part of the premises were open on a particular day did not thereby cease to be a "large shop" when on most other days the whole of the premises were open; see *Haskins Garden Centres Ltd v East Dorset District Council* (1998) Times, 7 May.

For penalty for contravention, see para 7, post. The Channel Tunnel (Sunday Trading Act 1994) (Disapplication) Order 1994, SI 1994/3286, excludes the application of para 2(1) of Sch 1 in relation to any shops situated in a specified part of the terminal area of the Channel Tunnel system at Cheriton, Folkestone.

3. The justices must ask themselves whether in the ordinary and natural use of language an item is capable of being a motor supply or accessory; evidence of capacity is not necessary; there is a difference between an object capable of being used as a motor accessory and an object which is properly speaking a motor accessory (*Hadley v Texas Homecare Ltd* (1987) 152 JP 268).

4. The Airports Shops Order 1977, SI 1977/1397, designates the following airports in England and Wales: Birmingham, Liverpool, London—Gatwick, Heathrow and Stansted—Manchester International and Southend, the Airports Shops Order 1985, SI 1985/654, similarly designates Leeds, Bradford, Luton and Southampton Airports and the Airports Shops (No 2) Order 1985, SI 1985/1739, designates Bournemouth (Hurn), Humberside, Liverpool, Norwich and Teesside, and orders have also been made for Exeter (SI 1986/981), London City (SI 1987/1983) and Manston (SI 1990/1044).

5. For statutory defence that goods were supplied to a customer who was in the shop before the end of permitted Sunday opening hours, see para 8, post.

6. For defence of due diligence, see Sch 2, para 7, post. For offences due to default of other person and for liability of director, manager etc for acts of a body corporate, see Sch 2, paras 5 and 6, post.

8–28543

Section 1(1)

SCHEDULE 2
Supplementary Provisions

Part I
General Enforcement Provisions

Duty to enforce Act

1. It shall be the duty[1] of every local authority to enforce within their area the provisions of Schedules 1 and 3 to this Act and Part II of this Schedule.

Inspectors

2. For the purposes of their duties under paragraph 1 above it shall be the duty of every local authority to appoint inspectors.

Powers of entry

3. An inspector appointed by a local authority under paragraph 2 above shall, on producing if so required some duly authenticated document showing his authority, have a right at all reasonable hours—

(*a*) to enter any premises within the area of the local authority, with or without a constable, for the purpose of ascertaining whether there is or has been on the premises any contravention of the provisions of Schedules 1 and 3 to this Act,

(*b*) to require the production of, inspect and take copies of any records (in whatever form they are held) relating to any business carried on on the premises which appear to him to be relevant for the purpose mentioned in paragraph (*a*) above,

(*c*) where those records are kept by means of a computer, to require the records to be produced in a form in which they may be taken away, and

(*d*) to take such measurements and photographs as he considers necessary for the purpose mentioned in paragraph (*a*) above.

Obstruction of inspectors

4. Any person who intentionally obstructs an inspector appointed under paragraph 2 above acting in the execution of his duty shall be liable on summary conviction to a fine not exceeding **level 3** on the standard scale.

Offences due to fault of other person

5. Where the commission by any person of an offence under this Act is due to the act or default of some other person, that other person shall be guilty of the offence, and a person may be charged with and convicted of the offence by virtue of this paragraph whether or not proceedings are taken against the first-mentioned person.

Offences by bodies corporate

6. (1) Where an offence under this Act committed by a body corporate is proved to have been committed with the consent or connivance of, or to be attributable to any neglect on the part of, any director, manager, secretary or other similar officer of the body corporate, or any person who was purporting to act in any such capacity, he as well as the body corporate shall be guilty of the offence and shall be liable to be proceeded against and punished accordingly.

(2) Where the affairs of a body corporate are managed by its members, sub-paragraph (1) above shall apply in relation to the acts and defaults of a member in connection with his functions of management as if he were a director of the body corporate.

Defence of due diligence

7. (1) In any proceedings for an offence under this Act it shall, subject to sub-paragraph (2) below, be a defence for the person charged to prove that he took all reasonable precautions and exercised all due diligence to avoid the commission of the offence by himself or by a person under his control.

(2) If in any case the defence provided by sub-paragraph (1) above involves the allegation that the commission of the offence was due to the act or default of another person, the person charged shall not, without leave of the court, be entitled to rely on that defence unless, at least seven clear days before the hearing, he has served on the prosecutor a notice in writing giving such information identifying or assisting in the identification of that other person as was then in his possession.

1. For the duty of a local authority and its powers to seek an injunction in the civil courts to restrain a person acting in contravention of the legislation. See *Stoke-on-Trent City Council v B & Q (Retail) Ltd* [1984] AC 754, [1984] 2 All ER 332, HL (decided under the Shops Act 1950).

8–28544

Part II
Shops occupied by Persons observing the Jewish Sabbath

Shops occupied by persons of the Jewish religion

8. (1) A person of the Jewish religion who is the occupier of a large shop may give to the local authority for the area in which the shop is situated a notice signed by him stating—

(*a*) that he is a person of the Jewish religion, and
(*b*) that he intends to keep the shop closed for the serving of customers on the Jewish Sabbath.

(2) For the purposes of this paragraph, a shop occupied by a partnership or company shall be taken to be occupied by a person of the Jewish religion if, and only if, the majority of the partners or of the directors, as the case may be, are persons of that religion.

(3) A notice under sub-paragraph (1) above shall be accompanied by a certificate signed by an authorised person that the person giving the notice is a person of the Jewish religion.

(4) Where the occupier of the shop is a partnership or company—

(*a*) any notice under sub-paragraph (1) above shall be given by the majority of the partners or directors and, if not given by all of them, shall specify the names of the other partners or directors;
(*b*) a certificate under sub-paragraph (3) above is required in relation to each of the persons by whom such a notice is given.

(5)–(6) *Register.*

(7) If there is any change—

(*a*) in the occupation of a shop in respect of which a notice under sub-paragraph (1) above has effect, or
(*b*) in any partnership or among the directors of any company by which such a shop is occupied,

the notice shall be taken to be cancelled at the end of the period of 14 days beginning with the day on which the change occurred, unless during that period, or within such further time as may be allowed by the local authority, a fresh notice is given under sub-paragraph (1) above in respect of the shop.

(8) Where a fresh notice is given under sub-paragraph (1) above by reason of a change of the kind mentioned in sub-paragraph (7) above, the local authority may dispense with the certificate required by sub-paragraph (3) above in the case of any person in respect of whom such a certificate has been provided in connection with a former notice in respect of that shop or any other shop in the area of the local authority.

(9) A notice given under sub-paragraph (1) above in respect of any shop shall be cancelled on application in that behalf being made to the local authority by the occupier of the shop.

(10) A person who, in a notice or certificate given for the purposes of this paragraph, makes a statement which is false in a material respect and which he knows to be false or does not believe to be true shall be liable on summary conviction to a fine not exceeding **level 5** on the standard scale.

(11) Where a person is convicted of an offence under sub-paragraph (10) above, the local authority may cancel any notice under sub-paragraph (1) above to which the offence relates.

(12) In this paragraph—

"authorised person", in relation to a notice under sub-paragraph (1) above, means—

(*a*) the Minister of the synagogue of which the person giving the notice is a member,
(*b*) the secretary of that synagogue, or
(*c*) any other person nominated for the purposes of this paragraph by the President of the London Committee of Deputies of the British Jews (otherwise known as the Board of Deputies of British Jews),

"large shop" and "shop" have the same meaning as in Schedule 1 to this Act, and
"secretary of a synagogue" has the same meaning as in Part IV of the Marriage Act 1949.

Members of other religious bodies observing the Jewish Sabbath

9. Paragraph 8 above shall apply to persons who are members of any religious body regularly observing the Jewish Sabbath as it applies to persons of the Jewish religion, and accordingly—

(*a*) references to persons of the Jewish religion shall be construed as including any person who is a member of such a body, and
(*b*) in the application of that paragraph to such persons "authorised person" means a Minister of the religious body concerned.

10. *Transitional provisions.*

8–28545

Section 2

SCHEDULE 3

LOADING AND UNLOADING AT LARGE SHOPS ON SUNDAY MORNING

(Amended by the Christmas Day (Trading) Act 2004, s 4.)

Shops to which Schedule applies

1. This Schedule applies to any shop—

(*a*) which is a large shop, within the meaning of Schedule 1 to this Act, in respect of which a notice under paragraph 4 of that Schedule has effect, and
(*b*) which is situated in an area designated as a loading control area under section 2 of this Act.

Consent required for early Sunday loading and unloading

2. The occupier of a shop to which this Schedule applies shall not load or unload, or permit any other person to load or unload, goods from a vehicle at the shop before 9 am on Sunday in connection with the trade or business carried on in the shop, unless the loading or unloading is carried on—

(*a*) with the consent of the local authority for the area in which the shop is situated granted under this Schedule, and
(*b*) in accordance with any conditions subject to which that consent is granted.

3. (1) A consent under this Schedule may be granted subject to such conditions as the local authority consider appropriate.

(2) The local authority may at any time vary the conditions subject to which a consent is granted, and shall give notice of the variation to the person to whom the consent was granted.

Offence

9. A person who contravenes paragraph 2 above shall be liable on summary conviction to a fine not exceeding **level 3** on the standard scale[1].

Christmas Day

10. Paragraph 2 does not apply where the Sunday is Christmas Day (loading and unloading at large shops on Christmas Day being regulated by section 2 of the Christmas Day (Trading) Act 2004).

1. For defence of due diligence, see Sch 2, para 7, ante. For offences due to default of other person and for liability of director, manager etc for acts of a body corporate, see Sch 2, paras 5 and 6, ante.

Christmas Day (Trading) Act 2004

(2004 c 26)

8–28546 1. Prohibition of opening of large shops on Christmas Day. (1) A large shop must not be open on Christmas Day for the serving of retail customers.

(2) Subsection (1) does not apply to any of the shops mentioned in paragraph 3(1) of Schedule 1 to the 1994 Act (shops exempt from restrictions on Sunday trading).

(3) If subsection (1) is contravened in relation to a shop, the occupier of the shop is liable on summary conviction to a fine not exceeding £50,000.

(4) In its application for the purposes of subsection (2), paragraph 3(2) of Schedule 1 to the 1994 Act (which relates to the interpretation of paragraph 3(1) of that Schedule) has effect as if—

(*a*) the reference to weekdays were a reference to days of the year other than Christmas Day, and

(*b*) the reference to Sunday were a reference to Christmas Day.

(5) In this section—

"large shop" has the same meaning as in Schedule 1 to the 1994 Act, except that for the purposes of this section the definition of "relevant floor area" in paragraph 1 of that Schedule is to be read as if the reference to the week ending with the Sunday in question were a reference to the period of seven days ending with the Christmas Day in question;

[Christmas Day (Trading) Act 2004, s 1.]

8–28546A 2. Loading and unloading early on Christmas Day. (1) Where a shop which is prohibited by section 1 from opening on Christmas Day is located in a loading control area, the occupier of the shop must not load or unload, or permit any other person to load or unload, goods from a vehicle at the shop before 9am on Christmas Day in connection with the trade or business carried on in the shop, unless the loading or unloading is carried on—

(*a*) with the consent of the local authority for the area in which the shop is situated, granted in accordance with this section, and

(*b*) in accordance with any conditions subject to which that consent is granted.

(2) The provisions of paragraphs 3 to 8 of Schedule 3 to the 1994 Act shall apply in relation to consent under subsection (1) as they apply in relation to consent under that Schedule, but as if—

(*a*) the reference in paragraph 6(1) to Sunday were a reference to Christmas Day, and

(*b*) the reference in paragraph 7(*a*) to an offence under paragraph 9 of that Schedule were a reference to an offence under subsection (3).

(3) A person who contravenes subsection (1) is liable on summary conviction to a fine not exceeding level 3 on the standard scale.

(4) In this section, "loading control area" means any area designated by a local authority as a loading control area in accordance with section 2 of the 1994 Act.

[Christmas Day (Trading) Act 2004, s 2.]

8–28546B 3. Enforcement. (1) It is the duty of every local authority to enforce within their area the provisions of sections 1 and 2.

(2) For the purposes of their duties under subsection (1), it is the duty of every local authority to appoint inspectors, who may be the same persons as those appointed as inspectors by the local authority under paragraph 2 of Schedule 2 to the 1994 Act.

(3) Paragraphs 3 and 4 of Schedule 2 to the 1994 Act (powers of entry and obstruction of inspectors) apply in respect of inspectors appointed under subsection (2) as they apply to inspectors appointed under paragraph 2 of that Schedule and, for the purposes of paragraph 3 of that Schedule as so applied, the reference in that paragraph to the provisions of Schedules 1 and 3 to the 1994 Act is to be taken to be a reference to the provisions of sections 1 and 2 of this Act.

(4) Paragraphs 5, 6 and 7 of Schedule 2 to the 1994 Act (offences due to fault of other person, offences by body corporate and defence of due diligence) apply in respect of the offences under sections 1 and 2 as they apply in respect of offences under the 1994 Act.

(5) In this section "local authority" has the meaning given by section 8 of the 1994 Act.
[Christmas Day (Trading) Act 2004, s 3.]

8–28546C 4. Consequential amendments. *Amends the 1994 Act.*

8–28546D 5. Expenses

8–28546E 6. Short title, interpretation, commencement and extent. (1) This Act may be cited as the Christmas Day (Trading) Act 2004.

(2) In this Act "the 1994 Act" means the Sunday Trading Act 1994 (c 20).

(3) This Act comes into force on such day as the Secretary of State may by order made by statutory instrument appoint.

(4) This Act extends to England and Wales only.
[Christmas Day (Trading) Act 2004, s 6.]

SOCIAL SECURITY

8–28550 This title includes the following statutes—

8–28559 NATIONAL ASSISTANCE ACT 1948
8–28820 NATIONAL ASSISTANCE (AMENDMENT) ACT 1951
8–29000 PNEUMOCONIOSIS ETC (WORKERS' COMPENSATION) ACT 1979
8–29030 HEALTH AND SOCIAL SERVICES AND SOCIAL SECURITY ADJUDICATIONS ACT 1983
8–29043 SOCIAL SECURITY ACT 1986
8–29049 NATIONAL HEALTH SERVICE AND COMMUNITY CARE ACT 1990
8–29060 SOCIAL SECURITY CONTRIBUTIONS AND BENEFITS ACT 1992
8–29070 SOCIAL SECURITY ADMINISTRATION ACT 1992
8–29110 PENSION SCHEMES ACT 1993
8–29120 JOBSEEKERS ACT 1995
8–29132A PENSIONS ACT 1995
8–29133 SOCIAL SECURITY CONTRIBUTIONS (TRANSFER OF FUNCTIONS, ETC) ACT 1999
8–29138 CHILD SUPPORT, PENSIONS AND SOCIAL SECURITY ACT 2000
8–29150 SOCIAL SECURITY FRAUD ACT 2001
8–29200 TAX CREDITS ACT 2002
8–29210 PENSIONS ACT 2004

The following statutory instruments are also reproduced here—

8–29280 Social Security (Claims and Payments) Regulations 1979
8–29290 Income Support (Liable Relatives) Regulations 1990

National Assistance Act 1948

(11 & 12 Geo 6 c 29)

PART III
LOCAL AUTHORITY SERVICES

Provision of Accommodation

8–28559 21. Duty of local authorities to provide accommodation. (1) Subject to and in accordance with the provisions of this Part of this Act[1], a local authority may with the approval of the Secretary of State, and to such extent as he may direct shall, make arrangements[2] for providing—

(*a*) residential accommodation[3] for persons aged eighteen or over who by reason of age, illness, disability or any other circumstances are in need of care and attention which is not otherwise available to them; and

(*aa*) residential accommodation for expectant and nursing mothers who are in need of care and attention which is not otherwise available to them.

(*b*) *Repealed.*

(1A) A person to whom section 115 of the Immigration and Asylum Act 1999 (exclusion from benefits) applies may not be provided with residential accommodation under subsection (1)(*a*) if his need for care and attention has arisen solely—

(*a*) because he is destitute; or

(*b*) because of the physical effects, or anticipated physical effects, of his being destitute.

(1B) Subsections (3) and (5) to (8) of section 95 of the Immigration and Asylum Act 1999, and paragraph 2 of Schedule 8 to that Act, apply for the purposes of subsection (1A) as they apply for the purposes of that section, but for the references in subsections (5) and (7) of that section and in that paragraph to the Secretary of State substitute references to a local authority.*

(2) In making any such arrangements a local authority shall have regard to the welfare of all persons for whom accommodation is provided, and in particular to the need for providing accommodation of different descriptions suited to different descriptions of such persons as are mentioned in the last foregoing subsection.

(2A) In determining for the purposes of paragraph (*a*) or (aa) of subsection (1) of this section whether care and attention are otherwise available to a person, a local authority shall disregard so much of the person's resources as may be specified in, or determined in accordance with, regulations[4] made by the Secretary of State for the purposes of this subsection.

(2B) In subsection (2A) of this section the reference to a person's resources is a reference to his resources within the meaning of regulations made for the purposes of that subsection.

(3) *Repealed.*

(4) Subject to the provisions of section 26 of this Act, accommodation provided by a local authority in the exercise of their functions under this section shall be provided in premises managed by the authority or, to such extent as may be determined in accordance with the arrangements under this section, in such premises managed by another local authority as may be agreed between the two authorities and on such terms, including terms as to the reimbursement of expenditure incurred by the said other authority, as may be so agreed.

(5) References in this Act to accommodation provided under this Part thereof shall be construed as references to accommodation provided in accordance with this and the five next following sections, and as including references to board and other services, amenities and requisites provided in connection with the accommodation except where in the opinion of the authority managing the premises their provision is unnecessary.

(6) References in this Act to a local authority providing accommodation shall be construed, in any case where a local authority agree with another local authority for the provision of accommodation in premises managed by the said other authority, as references to the first-mentioned local authority.

(7) Without prejudice to the generality of the foregoing provisions of this section, a local authority may—

(*a*) provide, in such cases as they may consider appropriate, for the conveyance of persons to and from premises in which accommodation is provided for them under this Part of the Act;

(*b*) make arrangements for the provision on the premises in which accommodation is being provided of such other services as appear to the authority to be required.

(8) Nothing in this section shall authorise or require a local authority to make any provision authorised or required to be made (whether by that or by any other authority) by or under any enactment not contained in this Part of this Act or authorised or required to be provided under the National Health Service Act 1977.

[National Assistance Act 1948, s 21, as amended by the Local Government Act 1972, Schs 23 and 30, the National Health Service Reorganisation Act 1973, Schs 4 and 5, the Housing (Homeless Persons) Act 1977, Sch, the Health Services Act 1980, Sch 1, the Children Act 1989, Sch 13, the National Health Service and Community Care Act 1990, s 42(1), Schs 9 and 10 and the Community Care (Residential Accommodation) Act 1998, s 1, the Immigration and Asylum Act 1999, s 116 and the Health and Social Care Act 2001, s 53.]

***Sub-section (1B) substituted by the Nationality, Immigration and Asylum Act 2002, s 45, from a date to be appointed.**

1. Section 26A, added by the National Health Service and Community Care Act 1990, s 43 excludes the power to provide accommodation in certain cases.

2. This duty may be discharged by arrangements made with third parties either wholly or in part under s 26, post (see *R v Wandsworth London Borough Council, ex p Beckwith* [1996] 1 All ER 129, [1996] 1 WLR 60, HL).

3. Power to make rules for the preservation of order is contained in s 23(1).

4. The National Assistance (Residential Accommodation) (Disregarding of Resources) (Wales) Regulations 2003, SI 2003/969 have been made.

8–28560 22. Charges to be made for accommodation. Such persons shall pay[1] for the accommodation in accordance with the rates provided by the Act and regulations[2] prescribed from time to time by the Secretary of State, giving effect to relevant provisions. In the case of a child under 16 years, accompanied by a person over that age, payment shall be made by the person by whom the child is accompanied.

[National Assistance Act 1948, s 22, amended by the Ministry of Social Security Act 1966, 6th Sch, the Social Security Act 1980, Sch 5, the Health and Social Services and Social Security Adjudications Act 1983, s 20, the Social Security Act 1986, Sch 10, the National Health Service and Community Care Act 1990, s 44 and Sch 10 and the Community Care (Delayed Discharges etc) Act 2003, s 17—summarised.]

1. For recovery of cost, see s 56, post. The Health and Social Services and Social Security Adjudications Act 1983, ss 21–24 makes further provision for the recovery of charges where persons in residential accommodation have disposed of assets or have a beneficial interest in land.

2. National Assistance (Assessment of Resources) Regulations 1992, SI 1992/2977 amended by SI 1993/964 and 2230, SI 1994/825 and 2386, SI 1995/858 and 3054, SI 1996/602, SI 1997/485, SI 1998/497 and 1730, SI 2001/276 (Wales), 1409 (Wales) and 3441 (England), SI 2002/410 (England), 814 (Wales) and 2531 (England), SI 2003/897 (W), 931 (W), 2343 (E) and 2530 (W),, SI 2004/2879 (W), SI 2005/662 (W), 708 (E), 3277 (E) and 3288 (W) and SI 2006/217have been made. See also the National Assistance (Residential Accommodation) (Disregarding of Resources) (England) Regulations 2001, SI 2001/3067 also the following regulations made under the Health and Social Care Act 2001: the National Assistance (Residential Accommodation) (Relevant Contributions) (England) Regulations 2001, SI 2001/3069; the National Assistance (Residential Accommodation) (Additional Payments and Assessment of Resources) (Amendment) (England) Regulations 2001, SI 2001/3441; the National Assistance (Sums for Personal Requirements) (England) Regulations 2003, SI 2003/628 amended by SI 2004/760 (E); the National Assistance (Sums for Personal Requirements) (Wales) Regulations 2003, SI 2003/892 amended by SI 2005/663; the National Assistance (Residential Accommodation) (Additional Payments, Relevant Contributions and Assessment of Resources) (Wales) Regulations 2003, SI 2003/931.

8–28561 **26. Provision of accommodation[1] in premises maintained by voluntary organisations.** (1) Subject to subsections (1A) and (1C) below, arrangements under section 21 of this Act may include arrangements with a voluntary organisation or with any other person who is not a local authority where—

(*a*) that organisation or person manages premises which provide for reward accommodation falling within subsection (1)(*a*) or (*aa*) of that section, and

(*b*) the arrangements are for the provision of such accommodation in those premises.

(1A) Arrangements must not be made by virtue of this section for the provision of accommodation together with nursing or personal care for persons such as are mentioned in section 3(2) of the Care Standards Act 2000 (care homes) unless—

(*a*) the accommodation is to be provided, under the arrangements, in a care home (within the meaning of that Act) which is managed by the organisation or person in question; and

(*b*) that organisation or person is registered under Part II of that Act in respect of the home.

(1C) Subject to subsection (1D) below, no arrangements may be made by virtue of this section for the provision of accommodation together with nursing without the consent of such Health Authority as may be determined in accordance with regulations.

(1D) Subsection (1C) above does not apply to the making by an authority of temporary arrangements for the accommodation of any person as a matter of urgency; but, as soon as practicable after any such temporary arrangements have been made, the authority shall seek the consent required by subsection (1C) above to the making of appropriate arrangements for the accommodation of the person concerned.

(1E) (*Repealed*).

(2) Any arrangements made by virtue of this section shall provide for the making by the local authority to [the other party thereto] of payments in respect of the accommodation provided at such rates as may be determined by or under the arrangements[2] and subject to subsection (3A) below the local authority shall recover from each person for whom accommodation is provided under the arrangements the amount of the refund which he is liable to make in accordance with the following provisions of this section.

(3) Subject to subsection (3A) below, a person for whom accommodation is provided under any such arrangements shall, in lieu of being liable to make payment therefor in accordance with section twenty-two of this Act, refund to the local authority any payments made in respect of him under the last foregoing subsection[3]:

Provided that where a person for whom accommodation is provided, or proposed to be provided, under any such arrangements satisfies the local authority that he is unable to make a refund at the full rate determined under that subsection, subsections (3) to (5) of section twenty-two of this Act shall, with the necessary modifications, apply as they apply where a person satisfies the local authority of his inability to pay at the standard rate as mentioned in the said subsection (3).

(3A) Where accommodation in any premises is provided for any person under arrangements made by virtue of this section and the local authority, the person concerned and the voluntary organisation or other person managing the premises (in this subsection referred to as "the provider") agree that this subsection shall apply—

(*a*) so long as the person concerned makes the payments for which he is liable under paragraph (*b*) below, he shall not be liable to make any refund under subsection (3) above and the local authority shall not be liable to make any payment under subsection (2) above in respect of the accommodation provided for him;

(*b*) the person concerned shall be liable to pay to the provider such sums as he would otherwise (under subsection (3) above) be liable to pay by way of refund to the local authority; and

(*c*) the local authority shall be liable to pay to the provider the difference between the sums paid by virtue of paragraph (*b*) above and the payments which, but for paragraph (*a*) above, the authority would be liable to pay under subsection (2) above.

(4) Subsections (5A), (7) and (9) of the said section twenty-two shall, with the necessary modifications, apply for the purposes of the last foregoing subsection as they apply for the purposes of the said section twenty-two.

(4A) Section 21(5) of this Act shall have effect as respects accommodation provided under arrangements made by virtue of this section with the substitution for the reference to the authority managing the premises of a reference to the authority making the arrangements.

(4AA) Subsections (2) to (4) shall have effect subject to any regulations under section 15 of the Community Care (Delayed Discharges etc) Act 2003 (power to require certain community care services and services for carers to be free of charge).

(5) Where in any premises accommodation is being provided under this section in accordance with arrangements made by any local authority, any person authorised in that behalf by the authority may at all reasonable times enter and inspect the premises.

(6) (*Repealed*).

(7) In this section the expression "voluntary organisation" includes any association which is a housing association for the purposes of the Housing Act, 1936; "small home" means an establishment falling within section 1(4) of the Registered Homes Act 1984 and "exempt body" means an authority or body constituted by an Act of Parliament or incorporated by Royal Charter.

[National Assistance Act 1948, s 26, as amended by the Health Services and Public Health Act 1968, s 44, the Social Work (Scotland) Act 1968, s 95 and Sch 9, the Local Government Act 1972, Sch 23, the Housing (Homeless Persons) Act 1977, s 20 and Sch, the Health and Social Services and Social Security Adjudications Act 1983, s 20, the Registered Homes (Amendment) Act 1991, s 2(5), the National Health Service and Community Care Act 1990, s 42 and Schs 9 and 10, the Community Care (Residential Accommodation) Act 1992, s 1 and the Health Authorities Act 1995, Sch 1, the Care Standards Act 2000, s 116 and the Community Care (Delayed Discharges etc) Act 2003, s 17.]

---

1. Section 26A, added by the National Health Service and Community Care Act 1990, s 43 excludes the power to provide accommodation in certain cases.

2. If the arrangements for transfer to a voluntary organization of the local authority's obligations to provide "residential accommodation" do not include arrangements for the local authority to make payments to the voluntary organization at rates determined by or under the arrangements, "residential accommodation" is not provided under Pt III of the Act. Accordingly the rate of benefit payable under the Social Security legislation will be at the rate applicable to claimants in a "residential care home" rather than to those in residential accommodation (*Chief Adjudication Officer v Quinn* [1996] 4 All ER 72, [1996] 1 WLR 1184, HL).

3. Section 26(3) is not to be construed as meaning that, whatever the figure and however wrongly a local authority may make payments for the provision of accommodation, the resident has to reimburse them under the section. The ordinary principles of construction involve putting in the words "any payments properly made in respect of him" (*Dorset County Council v Greenham* (1981) 145 JP 125).

8–28562 **42. Liability to maintain wife or husband and children.** (1) For the purposes of this Act—

(*a*) a man shall be liable to maintain his wife and his children[1], and

(*b*) a woman shall be liable to maintain her husband and her children[1].

(2) Any reference in subsection (1) of this section to a person's children shall be construed in accordance with section 1 of the Family Law Reform Act 1987[2].

[National Assistance Act 1948, s 42, as amended by the Family Law Reform Act 1987, Sch 2.]

---

1. The wife and her children of a polygamous marriage, valid according to the law of the country of the parties' domicile where the marriage was contracted, are a man's wife and his children for the purposes of this section (*Din v National Assistance Board* [1967] 2 QB 213, [1967] 1 All ER 750). "Child" means a person under the age of sixteen (s 64(1)). He shall not be deemed to have attained the age of sixteen until the commencement of the sixteenth anniversary of the day of his birth (s 64(3)). A father remains liable for the maintenance of his children notwithstanding that he may have entered into a deed of separation and covenanted thereby to pay to his wife a weekly sum for the maintenance of his children (*Westminster Union v Buckle* (1897) 61 JP 247).

2. See PART IV: FAMILY LAW, ante.

8–28563 **43. Recovery of cost of assistance from persons liable for maintenance.** (1) Where assistance is given or applied for by reference to the requirements of any person (in this section referred to as a person assisted), the local authority concerned may make a complaint[1] to the court against any other person who for the purposes of this Act is liable[2] to maintain the person assisted.

(2) On a complaint under this section the court shall have regard to all the circumstances[3] and in particular to the resources of the defendant, and may order[4] the defendant to pay such sum[5], weekly or otherwise, as the court may consider appropriate.

(3) For the purposes of the application of the last foregoing subsection to payments in respect of assistance given before the complaint was made, a person shall not be treated as having at the time when the complaint is heard any greater resources than he had at the time when the assistance was given.

(4) In this section the expression "assistance" means the provision of accommodation under Part III[6] of this Act (hereinafter referred to as "assistance under Part III of this Act"); and the expression "the court" means —

(*a*) in England and Wales, a magistrates' court acting in the local justice area where the assistance was given or applied for;

(*b*) in Scotland, the sheriff having jurisdiction in the place where the assistance was given or applied for.

(5) Payments under subsection (2) of this section shall be made—

(*a*) to the local authority concerned, in respect of the cost of assistance, whether given before or after the making of the order, or

(*b*) to the applicant for assistance or any other person being a person assisted, or

(*c*) to such other person as appears to the court expedient in the interests of the person assisted,

or as to part in one such manner and as to part in another, as may be provided by the order.

(6) An order under this section shall be enforceable as a magistrates, court maintenance order within the meaning of section 150(1) of the Magistrates' Courts Act 1980.

(7) *Repealed.*

(8) Subsections (6) and (7) of this section do not extend to Scotland.

[National Assistance Act 1948, s 43, amended by Ministry of Social Security Act 1966, 8th Sch, the Supplementary Benefits Act 1976, Sch 7, the Domestic Proceedings and Magistrates' Courts Act 1978, Schs 2 and 3, the Justices of the Peace Act 1979, Sch 2, the Social Security Act 1986, Schs 10 and 11, Family Law Reform Act 1987, Sch 2, and the Justices of the Peace Act 1997, Sch 5 and the Access to Justice Act 1999, Sch 15,.]

1. Legal representation may be granted in proceedings under this section, see Sch 2 to the Legal Aid Act 1988, ante.

2. That is, the liability of a man to maintain his wife and his children, and of a woman to maintain her husband and her children (s 42, supra).

3. Where a wife is in desertion, this is a circumstance that affords the husband an answer in law to a claim under s 43 (*National Assistance Board v Wilkinson* [1952] 2 QB 648, [1952] 2 All ER 255, 116 JP 428 (as explained in *National Assistance Board v Parkes*, infra)). The existence of a separation agreement providing that a wife shall claim no maintenance from her husband does not prevent an order being obtained (*National Assistance Board v Parkes* [1955] 2 QB 506, [1955] 3 All ER 1). A separation agreement containing no reference to maintenance has similar effect (*Stopher v National Assistance Board* [1955] 1 QB 486, [1955] 1 All ER 700, 119 JP 272). The existence of a maintenance order obtained by the wife is not, in itself, a bar to an order under this section, see *Birmingham Union v Timmins* [1918] 2 KB 189, 82 JP 279 (decided under the Poor Law Acts). The distinction between the obligation of a husband under this section and his obligation to maintain his wife under the former Summary Jurisdiction (Married Women) Acts 1895–1949 was discussed in *Lilley v Lilley* [1960] P 158, [1959] 3 All ER 283, 123 JP 525.

4. Costs may be awarded (Magistrates' Courts Act 1980, s 64 in PART I: MAGISTRATES' COURTS, PROCEDURE, ante). Provisions relating to orders against persons in Scotland and Northern Ireland are contained in the Maintenance Orders Act 1950, ante. See ss 4 and 16 of that Act. This will be a "maintenance order" within the meaning of the Maintenance Orders Act 1958, ante. Consequently, it may be registered in the High Court and an attachment of earnings order may be made to enforce payment. Guidance in the making of an order against a member of Her Majesty's forces is given in Home Office Circular No 251/1970, dated November 18th 1970 as amended by Circular No 61/1972 dated April 4th 1972 and Home Office Circular No 25/1986, dated 4 April 1986. For orders against members of the Royal Navy and the Royal Marines, see Home Office Circular No 12/1982, dated 10 February 1982.

5. This may be a larger sum than a husband is regularly paying to his wife under a separation deed, if that sum is not reasonable having regard to his means (*National Assistance Board v Prisk* [1954] 1 All ER 400, 118 JP 194).

6. See s 21 ante.

8–28564 **45. Recovery in cases of misrepresentation or non-disclosure.** (1) If, whether fraudulently or otherwise, any person misrepresents or fails to disclose any material fact, and in consequence of the misrepresentation or failure—

(*a*) a local authority incur any expenditure under Part III of this Act, or

(*b*) any sum recoverable under this Act by a local authority is not recovered, the authority shall be entitled to recover the amount thereof from the said person[1].

[National Assistance Act 1948, s 45, as amended by Ministry of Social Security Act 1966, 8th Sch.]

1. Recoverable summarily as a civil debt, see s 56(1), post.

8–28565 **47. Removal to suitable premises of persons in need of care and attention.** (1) The following provisions of this section shall have effect for the purposes of securing the necessary care and attention for persons who—

(*a*) are suffering from grave chronic disease or, being aged, infirm or physically incapacitated, are living in insanitary conditions, and

(*b*) are unable to devote to themselves, and are not receiving from other persons, proper care and attention.

(2) If the medical officer of health[1] certifies in writing to the appropriate authority[2] that he is satisfied after thorough inquiry and consideration that in the interests of any such person as aforesaid residing in the area of the authority or for preventing injury to the health of, or serious nuisance to, other persons, it is necessary to remove any such person as aforesaid from the premises in which he is residing, the appropriate authority may apply to the court of summary jurisdiction having jurisdiction in the place where the premises are situated for an order under the next following subsection.

(3)[3] On any such application the court may, if satisfied on oral evidence of the allegations in the certificate, and that it is expedient so to do, order the removal of the persons to whom the application relates by such officer of the appropriate authority as may be specified in the order, to a suitable hospital[4] or other place in, or within convenient distance of, the area of the appropriate authority, and his detention and maintenance therein:

Provided[3] that the court shall not order the removal of a person to any premises, unless either the person managing the premises has been heard in the proceedings or seven[5] clear days' notice has been given to him of the intended application and of the time and place at which it is proposed to be made.

(4)[3] An order under the last foregoing subsection may be made so as to authorise a person's detention for any period not exceeding three months, and the court may from time to time by order extend that period for such further period, not exceeding three months, as the court may determine.

(5)[3] An order under subsection (3) of this section may be varied by an order of the Court so as to substitute for the place referred to in that subsection such other suitable place in, or within convenient distance of, the area of the appropriate authority as the court may determine, so however that the proviso in the said subsection (3) shall with the necessary modification apply to any proceedings under this subsection.

(6)[3] At any time after the expiration of six clear weeks from the making of an order under subsection (3) or (4) of this section an application may be made to the court by or on behalf of the person in respect of whom the order was made, and on any such application the court may, if in the circumstances it appears expedient so to do, revoke the order.

(7)[3] No application under this section shall be entertained by the court unless, seven clear days before the making of the application, notice has been given of the intended application and of the time and place at which it is proposed to be made—

(*a*) where the application is for an order under subsection (3) or (4) of this section, to the person in respect of whom the application is made or to some person in charge of him;

(*b*) where the application is for the revocation of such an order, to the medical officer of health.

(8) Where in pursuance of an order under this section a person is maintained neither in hospital accommodation provided by the Minister of Health under the National Health Service Act 1977, nor by the Secretary of State under the National Health Service (Scotland) Act 1947, nor in premises where accommodation is provided by, or by arrangement with, a local authority under Part III[6] of this Act, the cost of his maintenance shall be borne by the appropriate authority.

(9) Any expenditure incurred under the last foregoing subsection shall be recoverable from the person maintained or from any person who for the purposes of this Act is liable to maintain that person[7]; and any expenditure incurred by virtue of this section in connection with the maintenance of a person in premises where accommodation is provided under Part III of this Act shall be recoverable[8] in like manner as expenditure incurred in providing accommodation under the said Part III.

(11) Any person who wilfully disobeys, or obstructs the execution of, an order under this section shall be guilty of an offence and liable on summary conviction to a fine not exceeding **level 1** on the standard scale.

(12) For the purposes of this section, the appropriate authorities shall be the councils of districts and London boroughs and the Common Council of the City of London, in Wales the councils of counties and county boroughs and in Scotland the councils of [regions and islands areas].

(13) The foregoing provisions of this section shall have effect in substitution for any provisions for the like purposes contained in, or having effect under, any public general or local Act passed before the passing of this Act: Provided that nothing in this subsection shall be construed as affecting any enactment providing for the removal to, or detention in, hospital of persons suffering from notifiable or infectious diseases[9].

(14) Any notice under this section may be served by post.

[National Assistance Act 1948, s 47, as amended by the Local Government Act 1972, Sch 29, the National Health Service Reorganisation Act 1973, Sch 5, the National Health Service Act 1977, Sch 15, the Criminal Law Act 1977, s 31, the Criminal Justice Act 1982, s 46, the Local Government (Scotland) Act 1973, s 214, Sch 7, Pt II and the Local Government (Wales) Act 1994, Sch 10.]

---

1. The reference to the medical officer of health must now be read as a reference to "the proper officer" by reason of the effect of the Local Government Act 1972, Sch 29, Pt I, paras 1 and 4.
2. "Appropriate authority" is defined in sub-s (12), infra.
3. Note amendments to this section appropriate to a case where it is certified by the medical officer of health and another registered medical practioner that in their opinion it is necessary in the interests of the person concerned to remove him without delay, contained in National Assistance (Amendment) Act 1951, post.
4. "Hospital" has the meaning assigned to it by s 79 of the National Health Service Act 1946 (s 64) (now s 128 of the National Health Service Act 1977)—that is, any institution for the reception and treatment of persons suffering from illness, any maternity home, and any institution for the reception and treatment of persons during convalescence or persons requiring medical rehabilitation, and includes clinics, dispensaries and out-patient departments, maintained in connection with any such institution or home as aforesaid.
5. That is, seven perfect intervening days (*Mitchell v Foster* (1840) 12 Ad & El 472).
6. See note 6 to s 43, ante.
7. That is, the liability of a man to maintain his wife and his children, and of a woman to maintain her husband and her children (see s 42, ante).
8. For procedure for recovery, see s 43, ante.
9. See the Public Health (Control of Disease) Act 1984, ss 37, 38 in this PART: title PUBLIC HEALTH, ante.

8–28566 48. Duty of councils to provide temporary protection for property of persons admitted to hospitals, etc. (1) Where a person—

(*a*) is admitted as a patient to any hospital[1], or

(*b*) is admitted to accommodation provided under Part III[2] of this Act, or

(*c*) is removed to any other place under an order made under subsection (3) of the last foregoing section;

and it appears to the council that there is danger of loss of, or damage to, any movable property of his by reason of his temporary or permanent inability to protect or deal with the property, and that no other suitable arrangements have been or are being made for the purposes of this subsection, it shall be the duty of the council to take reasonable steps to prevent or mitigate the loss or damage.

(2) For the purposes of discharging the said duty the council shall have power at all reasonable times to enter[3] any premises which immediately before the person was admitted or removed as aforesaid were his place of residence or usual place of residence, and to dealt with any movable property of his in any way which is reasonably necessary to prevent or mitigate loss thereof or damage thereto.

(3) A council may recover[4] from a person admitted or removed as aforesaid, or from any person who for the purposes of this Act is[5] liable to maintain him, any reasonable expenses incurred by the council in relation to him under the foregoing provisions of this section.

(4) In this section the expression "council" means in relation to any property the council which is the local authority for the purposes of the Local Authority Social Services Act 1970 and in the area of which the property is for the time being situated.

[National Assistance Act 1948, s 48, as amended by the Local Government Act 1972, Sch 23.]

1. For definition of "hospital" see note 4 to s 47, ante.
2. See note 6 to s 43, ante.
3. The person proposing to exercise the power to enter should have with him a written authority to do so (s 55(1)): for penalty for obstructing such a person, see s 55(2) post.
4. The sum is recoverable summarily as a civil debt, see s 56, post.
5. That is, the liability of a man to maintain his wife and his children, and of a woman to maintain her husband and her children (see s 42, ante).

8–28567 51. Failure to maintain. (1) Where a person persistently refuses or neglects to maintain himself or any person who he is liable to maintain for the purposes of this act[1], and in consequences of his refusal or neglect, accommodation under Part III[2] thereof is provided for himself or any other person, he shall be guilty of an offence.

(2) For the purposes of this section, a person shall not be deemed to refuse or neglect to maintain himself or any other person by reason only of anything done or omitted in furtherance of a trade dispute[3].

(3) A person guilty of an offence under this section shall be liable on summary conviction[4]—

(*a*) where the accommodation (*was*)[5] provided for him, to imprisonment for a term not exceeding **three months***[6];

(*b*) in any other case, to a fine not exceeding **level 3** on the standard scale or to imprisonment for a term not exceeding **three months*** or to **both** such imprisonment and such fine.

[National Assistance Act 1948, s 51, as amended by Ministry of Social Security Act 1966, 8th Sch and the Criminal Justice Act 1982, ss 38 and 46.]

***"51 weeks" substituted by the Criminal Justice Act 2003, Sch 26, from a date to be appointed.**

1. That is, the liability of a man to maintain his wife and his children, and of a woman to maintain her husband and her children (see s 42, ante).
2. See note 6 to s 43, ante.
3. "Trade dispute" has the same meaning as in (what is now) s 27(3)(*b*) of the Social Security Contributions and Benefits Act 1992; that is, any dispute between employers and employees or between employees and employees which is connected with the employment or non-employment or the terms of employment or the conditions of employment of any persons, whether employees in the employment of the employer with whom the dispute arises or not (s 64(1) amended by Sch 2 of the Social Security (Consequential Provisions) Act 1992).
4. While proceedings must be commenced within six months of the last refusal or neglect to maintain, evidence of earlier refusals or neglect may be given to prove persistence, cf *Donkin v Donkin* [1933] P 17, [1932] All ER Rep 582, 96 JP 472.
5. In the course of amendment this word was omitted.
6. A fine not exceeding **level 3** on the standard scale may be imposed (Magistrates' Courts Act 1980, s 34(3) in PART I: MAGISTRATES' COURTS, PROCEDURE, ante.

8–28568 52. False statements. (1) If any person—

(*a*) for the purpose of obtaining, either for himself or for another person, any benefit under Part III of this Act; or

(*b*) for the purpose of avoiding or reducing any liability under this Act,

makes any statement or representation which he knows to be false, he shall be guilty of an offence and liable on summary conviction to a fine not exceeding **level 3** on the standard scale or to imprisonment for a term not exceeding **three months*** or to both such imprisonment and such fine.

(2) Notwithstanding anything in any enactment, proceedings for an offence under this section may be begun at any time within three months from the date on which evidence sufficient in the opinion of the local authority concerned to justify a prosecution for an offence comes to the knowledge

of the local authority, or within twelve months from the commission of the offence, whichever period is the longer.

(3) For the purposes of the last foregoing subsection, a certificate of the local authority as to the date on which such evidence as aforesaid came to the knowledge of the local authority, as the case may be, shall be conclusive[1] proof thereof.

[National Assistance Act 1948, s 52, as amended by Ministry of Social Security Act 1966, 8th Sch and the Criminal Justice Act 1982, ss 38 and 46.]

***"51 weeks" substituted by the Criminal Justice Act 2003, Sch 26, from a date to be appointed.**

1. Therefore, where a proper certificate is produced, it will not be for the court to investigate, or to admit evidence casting doubt upon, its accuracy.

8–28569 55. Provisions as to entry and inspection. (1) A person who proposes to exercise any power of entry or inspection[1] conferred by this Act shall if so required produce some duly authenticated document showing his authority to exercise the power.

(2) Any person who obstructs the exercise of any such power as aforesaid shall be guilty of an offence and liable on summary conviction to a fine not exceeding **level 4** on the standard scale.

[National Assistance Act 1948, s 55, as amended by Criminal Law Act 1977, Sch 6 and the Criminal Justice Act 1982, ss 38 and 46.]

---

1. See s 26(5), premises maintained by voluntary organisations; s 39, ante, disabled persons' and old persons' homes; s 48(2), ante, to provide protection for property of persons admitted to hospitals, etc.

8–28570 56. Legal proceedings. (1) Without prejudice to any other method of recovery, any sum due under this Act[1] to a local authority (other than a sum due under an order made under section 43 of this Act) shall be recoverable summarily as a civil debt.

(2) Notwithstanding anything in any Act, proceedings for the recovery of any sum in the manner provided by the last foregoing subsection may be brought at any time within three years after the sum became due.

(3) Offences under this Act, other than offences under s 47(11) of this Act, may be prosecuted by any council which is a local authority for the purposes of the Local Authority Social Services Act 1970 and offences under s 47(11) of this Act may be prosecuted by the councils referred to in s. 47(12) of this Act.

(4) . . .

[National Assistance Act 1948, s 56, as amended by Ministry of Social Security Act 1966, 8th Sch, the Local Government Act 1972, Sch 23 and the Family Law Reform Act 1987, Sch 2.]

---

1. See eg s 22, ante, recovery of cost of accommodation provided by local authority; s 45, ante, recovery in cases of misrepresentation or non-disclosure; s 48, ante, recovery of reasonable expenses of providing protection for property of persons admitted to hospitals, etc. Recovery of cost of accommodation under Pt III of the Act from persons liable for maintenance (s 43, ante), is now enforceable as a magistrates' court maintenance order.

National Assistance (Amendment) Act 1951

(14 & 15 Geo 6 c 57)

8–28820 1. Amendments to section 47 of the National Assistance Act 1948. (1) An order under subsection (3) of section forty-seven of the National Assistance Act 1948, for the removal of any such person as is mentioned in subsection (1) of that section may be made without the notice required by subsection (7) of that section if it is certified by the medical officer of health[1] and another registered medical practitioner that in their opinion it is necessary in the interests of that person to remove him without delay.

(2) If in any such case it is shown by the applicant that the manager of any such hospital or place as is mentioned in the said subsection (3) agrees to accommodate therein the person in respect of whom the application is made, the proviso to that subsection (which requires that the manager of the premises to which a person is to be removed must be heard in the proceedings or receive notice of the application) shall not apply in relation to an order for the removal of that person to that hospital or place.

(3) Any such order as is authorised by this section may be made on the application either of the appropriate authority within the meaning of the said section forty-seven or, if the medical officer of health[1] is authorised by that authority to make such applications, by that officer, and may be made either by a court of summary jurisdiction having jurisdiction in the place where the premises are situated in which the person in respect of whom the application is made resides, or by a single justice having such jurisdiction; and the order may, if the court or justice thinks it necessary, be made *ex parte*.

(4) In relation to any such order as is authorised by this section the provision of the said section forty-seven shall have effect subject to the following modifications:

(*a*) in subsection (4) (which specifies the period for which a person may be detained pursuant to an order) for the words "three months" in the first place where those words occur, there shall be substituted the words "three weeks" and subsection (6) (which enables an application to be made for the revocation of an order) shall not apply:

(*b*) where the order is made by a single justice, any reference in subsections (4) and (5) to the court shall be construed as a reference to a court of summary jurisdiction having jurisdiction in the same place as that justice.

[National Assistance (Amendment) Act 1951, s 1.]

1. Now the "proper officer"; see footnote to the National Assistance Act 1948, s 47(2), ante.

Pneumoconiosis etc (Workers' Compensation) Act 1979

(1979 c 41)

8–29000 This Act makes provision for lump sum payments in respect of persons disabled by pneumoconiosis, byssinosis and diffuse mesothelioma. Knowingly making a false representation, or producing or furnishing or causing or knowingly allowing to be produced or furnished any document or information known to be false in a material particular; penalty on summary conviction a fine not exceeding **level 5** on the standard scale.

Health and Social Services and Social Security Adjudications Act 1983[1]

(1983 c 41)

PART VII[1]

CHARGES FOR LOCAL AUTHORITY SERVICES

8–29030 **17. Charges for local authority services in England and Wales..** (1) Subject to subsection (3) below, an authority providing a service to which this section applies may recover such charge (if any) for it as they consider reasonable.

(2) This section applies to services provided under the following enactments—

(*a*) section 29 of the National Assistance Act 1948 (welfare arrangements for blind, deaf, dumb and crippled persons etc);

(*b*) section 45(1) of the Health Services and Public Health Act 1968 (welfare of old people);

(*c*) Schedule 8 to the National Health Service Act 1977 (care of mothers and young children, prevention of illness and care and after-care and home help and laundry facilities);

(*d*) section 8 of the Residential Homes Act 1980 (meals and recreation for old people); and

(*e*) paragraph 1 of Part II of Schedule 9 to this Act other than the provision of services for which payment may be required under section 22 or 26 of the National Assistance Act 1948.

(*f*) section 2 of the Carers and Disabled Children Children Act 2000.

(3) If a person—

(*a*) avails himself of a service to which this section applies, and

(*b*) satisfies the authority providing the service that his means are insufficient for it to be reasonably practicable for him to pay for the service the amount which he would otherwise be obliged to pay for it,

the authority shall not require him to pay more for it than it appears to them that it is reasonably practicable for him to pay.

(4) Any charge under this section may, without prejudice to any other method of recovery, be recovered summarily[2] as a civil debt.

(5) This section has effect subject to any regulations under section 15 of the Community Care (Delayed Discharges etc) Act 2003 (power to require certain community care services and services for carers to be free of charge).

[Health and Social Services and Social Security Adjudications Act 1983, s 17, as amended by the National Health Service and Community Care Act 1990, Sch 9 and the Community Care (Delayed Discharges etc) Act 2003, s 17.]

1. Part VII contains 17–24.
2. See Magistrates' Courts Act 1980, s 58, in PART I: MAGISTRATES' COURTS, PROCEDURE, ante, for procedure to obtain order for payment of civil debt, and Magistrates' Courts Act 1980, s 96 for the enforcement of such order.

Social Security Act 1986

(1986 c 50)

8–29043 **54. Breach of regulations.** (1) Regulations under any of the benefit Acts may provide for contravention of, or failure to comply with, any provision contained in regulations made under that Act to be an offence under that Act and for the recovery, on summary conviction of any such offence, of penalties not exceeding—

(*a*) for any one offence, **level 3** on the standard scale; or
(*b*) for an offence of continuing any such contravention or failure after conviction, **£40 for each day** on which it is so continued.

(2) (*Repealed*).
[Social Security Act 1986, s 54 amended by the Social Security (Consequential Provisions) Act 1992, Sch 1.]

8–29045 56. Legal proceedings. (1) Any person authorised by the Secretary of State[1] in that behalf may conduct any proceedings under the benefit Acts before a magistrates' court although not a barrister or solicitor.

(2) Notwithstanding anything in any Act—

(*a*) proceedings for an offence under the benefit Acts may be begun[2] at any time within the period of three months from the date on which evidence, sufficient in the opinion of the Secretary of State to justify a prosecution for the offence, comes to his knowledge or within a period of twelve months from the commission of the offence, whichever period last expires;
(*b*) *Repealed.*

(3) For the purposes of subsection (2) above—

(*a*) a certificate purporting to be signed by or on behalf of the Secretary of State as to the date on which such evidence as is mentioned in paragraph (*a*) of that subsection came to his knowledge shall be conclusive evidence of that date;
(*b*) *Repealed.*

(4)–(5) *Repealed.*
[Social Security Act 1986, s 56, as amended by the Local Government Finance Act 1988, Sch 10 and the Social Security (Consequential Provisions) Act 1992, Sch 1.]

---

1. The authority to conduct proceedings is proved by the production of a copy of the original, certified under the Documentary Evidence Act 1868 (in PART II: EVIDENCE, ante) which Act is applied to any documents issued by the Secretary of State: see Secretary of State for Social Services Order 1968, art 5(3). An officer who did not lay the information may conduct the prosecution (*R v Northumberland Justices, ex p Thompson* (1923) 87 JP 95).
2. Proceedings begin when an information is laid or a complaint made (*Brooks v Bagshaw* [1904] 2 KB 798, 68 JP 514).

8–29046 57. Offences by bodies corporate. (1) Where an offence under any of the benefit Acts which has been committed by a body corporate is proved to have been committed with the consent or connivance of, or to be attributable to any neglect on the part of, a director[1], manager, secretary or other similar officer of the body corporate, or any person who was purporting to act in any such capacity, he, as well as the body corporate, shall be guilty of that offence and be liable to be proceeded against accordingly.

(2) Where the affairs of a body corporate are managed by its members, subsection (1) above applies in relation to the acts and defaults of a member in connection with his functions of management as if he were a director of the body corporate.
[Social Security Act 1986, s 57.]

---

1. This means a director properly appointed; in the case of a limited company, in accordance with the Companies Acts. It is not sufficient merely that he acted as a director (*Dean v Hiesler* [1942] 2 All ER 340, 106 JP 282). The director or other officer is liable to the same maximum penalty as the body corporate.

National Health Service and Community Care Act 1990

(1990 c 19)

8–29049 47. Assessment of needs for community care service[1]. (1) Subject to subsections (5) and (6) below, where it appears to a local authority that any person for whom they may provide or arrange for the provision of community care services may be in need of any such services, the authority—

(*a*) shall carry out an assessment of his needs for those services; and
(*b*) having regard to the results of that assessment, shall then decide whether his needs call for the provision by them of any such services.

(2)–(7) *Procedure on assessment.*
[National Health Service and Community Care Act 1990, s 47, as amended by the Health Authorities Act 1995, Sch 1.]

---

1. Where an authority have decided under s 47 of this Act that the needs of a person call for the provision of any community care services, and the person is of a description specified by regulations made by the Secretary of State, the authority may, if the person consents, make to him, in respect of his securing the provision of any of the services for which

they have decided his needs call, a payment of such amount as they think fit (Community Care (Direct Payments) Act 1996, s 1 (when in force)).

8–29050 **48. Inspection of premises used for provision of community care services.** (1) Any person authorised by the Secretary of State may at any reasonable time enter and inspect any premises (other than premises in respect of which any person is registered under Part II of the Care Standards Act 2000) in which community care services are or are proposed to be provided by a local authority, whether directly or under arrangements made with another person.

(2) Any person inspecting any premises under this section may—

(*a*) make such examination into the state and management of the premises and the facilities and services provided therein as he thinks fit;

(*b*) inspect any records (in whatever form they are held) relating to the premises, or any person for whom community care services have been or are to be provided there; and

(*c*) require the owner of, or any person employed in, the premises to furnish him with such information as he may request.

(3) Any person exercising the power to inspect records conferred by subsection (2)(*b*) above—

(*a*) shall be entitled at any reasonable time to have access to, and inspect and check the operation of, any computer and any associated apparatus or material which is or has been in use in connection with the records in question; and

(*b*) may require—

(i) the person by whom or on whose behalf the computer is or has been so used; or

(ii) any person having charge of or otherwise concerned with the operation of the computer, apparatus or material,

to give him such reasonable assistance as he may require.

(4) Any person inspecting any premises under this section—

(*a*) may interview any person residing there in private—

(i) for the purpose of investigating any complaint as to those premises or the community care services provided there, or

(ii) if he has reason to believe that the community care services being provided there for that person are not satisfactory; and

(*b*) may examine any such person in private.

(5) No person may—

(*a*) exercise the power conferred by subsection (2)(*b*) above so as to inspect medical records; or

(*b*) exercise the power conferred by subsection (4)(*b*) above,

unless he is a registered medical practitioner and, in the case of the power conferred by subsection (2)(*b*) above, the records relate to medical treatment given at the premises in question.

(6) Any person exercising the power of entry under subsection (1) above shall, if so required, produce some duly authenticated documented showing his authority to do so.

(7) Any person who intentionally obstructs another in the exercise of that power shall be guilty of an offence and liable on summary conviction to a fine not exceeding **level 3** on the standard scale.

(8) In this section "local authority" and "community care services" have the same meanings as in section 46 above.

[National Health Service and Community Care Act 1990, s 48, as amended by the Care Standards Act 2000, s 116.]

Social Security Contributions and Benefits Act 1992[1]

(1992 c 4)

8–29060 Part I (ss 1–19A) provides for contributions by earners, employers and others to funds for paying social security benefits and payments towards the National Health Service. There are six classes of contributions—

(*a*) Class 1, earnings-related, being—

(i) primary Class 1 contributions from employed earners; and

(ii) secondary Class 1 contributions from employers and other persons paying earnings;

(*b*) Class 1A, payable in respect of cars made available for private use and car fuel by persons liable to pay secondary Class 1 contributions and certain other persons;

(*bb*) Class 1B, payable under section 10A by persons who are accountable to the Inland Revenue in respect of income tax on emoluments in accordance with PAYE settlement agreement;

(*c*) Class 2, flat-rate, payable weekly by self-employed earners;

(*d*) Class 3, payable by earners and others voluntarily with a view to providing entitlement to benefit, or making up entitlement; and (*e*) Class 4, payable in respect of the profits or gains of a trade, profession or vocation, in respect of equivalent earnings.

8–29061 The Act defines limits and liability. Part II (ss 20–62) describes contributory benefits, being unemployment benefit, incapacity benefit maternity allowance, benefits for widows and widowers, retirement pensions, and child's special allowance.

8–29062 Part III (ss 63–79) describes non-contributory benefits, being attendance allowance, severe disablement allowance, invalid care allowance, disability living allowance, guardians allowance, and benefits for the aged.

8–29063 Part IV (ss 80–93) provides for benefit increases for child and adult dependants.

8–29064 Part V (ss 94–111) provides for benefit for industrial injuries.

8–29065 Part VII (ss 123–137) sets out income-related benefits, being income support, working families' tax credit, disabled person's tax credit, housing benefit, and community charge benefits.

8–29066 Part VIII (ss 138–140) governs the operation of the social fund.

8–29067 Part IX (ss 141–147) is concerned with child benefit, Part X (ss 148–150) with the Christmas bonus for pensioners, Part XI (ss 151–163) with statutory sick pay, and Part XII (ss 164–171) with statutory maternity pay.

S 175 enables the making of subordinate legislation under the Act.

---

1. This Act is part of a consolidation measure: the other two Acts are the Social Security Administration Act 1992 (post) and the Social Security (Consequential Provisions) Act 1992 (s 6) which provides for continuity of the law, repeals, and transitional, provision and savings.

Social Security Administration Act 1992

(1992 c 5)

Part III[1]

Overpayments and Adjustments of Benefit[2]

8–29070 **78. Recovery of social fund awards.** (1)–(5) *Recovery*.

(6) For the purposes of this section[3]—

(*a*) a man shall be liable to maintain his wife or civil partner and any children of whom he is the father;

(*b*) a woman shall be liable to maintain her husband or civil partner and any children of whom she is the mother;

(*c*) a person shall be liable to maintain another person throughout any period in respect of which the first-mentioned person has, on or after 23rd May 1980 (the date of the passing of the Social Security Act 1980) and either alone or jointly with a further person, given an undertaking in writing in pursuance of immigration rules within the meaning of the Immigration Act 1971 to be responsible for the maintenance and accommodation of the other person; and

(*d*) "child" includes a person who has attained the age of 16 but not the age of 19 and in respect of whom either parent, or some person acting in the place of either parent, is receiving income support or an income-based jobseeker's allowance.

(7) Any reference in subsection (6) above to children of whom the man or the woman is the father or the mother shall be construed in accordance with section 1 of the Family Law Reform Act 1987.

(8) Subsection (7) above does not apply in Scotland, and in the application of subsection (6) above to Scotland any reference to children of whom the man or the woman is the father or the mother shall be construed as a reference to any such children whether or not their parents have ever been married to one another.

(9) A document bearing a certificate which—

(*a*) is signed by a person authorised in that behalf by the Secretary of State; and

(*b*) states that the document apart from the certificate is, or is a copy of, such an undertaking as is mentioned in subsection (6)(*c*) above,

shall be conclusive of the undertaking in question for the purposes of this section; and a certificate purporting to be so signed shall be deemed to be so signed until the contrary is proved.

[Social Security Administration Act 1992, s 78 amended by the Jobseekers Act 1995, s 32 and Sch 2 and the Civil Partnership Act 2004, Sch 24.]

1. Part III contains ss 71–80.
2. Overpayment will usually be recovered by deduction from benefit, but other methods may sometimes be used.
3. Section 78(6)–(9) has effect for the purposes of Pt V, post, as well; see s 105, post.

PART V[1]
INCOME SUPPORT AND THE DUTY TO MAINTAIN

8–29080 **105. Failure to maintain—general.** (1) If—

(*a*) any person persistently refuses or neglects to maintain himself or any person whom he is liable to maintain; and

(*b*) in consequence of his refusal or neglect income support or an income-based jobseeker's allowance is paid to or in respect of him or such a person,

he shall be guilty of an offence and liable on summary conviction[2] to imprisonment for a term not exceeding **3 months** or to a fine of an amount not exceeding **level 4** on the standard scale or to **both**.

(2) For the purposes of subsection (1) above a person shall not be taken to refuse or neglect to maintain himself or any other person by reason only of anything done or omitted in furtherance of a trade dispute.

(3) Subject to subsection (4) below, subsections (6) to (9) of section 78 above[3] shall have effect for the purposes of this Part of this Act as they have effect for the purposes of that section.

(4) For the purposes of this section, in its application to an income-based jobseekers' allowance, a person is liable to maintain another if that other person is his or her spouse or civil partner.

[Social Security Administration Act 1992, s 105, as amended by the Jobseekers Act 1995, Sch 2 and the Civil Partnership Act 2004, Sch 24.]

1. Part V contains ss 105–109.
2. For legal proceedings see s 116, post.
3. Liability to maintain.

8–29081 **106. Recovery of expenditure on benefit from person liable for maintenance.** (1) Subject to the following provisions of this section, if income support is claimed by or in respect of a person whom another person is liable to maintain[1] or paid to or in respect of such a person, the Secretary of State may make a complaint[2] against the liable person to a magistrates' court for an order under this section.

(2) On the hearing of a complaint under this section the court shall have regard to all the circumstances[3] and, in particular, to the income of the liable person, and may order him to pay such sum, weekly or otherwise, as it may consider appropriate[4], except that in a case falling within section 78(6)(*c*) above that sum shall not include any amount which is not attributable to income support (whether paid before or after the making of the order).

(3) In determining whether to order any payments to be made in respect of income support for any period before the complaint was made, or the amount of any such payments, the court shall disregard any amount by which the liable person's income exceeds the income which was his during that period.

(4) Any payments ordered to be made under this section shall be made—

(*a*) to the Secretary of State in so far as they are attributable to any income support (whether paid before or after the making of the order);

(*b*) to the person claiming income support or (if different) the dependant; or

(*c*) to such other person as appears to the court expedient in the interests of the dependant.

(5) An order under this section shall be enforceable as a magistrates' court maintenance order within the meaning of section 150(1) of the Magistrates' Courts Act 1980[5].

(6)–(7) *Scotland.*

[Social Security Administration Act 1992, s 106.]

1. See ss 78 and 105(3), ante.
2. For legal proceedings see s 116, post; see also Legal Aid Act 1988, Sch 2, this provision replaces s 24 of the Social Security Act 1986 which in turn replaced s 18 of the Supplementary Benefits Act 1976.
3. See also notes to s 43 of the National Assistance Act 1948, ante, and *Windas v Bell* (1981) 2 FLR 109 (conduct of parents and delay in bringing proceedings are relevant).
4. For costs, see Magistrates' Courts Act 1980, s 64 in PART I: MAGISTRATES' COURTS, PROCEDURE, ante. A divorce consent order for no maintenance will not prevent an order under this section (*Hulley v Thompson* [1981] 1 All ER 1128, [1981] 1 WLR 159).
5. See PART I: MAGISTRATES' COURTS, PROCEDURE, ante. For relevant provisions relating to the enforcement of such an order, see Magistrates' Courts Act 1980, ss 93–95 in PART I: MAGISTRATES' COURTS, ante: see also Maintenance Orders Act 1950, ss 4 and 16 in PART IV: FAMILY LAW for enforcement in Scotland and Northern Ireland. This will be a "maintenance order" within the meaning of the Maintenance Orders Act 1958. Guidance for the making of Orders against a member of HM Forces is given in Home Office Circulars 251/1970 and 61/1972.

8–29082 107. Recovery of expenditure on income support: additional amounts and transfer of orders. (1) In any case where—

(*a*) the claim for income support referred to in section 106(1) above is or was made by the parent of one or more children in respect of both himself and those children; and
(*b*) the other parent is liable to maintain those children but, by virtue of not being the claimant's husband or wife or civil partner, is not liable to maintain the claimant,

the sum which the court may order that other parent to pay under subsection (2) of that section may include an amount, determined in accordance with regulations, in respect of any income support paid to or for the claimant by virtue of such provisions as may be prescribed.

(2) Where the sum which a court orders a person to pay under section 106 above includes by virtue of subsection (1) above an amount (in this section referred to as a "personal allowance element") in respect of income support by virtue of paragraph 1(2) of Schedule 2 to the Income Support (General) Regulations 1987 (personal allowance for lone parent) the order shall separately identify the amount of the personal allowance element.

(3) In any case where—

(*a*) there is in force an order under subsection (2) of section 106 above made against a person ("the liable parent") who is the parent of one or more children, in respect of the other parent or the children; and
(*b*) payments under the order fall to be made to the Secretary of State by virtue of subsection (4)(*a*) of that section; and
(*c*) that other parent ("the dependent parent") ceases to claim income support,

the Secretary of State may, by giving notice in writing to the court which made the order and to the liable parent and the dependent parent, transfer to the dependent parent the right to receive the payments under the order, exclusive of any personal allowance element, and to exercise the relevant rights in relation to the order, except so far as relating to that element.

(4) Notice under subsection (3) above shall not be given (and if purportedly given, shall be of no effect) at a time when there is in force a maintenance order made against the liable parent—

(*a*) in favour of the dependent parent or one or more of the children; or
(*b*) in favour of some other person for the benefit of the dependent parent or one or more of the children;

and if such a maintenance order is made at any time after notice under that subsection has been given, the order under section 106(2) above shall cease to have effect.

(5) In any case where—

(*a*) notice is given to a magistrates' court under subsection (3) above,
(*b*) payments under the order are required to be made by any method of payment falling within section 59(6) of the Magistrates' Courts Act 1980 (standing order, etc), and
(*c*) a justices' clerk decides that payment by that method is no longer possible,

the clerk shall amend the order to provide that payments under the order shall be made by the liable parent to the designated officer for the court.

(6) Except as provided by subsections (8) and (12) below, where the Secretary of State gives notice under subsection (3) above, he shall cease to be entitled—

(*a*) to receive any payment under the order in respect of any personal allowance element; or
(*b*) to exercise the relevant rights, so far as relating to any such element,

notwithstanding that the dependent parent does not become entitled to receive any payment in respect of that element or to exercise the relevant rights so far as so relating.

(7) If, in a case where the Secretary of State gives notice under subsection (3) above, a payment under the order is or has been made to him wholly or partly in respect of the whole or any part of the period beginning with the day on which the transfer takes effect and ending with the day on which the notice under subsection (3) above is given to the liable parent, the Secretary of State shall—

(*a*) repay to or for the liable parent so much of the payment as is referable to any personal allowance element in respect of that period or, as the case may be, the part of it in question; and
(*b*) pay to or for the dependent parent so much of any remaining balance of the payment as is referable to that period or part;

and a payment under paragraph (*b*) above shall be taken to discharge, to that extent, the liability of the liable parent to the dependent parent under the order in respect of that period or part.

(8) If, in a case where the Secretary of State has given notice under subsection (3) above, the dependent parent makes a further claim for income support, then—

(*a*) the Secretary of State may, by giving a further notice in writing to the court which made the order and to the liable parent and the dependent parent, transfer back from the dependent parent to himself the right to receive the payments and to exercise the relevant rights; and (*b*) that transfer shall revive the Secretary of State's right to receive payment under the order in respect of any personal allowance element and to exercise the relevant rights so far as relating to any such element.

(9) Subject to subsections (10) and (11) below, in any case where—

(*a*) notice is given to a magistrates' court under subsection (8) above, and

(*b*) the method of payment under the order which subsists immediately before the day on which the transfer under subsection (8) above takes effect differs from the method of payment which subsisted immediately before the day on which the transfer under subsection (3) above (or, if there has been more than one such transfer, the last such transfer) took effect,

a justices' clerk shall amend the order by reinstating the method of payment under the order which subsisted immediately before the day on which the transfer under subsection (3) above (or, as the case may be, the last such transfer) took effect.

(10) The clerk shall not amend the order under subsection (9) above if the Secretary of State gives notice in writing to the clerk, on or before the day on which the notice under subsection (8) above is given, that the method of payment under the order which subsists immediately before the day on which the transfer under subsection (8) above takes effect is to continue.

(11) In any case where—

(*a*) notice is given to a magistrates' court under subsection (8) above,

(*b*) the method of payment under the order which subsisted immediately before the day on which the transfer under subsection (3) above (or, if there has been more than one such transfer, the last such transfer) took effect was any method of payment falling within section 59(6) of the Magistrates' Courts Act 1980 (standing order, etc), and

(*c*) the clerk decides that payment by that method is no longer possible,

the clerk shall amend the order to provide that payments under the order shall be made by the liable parent to the designated officer for the court.

(12) A transfer under subsection (3) or (8) above does not transfer or otherwise affect the right of any person—

(*a*) to receive a payment which fell due to him at a time before the transfer took effect; or

(*b*) to exercise the relevant rights in relation to any such payment;

and, where notice is given under subsection (3), subsection (6) above does not deprive the Secretary of State of his right to receive such a payment in respect of any personal allowance element or to exercise the relevant rights in relation to such a payment.

(13) For the purposes of this section—

(*a*) a transfer under subsection (3) above takes effect on the day on which the dependent parent ceases to be in receipt of income support in consequence of the cessation referred to in paragraph (*c*) of that subsection, and

(*b*) a transfer under subsection (8) above takes effect on—

(i) the first day in respect of which the dependent parent receives income support after the transfer under subsection (3) above took effect, or

(ii) such later day as may be specified for the purpose in the notice under subsection (8),

irrespective of the day on which notice under the subsection in question is given.

(14) Any notice required to be given to the liable parent under subsection (3) or (8) above shall be taken to have been given if it has been sent to his last known address.

(15) In this section—

"child" means a person under the age of 16, notwithstanding section 78(6)(*d*) above;

"court" (where it occurs other than in the expression "magistrates' court") means in England and Wales a magistrates' court, and in Scotland the sheriff;

"maintenance order"—

(*a*) in England and Wales, means—

(i) any order for the making of periodical payments or for the payment of a lump sum which is, or has at any time been, a maintenance order within the meaning of the Attachment of Earnings Act 1971;

(ii) any order under Part III of the Matrimonial and Family Proceedings Act 1984 (overseas divorce) for the making of periodical payments or for the payment of a lump sum;

(iii) any order under Schedule 7 to the Civil Partnership Act 2004 for the making of periodical payments or for the payment of a lump sum;

(*b*) *Scotland*,

"the relevant rights", in relation to an order under section 106(2) above, means the right to bring any proceedings, take any steps or do any other thing under or in relation to the order which the Secretary of State could have brought, taken or done apart from any transfer under this section.

[Social Security Administration Act 1992, s 107, as amended by the Access to Justice Act 1999, s 90, the Courts Act 2003, Sch 8 and the Civil Partnership Act 2004, Sch 24.]

8–29083 108. Reduction of expenditure on income support: certain maintenance orders to be enforceable by the Secretary of State. (1) This section applies where—

(*a*) a person ("the claimant") who is the parent of one or more children is in receipt of income support either in respect of those children or in respect of both himself and those children; and

(*b*) there is in force a maintenance order made against the other parent ("the liable person")—

(i) in favour of the claimant or one or more of the children, or

(ii) in favour of some other person for the benefit of the claimant or one or more of the children;

and in this section "the primary recipient" means the person in whose favour that maintenance order was made.

(2) If, in a case where this section applies, the liable person fails to comply with any of the terms of the maintenance order—

(*a*) the Secretary of State may bring any proceedings or take any other steps to enforce the order that could have been brought or taken by or on behalf of the primary recipient; and

(*b*) any court before which proceedings are brought by the Secretary of State by virtue of paragraph (*a*) above shall have the same powers in connection with those proceedings as it would have had if they had been brought by the primary recipient.

(3) The Secretary of State's powers under this section are exercisable at his discretion and whether or not the primary recipient or any other person consents to their exercise; but any sums recovered by virtue of this section shall be payable to or for the primary recipient, as if the proceedings or steps in question had been brought or taken by him or on his behalf.

(4) The powers conferred on the Secretary of State by subsection (2)(*a*) above include power—

(*a*) to apply for the registration of the maintenance order under—

(i) section 17 of the Maintenance Orders Act 1950;

(ii) section 2 of the Maintenance Orders Act 1958;

(iii) the Civil Jurisdiction and Judgments Act 1982; or

(iv) Council regulation (EC) No 44/2001 of 22nd December 2000 on jurisdiction and the recognition and enforncement of judgments in civil and commercial matters; and

(*b*) to make an application under section 2 of the Maintenance Orders (Reciprocal Enforcement) Act 1972 (application for enforcement in reciprocating country).

(5) Where this section applies, the prescribed person shall in prescribed circumstances give the Secretary of State notice of any application—

(*a*) to alter, vary, suspend, discharge, revoke, revive or enforce the maintenance order in question; or

(*b*) to remit arrears under that maintenance order;

and the Secretary of State shall be entitled to appear and be heard on the application.

(6) Where, by virtue of this section, the Secretary of State commences any proceedings to enforce a maintenance order, he shall, in relation to those proceedings, be treated for the purposes of any enactment or instrument relating to maintenance orders as if he were a person entitled to payment under the maintenance order in question (but shall not thereby become entitled to any such payment).

(7) *Duty to notify Legal Services Commission.*

(8) In this section "maintenance order" has the same meaning as it has in section 107 above but does not include any such order for the payment of a lump sum.

[Social Security Administration Act 1992, s 108, as amended by the Access to Justice Act 1999, Sch 4 and SI 2001/3929.]

PART VI
ENFORCEMENT[1]

8–29084 109A. Authorisations for investigators. (1) An individual who for the time being has the Secretary of State's authorisation for the purposes of this Part shall be entitled, for any one or more of the purposes mentioned in subsection (2) below, to exercise any of the powers which are conferred on an authorised officer by sections 109B and 109C below.

(2) Those purposes are—

(*a*) ascertaining in relation to any case whether a benefit is or was payable in that case in accordance with any provision of the relevant social security legislation;

(*b*) investigating the circumstances in which any accident, injury or disease which has given rise, or may give rise, to a claim for—

(i) industrial injuries benefit, or

(ii) any benefit under any provision of the relevant social security legislation,

occurred or may have occurred, or was or may have been received or contracted;

(*c*) ascertaining whether provisions of the relevant social security legislation are being, have been or are likely to be contravened (whether by particular persons or more generally);
(*d*) preventing, detecting and securing evidence of the commission (whether by particular persons or more generally) of benefit offences.

(3) An individual has the Secretary of State's authorisation for the purposes of this Part if, and only if, the Secretary of State has granted him an authorisation for those purposes and he is—

(*a*) an official of a Government department;
(*b*) an individual employed by an authority administering housing benefit or council tax benefit;
(*c*) an individual employed by an authority or joint committee that carries out functions relating to housing benefit or council tax benefit on behalf of the authority administering that benefit; or
(*d*) an individual employed by a person authorised by or on behalf of any such authority or joint committee as is mentioned in paragraph (*b*) or (*c*) above to carry out functions relating to housing benefit or council tax benefit for that authority or committee.

(4) An authorisation granted for the purposes of this Part to an individual of any of the descriptions mentioned in subsection (3) above—

(*a*) must be contained in a certificate provided to that individual as evidence of his entitlement to exercise powers conferred by this Part;
(*b*) may contain provision as to the period for which the authorisation is to have effect; and
(*c*) may restrict the powers exercisable by virtue of the authorisation so as to prohibit their exercise except for particular purposes, in particular circumstances or in relation to particular benefits or particular provisions of the relevant social security legislation.

(5) An authorisation granted under this section may be withdrawn at any time by the Secretary of State.

(6) Where the Secretary of State grants an authorisation for the purposes of this Part to an individual employed by a local authority, or to an individual employed by a person who carries out functions relating to housing benefit or council tax benefit on behalf of a local authority—

(*a*) the Secretary of State and the local authority shall enter into such arrangements (if any) as they consider appropriate with respect to the carrying out of functions conferred on that individual by or in connection with the authorisation granted to him; and
(*b*) the Secretary of State may make to the local authority such payments (if any) as he thinks fit in respect of the carrying out by that individual of any such functions.

(7) The matters on which a person may be authorised to consider and report to the Secretary of State under section 139A below shall be taken to include the carrying out by any such individual as is mentioned in subsection (3)(*b*) to (*d*) above of any functions conferred on that individual by virtue of any grant by the Secretary of State of an authorisation for the purposes of this Part.

(8) The powers conferred by sections 109B and 109C below shall be exercisable in relation to persons holding office under the Crown and persons in the service of the Crown, and in relation to premises owned or occupied by the Crown, as they are exercisable in relation to other persons and premises.

[Social Security Administration Act 1992, s 109A as substituted by the Child Support, Pensions and Social Security Act 2000, Sch 6.]

1. Part VI comprises ss 109A–121.

8–29085 109B. Power to require information[1]**.** (1) An authorised officer who has reasonable grounds for suspecting that a person—

(*a*) is a person falling within subsection (2) or (2A) below, and
(*b*) has or may have possession of or access to any information about any matter that is relevant for any one or more of the purposes mentioned in section 109A(2) above,

may, by written notice, require that person to provide all such information described in the notice as is information of which he has possession, or to which he has access, and which it is reasonable for the authorised officer to require for a purpose so mentioned.

(2) The persons who fall within this subsection are—

(*a*) any person who is or has been an employer or employee within the meaning of any provision made by or under the Contributions and Benefits Act;
(*b*) any person who is or has been a self-employed earner within the meaning of any such provision;
(*c*) any person who by virtue of any provision made by or under that Act falls, or has fallen, to be treated for the purposes of any such provision as a person within paragraph (*a*) or (*b*) above;
(*d*) any person who is carrying on, or has carried on, any business involving the supply of goods for sale to the ultimate consumers by individuals not carrying on retail businesses from retail premises;

(*e*) any person who is carrying on, or has carried on, any business involving the supply of goods or services by the use of work done or services performed by persons other than employees of his;

(*f*) any person who is carrying on, or has carried on, an agency or other business for the introduction or supply, to persons requiring them, of persons available to do work or to perform services;

(*g*) any local authority acting in their capacity as an authority responsible for the granting of any licence;

(*h*) any person who is or has been a trustee or manager of a personal or occupational pension scheme;

(*i*) any person who is or has been liable to make a compensation payment or a payment to the Secretary of State under section 6 of the Social Security (Recovery of Benefits) Act 1997 (payments in respect of recoverable benefits); and

(*j*) the servants and agents of any such person as is specified in any of paragraphs (*a*) to (*i*) above.

(2A) The persons who fall within this subsection are—

(*a*) any bank;

(*aa*) the Director of National Savings;

(*b*) any person carrying on a business the whole or a significant part of which consists in the provision of credit (whether secured or unsecured) to members of the public;

(*c*) any insurer;

(*d*) any credit reference agency (within the meaning given by section 145(8) of the Consumer Credit Act 1974 (c 39));

(*e*) any body the principal activity of which is to facilitate the exchange of information for the purpose of preventing or detecting fraud;

(*f*) any person carrying on a business the whole or a significant part of which consists in the provision to members of the public of a service for transferring money from place to place;

(*g*) any water undertaker or sewerage undertaker, Scottish Water or any local authority which is to collect charges by virtue of an order under section 37 of the Water Industry (Scotland) Act 2002 (asp 3);

(*h*) any person who—

(i) is the holder of a licence under section 7 of the Gas Act 1986 (c 44) to convey gas through pipes, or

(ii) is the holder of a licence under section 7A(1) of that Act to supply gas through pipes;

(*i*) any person who (within the meaning of the Electricity Act 1989 (c 29)) distributes or supplies electricity;

(*j*) any person who provides a telecommunications service;

(*k*) any person conducting any educational establishment or institution;

(*l*) any body the principal activity of which is to provide services in connection with admissions to educational establishments or institutions;

(*m*) the Student Loans Company;

(*n*) any servant or agent of any person mentioned in any of the preceding paragraphs.

(2B) Subject to the following provisions of this section, the powers conferred by this section on an authorised officer to require information from any person by virtue of his falling within subsection (2A) above shall be exercisable for the purpose only of obtaining information relating to a particular person identified (by name or description) by the officer.

(2C) An authorised officer shall not, in exercise of those powers, require any information from any person by virtue of his falling within subsection (2A) above unless it appears to that officer that there are reasonable grounds for believing that the identified person to whom it relates is—

(*a*) a person who has committed, is committing or intends to commit a benefit offence; or

(*b*) a person who (within the meaning of Part 7 of the Contributions and Benefits Act) is a member of the family of a person falling within paragraph (*a*) above.

(2D) Nothing in subsection (2B) or (2C) above shall prevent an authorised officer who is an official of a Government department and whose authorisation states that his authorisation applies for the purposes of this subsection from exercising the powers conferred by this section for obtaining from—

(*a*) a water undertaker or Scottish Water,

(*b*) any person who (within the meaning of the Gas Act 1986) supplies gas conveyed through pipes,

(*c*) any person who (within the meaning of the Electricity Act 1989) supplies electricity conveyed by distribution systems, or

(*d*) any servant or agent of a person mentioned in any of the preceding paragraphs,

any information which relates exclusively to whether and in what quantities water, gas or electricity are being or have been supplied to residential premises specified or described in the notice by which the information is required.

(2E) The powers conferred by this section shall not be exercisable for obtaining from any person providing a telecommunications service any information other than information which (within the meaning of section 21 of the Regulation of Investigatory Powers Act 2000 (c 23)) is communications data but not traffic data.

(2F) Nothing in subsection (2B) or (2C) above shall prevent an authorised officer from exercising the powers conferred by this section for requiring information, from a person who provides a telecommunications service, about the identity and postal address of a person identified by the authorised officer solely by reference to a telephone number or electronic address used in connection with the provision of such a service.

(3) The obligation of a person to provide information in accordance with a notice under this section shall be discharged only by the provision of that information, at such reasonable time and in such form as may be specified in the notice, to the authorised officer who—

(*a*) is identified by or in accordance with the terms of the notice; or

(*b*) has been identified, since the giving of the notice, by a further written notice given by the authorised officer who imposed the original requirement or another authorised officer.

(4) The power of an authorised officer under this section to require the provision of information shall include a power to require the production and delivery up and (if necessary) creation of, or of copies of or extracts from, any such documents containing the information as may be specified or described in the notice imposing the requirement.

(5) No one shall be required under this section to provide—

(*a*) any information that tends to incriminate either himself or, in the case of a person who is married or is a civil partner, his spouse or civil partner; or

(*b*) any information in respect of which a claim to legal professional privilege or, in Scotland, confidentiality as between client and professional legal adviser, would be successful in any proceedings;

and for the purposes of this subsection it is immaterial whether the information is in documentary form or not.

(6) Provision may be made by order—

(*a*) adding any person to the list of persons falling within subsection (2A) above;

(*b*) removing any person from the list of persons falling within that subsection;

(*c*) modifying that subsection for the purpose of taking account of any change to the name of any person for the time being falling within that subsection.

(7) In this section—

"bank" means—

(*a*) a person who has permission under Part IV of the Financial Services and Markets Act 2000 (c 8) to accept deposits;

(*b*) an EEA firm of the kind mentioned in paragraph 5(*b*) of Schedule 3 to that Act which has permission under paragraph 15 of that Schedule (as a result of qualifying for authorisation under paragraph 12 of that Schedule) to accept deposits or other repayable funds from the public; or

(*c*) a person who does not require permission under that Act to accept deposits, in the course of his business in the United Kingdom;

"credit" includes a cash loan or any form of financial accommodation, including the cashing of a cheque;

"insurer" means—

(*a*) a person who has permission under Part IV of the Financial Services and Markets Act 2000 to effect or carry out contracts of insurance; or

(*b*) an EEA firm of the kind mentioned in paragraph 5(*d*) of Schedule 3 to that Act, which has permission under paragraph 15 of that Schedule (as a result of qualifying for authorisation under paragraph 12 of that Schedule) to effect or carry out contracts of insurance;

"residential premises", in relation to a supply of water, gas or electricity, means any premises which—

(*a*) at the time of the supply were premises occupied wholly or partly for residential purposes, or

(*b*) are premises to which that supply was provided as if they were so occupied; and

"telecommunications service" has the same meaning as in the Regulation of Investigatory Powers Act 2000 (c 23).

(7A) The definitions of "bank" and "insurer" in subsection (7) must be read with—

(*a*) section 22 of the Financial Services and Markets Act 2000;

(*b*) any relevant order under that section; and

(*c*) Schedule 2 to that Act.

[Social Security Administration Act 1992, s 109B, as amended by the Social Security Fraud Act 2001, s 1, SI 2004/1822 and the Civil Partnership Act 2004, Sch 2.]

1. The Secretary of State is required by s 3 of the Social Security Fraud Act 2001 to issue a Code of Practice relating to the exercise of the powers that are exercisable by an authorized officer under this section in relation to the persons mentioned in sub-s (2A) and the powers conferred on an authorized officer by ss 109BA and 110AA.

8–29085A 109BA. Power of Secretary of State to require electronic access to information[1]**.**

(1) Subject to subsection (2) below, where it appears to the Secretary of State—

(*a*) that a person falling within section 109B(2A) keeps any electronic records,

(*b*) that the records contain or are likely, from time to time, to contain information about any matter that is relevant for any one or more of the purposes mentioned in section 109A(2) above, and

(*c*) that facilities exist under which electronic access to those records is being provided, or is capable of being provided, by that person to other persons,

the Secretary of State may require that person to enter into arrangements under which authorised officers are allowed such access to those records.

(2) An authorised officer—

(*a*) shall be entitled to obtain information in accordance with arrangements entered into under subsection (1) above only if his authorisation states that his authorisation applies for the purposes of that subsection; and

(*b*) shall not seek to obtain any information in accordance with any such arrangements other than information which relates to a particular person and could be the subject of a requirement under section 109B above.

(3) The matters that may be included in the arrangements that a person is required to enter into under subsection (1) above may include—

(*a*) requirements as to the electronic access to records that is to be made available to authorised officers;

(*b*) requirements as to the keeping of records of the use that is made of the arrangements;

(*c*) requirements restricting the disclosure of information about the use that is made of the arrangements; and

(*d*) such other incidental requirements as the Secretary of State considers appropriate in connection with allowing access to records to authorised officers.

(4) An authorised officer who is allowed access in accordance with any arrangements entered into under subsection (1) above shall be entitled to make copies of, and to take extracts from, any records containing information which he is entitled to require under section 109B.

[Social Security Administration Act 1992, s 109BA, as inserted by the Social Security Fraud Act 2001, Sch.]

1. See note to s 109B ante.

8–29086 109C. Powers of entry. (1) An authorised officer shall be entitled, at any reasonable time and either alone or accompanied by such other persons as he thinks fit, to enter any premises which—

(*a*) are liable to inspection under this section; and

(*b*) are premises to which it is reasonable for him to require entry in order to exercise the powers conferred by this section.

(2) An authorised officer who has entered any premises liable to inspection under this section may—

(*a*) make such an examination of those premises, and

(*b*) conduct any such inquiry there,

as appears to him appropriate for any one or more of the purposes mentioned in section 109A(2) above.

(3) An authorised officer who has entered any premises liable to inspection under this section may—

(*a*) question any person whom he finds there;

(*b*) require any person whom he finds there to do any one or more of the following—

(i) to provide him with such information,

(ii) to produce and deliver up and (if necessary) create such documents or such copies of, or extracts from, documents,

as he may reasonably require for any one or more of the purposes mentioned in section 109A(2) above; and

(*c*) take possession of and either remove or make his own copies of any such documents as appear to him to contain information that is relevant for any of those purposes.

(4) The premises liable to inspection under this section are any premises (including premises

consisting in the whole or a part of a dwelling house) which an authorised officer has reasonable grounds for suspecting are—

(*a*) premises which are a person's place of employment;
(*b*) premises from which a trade or business is being carried on or where documents relating to a trade or business are kept by the person carrying it on or by another person on his behalf;
(*c*) premises from which a personal or occupational pension scheme is being administered or where documents relating to the administration of such a scheme are kept by the person administering the scheme or by another person on his behalf;
(*d*) premises where a person who is the compensator in relation to any such accident, injury or disease as is referred to in section 109A(2)(*b*) above is to be found;
(*e*) premises where a person on whose behalf any such compensator has made, may have made or may make a compensation payment is to be found.

(5) An authorised officer applying for admission to any premises in accordance with this section shall, if required to do so, produce the certificate containing his authorisation for the purposes of this Part.

(6) Subsection (5) of section 109B applies for the purposes of this section as it applies for the purposes of that section.*

[Social Security Administration Act 1992, s 109C.]

***As inserted by the Child Support, Pensions and Social Security Act 2000, Sch 6 from a date to be appointed.**

8–29086A 110ZA. Class 1, 1A, 1B or 2 contributions: powers to call for documents etc. (1) Section 20 of the Taxes Management Act 1970 (power to call for documents etc) applies (with sections 20B and 20BB) in relation to a person's liability to pay relevant contributions as it applies in relation to a person's tax liability (but subject to the modifications provided by subsection (2)).

(2) Those sections apply as if—

(*a*) the references to the taxpayer, a taxpayer or a class of taxpayers were to the person, a person or a class of persons required to pay relevant contributions,
(*b*) the references to an inspector were to an officer of the Inland Revenue,
(*c*) the references to any provision of the Taxes Acts were to any provision of this Act or the Contributions and Benefits Act relating to relevant contributions,
(*d*) the references to the assessment or collection of tax were to the assessment of liability for, and payment of, relevant contributions,
(*e*) the reference to an appeal relating to tax were to an appeal relating to relevant contributions, and
(*f*) the reference to believing that tax has been, or may have been, lost to the Crown were to believing that the Crown has, or may have, incurred a loss.

(3) In this section "relevant contributions" means Class 1, Class 1A, Class 1B or Class 2 contributions.

[Social Security Administration Act 1992, s 110ZA, as inserted by the Social Security Contributions (Transfer of Functions, etc) Act 1999, Sch 5 and substituted by the National Insurance Contributions and Statutory Payments Act 2004, s 7.]

8–29087 110A. Authorisations by local authorities. (1) An individual who for the time being has the authorisation for the purposes of this Part of an authority administering housing benefit or council tax benefit ("a local authority authorisation") shall be entitled, for any one or more of the purposes mentioned in subsection (2) below, to exercise any of the powers which, subject to subsection (8) below, are conferred on an authorised officer by sections 109B and 109C above.

(2) Those purposes are—

(*a*) ascertaining in relation to any case whether housing benefit or council tax benefit is or was payable in that case;
(*b*) ascertaining whether provisions of the relevant social security legislation that relate to housing benefit or council tax benefit are being, have been or are likely to be contravened (whether by particular persons or more generally);
(*c*) preventing, detecting and securing evidence of the commission (whether by particular persons or more generally) of benefit offences relating to housing benefit or council tax benefit.

(3) An individual has the authorisation for the purposes of this Part of an authority administering housing benefit or council tax benefit if, and only if, that authority have granted him an authorisation for those purposes and he is—

(*a*) an individual employed by that authority;
(*b*) an individual employed by another authority or joint committee that carries out functions relating to housing benefit or council tax benefit on behalf of that authority;
(*c*) an individual employed by a person authorised by or on behalf of—

(i) the authority in question,

(ii) any such authority or joint committee as is mentioned in paragraph (*b*) above,

to carry out functions relating to housing benefit or council tax benefit for that authority or committee;

(*d*) an official of a Government department.

(4) Subsection (4) of section 109A above shall apply in relation to a local authority authorisation as it applies in relation to an authorisation under that section.

(5) A local authority authorisation may be withdrawn at any time by the authority that granted it or by the Secretary of State.

(6) The certificate or other instrument containing the grant or withdrawal by any local authority of any local authority authorisation must be issued under the hand of either—

(*a*) the officer designated under section 4 of the Local Government and Housing Act 1989 as the head of the authority's paid service; or

(*b*) the officer who is the authority's chief finance officer (within the meaning of section 5 of that Act).

(7) It shall be the duty of any authority with power to grant local authority authorisations to comply with any directions of the Secretary of State as to—

(*a*) whether or not such authorisations are to be granted by that authority;

(*b*) the period for which authorisations granted by that authority are to have effect;

(*c*) the number of persons who may be granted authorisations by that authority at any one time; and

(*d*) the restrictions to be contained by virtue of subsection (4) above in the authorisations granted by that authority for those purposes.

(8) The powers conferred by sections 109B and 109C above shall have effect in the case of an individual who is an authorised officer by virtue of this section as if those sections had effect—

(*a*) with the substitution for every reference to the purposes mentioned in section 109A(2) above of a reference to the purposes mentioned in subsection (2) above;

(*b*) with the substitution for every reference to the relevant social security legislation of a reference to so much of it as relates to housing benefit or council tax benefit; and

(*c*) with the omission of section 109B(2D).

(9) Nothing in this section conferring any power on an authorised officer in relation to housing benefit or council tax benefit shall require that power to be exercised only in relation to cases in which the authority administering the benefit is the authority by whom that officer's authorisation was granted.

[Social Security Administration Act 1992, s 110A, as inserted by the Child Support, Pensions and Social Security Act 2000, Sch 6 and amended by the Socila Security Fraud Act 2001, s 1.]

8–29089A 110AA. Power of local authority to require electronic access to information[1]. (1) Subject to subsection (2) below, where it appears to an authority administering housing benefit or council tax benefit—

(*a*) that a person falling within section 109B(2A) keeps any electronic records,

(*b*) that the records contain or are likely, from time to time, to contain information about any matter that is relevant for any one or more of the purposes mentioned in section 110A(2) above, and

(*c*) that facilities exist under which electronic access to those records is being provided, or is capable of being provided, by that person to other persons,

that authority may require that person to enter into arrangements under which authorised officers are allowed such access to those records.

(2) An authorised officer—

(*a*) shall be entitled to obtain information in accordance with arrangements entered into under subsection (1) above only if his authorisation states that his authorisation applies for the purposes of that subsection; and

(*b*) shall not seek to obtain any information in accordance with any such arrangements other than information which—

(i) relates to a particular person; and

(ii) could be the subject of any such requirement under section 109B above as may be imposed in exercise of the powers conferred by section 110A(8) above.

(3) The matters that may be included in the arrangements that a person is required to enter into under subsection (1) above may include—

(*a*) requirements as to the electronic access to records that is to be made available to authorised officers;

(*b*) requirements as to the keeping of records of the use that is made of the arrangements;

(*c*) requirements restricting the disclosure of information about the use that is made of the arrangements; and

(*d*) such other incidental requirements as the authority in question considers appropriate in connection with allowing access to records to authorised officers.

(4) An authorised officer who is allowed access in accordance with any arrangements entered into under subsection (1) above shall be entitled to make copies of, and to take extracts from, any records containing information which he is entitled to make the subject of a requirement such as is mentioned in subsection (2)(*b*) above.

(5) An authority administering housing benefit or council tax benefit shall not—

(*a*) require any person to enter into arrangements for allowing authorised officers to have electronic access to any records; or

(*b*) otherwise than in pursuance of a requirement under this section, enter into any arrangements with a person specified in section 109B(2A) above for allowing anyone acting on behalf of the authority for purposes connected with any benefit to have electronic access to any private information contained in any records,

except with the consent of the Secretary of State and subject to any conditions imposed by the Secretary of State by the provisions of the consent.

(6) A consent for the purposes of subsection (5) may be given in relation to a particular case, or in relation to any case that falls within a particular description of cases.

(7) In this section "private information", in relation to an authority administering housing benefit or council tax benefit, means any information held by a person who is not entitled to disclose it to that authority except in compliance with a requirement imposed by the authority in exercise of their statutory powers.

[Social Security Administration Act 1992, s 110AA, as inserted by the Social Security Fraud Act 2001, s 2.]

8–29090 111. Delay, obstruction etc of inspector. (1) If a person—

(*a*) intentionally delays or obstructs an authorised officer in the exercise of any power under this Act other than an Inland Revenue power; or

(*ab*) refuses or neglects to comply with any requirement under section 109BA or 110AA or with the requirements of any arrangements entered into in accordance with subsection (1) of that section, or

(*b*) refuses or neglects to answer any question or to furnish any information or to produce any document when required to do so[1] under this Act otherwise than in the exercise of an Inland Revenue power,

he shall be guilty of an offence and liable on summary conviction to a fine not exceeding **level 3** on the standard scale.

(2) Where a person is convicted of an offence under subsection (1)(*ab*) or (*b*) above and the refusal or neglect is continued by him after his conviction, he shall be guilty of a further offence and liable on summary conviction to a fine not exceeding £40 for each day on which it is continued.

(3) In subsection (1) "Inland Revenue power" means any power conferred on an officer of the Inland Revenue by virtue of section 110ZA above or by virtue of an authorisation granted under section 109A or 110A above.

(4) *Repealed.*

[Social Security Administration Act 1992, s 111 as amended by Social Security Contributions (Transfer of Functions, etc) Act 1999, Sch 5 and the Child Support, Pensions and Social Security Act 2000, Sch 6 and the Social Security Fraud Act 2001, Sch and the National Insurance Contributions and Statutory Payments Act 2004, Sch 1.]

1. Section 110 (not printed here) defines the powers of the inspector, the premises liable to inspection by him, and the general duty to furnish information and produce documents; no one is required to answer questions tending to incriminate himself or a spouse. Similar provision is made for inspectors to be appointed by authorities administering housing benefit and officers of the Inland Revenue (ss 110A, 110ZA, 110B).

2. This section shall not apply in any case where the exercise of the power, or the question, information or document, relates to tax credit: see the Tax Credits Act 1999, Sch 2, para 12.

8–29090A 111A. Dishonest representations for obtaining benefit etc[1]. (1) If a person dishonestly—

(*a*) makes a false statement or representation or;

(*b*) produces or furnishes, or causes or allows to be produced or furnished, any document or information which is false in a material particular;

(*c*) (*repealed*);

(*d*) (*repealed*),

with a view to obtaining any benefit or other payment or advantage under the relevant social security legislation (whether for himself or for some other person), he shall be guilty of an offence.

(1A) A person shall be guilty of an offence if—

(*a*) there has been a change of circumstances affecting any entitlement of his to any benefit or other payment or advantage under any provision of the relevant social security legislation;
(*b*) the change is not a change that is excluded by regulations from the changes that are required to be notified;
(*c*) he knows that the change affects an entitlement of his to such a benefit or other payment or advantage; and
(*d*) he dishonestly fails to give a prompt notification of that change in the prescribed manner to the prescribed person.

(1B) A person shall be guilty of an offence if—
(*a*) there has been a change of circumstances affecting any entitlement of another person to any benefit or other payment or advantage under any provision of the relevant social security legislation;
(*b*) the change is not a change that is excluded by regulations from the changes that are required to be notified;
(*c*) he knows that the change affects an entitlement of that other person to such a benefit or other payment or advantage; and
(*d*) he dishonestly causes or allows that other person to fail to give a prompt notification of that change in the prescribed manner to the prescribed person.

(1C) This subsection applies where—
(*a*) there has been a change of circumstances affecting any entitlement of a person ("the claimant") to any benefit or other payment or advantage under any provision of the relevant social security legislation;
(*b*) the benefit, payment or advantage is one in respect of which there is another person ("the recipient") who for the time being has a right to receive payments to which the claimant has, or (but for the arrangements under which they are payable to the recipient) would have, an entitlement; and
(*c*) the change is not a change that is excluded by regulations from the changes that are required to be notified.

(1D) In a case where subsection (1C) above applies, the recipient is guilty of an offence if—
(*a*) he knows that the change affects an entitlement of the claimant to a benefit or other payment or advantage under a provision of the relevant social security legislation;
(*b*) the entitlement is one in respect of which he has a right to receive payments to which the claimant has, or (but for the arrangements under which they are payable to the recipient) would have, an entitlement; and
(*c*) he dishonestly fails to give a prompt notification of that change in the prescribed manner to the prescribed person.

(1E) In a case where that subsection applies, a person other than the recipient is guilty of an offence if—
(*a*) he knows that the change affects an entitlement of the claimant to a benefit or other payment or advantage under a provision of the relevant social security legislation;
(*b*) the entitlement is one in respect of which the recipient has a right to receive payments to which the claimant has, or (but for the arrangements under which they are payable to the recipient) would have, an entitlement; and
(*c*) he dishonestly causes or allows the recipient to fail to give a prompt notification of that change in the prescribed manner to the prescribed person.

(1F) In any case where subsection (1C) above applies but the right of the recipient is confined to a right, by reason of his being a person to whom the claimant is required to make payments in respect of a dwelling, to receive payments of housing benefit—
(*a*) a person shall not be guilty of an offence under subsection (1D) or (1E) above unless the change is one relating to one or both of the following—
   (i) the claimant's occupation of that dwelling;
   (ii) the claimant's liability to make payments in respect of that dwelling;

but

(*b*) subsections (1D)(*a*) and (1E)(*a*) above shall each have effect as if after "knows" there were inserted "or could reasonably be expected to know".

(1G) For the purposes of subsections (1A) to (1E) above a notification of a change is prompt if, and only if, it is given as soon as reasonably practicable after the change occurs.
(2) (*Repealed*).
(3) A person guilty of an offence under this section shall be liable[1]—
(*a*) on summary conviction, to imprisonment for a term not exceeding **six months**, or to a fine not exceeding the **statutory maximum**, or to **both**; or

(*b*) on conviction on indictment, to imprisonment for a term not exceeding **seven years**, or to a **fine**, or to **both**.

(4) *Scotland.*

[Social Security Administration Act 1992, s 111A, as inserted by the Social Security Administration (Fraud) Act 1997, s 13, as amended by the Child Support, Pensions and Social Security Act 2000, Sch 6, the Child Support, Pensions and Social Security Act 2000, Sch 6 and the Social Security Fraud Act 2001, Schedule.]

1. The provisions of this section do not apply in any case where the benefit or other payment or advantage is or relates to, or the failure to notify relates to, tax credit (Tax Credits Act 1999, Sch 2).

2. For procedure in respect of this offence which is triable either way, see the Magistrates' Courts Act 1980, ss 17A-21, in PART I: MAGISTRATES' COURTS, PROCEDURE, ante.

8–29091 **112. False representations for obtaining benefit etc[1].** (1) If a person for the purpose of obtaining any benefit or other payment under the relevant social security legislation whether for himself or some other person, or for any other purpose connected with that legislation—

(*a*) makes a statement or representation which he knows to be false[2]; or

(*b*) produces or furnishes, or knowingly causes or knowingly allows to be produced or furnished, any document or information which he knows to be false in a material particular,

he shall be guilty of an offence[3].

(1A) A person shall be guilty of an offence if—

(*a*) there has been a change of circumstances affecting any entitlement of his to any benefit or other payment or advantage under any provision of the relevant social security legislation;

(*b*) the change is not a change that is excluded by regulations from the changes that are required to be notified;

(*c*) he knows that the change affects an entitlement of his to such a benefit or other payment or advantage; and

(*d*) he fails to give a prompt notification of that change in the prescribed manner to the prescribed person.

(1B) A person is guilty of an offence under this section if—

(*a*) there has been a change of circumstances affecting any entitlement of another person to any benefit or other payment or advantage under any provision of the relevant social security legislation;

(*b*) the change is not a change that is excluded by regulations from the changes that are required to be notified;

(*c*) he knows that the change affects an entitlement of that other person to such a benefit or other payment or advantage; and

(*d*) he causes or allows that other person to fail to give a prompt notification of that change in the prescribed manner to the prescribed person.

(1C) In a case where subsection (1C) of section 111A above applies, the recipient is guilty of an offence if—

(*a*) he knows that the change affects an entitlement of the claimant to a benefit or other payment or advantage under a provision of the relevant social security legislation;

(*b*) the entitlement is one in respect of which he has a right to receive payments to which the claimant has, or (but for the arrangements under which they are payable to the recipient) would have, an entitlement; and

(*c*) he fails to give a prompt notification of that change in the prescribed manner to the prescribed person.

(1D) In a case where that subsection applies, a person other than the recipient is guilty of an offence if—

(*a*) he knows that the change affects an entitlement of the claimant to a benefit or other payment or advantage under a provision of the relevant social security legislation;

(*b*) the entitlement is one in respect of which the recipient has a right to receive payments to which the claimant has, or (but for the arrangements under which they are payable to the recipient) would have, an entitlement; and

(*c*) he causes or allows the recipient to fail to give a prompt notification of that change in the prescribed manner to the prescribed person.

(1E) Subsection (1F) of section 111A above applies in relation to subsections (1C) and (1D) above as it applies in relation to subsections (1D) and (1E) of that section.

(1F) For the purposes of subsections (1A) to (1D) above a notification of a change is prompt if, and only if, it is given as soon as reasonably practicable after the change occurs.

(2) A person guilty of an offence under this section shall be liable on summary conviction to a fine not exceeding **level 5** on the standard scale, or to imprisonment for a term not exceeding **3 months★**, or to **both**.

(3) *Repealed.*

[Social Security Administration Act 1992, s 112, as amended by the Social Security Administration (Fraud) Act 1997, s 14 and Sch 1, the Child Support, Pensions and Social Security Act 2000, Sch 6 and the Social Security Fraud Act 2001, s 16(3).]

***"51 weeks" substituted by the Criminal Justice Act 2003, Sch 26, from a date to be appointed.**

1. Para 13 of Sch 2 to the Tax Credit Act 1999 provides, inter alia, that ss 111A and 112 of the Social Security Administration Act 1992 shall not apply in any case where the benefit or other payment or advantage is or relates to, or the failure to notify relates to, tax credit. However, the "benefit" to which this refers is the benefit identified in s 112(1A), and the "failure to notify" identified in para 13 of Sch 2 to the 1999 Act refers to that in s 112(1A)(*d*). Consequently, where a person in receipt of housing benefit fails to notify promptly an increase in her tax credit which affects her entitlement to housing benefit, this can amount to an offence under s 112(1A): *Eyeson v Milton Keynes Council* [2005] All ER (D) 124 (Mar).

2. It is an offence under this section to obtain benefit by signing a postal draft on which the claimant represents he is entitled to the sum stated when he is not entitled to the whole sum even though the original award was not induced by any false statement or representation (*Tolfree v Florence* [1971] 1 All ER 125, [1971] 1 WLR 141). In cases decided under earlier legislation in similar terms it was established that the offence is committed when there is a false representation made which the person claiming benefit knows to be false; the proof of an intent to defraud is not necessary (*Barrass v Reeve* [1980] 3 All ER 705, [1981] 1 WLR 408; *Clear v Smith* [1981] 1 WLR 399). "Constructive knowledge" ie that the defendant neglected to make such inquiries as a reasonable and prudent person would make (as distinct from deliberately closing his eyes to an obvious means of knowledge) is insufficient to establish criminal liability for this offence (*Flintshire County Council v Reynolds* [2006] EWHC 195 (Admin), 170 JP 73).

3. The offence under s 112 does not require the prosecution to proved dishonesty (*Flintshire County Council v Reynolds* [2006] EWHC 195 (Admin), 170 JP 73). More serious offences may well be charged under the Theft Act 1968, s 15, post. As to sentencing, see comments in *R v Stewart* [1987] 2 All ER 383, [1987] 1 WLR 559, CA (noted in para **3–240**, ante).

8–29092 113. *Breach of Regulations.*

8–29092A 113A. *Statutory sick pay and statutory maternity pay: breach of regulations*

8–29092B 113B. *Statutory sick pay and statutory maternity pay: fraud and negligence*

8–29093 114. Offences relating to contributions. (1) Any person who is knowingly concerned in the fraudulent evasion of any contributions which he or any other person is liable to pay shall be guilty of an offence.

(2) A person guilty of an offence under this section shall be liable—

(*a*) on conviction on indictment, to imprisonment for a term not exceeding seven years or to a fine or to both;

(*b*) on summary conviction, to a fine not exceeding the statutory maximum.

[Social Security Administration Act 1992, s 114 as substituted by the Social Security Act 1998, s 61.]

8–29093A 114A

Repealed.

8–29094 115. Offences by bodies corporate. (1) Where an offence under this Act, or under the Jobseekers Act 1995, which has been committed by a body corporate is proved to have been committed with the consent or connivance of, or to be attributable to any neglect on the part of, a director[1], manager, secretary or other similar officer of the body corporate, or any person who was purporting to act in any such capacity, he, as well as the body corporate, shall be guilty of that offence and be liable to be proceeded against accordingly.

(2) Where the affairs of a body corporate are managed by its members, subsection (1) above applies in relation to the acts and defaults of a member in connection with his functions of management as if he were a director of the body corporate.

[Social Security Administration Act 1992, s 115, as amended by the Jobseekers Act 1995, Sch 2.]

---

1. This means a director properly appointed; in the case of a limited company, in accordance with the Companies Acts. It is not sufficient merely that he acted as a director (*Dean v Hiesler* [1942] 2 All ER 340, 106 JP 282). The director or other officer is liable to the same maximum penalty as the body corporate.

8–29094A 115A. *Penalty as alternative to prosecution.*

8–29094B 115B. *Penalty as alternative to prosecution: colluding employers etc*

Legal proceedings

8–29095 116. Legal proceedings. (1) Any person authorised by the Secretary of State[1] in that behalf may conduct any proceedings under this Act or under any provision of this Act other than section 114 or under any provision of the Jobseekers Act 1995 before a magistrates' court although not a barrister or solicitor.

(2) Notwithstanding anything in any Act—

(*a*) proceedings for an offence under this Act other than an offence relating to housing benefit or council tax benefit, or for an offence under the Jobseekers Act 1995, may be begun[2] at any time within the period of 3 months from the date on which evidence, sufficient in the opinion of the Secretary of State to justify a prosecution for the offence, comes to his knowledge or within a period of 12 months from the commission of the offence, whichever period last expires; and

(*b*) proceedings for an offence under this Act relating to housing benefit or council tax benefit may be begun at any time within the period of 3 months from the date on which evidence, sufficient in the opinion of the appropriate authority to justify a prosecution for the offence, comes to the authority's knowledge or within a period of 12 months from the commission of the offence, whichever period last expires.

(2A) Subsection (2) above shall not be taken to impose any restriction on the time when proceedings may be begun for an offence under section 111A above.

(3) For the purposes of subsection (2) above—

(*a*) a certificate purporting to be signed by or on behalf of the Secretary of State as to the date on which such evidence as is mentioned in paragraph (*a*) of that subsection came to his knowledge shall be conclusive evidence of that date; and

(*b*) a certificate of the appropriate authority as to the date on which such evidence as is mentioned in paragraph (*b*) of that subsection came to the authority's knowledge shall be conclusive evidence of that date.

(4) In subsections (2) and (3) above "the appropriate authority" means, in relation to an offence which relates to housing benefit and concerns any dwelling—

(*a*) if the offence relates to rate rebate, the authority who are the appropriate rating authority by virtue of section 134 below; and*

(*b*) if it relates to a rent rebate, the authority who are the appropriate housing authority by virtue of that subsection; and

(*c*) if it relates to rent allowance, the authority who are the appropriate local authority by virtue of that subsection.

(5) In subsections (2) and (3) above "the appropriate authority" means, in relation to an offence relating to council tax benefit, such authority as is prescribed in relation to the offence.

(5A) In relation to proceedings for an offence under section 114 above, the references in subsections (2)(*a*) and (3)(*a*) to the Secretary of State shall have effect as references to the Inland Revenue.

(6) Any proceedings in respect of any act or omission of an adjudication officer which, apart from this subsection, would fall to be brought against a person appointed by virtue of section 38(1)(*b*) above who is resident in Northern Ireland, other than proceedings for an offence, may instead be brought against the Chief Adjudication Officer; and, for the purposes of any proceedings so brought, the acts or omissions of the adjudication officer shall be treated as the acts or omissions of the Chief Adjudication Officer.**

(7) *Scotland.*

[Social Security Administration Act 1992, s 116, as amended by the Local Government Finance Act 1992, Sch 9, the Jobseekers Act 1995, Sch 2, the Social Security Administration (Fraud) Act 1997, Sch 1, the Social Security Contributions (Transfer of Functions, etc) Act 1999, Sch 1 and the Welfare Reform and Pensions Act 1999, Sch 11.]

***Sub-section (4A) repealed with savings by the Housing Act 1996, Sch 16. For savings, see SI 1997/618.**

****Sub-section 116(6) repealed by the Social Security Act 1998, Sch 7, when in force.**

1. The authority to conduct proceedings is proved by the production of a copy of the original, certified under the Documentary Evidence Act 1868 (in PART II: EVIDENCE, ante) which Act is applied to any documents issued by the Secretary of State: see Secretary of State for Social Services Order 1968, Art 5(3). An officer who did not lay the information may conduct the prosecution (*R v Northumberland Justices, ex p Thompson* (1923) 87 JP 95).

2. Proceedings begin when an information is laid or a complaint made (*Brooks v Bagshaw* [1904] 2 KB 798, 98 JP 514).

8–29096 117. Issues arising in proceedings. (1) This section applies to proceedings before a court—

(*a*) for an offence under this Act or the Jobseekers Act 1995; or

(*b*) involving any question as to the payment of contributions (other than a Class 4 contribution recoverable by the Inland Revenue); or

(*c*) for the recovery of any sums due to the Secretary of State, the Inland Revenue or the National Insurance Fund.

(2) A decision of the Secretary of State which—

(*a*) falls within Part II of Schedule 3 to the Social Security Act 1988 ("the 1998 Act"); and;

(*b*) relates to or affects an issue arising in the proceedings, shall be conclusive for the purposes of the proceedings.

(3) If—

(*a*) any such decision is necessary for the determination of the proceedings; and

(*b*) the decision of the Secretary of State has not been obtained or an application with respect to the decision has been made under section 9 or 10 of the 1998 Act;

the decision shall be referred to the Secretary of State to be made in accordance (subject to any necessary modification) with Chapter II of Part I of that Act.

(4) Subsection (2) above does not apply where, in relation to the decision—

(*a*) an appeal has been brought but not determined;

(*b*) an application for leave to appeal has been made but not determined;

(*c*) an appeal has not been brought (or, as the case may be, an application for leave to appeal has not been made) but the time for doing so has not yet expired; or

(*d*) an application has been made under section 9 or 10 of the 1998 Act.

(5) In a case falling within subsection (4) above the court shall adjourn the proceedings until such time as the final decision is known; and that decision shall be conclusive for the purposes of the proceedings*.

[Social Security Administration Act 1992, s 117, as amended by the Jobseekers Act 1995, Sch 2.]

***A new s 117 is substituted by the Social Security Act 1998, Sch 7 when in force. Until Chapter II of the Social Security Act 1998 is in force, s 117 has effect as if, in subsection (1) para (*b*) were omitted (SI 1999/978).**

1. The decision of the Inland Revenue is proved by the production of a copy of the original decision certified under the Documentary Evidence Act 1868, which Act is applied to any document issued by the Inland Revenue.

2. The court has no jurisdiction to determine questions as to insurability: they must be referred to the Inland Revenue (*Wood v Burke* (1927) 91 JP 144). This decision, under repealed enactments, is still good law: see *Ministry of Social Security v John Bryant & Co Ltd* [1968] 3 All ER 175, [1968] 1 WLR 1260, and also *Department of Health and Social Security v Walker Dean Walker Ltd* [1970] 2 QB 74, [1970] 1 All ER 757, where the question of whether National Insurance contributions had in fact been made by correctly affixing National Insurance stamps to employees' cards which were then delivered, duly stamped to the Department, was to be referred for the decision of the Inland Revenue. A form that may be used for the purpose of referring the question to the Inland Revenue is contained in *Oke's Magisterial Formulist*.

8–29096A 117A. Issues arising in proceedings: contributions, etc. (1) This section applies to proceedings before a court—

(*a*) for an offence under this Act or the Jobseekers Act 1995; or

(*b*) involving any question as to the payment of contributions (other than a Class 4 contribution recoverable in accordance with section 15 of the Contributions and Benefits Act); or

(*c*) for the recovery of any sums due to the Inland Revenue or the National Insurance Fund.

(2) A decision of an officer of the Inland Revenue which—

(*a*) falls within section 8(1) of the Social Security Contributions (Transfer of Functions, etc) Act 1999; and

(*b*) relates to or affects an issue arising in the proceedings,

shall be conclusive for the purposes of the proceedings.

(3) If—

(*a*) any such decision is necessary for the determination of the proceedings, and

(*b*) the decision of an officer of the Inland Revenue has not been obtained under section 8 of the Social Security Contributions (Transfer of Functions, etc) Act 1999,

the decision shall be referred to such an officer to be made in accordance (subject to any necessary modifications) with Part II of the Social Security Contributions (Transfer of Functions, etc) Act 1999.

(4) Subsection (2) above does not apply where, in relation to the decision—

(*a*) an appeal has been brought but not determined;

(*b*) an appeal has not been brought (or, as the case may be, an application for leave to appeal has not been made) but the time for doing so has not yet expired; or

(*c*) an application for variation of the decision has been made under regulations made under section 10 of the Social Security Contributions (Transfer of Functions, etc) Act 1999.

(5) In a case falling within subsection (4) above the court shall adjourn the proceedings until such time as the final decision is known; and that decision shall be conclusive for the purposes of the proceedings.

[Social Security Administration Act 1992, s 117A, as inserted by the Social Security Contributions (Transfer of Functions, etc) Act 1999, Sch 7.]

Unpaid contributions etc[1]

8–29097 118. Evidence of non-payment. (1) A certificate of an authorised officer that any amount by way of contributions, or by way of interest or penalty in respect of contributions, which a person is liable to pay to the Inland Revenue for any period has not been paid—

(*a*) to the officer; or

(*b*) to the best of his knowledge and belief, to any other person to whom it might lawfully be paid,

shall until the contrary is proved be sufficient evidence in any proceedings before any court that the sum mentioned in the certificate is unpaid and due.

(2) (*Repealed*).

(3) A document purporting to be such a certificate shall be deemed to be such a certificate until the contrary is proved.

(4) A statutory declaration by an officer of the Inland Revenue that the searches specified in the declaration for a record of the payment of a particular contribution have been made, and that a record of the payment of the contribution in question has not been found, is admissible in any proceedings for an offence as evidence of the facts stated in the declaration.

(5) Nothing in subsection (4) above makes a statutory declaration admissible as evidence in proceedings for an offence except in a case where, and to the extent to which, oral evidence to the like effect would have been admissible in those proceedings.

(6) Nothing in subsections (4) and (5) above makes a statutory declaration admissible as evidence in proceedings for an offence—

(*a*) unless a copy of it has, not less than 7 days before the hearing or trial, been served[3] on the person charged with the offence in any manner in which a summons or, in Scotland, a citation in a summary prosecution may be served; or

(*b*) if that person, not later than 3 days before the hearing or trial or within such further time as the court may in special circumstances allow, gives notice to the prosecutor requiring the attendance at the trial of the person by whom the declaration was made.

(7) In this section "authorised officer" means any officer of the Inland Revenue authorised by them for the purposes of this section.

[Social Security Administration Act 1992, s 118, as amended by the Social Security Contributions (Transfer of Functions, etc) Act 1999, Sch 5 and the Social Security Act 1998, S 63.]

1. Sections 118–120 and 121(1) to (4) apply to any secondary Class 1 contribution with which a surcharge under the National Insurance Surcharge Act 1976 is payable as if the surcharge were part of the contribution (National Insurance Surcharge Act 1976, s 1(3)).

2. See note to s 65 of the Taxes Management Act 1970, in this Part: Tax and Duties, post.

3. See Criminal Procedure Rules , Part 4, in PART I: MAGISTRATES' COURTS, PROCEDURE, ante.

8–29098 **119. Recovery of unpaid contributions on prosecution.** (1) Where—

(*a*) a person has been convicted of an offence under section 114(1) above of failing to pay a contribution at or within the time prescribed for the purpose; and

(*b*) the contribution remains unpaid at the date of the conviction,

he shall be liable to pay to the Inland Revenue a sum equal to the amount which he failed to pay.

(2) (*Repealed*).

[Social Security Administration Act 1992, s 119, as amended by the Social Security Act 1998, Sch 7 and the Social Security Contributions (Transfer of Functions, etc) Act 1999, Sch 1.]

8–29099 **120. Proof of previous offences.** (1) Subject to and in accordance with subsections (2) to (5) below, where a person is convicted of an offence mentioned in section 119(1) above, evidence may be given of any previous failure by him to pay contributions within the time prescribed for the purpose; and in those subsections "the conviction" and "the offence" mean respectively the conviction referred to in this subsection and the offence of which the person is convicted.

(2) Such evidence may be given only if notice of intention to give it is served with the summons or warrant or, in Scotland, the complaint on which the person appeared before the court which convicted him.

(3) If the offence is one of failure to pay a Class 1 contribution, evidence may be given of failure on his part to pay (whether or not in respect of the same person) such contributions or any Class 1A or Class 1B contributions or contributions equivalent premiums on the date of the offence, or during the 6 years preceding that date.

(4) If the offence is one of failure to pay Class 1A or Class 1B contribution, evidence may be given of failure on his part to pay (whether or not in respect of the same person or the same amount) such contributions, or any Class 1 contributions or contributions equivalent premiums, on the date of the offence, or during the 6 years preceding that date.

(4A) If the offence is one of failure to pay a Class 1B contribution, evidence may be given of failure on his part to pay such contributions, or any Class 1 or Class 1A contributions or contributions equivalent premiums, on the date of the offence, or during the 6 years preceding that date.

(5) If the offence—

(*a*) is one of failure to pay Class 2 contributions;

(*b*) (*Repealed*)

evidence may be given of his failure to pay such contributions during those 6 years.

(6) On proof of any matter of which evidence may be given under subsection (3), (4), (4A), or (5) above, the person convicted shall be liable to pay to the Inland Revenue a sum equal to the total

of all amounts which he is so proved to have failed to pay and which remain unpaid at the date of the conviction[1].

[Social Security Administration Act 1992, s 120, as amended by the Pensions Act 1995, Sch 5, the Social Security Act 1998, Sch 7, the Social Security Contributions (Transfer of Functions, etc) Act 1999, Sch 1 and the Child Support, Pensions and Social Security Act 2000, s 74.]

---

1. The sum ordered to be paid is recoverable as a penalty (see s 121(4), post). Where, following a conviction under s 14, evidence is given in accordance with s 120 of further arrears of contributions which the defendant has failed to pay, it is the duty of the magistrates to make an order for payment of those arrears. The words "shall be liable to pay" do not confer a discretion upon the magistrates. Once such an order has been made by the magistrates against a limited company, it is not appropriate for the prosecutor to be requested by the Court to commence civil proceedings against the company for the recovery of the arrears of contributions which have formed the subject of the order. This is because the Act gives a special remedy against the directors of a limited company which is a remedy which does not exist under the ordinary civil law. This additional remedy is available once the order has been made by the magistrates (*Morgan v Quality Tools Engineering (Stowbridge) Ltd* [1972] 1 All ER 744, [1972] 1 WLR 196, DC, followed in *R v Melksham Justices, ex p Williams* (1983) 147 JP 283). The justices have no power to mitigate any part of the contributions due (*Leach v Litchfield* [1960] 3 All ER 739, [1960] 1 WLR 1392, 125 JP 115); nor may they be remitted in accordance with s 85 of the Magistrates' Courts Act 1980 in PART I: MAGISTRATES' COURTS, PROCEDURE, ante.

8–29100 121. Unpaid contributions—supplementary. (1) Where in England and Wales a person charged with an offence mentioned in section 119(1) above is convicted of that offence in his absence under section 12(5) of the Magistrates' Courts Act 1980, then if—

(*a*) it is proved to the satisfaction of the court, on oath or in the manner prescribed by Criminal Procedure Rules, that notice under section 120(2) above has been duly served specifying the other contributions in respect of which the prosecutor intends to give evidence; and

(*b*) the designated officer for the court has received a statement in writing purporting to be made by the accused or by a solicitor acting on his behalf to the effect that if the accused is convicted in his absence of the offence charged he desires to admit failing to pay the other contributions so specified or any of them,

section 120 above shall have effect as if the evidence had been given and the failure so admitted had been proved, and the court shall proceed accordingly.

(2) In England and Wales, where a person is convicted of an offence mentioned in section 119(1) above and an order is made under section 12 of the Powers of Criminal Courts (Sentencing) Act 2000 placing the offender on probation or discharging him absolutely or conditionally, sections 119 and 120 above, and subsection (1) above, shall apply as if it were a conviction for all purposes.*

(3) *Scotland.*

(4) In England and Wales, any sum which a person is liable to pay under section 119 or 120 above or under subsection (1) above shall be recoverable from him as a penalty[1].

(5) Sums recovered by the Inland Revenue under the provisions mentioned in subsection (4) above, so far as representing contributions of any class, are to be treated for all purposes of the Contributions and Benefits Act and this Act (including in particular the application of section 162 below) as contributions of that class received by the Inland Revenue.

(6) Without prejudice to subsection (5) above, in so far as such sums represent primary Class 1 or Class 2 contributions, they are to be treated as contributions paid in respect of the person in respect of whom they were originally payable; and enactments relating to earnings factors shall apply accordingly.

[Social Security Administration Act 1992, s 121, as amended by the Magistrates' Courts (Procedure) Act 1998, s 4, the Social Security Act 1998, Sch 7, the Social Security Contributions (Transfer of Functions, etc) Act 1999, Sch 1, the Powers of Criminal Courts (Sentencing) Act 2000, Sch 9, the Access to Justice Act 1999, s 90 and the Courts Act 2004, Sch 8.]

---

1. This does not mean that the sum ordered to be paid is a penalty, but that it is recoverable in the same way as if it were a penalty; hence s 34(1) of the Magistrates' Courts Act 1980 (mitigation of penalties) does not apply and justices have no power to order an amount less than the full sum (*Leach v Litchfield*, ante). As to satisfaction and enforcement, see Magistrates' Courts Act 1980, Part III (s 75 et seq). Note that contributions due may not be remitted in accordance with s 85(1) of the Magistrates' Courts Act 1980 (Magistrates' Courts Act 1980, s 85(2), ante).

A sum so ordered to be paid is no longer enforceable as a civil debt (*R v Marlow (Bucks) Justices, ex p Schiller* [1957] 2 QB 508, [1957] 2 All ER 783, 121 JP 519) therefore a defendant who fails to comply with an order is liable to be committed to prison under the Magistrates' Courts Act 1980, Sch 4, ante in **PART I: MAGISTRATES' COURTS, PROCEDURE**.

8–29100A 121A. Recovery of contributions etc in England and Wales. (1) If—

(*a*) a person is served at any time with a copy of a certificate under section 118(1) above; and

(*b*) he neglects or refuses to pay the contributions, interest or penalty to which the certificate relates within 7 days of that time,

an authorised officer may distrain upon the goods and chattels of that person ("the person in default").

(2) For the purpose of levying any such distress, a justice of the peace, on being satisfied by information on oath that there is reasonable ground for believing that the conditions in subsection (1) above are fulfilled, may issue a warrant in writing authorising the authorised officer to enter in the

daytime, by force if necessary, any premises to which this section applies, calling on the assistance of any constable.

(3) Every such constable shall, when so required, assist the authorised officer in the execution of the warrant and in levying the distress in the premises.

(4) A warrant to enter premises by force shall be executed by the authorised officer, or under his direction and in his presence.

(5) A distress levied by the authorised officer shall be kept for five days, and any costs or charges shall be borne by the person in default.

(6) If the person in default does not pay the sum due, together with the costs and charges, the distress shall be appraised by one or more independent persons appointed by the authorised officer, and shall be sold by public auction by the authorised officer for payment of the sum due and all costs and charges.

(7) Any surplus arising from the distress, after the deduction of the costs and charges and of the sum due, shall be paid to the owner of the goods distrained.

(8) The Inland Revenue may by regulations make provision with respect to—

(*a*) the fees chargeable on or in connection with the levying of distress; and
(*b*) the costs and charges recoverable where distress has been levied.

(9) In this section "authorised officer" means an officer of the Inland Revenue authorised by them for the purposes of this section.

(10) The premises to which this section applies are premises where an authorised officer has reasonable grounds for believing that—

(*a*) any persons are employed; or
(*b*) a trade or business is being carried on;

but this section does not apply to a private dwelling-house unless an authorised officer has reasonable grounds for believing that a trade or business is being carried on from the dwelling-house and that the trade or business is not also being carried on from premises other than a dwelling-house.]

[Social Security Administration Act 1992, s 121A, as inserted by the Social Security Act 1998, s 63 and s 121e–f by the Social Security (Transfer of Functions, etc) Act 1999, Sch 6 and amended by the Social Security Contributions (Transfer of Functions, etc) Act 1999, Sch 5 and the National Insurance Contributions and Statutory Payments Act 2004, s 5.]

8–29100B 121B. Recovery of contributions etc in Scotland. (1) Where any contributions, interest or penalty remains unpaid 14 days after the service of a certificate under section 118(1) above, an authorised officer may apply to the sheriff for the grant of a summary warrant authorising the recovery of the amount remaining unpaid by any of the following diligences—

(*a*) an attachment;
(*b*) an earnings arrestment;
(*c*) an arrestment and action of forthcoming or sale.

(2) An application under subsection (1) above shall be accompanied by—

(*a*) a copy of the certificate served under section 118(1) above; and
(*b*) a certificate by the authorised officer—

(i) stating that the certificate was served on the person specified in the application;
(ii) stating that the amount specified in the certificate, or any part of that amount, remains unpaid at the date of the application.

(3) A summary warrant granted on an application under subsection (1) above shall be in such form as may be prescribed by Act of Sederunt.

(4) Subject to subsection (5) below and without prejudice to section 39 of the Debt Arrangement and Attachment (Scotland) Act 2002 (asp 17) (expenses of attachment), the sheriff officer's fees, together with the outlays necessarily incurred by him, in connection with the execution of a summary warrant granted on an application under subsection (1) above shall be chargeable against the debtor.

(5) No fee shall be chargeable by the sheriff officer against the debtor for collecting, and accounting to the Inland Revenue, for sums paid to him by the debtor in respect of the amount owing.

(6) In this section "authorised officer" means an officer of the Inland Revenue authorised by them for the purposes of this section.

[Social Security Administration Act 1992, s 121B, as inserted by the Social Security Act 1998, s 63 and amended by the Social Security Contributions (Transfer of Functions, etc) Act 1999, Sch 5, the Debt Arrangement and Attachment (Scotland) Act 2002, s 64 and the National Insurance Contributions and Statutory Payments Act 2004, s 5.]

8–29100C 121C. Liability of directors etc for company's contributions. (1) This section applies to contributions which a body corporate is liable to pay, where—

(*a*) the body corporate has failed to pay the contributions at or within the time prescribed for the purpose; and (*b*) the failure appears to the Inland Revenue to be attributable to fraud or neglect on the part of one or more individuals who, at the time of the fraud or neglect, were officers of the body corporate ("culpable officers").

(2) The Inland Revenue may issue and serve on any culpable officer a notice (a "personal liability notice")—

(*a*) specifying the amount of the contributions to which this section applies ("the specified amount");

(*b*) requiring the officer to pay to the Inland Revenue—

(i) a specified sum in respect of that amount; and

(ii) specified interest on that sum; and

(*c*) where that sum is given by paragraph (*b*) of subsection (3) below, specifying the proportion applied by the Inland Revenue for the purposes of that paragraph.

(3) The sum specified in the personal liability notice under subsection (2)(*b*)(I) above shall be—

(*a*) in a case where there is, in the opinion of the Inland Revenue, no other culpable officer, the whole of the specified amount; and

(*b*) in any other case, such proportion of the specified amount as, in the opinion of the Inland Revenue, the officer's culpability for the failure to pay that amount bears to that of all the culpable officers taken together.

(4) In assessing an officer's culpability for the purposes of subsection (3)(*b*) above, the Inland Revenue may have regard both to the gravity of the officer's fraud or neglect and to the consequences of it.

(5) The interest specified in the personal liability notice under subsection (2)(*b*) (ii) above shall be at the prescribed rate and shall run from the date on which the notice is issued.

(6) An officer who is served with a personal liability notice shall be liable to pay to the Inland Revenue the sum and the interest specified in the notice under subsection (2)(*b*) above.

(7) Where, after the issue of one or more personal liability notices, the amount of contributions to which this section applies is reduced by a payment made by the body corporate—

(*a*) the amount that each officer who has been served with such a notice is liable to pay under this section shall be reduced accordingly;

(*b*) the Inland Revenue shall serve on each such officer a notice to that effect; and

(*c*) where the reduced liability of any such officer is less than the amount that he has already paid under this section, the difference shall be repaid to him together with interest on it at the prescribed rate.

(8) Any amount paid under a personal liability notice shall be deducted from the liability of the body corporate in respect of the specified amount.

(8A) The amount which an officer is liable to pay under this section is to be recovered in the same manner as a Class 1 contribution to which regulations under paragraph 6 of Schedule 1 to the Contributions and Benfits Act apply and for this purpose references in those regulations to Class 1 contributions are to be construed accordingly.

(9) In this section—

"contributions" includes any interest or penalty in respect of contributions;

"officer", in relation to a body corporate, means—

(*a*) any director, manager, secretary or other similar officer of the body corporate, or any person purporting to act as such; and

(*b*) in a case where the affairs of the body corporate are managed by its members, any member of the body corporate exercising functions of management with respect to it or purporting to do so;

"the prescribed rate" means the rate from time to time prescribed by regulations under section 178 of the Finance Act 1989 for the purposes of the corresponding provision of Schedule 1 to the Contributions and Benefits Act, that is to say—

(*a*) in relation to subsection (5) above, paragraph 6(2)(*a*);

(*b*) in relation to subsection (7) above, paragraph 6(2)(*b*).

[Social Security Administration Act 1992, s 121C, as inserted by the Social Security Act 1998, s 64 and amended by the Social Security Contributions (Transfer of Functions, etc) Act 1999, Sch 5 and the National Insurance Contributions and Statutory Payments Act 2004, s 5.]

8–29100D 121D. Appeals in relation to personal liability notices. (1) No appeal shall lie in relation to a personal liability notice except as provided by this section.

(2) An individual who is served with a personal liability notice may appeal to the Special Commissioners against the Inland Revenue's decision as to the issue and content of the notice on the ground that—

(*a*) the whole or part of the amount specified under subsection (2)(*a*) of section 121C above (or the amount so specified as reduced under subsection (7) of that section) does not represent contributions to which that section applies;

(*b*) the failure to pay that amount was not attributable to any fraud or neglect on the part of the individual in question;

(*c*) the individual was not an officer of the body corporate at the time of the alleged fraud or neglect; or

(*d*) the opinion formed by the Inland Revenue under subsection (3)(*a*) or (*b*) of that section was unreasonable.

(3) The Inland Revenue shall give a copy of any notice of an appeal under this section, within 28 days of the giving of the notice, to each other individual who has been served with a personal liability notice.

(4) On an appeal under this section, the burden of proof as to any matter raised by a ground of appeal shall be on the Inland Revenue.

(5) Where an appeal under this section—

(*a*) is brought on the basis of evidence not considered by the Inland Revenue, or on the ground mentioned in subsection (2)(*d*) above; and

(*b*) is not allowed on some other basis or ground,

Special Commissioners shall either dismiss the appeal or remit the case to the Inland Revenue, with any recommendations the Special Commissioners see fit to make, for the Inland Revenue to consider whether to vary their decision as to the issue and content of the personal liability notice.

(6) In this section—

"officer", in relation to a body corporate, has the same meaning as in section 121C above;

"personal liability notice" has the meaning given by subsection (2) of that section;

"the Special Commissioners" means the Commissioners for the special purposes of the Income Tax Acts;

"vary" means vary under regulations made under section 10 of the Social Security Contributions (Transfer of Functions, etc) Act 1999.

[Social Security Administration Act 1992, s 121D, as inserted by the Social Security Act 1998, s 64 and amended by the Social Security Contributions (Transfer of Functions, etc) Act 1999, Sch 5.]

8–29100E 121DA. Interpretation of Part VI. (1) In this Part "the relevant social security legislation" means the provisions of any of the following, except so far as relating to contributions, statutory sick pay or statutory maternity pay, that is to say—

(*a*) the Contributions and Benefits Act;

(*b*) this Act;

(*c*) the Pensions Act, except Part III;

(*d*) section 4 of the Social Security (Incapacity for Work) Act 1994;

(*e*) the Jobseekers Act 1995;

(*f*) the Social Security (Recovery of Benefits) Act 1997;

(*g*) Parts I and IV of the Social Security Act 1998;

(*h*) Part V of the Welfare Reform and Pensions Act 1999;

(*hh*) the State Pension Credit Act 2002;

(*i*) the Social Security Pensions Act 1975;

(*j*) the Social Security Act 1973;

(*k*) any subordinate legislation made, or having effect as if made, under any enactment specified in paragraphs (*a*) to (*j*) above.

(2) In this Part "authorised officer" means a person acting in accordance with any authorisation for the purposes of this Part which is for the time being in force in relation to him.

(3) For the purposes of this Part—

(*a*) references to a document include references to anything in which information is recorded in electronic or any other form;

(*b*) the requirement that a notice given by an authorised officer be in writing shall be taken to be satisfied in any case where the contents of the notice—

(i) are transmitted to the recipient of the notice by electronic means; and

(ii) are received by him in a form that is legible and capable of being recorded for future reference.

(4) In this Part "premises" includes—

(*a*) moveable structures and vehicles, vessels, aircraft and hovercraft;

(*b*) installations that are offshore installations for the purposes of the Mineral Workings (Offshore Installations) Act 1971; and

(*c*) places of all other descriptions whether or not occupied as land or otherwise;

and references in this Part to the occupier of any premises shall be construed, in relation to premises that are not occupied as land, as references to any person for the time being present at the place in question.

(5) In this Part—

"benefit" includes any allowance, payment, credit or loan;

"benefit offence" means a criminal offence committed in connection with a claim for benefit under a provision of the relevant social security legislation, or in connection with the receipt or payment of such a benefit; and

"compensation payment" has the same meaning as in the Social Security (Recovery of Benefits) Act 1997.

(6) In this Part—

(*a*) any reference to a person authorised to carry out any function relating to housing benefit or council tax benefit shall include a reference to a person providing services relating to the benefit directly or indirectly to an authority administering it; and

(*b*) any reference to the carrying out of a function relating to such a benefit shall include a reference to the provision of any services relating to it.

(7) In this section—

"relevant social security benefit" means a benefit under any provision of the relevant social security legislation; and

"subordinate legislation" has the same meaning as in the Interpretation Act 1978.

[Social Security Administration Act 1992, s 121D, as inserted by the Child Support, Pensions and Social Security Act 2000, Sch 6, the Social Security Fraud Act 2001, Schedule, the Tax Credits Act 2002, 60 and the State Pension Credits Act 2002, Sch 2.]

PART VII[1]
INFORMATION

8–29101 Inland Revenue and Customs and Excise may disclose information to the Secretary of State or an authorised officer for use in the prevention, detection, investigation or prosecution of offences relating to social security, checking social security records or in connection with the operation of the Contributions and Benefits Act or this Act (**ss 122–122A**). Other government information relating to passports, immigration and emigration, nationality or prisoners and other prescribed matter may be disclosed for the purpose of social security fraud prevention or verification (**s 122B**). Social Security information may be disclosed to authorities administering housing benefit and council tax benefit (**s 122C**) and such authorities may make reciprocal disclosure for the purpose of preventing social security fraud (**s 122D**) and may make disclosure between themselves (**s 122E**). Unauthorised disclosure is an offence triable either way (with certain defences stated) (**s 123**). Further particular provisions are made for information to be provided to and by the Secretary of State (**ss 124–132**) including the furnishing of addresses for maintenance proceedings (**s 133**).

1. Part VII contains ss 122–133.

PART XV[1]
MISCELLANEOUS

Offences

8–29102 **181. Impersonation of officers.** If any person, with intent to deceive, falsely represents himself to be a person authorised by the Secretary of State for Work and Pensions to act in any capacity (whether under this Act or otherwise) he shall be guilty of an offence[2] and liable on summary conviction to a fine not exceeding **level 4** on the standard scale.

[Social Security Administration Act 1992, s 181, as amended by SI 2002/1397.]

1. Part XV contains ss 180–188.
2. As to legal proceedings see s 116, ante.

8–29103 **182. Illegal possession of documents.** (1) If any person—

(*a*) as a pledge or a security for a debt; or

(*b*) with a view to obtaining payment from the person entitled to it of a debt due either to himself or to any other person,

receives, detains or has in his possession any document issued by or on behalf of the Secretary of State for Work and Pensions in connection with any benefit, pension or allowance (whether payable under the Contributions and Benefits Act or otherwise) he shall be guilty of an offence.

(2) If any such person has such a document in his possession without lawful authority or excuse (the proof whereof shall lie on him) he shall be guilty of an offence.

(3) A person guilty of an offence[1] under this section shall be liable on summary conviction to

imprisonment for a term not exceeding **3 months** or to a fine not exceeding **level 4** on the standard scale or to **both**.
[Social Security Administration Act 1992, s 182, as amended by SI 2002/1397.]

1. As to legal proceedings see s 116, ante.

Pension Schemes Act 1993

(1993 c 48)

PART III[1]
CERTIFICATION OF PENSION SCHEMES AND EFFECTS ON MEMBERS' STATE SCHEME RIGHTS AND DUTIES

CHAPTER III[2]
TERMINATION OF CONTRACTED-OUT OR APPROPRIATE SCHEME STATUS: STATE SCHEME PREMIUMS

State scheme premiums

8–29110 67. Non-payment of contributions equivalent premiums. (1) If a person fails to pay[3] any contributions equivalent premium[4] which is payable by him at or within the time prescribed for the purpose, he shall be liable on summary conviction to a fine of not more than **level 3** on the standard scale.

(2) Where—

(*a*) a person is convicted of the offence under subsection (1) of failing to pay a premium, and
(*b*) the premium remains unpaid at the date of the conviction,

he shall be liable to pay to the Inland Revenue a sum equal to the amount which he failed to pay.

(3) Subject to subsection (4), where a person is convicted of an offence mentioned in subsection (2), evidence may be given of any previous failure by him to pay contributions equivalent premiums within the time prescribed for the purpose; and in that subsection "the conviction" and "the offence" mean respectively the conviction referred to in this subsection and the offence of which the person is convicted.

(4) Such evidence may be given only if notice of intention to give it is served with the summons or warrant or, in Scotland, the complaint on which the person appeared before the court which convicted him.
[Pension Schemes Act 1993, s 67, as amended by the Pensions Act 1995, Sch 5 and the Social Security Contributions (Transfer of Functions, etc) Act 1999, Sch 1.]

1. Part III contains ss 7–68.
2. Chapter III contains ss 50–68.
3. Where in any proceedings for an offence under this Act there arises any question as to whether a state scheme premium is payable or has been paid in any case or as to the amount of any such premium, the decision of the Secretary of State shall be conclusive for the purpose of the proceedings (ss 170(1) and 171(1), post).
4. "Contributions equivalent premium" means a contributions equivalent premium payable under Ch III of Pt III (s 181(1)).
A contributions equivalent premium is payable where an earner in contracted-out employment with reference to an occupational pension scheme (other than a contracted-out money purchase scheme) leaves the scheme within 2 years or the scheme ceases to be a contracted out scheme (whether by being wound up or otherwise (s 55(2)). The amount of the contributions equivalent premium is the difference between the amount of the Class 1 contributions payable in respect of the earner's employment which was contracted-out by reference to the scheme and the amount of those contributions which would have been payable if the employment had not been contracted-out (s 58(4)). The person paying the premium may deduct a specified amount (within defined limits) from the refund of contributions to the earner (s 61).

8–29111 68. Unpaid premiums: supplementary. (1) Where in England and Wales a person charged with an offence to which section 67(2) applies is convicted of that offence in his absence under section 12(5) of the Magistrates' Courts Act 1980[1], then if—

(*a*) it is proved to the satisfaction of the court, on oath or in the manner prescribed by rules under section 144 of that Act, that notice under section 67(4) has been duly served specifying the other premiums in respect of which the prosecutor intends to give evidence; and
(*b*) the justices' chief executive for court has received a statement in writing purporting to be made by the accused or by a solicitor acting on his behalf to the effect that if the accused is convicted in his absence of the offence charged he desires to admit failing to pay the other premiums so specified or any of them,

section 67(3) and (4) shall have effect as if the evidence had been given and the failure so admitted had been proved, and the court shall proceed accordingly.

(2) In England and Wales where—

(*a*) a person is convicted of an offence to which section 67(2) applies; and (*b*) an order is made under section 12 of the Powers of Criminal Courts (Sentencing) Act 2000 discharging him absolutely or conditionally,

subsection (1) and section 67(2) to (4) shall apply as if it were a conviction for all purposes.

(3) *Scotland.*

(4) In England or Wales any sum which a person is liable to pay under subsection (1) or section 67(2) to (4) shall be recoverable from him as a penalty.

(5) State scheme premiums recovered by the Inland Revenue under those provisions shall be treated for all purposes as premiums paid to the Inland Revenue in respect of the person in respect of whom they were originally payable.

[Pension Schemes Act 1993, s 68, as amended by the Magistrates' Courts (Procedure) Act 1998, s 4, the Social Security Contributions (Transfer of Functions, etc) Act 1999, Sch 1, the Powers of Criminal Courts (Sentencing) Act 2000, Sch 9 and the Access to Justice Act 1999, s 90.]

---

1. See PART I: MAGISTRATES' COURTS, PROCEDURE, ante.

PART IIIA
SAFEGUARDED RIGHTS

8–29111A 68A. Safeguarded rights. (1) Subject to subsection (2), the safeguarded rights of a member of an occupational pension scheme or a personal pension scheme are such of his rights to future benefits under the scheme as are attributable (directly or indirectly) to a pension credit in respect of which the reference rights are, or include, contracted-out rights or safeguarded rights.

(2) If the rules of an occupational pension scheme or a personal pension scheme so provide, a member's safeguarded rights are such of his rights falling within subsection (1) as—

(*a*) in the case of rights directly attributable to a pension credit, represent the safeguarded percentage of the rights acquired by virtue of the credit, and

(*b*) in the case of rights directly attributable to a transfer payment, represent the safeguarded percentage of the rights acquired by virtue of the payment.

(3) For the purposes of subsection (2)(*a*), the safeguarded percentage is the percentage of the rights by reference to which the amount of the credit is determined which are contracted-out rights or safeguarded rights.

(4) For the purposes of subsection (2)(*b*), the safeguarded percentage is the percentage of the rights in respect of which the transfer payment is made which are contracted-out rights or safeguarded rights.

(5) In this section—

"contracted-out rights" means such rights under, or derived from—

(*a*) an occupational pension scheme contracted-out by virtue of section 9(2) or (3), or

(*b*) an appropriate personal pension scheme,

as may be prescribed;

"reference rights", in relation to a pension credit, means the rights by reference to which the amount of the credit is determined.

[Pension Schemes Act 1993, s 68A, as inserted by the Welfare Reform and Pensions Act 1999, s 36.]

8–29111B 68B. Requirements relating to safeguarded rights. Regulations may prescribe requirements to be met in relation to safeguarded rights by an occupational pension scheme or a personal pension scheme including provision for such rights to be extinguished or reduced in consequence of a civil recovery order made in respect of such rights.

[Pension Schemes Act 1993, s 68B, as inserted by the Welfare Reform and Pensions Act 1999, s 36.]

8–29111C 68C. Reserve powers in relation to non-complying schemes. (1) This section applies to—

(*a*) any occupational pension scheme, other than a public service pension scheme, and

(*b*) any personal pension scheme.

(2) If any scheme to which this section applies does not comply with a requirement prescribed under section 68B and there are any persons who—

(*a*) have safeguarded rights under the scheme, or

(*b*) are entitled to any benefit giving effect to such rights under the scheme,

the Inland Revenue may direct the trustees or managers of the scheme to take or refrain from taking such steps as they may specify in writing for the purpose of safeguarding the rights of persons falling within paragraph (*a*) or (*b*).

(3) A direction under subsection (2) shall be final and binding on the trustees or managers to whom the direction is given and any person claiming under them.

(4) An appeal on a point of law shall lie to the High Court or, in Scotland, the Court of Session

from a direction under subsection (2) at the instance of the trustees or managers, or any person claiming under them.

(5) A direction under subsection (2) shall be enforceable—

(*a*) in England and Wales, in a county court, as if it were an order of that court, and

(*b*) in Scotland, by the sheriff, as if it were an order of the sheriff and whether or not the sheriff could himself have given such an order.

[Pension Schemes Act 1993, s 68C, as inserted by the Welfare Reform and Pensions Act 1999, s 36.]

8–29111D **68D. Power to control transfer or discharge of liability.** Regulations may prohibit or restrict the transfer or discharge of any liability under an occupational pension scheme or a personal pension scheme in respect of safeguarded rights except in prescribed circumstances or on prescribed conditions.

[Pension Schemes Act 1993, s 68D, as inserted by the Welfare Reform and Pensions Act 1999, s 36.]

PART XI[1]
GENERAL AND MISCELLANEOUS PROVISIONS

Information about schemes

8–29112 **157. Power of Secretary of State to obtain information in connection with applications under section 124.** (1) Where an application is made to the Secretary of State under section 124[2] in respect of contributions to an occupational pension scheme or personal pension scheme falling to be made, by an employer, the Secretary of State may require—

(*a*) the employer to provide him with such information as the Secretary of State may reasonably require for the purpose of determining whether the application is well founded; and

(*b*) any person having the custody or control of any relevant records or other documents to produce for examination on behalf of the Secretary of State any such document in that person's custody or under his control which is of such a description as the Secretary of State may require.

(2) Any such requirement shall be made in writing given to the person on whom the requirement is imposed and may be varied or revoked by a subsequent notice so given.

(3) If a person refuses or wilfully neglects to furnish any information or produce any document which he has been required to furnish or produce by a notice under this section he shall be liable on summary conviction to a fine not exceeding **level 3** on the standard scale.

(4) If a person, in purporting to comply with a requirement of a notice under this section, knowingly or recklessly makes any false statement, he shall be liable on summary conviction to a fine not exceeding **level 5** on the standard scale.

(5) This section shall be construed as if it were in Chapter II of Part VII.

[Pension Schemes Act 1993, s 157.]

---

1. Part XI contains ss 153–177.

2. Section 124 imposes, subject to the provisions of the section and s 125, a duty on the Secretary of State to pay into into the resources of an occupational pension scheme or a personal pension scheme a sum which in his opinion is payable in respect of unpaid relevant contributions. This obligation arises if, on an application made to him in writing by the persons competent to act in respect of the scheme, the Secretary of State is satisfied (*a*) that an employer has become insolvent; and (*b*) that at the time he did so there remained unpaid relevant contributions falling to be paid by him to the scheme.

General provisions as to offences

8–29113 **168. Breach of regulations.** (1) Regulations under any provision of this Act (other than Chapter II of Part VII) may make such provision as is referred to in subsection (2) or (4) for the contravention of any provision contained in regulations made or having effect as if made under any provision of this Act.

(2) The regulations may provide for the contravention to be an offence under this Act and for the recovery on summary conviction of a fine not exceeding **level 5** on the standard scale.

(3) An offence under any provision of the regulations may be charged by reference to any day or longer period of time; and a person may be convicted of a second or subsequent offence under such a provision by reference to any period of time following the preceding conviction of the offence.

(4)–(9) *Regulations may provide for a person in contravention of the provisions to pay a penalty to the Regulatory Authority.*

(10) Where by reason of the contravention of any provision contained in regulations made, or having effect as if made, under this Act—

(*a*) a person is convicted of an offence under this Act, or

(*b*) a person pays a penalty under subsection (4),

then, in respect of that contravention he shall not, in a case within paragraph (*a*), be liable to pay such a penalty or, in a case within paragraph (*b*), be convicted of such an offence.

(11) In this section "contravention" means a partnership constituted under the law of Scotland.
[Pension Schemes Act 1993, s 168 as substituted by the Pensions Act 1995, s 155.]

8–29113A 168A. Offence in connection with the Registrar. *Repealed.*

8–29114 169. Offences by bodies corporate. (1) Where an offence under this Act which has been committed by a body corporate is proved to have been committed with the consent or connivance of, or to be attributable to any neglect on the part of, a director, manager, secretary or other similar officer of the body corporate, or any person who was purporting to act in any such capacity, he as well as the body corporate shall be guilty of that offence and be liable to be proceeded against accordingly.

(2) Where the affairs of a body corporate are managed by its members, subsection (1) applies in relation to the acts and defaults of a member in connection with his functions of management as if he were a director of the body corporate.
[Pension Schemes Act 1993, s 169.]

General provisions as to determinations and appeals

8–29115 170. Decisions and appeals. (1) Section 2 (use of computers) of the Social Security Act 1998 ("the 1998 Act") applies as if, for the purposes of subsection (1) of that section, this Act were a relevant enactment.

(2) It shall be for an officer of the Inland Revenue—

(*a*) to make any decision that falls to be made under or by virtue of Part III of this Act, other than a decision which under or by virtue of that Part falls to be made by the Secretary of State;
(*b*) to decide any issue arising in connection with payments under section 7 of the Social Security Act 1986 (occupational pension schemes becoming contracted-out between 1986 and 1993); and
(*c*) to decide any issue arising by virtue of regulations made under paragraph 15 of Schedule 3 to the Social Security (Consequential Provisions) Act 1992 (continuing in force of certain enactments repealed by the Social Security Act 1973).

(3) In the following provisions of this section a "relevant decision" means any decision which under subsection (2) falls to be made by an officer of the Inland Revenue, other than a decision under section 53 or 54.

(4) Sections 9 and 10 of the 1998 Act (revision of decisions and decisions superseding earlier decisions) apply as if—

(*a*) any reference in those sections to a decision of the Secretary of State under section 8 of that Act included a reference to a relevant decision; and
(*b*) any other reference in those sections to the Secretary of State were, in relation to a relevant decision, a reference to an officer of the Inland Revenue.

(5) Regulations may make provision—

(*a*) generally with respect to the making of relevant decisions;
(*b*) with respect to the procedure to be adopted on any application made under section 9 or 10 of the 1998 Act by virtue of subsection (4); and
(*c*) generally with respect to such applications, revisions under section 9 and decisions under section 10;

but may not prevent a revision under section 9 or decision under section 10 being made without such an application.

(6) Section 12 of the 1998 Act (appeal to appeal tribunal) applies as if, for the purposes of subsection (1)(*b*) of that section, a relevant decision were a decision of the Secretary of State falling within Schedule 3 to the 1998 Act.

(7) The following provisions of the 1998 Act (which relate to decisions and appeals)—

sections 13 to 18,
sections 25 and 26,
section 28, and
Schedules 4 and 5,

shall apply in relation to any appeal under section 12 of the 1998 Act by virtue of subsection (6) above as if any reference to the Secretary of State were a reference to an officer of the Inland Revenue.
[Pension Schemes Act 1993, s 170, as amended by the Social Security Act 1998, Sch 7, the Social Security Contributions (Transfer of Functions, etc) Act 1999, s 16(2), the Welfare Reform and Pensions Act 1999, Sch 11 and SI 2001/3649.]

8–29116 171. Questions arising in proceedings. (1) Where in any proceedings—

(*a*) for an offence under this Act; or
(*b*) involving any question as to the payment of a contributions equivalent premium;

any relevant decision as defined by section 170(3) is made by the Inland Revenue, the decision shall be conclusive for the purpose of the proceedings.

(2) If—

(*a*) any such decision is necessary for the determination of the proceedings, and

(*b*) the decision of the Inland Revenue has not been obtained or an application with respect to the decision has been made under section 9 or 10 of the Social Security Act 1998,

the decision shall be referred to the Inland Revenue to be made in accordance (subject to any necessary modifications) with Chapter II of Part I of that Act.

(3) Subsection (1) does not apply where, in relation to the decision—

(*a*) an appeal has been brought but not determined,

(*b*) an application for leave to appeal has been made but not determined,

(*c*) an appeal has not been brought (or, as the case may be, an application for leave to appeal has not been made) but the time for doing so has not yet expired, or

(*d*) an application has been made under section 9 or 10 of that Act.

(4) In a case falling within subsection (3) the court shall adjourn the proceedings until such time as the final decision is known and that decision shall be conclusive for the purposes of the proceedings.

[Pension Schemes Act 1993, s 171, as amended by the Pensions Act 1995, Sch 5 and the Social Security Contributions (Transfer of Functions, etc) Act 1999, Sch 7.]

PART XII[1]

SUPPLEMENTARY PROVISIONS

8–29117 **181.** *General interpretation.*

1. Part XII contains ss 178–193.

8–29118 **182.** *Orders and regulations (general provisions).*

8–29119 **193.** *Short title and commencement.*

Jobseekers Act 1995[1]

(1995 c 18)

PART I[2]

THE JOBSEEKER'S ALLOWANCE

Entitlement

8–29120 **1. The jobseeker's allowance.** (1) An allowance, to be known as a jobseeker's allowance, shall be payable in accordance with the provisions of this Act.

(2) Subject to the provisions of this Act, a claimant is entitled to a jobseeker's allowance if he—

(*a*) is available for employment;

(*b*) has entered into a jobseeker's agreement which remains in force;

(*c*) is actively seeking employment;

(*d*) satisfies the conditions set out in section 2;

(*e*) is not engaged in remunerative work;

(*f*) is capable of work;

(*g*) is not receiving relevant education;

(*h*) is under pensionable age; and

(*i*) is in Great Britain.

(2A) Subject to the provisions of this Act, a claimant who is not a member of a joint-claim couple is entitled to a jobseeker's allowance if he satisfies—

(*a*) the conditions set out in paragraphs (*a*) to (*c*) and (*e*) to (*i*) of subsection (2); and

(*b*) the conditions set out in section 3.

(2B) Subject to the provisions of this Act, a joint-claim couple are entitled to a jobseeker's allowance if—

(*a*) a claim for the allowance is made jointly by the couple;

(*b*) each member of the couple satisfies the conditions set out in paragraphs (*a*) to (*c*) and (*e*) to (*i*) of subsection (2); and

(*c*) the conditions set out in section 3A are satisfied in relation to the couple.

(2C) Regulations may prescribe circumstances in which subsection (2A) is to apply to a claimant who is a member of a joint-claim couple.

(2D) Regulations may, in respect of cases where a person would (but for the regulations) be a member of two or more joint-claim couples, make provision for only one of those couples to be a joint-claim couple; and the provision which may be so made includes provision for the couple which is to be the joint-claim couple to be nominated—

(*a*) by the persons who are the members of the couples, or
(*b*) in default of one of the couples being so nominated, by the Secretary of State.

(3) A jobseeker's allowance is payable in respect of a week.
(4) In this Act—

"a contribution-based jobseeker's allowance" means a jobseeker's allowance entitlement to which is based on the claimant's satisfying conditions which include those set out in section 2;

"an income-based jobseeker's allowance" means a jobseeker's allowance entitlement to which is based on the claimant's satisfying conditions which include those set out in section 3 or a joint-claim jobseeker's allowance;

"a joint-claim couple" means a couple who—

(*a*) are not members of any family whose members include a person in respect of whom a member of the couple is entitled to child benefit, and
(*b*) are of a prescribed description;

"a joint-claim jobseeker's allowance" means a jobseeker's allowance entitlement to which arises by virtue of subsection (2B).

[Jobseekers Act 1995, s 1, as amended by the Welfare Reform and Pensions Act 1999, Sch 7 and the Civil Partnership Act 2004, Sch 24.]

---

1. The Jobseekers Act 1995 provides for a jobseeker's allowance and makes other provision to promote the employment of the unemployed and the assistance of persons without a settled way of life.
This Act shall come into force in accordance with the provisions of s 41, post.
Only those provisions of the Act which are relevant to the work of magistrates' courts are contained in this Manual.
2. Part I contains ss 1–25.

Miscellaneous

8–29121 23. Recovery of sums in respect of maintenance. (1) Regulations[1] may make provision for the court to have power to make a recovery order against any person where an award of income-based jobseeker's allowance has been made to that person's spouse or civil partner.

(2) In this section "recovery order" means an order requiring the person against whom it is made to make payments to the Secretary of State or to such other person or persons as the court may determine.

(3) Regulations[1] under this section may make provision for the transfer by the Secretary of State of the right to receive payments under, and to exercise rights in relation to, a recovery order.

(4) Regulations[1] made under this section may, in particular, include provision—

(*a*) as to the matters to which the court is, or is not, to have regard in determining any application under the regulations; and
(*b*) as to the enforcement of recovery orders.

(5) In this section, "the court" means—

(*a*) in relation to England and Wales, a magistrates' court; and
(*b*) in relation to Scotland, the sheriff.

[Jobseekers Act 1995, s 23 as amended by the Civil Partnership Act 2004, Sch 24.]

---

1. The Jobseeker's Allowance Regulations 1996, SI 1996/207 as amended have been made. Regulation 169 thereof—recovery orders—makes the following provision with respect to the recovery of maintenance under s 23 of the Act—

"**169. Recovery orders.**—(1) Where an award of income-based jobseeker's allowance has been made to a person ('the claimant'), the Secretary of State may apply to the court for a recovery order against the claimant's spouse ('the liable person').

(2) On making a recovery order the court may order the liable person to pay such amount at such intervals as it considers appropriate, having regard to all the circumstances of the liable person and in particular his income.

(3) Except in Scotland, a recovery order shall be treated for all purposes as if it were a maintenance order within the meaning of section 150(1) of the Magistrates Court Act 1980.

(4) Where a recovery order requires the liable person to make payments to the Secretary of State, the Secretary of State may, by giving notice in writing to the court which made the order, the liable person, and the claimant, transfer to the claimant the right to receive payments under the order and to exercise the relevant rights in relation to the order.

(5) In this regulation—

the expression 'the court' and 'recovery order' have the same meanings as in section 23 of the Act; and

'the relevant rights' means, in relation to a recovery order, the right to bring any proceedings, take any steps or do any other thing under or in relation to the order".

PART II[1]
BACK TO WORK SCHEMES

8–29122 **26. The back to work bonus.** (1) Regulations[2] may make provision for the payment, in prescribed circumstances, of sums to or in respect of persons who are or have been entitled to a jobseeker's allowance or to income support.

(2) A sum payable under the regulations shall be known as "a back to work bonus".

(3) Subject to section 677 of the Income Tax (Earnings and Pensions) Act 2003 (which provides for a back to work bonus not to be taxable), a back to work bonus shall be treated for all purposes as payable by way of a jobseeker's allowance or (as the case may be) income support.

(4) *Supplementary provisions as to regulations.*

[Jobseekers Act 1995, s 26, as amended by the Income Tax (Earnings and Pensions) Act 2003, Sch 6.]

1. Part II contains ss 26–29.
2. The Social Security (Back to Work Bonus) Regulations 1996, (No 2) Regulations 1996, SI 1996/2570 have been made.

8–29123 **27. Employment of long-term unemployed: deductions by employers.** (1) An employee is a "qualifying employee" in relation to his employer for the purposes of this section if, immediately before beginning his employment with that employer, he had been entitled to a jobseeker's allowance for a continuous period of not less than two years.

(2) An employee is also a "qualifying employee" in relation to his employer for the purposes of this section if—

(*a*) immediately before beginning his employment with that employer, he had been unemployed for a continuous period of not less than two years;
(*b*) he is under pensionable age; and
(*c*) he falls within a prescribed description of person.

(3) Regulations[1] may make provision for any employer who employs a person who is a qualifying employee in relation to him, to make deductions from the employer's contributions payments in accordance with the regulations and in prescribed circumstances.

(4) Those regulations may, in particular, make provision as to the period for which deductions may be made by an employer.

(5) Regulations[1] may provide, in relation to cases where an employee is a qualifying employee in relation to more than one employer at the same time, for the right to make deductions to be confined to one employer—

(*a*) determined in accordance with the regulations; and
(*b*) certified by the Commissioners of Inland Revenue, in accordance with the regulations, to be the employer entitled to make those deductions.

(6) *Supplementary provisions as to regulations.*

(7) Where, in accordance with any provision of regulations made under this section, an amount has been deducted from an employer's contributions payments, the amount so deducted shall (except in such cases as may be prescribed) be treated for the purposes of any provision made by or under any enactment in relation to primary or secondary Class 1 contributions as having been—

(*a*) paid (on such date as may be determined in accordance with the regulations); and
(*b*) received by the Commissioners of Inland Revenue,

towards discharging the employer's liability in respect of such contributions.

(8) In this section—

"contributions payments", in relation to an employer, means the aggregate of the payments which he is required to make by way of primary and secondary Class 1 contributions;
"deductions" means deductions made in accordance with regulations under subsection (3);
"employee" and "employer" have such meaning as may be prescribed;
"prescribed" means specified in or determined in accordance with regulations; and
"regulations" means regulations made by the Treasury.

[Jobseekers Act 1995, s 27, as amended by the Social Security Contributions (Transfer of Functions, etc) Act 1999, Sch 1, Sch 3.]

1. The Employers Contributions Re-imbursement Regulations 1996, SI 1996/195 amended by SI 1999/286 have been made.

PART III[1]
MISCELLANEOUS AND SUPPLEMENTAL

8–29127 **35. Interpretation.** (1) In this Act—

"the Administration Act" means the Social Security Administration Act 1992;
"applicable amount" means the applicable amount determined in accordance with regulations under section 4;

"benefit year" has the meaning given by section 2(4);
"the Benefits Act" means the Social Security Contributions and Benefits Act 1992;
"child" means a person under the age of 16;
"claimant" means a person who claims a jobseeker's allowance except that in relation to a joint-claim couple claiming a joint-claim jobseeker's allowance it means the couple, or each member of the couple, as the context requires;
"continental shelf operations" has the same meaning as in section 120 of the Benefits Act;
"contribution-based conditions" means the conditions set out in section 2;
"contribution-based jobseeker's allowance" has the meaning given in section 1(4);
"couple" means—

(*a*) a man and woman who are married to each other and are members of the same household;
(*b*) a man and woman who are not married to each other but are living together as husband and wife otherwise than in prescribed circumstances;
(*c*) two people of the same sex who are civil partners of each other and are members of the same household;
(*d*) two people of the same sex who are not civil partners but are living together as if they were civil partners otherwise than in prescribed circumstances;

"employed earner" has the meaning prescribed for the purposes of this Act;
"employment", except in section 7, has the meaning prescribed for the purposes of this Act;
"entitled", in relation to a jobseeker's allowance, is to be construed in accordance with—

(*a*) the provisions of this Act relating to entitlement; and
(*b*) section 1 of the Administration Act and section 27 of the Social Security Act 1998;

"family" means—

(*a*) a couple;
(*b*) a couple and a member of the same household for whom one of them is, or both are, responsible and who is a child or a person of a prescribed description;
(*c*) except in prescribed circumstances, a person who is not a member of a couple and a member of the same household for whom that person is responsible and who is a child or a person of a prescribed description;

"Great Britain" includes the territorial waters of the United Kingdom adjacent to Great Britain;
"income-based conditions" means the conditions set out in section 3;
"income-based jobseeker's allowance" has the meaning given in section 1(4);
"jobseeker's agreement" has the meaning given by section 9(1);
"jobseeking period" has the meaning prescribed for the purposes of this Act;
"joint-claim couple" and "joint-claim jobseeker's allowance" have the meanings given by section 1(4);
"the nominated member", in relation to a joint-claim couple, shall be construed in accordance with section 3B(4);
"occupational pension scheme" has the same meaning as it has in the Pension Schemes Act 1993 by virtue of section 1 of that Act;
"pensionable age" has the meaning prescribed for the purposes of this Act;
"pension payments" means—

(*a*) periodical payments made in relation to a person, under a personal pension scheme or, in connection with the coming to an end of an employment of his, under an occupational pension scheme or a public service pension scheme; and
(*b*) such other payments as may be prescribed;

"personal pension scheme" means—

(*a*) a personal pension scheme as defined by section 1 of the Pension Schemes Act 1993;
(*b*) a contract or trust scheme approved under Chapter III of Part XIV of the Income and Corporation Taxes Act 1988; and
(*c*) a personal pension scheme approved under Chapter IV of that Part of that Act;

"prescribed", except in section 27 (and in section 36 so far as relating to regulations under section 27), means specified in or determined in accordance with regulations;
"public service pension scheme" has the same meaning as it has in the Pension Schemes Act 1993 by virtue of section 1 of that Act;
"regulations", except in section 27 (and in section 36 so far as relating to regulations under section 27), means regulations made by the Secretary of State;
"tax year" means the 12 months beginning with 6th April in any year;
"trade dispute" means any dispute between employers and employees[2], or between employees and employees, which is connected with the employment or non-employment or the terms of employment or the conditions of employment of any persons, whether employees in the employment of the employer with whom the dispute arises, or not;
"training" has the meaning prescribed for the purposes of this Act and, in relation to prescribed provisions of this Act, if regulations so provide, includes assistance to find training or

employment, or to improve a person's prospects of being employed, of such a kind as may be prescribed;

"week" means a period of 7 days beginning with a Sunday or such other period of 7 days as may be prescribed;

"work" has the meaning prescribed for the purposes of this Act;

"year", except in the expression "benefit year", means a tax year.

(1A) For the purposes of this Act, two people of the same sex are to be regarded as living together as if they were civil partners if, but only if, they would be regarded as living together as husband and wife were they instead two people of the opposite sex.

(2) The expressions "capable of work", "linked period", "relevant education" and "remunerative work" are to be read with paragraphs 2, 3, 14 and 1 of Schedule 1.

(3) Subject to any regulations made for the purposes of this subsection, "earnings" is to be construed for the purposes of this Act in accordance with section 3 of the Benefits Act and paragraph 6 of Schedule 1 to this Act.

[Jobseekers Act 1995, s 35, as amended by the Social Security Contributions (Transfer of Functions, etc) Act 1999, Sch 3, the Welfare Reform and Pensions Act 1999, Sch 7, the Social Security Act 1998, Schs 7 and 8 and the Civil Partnership Act 2004, Sch 24.]

---

1. Part III contains ss 30–41.

2. Modified in respect of share fishermen by the Jobseeker's Allowance Regulations 1996, SI 1996/207, reg 160 to provide that the owner or managing owner shall be treated as the employer of the other share fishermen who for these purposes are to be treated as his employees.

8–29128 **36.** *Regulations and orders.*

8–29129 **41. Short title, commencement, extent etc.** (1) This Act may be cited as the Jobseekers Act 1995.

(2) Section 39 and this section (apart from subsections (4) and (5)) come into force on the passing of this Act, but otherwise the provisions of this Act come into force on such day as the Secretary of State may by order[1] appoint.

(3) Different days may be appointed for different purposes.

(4) Schedule 2 makes consequential amendments.

(5) The repeals set out in Schedule 3 shall have effect.

(6) Apart from this section, section 39 and paragraphs 11 to 16, 28, 67 and 68 of Schedule 2, this Act does not extend to Northern Ireland.

[Jobseekers Act 1995, s 41.]

---

1. At the date of going to press the Jobseekers Act 1995 (Commencement No 1) Order 1995, SI 1995/3228, Commencement No 2) Order 1996, SI 1996/1126, (Commencement No 3) Order 1996, SI 1996/1509, and (Commencement No 4) Order 1996, SI 1996/2208, had been made.

Pensions Act 1995[1]

(1995 c 26)

PART I
OCCUPATIONAL PENSIONS[2]

Supervision by the Authority

8–29132A (1) The Authority may by order prohibit a person from being a trustee of—

(*a*) a particular trust scheme,

(*b*) a particular description of trust schemes, or

(*c*) trust schemes in general,

if they are satisfied that he is not a fit and proper person to be a trustee of the scheme or schemes to which the order relates.

(2) Where a prohibition order is made under subsection (1) against a person in respect of one or more schemes of which he is a trustee, the order has the effect of removing him.

(3) The Authority may, on the application of any person prohibited under this section, by order revoke the order either generally or in relation to a particular scheme or description of schemes.

(4) An application under subsection (3) may not be made—

(*a*) during the period within which the determination to exercise the power to make the prohibition order may be referred to the Tribunal under section 96(3) or 99(7) of the Pensions Act 2004, and

(*b*) if the determination is so referred, until the reference, and any appeal against the Tribunal's determination, has been finally disposed of.

(5) A revocation made at any time under this section cannot affect anything done before that time.

(6) The Authority must prepare and publish a statement of the policies they intend to adopt in relation to the exercise of their powers under this section.

(7) The Authority may revise any statement published under subsection (6) and must publish any revised statement.

(8) In this section "the Tribunal" means the Pensions Regulator Tribunal established under section 102 of the Pensions Act 2004.

[Pensions Act 1995, s 3, as substituted by the Pensions Act 2004, s 33.]

1. The Act makes provision for amendment of the law relating to pensions. In particular, Pt I prescribes measures regulating the management of funds held by occupational pension schemes to protect the interests of the beneficiaries of such schemes. An Occupational Pensions Regulatory Authority is established (ss 1–2) which has wide powers over the appointment of trustees including powers to prohibit, suspend, and remove persons from appointment and to wind up schemes (ss 3–15). The description and functions of trustees are prescribed together with investment principles and the role of advisers and auditors (ss 16–61). There is a requirement for equal treatment of scheme members (ss 62–66) and restrictions on the power to modify schemes and for winding-up (ss 67–77). The Pensions Compensation Board is established (ss 78–80) which may make awards of compensation to members of an occupational scheme whose pension provision has suffered as a result of malpractice in the administration of the scheme (ss 81–86). The Authority and the Compensation Board are enabled to require and obtain information in order to fulfil their functions (ss 98–114). Pt II (ss 126–134) relates to state pensions and Pt III (ss 135–151) makes provision for the relationship between certified pension schemes and members' state scheme rights and duties. Part IV (ss 152–181) contains miscellaneous and general matters.

With some exceptions, the provisions of the Act are to be brought into force by orders made under s 180. At the time of going to press the following commencement orders had been made: Pensions Act 1995 (Commencement No 1) Order 1995, SI 1995/2548; (Commencement No 2) Order 1995, SI 1995/3104; (Commencement No 3) Order 1996, SI 1996/778; (Commencement No 4) Order 1996, SI 1996/1412; (Commencement No 5) Order 1996, SI 1996/1675; (Commencement No 6) Order 1996, SI 1996/1843 (*provisions applicable only to Scotland*); (Commencement No 7) Order 1996, SI 1996/1853 as amended by SI 1996/2150; Commencement (No 8) Order 1996, SI 1996/2637; Commencement (No 9) Order 1997, SI 1997/216; Commencement (No 10) Order 1997, SI 1997/664. All the provisions reproduced here are in force.

2. Part I contains ss 1–125.
3. The Occupational Pensions Regulatory Authority (s 1).
4. An occupational pension scheme established under a trust (s 124).
5. See the Occupational Pension Schemes (Prohibition of Trustees) Regulations 1997, SI 1997/663.

Trustees: general

8–29132B 27. Trustee not to be auditor or actuary of the scheme. (1) A trustee of a trust scheme[1], and any person who is connected with, or an associate of, such a trustee, is ineligible to act as an auditor or actuary of the scheme.

(2) Subsection (1) does not make a person who is a director, partner or employee of a firm of actuaries ineligible to act as an actuary of a trust scheme merely because another director, partner or employee of the firm is a trustee of the scheme.

(3) Subsection (1) does not make a person who falls within a prescribed class or description ineligible to act as an auditor or actuary of a trust scheme.

(4) A person must not act as an auditor or actuary of a trust scheme if he is ineligible under this section to do so[2].

(5) In this section and section 28 references to a trustee of a trust scheme do not include—

(*a*) a trustee, or
(*b*) a trustee of a scheme,

falling within a prescribed class or description.

[Pensions Act 1995, s 27.]

1. An occupational pension scheme established under a trust (s 124).
2. For provisions as to offences, see 28, post.

8–29132C 28. Section 27: consequences. (1) Any person[1] who acts as an auditor or actuary of a trust scheme in contravention of section 27(4) is guilty of an offence and liable—

(*a*) on summary conviction, to a fine not exceeding the **statutory maximum**, and
(*b*) on conviction on indictment, to **imprisonment** or a **fine**, or **both**[2].

(2) An offence under subsection (1) may be charged by reference to any day or longer period of time; and a person may be convicted of a second or subsequent offence under that subsection by reference to any period of time following the preceding conviction of the offence.

(3) Acts done as an auditor or actuary of a trust scheme by a person who is ineligible under section 27 to do so are not invalid merely because of that fact.

(4) *Repealed.*

[Pensions Act 1995, s 28 as amended by the Pensions Act 2004, Sch 12.]

1. For offences by bodies corporate and partnerships, see s 115, post.
2. For procedure in respect of an offence triable either way, see the Magistrates' Courts Act 1980, ss 17A–21, in PART I: MAGISTRATES' COURTS, PROCEDURE, ante.

8–29132D 29. Persons disqualified for being trustees. (1) Subject to subsection (5), a person is disqualified for being a trustee of any trust scheme[1] if—

(*a*) he has been convicted of any offence involving dishonesty or deception,

(*b*) he has been adjudged bankrupt or sequestration of his estate has been awarded and (in either case) he has not been discharged.

(*c*) where the person is a company, if any director of the company is disqualified under this section,

(*d*) where the person is a Scottish partnership, if any partner is disqualified under this section.

(*e*) he has made a composition contract or an arrangement with, or granted a trust deed for the behoof of, his creditors and has not been discharged in respect of it, or

(*f*) he is subject to a disqualification order or disqualification undertaking under the Company Directors Disqualification Act 1986 to a disqualification order under Part II of the Companies (Northern Ireland) Order 1989 or disqualification undertaking under the Company Directors Disqualifcation (Northern Ireland) Order 2002 or to an order made under section 429(2)(*b*) of the Insolvency Act 1986 (failure to pay under county court administration order).

(2) In subsection (1)—

(*a*) paragraph (*a*) applies whether the conviction occurred before or after the coming into force of that subsection, but does not apply in relation to any conviction which is a spent conviction for the purposes of the Rehabilitation of Offenders Act 1974,

(*b*) paragraph (*b*) applies whether the adjudication of bankruptcy or the sequestration occurred before or after the coming into force of that subsection,

(*c*) paragraph (*e*) applies whether the composition contract or arrangement was made, or the trust deed was granted, before or after the coming into force of that subsection, and

(*d*) paragraph (*f*) applies in relation to orders made before or after the coming into force of that subsection.

(3)–(6) *Disqualification by the Authority.*

[Pensions Act 1995, s 29 as amended by the Insolvency Act 2000, s 8, SI 2004/1941, the Pensions Act 2004, Schs 12 and 13.]

---

1. An occupational pension scheme established under a trust (s 124).

8–29132E 30. Persons disqualified: consequences. (1) Where a person who is a trustee of a trust scheme becomes disqualified under section 29 in relation to the scheme, his becoming so disqualified has the effect of removing him as a trustee.

(2) Where—

(*a*) a trustee of a trust scheme becomes disqualified under section 29,

(*b*) *repealed.*

the Authority[2] may exercise the same jurisdiction and powers as are exercisable by order by the High Court or, in relation to a trust scheme subject to the law of Scotland, the Court of Session for vesting any property in, or transferring any property to, the trustees.*

(3) A person[3] who purports to act as a trustee of a trust scheme while he is disqualified under section 29 is guilty of an offence and liable—

(*a*) on summary conviction to a fine not exceeding the **statutory maximum**, and

(*b*) on conviction on indictment, to a **fine** or **imprisonment** or **both**[4].

(4) An offence under subsection (3) may be charged by reference to any day or longer period of time; and a person may be convicted of a second or subsequent offence under that subsection by reference to any period of time following the preceding conviction of the offence.

(5) Things done by a person disqualified under section 29 while purporting to act as trustee of a trust scheme are not invalid merely because of that disqualification.

(6) Nothing in section 29 or this section affects the liability of any person for things done, or omitted to be done, by him while purporting to act as trustee of a trust scheme.

(7)–(8) *Repealed.*

[Pensions Act 1995, s 30, as amended by the Child Support, Pensions and Social Security Act 2000, Sch 5 and the Pensions Act 2004, s 37 and Sch 12, 13.]

---

1. An occupational pension scheme established under a trust (s 124).
2. The Occupational Pensions Regulatory Authority (s 1).
3. For offences by bodies corporate and partnerships, see s 115, post.
4. For procedure in respect of an offence triable either way, see the Magistrates' Courts Act 1980, ss 17A–21 in PART I: MAGISTRATES' COURTS, PROCEDURE, ante.

8–29132EA 30A. Accessibility of register of disqualified trustees. *Repealed.*

8–29132F 31. Trustees not to be indemnified for fines or civil penalties. *Repealed.*

Gathering information: the Authority

8–29132G 98–102. *Repealed.*

Disclosure of information: the Authority

8–29132L 104. Restricted information. *Repealed.*

Gathering information: the Compensation Board

8–29132M 110–112. *Repealed.*

General

8–29132Q 115. Offences by bodies corporate and partnerships. (1) Where an offence under this Part committed by a body corporate is proved to have been committed with the consent or connivance of, or to be attributable to any neglect on the part of, a director, manager, secretary or other similar officer of the body, or a person purporting to act in any such capacity, he as well as the body corporate is guilty of the offence and liable to be proceeded against and punished accordingly.

(2) Where the affairs of a body corporate are managed by its members, subsection (1) applies in relation to the acts and defaults of a member in connection with his functions of management as to a director of a body corporate.

(3) Where an offence under this Part committed by a Scottish partnership is proved to have been committed with the consent or connivance of, or to be attributable to any neglect on the part of, a partner, he as well as the partnership is guilty of the offence and liable to be proceeded against and punished accordingly.
[Pensions Act 1995, s 115.]

8–29132R 116. Breach of regulations. (1) *Regulations.*

(2) An offence under any provision of the regulations may be charged by reference to any day or longer period of time; and a person may be convicted of a second or subsequent offence under such a provision by reference to any period of time following the preceding conviction of the offence.

(3) Where by reason of the contravention of any provision contained in regulations made by virtue of this Part—

(*a*) a person is convicted of an offence under this Part, or
(*b*) a person pays a penalty under section 10,

then, in respect of that contravention, he shall not, in a case within paragraph (*a*), be liable to pay such a penalty or, in a case within paragraph (*b*), be convicted of such an offence.
[Pensions Act 1995, s 116.]

PART IV
MISCELLANEOUS AND GENERAL

General

8–29132S 176. Interpretation. In this Act—

"enactment" includes an enactment comprised in subordinate legislation (within the meaning of the Interpretation Act 1978),
"occupational pension scheme" and "personal pension scheme" have the meaning given by section 1 of the Pension Schemes Act 1993,

and the definition of "enactment" shall apply for the purposes of section 114 as if "Act" in section 21(1) of the Interpretation Act 1978 included any enactment.
[Pensions Act 1995, s 111.]

8–29132T 177. *Repeals.*

8–29132U 178. *Extent.*

8–29132V 180. Commencement. (1) Subject to the following provisions, this Act shall come into force on such day as the Secretary of State may by order[1] made by statutory instrument appoint and different days may be appointed for different purposes.

(2) The following provisions shall come into force on the day this Act is passed—

(*a*) subject to the provisions of Schedule 4, Part II,
(*b*) section 168,
(*c*) sections 170 and 171,
(*d*) section 179,

and any repeal in Schedule 7 for which there is a note shall come into force in accordance with that note.

(3) Section 166 shall come into force on such day as the Lord Chancellor may by order made by statutory instrument appoint and different days may be appointed for different purposes.

(4) Without prejudice to section 174(3), the power to make an order under this section includes power—

(*a*) to make transitional adaptations or modifications—

(i) of the provisions brought into force by the order, or

(ii) in connection with those provisions, of any provisions of this Act, or the Pension Schemes Act 1993, then in force, or

(*b*) to save the effect of any of the repealed provisions of that Act, or those provisions as adapted or modified by the order,

as it appears to the Secretary of State expedient, including different adaptations or modifications for different periods.

[Pensions Act 1995, s 180.]

1. As to commencement orders which had been made at the date of going to press, see note 1 to the short title of this Act, ante.

8–29132W 181. *Title.*

Social Security Contributions (Transfer of Functions, etc) Act 1999

(1999 c 2)

8–29133 4. Recovery of contributions where income tax recovery provisions not applicable[1]. The provisions of Schedule 4 shall have effect with respect to the recovery of—

(*a*) those Class 1, Class 1A, Class 1B and Class 2 contributions to which regulations under paragraph 6 or 7BZA of Schedule 1 to the Social Security Contributions and Benefits Act 1992 or paragraph 6 or 7BZA of Schedule 1 to the Social Security Contributions and Benefits (Northern Ireland) Act 1992 (power to combine collection of contributions with income tax) do not apply,

(*b*) Class 4 contributions payable by virtue of regulations under section 18 of the Social Security Contributions and Benefits Act 1992 or section 18 of the Social Security Contributions and Benefits (Northern Ireland) Act 1992, and

(*c*) interest or penalties payable under regulations made under paragraph 7A or 7B of Schedule 1 to the Social Security Contributions and Benefits Act 1992 or paragraph 7A or 7B of Schedule 1 to the Social Security Contributions and Benefits (Northern Ireland) Act 1992 and

(*d*) interest or penalties—

(i) payable under regulations made under paragraph 7B of Schedule 1 to the Social Security Contributions and Benefits Act 1992 and to which regulations under paragraph 7BZA of that Schedule do not apply, or

(ii) payable under regulations made under paragraph 7B of Schedule 1 to the Social Security Contributions and Benefits (Northern Ireland) Act 1992 and to which regulations under paragraph 7BZA of that Schedule do not apply.

[Social Security Contributions (Transfer of Functions, etc) Act 1999, s 4, as amended by the Welfare Reform and Pensions Act 1999, Sch 11 the National Insurance Contributions and Statutory Payments Act 2004, Sch 1.]

1. The Social Security Contributions (Transfer of Functions, etc) Act 1999 provides for the transfer of certain functions from the Secretary of State to the Commissioners of Inland Revenue or the Treasury relating to national insurance contributions, the National Insurance Fund, statutory sick pay, statutory maternity pay or pension schemes and certain associated functions relating to benefits and to make further provision, in connection with the functions transferred, as to the powers of the Commissioners of Inland Revenue, and the making of decisions and appeals. The Act is brought in to force in accordance with s 28.

PART III
MISCELLANEOUS AND SUPPLEMENTAL

8–29134 28. Short title, commencement and extent. (1) This Act may be cited as the Social Security Contributions (Transfer of Functions, etc) Act 1999.

(2) The following provisions of this Act—

(*a*) section 1(1) (with Schedule 1), so far as enabling the Secretary of State to make subordinate legislation conferring functions on the Board,

(*b*) sections 8 to 15, so far as conferring any power to make subordinate legislation,

(*c*) section 17,

(*d*) section 20,
(*e*) section 22(4), so far as conferring the power to make an order,
(*f*) sections 24 and 25,
(*g*) section 26(1) (with Schedule 8), and
(*h*) section 27 and this section,

shall come into force on the passing of this Act.

(3) Except as provided by subsection (2) above, the provisions of this Act shall come into force on such day as the Secretary of State may by order appoint; and different days may be appointed for different purposes[1].

(4)–(7) *Further provisions as to orders and extent*

[Social Security Contributions (Transfer of Functions, etc) Act 1999, s 4, as amended by the Welfare Reform and Pensions Act 1999, Sch 11.]

---

1. At the date of going the following orders had been made:
Social Security Contributions (Transfer of Functions, etc) Act 1999 (Commencement No 1 and Transitional Provisions) Order 1999, SI 1999/527;
Social Security Contributions (Transfer of Functions, etc) Act 1999 (Commencement No 2 and Consequential and Transitional Provisions) Order 1999, SI 1999/1662.

SCHEDULE 4

Recovery of Contributions where Income Tax Recovery Provisions not Applicable

Interpretation

8–29135 **1.** In any provision of this Schedule "authorised officer" means an officer of the Board authorised by them for the purposes of that provision.

Magistrates' courts

8–29136 **2.** (1) Any amount which—

(*a*) is due by way of contributions or by way of interest or penalty in respect of contributions, and
(*b*) does not exceed the prescribed sum,

shall, without prejudice to any other remedy, be recoverable summarily as a civil debt in proceedings commenced in the name of an authorised officer.

(2) All or any of the sums due from any one person in respect of contributions, or interest or penalties in respect of contributions, (being sums which are by law recoverable summarily) may be included in the same complaint, summons, order, warrant or other document required by law to be laid before justices or to be issued by justices, and every such document shall, as respects each such sum, be construed as a separate document and its invalidity as respects any one such sum shall not affect its validity as respects any other such sum.

(3) Proceedings under this paragraph in England and Wales may be brought—

(*a*) in the case of Class 2 contributions or interest or penalties in respect of such contributions, at any time before the end of the year following the tax year in which the contributor becomes liable to pay the contributions, and
(*b*) in any other case, not later than the first anniversary of the day on which the contributions became due.

(4) In sub-paragraph (1) above, the expression "recoverable summarily as a civil debt" in respect of proceedings in Northern Ireland means recoverable in proceedings under Article 62 of the Magistrates' Courts (Northern Ireland) Order 1981.

(5) In this paragraph—

"the prescribed sum" means the sum for the time being specified in section 65(1) of the Taxes Management Act 1970 (recovery of income tax, etc in magistrates' courts);
"tax year" means the twelve months beginning with 6th April in any year.

County courts

Sheriff courts in Scotland

General

8–29137 **5.** (1) Proceedings may be brought for the recovery of the total amount of Class 1 or Class 1A contributions which an employer has become liable to pay on a particular date and any sum due by way of interest or penalty in respect of those contributions without distinguishing the amounts which the employer is liable to pay in respect of each employee and without specifying the employees in question; and for the purposes of proceedings under any of paragraphs 2 to 4 above that total amount shall be one cause of action or one matter of complaint.

(2) Nothing in sub-paragraph (1) above shall prevent the bringing of separate proceedings for the recovery of each of the several amounts of Class 1 or Class 1A contributions which the employer is liable to pay.

Child Support, Pensions and Social Security Act 2000

(2000 c 19)

PART III[1]

SOCIAL SECURITY

Loss of benefit

8–29138 **62. Loss of benefit for breach of community order[2].** (1) If—

(*a*) a court makes a determination that a person ("the offender") has failed without reasonable excuse to comply with the requirements of a relevant community order made in respect of him,

(*b*) the Secretary of State is notified in accordance with regulations under section 64 of the determination, and

(*c*) the offender is a person with respect to whom the conditions for any entitlement to a relevant benefit are or become satisfied,

then, even though those conditions are satisfied, the following restrictions shall apply in relation to the payment of that benefit in the offender's case.

(2) Subject to subsections (3) to (5), the relevant benefit shall not be payable in the offender's case for the prescribed[3] period.

(3) Where the relevant benefit is income support, the benefit shall be payable in the offender's case for the prescribed[3] period as if the applicable amount used for the determination under section 124(4) of the Social Security Contributions and Benefits Act 1992 of the amount of the offender's entitlement for that period were reduced in such manner as may be prescribed.

(4) The Secretary of State may by regulations provide that, where the relevant benefit is jobseeker's allowance, any income-based jobseeker's allowance shall be payable, during the whole or a part of the prescribed[3] period, as if one or more of the following applied—

(*a*) the rate of the allowance were such reduced rate as may be prescribed;

(*b*) the allowance were payable only if there is compliance by the offender with such obligations with respect to the provision of information as may be imposed by the regulations;

(*c*) the allowance were payable only if the circumstances are otherwise such as may be prescribed.

(5) Where the relevant benefit is a payment under section 2 of the Employment and Training Act 1973 (under which training allowances are payable), that benefit shall not be payable for the prescribed[3] period except to such extent (if any) as may be prescribed.

(6) Where the determination by a court that was made in the offender's case is quashed or otherwise set aside by the decision of that or any other court, all such payments and other adjustments shall be made in his case as would be necessary if the restrictions imposed by or under this section in respect of that determination had not been imposed.

(7) The length of any period prescribed for the purposes of any of subsections (2) to (5) shall not exceed twenty-six weeks.

(8) In this section—

"income-based jobseeker's allowance" and "joint-claim jobseeker's allowance" have the same meanings as in the Jobseekers Act 1995;

"relevant benefit" means—

(*a*) income support;

(*b*) any jobseeker's allowance other than joint-claim jobseeker's allowance;

(*c*) any benefit under the Social Security Contributions and Benefits Act 1992 (other than income support) which is prescribed for the purposes of this section; or

(*d*) any prescribed payment under section 2 of the Employment and Training Act 1973 (under which training allowances are payable);

"relevant community order" means—

(*a*) a community order made under section 177 of the Criminal Jusitce Act 2003; or;

(*b*) any order falling in England and Wales to be treated as such an order.

(9) In relation to a relevant benefit falling within paragraph (*d*) of the definition of that expression in subsection (8), references in this section to the conditions for entitlement to that benefit being or becoming satisfied with respect to any person are references to there having been or, as the case may be, the taking of a decision to make a payment of such benefit to that person.

(10) In relation to any time before the coming into force of the Powers of Criminal Courts (Sentencing) Act 2000, the reference to that Act in subsection (8) shall be taken to be a reference to Part I of the Criminal Justice Act 1991.

(11) In the application to Scotland of this section—

(*a*) in subsection (1) after the word "excuse" insert "(or, in the case of a probation order, failed)";

(*b*) for paragraph (*b*) of that subsection substitute—

"(*b*) the Secretary of State is notified in accordance with an Act of Adjournal made under section 64 of the determination"; and

(*c*) in subsection (8)—

(i) in the definition of relevant benefit, paragraph (*d*) does not apply in the case of any payment made by or on behalf of the Scottish Ministers; and

(ii) in the definition of relevant community order, for paragraphs (*a*) and (*b*) substitute—

"(*a*) a community service order;

(*b*) a probation order;

(*c*) such other description of order made under the Criminal Procedure (Scotland) Act 1995 as may be prescribed for the purposes of this section; or

(*d*) any order falling in Scotland to be treated as an order specified in paragraphs (*a*) to (*c*)."

[Child Support, Pensions and Social Security Act 2000, s 62, as amended by the Criminal Justice and Court Services Act 2000, Sch 7 and the Criminal Justice Act 2003, Sch 32.]

---

1. Sections 62 to 66 (loss of benefit for breach of community order) have been brought fully into force for the purposes of their application to persons in relation to whom specified community orders have been made, and who fall to be supervised in the probation areas of Derbyshire, Hertfordshire, Teesside or West Midlands: Child Support, Pensions and Social Security Act 2000 (Commencement No 10) Order 2001, SI 2001/2619.
2. Part III comprises ss 62–73.
3. The Social Security (Breach of Community Order) Regulations 2001, SI 2001/1395 amended by SI 2005/2687 have been made.

8–29139 63. Loss of joint-claim jobseeker's allowance[1]. (1) Subsections (2) and (3) shall have effect, subject to the other provisions of this section, where—

(*a*) the conditions for the entitlement of any joint-claim couple to a joint-claim jobseeker's allowance are or become satisfied at any time; and

(*b*) the restriction in subsection (2) of section 62 would apply in the case of at least one of the members of the couple if the entitlement were an entitlement of that member to a relevant benefit.

(2) The allowance shall not be payable in the couple's case for so much of the prescribed period as is a period for which—

(*a*) in the case of each of the members of the couple, the restriction in subsection (2) of section 62 would apply if the entitlement were an entitlement of that member to a relevant benefit; or

(*b*) that restriction would apply in the case of one of the members of the couple and the other member of the couple—

(i) is subject to sanctions for the purposes of section 20A of the Jobseekers Act 1995 (c 18) (denial or reduction of joint-claim jobseeker's allowance); or

(ii) is a person in whose case the restriction in subsection (2) of section 8 of the Social Security Fraud Act 2001 (loss of benefit for offenders) would apply if the entitlement were an entitlement to a sanctionable benefit (within the meaning of that section)

(3) For any part of the period for which subsection (2) does not apply, the allowance—

(*a*) shall be payable in the couple's case as if the amount of the allowance were reduced to an amount calculated using the method prescribed for the purposes of this subsection; but

(*b*) shall be payable only to the member of the couple who is not the person in relation to whom the court has made a determination.

(4) The Secretary of State may by regulations[2] provide in relation to cases to which subsection (2) would otherwise apply that joint-claim jobseeker's allowance shall be payable in a couple's case, during the whole or a part of so much of the prescribed period as falls within paragraph (*a*) or (*b*) of that subsection, as if one or more of the following applied—

(*a*) the rate of the allowance were such reduced rate as may be prescribed;

(*b*) the allowance were payable only if there is compliance by each of the members of the couple with such obligations with respect to the provision of information as may be imposed by the regulations;

(*c*) the allowance were payable only if the circumstances are otherwise such as may be prescribed.

(5) Subsection (6) of section 20A of the Jobseekers Act 1995 (calculation of reduced amount) shall apply for the purposes of subsection (3) above as it applies for the purposes of subsection (5) of that section.

(6) Subsection (6) of section 62 shall apply for the purposes of this section in relation to any determination relating to one or both members of the joint-claim couple as it applies for the purposes of that section in relation to the determination relating to the offender.

(7) The length of any period prescribed for the purposes of subsection (2) or (3) shall not exceed twenty-six weeks.

(8) In this section—

"joint-claim couple" and "joint-claim jobseeker's allowance" have the same meanings as in the Jobseekers Act 1995; and

"relevant benefit" has the same meaning as in section 62.

[Child Support, Pensions and Social Security Act 2000, s 63, as amended by the Social Security Fraud Act 2001, s 12.]

1. Sections 62 to 66 (loss of benefit for breach of community order) have been brought fully into force for the purposes of their application to persons in relation to whom specified community orders have been made, and who fall to be supervised in the probation areas of Derbyshire, Hertfordshire, Teesside or West Midlands: Child Support, Pensions and Social Security Act 2000 (Commencement No 10) Order 2001, SI 2001/2619.

2. The Social Security (Breach of Community Order) Regulations 2001, SI 2001/1395 amended by SI 2005/2687 have been made.

8–29140 **64. Information provision**[1]. (1) A court in Great Britain shall, before making a relevant community order in relation to any person, explain to that person in ordinary language the consequences by virtue of sections 62 and 63 of a failure to comply with the order.

(2) The Secretary of State may by regulations[2] require the chief officer of a local probation board, or such other person as may be prescribed, to notify the Secretary of State at the prescribed time and in the prescribed manner—

(*a*) of the laying by an officer of a local probation board of any information that a person has failed to comply with the requirements of a relevant community order;

(*b*) of any such determination as is mentioned in section 62(1);

(*c*) of such information about the offender, and in the possession of the person giving the notification, as may be prescribed; and

(*d*) of any circumstances by virtue of which any payment or adjustment might fall to be made by virtue of section 62(6) or 63(6).

(3) The High Court of Justiciary may, by Act of Adjournal, make provision requiring the clerk of the court in which any proceedings are commenced that could result in a determination of a failure to comply with a relevant community order to notify the Secretary of State at such time and in such manner as may be specified in the Act of Adjournal of—

(*a*) the commencement of the proceedings;

(*b*) any such determination made in the proceedings;

(*c*) such information about the offender as may be so specified; and

(*d*) any circumstances by virtue of which any payment or adjustment might fall to be made by virtue of section 62(6) or 63(6).

(4) Where it appears to the Secretary of State that—

(*a*) the laying of any information that has been laid in England and Wales, or

(*b*) the commencement of any proceedings that have been commenced in Scotland,

could result in a determination the making of which would result in the imposition by or under one or both of sections 62 and 63 of any restrictions, it shall be the duty of the Secretary of State to notify the person in whose case those restrictions would be imposed, or (as the case may be) the members of any joint-claim couple in whose case they would be imposed, of the consequences under those sections of such a determination in the case of that person, or couple.

(5) A notification required to be given by the Secretary of State under subsection (4) must be given as soon as reasonably practicable after it first appears to the Secretary of State as mentioned in that subsection.

(6) The Secretary of State may by regulations[2] make such provision as he thinks fit for the purposes of sections 62 to 65 of this Act about—

(*a*) the use by a person within subsection (7) of information relating to community orders (as defined by section 177 of the Criminal Justice Act 2003) ;

(*b*) the supply of such information by a person within that subsection to any other person (whether or not within that subsection); and

(*c*) the purposes for which a person to whom such information is supplied under the regulations may use it.

(7) The persons within this subsection are—

(*a*) the Secretary of State;

(*b*) a person providing services to the Secretary of State;

(*c*) an officer of a local probation board;

(*d*) a person employed by a council constituted under section 2 of the Local Government etc (Scotland) Act 1994.

(8) Regulations[2] under subsection (6) may, in particular, authorise information supplied to a person under the regulations—

(*a*) to be used for the purpose of amending or supplementing other information held by that person; and (*b*) where so used, to be supplied to any other person to whom, and used for any purpose for which, the information amended or supplemented could be supplied or used.

(9) The explanation given to the offender by the court in pursuance of subsection (1) shall be treated as part of the explanation required to be given to the offender for the purposes of section 228(5) or 238(4) of the Criminal Procedure (Scotland) Act 1995.

(10) In this section "relevant community order" has the same meaning as in section 62 and "local probation board" means a local probation board established under section 4 of the Criminal Justice and Court Services Act 2000.

(11) For the purposes of this section proceedings that could result in such a determination as is mentioned in subsection (3) are commenced in Scotland when, and only when, a warrant to arrest the offender or to cite the offender to appear before a court is issued under section 232(1) or 239(4) of the Criminal Procedure (Scotland) Act 1995.

[Child Support, Pensions and Social Security Act 2000, s 64, as amended by the Criminal Justice and Court Services Act 2000, Sch 7 and the Criminal Justice Act 2003, Sch 32.]

---

1. Sections 62 to 66 (loss of benefit for breach of community order) have been brought fully into force for the purposes of their application to persons in relation to whom specified community orders have been made, and who fall to be supervised in the probation areas of Derbyshire, Hertfordshire, Teesside or West Midlands: Child Support, Pensions and Social Security Act 2000 (Commencement No 10) Order 2001, SI 2001/2619.

2. The Social Security (Breach of Community Order) Regulations 2001, SI 2001/1395 amended by SI 2005/2687 have been made.

8–29141 **65. Loss of benefit regulations**[1]. (1) In the loss of benefit provisions "prescribed" means prescribed by or determined in accordance with regulations made by the Secretary of State.

(2) Regulations prescribing a period for the purposes of any of the loss of benefit provisions may contain provision for determining the time from which the period is to run.

(3) Regulations under any of the loss of benefit provisions shall be made by statutory instrument which (except in the case of regulations to which subsection (4) applies) shall be subject to annulment in pursuance of a resolution of either House of Parliament.

(4) A statutory instrument containing (whether alone or with other provisions)—

(*a*) a provision prescribing the manner in which the applicable amount is to be reduced for the purposes of section 62(3),

(*b*) a provision prescribing the manner in which an amount of joint-claim jobseeker's allowance is to be reduced for the purposes of section 63(3)(*a*),

(*c*) a provision the making of which is authorised by section 62(4) or 63(4),

(*d*) a provision prescribing benefits under the Social Security Contributions and Benefits Act 1992 as benefits that are to be relevant benefits for the purposes of section 62, or

(*e*) a provision that any description of order is to be a relevant community order for the purposes of that section,

shall not be made unless a draft of the instrument has been laid before, and approved by a resolution of, each House of Parliament.

(5) Subsections (4) to (6) of section 189 of the Social Security Administration Act 1992 (supplemental and incidental powers etc) shall apply in relation to any power to make regulations that is conferred by the loss of benefit provisions as they apply in relation to the powers to make regulations that are conferred by that Act.

(6) The provision that may be made in exercise of the powers to make regulations that are conferred by the loss of benefit provisions shall include different provision for different areas.

(7) Where regulations made under section 62(8) prescribe a description of order made under the Criminal Procedure (Scotland) Act 1995 as a relevant community order for the purposes of that section, the regulations may make such modifications of that section as appear to the Secretary of State to be necessary in consequence of so prescribing.

(8) In this section "the loss of benefit provisions" means sections 62 to 64 of this Act.

[Child Support, Pensions and Social Security Act 2000, s 65.]

---

1. Sections 62 to 66 (loss of benefit for breach of community order) have been brought fully into force for the purposes of their application to persons in relation to whom specified community orders have been made, and who fall to be supervised in the probation areas of Derbyshire, Hertfordshire, Teesside or West Midlands: Child Support, Pensions and Social Security Act 2000 (Commencement No 10) Order 2001, SI 2001/2619.

PART V[1]
MISCELLANEOUS AND SUPPLEMENTAL

Supplemental

8–29142 **86. Commencement and transitional provisions.** (1) This section applies to the following provisions of this Act—

(*a*) Part I (other than section 24);

(*b*) Part II (other than sections 38 and 39 and paragraphs 4 to 6, 8(1), (3) and (4) and 13 of Schedule 5);
(*c*) Part III;
(*d*) sections 82 and 83 and Schedule 8;
(*e*) Parts I to VII and IX of Schedule 9.

(2) The provisions of this Act to which this section applies shall come into force on such day as may be appointed by order[2] made by statutory instrument; and different days may be appointed under this section for different purposes.

(3) The power to make an order under subsection (2) shall be exercisable—

(*a*) except in a case falling within paragraph (*b*), by the Secretary of State; and
(*b*) in the case of an order bringing into force any of the provisions of sections 82 and 83, Schedule 8 or Part IX of Schedule 9, by the Lord Chancellor.

(4) In the case of Part I (other than section 24) and of sections 62 to 66, the power under subsection (2) to appoint different days for different purposes includes power to appoint different days for different areas.

(5) The Secretary of State may by regulations make such transitional provision as he considers necessary or expedient in connection with the bringing into force of any of the following provisions of this Act—

(*a*) sections 43 to 46 and section (1) of Part III of Schedule 9;
(*b*) sections 68 to 70 and Schedule 7 and Part VII of Schedule 9.

(6) Regulations under subsection (5) shall be made by statutory instrument subject to annulment in pursuance of a resolution of either House of Parliament.

(7) Section 174(2) to (4) of the Pensions Act 1995 (supplementary provision in relation to powers to make subordinate legislation under that Act) shall apply in relation to the power to make regulations under subsection (5) as it applies to any power to make regulations under that Act.

(8) In this section "subordinate legislation" has the same meaning as in the Interpretation Act 1978.

[Child Support, Pensions and Social Security Act 2000, s 86.]

---

1. Part V comprises ss 82–87.
2. The following commencement orders have been made: Child Support, Pensions and Social Security Act 2000 (Commencement No 1) Order 2000, SI 2000/2666; Child Support, Pensions and Social Security Act 2000 (Commencement No 2) Order 2000, SI 2000/2950 (as amended by SI 2000/3166); Child Support, Pensions and Social Security Act 2000 (Commencement No 3) Order 2000, SI 2000/2994, Child Support, Pensions and Social Security Act 2000 (Commencement No 4) Order 2000, SI 2000/3166 (as amended by SI 2001/1252); Child Support, Pensions and Social Security Act 2000 (Commencement No 5) Order 2000, SI 2000/3354; Child Support, Pensions and Social Security Act 2000 (Commencement No 6) Order 2001, SI 2001/153; Child Support, Pensions and Social Security Act 2000 (Commencement No 7) Order 2001, SI 2001/774; Child Support, Pensions and Social Security Act 2000 (Commencement No 8) Order 2001, SI 2001/1252; Child Support, Pensions and Social Security Act 2000 (Commencement No 9) Order 2001, SI 2001/2295, as amended by SI 2002/437; Child Support, Pensions and Social Security Act 2000 (Commencement No 10) Order 2001, SI 2001/2619; Child Support, Pensions and Social Security Act 2000 (Commencement No 11) Order 2002, SI 2002/437; Child Support, Pensions and Social Security Act 2000 (Commencement No 12) Order 2003, SI 2003/192, as amended by SI 2003/346.

8–29143 **87. Short title and extent.** (1) This Act may be cited as the Child Support, Pensions and Social Security Act 2000.

(2) The following provisions of this Act extend to Northern Ireland—

(*a*) so much of section 46 as amends section 21(3) of the Pensions Act 1995;
(*b*) sections 57 to 61 (except section 60(5));
(*c*) section 73;
(*d*) sections 78 to 81;
(*e*) in Schedule 3, paragraphs 8 and 9, and in paragraph 11, sub-paragraph (2) (and sub-paragraph (1) so far as it relates to that sub-paragraph);
(*f*) paragraph 6 of Schedule 5; and
(*g*) this Part, except—
  (i) sections 82 and 83 and Schedule 8; and
  (ii) so much of this Part as gives effect to any repeal other than the repeals mentioned in subsection (3).

(3) The repeals mentioned in subsection (2)(*g*) (which extend to Northern Ireland) are—

(*a*) the repeals, in Part I of Schedule 9, that relate to the Tax Credits Act 1999;
(*b*) the repeals, in sections (1), (6) and (11) of Part III of that Schedule, that relate to—
  (i) section 21(3) of the Pensions Act 1995;
  (ii) paragraph 49(*a*)(ii) of Schedule 3 to the Pensions (Northern Ireland) Order 1995; and
  (iii) section 52(5) of the Pension Schemes (Northern Ireland) Act 1993;
(*c*) the repeals in Part IV of that Schedule (except so far as relating to the Courts and Legal Services Act 1990); and

(*d*) the repeals in section (2) of Part VIII of that Schedule.

(4) Subject to that, this Act does not extend to Northern Ireland.
[Child Support, Pensions and Social Security Act 2000, s 87.]

Social Security Fraud Act 2001[1]

(2001 c 11)

[11th May 2001]

Loss of benefit provisions

8–29150 **7. Loss of benefit for commission of benefit offences.** (1) If—

(*a*) a person ("the offender") is convicted of one or more benefit offences in each of two separate sets of proceedings,

(*b*) the benefit offence, or one of the benefit offences, of which he is convicted in the later proceedings is one committed within the period of three years after the date, or any of the dates, on which he was convicted of a benefit offence in the earlier proceedings,

(*c*) the later set of proceedings has not been taken into account for the purposes of any previous application of this section or section 8 or 9 in relation to the offender or any person who was then a member of his family,

(*d*) the earlier set of proceedings has not been taken into account as the earlier set of proceedings for the purposes of any previous application of this section or either of those sections in relation to the offender or any person who was then a member of his family, and

(*e*) the offender is a person with respect to whom the conditions for an entitlement to a sanctionable benefit are or become satisfied at any time within the disqualification period,

then, even though those conditions are satisfied, the following restrictions shall apply in relation to the payment of that benefit in the offender's case.

(2) Subject to subsections (3) to (5), the sanctionable benefit shall not be payable in the offender's case for any period comprised in the disqualification period.

(3) Where the sanctionable benefit is income support, the benefit shall be payable in the offender's case for any period comprised in the disqualification period as if the applicable amount used for the determination under section 124(4) of the Social Security Contributions and Benefits Act 1992 (c 4) of the amount of the offender's entitlement for that period were reduced in such manner as may be prescribed.

(4) The Secretary of State may by regulations provide that, where the sanctionable benefit is jobseeker's allowance, any income-based jobseeker's allowance shall be payable, during the whole or a part of any period comprised in the disqualification period, as if one or more of the following applied—

(*a*) the rate of the allowance were such reduced rate as may be prescribed;

(*b*) the allowance were payable only if there is compliance by the offender with such obligations with respect to the provision of information as may be imposed by the regulations;

(*c*) the allowance were payable only if the circumstances are otherwise such as may be prescribed.

(4A) The Secretary of State may by regulations provide that, where the sanctionable benefit is state pension credit, the benefit shall be payable in the offender's case for any period comprised in the disqualification period as if the rate of the benefit were reduced in such manner as may be prescribed.

(5) The Secretary of State may by regulations provide that, where the sanctionable benefit is housing benefit or council tax benefit, the benefit shall be payable, during the whole or a part of any period comprised in the disqualification period, as if one or both of the following applied—

(*a*) the rate of the benefit were reduced in such manner as may be prescribed;

(*b*) the benefit were payable only if the circumstances are such as may be prescribed.

(6) For the purposes of this section the disqualification period, in relation to the conviction of a person of one or more benefit offences in each of two separate sets of proceedings, means the period of thirteen weeks beginning with such date, falling after the date of the conviction in the later set of proceedings, as may be determined by or in accordance with regulations made by the Secretary of State.

(7) Where—

(*a*) the conviction of any person of any offence is taken into account for the purposes of the application of this section in relation to that person, and

(*b*) that conviction is subsequently quashed,

all such payments and other adjustments shall be made as would be necessary if no restriction had been imposed by or under this section that could not have been imposed if the conviction had not taken place.

(8) In this section—

"benefit offence" means—

(*a*) any post-commencement offence in connection with a claim for a disqualifying benefit;
(*b*) any post-commencement offence in connection with the receipt or payment of any amount by way of such a benefit;
(*c*) any post-commencement offence committed for the purpose of facilitating the commission (whether or not by the same person) of a benefit offence;
(*d*) any post-commencement offence consisting in an attempt or conspiracy to commit a benefit offence;

"disqualifying benefit" means (subject to any regulations under section 10(1))—

(*a*) any benefit under the Jobseekers Act 1995 (c 18) or the Jobseekers (Northern Ireland) Order 1995 (SI 1995/2705 (NI 15));
(*aa*) any benefit under the State Pension Credit Act 2002 or under any provision having effect in Northern Ireland corresponding to that Act;
(*b*) any benefit under the Social Security Contributions and Benefits Act 1992 (c 4) or the Social Security Contributions and Benefits (Northern Ireland) Act 1992 (c 7) other than—
  (i) maternity allowance;
  (ii) (*repealed*)
  (iii) (*repealed*)
  (iv) statutory sick pay and statutory maternity pay;
(*c*) any war pension;

"sanctionable benefit" means (subject to subsection (11) and to any regulations under section 10(1)) any disqualifying benefit other than—

(*a*) joint-claim jobseeker's allowance;
(*b*) any retirement pension;
(*c*) graduated retirement benefit;
(*d*) disability living allowance;
(*e*) attendance allowance;
(*f*) child benefit;
(*g*) guardian's allowance;
(*h*) a payment out of the social fund in accordance with Part 8 of the Social Security Contributions and Benefits Act 1992;
(i) a payment under Part X of that Act (Christmas bonuses).

(9) For the purposes of this section—

(*a*) the date of a person's conviction in any proceedings of a benefit offence shall be taken to be the date on which he was found guilty of that offence in those proceedings (whenever he was sentenced); and
(*b*) references to a conviction include references to a conviction in relation to which the court makes an order for a conditional discharge or a court in Scotland makes a probation order and to a conviction in Northern Ireland.

(10) In this section references to any previous application of this section or section 8 or 9—

(*a*) include references to any previous application of a provision having an effect in Northern Ireland corresponding to provision made by this section, or either of those sections; but
(*b*) do not include references to any previous application of this section, or of either of those sections, the effect of which was to impose a restriction for a period comprised in the same disqualification period.

(11) In its application to Northern Ireland this section shall have effect as if references to a sanctionable benefit were references only to a war pension.
[Social Security Fraud Act 2001, s 7, as amended by the Tax Credits Act 2002, s 14.]

1. As to commencement of this Act, see s 20 and commencement orders made thereunder, post.

8–29151 **8.** *Effect of offence on joint-claim jobseeker's allowance*

8–29152 **9.** *Effect of offence on benefits for members of offender's family*

8–29153 **10.** *Power to supplement and mitigate loss of benefit provisions*

8–29154 **11.** *Loss of benefit regulations*

8–29155 **12.** *Consequential amendments*

8–29156 **13. Interpretation of sections 7 to 12.** In this section and sections 7 to 12—

"benefit" includes any allowance, payment, credit or loan;

"disqualification period" has the meaning given by section 7(6);

"family" has the same meaning as in Part 7 of the Social Security Contributions and Benefits Act 1992 (c 4);

"income-based jobseeker's allowance", "joint-claim jobseeker's allowance" and "joint-claim couple" have the same meanings as in the Jobseekers Act 1995 (c 18);

"post-commencement offence" means any criminal offence committed after the commencement of section 7;

"sanctionable benefit" has the meaning given by section 7(8);

"state pension credit" means state pension credit under the State Pension Credit Act 2002;

"war pension" has the same meaning as in section 25 of the Social Security Act 1989 (c 24) (establishment and functions of war pensions committees).

[Social Security Fraud Act 2001, s 13, as amended by the State Pension Credit Act 2002, Sch 2.]

Supplemental

8–29157 **18. Meaning of "the Administration Act".** In this Act "the Administration Act" means the Social Security Administration Act 1992 (c 5).
[Social Security Fraud Act 2001, s 18.]

8–29158 **19.** *Repeals*

8–29159 **20. Commencement.** (1) The preceding provisions of this Act shall come into force on such day as the Secretary of State may by order[1] made by statutory instrument appoint.

(2) Subject to subsection (3), different days may be appointed under this section for different purposes.

(3) The power under this section to appoint a day for the coming into force of the provisions of sections 1 and 2 shall not authorise the appointment for those purposes of any day before the issue of the code of practice that must be issued under section 3.
[Social Security Fraud Act 2001, s 20.]

1. At the date of going to press the following commencement orders had been made: (No 1) SI 2001/3251; (No 2) SI 2001/3689; (No 3), SI 2002/117; (No 4) SI 2002/403; (No 5) SI 2002/1222; (No 6) SI 2003/273. All the provisions reproduced here are in force.

8–29160 **21.** *Short title and extent*

Tax Credits Act 2002[1]

(2002 c 21)

PART 1
TAX CREDITS

Fraud

8–29200 **35. Offence of fraud.** (1) A person commits an offence if he is knowingly concerned in any fraudulent activity undertaken with a view to obtaining payments of a tax credit by him or any other person.

(2) A person who commits an offence under subsection (1) is liable[2]—

(a) on summary conviction, to imprisonment for a term not exceeding six months, or a fine not exceeding the statutory maximum, or both, or

(b) on conviction on indictment, to imprisonment for a term not exceeding seven years, or a fine, or both.

[Tax Credits Act 2002, s 35.]

1. Administrative penalties may be levied under ss 31–34 in respect of incorrect statements, failure to comply with requirements and failure by employers to make correct payments. Provision is made for commencement of this Act by orders made under ss 61 and 62. At the date of going to press the following commencement orders had been made: (No 1) SI 2002/1727; (No 2) SI 2003/392. All the provisions reproduced here are in force.

2. For procedure in respect of this offence, which is triable either way, see the Magistrates' Courts Act 1980, ss 17A–21, in PART I: MAGISTRATES' COURTS, PROCEDURE, ante.

8–29201 **36. Powers in relation to documents.** (1) Section 20BA of the Taxes Management Act 1970 (c 9) (orders for delivery of documents) applies (with Schedule 1AA and section 20BB) in relation to offences involving fraud in connection with, or in relation to, tax credits as in relation to offences involving serious fraud in connection with, or in relation to, tax.

(2) Section 20C (entry with warrant to obtain documents) of that Act applies (with section 20CC) in relation to offences involving serious fraud in connection with, or in relation to, tax credits as in

relation to offences involving serious fraud in connection with, or in relation to, tax (but subject to the modification provided by subsection (3)).

(3) Subsection (1A) of section 20C applies by virtue of subsection (2) as if the references to the proper assessment or collection of tax were to the proper award or payment of a tax credit.

(4) Any regulations under Schedule 1AA to the Taxes Management Act 1970 which are in force immediately before the commencement of subsection (1) apply, subject to any necessary modifications, for the purposes of that Schedule as they apply by virtue of that subsection (until amended or revoked).
[Tax Credits Act 2002, s 36.]

Pensions Act 2004[1]

(2004 c 35)

Gathering information

8–29210 72. Provision of information. (1) The Regulator may, by notice in writing, require any person to whom subsection (2) applies to produce any document, or provide any other information, which is—

(*a*) of a description specified in the notice, and
(*b*) relevant to the exercise of the Regulator's functions.

(2) This subsection applies to—

(*a*) a trustee or manager of an occupational or personal pension scheme,
(*b*) a professional adviser in relation to an occupational pension scheme,
(*c*) the employer in relation to—
  (i) an occupational pension scheme, or
  (ii) a personal pension scheme where direct payment arrangements exist in respect of one or more members of the scheme who are employees, and
(*d*) any other person appearing to the Regulator to be a person who holds, or is likely to hold, information relevant to the exercise of the Regulator's functions.

(3) Where the production of a document, or the provision of information, is required by a notice given under subsection (1), the document must be produced, or information must be provided, in such a manner, at such a place and within such a period as may be specified in the notice.
[Pensions Act 2004, s 72.]

1. The provisions reproduced here are to be brought into force in accordance with commencement orders made under s 322. At the date of going to press, no such orders had been made.

8–29211 73. Inspection of premises. (1) An inspector may, for the purposes of investigating whether, in the case of any occupational pension scheme, the occupational scheme provisions are being, or have been, complied with, at any reasonable time enter premises liable to inspection.

(2) In subsection (1), the "occupational scheme provisions" means provisions contained in or made by virtue of—

(*a*) any of the following provisions of this Act—
this Part;
Part 3 (scheme funding);
sections 241 to 243 (member-nominated trustees and directors);
sections 247 to 249 (requirement for knowledge and understanding);
section 252 (UK-based scheme to be trust with effective rules);
section 253 (non-European scheme to be trust with UK-resident trustee);
section 255 (activities of occupational pension schemes);
section 256 (no indemnification for fines or civil penalties);
sections 259 and 261 (consultation by employers);
Part 7 (cross-border activities within European Union);
Part 9 (miscellaneous and supplementary);
(*b*) either of the following provisions of the Welfare Reform and Pensions Act 1999 (c 30)—
section 33 (time for discharge of pension credit liability);
section 45 (information);
(*c*) any of the provisions of Part 1 of the Pensions Act 1995 (c 26) (occupational pension schemes), other than—
  (i) sections 51 to 54 (indexation), and
  (ii) sections 62 to 65 (equal treatment);
(*d*) any of the following provisions of the Pension Schemes Act 1993 (c 48)—

Chapter 4 of Part 4 (transfer values);
Chapter 5 of Part 4 (early leavers: cash transfer sums and contribution refunds);
Chapter 2 of Part 4A (pension credit transfer values);
section 113 (information);
section 175 (levy);

(*e*) any provisions in force in Northern Ireland corresponding to any provisions within paragraphs (*a*) to (*d*).

(3) An inspector may, for the purposes of investigating whether, in the case of a stakeholder scheme—

(*a*) sections 1 and 2(4) of the Welfare Reform and Pensions Act 1999 (stakeholder pension schemes: registration etc), or
(*b*) any corresponding provisions in force in Northern Ireland,

are being, or have been, complied with, at any reasonable time enter premises liable to inspection.

(4) An inspector may, for the purposes of investigating whether, in the case of any trust-based personal stakeholder scheme, the trust-based scheme provisions are being, or have been, complied with, at any reasonable time enter premises liable to inspection.

(5) In subsection (4)—

"trust-based personal stakeholder scheme" means a personal pension scheme which—

(*a*) is a stakeholder scheme, and
(*b*) is established under a trust;

the "trust-based scheme provisions" means any provisions contained in or made by virtue of—

(*a*) any provision which applies in relation to trust-based personal stakeholder schemes by virtue of paragraph 1 of Schedule 1 to the Welfare Reform and Pensions Act 1999 (c 30); as the provision applies by virtue of that paragraph, or
(*b*) any corresponding provision in force in Northern Ireland.

(6) Premises are liable to inspection for the purposes of this section if the inspector has reasonable grounds to believe that—

(*a*) members of the scheme are employed there,
(*b*) documents relevant to the administration of the scheme are being kept there, or
(*c*) the administration of the scheme, or work connected with that administration, is being carried out there.

(7) In this section, "stakeholder scheme" means an occupational pension scheme or a personal pension scheme which is or has been registered under—

(*a*) section 2 of the Welfare Reform and Pensions Act 1999 (register of stakeholder schemes), or
(*b*) any corresponding provision in force in Northern Ireland.

[Pensions Act 2004, s 73.]

8–29212 74. Inspection of premises in respect of employers' obligations. (1) An inspector may, for the purposes of investigating whether an employer is complying, or has complied, with the requirements under—

(*a*) section 3 of the Welfare Reform and Pensions Act 1999 (duty of employers to facilitate access to stakeholder pension schemes), or
(*b*) any corresponding provision in force in Northern Ireland,

at any reasonable time enter premises liable to inspection.

(2) Premises are liable to inspection for the purposes of subsection (1) if the inspector has reasonable grounds to believe that—

(*a*) employees of the employer are employed there,
(*b*) documents relevant to the administration of the employer's business are being kept there, or
(*c*) the administration of the employer's business, or work connected with that administration, is being carried out there.

(3) In subsections (1) and (2), "employer" has the meaning given by section 3(9) of the Welfare Reform and Pensions Act 1999 (or, where subsection (1)(b) applies, by any corresponding provision in force in Northern Ireland).

(4) An inspector may, for the purposes of investigating whether, in the case of any direct payment arrangements relating to a personal pension scheme, any of the following provisions—

(*a*) regulations made by virtue of sections 260 and 261 (consultation by employers),
(*b*) section 111A of the Pension Schemes Act 1993 (c 48) (monitoring of employers' payments to personal pension schemes), or
(*c*) any corresponding provisions in force in Northern Ireland,

is being, or has been, complied with, at any reasonable time enter premises liable to inspection.

(5) Premises are liable to inspection for the purposes of subsection (4) if the inspector has reasonable grounds to believe that—

(*a*) employees of the employer are employed there,
(*b*) documents relevant to the administration of—

(i) the employer's business,
(ii) the direct payment arrangements, or
(iii) the scheme to which those arrangements relate,

are being kept there, or

(*c*) either of the following is being carried out there—
(i) the administration of the employer's business, the arrangements or the scheme;
(ii) work connected with that administration.

(6) In the application of subsections (4) and (5) in relation to any provision mentioned in subsection (4)(c) (a "corresponding Northern Ireland provision"), references in those subsections to—

direct payment arrangements,
a personal pension scheme,
the employer, or
employees of the employer,

are to be read as having the meanings that they have for the purposes of the corresponding Northern Ireland provision.
[Pensions Act 2004, s 74.]

8–29213 **75. Inspection of premises: powers of inspectors.** (1) Subsection (2) applies where, for a purpose mentioned in subsection (1), (3) or (4) of section 73 or subsection (1) or (4) of section 74, an inspector enters premises which are liable to inspection for the purposes of that provision.

(2) While there, the inspector—

(*a*) may make such examination and inquiry as may be necessary for the purpose for which he entered the premises,
(*b*) may require any person on the premises to produce, or secure the production of, any document relevant to compliance with the regulatory provisions for his inspection,
(*c*) may take copies of any such document,
(*d*) may take possession of any document appearing to be a document relevant to compliance with the regulatory provisions or take in relation to any such document any other steps which appear necessary for preserving it or preventing interference with it,
(*e*) may, in the case of any such document which consists of information which is stored in electronic form and is on, or accessible from, the premises, require the information to be produced in a form—

(i) in which it can be taken away, and
(ii) in which it is legible or from which it can readily be produced in a legible form, and

(*f*) may, as to any matter relevant to compliance with the regulatory provisions, examine, or require to be examined, either alone or in the presence of another person, any person on the premises whom he has reasonable cause to believe to be able to give information relevant to that matter.

[Pensions Act 2004, s 75.]

8–29214 **76. Inspection of premises: supplementary.** (1) This section applies for the purposes of sections 73 to 75.

(2) Premises which are a private dwelling-house not used by, or by permission of, the occupier for the purposes of a trade or business are not liable to inspection.

(3) Any question whether—

(*a*) anything is being or has been done or omitted which might by virtue of any of the regulatory provisions give rise to a liability for a civil penalty under or by virtue of section 10 of the Pensions Act 1995 (c 26) or section 168(4) of the Pension Schemes Act 1993 (c 48) (or under or by virtue of any provision in force in Northern Ireland corresponding to either of them), or
(*b*) an offence is being or has been committed under any of the regulatory provisions,

is to be treated as a question whether the regulatory provision is being, or has been, complied with.

(4) An inspector applying for admission to any premises for the purposes of section 73 or 74 must, if so required, produce his certificate of appointment.

(5) When exercising a power under section 73, 74 or 75 an inspector may be accompanied by such persons as he considers appropriate.

(6) Any document of which possession is taken under section 75 may be retained—

(*a*) if the document is relevant to proceedings against any person for any offence which are commenced before the end of the retention period, until the conclusion of those proceedings, and

(*b*) otherwise, until the end of the retention period.

(7) In subsection (6), "the retention period" means the period comprising—

(*a*) the period of 12 months beginning with the date on which possession was taken of the document, and

(*b*) any extension of that period under subsection (8).

(8) The Regulator may, by a direction made before the end of the retention period (including any extension of it under this subsection), extend it by such period not exceeding 12 months as the Regulator considers appropriate.

(9) "The regulatory provisions", in relation to an inspection under subsection (1), (3) or (4) of section 73 or subsection (1) or (4) of section 74, means the provision or provisions referred to in that subsection.

[Pensions Act 2004, s 76.]

8–29215 77. Penalties relating to sections 72 to 75. (1) A person who, without reasonable excuse, neglects or refuses to provide information or produce a document when required to do so under section 72 is guilty of an offence.

(2) A person who without reasonable excuse—

(*a*) intentionally delays or obstructs an inspector exercising any power under section 73, 74 or 75,

(*b*) neglects or refuses to produce, or secure the production of, any document when required to do so under section 75, or

(*c*) neglects or refuses to answer a question or to provide information when so required,

is guilty of an offence.

(3) A person guilty of an offence under subsection (1) or (2) is liable on summary conviction to a fine not exceeding level 5 on the standard scale.

(4) An offence under subsection (1) or (2)(b) or (c) may be charged by reference to any day or longer period of time; and a person may be convicted of a second or subsequent offence by reference to any period of time following the preceding conviction of the offence.

(5) Any person who intentionally and without reasonable excuse alters, suppresses, conceals or destroys any document which he is or is liable to be required to produce under section 72 or 75 is guilty of an offence.

(6) Any person guilty of an offence under subsection (5) is liable—

(*a*) on summary conviction, to a fine not exceeding the statutory maximum;

(*b*) on conviction on indictment, to a fine or imprisonment for a term not exceeding two years, or both.

[Pensions Act 2004, s 77.]

8–29216 78. Warrants. (1) A justice of the peace may issue a warrant under this section if satisfied on information on oath given by or on behalf of the Regulator that there are reasonable grounds for believing—

(*a*) that there is on, or accessible from, any premises any document—

- (i) whose production has been required under section 72 or 75, or any corresponding provision in force in Northern Ireland, and
- (ii) which has not been produced in compliance with that requirement,

(*b*) that there is on, or accessible from, any premises any document whose production could be so required and, if its production were so required, the document—

- (i) would not be produced, but
- (ii) would be removed, or made inaccessible, from the premises, hidden, tampered with or destroyed, or

(*c*) that—

- (i) an offence has been committed,
- (ii) a person will do any act which constitutes a misuse or misappropriation of the assets of an occupational pension scheme or a personal pension scheme,
- (iii) a person is liable to pay a penalty under or by virtue of section 10 of the Pensions Act 1995 (c 26) (civil penalties) or section 168(4) of the Pension Schemes Act 1993 (c 48) (civil penalties for breach of regulations), or under or by virtue of any provision in force in Northern Ireland corresponding to either of them, or

(iv) a person is liable to be prohibited from being a trustee of an occupational or personal pension scheme under section 3 of the Pensions Act 1995 (prohibition orders), including that section as it applies by virtue of paragraph 1 of Schedule 1 to the Welfare Reform and Pensions Act 1999 (c 30) (stakeholder schemes), or under or by virtue of any corresponding provisions in force in Northern Ireland,

and that there is on, or accessible from, any premises any document which relates to whether the offence has been committed, whether the act will be done or whether the person is so liable, and whose production could be required under section 72 or 75 or any corresponding provision in force in Northern Ireland.

(2) A warrant under this section shall authorise an inspector—

(*a*) to enter the premises specified in the information, using such force as is reasonably necessary for the purpose,

(*b*) to search the premises and—

(i) take possession of any document appearing to be such a document as is mentioned in subsection (1), or

(ii) take in relation to such a document any other steps which appear necessary for preserving it or preventing interference with it,

(*c*) to take copies of any such document,

(*d*) to require any person named in the warrant to provide an explanation of any such document or to state where it may be found or how access to it may be obtained, and

(*e*) in the case of any such document which consists of information which is stored in electronic form and is on, or accessible from, the premises, to require the information to be produced in a form—

(i) in which it can be taken away, and

(ii) in which it is legible or from which it can readily be produced in a legible form.

(3) In subsection (1), any reference in paragraph (a) or (b) to a document does not include any document which is relevant to whether a person has complied with—

(*a*) subsection (3) of section 238 (information and advice to employees) or regulations under subsection (4) of that section, or

(*b*) any provision in force in Northern Ireland which corresponds to that subsection (3) or is made under provision corresponding to that subsection (4),

and is not relevant to the exercise of the Regulator's functions for any other reason.

(4) For the purposes of subsection (1)(c)(iii), any liability to pay a penalty under—

(*a*) section 10 of the Pensions Act 1995 (c 26), or

(*b*) any corresponding provision in force in Northern Ireland,

which might arise out of a failure to comply with any provision within subsection (3)(a) or (b) is to be disregarded.

(5) References in subsection (2) to such a document as is mentioned in subsection (1) are to be read in accordance with subsections (3) and (4).

(6) When executing a warrant under this section, an inspector may be accompanied by such persons as he considers appropriate.

(7) A warrant under this section continues in force until the end of the period of one month beginning with the day on which it is issued.

(8) Any document of which possession is taken under this section may be retained—

(*a*) if the document is relevant to proceedings against any person for any offence which are commenced before the end of the retention period, until the conclusion of those proceedings, and

(*b*) otherwise, until the end of the retention period.

(9) In subsection (8), "the retention period" means the period comprising—

(*a*) the period of 12 months beginning with the date on which possession was taken of the document, and

(*b*) any extension of that period under subsection (10).

(10) The Regulator may, by a direction made before the end of the retention period (including any extension of it under this subsection), extend it by such period not exceeding 12 months as the Regulator considers appropriate.

(11) In the application of this section in Scotland—

(*a*) the reference to a justice of the peace is to be read as a reference to the sheriff, and

(*b*) the references in subsections (1) and (2)(a) to information are to be read as references to evidence.

[Pensions Act 2004, s 78.]

8–29217 **79. Sections 72 to 78: interpretation.** (1) This section applies for the purposes of sections 72 to 78.

(2) "Document" includes information recorded in any form, and any reference to production of a document, in relation to information recorded otherwise than in a legible form, is to producing a copy of the information—

(*a*) in a legible form, or
(*b*) in a form from which it can readily be produced in a legible form.

(3) "Inspector" means a person appointed by the Regulator as an inspector.
[Pensions Act 2004, s 79.]

8–29218 190. Information to be provided to the Board etc. (1) Regulations[1] may require such persons as may be prescribed to provide—

(*a*) to the Board, or
(*b*) to a person—

(i) with whom the Board has made arrangements under paragraph 18 of Schedule 5, and
(ii) who is authorised by the Board for the purposes of the regulations,

information of a prescribed description at such times, or in such circumstances, as may be prescribed.

(2) Regulations under subsection (1) may in particular make provision for requiring such persons as may be prescribed to provide any information or evidence needed for a determination of entitlement to compensation under Chapter 3 of this Part.

(3) Regulations made by virtue of paragraph (b) of that subsection must make provision regarding the manner in which the persons required to provide information are to be notified of the identity of the person authorised as mentioned in sub-paragraph (ii) of that paragraph.
[Pensions Act 2004, s 190.]

1. See the Pension Protection Fund (Provision of Information) Regulations 2005, SI 2005/674.

8–29219 191. Notices requiring provision of information. (1) Any person to whom subsection (3) applies may be required by a notice in writing to produce any document, or provide any other information, which is—

(*a*) of a description specified in the notice, and
(*b*) relevant to the exercise of the Board's functions in relation to an occupational pension scheme.

(2) A notice under subsection (1) may be given by—

(*a*) the Board, or
(*b*) a person authorised by the Board for the purposes of this section in relation to the scheme.

(3) This subsection applies to—

(*a*) a trustee or manager of the scheme,
(*b*) a professional adviser in relation to the scheme,
(*c*) the employer in relation to the scheme,
(*d*) an insolvency practitioner in relation to the employer, and
(*e*) any other person appearing to the Board, or person giving the notice, to be a person who holds, or is likely to hold, information relevant to the discharge of the Board's functions in relation to the scheme.

(4) Where the production of a document, or the provision of information, is required by a notice given under subsection (1), the document must be produced, or information must be provided, in such a manner, at such a place and within such a period as may be specified in the notice.
[Pensions Act 2004, s 191.]

8–29220 192. Entry of premises. (1) An appointed person may, for the purpose of enabling or facilitating the performance of any function of the Board in relation to an occupational pension scheme, at any reasonable time enter scheme premises and, while there—

(*a*) may make such examination and inquiry as may be necessary for such purpose,
(*b*) may require any person on the premises to produce, or secure the production of, any document relevant to that purpose for inspection by the appointed person,
(*c*) may take copies of any such document,
(*d*) may take possession of any document appearing to be such a document or take in relation to any such document any other steps which appear necessary for preserving it or preventing interference with it,

(*e*) may, in the case of any such document which consists of information which is stored in electronic form and is on, or accessible from, the premises, require the information to be produced in a form—

(i) in which it can be taken away, and
(ii) in which it is legible or from which it can readily be produced in a legible form, and

(*f*) may, as to any matter relevant to the exercise of the Board's functions in relation to the scheme, examine, or require to be examined, either alone or in the *presence* of another person, any person on the premises whom he has reasonable cause to believe to be able to give information relevant to that matter.

(2) Premises are scheme premises for the purposes of subsection (1) if the appointed person has reasonable grounds to believe that—

(*a*) they are being used for the business of the employer,
(*b*) an insolvency practitioner in relation to the employer is acting there in that capacity,
(*c*) documents relevant to—

(i) the administration of the scheme, or
(ii) the employer,

are being kept there, or

(*d*) the administration of the scheme, or work connected with the administration of the scheme, is being carried out there,

unless the premises are a private dwelling-house not used by, or by permission of, the occupier for the purposes of a trade or business.

(3) An appointed person applying for admission to any premises for the purposes of this section must, if so required, produce his certificate of appointment.

(4) When exercising a power under this section an appointed person may be accompanied by such persons as he considers appropriate.

(5) Any document of which possession is taken under this section may be retained until the end of the period comprising—

(*a*) the period of 12 months beginning with the date on which possession was taken of the document, and
(*b*) any extension of that period under subsection (6).

(6) The Board may before the end of the period mentioned in subsection (5) (including any extension of it under this subsection) extend it by such period not exceeding 12 months as the Board considers appropriate.

(7) In this section "appointed person" means a person appointed by the Board for the purposes of this section in relation to the scheme.

[Pensions Act 2004, s 192.]

8–29221 193. Penalties relating to sections 191 and 192. (1) A person who, without reasonable excuse, neglects or refuses to provide information or produce a document when required to do so under section 191 is guilty of an offence.

(2) A person who without reasonable excuse—

(*a*) intentionally delays or obstructs an appointed person exercising any power under section 192,
(*b*) neglects or refuses to produce, or secure the production of, any document when required to do so under that section, or
(*c*) neglects or refuses to answer a question or to provide information when so required,

is guilty of an offence.

(3) In subsection (2)(a) "appointed person" has the same meaning as it has in section 192.

(4) A person guilty of an offence under subsection (1) or (2) is liable on summary conviction to a fine not exceeding level 5 on the standard scale.

(5) An offence under subsection (1) or (2)(b) or (c) may be charged by reference to any day or longer period of time; and a person may be convicted of a second or subsequent offence by reference to any period of time following the preceding conviction of the offence.

(6) Any person who intentionally and without reasonable excuse alters, suppresses, conceals or destroys any document which he is or is liable to be required to produce under section 191 or 192 is guilty of an offence.

(7) Any person guilty of an offence under subsection (6) is liable—

(*a*) on summary conviction, to a fine not exceeding the statutory maximum;
(*b*) on conviction on indictment, to a fine or imprisonment for a term not exceeding two years, or both.

[Pensions Act 2004, s 193.]

8–29222 194. Warrants. (1) A justice of the peace may issue a warrant under this section if satisfied on information on oath given by or on behalf of the Board that there are reasonable grounds for believing—

(*a*) that there is on, or accessible from, any premises any document—

(i) whose production has been required under section 191 or 192, or any corresponding provision in force in Northern Ireland, and

(ii) which has not been produced in compliance with that requirement,

(*b*) that there is on, or accessible from, any premises any document relevant to the exercise of the Board's functions in relation to an occupational pension scheme whose production could be so required and, if its production were so required, the document—

(i) would not be produced, but

(ii) would be removed, or made inaccessible, from the premises, hidden, tampered with or destroyed, or

(*c*) that a person will do any act which constitutes a misuse or misappropriation of the assets of an occupational pension scheme and that there is on, or accessible from, any premises any document—

(i) which relates to whether the act will be done, and

(ii) whose production could be required under section 191 or 192, or any corresponding provision in force in Northern Ireland.

(2) A warrant under this section shall authorise an inspector—

(*a*) to enter the premises specified in the information, using such force as is reasonably necessary for the purpose,

(*b*) to search the premises and—

(i) take possession of any document appearing to be such a document as is mentioned in subsection (1), or

(ii) take in relation to such a document any other steps which appear necessary for preserving it or preventing interference with it,

(*c*) to take copies of any such document,

(*d*) to require any person named in the warrant to provide an explanation of any such document or to state where it may be found or how access to it may be obtained, and

(*e*) in the case of any such document which consists of information which is stored in electronic form and is on, or accessible from, the premises, to require the information to be produced in a form—

(i) in which it can be taken away, and

(ii) in which it is legible or from which it can readily be produced in a legible form.

(3) When executing a warrant under this section, an inspector may be accompanied by such persons as he considers appropriate.

(4) A warrant under this section continues in force until the end of the period of one month beginning with the day on which it is issued.

(5) Any document of which possession is taken under this section may be retained until the end of the period comprising—

(*a*) the period of 12 months beginning with the date on which possession was taken of the document, and

(*b*) any extension of that period under subsection (6).

(6) The Board may before the end of the period mentioned in subsection (5) (including any extension of it under this subsection) extend it by such period not exceeding 12 months as the Board considers appropriate.

(7) In this section "inspector" means a person appointed by the Board as an inspector.

(8) In the application of this section in Scotland—

(*a*) the reference to a justice of the peace is to be read as a reference to the sheriff, and

(*b*) the references in subsections (1) and (2)(a) to information are to be read as references to evidence.

[Pensions Act 2004, s 194.]

Provision of false or misleading information

8–29223 **195. Offence of providing false or misleading information to the Board.** (1) Any person who knowingly or recklessly provides information which is false or misleading in a material particular is guilty of an offence if the information—

(*a*) is provided in purported compliance with a requirement under—

(i) section 190 (information to be provided to the Board etc),

(ii) section 191 (notices requiring provision of information), or

(iii) section 192 (entry of premises), or

(*b*) is provided otherwise than as mentioned in paragraph (a) but in circumstances in which the person providing the information intends, or could reasonably be expected to know, that it would be used by the Board for the purposes of exercising its functions under this Act.

(2) Any person guilty of an offence under subsection (1) is liable—

(*a*) on summary conviction, to a fine not exceeding the statutory maximum;
(*b*) on conviction on indictment, to a fine or imprisonment for a term not exceeding two years, or both.

[Pensions Act 2004, s 195.]

Interpretation

8–29224 204. Sections 190 to 203: interpretation. (1) This section applies for the purposes of sections 190 to 203.

(2) "Document" includes information recorded in any form, and any reference to production of a document, in relation to information recorded otherwise than in a legible form, is to producing a copy of the information—

(*a*) in a legible form, or
(*b*) in a form from which it can readily be produced in a legible form.

(3) Where the Board has assumed responsibility for a scheme—

(*a*) any reference to the Board's functions in relation to the scheme includes a reference to the functions which it has by virtue of having assumed responsibility for the scheme, and
(*b*) any reference to a trustee, manager, professional adviser or employer in relation to the scheme is to be read as a reference to a person who held that position in relation to the scheme before the Board assumed responsibility for it.

[Pensions Act 2004, s 204.]

8–29225 322. Commencement. (1) Subject to subsections (2) to (4), the provisions of this Act come into force in accordance with provision made by the Secretary of State by order.

(2) The following provisions come into force on the day this Act is passed—

(*a*) in Part 4, sections 234, 235 and 236 and Schedule 10 (provisions relating to retirement planning);
(*b*) in Part 5, section 281 (exemption from statutory revaluation requirement);
(*c*) in Part 8—

(i) section 296 (entitlement to more than one state pension),
(ii) section 297(3) (commencement of amendments of state pension deferment provisions made by Pensions Act 1995),
(iii) section 298 (disclosure of state pension information), except subsections (4) and (5)(b), and
(iv) section 299 (claims for certain benefits following termination of reciprocal agreement with Australia);

(*d*) in this Part (miscellaneous and general)—

(i) sections 303 to 305 (service of notifications etc and electronic working), and
(ii) this section and sections 313, 315 (other than subsection (6)), 316, 317, 318 (other than subsections (4) and (5)) and 323 to 325;

(*e*) the repeal by this Act of section 50(2) of the Welfare Reform and Pensions Act 1999.

(3) Section 297 (and Schedule 11) (deferral of retirement pensions and shared additional pensions), other than the provisions coming into force in accordance with subsection (2)—

(*a*) come into force on the day this Act is passed so far as is necessary for enabling the making of any regulations for which they provide, and
(*b*) otherwise, come into force on 6th April 2005.

(4) The repeals by this Act of section 134(3) of, and paragraph 21(14) of Schedule 4 to, the Pensions Act 1995 (c 26) come into force on 6th April 2005.

(5) Without prejudice to section 315(5), the power to make an order under this section includes power—

(*a*) to make transitional adaptations or modifications—

(i) of the provisions brought into force by the order, or
(ii) in connection with those provisions, of any provisions of Parts 1 to 7 of this Act or of the Pension Schemes Act 1993 (c 48), the Pensions Act 1995, Parts 1, 2 or 4 of the Welfare Reform and Pensions Act 1999 (c 30) or Chapter 2 of Part 2 of the Child Support, Pensions and Social Security Act 2000 (c 19), or

(*b*) to save the effect of any of the repealed provisions of those Acts, or those provisions as adapted or modified by the order,

as it appears to the Secretary of State expedient, including different adaptations or modifications for different periods.
[Pensions Act 2004, s 322.]

Social Security (Claims and Payments) Regulations 1979[1]

(SI 1979/628, as amended by SI 1979/781 and 1199, SI 1980/1101, 1136, 1621, and 1943, SI 1982/699, 1241, 1344, and 1362, SI 1983/186, and 1015, SI 1984/458, 550, 1303, and 1699, SI 1985/600, SI 1986/903, SI 1993/495 and 405, SI 1993/2113 and SI 2002/1397)

Information to be given when making a claim for benefit

8–29280 **7.** (1) Every person who makes a claim for benefit[2] shall furnish such certificates, documents, information and evidence for the purpose of determining the claim as may be required by the Secretary of State and, if reasonably so required, shall for that purpose attend at such office or place as the Secretary of State may direct.

(2) Every person who makes a claim for a widowed mother's allowance, child's special allowance, benefit in respect of a child or for an increase of benefit in respect of a child, shall, in particular, furnish such certificate relating to the birth of the child and such other information to show that that person is entitled or may be treated by regulations as if he were entitled to child benefit in respect of that child as the Secretary of State may require.

(3) Every person who makes a claim for an increase of benefit in respect of an adult dependant shall, in particular, furnish, if required, the following information concerning such dependant—

(*a*) his identity, date of birth, usual place of residence, occupation and relationship to the claimant;

(*b*) his position in regard to benefit under the Act, available sources of income and the amounts contributed by any person towards his maintenance; and

(*c*) in the case of an increase in respect of a wife or a husband, a certificate of the marriage;

together with a declaration signed by the dependant confirming the information given.

(4) Every person who makes a claim for a death grant shall, in particular, furnish the following information—

(*a*) if required by the Secretary of State, a death certificate relating to the deceased; and, where the claim is in respect of the death of a child, such certificate relating to the birth of the child, and such other information as the Secretary of State may reasonably require in support of a contention that immediately before the death of the child or the person by whom the contribution condition is to be satisfied, as the case may be, that person was entitled to child benefit in respect of that child; in this sub-paragraph a child includes a person referred to in section 32(4) (*a*) or (*b*);

(*b*) if required by the Secretary of State, the estimate or account of the undertaker.

(5) In this regulation the expression "child benefit" means benefit under Part 1 of the Child Benefit Act 1975.

1. Made by the Secretary of State for Social Services under ss 45(4), 79–81, 88–90 and 146(5) of the Social Security Act 1975 and paras 9(1) (*a*) and (*c*) of Sch 3 to the Social Security (Consequential Provisions) Act 1975. Only those parts of the Regulations of direct concern to magistrates' courts are included here.

2. "Claim for benefit" includes an application for a declaration that an accident was an industrial accident and an application for the review of an award or a decision for the purpose of obtaining any increase of benefit mentioned in Schedule 1 to these regulations but does not include any other application for the review of an award or a decision; and the expression "claims benefit" and every reference to a claim shall be construed accordingly (reg 2(1)).

Information to be given when obtaining payment of benefit

8–29281 **23.** (1) Every beneficiary and every person by whom or on whose behalf sums payable by way of benefit are receivable shall furnish in such manner and at such times as the Secretary of State may determine such certificates and other documents and such information of facts affecting the right to benefit or to its receipt as the Secretary of State may require (either as a condition on which any sum or sums shall be receivable or otherwise), and in particular shall notify the Secretary of State in writing of any change of circumstances which he might reasonably be expected to know might affect the right to benefit, or to its receipt, as soon as reasonably practicable after the occurrence thereof.

(2) Where any sum is receivable on account of an increase of benefit in respect of an adult dependant the beneficiary shall, in such cases or classes of case as the Secretary of State may direct, furnish a declaration signed by such dependant confirming the particulars respecting him furnished by the claimant.

Breach of regulations

8–29282 **31.** If any person contravenes or fails to comply with any requirement of these regulations (not being a requirement to give notice of an accident or a requirement to submit himself to medical treatment or examination) in respect of which no special penalty is provided, he shall for such offence be liable on summary conviction to a penalty not exceeding **level 3** or, where the offence consists of continuing any such contravention or failure after conviction thereof, **£20** for each day on which it is so continued.

Income Support (Liable Relatives) Regulations 1990[1]

(SI 1990/1777, as amended by SI 2002/2497)

Citation, commencement and interpretation

8–29290 **1.** (1) *Citation and commencement.*

(2) In these Regulations—

"the Act" means the Social Security Act 1986; and
"the Income Support Regulations" means the Income Support (General) Regulations 1987.

1. Made by the Secretary of State for Social Security, in exercise of the powers conferred by section 166(1) to (3A) of the Social Security Act 1975 and ss 24A(1), 24B(5) and 84(1) of the Social Security Act 1986.

Prescribed amounts for the purposes of section 24A of the Act

8–29291 **2.** (1) For the purposes of section 24A of the Act (recovery of expenditure on income support: additional amounts and transfer of orders) the amount which may be included in the sum which the court may order the other parent to pay under section 24(4) of the Act shall be the whole of the following amounts which are payable to or for the claimant—

(*a*) any personal allowance under paragraph 2 of Part 1 of Schedule 2 to the Income Support Regulations for each of the children whom the other parent is liable to maintain;
(*b*) any family premium under paragraph 3 of Part II of that Schedule;
(*c*) any lone parent premium under paragraph 8 of Part III of that Schedule;
(*d*) any disabled child premium under paragraph 14 of Part III of that Schedule in respect of a child whom the other parent is liable to maintain; and
(*e*) any carer premium under paragraph 14ZA of Part III of that Schedule if, but only if, that premium is payable because the claimant is in receipt, or is treated as being in receipt, of carer's allowance by reason of the fact that he is caring for a severely disabled child or young person whom the other parent is liable to maintain.

(2) If the court is satisfied that in addition to the amounts specified in paragraph (1) above the liable parent has the means to pay, the sum which the court may order him to pay under section 24 of the Act may also include all or some of the amount of any personal allowance payable to or for the claimant under paragraph 1 of Part I of Schedule 2 to the Income Support Regulations.

Notice to the Secretary of State of applications to alter etc maintenance orders

8–29292 **3.** (1) For the purposes of section 24B(5) of the Act (prescribed person in prescribed circumstances to notify the Secretary of State of application to alter etc a maintenance order) the prescribed person is, and in paragraph (2) below that expression means—

(*a*) in England and Wales—

(i) in relation to the High Court, where the case is proceeding in the deputy principal registry the senior registrar of that registry, and where the case is proceeding in a district registry the district registrar;
(ii) in relation to a county court, the proper officer of that court within the meaning of Order 1, Rule 3 of the County Court Rules 1981; and
(iii) in relation to a magistrates' court, the clerk to the justices of that court; and

(*b*) in Scotland—

(i) in relation to the Court of Session, the deputy principal clerk of session; and
(ii) in relation to a sheriff court, the sheriff clerk.

(2) For the purposes of that subsection the prescribed circumstances are that before the final determination of the application the Secretary of State has made a written request to the prescribed person that he be notified of any such application, and has not made a written withdrawal of that request.

SOLICITORS

8–29309 This title contains the following statutes—

8–29309A European lawyers. The European Communities (Lawyer's Practice) Regulations 2000, SI 2000/1119 amended by SI 2001/644 and SI 2004/1628 made under s 2(2) of the European Communities Act 1972, give effect to European Communities Council Directive 98/5/EC. The purpose of the Directive is to facilitate the practice of the profession of lawyer on a permanent basis in a member State of the European Community other than the State in which the qualification was obtained. A European lawyer may apply to register with the solicitors' or the barristers' professional bodies. It is an offence punishable on summary conviction with a fine not exceeding **level 4** on the standard scale to pretend to be a registered European lawyer (reg 21). A certificate purporting to be signed by an officer of a professional body is evidence that a person is or is not registered with that professional body unless the contrary is proved (reg 23). A registered European lawyer is subject to the rules of professional conduct and disciplinary proceedings applicable to the professional body with which he is registered (regs 25 and 26). A registered European lawyer may apply for entry into the profession of solicitor or barrister (reg 29). Enactments relating to the provision of legal advice and assistance and legal aid, certain enactments reserving certain activities to solicitors, barristers and other qualified persons are modified accordingly (Sch 3); and certain enactments extended in relation to the registration of European lawyers with the Law Society (Sch 4).

8–29309B Apparent bias by legal representatives. Where a firm of solicitors has acted for one party in proceedings where they have previously acted for another party to them, an injunction may be issued to restrain the solicitors from acting based on the protection of confidential information, relevant to the proceedings, which the firm received when acting for the other party unless the solicitors establish that there is no real risk that the information is or will become known to those within the firm now proposing to act[1]. In care proceedings where the solicitor for the children had previously represented the father in the juvenile court and in other criminal proceedings but the solicitor had no recollection of the juvenile court proceedings nor any knowledge of the latter criminal proceedings, the court rightly refused not to continue to hear the solicitor[2]. It is generally undesirable for husband and wife, or other partners living together, to appear as advocates against each other in a contested criminal matter[3]. The particular sensitivity of care proceedings places a premium on impartiality and cohabitation by advocates for the local authority and one of the parties would give rise to a reasonable lay apprehension of bias in the other parties[4].

1. *Bolkiah (Prince Jefri) v KPMG (a firm)* [1999] 2 AC 222, [1999] 1 All ER 517, [1999] 2 WLR 215, HL.
2. *Re T and A (children) (risk of disclosure)* [2000] 1 FCR 659, [2000] 1 FLR 859, CA.
3. *R v Batt* [1996] Crim LR 910, CA.
4. *In re L (Minors) (care proceedings: solicitors)* [2001] 1 WLR 100, [2000] 3 FCR 71, [2000] 2 FLR 887, FD.

Solicitors Act 1974[1]

(1974 c 47)

8–29310 20. Unqualified person[2] not to act as solicitor. An unqualified person acting as a solicitor in any civil or criminal cause or matter is guilty of an offence punishable on indictment by imprisonment not exceeding two years and/or a fine, and may in addition be punished for contempt of court and proceeded against by the Law Society for an additional penalty.

[Solicitors Act 1974, s 20, as amended by the Courts and Legal Services Act 1990, Schs 18 and 20—summarised.]

1. See also PART I: MAGISTRATES' COURTS, PROCEDURE, para **1–139 Appearance by legal representative**, ante.
2. No person shall be qualified to act as a solicitor unless his name is on the roll—ie the list of solicitors kept in accordance with this Act, s 6(1)—and he has in force a practising certificate (s 1) and a person who is not so qualified is referred to in this Part as an "unqualified person" (s 87). A practising certificate has effect from the date which it bears until 31 October 31 (s 14). The certificate is suspended if an order is made by the Solicitors Disciplinary Tribunal (s 14) or the court suspending the solicitor from practice or if he is adjudicated bankrupt (s 15). Any list published by authority of the Law Society containing the names of solicitors holding practising certificates is *prima facie* evidence whether or not he holds a certificate (s 18). For European Lawyers see para **8–29309A**, ante.

8–29320 21. Unqualified person not to pretend to be a solicitor[1]. Any unqualified person[1], who wilfully pretends[2] to be, or takes or uses any name, title, addition or description implying that he is, qualified or recognised by law as qualified[3] to act as a solicitor, shall be guilty of an offence and liable on summary conviction to a fine not exceeding the **fourth level** on the standard scale.

[Solicitors Act 1974, s 214, as amended by the Criminal Justice Act 1982, ss 38 and 46 and the Administration of Justice Act 1985, Sch 1.]

---

1. See note 2 to s 20, supra.

2. B, a person in the employ of a tailor, was in the habit of issuing county court summonses for his employer, and applying for debts on a printed form sent from and bearing his own address, under the orders of his master, headed "Notice of intention to take proceedings in the county court for recovery of small debts," and ending with the words, "Unless you pay forthwith I shall proceed against you under the above Act." In a case where he demanded 9*s*. 6*d*. larger than the debt, and the receiver believed the letter came from a solicitor, the Queen's Bench Division held it was a question of fact whether B, intended falsely to represent himself as a solicitor, and the magistrate was not bound to convict upon the evidence (*Incorporated Law Society v Bedford* (1885) 49 JP 215). A notice in a printed form, "Final notice before proceeding in the county court," or "I hereby give you notice that unless the sum of £1 2*s*. 6*d*., due by you to Messrs. H and L, be paid on or before 21st inst., I shall proceed against you under the above Act," was sent by a partner of the firm, but did not on the face of it show he applied for payment of the debt as a member of the firm. The Queen's Bench Division held justices were wrong in convicting (*Symonds v Incorporated Law Society* (1884) 49 JP 212). Convictions were upheld when an unqualified person advertised that a society of which he was general secretary would do conveyancing business at cheap rates for any who would become members (*Carter v Butcher* [1966] 1 QB 326, [1965] 1 All ER 994).

3. Where a solicitor, while suspended from practice, on being approached on a matter of legal business, merely described himself as a solicitor, it was held that he held himself out as a person qualified to act as such. On the other hand, there may be occasions when the use of that word would not have that implication (*Taylor v Richardson* [1938] 2 All ER 681, 102 JP 341).

A person who not being duly qualified or authorised sues out any writ or process, or carries on any such proceeding as a solicitor is alone authorised to carry on, in effect acts as a solicitor, whether he acts in his own name or that of another (*Re Simmons* (1885) 15 QB 348, 49 JP 741). An unqualified person who gives notice of appearance on behalf of a defendant is carrying on a proceeding within what is now s 20(1) of the Solicitors Act 1974 (*Re Ainsworth, ex p Law Society* [1905] 2 KB 103).

4. See note 5 to s 22, below.

8–29321 **22. Unqualified person not to prepare certain instruments.** (1) Subject to subsections (2) and (2A), any unqualified person who directly or indirectly

(*a*) draws or prepares any instrument or transfer or charge for the purposes of the Land Registration Act 2002, or makes any application[1] or lodges any document for registration under that Act at the registry or,

(*b*) draws or prepares any instrument relating to real or personal estate or any legal proceeding[2] shall, unless he proves that the act was not done for or in expectation of any fee, gain or reward[3], be guilty of an offence and liable on summary conviction to a fine not exceeding **level 3** on the standard scale.

(2) Subsection (1) does not apply

(*a*) to a barrister or duly certificated notary public;

(*aa*) a registered trade mark agent drawing or preparing any instrument relating to any design or trade mark;

(*ab*) a registered patent agent drawing or preparing any instrument relating to any invention, design, technical information or trade mark;

(*ac*) any accredited person drawing or preparing any instrument—

(i) which creates, or which he believes on reasonable grounds will create, a farm business tenancy (within the meaning of the Agricultural Tenancies Act 1995), or

(ii) which relates to an existing tenancy which is, or which he believes on reasonable grounds to be, such a tenancy;

(*b*) any public officer[4] drawing or preparing instruments or applications in the course of his duty;

(*c*) any person employed merely to engross any instrument, application or proceeding, and paragraph

(*d*) of that subsection shall not apply to a duly certificated solicitor in Scotland.

(2A) Subsection (1) also does not apply to any act done by a person at the direction and under the supervision of another person if—

(*a*) that other person was at the time his employer, a partner of his employer or a fellow employee; and

(*b*) the act could have been done by that other person for or in expectation of any fee, gain or reward without committing an offence under this section.

(3) For the purposes of subsection (1)(*b*), "instrument" includes a contract for the sale or other disposition of land (except a contract to grant such a lease as is referred to in section 54(2) of the Law of Property Act 1925 (short leases)), but does not include:—

(*a*) a will or other testamentary instrument;

(*b*) an agreement not intended to be executed as a deed other than a contract that is included by virtue of the preceding provisions of this subsection;

(*c*) a letter or power of attorney; or

(*d*) a transfer of stock containing no trust or limitation thereof.

(3A) In subsection (2)—

"accredited person" means any person who is—

(*a*) a Full Member of the Central Association of Agricultural Valuers,
(*b*) an Associate or Fellow of the Incorporated Society of Valuers and Auctioneers, or
(*c*) an Associate or Fellow of the Royal Institution of Chartered Surveyors;

"registered trade mark agent" has the same meaning as in the Trade Marks Act 1994; and
"registered patent agent" has the same meaning as in section 275(1) of the Copyright, Designs and Patents Act 1988.

(4) A local weights and measures authority may institute proceedings[5] for an offence under this section.

[Solicitors Act 1974, s 22, as amended by the Criminal Justice Act 1982, ss 38 and 46, the Administration of Justice Act 1985, s 6, the Law of Property (Miscellaneous Provisions) Act 1989, Sch 1, the Courts and Legal Services Act 1990, s 68, the Trade Marks Act 1994, Sch 4, the Agricultural Tenancies Act 1995, s 35 and the Land Registration Act 2002, s 133.]

1. Ie, an application for registration (*Carter v Butcher* [1966] 1 QB 326, [1965] 1 All ER 994).

2. A rent or debt collector taking legal proceedings for no specific remuneration but in anticipation of a fixed commission on any moneys collected is guilty of an offence (*Pacey v Atkinson* [1950] 1 KB 539, [1950] 1 All ER 320, 114 JP 152).

3. Provided a fee, gain or reward is received by someone, it is immaterial that it does not go to the person who actually prepared the instrument (*Reynolds v Hoyle* [1975] 3 All ER 934, [1976] 1 WLR 207); nor does the fee have to be directly attributable to the instrument (*Reynolds v Hoyle (No 2)* (1980) 124 Sol Jo 543).

4. For definition of "public officer", cf *Beeston and Stapleford UDC v Smith* [1949] 1 KB 656, [1949] 1 All ER 394, 113 JP 160.

5. Proceedings under this section may be brought within two years next after the commission of the offence or within six months after the first discovery thereof by the prosecutor, whichever period expires first (Solicitors Act 1974, s 26).

8–29322 **22A. Powers of entry etc of local weights and measures authorities.** (1) Any authorised officer who has reasonable cause to suspect that an offence may have been committed under section 22 may, at any reasonable time—

(*a*) enter any premises which are not used solely as a dwelling;
(*b*) require any officer, agent or other competent person on the premises who is, or may be, in possession of information relevant to an investigation under section 22, to provide such information;
(*c*) require the production of any document which may be relevant to such an investigation;
(*d*) take copies, or extracts, of any such documents;
(*e*) seize and retain any document which he has reason to believe may be required as evidence in proceedings for an offence under section 22.

(2) Any person exercising any power given by subsection (1) shall, if asked to do so, produce evidence that he is an authorised officer.

(3) A justice of the peace may issue a warrant under this section if satisfied, on information on oath given by an authorised officer, that there is reasonable cause to believe that an offence may have been committed under section 22 and that—

(*a*) entry to the premises concerned, or production of any documents which may be relevant to an investigation under section 22, has been or is likely to be refused to an authorised officer; or
(*b*) there is reasonable cause to believe that, if production of any such document were to be required by the authorised officer without a warrant having been issued under this section, the document would not be produced but would be removed from the premises or hidden, tampered with or destroyed.

(4) A warrant issued under this section shall authorise the authorised officer accompanied, where he considers it appropriate, by a constable or any other person—

(*a*) to enter the premises specified in the information, using such force as is reasonably necessary; and
(*b*) to exercise any of the powers given to the authorised officer by subsection (1).

(5) If a person—

(*a*) intentionally obstructs an authorised officer in the exercise of any power under this section;
(*b*) intentionally fails to comply with any requirement properly imposed on him by an authorised officer in the exercise of any such power;
(*c*) fails, without reasonable excuse, to give to an authorised officer any assistance or information which he may reasonably require of him for the purpose of exercising any such power; or
(*d*) in giving to an authorised officer any information which he has been required to give to an authorised officer exercising any such power, makes any statement which he knows to be false or misleading in a material particular,

he shall be guilty of an offence.

(6) A person guilty of an offence under this section shall be liable on summary conviction to a fine not exceeding **level 3** on the standard scale.

(7) Nothing in this section shall be taken to require any person to answer any question put to him

by an authorised officer, or to give any information to an authorised officer, if to do so might incriminate him.

(8) In this section—

"authorised officer" means any officer of a local weights and measures authority who is authorised by the authority to exercise the powers given by subsection (1); and

"document" includes information recorded in any form.

(9) In relation to information recorded otherwise than in legible form, references in this section to its production include references to producing a copy of the information in legible form.

[Solicitors Act 1974, s 22A, as inserted by the Courts and Legal Services Act 1990, s 96.]

8–29323 **23. Unqualified person not to prepare papers for probate, etc.** (1) Subject to subsections (2) and (3) and unqualified person who, directly or indirectly, draws or prepares any papers on which to found or oppose—

(*a*) a grant of probate or

(*b*) a grant of letters of administration,

shall, unless he proves that the act was not done for or in expectation of any fee, gain or reward, be guilty of an offence and liable on summary conviction to a fine not exceeding the **first level** on the standard scale.

(2) Subsection (1) does not apply to a barrister or duly certified notary public[1].

(3) Subsection (1) also does not apply to any act done by a person at the direction and under the supervision of another person if—

(*a*) that other person was at the time his employer, a partner of his employer or a fellow employee; and

(*b*) the act could have been done by that other person for or in expectation of any fee, gain or reward without committing an offence under this section.*

[Solicitors Act 1974, s 23, as substituted by the Administration of Justice Act 1985, s 7.]

***Amended by the Courts and Legal Services Act 1990, s 54, and the Friendly Societies Act 1992, Sch 21, when in force.**

1. This subsection shall have effect as if the reference to an insurance company authorised under ss 3 or 4 of the Insurance Companies Act 1982 included a reference to an EC company lawfully carrying on insurance business in the United Kingdom (Insurance Companies (Third Insurance Directives) Regulations 1994, SI 1994/1696, Sch 8, para 4). For the meaning of "an EC company lawfully carrying on insurance business in the United Kingdom" see regs 68–71 and transitional provisions of the said Regulations.

8–29324 **24. Application of penal provisions to body corporate[1].** (1) If any act is done by a body corporate or by any director, officer, or servant of a body corporate, and is of such a nature or is done in such a manner as to be calculated[2] to imply that the body corporate is qualified or recognised by law as qualified to act as a solicitor, (*a*) the body corporate shall be guilty of an offence and liable on summary conviction to a fine not exceeding the **fourth level** on the standard scale, and (*b*), in the case of an act done by a director, officer, or servant of the body corporate, he shall be guilty of an offence and liable on summary conviction to a fine not exceeding the **fourth level** on the standard scale.

(2) For the avoidance of doubt it is hereby declared that in ss 20, 22 and 23 of this Act, references to unqualified persons and to persons include references to bodies corporate.

[Solicitors Act 1974, s 24, as amended by the Criminal Law Act 1977, s 31, the Criminal Justice Act 1982, ss 38 and 46 and the Administration of Justice Act 1985, Sch 1.]

1. See *Dean v Hiesler* [1942] 2 All ER 340, 106 JP 282. See also *Beeston and Stapleford UDC v Smith* [1949] 1 KB 656, [1949] 1 All ER 394, 113 JP 160.

2. This means likely to deceive—not intended to deceive (cf *Re London and Globe Finance Corpn Ltd* [1903] 1 Ch 728, 82 JP 447; *R v Wines* [1953] 2 All ER 1497, [1954] 1 WLR 64, 118 JP 49).

8–29325 **35–36. Intervention in solicitor's practice and Compensation Fund.** The Law Society has established and administers a Compensation Fund from which grants are paid to mitigate losses sustained in consequence of the dishonesty of a solicitor or his employees. The Law Society may intervene in a solicitor's practice in circumstances and to the extent set out in Schedule 1.

[Solicitors Act 1974, ss 35 and 36—summarised.]

Inadequate professional services

8–29326 **37A. Redress for inadequate professional services.** Schedule 1A[1] shall have effect with respect to the provision by solicitors of services which are not of the quality which it is reasonable to expect of them.

[Solicitors Act 1974, s 37A, as inserted by the Courts and Legal Services Act 1990, s 93.]

1. Schedule 1A is not printed in this work.

8–29327 38. Solicitor who is justice of the peace not to act in certain proceedings. (1) Subject to the provisions of this section, it shall not be lawful for any solicitor who is one of the justices of the peace for any area, or for any partner of his, to act in connection with proceedings before any of those justices as solicitor or agent for the solicitor of any person concerned in those proceedings.

(2) Where the area for which a solicitor is a justice of the peace consists of two or more petty sessions areas, his being a justice for the area shall not subject him or any partner of his to any disqualification under this section in relation to proceedings before justices acting for a petty sessions area for which he does not ordinarily act.

(3) Where a solicitor is a justice of the peace for any area, that shall not subject him or any partner of his to any disqualification under this section of his name is entered in the supplemental list kept under section 7 of the Justices of the Peace Act 1997.

(3A) Subsection (1) does not apply where a solicitor is a Deputy District Judge (Magistrates' Courts); but where a solicitor is acting as a Deputy District Judge (Magistrates' Courts) for any petty sessions area it shall not be lawful for him, or for any partner of his, to act in connection with proceedings before any justice of the peace acting for that area as solicitor or agent for the solicitor of any person concerned in those proceedings.

(4) *Repealed.*

[Solicitors Act 1974, s 38, as amended by the Justices of the Peace Act 1997, Sch 5 and the Access to Justice Act 1999, Schs 10, 11 and 15.]

8–29328 42. Failure to disclose fact of having been struck off or suspended. (1) Any person who, while he is disqualified from practising as a solicitor by reason of the fact that (*a*) his name has been struck off the roll, or (*b*) he is suspended from practising as a solicitor, or (*c*) his practising certificate is suspended while he is an undischarged bankrupt, seeks or accepts employment by a solicitor in connection with that solicitor's practice without previously informing him that he is so disqualified, shall be guilty of an offence and liable on summary conviction to a fine not exceeding **level 1** on the standard scale.

(1A) Any person—

(*a*) with respect to whom a direction is in force under section 47(2)(*g*); and

(*b*) who seeks or accepts employment by a solicitor in connection with that solicitor's practice without previously informing him of the direction,

shall be guilty of an offence and liable on summary conviction to a fine not exceeding **level three** on the standard scale.

(2) Notwithstanding anything in the Magistrates' Courts Act 1980, proceedings under this section may be commenced at any time before the expiration of six months after the first discovery of the offence by the prosecutor, but no such proceedings shall be commenced except by, or with the consent[1] of, the Attorney-General.

[Solicitors Act 1974, s 42, as amended by the Criminal Law Act 1977, s 31, the Magistrates' Courts Act 1980, Sch 7, the Criminal Justice Act 1982, s 46 and the Courts and Legal Services Act 1990, Sch 18.]

---

1. As to the consent of the Solicitor-General, see para **1–410 Criminal Prosecutions**, ante, and as to proof of such consent, see the Prosecution of Offences Act 1985, s 26 in PART I: MAGISTRATES' COURTS, PROCEDURE, ante.

8–29329 43. Control of solicitors' employees and consultants. (1) Where a person who is or was employed or remunerated by a solicitor in connection with his practice but is not himself a solicitor—

(*a*) has been convicted of a criminal offence which discloses such dishonesty that in the opinion of the Society[1] it would be undesirable for him to be employed or remunerated by a solicitor in connection with his practice; or

(*b*) has, in the opinion of the Society[1], occasioned or been a party to, with or without the connivance of the solicitor by whom he is or was employed or remunerated, an act or default in relation to that solicitor's practice which involved conduct on his part of such a nature that in the opinion of the Society it would be undesirable for him to be employed or remunerated by a solicitor in connection with his practice,

the Society may either make, or make an application to the Tribunal[2] for it to make, an order under subsection (2) with respect to him.

(1A) Where the Society investigates whether there are grounds for making, or making an application to the Tribunal for it to make, an order under subsection (2) with respect to a person, the Council may direct him to pay to the Council an amount which—

(*a*) is calculated by the Council as the cost to the Society of investigating the matter; or

(*b*) in the opinion of the Council represents a reasonable contribution towards that cost.

(2) An order under this subsection made by the Society or the Tribunal shall state that as from such date as may be specified in the order, no solicitor shall, except in accordance with permission in writing granted by the Society for such period and subject to such conditions as the Society may

think fit to specify in the permission, employ or remunerate, in connection with his practice as a solicitor, the person with respect to whom the order is made.

(3) Where an order has been made under subsection (2) with respect to a person by the Society or the Tribunal—

(*a*) that person or the Society may make an application to the Tribunal for it to be reviewed, and
(*b*) whichever of the Society and the Tribunal made it may at any time revoke it.

(3A) On the review of an order under subsection (3) the Tribunal may order—

(*a*) the quashing of the order;
(*b*) the variation of the order; or
(*c*) the confirmation of the order;

and where in the opinion of the Tribunal no prima facie case for quashing or varying the order is shown, the Tribunal may order its confirmation without hearing the applicant.

(4) The Tribunal, on the hearing of any application under this section, may make an order as to the payment of costs by any party to the application.

(7) For the purposes of this section an order discharging a person absolutely or conditionally shall, notwithstanding anything in section 14 of the Powers of Criminal Courts (Sentencing) Act 2000, be deemed to be a conviction of the offence for which the order was made.

[Solicitors Act 1974, s 43, as amended by the Administration of Justice Act 1985, Sch 1, the Criminal Justice Act 1991, Sch 11, the Access to Justice Act 1999, Sch 7 and the Powers of Criminal Courts (Sentencing) Act 2000, Sch 9.]

---

1. Ie, the Law Society (s 87).
2. The "Tribunal" is the Solicitors Disciplinary Tribunal appointed under s 46 of the Solicitors Act 1974.

8–29330 44. Offences in connection with orders controlling employment of certain clerks. (1) Any person who, while there is in force in respect of him an order under section 43(2), seeks or accepts any employment by or remuneration from a solicitor in connection with that solicitor's practice without previously informing him of that order shall on summary conviction be liable to a fine not exceeding **level 2** on the standard scale.

(2) Where an order under section 43(2) is in force in respect of a person, then, if any solicitor knowingly acts in contravention of that order or of any conditions subject to which permission for the employment of that person has been granted under it, a complaint in respect of that contravention may be made to the Tribunal by or on behalf of the Society.

(3) Any document purporting to be an order under section 43(2) and to be duly signed in accordance with s 48(1)[1] of this Act shall be received in evidence in any proceedings under this section and be deemed to be such an order without further proof unless the contrary is shown.

(4) Notwithstanding anything in the Magistrates' Courts Act 1980, proceedings under subsection (1) may be commenced at any time before the expiration of six months from the first discovery of the offence by the prosecutor, but no such proceedings shall be commenced, except with the consent[2] of the director of Public Prosecutions, by any person other than the Society or a person acting on behalf of the Society.

[Solicitors Act 1974, s. 44, as amended by the Magistrates' Courts Act 1980, Sch 7, the Criminal Justice Act 1982, ss 38 and 46 and the Access to Justice Act 1999, Sch 7.]

---

1. Section 48(1) requires that an order of the Tribunal shall be filed with the Society, and a statement of its findings signed by the Chairman or by some other member of the Tribunal authorised by him, shall be attached.
2. For proof of this consent, see the Prosecution of Offences Act 1985, s 26 in PART I: MAGISTRATES' COURTS, PROCEDURE, ante.

8–29331 44B. *Examination of files*

8–29331A 44C. *Payment of costs of investigations*

Disciplinary Proceedings before Solicitors Disciplinary Tribunal

8–29332 46. *Applications and complaints under the Act made to Solicitors Disciplinary Tribunal*[1].

---

1. The Solicitors (Disciplinary Proceedings) Rules 1994, SI 1994/288 made under s 46, specify the way in which applications are to be made and heard.

8–29333 47. Jurisdiction and powers of Tribunal. (1) Any application—

(*a*) to strike the name of a solicitor off the roll;
(*b*) to require a solicitor to answer allegations contained in an affidavit;
(*c*) to require a former solicitor whose name has been removed from or struck off the roll to answer allegations contained in an affidavit relating to a time when he was a solicitor;
(*d*) by a solicitor who has been suspended from practice for an unspecified period, by order of the Tribunal, for the termination of that suspension;

(*e*) by a former solicitor whose name has been struck off the roll to have his name restored to the roll;

(*f*) by a former solicitor in respect of whom a direction has been given under subsection (2)(*g*) to have his name restored to the roll.

shall be made to the Tribunal; but nothing in this subsection shall affect any jurisdiction over solicitors exercisable by the Master of the Rolls, or by any judge of the High Court, by virtue of section 50.

(2) Subject to subsection (3) and to section 54, on the hearing of any application or complaint made to the Tribunal under this Act, other than an application under section 43, the Tribunal shall have power to make such order as it may think fit, and any such order may in particular include provision for any of the following matters—

(*a*) the striking off the roll of the name of the solicitor to whom the application or complaint relates;

(*b*) the suspension of that solicitor from practice indefinitely or for a specified period;

(*c*) the payment by that solicitor or former solicitor of a penalty not exceeding £5,000, which shall be forfeit to Her Majesty;

(*d*) in the circumstances referred to in subsection (2A), the exclusion of that solicitor from providing representation funded by the Legal Services Commission as part of the Criminal Defence Service (either permanently or for a specified period);

(*e*) the termination of that solicitor's unspecified period of suspension from practice;

(*f*) the restoration to the roll of the name of a former solicitor whose name has been struck off the roll and to whom the application relates;

(*g*) in the case of a former solicitor whose name has been removed from the roll, a direction prohibiting the restoration of his name to the roll except by order of the Tribunal;

(*h*) in the case of an application under subsection (1)(*f*), the restoration of the applicant's name to the roll;

(*i*) the payment by any party of costs or a contribution towards, costs of such amount as the Tribunal may consider reasonable.

(2A) An order of the Tribunal may make provision for the exclusion of a solicitor from providing representation as mentioned in subsection (2)(*d*) where the Tribunal determines that there is good reason for doing so arising out of—

(*a*) his conduct, including conduct in the capacity of agent for another solicitor, in connection with the provision for any person of services funded by the Legal Services Commission as part of the Community Legal Service or Criminal Defence Service; or

(*b*) his professional conduct generally.

(2B) Where the Tribunal makes any such order as is referred to in subsection (2A) in the case of a solicitor who is a member of a firm of solicitors, the Tribunal may, if it thinks fit, order that any other person who is for the time being a member of the firm shall be excluded (either permanently or for a specified period) from providing representation funded by the Legal Services Commission as part of the Criminal Defence Service.

(2C) The Tribunal shall not make an order under subsection (2B) unless an opportunity is given to him to show cause why the order should not be made.

(2D) Any person excluded from providing representation funded by the Legal Services Commission as part of the Criminal Defence Service by an order under this section may make an application to the Tribunal for an order terminating his exclusion.

(3) On proof of the commission of an offence with respect to which express provision is made by any section of this Act, the Tribunal shall, without prejudice to its power of making an order as to costs, impose the punishment, or one of the punishments, specified in that section.

(3A) Where, on the hearing of any application or complaint under this Act, the Tribunal is satisfied that more than one allegation is proved against the person to whom the application or complaint relates it may impose a separate penalty (by virtue of subsection (2)(*c*)) with respect to each such allegation.

(4) If it appears to the Secretary of State that there has been a change in the value of money since the relevant date, he may by order made by statutory instrument subject to annulment in pursuance of a resolution by either House of Parliament substitute for the sum for the time being specified in subsection (2)(*c*) above such other sum as appears to him to be justified by the change.

(5) In subsection (4) above "the relevant date" means—

(*a*) in relation to the first order under that subsection, the date of the coming into force of section 56 of the Administration of Justice Act 1982; and

(*b*) in relation to each subsequent order, the last occasion when the sum specified in sub-s (2)(*c*) above was altered.

(6) *Repealed.*

[Solicitors Act 1974, s 47, as amended by the Administration of Justice Act 1982, s 56, the Administration of Justice Act 1985, s 44 and Sch 7, the Legal Aid Act 1988, Sch 5, the Courts and Legal Services Act 1990, s 92, the Access to Justice Act 1999, Schs 4 and 5 and SI 2003/1887.]

8–29334 48–55. *Orders of Tribunal; appeals from Tribunal; disciplinary proceedings and jurisdiction of the Supreme Court.*

8–29335 **88. Savings for solicitors to public departments and City of London.** Nothing in this Act shall prejudice or affect any rights or privileges of the solicitor to the Treasury[1], any other public department, the Church Comrs or the Duchy of Cornwall, or require any such officer or any clerk or officer appointed to act for him to be admitted or enrolled or to hold a practising certificate in any case where it would not have been necessary for him to be admitted or enrolled or to hold such a certificate if this Act had not been passed.
[Solicitors Act 1974, s 88(1)2.]

1. Where the Treasury solicitor acts under the directions of the Crown as solicitor for an individual, he is to be considered duly qualified for all purposes, including the right of his client to recover costs (*R v Archbishop of Canterbury* [1903] 1 KB 289).

2. There is a saving from the provisions of Pt I of the Act (Provisions relating to the right to practise as a solicitor) for unqualified persons empowered by any enactment to conduct, defend or otherwise act in relation to any legal proceedings (Solicitors Act 1974, s 27).

SCHEDULE 1

(*As amended by the Criminal Justice Act 1982, ss 38 and 46, the Administration of Justice Act 1985, Sch 1 and the Access to Justice Act 1999, Sch 7.*)

8–29336 9. (1) The Society may give notice to the solicitor or his firm requiring the production or delivery to any person appointed by the Society at a time and place to be fixed by the Society—

(*a*) where the powers conferred by this Part of this Schedule are exercisable by virtue of paragraph 1, of all documents in the possession of the solicitor or his firm in connection with his practice or with any controlled trust; and

(*b*) where they are exercisable by virtue of paragraph 3, of all documents in the possession of the solicitor or his firm in connection with the trust or other matters to which the complaint relates (whether or not they relate also to other matters).

(2) The person appointed by the Society may take possession of any such documents on behalf of the Society.

(3) Except in a case where an application has been made to the High Court under sub-paragraph (4), if the person having possession of any such documents refuses, neglects or otherwise fails to comply with a requirement under sub-paragraph (1), he shall be guilty of an offence and liable on summary conviction to a fine not exceeding **level 2** on the standard scale.

(4) The High Court, on the application of the Society, may order a person required to produce or deliver documents under sub-paragraph (1) to produce or deliver them to any person appointed by the Society at such time and place as may be specified in the order, and authorise him to take possession of them on behalf of the Society.
[Solicitors Act 1974, Sch 1, para 9(1)–(4).]

Administration of Justice Act 1985[1]

(1985 c 61)

PART I[2]

SOLICITORS

Incorporated practices

8–29440 **9. Incorporated practices.** (1) The Council may make rules—

(*a*) making provision as to the management and control by solicitors or solicitors and one or more registered foreign lawyers of bodies corporate carrying on businesses consisting of the provision of professional services such as are provided by individuals practising as solicitors or by multi-national partnerships;

(*b*) prescribing the circumstances in which such bodies may be recognised by the Council as being suitable bodies to undertake the provision of any such services;

(*c*) prescribing the conditions which (subject to any exceptions provided by the rules) must at all times be satisfied by bodies corporate so recognised if they are to remain so recognised; and

(*d*) regulating the conduct of the affairs of such bodies.

(2) *Supplementary provisions as to Rules*.

(3) Notwithstanding section 24(2) of the 1974 Act (application of penal provisions to bodies corporate), sections 20, 22(1) and 23(1) of that Act[3] (prohibition on unqualified person acting as solicitor, etc) shall not apply to a recognised body; and nothing in section 24(1) of that Act shall apply in relation to such a body.

(4) Section 22(1), or (as the case may be) section 23(1), of that Act[3] shall not apply to any act done by an officer or employee of a recognised body if—

(*a*) it was done by him at the direction and under the supervision of another person who was at the time an officer or employee of the body; and

(*b*) it could have been done by that other person for or in expectation of any fee, gain or reward without committing an offence under the said section 22 or (as the case may be) under the said section 23.

(5) A certificate signed by an officer of the Society and stating that any body corporate is or is not, or was or was not at any time, a recognised body shall, unless the contrary is proved, be evidence of the facts stated in the certificate; and a certificate purporting to be so signed shall be taken to have been so signed unless the contrary is proved.

(6) Schedule 2[4] (which makes provision with respect to the application of provisions of the 1974 Act to recognised bodies and with respect to other matters relating to such bodies) shall have effect.

(7) Subject to the provisions of that Schedule, the Secretary of State may by order[5] made by statutory instrument subject to annulment in pursuance of a resolution of either House of Parliament provide for any enactment or instrument passed or made before the commencement of this section and having effect in relation to solicitors to have effect in relation to recognised bodies with such additions, omissions or other modifications as appear to the Secretary of State to be necessary or expedient.

(8) In this section—

"the 1974 Act" means the Solicitors Act 1974;

"the Council" and "the Society" have the meaning given by section 87(1) of the 1974 Act;

"multi-national partnership" means a partnership whose members consist of one or more registered foreign lawyers and one or more solicitors;

"officer", in relation to a limited liability partnership, means a member of the limited liability partnership;

"recognised body" means a body corporate for the time being recognised under this section;

"registered foreign lawyer" means a person who is registered under section 89 of the Courts and Legal Services Act 1990.

(9) Any rules made by the Council under this section shall be made with the concurrence of the Master of the Rolls.

[Administration of Justice Act 1985, s 9, as amended by the Courts and Legal Services Act 1990, Schs 18 and 20, the Access to Justice Act 1999, Sch 15, SI 2001/1090 and SI 2003/1887.]

---

1. This Act is to be brought into force in accordance with s 69 post. At the date of going to press the following Commencement Orders had been made: SI 1986/364, 1503 and 2260, SI 1987/787, SI 1988/1341, SI 1989/287 and SI 1991/2683. Of the provisions referred to in this work, only ss 9 and 10, Pt II (ss 11–39) (except s 34(3)), ss 40, 41, 42 and 43 and 69 had been brought into force.
2. Part I contains ss 1–10.
3. See this title, ante.
4. Schedule 2 is not printed in this work.
5. The Solicitors Incorporated Practices Order 1991, SI 1991/2684 amended by SI 2001/645 has been made.

8–29441 10. Penalty for pretending to be a body recognised under s 9. (1) A body corporate shall not describe itself or hold itself out as a body corporate for the time being recognised under section 9 unless it is so recognised.

(2) Any body corporate which contravenes subsection (1) shall be guilty of an offence and liable on summary conviction to a fine not exceeding the **fourth level** on the standard scale.

(3) Where an offence under this section which has been committed by a body corporate is proved to have been committed with the consent or connivance of, or to be attributable to any neglect on the part of, any director, manager, secretary or other similar officer of the body corporate, or any person purporting to act in any such capacity, he as well as the body corporate shall be guilty of the offence and shall be liable to be proceeded against and punished accordingly.

(4) *Repealed.*

[Administration of Justice Act 1985, s 10 amended by the Statute Law (Repeals) Act 1993, Sch 1.]

PART II[1]
LICENSED CONVEYANCING

Preliminary

8–29442 11. Provision of conveyancing services by licensed conveyancers. (1) The provisions of this Part shall have effect for the purpose of regulating the provision of conveyancing services by persons who hold licences in force under this Part.

(2) In this Part—

"licence" means a licence to practise as a licensed conveyancer;

"licensed conveyancer" means a person who holds a licence in force under this Part;

and references in this Part to practising as a licensed conveyancer are references to providing, as the holder of such a licence, conveyancing services in accordance with the licence.

(3) References in this Part to conveyancing services are references to the preparation of transfers, conveyances, contracts and other documents in connection with, and other services ancillary to, the disposition or acquisition of estates or interests in land; and for the purposes of this subsection—

(*a*) "disposition"—

(i) does not include a testamentary disposition or any disposition in the case of such a lease as is referred to in section 54(2) of the Law of Property Act 1925 (short leases); but

(ii) subject to that, includes in the case of leases both their grant and their assignment; and

(*b*) "acquisition" has a corresponding meaning.

(4) Section 22(1) of the Solicitors Act 1974[2] (restriction on person preparing certain instruments when not qualified to act as a solicitor) shall not apply to any act done by a licensed conveyancer in the course of the provision of any conveyancing services if he is not precluded from providing those services as a licensed conveyancer by any conditions imposed as mentioned in section 16(3)(*a*).
[Administration of Justice Act 1985, s 11.]

1. Part II contains ss 11–39.
2. See this title, ante.

The Council for Licensed Conveyancers

8–29443 **12. Establishment of the Council.** (1) For the purposes of this Part there shall be a body to be known as the Council for Licensed Conveyancers.

(2) It shall be the general duty of the Council[1] to ensure that the standards of competence and professional conduct among persons who practise as licensed conveyancers are sufficient to secure adequate protection for consumers, and that the conveyancing services provided by such persons are provided both economically and efficiently.

(3) Schedule 3[2] shall have effect with respect to the Council.
[Administration of Justice Act 1985, s 12.]

1. The Council is required to establish and maintain, in such form as the Council may determine, a register containing the names and places of business of all persons who for the time being hold licences in force under Pt II of this Act. A certificate signed by an officer of the Council appointed for the purpose and stating—(*a*) that any person does or does not, or did or did not at any time, hold a licence in force under Pt II of the Act; or (*b*) that any licence held by any person is or was at any time either free of conditions or subject to any particular conditions, shall unless the contrary is proved, be evidence of the facts stated in the certificate; and a certificate purporting to be so signed shall be taken to have been so signed unless the contrary is proved (s 19).
2. Schedule 3 is not printed in this work.

8–29444 **13–31.** *Training and licensing of persons seeking to practise as licensed conveyancers; code of conduct, financial requirements and disciplinary and other proceedings.*

Recognised bodies

8–29445 **32. Provision of conveyancing services by recognised bodies.** (1) The Council may make rules—

(*a*) making provision as to the management and control by licensed conveyancers (or by licensed conveyancers together with persons who are not licensed conveyancers) of bodies corporate carrying on businesses consisting of the provision of conveyancing services;

(*b*) prescribing the circumstances in which such bodies may be recognised by the Council as being suitable bodies to undertake the provision of such services;

(*c*) prescribing the conditions which (subject to any exceptions provided by the rules) must at all times be satisfied by bodies so recognised if they are to remain so recognised; and

(*d*) regulating the conduct of the affairs of such bodies.

(2) In this Part "recognised body" means a body corporate for the time being recognised under this section.

(3) *Supplementary provisions as to Rules.*

(4) Notwithstanding section 24(2) of the Solicitors Act 1974[1] (application of penal provisions to bodies corporate), section 22(1)[1] of that Act shall not apply to a body corporate by reason of any act done by an officer or employee of the body if—

(*a*) at the time it was done the body was a recognised body; and

(*b*) it was done in the course of the provision of conveyancing services which the body was not precluded from undertaking to provide as a recognised body by any restrictions imposed in pursuance of subsection (3)(*d*) of this section.

(5) Section 22(1) of that Act shall also not apply to any officer or employee of a body corporate by reason of any act done by him if—

(*a*) the conditions specified in paragraphs (*a*) and (*b*) of the preceding subsection are satisfied in relation to that act; and

(*b*) it was done by him at the direction and under the supervision of another person who was at the time an officer or employee of the body; and

(*c*) it could have been done by that other person for or in expectation of any fee, gain or reward without committing an offence under the said section 22.

(6) A certificate signed by an officer of the Council and stating—

(*a*) that any body corporate is or is not, or was or was not at any time, a recognised body; or (*b*) that no restrictions were imposed in pursuance of subsection (3)(*d*) on the grant of a body corporate's recognition under this section or that any particular restrictions were so imposed,

shall, unless the contrary is proved, be evidence of the facts stated in the certificate; and a certificate purporting to be so signed shall be taken to have been so signed unless the contrary is proved.

(7) Schedule 6[2] shall have effect with respect to recognised bodies.
[Administration of Justice Act 1985, s 32.]

1. See this title, ante.
2. Schedule 6 is not printed in this work.

Miscellaneous and supplemental

8–29446 33. Legal professional privilege. Any communication made—

(*a*) to or by a licensed conveyancer in the course of his acting as such for a client; or
(*b*) to or by a recognised body in the course of its acting as such for a client,

shall in any legal proceedings be privileged from disclosure in like manner as if the licensed conveyancer or body had at all material times been acting as the client's solicitor.
[Administration of Justice Act 1985, s 33.]

8–29447 34. *Modification of existing enactments relating to conveyancing etc.*

8–29448 35. Penalty for pretending to be a licensed conveyancer or recognised body. (1) An individual shall not describe himself or hold himself out as a licensed conveyancer unless he holds a licence in force under this Part.

(2) A body corporate shall not describe itself or hold itself out as a recognised body unless it is for the time being recognised under section 32.

(3) Any person who contravenes subsection (1) or (2) shall be guilty of an offence and liable on summary conviction to a fine not exceeding the fourth level on the standard scale.
[Administration of Justice Act 1985, s 35.]

8–29449 36. Offences by bodies corporate. Where an offence under this Part which has been committed by a body corporate is proved to have been committed with the consent or connivance of, or to be attributable to any neglect on the part of, any director, manager, secretary or other similar officer of the body corporate, or any person purporting to act in any such capacity, he as well as the body corporate shall be guilty of the offence and shall be liable to be proceeded against and punished accordingly.
[Administration of Justice Act 1985, s 36.]

8–29450 39. Interpretation of Part II. (1) In this Part—

"associate" means, in the case of a licensed conveyancer practising in partnership with other persons, any partner of his not holding a licence in force under this Part or any employee of such a partner;

"client" means—

(*a*) in relation to a licensed conveyancer, any person by or on whose behalf instructions regarding the provision of conveyancing services are given to the licensed conveyancer or his firm;
(*b*) in relation to a recognised body, any person by whom or on whose behalf such instructions are given to the body;

and "client account" means an account in whose title the word "client" is required by rules under section 22(2);

"conveyancing services" shall be construed in accordance with section 11(3);
"the Council" means the Council for Licensed Conveyancers;
"director". In relation to a limited liability partnership, means a member of the limited liability partnership;
"fees" includes charges, disbursements, expenses and remuneration;
"functions" includes powers and duties;
"licence" and "licensed conveyancer" have the meaning given by section 11(2);
"officer", in relation to a recognised body, includes a director, manager or secretary;
"recognised body" means a body corporate for the time being recognised under section 32.

(2) Any reference in this Part to a licensed conveyancer practising as a sole practitioner is a reference to a licensed conveyancer practising either as the sole principal in the practice or in partnership with other persons of whom none are licensed conveyancers.
[Administration of Justice Act 1985, s 39 amended by SI 1991/1997, the Statute Law (Repeals) Act 1993, Sch 1 and SI 2001/1090.]

PART III[1]
LEGAL AID

Legal aid complaints

8–29451 **40. Legal aid complaints: preliminary.** (1) For the purposes of this Part of this Act a legal aid complaint is a complaint relating to the conduct of a barrister or solicitor in connection with the provision for any person of services funded by the Legal Services Commission as part of the Community Legal Service or Criminal Defence Service including, in the case of a solicitor, provision for any person of such services in the capacity of agent for that person's solicitor.

(2) In this Part—

"legally assisted person" means a person to whom aid is ordered to be given under section 28 of the Legal Aid Act 1974;

"the Senate" means the Senate of the Inns of Court and the Bar; and

"Senate Disciplinary Tribunal" means any committee of the Senate which in accordance with the regulations of the Senate is to be known as a Disciplinary Tribunal.

(3) *Repeals.*

[Administration of Justice Act 1985, s 40, as amended by the Legal Aid Act 1988, Sch 5 and the Access to Justice Act 1999, Sch 4.]

1. Part III contains ss 40–46.

8–29452 **41. Application to legal aid complaints against barristers of disciplinary provisions.** (1) The disciplinary provisions applicable to barristers shall apply to legal aid complaints relating to the conduct of barristers as they apply to other complaints about their conduct.

(2) Subject to any exclusion or restriction made by those provisions, any disciplinary tribunal which hears a legal aid complaint relating to the conduct of a barrister may, if it thinks fit and whether or not it makes any other order, order that any fees otherwise payable by the Legal Services Commission in connection with services provided by him as part of the Community Legal Service or Criminal Defence Service shall be reduced or cancelled.

(3) *Repealed.*

(4) An appeal shall lie in the case of an order under subsection (2) above in the same manner as an appeal would lie in the case of any other order of such a tribunal.

(5) The reference in subsection (2) above to a disciplinary tribunal is a reference to a tribunal acting under the disciplinary provisions applicable to barristers and it includes a reference to a member exercising any functions of the tribunal delegated to him.

[Administration of Justice Act 1985, s 41, as substituted by the Legal Aid Act 1988, s 33 and amended by the Access to Justice Act 1999, Sch 4 and 15.]

8–29453 **42. Exclusion of barristers from legal aid work.** (1) Subject to any exclusion or restriction made by the disciplinary provisions applicable to barristers, where a disciplinary tribunal hears a charge of professional misconduct or breach of professional standards against a barrister, it may order that he shall be excluded from providing representation funded by the Legal Services Commission as part of the Criminal Defence Service, either temporarily or for a specified period, if it determines that there is good reason for the exclusion arising out of—

(*a*) his conduct in connection with any such services as are mentioned in section 40(1), or

(*b*) his professional conduct generally.

(2) Subsection (4) of section 41 shall apply to an order under subsection (1) as it applies to an order under subsection (2) of that section.

(3) The disciplinary provisions applicable to barristers shall include provision enabling a barrister who has been excluded from providing representation funded by the Legal Services Commission as part of the Criminal Defence Service under this section to apply for an order terminating his exclusion.

(4) In this section—

(*a*) the reference to a disciplinary tribunal shall be construed in accordance with section 41(5); and

(*b*) *Repealed.*

[Administration of Justice Act 1985, s 42, as substituted by the Legal Aid Act 1988, s 33 and the Access to Justice Act 1999, Schs 4 and 15.]

8–29454 **43. Jurisdiction and powers of Solicitors Disciplinary Tribunal in relation to complaints against solicitors.** (1) The Solicitors Disciplinary Tribunal shall have jurisdiction to hear and determine any legal aid complaint relating to the conduct of a solicitor and made to the Tribunal under this section by or on behalf of the Law Society.

(2) In the following provisions of the Solicitors Act 1974, namely—

(*a*) subsections (7) to (11) of section 46 (procedure of Tribunal); and

(*b*) section 47(2) (powers of Tribunal),

any reference to a complaint or to a complaint made to the Tribunal under that Act shall be construed as including a reference to a legal aid complaint or to a legal aid complaint made to the Tribunal under this section.

(3) On the hearing of a legal aid complaint against a solicitor the Tribunal may, if it thinks fit and whether or not it makes any other order on the hearing, order that any costs otherwise payable by the Legal Services Commission in connection with services provided by the solicitor as part of the Community Legal Service or Criminal Defence Service shall be reduced or cancelled.

(4) *Repealed.*

(5) Without prejudice to the generality of subsection (1)(*b*) of section 49 of the Solicitors Act 1974, an appeal shall lie to the High Court under that section against an order of the Tribunal under subsection (3), but such an appeal shall lie only at the instance of the solicitor with respect to whom the legal aid complaint was made.

(6) In this section "costs" includes fees, charges, disbursements, expenses and remuneration.
[Administration of Justice Act 1985, s 43, as amended by the Access to Justice Act 1999, Schs 4 and 15.]

PART V[1]
MISCELLANEOUS AND SUPPLEMENTARY

Supplementary

8–29455 **69. Short title, commencement, transitional provisions and savings.** (1) This Act may be cited as the Administration of Justice Act 1985.

(2) Subject to subsections (3) and (4), this Act shall come into force on such day as the Secretary of State may by order[2] made by statutory instrument appoint; and an order under this subsection may appoint different days for different provisions and for different purposes.

(3) The following provisions of this Act shall come into force on the day this Act is passed—

(*a*) section 63;
(*b*) Part I of Schedule 8 and section 67(2) so far as relating thereto;
(*c*) section 68;
(*d*) this section and Schedule 9.

(4) The following provisions of this Act shall come into force at the end of the period of two months beginning with the day on which this Act is passed—

(*a*) sections 45, 49, 52, 54, 56 to 62 and 64 and 65;
(*b*) paragraph 8 of Schedule 7 and section 67(1) so far as relating thereto;
(*c*) Part II of Schedule 8 and section 67(2) so far as relating thereto.

(5) The transitional provisions and savings contained in Schedule 9 shall have effect; but nothing in that Schedule shall be taken as prejudicing the operation of sections 16 and 17 of the Interpretation Act 1978 (which relate to repeals).
[Administration of Justice Act 1985, s 69, as amended by SI 2003/1887.]

1. Part V contains ss 57–69.
2. See the Administration of Justice Act 1985 (Commencement No 1) Order 1986, SI 1986/364, (Commencement No 2) Order 1986, SI 1986/1503, (Commencement No 3) Order 1986, SI 1986/2260, (Commencement No 4) Order 1987, SI 1987/787, (Commencement No 5) Order 1988, SI 1988/1341 and (Commencement No 6) Order 1989, SI 1989/287.

Courts and Legal Services Act 1990[1]

(1990 c 41)

PART II[2] LEGAL SERVICES

Rights of audience and rights to conduct litigation

8–29560 **27. Rights of audience.** (1) The question whether a person has a right of audience before a court, or in relation to any proceedings, shall be determined solely in accordance with the provisions of this Part.

(2) A person shall have a right of audience before a court in relation to any proceedings only in the following cases—

(*a*) where—
(i) he has a right of audience before that court in relation to those proceedings granted by the appropriate authorised body; and
(ii) that body's qualification regulations and rules of conduct have been approved for the purposes of this section, in relation to that right;

(*b*) where paragraph (*a*) does not apply but he has a right of audience before that court in relation to those proceedings granted by or under any enactment;

(*c*) where paragraph (*a*) does not apply but he has a right of audience granted by that court in relation to those proceedings[3] (*d*) where he is a party to those proceedings and would have had a right of audience, in his capacity as such a party, if this Act had not been passed; or

(*e*) where[4]—

(i) he is employed (whether wholly or in part), or is otherwise engaged, to assist in the conduct of litigation and is doing so under instructions given (either generally or in relation to the proceedings) by a qualified litigator; and

(ii) the proceedings are being heard in chambers in the High Court or a county court and are not reserved family proceedings.

(2A) Every person who exercises before any court a right of audience granted by an authorised body has—

(a) a duty to the court to act with independence in the interests of justice; and

(b) a duty to comply with rules of conduct of the body relating to the right and approved for the purposes of this section;

and those duties shall override any obligation which the person may have (otherwise than under the criminal law) if it is inconsistent with them.

(3) *Repealed.*

(4) Nothing in this section affects the power of any court in any proceedings to refuse to hear a person (for reasons which apply to him as an individual) who would otherwise have a right of audience before the court in relation to those proceedings.

(5) Where a court refuses to hear a person as mentioned in subsection (4) it shall give its reasons for refusing.

(6) *Repealed.*

(7) Where, immediately before the commencement of this section, no restriction was placed on the persons entitled to exercise any right of audience in relation to any particular court or in relation to particular proceedings, nothing in this section shall be taken to place any such restriction on any person.

(8) Where—

(*a*) immediately before the commencement of this section; or

(*b*) by virtue of any provision made by or under an enactment passed subsequently,

a court does not permit the appearance of advocates, or permits the appearance of advocates only with leave, no person shall have a right of audience before that court, in relation to any proceedings, solely by virtue of the provisions of this section.

(8A) But a court may not limit the right to appear before the court in any proceedings to only some of those who have the right by virtue of the provisions of this section.

(9) In this section—

"advocate", in relation to any proceedings, means any person exercising a right of audience as a representative of, or on behalf of, any party to the proceedings;

"authorised body" means—

(*a*) the General Council of the Bar;

(*b*) the Law Society; and

(*c*) any professional or other body which has been designated by Order[5] in Council as an authorised body for the purposes of this section;

"appropriate authorised body", in relation to any person claiming to be entitled to any right of audience by virtue of subsection (2)(*a*), means the authorised body—

(*a*) granting that right; and

(*b*) of which that person is a member;

"family proceedings" has the same meaning as in the Matrimonial and Family Proceedings Act 1984 and also includes any other proceedings which are family proceedings for the purposes of the Children Act 1989;

"qualification regulations", in relation to an authorised body, means regulations (however they may be described) as to the education and training which members of that body must receive in order to be entitled to, or to exercise, any right of audience granted by it;

"qualified litigator" means—

(i) any practising solicitor (that is, one who has a practising certificate in force or is employed wholly or mainly for the purpose of providing legal services to his employer);

(ii) any recognised body; and

(iii) any person who is exempt from the requirement to hold a practising certificate by virtue of section 88 of the Solicitors Act 1974 (saving for solicitors to public departments and the City of London);

"recognised body" means any body recognised under section 9 of the Administration of Justice Act 1985 (incorporated practices);

"reserved family proceedings" means such category of family proceedings as the Secretary of State may, after consulting the President of the Law Society and with the concurrence of the President of the Family Division, by order prescribe; and "rules of conduct", in relation to an authorised body, means rules (however they may be described) as to the conduct required of members of that body in exercising any right of audience granted by it.

(10) Section 20 of the Solicitors Act 1974 (unqualified person not to act as a solicitor), section 22 of that Act (unqualified person not to prepare certain documents etc) and section 25 of that Act (costs where an unqualified person acts as a solicitor), shall not apply in relation to any act done in the exercise of a right of audience.

[Courts and Legal Services Act 1990, s 27, as amended by the Access to Justice Act 1999, s 42 and Schs 6 and 15 and SI 2003/1887.]

---

1. This Act is to be brought into force in accordance with s 124, post. For commencement orders, see s 124, post. Of the provisions of the Act printed below, ss 36, 37, 47, 48, 49, 50, 54, 55, 70, 104, 105, 106 and 107 had not been brought into force at the date of going to press.

2. Part II comprises ss 17–70.

3. The court, including the Crown Court, has the power in its discretion to grant a right of audience to any person in any proceedings (*R v Southwark Crown Court, ex p Tawfick*) (1994) Times, 1 December. However, those representing children and parties in children cases should be specially experienced in order that representation may be provided discreetly having regard to the overriding interests of the children; see *Re G (A Minor) (Rights of Audience)* [1997] 2 FCR 585. For the exercise of this discretion see *D v S* [1997] 1 FLR 724, [1997] 2 FCR 217 and note 1 to section 28(2)(*c*) post.

4. While the object of s 27 (2)(*e*) is to preserve the traditional right of solicitors' managing clerks to conduct proceedings in chambers on behalf of solicitors who employ them, it will also extend to other unqualified litigators who are engaged by a solicitor; see *Re H S (Chambers Proceedings: Rights of Audience)* [1998] 1 FLR 868.

5. The following orders have been made designating authorised bodies for the purposes of this section:

The Institute of Legal Executives Order 1998,
SI 1998/1077; the Chartered Institute of Patent Agents Order 1999, SI 1999/3137; Institute of Trade Mark Attorneys Order 2005, SI 2005/240.

8–29561 28. Rights to conduct litigation. (1) The question whether a person has a right to conduct litigation, or any category of litigation, shall be determined solely in accordance with the provisions of this Part.

(2) A person shall have a right to conduct litigation in relation to any proceedings only in the following cases—

(*a*) where—

(i) he has a right to conduct litigation in relation to those proceedings granted by the appropriate authorised body; and

(ii) that body's qualification regulations and rules of conduct have been approved for the purposes of this section, in relation to that right;

(*b*) where paragraph (*a*) does not apply but he has a right to conduct litigation in relation to those proceedings granted by or under any enactment;

(*c*) where paragraph (*a*) does not apply but he has a right to conduct litigation granted by that court in relation to those proceedings[1];

(*d*) where he is a party to those proceedings and would have had a right to conduct the litigation, in his capacity as such a party, if this Act had not been passed.

(2A) Every person who exercises in relation to proceedings in any court a right to conduct litigation granted by an authorised body has—

(*a*) a duty to the court to act with independence in the interests of justice; and

(*b*) a duty to comply with rules of conduct of the body relating to the right and approved for the purposes of this section;

and those duties shall override any obligation which the person may have (otherwise than under the criminal law) if it is inconsistent with them.

(3) *Repealed.*

(4) Where, immediately before the commencement of this section, no restriction was placed on the persons entitled to exercise any right to conduct litigation in relation to a particular court, or in relation to particular proceedings, nothing in this section shall be taken to place any such restriction on any person.

(4A) A court may not limit the right to conduct litigation in relation to proceedings before the court to only some of those who have the right by virtue of the provisions of this section.

(5) In this section—

"authorised body" means—

(*a*) the Law Society;

(*aa*) the General Council of the Bar;

(*ab*) the Institute of Legal Executives; and

(*b*) any professional or other body which has been designated by Order[2] in Council as an authorised body for the purposes of this section;

"appropriate authorised body", in relation to any person claiming to be entitled to any right to conduct litigation by virtue of subsection (2)(*a*), means the authorised body—

(*a*) granting that right; and
(*b*) of which that person is a member;

"qualification regulations", in relation to an authorised body, means regulations (however they may be described) as to the education and training which members of that body must receive in order to be entitled to, or to exercise, any right to conduct litigation granted by it; and

"rules of conduct", in relation to any authorised body, means rules (however they may be described) as to the conduct required of members of that body in exercising any right to conduct litigation granted by it.

(5A) Nothing in this section shall be taken to require the General Council of the Bar or the Institute of Legal Executives to grant a right to conduct litigation.

(6) Section 20 of the Solicitors Act 1974 (unqualified person not to act as a solicitor), section 22 of that Act (unqualified person not to prepare certain documents etc) and section 25 of that Act (costs where unqualified person acts as a solicitor) shall not apply in relation to any act done in the exercise of a right to conduct litigation.
[Courts and Legal Services Act 1990, s 28, as amended by the Access to Justice Act 1999, ss 40, 42, Sch 6, Sch 15.]

---

1. The discretion to grant the right to conduct litigation under this provision is that of the court and is not a matter for the consent of the parties. The discretion is to be exercised in each case individually and only in exceptional circumstances (*D v S* [1997] 1 FLR 724, [1997] 2 FCR 217; and see *Re Pelling (Rights of Audience)* [1997] 2 FLR 458). However, the objections which exist to granting rights of audience to an unqualified person who has set himself up as providing advocacy services do not apply to a husband who merely wishes to assist his wife by representing her in court (*Clarkson v Gilbert* [2000} 3 FCR 10, [2000] 2 FLR 839, CA).

2. The Chartered Institute of Patent Agents has been designated by The Chartered Institute of Patent Agents Order 1999, SI 1999/3137 and the Institute of Trade Mark Attorneys Order 2005, SI 2005/240 as an authorised body for the purposes of this section.

8–29562 **29. Authorised bodies: designation and approval of regulations and rules.** The provisions of Schedule 4[1] shall have effect with respect to the authorisation of bodies for the purposes of sections 27 and 28 and the approval and alteration of qualification regulations and rules of conduct.
[Courts and Legal Services Act 1990, s 29, as substituted by the Access to Justice Act 1999, Sch 5.]

---

1. Schedule 4 is not reproduced in this work.

8–29564 **31. Barristers and solicitors.** (1) Every barrister shall be deemed to have been granted by the General Council of the Bar a right of audience before every court in relation to all proceedings (exercisable in accordance with the qualification regulations and rules of conduct of the General Council of the Bar approved for the purposes of section 27 in relation to the right).

(2) Every solicitor shall be deemed to have been granted by the Law Society—

(*a*) a right of audience before every court in relation to all proceedings (exercisable in accordance with the qualification regulations and rules of conduct of the Law Society approved for the purposes of section 27 in relation to the right); and
(*b*) a right to conduct litigation in relation to every court and all proceedings (exercisable in accordance with the qualification regulations and rules of conduct of the Law Society approved for the purposes of section 28 in relation to the right).

(3) A person shall not have a right of audience by virtue of subsection (1) if—

(*a*) he has not been called to the Bar by an Inn of Court; or
(*b*) he has been disbarred, or is temporarily suspended from practice, by order of an Inn of Court.

[Courts and Legal Services Act 1990, s 31, as inserted by the Access to Justice Act 1999, s 36.]

8–29566A **31A. Employed advocates.** (1) Where a person who has a right of audience granted by an authorised body is employed as a Crown Prosecutor or in any other description of employment, any qualification regulations or rules of conduct of the body relating to that right which fall within subsection (2) shall not have effect in relation to him.

(2) Qualification regulations or rules of conduct relating to a right granted by a body fall within this subsection if—

(*a*) they limit the courts before which, or proceedings in which, that right may be exercised by members of the body who are employed or limit the circumstances in which that right may be exercised by them by requiring them to be accompanied by some other person when exercising it; and
(*b*) they do not impose the same limitation on members of the body who have the right but are not employed.*

[Courts and Legal Services Act 1990, s 31A as inserted by the Access to Justice Act 1999, s 37.]

8–29566B **31B. Advocates and litigators employed by Legal Services Commission*.** (1) Where a person who has a right of audience or right to conduct litigation granted by an authorised body is employed by the Legal Services Commission, or by any body established and maintained by the Legal Services Commission, any rules of the authorised body which fall within subsection (2) shall not have effect in relation to him.

(2) Rules of a body fall within this subsection if they are—

(*a*) rules of conduct prohibiting or limiting the exercise of the right on behalf of members of the public by members of the body who are employees; or

(*b*) rules of any other description prohibiting or limiting the provision of legal services to members of the public by such members of the body,

and either of the conditions specified in subsection (3) is satisfied.

(3) Those conditions are—

(*a*) that the prohibition or limitation is on the exercise of the right, or the provision of the services, otherwise than on the instructions of solicitors (or other persons acting for the members of the public); and

(*b*) that the rules do not impose the same prohibition or limitation on members of the body who have the right but are not employees.*

[Courts and Legal Services Act 1990, s 31B as inserted by the Access to Justice Act 1999, s 38.]

8–29566C 31C. Change of authorised body. (1) Where a person—

(*a*) has at any time had, and been entitled to exercise, a right of audience before a court in relation to proceedings of any description granted by one authorised body; and

(*b*) becomes a member of another authorised body and has a right of audience before that court in relation to that description of proceedings granted by that body,

any qualification regulations of that body relating to that right shall not have effect in relation to him.

(2) Subsection (1) does not apply in relation to any qualification regulations to the extent that they impose requirements relating to continuing education or training which have effect in relation to the exercise of the right by all members of the body who have the right.

(3) Subsection (1) does not apply to a person if he has been banned from exercising the right of audience by the body mentioned in paragraph (*a*) of that subsection as a result of disciplinary proceedings and that body has not lifted the ban.*

[Courts and Legal Services Act 1990, s 31C as inserted by the Access to Justice Act 1999, s 39.]

Extension of conveyancing services

8–29567 34. The Authorised Conveyancing Practitioners Board. (1) There shall be a body corporate to be known as the Authorised Conveyancing Practitioners Board (in this Act referred to as "the Board").

(2)–(8) *Constitution of the Board.*

[Courts and Legal Services Act 1990, s 34, amended by SI 2003/1887.]

8–29568 36. Provision of conveyancing services by authorised practitioners. (1) The restriction imposed by section 22 of the Solicitors Act 1974 (which has the effect of limiting the categories of person who may provide conveyancing services) shall not apply to any act done in connection with the provision of conveyancing services—

(*a*) by an individual at any time when he is an authorised practitioner;

(*b*) by a body corporate at any time when it is an authorised practitioner;

(*c*) by an officer or employee of a body corporate at any time when that body is an authorised practitioner; or

(*d*) by a member or employee of an unincorporated association at any time when that association is an authorised practitioner.

(2) In subsection (1)(*c*) and (*d*) "officer", "employee" and "member" mean respectively an officer, employee or member who (at the time of the act in question) satisfies, and is acting in accordance with, regulations under section 40.

(3) Any rule (however described) which is imposed by a professional or other body and which would, but for this subsection, result in restricting or preventing a qualified person from—

(*a*) providing any conveyancing services as an authorised practitioner;

(*b*) acting as an employee of an authorised practitioner in connection with the provision of any such services; or

(*c*) acting on behalf of an authorised practitioner in connection with the provision of any such services,

shall be of no effect unless it is given partial effect by subsection (4)(*a*) or full effect by subsection (4)(*b*).

(4) If the result mentioned in subsection (3) is not the main or only result of the rule in question, subsection (3)—

(*a*) shall apply only to the extent that the rule would have that result; but

(*b*) shall not apply if the rule is reasonably required as a rule of general application for the purpose of regulating the conduct or practice of all members of that body.

(5) Nothing in this section prevents a professional or other body from imposing a rule that any member of that body who is acting as mentioned in subsection (3)(*c*) may do so only on terms which allow him to give independent legal or financial advice to the person for whom conveyancing services are being provided by the authorised practitioner concerned.

(6) In this section "qualified person" means—

(*a*) any barrister, solicitor, duly certificated notary public or licensed conveyancer;
(*b*) any body recognised under section 9 of the Administration of Justice Act 1985 (incorporated practices); or
(*c*) any body recognised under section 32 of the Act of 1985 (incorporated bodies carrying on business of provision of conveyancing services).

[Courts and Legal Services Act 1990, s 36.]

8–29569 **37. Authorisation of practitioners.** (1) On an application duly made by a person who proposes to provide conveyancing services, the Board shall authorise that person to provide those services, if—

(*a*) it is satisfied that the applicant's business is, and is likely to continue to be, carried on by fit and proper persons or, in the case of an application by an individual, that he is a fit and proper person; and
(*b*) it is of the opinion that the applicant will comply with the requirements mentioned in subsection (7).

(2) Any such authorisation shall be given in writing and shall take effect on such date as the Board may specify.

(3) A person so authorised is referred to in this Act as "an authorised practitioner".

(4) An application for authorisation must be made in accordance with rules made by the Board, with the approval of the Secretary of State, for the purposes of this section.

(5) On making any such application, the applicant shall pay to the Board such fee as may be specified in the rules.

(6) The rules may, in particular, make provision—

(*a*) as to the form in which any application must be made; and
(*b*) for the furnishing by applicants of information required by the Board in connection with their applications.

(7) The requirements are that the applicant—

(*a*) complies with any rules made by the Board and any regulations made under section 40, so far as applicable;
(*b*) ensures that satisfactory arrangements are at all times in force for covering adequately the risk of any claim made against the applicant in connection with the provision of conveyancing services provided by the applicant, however arising;
(*c*) maintains satisfactory procedures for—
  (i) dealing with complaints made about any aspect of conveyancing services provided by the applicant; and
  (ii) the payment of compensation;
(*d*) has in force satisfactory arrangements to protect the applicant's clients in the event of the applicant ceasing to provide conveyancing services;
(*e*) is a member of the Conveyancing Ombudsman Scheme.

(8) Where the applicant is—

(*a*) an institution which is authorised under Part I of the Banking Act 1987, to carry on a deposit taking business[1];
(*b*) a building society which is authorised by the Building Societies Commission, under section 9 of the Building Societies Act 1986, to raise money from its members; or
(*c*) an insurance company which is authorised under section 3 or 4 of the Insurance Companies Act 1982[2],

the Board shall have regard to the fact that it is so authorised in determining whether the Board is satisfied as mentioned in subsection (1)(*a*).

(9) The Board shall maintain a register of authorised practitioners which shall be open to inspection, at all reasonable times, without charge.

(10) The Secretary of State may by order amend the provisions of subsection (7) by imposing any additional requirement or by varying or removing any requirement.

[Courts and Legal Services Act 1990, s 37, as amended by the Bank of England Act 1998, Schs 5 and 9 and SI 2003/1887.]

---

1. Includes a European deposit-taker (Banking Coordination (Second Council Directive) Regulations 1992, SI 1992/3218, Sch 10).

2. Includes an EC company which is lawfully carrying on insurance business in the United Kingdom (Insurance Companies (Third Insurance Directives) Regulations 1994, SI 1994/1696). For meaning of "an insurance company

lawfully carrying on insurance business in the United Kingdom" and transitional provisions see regs 68–71 of these regulations. (These regulations are not reproduced in this work.)

8–29570 **47. Power to obtain information and require production of documents.** (1) The Board may serve a notice on any—

(*a*) authorised practitioner;
(*b*) officer or employee of an authorised practitioner;
(*c*) qualified person who is acting, or has acted, on behalf of an authorised practitioner; or
(*d*) officer or employee of such a qualified person,

requiring him to provide the Board (within such time and at such place as may be specified in the notice) with such document, or documents of such a description, or with such information, as may be so specified.

(2) The Board shall not exercise its powers under subsection (1) except for the purpose of obtaining such information as it thinks reasonably necessary in connection with the discharge of any of its functions.

(3) The Board's power under this section to require a person to produce any document includes power—

(*a*) if the document is produced, to take copies of it or extracts from it and to require that person, or any other person who is or was a director or officer of, or is or was at any time employed by or acting as an employee of, the practitioner concerned, to provide an explanation of the document;
(*b*) if the document is not produced, to require the person who was required to produce it to state, to the best of his knowledge and belief, where it is.

(4) The Board's power under this section may be exercised in relation to a person who falls within subsection (1)(*c*) or (*d*) only in relation to the provision of conveyancing services on behalf of the authorised practitioner concerned.

(5) Any person who, without reasonable excuse, fails to comply with a requirement imposed on him under this section shall be guilty of an offence and liable on summary conviction to a fine not exceeding **level five** on the standard scale.

(6) Any person who, in response to any requirement imposed on him under this section, knowingly or recklessly provides any information or explanation or makes any statement which is false or misleading in a material particular shall be liable[1]—

(*a*) on summary conviction, to a fine not exceeding the **statutory maximum**; and
(*b*) on conviction on indictment, to imprisonment for a term not exceeding **two years** or to a **fine** or to **both**.

(7) Where any person from whom production of a document is required under this section claims a lien on the document, the production of it shall be without prejudice to the lien.

(8) Nothing in this section shall compel—

(*a*) the production of a document containing a communication which is privileged from disclosure in legal proceedings in England and Wales; or
(*b*) the furnishing of information contained in such a communication.

(9) In this section "document" includes any information recorded in any form and, in relation to information recorded otherwise than in legible form, references to its production include references to producing a copy in legible form.
[Courts and Legal Services Act 1990, s 47.]

---

1. For procedure in respect of an offence which is triable either way, see the Magistrates' Courts Act 1980, ss 17A–21, in PART I: MAGISTRATES' COURTS, PROCEDURE, ante.

8–29571 **48. Investigations on behalf of the Board.** (1) If it appears to the Board desirable to do so—

(*a*) in connection with the discharge of any of its functions; and
(*b*) in the interests of customers or potential customers of an authorised practitioner,

it may appoint one or more competent persons ("the investigators") to investigate and report to it on the state and conduct of the affairs of that authorised practitioner.

(2) The Board shall give written notice of any such appointment to the authorised practitioner concerned.

(3) If the investigators think it necessary for the purposes of their investigation, they may also investigate the affairs of any qualified person who is acting, or has acted, on behalf of the authorised practitioner (so far as concerns the provision of conveyancing services on behalf of the authorised practitioner), after giving the qualified person written notice of their investigation.

(4) Subsection (4A) applies if an authorised practitioner whose affairs are under investigation is—

(*a*) a person with permission under Part 4 of the Financial Services and Markets Act 2000 to accept deposits or to effect or carry out contracts of insurance; or

(*b*) an EEA firm of the kind mentioned in paragraph 5(*b*), (*c*) or (*d*) of Schedule 3 to that Act which has permission under paragraph 15 of that Schedule (as a result of qualifying for authorisation under paragraph 12(1) of that Schedule) either—
(i) to accept deposits; or
(ii) to effect or carry out contracts of insurance.

(4A) The Secretary of State may give a direction with a view to limiting the scope of the investigation to matters concerned with the provision of conveyancing services.

(4B) Subsection (4) must be read with—

(*a*) section 22 of the Financial Services and Markets Act 2000;
(*b*) any relevant order under that section; and
(*c*) Schedule 2 to that Act.

(5) Any such direction may be general or be given with respect to a particular investigation.

(6) It shall be the duty of every person whose affairs are being investigated and of any officer or employee of his—

(*a*) to produce to the investigators, within such time and at such place as they may reasonably require, all documents relating to the provision of conveyancing services by the practitioner which are in that person's custody or power;
(*b*) to provide the investigators, within such time as they may require, with such information as they may reasonably require with respect to the provision of those services; and
(*c*) to give the investigators such assistance in connection with the investigation as he is reasonably able to give.

(7) The investigators may take copies of, or extracts from, any document produced to them under subsection (6).

(8) This section applies in relation to a former authorised practitioner or former qualified person as it applies in relation to an authorised practitioner or qualified person.

(9) Any person who, without reasonable excuse, fails to produce any document, or provide any information, which it is his duty to produce under subsection (6) shall be guilty of an offence and liable on summary conviction to a fine not exceeding **level five** on the standard scale.

(10) Any person who, in response to any requirement imposed on him under this section, knowingly or recklessly provides any information or explanation or makes any statement which is false or misleading in a material particular shall be liable[3]—

(*a*) on summary conviction, to a fine not exceeding the **statutory maximum**; and
(*b*) on conviction on indictment, to imprisonment for a term not exceeding **two years** or to a **fine** or to **both**.

(11) Nothing in this section shall compel the production by an authorised practitioner or qualified person acting on his behalf of a document containing a privileged communication made by him or to him in that capacity.

[Courts and Legal Services Act 1990, s 48, as amended by the Bank of England Act 1998, Schs 5 and 9, SI 2001/3649 and SI 2003/1887.]

---

1. Includes a European deposit-taker (Banking Coordination (Second Council Directive) Regulations 1992, SI 1992/3218, Sch 10).
2. See note 2 to s 37 above.
3. For procedure in respect of an offence which is triable either way, see the Magistrates' Courts Act 1980, ss 17A–21, in PART I: MAGISTRATES' COURTS, PROCEDURE, ante.

8–29572 **49. Restrictions on disclosure of information.** (1) Subject to section 50, restricted information which relates to the business or other affairs of any person shall not be disclosed—

(*a*) by the Board or any member of its staff;
(*b*) by any person appointed as an investigator under section 48 or any officer or servant of his; or
(*c*) by any person obtaining it directly or indirectly from a person mentioned in paragraph (*a*) or (*b*),

without the consent of the person from whom it was obtained and, if they are different, the person to whom it relates.

(2) Subject to subsection (3), information is restricted information for the purposes of this section if it was obtained (whether or not in response to any requirement that it be provided) for the purposes of, or in the discharge of functions under, any provision made by or under this Act.

(3) Information shall not be treated as restricted information for the purposes of this section if it has been made available to the public by virtue of being disclosed in any circumstances in which, or for any purpose for which, disclosure is not prevented by this section.

(4) Any person who contravenes this section shall be guilty of an offence and liable[1]—

(*a*) on conviction on indictment, to imprisonment for a term not exceeding **two years** or to a **fine** or to **both**;

(*b*) on summary conviction, to a fine not exceeding the **statutory maximum**.
[Courts and Legal Services Act 1990, s 49.]

1. For procedure in respect of an offence which is triable either way, see the Magistrates' Courts Act 1980, ss 17A–21, in PART I: MAGISTRATES' COURTS, PROCEDURE, ante.

8–29573 **50. Exceptions from restrictions on disclosure.** (1) Section 49 shall not prevent the disclosure of information—

(*a*) with a view to the institution, or otherwise for the purposes, of any criminal proceedings;
(*b*) with a view to the institution, or otherwise for the purposes, of any civil proceedings arising under or by virtue of this Act;
(*c*) in a summary or collection of information framed in such a way as not to enable the identity of any person to whom the information relates to be ascertained; or
(*d*) in pursuance of any Community obligation.

(2) Section 49 shall not prevent the disclosure of information for the purpose of enabling or assisting—

(*a*) *repealed*;
(*b*) the Board to discharge any of its functions;
(*c*) the Law Society, the General Council of the Bar, the Council for Licensed Conveyancers or the Faculty Office of the Archbishop of Canterbury to discharge any of its functions;
(*d*) *repealed*;
(*e*) a recognised investment exchange or a recognised clearing house (both within the meaning given by section 285 of the Financial Services and Markets Act 2000) to discharge any of its functions;
(*f*) the Bank of England to discharge any of its functions;
(*fa*) the Financial Services Authority to discharge its functions under the legislation relating to friendly societies or to industrial and provident societies, under the Building Societies Act 1986 or under the Financial Services and Markets Act 2000;
(*g*) the Secretary of State or the Treasury to discharge any function conferred by this Act, the Financial Services and Markets Act 2000 or any enactment relating to competition, companies or insolvency;
(*h*) the competent authority for the purposes of Part 6 of the Financial Services and Markets Act 2000 to discharge its functions under that Part;
(*ha*) a person appointed under—

(i) section 167 of the Financial Services and Markets Act 2000 (general investigations),
(ii) section 168 of that Act (investigations in particular cases),
(iii) section 169(1)(*b*) of that Act (investigation in support of overseas regulator),
(iv) section 284 of that Act (investigations into affairs of certain collective investment schemes), or
(v) regulations made as a result of section 262(2)(k) of that Act (investigations into open-ended investment companies),

to conduct an investigation to discharge his functions;

(*hb*) any inspector appointed by the Secretary of State under this Act or any enactment relating to competition, companies or insolvency to discharge his functions under that enactment;
(*hc*) a body designated under section 326(1) of the Financial Services and Markets Act 2000 to discharge its functions in its capacity as a body designated under that section;
(*i*) an official receiver to discharge any of his functions under any enactment relating to insolvency;
(*j*) a body which is a recognised professional body under section 391 of the Insolvency Act 1986 to discharge any of its functions as such a body;
(*k*) *repealed*;
(*l*) *repealed*;
(*m*) the OFT to discharge any of its functions under—

(i) this Act;
(ii) the Fair Trading Act 1973 (other than Part II);
(iii) the Consumer Credit Act 1974;
(iv) (*repealed*);
(v) the Estate Agents Act 1979;
(vi) the Competition Act 1980;
(vii) *repealed*;
(viii) the Control of Misleading Advertisements Regulations 1988;
(ix) the Competition Act 1998;
(x) the Financial Services and Markets Act 2000;
(xi) the Enterprise Act 2002;

(*n*) the Competition Commission to discharge any of its functions under the Fair Trading Act 1973, the Competition Act 1980 and the Competition Act 1998;
(*o*) the Scottish Conveyancing and Executry Services Board to discharge any of its functions;
(*p*) an authority in a country or territory outside the United Kingdom to discharge any functions corresponding to—

(i) the functions of the Board, or the Financial Services Authority; or
(ii) those functions of the Secretary of State mentioned in paragraph (*g*);

(*q*) the Insolvency Practitioners Tribunal to discharge any of its functions under the Insolvency Act 1986;
(*r*) the Financial Services Tribunal to discharge any function it has in relation to proceedings before it by virtue of the Financial Services and Markets Act 2000 (Transitional Provisions) (Partly Completed Procedures) Order 2001;
(*s*) the Financial Services and Markets Tribunal to discharge any of its functions;
(*t*) the Pensions Regulator Tribunal to discharge any of its functions.

(3) Subject to subsection (4), section 49 shall not prevent the disclosure of information for the purpose of enabling or assisting any public or other authority for the time being designated for the purposes of this section by an order made by the Secretary of State to discharge any functions which are specified in the order.

(4) An order under subsection (3) designating an authority for the purposes of this section may—

(*a*) impose conditions subject to which the disclosure of information is permitted by subsection (3); and
(*b*) otherwise restrict the circumstances in which disclosure is permitted.

(5) Where information has been disclosed by one person ("the first person") to another, by virtue of subsection (2), section 49 shall not prevent that other person from disclosing that information to any person to whom it could have been disclosed by the first person by virtue of subsection (2).

(6) The Secretary of State may by order modify the application of any provision of this section so as—

(*a*) to prevent the disclosure of information by virtue of that provision; or
(*b*) to restrict the extent to which disclosure of information is permitted by virtue of that provision.

[Courts and Legal Services Act 1990, s 50, as amended by the Bank of England Act 1998, Sch 5, SI 1999/506, SI 2000/311, SI 2001/1283, SI 2001/3649, SI 2003/1398, SI 2003/1887, SI 2001/3649 and the Pensions Act 2004, Sch 4.]

Probate Services

8–29574 **54. Preparation of papers for probate etc.** (1)–(2) *Amendments.*

(3) If a person who applies for any grant of probate or letters of administration—

(*a*) makes a statement in his application, or supports his application with a document, which he knows to be false or misleading in a material particular; or
(*b*) recklessly makes a statement in his application, or supports his application with a document, which is false or misleading in a material particular,

he shall be guilty of an offence.

(4) Any person guilty of an offence under subsection (3) shall be liable[1]—

(*a*) on conviction on indictment, to imprisonment for a term not exceeding **two years** or to a **fine** or to **both**;
(*b*) on summary conviction, to imprisonment for a term not exceeding **six months** or to a fine not exceeding the **statutory maximum** or to **both**.

(5) In subsection (3) "letters of administration" includes all letters of administration of the effects of deceased persons, whether with or without a will annexed, and whether granted for general, special or limited purposes.

[Courts and Legal Services Act 1990, s 54, as amended by the Bank of England Act 1998, Schs 5 and 9, SI 2001/3649 and 2003/1887.]

---

1. For procedure in respect of an offence which is triable either way, see the Magistrates' Courts Act 1980, ss 17A–21, in PART I: MAGISTRATES' COURTS, PROCEDURE, ante.

8–29575 **55. Preparation of probate papers etc: exemption from section 23(1) of Solicitors Act 1974.** (1) The provisions of section 23(1) of the Solicitors Act 1974 (preparation of papers for probate etc by unqualified persons) shall not apply to any person to whom exemption from those provisions is granted by an approved body.

(2) An approved body may only grant such an exemption to a person who is one of its members and who satisfies it—

(*a*) that his business is, and is likely to continue to be, carried on by fit and proper persons or, in the case of an individual, that he is a fit and proper person;

(*b*) that he, and any person employed by him in the provision of probate services, is suitably trained;

(*c*) that satisfactory arrangements will at all times be in force for covering adequately the risk of any claim made against him in connection with the provision of probate services by him, however arising;

(*d*) that he is a member of, or otherwise subject to, a scheme which—

(i) has been established (whether or not exclusively) for the purpose of dealing with complaints about the provision of probate services; and

(ii) complies with such requirements as may be prescribed by regulations[1] made by the Secretary of State with respect to matters relating to such complaints; and

(*e*) that he has in force satisfactory arrangements to protect his clients in the event of his ceasing to provide probate services.

(3) In this section "approved body" means a professional or other body which is approved by the Secretary of State under Schedule 9[2].

(4) The approval of any body under Schedule 9 may be revoked under that Schedule.

[Courts and Legal Services Act 1990, s 55, as amended by SI 2003/1887.]

1. The Probate Services (Approved Body) Complaints Regulations 2004, SI 2004/2951 have been made.
2. Schedule 9 is not printed in this work.

8–29576 56. Administration of oaths etc by justices in certain probate business. (1) Every justice shall have power to administer any oath or take any affidavit which is required for the purposes of an application for a grant of probate or letters of administration made in any non-contentious or common form probate business.

(2) A justice before whom any oath or affidavit is taken or made under this section shall state in the jurat or attestation at what place and on what date the oath or affidavit is taken or made.

(3) No justice shall exercise the powers conferred by this section in any proceedings in which he is interested.

(4) A document purporting to be signed by a justice administering an oath or taking an affidavit shall be admitted in evidence without proof of the signature and without proof that he is a justice.

(5) In this section—

"affidavit" has the same meaning as in the Commissioners for Oaths Act 1889;

"justice" means a justice of the peace;

"letters of administration" includes all letters of administration of the effects of deceased persons, whether with or without a will annexed, and whether granted for general, special or limited purposes; and

"non-contentious or common form probate business" has the same meaning as in section 128 of the Supreme Court Act 1981.

[Courts and Legal Services Act 1990, s 56.]

1. Part II contains ss 17–70.

Miscellaneous

8–29577 58. Conditional fee agreements. (1) A conditional fee agreement which satisfies all of the conditions applicable to it by virtue of this section shall not be unenforceable by reason only of its being a conditional fee agreement; but (subject to subsection (5)) any other conditional fee agreement shall be unenforceable.

(2) For the purposes of this section and section 58A—

(*a*) a conditional fee agreement is an agreement with a person providing advocacy or litigation services which provides for his fees and expenses, or any part of them, to be payable only in specified circumstances; and

(*b*) a conditional fee agreement provides for a success fee if it provides for the amount of any fees to which it applies to be increased, in specified circumstances, above the amount which would be payable if it were not payable only in specified circumstances.

(3) The following conditions are applicable to every conditional fee agreement—

(*a*) it must be in writing;

(*b*) it must not relate to proceedings which cannot be the subject of an enforceable conditional fee agreement; and

(*c*) it must comply with such requirements (if any) as may be prescribed by the Secretary of State.

(4) The following further conditions are applicable to a conditional fee agreement which provides for a success fee—

(*a*) it must relate to proceedings of a description specified by order made by the Secretary of State;

(*b*) it must state the percentage by which the amount of the fees which would be payable if it were not a conditional fee agreement is to be increased; and

(*c*) that percentage must not exceed the percentage specified in relation to the description of proceedings to which the agreement relates by order made by the Secretary of State.

(5) If a conditional fee agreement is an agreement to which section 57 of the Solicitors Act 1974 (non-contentious business agreements between solicitor and client) applies, subsection (1) shall not make it unenforceable.

[Courts and Legal Services Act 1990, s 58, as substituted by the Access to Justice Act 1999, s 27 and amended by SI 2003/1887 and SI 2005/3429.]

8–29577A **58A. Conditional fee agreements: supplementary.** (1) The proceedings which cannot be the subject of an enforceable conditional fee agreement are—

(*a*) criminal proceedings, apart from proceedings under section 82 of the Environmental Protection Act 1990; and

(*b*) family proceedings.

(2) In subsection (1) "family proceedings" means proceedings under any one or more of the following—

(*a*) the Matrimonial Causes Act 1973;
(*b*) the Adoption and Children Act 2002;
(*c*) the Domestic Proceedings and Magistrates' Courts Act 1978;
(*d*) Part III of the Matrimonial and Family Proceedings Act 1984;
(*e*) Parts I, II and IV of the Children Act 1989;
(*f*) Part IV of the Family Law Act 1996;
(*fa*) Chapter 2 of Part 2 of the Civil Partnership Act 2004 (proceedings for dissolution etc of civil partnership);
(*fb*) Schedule 5 to the 2004 Act (financial relief in the High Court or a county court etc);
(*fc*) Schedule 6 to the 2004 Act (financial relief in magistrates' courts etc); and
(*fd*) Schedule 7 to the 2004 Act (financial relief in England and Wales after overseas dissolution etc of a partnership); and
(*g*) the inherent jurisdiction of the High Court in relation to children.

(3) The requirements which the Secretary of State may prescribe[1] under section 58(3)(*c*)—

(*a*) include requirements for the person providing advocacy or litigation services to have provided prescribed information before the agreement is made; and

(*b*) may be different for different descriptions of conditional fee agreements (and, in particular, may be different for those which provide for a success fee and those which do not).

(4) In section 58 and this section (and in the definitions of "advocacy services" and "litigation services" as they apply for their purposes) "proceedings" includes any sort of proceedings for resolving disputes (and not just proceedings in a court), whether commenced or contemplated.

(5) Before making an order under section 58(4), the Secretary of State shall consult—

(*a*) the designated judges;
(*b*) the General Council of the Bar;
(*c*) the Law Society; and
(*d*) such other bodies as he considers appropriate.

(6) A costs order made in any proceedings may, subject in the case of court proceedings to rules of court, include provision requiring the payment of any fees payable under a conditional fee agreement which provides for a success fee.

(7) Rules of court may make provision with respect to the assessment of any costs which include fees payable under a conditional fee agreement (including one which provides for a success fee).

[Courts and Legal Services Act 1990, s 58A, as substituted, together with s 58 for s 58 as originally enacted, by the Access to Justice Act 1999, s 27 and amended by SI 2003/1887, the Adoption and Children Act 2002, Sch 3, the Civil Partnership Act 2004, Sch 27 and SI 2005/3429.]

8–29577B **58B. Litigation funding agreements.** (1) A litigation funding agreement which satisfies all of the conditions applicable to it by virtue of this section shall not be unenforceable by reason only of its being a litigation funding agreement.

(2) For the purposes of this section a litigation funding agreement is an agreement under which—

(*a*) a person ("the funder") agrees to fund (in whole or in part) the provision of advocacy or litigation services (by someone other than the funder) to another person ("the litigant"); and

(*b*) the litigant agrees to pay a sum to the funder in specified circumstances.

(3) The following conditions are applicable to a litigation funding agreement—

(*a*) the funder must be a person, or person of a description, prescribed by the Lord Chancellor
(*b*) the agreement must be in writing;

(*c*) the agreement must not relate to proceedings which by virtue of section 58A(1) and (2) cannot be the subject of an enforceable conditional fee agreement or to proceedings of any such description as may be prescribed by the Lord Chancellor;

(*d*) the agreement must comply with such requirements (if any) as may be so prescribed;

(*e*) the sum to be paid by the litigant must consist of any costs payable to him in respect of the proceedings to which the agreement relates together with an amount calculated by reference to the funder's anticipated expenditure in funding the provision of the services; and

(*f*) that amount must not exceed such percentage of that anticipated expenditure as may be prescribed by the Lord Chancellor in relation to proceedings of the description to which the agreement relates.

(4) Regulations under subsection (3)(*a*) may require a person to be approved by the Secretary of State or by a prescribed person.

(5) The requirements which the Lord Chancellor may prescribe under subsection (3)(*d*)—

(*a*) include requirements for the funder to have provided prescribed information to the litigant before the agreement is made; and

(*b*) may be different for different descriptions of litigation funding agreements.

(6) In this section (and in the definitions of "advocacy services" and "litigation services" as they apply for its purposes) "proceedings" includes any sort of proceedings for resolving disputes (and not just proceedings in a court), whether commenced or contemplated.

(7) Before making regulations under this section, the Lord Chancellor shall consult—

(*a*) the designated judges;
(*b*) the General Council of the Bar;
(*c*) the Law Society; and
(*d*) such other bodies as he considers appropriate.

(8) A costs order made in any proceedings may, subject in the case of court proceedings to rules of court, include provision requiring the payment of any amount payable under a litigation funding agreement.

(9) Rules of court may make provision with respect to the assessment of any costs which include fees payable under a litigation funding agreement.*

[Courts and Legal Services Act 1990, s 58B, as inserted by the Access to Justice Act 1999, s 28 and amended by SI 2005/3429.]

***Printed as prospectively inserted by the Access to Justice Act 1999, s 28, when in force.**

8–29578 63. Legal professional privilege. (1) This section applies to any communication made to or by a person who is not a barrister or solicitor at any time when that person is—

(*a*) providing advocacy or litigation services as an authorised advocate or authorised litigator;
(*b*) providing conveyancing services as an authorised practitioner; or
(*c*) providing probate services as a probate practitioner.

(2) Any such communication shall in any legal proceedings be privileged from disclosure in like manner as if the person in question had at all material times been acting as his client's solicitor.

(3) In subsection (1), "probate practitioner" means a person to whom section 23(1) of the Solicitors Act 1974 (unqualified person not to prepare probate papers etc) does not apply.

[Courts and Legal Services Act 1990, s 63.]

Offences

8–29579 70. Offences. (1) If any person does any act in the purported exercise of a right of audience, or right to conduct litigation, in relation to any proceedings or contemplated proceedings when he is not entitled to exercise that right he shall be guilty of an offence.

(2) If any person does any act in the purported exercise of any right granted to authorised practitioners by virtue of this Act when he is not an authorised practitioner he shall be guilty of an offence.

(3) If any person—

(*a*) wilfully pretends—

(i) to be entitled to exercise any right of audience in relation to any proceedings, or contemplated proceedings; or

(ii) to be entitled to exercise any right to conduct litigation in relation to any proceedings, or contemplated proceedings,

when he is not so entitled;

(*b*) wilfully pretends to be an authorised practitioner when he is not; or

(*c*) with the intention of implying falsely that he is so entitled, or is such a practitioner, takes or uses any name, title or description,

he shall be guilty of an offence.

(4) A person guilty of an offence under subsection (1) or (2) shall be liable[1]—

(*a*) on summary conviction, to imprisonment for a term not exceeding **six months** or to a fine not exceeding the **statutory maximum** or to **both**; or

(*b*) on conviction on indictment, to imprisonment for a term not exceeding **two years** or to a **fine** or to **both**.

(5) A person guilty of an offence under subsection (3) shall be liable, on summary conviction, to a fine not exceeding **level 4** on the standard scale.

(6) A person guilty of an offence under this section, by virtue of subsection (1), shall also be guilty of contempt of the court concerned and may be punished accordingly.

(7) Subsection (8) applies where an offence under this section is committed by a body corporate.

(8) If the offence is proved to have been committed with the consent or connivance of or to be attributable to any neglect on the part of—

(*a*) any director, secretary or other similar officer of the body corporate; or

(*b*) any person who was purporting to act in any such capacity,

he (as well as the body corporate) shall be guilty of the offence and shall be liable to be proceeded against and punished accordingly.

[Courts and Legal Services Act 1990, s 70.]

---

1. For procedure in respect of an offence which is triable either way, see the Magistrates' Courts Act 1980, ss 17A–21, in PART I: MAGISTRATES' COURTS, PROCEDURE, ante.

PART VI[1]
MISCELLANEOUS AND SUPPLEMENTAL
Miscellaneous

Tying-in[1]

8–29580 **104. Tying-in arrangements in connection with residential property loans.** (1) In this section and sections 105 and 106 "residential property loan" means any loan which—

(*a*) is secured on land in the United Kingdom; and

(*b*) is made to an individual in respect of the acquisition of land which is for his residential use or the residential use of a dependant of his.

(2) No person ("the lender") shall provide a residential property loan together with one or more controlled services to another person ("the borrower") unless the conditions mentioned in subsection (3) are complied with before a relevant step is taken with respect to any of those services or the loan.

(3) The conditions are that the lender—

(*a*) informs the borrower by notice that the residential property loan, and each of the controlled services in question, are separate services;

(*b*) informs the borrower by notice whether the terms and conditions of the residential property loan will be capable of being varied by the lender after it is made;

(*c*) provides the borrower with a statement of—

(i) the price which will be payable by the borrower for each of the controlled services if they are all provided in accordance with the terms proposed by the lender; and

(ii) the extent to which (if at all) the terms and conditions of the residential property loan would differ if it were to be provided by the lender without the controlled services in question being provided by the lender; and

(*d*) informs the borrower by notice that, if the borrower declines to take from the lender any of the controlled services in question, the lender will not on that account refuse to provide the residential property loan.

(4) A person who—

(*a*) in the course of his business provides, or makes arrangements for the provision of, controlled services together with residential property loans; and

(*b*) advertises or in any other manner promotes—

(i) the provision of any controlled service or any residential property loan; or

(ii) the making by him of any such arrangements,

shall comply with such requirements as to the information to be given, or which may not be given, in any such advertisement or promotion as the Secretary of State may by regulations impose.

[Courts and Legal Services Act 1990, s 104.]

---

1. At the date of going to press, ss 104–107 had not been brought into force.

8–29581 **105. Tying-in arrangements: supplemental provisions.** (1) In section 104, this section and section 106 "controlled services" means any services of a description prescribed by order made by the Secretary of State.

(2) The order may, in particular, prescribe any description of—

(*a*) banking, insurance, investment, trusteeship, executorship or other financial services;
(*b*) services relating to the acquisition, valuation, surveying or disposal of property;
(*c*) conveyancing services; or
(*d*) removal services.

(3) For the purposes of section 104(1), the Secretary of State may by order specify—

(*a*) the circumstances in which land is to be treated as being for a person's residential use; and
(*b*) who are to be treated as a person's dependants.

(4) Section 104(2) shall not apply in relation to the provision of a controlled service if the lender proves—

(*a*) that the provision of that service was not connected with the transaction in respect of which the borrower required the residential property loan in question; or
(*b*) where it was so connected, that the lender did not know, and had no reasonable cause to know, that it was.

(5) For the purposes of section 104, this section and section 106—

(*a*) where the lender is a member of a group of companies, the lender and all the other members of the group shall be treated as one; and
(*b*) where the lender derives any financial benefit from the provision of a controlled service by any other person, the lender shall be treated as providing that service.

(6) In subsection (5), "a group of companies" means a holding company and its subsidiaries within the meaning of section 736 of the Companies Act 1985.

(7) The Secretary of State may by order provide that, in such cases or for such purposes as may be prescribed by the order, paragraph (*a*) or (*b*) of subsection (5) shall not have effect.

(8) For the purposes of section 104—

"notice" means a notice in writing given in the form prescribed by regulations made by the Secretary of State;
"price" shall have the meaning given by order made by the Secretary of State;
"relevant step", in relation to any controlled service or residential property loan, means such step as may be prescribed by order made by the Secretary of State in relation to that service or loan (taken by such person as may be so prescribed); and
"statement" means a statement in writing given in the form prescribed by regulations made by the Secretary of State.

(9) In relation to land in Scotland—

(*a*) "conveyancing services" has the same meaning as in the Law Reform (Miscellaneous Provisions) (Scotland) Act 1990; and
(*b*) the reference in section 104(1) to a loan being secured on land shall be read as a reference to its being secured over land by a standard security.

(10) Before making any order or regulations under section 104 or this section the Secretary of State shall consult the Director and such other persons as he considers appropriate.
[Courts and Legal Services Act 1990, s 105.]

8–29582 **106. Tying-in: offences.** (1) If any person contravenes section 104(2) or (4) he shall be guilty of an offence.

(2) Subsection (3) applies where—

(*a*) a person ("the lender") has, in relation to the proposed provision to any person ("the borrower") of a residential property loan together with one or more controlled services, complied with the conditions mentioned in section 104(3); and
(*b*) the borrower has declined to take from the lender one or more of the controlled services.

(3) The lender shall be guilty of an offence if he refuses to provide the borrower with the residential property loan or refuses to provide it to him—

(*a*) on the terms applicable if it were provided together with the controlled services; or
(*b*) where they differ, on terms which are compatible with the statement required by section 104(3)(*c*)(ii),

unless he proves that his reason for so refusing was unconnected with the borrower's having declined as mentioned in subsection (2)(*b*).

(4) Any person guilty of an offence under this section shall be liable[1]—

(*a*) on summary conviction, to a fine not exceeding the **statutory maximum**; and
(*b*) on conviction on indictment, to a **fine**.

(5) Subsection (6) applies where an offence under this section is committed by a body corporate.

(6) If the offence is proved to have been committed with the consent or connivance of or to be attributable to any neglect on the part of—

(*a*) any director, secretary or other similar officer of the body corporate; or

(*b*) any person who was purporting to act in any such capacity,

he (as well as the body corporate) shall be guilty of the offence and shall be liable to be proceeded against and punished accordingly.

(7) The fact that a person has committed an offence under this section in connection with any agreement shall not make the agreement void, or unenforceable (whether as a whole or in part) or otherwise affect its validity or give rise to any cause of action for breach of statutory duty.

[Courts and Legal Services Act 1990, s 106.]

1. For procedure in respect of an offence which is triable either way, see the Magistrates' Courts Act 1980, ss 17A–21, in PART I: MAGISTRATES' COURTS, PROCEDURE, ante.

8–29583 **107. Tying-in: enforcement.** (1) Every local weights and measures authority ("an authority") and the Director shall have the duty of enforcing sections 104 to 106 and any regulations made under them.

(2) Nothing in subsection (1) is to be taken as authorising a local weights and measures authority in Scotland to institute proceedings for an offence.

(3) Where an authority propose to institute proceedings for an offence under section 106 they shall give the Director notice of the intended proceedings together with a summary of the facts on which the charges are to be founded.

(4) Where an authority are under a duty to give such a notice and summary they shall not institute the proceedings until—

(*a*) the end of the period of 28 days beginning with the date on which they gave the required notice and summary; or

(*b*) if earlier, the date on which the Director notifies them of receipt of the notice and summary.

(5) Every authority shall, whenever the Director requires, report to him in such form and with such particulars as he requires on the exercise of their functions under this section.

(6) A duly authorised officer of the Director or of an authority ("an authorised officer") who has reasonable cause to suspect that an offence may have been committed under section 106 may, at any reasonable time—

(*a*) enter any premises which are not used solely as a dwelling;

(*b*) require any officer, agent or other competent person on the premises who is, or may be, in possession of information relevant to an investigation in connection with the provision made by section 104 or 105 to provide such information;

(*c*) require the production of any document which may be relevant to such an investigation;

(*d*) take copies, or extracts, of any such documents;

(*e*) seize and retain any document which he has reason to believe may be required as evidence in proceedings for an offence under section 106.

(7) Any authorised officer exercising any power given by subsection (6) shall, if asked to do so, produce evidence that he is such an officer.

(8) A justice of the peace may issue a warrant under this section if satisfied, on information on oath given by an authorised officer, that there is reasonable cause to believe that an offence may have been committed under section 106 and that—

(*a*) entry to the premises concerned, or production of any documents which may be relevant to an investigation in connection with the provision made by section 104 or 105, has been or is likely to be refused to the authorised officer; or

(*b*) there is reasonable cause to believe that, if production of any such document were to be required by the authorised officer without a warrant having been issued under this section, the document would not be produced but would be removed from the premises or hidden, tampered with or destroyed.

(9) In the application of this section to Scotland, "justice of the peace" includes a sheriff and "information on oath" shall be read as "evidence on oath".

(10) A warrant issued under this section shall authorise the authorised officer (accompanied, where he considers it appropriate, by a constable or any other person)—

(*a*) to enter the premises specified in the information, using such force as is reasonably necessary; and

(*b*) to exercise any of the powers given to the authorised officer by subsection (6).

(11) If a person—

(*a*) intentionally obstructs an authorised officer in the exercise of any power under this section;

(*b*) intentionally fails to comply with any requirement properly imposed on him by an authorised officer in the exercise of any such power;

(*c*) fails, without reasonable excuse, to give to an authorised officer any assistance or information which he may reasonably require of him for the purpose of exercising any such power; or

(*d*) in giving to an authorised officer any information which he has been required to give to an authorised officer exercising any such power, makes any statement which he knows to be false or misleading in a material particular,

he shall be guilty of an offence.

(12) A person guilty of an offence under subsection (11)(*a*), (*b*) or (*c*) shall be liable on summary conviction to a fine not exceeding **level 3** on the standard scale.

(13) A person guilty of an offence under subsection (11)(*d*) shall be liable on summary conviction to a fine not exceeding **level 4** on the standard scale.

(14) Nothing in this section shall be taken to require any person to answer any question put to him by an authorised officer, or to give any information to an authorised officer, if to do so might incriminate him.

(15) In this section "document" includes information recorded in any form.

(16) In relation to information recorded otherwise than in legible form, references in this section to its production include references to producing a copy of the information in legible form.

[Courts and Legal Services Act 1990, s 107.]

8–29584 113. Administration of oaths and taking of affidavits. (1) In this section—

"authorised person" means—

(*a*) any authorised advocate or authorised litigator, other than one who is a solicitor (in relation to whom provision similar to that made by this section is made by section 81 of the Solicitors Act 1974); or

(*b*) any person who is a member of a professional or other body prescribed[1] by the Secretary of State for the purposes of this section; and

"general notary" means any public notary other than

(*a*) an ecclesiastical notary;

(*b*) *Repealed.*

(2) *Repealed.*

(3) Subject to the provisions of this section, every authorised person shall have the powers conferred on a commissioner for oaths by the Commissioners for Oaths Acts 1889 and 1891 and section 24 of the Stamp Duties Management Act 1891; and any reference to such a commissioner in an enactment or instrument (including an enactment passed or instrument made after the commencement of this Act) shall include a reference to an authorised person unless the context otherwise requires.

(4) Subject to the provisions of this section, every general notary shall have the powers conferred on a commissioner for oaths by the Commissioners for Oaths Acts 1889 and 1891; and any reference to such a commissioner in an enactment or instrument (including an enactment passed or instrument made after the commencement of this Act) shall include a reference to a general notary unless the context otherwise requires.

(5) No person shall exercise the powers conferred by this section in any proceedings in which he is interested.

(6) A person exercising such powers and before whom any oath or affidavit is taken or made shall state in the jurat or attestation at which place and on what date the oath or affidavit is taken or made.

(7) A document containing such a statement and purporting to be sealed or signed by an authorised person or general notary shall be admitted in evidence without proof of the seal or signature, and without proof that he is an authorised person or general notary.

(8) The Secretary of State may, with the concurrence of the Lord Chief Justice and the Master of the Rolls, by order[2] prescribe the fees to be charged by authorised persons exercising the powers of commissioners for oaths by virtue of this section in respect of the administration of an oath or the taking of an affidavit.

(9) In this section "affidavit" has the same meaning as in the Commissioners for Oaths Act 1889.

(10) Every—

(*a*) solicitor who holds a practising certificate which is in force;

(*b*) authorised person;

(*c*) general notary;

(*d*) *Repealed,*

shall have the right to use the title "Commissioner for Oaths".*

[Courts and Legal Services Act 1990, s 113, as amended by the Access to Justice Act 1999, Sch 15 and SI 2003/1887.]

1. The Council for Licensed Conveyancers has been prescribed by the Commissioners for Oaths (Prescribed Bodies) Regulations 1994, SI 1994/1380, thereby enabling licensed conveyancers to act as commissioners for oaths; the Institute of Legal Executives has been similarly prescribed by SI 1995/1676.

2. The Commissioners for Oaths (Authorised Persons) (Fees) Order 1993, SI 1993/2298, has been made.

8–29585 **124. Commencement.** (1) The following provisions come into force on the passing of this Act—

(*a*) sections 1, 5, 119 to 123, this section and section 125(1); and
(*b*) paragraphs 2 and 3 of Schedule 17.

(2) The following provisions come into force at the end of the period of two months beginning on the day on which this Act is passed—

(*a*) sections 6, 8, 11, 16, 64, 65, 72, 73, 85, 87 and 88, 90 to 92, 94 to 97, 98 and 108 to 110;
(*b*) paragraphs 1, 11, 12, 16 and 20 of Schedule 17;
(*c*) paragraphs 7, 8, 14 to 16, 55 and 57 of Schedule 18; and
(*d*) paragraph 1 of Schedule 19.

(3) The other provisions of this Act shall come into force on such date as may be appointed by order[1] made by the Lord Chancellor or by the Secretary of State or by both, acting jointly.

(4) Different dates may be appointed for different provisions of this Act and for different purposes.
[Courts and Legal Services Act 1990, s 124.]

1. At the date of going to press the following commencement orders had been made: Courts and Legal Services Act 1990 (Commencement No 1) Order 1990, SI 1990/2170 (Commencement No 2) Order 1990, SI 1990/2484 (Commencement No 3) Order 1991, SI 1991/608 (Commencement No 4) Order 1991, SI 1991/985 (Commencement No 5) Order 1991, SI 1991/1364 (Commencement No 6) Order 1991, SI 1991/1883 (Commencement No 7) Order 1991, SI 1991/2730, Courts and Legal Services Act 1990 (Commencement No 8) Order 1992, SI 1992/1221, Courts and Legal Services Act 1990 (Commencement No 9) Order 1993, SI 1993/2132.

Access to Justice Act 1999[1]

(1999 c 22)

PART II[2]

OTHER FUNDING OF LEGAL SERVICES

8–29586 **27. Conditional fee agreements.** *Amends the Courts and Legal Services Act 1990.*

1. The Access to Justice Act 1999 is reproduced partly in PART VIII: SOLICITOR, and partly in PART I: MAGISTRATES' COURTS, PROCEDURE, ante.

2. Part II comprises ss 27–34. At the date of going to press, ss 27–31, which are set out here had not been brought into force. For commencement provisions, see s 108 in PART I: MAGISTRATES' COURTS, PROCEDURE, ante. The Access to Justice Act 1999 (Transitional Provisions) Order 2000, SI 2000/900 makes transitional and savings provisions in respect of conditional fee agreements, insurance policies or a body's undertaking to meet costs liabilities entered into before the coming into force of ss 27, 29 and 30 of the Access to Justice Act 1999 on 1 April 2000.

8–29586A **28. Litigation funding agreements.** *Amends the Courts and Legal Services Act 1990.*

Costs

8–29586B **29. Recovery of insurance premiums by way of costs.** Where in any proceedings a costs order is made in favour of any party who has taken out an insurance policy against the risk of incurring a liability in those proceedings, the costs payable to him may, subject in the case of court proceedings to rules of court, include costs in respect of the premium of the policy.
[Access to Justice Act 1999, s 29.]

8–29586C **30. Recovery where body undertakes to meet costs liabilities.** (1) This section applies where a body of a prescribed[1] description undertakes to meet (in accordance with arrangements satisfying prescribed conditions) liabilities which members of the body or other persons who are parties to proceedings may incur to pay the costs of other parties to the proceedings.

(2) If in any of the proceedings a costs order is made in favour of any of the members or other persons, the costs payable to him may, subject to subsection (3) and (in the case of court proceedings) to rules of court, include an additional amount in respect of any provision made by or on behalf of the body in connection with the proceedings against the risk of having to meet such liabilities.

(3) But the additional amount shall not exceed a sum determined in a prescribed[1] manner; and there may, in particular, be prescribed as a manner of determination one which takes into account the likely cost to the member or other person of the premium of an insurance policy against the risk of incurring a liability to pay the costs of other parties to the proceedings.

(4) In this section "prescribed" means prescribed by regulations[1] made by the Lord Chancellor by statutory instrument; and a statutory instrument containing such regulations shall be subject to annulment in pursuance of a resolution of either House of Parliament.

(5) Regulations under subsection (1) may, in particular, prescribe[1] as a description of body one which is for the time being approved by the Lord Chancellor or by a prescribed person.
[Access to Justice Act 1999, s 30, as amended by SI 2005/3249.]

1. The Access to Justice (Membership Organisations) Regulations 2000, SI 2000/693 have been made.

8–29586D 31. Rules as to costs. In section 51 of the Supreme Court Act 1981 (costs), in subsection (2) (rules regulating matters relating to costs), insert at the end "or for securing that the amount awarded to a party in respect of the costs to be paid by him to such representatives is not limited to what would have been payable by him to them if he had not been awarded costs."
[Access to Justice Act 1999, s 31.]

Legal aid in Scotland

8–29586E 32. Regulations about financial limits in certain proceedings.. In section 9(2) of the Legal Aid (Scotland) Act 1986 (application by regulations of Part II to assistance by way of representation), after paragraph (*d*) insert—

"(*dd*)provide that assistance by way of representation shall be available in relation to such proceedings as may be prescribed, without reference to the financial limits under section 8 of this Act;

(*de*) provide that section 11(2) of this Act shall not apply as respects assistance by way of representation received in relation to such proceedings as may be prescribed;".

[Access to Justice Act 1999, s 32.]

8–29586F 33. Recipients of disabled person's tax credit. *Repealed.*

8–29586G 34. References by Scottish Criminal Cases Review Commission. In section 25(7) of the Legal Aid (Scotland) Act 1986 (legal aid in appeals), for "Secretary of State under section 124" substitute "Scottish Criminal Cases Review Commission under section 194B".
[Access to Justice Act 1999, s 34.]

PART III[1]
PROVISION OF LEGAL SERVICES
Barristers and solicitors

8–29586Q 44. Barristers employed by solicitors etc. (1) Where a barrister is employed by—

(*a*) a solicitor or other authorised litigator (within the meaning of the Courts and Legal Services Act 1990), or

(*b*) a body recognised under section 9 of the Administration of Justice Act 1985 (incorporated solicitors' practices),

any rules of the General Council of the Bar which impose a prohibition or limitation on the provision of legal services shall not operate to prevent him from providing legal services to clients of his employer if either of the conditions specified in subsection (2) is satisfied.

(2) Those conditions are—

(*a*) that the prohibition or limitation is on the provision of the services otherwise than on the instructions of a solicitor (or other person acting for the client), and

(*b*) that the prohibition or limitation does not apply to barristers who provide legal services but are not employees.

[Access to Justice Act 1999, s 44.]

8–29586S 46. Bar practising certificates. (1) If the General Council of the Bar makes rules prohibiting barristers from practising as specified in the rules unless authorised by a certificate issued by the Council (a "practising certificate"), the rules may include provision requiring the payment of fees to the Council by applicants for practising certificates.

(2)–(6) *Rules*

[Access to Justice Act 1999, s 46 amended by SI 2001/135, art 2.]

8–29586T 47. Fees for solicitors' practising certificates. (1) The Secretary of State may by order made by statutory instrument amend section 11(3) of the Solicitors Act 1974 (power of Law Society to apply fees payable on issue of practising certificates for any of its purposes) by substituting for the purposes referred to in it (at any time)—

(*a*) the purposes of the regulation, education and training of solicitors and those wishing to become solicitors, or

(*b*) both those purposes and such other purposes as the Secretary of State considers appropriate.

(2) No order shall be made under this section unless—

(*a*) the Secretary of State has consulted the Master of the Rolls and the Law Society, and (*b*) a draft of the order has been laid before, and approved by a resolution of, each House of Parliament.

[Access to Justice Act 1999, s 47, as amended by SI 2003/1887.]

8–29586U 48. Law Society's powers in relation to conduct of solicitors etc. Schedule 7 (which extends the powers of the Law Society in relation to the conduct of solicitors and their employees and consultants) has effect.

[Access to Justice Act 1999, s 48.]

Legal Services Ombudsman

8–29586V 49. Powers of Ombudsman. (1) Section 23 of the Courts and Legal Services Act 1990 (recommendations of the Legal Services Ombudsman) is amended as follows.

(2) In subsection (1)(*c*) (written report of investigation to be sent to person with respect to whom recommendation is made), after "subsection (2)" insert "or an order under subsection (2A)".

(3) In paragraph (*e*) of subsection (2) (recommendation that costs be paid by person or body to which recommendation under paragraph (*c*) or (*d*) applies), for "which a recommendation under paragraph (*c*) or (*d*) applies" substitute "pay compensation under paragraph (*c*) or (*d*)".

(4) After that subsection insert—

"(2A) If after completing any investigation under this Act the Ombudsman considers that, rather than recommending the taking of any action by any person or professional body under paragraph (*c*), (*d*) or (*e*) of subsection (2), he should make an order requiring the taking of that action by the person or body—

(*a*) he shall afford the person or body, and the person who made the allegation, a reasonable opportunity of appearing before him to make representations; and

(*b*) having considered any representations from them, he may, in reporting his conclusions, make the order."

(5) In subsections (3) and (4) (reports), after "recommendation" (in each place) insert "or order".

(6) In subsection (6) (duty to have regard to Ombudsman's report), for "subsection (1)(*b*) or (*c*)" substitute "subsection (1)(*b*), (*c*) or (*d*)".

(7) For the sidenote substitute "Recommendations and orders."

[Access to Justice Act 1999, s 49.]

8–29586W 50. Funding of Ombudsman by professional bodies. In paragraph 7 of Schedule 3 to the Courts and Legal Services Act 1990 (financial provisions relating to Legal Services Ombudsman), for sub-paragraph (1) (Ombudsman's expenses to be defrayed by Secretary of State) substitute—

"(1) The Secretary of State may require any professional body (within the meaning of section 22 of this Act) to make payments of such amount as the Secretary of State considers appropriate to the Ombudsman towards meeting the expenditure incurred (or to be incurred) by him in the discharge of his functions.

(1A) To the extent that that expenditure is not met by payments under sub-paragraph (1), it shall be met by the Secretary of State out of money provided by Parliament."

[Access to Justice Act 1999, s 50, as amended by SI 2003/1887.]

Legal Services Complaints Commissioner

8–29586X 51. Commissioner. (1) The Secretary of State may appoint a person as Legal Services Complaints Commissioner.

(2) Any appointment of a person as Commissioner shall be for a period of not more than three years; and a person appointed as Commissioner shall hold and vacate office in accordance with the terms of his appointment.

(3) At the end of his term of appointment the Commissioner shall be eligible for re-appointment.

(4) The Commissioner shall not be an authorised advocate, authorised litigator, licensed conveyancer or authorised practitioner (within the meaning of the Courts and Legal Services Act 1990) or a notary.

(5) Schedule 8 (which makes further provision about the Commissioner) has effect.

[Access to Justice Act 1999, s 51, as amended by SI 2003/1887.]

8–29586Y 52. Commissioner's functions. (1) If it appears to the Secretary of State that complaints about members of any professional body are not being handled effectively and efficiently, he may by direction require the Legal Services Complaints Commissioner to consider exercising in relation to the body such of the powers in subsection (2) as are specified in the direction.

(2) Those powers are—

(*a*) to require a professional body to provide information, or make reports, to the Commissioner about the handling of complaints about its members,

(*b*) to investigate the handling of complaints about the members of a professional body,

(*c*) to make recommendations in relation to the handling of complaints about the members of a professional body,

(*d*) to set targets in relation to the handling of complaints about the members of a professional body, and

(*e*) to require a professional body to submit to the Commissioner a plan for the handling of complaints about its members.

(3) Where the Commissioner requires a professional body to submit to him a plan for the handling of complaints about its members but the body—

(*a*) fails to submit to him a plan which he considers adequate for securing that such complaints are handled effectively and efficiently, or

(*b*) submits to him such a plan but fails to handle complaints in accordance with it,

he may require the body to pay a penalty.

(4) Before requiring a professional body to pay a penalty under subsection (3) the Commissioner shall afford it a reasonable opportunity of appearing before him to make representations.

(5) The Secretary of State shall by order[1] made by statutory instrument specify the maximum amount of any penalty under subsection (3).

(6) In determining the amount of any penalty which a professional body is to be required to pay under subsection (3) the Commissioner shall have regard to all the circumstances of the case, including in particular—

(*a*) the total number of complaints about members of the body and, where the penalty is imposed in respect of a failure to handle complaints in accordance with a plan, the number of complaints not so handled, and

(*b*) the assets of the body and the number of its members.

(7) A penalty under subsection (3) shall be paid to the Commissioner who shall pay it to the Secretary of State.

(8) Where a direction under subsection (1) in relation to a professional body has been given (and not revoked), section 24(1) of the Courts and Legal Services Act 1990 (power of Legal Services Ombudsman to make recommendations about arrangements for investigation of complaints) shall not have effect in relation to the body.

(9) No order shall be made under subsection (5) unless a draft of the order has been laid before, and approved by a resolution of, each House of Parliament.

(10) In this section "professional body" has the same meaning as in section 22 of the Courts and Legal Services Act 1990.

[Access to Justice Act 1999, s 52, as amended by SI 2003/1887.]

---

1. The Legal Services Complaints Commissioner (Maximum Penalty) Order 2004, SI 2004 has fixed the penalty at whichever is the lesser of – (*a*) £1,000,000; and (*b*) 1 per cent. of the amount which is specified as the total income from all sources of the professional body in that body's most recent audited accounts at the date on which the penalty is imposed.

Public notaries

8–29586Z 53. Abolition of scriveners' monopoly. A public notary may practise as a notary in, or within three miles of, the City of London whether or not he is a member of the Incorporated Company of Scriveners of London (even if he is admitted to practise only outside that area).

[Access to Justice Act 1999, s 53.]

8–29587

SCHEDULE 5

AUTHORISED BODIES: DESIGNATION AND REGULATIONS AND RULES

8–29587A SCHEDULE 6

RIGHTS OF AUDIENCE AND RIGHTS TO CONDUCT LITIGATION

8–29587B SCHEDULE 7

POWERS OF LAW SOCIETY

STREET AND HOUSE TO HOUSE COLLECTIONS

8–29589 This title contains the following statutes—

8–29590 POLICE, FACTORIES, ETC (MISCELLANEOUS PROVISIONS) ACT 1916
8–29591 HOUSE TO HOUSE COLLECTIONS ACT 1939

Police, Factories, etc (Miscellaneous Provisions) Act 1916

(6 & 7 Geo 5 c 31)

8–29590 5. Regulations as to street collections. (1) Each of the authorities specified in subsection (1A) below may make regulations[1] with respect to the places where and the conditions under which persons may be permitted in any[2] street or public place[3], within their area, to collect money or sell articles for the benefit of charitable or other purposes, and any person who acts in contravention of any such regulation shall be liable on summary conviction to a fine not exceeding **level 1** on the standard scale.

Provided that—

(*a*) Regulations made under this section shall not come into operation until they have been confirmed by the Secretary of State, and published for such time and in such manner as the Secretary of State may direct; and

(*b*) Regulations made under this section shall not apply to the selling of articles in any street or public place where the articles are sold in the ordinary course of trade, and for the purpose of earning a livelihood, and no representation is made by or on behalf of the sellers that any part of the proceeds of sale will be devoted to any charitable purpose.

(1A) The authorities referred to in subsection (1) above are—

(*a*) the Common Council of the City of London
(*b*) the police authority for the Metropolitan Police District, and
(*c*) the council of each district

but any regulations made by a district council under that subsection shall not have effect with respect to any street or public place which is within the Metropolitan Police District as well as within the district.*

[Police, Factories, etc (Miscellaneous Provisions) Act 1916, s 5, as amended by the Local Government Act 1972, Sch 29, the Criminal Law Act 1977, s 31 and the Criminal Justice Act 1982, s 46.]

***Repealed by the Charities Act 1992, Sch 7, when in force.**

1. With the exception of those relating to the Metropolitan Police District, the regulations made under this section are not contained in the Statutory Instruments. For regulations covering the Metropolitan Police District, see the Street Collections (Metropolitan Police District) Regulations 1979, SI 1979/1230 amended by SI 1986/1696.

2. "Street" includes any highway and any public bridge, road, lane, footway, square, court, alley, or passage, whether a thoroughfare or not (s 5(4)).

3. The Act contains no definition of "public place". Cf the Licensing Act 1902, s 8, in PART VI: LICENSING, ante.

House to House Collections Act 1939[1]

(2 & 3 Geo 6 c 44)

8–29591 1. Charitable collections from house to house to be licensed. (1) Subject to the provisions of this Act, no collection[2] for charitable purpose[3] shall be made unless the requirements of this Act[4] as to a licence[5] for the promotion thereof are satisfied.

(2) If a person promotes[6] a collection for a charitable purpose, and a collection for that purpose is made in any locality pursuant to his promotion[6], then, unless there is in force, throughout the period during which the collection is made in that locality, a licence[5] authorising him, or authorising another under whose authority he acts, to promote[6] a collection therein for that purpose, he shall be guilty of an offence[7].

(3) If a person acts as a collector[8] in any locality[9] for the purposes of a collection for a charitable purpose, then, unless there is in force, at all times when he so acts, a licence[5] authorising a promoter[6] under whose authority he acts, or authorising the collector himself, to promote[6] a collection therein for that purpose, he shall be guilty of an offence[10].

(4) If the chief officer of police[11] for the police area[11] comprising a locality in which a collection for a charitable purpose is being, or is proposed to be, made is satisfied that that purpose is local in character and that the collection is likely to be completed within a short period of time, he may grant to the person who appears to him to be principally concerned in the promotion of the collection a certificate[12] in the prescribed[13] form, and, where a certificate is so granted, the provisions of this Act, except the provisions of sections five and six thereof and the provisions of section eight thereof in so far as they relate to those sections, shall not apply, in relation to a collection made for that purpose

within such locality and within such period as may be specified in the certificate, to the person to whom the certificate is granted or to any person authorised by him to promote[14] the collection or to act as a collector[8] for the purposes thereof.*
[House to House Collections Act 1939, s 1.]

***Repealed by the Charities Act 1992, Sch 7, when in force.**

1. This Act should be construed within its own ambit and not in conjunction with the provisions of the Trading Representations (Disabled Persons) Act 1958, title CONSUMER PROTECTION, ante; see *Cooper v Coles* [1987] QB 230, [1987] 1 All ER 91.

2. "Collection" means an appeal to the public, made by means of visits from house to house, to give, whether for consideration or not, money or other property; and "collector" means, in relation to a collection, a person who makes the appeal in the course of such visits as aforesaid (s 11(1)). For the purposes of this Act, a collection shall be deemed to be made for a particular purpose where the appeal is made in association with a representation that the money or other property appealed for, or part thereof, will be applied for that purpose (s 11(2)). See also *Emmanuel v Smith, Hird v Smith,* and *Carasu Ltd v Smith* [1968] 2 QB 383, [1968] 2 All ER 529. A promotion for a charitable purpose which involves the exchange of goods for money is a "collection" within the meaning of the Act (*Cooper v Coles* [1987] QB 230, [1987] 1 All ER 91).

3. "Charitable purpose" means any charitable, benevolent or philanthropic purpose, whether or not the purpose is charitable within the meaning of any rule of law (s 11(1)).

4. A licence is granted by the district council or, in the Metropolitan Police District, the Commissioner of Police for the Metropolis or, in the City of London, by the Common Council (s 2). An appeal lies to the Secretary of State against the refusal to grant a licence or its revocation (sub-s (4)).

5. "Licence" means a licence under this Act (s 11(1)). An order of exemption granted under s 3, post, has the same effect as a licence. An application for a licence is made to the licensing authority under s 2, which sets out the grounds on which the authority may refuse it, broadly speaking so as to ensure that a proper amount of the proceeds are applied to the charity and to exclude persons of bad character. Notification of the grounds of refusal must be given in writing by the authority.

6. "Promoter" means, in relation to a collection, a person who causes others to act, whether for remuneration or otherwise, as collectors for the purposes of the collection; and "promote" and "promotion" have corresponding meanings (s 11(1)). A promoter may be exempt from the provisions of s 1(2) (s 3, post).

7. As to penalty, see s 8(1), post; and as to an offence committed by a corporation, see s 8(7), post.

8. As to the meaning of "collector", see note 2, supra, and as to the effect where a promoter is exempted see s 3, post.

9. Collecting in one establishment on one occasion is not "collecting in a locality" unless there is evidence that the defendant was about to go on to other houses (*Hankinson v Dowland* [1974] 3 All ER 655, [1974] 1 WLR 1327). "Locality" can include two public houses a mile apart (*Davison v Richards* [1976] Crim LR 46).

10. As to penalty, see s 8(2), post.

11. These expressions are now defined by the Police Act 1964, Sch 8, in title POLICE, ante. A chief officer of police may delegate his functions to any police officer not below the rank of inspector (s 7). The Commissioner of Police is the police authority for the metropolitan police district. He cannot delegate his functions (s 9).

12. See the House to House Collections Regulations 1947, SR & O 1947/2662, as amended by SI 1963/684.

13. "Prescribed" means prescribed by regulations made under this Act (s 11(1)).

14. See note 6, supra.

8–29592 **3. Exemptions in the case of collections over wide areas.** (1) Where the Secretary of State is satisfied that a person pursues a charitable purpose[1] throughout the whole of England or a substantial part thereof and is desirous of promoting[2] collections[3] for that purpose, the Secretary of State may by order direct that he shall be exempt from the provisions of subsection (2) of section one of this Act as respects all collections for that purpose in such localities as may be described in the order, and whilst an order so made in the case of any person is in force as respects collections in any locality, the provisions of this Act shall have effect in relation to the person exempted, to a promoter[2] of a collection[3] in that locality for that purpose who acts under the authority of the person exempted, and to a person who so acts as a collector[3] for the purposes of any such collection, as if a licence[4] authorising the person exempted to promote[2] a collection in that locality for that purpose had been in force.

(2) Any order made under this section may be revoked or varied by a subsequent order made by the Secretary of State.*
[House to House Collections Act 1939, s 3.]

***Repealed by the Charities Act 1992, Sch 7, when in force.**

1. "Charitable purpose" means any charitable, benevolent or philanthropic purpose, whether or not the purpose is charitable within the meaning of any rule of law (s 11(1)).

2. See note 6 to s 1, supra.

3. See note 2 to s 1, supra.

4. See note 5 to s 1, supra.

8–29593 **4. Regulations.** (1) The Secretary of State may make regulations[1] for prescribing anything which by this Act is required to be prescribed, and for regulating the manner in which collections, in respect of which licences have been granted or orders have been made under the last foregoing section, may be carried out and the conduct of promoters and collectors in relation to such collections.

(2) Without prejudice to the generality of powers conferred by the foregoing subsection, regulations made thereunder may make provision for all or any of the following matters, that is to say—*(a)* to *(e)* (prescribing badges, minimum age for collectors and other matters).

(3) Any person who contravenes or fails to comply with the provisions of a regulation made under this Act shall be guilty of an offence[2].*
[House to House Collections Act 1939, s 4.]

***Repealed by the Charities Act 1992, Sch 7, when in force.**

1. See House to House Collections Regulations 1947, SR & O 1947/2662, as amended by SI 1963/684.
2. See s 8(3), post.

8–29594 **5. Unauthorised use of badges, &c.** If any person, in connection with any appeal[1] made by him, to the public in association with a representation that the appeal is for a charitable purpose[2], displays or uses—

(*a*) a prescribed badge[3] or a prescribed certificate of authority[3], not being a badge or certificate for the time being held by him for the purposes of the appeal pursuant to regulations made under this Act, or

(*b*) any badge or device, or any certificate or other document, so nearly resembling a prescribed badge[3] or, as the case may be, a prescribed certificate of authority as to be calculated to deceive[4],

he shall be guilty of an offence[5].*

[House to House Collections Act 1939, s 5.]

***Repealed by the Charities Act 1992, Sch 7, when in force.**

1. This section applies to any appeal made to the public in association with a representation which is for a charitable purpose and is not limited to house to house collections (*R v Davison* [1972] 3 All ER 1121, [1972] 1 WLR 1540).
2. See note 1 to s 3, supra.
3. See House to House Collections Regulations 1947, SR & O 1947 No 2662, as amended by SI 1963/684.
4. This means "likely to deceive" (*R v Davison* [1972] 3 All ER 1121, [1972] 1 WLR 1540).
5. See s 8(4), post.

8–29595 **6. Collector to give name, etc, to police on demand.** A police constable may require any person whom he believes to be acting as a collector[1] for the purposes of a collection[1] for a charitable purpose[2] to declare to him immediately his name and address and to sign his name, and if any person fails to comply with a requirement duly made to him under this section, he shall be guilty of an offence[3].*

[House to House Collections Act 1939, s 6.]

***Repealed by the Charities Act 1992, Sch 7, when in force.**

1. See note 2 to s 1, ante.
2. See note 1 to s 3, supra.
3. See s 8(5), post.

8–29596 **8. Penalties.** (1) Any promoter[1] guilty of an offence under subsection (2) of section one of this Act shall be liable, on summary conviction, to imprisonment for a term not exceeding six months or to a fine not exceeding **level 3** on the standard scale or to both[2] such imprisonment and such fine.

(2) Any collector guilty of an offence under subsection (3) of section one of this Act shall be liable, on summary conviction, to imprisonment for a term not exceeding three months** or to a fine not exceeding **level 2** on the standard scale or to both[2] such imprisonment and such fine.

(3) Any person guilty of an offence under subsection (3) of section four of this Act shall be liable, on summary conviction, to a fine not exceeding **level 1** on the standard scale.

(4) Any person guilty of an offence under section five of this Act shall be liable, on summary conviction, to imprisonment for a term not exceeding six months or to a fine not exceeding **level 3** on the standard scale, or to both[2] such imprisonment and such fine.

(5) Any person guilty of an offence under section six of this Act shall be liable, on summary conviction, to a fine not exceeding **level 1** on the standard scale.

(6) If any person in furnishing any information for the purposes of this Act knowingly or recklessly makes a statement false in a material particular, he shall be guilty of an offence, and shall be liable, on summary conviction, to imprisonment for a term not exceeding six months or to a fine not exceeding **level 3** on the standard scale, or to both[2] such imprisonment and such fine.

(7) Where an offence under this Act committed by a corporation is proved to have been committed with the consent or connivance of, or to be attributable to any culpable neglect of duty on the part of, any director[3], manager, secretary, or other officer of the corporation, he, as well as the corporation, shall be deemed to be guilty of that offence and shall be liable to be proceeded against and punished accordingly.*

[House to House Collections Act 1939, s 8, as amended by the Criminal Law Act 1977, s 31 and the Criminal Justice Act 1982, ss 35, 38 and 46.]

***Repealed by the Charities Act 1992 Sch 7 when in force.**
***"Three months" substituted by "51 weeks" by the Criminal Justice Act 2003, Sch 26, from a date to be appointed.**

1. See note 6 to s 1, ante.
2. As to consecutive sentences, see Magistrates' Courts Act 1980, s 133, ante.
3. See *Dean v Hiesler* [1942] 2 All ER 340, 106 JP 282.

TAX AND DUTIES

8–29670 This title includes relevant parts of the following statutes—

For customs and excise matters see in this Part: title Customs and Excise; for vehicles excise duty see Part VIII: title Transport, post.

For the statutory offence of fraudulent evasion of income tax, see the Finance Act 2000, s 144, in this Part, title Customs and Excise, ante.

CHEATING THE PUBLIC REVENUE

8–29680 Cheating is a common law offence punishable by imprisonment. Although s 32(1) of the Theft Act 1968[1] abolished cheating, it did so only "except as regards offences relating to the public revenue".

Hawkins[2] defined cheating as ". . . deceitful practices, in defrauding or endeavouring to defraud another of his own right by means of some artful device, contrary to the plain rules of common honesty." The offence may be committed not only by a public officer, but also by a private individual who acts in such a way as to defraud the Crown[3]. The Court of Criminal Appeal upheld a conviction on a charge of making false statements to the prejudice of the Crown and the public revenue with intent to defraud where the defendant had falsely stated to the Inland Revenue the profits of his business[3]. The offence does not necessarily require a false representation, either by words or conduct. Cheating can include any form of fraudulent conduct which results in diverting money from the Revenue and in depriving the Revenue of money to which it is entitled[4]. This will include omissions to act having the purpose and effect of depriving the revenue of money due to it (*R v Dimsey* [2000] QB 744, [2000] 3 WLR 273, CA (convictions confirmed by the House of Lords [2001] UKHL 46, [2002] 1 AC 509)).

1. See this PART: title THEFT, post.
2. 1 PC 318.
3. *R v Hudson* [1956] 2 QB 252, [1956] 1 All ER 814.
4. *R v Mavji* (1987) 84 Cr App Rep 34, [1987] Crim LR 39.

INCOME TAX AND MAINTENANCE ORDERS

8–29681 Section 65 of the Income and Corporation Taxes Act 1970 which made provision for the making of "small maintenance payments" without deduction of tax but enabled larger payments to be made less tax, has been repealed by the Income and Corporation Taxes Act 1988; s 351 of which, re-enacting the s 65 provisions, was in turn repealed by the Finance Act 1988.

For new maintenance orders, the Income and Corporation Taxes Act 1988 s 347A, this title, post, (added by the Finance Act 1988 s 36) provides that as a general rule annual payments (held to include a permanent order although expressed in weekly or monthly terms: see *Re Janes' Settlement, Wasmuth v Janes* [1918] 2 Ch 54; *Smith v Smith (No 2)* [1923] P 191) should not be deducted when computing the payer's income for tax purposes (ie there is no "tax relief"). The payment shall not form part of the income of the person to whom it is made or of any other person (ie the recipient is not liable to pay tax on such payments).

However, s 347B, this title, post, of the Income and Corporation Taxes Act 1988 (also added by the Finance Act 1988 s 36 and amended by the Finance (No 2) Act 1992, ss 61 and 62) allows the payer to deduct "qualifying maintenance payments" when assessing income for tax purposes (but *not* to deduct it from the payments made under an order). As a consequence of further amendments made to s 347B made by the Finance Act 1999, s 36, with respect to any payment falling due on or after 6 April 2000 a periodical payment is not a qualifying maintenance payment unless either of the parties to the marriage which has been dissolved or annulled was born before 6 April 1935.

Stamp Duties Management Act 1891

(54 & 55 Vict c 38)

8–29682 **13. Offences in relation to dies and stamps[1].** (1) A person commits an offence who does, or causes or procures to be done, or knowingly aids, abets, or assists in doing, any of the acts following; that is to say:

(1) and (2) (*Repealed*);

(3) fraudulently prints or makes an impression upon any material[2] from a genuine die[3];

(4) fraudulently cuts, tears, or in any way removes from any material any stamp[4] with intent that any use should be made of such stamp or of any part thereof;

(5) fraudulently mutilates any stamp, with intent that any use should be made of any part of such stamp;

(6) fraudulently fixes or places upon any material or upon any stamp, any stamp or part of a stamp which, whether fraudulently or not, has been cut, torn, or in any way removed from any other material, or out of or from any other stamp[5];

(7) fraudulently erases or otherwise either really or apparently removes from any stamped[6] material any name, sum, date, or other matter or thing whatsoever thereon written, with the intent that any use should be made of the stamp upon such material;

(8) knowingly sells or exposes for sale or utters or uses . . .[7] any stamp which has been fraudulently printed or impressed from a genuine die;

(9) knowingly[8] and without lawful excuse (the proof whereof shall lie on the person accused) has in his possession . . .[9] any stamp which has been fraudulently printed or impressed from a genuine die, or any stamp or part of a stamp which has been fraudulently cut, torn, or otherwise removed from any material, or any stamp which has been fraudulently mutilated, or any stamped material out of which any name, sum, date, or other matter or thing has been fraudulently erased or otherwise either really or apparently removed.

(10) A person guilty of an offence under this section is liable[10]—

(*a*) on summary conviction, to imprisonment for a term not exceeding six months or a fine not exceeding the statutory maximum, or both;

(*b*) on conviction on indictment, to imprisonment for a term not exceeding ten years or a fine, or both.

[Stamp Duties Management Act 1891, s 13, as amended by Forgery Act 1913, s 20, and Sch 1, the Criminal Justice Act 1948, s 1 and the Finance Act 1999, Schs 18 and 20.]

1. Section 13 is applied to offences in respect of contribution stamps by the Social Security (Contributions) Regulations 1979, this PART: title Social Security, ante. These Regulations also apply s 26 of the 1891 Act, relating to recovery of fines, to social security proceedings. For recovery of contributions in proceedings under the Social Security Administration Act 1992, see s 119 thereof.

2. "Material" includes every sort of material upon which words or figures can be expressed (Stamp Duties Management Act 1891, s 27).

3. "Die" includes any plate, type, tool, or implement whatever used under the direction of the Comrs (of Inland Revenue) for expressing or denoting any duty, or rate of duty, or the fact that any duty or rate of duty or penalty has been paid, or that an instrument is duly stamped, or is not chargeable with any duty or for denoting any fee, and also any part of any such plate, type, tool, or implement (Stamp Duties Management Act 1891, s 27). The reference to the Comrs of Inland Revenue is to be construed as including the Post Office and "duty" includes "postage" (Post Office Act 1969, s 118). The reference includes the Secretary of State in the case of proceedings under the Social Security Administration Act 1992, see s 119 thereof.

4. "Stamp" means as well a stamp impressed by means of a die as an adhesive stamp for denoting any duty or fee (Stamp Duties Management Act 1891, s 27).

5. For the offence of fixing a used social security contribution stamp to any contribution card, see Social Security Administration Act 1992, s 114.

6. The expression "stamped" is applicable as well to instruments and material impressed with stamps by means of a die as to instruments and material having adhesive stamps affixed thereto (Stamp Duties Management Act 1891, s 27).

7. The words "any forged stamp, or" here omitted are repealed by the Forgery Act 1913, s 20.

8. Knowledge is necessary both of the fact of possession and of the fraudulent removal etc (*R v Hallam* [1957] 1 QB 569, [1957] 1 All ER 665, 121 JP 254).

9. The words "any forged die or stamp or" here omitted are repealed by the Forgery Act 1913, s 20.

10. For procedure in respect of this offence which is triable either way, see the Magistrates, Courts Act 1980, ss 17A–21, in PART I: MAGISTRATES' COURTS, PROCEDURE, ante.

Finance Act 1931

(1931 c 28)

8–29700 **28. Production to commissioners of instruments transferring land[1].** (1) On the occasion of (*a*) any transfer on sale of the fee simple of land; (*b*) the grant of any lease of land for a term of seven or more years; (*c*) any transfer on sale of any such lease; it shall be the duty of the transferee, lessee, or proposed lessee to produce to the Commissioners the instrument by means of which the transfer is effected, or the lease granted or agreed to be granted, as the case may be, and to comply with the requirements of the Second Schedule to this Act, and if he fails so to produce any such instrument within thirty days after the execution thereof, or in the case of an instrument first executed at any place out of Great Britain, after the instrument is first received in Great Britain, or fails to comply with the requirements of the said Schedule, he shall be liable on summary conviction to a fine not exceeding **level 3** on the standard scale.

(3) This section shall not apply with respect to any instrument which relates—

(*a*) solely to incorporeal hereditaments or to a grave or right of burial; or (*b*) to an SDLT transaction within the meaning of paragraph 1(2) of Schedule 19 to the Finance Act 2003.

[Finance Act 1931, s 28, as amended by Sch 14 of the Land Commission Act 1967, the Criminal Justice Act 1982, ss 38 and 46 and SI 2003/2867.]

1. This section shall not apply in relation to any instrument (an "exempt instrument") which falls within any class prescribed for the purposes of s 89 of the Finance Act 1985 by regulations made by the Commissioners. Regulations under s 89 may provide that the particulars mentioned in Sch 2 to the Finance Act 1931 shall be furnished to the Commissioners, in accordance with the requirements of the regulations, in respect of exempt instruments or such descriptions of exempt instruments as may be prescribed by the regulations. Any person who fails to comply with any requirement imposed by regulations made under s 89 shall be liable on summary conviction to a fine not exceeding **level 3** on the standard scale (Finance Act 1985, s 89).

Taxes Management Act 1970

(1970 c 9)

Part III[1]

Other Returns and Information

Production of accounts, books and other information

8–29710 **20. Power to call for documents of taxpayer and others**[2]**.** (1) Subject to this section, an inspector may by notice in writing require a person—

(*a*) to deliver to him such documents as are in the person's possession or power and as (in the inspector's reasonable opinion) contain, or may contain, information relevant to—

(i) any tax liability to which the person is or may be subject, or

(ii) the amount of any such liability, or

(*b*) to furnish to him such particulars as the inspector may reasonably require as being relevant to, or to the amount of, any such liability.

(2) Subject to this section, the Board may by notice in writing require a person—

(*a*) to deliver to a named officer of the Board such documents as are in the person's possession or power and as (in the Board's reasonable opinion) contain, or may contain, information relevant to—

(i) any tax liability to which the person is or may be subject, or

(ii) the amount of any such liability, or

(*b*) to furnish to a named officer of the Board such particulars as the Board may reasonably require as being relevant to, or to the amount of, any such liability.

(3) Subject to this section, an inspector may, for the purpose of enquiring into the tax liability of any person ("the taxpayer"), by notice in writing require any other person to deliver to the inspector or, if the person to whom the notice is given so elects, to make available for inspection by a named officer of the Board, such documents as are in his possession or power and as (in the inspector's reasonable opinion) contain, or may contain, information relevant to any tax liability to which the taxpayer is or may be, or may have been, subject, or to the amount of any such liability; and the persons who may be required to deliver or make available a document under this subsection include the Director of Savings.

(4)–(5) (*Repealed*).

(6) The persons who may be treated as "the taxpayer" for the purposes of this section include a company which has ceased to exist and an individual who has died.

(7) Notices under subsection (1) or (3) above are not to be given by an inspector unless he is authorised by the Board for its purposes; and—

(*a*) a notice is not to be given by him except with the consent of a General or Special Commissioner; and

(*b*) the Commissioner is to give his consent only on being satisfied that in all the circumstances the inspector is justified in proceeding under this section.

(7A) A notice under subsection (2) above is not to be given unless the Board have reasonable grounds for believing—

(*a*) that the person to whom it relates may have failed or may fail to comply with any provision of the Taxes Acts; and

(*b*) that any such failure is likely to have led or to lead to serious prejudice to the proper assessment or collection of tax.

(7AB) A Commissioner who has given his consent under subsection (7) above shall neither take part in, nor be present at, any proceedings on, or related to, any appeal brought—

(*a*) in the case of a notice under subsection (1) above, by the person to whom the notice applies, or (*b*) in the case of a notice under subsection (3) above, by the taxpayer concerned,

if the Commissioner has reason to believe that any of the required information is likely to be adduced in evidence in those proceedings.

(7AC) In subsection (7AB) above "required information" means any document or particulars which were the subject of the proposed notice with respect to which the Commissioner gave his consent.

(8) Subject to subsection (8A) below, a notice under subsection (3) above shall name the taxpayer with whose liability the inspector (or, where section 20B(3) below applies, the Board) is concerned.

(8A) If, on an application made by an inspector and authorised by order of the Board, a Special Commissioner gives his consent, the inspector may give such a notice as is mentioned in subsection (3) above but without naming the taxpayer to whom the notice relates; but such a consent shall not be given unless the Special Commissioner is satisfied—

(*a*) that the notice relates to a taxpayer whose identity is not known to the inspector or to a class of taxpayers whose individual identities are not so known;

(*b*) that there are reasonable grounds for believing that the taxpayer or any of the class of taxpayers to whom the notice relates may have failed or may fail to comply with any provision of the Taxes Acts;

(*c*) that any such failure is likely to have led or to lead to serious prejudice to the proper assessment or collection of tax; and

(*d*) that the information which is likely to be contained in the documents to which the notice relates is not readily available from another source.

(8B) A person to whom there is given a notice under subsection (8A) above may, by notice in writing given to the inspector within thirty days after the date of the notice under that subsection, object to that notice on the ground that it would be onerous for him to comply with it; and if the matter is not resolved by agreement, it shall be referred to the Special Commissioners, who may confirm, vary or cancel that notice.

(8C) In this section references to documents do not include—

(*a*) personal records (as defined in section 12 of the Police and Criminal Evidence Act 1984), or

(*b*) journalistic material (as defined in section 13 of that Act),

and references to particulars do not include particulars contained in such personal records or journalistic material.

(8D) Subject to subsection (8C) above, references in this section to documents and particulars are to those specified or described in the notice in question; and—

(*a*) the notice shall require documents to be delivered (or delivered or made available), or particulars to be furnished, within such time (which, except in the case of a notice under subsection (2) above, shall not be less than thirty days after the date of the notice; and

(*b*) the person to whom they are delivered, made available or furnished may take copies of them or of extracts from them.

(8E) An inspector who gives a notice under subsection (1) or (3) above shall also give to—

(*a*) the person to whom the notice applies (in the case of a notice under subsection (1) above), or

(*b*) the taxpayer concerned (in the case of a notice under subsection (3) above),

a written summary of his reasons for applying for consent to the giving of the notice.

(8F) Subsection (8E) above does not apply, in the case of a notice under subsection (3) above, if by virtue of section 20B(1B) a copy of that notice need not be given to the taxpayer.

(8G) Subsection (8E) above does not require the disclosure of any information—

(*a*) which would, or might, identify any person who has provided the inspector with any information which he took into account in deciding whether to apply for consent; or

(*b*) if the Commissioner giving the required consent has given a direction that that information is not to be subject to the obligation imposed by that subsection.

(8H) A General or Special Commissioner shall not give a direction under subsection (8G) above unless he is satisfied that the inspector has reasonable grounds for believing that disclosure of the information in question would prejudice the assessment or collection of tax.

(9) To the extent specified in section 20B below, the above provisions are subject to the restrictions of that section.

[Taxes Management Act 1970, s 20, as substituted by the Finance Act 1976, s 57 and Sch 6 and amended by the Finance Act 1988, s 126, the Finance Act 1989, s 142 and Sch 17, the Finance Act 1990, s 93 and the Finance Act 1994, s 255.]

---

1. Part III contains ss 13–28.

2. Section 20(1) and the Hansard Procedure (which provides a mechanism for settling tax liabilities without recourse to criminal or civil proceedings) provide legitimate means of furthering the core function of the revenue to collect taxes in a prompt, fair and complete manner and they underpin the revenue's selective prosecution policy; both the s 20(1) notice and the Hansard Procedure are civil in nature, they do not constituted "criminal" proceedings for the purpose of the Convention and they belong to an investigative process to which art 6 does not apply; moreover, the notice under s 20(1) cannot constitute a violation of the right against self-incrimination (*R v Dimsey* [2001] UKHL 46, [2002] 1 AC 509, [2002]

1 Cr App Rep 167). Section 20(1) does not entitle an inspector of taxes to require a taxpayer to deliver to him material that is subject to legal professional privilege (*R (on the application of Morgan Grenfell & Co Ltd) v Special Comr of Income Tax* [2002] UKHL 21, [2002] 3 All ER 1).

8–29711 20A. Power to call for papers of tax accountant. (1) Where after the passing of the Finance Act 1976 a person—

(*a*) is convicted of an offence in relation to tax (whenever committed) by or before any court in the United Kingdom; or

(*b*) has a penalty imposed on him (whether before or after the passing of that Act) under section 99 of this Act.

and he has stood in relation to others as tax accountant, an inspector authorised by the Board for the purpose of this section may by notice in writing require the person to deliver to him such documents as are in his possession or power and as (in the inspector's reasonable opinion) contain information relevant to any tax liability to which any client of his is or has been, or may be or have been, subject, or to the amount of any such liability.

(1A) The reference to documents in subsection (1) above does not include—

(*a*) personal records (as defined in section 12 of the Police and Criminal Evidence Act 1984), or

(*b*) journalistic material (as defined in section 13 of that Act).

(1B) Subject to subsection (1A) above, the reference to documents in subsection (1) above is to those specified or described in the notice in question; and—

(*a*) the notice shall require documents to be delivered within such time (which shall not be less than thirty days after the date of the notice) as may be specified in the notice; and

(*b*) the inspector may take copies of them or of extracts from them.

(2) Subsection (1) above does not have effect in relation to a person convicted or penalised as there mentioned for so long as an appeal is pending against the conviction or penalty; and—

(*a*) for this purpose an appeal is to be treated as pending (where one is competent but has not been brought) until the expiration of the time for bringing it or, in the case of a conviction in Scotland, until the expiration of 28 days from the date of conviction; and

(*b*) references here to appeal include further appeal but, in relation to the imposition of a penalty, do not include appeal against the amount of the penalty.

(3) A notice is not to be given to any person under this section unless with the consent of the appropriate judicial authority; and that authority is to give his consent only on being satisfied that in all the circumstances the inspector is justified in so proceeding.

(4) The power to give a notice under this section, by reference to a person's conviction or the imposition on him of a penalty, ceases at the expiration of the period of 12 months beginning with the date on which it was first exercisable in his case by virtue of that conviction or penalty.

(5) To the extent specified in section 20B below, the above provisions are subject to the restrictions of that section.

[Taxes Management Act 1970, s 20A, as inserted by the Finance Act 1976, s 57 and Sch 6, and amended by the Finance Act 1989, ss 143 and 168.]

8–29712 20B. Restrictions on powers under sections 20 and 20A. (1) Before a notice is given to a person by an inspector under section 20(1), (3) or (8A) or under section 20A, the person must have been given a reasonable opportunity to deliver (or, in the case of section 20(3), to deliver or make available) the documents in question, or to furnish the particulars in question, and the inspector must not apply for consent under section 20(7) or (8A) or, as the case may be, section 20A(3), until the person has been given that opportunity.

(1A) Subject to subsection (1B) below, where a notice is given to any person under section 20(3) the inspector shall give a copy of the notice to the taxpayer to whom it relates.

(1B) If, on an application by the inspector, a General or Special Commissioner so directs, a copy of a notice under section 20(3) need not be given to the taxpayer to whom it relates; but such a direction shall not be given unless the Commissioner is satisfied that the inspector has reasonable grounds for suspecting the taxpayer of fraud.

(2) A notice under section 20(1) does not oblige a person to deliver documents or furnish particulars relating to the conduct of any pending appeal by him; a notice under section 20(3) or (8A) does not oblige a person to deliver or make available documents relating to the conduct of a pending appeal by the taxpayer; and a notice under section 20A does not oblige a person to deliver documents relating to the conduct of a pending appeal by the client.

"Appeal" means appeal relating to tax.

(3) An inspector cannot under section 20(1) or (3), or under section 20A(1), give notice to a barrister, advocate or solicitor, but the notice must in any such case be given (if at all) by the Board; and accordingly in relation to a barrister, advocate or solicitor for references in section 20(3) and (4) and section 20A to the inspector there are substituted references to the Board.

(4) To comply with a notice under section 20(1) or section 20A(1), and as an alternative to

delivering documents to comply with a notice under section 20(3) or (8A), copies of documents may be delivered instead of the originals; but—

(*a*) the copies must be photographic or otherwise by way of facsimile; and
(*b*) if so required by the inspector (or, as the case may be, the Board) in the case of any documents specified in the requirement, the originals must be made available for inspection by a named officer of the Board (failure to comply with this requirement counting as failure to comply with the notice).

(5) A notice under section 20(3), does not oblige a person to deliver or make available any document the whole of which originates more than 6 years before the date of the notice.

(6) But subsection (5) does not apply where the notice is so expressed as to exclude the restrictions of that subsection; and it can be so expressed where—

(*a*) the notice being given by an inspector with consent under section 20(7), the Commissioner giving consent has also given approval to the exclusion;
(*b*) the notice being given by the Board, they have applied to a General or Special Commissioner for, and obtained that approval.

For this purpose the Commissioner gives approval only if satisfied, on the inspector's or the Board's application, that there is reasonable ground for believing that tax has, or may have been, lost to the Crown owing to the fraud of the taxpayer.

(7) A notice under section 20(3) in relation to a taxpayer who has died cannot be given if more than 6 years have elapsed since the death.

(8) A notice under section 20(3) or (8A) or section 20A(1) does not oblige a barrister, advocate or a solicitor to deliver or make available, without his client's consent, any document with respect to which a claim to professional privilege could be maintained[1].

(9) Subject to subsections (11) and (12) below, a notice under section 20(3) or (8A)—

(*a*) does not oblige a person who has been appointed as an auditor for the purposes of any enactment to deliver or make available documents which are his property and were created by him or on his behalf for or in connection with the performance of his functions under that engagement, and
(*b*) does not oblige a tax adviser to deliver or make available documents which are his property and consist of relevant communications.

(10) In subsection (9) above "relevant communications" means communications between the tax adviser and—

(*a*) a person in relation to whose tax affairs he has been appointed, or
(*b*) any other tax adviser of such a person,

the purpose of which is the giving or obtaining of advice about any of those tax affairs; and in subsection (9) above and this subsection "tax adviser" means a person appointed to give advice about the tax affairs of another person (whether appointed directly by that other person or by another tax adviser of his).

(11) Subject to subsection (13) below, subsection (9) above shall not have effect in relation to any document which contains information explaining any information, return, accounts or other document which the person to whom the notice is given has, as tax accountant, assisted any client of his in preparing for, or delivering to, the inspector or the Board.

(12) Subject to subsection (13) below, in the case of a notice under section 20(8A) subsection (9) above shall not have effect in relation to any document which contains information given the identity or address of any taxpayer to whom the notice relates or of any person who has acted on behalf of any such person.

(13) Subsection (9) above is not disapplied by subsection (11) or (12) above in the case of any document if—

(*a*) the information within subsection (11) or (12) is contained in some other document, and
(*b*) either—
   (i) that other document, or a copy of it, has been delivered to the inspector or the Board, or
   (ii) that other document has been inspected by an officer of the Board.

(14) Where subsection (9) above is disapplied by subsection (11) or (12) above in the case of a document, the person to whom the notice is given either shall deliver the document to the inspector or make it available for inspection by an officer of the Board or shall—

(*a*) deliver to the inspector (or, where subsection (3) above applies, the Board) a copy (which is photographic or otherwise by way of facsimile) of any parts of the document which contain the information within subsection (11) or (12), and
(*b*) if so required by the inspector (or, as the case may be, the Board), make available for inspection by a named officer of the Board such parts of the document as contain that information;

and failure to comply with any requirement under paragraph (*b*) above shall constitute a failure to comply with the notice.

[Taxes Management Act 1970, s 20B, as inserted by the Finance Act 1976, s 57 and Sch 6, and amended by the Finance Act 1988, s 126, and the Finance Act 1989, s 144 and Sch 17.]

1. Neither this provision, nor s 20C(4) below, imports that Parliament intended to preserve legal professional privilege only when the documents were in the possession of the lawyer; therefore, s 20(1) above does not entitle an inspector of taxes to require a taxpayer to deliver to him material that is subject to legal professional privilege (*R (on the application of Morgan Grenfell & Co Ltd) v Special Comr of Income Tax* [2002] UKHL 21, [2002] 3 All ER 1).

8–29712A 20BA. Orders for the delivery of documents. (1) The appropriate judicial authority may make an order under this section if satisfied on information on oath given by an authorised officer of the Board—

(*a*) that there is reasonable ground for suspecting that an offence involving serious fraud in connection with, or in relation to, tax is being, has been or is about to be committed, and
(*b*) that documents which may be required as evidence for the purposes of any proceedings in respect of such an offence are or may be in the power or possession of any person.

(2) An order under this section is an order requiring the person who appears to the authority to have in his possession or power the documents specified or described in the order to deliver them to an officer of the Board within—

(*a*) ten working days after the day on which notice of the order is served on him, or
(*b*) such shorter or longer period as may be specified in the order.

For this purpose a "working day" means any day other than a Saturday, Sunday or public holiday.

(3) *Scotland.*

(4) Schedule 1AA[1] to this Act contains provisions supplementing this section.

[Taxes Management Act 1970, s 20BA, as inserted by the Finance Act 2000, s 149(1).]

1. See, post.

8–29713 20BB. Falsification etc of documents. (1) Subject to subsections (2) to (4) below, a person shall be guilty of an offence if he intentionally falsifies, conceals, destroys or otherwise disposes of, or causes or permits the falsification, concealment, destruction or disposal of, a document which—

(*a*) he has been required by a notice under section 20 or 20A above or an order under section 20BA above, or
(*b*) he has been given an opportunity in accordance with section 20B(1) above

to deliver, or to deliver or make available for inspection.

(2) A person does not commit an offence under subsection (1) above if he acts—

(*a*) with the written permission of a General or Special Commissioner, the inspector or an officer of the Board,
(*b*) after the document has been delivered or, in a case within section 20(3) or (8A) above, inspected or,
(*c*) after a copy has been delivered in accordance with section 20B(4) or (14) above and the original has been inspected.

(3) A person does not commit an offence under subsection (1)(*a*) above if he acts after the end of the period of two years beginning with the date on which the notice is given or the order is made, unless before the end of that period the inspector or an officer of the Board has notified the person in writing that the notice or order has not been complied with to his satisfaction.

(4) A person does not commit an offence under subsection (1)(*b*) above if he acts—

(*a*) after the end of the period of six months beginning with the date on which an opportunity to deliver the document was given, or
(*b*) after an application for consent to a notice being given in relation to the document has been refused.

(5) A person guilty of an offence under subsection (1) above shall be liable[1]—

(*a*) on summary conviction, to a fine not exceeding the **statutory maximum**;
(*b*) on conviction on indictment, to imprisonment for a term not exceeding **two years** or to a **fine** or to **both**.

[Taxes Management Act 1970, s 20BB, as inserted by the Finance Act 1989, s 145 and amended by the Finance Act 2000, s 149.]

1. For procedure in respect of an offence triable either way, see the Magistrates' Courts Act 1980, ss 17A–21, in PART I: MAGISTRATES' COURTS, PROCEDURE, ante.

8–29714 **20C. Entry with warrant to obtain documents.** (1) If the appropriate judicial authority[1] is satisfied on information on oath given by an officer of the Board that—

(*a*) there is reasonable ground for suspecting that an offence involving serious fraud in connection with, or in relation to, tax is being, has been or is about to be committed and that evidence of it is to be found on premises specified in the information; and

(*b*) in applying under this section, the officer acts with the approval of the Board given in relation to the particular case.

the authority may issue a warrant in writing authorising an officer of the Board to enter the premises, if necessary by force, at any time within 14 days from the time of issue of the warrant, and search them.

(1AA) The Board shall not approve an application for a warrant under this section unless they have reasonable grounds for believing that use of the procedure under section 20BA above and Schedule 1AA to this Act (order for production of documents) might seriously prejudice the investigation.

(1A) Without prejudice to the generality of the concept of serious fraud—

(*a*) any offence which involves fraud is for the purposes of this section an offence involving serious fraud if its commission had led, or is intended or likely to lead, either to substantial financial gain to any person or to serious prejudice to the proper assessment or collection of tax; and

(*b*) an offence which, if considered alone, would not be regarded as involving serious fraud may nevertheless be so regarded if there is reasonable ground for suspecting that it forms part of a course of conduct which is, or but for its detection would be, likely to result in serious prejudice to the proper assessment or collection of tax.

(1B) The powers conferred by a warrant under this section shall not be exercisable—

(*a*) by more than such number of officers of the Board as may be specified in the warrant[2];

(*b*) outside such times of day as may be so specified;

(*c*) if the warrant so provides, otherwise than in the presence of a constable in uniform.

(2) Section 4A of the Inland Revenue Regulation Act 1890 (Board's functions to be exercisable by an officer acting under their authority) does not apply to the giving of Board approval under this section.

(3) An officer who enters the premises under the authority of a warrant under this section may—

(*a*) take with him such other persons as appear to him to be necessary;

(*b*) seize[3] and remove any things whatsoever found there which he has reasonable cause to believe may be required as evidence for the purposes of proceedings in respect of such an offence as is mentioned in subsection (1) above; and

(*c*) search or cause to be searched any person found on the premises whom he has reasonable cause to believe to be in possession of any such things;

but no person shall be searched except by a person of the same sex.

(3A) In the case of any information contained in a computer stored in any electronic form which is information that—

(*a*) an officer who enters the premises as mentioned in subsection (3) above has reasonable cause to believe may be required as evidence for the purposes mentioned in paragraph (b) of that subsection, and

(*b*) is accessible from the premises,

the power of seizure under that subsection includes a power to require the information to be produced in a form in which it can be taken away and in which it is visible and legible or from which it can readily be produced in a visible and legible form.

(4) Nothing in subsection (3) above authorities the seizure and removal of items subject to legal privilege[4].

(4A) In subsection (4) "items subject to legal privilege" means—

(*a*) communications between a professional legal adviser and his client or any person representing his client made in connection with the giving of legal advice to the client;

(*b*) communications between a professional legal adviser and his client or any person representing his client or between such an adviser or his client or any such representative and any other person made in connection with or in contemplation of legal proceedings and for the purposes of such proceedings; and

(*c*) items enclosed with or referred to in such communications and made—

(i) in connection with the giving of legal advice; or

(ii) in connection with or in contemplation of legal proceedings and for the purposes of such proceedings,

when they are in the possession of a person who is entitled to possession of them.

(4B) Items held with the intention of furthering a criminal purpose are not subject to legal privilege.

(5) An officer of the Board seeking to exercise the powers conferred by a warrant under this section or, if there is more than one such officer, that one of them who is in charge of the search—

(*a*) if the occupier of the premises concerned is present at the time the search is to begin, shall supply a copy of the warrant endorsed with his name to the occupier;

(*b*) if at that time the occupier is not present but a person who appears to the officer to be in charge of the premises is present, shall supply such a copy to that person; and

(*c*) if neither paragraph (*a*) nor paragraph (*b*) above applies shall leave such a copy in a prominent place on the premises.

(6) Where entry to premises has been made with a warrant under this section, and the officer making the entry has seized any things under the authority of the warrant, he shall endorse on or attach to the warrant a list of the things seized.

(7) Subsections (10) to (12) of section 16 of the Police and Criminal Evidence Act 1984 (return, retention and inspection of warrants) apply to a warrant under this section (together with any list endorsed on or attached to it under subsection (6) above) as they apply to a warrant issued to a constable under any enactment.

(8) Subsection (7) above extends to England and Wales only.

(9) Where in Scotland the information mentioned in subsection (1) above relates to premises situated in different sheriffdoms—

(*a*) petitions for the issue of warrants in respect of all the premises to which the information relates may be made to the sheriff for a sheriffdom in which any of the premises is situated, and

(*b*) where the sheriff issues a warrant in respect of premises situated in his own sheriffdom, he shall also have jurisdiction to issue warrants in respect of all or any of the other premises to which the information relates.

This does not affect any power or jurisdiction of a sheriff to issue a warrant in respect of an offence committed within his own sheriffdom.

[Taxes Management Act 1970, s 20C, as inserted by the Finance Act 1976, s 57 and Sch 6, and amended by the Finance Act 1989, s 146, the Finance Act 2000, s 150 and the Criminal Justice and Police Act 2001, Sch 2.]

---

1. For the meaning of "the appropriate judicial authority", see s 20D, post.
2. It is not necessary for the officers to be named in the warrant (*R v Hunt* [1994] Crim LR 747).
3. The power of seizure is subject to the prohibition in subsection (4) on seizure and removal of documents in the possession of a barrister, advocate or solicitor "with respect to which a claim to professional privilege could be maintained". That prohibition does not depend upon whether an officer has reasonable grounds for believing that the documents were subject to legal professional privilege, but whether a claim could be maintained successfully (*R v Crown court at Middlesex, ex p Tamosius and Partners (a firm)* [2000] 1 WLR 453, DC, sub nom *R v IRC, ex p Tamosius and Partners (a firm)* [2000] Crim LR 390, DC).
4. Neither this provision, nor s 20B(8) above, imports that Parliament intended to preserve legal professional privilege only when the documents were in the possession of the lawyer; therefore, s 20(1) above does not entitle an inspector of taxes to require a taxpayer to deliver to him material that is subject to legal professional privilege (*R (on the application of Morgan Grenfell & Co Ltd) v Special Comr of Income Tax* [2002] UKHL 21, [2002] 3 All ER 1).

8–29715 **20CC. Procedure where documents etc are removed.** (1) An officer of the Board who removes anything in the exercise of the power conferred by section 20C above shall, if so requested by a person showing himself—

(*a*) to be the occupier of premises from which it was removed, or

(*b*) to have had custody or control of it immediately before the removal,

provide that person with a record of what he removed.

(2) The officer of the Board shall provide the record within a reasonable time from the making of the request for it.

(3) Where anything which has been removed by an officer of the Board as mentioned in subsection (1) above is of such a nature that a photograph or copy of it would be sufficient—

(*a*) for use as evidence at a trial for an offence, or

(*b*) for forensic examination or for investigation in connection with an offence,

it shall not be retained longer than is necessary to establish that fact and to obtain the photograph or copy[1].

(4) Subject to subsection (8) below, if a request for permission to be granted access to anything which—

(*a*) has been removed by an officer of the Board, and

(*b*) is retained by the Board for the purpose of investigating an offence,

is made to the officer in overall charge of the investigation by a person who had custody or control of the thing immediately before it was so removed or by someone acting on behalf of any such person, the officer shall allow the person who made the request access to it under the supervision of an officer of the Board.

(5) Subject to subsection (8) below, if a request for a photograph or copy of any such thing is made to the officer in overall charge of the investigation by a person who had custody or control of

the thing immediately before it was so removed, or by someone acting on behalf of any such person, the officer shall—

(*a*) allow the person who made the request access to it under the supervision of an officer of the Board for the purpose of photographing it or copying it, or

(*b*) photograph or copy it, or cause it to be photographed or copied.

(6) Where anything is photographed or copied under subsection (5)(*b*) above the photograph or copy shall be supplied to the person who made the request.

(7) The photograph or copy shall be supplied within a reasonable time from the making of the request.

(8) There is no duty under this section to grant access to, or to supply a photograph or copy of, anything if the officer in overall charge of the investigation for the purposes of which it was removed has reasonable grounds for believing that to do so would prejudice—

(*a*) that investigation;

(*b*) the investigation of an offence other than the offence for the purposes of the investigation of which the thing was removed; or

(*c*) any criminal proceedings which may be brought as a result of—

(i) the investigation of which he is in charge, or

(ii) any such investigation as is mentioned in paragraph (*b*) above.

(9) Any reference in this section to the officer in overall charge of the investigation is a reference to the person whose name and address are endorsed on the warrant concerned as being the officer so in charge.

[Taxes Management Act 1970, s 20CC, as inserted by the Finance Act 1989, s 147.]

---

1. See the Criminal Justice and Police Act 2001, Part 2 (PART I, ante). These provisions (summarised at para 1-180, ante) confer, by ss 50 and 51, additional powers of seizure of property in relation to searches carried out under existing powers. However, s 57 (retention of seized items) does not authorise the retention of any property which could not be retained under the provisions listed in s 57(1), which include s 20CC(3) of the Taxes Management Act 1970, if the property was seized under the new powers (ie those conferred by ss 50 and 51) in reliance on one of those powers (ie those conferred by the provisions listed in s 57(1)). Section 57(4) further provides that nothing in any of the provisions listed in s 57(1) authorises the retention of anything after an obligation to return it has arisen under Part 2.

8–29716 **20D. Interpretation of ss 20 to 20C.** (1) For the purposes of section 20A, 20BA and 20C above, "the appropriate judicial authority" is—

(*a*) in England and Wales, a Circuit judge;

(*b*) (*Scotland*); and

(*c*) (*Northern Ireland*).

(2) For the purposes of sections 20 and 20A, a person stands in relation to another as tax accountant at any time when he assists the other in the preparation or delivery of any information, return, accounts or other document which he knows will be, or is or are likely to be, used for any purpose of tax; and his clients are all those to whom he stands or has stood in that relationship.

(3) Without prejudice to section 127 of the Finance Act 1988, in sections 20 to 20CC above "document" means, subject to sections 20(8C) and 20A(1A), anything in which information of any description is recorded.

[Taxes Management Act 1970, s 20D, as inserted by the Finance Act 1976, s 57 and Sch 6, and amended by the Finance Act 1989, s 148, the Civil Evidence Act 1995, Sch 1 and the Finance Act 2000, s 149.]

PART VI[1]
COLLECTION AND RECOVERY

8–29717 **60. Issue of demand notes and receipts.** (1) Every collector shall, when the tax becomes due and payable, make demand of the respective sums given to him in charge to collect, from the persons charged therewith, or at the places of their last abode, or on the premises in respect of which the tax is charged, as the case may require.

(2) On payment of the tax, the collector shall if so requested give a receipt.

[Taxes Management Act 1970, s 60.]

---

1. Part VI contains ss 60–70.

Distraint and poinding

8–29718 **61. Distraint by collectors.** (1) If a person neglects or refuses to pay the sum charged, upon demand made by the collector, the collector may distrain upon the goods and chattels of the person charged (in this section referred to as "the person in default").

(2) For the purpose of levying any such distress, a justice of the peace, on being satisfied by information on oath that there is reasonable ground for believing that a person is neglecting or refusing to pay a sum charged, may issue a warrant in writing authorising a collector to break open, in the daytime, any house or premises, calling to his assistance any constable.

Every such constable shall when so required, aid and assist the collector in the execution of the warrant and in levying the distress in the house or premises.

(3) A levy or warrant to break open shall be executed by, or under the direction of, and in the presence of, the collector.

(4) A distress levied by the collector shall be kept for five days, at the costs and charges of the person in default.

(5) If the person in default does not pay the sum due, together with the costs and charges, the distress shall be appraised by one or more independent persons appointed by the collector, and shall be sold by public auction by the collector for payment of the sum due and all costs and charges.

Any overplus coming by the distress, after the deduction of the costs and charges and of the sum due, shall be restored to the owner of the goods distrained.

(6) The Treasury may by regulations[1] make provision with respect to—

(*a*) the fees chargeable on or in connection with the levying of distress, and

(*b*) the costs and charges recoverable where distress has been levied;

and any such regulations shall be made by statutory instrument which shall be subject to annulment in pursuance of a resolution of the House of Commons.

[Taxes Management Act 1970, s 61, as amended by the Finance Act 1989, s 152 and Sch 17.]

1. The Distraint by Collectors (Fees, Costs and Charges) Regulations 1994, SI 1994/236 amended by SI 1995/2151, have been made.

8–29719 62. Priority of claim for tax. (1) If at any time at which any goods or chattels belonging to any person (in this section referred to as "the person in default") are liable to be taken by virtue of any execution or other process, warrant, or authority whatever, or by virtue of any assignment, on any account or pretence whatever, except at the suit of the landlord for rent, the person in default is in arrears in respect of any such sums as are referred to in subsection (1A) below, the goods or chattels may not be taken unless on demand made by the collector the person at whose suit the execution or seizure is made, or to whom the assignment was made, pays or causes to be paid to the collector, before the sale or removal of the goods or chattels, all such sums as have fallen due at or before the date of seizure.

(1A) The sums referred to in subsection (1) above are—

(*a*) sums due from the person in default on account of deductions of income tax from taxable earnings (as defined by section 10 of ITEPA 2003) paid during the period of twelve months next before the date of seizure, being deductions which the person in default was liable to make under PAYE regulations less the amount of the repayments of income tax which he was liable to make during that period; and

(*b*) sums due from the person in default in respect of deductions required to be made by him for that period under section 559 of the principal Act* (sub-contractors in the construction industry).

(2) If the sums referred to in subsection (1) above are not paid within ten days of the date of the demand referred to in that subsection, the collector may distrain the goods and chattels notwithstanding the seizure or assignment, and may proceed to the sale thereof, as prescribed by this Act, for the purpose of obtaining payment of the whole of those sums, and the reasonable costs and charges attending such distress and sale, and every collector so doing shall be indemnified by virtue of this Act.

(3) (*Repealed*).

[Taxes Management Act 1970, s 62, as amended by the Finance Act 1989, s 153 and Sch 17, and the Income Tax (Earnings and Pensions) Act 2003, s 722.]

***Words substituted by the Finance Act 2004, Sch 12 from a date to be appointed.**

Court proceedings

8–29720 65. Magistrates' courts. (1) Any amount due and payable by way of income tax, capital gains tax or corporation tax which does not exceed £2,000 shall, without prejudice to any other remedy, be recoverable summarily as a civil debt[2] by proceedings commenced in the name of a collector[3].

(2) All or any of the sums due in respect of tax from any one person and payable to any one collector (being sums which are by law recoverable summarily) may, whether or not they are due under one assessment, be included in the same complaint, summons, order, warrant, or other document required by law to be laid before justices or to be issued by justices, and every such document as aforesaid shall, as respects each such sum, be construed as a separate document and its invalidity as respects any one such sum shall not affect its validity as respects any other such sum.

(3) Proceedings under this section may be brought in England and Wales at any time within one year from the time when the matter complained of arose.

(4) *Northern Ireland.*

(5) The Treasury may by order made by statutory instrument increase the sum specified in

subsection (1) above; and any such statutory instrument shall be subject to annulment in pursuance of a resolution of the Commons House of Parliament.

[Taxes Management Act 1970, s 65 as amended by the Finance Act 1984, s 57, SI 1989/1300, SI 1991/1625, the Finance Act 1994, Sch 19 and the Finance Act 1998, Schs 19 and 27.]

1. Section 203 of the Income and Corpn Taxes Act 1988 and the Income Tax (Employments) Regulations 1973 (SI 1973/334) provide for collecting tax due under Schedule E by means of deductions from current earnings (PAYE). Regulation 28 as amended by SI 1984/1858 and SI 1985/350 relates to the recovery of tax deducted by an employer; its purport is similar to that of s 65 of the Taxes Management Act 1970 and the maximum amount recoverable summarily is £500. A similar limit also applies to deductions from payment to sub-contractors in the construction industry made by contractors under the Income Tax (Sub-contractors in the Construction Industry) Regulations 1975, SI 1975/1960.

The Social Security Contributions and Benefits Act 1992, provides for the payment of earnings related contributions in respect of employed persons. The employer is liable to account therefor in the same manner as for deductions of tax. The Social Security (Contributions) Regulations 1979, SI 1979/591, apply reg 28 of the Income Tax (Employments) Regulations 1973, supra, so that any graduated contributions not accounted for may be recovered summarily. A certificate of non-payment given by a collector of taxes is admissible in evidence (Social Security Administration Act 1992, s 119); see this **PART**: title Social Security, ante.

2. See Magistrates' Courts Act 1980, ss 58, 96, in PART I, ante. See also in connection with the recovery in magistrates' courts of income tax or any other tax or liability recoverable under this section, the Administration of Justice Act 1970, s 12 and Sch 4, and the Magistrates' Courts Act 1980, s 92, in PART I: MAGISTRATES' COURTS, PROCEDURE, ante. An attachment of earnings order may be made only by a county court and not a magistrates' court; see Attachment of Earnings Act 1971, ss 1 and 2, in PART I: MAGISTRATES' COURTS, PROCEDURE, ante.

3. Proceedings begun by one collector may be continued by another and any collector may act for any division or area (s 1(3) of the Taxes Management Act 1970).

Supplemental

8–29721 **69. Recovery of penalty, surcharge or interest.** (1) This section applies to—

(*a*) penalties imposed under Part II, VA or X of this Act or Schedule 18 to the Finance Act 1998;
(*b*) surcharges imposed under Part VA of this Act; and
(*c*) interest charged under any provision of this Act (or recoverable as if it were interest so charged).

(2) An amount by way of penalty, surcharge or interest to which this section applies shall be treated for the purposes of the following provisions as if it were an amount of tax.

(3) Those provisions are—

(*a*) sections 61, 63 and 65 to 68 of this Act;
(*b*) section 35(2)(*g*)(i) of the Crown Proceedings Act 1947 (rules of court: restriction of set-off or counterclaim where proceedings, or set-off or counterclaim, relate to tax) and any rules of court imposing any such restriction;
(*c*) section 35(2)(*b*) of that Act as set out in section 50 of that Act (which imposes corresponding restrictions in Scotland).

[Taxes Management Act 1970, s 69 as substituted by the Finance Act 2001, s 89.]

8–29722 **70. Evidence.** (1) Where tax is in arrear, a certificate of the inspector or any other officer of the Board that tax has been charged and is due, together with a certificate of the collector that payment of the tax has not been made to him, or, to the best of his knowledge and belief, to any other collector, or to any person acting on his behalf or on behalf of another collector, shall be sufficient evidence that the sum mentioned in the certificate is unpaid and is due to the Crown; and any document purporting to be such a certificate as is mentioned in this subsection shall be deemed to be such a certificate until the contrary is proved.

(2) A certificate of a collector—

(*a*) that a penalty is payable under Part II, VA or X of this Act or under Schedule 18 to the Finance Act 1998, that a surcharge is payable under Part VA of this Act or that interest is payable under any provision or the principal Act, the principal Act or ITEPA 2003, and
(*b*) that payment of the penalty, surcharge or interest has not been made to him or, to the best of his knowledge and belief, to any other collector or to any person acting on his behalf or on behalf of another collector,

shall be sufficient evidence that the sum mentioned in the certificate is unpaid and is due to the Crown, and any document purporting to be such a certificate as is mentioned in this subsection shall be deemed to be such a certificate unless the contrary is proved.

(3) (*Repealed*).

(4) A written statement as to the wages, salaries, fees, and other earnings or amounts treated as earnings paid for any period to the person against whom proceedings are brought under section 65, 66 or 67 of this Act, purporting to be signed by his employer for that period, or by any responsible person in the employment of the employer, shall in such proceedings be *prima facie* evidence that the wages, salaries, fees and other earnings or amounts treated as earnings therein stated to have been paid to the person charged have in fact been so paid.

(5) In subsection (4) "earnings or amounts treated as earnings" means earnings or amounts

treated as earnings which constitute employment income (see section 7(2)(*a*) or (*b*) of ITEPA 2003).*

[Taxes Management Act 1970, s 70 as amended by the Finance Act 1985, s 93 and Sch 25, Part II, the Finance (No 2) Act 1987, s 84, the Finance Act 1989, s 160 and Sch 17, the Finance Act 1994, Sch 19, the Finance Act 1998, Sch 19 and the Finance Act 2001, s 89.]

***Sub-section (5) as originally enacted repealed, and second sub-section (5) inserted by the Income Tax (Earnings and Pensions) Act 2003, s 722. Amendment has effect, for the purposes of income tax for the year 2003–04 and subsequent years of assessment, and for the purpose of corporation tax for accounting periods ending after 5 April 2003.**

PART X[1]
PENALTIES, ETC

8–29723 **105. Admissibility of evidence not affected by offer of settlement etc.** (1) Statements made of documents produced by or on behalf of a person shall not be inadmissible[2] in any such proceedings as are mentioned in subsection (2) below by reason only that it has been drawn to his attention that—

(*a*) that where serious tax fraud had been committed the Board may accept a money settlement and that the Board will accept such a settlement, and will not pursue a criminal prosecution, if he makes a full confession of all tax irregularities, or

(*b*) that the extent to which he is helpful and volunteers information is a factor that will be taken into account in determining the amount of the penalty,

and that he was or may have been induced thereby to make the statements or produce the documents.

(2) The proceedings mentioned in subsection (1) above are—

(*a*) any criminal proceedings against the person in question for any form of fraudulent conduct in connection with or in relation to tax, and

(*b*) any proceedings against him for the recovery of any tax due from him, and

(*c*) any proceedings for a penalty or on appeal against the determination of a penalty.

[Taxes Management Act 1970, s 105 as amended by the Finance Act 1989, ss 149 and 168 and the Finance Act 2003, s 206.]

---

1. Part X contains ss 93–106.
2. If, in response to the Hansard statement (ie a statement made pursuant to the Hansard Procedure, which provides a mechanism for settling tax liabilities without recourse to criminal or civil proceedings) true and accurate information is disclosed that reveals earlier cheating, and the taxpayer is then prosecuted in respect of that earlier dishonesty, he will have a strong argument that the criminal proceedings are unfair and an even stronger argument that the Crown should not be able to rely on evidence of his admission; but that does not apply where the reverse occurs, ie the information that is provided is not true and accurate (*R v Dimsey* [2001] UKHL 46, [2002] 1 AC 509).

Section 20BA(4)

SCHEDULE 1AA
ORDERS FOR PRODUCTION OF DOCUMENTS

(*As inserted by the Finance Act 2000, s 149 and Sch 39.*)

Introduction

8–29724 **1.** The provisions of this Schedule supplement section 20BA.

Authorised officer of the Board

8–29725 **2.** (1) In section 20BA(1) an "authorised officer of the Board" means an officer of the Board authorised by the Board for the purposes of that section.

(2) The Board may make provision by regulations as to—

(*a*) the procedures for approving in any particular case the decision to apply for an order under that section, and

(*b*) the descriptions of officer by whom such approval may be given.

Notice of application for order

8–29726 **3.** (1) A person is entitled—

(*a*) to notice of the intention to apply for an order against him under section 20BA, and

(*b*) to appear and be heard at the hearing of the application,

unless the appropriate judicial authority is satisfied that this would seriously prejudice the investigation of the offence.

(2) The Board may make provision by regulations as to the notice to be given, the contents of the notice and the manner of giving it.

Obligations of person given notice of application

8–29727 **4.** (1) A person who has been given notice of intention to apply for an order under section 20BA(4) shall not—

(*a*) conceal, destroy, alter or dispose of any document to which the application relates, or
(*b*) disclose to any other person information or any other matter likely to prejudice the investigation of the offence to which the application relates.

This is subject to the following qualifications.

(2) Sub-paragraph (1)(*a*) does not prevent anything being done—

(*a*) with the leave of the appropriate judicial authority,
(*b*) with the written permission of an officer of the Board,
(*c*) after the application has been dismissed or abandoned, or
(*d*) after any order made on the application has been complied with.

(3) Sub-paragraph (1)(*b*) does not prevent a professional legal adviser from disclosing any information or other matter—

(*a*) to, or to a representative of, a client of his in connection with the giving by the adviser of legal advice to the client; or
(*b*) to any person—

(i) in contemplation of, or in connection with, legal proceedings; and
(ii) for the purpose of those proceedings.

This sub-paragraph does not apply in relation to any information or other matter which is disclosed with a view to furthering a criminal purpose.

(4) A person who fails to comply with the obligation in sub-paragraph (1)(a) or (b) above may be dealt with as if he had failed to comply with an order under section 20BA.

Exception of items subject to legal privilege

8–29728 **5.** (1) Section 20BA does not apply to items subject to legal privilege.

(2) For this purpose "items subject to legal privilege" means—

(*a*) communications between a professional legal adviser and his client or any person representing his client made in connection with the giving of legal advice to the client;
(*b*) communications between a professional legal adviser and his client or any person representing his client or between such an adviser or his client or any such representative and any other person made in connection with or in contemplation of legal proceedings and for the purposes of such proceedings; and
(*c*) items enclosed with or referred to in such communications and made—

(i) in connection with the giving of legal advice; or
(ii) in connection with or in contemplation of legal proceedings and for the purposes of such proceedings,

when they are in the possession of a person who is entitled to possession of them.

(3) Items held with the intention of furthering a criminal purpose are not subject to legal privilege.

Resolution of disputes as to legal privilege

8–29729 **6.** (1) The Board may make provision by regulations for the resolution of disputes as to whether a document, or part of a document, is an item subject to legal privilege.

(2) The regulations may, in particular, make provision as to—

(*a*) the custody of the document whilst its status is being decided;
(*b*) the appointment of an independent, legally qualified person to decide the matter;
(*c*) the procedures to be followed; and
(*d*) who is to meet the costs of the proceedings.

Complying with an order

8–29730 **7.** (1) The Board may make provision by regulations as to how a person is to comply with an order under section 20BA.

(2) The regulations may, in particular, make provision as to—

(*a*) the officer of the Board to whom the documents are to be produced,
(*b*) the address to which the documents are to be taken or sent, and
(*c*) the circumstances in which sending the documents by post complies with the order.

(3) Where an order under section 20BA applies to a document in electronic or magnetic form, the order shall be taken to require the person to deliver the information recorded in the document in a form in which it is visible and legible.

Procedure where documents are delivered

8–29731 **8.** (1) The provisions of section 20CC(3) to (9) apply in relation to a document delivered to an officer of the Board in accordance with an order under section 20BA as they apply to a thing removed by an officer of the Board as mentioned in subsection (1) of section 20CC.

(2) In section 20CC(9) as applied by sub-paragraph (1) above the reference to the warrant concerned shall be read as a reference to the order concerned.

Sanction for failure to comply with order

8–29732 **9.** (1) If a person fails to comply with an order made under section 20BA, he may be dealt with as if he had committed a contempt of the court.

(2) For this purpose "the court" means—

(*a*) in relation to an order made by a Circuit judge, the Crown Court;
(*b*) in relation to an order made by a sheriff, a sheriff court;
(*c*) in relation to an order made by a county court judge, a county court in Northern Ireland.

Notice of order etc

8–29733 **10.** The Board may make provision by regulations as to the circumstances in which notice of an order under section 20BA, or of an application for such an order, is to be treated as having been given.

General provisions about regulations

8–29734 **11.** Regulations under this Schedule—

(*a*) may contain such incidental, supplementary and transitional provision as appears to the Board to be appropriate, and
(*b*) shall be made by statutory instrument which shall be subject to annulment in pursuance of a resolution of either House of Parliament.]

Income and Corporation Taxes Act 1988

(1988 c 1)

PART IX[1]

ANNUAL PAYMENTS AND INTEREST

Annual payments

8–29850 **347A. General rule[2].** (1) A payment to which this section applies shall not be a charge on the income of the person liable to make it, and accordingly—

(*a*) his income shall be computed without any deduction being made on account of the payment, and
(*b*) the payment shall not, for the purposes of corporation tax, form part of the income of any company to whom it is made or of any other company.

(2) This section applies to any annual payment made by an individual which would otherwise be within the charge to tax under Case III of Schedule D except—

(*a*) a payment of interest;
(*b*) *Repealed*;
(*c*) a payment made for bona fide commercial reasons in connection with the individual's trade, profession or vocation; and
(*d*) a payment to which section 125(1) applies.

(2A) This section applies to any annual payment made by an individual which—

(*a*) arises in the United Kingdom, and
(*b*) is exempt from any charge under Part 5 of ITTOIA 2005 (miscellaneuos income) as a result of section 727 of that Act.

(3) This section applies to a payment made by personal representatives (within the meaning given in section 701(4)) where—

(*a*) the deceased would have been liable to make the payment if he had not died, and
(*b*) this section would have applied to the payment if he had made it.

(4)–(5) *Repealed.*
(6) *Applies to Scotland only.*
(7)–(8) *Repealed.*

[Income and Corporation Taxes Act 1988, s 347A, as inserted by the Finance Act 1988, s 36 and amended by the Finance (No 2) Act 1992, s 60, the Finance Act 1995, Sch 29, the Finance Act 2000, s 41 and Sch 40 and the Income Tax (Trading and Other Income) Act 2005, Sch 1.]

---

1. Part IX contains ss 347A–379.
2. Section 347A shall have effect in relation to payments becoming due on or after 6th April 1994 with the following modifications:

"Section 347A (which restricts the making of deductions) shall apply to any payment made—

(*a*) in pursuance of any obligation which falls within paragraphs (*a*) to (*c*) of subsection (4) of section 36 of the Finance Act 1988 (existing obligations) and is an obligation under an order made by a court, a written or oral agreement or a deed executed for giving effect to an agreement, and (*b*) for the benefit, maintenance or education of a person (whether or not the person to whom the payment is made) who attained the age of 21 on or before the day on which the payment became due but after 5th April 1994,

as if that obligation were not an existing obligation within the definition contained in that subsection."
[Finance Act 1994, s 79.]

8–29851 347B. Qualifying maintenance payments. (1) Subject to subsection (1A) below in this section "qualifying maintenance payment"[1] means a periodical payment which—

(*a*) is made under an order made by a court in a member State, or under a written agreement the law applicable to which is the law of a member State or of a part of a member State,

(*b*) is made—

(i) by one of the parties to a marriage or civil partnership (including a marriage or civil partnership which has been dissolved or annulled) to or for the benefit of the other party and for the maintenance of the other party, or

(ii) by one parent of a child to the child's other parent for the maintenance of the child by the other parent or by one person to another for the maintenance by the other of a relevant child of theirs,

(c) is due at a time when—

(i) in a case falling within paragraph (b)(i) above, the two parties are not a married couple, or civil partners of each other, living together and the party to whom or for whose benefit the payment is made has not subsequently entered into a marriage or civil partnership, and

(ii) in a case falling within paragraph (b)(ii) above, the person making the payment is not living together with the person to whom the payment is made, and

(*d*) is not a payment in respect of which relief from tax is available to the person making the payment under any provision of the Income Tax Acts other than this section.

(1A) A periodical payment is not a qualifying maintenance payment unless—

(*a*) in a case falling within subsection (1)(*b*)(i) above, either of the parties to the marriage or civil partnership was born before 6th April 1935, or

(*b*) in a case falling within subsection (1)(*b*)(ii) above, either the person by whom the payment is made, or the person to whom it is made, was born before that date.

(2) Subject to subsection (3) below, a person making a claim for the purpose shall be entitled, for a year of assessment* to an income tax reduction calculated by reference to an amount equal to the aggregate amount of any qualifying maintenance payments made by him which fall due in that year.

(3) The amount by reference to which any income tax reduction is to be calculated under this section shall be limited to the amount specified in section 257A(5A) for that year.

(4), (5) (*Repealed*).

(5A) Where any person is entitled under this section for any year of assessment* to an income tax reduction calculated by reference to the amount determined in accordance with subsections (2) and (3) above ("the relevant amount"), the amount of that person's liability for that year to income tax on his total income shall be the amount to which he would have been liable apart from this section less whichever is the smaller of—

(*a*) the amount equal to 10 per cent of the relevant amount; and

(*b*) the amount which reduces his liability to nil.

(5B) In determining for the purposes of subsection (5A) above the amount of income tax to which a person would be liable apart from any income tax reduction under this section, no account shall be taken of—

(*a*) any income tax reduction under Chapter I of Part VII;

(*b*) any relief by way of a reduction of liability to tax which is given in accordance with any arrangements having effect by virtue of section 788 or by way of a credit under section 790(1); or

(*c*) any tax at the basic rate on so much of that person's income as is income the income tax on which he is entitled to charge against any other person or to deduct, retain or satisfy out of any payment.

(6) (*Repealed*).

(7) In this section—

"child" means a person under 21 years of age;

"periodical payment" does not include an instalment of a lump sum.

"relevant child", in relation to any two persons, means a child who (not being a child who has been boarded out with them by a public authority or voluntary organisation) has been treated by both of them as a child of their family.

(8) In subsection (1)(*a*) above, the reference to an order made by a court in the United Kingdom includes a reference to a maintenance assessment*.

(9) Where—

(*a*) any periodical payment is made under a maintenance assessment* by any person,
(*b*) another person is, for the purposes of the Child Support Act 1991 or (as the case may be) the Child Support (Northern Ireland) Order 1991, a parent of the child or children with respect to whom the assessment* has effect,
(*c*) the assessment* was not made under section 7 of the Child Support Act 1991 (right of child in Scotland to apply for maintenance assessment*), and
(*d*) any of the conditions mentioned in subsection (10) below is satisfied,

this section shall have effect as if the payment had been made to the other person for the maintenance by that other person of that child or (as the case may be) those children.

(10) The conditions are that—

(*a*) the payment is made to the Secretary of State in accordance with regulations made under section 29 of the Child Support Act 1991, by virtue of subsection (3)(*a*)(ii) of that section;
(*b*) the payment is made to the Department of Health and Social Services for Northern Ireland in accordance with regulations made under Article 29 of the Child Support (Northern Ireland) Order 1991, by virtue of paragraph (3)(*a*)(ii) of that Article;
(*c*) the payment is retained by the Secretary of State in accordance with regulations made under section 41 of that Act;
(*d*) the payment is retained by the Department of Health and Social Services for Northern Ireland in accordance with regulations made under Article 38 of that Order.

(11) In this section "maintenance assessment" means a maintenance assessment made under the Child Support Act 1991 or the Child Support (Northern Ireland) Order 1991.**

(12) Where any periodical payment is made to the Secretary of State or to the Department of Health and Social Services for Northern Ireland—

(*a*) by any person, and
(*b*) under an order—
  (i) made under section 106 of the Social Security Administration Act 1992 or section 101 of the Social Security Administration (Northern Ireland) Act 1992 (recovery of expenditure on benefit from person liable for maintenance) in respect of income support claimed by any other person; or
  (ii) made by virtue of section 23 of the Jobseekers Act 1995 (recovery of sums in respect of maintenance), or any corresponding enactment in Northern Ireland, in respect of an income-based jobseeker's allowance claimed by any other person,

this section shall have effect as if the payment had been made to that other person to or for the benefit, and for the maintenance, of that other person or (as the case may be) to that other person for the maintenance of the child or children concerned.

(13) In subsection (12) above, "income-based jobseeker's allowance" has the same meaning as in the Jobseekers Act 1995 or, for Northern Ireland, the same meaning as in any corresponding enactment in Northern Ireland.

[Income and Corporation Taxes Act 1988, s 347B, as inserted by the Finance Act 1988, s 36, and amended by the Finance Act 1988, ss 35, 148, and Schs 3 and 14, the Contracts (Applicable Law) Act 1990, s 5 and Sch 4, the Finance (No 2) Act 1992, ss 61 and 62, the Finance Act 1994, s 79 and Sch 26, the Jobseekers Act 1995, Sch 2, the Finance Act 1998, s 27 and Sch 27, the Finance Act 1999, s 36 and Sch 20 and SI 2005/3229.]

***Prospectively amended by the Child Support, Pensions and Social Security Act 2000, Sch 3, from a date to be appointed.**

****Prospectively substituted by the Child Support, Pensions and Social Security Act 2000, Sch 3, from a date to be appointed.**

1. It should be noted that payments direct to a child are not "qualifying maintenance payments".

These provisions have effect in relation to any payment falling due on or after 15 March unless it is made in pursuance of an "existing obligation". There are thus savings for orders in existence on 15 March 1988, for orders for which application was made up to and including 15 March 1988 and which were made by 30 June 1988, and for orders varying any of these. By virtue of ss 37 and 38 of the Finance Act 1988, post, the payer will have tax relief and the recipient will have tax liability "frozen" at the 1988/89 level even if payments are increased in future. Recipients will not pay tax on the first £1,490 of such payments and will be able to use their full personal tax allowances for amounts over that. For such "existing obligation" orders, s 39 of the Finance Act 1988, enabled a person to elect to change to the rules for new orders. Section 39, however, has been repealed by the Finance Act 1999, Sch 20, in relation to any payment falling due on or after 6 April 2000. As a consequence of further amendments to s 347B made by the Finance Act 1999, s 36, with respect to any payment falling due on or after 6 April 2000 a periodical payment is not a qualifying maintenance payment unless either of the parties to the marriage which has been dissolved or annulled was born before 6 April 1935. This change has effect in relation to any payment falling due on or after 6 April 2000.

Finance Act 1988

(1988 c 39)

PART III[1]

INCOME TAX, CORPORATION TAX AND CAPITAL GAINS TAX

CHAPTER I

GENERAL

Annual payments

8–29860 **38. Maintenance payments under existing obligations: 1989–90 onwards.** (1) This section applies to any annual payment due in the year 1989–90 or any subsequent year of assessment* which—

(*a*) is made in pursuance of an existing obligation under an order made by a court (whether in the United Kingdom or elsewhere) or under a written or oral agreement,

(*b*) is made by an individual—

(i) as one of the parties to a marriage (including a marriage which has been dissolved or annulled) to or for the benefit of the other party to the marriage and for the maintenance of the other party, or

(ii) to any person under 21 years of age for his own benefit, maintenance or education, or

(iii) to any person for the benefit, maintenance or education of a person under 21 years of age, and

(*c*) is (apart from this section) within the charge to tax under Chapter 7 of Part 5 of the Income Tax (Trading and Other Income) Act 2005 (annual payments not otherwise charged) and is not, by virtue of Chapter 5 of that Part (settlements), treated for any purpose as the income of the person making it.

(2) A payment to which this section applies shall not be a charge on the income of the person liable to make it.

(3)–(6) *Repealed.*

(7) A payment to which this section applies shall be made without deduction of income tax.

(8) *Repealed.*

(8A) The reference in subsection (1)(*a*) above to an order made by a court includes a reference to a maintenance assessment* made under the Child Support Act 1991 or under the Child Support (Northern Ireland) Order 1991.

(9) No deduction shall be made under section 839 of the Income tax (Trading and Other Income Act 2005 (annual payments payable out of relvant foreign income) or section 335 of the Income Tax (Earnings and Pensions) Act 2003 on account of a payment to which this section applies.

[Finance Act 1988, s 38, as amended by the Finance Act 1988, s 35 and Sch 3, the Finance (No 2) Act 1992, ss 60 and 62, the Finance Act 1994, s 79, the Finance Act 1999, Sch 20, the Finance Act 2004, Sch 17 and the Income Tax (Trading and Other Income) Act 2005, Sch 1.]

***Prospectively amended by the Child Support, Pensions and Social Security Act 2000, s 1 and Sch 3 from a date to be appointed.**

****Section 38 is reproduced as amended by the Finance Act 1999, Sch 20, which has effect in relation to any payment falling due on or after 6 April 2000.**

1. Part III contains ss 23–73.

8–29861 **39. Maintenance payments under existing obligations: election for new rules.** *Repealed.**

***This repeal has effect in relation to any payment falling due on or after 6 April 2000: see the Finance Act 1999, Sch 20, Pt III(6).**

8–29862 **40. Provisions supplementary to sections 37 to 39.** (1) In sections 37 to 39 above—

"existing obligation"1 has the same meaning as in section 36(3) above.

(2), (3) *Repealed.**

[Finance Act 1988, s 40, as amended by the Finance Act 1988, s 148 and Sch 14 and the Finance Act 1999, Sch 20.]

***Section 40 is reproduced as amended by the Finance Act 1999, Sch 20, which has effect in relation to any payment falling due on or after the 6 April 2000.**

1. The meaning of "existing obligation" includes a binding obligation under an order made by a court (whether in the United Kingdom or elsewhere) before 15 March 1988, or before the end of June 1988 on an application made on or before 15 March 1988 (Finance Act 1988, s 36(3), (4)).

Finance Act 1989

(1989 c 26)

Part III[1]

Miscellaneous and General

Miscellaneous

8–30070 **182. Disclosure of information[2].** (1) A person who discloses any information which he holds or has held in the exercise of tax functions, tax credit functions, child trust fund functions or social security functions is guilty of an offence if it is information about any matter relevant, for the purposes of any of those functions—

(*a*) to tax or duty in the case of any identifiable person,
(*aa*) to a tax credit in respect of any identifiable person,
(*ab*) to a child trust fund of any identifiable person,
(*b*) to contributions payable by or in respect of any identifiable person, or
(*c*) to statutory sick pay, statutory maternity pay, statutory paternity pay or statutory adoption pay in respect of any identifiable person.

(2) In this section "tax functions" means functions relating to tax or duty—

(*a*) of the Commissioners, the Board and their officers,
(*b*) of any person carrying out the administrative work of any tribunal mentioned in subsection (3) below, and
(*c*) of any other person providing, or employed in the provision of, services to any person mentioned in paragraph (*a*) or (*b*) above.

(2ZA) In this section "tax credit functions" means the functions relating tax credits—

(*a*) of the Board,
(*b*) of any person carrying out the administrative work of the General Commissioners or the Special Commissioners, and
(*c*) of any other person providing, or employed in the provision of, services to any person mentioned in paragraph (*b*) above.

(2ZB) In this section "child trust fund functions" means the functions relating to child trust funds—

(*a*) of the Board and their officers,
(*b*) of any person carrying out the administrative work of the General Commissioners or the Special Commissioners, or
(*c*) of any person providing, or employed in the provision of, services to the Board or any person mentioned in paragraph (*b*) above.

(2A) In this section "social security functions" means—

(*a*) the functions relating to contributions, child benefit, guardian's allowance, statutory sick pay, statutory maternity pay, statutory paternity pay or statutory adoption pay—
  (i) of the Board and their officers,
  (ii) of any person carrying out the administrative work of the General Commissioners or the Special Commissioners, and
  (iii) of any other person providing, or employed in the provision of, services to any person mentioned in sub-paragraph (i) or (ii) above, and
(*b*) the functions under Part III of the Pension Schemes Act 1993 or Part III of the Pension Schemes (Northern Ireland) Act 1993 of the Board and their officers and any other person providing, or employed in the provision of, services to the Board or their officers.

(3) The tribunals referred to in subsection (2)(*b*) above are—

(*a*) the General Commissioners and the Special Commissioners,
(*b*) any value added tax tribunal,
(*c*) (*repealed*) and
(*d*) any tribunal established under section 463 of the Taxes Act 1970 or section 706 of the Taxes Act 1988.

(4) A person who discloses any information which—

(*a*) he holds or has held in the exercise of functions—
  (i) of the Comptroller and Auditor General and any member of the staff of the National Audit Office,
  (ii) of the Parliamentary Commissioner for Administration and his officers,
  (iii) of the Auditor General for Wales and any member of his staff, or
  (iv) of the Public Services Ombudsman for Wales and any member of his staff, or
  (v) of the Scottish Public Services Ombudsman and any member of his staff,

(*b*) is, or is derived from, information which was held by any person in the exercise of tax functions, tax credit functions, child trust fund functions or social security functions and
(*c*) is information about any matter relevant, for the purposes of tax functions, tax credit functions, child trust fund functions or social security functions—

(i) to tax or duty in the case of any identifiable person,
(ia) to a tax credit in respect of any identifiable person,
(ib) to a child trust fund of any identifiable person,
(ii) to contributions payable by or in respect of any identifiable person, or
(iii) to child benefit, guardian's allowance, statutory sick pay, statutory maternity pay, statutory paternity pay or statutory adoption pay in respect of any identifiable person]in respect of any identifiable person

is guilty of an offence.

(5) Subsections (1) and (4) above do not apply to any disclosure of information—

(*a*) with lawful authority,
(*b*) with the consent of any person in whose case the information is about a matter relevant to tax or duty, to a tax credit or to a child trust fund or to contributions, statutory sick pay, statutory maternity pay, statutory paternity pay or statutory adoption pay, or
(*c*) which has been lawfully made available to the public before the disclosure is made.

(6) For the purposes of this section a disclosure of any information is made with lawful authority if, and only if, it is made—

(*a*) by a Crown servant in accordance with his official duty,
(*b*) by any other person for the purposes of the function in the exercise of which he holds the information and without contravening any restriction duly imposed by the person responsible,
(*c*) to, or in accordance with an authorisation duly given by, the person responsible,
(*d*) in pursuance of any enactment or of any order of a court, or
(*e*) in connection with the institution of or otherwise for the purposes of any proceedings relating to any matter within the general responsibility of the Commissioners or, as the case requires, the Board,

and in this subsection "the person responsible" means the Commissioners, the Board, the Comptroller, the Parliamentary Commissioner, the Auditor General for Wales, the Public Services Ombudsman for Wales or the Scottish Public Services Ombudsman, as the case requires.

(7) It is a defence for a person charged with an offence under this section to prove that at the time of the alleged offence—

(*a*) he believed that he had lawful authority to make the disclosure in question and had no reasonable cause to believe otherwise, or
(*b*) he believed that the information in question had been lawfully made available to the public before the disclosure was made and had no reasonable cause to believe otherwise.

(8) A person of an offence under this section is liable[2]

(*a*) on conviction on indictment, to imprisonment for a term not exceeding **two years** or a **fine** or **both**, and
(*b*) on summary conviction, to imprisonment for a term not exceeding **six months** or a fine not exceeding the **statutory maximum** or **both**.

(9) No prosecution for an offence under this section shall be instituted in England and Wales or in Northern Ireland except—

(*a*) by the Commissioners or the Board, as the case requires, or
(*b*) by or with the consent of the Director of Public Prosecutions or, in Northern Ireland, the Director of Public Prosecutions for Northern Ireland.

(10) In this section—

"the Board" means the Commissioners of Inland Revenue,
"child trust fund" has the same meaning as in the Child Trust Funds Act 2004,
"the Commissioners" means the Commissioners of Customs and Excise,
"contributions" means contributions under Part I of the Social Security Contributions and Benefits Act 1992 or Part I of the Social Security Contributions and Benefits (Northern Ireland) Act 1992;
"Crown servant" has the same meaning as in the Official Secrets Act 1989,
"tax credit" means a tax credit under the Tax Credits Act 2002,
"tax or duty" means ant tax or duty within the general responsibility of the Commissioners or the Board.

(10A) In this section, inrelation to the disclosure of information "identifiable person" means a person whose identity is specifed in the disclosure or can be deduced from it.

(11) In this section—

(*a*) references to the Comptroller and Auditor General include the Comptroller and Auditor General for Northern Ireland,

(*b*) references to the National Audit Office include the Northern Ireland Audit Office, and

(*c*) reference to the Parliamentary Commissioner for Administration include the Health Service Commissioner for England, the Northern Ireland Parliamentary Commissioner for Administration and the Northern Ireland Commissioner for complaints.

(11A) In this section, references to statutory paternity pay or statutory adoption pay include statutory pay under Northern Ireland legislation corresponding to Part 12ZA or Part 12ZB of the Social Security Contributions and Benefits Act 1992 (c 4).

(12) *Commencement.*

[Finance Act 1989, s 182 as amended by the Finance Act 1995, Sch 29, the Government of Wales Act 1998, Sch 12 and Sch 18, the Tax Credits Act 1999, s 12, the Social Security Contributions (Transfer of Functions, etc) Act 1999, Sch 6, the Tax Credits Act 2002, s 59, the Employment Act 2002, Sch 7, the Statute Law (Repeals) Act 2004, SI 2004/1823, the Child Trust Funds Act 2004, s 18 and the Public Services Ombudsman (Wales) Act 2005, Sch 6.]

---

1. Part III contains ss 171–188.
2. For procedure in respect of an offence which is triable either way, see the Magistrates' Courts Act 1980, ss 17A–21, in PART I: MAGISTRATES' COURTS, PROCEDURE, ante.

8–30071 **182A. Double taxation: disclosure of information.** (1) A person who discloses any information acquired by him in the exercise of his functions as a member of an advisory commission set up under the Arbitration Convention is guilty of an offence.

(2) Subsection (1) above does not apply to any disclosure of information—

(*a*) with the consent of the person who supplied the information to the commission, or

(*b*) which has been lawfully made available to the public before the disclosure is made.

(3) It is a defence for a person charged with an offence under this section to prove that at the time of the alleged offence he believed that the information in question had been lawfully made available to the public before the disclosure was made and had no reasonable cause to believe otherwise.

(4) A person guilty of an offence under this section is liable[1]—

(*a*) on conviction on indictment to imprisonment for a term not exceeding **two years** or a **fine** or **both**;

(*b*) on summary conviction, to imprisonment for a term not exceeding **six months** or a fine not exceeding **the statutory maximum** or **both**.

(5) No prosecution for an offence under this section shall be instituted in England and Wales or in Northern Ireland except—

(*a*) by the Board, or

(*b*) by or with the consent of the Director of Public Prosecutions or, in Northern Ireland, the Director of Public Prosecutions for Northern Ireland.

(6) In this section—

"the Arbitration Convention" has the meaning given by section 815B(4) of the Taxes Act 1988;

"the Board" means the Commissioners of Inland Revenue."

[Finance Act 1989, s 182A, as inserted by the Finance (No 2) Act 1992, s 51.]

---

1. For procedure in respect of an offence which is triable either way, see the Magistrates' Courts Act 1980, ss 17A–21, in PART I: MAGISTRATES' COURTS, PROCEDURE, ante.

Value Added Tax Act 1994

(1994 c 23)

8–30080 Value added tax is charged on the supply of goods or services in the United Kingdom, the acquisition in the United Kingdom from other member states of any goods or on the importation of goods from places outside the member states (s 1). The scope of VAT on taxable supplies is defined by s 4 and the meaning of "supply" is defined by s 5 and Sch 4. The time of supply (and when VAT is due) is defined by s 6 and the place of supply by s 7. Further provision in respect of acquisition from member states is made by ss 10–14 and for goods imported from outside member states by ss 15–17. Specific provision is made for the determination of value by ss 19–23. The rate of tax is established by s 2.

A taxable person may offset VAT paid on goods supplied etc to him (input) against tax which he must pay (output tax) and must pay VAT in accordance with accounting periods prescribed by regulations.

Relief is available for zero rated supplies (s 30 and Sch 8), exempt supplies (s 31 and Sch 9) and certain second hand goods (s 32), capital goods (s 34) and other reliefs specified in Pt II. Application of the Act to particular cases such as the Crown and local authorities is provided for in Pt III (ss 41–57).

Administration, enforcement and collection is provided for by Pt IV (ss 58–81 and Sch 11). The Act contains extensive powers to make regulations under which, inter alia, the Value Added Tax Regulations 1995[1] have been made. The Commissioners of Customs and Excise may assess tax due where there has been failure to make proper returns; they may require the keeping of records, the furnishing of information and the production of documents by s 58 and Sch 11.

The Commissioners are empowered to impose surcharges in respect of default in payment (s 59) and penalties where there is evasion of VAT involving dishonesty (s 60). Other forms of misconduct liable to a penalty are prescribed by ss 62–69. Penalties may be mitigated by the Commissioners (s 70). Criminal liability may also arise under s 72.

Appeals in disputes including registration, assessment, tax chargeable and the deduction known as "input tax" lie to local value added tax tribunals (Pt V, ss 82–87, Sch 12); these and not magistrates' courts are the proper forum for the settlement of such disputes.

Only the parts of the Act concerned with entry and search facilities, and with offences and penalties, are included in this work.

Note that the comprehensive code governing proceedings, which is contained in ss 145–155 *of the Customs and Excise Management Act* 1979, *in this* PART: title CUSTOMS AND EXCISE, *ante, applies here.*

1. SI 1995/2518 amended by SI 1996/210, 1198, 1250, 2098 and 2960, SI 1997/1086, 1525, 1614, 2437 and 2887, SI 1998/59 and 765, SI 1999/438, 599, 1374, 3029 and 3114, SI 2000/258, 634 and 794, SI 2001/630, 677, and SI 2002/1074, 1142, 2918 and 3027, SI 2003/532, 1069, 1114, 1485, 2318 and 3220, SI 2004/767, 1082, 1675 and 3140 and SI 2005/762 and 2231.

PART I
THE CHARGE TO TAX

Imposition and rate of VAT

8–30081 1. Value added tax. (1) Value added tax shall be charged, in accordance with the provisions of this Act—

(*a*) on the supply of goods or services in the United Kingdom (including anything treated as such a supply),
(*b*) on the acquisition in the United Kingdom from other member States of any goods, and
(*c*) on the importation of goods from places outside the member States,

and references in this Act to VAT are references to value added tax.

(2) VAT on any supply of goods or services is a liability of the person making the supply and (subject to provisions about accounting and payment) becomes due at the time of supply.

(3) VAT on any acquisition of goods from another member State is a liability of the person who acquires the goods and (subject to provisions about accounting and payment) becomes due at the time of acquisition.

(4) VAT on the importation of goods from places outside the member States shall be charged and payable as if it were a duty of customs.
[Value Added Tax Act 1994, s 1.]

8–30082 3. Taxable persons and registration. (1) A person is a taxable person for the purposes of this Act while he is, or is required to be, registered[1] under this Act.

(2) Schedules 1 to 3A[2] shall have effect with respect to registration.

(3) Persons registered under any of those Schedules shall be registered in a single register kept by the Commissioners for the purposes of this Act; and, accordingly, references in this Act to being registered under this Act are references to being registered under any of those Schedules.

(4) The Commissioners may by regulations make provision as to the inclusion and correction of information in that register with respect to the Schedule under which any person is registered.
[Value Added Tax Act 1994, s 3, as amended by the Finance Act 2000, s 136.]

1. Registration of one firm name is registration of those who are carrying on business in partnership as such, and covers the taxable activities of the same individuals trading alternatively under another firm name (*Customs and Excise Comrs v Glassborow* [1975] QB 465, [1974] 1 All ER 1041).
2. Schedules 1–3A to this Act are not printed in this work.

8–30082A 3A. Supply of electronic services in member States: special accounting scheme. (1) Schedule 3B (scheme enabling persons who supply electronically supplied services in any member State but who are not established in a member State, to account for and pay VAT in the United Kingdom onthose supplies) has effect.

(2) The Treasury may by order amend Schdule 3B.

(3) The power of the Tresury by order to amend Schedule 3B includes power to make such incidental, supplemental, consequential and transitional provision in connection with any amendment of that Schedule as they think fit.

Supply of goods or services in the United Kingdom

8–30083 4. Scope of VAT on taxable supplies. (1) VAT shall be charged on any supply of goods or services made in the United Kingdom, where it is a taxable supply made by a taxable person in the course or furtherance of any business carried on by him.

(2) A taxable supply is a supply of goods or services made in the United Kingdom other than an exempt supply.
[Value Added Tax Act 1994, s 4.]

Acquisition of goods from member States

8–30084 10. Scope of VAT on acquisitions from member States. (1) VAT shall be charged on any acquisition from another member State of any goods where—

(*a*) the acquisition is a taxable acquisition and takes place in the United Kingdom;
(*b*) the acquisition is otherwise than in pursuance of a taxable supply; and
(*c*) the person who makes the acquisition is a taxable person or the goods are subject to a duty of excise or consist in a new means of transport.

(2) An acquisition of goods from another member State is a taxable acquisition if—

(*a*) it falls within subsection (3) below or the goods consist in a new means of transport; and
(*b*) it is not an exempt acquisition.

(3) An acquisition of goods from another member State falls within this subsection if—

(*a*) the goods are acquired in the course or furtherance of—

(i) any business carried on by any person; or
(ii) any activities carried on otherwise than by way of business by any body corporate or by any club, association, organisation or other unincorporated body;

(*b*) it is the person who carries on that business or, as the case may be, those activities who acquires the goods; and
(*c*) the supplier—

(i) is taxable in another member State at the time of the transaction in pursuance of which the goods are acquired; and
(ii) in participating in that transaction, acts in the course or furtherance of a business carried on by him.

[Value Added Tax Act 1994, s 10.]

Importation of goods from outside the member States

8–30085 15. General provisions relating to imported goods. (1) For the purposes of this Act goods are imported from a place outside the member States where—

(*a*) having been removed from a place outside the member States, they enter the territory of the Community;
(*b*) they enter that territory by being removed to the United Kingdom or are removed to the United Kingdom after entering that territory; and
(*c*) the circumstances are such that it is on their removal to the United Kingdom or subsequently while they are in the United Kingdom that any Community customs debt in respect of duty on their entry into the territory of the Community would be incurred.

(2) Accordingly—

(*a*) goods shall not be treated for the purposes of this Act as imported at any time before a Community customs debt in respect of duty on their entry into the territory of the Community would be incurred, and
(*b*) the person who is to be treated for the purposes of this Act as importing any goods from a place outside the member States is the person who would be liable to discharge any such Community customs debt.

(3) Subsections (1) and (2) above shall not apply, except in so far as the context otherwise requires or provision to the contrary is contained in regulations under section 16(1), for construing any references to importation or to an importer in any enactment or subordinate legislation applied for the purposes of this Act by section 16(1).
[Value Added Tax Act 1994, s 15.]

8–30086 60. VAT evasion: conduct involving dishonesty. (1) In any case where—

(*a*) for the purpose of evading VAT, a person does any act or omits to take any action, and
(*b*) his conduct involves dishonesty (whether or not it is such as to give rise to criminal liability),

he shall be liable, subject to subsection (6) below, to a penalty[1] equal to the amount of VAT evaded or, as the case may be, sought to be evaded, by his conduct.

(2) The reference in subsection (1)(*a*) above to evading VAT includes a reference to obtaining any of the following sums—

(*a*) a refund under any regulations made by virtue of section 13(5);
(*b*) a VAT credit;
(*c*) a refund under section 35, 36 or 40 of this Act or section 22 of the 1983 Act; and
(*d*) a repayment under section 39,

in circumstances where the person concerned is not entitled to that sum.

(3) The reference in subsection (1) above to the amount of the VAT evaded or sought to be evaded by a person's conduct shall be construed—

(*a*) in relation to VAT itself or a VAT credit as a reference to the aggregate of the amount (if any) falsely claimed by way of credit for input tax and the amount (if any) by which output tax was falsely understated; and
(*b*) in relation to the sums referred to in subsection (2)(*a*), (*c*) and (*e*)[2] above, as a reference to the amount falsely claimed by way of refund or repayment.

(4) Statements made or documents produced by or on behalf of a person shall not be inadmissible in any such proceedings as are mentioned in subsection (5) below by reason only that it has been drawn to his attention—

(*a*) that, in relation to VAT, the Commissioners may assess an amount due by way of a civil penalty instead of instituting criminal proceedings and, though no undertaking can be given as to whether the Commissioners will make such an assessment in the case of any person, it is their practice to be influenced by the fact that a person has made a full confession of any dishonest conduct to which he has been a party and has given full facilities for investigation, and
(*b*) that the Commissioners or, on appeal, a tribunal have power under section 70 to reduce a penalty under this section,

and that he was or may have been induced thereby to make the statements or produce the documents.

(5) The proceedings mentioned in subsection (4) above are—

(*a*) any criminal proceedings against the person concerned in respect of any offence in connection with or in relation to VAT, and
(*b*) any proceedings against him for the recovery of any sum due from him in connection with or in relation to VAT.

(6) Where, by reason of conduct falling within subsection (1) above, a person is convicted of an offence (whether under this Act or otherwise), that conduct shall not also give rise to liability to a penalty under this section.

(7) On an appeal against an assessment to a penalty under this section, the burden of proof as to the matters specified in subsection (1)(*a*) and (*b*) above shall lie upon the Commissioners.
[Value Added Tax Act 1994, s 60.]

---

1. The imposition of penalty pursuant to s 60(1) gave rise to a criminal charge within the meaning of art 6(1) of the European Convention on Human Rights; accordingly, a person made subject to such a penalty was entitled to the minimum rights provided by art 6(3): *Han v Customs and Excise Comrs, Martins v Customs and Excise Comrs, Morris v Customs and Excise Comrs* [2001] EWCA Civ 1040, [2001] 4 All ER 687, [2001] 1 WLR 2253.
2. This should refer to '(*d*)', see s 72(2)(*d*)(ii), below.

8–30087 72. Offences. (1) If any person is knowingly[1] concerned in, or in the taking of steps with a view to, the fraudulent evasion[2] of VAT by him or any other person, he shall be liable[3]—

(*a*) on summary conviction, to a penalty of the **statutory maximum or of three times the amount of the VAT, whichever is the greater**, or to imprisonment for a term not exceeding **6 months** or to **both**[4]; or
(*b*) on conviction on indictment, to a **penalty of any amount** or to imprisonment for a term not exceeding **7 years** or to **both**.

(2) Any reference in subsection (1) above or subsection (8) below to the evasion of VAT includes a reference to the obtaining of—

(*a*) the payment of a VAT credit; or
(*b*) a refund under section 35, 36 or 40 of this Act or section 22 of the 1983 Act; or
(*c*) a refund under any regulations made by virtue of section 13(5); or
(*d*) a repayment under section 39;

and any reference in those subsections to the amount of the VAT shall be construed—

(i) in relation to VAT itself or a VAT credit, as a reference to the aggregate of the amount (if any) falsely claimed by way of credit for input tax and the amount (if any) by which output tax was falsely understated, and
(ii) in relation to a refund or repayment falling within paragraph (*b*), (*c*) or (*d*) above, as a reference to the amount falsely claimed by way of refund or repayment.

(3) If any person—

(*a*) with intent to deceive produces, furnishes or sends for the purposes of this Act or otherwise makes use for those purposes of any document which is false in a material particular; or

(*b*) in furnishing any information for the purposes of this Act makes any statement which he knows to be false in a material particular or recklessly makes a statement which is false in a material particular,

he shall be liable[3]—

(i) on summary conviction, to a penalty of the **statutory maximum** or, where subsection (4) or (5) below applies, to the alternative penalty specified in that subsection if it is greater, or to imprisonment for a term not exceeding **6 months** or to **both**; or

(ii) on conviction on indictment, to a **penalty of any amount** or to imprisonment for a term not exceeding **7 years** or to **both**.

(4) In any case where—

(*a*) the document referred to in subsection (3)(*a*) above is a return required under this Act, or

(*b*) the information referred to in subsection (3)(*b*) above is contained in or otherwise relevant to such a return,

the alternative penalty referred to in subsection (3)(i) above is a penalty equal to three times the aggregate of the amount (if any) falsely claimed by way of credit for input tax and the amount (if any) by which output tax was falsely understated.

(5) In any case where—

(*a*) the document referred to in subsection (3)(*a*) above is a claim for a refund under section 35, 36 or 40 of this Act or section 22 of the 1983 Act, for a refund under any regulations made by virtue of section 13(5) or for a repayment under section 39, or

(*b*) the information referred to in subsection (3)(*b*) above is contained in or otherwise relevant to such a claim,

the alternative penalty referred to in subsection (3)(i) above is a penalty equal to 3 times the amount falsely claimed.

(6) The reference in subsection (3)(*a*) above to furnishing, sending or otherwise making use of a document which is false in a material particular, with intent to deceive, includes a reference to furnishing, sending or otherwise making use of such a document, with intent to secure that a machine will respond to the document as if it were a true document.

(7) Any reference in subsection (3)(*a*) or (6) above to producing, furnishing or sending a document includes a reference to causing a document to be produced, furnished or sent.

(8) Where a person's conduct during any specified period must have involved the commission by him of one or more offences under the preceding provisions of this section, then, whether or not the particulars of that offence or those offences are known, he shall, by virtue of this subsection, be guilty of an offence[4] and liable[3]—

(*a*) on summary conviction, to a penalty of the **statutory maximum or, if greater, 3 times the amount of any VAT** that was or was intended to be evaded by his conduct, or to imprisonment for a term not exceeding **6 months** or to **both**,[5] or

(*b*) on conviction on indictment to a penalty of any amount or to imprisonment for a term not exceeding **7 years** or to **both**.

(9) Where an authorised person has reasonable grounds for suspecting that an offence has been committed under the preceding provisions of this section, he may arrest anyone whom he has reasonable grounds for suspecting to be guilty of the offence.

(10) If any person acquires possession of or deals with any goods, or accepts the supply of any services, having reason to believe that VAT on the supply of the goods or services, on the accession of the goods from another member State or on the importation of the goods from a place outside the member States has been or will be evaded, he shall be liable on summary conviction to a penalty of **level 5** on the standard scale or **three times the amount of the VAT, whichever is the greater**.

(11) If any person supplies goods or services in contravention of paragraph 4(2) of Schedule 11, he shall be liable on summary conviction to a penalty of **level 5** on the standard scale.

(12) Subject to subsection (13) below, sections 145 to 155 of the Management Act (proceedings for offences, mitigation of penalties and certain other matters) shall apply in relation to offences under this Act (which include any act or omission in respect of which a penalty is imposed) and penalties imposed under this Act as they apply in relation to offences and penalties under the customs and excise Acts as defined in that Act; and accordingly in section 154(2) as it applies by virtue of this subsection the reference to duty shall be construed as a reference to VAT.

(13) In subsection (12) above the references to penalties do not include references to penalties under sections 60 to 70.

[Value Added Tax Act 1994, s 72.]

1. A person may act "knowingly" if, intending what is happening, he deliberately looks the other way (*Ross v Moss* [1965] 2 QB 396, [1965] 3 All ER 145, 129 JP 537). See also *R v Cohen* [1951] 1 KB 505, [1951] 1 All ER 203 (an offence of knowingly harbouring uncustomed goods).

2. Evasion in this section means a deliberate non-payment when payment is due. There is no need for the Crown to prove in addition an intention permanently to deprive (*R v Dealy* [1995] 1 WLR 658, [1995] 2 Cr App Rep 398, CA).

3. For procedure in respect of an offence triable either way, see the Magistrates' Courts Act 1980, ss 17A–21 in PART I: MAGISTRATES' COURTS, PROCEDURE, ante.

4. The offence under sub-s (8) relates to a person's conduct during a specified period, and creates one offence embracing the commission of numerous offences which themselves, if the details were known, could be individually charged under s 38(1) and (2) (*R v Asif* (1985) 82 Cr App Rep 123).

5. Where an offender is sentenced to imprisonment and a fine, with an alternative period of imprisonment in default of payment of the fine, the aggregate of the terms of imprisonment must not exceed 15 months (Customs and Excise Management Act 1979, s 149).

8–30088 94. Meaning of "business" etc. (1) In this Act "business" includes any trade, profession or vocation.

(2) Without prejudice to the generality of anything else in this Act, the following are deemed to be the carrying on of a business—

(*a*) the provision by a club, association or organisation (for a subscription or other consideration) of the facilities or advantages available to its members; and

(*b*) the admission, for a consideration, of persons to any premises.

(3) (*Repealed*).

(4) Where a person, in the course or furtherance of a trade, profession or vocation, accepts any office, services supplied by him as the holder of that office are treated as supplied in the course or furtherance of the trade, profession or vocation.

(5) Anything done in connection with the termination or intended termination of a business is treated as being done in the course or furtherance of that business.

(6) The disposition of a business as a going concern, or of its assets or liabilities (whether or not in connection with its reorganisation or winding up), is a supply made in the course or furtherance of the business.

[Value Added Tax Act 1994, s 94, as amended by the Finance Act 1999, s 20 and Sch 20.]

8–30089 96. Other interpretative provisions. (1) In this Act—

"the 1983 Act" means the Value Added Tax Act 1983;

"another member State" means, subject to section 93(1), any member State other than the United Kingdom, and "other member States" shall be construed accordingly;

"assignment", in relation to Scotland, means assignation;

"authorised person" means any person acting under the authority of the Commissioners;

"the Commissioners" means the Commissioners of Customs and Excise;

"copy", in relation to a document, means anything onto which information recorded in the document has been copied, by whatever means and whether directly or indirectly;

"document" means anything in which information of any description is recorded;

"fee simple"—

(*a*) in relation to Scotland, means the interest of the owner;

(*b*) in relation to Northern Ireland, includes the estate of a person who holds land under a fee farm grant;

"invoice" includes any document similar to an invoice;

"input tax" has the meaning given by section 24;

"interim trustee" has the same meaning as in the Bankruptcy (Scotland) Act 1985;

"local authority" has the meaning given by subsection (4) below;

"major interest", in relation to land, means the fee simple or a tenancy for a term certain of not less than 20 years, and in relation to Scotland means the interest of the owner, or the lessee's interest under a lease for a period of not less than 20 years;

"the Management Act" means the Customs and Excise Management Act 1979;

"money" includes currencies other than sterling;

"output tax" has the meaning given by section 24;

"permanent trustee" has the same meaning as in the Bankruptcy (Scotland) Act 1985;

"the Post Office company" has the same meaning as in Part IV of the Postal Services Act 2000;

"prescribed" means prescribed by regulations;

"prescribed accounting period" has the meaning given by section 25(1);

"quarter" means a period of 3 months ending at the end of March, June, September or December;

"regulations" means regulations made by the Commissioners under this Act;

"ship" includes hovercraft;

"subordinate legislation" has the same meaning as in the Interpretation Act 1978;

"tax" means VAT;

"taxable acquisition" has the meaning given by section 10(2);

"taxable person" means a person who is a taxable person under section 3;

"taxable supply" has the meaning given by section 4(2)

"the Taxes Act" means the Income and Corporation Taxes Act 1988;

"tribunal" has the meaning given by section 82;

"VAT" means value added tax charged in accordance with this Act or, where the context requires, with the law of another member State;

"VAT credit" has the meaning given by section 25(3);

"VAT invoice" has the meaning given by section 6(15);

"VAT representative" has the meaning given by section 48;

and any reference to a particular section, Part or Schedule is a reference to that section or Part of, or Schedule to, this Act.

(2) Any reference in this Act to being registered shall be construed in accordance with section 3(3).

(3) Subject to section 93—

(*a*) the question whether or not goods have entered the territory of the Community;

(*b*) the time when any Community customs debt in respect of duty on the entry of any goods into the territory of the Community would be incurred; and

(*c*) the person by whom any such debt would fall to be discharged,

shall for the purposes of this Act be determined (whether or not the goods in question are themselves subject to any such duties) according to the Community legislation applicable to goods which are in fact subject to such duties.

(4) In this Act "local authority" means the council of a county, county borough, district, London borough, parish or group of parishes (or, in Wales, community or group of communities), the Common Council of the City of London, the Council of the Isles of Scilly, and any joint committee or joint board established by two or more of the foregoing and, in relation to Scotland, a council constituted under section 2 of the Local Government etc (Scotland) Act 1994, any two or more such councils and any joint committee or joint board within the meaning of section 235(1) of the Local Government (Scotland) Act 1973.

established by of the foregoing and any joint board to which section 226 of that Act applies.

(5) Any reference in this Act to the amount of any duty of excise on any goods shall be taken to be a reference to the amount of duty charged on those goods with any addition or deduction falling to be made under section 1 of the Excise Duties (Surcharges or Rebates) Act 1979.

(6)–(7) (*Repealed*).

(8) The question whether, in relation to any supply of services, the supplier or the recipient of the supply belongs in one country or another shall be determined (subject to any provision made under section 8(6)) in accordance with section 9.

(9) Schedules 7A, 8 and 9 shall be interpreted in accordance with the notes contained in those Schedules; and accordingly the powers conferred by this Act to vary those Schedules include a power to add to, delete or vary those notes.

(10) The descriptions of Groups in those Schedules are for ease of reference only and shall not affect the interpretation of the descriptions of items in those Groups.

(10A) Where—

(*a*) the grant of any interest, right, licence or facilities gives rise for the purposes of this Act to supplies made at different times after the making of the grant, and

(*b*) a question whether any of those supplies is zero-rated or exempt falls to be determined according to whether or not the grant is a grant of a description specified in Schedule 8 or 9 or paragraph 2(2) or (3) of Schedule 10.

that question shall be determined according to whether the description is applicable as at the time of supply, rather than by reference to the time of the grant.

(10B) Notwithstanding subsection (10A) above—

(*a*) item 1 of Group 1 of Schedule 9 does not make exempt any supply that arises for the purposes of this Act from the prior grant of a fee simple falling within paragraph (*a*) of that item; and

(*b*) that paragraph does not prevent the exemption of a supply that arises for the purposes of this Act from the prior grant of a fee simple not falling within that paragraph.

(11) References in this Act to the United Kingdom include the territorial sea of the United Kingdom.

[Value Added Tax Act 1994, s 96 as amended by the Civil Evidence Act 1995, Schs 1 and 2, SI 1995/1510, SI 1996/739, the Finance Act 1997, s 35, the Finance Act 1998, s 19, SI 2001/1149, the Finance Act 2003, s 20 and the Abolition of Feudal Tenure etc (Scotland) Act 2000, Schs 12 and 13.]

Supplementary provisions

8–30090 **97. Orders, rules and regulations.** (1) Any order made by the Treasury or the Lord Chancellor under this Act and any regulations or rules under this Act shall be made by statutory instrument.

[Value Added Tax Act 1994, s 97, amended by the Finance Act 1995, s 21, the Finance Act 1996, s 33 and Sch 41 and the Finance Act 2004, ss 19, 20 and 22—summarised.]

8–30091 **101. Commencement and extent.** (1) This Act shall come into force on 1st September 1994 and Part I shall have effect in relation to the charge to VAT on supplies, acquisitions and importations in prescribed accounting periods ending on or after that date.

(2) Without prejudice to section 16 of the Interpretation Act 1978 (continuation of proceedings under repealed enactments) except in so far as it enables proceedings to be continued under repealed enactments, section 72 shall have effect on the commencement of this Act to the exclusion of section 39 of the 1983 Act.

(3) This Act extends to Northern Ireland.

(4) Paragraph 23 of Schedule 13 and paragraph 7 of Schedule 14 shall extend to the Isle of Man but no other provision of this Act shall extend there.

8–30092 **102. Short title.** This Act may be cited as the Value Added Tax Act 1994.

Section 58

SCHEDULE 11

ADMINISTRATION, COLLECTION AND ENFORCEMENT

(As amended by the Criminal Procedure (Consequential Provisions) (Scotland) Act 1995, Sch 4, the Finance Act 1996, s 38 and Sch 3, the Civil Evidence Act 1995, Sch 2, SI 1997/2983, the Finance Act 1999, the Youth Justice and Criminal Evidence Act 1999, Sch 6, the Finance Act 2002, s 24, the Criminal Justice and Police Act 2001, Sch 2 and the Commissioners for Revenue and Customs 2005, Sch 4.)

Power to require security and production of evidence

8–30093 **4.** (1) The Commissioners may, as a condition of allowing or repaying input tax[1] to any person, require the production of such evidence relating to VAT as they may specify.

(1A) If they think it necessary for the protection of the revenue, the Commissioners may require, as a condition of making any VAT credit, the giving of such security for the amount of the payment as appears to them appropriate.

(2) If they think it necessary for the protection of the revenue, the Commissioners may require a taxable person, as a condition of his supplying or being supplied with goods or services under a taxable supply, to give security, or further security, for the payment of any VAT that is or may become due from—

(*a*) the taxable person, or

(*b*) any person by or to whom relevant goods or services are supplied.

(3) In sub-paragraph (2) above "relevant goods or services" means goods or services supplied by or to the taxable person.

(4) Security under sub-paragraph (2) above shall be of such amount, and shall be given in such manner, as the Commissioners may determine.

(5) The powers conferred on the Commissioners by sub-paragraph (2) above are without prejudice to their powers under section 48(7).

1. Input tax is defined by s 24. It is tax already charged on goods or services acquired as part of his business (including goods imported); when he furnishes his return, and accounts for the tax due on supplies by him of goods or services, he is entitled to take credit for the input tax on supplies of goods or services made to him during the period to which the return relates. If input tax exceeds output tax, the Commissioners will repay the excess.

Section 24 also enables the Treasury by order to make provisions for exceptions to the entitlement to claim input tax, and this power has been extensively exercised.

Duty to keep records

8–30094 **6.** (1) Every taxable person shall keep such records as the Commissioners may by regulations require, and every person who, at a time when he is not a taxable person, acquires in the United Kingdom from another member State any goods which are subject to a duty of excise or consist in a new means of transport shall keep such records with respect to the acquisition (if it is a taxable acquisition and is not in pursuance of a taxable supply) as the Commissioners may so require.

(2) Regulations under sub-paragraph (1) above may make different provision for different cases and may be framed by reference to such records as may be specified in any notice published by the Commissioners in pursuance of the regulations and not withdrawn by a further notice.

(3) The Commissioners may require any records kept in pursuance of this paragraph to be preserved for such period not exceeding 6 years as they may require.

(4) The duty under this paragraph to preserve records may be discharged by the preservation of the information contained therein by such means as the Commissioners may approve; and where that information is so preserved a copy of any document forming part of the records shall, subject to the following provisions of this paragraph, be admissible in evidence in any proceedings, whether civil or criminal, to the same extent as the records themselves.

(5) The Commissioners may, as a condition of approving under sub-paragraph (4) above any means of preserving information contained in any records, impose such reasonable requirements as appear to them necessary for securing that the information will be as readily available to them as if the records themselves had been preserved.

(6) A statement contained in a document produced by a computer shall not by virtue of sub-paragraph (4) above be admissible in evidence—

(*a*) *(Repealed)*;

(*b*) in criminal proceedings in England and Wales except in accordance with Part II of the Criminal Justice Act 1988;

(*c*) *(Repealed)*;

(*d*) *Northern Ireland.*

This sub-paragraph does not apply in relation to Scotland.

Furnishing of information and production of documents

8–30095 **7.** (1) The Commissioners may be regulations make provision for requiring taxable persons to notify to the Commissioners such particulars of changes in circumstances relating to those persons or any business[1] carried on by them as appear to the Commissioners required for the purpose of keeping the register kept under this Act up to date.

(2) Every person who is concerned (in whatever capacity) in the supply of goods or services in the course or furtherance of a business or to whom such a supply is made, every person who is concerned (in whatever capacity) in the acquisition of goods from another member State and every person who is concerned (in whatever capacity) in the importation of goods from a place outside the member States in the course or furtherance of a business shall—

(*a*) furnish to the Commissioners, within such time and in such form as they may reasonably require, such information[2] relating[3] to the goods or services or to the supply, acquisition or importation as the Commissioners may reasonably specify; and

(*b*) upon demand made by an authorised person, produce or cause to be produced for inspection by that person—

(i) at the principal place of business of the person upon whom the demand is made or at such other place as the authorised person may reasonably require, and

(ii) at such time as the authorised person may reasonably require,

any documents relating to the goods or services or to the supply, acquisition or importation.

(3) Where, by virtue of sub-paragraph (2) above, an authorised person has power to require the production of any documents from any such person as is referred to in that sub-paragraph, he shall have the like power to require production of the documents concerned from any other person who appears to the authorised person to be in possession of them; but where any such other person claims a lien on any document produced by him, the production shall be without prejudice to the lien.

(4) For the purposes of this paragraph, the documents relating to the supply of goods or services, to the acquisition of goods from another member State or to the importation of goods from a place outside the member States shall be taken to include any profit and loss account and balance sheet relating to the business in the course of which the goods or services are supplied or the goods are imported or (in the case of an acquisition from another member State) relating to any business or other activities of the person by whom the goods are acquired.

(5) An authorised person may take copies of, or make extracts from, any document produced under sub-paragraph (2) or (3) above.

(6) If it appears to him to be necessary to do so, an authorised person may, at a reasonable time and for a reasonable period, remove any document produced under sub-paragraph (2) or (3) above and shall, on request, provide a receipt for any document so removed; and where a lien is claimed on a document produced under sub-paragraph (3) above the removal of the document under this sub-paragraph shall not be regarded as breaking the lien.

(7) Where a document removed by an authorised person under sub-paragraph (6) above is reasonably required for the proper conduct of a business he shall, as soon as practicable, provide a copy of the document, free of charge, to the person by whom it was produced or caused to be produced.

(8) Where any documents removed under the powers conferred by this paragraph are lost or damaged the Commissioners shall be liable to compensate their owner for any expenses reasonably incurred by him in replacing or repairing the documents.

(9) For the purposes of this paragraph a person to whom has been assigned a right to receive the whole or any part of the consideration for a supply of goods or services shall be treated as a person concerned in the supply.

1. See s 94, ante.

2. "If a demand for information is made in the proper manner the trader is bound to answer the demand within the time and in the form required whether or not the answer may tend to incriminate him", per Lord REID in *Customs and Excise Comrs v Harz* [1967] 1 AC 760 at 816, [1967] 1 All ER 177 at 181, HL (a case relating to purchase tax); compare *Customs and Excise Comrs v Ingram* [1948] 1 All ER 927 at 929 (also relating to purchase tax). "It is quite a commonplace of legislation designed to protect the revenue of the Crown . . . to put an onus on (the subject) or to oblige him to do certain things which may have the effect of incriminating him", per Lord GODDARD CJ.

3. "As a matter of ordinary English it is not easy to see why this phrase should not mean and include information not only as to the character of the goods but also what has happened to them", per EVERSHED LJ, in *Customs and Excise Comrs v Ingram* [1949] 2 KB 103, [1949] 1 All ER 896 at 900.

Power to take samples

8–30096 **8.** (1) An authorised person, if it appears to him necessary for the protection of the revenue against mistake or fraud, may at any time take, from the goods in the possession of any person who supplies goods or acquires goods from another member State, or in the possession of a fiscal warehousekeeper, such samples as the authorised person may require with a view to determining how the goods or the materials of which they are made ought to be or to have been treated for the purposes of VAT.

(2) Any sample taken under this paragraph shall be disposed of and accounted for in such manner as the Commissioners may direct.

(3) Where a sample is taken under this paragraph from the goods in any person's possession and is not returned to him within a reasonable time and in good condition the Commissioners shall pay him by way of compensation a sum equal to the cost of the sample to him or such larger sum as they may determine.

Power to require opening of gaming machines

8–30097 **9.** An authorised person may at any reasonable time require a person making such a supply as is referred to in section 23(1) or any person acting on his behalf—

(*a*) to open any gaming machine, within the meaning of that section; and

(*b*) to carry out any other operation which may be necessary to enable the authorised person to ascertain the amount which, in accordance with subsection (2) of that section, is to be taken as the value of supplies made in the circumstances mentioned in subsection (1) of that section in any period.

Entry and search of premises and persons

8–30098 **10.** (1) For the purpose of exercising any powers under this Act an authorised person[1] may at any reasonable time enter premises used in connection with the carrying on of a business[2].

(2) Where an authorised person has reasonable cause to believe that any premises are used in connection with the supply of goods under taxable supplies or with the acquisition of goods under taxable acquisitions from other member States and that goods to be so supplied or acquired are on those premises, or that any premises are used as a fiscal warehouse, he may at any reasonable time enter and inspect those premises and inspect any goods found on them.

(3) If a justice of the peace or in Scotland a justice (within the meaning of section 308 of the Criminal Procedure (Scotland) Act 1995) is satisfied on information on oath that there is reasonable ground for suspecting that a fraud offence which appears to be of a serious nature is being, has been or is about to be committed on any premises or that evidence of the commission of such an offence is to be found there[3], he may issue a warrant in writing authorising, subject to sub-paragraphs (5) and (6) below, any authorised person to enter those premises, if necessary by force, at any time[4] within one month from the time of the issue of the warrant and search them; and any person who enters the premises under the authority of the warrant may—

(*a*) take with him such other persons as appear to him to be necessary;

(*b*) seize[5] and remove any documents or other things whatsoever found on the premises which he has reasonable cause to believe may be required as evidence for the purposes of proceedings in respect of a fraud offence which appears to him to be of a serious nature; and

(*c*) search or cause to be searched any person found on the premises whom he has reasonable cause to believe to be in possession of any such documents or other things;

but no woman or girl shall be searched except by a woman.

(4) In sub-paragraph (3) above "a fraud offence" means an offence under any provision of section 72(1) to (8).

(5) The powers conferred by a warrant under this paragraph shall not be exercisable—

(*a*) by more than such number of authorised persons as may be specified in the warrant; nor

(*b*) outside such times of day as may be so specified; nor

(*c*) if the warrant so provides, otherwise than in the presence of a constable in uniform.

(6) An authorised person seeking to exercise the powers conferred by a warrant under this paragraph or, if there is more than one such authorised person, that one of them who is in charge of the search shall provide a copy of the warrant endorsed with his name as follows—

(*a*) if the occupier of the premises concerned is present at the time the search is to begin, the copy shall be supplied to the occupier;

(*b*) if at that time the occupier is not present but a person who appears to the authorised person to be in charge of the premises is present, the copy shall be supplied to that person; and

(*c*) if neither paragraph (*a*) nor paragraph (*b*) above applies, the copy shall be left in a prominent place on the premises.

---

1. "Authorised person" means any person acting under the authority of the Comrs of Customs and Excise (s 96) ante.
2. See s 94, ante.
3. The use of the word 'or' is not disjunctive and does not mean that the justice has to rely one access condition rather than the other (*R (Paul da Costa & Co (a firm) v Thames Magistrates' Court* [2002] EWHC 40 (Admin),[2002] Crim LR 504 and see the commentary thereto for the desirability of questioning the applicant about the operational detail of the proposed execution of the warrant).
4. This includes a Sunday (Magistrates' Courts Act 1980, s 125).
5. An officer of Customs and Excise has no power to seize an item which he has reasonable grounds for believing to be subject to legal privilege and, therefore, there can be no authorisation for a search for items subject to legal privilege. If, however, in the course of a legitimate search of a solicitor's office, particularly where the solicitor himself is alleged to be complicit in the offence being investigated, the officers inadvertently seize material which includes items subject to legal privilege, the seizure of those items will not render the execution of the warrant unlawful (*R v Customs and Excise Comrs, ex p Popely* [2000] Crim LR 388, DC).

Order for access to recorded information etc

8–30099 **11.** (1) Where, on an application[1] by an authorised person, a justice of the peace or, in Scotland, a justice (within the meaning of section 308 of the Criminal Procedure (Scotland) Act 1995) is satisfied[2] that there are reasonable grounds for believing—

(*a*) that an offence in connection with VAT is being, has been or is about to be committed, and

(*b*) that any recorded information (including any document of any nature whatsoever) which may be required as evidence for the purpose of any proceedings in respect of such an offence is in the possession of any person,

he may make an order[3] under this paragraph.

(2) An order under this paragraph is an order that the person who appears to the justice to be in possession of the recorded information to which the application relates shall—

(*a*) give an authorised person access to it, and

(*b*) permit an authorised person to remove and take away any of it which he reasonably considers necessary,

not later than the end of the period of 7 days beginning on the date of the order or the end of such longer period as the order may specify.

(3) The reference in sub-paragraph (2)(*a*) above to giving an authorised person access to the recorded information to which the application relates includes a reference to permitting the authorised person to take copies of it or to make extracts from it.

(4) Where the recorded information consists of information stored in any electronic form, an order under this paragraph shall have effect as an order to produce the information in a form in which it is visible and legible or

from which it can readily be produced in a visible and legible form and, if the authorised person wishes to remove it, in a form in which it can be removed.

(5) This paragraph is without prejudice to paragraphs 7 and 10 above.

---

1. In certain circumstances an *ex parte* application will be justified, even when a charge has been made. However, it is normally desirable that the application should be made on notice, even where a charge has not been made. In appropriate circumstances, instead of proceeding under para 11, resort should be had to the procedure under the Bankers' Books Evidence Act 1879 (in PART II: EVIDENCE, ante); see *R v Epsom Justices, ex p Bell* [1989] STC 169, [1988] Crim LR 684.

When an application is made for an order *ex parte*, the justice must consider whether it is appropriate to proceed in that way, bearing in mind that the balance is in favour of proceeding *inter partes* unless there is a real reason to believe something of value to the investigation may be lost. If it is decided to proceed *inter partes* it will normally be appropriate to give notice not only to those from whom access is sought but to others likely to be directly affected by the order, such as suspects (*R v City of London Magistrates' Court, ex p Asif* [1996] Crim LR 725).

2. The justice himself must be satisfied that there are reasonable grounds and not merely rely on a statement of belief by a customs officer. Any order made ought not to be without limit of subject-matter or time. Where an offence has been charged, the application should specify the grounds upon which it is believed that such an offence has been committed (*R v Epsom Justices, ex p Bell* [1989] STC 169, [1988] Crim LR 684, DC).

3. Where following an *inter partes* application an access order under paragraph 11 is made, the justice has no jurisdiction to make an order for costs in favour of the person against whom the order is made under s 19 of the Prosecution of Offences Act 1985 or regulation 3 of the Costs in Criminal Cases (General) Regulations 1986 because such application does not constitute criminal proceedings (*Customs and Excise Comrs v City of London Magistrates' Court* [2000] 1 WLR 2020, [2000] 2 Cr App Rep 348, [2000] Crim LR 841, DC).

Procedure where documents etc are removed

8–30100 **12.** (1) An authorised person who removes anything in the exercise of a power conferred by or under paragraph 10 or 11 above shall, if so requested by a person showing himself—

(*a*) to be the occupier of premises from which it was removed, or
(*b*) to have had custody or control of it immediately before the removal,

provide that person with a record of what he removed.

(2) The authorised person shall provide the record within a reasonable time from the making of the request for it.

(3) Subject to sub-paragraph (7) below, if a request for permission to be granted access to anything which—

(*a*) has been removed by an authorised person, and
(*b*) is retained by the Commissioners for the purposes of investigating an offence,

is made to the officer in overall charge of the investigation by a person who had custody or control of the thing immediately before it was so removed or by someone acting on behalf of such a person, the officer shall allow the person who made the request access to it under the supervision of an authorised person.

(4) Subject to sub-paragraph (7) below, if a request for a photograph or copy of any such thing is made to the officer in overall charge of the investigation by a person who had custody or control of the thing immediately before it was so removed, or by someone acting on behalf of such a person, the officer shall—

(*a*) allow the person who made the request access to it under the supervision of an authorised person for the purpose of photographing it or copying it, or
(*b*) photograph or copy it, or cause it to be photographed or copied.

(5) Where anything is photographed or copied under sub-paragraph (4)(*b*) above the photograph or copy shall be supplied to the person who made the request.

(6) The photograph or copy shall be supplied within a reasonable time from the making of the request.

(7) There is no duty under this paragraph to grant access to, or to supply a photograph or copy of, anything if the officer in overall charge of the investigation for the purposes of which it was removed has reasonable grounds for believing that to do so would prejudice—

(*a*) that investigation;
(*b*) the investigation of an offence other than the offence for the purposes of the investigation of which the thing was removed; or
(*c*) any criminal proceedings which may be brought as a result of—

(i) the investigation of which he is in charge, or
(ii) any such investigation as is mentioned in paragraph (*b*) above.

(8) Any reference in this paragraph to the officer in overall charge of the investigation is a reference to the person whose name and address are endorsed on the warrant or order concerned as being the officer so in charge.

8–30101 **13.** (1) Where, on an application made as mentioned in sub-paragraph (2) below, the appropriate judicial authority is satisfied that a person has failed to comply with a requirement imposed by paragraph 12 above, the authority may order that person to comply with the requirement within such time and in such manner as may be specified in the order.

(2) An application under sub-paragraph (1) above shall be made—

(*a*) in the case of a failure to comply with any of the requirements imposed by paragraph 12(1) and (2) above, by the occupier of the premises from which the thing in question was removed or by the person who had custody or control of it immediately before it was so removed, and
(*b*) in any other case, by the person who had such custody or control.

(3) In this paragraph "the appropriate judicial authority" means—

(*a*) in England and Wales, a magistrates' court;
(*b*) in Scotland, the sheriff; and
(*c*) in Northern Ireland, a court of summary jurisdiction.

(4) In England and Wales and Northern Ireland, an application for an order under this paragraph shall be made by way of complaint; and sections 21 and 42(2) of the Interpretation Act (Northern Ireland) 1954 shall apply as if any reference in those provisions to any enactment included a reference to this paragraph.

Evidence by certificate, etc

8–30102 **14.** (1) A certificate of the Commissioners—

(*a*) that a person was or was not, at any date, registered under this Act; or
(*b*) that any return required by or under this Act has not been made or had not been made at any date; or
(*c*) that any statement or notification required to be submitted or given to the Commissioners in accordance with any regulations under paragraph 2(3) or (4) above has not been submitted or given or had not been submitted or given at any date; or
(*d*) that any VAT shown as due in any return or assessment made in pursuance of this Act has not been paid;

shall be sufficient evidence of that fact until the contrary is proved.

(2) A photograph of any document furnished to the Commissioners for the purposes of this Act and certified by them to be such a photograph shall be admissible in any proceedings, whether civil or criminal, to the same extent as the document itself.

(3) Any document purporting to be a certificate under sub-paragraph (1) or (2) above shall be deemed to be such a certificate until the contrary is proved.

Commissioners for Revenue and Customs Act 2005

(2005 c 11)

Information

8–30102A **17. Use of information.** (1) Information acquired by the Revenue and Customs in connection with a function may be used by them in connection with any other function.

(2) Subsection (1) is subject to any provision which restricts or prohibits the use of information and which is contained in—

(*a*) this Act,
(*b*) any other enactment, or
(*c*) an international or other agreement to which the United Kingdom or Her Majesty's Government is party.

(3) In subsection (1) "the Revenue and Customs" means—

(*a*) the Commissioners,
(*b*) an officer of Revenue and Customs,
(*c*) a person acting on behalf of the Commissioners or an officer of Revenue and Customs,
(*d*) a committee established by the Commissioners,
(*e*) a member of a committee established by the Commissioners,
(*f*) the Commissioners of Inland Revenue (or any committee or staff of theirs or anyone acting on their behalf),
(*g*) the Commissioners of Customs and Excise (or any committee or staff of theirs or anyone acting on their behalf), and
(*h*) a person specified in section 6(2) or 7(3).

(4) In subsection (1) "function" means a function of any of the persons listed in subsection (3).

(5) In subsection (2) the reference to an enactment does not include—

(*a*) an Act of the Scottish Parliament or an instrument made under such an Act, or
(*b*) an Act of the Northern Ireland Assembly or an instrument made under such an Act.

(6) Part 2 of Schedule 2 (which makes provision about the supply and other use of information in specified circumstances) shall have effect.

[Commissioners for Revenue and Customs Act 2005, s 17.]

8–30102B **18. Confidentiality.** (1) Revenue and Customs officials may not disclose information which is held by the Revenue and Customs in connection with a function of the Revenue and Customs.

(2) But subsection (1) does not apply to a disclosure—

(*a*) which—

(i) is made for the purposes of a function of the Revenue and Customs, and
(ii) does not contravene any restriction imposed by the Commissioners,

(*b*) which is made in accordance with section 20 or 21,

(*c*) which is made for the purposes of civil proceedings (whether or not within the United Kingdom) relating to a matter in respect of which the Revenue and Customs have functions,

(*d*) which is made for the purposes of a criminal investigation or criminal proceedings (whether or not within the United Kingdom) relating to a matter in respect of which the Revenue and Customs have functions,

(*e*) which is made in pursuance of an order of a court,

(*f*) which is made to Her Majesty's Inspectors of Constabulary, the Scottish inspectors or the Northern Ireland inspectors for the purpose of an inspection by virtue of section 27,

(*g*) which is made to the Independent Police Complaints Commission, or a person acting on its behalf, for the purpose of the exercise of a function by virtue of section 28, or

(*h*) which is made with the consent of each person to whom the information relates.

(3) Subsection (1) is subject to any other enactment permitting disclosure.

(4) In this section—

(*a*) a reference to Revenue and Customs officials is a reference to any person who is or was—

(i) a Commissioner,
(ii) an officer of Revenue and Customs,
(iii) a person acting on behalf of the Commissioners or an officer of Revenue and Customs, or
(iv) a member of a committee established by the Commissioners,

(*b*) a reference to the Revenue and Customs has the same meaning as in section 17,

(*c*) a reference to a function of the Revenue and Customs is a reference to a function of—

(i) the Commissioners, or
(ii) an officer of Revenue and Customs,

(*d*) a reference to the Scottish inspectors or the Northern Ireland inspectors has the same meaning as in section 27, and

(*e*) a reference to an enactment does not include—

(i) an Act of the Scottish Parliament or an instrument made under such an Act, or
(ii) an Act of the Northern Ireland Assembly or an instrument made under such an Act.

[Commissioners for Revenue and Customs Act 2005, s 18.]

8–30102C 19. Wrongful disclosure. (1) A person commits an offence if he contravenes section 18(1) or 20(9) by disclosing revenue and customs information relating to a person whose identity—

(*a*) is specified in the disclosure, or
(*b*) can be deduced from it.

(2) In subsection (1) "revenue and customs information relating to a person" means information about, acquired as a result of, or held in connection with the exercise of a function of the Revenue and Customs (within the meaning given by section 18(4)(*c*)) in respect of the person; but it does not include information about internal administrative arrangements of Her Majesty's Revenue and Customs (whether relating to Commissioners, officers or others).

(3) It is a defence for a person charged with an offence under this section of disclosing information to prove that he reasonably believed—

(*a*) that the disclosure was lawful, or
(*b*) that the information had already and lawfully been made available to the public.

(4) A person guilty of an offence under this section shall be liable—

(*a*) on conviction on indictment, to imprisonment for a term not exceeding two years, to a fine or to both, or

(*b*) on summary conviction, to imprisonment for a term not exceeding 12 months, to a fine not exceeding the statutory maximum or to both.

(5) A prosecution for an offence under this section may be instituted in England and Wales only—

(*a*) by the Director of Revenue and Customs Prosecutions, or
(*b*) with the consent of the Director of Public Prosecutions.

(6) A prosecution for an offence under this section may be instituted in Northern Ireland only—

(*a*) by the Commissioners, or
(*b*) with the consent of the Director of Public Prosecutions for Northern Ireland.

(7) In the application of this section to Scotland or Northern Ireland the reference in subsection (4)(*b*) to 12 months shall be taken as a reference to six months.

(8) This section is without prejudice to the pursuit of any remedy or the taking of any action in relation to a contravention of section 18(1) or 20(9) (whether or not this section applies to the contravention).

[Commissioners for Revenue and Customs Act 2005, s 19.]

8–30102D 20. Public interest disclosure. (1) Disclosure is in accordance with this section (as mentioned in section 18(2)(*b*)) if—

(*a*) it is made on the instructions of the Commissioners (which may be general or specific),
(*b*) it is of a kind—

(i) to which any of subsections (2) to (7) applies, or
(ii) specified in regulations made by the Treasury, and

(*c*) the Commissioners are satisfied that it is in the public interest.

(2) This subsection applies to a disclosure made—

(*a*) to a person exercising public functions (whether or not within the United Kingdom),
(*b*) for the purposes of the prevention or detection of crime, and
(*c*) in order to comply with an obligation of the United Kingdom, or Her Majesty's Government, under an international or other agreement relating to the movement of persons, goods or services.

(3) This subsection applies to a disclosure if—

(*a*) it is made to a body which has responsibility for the regulation of a profession,
(*b*) it relates to misconduct on the part of a member of the profession, and
(*c*) the misconduct relates to a function of the Revenue and Customs.

(4) This subsection applies to a disclosure if—

(*a*) it is made to a constable, and
(*b*) either—

(i) the constable is exercising functions which relate to the movement of persons or goods into or out of the United Kingdom, or
(ii) the disclosure is made for the purposes of the prevention or detection of crime.

(5) This subsection applies to a disclosure if it is made—

(*a*) to the National Criminal Intelligence Service, and
(*b*) for a purpose connected with its functions under section 2(2) of the Police Act 1997 (c 50) (criminal intelligence).

(6) This subsection applies to a disclosure if it is made—

(*a*) to a person exercising public functions in relation to public safety or public health, and
(*b*) for the purposes of those functions.

(7) This subsection applies to a disclosure if it—

(*a*) is made to the Police Information Technology Organisation for the purpose of enabling information to be entered in a computerised database, and
(*b*) relates to—

(i) a person suspected of an offence,
(ii) a person arrested for an offence,
(iii) the results of an investigation, or
(iv) anything seized.

(8) Regulations under subsection (1)(*b*)(ii)—

(*a*) may specify a kind of disclosure only if the Treasury are satisfied that it relates to—

(i) national security,
(ii) public safety,
(iii) public health, or
(iv) the prevention or detection of crime;

(*b*) may make provision limiting or restricting the disclosures that may be made in reliance on the regulations; and that provision may, in particular, operate by reference to—

(i) the nature of information,
(ii) the person or class of person to whom the disclosure is made,
(iii) the person or class of person by whom the disclosure is made,
(iv) any other factor, or
(v) a combination of factors;

(*c*) shall be made by statutory instrument;
(*d*) may not be made unless a draft has been laid before and approved by resolution of each House of Parliament.

(9) Information disclosed in reliance on this section may not be further disclosed without the consent of the Commissioners (which may be general or specific); (but the Commissioners shall be taken to have consented to further disclosure by use of the computerised database of information disclosed by virtue of subsection (7)).

[Commissioners for Revenue and Customs Act 2005, s 20.]

8–30102E 21. Disclosure to prosecuting authority. (1) Disclosure is in accordance with this section (as mentioned in section 18(2)(*b*)) if made—

(*a*) to a prosecuting authority, and
(*b*) for the purpose of enabling the authority—

(i) to consider whether to institute criminal proceedings in respect of a matter considered in the course of an investigation conducted by or on behalf of Her Majesty's Revenue and Customs, or
(ii) to give advice in connection with a criminal investigation (within the meaning of section 35(5)(*b*)) or criminal proceedings.

(2) In subsection (1) "prosecuting authority" means—

(*a*) the Director of Revenue and Customs Prosecutions,
(*b*) in Scotland, the Lord Advocate or a procurator fiscal, and
(*c*) in Northern Ireland, the Director of Public Prosecutions for Northern Ireland.

(3) Information disclosed to a prosecuting authority in accordance with this section may not be further disclosed except—

(*a*) for a purpose connected with the exercise of the prosecuting authority's functions, or
(*b*) with the consent of the Commissioners (which may be general or specific).

(4) A person commits an offence if he contravenes subsection (3).

(5) It is a defence for a person charged with an offence under this section to prove that he reasonably believed—

(*a*) that the disclosure was lawful, or
(*b*) that the information had already and lawfully been made available to the public.

(6) A person guilty of an offence under this section shall be liable—

(*a*) on conviction on indictment, to imprisonment for a term not exceeding two years, to a fine or to both, or
(*b*) on summary conviction, to imprisonment for a term not exceeding 12 months, to a fine not exceeding the statutory maximum or to both[1].

(7) A prosecution for an offence under this section may be instituted in England and Wales only—

(*a*) by the Director of Revenue and Customs Prosecutions, or
(*b*) with the consent of the Director of Public Prosecutions.

(8) A prosecution for an offence under this section may be instituted in Northern Ireland only—

(*a*) by the Commissioners, or
(*b*) with the consent of the Director of Public Prosecutions for Northern Ireland.

(9) In the application of this section to Scotland or Northern Ireland the reference in subsection (6)(*b*) to 12 months shall be taken as a reference to six months.
[Commissioners for Revenue and Customs Act 2005, s 21.]

---

1. For procedure in respect of an offence triable either way, see the Magistrates' Courts Act 1908, ss 17A–21, in PART I: MAGISTRATES' COURTS, PROCEDURE, ante.

8–30102F 22. Data protection, &c. Nothing in sections 17 to 21 authorises the making of a disclosure which—

(*a*) contravenes the Data Protection Act 1998 (c 29), or
(*b*) is prohibited by Part 1 of the Regulation of Investigatory Powers Act 2000 (c 23).
[Commissioners for Revenue and Customs Act 2005, s 22.]

8–30102G 23. Freedom of information. (1) Revenue and customs information relating to a person, the disclosure of which is prohibited by section 18(1), is exempt information by virtue of section 44(1)(*a*) of the Freedom of Information Act 2000 (c 36) (prohibitions on disclosure) if its disclosure—

(*a*) would specify the identity of the person to whom the information relates, or
(*b*) would enable the identity of such a person to be deduced.

(2) Except as specified in subsection (1), information the disclosure of which is prohibited by section 18(1) is not exempt information for the purposes of section 44(1)(*a*) of the Freedom of Information Act 2000.

(3) In subsection (1) "revenue and customs information relating to a person" has the same meaning as in section 19.
[Commissioners for Revenue and Customs Act 2005, s 23.]

Proceedings

8–30102H 24. Evidence. (1) A document that purports to have been issued or signed by or with the authority of the Commissioners—

(*a*) shall be treated as having been so issued or signed unless the contrary is proved, and
(*b*) shall be admissible in any legal proceedings.

(2) A document that purports to have been issued by the Commissioners and which certifies any of the matters specified in subsection (3) shall (in addition to the matters provided for by subsection (1)(*a*) and (*b*)) be treated as accurate unless the contrary is proved.

(3) The matters mentioned in subsection (2) are—

(*a*) that a specified person was appointed as a commissioner on a specified date,
(*b*) that a specified person was appointed as an officer of Revenue and Customs on a specified date,
(*c*) that at a specified time or for a specified purpose (or both) a function was delegated to a specified Commissioner,
(*d*) that at a specified time or for a specified purpose (or both) a function was delegated to a specified committee, and
(*e*) that at a specified time or for a specified purpose (or both) a function was delegated to another specified person.

(4) A photographic or other copy of a document acquired by the Commissioners shall, if certified by them to be an accurate copy, be admissible in any legal proceedings to the same extent as the document itself.

(5) Section 2 of the Documentary Evidence Act 1868 (c 37) (proof of documents) shall apply to a Revenue and Customs document as it applies in relation to the documents mentioned in that section.

(6) In the application of that section to a Revenue and Customs document the Schedule to that Act shall be treated as if—

(*a*) the first column contained a reference to the Commissioners, and
(*b*) the second column contained a reference to a Commissioner or a person acting on his authority.

(7) In this section—

(*a*) "Revenue and Customs document" means a document issued by or on behalf of the Commissioners, and
(*b*) a reference to the Commissioners includes a reference to the Commissioners of Inland Revenue and to the Commissioners of Customs and Excise.

[Commissioners for Revenue and Customs Act 2005, s 24.]

8–30102I 25. Conduct of civil proceedings. (1) An officer of Revenue and Customs or a person authorised by the Commissioners may conduct civil proceedings, in a magistrates' court or in the sheriff court, relating to a function of the Revenue and Customs.

(2) A solicitor member of the Commissioners' staff may act as a solicitor in connection with civil proceedings relating to a function of the Revenue and Customs.

(3) A legally qualified member of the Commissioners' staff may conduct county court proceedings relating to a matter specified in section 7.

(4) A court shall grant any rights of audience necessary to enable a person to exercise a function under this section.

(5) In this section—

(*a*) a reference to a function of the Revenue and Customs is a reference to a function of—
  (i) the Commissioners, or
  (ii) an officer of Revenue and Customs,
(*b*) a reference to civil proceedings is a reference to proceedings other than proceedings in respect of an offence,
(*c*) a reference to county court proceedings is a reference to civil proceedings in a county court,
(*d*) the reference to a legally qualified member of the Commissioners' staff is a reference to a member of staff who has been admitted as a solicitor, or called to the Bar, whether or not he holds a practising certificate, and
(*e*) the reference to a solicitor member of the Commissioners' staff—
  (i) except in relation to Scotland, is a reference to a member of staff who has been admitted as a solicitor, whether or not he holds a practising certificate,
  (ii) in relation to Scotland, is a reference to a member of staff who has been admitted as a solicitor and who holds a practising certificate.

[Commissioners for Revenue and Customs Act 2005, s 25.]

8–30102J **26. Rewards.** The Commissioners may pay a reward to a person in return for a service which relates to a function of—

(*a*) the Commissioners, or
(*b*) an officer of Revenue and Customs.

[Commissioners for Revenue and Customs Act 2005, s 26.]

8–30102K

Inspection and complaints

27. Inspection. (1) The Treasury may make regulations conferring functions on Her Majesty's Inspectors of Constabulary, the Scottish inspectors or the Northern Ireland inspectors in relation to—

(*a*) the Commissioners for Her Majesty's Revenue and Customs, and
(*b*) officers of Revenue and Customs.

(2) Regulations under subsection (1)—

(*a*) may—

(i) in relation to Her Majesty's Inspectors of Constabulary, apply (with or without modification) or make provision similar to any provision of sections 54 to 56 of the Police Act 1996 (c 16) (inspection);
(ii) in relation to the Scottish inspectors, apply (with or without modification) or make provision similar to any provision of section 33 or 34 of the Police (Scotland) Act 1967 (c 77) (inspection);
(iii) in relation to the Northern Ireland inspectors, apply (with or without modification) or make provision similar to any provision of section 41 or 42 of the Police (Northern Ireland) Act 1998 (c 32) (inspection);

(*b*) may enable a Minister of the Crown or the Commissioners to require an inspection to be carried out;
(*c*) shall provide for a report of an inspection to be made and, subject to any exceptions required or permitted by the regulations, published;
(*d*) shall provide for an annual report by Her Majesty's Inspectors of Constabulary;
(*e*) may make provision for payment by the Commissioners to or in respect of Her Majesty's Inspectors of Constabulary, the Scottish inspectors or the Northern Ireland inspectors.

(3) An inspection carried out by virtue of this section may not address a matter of a kind which the Comptroller and Auditor General may examine under section 6 of the National Audit Act 1983 (c 44).

(4) An inspection carried out by virtue of this section shall be carried out jointly by Her Majesty's Inspectors of Constabulary and the Scottish inspectors—

(*a*) if it is carried out wholly in Scotland, or
(*b*) in a case where it is carried out partly in Scotland, to the extent that it is carried out there.

(5) Regulations under subsection (1)—

(*a*) shall be made by statutory instrument, and
(*b*) shall be subject to annulment in pursuance of a resolution of either House of Parliament.

(6) In this section—

(*a*) "the Scottish inspectors" means the inspectors of constabulary appointed under section 33(1) of the Police (Scotland) Act 1967, and
(*b*) "the Northern Ireland inspectors" means the inspectors of constabulary appointed under section 41(1) of the Police (Northern Ireland) Act 1998.

[Commissioners for Revenue and Customs Act 2005, s 27.]

8–30102L **28. Complaints and misconduct: England and Wales.** (1) The Treasury may make regulations conferring functions on the Independent Police Complaints Commission in relation to—

(*a*) the Commissioners for Her Majesty's Revenue and Customs, and
(*b*) officers of Revenue and Customs.

(2) Regulations under subsection (1)—

(*a*) may apply (with or without modification) or make provision similar to any provision of or made under Part 2 of the Police Reform Act 2002 (c 30) (complaints);
(*b*) may confer on the Independent Police Complaints Commission, or on a person acting on its behalf, a power of a kind conferred by this Act or another enactment on an officer of Revenue and Customs;
(*c*) may make provision for payment by the Commissioners to or in respect of the Independent Police Complaints Commission.

(3) The Independent Police Complaints Commission and the Parliamentary Commissioner for Administration may disclose information to each other for the purposes of the exercise of a function—

(*a*) by virtue of this section, or
(*b*) under the Parliamentary Commissioner Act 1967 (c 13).

(4) The Independent Police Complaints Commission and the Parliamentary Commissioner for Administration may jointly investigate a matter in relation to which—

(*a*) the Independent Police Complaints Commission has functions by virtue of this section, and
(*b*) the Parliamentary Commissioner for Administration has functions by virtue of the Parliamentary Commissioner Act 1967.

(5) Regulations under subsection (1)—

(*a*) shall be made by statutory instrument, and
(*b*) shall be subject to annulment in pursuance of a resolution of either House of Parliament.

(6) Regulations under subsection (1) shall relate to the Commissioners or officers of Revenue and Customs only in so far as their functions are exercised in or in relation to England and Wales.
[Commissioners for Revenue and Customs Act 2005, s 28.]

8–30102M 29. Confidentiality, &c. (1) Where Her Majesty's Inspectors of Constabulary, the Scottish inspectors or the Northern Ireland inspectors obtain information in the course of exercising a function by virtue of section 27—

(*a*) they may not disclose it without the consent of the Commissioners, and
(*b*) they may not use it for any purpose other than the exercise of the function by virtue of section 27.

(2) A report of an inspection by virtue of section 27 may not include information relating to a specified person without his consent.

(3) Where the Independent Police Complaints Commission or a person acting on its behalf obtains information from the Commissioners or an officer of Revenue and Customs, or from the Parliamentary Commissioner for Administration, in the course of exercising a function by virtue of section 28—

(*a*) the Commission or person shall comply with any restriction on disclosure imposed by regulations under that section (and those regulations may, in particular, prohibit disclosure generally or only in specified circumstances or only without the consent of the Commissioners), and
(*b*) the Commission or person may not use the information for any purpose other than the exercise of the function by virtue of that section.

(4) A person commits an offence if he contravenes a provision of this section.

(5) It is a defence for a person charged with an offence under this section of disclosing or using information to prove that he reasonably believed—

(*a*) that the disclosure or use was lawful, or
(*b*) that the information had already and lawfully been made available to the public.

(6) A person guilty of an offence under this section shall be liable—

(*a*) on conviction on indictment, to imprisonment for a term not exceeding two years, to a fine or to both, or
(*b*) on summary conviction, to imprisonment for a term not exceeding 12 months, to a fine not exceeding the statutory maximum or to both[1].

(7) A prosecution for an offence under this section may be instituted in England and Wales only—

(*a*) by the Director of Revenue and Customs Prosecutions, or
(*b*) with the consent of the Director of Public Prosecutions.

(8) A prosecution for an offence under this section may be instituted in Northern Ireland only—

(*a*) by the Commissioners, or
(*b*) with the consent of the Director of Public Prosecutions for Northern Ireland.

(9) In the application of this section to Scotland or Northern Ireland the reference in subsection (6)(*b*) to 12 months shall be taken as a reference to six months.

(10) In this section a reference to the Scottish inspectors or the Northern Ireland inspectors has the same meaning as in section 27.
[Commissioners for Revenue and Customs Act 2005, s 29.]

---

1. For procedure in respect of an offence triable either way, see the Magistrates' Courts Act 1908, ss 17A–21, in PART I: MAGISTRATES' COURTS, PROCEDURE, ante.

8–30102N

Offences

30. Impersonation. (1) A person commits an offence if he pretends to be a Commissioner or an officer of Revenue and Customs with a view to obtaining—

(*a*) admission to premises,
(*b*) information, or
(*c*) any other benefit.

(2) A person guilty of an offence under this section shall be liable on summary conviction to—

(*a*) imprisonment for a period not exceeding 51 weeks,
(*b*) a fine not exceeding level 5 on the standard scale, or
(*c*) both.

(3) In the application of this section to Scotland or Northern Ireland the reference in subsection (2)(*a*) to 51 weeks shall be taken as a reference to six months.
[Commissioners for Revenue and Customs Act 2005, s 30.]

8–30102O 31. Obstruction. (1) A person commits an offence if without reasonable excuse he obstructs—

(*a*) an officer of Revenue and Customs,
(*b*) a person acting on behalf of the Commissioners or an officer of Revenue and Customs, or
(*c*) a person assisting an officer of Revenue and Customs.

(2) A person guilty of an offence under this section shall be liable on summary conviction to—

(*a*) imprisonment for a period not exceeding 51 weeks,
(*b*) a fine not exceeding level 3 on the standard scale, or
(*c*) both.

(3) In the application of this section to Scotland or Northern Ireland the reference in subsection (2)(*a*) to 51 weeks shall be taken as a reference to six months.
[Commissioners for Revenue and Customs Act 2005, s 31.]

8–30102P 32. Assault. (1) A person commits an offence if he assaults an officer of Revenue and Customs.

(2) A person guilty of an offence under this section shall be liable on summary conviction to—

(*a*) imprisonment for a period not exceeding 51 weeks,
(*b*) a fine not exceeding level 5 on the standard scale, or
(*c*) both.

(3) In the application of this section to Scotland or Northern Ireland the reference in subsection (2)(*a*) to 51 weeks shall be taken as a reference to six months.
[Commissioners for Revenue and Customs Act 2005, s 32.]

8–30102Q 33. Power of arrest. (1) An authorised officer of Revenue and Customs may arrest a person without warrant if the officer reasonably suspects that the person—

(*a*) has committed an offence under section 30, 31 or 32,
(*b*) is committing an offence under any of those sections, or
(*c*) is about to commit an offence under any of those sections.

(2) In subsection (1) "authorised" means authorised by the Commissioners.

(3) Authorisation for the purposes of this section may be specific or general.

(4) In Scotland or Northern Ireland, a constable may arrest a person without warrant if the constable reasonably suspects that the person—

(*a*) has committed an offence under this Act,
(*b*) is committing an offence under this Act, or
(*c*) is about to commit an offence under this Act.

[Commissioners for Revenue and Customs Act 2005, s 33.]

Prosecutions

8–30102R 34. The Revenue and Customs Prosecutions Office. (1) The Attorney General shall appoint an individual as Director of Revenue and Customs Prosecutions.

(2) The Director may, with the approval of the Minister for the Civil Service as to terms and conditions of service, appoint staff.

(3) The Director and his staff may together be referred to as the Revenue and Customs Prosecutions Office.

(4) Schedule 3 (which makes provision about the Office) shall have effect.
[Commissioners for Revenue and Customs Act 2005, s 34.]

8–30102S 35. Functions. (1) The Director—

(*a*) may institute and conduct criminal proceedings in England and Wales relating to a criminal investigation by the Revenue and Customs, and
(*b*) shall take over the conduct of criminal proceedings instituted in England and Wales by the Revenue and Customs.

(2) The Director shall provide such advice as he thinks appropriate, to such persons as he thinks appropriate, in relation to—

(*a*) a criminal investigation by the Revenue and Customs, or
(*b*) criminal proceedings instituted in England and Wales relating to a criminal investigation by the Revenue and Customs.

(3) In this section a reference to the Revenue and Customs is a reference to—

(*a*) the Commissioners,
(*b*) an officer of Revenue and Customs, and
(*c*) a person acting on behalf of the Commissioners or an officer of Revenue and Customs.

(4) The Attorney General may by order assign to the Director a function of—

(*a*) instituting criminal proceedings,
(*b*) assuming the conduct of criminal proceedings, or
(*c*) providing legal advice.

(5) In this section—

(*a*) a reference to the institution of criminal proceedings shall be construed in accordance with section 15(2) of the Prosecution of Offences Act 1985 (c 23), and
(*b*) "criminal investigation" means any process—

(i) for considering whether an offence has been committed,
(ii) for discovering by whom an offence has been committed, or
(iii) as a result of which an offence is alleged to have been committed.

[Commissioners for Revenue and Customs Act 2005, s 35.]

8–30102T 36. Functions: supplemental. (1) The Director shall discharge his functions under the superintendence of the Attorney General.

(2) The Director or an individual designated under section 37 or 39 or appointed under section 38 must have regard to the Code for Crown Prosecutors issued by the Director of Public Prosecutions under section 10 of the Prosecution of Offences Act 1985 (c 23)—

(*a*) in determining whether proceedings for an offence should be instituted,
(*b*) in determining what charges should be preferred,
(*c*) in considering what representations to make to a magistrates' court about mode of trial, and
(*d*) in determining whether to discontinue proceedings.

(3) Sections 23 and 23A of the Prosecution of Offences Act 1985 (power to discontinue proceedings) shall apply (with any necessary modifications) to proceedings conducted by the Director under this Act as they apply to proceedings conducted by the Director of Public Prosecutions.

(4) A power of the Director under an enactment to institute proceedings may be exercised to institute proceedings in England and Wales only.

[Commissioners for Revenue and Customs Act 2005, s 36.]

8–30102U 37. Prosecutors. (1) The Director may designate a member of the Office (to be known as a "Revenue and Customs Prosecutor") to exercise any function of the Director under or by virtue of section 35.

(2) An individual may be designated as a Prosecutor only if he has a general qualification within the meaning of section 71 of the Courts and Legal Services Act 1990 (c 41) (qualification for judicial appointments).

(3) A Prosecutor shall act in accordance with any instructions of the Director.

[Commissioners for Revenue and Customs Act 2005, s 37.]

8–30102V 38. Conduct of prosecutions on behalf of the Office. (1) An individual who is not a member of the Office may be appointed by the Director to exercise any function of the Director under or by virtue of section 35 in relation to—

(*a*) specified criminal proceedings, or
(*b*) a specified class or description of criminal proceedings.

(2) An individual may be appointed under this section only if he has a general qualification within the meaning of section 71 of the Courts and Legal Services Act 1990 (qualifications for judicial appointments).

(3) An individual appointed under this section shall act in accordance with any instructions of—

(*a*) the Director, or

(*b*) a Prosecutor.

[Commissioners for Revenue and Customs Act 2005, s 38.]

8–30102W 39. Designation of non-legal staff. (1) The Director may designate a member of the Office—

(*a*) to conduct summary bail applications, and
(*b*) to conduct other ancillary magistrates' criminal proceedings.

(2) In carrying out a function for which he is designated under this section an individual shall have the same powers and rights of audience as a Prosecutor.

(3) In subsection (1)—

(*a*) "summary bail application" means an application for bail made in connection with an offence—

(i) which is not triable only on indictment, and
(ii) in respect of which the accused has not been sent to the Crown Court for trial, and

(*b*) "ancillary magistrates' criminal proceedings" means criminal proceedings other than trials in a magistrates' court.

(4) An individual designated under this section shall act in accordance with any instructions of—

(*a*) the Director, or
(*b*) a Prosecutor.

[Commissioners for Revenue and Customs Act 2005, s 39.]

8–30102X 40. Confidentiality. (1) The Revenue and Customs Prosecutions Office may not disclose information which—

(*a*) is held by the Prosecutions Office in connection with any of its functions, and
(*b*) relates to a person whose identity is specified in the disclosure or can be deduced from it.

(2) But subsection (1)—

(*a*) does not apply to a disclosure which—

(i) is made for the purposes of a function of the Prosecutions Office, and
(ii) does not contravene any restriction imposed by the Director,

(*b*) does not apply to a disclosure made to Her Majesty's Revenue and Customs in connection with a function of the Revenue and Customs (within the meaning of section 25),
(*c*) does not apply to a disclosure made for the purposes of a criminal investigation or criminal proceedings (whether or not within the United Kingdom),
(*d*) does not apply to a disclosure which in the opinion of the Director is desirable for the purpose of safeguarding national security,
(*e*) does not apply to a disclosure made in pursuance of an order of a court,
(*f*) does not apply to a disclosure made with the consent of each person to whom the information relates, and
(*g*) is subject to any other enactment.

(3) A person commits an offence if he contravenes subsection (1).

(4) Subsection (3) does not apply to the disclosure of information about internal administrative arrangements of the Revenue and Customs Prosecutions Office (whether relating to a member of the Office or to another person).

(5) It is a defence for a person charged with an offence under this section of disclosing information to prove that he reasonably believed—

(*a*) that the disclosure was lawful, or
(*b*) that the information had already and lawfully been made available to the public.

(6) In this section a reference to the Revenue and Customs Prosecutions Office includes a reference to—

(*a*) former members of the Office, and
(*b*) persons who hold or have held appointment under section 38.

(7) A person guilty of an offence under this section shall be liable—

(*a*) on conviction on indictment, to imprisonment for a term not exceeding two years, to a fine or to both, or
(*b*) on summary conviction, to imprisonment for a term not exceeding 12 months, to a fine not exceeding the statutory maximum or to both[1].

(8) A prosecution for an offence under this section may be instituted in England and Wales only—

(*a*) by the Director of Revenue and Customs Prosecutions, or
(*b*) with the consent of the Director of Public Prosecutions.

(9) A prosecution for an offence under this section may be instituted in Northern Ireland only—

(*a*) by the Commissioners, or
(*b*) with the consent of the Director of Public Prosecutions for Northern Ireland.

(10) In the application of this section to Scotland or Northern Ireland the reference in subsection (7)(*b*) to 12 months shall be taken as a reference to six months.

(11) In subsection (2) the reference to an enactment does not include—

(*a*) an Act of the Scottish Parliament or an instrument made under such an Act, or
(*b*) an Act of the Northern Ireland Assembly or an instrument made under such an Act.

[Commissioners for Revenue and Customs Act 2005, s 40.]

---

1. For procedure in respect of an offence triable either way, see the Magistrates' Courts Act 1908, ss 17A–21, in PART I: MAGISTRATES' COURTS, PROCEDURE, ante.

8–30102Y 41. Disclosure of information to Director of Revenue and Customs Prosecutions. (1) A person specified in subsection (2) may disclose information held by him to the Director for a purpose connected with a specified investigation or prosecution.

(2) Those persons are—

(*a*) a constable,
(*b*) the Director General of the National Criminal Intelligence Service,
(*c*) the Director General of the National Crime Squad,
(*d*) the Director of the Serious Fraud Office,
(*e*) the Director General of the Serious Organised Crime Agency,
(*f*) the Director of Public Prosecutions,
(*g*) the Director of Public Prosecutions for Northern Ireland, and
(*h*) such other persons as the Attorney General may specify by order.

(3) An order under subsection (2)(*h*)—

(*a*) may specify a person only if, or in so far as, he appears to the Attorney General to be exercising public functions,
(*b*) may include transitional or incidental provision,
(*c*) shall be made by statutory instrument, and
(d) shall not be made unless a draft has been laid before, and approved by resolution of, each House of Parliament.

(4) In relation to a person if or in so far as he exercises functions in respect of Northern Ireland subsections (2)(*h*) and (3)(*a*) shall have effect as if a reference to the Attorney General were a reference to—

(*a*) the Advocate General for Northern Ireland, or
(*b*) before the commencement of section 27(1) of the Justice (Northern Ireland) Act 2002 (c 26), the Attorney General for Northern Ireland.

(5) In the application of this section to Scotland, references to the Attorney General are to be read as references to a Minister of the Crown (including the Treasury).

(6) Nothing in this section authorises the making of a disclosure which—

(*a*) contravenes the Data Protection Act 1998 (c 29), or
(*b*) is prohibited by Part 1 of the Regulation of Investigatory Powers Act 2000 (c 23).

[Commissioners for Revenue and Customs Act 2005, s 41.]

8–30102Z 42. Inspection. Section 2 of the Crown Prosecution Service Inspectorate Act 2000 (c 10) shall apply to the Revenue and Customs Prosecutions Office as it applies to the Crown Prosecution Service.

Money and property

[Commissioners for Revenue and Customs Act 2005, s 42.]

8–30103 43–50. *These provisions are concerned with transfer of property, money, and consequential amendments.*

General

[Commissioners for Revenue and Customs Act 2005, s 43.]

8–30103A 51. Interpretation. (1) In this Act—

except where otherwise expressly provided, "enactment" includes—

(*a*) an Act of the Scottish Parliament,
(*b*) an instrument made under an Act of the Scottish Parliament,
(*c*) Northern Ireland legislation, and
(d) an instrument made under Northern Ireland legislation,

"officer of Revenue and Customs" means a person appointed under section 2, and
"revenue" has the meaning given by section 5(4).

(2) In this Act—

(*a*) "function" means any power or duty (including a power or duty that is ancillary to another power or duty), and

(*b*) a reference to the functions of the Commissioners or of officers of Revenue and Customs is a reference to the functions conferred—

(i) by or by virtue of this Act, or

(ii) by or by virtue of any enactment passed or made after the commencement of this Act.

(3) A reference in this Act, in an enactment amended by this Act or, subject to express provision to the contrary, in any future enactment, to responsibility for collection and management of revenue has the same meaning as references to responsibility for care and management of revenue in enactments passed before this Act.

(4) In this Act a reference to information acquired in connection with a matter includes a reference to information held in connection with that matter.

[Commissioners for Revenue and Customs Act 2005, s 51.]

8–30103B 52. Repeals. (1) The following shall cease to have effect—

(*a*) the following provisions of the Customs and Excise Management Act 1979 (c 2)—

(i) section 12 (inquiries),
(ii) section 15 (bribery and collusion),
(iii) section 32 (kidnapping officers),
(iv) section 84 (signalling to smugglers),
(v) section 86 (higher penalty where offender armed, &c),
(vi) section 152(*c*) (mitigation and remission of penalties, &c),
(vii) section 152(d) (early discharge from prison), and
(viii) section 169 (false scales, &c), and

(*b*) section 111(2) of the Taxes Management Act 1970 (c 9) (valuation: obstruction).

(2) The enactments specified in Schedule 5 are hereby repealed to the extent specified.

[Commissioners for Revenue and Customs Act 2005, s 52.]

8–30103C 53. Commencement. (1) This Act shall come into force in accordance with provision made by order of the Treasury.

(2) An order under subsection (1)—

(*a*) may make provision generally or only in relation to specified provisions or purposes,
(*b*) may include transitional, consequential or incidental provision or savings, and
(*c*) shall be made by statutory instrument.

[Commissioners for Revenue and Customs Act 2005, s 53.]

8–30103D 54. Transitional: general. (1) In the application of section 5—

(*a*) a reference to responsibility before commencement of that section includes a reference to responsibility under an enactment passed or made, but not yet in force, before commencement, and

(*b*) a reference to a function vesting includes a reference to a function which is to vest under an enactment passed or made, but not yet in force, before commencement of that section.

(2) In the application of section 6 or 7 a reference to a function conferred by an enactment includes a reference to a function conferred by an enactment passed or made, but not yet in force, before commencement of that section.

(3) Where immediately before the commencement of section 6 a person holds appointment as a member of the staff of the Commissioners of Inland Revenue or of the Commissioners of Customs and Excise, his appointment shall have effect on commencement as if made by the Commissioners for Her Majesty's Revenue and Customs under section 2.

(4) The following shall be treated as being included in the list in Schedule 1—

(*a*) development land tax,
(*b*) disabled person's tax credit,
(*c*) estate duty,
(d) the national defence contribution under Part III of the Finance Act 1937 (c 54),
(*e*) the special tax on banking deposits under section 134 of the Finance Act 1981 (c 35), and
(*f*) working families tax credit.

(5) The Treasury may by order made by statutory instrument add to the list in subsection (4) an item relating to a matter for which the Commissioners of Inland Revenue or a person listed in section 7(3) had responsibility before the commencement of section 5, if it appears to the Treasury that the law relating to that matter has lapsed or ceased to have effect but that transitional matters may continue to arise in respect of it.

(6) An order under subsection (5)—

(*a*) may include consequential, transitional or incidental provision,
(*b*) shall be made by statutory instrument, and
(*c*) shall be subject to annulment in pursuance of a resolution of either House of Parliament.

(7) A reference in this Act to anything done by, on behalf of or in relation to a specified person or class of person includes a reference to anything treated as if done by, on behalf of or in relation to that person by virtue of transitional provision of an enactment passed or made before this Act.
[Commissioners for Revenue and Customs Act 2005, s 54.]

8–30103E 55. Transitional: penalties. (1) In relation to an offence under section 19 committed before the commencement of section 282 of the Criminal Justice Act 2003 (c 44) (short sentences) the reference in section 19(4)(*b*) to 12 months shall have effect as if it were a reference to six months.

(2) In relation to an offence under section 21 committed before the commencement of section 282 of the Criminal Justice Act (short sentences), the reference in section 21(6)(*b*) to 12 months shall have effect as if it were a reference to six months.

(3) In relation to an offence under section 29 committed before the commencement of section 282 of the Criminal Justice Act 2003 (c 44) (short sentences) the reference in section 29(6)(*b*) to 12 months shall have effect as if it were a reference to six months.

(4) In relation to an offence under section 30 committed before the commencement of section 281(4) and (5) of the Criminal Justice Act 2003 (51 week maximum term of sentences) the reference in section 30(2)(*a*) to 51 weeks shall have effect as if it were a reference to six months.

(5) In relation to an offence under section 31 committed before the commencement of section 281(4) and (5) of the Criminal Justice Act 2003 (51 week maximum term of sentences) the reference in section 31(2)(*a*) to 51 weeks shall have effect as if it were a reference to one month.

(6) In relation to an offence under section 32 committed before the commencement of section 281(4) and (5) of the Criminal Justice Act 2003 (51 week maximum term of sentences) the reference in section 32(2)(*a*) to 51 weeks shall have effect as if it were a reference to six months.

(7) In relation to an offence under section 40 committed before the commencement of section 282 of the Criminal Justice Act 2003 (short sentences) the reference in section 40(7)(*b*) to 12 months shall have effect as if it were a reference to six months.
[Commissioners for Revenue and Customs Act 2005, s 55.]

8–30103F 56. Extent. (1) This Act extends to the United Kingdom.

(2) But an amendment, modification or repeal effected by this Act has the same extent as the enactment (or the relevant part of the enactment) to which it relates.
[Commissioners for Revenue and Customs Act 2005, s 56.]

8–30103G 57. Short title. This Act may be cited as the Commissioners for Revenue and Customs Act 2005.
[Commissioners for Revenue and Customs Act 2005, s 57.]

TELECOMMUNICATIONS AND BROADCASTING

8–30105 This title contains references to the following statutes—

8–30105A Privacy and Electronic Communications (EC Directive) Regulations 2003, SI 2003/2426 amended by SI 2004/1039. These Regulations implement arts 2, 4, 5(3), 6 to 13, 15 and 16 of Directive 2002/58/EC of the European Parliament and of the Council of 12 July 2002 concerning the processing of personal data and the protection of privacy in the electronic communications sector (Directive on privacy and electronic communications). No criminal offences are created but remedies for non compliance are provided in damages (reg 30). Further, the Regulations do not relieve a person of any of his obligations under the Data Protection Act 1998.

A provider of a public electronic communications service has a duty to take measures to safeguard the security of the service, and to comply with the service provider's reasonable requests made for the purposes of taking the measures (reg 5).

An electronic communications network may not be used to store or gain access to information in the terminal equipment of a subscriber or user ("user" is defined as "any individual using a public electronic communications service") unless the subscriber or user is provided with certain information and is given the opportunity to refuse the storage of or access to the information in his terminal equipment (reg 6). Certain restrictions on the processing of traffic data relating to a subscriber or user are imposed on a public communications provider (regs 7 and 8).

Providers of public electronic communications services are to provide subscribers with non-itemised bills on request; with a means of preventing the presentation of calling line identification on a call-by-call basis; and with a means of preventing the presentation of such identification on a per-line basis (regs 9–11).

Restrictions are imposed on the processing of location data, i.e. data which indicates the geographical position of the terminal equipment of a user of a public electronic communications service (reg 14).

Provision is made for the tracing of malicious or nuisance calls and there is provision in relation to emergency calls, i.e. 999 or the European emergency call number 112 (regs 15 and 16).

The provider of an electronic communications service is required to stop, on request, the automatic forwarding of calls to a subscriber's line and conditions are set out in relation to directories of subscribers including rights for subscribers to verify, correct or withdraw their data in directories (regs 17 and 18).

Provision is made which prevents calls for direct marketing purposes by an automated calling system without the consent of the subscriber, similarly there are restrictions on the unsolicited use for direct marketing of facsimile machines, unsolicited calls or unsolicited e-mails for these purposes (regs 19–22). Also, direct marketing by e-mail is prohibited where the identity of the person on whose behalf the communication is made has been disguised or concealed or an address to which requests for such communications to cease may be sent has not been provided (reg 23).

8-30105B European Communities Act 1972: regulations. Within the scope of the title Telecommunications and Broadcasting would logically fall the subject matter of a number of regulations made under the very wide enabling power provided in section 2(2) of the European Communities Act 1972. Where such regulations create offences they are noted below.

Radio Equipment and Telecommunications Terminal Equipment Regulations 2000, SI 2000/730 amended by SI 2003/1903 and 3144, SI 2004/693 and SI 2005/281;

Electromagnetic Compatibility Regulations 2005, SI 2005/281.

Telegraph Act 1863

(26 & 27 Vict 2 c 112)

8-30105C 45. Misconduct of servants. If any person in the employment of the company[1]—Wilfully or negligently omits or delays to transmit or deliver any message; Or by any wilful or negligent act or omission prevents or delays the transmission or delivery of any message; Or improperly divulges to any person the purport of any message;—He shall for every such offence be liable on summary conviction to a fine not exceeding **level 3** on the standard scale.

[Telegraph Act 1863, s 45, amended by Criminal Justice Act 1967, 3rd Sch, the Criminal Justice Act 1982, ss 38 and 46 and the Telecommunications Act 1984, Sch 4.]

1. To be construed as a reference to the Post Office authority (Post Office Act 1969, Sch 4). Reference to the Post Office is now to be construed as including a reference to the public corporation called British Telecommunications (British Telecommunications Act 1981, Sch 3, Pt II).

Telegraph Act 1868

(31 & 32 Vict c 110)

8-30105D 20. Punishment of officials for disclosing messages. Any person having official duties connected with the Post Office, or acting on behalf of the Postmaster General[1], who shall, contrary to his duty, disclose or in any way make known or intercept the contents or any part of the contents of any telegraph messages or any message intrusted to the Postmaster General for the purpose of transmission, shall in England . . . be guilty of a misdemeanour[2], and shall upon conviction be subject to imprisonment for a term not exceeding **twelve calendar months** . . .

[Telegraph Act 1868, s 20, as amended by Post Office Act 1969, Sch 8.]

1. To be construed as a reference to the Post Office authority (Post Office Act 1969, Sch 4).
2. Triable either way; see Magistrates' Courts Act 1980, s 17 and Sch 1; also ss 17A–21 (procedure) and s 32 (penalty) in PART I: MAGISTRATES' COURTS, PROCEDURE, ante.

Wireless Telegraphy Act 1949[1]

(12, 13 & 14 Geo 6 c 54)

PART I[2]

Regulation of Wireless Telegraphy

8–30105E 1. Licensing of wireless telegraphy[3]. (1) No person shall establish or use any station for wireless telegraphy[3] or install or use any apparatus for wireless telegraphy[4] except under the authority of a licence[5] in that behalf granted under this section by OFCOM and any person who establishes or uses any station for wireless telegraphy or installs or uses apparatus for wireless telegraphy except under and in accordance with such a licence shall be guilty of an offence[6] under this Act:

Provided that OFCOM may by regulations exempt[7] from the provisions of this subsection the establishment, installation use of stations for wireless telegraphy or wireless telegraphy apparatus of such classes or descriptions as may be specified in the regulations, either absolutely or subject to such terms, provisions and limitations as may be so specified.

(1AA) Subsection (1) shall not apply to the use of a television receiver (within the meaning of Part 4 of the Communications Act 2003) for receiving a television programme or to the installation of a television receiver for use solely for that purpose.

(1A) *Repealed.*

(2) A licence granted under this section (hereafter in this Act referred to as a wireless telegraphy licence) may be issued subject to such terms, provisions and limitations as OFCOM think fit, including in particular in the case of a licence to establish a station, limitations as to the position and nature of the station, the purposes for which, the circumstances in which, and the persons by whom the station may be used, and the apparatus which may be installed or used therein, and, in the case of any other licence, limitations as to the apparatus which may be installed or used, and the places where the purposes for which, the circumstances in which[8] and the persons by whom the apparatus may be used.

(2A) Those terms, provisions and limitations may also include, in particular—

(*a*) terms, provisions and limitations as to strength or type of signal, as to times of use and as to the sharing of frequencies;

(*b*) terms, provisions or limitations imposing prohibitions on the transmission or broadcasting of particular matters by the holder of the licence; and

(*c*) terms or provisions requiring the transmission or broadcasting of particular matters by that person.

(2B) A licence under this section may be granted either—

(*a*) in relation to a particular station or particular apparatus; or

(*b*) in relation to any station or apparatus falling within a description specified in the licence;

and such a description may be expressed by reference to such factors (including factors confined to the manner in which it is established, installed or used) as OFCOM think fit.

(2C) The terms, provisions and limitations of a licence granted under this section to a person must not duplicate obligations already imposed on him by general conditions set under section 45 of the Communications Act 2003.

(3) A wireless telegraphy licence shall, unless previously revoked by the Secretary of State, or (if it is a television licence) by the BBC continue in force for such period as may be specified in the licence.

(4) A wireless telegraphy licence may be revoked[9], or the terms, provisions or limitations thereof varied, by a notice in writing from OFCOM served by them on the holder of the licence or by a general notice applicable to licences of the class to which the licence in question belongs published in such manner as may be specified in the licence.

(5) Where a wireless telegraphy licence has expired or has been revoked, it shall be the duty of the person to whom the licence was issued, and of every other person in whose possession or under whose control the licence may be, to cause the licence to be surrendered to the Secretary of State if required by the Secretary of State so to do, and any person who without reasonable excuse fails or refuses to comply with the provisions of this subsection shall be guilty of an offence[10] under this Act: Provided that this subsection shall not apply to a licence relating solely to apparatus not designed or adapted for emission (as opposed to reception)[11].

(6) *Repealed.*

(7) *Repealed.*

[Wireless Telegraphy Act 1949, s 1, as amended by the Broadcasting Act 1990, Sch 18, SI 1996/1864 and the Communications Act 2003, s 406.]

---

1. References in this Act to the Postmaster General are to be construed as references to the Secretary of State. See the Post Office Act 1969, s 3, and the Ministry of Posts and Telecommunications (Dissolution) Order 1974, SI 1974/691. Appropriate alterations to the text have been made.

2. The establishment and installation of stations and apparatus for use by members of visiting forces or international headquarters for service purposes in the course of their duty as such, and the use as aforesaid of such stations or apparatus, are excepted from the provisions of this Part of the Act (Visiting Forces and International Headquarters (Application of Law) Order 1965, SI 1965/1536, art 7.

3. For meaning of "wireless telegraphy," "station for wireless telegraphy", see s 19, post. Provision for the grant of licences under this Act other than television licences and about the promotion of the efficient use and management of the electro-magnetic spectrum for wireless telegraphy is made in the Wireless Telegraphy Act 1998 which is not reproduced in this work.

4. The installation and use of cordless telephone apparatus, metal detectors and model control equipment are exempted from the requirements of a licence; see note 9 below.

5. The prosecution does not have to prove the defendant had no licence; see the Magistrates' Courts Act 1980, s 101, ante.

6. To prove an offence under s 1(1) of the Act the prosecution must establish merely that the defendant knew he was making use of apparatus, and do not need to show that he was doing so with a guilty mind because the section creates an absolute offence (*R v Blake* [1997] 1 All ER 963, [1997] 1 WLR 1167, [1997] 1 Cr App Rep 209; [1997] Crim LR 207). For penalty, procedure where offence is by a body corporate, and power to order forfeiture of apparatus, see s 14, post. Offences under s 1(1), other than one falling within s 14(1A)(*a*), post, are triable either way; see s 14(1), post. The offence under s 1(1) of the Act involving the installation or use of any apparatus not designed or adapted for emission (as opposed to reception) attracts a maximum penalty on summary conviction not exceeding **level 3** on the standard scale (s 14(1A)(*a*), post). For power to issue search warrant, see s 15, post.

7. Exemptions are provided under the following regulations:

Wireless Telegraphy (Reciprocal Exemption of European Radio Amateurs) Regulations 1988, 1988/2090;
Wireless Telegraphy Apparatus (Receivers) (Exemption) Regulations 1989, SI 1989/123;
Wireless Telegraphy Apparatus (Citizens' Band European Users) (Exemption) Regulations 1989, SI 1989/943;
Wireless Telegraphy (Testing and Development Under Suppressed Radiation Conditions) (Exemption) Regulations 1989, SI 1989/1842;
Wireless Telegraphy (Exemption) Regulations 2003, SI 2003/74 amended by SI 2003/2155 and SI 2005/3481;
Wireless Telegraphy (Automotive Short Range Radar) (Exemption) Order 2005, SI 2005/353 and (No 2) Order 2005, SI 2005/1585;
Wireless Telegraphy (Radio Frequency Identification Equipment) (Exemption) Regulations 2005, SI 2005/3471.

8. The use of an amplifier connected with wires to a socket in a tenant's flat from a licensed wireless set of the landlord was held, under a repealed Act, to be "working" apparatus for wireless telegraphy (*King v Bull* [1937] 1 KB 810, [1937] 1 All ER 585, 101 JP 169).

9. The Secretary of State does not have an unfettered right to revoke a licence: see *Congreve v Home Office* [1976] QB 629, [1976] 1 All ER 697.

10. For penalty, procedure where an offence is by a body corporate, and power to order forfeiture of apparatus, see s 14, post. For power to issue search warrant, see s 15, post.

11. For construction of the expression "emission (as opposed to reception)", see s 19, post.

8–30105EA 1AA. Exemption from need for wireless telegraphy licence. (1) If OFCOM are satisfied that the condition in subsection (2) is satisfied as respects the use of stations or apparatus of any particular description, they shall make regulations under section 1 of this Act exempting the establishment, installation and use of any station or apparatus of that description from the prohibition in that section.

(2) That condition is that the use of stations or apparatus of that description is not likely to involve any undue interference with wireless telegraphy.
[Wireless Telegraphy Act 1949, s 1, as inserted by the Communications Act 2003, s 166.]

8–30105F 1A. Offence of keeping wireless telegraphy station or apparatus available for unauthorised use. Any person who has any station for wireless telegraphy or apparatus for wireless telegraphy in his possession or under his control and either—

(*a*) intends to use it in contravention of section 1 of this Act; or
(*b*) knows, or has reasonable cause to believe, that another person intends to use it in contravention of that section,

shall be guilty of an offence[1].
[Wireless Telegraphy Act 1949, s 1A, as inserted by the Broadcasting Act 1990, s 168.]

---

1. For penalty, see s 14, post.

8–30105G 1B. Offence of allowing premises to be used for purpose of unlawful broadcasting. (1) A person who is in charge of any premises which are used for making an unlawful broadcast, or for sending signals for the operation or control of any apparatus used for the purpose of making an unlawful broadcast from any other place, shall be guilty of an offence[1] if—

(*a*) he knowingly causes or permits the premises to be so used; or
(*b*) having reasonable cause to believe that the premises are being so used, he fails to take such steps as are reasonable in the circumstances of the case to prevent the premises from being so used.

(2) For the purposes of this section a person is in charge of any premises if he—

(*a*) is the owner or occupier of the premises; or
(*b*) has, or acts or assists in, the management or control of the premises.

(3) For the purposes of this section a broadcast is unlawful if—

(*a*) it is made by means of the use of any station for wireless telegraphy or apparatus for wireless telegraphy in contravention of section 1 of this Act; or
(*b*) the making of the broadcast contravenes any provision of the Marine, &c, Broadcasting (Offences) Act 1967.

(4) In this section—

"broadcast" has the same meaning as in the Marine, &c, Broadcasting (Offences) Act 1967;

"premises" includes any place and, in particular, includes—

(*a*) any vehicle, vessel or aircraft; and
(*b*) any structure or other object (whether movable or otherwise and whether on land or otherwise).

[Wireless Telegraphy Act 1949, s 1B, as inserted by the Broadcasting Act 1990, s 169.]

1. For penalty, see s 14, post.

8–30105H 1C. Prohibition of acts facilitating unauthorised broadcasting. (1) If a person—

(*a*) does any of the acts mentioned in subsection (2) in relation to a broadcasting station by which unauthorised broadcasts are made, and
(*b*) if any knowledge or belief or any circumstances is or are specified in relation to the act, does it with that knowledge or belief or in those circumstances,

he shall be guilty of an offence[1].

(2) The acts referred to in subsection (1) are—

(*a*) participating in the management, financing, operation or day-to-day running of the station knowing, or having reasonable cause to believe, that unauthorised broadcasts are made by the station;
(*b*) supplying, installing, repairing or maintaining any wireless telegraphy apparatus or any other item knowing, or having reasonable cause to believe, that the apparatus or other item is to be, or is, used for the purpose of facilitating the operation or day-to-day running of the station and that unauthorised broadcasts are made by the station;
(*c*) rendering any other service to any person knowing, or having reasonable cause to believe, that the rendering of that service to that person will facilitate the operation or day-to-day running of the station and that unauthorised broadcasts are so made;
(*d*) supplying a film or sound recording knowing, or having reasonable cause to believe, that an unauthorised broadcast of the film or recording is to be so made;
(*e*) making a literary, dramatic or musical work knowing, or having reasonable cause to believe, that an unauthorised broadcast of the work is to be so made;
(*f*) making an artistic work knowing, or having reasonable cause to believe, that an unauthorised broadcast including that work is to be so made;
(*g*) doing any of the following acts, namely—

(i) participating in an unauthorised broadcast made by the station, being actually present as an announcer, as a performer or one of the performers concerned in an entertainment given, or as the deliverer of a speech;
(ii) advertising, or inviting another to advertise, by means of an unauthorised broadcast made by the station; or
(iii) publishing the times or other details of any unauthorised broadcasts made by the station or (otherwise than by publishing such details) publishing an advertisement of matter calculated to promote the station (whether directly or indirectly),

knowing, or having reasonable cause to believe, that unauthorised broadcasts are made by the station.

(3) In any proceedings against a person for an offence under this section consisting in the supplying of any thing or the rendering of any service, it shall be a defence for him to prove that he was obliged, under or by virtue of any enactment, to supply that thing or render that service.

(4) The cases in which a person is to be taken for the purposes of this section as advertising by means of a broadcast include any case in which he causes or allows it to be stated, suggested or implied that entertainment included in the broadcast—

(*a*) has been supplied by him; or
(*b*) is provided wholly or partly at his expense.

(5) Section 46 of the Consumer Protection Act 1987 shall have effect for the purpose of construing references in this section to the supply of any thing as it has effect for the purpose of construing references in that Act to the supply of any goods.

(6) In this section—

"broadcast" has the same meaning as in the Marine, &c, Broadcasting (Offences) Act 1967;

"broadcasting station" means any business or other operation (whether or not in the nature of a commercial venture) which is engaged in the making of broadcasts;

"film", "sound recording", "literary, dramatic or musical work" and "artistic work" have the same meaning as in Part I of the Copyright, Designs and Patents Act 1988;

"speech" includes lecture, address and sermon; and

"unauthorised broadcast" means a broadcast made by means of the use of a station for wireless telegraphy or wireless telegraphy apparatus in contravention of section 1 of this Act.

[Wireless Telegraphy Act 1949, s 1C, as inserted by the Broadcasting Act 1990, s 170 and amended by the Communications Act 2003, s 406.]

1. For penalty, see s 14, post.

8–30105I 1D–1E. *Procedures for the grant, variation and revocation of licences providing a telecommunications service*[1].

1. These sections were inserted by the Telecommunications (Licensing) Regulations 1997, SI 1997/2930.

8–30105J 2. *Fees and charges for telegraphy licences.*
Repealed by the Communications Act 2003, s 406[1].

1. For regulations which prescribe licence fees, see the Communications (Television Licensing) Regulations 2004, in this title, post.

8–30105K 3. Regulations as to wireless telegraphy. (1) OFCOM may make regulations[1]—

(*a*) prescribing the things which are to be done or are not to be done in connection with the use of any station for wireless telegraphy or wireless telegraphy apparatus, and, in particular, requiring the use of any such station or apparatus to cease on the demand in that behalf of any such persons as may be prescribed by or under the regulations;

(*b*) imposing on the persons to whom a wireless telegraphy licence is issued with respect to any station for wireless telegraphy or wireless telegraphy apparatus, or who is in possession or control of any station for wireless telegraphy or wireless telegraphy apparatus, obligations as to permitting and facilitating the inspection of the station and apparatus, as to the condition in which the station and apparatus are to be kept and, in the case of a station or apparatus for the establishment, installation or use of which a wireless telegraphy licence is necessary, as to the production of the licence, or of such other evidence of the licensing of the station or apparatus as may be prescribed by the regulations;

(*c*) where sums are or may become due from the person to whom a wireless telegraphy licence is issued after the issue or renewal thereof, requiring that person to keep and produce such accounts and records as may be specified in the regulations; and

(*d*) requiring the person to whom a wireless telegraphy licence authorising the establishment or use of a station has been issued to exhibit at the station such notices as may be specified in the regulations,

Provided that nothing in any such regulations shall require any person to concede any form of right of entry into a private dwelling-house for the purpose of permitting or facilitating the inspection of any apparatus not designed or adapted for emission (as opposed to reception).

(2) Any person who contravenes any regulations made under this section, or causes or permits any station for wireless telegraphy or wireless telegraphy apparatus to be used in contravention of any such regulations, shall be guilty of an offence[2] under this Act.

(2A) The approval of the Secretary of State is required for the making by OFCOM of any regulations under this section.

(2B) A statutory instrument containing regulations made by OFCOM under this section shall be subject to annulment in pursuance of a resolution of either House of Parliament.

[Wireless Telegraphy Act 1949, s 3, as amended by the Communications Act 2003, s 406.]

1. The Wireless Telegraphy (Content of Transmission) Regulations 1988, SI 1988/47 amended by SI 2003/2155 prohibits the use of apparatus to send messages etc of a grossly offensive, indecent, obscene or menacing nature. The Wireless Telegraphy (Inspections and Restrictions on Use of Exempt Stations and Apparatus) Regulations 2005, SI 2005/3481 have also been made.

2. For penalty, see s 14, post.

8–30105L 5. Misleading messages and interception and disclosure of messages. (1) Any person who—

(*a*) by means of wireless telegraphy, sends or attempts to send, any message which, to his knowledge, is false or misleading and is, to this knowledge, likely to prejudice the efficiency of any safety of life service or endanger the safety of any person or of any vessel, aircraft or vehicle, and, in particular, any message which, to his knowledge, falsely suggests that a vessel or aircraft is in distress or in need of assistance or is not in distress or not in need of assistance; or

(*b*) otherwise than under the authority of a designated person either—

(i) uses[1] any wireless telegraphy apparatus with intent to obtain information[2] as to the contents, sender or addressee of any message[3] (whether sent by means of wireless telegraphy or not) of which neither the person using the apparatus nor a person on whose behalf he is acting is an intended recipient; or

(ii) except in the course of legal proceedings or for the purpose of any report thereof, discloses any information as to the contents, sender or addressee of any such message, being information which would not have come to his knowledge but for the use of wireless telegraphy apparatus by him or by another person,

shall be guilty of an offence[4] under this Act.

(2) The conduct in relation to which a designated person may give a separate authority for the purposes of this section shall not, except where he believes the conduct to be necessary on grounds falling within subsection (5) of this section, include—

(*a*) any conduct which, if engaged in without lawful authority, constitutes an offence under section 1(1) or (2) of the Regulation of Investigatory Powers Act 2000;

(*b*) any conduct which, if engaged in without lawful authority, is actionable under section 1(3) of that Act;

(*c*) any conduct which is capable of being authorised by an authorisation or notice granted by any person under Chapter II of Part I of that Act (communications data);

(*d*) any conduct which is capable of being authorised by an authorisation granted by any person under Part II of that Act (surveillance etc).

(3) A designated person shall not exercise his power to give a separate authority for the purposes of this section except where he believes—

(*a*) that the giving of his authority is necessary on grounds falling within subsection (4) or (5) of this section; and

(*b*) that the conduct authorised by him is proportionate to what is sought to be achieved by that conduct.

(4) A separate authority for the purposes of this section is necessary on grounds falling within this subsection if it is necessary—

(*a*) in the interests of national security;

(*b*) for the purpose of preventing or detecting crime (within the meaning of the Regulation of Investigatory Powers Act 2000) or of preventing disorder;

(*c*) in the interests of the economic well-being of the United Kingdom;

(*d*) in the interests of public safety;

(*e*) for the purpose of protecting public health;

(*f*) for the purpose of assessing or collecting any tax, duty, levy or other imposition, contribution or charge payable to a government department; or

(*g*) for any purpose (not falling within paragraphs (*a*) to (*f*)) which is specified for the purposes of this subsection by regulations made by the Secretary of State.

(5) A separate authority for the purposes of this section is necessary on grounds falling within this subsection if it is not necessary on grounds falling within subsection (4)(*a*) or (*c*) to (*g*) but is necessary for purposes connected with—

(*a*) the issue of licences under this Act;

(*b*) the prevention or detection of anything which constitutes interference with wireless telegraphy; or

(*c*) the enforcement of any enactment contained in this Act or of any enactment not so contained that relates to such interference.

(6) The matters to be taken into account in considering whether the requirements of subsection (3) of this section are satisfied in the case of the giving of any separate authority for the purposes of this section shall include whether what it is thought necessary to achieve by the authorised conduct could reasonably be achieved by other means.

(7) A separate authority for the purposes of this section must be in writing and under the hand of—

(*a*) the Secretary of State;

(*b*) one of the Commissioners of Customs and Excise; or

(*c*) a person not falling within paragraph (*a*) or (*b*) who is designated for the purposes of this subsection by regulations made by the Secretary of State[5].

(8) A separate authority for the purposes of this section may be general or specific and may be given—

(*a*) to such person or persons, or description of persons,

(*b*) for such period, and

(*c*) subject to such restrictions and limitations,

as the designated person thinks fit.

(9) No regulations shall be made under subsection (4)(*g*) unless a draft of them has first been laid before Parliament and approved by a resolution of each House.

(10) For the purposes of this section the question whether conduct is capable of being authorised under Chapter II of Part I of the Regulation of Investigatory Powers Act 2000 or under Part II of that Act shall be determined without reference—

(*a*) to whether the person whose conduct it is is a person on whom any power or duty is or may be conferred or imposed by or under Chapter II of Part I or Part II of that Act; or

(*b*) to whether there are grounds for believing that the requirements for the grant of an authorisation or the giving of a notice under Chapter II of Part I or Part II of that Act are satisfied.

(11) References in this section to a separate authority for the purposes of this section are references to any authority for the purposes of this section given otherwise than by way of the issue or renewal of a warrant, authorisation or notice under Part I or II of the Regulation of Investigatory Powers Act 2000.

(12) In this section "designated person" means—

(*a*) the Secretary of State;

(*b*) the Commissioners of Customs and Excise; or

(*c*) any other person designated for the purposes of this section by regulations made by the Secretary of State[5].

[Wireless Telegraphy Act 1949, s 5, as amended by the Regulation of Investigatory Powers Act 2000, s 73.]

---

1. It is a question of fact whether or not the apparatus has been used unlawfully. "Use" must bear its normal meaning and is not to be construed as meaning merely available for use (*Whiley v DPP* [1995] Crim LR 39).

2. Evidence of mischievous or improper intentions is not necessary; all that is required is evidence of the intent to do the prohibited act (*Paul v Ministry of Posts and Telecommunications* [1973] Crim LR 322). Tuning to a police frequency and listening to police messages is an offence since it is impossible to listen to the channel without obtaining information as the messages transmitted on it. It is otherwise where the listener chances on the channel while tuning a radio and passes over it since he does not intend to obtain information (*DPP v White* (1996) 160 JP 726, sub nom *DPP v Waite* [1997] Crim LR 123, DC).

3. As microwave radio emissions from a police radar speed gun do not constitue a "message" for the purposes of this section, the use by a motorist of an electrical field meter to detect such emissions is not an offence under this provision (*R v Knightsbridge Crown Court, ex p Foot* [1999] RTR 21, DC).

4. The penalty is that prescribed by s 14(1)(*a*), post, for an offence under s 5(*a*); or s 14(1C) post for any other offence under s 5. For procedure where offence is by a body corporate, and power to order forfeiture of apparatus, see s 14, post. For power to issue search warrant, see s 15, post.

5. See the Wireless Telegraphy (Interception and Disclosure of Messages) (Designation) Regulations 2003, SI 2003/3104.

8–30105M 6. Territorial extent of preceding provisions. (1) Subject to the provisions of this section, the preceding provisions of this Part[1] of this Act shall apply—

(*a*) to all stations and apparatus in or over, or for the time being in or over, the United Kingdom or the territorial waters adjacent thereto[2]; and

(*b*) subject to any limitations which the Secretary of State may by regulations determine, to all stations and apparatus on board any ship or aircraft which is registered in the United Kingdom but is not for the time being in or over the United Kingdom or the said territorial waters; and

(*c*) subject to any limitations which the Secretary of State may by regulations determine, to all apparatus which is not in or over the United Kingdom or the said territorial waters but was released from within the United Kingdom or the said territorial waters, or from any ship or aircraft which is registered in the United Kingdom,

and, without prejudice to the liability of any other person, in the event of any contravention of the said preceding provisions or of any regulations made thereunder occurring in relation to any station or apparatus on board or released from any vessel or aircraft, the captain or the person for the time being in charge of the vessel or aircraft shall be guilty of an offence[3] under this Act: Provided that the captain or person for the time being in charge of a vessel or aircraft shall not be guilty of any offence under this Act by reason of any contravention of the said provisions or regulations occurring in relation to apparatus on board the vessel or aircraft if the contravention consists of the use by a passenger on board the ship or aircraft of apparatus not designed or adapted for emission (as opposed to reception)[4] which is not part of the wireless telegraphy apparatus, if any, of the ship or aircraft.

(2) The Secretary of State may make regulations[5] for regulating the use, on board any ship or aircraft which, not being registered in the United Kingdom, is registered in a country other than the United Kingdom, the Isle of Man or any of the Channel Islands while that ship or aircraft is within the limits of the United Kingdom and the territorial waters adjacent thereto, of wireless telegraphy apparatus on board the ship or aircraft, and such regulations may provide for the punishment of persons contravening the regulations by a maximum fine for each offence of an amount not exceeding **level 5** on the standard scale, or of a lesser amount, and for the forfeiture of any wireless telegraphy apparatus in respect of which an offence under such regulations is committed; but, save as aforesaid or by virtue of an Order in Council under subsection (3) of this section, nothing in this Part of this

Act shall operate so as to impose any prohibition or restriction on persons using wireless telegraphy apparatus on board any such ship or aircraft as aforesaid.

(3) Her Majesty may by Order in Council direct that any reference in this section to any ship or aircraft registered in the United Kingdom shall be construed as including a reference to any ship or aircraft registered in the Isle of Man, in any of the Channel Islands, or in any colony, British protectorate or British protected state, or registered under the law of any other country or territory outside the United Kingdom which is for the time being administered by Her Majesty's Government in the United Kingdom.

(4) *Northern Ireland.*

[Wireless Telegraphy Act 1949, s 6, as amended by the Wireless Telegraphy Act 1967, s 9, the Criminal Justice Act 1982, s 50 and the Statute Law (Repeals) Act 1993, Sch 1.]

---

1. This expression has effect as if it included a reference to the provisions of any regulations made under s 10, post, and the provisions of ss 11–13, post (Wireless Telegraphy Act 1967, s 10(3)).

2. See the Territorial Waters Jurisdiction Act 1878 and the Territorial Sea Act 1987 (12 miles). For provision regarding venue of proceedings, see the Wireless Telegraphy Act 1967, s 12, post. Installations in the English part of the Continental Shelf adjacent to the United Kingdom are treated for the purposes of the civil jurisdiction of the High Court as being in England for the purposes of this Act (Civil Jurisdiction (Offshore Activities) Order 1987, SI 1987/2197 (made under the Continental Shelf Act 1964, ss 6 and 7)). For criminal jurisdiction see note to s 2 of the Magistrates' Courts Act 1980, in PART I: MAGISTRATES' COURTS, PROCEDURE, ante.

3. Section 143 of the Powers of Criminal Courts (Sentencing) Act 2000 (deprivation order) does not apply to a conviction of an offence under the 1949 Act (Telecommunications Act 1984, Sch 3, para 3).

4. For construction of the expression "emission (as opposed to reception)", see s 19, post.

5. Regulations may make different provision for different cases or for ships or aircraft registered in different countries (Wireless Telegraphy Act 1967, s 9(4)). The Wireless Telegraphy (Visiting Ships and Aircraft) Regulations 1998, SI 1998/2970 have been made.

PART II

8–30105N **10. Regulations as to radiation of electro-magnetic energy, etc.** (1) OFCOM may make regulations1 for either or both of the following purposes—

(*a*) for prescribing the requirements to be complied with in the case of any apparatus to which this section applies if the apparatus is to be used;

(*b*) for prescribing the requirements to be complied with in the case of any apparatus to which this section applies if the apparatus is to be sold otherwise than for export, or offered or advertised for sale otherwise than for export, or let on hire or offered or advertised for letting on hire, by any person who in the course of business manufactures, assembles or imports such apparatus.

(2) The requirements prescribed under subsection (1) shall be such as OFCOM think fit for the purpose of ensuring that the use of the apparatus does not cause undue interference[2] with wireless telegraphy[4], and may in particular include—

(*a*) requirements as to the maximum intensity of electro-magnetic energy of any specified frequencies which may be radiated in any direction from the apparatus while it is being used; and

(*b*) in the case of an apparatus the power for which is supplied from electric lines, requirements as to the maximum electro-magnetic energy of any specified frequencies which may be injected into those lines by the apparatus.

(3) The apparatus to which this section applies shall be such apparatus as may be specified in the regulations made thereunder, being apparatus, generating, or designed to generate, or liable to generate fortuitously, electro-magnetic energy at frequencies of not more than three million megacycles per second.

The references in this subsection to apparatus include references to any form of electric line, and other references in the Act to apparatus shall be construed accordingly.

(4) It shall not be unlawful for any person to use any apparatus to which this section applies or to sell any such apparatus or offer or advertise it for sale or let it on hire or offer or advertise it for letting on hire by reason only that it does not comply with the requirements applicable under any regulations made under this section, but the non-compliance shall be a ground for the giving of a notice under the next succeeding section or under section twelve of this Act, as the case may be.

(4A) The approval of the Secretary of State is required for the making by OFCOM of any regulations under this section.

(4B) A statutory instrument containing regulations made by OFCOM under this section shall be subject to annulment in pursuance of a resolution of either House of Parliament.

[Wireless Telegraphy Act 1949, s 10, as amended by the Wireless Telegraphy Act 1967, s 10(2)4 and the Communications Act 2003, s 406.]

---

1. Regulations have been made as follows:

Wireless Telegraphy (Control of Interference from Ignition Apparatus) Regulations 1952, SI 1952/2023 amended by SI 1957/347;

Wireless Telegraphy (Control of Interference from Electro-Medical Apparatus) Regulations 1963, SI 1963/1895;
Wireless Telegraphy (Control of Interference from Radio-Frequency Heating Apparatus) Regulations 1971, SI 1971/1675;
Wireless Telegraphy (Control of Interference from Ignition Apparatus) Regulations 1973, SI 1973/1217;
Wireless Telegraphy (Control of Interference from Household Appliances, Portable Tools etc) Regulations 1978, SI 1978/1267 amended by SI 1985/808 and SI 1989/562;
Wireless Telegraphy (Control of Interference from Fluorescent Lighting Apparatus) Regulations 1979, SI 1979/1268 amended by SI 1985/807 and SI 1989/561;
Wireless Telegraphy (Control of Interference from Citizens Band Radio Apparatus) Regulations 1982, SI 1982/635 amended by SI 1988/1216.

The above regulations ceased to have effect by virtue of the Electromagnetic Compatibility Regulations 2005, SI 2005 except to the extent that they impose requirements for radio frequency spectrum planning or for the prevention of undue interference to wireless telegraphy from relevant apparatus in use.

2. For meaning of "interference," "wireless telegraphy," see s 19, post.

3. The use of any apparatus by members of visiting forces or international headquarters for service purposes, in the course of their duty as such, is excepted from this section and any regulations made thereunder (Visiting Forces and International Headquarters (Application of Law) Order 1965, SI 1965/1586, art 7.

8–30105O 11. Enforcement of regulations as to use of apparatus. (1) If OFCOM are of the opinion—

(*a*) that any apparatus does not comply with the requirements applicable to it under regulations made for the purpose specified in paragraph (*a*) of subsection (1) of the last preceding section; and

(*b*) that either—

(i) the use of the apparatus is likely to cause undue interference[1] with any wireless telegraphy[1] used for the purposes of any safety of life service or for any purpose on which the safety of any person or of any vessel, aircraft or vehicle may depend; or

(ii) the use of the apparatus is likely to cause undue interference with any other wireless telegraphy and in fact has caused or is causing such interference in a case where he considers that all reasonable steps to minimise interference have been taken in relation to the station or apparatus receiving the telegraphy,

OFCOM may serve on the person in whose possession the apparatus is a notice[2] in writing requiring that, after a date fixed by the notice, not being less than twenty-eight days from the date of the service thereof, the apparatus shall not be used, whether by the person to whom the notice is given or otherwise, or, if OFCOM think fit so to frame the notice, shall only be used in such manner, at such times and in such circumstances as may be specified in the notice:

Provided that—

(i) *repealed*

(ii) if OFCOM are satisfied that the use of the apparatus in question is likely to cause undue interference with any wireless telegraphy used for the purposes of any safety of life service or for any purpose on which the safety of any person or of any vessel, aircraft or vehicle may depend, the date to be fixed by the notice may be the date of the service thereof.

(2) A notice under subsection (1) of this section may be revoked or varied by a subsequent notice in writing from OFCOM served by them on the person in whose possession the apparatus then is: Provided that where a notice under this subsection has the effect of imposing any additional restrictions on the use of the apparatus, the provisions of subsection (1) of this section relating to the coming into force of notices shall apply in relation to the notice as if it had been a notice served under the said subsection (1).

(2A) Where an appeal with respect to a notice under this section is pending—

(*a*) proceedings for an offence of contravening that notice (whether instituted before or after the bringing of the appeal) shall be stayed until the appeal has been finally determined; and

(*b*) any such proceedings shall be discharged if the notice is set aside in consequence of the appeal;

but this subsection does not affect proceedings in which a person has been convicted at a time when there was no pending appeal.

(2B) For the purposes of this section an appeal under section 192 of the Communications Act 2003 with respect to a notice under this section or a further appeal relating to the decision on such an appeal is pending unless—

(*a*) that appeal has been brought to a conclusion or withdrawn and there is no further appeal pending in relation to the decision on the appeal; or

(*b*) no further appeal against a decision made on the appeal or on any such further appeal may be brought without the permission of the court and—

(i) in a case where there is no fixed period within which that permission can be sought, that permission has been refused or has not been sought; or

(ii) in a case where there is a fixed period within which that permission can be sought, that permission has been refused or that period has expired without permission having been sought.

(2C) No proceedings for an offence of contravening a notice under this section may be commenced in Scotland—

(*a*) until the time during which an appeal against such a notice may be brought has expired; or
(*b*) where such an appeal has been brought, until that appeal has been determined.

(2D) Such proceedings in Scotland must be commenced within six months of—

(*a*) where no appeal has been brought, the time referred to in paragraph (*a*) of subsection (2C); and
(*b*) where an appeal has been brought and determined, the date of that determination.

(7) Any person who, knowing that a notice from OFCOM under this section is in force with respect to any apparatus, uses that apparatus, or causes or permits it to be used, in contravention of the notice, shall be guilty of an offence[4] under this Act.*
[Wireless Telegraphy Act 1949, s 11, as amended by the Communications Act 2003, s 406.]

1. Defined in s 19, post.
2. The notice may be served by registered post (or recorded delivery) (s 19(9), post).
3. The appeal tribunal is appointed under s 9.
4. For penalty, and procedure where offence is by a body corporate, see s 14, post. For power to issue search warrant, see s 15, post. Proceedings shall not be instituted except with the consent of the Secretary of State (s 14, post).

8–30105P 12. Enforcement of regulations as to sales, etc, by manufacturers and others. (1) If OFCOM are of the opinion that any apparatus does not comply with the requirements applicable to it under regulations made for the purpose specified in paragraph (b) of subsection (1) of section ten of this Act, OFCOM may serve on any person who has manufactured, assembled or imported the apparatus in the course of business a notice in writing prohibiting him from selling the apparatus, otherwise than for export, or offering or advertising it for sale, otherwise than for export, or letting it on hire or offering or advertising it for letting on hire.

(1A) Where an appeal with respect to a notice under subsection (1) of this section is pending—

(*a*) proceedings for an offence of contravening that notice (whether instituted before or after the bringing of the appeal) shall be stayed until the appeal has been finally determined; and
(*b*) any such proceedings shall be discharged if the notice is set aside in consequence of the appeal;

but this subsection does not affect proceedings in which a person has been convicted at a time when there was no pending appeal.

(1B) For the purposes of this section any appeal under section 192 of the Communications Act 2003 with respect to a notice under this section or a further appeal relating to the decision on that appeal is pending unless—

(*a*) that appeal has been brought to a conclusion or withdrawn and there is no further appeal pending in relation to the decision; or
(*b*) no further appeal against any decision made on the appeal or on any such further appeal may be brought without the permission of the court and—
  (i) in a case where there is no fixed period within which that permission can be sought, that permission has been refused or has not been sought; or
  (ii) in a case where there is a fixed period within which that permission can be sought, that permission has been refused or that period has expired without permission having been sought.

(1C) No proceedings for an offence of contravening a notice under this section may be commenced in Scotland—

(*a*) until the time during which an appeal against such a notice may be brought has expired; or
(*b*) where such an appeal has been brought, until that appeal has been determined.

(1D) Such proceedings in Scotland must be commenced within six months of—

(*a*) where no appeal has been brought, the time referred to in paragraph (a) of subsection (1C); and
(*b*) where an appeal has been brought and determined, the date of that determination.

(5) Where a notice has been served under subsection (1) of this section, the person on whom the notice has been served shall, if he contravenes the provisions of the notice without the notice having been previously revoked [by OFCOM, be guilty of an offence.
[Wireless Telegraphy Act 1949, s 12 as amended by by the Communications Act 2003, ss 178 and 406.]

8–30105Q 12A. *Repealed.*

8–30105R 13. Deliberate interference. (1) Any person who uses any apparatus for the purpose of interfering with any wireless telegraphy[1] shall be guilty of an offence[2] under this Act.

(2) This section shall whether or not the apparatus in question is wireless telegraphy apparatus or apparatus to which any of the preceding provisions of this Part[3] of this Act apply, and whether or not

any notice under section eleven or section twelve of this Act has been given with respect to the apparatus, or, if given, has been varied or revoked.
[Wireless Telegraphy Act 1949, s 13.]

1. For meaning of "interfering", "wireless telegraphy", see s 19, post.
2. For penalty, etc, see s 14, post.
3. Part II, ss 9–13, ante.

PART III
Supplemental

8–30105RA 13A. Information requirements. (1) Subject to the following provisions of this section, OFCOM may require a person who is using or has established, installed or used a station or apparatus for wireless telegraphy to provide OFCOM with all such information relating to—

(*a*) the establishment, installation or use of the station or apparatus, and
(*b*) any related matters,

as OFCOM may require for statistical purposes.

(2) OFCOM are not to require the provision of information under this section except—

(*a*) by a demand for the information that sets out OFCOM's reasons for requiring the information and the statistical purposes for which it is required; and
(*b*) where the making of a demand for that information is proportionate to the use to which the information is to be put in the carrying out of OFCOM's functions.

(3) A demand for information required under this section must be contained in the notice served on the person from whom the information is required.

(4) A person required to provide information under this section must provide it in such manner and within such reasonable period as may be specified by OFCOM.

(5) A person who fails to provide information in accordance with a requirement of OFCOM under this section is guilty of an offence.

(6) In proceedings against a person for an offence under subsection (1) it shall be a defence for that person to show—

(*a*) that it was not reasonably practicable for him to comply with the requirement within the period specified by OFCOM; but
(*b*) that he has taken all reasonable steps to provide the required information after the end of that period.

(7) A person is guilty of an offence if—

(*a*) in pursuance of any requirement under this section, he provides information that is false in any material particular; and
(*b*) at the time he provides it, he either knows it to be false or is reckless as to whether or not it is false.

[Wireless Telegraphy Act 1949, s 13A as inserted by the Communications Act 2003, s 171.]

8–30105RB 13B. Statement of policy on information gathering. (1) It shall be the duty of OFCOM to prepare and publish a statement of their general policy with respect to—

(*a*) the exercise of their powers under section 13A; and
(*b*) the uses to which they are proposing to put information obtained under that section.

(2) OFCOM may from time to time revise that statement as they think fit.

(3) Where OFCOM make or revise their statement of policy under this section, they must publish that statement or (as the case may be) the revised statement in such manner as they consider appropriate for bringing it to the attention of the persons who, in their opinion, are likely to be affected by it.

(4) It shall be the duty of OFCOM, in exercising the powers conferred on them by section 13A, to have regard to the statement for the time being in force under this section.

[Wireless Telegraphy Act 1949, s 13B as inserted by the Communications Act 2003, s 171.]

8–30105S 14. Penalties and legal proceedings[1]. (1) Any person committing—

(*aa*) any offence under section 1(1) of this Act consisting in the establishment or use of a station for wireless telegraphy, or the installation or use of wireless telegraphy apparatus, for the purpose of making a broadcast (within the meaning of section 9 of the Marine, &c., Broadcasting (Offences) Act 1967 (c 41));
(*ab*) any offence under section 1A of this Act where the relevant contravention of section 1 would constitute an offence falling within paragraph (*aa*);
(*ac*) any offence under section 1B or 1C of this Act;
(*a*) any offence under section 5(1)(*a*) of this Act; or
(*b*) any offence under section 13 of this Act;

shall be liable on summary conviction to imprisonment for a term not exceeding **six months** or a fine not exceeding the **statutory maximum** or **both**, or on conviction on indictment to imprisonment for a term not exceeding two years or a fine or both[2].

(1A) Any person committing—

(*a*) any offence under section 1(1) of this Act consisting in the installation or use, otherwise than under and in accordance with a wireless telegraphy licence, of any apparatus not designed or adapted for emission (as opposed to reception); or

(*aa*) any offence under section 1A of this Act committed in relation to any wireless telegraphy apparatus not designed or adapted for emission (as opposed to reception);

(*b*) any offence under section 3(2) of this Act consisting in a contravention, in relation to any such apparatus, of any regulations made under that section; or

(*c*) any offence under section 11(7) or 12(5) of this Act involving or consisting in a contravention of a notice from OFCOM in relation to any apparatus, not being apparatus the use of which is likely to cause undue interference with any wireless telegraphy used for the purpose of any safety of life service or any purpose on which the safety of any person or of any vessel, aircraft or vehicle may depend; or

(*d*) any offence under section 1(5) or 7(4) of this Act; or

(*e*) *repealed*

(*ea*) any offence under section 13A(1) of this Act; or

(*f*) any offence under this Act which is an offence under section 5 or 8(2) of the Wireless Telegraphy Act 1967 (failure to comply with notices under Part I of that Act, giving false information, etc);

shall be liable on summary conviction to a fine not exceeding **level 3** on the standard scale.

(1AA) A person committing—

(*a*) an offence under section 1(1) of this Act other than—

(i) one which falls within subsection (1)(*aa*), or

(ii) one which falls within subsection (1A)(*a*), or

(*b*) an offence under section 1A of this Act other than—

(i) one which falls within subsection (1)(*ab*), or

(ii) one which falls within subsection (1A)(*aa*),

shall be liable, on summary conviction, to imprisonment for a term not exceeding six months or to a fine not exceeding level 5 on the standard scale, or to both.

(1B) any person committing—

(*a*) *repealed*;

(*b*) any offence under section 11(7) of this Act other than one within subsection (1A)(*c*) of this section;

shall be liable on summary conviction to imprisonment for a term not exceeding **three months** or to a fine not exceeding **level 5** on the standard scale, or **both**.

(1C) Any person committing any other offence under this Act shall be liable on summary conviction to a fine not exceeding **level 5** on the standard scale.*

(2) *Repealed.*

(3) Where a person is convicted of—

(*a*) an offence under this Act consisting in any contravention of any of the provisions of Part I of this Act in relation to any station for wireless telegraphy or any wireless telegraphy apparatus (including an offence under section 1B or 1C of this Act) or in the use of any apparatus for the purpose of interfering with any wireless telegraphy;

(*b*) *repealed*;

(*c*) any offence under the Marine, &c, Broadcasting (Offences) Act 1967; or

(*d*) any offence under this Act which is an offence under section 7 of the Wireless Telegraphy Act 1967 (whether as originally enacted or as substituted by section 77 of the Telecommunications Act 1984),

the court may, in addition to any other penalty, order such of the following things to be forfeited to the OFCOM as the court considers appropriate, that is to say—

(i) any vehicle, vessel or aircraft, or any structure or other object, which was used in connection with the commission of the offence;

(ii) any wireless telegraphy apparatus or other apparatus in relation to which the offence was committed or which was used in connection with the commission of it;

(iii) any wireless telegraphy apparatus or other apparatus not falling within paragraph (ii) above which was, at the time of the commission of the offence, in the possession or under the control of the person convicted of the offence and was intended to be used (whether or not by that person) in connection with the making of any broadcast or other transmission that would contravene section 1 of this Act or any provision of the Marine, &c, Broadcasting (Offences) Act 1967.

(3AA) The power conferred by virtue of subsection (3)(*a*) above does not apply in a case where the offence is any such offence as is mentioned in subsection (1A)(*a*) or (*aa*) above.

(3AB) References in subsection (3)(ii) or (iii) above to apparatus other than wireless telegraphy apparatus include references to—

(*a*) recordings;

(*b*) equipment designed or adapted for use—

(i) in making recordings; or

(ii) in reproducing from recordings any sounds or visual images; and

(*c*) equipment not falling within paragraphs (*a*) and (*b*) above but connected, directly or indirectly, to wireless telegraphy apparatus.

(3A) Without prejudice to the operation of subsection (3) of this section in relation to any other apparatus, where a person is convicted of an offence under this Act involving restricted apparatus, the court shall order the apparatus to be forfeited to OFCOM unless the accused or any person claiming to be the owner of or otherwise interested in the apparatus shows cause why the apparatus should not be forfeited.

Apparatus is restricted apparatus for the purpose of this subsection if custody or control of apparatus of any class or description to which it belongs is for the time being restricted by an order under section 7 of the Wireless Telegraphy Act 1967.

(3B) Apparatus may be ordered to be forfeited under this section notwithstanding that it is not the property of the person by whom the offence giving rise to the forfeiture was committed, and any apparatus ordered to be forfeited under this section may be disposed of by the OFCOM in such manner as they think fit.

(3C) Subsections (3) to (3B) of this section have effect notwithstanding anything in section 140 of the Magistrates' Courts Act 1980 or (*Northern Ireland*).

(3D) The court by whom any apparatus is ordered to be forfeited under this section may also order the person by whom the offence giving rise to the forfeiture was committed not to dispose of that apparatus except by delivering it up to OFCOM within forty-eight hours of being so required by him.

(3E) If a person against whom an order is made under subsection (3D) of this section contravenes that order or fails to deliver up the apparatus to OFCOM as required he shall be guilty of a further offence under this Act which, for the purpose of determining the appropriate penalty in accordance with the provisions of this section relating to penalties, shall be treated as an offence committed under the same provision, and at the same time, as the offence for which the forfeiture was ordered.

(4), (5) *Repealed.*

(6) Without prejudice to the right to bring separate proceedings for contraventions of this Act taking place on separate occasions, a person who is convicted of an offence under this Act consisting in the use of any station or apparatus, or in a failure or refusal to cause any licence or authority to be surrendered, shall where the use, or failure or refusal continues after the conviction, be deemed to commit a separate offence in respect of every day on which the use, failure or refusal so continues.

(7) Nothing in the preceding provisions of this section shall limit any right of any person to bring civil proceedings in respect of the doing or apprehended doing of anything rendered unlawful by any provision of this Act, and, without prejudice to the generality of the preceding words, compliance with the provisions of this Act contraventions of which are declared to be offences under this Act shall be enforceable by civil proceedings by the Crown or by OFCOM for an injunction or for any other appropriate relief.

Scotland.

(8), (9) *Repealed.*

[Wireless Telegraphy Act 1949, s 14, as amended by the Wireless Telegraphy Act 1967, ss 9(3), 11(1), (2), the Post Office Act 1969, the Criminal Law Act 1977, Sch 6, the Criminal Justice Act 1982, ss 35, 38 and 46, the Telecommunications Act 1984, s 82 and Sch 3, the Broadcasting Act 1990, s 172 and Sch 21, the Statute Law (Repeals) Act 1993, Sch 1 and the Communications Act 2003, s 179 and the Communications Act 2003, ss 179 and 406.]

---

1. The Telecommunications Act 1984 s 76 provides that in relation to any indictable offence under the 1949 Act and any offence under s 1(1) other than one consisting in the installation or use, otherwise than under and in accordance with a wireless telegraphy licence, of any apparatus not designed or adapted for emission (as opposed to reception), a constable may arrest without warrant a person who has committed, or whom the constable with reasonable cause suspects to have committed, an offence to which this section applies, if the name and address of that person are unknown to, and cannot be ascertained by, the constable or the constable has reasonable grounds for doubting—

(*a*) Whether a name and address furnished by that person as his name and address are his real name and address; or

(*b*) Whether that person will be at an address furnished by him for a sufficiently long period for it to be possible to serve him with a summons.

2. For procedure in respect of an offence triable either way, see the Magistrates' Courts Act 1980, ss 17A–21 in PART I: MAGISTRATES' COURTS, PROCEDURE, ante. Section 143 of the Powers of Criminal Courts (Sentencing) Act 2000 (deprivation order) does not apply to a conviction of an offence under the 1949 Act (Telecommunications Act 1984, Sch 3, para 3).

8–30105T 15. Entry and search of premises, etc. (1) If, in England, Wales or Northern Ireland, a justice of the peace, or, in Scotland, the sheriff, is satisfied by information on oath that there is reasonable ground for suspecting that an offence under this Act or under the Marine, &c., Broadcasting (Offences) Act 1967 has been or is being committed, and that evidence of the commission of the offence is to be found on any premises specified in the information, or in any vehicle, vessel or aircraft so specified, he may grant a search warrant authorising any constable or any person or persons authorised for the purpose by OFCOM or the Secretary of State to enter, at any time within three months from the date of the warrant, the premises specified in the information or, as the case may be, the vehicle, vessel or aircraft so specified and any premises upon which it may be, and to search the premises, or, as the case may be, the vehicle, vessel or aircraft, and to examine and test any apparatus found on the premises, vessel, vehicle or aircraft.

(1A) Where a person authorised by OFCOM or the Secretary of State is authorised by a warrant under subsection (1) to enter any premises, he is to be entitled to exercise that warrant alone or to exercise it accompanied by one or more constables.

(2) If, in England, Wales or Northern Ireland, a justice of the peace, or, in Scotland, the sheriff, is satisfied upon an application supported by sworn evidence—

(*a*) that there is reasonable ground for believing that, on any specified premises or in any specified vessel, aircraft or vehicle, apparatus to which section ten of this Act applies is to be found which does not comply with the requirements applicable to it under regulations made under that section; and

(*b*) that it is necessary to enter those premises, or that vessel, aircraft or vehicle, for the purpose of obtaining such information as will enable OF to decide whether or not to serve a notice under section eleven or section twelve of this Act; and

(*c*) that access to the premises, vessel, aircraft or vehicle for the purpose of obtaining such information as aforesaid has, within fourteen days before the date of the application to the justice or sheriff, been demanded by a person authorised in that behalf by the Secretary of State and producing sufficient documentary evidence of his identity and authority, but has been refused,

the justice or sheriff may issue a written authorisation under his hand empowering any person or persons authorised in that behalf by the Secretary of State and named in the authorisation, with or without any constables, to enter the premises or, as the case may be, the vessel, aircraft or vehicle and any premises on which it may be and to search the premises, vessel, aircraft or vehicle with a view to discovering whether any such apparatus as aforesaid is situate thereon or therein, and, if he finds or they find any such apparatus thereon, or therein, to examine and test it with a view to obtaining such information as aforesaid: Provided that an authorisation shall not be issued under this subsection unless either—

(i) it is shown to the justice or sheriff that the Secretary of State is satisfied that there is reasonable ground for believing that the use of the apparatus in question is likely to cause undue interference with any wireless telegraphy used for the purposes of any safety of life service or any purpose on which the safety of any person or of any vessels, aircraft or vehicle may depend; or

(ii) it is shown to the justice or sheriff that not less than seven days' notice of the demand for access was served on the occupier of the premises, or, as the case may be, the person in possession or the person in charge of the vessel, aircraft or vehicle, and that the demand was made at a reasonable hour and was unreasonably refused.

(2A) Without prejudice to any power exercisable by him apart from this subsection, a person authorised by the Secretary of State or (as the case may be) by OFCOM to exercise any power conferred by this section may use reasonable force, if necessary, in the exercise of that power.

(3) Where under this section a person has a right to examine and test any apparatus on any premises or in any vessel, aircraft or vehicle, it shall be the duty of any person who is on the premises, or is in charge of, or in or in attendance on, the vessel, aircraft or vehicle, to give him any such assistance as he may reasonably require in the examination or testing of the apparatus.

(4) Any person who—

(*a*) intentionally obstructs any person in the exercise of the powers conferred on him under this section; or

(*b*) without reasonable excuse fails or refuses to give any such person assistance which he is under this section under a duty to give to him;

(*c*) *repealed*

shall be guilty of an offence[3] under this Act.

[Wireless Telegraphy Act 1949, s 15, as amended by Post Office Act 1969, 8th Sch, the Telecommunications Act 1984, s 92 and the Broadcasting Act 1990, s 173 and Schs 18, 21, the Communications Act 2003, s 406 and the Serious Organised Crime and Police Act 2005, Sch 16.]

---

1. The Telecommunications Act 1984 s 79, as amended by the Broadcasting Act 1990, s 173, provides that where a warrant is issued and the suspected offence is any indictable offence under the 1949 Act or any offence under s 1(1) thereof other than one consisting in the installation or use, otherwise than under and in accordance with a wireless telegraphy licence, of any apparatus not designed or adapted for emission (as opposed to reception), or s 5(*b*) thereof, or under the Marine &c, Broadcasting (Offences) Act 1967, the warrant may authorise any person authorised by the Secretary

of State to seize and detain, for the purposes of any relevant proceedings, any apparatus or other thing found in the course of the search carried out in pursuance of the warrant which appears to him to have been used in connection with or to be evidence of the commission of any such offence; also if a constable or any person authorised by the Secretary of State to exercise the power has reasonable grounds to suspect that an offence to which this section applies has been or is being committed, he may seize and detain, for the purposes of any relevant proceedings, any apparatus or other thing which appears to him to have been used in connection or to be evidence of the commission of any such offence. Obstruction is an offence punishable under the 1949 Act. Relevant proceedings are proceedings for an offence as indicated above, and also proceedings for forfeiture under s 80 of the Telecommunications Act 1984 (see in this title, post). Property seized is retained for six months or until the conclusion of proceedings for forfeiture under s 80 of the Telecommunications Act 1984, see s 83 thereof, time for any appeal should also be allowed for (s 91).

2. In our opinion, the authority to enter "at any time" empowers the entry by virtue of the warrant to be by day or by night, on a weekday or a Sunday; see *Magee v Morris* [1954] 2 All ER 276, 118 JP 360.

3. For penalty, etc, see s 14, ante.

8–30105U 19. Interpretation. (1) In this Act, except where the context otherwise requires, the expression "wireless telegraphy" means the emitting or receiving, over paths which are not provided by any material substance constructed or arranged for that purpose, of electro-magnetic energy of a frequency not exceeding three million megacycles a second, being energy which either—

(*a*) serves for the conveying of messages, sound or visual images (whether the messages, sound or images are actually received by any person or not), or for the actuation or control of machinery or apparatus; or

(*b*) is used in connection with the determination of position, bearing or distance, or for the gaining of information as to the presence, absence, position or motion of any object or of any objects of any class,

and references to stations for wireless telegraphy and apparatus for wireless telegraphy or wireless telegraphy apparatus shall be construed as references to stations and apparatus for the emitting or receiving as aforesaid of such electro-magnetic energy as aforesaid.

(2) In this Act, the expression "station for wireless telegraphy" includes the wireless telegraphy apparatus of a ship or aircraft, and the expression "electric line" has the same meaning as in the Electricity Act 1989[1].

(2A) *Repealed.*

(2AA) In this Act "OFCOM" means the Office of Communications.

(3) Any reference in this Act to the emission of electro-magnetic energy, or to emission (as opposed to reception), shall be construed as including a reference to the deliberate reflection of electro-magnetic energy by means of any apparatus designed or specially adapted for that purpose, whether the reflection is continuous or intermittent.

(4) In this Act, the expression "interference," in relation to wireless telegraphy, means the prejudicing by any emission or reflection of electro-magnetic energy of the fulfilment of the purposes of the telegraphy (either generally or in part, and, without prejudice to that generality of the preceding words, as respects all, or as respects any, of the recipients or intended recipients of any message, sound or visual image intended to be conveyed by the telegraphy), and the expression "interfere" shall be construed accordingly.

(5) Interference with any wireless telegraphy is not to be regarded as undue for the purposes of this Act unless it is also harmful.

(5A) For the purposes of this Act interference is harmful if—

(*a*) it creates dangers, or risks of danger, in relation to the functioning of any service provided by means of wireless telegraphy for the purposes of navigation or otherwise for safety purposes; or

(*b*) it degrades, obstructs or repeatedly interrupts anything which is being broadcast or otherwise transmitted—

(i) by means of wireless telegraphy; and

(ii) in accordance with a licence under this Act, regulations under the proviso to section 1(1) of this Act or a grant of recognised spectrum access under Chapter 2 of Part 2 of the Communications Act 2003 or otherwise lawfully.

(6) Any reference in this Act to the sending or the conveying of messages including a reference to the making of any signal or the sending or conveying of any warning or information, and any reference to the reception of messages shall be construed accordingly.

(7) In this Act, the expressions "ship" and "vessel" have the same meaning as "ship" in the Merchant Shipping Act 1995[2].

(8) References in this Act to apparatus on board a ship or vessel include references to apparatus on a kite or captive balloon flown from a ship or vessel.

(9) *Repealed.*

(10) Any reference in this Act to any other enactment shall, except so far as the context otherwise requires, be construed as a reference to that enactment as amended by or under any other enactment, including this Act.

[Wireless Telegraphy Act 1949, s 19, as amended by the Cable and Broadcasting Act 1984, Sch 6, the Electricity Act 1989, Sch 16, the Broadcasting Act 1990, Sch 18, the Merchant Shipping Act 1995, Sch 13 and the Communications Act 2003, ss 183 and 406.]

1. For the meaning of "electric line" see s 64 of the Electricity Act 1989, in this PART: title ENERGY, ante.
2. "Ship" includes every description of vessel used in navigation (Merchant Shipping Act 1995, s 313(1)).
3. The recorded delivery service may be used (Recorded Delivery Service Act 1962, s 1).

Wireless Telegraphy Act 1967

(1967 c 72)

PART I
INFORMATION AS TO SALE AND HIRE OF TELEVISION SETS

8–30105V 1. Registration of dealers. *Repealed.*

8–30105W 2. Notification and recording of transactions. (1) Subject to subsections (1A) and (2) of this section, every television dealer who, after the end of twenty-eight days from the date on which he became such a dealer—

(*a*) sells a television set[1] by retail;
(*b*) lets a television set on hire or hire-purchase; or
(*c*) arranges for a television set to be sold or let as aforesaid to any person by another television dealer,

shall, in relation to that sale or letting, give to the BBC a notification[2] containing the particulars specified in Part I of the Schedule to this Act[1] and make a record[2] of the particulars specified in Part II of the Schedule.

(1A) Subsection (1) of this section shall not apply to a television dealer in whose case the following conditions are satisfied, that is to say—

(*a*) that he is such a dealer by reason only that he sells or lets, or holds himself out as willing to sell or let, television sets in pursuance of arrangements made by another television dealer; and
(*b*) that all payments of or towards the price or by way of rent in respect of any television set sold or let by him are received or collected on his behalf by the dealer who arranged for the sale or letting to be made.

(1B) A television dealer in whose case the conditions specified in subsection (1A) of this section cease to be satisfied shall be treated for the purposes of subsection (1) of this section as having become a television dealer when those conditions ceased to be satisfied in his case.

(2) In relation to any sale or letting as respects which subsection (1) of this section is required to be complied with by the dealer who arranges for the sale or letting to be made, the other dealer concerned—

(*a*) shall not be required to comply with that subsection; but
(*b*) shall, unless all payments of or towards the price or by way of rent in respect of the sale or letting are to be received or collected on his behalf by the first-mentioned dealer, make a record of the particulars specified in Part III of the Schedule to this Act.

(3) Any notification to be given to the BBC under this section shall be in the prescribed form and shall be given to them within twenty-eight days from the date of the sale or letting to which it relates; and any such notification to be given by any dealer shall be given to the BBC at such address as they may have directed by a notice in writing given to that dealer or, if no such notice has been given, at the prescribed address[2].

(4) Any record under this section may be made either in the prescribed form or in any other form which enables the matters recorded to be readily ascertained by any person to whom the record is produced for inspection; and any matter required to be recorded by virtue of Part II or III of the Schedule to this Act shall be recorded within the time specified in relation thereto in that Part of the Schedule.

(5) Any record made under this section by any person shall be kept at a place at which he carries on business and, unless he previously ceases to be a television dealer, shall be preserved by him—

(*a*) if it relates to a sale and the price is not payable by instalments, for twelve months from the date of the sale;
(*b*) if it relates to a sale and the price is payable by instalments or to a letting, for twelve months from the date when the last instalment or payment of rent is due.

(6) The person having charge of any place where records are kept under this section shall at any time during normal business hours, if so required by a person duly authorised in that behalf by the BBC, produce the records for inspection.

(7) The [Secretary of State] may by regulations amend or delete any provision of the Schedule to this Act or add any further provision thereto.

[Wireless Telegraphy Act 1967, s 2, as amended by the Broadcasting Act 1990, Sch 18 and SI 1996/1864.]

1. "Television set" is defined in s 6(1), post.
2. See the Wireless Telegraphy Act 1967 (Prescribed Forms etc) Regulations 1979, SI 1979/563.

8–30105X **3. Power to call for additional information.** (1) The BBC may by notice in writing require a television dealer to furnish to them, at the specified address and within twenty-eight days from the date of the notice, a statement containing the following information—

(*a*) whether, in the case of any specified credit-sale contract, hire contract or hire-purchase contract[1] made after the expiration of twenty-eight days from the appointed day, any instalment of the price or payment of rent will fall to be received or collected by him from the buyer or hirer after the date of the notice;

(*b*) if so, the present or last-known address of the buyer or hirer.

(2) *Repealed.*

(3) In this section "credit-sale contract" means a contract for the sale of a television set by retail on terms providing for the price to be paid by instalments, "hire contract" means a contract for the letting of a television set on hire, "hire-purchase contract" means a contract for the letting of a television set on hire-purchase and "specified" means specified in the notice in question.

[Wireless Telegraphy Act 1967, s 3, as amended by the Broadcasting Act 1990, Schs 18 and 21.]

1. For definitions of these terms, see sub-s (3), post.

8–30105Y **4. Service of notices, etc.** *Repealed.*

8–30105Z **5. Offences and enforcement.** (1) Any person who—

(*a*) without reasonable excuse, fails to comply with, or with any notice given under, any of the foregoing provisions of this Part of this Act; or

(*b*) in purported compliance therewith—

(i) knowingly or recklessly furnishes any information which is false in a material particular; or

(ii) makes or causes to be made or knowingly allows to be made any record which he knows to be false in a material particular,

shall be guilty of an offence under the principle Act[1].

(2) *Repealed.*

(3) Summary proceedings in England, Wales or Northern Ireland for an offence under this section may be taken on behalf of the BBC at any time within six months from the date on which evidence sufficient in their opinion to justify the proceedings comes to his knowledge:

Provided that proceedings shall not be so taken more than three years after the commission of the offence.

(4) *Scotland.*

(5) For the purpose of subsections (3) and (4) of this section, a certificate of the BBC or the Lord Advocate, as the case may be, as to the date on which such evidence as aforesaid came to their or his knowledge shall be conclusive evidence of that fact.

[Wireless Telegraphy Act 1967, s 5, as amended by the Broadcasting Act 1990, Schs 18 and 21.]

1. For penalties, see the Wireless Telegraphy Act 1949, s 14, ante.

8–30106 **6. Interpretation of Part I.** (1) In this Part of this Act—

"appointed day" means such day as the Secretary of State may by order appoint;

"the BBC" means the British Broadcasting Corporation;

"prescribed" means prescribed by regulations made by the Secretary of State after consultation with the BBC;

"television dealer" means a person of any description specified in regulations made by the Secretary of State setting out the descriptions of persons who are to be television dealers for the purposes of this Part;

"television set" means any apparatus of a description specified in regulations made by the Secretary of State setting out the descriptions of apparatus that are to be television sets for the purposes of this Part.

(1A) Regulations under subsection (1) defining a television set may provide for references to such a set to include references to software used in association with apparatus.

(2) In this Part of this Act references to sale by retail do not include references to such sales by auction unless the auctioneer is selling as principal; and references to letting on hire or hire-purchase do not include references to letting as aforesaid for the purpose of re-sale or re-letting.

(3) For the purposes of this Part of this Act a television set is sold or let on hire or hire-purchase when the contract of sale or, as the case may be, the contract of hire or hire-purchase is made.

[Wireless Telegraphy Act 1967, s 6, as amended by the Cable and Broadcasting Act 1984, Schs 5 and 6, the Broadcasting Act 1990, Schs 18 and 20 and the Communications Act 2003, s 367,.]

PART II
MISCELLANEOUS

8–30106A **7. Restriction on dealings in and custody of certain apparatus.** In order to reduce or prevent the risk of interference[1], OFCOM may make an order[2] restricting manufacture, selling, hiring, advertising, having in one's custody or control or importation[3] of wireless telegraphy apparatus[1] or apparatus used with it; any person contravening the order may be liable to a penalty under the Customs and Excise Management 1979 or the Wireless Telegraphy Act 1949[4].*

[Wireless Telegraphy Act 1967, s 7 as substituted by the Telecommunications Act 1984, s 77 and amended by the Communications Act 2003, s 406—summarised.]

1. In this Act, "wireless telegraphy", "wireless telegraphy apparatus", "apparatus for wireless telegraphy" and "interference" have the same meanings as in the Wireless Telegraphy Act 1949 (s 15(3)). See s 19 of that Act, ante.

2. The Wireless Telegraphy (Control of Interference from Videosenders) Order 1998, SI 1998/722, the Wireless Telegraphy (Citizen Band and Amateur Apparatus) (Various Provisions) Order 1998, SI 1998/2531 amended by SI 2000/1013 and the Wireless Telegraphy (Cordless Telephone Apparatus) (Restriction and Marking) Order 1999, SI 1999/2934 amended by SI 2000/1014 have been made.

3. In *R v Goldstein* [1982] 3 All ER 53, [1982] 1 WLR 804 (affirmed House of Lords [1983] 1 All ER 434, [1983] 1 WLR 151), the prohibition on importation of certain radiotelephonic apparatus imposed pursuant to this section and the Radiotelephonic Transmitters (Control of Manufacture and Importation) Order 1968, reg 3, was held not to be precluded by article 30 of the EEC Treaty since on the facts of that case it was justified under article 36 of the EEC Treaty.

4. For penalties, see the Wireless Telegraphy Act 1949, s 14(1)(*c*), ante. As to forfeiture of apparatus, see s 11(3), post.

8–30106B 8. Provisions for securing enforcement of s 1[1] of principal Act in relation to vehicles. (1) The power of the Secretary of State under section 7(1) of the Vehicle Excise and Registration Act 1994 to specify declaration to be made and particulars to be furnished by a person applying for a licence under that Act in respect of a vehicle shall include power to require the declaration and particulars to extend to any matters relevant for the enforcement of s 1(1) of the principal Act in respect of any apparatus for wireless telegraphy installed in the vehicle; and the appropriate authority shall accordingly not be required to issue a licence under the Vehicle Excise and Registration Act 1994 where the applicant fails to comply with provisions included in the regulations by virtue of this subsection.*

(2) If any person, in furnishing any information for the purpose of a requirement imposed by virtue of subsection (1) of this section, makes any statement which he knows to be false in a material particular, or recklessly makes any statement which is false in a material particular, he shall be guilty of an offence under the principal Act[2].*

(3) Subsection (2) of this section shall have effect to the exclusion of any provision for corresponding purposes contained in the Vehicle Excise and Registration Act 1994.

(4) *Repealed.*

[Wireless Telegraphy Act 1967, s 8 as amended by the Vehicle Excise and Registration Act 1994, Schs 3 and 5 and the Communications Act 2003, s 406.]

1. See PART VII: TRANSPORT, title ROAD TRAFFIC, ante.

2. For penalties, see the Wireless Telegraphy Act 1949, s 14, ante.

8–30106C 12. Enforcement of principal Act. (1) For the purposes of any offence under the principal Act committed within the seaward limits referred to in s 9(1)[1] of this Act but not within the United Kingdom, proceedings for that offence may be taken, and the offence may for all incidental purposes be treated as having been committed, in any place in the United Kingdom.

(2) For the purpose of the enforcement of the principal Act, a member of a police force shall have in any area of the sea within the seaward limits aforesaid all the powers, protection and privileges which he has in the area for which he acts as constable.

[Wireless Telegraphy Act 1967, s 12.]

1. Repealed; see now the Territorial Waters Jurisdiction Act 1878 and the Territorial Sea Act 1987 (12 miles).

Section 2

SCHEDULE

NOTIFICATIONS AND RECORDS

(As amended by the Wireless Telegraphy Act 1967 (Prescribed Forms, etc) Regulations 1979, SI 1979/563.)

PART I

PARTICULARS TO BE NOTIFIED

8–30106D 1. The date of the sale or letting.

2. The name and address of the buyer or hirer.

3. The address of the premises where the set is to be installed.

4. Whether the set is designed for reception in colour.

5. The name, address and registration number of the dealer selling or letting the set.

PART II

PARTICULARS TO BE RECORDED BY NOTIFYING DEALER

Within 28 days from the date of the sale or letting

1. The date of the sale or letting.

2. The name and address of the buyer or hirer.

3. The address of the premises where the set is to be installed.

4. Whether the set is designed for reception in colour.
5. The name, address and registration number of the dealer selling or letting the set.

PART III
PARTICULARS TO BE RECORDED BY OTHER DEALER

Within 28 days from the date of the sale or letting

1. The date of the sale or letting.
2. The name and address of the buyer or hirer.
3. The name and address of the dealer who arranged the sale or letting.
4. The address (if known) of the premises where the set is to be installed.
5. Whether the set is designed for reception in colour.

Marine etc Broadcasting (Offences) Act 1967

(1967 c 41)

8–30106E 1. Prohibition of broadcasting from ships and aircraft. (1) It shall not be lawful for a broadcast[1] to be made from a ship[1] or aircraft while it is in or over the United Kingdom or external waters[1], nor shall it be lawful for a broadcast to be made from a ship registered in the United Kingdom, the Isle of Man or any of the Channel Islands or an aircraft so registered while the ship or aircraft is elsewhere than in or over the United Kingdom or external waters[1].

(2) If a broadcast is made from a ship in contravention of the foregoing subsection, the owner of the ship, the master of the ship and every person who operates, or participates in the operation of, the apparatus by means of which the broadcast is made shall be guilty of an offence[2]; and if a broadcast is made from an aircraft in contravention of that subsection, the operator of the aircraft, the commander of the aircraft and every person who operates, or participates in the operation of, the apparatus by means of which the broadcast is made shall be guilty of an offence[2].

(3) A person who procures the making of a broadcast in contravention of subsection (1) above shall be guilty of an offence[2].

(4) In subsection (2) above—

(*a*) "master", in relation to a ship, includes any other person (except a pilot) having command or charge of the ship;

(*b*) "operator", in relation to an aircraft, means the person for the time being having the management of the aircraft.

[Marine etc Broadcasting (Offences) Act 1967, s 1.]

1. "Broadcast", "ship", "external waters", are defined in s 9(1), post.
2. For penalty and provisions regarding prosecutions, see s 6, post.

8–30106F 2. Prohibition of a broadcasting from marine structures. (1) It shall not be lawful for a broadcast[1] to be made from—

(*a*) a structure in any waters to which this section applies, being a structure affixed to, or supported by, the bed of those waters and not being a ship; or

(*b*) any other object in such waters, being neither a structure affixed or supported as aforesaid nor a ship or aircraft;

and if a broadcast is made in contravention of the foregoing provision, every person who operates, or participates in the operation of, the apparatus by means of which the broadcast is made shall be guilty of an offence[1].

(2) A person who procures the making of a broadcast in contravention of the foregoing subsection shall be guilty of an offence[2].

(3) This section applies to—

(*a*) tidal waters in the United Kingdom;

(*b*) external waters; and

(*c*) waters in a designated area within the meaning of the Continental Shelf Act 1964.

[Marine etc Broadcasting (Offences) Act 1967, s 2, as amended by the Broadcasting Act 1990, Sch 16.]

1. For penalty and provisions regarding prosecutions, see s 6, post.

8–30106G 2A. Unlawful broadcasting from within prescribed areas of the high seas. (1) Subject to subsection (4) below, it shall not be lawful to make a broadcast which—

(*a*) is made from a ship (other than one registered in the United Kingdom, the Isle of Man or any of the Channel Islands) while the ship is within any area of the high seas prescribed for the purposes of this section by an order[1] made by the Secretary of State; and

(*b*) is capable of being received in, or causes interference with any wireless telegraphy in, the United Kingdom.

(2) If a broadcast is made from a ship in contravention of subsection (1) above, the owner of the ship, the master of the ship and every person who operates, or participates in the operation of, the apparatus by means of which the broadcast is made shall be guilty of an offence[2].

(3) A person who procures the making of a broadcast in contravention of subsection (1) above shall be guilty of an offence[2].

(4) The making of a broadcast does not contravene subsection (1) above if it is shown to have been authorised under the law of any country or territory outside the United Kingdom.

(5) Any order under this section shall be made by statutory instrument subject to annulment in pursuance of a resolution of either House of Parliament.

[Marine etc Broadcasting (Offences) Act 1967, s 2A, as inserted by the Broadcasting Act 1990, Sch 16.]

---

1. See the Marine, etc, Broadcasting (Offences) (Prescribed Areas of the High Seas) Order 1990, SI 1990/2503.
2. For penalty, see s 6, post.

8-30106H 3. Prohibition of acts connected with broadcasting from certain ships and aircraft, and from marine structures outside United Kingdom. (1) Subject to subsection (1A) below, if a broadcast is made—

(*a*) from a ship other than one registered in the United Kingdom, the Isle of Man or any of the Channel Islands while the ship is on the high seas[1]; or

(*b*) from an aircraft other than one so registered while the aircraft is on or over the high seas[1]; or

(*c*) from a structure on the high seas[1], being a structure affixed to, or supported by, the bed of those seas not being a ship; or

(*d*) from any other object on those seas, being neither a structure affixed or supported as aforesaid nor a ship or aircraft;

any of the persons mentioned in subsection (3) below who operates, or participates in the operation of, the apparatus by means of which the broadcast is made shall be guilty of an offence[2].

(1A) Subsection (1)(*a*) above does not apply to any broadcast made in contravention of section 2A(1) of this Act, and subsections (1)(*c*) and (*d*) above do not apply to structures or other objects in waters falling within section 2(3)(*c*) of this Act.

(2) Any person who procures a broadcast to be made as mentioned in the foregoing subsection[2] shall be guilty of an offence[3].

(3) The persons referred to in subsection (1) above are the following, namely—

(*a*) a British citizen, a British overseas territories citizen or a British Overseas citizen;

(*b*) a person who under the British Nationality Act 1981 is a British subject; or

(*c*) a British protected person (within the meaning of that Act).

[Marine etc Broadcasting (Offences) Act 1967, s 3, as amended by the British Nationality Act 1981, Sch 7, the Broadcasting Act 1990, Sch 16 and the British Overseas Territories Act 2002, s 2(3).]

---

1. "High seas" is defined in s 9(1), post.
2. It is not a necessary ingredient of the offence that the broadcast should be made by UK citizens or British subjects (*R v Murray* [1990] 1 WLR 1360, CA).
3. For penalty and provisions regarding prosecutions, see s 6, post.

8-30106I 3A. Prohibition of management of stations broadcasting from ships, aircraft etc. (1) Any person who, from any place in the United Kingdom or external waters, participates in the management, financing, operation or day-to-day running of any broadcasting station by which broadcasts are made—

(*a*) in contravention of section 1, 2 or 2A(1) of this Act, or

(*b*) as mentioned in section 3(1)(*a*) of this Act,

shall be guilty of an offence.

(2) In this section "broadcasting station" means any business or other operation (whether or not in the nature of a commercial venture) which is engaged in the making of broadcasts.

[Marine etc Broadcasting (Offences) Act 1967, s 3A, as inserted by the Broadcasting Act 1990, Sch 16.]

8-30106J 4. Prohibition of acts facilitating broadcasting from ships, aircraft, etc[1]. (1) A person who does any of the acts mentioned in subsection (3) below, while satisfying the condition as to knowledge or belief mentioned in the case of that act, shall be guilty of an offence[2] if—

(*a*) he does the act in the United Kingdom or external waters or in a ship registered in the United Kingdom, the Isle of Man or any of the Channel Islands or an aircraft so registered while the ship or aircraft is elsewhere than in or over the United Kingdom or external waters; or

(*aa*) where paragraph (*a*) above does not apply but the broadcasts in question are made, or are to be made, from any structure or other object (not being a ship or aircraft) in waters falling within section 2(3)(*c*) of this Act, he does the act on that structure or other object within those waters; or (*ab*) where paragraph (*a*) above does not apply but the broadcasts in question are made, or are to be made, from a ship in contravention of section 2A(1) of this Act, he does the act in that ship within any such area of the high seas as is mentioned in paragraph (*a*) of that provision; or

(*b*) being a person mentioned in s 3(3) of this Act, he does the act on or over the high seas.

(2) A person who, in the United Kingdom, procures another person to do, outside the United Kingdom, anything which, if it had been done in the United Kingdom by the last-mentioned person, would have constituted an offence under the foregoing subsection, shall be guilty of an offence[2].

(3) The acts, and conditions as to knowledge or belief, referred to in subsection (1) above are the following, namely—

(*a*) furnishing or agreeing to furnish to another ship[1] or aircraft knowing, or having reasonable cause to believe, that broadcasts are to be made from it in contravention of s 1(1) of this Act or while it is on or over the high seas;

(*b*) carrying or agreeing to carry in a ship or aircraft wireless telegraphy apparatus[3] knowing, or having reasonable cause to believe, that by means thereof broadcasts are to be made from the ship or aircraft as aforesaid;

(*c*) supplying to, or installing in, a ship or aircraft wireless telegraphy apparatus knowing, or having reasonable cause to believe that, by means thereof broadcasts are to be made from the ship or aircraft as aforesaid;

(*d*) supplying any wireless telegraphy apparatus for installation on or in, or installing any such apparatus on or in, any structure or other object (not being, in either case, a ship or aircraft) knowing, or having reasonable cause to believe, that by means of that apparatus broadcasts are to be made from the object in contravention of s 2(1) of this Act or while the object is on the high seas;

(*e*) repairing or maintaining any wireless telegraphy apparatus knowing, or having reasonable cause to believe that, by means thereof, broadcasts are made, or are to be made, in contravention of s 1(1), 2(1) or 2A(1) of this Act or as mentioned in s 3(1) of this Act;

(*f*) knowing, or having reasonable cause to believe, in the case of a ship or aircraft, that broadcasts are made, or are to be made, from it in contravention of s 1(1) of this Act or while it is on or over the high seas—

   (i) supplying any goods or materials for its operation or maintenance, for the operation or maintenance of wireless telegraphy apparatus installed therein or for the sustentation or comfort of the persons on board of it;
   (ii) carrying by water or air goods or persons to or from it;
   (iii) engaging a person as an officer or one of the crew of it;

(*g*) knowing, or having reasonable cause to believe, in the case of a structure or other object (not being, in either case, a ship or aircraft), that broadcasts are made, or are to be made, from it in contravention of s 2(1) of this Act or while it is on the high seas—

   (i) supplying any goods or materials for its maintenance, for the operation or maintenance of wireless telegraphy apparatus installed therein or thereon or for the sustentation or comfort of the persons therein or thereon;
   (ii) carrying by water or air goods or persons thereto or therefrom;
   (iii) engaging a person to render services therein or thereon.

(3A) Section 46 of the Consumer Protection Act 1987 (meaning of supply) shall have effect for construing references in this section to the supply of any thing as it has effect for the purpose of construing references in that Act to the supply of goods.]

[Marine etc Broadcasting (Offences) Act 1967, s 4 amended by the Broadcasting Act 1990, Sch 16 and the Communications Act 2003, Sch 17.]

---

1. For special defences in relation to contraventions of this section, see s 7, post.
2. For penalty and provisions regarding prosecutions, see s 6, post.
3. "Wireless telegraphy apparatus" has the same meaning as in the Wireless Telegraphy Act 1949, ante (s 9(1)).

8–30106K 5. Prohibition of acts relating to matter broadcast from ships, aircraft, etc. (1) A person who does any of the acts mentioned in subsection (3) below, and, if any intent or circumstances is or are specified in relation to the act, does it with that intent or in those circumstances, shall be guilty of an offence[1] if—

(*a*) he does the act in the United Kingdom or external waters or in a ship registered in the United Kingdom, the Isle of Man, or any of the Channel Islands or an aircraft so registered while the ship or aircraft is elsewhere than in or over the United Kingdom or external waters; or

(*aa*) where paragraph (*a*) above does not apply but the broadcasts in question are made, or are to be made, from any structure or other object (not being a ship or aircraft) in waters falling within section 2(3)(*c*) of this Act, he does the act on that structure or other object within those waters; or

(*ab*) where paragraph (*a*) above does not apply but the broadcasts in question are made, or are to be made, from a ship in contravention of section 2A(1) of this Act, he does the act in that ship within any such area of the high seas as is mentioned in paragraph (*a*) of that provision; or (*b*) being a person mentioned in s 3(3) of this Act, he does the act on or over the high seas.

(2) A person who, in the United Kingdom, procures another person to do, outside the United Kingdom, anything which, if it had been done in the United Kingdom by the last-mentioned person, would have constituted an offence under the foregoing subsection, shall be guilty of an offence[1].

(3) The acts, and, where relevant, the intent and circumstances, referred to in subsection (1) above are the following namely—

(*a*) supplying a film or sound recording knowing, or having reasonable cause to believe, that a broadcast of it is to be made in contravention of s 1(1), 2(1) or 2A(1) of this Act or as mentioned in s 3(1) thereof;

(*b*) making a literary, dramatic or musical work knowing, or having reasonable cause to believe, that a broadcast of it is to be made as aforesaid;

(*c*) making an artistic work knowing, or having reasonable cause to believe, that a broadcast of it is to be included in a television broadcast made as aforesaid;

(*d*) participating in a broadcast made as aforesaid, being actually present as an announcer, as a performer or one of the performers concerned in an entertainment given, or as the deliverer of a speech;

(*e*) advertising by means of a broadcast made as aforesaid or inviting another to advertise by means of a broadcast to be so made;

(*f*) publishing the times or other details of any broadcasts which are to be so made, or (otherwise than by publishing such details) publishing an advertisement of matter calculated to promote, directly or indirectly, the interests of a business whose activities consist in or include the operation of a station from which broadcasts are or are to be so made.*

(3A) Section 46 of the Consumer Protection Act 1987 (meaning of supply) shall have effect for construing references in this section to the supply of any thing as it has effect for the purpose of construing references in that Act to the supply of goods.

(4) The cases in which a person is to be taken for the purposes of this section as advertising by means of a broadcast include any case in which he causes or allows it to be stated, suggested or implied that entertainment included in the broadcast—

(*a*) has been supplied by him; or

(*b*) is provided wholly or partly at his expense.

(5) For the purposes of this section advertising by means of a broadcast shall be deemed to take place as well wherever the broadcast is received as where it is made.

(6) In this section "speech" includes lecture, address and sermon, and "film", "sound recording", "literary, dramatic or musical work" and "artistic work" have the same meaning as in Part I of the Copyright, Designs and Patents Act 1988 (copyright).

[Marine etc Broadcasting (Offences) Act 1967, s 5, as amended by the Copyright, Designs and Patents Act 1988, Sch 7, the Broadcasting Act 1990, Sch 16 and the Communications Act 2003, Sch 17.]

1. For penalty and provisions regarding prosecutions, see s 6, post. Nothing in this Act restricts the activities prohibited by s 5 to those done with the knowledge that the broadcast was to be made by British subjects (*R v Murray* [1990] 1 WLR 1360, CA).

8–30106L 6. Penalties and legal proceedings. (1) A person guilty of an offence under this Act shall be liable[1]—

(*a*) on summary conviction, to imprisonment for term not exceeding **six months** or to a fine exceeding the **statutory maximum**, or to **both**;

(*b*) on conviction on indictment, to imprisonment for a term not exceeding **two years** or to a **fine**, or to **both**.

(2) *Repealed.*

(3) Proceedings for an offence under this Act may be taken, and the offence may for all incidental purposes be treated as having been committed, in any place in the United Kingdom.

(4) Notwithstanding anything in any enactment relating to courts of summary jurisdiction, summary proceedings for an offence under this Act may be instituted at any time within two years[2] from the time when the offence was committed.

(5) Proceedings for an offence under this Act shall not, in England or Wales, be instituted otherwise than by OFCOM or by or with the consent of the Secretary of State or the Director of Public Prosecutions and shall not, in Northern Ireland, be instituted otherwise than by OFCOM or by or with the consent of the Secretary of State or the Attorney General for Northern Ireland.* **

(6) A member of a police force shall, for the purpose of the enforcement of this Act, have in external waters all the powers, protection and privileges which he has in the area for which he acts as constable.

(7) *Repealed.*

[Marine etc Broadcasting (Offences) Act 1967, s 6, as amended by the Criminal Jurisdiction Act 1975, Sch 6, the Broadcasting Act 1990, Sch 16 and the Communications Act 2003, Schs 17 and 19.]

***Subsection (5) words repealed and substituted by the Justice (Northern Ireland) Act 2002, s 28(2) from a date to be appointed.**

1. For procedure in respect of an offence triable either way, see the Magistrates' Courts Act 1980, ss 17A–21 in PART I: MAGISTRATES' COURTS, PROCEDURE, ante.

8–30106M 7. Special defence available in proceedings for carrying goods or persons in contravention of s 4. (1) In any proceedings against a person for an offence under s 4 of this Act consisting in the carriage of goods or persons to or from a ship or aircraft it shall be a defence for him to prove—

(*a*) that the ship or aircraft was, or was believed to be, wrecked, stranded or in distress, and that the goods or persons carried were carried for the purpose of preserving the ship or aircraft, or its cargo or apparel, or saving the lives of persons on board of it; or

(*b*) that a person on board of the ship or aircraft was, or was believed to be, suffering from hurt, injury or illness, and that the goods or persons were carried for the purpose of securing that the necessary surgical or medical advice and attendance were rendered to him.

(2) In any proceedings against a person for an offence under s 4 of this Act consisting in the carriage of goods or persons to or from an object other than a ship or aircraft it shall be a defence for him to prove—

(*a*) that the object was, or was believed to be, unsafe, and that the goods or persons carried were carried for the purpose of saving the lives of persons therein or thereon; or

(*b*) that a person therein or thereon was, or was believed to be, suffering from hurt, injury or illness, and that the goods or persons were carried for the purpose of securing that the necessary surgical or medical advice and attendance were rendered to him.

(3) In any proceedings against a person for an offence under s 4 of this Act consisting in the carriage of a person to or from a ship or aircraft or to or from an object other than a ship or aircraft, it shall be a defence for him to prove that the person carried was visiting the ship, aircraft or object, as the case may be, for the purpose of exercising or performing any power or duty conferred or imposed on him by law.

(4) The references in subsections (1)(*a*) and (2)(*a*) above to persons having been carried for the purpose of saving lives shall not be construed so as to exclude the persons whose lives it was the purpose to save and the references in subsections (1)(*b*) and (2)(*b*) above to persons having been carried as therein mentioned shall not be construed so as to exclude the person who was, or was believed to be, suffering as so mentioned.

[Marine etc Broadcasting (Offences) Act 1967, s 7.]

8–30106N 7A. Powers of enforcement in relation to marine offences under this Act. (1) The following persons are enforcement officers for the purposes of this section—

(*a*) persons authorised by the Secretary of State or OFCOM to exercise the powers conferred by subsection (5) below;*

(*b*) police officers;

(*c*) commissioned officers of Her Majesty's armed forces;

(*d*) officers commissioned by the Commissioners of Customs and Excise under section 6(3) of the Customs and Excise Management Act 1979; and

(*e*) persons not falling within any of the preceding paragraphs who are British sea-fishery officers by virtue of section 7(1) of the Sea Fisheries Act 1968;

and in this subsection "armed forces" means the Royal Navy, the Royal Marines, the regular army and the regular air force, and any reserve or auxiliary force of any of those services which has been called out on permanent service, or embodied.

(2) If an enforcement officer has reasonable grounds for suspecting—

(*a*) that an offence under this Act has been or is being committed by the making of a broadcast from any ship, structure or other object in external waters or in tidal waters in the United Kingdom or from a ship registered in the United Kingdom, the Isle of Man or any of the Channel Islands while on the high seas,

(*b*) that an offence under section 2 of this Act has been or is being committed by the making of a broadcast from a structure or other object in waters falling within subsection (3)(*c*) of that section, or

(*c*) that an offence under section 2A of this Act has been or is being committed by the making of a broadcast from a ship,

and a written authorisation has been issued by the Secretary of State or OFCOM for the exercise of the powers conferred by subsection (5) below in relation to that ship, structure or other object, then (subject to subsections (6) and (7) below) the officer may, with or without persons assigned to assist him in his duties, so exercise those powers.

(3) If—

(*a*) an authorisation has been issued by the Secretary of State or OFCOM under subsection (2) above for the exercise of the powers conferred by subsection (5) below in relation to any ship, structure or other object, and

(*b*) an enforcement officer has reasonable grounds for suspecting that an offence under section 4 or 5 of this Act has been or is being committed in connection with the making of a broadcast from that ship, structure or other object,

then (subject to subsections (6) and (7) below) the officer may, with or without persons assigned to assist him in his duties, also exercise those powers in relation to any ship, structure or other object which he has reasonable grounds to suspect has been or is being used in connection with the commission of that offence.

(4) Where—

(*a*) an enforcement officer has reasonable grounds for suspecting that an offence under section 4 or 5 of this Act has been or is being committed in connection with the making of a broadcast from a ship, structure or other object, but

(*b*) an authorisation has not been issued under subsection (2) above for the exercise of the powers conferred by subsection (5) below in relation to that ship, structure or other object,

then (subject to subsections (6) and (7) below) the officer may, with or without persons assigned to assist him in his duties, nevertheless exercise those powers in relation to any ship, structure or other object which he has reasonable grounds to suspect has been or is being used in connection with the commission of that offence if a written authorisation has been issued by the Secretary of State or OFCOM for the exercise of those powers in relation to that ship, structure or other object.

(5) The powers conferred by this subsection on an enforcement officer in relation to any ship, structure or other object are—

(*a*) to board and search the ship, structure or other object;

(*b*) to seize and detain the ship, structure or other object and any apparatus or other thing found in the course of the search which appears to him to have been used, or to have been intended to be used, in connection with, or to be evidence of, the commission of the suspected offence;

(*c*) to arrest and search any person who he has reasonable grounds to suspect has committed or is committing an offence under this Act if—

(i) that person is on board the ship, structure or other object, or

(ii) the officer has reasonable grounds for suspecting that that person was so on board at, or shortly before, the time when the officer boarded the ship, structure or other object;

(*d*) to arrest any person who assaults him, or a person assigned to assist him in his duties, while exercising any of the powers conferred by this subsection or who intentionally obstructs him or any such person in the exercise of any of those powers;

(*e*) to require any person on board the ship, structure or other object to produce any documents or other items which are in his custody or possession and are or may be evidence of the commission of any offence under this Act;

(*f*) to require any such person to do anything for the purpose of facilitating the exercise of any of the powers conferred by this subsection, including enabling any apparatus or other thing to be rendered safe and, in the case of a ship, enabling the ship to be taken to a port;

(*g*) to use reasonable force, if necessary, in exercising any of those powers;

and references in paragraphs (*a*) to (*c*) and (*e*) above to the ship, structure or other object include references to any ship's boat or other vessel used from the ship, structure or other object.

(6) Except as provided in subsection (7) below, the powers conferred by subsection (5) above shall only be exercised in tidal waters in the United Kingdom or in external waters.

(7) Those powers except so far as exercisable by virtue of an authorisation issued by OFCOM may in addition—

(*a*) in relation to a suspected offence under this Act committed in a ship registered in the United Kingdom, the Isle of Man or any of the Channel Islands while on the high seas, be exercised in relation to that ship on the high seas;

(*b*) in relation to a suspected offence under section 2 of this Act committed on a structure or other object within waters falling within subsection (3)(*c*) of that section, be exercised in relation to that structure or other object within those waters; and

(*c*) in relation to a suspected offence under section 2A of this Act committed in a ship within any such area of the high seas as is mentioned in subsection (1)(*a*) of that section, be exercised in relation to that ship within that area of the high seas.

(8) Any person who—

(*a*) assaults an enforcement officer, or a person assigned to assist him in his duties, while exercising any of the powers conferred by subsection (5) above or intentionally obstructs him or any such person in the exercise of any of those powers, or

(*b*) without reasonable excuse fails or refuses to comply with any such requirement as is mentioned in paragraph (*e*) or (*f*) of that subsection, shall be guilty of an offence[1] under this Act.

(9) Neither an enforcement officer nor a person assigned to assist him in his duties shall be liable in any civil or criminal proceedings for anything done in purported exercise of any of the powers conferred by subsection (5) above if the court is satisfied that the act was done in good faith and that there were reasonable grounds for doing it.

(10) Nothing in this section shall have effect so as to prejudice the exercise of any powers exercisable apart from this section.

(11) Any reference in this section, in relation to a person assigned to assist an enforcement officer in his duties, to the exercise of any of the powers conferred by subsection (5) above is a reference to the exercise by that person of any of those powers on behalf of that officer.

[Marine etc Broadcasting (Offences) Act 1967, s 7A, as inserted by the Broadcasting Act 1990, Sch 16 and amended by SI 1998/3086 and the Communications Act 2003, Sch 17.]

---

1. For penalty, see s 6, ante.

8–30106O 8. Saving for things done under wireless telegraphy licence. Nothing in this Act shall render it unlawful to do anything under and in accordance with a wireless telegraphy licence, or to procure anything to be so done.

[Marine etc Broadcasting (Offences) Act 1967, s 8.]

8–30106P 9. Interpretation. (1) In this Act—

"broadcast" means a broadcast by wireless telegraphy of sounds or visual images intended for general reception (whether the sounds or images are actually received by any person or not), but does not include a broadcast consisting in a message or signal sent in connection with navigation or for the purpose of securing safety;

"external waters" means the whole of the sea adjacent to the United Kingdom which is within the seaward limits of the territorial waters adjacent thereto;

"the high seas" means the seas outside the seaward limits of the territorial waters adjacent to the United Kingdom or to any country or territory outside the United Kingdom;*

"OFCOM" means the Office of Communications;

"ship" includes every description of vessel used in navigation;

"wireless telegraphy," "wireless telegraphy apparatus" and "wireless telegraphy licence" have the same meanings respectively as in the Wireless Telegraphy Act 1949[1].

(2) *Repealed.*

[Marine etc Broadcasting (Offences) Act 1967, s 9 amended by the Territorial Sea Act 1987, Sch 2 and the Communications Act 2003, Sch 17.]

---

1. See s 19 thereof, ante.

British Telecommunications Act 1981

(1981 c 38)

PART II[1]
THE POST OFFICE

Exclusive privilege of the Post Office with respect to the conveyance etc of letters

8–30106Q 66. Exclusive privilege of the Post Office with respect to the conveyance etc of letters. *Repealed.*

---

1. Includes a European deposit-taker (Banking Coordination (Second Council Directive) Regulation 1992)

8–30106R 67. General classes of acts not infringing the postal privilege. *Repealed.*

8–30106S 68 Saving for things done under a licence. *Repealed.*

PART III[1]
MISCELLANEOUS AND GENERAL

8–30106T 85. General interpretation. (1) In this Act—

"the 1953 Act" means the Post Office Act 1953;

"the 1969 Act" means the Post Office Act 1969;

"the appointed day" has the meaning given by section 1(2);

"the Corporation" means British Telecommunications;

"pension" includes allowances and gratuity;

"statutory provisions", except in relation to Northern Ireland or the Isle of Man, has the same meaning as in section 57(1) of the Harbours Act 1964, in relation to Northern Ireland, has the same meaning as in section 1(*f*) of the Interpretation Act (Northern Ireland) 1954 and, in relation to the Isle of Man, means an Act of Tynwald.

(2) Any reference in this Act to a subsidiary or wholly-owned subsidiary shall be construed in accordance with section 736 of the Companies Act 1985.

(3) This section shall extend to the Isle of Man and the Channel Islands.

[British Telecommunications Act 1981, s 85 as amended by the Companies Consolidation (Consequential Provisions) Act 1985, Sch 2, the Telecommunications Act 1984, Sch 7, the Companies Act 1989, Sch 18 amended by the Statute Law (Repeals) Act 1993, Sch 1.]

1. Part III contains ss 79–90.

Telecommunications Act 1984

(1984 c 12)

PART I[1]

INTRODUCTORY

8–30106U 4. Meaning of "telecommunication system" and related expressions. (1) In this Act "telecommunication system" means a system for the conveyance, through the agency of electric, magnetic, electro-magnetic, electro-chemical or electro-mechanical energy, of—

(*a*) speech, music and other sounds;

(*b*) visual images;

(*c*) signals serving for the impartation (whether as between persons and persons, things and things or persons and things) of any matter otherwise than in the form of sounds or visual images; or

(*d*) signals serving for the actuation or control of machinery or apparatus.

(2) For the purposes of this Act telecommunication apparatus which is situated in the United Kingdom and—

(*a*) is connected to but not comprised in a telecommunication system; or

(*b*) is connected to and comprised in a telecommunication system which extends beyond the United Kingdom.

shall be regarded as a telecommunication system and any person who controls the apparatus shall be regarded as running the system.

(3) In this Act—

"commercial activities connected with telecommunications" means any of the following, that is to say, the provision of telecommunication services, the supply or export of telecommunication apparatus and the production or acquisition of such apparatus for supply or export;

"telecommunication apparatus" means (except where the extended definition in Schedule 2 to this Act applies) apparatus constructed or adapted for use—

(*a*) in transmitting or receiving anything falling within paragraphs (*a*) to (*d*) of subsection (1) above which is to be or has been conveyed by means of a telecommunication system; or

(*b*) in conveying, for the purposes of such a system, anything falling within those paragraphs;

"telecommunication service" means any of the following, that is to say—

(*a*) a service consisting in the conveyance by means of a telecommunication system of anything falling within paragraphs (*a*) to (*d*) of subsection (1) above;

(*b*) a directory information service, that is to say, a service consisting in the provision by means of a telecommunication system of directory information for the purpose of facilitating the use of a service falling within paragraph (*a*) above and provided by means of that system; and

(*c*) a service consisting in the installation, maintenance, adjustment, repair, alteration, moving, removal or replacement of apparatus which is or is to be connected to a telecommunication system.

(4) Subject to subsection (6) below, a telecommunication system is connected to another telecommunication system for the purposes of this Act if it is being used, or is installed or connected for use, in conveying anything falling within paragraphs (*a*) to (*d*) of subsection (1) above which is to be or has been conveyed by means of that other system.

(5) Subject to subsection (6) below, apparatus is connected to a telecommunication system for the purposes of this Act if it is being used, or is installed or connected for use—

(*a*) in transmitting or receiving anything falling within paragraphs (*a*) to (*d*) of subsection (1) above which is to be or has been conveyed by means of that system; or

(*b*) in conveying, for the purposes of that system, anything falling within those paragraphs;

and references in this subsection to anything falling within those paragraphs shall include references to energy of any kind mentioned in that subsection.

(6) The connection to a telecommunication system of any other telecommunication system or any apparatus shall not be regarded as a connection for the purposes of this Act if that other telecommunication system or that apparatus would not be so connected but for its connection to another telecommunication system.

(7) In this section, except subsection (1) above, "convey" includes transmit, switch and receive and cognate expressions shall be construed accordingly.
[Telecommunications Act 1984, s 4.]

1. Part I comprises ss 1–4.

PART II[1]

PROVISION OF TELECOMMUNICATION SERVICES

Licensing etc of telecommunication systems

8–30106V 5. Prohibition on running unlicensed systems. (1) Subject to the provisions of this section and section 6 below, a person who runs a telecommunication system within the United Kingdom shall be guilty of an offence unless he is authorised to run the system by a licence granted under section 7[2] below.

(2) Subject to the provisions of this section, a person who runs within the United Kingdom a telecommunication system which he is authorised to run by a licence granted under section 7 below shall be guilty of an offence if—

(*a*) there is connected to the system—

(i) any other telecommunication system; or
(ii) any apparatus,

which is not authorised by the licence to be so connected; or

(*b*) there are provided by means of the system any telecommunication services which are not authorised by the licence to be so provided.

(3) A person guilty of an offence under this section shall be liable[3]—

(*a*) on summary conviction, to a fine not exceeding **the statutory maximum**;
(*b*) on conviction on indictment, to a **fine**.

(4) Where the commission by any person of an offence under this section is due to the act or default of some other person, that other person shall be guilty of the offence; and a person may be charged with and convicted of the offence by virtue of this subsection whether or not proceedings are taken against the first-mentioned person.

(5) In any proceedings for an offence under this section it shall, subject to subsection (6) below, be a defence for the person charged to prove that he took all reasonable steps and exercised all due diligence to avoid committing the offence.

(6) Where the defence provided by subsection (5) above involves an allegation that the commission of the offence was due to the act or default of another person, the person charged shall not, without leave of the court, be entitled to rely on that defence unless, within a period ending seven clear days before the hearing, he has served on the prosecutor a notice in writing giving such information identifying or assisting in the identification of that other person as was then in his possession.

(7) No proceedings shall be instituted in England and Wales or Northern Ireland in respect of an offence under this section except by or on behalf of the Secretary of State or the Director.
[Telecommunications Act 1984, s 5.]

1. Part II comprises ss 5–46.
2. Sections 7–27 are concerned with the licensing and approval of systems, contractors and apparatus.
3. For procedure in respect of an offence triable either way, see Magistrates' Courts Act 1980, ss 17A–21 in PART I: MAGISTRATES' COURTS PROCEDURE, ante.

8–30106W 6. Exceptions to section 5. (1) *Repealed.*

(2) Section 5(1) above is not contravened by—

(*a*) the running of a telecommunication system in the case of which the only agency involved in the conveyance of things thereby conveyed is light and the things thereby conveyed are so conveyed as to be capable of being received or perceived by the eye and without more;
(*b*) the running by a person of a telecommunication system which is not connected to another telecommunication system and in the case of which all the apparatus comprised therein is situated either—

(i) on a single set of premises in single occupation; or
(ii) in a vehicle, vessel, aircraft or hovercraft or in two or more vehicles, vessels, aircraft or hovercraft mechanically coupled together; or

(*c*) the running by a single individual of a telecommunication system which is not connected to another telecommunication system and in the case of which—

(i) all the apparatus comprised therein is under his control; and

(ii) everything conveyed by it that falls within paragraphs (*a*) to (*d*) of section 4(1) above is conveyed solely for domestic purposes of his;

and references in paragraphs (*b*) and (*c*) above to another telecommunication system do not include references to a telecommunication system to which subsection (2A) below applies (whether run by a broadcasting authority or by any other person).

(2A) This subsection applies to a telecommunication system in the case of which every conveyance made by it is either—

(*a*) a transmission, by wireless telegraphy, from a transmitting station for general reception of sounds, visual images or such signals as are mentioned in paragraph (*c*) of section 4(1) above; or

(*b*) a conveyance within a single set of premises of sounds, visual images or such signals which are to be or have been so transmitted.

(3) In the case of a business carried on by a person, section 5(1) above is not contravened by the running, for the purposes of that business, of a telecommunication system which is not connected to another telecommunication system and with respect to which the conditions specified in subsection (4) below are satisfied.

(4) The said conditions are—

(*a*) that no person except the person carrying on the business is concerned in the control of the apparatus comprised in the system;

(*b*) that nothing falling within paragraphs (*a*) to (*d*) of section 4(1) above is conveyed by the system by way of rendering a service to another;

(*c*) that, in so far as sounds or visual images are conveyed by the system, they are not conveyed for the purpose of their being heard or seen by persons other than the person carrying on the business or any employees of his engaged in the conduct thereof;

(*d*) that in so far as such signals as are mentioned in paragraph (*c*) of section 4(1) above are conveyed by the system, they are not conveyed for the purpose of imparting matter otherwise than to the person carrying on the business, any employees of his engaged in the conduct thereof or things used in the course of the business and controlled by him; and

(*e*) that, in so far as such signals as are mentioned in paragraph (*d*) of section 4(1) above are conveyed by the system, they are not conveyed for the purpose of actuating or controlling machinery or apparatus used otherwise than in the course of the business.

(5) In this section—

"broadcasting authority" means a person licensed under the Wireless Telegraphy Act 1949 to broadcast programmes for general reception;

"business" includes a trade, profession or employment and includes any activity carried on by a body of persons, whether corporate or unincorporate;

"vessel" means a vessel of any description used in navigation;

"wireless telegraphy" has the same meaning as in the said Act of 1949.

[Telecommunications Act 1984, s 6 as amended by the Broadcasting Act 1990, Schs 20 and 21.]

8–30106X 27A–27L. *Standards of Performance*[1].

1. These sections were inserted by the Competition and Service (Utilities) Act 1992, ss 1–10.

Marking etc of telecommunication apparatus

8–30106Y 28. Information etc to be marked on or to accompany telecommunication apparatus. (1) Where it appears to the Secretary of State expedient that any description of telecommunication apparatus should be marked with or accompanied by any information or instruction relating to the apparatus or its connection or use, the Secretary of State may by order[1] impose requirements for securing that apparatus of that description is so marked or accompanied, and regulate or prohibit the supply of any such apparatus with respect to which the requirements are not complied with; and the requirements may extend to the form and manner in which the information or instruction is to be given.

(2) Where an order under this section is in force with respect to telecommunication apparatus of any description, any person who, in the course of any trade or business, supplies or offers to supply telecommunication apparatus of that description in contravention of the order shall, subject to subsection (3) below, be guilty of an offence and liable[2]—

(*a*) on summary conviction, to a fine not exceeding **the statutory maximum**;

(*b*) on conviction on indictment, to a **fine**.

(3) Subsections (4) to (6) of section 5 above shall apply for the purposes of this section as they apply for the purposes of that section.

(4) An order under this section may, in the case of telecommunication apparatus supplied in circumstances where the information or instruction required by the order would not be conveyed until after delivery, require the whole or part thereof to be also displayed near the apparatus.

(5) For the purposes of this section a person exposing telecommunication apparatus for supply or having telecommunication apparatus in his possession for supply shall be deemed to offer to supply it.

(6) In this section and section 29 below "supply" shall have the same meaning as it has in Part II of the Consumer Protection Act 1987.

[Telecommunications Act 1984, s 28 as amended by the Consumer Protection Act 1987, Sch 4.]

---

1. See the Radio Equipment and Telecommunications Terminal Equipment Regulations 2000, SI 2000/730 amended by SI 2003/1903 and 3144, SI 2004/693 and SI 2005/281 made under s 2 of the European Communities Act 1972.

2. For procedure in respect of an offence triable either way, see Magistrates' Courts Act 1980, ss 17A–21 in PART I: MAGISTRATES' COURTS, PROCEDURE, ante. The enforcing authority is the Director or a local weights and measures authority within their area (s 30).

8–30106Z 29. Information etc to be given in advertisements. (1) Where it appears to the Secretary of State expedient that any description of advertisements of telecommunication apparatus should contain or refer to any information relating to the apparatus or its connection or use, the Secretary of State may by order[1] impose requirements as to the inclusion of that information, or an indication of the means by which it may be obtained, in advertisements of that description.

(2) Where an advertisement of any telecommunication apparatus to be supplied in the course of any trade or business fails to comply with any requirement imposed under this section, any person who publishes the advertisement shall, subject to subsections (3) and (4) below, be guilty of an offence and liable[2]—

(*a*) on summary conviction, to a fine not exceeding **the statutory maximum**;

(*b*) on conviction on indictment, to a **fine**.

(3) Subsections (4) to (6) of section 5 above shall apply for the purposes of this section as they apply for the purposes of that section.

(4) In any proceedings for an offence under this section it shall be a defence for the person charged to prove that he is a person whose business it is to publish or arrange for the publication of advertisements and that he received the advertisement for publication in the ordinary course of business and did not know and had no reason to suspect that its publication would amount to an offence under this section.

(5) An order under this section may specify the form and manner in which any information or indication required by the order is to be included in advertisements of any description.

(6) In this section "advertisement" includes a catalogue, a circular and a price list.

[Telecommunications Act 1984, s 29.]

---

1. See the Radio Equipment and Telecommunications Terminal Equipment Regulations 2000, SI 2000/730 amended by SI 2003/1903 and 3144, SI 2004/693 and SI 2005/281 made under s 2 of the European Communities Act 1972.

2. For procedure in respect of an offence triable either way, see Magistrates' Courts Act 1980, ss 17A–21 in PART I: MAGISTRATES' COURTS, PROCEDURE, ante. The enforcing authority is the Director or a local weights and measures authority within their area (s 30).

Offences

8–30107 42. Fraudulent use of telecommunication system. (1) A person who dishonestly obtains a service to which this subsection applies with intent to avoid payment of any charge applicable to the provision of that service shall be guilty of an offence and liable[1]—

(*a*) on summary conviction, to imprisonment for a term not exceeding **six months** or to a fine not exceeding **the statutory maximum** or to **both**;

(*b*) on conviction on indictment, to imprisonment for a term not exceeding **five years** or to a **fine** or to **both**.

(2) Subsection (1) above applies to any service (other than a service such as is mentioned in section 297(1) of the Copyright, Designs and Patents Act 1988) which is provided by means of telecommunication system the running of which is authorised by a licence granted under section 7 above.

[Telecommunications Act 1984, s 42 as amended by the Cable and Broadcasting Act 1984, Sch 5, the Broadcasting Act 1990, Sch 20 and the Telecommunications (Fraud) Act 1997, s 2.]

---

1. For procedure in respect of an offence triable either way, see Magistrates' Courts Act 1980, ss 17A–21 in PART I: MAGISTRATES' COURTS, PROCEDURE, ante.

8–30107A 42A. Possession or supply of anything for fraudulent purpose in connection with use of telecommunication system. (1) Subsection (2) below applies if a person has in his custody or under his control anything (other than an unauthorised decoder as defined in section 297A(4) of the Copyright, Designs and Patents Act 1988) which may be used for the purpose of obtaining, or for a purpose connected with the obtaining of, a service to which section 42(1) above applies.

(2) If the person intends—

(*a*) to use the thing—

(i) to obtain such a service dishonestly, or

(ii) for a purpose connected with the dishonest obtaining of such a service,

(*b*) dishonestly to allow the thing to be used to obtain such a service, or

(*c*) to allow the thing to be used for a purpose connected with the dishonest obtaining of such a service,

he shall be guilty of an offence.

(3) Subsection (4) below applies if a person supplies or offers to supply anything (other than an unauthorised decoder as defined in section 297A(4) of the Copyright, Designs and Patents Act 1988) which may be used for the purpose of obtaining, or for a purpose connected with the obtaining of, a service to which section 42(1) above applies.

(4) If the person supplying or offering to supply the thing knows or believes that the person to whom it is supplied or offered intends or intends if it is supplied to him—

(*a*) to use it—

(i) to obtain such a service dishonestly, or

(ii) for a purpose connected with the dishonest obtaining of such a service,

(*b*) dishonestly to allow it to be used to obtain such a service, or

(*c*) to allow it to be used for a purpose connected with the dishonest obtaining of such a service,

he shall be guilty of an offence.

(5) A person guilty of an offence under this section shall be liable[1]—

(*a*) on summary conviction, to imprisonment for a term not exceeding **six months** or to a fine not exceeding the **statutory maximum** or to **both**, and

(*b*) on conviction on indictment, to imprisonment for a term not exceeding **five years** or to a **fine** or to **both**.

(6) In this section, references to use of a thing include, in the case of a thing which is used to record any data, use of any of the data.

[Telecommunications Act 1984, s 42A as inserted by the Telecommunications (Fraud) Act 1997, s 1 and amended by SI 2000/1175.]

---

1. For procedure in respect of this offence which is triable either way, see the Magistrates' Courts Act 1980, ss 17A–21 in PART I: MAGISTRATES' COURTS, PROCEDURE, ante.

8–30107B 43. Improper use of public telecommunication system. (1) A person who—

(*a*) sends, by means of a public telecommunication system, a message or other matter that is grossly offensive or of an indecent, obscene or menacing character; or

(*b*) sends by those means, for the purpose of causing annoyance, inconvenience or needless anxiety to another, a message that he knows to be false or persistently makes use for that purpose of a public telecommunication system,

shall be guilty of an offence and liable on summary conviction to imprisonment for a term not exceeding **six months** or a fine not exceeding **level 5** on the standard scale or **both**.

(2) Subsection (1) above does not apply to anything done in the course of providing a programme service (within the meaning of the Broadcasting Act 1990).

[Telecommunications Act 1984, s 43 as amended by the Cable and Broadcasting Act 1984, Schs 5 and 6, the Broadcasting Act 1990, Sch 20 and the Criminal Justice and Public Order Act 1994, s 92.]

8–30107C 44. Modification etc of messages. (1) A person engaged in the running of a public telecommunication system who otherwise than in the course of his duty intentionally modifies or interferes with the contents of a message sent by means of that system shall be guilty of an offence.

(2) A person guilty of an offence under subsection (1) above shall be liable[1]—

(*a*) on summary conviction, to imprisonment for a term not exceeding **six months** or to a fine not exceeding **the statutory maximum** or to **both**;

(*b*) on conviction on indictment, to imprisonment for a term not exceeding **two years** or to a **fine** or to **both**.

[Telecommunications Act 1984, s 44.]

---

1. For procedure in respect of an offence triable either way, see Magistrates' Courts Act 1980, ss 17A–21 in PART I: MAGISTRATES' COURTS, PROCEDURE, ante.

8–30107D 45. Disclosure of messages etc. (1) A person engaged in the running of a public telecommunication system who otherwise than in the course of his duty intentionally discloses to any person—

(*a*) the contents of any message which has been intercepted in the course of its transmission by means of that system; or

(*b*) any information concerning the use made of telecommunication services provided for any other person by means of that system,

shall be guilty of an offence.

(2) Subsection (1) above does not apply to any disclosure made—

(*a*) in accordance with the order of any court or for the purposes of any criminal proceedings;

(*b*) in accordance with any warrant, authorisation or notice issued, granted or given under any provision of the Regulation of Investigatory Powers Act 2000;

(*c*) in compliance with any requirement imposed (apart from that Act) in consequence of the exercise by any person of any statutory power exercisable by him for the purpose of obtaining any document or other information; or

(*d*) in pursuance of any duty under that Act of 2000, or under Part III of the Police Act 1997, to provide information or produce any document to the Interception of Communications Commissioner or to the tribunal established under section 65 of that Act of 2000.

(3) In subsection (2) above "criminal proceedings" and "statutory power" have the same meanings as in the Regulation of Investigatory Powers Act 2000.

(4) A person guilty of an offence under this section shall be liable[1]—

(*a*) on summary conviction, to a fine not exceeding the **statutory maximum**;

(*b*) on conviction on indictment, to a **fine**.

[Telecommunications Act 1984, s 45 as substituted by the Interception of Communications Act 1985, s 11 and Sch 2 and amended by SI 2000/2543.]

1. For procedure in respect of an offence triable either way, see Magistrates' Courts Act 1980, ss 17A–21 in PART I: MAGISTRATES' COURTS, PROCEDURE, ante.

8–30107E 46. Assaults etc on persons engaged in the business of public telecommunications operator. (1) A person who—

(*a*) assaults or intentionally obstructs a person engaged in the business of a public telecommunications operator; or

(*b*) whilst in any premises used for the purposes of the business of such an operator, intentionally obstructs the course of business of the operator,

shall be guilty of an offence and liable on summary conviction to a fine not exceeding **level 3** on the standard scale.

(2) Any person engaged in the business of a public telecommunications operator may require any person guilty of an offence under subsection (1) above to leave premises used for the purposes of that business and, if any such offender who is so required refuses or fails to comply with the requirement, he shall be liable on summary conviction to a further fine not exceeding **level 3** on the standard scale and may be removed by a person engaged in that business; and any constable shall on demand remove or assist in removing any such offender.

[Telecommunications Act 1984, s 46.]

8–30107F 46A. *Powers to make regulations.*

PART III[1]
OTHER FUNCTIONS OF DIRECTOR

8–30107G 53. Power to require information etc. (1) The Director may, for any relevant purpose, by notice in writing signed by him—

(*a*) require any person to produce, at a time and place specified in the notice, to the Director or to any person appointed by him for the purpose, any documents which are specified or described in the notice and are in that person's custody or under his control; or

(*b*) require any person carrying on any business to furnish to the Director such estimates, returns or other information as may be specified or described in the notice, and specify the time, the manner and the form in which any such estimates, returns or information are to be furnished;

but no person shall be compelled for any such purpose to produce any documents which he could not be compelled to produce in civil proceedings before the court or, in complying with any requirement for the furnishing of information, to give any information which he could not be compelled to give in evidence in such proceedings.

(2) A person who refuses or, without reasonable excuse, fails to do anything duly required of him by a notice under subsection (1) above shall be guilty of an offence and liable on summary conviction to a fine not exceeding level 5 on the standard scale.

(3) A person who—

(*a*) intentionally alters, suppresses or destroys any document which he has been required by any such notice to produce; or (*b*) in furnishing any estimate, return or other information required of him under any such notice, makes any statement which he knows to be false in a material particular, or recklessly makes any statement which is false in a material particular,

shall be guilty of an offence.

(4) A person guilty of an offence under subsection (3) above shall be liable[2]—

(*a*) on summary conviction, to a fine not exceeding **the statutory maximum**;

(*b*) on conviction on indictment, to a **fine**.

(5) If a person makes default in complying with a notice under subsection (1) of this section, the court may, on the application of the Director, make such order as the court thinks fit for requiring the default to be made good; and any such order may provide that all the costs or expenses of and incidental to the application shall be borne by the person in default or by any officers of a company or other association who are responsible for its default.

(6) In this section—

"the court" has the same meaning as in section 18 above[3];

"relevant purpose" means any purpose connected with—

(*a*) the investigation of any offence under section 5, 28 or 29 above or any proceedings for any such offence,

(*aa*) the determination of any dispute referred to the Director under section 27F above,

(*ab*) the determination of any dispute referred to the Director in accordance with regulations made under section 27G above, or

(*b*) the exercise of the Director's functions under section 16, 27E, 27H, 27I, 47, 49, 50, 51 or 52[4] above or under the Telecommunications (Open Network Provision) (Voice Telephony) Regulations 1998[5].

[Telecommunications Act 1984, s 53, as amended by the Competition and Service (Utilities) Act 1992, ss 5 and 6, and Sch 1 and the Telecommunications (Licensing) Regulations 1997, SI 1997/2930 and SI 1998/1580.]

1. PART III comprises ss 47–55.
2. For procedure in respect of an offence triable either way, see the Magistrates' Courts Act 1980, ss 17A–21 in PART I: MAGISTRATES' COURTS, PROCEDURE, ante.
3. That is, the High Court.
4. Section 16 is concerned with securing compliance with licence conditions; s 49 with the investigation of complaints.
5. Telecommunications (Open Network Provision) (Voice Telephony) Regulations 1998, SI 1998/1580 amended by SI 1999/2093.

PART VI[1]

PROVISIONS RELATING TO WIRELESS TELEGRAPHY

8–30107H 80. Proceedings in England and Wales or Northern Ireland for forfeiture of restricted apparatus. (1) Apparatus is restricted apparatus for the purposes of this section and section 81 below if custody or control of apparatus of any class or description to which it belongs is for the time being restricted by an order under section 7 of the 1967 Act.

(2) Where any restricted apparatus is seized in pursuance of a warrant under section 15(1) of the 1949 Act or in exercise of the power conferred by section 79(3)[2] above, a constable or any person authorised by the Secretary of State for the purpose may apply to a justice of the peace acting for the petty sessions area in which the apparatus was seized (referred to below in this section as the relevant petty sessions area) to initiate proceedings for forfeiture of the apparatus under this section.

(3) An application under this section must be made within the period of six months beginning with the date on which the apparatus to which it relates was seized.

(4) A justice of the peace to whom an application under this section is made may issue a summons to any person appearing to him to be the owner of or otherwise interested in the apparatus to which the application relates requiring him to appear on a day specified in the summons before a magistrates' court acting for the relevant petty sessions area to show cause why the apparatus should not be forfeited.

(5) In addition to the person summoned, any other person claiming to be the owner of or otherwise interested in any apparatus to which an application under this section relates shall be entitled to appear before the court on the day specified in the summons to show cause why it should not be forfeited.

(6) Subject to the following provisions of this section, where any apparatus is brought before a magistrates' court in proceedings under this section and the court is satisfied that the apparatus is restricted apparatus, the court shall order the apparatus to be forfeited to the Secretary of State, unless the person summoned or any other person entitled to appear before the court for that purpose shows cause why the apparatus should not be forfeited.

(7) If the person summoned does not appear, the court shall not make an order under this section unless service of the summons is proved.

(8) Where in any proceedings under this section an order is made for the forfeiture of any apparatus, any person who appeared, or was entitled to appear, to show cause against the making of the order may appeal to the Crown Court.

(9) No order for the forfeiture of any apparatus made under this section shall take effect—

(*a*) until the end of the period of twenty-one days after the day on which the order is made; or

(*b*) if appeal proceedings are brought in respect of the order within that period (whether by way of appeal to the Crown Court or by way of case stated for the opinion of the High Court), until the conclusion of those proceedings.

(10) If a magistrates' court does not order forfeiture of any apparatus brought before it in proceedings under this section the court may if it thinks fit order the person on whose application the proceedings were initiated to pay such costs as the court thinks reasonable to any person who has appeared before the court to show cause why the apparatus should not be forfeited; and costs ordered to be paid under this subsection shall be enforceable as a civil debt.

(11) Any apparatus ordered to be forfeited under this section may be disposed of by the Secretary of State in such manner as he thinks fit.

(12) This section has effect notwithstanding anything in section 140 of the Magistrates' Courts Act 1980 or (*Northern Ireland*).

(13) *Northern Ireland.*

(14) *Scotland.*

[Telecommunications Act 1984, s 80.]

1. Part VI comprises ss 74–92.
In this Part—
"the 1949 Act" means the Wireless Telegraphy Act 1949;
"the 1967 Act" means the Wireless Telegraphy Act 1967; and
"wireless telegraphy", "wireless telegraphy apparatus", "emission" and "interference" have the same meanings as in the 1949 Act.

2. Section 79 of this Act is noted to s 15(1) of the Wireless Telegraphy Act 1949, in this title, ante.

8–30107I 84. *Approval of wireless apparatus etc.*

8–30107J 85. Information etc to be marked on or to accompany apparatus. (1), (2) Secretary of State may make regulations[1] about marking and display of apparatus.

(3) Where an order under this section is in force with respect to relevant apparatus of any description, any person who, in the course of any trade or business, supplies or offers to supply relevant apparatus of that description in contravention of the order shall, subject to section 87 below, be guilty of an offence and liable on summary conviction to a fine not exceeding **level 5** on the standard scale.

(4) For the purposes of this section a person exposing relevant apparatus for supply or having such apparatus in his possession for supply shall be deemed to offer to supply it.

(5) In this section and section 86 below—

(*a*) "relevant apparatus" means wireless telegraphy apparatus or apparatus designed or adapted for use in connection with wireless telegraphy apparatus; and

(*b*) "supply" shall have the same meaning as it has in Part II of the Consumer Protection Act 1987.

[Telecommunications Act 1984, s 85 as amended by the Consumer Protection Act 1987, Sch 4.]

1. See the Wireless Telegraphy (Cordless Telephone Apparatus) (Restriction and Marking) Order 1999, SI 1999/2834 amended by SI 2000/1013 and SI 2003/2155.

8–30107K 86. Information etc to be given in advertisements. (1), (2) Secretary of State may make regulations about information to be given in advertisements.

(3) Where an advertisement of any relevant apparatus which is to be supplied in the course of any trade or business fails to comply with any requirement imposed under this section, any person who publishes the advertisement shall, subject to section 87 below, be guilty of an offence and liable on summary conviction to a fine not exceeding level 5 on the standard scale.

(4) Section 85(5) above applies for the purposes of this section; and in this section "advertisement" includes a catalogue, a circular and a price list.

[Telecommunications Act 1984, s 86.]

8–30107L 87. Offences under section 85 or 86 due to default of third person. (1) Where the commission by any person of an offence under section 85 or 86 above is due to the act or default of some other person, that other person shall be guilty of the offence; and a person may be charged with and convicted of the offence by virtue of this subsection whether or not proceedings are taken against the first-mentioned person.

(2) In any proceedings for an offence under either of those sections it shall, subject to subsection (3) below, be a defence for the person charged to prove that he took all reasonable steps and exercised all due diligence to avoid committing the offence.

(3) Where the defence provided by subsection (2) above involves an allegation that the commission of the offence was due to the act or default of another person, the person charged shall not, without

leave of the court, be entitled to rely on that defence unless, within a period ending seven clear days before the hearing, he has served on the prosecutor a notice in writing giving such information identifying or assisting in the identification of that other person as was then in his possession.

(4) In any proceedings for an offence under section 86 above it shall be a defence for the person charged to prove that he is a person whose business it is to publish or arrange for the publication of advertisements and that he received the advertisement for publication in the ordinary course of business and did not know and had no reason to suspect that its publication would amount to an offence under that section.

[Telecommunications Act 1984, s 87.]

PART VII[1]

MISCELLANEOUS AND SUPPLEMENTAL

Supplemental

8–30107M 101. General restrictions on disclosure of information. (1) Subject to the following provisions of this section, no information with respect to any particular business which—

(*a*) has been obtained under or by virtue of the provisions of this Act except Part 6; and
(*b*) relates to the private affairs of any individual or to any particular business,

shall during the lifetime of that individual or so long as that business continues to be carried on, be disclosed without the consent of that individual or the person for the time being carrying on that business.

(2) Subsection (1) above does not apply to any disclosure of information which is made—

(*a*) for the purpose of facilitating the performance of any functions assigned to the Secretary of State, the Director or the Commission by or under this Act;
(*b*) for the purpose of facilitating the performance of any functions of any Minister, any Northern Ireland department, the head of any such department, the Office of Fair Trading, the Commission, the Water Services Regulation Authority, the Gas and Electricity Markets Authority, (*Northern Ireland*), the Office of Rail Regulation, OFCOM, the Civil Aviation Authority or a local weights and measures authority in Great Britain under any of the enactments or subordinate legislation specified in subsection (3) below;
(*bb*) for the purpose of facilitating the carrying out by the Comptroller and Auditor General of any of his functions under any enactment;
(*c*) in connection with the investigation of any criminal offence or for the purposes of any criminal proceedings;
(*d*) for the purpose of any civil proceedings brought under or by virtue of this Act or any of the enactments or subordinate legislation specified in subsection (3) below; or
(*e*) in pursuance of a Community obligation.

(3) The enactments or subordinate legislation referred to in subsection (2) above are—

(*a*) the Trade Descriptions Act 1968;
(*b*) the 1973 Act;
(*c*) the Consumer Credit Act 1974;
(*d*)–(*e*) *Repealed*;
(*f*) the Estate Agents Act 1979;
(*g*) the 1980 Act;
(*h*) the Consumer Protection Act 1987;
(*i*) the Control of Misleading Advertisements Regulations 1988;
(*j*) the Water Act 1989, the Water Industry Act 1991 or any of the other consolidation Acts (within the meaning of section 206 of that Act of 1991);
(*k*) the Electricity Act 1989;
(*l*) *Northern Ireland*;
(*m*) the Railways Act 1993;
(*n*) the Competition Act 1998;
(*o*) Part I of the Transport Act 2000;
(*p*) the Enterprise Act 2002;
(*q*) the Communications Act 2003 (excluding the provisions of that Act which are enactments relating to the management of the radio spectrum within the meaning of that Act);
(*r*) the Railways Act 2005.

(4) *Repealed.*

(5) Any person who discloses any information in contravention of this section shall be guilty of an offence[2] and liable—

(*a*) on summary conviction, to a fine not exceeding **the statutory maximum**;
(*b*) on conviction on indictment, to imprisonment for a term not exceeding **two years** or to a **fine** or to **both**.

(6) Information obtained by OFCOM in the exercise of functions which are exercisable

concurrently with the Office of Fair Trading under Part I of the Competition Act 1998 is subject to Part 9 of the Enterprise Act 2002 (information) and not to subsections (1) to (5) of this section.
[Telecommunications Act 1984, s 101 as amended by the Consumer Protection Act 1987, Schs 4 and 5, SI 1988/915, the Water Act 1989, Sch 25, the Electricity Act 1989, Sch 16, the Water Consolidation (Consequential Provisions) Act 1991, Sch 1, the Competition and Service (Utilities) Act 1992, Sch 1, the Railways Act 1993, Sch 12, the Competition Act 1998, Schs 10 and 14, SI 1999/506, the Utilities Act 2000, s 3(2), SI 2001/4050, the Communications Act 2003, s 406, the Enterprise Act 2002, Sch 25 and the Railways Act 2005, Sch 12 and the Water Act 2003, Sch 7.]

---

1. Part VII comprises ss 93–110.
2. For procedure in respect of an offence triable either way, see Magistrates' Courts Act 1980, ss 17A–21 of the Magistrates' Courts Act 1980 in PART I: MAGISTRATES' COURTS, PROCEDURE, ante.

8–30107N 102. Offences by bodies corporate. (1) Where a body corporate is guilty of an offence under this Act and that offence is proved to have been committed with the consent or connivance of, or to be attributable to any neglect on the part of, any director, manager, secretary or other similar officer of the body corporate or any person who was purporting to act in any such capacity he, as well as the body corporate, shall be guilty of that offence and shall be liable to be proceeded against and punished accordingly.

(2) Where the affairs of a body corporate are managed by its members, subsection (1) above shall apply in relation to the acts and defaults of a member in connection with his functions of management as if he were a director of the body corporate.
[Telecommunications Act 1984, s 102.]

8–30107O 103. Summary proceedings. Proceedings for any offence under this Act which is punishable on summary conviction may be commenced at any time within twelve months next after the commission of the offence.
[Telecommunications Act 1984, s 103.]

8–30107P 106. General interpretation. (1) In this Act, unless the context otherwise requires—

"the 1973 Act" means the Fair Trading Act 1973;
"the 1980 Act" means the Competition Act 1980;
"the 1981 Act" means the British Telecommunications Act 1981;
"commercial activities connected with telecommunications" has the meaning given by section 4(3) above;
"the Commission" means the Competition Commission;
"consumer", "monopoly situation", "practice" and "supply" have the meanings given by section 137 of the 1973 Act;
"the Director" means the Director General of Telecommunications;
"directory information service" has the meaning given by section 4(3) above;
"disabled person" means any person who is blind, deaf or dumb or who is substantially and permanently handicapped by illness, injury, congenital deformity or any other disability and "disabled" shall be construed accordingly;
"modifications" includes additions, alterations and omissions and cognate expressions shall be construed accordingly;
"telecommunication apparatus" (except where the extended definition in Schedule 2 to this Act applies) has the meaning given by section 4(3) above;
"telecommunication service" has the meaning given by section 4(3) above;
"telecommunication system" has the meaning given by subsection (1) of section 4 above (read with subsection (2) of that section).

(2), (3) *Repealed.*

(4) Any power conferred on the Secretary of State by this Act to give a direction if it appears to him to be requisite or expedient to do so in the interests of national security or relations with the government of a country or territory outside the United Kingdom includes power to give the direction if it appears to him to be requisite or expedient to do so in order—

(*a*) to discharge, or facilitate the discharge of, an obligation binding on Her Majesty's Government in the United Kingdom by virtue of it being a member of an international organisation or a party to an international agreement;
(*b*) to attain, or facilitate the attainment of, any other objects the attainment of which is, in the Secretary of State's opinion, requisite or expedient in view of Her Majesty's Government in the United Kingdom being a member of such an organisation or a party to such an agreement; or
(*c*) to enable Her Majesty's Government in the United Kingdom to become a member of such an organisation or a party to such an agreement.

(5) For the purposes of any licence granted, approval given or order made under this Act any description or class may be framed by reference to any circumstances whatsoever.
[Telecommunications Act 1984, s 106 as amended by the Statute Law (Repeals) Act 1993, Sch 1 and SI 1999/506.]

Broadcasting Act 1990

(1990 c 42)

PART I[1]
INDEPENDENT TELEVISION SERVICES

CHAPTER I
REGULATION BY COMMISSION OF TELEVISION SERVICES GENERALLY

Establishment of Independent Television Commission

8–30107Q 1. The Independent Television Commission. *Repealed.*

Function of Commission

8–30107R 2. Regulation by Commission of provision of television services. *Repealed.*

Prohibition on providing unlicensed television services

8–30107S 13. Prohibition on providing television services without a licence. (1) Subject to subsection (2), any person who provides any relevant regulated television service without being authorised to do so by or under a licence under this Part or Part I of the Broadcasting Act 1996 shall be guilty of an offence.

(1A) In subsection (1) "relevant regulated television service" means a service falling, in pursuance of section 211(1) of the Communications Act 2003, to be regulated by OFCOM, other than a television multiplex service.

(2) The Secretary of State may, after consultation with OFCOM by order[1] provide that subsection (1) shall not apply to such services or descriptions of services as are specified in the order.

(3) A person guilty of an offence under this section shall be liable[2]—

(*a*) on summary conviction, to a fine not exceeding the **statutory maximum**;
(*b*) on conviction on indictment, to a **fine**.

(4) No proceedings in respect of an offence under this section shall be instituted—

(*a*) in England and Wales, except by or with the consent of the Director of Public Prosecutions;
(*b*) *Northern Ireland.*

(5) Without prejudice to subsection (3), compliance with this section shall be enforceable by civil proceedings by the Crown for an injunction or interdict or for any other appropriate relief.

(6) Any order under this section shall be subject to annulment in pursuance of a resolution of either House of Parliament.

[Broadcasting Act 1990, s 13, as amended by the Broadcasting Act 1996, Sch 10, SI 1997/1682, SI 2000/54 and the Communications Act 2003, Sch 15.]

---

1. See the Broadcasting Act 1990 (Independent Television Services: Exceptions) Order 1990, SI 1990/2537 and the Broadcasting and (Unlicensed Television Services) Exemption (Revocation) Order 1999, SI 1999/2628.

2. For procedure in respect of an offence which is triable either way, see the Magistrates' Courts Act 1980, ss 17A–21, in PART I: MAGISTRATES' COURTS, PROCEDURE, ante.

CHAPTER VII
SUPPLEMENTAL

8–30107T 71. Interpretation of Part I. (1) In this Part (unless the context otherwise requires)—

"the 1981 Act" means the Broadcasting Act 1981;

"additional service" and "additional services licence" have the meaning given by section 48(1) and section 49(10) respectively;

"the appropriate percentage", in relation to any year, has the meaning given by section 19(10);

"cash bid", in relation to a licence, has the meaning given by section 15(7);

"Channel 3" means the system of television broadcasting services established by the Commission under section 14, and "a Channel 3 licence" means a licence to provide one of the services comprised within that system;

"Channel 4" means the television broadcasting service referred to in section 24(1), and "on Channel 4" means in that service;

"Channel 5" means the television broadcasting service referred to in section 28(1), and "a Channel 5 licence" means a licence to provide that service;

"the Corporation" means the Channel Four Television Corporation established by section 23;

"licence" means a licence under this Part, and "licensed" shall be construed accordingly;

"national Channel 3 service" has the meaning given by section 14(6), and "a national Channel 3 licence" means a licence to provide a national Channel 3 service;

"regional Channel 3 service" has the meaning given by section 14(6), and "a regional Channel 3 licence" means a licence to provide a regional Channel 3 service;

"restricted service" has the meaning given by section 42A;

"S4C" has the same meaning as in Part 3 of the Communications Act 2003;

"spare capacity" shall be construed in accordance with section 48(2);

"television broadcasting service", "television licensable content service" and "television programme service" each has the same meaning as in Part 3 of the Communications Act 2003.

(2) Where the person who is for the time being the holder of any licence ("the present licence holder") is not the person to whom the licence was originally granted, any reference in this Part (however expressed) to the holder of the licence shall be construed, in relation to any time falling before the date when the present licence holder became the holder of it, as including a reference to a person who was previously the holder of the licence.

[Broadcasting Act 1990, s 71, as amended by the Broadcasting Act 1996, Sch 10 and SI 1997/1682 and the Communications Act 2003, Schs 15 and 19.]

PART II[1]
LOCAL DELIVERY SERVICES

Preliminary

8–30107U 72. Local delivery services. *Repealed.*

1. Part II contains ss 72–82.

Prohibition on providing unlicensed local delivery services

8–30107V 82. Prohibition on providing local delivery services without a licence. *Repealed.*

PART III[1]
INDEPENDENT RADIO SERVICES

CHAPTER I
REGULATIONS BY AUTHORITY OF INDEPENDENT RADIO SERVICES GENERALLY

Establishment of Radio Authority

8–30107W 83. The Radio Authority. *Repealed.*

1. Part III contains Chs I–V, ss 83–126.

Function of Authority

8–30107X 84. Regulation by Authority of independent radio services. *Repealed.*

Prohibition on providing unlicensed independent radio services

8–30107Y 97. Prohibition on providing independent radio services without a licence. (1) Subject to subsection (2), any person who provides any relevant regulated radio service without being authorised to do so by or under a licence under this Part or Part II of the Broadcasting Act 1996 shall be guilty of an offence.*

(1A) In subsection (1) "relevant regulated radio service" means a service falling to be regulated by OFCOM under section 245 of the Communications Act 2003, other than a radio multiplex service.

(2) The Secretary of State may, after consultation with OFCOM, by order[1] provide that subsection (1) shall not apply to such services or descriptions of services as are specified in the order.

(3) A person guilty of an offence under this section shall be liable[2]—

(*a*) on summary conviction, to a fine not exceeding the **statutory maximum;**
(*b*) on conviction on indictment, to a **fine**.

(4) No proceedings in respect of an offence under this section shall be instituted—

(*a*) in England and Wales, except by or with the consent of the Director of Public Prosecutions;
(*b*) *Northern Ireland.*

(5) Without prejudice to subsection (3) above, compliance with this section shall be enforceable by civil proceedings by the Crown for an injunction or interdict or for any other appropriate relief.

(6) Any order under this section shall be subject to annulment in pursuance of a resolution of either House of Parliament.

[Broadcasting Act 1990, s 97, as amended by the Broadcasting Act 1996, Sch 10 and the Communications Act 2003, Sch 15.]

1. See the Broadcasting Act 1990 (Independent Radio Services: Exceptions) Order 1990, SI 1990/2536.
2. For procedure in respect of an offence which is triable either way, see the Magistrates' Courts Act 1980, ss 17A–21, in PART I: MAGISTRATES' COURTS, PROCEDURE, ante.

PART VII[1]

PROHIBITION ON INCLUSION OF OBSCENE AND OTHER MATERIAL IN PROGRAMME SERVICES

Supplementary

8–30107Z 167. Power to make copies of recordings. (1) If a justice of the peace is satisfied by information on oath laid by a constable that there is reasonable ground for suspecting that a relevant offence has been committed by any person in respect of a programme included in a programme service, he may make an order authorising any constable to require that person—

(*a*) to produce to the constable a visual or sound recording of any matter included in that programme, if and so far as that person is able to do so; and

(*b*) on the production of such a recording, to afford the constable an opportunity of causing of copy of it to be made.

(2) An order made under this section shall describe the programme to which it relates in a manner sufficient to enable that programme to be identified.

(3) A person who without reasonable excuse fails to comply with any requirement of a constable made by virtue of subsection (1) shall be guilty of an offence and liable on summary conviction to a fine not exceeding the **third level** on the standard scale.

(4) No order shall be made under this section in respect of any recording in respect of which a warrant could be granted under any of the following provisions, namely—

(*a*) section 3 of the Obscene Publications Act 1959;

(*b*) section 24 of the Public Order Act 1986; and

(*c*) Article 14 of the Public Order (Northern Ireland) Order 1987.

(5) In the application of subsection (1) to England and Wales "relevant offence" means an offence under—

(*a*) section 2 of the Obscene Publications Act 1959; or

(*b*) section 22 of the Public Order Act 1986.

(6)–(7) *Scotland and Northern Ireland.*

[Broadcasting Act 1990, s 167.]

---

1. Part VII contains ss 162–167.

PART X[1]

MISCELLANEOUS AND GENERAL

Foreign satellite services

8–30108 177. Orders proscribing unacceptable foreign satellite services. (1) Subject to the following provisions of this section, the Secretary of State may make an order[2] proscribing a foreign satellite service for the purposes of section 178.

(2) If OFCOM consider that the quality of any relevant foreign satellite service which is brought to their attention is unacceptable and that the service should be the subject of an order under this section, they shall notify to the Secretary of State details of the service and their reasons why they consider such an order should be made.

(3) OFCOM shall not consider a foreign satellite service to be unacceptable for the purposes of subsection (2) unless they are satisfied that there is repeatedly contained in programmes included in the service matter which offends against good taste or decency or is likely to encourage or incite to crime or to lead to disorder or to be offensive to public feeling.

(4) Where the Secretary of State has been notified under subsection (2), he shall not make an order under this section unless he is satisfied that the making of the order—

(*a*) is in the public interest; and

(*b*) is compatible with any international obligations of the United Kingdom.

(5) An order under this section—

(*a*) may make such provision for the purpose of identifying a particular foreign satellite service as the Secretary of State thinks fit; and

(*b*) shall be subject to annulment in pursuance of a resolution of either House of Parliament.

(6) In this section and section 178—

"foreign satellite service" means—

(*a*) a service which is provided by a person who is not for the purposes of Council Directive 89/552/EEC under the jurisdiction of the United Kingdom and which consists wholly or mainly in the transmission by satellite of television programmes which are capable of being received in the United Kingdom, or

(*b*) a service which consists wholly or mainly in the transmission by satellite from a place outside the United Kingdom of sound programmes which are capable of being received in the United Kingdom.

[Broadcasting Act 1990, s 177, as amended by SI 1997/1682, SI 1998/3196 and the Communications Act 2003, Sch 15.]

---

1. Part X contains ss 177–204.
2. The following Foreign Satellite Service Proscription Orders have been made: 1993, SI 1993/1024; 1995, SI 1995/2917; 1996, SI 1996/2557 and 1997, SI 1997/1150, SI 1998/1865 and 3083, SI 2005/220.

8–30108A 178. Offence of supporting proscribed foreign satellite services. (1) This section applies to any foreign satellite service which is proscribed for the purposes of this section by virtue of an order under section 177; and references in this section to a proscribed service are references to any such service.

(2) Any person who in the United Kingdom does any of the acts specified in subsection (3) shall be guilty of an offence.

(3) Those acts are—

(*a*) supplying any equipment or other goods for use in connection with the operation or day-to-day running of a proscribed service;
(*b*) supplying, or offering to supply, programme material to be included in any programme transmitted in the provision of a proscribed service;
(*c*) arranging for, or inviting, any other person to supply programme material to be so included;
(*d*) advertising, by means of programmes transmitted in the provision of a proscribed service, goods supplied by him or services provided by him;
(*e*) publishing the times or other details of any programmes which are to be transmitted in the provision of a proscribed service or (otherwise than by publishing such details) publishing an advertisement of matter calculated to promote a proscribed service (whether directly or indirectly);
(*f*) supplying or offering to supply any decoding equipment which is designed or adapted to be used primarily for the purpose of enabling the reception of programmes transmitted in the provision of a proscribed service.

(4) In any proceedings against a person for an offence under this section, it is a defence for him to prove that he did not know, and had no reasonable cause to suspect, that the service in connection with which the act was done was a proscribed service.

(5) A person who is guilty of an offence under this section shall be liable[1]—

(*a*) on summary conviction, to imprisonment for a term not exceeding **six months** or to a fine not exceeding the **statutory maximum**, or **both**;
(*b*) on conviction on indictment, to imprisonment for a term not exceeding **two years** or to a **fine**, or **both**.

(6) For the purposes of this section a person exposing decoding equipment for supply or having such equipment in his possession for supply shall be deemed to offer to supply it.

(7) Section 46 of the Consumer Protection Act 1987 shall have effect for the purpose of construing references in this section to the supply of any thing as it has effect for the purpose of construing references in that Act to the supply of any goods.

(8) In this section "programme material" includes—

(*a*) a film (within the meaning of Part I of the Copyright, Designs and Patents Act 1988);
(*b*) any other recording; and
(*c*) any advertisement or other advertising material.

[Broadcasting Act 1990, s 178.]

---

1. For procedure in respect of an offence which is triable either way, see the Magistrates' Courts Act 1980, ss 17A–21, in PART I: MAGISTRATES' COURTS, PROCEDURE, ante.

8–30108B 181. Certain apparatus to be deemed to be apparatus for wireless telegraphy. *Repealed.*

General

8–30108C 195. Offences by bodies corporate. (1) Where a body corporate is guilty of an offence under this Act and that offence is proved to have been committed with the consent or connivance of, or to be attributable to any neglect on the part of, any director, manager, secretary or other similar officer of the body corporate or any person who was purporting to act in any such capacity, then he, as well as the body corporate, shall be guilty of that offence and shall be liable to be proceeded against and punished accordingly.

(2) Where the affairs of a body corporate are managed by its members, subsection (1) above shall apply in relation to the acts and defaults of a member in connection with his functions of management as if he were a director of the body corporate.

[Broadcasting Act 1990, s 195.]

8–30108D 196. Entry and search of premises. (1) If a justice of the peace is satisfied by information on oath—

(*a*) that there is reasonable ground for suspecting that an offence under section 13, 82 or 97 has been or is being committed on any premises specified in the information, and
(*b*) that evidence of the commission of the offence is to be found on those premises,

he may grant a search warrant conferring power on any person or persons authorised in that behalf by OFCOM to enter and search the premises specified in the information at any time within one month from the date of the warrant.

(2) *Repealed.*

(3) A person who intentionally obstructs a person in the exercise of powers conferred on him under this section shall be guilty of an offence and liable on summary conviction to a fine not exceeding the fifth level on the standard scale.

(4) A person who discloses, otherwise than for the purposes of any legal proceedings or of a report of any such proceedings, any information obtained by means of an exercise of powers conferred by this section shall be guilty of an offence and liable[1]—

(*a*) on summary conviction, to a fine not exceeding the **statutory maximum**;
(*b*) on conviction on indictment, to imprisonment for a term not exceeding **two years** or to a **fine**, or **both**.

(5) *Scotland.*

(6) *Northern Ireland.*

[Broadcasting Act 1990, s 196 as amended by the Communications Act 2003, Schs 15 and 19.]

1. For procedure in respect of an offence which is triable either way, see ss 18–21 of the Magistrates' Courts Act 1980, ss 17A–21 in PART I: MAGISTRATES' COURTS, PROCEDURE, ante.

8–30108E 197. Restriction on disclosure of information. *Repealed.*

8–30108F 199. *Notices.*

8–30108G 200. *Regulations and orders.*

8–30108H 201. Programme services. (1) In this Act "programme service" means any of the following services (whether or not it is, or it requires to be, licensed under this Act), namely—

(*aa*) any service which is a programme service within the meaning of the Communications Act 2003;
(*c*) any other service which consists in the sending, by means of an electronic communications network (within the meaning of the Communications Act 2003), of sounds or visual images or both either—
(i) for reception at two or more places in the United Kingdom (whether they are so sent for simultaneous reception or at different times in response to requests made by different users of the service); or
(ii) for reception at a place in the United Kingdom for the purpose of being presented there to members of the public or to any group of persons.

(2A) Subsection (1)(c) does not apply to so much of a service consisting only of sound programmes as—

(*a*) is a two-way service (within the meaning of section 248(4) of the Communications Act 2003);
(*b*) satisfies the conditions in section 248(5) of that Act; or
(*c*) is provided for the purpose only of being received by persons who have qualified as users of the service by reason of being persons who fall within paragraph (a) or (b) of section 248(7) of that Act.

(2B) Subsection (1)(c) does not apply to so much of a service not consisting only of sound programmes as—

(*a*) is a two-way service (within the meaning of section 232 of the Communications Act 2003);
(*b*) satisfies the conditions in section 233(5) of that Act; or
(*c*) is provided for the purpose only of being received by persons who have qualified as users of the service by reason of being persons who fall within paragraph (a) or (b) of section 233(7) of that Act.

[Broadcasting Act 1990, s 201, as amended by the Broadcasting Act 1996, Sch 10 and the Communications Act 2003, s 360 and Sch 19.]

8–30108I 202. General interpretation. (1) In this Act (unless the context otherwise requires)—

"advertising agent" shall be construed in accordance with subsection (7);
"the BBC" means the British Broadcasting Corporation;
"a BBC company" means—

(*a*) any body corporate which is controlled by the BBC, or

(*b*) any body corporate in which the BBC or any body corporate falling within paragraph (*a*) above is (to any extent) a participant (as defined in paragraph 1(1) of Part I of Schedule 2);

"body", without more, means a body of persons whether incorporated or not, and includes a partnership;

"broadcast" means broadcast by wireless telegraphy;

"a Channel 4 company" means—

(*a*) any body corporate which is controlled by the Channel Four Television Corporation, or

(*b*) any body corporate in which the Corporation or any body corporate falling within paragraph (*a*) above is (to any extent) a participant (as defined in paragraph 1(1) of Part I of Schedule 2);

"connected", in relation to any person, shall be construed in accordance with paragraph 3 in Part I of Schedule 2;

"control", in relation to a body, has the meaning given by paragraph 1(1) in that Part of that Schedule;

"dwelling-house" includes a hotel, inn, boarding-house or other similar establishment;

"EEA Agreement" means the Agreement on the European Economic Area signed at Oporto on 2 May 1992 as adjusted by the Protocol signed at Brussels on 17 March 1993;

"EEA State" means a State which is a contracting party to the EEA Agreement;

"financial year" shall be construed in accordance with subsection (2);

"frequency" includes frequency band;

"modifications" includes additions, alterations and omissions;

"OFCOM" means the Office of Communications;

"pension scheme" means a scheme for the payment of pensions, allowances or gratuities;

"programme" includes an advertisement and, in relation to any service, includes any item included in that service;

"an S4C company" means—

(*a*) any body corporate which is controlled by the Welsh Authority, or

(*b*) any body corporate in which the Welsh Authority or any body corporate falling within paragraph (*a*) above is (to any extent) a participant (as defined in paragraph 1(1) of Part I of Schedule 2);

"the Welsh Authority" means the authority renamed Sianel Pedwar Cymru by section 56(1);

"wireless telegraphy" and "station for wireless telegraphy" have the same meaning as in the Wireless Telegraphy Act 1949.

(2) In any provision of—

(*a*) *Repealed*; or

(*b*) Schedule 1*, 2, 3, 6, 8* or 19,

"financial year" means a financial year of the body with which that provision is concerned; and in any other provision of this Act "financial year" means the twelve months ending with 31st March.

(3) In this Act—

(*a*) references to pensions, allowances or gratuities include references to like benefits to be given on death or retirement; and

(*b*) any reference to the payment of pensions, allowances or gratuities to or in respect of any persons includes a reference to the making of payments towards provision for the payment of pensions, allowances or gratuities to or in respect of those persons.

(4) Any reference in this Act (however expressed) to a licence under this Act being in force is a reference to its being in force so as to authorise the provision under the licence of the licensed service; and any such reference shall accordingly not be construed as prejudicing the operation of any provisions of such a licence which are intended to have effect otherwise than at a time when the licensed service is authorised to be so provided.

(4A) Any reference in this Act to Council Directive 89/552/EEC is a reference to that Directive as amended by Directive 97/36/EC of the European Parliament and the Council.

(5) It is hereby declared that, for the purpose of determining for the purposes of any provision of this Act whether a service is—

(*a*) capable of being received, within the United Kingdom or elsewhere, or

(*b*) for reception at any place or places, or in any area, in the United Kingdom,

the fact that the service has been encrypted to any extent shall be disregarded.

(6) Any reference in this Act, in relation to a service consisting of programmes transmitted by satellite—

(*a*) to a person by whom the programmes are transmitted, or

(*b*) to a place from which the programmes are transmitted,

is a reference to a person by whom, or a place from which, the programmes are transmitted to the satellite by means of which the service is provided.*

(7) For the purposes of this Act—

(*a*) a person shall not be regarded as carrying on business as an advertising agent, or as acting as such an agent, unless he carries on a business involving the selection and purchase of advertising time or space for persons wishing to advertise;

(*b*) a person who carries on such a business shall be regarded as carrying on business as an advertising agent irrespective of whether in law he is the agent of those for whom he acts;

(*c*) a person who is the proprietor of a newspaper shall not be regarded as carrying on business as an advertising agent by reason only that he makes arrangements on behalf of advertisers whereby advertisements appearing in the newspaper are also to appear in one or more other newspapers;

(*d*) a company or other body corporate shall not be regarded as carrying on business as an advertising agent by reason only that its objects or powers include or authorise that activity.

[Broadcasting Act 1990, s 202, as amended by the Broadcasting Act 1996, Schs 10 and 11, SI 1997/1682, SI 1998/3196 and the Communications Act 2003, Sch 5.]

8–30108J 203. Consequential and transitional provisions. *Consequential amendments.*

(2) Unless the context otherwise requires, in any enactment amended by this Act—

"programme", in relation to a programme service, includes any item included in that service; and "television programme" includes a teletext transmission.

(3)–(4) *Repeals and transitional provisions.*

[Broadcasting Act 1990, s 203.]

8–30108K 204. *Short title, commencement and extent.*

8–30108L

Section 162

SCHEDULE 15

APPLICATION OF 1959 ACT TO TELEVISION AND SOUND PROGRAMMES

Interpretation

1. In this Schedule—

"the 1959 Act" means the Obscene Publications Act 1959;

"relevant programme" means a programme included in a programme service;

and other expressions used in this Schedule which are also used in the 1959 Act have the same meaning as in that Act.

Liability of person providing live programme material

2. Where—

(*a*) any matter is included by any person in a relevant programme in circumstances falling within section 1(5) of the 1959 Act, and

(*b*) that matter has been provided, for inclusion in that programme, by some other person,

the 1959 Act shall have effect as if that matter had been included in that programme by that other person (as well as by the person referred to in sub-paragraph (*a*)).

Obscene articles kept for inclusion in programmes

3. It is hereby declared that where a person has an obscene article in his ownership, possession or control with a view to the matter recorded on it being included in a relevant programme, the article shall be taken for the purposes of the 1959 Act to be an obscene article had or kept by that person for publication for gain.

Requirement for consent of Director of Public Prosecutions

4. (1) Proceedings for an offence under section 2 of the 1959 Act for publishing an obscene article shall not be instituted except by or with the consent of the Director of Public Prosecutions in any case where—

(*a*) the relevant publication, or

(*b*) the only other publication which followed from the relevant publication,

took place in the course of the inclusion of a programme in a programme service; and in this sub-paragraph "the relevant publication" means the publication in respect of which the defendant would be charged if the proceedings were brought.

(2) Proceedings for an offence under section 2 of the 1959 Act for having an obscene article for publication for gain shall not be instituted except by or with the consent of the Director of Public Prosecutions in any case where—

(*a*) the relevant publication, or

(*b*) the only other publication which could reasonably have been expected to follow from the relevant publication,

was to take place in the course of the inclusion of a programme in a programme service; and in this sub-paragraph "the relevant publication" means the publication which, if the proceedings were brought, the defendant would be alleged to have had in contemplation.

(3) Without prejudice to the duty of a court to make an order for the forfeiture of an article under section 1(4)

of the Obscene Publications Act 1964 (orders on conviction), in a case where by virtue of sub-paragraph (2) above proceedings under section 2 of the 1959 Act for having an article for publication for gain could not be instituted except by or with the consent of the Director of Public Prosecutions, no order for the forfeiture of the article shall be made under section 3 of the 1959 Act (power of search and seizure) unless the warrant under which the article was seized was issued on an information laid by or on behalf of the Director of Public Prosecutions.

Defences

5. (1) A person shall not be convicted of an offence under section 2 of the 1959 Act in respect of the inclusion of any matter in a relevant programme if he proves that he did not know and had no reason to suspect that the programme would include matter rendering him liable to be convicted of such an offence.

(2) Where the publication in issue in any proceedings under that Act consists of the inclusion of any matter in a relevant programme, section 4(1) of that Act (general defence of public good) shall not apply; but—

(*a*) a person shall not be convicted of an offence under section 2 of that Act, and
(*b*) an order for forfeiture shall not be made under section 3 of that Act,

if it is proved that the inclusion of the matter in question in a relevant programme is justified as being for the public good on the ground that it is in the interests of—

(i) drama, opera, ballet or any other art,
(ii) science, literature or learning, or
(iii) any other objects of general concern.

(3) Section 4(2) of that Act (admissibility of opinions of experts) shall apply for the purposes of sub-paragraph (2) above as it applies for the purposes of section 4(1) and (1A) of that Act.

Exclusion of proceedings under common law

6. Without prejudice to section 2(4) of the 1959 Act, a person shall not be proceeded against for an offence at common law—

(*a*) in respect of a relevant programme or anything said or done in the course of a such a programme, where it is of the essence of the common law offence that the programme or (as the case may be) what was said or done was obscene, indecent, offensive, disgusting or injurious to morality; or
(*b*) in respect of an agreement to cause a programme to be included in a programme service or to cause anything to be said or done in the course of a programme which is to be so included, where the common law offence consists of conspiring to corrupt public morals or to do any act contrary to public morals or decency.

Broadcasting Act 1996

(1996 c 55)

PART VIII[1]

MISCELLANEOUS AND GENERAL

Provision of false information, etc.

8–30108M 144. Offence of providing false information in certain circumstances. (1) A person who, in connection with an application by him for, or his continued holding of, a licence under the 1990 Act or this Act—

(*a*) makes to the relevant authority a statement which he knows to be false in a material particular, or
(*b*) recklessly makes to the relevant authority a statement which is false in a material particular,

is guilty of an offence if the statement relates to a matter which would be relevant in determining whether he is by virtue of any of the provisions specified in subsection (3) a disqualified person, and he is by virtue of any of those provisions a disqualified person in relation to that licence.

(2) A person who, in connection with an application by him for, or his continued holding of, a licence under the 1990 Act or this Act, withholds any information with the intention of causing the relevant authority to be misled is guilty of an offence if—

(*a*) the information would be relevant in determining whether he is by virtue of any of the provisions specified in subsection (3) a disqualified person, and
(*b*) he is by virtue of any of those provisions a disqualified person in relation to that licence.

(3) The provisions referred to in subsection (1) and (2) are the following provisions of paragraph 1(1) of Part II of Schedule 2 to the 1990 Act—

(*a*) paragraphs (*d*) to (*g*),
(*b*) paragraph (*h*) so far as relating to participating by bodies falling within paragraph (*d*), (*e*) or (*g*),
(*c*) paragraph (*hh*) so far as relating to a body corporate controlled by a body corporate in which a body falling within paragraph (*d*), (*e*) or (*g*) is a participant with more than a 5 per cent. interest,
(*d*) paragraph (i) so far as relating to control by a person falling within any of paragraphs (*d*) to (*g*) or by two or more such persons, and

(*e*) paragraph (*j*) so far as relating to participation by a body corporate which is controlled by a person falling within any of paragraphs (*d*) to (*g*) or by two or more such persons.

(4) A person guilty of an offence under this section is liable on summary conviction to imprisonment for a term not exceeding **three months** or to a fine not exceeding **level 5** on the standard scale or to **both**.

(5) In this section "the relevant authority" means—

(*a*) in relation to any licence under Part I or II of the 1990 Act or Part I of this Act, the Independent Television Commission, and

(*b*) in relation to any licence under Part III of the 1990 Act or Part II of this Act, the Radio Authority.

[Broadcasting Act 1996, s 144.]

---

1. Part VIII contains ss 142–150.

8–30108N 145. Disqualification for offence of supplying false information, etc. (1) Where a person is convicted of an offence under section 144 the court by which he is convicted may make an order (in this section referred to as a "disqualification order") disqualifying him from holding a licence during a period specified in the order.

(2) The period specified in a disqualification order shall not exceed five years beginning with the date on which the order takes effect.

(3) Where an individual is disqualified from holding a licence by virtue of a disqualification order, any body corporate—

(*a*) of which he is a director, or

(*b*) in the management of which he is directly or indirectly concerned,

is also disqualified from holding a licence.

(4) Where the holder of a licence is disqualified by virtue of a disqualification order, the licence shall be treated as being revoked with effect from the time when the order takes effect.

(5) For the purposes of any of the provisions specified in subsection (6) (which relate to the imposition of a financial penalty on the revocation of a licence), a licence which is revoked by virtue of subsection (4) shall be taken to have been revoked by the relevant authority as mentioned in that provision.

(6) The provisions referred to in subsection (5) are as follows—

(*a*) section 18(3) of the 1990 Act,

(*b*) section 101(3) of the 1990 Act,

(*c*) section 11(5), and

(*d*) section 53(5)

(7) In sections 5(1)(*a*) and 88(1)(*a*) of the 1990 Act and sections 5(1)(*a*) and 44(1)(*a*) of this Act, the reference to a person who is a disqualified person by virtue of Part II of Schedule 2 to the 1990 Act includes a reference to a person who is disqualified by virtue of a disqualification order.

(8) In this section—

"licence" means any licence granted by the Independent Television Commission or the Radio Authority under the 1990 Act or this Act;

"the relevant authority" has the same meaning as in section 144.

[Broadcasting Act 1996, s 145.]

8–30108O 146. Supplementary provisions as to disqualification orders. (1) A person disqualified by a disqualification order may appeal against the order in the same manner as against a conviction.

(2) A disqualification order made by a court in England and Wales or Northern Ireland—

(*a*) shall not take effect until the end of the period within which the person on whose conviction the order was made can appeal against the order, and

(*b*) if he so appeals, shall not take effect until the appeal has been determined or abandoned.

(3) A disqualification order made by a court in Scotland—

(*a*) shall not take effect until the end of the period within which the person on whose conviction the order was made can appeal against the order, and

(*b*) if an appeal against the order or the conviction is taken within that period, shall not take effect until the date when that appeal is determined or abandoned or deemed to have been abandoned.

(4) In this section "disqualification order" means an order under section 145.

[Broadcasting Act 1996, s 146.]

General

8–30108P 147. General interpretation. (1) In this Act—

"the 1990 Act" means the Broadcasting Act 1990;

"the BBC" means the British Broadcasting Corporation.

(2) The 1990 Act and the following provisions of this Act—

(*a*) Parts I and II and Schedule 1,

(*b*) Part IV,

(*c*) Part V and Schedules 3 and 4, and

(*d*) sections 142 to 146,

shall be construed as if those provisions were contained in that Act.

[Broadcasting Act 1996, s 147.]

8–30108Q 149. *Commencement and transitional provisions.*

8–30108R 150. *Short title and extent.*

Electronic Communications Act 2000[1]

(2000 c 7)

8–30108S 1–6. *Repealed.*

1. This Act makes provision to facilitate the use of electronic communications and electronic data storage, and makes provision about the modification of licences granted under s 7 of the Telecommunications Act 1984. Only those provisions of the Act that are relevant to the work of magistrates' courts are included in this Manual. The Act is to be brought into force in accordance with the provisions of s 16, post.

PART II[1]

FACILITATION OF ELECTRONIC COMMERCE, DATA STORAGE, ETC

8–30108W 7. Electronic signatures and related certificates. (1) In any legal proceedings—

(*a*) an electronic signature[2] incorporated into or logically associated with a particular electronic communication or particular electronic data, and

(*b*) the certification by any person of such a signature,

shall each be admissible in evidence in relation to any question as to the authenticity of the communication or data or as to the integrity of the communication or data.

(2) For the purposes of this section an electronic signature is so much of anything in electronic form as—

(*a*) is incorporated into or otherwise logically associated with any electronic communication or electronic data; and

(*b*) purports to be so incorporated or associated for the purpose of being used in establishing the authenticity of the communication or data, the integrity of the communication or data, or both.

(3) For the purposes of this section an electronic signature incorporated into or associated with a particular electronic communication or particular electronic data is certified by any person if that person (whether before or after the making of the communication) has made a statement confirming that—

(*a*) the signature,

(*b*) a means of producing, communicating or verifying the signature, or

(*c*) a procedure applied to the signature,

is (either alone or in combination with other factors) a valid means of establishing the authenticity of the communication or data, the integrity of the communication or data, or both.

[Electronic Communications Act 2000, s 7.]

1. Part II comprises ss 7–10.
2. For regulation of electronic signature certificate providers, see the Electronic Signatures Regulations 2002, SI 2002/318 made under s 2 of the European Communities Act 1972.

PART III[1]

MISCELLANEOUS AND SUPPLEMENTAL

Supplemental

8–30108X 15. General interpretation. (1) In this Act, except in so far as the context otherwise requires—

"document" includes a map, plan, design, drawing, picture or other image;

"communication" includes a communication comprising sounds or images or both and a communication effecting a payment;

"electronic communication" means a communication transmitted (whether from one person to another, from one device to another or from a person to a device or vice versa)—

(a) by means of a telecommunication system (within the meaning of the Telecommunications Act 1984); or

(b) by other means but while in an electronic form;

"enactment" includes—

(a) an enactment passed after the passing of this Act,

(b) an enactment comprised in an Act of the Scottish Parliament, and

(c) an enactment contained in Northern Ireland legislation,

but does not include an enactment contained in Part I or II of this Act;

"modification" includes any alteration, addition or omission, and cognate expressions shall be construed accordingly;

"record" includes an electronic record; and

"subordinate legislation" means—

(*a*) any subordinate legislation (within the meaning of the Interpretation Act 1978);

(*b*) any instrument made under an Act of the Scottish Parliament; or

(*c*) any statutory rules (within the meaning of the Statutory Rules (Northern Ireland) Order 1979).

(2) In this Act—

(*a*) references to the authenticity of any communication or data are references to any one or more of the following—

(i) whether the communication or data comes from a particular person or other source;

(ii) whether it is accurately timed and dated;

(iii) whether it is intended to have legal effect;

and

(*b*) references to the integrity of any communication or data are references to whether there has been any tampering with or other modification of the communication or data.

(3) References in this Act to something's being put into an intelligible form include references to its being restored to the condition in which it was before any encryption or similar process was applied to it.

[Electronic Communications Act 2000, s 15.]

1. Part III comprises ss 11–16.

8–30108Y 16. Short title, commencement, extent. (1) This Act may be cited as the Electronic Communications Act 2000.

(2) Part I of this Act and sections 7, 11 and 12 shall come into force on such day as the Secretary of State may by order[1] made by statutory instrument appoint; and different days may be appointed under this subsection for different purposes.

(3) An order shall not be made for bringing any of Part I of this Act into force for any purpose unless a draft of the order has been laid before Parliament and approved by a resolution of each House.

(4) If no order for bringing Part I of this Act into force has been made under subsection (2) by the end of the period of five years beginning with the day on which this Act is passed, that Part shall, by virtue of this subsection, be repealed at the end of that period.

(5) This Act extends to Northern Ireland.

[Electronic Communications Act 2000, s 16.]

1. At the date of going to press, the Electronic Communications Act 2000 (Commencement No 1) Order, SI 2000/1798, had been made, bringing ss 7, 11 and 12 of the Act into force on 25 July 2000.

Regulation of Investigatory Powers Act 2000[1]

(2000 c 23)

PART I[2]
COMMUNICATIONS

CHAPTER I[3]
INTERCEPTION

Unlawful and authorised interception

8–30108Z 1. Unlawful interception. (1) It shall be an offence for a person intentionally and without lawful authority to intercept, at any place in the United Kingdom, any communication in the course of its transmission by means of—

(*a*) a public postal service; or
(*b*) a public telecommunication system.

(2) It shall be an offence for a person—

(*a*) intentionally and without lawful authority, and
(*b*) otherwise than in circumstances in which his conduct is excluded by subsection (6) from criminal liability under this subsection,

to intercept, at any place in the United Kingdom, any communication in the course of its transmission by means of a private telecommunication system.

(3) Any interception of a communication which is carried out at any place in the United Kingdom by, or with the express or implied consent of, a person having the right to control the operation or the use of a private telecommunication system shall be actionable at the suit or instance of the sender or recipient, or intended recipient, of the communication if it is without lawful authority and is either—

(*a*) an interception of that communication in the course of its transmission by means of that private system; or
(*b*) an interception of that communication in the course of its transmission, by means of a public telecommunication system, to or from apparatus comprised in that private telecommunication system.

(4) Where the United Kingdom is a party to an international agreement which—

(*a*) relates to the provision of mutual assistance in connection with, or in the form of, the interception of communications,
(*b*) requires the issue of a warrant, order or equivalent instrument in cases in which assistance is given, and
(*c*) is designated for the purposes of this subsection by an order[4] made by the Secretary of State,

it shall be the duty of the Secretary of State to secure that no request for assistance in accordance with the agreement is made on behalf of a person in the United Kingdom to the competent authorities of a country or territory outside the United Kingdom except with lawful authority.

(5) Conduct has lawful authority[5] for the purposes of this section if, and only if—

(*a*) it is authorised by or under section 3 or 4;
(*b*) it takes place in accordance with a warrant under section 5 ("an interception warrant"); or
(*c*) it is in exercise, in relation to any stored communication, of any statutory power that is exercised (apart from this section) for the purpose of obtaining information or of taking possession of any document or other property;

and conduct (whether or not prohibited by this section) which has lawful authority for the purposes of this section by virtue of paragraph (a) or (b) shall also be taken to be lawful for all other purposes.

(6) The circumstances in which a person makes an interception of a communication in the course of its transmission by means of a private telecommunication system are such that his conduct is excluded from criminal liability under subsection (2) if—

(*a*) he is a person with a right to control[6] the operation or the use of the system; or
(*b*) he has the express or implied consent of such a person to make the interception.

(7) A person who is guilty of an offence under subsection (1) or (2) shall be liable[7]—

(*a*) on conviction on indictment, to imprisonment for a term not exceeding two years or to a fine, or to both;
(*b*) on summary conviction, to a fine not exceeding the statutory maximum.

(8) No proceedings for any offence which is an offence by virtue of this section shall be instituted—

(*a*) in England and Wales, except by or with the consent of the Director of Public Prosecutions;
(*b*) in Northern Ireland, except by or with the consent of the Director of Public Prosecutions for Northern Ireland.

[Regulation of Investigatory Powers Act 2000, s 1.]

1. The main purpose of this Act is to ensure that relevant investigatory powers are used in accordance with the European Convention on Human Rights namely: interception of communications; acquisition of communications data (eg billing data); intrusive surveillance on residential premises or in private vehicles; covert surveillance in the course of specific operations; use of agents, informants, undercover officers; access to encrypted data. The background to this Act was fully considered in *A-G's Reference (No 5 of 2002)* UKHL 40, [2005] 1 AC 167, [2004] 3 WLR 957, [2004] 4 All ER 901 (see Note 1 to s 17, post). The Act works in conjunction with other legislation such as the Intelligence Services Act 1994, the Police Act 1997 and the Human Rights Act 1998. The provisions of the Act implement art 5 of the Telecommunications Data Protection Directive 97/66, and are to be brought into force in accordance with commencement orders made under section 83. At the date of going to press the following orders had been made: Commencement (No 1 and Transitional Provisions) Order 2000, SI 2000/2543 which brought into effect s 1 (except (3)), 2–20, 21(4) (partially), 26–48, 57–59 (all partially), 60, s 61, 62 (except (1)(*b*) and (*c*)), 63, 64, 65 (partially), 67 (partially), 68 (partially), 69, 70, 71 and 72 (partially), 73, 74–78, 79, 80, 81, 82, Schs 1, 3, 4, 5; Commencement (No 2) Order 2001, SI 2001/2684 which brought into force ss 71 and 72 to the extent they relate to Chapter II of Part I of the Act; Commencement (No 3) Order 2003, SI 2003/3140 which brought into force 5 January 2004: Chapter II of Part I (Acquisition and disclosure of communications data) (ss 21–25); s 57(2)(*b*); s 58(1)(*g*), (*h*) and (*j*); ss 65(5)(*c*) and (8)(*b*); and s 68(7)(*g*) and (*h*).
2. Part I contains ss 1–25.

3. Chapter I contains ss 1–20.

4. The Regulation of Investigatory Powers (Designation of an International Agreement) Order 2004, SI 2004/158 has been made which designates the Convention on Mutual Assistance in Criminal Matters between the Member States of the European Union established by Council Act of 29 May 2000 (2000/C197/01).

5. Where a company is served with notice of an application pursuant to s 9 of and Sch 1 to the Police and Criminal Evidence Act 1984 for an order to produce special procedure material in the form of e-mails addressed to a particular customer and the notice warns that the company cannot destroy or dispose of that material except with the leave of the court and, due to its auto deletion system (for reasons of storage) the company can only comply by transferring copies of the e-mails to another e-mail address, which amounts to an offence under s 1 above, the company has implicit power to preserve the e-mails and this provides it with lawful authority for the purposes of s 1(5)(c) below (*R (NTL Group Ltd) v Crown Court at Ipswich* [2002] EWHC 1585 (Admin), [2002] QB 131).

6. "Control" extends to controlling how the system is used and operated by others and not to those who merely have the right to access or to operate the system (*R v Stanford* (2006) Times, 7 February, CA).

7. For procedure in respect of an offence triable either way, see Magistrates' Courts Act 1980, ss 17A–21, in PART I: MAGISTRATES' COURTS, PROCEDURE, ante.

8–30109 2. Meaning and location of "interception" etc. (1) In this Act—

"postal service" means any service which—

(a) consists in the following, or in any one or more of them, namely, the collection, sorting, conveyance, distribution and delivery (whether in the United Kingdom or elsewhere) of postal items; and

(b) is offered or provided as a service the main purpose of which, or one of the main purposes of which, is to make available, or to facilitate, a means of transmission from place to place of postal items containing communications;

"private telecommunication system" means any telecommunication system which, without itself being a public telecommunication system, is a system in relation to which the following conditions are satisfied—

(a) it is attached, directly or indirectly and whether or not for the purposes of the communication in question, to a public telecommunication system; and

(b) there is apparatus comprised in the system which is both located in the United Kingdom and used (with or without other apparatus) for making the attachment to the public telecommunication system;

"public postal service" means any postal service which is offered or provided to, or to a substantial section of, the public in any one or more parts of the United Kingdom;

"public telecommunications service" means any telecommunications service which is offered or provided to, or to a substantial section of, the public in any one or more parts of the United Kingdom;

"public telecommunication system" means any such parts of a telecommunication system by means of which any public telecommunications service is provided as are located in the United Kingdom;

"telecommunications service" means any service that consists in the provision of access to, and of facilities for making use of, any telecommunication system (whether or not one provided by the person providing the service); and

"telecommunication system" means any system (including the apparatus comprised in it) which exists (whether wholly or partly in the United Kingdom or elsewhere) for the purpose of facilitating the transmission of communications by any means involving the use of electrical or electro-magnetic energy.

(2) For the purposes of this Act, but subject to the following provisions of this section, a person intercepts a communication in the course of its transmission by means of a telecommunication system if, and only if, he—

(*a*) so modifies or interferes with the system, or its operation,

(*b*) so monitors transmissions made by means of the system, or

(*c*) so monitors transmissions made by wireless telegraphy to or from apparatus comprised in the system,

as to make some or all of the contents of the communication available, while being transmitted, to a person other than the sender or intended recipient[2] of the communication.

(3) References in this Act to the interception of a communication do not include references to the interception of any communication broadcast for general reception.

(4) For the purposes of this Act the interception of a communication takes place in the United Kingdom if, and only if, the modification, interference or monitoring or, in the case of a postal item, the interception is effected by conduct within the United Kingdom and the communication is either—

(*a*) intercepted in the course of its transmission by means of a public postal service or public telecommunication system; or

(*b*) intercepted in the course of its transmission by means of a private telecommunication system in a case in which the sender or intended recipient of the communication is in the United Kingdom.

(5) References in this Act to the interception of a communication in the course of its transmission by means of a postal service or telecommunication system do not include references to—

(*a*) any conduct that takes place in relation only to so much of the communication as consists in any traffic data comprised in or attached to a communication (whether by the sender or otherwise) for the purposes of any postal service or telecommunication system by means of which it is being or may be transmitted; or

(*b*) any such conduct, in connection with conduct falling within paragraph (*a*), as gives a person who is neither the sender nor the intended recipient only so much access to a communication as is necessary for the purpose of identifying traffic data so comprised or attached.

(6) For the purposes of this section references to the modification of a telecommunication system include references to the attachment of any apparatus to, or other modification of or interference with—

(*a*) any part of the system; or

(*b*) any wireless telegraphy apparatus used for making transmissions to or from apparatus comprised in the system.

(7) For the purposes of this section the times while a communication is being transmitted by means of a telecommunication system shall be taken to include any time when the system by means of which the communication is being, or has been, transmitted is used for storing it in a manner that enables the intended recipient to collect it or otherwise to have access to it.

(8) For the purposes of this section the cases in which any contents of a communication are to be taken to be made available to a person while being transmitted shall include any case in which any of the contents of the communication, while being transmitted, are diverted or recorded so as to be available to a person subsequently.

(9) In this section "traffic data", in relation to any communication, means—

(*a*) any data identifying, or purporting to identify, any person, apparatus or location to or from which the communication is or may be transmitted,

(*b*) any data identifying or selecting, or purporting to identify or select, apparatus through which, or by means of which, the communication is or may be transmitted,

(*c*) any data comprising signals for the actuation of apparatus used for the purposes of a telecommunication system for effecting (in whole or in part) the transmission of any communication, and

(*d*) any data identifying the data or other data as data comprised in or attached to a particular communication,

but that expression includes data identifying a computer file or computer program access to which is obtained, or which is run, by means of the communication to the extent only that the file or program is identified by reference to the apparatus in which it is stored.

(10) In this section—

(*a*) references, in relation to traffic data comprising signals for the actuation of apparatus, to a telecommunication system by means of which a communication is being or may be transmitted include references to any telecommunication system in which that apparatus is comprised; and

(*b*) references to traffic data being attached to a communication include references to the data and the communication being logically associated with each other;

and in this section "data", in relation to a postal item, means anything written on the outside of the item.

(11) In this section "postal item" means any letter, postcard or other such thing in writing as may be used by the sender for imparting information to the recipient, or any packet or parcel.
[Regulation of Investigatory Powers Act 2000, s 2.]

---

1. The natural meaning of "interception" denotes some interference or abstraction of the signal, whether it is passing along wires or by wireless telegraphy, during the process of transmission; accordingly, a listening device (fitted in a car) that picked up what a person said, including words spoken on his mobile telephone, but not what was said by persons at the other end of the telephone, was not an 'interception': *R v E* [2004] EWCA Crim 1243, [2004] Cr App R 29.

2. The tape recording by undercover police officers of their telephone conversations with a suspect does not constitute the interception of a communication within the meaning of s 2(2); it is not telephone tapping by a third party, but the same as a secret recording of a face-to-face meeting of a suspect (*R v Hardy* [2002] EWCA Crim 3012, [2003] 1 Cr App Rep 494).

8–30109A 3. Lawful interception without an interception warrant. (1) Conduct by any person consisting in the interception of a communication is authorised by this section if the communication is one which, or which that person has reasonable grounds for believing, is both—

(*a*) a communication sent by a person who has consented to the interception; and

(*b*) a communication the intended recipient of which has so consented.

(2) Conduct by any person consisting in the interception of a communication is authorised by this section if—

(*a*) the communication is one sent by, or intended for, a person who has consented to the interception; and

(*b*) surveillance by means of that interception has been authorised under Part II.

(3) Conduct consisting in the interception of a communication is authorised by this section if—

(*a*) it is conduct by or on behalf of a person who provides a postal service or a telecommunications service; and

(*b*) it takes place for purposes connected with the provision or operation of that service or with the enforcement, in relation to that service, of any enactment relating to the use of postal services or telecommunications services.

(4) Conduct by any person consisting in the interception of a communication in the course of its transmission by means of wireless telegraphy is authorised by this section if it takes place—

(*a*) with the authority of a designated person under section 5 of the Wireless Telegraphy Act 1949[1] (misleading messages and interception and disclosure of wireless telegraphy messages); and

(*b*) for purposes connected with anything falling within subsection (5).

(5) Each of the following falls within this subsection—

(*a*) the issue of licences under the Wireless Telegraphy Act 1949;

(*b*) the prevention or detection of anything which constitutes interference with wireless telegraphy; and

(*c*) the enforcement of any enactment contained in that Act or of any enactment not so contained that relates to such interference.

[Regulation of Investigatory Powers Act 2000, s 3.]

---

1. In this title, ante.

8–30109B 4. Power to provide for lawful interception. (1) Conduct by any person ("the interceptor") consisting in the interception of a communication in the course of its transmission by means of a telecommunication system is authorised by this section if—

(*a*) the interception is carried out for the purpose of obtaining information about the communications of a person who, or who the interceptor has reasonable grounds for believing, is in a country or territory outside the United Kingdom;

(*b*) the interception relates to the use of a telecommunications service provided to persons in that country or territory which is either—

(i) a public telecommunications service; or

(ii) a telecommunications service that would be a public telecommunications service if the persons to whom it is offered or provided were members of the public in a part of the United Kingdom;

(*c*) the person who provides that service (whether the interceptor or another person) is required by the law of that country or territory to carry out, secure or facilitate the interception in question;

(*d*) the situation is one in relation to which such further conditions as may be prescribed by regulations made by the Secretary of State are required to be satisfied before conduct may be treated as authorised by virtue of this subsection; and

(*e*) the conditions so prescribed are satisfied in relation to that situation.

(2) Subject to subsection (3), the Secretary of State may by regulations[1] authorise any such conduct described in the regulations as appears to him to constitute a legitimate practice reasonably required for the purpose, in connection with the carrying on of any business, of monitoring or keeping a record of—

(*a*) communications by means of which transactions are entered into in the course of that business; or

(*b*) other communications relating to that business or taking place in the course of its being carried on.

(3) Nothing in any regulations under subsection (2) shall authorise the interception of any communication except in the course of its transmission using apparatus or services provided by or to the person carrying on the business for use wholly or partly in connection with that business.

(4) Conduct taking place in a prison is authorised by this section if it is conduct in exercise of any power conferred by or under any rules made under section 47 of the Prison Act 1952[2], section 39 of the Prisons (Scotland) Act 1989 or section 13 of the Prison Act (Northern Ireland) 1953 (prison rules).

(5) Conduct taking place in any hospital premises where high security psychiatric services are provided is authorised by this section if it is conduct in pursuance of, and in accordance with, any direction given under section 17 of the National Health Service Act 1977 (directions as to the carrying out of their functions by health bodies) to the body providing those services at those premises.

(6) Conduct taking place in a state hospital is authorised by this section if it is conduct in pursuance of, and in accordance with, any direction given to the State Hospitals Board for Scotland under section 2(5) of the National Health Service (Scotland) Act 1978 (regulations and directions as to the exercise of their functions by health boards) as applied by Article 5(1) of and the Schedule to The State Hospitals Board for Scotland Order 1995 (which applies certain provisions of that Act of 1978 to the State Hospitals Board).

(7) In this section references to a business include references to any activities of a government department, of any public authority or of any person or office holder on whom functions are conferred by or under any enactment.

(8) In this section—

"government department" includes any part of the Scottish Administration, a Northern Ireland department and the National Assembly for Wales;

"high security psychiatric services" has the same meaning as in the National Health Service Act 1977;

"hospital premises" has the same meaning as in section 4(3) of that Act; and

"state hospital" has the same meaning as in the National Health Service (Scotland) Act 1978.

(9) In this section "prison" means—

(*a*) any prison, young offender institution, young offenders centre or remand centre which is under the general superintendence of, or is provided by, the Secretary of State under the Prison Act 1952 or the Prison Act (Northern Ireland) 1953, or

(*b*) any prison, young offenders institution or remand centre which is under the general superintendence of the Scottish Ministers under the Prisons (Scotland) Act 1989,

and includes any contracted out prison, within the meaning of Part IV of the Criminal Justice Act 1991 or section 106(4) of the Criminal Justice and Public Order Act 1994, and any legalised police cells within the meaning of section 14 of the Prisons (Scotland) Act 1989.

[Regulation of Investigatory Powers Act 2000, s 4.]

---

1. The Telecommunications (Lawful Business Practice) (Interception of Communications) Regulations 2000 have been made, in this title, post.
2. For the rules made under s 47 of the Prison Act 1952, see PART VIII, title PRISONS, post.

8–30109C 5. Interception with a warrant. (1) Subject to the following provisions of this Chapter, the Secretary of State may issue a warrant authorising or requiring the person to whom it is addressed, by any such conduct as may be described in the warrant, to secure any one or more of the following—

(*a*) the interception in the course of their transmission by means of a postal service or telecommunication system of the communications described in the warrant;

(*b*) the making, in accordance with an international mutual assistance agreement, of a request for the provision of such assistance in connection with, or in the form of, an interception of communications as may be so described;

(*c*) the provision, in accordance with an international mutual assistance agreement, to the competent authorities of a country or territory outside the United Kingdom of any such assistance in connection with, or in the form of, an interception of communications as may be so described;

(*d*) the disclosure, in such manner as may be so described, of intercepted material obtained by any interception authorised or required by the warrant, and of related communications data.

(2) The Secretary of State shall not issue an interception warrant unless he believes—

(*a*) that the warrant is necessary on grounds falling within subsection (3); and

(*b*) that the conduct authorised by the warrant is proportionate to what is sought to be achieved by that conduct.

(3) Subject to the following provisions of this section, a warrant is necessary on grounds falling within this subsection if it is necessary—

(*a*) in the interests of national security;

(*b*) for the purpose of preventing or detecting serious crime;

(*c*) for the purpose of safeguarding the economic well-being of the United Kingdom; or

(*d*) for the purpose, in circumstances appearing to the Secretary of State to be equivalent to those in which he would issue a warrant by virtue of paragraph (*b*), of giving effect to the provisions of any international mutual assistance agreement.

(4) The matters to be taken into account in considering whether the requirements of subsection (2) are satisfied in the case of any warrant shall include whether the information which it is thought necessary to obtain under the warrant could reasonably be obtained by other means.

(5) A warrant shall not be considered necessary on the ground falling within subsection (3)(c) unless the information which it is thought necessary to obtain is information relating to the acts or intentions of persons outside the British Islands.

(6) The conduct authorised by an interception warrant shall be taken to include—

(*a*) all such conduct (including the interception of communications not identified by the warrant) as it is necessary to undertake in order to do what is expressly authorised or required by the warrant;

(*b*) conduct for obtaining related communications data; and

(*c*) conduct by any person which is conduct in pursuance of a requirement imposed by or on behalf of the person to whom the warrant is addressed to be provided with assistance with giving effect to the warrant.

[Regulation of Investigatory Powers Act 2000, s 5.]

Interception warrants

An interception warrant may only be made on application by specified persons (**s 6**) and may only be issued by the Secretary of State or, in prescribed circumstances, under the hand of a senior official (**s 7**). An interception warrant must contain prescribed particulars including the name or description of one person as the interception subject or a single set of premises in relation to which the interception is to take place (**s 8**). A warrant ceases to have effect at the end of the 'relevant period' as defined but may be renewed on certain grounds (**s 9**), and may be modified (**s 10**). The person to whom the warrant is addressed may give effect to the warrant himself or with persons he may require to assist him (**s 11**).

Interception capability

The Secretary of State may by order provide for the imposition by him on persons who are providing public postal services or public telecommunications services of reasonable obligations to provide assistance in relation to interception warrants (**s 12**). A Technical Advisory Board is established (**s 13**) and grants may be made for fair contributions towards the costs imposed (**s 14**).]

Restrictions on use of intercepted material etc

8–30109D 15. General safeguards. (1) Subject to subsection (6), it shall be the duty of the Secretary of State to ensure, in relation to all interception warrants, that such arrangements are in force as he considers necessary for securing—

(*a*) that the requirements of subsections (2) and (3) are satisfied in relation to the intercepted material and any related communications data; and

(*b*) in the case of warrants in relation to which there are section 8(4) certificates, that the requirements of section 16 are also satisfied.

(2) The requirements of this subsection are satisfied in relation to the intercepted material and any related communications data if each of the following—

(*a*) the number of persons to whom any of the material or data is disclosed or otherwise made available,

(*b*) the extent to which any of the material or data is disclosed or otherwise made available,

(*c*) the extent to which any of the material or data is copied, and

(*d*) the number of copies that are made,

is limited to the minimum that is necessary for the authorised purposes.

(3) The requirements of this subsection are satisfied in relation to the intercepted material and any related communications data if each copy made of any of the material or data (if not destroyed earlier) is destroyed as soon as there are no longer any grounds for retaining it as necessary for any of the authorised purposes.

(4) For the purposes of this section something is necessary for the authorised purposes if, and only if—

(*a*) it continues to be, or is likely to become, necessary as mentioned in section 5(3);

(*b*) it is necessary for facilitating the carrying out of any of the functions under this Chapter of the Secretary of State;

(*c*) it is necessary for facilitating the carrying out of any functions in relation to this Part of the Interception of Communications Commissioner or of the Tribunal;

(*d*) it is necessary to ensure that a person conducting a criminal prosecution has the information he needs to determine what is required of him by his duty to secure the fairness of the prosecution; or

(*e*) it is necessary for the performance of any duty imposed on any person by the Public Records Act 1958 or the Public Records Act (Northern Ireland) 1923.

(5) The arrangements for the time being in force under this section for securing that the requirements of subsection (2) are satisfied in relation to the intercepted material or any related communications data must include such arrangements as the Secretary of State considers necessary for securing that every copy of the material or data that is made is stored, for so long as it is retained, in a secure manner.

(6) Arrangements in relation to interception warrants which are made for the purposes of subsection (1)—

(*a*) shall not be required to secure that the requirements of subsections (2) and (3) are satisfied in so far as they relate to any of the intercepted material or related communications data, or any copy of any such material or data, possession of which has been surrendered to any authorities of a country or territory outside the United Kingdom; but

(*b*) shall be required to secure, in the case of every such warrant, that possession of the intercepted material and data and of copies of the material or data is surrendered to authorities of a country or territory outside the United Kingdom only if the requirements of subsection (7) are satisfied.

(7) The requirements of this subsection are satisfied in the case of a warrant if it appears to the Secretary of State—

(*a*) that requirements corresponding to those of subsections (2) and (3) will apply, to such extent (if any) as the Secretary of State thinks fit, in relation to any of the intercepted material or related communications data possession of which, or of any copy of which, is surrendered to the authorities in question; and

(*b*) that restrictions are in force which would prevent, to such extent (if any) as the Secretary of State thinks fit, the doing of anything in, for the purposes of or in connection with any proceedings outside the United Kingdom which would result in such a disclosure as, by virtue of section 17, could not be made in the United Kingdom.

(8) In this section "copy", in relation to intercepted material or related communications data, means any of the following (whether or not in documentary form)—

(*a*) any copy, extract or summary of the material or data which identifies itself as the product of an interception, and

(*b*) any record referring to an interception which is a record of the identities of the persons to or by whom the intercepted material was sent, or to whom the communications data relates,

and "copied" shall be construed accordingly.
[Regulation of Investigatory Powers Act 2000, s 15.]

8–30109E 16. Extra safeguards in the case of certificated warrants. (1) For the purposes of section 15 the requirements of this section, in the case of a warrant in relation to which there is a section 8(4) certificate, are that the intercepted material is read, looked at or listened to by the persons to whom it becomes available by virtue of the warrant to the extent only that it—

(*a*) has been certified as material the examination of which is necessary as mentioned in section 5(3)(*a*), (*b*) or (*c*); and

(*b*) falls within subsection (2).

(2) Subject to subsections (3) and (4), intercepted material falls within this subsection so far only as it is selected to be read, looked at or listened to otherwise than according to a factor which—

(*a*) is referable to an individual who is known to be for the time being in the British Islands; and

(*b*) has as its purpose, or one of its purposes, the identification of material contained in communications sent by him, or intended for him.

(3) Intercepted material falls within subsection (2), notwithstanding that it is selected by reference to any such factor as is mentioned in paragraph (*a*) and (b) of that subsection, if—

(*a*) it is certified by the Secretary of State for the purposes of section 8(4) that the examination of material selected according to factors referable to the individual in question is necessary as mentioned in subsection 5(3)(*a*), (*b*) or (*c*); and

(*b*) the material relates only to communications sent during a period of not more than three months specified in the certificate.

(4) Intercepted material also falls within subsection (2), notwithstanding that it is selected by reference to any such factor as is mentioned in paragraph (*a*) and (b) of that subsection, if—

(*a*) the person to whom the warrant is addressed believes, on reasonable grounds, that the circumstances are such that the material would fall within that subsection; or

(*b*) the conditions set out in subsection (5) below are satisfied in relation to the selection of the material.

(5) Those conditions are satisfied in relation to the selection of intercepted material if—

(*a*) it has appeared to the person to whom the warrant is addressed that there has been such a relevant change of circumstances as, but for subsection (4)(*b*), would prevent the intercepted material from falling within subsection (2);

(*b*) since it first so appeared, a written authorisation to read, look at or listen to the material has been given by a senior official; and

(*c*) the selection is made before the end of the first working day after the day on which it first so appeared to that person.

(6) References in this section to its appearing that there has been a relevant change of circumstances are references to its appearing either—

(*a*) that the individual in question has entered the British Islands; or

(*b*) that a belief by the person to whom the warrant is addressed in the individual's presence outside the British Islands was in fact mistaken.

[Regulation of Investigatory Powers Act 2000, s 16.]

8–30109F 17. Exclusion of matters from legal proceedings[1]. (1) Subject to section 18, no evidence shall be adduced, question asked, assertion or disclosure made or other thing done in, for the purposes of or in connection with any legal proceedings or Inquiries Act proceedings which (in any manner)—

(*a*) discloses, in circumstances from which its origin in anything falling within subsection (2) may be inferred, any of the contents of an intercepted communication or any related communications data; or

(*b*) tends (apart from any such disclosure) to suggest that anything falling within subsection (2) has or may have occurred or be going to occur[2].

(2) The following fall within this subsection—

(*a*) conduct by a person falling within subsection (3) that was or would be an offence under section 1(1) or (2) of this Act or under section 1 of the Interception of Communications Act 1985;

(*b*) a breach by the Secretary of State of his duty under section 1(4) of this Act;

(*c*) the issue of an interception warrant or of a warrant under the Interception of Communications Act 1985;

(*d*) the making of an application by any person for an interception warrant, or for a warrant under that Act;

(*e*) the imposition of any requirement on any person to provide assistance with giving effect to an interception warrant.

(3) The persons referred to in subsection (2)(*a*) are—

(*a*) any person to whom a warrant under this Chapter may be addressed;

(*b*) any person holding office under the Crown;

(*c*) any member of the staff of the Serious Organised Crime Agency;

(*e*) any person employed by or for the purposes of a police force;

(*f*) any person providing a postal service or employed for the purposes of any business of providing such a service; and

(*g*) any person providing a public telecommunications service or employed for the purposes of any business of providing such a service.

(4) In this section—

"Inquiries Act proceedings" means proceedings of an inquiry under the Inquiries Act 2005;

"intercepted communication" means any communication intercepted in the course of its transmission by means of a postal service or telecommunication system.

[Regulation of Investigatory Powers Act 2000, s 17 as amended by the Inquiries Act 2005, s 48 and the Serious Organised Crime and Police Act 2005, Sch 4.]

---

1. In *A-G's Reference (No 5 of 2002)* [2004] UKHL 40, [2005] 1 AC 167, [2004] 3 WLR 957 the following questions were referred by the Attorney-General: (1) whether s 17(1) operated so as to prevent, in criminal proceedings, any evidence being adduced, question asked, assertion or disclosure made or other thing done so as to ascertain whether a telecommunications system was a public or a private telecommunications system; (2) whether the answer to question (1) was different if the evidence being adduced or question asked related to events which took place before the 2000 Act came into force; (3) whether, where an interception of a communication had taken place on a private telecommunications system, it was permissible in criminal proceedings to ask questions or adduce evidence to establish that the interception had been carried out by or on behalf of the person with the right to control the operation or use of the system (*a*) where the interception took place before the 2000 Act came into force and (*b*) where the interception took place after the 2000 Act came into force. Their lordships upheld the answers to those questions given by the Court of Appeal, namely "No" to questions 1 and 2, "Yes" to question 3(*a*) and "Yes, subject to the facts of the particular case", to question 3(*b*) (adding, however, that the latter qualification might not have been necessary).

2. It was held in *A-G's Reference (No 5 of 2002)* [2004] UKHL 40, [2004] 3 WLR 957 that s 17(1) did not operate so as to prevent, in criminal proceedings, any evidence being adduced, question asked, assertion or disclosure made or other thing done so as to ascertain whether a telecommunications system was a public or private telecommunications system, whether or not the evidence being adduced or question asked related to events which had taken place before the 2000 Act came into force; where an interception of a communication had taken place on a private telecommunications system, it was permissible to in criminal proceedings to ask questions or adduce evidence to establish that the interception had been carried out by or on behalf of the person with the right to control the operation of the system (*a*) where the interception had taken place before the 2000 Act came into force, and (*b*) possibly where it had taken place after that date, subject to the facts of the particular case.

8–30109G 18. Exceptions to section 17. (1) Section 17(1) shall not apply in relation to—

(*a*) any proceedings for a relevant offence;

(*b*) any civil proceedings under section 11(8);

(*c*) any proceedings before the Tribunal;
(*d*) any proceedings on an appeal or review for which provision is made by an order under section 67(8);
(*da*) any control order proceedings (within the meaning of the Prevention of Terrorism Act 2005) or any proceedings arising out of such proceedings;
(*e*) any proceedings before the Special Immigration Appeals Commission or any proceedings arising out of proceedings before that Commission; or
(*f*) any proceedings before the Proscribed Organisations Appeal Commission or any proceedings arising out of proceedings before that Commission.

(2) Subsection (1) shall not, by virtue of paragraphs (*da*) to (*f*), authorise the disclosure of anything—

(*za*) in the case of any proceedings falling within paragraph (da) to—

(i) a person who, within the meaning of the Schedule to the Prevention of Terrorism Act 2005, is or was a relevant party to the control order proceedings; or
(ii) any person who for the purposes of any proceedings so falling (but otherwise than by virtue of an appointment under paragraph 7 of that Schedule) represents a person falling within sub-paragraph (i);

(*a*) in the case of any proceedings falling within paragraph (*e*), to—

(i) the appellant to the Special Immigration Appeals Commission; or
(ii) any person who for the purposes of any proceedings so falling (but otherwise than by virtue of an appointment under section 6 of the Special Immigration Appeals Commission Act 1997) represents that appellant;

or

(*b*) in the case of proceedings falling within paragraph (*f*), to—

(i) the applicant to the Proscribed Organisations Appeal Commission;
(ii) the organisation concerned (if different);
(iii) any person designated under paragraph 6 of Schedule 3 to the Terrorism Act 2000 to conduct proceedings so falling on behalf of that organisation; or
(iv) any person who for the purposes of any proceedings so falling (but otherwise than by virtue of an appointment under paragraph 7 of that Schedule) represents that applicant or that organisation.

(3) Section 17(1) shall not prohibit anything done in, for the purposes of, or in connection with, so much of any legal proceedings as relates to the fairness or unfairness of a dismissal on the grounds of any conduct constituting an offence under section 1(1) or (2), 11(7) or 19 of this Act, or section 1 of the Interception of Communications Act 1985.

(4) Section 17(1)(*a*) shall not prohibit the disclosure of any of the contents of a communication if the interception of that communication was lawful by virtue of section 1(5)(*c*), 3 or 4.

(5) Where any disclosure is proposed to be or has been made on the grounds that it is authorised by subsection (4), section 17(1) shall not prohibit the doing of anything in, or for the purposes of, so much of any legal proceedings as relates to the question whether that disclosure is or was so authorised.

(6) Section 17(1)(*b*) shall not prohibit the doing of anything that discloses any conduct of a person for which he has been convicted of an offence under section 1(1) or (2), 11(7) or 19 of this Act, or section 1 of the Interception of Communications Act 1985.

(7) Nothing in section 17(1) shall prohibit any such disclosure of any information that continues to be available for disclosure as is confined to—

(*a*) a disclosure to a person conducting a criminal prosecution for the purpose only of enabling that person to determine what is required of him by his duty to secure the fairness of the prosecution; or
(*b*) a disclosure to a relevant judge in a case in which that judge has ordered the disclosure to be made to him alone; or
(*c*) a disclosure to the panel of an inquiry held under the Inquiries Act 2005 in the course of which the panel has ordered the disclosure to be made to the panel alone.

(8) A relevant judge shall not order a disclosure under subsection (7)(b) except where he is satisfied that the exceptional circumstances of the case make the disclosure essential in the interests of justice.

(8A) The panel of an inquiry shall not order a disclosure under subsection (7)(c) except where it is satisfied that the exceptional circumstances of the case make the disclosure essential to enable the inquiry to fulfil its terms of reference.

(9) Subject to subsection (10), where in any criminal proceedings—

(*a*) a relevant judge does order a disclosure under subsection (7)(*b*), and
(*b*) in consequence of that disclosure he is of the opinion that there are exceptional circumstances requiring him to do so,

he may direct the person conducting the prosecution to make for the purposes of the proceedings any such admission of fact as that judge thinks essential in the interests of justice.

(10) Nothing in any direction under subsection (9) shall authorise or require anything to be done in contravention of section 17(1).

(11) In this section "a relevant judge" means—

(*a*) any judge of the High Court or of the Crown Court or any Circuit judge;
(*b*) any judge of the High Court of Justiciary or any sheriff;
(*c*) in relation to a court-martial, the judge advocate appointed in relation to that court-martial under section 84B of the Army Act 1955, section 84B of the Air Force Act 1955 or section 53B of the Naval Discipline Act 1957; or
(*d*) any person holding any such judicial office as entitles him to exercise the jurisdiction of a judge falling within paragraph (*a*) or (*b*).

(12) In this section "relevant offence" means—

(*a*) an offence under any provision of this Act;
(*b*) an offence under section 1 of the Interception of Communications Act 1985;
(*c*) an offence under section 5 of the Wireless Telegraphy Act 1949;
(*d*) an offence under section 83 or 84 of the Postal Services Act 2000;
(*e*) *repealed*;
(*f*) an offence under section 4 of the Official Secrets Act 1989 relating to any such information, document or article as is mentioned in subsection (3)(*a*) of that section;
(*g*) an offence under section 1 or 2 of the Official Secrets Act 1911 relating to any sketch, plan, model, article, note, document or information which incorporates or relates to the contents of any intercepted communication or any related communications data or tends to suggest as mentioned in section 17(1)(*b*) of this Act;
(*h*) perjury committed in the course of any proceedings mentioned in subsection (1) or (3) of this section;
(*i*) attempting or conspiring to commit, or aiding, abetting, counselling or procuring the commission of, an offence falling within any of the preceding paragraphs; and
(*j*) contempt of court committed in the course of, or in relation to, any proceedings mentioned in subsection (1) or (3) of this section.

(13) In subsection (12) "intercepted communication" has the same meaning as in section 17.

[Regulation of Investigatory Powers Act 2000, s 18 as amended by the Inquiries Act 2005, Schs 2 and 3 and the Prevention of Terrorism Act 2005, Schedule.]

8–30109H 19. Offence for unauthorised disclosures. (1) Where an interception warrant has been issued or renewed, it shall be the duty of every person falling within subsection (2) to keep secret all the matters mentioned in subsection (3).

(2) The persons falling within this subsection are—

(*a*) the persons specified in section 6(2);
(*b*) every person holding office under the Crown;
(*c*) every member of the staff of the Serious Organised Crime Agency;
(*e*) every person employed by or for the purposes of a police force;
(*f*) persons providing postal services or employed for the purposes of any business of providing such a service;
(*g*) persons providing public telecommunications services or employed for the purposes of any business of providing such a service;
(*h*) persons having control of the whole or any part of a telecommunication system located wholly or partly in the United Kingdom.

(3) Those matters are—

(*a*) the existence and contents of the warrant and of any section 8(4) certificate in relation to the warrant;
(*b*) the details of the issue of the warrant and of any renewal or modification of the warrant or of any such certificate;
(*c*) the existence and contents of any requirement to provide assistance with giving effect to the warrant;
(*d*) the steps taken in pursuance of the warrant or of any such requirement; and
(*e*) everything in the intercepted material, together with any related communications data.

(4) A person who makes a disclosure to another of anything that he is required to keep secret under this section shall be guilty of an offence and liable[1]—

(*a*) on conviction on indictment, to imprisonment for a term not exceeding five years or to a fine, or to both;
(*b*) on summary conviction, to imprisonment for a term not exceeding six months or to a fine not exceeding the statutory maximum, or to both.

(5) In proceedings against any person for an offence under this section in respect of any disclosure,

it shall be a defence for that person to show that he could not reasonably have been expected, after first becoming aware of the matter disclosed, to take steps to prevent the disclosure.

(6) In proceedings against any person for an offence under this section in respect of any disclosure, it shall be a defence for that person to show that—

(*a*) the disclosure was made by or to a professional legal adviser in connection with the giving, by the adviser to any client of his, of advice about the effect of provisions of this Chapter; and

(*b*) the person to whom or, as the case may be, by whom it was made was the client or a representative of the client.

(7) In proceedings against any person for an offence under this section in respect of any disclosure, it shall be a defence for that person to show that the disclosure was made by a legal adviser—

(*a*) in contemplation of, or in connection with, any legal proceedings; and

(*b*) for the purposes of those proceedings.

(8) Neither subsection (6) nor subsection (7) applies in the case of a disclosure made with a view to furthering any criminal purpose.

(9) In proceedings against any person for an offence under this section in respect of any disclosure, it shall be a defence for that person to show that the disclosure was confined to a disclosure made to the Interception of Communications Commissioner or authorised—

(*a*) by that Commissioner;

(*b*) by the warrant or the person to whom the warrant is or was addressed;

(*c*) by the terms of the requirement to provide assistance; or

(*d*) by section 11(9).

[Regulation of Investigatory Powers Act 2000, s 19 as amended by the Serious Organised Crime and Police Act 2005, Sch 4.]

---

1. For procedure in respect of an offence triable either way, see Magistrates' Courts Act 1980, ss 17A–21, in PART I: MAGISTRATES' COURTS, PROCEDURE, ante.

Interpretation of Chapter I

8–30109I 20. Interpretation of Chapter I. In this Chapter—

"certified", in relation to a section 8(4) certificate, means of a description certified by the certificate as a description of material the examination of which the Secretary of State considers necessary;

"external communication" means a communication sent or received outside the British Islands;

"intercepted material", in relation to an interception warrant, means the contents of any communications intercepted by an interception to which the warrant relates;

"the interception subject", in relation to an interception warrant, means the person about whose communications information is sought by the interception to which the warrant relates;

"international mutual assistance agreement" means an international agreement designated for the purposes of section 1(4);

"related communications data", in relation to a communication intercepted in the course of its transmission by means of a postal service or telecommunication system, means so much of any communications data (within the meaning of Chapter II of this Part) as—

(a) is obtained by, or in connection with, the interception; and

(b) relates to the communication or to the sender or recipient, or intended recipient, of the communication;

"section 8(4) certificate" means any certificate issued for the purposes of section 8(4).

[Regulation of Investigatory Powers Act 2000, s 20.]

CHAPTER II[1]

ACQUISITION AND DISCLOSURE OF COMMUNICATIONS DATA

8–30109J 21. Lawful acquisition and disclosure of communications data. (1) This Chapter applies to—

(*a*) any conduct in relation to a postal service or telecommunication system for obtaining communications data, other than conduct consisting in the interception of communications in the course of their transmission by means of such a service or system; and

(*b*) the disclosure to any person of communications data.

(2) Conduct to which this Chapter applies shall be lawful for all purposes if—

(*a*) it is conduct in which any person is authorised or required to engage by an authorisation or notice granted or given under this Chapter; and

(*b*) the conduct is in accordance with, or in pursuance of, the authorisation or requirement.

(3) A person shall not be subject to any civil liability in respect of any conduct of his which—

(*a*) is incidental to any conduct that is lawful by virtue of subsection (2); and (*b*) is not itself conduct an authorisation or warrant for which is capable of being granted under a relevant enactment and might reasonably have been expected to have been sought in the case in question.

(4) In this Chapter "communications data" means any of the following—

(*a*) any traffic data comprised in or attached to a communication (whether by the sender or otherwise) for the purposes of any postal service or telecommunication system by means of which it is being or may be transmitted;

(*b*) any information which includes none of the contents of a communication (apart from any information falling within paragraph (*a*)) and is about the use made by any person—

(i) of any postal service or telecommunications service; or

(ii) in connection with the provision to or use by any person of any telecommunications service, of any part of a telecommunication system;

(*c*) any information not falling within paragraph (*a*) or (*b*) that is held or obtained, in relation to persons to whom he provides the service, by a person providing a postal service or telecommunications service.

(5) In this section "relevant enactment" means—

(*a*) an enactment contained in this Act;

(*b*) section 5 of the Intelligence Services Act 1994 (warrants for the intelligence services); or

(*c*) an enactment contained in Part III of the Police Act 1997 (powers of the police and of customs officers).

(6) In this section "traffic data", in relation to any communication, means—

(*a*) any data identifying, or purporting to identify, any person, apparatus or location to or from which the communication is or may be transmitted,

(*b*) any data identifying or selecting, or purporting to identify or select, apparatus through which, or by means of which, the communication is or may be transmitted,

(*c*) any data comprising signals for the actuation of apparatus used for the purposes of a telecommunication system for effecting (in whole or in part) the transmission of any communication, and

(*d*) any data identifying the data or other data as data comprised in or attached to a particular communication,

but that expression includes data identifying a computer file or computer program access to which is obtained, or which is run, by means of the communication to the extent only that the file or program is identified by reference to the apparatus in which it is stored.

(7) In this section—

(*a*) references, in relation to traffic data comprising signals for the actuation of apparatus, to a telecommunication system by means of which a communication is being or may be transmitted include references to any telecommunication system in which that apparatus is comprised; and

(*b*) references to traffic data being attached to a communication include references to the data and the communication being logically associated with each other;

and in this section "data", in relation to a postal item, means anything written on the outside of the item.

[Regulation of Investigatory Powers Act 2000, s 21.]

---

1. Chapter II contains ss 21–25.

8–30109K 22. Obtaining and disclosing communications data. (1) This section applies where a person designated for the purposes of this Chapter believes that it is necessary on grounds falling within subsection (2) to obtain any communications data.

(2) It is necessary on grounds falling within this subsection to obtain communications data if it is necessary—

(*a*) in the interests of national security;

(*b*) for the purpose of preventing or detecting crime or of preventing disorder;

(*c*) in the interests of the economic well-being of the United Kingdom;

(*d*) in the interests of public safety;

(*e*) for the purpose of protecting public health;

(*f*) for the purpose of assessing or collecting any tax, duty, levy or other imposition, contribution or charge payable to a government department;

(*g*) for the purpose, in an emergency, of preventing death or injury or any damage to a person's physical or mental health, or of mitigating any injury or damage to a person's physical or mental health; or

(*h*) for any purpose (not falling within paragraphs (*a*) to (*g*)) which is specified for the purposes of this subsection by an order made by the Secretary of State.

(3) Subject to subsection (5), the designated person may grant an authorisation for persons holding offices, ranks or positions with the same relevant public authority as the designated person to engage in any conduct to which this Chapter applies.

(4) Subject to subsection (5), where it appears to the designated person that a postal or telecommunications operator is or may be in possession of, or be capable of obtaining, any communications data, the designated person may, by notice to the postal or telecommunications operator, require the operator—

(*a*) if the operator is not already in possession of the data, to obtain the data; and

(*b*) in any case, to disclose all of the data in his possession or subsequently obtained by him.

(5) The designated person shall not grant an authorisation under subsection (3), or give a notice under subsection (4), unless he believes that obtaining the data in question by the conduct authorised or required by the authorisation or notice is proportionate to what is sought to be achieved by so obtaining the data.

(6) It shall be the duty of the postal or telecommunications operator to comply with the requirements of any notice given to him under subsection (4).

(7) A person who is under a duty by virtue of subsection (6) shall not be required to do anything in pursuance of that duty which it is not reasonably practicable for him to do.

(8) The duty imposed by subsection (6) shall be enforceable by civil proceedings by the Secretary of State for an injunction, or for specific performance of a statutory duty under section 45 of the Court of Session Act 1988, or for any other appropriate relief.

(9) The Secretary of State shall not make an order under subsection (2)(*h*) unless a draft of the order has been laid before Parliament and approved by a resolution of each House.

[Regulation of Investigatory Powers Act 2000, s 22.]

8–30109L 23. *Form and duration of authorisations and notices*

8–30109M 24. *Arrangements for payments*

8–30109N 25. Interpretation of Chapter II. (1) In this Chapter—

"communications data" has the meaning given by section 21(4);

"designated" shall be construed in accordance with subsection (2);

"postal or telecommunications operator" means a person who provides a postal service or telecommunications service;

"relevant public authority" means (subject to subsection (4)) any of the following—

(*a*) a police force;

(*b*) the Serious Organised Crime Agency;

(*d*) the Commissioners of Customs and Excise;

(*e*) the Commissioners of Inland Revenue;

(*f*) any of the intelligence services;

(*g*) any such public authority not falling within paragraphs (*a*) to (*f*) as may be specified for the purposes of this subsection by an order made by the Secretary of State.

(2) Subject to subsection (3), the persons designated for the purposes of this Chapter are the individuals holding such offices, ranks or positions with relevant public authorities as are prescribed for the purposes of this subsection by an order[1] made by the Secretary of State.

(3) The Secretary of State may by order[1] impose restrictions—

(*a*) on the authorisations and notices under this Chapter that may be granted or given by any individual holding an office, rank or position with a specified public authority; and

(*b*) on the circumstances in which, or the purposes for which, such authorisations may be granted or notices given by any such individual.*

(3A) References in this Chapter to an individual holding an office or position with the Serious Organised Crime Agency include references to any member of the staff of that Agency.

(4) The Secretary of State may by order—

(*a*) remove any person from the list of persons who are for the time being relevant public authorities for the purposes of this Chapter; and

(*b*) make such consequential amendments, repeals or revocations in this or any other enactment as appear to him to be necessary or expedient.

(5) The Secretary of State shall not make an order under this section—

(*a*) that adds any person to the list of persons who are for the time being relevant public authorities for the purposes of this Chapter, or

(*b*) that by virtue of subsection (4)(*b*) amends or repeals any provision of an Act,

unless a draft of the order has been laid before Parliament and approved by a resolution of each House.

[Regulation of Investigatory Powers Act 2000, s 25 as amended by the Serious Organised Crime and Police Act 2005, Sch 4.]

1. The Regulation of Investigatory Powers (Communications Data) Order 2003, SI 2003/3172 amended by SI 2005/1083 and 2929 (W) has been made.

PART II[1]

SURVEILLANCE AND COVERT HUMAN INTELLIGENCE SOURCES

Introductory

8–30109O 26. Conduct to which Part II applies. (1) This Part applies to the following conduct—

(*a*) directed surveillance;

(*b*) intrusive surveillance; and

(*c*) the conduct and use of covert human intelligence sources.

(2) Subject to subsection (6), surveillance is directed for the purposes of this Part if it is covert but not intrusive and is undertaken—

(*a*) for the purposes of a specific investigation or a specific operation;

(*b*) in such a manner as is likely to result in the obtaining of private information about a person (whether or not one specifically identified for the purposes of the investigation or operation); and

(*c*) otherwise than by way of an immediate response to events or circumstances the nature of which is such that it would not be reasonably practicable for an authorisation under this Part to be sought for the carrying out of the surveillance.

(3) Subject to subsections (4) to (6), surveillance is intrusive for the purposes of this Part if, and only if, it is covert surveillance that—

(*a*) is carried out in relation to anything taking place on any residential premises or in any private vehicle; and

(*b*) involves the presence of an individual on the premises or in the vehicle or is carried out by means of a surveillance device.

(4) For the purposes of this Part surveillance is not intrusive to the extent that—

(*a*) it is carried out by means only of a surveillance device designed or adapted principally for the purpose of providing information about the location of a vehicle; or

(*b*) it is surveillance consisting in any such interception of a communication as falls within section 48(4).

(5) For the purposes of this Part surveillance which—

(*a*) is carried out by means of a surveillance device in relation to anything taking place on any residential premises or in any private vehicle, but

(*b*) is carried out without that device being present on the premises or in the vehicle,

is not intrusive unless the device is such that it consistently provides information of the same quality and detail as might be expected to be obtained from a device actually present on the premises or in the vehicle.

(6) For the purposes of this Part surveillance which—

(*a*) is carried out by means of apparatus designed or adapted for the purpose of detecting the installation or use in any residential or other premises of a television receiver (within the meaning of section 1 of the Wireless Telegraphy Act 1949), and

(*b*) is carried out from outside those premises exclusively for that purpose,

is neither directed nor intrusive.

(7) In this Part—

(*a*) references to the conduct of a covert human intelligence source are references to any conduct of such a source which falls within any of paragraphs (*a*) to (*c*) of subsection (8), or is incidental to anything falling within any of those paragraphs; and

(*b*) references to the use of a covert human intelligence source are references to inducing, asking or assisting a person to engage in the conduct of such a source, or to obtain information by means of the conduct of such a source.

(8) For the purposes of this Part a person is a covert human intelligence source[2] if—

(*a*) he establishes or maintains a personal or other relationship with a person for the covert purpose of facilitating the doing of anything falling within paragraph (*b*) or (*c*);

(*b*) he covertly uses such a relationship to obtain information or to provide access to any information to another person; or

(*c*) he covertly discloses information obtained by the use of such a relationship, or as a consequence of the existence of such a relationship.

(9) For the purposes of this section—

(*a*) surveillance is covert if, and only if, it is carried out in a manner that is calculated to ensure that persons who are subject to the surveillance are unaware that it is or may be taking place;

(*b*) a purpose is covert, in relation to the establishment or maintenance of a personal or other relationship, if and only if the relationship is conducted in a manner that is calculated to ensure that one of the parties to the relationship is unaware of the purpose; and

(*c*) a relationship is used covertly, and information obtained as mentioned in subsection (8)(*c*) is disclosed covertly, if and only if it is used or, as the case may be, disclosed in a manner that is calculated to ensure that one of the parties to the relationship is unaware of the use or disclosure in question.

(10) In this section "private information", in relation to a person, includes any information relating to his private or family life.

(11) References in this section, in relation to a vehicle, to the presence of a surveillance device in the vehicle include references to its being located on or under the vehicle and also include references to its being attached to it.

[Regulation of Investigatory Powers Act 2000, s 26.]

---

1. Part II contains ss 26–48 and Sch 1.
2. The tape recording by undercover police officers of their telephone conversations with a suspect constitutes the use of "a covert human intelligence source" within the meaning of s 26(8), but the complex framework provided for authority for surveillance under the 2000 Act was in no way contrary to the provisions of the European Convention (*R v Hardy* [2002] EWCA Crim 3012, [2003] 1 Cr App R 30).

Authorisation of surveillance and human intelligence sources

8–30109P 27. Lawful surveillance etc. (1) Conduct to which this Part applies shall be lawful for all purposes if—

(*a*) an authorisation[1] under this Part confers an entitlement to engage in that conduct on the person whose conduct it is; and

(*b*) his conduct is in accordance with the authorisation.

(2) A person shall not be subject to any civil liability in respect of any conduct of his which—

(*a*) is incidental to any conduct that is lawful by virtue of subsection (1); and

(*b*) is not itself conduct an authorisation or warrant for which is capable of being granted under a relevant enactment and might reasonably have been expected to have been sought in the case in question.

(3) The conduct that may be authorised under this Part includes conduct outside the United Kingdom.

(4) In this section "relevant enactment" means—

(*a*) an enactment contained in this Act;

(*b*) section 5 of the Intelligence Services Act 1994 (warrants for the intelligence services); or

(*c*) an enactment contained in Part III of the Police Act 1997 (powers of the police and of customs officers).

[Regulation of Investigatory Powers Act 2000, s 27.]

---

1. The authorisation and the terms of it do not attract public interest immunity, see *R v Hardy* [2002] EWCA Crim 3012, [2003] 1 Cr App Rep 494 (an application to exclude the evidence obtained by the surveillance was foreseeable; therefore, this was material that could assist the defence and it should have been disclosed).

28–46. *Powers to grant authorisation of surveillance and human intelligence sources; intrusive surveillance; police and customs authorisations; notifications to an ordinary surveillance commissioner; appeals against decisions of Surveillance Commissioners; authorisation by Secretary of State of intrusive surveillance; authorisation on application by Intelligence Services; general rules about grant, renewal and duration.*

Supplemental provision for Part II

8–30109Q 47. Power to extend or modify authorisation provisions. (1) The Secretary of State may by order[1] do one or both of the following—

(*a*) apply this Part, with such modifications as he thinks fit, to any such surveillance that is neither directed nor intrusive as may be described in the order;

(*b*) provide for any description of directed surveillance to be treated for the purposes of this Part as intrusive surveillance.

(2) No order shall be made under this section unless a draft of it has been laid before Parliament and approved by a resolution of each House.

[Regulation of Investigatory Powers Act 2000, s 47.]

---

1. The Regulation of Investigatory Powers (British Broadcasting Corporation) Order 2001, SI 2001/1057 has been made which applies Part II of the 2000 Act with modifications, to the carrying out of surveillance to detect whether a television is being used in any residential or other premises.

8–30109R 48. Interpretation of Part II. (1) In this Part—

"covert human intelligence source" shall be construed in accordance with section 26(8);

"directed" and "intrusive", in relation to surveillance, shall be construed in accordance with section 26(2) to (6);

"private vehicle" means (subject to subsection (7)(*a*)) any vehicle which is used primarily for the private purposes of the person who owns it or of a person otherwise having the right to use it;

"residential premises" means (subject to subsection (7)(*b*)) so much of any premises as is for the time being occupied or used by any person, however temporarily, for residential purposes or otherwise as living accommodation (including hotel or prison accommodation that is so occupied or used);

"senior authorising officer" means a person who by virtue of subsection (6) of section 32 is a senior authorising officer for the purposes of that section;

"surveillance" shall be construed in accordance with subsections (2) to (4);

"surveillance device" means any apparatus designed or adapted for use in surveillance.

(2) Subject to subsection (3), in this Part "surveillance" includes—

(*a*) monitoring, observing or listening to persons, their movements, their conversations or their other activities or communications;

(*b*) recording anything monitored, observed or listened to in the course of surveillance; and

(*c*) surveillance by or with the assistance of a surveillance device.

(3) References in this Part to surveillance do not include references to—

(*a*) any conduct of a covert human intelligence source for obtaining or recording (whether or not using a surveillance device) any information which is disclosed in the presence of the source;

(*b*) the use of a covert human intelligence source for so obtaining or recording information; or

(*c*) any such entry on or interference with property or with wireless telegraphy as would be unlawful unless authorised under—

(i) section 5 of the Intelligence Services Act 1994 (warrants for the intelligence services); or

(ii) Part III of the Police Act 1997 (powers of the police and of customs officers).

(4) References in this Part to surveillance include references to the interception of a communication in the course of its transmission by means of a postal service or telecommunication system if, and only if—

(*a*) the communication is one sent by or intended for a person who has consented to the interception of communications sent by or to him; and

(*b*) there is no interception warrant authorising the interception.

(5) References in this Part to an individual holding an office or position with a public authority include references to any member, official or employee of that authority.

(6) For the purposes of this Part the activities of a covert human intelligence source which are to be taken as activities for the benefit of a particular public authority include any conduct of his as such a source which is in response to inducements or requests made by or on behalf of that authority.

(7) In subsection (1)—

(*a*) the reference to a person having the right to use a vehicle does not, in relation to a motor vehicle, include a reference to a person whose right to use the vehicle derives only from his having paid, or undertaken to pay, for the use of the vehicle and its driver for a particular journey; and

(*b*) the reference to premises occupied or used by any person for residential purposes or otherwise as living accommodation does not include a reference to so much of any premises as constitutes any common area to which he has or is allowed access in connection with his use or occupation of any accommodation.

(8) In this section—

"premises" includes any vehicle or moveable structure and any other place whatever, whether or not occupied as land;

"vehicle" includes any vessel, aircraft or hovercraft.

[Regulation of Investigatory Powers Act 2000, s 48.]

8–30109S

PART III[1]

INVESTIGATION OF ELECTRONIC DATA PROTECTED BY ENCRYPTION ETC

1. Part III contains ss 49–56 and Sch 2.

8–30109T

PART IV[1]

SCRUTINY ETC OF INVESTIGATORY POWERS AND OF THE FUNCTIONS OF THE INTELLIGENCE SERVICES

1. Part IV contains ss 57–72 and Sch 3.

Codes of practice

8–30109U **71.** *Issue and revision of Codes of Practice*[1]

1. The Regulation of Investigatory Powers (Interception of Communications: Code of Practice) Order 2002, SI 2002/1693 has been made which brought into force the code of practice entitled "Interception of Communications", laid before each House of Parliament on 8 May 2002, relating to the interception of communications under Chapter I of Part I of the 2000 Act, on 1 July 2002.

The Regulation of Investigatory Powers (Covert Human Intelligence Sources: Code of Practice) Order 2002, SI 2002/1932 has been made which brought into force the code of practice entitled "Covert Human Intelligence Sources", laid before each House of Parliament on 10 June 2002, relating to the conduct and use of covert human intelligence sources under Part II of the 2000 Act, on 1 August 2002.

The Regulation of Investigatory Powers (Covert Surveillance: Code of Practice) Order 2002, SI 2002/1933 has been made which brought into force the code of practice entitled "Covert Surveillance", laid before each House of Parliament on 10 June 2002, relating to covert surveillance under Part II of the 2000 Act, on 1 August 2002.

8–30109V **72. Effect of codes of practice.** (1) A person exercising or performing any power or duty in relation to which provision may be made by a code of practice under section 71 shall, in doing so, have regard to the provisions (so far as they are applicable) of every code of practice for the time being in force under that section.

(2) A failure on the part of any person to comply with any provision of a code of practice for the time being in force under section 71 shall not of itself render him liable to any criminal or civil proceedings.

(3) A code of practice in force at any time under section 71 shall be admissible in evidence in any criminal or civil proceedings.

(4) If any provision of a code of practice issued or revised under section 71 appears to—

(*a*) the court or tribunal conducting any civil or criminal proceedings,
(*b*) the Tribunal,
(*c*) a relevant Commissioner carrying out any of his functions under this Act,
(*d*) a Surveillance Commissioner carrying out his functions under this Act or the Police Act 1997, or
(*e*) any Assistant Surveillance Commissioner carrying out any functions of his under section 63 of this Act,

to be relevant to any question arising in the proceedings, or in connection with the exercise of that jurisdiction or the carrying out of those functions, in relation to a time when it was in force, that provision of the code shall be taken into account in determining that question.

(5) In this section "relevant Commissioner" means the Interception of Communications Commissioner, the Intelligence Services Commissioner or the Investigatory Powers Commissioner for Northern Ireland.

[Regulation of Investigatory Powers Act 2000, s 72.]

PART V[1]
MISCELLANEOUS AND SUPPLEMENTAL

1. Part V contains ss 73–83 and Schs 4 and 5.

Mobile Telephones (Re-programming) Act 2002[1]

(2002 c 31)

8–30109W **1. Re-programming mobile telephone etc.** (1) A person commits an offence if—

(*a*) he changes a unique device identifier, or
(*b*) he interferes with the operation of a unique device identifier.

(2) A unique device identifier is an electronic equipment identifier which is unique to a mobile wireless communications device.

(3) But a person does not commit an offence under this section if—

(*a*) he is the manufacturer of the device, or
(*b*) he does the act mentioned in subsection (1) with the written consent of the manufacturer of the device.

(4) A person guilty of an offence under this section is liable[2]—

(*a*) on summary conviction, to imprisonment for a term not exceeding 6 months or to a fine not exceeding the statutory maximum or to both, or
(*b*) on conviction on indictment, to imprisonment for a term not exceeding 5 years or to a fine or to both.

[Mobile Telephones (Re-programming) Act 2002, s 1.]

1. Sections 1 and 2 of this Act were brought into effect on 4 October 2002 in accordance with the Mobile Telephones (Re-programming) Act 2002 (Commencement) Order 2002, SI 2002/2294 made under s 3.

2. For mode of trial of this offence which is triable either way, see the Magistrates' Courts Act 1980, ss 17A–21 in PART I, MAGISTRATES' COURTS, PROCEDURE, ante.

8–30109X 2. Possession or supply of anything for re-programming purposes. (1) A person commits an offence if—

(*a*) he has in his custody or under his control anything which may be used for the purpose of changing or interfering with the operation of a unique device identifier, and

(*b*) he intends to use the thing unlawfully for that purpose or to allow it to be used unlawfully for that purpose.

(2) A person commits an offence if—

(*a*) he supplies anything which may be used for the purpose of changing or interfering with the operation of a unique device identifier, and

(*b*) he knows or believes that the person to whom the thing is supplied intends to use it unlawfully for that purpose or to allow it to be used unlawfully for that purpose.

(3) A person commits an offence if—

(*a*) he offers to supply anything which may be used for the purpose of changing or interfering with the operation of a unique device identifier, and

(*b*) he knows or believes that the person to whom the thing is offered intends if it is supplied to him to use it unlawfully for that purpose or to allow it to be used unlawfully for that purpose.

(4) A unique device identifier is an electronic equipment identifier which is unique to a mobile wireless communications device.

(5) A thing is used by a person unlawfully for a purpose if in using it for that purpose he commits an offence under section 1.

(6) A person guilty of an offence under this section is liable[1]—

(*a*) on summary conviction, to imprisonment for a term not exceeding 6 months or to a fine not exceeding the statutory maximum or to both, or

(*b*) on conviction on indictment, to imprisonment for a term not exceeding 5 years or to a fine or to both.

[Mobile Telephones (Re-programming) Act 2002, s 2.]

1. For mode of trial of this offence which is triable either way, see the Magistrates' Courts Act 1980, For mode of trial of this offence which is triable either way, see the Magistrates' Courts Act 1980, ss 17A–21 in PART I, MAGISTRATES' COURTS, PROCEDURE, ante.

8–30109Y 3. *Citation etc*

Communications Act 2003[1]

(2003 c 21)

8–30110

Offences relating to networks and services

125. Dishonestly obtaining electronic communications services. (1) A person who—

(*a*) dishonestly obtains an electronic communications service, and

(*b*) does so with intent to avoid payment of a charge applicable to the provision of that service,

is guilty of an offence.

(2) It is not an offence under this section to obtain a service mentioned in section 297(1) of the Copyright, Designs and Patents Act 1988 (c 48) (dishonestly obtaining a broadcasting or cable programme service provided from a place in the UK).

(3) A person guilty of an offence under this section shall be liable—

(*a*) on summary conviction, to imprisonment for a term not exceeding six months or to a fine not exceeding the statutory maximum, or to both;

(*b*) on conviction on indictment, to imprisonment for a term not exceeding five years or to a fine, or to both.

[Communications Act 2003, s 125.]

1. The Act provides a regulatory framework for the communications sector, reflecting the proposals made in the Communications White Paper – A New Future for Communications (Cm 5010) – published on 12 December 2000.

The main provisions of the Act provide for: the transfer of functions to the Office of Communications (OFCOM) from the bodies and office holders that previously regulated the telecommunications and broadcasting and managed the radio spectrum; namely: the Broadcasting Standards Commission; the Director General of Telecommunications; the Independent

Television Commission; the Radio Authority; and the Secretary of State, as far as the office included (through the Radio Communications Agency) a regulatory role in respect of the allocation, maintenance and supervision of non-military radio spectrum in the UK.

The Office of Communications Act 2002 established OFCOM and gave it a single initial function – to prepare to assume regulatory functions at a later stage. It also gave the existing regulators additional functions and duties to assist OFCOM to prepare.

Once the transfer to OFCOM of the functions, property, rights and liabilities of the bodies and office holders that previously regulated the communications sector has taken effect OFCOM will develop and maintain new regulatory rules for the communications sector within the context of a single set of regulatory objectives, and in the light of the changing market environment.

In February 2002 the European Parliament and the Council of Ministers adopted four Directives ("the EC Communications Directives"), which set out a package of measures for a common regulatory framework for electronic communications networks and services. Provisions in the Act implement a significant proportion of this new regulatory package in the UK.

8–30110A 126. Possession or supply of apparatus etc for contravening s 125. (1) A person is guilty of an offence if, with an intention falling within subsection (3), he has in his possession or under his control anything that may be used—

(*a*) for obtaining an electronic communications service; or
(*b*) in connection with obtaining such a service.

(2) A person is guilty of an offence if—

(*a*) he supplies or offers to supply anything which may be used as mentioned in subsection (1); and
(*b*) he knows or believes that the intentions in relation to that thing of the person to whom it is supplied or offered fall within subsection (3).

(3) A person's intentions fall within this subsection if he intends—

(*a*) to use the thing to obtain an electronic communications service dishonestly;
(*b*) to use the thing for a purpose connected with the dishonest obtaining of such a service;
(*c*) dishonestly to allow the thing to be used to obtain such a service; or
(*d*) to allow the thing to be used for a purpose connected with the dishonest obtaining of such a service.

(4) An intention does not fall within subsection (3) if it relates exclusively to the obtaining of a service mentioned in section 297(1) of the Copyright, Designs and Patents Act 1988 (c 48).

(5) A person guilty of an offence under this section shall be liable—

(*a*) on summary conviction, to imprisonment for a term not exceeding six months or to a fine not exceeding the statutory maximum, or to both; and
(*b*) on conviction on indictment, to imprisonment for a term not exceeding five years or to a fine, or to both.

(6) In this section, references, in the case of a thing used for recording data, to the use of that thing include references to the use of data recorded by it.
[Communications Act 2003, s 126.]

8–30110B 127. Improper use of public electronic communications network. (1) A person is guilty of an offence if he—

(*a*) sends by means of a public electronic communications network a message or other matter that is grossly offensive[1] or of an indecent, obscene or menacing character; or
(*b*) causes any such message or matter to be so sent.

(2) A person is guilty of an offence if, for the purpose of causing annoyance, inconvenience or needless anxiety to another, he—

(*a*) sends by means of a public electronic communications network, a message that he knows to be false,
(*b*) causes such a message to be sent; or
(*c*) persistently makes use of a public electronic communications network.

(3) A person guilty of an offence under this section shall be liable, on summary conviction, to imprisonment for a term not exceeding six months or to a fine not exceeding level 5 on the standard scale, or to both.

(4) Subsections (1) and (2) do not apply to anything done in the course of providing a programme service (within the meaning of the Broadcasting Act 1990 (c 42)).
[Communications Act 2003, s 127.]

1. "Offensive" and thus "grossly offensive", must be judged by the standards of an open and just multi-racial society. Whether a telephone message falls into the category of grossly offensive depends on its content, on the circumstances in which the message was sent and, at least as background, on the objective of Parliament of protecting people from being involuntarily subjected to messages which they might find seriously objectionable. If a recorded message contains abusive and intemperate language, and the defendant had no idea or concern as to whether the intended recipient or anybody else who might pick up the message would be personally grossly offended, it would be his good fortune if nobody were so affected; nevertheless, such

absence of actual offence is a fact which the court is entitled to take into account: *DPP v Collins* [2005] EWHC 1308 (Admin), [2005] 3 All ER 326, [2005] 2 Cr App R 39. [2005] Crim LR 794.

Powers to deal with emergencies

8–30110C 132. Powers to require suspension or restriction of a provider's entitlement. (1) If the Secretary of State has reasonable grounds for believing that it is necessary to do so—

(*a*) to protect the public from any threat to public safety or public health, or
(*b*) in the interests of national security,

he may, by a direction to OFCOM, require them to give a direction under subsection (3) to a person ("the relevant provider") who provides an electronic communications network or electronic communications service or who makes associated facilities available.

(2) OFCOM must comply with a requirement of the Secretary of State under subsection (1) by giving to the relevant provider such direction under subsection (3) as they consider necessary for the purpose of complying with the Secretary of State's direction.

(3) A direction under this section is—

(*a*) a direction that the entitlement of the relevant provider to provide electronic communications networks or electronic communications services, or to make associated facilities available, is suspended (either generally or in relation to particular networks, services or facilities); or
(*b*) a direction that that entitlement is restricted in the respects set out in the direction.

(4) A direction under subsection (3)—

(*a*) must specify the networks, services and facilities to which it relates; and
(*b*) except so far as it otherwise provides, takes effect for an indefinite period beginning with the time at which it is notified to the person to whom it is given.

(5) A direction under subsection (3)—

(*a*) in providing for the effect of a suspension or restriction to be postponed, may provide for it to take effect only at a time determined by or in accordance with the terms of the direction; and
(*b*) in connection with the suspension or restriction contained in the direction or with the postponement of its effect, may impose such conditions on the relevant provider as appear to OFCOM to be appropriate for the purpose of protecting that provider's customers.

(6) Those conditions may include a condition requiring the making of payments—

(*a*) by way of compensation for loss or damage suffered by the relevant provider's customers as a result of the direction; or
(*b*) in respect of annoyance, inconvenience or anxiety to which they have been put in consequence of the direction.

(7) Where OFCOM give a direction under subsection (3), they shall, as soon as practicable after doing so, provide that person with an opportunity of—

(*a*) making representations about the effect of the direction; and
(*b*) proposing steps for remedying the situation.

(8) If OFCOM consider it appropriate to do so (whether in consequence of any representations or proposals made to them under subsection (3) or otherwise), they may, without revoking it, at any time modify the terms of a direction under subsection (3) in such manner as they consider appropriate.

(9) If the Secretary of State considers it appropriate to do so, he may, by a direction to OFCOM, require them to revoke a direction under subsection (3).

(10) Where OFCOM modify or revoke a direction they have given under subsection (3), they may do so—

(*a*) with effect from such time as they may direct;
(*b*) subject to compliance with such requirements as they may specify; and
(*c*) to such extent and in relation to such networks, services or facilities, or parts of a network, service or facility, as they may determine.

(11) It shall be the duty of OFCOM to comply with—

(*a*) a requirement under subsection (9) to revoke a direction; and
(*b*) a requirement contained in that direction as to how they should exercise their powers under subsection (10) in the case of the required revocation.

[Communications Act 2003, s 132.]

8–30110D 133. Enforcement of directions under s 132. (1) A person is guilty of an offence if he provides an electronic communications network or electronic communications service, or makes available any associated facility—

(*a*) while his entitlement to do so is suspended by a direction under section 132; or
(*b*) in contravention of a restriction contained in such a direction.

(2) A person guilty of an offence under subsection (1) shall be liable—

(*a*) on summary conviction, to a fine not exceeding the statutory maximum;

(*b*) on conviction on indictment, to a fine.

(3) The duty of a person to comply with a condition of a direction under section 132 shall be a duty owed to every person who may be affected by a contravention of the condition.

(4) Where a duty is owed by virtue of subsection (3) to a person—

(*a*) a breach of the duty that causes that person to sustain loss or damage, and

(*b*) an act which—

(i) by inducing a breach of the duty or interfering with its performance, causes that person to sustain loss or damage, and

(ii) is done wholly or partly for achieving that result,

shall be actionable at the suit or instance of that person.

(5) In proceedings brought against a person by virtue of subsection (4)(*a*) it shall be a defence for that person to show that he took all reasonable steps and exercised all due diligence to avoid contravening the condition in question.

(6) Sections 94 to 99 apply in relation to a contravention of conditions imposed by a direction under section 132 as they apply in relation to a contravention of conditions set under section 45.
[Communications Act 2003, s 133.]

8–30110E 140. Suspending service provision for information contraventions. (1) OFCOM may give a direction under this section to a person who is a communications provider or who makes associated facilities available ("the contravening provider") if they are satisfied—

(*a*) that he is or has been in serious and repeated contravention of requirements imposed under sections 135 and 136, or either of them;

(*b*) the requirements are not requirements imposed for purposes connected with the carrying out of OFCOM's functions in relation to SMP apparatus conditions;

(*c*) that an attempt, by the imposition of penalties under section 139 or the bringing of proceedings for an offence under section 144, to secure compliance with the contravened requirements has failed; and

(*d*) that the giving of the direction is appropriate and proportionate to the seriousness (when repeated as they have been) of the contraventions.

(2) A direction under this section is—

(*a*) a direction that the entitlement of the contravening provider to provide electronic communications networks or electronic communications services, or to make associated facilities available, is suspended (either generally or in relation to particular networks, services or facilities); or

(*b*) a direction that that entitlement is restricted in the respects set out in the direction.

(3) A direction under this section—

(*a*) must specify the networks, services and facilities to which it relates; and

(*b*) except so far as it otherwise provides, takes effect for an indefinite period beginning with the time at which it is notified to the person to whom it is given.

(4) A direction under this section—

(*a*) in providing for the effect of a suspension or restriction to be postponed, may provide for it to take effect only at a time determined by or in accordance with the terms of the direction; and

(*b*) in connection with the suspension or restriction contained in the direction or with the postponement of its effect, may impose such conditions on the contravening provider as appear to OFCOM to be appropriate for the purpose of protecting that provider's customers.

(5) Those conditions may include a condition requiring the making of payments—

(*a*) by way of compensation for loss or damage suffered by the contravening provider's customers as a result of the direction; or

(*b*) in respect of annoyance, inconvenience or anxiety to which they have been put in consequence of the direction.

(6) If OFCOM consider it appropriate to do so (whether or not in consequence of any representations or proposals made to them), they may revoke a direction under this section or modify its conditions—

(*a*) with effect from such time as they may direct;

(*b*) subject to compliance with such requirements as they may specify; and

(*c*) to such extent and in relation to such networks, services or facilities, or parts of a network, service or facility, as they may determine.

(7) For the purposes of this section there are repeated contraventions by a person of requirements imposed under sections 135 and 136, or either of them, to the extent that—

(*a*) in the case of a previous notification given to that person under section 138, OFCOM have determined for the purposes of section 139(2) that such a contravention did occur; and

(*b*) in the period of twelve months following the day of the making of that determination, one or more further notifications have been given to that person in respect of contraventions of such requirements;

and for the purposes of this subsection it shall be immaterial whether the notifications related to the same contravention or to different contraventions of the same or different requirements or of requirements under different sections.
[Communications Act 2003, s 140.]

8–30110F 141. Suspending apparatus supply for information contraventions. (1) OFCOM may give a direction under this section to a person who supplies electronic communications apparatus ("the contravening supplier") if they are satisfied—

(*a*) that he is or has been in serious and repeated contravention of requirements imposed under section 135;

(*b*) that an attempt, by the imposition of penalties under section 139 or the bringing of proceedings for an offence under section 144, to secure compliance with the contravened requirements has failed; and

(*c*) that the giving of the direction is appropriate and proportionate to the seriousness (when repeated as they have been) of the contraventions.

(2) A direction under this section is—

(*a*) a direction to the contravening supplier to cease to act as a supplier of electronic communications apparatus (either generally or in relation to apparatus of a particular description); or

(*b*) a direction imposing such restrictions as may be set out in the direction on the supply by that supplier of electronic communications apparatus (either generally or in relation to apparatus of a particular description).

(3) A direction under this section takes effect, except so far as it otherwise provides, for an indefinite period beginning with the time at which it is notified to the person to whom it is given.

(4) A direction under this section—

(*a*) may provide for a prohibition or restriction to take effect only at a time determined by or in accordance with the terms of the direction; and

(*b*) in connection with a prohibition or restriction contained in the direction or with the postponement of its effect, may impose such conditions on the contravening supplier as appear to OFCOM to be appropriate for the purpose of protecting that supplier's customers.

(5) Those conditions may include a condition requiring the making of payments—

(*a*) by way of compensation for loss or damage suffered by the contravening supplier's customers as a result of the direction; or

(*b*) in respect of annoyance, inconvenience or anxiety to which they have been put in consequence of the direction.

(6) If OFCOM consider it appropriate to do so (whether or not in consequence of representations or proposals made to them), they may revoke a direction under this section or modify its conditions—

(*a*) with effect from such time as they may direct;

(*b*) subject to compliance with such requirements as they may specify; and

(*c*) to such extent and in relation to such apparatus or descriptions of apparatus as they may determine.

(7) For the purposes of this section contraventions by a person of requirements imposed under section 135 are repeated contraventions if—

(*a*) in the case of a previous notification given to that person under section 138, OFCOM have determined for the purposes of section 139(2) that such a contravention did occur; and

(*b*) in the period of twelve months following the day of the making of that determination, one or more further notifications have been given to that person in respect of contraventions of such requirements;

and for the purposes of this subsection it shall be immaterial whether the notifications related to the same contravention or to different contraventions of the same or different requirements.
[Communications Act 2003, s 141.]

8–30110G 142. Procedure for directions under ss 140 and 141. (1) Except in an urgent case, OFCOM are not to give a direction under section 140 or 141 unless they have—

(*a*) notified the contravening provider or contravening supplier of the proposed direction and of the conditions (if any) which they are proposing to impose by that direction;

(*b*) provided him with an opportunity of making representations about the proposals and of proposing steps for remedying the situation; and (*c*) considered every representation and proposal made to them during the period allowed by them for the contravening provider or the contravening supplier to take advantage of that opportunity.

(2) That period must be one ending not less than one month after the day of the giving of the notification.

(3) As soon as practicable after giving a direction under section 140 or 141 in an urgent case, OFCOM must provide the contravening provider or contravening supplier with an opportunity of—

(*a*) making representations about the effect of the direction and of any of its conditions; and
(*b*) proposing steps for remedying the situation.

(4) A case is an urgent case for the purposes of this section if OFCOM—

(*a*) consider that it would be inappropriate, because the contraventions in question fall within subsection (5), to allow time, before giving a direction under section 140 or 141, for the making and consideration of representations; and
(*b*) decide for that reason to act in accordance with subsection (3), instead of subsection (1).

(5) The contraventions fall within this subsection if they have resulted in, or create an immediate risk of—

(*a*) a serious threat to the safety of the public, to public health or to national security;
(*b*) serious economic or operational problems for persons (apart from the contravening provider or contravening supplier) who are communications providers or persons who make associated facilities available; or
(*c*) serious economic or operational problems for persons who make use of electronic communications networks, electronic communications services or associated facilities.

(6) In this section—

"contravening provider" has the same meaning as in section 140; and
"contravening supplier" has the same meaning as in section 141.

[Communications Act 2003, s 142.]

8–30110H 143. Enforcement of directions under ss 140 and 141. (1) A person is guilty of an offence if he provides an electronic communications network or electronic communications service, or makes available any associated facility—

(*a*) while his entitlement to do so is suspended by a direction under section 140; or
(*b*) in contravention of a restriction contained in such a direction.

(2) A person is guilty of an offence if he supplies electronic communications apparatus—

(*a*) while prohibited from doing so by a direction under section 141; or
(*b*) in contravention of a restriction contained in such a direction.

(3) A person guilty of an offence under this section shall be liable—

(*a*) on summary conviction, to a fine not exceeding the statutory maximum;
(*b*) on conviction on indictment, to a fine.

(4) Sections 94 to 99 apply in relation to a contravention of conditions imposed by a direction under section 140 or 141 as they apply in relation to a contravention of conditions set under section 45.

[Communications Act 2003, s 143.]

Abolition of telecommunications licensing etc

8–30110I 147. Repeal of provisions of Telecommunications Act 1984. The following provisions of the Telecommunications Act 1984 (c 12) shall cease to have effect—

(*a*) sections 5 to 8 (licensing provisions);
(*b*) sections 9 to 11 (public telecommunications systems);
(*c*) sections 12 to 15 (modification of licences);
(*d*) sections 16 to 19 (enforcement of licences); and
(e) sections 27A to 27L (standards of performance of designated public telecommunications operators).

[Communications Act 2003, s 147.]

Interpretation of Chapter 1

8–30110J 151. Interpretation of Chapter 1. (1) In this Chapter—

"the Access Directive" means Directive 2002/19/EC of the European Parliament and of the Council on access to, and interconnection of, electronic communications networks and associated facilities;
"access-related condition" means a condition set as an access-related condition under section 45;

"allocation" and "adoption", in relation to telephone numbers, and cognate expressions, are to be construed in accordance with section 56;

"apparatus market", in relation to a market power determination, is to be construed in accordance with section 46(9)(*b*);

"designated universal service provider" means a person who is for the time being designated in accordance with regulations under section 66 as a person to whom universal service conditions are applicable;

"electronic communications apparatus"—

(*a*) in relation to SMP apparatus conditions and in section 141, means apparatus that is designed or adapted for a use which consists of or includes the sending or receiving of communications or other signals (within the meaning of section 32) that are transmitted by means of an electronic communications network; and

(*b*) in all other contexts, has the same meaning as in the electronic communications code;

"the electronic communications code" has the meaning given by section 106(1);

"end-user", in relation to a public electronic communications service, means—

(*a*) a person who, otherwise than as a communications provider, is a customer of the provider of that service;

(*b*) a person who makes use of the service otherwise than as a communications provider; or

(*c*) a person who may be authorised, by a person falling within paragraph (*a*), so to make use of the service;

"the Framework Directive" means Directive 2002/21/EC of the European Parliament and of the Council on a common regulatory framework for electronic communications networks and services;

"general condition" means a condition set as a general condition under section 45;

"interconnection" is to be construed in accordance with subsection (2);

"market power determination" means—

(*a*) a determination, for the purposes of provisions of this Chapter, that a person has significant market power in an identified services market or an identified apparatus market, or

(*b*) a confirmation for such purposes of a market power determination reviewed on a further analysis under section 84 or 85;

"misuse", in relation to an electronic communications network or electronic communications service, is to be construed in accordance with section 128(5) and (8), and cognate expressions are to be construed accordingly;

"network access" is to be construed in accordance with subsection (3);

"persistent" and "persistently", in relation to misuse of an electronic communications network or electronic communications service, are to be construed in accordance with section 128(6) and (7);

"premium rate service" is to be construed in accordance with section 120(7);

"privileged supplier condition" means a condition set as a privileged supplier condition under section 45;

"provider", in relation to a premium rate service, is to be construed in accordance with section 120(9) to (12), and cognate expressions are to be construed accordingly;

"public communications provider" means—

(*a*) a provider of a public electronic communications network;

(*b*) a provider of a public electronic communications service; or

(*c*) a person who makes available facilities that are associated facilities by reference to a public electronic communications network or a public electronic communications service;

"public electronic communications network" means an electronic communications network provided wholly or mainly for the purpose of making electronic communications services available to members of the public;

"public electronic communications service" means any electronic communications service that is provided so as to be available for use by members of the public;

"regulatory authorities" is to be construed in accordance with subsection (5);

"relevant international standards" means—

(*a*) any standards or specifications from time to time drawn up and published in accordance with Article 17 of the Framework Directive;

(*b*) the standards and specifications from time to time adopted by—

(i) the European Committee for Standardisation,

(ii) the European Committee for Electrotechnical Standardisation; or

(iii) the European Telecommunications Standards Institute; and

(*c*) the international standards and recommendations from time to time adopted by—

(i) the International Telecommunication Union;
(ii) the International Organisation for Standardisation; or
(iii) the International Electrotechnical Committee;

"service interoperability" means interoperability between different electronic communications services;

"services market", in relation to a market power determination or market identification, is to be construed in accordance with section 46(8)(*a*);

"significant market power" is to be construed in accordance with section 78;

"SMP condition" means a condition set as an SMP condition under section 45, and "SMP services condition" and "SMP apparatus condition" are to be construed in accordance with subsections (8) and (9) of that section respectively;

"telephone number" has the meaning given by section 56(5);

"the Universal Service Directive" means Directive 2002/22/EC of the European Parliament and of the Council on universal service and users' rights relating to electronic communications networks and services;

"universal service condition" means a condition set as a universal service condition under section 45;

"the universal service order" means the order for the time being in force under section 65.

(2) In this Chapter references to interconnection are references to the linking (whether directly or indirectly by physical or logical means, or by a combination of physical and logical means) of one public electronic communications network to another for the purpose of enabling the persons using one of them to be able—

(*a*) to communicate with users of the other one; or
(*b*) to make use of services provided by means of the other one (whether by the provider of that network or by another person).

(3) In this Chapter references to network access are references to—

(*a*) interconnection of public electronic communications networks; or
(*b*) any services, facilities or arrangements which—
(i) are not comprised in interconnection; but
(ii) are services, facilities or arrangements by means of which a communications provider or person making available associated facilities is able, for the purposes of the provision of an electronic communications service (whether by him or by another), to make use of anything mentioned in subsection (4);

and references to providing network access include references to providing any such services, making available any such facilities or entering into any such arrangements.

(4) The things referred to in subsection (3)(*b*) are—

(*a*) any electronic communications network or electronic communications service provided by another communications provider;
(*b*) any apparatus comprised in such a network or used for the purposes of such a network or service;
(*c*) any facilities made available by another that are associated facilities by reference to any network or service (whether one provided by that provider or by another);
(*d*) any other services or facilities which are provided or made available by another person and are capable of being used for the provision of an electronic communications service.

(5) References in this Chapter to the regulatory authorities of member States are references to such of the authorities of the member States as have been notified to the European Commission as the regulatory authorities of those States for the purposes of the Framework Directive.

(6) For the purposes of this Chapter, where there is a contravention of an obligation that requires a person to do anything within a particular period or before a particular time, that contravention shall be taken to continue after the end of that period, or after that time, until that thing is done.

(7) References in this Chapter to remedying the consequences of a contravention include references to paying an amount to a person—

(*a*) by way of compensation for loss or damage suffered by that person; or
(*b*) in respect of annoyance, inconvenience or anxiety to which he has been put.

(8) In determining for the purposes of provisions of this Chapter whether a contravention is a repeated contravention for any purposes, a notification of a contravention under that provision shall be disregarded if it has been withdrawn before the imposition of a penalty in respect of the matters notified.

(9) For the purposes of this section a service is made available to members of the public if members of the public are customers, in respect of that service, of the provider of that service.
[Communications Act 2003, s 151.]

Limitations and exemptions applied to spectrum use

8–30110K 165. Terms etc of wireless telegraphy licences. *Amends s 1 of the Wireless Telegraphy Act 1949.*

8–30110L 166. Exemption from need for wireless telegraphy licence. *Inserts s 1AA into the Wireless Telegraphy Act 1949.*

Criminal proceedings etc

8–30110M 178. Proceedings for an offence relating to apparatus use. *Amends ss 11 and 12 of the Wireless Telegraphy Act 1949.*

8–30110N 179. Modification of penalties for certain wireless telegraphy offences. *Amends s 14 of the Wireless Telegraphy Act 1949 and s 79(1) of the Telecommunications Act 1984.*

8–30110O 180. Fixed penalties for certain wireless telegraphy offences. Schedule 6 (which makes provision as respects fixed penalty notices for summary offences under the Wireless Telegraphy Act 1949 (c 54)) shall have effect.
[Communications Act 2003, s 180.]

8–30110P 181. Power of arrest. *Inserts para 2A into Sch 1A to the Police and Criminal Evidence Act 1984.*

8–30110Q 182. Forfeiture etc of restricted apparatus. (1) Apparatus to which this section applies shall be liable to forfeiture if, immediately before being seized, it was in a person's custody or control in contravention of a prohibition imposed by an order under section 7 of the Wireless Telegraphy Act 1967 (c 72) (restriction on dealings in and custody of certain apparatus).

(2) This section applies to apparatus if it has been seized—

(*a*) in pursuance of a warrant granted under section 15(1) of the Wireless Telegraphy Act 1949; or

(*b*) in the exercise of the power conferred by section 79(3) of the Telecommunications Act 1984 (c 12).

(3) Apparatus forfeited under this section is to be forfeited to OFCOM and may be disposed of by them in any manner they think fit.

(4) Schedule 7 (which makes provision in relation to the seizure and forfeiture of apparatus) shall have effect.

(5) The preceding provisions of this section and Schedule 7 apply only in relation to apparatus seized after the commencement of this section.

(6) Sections 80 and 81 of the Telecommunications Act 1984 (c 12) (which make provision for forfeiture of apparatus) are not to apply in relation to apparatus seized after the commencement of this section.

(7) In section 7(5) of the Wireless Telegraphy Act 1967 (c 72), paragraph (*b*) (which allows a person to have custody or control of restricted apparatus when authorised otherwise than by the Secretary of State) shall cease to have effect.*
[Communications Act 2003, s 182.]

Construction of 1949 Act

8–30110R 183. Modification of definition of "undue interference". *Substitutes new sub-ss (5) and (5A) into s 19 of the Wireless Telegraphy Act 1949.*

8–30110S 184. Modification of definition of "wireless telegraphy". (1) The Secretary of State may by order modify the definition of "wireless telegraphy" in section 19(1) of the Wireless Telegraphy Act 1949 by substituting a different frequency for the frequency (at the passing of this Act, 3,000 GHz) that is for the time being specified in that definition.

(2) No order is to be made containing provision authorised by this section unless a draft of the order has been laid before Parliament and approved by a resolution of each House.
[Communications Act 2003, s 184.]

PART 4[1]
LICENSING OF TV RECEPTION

8–30110T 363. Licence required for use of TV receiver. (1) A television receiver must not be installed or used unless the installation and use of the receiver is authorised by a licence under this Part.

(2) A person who installs or uses a television receiver in contravention of subsection (1) is guilty of an offence.

(3) A person with a television receiver in his possession or under his control who—

(*a*) intends to install or use it in contravention of subsection (1), or

(*b*) knows, or has reasonable grounds for believing, that another person intends to install or use it in contravention of that subsection,

is guilty of an offence.

(4) A person guilty of an offence under this section shall be liable, on summary conviction, to a fine not exceeding level 3 on the standard scale.

(5) Subsection (1) is not contravened by anything done in the course of the business of a dealer in television receivers solely for one or more of the following purposes—

(*a*) installing a television receiver on delivery;
(*b*) demonstrating, testing or repairing a television receiver.

(6) The Secretary of State may by regulations exempt from the requirement of a licence under subsection (1) the installation or use of television receivers—

(*a*) of such descriptions,
(*b*) by such persons,
(*c*) in such circumstances, and
(*d*) for such purposes,

as may be provided for in the regulations.

(7) Regulations under subsection (6) may make any exemption for which such regulations provide subject to compliance with such conditions as may be specified in the regulations.
[Communications Act 2003, s 363.]

1. Part 4 comprises ss 363–368.

8–30110U 364. TV licences. *May be issued by the BBC and must be subject to such restrictions and conditions as the BBC think fit and the Secretary of State may require. A TV licence shall continue in force, unless previously revoked by the BBC, for such period as may be specified in the licence.*

8–30110V 365. TV licence fees. (1) A person to whom a TV licence is issued shall be liable to pay—

(*a*) on the issue of the licence (whether initially or by way of renewal), and
(*b*) in such other circumstances as regulations[1] made by the Secretary of State may provide,

such sum (if any) as may be provided for by any such regulations.

(2) Sums which a person is liable to pay by virtue of regulations under subsection (1) must be paid to the BBC and are to be recoverable by them accordingly.

(3) The BBC are entitled, in such cases as they may determine, to make refunds of sums received by them by virtue of regulations under this section.

(4)–(8) *Concessions and further provisions as to Regulations.*
[Communications Act 2003, s 365.]

1. The Communications (Television Licensing) Regulations 2004 have been made, in this title, post.

8–30110W 366. Powers to enforce TV licensing. (1) If a justice of the peace, a sheriff in Scotland or a lay magistrate in Northern Ireland is satisfied by information on oath that there are reasonable grounds for believing—

(*a*) that an offence under section 363 has been or is being committed,
(*b*) that evidence of the commission of the offence is likely to be on premises specified in the information, or in a vehicle so specified, and
(*c*) that one or more of the conditions set out in subsection (3) is satisfied,

he may grant a warrant under this section.

(2) A warrant under this section is a warrant authorising any one or more persons authorised for the purpose by the BBC or by OFCOM—

(*a*) to enter the premises or vehicle at any time (either alone or in the company of one or more constables); and
(*b*) to search the premises or vehicle and examine and test any television receiver found there.

(3) Those conditions are—

(*a*) that there is no person entitled to grant entry to the premises or vehicle with whom it is practicable to communicate;
(*b*) that there is no person entitled to grant access to the evidence with whom it is practicable to communicate;
(*c*) that entry to the premises or vehicle will not be granted unless a warrant is produced;
(*d*) that the purpose of the search may be frustrated or seriously prejudiced unless the search is carried out by a person who secures entry immediately upon arriving at the premises or vehicle.

(4) A person is not to enter premises or a vehicle in pursuance of a warrant under this section at any time more than one month after the day on which the warrant was granted.

(5) The powers conferred by a warrant under this section on a person authorised by OFCOM are

exercisable in relation only to a contravention or suspected contravention of a condition of a TV licence relating to interference with wireless telegraphy.

(6) A person authorised by the BBC, or by OFCOM, to exercise a power conferred by a warrant under this section may (if necessary) use such force as may be reasonable in the exercise of that power.

(7) Where a person has the power by virtue of a warrant under this section to examine or test any television receiver found on any premises, or in any vehicle, it shall be the duty—

(*a*) of a person who is on the premises or in the vehicle, and

(*b*) in the case of a vehicle, of a person who has charge of it or is present when it is searched,

to give the person carrying out the examination or test all such assistance as that person may reasonably require for carrying it out.

(8) A person is guilty of an offence if he—

(*a*) intentionally obstructs a person in the exercise of any power conferred on that person by virtue of a warrant under this section; or

(*b*) without reasonable excuse, fails to give any assistance that he is under a duty to give by virtue of subsection (7).

(9) A person guilty of an offence under subsection (8) shall be liable, on summary conviction, to a fine not exceeding level 5 on the standard scale.

(10) In this section—

"interference", in relation to wireless telegraphy, has the same meaning as in the Wireless Telegraphy Act 1949 (c 54); and

"vehicle" includes vessel, aircraft or hovercraft.

(11) *Scotland*

(12) *Northern Ireland*

[Communications Act 2003, s 366.]

8–30110X 367. Interpretation of provisions about dealer notification. *Amends the Wireless Telegraphy Act 1967, s 6.*

8–30110Y 368. Meanings of "television receiver" and "use". (1) In this Part "television receiver" means any apparatus of a description specified in regulations[1] made by the Secretary of State setting out the descriptions of apparatus that are to be television receivers for the purposes of this Part.

(2) Regulations under this section defining a television receiver may provide for references to such a receiver to include references to software used in association with apparatus.

(3) References in this Part to using a television receiver are references to using it for receiving television programmes.

(4) The power to make regulations under this section defining a television receiver includes power to modify subsection (3).

[Communications Act 2003, s 368.]

1. The Communications (Television Licensing) Regulations 2004 have been made, in this title, post.

8–30110Z 411. Short title, commencement and extent. (1) This Act may be cited as the Communications Act 2003.

(2) This Act (except the provisions listed in subsection (3), which come into force on the passing of this Act) shall come into force on such day as the Secretary of State may by order[1] appoint; and different days may be appointed under this subsection for different purposes.

(3) Those provisions are sections 31(1) to (4) and (6) and 405 and this section.

(4) An order under subsection (2) may include provision making such transitional or transitory provision, in addition to that made by Schedule 18, as the Secretary of State considers appropriate in connection with the bringing into force of any provisions of this Act; and the power to make transitional or transitory provision includes power to make—

(*a*) different provision for different cases (including different provision in respect of different areas);

(*b*) provision subject to such exemptions and exceptions as the Secretary of State thinks fit; and

(*c*) such incidental, supplemental and consequential provision as he thinks fit.

(5) This Act extends to Northern Ireland.

(6) Subject to subsection (7), Her Majesty may by Order in Council[2] extend the provisions of this Act, with such modifications as appear to Her Majesty in Council to be appropriate, to any of the Channel Islands or to the Isle of Man.

(7) Subsection (6) does not authorise the extension to any place of a provision of this Act so far as it gives effect to an amendment of an enactment that is not itself capable of being extended there in exercise of a power conferred on Her Majesty in Council.

(8) Subsection (3) of section 402 applies to the power to make an Order in Council under this

section as it applies to any power of the Secretary of State to make an order under this Act, but as if references in that subsection to the Secretary of State were references to Her Majesty in Council.
[Communications Act 2003, s 411.]

---

1. At the time of going to press the following commencement orders had been made: Communications Act 2003 (Commencement No 1) Order 2003, SI 2003/1900, as amended by SI 2003/3142; Office of Communications Act 2002 (Commencement No 3) and Communications Act 2003 (Commencement No 2) Order 2003, SI 2003/3142, as amended by SI 2004/545, SI 2004/697, SI 2004/1492; and Communications Act 2003 (Commencement No 3) Order 2004, SI 2004/3309.

2. The following orders have been made under this provision: Communications (Bailiwick of Guernsey) Order 2003, SI 2003/3195 amended by SI 2005/856; (No 2) Order 2004, SI 2004/715; (No 3) Order 2004, SI 2004/1116; Broadcasting and Communications (Jersey) Order 2003, SI 2003/3197 amended by SI 2005/855, (No 2) Order 2004, SI 2004/716; (No 3) Order 2004, SI 2004/1114; Broadcasting and Communications (Isle of Man) Order 2003, SI 2003/3198, (No 2) Order 2004, SI 2004/718; (No 3) Order 2004, SI 2004/1115.

Section 180

SCHEDULE 6
FIXED PENALTIES FOR WIRELESS TELEGRAPHY OFFENCES

8–30111

Offences to which this Schedule applies

1. (1) This Schedule applies to an offence under the Wireless Telegraphy Act 1949 which—

(*a*) is a summary offence; and
(*b*) is committed after the coming into force of section 180.

(2) Such an offence is referred to in this Schedule as a "relevant offence".

Fixed penalties and fixed penalty notices

2. (1) The fixed penalty for a relevant offence is such amount as may be prescribed in relation to that offence by regulations made by the Secretary of State.

(2) The amount prescribed by regulations under sub-paragraph (1) is not to be more than 25 per cent of the maximum fine on summary conviction for the offence in question.

(3) In this Schedule "fixed penalty notice" means a notice offering the opportunity of the discharge of any liability to conviction of the offence to which the notice relates by payment of a fixed penalty in accordance with this Schedule.

Issuing of fixed penalty notice

3. (1) If OFCOM have reason to believe that a person has committed a relevant offence, they may send a fixed penalty notice to that person.

(2) If a procurator fiscal receives a report that a person has committed a relevant offence in Scotland, he also shall have power to send a fixed penalty notice to that person.

(3) If an authorised person has, on any occasion, reason to believe that a person—

(*a*) is committing a relevant offence, or
(*b*) has on that occasion committed a relevant offence,

he may hand that person a fixed penalty notice.

(4) In this paragraph "authorised person" means a person authorised by OFCOM, for the purposes of sub-paragraph (3), to issue fixed penalty notices on OFCOM's behalf.

(5) References in this Schedule to the person by whom a fixed penalty notice is issued, in relation to a notice handed to a person in accordance with sub-paragraph (3), are references to OFCOM.

Content of fixed penalty notice

4. (1) A fixed penalty notice must—

(*a*) state the alleged offence;
(*b*) give such particulars of the circumstances alleged to constitute that offence as are necessary for giving reasonable information about it;
(*c*) state the fixed penalty for that offence;
(*d*) specify the relevant officer to whom the fixed penalty may be paid and the address at which it may be paid;
(*e*) state that proceedings against the person to whom it is issued cannot be commenced in respect of the offence until the end of the suspended enforcement period;
(*f*) state that such proceedings cannot be commenced if the penalty is paid within the suspended enforcement period;
(*g*) inform the person to whom it is issued of his right to ask to be tried for the alleged offence; and
(*h*) explain how that right may be exercised and the effect of exercising it.

(2) The suspended enforcement period for the purposes of this Schedule is—

(*a*) the period of one month beginning with the day after that on which the fixed penalty notice was issued; or
(*b*) such longer period as may be specified in the notice.

Withdrawal of fixed penalty notice

5. If it appears to a person who has issued a fixed penalty notice that it was wrongly issued—

(*a*) he may withdraw the notice by a further notice to the person to whom it was issued; and
(*b*) if he does so, the relevant officer must repay any amount paid in respect of the penalty.

Notification to person to whom payment is to be made

6. A person who issues or withdraws a fixed penalty notice shall send a copy of the notice or (as the case may be) of the notice of withdrawal to the relevant officer specified in the notice being issued or withdrawn.

Effect of fixed penalty notice

7. (1) This paragraph applies if a fixed penalty notice is issued to a person ("the alleged offender").

(2) Proceedings for the offence to which the notice relates cannot be brought against the alleged offender until the person who issued the notice has been notified by the relevant officer specified in the notice that payment of the fixed penalty has not been made within the suspended enforcement period.

(3) If the alleged offender asks to be tried for the alleged offence—

(*a*) sub-paragraph (2) does not apply; and
(*b*) proceedings may be brought against him.

(4) Such a request must be made by a notice given by the alleged offender—

(*a*) in the manner specified in the fixed penalty notice; and
(*b*) before the end of the suspended enforcement period.

(5) A request which is made in accordance with sub-paragraph (3) is referred to in this Schedule as a "request to be tried".

Payment of fixed penalty

8. (1) If the alleged offender decides to pay the fixed penalty, he must pay it to the relevant officer specified in the notice.

(2) Payment of the penalty may be made by properly addressing, pre-paying and posting a letter containing the amount of the penalty (in cash or otherwise).

(3) Sub-paragraph (4) applies if a person—

(*a*) claims to have made payment by that method; and
(*b*) shows that his letter was posted.

(4) Unless the contrary is proved, payment is to be regarded as made at the time at which the letter would be delivered in the ordinary course of post.

(5) Sub-paragraph (2) is not to be read as preventing the payment of a penalty by other means.

(6) A letter is properly addressed for the purposes of sub-paragraph (2) if it is addressed in accordance with the requirements specified in the fixed penalty notice.

Effect of payment

9. If the fixed penalty specified in a fixed penalty notice is paid within the period specified in that notice, no proceedings for the offence to which that notice relates may be brought against the alleged offender.

Service of statement and proof of service

10. (1) This paragraph applies to proceedings for a relevant offence.

(2) A certificate by OFCOM—

(*a*) that a copy of a statement by a person authorised by OFCOM was included in, or given with, a fixed penalty notice,
(*b*) that the notice was a notice with respect to the relevant offence, and
(*c*) that that notice was issued to the accused on a date specified in the certificate,

is evidence that a copy of the statement was served on the alleged offender by delivery to him on that date.

(3) The statement is to be treated as properly served for the purposes of—

(*a*) section 9 of the Criminal Justice Act 1967 (c 80) (proof by written statement), and
(*b*) section 1 of the Criminal Justice (Miscellaneous Provisions) Act (Northern Ireland) 1968 (c 28 (NI)) (which contains corresponding provision for Northern Ireland),

even though the manner of service is not authorised by subsection (8) of either of those sections.

(4) Sub-paragraphs (5) and (6) apply to any proceedings in which service of a statement is proved by a certificate under this paragraph.

(5) For the purposes of—

(*a*) section 9(2)(*c*) of the Criminal Justice Act 1967 (copy of statement to be tendered in evidence to be served before hearing on other parties to the proceedings by or on behalf of the party proposing to tender it), and
(*b*) section 1(2)(*c*) of the Criminal Justice (Miscellaneous Provisions) Act (Northern Ireland) 1968 (which contains corresponding provision for Northern Ireland),

service of the statement is to be taken to have been effected by or on behalf of the prosecutor.

(6) If the alleged offender makes a request to be tried—

(*a*) section 9(2)(*d*) of the Criminal Justice Act 1967 (time for objection), and
(*b*) section 1(2)(*d*) of the Criminal Justice (Miscellaneous Provisions) Act (Northern Ireland) 1968 (which contains corresponding provision for Northern Ireland),

are to apply with the substitution, for the reference to seven days from the service of the copy of the statement, of a reference to seven days beginning with the day after the one on which the request to be tried was made.

(7) This paragraph does not extend to Scotland.

Certificate about payment

11. In any proceedings, a certificate—

(*a*) that payment of a fixed penalty was, or was not, received by the relevant officer specified in the fixed penalty notice by a date specified in the certificate, or

(*b*) that a letter containing an amount sent by post in payment of a fixed penalty was marked as posted on a date specified in the certificate,

shall, if the certificate purports to be signed by that officer, be evidence (and in Scotland sufficient evidence) of the facts stated.

Regulations

12. The Secretary of State may by regulations make provision as to any matter incidental to the operation of this Schedule, and in particular—

(*a*) for prescribing any information or further information to be provided in a notice, notification, certificate or receipt;

(*b*) for prescribing the duties of relevant officers and the information to be supplied to and by them.

Interpretation

13. In this Schedule "relevant officer" means—

(*a*) in relation to England and Wales, the justices' chief executive;

(*b*) in relation to Scotland, the clerk of court; and

(*c*) in relation to Northern Ireland, the clerk of petty sessions.

Section 182

SCHEDULE 7
SEIZURE AND FORFEITURE OF APPARATUS

8–30111A

Application of Schedule

1. (1) This Schedule applies to restricted apparatus seized, after the coming into force of this Schedule—

(*a*) in pursuance of a warrant granted under section 15(1) of the Wireless Telegraphy Act 1949 (c 54); or

(*b*) in the exercise of the power conferred by section 79(3) of the Telecommunications Act 1984 (c 12).

(2) Apparatus is restricted apparatus for the purposes of this Schedule if custody or control of apparatus of any class or description to which it belongs is for the time being restricted by an order under section 7 of the Wireless Telegraphy Act 1967 (c 72).

Notice of seizure

2. (1) OFCOM must give notice of the seizure of the restricted apparatus to every person who, to their knowledge, was at the time of the seizure the owner or one of the owners of the apparatus.

(2) The notice must set out the grounds of the seizure.

(3) Where there is no proper address for the purposes of the service of a notice under sub-paragraph (1) in a manner authorised by section 394, the requirements of that sub-paragraph shall be satisfied by the publication of a notice of the seizure (according to the part of the United Kingdom where the seizure took place) in the London, Edinburgh or Belfast Gazette.

(4) Apparatus may be condemned or taken to have been condemned under this Schedule only if the requirements of this paragraph have been complied with in the case of that apparatus.

Notice of claim

3. A person claiming that the restricted apparatus is not liable to forfeiture must give written notice of his claim to OFCOM.

4. (1) A notice of claim must be given within one month after the day of the giving of the notice of seizure.

(2) A notice of claim must specify—

(*a*) the name and address of the claimant; and

(*b*) in the case of a claimant who is outside the United Kingdom, the name and address of a solicitor in the United Kingdom who is authorised to accept service of process and to act on behalf of the claimant.

(3) Service of process upon a solicitor so specified is to be taken to be proper service upon the claimant.

Condemnation

5. The restricted apparatus is to be taken to have been duly condemned as forfeited if—

(*a*) by the end of the period for the giving of a notice of claim in respect of the apparatus, no such notice has been given to OFCOM; or

(*b*) a notice of claim is given which does not comply with the requirements of paragraphs 3 and 4.

6. (1) Where a notice of claim in respect of the restricted apparatus is duly given in accordance with paragraphs 3 and 4, OFCOM may take proceedings for the condemnation of that apparatus by the court.

(2) In any such proceedings—

(*a*) if the court finds that the apparatus was liable to forfeiture at the time of seizure, it must condemn the apparatus as forfeited unless cause is shown why it should not; and (*b*) if the court finds that the apparatus was not liable to forfeiture at that time, or cause is shown why it should not be forfeited, the court must order the return of the apparatus to the person appearing to the court to be entitled to it.

(3) If OFCOM decide not to take proceedings for condemnation in a case in which a notice of claim has been so given, they must return the apparatus to the person appearing to them to be the owner of the apparatus, or to one of the persons appearing to them to be the owners of it.

(4) Apparatus required to be returned in accordance with sub-paragraph (3) must be returned as soon as reasonably practicable after the decision not to take proceedings for condemnation.

(5) OFCOM's decision whether to take such proceedings must be taken as soon as reasonably practicable after the receipt of the notice of claim.

7. Where the restricted apparatus is condemned or taken to have been condemned as forfeited, the forfeiture is to have effect as from the time of the seizure.

Proceedings for condemnation by court

8. Proceedings for condemnation are civil proceedings and may be instituted—

(*a*) in England or Wales, either in the High Court or in a magistrates' court;
(*b*) in Scotland, either in the Court of Session or in the sheriff court;
(*c*) in Northern Ireland, either in the High Court or in a court of summary jurisdiction.

9. Proceedings for the condemnation of restricted apparatus instituted in a magistrates' court in England or Wales, in the sheriff court in Scotland or in a court of summary jurisdiction in Northern Ireland may be so instituted—

(*a*) in any such court having jurisdiction in a place where an offence under section 7 of the Wireless Telegraphy Act 1967 (c 72) involving that apparatus was committed;
(*b*) in any such court having jurisdiction in proceedings for such an offence;
(*c*) in any such court having jurisdiction in the place where the claimant resides or, if the claimant has specified a solicitor under paragraph 4, in the place where that solicitor has his office; or
(*d*) in any such court having jurisdiction in the place where that apparatus was seized or to which it was first brought after being seized.

10. (1) In proceedings for condemnation that are instituted in England and Wales or Northern Ireland, the claimant or his solicitor must make his oath that the seized apparatus was, or was to the best of his knowledge and belief, the property of the claimant at the time of the seizure.

(2) In proceedings for condemnation instituted in the High Court—

(*a*) the court may require the claimant to give such security for the costs of the proceedings as may be determined by the court; and
(*b*) the claimant must comply with any such requirement.

(3) If a requirement of this paragraph is not complied with, the court shall give judgement for OFCOM.

11. (1) In the case of proceedings for condemnation instituted in a magistrates' court in England or Wales, either party may appeal against the decision of that court to the Crown Court.

(2) In the case of proceedings for condemnation instituted in a court of summary jurisdiction in Northern Ireland, either party may appeal against the decision of that court to the county court.

(3) This paragraph does not affect any right to require the statement of a case for the opinion of the High Court.

12. Where an appeal has been made (whether by case stated or otherwise) against the decision of the court in proceedings for the condemnation of restricted apparatus, that apparatus is to be left with OFCOM pending the final determination of the matter.

Disposal of unclaimed property

13. (1) This paragraph applies where a requirement is imposed by or under this Schedule for apparatus to be returned to a person.

(2) If the apparatus is still in OFCOM's possession after the end of the period of twelve months beginning with the day after the requirement to return it arose, OFCOM may dispose of it in any manner they think fit.

(3) OFCOM may exercise their power under this paragraph to dispose of apparatus only if it is not practicable at the time when the power is exercised to dispose of the apparatus by returning it immediately to the person to whom it is required to be returned.

Provisions as to proof

14. In proceedings arising out of the seizure of restricted apparatus, the fact, form and manner of the seizure is to be taken, without further evidence and unless the contrary is shown, to have been as set forth in the process.

15. In any proceedings, the condemnation by a court of restricted apparatus as forfeited may be proved by the production of either—

(*a*) the order or certificate of condemnation; or
(*b*) a certified copy of the order purporting to be signed by an officer of the court by which the order or certificate was made or granted.

Special provisions as to certain claimants

16. (1) This paragraph applies for the purposes of a claim to the restricted apparatus, and of proceedings for its condemnation.

(2) Where, at the time of the seizure, the apparatus is—

(*a*) the property of a body corporate,
(*b*) the property of two or more partners, or
(*c*) the property of more than five persons,

the oath required by paragraph 10 to be taken by the claimant, and any other thing required by this Schedule or by rules of court to be done by the owner of the apparatus, may be done by a person falling within sub-paragraph (3) or by a person authorised to act on his behalf.

(3) The persons falling within this sub-paragraph are—

(*a*) where the owner is a body corporate, the secretary or some duly authorised officer of that body;
(*b*) where the owners are in partnership, any one or more of the owners;
(*c*) where there are more than five owners and they are not in partnership, any two or more of the owners acting on behalf of themselves and any of their co-owners who are not acting on their own behalf.

Saving for owner's rights

17. Neither the imposition of a requirement by or under this Schedule to return apparatus to a person nor the return of apparatus to a person in accordance with such a requirement affects—

(*a*) the rights in relation to that apparatus of any other person; or
(*b*) the right of any other person to enforce his rights against the person to whom it is returned.

Section 192

SCHEDULE 8
Decisions not Subject to Appeal

8–30111B

Prosecutions and civil proceedings

1. A decision to institute, bring or carry on any criminal or civil proceedings.
2. A decision (other than one under section 119) to take preliminary steps for the purpose of enabling any such proceedings to be instituted.

This Act

3. A decision relating to the making or revision of a statement under section 38.
4. A decision required to be published in a notification under section 44(4).
5. A decision given effect to by an order under section 55.
6. A decision given effect to by regulations under section 66.
7. A decision given effect to by regulations under section 71.
8. A decision required to be published in a notification under section 108(4).
9. A decision given effect to by an order under section 122.
10. A decision relating to the making or revision of a statement under section 131.
11. A decision given effect to by an order under section 134(6).
12. A decision relating to the making or revision of a statement under section 145.
13. A decision relating to the publication of the United Kingdom Plan for Frequency Authorisation.
14. A decision in exercise of the functions conferred on OFCOM by section 152 as to—

(*a*) the services, records and advice to be provided, maintained or given by them;
(*b*) the research to be carried out or the arrangements made for carrying it out; or
(*c*) the making or terms of any grant.

15. A decision under section 155.
16. A decision under section 158.
17. A decision given effect to by regulations under section 159.
18. A decision given effect to by regulations under section 162.
19. A decision given effect to by an order under section 164.
20. A decision given effect to by regulations under section 168.
21. A decision given effect to by regulations under section 170 and any decision under any such regulations.
22. A decision to impose a penalty under section 175(1).
23. A decision relating to the making or revision of a statement under section 177.
24. A decision given effect to by regulations under paragraph 1 of Schedule 5.
25. A decision under any provision of Schedule 6.
26. A decision under any provision of Schedule 7.

Wireless Telegraphy Act 1949

27. A decision given effect to by regulations under the proviso to section 1(1) of the Wireless Telegraphy Act 1949 (c 54).
28. A decision given effect to by regulations under section 1D(3) of that Act.
29. A decision given effect to by regulations under section 3 of that Act.
30. A decision given effect to by regulations under section 10 of that Act.
31. A decision relating to the making or revision of a statement under section 13B of that Act.
32. A decision for the purposes of section 15 of that Act.

Wireless Telegraphy Act 1998

33. A decision given effect to by regulations under section 1 of the Wireless Telegraphy Act 1998 (c 6).
34. A decision given effect to by regulations under section 3 of that Act.
35. A decision given effect to by regulations under section 3A of that Act.
36. A decision relating to the recovery of a sum payable to OFCOM under section 4A of that Act.

Telecommunications (Lawful Business Practice) (Interception of Communications) Regulations 2000[1]

(SI 2000/2699 amended by SI 2003/2426)

8–30115 1. Citation and commencement. These Regulations may be cited as the Telecommunications (Lawful Business Practice) (Interception of Communications) Regulations 2000 and shall come into force on 24th October 2000.

---

1. Made by the Secretary of State in exercise of the powers conferred by ss 4(2) and 78(5) of the Regulation of Investigatory Powers Act 2000.

8–30115A 2. Interpretation. In these Regulations—

(*a*) references to a business include references to activities of a government department, of any public authority or of any person or office holder on whom functions are conferred by or under any enactment;

(*b*) a reference to a communication as relevant to a business is a reference to—

(i) a communication—

(*aa*) by means of which a transaction is entered into in the course of that business, or

(*bb*) which otherwise relates to that business, or

(ii) a communication which otherwise takes place in the course of the carrying on of that business;

(*c*) "regulatory or self-regulatory practices or procedures" means practices or procedures—

(i) compliance with which is required or recommended by, under or by virtue of—

(*aa*) any provision of the law of a member state or other state within the European Economic Area, or

(*bb*) any standard or code of practice published by or on behalf of a body established in a member state or other state within the European Economic Area which includes amongst its objectives the publication of standards or codes of practice for the conduct of business, or

(ii) which are otherwise applied for the purpose of ensuring compliance with anything so required or recommended;

(*d*) "system controller" means, in relation to a particular telecommunication system, a person with a right to control its operation or use.

8–30115B 3. Lawful interception of a communication. (1) For the purpose of section 1(5)(*a*) of the Act, conduct is authorised, subject to paragraphs (2) and (3) below, if it consists of interception of a communication, in the course of its transmission by means of a telecommunication system, which is effected by or with the express or implied consent of the system controller for the purpose of—

(*a*) monitoring or keeping a record of communications—

(i) in order to—

(*aa*) establish the existence of facts, or

(*bb*) ascertain compliance with regulatory or self-regulatory practices or procedures which are—

applicable to the system controller in the carrying on of his business or

applicable to another person in the carrying on of his business where that person is supervised by the system controller in respect of those practices or procedures, or

(*cc*) ascertain or demonstrate the standards which are achieved or ought to be achieved by persons using the system in the course of their duties, or

(ii) in the interests of national security, or

(iii) for the purpose of preventing or detecting crime, or

(iv) for the purpose of investigating or detecting the unauthorised use of that or any other telecommunication system, or

(v) where that is undertaken—

(*aa*) in order to secure, or

(*bb*) as an inherent part of,

the effective operation of the system (including any monitoring or keeping of a record which would be authorised by section 3(3) of the Act if the conditions in paragraphs (*a*) and (*b*) thereof were satisfied); or

(*b*) monitoring communications for the purpose of determining whether they are communications relevant to the system controller's business which fall within regulation 2(*b*)(i) above; or (*c*) monitoring communications made to a confidential voice-telephony counselling or support service which is free of charge (other than the cost, if any, of making a telephone call) and operated in such a way that users may remain anonymous if they so choose.

(2) Conduct is authorised by paragraph (1) of this regulation only if—

(*a*) the interception in question is effected solely for the purpose of monitoring or (where appropriate) keeping a record of communications relevant to the system controller's business;

(*b*) the telecommunication system in question is provided for use wholly or partly in connection with that business;

(*c*) the system controller has made all reasonable efforts to inform every person who may use the telecommunication system in question that communications transmitted by means thereof may be intercepted; and

(*d*) in a case falling within—

(i) paragraph (1)(*a*)(ii) above, the person by or on whose behalf the interception is effected is a person specified in section 6(2)(*a*) to (*i*) of the Act;

(ii) paragraph (1)(*b*) above, the communication is one which is intended to be received (whether or not it has been actually received) by a person using the telecommunication system in question.

(3) Conduct falling within paragraph (1)(a)(i) above is authorised only to the extent that Article 5 of Directive 2002/58/EC of the European Parliament and of the Council of 12 July 2002 concerning the processing of personal data and the protection of privacy in the electronic communications sector so permits.

Communications (Television Licensing) Regulations 2004[1]

(SI 2004/692 amended by SI 2005/606[2])

Part 1
General

8–30115C 1. Citation, commencement, extent and interpretation. (1) These Regulations may be cited as the Communications (Television Licensing) Regulations 2004 and shall come into force on 1st April 2004.

(2) These Regulations, except regulations 10 and 11, extend to the Channel Islands and the Isle of Man.

(3) In these Regulations "the Act" means the Communications Act 2003.

1. Made by the Secretary of State, in exercise of the powers conferred by s 6(1) of the Wireless Telegraphy Act 1967 and ss 365(1) and (4), 368 and 402(3) of the Communications Act 2003, as extended by the Broadcasting and Communications (Jersey) Order 2004, the Communications (Bailiwick of Guernsey) Order 2004 and the Communications (Isle of Man) Order 2003, with the consent of the Treasury (to the extent that the Regulations are made in exercise of the powers conferred by s 365 of the Communications Act 2003).

2. Reference is made only to those instruments which amend the provisions reproduced in this work.

Part 2
TV Licence Fees

8–30115D 2. Interpretation of Part 2. (1) In this Part—

"caravan" means any structure designed or adapted for habitation which is capable of being moved from one place to another (whether by being towed, or by being transported on a motor vehicle or trailer) and any motor vehicle so designed or adapted;

"the due date" in relation to any TV licence means the date on which the licensee is required to obtain the licence in accordance with the Act whether in consequence of the expiry of a previous licence or otherwise; and

"touring caravan" means a caravan normally used for touring from place to place.

(2) Any reference to—

(*a*) the issue of a TV licence includes a reference to the renewal of such a licence;

(*b*) a person's residence includes any place provided for that person's private occupation.

8–30115E 3. TV licence fees. (1) Subject to regulations 5 and 6—

(*a*) on the issue of a TV licence of a type specified in an entry in column 1 of the table in Schedule 1, the fee payable shall be that specified in column 3 in relation to that type of licence;

(*b*) on the issue of a TV licence of a type specified in paragraph 1, 3 or 8 of Schedule 2, the person to whom the licence is issued shall be liable to make payments as provided by (as the case may be) Part 1, 2 or 3 of that Schedule;

(*c*) on the issue of a TV licence of a type specified in an entry in column 1 of the table in Part 1 of Schedule 3, the fee payable shall (subject to paragraph (2)) be determined in accordance with the entry in column 3 in relation to that type of licence;

(*d*) on the issue of a TV licence of the type specified in paragraph 1 of Schedule 4, the fee payable shall be determined in accordance with paragraph 2 of that Schedule;

(*e*) on the issue of a TV licence of the type specified in paragraph 2 of Schedule 5, the fee payable shall be determined in accordance with paragraph 3 of that Schedule.

(2) In relation to a TV licence of the type specified in the second entry in column 1 of the table in Part 1 of Schedule 3, the fee is to be payable in instalments in the circumstances specified in Part 2 of that Schedule; and the amount of each of the instalments, and the dates on which they are payable, are to be determined in accordance with that Part.

(3) Any sum payable by virtue of paragraph (1) or (2) shall be payable irrespective of the duration of the TV licence.

8–30115F **4. Duplicate licences.** Where a TV licence has been lost or destroyed, the sum of £3.25 shall be paid on the issue of a duplicate of such a licence; but no such sum shall be payable on the issue of a duplicate of a TV licence that was issued free of charge.

8–30115G **5. Concessions for blind persons.** (1) Where—

(*a*) a TV licence is issued to a blind person, authorising the installation or use of a television receiver at one or more places or in one or more vehicles, vessels or caravans specified in the licence; and

(*b*) each place, vehicle, vessel or caravan so specified is a residence of that person,

the fee payable (including the amount of any instalment payments) shall be 50 per cent of the amount which would otherwise be payable for the licence in accordance with regulation 3.

This reduction in the amount payable is referred to in this paragraph as the "blind concession".

(2) In order to establish an entitlement to the blind concession a person must—

(*a*) show that he is registered as blind with—

(i) a local authority in the United Kingdom, or

(ii) the Department of Health and Social Security for the Isle of Man,

by way of a certificate or other document issued by or on behalf of the authority concerned; or

(*b*) provide evidence that he is blind by way of a certificate signed by an ophthalmologist.

(3) A person is not required to provide the evidence referred to in paragraph (2) to obtain the blind concession in respect of a TV licence where—

(*a*) that person has previously established an entitlement to the concession by providing the evidence referred to in that paragraph; and

(*b*) that evidence was provided within the period of 5 years ending on the date on which the licence is issued.

(4) This regulation does not apply where the TV licence is of a type and description specified in paragraph 1 of Schedule 4 or paragraph 2 of Schedule 5.

(5) In these Regulations—

"blind" means that the person concerned is so blind as to be unable to perform any work for which eyesight is essential;

"local authority" means—

(*a*) in England, a county council, a district council, a London borough council, the Common Council of the City of London, and the Council of the Isles of Scilly;

(*b*) in Wales, a county council or a county borough council;

(*c*) in Scotland, a council constituted under section 2 of the Local Government etc (Scotland) Act 1994; and

(*d*) in Northern Ireland, a district council;

"ophthalmologist" means a doctor whose name is included in the register of specialists kept by the General Medical Council under article 8 of the European Specialist Medical Qualifications Order 1995 and in respect of whom that register indicates his speciality to be ophthalmology.

8–30115H **6. Concessions for persons aged 75 years or more.** (1) No fee shall be payable for a TV licence of a type referred to in the first or second entry in column 1 of the table in Schedule 1 where—

(*a*) the licence is issued to a person aged 75 years or more or to a person who will attain that age in the calendar month in which the licence is issued; and

(*b*) the single place, vehicle, vessel or caravan specified in the licence is the sole or main residence of that person.

(2) Paragraph (1) only applies where the residence referred to in that paragraph is in the United Kingdom, the Isle of Man or the Bailiwick of Guernsey (but excluding Sark).

(3) Where a TV licence of the type referred to in paragraph 1 of Schedule 4 is issued in respect of accommodation for residential care, in calculating the fee payable no account shall be taken of any unit of accommodation or, as the case may be, residential care dwelling that is the sole or main residence of a resident who is aged 75 years or more on the date on which the licence is issued.

(4) In paragraph (3), the expressions "accommodation for residential care", "resident" and "residential care dwelling" shall have the meanings given to them by Part 2 of Schedule 4.

(5) Paragraph (3) only applies where the accommodation to which the licence relates is in the United Kingdom.

8–30115I 7. Revocation and savings

PART 3

DEFINITIONS FOR THE PURPOSES OF THE COMMUNICATIONS ACT 2003 AND THE WIRELESS TELEGRAPHY ACT 1967

8–30115J 8. Interpretation of Part 3. In this Part—

"members of the public" means members of the public in the United Kingdom, the Channel Islands and the Isle of Man;

"programme" has the same meaning as in the Act; and

"television programme service" has the same meaning as in Part 3 of the Act.

8–30115K 9. Meaning of "television receiver". (1) In Part 4 of the Act (licensing of TV reception), "television receiver" means any apparatus installed or used for the purpose of receiving (whether by means of wireless telegraphy or otherwise) any television programme service, whether or not it is installed or used for any other purpose.

(2) In this regulation, any reference to receiving a television programme service includes a reference to receiving by any means any programme included in that service, where that programme is received at the same time (or virtually the same time) as it is received by members of the public by virtue of its being broadcast or distributed as part of that service.

8–30115L 10. Meaning of "television dealer". In Part 1 of the Wireless Telegraphy Act 1967, "television dealer" means a person who by way of trade or business—

(*a*) sells television sets by retail;
(*b*) lets such sets on hire or hire-purchase;
(*c*) arranges for such sets to be sold or let as aforesaid by another television dealer; or
(*d*) holds himself out as willing to engage in any of the foregoing activities.

8–30115M 11. Meaning of "television set". (1) In Part 1 of the Wireless Telegraphy Act 1967, "television set" means any apparatus which (either alone or in association with other apparatus) is capable of receiving (whether by means of wireless telegraphy or otherwise) any television programme service but is not computer apparatus.

(2) In this regulation, "computer apparatus" means apparatus which—

(*a*) is designed or adapted to be used (either alone or in association with other apparatus) for storing or processing data, but not for doing so in connection with the reception by means of wireless telegraphy of television programme services; and
(*b*) is not offered for sale or letting as apparatus for use (either alone or in association with other apparatus) primarily for or in connection with the reception (whether by means of wireless telegraphy or otherwise) of such services;

and "processing" includes displaying.

8–30115N

Regulation 3(1)( )

SCHEDULE 1

ISSUE FEES FOR TV LICENCES

TABLE

Type of licence	*Description of licence*	*Issue fee*
1 TV licence (black and white only) General Form	A licence— (*a*) to install and use black and white television receivers at the single place specified in the licence or, as the case may be, in the single vehicle, vessel or caravan so specified ("the specified location"); (*b*) to install and use black and white television receivers in any vehicle, vessel or caravan being used or occupied by the licensee or by a person normally living with the licensee at the specified location, being installation or use not covered by a licence described in Schedule 5, provided that a receiver may not be used in a caravan, other than a touring caravan, at the same time as a receiver is being used at the specified location; and (*c*) for the use anywhere of any black and white television receiver powered solely by its own internal batteries by the licensee or by a person normally living with the licensee at the specified location.	£40.50

Type of licence	*Description of licence*	*Issue fee*
2 TV licence (including colour) General Form	A licence— (*a*) to install and use television receivers at the single place specified in the licence or, as the case may be, in the single vehicle, vessel or caravan so specified ("the specified location"); (*b*) to install and use television receivers in any vehicle, vessel or caravan being used or occupied by the licensee or by a person normally living with the licensee at the specified location, being installation or use not covered by a licence described in Schedule 5, provided that a receiver may not be used in a caravan, other than a touring caravan, at the same time as a receiver is being used at the specified location; and (*c*) for the use anywhere of any television receiver powered solely by its own internal batteries by the licensee or by a person normally living with the licensee at the specified location.	£121.00
3 TV licence (black and white only) Multiple Form	A licence— (*a*) to install and use black and white television receivers at each of the places specified in the licence or, as the case may be, in each of the vehicles, vessels or caravans so specified ("the specified locations"); (*b*) to install and use black and white television receivers in any vehicle, vessel or caravan being used or occupied by the licensee or by a person normally living at one of the specified locations, being installation or use not covered by a licence described in Schedule 5, provided that a receiver may not be used in a caravan, other than a touring caravan, at the same time as a receiver is being used at the specified location at which the person using the receiver normally lives; and (*c*) for the use anywhere of any black and white television receiver powered solely by its own internal batteries by the licensee or by a person normally living at one of the specified locations.	£40.50 for each place, vehicle, vessel or caravan specified in the licence.
4 TV licence (including colour) Multiple Form	A licence— (*a*) to install and use television receivers at each of the places specified in the licence or, as the case may be, in each of the vehicles, vessels or caravans so specified ("the specified locations"); (*b*) to install and use television receivers in any vehicle, vessel or caravan being used or occupied by the licensee or by a person normally living at one of the specified locations, being installation or use not covered by a licence described in Schedule 5, provided that a receiver may not be used in a caravan, other than a touring caravan, at the same time as a receiver is being used at the specified location at which the person using the receiver normally lives; and (*c*) for the use anywhere of any television receiver powered solely by its own internal batteries by the licensee or by a person normally living at one of the specified locations.	£121.00 for each place, vehicle, vessel or caravan specified in the licence.

8–30115O

Regulation 3(1)(*b*)

SCHEDULE 2
FEES FOR TV LICENCES PAYABLE BY INSTALMENTS

8–30115P

Regulation 3(1)(*c*)

SCHEDULE 3
FEES FOR INTERIM TV LICENCES

8–30115Q

Regulation 3(1)(*d*)

SCHEDULE 4
ACCOMMODATION FOR RESIDENTIAL CARE LICENCES

8–30115R

Regulation 3(1)(*e*)

SCHEDULE 5
TV LICENCE FEES FOR HOTELS AND HOSPITALITY AREAS AND MOBILE UNITS

8–30115S

Regulation 7(1)

SCHEDULE 6
REVOCATIONS

THEATRE, CINEMATOGRAPH AND VIDEO

8–30120 This title contains the following statutes—

and the following statutory instrument—

8–30121 Licensing of plays, exhibition of films, indoor sporting events, performance of live music, playing of recorded music etc and the use of premises for the supply and consumption of alcohol. Licensing by licensing authorities of 'regulated entertainments' and premises for the supply and consumption of alcohol is now governed by the Licensing Act 2003 which is reproduced in PART VIII: LOCAL GOVERNMENT, ante.

Celluloid and Cinematograph Film Act 1922

(12 & 13 Geo 5 c 35)

8–30139 1. General safety provisions. (1) No premises[1] shall be used for any purpose to which this Act applies[2]

(*a*) *repealed*;

(*b*) unless the premises are provided with such means of escape[4] in case of fire as the local authority[3] may reasonably require, and such means of escape are maintained in good condition and free from obstruction;

(*c*) if the premises are situated underneath premises used for residential purposes;

(*d*) if the premises are so situated that a fire occurring therein might interfere with the means of escape from the building of which they form part or from any adjoining building;

(*e*) where the premises form part of a building, unless such part either

(i) is separated from any other part of the building by fire-resisting partitions (including fire-resisting ceilings and floors) and fire-resisting self-closing doors; or

(ii) is so situated and constructed that a fire occurring therein is not likely to spread to other parts of the building, and its use for the purposes to which this Act applies[2] is sanctioned in writing by the local authority and any conditions attached to such sanctions are complied with;

(*f*) unless the regulations[5] set out in the First Schedule to this Act are duly observed;

(*g*) unless any regulations[6] are duly observed which may be made by the Secretary of State with respect to the use upon the premises of any cinematograph or other similar apparatus.

(3) Any person aggrieved by any requirement of a local authority, or the refusal of the local authority to grant any sanction, or by the conditions attached to any such sanction, may, within seven[7] days after being notified of such requirement, refusal, or conditions, appeal to a court of summary jurisdiction, provided that he has given not less than twenty-four hours' notice in writing of such appeal and of the grounds thereof to the local authority, and the court on any such appeal may make such order as appears to the court to be just, including any order for the payment of costs.
[Celluloid and Cinematograph Film Act 1922, s 1 as amended by SI 1974/1841 and the Employment Act 1989, s 21 and Sch 7.]

---

1. An artificially formed cave closed by a wooden door has been held to be "premises" within the meaning of this section (*Gardiner v Sevenoaks RDC* [1950] 2 All ER 84, 114 JP 352).
2. See s 2.
3. The expression "local authority" means the council of a county or London borough or the Common Council of the City of London and in a metropolitan county means the fire authority (s 9, amended by the Local Government Act 1985, Sch 11, para 6). London borough councils and the Common Council for the City of London shall be local authorities for the purposes of this Act (London Government Act 1963, s 62). It is the duty of such authority to see that the provisions of this Act are duly complied with (s 4(1)). The occupier must pay the prescribed fees to the local authority (s 4(3)).
4. As to the provision against fire in factories and the duties of the fire authority, see the Fire Precautions Act 1971, in this PART: title HEALTH AND SAFETY, ante.
5. Part 1 relates to raw celluloid stores, Pt II to premises where cinematograph film is kept or stored, and Pt III to fire-resisting storerooms.
6. See Order, SR & O 1924 No 403.
7. We think that the hearing need not be within the seven days provided that the complaint was made in time. For procedure, see the Magistrates' Courts Rules 1981, r 34, in PART I: MAGISTRATES' COURTS, PROCEDURE, ante.

8–30140 2. Purposes to which the Act applies[1]. The purposes to which this Act applies are—

(1) the keeping or storing of raw celluloid[2]—

(*a*) in quantities exceeding at any time 50 kilograms; or
(*b*) in smaller quantities unless kept (except when required to be exposed for the purpose of the work carried on in the premises) in a properly closed metal box or case; and

(2) the keeping or storing of cinematograph film[3]—

(*a*) in quantities exceeding at any one time twenty reels, or 37 kilograms in weight; or
(*b*) in smaller quantities unless each reel is kept (except when required to be exposed for the purpose of the work carried on in the premises) in a separate and properly closed metal box or case:

Provided that—

(i) for the purposes of this Act, cinematograph film[3] shall be deemed to be kept in any premises where it is temporarily deposited for the purpose of examination, cleaning, packing, re-winding or repair, but celluloid or cinematograph film shall not be deemed to be kept or stored in any premises where it is temporarily deposited whilst in the course of delivery, conveyance or transport; and
(ii) the provisions of this Act shall not, except in the cases referred to in paragraphs (*c*), (*d*) and (*e*) of subsection (1) of s 1 thereof, apply to premises to which the Factory and Workshops Acts 1901 to 1920[4] apply; and
(iii) the provisions of this Act shall not apply to premises licensed in accordance with the provisions of section 1 of the Cinemas Act 1985; and
(iv) the provisions of this Act shall not apply to a workplace within the meaning of the Regulatory Reform (Fire Safety) Order 2005 or which may, by virtue of an authorisation (within the meaning of section 136 of the Licensing Act 2003), be used for an exhibition of a film (within the meaning of paragraph 15 of Schedule 1 to that Act).

[Celluloid and Cinematograph Film Act 1922, s 2 as amended by the Cinemas Act 1985, Sch 2, SI 1992/1811, SI 2002/2776, the Licensing Act 2003, Sch 6 and SI 2005/1541.]

1. See also Regulations (SR & O 1921 No 1825 and 1928 No 82), made under s 79 of the Factory and Workshop Act 1901 and continued in force by Factories Act 1937 (now the Factories Act 1961), as to factories and workshops in which celluloid articles, etc, are manufactured, manipulated, or stored.
2. "Celluloid" means and includes the substances known as celluloid and xylonite and other similar substances, containing nitrated cellulose or other nitrated products, but does not include any substances which are explosives within the meaning of the Explosives Act 1875. "Raw celluloid" means (*a*) celluloid which has not been subjected to any process of manufacture; and (*b*) celluloid scrap or waste (s 9).
3. "Cinematograph film" means any film containing celluloid which is intended for use in a cinematograph or any similar apparatus (s 9).
4. See now the Factories Act 1961, in this PART: title HEALTH AND SAFETY, ante.

8–30141 3. Penalties. (1) In the event of any contravention in or in connection with any premises of the foregoing provisions of this Act, the occupier shall be guilty of an offence[1].

(2) In the event of the contravention by any other person employed on any premises of any regulation contained in the First Schedule to this Act or of any regulation made under this Act, he shall be guilty of an offence[1].

[Celluloid and Cinematograph Film Act 1922, s 3, as amended by SI 1974/1841, the Criminal Law Act 1977, s 31 and the Criminal Justice Act 1982, s 46.]

1. These are "existing statutory provisions" under the Health and Safety at Work etc Act 1974 with a penalty provided under s 33(3) thereof; see this PART: title HEALTH AND SAFETY, ante.

Cinematograph Films (Animals) Act 1937

(1 Edw 8 & 1 Geo 6 c 59)

8–30160 1. Prohibition of films involving cruelty to animals. (1) No person shall exhibit to the public, or supply to any person for public exhibition (whether by him or by another person) any cinematograph film (whether produced in Great Britain or elsewhere) if in connection with the production of the film any scene represented in the film was organised or directed in such way as to involve the cruel infliction of pain or terror on any animal or the cruel goading of any animal[1] to fury.

(2) In any proceedings brought under this Act in respect of any film, the court may (without prejudice to any other mode of proof) infer from the film as exhibited to the public or supplied for public exhibition, as the case may be, that a scene represented in the film as so exhibited or supplied was organised or directed in such way as to involve the cruel infliction of pain or terror on an animal or the cruel goading of an animal to fury, but (whether the court draws such an inference or not) it shall be a defence for the defendant to prove that he believed, and had reasonable cause to believe, that no scene so represented was so organised or directed.

(3) Any person contravening the provisions of this section shall be liable on summary conviction to a fine not exceeding **level 3** on the standard scale, or to imprisonment for a term not exceeding **three months*** or to **both** such fine and imprisonment.

(4) For the purpose of this Act—(*a*) a cinematograph film shall be deemed to be exhibited to the public when, and only when, it is exhibited in a place to which for the time being members of the general public as such have access, whether on payment of money or otherwise, and the expression "public exhibition" shall be construed accordingly; and (*b*) the expression "animal" has the same meaning as in the Protection of Animals Act 1911 and the Protection of Animals (Scotland) Act 1912.

[Cinematograph Films (Animals) Act 1937, s 1, as amended by the Criminal Law Act 1977, Sch 6 and the Criminal Justice Act 1982, s 46.]

***"51 weeks" aubstituted by the Criminal Justice Act 2003, Sch 26, from a date to be appointed.**

1. The expression "animal" means any domestic or captive animal (Protection of Animals Act 1911, s 15, in this PART: title ANIMALS, ante).

Theatres Act 1968

(1968 c 54)

Provisions with respect to performances of plays

8–30170 **2. Prohibition of presentation of obscene performances of plays.** (1) For the purposes of this section a performance of a play[1] shall be deemed to be obscene if, taken as a whole, its effect was such as to tend to deprave and corrupt persons who were likely, having regard to all relevant circumstances, to attend it[2].

(2) Subject to sections 3 and 7 of this Act, if an obscene performance of a play[1] is given, whether in public or private, any person who (whether for gain or not) presented[3] or directed[3] that performance shall be liable[4]—

(*a*) on summary conviction, to a fine not exceeding the **statutory maximum** or to imprisonment for a term not exceeding **six months**;

(*b*) on conviction on indictment, to a fine or to imprisonment for a term not exceeding **three years**, or **both**.

(3) A prosecution on indictment for an offence under this section shall not be commenced more than two years after the commission of the offence.

(4) No person shall be proceeded against in respect of a performance of a play[1] or any thing said or done in the course of such a performance—

(*a*) for an offence at common law where it is of the essence of the offence that the performance or, as the case may be, what was said or done was obscene, indecent, offensive, disgusting or injurious to morality; or

(*b*) *(Repealed)*.

and no person shall be proceeded against for an offence at common law of conspiring to corrupt public morals, or to do any act contrary to public morals or decency, in respect of an agreement to present or give a performance of a play, or to cause anything to be said or done in the course of such a performance.

[Theatres Act 1968, s 2, as amended by the Criminal Law Act 1977, s 28 and the Indecent Displays (Control) Act 1981, Sch.]

---

1. See s 18, post.
2. See note 2 to the Obscene Publications Act 1959, s 1, this PART: title OBSCENE PUBLICATIONS, ante.
3. See s 18, post.
4. For procedure in respect of an offence triable either way, see Magistrates' Courts Act 1980, ss 17A–21, in PART I: MAGISTRATES' COURTS, PROCEDURE, ante. Proceedings may not be instituted except with the consent of the Attorney General (s 8, post).

8–30171 **3. Defence of public good.** (1) A person shall not be convicted of an offence under section 2 of this Act if it is proved that the giving of the performance in question was justified as being for the public good on the ground that it was in the interest of drama, opera, ballet or any other art, or of literature or learning.

(2) It is hereby declared that the opinion of experts as to the artistic, literary or other merits of a performance of a play may be admitted in any proceedings for an offence under section 2 of this Act either to establish or negative the said ground[1].

[Theatres Act 1968, s 3.]

---

1. See note 4 to the Obscene Publications Act 1959, s 4, this PART: title OBSCENE PUBLICATIONS, ante.

8–30172 **6. Provocation of breach of peace by means of public performance of a play.** (1) Subject to section 7 of this Act, if there is given a public performance of a play[1] involving the use of threatening, abusive or insulting words or behaviour, any person who (whether for gain or not) presented[1] that performance shall be guilty of an offence under this section if—

(*a*) he did so with intent to provoke a breach of the peace; or

(*b*) the performance, taken as whole, was likely to occasion a breach of the peace.

(2) A person guilty of an offence under this section shall be liable on summary conviction to a fine not exceeding **level 5** on the standard scale or to imprisonment for a term not exceeding **six months** or to **both**.

[Theatres Act 1968, s 6, as amended by the Criminal Law Act 1977, Sch 1 and the Criminal Justice Act 1982, s 46.]

---

1. See s 18, post.

8–30173 **7. Exceptions for performances given in certain circumstances.** (1) Nothing in sections 2 to 4 of this Act shall apply in relation to a performance of a play[1] given on a domestic occasion in a private dwelling.

(2) Nothing in sections 2 to 6 of this Act shall apply in relation to a performance of a play given solely or primarily for one or more of the following purposes, that is to say—

(*a*) rehearsal; or

(*b*) to enable—

(i) a record or cinematograph film to be made from or by means of the performance; or

(ii) the performance to be broadcast; or

(iii) the performance to be included in a programme service (within the meaning of the Broadcasting Act 1990) other than a sound or television broadcasting service;

but in any proceedings for an offence under section 2 or 6 of this Act alleged to have been committed in respect of a performance of a play or an offence at common law alleged to have been committed in England and Wales by the publication of defamatory matter in the course of a performance of a play, if it is proved that the performance was attended by persons other than persons directly connected with the giving of the performance or the doing in relation thereto of any of the things mentioned in paragraph (*b*) above, the performance shall be taken not to have been given solely or primarily for one or more of the said purposes unless the contrary is shown.

(3) In this section—

"broadcast" means broadcast by wireless telegraphy (within the meaning of the Wireless Telegraphy Act 1949), whether by way of sound broadcasting or television;

"cinematograph film" means any print, negative, tape or other article on which a performance of a play or any part of such a performance is recorded for the purposes of visual reproduction;

"record" means any record or similar contrivance for reproducing sound, including the sound-track of a cinematograph film;

[Theatres Act 1968, s. 7 as amended by the Cable and Broadcasting Act 1984, Schs 5 and 6, the Public Order Act 1986, Sch 3 and the Broadcasting Act 1990, Sch 20.]

---

1. See s 18, post.

8–30174 **8. Restriction on institution of proceedings.** Proceedings for an offence under section 2 or 6 of this Act or an offence at common law committed by the publication of defamatory matter in the course of a performance of a play shall not be instituted in England and Wales except by or with the consent of the Attorney-General.

[Theatres Act 1968, s 8 amended by the Public Order Act 1986 Sch 3.]

8–30175 **9. Script as evidence of what was performed.** (1) Where a performance of a play[1] was based on a script, then, in any proceedings for an offence under section 2 or 6 of this Act alleged to have been committed in respect of that performance—

(*a*) an actual script on which that performance was based shall be admissible as evidence of what was performed and of the manner in which the performance or any part of it was given; and

(*b*) if such a script is given in evidence on behalf of any party to the proceedings then, except in so far as the contrary is shown, whether by evidence given on behalf of the same or any other party, the performance shall be taken to have been given in accordance with that script.

(2) In this Act "script", in relation to a performance of a play, means the text of the play (whether expressed in words or in musical or other notation) together with any stage or other directions for its performance, whether contained in a single document or not.

[Theatres Act 1968, s 9 amended by the Public Order Act 1986 Sch 3.]

---

1. See s 18, post.

8–30176 **10. Power to make copies of scripts.** (1) If a police officer of or above the rank of superintendent has reasonable grounds for suspecting—

(*a*) that an offence under section 2 or 6 of this Act has been committed by any person in respect of a performance of a play[1]; or (*b*) that a performance of a play is to be given and that an offence under the said section 2 or 6 is likely to be committed by any person in respect of that performance,

he may make an order in writing under this section relating to that person and that performance.

(2) Every order made under this section shall be signed by the police officer by whom it is made, shall name the person to whom it relates, and shall describe the performance to which it relates in a manner sufficient to enable that performance to be identified.

(3) Where an order under this section has been made, any police officer, on production if so required of the order—

(*a*) may require the person named in the order to produce, if such a thing exists, an actual script[2] on which the performance was or, as the case may be, will be based; and

(*b*) if such a script is produced to him, may require the person so named to afford him an opportunity of causing a copy thereof to be made.

(4) Any person who without reasonable excuse fails to comply with a requirement under subsection (3) above shall be liable on summary conviction to a fine not exceeding **level 3** on the standard scale.

(5) Where, in the case of a performance of a play based on a script, a copy of an actual script on which that performance was based has been made by or on behalf of a police officer by virtue of an order under this section relating to that performance, section 9(1) of this Act shall apply in relation to that copy as it applies in relation to an actual script on which the performance was based.

[Theatres Act 1968, s 10 as amended by the Criminal Justice Act 1982, ss 38 and 46 and the Public Order Act 1986, Sch 3.]

---

1. See s 18, post.
2. See s 9(2), ante.

8–30177 11. Delivery of scripts of new plays to British Museum. (1) Where after the coming into force of this section there is given in Great Britain a public performance of a new play[1], being a performance based on a script[2], a copy of the actual script on which that performance was based shall be delivered to the Trustees of the British Museum free of charge within the period of one month beginning with the date of the performance; and the Trustees shall give a written receipt for every script delivered to them pursuant to this section.

(2) If the requirements of subsection (1) above are not complied with in the case of any performance to which that subsection applies, any person who presented that performance shall be liable on summary conviction to a fine not exceeding **level 1** on the standard scale.

(3) In this section "public performance of a new play" means a public performance of a play of which no previous public performance has ever been given in Great Britain, but does not include a public performance of a play which—

(*a*) is based on a script substantially the same as that on which a previous public performance of a play given there was based; or

(*b*) is based substantially on a text of the play which has been published in the United Kingdom.

(4) For the purposes of this section a performance of a play given solely or primarily for one or more of the purposes mentioned in section 7(2)(*a*) and (*b*) of this Act shall be disregarded.

[Theatres Act 1968, s 11 as amended by the Criminal Justice Act 1982, ss 38 and 46.]

---

1. See s 18, post.
2. See s 9(2), ante.

Licensing of premises for public performance of plays

8–30178 12. Licensing of premises for public performance of plays. *Repealed.*

8–30179 13. Enforcement of s 12. *Repealed.*

8–30180 14. Appeals in respect of licences. *Repealed.*

Miscellaneous and general

8–30181 15. Powers of entry and inspection. (1) If a justice of the peace is satisfied by information on oath that there are reasonable grounds for suspecting, as regards any premises[1] specified in the information—

(*a*) that a performance of a play[1] is to be given at those premises, and that an offence under section 2 or 6 of this Act is likely to be committed in respect of that performance;

(*b*) *repealed*

the justice may issue a warrant under his hand empowering any police officer at any time within one month from the date of the warrant to enter the premises and—

(i) in a case falling within paragraph (*a*) above, to attend any performance of a play which may be given there;

(ii) in a case falling within paragraph (*b*) above, to inspect the premises.

. . . (*Scotland*).

(2)–(6) *Repealed.*

(7) *Scotland.*

[Theatres Act 1968, s 15 as amended by the Criminal Justice Act 1982, ss 38 and 46, the Police and Criminal Evidence Act 1984, Sch 6, the Public Order Act 1986, Sch 3, the Licensing Act 2003, Sch 6 and SSI 2005/383.]

---

1. See s 18, post.

8–30182 16. Offences by bodies corporate. Where any offence under this Act committed by a body corporate is proved to have been committed with the consent or connivance of, or to be attributable to any neglect on the part of, any director, manager, secretary or other similar officer of the body corporate, or any person purporting to act in any such capacity, he as well as the body corporate shall be guilty of that offence and shall be liable to be proceeded against and punished accordingly.

[Theatres Act 1968, s 16.]

8–30183 18. Interpretation. (1) In this Act—

"licensing authority" means—

(*a*)–(*bb*) *repealed*

(*c*) *Scotland*;

"play" means—

(*a*) any dramatic piece, whether involving improvisation or not, which is given wholly or in part by one or more persons actually present and performing and in which the whole or a major proportion of what is done by the person or persons performing, whether by way of speech, singing or action, involves the playing of a role; and

(*b*) any ballet given wholly or in part by one or more persons actually present and performing, whether or not it falls within paragraph (*a*) of this definition;

"police officer" means a member, or in Scotland a constable, of a police force;

"premises" includes any place;

"public performance" includes any performance in a public place within the meaning of the Public Order Act 1936, and any performance which the public or any section thereof are permitted to attend, whether on payment or otherwise;

"script" has the meaning assigned by section 9(2) of this Act.

(2) For the purposes of this Act—

(*a*) a person shall not be treated as presenting a performance of a play by reason only of his taking part therein as performer;

(*b*) a person taking part as a performer in a performance of a play directed by another person shall be treated as a person who directed the performance if without reasonable excuse he performs otherwise than in accordance with that person's direction; and

(*c*) a person shall be taken to have directed a performance of a play given under his direction notwithstanding that he was not present during the performance[1];

and a person shall not be treated as aiding or abetting the commission of an offence under section 2 or 6 of this Act in respect of a performance of a play by reason only of his taking part in that performance as a performer.

[Theatres Act 1968, s 18 as amended by the Local Government Act 1985, Sch 8, the Public Order Act 1986, Sch 3 and the Local Government (Wales) Act 1994, Sch 16 and the Licensing Act 2003, Sch 6.]

---

1. But under previous legislation a theatre licence did not "cause to be presented" an unauthorised interpolation for which a performer was solely responsible (*Lovelace v DPP* [1954] 3 All ER 481, 119 JP 21).

Video Recordings Act 1984

(1984 c 39)

Preliminary

8–30390 1. Interpretation of terms. (1) The provisions of this section shall have effect for the interpretation of terms used in this Act.

(2) "Video work" means any series of visual images (with or without sound)—

(*a*) produced electronically by the use of information contained on any disc, magnetic tape or any other device capable of storing data electronically, and

(*b*) shown as a moving picture[1].

(3) "Video recording" means any disc, magnetic tape or any other device capable of storing data electronically containing information by the use of which the whole or a part of a video work may be produced.

(4) "Supply" means supply in any manner, whether or not for reward, and, therefore, includes supply by way of sale, letting on hire, exchange or loan; and references to a supply are to be interpreted accordingly.

[Video Recordings Act 1984, s 1 as amended by the Criminal Justice and Public Order Act 1994, Schs 9 and 11.]

1. It is inappropriate to take account of the brevity of the display. Provided the sequence is long enough to show continuing movement, it can properly be described as a moving picture (*Kent County Council v Multi Media Marketing (Canterbury) Ltd* (1995) Times, 9 May).

8–30391 **2. Exempted works.** (1) Subject to subsection (2) or (3) below, a video work is for the purposes of this Act an exempted work if, taken as a whole—

(*a*) it is designed to inform, educate or instruct;
(*b*) it is concerned with sport, religion or music; or
(*c*) it is a video game.

(2) A video work is not an exempted work for those purposes if, to any significant extent, it depicts—

(*a*) human sexual activity[1] or acts of force or restraint associated with such activity;
(*b*) mutilation or torture of, or other acts of gross violence towards, humans or animals;
(*c*) human genital organs[1] or human urinary or excretory functions;
(*d*) techniques likely[1] to be useful in the commission of offences;

or is likely to any significant extent to stimulate or encourage anything falling within paragraph (*a*) or, in the case of anything falling within paragraph (*b*), is likely to any extent to do so.

(3) A video work is not an exempted work for those purposes if, to any significant extent, it depicts criminal activity which is likely to any significant extent to stimulate or encourage the commission of offences.

[Video Recordings Act 1984, s 2 as amended by the Criminal Justice and Public Order Act 1994, s 89.]

1. Activity short of masturbation might amount to "human sexual activity". Female genitalia need not be confined to internal organs. In considering whether a work is designed to encourage human sexual activity it is unnecessary that any video clips be regarded as hard pornography or offensive (*Kent County Council v Multi Media Marketing (Canterbury) Ltd* (1995) Times, 9 May).

8–30392 **3. Exempted supplies.** (1) The provisions of this section apply to determine whether or not a supply of a video recording is an exempted supply for the purposes of this Act.

(2) The supply of a video recording by any person is an exempted supply if it is neither—

(*a*) a supply for reward, nor
(*b*) a supply in the course or furtherance of a business.

(3) Where on any premises facilities are provided in the course or furtherance of a business for supplying video recordings, the supply by any person of a video recording on those premises is to be treated for the purposes of subsection (2) above as a supply in the course or furtherance of a business.

(4) Where a person (in this subsection referred to as the "original supplier") supplies a video recording to a person who, in the course of a business, makes video works or supplies video recordings the supply is an exempted supply—

(*a*) if it is not made with a view to any further supply of that recording, or
(*b*) if it is so made, but is not made with a view to the eventual supply of that recording to the public or is made with a view to the eventual supply of that recording to the original supplier.

For the purposes of this subsection, any supply is a supply to the public unless it is—

(i) a supply to a person who, in the course of a business, makes video works or supplies video recordings,
(ii) an exempted supply by virtue of subsection (2) above or subsections (5) to (10) below, or
(iii) a supply outside the United Kingdom.

(5) Where a video work—

(*a*) is designed to provide a record of an event or occasion for those who took part in the event or occasion or are connected with those who did so,
(*b*) does not, to any significant extent, depict anything falling within paragraph (*a*), (*b*) or (*c*) of section 2(2) of this Act, and
(*c*) is not designed to any significant extent to stimulate or encourage anything falling within paragraph (*a*) of that subsection or, in the case of anything falling within paragraph (*b*) of that subsection, is not designed to any extent to do so,

the supply of a video recording containing only that work to a person who took part in the event or occasion or is connected with someone who did so is an exempted supply.

(6) The supply of a video recording for the purpose only of the exhibition of any video work contained in the recording in premises other than a dwelling-house—

(*a*) being premises mentioned in subsection (7) below, or
(*b*) being an exhibition which in England and Wales or Scotland would be a film exhibition to which section 6 of the Cinemas Act 1985 applies (film exhibition to which public not admitted or are admitted without payment), or (*Northern Ireland*).

is an exempted supply.

(7) The premises referred to in subsection (6) above are—

(*za*) premises in England and Wales which, by virtue of an authorisation within the meaning of section 136 of the Licensing Act 2003, may be used for the exhibition of a film within the meaning of paragraph 15 of Schedule 1 to that Act,
(*a*) premises in Scotland in respect of which a licence under section 1 of the Cinemas Act 1985 is in force,
(*b*) premises in Scotland falling within section 7 of that Act (premises used only occasionally and exceptionally for film exhibitions), or
(*c*) premises in Scotland falling within section 8 of that Act (building or structure of a movable character) in respect of which such a licence as is mentioned in subsection (1)(*a*) of that section has been granted.*

(8) The supply of a video recording with a view only to its use for or in connection with a programme service (within the meaning of the Broadcasting Act 1990) is an exempted supply.

(9) The supply of a video recording for the purpose only of submitting a video work contained in the recording for the issue of a classification certificate or otherwise only for purposes of arrangements made by the designated authority is an exempted supply.

(10) The supply of a video recording with a view only to its use—

(*a*) in training for or carrying on any medical or related occupation,
(*b*) for the purpose of—
    (i) services provided in pursuance of the National Health Service Act 1977 or the National Health Service (Scotland) Act 1978, or
    (ii) (*Northern Ireland*)
(*c*) in training persons employed in the course of services falling within paragraph (*b*) above,

is an exempted supply.

(11) For the purposes of subsection (10) above, an occupation is a medical or related occupation if, to carry on the occupation, a person is required to be registered under the the Health Professions Order 2001, the Nursing and Midwifery Order 2001, the Medical Act 1983, the Osteopaths Act 1993 or the Chiropractors Act 1994.

(12) The supply of a video recording otherwise than for reward, being a supply made for the purpose only of supplying it to a person who previously made an exempted supply of the recording, is also an exempted supply.

[Video Recordings Act 1984, s 3 as amended by the Cable and Broadcasting Act 1984, Sch 5, the Cinemas Act 1985, Sch 2, the Broadcasting Act 1990, Sch 20, the Chiropractors Act 1994, s 39, the Nurses, Midwives and Health Visitors Act 1997, Sch 4, SI 2002/254 and the Licensing Act 2003, Sch 6.]

8–30393 **4–7.** *Classification and labelling of video works by authority designated by the Secretary of State.*

8–30394 **8. Requirements as to labelling etc.** Secretary of State may make regulations[1] to labelling of video works.
[Video Recordings Act 1984, s 8—summarised.]

1. See the Video Recordings (Labelling) Regulations 1985, post.

Offences and penalties

8–30395 **9. Supplying video recording of unclassified work.** (1) A person who supplies or offers to supply a video recording containing a video work in respect of which no classification certificate has been issued is guilty of an offence unless—

(*a*) the supply is, or would if it took place be, an exempted supply, or
(*b*) the video work is an exempted work.

(2) It is a defence to a charge of committing an offence under this section to prove that the accused believed on reasonable grounds—

(*a*) that the video work concerned or, if the video recording contained more than one work to which the charge relates, each of those works was either an exempted work or a work in respect of which a classification certificate had been issued, or
(*b*) that the supply was, or would if it took place be, an exempted supply by virtue of section 3(4) or (5) of this Act.

(3) A person guilty of an offence under this section shall be liable[1]—

(*a*) on conviction on indictment, to imprisonment for a term not exceeding **two years** or a **fine** or **both**,

(*b*) on summary conviction, to imprisonment for a term not exceeding **six months** or a fine not exceeding **£20,000** or **both**.

[Video Recordings Act 1984, s 9 as amended by the Criminal Justice and Public Order Act 1994, s 88.]

1. For procedure in respect of this offence which is triable either way, see the Magistrates' Courts Act 1980, ss 17A–21, in PART I: MAGISTRATES' COURTS, PROCEDURE, ante.

8–30396 10. Possession of video recording of unclassified work for the purposes of supply. (1) Where a video recording contains a video work in respect of which no classification certificate has been issued, a person who has the recording in his possession for the purposes of supplying it is guilty of an offence unless—

(*a*) he has it in his possession for the purpose only of a supply which, if it took place, would be an exempted supply, or

(*b*) the video work is an exempted work.

(2) It is a defence to a charge of committing an offence under this section to prove—

(*a*) that the accused believed on reasonable grounds that the video work concerned or, if the video recording contained more than one work to which the charge relates, each of those works was either an exempted work or a work in respect of which a classification certificate had been issued,

(*b*) that the accused had the video recording in his possession for the purposes only of a supply which he believed on reasonable grounds would, if it took place, be an exempted supply by virtue of section 3(4) or (5) of this Act, or

(*c*) that the accused did not intend to supply the video recording until a classification certificate had been issued in respect of the video work concerned.

(3) A person guilty of an offence under this section shall be liable[1]—

(*a*) on conviction on indictment, to imprisonment for a term not exceeding **two years** or a **fine** or **both**,

(*b*) on summary conviction, to imprisonment for a term not exceeding **six months** or a fine not exceeding **£20,000** or **both**.

[Video Recordings Act 1984, s 10 as amended by the Criminal Justice and Public Order Act 1994, s 88.]

1. For procedure in respect of this offence which is triable either way, see the Magistrates' Courts Act 1980, ss 17A–21, in PART I: MAGISTRATES' COURTS, PROCEDURE, ante.

8–30397 11. Supplying video recording of classified work in breach of classification. (1) Where a classification certificate issued in respect of a video work states that no video recording containing that work is to be supplied to any person who has not attained the age[1] specified in the certificate, a person who supplies or offers to supply a video recording containing that work to a person who has not attained the age so specified is guilty of an offence unless the supply is, or would if it took place be, an exempted supply.

(2) It is a defence to a charge of committing an offence under this section to prove[2]—

(*a*) that the accused neither knew nor had reasonable grounds to believe that the classification certificate contained the statement concerned,

(*b*) that the accused neither knew nor had reasonable grounds to believe that the person concerned had not attained that age, or

(*c*) that the accused believed on reasonable grounds that the supply was, or would if it took place be, an exempted supply by virtue of section 3(4) or (5) of this Act.

(3) A person guilty of an offence under this section shall be liable, on summary conviction, to imprisonment for a term not exceeding **six months** or a fine not exceeding **level 5** on the standard scale or both.

[Video Recordings Act 1984, s 11 as amended by the Criminal Justice and Public Order Act 1994, s 88.]

1. Evidence of the 11-year-old son of a Trading Standards Officer acting under instructions to purchase an 18 category video was, in the absence of his acting as an agent provocateur, held to have been rightly admitted (*Ealing London Borough v Woolworths plc* [1995] Crim LR 58).

2. For this purpose, s 11(2) refers to the knowledge or reasonable grounds for belief of the employee through whom a company effects a supply (*Tesco Stores Ltd v Brent London Borough Council* [1993] 2 All ER 718, [1993] 1 WLR 1037, 158 JP 121).

8–30398 12. Certain video recordings only to be supplied in licensed sex shops. (1) Where a classification certificate issued in respect of a video work states that no video recording containing that work is to be supplied other than in a licensed sex shop, a person who at any place other than in a sex shop for which a licence is in force under the relevant enactment—

(*a*) supplies[1] a video recording containing the work, or

(*b*) offers to do so[2],

is guilty of an offence unless the supply is, or would if it took place be, an exempted supply.

(2) It is a defence to a charge of committing an offence under subsection (1) above to prove—

(*a*) that the accused neither knew nor had reasonable grounds to believe that the classification certificate contained the statement concerned,

(*b*) that the accused believed on reasonable grounds that the place concerned was a sex shop for which a licence was in force under the relevant enactment, or

(*c*) that the accused believed on reasonable grounds that the supply was, or would if it took place be, an exempted supply by virtue of section 3(4) of this Act or subsection (6) below.

(3) Where a classification certificate issued in respect of a video work states that no video recording containing that work is to be supplied other than in a licensed sex shop, a person who has a video recording containing the work in his possession for the purposes of supplying it at any place other than in such a sex shop is guilty of an offence, unless he has it in his possession for the purpose only of a supply which, if it took place, would be an exempted supply.

(4) It is a defence to a charge of committing an offence under subsection (3) above to prove—

(*a*) that the accused neither knew nor had reasonable grounds to believe that the classification certificate contained the statement concerned,

(*b*) that the accused believed on reasonable grounds that the place concerned was a sex shop for which a licence was in force under the relevant enactment, or

(*c*) that the accused had the video recording in his possession for the purpose only of a supply which he believed on reasonable grounds would, if it took place, be an exempted supply by virtue of section 3(4) of this Act or subsection (6) below.

(4A) A person guilty of an offence under subsection (1) or (3) above shall be liable, on summary conviction, to imprisonment for a term not exceeding **six months** or a fine not exceeding **level 5** on the standard scale or both.

(5) In this section "relevant enactment" means Schedule 3 to the Local Government (Miscellaneous Provisions) Act 1982 or, in Scotland, Schedule 2 to the Civic Government (Scotland) Act 1982, and "sex shop" has the same meaning as in the relevant enactment.

(6) For the purposes of this section, where a classification certificate issued in respect of a video work states that no video recording containing that work is to be supplied other than in a licensed sex shop, the supply of a video recording containing that work—

(*a*) to a person who, in the course of a business, makes video works or supplies video recordings, and

(*b*) with a view to its eventual supply in sex shops, being sex shops for which licences are in force under the relevant enactment,

is an exempted supply.

[Video Recordings Act 1984, s 12 as amended by the Criminal Justice and Public Order Act 1994, s 88.]

1. The restriction is not directed simply to ensure a supply takes place "by" a licensed sex shop proprietor but to ensure that the "supply" of restricted material only takes place at licensed establishments. The customer must come face to face with the supplier. Accordingly, it is an offence to supply restricted videos by post in response to telephone, postal or internet orders (*Interfact Ltd v Liverpool City Council* [2005] EWHC 995 (Admin), [2005] 1 WLR 3118, 169 JP 353).

2. The offence consists of the offer to make the supply, not to make the offer, other than in a licensed sex shop. As regards what amounts to an "offer", the issue is not whether a catalogue amounts to an offer to sell videos or an invitation to treat but whether it amounts to an offer to supply videos, namely to supply outside a licensed sex shop. An offer to supply under s 1(4) need not be underpinned by a contract of sale or contractually binding relationship. A gratuitous offer to supply without any consideration is equally an offer to supply a video recording (*Interfact Ltd v Liverpool City Council* [2005] EWHC 995 (Admin), [2005] 1 WLR 3118, 169 JP 353).

8–30399 13. Supply of video recording not complying with requirements as to labels, etc. (1) A person who supplies or offers to supply a video recording or any spool, case or other thing on or in which the recording is kept which does not satisfy any requirement imposed by regulations under section 8 of this Act is guilty of an offence unless the supply is, or would if it took place be, an exempted supply.

(2) It is a defence to a charge of committing an offence under this section to prove that the accused—

(*a*) believed on reasonable grounds that the supply was, or would if it took place be, an exempted supply by virtue of section 3(4) or (5) of this Act, or

(*b*) neither knew nor had reasonable grounds to believe that the recording, spool, case or other thing (as the case may be) did not satisfy the requirement concerned.

(3) A person guilty of an offence under this section shall be liable, on summary conviction, to a fine not exceeding **level 5** on the standard scale.

[Video Recordings Act 1984, s 13 as amended by the Criminal Justice and Public Order Act 1994, Sch 10.]

8–30400 14. Supply of video recording containing false indication as to classification. (1) A person who supplies or offers to supply a video recording containing a video work in respect of which no classification certificate has been issued is guilty of an offence if the video recording or any spool, case or other thing on or in which the recording is kept contains any indication that a classification certificate has been issued in respect of that work unless the supply is, or would if it took place be, an exempted supply.

(2) It is a defence to a charge of committing an offence under subsection (1) above to prove—

(*a*) that the accused believed on reasonable grounds—

(i) that a classification certificate had been issued in respect of the video work concerned, or
(ii) that the supply was, or would if it took place be, an exempted supply by virtue of section 3(4) or (5) of this Act, or

(*b*) that the accused neither knew nor had reasonable grounds to believe that the recording, spool, case or other thing (as the case may be) contained the indication concerned.

(3) A person who supplies or offers to supply a video recording containing a video work in respect of which a classification certificate has been issued is guilty of an offence if the video recording or any spool, case or other thing on or in which the recording is kept contains any indication that is false in a material particular of any statement falling within section 7(2) of this Act[1] (including any advice falling within paragraph (*a*) of that subsection) contained in the certificate, unless the supply is, or would if it took place be, an exempted supply.

(4) It is a defence to a charge of committing an offence under subsection (3) above to prove—

(*a*) that the accused believed on reasonable grounds—

(i) that the supply was, or would if it took place be, an exempted supply by virtue of section 3(4) or (5) of this Act, or
(ii) that the certificate concerned contained the statement indicated, or

(*b*) that the accused neither knew nor had reasonable grounds to believe that the recording, spool, case or other thing (as the case may be) contained the indication concerned.

(5) A person guilty of an offence under subsection (1) or (3) above shall be liable, on summary conviction, to imprisonment for a term not exceeding **six months** or a fine not exceeding **level 5** on the standard scale.

[Video Recordings Act 1984, s 14 as amended by the Criminal Justice and Public Order Act 1994, s 88.]

1. Those requirements are that the certificate must contain—

(*a*) a statement that the video work concerned is suitable for general viewing and unrestricted supply (with or without any advice as to the desirability of parental guidance with regard to the viewing of the work by young children or as to the particular suitability of the work for viewing by children); or
(*b*) a statement that the video work concerned is suitable for viewing only by persons who have attained the age (not being more than eighteen years) specified in the certificate and that no video recording containing that work is to be supplied to any person who has not attained the age so specified; or
(*c*) the statement mentioned in paragraph (*b*) above together with a statement that no video recording containing that work is to be supplied other than in a licensed sex shop; (s 7(2), Video Recordings Act 1994).

8–30400A 14A. General defences to offences under this Act. Without prejudice to any defence specified in the preceding provisions of this Act in relation to a particular offence, it is a defence to a charge of committing any offence under this Act to prove—

(*a*) that the commission of the offence was due to the act or default of a person other than the accused, and
(*b*) that the accused took all reasonable precautions and exercised all due diligence[1] to avoid the commission of the offence by any person under his control.

[Video Recording Act 1984, s 14A inserted by the Video Recording Act 1993, s 2.]

1. The 'due diligence' defence was established where a company had been dealing with a reputable supplier for 20 years without problems which was clearly aware of its statutory obligations and it was not necessary for the company to make checks (*Bilon v WH Smith Trading Ltd* [2001] EWHC Admin 469, 165 JP 701, [2001] Crim LR 850).

8–30401 15. Time limit for prosecutions. (1) No prosecution for an offence under this Act shall be brought after the expiry of the period of three years beginning with the date of the commission of the offence or one year beginning with the date of its discovery by the prosecutor, whichever is earlier.

(2)–(3) *Scotland.*

[Video Recordings Act 1984, s 15, as substituted by the Criminal Justice and Public Order Act 1994, Sch 10.]

Miscellaneous and supplementary

8–30402 16. Offences by bodies corporate. (1) Where an offence under this Act committed by a body corporate is proved to have been committed with the consent or connivance of, or to be attributable to any neglect on the part of, any director, manager, secretary or other similar officer of the body corporate, or any person who was purporting to act in any such capacity, he as well as the body corporate shall be guilty of the offence and shall be liable to be proceeded against and punished accordingly.

(2) Where the affairs of a body corporate are managed by its members, subsection (1) above shall apply in relation to the acts and defaults of a member in connection with his functions of management as if he were a director of the body corporate.

[Video Recordings Act 1984, s 16.]

8–30403 16A. Enforcement. (1) The functions of a local weights and measures authority include the enforcement in their area of this Act.

(1A) Subject to subsection (1B) below, the functions of a local weights and measures authority shall also include the investigation and prosecution outside their area of offences under this Act suspected to be linked to their area as well as the investigation outside their area of offences suspected to have been committed within it.

(1B) The functions available to an authority under subsection (1A) above shall not be exercisable in relation to any circumstances suspected to have arisen within the area of another local weights and measures authority without the consent of that authority.

(2) The following provisions of the Trade Descriptions Act 1968 apply in relation to the enforcement of this Act by such an authority as in relation to the enforcement of that Act—

section 27 (power to make test purchases),
section 28 (power to enter premises and inspect and seize goods and documents),
section 29 (obstruction of authorised officers), and
section 33 (compensation for loss, &c of goods seized under s 28).

(3) Nothing in this section shall be taken as authorising a local weights and measures authority in Scotland to initiate proceedings for an offence.

(4) *Northern Ireland.*

(4A) For the purposes of subsections (1A), (1B) and (2) above—

(*a*) offences in another area are "linked" to the area of a local weights and measures authority if—

(i) the supply or possession of video recordings in contravention of this Act within their area is likely to be or to have been the result of the supply or possession of those recordings in the other area; or

(ii) the supply or possession of video recordings in contravention of this Act in the other area is likely to be or to have been the result of the supply or possession of those recordings in their area; and

(*b*) "investigation" includes the exercise of the powers conferred by sections 27 and 28 of the Trade Descriptions Act 1968 as applied by subsection (2) above;

and sections 29 and 33 of that Act shall apply accordingly.

(5) Any enactment which authorises the disclosure of information for the purpose of facilitating the enforcement of the Trade Descriptions Act 1968 shall apply as if the provisions of this Act were contained in that Act and as if the functions of any person in relation to the enforcement of this Act were functions under that Act.

[Video Recordings Act 1984, s 16A, as inserted by the Criminal Justice Act 1988, s 162 as amended by the Criminal Justice and Public Order Act 1994, s 91.]

8–30403A 16B. Extension of jurisdiction of magistrates' courts in linked cases. (1) A justice of the peace for an area to which section 1 of the Magistrates' Courts Act 1980 applies may issue a summons or warrant under and in accordance with that section as respects an offence under this Act committed or suspected of having been committed outside the area for which he acts if it appears to the justice that the offence is linked to the supply or possession of video recordings within the area for which he acts.

(2) Where a person charged with an offence under this Act appears or is brought before a magistrates' court in answer to a summons issued by virtue of subsection (1) above, or under a warrant issued under subsection (1) above, the court shall have jurisdiction to try the offence.

(3) For the purposes of this section an offence is "linked" to the supply or possession of video recordings within the area for which a justice acts if—

(*a*) the supply or possession of video recordings within his area is likely to be or to have been the result of the offence; or

(*b*) the offence is likely to be or to have been the result of the supply or possession of video recordings in his area.

[Video Recordings Act 1984, s 16B, as inserted by the Criminal Justice and Public Order Act 1994, s 91.]

8–30403B 16C–16D. *Scotland; Northern Ireland.*

8–30404 17. Entry, search and seizure. (1) If a justice of the peace is satisfied by information on oath that there are reasonable grounds for suspecting—

(*a*) that an offence under this Act has been or is being committed on any premises, and
(*b*) that evidence that the offence has been or is being committed is on those premises,

he may issue a warrant under his hand authorising any constable to enter and search the premises.

(2) A constable entering or searching any premises in pursuance of a warrant under subsection (1) above may use reasonable force if necessary and may seize anything found there which he has reasonable grounds to believe may be required to be used in evidence in any proceedings for an offence under this Act.

(3) Reference to Scotland and Northern Ireland.

[Video Recordings Act 1984, s 17 as amended by the Criminal Justice and Public Order Act 1994, Schs 9 and 11.]

8–30405 18. Arrest. (1) If a constable has reasonable grounds for suspecting that a person has committed an offence under this Act, he may require him to give his name and address and, if that person refuses or fails to do so or gives a name and address which the constable reasonably suspects to be false, the constable may arrest him without warrant.

(2) This section does not extend to Scotland.

[Video Recordings Act 1984, s 18.]

8–30406 19. Evidence by certificate. (1) In any proceedings in England and Wales or Northern Ireland for an offence under this Act, a certificate purporting to be signed by a person authorised in that behalf by the Secretary of State and stating—

(*a*) that he has examined—

  (i) the record maintained in pursuance of arrangements made by the designated authority, and
  (ii) a video work (or part of a video work) contained in a video recording identified by the certificate, and

(*b*) that the record shows that, on the date specified in the certificate, no classification certificate had been issued in respect of the video work concerned,

shall be admissible as evidence of the fact that, on that day, no classification certificate had been issued in respect of the video work concerned.

(2) A certificate under subsection (1) above may also state—

(*a*) that the video work concerned differs in such respects as may be specified from another video work examined by the person so authorised and identified by the certificate, and
(*b*) that the record shows that, on a date specified in the certificate under subsection (1) above, a classification certificate was issued in respect of that other video work;

and, if it does so, shall be admissible as evidence of the fact that the video work concerned differs in those respects from the other video work.

(3) In any proceedings in England and Wales or Northern Ireland for an offence under this Act, a certificate purporting to be signed by a person authorised in that behalf by the Secretary of State and stating—

(*a*) that he has examined—

  (i) the record maintained in pursuance of arrangements made by the designated authority, and
  (ii) a video work (or part of a video work) contained in a video recording identified by the certificate, and

(*b*) that the record shows that, on the date specified in the certificate under this subsection, a classification certificate was issued in respect of the video work concerned and that a document identified by the certificate under this subsection is a copy of the classification certificate so issued,

shall be admissible as evidence of the fact that, on that date, a classification certificate in terms of the document so identified was issued in respect of the video work concerned.

(3A) In any proceedings in England and Wales or Northern Ireland for an offence under this Act, a certificate purporting to be signed by a person authorised in that behalf by the Secretary of State and stating—

(*a*) that he has examined the record maintained in pursuance of arrangements made by the designated authority, and
(*b*) that the record shows that, on the date specified in the certificate, no classification certificate had been issued in respect of a video work having a particular title,

shall be admissible as evidence of the fact that, on that date, no classification certificate had been issued in respect of a work of that title.

(3B) In any proceedings in England and Wales or Northern Ireland for an offence under this Act, a certificate purporting to be signed by a person authorised in that behalf by the Secretary of State and stating—

(*a*) that he has examined the record maintained in pursuance of arrangements made by the designated authority, and

(*b*) that the record shows that, on the date specified in the certificate under this subsection, a classification certificate was issued in respect of a video work having a particular title and that a document identified by the certificate under this subsection is a copy of the classification certificate so issued,

shall be admissible as evidence of the fact that, on that date, a classification certificate in terms of the document so identified was issued in respect of a work of that title.

(4) Any document or video recording identified in a certificate tendered in evidence under this section shall be treated as if it had been produced as an exhibit and identified in court by the person signing the certificate.

(5) This section does not make a certificate admissible as evidence in proceedings for an offence unless a copy of the certificate has, not less than seven days before the hearing, been served on the person charged with the offence in one of the following ways—

(*a*) by delivering it to him or to his solicitor, or

(*b*) by addressing it to him and leaving it at his usual or last known place of abode or place of business or by addressing it to his solicitor and leaving it at his office, or

(*c*) by sending it in a registered letter or by the recorded delivery service addressed to him at his usual or last known place of abode or place of business or addressed to his solicitor at his office, or

(*d*) in the case of a body corporate, by delivering it to the secretary or clerk of the body at its registered or principal office or sending it in a registered letter or by the recorded delivery service addressed to the secretary or clerk of that body at that office.

[Video Recordings Act 1984, s 19 amended by the Video Recording Act 1993, s 4.]

8–30407 21. Forfeiture. (1) Where a person is convicted of any offence under this Act, the court may order any video recording—

(*a*) produced to the court, and

(*b*) shown to the satisfaction of the court to relate to the offence,

to be forfeited.

(2) The court shall not order any video recording to be forfeited under subsection (1) above if a person claiming to be the owner of it or otherwise interested in it applies to be heard by the court, unless an opportunity has been given to him to show cause why the order should not be made.

(3) References in this section to a video recording include a reference to any spool, case or other thing on or in which the recording is kept.

(4) An order made under subsection (1) above in any proceedings in England and Wales or Northern Ireland shall not take effect until the expiration of the ordinary time within which an appeal may be instituted or, where such an appeal is duly instituted, until the appeal is finally decided or abandoned; and for this purpose—

(*a*) an application for a case to be stated or for leave to appeal shall be treated as the institution of an appeal; and

(*b*) where a decision on appeal is subject to a further appeal, the appeal is not finally decided until the expiration of the ordinary time within which a further appeal may be instituted or, where a further appeal is duly instituted, until the further appeal is finally decided or abandoned.

(5) *Scotland.*

[Video Recordings Act 1984, s 21.]

8–30408 22. Other interpretation. (1) In this Act—

"business", except in section 3(4), includes any activity carried on by a club; and

"premises" includes any vehicle, vessel or stall.

(2) For the purposes of this Act, a video recording contains a video work if it contains information by the use of which the whole or a part of the work may be produced; but where a video work includes any extract from another video work, that extract is not to be regarded for the purposes of this subsection as a part of that other work.

(3) Where any alteration is made to a video work in respect of which a classification certificate has been issued, the classification certificate is not to be treated for the purposes of this Act as issued in respect of the altered work.

In this subsection, "alteration" includes addition.

[Video Recordings Act 1984, s 22.]

Video Recording (Labelling) Regulations 1985[1]

(SI 1985/911 as amended by SI 1995/2550 and SI 1998/852)

8–30650 **1.** *Citation and commencement.*

1. Made by the Secretary of State in exercise of the powers then conferred on him under s 8 of the Video Recording Act 1984.

8–30651 **2.** (1) In these Regulations—

"the Act" means the Video Recordings Act 1984;

"disc" and "magnetic tape" mean, respectively, a disc or magnetic tape containing information by the use of which the whole or a part of a video work may be produced;

"double sided disc" means a disc containing on both faces the information by the use of which the whole or part of the video may be produced;

"spine" means in relation to a case or cover in which a video recording is kept the next largest face, or one of them, after the first largest pair of faces.

"unique title" means the title assigned to a video work under section 4(1)(*b*)(ia) of the Act.

(2) In these Regulations, "the appropriate explanatory statement" means—

(*a*) in relation to a classification certificate which contains a statement of a kind described in column (1) below, the explanatory statement set out opposite thereto in column (2)—

(1) *Statement contained in classification certificate*	(2) *Explanatory statement*
A1. A statement within section 7(2)(*a*) of the Act with advice as to the particular suitability of the video work for viewing by young children.	UNIVERSAL. Particularly suitable for young children.
1. A statement within section 7(2)(*a*) of the Act with advice as to the particular suitability of the video work for viewing by children.	UNIVERSAL. Particularly suitable for children.
2. A statement within section 7(2)(*a*) of the Act without the advice mentioned in [item A1 or] item 1 above or item 3 below.	UNIVERSAL. Suitable for all.
3. A statement within section 7(2)(*a*) of the Act with advice as to the desirability of parental guidance with regard to the viewing of the work by young children.	PARENTAL GUIDANCE. General viewing but some scenes may be unsuitable for young children.

(*b*) in relation to a classification certificate which contains a statement within section 7(2)(*b*) of the Act without the other statement within section 7(2)(*c*) of the Act, a statement in the following terms:—

"Suitable only for persons of .... years and over.
Not to be supplied to any person below that age.",

with the inclusion (in numbers) of the age specified in the certificate in the explanatory statement before the word "years";

(*c*) in relation to a classification certificate which contains the statements within section 7(2)(*c*) of the Act, a statement in the following terms:—

"RESTRICTED. To be supplied only in licensed sex shops to persons of not less than .... years.",

with the inclusion (in numbers) of the age specified in the certificate in the explanatory statement before the word "years".

(3) In these Regulations, "the appropriate symbol" means—

(*a*) in relation to a classification certificate which contains a statement of the kind described in item 1 of the Table in paragraph (2)(*a*) above, the letters "Uc";

(*b*) in relation to a classification certificate which contains a statement of the kind described in item 2 of the said Table, the letter "U";

(*c*) in relation to a classification certificate which contains a statement of the kind described in item 3 of the said Table, the letters "PG";

(*d*) in relation to a classification certificate which contains a statement within section 7(2)(*b*) of the Act without the other statement within section 7(2)(*c*) of the Act, the numbers representing the age specified in the certificate;

(*e*) in relation to a classification certificate which contains the statements within section 7(2)(*c*) of the Act, the word "Restricted" with the inclusion (in numbers) of the age specified in the certificate after the word "Restricted".

(4) In these Regulations, "case" does not include a case or other article from which a video recording need not be removed in order for the video work contained on the recording to be produced; but such a case or other article is, for the purpose of these Regulations, to be treated as if it were a spool.

(5) A reference in these Regulations to a face of a case or cover in which a video recording is kept and to a spine of such a case or cover is a reference to the outer face of such a case or cover and to the outer face of the spine, respectively.

(6) For the purposes of these Regulations—

(*a*) where a video recording contains more than one video work and all or some of those works are works in respect of which classification certificates which are equally restrictive have been issued, those video works shall be taken to be one video work comprising any one of them;

(*b*) where a video recording contains more than one video work in respect of which classification certificates which are not equally restrictive have been issued, the video recording shall be taken to contain only the most restrictively classified video work of those works.

(7)(*a*) For the purposes of paragraph (6) above—

(i) a classification certificate is equally restrictive as another such certificate if either they both contain the same statement within section 7(2) of the Act or one contains a statement within paragraph (*a*) of that sub-section with which is included advice as to the particular suitability of the work for viewing by children and the other contains such a statement with which is included no advice falling within the said paragraph (*a*);

(ii) "the most restrictively classified video work" means the work in respect of which the classification certificate issued in respect of it contains the most restrictive statement.

(*b*) For the purposes of this paragraph—

(i) the statements within paragraphs (*a*), (*b*) and (*c*) of section 7(2) of the Act are to be regarded as being progressively more restrictive so that the statement within the said paragraph (*a*) is the least restrictive and the statement within the said paragraph (*c*) that no video recording containing the video work in respect of which the certificate was issued is to be supplied other than in a licensed sex shop is the most restrictive;

(ii) a statement within paragraph (*a*) of that subsection with which is included advice as to the desirability of parental guidance with regard to the viewing of the video work by young children is to be regarded as more restrictive than such a statement with which is included advice as to the particular suitability of the video work for viewing by children or with which is included no advice falling within the said paragraph (*a*);

(iii) a statement within paragraph (*b*) of that subsection is to be regarded as more restrictive than another statement within that paragraph if the age included in the first statement is greater than that included in the other statement.

8–30652 3. These Regulations apply in relation to video works in respect of which classification certificates have been issued.

8–30653 4. (1) Subject to the following provisions of these Regulations, the appropriate symbol and the unique title shall be shown—

(*a*) on one face of every disc;
(*b*) on every magnetic tape which is not kept on a spool;
(*c*) on one face of every spool on which a magnetic tape is kept or, in the case of a case which, by virtue of Regulation 2(4), is to be treated as a spool, on one of its largest faces.

(2) Subject as aforesaid, the appropriate symbol shall be shown on the spine or one spine, as appropriate, of every case or cover in which a video recording is kept unless one of the dimensions of the spine is less than 2 centimetres.

(3) Where the title of any video work or works contained on a video recording is visible on or through one spine of the case or cover in which the recording is kept, paragraph (2) above shall apply as if the requirement in that paragraph was for the appropriate symbol to be shown on that spine.

(4) Paragraph (2) above does not apply where the appropriate symbol is clearly visible through the spine or one spine, as appropriate, of the case or cover or, in a case falling within paragraph (3) above, through the spine of the case or cover on or through which the title of any video work or works contained on the video recording is visible and it is shown in the manner provided for in Regulations 7 and 9 as if it was required to be shown under these Regulations.

(5) Subject as aforesaid, the appropriate symbol shall be shown on one of the largest faces or the largest face, as appropriate, of the case or cover in which a video recording is kept and the appropriate explanatory statement and the appropriate symbol shall be shown together on another of the largest faces or another face other than the spine, as appropriate, of the case or cover unless—

(*a*) the appropriate symbol is clearly visible through one of the largest faces or the largest face, as appropriate, of the case or cover in which the disc, tape or spool is kept;

(*b*) the appropriate symbol and the appropriate explanatory statement are together clearly visible through another of the largest faces or another face other than the spine, as appropriate, of the case or cover; and

(*c*) the appropriate symbol and the appropriate explanatory statement referred to in sub-paragraph (*b*) above are shown together in the manner provided for in Regulation 6, the appropriate symbol referred to in sub-paragraph (*a*) above is shown in the manner provided for in Regulation 7 and the said symbol or symbol and statement is or are shown in the manner provided for in Regulation 9 as if it was or they were required to be shown under these Regulations.

8–30653A **4A.** (1) In relation to a double-sided disc, the requirement in regulation 4(1)(a) above to show the appropriate symbol on one face of every disc shall have effect as if these Regulations were amended in accordance with paragraphs (2) and (3) below.

(2) In regulation 2(3), after "means" add "the letters "UK", followed by".

(3) In regulation 7:

(*a*) omit paragraphs (a) to (d);

(*b*) in paragraph (e), for "5" substitute "2"; and

(*c*) in paragraph (f), before sub-paragraph (i) insert:

"(ai) the letters "U" and "K" before the letters, numbers or word and numbers, as the case may be, specified in sub-paragraphs (a) to (e) of regulation 2(3);".

8–30653B **4B.** (1) In relation to a disc which is not a double-sided disc, the requirement in regulation 4(1)(*a*) above to show the appropriate symbol on one face of every disc shall have effect as if regulation 7 were amended in accordance with paragraph (2) below.

(2) In regulation 7:

(*a*) in paragraph (*a*), omit the words "green coloured";

(*b*) in paragraph (*b*), omit the words "yellow coloured";

(*c*) in paragraph (*c*)(i), omit the words "red coloured";

(*d*) in paragraph (*c*)(ii),

(i) add after the word "red" the words "or black"; and

(ii) omit the words "white coloured"; and

(*e*) in paragraph (*d*) omit the words "blue coloured".

8–30654 **5.** Where under these Regulations *the appropriate symbol, the unique title or the appropriate explanatory statement, or any combination of them, is or are** required to be shown it or they shall be shown by means of a label affixed to or a marking on the disc, magnetic tape, spool, spine, case or cover in which a video recording is kept, as the case may be, which satisfies the requirements of Regulations 6, 7, 8 and 9 as appropriate.

8–30655 **6.** Where under these Regulations the appropriate explanatory statement and the appropriate symbol are required to be shown together on the same face of a case or cover in which a video recording is kept, the symbol shall be shown in the manner provided for in Regulation 7, the explanatory statement shall, if appropriate, be shown in the manner provided for in Regulation 8 and both the symbol as so shown and the explanatory statement as so shown, if appropriate shall be shown within a single rectangular shaped frame.

8–30656 **7.** Where under these Regulations the appropriate symbol is required to be shown, it shall be shown in the following manner:—

(*a*) in the case of a symbol referred to in Regulation 2(3)(*a*) and (*b*) the symbol shall be black or white, and set on a green coloured triangular shaped background;

(*b*) in the case of the symbol referred to in Regulation 2(3)(*c*) the symbol shall be black or white, and set on a yellow coloured triangular shaped background;

(*c*) in the case of the symbol referred to in Regulation 2(3)(*d*) the symbol shall be—

(i) where the age specified in the classification certificate is 18 years, black or white, and set on a red coloured circular shaped background;

(ii) where the age specified in the classification certificate is less than 18 years, red and set on a white coloured circular shaped background;

(*d*) in the case of the symbol referred to in Regulation 2(3)(*e*) the symbol shall be black or white, and set on a blue coloured rectangular shaped background;

(*e*) except in the case of the letter "c" in the symbol referred to in Regulation 2(3)(*a*) and the letters following "R" in the symbol referred to in Regulation 2(3)(*e*), the letters and numbers contained in a symbol shall be of a minimum height of 5 millimetres;

(*f*) the following letters shall be shown as capitals:

(i) the letter "U" in the symbols referred to in Regulation 2(3)(*a*) and (*b*);

(ii) the letters "P" and "G" in the symbol referred to in Regulation 2(3)(*c*);

(iii) all the letters in the word "Restricted" in the symbol referred to in Regulation 2(3)(*e*).

8–30657 **8.** Where under these Regulations there is a requirement to show the appropriate explanatory statement described in items 1, 2 or 3 of the Table in Regulation 2(2)(*a*) or in Regulation 2(2)(*c*), it shall be shown so that—

(*a*) in relation to the statements described in items 1 and 2 of the said Table, all the letters in the word "Universal", (*b*) in relation to the statement described in item 3 of the said Table, all the letters in the words "Parental Guidance", and

(*c*) in relation to the statement described in Regulation 2(2)(*c*), all the letters in the word "Restricted",

are shown in capitals.

8–30658 **9.** (1) Where under these Regulations *the appropriate symbol, the unique title or the appropriate explanatory statement, or combination of them, is or are** required to be shown it or they shall be clearly legible and indelible and no part of it or them shall be hidden or obscured by any other written or pictorial matter or by any other matter.

(2) Where under these Regulations the appropriate symbol is or the appropriate explanatory statement and the appropriate symbol are required to be shown on a case or cover in which a video recording is kept or on the spine or one spine, as appropriate, of such a case or cover it or they shall be shown in such manner as it remains or they remain clearly visible where that case or cover is kept in a cover.

***This amendment only has effect with respect to a video recording if it contains a video work which has not been included in a video recording lawfully supplied or offered for supply in the United Kingdom before 1 November 1995 (SI 1995/2550, reg 3).**

THEFT

8–30659 This title contains the following statutes—

INTRODUCTION

8–30660 **Statutory definition of theft.** A person is guilty of theft if he dishonestly appropriates property belonging to another with the intention of permanently depriving the other of it (Theft Act 1968, s 1).

The words "dishonestly", "appropriates" and "property" and the phrases "belonging to another" and "with the intention of permanently depriving the other of it" are amplified and partially defined in ss 2 to 6.

Much of the case law that built up over many years in respect of the offences under the Larceny Acts has no bearing on the offences against the Theft Act 1968 but those decisions which it is submitted remain appropriate have been annotated to the text of the Act.

8–30669 **The doctrine of recent possession is as applicable to offences of theft as it was to offences of larceny.** Possession of stolen property recently after the date of the theft, if unexplained, is presumptive evidence that the possessor stole it or had received it well knowing that it had been previously stolen. Proof must be given that the property has actually been stolen. Where a person is found in possession of property recently stolen and there is no positive evidence of stealing, but the evidence is as consistent with theft as with receiving, he should be charged with both offences and the court will then determine whether he was the thief or the handler (*R v Seymour* [1954] 1 All ER 1006, 118 JP 311). For possession to be "recent", the time varies according to the nature of the article stolen. For articles that pass readily from hand to hand, the time must be short. Four months have been held to be recent for a debenture bond (*R v Livock* (1914) 10 Cr App Rep 264); but not six months for a horse (*R v Cooper* (1852) 3 Car & Kir 318), nor eight months for a bale of silk (*R v Marcus* (1923) 17 Cr App Rep 191). Any short time, ie twenty minutes after the theft will suffice (*R v Proctor* (1923) 17 Cr App Rep 124). Where the only evidence on a charge of handling stolen goods is that an accused person is in possession of property recently stolen, a court may infer guilty knowledge (*a*) if the accused offers no explanation to account for his possession, or (*b*) if the court is satisfied that the explanation he does offer is untrue. If, however, the explanation offered is one which leaves the court in doubt whether he believed the property was stolen the case has not been proved, and, therefore, the verdict should be not guilty (*R v Aves* [1950] 2 All ER 330, 114 JP 402; explaining *R v Schama, R v Abramovitch* (1914) 79 JP 184). See also *R v Garth* [1949] 1 All ER 773, 113 JP 222; *R v Norris* (1916) 86 LJKB 810; *R v Grinberg* (1917) 33 TLR 428; *R v Badash* (1917) 87 LJKB 732; *R v Sanders* (*No* 2) (1919) 14 Cr App Rep 11; *R v Currell* (1935) 25 Cr App Rep 116, CCA; *Mancini v DPP* [1942] AC 1, [1941] 3 All ER 272; *R v Smith* (1983) 148 JP 215. Therefore where the prisoner gives a reasonable explanation, it is incumbent on the prosecution to prove that such account is false unless there are other circumstances from which the jury may fairly infer the falsehood of the story (*R v Ritson* (1884) 48 JP 630; *R v Barnes* (1942) 86 Sol Jo 341), such as making different statements as to the manner in which he came by the property (*R v Harmer* (1848) 2 Cox CC 487). Although the alleged stolen property had not been seen by the owner for fifteen months before it was missed, where the prisoner admitted that it was in his possession immediately after the theft but alleged that he bought it some considerable time before at a sale, it was held that there was evidence of recent possession and the question was simply one of identity (*R v Evans* (1847) 2 Cox CC 270). On a charge of theft of Kruger gold sovereigns, evidence of similar sovereigns having been found in defendant's house is admissible (*R v Kurasch* [1937] 2 All ER 130).

8–30670 Admissibility of documentary evidence. In any proceedings for an offence of theft of goods in the course of transmission (whether by post or otherwise) or of handling stolen goods from such a theft, a statutory declaration is admissible as proof of the fact that the goods were dispatched or received or not so received as the case may be, or that they were in a particular state or condition when dispatched or received.

(Theft Act 1968, s 27, post.)

8–30671 Ownership. The word "owner" does not appear in the definition of theft but the decisions that have been made on the question of ownership can be regarded as appropriate in the consideration of the phrase "belonging to another". There can be no theft of things which have no owner at all, or perhaps more correctly where there is not such a possession as would support an action of trespass. Actual proof as to the ownership of goods may be dispensed with (*R v Fuschillo* [1940] 2 All ER 489). A prisoner may be indicted for stealing the property of some person unknown, if facts be proved from which the jury may fairly presume that the goods were stolen. Things of which the ownership has been abandoned are not capable of being stolen; where something is taken in the belief that it had been abandoned, the court must consider whether, according to the standards of reasonable and honest people, what was done was dishonest, and if it is so considered, whether the defendant himself must have realised that what he was doing was dishonest by those standards (*R v Small* [1988] RTR 32, 86 Cr App Rep 170, CA). Where the diseased carcases of pigs had been buried to prevent them being made use of, it was held that the ownership had not been abandoned (*R v Edwards and Stacey* (1877) 41 JP 212). If the evidence shows that the accused believed that they had been abandoned and belonged to nobody he is not guilty of theft (*R v White* (1912) 76 JP 384; *Ellerman's Wilson Line Ltd v Webster* [1952] 1 Lloyd's Rep 179). Running or standing water is not capable of being stolen, unlike water under control such as water in stand pipes (*Ferens v O'Brien* (1883) 11 QBD 21, 47 JP 472), as also gas (*R v Firth* (1869) LR 1 CCR 172, 33 JP 212; *R v White* (1853) Dears CC 203, 17 JP 391). At common law every co-owner is lawfully entitled to possession of the property and could not commit theft by taking it. Now he may be guilty of stealing from his co-owner (Theft Act 1968, s 5(1), post and see *R v Bonner* [1970] 2 All ER 97, 134 JP 429). A domestic servant left in charge of her master's property is included as she has the control of it (*R v Harding* (1929) 94 JP 55). Property stolen out of the possession of a bailee, pawnee, carrier or the like, may be described as the property of such bailee, etc, or of the actual owner. The property of a joint-stock company on winding up must not be described as belonging to the liquidator until he has taken actual possession of it (*R v Bell* (1877) 41 JP 455). A bailee has a special property in the article bailed even if the bailor had no intention of charging him with its loss; if the bailor fraudulently removes the goods from the possession of the bailee he may be charged with theft (*Rose v Matt* [1951] 1 KB 810, [1951] 1 All ER 361, 115 JP 122).

A person who obtains a mortgage advance by deception does not commit the offence of dishonestly obtaining property belonging to another contrary to s 15 of the Theft Act 1968. The original sum in the lender's bank account constitutes a chose in action enforceable by the lending institution against its own bank. Where the advance by way of mortgage is paid either by way of electronic transfer or by cheque to the borrower's or his solicitor's account, the lender's chose in action vis à vis its bank is extinguished pro tanto and a new chose in action is created owned by the borrower or his solicitor. Accordingly the defendant has not obtained the lender's chose in action, rather a new chose has been created which did not exist before. Similarly where a drawer writes a cheque in favour of the defendant a chose is thereby created in his favour. Prior to its drawing, the cheque did not constitute a chose in favour of the drawer and the defendant does not obtain a chose or property which belongs to another. Therefore whilst a third party might steal the chose belonging to the defendant, he did not obtain a chose belonging to the drawer (*R v Preddy* [1996] AC 815, [1996] 3 All ER 481, [1996] 2 Cr App Rep 524, HL)[1]. In such circumstances a dishonest defendant will commit an offence of obtaining a money transfer by deception contrary to s 15A of the Theft Act 1968 as inserted by the Theft (Amendment) Act 1996, s 1.

---

1. In *R v Clark (Brian James Hemmings)* [2001] EWCA Crim 884, [2002] 1 Cr App Rep 14, the Court of Appeal, though sympathetic with the argument, held it was inappropriate to hold, in view of the observations of Lord Goff in *R v Preddy* (supra), that a cheque form was a tangible thing and was, therefore, property capable of being obtained.

Theft Act 1968

(1968 c 60)

Definition of "theft"

8–30690 1. Basic definition of theft. (1) A person is guilty of theft[1] if he[2] dishonestly[3] appropriates[4] property belonging to another[5] with the intention of permanently depriving the other of it[6]; and "thief" and "steal" shall be construed accordingly.

(2) It is immaterial whether the appropriation is made with a view to gain, or is made for the thief's own benefit.

(3) The five following sections of this Act shall have effect as regards the interpretation and operation of this section (and, except as otherwise provided by this Act, shall apply only for purposes of this section).

[Theft Act 1968, s 1.]

---

1. This subsection and s 15(1) are not mutually exclusive (*Lawrence v Metropolitan Police Comr* [1972] AC 626, [1971] 2 All ER 1253).

2. Appropriation can occur through the acts of innocent agents; see *R v Stringer and Banks* [1991] Crim LR 639.

3. Defined in s 2. See note 5 to s 2(2), post. Where the accused gives evidence of his state of mind at the time of the alleged offence, the justices should give that evidence such weight as they think right in the circumstances and apply their own standards when deciding whether the appropriation was dishonest (*R v McIvor* [1982] 1 All ER 491, 146 JP 193).

4. Defined in s 3. This subsection should not be read as if it contained the words "without the consent of the owner", and it is not necessary for the prosecution to prove that the taking was without the owner's consent; that is no longer an ingredient of the offence (*Lawrence v Metropolitan Police Comr*, supra). The issue of consent is dealt with in s 2(1) below.

5. These words "belonging to another" signify no more than that at the time of appropriation the property belonged to another (*Lawrence v Metropolitan Police Comr*, supra). See further s 5, post. If a bookmaker pays out money in the mistaken belief that a horse has won it is unnecessary for the prosecution to rely on s 5(4), post, because the property in the money does not pass to the payee (*R v Gilks* [1972] 3 All ER 280, 136 JP 777). By virtue of s 18, r 5 of (what is now) the Sale of Goods Act 1979 the property in petrol passes from the garage to the customer when it is poured into the tank of his car, and the customer does not appropriate property belonging to another if he drives away without paying (*Edwards v Ddin* [1976] 3 All ER 705, 121 JP 27); but see now the Theft Act 1978, s 3, post (making off without payment). Where a purchaser returns an unsatisfactory video recorder to the seller for repair, and afterwards issues a summons claiming the return of money paid for defective goods, the court must have recourse to the civil law as to the passing of property, rescission of contract etc in deciding ownership for the purpose of this section (*R v Walker* [1984] Crim LR 112).

In relation to goods in a supermarket, the general rule is that the property in them does not pass to a customer until he pays the price. This will normally be so even where goods have not only been bagged but also weighed according to the customer's requirements; see *Davies v Leighton* [1978] Crim LR 575, and commentary thereon; (1979) 68 Cr App Rep 4.

6. The essence of this offence is the dishonest appropriation of property. The "taking" required under previous law is not an element of the offence of theft. The words "dishonestly", "appropriates", "property" and the phrases "belonging to another" and "with the intention of permanently depriving the other of it" are amplified and partially defined in the following sections. See *R v Easom* [1971] 2 QB 315, [1971] 2 All ER 945; for a case in which a dishonest appropriation followed by replacement was held not to be theft but see also *R v Velumyl* [1989] Crim LR 299, CA, for an unauthorised temporary borrowing held to be dishonest.

The section does not distinguish between acts of essentially similar character which under previous law, would, according to circumstances, have been different offences. The offence of theft depends on the dishonest achievement of the accused and not on the means used to achieve it. If, when a person takes goods from a display stand in a supermarket, he intends to steal them, that is a dishonest appropriation; there can be a dishonest appropriation (and a theft) in a supermarket *before* the goods are taken past the point for payment; see *R v McPherson* [1973] Crim LR 191; distinguished in *Eddy v Niman* (1981) 73 Cr App Rep 237, where it was held that there had been no appropriation when goods were placed in a receptacle provided by the store. A cashier who received money from a customer without ringing it up on the till and intended to steal it was held guilty of a dishonest appropriation notwithstanding that she was arrested before the money could be removed from the till (*R v Monaghan* [1979] Crim LR 673).

8-30691 2. "Dishonestly". (1) A person's appropriation of property belonging to another is not to be regarded as dishonest—

- (*a*) if he appropriates the property in the belief[1] that he has in law the right to deprive[2] the other of it, on behalf of himself or of a third person; or
- (*b*) if he appropriates the property in the belief[3] that he would have the other's consent if the other knew of the appropriation and the circumstances of it; or
- (*c*) (except where the property came to him as trustee or personal representative)[4] if he appropriates the property in the belief that the person to whom the property belongs cannot be discovered by taking reasonable steps.

(2) A person's appropriation of property belonging to another may be dishonest[5] notwithstanding that he is willing to pay for the property.

[Theft Act 1968, s 2.]

---

1. It is immaterial that there exists no basis in law for such belief; if the defendant believed he had a right, even if there were none, he would fall to be acquitted (*R v Turner (No 2)* [1971] 2 All ER 441, 135 JP 419).

2. Where such a defendant uses a knife in order to "recover" money owed to him, this will not be theft (nor robbery under s 9, post) even if he knew it was wrong to use the knife (*R v Robinson* [1977] Crim LR 173).

3. A defendant's "belief that he would have the other's consent . . ." must be an honest belief, and it must be an honest belief in a true consent, honestly obtained; see *A-G's Reference (No 2 of 1982)* [1984] QB 624, [1984] 2 All ER 216, 78 Cr App Rep 131).

4. This exception preserves the requirement that a trustee or personal representative is to obtain a direction of the court for the disposal of property coming to him in that capacity of which he believes that the owner cannot be traced.

5. See *R v Feely* [1973] QB 530, [1973] 1 All ER 341, 137 JP 157, and *Boggeln v Williams* [1978] 2 All ER 1061. "Dishonestly" in section 1 describes something in the mind of the accused and not his conduct; therefore, the test of dishonesty is subjective, but the standard of honesty to be applied is the standard of reasonable and honest people and not that of the accused (*R v Ghosh* [1982] QB 1053, [1982] 2 All ER 689, 75 Cr App Rep 154). The questions to be asked, based on *R v Feely* and *R v Ghosh* are (1) was what was done dishonest according to the ordinary standards of reasonable and honest people? And (2) must the defendant have realised that what he was doing was dishonest according to those standards? See however an article at [1985] Crim LR 341. An intention to repay or perform contractual obligations cannot

of itself amount to a defence to deception, but may be some evidence of honesty (*R v O'Connell* (1991) 94 Cr App Rep 39, [1991] Crim LR 771).

8–30692 3. "Appropriates". (1) Any assumption by a person of the rights of an owner amounts to an appropriation[1], and this includes, where he has come by the property (innocently or not) without stealing it, any later assumption of a right to it by keeping or dealing with it as owner[2].

(2) Where property or a right or interest in property is or purports to be transferred for value[3] to a person acting in good faith, no later assumption by him of rights which he believed himself to be acquiring[4] shall, by reason of any defect in the transferor's title[5], amount to theft of the property.
[Theft Act 1968, s 3.]

---

1. The prosecution do not need to establish that the appropriation was without the owner's consent; even if consent is shown this will not mean that there was no dishonesty if consent was given without full knowledge of the circumstances; *Lawrence v Metropolitan Police Comr* [1972] AC 626, [1971] 2 All ER 1253, HL, taxi driver taking excessive fare out of foreigner's wallet. When theft is alleged and that which is alleged to be stolen passes to the defendant with the consent of the owner, but that consent has been obtained by a false representation, an appropriation within the meaning of s 1(1) of the Theft Act 1968 has taken place (*R v Gomez* [1993] 1 All ER 1 [1993] Crim LR 304 HL—owner of electrical goods induced by fraudulent misrepresentation, namely that cheques presented in payment were as good as cash, to consent to electrical goods being removed from his shop—cheques were in fact stolen and were dishonoured on presentation—held that there had been a dishonest appropriation of the goods). Appropriation is an objective description of the act done irrespective of the mental state either of the owner or the accused (*R v Gallasso* (1992) 98 Cr App Rep 284). For the relevance of a donor's mental capacity where the defendant maintains that the appropriation was the result of a gift *inter vivos*, see *R v Kendrick and Hopkins* [1997] 2 Cr App Rep 252, CA and *R v Hinks* [2000] 4 All ER 833,[2000] 3 WLR 1590,[2001] 1 Cr App Rep 1, HL; in the latter case, the House of Lords held that the acquisition of an indefeasible title to property from a person who no longer retained any proprietary interest or any right to resume or recover any proprietary interest in the property was capable of amounting to appropriation of that property.

A director can be guilty of theft from his own company where there is an appropriation within the meaning of s 3, provided the appropriation is dishonest ie directed at the company: *R (on the application of A) v Crown Court at Snaresbrook* (2001) 165 JPN 495, DC (director used resources of the company to bribe the managers of another company to secure an early renewal of a supply agreement; such conduct may be found not to be the conduct of the company, especially where the director does not own all the shares and the scheme involves concealment from the board of the company).

The use of a cheque card to guarantee payment of a cheque delivered to a payee and drawn on an account with inadequate funds was held not to be an assumption of the rights of the bank and thus not an appropriation within s 3(1), because the use of the cheque card and delivery of the cheque did no more than give the payee a contractual right, as against the bank, to be paid a specified sum from the banks' funds on presentation of the guaranteed cheque (*R v Navvabi* [1986] 3 All ER 102, [1986] 1 WLR 1311, 150 JP 474, CA).

'Appropriate' should be distinguished from obtains by deception. Where the defendant presented for payment cheques drawn by another person upon the credit balance of the drawer's account in respect of building work for which the defendant had dishonestly overbilled, the defendant had appropriated the chose in action by diminishing the relevant bank balance. (*R v Kohn* (1979) 69 Cr App Rep 395 *R v Williams* [2001] 1 Cr App Rep 23, [2001] Crim LR 253, CA). This should be contrasted with the situation in *R v Preddy* [1996] AC 815, where it had been difficult to discover the relevant obtaining of property belonging to another where on the facts a new chose in action had come into existence on the presentation of the relevant cheques (*R v Williams* [2001] 1 Cr App Rep 23, [2001] Crim LR 253,CA).

In a criminal enterprise involving theft there need not necessarily be only one "appropriation"; in the case of burglary in a dwelling house before any property is removed from the house there might be a number of appropriations by several persons at different times during the same incident, see *R v Gregory* (1982) 77 Cr App Rep 41, [1982] Crim LR 229, CA.

If goods have once been stolen, even if stolen abroad, they cannot be stolen again by the same thief exercising the same or other rights of ownership over the property. Accordingly, if a person steals property abroad and brings it into England for dishonest gain, the theft is nevertheless, committed abroad and cannot be charged with theft in England (*R v Atakpu* [1993] 4 All ER 215, [1994] RTR 23). "Appropriate" connotes a physical act; thus, where a victim caused a payment to be made, in reliance on deceptive conduct by the defendant, there was no "appropriation" by the defendant; he had done no more than a remote act to trigger the payment: *R v Briggs* [2003] EWCA Crim 3662, [2004] Cr App R 34, [2004] Crim LR 495. Where money has been wrongly credited to the defendant's bank account in England and the defendant signs blank cheques and sends them to a person who lives in Scotland, appropriation takes place within the jurisdiction when the cheques are presented for payment in England (*R v Ngan* [1998] 1 Cr App Rep 331.).

2. This subsection and s 5(4), post, together make it clear that a person coming into possession of property innocently can be guilty of theft if he later keeps it or otherwise deals with it as owner. But the position may be different if after discovering that the property was stolen, the defendant has not come to any decision as to what to do with it, and has not kept it for a long time or attempted to dispose of it; see *Broom v Crowther* (1984) 148 JP 592. The lacuna in the previous law which required the intention to deprive the owner to exist at the time of taking, is no longer present. An appropriation takes place where a bag is snatched and then immediately dropped, allowing the owner to recover it (*Corcoran v Anderton* (1980) 71 Cr App Rep 104, [1980] Crim LR 385). Where however there was no dishonesty at the time of acquisition and fitting of a gas cooker, there was a sale, and property passed; it was not possible to have a subsequent dishonest appropriation within s 3 (*R v Stuart* (1982) 147 JP 221). Drawing and issuing cheques on a company's account by a director who used the proceeds for his own purposes constitutes an appropriation; the fact that the cheques were honoured in contradiction of the terms of a mandate to the bank did not prevent the debt arising (*R v Wille* (1987) 86 Cr App Rep 296, CA). No offence was committed by a dealer who agreed to sell a medal and to keep it for the purchaser until later in the day and who then accepted the purchaser's cheque although meanwhile he has learnt that the medal was stolen (*R v Wheeler* (1990) 92 Cr App Rep 279).

3. This subsection will not apply to property transferred as a gift.

4. This refers to the moment when the person purchases for value (*R v Adams* [1993] Crim LR 72, CA).

5. For example, because it was stolen.

8–30693 4. "Property". (1) "Property" includes money and all other property[1], real or personal, including things in action[2] and other intangible property[3].

(2) A person cannot steal land, or things forming part of land and severed from it by him or by his directions, except in the following cases, that is to say—

(*a*) when he is a trustee or personal representative, or is authorised by power of attorney, or as liquidator of a company, or otherwise, to sell or dispose of land belonging to another, and he appropriates the land or anything forming part of it by dealing with it in breach of the confidence reposed in him; or
(*b*) when he is not in possession of the land and appropriates anything forming part of the land by severing it or causing it to be severed, or after it has been severed; or
(*c*) when, being in possession of the land under a tenancy, he appropriates the whole or part of any fixture or structure let to be used with the land.

For purposes of this subsection "land" does not include incorporeal hereditaments; "tenancy" means a tenancy for years or any less period and includes an agreement for such a tenancy, but a person who after the end of a tenancy remains in possession as statutory tenant or otherwise is to be treated as having possession under the tenancy, and "let" shall be construed accordingly.

(3) A person who picks[4] mushrooms growing wild on any land, or who picks[4] flowers, fruit or foliage from a plant growing wild on any land, does not (although not in possession of the land) steal what he picks, unless he does it for reward or for sale or other commercial purpose.

For purposes of this subsection "mushroom" includes any fungus, and "plant" includes any shrub or tree.

(4) Wild creatures, tamed or untamed, shall be regarded as property; but a person cannot steal a wild creature not tamed nor ordinarily kept in captivity, or the carcase of any such creature, unless either it has been reduced into possession[5] by or on behalf of another person and possession of it has not since been lost or abandoned, or another person is in course of reducing it into possession.
[Theft Act 1968, s 4.]

1. At common law a corpse and parts of a corpse are not property and therefore cannot be stolen. However they may become "property" within the meaning of s 4 if they have acquired different attributes by virtue of the application of skill, such as dissection and preservation techniques, for exhibition and teaching purposes: *R v Kelly* [1998] 3 All ER 741, [1999] 2 WLR 384, CA. In alcohol and driving cases there have been convictions for theft of urine and blood specimens: *R v Welsh* [1974] RTR 478; *R v Rothery* [1976] Crim LR 691. In *Oxford v Moss* (1978) 68 Cr App Rep 183, [1979] Crim LR 119; confidential information in an examination paper was held not to be intangible property for the purposes of this section.

2. Where a cheque is made out in favour of the payee it constitutes a chose in action belonging to the payee which he can enforce against the payer and therefore constitutes "property" of the payee within s 4(1) (*R v Preddy* [1996] AC 815, [1996] 3 All ER 481, [1996] 2 Cr App Rep 524, HL). In *R v Clark (Brian James Hemmings)* [2001] EWCA Crim 884, [2002] 1 Cr App Rep 141, the Court of Appeal, though sympathetic with the argument, held it was inappropriate to hold, in view of the observations of Lord Goff in *R v Preddy* (supra), that a cheque form was a tangible thing and was, therefore, capable of being obtained. Theft of a bank debt may constitute theft of a chose in action (*R v Kohn* (1979) 69 Cr App R 395, [1979] Crim LR 675, CA, applied in *R v Graham* [1997] Crim LR 358). See also the *A-G's Reference (No 1 of 1983)* [1985] QB 182, [1984] 3 All ER 369, *Chan Man-sin v A-G of Hong Kong* [1988] 1 All ER 1, [1988] 1 WLR 196, 86 Cr App Rep 303, PC and *R v Stalham* [1993] Crim LR 310, CA.

3. This subsection applies throughout this Act (s 34(1), post). However, electricity cannot be described as property; s 13, post, deals with the offence of dishonestly using electricity; see *Low v Blease* (1975) 119 Sol Jo 695. As to "intangible property" including patents, applications for patents, copyright, see commentary at [1983] Crim LR 332 on *R v Storrow and Poole*. Proof that only some of the property specified was stolen is enough for a conviction (*Machent v Quinn* [1970] 2 All ER 255, 134 JP 501); nor is it necessary to prove the precise sum of money involved (*Levene v Pearcey* [1976] Crim LR 63—taxi driver dishonestly taking longer route). It does not matter that theft of only part of the goods is charged and theft of the whole is proved (*Pilgram v Rice-Smith* [1977] 2 All ER 658, 141 JP 427).

4. The expression "picks" would probably not include a complete uprooting of the plant.

5. The ruling that there is no property in a swarm of bees until hived (*Kearry v Pattinson* [1939] 1 KB 471, [1939] 1 All ER 65) can be construed in the context of this section as meaning that until hived the swarm is not reduced into possession.

8–30694 **5. "Belonging to another[1]".** (1) Property[2] shall be regarded as belonging to any person having possession or control of it[3], or having in it any proprietary right or interest[4] (not being an equitable interest arising only from an agreement to transfer or grant an interest)[5].

(2) Where property is subject to a trust, the persons to whom it belongs shall be regarded as including any person having a right to enforce the trust, and an intention to defeat the trust shall be regarded accordingly as an intention to deprive of the property any person having that right.

(3) Where a person receives property[6] from or on account of another[7], and is under an obligation[8] to the other to retain and deal with that property or its proceeds in a particular way[9], the property or proceeds shall be regarded (as against him) as belonging to the other[10].

(4) Where a person gets property by another's mistake, and is under an obligation[11] to make restoration (in whole or in part) of the property or its proceeds or of the value thereof, then to the extent of that obligation the property or proceeds shall be regarded (as against him) as belonging to the person entitled to restoration, and an intention not to make restoration shall be regarded accordingly as an intention to deprive that person of the property or proceeds[12].

(5) Property of a corporation sole[13] shall be regarded as belonging to the corporation notwithstanding a vacancy in the corporation.
[Theft Act 1968, s 5.]

1. See headnote to this title, ante, "Ownership".

2. See s 4, ante.

3. Such as a domestic servant left in charge of her master's property (*R v Harding* (1929) 94 JP 55). The words "possession or control" are not to be qualified in any way; it is sufficient if it is found that the person from whom the

property was taken (or "appropriated") was at the time in fact in possession or control (*R v Turner (No 2)* [1971] 2 All ER 441, 135 JP 419). A person can be in possession or control of property without knowing of its existence (*R v Woodman* [1974] QB 754, [1974] 2 All ER 955, 138 JP 567). The lack of a coroner's inquisition determining the status and ownership of coins found does not prevent a conviction of theft of the coins as treasure trove if the jury determines that they were treasure trove (*R v Hancock* [1990] 2 QB 242, [1990] 3 All ER 183, 90 Cr App Rep 422, CA). Personal representatives appointed under a will do not have an interest in property under the will so as to enable a charge of theft of their property to be brought where it is said that the testator was induced to execute a new will by unlawful means (*R v Tillings and Tillings* [1985] Crim LR 393). It is possible in law for the directors and shareholders of a company to steal from their own company (*R v Philippou* (1989) 89 Cr App Rep 290, CA).

4. The phrase "proprietory right or interest" was considered in *Re A-G's Reference (No 1 of 1985)* [1986] QB 491, [1986] 2 All ER 219. Where a bank mistakenly credits an account in another bank, and the defendant arranges for banker's drafts to be drawn in favour of himself, the bank retains rights by reason of the mistake, being an equitable proprietary interest, and on that basis the defendant is under a duty to make restoration of the instruments (*R v Shadrokh-Cigari* [1988] Crim LR 465).

5. This subsection applies throughout this Act (s 34(1), post).

6. Section 5(3) covers property received from another under an obligation short of actual trusteeship. Accordingly, provided that the obligation was one which clearly required the recipient to retain and deal with that property or its proceeds in a particular way, there is no good reason to introduce words of limitation in relation to the interest of the transferor, save that at the time of the handing over of the property he had lawful possession of it in circumstances which gave him a legal right vis-à-vis the recipient to require that it be retained or dealt with in a particular way for his benefit (*R v Arnold* [1997] 4 All ER 1, CA).

7. Eg, a person acting as treasurer of a Christmas or holiday fund. An employee does not receive moneys *on account of* his employer when they are paid to him by customers for goods he has secretly obtained from someone other than his employer and sold to them, notwithstanding that the employee has contracted with the employer to sell only goods supplied by the employer (*Re A-G's Reference* (No 1 of 1985) [1986] QB 491, [1986] 2 All ER 219).

8. Where money was collected for a charity, the defendant is under an obligation in the nature of a trust to the sponsors. Accordingly, he is under an obligation to retain, if not the actual notes and coins, at least their proceeds such as where he has credited the money to a bank account. Whether the defendant is a trustee is to be judged on an objective basis; it is not essential that he realised he was a trustee (*R v Wain* [1995] 2 Cr App Rep 660, CA). Where money is given by donors to a charity collector, a trust is imposed and the money belongs to the beneficiaries of that trust (ie the charity) and property in the money passes from the donors to the charity when it is put into the tin; accordingly any subsequent misappropriation of the money by the collector is theft from the charity, not from the donors, and the charge should be so drafted (*R v Dyke and Munro* [2001] EWCA 2184, [2002] 1 Cr App Rep 404, [2002] Crim LR 153). The obligation is a legal, not a moral or social, obligation; see *DPP v Huskinson* (1988) 152 JP 582, [1988] Crim LR 620, and commentary thereto. Money received by a timeshare company from purchasers on implied terms that the money would be paid to a trust company which would act as a stakeholder to protect the purchasers, belonged to the purchasers when it was misapplied by the timeshare company. What was done was in breach of the obligation to deal with the money in a particular way so that s 5(3) applied. Although monies paid into the time share company's bank account might be replaced by a chose in action, s 5(3) deemed the money to belong to the purchasers. This situation is distinguishable from *R v Preddy* [1996] AC 815, HL where the money had been applied to the intended use, namely the purchase of property (*R v Klineberg* [1999] 1 Cr App Rep 427, CA).

9. These words were considered in *R v Hall* [1973] 1 QB 126, [1972] 2 All ER 1009, 136 JP 593, *R v Hayes* (1976) 64 Cr App Rep 82 and *R v Wills* (1990) 92 Cr App Rep 297.

10. And he will be guilty of theft if he misapplies it or the proceeds thereof. This will be so, even if the property had been acquired by the other (the bailor) illegally, if the defendant (as bailee) acts dishonestly (*R v Meech* [1974] QB 549, [1973] 3 All ER 939, 138 JP 6).

11. The obligation must be a legal one; a social or moral obligation is not sufficient (*R v Gilks* [1972] 3 All ER 280 at 283).

12. See note 2 to s 3, supra. This subsection was considered in detail in the *A-G's Reference (No 1 of 1983)* [1985] QB 182, [1984] 3 All ER 369, CA, where an opinion was expressed that a person who receives overpayment of a debt due to him by way of a credit to his bank account through the "direct debit" system and who knowing of that overpayment intentionally fails to repay the amount of the overpayment may be guilty of theft of the sum credited. When considering a financial consultant's treatment of money invested it has been said that the section applied if the defendant and the investor clearly understood that the investment or its proceeds was to be kept separate from the defendant's money or that of his business (*R v McHugh* (1993) 97 Cr App R 335).

13. Eg, the Rector of a parish who holds parish property in that capacity.

8–30695 6. "With the intention of permanently depriving the other of it". (1) A person appropriating[1] property[2] belonging to another without meaning the other permanently to lose the thing itself is[3] nevertheless to be regarded as having the intention of permanently depriving the other of it if his intention is to treat the thing as his own to dispose of regardless of the other's rights[4]; and a borrowing[5] or lending of it may amount to so treating it if, but only if, the borrowing or lending is for a period and in circumstances making it equivalent to an outright taking or disposal.

(2) Without prejudice to the generality of subsection (1) above, where a person, having possession or control (lawfully or not) of property belonging to another, parts with the property under a condition as to its return which he may not be able to perform[6], this (if done for purposes of his own and without the other's authority) amounts to treating the property as his own to dispose of regardless of the other's rights.

[Theft Act 1968, s 6.]

---

1. See s 3, ante.
2. See s 4, ante.
3. See s 5, ante.
4. Thus a company director was properly convicted where he stole company cheques to pay his debts because even though they were company liabilities they had been incurred for his personal purposes and were unauthorised (*R v Sobel* [1986] Crim LR 261). A council tenant who removed doors which were the council's responsibility and substituted them for doors for which he was responsible had treated the doors as his own regardless of the council's rights (*DPP v Lavender* [1994] Crim LR 297). Section 6 may apply to a person in possession or control of another's property who, dishonestly

and for his own purpose, deals with that property in such a manner that he knows he is risking its loss (*R v Fernandes* [1996] 1 Cr App Rep 175, CA (dishonest disposal of another's money on an obviously insecure investment)) A defendant who obtained used tickets for travel on London Underground whose usefulness had not been exhausted and sold them at a reduced price to persons intending to travel had an intention to treat the tickets as his own to dispose of regardless of the exclusive right of London Underground to sell tickets. The fact that the tickets might find their way back into the possession of London Underground Limited, albeit with their usefulness or "virtue" exhausted is not material (*R v Marshall* [1998] 2 Cr App Rep 282, 162 JP 488, [1999] Crim LR 317, CA).

5. Mere borrowing is insufficient to constitute the necessary guilty mind unless the intention is to return the thing in such a changed state that it has lost all its goodness or virtue; accordingly, feature films temporarily borrowed for copying in breach of copyright were held not to have been stolen since they had not diminished in value; see *R v Lloyd* [1985] QB 829, [1985] 2 All ER 661, CA.

6. Eg, by pawning it.

Theft, robbery, burglary, etc

8–30696 **7. Theft.** A person guilty of theft[1] shall on conviction on indictment be liable to imprisonment for a term not exceeding seven years[2].
[Theft Act 1968, s 7, as amended by the Criminal Justice Act 1991, s 26.]

1. As defined in s 1, ante.

A person charged on indictment with theft of a conveyance (as defined in s 12(7)(*a*), post) may be convicted instead of an offence under s 12(1), post (s 12(4)).

2. Triable either way; see Magistrates' Courts Act 1980, s 17 and Sch 1, also ss 17A–21 (procedure) and s 32 (penalty) in PART I: MAGISTRATES' COURTS, PROCEDURE, ante. In respect of offences of stealing or attempting to steal a motor vehicle, see note to s 12(2) post, for the powers and duties of a Court as to endorsements and disqualifications.

A person who has in his possession any firearm or imitation firearm at the time of committing or at the time of his apprehension for this offence (or aiding and abetting or attempting to commit this offence) is subject to the provisions of the Firearms Act 1968, s 17(2), ante.

8–30697 **8. Robbery.** (1) A person is guilty of robbery if he steals[1], and immediately before or at the time of doing so[2], and in order to do so, he uses force[3] on any person or puts or seeks to put any person[4] in fear of being then and there[5] subjected to force[6].

(2) A person guilty of robbery, or of an assault with intent to rob, shall on conviction on indictment be liable to imprisonment for life[7].
[Theft Act 1968, s 8.]

1. Where the "robbery" was an attempt to recover money owed, see *R v Robinson* [1977] Crim LR 173; an appropriate charge could be under s 21, blackmail, post.

2. It should be noted that force used after the theft is no longer within the offence of robbery. However, it should be noted that appropriation is a continuing act and accordingly a defendant who appropriated goods from the shelf of a shop and used violence on the shopkeeper when he approached, was guilty of robbery (*R v Hale* (1978) 68 Cr App Rep 415, CA, *R v Lockley* [1995] Crim LR 656).

3. It is not an acceptable proposition to seek to show that if one robber does violence, his confederates could not be held responsible for the consequences of that violence unless it was proved that they had agreed in advance to the use of that degree of violence to further their design (*R v Penfold* (1979) 71 Cr App Rep 4).

4. The person on whom the force is used or who is threatened need not be the person from whom the property is stolen.

5. Ie immediately.

6. The assault is nothing more than an attempt to commit a robbery. It is not necessary to prove more than that the accused intended to rob the prosecutor and did some act in his presence with reference to him for that purpose.

7. A claim of right made in good faith was held to be defence to a charge of robbery under previous legislation (*R v Skivington* [1968] 1 QB 166, [1967] 1 All ER 483, 131 JP 265).

8–30698 **9. Burglary.** (1) A person is guilty of burglary[1] if—

(*a*) he enters[2] any building[3] or part of a building[4] as a trespasser[5] and with intent[6] to commit any such offence as is mentioned in subsection (2) below; or

(*b*) having entered[2] any building[3] or part of a building[4] as a trespasser[5] he steals or attempts to steal anything in the building or that part of it or inflicts or attempts to inflict on any person therein any grievous bodily harm[7].

(2) The offences referred to in subsection (1)(*a*) above are offences of stealing anything in the building or part of a building in question, of inflicting on any person therein any grievous bodily harm or raping any person★ therein, and of doing unlawful damage to the building or anything therein.

(3) A person guilty of burglary shall on conviction on indictment be liable to imprisonment for a term not exceeding—

(*a*) where the offence was committed in respect of a building or part of a building which is a dwelling, fourteen years[8];

(*b*) in any other case, ten years[8].

(4) References in subsections (1) and (2) above to a building, and the reference in subsection (3) above to a building which is a dwelling, shall apply also to an inhabited vehicle or vessel, and shall apply to any such vehicle or vessel at times when the person having a habitation in it is not there as well as at times when he is.

[Theft Act 1968, s 9, as amended by the Criminal Justice Act 1991, s 26 and the Criminal Justice and Public Order Act 1994, Sch 10.]

***Words repealed by the Sexual Offences Act 2003, Sch 6, from a date to be appointed.**

1. The offence of burglary makes no distinction between offences committed during the night or in the daytime or between different types of buildings attacked. No element of breaking is required, instead it must be proved that entry was made as a trespasser.

2. The least degree of entry, with the hand or any part of the person is sufficient (*R v Davis* (1823) Russ & Ry 499) and does not require that the whole of the defendant's body be within the building (*R v Brown* [1985] Crim LR 212, CA). It would seem that the entry need not be effective (see *R v Brown* ante, and *R v Ryan* (1995) 160 JP 610, [1996] Crim LR 320, CA).

3. "Building" includes an inhabited vehicle or vessel (s 9(3), infra).

4. A person lawfully within one part of a building who enters another part as a trespasser is within the section; *R v Walkington* [1979] 2 All ER 716, 143 JP 542 (behind unattended counter in a shop).

5. In civil law an unauthorised, intentional, reckless or negligent entry into a building in another's possession is a trespass even though the entry is made, eg, in the mistaken impression that it is a different building. However, entry as a result of such a mistake will not amount to a trespass such as is contemplated by s 9 to form the basis of an offence of burglary. In criminal law "mens rea" is a necessary ingredient of trespass and therefore a knowledge of the fact of being a trespasser, or, at the very least, recklessness as to whether or not entering the premises of another is without that other's consent, is essential. The doctrine of "trespass ab initio" which in civil law renders an originally lawful entry into a trespass as a result of subsequent hostile action, has no place in consideration of the offence of burglary. The accused must be a trespasser at the actual time of entry. See *R v Collins* [1973] QB 100, [1972] 2 All ER 1105, 136 JP 605; and *R v John Jones* [1976] 3 All ER 54, 140 JP 515 (entry in excess of permission).

6. It is not necessary that the original intention should have been completed: it is enough that the intention existed at the time of entry. In *R v Walkington* [1979] 2 All ER 716, 143 JP 542, the fact that a till in a shop was empty did not destroy the defendant's intention to steal. In *Re A-G's Reference (Nos 1 and 2 of 1979)* [1980] QB 180, 143 JP 708,CA, it was held that the fact that the intention to steal was conditional on finding money in the house which had been unlawfully entered did not entitle a person to be acquitted of a charge under s 9(1)(*a*). Similar considerations apply where the charge relates to attempted burglary.

7. Under this paragraph the accused need not have had any specific intention at the time of entry if he commits such an offence having entered.

8. Triable either way unless burglary comprising the commission of, or an intention to commit, an offence which is triable only on indictment, or burglary in a dwelling if any person in the dwelling was subjected to violence or the threat of violence; see Magistrates' Courts Act 1980, s 17 and Sch 1; also ss 17A–21 (procedure) and s 32 (penalty) in PART I: MAGISTRATES' COURTS, PROCEDURE, ante. A person who has in his possession any firearm or imitation firearm at the time of committing or at the time of his apprehension for this offence (or aiding and abetting or attempting to commit this offence) is subject to the provisions of the Firearms Act 1968, s 17(2), ante.

8–30699 10. Aggravated burglary. (1) A person is guilty of aggravated burglary if he commits any burglary[1] and at the time has with him[2] any firearm or imitation firearm, any weapon of offence[3], or any explosive; and for this purpose—

(*a*) "firearm" includes an airgun or air pistol, and "imitation firearm" means anything which has the appearance of being a firearm, whether capable of being discharged or not[4]; and

(*b*) "weapon of offence" means any article made or adapted for use for causing injury to or incapacitating a person, or intended by the person having it with him for such use[5]; and

(*c*) "explosive" means any article manufactured for the purpose of producing a practical effect by explosion, or intended by the person having it with him for that purpose.

(2) A person guilty of aggravated burglary shall on conviction on indictment be liable to imprisonment for life.

[Theft Act 1968, s 10.]

---

1. As defined in s 9, ante.

2. The gravaman of the offence is entry into a building with a weapon. Therefore where there is only one weapon and that weapon is with an accomplice who remains on the outside, although he may be guilty of aiding and abetting his co-accused who effects entry to the building, neither is guilty of the offence in its aggravated form (*R v Klass* [1998] 1 Cr App Rep 453, 162 JP 105, CA).

3. The time at which the defendant must be proved to have had with him a weapon of offence to make him guilty of aggravated burglary, is, in the case of a charge under s 9(1)(*a*) the time when he entered, and in the case of a charge under s 9(1)(*b*) the time at which he actually stole etc; see *R v O'Leary* (1986) 82 Cr App Rep 341. It is not necessary to prove intention to use the weapon during the course of the burglary (*R v Stones* [1989] 1 WLR 156, CA).

4. Cf the definition in Firearms Act 1968, s 57(4), ante.

5. Cf the definition of "offensive weapon" in Prevention of Crimes Act 1953, s 1(4), ante.

8–30700 11. Removal of articles from places open to the public. (1) Subject to subsections (2) and (3) below, where the public have access to a building[1] in order to view the building or part of it, or a collection or part of a collection housed in it, any person who without lawful authority removes[2] from the building or its grounds the whole or part of any article displayed or kept for display to the public in the building or that part of it or in its grounds shall be guilty of an offence.

For this purpose "collection" includes a collection got together for a temporary purpose, but references in this section to a collection do not apply to a collection made or exhibited for the purpose of effecting sales or other commercial dealings.

(2) It is immaterial for purposes of subsection (1) above, that the public's access to a building is limited to a particular period or particular occasion; but where anything removed from a building or its grounds is there otherwise than as forming part of, or being on loan for exhibition with, a collection

intended for permanent exhibition to the public[3] the person removing it does not thereby commit an offence under this section[4] unless he removes it on a day when the public have access to the building as mentioned in subsection (1) above.

(3) A person does not commit an offence under this section if he believes that he has lawful authority for the removal of the thing in question or that he would have it if the person entitled to give it knew of the removal and the circumstances of it.

(4) A person guilty of an offence under this section shall, on conviction on indictment, be liable to imprisonment for a term not exceeding five years[5].

[Theft Act 1968, s 11.]

---

1. Access to the grounds of a building is not thought to be sufficient: thus a person removing an article from a collection displayed in the grounds of a building to which the public have no access although there is access to the collection, is not liable to prosecution under this section, but might very well be liable under s 1, ante.

2. The offence under this section is "removes" and not "appropriates". It is not necessary that there is an intent to permanently deprive the owner of it. The building may either be open or closed to the public at the time of removal; see sub-s (2), post.

3. This means intended to be permanently *available* for exhibition to the public, and would therefore include pictures only intermittently on display in an art gallery (*R v Durkin* [1973] QB 786, [1973] 2 All ER 872).

4. But might very well be liable under s 1, ante.

5. Triable either way; see Magistrates' Courts Act 1980, s 17 and Sch 1; also ss 17A–21 (procedure) and s 32 (penalty) in PART I: MAGISTRATES' COURTS, PROCEDURE, ante.

8–30701 **12. Taking motor vehicle or other conveyance without authority[1].** (1) Subject to subsections (5) and (6) below, a person shall be guilty of an offence[2] if, without having the consent[3] of the owner[4] or other lawful authority, he takes[5] any conveyance[5] for his own or another's use or, knowing that any conveyance[6] has been taken without such authority, drives[7] it or allows himself to be carried[8] in or on it.

(2) A person guilty of an offence under subsection (1) above shall be liable on summary conviction to a fine not exceeding **level 5** on the standard scale, to imprisonment for a term not exceeding **six months**, or to **both**[9].

(3) *Repealed.*

(4) If on the trial of an indictment[10] for theft the jury are not satisfied that the accused committed theft, but it is proved that the accused committed an offence under subsection (1) above, the jury may find him guilty of the offence under subsection (1) and if he is found guilty of it, he shall be liable as he would have been liable under subsection (2) above on summary conviction.

(4A) Proceedings for an offence under subsection (1) above (but not proceedings of a kind falling within subsection (4) above) in relation to a mechanically propelled vehicle—

(*a*) shall not be commenced after the end of the period of three years beginning with the day on which the offence was committed; but

(*b*) subject to that, may be commenced at any time within the period of six months beginning with the relevant day.

(4B) In subsection (4A)(*b*) above "the relevant day" means—

(*a*) in the case of a prosecution for an offence under subsection (1) above by a public prosecutor, the day on which sufficient evidence to justify the proceedings came to the knowledge of any person responsible for deciding whether to commence any such prosecution;

(*b*) in the case of a prosecution for an offence under subsection (1) above which is commenced by a person other than a public prosecutor after the discontinuance of a prosecution falling within paragraph (*a*) above which relates to the same facts, the day on which sufficient evidence to justify the proceedings came to the knowledge of the person who has decided to commence the prosecution or (if later) the discontinuance of the other prosecution;

(*c*) in the case of any other prosecution for an offence under subsection (1) above, the day on which sufficient evidence to justify the proceedings came to the knowledge of the person who has decided to commence the prosecution.

(4C) For the purposes of subsection (4A)(*b*) above a certificate of a person responsible for deciding whether to commence a prosecution of a kind mentioned in subsection (4B)(*a*) above as to the date on which such evidence as is mentioned in the certificate came to the knowledge of any person responsible for deciding whether to commence any such prosecution shall be conclusive evidence of that fact.

(5) Subsection (1) above shall not apply in relation to pedal cycles; but, subject to subsection (6) below, a person who, without having the consent of the owner[11] or other lawful authority, takes a pedal cycle for his own or another's use, or rides a pedal cycle knowing it to have been taken without such authority, shall on summary conviction be liable to a fine not exceeding **level 3** on the standard scale.

(6) A person does not commit an offence under this section by anything done in the belief that he has lawful authority to do it or that he would have the owner's consent if the owner knew of his doing it and the circumstances of it.

(7) For purposes of this section—

(*a*) "conveyance" means any conveyance[12] constructed or adapted for the carriage of a person or persons whether by land, water or air, except that it does not include a conveyance constructed or adapted for use only under the control of a person not carried in or on it, and "drive" shall be construed accordingly; and

(*b*) "owner", in relation to a conveyance which is the subject of a hiring agreement or hire-purchase agreement, means the person in possession of the conveyance under that agreement.

[Theft Act 1968, s 12, as amended by the Criminal Justice Act 1982, ss 38 and 46, the Police and Criminal Evidence Act 1984, Sch 7, the Criminal Justice Act 1988, s 37 and the Vehicles (Crimes) Act 2001, s 37.]

---

1. For the offence of interference with a motor vehicle or trailer, see the Criminal Attempts Act 1981, s 9, in PART I: MAGISTRATES' COURTS, PROCEDURE, ante.

2. A person who has in his possession any firearm or imitation firearm at the time of committing or at the time of his apprehension for this offence (or aiding and abetting or attempting to commit this offence) is subject to the provisions of the Firearms Act 1968, s 17(2), ante.

3. Consent is not vitiated by the fact that consent is obtained by a false pretence as to the destination and purpose of the journey (*R v Peart* [1970] 2 QB 672, [1970] 2 All ER 823, 134 JP 547). The consent of an owner to allow a vehicle to be hired was held not to have been vitiated where that consent was obtained by the fraudulent misrepresentations of the hirer as to his identity and the holding of a full driving licence (*Whittaker v Campbell* [1984] QB 318, [1983] 3 All ER 582, 77 Cr App Rep 267).

4. A person in possession of a conveyance under a hire purchase agreement is the owner for the purposes of this section. See also note 2 to s 5, ante.

5. Possession of a motor vehicle proved to have recently been "taken" would, no doubt, give rise to a rebuttable presumption (as in theft) of a "taking" for the purposes of this section. The evidence necessary to support a conviction where two or more persons are acting in concert was considered in *Ross v Rivenall* [1959] 2 All ER 376, 123 JP 352; and in *R v Stally* [1959] 3 All ER 814, 124 JP 65; in the latter case it was held that no offence was committed by a second defendant who was a passenger in a vehicle which had previously been taken by a first defendant, in his absence and without his knowledge; applied in *D (an infant) v Parsons* [1960] 2 All ER 493, 124 JP 375. However, the cases of a "second taking" need to be considered together with *DPP v Spriggs* [1993] Crim LR 622, [1994] RTR 1 when a defendant was convicted after taking a vehicle abandoned by an earlier taker. It should be noted that it is now not necessary that the conveyance taken should be "driven away". There still remains the need to show some movement, however small, of the conveyance, following the unauthorised taking of possession or control of it, before there can be a conviction of the completed offence rather than an attempt (*R v Bogacki* [1973] QB 832, [1973] 2 All ER 864, 137 JP 676). The offence does not require the propelling of the conveyance "in its own element"; thus a conviction was upheld where a defendant had loaded an inflatable rubber dinghy on a trailer which he then drove away (*R v Pearce* [1973] Crim LR 321). But in *R v Bow* [1977] RTR 6, [1977] Crim LR 176, where a vehicle which had caused an obstruction was moved 200 yards by allowing it to coast downhill, it was held that, as the vehicle was taken in a way which involved its use as a conveyance, the taker could not be heard to say that the taking was not for that use. An accidental movement of a vehicle is not a "taking", see *Blayney v Knight* [1975] Crim LR 237, nor did the moving of a motorcar round the corner as a practical joke where it was not established that anyone rode inside it (*R v Stokes* [1982] Crim LR 695).

An unauthorised deviation by an authorised driver was not an offence against previous corresponding legislation (*Mowe v Perraton* [1952] 1 All ER 423, 116 JP 739). A person having custody without authority to drive might have been guilty however (*R v Wibberley* [1966] 2 QB 214, [1965] 3 All ER 718, 130 JP 58). The circumstances of these two contrasting cases may be considered where a servant of the owner is charged. It will be no defence to prove that the conveyance was stolen rather than merely taken (*Tolley v Giddings* [1964] 2 QB 354, [1964] 1 All ER 201, 128 JP 182), nor is self-induced drunkenness a defence (*R v MacPherson* [1973] Crim LR 457).

6. Conveyance is defined at s 12(7)(*a*). See s 12(5) for the offence of taking pedal cycles without authority.

7. The word "drive" is to be construed according to the nature of the conveyance taken, and would include for example rowing a boat or piloting an aircraft.

8. This involves some movement of the conveyance (*R v Miller* [1976] Crim LR 147).

9. Disqualification may be ordered (Road Traffic Offenders Act 1988, Sch 2, PART VII: TRANSPORT, ante). The defendant must deliver his driving licence to the clerk of the court prior to the hearing or have it with him at the hearing (Road Traffic Offenders Act 1988, ss 7 and 27, ante).

10. There is no power given to a magistrates' court to convict of an offence under this section in substitution of a conviction for theft. In such a court there may be no conviction under this section except where the accused has been charged with an offence thereunder.

11. Where there are admissions that a bicycle has been taken without the owner's consent and does not belong to the defendant, the court is entitled to find that the bicycle had not been abandoned and had an owner without the need of a formal statement from the owner (*Sturrock v DPP* (1995) Times, 9 February).

12. A horse to which a halter or bridle has been attached is not a conveyance for the purposes of this section (*Neal v Gribble* (1978) 68 Cr App Rep 9, [1978] Crim LR 500).

8–30701A 12A. Aggravated vehicle-taking[1]. (1) Subject to subsection (3) below a person is guilty of aggravated taking of a vehicle if—

(*a*) he commits an offence under section 12(1) above (in this section referred to as a "basic offence") in relation to a mechanically propelled vehicle; and

(*b*) it is proved that, at any time after the vehicle was unlawfully taken (whether by him or another) and before it was recovered, the vehicle was driven, or injury or damage was caused, in one or more of the circumstances set out in paragraphs (*a*) to (*d*) of subsection (2) below.

(2) The circumstances referred to in subsection (1)(*b*) above are—

(*a*) that the vehicle was driven dangerously on a road or other public place;

(*b*) that, owing to the driving of the vehicle, an accident[2] occurred by which injury was caused to any person[3];

(*c*) that, owing to the driving of the vehicle, an accident occurred by which damage was caused to any property, other than the vehicle;

(*d*) that damage[4] was caused to the vehicle.

(3) A person is not guilty of an offence under this section if he proves that, as regards any such proven driving, injury or damage as is referred to in subsection (1)(*b*) above, either—

(*a*) the driving, accident or damage referred to in subsection (2) above occurred before he committed the basic offence; or

(*b*) he was neither in nor on nor in the immediate vicinity of the vehicle when that driving, accident or damage occurred.

(4) A person guilty of an offence[5] under this section shall be liable on conviction on indictment to imprisonment for a term not exceeding **two years** or, if it is proved that, in circumstances falling within subsection (2)(*b*) above, the accident caused the death of the person concerned, **fourteen years**.

(5) If a person who is charged with an offence under this section is found not guilty of that offence but it is proved that he committed a basic[6] offence, he may be convicted of the basic offence.

(6) If by virtue of subsection (5) above a person is convicted of a basic offence before the Crown Court, that court shall have the same powers and duties as a magistrates' court would have had on convicting him of such an offence.

(7) For the purposes of this section a vehicle is driven dangerously[7] if—

(*a*) it is driven in a way which falls far below what would be expected of a competent and careful driver; and

(*b*) it would be obvious to a competent and careful driver that driving the vehicle in that way would be dangerous.

(8) For the purposes of this section a vehicle is recovered when it is restored to its owner or to other lawful possession or custody; and in this subsection "owner" has the same meaning as in section 12 above.

[Theft Act 1968, s 12A, as inserted by the Aggravated Vehicle-Taking Act 1992, s 1.]

---

1. Nothing in s 12A applies to an offence under s 12(1) of the Theft Act 1968 which was committed before s 12A came into force on 1 April 1992, or to any driving, injury or damage which occurred before that date (Aggravated Vehicle-Taking Act 1992, s 1(3)).

2. The term "accident" is concerned with the consequences of what occurred and not the way in which those consequences came about; thus, a deliberate result is included: *R v Branchflower* [2004] EWCA Crim 2042, 1 Cr App R 10, [2005] RTR 13, [2005] Crim RT 388.

3. The words "owing to the driving of the vehicle, an accident occurred by which injury was caused to any person" do not import a requirement of fault in the driving (*R v Marsh* [1997] 1 Cr App Rep 67, 160 JP 721, [1997] RTR 195, CA).

4. Damage caused to a vehicle by a defendant in an attempt to escape from the vehicle is sufficient to establish the circumstances set out in paragraph (*d*) (*Dawes v DPP* [1994] RTR 209, [1995] 1 Cr App Rep 65).

5. This offence is triable either way (Magistrates' Courts Act 1980, s 17 and Sch 1, in PART I: MAGISTRATES' COURTS, PROCEDURE, ante. For procedure in relation to a triable either way offence, see Magistrates' Courts Act 1980, ss 17A–21, ante, and for penalty, see Magistrates' Courts Act 1980, s 32, ante. Nevertheless, if the only aggravating circumstances are damage, the total value of which is below the specified amount, ie £5,000, the offence is to be tried summarily (Magistrates' Courts Act 1980, s 22 and Sch 2, in PART I: MAGISTRATES' COURTS, PROCEDURE, ante.

When sentencing co-accused, differentiation should be made between a defendant who was the driver and a defendant passenger who had asked the driver to desist from the dangerous driving. (*R v Wiggins* (2000) 165 JP 210, [2001] RTR 37, CA). On conviction this offence carries obligatory disqualification; the court must order the offender to be disqualified for such period not less than 12 months as the court thinks fit, unless the court for special reasons thinks fit to order him to be disqualified for a shorter period. However, for the purposes of an offence of aggravated vehicle-taking the fact that the offender did not drive the vehicle in question at any particular time or at all shall not be regarded as a special reason; see the Road Traffic Offenders Act 1988, s 34(1)–(1A) and Sch 2, Pt II, in **PART VII**: title TRANSPORT, post. It is inappropriate to order the passenger convicted of an offence of aggravated vehicle taking to take an extended test (*R v Bradshaw* (1994) Times, 31 December).

6. This power is exercisable by the Magistrates' court and for the court should generally indicate its intention as to the basic offence before dismissing the aggravated offence (*R on the application of H) v Liverpool City Youth Court* [2001] Crim LR 897, DC).

7. Sub-section (7) reflects the meaning of "dangerous driving" provided by s 2A of the Road Traffic Act 1988 for the purposes of that Act; see PART VII: title TRANSPORT: ROAD TRAFFIC, post.

8–30702 13. Abstracting of electricity. A person who dishonestly[1] uses without due authority, or dishonestly causes to be wasted or diverted, any electricity shall on conviction on indictment be liable to imprisonment for a term not exceeding **five years**[2].

[Theft Act 1968, s 13.]

---

1. See s 2, ante. It is sufficient for the prosecution to establish electricity was used without the authority of the Electricity Board and with no intention to pay (*R v McCreadie and Tume* (1992) 96 Cr App Rep 143, 157 JP 541, [1992] Crim LR 872 CA, where an officially disconnected meter was unlawfully reconnected by a third party and electricity used by squatters).

2. Triable either way; see Magistrates' Courts Act 1980, s 17 and Sch 1; also ss 17A–21 (procedure) and s 32 (penalty) in PART I: MAGISTRATES' COURTS, PROCEDURE, ante.

8–30703 **14. Extension to thefts from mails outside England and Wales, and robbery, etc, on such a theft**[1]**.** (1) Where a person—

(*a*) steals or attempts to steal any mail bag[2] or postal packet in the course of transmission as such between places in different jurisdictions in the British postal area, or any of the contents of such a mail bag or postal packet; or

(*b*) in stealing or with intent to steal any such mail bag or postal packet or any of its contents, commits any robbery, attempted robbery or assault with intent to rob;

then, notwithstanding that he does so outside England and Wales, he shall be guilty of committing or attempting to commit the offence against this Act as if he had done so in England or Wales, and he shall accordingly be liable to be prosecuted, tried and punished in England and Wales without proof that the offence was committed there.

(2) In subsection (1) above the reference to different jurisdictions in the British postal area is to be construed as referring to the several jurisdictions of England and Wales, of Scotland, of Northern Ireland, of the Isle of Man and of the Channel Islands.

(3) *Repealed.*

[Theft Act 1968, s 14, as amended by SI 2003/2908.]

1. Section 14 secures that theft from mail in transmission between different parts of the British postal areas and related offences against such mail will be criminal and so may be prosecuted even though the offence took place outside England and Wales.

2. See s 14(3), infra.

Fraud and blackmail

8–30704 **15. Obtaining property by deception**[1]**.** (1)[2] A person who by any deception[3] dishonestly[4] obtains property[5] belonging to another[6], with the intention of permanently depriving the other of it[7], shall on conviction on indictment be liable to imprisonment for a term not exceeding **ten years**[8].

(2) For purposes of this section a person is to be treated as obtaining property if he obtains ownership, possession or control of it, and "obtain" includes obtaining for another[9] or enabling another to obtain or to retain.

(3) Section 6[10] above shall apply for purposes of this section, with the necessary adaptation of the reference to appropriating, as it applies for purposes of section 1[11].

(4) For purposes of this section "deception" means any deception (whether deliberate or reckless)[12] by words or conduct[13] as to fact or as to law, including a deception as to the present intentions of the person using the deception or any other person.

[Theft Act 1968, s 15.]

1. Even if the facts proved justify a conviction under this section, a conviction under s 1, ante, may still be sustained (*Lawrence v Metropolitan Police Comr* [1972] AC 626, [1971] 2 All ER 1253, HL; followed in *R v Hircock* (1978) 67 Cr App Rep 278, [1979] Crim LR 184).

2. These sections replace previous law concerned with obtaining something by false pretences. Offences under s 15 are wider than in previous legislation applying to "property" generally including land. It is only necessary for the accused to obtain possession or control of property, not necessarily ownership as hitherto.

3. See s 15(4), infra. The prosecution must prove that the deception acted on the mind of the person from whom the property was obtained (*R v Laverty* [1970] 3 All ER 432) unless there is a necessary inference that the deception was the cause of the obtaining (*Etim v Hatfield* [1975] Crim LR 234). A cheque is only dishonestly obtained from a company if a person whose state of mind stood for that of the company and who signed the cheque was actually deceived. It is not relevant that other employees who prepared the cheque were deceived (*R v Rozeik* [1996] 3 All ER 281, [1996] 1 WLR 159, [1996] Crim LR 271, CA). Defendants who sought by false representations to induce a person to have trees in her garden cut down, were held to have been properly convicted of attempting to obtain money by deception because the deception would have been an operative cause of obtaining the money, and not the work which they would have done if they had actually cut them down (*R v King* [1987] QB 547, [1987] 1 All ER 547). An excessively high quotation for work will not of itself amount to a false representation, but on the facts (where, for example there were circumstances of trust) it may be so (*R v Silverman* [1987] Crim LR 574). Where an exorbitant fare was paid by foreigners who had believed a defendant to be a taxi driver when entering his vehicle the offence was made out even though at the time money changed hands the victim knew the defendant to be lying (*R v Miller* [1993] RTR 6). A claim containing deliberate misrepresentations for housing benefit for which the claimant was qualified was a deception since the housing authority needed to know the truth before paying it (*R v Talbott* [1995] Crim LR 396, CA).

The basis of English courts' jurisdiction is that the physical acts of the accused, wherever they were done, had caused the intended consequence in England that property belonging to another had been obtained by deception, and *not* that the accused had done some physical act in England (*DPP v Stonehouse* [1977] 2 All ER 909); the *obtaining* must happen within the jurisdiction, thus where a computer in Kuwait had been programmed to debit a bank customers' accounts and credit accounts opened by the accused, the obtaining occurred when the bank transferred credit balance into English accounts by telex following the accused's letters requesting this (*R v Thompson* [1984] 3 All ER 565, [1984] 1 WLR 962, CA). The acquiring of ownership and control does not have to be tied to the physical location of the property in respect of a bank account. Therefore an English company obtained property at the place where it was registered where money was transferred into its account in a bank outside the jurisdiction (*R v Smith (Wallace Duncan)* [1996] 2 Cr App Rep 1, [1996] Crim LR 329, CA). See further the Criminal Justice Act 1993 ss 1–6 in PART I: MAGISTRATES' COURTS, PROCEDURE, ante.

4. It should be noted that the partial definition of "dishonestly" in s 2 ante applies only for the purposes of s 1 (Theft Act 1968, s 1(3)). In general terms, however, the test to be applied in deciding whether someone had acted "dishonestly" is set out in *R v Ghosh* [1982] QB 1053, [1982] 2 All ER 689, 146 JP 376; the court must decide whether according to the ordinary standards of reasonable and honest people what was done was dishonest. If it was dishonest by those standards, the court must consider whether the defendant himself must have realised that what he was doing was by those standards

dishonest. It is dishonest for a defendant to act in a way which he knows ordinary people consider to be dishonest, even if he asserts or genuinely believes that he is morally justified in acting as he did. This approach is likely to cover all occasions when a reference to s 2(1)(*a*) might otherwise (and but for s 1(3)) have been appropriate; see *R v Woolven*, [1983] Crim LR 623. The onus of proving that a false representation acted on the mind of the alleged victim falls on the prosecution and in the ordinary way should be proved by direct evidence (*R v Laverty* [1970] 3 All ER 432 but cf. *Etim v Hatfield* [1975] Crim LR 234).

5. Section 4(1), ante (definition of "property") applies; see s 34(1), post. As to obtaining services, or evading liability by deception, or making off without payment, see the Theft Act 1978, post. Offences of fraud on the public purse were commented on in *R v Stewart* [1987] 2 All ER 383, [1987] 1 WLR 559, CA (noted in PART III: SENTENCING, para **3–240** ante).

6. Section 5(1) ante defines "belonging to another"; see s 34(1), post.

7. See s 6, ante.

8. Triable either way; see Magistrates' Courts Act 1980, s 17 and Sch 1; also ss 17A–21 (procedure) and s 32 (penalty) in PART I: MAGISTRATES' COURTS, PROCEDURE, ante.

9. It is irrelevant that there is no dishonesty or deception or knowledge thereof by the other person (*R v Duru* [1973] 3 All ER 715).

10. Section 6 partially defines the expression "with the intention of permanently depriving the other of it".

11. Section 1 is the general definition of the offence of theft.

12. "Reckless" means more than being careless or negligent and involves an indifference to whether the statement is true or false (*R v Staines* (1974) 60 Cr App Rep 160).

13. This can include "positive acquiescence" so that a defendant who had applied for and been granted a grant towards providing a downstairs bathroom at his house for his elderly and infirm mother, was guilty of deception in failing to notify the council of her death being aware that the council were still of the mind that the mother would occupy his premises, *R v Rai* [2000] 1 Cr App Rep 242, 164 JP 121, [2000] Crim LR 192, CA.

8–30704A 15A. Obtaining a money transfer by deception. (1) A person is guilty of an offence if by any deception he dishonestly obtains a money transfer for himself or another.

(2) A money transfer occurs when—

(*a*) a debit[1] is made to one account,
(*b*) a credit[1] is made to another, and
(*c*) the credit results from the debit or the debit results from the credit[1].

(3) References to a credit and to a debit are to a credit of an amount of money and to a debit of an amount of money.

(4) It is immaterial (in particular)—

(*a*) whether the amount credited is the same as the amount debited;
(*b*) whether the money transfer is effected on presentment of a cheque or by another method;
(*c*) whether any delay occurs in the process by which the money transfer is effected;
(*d*) whether any intermediate credits or debits are made in the course of the money transfer;
(*e*) whether either of the accounts is overdrawn before or after the money transfer is effected.

(5) A person guilty of an offence under this section shall be liable on conviction on indictment to imprisonment for a term not exceeding **ten years**[2].

[Theft Act 1968, s 15A, as inserted by the Theft (Amendment) Act 1996, s 1.]

---

1. "Credited" in that context of s 15A, means credited unconditionally and s 15A, furthermore, requires that, in addition to a credit to a bank account, there has to be a debit made to an account, and that the credit results from the debit or vice versa; however, the court is entitled to take judicial notice of invariable banking and accountancy practice that a money transfer cannot be made without an account being debited with the amount of the transfer and the debit and credit must be causally connected, and it is unnecessary to specify what account was debited as the concomitant to the credit or whether the former was overdrawn or in credit provided there was a debiting of an account and that debiting was causally connected with the credit: *Re Holmes* [2004] EWHC 2020 (Admin), [2005] 1 Cr App R 16, [2005] Crim LR 229.

2. Triable either way; see Magistrates' Courts Act 1980, s 17 and Sch 1; also ss 17A–21 (procedure) and s 32 (penalty) in PART I: MAGISTRATES' COURTS, PROCEDURE, ante.

8–30704B 15B. Section 15A: supplementary. (1) The following provisions have effect for the interpretation of section 15A of this Act.

(2) "Deception" has the same meaning as in section 15 of this Act.

(3) "Account" means an account kept with—

(*a*) a bank; or
(*b*) a person carrying on a business which falls within subsection (4) below.

(4) A business falls within this subsection if—

(*a*) in the course of the business money received by way of deposit is lent to others; or
(*b*) any other activity of the business is financed, wholly or to any material extent, out of the capital of or the interest on money received by way of deposit;

and "deposit" here has the same meaning as in section 35 of the Banking Act 1987 (fraudulent inducement to make a deposit).

(5) For the purposes of subsection (4) above—

(*a*) all the activities which a person carries on by way of business shall be regarded as a single business carried on by him; and (*b*) "money" includes money expressed in a currency other than sterling or in the European currency unit (as defined in Council Regulation No. 3320/94/EC or any Community instrument replacing it).

[Theft Act 1968, s 15B, as inserted by the Theft (Amendment) Act 1996, s 1.]

8–30705 **16. Obtaining pecuniary advantage by deception**[1]. (1) A person who by any deception[2] dishonestly[3] obtains for himself or another any pecuniary advantage[4] shall on conviction on indictment be liable to imprisonment for a term not exceeding **five years**[5].

(2) The cases in which a pecuniary advantage within the meaning of this section is to be regarded as obtained for a person[6] are cases where—

(*a*) *Repealed*[7];

(*b*) he is allowed[8] to borrow by way of overdraft[9], or to take out any policy of insurance or annuity contract, or obtains an improvement of the terms on which he is allowed to do so; or

(*c*) he is given the opportunity to earn remuneration or greater remuneration in an office[10] or employment[11], or to win money by betting.

(3) For purposes of this section "deception" has the same meaning as in section 15 of this Act.

[Theft Act 1968, s 16, as amended by the Theft Act 1978, s 5.]

1. See s 16(3), infra.

2. Although there must be a causal connection between the deception used and the pecuniary advantage obtained, it is not necessary that the person deceived suffered any loss arising from the deception: see *R v Kovacs* [1974] 1 All ER 1236, 138 JP 425.

The drawer of a cheque represents to the payee (i) that he has an account with the bank, and (ii) that the cheque, as drawn, is a valid order for the payment of that amount (ie that it will be met on presentment). Where the drawer of a cheque uses a cheque card in compliance with the conditions endorsed on the card, he makes to the payee the representations mentioned above and further represents that he has the actual authority of the bank to create a contract with the payee on the bank's behalf that it will honour the cheque on presentment for payment (*Metropolitan Police Comr v Charles* [1977] AC 177, [1976] 3 All ER 112, 140 JP 531, HL). If the cheque given is post dated, the drawer impliedly represents that the state of facts existing at the date of delivery are such that in the ordinary course of events it will, on presentation for payment on or after the date specified in the cheque, be met (*R v Gilmartin* [1983] QB 953, [1983] 1 All ER 829, 147 JP 183, CA). The presentation of a credit card as a means of payment implies a representation on the part of the holder of the card that he has actual authority to make, on behalf of the bank or credit card company which issued the card, a contract with the payee to the effect that the bank or company will honour the voucher on presentation (*R v Lambie* [1982] AC 449, [1981] 2 All ER 776, 145 JP 364, HL).

Where no one can reasonably be expected to remember a particular transaction in detail, reliance on a dishonest representation may be established by proof of facts from which an irresistible inference of inducement can be drawn, see *R v Lambie*, supra.

3. See s 2, ante, and *R v Royle* [1971] 3 All ER 1359; *R v Nordeng* [1975] Crim LR 194.

4. Section 16(1) creates only one offence, which can be committed in the various ways specified in s 16(2): stating more than one such way (eg evasion *or* deferment) in the charge does not make it bad for duplicity (*Bale v Rosier* [1977] 2 All ER 160, 141 JP 292).

5. Triable either way; see Magistrates' Courts Act 1980, s 17 and Sch 1; also ss 17A–21 (procedure) and s 32 (penalty) in PART I: MAGISTRATES' COURTS, PROCEDURE, ante.

6. This refers not only to the person using the deception but also to the other person mentioned in sub-s (1) for whom the pecuniary advantage is obtained (*Richardson v Skells* [1976] Crim LR 448).

7. Section 16(2)(*a*) has been replaced by the Theft Act 1978, post, which makes separate provision for offences of obtaining services by deception, evasion of liability by deception, and making off without payment.

8. A person may be so "allowed" even though a bank imposed limits on the use of a cheque book and cheque card which were breached by the person: the circumstances of s 12, ante are so different that the use of "allow" there does not help in defining its use in s 16(2)(*b*) (*R v Waites* [1982] Crim LR 369, [1982] LS Gaz R 535; such offence can be tried in England even when the use of the cheque card took place abroad (*R v Bevan* (1986) 84 Cr App Rep 143, [1987] Crim LR 129).

9. A customer obtains the pecuniary advantage at the moment when the overdraft facility is granted to him, without need for proof that he drew on that facility (*R v Watkins* [1976] 1 All ER 578, 140 JP 197).

10. A tenancy is not an "office" or "employment" within s 16(2)(*c*) (*R v McNiff* [1986] Crim LR 57).

11. An independent contractor, who held himself out to be a self-employed accountant, and who was engaged to render services under a contract for services was held, for the purposes of s 16(2)(*c*), to have been "employed" by the person who engaged him (*R v Callender* [1992] 3 All ER 51, [1992] Crim LR 591).

8–30706 **17. False accounting.** (1) Where a person dishonestly[1] with a view to gain[2] for himself or another or with intent to cause loss[2] to another—

(*a*) destroys, defaces, conceals or falsifies any account or any record[3] or document made or required[4] for any accounting purpose; or

(*b*) in furnishing information for any purpose produces or makes use of any account, or any such record or document as aforesaid, which to his knowledge is or may be misleading, false or deceptive in a material particular[5]

he shall, on conviction on indictment, be liable to imprisonment for a term not exceeding **seven years**[6].

(2) For purposes of this section a person who makes or concurs in making in an account or other document an entry which is or may be misleading, false or deceptive in a material particular, or who omits or concurs in omitting a material particular from an account or other document, is to be treated as falsifying the account or document.

[Theft Act 1968, s 17.]

1. "Dishonestly" is to be interpreted in the terms set out in *R v Ghosh* [1982] QB 1053, [1982] 2 All ER 689, 75 Cr App Rep 154 (*R v Wood* [1999] Crim LR 564, CA). See notes to s 2, ante.

2. For definition of "gain" and "loss", see s 34(2)(*a*), post. The use of falsified bills of exchange with a view to securing a bank's forbearance from enforcing repayment of existing debts does not constitute falsification with a view to "gain" within the meaning of this section (*R v Golechha* [1989] 3 All ER 908, [1989] 1 WLR 1050, CA).

3. A "record" may include a taximeter (*R v Solomons* [1909] 2 KB 980, 73 JP 467); a turnstile meter (*Edwards v Toombs* [1983] Crim LR 43).

4. In *Re A-G's Reference (No 1 of 1980)* [1981] 1 All ER 366, [1981] 1 WLR 34; it was held, on the facts of that reference, that a personal loan proposal form was a document "required for any accounting purpose". See also *Osinuga v DPP* (1997) 162 JP 120, [1998] Crim LR 216. Failure to complete any documents when required can be an offence under this section (*R v Shama* [1990] 2 All ER 602, [1990] 1 WLR 661, CA). A claim form submitted in respect of a home insurance policy may be a document made or required for an accounting purpose in that the insurance company may use the form as a basis for keeping its accounting records but the court must receive some evidence that it is in fact used for this purpose and the court cannot draw its own conclusion from the nature and form of the claim form (*R v Sundhers* [1998] Crim LR 497, CA). See also *R v Manning* [1999] QB 980, [1998] 4 All ER 876, [1998] 2 Cr App Rep 461, CA (court entitled to conclude that insurance cover note an accounting document as it set out on the document what was owed by the client), and *Re Baxter* [2002] All ER (D) 218 (Jan), (2002) JPN 99 (a certificate, included in an application pack for an investment scheme, by which an insurance company purportedly stood behind the investment programme concerned could be regarded as a document made or required for an accounting purpose, but another document that was a general solicitation, any response to which would have resulted in the issue of accounting documents, could not be so regarded)..

5. Where an accused has used a false instrument or furnished false information with a view to obtaining money or other property, the prosecution does not have to prove, either in relation to this offence or in relation to an offence under s 3 of the Forgery and Counterfeiting Act 1981, that the accused had no legal entitlement to the money or property in question (*A-G's Reference (No 1 of 2001)* [2002] EWCA Crim 1768, [2002] 3 All ER 840, [2002] Crim LR 844). Although the document itself must be made or required for an accounting purpose, the material particular in question does not have to be one which is directly connected with the accounting purpose of the document (*R v Mallett* [1978] 3 All ER 10).

6. Triable either way; see Magistrates' Courts Act 1980, s 17 and Sch 1; also ss 17A–21 (procedure) and s 32 (penalty) in PART I: MAGISTRATES' COURTS, PROCEDURE, ante.

8–30707 **18. Liability of company officers for certain offences by company.** (1) Where an offence committed by a body corporate under section 15, 16 or 17 of this Act is proved to have been committed with the consent or connivance of any director, manager, secretary or other similar officer of the body corporate, or any person who was purporting to act in any such capacity, he as well as the body corporate shall be guilty of that offence, and shall be liable to be proceeded against and punished accordingly.

(2) Where the affairs of a body corporate are managed by its members, this section shall apply in relation to the acts and defaults of a member in connection with his functions of management as if he were a director of the body corporate.

[Theft Act 1968, s 18.]

8–30708 **19. False statements by company directors, etc.** (1) Where an officer of a body corporate or unincorporated association (or person purporting to act as such), with intent to deceive members or creditors of the body corporate or association about its affairs, publishes or concurs in publishing a written statement or account which to his knowledge is or may be misleading, false or deceptive in a material particular, he shall on conviction on indictment be liable to imprisonment for a term not exceeding **seven years**[1].

(2) For purposes of this section a person who has entered into a security for the benefit of a body corporate or association is to be treated as a creditor of it.

(3) Where the affairs of a body corporate or association are managed by its members, this section shall apply to any statement which a member publishes or concurs in publishing in connection with his functions of management as if he were an officer of the body corporate or association.

[Theft Act 1968, s 19.]

1. Triable either way; see Magistrates' Courts Act 1980, s 17 and Sch 1; also ss 17A–21 (procedure) and s 32 (penalty) in PART I: MAGISTRATES' COURTS, PROCEDURE, ante.

8–30709 **20. Suppression, etc, of documents.** (1) A person who dishonestly[1], with a view to gain[2] for himself or another or with intent to cause loss[2] to another, destroys, defaces or conceals any valuable security[3], any will or other testamentary document or any original document of or belonging to, or filed or deposited in, any court of justice or any government department shall on conviction on indictment be liable to imprisonment for a term not exceeding **seven years**[4].

(2) A person who dishonestly[1], with a view to gain[2] for himself or another or with intent to cause loss[2] to another, by any deception[3] procures[5] the execution[6] of a valuable security shall on conviction on indictment be liable to imprisonment for a term not exceeding **seven years**[4], and this subsection shall apply in relation to the making, acceptance[7], indorsement, alteration, cancellation or destruction in whole or in part of a valuable security, and in relation to the signing or sealing of any paper or other material in order that it may be made or converted into, or used or dealt with as, a valuable security, as if that were the execution[8] of a valuable security.

(3) For purposes of this section "deception" has the same meaning as in section 15 of this Act, and "valuable security"[9] means any document creating, transferring, surrendering or releasing any right to, in or over property, or authorising the payment of money or delivery of any property, or

evidencing the creation, transfer, surrender or release of any such right, or the payment of money or delivery of any property, or the satisfaction of any obligation.
[Theft Act 1968, s 20.]

1. "Dishonestly" is to be interpreted in the terms set out in *R v Ghosh* [1982] QB 1053, [1982] 2 All ER 689, 75 Cr App Rep 154 (*R v Wood* [1999] Crim LR 564, CA). See notes to s 2, ante.
2. The words "gain" and "loss" are defined in s 34(2)(*a*), post.
3. See s 20(3), infra.
4. Triable either way; see Magistrates' Courts Act 1980, s 17 and Sch 1; also ss 17A–21 (procedure) and s 32 (penalty).
5. "Procure" for this purpose means to cause or bring about (*R v Beck* [1985] 1 All ER 571, [1985] 1 WLR 22, 149 JP 260, CA).
6. The execution of a valuable security contemplates acts done to or in connection with the document, and not the giving effect to the document by carrying out the instructions which it might contain, such as the payment of money. Thus payment on a cheque or credit voucher is not such an execution (*R v Kassim* [1991] 3 All ER 713).
7. "Acceptance" is to be given its proper commercial meaning, derived from the Bills of Exchange Act 1882, s 17, of a written and signed signification by the drawee of his assent to the order of the drawer; accordingly, the mere handing over to and receipt of orders to a bank did not amount to an acceptance within s 20(2) (*R v Nanayakkara* [1987] 1 All ER 650, [1987] 1 WLR 265, 84 Cr App Rep 125, CA).
8. Where the final acceptance of a valuable security which was a traveller's cheque occurred in England, even though there had been an earlier acceptance abroad, that final acceptance constituted execution of the security within the jurisdiction (*R v Beck* [1985] 1 All ER 571, [1985] 1 WLR 22, 149 JP 260, CA). See also *R v Manning* [1999] QB 980, [1998] 4 All ER 876, [1998] 2 Cr App Rep 461 (actus reus of procuring of a valuable security by deception occurred in Greece where cheques were signed in Athens) not followed as to jurisdiction by *R v Smith (Wallace) (No 4)* [2004] EWCA Crim 631, [2004] Crim LR 951 and see the Criminal Justice Act 1993, Part I in PART I: MAGISTRATES' COURTS PROCEDURE, ante.
9. An irrevocable letter of credit is a valuable security within the meaning of this section (*R v Benstead and Taylor* [1982] Crim LR 456) as is a clearing house automated payment system ("CHAPS") order (*R v King* [1992] 1 QB 20, [1991] 3 All ER 705), but a telegraphic transfer of funds may be made without the execution of any document (*R v Manjdadria* [1993] Crim LR 73, CA).

8–30720 **21. Blackmail.** (1) A person is guilty of blackmail[1] if, with a view to gain[2] for himself or another or with intent to cause loss[2] to another, he makes[3] any unwarranted demand with menaces[4]; and for this purpose a demand with menaces is unwarranted unless the person making it does so in the belief—

(*a*) that he has reasonable grounds for making the demand; and
(*b*) that the use of the menaces is a proper means of reinforcing the demand.

(2) The nature of the act or omission demanded is immaterial, and it is also immaterial whether the menaces relate to action to be taken by the person making the demand.

(3) A person guilty of blackmail shall on conviction on indictment be liable to imprisonment for a term not exceeding **fourteen years**.
[Theft Act 1968, s 21.]

1. This is a new offence replacing the offences of demanding property with menaces, the essence of this offence is that the accused knows either that he has no right to make the demand or that the use of menaces to reinforce it is improper.
2. The words "gain" and "loss" are defined in s 34(2)(*a*), post.
3. A person makes a demand when he utters threatening words, and when the demand is by letter it is made when the letter is posted. If posted in England to an intended victim abroad the offence is triable in England (*Treacy v DPP* [1971] AC 537, [1971] 1 All ER 110; distinguished by the Court of Appeal in *R v Baxter* [1972] 2 QB 1 [1971] 2 All ER 359; where the offence of attempting to obtain property by deception was held to be committed in England although the letters by which the attempt was made were posted abroad).
4. The word "menace" is not limited to threats of violence but includes threats of any action detrimental to or unpleasant to the person addressed, even if the accused is entitled to carry it out (*Thorne v Motor Trade Association* [1937] AC 797, [1937] 3 All ER 157; *R v Tomlinson* [1895] 1 QB 706 and *R v Boyle and Merchant* [1914] 3 KB 339, 78 JP 390, approved). It seems to be immaterial whether money was wholly or only in part obtained (*R v Robertson* (1864) 28 JP 821). A threat to injure a man's property may be a menace within the section (*R v Boyle and Merchant*, supra). The language used may be only a request; it need not necessarily be a specified demand. A request imposing conditions may be evidence of a demand (*R v Studer* (1915) 85 LJKB 1017). A threat to report a betting defaulter to Tattersalls was not a menace within corresponding legislation (*Burden v Harris* [1937] 4 All ER 559). It is submitted on the authority of *R v Moran* [1952] 1 All ER 803, 116 JP 216 that there can be no such offence as attempted blackmail.

Words or conduct are menaces if they are such as are likely to operate on the mind of a person of ordinary courage and firmness so as to make him accede unwillingly to the demand. It is not necessary that the intended victim is himself alarmed (*R v Clear* [1968] 1 QB 670, [1968] 1 All ER 75, 132 JP 103). See also *R v Garwood* [1987] 1 All ER 1032, [1987] 1 WLR 319.

Offences relating to goods stolen, etc

8–30721 **22. Handling stolen goods.** (1)[1] A person handles stolen[2] goods if (otherwise than in the course of the stealing[3]) knowing or believing[4] them to be stolen goods[5] he dishonestly receives[6] the goods, or dishonestly undertakes or assists[7] in their retention[8], removal, disposal or realisation[9] by or for the benefit of another person[10], or if he arranges to do so[11].

(2) A person guilty of handling stolen[2] goods shall on conviction on indictment be liable to imprisonment for a term not exceeding **fourteen years**[12].
[Theft Act 1968, s 22.]

1. This section replaces the previous offence of receiving stolen property. It creates only one offence, namely, handling stolen goods, and it is not necessary for the information to state whether the alleged handling was by receiving, undertaking retention or removal, etc but in the ordinary way these particulars should be given (*Griffiths v Freeman* [1970] 1 All ER 1117, 134 JP 394). See also *R v Willis* [1972] 3 All ER 797, [1972] 1 WLR 1605; *R v Deakin* [1972] 3 All ER 803, [1972] 1 WLR 1618; and *R v Pitchley* (1972) 57 Cr App Rep 30. But where the form of handling is particularised in the charge the defendant cannot be convicted of another form of handling with which he has not been charged (*R v Nicklin* [1977] 2 All ER 444, 141 JP 391). In the absence of evidence showing a preconcerted arrangement between husband and wife the receipt by the wife does not amount to a dishonest receiving by the husband of goods stolen (*R v Pritchard* (1913) 109 LT 911).

2. Goods obtained by deception or blackmail are within this offence (s 24(4), post). Goods are not to be regarded as stolen after they have been restored to the person from whom they were stolen: see s 24(3), post and note thereto.

3. If a person handles goods he has stolen subsequent to the theft he *may* be guilty of both theft and handling, though normally theft and handling will be alternative charges; see *R v Dolan* [1976] Crim LR 145 and *R v Sainthouse* [1980] Crim LR 506. See also *R v Pitham and Hehl* [1977] Crim LR 285, where the defendants were convicted of handling, having been taken to a house and sold furniture by the thief who thereby appropriated furniture left in his care: their buying was nevertheless not "in the course of the stealing". Where there are several charges of robbery and burglary, there are problems with one compendious charge of handling as an alternative: see *R v Smythe* (1980) 72 Cr App Rep 8.

In the ordinary case where there is no evidence that the defendant was the thief, the prosecution is not required to prove affirmatively that the defendant was not the thief, because handling the goods "otherwise than in the course of the stealing" is not an essential ingredient of the offence. However, where the defendant is in possession of stolen goods so recently after they are stolen that the inevitable inference is that he is the thief then, if he is charged only with handling, the words "otherwise than in the course of the stealing" are relevant since the prosecution can only prove the offence of handling if it proves affirmatively that the defendant was not the thief (*R v Cash* [1985] QB 801, [1985] 2 All ER 128, CA).

4. The question is a subjective one and it must be proved that the defendant was aware of the theft or that he believed the goods to be stolen. Suspicion that they were stolen, even coupled with the fact that he shut his eyes to the circumstances, is not enough, although those matters may be taken into account by a court when deciding whether or not the necessary knowledge or belief existed; see *R v Moys* (1984) 79 Cr App Rep 72. The prosecution need not go further and show that the defendant knew the identity of the goods (*R v McCullum* (1973) 117 Sol Jo 525).

The Court of Appeal has laid down guidelines to be followed on the approach to the phrase "knowing or believing" when directing juries. The guidelines, which will be equally relevant to justices, can be summarised as follows: A man may be said to know that goods are stolen when he is told by someone with first hand knowledge (ie such as the thief or burglar) that such is the case. Belief, which is something short of knowledge, may be said to be the state of mind of a person who says to himself, "I cannot say I know for certain that these goods are stolen, but there can be no other reasonable conclusion in the light of all the circumstances, in the light of all that I have heard and seen". Either of those two states of mind is enough to satisfy the words of the statute (*R v Hall* (1985) 81 Cr App Rep 260).

5. Section 27 post makes provision for evidence admissible for the purpose of proving that the accused knew or believed the goods to be stolen goods.

6. It has been stated that guilty knowledge must be proved at the moment of receipt and not at any time during the handling thereafter: see *Atwal v Massey* [1971] 3 All ER 881, *per* LORD WIDGERY, CJ at 882; and *R v Grainge* [1974] 1 All ER 928 at 932, *per* EVERLEIGH, J; but note s 3(1), ante, whereby a subsequent guilty knowledge might amount to a dishonest appropriation and, therefore, theft.

7. Assists means helping or encouraging amongst other things; there must be either affirmative or circumstantial evidence of help or encouragement (*R v Coleman* (1985) 150 JP 175, [1986] Crim LR 56. Something must be done by the defendant; a mere failure to act, where no duty to act existed in law, does not amount to an offence: *R v Burroughes* [2000] All ER (D) 2032, CA.

8. The words "by or for the benefit of another person", govern "retention", "removal", "disposal" and "realisation", and should be included in the charge where retention, removal, disposal or realisation is alleged (*R v Sloggett* [1972] 1 QB 430, [1971] 3 All ER 264, 135 JP 539). See *R v Deakin* [1972] 3 All ER 803, 137 JP 19. If the accused knows that the stolen goods are hidden on his property, mere failure to reveal their presence does not in itself amount to assisting in their retention but would afford strong evidence of providing accommodation for the goods which may amount to assisting in their retention (*R v Brown* [1970] 1 QB 105, [1969] 3 All ER 198, 133 JP 592). Merely using stolen goods in the possession of another does not constitute the offence of assisting in their retention, because something must be done by the offender, and done intentionally and dishonestly, for the purpose of enabling the goods to be retained (*R v Kanwar* [1982] 2 All ER 528, 146 JP 283; *R v Sanders* [1982] Crim LR 695).

9. "Realisation" merely involves the exchange of the goods for money; and he who pays is just as much involved in the realisation as he who receives the payment (*R v Deakin* [1972] 3 All ER 803, 137 JP 19).

10. A person who has *bona fide* acquired goods for value does not commit an offence of dishonestly undertaking the disposal or realisation of stolen property for the benefit of another if when he sells the goods he knows or believes them to be stolen, because it is the purchase, not the sale, which is for the purchaser's benefit (*R v Bloxham* [1983] 1 AC 109, [1982] 1 All ER 582, 146 JP 201). The word "another" in s 22(1) cannot be construed to embrace a co-accused on the same charge (*R v Gingell* (1999) 163 JP 648, [2000] 1 Cr App Rep 88, CA).

11. This does not cover the situation where the goods are not yet stolen (*R v Park* [1988] Crim LR 238).

12. Triable either way; see Magistrates' Courts Act 1980, s 17 and Sch 1; also ss 17A–21 (procedure) and s 32 (penalty) in PART I: MAGISTRATES' COURTS, PROCEDURE, ante.

8-30722 23. Advertising rewards for return of goods stolen or lost. Where any public advertisement of a reward for the return of any goods which have been stolen[1] or lost uses any words to the effect that no questions will be asked, or that the person producing the goods will be safe from apprehension or inquiry, or that any money paid for the purchase of the goods or advanced by way of loan on them will be repaid, the person advertising the reward and any person who prints or publishes the advertisement shall on summary conviction be liable[2] to a fine not exceeding **level 3** on the standard scale.

[Theft Act 1968, s 23, as amended by the Criminal Justice Act 1982, ss 35 and 46.]

1. See s 24(4), post.

2. This is an offence of strict liability requiring no *mens rea* (*Denham v Scott* [1983] Crim LR 558).

8-30723 24. Scope of offences relating to stolen goods. (1) The provisions of this Act relating to goods which have been stolen shall apply whether the stealing occurred in England or Wales or elsewhere, and whether it occurred before or after the commencement of this Act, provided that the stealing (if not an offence under this Act) amounted to an offence where and at the time when the goods were stolen; and references to stolen goods shall be construed accordingly.

(2) For purposes of those provisions references to stolen goods shall include, in addition to the goods originally stolen and parts of them (whether in their original state or not)—

(*a*) any other goods which directly or indirectly represent or have at any time represented the stolen goods in the hands of the thief[1] as being the proceeds of any disposal or realisation of the whole or part of the goods stolen[2] or of goods so representing the stolen goods; and

(*b*) any other goods which directly or indirectly represent or have at any time represented the stolen goods in the hands of a handler of the stolen goods or any part of them as being the proceeds of any disposal or realisation of the whole or part of the stolen goods handled by him or of goods so representing them.

(3) But no goods shall be regarded as having continued to be stolen goods after they have been restored[3] to the person from whom they were stolen or to other lawful possession or custody, or after that person and any other person claiming through him have otherwise ceased as regards those goods to have any right to restitution in respect of the theft.

(4) For purposes of the provisions of this Act relating to goods which have been stolen (including subsections (1) to (3) above) goods obtained in England or Wales or elsewhere either by blackmail or in the circumstances described in section 15(1) of this Act shall be regarded as stolen; and "steal", "theft" and "thief" shall be construed accordingly.

[Theft Act 1968, s 24.]

---

1. The words "in the hands of the thief" mean in the possession or under the control of the thief (*R v Forsyth* [1997] 2 Crim App Rep 299, CA).

2. Where a person is tried on a charge of handling stolen goods, the jury is not entitled to infer that a sum of money paid by cheque to the receiver by the thief represents stolen goods within s 24(2)(*a*), if the inference is to be drawn merely from the receiver's intention or belief that the money should or did represent stolen goods (*Re A-G's Reference (No 4 of 1979)* [1981] 1 All ER 1193, [1981] Crim LR 51).

3. This means taken into possession and not merely kept under observation: see *A-G's Reference (No 1 of 1974)* [1974] QB 744, [1974] 2 All ER 899, 138 JP 570. See also *Greater London Metropolitan Police Comr v Streeter* (1980) 71 Cr App Rep 113 (carton initialled by security officer and kept under observation).

8–30723A 24A. Dishonestly retaining a wrongful credit. (1) A person is guilty of an offence[1] if—

(*a*) a wrongful credit has been made to an account kept by him or in respect of which he has any right or interest;

(*b*) he knows or believes that the credit is wrongful; and

(*c*) he dishonestly fails to take such steps as are reasonable in the circumstances to secure that the credit is cancelled.

(2) References to a credit are to a credit of an amount of money.

(3) A credit to an account is wrongful if it is the credit side of a money transfer obtained contrary to section 15A of this Act.

(4) A credit to an account is also wrongful to the extent that it derives from—

(*a*) theft;

(*b*) an offence under section 15A of this Act;

(*c*) blackmail; or

(*d*) stolen goods.

(5) In determining whether a credit to an account is wrongful, it is immaterial (in particular) whether the account is overdrawn before or after the credit is made.

(6) A person guilty of an offence under this section shall be liable on conviction on indictment to imprisonment for a term not exceeding **ten years**[1].

(7) Subsection (8) below applies for purposes of provisions of this Act relating to stolen goods (including subsection (4) above).

(8) References to stolen goods include money which is dishonestly withdrawn from an account to which a wrongful credit has been made, but only to the extent that the money derives from the credit.

(9) In this section "account" and "money" shall be construed in accordance with section 15B of this Act.

[Theft Act 1968, s 24A, as inserted by the Theft (Amendment) Act 1996, s 2.]

---

1. Triable either way; see Magistrates' Courts Act 1980, s 17 and Sch 1; also ss 17A–21 (procedure) and s 32 (penalty) in PART I: MAGISTRATES' COURTS, PROCEDURE, ante.

Possession of housebreaking implements, etc

8–30724 25. Going equipped for stealing, etc[1]. (1) A person shall be guilty of an offence if, when not at his place of abode[2], he has with him[3] any article for use[4] in the course of or in connection with any burglary, theft[5] or cheat[5].

(2) A person guilty of an offence under this section shall on conviction on indictment be liable to imprisonment for a term not exceeding **three years**[6].

(3) Where a person is charged with an offence under this section, proof that he had with him any article made or adapted for use in committing a burglary, theft[5] or cheat shall be evidence that he had it with him for such use[7].

(4) *Repealed.*

(5) For purposes of this section an offence under section 12(1) of this Act of taking a conveyance shall be treated as theft, and "cheat" means an offence under section 15 of this Act.

[Theft Act 1968, s 25 as amended by the Serious Organised Crime and Police Act 2005, Sch 7.]

---

1. This offence can be committed at any time of the day or night.

2. The phrase "place of abode" means a site at which the occupier intends to abide. Therefore, a person who is living rough in a car is at his place of abode when on a site with the intention of abiding there, but not when the vehicle is in transit from one site to another (*R v Bundy* [1977] 2 All ER 382, 141 JP 345).

3. In a case under the equivalent provisions of previous legislation it was held that possession must be actual and not constructive and possession after arrest was not sufficient (*R v Harris* (1925) 89 JP 37); see also *R v Hatch* (1933) 24 Cr App Rep 100. A person in possession of counterfeit shirts at a bonded warehouse had them "with him" when in person he displayed them to undercover agents (*Re McAngus* [1994] Crim LR 602). The possession of housebreaking implements by one of two or more persons acting in concert was held to be possession by all (*R v Thompson* (1869) 33 JP 791).

4. The prosecution must prove that the defendant had the article for use in some *future* burglary, theft or cheat, though it is not necessary to prove that the defendant intended to use it himself (*R v Ellames* [1974] 3 All ER 130, 138 JP 682). There is no reason why a person should not be charged with an offence under this section as well as with attempted theft or theft where the circumstances in which he was in possession of the article were those of an attempt or of the completed crime; see *Minor v DPP* (1987) 152 JP 30, 86 Cr App Rep 378. A person who has not decided whether to use an article, which he has with him, should an opportunity present itself, does not have the necessary intention required for an offence under this section (*R v Hargreaves* [1985] Crim LR 243, CA).

5. See s 25(5), *infra*. In *R v Rashid* [1977] 2 All ER 237, 141 JP 305, because of a misdirection to the jury, the defendant was held to have been wrongly convicted of possession of bread and tomatoes with which he intended to make sandwiches for sale to passengers on a train on which he was a steward. In that case the Court of Appeal, in an *obiter dicta*, expressed the view that on the facts of the case there was probably no obtaining by deception and that it was not appropriate to exalt a breach of contractual duty owed to the defendant's employers into a criminal offence. But *R v Rashid*, *supra*, was distinguished in *R v Doukas* [1978] 1 All ER 1061, where a wine waiter in an hotel was held to have been properly convicted of having with him his own wine which he dishonestly intended to sell to customers as property of his employers. In the latter case it was held that it had to be assumed that the hypothetical customer against whom the intended deception was to be practised was reasonably honest and intelligent, and that it was unlikely that any customer to whom the true situation was made clear would willingly make himself a party to what was a fraud by the waiter on his employer. See also *R v Corboz* [1984] Crim LR 629 and *R v Whiteside and R v Antoniou* [1989] Crim LR 436, CA.

6. Triable either way; see Magistrates' Courts Act 1980, s 17 and Sch 1; also ss 17A–21 (procedure) and s 32 (penalty) in PART I: MAGISTRATES' COURTS, PROCEDURE, ante. Disqualification *may* be ordered (Road Traffic Offenders Act 1988, Sch 2, in PART VII: TRANSPORT, ante).

7. Once possession of this sort of article has been proved the accused has an evidential burden to show that the article was in his possession for purposes other than burglary, theft or cheat.

Enforcement and procedure

8–30725 **26. Search for stolen goods.** (1) If it is made to appear by information[1] on oath before a justice of the peace that there is reasonable cause to believe that any person has in his custody or possession or on his premises any stolen goods, the justice[2] may grant a warrant[2] to search for and seize the same[3]; but no warrant to search for stolen goods shall be addressed to a person other than a constable except under the authority of an enactment expressly so providing.

(2) *Repealed.*

(3) Where under this section a person is authorised to search premises for stolen goods, he may enter and search the premises accordingly, and may seize any goods[4], he believes to be stolen goods[5].

(5) This section is to be construed in accordance with section 24 of this Act; and in subsection (2) above the references to handling stolen goods shall include any corresponding offence committed before the commencement of this Act[6].

[Theft Act 1968, s 26, as amended by the Criminal Justice Act 1972, Sch 6 and the Police and Criminal Evidence Act 1984, Sch 7.]

---

1. The information that a person has stolen goods in his possession may be sworn by any person. It is not necessary to state in the information that an offence has been actually committed (*Elsee v Smith* (1822) 1 Dow & Ry KB 97), or to specify the particular goods to be searched for (*Jones v German* [1897] 1 QB 374, 61 JP 180).

2. The issue and execution of this warrant must conform to the Police and Criminal Evidence Act 1984, ss 15 and 16 in PART I: MAGISTRATES' COURTS, PROCEDURE, ante.

3. See Precedent for search warrant in PART IX: PRECEDENTS AND FORMS, post.

4. Even if they are not the suspected stolen goods. This provision preserves the law as laid down in *Chic Fashions (West Wales) Ltd v Jones* [1968] 2 QB 299, [1968] 1 All ER 229, 132 JP 175.

5. Section 26 is not limited solely to the purpose of enabling the police or other authorities to recover stolen property and the provisions are to be read as they are set out; the warrant is concerned primarily with search, seizure is permitted by subsection (3) and the fact that the warrant does not expressly state that property can be seized does not in any way invalidate it. The applicant is obliged to provide the material required by s 15 of PACE and it is that material which the justice has to consider in determining whether or not he is persuaded to grant the warrant: *R (on the application of R Cruickshank Ltd) v Chief Constable of Kent* [2001] EWHC Admin 123, [2001] Crim LR 990.

6. Ie, offences of receiving under the Larceny Act 1916.

8–30726 **27. Evidence and procedure on charge of theft or handling stolen goods.** (1) Any number of persons may be charged in one indictment[1], with reference to the same theft, with having at different times or at the same time handled all or any of the stolen goods, and the persons so charged may be tried together.

(2) On the trial of two or more persons indicted[1] for jointly handling any stolen goods the jury may find any of the accused guilty if the jury are satisfied that he handled all or any of the stolen goods, whether or not he did so jointly with the other accused or any of them.

(3) Where a person is being proceeded against for handling stolen goods (but not for any offence other than handling stolen goods)[2], then at any stage of the proceedings, if evidence has been given of his having or arranging to have in his possession the goods the subject of the charge, or of his undertaking or assisting in, or arranging to undertake or assist in, their retention, removal, disposal or realisation, the following evidence shall be admissible for the purpose of proving that he knew or believed the goods to be stolen goods:

(*a*) evidence that he has had in his possession[3], or has undertaken or assisted in the retention, removal, disposal or realisation of, stolen goods from any theft taking place not earlier than twelve months before the offence charged; and

(*b*) (provided that seven days' notice in writing has been given to him of the intention to prove the conviction) evidence that he has within the five years preceding the date of the offence charged been convicted of theft or of handling stolen goods[4].

(4) In any proceedings for the theft of anything in the course of transmission (whether by post or otherwise), or for handling stolen goods from such a theft, a statutory declaration made by any person that he despatched or received or failed to receive any goods or postal packet, or that any goods or postal packet when despatched or received by him were in a particular state or condition, shall be admissible as evidence of the facts stated in the declaration, subject to the following conditions:

(*a*) a statutory declaration shall only be admissible where and to the extent to which oral evidence to the like effect would have been admissible in the proceedings; and

(*b*) a statutory declaration shall only be admissible if at least seven days before the hearing or trial a copy of it has been given to the person charged, and he has not, at least three days before the hearing or trial or within such further time as the court may in special circumstances allow, given the prosecutor written notice requiring the attendance at the hearing or trial of the person making the declaration.

(4A) Where the proceedings mentioned in subsection (4) above are proceedings before a magistrates' court inquiring into an offence as examining justices that subsection shall have effect with the omission of the words from "subject to the following conditions" to the end of the subsection.

(5) This section is to be construed in accordance with section 24 of this Act; and in subsection (3)(*b*) above the reference to handling stolen goods shall include any corresponding offence committed before the commencement of this Act[5].

[Theft Act 1968, s 27, as amended by the Criminal Procedure and Investigations Act 1996, Sch 1.]

1. These provisions do not apply to summary trial.
2. This exclusion preserves the principle laid down in *R v Davies* [1953] 1 QB 489, [1953] 1 All ER 341, 117 JP 121.
3. Proof may be by circumstantial evidence; see for example *R v Sbarra* (1919) 13 Cr App Rep 118 (goods delivered in the middle of the night to a side door); *R v Fuschillo* [1940] 2 All ER 489 ("This means going away"). A lie told by the accused as to where he acquired property is insufficient evidence that it was stolen (*Cohen v March* [1951] 2 TLR 402).

This section does not authorise the introduction of evidence as to the circumstances in which the stolen goods were found, nor explanations made by the defendant at that time (*R v Wood* [1987] 1 WLR 779). Such evidence ought not to be admitted if the real offence charged is theft and not handling, or if there is no evidence that the property found was stolen (*R v Girod and Girod* (1906) 70 JP 514; *R v Harding* (1909) 53 Sol Jo 762). Evidence of the thief that he has sold stolen property to the defendant at any previous time is admissible to prove guilty knowledge; it is not affected by the time limit in this subsection (*R v Powell* (1909) 3 Cr App Rep 1).

4. Admissibility under this subsection is directed to proof of guilty knowledge; if guilty knowledge is not a live issue in the trial the evidence may not be admitted (*R v Herron* [1967] 1 QB 107, [1966] 2 All ER 26, 130 JP 266); nor should it be admitted where it would be only of minimal assistance (*R v Perry* [1984] Crim LR 680 or where the only issue is one of dishonesty (*R v Duffus* (1993) 158 JP 224). Where the defence is based on a substantial additional point, eg, that the accused did not have possession of the property alleged to have been received or that property of which he had possession is not clearly identified as that which was stolen, evidence under this subsection may be excluded, at the court's discretion, on the ground that its prejudicial effect would outweigh its probative value (*R v Herron, supra*; *R v List* [1965] 3 All ER 710, 130 JP 30; *R v Wilkins* [1975] 2 All ER 734, 139 JP 543).

A certificate of a previous conviction adduced and admitted in evidence should, where the conviction was on indictment, state the substance and effect, omitting the formal parts, of the indictment and conviction, and where the previous indictment and conviction were for stealing or handling a car, the reference to the car is not a formal part but is of the substance of the indictment and the conviction. If a conviction on summary trial was for stealing or handling a car, the certificate should record that fact, and the whole of the certificate is admissible (*R v Hacker* [1995] 1 All ER 45, [1994] 1 WLR 1659, 159 JP 62, HL).

5. Ie offences of receiving under the Larceny Act 1916.

8–30727 28. *Repealed.*

8–30728 30. Spouses and civil partners. (1) This Act shall apply in relation to the parties to a marriage, and to property belonging to the wife or husband whether or not by reason of an interest derived from the marriage, as it would apply if they were not married and any such interest subsisted independently of the marriage[1].

(2) Subject to subsection (4) below, a person shall have the same right to bring proceedings against that person's wife or husband for any offence (whether under this Act or otherwise) as if they were not married[2], and a person bringing any such proceedings shall be competent to give evidence for the prosecution at every stage of the proceedings.★

(3) *Repealed.*

(4) Proceedings shall not be instituted against a person for any offence of stealing or doing unlawful damage to property[3] which at the time of the offence belongs to that person's wife or husband or civil partner, or for any attempt, incitement or conspiracy to commit such an offence, unless the proceedings are instituted by or with the consent[4] of the Director of Public Prosecutions.

Provided that—

(*a*) this subsection shall not apply to proceedings against a person for an offence—

(i) if that person is charged with committing the offence jointly with the wife or husband or civil partner;

(ii) if by virtue of any judicial decree or order (wherever made) that person and the wife or husband are at the time of the offence under no obligation to cohabit; or

(iii) an order (wherever made) is in force providing for the separation of that person and his or her civil partner.

(*b*) *Repealed.*

(5) Notwithstanding section 6 of the Prosecution of Offences Act 1979[5] subsection (4) of this section shall apply—

(*a*) to an arrest (if without warrant) made by the wife or husband or civil partner, and

(*b*) to a warrant of arrest issued on an information laid by the wife or husband or civil partner.

[Theft Act 1968, s 30, as amended by the Criminal Jurisdiction Act 1975, Sch 5, the Prosecution of Offences Act 1979, Sch 1, the Police and Criminal Evidence Act 1984, Sch 7 and the Civil Partnership Act 2004, Sch 27.]

★Section 30(2) is amended by the Youth Justice and Criminal Evidence Act 1999, Sch 6, when in force.

1. The effect of this provision is to enable one spouse to prosecute the other for an offence under the Act even if they are living together.

2. The effect of this provision is to enable one spouse to prosecute the other for *any* offence (whether under the Theft Act or otherwise).

3. For example, under s 1(1) of the Criminal Damage Act 1971; see *R v Withers* [1975] Crim LR 647.

4. Consent is not required if the husband and wife are, by virtue of a judicial decree or order, no longer bound to cohabit (*Woodley v Woodley* [1978] Crim LR 629).

5. The effect of this would appear to be that the appropriate consent must be obtained before arrest, issue or execution of a warrant or remand. The 1979 Act has been repealed and replaced by the Prosecution of Offences Act 1985, s 25(2) in PART I: MAGISTRATES' COURTS, PROCEDURE, ante.

8–30729 31. Effect on civil proceedings and rights. (1) A person shall not be excused, by reason that to do so may incriminate that person or the spouse or civil partner of that person of an offence under this Act—

(*a*) from answering any question put to that person in proceedings for the recovery or administration of any property[1], for the execution of any trust or for an account of any property or dealings with property; or

(*b*) from complying with any order made in any such proceedings;

but no statement or admission made by a person in answering a question put or complying with an order made as aforesaid shall, in proceedings for an offence under this Act, be admissible in evidence against that person or (unless they married or became civil partners after the making of the statement or admission) against thespouse or civil partner of that person.

(2) Notwithstanding any enactment to the contrary, where property has been stolen or obtained by fraud or other wrongful means, the title to that or any other property shall not be affected by reason only of the conviction of the offender[2].

[Theft Act 1968, s 31 as amended by the Civil Partnership Act 2004, Sch 27.]

---

1. Self-incriminating statements made by a bankrupt during his public examination can be used against him in criminal proceedings (*R v Kansal* [1993] QB 244, [1992] 3 All ER 844).

2. Under the provisions of this section, questions of title to property will be left to the Civil Law.

8–30730 32. Effect on existing law and construction of references to offences. (1) The following offences are hereby abolished for all purposes not relating to offences committed before the commencement of this Act, that is to say—

(*a*) any offence at common law of larceny, robbery, burglary, receiving stolen property, obtaining property by threats, extortion by colour of office or franchise, false accounting by public officers, concealment of treasure trove and, except as regards offences relating to the public revenue[1], cheating[2]; and

(*b*) any offence under an enactment mentioned in Part I of Schedule 3 to this Act, to the extent to which the offence depends on any section or part of a section included in column 3 of that Schedule;

but so that the provisions in Schedule 1 to this Act (which preserve with modifications certain offences under the Larceny Act 1861 of taking or killing deer and taking or destroying fish) shall have effect as there set out.

(2) Except as regards offences committed before the commencement of this Act, and except in so far as the context otherwise requires—

(*a*) references in any enactment passed before this Act to an offence abolished by this Act shall, subject to any express amendment or repeal made by this Act, have effect as references to the corresponding offence under this Act, and in any such enactment the expression "receive" (when it relates to an offence of receiving) shall mean handle, and "receiver" shall be construed accordingly; and

(*b*) without prejudice to paragraph (*a*) above, references in any enactment, whenever passed, to theft or stealing (including references to stolen goods), and references to robbery, blackmail, burglary, aggravated burglary or handling stolen goods, shall be construed in accordance with the provisions of this Act, including those of section 24.

[Theft Act 1968, s 32.]

---

1. The common law offence of cheating the revenue is still available even when the facts show that a statutory offence has ben committed; the common law offence may be satisfied by matters of omission, a positive act of deception directed against the revenue is not required (*R v Redford* (1988) 89 Cr App Rep 1, CA). See also *R v Mulligan* [1990] STC 220, [1990] Crim LR 427, CA.

2. This subsection is not to be construed as meaning that cheating at common law could not be charged where there was available a statutory offence; also, one can cheat by omission (*R v Redford* [1988] STC 845, 89 Cr App Rep 1, CA).

8–30731 **33. Miscellaneous and consequential amendments, and repeal.** (1) *Repealed.*

(2) The enactments mentioned in Parts II and III of Schedule 2 to this Act shall have effect subject to the amendments there provided for, and (subject to subsection (4) below) the amendments made by Part II to enactments extending beyond England and Wales shall have the like extent as the enactment amended.

(3) The enactments mentioned in Schedule 3 to this Act (which include in Part II certain enactments related to the subject matter of this Act but already obsolete or redundant apart from this Act) are hereby repealed to the extent specified in column 3 of that Schedule; and, notwithstanding that the foregoing sections of this Act do not extend to Scotland, where any enactment expressed to be repealed by Schedule 3 does so extend, the Schedule shall have effect to repeal it in its application to Scotland except in so far as the repeal is expressed not to extend to Scotland.

(4) No amendment or repeal made by this Act in Schedule 1 to the Extradition Act 1870 or in the Schedule to the Extradition Act 1873 shall affect the operation of that Schedule by reference to the law of a British Possession; but the repeal made in Schedule 1 to the Extradition Act 1870 shall extend throughout the United Kingdom.

[Theft Act 1968, s 33, as amended by SI 2001/1149.]

Supplementary

8–30732 **34. Interpretation.** (1) Sections 4(1) and 5(1) of this Act shall apply generally for purposes of this Act as they apply for purposes of section 1[1].

(2) For purposes of this Act—

(*a*) "gain" and "loss" are to be construed[2] as extending only to gain or loss in money or other property, but as extending to any such gain or loss whether temporary or permanent; and—

(i) "gain" includes a gain by keeping what one has, as well as a gain by getting what one has not; and

(ii) "loss" includes a loss by not getting what one might get, as well as a loss by parting with what one has;

(*b*) "goods", except in so far as the context otherwise requires, includes[3] money and every other description of property except land[4], and includes things severed from the land by stealing; and

(*c*) "mail bag" and "postal packet" have the meanings given by section 125(1) of the Postal Services Act 2000.

[Theft Act 1968, s 34, as amended by SI 2003/2908.]

---

1. Section 1 is the general definition of the offence of theft.

2. The definitions of "gain" and "loss" are material to the offences under ss 17(1) (destroying or defacing accounts or producing a false misleading or deceptive account), 20(1) and (2) (suppression, etc, of documents) and 21(1) (blackmail). A person who demands money that is undoubtedly owed to him does so with a view to gain by intending to obtain hard cash as opposed to a mere right of action in respect of the debt (*R v Parkes* [1973] Crim LR 358, followed in *A-G's Reference (No 1 of 2001)* [2002] EWCA Crim 1768, [2002] 3 All ER 840, [2002] Crim LR 844).

3. The definition of "goods" is material for the purposes of the offence of handling stolen goods under s 22 and the related ss 23, 24, 26 and 27. It also applies to the word "goods" in the provisions as to restitution orders in s 28.

4. Since land is excluded from the definition of goods, the offence of "handling" does not apply to land or the proceeds of stolen land.

SCHEDULES

Section 32.

SCHEDULE 1

OFFENCES OF TAKING, ETC DEER OR FISH

(*As amended by the Deer Act 1980, s 9 and the Criminal Justice Act 1982, ss 35, 38 and 46.*)

Taking or killing deer

8–30733 **1.** *Repealed.*

Taking or destroying fish

2. (1) Subject to subparagraph (2) below, a person who unlawfully takes[1] or destroys, or attempts to take[1] or destroy, any fish[2] in water which is private property[3] or in which there is any private[4] right of fishery on summary conviction be liable to imprisonment for a term not exceeding **three months** or* to a fine not exceeding **level 3** on the standard scale or to **both**.

(2) Subparagraph (1) above shall not apply to taking or destroying fish by angling in the daytime (that is to say, in the period beginning one hour before sunrise and ending one hour after sunset); but a person who by angling in the daytime unlawfully takes[1] or destroys, or attempts to take[1] or destroy, any fish[2] in water which is private property[3] or in which there is any private right of fishery[4] shall on summary conviction be liable to a fine not exceeding **level 1** on the standard scale.

(3) The court by which a person is convicted of an offence under this paragraph may order the forfeiture of anything which, at the time of the offence, he had with him for use for taking or destroying fish.

(4) Any person may arrest without warrant anyone who is, or whom he, with reasonable cause, suspects to be, committing an offence under subparagraph (1) above, and may seize from any person who is, or whom he, with reasonable cause, suspects to be, committing any offence under this paragraph anything which on that person's conviction of the offence would be liable to be forfeited under subparagraph (3) above.**

***Repealed by the Criminal Justice Act 2003, Sch 37 from a date to be appointed.**
****Repealed by the Serious Organised Crime and Police Act 2005, Sch 7 in so far as it confers a power of arrest without warrant on a constable or persons in general.**

1. There need be no "*mens rea*", no asportation: the taker may intend to keep the fish in a keep net and return them to the water at the end of his fishing (*Wells v Hardy* [1964] 2 QB 447, [1964] 1 All ER 953, 128 JP 238).

2. Crayfish are included (*Caygill v Thwaite* (1885) 49 JP 614). So are winkles (*Leavett v Clark* [1915] 3 KB 9, 79 JP 396).

3. The public cannot by prescription or otherwise obtain a legal right to fish in a non-tidal river even though it be navigable (*Smith v Andrews* [1891] 2 Ch 678). Proof of uninterrupted custom for sixty years and upwards to fish by angling from a public footpath running along the river bank of a non-navigable and non-tidal river did not support a claim on the part of the defendant, as one of the public, to fish in the river, as such a right could not possibly be acquired (*Hudson v MacRae* (1863) 4 B & S 585, 28 JP 436). But in *R v Stimpson* (1863) 4 B & S 301, where the defendant contended that he and the public had a right of fishing in a navigable *tidal* river, and proved by witnesses they had fished it for many years without interruption, it was held there was reasonable evidence to show that the question of title raised by the defendant was *bonâ fide*.

The public have no right to fish in a river made navigable by Act of Parliament but not tidal, although they have fished in it as of right for many years without interruption; the navigation is private property, subject to certain limited rights on the part of the public (*Hargreaves v Diddams* (1875) LR 10 QB 582, 40 JP 167). "That is called an arm of the sea where the sea flows and reflows and so far only as the sea flows and reflows;" "and only in such waters is there *prima facie* a right of fishing common to all" (HALE, *De jure Maris*, p 12). Upon exceptionally high tides the rising of the salt water in the lower part of the river Wye dammed back the fresh water and caused it to rise and fall with the flow and ebb of the tide, but the salt water did not reach the place where the public claimed a right to fish, and it was held that the place was not a tidal river within the meaning of the rule of law (*Reece v Miller* (1882) 8 QBD 626). KEKEWICH, J, held that a creek to be navigable in the legal sense of the term must be affected by the ebb and flow of ordinary or mean tides (*Earl of Ilchester v Raishleigh* (1890) 61 LT 477). Where there was some evidence to support the finding of the justices that the water of a Norfolk Broad (Wroxham) was not part of a tidal navigable river, the QB Division would not interfere with a conviction (*Blower v Ellis* (1886) 50 JP 326, Treat 338). A similar question was raised as to another Norfolk Broad (Hickling), when ROMER, J, held the public had a right of way over it, but no right to shoot or fish (*Mickelthwait v Vincent* (1892) 67 LT 225). It was expressly decided in the case of *Murphy v Ryan* (1868) IR 2 CL 143, that the public cannot acquire by immemorial usage any right to fish in a navigable river above the flow of the tide, and that the fishery belonged to the riparian owners, who could, if they pleased, prohibit the public any longer going there. But COCKBURN, CJ, in *R v Burrow* (1869) 34 JP 53, was not prepared to assent to that decision without further argument, and the conviction, which was for fishing in the Ullswater lake, was quashed. The QB Division has, however, since confirmed *Murphy v Ryan*, and held that *Hargreaves v Diddams, supra*, in which upon the argument reference was made to *Murphy v Ryan* and *R v Burrow*, put an end to any doubt thrown upon the Irish case (*Mussett v Burch* (1876) 41 JP 72). The last quoted case was for fishing from private land in the river Stour, a navigable river used by means of locks. The same rule of law was followed as to the Dee at Craigpool, Denbighshire, about 30 miles above the tidal flow, where the river is public and navigable for small craft; a *bonâ fide* claim of right was set up, and evidence was given that the public had not been interfered with for forty years and upwards when fishing in this part of the river, but the QB Division held justices were wrong in not convicting, for it was impossible that the public could acquire such a right (*Pearce v Scotcher* (1882) 9 QBD 162, 46 JP 248). The case of *R v Burrows, supra*, was again quoted and relied on, but was disregarded by the court: the *dictum* of COCKBURN, CJ, in that case may, therefore, be considered erroneous. The point has been, moreover, conclusively settled by *Reece v Miller, supra*, where the actual point argued was whether the river Wye was tidal at the spot in question, but the court being of opinion that the river was not tidal there, affirmed the conviction for unlawful fishing. An injunction was granted restraining a person from interfering with posts and chains which the owner of the bed of the river Mole, a non-tidal river running into the Thames, had placed in the river to stop the waterway. Evidence was given of the long use of the river for boating purposes, but the court held the use had been permissive (*Bourke v Davis* (1889) 44 Ch D 110).

The "dwellers" in a parish or manor cannot acquire a right of piscary, but the commoners of a manor, and probably the occupiers of their customary tenements may have such a right by custom of the manor (*Allgood v Gibson* (1876) 34 LT 883; see also *Lord Rivers v Adam* (1878) 3 Ex D 361); and it has been held by the House of Lords that the "uninterrupted enjoyment from time immemorial by the free inhabitants of ancient tenements", within a borough of dredging for oysters on certain days in a year, was sufficient to raise a presumption of the lawful origin of the usage (*Goodman v Saltash Corpn* (1882) 7 App Cas 633, 47 JP 276). As far back as living memory extended outfishing had been carried on in a tidal navigable river without interference from the plaintiff or his predecessors; but it was held this did not take away the right to a several fishery, which could only pass by deed (*Neill v Duke of Devonshire* (1882) 8 App Cas 135, HL).

The Crown has no *de jure* right to the soil or fisheries of an inland non-tidal lake (*Bristow v Cormican* (1878) 3 App Cas 641). The Court of Appeal has also held that the Crown never had anything to do with private fisheries; and as it could not exclude the owner of the soil from a private river, it certainly could not grant the fishery as a separate tenement to another. The presumption that half of the river fishery in a non-tidal river passes with the grant of the riparian lands may be rebutted (*Duke of Devonshire v Pattison* (1887) 20 QBD 263, 52 JP 276, Treat, 306). The executive right of fishing in tidal waters vested in the Crown is no more than an incidence of the soil over which the water flows (*Duke of Devonshire v Neill* (1876) 2 LR Ir 132). The grant of an exclusive right to fish in a river conveys the right irrespective of the ownership of the soil over which the water flows (*Foster v Wright* (1878) 4 CPD 438, 44 JP 7). The Crown or an individual can grant by deed a several fishery held by the Crown, or the individual before Magna Carta (*Neill v Duke of Devonshire, supra*). A several fishery in a navigable tidal river could only have been legally created by grant from the Crown before Magna Carta; the use of stop nets in such rivers was prohibited by 2 Hen 6, c 15, and such nets are illegal unless they were lawfully used before that statute. For an instance of such a grant, see *Stephens v Snell* [1939] 3 All ER 622. See *Holford v George* (1868) LR 3 QB 639, 32 JP 468; as to evidence of a several fishery in a public navigable river, see *Edgar v English Fisheries Special Comrs* (1870) 35 JP 822, and *Goodman v Saltash Corpn* (1882) 7 App Cas 633, 47 JP 276, HL; and as to evidence of a several fishery in the non-tidal part of a river, see *Powell v Heffernan* (1881) 8 LR Ir 130. The cases dealing with the right of owners of several fisheries were considered by the Court of Appeal in *Hindson v Ashby* [1896] 2 Ch 1, 60 JP 484, where a question was argued as to the ownership of the bed of a river upon recession of the water. See also *Hanbury v Jenkins* [1901] 2 Ch 401, 65 JP 631.

4. A right of fishery can be conveyed only by deed; the ownership of the right must be proved (*Halse v Alder* (1874) 38 JP 407).

By a lease of land through which a river flows, the right of fishing, unless expressly reserved to the lessor, passes to the tenant, and the lessor cannot prosecute persons for unlawfully taking fish (*Jones v Davies* (1902) 66 JP 439).

Theft Act 1978

(1978 c 31)

8–30840 1. Obtaining services by deception. (1) A person who by any deception dishonestly obtains services from another shall be guilty of an offence.

(2) It is an obtaining of services[1] where the other is induced to confer a benefit by doing some act, or causing or permitting some act to be done, on the understanding[2] that the benefit has been or will be paid for.

(3) Without prejudice to the generality of subsection (2) above, it is an obtaining of services where the other is induced to make a loan, or to cause or permit a loan to be made, on the understanding that any payment (whether by way of interest or otherwise) will be or has been made in respect of the loan.

[Theft Act 1978, s 1, as amended by the Theft (Amendment) Act 1996, s 4.]

---

1. Obtaining a credit card or the opening of a bank account provides access to bank services which underlie the use of an account or a credit card. Therefore, the dishonest opening of a bank account or the obtaining of a credit card by deception can constitute obtaining services by deception as can the dishonest operation of a bank account over a period or the dishonest use of a credit card (*R v Sofroniou* [2003] EWCA Crim 3681, [2004] QB 1218, [2004] 1 Cr App R 35, [2004] Crim LR 381).

2. This is intended to cover situations where nothing explicitly is said about payment, but where there is a common, objective, understanding that the service will not be provided gratuitously (even though the defendant might not have a subjective intention to make payment) (*R v Sofroniou* [2003] EWCA Crim 3681, [2004] QB 1218, [2004] 1 Cr App R 35, [2004] Crim LR 381).

8–30841 2. Evasion of liability by deception. (1)[1] Subject to subsection (2) below, where a person by any deception—

(*a*) dishonestly secures the remission of the whole or part of any existing liability to make a payment, whether his own liability or another's; or

(*b*) with intent to make permanent default in whole or in part on any existing liability[2] to make a payment, or with intent to let another do so, dishonestly induces the creditor or any person claiming payment on behalf of the creditor to wait for payment (whether or not the due date for payment is deferred) or to forgo payment; or

(*c*) dishonestly obtains any exemption from or abatement of liability to make a payment[3];

he shall be guilty of an offence.

(2) For purposes of this section "liability" means legally enforceable liability; and subsection (1) shall not apply in relation to a liability that has not been accepted or established to pay compensation for a wrongful act or omission.

(3) For purposes of subsection (1)(*b*) a person induced to take in payment a cheque or other security for money by way of conditional satisfaction of a pre-existing liability is to be treated not as being paid but as being induced to wait for payment.

(4) For purposes of subsection (1)(*c*) "obtains" includes obtaining for another or enabling another to obtain.

[Theft Act 1978, s 2.]

1. For consideration of the provisions of s 2(1), see *R v Holt* [1981] 2 All ER 854, [1981] 1 WLR 1000; considered in *R v Jackson* [1983] Crim LR 617.

2. The fact that an agreement is not enforceable without a court order does not mean there is no existing liability (*R v Modupe* [1991] Crim LR 530—improperly executed consumer credit agreement). An offence may be committed by a defendant either intending to make permanent default in respect of a personal liability or by intending to enable another to make permanent default in respect of that other's liability (*R v Attewell-Hughes* [1991] 4 All ER 810, [1991] 1 WLR 955, 155 JP 828, CA).

3. As to the relationship of paragraphs (*a*), (*b*) and (*c*), see *R v Sibartie* [1983] Crim LR 470. For the purpose of paragraph (*c*), the deception may take the form of an act of commission or omission; see *R v Firth* (1989) 154 JP 576, 91 Cr App Rep 217, CA.

8–30842 **3. Making off without payment.** (1) Subject to subsection (3) below, a person who, knowing that payment on the spot for any goods supplied or service done is required or expected[1] from him, dishonestly makes off[2] without having paid as required or expected and with intent[3] to avoid payment of the amount due shall be guilty of an offence[3].

(2) For purposes of this section "payment on the spot" includes payment at the time of collecting goods on which work has been done or in respect of which service has been provided.

(3) Subsection (1) above shall not apply where the supply of the goods or the doing of the service is contrary to law, or where the service done is such that payment is not legally enforceable[4].

(4) *Repealed.*

[Theft Act 1978, s 3 as amended by the Serious Organised Crime and Police Act 2005, Sch 7.]

1. Where an agreement has been made to defer payment, that agreement will defeat the normal expectation of payment on the spot. As this subsection is intended to create a simple and straightforward offence, an analysis of whether the agreement was obtained by deception is neither required nor permitted. The fact that the agreement was obtained dishonestly does not reinstate the expectation (*R v Vincent* [2001] EWCA Crim 295, [2001] 1 WLR 1172, [2001] 2 Cr App Rep 150, CA).

2. "Making off" involves a departure from the spot where payment is required (*R v Brooks* (1983) 76 Cr App Rep 66); a breach of contract by the party claiming payment may mean that the defendant may not have been in a situation in which he was bound to pay or even tender the money, thus cannot be charged with making off (*Troughton v Metropolitan Police* [1987] Crim LR 138).

3. There must be an intention permanently to avoid payment or to avoid payment altogether and not merely an intent to delay or defer payment (*R v Allen* [1985] AC 1029, [1985] 2 All ER 641, 149 JP 587, HL).

4. For example, where the person providing a service is in breach of contract; see *Troughton v Metropolitan Police* [1987] Crim LR 138 (taxi driver not completing journey).

5. This power of arrest would seem to be consumed in the power of arrest in s 24 of and Sch 1A to the Police and Criminal Evidence Act 1984, in PART I: MAGISTRATES' COURTS, PROCEDURE, ante. It has been held that this power of arrest may be exercised by a railway ticket collector to prevent a passenger passing through the exit barrier at the end of a journey and making off without payment of the fare, notwithstanding the specific statutory powers in s 5 of the Regulation of Railways Act 1889, in PART VIII: TRANSPORT—Railways, post; see *Moberly v Allsop* (1991) 156 JP 514.

8–30843 **4. Punishments.** (1) Offences under this Act shall be punishable either on conviction on indictment or on summary conviction.

(2) A person convicted on indictment shall be liable—

(*a*) for an offence under section 1 or section 2 of this Act, to imprisonment for a term not exceeding **five years**; and

(*b*) for an offence under section 3 of this Act, to imprisonment for a term not exceeding **two years**.

(3) A person convicted summarily of any offence under this Act shall be liable[1]—

(*a*) to imprisonment for a term not exceeding **six months**; or

(*b*) to a fine not exceeding **the prescribed sum** for the purposes of section 32 of the Magistrates' Courts Act 1980 (punishment on summary conviction of offences triable either way: £1,000[2] or other sum substituted by order under that Act), or to **both**.

[Theft Act 1978, s 4, as amended by the Magistrates' Courts Act 1980, Sch 7.]

1. For procedure in respect of an offence triable either way, see the Magistrates' Courts Act 1980, ss 17A–21, in PART I: MAGISTRATES' COURTS, PROCEDURE, ante.

2. For the current amount of "the prescribed sum", see the Magistrates' Courts Act 1980, s 32(9), in PART I: MAGISTRATES' COURTS, PROCEDURE, ante.

8–30844 **5. Supplementary.** (1) For purposes of sections 1 and 2 above "deception" has the same meaning as in section 15 of the Theft Act 1968, that is to say, it means any deception (whether deliberate or reckless) by words or conduct as to fact or as to law, including a deception as to the present intentions of the person using the deception or any other person; and section 18 of that Act (liability of company officers for offences by the company) shall apply in relation to sections 1 and 2 above as it applies in relation to section 15 of that Act.

(2) Sections 30(1) (husband and wife), 31(1) (effect on civil proceedings) and 34 (interpretation) of the Theft Act 1968, so far as they are applicable in relation to this Act, shall apply as they apply in relation to that Act.

(4)–(5) *Visiting Forces Act 1952; Repeal provisions.*

[Theft Act 1978, s 5, as amended by the Criminal Justice Act 1988, Sch 16 and the Extradition Act Sch 2.]

TOWN AND COUNTRY PLANNING

8–30860 This title comprises the following statutes—

The following statutory instrument is also printed—

Caravan Sites and Control of Development Act 1960

(8 & 9 Eliz 2 c 62)

PART I
CARAVAN SITES

Licensing of caravan sites

8–30890 1. Prohibition of use of land as caravan site without site licence. (1) Subject to the provisions of this Part of this Act, no occupier[1] of land shall after the commencement of this Act[2] cause or permit any part of the land to be used as a caravan site[3] unless he is the holder of a site licence (that is to say, a licence under this Part of this Act authorising the use of land as a caravan site) for the time being in force as respects the land so used.

(2) If the occupier of any land contravenes subsection (1) of this section he shall be guilty of an offence and liable on summary conviction, to a fine not exceeding **level 4** on the standard scale.

(3) In this Part of this Act the expression "occupier" means, in relation to any land, the person who, by virtue of an estate or interest therein held by him, is entitled to possession thereof or would be so entitled but for the rights of any other person under any licence granted in respect of the land:

Provided that where land amounting to not more than four hundred square yards in area is let under a tenancy entered into with a view to the use of the land as a caravan site, the expression "occupier" means in relation to that land the person who would be entitled to possession of the land but for the rights of any person under that tenancy.

(4) In this Part of this Act the expression "caravan site" means land on which a caravan is stationed for the purposes of human habitation and land which is used in conjunction with land on which a caravan is so stationed.

[Caravan Sites and Control of Development Act 1960, s 1, as amended by the Criminal Justice Act 1982, ss 35, 38 and 46.]

1. "Occupier" is defined by s 1(3), *infra*.
2. This Act commenced on 29 August 1960.
3. "Caravan site" is defined by s 1(4), *infra*. "Caravan" means any structure designed or adapted for human habitation which is capable of being moved from one place to another whether by being towed, or by being transported on a motor vehicle or trailer, and any motor vehicle so designed or adapted, but does not include—(*a*) any railway rolling stock which is for the time being on rails forming part of a railway system, or, (*b*) any tent (s 29(1)). The definition of "caravan" contemplates that the structure has to be capable of being moved from one place to another as a single unit; accordingly, a prefabricated structure which was delivered to a site by lorry, had to be bolted together and which lacked wheels so that it had to be dismantled to be moved was held not to be a caravan; see *Carter v Secretary of State for the Environment* [1994] 1 WLR 1212.

8–30891 2. Exemptions from licensing requirements. No site licence shall be required for the use of land as a caravan site in any of the circumstances specified in the First Schedule to this Act[1] and that Schedule shall have effect accordingly.

[Caravan Sites and Control of Development Act 1960, s 2.]

1. For the purposes of this work, the First Schedule may be summarised as follows: A licence is not required, in the circumstances set out in the Schedule, for (1) use within curtilage of a dwelling-house, (2) use for not more than two nights, (3) use of holdings of five acres or more in certain circumstances, (4) sites occupied or approved by exempted organisations, (5) agricultural and forestry workers, (6), building and engineering sites, (7) travelling showmen, (8) sites occupied by local authority.

As to the exemption for travelling showmen, see *Holmes v Cooper* [1985] 3 All ER 114, [1985] 1 WLR 1060, CA.

8–30892 3, 4. Issue of site licences by local authorities.—The council of a borough or urban or rural district or the Common Council of the City of London may, and in prescribed circumstances shall[1] issue to applicants a site licence, the duration of which is unlimited except where permission to use the land as a caravan site has been granted under Part III of the Town and Country Planning Act [1990], otherwise than by a development order. [Caravan Sites and Control of Development Act

1960, ss 3, 4, amended by the Local Government, Planning and Land Act 1980, Sch 3 *summarised.*] The application of the Act to Greater London is modified by the London Government Act 1963, 17th Sch, para 21.

1. Where a local authority being required to issue a licence, fail to do so, no offence is committed under s 1 by a person by whom an application has been made (s 6).

8–30893 **5. Power of local authority to attach conditions to site licences.** (1) A site licence issued by a local authority in respect of any land may be so issued subject to such conditions as the authority may think it necessary or desirable to impose on the occupier of the land in the interests of persons dwelling thereon in caravans, or of any other class of persons, or of the public at large; and in particular, but without prejudice to the generality of the foregoing, a site licence may be issued subject to conditions—

(*a*) for restricting the occasions on which caravans are stationed on the land for the purposes of human habitation, or the total number of caravans which are so stationed at any one time;
(*b*) for controlling (whether by reference to their size, the state of their repair or, subject to the provisions of subsection (2) of this section, any other feature) the type of caravan which are stationed on the land;
(*c*) for regulating the positions in which caravans are stationed on the land for the purposes of human habitation and for prohibiting, restricting, or otherwise regulating, the placing or erection on the land, at any time when caravans are so stationed, of structures and vehicles of any description whatsoever and of tents;
(*d*) for securing the taking of any steps for preserving or enhancing the amenity of the land, including the planting and replanting thereof with trees and bushes;
(*e*) for securing that, at all times when caravans are stationed on the land, proper measures are taken for preventing and detecting the outbreak of fire and adequate means of fighting fire are provided and maintained;
(*f*) for securing that adequate sanitary facilities, and such other facilities, services or equipment as may be specified, are provided for the use of persons dwelling on the land in caravans and that, at all times when caravans are stationed thereon for the purposes of human habitation, any facilities and equipment so provided are properly maintained.

(2) No condition shall be attached to a site licence controlling the types of caravans which are stationed on the land by reference to the materials used in their construction.

(2A) Where the Regulatory Reform (Fire Safety) Order 2005 applies to the land, no condition is to be attached to a site licence in so far as it relates to any matter in relation to which requirements or prohibitions are or could be imposed by or under that Order.[1]

(3) A site licence issued in respect of any land shall, unless it is issued subject to a condition restricting to three or less the total number of caravans which may be stationed on the land at any one time, contain an express condition that, at all times when caravans are stationed on the land for the purposes of human habitation, a copy of the licence as for the time being in force shall be displayed on the land in some conspicuous place.

(3A) The local authority shall consult the fire and rescue authority as to the extent to which any model standards relating to fire precautions which have been specified under subsection (6) of this section are appropriate to the land.

(3B) If—

(*a*) no such standards have been specified; or
(*b*) any standard that has been specified appears to the fire and rescue authority to be inappropriate to the land,

the local authority shall consult the fire and rescue authority as to what conditions relating to fire precautions ought to be attached to the site licence instead.

(3C) Subsections (3A) and (3B) of this section do not apply where the Regulatory Reform (Fire Safety) Order 2005 applies to the land.[1]

(4) A condition attached to a site licence may, if it requires the carrying out of any works on the land in respect of which the licence is issued, prohibit or restrict the bringing of caravans on to the land for the purposes of human habitation until such time as the local authority have certified in writing that the works have been completed to their satisfaction; and where the land to which the site licence relates is at the time in use as a caravan site, the condition may, whether or not it contains any such prohibition or restriction as aforesaid, require the works to be completed to the satisfaction of the authority within a stated period[2].

(5) For the avoidance of doubt, it is hereby declared that a condition attached to a site licence shall be valid notwithstanding that it can be complied with only by the carrying out of works which the holder of the site licence is not entitled to carry out as of right.

(6) The Minister[3] may from time to time specify for the purposes of this section model standards[4] with respect to the layout of, and the provision of facilities, services and equipment for, caravan sites or particular types of caravan site; and in deciding what (if any) conditions to attach to a site licence, a local authority shall have regard to any standards so specified.

(6A) No model standards may be specified under subsection (6) of this section in relation to land to which the Regulatory Reform (Fire Safety) Order 2005 applies in so far as the standards relate to any matter in relation to which requirements or prohibitions are or could be imposed by or under that Order.[1]

(7) The duty imposed on a local authority by subsection (6) of this section to have regard to standards specified under that subsection is to be construed, as regards standards relating to fire precautions which are so specified, as a duty to have regard to them subject to any advice given by the fire and rescue authority[2] under subsection (3A) or (3B) of this section.

(8) In this section "fire precautions" means precautions to be taken for any of the purposes specified in paragraph (*e*) of subsection (1) of this section for which conditions may be imposed by virtue of this section[1].

[Caravan Sites and Control of Development Act 1960, s 5, as amended by the Local Government (Miscellaneous Provisions) Act 1982, s 8, the Fire and Rescue Services Act 2004, Sch 1 and SI 2005/1541.]

---

1. Subsections (2A), (3C) and (6A) and words "this section" inserted in relation to England and Wales by SI 2005/1541.
2. Failure to complete the works after the end of the stated period is a continuing offence under s 9, post (*Penton Park Homes Ltd v Chertsey UDC* (1973) 72 LGR 115, 26 P & CR 531).
3. "The Minister" is the Secretary of State for the Environment (s 29(1)).
4. Model Standards were specified by the Minister of Housing and Local Government in 1960 and are obtainable from HM Stationery Office.

8–30894 **7. Appeal to magistrates' court against conditions attached to site licence.** (1) Any person aggrieved by any condition (other than the condition referred to in s 5(3) of this Act) subject to which a site licence has been issued to him in respect of any land may, within twenty-eight days of the date on which the licence was so issued, appeal to a magistrates' court[1] acting for the petty sessions area in which the land is situated; and the court, if satisfied (having regard amongst other things[2] to any standards which may have been specified by the Minister under subsection (6) of the said section five[2]) that the condition is unduly burdensome[3], may vary or cancel the condition.

(2) In so far as the effect of a condition (in whatever words expressed) subject to which a site licence is issued in respect of any land is to require the carrying out on the land of any works, the condition shall not have effect during the period within which the person to whom the site licence is issued is entitled by virtue of the foregoing subsection to appeal against the condition nor, thereafter, whilst an appeal against the condition is pending.

[Caravan Sites and Control of Development Act 1960, s 7.]

---

1. Appeal is by way of complaint (Magistrates' Courts Rules 1981, r 34, in PART I: MAGISTRATES' COURTS, PROCEDURE, ante).
2. Visual amenity of an area is a matter to which magistrates can lawfully have regard (*Babbage v North Norfolk District Council* (1988) 153 JP 278).
3. "The Minister" is the Secretary of State for the Environment (s 29(1)).
4. The site licence must be confined within the limits of the planning permission: a magistrates' court has no jurisdiction to vary a condition of a site licence, beyond the scope of this permission (*R v Kent Justices, ex p Crittenden* [1964] 1 QB 144, [1963] 2 All ER 245, 127 JP 359). On the other hand, conditions which seek to impose a substantial limitation on the licensee, beyond the scope and object of the Act (ie control of the physical condition or use of the site) may be invalid and therefore unduly burdensome, see *Mixnam's Properties Ltd v Chertsey UDC* [1965] AC 735, [1964] 2 All ER 627, 128 JP 405, HL.

Section 17 of the Act contains provisions whereby planning permission is deemed to have been granted in respect of existing sites (defined in s 13, post). The licensing authority may not impose conditions derogating from existing user rights; *Minister of Housing and Local Government v Hartnell* [1965] AC 1134, [1965] 1 All ER 490, 129 JP 234, HL. Whether any such conditions are "unduly burdensome" is a question of fact for the magistrates (*Esdell Caravan Parks Ltd v Hemel Hempstead RDC* [1966] 1 QB 895, [1965] 3 All ER 737, 130 JP 66).

8–30895 **8. Power of local authority to alter conditions attached to site licences.** (1) The conditions attached to a site licence may be altered at any time (whether by the variation or cancellation of existing conditions, or by the addition of new conditions, or by a combination of any such methods) by the local authority, but before exercising their powers under this subsection the local authority shall afford to the holder of the licence an opportunity of making representations.

(1A) Where the Regulatory Reform (Fire Safety) Order 2005 applies to the land to which the site licence relates, no condition may be attached to a site licence under subsection (1) of this section in so far as it relates to any matter in relation to which requirements or prohibitions are or could be imposed by or under that Order.[1]

(2) Where the holder of a site licence is aggrieved by any alteration of the conditions attached thereto or by the refusal of the local authority of an application by him for the alteration of those conditions[2], he may within twenty-eight days of the date on which written notification of the alteration or refusal is received by him, appeal to a magistrates' court[2] acting for the petty sessions area in which the land to which the site licence relates is situated; and the court may, if they allow the appeal, give to the local authority such directions as may be necessary to give effect to their decision.

(3) The alteration by a local authority of the conditions attached to any site licence shall not have effect until written notification thereof has been received by the holder of the licence.

(5) The local authority shall consult the fire and rescue authority before exercising the powers

conferred upon them by subsection (1) of this section in relation to a condition attached to a site licence for the purposes set out in section 5(1)(*e*) of this Act.

(5A) Subsection (5) of this section does not apply where the Regulatory Reform (Fire Safety) Order 2005 applies to the land.[1]

[Caravan Sites and Control of Development Act 1960, s 8, as amended by the Local Government (Miscellaneous Provisions) Act 1982, s 8, the Fire and Rescue Services Act 2004, Sch 1 and SI 2005/1541.]

---

1. Subsections (1A) and (5A) inserted in relation to England and Wales by SI 2005/1541.

2. The expression "those conditions" includes the conditions originally imposed on the grant of the licence and is not limited to the conditions that the local authority propose to alter (*Peters v Yiewsley and West Drayton UDC* [1963] 2 QB 133, [1963] 1 All ER 843, 127 JP 277).

8–30896 9. Provisions as to breaches of condition. (1) If an occupier of land fails to comply with any condition for the time being attached to a site licence held by him in respect of the land, he shall be guilty of an offence and liable on summary conviction, to a fine not exceeding **level 4** on the standard scale.

(2) Where a person convicted under this section for failing to comply with a condition attached to a site licence has on two or more previous occasions been convicted thereunder for failing to comply with a condition attached to that licence, the court before whom he is convicted may, if an application in that behalf is made at the hearing by the local authority in whose area the land is situated, make an order for the revocation of the said site licence to come into force on such date as the court may specify in the order, being a date not earlier than the expiration of any period within which notice of appeal (whether by case stated or otherwise) may be given against the conviction[1] and if before the date so specified an appeal is so brought the order shall be of no effect pending the final determination or withdrawal of the appeal.

The person convicted or the local authority who issued the site licence may apply to the magistrates' court which has made such an order revoking a site licence for an order extending the period at the end of which the revocation is to come into force, and the magistrates' court may, if satisfied that adequate notice of the application has been given to the local authority or, as the case may be, the person convicted, make an order extending that period.

(3) Where an occupier of land fails within the time specified in a condition attached to a site licence held by him to complete to the satisfaction of the local authority in whose area the land is situated any works required by the condition to be so completed, the local authority may carry out those works, and may recover as a simple contract debt in any court of competent jurisdiction from that person any expenses reasonably incurred by them in that behalf.

[Caravan Sites and Control of Development Act 1960, s 9, as amended by the Courts Act 1971, Sch 8 and the Criminal Justice Act 1982, ss 35, 38 and 46.]

---

1. See the Magistrates' Court Act 1980, s 111(2), and the Crown Court Rules 1982 in PART I: MAGISTRATES' COURTS, PROCEDURE, ante.

8–30897 10. Transfer of site licences and transmission on death, etc. Provision is made for transfer of a site licence and for its devolution to a person becoming the occupier of the land.

[Caravan Sites and Control of Development Act 1960, s 10—summarised.]

8–30898 11. Duty of licence holder to surrender licence for alteration. (1) A local authority who have issued a site licence may at any time require the holder to deliver it up so as to enable them to enter in it any alteration of the conditions or other terms of the licence made in pursuance of the provisions of this Part of this Act.

(2) If the holder of a site licence fails without reasonable excuse to comply with a requirement duly made under this section he shall be liable on summary conviction to a fine not exceeding **level 1** on the standard scale.

[Caravan Sites and Control of Development Act 1960, s 11, as amended by the Criminal Justice Act 1982, ss 38 and 46.]

Special Provisions as to existing sites

8–30899 13–20. (*Repealed.*)

[Caravan Sites and Control of Development Act 1960, ss 13–20, repealed by the Statute Law (Repeals) Act 1993.]

Caravans on commons

8–30901 23. A district council may make an order with respect to prescribed commons in their area prohibiting the stationing of caravans on the land for the purposes of human habitation. Contravention of such an order is punishable on summary conviction by a fine not exceeding **level 1** on the standard scale.

[Caravan Sites and Control of Development Act 1960, s 23, as amended by the Local Government Act 1972, Sch 29, the Criminal Justice Act 1982, ss 38 and 46 and the Local Government (Wales) Act 1994, Sch 16—summarised.]

Miscellaneous and supplemental

8-30902 **26. Power of entry of officers of local authorities.** (1) Subject to the provisions of this section, any authorised officer of a local authority shall, on producing, if so required, some duly authenticated document showing his authority, have a right at all reasonable hours to enter any land which is used as a caravan site or in respect of which an application for a site licence has been made—

(*a*) for the purpose of enabling the local authority to determine what conditions should be attached to a site licence or whether conditions attached to a site licence should be altered;
(*b*) for the purpose of ascertaining whether there is, or has been, on or in connection with the land any contravention of the provisions of this part of this Act;
(*c*) for the purpose of ascertaining whether or not circumstances exist which would authorise the local authority to take any action, or execute any work, under this Part of this Act;
(*d*) for the purpose of taking any action, or executing any work, authorised by this Part of this Act to be taken or executed by the local authority:

Provided that admission to any land shall not be demanded as of right unless twenty-four hours notice of the intended entry has been given to the occupier.

(2) If it is shown to the satisfaction of a justice of the peace—

(*a*) that admission to any land has been refused, or that refusal is apprehended, or that the occupier of the land is temporarily absent and the case is one of urgency, or that an application for admission would defeat the object of the entry; and
(*b*) that there is reasonable ground for entering on the land for any such purpose as is mentioned in subsection (1) of this section,

the justice may by warrant under his hand authorise the local authority by any authorised officer to enter the land, if need be by force:

Provided that such a warrant shall not be issued unless the justice is satisfied either that notice of the intention to apply for the warrant has been given to the occupier, or that the occupier is temporarily absent and the case is one of urgency, or that the giving of such notice would defeat the object of the entry.

(3) An authorised officer entering any land by virtue of this section, or of a warrant issued thereunder, may take with him such other persons as may be necessary.

(4) Every warrant granted under this section shall continue in force until the purpose for which the entry is necessary has been satisfied.

(5) A person who wilfully obstructs any person acting in the execution of this section, or of a warrant under this section, shall be liable on summary conviction to a fine not exceeding **level 1** on the standard scale.

[Caravan Sites and Control of Development Act 1960, s 26, as amended by the Criminal Justice Act 1982, ss 38 and 46.]

Caravan Sites Act 1968

(1968 c 52)

Part I

Provisions for Protection of Residential Occupiers

8-31010 **1. Application of Part I.** (1) This Part of this Act applies in relation to any licence or contract (whether made before or after the passing of this Act) under which a person is entitled to station a caravan on a protected site (as defined by subsection (2) below) and occupy it at his residence, or to occupy as his residence a caravan stationed on any such site; and any such licence or contract is in this Part referred to as a residential contract, and the person so entitled as the occupier.

(2) For the purposes of this Part of this Act a protected site is any land in respect of which a site licence is required under Part I of the Caravan Sites and Control of Development Act 1960 or would be so required if paragraph 11 or 11A of Schedule 1 to that Act (exemption of gypsy and other* local authority sites) were omitted, not being land in respect of which the relevant planning permission or site licence—

(*a*) is expressed to be granted for holiday use only; or
(*b*) is otherwise so expressed or subject to such conditions that there are times of the year when no caravan may be stationed on the land for human habitation.

(3) References in this Part of this Act to the owner of a protected site are references to the person who is or would apart from any residential contract be entitled to possession of the land.

[Caravan Sites Act 1968, s 1, as amended by the Housing Act 2004, s 209.]

***Amended by the Housing (Scotland) Act 2006, s 171 from a date to be appointed.**

8-31011 **2.** *Minimum length of notice determining a residential contract.*

8–31012 **3. Protection of occupiers against eviction and harassment.** (1) Subject to the provisions of this section, a person shall be guilty of an offence under this section—

(*a*) if, during the subsistence of a residential contract, he unlawfully deprives the occupier of his occupation on the protected site of any caravan which the occupier is entitled by the contract to station and occupy, or to occupy, as his residence thereon;

(*b*) if, after the expiration or determination of a residential contract, he enforces, otherwise than by proceedings in the court, any right to exclude the occupier from the protected site or from any such caravan, or to remove or exclude any such caravan from the site;

(*c*) if, whether during the subsistence or after the expiration or determination of a residential contract, with intent to cause the occupier—

(i) to abandon the occupation of the caravan or remove it from the site, or

(ii) to refrain from exercising any right or pursuing any remedy in respect thereof,

he does acts likely to interfere with the peace or comfort of the occupier or persons residing with him, or persistently withdraws or withholds services or facilities reasonably required for the occupation of the caravan as a residence on the site.*

(1A) Subject to the provisions of this section, the owner of a protected site or his agent shall be guilty of an offence under this section if, whether during the subsistence or after the expiration or determination of a residential contract—

(*a*) he does acts likely to interfere with the peace or comfort of the occupier or persons residing with him, or

(*b*) he persistently withdraws or withholds services or facilities reasonably required for the occupation of the caravan as a residence on the site,

and (in either case) he knows, or has reasonable cause to believe, that that conduct is likely to cause the occupier to do any of the things mentioned in subsection (1)(*c*)(i) or (ii) of this section.*

(1B) References in subsection (1A) of this section to the owner of a protected site include references to a person with an estate or interest in the site which is superior to that of the owner.*

(2) References in this section to the occupier include references to the person who was the occupier under a residential contract which has expired or been determined and, in the case of the death of the occupier (whether during the subsistence or after the expiration or determination of the contract), to any person then residing with the occupier being—

(*a*) The widow, widower or surviving civil partner of the occupier; or

(*b*) in default of a widow, widower or surviving civil partner so residing, any member of the occupier's family.

(3) A person guilty of an offence under this section shall, without prejudice to any liability or remedy to which he may be subject in civil proceedings, be liable—

(*a*) on summary conviction, to a fine not exceeding the statutory maximum or to imprisonment for a term not exceeding 12 months, or to both;

(*b*) on conviction on indictment, to a fine or to imprisonment for a term not exceeding 2 years, or to both.*

(4) In proceedings for an offence under paragraph (*a*) or (*b*) of subsection (1) of this section it shall be a defence to prove that the accused believed, and had reasonable cause to believe, that the occupier of the caravan had ceased to reside on the site.

(4A) In proceedings for an offence under subsection (1A) of this section it shall be a defence to prove that the accused had reasonable grounds for doing the acts or withdrawing or withholding the services or facilities in question.*

(5) Nothing in this section applies to the exercise by any person of a right to take possession of a caravan of which he is the owner, other than a right conferred by or arising on the expiration or determination of a residential contract, or to anything done pursuant to the order of any court.

[Caravan Sites Act 1968, s 3, as amended by the Criminal Justice Act 1982, ss 35, 38 and 46, the Housing Act 2004, s 210 and the Civil Partnership Act 2004, Sch 27.]

***Amended by the Housing (Scotland) Act 2006, s 171 from a date to be appointed.**

8–31013 **4.** *Provision for suspension of eviction orders.*

PART III

8–31017 **13. Twin-unit caravans.** (1) A structure designed or adapted for human habitation which—

(*a*) is composed of not more than two sections separately constructed and designed to be assembled on a site by means of bolts, clamps or other devices; and

(*b*) is, when assembled, physically capable of being moved by road from one place to another (whether by being towed, or by being transported on a motor vehicle or trailer),

shall not be treated as not being (or as not having been) a caravan within the meaning of Part I of the

Caravan Sites and Control of Development Act 1960 by reason only that it cannot lawfully be so moved on a highway when assembled.

(2) For the purposes of Part I of the Caravan Sites and Control of Development Act 1960, the expression "caravan" shall not include a structure designed or adapted for human habitation which falls within paragraphs (*a*) and (*b*) of the foregoing subsection if its dimensions when assembled exceed any of the following limits, namely—

(*a*) length (exclusive of any drawbar): 60 feet (18·288 metres);
(*b*) width: 20 feet (6·096 metres);
(*c*) overall height of living accommodation (measured internally from the floor at the lowest level to the ceiling at the highest level): 10 feet (3·048 metres).

(3) The Minister may by order made by statutory instrument after consultation with such persons or bodies as appear to him to be concerned substitute for any figure mentioned in subsection (2) of this section such other figure as may be specified in the order.

(4) Any statutory instrument made by virtue of subsection (3) of this section shall be subject to annulment in pursuance of a resolution of either House of Parliament.
[Caravan Sites Act 1968, s 13.]

8–31018 14. Offences. (1) Where an offence under this Act committed by a body corporate is proved to have been committed with the consent or connivance of or to be attributable to any neglect on the part of, any director, manager, secretary or other similar officer of the body corporate or any person who is purporting to act in any such capacity, he as well as the body corporate shall be guilty of that offence and shall be liable to be proceeded against and punished accordingly.

(2) Proceedings for an offence under this Act may be instituted by any local authority.
[Caravan Sites Act 1968, s 14.]

8–31019 16. Interpretation. In this Act the following expressions have the following meanings that is to say—

"caravan" has the same meaning as in Part I of the Caravan Sites and Control of Development Act 1960, as amended by this Act;

"local authority" has the same meaning as in section 24 of the Caravan Sites and Control of Development Act 1960;

"the Minister" means, in England other than Monmouthshire, the Minister of Housing and Local Government, and in Wales and Monmouthshire the Secretary of State;

"planning permission" means permission under Part III of the Town and Country Planning Act 1990.

[Caravan Sites Act 1968, s 16, as amended by the Town and Country Planning Act 1971, Sch 23, the Planning (Consequential Provisions) Act 1990, Sch 2 and the Criminal Justice and Public Order Act 1994, Sch 11.]

Town and Country Planning Act 1990

(1990 c 8)

PART III[1]

CONTROL OVER DEVELOPMENT

Meaning of development

8–31030 55. Meaning of "development" and "new development". (1) Subject to the following provisions of this section, in this Act, except where the context otherwise requires, "development," means the carrying out of building, engineering, mining or other operations in, on, over or under land, or the making of any material change in the use of any buildings or other land.

(1A) For the purposes of this Act "building operations" includes—

(*a*) demolition of buildings;
(*b*) rebuilding;
(*c*) structural alterations of or additions to buildings; and
(*d*) other operations normally undertaken by a person carrying on business as a builder.

(2) The following operations or uses of land shall not be taken for the purposes of this Act to involve development of the land—

(*a*) the carrying out for the maintenance, improvement or other alteration of any building of works which—

(i) affect only the interior of the building, or
(ii) do not materially affect the external appearance of the building,

and are not works for making good war damage or works begun after 5th December 1968 for the alteration of a building by providing additional space in it underground;

(*b*) the carrying out on land within the boundaries of a road by a local highway authority of any works required for the maintenance or improvement of the road but, in the case of any such works which are not exclusively for the maintenance of the road, not including any works which may have significant adverse effects on the environment;

(*c*) the carrying out by a local authority or statutory undertakers of any works for the purpose of inspecting, repairing or renewing any sewers, mains, pipes, cables or other apparatus, including the breaking open of any street or other land for that purpose;

(*d*) the use of any buildings or other land within the curtilage of a dwellinghouse for any purpose incidental to the enjoyment of the dwellinghouse as such;

(*e*) the use of any land for the purposes of agriculture or forestry (including afforestation) and the use for any of those purposes of any building occupied together with land so used;

(*f*) in the case of buildings or other land which are used for a purpose of any class specified in an order[2] made by the Secretary of State under this section, the use of the buildings or other land or, subject to the provisions of the order, of any part of the buildings or the other land, for any other purpose of the same class;

(*g*) the demolition of any description of building specified in a direction given by the Secretary of State to local planning authorities generally or to a particular local planning authority.

(2A) The Secretary of State may in a development order specify any circumstances or description of circumstances in which subsection (2) does not apply to operations mentioned in paragraph (*a*) of that subsection which have the effect of increasing the gross floor space of the building by such amount or percentage amount as is so specified.

(2B) The development order may make different provision for different purposes.

(3) For the avoidance of doubt it is hereby declared that for the purposes of this section—

(*a*) the use as two or more separate dwellinghouses of any building previously used as a single dwellinghouse involves a material change in the use of the building and of each part of it which is so used;

(*b*) the deposit of refuse or waste materials on land involves a material change in its use, notwithstanding that the land is comprised in a site already used for that purpose, if—

(i) the superficial area of the deposit is extended, or

(ii) the height of the deposit is extended and exceeds the level of the land adjoining the site.

(4) For the purposes of this Act mining operations include—

(*a*) the removal of material of any description—

(i) from a mineral-working deposit;

(ii) from a deposit of pulverised fuel ash or other furnace ash or clinker; or

(iii) from a deposit of iron, steel or other metallic slags; and

(*b*) the extraction of minerals from a disused railway embankment.

(4A) Where the placing or assembly of any tank in any part of any inland waters for the purpose of fish farming there would not, apart from this subsection, involve development of the land below, this Act shall have effect as if the tank resulted from carrying out engineering operations over that land; and in this subsection—

"fish farming" means the breeding, rearing or keeping of fish or shellfish (which includes any kind of crustacean and mollusc);

"inland waters" means waters which do not form part of the sea or of any creek, bay or estuary or of any river as far as the tide flows; and

"tank" includes any cage and any other structure for use in fish farming.

(5) Without prejudice to any regulations made under the provisions of this Act relating to the control of advertisements, the use for the display of advertisements of any external part of a building which is not normally used for that purpose shall be treated for the purposes of this section as involving a material change in the use of that part of the building.

(6) (*Repealed*).

[Town and Country Planning Act 1990, s 55, as amended by the Planning and Compensation Act 1991, ss 13, 14 and Sch 19, SI 1999/293 and the Planning and Compulsory Purchase Act 2004, s 49.]

8–31030A 65. Notice etc of applications for planning permission. (1) A development order may make provision requiring—

(*a*) notice to be given of any application for planning permission, and

(*b*) any applicant for such permission to issue a certificate as to the interests in the land to which the application relates or the purpose for which it is used,

and provide for publicising such applications and for the form, content and service of such notices and certificates.

(2) Provision shall be made by a development order for the purpose of securing that, in the case of any application for planning permission, any person (other than the applicant) who on such date as may be prescribed by the order is an owner of the land to which the application relates, or an

agricultural tenant of that land, is given notice of the application in such manner as may be required by the order.

(3) A development order may require an applicant for planning permission to certify, in such form as may be prescribed by the order, or to provide evidence, that any requirements of the order have been satisfied.

(4) A development order making any provision by virtue of this section may make different provision for different cases or different classes of development.

(5) A local planning authority shall not entertain an application for planning permission unless any requirements imposed by virtue of this section have been satisfied.

(6) If any person—

(*a*) issues a certificate which purports to comply with any requirement imposed by virtue of this section and contains a statement which he knows to be false or misleading in a material particular; or

(*b*) recklessly issues a certificate which purports to comply with any such requirement and contains a statement which is false or misleading in a material particular;

he shall be guilty of an offence.

(7) A person guilty of an offence under this section shall be liable on summary conviction to a fine not exceeding **level 5** on the standard scale.

(8) In this section—

"agricultural tenant", in relation to any land, means any person who—

(*a*) is the tenant, under a tenancy in relation to which the Agricultural Holdings Act 1986 applies, of an agricultural holding within the meaning of that Act any part of which is comprised in that land; or

(*b*) is the tenant, under a farm business tenancy (within the meaning of the Agricultural Tenancies Act 1995), of land any part of which is comprised in that land;

"owner" in relation to any land means any person who—

(*a*) is the estate owner in respect of the fee simple;

(*b*) is entitled to a tenancy granted or extended for a term of years certain of which not less than seven years remain unexpired; or

(*c*) in the case of such applications as may be prescribed by a development order, is entitled to an interest in any mineral so prescribed,

and the reference to the interests in the land to which an application for planning permission relates includes any interest in any mineral in, on or under the land.

(9) Notwithstanding section 127 of the Magistrates' Courts Act 1980, a magistrates' court may try an information in respect of an offence under this section whenever laid."

[Town and Country Planning Act 1990, s 65, as substituted by the Planning and Compensation Act 1991, s 16 and amended by the Agricultural Tenancies Act 1995, Sch.]

8–31031 102. Orders requiring discontinuance of use or alteration or removal of buildings or works. [1] A local planning authority, if it appears expedient so to do in the interests of the proper planning, may by order require that any use of land should be discontinued, or that any conditions be imposed on the continuance thereof, or that any buildings or works should be altered or removed. Such an order requires to be confirmed by the Secretary of State after the owner and occupier and any other person affected has been given an opportunity of being heard. Where such an order involves the displacement of persons residing in any premises, provision is made for their being provided with alternative accommodation.

[Town and Country Planning Act 1990, s 102, as amended by the Planning and Compensation Act 1991, Schs 1, 7—summarised.]

1. Schedule 9 to this Act makes provision for the discontinuance of mineral working. For enforcement of orders under this section see s 172 et seq.

PART VII
ENFORCEMENT

Enforcement notices[1]

Introductory

8–31032 171A. Expressions used in connection with enforcement[2]**.** (1) For the purposes of this Act—

(*a*) carrying out development without the required planning permission; or

(*b*) failing to comply with any condition or limitation subject to which planning permission has been granted,

constitutes a breach of planning control.

(2) For the purposes of this Act—

(*a*) the issue of an enforcement notice (defined in section 172); or

(*b*) the service of a breach of condition notice (defined in section 187A),

constitutes taking enforcement action.

(3) In this Part "planning permission" includes permission under Part III of the 1947 Act, of the 1962 Act or of the 1971 Act.

[Town and Country Planning Act 1990, s 171A added by the Planning and Compensation Act 1991, s 4.]

1. Part VII contains ss 171A–196.
2. Control of development on Crown land is provided by s 294 of this Act.

8–31033 171B. Time limits. (1) Where there has been a breach of planning control consisting in the carrying out without planning permission of building, engineering, mining or other operations in, on, over or under land, no enforcement action may be taken after the end of the period of four years beginning with the date on which the operations were substantially completed[1].

(2) Where there has been a breach of planning control consisting in the change of use of any building to use as a single dwellinghouse, no enforcement action may be taken after the end of the period of four years beginning with the date of the breach[2].

(3) In the case of any other breach of planning control, no enforcement action may be taken after the end of the period of ten years beginning with the date of the breach.

(4) The preceding subsections do not prevent—

(*a*) the service of a breach of condition notice in respect of any breach of planning control if an enforcement notice in respect of the breach is in effect; or

(*b*) taking further enforcement action in respect of any breach of planning control if, during the period of four years ending with that action being taken, the local planning authority have taken or purported to take enforcement action in respect of that breach[3].

[Town and Country Planning Act 1990, s 171B added by the Planning and Compensation Act 1991, s 4.]

1. The purpose of this provision is to provide a single easily-applied limitation period for operations. In considering whether a building is "substantially completed" it is appropriate to adopt a holistic approach and the question is not confined to those aspects of the development which require planning consent and includes the remainder of the works, such as interior works, which fall outside the definition of development in s 55(2) of the Act (*Sage v Secretary of State for the Environment, Transport and the Regions* [2003] UKHL 22, [2003] 2 All ER 689).

2. If, in the case of any breach of planning control, the time for issuing an enforcement notice has expired, before the coming into force of this section, by virtue of section 172(4)(*b*) of the principal Act (as originally enacted), nothing in this section enables any enforcement action to be taken in respect of the breach; (Planning and Compensation Act 1991, s 4(2)).

3. The breach does not have to be identically described on both occasions. Accordingly where the first enforcement notice referred to a mobile home which the defendant subsequently transformed into a single storey dwelling, the second enforcement notice referring to it or such, was directed at the same development and was within the terms of the subsection (*Jarmain v Secretary of State for the Environment, Transport and the Regions* [1999] 15 LS Gaz R 30).

Planning contravention notices

8–31034 171C. Power to require information about activities on land. (1) Where it appears to the local planning authority that there may have been a breach of planning control in respect of any land, they may serve notice to that effect (referred to in this Act as a "planning contravention notice") on any person who—

(*a*) is the owner or occupier of the land or has any other interest in it; or

(*b*) is carrying out operations on the land or is using it for any purpose.

(2) A planning contravention notice may require the person on whom it is served to give such information as to—

(*a*) any operations being carried out on the land, any use of the land and any other activities being carried out on the land; and

(*b*) any matter relating to the conditions or limitations subject to which any planning permission in respect of the land has been granted,

as may be specified in the notice.

(3) Without prejudice to the generality of subsection (2), the notice may require the person on whom it is served, so far as he is able—

(*a*) to state whether or not the land is being used for any purpose specified in the notice or any operations or activities specified in the notice are being or have been carried out on the land;

(*b*) to state when any use, operations or activities began;

(*c*) to give the name and postal address of any person known to him to use or have used the land for any purpose or to be carrying out, or have carried out, any operations or activities on the land;

(*d*) to give any information he holds as to any planning permission for any use or operations or any reason for planning permission not being required for any use or operations;

(*e*) to state the nature of his interest (if any) in the land and the name and postal address of any other person known to him to have an interest in the land.

(4) A planning contravention notice may give notice of a time and place at which—

(*a*) any offer which the person on whom the notice is served may wish to make to apply for planning permission, to refrain from carrying out any operations or activities or to undertake remedial works; and

(*b*) any representations which he may wish to make about the notice,

will be considered by the authority, and the authority shall give him an opportunity to make in person any such offer or representations at that time and place.

(5) A planning contravention notice must inform the person on whom it is served—

(*a*) of the likely consequences of his failing to respond to the notice and, in particular, that enforcement action may be taken; and

(*b*) of the effect of section 186(5)(*b*).

(6) Any requirement of a planning contravention notice shall be complied with by giving information in writing to the local planning authority.

(7) The service of a planning contravention notice does not affect any other power exercisable in respect of any breach of planning control.

(8) In this section references to operations or activities on land include operations or activities in, under or over the land.

[Town and Country Planning Act 1990, s 171C as added by the Planning and Compensation Act 1991, s 1 and amended by SI 2003/956.]

8–31035 **171D. Penalties for non-compliance with planning contravention notice.** (1) If, at any time after the end of the period of twenty-one days beginning with the day on which a planning contravention notice has been served on any person, he has not complied with any requirement of the notice, he shall be guilty of an offence.

(2) An offence under subsection (1) may be charged by reference to any day or longer period of time and a person may be convicted of a second or subsequent offence under that subsection by reference to any period of time following the preceding conviction for such an offence.

(3) It shall be a defence for a person charged with an offence under subsection (1) to prove that he had a reasonable excuse for failing to comply with the requirement.

(4) A person guilty of an offence under subsection (1) shall be liable on summary conviction to a fine not exceeding **level 3** on the standard scale.

(5) If any person—

(*a*) makes any statement purporting to comply with a requirement of a planning contravention notice which he knows to be false or misleading in a material particular; or

(*b*) recklessly makes such a statement which is false or misleading in a material particular,

he shall be guilty of an offence.

(6) A person guilty of an offence under subsection (5) shall be liable on summary conviction to a fine not exceeding **level 5** on the standard scale.

[Town and Country Planning Act 1990, s 171D as added by the Planning and Compensation Act 1991, s 1.]

8–31035A **171E. Temporary stop notice.** (1) This section applies if the local planning authority think—

(*a*) that there has been a breach of planning control in relation to any land, and

(*b*) that it is expedient that the activity (or any part of the activity) which amounts to the breach is stopped immediately.

(2) The authority may issue a temporary stop notice.

(3) The notice must be in writing and must—

(*a*) specify the activity which the authority think amounts to the breach;

(*b*) prohibit the carrying on of the activity (or of so much of the activity as is specified in the notice);

(*c*) set out the authority's reasons for issuing the notice.

(4) A temporary stop notice may be served on any of the following—

(*a*) the person who the authority think is carrying on the activity;

(*b*) a person who the authority think is an occupier of the land;

(*c*) a person who the authority think has an interest in the land.

(5) The authority must display on the land—

(*a*) a copy of the notice;

(*b*) a statement of the effect of the notice and of section 171G.

(6) A temporary stop notice has effect from the time a copy of it is first displayed in pursuance of subsection (5).

(7) A temporary stop notice ceases to have effect—

(*a*) at the end of the period of 28 days starting on the day the copy notice is so displayed,
(*b*) at the end of such shorter period starting on that day as is specified in the notice, or
(*c*) if it is withdrawn by the local planning authority.*

[Town and Country Planning Act 1990, s 171E as added by the Planning and Compulsory Purchase Act 2004, s 52.]

***In force in relation to England 7 March 2005; and in relation to Wales in force for purposes of regulation making only, to be appointed for remaining purposes.**

8–31035B 171F. Temporary stop notice: restrictions. (1) A temporary stop notice does not prohibit—

(*a*) the use of a building as a dwelling house;
(*b*) the carrying out of an activity of such description or in such circumstances as is prescribed.

(2) A temporary stop notice does not prohibit the carrying out of any activity which has been carried out (whether or not continuously) for a period of four years ending with the day on which the copy of the notice is first displayed as mentioned in section 171E(6).

(3) Subsection (2) does not prevent a temporary stop notice prohibiting—

(*a*) activity consisting of or incidental to building, engineering, mining or other operations, or
(*b*) the deposit of refuse or waste materials.

(4) For the purposes of subsection (2) any period during which the activity is authorised by planning permission must be ignored.

(5) A second or subsequent temporary stop notice must not be issued in respect of the same activity unless the local planning authority has first taken some other enforcement action in relation to the breach of planning control which is constituted by the activity.

(6) In subsection (5) enforcement action includes obtaining the grant of an injunction under section 187B.*

[Town and Country Planning Act 1990, s 171F as added by the Planning and Compulsory Purchase Act 2004, s 52.]

***In force in relation to England 7 March 2005; and in relation to Wales in force for purposes of regulation making only, to be appointed for remaining purposes.**

8–31035C 171G. Temporary stop notice: offences. (1) A person commits an offence if he contravenes a temporary stop notice—

(*a*) which has been served on him, or
(*b*) a copy of which has been displayed in accordance with section 171E(5).

(2) Contravention of a temporary stop notice includes causing or permitting the contravention of the notice.

(3) An offence under this section may be charged by reference to a day or a longer period of time.

(4) A person may be convicted of more than one such offence in relation to the same temporary stop notice by reference to different days or periods of time.

(5) A person does not commit an offence under this section if he proves—

(*a*) that the temporary stop notice was not served on him, and
(*b*) that he did not know, and could not reasonably have been expected to know, of its existence.

(6) A person convicted of an offence under this section is liable—

(*a*) on summary conviction, to a fine not exceeding £20,000;
(*b*) on conviction on indictment, to a fine.

(7) In determining the amount of the fine the court must have regard in particular to any financial benefit which has accrued or has appeared to accrue to the person convicted in consequence of the offence.*

[Town and Country Planning Act 1990, s 171G as added by the Planning and Compulsory Purchase Act 2004, s 52.]

***In force in relation to England 7 March 2005; and in relation to Wales in force for purposes of regulation making only, to be appointed for remaining purposes.**

8–31035D 171H. Temporary stop notice: compensation. (1) This section applies if and only if a temporary stop notice is issued and at least one of the following paragraphs applies—

(*a*) the activity which is specified in the notice is authorised by planning permission or a development order or local development order;
(*b*) a certificate in respect of the activity is issued under section 191 or granted under that section by virtue of section 195;
(*c*) the authority withdraws the notice.

(2) Subsection (1)(*a*) does not apply if the planning permission is granted on or after the date on which a copy of the notice is first displayed as mentioned in section 171E(6).

(3) Subsection (1)(*c*) does not apply if the notice is withdrawn following the grant of planning permission as mentioned in subsection (2).

(4) A person who at the time the notice is served has an interest in the land to which the notice relates is entitled to be compensated by the local planning authority in respect of any loss or damage directly attributable to the prohibition effected by the notice.

(5) Subsections (3) to (7) of section 186 apply to compensation payable under this section as they apply to compensation payable under that section; and for that purpose references in those subsections to a stop notice must be taken to be references to a temporary stop notice.*

[Town and Country Planning Act 1990, s 171H as added by the Planning and Compulsory Purchase Act 2004, s 52.]

***In force in relation to England 7 March 2005; and in relation to Wales in force for purposes of regulation making only, to be appointed for remaining purposes.**

8–31036 **172. Issue of enforcement notice.** (1) The local planning authority may issue a notice (in this Act referred to as an "enforcement notice") where it appears to them—

(*a*) that there has been a breach of planning control[1], and

(*b*) that it is expedient to issue the notice, having regard to the provisions of the development plan and to any other material considerations.

(2) A copy of an enforcement notice shall be served[2]—

(*a*) on the owner[3] and on the occupier of the land[3] to which it relates; and

(*b*) on any other person having an interest in the land, being an interest which, in the opinion of the authority, is materially affected by the notice.

(3) The service[2] of the notice shall take place—

(*a*) not more than twenty-eight days after its date of issue; and

(*b*) not less than twenty-eight days before the date specified in it as the date on which it is to take effect.

[Town and Country Planning Act 1990, s 172, as substituted by the Planning and Compensation Act 1991, s 5.]

---

1. Control of development on Crown land is provided by s 294 of this Act. "Development" is defined by s 55 ante.

2. For mode of service see s 329 post, and *Moody v Godstone RDC* [1966] 2 All ER 696, 130 JP 332. The validity of an enforcement notice may generally be questioned only by way of an appeal; see s 285.

Notice must be served on all the occupiers (*Caravans and Automobiles Ltd v Southall Borough Council* [1963] 2 All ER 533, 127 JP 415), which may include squatters (*Scarborough Borough Council v Adams and Adams* (1983) 147 JP 449); this case also sanctioned the service of a notice on someone not categorised in sub-s (6)(*a*) or (*b*), although service on someone not within the definition of "owners" has been held to be invalid (*Courtney-Southan v Crawley UDC* [1967] 2 QB 930, [1967] 2 All ER 246, 131 JP 330. Failure to serve a notice in accordance with the Act's requirements may not render the notice a nullity (*R v Greenwich London Borough Council, ex p Patel* (1985) 84 LGR 241, 51 P & CR 232, CA).

3. "Owner" and "land" are defined in s 336, post. The phrase "multiple paying occupation" was considered in *Duffy v Pilling* (1976) 120 Sol Jo 504.

8–31037 **173.** *Contents and effect of notice.*

8–31037A **173A.** *Variation and withdrawal of enforcement notices.*

8–31038 **174–177.** *Appeal against enforcement notice.*

8–31039 **178.** *Execution and costs of works required by enforcement notice.*

8–31040 **179. Offence where enforcement notice not complied with.** (1) Where, at any time after the end of the period for compliance with an enforcement notice,[1]any step required by the notice to be taken has not been taken or any activity required by the notice to cease is being carried on, the person who is then the owner of the land is in breach of the notice.

(2) Where the owner of the land is in breach of an enforcement notice he shall be guilty of an offence.

(3) In proceedings against any person for an offence under subsection (2), it shall be a defence for him to show that he did everything he could be expected to do to secure compliance with the notice[2].

(4) A person who has control of or an interest in the land to which an enforcement notice relates (other than the owner) must not carry on any activity which is required by the notice to cease or cause[3] or permit such an activity to be carried on.

(5) A person who, at any time after the end of the period for compliance with the notice, contravenes subsection (4) shall be guilty of an offence.

(6) An offence under subsection (2) or (5) may be charged by reference to any day or longer period of time and a person may be convicted of a second or subsequent offence under the subsection in question by reference to any period of time following the preceding conviction for such an offence.

(7) Where—

(*a*) a person charged with an offence under this section has not been served with a copy of the enforcement notice; and

(*b*) the notice is not contained in the appropriate register kept under section 188,

it shall be a defence for him to show that he was not aware of the existence of the notice.

(8) A person guilty of an offence under this section shall be liable[4]—

(*a*) on summary conviction, to a fine not exceeding **£20,000**; and

(*b*) on conviction on indictment, to a **fine**.

(9) In determining the amount of any fine to be imposed on a person convicted of an offence under this section, the court shall in particular have regard to any financial benefit which has accrued or appears likely to accrue to him in consequence of the offence.

[Town and Country Planning Act 1990, s 179, as substituted by the Planning and Compensation Act 1991, s 8.]

---

1. A defect in an enforcement notice does not render the notice invalid unless it amounts to a material error which causes an injustice (*Patel v Betts* (1977) 243 Estates Gazette 1003). An 'enforcement notice' means a notice issued by a planning authority which on its face complies with the requirements of the Act and has not actually been quashed on appeal or by judicial review. Therefore a defendant in criminal proceedings is not entitled as a matter of right to put forward the defence that the decision to issue the enforcement notice was ultra vires such as where it is alleged the local authority's decision was influenced by bias or improper motives (*R v Wicks* [1997] 2 All ER 801, [1997] 2 WLR 876, 161 JP 433, HL). (See also the decision of the Court of Appeal in the same case where it was held that so long as the enforcement notice is not a nullity, patently defective on its face, it will remain valid until quashed. The prosecutor is under no requirement to establish that the decision of the local planning authority to issue the notice was valid and within its powers. Only the High Court has power to quash the notice. In an exceptional case where proper ground to challenge the validity of the notice came to light as a prosecution was about to be pursued, the appropriate procedure would be for the defendant to apply for an adjournment of the trial on an undertaking to apply for judicial review to quash the notice. If there is a sound basis for such an adjournment the court in its discretion might grant it (*R v Wicks* (1995) 160 JP 46, CA)). An information alleging an offence under sub-ss (1) and (6) must aver to the compliance period which is an essential element of the offence (*Maltedge Ltd v Wokingham District Council* [1993] Crim LR 400).

2. The court is permitted to take into account the defendant's personal and financial circumstances in determining whether he has done everything he could be expected to do to secure compliance with the notice (*Kent County Council v Brockman* [1994] Crim LR 296).

3. To "cause" involves some express or positive mandate from the person causing (*McLeod (or Houston) v Buchanan* [1940] 2 All ER 179, approved in *Shave v Rosner* [1954] 2 QB 113, [1954] 2 All ER 280, 118 JP 364, but see *Sopp v Long* [1969] 1 All ER 855, 133 JP 261): to "permit" involves being in a position to forbid the user (*Goodbarne v Buck* [1940] 1 KB 771, [1940] 1 All ER 613). See introductory note to PART IV title ROAD TRAFFIC, ante on causing, permitting etc. A perpetual injunction was granted at the suit of the Attorney-General to restrain use of land in contravention of an enforcement notice after the defendant had been fined repeatedly by a magistrates' court (*A-G (on relation of Hornchurch UDC) v Bastow* [1957] 1 QB 514, [1957] 1 All ER 497, 121 JP 171; (*A-G v Smith* [1958] 2 QB 173, [1958] 2 All ER 557, 122 JP 367). When deciding whether a failure to take legal action for eviction to prevent an unlawful use from continuing can be said to amount permitting that use, regard must be had to the reasonableness or otherwise of taking that action (*Ragsdale v Creswick* (1984) 148 JP 564). An offence under s 179(6) may be committed by anyone who contravenes the enforcement notice, whether they be occupiers, squatters or other trespassers (*Scarborough Borough Council v Adams and Adams* (1983) 147 JP 449).

4. For procedure in respect of an offence triable either way, see Magistrates' Courts Act 1980, ss 17A–21 in PART I: MAGISTRATES' COURTS, PROCEDURE, ante. As a general rule, the court should proceed to hear and determine an information alleging an offence under this section notwithstanding that a planning application has recently been submitted, unless there is a prospect that the planning application's fate will be known shortly; see *R v Beaconsfield Magistrates, ex p South Buckinghamshire District Council* (1993) 157 JP 1073.

Where a summons for failure to comply with an enforcement notice was marked withdrawn in contemplation of the imminent grant of a certificate of lawful development after a not guilty plea had been entered, but that certificate was later revoked due to non-disclosure and misrepresentation, the authority was entitled to bring identical, fresh proceedings and the principle of autrefois acquit did not arise: *Islington London Borough Council v Andreas Michaelides* [2001] EWHC 468, [2001] 26 LS Gaz R 46, [2001] Crim LR 84.

This subsection creates a continuing offence and hence a previous acquittal in respect of an earlier period will not bar proceedings in relation to a later period; see *Tandridge District Council v Powers* [1982] Crim LR 373. An information which alleges a failure to comply with an enforcement notice over a period of time is not bad for duplicity since subsection (5) creates a single offence; see *Hodgetts v Chiltern District Council* [1983] 2 AC 120, [1983] 1 All ER 1057, 147 JP 372, HL.

Section 175(4) provides that where an appeal is brought under that section, the enforcement notice shall be of no effect pending the final determination or the withdrawal of the appeal. Where however no such appeal has been brought, courts should beware of adjourning simply because planning permission is being sought. S 180(3) of the Act makes it clear that even if planning permission is later granted, this is without prejudice to the liability of any person for an offence in respect of a failure to comply with an enforcement notice prior to that.

8–31041 180. Effect of planning permission, etc, on enforcement or breach of condition notice. (1) Where, after the service of—

(*a*) a copy of an enforcement notice; or

(*b*) a breach of condition notice,

planning permission is granted for any development carried out before the grant of that permission, the notice shall cease to have effect so far as inconsistent with that permission.

(2) Where after a breach of condition notice has been served any condition to which the notice relates is discharged, the notice shall cease to have effect so far as it requires any person to secure compliance with the condition in question.

(3) The fact that an enforcement notice or breach of condition notice has wholly or partly ceased to have effect by virtue of this section shall not affect the liability of any person for an offence in respect of a previous failure to comply, or secure compliance, with the notice.
[Town and Country Planning Act 1990, s 180, as substituted by the Planning and Compensation Act 1991, Sch 7.]

8–31042 **181. Enforcement notice to have effect against subsequent development.** (1) Compliance with an enforcement notice, whether in respect of—

(*a*) the completion, removal or alteration of any buildings or works;
(*b*) the discontinuance of any use of land; or
(*c*) any other requirements contained in the notice,

shall not discharge the notice.

(2) Without prejudice to subsection (1), any provision of an enforcement notice requiring a use of land to be discontinued shall operate as a requirement that it shall be discontinued permanently, to the extent that it is in contravention of Part III; and accordingly the resumption of that use at any time after it has been discontinued in compliance with the enforcement notice shall to that extent be in contravention of the enforcement notice.

(3) Without prejudice to subsection (1), if any development is carried out on land by way of reinstating or restoring buildings or works which have been removed or altered in compliance with an enforcement notice, the notice shall, notwithstanding that its terms are not apt for the purpose, be deemed to apply in relation to the buildings or works as reinstated or restored as it applied in relation to the buildings or works before they were removed or altered; and, subject to subsection (4), the provisions of section 178(1) and (2) shall apply accordingly.

(4) here, at any time after an enforcement notice takes effect—

(*a*) any development is carried out on land by way of reinstating or restoring buildings or works which have been removed or altered in compliance with the notice; and
(*b*) the local planning authority propose, under section 178(1), to take any steps required by the enforcement notice for the removal or alteration of the buildings or works in consequence of the reinstatement or restoration,

the local planning authority shall, not less than 28 days before taking any such steps, serve on the owner and occupier of the land a notice of their intention to do so.

(5) Where without planning permission a person carries out any development on land by way of reinstating or restoring buildings or works which have been removed or altered in compliance with an enforcement notice—

(*a*) he shall be guilty of an offence and shall be liable on summary conviction to a fine not exceeding **level 5** on the standard scale, and
(*b*) no person shall be liable under section 179(2) for failure to take any steps required to be taken by an enforcement notice by way of removal or alteration of what has been so reinstated or restored.

[Town and Country Planning Act 1990, s 181, as amended by the Planning and Compensation Act 1991, Sch 7.]

8–31043 **182.** *Enforcement by the Secretary of State.*

Stop notices

8–31044 **183. Stop notices.** (1) Where the local planning authority considers it expedient that any relevant activity should cease before the expiry of the period for compliance with an enforcement notice, they may, when they serve the copy of the enforcement notice or afterwards, serve a notice (in this Act referred to as a "stop notice") prohibiting the carrying out of that activity on the land to which the enforcement notice relates, or any part of that land specified in the stop notice.

(2) In this section and sections 184 and 186 "relevant activity" means any activity[1] specified in the enforcement notice as an activity which the local planning authority require to cease and any activity carried out as part of that activity or associated with that activity.

(3) A stop notice may not be served where the enforcement notice has taken effect.

(4) A stop notice shall not prohibit the use of any building as a dwellinghouse[2].

(5) A stop notice shall not prohibit the carrying out of any activity if the activity has been carried out (whether continuously or not) for a period of more than four years ending with the service of the notice; and for the purposes of this subsection no account is to be taken of any period during which the activity was authorised by planning permission.

(5A) Subsection (5) does not prevent a stop notice prohibiting any activity consisting of, or incidental to, building, engineering, mining or other operations or the deposit of refuse or waste materials.

(6) A stop notice may be served by the local planning authority on any person who appears to them to have an interest in the land or to be engaged in any activity prohibited by the notice.

(7) The local planning authority may at any time withdraw a stop notice (without prejudice to their power to serve another) by serving notice to that effect on persons served with the stop notice.
[Town and Country Planning Act 1990, s 183, as amended by the Planning and Compensation Act 1991, s 9.]

1. "Activity" can be restricted in its meaning so as to comprehend merely a particular kind of advertisement; see *Arora v Hackney London Borough Council* (1990) 155 JP 808, DC.

2. Although the exemption applies only to dwellinghouses and does not extend to caravans, whilst amounting indirectly to discrimination against gypsies and an infringement of their human rights, it is objectively justified and proportionate and thereby valid (*Wilson v Wychavon District Council* (2006) Times, 18 January, QBD).

8–31045 **184. Stop notices: supplementary provisions.** (1) A stop notice must refer to the enforcement notice to which it relates and have a copy of that notice annexed to it.

(2) A stop notice must specify the date on which it will take effect (and it cannot be contravened until that date).

(3) That date—

(*a*) must not be earlier than three days after the date when the notice is served, unless the local planning authority consider that there are special reasons for specifying an earlier date and a statement of those reasons is served with the stop notice; and

(*b*) must not be later than twenty-eight days from the date when the notice is first served on any person.

(4) A stop notice shall cease to have effect when—

(*a*) the enforcement notice to which it relates is withdrawn or quashed; or

(*b*) the period of compliance with the enforcement notice expires; or

(*c*) notice of the withdrawal of the stop notice is first served under section 183(7).

(5) A stop notice shall also cease to have effect if or to the extent that the activities prohibited by it cease, on a variation of the enforcement notice, to be relevant activities.

(6) Where a stop notice has been served in respect of any land, the local planning authority may display there a notice (in this section and section 187 referred to as a "site notice")—

(*a*) stating that a stop notice has been served and that any person contravening it may be prosecuted for an offence under section 187,

(*b*) giving the date when the stop notice takes effect, and

(*c*) indicating its requirements.

(7) If under section 183(7) the local planning authority withdraw a stop notice in respect of which a site notice was displayed they must display a notice of the withdrawal in place of the site notice.

(8) A stop notice shall not be invalid by reason that a copy of the enforcement notice to which it relates was not served as required by section 172 if it is shown that the local planning authority took all such steps as were reasonably practicable to effect proper service.

[Town and Country Planning Act 1990, s 184, as amended by the Planning and Compensation Act 1991, s 9 and Sch 7.]

8–31046 **187. Penalties for contravention of stop notice.** (1) If any person contravenes a stop notice after a site notice has been displayed or the stop notice has been served on him he shall be guilty of an offence.

(1A) An offence under this section may be charged by reference to any day or longer period of time and a person may be convicted of a second or subsequent offence under this section by reference to any period of time following the preceding conviction for such an offence.

(1B) References in this section to contravening a stop notice include causing or permitting its contravention.

(2) A person guilty of an offence under this section shall be liable[1]—

(*a*) on summary conviction, to a fine not exceeding **£20,000**; and

(*b*) on conviction on indictment, to a **fine**.

(2A) In determining the amount of any fine to be imposed on a person convicted of an offence under this section, the court shall in particular have regard to any financial benefit which has accrued or appears likely to accrue to him in consequence of the offence.

(3) In proceedings for an offence under this section it shall be a defence for the accused to prove—

(*a*) that the stop notice was not served on him, and

(*b*) that he did not know, and could not reasonably have been expected to know, of its existence.

[Town and Country Planning Act 1990, s 187, as amended by the Planning and Compensation Act 1991, s 9.]

1. For procedure in respect of an offence triable either way, see the Magistrates' Courts Act 1980, ss 17A–21 in PART I: MAGISTRATES' COURTS, PROCEDURE, ante. The defendant is entitled to attempt to establish that he is not in fact prohibited from carrying on his activities by the terms of the prohibition contained on the face of the stop order (*R v Jenner* [1983] 2 All ER 46, [1983] 1 WLR 873).

Breach of condition

8–31047 **187A. Enforcement of conditions.** (1) This section applies where planning permission for carrying out any development of land has been granted subject to conditions.

(2) The local planning authority may, if any of the conditions is not complied with, serve a notice (in this Act referred to as a "breach of condition notice") on—

(*a*) any person who is carrying out or has carried out the development; or
(*b*) any person having control of the land,

requiring him to secure compliance with such of the conditions as are specified in the notice.

(3) References in this section to the person responsible are to the person on whom the breach of condition notice has been served.

(4) The conditions which may be specified in a notice served by virtue of subsection (2)(*b*) are any of the conditions regulating the use of the land.

(5) A breach condition notice shall specify the steps which the authority consider ought to be taken, or the activities which the authority consider ought to cease, to secure compliance with the conditions specified in the notice.

(6) The authority may by notice served on the person responsible withdraw the breach of condition notice, but its withdrawal shall not affect the power to serve on him a further breach of condition notice in respect of the conditions specified in the earlier notice or any other conditions.

(7) The period allowed for compliance with the notice is—

(*a*) such period of not less than twenty-eight days beginning with the date of service of the notice as may be specified in the notice; or
(*b*) that period as extended by a further notice served by the local planning authority on the person responsible.

(8) If, at any time after the end of the period allowed for compliance with the notice—

(*a*) any of the conditions specified in the notice is not complied with; and
(*b*) the steps specified in the notice have not been taken or, as the case may be, the activities specified in the notice have not ceased,

the person responsible is in breach of the notice.

(9) If the person responsible is in breach of the notice he shall be guilty of an offence[1].

(10) An offence under subsection (9) may be charged by reference to any day or longer period of time and a person may be convicted of a second or subsequent offence under that subsection by reference to any period of time following the preceding conviction for such an offence.

(11) It shall be a defence for a person charged with an offence under subsection (9) to prove—

(*a*) that he took all reasonable measures to secure compliance with the conditions specified in the notice; or
(*b*) where the notice was served on him by virtue of subsection (2)(*b*), that he no longer had control of the land.

(12) A person who is guilty of an offence under subsection (9) shall be liable on summary conviction to a fine not exceeding **level 3** on the standard scale.

(13) In this section—

(*a*) "conditions" includes limitations; and
(*b*) references to carrying out any development include causing or permitting another to do so.

[Town and Country Planning Act 1990, s 187A added by the Planning and Compensation Act 1991, s 2.]

---

1. A "breach of condition notice" means a breach of condition notice which has been served within the limits prescribed by s 171B, ante. Accordingly a defendant charged with failing to comply with such a notice is entitled by way of defence in criminal proceedings to challenge the validity of the notice on the ground that it was served out of time under s 171B(3), ante. Furthermore the defendant is also entitled by way of defence in such proceedings to challenge the lawfulness of the planning condition (*Dilieto v Ealing London Borough Council* [2000] QB 381, [1998] 2 All ER 885, [1998] 3 WLR 1403).

8–31048 187B. *Injunctions restraining breaches of planning control.*

Enforcement of orders for discontinuance of use etc

8–31049 189. Penalties for contravention of orders under section 102 and Schedule 9.

(1) Any person who without planning permission—

(*a*) uses land, or causes or permits land to be used—
  (i) for any purpose for which an order under section 102 or paragraph 1 of Schedule 9 has required that its use shall be discontinued; or
  (ii) in contravention of any condition imposed by such an order by virtue of subsection (1) of that section or, as the case may be, sub-paragraph (1) of that paragraph; or
(*b*) resumes, or causes or permits to be resumed, development consisting of the winning and working of minerals or involving the depositing of mineral waste the resumption of which an order under paragraph 3 of that Schedule has prohibited; or
(*c*) contravenes, or causes or permits to be contravened, any such requirement as is specified in sub-paragraph (3) or (4) of that paragraph,

shall be guilty of an offence.

(2) Any person who contravenes any requirement of an order under paragraph 5 or 6 of that

Schedule or who causes or permits any requirement of such an order to be contravened shall be guilty of an offence.

(3) Any person guilty of an offence under this section shall be liable[1]—

(*a*) on summary conviction to a fine not exceeding the **statutory maximum**; and

(*b*) on conviction on indictment, to a **fine**.

(4) It shall be a defence for a person charged with an offence under this section to prove that he took all reasonable measures and exercised all due diligence to avoid commission of the offence by himself or by any person under his control.

(5) If in any case the defence provided by subsection (4) involves an allegation that the commission of the offence was due to the act or default of another person or due to reliance on information supplied by another person, the person charged shall not, without the leave of the court, be entitled to rely on the defence unless, within a period ending seven clear days before the hearing, he has served on the prosecutor a notice in writing giving such information identifying or assisting in the identification of the other person as was then in his possession.

[Town and Country Planning Act 1990, s 189, as amended by the Planning and Compensation Act 1991, Sch 1.]

---

1. For procedure in respect of an offence triable either way, see the Magistrates' Courts Act 1980, ss 17A–21, in PART I: MAGISTRATES' COURTS, PROCEDURE, ante.

Certificate of lawful use or development

8–31050 191. Certificate of lawfulness of existing use or development. (1) If any person wishes to ascertain whether—

(*a*) any existing[1] use of buildings or other land is lawful;

(*b*) any operations which have been carried out in, on, over or under land are lawful; or

(*c*) any other matter constituting a failure to comply with any condition or limitation subject to which planning permission has been granted is lawful,

he may make an application for the purpose to the local planning authority specifying the land and describing the use, operations or other matter.

(2) For the purposes of this Act uses and operations are lawful at any time if—

(*a*) no enforcement action may then be taken in respect of them (whether because they did not involve development or require planning permission or because the time for enforcement action has expired or for any other reason); and

(*b*) they do not constitute a contravention of any of the requirements of any enforcement notice then in force.

(3) For the purposes of this Act any matter constituting a failure to comply with any condition or limitation subject to which planning permission has been granted is lawful at any time if—

(*a*) the time for taking enforcement action in respect of the failure has then expired; and

(*b*) it does not constitute a contravention of any of the requirements of any enforcement notice or breach of condition notice then in force.

(4) If, on an application under this section, the local planning authority are provided with information satisfying them of the lawfulness at the time of the application of the use, operations or other matter described in the application or that description as modified by the local planning authority or a description substituted by them, they shall issue a certificate to that effect; and in any other case they shall refuse the application.

(5) A certificate under this section shall—

(*a*) specify the land to which it relates;

(*b*) describe the use, operations or other matter in question (in the case of any use falling within one of the classes specified in an order under section 55(2)(*f*), identifying it by reference to that class);

(*c*) give the reasons for determining the use, operations or other matter to be lawful; and

(*d*) specify the date of the application for the certificate.

(6) The lawfulness of any use, operations or other matter for which a certificate is in force under this section shall be conclusively presumed.

(7) A certificate under this section in respect of any use shall also have effect, for the purposes of the following enactments, as if it were a grant of planning permission—

(*a*) section 3(3) of the Caravan Sites and Control of Development Act 1960;

(*b*) section 5(2) of the Control of Pollution Act 1974; and

(*c*) section 36(2)(*a*) of the Environmental Protection Act 1990.

[Town and Country Planning Act 1990, s 191, as substituted by the Planning and Compensation Act 1991, s 10.]

---

1. The uses for which the certificate is requested may include uses which although not physically active at the time of the application, are dormant uses (*Panton and Farmer v Secretary of State for the Environment, Transport and the Regions* (1998) 78 P & CR 186).

8–31051 **192. Certificate of lawfulness of proposed use or development.** (1) If any person wishes to ascertain whether—

(*a*) any proposed use of buildings or other land; or
(*b*) any operations proposed to be carried out in, on, over or under land,

would be lawful, he may make an application for the purpose to the local planning authority specifying the land and describing the use or operations in question.

(2) If, on an application under this section, the local planning authority are provided with information satisfying them that the use or operations described in the application would be lawful if instituted or begun at the time of the application, they shall issue a certificate to that effect; and in any other case they shall refuse the application.

(3) A certificate under this section shall—

(*a*) specify the land to which it relates;
(*b*) describe the use or operations in question (in the case of any use falling within one of the classes specified in an order under section 55(2)(*f*), identifying it by reference to that class);
(*c*) give the reasons for determining the use or operations to be lawful; and
(*d*) specify the date of the application for the certificate.

(4) The lawfulness of any use or operations for which a certificate is in force under this section shall be conclusively presumed unless there is a material change, before the use is instituted or the operations are begun, in any of the matters relevant to determining such lawfulness.
[Town and Country Planning Act 1990, s 192, as substituted by the Planning and Compensation Act 1991, s 10.]

8–31051A **193.** *Certificates under sections 191 and 192: supplementary provisions.*

8–31052 **194. Offences.** (1) If any person, for the purpose of procuring a particular decision on an application (whether by himself or another) for the issue of a certificate under section 191 or 192—

(*a*) knowingly or recklessly makes a statement which is false or misleading in a material particular;
(*b*) with intent to deceive, uses any document which is false or misleading in a material particular; or
(*c*) with intent to deceive, withholds any material information,

he shall be guilty of an offence.

(2) A person guilty of an offence under subsection (1) shall be liable[1]—

(*a*) on summary conviction, to a fine not exceeding the **statutory maximum**; or
(*b*) on conviction on indictment, to imprisonment for a term not exceeding **two years**, or a **fine**, or **both**

(3) Notwithstanding section 127 of the Magistrates' Courts Act 1980, a magistrates' court may try an information in respect of an offence under subsection (1) whenever laid.
[Town and Country Planning Act 1990, s 194, as substituted by the Planning and Compensation Act 1991, s 10.]

1. For procedure in respect of an offence triable either way, see the Magistrates' Courts Act 1980, ss 17A–21, in PART I: MAGISTRATES' COURTS, PROCEDURE, ante.

Rights of entry for enforcement purposes

8–31052A **196A. Rights to enter without warrant.** (1) Any person duly authorised in writing by a local planning authority may at any reasonable hour enter any land—

(*a*) to ascertain whether there is or has been any breach of planning control on the land or any other land;
(*b*) to determine whether any of the powers conferred on a local planning authority by this Part should be exercised in relation to the land or any other land;
(*c*) to determine how any such power should be exercised in relation to the land or any other land;
(*d*) to ascertain whether there has been compliance with any requirement imposed as a result of any such power having been exercised in relation to the land or any other land,

if there are reasonable grounds for entering for the purpose in question.

(2) Any person duly authorised in writing by the Secretary of State may at any reasonable hour enter any land to determine whether an enforcement notice should be issued in relation to the land or any other land, if there are reasonable grounds for entering for that purpose.

(3) The Secretary of State shall not so authorise any person without consulting the local planning authority.

(4) Admission to any building used as a dwellinghouse shall not be demanded as of right by virtue of subsection (1) or (2) unless twenty-four hours' notice of the intended entry has been given to the occupier of the building.
[Town and Country Planning Act 1990, s 196A added by the Planning and Compensation Act 1991, s 11.]

8–31052B 196B. Right to enter under warrant. (1) If it is shown to the satisfaction of a justice of the peace on sworn information in writing—

(*a*) that there are reasonable grounds for entering any land for any of the purposes mentioned in section 196A(1) or (2); and

(*b*) that—

(i) admission to the land has been refused, or a refusal is reasonably apprehended; or

(ii) the case is one of urgency,

the justice may issue a warrant authorising any person duly authorised in writing by a local planning authority or, as the case may be, the Secretary of State to enter the land.

(2) For the purposes of subsection (1)(*b*)(i) admission to land shall be regarded as having been refused if no reply is received to a request for admission within a reasonable period.

(3) A warrant authorises entry on one occasion only and that entry must be—

(*a*) within one month from the date of the issue of the warrant; and

(*b*) at a reasonable hour, unless the case is one of urgency.

[Town and Country Planning Act 1990, s 196B added by the Planning and Compensation Act 1991, s 11.]

8–31052C 196C. Rights of entry: supplementary provisions. (1) A person authorised to enter any land in pursuance of a right of entry conferred under or by virtue of section 196A or 196B (referred to in this section as "a right of entry")—

(*a*) shall, if so required, produce evidence of his authority and state the purpose of his entry before so entering;

(*b*) may take with him such other persons as may be necessary; and

(*c*) on leaving the land shall, if the owner or occupier is not then present, leave it as effectively secured against trespassers as he found it.

(2) Any person who wilfully obstructs a person acting in the exercise of a right of entry shall be guilty of an offence and liable on summary conviction to a fine not exceeding **level 3** on the standard scale.

(3) If any damage is caused to land or chattels in the exercise of a right of entry, compensation may be recovered by any person suffering the damage from the authority who gave the written authority for the entry or, as the case may be, the Secretary of State.

(4) The provisions of section 118 shall apply in relation to compensation under subsection (3) as they apply in relation to compensation under Part IV.

(5) If any person who enters any land, in exercise of a right of entry, discloses to any person any information obtained by him while on the land as to any manufacturing process or trade secret, he shall be guilty of an offence.

(6) Subsection (5) does not apply if the disclosure is made by a person in the course of performing his duty in connection with the purpose for which he was authorised to enter the land.

(7) A person who is guilty of an offence under subsection (5) shall be liable[1] on summary conviction to a fine not exceeding the **statutory maximum** or on conviction on indictment to imprisonment for a term not exceeding **two years** or a **fine** or **both**.

(8) In sections 196A and 196B and this section references to a local planning authority include, in relation to a building situated in Greater London, a reference to the Historic Buildings and Monuments Commission for England.

[Town and Country Planning Act 1990, s 196C added by the Planning and Compensation Act 1991, s 11.]

---

1. For procedure in respect of an offence triable either way, see the Magistrates' Courts Act 1980, ss 17A–21 in PART I: MAGISTRATES' COURTS, PROCEDURE, ante.

PART VIII[1]
SPECIAL CONTROLS

CHAPTER I
TREES

Tree preservation orders

8–31053 198. Power to make tree preservation orders. If it appears to a local planning authority that it is expedient in the interests of amenity they may make an order prohibiting cutting down, topping, lopping, uprooting, wilful damage or wilful destruction of trees except with consent, and to secure replanting after forestry operations. Such order not to apply to cutting down, uprooting, topping or lopping of trees which are dying or dead or have become dangerous or such work done in compliance with an Act of Parliament or to prevent or abate a nuisance[2].

[Town and Country Planning Act 1990, s 198—summarised.]

---

1. Part VIII contains sections 197–225.
2. Additionally this section has effect subject to s 39(2) of the Housing and Planning Act 1986 (saving s 2(4) of the

repealed Opencast Coal Act 1958) and s 15 of the Forestry Act 1967 (licence to fell) Town and Country Planning Act 1990, s 198(7).

For procedure in respect of the making of tree preservation orders see the Town and Country Planning (Trees) Regulations 1999, SI 1999/1892 amended by SI 2001/4050. In proceedings alleging commission of an offence under s 210(1), post, it will be for the defendant to prove on the balance of probabilities that the conditions creating an exemption under this section existed at the time; see *R v Alath Construction Ltd* [1990] 1 WLR 1255, CA (decided under s 102(1) of the repealed 1971 Act). The burden of proof on the issue of whether the tree was dying, or dead or had become dangerous, so as to justify its felling without the local auithority's consent, falls on the defendant who asserts such exemption from the preservation order (*R v Alath Construction Ltd* supra).

8–31054 207–209. *Replacement of trees*[1].

1. By s 209(6) any person wilfully obstructing the exercise of a power under s 209(1)(*a*) is punishable on summary conviction to a fine not exceeding **level 3** on the standard scale.

8–31055 210. Penalties for non-compliance with tree preservation order. (1) If any person, in contravention of a tree preservation order—

(*a*) cuts down, uproots or wilfully destroys[1] a tree, or

(*b*) wilfully damages, tops or lops a tree in such a manner as to be likely to destroy it,

he shall be guilty of an offence.

(2) A person guilty of an offence under subsection (1) shall be liable[2]—

(*a*) on summary conviction to a fine not exceeding **£20,000**;

(*b*) on conviction on indictment, to a **fine**.

(3) In determining the amount of any fine to be imposed on a person convicted of an offence under subsection (1), the court shall in particular have regard to any financial benefit which has accrued or appears likely to accrue to him in consequence of the offence.

(4) If any person contravenes the provisions of a tree preservation order otherwise than as mentioned in subsection (1), he shall be guilty of an offence and liable on summary conviction to a fine not exceeding **level 4** on the standard scale.

(5) (*Repealed*).

[Town and Country Planning Act 1990, s 210, as amended by the Planning and Compensation Act 1991, s 23.]

1. A tree is "destroyed" if it ceases to have any use as an amenity, or as something worth preserving, and if a competent forester, taking into account its situation, would decide it ought to be felled (*Barnet London Borough Council v Eastern Electricity Board* [1973] 2 All ER 319, 137 JP 486). It is not necessary for the prosecutor to prove that the accused knew of the existence of the preservation order (*Maidstone Borough Council v Mortimer* [1980] 3 All ER 552). The prosecutor must adduce evidence of the age of the tree to establish that it was subject to the tree preservation order and it is not permissible for the justices to act on personal knowledge of facts after looking at photographs tendered in evidence (*Carter v Eastbourne Borough Council* (2000) 164 JP 273).

2. For procedure in respect of an offence triable either way, see the Magistrates' Courts Act 1980, ss 17A–21, in PART I: MAGISTRATES' COURTS, PROCEDURE, ante.

3. A local authority acting under s 222 of the Local Government Act 1972 may apply for an injunction. However, the discretion to grant an injunction in support of the criminal law in such cases will be exercised sparingly and with great caution, see *Newport Borough Council v Khan* [1990] 1 WLR 1185, [1991] 1 EGLR 287, CA.

Trees in conservation areas

8–31056 211. Preservation of trees in conservation areas. (1) Subject to the provisions of this section and section 212[1], any person who, in relation to a tree to which this section applies, does any act which might by virtue of section 198(3)(a) be prohibited by a tree preservation order shall be guilty of an offence.

(2) Subject to section 212, this section applies to any tree in a conservation area in respect of which no tree preservation order is for the time being in force.

(3) It shall be a defence for a person charged with an offence under subsection (1) to prove—

(*a*) that he served notice of his intention to do the act in question (with sufficient particulars to identify the tree) on the local planning authority in whose area the tree is or was situated; and

(*b*) that he did the act in question—

(i) with the consent of the local planning authority in whose area the tree is or was situated, or

(ii) after the expiry of the period of six weeks from the date of the notice but before the expiry of the period of two years from that date.

(4) Section 210 shall apply to an offence under this section as it applies to a contravention of a tree preservation order.

[Town and Country Planning Act 1990, s 211.]

1. Under s 212 the Secretary of State may disapply s 211 in specified cases. Exceptions are contained in the Town and Country Planning (Trees) Regulations 1999, SI 1999/1892 amended by SI 2001/4050.

8–31056A 214A. *Injunctions.*

Rights of entry

8–31056B 214B. Rights to enter without warrant. (1) Any person duly authorised in writing by a local planning authority may enter any land for the purpose of—

(*a*) surveying it in connection with making or confirming a tree preservation order with respect to the land;

(*b*) ascertaining whether an offence under section 210 or 211 has been committed on the land; or

(*c*) determining whether a notice under section 207 should be served on the owner of the land,

if there are reasonable grounds for entering for the purpose in question.

(2) Any person duly authorised in writing by the Secretary of State may enter any land for the purpose of surveying it in connection with making, amending or revoking a tree preservation order with respect to the land, if there are reasonable grounds for entering for that purpose.

(3) Any person who is duly authorised in writing by a local planning authority may enter any land in connection with the exercise of any functions conferred on the authority by or under this Chapter.

(4) Any person who is an officer of the Valuation Office may enter any land for the purpose of surveying it, or estimating its value, in connection with a claim for compensation in respect of any land which is payable by the local planning authority under this Chapter (other than section 204).

(5) Any person who is duly authorised in writing by the Secretary of State may enter any land in connection with the exercise of any functions conferred on the Secretary of State by or under this Chapter.

(6) The Secretary of State shall not authorise any person as mentioned in subsection (2) without consulting the local planning authority.

(7) Admission shall not be demanded as of right—

(*a*) by virtue of subsection (1) or (2) to any building used as a dwellinghouse; or

(*b*) by virtue of subsection (3), (4) or (5) to any land which is occupied,

unless twenty-four hours' notice of the intended entry has been given to the occupier.

(8) Any right to enter by virtue of this section shall be exercised at a reasonable hour.

[Town and Country Planning Act 1990, s 214B as added by the Planning and Compensation Act 1991, s 23.]

8–31056C 214C. Right to enter under warrant. (1) If it is shown to the satisfaction of a justice of the peace on sworn information in writing—

(*a*) that there are reasonable grounds for entering any land for any of the purposes mentioned in section 214B(1) or (2); and

(*b*) that—

(i) admission to the land has been refused, or a refusal is reasonably apprehended; or

(ii) the case is one of urgency,

the justice may issue a warrant authorising any person duly authorised in writing by a local planning authority or, as the case may be, the Secretary of State to enter the land.

(2) For the purposes of subsection (1)(*b*)(i) admission to land shall be regarded as having been refused if no reply is received to a request for admission within a reasonable period.

(3) A warrant authorises entry on one occasion only and that entry must be—

(*a*) within one month from the date of the issue of the warrant; and

(*b*) at a reasonable hour, unless the case is one of urgency.

[Town and Country Planning Act 1990, s 214C as added by the Planning and Compensation Act 1991, s 23.]

8–31056D 214D. Rights of entry supplementary provisions. (1) Any power conferred under or by virtue of section 214B to 214C to enter land (referred to in this section as "a right of entry") shall be construed as including power to take samples from any tree and samples of the soil.

(2) A person authorised to enter land in the exercise of a right of entry—

(*a*) shall, if so required, produce evidence of his authority and state the purpose of his entry before so entering;

(*b*) may take with him such other persons as may be necessary; and

(*c*) on leaving the land shall, if the owner or occupier is not then present, leave it as effectively secured against trespassers as he found it.

(3) Any person who wilfully obstructs a person acting in the exercise of a right of entry shall be guilty of an offence and liable on summary conviction to a fine not exceeding **level 3** on the standard scale.

(4) If any damage is caused to land or chattels in the exercise of a right of entry, compensation may be recovered by any person suffering the damage from the authority who gave the written authority for the entry or, as the case may be, the Secretary of State.

(5) The provisions of section 118 shall apply in relation to compensation under subsection (4) as they apply in relation to compensation under Part IV.

[Town and Country Planning Act 1990, s 214D as added by the Planning and Compensation Act 1991, s 23.]

CHAPTER II
LAND ADVERSELY AFFECTING AMENITY OF NEIGHBOURHOOD

8–31057 **215. Power to require proper maintenance of land.** (1) If it appears to the local planning authority that the amenity of a part of their area, or of an adjoining area, is adversely affected by the condition of land in their area, they may serve on the owner and occupier of the land a notice under this section.

(2) The notice shall require such steps for remedying the condition of the land as may be specified in the notice to be taken within such period as may be so specified.

(3) Subject to the following provisions of this Chapter, the notice shall take effect at the end of such period as may be specified in the notice.

(4) That period shall not be less than 28 days after the service of the notice.

[Town and Country Planning Act 1990, s 215.]

8–31058 **216. Penalty for non-compliance with s 215 notice.** (1) The provisions of this section shall have effect where a notice has been served under section 215.

(2) If any owner or occupier of the land on whom the notice was served fails to take steps required by the notice within the period specified in it for compliance with it, he shall be guilty of an offence and liable on summary conviction to a fine not exceeding **level 3** on the standard scale.

(3) Where proceedings have been brought under subsection (2) against a person as the owner of the land and he has, at some time before the end of the compliance period, ceased to be the owner of the land, if he—

(*a*) duly lays information to that effect, and
(*b*) gives the prosecution not less than three clear day's notice of his intention,

he shall be entitled to have the person who then became the owner of the land brought before the court in the proceedings.

(4) Where proceedings have been brought under subsection (2) against a person as the occupier of the land and he has, at some time before the end of the compliance period, ceased to be the occupier of the land, if he—

(*a*) duly lays information to that effect, and
(*b*) gives the prosecution not less than three clear days' notice of his intention,

he shall be entitled to have brought before the court in the proceedings the person who then became the occupier of the land or, if nobody then became the occupier, the person who is the owner at the date of the notice.

(5) Where in such proceedings—

(*a*) it has been proved that any steps required by the notice under section 215 have not been taken within the compliance period, and
(*b*) the original defendant proves that the failure to take those steps was attributable, in whole or in part, to the default of a person specified in a notice under subsection (3) or (4),

then—

(i) that person may be convicted of the offence; and
(ii) if the original defendant also proves that he took all reasonable steps to ensure compliance with the notice, he shall be acquitted of the offence.

(6) If, after a person has been convicted under the previous provisions of this section, he does not as soon as practicable do everything in his power to secure compliance with the notice, he shall be guilty of a further offence and liable on summary conviction to a fine not exceeding **one-tenth of level 3 on the standard scale for each day** following his first conviction on which any of the requirements of the notice remain unfulfilled.

(7) Any reference in this section to the compliance period, in relation to a notice, is a reference to the period specified in the notice for compliance with it or such extended period as the local planning authority who served the notice may allow for compliance.

[Town and Country Planning Act 1990, s 216, as amended by the Planning and Compensation Act 1991, Sch 7.]

8–31059 **217. Appeal to magistrates' court against s 215 notice.** (1) A person on whom a notice under section 215 is served, or any other person having an interest in the land to which the notice relates, may, at any time within the period specified in the notice as the period at the end of which it is to take effect, appeal against the notice on any of the following grounds—

(*a*) that the condition of the land to which the notice relates does not adversely affect the amenity of any part of the area of the local planning authority who served the notice, or of any adjoining area;
(*b*) that the condition of the land to which the notice relates is attributable to, and such as results in the ordinary course of events from, the carrying on of operations or a use of land which is not in contravention of Part III;

(*c*) that the requirements of the notice exceed what is necessary for preventing the condition of the land from adversely affecting the amenity of any part of the area of the local planning authority who served the notice, or of any adjoining area;

(*d*) that the period specified in the notice as the period within which any steps required by the notice are to be taken falls short of what should reasonably be allowed.

(2) Any appeal under this section shall be made to a magistrates' court[1] acting for the petty sessions area in which the land in question is situated.

(3) Where such an appeal is brought, the notice to which it relates shall be of no effect pending the final determination or withdrawal of the appeal.

(4) On such an appeal the magistrates' court may correct any informality, defect or error in the notice if satisfied that the informality, defect or error is not material.

(5) On the determination of such an appeal the magistrates' court shall give directions for giving effect to their determination, including, where appropriate, directions for quashing the notice or for varying the terms of the notice in favour of the appellant.

(6) Where any person has appealed to a magistrates' court under this section against a notice, neither that person nor any other shall be entitled, in any other proceedings instituted after the making of the appeal, to claim that the notice was not duly served on the person who appealed.

[Town and Country Planning Act 1990, s 217.]

1. Appeal is by way of complaint (Magistrates' Courts Rules 1981, r 34 in PART I: MAGISTRATES' COURTS, PROCEDURE, ante. The appellant or the local planning authority who served the notice under s 215 may thereafter appeal to the Crown Court (s 218); the Magistrates' Courts Act 1980, ss 109 and 110 ante and the Crown Court Rules 1982 in PART I: MAGISTRATES' COURTS, PROCEDURE will apply.

CHAPTER III
ADVERTISEMENTS

8–31060 220. *Regulations controlling display of advertisements.*

8–31061 221. *Power to make different advertisement regulations for different areas.*

Enforcement of control over advertisements

8–31062 224. Enforcement of control as to advertisements. (1) Regulations[1] under section 220 may make provision for enabling the local planning authority to require—

(*a*) the removal of any advertisement which is displayed in contravention of the regulations, or

(*b*) the discontinuance of the use for the display of advertisements of any site which is being so used in contravention of the regulations.

(2) For that purpose the regulations may apply any of the provisions of Part VII with respect to enforcement notices or the provisions of section 186, subject to such adaptations and modifications as may be specified in the regulations.

(3) Without prejudice to any provisions included in such regulations by virtue of subsection (1) or (2), if any person displays an advertisement in contravention of the regulations he shall be guilty of an offence[2] and liable on summary conviction to a fine of such amount as may be prescribed, not exceeding **level 3** on the standard scale and, in the case of a continuing offence, **one-tenth of level 3 on the standard scale for each day** during which the offence continues after conviction.

(4) Without prejudice to the generality of subsection (3), a person shall be deemed to display an advertisement for the purposes of that subsection if—

(*a*) he is the owner or occupier of the land on which the advertisement is displayed; or

(*b*) the advertisement gives publicity to his goods, trade, business or other concerns[3].

(5) A person shall not be guilty of an offence under subsection (3) by reason only—

(*a*) of his being the owner or occupier of the land on which an advertisement is displayed, or

(*b*) of his goods, trade, business or other concerns being given publicity by the advertisement,

if he proves either of the matters specified in subsection (6).

(6) The matters are that—

(*a*) the advertisment was displayed without his knowlegde; or

(*b*) he took all reasonable steps to prevent the display or, after the advertisement had been displayed, to secure its removal.

[Town and Country Planning Act 1990, s 224, as amended by the Planning and Compensation Act 1991, Sch 7 and the Clean Neighbourhoods and Environment Act 2005, s 33.]

1. See Town and Country Planning (Control of Advertisements) Regulations 1992, PART VII, post. For application of the predecessor regulations to advertisements on a petrol station forecourt, see *Heron Service Stations Ltd v Coupe* [1973] 2 All ER 110, 137 JP 415.

2. This is an absolute offence; see *Porter v Honey* [1988] 2 All ER 449. The display of different posters on a hoarding on different dates has been held to constitute separate offences for each display, contrary to reg 27 of the Town and Country Planning (Control of Advertisements) Regulations 1992, this PART, post (*Kingston-upon-Thames London Borough*

Council v National Solus Sites Ltd (1993) 158 JP 70). The regulations under s 220 provide a code for control of advertisements which does not depend on the breach of planning and control and enforcement procedures under Pts III and VII of this Act. Accordingly, the defence in s 171B(3), ante, is not available in a prosecution under s 224(3) of the Act (*Torridge District Council v Jarrad* (1998) Times, 13 April.)

3. Whether an advertisement gives publicity to the "goods, trade, business or other concerns" of the defendant is a mixed question of fact and law (*Merton London Borough Council v Edmonds* (1993) 157 JP 1129).

8-31063 **225.** *Power to remove or obliterate placards and posters.*

PART XII[1]
VALIDITY

8-31064 **284. Validity of development plans and certain orders, decisions and directions.** The validity of these is not to be questioned in any legal proceedings whatsoever; these matters include orders under ss 102, 221(5), Sch 9, paras 1, 3, 5 and 6, a tree preservation order, a decision under s 177(1)(*a*) or (*b*), and under s 192(5) and 195(1), and any decision relating—

(i) to an application for consent under a tree preservation order,
(ii) to an application for consent under any regulations made in accordance with section 220 or 221, or
(iii) to any certificate or direction under any such order or regulations, whether it is a decision on appeal or a decision on an application referred to the Secretary of State for determination in the first instance.

[Town and Country Planning Act 1990, s 284 amended by the Planning and Compensation Act 1991, Schs 4, 7 and 19 and the Planning and Compulsory Purchase Act 2004, s 82—summarised.]

1. Part XII contains ss 284–292.

8-31065 **285. Validity of enforcement notices and similar notices.** (1) The validity of an enforcement notice shall not, except by way of an appeal under Part VII, be questioned in any proceedings whatsoever on any of the grounds on which such an appeal may be brought.

(2) Subsection (1) shall not apply to proceedings brought under section 179 against a person who—

(*a*) has held an interest in the land since before the enforcement notice was issued under that Part;
(*b*) did not have a copy of the enforcement notice served on him under that Part; and
(*c*) satisfies the court—
  (i) that he did not know and could not reasonably have been expected to know that the enforcement notice had been issued; and
  (ii) that his interests have been substantially prejudiced by the failure to serve him with a copy of it.

(3) Subject to subsection (4), the validity of a notice which has been served under section 215 on the owner and occupier of the land shall not, except by way of an appeal under Chapter II of Part VIII, be questioned in any proceedings whatsoever on either of the grounds specified in section 217(1)(*a*) or (*b*).

(4) Subsection (3) shall not prevent the validity of such a notice being questioned on either of those grounds in proceedings[1] brought under section 216 against a person on whom the notice was not served, but who has held an interest in the land since before the notice was served on the owner and occupier of the land, if he did not appeal against the notice under that Chapter.

(5)–(6) (*Repealed*).

[Town and Country Planning Act 1990, s 285, as amended by the Planning and Compensation Act 1991, Sch 7.]

1. "Proceedings" includes criminal proceedings (*R v Thomas George Smith* [1984] Crim LR 630). A person who has no right of appeal to the Secretary of State against the enforcement notice may in subsequent criminal proceedings challenge the validity of the enforcement notice (*Scarborough Borough Council v Adams and Adams* (1983) 147 JP 449).

8-31066 **286. Challenges to validity on ground of authority's powers.** (1) The validity of any permission, determination or certificate granted, made or issued or purporting to have been granted, made or issued by a local planning authority in respect of—

(*a*) an application for planning permission;
(*b*) *Repealed*;
(*c*) an application for a certificate under section 191 or 192;
(*d*) an application for consent to the display of advertisements under section 220; or
(*e*) a determination under section 302 or Schedule 15,

shall not be called in question in any legal proceedings, or in any proceedings under this Act which are not legal proceedings, on the ground that the permission, determination or certificate should have been granted, made or given by some other local planning authority.

(2) The validity of any order under section 97 revoking or modifying planning permission, any order under section 102 or paragraph 1 of Schedule 9 requiring discontinuance of use, or imposing

conditions on continuance of use, or requiring the alteration or removal of buildings or works, or any enforcement notice under section 172 or stop notice under section 183 or a breach of condition notice under section 187A, being an order or notice purporting to have been made, issued or served by a local planning authority, shall not be called in question in any such proceedings on the ground—

(*a*) in the case of an order or notice purporting to have been made, issued or served by a district planning authority, that they failed to comply with paragraph 11(2) of Schedule 1;

(*b*) in the case of an order or notice purporting to have been made, issued or served by a county planning authority, that they had no power to make, issue or serve it because it did not relate to a county matter within the meaning of that Schedule.

[Town and Country Planning Act 1990, s 286, as amended by the Planning and Compensation Act 1991, Schs 7 and 19.]

PART XV[1]
MISCELLANEOUS AND GENERAL PROVISIONS

Application of Act in special cases

8–31067 315. Power to modify Act in relation to minerals. Many provisions, including practically all those included in this work, may be subject to prescribed adaptations and modifications in relation to development consisting of the winning and working of minerals.

[Town and Country Planning Act 1990, s 315 amended by the Planning and Compensation Act 1991, Schs 1, 6 and 19 and the Coal Industry Act 1994, Schs 9 and 11—summarised.]

1. Part XV comprises ss 315–337.

Rights of entry

8–31068 324. *Rights of entry*[1].

1. Section 324 enables the Secretary of State or a local planning authority to give written authority to enter land to survey it, or for the purposes of ss 207–209, or 225, or valuation purposes, or to ascertain compliance with an order or notice, or to ascertain the nature of the subsoil or the presence of minerals.

8–31069 325. Supplementary provisions as to rights of entry[1]. (1) A person authorised under section 324 to enter any land—

(*a*) shall, if so required, produce evidence of his authority and state the purpose of his entry before so entering, and

(*b*) shall not demand admission as of right to any land which is occupied unless 24 hours notice of the intended entry has been given to the occupier.

(2) Any person who wilfully obstructs a person acting in the exercise of his powers under section 324 shall be guilty of an offence and liable on summary conviction to a fine not exceeding **level 3** on the standard scale.

(3) If any person who, in compliance with the provisions of section 324, is admitted into a factory, workshop or workplace discloses to any person any information obtained by him in it as to any manufacturing process or trade secret, he shall be guilty of an offence.

(4) Subsection (3) does not apply if the disclosure is made by a person in the course of performing his duty in connection with the purpose for which he was authorised to enter the land.

(5) A person who is guilty of an offence under subsection (3) shall be liable[2] on summary conviction to a fine not exceeding the **statutory maximum** or on conviction on indictment to imprisonment for a term not exceeding **two years** or a **fine** or **both**.

(6)–(9) *Compensation for damage to land; notice required to search and bore; Minister's consent for land held by statutory undertakers.*

[Town and Country Planning Act 1990, s 325, as amended by the Planning and Compensation Act 1991, s 11 and Sch 7.]

1. This section applies as well to s 88 of the Planning (Listed Buildings and Conservation Areas) Act 1990 (rights of entry under that Act), post.

2. For procedure in respect of an offence triable either way, see the Magistrates' Courts Act, 1980 ss 17A–21, in PART I: MAGISTRATES' COURTS, PROCEDURE, ante.

8–31070 329. Service of notices. (1) Any notice or other document required or authorised to be served or given under this Act may be served or given either—

(*a*) by delivering it to the person on whom it is to be served or to whom it is to be given; or

(*b*) by leaving it at the usual or last known place of abode of that person or, in a case where an address for service has been given by that person, at that address; or

(*c*) by sending it in a prepaid registered letter, or by the recorded delivery service, addressed to that person at his usual or last known place of abode or, in a case where an address for service has been given by that person, at that address; or (*cc*) in a case where an address for service using electronic communications has been given by that person, by sending it using electronic communications, in accordance with the condition set out in subsection (3A), to that person at that address (subject to subsection (3B)); or

(*d*) in the case of an incorporated company or body, by delivering it to the secretary or clerk of the company or body at their registered or principal office or sending it in a prepaid registered letter, or by the recorded delivery service, addressed to the secretary or clerk of the company or body at that office.

(2) Where the notice or document is required or authorised to be served on any person as having an interest in premises, and the name of that person cannot be ascertained after reasonable inquiry, or where the notice or document is required or authorised to be served on any person as an occupier of premises, the notice or document shall be taken to be duly served if—

(*a*) it is addressed to him either by name or by the description of "the owner" or, as the case may be, "the occupier" of the premises (describing them) and is delivered or sent in the manner specified in subsection (1)(*a*), (*b*) or (*c*); or

(*b*) it is so addressed and is marked in such a manner as may be prescribed for securing that it is plainly identifiable as a communication of importance and—

(i) it is sent to the premises in a prepaid registered letter or by the recorded delivery service and is not returned to the authority sending it, or

(ii) it is delivered to some person on those premises, or is affixed conspicuously to some object on those premises.

(3) Where—

(*a*) the notice or other document is required to be served on or given to all persons who have interests in or are occupiers of premises comprised in any land, and

(*b*) it appears to the authority required or authorised to serve or give the notice or other document that any part of that land is unoccupied,

the notice or document shall be taken to be duly served on all persons having interests in, and on any occupiers of, premises comprised in that part of the land (other than a person who has given to that authority an address for the service of the notice or document on him) if it is addressed to "the owners and any occupiers" of that part of the land (describing it) and is affixed conspicuously to some object on the land.

(3A) The condition mentioned in subsection (1)(cc) is that the notice or other document shall be—

(*a*) capable of being accessed by the person mentioned in that provision;

(*b*) legible in all material respects; and

(*c*) in a form sufficiently permanent to be used for subsequent reference;

and for this purpose "legible in all material respects" means that the information contained in the notice or document is available to that person to no lesser extent than it would be if served or given by means of a notice or document in printed form.

(3B) Subsection (1)(*cc*) shall not apply to—

(*a*) service of a planning contravention notice;

(*b*) service of a copy of an enforcement notice by a local planning authority;

(*c*) giving of notice under section 173A of the exercise of powers conferred by subsection (1) of that section;

(*d*) service under section 181(4) of notice of a local planning authority's intention to take steps required by an enforcement notice;

(*e*) service of an enforcement notice issued by the Secretary of State;

(*f*) service of a stop notice, or of notice of withdrawal of a stop notice, by a local planning authority;

(*g*) service of a stop notice by the Secretary of State;

(*h*) service of a breach of condition notice or of notice of withdrawal of a breach of condition notice;

(*i*) giving of notice of the making of a tree preservation order, or service of a copy of such an order, in accordance with regulations under section 199;

(*j*) service of a notice under section 215 requiring steps to be taken to remedy the condition of any land;

(*k*) service of a notice under section 330 requiring information as to interests in land.

(4) This section is without prejudice to section 233 of the Local Government Act 1972 (general provisions as to services of notices by local authorities).

[Town and Country Planning Act 1990, s 329, as amended by the Planning and Compensation Act 1991, Sch 7, SI 2003/956 and SI 2004/3156.]

8–31071 **330. Power to require information as to interests in land.** (1) For the purpose of enabling the Secretary of State or a local authority to make an order or issue or serve any notice or other document which, by any of the provisions of this Act, he or they are authorised or required to make, issue or serve, the Secretary of State or the local authority may by notice in writing require the occupier of any premises and any person who, either directly or indirectly, receives rent in respect of any premises to give in writing such information as to the matters mentioned in subsection (2) as may be so specified.

(2) Those matters are—

(*a*) the nature of the interest in the premises of the person on whom the notice is served;
(*b*) the name and postal address of any other person known to him as having an interest in the premises;
(*c*) the purpose for which the premises are being used;
(*d*) the time when that use began;
(*e*) the name and postal address of any person known to the person on whom the notice is served as having used the premises for that purpose;
(*f*) the time when any activities being carried out on the premises began.

(3) A notice under subsection (1) may require information to be given within 21 days after the date on which it is served, or such longer time as may be specified in it, or as the Secretary of State or, as the case may be, the local authority may allow.

(4) Any person who, without reasonable excuse, fails to comply with a notice served on him under subsection (1) shall be guilty of an offence and liable on summary conviction to a fine not exceeding **level 3** on the standard scale.

(5) Any person who, having been required by a notice under subsection (1) to give any information, knowingly makes any misstatement in respect of it shall be guilty of an offence and liable[1] on summary conviction to a fine not exceeding the **statutory maximum** or on conviction on indictment to imprisonment for a term not exceeding **two years** or to a **fine**, or **both**.

(6) This section shall have effect as if the references to a local authority included references to a National Park authority.

[Town and Country Planning Act 1990, s 330, as amended by the Environment Act 1995, Sch 10, SI 2003/956 and SI 2004/3156.]

---

1. For procedure in respect of an offence triable either way see the Magistrates' Courts Act 1980, ss 17A–21 in PART I: MAGISTRATES' COURTS, PROCEDURE, ante.

8–31072 331. Offences by corporations. (1) Where an offence under this Act[1] which has been committed by a body corporate is proved to have been committed with the consent or connivance of, or to be attributable to any neglect on the part of—

(*a*) a director, manager, secretary or other similar officer of the body corporate, or
(*b*) any person who was purporting to act in any such capacity,

he as well as the body corporate shall be guilty of that offence and be liable to be proceeded against accordingly.

(2) In subsection (1) "director", in relation to any body corporate—

(*a*) which was established by or under an enactment for the purpose of carrying on under national ownership an industry or part of an industry or undertaking, and
(*b*) whose affairs are managed by its members,

means a member of that body corporate.

[Town and Country Planning Act 1990, s 331.]

---

1. This section applies for the purposes of the Planning (Listed Buildings and Conservation Areas) Act 1990 post (with the exception of s 59 thereof) as well: Planning (Listed Buildings and Conservation Areas) Act 1990, s 89.

8–31073 333. *Regulations and orders.*

8–31074 336. Interpretation. (1) In this Act, except in so far as the context otherwise requires and subject to the following provisions of this section and to any transitional provision made by the Planning (Consequential Provisions) Act 1990—

"address", in relation to electronic communications, means any number or address used for the purposes of such communications;

"advertisement" means any word, letter, model, sign, placard, board, notice, awning, blind, device or representation, whether illuminated or not, in the nature of, and employed wholly or partly for the purposes of, advertisement, announcement or direction, and (without prejudice to the previous provisions of this definition), includes any hoarding or similar structure used or designed, or adapted for use and anything else principally used, or designed or adapted principally for use, for the display of advertisements, and references to the display of advertisements shall be construed accordingly;

"agriculture" includes horticulture, fruit growing, seed growing, dairy farming, the breeding and keeping of livestock (including any creature kept for the production of food, wool, skins or fur, or for the purpose of its use in the farming of land), the use of land as grazing land, meadow land, osier land, market gardens and nursery grounds, and the use of land for woodlands where that use is ancillary to the farming of land for other agricultural purposes, and "agricultural" shall be construed accordingly;

"breach of condition notice" has the meaning given in section 187A;

"breach of planning control" has the meaning given in section 171A;

"building" includes any structure or erection, and any part of a building, as so defined, but does not include plant or machinery comprised in a building;

"buildings or works" includes waste materials, refuse and other matters deposited on land, and references to the erection or construction of buildings or works shall be construed accordingly and references to the removal of buildings or works include demolition of buildings and filling in of trenches;

"building operations" has the meaning given by section 55;

"depositing of mineral waste" means any process whereby a mineral-working deposit is created or enlarged and "depositing of refuse or waste materials" includes the depositing of mineral waste;

"development" has the meaning given in section 55, and "develop" shall be construed accordingly;

"development plan" must be construed in accordance with section 38 of the Planning and Compulsory Purchase Act 2004;

"electronic communication" has the same meaning as in the Electronic Communications Act 2000;

"enforcement notice" means a notice under section 172;

"engineering operations" includes the formation or laying out of means of access to highways;

"land" means any corporeal hereditament, including a building, and, in relation to the acquisition of land under Part IX, includes any interest in or right over land;

"local authority" (except in section 252 and subject to subsection (10) below and section 71(7) of the Environment Act 1995) means—

(*a*) a billing authority or a precepting authority (except the Receiver for the Metropolitan Police District)*, as defined in section 69 of the Local Government Finance Act 1992 or the Metropolitan Police Authority;

(*aa*) a fire and rescue authority in Wales constituted by a scheme under section 2 of the Fire and Rescue Services Act 2004 or a scheme to which section 4 of that Act applies;

(*b*) a levying body within the meaning of section 74 of the Local Government Finance Act 1988; and

(*c*) a body as regards which section 75 of that Act applies;

and includes any joint board or joint committee if all the constituent authorities are local authorities within paragraph (*a*), (*b*) or (*c*);

"local highway authority" means a highway authority other than the Secretary of State;

"local planning authority" shall be construed in accordance with Part I;

"owner", in relation to any land, means a person, other than a mortgagee not in possession, who, whether in his own right or as trustee for any other person, is entitled to receive the rack rent of the land, or, where the land is not let at a rack rent, would be so entitled if it were so let;

"the planning Acts" means this Act, the Planning (Listed Buildings and Conservation Areas) Act 1990, the Planning (Hazardous Substances) Act 1990 and the Planning (Consequential Provisions) Act 1990;

"planning contravention notice" has the meaning given in section 171C;

"planning decision" means a decision made on an application under Part III;

"planning permission" means permission under Part III;

"planning permission granted for a limited period" has the meaning given in section 72(2);

"spatial development strategy" shall be construed in accordance with Part VIII of the Greater London Authority Act 1999 (planning);

"stop notice" has the meaning given in section 183;

"tree preservation order" has the meaning given in section 198;

"universal postal service provider" means a universal service provider within the meaning of the Postal Services Act 2000; and references to the provision of a universal postal service shall be construed in accordance with that Act;

"use", in relation to land, does not include the use of land for the carrying out of any building or other operations on it;

(1A) In this Act—

(*a*) any reference to a county (other than one to a county planning authority) shall be construed, in relation to Wales, as including a reference to a county borough;

(*b*) any reference to a county council shall be construed, in relation to Wales, as including a reference to a county borough council; and

(*c*) section 17(4) and (5) of the Local Government (Wales) Act 1994 (references to counties and districts to be construed generally in relation to Wales as references to counties and county boroughs) shall not apply.

(2)–(9) *Further references.*

(10) In section 90, Chapter I of Part VI, and sections 324(2) and 330 "local authority", in relation to land in the Broads, includes the Broads Authority.

[Town and Country Planning Act 1990, s 336, as amended by the Planning and Compensation Act 1991, s 24, Schs 1, 4, 7 and 19, the Local Government Finance Act 1992, Sch 13, the Police and Magistrates' Courts Act 1994, Sch 9, the Local Government (Wales) Act 1994, Sch 6, the Environment Act 1995, Sch 10, the Gas Act 1995, Sch 4, the Greater London Authority Act 1999, s 344 and Sch 27, SI 2001/1149, SI 2003/956, SI 2004/3156, the Planning and Compulsory Purchase Act 2004, Sch 6 and the Fire and Rescue Services Act 2004, Sch1.]

***Repealed by the Greater London Authority Act 1999, Sch 27, from a date to be appointed.**

1. Only selected definitions are printed here, relevant to the parts of the Act appearing in this work.

Planning (Listed Buildings and Conservation Areas) Act 1990

(1990 c 9)

PART I[1]
LISTED BUILDINGS

CHAPTER I
LISTING OF SPECIAL BUILDINGS

8–31075 **1. Listing of buildings of special architectural or historic interest.** (1)–(4) *Secretary of State to compile or approve lists*

(5) In this Act "listed building"[2] means a building which is for the time being included in a list compiled or approved by the Secretary of State under this section; and for the purposes of this Act—

(*a*) any object or structure fixed to the building;
(*b*) any object or structure within the curtilage of the building which, although not fixed to the building, forms part of the land and has done so since before 1st July 1948,

shall be treated as part of the building.

(6) *Former building preservation orders.*

[Planning (Listed Buildings and Conservation Areas) Act 1990, s 1.]

1. Part I comprises ss 1–68.

2. Notwithstanding the definition of "building" in s 336 of the Town and Country Planning Act 1990 which includes "any part of a building" unless the context otherwise requires, the term "listed building" in this Act is not required to include part of a building. Accordingly whether work amounts to alteration of a listed building has to be considered in the context of the whole, and not part only of the building. Since "demolition" means the complete destruction of a building, the pulling down of a part falls within the expression "alteration" for the purposes of the Act, *Shimizu (UK) Ltd v Westminster City Council* [1997] 1 All ER 481, [1997] 1 WLR 168, HL.

CHAPTER II
AUTHORISATION OF WORKS AFFECTING LISTED BUILDINGS

Control of works in respect of listed buildings

8–31076 **7. Restriction on works affecting listed buildings.** Subject to the following provisions of this Act, no person shall execute or cause to be executed any works for the demolition of a listed building or for its alteration or extension in any manner which would affect its character as a building of special architectural or historic interest, unless the works are authorised.

[Planning (Listed Buildings and Conservation Areas) Act 1990, s 7.]

8–31077 **8. Authorisation of works: listed building consent.** (1) Works for the alteration or extension of a listed building are authorised if—

(*a*) written consent for their execution has been granted by the local planning authority or the Secretary of State; and
(*b*) they are executed in accordance with the terms of the consent and of any conditions attached to it.

(2) Works for the demolition of a listed building are authorised if—

(*a*) such consent has been granted for their execution;
(*b*) notice of the proposal to execute the works has been given to the Commission;*
(*c*) after such notice has been given either—
  (i) for a period of at least one month following the grant of such consent, and before the commencement of the works, reasonable access to the building has been made available to members or officers of the Commission* for the purpose of recording it; or
  (ii) the Secretary of the Commission*, or another officer of theirs with authority to act on their behalf for the purposes of this section, has stated in writing that they have completed their recording of the building or that they do not wish to record it; and
(*d*) the works are executed in accordance with the terms of the consent and of any conditions attached to it.

(3) Where—

(*a*) works for the demolition of a listed building or for its alteration or extension are executed without such consent; and

(*b*) written consent is granted by the local planning authority or the Secretary of State for the retention of the works,

the works are authorised from the grant of that consent.

(4) In this section "the Royal Commission" means—

(*a*) in relation to England, the Royal Commission on the Historical Monuments of England; and

(*b*) in relation to Wales, the Royal Commission on Ancient and Historical Monuments in Wales.

(5) The Secretary of State may by order provide that subsection (2) shall have effect with the substitution for the references to the Royal Commission of references to such other body as may be so specified.

(6) Such an order—

(*a*) shall apply in the case of works executed or to be executed on or after such date as may be specified in the order; and

(*b*) may apply in relation to either England or Wales, or both.

(7) Consent under subsection (1), (2) or (3) is referred to in this Act as "listed building consent".

[Planning (Listed Buildings and Conservation Areas) Act 1990, s 8.]

***In relation to works for the demolition of a listed building executed or to be executed on or after that date): see SI 2001/24, art 1(1).**

8–31078 9. Offences. (1) If a person contravenes section 7 he shall be guilty of an offence[1].

(2) Without prejudice to subsection (1), if a person executing or causing to be executed any works in relation to a listed building under a listed building consent fails to comply with any condition attached to the consent, he shall be guilty of an offence.

(3) In proceedings for an offence under this section it shall be a defence to prove the following matters—

(*a*) that works to the building were urgently necessary in the interests of safety or health or for the preservation of the building;

(*b*) that it was not practicable to secure safety or health or, as the case may be, the preservation of the building by works of repair or works for affording temporary support or shelter;

(*c*) that the works carried out were limited to the minimum measures immediately necessary; and

(*d*) that notice in writing justifying in detail the carrying out of the works was given to the local planning authority as soon as reasonably practicable.

(4) A person who is guilty of an offence under this section shall be liable[2]—

(*a*) on summary conviction, to imprisonment for a term not exceeding **six months** or a fine not exceeding **£20,000**, or **both**; or

(*b*) on conviction on indictment, to imprisonment for a term not exceeding **two years** or a **fine**, or **both**.

(5) In determining the amount of any fine to be imposed on a person convicted of an offence under this section, the court shall in particular have regard to any financial benefit which has accrued or appears likely to accrue to him in consequence of the offence.

[Planning (Listed Buildings and Conservation Areas) Act 1990, s 9, as amended by the Planning and Compensation Act 1991, Sch 3.]

---

1. This is an offence of strict liability and does not require the prosecution to prove intent (*R v Wells Street Metropolitan Stipendiary Magistrate, ex p Westminster City Council* [1986] 3 All ER 4, [1986] 1 WLR 1046. Section 7 does not apply to the demolition of a redundant building in pursuance of a pastoral or redundancy scheme within the meaning of the Pastoral Measure 1968 (Redundant Churches and other Religious Buildings Act 1969, s 2).

2. For procedure in respect of an offence triable either way, see Magistrates' Courts Act 1980, ss 17A–21 in PART I: MAGISTRATES' COURTS, PROCEDURE, ante.

8–31079 10. *Making of applications for listed building consent*[1].

8–31080 11. Certificates as to applicant's status etc. (1)–(5) *Applications may need to be accompanied by certificates as prescribed by regulations*[1] *as to ownership etc.*

(6) If any person—

(*a*) issues a certificate which purports to comply with the requirements of regulations made by virtue of this section and contains a statement which he knows to be false or misleading in a material particular; or

(*b*) recklessly issues a certificate which purports to comply with those requirements and contains a statement which is false or misleading in a material particular, he shall be guilty of an offence and liable on summary conviction to a fine not exceeding **level 3** on the standard scale.

(7) Subject to subsection (5), in this section "owner" means a person who is for the time being the estate owner in respect of the fee simple or is entitled to a tenancy granted or extended for a term of years certain of which not less than seven years remain unexpired.
[Planning (Listed Buildings and Conservation Areas) Act 1990, s 11.]

---

1. The Planning (Listed Buildings and Conservation Areas) Act Regulations 1990, SI 1990/1519 amended by SI 2003/2048 (E), SI 2004/2210 (E) and 3341 (E) and SI 2005/108 (E), have been made. See also the Transport and Works Applications (Listed Buildings, Conservation Areas and Ancient Monuments Procedure) Regulations 1992, SI 1992/3138. See also the Transport and Works Applications (Listed Buildings, Conservation Areas and Ancient Monuments Procedure) Regulations 1992, SI 1992/3138.

CHAPTER IV
ENFORCEMENT

8-31081 **38. Power to issue listed building enforcement notice**[1]**.** (1) Where it appears to the local planning authority—

(*a*) that any works have been or are being executed to a listed building in their area; and
(*b*) that the works are such as to involve a contravention of section 9(1) or (2),

they may, if they consider it expedient to do so having regard to the effect of the works on the character of the building as one of special architectural or historic interest, issue a notice under this section (in this Act referred to as a "listed building enforcement notice").

(2) A listed building enforcement notice shall specify the alleged contravention and require such steps as may be specified in the notice to be taken—

(*a*) for restoring the building to its former state; or
(*b*) if the authority consider that such restoration would not be reasonably practicable or would be undesirable, for executing such further works specified in the notice as they consider necessary to alleviate the effect of the works which were carried out without listed building consent; or
(*c*) for bringing the building to the state in which it would have been if the terms and conditions of any listed building consent which has been granted for the works had been complied with.

(3) A listed building enforcement notice—

(*a*) shall specify the date on which it is to take effect and, subject to sections 39(3) and 65(3A) shall take effect on that date, and
(*b*) shall specify the period within which any steps are required to be taken and may specify different periods for different steps,

and, where different periods apply to different steps, references in this Part to the period for compliance with a listed building enforcement notice, in relation to any step, are to the period within which the step is required to be taken.

(4) copy of a listed building enforcement notice shall be served, not later than 28 days after the date of its issue and not later than 28 days before the date specified in it as the date on which it is to take effect—

(*a*) on the owner and on the occupier of the building to which it relates; and
(*b*) on any other person having an interest in that building which in the opinion of the authority is materially affected by the notice.

(5), (6) *Withdrawal of notices.*

(7) Where a listed building enforcement notice imposes any such requirement as is mentioned in subsection (2)(*b*), listed building consent shall be deemed to be granted for any works of demolition, alteration or extension of the building executed as a result of compliance with the notice.
[Planning (Listed Buildings and Conservation Areas) Act 1990, s 38 amended by the Planning and Compensation Act 1991, Sch 3.]

---

1. There are similar provisions in s 172 of the Town and Country Planning Act 1990, ante.

8-31082 **39–42.** *Appeals, execution of works.*

8-31083 **43. Offence where listed building enforcement notice not complied with.** (1) Where, at any time after the end of the period for compliance with the notice, any step required by a listed building enforcement notice to be taken has not been taken, the person who is then owner of the land is in breach of the notice.

(2) If at any time the owner of the land is in breach of a listed building enforcement notice he shall be guilty of an offence.

(3) An offence under this section may be charged by reference to any day or longer period of time and a person may be convicted of a second or subsequent offence under this section by reference to any period of time following the preceding conviction for such an offence.

(4) In proceedings against any person for an offence under this section it shall be a defence for him to show—

(*a*) that he did everything he could be expected to do to secure that all the steps required by the notice were taken; or

(*b*) that he was not served with a copy of the listed building enforcement notice and was not aware of its existence.

(5) A person guilty of an offence under this section shall be liable[1]—

(*a*) on summary conviction, to a fine not exceeding **£20,000**; and

(*b*) on conviction on indictment, to a **fine**.

(6) In determining the amount of any fine to be imposed on a person convicted of an offence under this section, the court shall in particular have regard to any financial benefit which has accrued or appears likely to accrue to him in consequence of the offence.

[Planning (Listed Buildings and Conservation Areas) Act 1990, s 43, as substituted by the Planning and Compensation Act 1991, Sch 3.]

---

1. For procedure in respect of an offence triable either way, see the Magistrates' Courts Act 1980, ss 17A–21 in PART I: MAGISTRATES' COURTS, PROCEDURE, ante.

8–31084 **44. Effect of listed building consent on listed building enforcement notice.** (1) If, after the issue of a listed building enforcement notice, consent is granted under section 8(3)—

(*a*) for the retention of any work to which the notice relates; or

(*b*) permitting the retention of works without compliance with some condition subject to which a previous listed building consent was granted,

the notice shall cease to have effect in so far as it requires steps to be taken involving the works not being retained or, as the case may be, for complying with that condition.

(2) The fact that such a notice has wholly or partly ceased to have effect under subsection (1) shall not affect the liability of any person for an offence in respect of a previous failure to comply with that notice.

[Planning (Listed Buildings and Conservation Areas) Act 1990, s 44.]

CHAPTER V
PREVENTION OF DETERIORATION AND DAMAGE

Compulsory acquisition of listed building in need of repair

8–31085 **47–58.** *Compulsory acquisition of listed building in need of repair, compensation, acquisition of land by agreement, management of listed buildings, urgent works for unoccupied listed buildings, dangerous structures orders, etc.*

Damage to listed buildings

8–31086 **59. Acts causing or likely to result in damage to listed buildings.** (1) If, with the intention of causing damage to a listed building, any relevant person does or permits the doing of any act which causes or is likely to result in damage to the building, he shall be guilty of an offence and liable on summary conviction to a fine not exceeding **level 3** on the standard scale.

(2) A person is a relevant person for the purpose of subsection (1) if apart from that subsection he would be entitled to do or permit the act in question.

(3) Subsection (1) does not apply to an act for the execution—

(*a*) of works authorised by planning permission granted or deemed to be granted in pursuance of an application under the principal Act; or

(*b*) of works for which listed building consent has been given under this Act.

(4) If a person convicted of an offence under this section fails to take such reasonable steps as may be necessary to prevent any damage or further damage resulting from the offence, he shall be guilty of a further offence and liable on summary conviction to a fine not exceeding £40 for each day on which the failure continues.

[Planning (Listed Buildings and Conservation Areas) Act 1990, s 59.]

CHAPTER VI
MISCELLANEOUS AND SUPPLEMENTAL

Exceptions for church buildings and ancient monuments

8–31087 **60. Exceptions for ecclesiastical buildings and redundant churches.** (1) The provisions mentioned in subsection (2) shall not apply to any ecclesiastical building which is for the time being used for ecclesiastical purposes.

(2) Those provisions are sections 3, 4, 7 to 9, 47, 54 and 59.

(3) For the purposes of subsection (1), a building used or available for use by a minister of religion

wholly or mainly as a residence from which to perform the duties of his office shall be treated as not being an ecclesiastical building.

(4) For the purposes of sections 7 to 9 a building shall be taken to be used for the time being for ecclesiastical purposes if it would be so used but for the works in question.

(5), (6) *Orders*[1] *of Secretary of State restricting or excluding sub-ss (1)–(3).*

(7) Sections 7 to 9 shall not apply to the execution of works for the demolition, in pursuance of a pastoral or redundancy scheme (within the meaning of the Pastoral Measure 1983), of a redundant building (within the meaning of that Measure) or a part of such a building.

[Planning (Listed Buildings and Conservation Areas) Act 1990, s 60.]

1. The Ecclesiastical Exemption (Listed Buildings and Conservation Areas) Order 1994, SI 1994/1771 has been made.

8-31088 61. Exceptions for ancient monuments etc. (1) The provisions mentioned in subsection (2) shall not apply to any building for the time being included in the schedule of monuments compiled and maintained under section 1 of the Ancient Monuments and Archaeological Areas Act 1979.

(2) Those provisions are sections 3, 4, 7 to 9, 47, 54 and 59.

[Planning (Listed Buildings and Conservation Areas) Act 1990, s 61.]

Validity of instruments, decisions and proceedings

8-31089 62–65. *Validity of certain orders, decisions, notices; appeals to High Court*[1].

1. These provisions restricting challenges in legal proceedings to the validity of steps taken by various authorities are comparable with those contained in ss 284–290 of the Town and Country Planning Act 1990, ante.

8-31089A 88–88B. *Rights of entry, warrants to enter land*[1].

1. These provisions are similar to those in s 214C of the Town and Country Planning Act 1990, ante.

Planning (Hazardous Substances) Act 1990

(1990 c 10)

8-31090 4. *Requirement of hazardous substances consent*[1].

1. Sections 1–3 of the Act state who are the hazardous substances authorities for a variety of circumstances; in most instances the authority will be the council of the district or London Borough.

8-31091 5. *Power to prescribe hazardous substances*[1].

1. The Planning (Hazardous Substances) Regulations 1992, SI 1992/656, amended by SI 1994/2567, SI 1996/252, SI 1999/981 and SI 2005/1082 have been made under inter alia, ss 4, 5 and 8. See also the Planning (Control of Major-Accident Hazards) Regulations 1999, SI 1999/981.

8-31092 8. Certificates as to applicant's status etc. (1)–(5) *Regulations may provide that applications for hazardous substances consent shall be accompanied by certificates in prescribed form.*

(6) If any person—

(*a*) issues a certificate which purports to comply with the requirements of regulations made by virtue of this section and contains a statement which he knows to be false or misleading in a material particular; or

(*b*) recklessly issues a certificate which purports to comply with those requirements and contains such a statement,

he shall be guilty of an offence and liable on summary conviction to a fine not exceeding **level 3** on the standard scale.

(7), (8) Regulations. Meaning of "owner".

[Planning (Hazardous Substances) Act 1990, s 8.]

Contraventions of hazardous substances control

8-31093 23. Offences. (1) Subject to the following provisions of this section, if there is a contravention of hazardous substances control, the appropriate person shall be guilty of an offence.

(2) There is a contravention of hazardous substances control—

(*a*) if a quantity of a hazardous substance equal to or exceeding the controlled quantity is or has been present on, over or under land and either—

(i) there is no hazardous substances consent for the presence of the substance; or

(ii) there is hazardous substances consent for its presence but the quantity present exceeds the maximum quantity permitted by the consent;

(*b*) if there is or has been a failure to comply with a condition subject to which a hazardous substances consent was granted.

(3) In subsection (1) "the appropriate person" means—

(*a*) in relation to a contravention falling within paragraph (*a*) of subsection (2)—

(i) any person knowingly causing the substance to be present on, over or under the land;

(ii) any person allowing it to be so present; and

(*b*) in relation to a contravention falling within paragraph (*a*) or (*b*) of that subsection, the person in control of the land.

(4) A person guilty of an offence under this section shall be liable[1]—

(*a*) on summary conviction, to a fine not exceeding the **£20,000**; or

(*b*) on conviction on indictment, to a **fine**,

(4A) In determining the amount of any fine to be imposed on a person convicted of an offence under this section, the court shall in particular have regard to any financial benefit which has accrued or appears likely to accrue to him in consequence of the offence.

(5) In any proceedings for an offence under this section it shall be a defence for the accused to prove—

(*a*) that he took all reasonable precautions and exercised all due diligence to avoid commission of the offence, or

(*b*) that commission of the offence could be avoided only by the taking of action amounting to a breach of a statutory duty.

(6) In any proceedings for an offence consisting of a contravention falling within subsection (2)(*a*), it shall be a defence for the accused to prove that at the time of the alleged commission of the offence he did not know, and had no reason to believe—

(*a*) if the case falls within paragraph (*a*)(i)—

(i) that the substance was present; or

(ii) that it was present in a quantity equal to or exceeding the controlled quantity;

(*b*) if the case falls within paragraph (*a*)(ii), that the substance was present in a quantity exceeding the maximum quantity permitted by the consent.

(7) In any proceedings for an offence consisting of a contravention falling within subsection (2)(*b*), it shall be a defence for the accused to prove that he did not know, and had no reason to believe, that there was a failure to comply with a condition subject to which hazardous substances consent had been granted.

[Planning (Hazardous Substances) Act 1990, s 23, as amended by the Planning and Compensation Act 1991, Sch 3.]

---

1. For procedure in respect of an offence triable either way, see the Magistrates' Courts Act 1990, ss 17A–21 in PART I: MAGISTRATES' COURTS, ante.

8–31094 24. Power to issue hazardous substances contravention notice. (1) Where it appears to the hazardous substances authority that there is or has been a contravention of hazardous substances control, they may issue a notice—

(*a*) specifying an alleged contravention of hazardous substances control; and

(*b*) requiring such steps as may be specified in the notice to be taken to remedy wholly or partly the contravention,

if they consider it expedient to do so having regard to any material consideration.

(2) Such a notice is referred to in this Act as a "hazardous substances contravention notice".

(3) A hazardous substances authority shall not issue a hazardous substances contravention notice where it appears to them that a contravention of hazardous substances control can be avoided only by the taking of action amounting to a breach of statutory duty.

(4) A copy of a hazardous substances contravention notice shall be served—

(*a*) on the owner of the land to which it relates;

(*b*) on any person other than the owner who appears to the hazardous substances authority to be in control of the land; and

(*c*) on such other persons as may be prescribed.

(5) A hazardous substances contravention notice shall also specify—

(*a*) a date not less than 28 days from the date of service of copies of the notice as the date on which it is to take effect;

(*b*) in respect of each of the steps required to be taken to remedy the contravention of hazardous substances control, the period from the notice taking effect within which the step is to be taken.

(6) Where a hazardous substances authority issue a hazardous substances contravention notice the steps required by the notice may, without prejudice to the generality of subsection (1)(*b*), if the authority think it expedient, include a requirement that the hazardous substance be removed from the land.

(7) Where a notice includes such a requirement, it may also contain a direction that at the end of such period as may be specified in the notice any hazardous substances consent for the presence of the substance shall cease to have effect or, if it relates to more than one substance, shall cease to have effect so far as it relates to the substances which are required to be removed.

(8) The hazardous substances authority may withdraw a hazardous substances contravention notice (without prejudice to their power to issue another) at any time before or after it takes effect.

(9) If they do so, they shall immediately give notice of the withdrawal to every person who was served with a copy of the notice or would, if the notice were re-issued, be served with a copy of it.

[Planning (Hazardous Substances) Act 1990, s 24 amended by the Planning and Compensation Act 1991, Sch 3.]

1. Section 25 makes supplementary provision for hazardous substances contravention notices, in particular the making of regulations by the Secretary of State, which may direct that any of the provisions of ss 178(1) to (5) and (7), 179–181, 183, 184, 187 and 188 of the Town and Country Planning Act 1990 (ante) shall have effect, with appropriate modifications, to notices under this Act.

8–31095 26. Transitional exemptions. (1) No offence is committed under section 23 and no hazardous substances contravention notice may be issued in relation to a hazardous substance which is on, over or under any land, if—

(*a*) the substance was present on, over or under the land at any time within the establishment period; and

(*b*) in a case in which at the relevant date notification in respect of that substance was required by any of the Notification Regulations, both the conditions specified in subsection (2) were satisfied; and

(*c*) in a case in which at that date such notification was not so required, the condition specified in paragraph (*b*) of that subsection is satisfied.

(2) The conditions mentioned in subsection (1) are—

(*a*) that notification required by the Notification Regulations was given before the relevant date; and

(*b*) that the substance has not been present during the transitional period in a quantity greater in aggregate than the established quantity.

(2A) This section shall have effect until the end of the transitional period.

(3) Expressions used in this section and in section 11[1] have the same meanings as in that section.

[Planning (Hazardous Substances) Act 1990, s 26 amended by the Planning and Compensation Act 1991, Sch 3.]

1. Section 11(8) contains the following definitions:

"establishment period" means the period of 12 months immediately preceding the relevant date;

"established quantity" means, in relation to any land—

(*a*) where before the relevant date there was a notification in respect of a substance in accordance with any of the Notification Regulations—

(i) the quantity notified or last notified before that date; or

(ii) a quantity equal to twice the quantity which was so notified or last notified before the start of the establishment period,

whichever is the greater;

(*b*) where a notification was not required before that date by any of those regulations, a quantity exceeding by 50 per cent the maximum quantity which was present on, over or under the land at any one time within that period;

"Notification Regulations" means the Notification of Installations Handling Hazardous Substances Regulations 1982;

"the relevant date" means the date on which Part IV of the Housing and Planning Act 1986 came into force or, if that Part of that Act is not in force immediately before the date on which this Act comes into force, that date;

"the transitional period" means the period of 6 months beginning with the relevant date.

8–31096 36–36B. *Rights of entry, warrants to enter land*[1].

1. These provisions are similar to those in s 214C of the Town and Country Planning Act 1990, ante.

Town and Country Planning (Control of Advertisements) Regulations 1992[1]

(SI 1992/666 amended by SI 1994/2351, SI 1996/252, SI 1996/525, SI 1999/1810, SI 2001/1149 and 4050, SI 2003/2155 and SI 2005/3050)

PART I
GENERAL

8–31180 1. *Citation and commencement.*

---

1. Made by the Secretary of State for the Environment, as respects England, and the Secretary of State for Wales, as respects Wales, in exercise of the powers conferred upon them by ss 220, 221, 223(1), 224(3) and 333(1) of the Town and Country Planning Act 1990.

Interpretation

8–31181 2. (1) In these Regulations—

"the Act" means the Town and Country Planning Act 1990;

"advertisement" does not include anything employed wholly as a memorial or as a railway signal;

"area of outstanding natural beauty" means an area designated as such by an order made under section 87 of the National Parks and Access to the Countryside Act 1949;

"area of special control" means an area designated by an order under regulation 18;

"balloon" means a tethered balloon or similar object;

"deemed consent" has the meaning given by regulation 5;

"discontinuance notice" means a notice served under regulation 8;

"EEA State" means a member State, Norway, Iceland or Liechtenstein,

"express consent" has the meaning given by regulation 5;

"illuminated advertisement" means an advertisement which is designed or adapted to be illuminated by artificial lighting, directly or by reflection, and which is so illuminated;

"National Park" has the meaning given by section 5 of the National Parks and Access to the Countryside Act 1949;

"site" means any land or building, other than an advertisement, on which an advertisement is displayed;

"standard conditions" means the conditions specified in Schedule 1;

"statutory undertaker" includes, in addition to any person mentioned in section 262(1) of the Act, the Civil Aviation Authority, a person who holds a licence under Chapter I of Part I of the Transport Act 2000 (air traffic services), the British Airports Authority, the Coal Authority or any licensed operator within the meaning of section 65(1) of the Coal Industry Act 1994, any gas transporter within the meaning of Part I of the Gas Act 1986, any public electricity supplier within the meaning of Part I of the Electricity Act 1989, any person who is a licence holder, or who has the benefit of a licence exemption, within the meaning of Part I of the Railways Act 1993, any person who holds a European licence granted pursuant to the Railway (Licensing of Railway Undertaking) Regulations 2005 or pursuant to any action taken by an EEA State for the purpose of implementing Council Directive 1995/18/EC dated 19th June 1995 on the licensing of railway undertakings, as amended by Directive 2001/13/EC dated 26th February 2001 and Directive 2004/49/EC dated 29th April 2004, both of the European Parliament and of the Council, a universal postal service provider in connection with the provision of a universal postal service, the Environment Agency, any water or sewerage undertaker and any electronic communications code operator; and, subject to paragraph (1A), statutory undertaking shall be interpreted accordingly;

"vehicle" includes a vessel on any inland waterway; and

"waterway" includes coastal waters.

(1A) The undertaking of a universal postal service provider so far as relating to the provision of a universal postal service shall be taken to be his statutory undertaking for the purposes of these regulations; and references in these regulations to his undertaking shall be construed accordingly.

(2) In the application of these Regulations in England, "local planning authority" means—

(*a*) for land in the area of an urban development corporation, except in regulation 18, that corporation where it is the local planning authority for the purposes of sections 220 and 224 of the Act;

(*b*) for land in a National Park which is land that is not in a metropolitan county, the county planning authority for the area where the land is situated; and

(*c*) in any other case, the relevant district planning authority or metropolitan district or London borough council.

(2A) In the application of these Regulations in Wales "local planning authority" means—

(*a*) subject to sub-paragraph (*b*) below, the local planning authority for the area in which the land in question is situated;

(*b*) for land in the area of any urban development corporation, except in regulation 18, that corporation where it is the local planning authority for the purposes of sections 220 and 224 of the Act.

(2B) For the purposes of these Regulations—

(*a*) a person who holds a licence under Chapter I of Part I of the Transport Act 2000 shall not be considered to be a statutory undertaker unless the person is carrying out activities authorised by the licence; and

(*b*) the person's undertaking shall not be considered to be a statutory undertaking except to the extent that it is the person's undertaking as licence holder.

(3) Any reference in these Regulations to a person displaying an advertisement includes—

(*a*) the owner and occupier of the land on which the advertisement is displayed;

(*b*) any person to whose goods, trade, business or other concerns publicity is given by the advertisement; and

(*c*) the person who undertakes or maintains the display of the advertisement.

(4) Except in Class A in Schedule 2, any reference in these Regulations to the land, the building, the site or the premises on which an advertisement is displayed includes, in the case of an advertisement which is displayed on, or which consists of, a balloon, a reference to the land, the building, the site or other premises to which the balloon is attached[1] and to all land, buildings or other premises normally occupied therewith.

---

1. A balloon is attached to land if it is attached to something on the land such as a tree, or to something laid on the land, of sufficient weight to prevent it from blowing away (*Wadham Stringer (Fareham) Ltd v Fareham Borough Council* (1986) 151 JP 140).

Application

8–31182 **3.** (1) These Regulations apply to the display on any site in England and Wales of any advertisement.

(2) Parts II and III of these Regulations do not apply to any advertisement falling within a description set out in Schedule 2 provided it complies with any conditions and limitations specified in that Schedule; and—

(*a*) in the case of an advertisement falling within Class G, it complies with the standard conditions set out in paragraphs 1, 2, 3, and 5 of Schedule 1; or

(*b*) in any other case, it complies with all the standard conditions.

Powers to be exercised in the interests of amenity and public safety

8–31183 **4.** (1)[1] A local planning authority shall exercise their powers under these Regulations only in the interests of amenity and public safety, taking account of any material factors, and in particular—

(*a*) in the case of amenity, the general characteristics of the locality, including the presence of any feature of historic, architectural, cultural or similar interest, disregarding, if they think fit, any advertisement being displayed there;

(*b*) in the case of public safety—

(i) the safety of any person who may use any road, railway, waterway, dock, harbour or aerodrome;

(ii) whether any display of advertisements is likely to obscure, or hinder the ready interpretation of, any road traffic sign, railway signal or aid to navigation by water or air.

(2) In determining an application for consent for the display of advertisements, or considering whether to make an order revoking or modifying a consent, the local planning authority may have regard to any material change in circumstances likely to occur within the period for which the consent is required or granted.

(3) Unless it appears to the local planning authority to be required in the interests of amenity or public safety, an express consent for the display of advertisements shall not contain any limitation or restriction relating to the subject matter, content or design of what is to be displayed.

(4) A consent for the display of advertisements shall take effect as consent for the use of the site for the purposes of the display, whether by the erection of structures or otherwise, and for the benefit of any person interested in the site.

---

1. The exercise of the power to prosecute under s 224 of the Town and Country Planning Act 1990 for a contravention of these regulations is not subject to the duties specified in Regulation 4 (*Kingsley and Kingsley v Hammersmith and Fulham London Borough Council* (1991) 156 JP 372) (decided under the corresponding 1989 regulation).

Requirement for consent

8–31184 **5.** (1) No advertisement may be displayed without consent granted by the local planning authority or by the Secretary of State on an application in that behalf (referred to in these Regulations as "express consent"), or granted by regulation 6 (referred to in these Regulations as "deemed consent"), except an advertisement displayed in accordance with paragraph (2) below.

(2) The display—

(*a*) outside any area of special control, of such an advertisement as is mentioned in regulation 3(2); or

(*b*) within an area of special control, of such an advertisement as is so mentioned, other than one falling within Class A in Schedule 2,

is in accordance with this paragraph.

PART II
DEEMED CONSENT

Deemed consent for the display of advertisements

8–31185 **6.** (1) Subject to regulations 7 and 8, and in the case of an area of special control also to regulation 19, deemed consent is hereby granted for the display of an advertisement falling within any class specified in Part I of Schedule 3, subject—

(*a*) to any conditions and limitations specified in that Part in relation to that class; and

(*b*) to the standard conditions.

(2) Part II of Schedule 3 applies for the interpretation of that Schedule.

Directions restricting deemed consent

8–31186 **7.** (1) If the Secretary of State is satisfied, upon a proposal made to him by the local planning authority, that the display of advertisements of any class or description specified in Schedule 3, other than Class 12 or 13, should not be undertaken in any particular area or in any particular case without express consent, he may direct that the consent granted by regulation 6 for that class or description shall not apply in that area or in that case, for a specified period or indefinitely.

(2) Before making any such direction, the Secretary of State shall—

(*a*) where the proposal relates to a particular area, publish, or cause to be published, in at least one newspaper circulating in the locality, and on the same or a subsequent date in the London Gazette, a notice that such a proposal has been made, naming a place or places in the locality where a map or maps defining the area concerned may be inspected at all reasonable hours; and

(*b*) where the proposal relates to a particular case, serve, or cause to be served, on the owner and occupier of the land affected and on any other person who, to his knowledge, proposes to display on such land an advertisement of the class or description concerned, a notice that a proposal has been made, specifying the land and the class or description of advertisement in question.

(3) Any notice under paragraph (2) above shall state that any objection to the making of a direction may be made to the Secretary of State in writing within such period (not being less than 21 days from the date when the notice was given) as is specified in the notice.

(4) The Secretary of State shall not make a direction under this regulation until after the expiry of the specified period.

(5) In determining whether to make a direction, the Secretary of State—

(*a*) shall take into account any objections made in accordance with paragraph (3) above;

(*b*) may modify the proposal of the local planning authority if—

(i) he has notified, in writing, that authority and any person who has made an objection or representation to him of his intention and his reasons for it and has given them a reasonable opportunity to respond; and

(ii) the intended modification does not extend the area of land specified in the proposal.

(6) Where the Secretary of State makes a direction, he shall send it to the local planning authority, with a statement of his reasons for making it, and shall send a copy of that statement to any person who has made an objection in accordance with paragraph (3) above.

(7) Notice of the making of any direction for a particular area shall be published by the local planning authority in at least one newspaper circulating in the locality and, unless the Secretary of State otherwise directs, on the same or a subsequent date in the London Gazette, and such notice shall—

(*a*) contain a full statement of the effect of the direction;

(*b*) name a place or places in the locality where a copy of the direction and of a map defining the area concerned may be seen at all reasonable hours; and

(*c*) specify a date when the direction shall come into force, being at least 14 and not more than 28 days after the first publication of the notice.

(8) Notice of the making of any direction for a particular case shall be served by the local planning authority on the owner and on any occupier of the land to which the direction relates, and on any other person who, to the knowledge of the authority, proposes to display on such land an advertisement of the class or description affected.

(9) A direction for an area shall come into force on the date specified in the notice given under

paragraph (7) above; and a direction for a particular case shall come into force on the date on which notice is served on the occupier or, if there is no occupier, on the owner of the land affected.

Discontinuance of deemed consent

8-31187 **8.** (1) The local planning authority may serve a notice requiring the discontinuance of the display of an advertisement, or of the use of a site for the display of an advertisement, for which deemed consent is granted under regulation 6 if they are satisfied that it is necessary to do so to remedy a substantial injury to the amenity of the locality or a danger to members of the public: but in the case of an advertisement within Class 12 in Schedule 3, they may not do so if the advertisement is also within Class F or Class G in Schedule 2.

(2) A discontinuance notice—

(*a*) shall be served on the advertiser[1] and on the owner and occupier of the site on which the advertisement is displayed;

(*b*) may, if the local planning authority think fit, also be served on any other person displaying the advertisement;

(*c*) shall specify the advertisement or the site to which it relates;

(*d*) shall specify a period within which the display or the use of the site (as the case may be) is to be discontinued; and

(*e*) shall contain a full statement of the reasons why action has been taken under this regulation.

(3) Subject to paragraphs (4) and (5) below, a discontinuance notice shall take effect at the end of the period (being at least 8 weeks after the date on which it is served) specified in the notice.

(4) If an appeal is made to the Secretary of State under regulation 15, the notice shall be of no effect pending the final determination or withdrawal of the appeal.

(5) The local planning authority, by a notice served on the advertiser, may withdraw a discontinuance notice at any time before it takes effect or may, where no appeal to the Secretary of State is pending, from time to time vary a discontinuance notice by extending the period specified for the taking effect of the notice.

(6) The local planning authority shall, on serving on the advertiser a notice of withdrawal or variation under paragraph (5) above, send a copy to every other person served with the discontinuance notice.

1. "Advertiser" includes the person whose goods are advertised and it is necessary that he also is served with an notice requiring the discontinuance of the display of an advertisement (*O'Brien v Croydon London Borough Council* [1998] EGCS 112).

PART III
EXPRESS CONSENT

Applications for express consent

8-31188 **9.** (1) An application for express consent shall be made to the local planning authority.

(2) Such an application shall be made on a form provided by the local planning authority and give the particulars required by that form. There shall be annexed to the form such plans as the authority require.

(3) An applicant shall provide the local planning authority with 2 additional copies of the completed form and the annexed plans.

(4) The local planning authority may, if they think fit, accept an application notwithstanding that the requirements of paragraph (2) or (3) above are not complied with, provided the application is in writing.

(5) A local planning authority shall not employ a form or require the submission of plans or information inconsistently with any direction which the Secretary of State may have given as to the matter.

(6) An application for the renewal of an express consent may not be made at a date earlier than 6 months before the expiry of that consent.

8-31188A **9A.** ***Application of section 77 of the Act to applications for express consent.***

8-31189 **10.** *Secretary of State's directions.*

8-31190 **11.** *Receipt of applications.*

8-31191 **12.** *Duty to consult.*

Power to deal with applications

8-31192 **13.** (1) Subject to regulation 19 below, where an application for express consent is made to the local planning authority, they may—

(*a*) grant consent, in whole or in part, subject to the standard conditions and, subject to paragraphs (3) to (6) below, to such additional conditions as they think fit; or (*b*) refuse consent; or

(*c*) decline to determine the application in accordance with section 70A of the Act, which shall apply in relation to the application subject to the modifications specified in Part I of Schedule 4[1], the provisions of that section as modified being set out in Part II of that Schedule.

(2) An express consent may be—

(*a*) for the display of a particular advertisement or advertisements with or without illumination, as the applicant specifies;

(*b*) for the use of a particular site for the display of advertisements in a specified manner, whether by reference to the number, siting, size or illumination of the advertisements, or the structures intended for such display, or the design or appearance of any such structure, or otherwise; or

(*c*) for the retention of any display of advertisements or the continuation of the use of a site begun before the date of the application.

(3) The conditions imposed under paragraph (1)(*b*) above may in particular include conditions—

(*a*) regulating the display of advertisements to which the consent relates;

(*b*) regulating the use for the display of advertisements of the site to which the application relates or any adjacent land under the control of the applicant, or requiring the carrying out of works on any such land;

(*c*) requiring the removal of any advertisement or the discontinuance of any use of land authorised by the consent, at the end of a specified period, and the carrying out of any works required for the reinstatement of the land.

(4) The local planning authority shall not, under paragraph (1)(*b*) above, impose any conditions in relation to the display of an advertisement within any class specified in Schedule 3 more restrictive than those imposed by that Schedule in relation to that class.

(5) Subject to paragraph (4) above, an express consent shall be subject to the condition that it expires at the end of—

(*a*) such period as the local planning authority may specify in granting the consent; or

(*b*) where no period is so specified, a period of 5 years.

(6) A local planning authority may specify a period under paragraph (5)(*a*) above as a period running from the earlier of the following, namely the date of the commencement of the display or a specified date not later than 6 months after the date on which the consent is granted.

---

1. Schedule 4 is not reproduced.

8–31192A 13A. ***Applications by an interested planning authority.***

Notification of decision

8–31193 14. (1) The grant or refusal of an express consent by a local planning authority shall be notified in writing to the applicant within a period of 8 weeks from the date of the receipt of the application or such longer period as the applicant may, before the expiry of that period, agree in writing.

(2) The authority shall state in writing their reasons for—

(*a*) any refusal of consent in whole or in part;

(*b*) any decision to impose any condition under regulation 13(1)(*a*) on a consent, except a condition specified in Schedule 3 in relation to a class within which the advertisement falls; and

(*c*) any condition whereby the consent expires before the expiry of 5 years from the date on which it is granted, except when the consent is granted for the period for which it was applied for.

8–31194 15. *Appeals to the Secretary of State.*

Revocation or modification of express consent

8–31195 16. (1) If a local planning authority are satisfied that it is expedient, they may by order revoke or modify an express consent, subject to paragraphs (2) to (7) below.

(2) An order under paragraph (1) above shall not take effect without the approval of the Secretary of State.

(3) When an authority submit an order under paragraph (1) above to the Secretary of State for approval, they shall serve notice on the person who applied for the express consent, the owner and the occupier of the land affected and any other person who, in their opinion, will be affected by the order, specifying a period of at least 28 days from the service of the notice within which objection may be made.

(4) If, within the period specified in the notice, an objection to the order is received by the Secretary of State from any person on whom notice was served, the Secretary of State shall, before approving the order, give to that person and to the local planning authority an opportunity of appearing before and being heard by a person appointed by him.

(5) The power to make an order under this regulation may be exercised—

(*a*) in a case which involves the carrying out of building or other operations, at any time before those operations have been completed;

(*b*) in any other case, at any time before the display of advertisements is begun.

(6) In a case to which paragraph (5)(*a*) above applies, the revocation or modification of consent shall not affect such operations as have already been carried out.

(7) The Secretary of State may approve an order submitted to him under this regulation either without modification or subject to such modifications as he considers expedient.

8–31196 **17.** *Compensation for revocation or modification.*

PART IV
AREAS OF SPECIAL CONTROL

Area of Special Control Orders

8–31197 **18.** (1) Every local planning authority shall from time to time consider whether any part or additional part of their area should be designated as an area of special control.

(2) An area of special control shall be designated by an area of special control order made by the local planning authority and approved by the Secretary of State, in accordance with the provisions of Schedule 5[1].

(3) An area of special control order may be revoked or modified by a subsequent order made by the authority and approved by the Secretary of State, in accordance with the provisions of Schedule 5[1].

(4) Where an area of special control order is in force, the local planning authority shall consider at least once in every 5 years whether it should be revoked or modified.

(5) Before making an order under this regulation, a local planning authority shall consult—

(*a*) where it appears to them that the order will be likely to affect any part of the area of a neighbouring local planning authority, that authority;

(*b*) where the order will relate to any land in a National Park which is land that is not in a metropolitan county, any district planning authority within whose area any of that land is situated.

(6) A local planning authority shall not exercise their power under this regulation in the interests of public safety within the meaning of regulation 4(1).

---

1. Schedule 5 is not reproduced.

Control in areas of special control

8–31198 **19.** (1) Subject to the provisions of this regulation, no advertisements may be displayed in an area of special control unless they fall within—

(*a*) Classes B to J in Schedule 2;

(*b*) Classes 1 to 3, 5 to 7 and 9 to 14 in Schedule 3;

(*c*) paragraph (2) below.

(2) Advertisements of the following descriptions displayed with express consent come within this paragraph—

(*a*) hoardings or similar structures to be used only for the display of notices relating to local events, activities or entertainments;

(*b*) any advertisement for the purpose of announcement or direction in relation to buildings or other land in the locality, where reasonably required having regard to the nature and situation of such buildings or other land;

(*c*) any advertisement required in the interests of public safety;

(*d*) any advertisement which could be displayed by virtue of paragraph (1)(*b*) above but for some non-compliance with a condition or limitation imposed by Schedule 3 as respects size, height from the ground, number or illumination or but for a direction under regulation 7;

(*e*) any advertisement within Class 4A, 4B or 8 in Schedule 3.

(3) Express consent may not be given for the display in an area of special control of an illuminated advertisement falling within sub-paragraph (2)(*a*) or (*b*) above.

(4) Without prejudice to paragraph (2) above, where an area is designated as an area of special control, advertisements within paragraph (5) below which are being displayed immediately before the relevant order comes into force may continue to be displayed, but only for the period specified in relation thereto in that paragraph.

(5) The advertisements and specified periods mentioned in paragraph (4) above are—

(*a*) any advertisement within Class 4A or 4B in Schedule 3 for which express consent has not been granted, 5 years from the date on which the order comes into force;

(*b*) any advertisement within Class 8 for which express consent has not been granted, 1 year from the date on which the order comes into force or 2 years from the date on which the advertisement was first displayed, whichever period expires later;

(*c*) any advertisement for which express consent has been granted, 6 months from the date on which the order comes into force or for the remainder of the period of the express consent, whichever period expires later.

(6) Nothing in paragraphs (1) to (5) above shall—

(*a*) affect a notice served at any time under regulation 8;
(*b*) override any condition imposed on a consent, whereby an advertisement is required to be removed;
(*c*) restrict the powers of a local planning authority, or of the Secretary of State, in regard to any contravention of these Regulations;
(*d*) render unlawful the display, pursuant to express consent or to Class 14 in Schedule 3, of an advertisement mentioned in paragraph 2(*d*) or (*e*) above.

PART V
MISCELLANEOUS

8–31199 **20.** *Repayment of expense of removing prohibited advertisements.*

8–31210 **21.** *Register of applications.*

8–31211 **22.** *Directions requiring information.*

8–31212 **23.** *Exercise of powers by the Secretary of State.*

Discontinuance notice in respect of authority's advertisement

8–31213 **24.** (1) If the Secretary of State is satisfied that it is necessary to remedy a substantial injury to the amenity of the locality or a danger to members of the public, he may serve a discontinuance notice under regulation 8 in relation to an advertisement displayed by an interested planning authority.

(2) Paragraphs (2), (5) and (6) of regulation 8 shall apply to a discontinuance notice to which paragraph (1) above applies as if references to the local planning authority were references to the Secretary of State.

(3) Paragraph (3) of regulation 15 shall apply to a discontinuance notice to which paragraph (1) above applies, with such modifications as may be necessary.

Extension of time limits

8–31214 **25.** The Secretary of State may, in any particular case, extend the time within which anything is required to be done under these Regulations or within which any objection, representation or claim for compensation may be made.

Cancellation or variation of directions

8–31215 **26.** Any power conferred by these Regulations to give a direction includes power to cancel or vary the direction by a subsequent direction.

Contravention of Regulations

8–31216 **27.** A person displaying an advertisement in contravention of these Regulations shall be liable on summary conviction of an offence[1] under section 224(3) of the Act to a fine of an amount not exceeding **level 3** on the standard scale and, in the case of a continuing offence, **one-tenth of level 3** on the standard scale for each day during which the offence continues after conviction.

1. The display of an advertising poster on a hoarding without consent constitutes a single offence; accordingly, the display of 11 different posters on a variety of dates was held to constitute 11 separate offences (*Kingston-upon-Thames London Borough Council v National Solus Sites Ltd* (1993) 158 JP 70).

8–31217 **28.** *Revocation.*

Regulation 2(1)

SCHEDULE 1
STANDARD CONDITIONS

8–31218 **1.** Any advertisements displayed, and any site used for the display of advertisements, shall be maintained in a clean and tidy condition to the reasonable satisfaction of the local planning authority.

2. Any structure or hoarding erected or used principally for the purpose of displaying advertisements shall be maintained in a safe condition.

3. Where an advertisement is required under these Regulations to be removed, the removal shall be carried out to the reasonable satisfaction of the local planning authority.

4. No advertisement is to be displayed without the permission of the owner of the site or any other person with an interest in the site entitled to grant permission.

5. No advertisement shall be sited or displayed so as to obscure, or hinder the ready interpretation of, any road traffic sign, railway signal or aid to navigation by water or air, or so as otherwise to render hazardous the use of any highway, railway, waterway or aerodrome (civil or military).

8–31219

Regulation 3(2)

SCHEDULE 2

CLASSES OF ADVERTISEMENTS TO WHICH PARTS II AND III OF THESE REGULATIONS DO NOT APPLY

Description of advertisement	*Conditions, limitations and interpretation*
CLASS A The display of an advertisement on or consisting of a balloon not more than 60 metres above ground level.	1 The site of the advertisement is not within an area of outstanding natural beauty, a conservation area, a National Park, the Broads or an area of special control. 2 Not more than one such advertisement may be displayed on the site at any one time. 3 The site may not be used for the display of advertisements on more than 10 days in total in any calendar year. 4 For the purposes of Class A, "the site" means— (*a*) in a case where the advertisement is being displayed by a person (other than the occupier of the land) who is using, or proposing to use, the land to which the balloon is attached for a particular activity (other than the display of advertisements) for a temporary period, the whole of the land used, or to be used, for that activity; or (*b*) in any other case, the land to which the balloon is attached and all land normally occupied together therewith.
CLASS B An advertisement displayed on enclosed land.	1 The advertisement is not readily visible from outside the enclosed land or from any place to which the public have a right of access. 2 For the purposes of Class B, "enclosed land" includes any railway station (and its yards) or bus station, together with its forecourt, whether enclosed or not; but does not include any public park, public garden or other land held for the use or enjoyment of the public, or (save as herein specified) any enclosed railway land normally used for the carriage of passengers or goods by rail.
CLASS C An advertisement displayed on or in a vehicle.	1 The vehicle is not— (*a*) normally employed except as a moving vehicle; or (*b*) used principally for the display of advertisements.
CLASS D An advertisement incorporated in the fabric of a building.	1 The building or any external face of it is not used principally for the display of advertisements. 2 For the purposes of Class D— (*a*) an advertisement fixed to, or painted on, a building is not to be regarded as incorporated in its fabric; (*b*) a hoarding or similar structure is to be regarded as a building used principally for the display of advertisements.
CLASS E An advertisement displayed on an article for sale or on the container in, or from which, an article is sold.	1 The advertisement refers only to the article for sale. 2 The advertisement may not be illuminated. 3 It may not exceed 0.1 square metre in area. 4 For the purposes of Class E, "article" includes a gas or liquid.
CLASS F An advertisement relating specifically to a pending Parliamentary, [European Parliamentary] or local government election.	1 The advertisement shall be removed within 14 days after the close of the poll in the election to which it relates.
CLASS G An advertisement required to be displayed by Standing Orders of either House of Parliament or by any enactment or any condition imposed by any enactment on the exercise of any power or function.	1 If the advertisement would, if it were not within this Class, fall within any Class in Schedule 3, any conditions imposed on that Class as to size, height or number of advertisements displayed shall apply to it.

Description of advertisement	*Conditions, limitations and interpretation*
	2 In a case to which paragraph 1 does not apply, the size, height, and number of advertisements displayed shall not exceed what is necessary to achieve the purpose for which the advertisement is required. 3 The advertisement may not be displayed after the expiry of the period during which it is required or authorised to be displayed, or if there is no such period, the expiry of a reasonable time after its purpose has been satisfied.
CLASS H A traffic sign.	1 For the purposes of Class H, a traffic sign means a traffic sign as defined in section 64(1) of the Road Traffic Regulation Act 1984.
CLASS I The national flag of any country.	1 Each flag is to be displayed on a single vertical flagstaff. 2 Neither the flag nor the flagstaff may display any advertisement or subject matter additional to the design of the flag.
CLASS J An advertisement displayed inside a building.	1 The advertisement may not be illuminated. 2 The building in which the advertisement is displayed is not used principally for the display of advertisements. 3 No part of the advertisement may be within 1 metre of any external door, window or other opening, through which it is visible from outside the building.

8–31220

Regulation 6

SCHEDULE 3

CLASSES OF ADVERTISEMENTS WHICH MAY BE DISPLAYED WITH DEEMED CONSENT

PART I

SPECIFIED CLASSES AND CONDITIONS

Class 1—Functional advertisements of local authorities, statutory undertakers and public transport undertakers

1A. Description. An advertisement displayed wholly for the purpose of announcement or direction in relation to any of the functions of a local authority or to the operation of a statutory undertaking or a public transport undertaking, which—

(*a*) is reasonably required to be displayed for the safe or efficient performance of those functions, or operation of that undertaking, and

(*b*) cannot be displayed by virtue of any other specified class.

1A. Conditions and Limitations. (1) Illumination is not permitted unless reasonably required for the purpose of the advertisement.

1B. Description. An advertisement displayed by a local planning authority on land in their area.

1B. Conditions and Limitations. (1) In an area of special control, such an advertisement may be displayed only if the authority could have granted express consent for its display.

Class 2—Miscellaneous advertisements relating to the premises on which they are displayed

2A. Description. An advertisement displayed for the purpose of identification, direction or warning, with respect to the land or building on which it is displayed.

2A. Conditions and Limitations. (1) No such advertisement may exceed 0.3 square metre in area.

(2) Illumination is not permitted.

(3) No character or symbol on the advertisement may be more than 0.75 metre in height, or 0.3 metre in an area of special control.

(4) No part of the advertisement may be more than 4.6 metres above ground level, or 3.6 metres in an area of special control.

2B. Description. An advertisement relating to any person, partnership or company separately carrying on a profession, business or trade at the premises where it is displayed.

2B. Conditions and Limitations. (1) No advertisement may exceed 0.3 square metre in area.

(2) No character or symbol on the advertisement may be more than 0.75 metre in height, or 0.3 metre in an area of special control.

(3) No part of the advertisement may be more than 4.6 metres above ground level, or 3.6 metres in an area of special control.

(4) Not more than one such advertisement is permitted for each person, partnership or company or, in the

case of premises with entrances on different road frontages, one such advertisement at each of two such entrances.

(5) Illumination is not permitted unless the advertisement states that medical or similar services or supplies are available on the premises and the illumination is in a manner reasonably required to fulfil the purpose of the advertisement.

2C. Description. An advertisement relating to any institution of a religious, educational, cultural, recreational or medical or similar character, or to any hotel, inn or public house, block of flats, club, boarding house or hostel, at the premises where it is displayed.

2C. Conditions and Limitations. (1) Not more than one such advertisement is permitted in respect of each premises or, in the case of premises with entrances on different road frontages, one such advertisement at each of two such entrances.

(2) No such advertisement may exceed 1.2 square metres in area.

(3) No character or symbol on the advertisement may be more than 0.75 metre in height, or 0.3 metre in an area of special control.

(4) No part of the advertisement may be more than 4.6 metres above ground level, or 3.6 metres in an area of special control.

(5) Illumination is not permitted unless the advertisement states that medical or similar services or supplies are available at the premises and the illumination is in a manner reasonably required to fulfil the purpose of the advertisement.

Class 3—Miscellaneous temporary advertisements

3A. Description. An advertisement relating to the sale or letting, for residential, agricultural, industrial or commercial use or for development for such use, of the land or premises on which it is displayed.

3A. Conditions and Limitations. (1)

(*a*) Not more than one such advertisement, consisting of a single board or two joined boards, is permitted.

(*b*) Where more than one such advertisement is displayed, the first to be displayed shall be taken to be the one permitted.

(2) No advertisement may be displayed indicating that land or premises have been sold or let, other than by the addition to an existing advertisement of a statement that a sale or letting has been agreed, or that the land or premises have been sold or let, subject to contract.

(3) Any such advertisement shall be removed within 14 days after the sale is completed or a tenancy is granted.

(4) No such advertisement may exceed in area—

(*a*) where the advertisement relates to residential use or development, 0.5 square metre or, in the case of two joined boards together, 0.6 square metre in aggregate;

(*b*) where the advertisement relates to any other use or development, 2 square metres or, in the case of two joined boards together, 2.3 square metres in aggregate.

(5) Where the advertisement is displayed on a building, the maximum projection permitted from the face of the building is 1 metre.

(6) Illumination is not permitted.

(7) No character or symbol on the advertisement may be more than 0.75 metre in height, or 0.3 metre in an area of special control.

(8) No part of the advertisement may be higher above ground level than 4.6 metres, or 3.6 metres in an area of special control or, in the case of a sale or letting of part only of a building, the lowest level of that part of the building on which display is reasonably practicable.

3B. Description. An advertisement announcing the sale of goods or livestock, and displayed on the land where the goods or livestock are situated or where the sale is held, not being land which is normally used, whether at regular intervals or otherwise, for the purpose of holding such sales.

3B. Conditions and Limitations. (1)

(*a*) Not more than one such advertisement may be displayed at any one time on the land concerned.

(*b*) Where more than one such advertisement is displayed, the first to be displayed shall be taken to be the one permitted.

(2) No such advertisement may be displayed earlier than 28 days before the day (or first day) on which the sale is due to take place.

(3) Any such advertisement shall be removed within 14 days after the sale is completed.

(4) No such advertisement may exceed 1.2 square metres in area.

(5) Illumination is not permitted.

(6) No character or symbol on the advertisement may be more than 0.75 metre in height, or 0.3 metre in an area of special control.

(7) No part of the advertisement may be more than 4.6 metres above ground level, or 3.6 metres in an area of special control.

3C. Description. An advertisement relating to the carrying out of building or similar work on the land on which it is displayed, not being land which is normally used, whether at regular intervals or otherwise, for the purposes of carrying out such work.

3C. Conditions and Limitations. (1)

(*a*) Not more than one such advertisement shall be displayed at any one time, on each road frontage of the land, in respect of each separate development project, except in the case mentioned in paragraph (4) below.

(*b*) Where more than one such advertisement is displayed, the first to be displayed on any frontage shall be taken to be the one permitted.

(2) No such advertisement may be displayed except while the relevant works are being carried out.

(3) No such advertisement may exceed in aggregate—

(*a*) in the case of an advertisement referring to one person—

(i) if the display is more than 10 metres from a highway, 3 square metres in area; or

(ii) in any other case, 2 square metres;

(*b*) in the case of an advertisement referring to more than one person—

(i) if the display is more than 10 metres from a highway, 3 square metres plus 0.6 square metre for each additional person, or

(ii) in any other case, 2 square metres plus 0.4 square metre for each additional person,

together with 0.2 of the area permitted under sub-paragraph (a) or (b) above for the name, if any, of the development project.

(4) Where any such advertisement does not refer to any person carrying out such work, that person may display a separate advertisement with a maximum area of 0.5 square metre, which does so refer, on each frontage of the land for a maximum period of 3 months.

(5) Illumination is not permitted.

(6) No character or symbol on the advertisement may be more than 0.75 metre in height, or 0.3 metre in an area of special control.

(7) No part of the advertisement may be more than 4.6 metres above ground level, or 3.6 metres in an area of special control.

3D. Description. An advertisement—

(i) announcing any local event of a religious, educational, cultural, political, social or recreational character,

(ii) relating to any temporary matter in connection with an event or local activity of such a character,

not being an event or activity promoted or carried on for commercial purposes.

3D. Conditions and Limitations. (1) No such advertisement may exceed 0.6 square metre in area.

(2) No such advertisement may be displayed earlier than 28 days before the day (or first day) on which the event or activity is due to take place.

(3) Any such advertisement shall be removed within 14 days after the end of the event or activity.

(4) Illumination is not permitted.

(5) No character or symbol on the advertisement may be more than 0.75 metre in height, or 0.3 metre in an area of special control.

(6) No part of the advertisement may be more than 4.6 metres above ground level, or 3.6 metres in an area of special control.

3E. Description. An advertisement relating to any demonstration of agricultural methods or processes, on the land on which it is displayed.

3E. Conditions and Limitations. (1) Advertisements of this Class may not be displayed on any land for more than 6 months in any period of 12 months.

(2) The maximum area of display permitted in respect of each demonstration is 1.2 square metres.

(3) No single advertisement within such a display may exceed 0.4 square metre in area.

(4) No such advertisement may be displayed earlier than 28 days before the day (or first day) on which the demonstration is due to take place and shall be removed within 14 days after the end of the demonstration.

(5) Illumination is not permitted.

(6) No character or symbol on the advertisement may be more than 0.75 metre in height, or 0.3 metre in an area of special control.

(7) No part of the advertisement may be more than 4.6 metres above ground level, or 3.6 metres in an area of special control.

3F. Description. An advertisement relating to the visit of a travelling circus, fair or similar travelling entertainment to any specified place in the district.

3F. Conditions and Limitations. (1) No such advertisement may exceed 0.6 square metre in area.

(2) No such advertisement may be displayed earlier than 14 days before the first performance or opening of the entertainment at the place specified.

(3) Any such advertisement shall be removed within 7 days after the last performance or closing of the specified entertainment.

(4) At least 14 days before the advertisement is first displayed, the local planning authority are to be notified in writing of the first date on which, and of the site at which, it is to be displayed.

(5) Illumination is not permitted.

(6) No part of the advertisement may be more than 3.6 metres above ground level.

Class 4—Illuminated advertisements on business premises

4A. Description. An illuminated advertisement displayed on the frontage of premises within a retail park, which overlook or face on to a communal car park wholly bounded by the retail park, where the advertisement refers wholly to any or all of the following matters, namely the business carried on, the goods sold or services provided, or the name or qualifications of the person carrying on the business, or supplying the goods or services, on those premises.

4A. Conditions and Limitations. (1) Subject to paragraph (11) below, no such advertisement is permitted within a conservation area, an area of outstanding natural beauty, a National Park or the Broads.

(2) In the case of a shop, no such advertisement may be displayed except on a wall containing a shop window.

(3) Not more than one such advertisement parallel to a wall and one projecting at right angles from such a wall is permitted, and in the case of any projecting advertisement—

(*a*) no surface may be greater than 1 square metre in area;
(*b*) the advertisement may not project more than 1 metre from the wall; and
(*c*) it may not be more than 1.5 metres high.

(4) Illumination may be—

(*a*) by halo illumination, or
(*b*) so long as no part of the background of the advertisement is illuminated, by illumination of each character or symbol of the advertisement from within.

(5) No such advertisement may include any intermittent light source, moving feature, exposed cold cathode tubing, or animation.

(6) Where the method of illumination is that described in paragraph (4)(*b*), the luminance of any such advertisement may not exceed the limits specified in paragraph 2 of Part II of this Schedule.

(7) In the case of any advertisement consisting of a built-up box containing the light source, the distance between—

(*a*) the face of the advertisement and any wall parallel to which it is displayed, at the point where it is affixed, or
(*b*) the two faces of an advertisement projecting from a wall,

may not exceed 0.25 metre.

(8) The lowest part of any such advertisement must be at least 2.5 metres above ground level.

(9) No character or symbol on the advertisement may be more than 0.75 metre in height.

(10) No part of the advertisement may be higher above ground level than 4.6 metres or the bottom level of any first floor window in the wall on which the advertisement is displayed, whichever is the lower.

(11) Paragraph (1) above does not preclude the continued display of an advertisement being displayed at the date of designation of the relevant area until the expiry of 5 years from that date.

4B. Description. An illuminated advertisement, other than one falling within Class 4A, displayed on business premises wholly with reference to any or all of the following matters, namely the business carried on, the goods sold or services provided, or the name or qualifications of the person carrying on the business, or supplying the goods or services, on those premises.

4B. Conditions and Limitations. (1) Subject to paragraph (12) below, no such advertisement is permitted within a conservation area, an area of outstanding natural beauty, a National Park or the Broads.

(2) In the case of a shop, no such advertisement may be displayed except on a wall containing a shop window.

(3) Not more than one such advertisement parallel to a wall and one projecting at right angles from such a wall is permitted, and in the case of any projecting advertisement—

(*a*) no surface may be greater than 0.75 square metre in area;
(*b*) the advertisement may not project more than 1 metre from the wall or two-thirds of the width of any footway or pavement below, whichever is the less;
(*c*) it may not be more than 1 metre high; and
(*d*) it may not project over any carriageway.

(4) Illumination may be—

(*a*) by halo illumination, or
(*b*) so long as no part of the background of the advertisement is illuminated, by illumination of each character or symbol of the advertisement from within.

(5) No such advertisement may include any intermittent light source, moving feature, exposed cold cathode tubing, or animation.

(6) Where the method of illumination is that described in paragraph (4)(*b*), the luminance of any such advertisement may not exceed the limits specified in paragraph 2 of Part II of this Schedule.

(7) In the case of any such advertisement consisting of a built-up box containing the light source, the distance between—

(*a*) the face of the advertisement and any wall parallel to which it is displayed, at the point where it is affixed, or
(*b*) the 2 faces of an advertisement projecting from a wall,

may not exceed 0.25 metre.

(8) The lowest part of any such advertisement shall be at least 2.5 metres above ground level.

(9) No surface of any advertisement may exceed one-sixth of the frontage on which it is displayed, measured up to a height of 4.6 metres from ground level or 0.2 of the frontage measured to the top of the advertisement, whichever is the less.

(10) No character or symbol on the advertisement may be more than 0.75 metre in height.

(11) No part of the advertisement may be higher above ground level than 4.6 metres or the bottom level of any first floor window in the wall on which the advertisement is displayed, whichever is the lower.

(12) Paragraph (1) above does not preclude the continued display of an advertisement being displayed at the date of designation of the relevant area until the expiry of 5 years from that date.

Class 5—Advertisements on business premises

5. Description. Any advertisement which does not fall within Class 4A or 4B displayed on business premises wholly with reference to any or all of the following matters, namely the business carried on, the goods sold or services provided, or the name or qualifications of the person carrying on the business, or supplying the goods or services, on those premises.

5. Conditions and Limitations. (1) In the case of a shop, no such advertisement may be displayed, except on a wall containing a shop window.

(2) In an area of special control, the space occupied by any such advertisement may not exceed 0.1 of the overall area of the face of the building on which it is displayed, up to a height of 3.6 metres from ground level; and the area occupied by any such advertisement shall, notwithstanding that it is displayed in some other manner, be calculated as if the whole advertisement were displayed flat against the face of the building.

(3) Illumination is not permitted unless the advertisement states that medical or similar services or supplies are available at the premises on which the advertisement is displayed and the illumination is in a manner reasonably required to fulfil the purpose of the advertisement.

(4) No character or symbol on the advertisement may be more than 0.75 metre in height, or 0.3 metre in an area of special control.

(5) No part of the advertisement may be higher above ground level than whichever is the lower of—

(*a*) 4.6 metres, or 3.6 metres in an area of special control; or
(*b*) the bottom level of any first floor window in the wall on which the advertisement is displayed.

Class 6—An advertisement on a forecourt of business premises

6. Description. An advertisement displayed on any forecourt of business premises, wholly with reference to all or any of the matters specified in Class 5.

6. Conditions and Limitations. (1) Advertisements displayed on any such forecourt or, in the case of a building with a forecourt on two or more frontages on each of those frontages, shall not exceed in aggregate 4.5 square metres in area.

(2) Illumination is not permitted.

(3) No character or symbol on the advertisement may be more than 0.75 metre in height, or 0.3 metre in an area of special control.

(4) No part of the advertisement may be more than 4.6 metres above ground level, or 3.6 metres in an area of special control.

Class 7—Flag advertisements

7A. Description. An advertisement in the form of a flag attached to a single flagstaff projecting vertically from the roof of a building.

7A. Conditions and Limitations. (1) No such advertisement is permitted other than one—

(*a*) bearing the name or device of any person occupying the building; or
(*b*) referring to a specific event (other than the offering of named goods for sale) of limited duration, which is taking place in the building, for the duration of that event.

(2) No character or symbol on the flag may be more than 0.75 metre in height, or 0.3 metre in an area of special control.

7B. Description. An advertisement in the form of a flag attached to a single vertical flagstaff erected on a site which forms part of an area of land in respect of which planning permission has been granted for development of which the only or principal component is residential development and on which—

(*a*) operations for the construction of houses are in progress pursuant to that permission, or
(*b*) such operations having been completed, at least one of the houses remains unsold.

7B. Conditions and Limitations. (1) No such advertisement is permitted within a conservation area, an area of outstanding natural beauty, a National Park, the Broads or an area of special control.

(2) The number of such advertisements on the land concerned shall not exceed—

(*a*) where the aggregate number of houses on that land does not exceed 10, one;
(*b*) where the aggregate number of houses on that land exceeds 10 but does not exceed 100, two;
(*c*) where the aggregate number of houses on that land exceeds 100, three.

(3) No part of the flagstaff may be more than 4.6 metres above ground level.

(4) No flag shall exceed 2 square metres in area.

(5) No such advertisement shall be displayed after the expiration of the period of 1 year commencing on the day on which building operations on the land concerned have been substantially completed.

Class 8—Advertisements on hoardings

8. Description. An advertisement on a hoarding which encloses, either wholly or in part, land on which building operations are taking place or are about to take place, if those operations are in accordance with a grant of planning permission (other than outline permission) for development primarily for use for commercial, industrial or business purposes.

8. Conditions and Limitations. (1) Subject to paragraph (7) below, no such advertisement shall be displayed in a conservation area, a National Park, an area of outstanding natural beauty or the Broads.

(2) No such advertisement may be displayed earlier than [three months] before the commencement of the building operations.

(3) Any such advertisement shall be at least 1.5 metres high and 1 metre long and not more than 3.1 metres high and 12.1 metres long.

(4) At least 14 days before the advertisement is first displayed, the local planning authority shall be notified in writing by the person displaying it of the date on which it will first be displayed and shall be sent a copy of the relevant planning permission.

(5) No such advertisement shall be displayed for more than 3 years.

(6) Illumination is permitted in a manner and to the extent reasonably required to achieve the purpose of the advertisement.

(7) Paragraph (1) above does not preclude the continued display of an advertisement being displayed at the date of designation of the relevant area until the expiry of 1 year from that date or 2 years from the date of commencement of the display, whichever is the later.

Class 9—Advertisements on highway structures

9. Description. An advertisement displayed on a part of an object or structure designed to accommodate four-sheet panel displays, the use of which for the display of such advertisements is authorised under section 115E(1)(*a*) of the Highways Act 1980.

9. Conditions and Limitations. (1) No such advertisement may exceed 2.16 square metres in area.
(2) Illumination is not permitted.
(3) No character or symbol on the advertisement may be more than 0.75 metre in height, or 0.3 metre in an area of special control.
(4) No part of the advertisement may be more than 4.6 metres above ground level, or 3.6 metres in an area of special control.

Class 10—Advertisements for neighbourhood watch and similar schemes

10. Description. An advertisement displayed on or near highway land (but not in the window of a building), to give notice that a neighbourhood watch scheme or a similar scheme established jointly by the police authority and a local committee or other body of persons is in operation in the area.

10. Conditions and Limitations. (1) No such advertisement may exceed 0.2 square metre in area.
(2) No such advertisement may be displayed on highway land without the consent of the highway authority.
(3) The local planning authority shall, at least 14 days before the advertisement is first displayed, be given particulars in writing of the place at which it is to be displayed and a certificate—

(*a*) that the scheme has been properly established;
(*b*) that the police authority have agreed to the display of the advertisement; and
(*c*) where relevant, that the consent of the highway authority has been given.

(4) Any such advertisement shall be removed within 14 days after—

(*a*) the relevant scheme ceases to operate;
(*b*) the relevant scheme ceases to be approved by the police authority; or
(*c*) the highway authority withdraw their consent to its display.

(5) Illumination is not permitted.
(6) No character or symbol on the advertisement may be more than 0.75 metre in height, or 0.3 metre in an area of special control.
(7) No part of the advertisement may be more than 3.6 metres above ground level.

Class 11—Directional advertisements

11. Description. An advertisement on a single flat surface directing potential buyers and others to a site where residential development is taking place.

11. Conditions and Limitations. (1) No such advertisement may exceed 0.15 square metre in area.
(2) No part of the advertisement may be of a reflective material.
(3) The design of the advertisement may not be similar to that of a traffic sign.
(4) The advertisement is to be displayed on land adjacent to highway land, in a manner which makes it reasonably visible to an approaching driver, but not within 50 metres of a traffic sign intended to be observed by persons approaching from the same direction.
(5) No advertisement may be more than two miles from the main entrance of the site.
(6) The local planning authority shall, at least 14 days before the advertisement is first displayed, be notified in writing of the place at which, and the first date on which, it will be displayed.
(7) No such advertisement may be displayed after the development of the site is completed or, in any event, for more than 2 years.
(8) Illumination is not permitted.
(9) Any character or symbol on the advertisement shall be at least 0.04 metre high.
(10) No character or symbol on the advertisement may be more than 0.25 metre high.
(11) No part of the advertisement may be more than 4.6 metres above ground level, or 3.6 metres in an area of special control.

Class 12—Advertisements inside buildings

12. Description. An advertisement displayed inside a building which does not fall within Class J in Schedule 2.

Class 13—Sites used for the display of advertisements on 1st April 1974

13. Description. An advertisement displayed on a site which was used for the display of advertisements without express consent on 1st April 1974 and has been so used continually since that date.

13. Conditions and Limitations. (1) No substantial increase in the extent, or substantial alteration in the manner, of the use of the site for the display of advertisements on 1st April 1974 is permitted.
(2) If any building or structure on which such an advertisement is displayed is required by or under any enactment to be removed, no erection of any building or structure to continue the display is permitted.

Class 14—Advertisements displayed after expiry of express consent

14. Description. An advertisement displayed with express consent, after the expiry of that consent, unless—

(*a*) a condition to the contrary was imposed on the consent,

(*b*) a renewal of consent was applied for and refused.

14. Conditions and Limitations. (1) Any condition imposed on the relevant express consent is to continue to apply to any such advertisement.

(2) No advertisement may be displayed under this class except on a site which has been continually used for the purpose since the expiry of the express consent.

---

1. This means that deemed consent is limited to one board at any one time; the first advertisement attracts the deemed consent and this is not lost by the unlawful erection of subsequent sale boards: see *Porter v Honey* [1988] 3 All ER 1045, [1988] 1 WLR 1420, HL.

2. An advertisement displayed on business premises may advertise goods sold on the premises notwithstanding the fact that the goods are unrelated to the principal business carried on, goods sold or services provided on the premises (*Berridge v Vision Posters Ltd* (1994) 159 JP 218, *sub nom Waverley District Council v Vision Posters Ltd* [1994] Crim LR 940).

3. This means a window through which one can see a shop or see shopwares displayed therein. Accordingly an advertising hoarding on a flank wall which had five small windows in it each seven feet above the ground, two of which had extractor fans in them and the other three let light into a store room was erected in breach of the regulations (*Havering London Borough Council v Network Sites Ltd* (1998) Times, 2 January, DC.

4. An advertisment board which had been placed regularly but not continuously on the highway outside a public house since 1974 without objection had been displayed "continuously" for the purpose of clause 13 (*Westminster City Council v Moran* (1998) 77 P & CR 294.)

PART II

INTERPRETATION

8–31221 1. (1) In this Schedule—

"business premises" means any building or part of a building normally used for the purpose of any professional, commercial or industrial undertaking, or for providing services to members of the public or of any association, and includes a public restaurant, licensed premises and a place of public entertainment, but not—

(*a*) a building used as an institution of a religious, educational, cultural, recreational, or medical or similar character;

(*b*) a building designed for use as one or more separate dwellings, unless it was normally used, immediately before 1st September 1949, for any such purpose or has been adapted for use for any such purpose by the construction of a shop front or the making of a material alteration of a similar kind to its external appearance;

(*c*) any forecourt or other land forming part of the curtilage of a building;

(*d*) any fence, wall or similar screen or structure, unless it forms part of the fabric of a building;

"forecourt" includes any fence, wall or similar screen or structure enclosing a forecourt and not forming part of the fabric of a building constituting business premises:

"ground level", in relation to the display of advertisements on any building, means the ground-floor level of that building;

"highway land" means any land within the boundaries of a highway;

"joined boards" means boards joined at an angle, so that only one surface of each is usable for advertising;

"public transport undertaking" means an undertaking engaged in the carriage of passengers in a manner similar to that of a statutory undertaking;

"retail park" means a group of 3 or more retail stores, at least one of which has a minimum internal floor area of 1,000 square metres and which—

(*a*) are set apart from existing shopping centres but within an existing or proposed urban area;

(*b*) sell primarily goods other than food;

(*c*) share one or more communal car parks.

"traffic sign" means a sign falling within Class H of Schedule 2 to these Regulations.

(2) Where a maximum area is specified, in relation to any class in this Schedule, in the case of a double-sided board, the area of one side only shall be taken into account.

2. (1) Subject to sub-paragraph (2), the permitted limits of luminance for advertisements falling within Class 4A or 4B are, for an illuminated area measuring not more than—

(*a*) 0·5 square metres, 1,000 candela per square metre,

(*b*) 2 square metres, 800 candela per square metre,

(*c*) 10 square metres, 600 candela per square metre,

and for any greater area, 400 candela per square metre.

(2) For the purposes of calculating the relevant area for the permitted limits—

(*a*) each advertisement, or in the case of a double-sided projecting advertisement, each side of the advertisement is to be taken separately;

(*b*) no unilluminated part of the advertisement is to be taken into account.

3. In relation to advertisements within Class 4A or Class 4B "halo illumination" means illumination from within built-up boxes comprising characters or symbols where the only source of light is directed through the back of the box onto an otherwise unilluminated backing panel.

4. (1) For the purposes of Class 7B—

"aggregate number" means the aggregate of the number of houses constructed, in the course of construction or proposed to be constructed on the land concerned;

"flat" means a separate and self-contained set of premises constructed for the purpose of a dwelling and forming part of a building from some other part of which it is divided horizontally;

"house" includes a flat;

"planning permission" does not include any outline planning permission in relation to which some or all of the matters reserved for subsequent approval remain to be approved; and "the land concerned", in relation to any development, means—

(*a*) except in a case to which sub-paragraph (2) or (3) applies, the land to which the planning permission for the development relates;

(*b*) in a case to which sub-paragraph (2) applies, the land on which a particular phase of that development was or, as the case may be, is being or is about to be carried out;

(*c*) in a case to which sub-paragraph (3) applies, the part of the land to which the permission relates on which a person has carried out part of that development, or, as the case may be, is carrying it out or is about to carry it out.

(2) Subject to sub-paragraph (3), this sub-paragraph applies where the development is carried out in phases.

(3) This sub-paragraph applies where the development is carried out by two or more persons who each carry out part of it on a discrete part of the land to which the planning permission relates (whether the whole of the development or any part of it is carried out in phases or otherwise).

8–31222

Regulations 13 and 15

SCHEDULE 4

MODIFICATIONS OF THE ACT

PART I

MODIFICATIONS OF SECTION 70A OF THE ACT (POWER OF LOCAL PLANNING AUTHORITY TO DECLINE TO DETERMINE APPLICATIONS)

1. In section 70A of the Act—

(*a*) in subsection (1)—

(i) for "planning permission for the development of any land" substitute "express consent";

(ii) in paragraph (*a*), omit the words "has refused a similar application referred to him under section 77 or"; and

(iii) for paragraph (*b*) substitute—

"(*b*) in the opinion of the authority there has been no significant change since the dismissal mentioned in paragraph (*a*) in any material consideration.";

(*b*) in subsection (2)—

(i) for "planning permission for the development of any land" substitute "express consent";

(ii) for "development" substitute "subject matter of the applications"; and

(iii) for "the applications" substitute "they".

PART II

SECTION 70A OF THE ACT AS MODIFIED

8–31223 **70A.** (1) A local planning authority may decline to determine an application for express consent if—

(*a*) within the period of two years ending with the date on which the application is received, and

(*b*) in the opinion of the authority there has been no significant change since the dismissal mentioned in paragraph (*a*) in any material consideration.

(2) For the purposes of this section an application for express consent shall be taken to be similar to a later application if the subject matter of the applications and the land to which they relate are in the opinion of the local planning authority the same or substantially the same.

PART III

MODIFICATIONS OF SECTIONS 78 AND 79 OF THE ACT (APPLICATIONS FOR EXPRESS CONSENT)

8–31224 **1.** In section 78 of the Act—

(*a*) in subsection (1), for paragraphs (*a*), (*b*) and (*c*) substitute "refuse an application for express consent or grant it subject to conditions,";

(*b*) for subsection (2) substitute—

"(2) A person who has made an application for express consent may also appeal to the Secretary of State if within the period of 8 weeks from the date when the application was received by the local planning authority, that authority have neither given him notice of their decision on it nor given him notice that they have exercised their power under section 70A to decline to determine the application.";

(*c*) for subsection (3) substitute the following subsections—

"(3) Any appeal under subsection (1) or (2) shall be made by notice served within 8 weeks from the date of receipt of the local planning authority's decision, or, as the case may be, within 8 weeks from the expiry of the period mentioned in subsection (2), or within such longer period as the Secretary of State may in either case at any time allow.

(3A) The notice mentioned in subsection (3) shall be accompanied by a copy of each of the following documents—

(*a*) the application made to the local planning authority;

(*b*) all relevant plans and particulars submitted to them;

(*c*) any notice of decision; and

(*d*) any other relevant correspondence with the authority.";

(*d*) for subsection (4) substitute—

"(4) Where an appeal is made to the Secretary of State as mentioned in subsection (3), he may require the appellant or the local planning authority to submit to him, within such period as he may specify, a statement in writing in respect of such matters relating to the application as he may specify, and if, after considering the grounds of appeal and any such statement, the Secretary of State is satisfied that he has sufficient information to enable him to determine the appeal he may, with the agreement in writing of both the appellant and the local planning authority, determine the appeal without complying with section 79(2).";

(*e*) in subsection (5), omit references to sections 253(2)(*c*) and 266(1)(*b*).

2. In section 79 of the Act—

(*a*) after subsection (1) insert—

"(1A) The Secretary of State may, in granting an express consent, specify that the term thereof shall run for such longer or shorter period than 5 years as he considers expedient, having regard to regulation 4 of the Town and Country Planning (Control of Advertisements) Regulations 1992 and to any period specified in the application for consent.";

(*b*) omit subsection (4);
(*c*) in subsection (5), for "such an appeal shall be final", substitute "an appeal under section 78 shall be final, and shall otherwise have effect as if it were a decision of the local planning authority.";
(*d*) in subsection (6), for the words from "in respect of an application for planning permission" to "planning permission for that development", substitute "in respect of an application for express consent, the Secretary of State forms the opinion that, having regard to the Regulations mentioned in subsection (1A) and to any direction given under them, consent";
(*e*) in subsection (6A), after the word "appeal" the first time it appears, insert "as is mentioned in subsection (6)".

PART IV
SECTIONS 78 AND 79 OF THE ACT AS MODIFIED (APPLICATIONS FOR EXPRESS CONSENT)

8–31225 **78.** (1) Where a local planning authority refuse an application for express consent or grant it subject to conditions, the application may by notice appeal to the Secretary of State.

(2) A person who has made an application for express consent may also appeal to the Secretary of State if within the period of 8 weeks from the date when the application was received by the local planning authority, that authority have neither given him notice of their decision on it nor given him notice that they have exercised their power under section 70A to decline to determine the application.

(3) Any appeal under subsection (1) or (2) shall be made by notice served within 8 weeks from the date of receipt of the local planning authority's decision, or, as the case may be, within 8 weeks from the expiry of the period mentioned in subsection (2), or within such longer period as the Secretary of State may in either case at any time allow.

(3A) The notice mentioned in subsection (3) shall be accompanied by a copy of each of the following documents—

(*a*) the application made to the local planning authority;
(*b*) all relevant plans and particulars submitted to them;
(*c*) any notice of decision; and
(*d*) any other relevant correspondence with the authority.

(4) Where an appeal is made to the Secretary of State as mentioned in subsection (3), he may require the appellant or the local planning authority to submit to him, within such period as he may specify, a statement in writing in respect of such matters relating to the application as he may specify, and if, after considering the grounds of appeal and any such statement, the Secretary of State is satisfied that he has sufficient information to enable him to determine the appeal he may, with the agreement in writing of both the appellant and the local planning authority, determine the appeal without complying with section 79(2).

(5) For the purposes of the application of sections 79(1) and 288(10)(*b*) in relation to an appeal under subsection (2), it shall be assumed that the authority decided to refuse the application in question.

79. (1) On an appeal under section 78 the Secretary of State may—

(*a*) allow or dismiss the appeal, or
(*b*) reverse or vary any part of the decision of the local planning authority (whether the appeal relates to that part of it or not),

and may deal with the application as if it had been made to him in the first instance.

(1A) The Secretary of State may, in granting an express consent, specify that the term thereof shall run for such longer or shorter period than 5 years as he considers expedient, having regard to regulation 4 of the Town and Country Planning (Control of Advertisements) Regulations 1992 and to any period specified in the application for consent.

(2) Before determining an appeal under section 78 the Secretary of State shall, if either the appellant or the local planning authority so wish, give each of them an opportunity of appearing before and being heard by a person appointed by the Secretary of State for the purpose.

(3) Subsection (2) does not apply to an appeal referred to a Planning Inquiry Commission under section 101.

(5) The decision of the Secretary of State on an appeal under section 78 shall be final, and shall otherwise have effect as if it were a decision of the local planning authority.

(6) If, before or during the determination of such an appeal in respect of an application for express consent, the Secretary of State forms the opinion that, having regard to the Regulations mentioned in subsection (1A) and to any direction given under them, consent—

(*a*) could not have been granted by the local planning authority, or
(*b*) could not have been granted otherwise than subject to the conditions imposed,

he may decline to determine the appeal or to proceed with the determination.

(6A) If at any time before or during the determination of such an appeal as in mentioned in subsection (6) it appears to the Secretary of State that the appellant is responsible for undue delay in the progress of the appeal, he may—

(*a*) give the appellant notice that the appeal will be dismissed unless the appellant takes, within the period specified in the notice, such steps as are specified in the notice for the expedition of the appeal; and
(*b*) if the appellant fails to take those steps within that period, dismiss the appeal accordingly.

(7) Schedule 6 applies to appeals under section 78, including appeals under that section as applied by or under any other provision of this Act.

PART V
MODIFICATIONS OF THE ACT (DISCONTINUANCE NOTICES)

8–31226 **1.** In section 78 for subsections (1) to (5) substitute—

"(1) Where a discontinuance notice has been served on any person by a local planning authority under regulation 8 of the Town and Country Planning (Control of Advertisements) Regulations 1992 that person may, if he is aggrieved by the notice, appeal by notice under this section to the Secretary of State.

(2) Notice of appeal shall be given in writing to the Secretary of State at any time before the date on which the discontinuance notice is due to take effect under regulation 8(3), taking account where appropriate of any extension of time under regulation 8(5), of those Regulations, or such longer period as the Secretary of State may allow, and the notice shall be accompanied by a copy of each of the following documents—

(*a*) the discontinuance notice;
(*b*) any notice of variation thereof; and
(*c*) any relevant correspondence with the authority.

(3) Where an appeal is brought under this section, the Secretary of State may require the appellant or the local planning authority to submit to him, within such period as he may specify, a statement in writing in respect of such matters relating to the discontinuance notice as he may specify and if, after considering the grounds of appeal and any such statement, the Secretary of State is satisfied that he has sufficient information to enable him to determine the appeal, he may, with the agreement in writing of both the appellant and the local planning authority, determine the appeal without complying with section 79(2).".

2. In section 79—

(*a*) for subsection (1) substitute—

"(1) Where an appeal is brought in respect of a discontinuance notice the Secretary of State may—

(*a*) allow or dismiss the appeal, or
(*b*) reverse or vary any part of the discontinuance notice (whether the appeal relates to that part of it or not),

and may deal with the matter as if an application for express consent had been made and refused for the reasons stated for the taking of discontinuance action.";

(*b*) for subsection (4) substitute—

"(4) On the determination of an appeal under section 78 the Secretary of State shall give such directions as may be necessary for giving effect to his determination, including, where appropriate, directions for quashing the discontinuance notice or for varying its terms in favour of the appellant.";

(*c*) omit subsection (6);
(*d*) in subsection (6A), after the word "appeal" the first time it appears, insert "in respect of a discontinuance notice".

Regulation 18

SCHEDULE 5
AREA OF SPECIAL CONTROL ORDERS

PART I
PROCEDURE FOR AREA OF SPECIAL CONTROL ORDERS

8–31227 **1.** A local planning authority who propose—

(*a*) to designate an area of special control; or
(*b*) to modify an area of special control order,

shall make an area of special control order designating the area or indicating the modifications by reference to an annexed map.

2. If an area of special control order contains any descriptive matter relating to the area or the modifications in question, that descriptive matter shall prevail, in the case of any discrepancy with the map, unless the order provides to the contrary.

3. As soon as may be after the making of an area of special control order, the authority shall submit it to the Secretary of State for approval, together with—

(*a*) two certified copies of the order;
(*b*) a full statement of their reasons for making it;
(*c*) in the case of an order modifying an existing order, unless the boundaries of the existing area of special control are indicated on the map annexed to the order, a plan showing both these boundaries and the proposed modifications; and
(*d*) any additional certified copy of any of the material in subparagraphs (*a*) to (*c*) above, which the Secretary of State requires.

4. The authority shall forthwith publish in the London Gazette, and in two successive weeks in at least one newspaper circulating in the locality, a notice in prescribed Form 1.

5. If any objection is made to an order, in the manner and within the time provided for in the prescribed form, the Secretary of State—

(*a*) may offer all interested parties an opportunity to make representations to him in writing about any such objection before such date as he may specify;
(*b*) may, and at the request of any interested party shall, either provide for a local inquiry to be held or afford to the parties an opportunity of a hearing before a person appointed by him.

6. After considering any representations or objections duly made and not withdrawn and, where applicable, the report of any person holding an inquiry or hearing, the Secretary of State may, subject to paragraph 7 below, approve the order with or without modifications.

7. If the Secretary of State proposes to make a modification for the inclusion of additional land in an order, he shall—

(*a*) publish notice of his intention to do so;

(*b*) afford an opportunity for the making of objections to, or representations about, the proposed modification; and

(*c*) if he considers it expedient, provide for a further inquiry or hearing to be held.

8. As soon as may be after the order has been approved, the local planning authority shall publish in the London Gazette, and in two successive weeks in at least one newspaper circulating in the locality, a notice of its approval in prescribed Form 2.

9. An area of special control order shall come into force on the date on which the notice of its approval is published in the London Gazette.

10. Where a local planning authority propose to make an order revoking an area of special control order, a map showing the existing area shall be annexed to the order, and the procedure prescribed in paragraphs 2 to 9 of this Schedule in relation to an order modifying an existing order shall be followed, subject to the modification that the prescribed forms of notice under paragraphs 4 and 8 respectively are prescribed Forms 3 and 4.

11. Any reference in this Part of this Schedule to a prescribed form is to the form bearing that number in Part II of this Schedule or a form substantially to the like effect.

PART II
FORMS OF NOTICE

FORM 1
NOTICE OF AN AREA OF SPECIAL CONTROL ORDER
Town and Country Planning Act 1990

8–31228 Town and Country Planning (Control of Advertisements) Regulations 1992

FORM 1
NOTICE OF AN AREA OF SPECIAL CONTROL ORDER
Town and Country Planning Act 1990

Town and Country Planning (Control of Advertisements) Regulations 1992

1. We, the (insert name of Council) give notice that we have submitted an area of special control order, made under regulation 18 of the Town and Country Planning (Control of Advertisements) Regulations 1992, to the Secretary of State for the [Environment, Transport and the Regions]/for Wales (delete whichever is inappropriate) for approval under Schedule 5 to the Regulations.

2. The order designates the area of land described in the Schedule hereto and shown on the map accompanying the order.

OR

The order modifies the (insert name of relevant order) by adding/removing (delete whichever is inappropriate) the area of land described in the Schedule hereto and shown on the map accompanying the order.

(delete whichever is inappropriate)

3. A copy of the order and of the statement of the reasons for making it have been deposited at and will be available for inspection free of charge between the hours of .

4. The order is about to be considered by the Secretary of State. Any objection to it must be made in writing, stating the grounds of objection, and sent to the Department of the [Environment, Transport and the Regions]/ Welsh Office (delete whichever is inappropriate) at before (insert a date at least 28 days from the date of first publication of the local advertisement).

Signed ....

On behalf of ....

Date ....

SCHEDULE

(insert description of land)

FORM 2
NOTICE OF APPROVAL OF AN AREA OF SPECIAL CONTROL ORDER
Town and Country Planning Act 1990

Town and Country Planning (Control of Advertisements) Regulations 1992

1. We, the (insert name of Council) give notice that the Secretary of State for the [Environment, Transport and the Regions]/for Wales (delete inappropriate words) has approved with modifications (delete inappropriate words) the (insert name of order) for the purposes of Schedule 5 to the Town and Country Planning (Control of Advertisements) Regulations 1992.

2. The order designates as an area of special control the land described in the Schedule hereto/modifies the (insert name of relevant order) by adding/removing the land described in the Schedule hereto (delete inappropriate words).

3. The order comes into force on (insert date of publication in London Gazette).

4. A copy of the order as approved has been deposited at................. and will be available for inspection free of charge between the hours of ....

IMPORTANT. Regulation 19 of the 1992 Regulations contains important provisions about—

The advertisements permitted in an area of special control.

The circumstances in which existing advertisements must be removed after this order comes into force.

Signed ....

On behalf of ....

Date ....

(Delete inappropriate words)

SCHEDULE

(insert description of land)

FORM 3

NOTICE OF REVOCATION OF AN AREA OF SPECIAL CONTROL ORDER

Town and Country Planning Act 1990

Town and Country Planning (Control of Advertisements) Regulations 1992

1. We, the (insert name of Council) give notice that we have submitted an order revoking the (insert name of relevant order) made under regulation 18 of the Town and Country Planning (Control of Advertisements) Regulations 1992 to the Secretary of State for the [Environment, Transport and the Regions]/for Wales (delete whichever is inappropriate) for approval under Schedule 5 to the Regulations.

2. A copy of the revocation order and of the statement of the reasons for making it have been deposited at.......................and will be available for inspection free of charge between the hours of ....

3. The revocation order is about to be considered by the Secretary of State. Any objection to it must be made in writing, stating the grounds of objection, and sent to the Department of the [Environment, Transport and the Regions]/Welsh Office (delete whichever is inappropriate) at .... before (insert a date at least 28 days after the first publication of the local advertisement).

Signed ....
On behalf of ....
Date ....

FORM 4

NOTICE OF APPROVAL OF AN ORDER REVOKING AN AREA OF SPECIAL CONTROL ORDER

Town and Country Planning Act 1990

Town and Country Planning (Control of Advertisements) Regulations 1992

1. We, the (insert name of Council) give notice that the Secretary of State for the [Environment, Transport and the Regions]/for Wales (delete whichever is inappropriate) has approved an order revoking the (insert name of order revoked) for the purposes of Schedule 5 to the Town and Country Planning (Control of Advertisements) Regulations 1992.

2. The revocation order comes into force on (insert date of publication in London Gazette).

3. A copy of the revocation order as approved has been deposited at......................and will be available for inspection free of charge between the hours of..................

Signed ....
On behalf of ....
Date ....

TOWNS IMPROVEMENT; TOWN POLICE

8–31319 This title contains the following statutes—

Towns Improvement Clauses Act 1847[1]

(10 & 11 Vict c 34)

OFFENCES

8–31320 64. Defacing numbers etc. Every person who destroys, pulls down, or defaces any number of a house, or name of a street[2] put up by the local authority or puts up any number or name different from the number or name put up by the authority—*Penalty*, not exceeding **level 1** on the standard scale.

[Towns Improvement Clauses Act 1847, s 64, as amended by the Criminal Law Act 1977, s 31 as amended by the Criminal Justice Act 1982, s 46—summarised.]

1. This Act was originally intended for incorporation in local Acts. The sections here contained were incorporated by the Public Health Act 1875, s 160, and are of general application except for Greater London. By virtue of the Highways Act 1959, Sch 25, s 160 of the Public Health Act 1875 now incorporates only the provisions of this Act relating to naming streets and numbering houses. Section 251 of the 1875 Act provides for summary procedure and remains in force for incorporated provisions although otherwise repealed by the Public Health Act 1936. S 253 of the 1875 Act, which required written consent of the Attorney General for proceedings to be taken by a person other than the party aggrieved or the local authority, was repealed by the Local Government (Miscellaneous Provisions) Act 1976, s 27. Where the Public Health Act 1875 is incorporated in a local Act, publication of bye-laws in conformity with that Act is sufficient (*Fielding v Rhyl Improvement Comrs* (1878) 3 CPD 272, 42 JP 311).

2. Where Pt II of the Public Health Act 1925 is in force, see ss 17–19, thereof, ante. The local authority has a right to name a street, and if an owner or other person obliterates or removes the name affixed by the authority, he is liable to be convicted under this section. But the section does not give the local authority a right to alter the well-known name of an old street (*Collins v Hornsey UDC* [1901] 2 KB 180, 65 JP 600). For power to alter street name, and penalties for obliterating same, etc, see the Public Health Acts Amendment Act 1907, s 21 in this PART: title PUBLIC HEALTH, ante.

8–31330 **65. Renewing numbers.** Every occupier who fails within one week after notice from the local authority to mark his house with a number approved by the authority, or to renew such number when obliterated—*Penalty*, not exceeding **level 1** on the standard scale, with power for the authority to do the work at the expense of the occupier.

[Towns Improvement Clauses Act 1847, s 65, as amended by the Criminal Justice Act 1967, Sch 3 as amended by the Criminal Justice Act 1982, ss 38 and 46—summarised.]

Town Police Clauses Act 1847[1]

(10 & 11 Vict c 89)

8–31341 **1. Incorporation with special Act.** This Act shall extend only to such towns or districts in England or Ireland as shall be comprised in any Act of Parliament hereafter to be passed which shall declare that this Act shall be incorporated therewith; and all the clauses of this Act, save so far as they shall be expressly varied or excepted by any such Act, shall apply to the town or district which shall be comprised in such Act, and to the commissioners appointed for improving and regulating the same, so far as such clauses shall be applicable thereto respectively, and shall, with the clauses of every other Act which shall be incorporated therewith, form part of such Act, and be construed therewith as forming one Act.

[Town Police Clauses Act 1847, s 1.]

1. Although originally adoptive, this Act has had ss 21–36 applied throughout England and Wales by virtue of s 171 of the Public Health Act 1875, as amended by the Local Government Act 1972, s 179 and Sch 14, and by virtue of para 23 of the said Sch 14. Paragraph 24 of Sch 14 does, however, exclude s 171(4) of the 1875 Act (Hackney carriages) with the saving that those provisions will apply to those areas to which they applied immediately before 1 April 1974. Paragraph 25 takes this a stage further by enabling local authorities to apply or disapply provisions in para 24 to their area. Proceedings are those appropriate to summary jurisdiction; prosecutions must be taken before two or more justices (Public Health Act 1875, s 251). Since the nullifying of s 253 of the Public Health Act 1875 by s 27 of the Local Government (Miscellaneous Provisions) Act 1976, the power to prosecute is not limited to the local authority.

Interpretation

8–31341A **2. "The special Act"—"Prescribed"—"The commissioners".** And with respect to the construction of this Act, whether incorporated in whole or in part with any other Act, and of any Act incorporated therewith, be it enacted as follows:

The expression "the special Act" used in this Act shall be construed to mean any Act which shall be hereafter passed for the improvement or regulation of any town or district defined or comprised therein, and with which this Act shall be incorporated; and the word "prescribed" used in this Act in reference to any matter herein stated shall be construed to refer to such matter as the same shall be prescribed or provided for in the special Act, and the sentence in which such word shall occur shall be construed as if instead of the word "prescribed" the expression "prescribed for that purpose in the special Act" had been used; and the expression "the commissioners" shall mean the commissioners, trustees, or other persons or body corporate instrusted by the special Act with powers for executing the purposes thereof.

[Town Police Clauses Act 1847, s 2.]

8–31341B **3. Interpretations in this and the special Act.** The following words and expressions in both this and the special Act, and any Act incorporated therewith, shall have the meanings hereby assigned to them, unless there be something in the subject or context repugnant to such construction; (that is to say,)

NUMBER: Words importing the singular number shall include the plural number, and words importing the plural number shall include the singular number:

GENDER: Words importing the masculine gender shall include females;

"PERSON": The word "person" shall include a corporation, whether aggregate or sole:

"LANDS": The words "lands" shall include messuages, lands, tenements, and hereditaments, of any tenure:

"STREET": The word "street" shall extend to and include any road, square, court, alley, and thoroughfare, or public passage, within the limits of the special Act:

"MONTH": The word "month" shall mean a calendar month:

"JUSTICE": The word "justice" shall mean justice of the peace acting for the . . . place where the matter requiring the cognizance of any such justice arises; and where any matter shall be authorized or required to be done by two justices, the expression "two justices" shall be understood to mean two or more justices met and acting together:

"CATTLE": The word "cattle" shall include horses, asses, mules, sheep, goats, and swine.

[Town Police Clauses Act 1847, s 3.]

Citing the Act

8–31341C **4.** *Short title of this Act*

8–31341D 5–20. *Repealed.*

Obstructions and Nuisances in Streets

8–31341E 21. Power to make orders for preventing obstructions in the streets during public processions, etc. The local authority may from time to time make orders[1] for the route to be observed by all carts, carriages, horses and persons, and for preventing obstruction of the streets in all times of public processions, rejoicings, or illuminations, and in any case when the streets are thronged or liable to be obstructed[2], and may also give directions to the constables for keeping order and preventing any obstruction of the streets in the neighbourhood of theatres and other places of public resort; and every wilful breach of any such order shall be deemed a separate offence against this Act, and every person committing any such offence shall be liable to a penalty not exceeding **level 3** on the standard scale.

[Town Police Clauses Act 1847, s 21, as amended by the Criminal Justice Act 1967, Sch 3 and the Criminal Justice Act 1982, ss 39 and 46 and Sch 3.]

1. Where an order was made that constables stationed at certain crossings should give directions to drivers of vehicles, it was held that there was an implied obligation on the part of the drivers to obey such directions (*Dudderidge v Rawlings* (1912) 77 JP 167). For power to erect appropriate traffic signs, see the Road Traffic Regulation Act 1984, s 66, ante. See also the Road Traffic Regulation Act 1984, ss 1, 14 (orders restricting use of roads and for one way traffic), the Road Traffic Act 1988, ss 35, 36 (neglect of traffic directions by a police constable or traffic sign), ante, and the "Highway Code". Nothing contained in the Roman Catholic Relief Act 1926 shall affect any power conferred by any Act or byelaw upon any local authority to make byelaws or regulations relating to, or otherwise to control, any meeting or procession in streets or public places, or adjoining or abutting unfenced grounds (Roman Catholic Relief Act 1926, s 2). No local authority shall exercise these powers in relation to the Greater London area; see the Public Health Act 1875, s 171 and the Local Government Act 1972, Sch 14, para 26.

2. This expression is limited to cases of the same class or *genus* as the three preceding instances; a more general order is invalid (*Brownsea Haven Properties Ltd v Poole Corpn* (supra), overruling *Teale v Williams* [1914] 3 KB 395, 78 JP 383; *Edwards v Wanstall* (1929) 94 JP 51; *Etherington v Carter* [1937] 2 All ER 528). A breach of an order must be alleged and proved to have been "wilful" (*Waring v Wheatley* (1951) 115 JP 630).

8–31341F 22. *Repealed.*

8–31341G 23. *Power to stage carriages to deviate from route under order of commissioners*

8–31342 24. Power to impound stray cattle[1]. If any cattle be at any time found at large in any street without any person having the charge thereof any constable or any person residing within the [jurisdiction] may seize and impound such cattle in any common pound within the said limits, or in such other place as the commissioners appoint for that purpose and may detain the same therein until the owner thereof pay to the [authority] a penalty not exceeding **level 1** on the standard scale, besides the reasonable expenses of impounding and keeping such cattle.

[Town Police Clauses Act 1847, s 24, as amended by the Criminal Law Act 1977, s 31 and the Criminal Justice Act 1982, s 46.]

1. See Protection of Animals Act 1911, s 7(1), title ANIMALS—*Protection*, ante (feeding impounded cattle); also this PART: title POUND BREACH, ante.

8–31343 25. Power to sell cattle impounded for payment of penalty and expenses, after notice and advertisement. If the said penalty and expenses be not paid within three days after such impounding[1], the pound-keeper or other person appointed by the commissioners for that purpose may proceed to sell or cause to be sold any such cattle; but previous to such sale seven days notice thereof shall be given to or left at the dwelling house or place of abode of the owner of such cattle, if he be known, or if not, then notice of such intended sale shall be given by advertisement, to be inserted seven days before such sale in some newspaper published or circulated within the limits of the special Act; and the money arising from such sale, after deducting the said sums, and the expenses aforesaid, and all other expenses attending the impounding, advertising, keeping, and sale of any such cattle so impounded, shall be paid to the commissioners, and shall be by them paid, on demand, to the owner of the cattle so sold.

[Town Police Clauses Act 1847, s 25.]

1. This time limit will not nowadays always fit the time-scale of the summary proceedings required by s 251 of the Public Health Act 1875.

8–31344 26. Persons guilty of pound-breach to be committed for three months[1]. Every person who releases or attempts to release any cattle from any pound or place where the same are impounded under the authority of this or the special Act, or who pulls down, damages, or destroys the same pound or place, or any part thereof, with intent to procure the unlawful release of such cattle, shall, upon conviction of such offence before any two justices, be committed by them to some common gaol or house of correction for any time not exceeding three months.

[Town Police Clauses Act 1847, s 26.]

1. By the provisions of the Magistrates' Courts Act 1980, s 34(3), may in the alternative impose a fine not exceeding **level 3** on the standard scale.

8–31345 **27.** *Power to provide a pound.*

8–31345A **28. Penalty on persons committing any of the offences herein named.** Every person[1] who in any[2] street to the obstruction, annoyance[3] or danger[4], of the residents or[5] passengers[6], commits any of the following offences[7], shall be liable to a penalty not exceeding **level 3** on the standard scale for each offence, or, in the discretion of the justice[8] before whom he is convicted, may be committed to prison for a period not exceeding **fourteen days**; (that is to say,)

Every person who exposes for show, hire, or sale (except in a market or market-place or fair lawfully appointed for that purpose) any horse or other animal, or exhibits in a caravan or otherwise any show or public entertainment, or shoes, bleeds, or farries any horse or animal (except in cases of accident), or cleans, dresses, exercises, trains, or breaks, or turns loose any horse or animal, or makes or repairs any part of any cart or carriage (except in cases of accident where repair on the spot is necessary);

Every person who suffers to be at large any unmuzzled ferocious[9] dog, or sets on or urges any dog or other animal to attack, worry, or put in fear any person or animal[10];

Every person who slaughters[11] or dresses any cattle[12], or any part thereof, except in the case of any cattle overdriven which may have met with any accident, and which for the public safety or other reasonable cause ought to be killed on the spot;

Every person having the care of any waggon, cart, or carriage, who rides on the shafts thereof, or without having reins and holding the same rides upon such waggon, cart, or carriage, or on any animal drawing the same, or is at such a distance from such waggon, cart, or carriage, as not to have due control over every animal drawing the same, or who does not in meeting any other carriage, keep his waggon, cart, or carriage[13] to the left or near side, or who in passing any other carriage does not keep his waggon, cart, or carriage, on the right or off side (except in cases of[14] actual necessity, or some sufficient reason for deviation), or who, by obstructing the street, wilfully prevents any person or carriage from passing him, or any waggon, cart, or carriage under his care;

Every person who rides or drives furiously[10] any horse or carriage[13] or drives furiously any cattle[12];

Every person who causes any public carriage, sledge, truck, or barrow, with or without horses, or any beast of burden, to stand longer[17] than is necessary for loading or unloading goods, or for taking up or setting down passengers (except hackney carriages and horses and other beasts of draught or burthen standing for hire in any place appointed for that purpose by lawful authority), and every person who by means of any cart, carriage, sledge, truck, or barrow, or any animal, or other means[18], wilfully interrupts any public crossing, or wilfully causes any obstruction[19] in any public footpath, or other public thoroughfare;

Every person who causes any tree, or timber, or iron beam, to be drawn in or upon any carriage without having sufficient means of safely guiding the same;

Every person who leads or rides any horse or other animal, or draws or drives any cart or carriage[20], sledge, truck, or barrow, upon any footway of any street, or fastens any horse or other animal, so that it stands across or upon any footway;

Every person who places or leaves any furniture, goods, wares, or merchandise, or any cask, tub, basket, pail, or bucket, or places or uses any standing place, stool, bench, stall, or show-board on any footway, or places any blind, shade, covering, awning, or other projection, over or along any such footway unless such blind, shade, covering, awning or other projection is eight feet in height at least in every part thereof from the ground;

Every person who places, hangs up, or otherwise exposes to sale any goods, wares, merchandise[21], matter, or thing whatsoever, so that the same project[22] into or over any footway, or beyond the line of any house, shop, or building at which the same are so exposed, so as to obstruct or incommode[23] the passage of any person over or along such footway;

Every person who rolls or carries any cask, tub, hoop, or wheel, or any ladder, plank, pole, timber, or log of wood upon any footway, except for the purpose of loading or unloading any cart or carriage, or for crossing the footway;

Every person who places any line, cord, or pole across any street, or hangs or places any clothes thereon;

Every person who wilfully and indecently exposes his person;

Every person who publicly offers for sale or distribution or exhibits to public view any profane book, paper, print, drawing, painting, or representation, or sings any profane or obscene song or ballad, or uses any profane or obscene language;

Every person who wantonly discharges any firearm, or throws or discharges any stone, or other missile, or makes any bonfire, or throws or sets fire to any firework[24];

Every person who wilfully and wantonly disturbs any inhabitant by pulling or ringing any door-bell[27], or knocking at any door, or wilfully and unlawfully extinguishes the light of any lamp;

Every person who flies any kite, or makes or uses any slide upon ice or snow;

Every person who cleanses, hoops, fires, washes, or scalds any cask or tub, or hews, saws, bores, or cuts any timber or stone, or slacks, sifts, or screens any lime;

Every person who throws or lays down any[26] stones, coal, slate, shells, lime, bricks, timber, iron, or other materials (except building material so enclosed as to prevent mischief to passengers);

Every person who beats or shakes any carpet, rug, or mat (except door-mats before 8 am);

Every person who fixes or places any flower-pot or box or other heavy article in any upper window without sufficiently guarding the same from being blown down;

Every person who throws from the roof or any part of any house or other building any slate, brick, wood, rubbish, or other thing (except snow thrown so as not to fall on any passenger);

Every occupier of any house or other building or other person[27] who orders or permits any person in his service to stand on the sill of any window in order to clean, paint, or perform any other operation upon the outside of such window, or upon any house or other building, unless such window be in the sunk or basement storey;

Every person who leaves open any vault or cellar, or the entrance from any street to any cellar or room underground, without a sufficient fence or handrail, or leaves defective the door, window or other covering of any vault or cellar, or does not sufficiently fence any area, pit, or sewer left open, or who leaves such open area, pit or sewer without a sufficient light after sunset to warn and prevent persons from falling thereinto;

Every person who throws or lays any dirt, litter, or ashes, or nightsoil, or any carrion, fish, offal, or rubbish on any street[28], or causes any offensive matter to run from any manufactory, brewery, slaughterhouse, butcher's shop, or dung-hill into any street:

Provided always that it shall not be an offence to lay sand or other materials in any street in time of frost to prevent accidents, or litter or other suitable materials to prevent the freezing of water in pipes, or in case of sickness to prevent noise, if the party laying any such things causes them to be removed as soon as the occasion for them ceases;

Every person who keeps any pigstye to the front of any street not being shut out from such street by a sufficient wall or fence, or who keeps any[29] swine in or near any street so as to be a common nuisance.

[Town Police Clauses Act 1847, s 28, as amended by the Street Offences Act 1959, Sch, the Police Act 1964, Sch 9, the Criminal Justice Act 1967, Sch 3, the Rabies Act 1974, s 9, the Statute Law (Repeals) Act 1975, Sch, Part X, the Indecent Displays (Control) Act 1981, Sch, the Criminal Justice Act 1982, ss 39 and 46 and Sch 3 and the Police and Criminal Evidence Act 1984, Sch 7.]

---

1. "Person" includes a corporation, whether aggregate or sole (s 3).

2. The word "street" includes any road, square, court, alley and thoroughfare, or public passage (s 3). The street includes the carriageway and the footways at the sides. The offence must be committed in the street, but the annoyance may be to "residents", meaning, it seems, the occupiers of houses in the street although they may not be in the street at the time. See *Mantle v Jordan* [1897] 1 QB 248, 61 JP 119. As to the definition of "street" for the purpose of certain offences within this section where the Public Health Acts Amendment Act 1907 is in force, see s 81 of that Act, ante.

3. There is no offence merely for shouting in connection with selling newspapers without evidence that any person was annoyed (*Stanley v Farndale* (1892) 56 JP Jo 709). But see *Innes v Newman* [1894] 2 QB 292, 58 JP 543, where it was held that, as the act complained of was calculated to annoy the inhabitants generally, annoyance of one inhabitant by a similar outcry was sufficient to justify a conviction under a byelaw. See also *Brabham v Wookey* (1901) 18 TLR 99, where under a local Act the appellant was convicted for using indecent language "to the annoyance of the inhabitants or passengers", he at the time being inside his house, the door of which was open, and there being no evidence of annoyance save that of two constables.

4. These words govern the whole of the section, and restrict the offences to cases where obstruction, annoyance, or danger can be proved (see *Stinson v Browning* (1866) LR 1 CP 321, 30 JP 312). But it will not be necessary to call any person who has been annoyed, etc, as a witness (*Woolley v Corbishley* (1860) 24 JP 773; *Read v Perrett* (1876) 1 Ex D 349, 41 JP 135) or to prove that any particular passenger was endangered (*West Riding Cleaning Co Ltd v Jowett* [1938] 4 All ER 21). Several of the offences mentioned in this section are punishable under the Highways, Vagrancy and other Acts.

5. The conviction must specify against which class the offence has been committed (*Cotterill v Lampriere* (1890) 24 QBD 684, 54 JP 588).

6. For the purposes of an information alleging that the defendant wilfully and indecently exposed his person, it was held that police officers who witnessed the defendant masturbating in a public lavatory were not "passengers" when they had been stationed in the lavatory following complaints (*Cheeseman v DPP* [1992] QB 83, 93 Cr App Rep 145, [1991] Crim LR 296).

7. A failure on the part of any person to observe any provision of the "Highway Code", may in any proceedings be relied upon by any party to the proceedings as tending to establish or to negative any liability which is in question in those proceedings (Road Traffic Act 1988, s 38, ante).

8. Where the provisions of this section are in force under the Public Health Act, the conviction must be by two justices (Public Health Act 1875, s 251). If the case is heard before one justice the sum adjudged to be paid must not exceed **£1** (Magistrates' Courts Act 1980, s 121(5), ante).

9. WILLS J, held in a civil action that it was not a necessary inference because a dog was accustomed to attack sheep that it was, *ipso facto*, liable to attack men (*Osborne v Chocqueel* [1896] 2 QB 109). It is not necessary to show that the dog has, to the knowledge of its owner, actually bitten or attempted to bite anybody. It is sufficient to prove that the dog is, to the knowledge of its master, ferocious, which may be of an intermittent character, as when a bitch has pups (*Barnes v Lucille Ltd* (1907) 96 LT 680). Complaints to servants of owner at his house are some evidence of *scienter* (*Applebee v Percy* (1874) 38 JP 567). In the case of a corporation, knowledge of a servant is ineffectual, unless communicated to the directors or others in control. There is no absolute duty imposed on the occupier of premises because he allowed a dog to be kept there. It is the person who controls and harbours the dog who is liable (*Knott v LCC* [1934] 1 KB 126, 97 JP 335, CA). An opinion is given at 54 JP 639, that there must be evidence that the defendant suffered, ie knowingly permitted, the dog to be at large, but that it is not necessary to prove the defendant knew the dog to be ferocious. A dog on a lead is not "at large" (*Ross v Evans* [1959] 2 QB 79, [1959] 2 All ER 222, 123 JP 320). As to dangerous dogs, see the Dogs Act 1871, s 2, ante, under which proceedings may be taken in the proper case despite the dismissal of an information under this section. Cf *Keddle v Payn* [1964] 1 All ER 189, 128 JP 144.

10. For extended meaning of "street" in relation to offences as to dogs, where the Public Health Acts Amendment Act 1907 is in force, see s 81 of that Act, ante.

11. The Protection of Animals Act 1911, s 11, ante, enables the police on veterinary certificate to order the slaughter of horses, mules, asses, bulls, sheep, goats, or pigs severely injured in street accidents.

12. "Cattle" includes horses, asses, mules, sheep, goats and swine (s 3).

13. A bicycle is a carriage (*Taylor v Goodwin* (1879) 4 QBD 228, 43 JP 653).

17. What is a reasonable user depends on the facts in each case (*A-G v Brighton and Hove Co-operative Supply Association* [1900] 1 Ch 276, 64 JPJo 68). See also *Drapers' Co v Hadder* (1892) 57 JP 200; *Dunn v Holt* (1904) 68 JP 271; *A-G v WH Smith & Son* (1910) 74 JP 313. The occupier of premises abutting on a highway is entitled to make a reasonable use of the highway for the purpose of obtaining access to his premises and of loading and unloading goods there, but the right of the public is higher than the right of the occupier. Whether the public right has been unduly interfered with is a question of degree (*Vanderpant v Mayfair Hotel Co Ltd* [1930] 1 Ch 138, 94 JP 23).

18. The words "or other means" do not apply to persons not using a carriage, etc, to obstruct (*R v Long* (1888) 52 JP 630; *R v Williams* (1891) 55 JP 406). See however the Highways Act 1980, s 137 providing for persons who "in any way wilfully obstruct the free passage along a highway."

19. Attracting a crowd by selling goods by auction from a hawker's caravan in a market-place, about three feet from the paved street, and thereby obstructing the public carriage and footway, is not an obstruction within these words (*Ball v Ward* (1875) 40 JP 213; see 46 JP 19). But this case has no bearing upon an obstruction upon a highway where the Highways Act is in force. See *Horner v Cadman* (1886) 50 JP 454, where a conviction for causing a partial obstruction of the highway was upheld. As to obstruction by attracting crowds, see this PART: title NUISANCE, ante. A highway may be dedicated to the public subject to rights, privileges, and immunity, and even to such an occasional obstruction as washing carriages upon it (*Chelsea Vestry v Stoddard* (1879) 43 JP 782). See note 3, to s 21, ante. See also *Gill v Carson and Nield* [1917] 2 KB 674, 81 JP 250. The obstruction must be intentional (*Eatan v Cobb* [1950] 1 All ER 1016, 114 JP 271) but it need not be an intention to do wrong (*Arrowsmith v Jenkins* [1963] 2 QB 561, [1963] 2 All ER 210, 127 JP 289).

For a case under a similarly worded provision of the Metropolitan Police Act 1839, s 54, where the obstruction was to the access way of a public market, see *Brandon v Barnes* [1966] 3 All ER 296, 130 JP 389.

20. Apparently a perambulator is not a carriage; see *R v Mathias* (1861) 2 F & F 570. Local authority vehicles cleansing, maintaining or improving footpaths may be exempt from this prohibition (Public Health Act 1961, s 49).

21. Similar words in s 65 of the Metropolitan Paving Act 1817 were held to refer only to things temporarily hung out and to removable things, and not to things fixed to the walls, such as reflector lights (*Winsborrow v London Joint Stock Bank* (1903) 67 JP 289).

22. It would appear that justices are not prevented from deciding whether parts of the footway were dedicated to public use or not, by the principle of ouster of jurisdiction (*Leicester Urban Sanitary Authority v Holland* (1888) 52 JP 788 at 818). Cases decided under this, and similar, local statutes are *Whittaker v Rhodes* (1881) 46 JP 182; *Hitchman v Watt* (1894) 58 JP 720; *Robinson v Cowpen Local Board* (1893) 63 LJQB 235; *R v Berger* [1894] 1 QB 823, 58 JP 416; *Piggott v Goldstraw* (1901) 65 JP 259; *Openshaw v Pickering* (1913) 77 JP 27 (which stated that dedication may be presumed).

23. An unauthorised encroachment restricting access to any part of the footway contravenes this provision and the prosecution is not obliged to allege or prove that any particular person was incommoded: see *Wolverton UDC v Willis* [1962] 1 All ER 243, 126 JP 84, in which it was held, on the facts, that justices were wrong in applying the *de minimis* principle.

24. See also the Explosives Act 1875, s 80, in this PART: title HEALTH AND SAFTY, ante.

25. The mere fact of being employed to deliver papers at the house is no answer to a complaint for thus disturbing the family at a late hour of the night, or for an unreasonable time (*Clark v Hoggins* (1862) 11 CBNS 545).

26. The jurisdiction is not ousted by a *bona fide* claim that the spot is private property, free from any right of way (*R v Young* (1883) 47 JP 519; *Leicester Urban Sanitary Authority v Holland* (1888) 52 JP 788, 818). For offences relating to throwing down, etc, litter, see the Litter Act 1983, in this PART: title PUBLIC HEALTH, ante.

27. The *ejusdem generis* rule does not apply here. The other person need not be akin to an occupier (*West Riding Cleaning Co Ltd v Jewett* [1938] 4 All ER 21).

28. For extended meaning of "street" in relation to offences of throwing dirt, etc, on a street, see the Public Health Acts Amendment Act 1907, s 81, ante (where in force).

29. Statutory nuisances are also dealt with by the Environmental Protection Act 1990, ss 80 et seq, in this PART: title PUBLIC HEALTH, ante.

8–31346 29. Penalty on [persons] guilty of riotous or indecent behaviour[1]. Every person guilty of any violent or indecent behaviour in any police office or any police station-house shall be liable to a penalty not exceeding **level 1** on the standard scale for every such offence, or, in the discretion of the justice before whom he is convicted to imprisonment for a period not exceeding **one month**.

[Town Police Clauses Act 1847, s 29, as amended by the Penalties for Drunkenness Act 1962, s 1, the Criminal Justice Act 1967, Sch 7 and the Criminal Justice Act 1982, ss 38 and 46.]

---

1. The Criminal Justice Act 1967, s 91 in PART VI: LICENSING, ante has effect in place of this section where a person is guilty whilst drunk of disorderly behaviour (Criminal Justice Act 1967, s 91(2)).

Fires

8–31346A 30. *Repealed.*

8–31347 31. Penalty for accidentally allowing chimneys to catch fire. If any chimney accidentally catch or be on fire . . . the persons occupying or using the premises in which such chimney is situated shall be liable to a penalty not exceeding **level 1** on the standard scale:

Provided always, that such forfeiture shall not be incurred if such person prove to the satisfaction of the justice before whom the case is heard that such fire was in no wise owing to omission, neglect, or carelessness of himself or servant.

[Town Police Clauses Act 1847, s 31, as amended by the Criminal Law Act 1977, s 31 and the Criminal Justice Act 1982, s 46.]

8–31347A 32–33. *Repealed.*

Places of Public Resort

8–31347B 34. *Repealed.*

8–31348 35. *Repealed.*

8–31349 36. Penalty on persons keeping places for bear-baiting, cock-fighting etc[1]. Every person who . . . keeps or uses, or acts in the management of any house, room, pit, or other place for the purpose of fighting, baiting or worrying any animals shall be liable to a penalty of not more than **level 4** on the standard scale, or, in discretion of the justices before whom he is convicted, to imprisonment . . . for a time not exceeding **one month**; and the [authority] may, by order in writing, authorise the [police][2] to enter any premises kept or used for any of the purposes aforesaid, and all persons found therein without lawful excuse, shall be liable to a penalty not exceeding **level 4** on the standard scale, and a conviction for this offence shall not exempt the owner, keeper or manager of any such house, room, pit or place from any penal consequences to which he is liable for the nuisance thereby occasioned.

[Town Police Clauses Act 1847, s 36, as amended by the Criminal Law Act 1977, s 31 and the Criminal Justice Act 1982, s 46, the Protection of Animals (Amendment) Act 1988, s 2 and the Statute Law (Repeals) Act 1989, Sch 1.]

---

1. Similar provision with similar penalties is made in the Metropolitan Police Act 1839 s 47 and the City of London Police Act 1839, s 36 for the metropolis.

2. The original working of this section has been adapted so as to accord with modern police arrangements. We are of the opinion that the modern successors to the 1847 Act Comrs for this purpose are the police authority and the chief constable, and there does not arise any requirement for a formal warrant of entry from any outside authority here, as under other legislation.

Hackney Carriages[1]

8–31350 37. Local authority may licence hackney carriages.—Local authority may from time to time license[2] to ply for hire within the prescribed distance[3] or if no distance is prescribed, within five miles from the General Post Office of the city, town, or place to which the special Act refers, (which in that case shall be deemed the prescribed distance,) hackney coaches or carriages of any kind or description adapted to the carriage of persons.

[Town Police Clauses Act 1847, s 37 as amended by the Transport Act 1985, s 16.]

---

1. The 1847 Act is to be construed as one with the Town Police Clauses Act 1889; both Acts are incorporated with the Public Health Act 1875. The hackney carriage provisions were adoptive (Local Government Act 1972, Sch 14, para 25) and applied in conjunction with Part II of the Local Government (Miscellaneous Provisions) Act 1976, in this PART: title LOCAL GOVERNMENT, ante. The Transport Act 1985, s 15 has applied the hackney carriage provisions of the 1847 Act throughout England and Wales. The police are now, despite s 253 of the Public Health Act 1875, enabled to prosecute for hackney carriage offences under this Act. See the Public Health Act 1875, ss 171(4) and 253, the Local Government Act 1972, Sch 14, paras 23–25, and the Local Government (Miscellaneous Provisions) Act 1976, s 27. The 1847 Act provisions do not apply in London (see the Public Passenger Vehicles Act 1981, s 64, the Metropolitan Public Carriage Act 1869 and, as to the metropolitan traffic area the London Passenger Transport Act 1933, s 51(7)).

Sections 37–65 of the Act, to the extent to which they are part of the taxi code, shall apply, subject to modifications and exceptions, to a licensed taxi which is being used to provide a local service under a special licence under s 12 of the Transport Act 1985 (Local Services (Operation by Taxis) Regulations 1986, SI 1986/567).

Sections 52–59 of the Act are modified or disapplied in relation to the hiring of taxis at separate fares under ss 10 and 11 of the Transport Act 1985 (Licensed Taxis (Hiring at Separate Fares) Order 1986, SI 1986/1386).

2. The Transport Act 1985, s 16 provides that where the hackney carriage provisions of the 1847 Act are incorporated in any enactment, the person considering licence applications may refuse only if satisfied that there is no significant unmet demand, as to which see *R v Reading Borough Council, ex p Egan and Sullman* [1990] RTR 399n (a note of 1987 cases); also *Stevenage Borough Council v Younas* [1990] RTR 405n (a note of a 1988 case) and *Ghafoor v Wakefield Metropolitan District Council* [1990] RTR 389. As to appeal, see the Public Health Acts Amendment Act 1890, s 7(1). A failure to determine an application for a hackney carriage licence amounts to "withholding" for the purpose of affording a right of appeal under s 107(1) of the 1890 Act, in this PART: title PUBLIC HEALTH, ante. Where, on appeal, the crown court determines that there is a significant unmet demand, further inquiry must be made to determine its extent and how it is to be matched with all the current competing applications before granting the application before it. The crown court may do this itself or remit the matter to the local authority for reconsideration (*Kelly v Wirral Metropolitan Borough Council* (1996) Times, 13 May, CA).

3. The Public Health Act 1875, s 171, defines this as within any urban district.

8–31351 38. What vehicles to be deemed hackney carriages. Every wheeled carriage[1], whatever may be its form or construction, used in standing or plying for hire[2] in any street[3] within the prescribed distance, and every carriage standing upon any street within the prescribed distance, having thereon any numbered plate required by this or the special Act to be fixed upon a hackney carriage, or having thereon any plate resembling or intended to resemble any such plate as aforesaid, shall be deemed to be a hackney carriage within the meaning of this Act; and in all proceedings at law or otherwise the term "hackney carriage" shall be sufficient to describe any such carriage:

Provided always, that no stage coach[4] used for the purpose of standing or plying for passengers to be carried for hire at separate fares, and duly licensed for that purpose, and having thereon the proper

numbered plates required by law to be placed on such stage coaches, shall be deemed to be a hackney carriage[4] within the meaning of this Act.
[Town Police Clauses Act 1847, s 38.]

1. The Town Police Clauses Act 1889 provides:—The several terms "hackney carriages", "hackney coach", "carriages", and "carriage", whenever used in sections thirty-seven, forty to fifty-two (both inclusive), fifty-four, fifty-eight, and sixty to sixty-seven (both inclusive) of the principal Act shall, notwithstanding anything contained in section thirty-eight of that Act, be deemed to include every omnibus (s 4(1));

Notwithstanding the above provisions, it has been held that Parliament's intention must have been to attribute the same meaning to the term "hackney carriage" throughout the 1847 Act and this necessarily limited the meaning to that within s 38 of the 1847 Act without incorporation of the 1889 Act amendments. Accordingly, a trishaw was held to be a hackney carriage and not a stage coach for the purposes of the licensing provisions under s 37, ante and ss 47 and 59 of the Local Government (Miscellaneous Provisions) Act 1976 (*R v Cambridge City Council, ex p Lane* [1999] RTR 182).

The term "omnibus," where used in this Act, shall include—

Every omnibus, char-à-banc, wagonette, brake, stage coach, and other carriage plying or standing for hire by or used to carry passengers at separate fares, to, from, or in any part of the prescribed distance;

but shall not include—

Any tramcar or tram carriage duly licensed under the provisions of the Tramways Act 1870, or of any Provisional Order made thereunder and confirmed by Parliament, or under the provisions of any local Act of Parliament:

Any carriage starting from and previously hired for the particular passengers thereby carried at any livery stable yard (within the prescribed distance) whereat horses are stabled and carriages let for hire, the said carriage starting from the said stable yard and being bona fide the property of the occupier thereof, and not standing or plying for hire within the prescribed distance:

Any omnibus belonging to or hired or used by any railway company for conveying passengers and their luggage to or from any railway station of that company, and not standing or plying for hire within the prescribed distance:

Any omnibus starting from outside the prescribed distance, and bringing passengers within the prescribed distance, and not standing or plying for hire within the prescribed distance (s 3).

As to tramcars and trolley vehicles, see the Tramways Act 1870, s 48; and as to carriages as a light railway, see *Yorkshire (Woollen District) Electric Tramways Ltd v Ellis* [1905] 1 KB 396, 69 JP 67. The provisions of the 1847 Act do not apply to motor public service vehicles (Road Traffic Act 1930, ss 121(1), 122 and Sch 5), but do apply to a motor "contract carriage" (Road Traffic Act 1930). Note also the definition of "hackney carriage" for use purposes in the Vehicle Excise and Registration Act 1994, Sch 1, Part III.

2. With regard to cases on the meaning of "plying for hire", see also footnote 3, post. "Plying for hire" involves being on view to the public and inviting the public to use it; it can be inferred from the appearance of the vehicle, the place where it was on view and its conduct; see *Rose v Welbeck Motors Ltd* [1962] 2 All ER 801, 126 JP 413, and cases quoted therein. See also *Cogley v Sherwood* [1959] 2 All ER 313, 123 JP 377; *Greyhound Motors Ltd v Lambert* [1928] 1 KB 322, 91 JP 198; *Sales v Lake* (1922) 1 KB 553, 86 JP 80; *Cocks v Mayner* (1894) 58 JP 104 ("voluntary contributions").

3. The word "street" shall extend to and include any road, square, court, alley and thoroughfare, or public passage, within the limits of the special Act (Town Police Clauses Act 1847, s 3). A number of cases on the meaning of "plying for hire" were decided under London legislation; although the cases are relevant, the actual wording of the section differs from that in the 1847 Act and this should be duly noted; "any carriage for the conveyance of passengers which plies for hire within the limits of this Act, and is not a stage carriage" (Metropolitan Public Carriage Act 1869, s 4).

Special provision is made for railway premises by the Public Health Act 1925, s 76, as follows;

"In any area within which the provisions of the Town Police Clauses Act 1847 with respect to hackney carriages are in force, those provisions and any byelaws of the local authority with respect to hackney carriages shall be as fully applicable in all respects to hackney carriages standing or plying for hire at any railway station or railway premises within such area, as if such railway station or railway premises were a stand for hackney carriages or a street:

Provided that—

(a) the provisions of this section shall not apply to any vehicle belonging to or used by any railway company for the purpose of carrying passengers and their luggage to or from any of their railway stations or railway premises, or to the driver or conductor of such vehicle;

(b) nothing in this section shall empower the local authority to fix the site of the stand or starting place of any hackney carriage in any railway station or railway premises, or in any yard belonging to a railway company, except with the consent of that company."

The word "street" does not include an airport private road (*Young v Scampion* [1989] RTR 95, 87 LGR 240) but a vehicle positioned on private land in order to draw custom from the general public in an adjoining public street can be "plying for hire in any street" (*Eastbourne Borough Council v Stirling and Morley* [2001] RTR 65, [2001] Crim LR 42, DC).

4. See note 1, ante.

8–31351A 39. *Repealed.*

8–31352 40. Persons applying for licence to sign a requisition. Before any such licence is granted a requisition for the same, in such form as the commissioners from time to time provide for that purpose, shall be made and signed by the proprietor or one of the proprietors of the hackney carriage in respect of which such licence is applied for; and in every such requisition shall be truly stated the name and surname and place of abode of the person applying for such licence, and of every proprietor or part proprietor of such carriage, or person concerned, either solely or in partnership with any other person, in the keeping, employing, or letting to hire of such carriage; and any person who, on applying for such licence, states in such requisition the name of any person who is not a proprietor or part proprietor of such carriage, or who is not concerned as aforesaid in the keeping, employing, or letting to hire of such carriage, and also any person who wilfully omits to specify truly in such requisition as aforesaid the name of any person who is a proprietor or part proprietor of such carriage, or who is concerned as aforesaid in the keeping, employing, or letting to hire of such carriage, shall be liable to a penalty not exceeding **level 1** on the standard scale.

[Town Police Clauses Act 1847, s 40, as amended by the Criminal Justice Act 1967, Sch 3 and the Criminal Justice Act 1982, ss 38 and 46.]

8–31352A **41. What shall be specified in the licences.** In every such licence shall be specified the name and surname and place of abode of every person who is a proprietor or part proprietor of the hackney carriage in respect of which such licence is granted, or who is concerned, either solely or in partnership with any other person, in the keeping, employing, or letting to hire of any such carriage, and also the number of such licence which shall correspond with the number to be painted or marked on the plates to be fixed on such carriage, together with such other particulars as the commissioners think fit.
[Town Police Clauses Act 1847, s 41.]

8–31352B **42. Licences to be registered.** Every licence shall be made out by the clerk of the commissioners, and duly entered in a book to be provided by him for that purpose; and in such book shall be contained columns or places for entries to be made of every offence committed by any proprietor or driver or person attending such carriage; and any person may at any reasonable time inspect such book, without fee or reward.
[Town Police Clauses Act 1847, s 42.]

8–31352C **43. Licence to be in force for one year only.** Every licence so to be granted shall be under the common seal of the commissioners, if incorporated, or, if not incorporated, shall be signed by two or more of the commissioners, and shall not include more than one carriage so licensed, and shall be in force for one year only from the day of the date of such licence or until the next general licensing meeting, in case any general licensing day be appointed by the commissioners.
[Town Police Clauses Act 1847, s 43.]

8–31353 **44. Notice to be given by proprietors of hackney carriage of any change of abode.** So often as any person named in any such licence as the proprietor or one of the proprietors, or as being concerned, either solely or in partnership with any person, in the keeping, employing, or letting to hire of any such carriage, changes his place of abode, he shall, within seven days next after such change, give notice thereof in writing, signed by him, to the commissioners, specifying in such notice his new place of abode; and he shall at the same time produce such licence at the office of the commissioners, who shall by their clerk, or some other officer, endorse thereon and sign a memorandum specifying the particulars of such change; and any person named in any such licence as aforesaid as the proprietor, or one of the proprietors, of any hackney carriage, or as being concerned as aforesaid, who changes his place of abode and neglects or wilfully omits to give notice of such change, or to produce such licence in order that such memorandum as aforesaid may be endorsed thereon, within the time and in the manner limited and directed by this or the special Act, shall be liable to a penalty not exceeding **level 1** on the standard scale.
[Town Police Clauses Act 1847, s 44, as amended by the Criminal Law Act 1977, s 31 and the Criminal Justice Act 1982, s 46.]

8–31354 **45. Penalty for plying for hire without a licence.** If the proprietor or part proprietor of any carriage, or any person so concerned as aforesaid, permits the same to be used as a hackney carriage plying for hire within the prescribed distance without having obtained a licence as aforesaid for such carriage, or during the time that such licence is suspended as hereinafter provided, or if any person be found driving, standing, or plying for hire[1] with any carriage within the prescribed distance for which such licence as aforesaid has not been previously obtained, or without having the number of such carriage corresponding with the number of the licence openly displayed on such carriage, every such person so offending shall for every such offence be liable to a penalty not exceeding **level 4** on the standard scale.
[Town Police Clauses Act 1847, s 45, as amended by the Criminal Justice Act 1967, Sch 3 and the Criminal Justice Act 1982, ss 39 and 46 and Sch 3.]

1. The driver of a marked mini-cab, not licensed to ply for hire as a hackney carriage did ply for hire when telling a prospective passenger that he was free (*Nottingham City Council v Woodings* [1994] RTR 72).

8–31354A **46. Drivers not to act without first obtaining a licence.** No person shall act as driver of any hackney carriage licensed in pursuance of this or the special Act to ply for hire within the prescribed distance without first obtaining a licence from the commissioners, which licence shall be registered by the clerk to the commissioners, [and such fee as the commissioners may determine shall be paid] for the same; and every such licence shall be in force until the same is revoked except during the time that the same may be suspended as after mentioned.
[Town Police Clauses Act 1847, s 46, as amended by the Local Government, Planning and Land Act 1980, s 1(6), Sch 6.]

8–31355 **47. Penalty on drivers[1] acting without licence, or proprietors employing unlicensed drivers.** If any person acts as such driver as aforesaid without having obtained such licence, or during the time that his licence is suspended, or if he lend or part with his licence, except to the proprietor of the hackney carriage, or if the proprietor of any such hackney carriage employ any person as the driver thereof who has not obtained such licence, or during the time that his licence is suspended, as herein-after provided, every such driver and every such proprietor shall for every such offence respectively be liable to a penalty not exceeding **level 3** on the standard scale.

[Town Police Clauses Act 1847, s 47, as amended by the Criminal Justice Act 1967, Sch 3 and the Criminal Justice Act 1982, ss 35, 38 and 46.]

1. This offence is committed if the vehicle is licensed as a hackney carriage even if it is not, at the time, plying for hire (*Yates v Gates* [1970] 2 QB 27, [1970] 1 All ER 754, 134 JP 274). The Town Police Clauses Act 1889, s 4(2), provides that the word "driver" or "drivers", when used in ss 37, 40–52, 54, 58 and 60–67, shall be deemed to include every conductor of any omnibus.

8–31356 **48. Proprietor to retain licences of drivers,[1] and to produce the same before justices on complaint.** In every case in which the proprietor of any such hackney carriage permits or employs any licensed person to act as the driver thereof, such proprietor shall cause to be delivered to him, and shall retain in his possession, the licence of such driver, while such driver remains in his employ; and in all cases of complaint, where the proprietor of a hackney carriage is summoned to attend before a justice, or to produce the driver, the proprietor so summoned shall also produce the licence of such driver, if he be then in his employ; and if any driver complained of be adjudged guilty of the offence alleged against him, such justice shall make an endorsement upon the licence of such driver, stating the nature of the offence and amount of the penalty inflicted; and if any such proprietor neglect to have delivered to him and to retain in his possession the licence of any driver while such driver remains in his employ, or if he refuse or neglect to produce such licence as aforesaid, such proprietor shall for every such offence be liable to a penalty not exceeding **level 1** on the standard scale.

[Town Police Clauses Act 1847, s 48, as amended by the Criminal Law Act 1977, s 31 and the Criminal Justice Act 1982, s 46.]

1. See definition of "driver" noted to s 47, ante.

8–31357 **49. Proprietor to return licence to drivers except in case of misconduct.** When any driver leaves the service of the proprietor by whom he is employed without having been guilty of any misconduct, such proprietor shall forthwith return to such driver the licence belonging to him; but if such driver have been guilty of any misconduct, the proprietor shall not return his licence, but shall give him notice of the complaint which he intends to prefer against him, and shall forthwith summon such driver to appear before any justice to answer the said complaint; and such justice, having the necessary parties before him, shall inquire into and determine the matter of complaint, and if upon inquiry it appear that the licence of such driver has been improperly withheld, such justice shall direct the immediate re-delivery of such licence, and award such sum of money as he thinks proper to be paid by such proprietor to such driver by way of compensation.

[Town Police Clauses Act 1847, s 49.]

8–31357A **50. Revocation of licences of proprietors or drivers.** The commissioners may, upon the conviction for the second time of the proprietor or driver of any such hackney carriage for any offence under the provisions of this or the special Act with respect to hackney carriages, or any byelaw made in pursuance thereof, suspend or revoke, as they deem right, the licence of any such proprietor or driver.

[Town Police Clauses Act 1847, s 50.]

8–31357B **51. Number of persons to be carried in a hackney carriage to be painted thereon.** No hackney carriage shall be used or employed or let to hire, or shall stand or ply for hire, within the prescribed distance, unless the number of persons to be carried by such hackney carriage, in words at length, and in form following, (that is to say,) "To carry .... persons," be painted on a plate placed on some conspicuous place on the outside of such carriage, and in legible letters, so as to be clearly distinguishable from the colour of the ground whereon the same are painted, one inch in length, and of a proportionate breadth; and the driver of any such hackney carriage shall not be required to carry in or by such hackney carriage a greater number of persons than the number painted thereon.*

[Town Police Clauses Act 1847, s 51.]

***Repealed, in relation to tramcars and trolley vehicles, by the Transport Charges &c (Miscellaneous Provisions) Act 1954, ss 14(1), 15(2), Sch 2, Part IV.**

8–31358 **52. Penalty for neglect to exhibit the number, or for refusal to carry the prescribed number[1].** If the proprietor of any hackney carriage permit the same to be used, employed, or let to hire, or if any person stand or ply for hire with such carriage, without having the number of persons to be carried thereby painted and exhibited in manner aforesaid, or if the driver[2] of any such hackney carriage refuse, when required by the hirer thereof, to carry in or by such hackney carriage the

number of persons painted thereon, or any less number, every proprietor or driver so offending shall be liable to a penalty not exceeding **level 1** on the standard scale.*
[Town Police Clauses Act 1847, s 52, as amended by the Criminal Law Act 1977, s 31 and the Criminal Justice Act 1982, s 46.]

***Repealed, in relation to tramcars and trolley vehicles, by the Transport Charges &c (Miscellaneous Provisions) Act 1954, ss 14(1), 15(2), Sch 2, Part IV.**

1. Section 52 does not apply to tramcars or trolley vehicles (Transport Charges, etc (Miscellaneous Provisions) Act 1954, Sch 2, Pt. IV).
2. See definition of "driver" noted to s 47 ante.

8–31359 **53. Penalty on driver for refusing to drive.** A driver of a hackney carriage standing at any of the stands for hackney carriages appointed by the commissioners, or in any street, who refuses or neglects, without reasonable excuse, to drive such carriage to any place within the prescribed distance, or the distance to be appointed by any byelaw of the commissioners, not exceeding the prescribed distance, to which he is directed to drive by the person hiring or wishing to hire such carriage, shall for every such offence be liable to a penalty not exceeding **level 2** on the standard scale.
[Town Police Clauses Act 1847, s 53, as amended by the Criminal Justice Act 1967, Sch 3 and the Criminal Justice Act 1982, ss 39 and 46 and Sch 3.]

8–31370 **54. Penalty for demanding[1] more than the sum[2] agreed for.** If the proprietor or driver of any such hackney carriage, or if any other person on his behalf, agree beforehand with any person hiring such hackney carriage to take for any job a sum less than the fare allowed by this or the special Act, or any byelaw made thereunder, such proprietor or driver shall be liable to a penalty not exceeding **level 1** on the standard scale if he exact or demand for such job more than the fare so agreed upon.
[Town Police Clauses Act 1847, s 54, as amended by the Criminal Law Act 1977, s 31 and the Criminal Justice Act 1982, s 46.]

1. See definition of "driver" noted to s 47, ante.
2. The Town Police Clauses Act 1889, s 4(3), provides that for the purposes of ss 54, 58 and 66, the fare is deemed to be that allowed by the 1847 Act or a byelaw thereunder.

8–31371 **55. Agreement to pay more than the legal fare.** No agreement whatever made with the driver, or with any person having or pretending to have the care of any such hackney carriage, for the payment of more than the fare allowed by any byelaw made under this or the special Act, shall be binding on the person making the same; and any such person may, notwithstanding such agreement, refuse, on discharging such hackney carriage, to pay any sum beyond the fare allowed as aforesaid; and if any person actually pay to the driver of any such hackney carriage, whether in pursuance of any such agreement or otherwise, any sum exceeding the fare to which such driver was entitled, the person paying the same shall be entitled, on complaint made against such driver before any justice of the peace, to recover back the sum paid beyond the proper fare, and moreover such driver shall be liable to a penalty for such exaction not exceeding **level 3** on the standard scale[1]; and in default of the repayment by such driver of such excess of fare, or of payment of the said penalty, such justice shall forthwith commit such driver to prison, there to remain for any time not exceeding one month, unless the said excess of fare and the said penalty be sooner paid.
[Town Police Clauses Act 1847, s 55, as amended by the Criminal Law Act 1977, s 31 and the Criminal Justice Act 1982, ss 39 and 46 and Sch 3.]

1. The excess fare is recoverable as a civil debt; provision in the section for imprisonment in default of paying the fine is now superseded by the provisions of the Magistrates' Courts Act 1980, Pt III. The power of fixing the fare is, by s 37 and the Public Health Act 1875, s 171, limited to the fare for drivers within the urban district. The offence of taking more than the proper fare is committed at the arrival point, which may be outside the jurisdiction of the justices (*Ely v Godfrey* (1922) 86 JP 82). As to public service vehicle fares, see the Public Passenger Vehicles Act 1981, s 33. In *House v Reynolds* [1977] 1 All ER 689, 141 JP 202, a defendant who required persons telephoning to hire a taxicab to pay a "booking fee" in addition to the fare was properly convicted under s 55, but his appeal allowed against a conviction under s 58.

8–31372 **56. Agreements to carry passengers a discretionary distance for a fixed sum.** If the proprietor or driver of any such hackney carriage, or if any other person on his behalf, agree with any person to carry in or by such hackney carriage persons not exceeding in number the number so painted on such carriage as aforesaid, for a distance to be in the discretion of such proprietor or driver, and for a sum agreed upon, such proprietor or driver shall be liable to a penalty not exceeding **level 1** on the standard scale if the distance which he carries such persons be under that to which they were entitled to be carried for the sum so agreed upon, according to the fare allowed by this or the special Act, or any byelaw made in pursuance thereof.
[Town Police Clauses Act 1847, s 56, as amended by the Criminal Law Act 1977, s 31 and the Criminal Justice Act 1982, s 46.]

8–31373 **57. Deposit to be made for carriages required to wait.** When any hackney carriage is hired and taken to any place, and the driver thereof is required by the hirer there to wait with such hackney carriage, such driver may demand and receive from such hirer his fare for driving to such place, and also a sum equal to the fare of such carriage for the period, as a deposit over and above such fare, during which he is required to wait as aforesaid, or if no fare for time be fixed by the byelaws, then the sum of [7p] for every half hour during which he is so required to wait, which deposit shall be accounted for by such driver when such hackney carriage is finally discharged by such hirer; and if any such driver who has received any such deposit as aforesaid refuses to wait as aforesaid, or goes away or permits such hackney carriage to be driven or taken away without the consent of such hirer, before the expiration of the time for which such deposit was made, or if such driver on the final discharge of such hackney carriage refuse duly to account for such deposit, every such driver so offending shall be liable to a penalty not exceeding **level 1** on the standard scale.
[Town Police Clauses Act 1847, s 57, as amended by the Criminal Law Act 1977, s 31 and the Criminal Justice Act 1982, s 46.]

8–31374 **58. Penalty on proprietors etc convicted of overcharging.** Every proprietor or driver[1] of any such hackney carriage who is convicted of taking as a fare a greater sum than is authorized[2] by any byelaw made under this or the special Act shall be liable to a penalty not exceeding **level 3** on the standard scale, and such penalty may be recovered before one justice; and in the conviction of such proprietor or driver an order may be included for payment of the sum so overcharged, over and above the penalty and costs; and such overcharge shall be returned to the party aggrieved.
[Town Police Clauses Act 1847, s 58, as amended by the Criminal Justice Act 1967, Sch 3 and the Criminal Justice Act 1982, ss 39 and 46 and Sch 3.]

1. See definition of "driver" noted to s 47, ante.
2. The excess fare is recoverable as a civil debt; provision in the section for imprisonment in default of paying the fine is now superseded by the provisions of the Magistrates' Courts Act 1980, Pt III. The power of fixing the fare is, by s 37 and the Public Health Act 1875, s 171, limited to the fare for drivers within the urban district. The offence of taking more than the proper fare is committed at the arrival point, which may be outside the jurisdiction of the justices (*Ely v Godfrey* (1922) 86 JP 82). As to public service vehicle fares, see the Public Passenger Vehicles Act 1981, s 33. In *House v Reynolds* [1977] 1 All ER 689, 141 JP 202, a defendant who required persons telephoning to hire a taxicab to pay a "booking fee" in addition to the fare was properly convicted under s 55, but his appeal allowed against a conviction under s 58.

8–31375 **59. Penalty for permitting persons to ride without consent[1] of hirer.** Any proprietor or driver of any such hackney carriage which is hired who permits or suffers any person to be carried in or upon or about such hackney carriage during such hire, without the express consent of the person hiring the same, shall be liable to a penalty not exceeding **level 1** on the standard scale.
[Town Police Clauses Act 1847, s 59, as amended by the Criminal Law Act 1977, s 31 and the Criminal Justice Act 1982, s 46.]

1. This means positive consent not mere acquiescence (*Yates v Gates* [1970] 2 QB 27, [1970] 1 All ER 754, 134 JP 274).

8–31376 **60. No unauthorised person to act as driver.** No person authorized by the proprietor of any hackney carriage to act as driver[1] of such carriage shall suffer any other person to act as driver of such carriage without the consent of the proprietor thereof; and no person, whether licensed or not, shall act as driver of any such carriage without the consent of the proprietor; and any person so suffering another person to act as driver, and any person so acting as driver without such consent as aforesaid, shall be liable to a penalty not exceeding **level 1** on the standard scale for every such offence.
[Town Police Clauses Act 1847, s 60, as amended by the Criminal Law Act 1977, s 31 and the Criminal Justice Act 1982, s 46.]

1. See definition of "driver" noted to s 47, ante.

8–31377 **61. Penalty on drivers for drunkenness, furious driving, etc.** If the driver[1] or any other person having or pretending to have the care of any such hackney carriage be intoxicated while driving, or if any such driver or other person by wanton and furious driving, or by any other wilful misconduct, injure or endanger any person in his life, limbs, or property, he shall be liable to a penalty not exceeding **level 1** on the standard scale[2]; . . .
[Town Police Clauses Act 1847, s 61, as amended by the Criminal Law Act 1977, s 31, the Criminal Justice Act 1982, s 46 and the Statute Law (Repeals) Act 1989, Sch 1.]

1. See definition of "driver" noted to s 47, ante.
2. Provisions in the section, as originally enacted, for imprisonment in default of paying the fine, are now superseded by provisions in the Magistrates' Courts Act 1980, Pt III in PART I: MAGISTRATES' COURTS, PROCEDURE, ante.

8–31378 **62. Penalties in case of carriages being unattended at places of public resort.** If the driver[1] of any such hackney carriage leave it in any street or at any place of public resort or entertainment, whether it be hired or not, without some one proper to take care of it, any constable

may drive away such hackney carriage and deposit it, and the horse or horses harnessed thereto, at some neighbouring livery stable or other place of safe custody; and such driver shall be liable to a penalty not exceeding **level 1** on the standard scale for such offence; and in default of payment of the said penalty upon conviction, and of the expences of taking and keeping the said hackney carriage and horse or horses, the same, together with the harness belonging thereto, or any of them, shall be sold by order of the justice before whom such conviction is made, and after deducting from the produce of such sale the amount of the said penalty, and of all costs and expences, as well of the proceedings before such justice as of the taking, keeping, and sale of the said hackney carriage, and of the said horse or horses and harness, the surplus (if any) of the said produce shall be paid to the proprietor of such hackney carriage.
[Town Police Clauses Act 1847, s 62, as amended by the Criminal Law Act 1977, s 31 and the Criminal Justice Act 1982, s 46.]

1. See definition of "driver" noted to s 47, ante.

8–31379 **63. Compensation for damage done by driver.** In every case in which any hurt or damage has been caused to any person or property as aforesaid by the driver[1] of any carriage let to hire, the justice before whom such driver has been convicted may direct that the proprietor of such carriage shall pay such a sum, not exceeding five pounds, as appears to the justice a reasonable compensation for such hurt or damage; and every proprietor who pays any such compensation as aforesaid may recover the same from the driver, and such compensation shall be recoverable from such proprietor, and by him from such driver, as damages.
[Town Police Clauses Act 1847, s 63 as amended by the Criminal Justice Act 1982, ss 38 and 46.]

1. See definition of "driver" noted to s 47, ante.

8–31380 **64.** Any driver of any hackney carriage who suffers the same to stand for hire across any street or alongside of any other hackney carriage, or who refuses to give way, if he conveniently can, to any other carriage, or who obstructs or hinders the driver of any other carriage in taking up or setting down any person into or from such other carriage, or who wrongfully in a forcible manner prevents or endeavours to prevent the driver[1] of any other hackney carriage from being hired, shall be liable to a penalty not exceeding level 1 on the standard scale.
[Town Police Clauses Act 1847, s 64, as amended by the Criminal Law Act 1977, s 31 and the Criminal Justice Act 1982, s 46.]

1. See definition of "driver" noted to s 47, ante.

8–31381 **65. Compensation to drivers attending to answer complaints not substantiated.** If the driver of any such hackney carriage be summoned or brought before any justice to answer any complaint or information touching or concerning any offence alleged to have been committed by such driver against the provisions of this or the special Act, or any byelaw made thereunder, and such complaint or information be afterwards withdrawn or quashed or dismissed, or if such driver be acquitted of the offence charged against him, the said justice, if he think fit, may order the complainant or informant to pay to the said driver such compensation for his loss of time in attending the said justice touching or concerning such complaint or information as to the said justice seems reasonable;
[Town Police Clauses Act 1847, s 65 amended by the Statute Law (Repeals) Act 1989, Sch 1.]

8–31382 **66. Fare unpaid may be recovered as a penalty.** If any person refuse to pay on demand to any proprietor or driver of any hackney carriage the fare allowed by this or the special Act, or any byelaw made thereunder, such fare may, together with costs, be recovered before one justice[1] as a penalty.
[Town Police Clauses Act 1847, s 66.]

1. The fare, though recoverable as a penalty, is really only a debt. The amount is recoverable as a civil debt under the Magistrates' Courts Act 1980, s 58, and not by conviction under s 76 (*R v Kerswill* [1895] 1 QB 1, 59 JP 342). See also *R v Master* (*or Martin*) (1869) LR 4 QB 285. The demand may be by the proprietor, driver or conductor to see note 1 to s 47, ante. The fare is deemed to be the fare allowed by the 1847 Act or byelaws thereunder (Town Police Clauses Act 1889, s 4(3)).

8–31382A 67. *Repealed.*

8–31383 **68. Byelaws for regulating hackney carriages.** The commissioners may from time to time (subject to the restrictions of this and the special Act) make byelaws[1] for all or any of the purposes following; (that is to say,)

For regulating the conduct of the proprietors and drivers of hackney carriages plying within the prescribed distance in their several employments, and determining whether such drivers shall wear any and what badges, and for regulating the hours within which they may exercise their calling:

For regulating the manner in which the number of each carriage, corresponding with the number of its licence, shall be displayed:

For regulating the number of persons to be carried by such hackney carriages, and in what manner such number is to be shown on such carriage, and* what number of horses or other animals is to draw the same, and the placing of check strings to the carriages, and the holding of the same by the driver, and how such hackney carriages are to be furnished or provided:

For fixing the stands of such hackney carriages, and the distance to which they may be compelled to take passengers, not exceeding the prescribed distance:

For fixing the rates or fares, as well for time as distance, to be paid for such hackney carriages within the prescribed distance, and for securing the due publication of such fares:

For securing the safe custody and re-delivery of any property accidentally left in hackney carriages, and fixing the charges to be made in respect thereof.

***Repealed, in relation to tramcars and trolley vehicles, by the Transport Charges &c (Miscellaneous Provisions) Act 1954, ss 14(1), 15(2), Sch 2, Part IV.**

1. This section gives power to make byelaws, and it is supplemented by s 6 of the Town Police Clauses Act 1889. Maximum fine for a breach of the byelaws is **level 2** on the standard scale and in case of a continuing offence a further penalty not exceeding £2 for each day after written notice of the offence from the local authority (Public Health Act 1875, s 183, as amended by the Criminal Law Act 1977, s 31(2) and the Criminal Justice Act 1982, s 46. Some of these byelaws may relate to horse-drawn vehicles only and some to motor vehicles as well (*Neal v Guy* [1923] 2 KB 451, 92 JP 119). A committee of a town council have no power to cause summonses to be issued to cabdrivers to appear before them and answer complaints of offences against byelaws (*Wiseman v Manchester Corpn* (1886) 3 TLR 12). As to tramcars or trolley vehicles, see the Transport Charges, etc, (Miscellaneous Provisions) Act 1954, Sch 2, Pt IV. As to plying for hire while a vehicle is in a parking place, and byelaws as to persons waiting to enter public service vehicles, see the Road Traffic Regulation Act 1984, and the Public Health Act 1925, s 75.

8–31383A 69–79. *Repealed.*

UNIFORMS

8–31384 This title contains the following statute—

8–31385 UNIFORMS ACT 1894

Uniforms Act 1894

(57 & 58 Vict c 45)

8–31385 2. Military uniforms not to be worn without authority. (1) It shall not be lawful for any person not serving in Her Majesty's military forces[1] to wear without Her Majesty's permission the uniform of any of those forces, or any dress having the appearance or bearing any of the regimental or other distinctive marks of any such uniform:

Provided that this enactment shall not prevent . . . any persons from wearing any uniform or dress in the course of a stage play performed in a place duly licensed or authorised for the public performance of stage plays, or in the course of a music hall or circus performance, or in the course of any *bona fide* military representation.

(2) If any person contravenes this section he shall be liable on summary conviction to a fine not exceeding **level 3** on the standard scale.

[Uniforms Act 1894, s 2, as amended by the Statute Law Revision Act 1908, Sch, the Criminal Justice Act 1967, Sch 3 and the Criminal Justice Act 1982, ss 38 and 46.]

---

1. Sections 2 and 3 apply also to the Air Force (SR & O 1918 No 548).

8–31386 3. Penalty for bringing contempt on uniform. If any person not serving in Her Majesty's naval or military forces[1] wears without Her Majesty's permission the uniform of any of those forces, or any dress having the appearance or bearing any of the regimental or other distinctive marks of any such uniform, in such a manner and under such circumstances as to be likely to bring contempt upon that uniform, or employs any other person so to wear that uniform or dress, he shall be liable on summary conviction to a fine not exceeding **level 3** on the standard scale, or to imprisonment for a term not exceeding **one month**.

[Uniforms Act 1894, s 3, as amended by the Criminal Justice Act 1967, Sch 3 and the Criminal Justice Act 1982, ss 38 and 46.]

---

1. Sections 2 and 3 apply also to the Air Force (SR & O 1918 No 548).

8–31387 4. In this Act—

"Her Majesty's Military Forces" has the same meaning as in the Army Act 1955;

"Her Majesty's Naval Forces" has the same meaning as in the Naval Discipline Act 1957.

[Uniforms Act 1894, s 4, as substituted by the Armed Forces Act 1981, Sch 3.]

Other Uniforms

8–31420 Official Secrets Act 1920. The unauthorised use of any official uniform used for gaining admission to a "prohibited place" is an offence under s 1 of this Act (this PART: title OFFICIAL SECRETS ante).

8–31421 British Transport Commission Act 1962, Police Act 1996. Impersonation of a member of a police force or a BTC constable is an offence against these Acts (ss 43 and 90 respectively, this PART: title POLICE) ante.

8–31422 Chartered Associations (Protection of Names and Uniforms) Act 1926. Unauthorised use of uniform, etc, of an association protected by Order in Council under this Act is prohibited (this PART: title COPYRIGHT, DESIGNS AND PATENTS) ante.

8–31423 Merchant Shipping Act 1995. Unauthorised wearing of merchant navy uniform is an offence under s 57 of this Act (see the Merchant Shipping Act 1995 in PART VII: TRANSPORT, title MERCHANT SHIPPING ante).

VAGRANTS

Vagrancy Act 1824

(5 Geo 4 c 83)

8–31440 3. Persons committing certain offences, how to be punished. Every person wandering abroad, or placing himself or herself in any public[1] place, street, highway, court, or passage, to beg[2] or gather alms, or causing or procuring or encouraging any child or children[3] so to do; shall be deemed an idle and disorderly person within the true intent and meaning of this Act; and, subject to section 70 of the Criminal Justice Act 1982[4], it shall be lawful for any justice of the peace to commit such offender (being thereof convicted before him by his own view, or by the confession of such offender, or by the evidence on oath of one or more credible witness or witnesses) to imprisonment[5] for any time not exceeding **one calendar month**[4].

[Vagrancy Act 1824, s 3, as amended by the Prison Act 1865, s 56, the Statute Law Revision (No 2) Act 1888, the National Assistance Act 1948, Sch 7, the Criminal Justice Act 1948, s 1(2) and the Criminal Justice Act 1982, Sch 14 and the Statute Law (Repeals) Act 1989, Sch 1.]

---

1. Any place of public resort or recreation ground belonging to, or under the control of, the local authority, and any unfenced ground adjoining or abutting upon any street in an urban district, shall be deemed to be an open and public space (Public Health Acts Amendment Act 1907, s 81).

2. Workmen on strike seeking assistance are not begging (*Pointon v Hill* (1884) 12 QBD 306, 48 JP 341; *Mathers v Penfold* [1915] 1 KB 514, 79 JP 225).

3. See also Children and Young Persons Act 1933, s 4, ante. As to age and appearance of a child, see *R v Viasani* (1867) 31 JP 260.

4. For certain of the offences in this section the power to sentence a person to imprisonment has been abolished by the Criminal Justice Act 1982, s 70; see note 11 to s 4, post.

5. The Magistrates' Courts Act 1980, s 34(3), as amended, provides an alternative to imprisonment of a fine not exceeding **level 3** on the standard scale. If the conviction is before a single justice, s 121(5) of the 1980 Act limits imprisonment to fourteen days and a fine to £1. See also note 5 supra as to limitation of the power to imprison.

8–31441 4. Persons committing certain offences to be deemed rogues and vagabonds. Every person committing any of the offences[1] herein-before mentioned, after having been convicted as an idle and disorderly person; every person wandering abroad and lodging[2] in any barn or outhouse, or in any deserted or unoccupied building, or in the open air, or under a tent, or in any cart or waggon[3] and not giving a good account of himself or herself; every person wilfully, openly, lewdly, and obscenely exposing his person, with intent to insult any female, every person wandering abroad, and endeavouring by the exposure of wounds or deformities to obtain or gather alms; every person going about as a gatherer or collector of alms, or endeavouring to procure charitable contributions of any nature or kind, under any false or fraudulent pretence; every person being found in or upon any dwelling house[4], warehouse, coach-house, stable, or outhouse, or in any enclosed[5] yard, garden, or , for any unlawful purpose[6] and every person apprehended as an idle and disorderly person, and violently resisting any constable, or other peace officer so apprehending him or her, and being subsequently convicted of the offence for which he or she shall have been so apprehended; shall be deemed a rogue and vagabond[7] within the true intent and meaning of this Act: and, subject to section

70 of the Criminal Justice Act 1982[8], it shall be lawful for any justice of the peace to commit such offender (being thereof convicted before him by the confession of such offender, or by the evidence on oath of one or more credible witness or witnesses) to imprisonment[9] for any time not exceeding **three calendar months**[9].*

[Vagrancy Act 1824, s 4, as amended by the Prison Act 1865, s 56, the Prevention of Crimes Act 1871, s 15, the Statute Law Revision (No 2) Act 1888, the Criminal Justice Act 1925, Sch 3, the Vagrancy Act 1935, s 1(2), the National Assistance Act 1948, Sch 7, the Criminal Justice Act 1948, s 1(2), the Criminal Law Act 1967, Sch 2, the Theft Act 1968, Sch 3, the Indecent Displays (Control) Act 1981, Sch, the Criminal Attempts Act 1981, s 8 and Sch, the Criminal Justice Act 1982, Sch 14, the Public Order Act 1986 Sch 3 and the Statute Law (Repeals) Act 1989, Sch 1.]

***Amended by the Sexual Offences Act 2003, Sch 6, from a date to be appointed.**

1. This section can properly be applied to an occupier of premises in respect of an offence on those premises, if he falls within the language of the relevant charging provisions; see *Wood v Metropolitan Police Comr* [1986] 2 All ER 570, [1986] 1 WLR 796.

2. This section has been amended by the Vagrancy Act 1935 to have effect as follows; a person wandering abroad and lodging as aforesaid shall not be deemed by virtue of the said enactment a rogue and vagabond within the meaning of the said Act unless it is proved either—

(*a*) that, in relation to the occasion on which he lodged as aforesaid, he had been directed to a reasonably accessible place of shelter and failed to apply for, or refused, accommodation there;

(*b*) that he is a person who persistently wanders abroad and, notwithstanding that a place of shelter is reasonably accessible, lodges or attempts to lodge as aforesaid; or

(*c*) that by, or in the course of, lodging as aforesaid he caused damage to property, infection with vermin, or other offensive consequence, or that he lodged as aforesaid in such circumstances as to appear to be likely so to do.

In this subsection the expression "a place of shelter" means a place where provision is regularly made for giving (free of charge) accommodation for the night to such persons as apply therefor.

3. The Vagrancy Act 1935, s 1(4), provides that the reference to a person lodging under a tent or in a cart or waggon shall not be deemed to include a person lodging under a tent or in a cart or waggon with or in which he travels.

4. The occupier's name need not be given in the information but the address must be (*Hollyhomes v Hind* [1944] KB 571, [1944] 2 All ER 8, 108 JP 190). "Dwellinghouse" includes an entrance hall common to several dwellings (ibid).

5. A yard, garden or area may be enclosed although access can be gained through spaces left between buildings, an archway, an open gate, etc (*Goodhew v Morton* [1962] 2 All ER 771, 126 JP 369). Railway sidings or a railway yard a mile long and a quarter mile wide are not within the section; the essential feature of a yard is that it should be a relatively small area ancillary to a building (*Knott v Blackburn* [1944] KB 77, [1944] 1 All ER 116, 108 JP 19; *Quatromini v Peck* [1972] 3 All ER 521, 136 JP 854). The words "enclosed yard, garden or area" connote an area which is in the open air; accordingly, enclosed area does not include a room within a building (*Talbot v DPP* [2000] 1 WLR 1102, [2000] 2 Cr App Rep 60, 164 JP 169, DC).

6. The unlawful purpose must be the commission of some offence which would subject the party to criminal proceedings, and not an act of immorality (*Hayes v Stevenson* (1860) 25 JP 39). The unlawful purpose need not be to commit a crime at the time or place where the defendant is found (*Re Joy* (1853) 22 LT Jo 80). The accused must be found on the premises but may be arrested elsewhere (*Moran v Jones* (1911) 75 JP 411; *R v Goodwin* [1944] KB 518, [1944] 1 All ER 506, 108 JP 159; *R v Lumsden* [1951] 2 KB 513, [1951] 1 All ER 1101, 115 JP 364). The actions of a man who at night looked through the windows of a ground floor bed sitting room with the intention of frightening a woman inside and causing her to fear some act of immediate violence were held to constitute an assault, and therefore amounted to an "unlawful purpose" (*Smith v Chief Superintendent, Woking Police Station* (1983) 76 Cr App Rep 234).

7. It is not necessary to constitute a man a rogue and vagabond that he should lead a wandering and vagabond life (*Monck v Hilton* (1877) 2 Ex D 268, 41 JP 214).

8. The Criminal Justice Act 1982, s 70 provides that where a person is convicted.

(*a*) under section 3 or 4 of this Act, of wandering abroad, or placing himself in any public place, street, highway, court, or passage, to beg or gather alms; or

(*b*) under section 4 of this Act—

(i) of wandering abroad and lodging in any barn or outhouse, or in any deserted or unoccupied building, or in the open air, or under a tent, or in any cart or waggon, and not giving a good account of himself; or

(ii) of wandering abroad, and endeavouring by the exposure of wounds and deformities to obtain or gather alms,

the court shall not have power to sentence him to imprisonment but shall have the power to fine him.

If a person deemed a rogue and vagabond by virtue of section 4 of the Act is thereafter guilty of an offence mentioned above, he shall be convicted of that offence under section 4 of the Act and accordingly—

(*a*) shall not be deemed an incorrigible rogue; and

(*b*) shall not be committed to the Crown Court,

by reason only of that conviction.

9. The Magistrates' Courts Act 1980, s 34(3), as amended, provided an alternative to imprisonment of a fine not exceeding **level 3** on the standard scale. If the conviction is before a single justice, s 121(5) of the 1980 Act limits imprisonment to fourteen days and a fine to £1. The Criminal Justice Act 1982, s 70, removes the power to imprison for certain offences under this section; see note 11 supra. The Criminal Justice Act 1991, s 26(5), limits the fine for sleeping rough (see s 70(*b*)(i) of the 1982 Act in note 11 supra) to **level 1** on the standard scale.

8–31442 **5. Who shall be deemed incorrigible rogues.** Every person committing any offence against this Act which shall subject him or her to be dealt with as a rogue and vagabond, such person having been at some former time adjudged so to be, and duly convicted thereof[1]; shall, subject to section 70 of the Criminal Justice Act 1982[2], be deemed an incorrigible rogue within the true intent and meaning of this Act; and subject to section 70 of the Criminal Justice Act 1982[2], it shall be lawful for any justice of the peace to commit[3] such offender (being thereof convicted before him by the confession of such offender, or by the evidence on oath of one or more credible witness or witnesses,) to the Crown Court[4] either in custody or on bail.

[Vagrancy Act 1824, s 5, as amended by the Criminal Justice Act 1948, Sch 10, the Criminal Justice Act 1967, s 20 and Sch 6, the Courts Act 1971, Sch 8, the Criminal Justice Act 1982, Sch 14 and the Statute Law (Repeals) Act 1989, Sch 1.]

---

1. Before a person can be dealt with as an incorrigible rogue, proof must be furnished of a previous conviction either for an offence for which he is deemed an idle and disorderly person, recording his previous conviction for a similar offence (*R v Johnson* [1909] 1 KB 439, 73 JP 135), or for an offence which brought him within the category of rogues and vagabonds (*R v Teesdale* (1927) 44 TLR 30, 91 JP 184). Two separate convictions as an idle and disorderly person without stating that the latter was for a second offence will not suffice (*R v Johnson* supra). Proof will usually be by an extract from the court register (Criminal Procedure Rules 2005, Part 6, in PART I: MAGISTRATES' COURTS, PROCEDURE, ante); see also the Criminal Justice Act, 1948, s 39, ante (finger-prints).

2. The Criminal Justice Act 1982, s 70 provides that where a person is convicted:

(*a*) under section 3 or 4 of this Act, of wandering abroad, or placing himself in any public place, street, highway, court, or passage, to beg or gather alms; or

(*b*) under section 4 of this Act—

(i) of wandering abroad and lodging in any barn or outhouse, or in any deserted or unoccupied building, or in the open air, or under a tent, or in any cart or waggon, and not giving a good account of himself; or

(ii) of wandering abroad, and endeavouring by the exposure of wounds and deformities to obtain or gather alms,

the court shall not have power to sentence him to imprisonment but shall have the power to fine him.

If a person deemed a rogue and vagabond by virtue of section 4 of the Act is thereafter guilty of an offence mentioned above, he shall be convicted of that offence under section 4 of the Act and accordingly—

(*a*) shall not be deemed an incorrigible rogue; and

(*b*) shall not be committed to the Crown Court,

by reason only of that conviction.

3. The Criminal Justice Act 1967, s 56, ante, applies; for documents see the Criminal Procedure Rules 2005, r 43.1, in PART I: MAGISTRATES' COURTS, PROCEDURE, ante.

4. See s 10, post.

8–31443 **6. Any person may apprehend offenders.** *Repealed.*

8–31444 **10. Power of Crown Court to punish rogues and vagabonds and incorrigible rogues.** When any incorrigible rogues shall have been committed to the Crown Court, it shall be lawful for the Crown Court to examine into the circumstances of the case, and to order, if they think fit, that such offender be imprisoned[1] for any time not exceeding one year from the time of making such order.

[Vagrancy Act 1824, s 10, as amended by the Criminal Justice Act 1948, Sch 10, the Criminal Justice Act 1967, Sch 7, the Courts Act 1971, Sch 8 and the Statute Law (Repeals) Act 1989, Sch 1.]

---

1. The Crown Court has no power to adjudge whether the accused is an incorrigible rogue; the magistrates will have decided that (*R v Evans* [1915] 2 KB 762, 79 JP 415). Nor will the Crown Court have power to sentence for the offences on which the defendant was deemed to be an incorrigible rogue (*R v Walters* [1969] 1 QB 255, [1968] 3 All ER 863, 133 JP 73). For observations as to limits of Crown Court powers see *R v Jackson* [1974] QB 517, [1974] 2 All ER 211, 138 JP 363. As to procedure in the Crown Court see *R v Cope* (1925) 89 JP 100; *R v Holding, R v Long* (1935) 98 JP 459; *R v Billington* (1942) 28 Cr App Rep 180. Although there is no appeal from the conviction by the magistrates under s 10 of the Criminal Appeal Act 1968; appeal will lie from the decision of the Crown Court; see *R v Brown* (1908) 72 JP 427; *R v Dean* (1924) 18 Cr App Rep 133; *R v Cadwell* (1927) 20 Cr App Rep 60. As to appeal to the Crown Court from the magistrates' court, see s 14, post.

8–31445 **14. Persons aggrieved may appeal to the Crown Court.** Any person aggrieved by any act or determination of any justice or justices of the peace out of sessions[1], in or concerning the execution of this Act, may appeal[2] to the Crown Court.

[Vagrancy Act 1824, s 14, as amended by the Summary Jurisdiction Act 1884, Sch, and the Courts Act 1971, Sch 8.]

---

1. That is, where the decision was of a single justice, or at an occasional court house, or in petty sessions.

2. See the Magistrates' Courts Act 1980, ss 108–110, ante; the Criminal Procedure Rules 2005, Part 63, in PART I: MAGISTRATES' COURTS, PROCEDURE, ante.

WAR CRIMES

War Crimes Act 1991[1]

(1991 c 13)

8–31450 **1. Jurisdiction over certain war crimes.** (1) Subject to the provisions of this section, proceedings for murder, manslaughter or culpable homicide may be brought against a person in the United Kingdom irrespective of his nationality at the time of the alleged offence if that offence—

(*a*) was committed during the period beginning with 1st September 1939 and ending with 5th June 1945 in a place which at the time was part of Germany or under German occupation; and

(*b*) constituted a violation of the laws and customs of war.

(2) No proceedings shall by virtue of this section be brought against any person unless he was on 8th March 1990, or has subsequently become, a British citizen or resident in the United Kingdom, the Isle of Man or any of the Channel Islands.

(3) No proceedings shall by virtue of this section be brought in England and Wales or in Northern Ireland except by or with the consent of the Attorney General or, as the case may be, the Attorney General for Northern Ireland.

(4) The Schedule[2] to this Act provides a procedure for use instead of committal proceedings where a person is charged in Northern Ireland with an offence to which this section applies.

[War Crimes Act 1991, s 1 as amended by the Criminal Procedure and Investigations Act 1996, s 46 and Sch 5.]

---

1. This Act is protected from challenge under art 7(1) of the European Convention on Human Rights (the prohibition on retrospective criminal penalties) by art 7(2) which provides for the trial and punishment of any person for any act or omission which, at the time when it was committed, was criminal according to the general principles of law recognised by civilised nations.

2. The Schedule has been repealed in so far as it applied to England and Wales by the Criminal Procedure and Investigations Act 1996, s 46.

WATER

8–31469 This title includes sections of the following statutes, relevant to proceedings in magistrates' courts—

This title also contains the following statutory instrument—

See also titles Salmon and Freshwater Fisheries ante, Sea Fisheries ante, Public Health ante (cleansing and repairing etc of drains in Part II of the Public Health Act 1936, pollution in the Control of Pollution Act 1974 Part II).

The Water Act 1989 reorganised arrangements for water matters. Schedule 26 thereto made transitional provisions and savings with respect to water authorities, water and sewerage services, control of pollution, water resources, flood defence and fisheries as well as various miscellaneous matters.

Reservoirs Act 1975

(1975 c 23)

8–31505 The enforcement authority for the purposes of this Act is the local authority, with supervisory powers to the Secretary of State[1] [ss 2 and 3].

A qualified civil engineer must design and supervise the construction or enlargement of a reservoir, which can only then be filled in accordance with his certificate [s 6]. The undertakers are to carry into effect any safety recommendations of an engineer appointed in place of a construction engineer [s 8(3)]. Re-use of abandoned reservoirs is subject to inspection, supervision, certification and implementation of safety recommendations [s 9]. Undertakers must have any large raised reservoir inspected periodically by an independent qualified civil engineer, implement and have certified any safety recommendations in his report [s 10]. Water levels etc must be recorded [s 11]. A supervising engineer must be employed for any large raised reservoir to advise on safety and compliance with provisions [s 12(1)]. Discontinuance and abandonment of reservoirs must also be under qualified supervision and subject to a safety report [ss 13 and 14].

A person duly authorised in writing by an enforcement authority has power to enter on reservoir land at any reasonable time. A Justice may issue a warrant to enter in the event of refusal or apprehended refusal or in the occupier's absence, where there is reasonable ground for entry and where notice in writing of intention to apply has been given to the occupier. Warrant continues in force until purpose satisfied: penalty for wilful obstruction **level 3** on the standard scale [s 17 as amended by the Criminal Justice Act 1982, ss 38 and 46].

---

1. An index of general definitions appears in Sch 1 to the Act. The Reservoirs Act 1975 (Registers, Reports and Records) Regulations 1985, SI 1985/177 amended by SI 1985/548 have been made.

8–31506 **22. Criminal liability of undertakers and their employees.** (1) If—

(*a*) by the wilful default of the undertakers any of the provisions of section 6, 8(3), 9(1), (2) or (3), 10(1) or (6), 11, 12(1), 13 or 14(1) or (2) above is not observed or complied with in relation to a large raised reservoir;

(*b*) the undertakers fail to comply with a notice from the enforcement authority under section 8, 9, 10, 12 or 14 above; or

(*c*) the undertakers fail to comply with a direction under section 12A above;

then unless there is reasonable excuse for the default or failure, the undertakers shall be guilty of an offence and liable on conviction[1] on indictment or on summary conviction to a **fine**, which on summary conviction shall not exceed the **statutory maximum**.

(1A) If the undertakers fail without reasonable excuse to comply with a notice under section 12B above, they shall be guilty of an offence and liable—

(*a*) on summary conviction, to a fine not exceeding the statutory maximum;

(*b*) on conviction on indictment, to imprisonment for a term not exceeding two years, or to a fine, or to both.

(2) If, in the case of any large raised reservoir, the undertakers fail without reasonable excuse to give the enforcement authority in due time any notice required by this Act to be given by them to that authority, the undertakers shall be guilty of an offence and liable on summary conviction to a fine not exceeding **level 4** on the standard scale.

(3) If, in the case of any large raised reservoir, the undertakers or persons employed by them without reasonable excuse refuse or knowingly fail to afford to any person the facilities required by section 21(5) above or to furnish to any person the information and particulars so required, the undertakers shall be guilty of an offence and liable on summary conviction to a fine not exceeding **level 4** on the standard scale.

(4) If for the purposes of section 21(5) above a person makes use of any document or furnishes any information or particulars which he knows to be false in a material respect, or recklessly makes use of any document or furnishes any information or particulars which is or are false in a material respect, he shall be guilty of an offence and liable on summary conviction to a fine not exceeding **level 5** on the standard scale.

(5) Where an offence committed by a body corporate under this section is proved to have been committed with the consent or connivance of any director, manager, secretary or other similar officer of the body corporate, or any person who was purporting to act in any such capacity, he as well as the body corporate shall be guilty of that offence, and shall be liable to be proceeded against and punished accordingly.

Where the affairs of a body corporate are managed by its members, this section shall apply in relation to the acts and defaults of a member in connection with his functions of management as if he were a director of the body corporate.

(6) In England and Wales proceedings for an offence under this section may be instituted only by the Environment Agency or the Secretary of State or by or with the consent of the Director of Public Prosecutions.

[Reservoirs Act 1975, s 22, as amended by the Criminal Law Act 1977, s 28, the Criminal Justice Act 1982, ss 38 and 46 and the Water Act 2003, ss 74 and 79.]

---

1. For procedure in respect of an offence triable either way, see the Magistrates' Courts Act 1980, ss 17A–21 in PART I: MAGISTRATES' COURTS, PROCEDURE, ante.

8–31506A **22A. Service of notices by the Environment Agency.** Section 123 of the Environment Act 1995 (service of documents) applies to any document authorised or required by virtue of any provision of this Act to be served or given by the Environment Agency as if it were authorised or required to be served or given by or under that Act.

[Reservoirs Act 1975, s 22A, as inserted by the Water Act 2003, s 76.]

Water Act 1989

(1989 c 15)

8–31630 This Act has been extensively repealed by the Water Consolidation (Consequential Provisions) Act 1991, Sch 3. Preserved sections include s 174 (General restrictions on disclosure of information), 175 (Making false statements etc), which have penal provisions providing for offences triable either way, 177 (Offences by bodies corporate), and 189 (General interpretation, of which definitions relevant to the above preserved sections are retained and listed in Sch 3 of the 1991 Act).

Water Industry Act 1991

(1991 c 56)

PART III[1]

WATER SUPPLY

8–31631 **57. Duty to provide a supply of water etc for fire-fighting.** Water undertaker to allow any person to take water for extinguishing fires from mains or pipes fitted with a fire-hydrant; duty to fix fire-hydrants at request of fire and rescue authority, to keep same in good working order and replace when necessary, to supply keys to fire and rescue authority; breach punishable on summary conviction with fine not exceeding **statutory maximum** or on conviction on indictment by **fine**[2]; defence of being unable to do something by reason of carrying out necessary works, also took all reasonable steps and exercised all due diligence.

[Water Industry Act 1991, s 57—summarised.]

1. Part III comprises ss 37–93.
2. For procedure in respect of an offence triable either way, see the Magistrates' Courts Act 1980, ss 17A–21 in PART I: MAGISTRATES' COURTS, PROCEDURE, ante.

Disconnections

8–31632 **60. Disconnections for the carrying out of necessary works.** Water undertaker may disconnect or reduce supply if it is reasonable to do so for the carrying out of necessary works; it must serve reasonable notice on the consumer, carry out the works with reasonable dispatch, make available an emergency supply within a reasonable distance for domestic purposes.

[Water Industry Act 1991, s 60—summarised.]

8–31633 **61. Disconnections for non-payment of charges.** Water undertaker may disconnect supply if occupier of premises liable to pay and has failed to do so within seven days beginning with the day he is served with a notice; provision is made for disputed liability and to preserve supply to other premises on same service pipe.

[Water Industry Act 1991, s 61—summarised.]

8–31634 **62.** *Disconnections at request of customer.*

8–31635 **63. General duties of undertakers with respect to disconnections.** Where a water undertaker disconnects or cuts off supply of water to any inhabited house for longer than 24 hours, it must serve notice on the local authority within 48 hours; if it disconnects other than under powers in ss 60–62 above or s 75 or any other enactment or fails to comply with requirements under which it disconnects, it is liable of summary conviction to a fine not exceeding **level 3** on the standard scale.

[Water Industry Act 1991, s 63—summarised.]

Use of limiting devices

8–31635A **63A. Prohibition of use of limiting devices.** (1) A water undertaker shall be guilty of an offence under this section if it uses a limiting device in relation to any premises specified in Schedule 4A to this Act, with the intention of enforcing payment of charges which are or may become due to the undertaker in respect of the supply of water to the premises.

(2) For the purposes of this section "a limiting device", in relation to any premises, means any device or apparatus which—

(*a*) is fitted to any pipe by which water is supplied to the premises or a part of the premises, whether that pipe belongs to the undertaker or to any other person, and

(*b*) is designed to restrict the use which may be made of water supplied to the premises by the undertaker.

(3) An undertaker does not commit an offence under this section by disconnecting a service pipe to any premises or otherwise cutting off a supply of water to the premises.

(4) An undertaker guilty of an offence under this section shall be liable on summary conviction to a fine not exceeding level 3 on the standard scale.

[As inserted by the Water Industry Act 1999, s 2.]

Means of supply

8–31636 **65. Duties of undertakers as respects constancy and pressure.** Duty of water undertaker to cause water in mains and pipes used for domestic purposes or fire-hydrants to be paid on constantly and at such pressure as will cause it to reach to top of every building except when necessary works being carried out; breach punishable on summary conviction by a fine not exceeding the **statutory maximum** or on conviction on indictment to a **fine**[1].

[Water Industry Act 1991, s 65 amended by the Competition and Service (Utilities) Act 1992, Sch 1—summarised.]

1. For procedure in respect of an offence triable either way, see the Magistrates' Courts Act 1980, ss 17A–21 in PART I: MAGISTRATES' COURTS, PROCEDURE, ante.

Standards of wholesomeness

8–31637 69. *Regulations for preserving water quality*[1].

1. The Water Supply (Water Quality) Regulations 1989, SI 1989/1147 amended by SI 1989/1384 , SI 1991/1837 and 2790, SI 1996/3001, SI 1999/1524, SI 2000/3184, SI 2001/2885 and 3911 and SI 2002/2469 have been made under the previously corresponding Water Act 1989, s 53. They are revoked and replaced by the Water Supply (Water Quality) Regulations 2000, SI 2000/3184 amended by SI 2001/2885, SI 2002/2469 and SI 2005/2035 as from 1 January 2004. They create offences (triable either way) of applying or introducing unauthorised substances, with statutory defences, and making false statements. For Wales, see the Water Supply (Water Quality) Regulations 2001, SI 2001/3911 amended by SI 2005/2035. Consent of the Secretary of State (in Wales, the National Assembly) or the DPP is required for prosecution.

8–31638 70. Offence of supplying water unfit for human consumption. (1) Subject to subsection (3) below, where a water undertaker's supply system is used for the purposes of supplying water to any premises and that water is unfit for human consumption, the relevant persons shall be guilty of an offence and liable[1]—

(*a*) on summary conviction, to a fine not exceeding £20,000;
(*b*) on conviction on indictment, to a **fine**.

(1A) For the purposes of subsection (1) above, the relevant persons are—

(*a*) the water undertaker whose supply system is used for the purposes of supplying the water (in this section referred to as the "primary water undertaker"); and
(*b*) any employer of persons, or any self-employed person, who is concerned in the supply of the water.

(2) For the purposes of section 210 below and any other enactment under which an individual is guilty of an offence by virtue of subsection (1) above the penalty on conviction on indictment of an offence under this section shall be deemed to include imprisonment (in addition to or instead of a fine) for a term not exceeding two years.

(3) In any proceedings against any relevant person for an offence under this section it shall be a defence for that person to show that it—

(*a*) had no reasonable grounds for suspecting that the water would be used for human consumption; or
(*b*) took all reasonable steps and exercised all due diligence for securing that the water was fit for human consumption on leaving the primary water undertaker's pipes or was not used for human consumption.

(3A) For the purposes of paragraph (*b*) of subsection (3) above—

(*a*) in the case of proceedings against a primary water undertaker, showing that the undertaker took all reasonable steps and exercised all due diligence as mentioned in that paragraph includes (among other things) showing that the relevant arrangements were reasonable in all the circumstances; and
(*b*) in the case of proceedings against any other relevant person, showing that the person took all reasonable steps and exercised all due diligence as mentioned in that paragraph includes (among other things) showing that it took all reasonable steps and exercised all due diligence for securing that all aspects of the relevant arrangements for which it was responsible were properly carried out.

(3B) In subsection (3A) above, "relevant arrangements" means arrangements made by the primary water undertaker to ensure that all other relevant persons were required to take all reasonable steps and exercise all due diligence for securing that the water was fit for human consumption on leaving the undertaker's pipes or was not used for human consumption.

(4) Proceedings for an offence under this section shall not be instituted except by the Secretary of State or the Director of Public Prosecutions.

[Water Industry Act 1991, s 70, as amended by the Water Act 2003, s 60 and Sch 8.]

1. For procedure in respect of an offence triable either way, see the Magistrates' Courts Act 1980, ss 17A–21 in PART I: MAGISTRATES' COURTS, PROCEDURE, ante.

Waste, contamination, misuse etc

8–31639 71. Waste from water sources. (1) Subject to subsections (2) and (3) below, a person shall be guilty of an offence under this section if—

(*a*) he causes or allows any underground water to run to waste from any well, borehole or other work; or
(*b*) he abstracts from any well, borehole or other work water in excess of his reasonable requirements.

(2) A person shall not be guilty of an offence by virtue of subsection (1)(*a*) above in respect of anything done for the purpose—

(*a*) of testing the extent or quality of the supply; or
(*b*) of cleaning, sterilising, examining or repairing the well, borehole or other work in question.

(3) Where underground water interferes or threatens to interfere with the carrying out or operation of any underground works (whether waterworks or not), it shall not be an offence under this section, if no other method of disposing of the water is reasonably practicable, to cause or allow the water to run to waste so far as may be necessary for enabling the works to be carried out or operated.

(4) A person who is guilty of an offence under this section shall be liable, on summary conviction, to a fine not exceeding **level 3** on the standard scale.

(5) On the conviction of a person under this section, the court may—

(*a*) order that the well, borehole or other work to which the offence relates shall be effectively sealed; or
(*b*) make such other order as appears to the court to be necessary to prevent waste of water.

(6) If any person fails to comply with an order under subsection (5) above, then, without prejudice to any penalty for contempt of court, the court may, on the application of the Environment Agency, authorise the Agency to take such steps as may be necessary to execute the order; and any expenses incurred in taking any such steps shall be recoverable summarily as a civil debt from the person convicted.

(7) Any person designated for the purpose by the Environment Agency shall, on producing some duly authenticated document showing his authority, have a right at all reasonable times—

(*a*) to enter any premises for the purpose of ascertaining whether there is, or has been, any contravention of the provisions of this section on or in connection with the premises;
(*b*) to enter any premises for the purpose of executing any order of the court under this section which the Environment Agency has been authorised to execute in those premises.

(8) Part I of Schedule 6 to this Act shall apply to the rights of entry conferred by subsection (7) above.

[Water Industry Act 1991, s 71, as amended by the Environment Act 1995, Sch 22.]

8–31640 72. Contamination of water sources. (1) Subject to subsections (2) and (3) below, a person is guilty of an offence under this section if he is guilty of any act or neglect whereby the water in any waterworks which is used or likely to be used—

(*a*) for human consumption or domestic purposes; or
(*b*) for manufacturing food or drink for human consumption,

is polluted or likely to be polluted.

(2) Nothing in this section shall be construed as restricting or prohibiting any method of cultivation of land which is in accordance with the principles of good husbandry.

(3) Nothing in this section shall be construed as restricting or prohibiting the reasonable use of oil or tar on any highway maintainable at public expense so long as the highway authority take all reasonable steps for preventing—

(*a*) the oil or tar; and
(*b*) any liquid or matter resulting from the use of the oil or tar,

from polluting the water in any waterworks.

(4) A person who is guilty of an offence under this section shall be liable[1]—

(*a*) on summary conviction, to a fine not exceeding the **statutory maximum** and, in the case of a continuing offence, to a further fine not exceeding **£50 for every day during which the offence is continued** after conviction;
(*b*) on conviction on indictment, to imprisonment for a term not exceeding **two years** or to a **fine** or to **both**.

(5) In this section "waterworks" includes—

(*a*) any spring, well, adit, borehole, service reservoir or tank; and
(*b*) any main or other pipe or conduit of a water undertaker.

[Water Industry Act 1991, s 72.]

---

1. For procedure in respect of an offence triable either way, see the Magistrates' Courts Act 1980, ss 17A–21 in PART I: MAGISTRATES' COURTS, PROCEDURE, ante.

8–31641 73. Offences of contaminating, wasting and misusing water etc. (1) If any person who is the owner or occupier of any premises to which a supply of water is provided by a water undertaker intentionally or negligently causes or suffers any water fitting for which he is responsible to be or remain so out of order, so in need of repair or so constructed or adapted, or to be so used—

(*a*) that water in a water main or other pipe of a water undertaker, or in a pipe connected with such a water main or pipe, is or is likely to be contaminated by the return of any substance from those premises to that main or pipe;

(*b*) that water that has been supplied by the undertaker to those premises is or is likely to be contaminated before it is used; or

(*c*) that water so supplied is or is likely to be wasted or, having regard to the purposes for which it is supplied, misused or unduly consumed,

that person shall be guilty of an offence and liable, on summary conviction, to a fine not exceeding **level 3** on the standard scale.

(1A) In any proceedings under subsection (1) above it shall be a defence to prove—

(*a*) that the contamination or likely contamination, or the wastage, misuse or undue consumption, was caused (wholly or mainly) by the installation, alteration, repair or connection of the water fitting on or after 1st July 1999;

(*b*) that the works were carried out by or under the direction of an approved contractor within the meaning of the Water Supply (Water Fittings) Regulations 1999; and

(*c*) that the contractor certified to the person who commissioned those works that the water fitting complied with the requirements of those regulations.

(2) Any person who uses any water supplied to any premises by a water undertaker for a purpose other than one for which it is supplied to those premises shall, unless the other purpose is the extinguishment of a fire, be guilty of an offence and liable, on summary conviction, to a fine not exceeding **level 3** on the standard scale.

(3) Where a person has committed an offence under subsection (2) above, the water undertaker in question shall be entitled to recover from that person such amount as may be reasonable in respect of any water wasted, misused or improperly consumed in consequence of the commission of the offence.

(4) For the purposes of this section the owner or occupier of any premises shall be regarded as responsible for every water fitting on the premises which is not a water fitting which a person other than the owner or, as the case may be, occupier is liable to maintain.

[Water Industry Act 1991, s 73, as amended by SI 1999/1148.]

8–31642 **74.** *Regulations for preventing contamination, waste etc and with respect to water fittings.*

8–31643 **75. Power to prevent damage and to take steps to prevent contamination, waste etc.** In specified circumstances the water undertaker may in an emergency cut off the supply, and serve notice on the customer as soon as reasonably practicable thereafter specifying steps to be taken before supply is restored; failure by undertaker to serve notice punishable summarily by a fine not exceeding **level 3** on the standard scale.

[Water Industry Act 1991, s 75—summarised.]

8–31644 **76. Temporary hosepipe bans.** (1) If a water undertaker is of the opinion that a serious deficiency of water available for distribution by that undertaker exists or is threatened, that undertaker may, for such period as it thinks necessary, prohibit or restrict, as respects the whole or any part of its area, the use for the purpose of—

(*a*) watering private gardens; or

(*b*) washing private motor cars,

of any water supplied by that undertaker and drawn through a hosepipe or similar apparatus.

(2) A water undertaker imposing a prohibition or restriction under this section shall, before it comes into force, give public notice of it, and of the date on which it will come into force, in two or more newspapers circulating in the locality affected by the prohibition or restriction.

(3) Any person who, at a time when a prohibition or restriction under this section is in force, contravenes its provisions shall be guilty of an offence and liable, on summary conviction, to a fine not exceeding **level 3** on the standard scale.

(4) Where a prohibition or restriction is imposed by a water undertaker under this section, charges made by the undertaker for the use of a hosepipe or similar apparatus shall be subject to a reasonable reduction and, in the case of a charge paid in advance, the undertaker shall make any necessary repayment or adjustment.

(5) In this section "private motor car" means any mechanically propelled vehicle intended or adapted for use on roads other than—

(*a*) a public service vehicle, within the meaning of the Public Passenger Vehicles Act 1981; or

(*b*) a goods vehicle within the meaning of the Road Traffic Act 1988,

and includes any vehicle drawn by a private motor car.

[Water Industry Act 1991, s 76.]

Local authority functions

8–31645 **78–84.** *Local authorities are to keep themselves informed about the wholesomeness and sufficiency of water supplies and to give appropriate notice to water undertakers and exercise remedial powers. Similar duties and powers are given in relation to private supplies. Rights of entry are regulated by Sch 6.*

8–31646 **85. Local authority power to obtain information for the purposes of functions under Chapter III**[1]**.** (1) Subject to subsection (2) below, a local authority may serve on any person a notice requiring him to furnish that authority, within a period or at times specified in the notice and in a form and manner so specified, with such information as is reasonably required by that authority for the purpose of exercising or performing any power or duty conferred or imposed on that authority by or under any of sections 77 to 82 above.

(2) The Secretary of State may by regulations make provision for restricting the information which may be required under subsection (1) above and for determining the form in which the information is to be so required.

(3) A person who fails without reasonable excuse to comply with the requirements of a notice served on him under subsection (1) above shall be guilty of an offence and liable, on summary conviction, to a fine not exceeding **level 5** on the standard scale.

[Water Industry Act 1991, s 85.]

---

1. Chapter III of Pt III of this Act comprises ss 67–86.

8–31647 **86. Assessors for the enforcement of water quality.** (1) The Secretary of State may for the purposes of this section appoint persons to act on his behalf in relation to some or all of—

(*a*) the powers and duties conferred or imposed on him by or under sections 67 to 70 and 77 to 82 above; and

(*b*) such other powers and duties in relation to the quality and sufficiency of water supplied by a water undertaker as are conferred or imposed on him by or under any other enactments.*

(1A) Subject to subsection (1B) below, the Secretary of State shall designate one such person as the Chief Inspector of Drinking Water.

(1B) If the function of the Secretary of State under subsection (1) above is transferred to any extent to the Assembly—

(*a*) subject to paragraph (*b*) below, the Assembly may designate one such person appointed by it as the Chief Inspector of Drinking Water for Wales; but

(*b*) if the person designated by the Assembly is the same as the person designated by the Secretary of State as the Chief Inspector of Drinking Water, he shall be known as such in both capacities.

(2) An inspector appointed under this section shall—

(*a*) carry out such investigations as the Secretary of State may require him to carry out for the purpose of—

(i) ascertaining whether any duty or other requirement imposed on that undertaker by or under any of sections 68 to 70 or section 79 above is being, has been or is likely to be contravened; or*

(ii) advising the Secretary of State as to whether, and if so in what manner, any of the powers of the Secretary of State in relation to such a contravention, or any of the powers (including the powers to make regulations) which are conferred on him by or under any of sections 67 to 70 and 77 to 82 above should be exercised;

and

(*b*) make such reports to the Secretary of state with respect to any such investigation as the Secretary of State may require.

(3) Without prejudice to the powers conferred by subsection (4) below, it shall be the duty of a water undertaker—

(*a*) to give an inspector appointed under this section all such assistance; and

(*b*) to provide an inspector so appointed with all such information,

as that person may reasonably require for the purpose of carrying out any such investigation as is mentioned in subsection (2) above.*

(4) Any inspector appointed under this section who is designated in writing for the purpose by the Secretary of State may—

(*a*) enter any premises for the purpose of carrying out any such investigation as is mentioned in subsection (2) above;

(*b*) carry out such inspections, measurements and tests on premises entered by that inspector or of articles or records found on any such premises, and take away such samples of water or of any land or articles, as that inspector considers appropriate for the purpose of enabling him to carry out any such investigation; or

(*c*) at any reasonable time require any water undertaker to supply him with copies of, or of extracts from, the contents of any records kept for the purpose of complying with any duty or other requirement imposed on that undertaker by or under any of sections 68 to 70 or section 79 above.*

(5) Part II of Schedule 6 to this Act shall apply to the rights and powers conferred by subsection (4) above.

(6) Any water undertaker which fails to comply with the duty imposed on it by virtue of subsection (3) above shall be guilty of an offence and liable[1]—*

(*a*) on summary conviction, to a fine not exceeding £20,000;
(*b*) on conviction on indictment, to a fine.

(7) Proceedings by the Secretary of State for an offence under this section or in relation to the quality and sufficiency of water supplied using a water undertaker's supply system may be instituted and carried on in the name of the Chief Inspector of Drinking Water.

(8) Any such proceedings by the Assembly may be instituted and carried on in the name of the Chief Inspector of Drinking Water for Wales, if there is one (or, if subsection (1B)(*b*) above applies, in the name of the Chief Inspector of Drinking Water).

(9) In this section "inspector" means the Chief Inspector of Drinking Water or any other person appointed under subsection (1) above.

[Water Industry Act 1991, s 86 as amended by the Water Act 2003, s 57.]

***Amended by the Water Act 2003, Sch 8 from a date to be appointed.**

1. For procedure in respect of this offence which is triable either way, see the Magistrates' Courts Act 1980, ss 17A–21 in PART I: Magistrates' COURTS, PROCEDURE, ante

8–31648 93. Interpretation of Part III. (1) In this Part—

"connection notice" shall be construed in accordance with section 45(8) above;

"consumer", in relation to a supply of water provided by a water undertaker to any premises, means (except in Chapter IV) a person who is for the time being the person on whom liability to pay charges to the undertaker in respect of that supply of water would fall;

"food production purposes" means the manufacturing, processing, preserving or marketing purposes with respect to food or drink for which water supplied to food production premises may be used, and for the purposes of this definition "food production premises" means premises used for the purposes of a business of preparing food or drink for consumption otherwise than on the premises;

"necessary works" includes works carried out, in exercise of any power conferred by or under any enactment, by a person other than a water undertaker;

"private supply" means, subject to subsection (2) below, a supply of water provided otherwise than by a water undertaker (including a supply provided for the purposes of the bottling of water), and cognate expressions shall be construed accordingly;

"private supply notice" shall be construed in accordance with section 80(7) above;

"water fittings" includes pipes (other than water mains), taps, cocks, valves, ferrules, meters, cisterns, baths, water closets, soil pans and other similar apparatus used in connection with the supply and use of water;

"wholesome" and cognate expressions shall be construed subject to the provisions of any regulations made under section 67 above.

(2) For the purposes of any reference in this Part to a private supply, or to supplying water by means of a private supply, water shall be treated as supplied to any premises not only where it is supplied from outside those premises, but also where it is abstracted, for the purpose of being used or consumed on those premises, from a source which is situated on the premises themselves; and for the purposes of this subsection water shall be treated as used on any premises where it is bottled on those premises for use or consumption elsewhere.

(3) For the purposes of this Part a service pipe shall be treated as connected with a water main other than a trunk main even if the connection is an indirect connection made by virtue of a connection with another service pipe.

(4) The rights conferred by virtue of this Part as against the owner or occupier of any premises shall be without prejudice to any rights and obligations, as between themselves, of the owner and occupier of the premises.

[Water Industry Act 1991, s 93.]

PART IV[1]

SEWERAGE SERVICES

Communication of drains and private sewers with public sewers

8–31649 106. Right to communicate with public sewers. (1) Subject to the provisions of this section—

(*a*) the owner or occupier of any premises, or
(*b*) the owner of any private sewer which drains premises,

shall be entitled to have his drains or sewer communicate with the public sewer of any sewerage undertaker and thereby to discharge foul water and surface water from those premises or that private sewer.

(2) Subject to the provisions of Chapter III of this Part[2], nothing in subsection (1) above shall entitle any person—

(*a*) to discharge directly or indirectly into any public sewer—

(i) any liquid from a factory, other than domestic sewage or surface or storm water, or any liquid from a manufacturing process; or

(ii) any liquid or other matter the discharge of which into public sewers is prohibited by or under any enactment; or

(*b*) where separate public sewers are provided for foul water and for surface water, to discharge directly or indirectly—

(i) foul water into a sewer provided for surface water; or

(ii) except with the approval of the undertaker, surface water into a sewer provided for foul water; or

(*c*) to have his drains or sewer made to communicate directly with a storm-water overflow sewer.

(3) A person desirous of availing himself of his entitlement under this section shall give notice of his proposals to the sewerage undertaker in question.

(4) At any time within twenty-one days after a sewerage undertaker receives a notice under subsection (3) above, the undertaker may by notice to the person who gave the notice refuse to permit the communication to be made, if it appears to the undertaker that the mode of construction or condition of the drain or sewer is such that the making of the communication would be prejudicial to the undertaker's sewerage system.

(5) For the purpose of examining the mode of construction and condition of a drain or sewer to which a notice under subsection (3) above relates a sewerage undertaker may, if necessary, require it to be laid open for inspection.

(6) Any question arising under subsections (3) to (5) above between a sewerage undertaker and a person proposing to make a communication as to—

(*a*) the reasonableness of the undertaker's refusal to permit a communication to be made; or

(*b*) as to the reasonableness of any requirement under subsection (5) above,

may, on the application of that person, be determined by the Director under section 30A above.

(7) (*Repealed*).

(8) Where a person proposes under this section to make a communication between a drain or sewer and such a public sewer in Greater London as is used for the general reception of sewage from other public sewers and is not substantially used for the reception of sewage from private sewers and drains—

(*a*) the grounds on which a sewerage undertaker may refuse to permit the communication shall be such grounds as the undertaker thinks fit; and

(*b*) no application to the Director may be made under subsection (6) above in respect of any refusal under this subsection.

(9) In this section "factory" has the same meaning as in the Factories Act 1961.

[Water Industry Act 1991, s 106, as amended by the Competition and Service (Utilities) Act 1992, ss 35 and 43, and Sch 2.]

---

1. Part IV comprises ss 94–141.
2. Chapter II of Pt IV comprises ss 118–141.

8–31650 **107. Right of sewerage undertaker to undertake the making of communications with public sewers.** (1) Where a person gives to a sewerage undertaker notice under section 106 above of his proposal to have his drains or sewer made to communicate with a public sewer of that undertaker, the undertaker may—

(*a*) within fourteen days after the receipt of the notice; or

(*b*) if any question arising under the notice requires to be determined by the Director within fourteen days after the determination of that question,

give notice to that person that the undertaker intends itself to make the communication.

(2) If, after a notice has been given to any person under subsection (1) above, that person proceeds himself to make the communication, he shall be guilty of an offence and liable, on summary conviction, to a fine not exceeding **level 4** on the standard scale.

(3) Where a sewerage undertaker has given a notice under subsection (1) above—

(*a*) the undertaker shall have all such rights in respect of the making of the communication as the person desiring it to be made would have; but

(*b*) it shall not be obligatory on the undertaker to make the communication until either—

(i) there has been paid to the sewerage undertaker any such sum, not exceeding the undertaker's reasonable estimate of the cost of the work, as the undertaker may have required to be paid to it; or

(ii) there has been given to the undertaker such security for the payment of the cost of the work as it may reasonably have required.

(4) If any payment made to a sewerage undertaker under subsection (3) above exceeds the

expenses reasonably incurred by it in the carrying out of the work in question, the excess shall be repaid by the undertaker; and, if and so far as those expenses are not covered by such a payment, the undertaker may recover the expenses, or the balance of them, from the person for whom the work was done.

(4A) *Referral of any dispute between a sewerage* undertaker and any other person to the Director.

(5) Sections 291, 293 and 294 of the Public Health Act 1936 (which provide for the means of, and for limitations on, the recovery of expenses incurred by a local authority) shall apply in relation to the recovery by a sewerage undertaker of any sums under this section as they apply in relation to the recovery of expenses under that Act by a local authority.

(6) For the purposes of this section, the making of the communication between a drain or private sewer and a public sewer includes all such work as involves the breaking open of a street.

[Water Industry Act 1991, s 107, as amended by the Competition and Service (Utilities) Act 1992, s 35.]

8–31651 108. Communication works by person entitled to communication. (1) Where a sewerage undertaker does not under section 107 above elect itself to make a communication to which a person is entitled under section 106 above, the person making it shall—

(*a*) before commencing the work, give reasonable notice to any person directed by the undertaker to superintend the carrying out of the work; and

(*b*) afford any such person all reasonable facilities for superintending the carrying out of the work.

(2) For the purpose—

(*a*) of exercising his rights under section 106 above; or

(*b*) of examining, repairing or renewing any drain or private sewer draining his premises into a public sewer,

the owner or occupier of any premises shall be entitled to exercise the same powers as, for the purpose of carrying out its functions, are conferred on a sewerage undertaker by sections 158 and 161(1) below.

(3) The provisions of Part VI of this Act shall apply, with the necessary modifications, in relation to the power conferred by subsection (2) above as they apply in relation to the power conferred by sections 158 and 161(1) below.

[Water Industry Act 1991, s 108.]

8–31652 109. Unlawful communications. (1) Any person who causes a drain or sewer to communicate with a public sewer—

(*a*) in contravention of any of the provisions of section 106 or 108 above; or

(*b*) before the end of the period mentioned in subsection (4) of that section 106,

shall be guilty of an offence and liable, on summary conviction, to a fine not exceeding **level 4** on the standard scale.

(2) Whether proceedings have or have not been taken by a sewerage undertaker in respect of an offence under this section, such an undertaker may—

(*a*) close any communication made in contravention of any of the provisions of section 106 or 108 above; and

(*b*) recover from the offender any expenses reasonably incurred by the undertaker in so doing.

(3) Sections 291, 293 and 294 of the Public Health Act 1936 (which provide for the means of, and for limitations on, the recovery of expenses incurred by a local authority) shall apply in relation to the recovery by a sewerage undertaker of any sums under this section as they apply in relation to the recovery of expenses under that Act by a local authority.

[Water Industry Act 1991, s 109.]

Provisions protecting sewerage system

8–31653 111. Restrictions on use of public sewers. (1) Subject to the provisions of Chapter III of this Part, no person shall throw, empty or turn, or suffer or permit to be thrown or emptied or to pass, into any public sewer, or into any drain or sewer communicating with a public sewer—

(*a*) any matter likely to injure the sewer or drain, to interfere with the free flow of its contents or to affect prejudicially the treatment and disposal of its contents; or

(*b*) any such chemical refuse or waste steam, or any such liquid of a temperature higher than one hundred and ten degrees Fahrenheit, as by virtue of subsection (2) below is a prohibited substance; or

(*c*) any petroleum spirit or carbide of calcium.

(2) For the purposes of subsection (1) above, chemical refuse, waste steam or a liquid of a temperature higher than that mentioned in that subsection is a prohibited substance if (either alone or in combination with the contents of the sewer or drain in question) it is or, in the case of the liquid, is when so heated—

(*a*) dangerous;

(*b*) the cause of a nuisance; or

(*c*) injurious, or likely to cause injury, to health.

(3) A person who contravenes any of the provisions of this section shall be guilty of an offence and liable[1]—

(*a*) on summary conviction, to a fine not exceeding the **statutory maximum** and to a further fine not exceeding **£50 for each day on which the offence continues** after conviction;

(*b*) on conviction on indictment, to imprisonment for a term not exceeding **two years** or to a **fine** or to **both**.

(4) For the purposes of so much of subsection (3) above as makes provision for the imposition of a daily penalty—

(*a*) the court by which a person is convicted of the original offence may fix a reasonable date from the date of conviction for compliance by the defendant with any directions given by the court; and

(*b*) where a court has fixed such a period, the daily penalty shall not be imposed in respect of any day before the end of that period.

(5) In this section the expression "petroleum spirit" means any such—

(*a*) crude petroleum;

(*b*) oil made from petroleum or from coal, shale, peat or other bituminous substances; or

(*c*) product of petroleum or mixture containing petroleum,

as, when tested in the manner prescribed by or under the Petroleum (Consolidation) Act 1928, gives off an inflammable vapour at a temperature of less than seventy-three degrees Fahrenheit.

[Water Industry Act 1991, s 111.]

1. For procedure in respect of an offence triable either way, see the Magistrates' Courts Act 1980, ss 17A–21 in PART I: MAGISTRATES' COURTS, PROCEDURE, ante.

Interpretation of Chapter II[1]

8–31655 **117. Interpretation of Chapter II.** (1) In this Chapter[1], except in so far as the context otherwise requires—

"dock undertakers" means persons authorised by any enactment, or by any order, rule or regulation made under any enactment, to construct, work or carry on any dock, harbour, canal or inland navigation;

"domestic sewerage purposes", in relation to any premises, means any one or more of the following purposes, that is to say—

(*a*) the removal, from buildings on the premises and from land occupied with and appurtenant to the buildings, of the contents of lavatories;

(*b*) the removal, from such buildings and from such land, of water which has been used for cooking or washing; and

(*c*) the removal, from such buildings and such land, of surface water;

but does not, by virtue of paragraph (*b*) of this definition, include the removal of any water used for the business of a laundry or for a business of preparing food or drink for consumption otherwise than on the premises.

(2) References in this Chapter to the construction of a sewer or of any sewage disposal works include references to the extension of any existing sewer or works.

(3) In this Chapter "local authority", in relation to the Inner Temple and the Middle Temple, includes, respectively, the Sub-Treasurer of the Inner Temple and the Under-Treasurer of the Middle Temple.

(4) Every application made or consent given under this Chapter shall be made or given in writing.

(5) Nothing in sections 102 to 109 above or in sections 111 to 116 above shall be construed as authorising a sewerage undertaker to construct or use any public or other sewer, or any drain or outfall—

(*a*) in contravention of any applicable provision of the Water Resources Act 1991; or

(*b*) for the purpose of conveying foul water into any natural or artificial stream, watercourse, canal, pond or lake, without the water having been so treated as not to affect prejudicially the purity and quality of the water in the stream, watercourse, canal, pond or lake.

(6) A sewerage undertaker shall so carry out its functions under sections 102 to 105, 112, 115 and 116 above as not to create a nuisance.

[Water Industry Act 1991, s 117.]

1. Chapter II comprises ss 98–117.

CHAPTER III[1]
TRADE EFFLUENT

Consent for discharge of trade effluent into public sewer

8–31656 **118. Consent required for discharge of trade effluent into public sewer.** (1) Subject to the following provisions of this Chapter[1], the occupier of any trade premises in the area of a sewerage undertaker may discharge any trade effluent proceeding from those premises into the undertaker's public sewers if he does so with the undertaker's consent.

(2) Nothing in this Chapter shall authorise the discharge of any effluent into a public sewer otherwise than by means of a drain or sewer.

(3) The following, that is to say—

(*a*) the restrictions imposed by paragraphs (*a*) and (*b*) of section 106(2) above; and

(*b*) section 111 above so far as it relates to anything falling within paragraph (*a*) or (*b*) of subsection (1) of that section,

shall not apply to any discharge of trade effluent which is lawfully made by virtue of this Chapter.

(4) Accordingly, subsections (3) to (8) of section 106 above and sections 108 and 109 above shall have effect in relation to communication with a sewer for the purpose of making any discharge which is lawfully made by virtue of this Chapter as they have effect in relation to communication with a sewer for the purpose of making discharges which are authorised by subsection (1) of section 106 above.

(5) If, in the case of any trade premises, any trade effluent is discharged without such consent or other authorisation as is necessary for the purposes of this Chapter, the occupier of the premises shall be guilty of an offence and liable[2]—

(*a*) on summary conviction, to a fine not exceeding the **statutory maximum**; and

(*b*) on conviction on indictment, to a **fine**.

[Water Industry Act 1991, s 118.]

1. Chapter III of Pt IV comprises ss 118–141.
2. For procedure in respect of an offence triable either way, see the Magistrates' Courts Act 1980, ss 17A–21 in PART I: MAGISTRATES' COURTS, ante.

8–31657 **119. Application for consent.** (1) An application to a sewerage undertaker for a consent to discharge trade effluent from any trade premises into a public sewer of that undertaker shall be by notice served on the undertaker by the owner of occupier of the premises.

(2) An application under this section with respect to a proposed discharge of any such effluent shall state—

(*a*) the nature or composition of the trade effluent;

(*b*) the maximum quantity of the trade effluent which it is proposed to discharge on any one day; and

(*c*) the highest rate at which it is proposed to discharge the trade effluent.

[Water Industry Act 1991, s 119.]

8–31658 **120. Applications for the discharge of special category effluent.** (1) Subject to subsection (3) below, where a notice containing an application under section 119 above is served on a sewerage undertaker with respect to discharges of any special category effluent, it shall be the duty of the undertaker to refer to the Environment Agency the questions—

(*a*) whether the discharges to which the notice relates should be prohibited; and

(*b*) whether, if they are not prohibited, any requirements should be imposed as to the conditions on which they are made.

(2) Subject to subsection (3) below, a reference which is required to be made by a sewerage undertaker by virtue of subsection (1) above shall be made before the end of the period of two months beginning with the day after the notice containing the application is served on the undertaker.

(3) There shall be no obligation on a sewerage undertaker to make a reference under this section in respect of any application if, before the end of the period mentioned in subsection (2) above, there is a refusal by the undertaker to give any consent on the application.

(4) It shall be the duty of a sewerage undertaker where it has made a reference under this section not to give any consent, or enter into any agreement, with respect to the discharges to which the reference relates at any time before the Environment Agency serves notice on the undertaker of his determination on the reference.

(5) Every reference under this section shall be made in writing and shall be accompanied by a copy of the notice containing the application in respect of which it is made.

(6) It shall be the duty of a sewerage undertaker, on making a reference under this section, to serve a copy of the reference on the owner or the occupier of the trade premises in question, according to whether the discharges to which the reference relates are to be by the owner or by the occupier.

(7)–(8) (*Repealed*).

(9) If a sewerage undertaker fails, within the period provided by subsection (2) above, to refer to the Environment Agency any question which he is required by subsection (1) above to refer to the Agency, the undertaker shall be guilty of an offence and liable[1]—

(*a*) on summary conviction, to a fine not exceeding the **statutory maximum;**

(*b*) on conviction on indictment, to a **fine**.

(10) If the Environment Agency becomes aware of any such failure as is mentioned in subsection (9) above, the Agency may—

(*a*) if a consent under this Chapter to make discharges of any special category effluent has been granted on the application in question, exercise its powers to review under section 127 or 131 below, notwithstanding anything in subsection (2) of the section in question; or

(*b*) in any other case, proceed as if the reference required by this section had been made.

[Water Industry Act 1991, s 120, as amended by the Environment Act 1995, Sch 22.]

---

1. For procedure in respect of this offence which is triable either way, see the Magistrates' Courts Act 1980, ss 17A–21, in PART I: MAGISTRATES' COURTS, PROCEDURE ante.

8–31659 **121. Conditions of consent.** (1) The power of a sewerage undertaker, on an application under section 119 above, to give a consent with respect to the discharge of any trade effluent shall be a power to give a consent either unconditionally or subject to such conditions as the sewerage undertaker thinks fit to impose with respect to—

(*a*) the sewer or sewers into which the trade effluent may be discharged;

(*b*) the nature or composition of the trade effluent which may be discharged;

(*c*) the maximum quantity of trade effluent which may be discharged on any one day, either generally or into a particular sewer; and

(*d*) the highest rate at which trade effluent may be discharged, either generally or into a particular sewer.

(2) Conditions with respect to all or any of the following matters may also be attached under this section to a consent to the discharge of trade effluent from any trade premises—

(*a*) the period or periods of the day during which the trade effluent may be discharged from the trade premises into the sewer;

(*b*) the exclusion from the trade effluent of all condensing water;

(*c*) the elimination or diminution, in cases falling within subsection (3) below, of any specified constituent of the trade effluent, before it enters the sewer;

(*d*) the temperature of the trade effluent at the time when it is discharged into the sewer, and its acidity or alkalinity at that time;

(*e*) the payment by the occupier of the trade premises to the undertaker of charges for the reception of the trade effluent into the sewer and for the disposal of the effluent;

(*f*) the provision and maintenance of such an inspection chamber or manhole as will enable a person readily to take samples, at any time, of what is passing into the sewer from the trade premises;

(*g*) the provision, testing and maintenance of such meters as may be required to measure the volume and rate of discharge of any trade effluent being discharged from the trade premises into the sewer;

(*h*) the provision, testing and maintenance of apparatus for determining the nature and composition of any trade effluent being discharged from the premises into the sewer;

(*i*) the keeping of records of the volume, rate of discharge, nature and composition of any trade effluent being discharged and, in particular, the keeping of records of readings of meters and other recording apparatus provided in compliance with any other condition attached to the consent; and

(*j*) the making of returns and giving of other information to the sewerage undertaker concerning the volume, rate of discharge, nature and composition of any trade effluent discharged from the trade premises into the sewer.

(3) A case falls within this subsection where the sewerage undertaker is satisfied that the constituent in question, either alone or in combination with any matter with which it is likely to come into contact while passing through any sewers—

(*a*) would injure or obstruct those sewers, or make the treatment or disposal of the sewage from those sewers specially difficult or expensive; or

(*b*) in the case of trade effluent which is to be or is discharged—

(i) into a sewer having an outfall in any harbour or tidal water; or

(ii) into a sewer which connects directly or indirectly with a sewer or sewage disposal works having such an outfall,

would cause or tend to cause injury or obstruction to the navigation on, or the use of, the harbour or tidal water.

(4) In the exercise of the power conferred by virtue of subsection (2)(*e*) above, regard shall be had—

(*a*) to the nature and composition and to the volume and rate of discharge of the trade effluent discharged;

(*b*) to any additional expense incurred or likely to be incurred by a sewerage undertaker in connection with the reception or disposal of the trade effluent; and (*c*) to any revenue likely to be derived by the undertaker from the trade effluent.

(5) If, in the case of any trade premises, a condition imposed under this section is contravened, the occupier of the premises shall be guilty of an offence and liable[1]—

(*a*) on summary conviction, to a fine not exceeding the **statutory maximum**; and
(*b*) on conviction on indictment, to a **fine**.

(6) In this section "harbour" and "tidal water" have the same meanings as in the Merchant Shipping Act 1995.

(7) This section has effect subject to the provisions of sections 133 and 135(3) below[2].

[Water Industry Act 1991, s 121, as amended by the Merchant Shipping Act 1995, Sch 13.]

1. For procedure in respect of an offence triable either way, see the Magistrates' Courts Act 1980, ss 17A–21 in PART I: MAGISTRATES' COURTS, PROCEDURE, ante.

2. Sections 133 and 135(3) deal respectively with the duty of an undertaker to secure compliance with conditions under this section or s 132, and to the fixing of charges only under a charges scheme.

8–31660 **132. Powers and procedure on references and reviews.** (1) This section applies to—

(*a*) any reference to the Environment Agency under section 120, 123 or 130 above;
(*b*) any review by the Environment Agency under section 127 or 131 above.

(2) On a reference or review to which this section applies, it shall be the duty of the Environment Agency, before determining the questions which are the subject-matter of the reference or review—

(*a*) to give an opportunity of making representations or objections to the Environment Agency—

(i) to the sewerage undertaker in question; and
(ii) to the following person, that is to say, the owner or the occupier of the trade premises in question, according to whether it is the owner or the occupier of those premises who is proposing to be, or is, the person making the discharges or, as the case may be, a party to the agreement;

and

(*b*) to consider any representations or objections which are duly made to the Agency with respect to those questions by a person to whom the Agency is required to give such an opportunity and which are not withdrawn.

(3) On determining any question on a reference or review to which this section applies, the Environment Agency shall serve notice on the sewerage undertaker in question and on the person specified in subsection (2)(*a*)(ii) above.

(4) A notice under this section shall state, according to what has been determined—

(*a*) that the discharges or operations to which, or to the proposals for which, the reference or review relates, or such of them as are specified in the notice, are to be prohibited; or
(*b*) that those discharges or operations, or such of them as are so specified, are to be prohibited except in so far as they are made or carried out in accordance with conditions which consist in or include conditions so specified; or
(*c*) that the Environment Agency has no objection to those discharges or operations and does not intend to impose any requirements as to the conditions on which they are made or carried out.

(5) Without prejudice to section 133 below, a notice under this section, in addition to containing such provision as is specified in sub-paragraph (4) above, may do one or both of the following, that is to say—

(*a*) vary or revoke the provisions of a previous notice with respect to the discharges or operations in question; and
(*b*) for the purpose of giving effect to any prohibition or other requirement contained in this notice, vary or revoke any consent under this Chapter or any agreement under section 129 above.

(6) Nothing in subsection (1) or (2) of section 121 above shall be construed as restricting the power of the Environment Agency, by virtue of subsection (4)(*b*) above, to specify such conditions as the Agency considers appropriate in a notice under this section.

(7) (*Repealed*).

(8) The Secretary of State shall send a copy of every notice served under this section to the Director.

[Water Industry Act 1991, s 132, as amended by the Environment Act 1995, Schs 22 and 24.]

8–31661 **133. Effect of determination on reference or review.** (1) Where a notice under section 132 above has been served on a sewerage undertaker, it shall be the duty—

(*a*) of the undertaker; and
(*b*) in relation to that undertaker, of the Director,

so to exercise the powers to which this section applies as to secure compliance with the provisions of the notice.

(2) This paragraph applies to the following powers, that is to say—

(*a*) in relation to a sewerage undertaker, its power to give a consent under this Chapter, any of its powers under section 121 or 124 above and any power to enter into or vary an agreement under section 129 above; and

(*b*) in relation to the Director, any of his powers under this Chapter.

(3) Nothing in subsection (1) or (2) of section 121 above shall be construed as restricting the power of a sewerage undertaker, for the purpose of complying with this section, to impose any condition specified in a notice under section 132 above.

(4) (*Repealed*).

(5) A sewerage undertaker which fails to perform its duty under subsection (1) above shall be guilty of an offence and liable[1]—

(*a*) on summary conviction, to a fine not exceeding the **statutory maximum;**

(*b*) on conviction on indictment, to a **fine**.

(6) The Environment Agency may, for the purpose of securing compliance with the provisions of a notice under section 132 above, by serving notice on the sewerage undertaker in question and on the person specified in section 132(2)(*a*)(ii) above, vary or revoke—

(*a*) any consent given under this Chapter to make discharges of any special category effluent, or

(*b*) any agreement under section 129 above.

[Water Industry Act 1991, s 133, as amended by the Environment Act 1995, Sch 22.]

1. For procedure in respect of an offence which is triable either way, see the Magistrates' Courts Act 1980, ss 17A–21, in PART I: MAGISTRATES' COURTS, PROCEDURE, ante.

Supplemental provisions of Chapter III

8-31662 135A. Power of the Environment Agency to acquire information for the purpose of its functions in relation to special category effluent. (1) For the purpose of the discharge of its functions under this Chapter, the Environment Agency may, by notice in writing served on any person, require that person to furnish such information specified in the notice as that Agency reasonably considers it needs, in such form and within such period following service of the notice, or at such time, as is so specified.

(2) A person who—

(*a*) fails, without reasonable excuse, to comply with a requirement imposed under subsection (1) above, or

(*b*) in furnishing any information in compliance with such a requirement, makes any statement which he knows to be false or misleading in a material particular, or recklessly makes a statement which is false or misleading in a material particular,

shall be guilty of an offence.

(3) A person guilty of an offence under subsection (2) above shall be liable[1]—

(*a*) on summary conviction, to a fine not exceeding the **statutory maximum;**

(*b*) on conviction on indictment, to a **fine** or to imprisonment for a term not exceeding **two years**, or to **both**.

[Water Industry Act 1991, s 135A, as inserted by the Environment Act 1995, Sch 22.]

1. For procedure in respect of an offence which is triable either way, see the Magistrates' Courts Act 1980, ss 17A–21, in PART I: MAGISTRATES' COURTS, PROCEDURE, ante.

8-31663 138. Meaning of "special category effluent". (1) Subject to subsections (1A) and (2) below, trade effluent shall be special category effluent for the purposes of this Chapter if—

(*a*) such substances as may be prescribed[1] under this Act are present in the effluent or are present in the effluent in prescribed concentrations; or

(*b*) the effluent derives from any such process as may be so prescribed or from a process involving the use of prescribed substances or the use of such substances in quantities which exceed the prescribed amounts.

(1A) If trade effluent is produced, or to be produced, by operating any installation or plant or othetwise carrying on any activity, the operation or carrying on of which requires a permit, that effluent shall not be special category effluent for the purposes of this Chapter as from the determination date relating to the installation, plant or activity in question.

(1B) In subsection (1A)—

(a) "determination date", in relation to an installation, plant or activity, means—

(i) in the case of an installation, plant or activity in relation to which a permit is granted, the date on which it is granted, whether in pursuance of the application, or on an appeal, of a direction to grant it;

(ii) in the case of an installation, plant or activity in relation to which the grant of a permit is refused, the date of refusal or, on appeal, of the affirmation of the refusal,

and in this paragraph the references to an appeal are references to an appeal under regulations under section 2 of the Pollution Prevention and Control Act 1999;

(b) "permit" means a permit granted, under regulations under that section, by an authority exercising functions under the regulations that are exercisable for the purpose of preventing or reducing emissions into the air, water and land.

(2) Trade effluent shall not be special category effluent for the purposes of this Chapter if it is produced, or to be produced, in any process which is a prescribed process designated for central control as from the date which is the determination date for that process.

(3) In subsection (2) above "determination date", in relation to a prescribed process, means—

(*a*) in the case of a process for which authorisation is granted, the date on which the enforcing authority grants it, whether in pursuance of the application or, on an appeal, of a direction to grant it;

(*b*) in the case of a process for which authorisation is refused, the date of refusal or, on appeal, of the affirmation of the refusal.

(4) In subsection (2) and (3) above—

(*a*) "authorisation", "enforcing authority" and "prescribed process" have the meanings given by section 1 of the Environmental Protection Act 1990; and

(*b*) the references to designation for central control and to an appeal are references, respectively, to designation under section 4 of that Act and to an appeal under section 15 of that Act.*

(5) Without prejudice to the power in subsection (3) of section 139 below, nothing in this Chapter shall enable regulations under this section to prescribe as special category effluent any liquid or matter which is not trade effluent but falls to be treated as such for the purposes of this Chapter by virtue of an order under that section.

[Water Industry Act 1991, s 138, as amended by SI 2000/1973.]

***Sub-sections 138(2)–(4) are repealed by the Pollution Prevention and Control Act 1999, Sch 3, when in force.**

1. See the Trade Effluent (Prescribed Processes and Substances) Regulations 1992, SI 1992/339.

8–31664 139. *Power to apply Chapter III to other effluents.*

Interpretation of Chapter III

8–31665 141. Interpretation of Chapter III. (1) In this Chapter, except in so far as the context otherwise requires—

"special category effluent" has the meaning given by section 138 above;

"trade effluent"—

(*a*) means any liquid, either with or without particles of matter in suspension in the liquid, which is wholly or partly produced in the course of any trade or industry carried on at trade premises; and

(*b*) in relation to any trade premises, means any such liquid which is so produced in the course of any trade or industry carried on at those premises,

but does not include domestic sewage;

"trade premises" means, subject to subsection (2) below, any premises used or intended to be used for carrying on any trade or industry.

(2) For the purposes of this Chapter any land or premises used or intended for use (in whole or in part and whether or not for profit)—

(*a*) for agricultural or horticultural purposes or for the purposes of fish farming; or

(*b*) for scientific research or experiment,

shall be deemed to be premises used for carrying on a trade or industry; and the references to a trade or industry in the definition of "trade effluent" in subsection (1) above shall include references to agriculture, horticulture, fish farming and scientific research or experiment.

(3) Every application or consent made or given under this Chapter shall be made or given in writing.

(4) Nothing in this Chapter shall affect any right with respect to water in a river stream or watercourse, or authorise any infringement of such a right, except in so far as any such right would dispense with the requirements of this Chapter so far as they have effect by virtue of any regulations under section 138 above.

[Water Industry Act 1991, s 141.]

PART V[1]
FINANCIAL PROVISIONS

8–31666 *The powers of undertakers include the power to fix charges for services including, in the case of a sewerage undertaker, charges for its trade effluent functions, and to demand and recover charges* (s 142). *Occupiers of premises are liable for charges for water supply and sewerage services; provision is made for notice on ceasing to occupy premises* (s 144). Charging by reference to volume (s 144A–144B). *Provision is made for limiting connection charges* (s 146) *and emergency use of water* (s 147), *as well as restriction on charging for metering works* (s 148, amended by the Competition and Service (Utilities) Act 1992, s 53). *Regulations may be made relating to charging by volume* (s 149, amended by the Competition and Service (Utilities) Act 1992, s 53). *Billing disputes: Secretary of State may by regulations make provision for billing disputes to be referred to the Director for determination* (s 150A).

1. Part V comprises ss 142–154. The Water Industry (Charges) (Vulnerable Groups) Regulations 1999, SI 1999/3441 amended by SI 2003/552 and SI 2005/59 and 2035 have been made which define vulnerable groups, ie persons who are in receipt of, or reside with a person in receipt of, certain benefits or tax credits, who are to be given assistance with water and sewerage charges by water and sewerage undertakers.

PART VI[1]
UNDERTAKERS' POWERS AND WORKS

8–31667 157. *Byelaws with respect of undertakers' waterways and land.*

1. Part VI comprises ss 155–192.

Powers to discharge water

8–31668 165. Discharges for works purposes. (1) Subject to the following provisions of this section and to section 166 below, where any water undertaker—

(*a*) is exercising or about to exercise any power conferred by section 158, 159, 161 or 163[1] above (other than the power conferred by section 161(3) above); or

(*b*) is carrying out, or is about to carry out, the construction, alteration, repair, cleaning, or examination of any reservoir, well, borehole, or other work belonging to or used by that undertaker for the purposes of, or in connection with, the carrying out of any of its functions,

the undertaker may cause the water in any relevant pipe or in any such reservoir, well, borehole or other work to be discharged into any available watercourse.

(2) Nothing in this section shall authorise any discharge which—

(*a*) damages or injuriously affects the works or property of any railway undertakers or navigation authority; or

(*b*) floods or damages any highway.

(3) If any water undertaker fails to take all necessary steps to secure that any water discharged by it under this section is as free as may be reasonably practicable from—

(*a*) mud and silt;

(*b*) solid, polluting, offensive or injurious substances; and

(*c*) any substances prejudicial to fish or spawn, or to spawning beds or food of fish,

the undertaker shall be guilty of an offence and liable, on summary conviction, to a fine not exceeding **level 3** on the standard scale.

(4) In this section "relevant pipe" means any water main (including a trunk main), resource main, discharge pipe or service pipe.

[Water Industry Act 1991, s 165.]

1. Section 158 provides powers to lay pipes in streets, s 159 power to lay pipes in other land, s 161 power to deal with foul water and pollution (s 161(3) deals with the construction and maintenance of drains etc to deal with foul water or of otherwise preventing the pollution of waters, reservoir or underground strata from which the NRA or a water undertaker will take water) and s 163 is the power to fit stopcocks.

8–31669 166. Consents for certain discharges under section 165. No discharge through any pipe exceeding 229 mm shall be made except with consent of the Environment Agency and any relevant navigation authority; water undertaker contravening is liable on summary conviction to fine not exceeding **level 3** on the standard scale.

[Water Industry Act 1991, s 166 amended by the Environment Act 1995, Sch 22—summarised.]

Entry to land etc by water undertakers

8–31670 168–172. *Entry to land etc*[1].

1. Part II of Sch 6 applies for the purposes of ss 168, 169, 172 and Pt I thereof for ss 170 and 171.

8–31671 **173. Impersonation of persons entitled to entry.** (1) A person who, without having been designated or authorised for the purpose by a relevant undertaker, purports to be entitled to enter any premises or vessel in exercise of a power exercisable in pursuance of any such designation or authorisation shall be guilty of an offence and liable, on summary conviction, to a fine not exceeding **level 4** on the standard scale.

(2) For the purposes of this section it shall be immaterial, where a person purports to be entitled to enter any premises or vessel, that the power which that person purports to be entitled to exercise does not exist or would not be exercisable even if that person had been designated or authorised by a relevant undertaker.

[Water Industry Act 1991, s 173.]

CHAPTER II

PROTECTION OF UNDERTAKERS' WORKS, APPARATUS ETC

Protection of apparatus in general

8–31672 **174. Offences of interference with works etc.** (1) Subject to subsection (2) below, if any person without the consent of the water undertaker—

(*a*) intentionally or recklessly interferes with any resource main, water main or other pipe vested in any water undertaker or with any structure, installation or apparatus belonging to any water undertaker; or

(*b*) by any act or omission negligently interferes with any such main or other pipe or with any such structure, installation or apparatus so as to damage it or so as to have an effect on its use or operation,

that person shall be guilty of an offence and liable, on summary conviction, to a fine not exceeding **level 3** on the standard scale.

(2) A person shall not be guilty of an offence under subsection (1) above—

(*a*) by reason of anything done in an emergency to prevent loss or damage to persons or property; or

(*b*) by reason of his opening or closing the stopcock fitted to a service pipe by means of which water is supplied to any premises by a water undertaker if—

(i) he has obtained the consent of every consumer whose supply is affected by the opening or closing of that stopcock or, as the case may be, of every other consumer whose supply is so affected; and

(ii) in the case of opening a stopcock, the stopcock was closed otherwise than by the undertaker.

(3) Any person who, without the consent of the water undertaker—

(*a*) attaches any pipe or apparatus—

(i) to any resource main, water main or other pipe vested in a water undertaker; or

(ii) to any service pipe which does not belong to such an undertaker but which is a pipe by means of which water is supplied by such an undertaker to any premises;

(*b*) makes any alteration in a service pipe by means of which water is so supplied, or in any apparatus attached to any such pipe; or

(*c*) subject to subsection (4) below, uses any pipe or apparatus which has been attached or altered in contravention of this section,

shall be guilty of an offence and liable, on summary conviction, to a fine not exceeding **level 3** on the standard scale.

(4) In proceedings against any person for an offence by virtue of paragraph (*c*) of subsection (3) above it shall be a defence for that person to show that he did not know, and had no grounds for suspecting, that the pipe or apparatus in question had been attached or altered as mentioned in that subsection.

(5) If any person wilfully or negligently injures or suffers to be injured any water fitting belonging to a water undertaker, he shall be guilty of an offence and liable, on summary conviction, to a fine not exceeding **level 1** on the standard scale.

(6) An offence under subsection (1) or (3) above shall constitute a breach of a duty owed to the water undertaker in question; and any such breach of duty which causes the undertaker to sustain loss or damage shall be actionable at the suit of the undertaker.

(7) The amount recoverable by virtue of subsection (6) above from a person who has committed an offence under subsection (3) above shall include such amount as may be reasonable in respect of any water wasted, misused or improperly consumed in consequence of the commission of the offence.

(8) A water undertaker may—

(*a*) do all such work as is necessary for repairing any injury done in contravention of subsection (5) above; and

(*b*) recover the expenses reasonably incurred by the undertaker in doing so from the offender summarily as a civil debt[1].

(9) In this section "consumer" and "water fitting" have the same meanings as in Part III of this Act[2]; and in subsection (1) above the references to apparatus belonging to a water undertaker do not include references to any meter which belongs to such an undertaker and is used by it for the purpose of determining the amount of any charges which have been fixed by the undertaker by reference to volume.
[Water Industry Act 1991, s 174.]

1. For enforcement of a civil debt, see the Magistrates' Courts Act 1980, s 96, in PART I: MAGISTRATES' COURTS, PROCEDURE, ante.
2. See s 93, ante.

Protection of meters

8–31673 **175. Offence of tampering with meter.** (1) If any person—

(*a*) so interferes with a meter used by any relevant undertaker in determining the amount of any charges fixed in relation to any premises as intentionally or recklessly to prevent the meter from showing, or from accurately showing, the volume of water supplied to, or of effluent discharged from, those premises; or

(*b*) carries out any works which he knows are likely to affect the operation of such a meter or which require the disconnection of such a meter,

he shall be guilty of an offence and liable, on summary conviction, to a fine not exceeding **level 3** on the standard scale.

(2) A person shall not be guilty of an offence under this section in respect of anything done by him with the consent under section 176 below of the undertaker which uses the meter.
[Water Industry Act 1991, s 175.]

8–31673A **176. Consent for the purposes of section 175.** (1) Where an application is made to any relevant undertaker for a consent for the purposes of section 175 above, the undertaker—

(*a*) shall give notice of its decision with respect to the application as soon as reasonably practicable after receiving it; and

(*b*) subject to subsection (2) below, may make it a condition of giving any consent that the undertaker itself should carry out so much of any works to which the application relates as is specified in the notice of its decision.

(2) On such an application a relevant undertaker shall not refuse its consent, or impose any such condition as is mentioned in subsection (1)(*b*) above, unless it is reasonable to do so.

(3) Where any relevant undertaker has given a notice to any person imposing any such condition as is mentioned in subsection (1)(*b*) above, the undertaker—

(*a*) shall carry out those works as soon as reasonably practicable after giving the notice; and
(*b*) may recover from that person any expenses reasonably incurred by it in doing so.

(4) Any dispute between a relevant undertaker and any other person (including another such undertaker)—

(*a*) as to whether the undertaker or that other person should bear any expenses under subsection (3) above; or

(*b*) as to the amount of any expenses to be borne by any person under that subsection,

shall be referred to the arbitration of a single arbitrator appointed by agreement between the undertaker and that person or, in default of agreement, by the Director.

(5) Subsection (3) above shall not apply where the person who was given the notice notifies the undertaker that the carrying out of the works to which the condition relates is no longer required.
[Water Industry Act 1991, s 176.]

8–31673B **177. Financial obligations with respect to any interference with a meter.** (1) A relevant undertaker which carries out any works made necessary by the commission of an offence under section 175 above shall be entitled to recover any expenses reasonably incurred in carrying out those works from the person who committed the offence.

(2) Any person who sustains any loss or damage in consequence of any failure by any relevant undertaker—

(*a*) to comply with any obligation imposed on it by section 176 above; or

(*b*) to exercise reasonable care in the performance of the duty imposed by subsection (3)(*a*) of that section,

shall be entitled to recover compensation from the undertaker.

(3) Any dispute between a relevant undertaker and any other person (including another such undertaker)—

(*a*) as to whether the undertaker or that other person should bear any expenses under this section;
(*b*) as to whether the undertaker should pay any compensation under this section; or

(*c*) as to the amount of any expenses to be borne by any person under this section or as to the amount of any such compensation,

shall be referred to the arbitration of a single arbitrator appointed by agreement between the undertaker and that person or, in default of agreement, by the Director.
[Water Industry Act 1991, s 177.]

Obstruction of sewerage works etc

8–31674 **178. Obstruction of sewerage works etc.** (1) A person who wilfully obstructs any person acting in the execution of any of the relevant sewerage provisions shall be guilty of an offence and liable, on summary conviction, to a fine not exceeding **level 1** on the standard scale.

(2) If on a complaint made by the owner of any premises, it appears to a magistrates' court that the occupier of those premises is preventing the owner of those premises from carrying out any work which he is required to carry out by or under any of the relevant sewerage provisions, the court may order the occupier to permit the carrying out of the work.

(3) Sections 300 to 302 of the Public Health Act 1936 (which relate to the determination of questions by courts of summary jurisdiction and to appeals against such determinations) shall apply for the purposes of and in relation to the determination under subsection (2) above of any matter by a magistrates' court—

(*a*) as they apply for the purposes of or in relation to a determination by such a court under that Act; and

(*b*) in the case of section 302, as if the reference to a decision of a local authority included a reference to a decision of a sewerage undertaker.

[Water Industry Act 1991, s 178.]

8–31675 **203. Power to acquire information for enforcement purposes.** (1) Where it appears to the Secretary of State or the Director that a company which holds an appointment as a relevant undertaker may be contravening, or may have contravened—

(*a*) any condition of its appointment; or

(*b*) any statutory or other requirement enforceable under section 18 above,

he may, for any purpose connected with such of his powers under Chapter II of Part II of this Act as are exercisable in relation to that matter, serve a notice under subsection (2) below on any person.

(2) A notice under this subsection is a notice signed by the Secretary of State or the Director and—

(*a*) requiring the person on whom it is served to produce, at a time and place specified in the notice, to—

(i) the Secretary of State or the Director; or

(ii) any person appointed by the Secretary of State or the Director for the purpose,

any documents which are specified or described in the notice and are in that person's custody or under his control; or

(*b*) requiring that person, if he is carrying on a business, to furnish, at the time and place and in the form and manner specified in the notice, the Secretary of State or the Director with such information as may be specified or described in the notice.

(3) No person shall be required under this section to produce any documents which he could not be compelled to produce in civil proceedings in the High Court or, in complying with any requirement for the furnishing of information, to give any information which he could not be compelled to give in evidence in any such proceedings.

(4) A person who, without reasonable excuse, fails to do anything required of him by a notice under subsection (2) above shall be guilty of an offence and liable, on summary conviction, to a fine not exceeding **level 5** on the standard scale.

(5) A person who intentionally alters, suppresses or destroys any document which he has been required by any notice under subsection (2) above to produce shall be guilty of an offence and liable[1]—

(*a*) on summary conviction, to a fine not exceeding the **statutory maximum**;

(*b*) on conviction on indictment, to a **fine**.

(6) If a person makes default in complying with a notice under subsection (2) above, the High Court may, on the application of the Secretary of State or the Director, make such order as the Court thinks fit for requiring the default to be made good; and any such order may provide that all the costs or expenses of and incidental to the application shall be borne by the person in default or by any officers of a company or other association who are responsible for its default.

(7) Nothing in this section shall be construed as restricting any power of the Secretary of State or the Director under section 202 above or the conditions of an appointment under Chapter I of Part II of this Act to require a company holding such an appointment to produce any document to him or to furnish him with any information.

[Water Industry Act 1991, s 203.]

1. For procedure in respect of an offence triable either way, see the Magistrates' Courts Act 1980, ss 17A–21 in PART I: MAGISTRATES' COURTS, PROCEDURE, ante.

8–31676 204. Provision of information to sewerage undertakers with respect to trade effluent discharges. (1) The owner or occupier of any land on or under which is situated any sewer, drain, pipe, channel or outlet used or intended to be used for discharging any trade effluent into a sewer of a sewerage undertaker shall, when requested to do so by the undertaker—

(*a*) produce to the undertaker all such plans of the sewer, drain, pipe, channel or outlet as the owner or, as the case may be, occupier possesses or is able without expense to obtain;

(*b*) allow copies of the plans so produced by him to be made by, or under the directions of, the undertaker; and

(*c*) furnish to the undertaker all such information as the owner or, as the case may be, occupier can reasonably be expected to supply with respect to the sewer, drain, pipe, channel or outlet.

(2) A request by a sewerage undertaker for the purposes of this section shall be made in writing.

(3) Every person who fails to comply with this section shall be guilty of an offence and liable, on summary conviction to a fine not exceeding **level 3** on the standard scale.

(4) Expressions used in this section and in Chapter III of Part IV of this Act have the same meanings in this section as in that Chapter; and, accordingly, section 139 above shall have effect for the purposes of this section as it has effect for the purposes of that Chapter.

[Water Industry Act 1991, s 204.]

Restriction on disclosure of information

8–31677 206. Restriction on disclosure of information. (1) Subject to the following provisions of this section, no information with respect to any particular business which—

(*a*) has been obtained by virtue of any of the provisions of this Act; and

(*b*) relates to the affairs of any individual or to any particular business,

shall, during the lifetime of that individual or so long as that business continues to be carried on, be disclosed without the consent of that individual or the person for the time being carrying on that business.

(2) No person shall disclose any information furnished to him under section 204 above or under Chapter III of Part IV of this Act except—

(*a*) with the consent of the person by whom the information was furnished;

(*b*) in connection with the execution of that Chapter;

(*c*) for the purposes of any proceedings arising under that Chapter (including any appeal, application to the Secretary of State or the Director or an arbitration);

(*d*) for the purposes of any criminal proceedings (whether or not so arising); or

(*e*) for the purposes of any report of any proceedings falling within paragraph (*c*) or (*d*) above.

(3) Subsection (1) above does not apply to any disclosure of information which is made—

(*a*) for the purpose of facilitating the carrying out by the Secretary of State, the Minister, the Environment Agency, the Scottish Environment Protection Agency, the Director, the Competition Commission or a county council or local authority of any of his, its or, as the case may be, their functions by virtue of this Act, any of the other consolidation Acts, the Water Act 1989, Part I or IIA of the Environmental Protection Act 1990, the Environment Act 1995 or regulations under section 2 of the Pollution Prevention and Control Act 1999;*

(*b*) for the purpose of facilitating the performance by a relevant undertaker of any of the duties imposed on it by or under this Act, any of the other consolidation Acts or the Water Act 1989;

(*c*) in pursuance of any arrangements made by the Director under section 29(6) above or of any duty imposed by section 197(1)(*a*) or (2) or 203(1) or (2) of the Water Resources Act 1991 (information about water flow and pollution);

(*d*) for the purpose of facilitating the carrying out by any person mentioned in Part I of Schedule 15 to this Act of any of his functions under any of the enactments or instruments specified in Part II of that Schedule;

(*e*) for the purpose of enabling or assisting the Secretary of State, the Treasury or the Financial Services Authority to exercise any powers conferred by or under the Financial Services and Markets Act 2000 or by the enactments relating to companies or insolvency;

(*ea*) for the purpose of enabling or assisting any inspector appointed under enactments relating to companies to carry out his functions;

(*f*) for the purpose of enabling an official receiver to carry out his functions under the enactments relating to insolvency or for the purpose of enabling or assisting a recognised professional body for the purposes of section 391 of the Insolvency Act 1986 to carry out its functions as such;

(*g*) for the purpose of facilitating the carrying out by the Health and Safety Commission or the Health and Safety Executive of any of its functions under any enactment or of facilitating the carrying out by any enforcing authority, within the meaning of Part I of the Health and Safety at Work etc Act 1974, of any functions under a relevant statutory provision, within the meaning of that Act;

(*h*) for the purpose of facilitating the carrying out by the Comptroller and Auditor General of any of his functions under any enactment;

(*i*) in connection with the investigation of any criminal offence or for the purposes of any criminal proceedings;

(*j*) for the purposes of any civil proceedings brought under or by virtue of this Act, any of the other consolidation Acts, the Water Act 1989 or any of the enactments or instruments specified in Part II of Schedule 15 to this Act, or of any arbitration under this Act, any of the other consolidation Acts or that Act of 1989; or

(*k*) in pursuance of a Community obligation.

(4) Nothing in subsection (1) above shall be construed—

(*a*) as limiting the matters which may be published under section 38A, 95A or 201 above or may be included in, or made public as part of, a report of the Environment Agency, the Scottish Environment Protection Agency, the Director, a customer service committee or the Competition Commission under any provision of this Act, Part I or IIA of the Environmental Protection Act 1990, the Water Resources Act 1991, the Environment Act 1995 or regulations under section 2 of the Pollution Prevention and Control Act 1999; or*

(*b*) as applying to any information which has been so published or has been made public as part of such a report or to any information exclusively of a statistical nature.

(5) Subject to subsection (6) below, nothing in subsection (1) above shall preclude the disclosure of information—

(*a*) if the disclosure is of information relating to a matter connected with the carrying out of the functions of a relevant undertaker and is made by one Minister of the Crown or government department to another; or

(*b*) if the disclosure is for the purpose of enabling or assisting any public or other authority for the time being designated for the purposes of this section by an order made by the Secretary of State to discharge any functions which are specified in the order.

(6) The power to make an order under subsection (5) above shall be exercisable by statutory instrument subject to annulment in pursuance of a resolution of either House of Parliament; and where such an order designates an authority for the purposes of paragraph (*b*) of that subsection, the order may—

(*a*) impose conditions subject to which the disclosure of information is permitted by virtue of that paragraph; and

(*b*) otherwise restrict the circumstances in which disclosure is so permitted.

(7) Any person who discloses any information in contravention of the preceding provisions of this section shall be guilty of an offence.

(8) A person who is guilty of an offence under this section by virtue of subsection (1) above shall be liable[1]—

(*a*) on summary conviction, to a fine not exceeding the **statutory maximum**;

(*b*) on conviction on indictment, to imprisonment for a term not exceeding **two years** or to a **fine** or to **both**.

(9) A person who is guilty of an offence under this section by virtue of subsection (2) above shall be liable, on summary conviction, to imprisonment for a term not exceeding **three months** or to a fine not exceeding **level 3** on the standard scale or to both.

(9A) Information obtained by the Director in the exercise of functions which are exercisable concurrently with the Director General of Fair Trading under Part I of the Competition Act 1998 is subject to Part 9 of the Enterprise Act 2002 (Information) and not to subsections (1) to (9) of this section.

(10) In this section "the other consolidation Acts" means the Water Resources Act 1991, the Statutory Water Companies Act 1991, the Land Drainage Act 1991 and the Water Consolidation (Consequential Provisions) Act 1991.

[Water Industry Act 1991, s 206, as amended by the Competition and Service (Utilities) Act 1992, Sch 1, the Environment Act 1995, Schs 22 and 24, the Competition Act 1998, Sch 10, SI 1999/506, the Pollution Prevention and Control Act 1999, Sch 2, SI 2001/3649 and the Enterprise Act 2002, Sch 25.]

***Section 206(3)(*a*) and (4)(*a*) further amended by the Pollution Prevention and Control Act 1999, Sch 3, when in force.**

1. For procedure in respect of an offence triable either way, see the Magistrates' Courts Act 1980, ss 17A–21 in PART I: MAGISTRATES' COURTS, PROCEDURE, ante.

Provision of false information

8–31678 207. Provision of false information. (1) If any person, in furnishing any information or making any application under or for the purposes of any provision of this Act, makes any statement which he knows to be false in a material particular, or recklessly makes any statement which is false in a material particular, he shall be guilty of an offence and liable[1]—

(*a*) on summary conviction, to a fine not exceeding the **statutory maximum**;
(*b*) on conviction on indictment, to a **fine**.

(2) Proceedings for an offence under subsection (1) above shall not be instituted except by or with the consent of the Secretary of State or the Director of Public Prosecutions.
[Water Industry Act 1991, s 207 as amended by SI 2002/794.]

1. For procedure in respect of an offence triable either way, see the Magistrates' Courts Act 1980, ss 17A–21, in PART I: MAGISTRATES' COURTS, PROCEDURE, ante.

PART VIII[1]

MISCELLANEOUS AND SUPPLEMENTAL

Miscellaneous

8–31679 208. Directions in the interests of national security. Person disclosing something when the Secretary of State has notified him that disclosure against the interests of national security: liable on conviction on indictment to two years imprisonment and/or a fine.
[Water Industry Act 1991, s 208(5), (6)—summarised.]

1. Part VIII comprises ss 208–223.

Offences

8–31680 210. Offences by bodies corporate. (1) Where a body corporate is guilty of an offence under this Act and that offence is proved to have been committed with the consent or connivance of, or to be attributable to any neglect on the part of, any director, manager, secretary or other similar officer of the body corporate or any person who was purporting to act in any such capacity, then he, as well as the body corporate, shall be guilty of that offence and shall be liable to be proceeded against and punished accordingly.

(2) Where the affairs of a body corporate are managed by its members, subsection (1) above shall apply in relation to the acts and defaults of a member in connection with his functions of management as if he were a director of the body corporate.
[Water Industry Act 1991, s 210.]

8–31681 211. Limitation on right to prosecute in respect of sewerage offences. Proceedings in respect of an offence created by or under any of the relevant sewerage provisions shall not, without the written consent of the Attorney-General, be taken by any person other than—

(*a*) a party aggrieved;
(*b*) a sewerage undertaker; or
(*c*) a body whose function it is to enforce the provisions in question.

[Water Industry Act 1991, s 211.]

Judicial disqualification

8–31682 212. Judicial disqualification. No judge of any court or justice of the peace shall be disqualified from acting in relation to any proceedings to which a relevant undertaker is a party by reason only that he is or may become liable to pay a charge to that undertaker in respect of any service that is not the subject-matter of the proceedings.
[Water Industry Act 1991, s 212.]

8–31683 216. *Provisions relating to the service of documents.*

8–31684 218. Meaning of "domestic purposes" in relation to water supply. (1) Subject to the following provisions of this section, in this Act references to domestic purposes, in relation to a supply of water to any premises or in relation to any cognate expression, are references to the drinking, washing, cooking, central heating and sanitary purposes for which water supplied to those premises may be used.

(2) Where the whole or any part of the premises are or are to be occupied as a house, those purposes shall be taken to include—

(*a*) the purposes of a profession carried on in that house or, where—
  (i) that house and another part of the premises are occupied together; and
  (ii) the house comprises the greater part of what is so occupied,

  in that other part; and

(*b*) such purposes outside the house (including the washing of vehicles and the watering of gardens) as are connected with the occupation of the house and may be satisfied by a supply of water drawn from a tap inside the house and without the use of a hosepipe or similar apparatus.

(3) No such reference to domestic purposes shall be taken to include a reference—

(*a*) to the use of a bath having a capacity, measured to the centre line of overflow or in such other manner as may be prescribed, of more than two hundred and thirty litres;
(*b*) to the purposes of the business of a laundry; or
(*c*) to any purpose of a business of preparing food or drink for consumption otherwise than on the premises.

[Water Industry Act 1991, s 218.]

8–31685 **219. General interpretation.** (1) In this Act, except in so far as the context otherwise requires—

"accessories", in relation to a water main, sewer or other pipe, includes any manholes, ventilating shafts, inspection chambers, settling tanks, wash-out pipes, pumps, ferrules or stopcocks for the main, sewer or other pipe, or any machinery or other apparatus which is designed or adapted for use in connection with the use or maintenance of the main, sewer or other pipe or of another accessory for it, but does not include any electronic communications apparatus unless it—

(*a*) is or is to be situated inside or in the close vicinity of the main, sewer or other pipe or inside or in the close vicinity of another accessory for it; and
(*b*) is intended to be used only in connection with the use or maintenance of the main, sewer or other pipe or of another accessory for it;

"analyse", in relation to any sample of land, water or effluent, includes subjecting the sample to a test of any description, and cognate expressions shall be construed accordingly;
"conservancy authority" means any person who has a duty or power under any enactment to conserve, maintain or improve the navigation of a tidal water, and is not a harbour authority or navigation authority;
"contravention" includes a failure to comply, and cognate expressions shall be construed accordingly;
"the Council" means the Consumer Council for Water;
"damage", in relation to individuals, includes death and any personal injury, including any disease or impairment of physical or mental condition;
"disposal"—

(*a*) in relation to land or any interest or right in or over land, includes the creation of such an interest or right and a disposal effected by means of the surrender or other termination of any such interest or right; and
(*b*) in relation to sewage, includes treatment;

and cognate expressions shall be construed accordingly;

"disposal main" means (subject to subsection (2) below) any outfall pipe or other pipe which—

(*a*) is a pipe for the conveyance of effluent to or from any sewage disposal works, whether of a sewerage undertaker or of any other person; and
(*b*) is not a public sewer;

"domestic purposes", except in relation to sewers, shall be construed in accordance with section 218 above;
"drain" means (subject to subsection (2) below) a drain used for the drainage of one building or of any buildings or yards appurtenant to buildings within the same curtilage;
"effluent" means any liquid, including particles of matter and other substances in suspension in the liquid;
"enactment" includes an enactment contained in this Act or in any Act passed after this Act;
"engineering or building operations", without prejudice to the generality of that expression, includes—

(*a*) the construction, alteration, improvement, maintenance or demolition of any building or structure or of any reservoir, watercourse, dam, weir, well, borehole or other works; and
(*b*) the installation, modification or removal of any machinery or apparatus;

"harbour authority" means a person who is a harbour authority within the meaning of Chapter II of Part VI of the Merchant Shipping Act 1995 and is not a navigation authority;
"highway" and "highway authority" have the same meanings as in the Highways Act 1980;
"house" means any building or part of a building which is occupied as a dwelling-house, whether or not a private dwelling-house, or which, if unoccupied, is likely to be so occupied;
"information" includes anything contained in any records, accounts, estimates or returns;
"inland waters", has the same meaning as in the Water Resources Act 1991;
"lateral drain" means—

(*a*) that part of a drain which runs from the curtilage of a building (or buildings or yards within the same curtilage) to the sewer with which the drain communicates or is to communicate; or

(*b*) (if different and the context so requires) the part of a drain identified in a declaration of vesting made under section 102 above or in an agreement made under section 104 above;

"licensed water supplier" shall be construed in accordance with section 17B(9) above;

"limited company" means a company within the meaning of the Companies Act 1985 which is limited by shares;

"local authority" means the council of a district or of a London borough or the Common Council of the City of London but, in relation to Wales, means the council of a county or county borough;

"local statutory provision" means—

(*a*) a provision of a local Act (including an Act confirming a provisional order);

(*b*) a provision of so much of any public general Act as has effect with respect to a particular area, with respect to particular persons or works or with respect to particular provisions falling within any paragraph of this definition;

(*c*) a provision of an instrument made under any provision falling within paragraph (*a*) or (*b*) above; or

(*d*) a provision of any other instrument which is in the nature of a local enactment;

"meter" means any apparatus for measuring or showing the volume of water supplied to, or of effluent discharged from, any premises;

"micro-organism" includes any microscopic biological entity which is capable of replication;

"modifications" includes additions, alterations and omissions, and cognate expressions shall be construed accordingly;

"navigation authority" means any person who has a duty or power under any enactment to work, maintain, conserve, improve or control any canal or other inland navigation, navigable river, estuary, harbour or dock;

"notice" means notice in writing;

"the OFT" means the Office of Fair Trading;

"owner", in relation to any premises, means the person who—

(*a*) is for the time being receiving the rack-rent of the premises, whether on his own account or as agent or trustee for another person; or

(*b*) would receive the rack-rent if the premises were let at a rack-rent,

and cognate expressions shall be construed accordingly;

"prescribed" means prescribed by regulations made by the Secretary of State;

"public authority" means any Minister of the Crown or government department, the Environment Agency, any local authority or county council or any person certified by the Secretary of State to be a public authority for the purposes of this Act;

"public sewer" means (subject to section 106 (1A) above) a sewer for the time being vested in a sewerage undertaker in its capacity as such, whether vested in that undertaker by virtue of a scheme under Schedule 2 to the Water Act 1989 or Schedule 2 to this Act or under section 179 above or otherwise, and "private sewer" shall be construed accordingly;

"railway undertakers" means the British Railways Board, Transport for London or any subsidiary (within the meaning of the Greater London Authority Act 1999) of Transport for London, or any other person authorised by any enactment, or by any order, rule or regulation made under any enactment, to construct, work or carry on any railway;

"records" includes computer records and any other records kept otherwise than in a document;

"the relevant sewerage provisions" means the following provisions of this Act, that is to say—

(*a*) Chapters II and III of Part IV (except sections 98 to 101 and 110 and so much of Chapter III of that Part as provides for regulations under section 138 or has effect by virtue of any such regulations);

(*b*) sections 160, 171, 172(4), 178, 184, 189, 196 and 204 and paragraph 4 of Schedule 12; and

(*c*) the other provisions of this Act so far as they have effect for the purposes of any provision falling within paragraph (*a*) or (*b*) of this definition;

"relevant undertaker" means a water undertaker or sewerage undertaker;

"resource main" means (subject to subsection (2) below) any pipe, not being a trunk main, which is or is to be used for the purpose of—

(*a*) conveying water from one source of supply to another, from a source of supply to a regulating reservoir or from a regulating reservoir to a source of supply; or

(*b*) giving or taking a supply of water in bulk;

"service pipe" means (subject to subsection (2) below) so much of a pipe which is, or is to be, connected with a water main for supplying water from that main to any premises as—

(*a*) is or is to be subject to water pressure from that main; or (*b*) would be so subject but for the closing of some valve,

and includes part of any service pipe;

"services" includes facilities;

"sewer" includes (without prejudice to subsection (2) below) all sewers and drains (not being drains within the meaning given by this subsection) which are used for the drainage of buildings and yards appurtenant to buildings;

"sewerage services" includes the disposal of sewage and any other services which are required to be provided by a sewerage undertaker for the purpose of carrying out its functions;

"special administration order" has the meaning given by section 23 above;

"statutory water company" means any company which was a statutory water company for the purposes of the Water Act 1973 immediately before 1st September 1989;

"stopcock" includes any box or pit in which a stopcock is enclosed and the cover to any such box or pit;

"street" has, subject to subsection (5) below, the same meaning as in Part III of the New Roads and Street Works Act 1991;

"subordinate legislation" has the same meaning as in the Interpretation Act 1978;

"substance" includes micro-organisms and any natural or artificial substance or other matter, whether it is in solid or liquid form or in the form of a gas or vapour;

"supply of water in bulk" means a supply of water for distribution by a water undertaker taking the supply;

"surface water" includes water from roofs;

"trunk main" means a water main which is or is to be used by a water undertaker for the purpose of—

(*a*) conveying water from a source of supply to a filter or reservoir or from one filter or reservoir to another filter or reservoir; or

(*b*) conveying water in bulk, whether in the course of taking a supply of water in bulk or otherwise, between different places outside the area of the undertaker, from such a place to any part of that area or from one part of that area to another part of that area;

"underground strata" means strata subjacent to the surface of any land;

"vessel" includes a hovercraft within the meaning of the Hovercraft Act 1968;

"water main" means (subject to subsection (2) below) any pipe, not being a pipe for the time being vested in a person other than the undertaker, which is used or to be used by a water undertaker or licensed water supplier for the purpose of making a general supply of water available to customers or potential customers of the undertaker or supplier, as distinct from for the purpose of providing a supply to particular customers;

"watercourse" includes all rivers, streams, ditches, drains, cuts, culverts, dykes, sluices, sewers and passages through which water flows except mains and other pipes which belong to the Environment Agency or a water undertaker or are used by a water undertaker or any other person for the purpose only of providing a supply of water to any premises.

(2) In this Act—

(*a*) references to a pipe, including references to a main, a drain or a sewer, shall include references to a tunnel or conduit which serves or is to serve as the pipe in question and to any accessories for the pipe; and

(*b*) references to any sewage disposal works shall include references to the machinery and equipment of those works and any necessary pumping stations and outfall pipes;

and, accordingly, references to the laying of a pipe shall include references to the construction of such a tunnel or conduit, to the construction or installation of any such accessories and to the making of a connection between one pipe and another.

(3) Nothing in Part III or IV of this Act by virtue of which a relevant undertaker owes a duty to any particular person to lay any water main, resource main or service pipe or any sewer, disposal main or discharge pipe shall be construed—

(*a*) as conferring any power in addition to the powers conferred apart from those Parts; or

(*b*) as requiring the undertaker to carry out any works which it has no power to carry out.

(4) References in this Act to the fixing of charges in relation to any premises by reference to volume are references to the fixing of those charges by reference to the volume of water supplied to those premises, to the volume of effluent discharged from those premises, to both of those factors or to one or both of those factors taken together with other factors.

(4A) In this Act, unless otherwise stated, references to the supply system of a water undertaker are to the water mains and other pipes which it is the undertaker's duty to develop and maintain by virtue of section 37 above.

(5) Until the coming into force of Part III of the New Roads and Street Works Act 1991, the definition of "street" in subsection (1) above shall have effect as if the reference to that Part were a reference to the Public Utilities Street Works Act 1950; but nothing in this section shall be taken—

(*a*) to prejudice the power of the Secretary of State under that Act of 1991 to make an order bringing Part III of that Act into force on different days for different purposes (including the purposes of this section); or

(*b*) in the period before the coming into force of that Part, to prevent references in this Act to a street, where the street is a highway which passes over a bridge or through a tunnel, from including that bridge or tunnel.

(6) For the purposes of any provision of this Act by or under which power is or may be conferred on any person to recover the expenses incurred by that person in doing anything, those expenses shall be assumed to include such sum as may be reasonable in respect of establishment charges or overheads.

(7) References in this Act to the later or latest of two or more different times or days are, in a case where those times or days coincide, references to the time at which or, as the case may be, the day on which they coincide.

(8) Where by virtue of any provision of this Act any function of a Minister of the Crown is exercisable concurrently by different Ministers, that function shall also be exercisable jointly by any two or more of those Ministers.

(9) Sub-paragraph (1) of paragraph 1 of Schedule 2 to the Water Consolidation (Consequential Provisions) Act 1991 has effect (by virtue of sub-paragraph (2)(*b*) of that paragraph) so that references in this Act to things done under or for the purposes of provisions of this Act or the Water Resources Act 1991 include references to things done, or treated as done, under or for the purposes of the corresponding provisions of the law in force before the commencement of this Act[1].

(10) If the Assembly designates a person as Chief Inspector of Drinking Water for Wales under section 86(1B) above, references in this Act to the Chief Inspector of Drinking Water, as respects anything to be done in relation to him, shall be taken as references to the person designated as the Chief Inspector of Drinking Water by the Secretary of State and also the person designated by the Assembly as the Chief Inspector of Drinking Water for Wales.

[Water Industry Act 1991, s 219, as amended by the Local Government (Wales) Act 1994, Sch 11, the Merchant Shipping Act 1995, Sch 13, the Environment Act 1995, Schs 22 and 24, SI 1999/506, the Enterprise Act 2002, Sch 25 SI 2003/1615, the Communications Act 2003, Sch 17 and the Water Act 2003, ss 57, 97, 99 and Sch 8 and the Water Act 2003, Sch 7.]

1. Definitions not relevant to the parts of this Act printed here have been omitted.

8–31686 **220.** *Effect of local Acts.*

8–31687 **221.** *Crown application.*

8–31687A

Section 63A

SCHEDULE 4A

PREMISES THAT ARE NOT TO BE DISCONNECTED FOR NON-PAYMENT OF CHARGES

(*Amended by the Care Standards Act 2000, s 116, the Health and Social Care (Community Health and Standards Act 2002, Sch 11 and the Fire and Rescue Services Act 2004, Sch 1.*)

1. (1) Any dwelling which is occupied by a person as his only or principal home.

(2) In this paragraph "dwelling" means—

(*a*) a private dwelling-house (which may be a building or part of a building),

(*b*) a caravan within the meaning of Part I of the Caravan Sites and Control of Development Act 1960 (disregarding the amendment made by section 13(2) of the Caravan Sites Act 1968), or

(*c*) a boat or similar structure designed or adapted for use as a place of permanent habitation.

2. (1) Any house in multiple occupation which does not constitute a dwelling within the meaning of paragraph 1 above and in which any person has his only or principal home.

(2) In this paragraph "house in multiple occupation" has the meaning given by section 345(1) of the Housing Act 1985.*

3. (1) Accommodation for the elderly in which a person has his only or principal home.

(2) In this paragraph "accommodation for the elderly" means residential accommodation to which sub-paragraph (3) or (4) below applies, but which is not a dwelling within the meaning of paragraph 1 above or a house in multiple occupation within the meaning of paragraph 2 above.

(3) This sub-paragraph applies to residential accommodation—

(*a*) which is particularly suitable, having regard to its location, size, design, heating systems and other features, for occupation by elderly persons,

(*b*) which it is the practice of the landlord to let for occupation by persons aged 60 or more, and

(*c*) where the services of a warden are provided.

(4) This sub-paragraph applies to any building or part of a building designed or adapted for use as residential accommodation for elderly persons.

4. A hospital within the meaning of section 11 of the Public Health (Control of Disease) Act 1984.

5. Premises used for the provision of medical services by a registered medical practitioner.

6. Premises used for the provision of dental services by a person who under the Dentists Act 1984 is permitted to practise dentistry.

7. Premises not falling within paragraph 5 or 6 above which are used for the provision of primary medical services under Part 1 of the National Health Service Act 1977 or personal dental services under a pilot scheme (within the meaning of Part 1 of the National Health Service (Primary Care) Act 1997).

***Sub-paragraph (2) substituted by the Housing Act 2004, Sch 15 from a date to be appointed.**

8. (1) A care home or independent hospital.

(2) In this paragraph—

"care home" means—

(*a*) a care home within the meaning of the Care Standards Act 2000;
(*b*) a building or part of a building in which residential accommodation is provided under section 21 of the National Assistance Act 1948;

"independent hospital" means an independent hospital within the meaning of the Care Standards Act 2000.

9. A children's home within the meaning of the Care Standards Act 2000.

10. A school within the meaning of the Education Act 1996.

11. (1) Premises used by an institution within the further education sector or an institution within the higher education sector for, or in connection with, the provision of education.

(2) In this paragraph the references to an institution within the further education sector or within the higher education sector are to be construed in accordance with section 91 of the Further and Higher Education Act 1992.

12. Premises used for the provision of day care for children by a person who is registered under Part XA of the Children Act 1989 in respect of the premises.

13. (1) A prison or removal centre.

(2) In this paragraph "prison" means—

(*a*) any prison, young offender institution or remand centre* which is under the general superintendence of, or is provided by, the Secretary of State under the Prison Act 1952, including a contracted out prison within the meaning of Part IV of the Criminal Justice Act 1991,
(*b*) any secure training centre within the meaning of section 43(1)(*d*) of the Prison Act 1952, or
(*c*) a naval, military or air force prison.

(3) In this paragraph "removal centre" means any premises which are used solely for detaining persons under the Immigration Act 1971 or the Asylum and Immigration Appeals Act 1993, but which are not a part of a prison.

***Amended by the Criminal Justice and Court Services Act 2000, Sch 7 from a date to be appointed.**

14. Premises occupied for the purposes of a police force.

15. Premises occupied for the purposes of a fire and resuce authority.

16. Premises occupied for the purposes of the provision of an ambulance service by a National Health Service trust established under Part I of the National Health Service and Community Care Act 1990 or by an NHS foundation trust.

8–31688

Sections 71 to 84 and 162 to 172

SCHEDULE 6

SUPPLEMENTAL PROVISIONS RELATING TO RIGHTS OF ENTRY

PART I

RIGHTS REQUIRING NOTICE FOR ENTRY TO NON-BUSINESS PREMISES

Notice of entry

1. (1) Where this Part of this Schedule applies to any right of entry conferred by a provision of this Act, admission to any premises which are not business premises shall not be demanded as of right by virtue of that provision, unless twenty-four hours notice of the intended entry has been given to the occupier of the premises.

(2) In this paragraph "business premises" means—

(*a*) any factory; or
(*b*) any place in which persons are employed otherwise than in domestic service;

and in this sub-paragraph "factory" has the same meaning as in the Factories Act 1961.

Warrants to exercise right

2. (1) Subject to sub-paragraph (3) below, if it is shown to the satisfaction of a justice of the peace, on sworn information in writing—

(*a*) that any one or more of the conditions specified in sub-paragraph (2) below is fulfilled in relation to any premises which a person is entitled to enter by virtue of a right of entry to which this Part of this Schedule applies; and
(*b*) that there is reasonable ground for entry to the premises for any purpose for which the right is exercisable,

the justice may by a warrant under his hand authorise that person to enter the premises, if need be by force.

(2) The conditions mentioned in sub-paragraph (1) above are—

(*a*) that admission to the premises has been refused to the person having the right to enter them;
(*b*) that such refusal is apprehended;
(*c*) that the premises are unoccupied or the occupier is temporarily absent;
(*d*) that the case is one of urgency;
(*e*) that an application for admission would defeat the object of the entry.

(3) A warrant under this Part of this Schedule shall not be issued by a justice of the peace in a case in which he is satisfied that the condition mentioned in paragraph (*a*) or (*b*) of sub-paragraph (2) above is fulfilled unless he is also satisfied—

(*a*) that notice of the intention to apply for a warrant has been given to the occupier;
(*b*) that a condition mentioned in either of paragraphs (*c*) and (*d*) of that sub-paragraph is also fulfilled in relation to the premises; or
(*c*) that the giving of such notice as is mentioned in paragraph (*a*) above would defeat the object of the entry.

(4) Every warrant under this Part of this Schedule shall continue in force until the purpose for which the entry is necessary has been fulfilled.

(5) A person leaving any unoccupied premises which he has entered by virtue of a warrant under this Part of this Schedule shall leave them as effectually secured against trespassers as he found them.

Supplementary power of person making entry

3. Any person entitled to enter any premises by virtue of a right to which this Part of this Schedule applies, or of a warrant under this Part of this Schedule, may take with him such other persons as may be necessary.

Obstruction of person exercising right

4. Any person who wilfully obstructs any person upon whom a right of entry has been conferred by virtue of—

(*a*) any provision of this Act relating to a right of entry to which this Part of this Schedule applies; or
(*b*) a warrant under this Part of this Schedule,

shall be guilty of an offence and liable, on summary conviction, to a fine not exceeding **level 1** on the standard scale.

Duty of persons exercising rights to maintain confidentiality

5. (1) Without prejudice to section 206 of this Act and subject to sub-paragraphs (2) and (3) below, any person who is admitted to any premises in compliance—

(*a*) with any provision of this Act relating to a right of entry to which this Part of this Schedule applies; or
(*b*) with a warrant under this Part of this Schedule,

shall be guilty of an offence under this paragraph if he discloses to any person any information obtained by him there with regard to any manufacturing process or trade secret.

(2) A person shall not be guilty of an offence under this paragraph in respect of any disclosure made in the performance of his duty.

(3) For the purposes of the application of this Part of this Schedule to the right conferred by section 171 of this Act, the reference to premises in subsection (1) above shall have effect as a reference only to business premises, within the meaning of paragraph 1 above.

(4) A person who is guilty of an offence under this paragraph, other than such a person as is mentioned in sub-paragraph (5) below, shall be liable[1]—

(*a*) on summary conviction, to imprisonment for a term not exceeding **three months** or to a fine not exceeding the **statutory maximum** or to **both**;
(*b*) on conviction on indictment, to imprisonment for a term not exceeding **three months** or to a **fine** or to **both**.

(5) A person who is guilty of an offence under this paragraph by virtue of the application of this Part of this Schedule to the rights conferred by section 171 of this Act shall be liable, on summary conviction, to imprisonment for a term not exceeding **three months** or to a fine not exceeding **level 3** on the standard scale or to **both**.

---

1. For procedure in respect of an offence triable either way, see the Magistrates' Courts Act 1980, ss 17A–21 in PART I: MAGISTRATES' COURTS, PROCEDURE, ante.

PART II
OTHER RIGHTS OF ENTRY AND RELATED POWERS

Notice of entry

6. (1) Without prejudice to any power exercisable by virtue of a warrant under this Part of this Schedule, no person shall make an entry into any premises by virtue of any right or power to which this Part of this Schedule applies except—

(*a*) in an emergency; or
(*b*) at a reasonable time and after the required notice of the intended entry has been given to the occupier of the premises.

(2) For the purposes of this paragraph the required notice is—

(*a*) in the case of the rights and powers conferred by virtue of any of sections 74(4), 84(2) and (3), 86(4) and 170(1)(*c*) and (3) of this Act, twenty-four hours' notice; and
(*b*) in any other case, seven days' notice.

(3) For the purposes of the application of this Part of this Schedule to any right or power conferred by section 168 of this Act the reference in sub-paragraph (1) above to an emergency—

(*a*) in relation to any entry to premises for the purposes of, or for purposes connected with, the exercise or proposed exercise of any power in relation to a street, includes a reference to any circumstances requiring the carrying out of emergency works within the meaning of Part III of the New Roads and Street Works Act 1991; and
(*b*) in relation to any other entry to premises, includes a reference to any danger to property and to any interruption of a supply of water provided to any premises by any person and to any interruption of the provision of sewerage services to any premises.

(4) Until the coming into force of section 52 of the New Roads and Street Works Act 1991, sub-paragraph (3)(*a*) above shall have effect as if the reference to Part III of that Act were a reference to the Public Utilities Street Works Act 1950; but nothing in this sub-paragraph shall be taken to prejudice the power of the Secretary of State under that Act of 1991 to make an order bringing that section 52 into force on different days for different purposes (including the purposes of this paragraph).

(5) For the purposes of the application of this Part of this Schedule to the rights and other powers conferred by section 172 of this Act sub-paragraph (1) above shall have effect as if the power in an emergency to make an entry to any premises otherwise than at a reasonable time and after the required notice were omitted.

Warrant to exercise right or power

7. (1) If it is shown to the satisfaction of a justice of the peace on sworn information in writing—

(*a*) that there are reasonable grounds for the exercise in relation to any premises of a right or power to which this Part of this Schedule applies; and

(*b*) that one or more of the conditions specified in sub-paragraph (2) below is fulfilled in relation to those premises,

the justice may by warrant authorise the relevant authority to designate a person who shall be authorised to exercise the right or power in relation to those premises in accordance with the warrant and, if need be, by force.

(2) The conditions mentioned in sub-paragraph (1)(*b*) above are—

(*a*) that the exercise of the right or power in relation to the premises has been refused;
(*b*) that such a refusal is reasonably apprehended;
(*c*) that the premises are unoccupied;
(*d*) that the occupier is temporarily absent from the premises;
(*e*) that the case is one of urgency; or
(*f*) that an application for admission to the premises would defeat the object of the proposed entry.

(3) A justice of the peace shall not issue a warrant under this Part of this Schedule by virtue only of being satisfied that the exercise of a right or power in relation to any premises has been refused, or that a refusal is reasonably apprehended, unless he is also satisfied—

(*a*) that notice of the intention to apply for the warrant has been given to the occupier of the premises; or
(*b*) that the giving of such a notice would defeat the object of the proposed entry.

(4) For the purposes of the application of this Part of this Schedule to the rights and powers conferred by section 169 of this Act in a case to which subsection (4) of that section applies, a justice of the peace shall not issue a warrant under this Part of this Schedule unless he is satisfied that the Secretary of State has given his authorisation for the purposes of that subsection in relation to that case.

(5) Every warrant under this Part of this Schedule shall continue in force until the purposes for which the warrant was issued have been fulfilled.

Manner of exercise of right or power

8. A person designated as the person who may exercise any right or power to which this Part of this Schedule applies shall produce evidence of his designation and other authority before he exercises the right or power.

Supplementary powers of person making entry etc

9. A person authorised to enter any premises by virtue of any right or power to which this Part of this Schedule applies shall be entitled, subject in the case of a right or power exercisable under a warrant to the terms of the warrant, to take with him on to the premises such other persons and such equipment as may be necessary.

Duty to secure premises

10. A person who enters any premises in the exercise of any right or power to which this Part of this Schedule applies shall leave the premises as effectually secured against trespassers as he found them.

Compensation

11. (1) Where any person exercises any right or power to which this Part of this Schedule applies, it shall be the duty of the relevant authority to make full compensation to any person who has sustained loss or damage by reason of—

(*a*) the exercise by the designated person of that right or power or of any power to take any person or equipment with him when entering the premises in relation to which the right or power is exercised; or

(*b*) the performance of, or failure of the designated person to perform, the duty imposed by paragraph 10 above.

(2) Compensation shall not be payable by virtue of sub-paragraph (1) above in respect of any loss or damage if the loss or damage—

(*a*) is attributable to the default of the person who sustained it; or
(*b*) is loss or damage in respect of which compensation is payable by virtue of any other provision of this Act.

(3) Any dispute as to a person's entitlement to compensation under this paragraph or as to the amount of any such compensation, shall be referred to the arbitration of a single arbitrator appointed by agreement between the relevant authority and the person who claims to have sustained the loss or damage or, in default of agreement—

(*a*) by the President of the Lands Tribunal where the relevant authority is the Secretary of State; and
(*b*) by the Secretary of State, in any other case.

Obstruction of person exercising right or power

12. A person who intentionally obstructs another person acting in the exercise of any right or power to which this Part of this Schedule applies shall be guilty of an offence and liable, on summary conviction, to a fine not exceeding **level 3** on the standard scale.

Interpretation of Part II

13. (1) In this Part of this Schedule "relevant authority", in relation to a right or power to which this Part of this Schedule applies, means the person who, by virtue of—

(*a*) the provision by which the right or power is conferred; or
(*b*) (except in paragraph 7 above) the warrant,

is entitled to designate the person by whom the right or power may be exercised.

(2) References in this Part of this Schedule, except in paragraph 7 above, to a right or power to which this Part of this Schedule applies include references to a right or power exercisable by virtue of a warrant under this Part of this Schedule.

(3) For the purposes of paragraphs 10 and 11 above a person enters any premises by virtue of a right or power to which this Part of this Schedule applies notwithstanding that he has failed (whether by virtue of the waiver of the requirement by the occupier of the premises or otherwise) to comply with—

(*a*) any requirement to enter those premises at a reasonable time or after giving notice of his intended entry; or
(*b*) the requirement imposed by paragraph 8 above.

Water Resources Act 1991

(1991 c 57)

PART II[1]
WATER RESOURCES MANAGEMENT

CHAPTER II
ABSTRACTION AND IMPOUNDING

Restrictions on abstraction and impounding

8–31690 24. Restrictions on abstraction. No person shall, or cause or permit any other person, to abstract water or construct or extend any well, borehole or other work or install or modify machinery to abstract additional quantities of water, except with, and complying with conditions on, a licence; offence punishable on summary conviction by a fine not exceeding **£20,000** and on conviction on indictment by a **fine**[2].*

[Water Resources Act 1991, s 24 as amended by the Water Act 2003, s 60—summarised.]

1. Part II comprises ss 19–81.
2. For procedure in respect of an offence triable either way, see the Magistrates' Courts Act 1980, ss 17A–21 in PART I: MAGISTRATES' COURTS, PROCEDURE, ante.

8–31690A 24A. Abstraction licences

8–31691 25. Restrictions on impounding. No person shall, or cause or permit any other person, to begin construct or alter impounding works at any point in any inland waters which are not discrete waters except with, and complying with requirements of, a licence; offence punishable on summary conviction by a fine not exceeding the **statutory maximum**, and on conviction on indictment by a **fine**[1].*

[Water Resources Act 1991, s 25—summarised.]

***Section amended and new ss 25A–25C inserted by the Water Act 2003, ss 2 and 30, from a date to be appointed.**

1. For procedure in respect of an offence triable either way, see the Magistrates' Courts Act 1980, ss 17A–21 in PART I: MAGISTRATES' COURTS, PROCEDURE, ante.

Rights to abstract or impound

8–31692 26. *Rights of navigation, harbour and conservancy authorities.*

8–31693 27. Rights to abstract small quantities. Exception for abstraction not exceeding 20 cubic metres if not part of a continuous operation or series of operations, or not exceeding 20 cubic metres in 24 hours.*

[Water Resources Act 1991, s 27 amended by the Environment Act 1995, Sch 22—summarised.]

***Section substituted, by new ss 27 and 27A, by the Water Act 2003, s 6, from a date to be appointed.**

8–31694 **29.** *Rights to abstract for drainage purposes etc.*

CHAPTER III
DROUGHT

8–31694A **73–77.** *Power to make ordinary and emergency drought orders; provisions and duration of drought orders.*

8–31694B **78.** *Works under drought orders.*

8–31694C **79A.** *Drought permits.*

8–31695 **80. Offences against drought order.** (1) If any person—

(*a*) takes or uses water in contravention of a prohibition or limitation imposed by or under any drought order or takes or uses water otherwise than in accordance with any condition or restriction imposed by or under any drought order or by any drought permit; or
(*b*) discharges water otherwise than in accordance with any condition or restriction imposed by or under such an order,

he shall be guilty of an offence under this section.

(2) If any person—

(*a*) fails to construct or maintain in good order a gauge, weir or other apparatus for measuring the flow of water which he was required to construct or maintain by any drought order or drought permit; or
(*b*) fails to allow some person authorised for the purpose by or under any such order or by virtue of any such permit to inspect and examine any such apparatus or any records made thereby or kept by that person in connection therewith or to take copies of any such records,

he shall be guilty of an offence under this section.

(3) In any proceedings against any person for an offence under this section it shall be a defence for that person to show that he took all reasonable precautions and exercised all due diligence to avoid the commission of the offence.

(4) A person who is guilty of an offence under this section shall be liable—

(*a*) on summary conviction, to a fine not exceeding the **statutory maximum**;
(*b*) on conviction on indictment, to a **fine**.

[Water Resources Act 1991, s 80, as amended by the Environment Act 1995, Sch 22.]

1. For procedure in respect of an offence triable either way, see the Magistrates' Courts Act 1980, ss 17A–21 in PART I: MAGISTRATES' COURTS, PROCEDURE, ante.

8–31696 **81. Interpretation of Chapter III.** In this Chapter—

(*a*) references to the taking of water include references to the collection, impounding, diversion or appropriation of water; and
(*b*) references to an obligation or to a restriction include references to an obligation or, as the case may be, to a restriction which is imposed by or under any enactment or agreement.

[Water Resources Act 1991, s 81.]

1. Chapter III of Pt II comprises ss 73–81.

PART III[1]
CONTROL OF POLLUTION OF WATER RESOURCES

Principal offences

8–31697 **85. Offences of polluting controlled waters.** (1) A person contravenes this section if he causes[2] or knowingly permits any poisonous, noxious or polluting[3] matter or any solid waste matter to enter any controlled waters[4].

(2) A person contravenes this section if he causes[2] or knowingly permits any matter, other than trade effluent or sewage effluent, to enter controlled waters by being discharged from a drain or sewer in contravention of a prohibition imposed under section 86 below.

(3) A person contravenes this section if he causes[2] or knowingly permits any trade effluent or sewage effluent to be discharged—

(*a*) into any controlled waters; or
(*b*) from land in England and Wales, through a pipe, into the sea outside the seaward limits of controlled waters.

(4) A person contravenes this section if he causes[2] or knowingly permits any trade effluent or sewage effluent to be discharged, in contravention of any prohibition imposed under section 86 below, from a building or from any fixed plant—

(*a*) on to or into any land; or
(*b*) into any waters of a lake or pond which are not inland freshwaters.

(5) A person contravenes this section if he causes[3] or knowingly permits any matter whatever to enter any inland freshwaters so as to tend (either directly or in combination with other matter which he or another person causes or permits to enter those waters) to impede the proper flow of the waters in a manner leading, or likely to lead, to a substantial aggravation of—

(*a*) pollution due to other causes; or
(*c*) the consequences of such pollution.

(6) Subject to the following provisions of this Chapter, a person who contravenes this section or the conditions of any consent[5] given under this Chapter for the purposes of this section shall be guilty of an offence and liable[6]—

(*a*) on summary conviction, to imprisonment for a term not exceeding **three months** or to a fine not exceeding **£20,000** or to **both**;
(*b*) on conviction on indictment, to imprisonment for a term not exceeding **two years** or to a **fine** or to **both**.

[Water Resources Act 1991, s 85.]

---

1. Part III comprises ss 82–104.
2. "Causing" involves some active operation or chain of operations involving as a result the pollution of controlled waters; "knowingly permitting" involves a failure to prevent the pollution, which failure, however, must be accompanied by knowledge (*Alphacell Ltd v Woodward* [1972] AC 824, [1972] 2 All ER 475, HL). Accordingly, on a charge brought against a sewage undertaker under s 107(1)(*a*) of the Water Act 1989 (now s 85(1) of the Water Resources Act 1991) whereby it was alleged that the undertaker had caused poisonous, noxious or polluting matter to enter controlled waters from a sewage treatment works, it was held that the undertaker had "caused" the entry of such polluting matter into controlled waters, notwithstanding that the controlled waters had been rendered poisonous, noxious or polluting by the discharge into the sewer by an unidentified third party of iso-octanol, a prohibited chemical, in circumstances which could not have reasonably been prevented by the undertaker (*National Rivers Authority v Yorkshire Water Services Ltd* [1995] 1 All ER 225, [1994] 3 WLR 1202, 158 JP 709, HL).

In *A-G's Reference (No 1 of 1994)* [1995] 1 WLR 599, 159 JP 584, CA, the following propositions were established:

(*a*) The offence of causing polluting matter to enter controlled waters may be committed by more than one person and by separate acts.
(*b*) Where a sewerage company sets up and owns a plant or system to carry out its statutory duties, then, if the sewerage passing through that system pollutes controlled waters, the company has participated in an active operation or chain of operations involving as the result the pollution of controlled waters sufficient to constitute "causing", unless it can rely on the defence in s 87(2), post.
(*c*) Where a party has undertaken the day-to-day running of maintenance of a sewerage system, if it fails properly to maintain the system and runs it in an unmaintained state, that will be sufficient to entitle the court to find that party guilty of "causing" pollution to controlled waters resulting from lack of maintenance.

In *Empress Car Co (Abertillery) Ltd v National Rivers Authority* [1998] 1 All ER 481, sub nom *Environment Agency v Empress Car Co (Abertillery) Ltd* [1998] 2 WLR 350, the House of Lords gave the following guidance to assist courts to determine whether a defendant has "caused" the pollution which is being alleged:

(1) Justices dealing with prosecutions for "causing" pollution under section 85 (1) should first require the prosecution to identify what it says the defendant did to cause the pollution. If the defendant cannot be said to have done anything at all, the prosecution must fail: the defendant may have "Knowingly permitted" pollution but cannot have caused it.
(2) The prosecution need not prove that the defendant did something which was the immediate cause of the pollution: maintaining tanks, lagoons or sewage systems full of noxious liquid is doing something, even if the immediate cause of the pollution was lack of maintenance, a natural event or the act of a third party.
(3) When the prosecution has identified something which the defendant did, the justices must decide whether it caused the pollution. They should not be diverted by questions like "What was the cause of the pollution?" or "Did something else cause the pollution?" because to say that something else caused the pollution (like brambles clogging the pumps or vandalism by third parties) is not inconsistent with the defendant having caused it as well.
(4) If the defendant did something which produced a situation in which the polluting matter could escape but a necessary condition of the actual escape which happened was also the act of a third party or a natural event, the justices should consider whether that act or event should be regarded as a normal fact of life or something extraordinary. If it was in the general run of things a matter of ordinary occurrence, it will not negative the causal effect of the defendant's actions, even if it was not foreseeable that it would happen to that defendant or take that form. If it can be regarded as something extraordinary, it will be open to the justices to hold that the defendant did not cause the pollution.
(5) The distinction between ordinary and extraordinary is one of fact and degree to which the justices must apply their common sense and knowledge of what happens in the area.

3. "Polluting" bears the definition in the *Oxford English Dictionary* ie "to make physically impure, foul or filthy: to dirty, stain, taint, befoul". Whether the introduction of polluting matter into controlled waters has any polluting effect depends on the relative quantities of the polluting matter and the controlled waters, and is a matter of fact (*R v Dovermoss Ltd* (1995) 159 JP 448, CA. The polluting matter does not need to be either poisonous or noxious; it is sufficient if it, for example, stains or taints: *Express Ltd v Environment Agency* [2004] EWHC Admin 1710, [2005] 1 WLR 223, (2004) 168 JPN 586. If a landowner permits an operation on his land which gives rise a risk of pollution then, to avoid falling foul of s 85(1), he must carry out a risk assessment and respond to whatever that assessment reveals; otherwise, if pollution does occur, it might be impossible for him to say that the offence committed by those using his land was not due to his act or default: *Express Ltd v Environment Agency*, supra.

4. For the meaning of "controlled waters", see s 104, post. A river bed is part of controlled waters; accordingly, where mud and silt from the river bed were churned up into the water, it was held no offence under s 85 was committed because the mud and silt were already present (*National Rivers Authority v Biffa Waste Services Ltd* (1995) 160 JP 497). Where a company is prosecuted under this section, the question in all cases is whether as a matter of common sense the company, by some active operation or chain of operations carried out under its essential control, caused the pollution of controlled

water. Accordingly, a company will be criminally liable for causing pollution which results from the acts or omissions of its employees acting within the course and scope of their employment when the pollution occurred, regardless of whether they can be said to be exercising the controlling mind and will of the company, save only where some third party has acted in such a way as to interrupt the chain of causation (*National Rivers Authority v Alfred McAlpine Homes (East) Ltd* [1994] 4 All ER 286, 158 JP 628).

5. Where a consent is granted, subject to a positive obligation contained in a lawfully applicable condition to ensure that discharged matter shall be non-polluting, a defendant who has the benefit of the consent may be properly convicted in respect of a failure to comply with that positive obligation, even though he has not committed an act of discharge (*Taylor Woodrow Property Management Ltd v National Rivers Authority* (1994) 158 JP 1101).

6. For procedure in respect of an offence triable either way, see the Magistrates' Courts Act 1980, ss 17A–21 in PART I: MAGISTRATES' COURTS, PROCEDURE, ante.

8–31698 **86. Prohibition of certain discharges by notice or regulations.** (1) For the purposes of section 85 above a discharge of any effluent or other matter is, in relation to any person, in contravention of a prohibition imposed under this section if, subject to the following provisions of this section—

(*a*) the Agency has given that person notice prohibiting him from making or, as the case may be, continuing the discharge; or

(*b*) the Agency has given that person notice prohibiting him from making or, as the case may be, continuing the discharge unless specified conditions are observed, and those conditions are not observed.

(2) For the purposes of section 85 above a discharge of any effluent or other matter is also in contravention of a prohibition imposed under this section if the effluent or matter discharged—

(*a*) contains a prescribed substance or a prescribed concentration of such a substance; or

(*b*) derives from a prescribed process or from a process involving the use of prescribed substances or the use of such substances in quantities which exceed the prescribed amounts.

(3) Nothing in subsection (1) above shall authorise the giving of a notice for the purposes of that subsection in respect of discharges from a vessel; and nothing in any regulations made by virtue of subsection (2) above shall require any discharge from a vessel to be treated as a discharge in contravention of a prohibition imposed under this section.

(4) A notice given for the purposes of subsection (1) above shall expire at such time as may be specified in the notice.

(5) The time specified for the purposes of subsection (4) above shall not be before the end of the period of three months beginning with the day on which the notice is given, except in a case where the Agency is satisfied that there is an emergency which requires the prohibition in question to come into force at such time before the end of that period as may be so specified.

(6) Where, in the case of such a notice for the purposes of subsection (1) above as (but for this subsection) would expire at a time at or after the end of the said period of three months, an application is made before that time for a consent under this Chapter in respect of the discharge to which the notice relates, that notice shall be deemed not to expire until the result of the application becomes final—

(*a*) on the grant or withdrawal of the application;

(*b*) on the expiration, without the bringing of an appeal with respect to the decision on the application, of any period prescribed as the period within which any such appeal must be brought; or

(*c*) on the withdrawal or determination of any such appeal.

[Water Resources Act 1991, s 86, as amended by the Environment Act 1995, Sch 22.]

8–31699 **87. Discharges into and from public sewers etc.** (1) This section applies for the purpose of determining liability where sewage effluent is discharged as mentioned in subsection (3) or (4) of section 85 above from any sewer or works ("the discharging sewer") vested in a sewerage undertaker ("the discharging undertaker").

(1A) If the discharging undertaker did not cause, or knowingly permit, the discharge it shall nevertheless be deemed[1] to have caused the discharge if—

(*a*) matter included in the discharge was received by it into the discharging sewer or any other sewer or works vested in it;

(*b*) it was bound (either unconditionally or subject to conditions which were observed) to receive that matter into that sewer or works; and

(*c*) subsection (1B) below does not apply.

(1B) This subsection applies where the sewage effluent was, before being discharged from the discharging sewer, discharged through a main connection into that sewer or into any other sewer or works vested in the discharging undertaker by another sewerage undertaker ("the sending undertaker") under an agreement having effect between the discharging undertaker and the sending undertaker under section 110A of the Water Industry Act 1991.

(1C) Where subsection (1B) above applies, the sending undertaker shall be deemed to have caused the discharge if, although it did not cause, or knowingly permit, the sewage effluent to be discharged into the discharging sewer, or into any other sewer or works of the discharging undertaker—

(*a*) matter included in the discharge was received by it into a sewer or works vested in it; and

(*b*) it was bound (either unconditionally or subject to conditions which were observed) to receive that matter into that sewer or works.

(2) A sewerage undertaker shall not be guilty of an offence under section 85[2] above by reason only of the fact that a discharge from a sewer or works vested in the undertaker contravenes conditions of a consent relating to the discharge if—

(*a*) the contravention is attributable to a discharge which another person caused or permitted to be made into the sewer or works;

(*b*) the undertaker either was not bound to receive the discharge into the sewer or works or was bound to receive it there subject to conditions which were not observed; and

(*c*) the undertaker could not reasonably have been expected to prevent the discharge into the sewer or works.

(3) A person shall not be guilty of an offence under section 85 above in respect of a discharge which he caused or permitted to be made into a sewer or works vested in a sewerage undertaker if the undertaker was bound to receive the discharge there either unconditionally or subject to conditions which were observed.

(4) In this section "main connection" has the same meaning as in section 110A of the Water Industry Act 1991.

[Water Resources Act 1991, s 87, as amended by the Competition and Service (Utilities) Act 1992, s 46.]

1. Although the offence is one of strict liability, in considering sentence the court will have regard to the fact that it is the responsibility of the undertaker to ensure through powers of instruction and supervision of an agent with day-to-day management of sewers that discharges of effluent into controlled waters do not occur (*R v Yorkshire Water Services Ltd* (1994) Times, 19 July, CA).

2. In *National Rivers Authority v Yorkshire Water Services Ltd* [1995] 1 All ER 225 it was held in respect of an offence under s 107(1)(*a*) of the Water Act 1989 (now s 85(1) of the Water Resources Act 1991) that the defence in s 108(7) of the 1989 Act (now s 87(2) of the 1991 Act) is available to an offence of causing poisonous, noxious or polluting matter to enter controlled waters where on the facts of the case the offence is not committed by reason only of the fact that a discharge contravened conditions of a consent.

8–31700 **88. Defence to principal offences in respect of authorised discharges.** (1) Subject to the following provisions of this section, a person shall not be guilty of an offence under section 85 above in respect of the entry of any matter into any waters or any discharge if the entry occurs or the discharge is made under and in accordance with, or as a result of any act or omission under and in accordance with—

(*a*) a consent given under this Chapter or under Part II of the Control of Pollution Act 1974 (which makes corresponding provision for Scotland);

(*aa*) a permit granted, under regulations under section 2 of the Pollution Prevention and Control Act 1999, by an authority exercising functions under the regulations that are exercisable for the purpose of preventing or reducing emissions in to the air, water and land;

(*b*) an authorisation for a prescribed process designated for central control granted under Part I of the Environmental Protection Act 1990;*

(*c*) a waste management or disposal licence;

(*d*) a licence granted under Part II of the Food and Environment Protection Act 1985;

(*e*) section 163 below or section 165 of the Water Industry Act 1991 (discharges for works purposes);

(*f*) any local statutory provision or statutory order which expressly confers power to discharge effluent into water; or

(*g*) any prescribed enactment.

(2) Schedule 10 to this Act shall have effect, subject to section 91 below, with respect to the making of applications for consents under this Chapter for the purposes of subsection (1)(*a*) above and with respect to the giving, revocation and modification of such consents.

(3) Nothing in any disposal licence shall be treated for the purposes of subsection (1) above as authorising—

(*a*) any such entry or discharge as is mentioned in subsections (2) to (4) of section 85 above; or

(*b*) any act or omission so far as it results in any such entry or discharge.

(4) In this section—

"disposal licence" means a licence issued in pursuance of section 5 of the Control of Pollution Act 1974;

"statutory order" means—

(*a*) any order under section 168 below or section 167 of the Water Industry Act 1991 (compulsory works orders); or (*b*) any order, byelaw, scheme or award made under any other enactment, including an order or scheme confirmed by Parliament or brought into operation in accordance with special parliamentary procedure;

and

"waste management licence" means such a licence granted under Part II of the Environmental Protection Act 1990.

[Water Resources Act 1991, s 88, as amended by SI 2000/1973.]

***Section 88(1)(*b*) is repealed by the Pollution Prevention and Control Act 1999, Sch 3, when in force.**

8–31701 **89. Other defences to principal offences.** (1) A person shall not be guilty of an offence under section 85 above in respect of the entry of any matter into any waters or any discharge if—

(*a*) the entry is caused or permitted, or the discharge is made, in an emergency[1] in order to avoid danger to life or health;

(*b*) that person takes all such steps as are reasonably practicable in the circumstances for minimising the extent of the entry or discharge and of its polluting effects; and

(*c*) particulars of the entry or discharge are furnished to the Agency as soon as reasonably practicable after the entry occurs.

(2) A person shall not be guilty of an offence under section 85 above by reason of his causing or permitting any discharge of trade or sewage effluent from a vessel.

(3) A person shall not be guilty of an offence under section 85 above by reason only of his permitting water from an abandoned mine or an abandoned part of a mine to enter controlled waters.

(3A) Subsection (3) above shall not apply to the owner or former operator of any mine or part of a mine if the mine or part in question became abandoned after 31st December 1999.

(3B) In determining for the purposes of subsection (3A) above whether a mine or part of a mine became abandoned before, on or after 31st December 1999 in a case where the mine or part has become abandoned on two or more occasions, of which—

(*a*) at least one falls on or before that date, and

(*b*) at least one falls after that date,

the mine or part shall be regarded as becoming abandoned after that date (but without prejudice to the operation of subsection (3) above in relation to that mine or part at, or in relation to, any time before the first of those occasions which falls after that date).

(3C) Where, immediately before a part of a mine becomes abandoned, that part is the only part of the mine not falling to be regarded as abandoned for the time being, the abandonment of that part shall not be regarded for the purposes of subsection (3A) or (3B) above as constituting the abandonment of the mine, but only of that part of it.

(4) A person shall not, otherwise than in respect of the entry of any poisonous, noxious or polluting matter into any controlled waters, be guilty of an offence under section 85 above by reason of his depositing the solid refuse of a mine or quarry on any land so that it falls or is carried into inland freshwaters if—

(*a*) he deposits the refuse on the land with the consent of the Agency;

(*b*) no other site for the deposit is reasonably practicable; and

(*c*) he takes all reasonably practicable steps to prevent the refuse from entering those inland freshwaters.

(5) A highway authority or other person entitled to keep open a drain by virtue of section 100 of the Highways Act 1980 shall not be guilty of an offence under section 85 above by reason of his causing or permitting any discharge to be made from a drain kept open by virtue of that section unless the discharge is made in contravention of a prohibition imposed under section 86 above.

(6) In this section "mine" and "quarry" have the same meanings as in the Mines and Quarries Act 1954.

[Water Resources Act 1991, s 89, as amended by the Environment Act 1995, s 60 and Sch 22.]

---

1. Since discharge is not involved in the offence, the reason for it (see infra) is not of concern; the court is entitled to focus on the chain of causation and ask whether the act which caused the entry was done in an emergency in order to save life or health; so that where a tanker being driven by the defendants suffered a tyre blow out which caused milk to escape from a delivery pipe and he stopped the vehicle where drains were situated and this led to milk entering controlled waters his action could have been for the aforementioned purpose of saving life or health and, accordingly, the defendants could rely on the defence in s 89(1): *Express Ltd (trading as Express Dairies Distribution) v Environment Agency* [2004] EWHC 448 (Admin), [2004] 1 WLR 579.

Offences in connection with deposits and vegetation in rivers

8–31702 **90. Offences in connection with deposits and vegetation in rivers.** (1) A person shall be guilty of an offence under this section if, without the consent of the Agency, he—

(*a*) removes from any part of the bottom, channel or bed of any inland freshwaters a deposit accumulated by reason of any dam, weir or sluice holding back the waters; and (*b*) does so by causing the deposit to be carried away in suspension in the waters.

(2) A person shall be guilty of an offence under this section if, without the consent of the Agency, he—

(*a*) causes or permits a substantial amount of vegetation to be cut or uprooted in any inland freshwaters, or to be cut or uprooted so near to any such waters that it falls into them; and

(*b*) fails to take all reasonable steps to remove the vegetation from those waters.

(3) A person guilty of an offence under this section shall be liable, on summary conviction, to a fine not exceeding **level 4** on the standard scale.

(4) Nothing in subsection (1) above applies to anything done in the exercise of any power conferred by or under any enactment relating to land drainage, flood prevention or navigation.

(5) In giving a consent for the purposes of this section the Agency may make the consent subject to such conditions as it considers appropriate.

(6) The Secretary of State may by regulations provide that any reference to inland freshwaters in subsection (1) or (2) above shall be construed as including a reference to such coastal waters as may be prescribed.

[Water Resources Act 1991, s 90, as amended by the Environment Act 1995, Sch 22.]

Consents for the purposes of sections 88 to 90

8–31702A **90A. Applications for consent under section 89 or 90[1].** (1) Any application for a consent for the purposes of section 89(4)(*a*) or 90(1) or (2) above—

(*a*) must be made on a form provided for the purpose by the Agency, and

(*b*) must be advertised in such manner as may be required by regulations[2] made by the Secretary of State,

except that paragraph (*b*) above shall not have effect in the case of an application of any class or description specified in the regulations[2] as being exempt from the requirements of that paragraph.

(2) The applicant for such a consent must, at the time when he makes his application, provide the Agency—

(*a*) with all such information as it reasonably requires; and

(*b*) with all such information as may be prescribed[2] for the purpose by the Secretary of State.

(3) The information required by subsection (2) above must be provided either on, or together with, the form mentioned in subsection (1) above.

(4) The Agency may give the applicant notice requiring him to provide it with all such further information of any description specified in the notice as it may require for the purpose of determining the application.

(5) If the applicant fails to provide the Agency with any information required under subsection (4) above, the Agency may refuse to proceed with the application or refuse to proceed with it until the information is provided.

[Water Resources Act 1991, s 90A, as inserted by the Environment Act 1995, Sch 22.]

---

1. At the date of going to press, s 90A which is to be inserted in this Act by the Environment Act 1995, Sch 22, para 142, had not been brought into force.

2. The Control of Pollution (Applications, Appeals and Registers) Regulations 1996, SI 1996/2971, as amended by SI 1999/1006 have been made.

8–31702B **90B. Enforcement notices[1].** (1) If the Agency is of the opinion that the holder of a relevant consent is contravening any condition of the consent, or is likely to contravene any such condition, the Agency may serve on him a notice (an "enforcement notice").

(2) An enforcement notice shall—

(*a*) state that the Agency is of the said opinion;

(*b*) specify the matters constituting the contravention or the matters making it likely that the contravention will arise;

(*c*) specify the steps that must be taken to remedy the contravention or, as the case may be, to remedy the matters making it likely that the contravention will arise; and

(*d*) specify the period within which those steps must be taken.

(3) Any person who fails to comply with any requirement imposed by an enforcement notice shall be guilty of an offence and liable[2]—

(*a*) on summary conviction, to imprisonment for a term not exceeding **three months** or to a fine not exceeding **£20,000** or to **both**;

(*b*) on conviction on indictment, to imprisonment for a term not exceeding **two years** or to a **fine** or to **both**.

(4) If the Agency is of the opinion that proceedings for an offence under subsection (3) above would afford an ineffectual remedy against a person who has failed to comply with the requirements of an enforcement notice, the Agency may take proceedings in the High Court for the purpose of securing compliance with the notice.

(5) The Secretary of State may, if he thinks fit in relation to any person, give to the Agency directions as to whether the Agency should exercise its powers under this section and as to the steps which must be taken.

(6) In this section—

"relevant consent" means—

(*a*) a consent for the purposes of section 89(4)(*a*) or 90(1) or (2) above; or

(*b*) a discharge consent, within the meaning of section 91 below; and

"the holder", in relation to a relevant consent, is the person who has the consent in question.

[Water Resources Act 1991, s 90B, as inserted by the Environment Act 1995, Sch 22.]

---

1. At the date of going to press, s 90B which is to be inserted in this Act by the Environment Act 1995, Sch 22, para 142, had not been brought into force.

2. For procedure in respect of this offence which is triable either way, see the Magistrates' Courts Act 1980, ss 17A–21, in PART I: MAGISTRATES' COURTS, PROCEDURE, ante.

8–31702C 91. *Appeals in respect of consents under Chapter II.*

CHAPTER IIA[1]
ABANDONED MINES

8–31702D 91A. Introductory. (1) For the purposes of this Chapter, "abandonment", in relation to a mine,—

(*a*) subject to paragraph (*b*) below, includes—

(i) the discontinuance of any or all of the operations for the removal of water from the mine;

(ii) the cessation of working of any relevant seam, vein or vein-system;

(iii) the cessation of use of any shaft or outlet of the mine;

(iv) in the case of a mine in which activities other than mining activities are carried on (whether or not mining activities are also carried on in the mine)—

(A) the discontinuance of some or all of those other activities in the mine; and

(B) any substantial change in the operations for the removal of water from the mine; but

(*b*) does not include—

(i) any disclaimer under section 178 or 315 of the Insolvency Act 1986 (power of liquidator, or trustee of a bankrupt's estate, to disclaim onerous property) by the official receiver acting in a compulsory capacity; or

(ii) the abandonment of any rights, interests or liabilities by the Accountant in Bankruptcy acting as permanent or interim trustee in a sequestration (within the meaning of the Bankruptcy (Scotland) Act 1985);

and cognate expressions shall be construed accordingly.

(2) In this Chapter, except where the context otherwise requires—

"the 1954 Act" means the Mines and Quarries Act 1954;

"acting in a compulsory capacity", in the case of the official receiver, means acting as—

(*a*) liquidator of a company;

(*b*) receiver or manager of a bankrupt's estate, pursuant to section 287 of the Insolvency Act 1986;

(*c*) trustee of a bankrupt's estate;

(*d*) liquidator of an insolvent partnership;

(*e*) trustee of an insolvent partnership;

(*f*) trustee, or receiver or manager, of the insolvent estate of a deceased person;

"mine" has the same meaning as in the 1954 Act;

"the official receiver" has the same meaning as it has in the Insolvency Act 1986 by virtue of section 399(1) of that Act;

"prescribed" means prescribed in regulations;

"regulations" means regulations made by the Secretary of State;

"relevant seam, vein or vein-system", in the case of any mine, means any seam, vein or vein-system for the purpose of, or in connection with, whose working any excavation constituting or comprised in the mine was made.

[Water Resources Act 1991, s 91A, as inserted by the Environment Act 1995, s 58.]

---

1. Chapter IIA contains ss 91A and 91B.

8–31702E 91B Mine operators to give the Agency six months' notice of any proposed abandonment. (1) If, in the case of any mine, there is to be an abandonment at any time after the expiration of the initial period, it shall be the duty of the operator of the mine to give notice of the proposed abandonment to the Agency at least six months before the abandonment takes effect.

(2) A notice under subsection (1) above shall contain such information (if any) as is prescribed[1] for the purpose, which may include information about the operator's opinion as to any consequences of the abandonment.

(3) A person who fails to give the notice required by subsection (1) above shall be guilty of an offence and liable[2]—

(*a*) on summary conviction, to a fine not exceeding the **statutory maximum;**
(*b*) on conviction on indictment, to a **fine**.

(4) A person shall not be guilty of an offence under subsection (3) above if—

(*a*) the abandonment happens in an emergency in order to avoid danger to life or health; and
(*b*) notice of the abandonment, containing such information as may be prescribed[1], is given as soon as reasonably practicable after the abandonment has happened.

(5) Where the operator of a mine is—

(*a*) the official receiver acting in a compulsory capacity, or
(*b*) the Accountant in Bankruptcy acting as permanent or interim trustee in a sequestration (within the meaning of the Bankruptcy (Scotland) Act 1985),

he shall not be guilty of an offence under subsection (3) above by reason of any failure to give the notice required by subsection (1) above if, as soon as reasonably practicable (whether before or after the abandonment), he gives to the Agency notice of the abandonment or proposed abandonment, containing such information as may be prescribed[1].

(6) Where a person gives notice under subsection (1), 4(*b*) or (5) above, he shall publish prescribed[1] particulars of, or relating to, the notice in one or more local newspapers circulating in the locality where the mine is situated.

(7) Where the Agency—

(*a*) receives notice under this section or otherwise learns of an abandonment or proposed abandonment in the case of any mine, and
(*b*) considers that, in consequence of the abandonment or proposed abandonment taking effect, any land has or is likely to become contaminated land, within the meaning of Part IIA of the Environmental Protection Act 1990,

it shall be the duty of the Agency to inform the local authority in whose area that land is situated of the abandonment or proposed abandonment.

(8) In this section—

"the initial period" means the period of six months beginning with the day on which subsection (1) above comes into force;

"local authority" means—

(*a*) any unitary authority;
(*b*) any district council, so far as it is not a unitary authority;
(*c*) the Common Council of the City of London and, as respects the Temples, the Sub-Treasurer of the Inner Temple and the Under-Treasurer of the Middle Temple respectively;

"unitary authority" means—

(*a*) the council of a county, so far as it is the council of an area for which there are no district councils;
(*b*) the council of any district comprised in an area for which there is no county council;
(*c*) the council of a London borough;
(*d*) the council of a county borough in Wales.

[Water Resources Act 1991, s 91B, as inserted by the Environment Act 1995, s 58.]

1. See the Mines (Notice of Abandonment) Regulations 1998, SI 1998/892.
2. For procedure in respect of this offence which is triable either way, see the Magistrates' Courts Act 1980, ss 17A–21, in PART I: MAGISTRATES' COURTS, PROCEDURE, ante.

CHAPTER IV
SUPPLEMENTAL PROVISIONS WITH RESPECT TO WATER POLLUTION

8–31703 **101. Limitation for summary offences under Part III.** Notwithstanding anything in section 127 of the Magistrates' Courts Act 1980 (time limit for summary proceedings), a magistrates' court may try any summary offence under this Part, or under any subordinate legislation made under this Part, if the information is laid not more than twelve months after the commission of the offence.
[Water Resources Act 1991, s 101.]

8–31704 **104. Meaning of "controlled waters" etc in Part III.** (1) References in this Part to controlled waters are references to waters of any of the following classes—

(*a*) relevant territorial waters, that is to say, subject to subsection (4) below, the waters which extend seaward for three miles from the baselines from which the breadth of the territorial sea adjacent to England and Wales is measured;

(*b*) coastal waters, that is to say, any waters which are within the area which extends landward from those baselines as far as—

(*a*) the limit of the highest tide; or

(*b*) in the case of the waters of any relevant river or watercourse, the fresh-water limit of the river or watercourse,

together with the waters of any enclosed dock which adjoins waters within that area:

(*c*) inland freshwaters, that is to say, the waters of any relevant lake or pond or of so much of any relevant river or watercourse[1] as is above the fresh-water limit;

(*d*) ground waters, that is to say, any waters contained in underground strata;

and, accordingly, in this Part "coastal waters", "controlled waters", "ground waters", "inland freshwaters" and "relevant territorial waters" have the meanings given by this subsection.

(2) In this Part any reference to the waters of any lake or pond or of any river or watercourse includes a reference to the bottom, channel or bed of any lake, pond, river or, as the case may be, watercourse which is for the time being dry.

(3) In this section—

"fresh-water limit", in relation to any river or watercourse, means the place for the time being shown as the fresh-water limit of that river or watercourse in the latest map deposited for that river or watercourse under section 192 below;

"miles" means international nautical miles of 1,852 metres:

"lake or pond" includes a reservoir of any description:

"relevant lake or pond" means (subject to subsection (4) below) any lake or pond which (whether it is natural or artificial or above or below ground) discharges into a relevant river or watercourse or into another lake or pond which is itself a relevant lake or pond;

"relevant river or watercourse" means (subject to subsection (4) below) any river or watercourse (including an underground river or watercourse and an artificial river or watercourse) which is neither a public sewer nor a sewer or drain which drains into a public sewer.

(4)–(6) Secretary of State's power to make orders.

[Water Resources Act 1991, s 104.]

1. Waters which are within the definition of "controlled waters" for the purposes of this Act because they are "waters . . . of [a] . . . watercourse" do not cease to be controlled waters merely because they leave the watercourse as a result of diversion or flooding (*R v Dovermoss Ltd* (1995) 159 JP 448, CA).

PART VII[1]
LAND AND WORKS POWERS

CHAPTER I
POWERS OF THE AUTHORITY

Anti-pollution works

8–31704A **161. Anti-pollution works and operations.** (1) Subject to subsections (1A) and (2) below, where it appears to the Agency that any poisonous, noxious or polluting matter or any solid waste matter is likely to enter, or to be or to have been present in, any controlled waters, the Agency shall be entitled to carry out the following works and operations, that is to say—

(*a*) in a case where the matter appears likely to enter any controlled waters, works and operations for the purpose of preventing it from doing so; or

(*b*) in a case where the matter appears to be or to have been present in any controlled waters, works and operations for the purpose—

(i) of removing or disposing of the matter;

(ii) of remedying or mitigating any pollution caused by its presence in the waters; or

(iii) so far as it is reasonably practicable to do so, of restoring the waters, including any flora and fauna dependent on the aquatic environment of the waters, to their state immediately before the matter became present in the waters,

and, in either case, the Agency shall be entitled to carry out investigations for the purpose of establishing the source of the matter and the identity of the person who has caused or knowingly permitted it to be present in controlled waters or at a place from which it was likely, in the opinion of the Agency, to enter controlled waters,

(1A) Without prejudice to the power of the Agency to carry out investigations under subsection

(1) above, the power conferred by that subsection to carry out works and operations shall only be exercisable in a case where—

(*a*) the Agency considers it necessary to carry out forthwith any works or operations falling within paragraph (*a*) or (*b*) of that subsection; or

(*b*) it appears to the Agency, after reasonable inquiry, that no person can be found on whom to serve a works notice under section 161A below.

(2) Nothing in subsection (1) above shall entitle the Agency to impede or prevent the making of any discharge in pursuance of a consent given under Chapter I of Part III of this Act.

(3) Where the Agency carries out any such works, operations or investigations as are mentioned in subsection (1) above, it shall, subject to subsection (4) below, be entitled to recover the expenses reasonably incurred in doing so from any person who, as the case may be—

(*a*) caused or knowingly permitted the matter in question to be present at the place from which it was likely, in the opinion of the Agency, to enter any controlled waters; or

(*b*) caused or knowingly permitted the matter in question to be present in any controlled waters.

(4) No such expenses shall be recoverable from a person for any works, operations or investigations in respect of water from an abandoned mine or an abandoned part of a mine which that person permitted to reach such a place as is mentioned in subsection (3) above or to enter any controlled waters.

(4A) Subsection (4) above shall not apply to the owner or former operator of any mine or part of a mine if the mine or part in question became abandoned after 31 December 1999.

(4B) Subsections (3B) and (3C) of section 89 above shall apply in relation to subsections (4) and (4A) above as they apply in relation to subsections (3) and (3A) of that section.

(5) Nothing in this section—

(*a*) derogates from any right of action or other remedy (whether civil or criminal) in proceedings instituted otherwise than under this section; or

(*b*) affects any restriction imposed by or under any other enactment, whether public, local or private.

(6) In this section—

"controlled waters" has the same meaning as in Part III of this Act; and
"expenses" includes costs;
"mine" has the same meaning as in the Mines and Quarries Act 1954.

[Water Resources Act 1991, s 161, as amended by the Environment Act 1995, s 60 and Sch 22.]

1. Part VII comprises ss 154–186.

8–31704B 161A. Notices requiring persons to carry out anti-pollution works and operations. (1) Subject to the following provisions of this section, where it appears to the Agency that any poisonous, noxious or polluting matter or any solid waste matter is likely to enter, or to be or to have been present in, any controlled waters, the Agency shall be entitled to serve a works notice on any person who, as the case may be,—

(*a*) caused or knowingly permitted the matter in question to be present at the place from which it is likely, in the opinion of the Agency, to enter any controlled waters; or

(*b*) caused or knowingly permitted the matter in question to be present in any controlled waters.

(2) For the purposes of this section, a "works notice" is a notice requiring the person on whom it is served to carry out such of the following works or operations as may be specified in the notice, that is to say—

(*a*) in a case where the matter in question appears likely to enter any controlled waters, works or operations for the purpose of preventing it from doing so; or

(*b*) in a case where the matter appears to be or to have been present in any controlled waters, works or operations for the purpose—

(i) of removing or disposing of the matter;

(ii) of remedying or mitigating any pollution caused by its presence in the waters; or

(iii) so far as it is reasonably practicable to do so, of restoring the waters, including any flora and fauna dependent on the aquatic environment of the waters, to their state immediately before the matter became present in the waters.

(3) A works notice—

(*a*) must specify the periods within which the person on whom it is served is required to do each of the things specified in the notice; and

(*b*) is without prejudice to the powers of the Agency by virtue of section 161(1A)(*a*) above.

(4) Before serving a works notice on any person, the Agency shall reasonably endeavour to consult that person concerning the works or operations which are to be specified in the notice.

(5) *Power of Secretary of State to make regulations*[1] *with respect to form of works notices and procedure.*

(6) A works notice shall not be regarded as invalid, or as invalidly served, by reason only of any failure to comply with the requirements of subsection (4) above or of regulations made by virtue of paragraph (*b*) of subsection (5) above.

(7) Nothing in subsection (1) above shall entitle the Agency to require the carrying out of any works or operations which would impede or prevent the making of any discharge in pursuance of a consent given under Chapter II of Part III of this Act.

(8) No works notice shall be served on any person requiring him to carry out any works or operations in respect of water from an abandoned mine or an abandoned part of a mine which that person permitted to reach such a place as is mentioned in subsection (1)(*a*) above or to enter any controlled waters.

(9) Subsection (8) above shall not apply to the owner or former operator of any mine or part of a mine if the mine or part in question became abandoned after 31st December 1999.

(10) Subsections (3B) and (3C) of section 89 above shall apply in relation to subsections (8) and (9) above as they apply in relation to subsections (3) and (3A) of that section.

(11) Where the Agency—

(*a*) carries out any such investigations as are mentioned in section 161(1) above, and

(*b*) serves a works notice on a person in connection with the matter to which the investigations relate,

it shall (unless the notice is quashed or withdrawn) be entitled to recover the costs or expenses reasonably incurred in carrying out those investigations from that person.

(12) The Secretary of State may, if he thinks fit in relation to any person, give directions to the Agency as to whether or how it should exercise its powers under this section.

(13) In this section—

"controlled waters" has the same meaning as in Part III of this Act;

"mine" has the same meaning as in the Mines and Quarries Act 1954.

[Water Resources Act 1991, s 161A, as inserted by the Environment Act 1995, Sch 22.]

1. The Anti-Pollution Works Regulations 1999, SI 1999/1006 have been made.

8–31704C 161B. Grant of, and compensation for, rights of entry etc. (1) A works notice may require a person to carry out works or operations in relation to any land or waters notwithstanding that he is not entitled to carry out those works or operations.

(2) Any person whose consent is required before any works or operations required by a works notice may be carried out shall grant, or join in granting, such rights in relation to any land or waters as will enable the person on whom the works notice is served to comply with any requirements imposed by the works notice.

(3) Before serving a works notice, the Agency shall reasonably endeavour to consult every person who appears to it—

(*a*) to be the owner or occupier of any relevant land, and

(*b*) to be a person who might be required by subsection (2) above to grant, or join in granting, any rights,

concerning the rights which that person may be so required to grant.

(4) A works notice shall not be regarded as invalid, or as invalidly served, by reason only of any failure to comply with the requirements of subsection (3) above.

(5) A person who grants, or joins in granting, any rights pursuant to subsection (2) above shall be entitled, on making an application within such period as may be prescribed and in such manner as may be prescribed to such person as may be prescribed, to be paid by the person on whom the works notice in question is served compensation of such amount as may be determined in such manner as may be prescribed.

(6) Without prejudice to the generality of the regulations that may be made by virtue of subsection (5) above, regulations by virtue of that subjection may make such provision in relation to compensation under this section as may be made by regulations by virtue of subsection (4) of section 35A of the Environmental Protection Act 1990 in relation to compensation under that section.

(7) In this section—

"prescribed" means prescribed in regulations[1] made by the Secretary of State;

"relevant land" means—

(*a*) any land or waters in relation to which the works notice in question requires, or may require, works or operations to be carried out; or

(*b*) any land adjoining or adjacent to that land or those waters;

"works notice" means a works notice under section 161A above.

[Water Resources Act 1991, s 161B, as inserted by the Environment Act 1995, Sch 22.]

1. The Anti-Pollution Works Regulations 1999, SI 1999/1006 have been made.

8–31704D 161C. Appeals against works notices. (1) A person on whom a works notice is served may, within the period of twenty-one days beginning with the day on which the notice is served, appeal against the notice to the Secretary of State.

(2) On any appeal under this section the Secretary of State—

(*a*) shall quash the notice, if he is satisfied that there is a material defect in the notice; but
(*b*) subject to that, may confirm the notice, with or without modification, or quash it.

(3) The Secretary of State may by regulations[1] make provision with respect to—

(*a*) the grounds on which appeals under this section may be made; or
(*b*) the procedure on any such appeal.

(4) Regulations[1] under subsection (3) above may (among other things)—

(*a*) include provisions comparable to those in section 290 of the Public Health Act 1936 (appeals against notices requiring the execution of works);
(*b*) prescribe the cases in which a works notice is, or is not, to be suspended until the appeal is decided, or until some other stage in the proceedings;
(*c*) prescribe the cases in which the decision on an appeal may in some respects be less favourable to the appellant than the works notice against which he is appealing;
(*d*) prescribe the cases in which the appellant may claim that a works notice should have been served on some other person and prescribe the procedure to be followed in those cases;
(*e*) make provision as respects—
  (i) the particulars to be included in the notice of appeal;
  (ii) the persons on whom notice of appeal is to be served and the particulars, if any, which are to accompany the notice; or
  (iii) the abandonment of an appeal.

(5) In this section "works notice" means a works notice under section 161A above.

(6) This section is subject to section 114 of the 1995 Act (delegation or reference of appeals).

[Water Resources Act 1991, s 161C, as inserted by the Environment Act 1995, Sch 22.]

---

1. The Anti-Pollution Works Regulations 1999, SI 1999/1006 have been made.

8–31704E 161D. Consequences of not complying with a works notice. (1) If a person on whom the Agency serves a works notice fails to comply with any of the requirements of the notice, he shall be guilty of an offence.

(2) A person who commits an offence under subsection (1) above shall be liable[1]—

(*a*) on summary conviction, to imprisonment for a term not exceeding **three months** or to a fine not exceeding **£20,000** or to **both**;
(*b*) on conviction on indictment to imprisonment for a term not exceeding **two years** or to a **fine** or to **both**.

(3) If a person on whom a works notice has been served fails to comply with any of the requirements of the notice, the Agency may do what that person was required to do and may recover from him any costs or expenses reasonably incurred by the Agency in doing it.

(4) If the Agency is of the opinion that proceedings for an offence under subsection (1) above would afford an ineffectual remedy against a person who has failed to comply with the requirements of a works notice, the Agency may take proceedings in the High Court for the purpose of securing compliance with the notice.

(5) In this section "works notice" means a works notice under section 161A above.

[Water Resources Act 1991, s 161D, as inserted by the Environment Act 1995, Sch 22.]

---

1. For procedure in respect of this offence which is triable either way, see the Magistrates' Courts Act 1980, ss 17A–21, in PART I: MAGISTRATES' COURTS, PROCEDURE, ante.

Powers to discharge water

8–31705 163. Discharges for works purposes. The Agency working on reservoir, well, borehole etc may discharge water into any available watercourse but must take steps to secure that the discharge is reasonably free from pollutants; failure punishable on summary conviction by fine not exceeding **level 3** on the standard scale[1].

[Water Resources Act 1991, s 163 amended by the Environment Act 1995, Sch 22 and SI 2003/1615—summarised.]

---

1. Section 163 is expressed in terms similar to s 165 of the Water Industry Act 1991, ante.

8–31706 164. *Consents for certain discharges under section 163.*

CHAPTER II
POWERS OF ENTRY

8–31707 169. Powers of entry for enforcement purposes. (1) Any person designated in writing for the purpose by either of the Ministers or by the Agency may—

(*a*) enter any premises or vessel for the purpose of ascertaining whether any provision of an enactment to which this section applies, of any subordinate legislation or other instrument made by virtue of any such enactment or of any byelaws made by the Agency is being or has been contravened; and

(*b*) carry out such inspections, measurements and tests on any premises or vessel entered by that person or of any articles found on any such premises or vessel, and take away such samples of water or effluent or of any land or articles, as that Minister or the Agency—

(i) considers appropriate for the purpose mentioned in paragraph (*a*) above; and
(ii) has authorised that person to carry out or take away.

(2) The powers conferred by subsection (1) above in relation to any premises shall include power, in order to obtain information for the purpose mentioned in subsection (1)(a) above—

(*a*) to carry out experimental borings or other works on those premises; and
(*b*) to install and keep monitoring and other apparatus there.

(3) Subject to subsection (4) below, this section applies to any enactment contained in this Act and to any other enactment under or for the purposes of which the Agency carries out functions.

(4) The powers conferred by this section shall not have effect for the purposes of any of the Agency's pollution control functions, within the meaning of section 108 of the 1995 Act.

[Water Resources Act 1991, s 169, as amended by the Environment Act 1995, Sch 22 and the Water Act 2003, s 71.]

8–31707A 170. Power of entry for certain works purposes. (1) Any person designated in writing for the purpose by the Agency may enter any premises for any of the purposes specified in subsection (2) below.

(2) The purposes mentioned in subsection (1) above are—

(*a*) the carrying out of any survey or tests for the purpose of determining—

(i) whether it is appropriate and practicable for the Agency to exercise any relevant works power; or
(ii) how any such power should be exercised;

(*b*) the exercise of any such power.

(3) The power by virtue of subsection (1) above of a person designated by the Agency to enter any premises for the purposes of carrying out any survey or tests shall include power—

(*a*) to carry out experimental borings or other works for the purpose of ascertaining the nature of the sub-soil; and

(*b*) to take away and analyse such samples of water or effluent or of any land or article as the agency considers necessary for the purpose of determining either of the matters mentioned in subsection (2)(*a*) above and has authorised that person to take away and analyse.

(4) In this section "relevant works power" means any power conferred by any of the provisions of sections 159, 160, 162(2) and (3) and 163 above.

[Water Resources Act 1991, s 170, as amended by the Environment Act 1995, Sch 22.]

8–31707B 171. Power to carry out surveys and to search for water. (1) Without prejudice to the rights and powers conferred by the other provisions of this Chapter, any person designated in writing under this section by the Agency may enter any premises for any of the purposes specified in subsection (2) below.

(2) The purposes mentioned in subsection (1) above are the carrying out of any survey or tests for the purpose of determining—

(*a*) whether it would be appropriate for the Agency to acquire any land, or any interest or right in or over land, for purposes connected with the carrying out of its functions; or

(*b*) whether it would be appropriate for the Agency to apply for an order under section 168 above and what compulsory powers it would be appropriate to apply for under that section.

(3) The power by virtue of subsection (1) above of a person designated under this section to enter any premises for the purpose of carrying out any survey or tests shall include power—

(*a*) to carry out experimental borings or other works for the purpose of ascertaining the nature of the sub-soil, the presence of underground water in the sub-soil or the quantity or quality of any such water;

(*b*) to install and keep monitoring or other apparatus on the premises for the purpose of obtaining the information on which any such determination as is mentioned in subsection (2) above may be made; and (*c*) to take away and analyse such samples of water or of any land or articles as the Agency considers necessary for any of the purposes so mentioned and has authorised that person to take away and analyse.

(4) The powers conferred by this section shall not be exercised in any case for purposes connected with the determination of—

(*a*) whether, where or how a reservoir should be constructed; or
(*b*) whether, where or how a borehole should be sunk for the purpose of abstracting water from or discharging water into any underground strata,

unless the Secretary of State has, in accordance with subsection (5) below, given his written authorisation in relation to that case for the exercise of those powers for those purposes.

(5) The Secretary of State shall not give his authorisation for the purposes of subsection (4) above unless—

(*a*) he is satisfied that notice of the proposal to apply for the authorisation has been given to the owner and to the occupier of the premises in question; and
(*b*) he has considered any representation or objections with respect to the proposed exercise of the powers under this section which—
   (i) have been duly made to him by the owner or occupier of those premises, within the period of fourteen days beginning with the day after the giving of the notice; and
   (ii) have not been withdrawn.

[Water Resources Act 1991, s 171, as amended by the Environment Act 1995, Sch 22.]

8–31707C 172. Powers of entry for other purposes. (1) Any person designated in writing for the purpose by either of the Ministers of the Agency may enter any premises or vessel for the purpose of—

(*a*) determining whether, and if so in what manner, any power or duty conferred or imposed on either of the Ministers or on the Agency by virtue of any enactment to which this section applies (including a power of either or both of the Ministers to make subordinate legislation) should be exercised or, as the case may be, performed; or
(*b*) exercising or performing any power or duty which is so conferred or imposed.

(2) Any person designated in writing for the purpose by either of the Ministers or the Agency may—

(*a*) carry out such inspections, measurements and tests on any premises or vessel entered by that person under this section or of any articles found on any such premises or vessel; and
(*b*) take away such samples of water or effluent or of any land or articles,

as that Minister or the Agency considers appropriate for any purpose mentioned in subsection (1) above and has authorised that person to carry out or take away.

(3) Subject to subsection (3A) below the powers which by virtue of subsections (1) and (2) above are conferred in relation to any premises for the purpose of enabling either of the Ministers or the Agency to determine whether or in what manner to exercise or perform any power or duty conferred or imposed on him or it by or under the water pollution provisions of this Act shall include power, in order to obtain the information on which that determination may be made—

(*a*) to carry out experimental borings or other works on those premises; and
(*b*) to install and keep monitoring and other apparatus there.

(3A) The powers conferred by this section shall not have effect for the purposes of any of the Agency's pollution control functions, within the meaning of section 108 of the 1995 Act.

(4) This section applies to any enactment contained in this Act and to any other enactment under or for the purposes of which the Agency carries out functions.

[Water Resources Act 1991, s 172, as amended by the Environment Act 1995, Sch 22.]

8–31707D 173. Powers of entry: supplemental provisions. Schedule 20[1] to this Act shall have effect with respect to the powers of entry and related powers which are conferred by the preceding provisions of this Chapter.

[Water Resources Act 1991, s 173.]

---

1. See Sch 20, post, for supplemental provisions including the issue of warrants.

8–31708 174. Impersonation of persons exercising powers of entry. (1) A person who, without having been designated or authorised for the purpose by the Agency, purports to be entitled to enter any premises or vessel in exercise of a power exercisable in pursuance of any such designation or authorisation shall be guilty of an offence and liable[1]—

(*a*) on summary conviction, to a fine not exceeding the **statutory maximum;**
(*b*) on conviction on indictment, to a **fine** or to imprisonment for a term not exceeding **two years**, or to **both**.

(2) For the purposes of this section it shall be immaterial, where a person purports to be entitled to enter any premises or vessel, that the power which that person purports to be entitled to exercise does not exist, or would not be exercisable, even if that person had been designated or authorised by the Agency.
[Water Resources Act 1991, s 174, as amended by the Environment Act 1995, Sch 22.]

---

1. For procedure in respect of an offence which is triable either way, see the Magistrates' Courts Act 1980, ss 17A–21, in PART I: MAGISTRATES' COURTS, PROCEDURE.

Offence of interference with works etc

8–31709 176. Offence of interference with works etc. (1) Subject to subsection (2) below, if any person without the consent of the Agency—

(*a*) intentionally or recklessly interferes with any resource main or other pipe vested in the Agency or with any structure, installation or apparatus belonging to the Agency; or
(*b*) by any act or omission negligently interferes with any such main or other pipe or with any such structure, installation or apparatus so as to damage it or so as to have an effect on its use or operation,

that person shall be guilty of an offence and liable, on summary conviction, to a fine not exceeding **level 3** on the standard scale.

(2) A person shall not be guilty of an offence under subsection (1) above—

(*a*) by reason of anything done in an emergency to prevent loss or damage to persons or property; or
(*b*) by reason of his opening or closing the stopcock fitted to a service pipe by means of which water is supplied to any premises by a water undertaker if—
  (i) he has obtained the consent of every consumer whose supply is affected by the opening or closing of that stopcock or, as the case may be, of every other consumer whose supply is so affected; and
  (ii) in the case of opening a stopcock, the stopcock was closed otherwise than by the undertaker.

(3) Any person who without the consent of the Agency—

(*a*) attaches any pipe or apparatus to any resource main or other pipe vested in the Agency; or
(*b*) subject to subsection (4) below, uses any pipe or apparatus which has been attached or altered in contravention of this section,

shall be guilty of an offence and liable, on summary conviction, to a fine not exceeding **level 3** on the standard scale.

(4) In proceedings against any person for an offence by virtue of paragraph (*b*) of subsection (3) above it shall be a defence for that person to show that he did not know, and had no grounds for suspecting, that the pipe or apparatus in question had been attached or altered as mentioned in that subsection.

(5), (6) *Action by Agency for loss or damage.*

(7) In this section "service pipe" and "stopcock" have the same meanings as in the Water Industry Act 1991, and "consumer" has the same meaning as in Part III of that Act.
[Water Resources Act 1991, s 176, as amended by the Environment Act 1995, Sch 22.]

Interpretation of Part VII

8–31710 186. Interpretation of Part VII. (1) In this Part—

"discharge pipe" means a pipe from which discharges are or are to be made under section 163 above;
"resource main" means any pipe, not being a trunk main within the meaning of the Water Industry Act 1991, which is or is to be used for the purpose of—

(*a*) conveying water from one source of supply to another, from a source of supply to a regulating reservoir or from a regulating reservoir to a source of supply; or
(*b*) giving or taking a supply of water in bulk.

(2) In subsection (1) above—

"source of supply" shall be construed without reference to the definition of that expression in section 221 below; and
"supply of water in bulk" has the same meaning as in section 3 above[1].

(3) The powers conferred by Chapter I of this Part[2] shall be without prejudice to the powers conferred on the Agency by any other enactment or by any agreement.
[Water Resources Act 1991, s 186, as amended by the Environment Act 1995, Sch 22.]

1. Section 3 defines "supply of water in bulk" as a supply of water for distribution by a water undertaker taking the supply.
2. Chapter I of Part VII comprises ss 154.

PART VIII[1]
INFORMATION PROVISIONS

Provision and acquisition of information etc

8–31711 198. Information about underground water. Any person searching for or abstracting water by sinking a well or borehole deeper than 50 feet to notify, keep journal for, and supply particulars to the Natural Environment Research Council; he (and the occupier if different person) to allow access etc; failure is summary offence punishable by fine not exceeding **level 3** on the standard scale and a fine of £20 a day thereafter for continuing offence.
[Water Resources Act 1991, s 198—summarised.]

1. Part VII comprises ss 187–206.

8–31712 199. Notice etc of mining operations which may affect water conservation. Failure to give notice or fail to comply with conservation notice is an offence punishable on summary conviction by a fine not exceeding the **statutory maximum** and on conviction on indictment by a **fine**[1].*
[Water Resources Act 1991, s 199—summarised.]

***Section amended by the Water Act 2003, s 8, from a date to be appointed.**
1. For procedure in respect of an offence triable either way, see the Magistrates' Courts Act 1980, ss 17A–21 in PART I: MAGISTRATES' COURTS, PROCEDURE, ante.

8–31712A 199A. Appeals against conservation notices under section 199

8–31713 200. Gauges and records kept by other persons. Person proposing to install gauge on inland waters other than discrete waters to notify Agency, allow three months to elapse before installation, and state where records to be kept: contravention punishable on summary conviction by a fine not exceeding **level 1** on the standard scale.
[Water Resources Act 1991, s 200 amended by the Environment Act, Sch 22—summarised.]

8–31714 201. Power to require information with respect of water resouces functions. Person failing to comply with directions liable on summary conviction to fine not exceeding the statutory maximum and on conviction on indictment to a fine or imprisonment for a term not exceeding two years, or both.
[Water Resources Act 1991, s 201 as amended by the Water Act 2003, s 70—summarised.]

8–31715 202. Information and assistance required in connection with the control of pollution. (1) It shall be the duty of the Agency, if and so far as it is requested to do so by either of the Ministers, to give him all such advice and assistance as appears to it to be appropriate for facilitating the carrying out by him of his functions under the water pollution provisions of this Act.

(2) Subject to subsection (3) below, either of the Ministers of the Agency may serve on any person a notice requiring that person to furnish him or, as the case may be, it, within a period or at times specified in the notice and in a form and manner so specified, with such information as is reasonably required by the Minister in question or by the Agency for the purpose of carrying out any of his or, as the case may be, its functions under the water pollution provisions of this Act.

(3) Each of the Ministers shall have power by regulations to make provision for restricting the information which may be required under subsection (2) above and for determining the form in which the information is to be so required.

(4) A person who fails without reasonable excuse to comply with the requirements of a notice served on him under this section shall be guilty of an offence and liable[1]—

(*a*) on summary conviction, to a fine not exceeding the **statutory maximum;**
(*b*) on conviction on indictment, to a **fine** or to imprisonment for a term not exceeding **two years**, or to **both**.

(5) (*Repealed*).
[Water Resources Act 1991, s 202, as amended by the Environment Act 1995, Schs 22 and 24.]

1. For procedure in respect of this offence which is triable either way, see the Magistrates' Courts Act 1980, ss 17A–21, in PART I: MAGISTRATES' COURTS, PROCEDURE, ante.

Restriction on disclosure of information

8–31716 **204. Restriction on disclosure of information.** Subject to the following provisions of this section, no information with respect to any particular business which—

(*a*) has been obtained by virtue of any of the provisions of this Act; and
(*b*) relates to the affairs of any individual or to any particular business,

shall, during the lifetime of that individual or so long as that business continues to be carried on, be disclosed without the consent of that individual or the person for the time being carrying on that business.

(2) Subsection (1) above does not apply to any disclosure of information which is made—

(*a*) for the purpose of facilitating the carrying out by either of the Ministers, the Agency, the Scottish Environment Protection Agency, the Water Services Regulation Authority, the Consumer Council for Water, the Competition Commission or a local authority of any of his, its or, as the case may be, their functions by virtue of this Act, any of the other consolidation Acts or the Water Act 1989 Part I or IIA of the Environmental Protection Act 1990, the 1995 Act, regulations under section 2 of the Pollution Prevention and Control Act 1999, or the Water Act 2003;
(*b*) for the purpose of facilitating the performance by a water undertaker, sewerage undertaker or company holding a licence under Chapter 1A of Part 2 of the Water Industry Act 1991 of any of the duties imposed on it by or under this Act, any of the other consolidation Acts, the Water Act 1989 or the Water Act 2003;
(*c*) in pursuance of any duty imposed by section 197(1)(*a*) or (2) or 203(1), (1A), (2) or (2A) above or of any duty imposed by section 27H of the Water Industry Act 1991;
(*d*) for the purpose of facilitating the carrying out by any person mentioned in Part I of Schedule 24 to this Act of any of his functions under any of the enactments or instruments specified in Part II of that Schedule;
(*e*) for the purpose of enabling or assisting the Secretary of State, the Treasury or the Financial Services Authority to exercise any powers conferred by or under the Financial Services and Markets Act 2000 or by the enactments relating to companies or insolvency;
(*ea*) for the purpose of enabling or assisting any inspector appointed under enactments relating to companies to carry out his functions;
(*f*) for the purpose of enabling an official receiver to carry out his functions under the enactments relating to insolvency or for the purpose of enabling or assisting a recognised professional body for the purposes of section 391 of the Insolvency Act 1986 to carry out its functions as such;
(*g*) for the purpose of facilitating the carrying out by the Health and Safety Commission or the Health and Safety Executive of any of its functions under any enactment or of facilitating the carrying out by any enforcing authority, within the meaning of Part I of the Health and Safety at Work etc Act 1974, of any functions under a relevant statutory provision, within the meaning of that Act;
(*h*) for the purpose of facilitating the carrying out by the Comptroller and Auditor General of any of his functions under any enactment;
(*i*) in connection with the investigation of any criminal offence or for the purposes of any criminal proceedings;
(*j*) for the purposes of any civil proceedings brought under or by virtue of this Act, any of the other consolidation Acts, the Water Act 1989, the Water Act 2003 or any of the enactments or instruments specified in Part II of Schedule 24 to this Act, or of any arbitration under this Act, any of the other consolidation Acts, the Water Act 1989 or the Water Act 2003; or
(*k*) in pursuance of a Community obligation.

(3) Nothing in subsection (1) above shall be construed—

(*a*) as limiting the matters which may be included in, or made public as part of, a report of—

(i) the Agency;
(ia) the Scottish Environment Protection Agency;
(ii) the Water Services Regulation Authority;
(iii) the Consumer Council for Water (or any regional committee of that Council established under section 27A of the Water Industry Act 1991); or
(iv) the Competition Commission,

under any provision of this Act, Part I or IIA of the Environmental Protection Act 1990, that Act of 1991, the 1995 Act, regulations under section 2 of the Pollution Prevention and Control Act 1999, or the Water Act 2003;

(*b*) as limiting the matters which may be published under section 201 of that Act of 1991; or
(*c*) as applying to any information which has been made public as part of such a report or has been so published or to any information exclusively of a statistical nature.

(4) Subject to subsection (5) below, nothing in subsection (1) above shall preclude the disclosure of information—

(*a*) if the disclosure is of information relating to a matter connected with the carrying out of the functions of a water undertaker or sewerage undertaker, or with the carrying on by a company holding a licence under Chapter 1A of Part 2 of the Water Industry Act 1991 of activities under its licence, and is made by one Minister of the Crown or government department to another; or

(*b*) if the disclosure is for the purpose of enabling or assisting any public or other authority for the time being designated for the purposes of this section by an order made by the Secretary of State to discharge any functions which are specified in the order.

(5) The power to make an order under subsection (4) above shall be exercisable by statutory instrument subject to annulment in pursuance of a resolution of either House of Parliament; and where such an order designates an authority for the purposes of paragraph (*b*) of that subsection, the order may—

(*a*) impose conditions subject to which the disclosure of information is permitted by virtue of that paragraph; and

(*b*) otherwise restrict the circumstances in which disclosure is so permitted.

(6) Any person who discloses any information in contravention of the preceding provisions of this section shall be guilty of an offence and liable[1]—

(*a*) on summary conviction, to a fine not exceeding the **statutory maximum**;

(*b*) on conviction on indictment, to imprisonment for a term not exceeding **two years** or to a **fine** or to **both**.

(7) In this section "the other consolidation Acts" means the Water Industry Act 1991, the Statutory Water Companies Act 1991, the Land Drainage Act 1991 and the Water Consolidation (Consequential Provisions) Act 1991.

[Water Resources Act 1991, s 204, as amended by the Environment Act 1995, Sch 22, SI 1999/506, the Pollution Prevention and Control Act 1999, Sch 2, SI 2001/3649, the Pollution Prevention and Control Act 1999, Sch 3 and the Water Act 2003, Sch 7.]

1. For procedure in respect of an offence triable either way, see the Magistrates' Courts Act 1980, ss 17A–21 in PART I: MAGISTRATES' COURTS, PROCEDURE, ante.

8–31717 205. Confidentiality of information relating to underground water etc. (1) The person sinking any such well or borehole as is mentioned in section 198 above or, if it is a different person, the owner or occupier of the land on which any such well or borehole is sunk may by notice to the Natural Environment Research Council require that Council to treat as confidential—

(*a*) any copy of or extract from the journal required to be kept under that section; or

(*b*) any specimen taken in exercise of the rights specified in subsection (5) of that section.

(2) Subject to subsections (3) and (4) below, the Natural Environment Research Council shall not, without the consent of the person giving the notice, allow any matter to which any notice under subsection (1) above relates to be published or shown to any person who is not an officer of that Council or of a department of the Secretary of State.

(3) Subsection (2) above shall not prohibit any matter from being published or shown to any person in so far as it contains or affords information as to water resources and supplies.

(4) If at any time the Natural Environment Research Council give notice to any person that in their opinion his consent for the purposes of subsection (2) above is being unreasonably withheld—

(*a*) that person may, within three months after the giving of the notice, appeal to the High Court for an order restraining that Council from acting as if consent had been given; and

(*b*) that Council may proceed as if consent had been given if either no such appeal is brought within that period or the High Court, after hearing the appeal, do not make such an order.

(5) Any person who fails to comply with any obligation imposed on him by the preceding provisions of this section shall be guilty of an offence and liable, on summary conviction—

(*a*) to a fine not exceeding **level 3** on the standard scale; and

(*b*) where the offence continues after conviction, to a further fine of £20 for every day during which it so continues.

(6) If any person who is admitted to any premises in compliance with section 198(2)(*c*) above discloses to any person any information obtained by him there with regard to any manufacturing process or trade secret, he shall, unless the disclosure is in performance of his duty, be guilty of an offence and liable[1]—

(*a*) on summary conviction, to imprisonment for a term not exceeding **three months** or to a fine not exceeding the **statutory maximum** or to **both**;

(*b*) on conviction on indictment, to imprisonment for a term not exceeding **three months** or to a **fine** or to **both**.

[Water Resources Act 1991, s 205.]

1. For procedure in respect of an offence triable either way, see the Magistrates' Courts Act 1980, ss 17A–21 in PART I: MAGISTRATES' COURTS, PROCEDURE, ante.

Making of false statements etc

8–31718 206. Making of false statements etc. (1) If, in furnishing any information or making any application under or for the purposes of any provision of this Act, any person makes a statement which he knows to be false or misleading in a material particular, or recklessly makes any statement which is false or misleading in a material particular, he shall be guilty of an offence under this section.

(2) (*Repealed*).

(3) Where—

(*a*) the provisions contained in a licence under Chapter II of Part II of this Act in pursuance of paragraph (*b*) of subsection (2) of section 46 above, or of that paragraph as modified by subsection (6) of that section, require the use of a meter, gauge or other device; and

(*b*) such a device is used for the purposes of those provisions,

any person who wilfully alters or interferes with that device so as to prevent it from measuring correctly shall be guilty of an offence under this section.

(3A) If a person intentionally makes a false entry in any record required to be kept by virtue of a licence under Chapter II of Part II of this Act, or a consent under Chapter II of Part III of this Act, he shall be guilty of an offence under this section.

(4) If, in keeping any record or journal or in furnishing any information which he is required to keep or furnish under section 198 or 205 above, any person knowingly or recklessly makes any statement which is false in a material particular, he shall be guilty of an offence under this section.

(5) A person who is guilty of an offence under this section shall be liable[1]—

(*a*) on summary conviction, to a fine not exceeding the **statutory maximum;**

(*b*) on conviction on indictment, to a **fine** or to imprisonment for a term not exceeding **two years**, or to **both**.

[Water Resources Act 1991, s 206, as amended by the Environment Act 1995, Schs 19 and 24.]

1. For procedure in respect of an offence triable either way, see the Magistrates' Courts Act 1980, ss 17A–21 in PART I: MAGISTRATES' COURTS, PROCEDURE, ante.

PART IX[1]
MISCELLANEOUS AND SUPPLEMENTAL

Miscellaneous

8–31719 209. Evidence of samples and abstractions. (1)–(2) (*Repealed*).

(3) Where, in accordance with the provisions contained in a licence in pursuance of paragraph (*b*) of subsection (2) of section 46 above, or in pursuance of that paragraph as read with subsection (6) of that section, it has been determined what quantity of water is to be taken—

(*a*) to have been abstracted during any period from a source of supply by the holder of the licence; or

(*b*) to have been so abstracted at a particular point or by particular means, or for use for particular purposes,

that determination shall, for the purposes of any proceedings under Chapter II of Part II of this Act or any of the related water resources provisions, be conclusive evidence of the matters to which it relates.

(4) (*Repealed*).

[Water Resources Act 1991, s 209, as amended by the Environment Act 1995, Sch 24.]

1. Part IX comprises ss 207–225.

Byelaws

8–31720 210. Byelaw-making powers of the Agency. (1) Schedule 25[1] to this Act shall have effect for conferring powers on the Agency to make byelaws for purposes connected with the carrying out of its functions.

(2) Schedule 26[1] to this Act shall have effect in relation to byelaws made by the Agency, whether by virtue of subsection (1) above or by virtue of any other enactment.

[Water Resources Act 1991, s 210, as amended by the Environment Act 1995, Sch 22.]

1. See, post.

8–31720A 211. Enforcement of byelaws. (1) If any person contravenes any byelaws made by virtue of paragraph 1 of Schedule 25[1] to this Act, he shall be guilty of an offence and liable, on summary conviction—

(*a*) to a fine not exceeding **level 1** on the standard scale; and (*b*) if the contravention is continued after conviction, to a fine not exceeding **£5** for each day on which it is so continued.

(2) Byelaws made by virtue of paragraph 2 or 3 of that Schedule may contain provision providing for a contravention of the byelaws to constitute a summary offence punishable, on summary conviction, by a fine not exceeding **level 5** on the standard scale or such smaller sum as may be specified in the byelaws.

(3) A person who contravenes any byelaws made by virtue of paragraph 4 or 6 of that Schedule shall be guilty of an offence and liable, on summary conviction, to a fine not exceeding **level 4** on the standard scale or, in the case of byelaws made by virtue of paragraph 4, such smaller sum as may be specified in the byelaws.

(4) If any person acts in contravention of any byelaw made by virtue of paragraph 5 of that Schedule he shall be guilty of an offence and liable, on summary conviction—

(*a*) to a fine not exceeding **level 5** on the standard scale; and

(*b*) if the contravention is continued after conviction, to a further fine not exceeding **£40** for each day on which it is so continued.

(5) Without prejudice to any proceedings by virtue of subsection (1) or (4) above, the Agency may—

(*a*) take such action as it considers necessary to remedy the effect of any contravention of byelaws made by virtue of paragraph 1 of Schedule 25 to this Act;

(*b*) take such action as may be necessary to remedy the effect of any person's contravention of byelaws made by virtue of paragraph 5 of that Schedule; and

(*c*) recover the expenses reasonably incurred by the Agency in taking any action under paragraph (*a*) or (*b*) above from the person in default.

(6) So much of the Salmon and Freshwater Fisheries Act 1975[2] as makes provision with respect to or by reference to offences under that Act shall have effect as if an offence consisting in a contravention of byelaws made by virtue of paragraph 6 of Schedule 25 to this Act were an offence under that Act.

(7) Section 70 above shall apply in relation to any restrictions imposed by byelaws made by virtue of paragraph 1 of Schedule 25 to this Act as it applies in relation to restrictions imposed by the provisions of Chapter II of Part II of this Act which are mentioned in that section; and sections 100 and 101 above shall have effect in relation to contraventions of byelaws made by virtue of paragraph 4 of that Schedule as they have effect in relation to contraventions of provisions of Part III of this Act.

[Water Resources Act 1991, s 211, as amended by the Environment Act 1995, Sch 22.]

---

1. See, post.
2. See this Part: title, FISHERIES, ante.

Offences etc

8–31721 **216. Enforcement: powers and duties.** (1) Without prejudice to its powers of enforcement in relation to the other provisions of this Act, it shall be the duty of the Agency to enforce the provisions to which this section applies.

(2) No proceedings for any offence under any provision to which this section applies shall be instituted except—

(*a*) by the Agency; or

(*b*) by, or with the consent of, the Director of Public Prosecutions.

(3) This section applies to Chapter II of Part II[1] of this Act and the related water resources provisions.

[Water Resources Act 1991, s 216, as amended by the Environment Act 1995, Sch 22.]

---

1. Part II, Ch II comprises ss 24–72.

8–31722 **217. Criminal liabilities of directors and other third parties.** (1) Where a body corporate is guilty of an offence under this Act and that offence is proved to have been committed with the consent or connivance of, or to be attributable to any neglect on the part of, any director, manager, secretary or other similar officer of the body corporate or any person who was purporting to act in any such capacity, then he, as well as the body corporate, shall be guilty of that offence and shall be liable to be proceeded against and punished accordingly.

(2) Where the affairs of a body corporate are managed by its members, subsection (1) above shall apply in relation to the acts and defaults of a member in connection with his functions of management as if he were a director of the body corporate.

(3) Without prejudice to subsections (1) and (2) above, where the commission by any person of an offence under the water pollution provisions of this Act is due to the act or default of some other

person, that other person may be charged with and convicted of the offence whether or not proceedings for the offence are taken against the first-mentioned person.
[Water Resources Act 1991, s 217.]

8–31723 220. *Provisions relating to service of documents.*

8–31724 221. General interpretation[1]. (1) In this Act, except in so far as the context otherwise requires—

"the 1995 Act" means the Environment Act 1995;

"abstraction", in relation to water contained in any source of supply, means the doing of anything whereby any of that water is removed from that source of supply, whether temporarily or permanently, including anything whereby the water is so removed for the purpose of being transferred to another source of supply; and "abstract" shall be construed accordingly;

"accessories", in relation to a main, sewer or other pipe, includes any manholes, ventilating shafts, inspection chambers, settling tanks, wash-out pipes, pumps, ferrules or stopcocks for the main, sewer or other pipe, or any machinery or other apparatus which is designed or adapted for use in connection with the use or maintenance of the main, sewer or other pipe or of another accessory for it, but does not include any electronic communications apparatus unless it—

(*a*) is or is to be situated inside or in the close vicinity of the main, sewer or other pipe or inside or in the close vicinity of another accessory for it; and
(*b*) is intended to be used only in connection with the use or maintenance of the main, sewer or other pipe or of another accessory for it;

and in this definition "stopcock" has the same meaning as in the Water Industry Act 1991;

"the Agency" means the Environment Agency;

"agriculture" has the same meaning as in the Agriculture Act 1947 and "agricultural" shall be construed accordingly;

"analyse", in relation to any sample of land, water or effluent, includes subjecting the sample to a test of any description, and cognate expressions shall be construed accordingly;

"conservancy authority" means any person who has a duty or power under any enactment to conserve, maintain or improve the navigation of a tidal water and is not a navigation authority or harbour authority;

"contravention" includes a failure to comply, and cognate expressions shall be construed accordingly;

"damage", in relation to individuals, includes death and any personal injury (including any disease or impairment of physical or mental condition);

"discrete waters" means inland waters so far as they comprise—

(*a*) a lake, pond or reservoir which does not discharge to any other inland waters; or
(*b*) one of a group of two or more lakes, ponds or reservoirs (whether near to or distant from each other) and of watercourses or mains connecting them, where none of the inland waters in the group discharges to any inland waters outside the group;

"disposal"—

(*a*) in relation to land or any interest or right in or over land, includes the creation of such an interest or right and a disposal effected by means of the surrender or other termination of any such interest or right; and
(*b*) in relation to sewage, includes treatment;

and cognate expressions shall be construed accordingly;

"drain" has, subject to subsection (2) below, the same meaning as in the Water Industry Act 1991;

"drainage" in the expression "drainage works" has the meaning given by section 113 above for the purposes of Part IV of this Act;

"drought order" means an ordinary drought order under subsection (1) of section 73 above or an emergency drought order under subsection (2) of that section;

"effluent" means any liquid, including particles of matter and other substances in suspension in the liquid;

"enactment" includes an enactment contained in this Act or in any Act passed after this Act;

"enforcement notice" has the meaning given by section 90B above;

"engineering or building operations", without prejudice to the generality of that expression, includes—

(*a*) the construction, alteration, improvement, maintenance or demolition of any building or structure or of any reservoir, watercourse, dam, weir, well, borehole or other works; and
(*b*) the installation, modification or removal of any machinery or apparatus;

"harbour authority" (except in the flood defence provisions of this Act, in which it has the same meaning as in section 313 of the Merchant Shipping Act 1995) means a person who is a harbour authority as defined in section 151 for the purposes of Chapter II of Part VI of that Act and is not a navigation authority;

"highway" has the same meaning as in the Highways Act 1980;

"information" includes anything contained in any records, accounts, estimates or returns;

"inland waters" means the whole or any part of—

(*a*) any river, stream or other watercourse (within the meaning of Chapter II of Part II of this Act), whether natural or artificial and whether tidal or not;

(*b*) any lake or pond, whether natural or artificial, or any reservoir or dock, in so far as the lake, pond, reservoir or dock does not fall within paragraph (*a*) of this definition; and

(*c*) so much of any channel, creek, bay, estuary or arm of the sea as does not fall within paragraph (*a*) or (*b*) of this definition;

"joint planning board" has the same meaning as in the Town and Country Planning Act 1990;

"local authority" means the council of any county, county borough, district or London borough or the Common Council of the City of London;

"local statutory provision" means—

(*a*) a provision of a local Act (including an Act confirming a provisional order);

(*b*) a provision of so much of any public general Act as has effect with respect to a particular area, with respect to particular persons or works or with respect to particular provisions falling within any paragraph of this definition;

(*c*) a provision of an instrument made under any provision falling within paragraph (*a*) or (*b*) above; or

(*d*) a provision of any other instrument which is in the nature of a local enactment;

"main river map" has, subject to section 194 above, the meaning given by section 193(2) above;

"micro-organism" includes any microscopic, biological entity which is capable of replication;

"the Minister" means the Minister of Agriculture, Fisheries and Food;

"the Ministers" means the Secretary of State and the Minister;

"modifications" includes additions, alterations and omissions, and cognate expressions shall be construed accordingly;

"navigation authority" means any person who has a duty or power under any enactment to work, maintain, conserve, improve or control any canal or other inland navigation, navigable river, estuary, harbour or dock;

"notice" means notice in writing;

"owner", in relation to any premises, means the person who—

(*a*) is for the time being receiving the rack-rent of the premises, whether on his own account or as agent or trustee for another person; or

(*b*) would receive the rack-rent if the premises were let at a rack-rent,

but for the purposes of Schedule 2 to this Act, Chapter II of Part II of this Act and the related water resources provisions does not include a mortgagee not in possession, and cognate expressions shall be construed accordingly;

"prescribed" means prescribed by regulations made by the Secretary of State or, in relation to regulations made by the Minister, by those regulations;

"public authority" means any Minister of the Crown or government department, the Authority, any local authority or any person certified by the Secretary of State to be a public authority for the purposes of this Act;

"public sewer" means a sewer for the time being vested in a sewerage undertaker in its capacity as such, whether vested in that undertaker by virtue of a scheme under Schedule 2 to the Water Act 1989, section 179 of or Schedule 2 to the Water Industry Act 1991 or otherwise;

"records" includes computer records and any other records kept otherwise than in a document;

"the related water resources provisions", in relation to Chapter II of Part II of this Act, means—

(*a*) the following provisions of this Act, that is to say, the provisions—

(i) of sections 21 to 23 (including Schedule 5);

(ii) of sections 120, 125 to 130, 158, 189, 199 to 201, 206(3), 209(3), 211(1) and 216; and

(iii) of paragraph 1 of Schedule 25; and

(*b*) the following provisions of the 1995 Act, that is to say, the provisions—

(i) of sections 41 and 42 (charging schemes) as they have effect by virtue of subsection (1)(*a*) of section 41 (licences under Chapter II of Part II of this Act); and

(ii) of subsections (1) and (2) of section 53 (inquiries and other hearings);

"sewage effluent" includes any effluent from the sewage disposal or sewerage works of a sewerage undertaker but does not include surface water;

"sewer" has, subject to subsection (2) below, the same meaning as in the Water Industry Act 1991;

"source of supply" means—

(*a*) any inland waters except, without prejudice to subsection (3) below in its application to paragraph (*b*) of this definition, any which are discrete waters; or

(*b*) any underground strata in which water is or at any time may be contained;

"street" has, subject to subsection (4) below, the same meaning as in Part III of the New Roads and Street Works 1991;

"subordinate legislation" has the same meaning as in the Interpretation Act 1978;

"substance" includes micro-organisms and any natural or artificial substance or other matter, whether it is in solid or liquid form or in the form of a gas or vapour;

"surface water" includes water from roofs;

"trade effluent" includes any effluent which is discharged from premises used for carrying on any trade or industry, other than surface water and domestic sewage, and for the purposes of this definition any premises wholly or mainly used (whether for profit or not) for agricultural purposes or for the purposes of fish farming or for scientific research or experiment shall be deemed to be premises used for carrying on a trade;

"underground strata" means strata subjacent to the surface of any land;

"vessel" includes a hovercraft within the meaning of the Hovercraft Act 1968;

"watercourse" includes (subject to sections 72(2) and 113(1) above) all rivers, streams, ditches, drains, cuts, culverts, dykes, sluices, sewers and passages through which water flows[2], except mains and other pipes which—

(*a*) belong to the Authority or a water undertaker; or

(*b*) are used by a water undertaker or any other person for the purpose only of providing a supply of water to any premises;

"water pollution provisions" in relation to this Act, means the following provisions of this Act—

(*a*) the provisions of Part III of this Act;

(*b*) sections 161 to 161D, 190, 202 and 203; and

(*c*) paragraph 4 of Schedule 25 to this Act and section 211 above so far as it relates to byelaws made under that paragraph.

and the following provisions of the 1995 Act, that is to say the provisions of subsections (1) and (2) of section 53.

(2) References in this Act to a pipe, including references to a main, a drain or a sewer, shall include references to a tunnel or conduit which serves or is to serve as the pipe in question and to any accessories for the pipe; and, accordingly, references to the laying of a pipe shall include references to the construction of such a tunnel or conduit, to the construction or installation of any such accessories and to the making of a connection between one pipe and another.

(3) Any reference in this Act to water contained in underground strata is a reference to water so contained otherwise than in a sewer, pipe, reservoir, tank or other underground works constructed in any such strata; but for the purposes of this Act water for the time being contained in—

(*a*) a well, borehole or similar work, including any adit or passage constructed in connection with the well, borehole or work for facilitating the collection of water in the well, borehole or work; or

(*b*) any excavation into underground strata, where the level of water in the excavation depends wholly or mainly on water entering it from those strata,

shall be treated as water contained in the underground strata into which the well, borehole or work was sunk or, as the case may be, the excavation was made.

(4) Until the coming into force of Part III of the New Roads and Street Works Act 1991, the definition of "street" in subsection (1) above shall have effect as if the reference to that Part were a reference to the Public Utilities Street Works Act 1950; but nothing in this section shall be taken—

(*a*) to prejudice the power of the Secretary of State under that Act of 1991 to make an order bringing Part III of that Act into force on different days for different purposes (including the purposes of this section); or

(*b*) in the period before the coming into force of that Part, to prevent references in this Act to a street, where the street is a highway which passes over a bridge or through a tunnel, from including that bridge or tunnel.

(5) For the purposes of any provision of this Act by or under which power is or may be conferred on any person to recover the expenses incurred by that person in doing anything, those expenses shall be assumed to include such sum as may be reasonable in respect of establishment charges or overheads.

(6) References in this Act to the later or latest of two or more different times or days are, in a case where those times or days coincide, references to the time at which or, as the case may be, the day on which they coincide.

(7) For the purposes of this Act—

(*a*) references in this Act to more than one Minister of the Crown, in relation to anything falling to be done by those Ministers, are references to those Ministers acting jointly; and

(*b*) any provision of this Act by virtue of which any function of a Minister of the Crown is exercisable concurrently by different Ministers, shall have effect as providing for that function also to be exercisable jointly by any two or more of those Ministers.

(8) Sub-paragraph (1) of paragraph 1 of Schedule 2 to the Water Consolidation (Consequential Provisions) Act 1991 has effect (by virtue of sub-paragraph (2)(*b*) of that paragraph) so that

references in this Act to things done under or for the purposes of provisions of this Act, the Water Industry Act 1991 or the Land Drainage Act 1991 include references to things done, or treated as done, under or for the purposes of the corresponding provisions of the law in force before the commencement of this Act.

(9) Subject to any provision to the contrary which is contained in Schedule 26 to the Water Act 1989 or in the Water Consolidation (Consequential Provisions) Act 1991, nothing in any local statutory provision passed or made before 1st September 1989 shall be construed as relieving any water undertaker or sewerage undertaker from any liability arising by virtue of this Act in respect of any act or omission occurring on or after that date.

[Water Resources Act 1991, s 221, as amended by the Local Government (Wales) Act 1994, Sch 11, the Merchant Shipping Act 1995, Sch 13, the Environment Act 1995, Schs 22 and 24 and the Communications Act 2003, Sch 17.]

---

1. Section 221(1) is reproduced in an abridged form and contains only those definitions which are likely to be relevant to the provisions of the Act which are contained in this Manual.

2. The words "through which water flows" qualify only the words immediately preceding them ie "sewers and passages". Watercourses do not cease to be such because they are dry at the particular time (*R v Dovermoss Ltd* (1995) 159 JP 448, CA) and see s 104(2), this PART, ante.

Other supplemental provisions

8–31725 222. *Crown application.*

8–31726 223. *Exemption for visiting forces.*

8–31727

Section 88

SCHEDULE 10[1]

DISCHARGE CONSENTS

(*As substituted by the Environment Act 1995, Sch 22 and the Water Act 2003, Sch 9.*)

Application for consent

1. (1) An application for a consent, for the purposes of section 88(1)(*a*) of this Act, for any discharges—

(*a*) shall be made to the Agency on a form provided for the purpose by the Agency; and
(*b*) must be advertised by or on behalf of the applicant in such manner as may be required by regulations[2] made by the Secretary of State.

(2) Regulations made by the Secretary of State may make provision for enabling the Agency to direct or determine that any such advertising of an application as is required under sub-paragraph (1)(*b*) above may, in any case, be dispensed with if, in that case, it appears to the Agency to be appropriate for that advertising to be dispensed with.

(3) The applicant for such a consent must provide to the Agency, either on, or together with, the form mentioned in sub-paragraph (1) above—

(*a*) such information as the Agency may reasonably require; and
(*b*) such information as may be prescribed for the purpose by the Secretary of State;

but, subject to paragraph 3(3) below and without prejudice to the effect (if any) of any other contravention of the requirements of this Schedule in relation to an application under this paragraph, a failure to provide information in pursuance of this sub-paragraph shall not invalidate an application.

(4) The Agency may give the applicant notice requiring him to provide it with such further information of any description specified in the notice as it may require for the purpose of determining the application.

(5) An application made in accordance with this paragraph which relates to proposed discharges at two or more places may be treated by the Agency as separate applications for consents for discharges at each of those places.

---

1. Schedule 10 is printed as prospectively substituted by the Environment Act 1995, Sch 22, para 183; at the date of going to press para 183 had not been brought into force.

2. The Control of Pollution (Channel Tunnel Rail Link) Regulations 1998, SI 1998/1649 have been made.

Transfer of consents

11. (1) A consent under paragraph 3 or 6 above may be transferred by the holder to a person who proposes to carry on the discharges in place of the holder.

(2) On the death of the holder of a consent under paragraph 3 or 6 above, the consent shall, subject to sub-paragraph (4) below, be regarded as property forming part of the deceased's personal estate, whether or not it would be so regarded apart from this sub-paragraph, and shall accordingly vest in his personal representatives.

(3) If a bankruptcy order is made against the holder of a consent under paragraph 3 or 6 above, the consent shall, subject to sub-paragraph (4) below, be regarded for the purposes of any of the Second Group of Parts of the Insolvency Act 1986 (insolvency of individuals; bankruptcy), as property forming part of the bankrupt's estate, whether or not it would be so regarded apart from this sub-paragraph, and shall accordingly vest as such in the trustee in bankruptcy.

(4) Notwithstanding anything in the foregoing provisions of this paragraph, a consent under paragraph 3 or 6 above (and the obligations arising out of, or incidental to, such a consent) shall not be capable of being disclaimed.

(5) A consent under paragraph 3 or 6 above which is transferred to, or which vests in, a person under this section shall have effect on and after the date of the transfer or vesting as if it had been granted to that person under paragraph 3 or 6 above, subject to the same conditions as were attached to it immediately before that date.

(6) Where a consent under paragraph 3 or 6 above is to be transferred under sub-paragraph (1) above—

(*a*) the person from whom and the person to whom the consent is to be transferred shall give joint notice to the Agency of the proposed transfer;

(*b*) the notice may specify the date on which it is proposed that the transfer should take effect;

(*c*) within twenty-one days beginning with the date of receipt of the notice duly given in accordance with sub-paragraph (6A) below, the Agency shall—

(i) arrange to amend the consent by substituting the name of the transferee as holder of the consent; and

(ii) serve notice on the transferor and the transferee that the amendment has been made; and

(*d*) the transfer shall take effect from the later of—

(i) the date on which the Agency amends the consent; and

(ii) the date (if any) specified in the joint notice under paragraph (a) above.

(6A) A joint notice under sub-paragraph (6)(*a*) above shall include such information as may be prescribed.

(6B) If the person from whom the consent is to be transferred is a person in whom the consent has vested by virtue of sub-paragraph (2) or (3) above, a joint notice given under sub-paragraph (6)(*a*) above shall be of no effect unless the notice required by sub-paragraph (7) below has been given.

(6C) A notice or other instrument given by or on behalf of the Agency pursuant to sub-paragraph (6) above shall not constitute an instrument signifying the consent of the Agency for the purposes of paragraph 8 above.

(7) Where a consent under paragraph 3 or 6 above vests in any person as mentioned in sub-paragraph (2) or (3) above, that person shall give notice of that fact to the Agency not later than the end of the period of fifteen months beginning with the date of the vesting.

(8) If—

(*a*) a consent under paragraph 3 or 6 above vests in any person as mentioned in sub-paragraph (2) or (3) above, but

(*b*) that person fails to give the notice required by sub-paragraph (7) above within the period there mentioned,

the consent, to the extent that it permits the making of any discharges, shall cease to have effect.

(9) A person who fails to give a notice which he is required by sub-paragraph (6) or (7) above to give shall be guilty of an offence and liable[1]—

(*a*) on summary conviction, to a fine not exceeding the **statutory maximum;**

(*b*) on conviction on indictment, to a **fine** or to imprisonment for a term not exceeding **two years**, or to **both**.

---

1. For procedure in respect of this offence which is triable either way, see the Magistrates' Courts Act 1980, ss 17A–21, in PART I: MAGISTRATES' COURTS, PROCEDURE, ante.

8–31728

Section 173

SCHEDULE 20
SUPPLEMENTAL PROVISIONS WITH RESPECT TO POWERS OF ENTRY

(*As amended by the Environment Act 1995, Sch 22.*)

Notice of entry

1. (1) Without prejudice to any power exercisable by virtue of a warrant under this Schedule, no person shall make an entry into any premises or vessel by virtue of any power conferred by sections 169 to 172 of this Act except—

(*a*) in an emergency; or

(*b*) at a reasonable time and after the required notice of the intended entry has been given to the occupier of the premises or vessel.

(2) For the purposes of this paragraph the required notice is seven days' notice; but such notice shall not be required in the case of an exercise of a power conferred by section 169 or 172 above, except where the premises in question are residential premises, the vessel in question is used for residential purposes or the entry in question is to be with heavy equipment.

(3) For the purposes of the application of this paragraph to the power conferred by section 170 of this Act the reference in sub-paragraph (1) above to an emergency—

(*a*) in relation to any entry to premises for the purposes of, or for purposes connected with, the exercise or proposed exercise of any power in relation to a street, includes a reference to any circumstances requiring the carrying out of emergency works within the meaning of Part III of the New Roads and Street Works Act 1991; and

(*b*) in relation to any other entry to premises, includes a reference to any danger to property and to any interruption of a supply of water provided to any premises by any person and to any interruption of the provision of sewerage services to any premises.

(4) Until the coming into force of section 52 of the New Roads and Street Works Act 1991, sub-paragraph (3) above shall have effect as if the reference to Part III of that Act were a reference to the Public Utilities Street Works Act 1950; but nothing in this sub-paragraph shall be taken to prejudice the power of the Secretary of State under that Act of 1991 to make an order bringing that section 52 into force on different days for different purposes (including the purposes of this paragraph).

Warrant to exercise power

2. (1) If it is shown to the satisfaction of a justice of the peace on sworn information in writing—

(*a*) that there are reasonable grounds for the exercise in relation to any premises or vessel of a power conferred by sections 169 to 172 of this Act; and (*b*) that one or more of the conditions specified in sub-paragraph (2) below is fulfilled in relation to those premises or that vessel,

the justice may by warrant authorise the relevant authority to designate a person who shall be authorised to exercise the power in relation to those premises, or that vessel, in accordance with the warrant and, if need be, by force.

(2) The conditions mentioned in sub-paragraph (1)(*b*) above are—

(*a*) that the exercise of the power in relation to the premises or vessel has been refused;
(*b*) that such a refusal is reasonably apprehended;
(*c*) that the premises are unoccupied or the vessel is unoccupied;
(*d*) that the occupier is temporarily absent from the premises or vessel;
(*e*) that the case is one of urgency; or
(*f*) that an application for admission to the premises or vessel would defeat the object of the proposed entry.

(3) A justice of the peace shall not issue a warrant under this Schedule by virtue only of being satisfied that the exercise of a power in relation to any premises or vessel has been refused, or that a refusal is reasonably apprehended, unless he is also satisfied—

(*a*) that notice of the intention to apply for the warrant has been given to the occupier of the premises or vessel; or
(*b*) that the giving of such a notice would defeat the object of the proposed entry.

(4) For the purposes of the application of this Schedule to the powers conferred by section 171 of this Act in a case to which subsection (4) of that section applies, a justice of the peace shall not issue a warrant under this Schedule unless he is satisfied that the Secretary of State has given his authorisation for the purposes of that subsection in relation to that case.

(5) Every warrant under this Schedule shall continue in force until the purposes for which the warrant was issued have been fulfilled.

Manner of exercise of powers

3. A person designated as the person who may exercise any power to which this Schedule applies shall produce evidence of his designation and other authority before he exercises the power.

Supplementary powers of person making entry etc

4. A person authorised to enter any premises or vessel by virtue of any power to which this Schedule applies shall be entitled, subject in the case of a power exercisable under a warrant to the terms of the warrant, to take with him on to the premises or vessel such other persons and such equipment as may be necessary.

Duty to secure premises

5. A person who enters any premises or vessel in the exercise of any power to which this Schedule applies shall leave the premises or vessel as effectually secured against trespassers as he found them.

Compensation

6. (1) Where any person exercises any power to which this Schedule applies, it shall be the duty of the relevant authority to make full compensation to any person who has sustained loss or damage by reason of—

(*a*) the exercise by the designated person of that power or of any power to take any person or equipment with him when entering the premises or vessel in relation to which the power is exercised; or
(*b*) the performance of, or failure of the designated person to perform, the duty imposed by paragraph 5 above.

(2) Compensation shall not be payable by virtue of sub-paragraph (1) above in respect of any loss or damage if the loss or damage—

(*a*) is attributable to the default of the person who sustained it; or
(*b*) is loss or damage in respect of which compensation is payable by virtue of any other provision of this Act.

(3) Any dispute as to a person's entitlement to compensation under this paragraph, or as to the amount of any such compensation, shall be referred to the arbitration of a single arbitrator appointed by agreement between the relevant authority and the person who claims to have sustained the loss or damage or, in default of agreement—

(*a*) by the President of the Lands Tribunal where the relevant authority is one of the Ministers; and
(*b*) by one of the Ministers, where the Authority is the relevant authority.

Obstruction of person exercising power

7. A person who intentionally obstructs another person acting in the exercise of any power to which this Schedule applies shall be guilty of an offence and liable[1]—

(*a*) on summary conviction, to a **fine** not exceeding the **statutory maximum;**
(*b*) on conviction on indictment, to a **fine** or to imprisonment for a term not exceeding **two years**, or to **both**.

---

1. For procedure in respect of this offence which is triable either way, see the Magistrates' Courts act 1980, ss 17A–21, in PART I: MAGISTRATES' COURTS, PROCEDURE, ante.

Interpretation

8. (1) In this Schedule—

"relevant authority", in relation to a power to which this Schedule applies, means one of the Ministers or the Authority, according to who is entitled, by virtue of the provision by which the power is conferred or, as the case may be, the warrant, to designate the person by whom the power may be exercised; and "sewerage services" has the same meaning as in the Water Industry Act 1991.

(2) References in this Schedule to a power to which this Schedule applies are references to any power conferred by Chapter II of Part VI of this Act, including a power exercisable by virtue of a warrant under this Schedule.

(3) For the purposes of paragraphs 5 and 6 above a person enters any premises or vessel by virtue of a power to which this Schedule applies notwithstanding that he has failed (whether by virtue of the waiver of the requirement by the occupier of the premises or otherwise) to comply with—

(*a*) any requirement to enter those premises at a reasonable time or after giving notice of his intended entry; or

(*b*) the requirement imposed by paragraph 3 above.

8–31729

Section 210

SCHEDULE 25

BYELAW-MAKING POWERS OF THE AUTHORITY

(*As amended by the Environment Act 1995, s 103 and Schs 15 and 22.*)

Byelaws for regulating use of inland waters

1. (1) Subject to the following provisions of this paragraph but without prejudice to the powers conferred by the following provisions of this Schedule, where it appears to the Authority to be necessary or expedient to do so for the purposes of any of the functions specified in sub-paragraphs (i), (iii) and (v) of section 2(1)(*a*) of the 1995 Act, the Authority may make byelaws—

(*a*) prohibiting such inland waters as may be specified in the byelaws from being used for boating (whether with mechanically propelled boats or otherwise), swimming or other recreational purposes; or

(*b*) regulating the way in which any inland waters so specified may be used for any of those purposes.

(2) Byelaws made by the Authority under this paragraph shall not apply to—

(*a*) any tidal waters or any discrete waters;

(*b*) any inland waters in relation to which functions are exercisable by a navigation authority, harbour authority or conservancy authority other than the Authority; or

(*c*) any reservoir belonging to, and operated by, a water undertaker.

(3) Byelaws made in respect of any inland waters by virtue of this paragraph may—

(*a*) include provision prohibiting the use of the inland waters by boats which are not for the time being registered with the Authority in such manner as the byelaws may provide; and

(*b*) authorise the Authority to make reasonable charges in respect of the registration of boats in pursuance of the byelaws.

Byelaws for regulating the use of navigable waters etc

2. (1) The Authority shall have power to make such byelaws as are mentioned in sub-paragraph (3) below with respect to any inland waters in relation to which—

(*a*) there is a public right of navigation; and

(*b*) the condition specified in sub-paragraph (2) below is satisfied,

and with respect to any land associated with such waters.

(2) For the purposes of this paragraph the condition mentioned in sub-paragraph (1) above is satisfied in relation to any waters if navigation in those waters—

(*a*) is not for the time being subject to the control of any navigation authority, harbour authority or conservancy authority; or

(*b*) is subject to the control of such a navigation authority, harbour authority or conservancy authority as is prescribed for the purposes of this paragraph by reason of its appearing to the Secretary of State to be unable for the time being to carry out its functions.

(3) The byelaws referred to in sub-paragraph (1) above in relation to any inland waters or to any land associated with any such waters are byelaws for any of the following purposes, that is to say—

(*a*) the preservation of order in or on any such waters or land;

(*b*) the prevention of damage to anything in or on any such waters or land or to any such land:

(*c*) securing that persons resorting to any such waters or land so behave as to avoid undue interference with the enjoyment of the waters or land by others.

(4) Without prejudice to the generality of any of the paragraphs of sub-paragraph (3) above or to the power conferred on the Authority by virtue of paragraph 4 below, the byelaws mentioned in that sub-paragraph include byelaws—

(*a*) regulating sailing, boating, bathing and fishing and other forms of recreation;

(*b*) prohibiting the use of the inland waters in question by boats which are not for the time being registered, in such manner as may be required by the byelaws, with the Authority;

(*c*) requiring the provision of such sanitary appliances as may be necessary for the purpose of preventing pollution; and

(*d*) authorising the making of reasonable charges in respect of the registration of boats for the purposes of the byelaws.

(5) In this paragraph "boat" includes a vessel of any description, and "boating" shall be construed accordingly.

Byelaws for regulating the use of the Authority's waterways etc

3. (1) The Authority shall have power to make such byelaws as are mentioned in sub-paragraph (2) below with respect to any waterway owned or managed by the Authority and with respect to any land held or managed with the waterway.

(2) The byelaws referred to in sub-paragraph (1) above in relation to any waterway or to any land held or managed with any such waterway are byelaws for any of the following purposes, that is to say—

(*a*) the preservation of order on or in such waterway or land;
(*b*) the prevention of damage to anything on or in any such waterway or land or to any such land;
(*c*) securing that persons resorting to any such waterway or land so behave as to avoid undue interference with the enjoyment of the waterway or land by others.

(3) Without prejudice to the generality of any of the paragraphs of sub-paragraph (2) above or to the power conferred on the Authority by virtue of paragraph 4 below, the byelaws mentioned in that sub-paragraph include byelaws—

(*a*) regulating sailing, boating, bathing and fishing and other forms of recreation;
(*b*) prohibiting the use of the waterway in question by boats which are not for the time being registered, in such manner as may be required by the byelaws, with the Authority;
(*c*) requiring the provision of such sanitary appliances as may be necessary for the purpose of preventing pollution; and
(*d*) authorising the making of reasonable charges in respect of the registration of boats for the purposes of the byelaws.

(4) In this paragraph—

"boat" and "boating" have the same meanings as in paragraph 2 above; and
"waterway" has the same meaning as in the National Parks and Access to the Countryside Act 1949.

Byelaws for controlling certain forms of pollution

4. (1) The Authority may by byelaws make such provision as the Authority considers appropriate—

(*a*) for prohibiting or regulating the washing or cleaning in any controlled waters of things of a description specified in the byelaws;
(*b*) for prohibiting or regulating the keeping or use on any controlled waters of vessels of a description specified in the byelaws which are provided with water closets or other sanitary appliances.

(2) In this paragraph—

"controlled waters" has the same meaning as in Part III of this Act; and
"sanitary appliance", in relation to a vessel, means any appliance which—

(*a*) not being a sink, bath or shower bath, is designed to permit polluting matter to pass into the water where the vessel is situated; and
(*b*) is prescribed for the purposes of this paragraph.

Byelaws for flood defence and drainage purposes

5. (1) The Authority may make such byelaws in relation to any particular locality or localities as it considers necessary for securing the efficient working of any drainage system including the proper defence of any land against sea or tidal water.

(2) Without prejudice to the generality of sub-paragraph (1) above and subject to sub-paragraph (3) below, the Authority may, in particular, make byelaws for any of the following purposes, that is to say—

(*a*) regulating the use and preventing the improper use of any watercourses, banks or works vested in the Authority or under its control or for preserving any such watercourses, banks or works from damage or destruction;
(*b*) regulating the opening of sluices and flood gates in connection with any such works as are mentioned in paragraph (*a*) above;
(*c*) preventing the obstruction of any watercourse vested in the Authority or under its control by the discharge into it of any liquid or solid matter or by reason of any such matter being allowed to flow or fall into it;
(*d*) compelling the persons having control of any watercourse vested in the Authority or under its control, or of any watercourse flowing into any such watercourse, to cut the vegetable growths in or on the bank of the watercourse and, when cut, to remove them.

(3) No byelaw for any purpose specified in sub-paragraph (2)(*a*) above shall be valid if it would prevent reasonable facilities being afforded for enabling a watercourse to be used by stock for drinking purposes.

(4) Notwithstanding anything in this Act, no byelaw made by the Authority under this paragraph shall conflict with or interfere with the operation of any byelaw made by a navigation authority, harbour authority or conservancy authority.

(5) In this paragraph "banks" and "watercourse" have the same meanings as in Part IV of this Act.

Byelaws for purposes of fisheries functions

6. (1) The Authority shall have power, in relation to the whole or any part or parts of the area in relation to which it carries out its functions relating to fisheries under Part V of this Act, to make byelaws generally for the purposes of—

(*a*) the better execution of the Salmon and Freshwater Fisheries Act 1975; and
(*b*) the better protection, preservation and improvement of any salmon fisheries, trout fisheries, freshwater fisheries and eel fisheries.

(2) Subject to paragraph 7(1) below, the Authority shall have power, in relation to the whole or any part or parts of the area mentioned in sub-paragraph (1) above, to make byelaws for any of the following purposes, that is to say—

(*a*) prohibiting the taking or removal from any water without lawful authority, of any fish, whether alive or dead;

(*b*) prohibiting or regulating—

(i) the taking of trout or any freshwater fish of a size less than such as may be prescribed by the byelaw; or

(ii) the taking of fish by any means within such distance as is specified in the byelaw above or below any dam or any other obstruction, whether artificial or natural;

(*c*) prohibiting the use for taking salmon, trout, or freshwater fish of any instrument (not being a fixed engine) in such waters and at such times as may be prescribed by the byelaws;

(*d*) specifying the nets and other instruments (not being fixed engines) which may be used for taking salmon, trout, freshwater fish and eels, imposing requirements as to the use of such nets and other instruments and regulating the use, in connection with fishing with rod and line, of any lure or bait specified in the byelaw;

(*e*) authorising the placing and use of fixed engines at such places, at such times and in such manner as may be prescribed by the byelaws:

(*f*) imposing requirements as to the construction, design, material and dimensions of any such nets, instruments or engines as are mentioned in paragraphs (*d*) and (*e*) above, including in the case of nets the size of mesh:

(*g*) requiring and regulating the attachment to licensed nets and instruments of marks, labels or numbers, or the painting of marks or numbers or the affixing of labels or numbers to boats, coracles or other vessels used in fishing;

(*h*) prohibiting the carrying in any boat or vessel whilst being used in fishing for salmon or trout of any net which is not licensed, or which is without the mark, label or number prescribed by the byelaws; and

(*i*) prohibiting or regulating the carrying in a boat or vessel during the annual close season for salmon of a net capable of taking salmon, other than a net commonly used in the area to which the byelaw applies for sea fishing and carried in a boat or vessel commonly used for that purpose.

(3) Subject to the provisions of Schedule 1 to the Salmon and Freshwater Fisheries Act 1975 (duty to make byelaws about close season), the Authority shall have power, in relation to the whole or any part or parts of the area mentioned in sub-paragraph (1) above, to make byelaws for any of the following purposes, that is to say—

(*a*) fixing or altering any such close season or close time as is mentioned in paragraph 3 of that Schedule;

(*b*) dispensing with a close season for freshwater fish or rainbow trout;

(c) determining for the purposes of the Salmon and Freshwater Fisheries Act 1975 the period of the year during which screens need not be maintained;

(*d*) prohibiting or regulating fishing with rod and line between the end of the first hour after sunset on any day and the beginning of the last hour before sunrise on the following morning;

(*e*) determining the time during which it shall be lawful to use a gaff in connection with fishing with rod and line for salmon or migratory trout;

(*f*) authorising fishing with rod and line for eels during the annual close season for freshwater fish.

(4) Subject to paragraph 7(2) below, the Authority shall have power, in relation to the whole or any part or parts of the area mentioned in sub-paragraph (1) above, to make byelaws for the purpose of regulating the deposit or discharge in any waters containing fish of any liquid or solid matter specified in the byelaw which is detrimental to salmon, trout or freshwater fish, or the spawn or food of fish.

(5) The Authority shall have power, in relation to the whole or any part of parts of the area mentioned in sub-paragraph (1) above, to make byelaws for the purpose of requiring persons to send to the Authority returns, in such form, giving such particulars and at such times as may be specified in the byelaws—

(*a*) of the period or periods during which they have fished for salmon, trout, freshwater fish or eels,

(*b*) of whether they have taken any; and

(*c*) if they have, of what they have taken.

(6) Byelaws made under this paragraph may be made to apply to the whole or any part of parts of the year.

(7) Expressions used in this paragraph and in the Salmon and Freshwater Fisheries Act 1975 have the same meanings in this paragraph as in that Act.

Fisheries byelaws for marine or aquatic environmental purposes

6A. (1) Any power to make byelaws conferred by paragraph 6 above may be exercised for marine or aquatic environmental purposes.

(2) The power to make byelaws under paragraph 6 above by virtue of this paragraph is in addition to, and not in derogation from, the power to make byelaws under that paragraph otherwise than by virtue of this paragraph.

(3) In this paragraph "marine or aquatic environmental purposes" means—

(*a*) the conservation or enhancement of the natural beauty or amenity of marine or coastal, or aquatic or waterside, areas (including their geological or physiographical features) or of any features of archaeological or historic interest in such areas; or

(*b*) the conservation of flora or fauna which are dependent on, or associated with, a marine or coastal, or aquatic or waterside, environment.

Restrictions on powers to make byelaws for fisheries purposes

7. (1) The Authority shall not make any byelaws by virtue of paragraph 6(2)(*e*) above in relation to any place within the sea fisheries district of a local fisheries committee except with the consent of that committee.

(2) The Authority shall not make byelaws by virtue of paragraph 6(4) above so as to prejudice any powers of a sewerage undertaker to discharge sewage in pursuance of any power given by a public general Act, a local Act or a provisional order confirmed by Parliament.

8–31729A Section 210

SCHEDULE 26

PROCEDURE RELATING TO BYELAWS MADE BY THE AUTHORITY

Confirmation of byelaws

1. (1) No byelaw made by the Authority shall have effect until confirmed by the relevant Minister under this Schedule.

(2) At least one month before it applies for the confirmation of any byelaw, the Authority shall—

(*a*) cause a notice of its intention to make the application to be published in the London Gazette and in such other manner as it considers appropriate for the purpose of bringing the proposed byelaw to the attention of persons likely to be affected by it; and

(*b*) cause copies of the notice to be served on any persons carrying out functions under any enactment who appear to it to be concerned.

(3) For at least one month before an application is made by the Authority for the confirmation of any byelaw, a copy of it shall be deposited at one or more of the offices of the Authority, including (if there is one) at an office in the area to which the byelaw would apply.

(4) The Authority shall provide reasonable facilities for the inspection free of charge of a byelaw deposited under sub-paragraph (3) above.

(5) Every person shall be entitled, on application to the Authority, to be furnished free of charge with a printed copy of a byelaw so deposited.

2. *Confirmation with or without modifications.*

Commencement of byelaw

3. (1) The relevant Minister may fix the date on which any byelaw confirmed under this Schedule is to come into force.

(2) If no date is so fixed in relation to a byelaw, it shall come into force at the end of the period of one month beginning with the date of confirmation.

Availability of confirmed byelaws

4. (1) Every byelaw made by the Authority and confirmed under this Schedule shall be printed and deposited at one or more of the offices of the Authority, including (if there is one) at an office in the area to which the byelaw applies; and copies of the byelaw shall be available at those offices, at all reasonable times, for inspection by the public free of charge.

(2) Every person shall be entitled, on application to the Authority and on payment of such reasonable sum as the Authority may determine, to be furnished with a copy of any byelaw so deposited by the Authority.

5. *Revocation of byelaws by Minister.*

Proof of byelaws

6. The production of a printed copy of a byelaw purporting to be made by the Authority upon which is endorsed a certificate, purporting to be signed on its behalf, stating—

(*a*) that the byelaw was made by the Authority;

(*b*) that the copy is a true copy of the byelaw;

(*c*) that on a specified date the byelaw was confirmed under this Schedule; and

(*d*) the date, if any, fixed under paragraph 3 above for the coming into force of the byelaw,

shall be prima facie evidence of the facts stated in the certificate, and without proof of the handwriting or official position of any person purporting to sign the certificate.

7. *Meaning of "the relevant Minister".*

Land Drainage Act 1991

(1991 c 59)

PART II[1]

PROVISIONS FOR FACILITATING OR SECURING THE DRAINAGE OF LAND

Control of flow of watercourses etc

8–31730 **23. Prohibition on obstructions etc in watercourses.** Consent in writing of drainage board required before erection of mill dam, weir or other like obstruction or erection or alteration of culvert.

[Land Drainage Act 1991, s 23 amended by the Environment Act 1995, Sch 22—summarised.]

1. Part II comprises ss 14–31.

8–31731 **24. Contraventions of prohibition on obstructions etc.** (1) If any obstruction is erected or raised or otherwise altered, or any culvert is erected or altered, in contravention of section 23 above, it shall constitute a nuisance in respect of which the drainage board concerned may serve upon such person as is specified in subsection (2) below a notice requiring him to abate the nuisance within a period to be specified in the notice.

(2) The person upon whom a notice may be served under subsection (1) above is—

(*a*) in a case where the person by whom the obstruction has been erected or raised or otherwise altered has, at the time when the notice is served, power to remove the obstruction, that person; and

(*b*) in any other case, any person having power to remove the obstruction.

(3) If any person acts in contravention of, or fails to comply with, any notice served under subsection (1) above he shall be guilty of an offence and liable, on summary conviction—

(*a*) to a fine not exceeding **level 5** on the standard scale; and

(*b*) if the contravention or failure is continued after conviction, to a further fine not exceeding **£40 for every day on which the contravention or failure is so continued**.

(4) If any person acts in contravention of, or fails to comply with, any notice served under subsection (1) above, the drainage board concerned may, without prejudice to any proceedings under subsection (3) above—

(*a*) take such action as may be necessary to remedy the effect of the contravention or failure; and

(*b*) recover the expenses reasonably incurred by them in doing so from the person in default.

[Land Drainage Act 1991, s 24.]

8–31732 **25. Powers to require works for maintaining flow of watercourse.** (1) Subject to section 26 below, where any ordinary watercourse is in such a condition that the proper flow of water is impeded, then, unless the condition is attributable to subsidence due to mining operations (including brine pumping), the drainage board or local authority concerned may, by notice served on a person falling within subsection (3) below, require that person to remedy that condition.

(2) For the purposes of this section in its application in relation to any watercourse—

(*a*) the drainage board concerned is the drainage board for the internal drainage district in which the watercourse is situated; and

(*b*) the local authority concerned is the local authority for the area where the land as respects which the powers under this section are exercisable is situated;

but references in this section to the drainage board concerned shall, in relation to a watercourse which is not in an internal drainage district, be construed as references to the Agency.

(3) Subject to subsection (4) below, a notice under this section in relation to a watercourse may be served on—

(*a*) any person having control of the part of the watercourse where any impediment occurs; or

(*b*) any person owning or occupying land adjoining that part; or

(*c*) any person to whose act or default the condition of the watercourse mentioned in subsection (1) above is due.

(4) No notice under this section requiring any person to carry out any work on land not owned or occupied by him shall be served without the consent of the owner and the occupier of the land, except in a case where it is not practicable, after reasonable inquiry, to ascertain the name and address of the owner or occupier.

(5) A notice under this section shall indicate—

(*a*) the nature of the works to be carried out and the period within which they are to be carried out; and

(*b*) the right of appeal to a magistrates' court and the period within which such an appeal may be brought under section 27 below.

(6) Subject to the right of appeal provided by section 27 below, if the person upon whom a notice is served under this section fails to carry out the works indicated by the notice within the period so indicated—

(*a*) the drainage board or local authority concerned may themselves carry out the works and recover from that person the expenses reasonably incurred by them in doing so; and

(*b*) without prejudice to their right to exercise that power, that person shall be guilty of an offence and liable, on summary conviction, to a fine not exceeding **level 4** on the standard scale.

(7) In proceedings by the drainage board or local authority concerned for the recovery of any expenses under subsection (6) above it shall not be open to the defendant to raise any question which he could not have raised on an appeal under section 27 below.

(8) Nothing in this section shall affect the right of an owner or occupier to recover from the other, under the terms of any lease or other contract, the amount of any expenses incurred by him under this section or recovered from him by the drainage board or local authority concerned.

[Land Drainage Act 1991, s 25, as amended by the Environment Act 1995, Sch 22.]

8–31733 **26. Competing jurisdictions under section 25.** (1) Before exercising their powers under section 25 above in relation to any watercourse or part of a watercourse a local authority shall, according to whether or not the watercourse or part is in an internal drainage district, notify either the drainage board for that district or the Agency.

(2) Where a local authority have powers (otherwise than under section 25 above) for securing the appropriate flow of water in any watercourse under their jurisdiction, the powers conferred by section 25 above shall not be exercised by any body in relation to that watercourse except—

(*a*) by agreement with the local authority; or

(*b*) where, after reasonable notice from that body, the local authority either fail to exercise their powers or exercise them improperly.

(3) Where any watercourse is under the jurisdiction of a navigation authority, harbour authority,

conservancy authority or board of conservators which are exercising their powers, section 25 above shall not apply to the watercourse except with the consent of that authority or board.

(4) Nothing in this section shall apply in relation to section 25 above in its application to main rivers by virtue section 107(3) of the Water Resources Act 1991 (main river functions of Agency).
[Land Drainage Act 1991, s 26, as amended by the Environment Act 1995, Sch 22.]

8–31734 **27. Appeals against notices under section 25.** (1) A person served with a notice under section 25 above may, within twenty-one days from the date on which the notice is served on him, appeal to a magistrates' court on any of the following grounds, that is to say—

(*a*) that the notice or requirement is not justified by that section;
(*b*) that there has been some informality, defect or error in, or in connection with, the notice;
(*c*) that the body which served the notice has refused unreasonably to approve the carrying out of alternative works, or that the works required by the notice to be carried out are otherwise unreasonable in character or extent, or are unnecessary;
(*d*) that the period within which the works are to be carried out is not reasonably sufficient for the purpose;
(*e*) that the notice might lawfully have been served on another person and that it would have been equitable for it to have been so served;
(*f*) that some other person ought to contribute towards the expenses of carrying out any works required by the notice.

(2) The procedure on an appeal under this section shall be by way of complaint for an order and in accordance with the Magistrates' Courts Act 1980.

(3) For the purposes of the time limit for bringing an appeal under this section the making of the complaint shall be treated as the bringing of the appeal.

(4) In so far as an appeal under this section is based on the ground of some informality, defect or error in, or in connection with, the notice, the court shall dismiss the appeal if it is satisfied that the informality, defect or error was not a material one.

(5) In the case of an appeal under this section, the appellant—

(*a*) may serve a copy of his notice of appeal on any person having an estate or interest in the part of the watercourse where the impediment occurs or land adjoining that part; and
(*b*) shall, where the grounds upon which the appeal under this section is brought include a ground specified in subsection (1)(*e*) or (*f*) above, serve a copy of his notice of appeal on each other person referred to.

(6) On the hearing of an appeal under this section the court may make such order as it thinks fit—

(*a*) with respect to the person by whom any work is to be carried out and the contribution to be made by any other person towards the cost of the work; or
(*b*) as to the proportions in which any expenses which may become recoverable by the body which served the notice are to be borne by the appellant and such other person.

(7) In exercising its powers under subsection (6) above the court shall have regard—

(*a*) as between an owner and an occupier, to the terms and conditions (whether contractual or statutory) of the tenancy and to the nature of the works required; and
(*b*) in any case, to the degree of benefit to be derived by the different persons concerned.

(8) A person aggrieved by an order, determination or other decision of a magistrates' court under this section may appeal to the Crown Court.

(9) Where upon an appeal under this section a court varies or reverses any decision of a body which has served a notice under section 25 above, it shall be the duty of that body to give effect to the order of the court.
[Land Drainage Act 1991, s 27.]

PART IV[1]

FINANCIAL PROVISIONS

8–31735 **53. Power to require information.** (1) The drainage board for an internal drainage district may serve on the owner of any hereditament in the district in respect of which a drainage rate is levied a notice requiring him to state in writing the name and address of any person known to him as being an occupier of that hereditament.

(2) A person shall be guilty of an offence under this section if, where a notice is served on him under subsection (1) above, he—

(*a*) fails without reasonable excuse to comply with the notice; or
(*b*) in pursuance of the notice—
  (i) makes any statement in respect of the information required which he knows to be false in a material particular; or
  (ii) recklessly makes any statement in respect of that information which is false in a material particular.

(3) A person guilty of an offence under this section shall be liable, on summary conviction, to a fine not exceeding **level 4** on the standard scale.

(4) Where—

(*a*) a person is convicted of an offence under this section in respect of a failure to comply with a notice; and

(*b*) the failure continues after conviction,

then, unless he has a reasonable excuse for the continuance of the failure, he shall be guilty of a further offence under this section and shall be liable, on summary conviction, to be punished accordingly.
[Land Drainage Act 1991, s 53.]

1. Part IV contains ss 36–54.

8–31736 **54. Powers for enforcing payment.** (1) Arrears of any drainage rates made under this Chapter may be recovered by the drainage board for an internal drainage district in the same manner in which arrears of a non-domestic rate may be recovered under the Local Government Finance Act 1988 by a charging authority.

(2) The drainage board for an internal drainage district may by resolution authorise any member or officer of the board, either generally or in respect of particular proceedings—

(*a*) to institute or defend on their behalf proceedings in relation to a drainage rate; or

(*b*) notwithstanding that he is not qualified to act as a solicitor, to appear on their behalf in any proceedings before a magistrates' court for the issue of a warrant of distress for failure to pay a drainage rate.

(3) In proceedings for the recovery of arrears of a drainage rate the defendant shall not be entitled to raise by way of defence any matter which might have been raised on an appeal under section 45 or 51 above[1].

(4) The powers conferred by this section are in addition to, and not in substitution for, the powers conferred by any provision of any local Act on any drainage board in relation to arrears of drainage rates; and for the purposes of any such provisions a rate made under this Chapter shall be treated, subject to subsection (5) below, as a rate to which those provisions apply.

(5) Notwithstanding anything in any local Act—

(*a*) no distress for arrears of any rate made under this Chapter shall be levied on the goods or chattels of any person other than a person from whom the arrears may be recovered by virtue of subsection (1) above; and

(*b*) no proceedings shall be taken, whether by action or otherwise, for the enforcement of any charge on land created by a local Act for securing payment of arrears of any rate made under this Chapter.

(6) The drainage board for an internal drainage district shall not be required to enforce payment of any drainage rate in any case where the amount payable is, in their opinion, insufficient to justify the expense of collection.
[Land Drainage Act 1991, s 54.]

1. Sections 45 and 51 enable appeals against determinations of annual value by a valuation and community charge tribunal, and on any other ground to the Crown Court.

8–31737 **64. Powers of entry for internal drainage boards and local authorities.** Authorised person may at all reasonable times enter etc after notice: penalty on summary conviction for person intentionally obstructing or impeding is fine not exceeding **level 4** on the standard scale.
[Land Drainage Act 1991, s 64—summarised.]

8–31738 **72. Interpretation[1].** (1) In this Act, unless the context otherwise requires—

"the Agency" means the Environment Agency;

"charging authority" has the same meaning as in the Local Government Finance Act 1988;

"drainage" includes—

(*a*) defence against water (including sea water);

(*b*) irrigation, other than spray irrigation;

(*c*) warping; and

(*d*) the carrying on, for any purpose, of any other practice which involves management of the level or water in a watercourse;

"drainage body" means the Agency, an internal drainage board or any other body having power to make or maintain works for the drainage of land;

"land" includes water and any interests in land or water and any easement or right in, to or over land or water;

"local authority" means the council of a county, county borough, district or London borough or the Common Council of the City of London;

"main river" has the same meaning as in the Water Resources Act 1991;
"the Minister" means the Minister of Agriculture, Fisheries and Food;
"the Ministers" means the Minister and the Secretary of State, and in relation to anything which falls to be done by the Ministers, means those Ministers acting jointly;
"ordinary watercourse" means a watercourse that does not form part of a main river;
"prescribed" means prescribed by regulations under section 65 above;
"qualified authority", in relation to an internal drainage district, means a charging authority for an area wholly or partly included in that district;
"qualified persons" shall be construed in accordance with subsection (2) below;
"the relevant Minister"—

(*a*) in relation to internal drainage districts which are neither wholly nor partly in Wales or to the boards for such districts, means the Minister;
(*b*) in relation to internal drainage districts which are partly in Wales or to the boards for such districts, means the Ministers; and
(*c*) in relation to internal drainage districts which are wholly in Wales or to the boards for such districts, means the Secretary of State;

"watercourse" includes all rivers and streams and all ditches, drains, cuts, culverts, dikes, sluices, sewers (other than public sewers within the meaning of the Water Industry Act 1991) and passages, through which water flows.

(2) Subject to the provisions of paragraph 19 of Schedule 2 to the Water Consolidation (Consequential Provisions) Act 1991 (which makes provision with respect to qualification under this subsection by reference to drainage rates levied on land in respect of years beginning before 1993), where any provision of this Act refers, in relation to an internal drainage district, to the making of any appeal or petition by a sufficient number of qualified persons—

(*a*) the persons who are qualified are the occupiers of any land in the district in respect of which a drainage rate is levied; and
(*b*) subject to subsection (3) below, their number shall be sufficient if (but only if)—

(i) they are not less than forty; or
(ii) they are not less than one-fifth of the number of persons who are qualified to make the petition or appeal; or
(iii) the assessable value for the purposes of the last drainage rate levied in the district of all the land in respect of which they are qualified persons is not less than one-fifth of the assessable value of all the land in respect of which that rate was levied.

(3) In relation to a district divided into sub-districts the persons qualified to make a petition under section 39 above as being the occupiers of land in one of the sub-districts shall also be sufficient in any case where the condition in subsection (2)(*b*)(ii) or (iii) above would be satisfied if the sub-district were an internal drainage district.

(4) The references to the assessable value of any land in paragraph (*b*) of subsection (2) above are references to the amount which for the purposes of the drainage rate mentioned in that paragraph would be the annual value of the land.

(5) References in this Act to the carrying out of drainage works include references to the improvement of drainage works.

(6) Nothing in this Act shall operate to release any person from an obligation to which section 21 above applies; and the functions of the Agency or any internal drainage board as respects the doing of any work under this Act are not to be treated as in any way limited by the fact that some other person is under an obligation, by reason of tenure, custom, prescription or otherwise, to do that work.

(7) Where by virtue of any provision of this Act any function of a Minister of the Crown is exercisable concurrently by different Ministers, that function shall also be exercisable jointly by any two or more of those Ministers.

(8) This Act so far as it confers any powers on the Agency shall have effect subject to the provisions of the Water Resources Act 1991.

(9) The powers conferred by this Act on the Common Council of the City of London shall be exercisable as respects that City.

(10) Sub-paragraph (1) of paragraph 1 of Schedule 2 to the Water Consolidation (Consequential Provisions) Act 1991 has effect (by virtue of sub-paragraph (2)(*b*) of that paragraph) so that references in this Act to things done under or for the purposes of provisions of this Act or the Water Resources Act 1991 include references to things done, or treated as done, under or for the purposes of the corresponding provisions of the law in force before the commencement of this Act.

[Land Drainage Act 1991, s 72, as amended by the Local Government (Wales) Act 1994, Sch 11, the Merchant Shipping Act 1995, Sch 13, the Environment Act 1995, s 100 and the Environment Act 1995, Schs 22 and 24.]

---

1. Only definitions relevant to the parts of this Act printed in this work are included here.

Water Act 2003[1]

(2003 c 37)

PART 1[2]
ABSTRACTION AND IMPOUNDING

Restrictions on abstraction and impounding

8–31739A 3. Existing impounding works. (1) Except as provided in subsection (3), the restriction in section 25(1)(b) of the WRA (as substituted by section 2 of this Act) does not apply in respect of any existing unlicensed impounding works.

(2) With respect to any existing unlicensed impounding works to which, but for subsection (1), that restriction would apply, the Environment Agency may serve a notice on any relevant person requiring him to apply for a licence.

(3) If that person fails to apply for such a licence within—

(*a*) the period of 28 days beginning with—

(i) the date of service of the notice, or

(ii) if an appeal is brought under subsection (4) and the appeal is dismissed, the date when the decision of the appropriate authority is notified to that person, or

(*b*) such extended period as may be agreed in writing between the Agency and that person,

the restriction in section 25(1)(b) of the WRA applies in respect of the impounding works from the expiry of that period.

(4) If the relevant person on whom a notice is served under subsection (2) is aggrieved by the service of that notice, he may by notice appeal to the appropriate authority.

(5)–(13) *Appeals.*

[Water Act 2003, s 3.]

---

1. This Act is to be brought into force in accordance with orders made under s 105. At the date of going to press the following commencement orders had been made: (No 1 and Transitional Provisions) 2004, SI 2004/641; (Wales) 2004, SI 2004/910 (ss 3 and 4 had not been brought into force); (No 2, Transitional Provisions and Savings) 2004, SI 2004/2528; (No 2) (Wales) SI 2004/2916; (No 3) (England) 2005, SI 2005/344; (No 4 Transitional Provisions and Savings) 2005, SI 2005/968; (No 5 Transitional Provisions and Savings) 2005, SI 2005/2714. At the date of going to press ss 3 and 4 had not been brought into force.

2. Part 1 comprises ss 1–33.

8–31739B 4. Existing impounding works: works notices. (1) Without prejudice to the Environment Agency's power under subsection (2) of section 3, where it appears to the Agency to be necessary for—

(*a*) the protection of the environment, or

(*b*) the performance of its functions in connection with the management of water resources,

the Agency may serve a works notice on any relevant person with respect to any existing unlicensed impounding works of the kind mentioned in subsection (2) of that section.

(2) For the purposes of subsection (1), a works notice is a notice requiring the person on whom it is served to carry out such works or operations in relation to the impounding works as—

(*a*) appear to the Environment Agency to be required for the purposes mentioned in subsection (1)(a) or (b), and

(*b*) are specified in the notice.

(3) The following provisions of the WRA apply in relation to works notices under this section as they apply in relation to notices referred to in those provisions—

(*a*) subsections (5) to (9) of section 25A (as inserted by section 30 of this Act), and

(*b*) sections 161B and 161C,

including any power to make regulations or give directions, but references in those provisions to the Secretary of State shall be treated as references to the appropriate authority.

(4) If a person on whom the Agency serves a notice under this section fails to comply with any of its requirements, he shall be guilty of an offence.

(5) A person who commits an offence under subsection (4) shall be liable—

(*a*) on summary conviction, to a fine not exceeding £20,000,

(*b*) on conviction on indictment, to a fine.

(6) If a person on whom a works notice has been served under this section fails to comply with any of its requirements, the Agency may do what that person was required to do and may recover from him any costs or expenses reasonably incurred by the Agency in doing it.

(7) If the Agency is of the opinion that proceedings for an offence under subsection (4) would afford an ineffectual remedy against a person who has failed to comply with the requirements of a works notice, the Agency may take proceedings in the High Court for the purpose of securing compliance with the notice.

(8) In this section, "the appropriate authority", "existing unlicensed impounding works" and "relevant person" have the meanings given in section 3.
[Water Act 2003, s 4.]

Control of Pollution (Silage, Slurry and Agricultural Fuel Oil) Regulations 1991[1]

(SI 1991/324)

8–31740 **1.** *Citation and commencement.*

1. Made by Secretary of State for the Environment as respects England and the Secretary of State for Wales as respects Wales, in exercise of the powers conferred on them by ss 110 and 185(2)(*c*)–(*e*) of the Water Act 1989.

Interpretation

8–31741 **2.** In these Regulations, unless the context otherwise requires—

"construct" includes install and cognate expressions shall be construed accordingly;

"fuel oil" means oil intended for use as a fuel for the production of heat or power but does not include oil intended for use exclusively as a fuel for heating a farmhouse or other residential premises on a farm and stored separately from other oil;

"livestock" means—

(*a*) any animals kept for the production of food or wool; or

(*b*) any birds kept for the production of food;

"reception pit" means a pit used for the collection of slurry before it is transferred into a slurry storage tank or for the collection of slurry discharged from such a tank;

"relevant substance" means slurry, fuel oil or, as the case may be, the crop being made into silage;

"slurry" means—

(*a*) excreta produced by livestock whilst in a yard or building; or

(*b*) a mixture consisting wholly or mainly of such excreta, bedding, rainwater and washings from a building or yard used by livestock or any combination of these,

of a consistency that allows it to be pumped or discharged by gravity at any stage in the handling process;

"slurry storage system" means—

(*a*) a slurry storage tank;

(*b*) any reception pit and any effluent tank used in connection with the slurry storage tank; and

(*c*) any channels and pipes used in connection with the slurry storage tank, any reception pit or any effluent tank; and

"slurry storage tank" includes a lagoon, pit (other than a reception pit) or tower used for the storage of slurry.

Making of silage

8–31742 **3.** (1) Subject to regulation 7 below, no person shall have custody or control of any crop which is being made into silage unless—

(*a*) it is kept in a silo in relation to which the requirements of Schedule 1 are satisfied or which is an exempt structure by virtue of regulation 6 below; or

(*b*) it is compressed in the form of bales which are wrapped and sealed within impermeable membranes (or are enclosed in impermeable bags) and are stored at least 10 metres from any inland or coastal waters which effluent escaping from the bales could enter.

(2) No person having custody or control of any crop which is being, or has been, made into silage in the manner described in paragraph (1)(*b*) above shall open or remove the wrapping of any bales unless he does so at a place at least 10 metres from any inland or coastal waters which silage effluent could enter as a result.

Storage of slurry

8–31743 **4.** (1) Subject to paragraph (2) below, a person having custody or control of slurry shall store it only in a slurry storage system in relation to which the requirements of Schedule 2 are satisfied or which is an exempt structure by virtue of regulation 6 below.

(2) Paragraph (1) above shall not apply to slurry whilst it is stored temporarily in a tanker with a capacity not exceeding 18,000 litres which is used for transporting slurry on roads or about a farm.

Storage of fuel oil on farms

8–31744 **5.** (1) Subject to paragraph (2) below, no person shall have custody or control of fuel oil on a farm unless it is stored—

(*a*) in a fuel storage tank within a storage area in relation to which the requirements of Schedule 3 are satisfied;
(*b*) in drums within such a storage area;
(*c*) temporarily in a tanker used for transporting fuel oil on roads or about the farm;
(*d*) in a fuel storage tank which is an exempt structure by virtue of regulation 6 below; or
(*e*) in an underground fuel storage tank.

(2) Paragraph (1) above shall not apply if the total quantity of fuel stored on the farm does not exceed 1,500 litres.

Exemptions

8–31745 **6.** A silo, slurry storage system or fuel storage tank is for the time being an exempt structure if—

(*a*) it was used before 1st March 1991 for the purpose of making silage, storing slurry or, as the case may be, storing fuel oil;
(*b*) where it was not used before 1st March 1991 for that purpose, it was constructed before that date for such use; or
(*c*) a contract for its construction was entered into before 1st March 1991 or its construction was commenced before that date and in either case was completed before 1st September 1991,

and it has not ceased to be an exempt structure by virtue of regulation 8(1) below.

8–31746 **7.** (1) Subject to the following provisions of this regulation and regulation 8(2) below, regulation 3 above shall not apply where a person makes silage on a farm—

(*a*) otherwise than in a silo;
(*b*) by a method different from that described in regulation 3(1)(*b*) above,

and made the majority of his silage on that farm by that method in the period of 3 years immediately before 1st March 1991.

(2) A person shall not be entitled to rely on the exemption conferred by paragraph (1) above—

(*a*) unless he has given notice to the Authority before 1st September 1991 of his intention to do so and he keeps any crop which is being made into silage in a place at least 10 metres from any inland or coastal waters which silage effluent could enter if it were to escape;
(*b*) on or after 1st September 1996.

Loss of exemption

8–31747 **8.** (1) A structure which is an exempt structure by virtue of regulation 6 above shall cease to be an exempt structure if—

(*a*) any requirement of a notice under regulation 9 below is not complied with within the period stated in the notice; or
(*b*) at any time on or after 1st March 1991 it is substantially enlarged or substantially reconstructed unless a contract for the work was entered into or the work was commenced before that date and in either case the work was completed before 1st September 1991.

(2) The exemption conferred by regulation 7 above shall cease if any requirement of a notice under regulation 9 below is not complied with within the period stated in the notice.

(3) Any reference in paragraphs (1) and (2) above to the period stated in a notice is to that period as extended if it has been extended under regulation 9(4) below or by virtue of regulation 10(5) below; and any reference in those paragraphs to a requirement of a notice is to that requirement as modified if it has been modified under regulation 9(4) below.

Notice requiring works etc

8–31748 **9.** (1) Where the Authority is satisfied that there is a significant risk of pollution of controlled waters as a result of—

(*a*) the use of an exempt structure mentioned in regulation 6 above for storage of a relevant substance; or
(*b*) the making of silage in circumstances in which the exemption conferred by regulation 7 above applies,

it may serve notice on the person having custody or control of the relevant substance requiring him to carry out such works and to take such precautions and other steps as it considers appropriate, having regard to the requirements of Schedule 1, Schedule 2 or, as the case may be, Schedule 3, for reducing that risk to a minimum.

(2) The notice shall specify or describe the works, precautions or other steps which the person is required to carry out or take, state the period within which any such requirement is to be complied with and inform him of the effect in relation to the notice of regulation 10 below.

(3) The period for compliance stated in the notice shall be such period as is reasonable in the circumstances and shall not in any case be less than 28 days.

(4) The Authority may at any time—

(*a*) withdraw the notice;
(*b*) extend the period for compliance with any requirement of the notice;
(*c*) with the consent of the person on whom the notice is served, modify the requirements of the notice,

and shall do so if so directed by the Secretary of State under regulation 10(4) below.

Appeals against notices requiring works etc

8–31749 10. (1)–(4) *Appeals to Secret of State.*

(5) The period for compliance with a notice under regulation 9 above shall, subject to any direction under paragraph (4) above, be extended by a period equal to the period beginning with the date on which notice of appeal is served and ending on the date on which the Secretary of State finally determines the appeal or, if the appeal is withdrawn, the date on which it is withdrawn.

Notice of construction etc

8–31750 11. A person who proposes to have custody or control of any relevant substance which is to be kept or stored on a farm in a silo, slurry storage system or, as the case may be, fuel storage area constructed, substantially enlarged or substantially reconstructed on or after 1st September 1991 shall serve notice on the Authority specifying the type of structure to be used and its location at least 14 days before it is to be used for such keeping or storage.

Criminal offences

8–31751 12. (1) A person who contravenes regulation 3(1) or (2), 4(1) or 5(1) above shall be guilty of an offence and liable[1]—

(*a*) on summary conviction, to a fine not exceeding the **statutory maximum;**
(*b*) on conviction on indictment, to a **fine.**

(2) A person who contravenes regulation 11 above shall be guilty of an offence and liable on summary conviction to a fine not exceeding **level 2** on the standard scale.

---

1. For procedure in respect of an offence which is triable either way, see Magistrates' Courts Act 1980, ss 17A–21, in PART I: MAGISTRATES' COURTS, PROCEDURE, ante.

8–31752

Regulation 3(1)(*a*)

SCHEDULE 1

REQUIREMENTS FOR SILOS

1. The requirements which have to be satisfied in relation to a silo are that—

(*a*) it complies with the following provisions of this Schedule; or
(*b*) it is designed and constructed in accordance with the standard on cylindrical forage tower silos published by the British Standards Institution and numbered BS 5061: 1974.

2. The base of the silo shall extend beyond any walls of the silo and shall be provided at its perimeter with channels designed and constructed so as to collect any silage effluent which may escape from the silo and adequate provision shall be made for the drainage of that effluent from those channels to an effluent tank through a channel or pipe.

3. The capacity of the effluent tank—

(*a*) in the case of a silo with a capacity of less than 1,500 cubic metres, shall be not less than 20 litres for each cubic metre of silo capacity; and
(*b*) in the case of a silo with a capacity of 1,500 cubic metres or more, shall be not less than 30 cubic metres plus 6·7 litres for each cubic metre of silo capacity in excess of 1,500 cubic metres.

4. The base of the silo, the base and walls of its effluent tank and channels and the walls of any pipes shall be impermeable.

5. The base and any walls of the silo, its effluent tank and channels and the walls of any pipes shall, so far as reasonably practicable, be resistant to attack by silage effluent.

6. No part of the silo, its effluent tank or channels or any pipes shall be situated within 10 metres of any inland or coastal waters which silage effluent could enter if it were to escape.

7. If the silo has retaining walls—

(*a*) the retaining walls shall be capable of withstanding minimum wall loadings calculated on the assumptions and in the manner indicated by paragraphs 13.9.1 to 13.9.9 of the code of practice on buildings and structures for agriculture published by the British Standards Institution and numbered BS 5502: Part 22: 1987;
(*b*) the silo shall at no time be loaded to a depth exceeding the maximum depth consistent with the design assumption made in respect of the loadings of the retaining walls; and
(*c*) notices shall be displayed on the retaining walls in accordance with paragraph 13.9.9 of that code of practice.

8. Subject to paragraph 9 below, the silo, its effluent tank and channels and any pipes shall be designed and constructed so that with proper maintenance they are likely to satisfy the requirements of paragraphs 2 to 5 and, if applicable, 7(*a*) above for a period of at least 20 years.

9. Where any part of an effluent tank is installed below ground level, the tank shall be designed and constructed so that without maintenance it is likely to satisfy the requirements of paragraphs 4 and 5 above for a period of at least 20 years.

8–31753

Regulation 4(1)

SCHEDULE 2
REQUIREMENTS FOR SLURRY STORAGE SYSTEMS

1. The requirements which have to be satisfied in relation to a slurry storage system are as follows.

2. The base of the slurry storage tank, the base and walls of any effluent tank, channels and reception pit and the walls of any pipes shall be impermeable.

3. The base and walls of the slurry storage tank, any effluent tank, channels and reception pit and the walls of any pipes shall be protected against corrosion in accordance with paragraph 7.2 of the code of practice on buildings and structures for agriculture published by the British Standards Institution and numbered BS 5502: Part 50: 1989.

4. The base and walls of the slurry storage tank and of any reception pit shall be capable of withstanding characteristic loads calculated on the assumptions and in the manner indicated by paragraph 5 of that code of practice.

5. (1) Any facilities used for the temporary storage of slurry before it is transferred to a slurry storage tank shall have adequate capacity to store the maximum quantity of slurry which (disregarding any slurry which will be transferred directly into a slurry storage tank) is likely to be produced on the premises in any two day period.

(2) Where slurry flows into a channel before discharging into a reception pit and the flow of slurry out of the channel is controlled by means of a sluice, the capacity of the reception pit shall be adequate to store the maximum quantity of slurry which can be released by opening the sluice.

6. (1) Subject to sub-paragraph (2) below, the slurry storage tank shall have adequate storage capacity for the likely quantities of slurry produced from time to time on the premises in question having regard to—

(*a*) the proposed method of disposal of the slurry (including the likely rates and times of disposal); and
(*b*) the matters mentioned in sub-paragraph (3) below.

(2) Where it is proposed to dispose of the slurry on the premises by spreading it on the land nothing in sub-paragraph (1) above shall require the tank to have a greater storage capacity than is adequate, having regard to the matters mentioned in sub-paragraph (3) below, to store the maximum quantity of slurry which is likely to be produced in any continuous four month period.

(3) The matters to which regard is to be had under sub-paragraphs (1) and (2) above are—

(*a*) the storage capacity of any other slurry storage tank on the premises in question;
(*b*) the likely quantities of rainfall (including any fall of snow, hail or sleet) which may fall or drain into the slurry storage tank during the likely maximum storage period; and
(*c*) the need to make provision for not less than 750 millimetres of freeboard in the case of a tank with walls made of earth and 300 millimetres of freeboard in all other cases.

7. No part of the slurry storage tank or any effluent tank, channels or reception pit shall be situated within 10 metres of any inland or coastal waters which slurry could enter if it were to escape.

8. The slurry storage tank and any effluent tank, channels, pipes and reception pit shall be designed and constructed so that with proper maintenance they are likely to satisfy the requirements of paragraphs 2 to 4 above for a period of at least 20 years.

9. Where the walls of the slurry storage tank are not impermeable, the base of the tank shall extend beyond its walls and shall be provided with channels designed and constructed so as to collect any slurry which may escape from the tank and adequate provision shall be made for the drainage of the slurry from those channels to an effluent tank through a channel or pipe.

10. (1) Subject to sub-paragraph (2) below, where the slurry storage tank, any effluent tank or reception pit is fitted with a drainage pipe there shall be two valves in series on the pipe and each valve shall be capable of shutting off the flow of slurry through the pipe and shall be kept shut and locked in that position when not in use.

(2) Sub-paragraph (1) above does not apply in relation to a slurry storage tank which drains through the pipe into another slurry storage tank of equal or greater capacity or where the tops of the tanks are at the same level.

11. In the case of a slurry storage tank with walls which are made of earth the tank shall not be filled to a level which allows less than 750 millimetres of freeboard.

8–31754

Regulation 5(1)(*a*)

SCHEDULE 3
REQUIREMENTS FOR FUEL OIL STORAGE AREAS

1. The requirements which have to be satisfied in relation to a fuel oil storage area are as follows.

2. The fuel storage area shall be surrounded by a bund capable of retaining within the area—

(*a*) in a case where there is only one fuel storage tank within the fuel storage area and fuel oil is not otherwise stored there, a volume of fuel oil not less than 110 per cent of the capacity of the tank;
(*b*) in a case where there is more than one fuel storage tank within the fuel storage area and fuel oil is not otherwise stored there, a volume of fuel oil not less than whichever is the greater of—

(i) 110 per cent of the capacity of the largest tank within the storage area; and
(ii) 25 per cent of the total volume of such oil which could be stored in the tanks within the area;

(*c*) in a case where there is no fuel storage tank within the fuel storage area, a volume of fuel oil not less than 25 per cent of the total of such oil at any time stored within the area;
(*d*) in any other case, a volume of fuel oil not less than any of the following—

(i) 110 per cent of the capacity of the fuel storage tank or, as the case may be, of the largest tank within the fuel storage area;
(ii) where there is more than one fuel storage tank within the fuel storage area, 25 per cent of the total volume of such oil which could be stored in the tanks within the area;

(iii) 25 per cent of the total volume of such oil at any time stored within the area.

3. The bund and the base of the storage area shall be impermeable and shall be designed and constructed so that with proper maintenance they are likely to remain so for a period of at least 20 years.

4. Every part of any fuel storage tank shall be within the bund.

5. Any tap or valve permanently fixed to the tank through which fuel oil can be discharged to the open shall also be within the bund, shall be so arranged as to discharge vertically downwards and shall be shut and locked in that position when not in use.

6. Where fuel from the tank is delivered through a flexible pipe which is permanently attached to the tank—

(*a*) it shall be fitted with a tap or valve at its end which closes automatically when not in use; and
(*b*) it shall be locked in a way which ensures that it is kept within the bund when not in use.

7. No part of the fuel storage area or the bund enclosing it shall be situated within 10 metres of any inland or coastal waters which fuel oil could enter if it were to escape.

WEIGHTS AND MEASURES

8–31799 This title contains the following statute—

8–31819 Weights and Measures Act 1985

and the following statutory instruments—

8–32140 Weights and Measures (Solid Fuel) Regulations 1978
8–32160 Weights and Measures Act 1963 (Cheese, Fish, Fresh Fruits and Vegetables, Meat and Poultry) Order 1984
8–32320 Weights and Measures Act 1963 (Intoxicating Liquor) Order 1988
8–32340 Weights and Measures (Miscellaneous Foods) Order 1988
8–32360 Units of Measurement Regulations 1995

8–31800 European Communities Act 1972: regulations. Within the scope of the title Weights and Measures would logically fall the subject matter of a number of regulations made under the very wide enabling powers provided in s 2(2) of the European Communities Act 1972. Regulations may validly be made under this provision for the purpose of implementing the 'Metrication Directive' (Council Directive 80/181/EEC)[1].

The Units of Measurement Regulations 1995, are contained, post; other such regulations which create offences are noted below in chronological order:

Calibration of Tanks of Vessels (EEC Requirements) Regulations 1975, SI 1975/2125 amended by SI 1988/1128;
Measuring Container Bottles (EEC Requirements) Regulations 1977, SI 1977/932 amended by SI 1985/306;
Alcoholometers and Alcohol Hydrometers (EEC Requirements) Regulations 1977, SI 1977/1753 amended by SI 1983/530 and SI 1988/1128;
Prepackaging and Labelling of Wine and Grape Must (EEC Requirements) Regulations 1978, SI 1978/463;
Alcohol Tables Regulations 1979, SI 1979/132;
Taximeters (EEC Requirements) Regulations 1979, SI 1979/1379 amended by SI 1988/1128;
Units of Measurement Regulations 1986, SI 1986/1082 amended by SI 1994/2867, SI 1995/1804 and SI 2001/55;
Measuring Instruments (EEC Requirements) Regulations 1988, SI 1988/186 amended by SI 1988/1128 and SI 1996/319;
Measuring Instruments (EEC Requirements) (Gas Volume Meters) Regulations 1988, SI 1988/296; amended by SI 1996/319;
Clinical Thermometers (EEC Requirements) Regulations 1993, SI 1993/2360;
Measuring Instruments (EC Requirements) (Electrical Energy Meters) Regulations 1995, SI 1995/2607 amended by SI 2002/3082.

1. *Thoburn v Sunderland City Council* [2002] EWHC 195 (Admin), [2003] QB 151, [2002] 4 All ER 156, 166 JP 257.

Weights and Measures Act 1985

(1985 c 72)

Part I

Units and Standards of Measurement

8–31819 This Part prescribes units of measurement[1] and provides for the maintenance of United Kingdom, Board of Trade and Local standards, and the provision of working standards and texting and stamping equipment. It gives effect to Schedule 1.

1. Certain units of measurement are authorised by the Units of Measurement Regulations 1986, SI 1986/1082 amended by SI 1994/2867, SI 1995/1804 and SI 2001/55. See also the Units of Measurement Regulations 1995, this title, post.

PART II[1]
WEIGHING AND MEASURING FOR TRADE

General

8–31820 **7. Meaning of "use for trade".** (1) In this Act "use for trade" means, subject to subsection (3) below, use in Great Britain in connection with, or with a view to, a transaction falling within subsection (2) below where—

(*a*) the transaction is by reference to quantity or is a transaction for the purposes of which there is made or implied a statement of the quantity of goods to which the transaction relates, and
(*b*) the use is for the purpose of the determination or statement of that quantity.

(2) A transaction falls within this subsection if it is a transaction for—

(*a*) the transferring or rendering of money or money's worth in consideration of money or money's worth, or
(*b*) the making of a payment in respect of any toll or duty.

(3) Use for trade does not include use in a case where—

(*a*) the determination or statement is a determination or statement of the quantity of goods required for despatch to a destination outside Great Britain and any designated country, and
(*b*) the transaction is not a sale by retail, and
(*c*) no transfer or rendering of money or money's worth is involved other than the passing of the title to the goods and the consideration for them.

(4) The following equipment, that is to say—

(*a*) any weighing or measuring equipment which is made available in Great Britain for use by the public, whether on payment or otherwise, and
(*b*) any equipment which is used in Great Britain for the grading by reference to their weight, for the purposes of trading transactions by reference to that grading, of hens' eggs in shell which are intended for human consumption,

shall be treated for the purposes of this Part of this Act as weighing or measuring equipment in use for trade, whether or not it would apart from this subsection be so treated.

(5) Where any weighing or measuring equipment is found in the possession of any person carrying on trade or on any premises which are used for trade, that person or, as the case may be, the occupier of those premises shall be deemed for the purposes of this Act, unless the contrary is proved, to have that equipment in his possession for use for trade.
[Weights and Measures Act 1985, s 7.]

1. Part II comprises ss 8–17.

8–31821 **8. Units of measurement, weights and measures lawful for use for trade.** (1) No person shall—

(*a*) use for trade any unit of measurement which is not included in Parts I to V of Schedule 1 to this Act, or
(*b*) use for trade, or have in his possession for use for trade, any linear, square, cubic or capacity[1] measure which is not included in Schedule 3 to this Act, or any weight which is not so included.

(2) No person shall use for trade—

(a) the ounce troy, except for the purposes of transactions in, or in articles made from, gold, silver or other precious metals, including transactions in gold or silver thread, lace or fringe, or
(b) the carat (metric), except for the purposes of transactions in precious stones or pearls, or
(c) a capacity measure of 35, 70, 125, 150 or 175 millilitres, except for the purposes of transactions in intoxicating liquor, or
(d) the pint except for—

(i) the purposes of the sale of draught beer or cider, or
(ii) the purposes of the sale of milk in returnable containers.

(e), (f) *Repealed.*

(3) Subsection (1)(*a*) above shall not apply to the prescribing of, or the dispensing of a prescription for, drugs.

(4) A person who contravenes subsection (1) or (2) above shall be guilty of an offence[2], and any measure or weight used, or in any person's possession for use, in contravention of that subsection shall be liable to be forfeited.

(5) The preceding provisions have effect subject to—

(*a*) subsection (5A) below, and
(*b*) sections 9 and 89 below.

(5A) Nothing in this section precludes the use for trade up to and including 31 December 2009, of any supplementary indication; and for this purpose any indication of quantity ("the imperial indication") is a supplementary indication if—

(*a*) it is expressed in a unit of measurement other than a metric unit,
(*b*) it accompanies an indication of quantity expressed in a metric unit ("the metric indication") and is not itself authorised for use in the circumstances as a primary indication of quantity, and
(*c*) the metric indication is the more prominent, the imperial indication being, in particular, expressed in characters no larger than those of the metric indication.

(6) The Secretary of State may by order—

(*a*) amend Schedule 3 to this Act by adding to or removing from it any linear, square, cubic or capacity measure, or any weight;
(*b*) add to, vary or remove from subsection (2) above any restriction on the cases or circumstances in which, or the conditions subject to which, a unit of measurement, measure or weight may be used for trade or possessed for use for trade.

(7) An order under subsection (6) above may contain such transitional or other supplemental or incidental provisions as appear to the Secretary of State expedient.

(8) In this section "unit of measurement" means a unit of measurement of length, area, volume, capacity, mass or weight.

[Weights and Measures Act 1985, s 8 amended by SI 1994/1883, 2866 and 2867, and SI 2001/55 and 1322.]

1. In relation to wine and grape must, see SI 1978/463 (referring to s 9A(1)(*b*) of the 1963 Act which s 8 of the 1985 Act replaces).
2. For penalty see s 84, post.

8–31822 9. Dual marking and conversion charts. (1) The Secretary of State may make regulations—

(*a*) requiring or authorising a person who uses a metric unit for trade to afford, for explanatory purposes, information giving the equivalent in the imperial system of the relevant quantity in the metric system, and
(*b*) specifying the manner in which the information is to be given, and in particular specifying the cases in which any obligation to give information in metric units is to be extended to include the same information in imperial units.

(2) The Secretary of State may make regulations requiring or authorising the display on premises where metric units are used for trade of conversion tables or other material for converting metric units into imperial units.

(3) Regulations under this section—

(*a*) may prescribe the form and manner in which any information or other material is to be given or displayed,
(*b*) may prescribe appropriate conversion factors by reference to which, in prescribed cases or circumstances, an amount expressed in imperial units is to be treated as equivalent to a given amount expressed in metric units,
(*c*) may prescribe the persons to whom, and the cases and circumstances in which, the regulations apply and may make different provision for different persons, cases or circumstances,
(*d*) may contain such consequential, incidental or supplementary provisions as appear to the Secretary of State to be expedient.

(4) A person contravening regulations made under this section shall be guilty of an offence[1].

(5) In this section "unit" in the expressions "metric unit" and "imperial unit" means any unit of measurement of length, area, volume, capacity, mass or weight.

(6) Regulations under this section imposing obligations apply whether or not the relevant imperial unit may lawfully be used for trade, and regulations authorising, but not requiring, anything to be done authorise it to be done notwithstanding that the relevant imperial unit may not be lawfully used for trade, but do not in any other respect authorise what is unlawful.

[Weights and Measures Act 1985, s 9.]

1. For penalty see s 84, post.

8–31823 10. Multiples and fractions of measures and units. (1) Except as may be prescribed[1], and subject to any regulations made under section 15 below—

(*a*) a linear measure specified in Part I of Schedule 3 to this Act may be marked in whole or in part with divisions and sub-divisions representing any shorter length or lengths; but (*b*) no capacity measure specified in Part IV of that Schedule shall be used for trade by means of any division or sub-division marked on it as a capacity measure of any lesser quantity.

(2) Any person who contravenes paragraph (*b*) of subsection (1) above shall be guilty of an offence[2], and any measure used, or in any person's possession for use, in contravention of that paragraph, shall be liable to be forfeited.

(3) The Secretary of State may by regulations prescribe what may be treated for the purposes of use for trade as the equivalent of, or of any multiple or fraction of, any unit of measurement included in Schedule 1 to this Act in terms of any other such unit.

(4) Nothing in any regulations under subsection (3) above shall apply to any transaction in drugs.

(5) *Saving*[3] *for prescribing or dealing in drugs.*

[Weights and Measures Act 1985, s 10.]

1. See the Weights and Measures Regulations 1963 as amended (noted to s 15, post) and the Capacity Serving Measures (Intoxicating Liquor) Regulations 1988, SI 1988/120 amended by SI 1993/2060.
2. For penalty see s 84, post.
3. The Weights and Measures (Equivalents for Dealing with Drugs) Regulations 1970, SI 1970/1897 amended by SI 1976/1664 were made under s 10 of the 1963 Act which this replaces. See also exemptions in the Measuring Instruments (EEC Requirements) Regulations, post.

Weighing or measuring equipment for use for trade

8–31824 11. Certain equipment to be passed and stamped by inspector. (1) The provisions of this section shall apply to the use for trade[1] of weighing or measuring equipment of such classes or descriptions as may be prescribed[2].

(2) No person shall use[3] any article for trade as equipment to which this section applies, or have any article in his possession for such use, unless that article, or equipment to which this section applies in which that article is incorporated or to the operation of which the use of that article is incidental—

(*a*) has been passed by an inspector or approved verifier as fit for such use, and
(*b*) except as otherwise expressly provided by or under this Act, bears a stamp indicating that it has been so passed which remains undefaced otherwise than by reason of fair wear and tear.

(3) If any person contravenes subsection (2) above, he shall be guilty of an offence[4] and any article in respect of which the offence was committed shall be liable to be forfeited.

(4)–(10) *Testing, stamping, marking (summarised).*

(11) Where a person submits equipment to an inspector under this section, the inspector may require the person to provide the inspector with such assistance in connection with the testing of the equipment as the inspector reasonably considers it necessary for the person to provide and shall not be obliged to proceed with the test until the person provides it; but a failure to provide the assistance shall not constitute an offence under section 81 below.

(12) If an inspector refuses to pass as fit for use for trade any equipment submitted to him under this section and is requested by the person by whom the equipment was submitted to give reasons for the refusal, the inspector shall give to that person a statement of those reasons in writing.

(13) In the case of any equipment which is required by regulations made under section 15 below to be passed and stamped under this section only after it has been installed at the place where it is to be used for trade, if after the equipment has been so passed and stamped it is dismantled and reinstalled, whether in the same or some other place, it shall not be used for trade after being so reinstalled until it has again been passed under this section.

(14) If any person—

(*a*) knowingly uses any equipment in contravention of subsection (13) above, or
(*b*) knowingly causes or permits any other person so to use it, or
(*c*) knowing that the equipment is required by virtue of subsection (13) above to be again passed under this section, disposes of it to some other person without informing him of that requirement,

he shall be guilty of an offence[4] and the equipment shall be liable to be forfeited[5].

(15), (16) *Validity of stamping (summarised).*

[Weights and Measures Act 1985, s 11, as amended by SI 1999/503.]

1. Defined by s 7, ante.
2. See the text of Regulations noted to s 15, post.
3. This included the use of a vehicle in *FE Charman Ltd v Clow* [1974] 3 All ER 371, [1974] 1 WLR 384, 138 JP 728. Use of unstamped equipment for the sale of intoxicating liquor by the licensee of a public house in the course of his employment was held *prima facie* to be use by the employers for the purposes of s 11(2) (*Evans v Clifton Inns Ltd* (1986) 150 JP 639, 85 LGR 119).
4. For penalty see s 84, post.
5. For disposal of forfeiture see Magistrates' Courts Act 1980, s 140, ante.

8–31824A 11A. Approval of persons to verify equipment manufactured etc by them [Weights and Measures Act 1985, s 11A, as inserted by SI 1999/503.]

8–31824B 11B. Testing by official EEA testers[Weights and Measures Act 1985, s 11B, as inserted by SI 1999/503.]

8–31825 12. Approved patterns of equipment. Secretary of State may examine any pattern of weighing or measuring equipment and issue a certificate of approval which may be revoked.
[Weights and Measures Act 1985, s 12—summarised.]

8–31826 13. Offences in connection with approved patterns of equipment. (1) Where one or more conditions are imposed by the Secretary of State on the grant or renewal of a certificate of approval, then if any person—

(*a*) knowing that a condition, other than such a condition as is mentioned in section 12(6) above, has been imposed with respect to any equipment, uses, or causes or permits any other person to use, that equipment in contravention of that condition, or

(*b*) knowing that any condition has been imposed with respect to any equipment, disposes of that equipment to any other person in a state in which it could be used for trade without informing that other person of that condition,

he shall be guilty of an offence[1] and the equipment shall be liable to be forfeited[2].

(2) Where a certificate of approval in respect of any pattern of equipment—

(*a*) expires (whether at the end of a period or by virtue of a notice under section 12(9) above), or

(*b*) is revoked in a case falling within section 12(11)(*b*) above,

then if any person, knowing that the certificate has expired or has been so revoked, supplies to another person any equipment of the pattern in question which is marked with a stamp and which was not used for trade at a time when the certificate was in force otherwise than by virtue of section 12(11) above, he shall be guilty of an offence[1] and the equipment supplied shall be liable to be forfeited[2].

(3) Where a certificate of approval in respect of any pattern of equipment is revoked in a case not falling within section 12(11)(*b*) above, then if any person, knowing that the certificate has been so revoked (and except as may be permitted by any fresh certificate granted in respect of that pattern)—

(*a*) uses for trade, or has in his possession for such use, any equipment of that pattern,

(*b*) causes or permits any other person to use any such equipment for trade, or

(*c*) disposes of any such equipment to any such person in a state in which it could be used for trade without informing that other person of the revocation,

he shall be guilty of an offence[1] and the equipment shall be liable to be forfeited[2].

(4) In this section "certificate of approval" means a certificate of approval of a pattern of weighing or measuring equipment granted under section 12 above; and subsections (1) and (3) above have effect in relation to a certificate of approval remaining in force by virtue of subsection (9) or (11) of section 12 above as they have effect in relation to other certificates of approval.
[Weights and Measures Act 1985, s 13.]

1. For penalty see s 84, post.
2. For disposal of forfeiture see Magistrates' Courts Act 1980, s 140, ante.

8–31827 14. General specifications of equipment. (1) The Secretary of State may by regulations prescribe general specifications for the construction of equipment to which section 11 above applies and, subject to subsection (4) below, while any such specification is for the time being so prescribed no equipment which does not conform with it shall be passed or stamped by an inspector or approved verifier under that section unless it is of a pattern in respect of which a certificate of approval under section 12 above is in force.

(2) If the Secretary of State is satisfied that any pattern submitted to him under section 12(1) above conforms with any general specification for the time being prescribed under this section he may, instead of issuing a certificate of approval under that section, cause to be published a declaration to that effect together with particulars of that pattern.

(3) Where a specification prescribed by regulations under this section is varied or revoked by further regulations under this section, then if any person—

(*a*) uses for trade[1] any equipment which conformed with that specification but which to his knowledge no longer conforms with any specification prescribed by regulations under this section,

(*b*) has any such equipment in his possession for use for trade,

(*c*) causes or permits any other person to use any such equipment for trade, or

(*d*) disposes of any such equipment to any other person in a state in which it could be used for trade without informing that other person that it no longer conforms with any specification prescribed by regulations under this section,

he shall be guilty of an offence[2] and the equipment shall be liable to be forfeited[3].

(4) Where, in the case of any particular equipment, the Secretary of State is of opinion that there are special circumstances which make it impracticable or unnecessary for that equipment to comply

with any particular requirement of any specification prescribed under this section, the Secretary of State may exempt that equipment from that requirement subject to compliance with such conditions, if any, as he thinks fit.

(5) If any person knowingly contravenes any condition imposed with respect to any equipment by virtue of subsection (4) above, he shall be guilty of an offence[2] and the equipment shall be liable to be forfeited[3].

(6) If any difference arises between an inspector and any other person as to the interpretation of any specification prescribed under this section, or as to whether or not any equipment conforms with such a specification, that difference may with the consent of that other person, and shall at the request of that other person, be referred to the Secretary of State, whose decision shall be final.
[Weights and Measures Act 1985, s 14, as amended by SI 1999/503.]

1. "Use for trade" is defined by s 7, ante.
2. For penalty see s 84, post.
3. For disposal of forfeiture see Magistrates' Courts Act 1980, s 140, ante.

Miscellaneous

8–31828 **15. Regulations relating to weighing or measuring for trade.** (1) The Secretary of State may make regulations[1] with respect to—

(*a*) the materials and principles of construction of weighing or measuring equipment for use for trade,
(*b*) the inspection, testing, passing as fit for use for trade and stamping of such equipment, including—
  (i) the prohibition of the stamping of such equipment in such circumstances as may be specified in the regulations,
  (ii) the circumstances in which an inspector may remove or detain any such equipment for inspection or testing,
  (iii) the marking of any such equipment found unfit for use for trade,
(*c*) the circumstances in which, conditions under which and manner in which stamps may be destroyed, obliterated or defaced,
(*d*) where any stamp on weighing or measuring equipment is lawfully destroyed, obliterated or defaced, the circumstances in which, and conditions subject to which, the equipment may be used for trade without contravening section 11(2) above,
(*e*) the purposes for which particular types of weighing or measuring equipment may be used for trade,
(*f*) the manner of erection or use of weighing or measuring equipment used for trade,
(*g*) the abbreviations of or symbols for units of measurement which may be used for trade, and
(*h*) the manner in which the tare weight of road vehicles, or of road vehicles of any particular class or description, is to be determined.

(2) Regulations under subsection (1) above with respect to the testing of equipment may provide—

(*a*) that where a group of items of equipment of the same kind is submitted for testing and prescribed conditions are satisfied with respect to the group, the testing may be confined to a number of items determined by or under the regulations and selected in the prescribed manner, and
(*b*) that if items so selected satisfy the test other items in the group shall be treated as having satisfied it.

(3) Subject to subsection (5) below, if any person contravenes any regulation made by virtue of subsection 1(*e*), (*f*), (*g*) or (*h*) above, he shall be guilty of an offence[2], and any weighing or measuring equipment in respect of which the contravention was committed shall be liable to be forfeited[3].

(4) If any difference arises between an inspector and any other person as to the interpretation of any regulations made under this section or as to the method of testing any weighing or measuring equipment, that difference may with the consent or that other person, and shall at the request of that other person, be referred to the Secretary of State, whose decision shall be final.

(5) Where in the special circumstances of any particular case it appears to be impracticable or unnecessary that any requirement of any regulations made under this section should be complied with, the Secretary of State may if he thinks fit dispense with the observance of that requirement subject to compliance with such conditions, if any, as he thinks fit to impose; and if any person knowingly contravenes any condition imposed with respect to any equipment by virtue of this subsection he shall be guilty of an offence[2] and the equipment shall be liable to be forfeited[3].
[Weights and Measures Act 1985, s 15.]

1. The Weights and Measures Regulations 1963, SI 1963/1710 amended by SI 1972/767, SI 1979/1612, SI 1983/914, SI 1986/1320 and 1682, SI 1988/876 and 120, SI 1994/1259, SI 1995/735, SI 2000/388, SI 2001/599 and 1208 and SI 2003/2454 and 2761 were made under s 14 of the Weights and Measures Act 1963 which this section replaces.
The following regulations were made under the Weights and Measures Act 1963 and now have effect under s 15:

Cubic Measures (Ballast and Agricultural Materials) Regulations 1978, SI 1978/1962 amended by SI 1988/765;
Liquid Fuel Deliveries from Road Tankers Regulations 1983, SI 1983/1390 amended by SI 1986/1210, SI 1994/1851, SI 1995/3117, SI 2001/85 and SI 2003/214;
Intoxicating Liquor Regulations 1983, SI 1983/1656 amended by SI 1984/273, SI 1994/1851 and SI 2001/85;
The following regulations have been made under this section:
Filling and Discontinuous Totalising Automatic Weighing Machines Regulations 1986, SI 1986/1320 amended by SI 1994/1851, SI 1996/797, SI 2000/387, SI 2001/85 and SI 2003/214;
Measuring Equipment (Measures of Length) Regulations 1986, SI 1986/1682 amended by SI 1986/2109, SI 1994/1851, SI 1996/2636 and 3020, SI 2001/85 and SI 2003/214;
Weights Regulations 1986, SI 1986/1683 amended by SI 1994/1851;
Quantity Marking and Abbreviation of Units Regulations 1987, SI 1987/1538 amended by SI 1988/627 and SI 1994/1852;
Capacity Serving Measures (Intoxicating Liquor) Regulations 1988, SI 1988/120 amended by SI 1993/2060, SI 1994/1851, SI 2001/85 and SI 2003/214;
Cold Water Meters Regulations 1988, SI 1988/997 amended by SI 2001/1229 and SI 2003/214;
Measuring Equipment (Capacity Measures and Testing Equipment) Regulations 1995, SI 1995/735 amended by SI 2001/599 amended by SI 2001/85 and SI 2003/214;
Measuring Equipment (Liquid Fuel and Lubricants) Regulations 1995, SI 1995/1014 amended by SI 1998/2218, SI 2001/85 and SI 2003/214 and 2110;
Weighing Equipment (Automatic Gravimetric Filling Instruments) Regulations 2000, SI 2000/388 and SI 2001/85 and SI 2003/214;
Weighing Equipment (Non-automatic Weighing Machines) Regulations 2000, SI 2000/932 amended by SI 2000/3236, SI 2001/85 and SI 2003/214 and 2761;
Non-automatic Weighing Instruments Regulations 2000, SI 2000/3236;
Weighing Equipment (Beltweighers) Regulations 2001, SI 2001/1208 amended by SI 2003/214;
Weighing Equipment (Automatic Rail-weighbridges) Regulations 2003, SI 2003/2454;
Weighing Equipment (Automatic Catchweighing Instruments) Regulations 2003, SI 2003/2761.

2. For penalty see s 84, post.
3. For disposal of forfeiture see Magistrates' Courts Act 1980, s 140 ante.

8–31828A 15A. Pre-test stamping by certain manufacturers. (1) Subject to subsection (2) below, an approved verifier who is the manufacturer of any equipment to which section 11 above applies may apply the prescribed stamp to the equipment, notwithstanding that it has not been passed as fit for use for trade, if he is satisfied on reasonable grounds that it will not be used (whether for trade or otherwise) unless either—

(*a*) the equipment has been passed as fit for use for trade, or
(*b*) the stamp has been destroyed, obliterated or defaced.

(2) A prescribed stamp shall not be applied under subsection (1) above unless the stamp includes the approved verifier's number.

(3) If any person contravenes subsection (2) above, he shall be guilty of an offence and any equipment in respect of which the offence[1] was committed shall be liable to be forfeited.

(4) A prescribed stamp which has been duly applied to any equipment under subsection (1) above shall have effect as follows—

(*a*) at any time before the equipment is passed as fit for use for trade, as an indication that, at the time when the stamp was applied, the approved verifier was satisfied as mentioned in subsection (1) above, and
(*b*) at any time after the equipment is so passed, as evidence of the passing of the equipment as fit for such use.

(5) Where equipment to which a prescribed stamp has been duly applied under subsection (1) above is passed as fit for use for trade, nothing in section 11(4)(*c*) or (4A)(*c*) above shall require another such stamp to be applied to it.

(6) Where the approved verifier fails to pass as fit for use for trade equipment to which a prescribed stamp has been applied under subsection (1) above, he may destroy, obliterate or deface the stamp—

(*a*) in any case where there is a prescribed manner of doing so, in that manner, and
(*b*) in any other case, in such reasonable manner as will leave no doubt that the stamp has been intentionally destroyed, obliterated or defaced.

(7) References in subsections (4) to (6) above to prescribed stamps which have been applied do not include references to such stamps which have subsequently been destroyed, obliterated or defaced.
[Weights and Measures Act 1985, s 15A, as inserted by SI 1999/503.]

1. For penalty see s 84, post.

8–31829 16. Offences in connection with stamping of equipment. (1) Subject to subsection (2) below, any person who, in the case of any weighing or measuring equipment used or intended to be used for trade—

(*a*) not being an inspector or approved verifier or a person acting under the instructions of an inspector or approved verifier, marks in any manner any plug or seal used or designed for use for the reception of a stamp, (*b*) forges, counterfeits or, except as permitted by or under this Act, in any way alters or defaces any stamp,

(*c*) removes any stamp and inserts it into any other such equipment,

(*d*) makes any alteration in the equipment after it has been stamped such as to make it false or unjust, or

(*e*) severs or otherwise tampers with any wire, cord or other thing by means of which a stamp is attached to the equipment,

shall be guilty of an offence[1].

(2) Paragraphs (*a*) and (*b*) of subsection (1) above shall not apply to the destruction or obliteration of any stamp, plug or seal, and paragraph (*e*) of that subsection shall not apply to anything done, in the course of the adjustment or repair of weighing or measuring equipment by, or by the duly authorised agent of, a person who is a manufacturer of, or regularly engaged in the business of repairing, such equipment.

(3) Any person who uses for trade, sells, or exposes or offers for sale any weighing or measuring equipment which to his knowledge—

(*a*) bears a stamp which is a forgery or counterfeit, or which has been transferred from other equipment, or which has been altered or defaced otherwise than as permitted by or under this Act, or

(*b*) is false or unjust as the result of an alteration made in the equipment after it has been stamped,

shall be guilty of an offence[1].

(4) Any weighing or measuring equipment in respect of which an offence under this section is committed, and any stamp or stamping implement used in the commission of the offence, shall be liable to be forfeited[2].

[Weights and Measures Act 1985, s 16, as amended by SI 1999/503.]

1. For penalty see s 84, post.
2. For disposal of a forfeiture, see the Magistrates' Courts Act 1980, s 140, ante.

8–31830 **17. Offences relating to false or unjust equipment or fraud.** (1) If any person uses for trade, or has in his possession[1] for use for trade[2], any weighing or measuring equipment which is false or unjust, he shall be guilty of an offence[3] and the equipment shall be liable to be forfeited[4].

(2) Without prejudice to the liability of any equipment to be forfeited, it shall be a defence for any person charged with an offence under subsection (1) above in respect of the use for trade of any equipment to show—

(*a*) that he used the equipment only in the course of his employment by some other person, and

(*b*) that he neither knew, nor might reasonably have been expected to know, nor had any reason to suspect, the equipment to be false or unjust.

(3) If any fraud is committed in the using of any weighing or measuring equipment for trade, the person committing the fraud and any other person party to it shall be guilty of an offence[3] and the equipment shall be liable to be forfeited[4].

[Weights and Measures Act 1985, s 17.]

1. For a person to have weighing or measuring equipment "in his possession", he must have at least some degree of control over it; and the mere fact that, as licensee, he is the only person lawfully entitled by himself or his agents, to use the equipment in question for selling intoxicating liquor to customers does not necessarily, or of itself, create a situation in which he "has possession of" such equipment (*Bellerby v Carle* [1983] 2 AC 101, [1983] 1 All ER 1031).
2. "Use for trade" is defined by s 7, ante.
3. For penalty see s 84, post.
4. For disposal of a forfeiture, see the Magistrates' Courts Act 1980, s 140.

PART III[1]

PUBLIC WEIGHING OR MEASURING EQUIPMENT

8–31831 **18. Keepers of public equipment to hold certificate.** (1) No person shall attend to any weighing or measuring by means of weighing or measuring equipment available for use by the public, being a weighing or measuring demanded by a member of the public and for which a charge is made, other than a weighing or measuring of a person, unless he holds a certificate from a chief inspector that he has sufficient knowledge for the proper performance of his duties.

(2) Any person refused such a certificate by a chief inspector may appeal against the refusal to the Secretary of State, who may if he thinks fit direct the chief inspector to grant the certificate.

(3) Any person who contravenes, or who causes or permits any other person to contravene, subsection (1) above shall be guilty of an offence[2].

[Weights and Measures Act 1985, s 18.]

1. Part III comprises ss 18–20.
2. For penalty see s 84, post.

8–31832 19. Provision of public equipment by local authorities. Local authority may provide and maintain weighing or measuring equipment.
[Weights and Measures Act 1985, s 19—summarised.]

8–31833 20. Offences in connection with public equipment. (1) Subsection (2) below shall apply where any article, vehicle (whether loaded or unloaded) or animal has been brought for weighing or measuring by means of weighing or measuring equipment which is available for use by the public and is provided for the purpose of weighing or measuring articles, vehicles or animals of the description in question.

(2) If any person appointed to attend to weighing or measuring by means of the equipment in question—

(*a*) without reasonable cause fails to carry out the weighing or measuring on demand,
(*b*) carries out the weighing or measuring unfairly,
(*c*) fails to deliver to the person demanding the weighing or measuring or to his agent a statement in writing of the weight or other measurement found, or
(*d*) fails to make a record of the weighing or measuring, including the time and date of it and, in the case of the weighing of a vehicle, such particulars of the vehicle and of any load on the vehicle as will identify that vehicle and that load,

he shall be guilty of an offence[1].

(3) If in connection with any such equipment as is mentioned in subsection (1) above—

(*a*) any person appointed to attend to weighing or measuring by means of the equipment delivers a false statement of any weight or other measurement found or makes a false record of any weighing or measuring, or
(*b*) any person commits any fraud in connection with any, or any purported, weighing or measuring by means of that equipment,

he shall be guilty of an offence[1].

(4) If, in the case of a weighing or measuring of any article, vehicle or animal carried out by means of any such equipment as is mentioned in subsection (1) above, the person bringing the article, vehicle or animal for weighing or measuring, on being required by the person attending to the weighing or measuring to give his name and address, fails to do so or gives a name or address which is incorrect, he shall be guilty of an offence[1].

(5) The person making any weighing or measuring equipment available for use by the public (in this section referred to as "the responsible person") shall retain for a period of not less than two years any record of any weighing or measuring by means of that equipment made by any person appointed to attend to the weighing or measuring.

(6) An inspector, subject to the production of his credentials if so requested, may require the responsible person to produce any such record as is mentioned in subsection (5) above for inspection at any time while it is retained by him.

(7) If the responsible person fails to retain any such record as is mentioned in subsection (5) above in accordance with that subsection or fails to produce it in accordance with subsection (6) above, he shall be guilty of an offence[1].

(8) If any person wilfully destroys or defaces any such record as is mentioned in subsection (5) above before the expiration of two years from the date when it was made, he shall be guilty of an offence[1].
[Weights and Measures Act 1985, s 20.]

---

1. For penalty see s 84, post.

PART IV[1]
REGULATION OF TRANSACTIONS IN GOODS

Transactions in particular goods

8–31834 21–24. Effect is given to Schedules 4–7 relating to transactions in goods. Secretary of State may make Orders[2] relating to transactions in particular goods and the information which is to be displayed: contravention is an offence[3]; provision is made for exemptions.
[Weights and Measures Act 1985, ss 21–24—summarised.]

---

1. Part IV comprises ss 21–46.
2. The following regulations and orders have been made under s 21 of the Weights and Measures Act 1963 and now have effect under ss 21–24 of the 1985 Act: Weights and Measures (Solid Fuel) Regulations 1987, in this title, post; Weights and Measures (Milk and Solid Fuel Vending Machines) Regulations 1980, SI 1980/246; Weights and Measures Act 1963 (Cheese, Fish, Fresh Fruits and Vegetables, Meat and Poultry) Order 1984, in this title, post; Weights and Measures (Liquid Fuel Carried by Road Tanker) Order 1985, SI 1985/778; the following orders and regulations have been made under ss 21–24 of the following Act: Weights and Measures (Knitting Yarn) Order 1988, SI 1988/895; Weights and Measures Act 1963 (Intoxicating Liquor) Order 1988, SI 1988/2039, in this title, post; Weights and Measures (Miscellaneous Foods) Order 1988, SI 1988/2040, in this title, post.
3. For penalty see s 84, post. The Weights and Measures (Intoxicating Liquor) Order 1988 and the Weights and Measures (Miscellaneous Foods) Order 1988 are also reproduced in this PART, post.

8–31835 **25. Offences relating to transactions in particular goods.** (1) Subject to section 44 below, where any goods are required, when not pre-packed, to be sold only by quantity expressed in a particular manner[1] or only in a particular quantity, any person shall be guilty of an offence[2] who—

(*a*) whether on his own behalf or on behalf of another person, offers[3] or exposes for sale[4], sells or agrees to sell, or

(*b*) causes or suffers any other person to offer or expose for sale, sell or agree to sell on his behalf,

those goods otherwise than by quantity expressed in that manner or, as the case may be, otherwise than in that quantity.

(2) Any person shall be guilty of an offence[2] who—

(*a*) whether on his own behalf or on behalf of another person has in his possession for sale[5], sells or agrees to sell,

(*b*) except in the course of carriage of the goods for reward, has in his possession for delivery after sale, or

(*c*) causes or suffers any other person to have in his possession for sale or for delivery after sale, sell or agree to sell on behalf of the first-mentioned person,

any goods to which subsection (3) below applies, whether the sale is, or is to be, by retail or otherwise.

(3) This subsection applies to any goods—

(*a*) which are required to be pre-packed only in particular quantities but are not so pre-packed,

(*b*) which are required to be otherwise made up in or on a container for sale or for delivery after sale only in particular quantities but are not so made up,

(*c*) which are required to be made for sale only in particular quantities but are not so made,

(*d*) which are required to be pre-packed only if the container is marked with particular information but are pre-packed otherwise than in or on a container so marked,

(*e*) which are required to be otherwise made up in or on a container for sale or for delivery after sale only if the container is marked with particular information but are so made up otherwise than in or on a container so marked,

(*f*) which are required to be pre-packed only in or on a container of a particular description but are not pre-packed in or on a container of that description, or

(*g*) which are required to be otherwise made up in or on a container for sale or for delivery after sale only in or on a container of a particular description but are not so made up in or on a container of that description.

(4) In the case of any sale where the quantity of the goods sold expressed in a particular manner[1] is required to be made known to the buyer at or before a particular time and that quantity is not so made known, the person by whom, and any other person on whose behalf, the goods were sold shall be guilty of an offence[2].

(5) Where any goods required to be sold by means of, or to be offered or exposed for sale in, a vending machine only if certain requirements are complied with are so sold, offered or exposed without those requirements being complied with, the seller or person causing the goods to be offered or exposed shall be guilty of an offence[2].

(6) The preceding provisions of this section have effect subject to sections 33 to 37 below.

(7) For the purposes of this section the quantity of the goods in a regulated package (as defined by section 68(1) below) shall be deemed to be the nominal quantity (as so defined) on the package.

(8) In this section "required" means required by or under this Part of this Act.

[Weights and Measures Act 1985, s 25.]

1. For extended use of this expression, see s 44, post.
2. For penalty see s 84, post.
3. See *Fisher v Bell* [1961] 1 QB 394; [1960] 3 All ER 731; 125 JP 201.
4. There is an exposure for sale when goods are sent to a purchaser who, by agreement, is entitled to accept or reject them, and he rejects them (*Ollett v Jordan* [1918] 2 KB 41, 82 JP 221).
5. This means possession with a sale in contemplation (*Birkett v McGlassons Ltd* [1957] 1 All ER 369, 121 JP 126), not during an intermediate stage between the completion of manufacture and the time when, eg, in the case of loaves of bread, it has been decided after checking and sorting which particular goods are to be offered for sale (*Ben Worsley Ltd v Harvey* [1967] 2 All ER 507, 131 JP 376). Unascertained goods such as coal are in the possession for sale of the vendors or their agent until delivery of the goods is completed so as to perform the contract for sale (*Church v Lee and Co-operative Retail Services* (1985) 150 JP 300).

Quantity to be stated in writing

8–31836 **26. Quantity to be stated in writing in certain cases.** (1) Subject to section 27 below, the provisions of this section shall have effect on any sale of goods—

(*a*) which is required by or under this Part of this Act to be a sale by quantity expressed in a particular manner[1],

(*b*) in the case of which the quantity of the goods sold expressed in a particular manner is so required to be made known to the buyer at or before a particular time, or

(*c*) which, being a sale by retail[2] not falling within paragraph (*a*) or (*b*) above, is, or purports to be, a sale by quantity expressed in a particular manner other than by number.

(2) Subject to subsections (4) to (6) below, unless the quantity of the goods sold expressed in the manner in question is made known to the buyer at the premises of the seller and the goods are delivered to the buyer at those premises on the same occasion as, and at or after the time when, that quantity is so made known to him, a statement in writing of that quantity shall be delivered to the consignee at or before delivery of the goods to him.

(3) If subsection (2) above is contravened then, subject to sections 33 to 37 below, the person by whom, and any other person on whose behalf, the goods were sold shall be guilty of an offence[3].

(4) If at the time when the goods are delivered the consignee is absent, it shall be sufficient compliance with subsection (2) above if the statement is left at some suitable place at the premises at which the goods are delivered.

(5) Subsection (2) above shall not apply to any sale otherwise than by retail where, by agreement with the buyer, the quantity of the goods sold is to be determined after their delivery to the consignee.

(6) Where any liquid goods are sold by capacity measurement and the quantity sold is measured at the time of delivery and elsewhere than at the premises of the seller, subsection (2) above shall not apply but, unless the quantity by capacity measurement of the goods sold is measured in the presence of the buyer, the person by whom the goods are delivered shall immediately after the delivery hand to the buyer, or if the buyer is not present leave at some suitable place at the premises at which the goods are delivered, a statement in writing of the quantity by capacity measurement delivered, and if without reasonable cause he fails so to do he shall be guilty of an offence[3].

[Weights and Measures Act 1985, s 26.]

---

1. For extended use of this expression, see s 44, post.
2. This means a sale to a consuming member of the public; contrasted with a sale wholesale to a purchaser who proposes himself to sell the goods by retail (*Chappell & Co Ltd v Nestlé Co Ltd* [1960] AC 87, [1959] 2 All ER 701, HL, *Treacher v Treacher* [1874] WN 4; *Phillips v Parnaby* [1934] 2 KB 299, 98 JP 388).
3. For penalty see s 84, post.

8–31837 **27. Exemption from requirements of section 26.** (1) The Secretary of State may by order grant, with respect to goods or sales of such descriptions as may be specified in the order, exemption, either generally or in such circumstances as may be so specified, from all or any of the requirements of section 26 above.

(2) Until otherwise provided by an order under subsection (1) above, nothing in section 26 above shall apply to —

(*a*) a sale by retail from a vehicle of—

(i) any of the following in a quantity not exceeding 110 kilograms, that is to say, any solid fuel within the meaning of Schedule 5 to this Act, and wood fuel, or
(ii) any of the following in a quantity not exceeding 25 litres, that is to say, liquid fuel, lubricating oil, and any mixture of such fuel and oil,

(*b*) a sale by retail of bread within the meaning of the Weights and Measures Act 1963 (Miscellaneous Foods) Order 1984[1],
(*c*) goods made up for sale (whether by way of pre-packing or otherwise) in or on a container marked with a statement in writing with respect to the quantity of the goods expressed in the manner in question, being a container which is delivered with the goods,
(*d*) a sale of goods in the case of which a document stating the quantity of the goods expressed in the manner in question is required to be delivered to the buyer or consignee of the goods by or under any other provision of this Part of this Act,
(*e*) any such goods or sales as are mentioned in section 24(2)(*a*) to (*d*) above,
(*f*) a sale of intoxicating liquor for consumption at the premises of the seller,
(*g*) a sale by means of a vending machine, or
(*h*) goods delivered at premises of the buyer by means of an installation providing a connection of a permanent nature between those premises and premises of the seller.

[Weights and Measures Act 1985, s 27 as amended by SI 1994/2867.]

---

1. SI 1984/1316.

General offences

8–31838 **28. Short weight, etc.** (1) Subject to sections 33 to 37 below, any person who, in selling or purporting to sell any goods[1] by weight or other measurement or by number, delivers or causes to be delivered[2] to the buyer—

(*a*) a lesser quantity[1] than that purported to be sold, or
(*b*) a lesser quantity than corresponds with the price charged,

shall be guilty of an offence[3].

(2) For the purposes of this section—

(*a*) the quantity of the goods in a regulated package (as defined by section 68(1) below) shall be deemed to be the nominal quantity (as so defined) on the package, and (*b*) any statement, whether oral or in writing, as to the weight of any goods shall be taken, unless otherwise expressed, to be a statement as to the net weight of the goods.

(3) Nothing in this section shall apply in relation to any such goods or sales as are mentioned in section 24(2)(*a*) or (*b*) above.
[Weights and Measures Act 1985, s 28.]

1. As to wine and grape must, see SI 1984/1318; as to beer and cider see s 43, post.
2. The licensee is the only person who can sell intoxicating liquor and thus an absent licensee was rightly convicted of causing the delivery to a purchaser of a short measure of whisky which was supplied to a customer by his servant. Active causation or counselling the delivery of a short measure was not necessary for the offence to be complete (*Sopp v Long* [1970] 1 QB 518, [1969] 1 All ER 855, 133 JP 261). Where an order for 15 lbs of meat was made and joints were delivered with a delivery note stating the meat weight as 14·35 lbs whereas the lamb when delivered weighed just over 9·25 lbs, it was held that no offence had been committed because the defendants had, as was their normal practice, removed the bone and the customer was only entitled to expect what was delivered (*North Yorkshire County Council v Holmesterne Farm Co Ltd* (1985) 150 JP 124).
3. For penalty see s 84, post.

8–31849 29. Misrepresentation. (1) Subject to sections 33 to 37 below, any person who—

(*a*) on or in connection with the sale[1] or purchase of any goods,
(*b*) in exposing or offering any goods for sale,
(*c*) in purporting to make known to the buyer the quantity of any goods sold, or
(*d*) in offering to purchase any goods,

makes any misrepresentation whether oral or otherwise as to the quantity of the goods, or does any other act calculated to mislead a person buying or selling the goods as to the quantity of the goods, shall be guilty of an offence[2].

(2) Subsection (2) of section 28 above shall have effect for the purposes of this section as it has effect for the purposes of that section.

(3) Nothing in this section shall apply in relation to any such goods or sales as are mentioned in section 24(2)(*a*) or (*b*) above.
[Weights and Measures Act 1985, s 29.]

1. The misrepresentation need not be made by one of the parties to the contract, but must be made to the buyer or seller and be calculated to mislead him (*Collett v Co-operative Wholesale Society Ltd* [1970] 1 All ER 274, 134 JP 277).
2. For penalty see s 84, post.

8–31850 30. Quantity less than stated. (1) If, in the case of any goods pre-packed in or on a container marked with a statement in writing with respect to the quantity of the goods, the quantity of the goods is at any time found to be less than that stated, then, subject to sections 33 to 37 below—

(*a*) any person who has those goods in his possession for sale shall be guilty of an offence[1], and
(*b*) if it is shown that the deficiency cannot be accounted for by anything occurring after the goods had been sold by retail and delivered to, or to a person nominated in that behalf by, the buyer, any person by whom or on whose behalf those goods have been sold or agreed to be sold at any time while they were pre-packed in or on the container in question, shall be guilty of an offence[1].

(2) If—

(*a*) in the case of a sale of or agreement to sell any goods which, not being pre-packed, are made up for sale or for delivery after sale in or on a container marked with a statement in writing with respect to the quantity of the goods, or
(*b*) in the case of any goods which, in connection with their sale or an agreement for their sale, have associated with them a document containing such a statement,

the quantity of the goods is at any time found to be less than that stated, then, if it is shown that the deficiency cannot be accounted for by anything occurring after the goods had been delivered to, or to a person nominated in that behalf by, the buyer, and subject to sections 33 to 37 below and paragraph 10 of Schedule 4 to this Act, the person by whom, and any other person on whose behalf, the goods were sold or agreed to be sold shall be guilty of an offence[1].

(3) Subsections (1) and (2) above shall have effect notwithstanding that the quantity stated is expressed to be the quantity of the goods at a specified time falling before the time in question, or is expressed with some other qualification of whatever description, except where—

(*a*) that quantity is so expressed in pursuance of an express requirement of this Part of this Act or any instrument made under this Part, or
(*b*) the goods, although falling within subsection (1) or subsection (2)(*a*) above—

(i) are not required by or under this Part of this Act to be pre-packed as mentioned in subsection (1) or, as the case may be, to be made up for sale or for delivery after sale in or on a container only if the container is marked as mentioned in subsection (2)(*a*), and

(ii) are not goods on a sale of which (whether any sale or a sale of any particular description) the quantity sold is required by or under any provision of this Part of this Act other than section 26, to be made known to the buyer at or before a particular time, or

(*c*) the goods, although falling within subsection (2)(*b*) above, are not required by or under this Part of this Act to have associated with them such a document as is mentioned in that provision.

(4) In any case to which, by virtue of paragraph (*a*), (*b*) or (*c*) of subsection (3) above, the provisions of subsection (1) or (2) above do not apply, if it is found at any time that the quantity of the goods in question is less than that stated and it is shown that the deficiency is greater than can be reasonably justified on the ground justifying the qualification in question, then, subject to sections 33 to 37 below—

(*a*) in the case of goods such as are mentioned in subsection (1) above, if it is further shown as mentioned in that subsection, then—

(i) where the container in question was marked in Great Britain, the person by whom, and any other person on whose behalf, the container was marked, or

(ii) where the container in question was marked outside Great Britain, the person by whom, and any other person on whose behalf, the goods were first sold in Great Britain,

shall be guilty of an offence[1];

(*b*) in the case of goods such as are mentioned in subsection (2) above, the person by whom, and any other person on whose behalf, the goods were sold or agreed to be sold shall be guilty of an offence if, but only if, he would, but for paragraph (*a*), (*b*) or (*c*) of subsection (3) above have been guilty of an offence under subsection (2).

(5) Subsection (2) of section 28 above shall have effect for the purposes of this section as it has effect for the purposes of that section.

(6) Nothing in this section shall apply in relation to any such goods or sales as are mentioned in section 24(2)(*a*) or (*b*) above.

[Weights and Measures Act 1985, s 30.]

1. For penalty see s 84, post.

8–31851 **31. Incorrect statements.** (1) Without prejudice to section 30(2) to (4) above, if in the case of any goods required by or under this Part of this Act to have associated with them a document containing particular statements, that document is found to contain any such statement which is materially incorrect, any person who, knowing or having reasonable cause to suspect that statement to be materially incorrect, inserted it or caused it to be inserted in the document, or used the document for the purposes of this Part of this Act while that statement was contained in the document, shall be guilty of an offence[1].

(2) Subsection (2) of section 28 above shall have effect for the purposes of this section as it has effect for the purposes of that section.

(3) Nothing in this section shall apply in relation to any such goods or sales as are mentioned in section 24(2)(*a*) or (*b*) above.

[Weights and Measures Act 1985, s 31.]

1. For penalty see s 84, post.

8–31852 **32. Offences due to default of third person.** Where the commission by any person of an offence under this Part of this Act or an instrument made under this Part is due to the act or default[1] of some other person, the other person shall be guilty of an offence and may be charged with and convicted[2] of the offence whether or not proceedings are taken against the first-mentioned person.

[Weights and Measures Act 1985, s 32.]

1. The prosecution must identify the "act or default" of the third person to which the commission of the offence was said to be due. Where the third person was a company which owned a public house and an employee of the company caused a short measure of beer to be served to a purchaser, it was held that an assumption that the owner could not adequately have trained their staff was insufficient to establish the offence was due to the "act or default" of the company (*Allied Domecq Leisure Ltd v Cooper* (1998) 163 JP 1, [1999] Crim LR 230).

2. A person convicted, whether the original defendant or "third party" may appeal to the Crown Court; see *R v Epsom Justices, ex p Dawnier Motors Ltd* [1961] 1 QB 201, [1960] 3 All ER 635, 125 JP 40, in which previous decisions on the subject are reviewed. Where the "third party" appeals, he must serve notice on both the prosecutor and the defendant (*Oxo Ltd v Chappell and Turner* [1966] 2 QB 228, [1966] 3 All ER 1968, 130 JP 356).

Defences

8–31853 **33. Warranty.** (1) Subject to the following provisions of this section, in any proceedings for an offence under this Part of this Act or any instrument made under this Part, being an offence relating to the quantity or pre-packing of any goods, it shall be a defence for the person charged to prove—

(*a*) that he bought the goods from some other person—

(i) as being of the quantity which the person charged purported to sell or represented, or which was marked on any container or stated in any document to which the proceedings relate, or

(ii) as conforming with the statement marked on any container to which the proceedings relate, or with the requirements with respect to the pre-packing of goods of this Part of this Act or any instrument made under this Part,

as the case may require, and

(*b*) that he so bought the goods with a written warranty from that other person that they were of that quantity or, as the case may be, did so conform, and

(*c*) that at the time of the commission of the offence he did in fact believe the statement contained in the warranty to be accurate and had no reason to believe it to be inaccurate, and

(*d*) if the warranty was given by a person who at the time he gave it was resident outside Great Britain and any designated country, that the person charged had taken reasonable steps to check the accuracy of the statement contained in the warranty, and

(*e*) in the case of proceedings relating to the quantity of any goods, that he took all reasonable steps to ensure that, while in his possession, the quantity of the goods remained unchanged and, in the case of such or any other proceedings, that apart from any change in their quantity the goods were at the time of the commission of the offence in the same state as when he bought them.

(2) A warranty shall not be a defence in any such proceedings as are mentioned in subsection (1) above unless, not later than three days before the date of the hearing, the person charged has sent to the prosecutor a copy of the warranty with a notice stating that he intends to rely on it and specifying the name and address of the person from whom the warranty was received, and has also sent a like notice to that person.

(3) Where the person charged is the employee of a person who, if he had been charged, would have been entitled to plead a warranty as a defence under this section, subsection (1) above shall have effect—

(*a*) with the substitution, for any reference (however expressed) in paragraphs (*a*), (*b*), (*d*) and (*e*) to the person charged, of a reference to his employer, and

(*b*) with the substitution for paragraph (*c*) of the following—

"(*c*) that at the time of the commission of the offence his employer did in fact believe the statement contained in the warranty to be accurate and the person charged had no reason to believe it to be inaccurate,".

(4) The person by whom the warranty is alleged to have been given shall be entitled to appear at the hearing and to give evidence.

(5) If the person charged in any such proceedings as are mentioned in subsection (1) above wilfully attributes to any goods a warranty given in relation to any other goods, he shall be guilty of an offence[1].

(6) A person who, in respect of any goods sold by him in respect of which a warranty might be pleaded under this section, gives to the buyer a false warranty in writing shall be guilty of an offence[1] unless he proves that when he gave the warranty he took all reasonable steps to ensure that the statements contained in it were, and would continue at all relevant times to be, accurate.

(7) Where in any such proceedings as are mentioned in subsection (1) above ("the original proceedings") the person charged relies successfully on a warranty given to him or to his employer, any proceedings under subsection (6) above in respect of the warranty may, at the option of the prosecutor, be taken either before a court having jurisdiction in the place where the original proceedings were taken or before a court having jurisdiction in the place where the warranty was given.

(8) For the purposes of this section, any statement with respect to any goods which is contained in any document required by or under this Part of this Act to be associated with the goods or in any invoice, and, in the case of goods made up in or on a container for sale or for delivery after sale, any statement with respect to those goods with which that container is marked, shall be taken to be a written warranty of the accuracy of that statement.

[Weights and Measures Act 1985, s 33.]

---

1. For penalty see s 84, post.

8–31854 34. Reasonable precautions and due diligence. (1) In any proceedings for an offence under this Part of this Act or any instrument made under this Part, it shall be a defence for the person charged to prove[1] that he took all reasonable precautions[2] and exercised all due diligence[3] to avoid the commission of the offence.

(2) If in any case the defence provided by subsection (1) above involves an allegation that the

commission of the offence in question was due to the act or default of another person[4] or due to reliance on information supplied by another person, the person charged shall not, without the leave of the court, be entitled[5] to rely on the defence unless, before the beginning of the period of seven days ending with the date when the hearing of the charge began, he served on the prosecutor a notice giving such information identifying or assisting in the identification of the other person as was then in his possession.
[Weights and Measures Act 1985, s 34.]

---

1. The onus of proof is on the defendant; but is less than is required of the prosecution in proving case beyond reasonable doubt and may be discharged by evidence of probability (*R v Carr-Briant* [1943] 2 All ER 156, 107 JP 167). The somewhat narrow extent of this defence is illustrated by *Urwin v Toole* [1976] Crim LR 583.
2. The court must require proof of all the prescribed elements, not, eg, merely that the defendant in the court's opinion took all reasonable precautions; see *Marshall v Matthews* [1939] 1 All ER 156.
3. There is no legal standard of diligence; therefore the question of what is due diligence falls to be decided as a question of fact (*R C Hammett Ltd v Crabb, R C Hammett Ltd v Beldam* (1931) 95 JP 180). Due diligence of a limited company means that of those who represent the directing mind and will of the company and control what it does; it does not refer to that of a subordinate unless some part of the functions of management has been delegated to him, and it does not refer to shop managers who act under the control of directions from their superiors (*Tesco Supermarkets Ltd v Nattrass* [1972] AC 153, [1971] 2 All ER 127, 135 JP 289).
4. See *Melias Ltd v Preston* [1957] 2 QB 380, [1957] 2 All ER 449, 121 JP 444.
5. See *Thomas v Thomas Bolton & Sons Ltd* (1928) 92 JP 147; cf Factories Act 1961, s 162; *R v Derby Recorder, ex p Spalton* [1944] KB 611, [1944] 1 All ER 721, 108 JP 193; *R v Epsom Justices, ex p Dawnier Motors Ltd* [1951] 1 QB 201, [1960] 3 All ER 635, 125 JP 40; *Oxo Ltd v Chappell and Tunner* [1966] 2 QB 228, [1966] 3 All ER 168, 130 JP 356.

8–31855 35. Subsequent deficiency. (1) This subsection applies to any proceedings for an offence under this Part of this Act, or any instrument made under this Part, by reason of the quantity—

(*a*) of any goods made up for sale or for delivery after sale (whether by way of pre-packing or otherwise) in or on a container marked with an indication of quantity,
(*b*) of any goods which, in connection with their sale or an agreement for their sale, have associated with them a document purporting to state the quantity of the goods, or
(*c*) of any goods required by or under this Part of this Act to be pre-packed, or to be otherwise made up in or on a container for sale or for delivery after sale, or to be made for sale, only in particular quantities,

being less than that marked on the container or stated in the document in question or than the relevant particular quantity, as the case may be.

(2) In any proceedings to which subsection (1) above applies, it shall be a defence for the person charged[1] to prove[2] that the deficiency arose—

(*a*) in a case falling within paragraph (*a*) of subsection (1) above, after the making up of the goods and the marking of the container,
(*b*) in a case falling within paragraph (*b*) of that subsection, after the preparation of the goods for delivery in pursuance of the sale or agreement and after the completion of the document,
(*c*) in a case falling within paragraph (*c*) of that subsection, after the making up or making, as the case may be, of the goods for sale,

and was attributable wholly to factors for which reasonable allowance was made in stating the quantity of the goods in the marking or document or in making up or making the goods for sale, as the case may be.

(3) In the case of a sale by retail of food, other than food pre-packed in a container which is, or is required by or under this Part of this Act to be, marked with an indication of quantity, in any proceedings for an offence under this Part of this Act or any instrument made under this Part, by reason of the quantity delivered to the buyer being less than that purported to be sold, it shall be a defence for the person charged to prove[2] that the deficiency was due wholly to unavoidable evaporation or drainage since the sale and that due care and precaution were taken to minimise any such evaporation or drainage.

(4) If in any proceedings for an offence under this Part of this Act or any instrument made under this Part, being an offence in respect of any deficiency in the quantity of any goods sold, it is shown that between the sale and the discovery of the deficiency the goods were with the consent of the buyer subjected to treatment which could result in a reduction in the quantity of those goods for delivery to, or to any person nominated in that behalf by, the buyer, the person charged shall not be found guilty of that offence unless it is shown that the deficiency cannot be accounted for by the subjecting of the goods to that treatment.
[Weights and Measures Act 1985, s 35.]

---

1. The defence in this subsection is not restricted to the person who has packed and marked the goods but is also available to the retailer (*F W Woolworth & Co Ltd v Gray* [1970] 1 All ER 953, 134 P 324).
2. See note to "prove" in s 34 above.

8–31856 36. Excess due to precautions. In any proceedings for an offence under this Part of this Act or any instrument made under this Part, being an offence in respect of any excess in the quantity

of any goods, it shall be a defence for the person charged to prove[1] that the excess was attributable to the taking of measures reasonably necessary in order to avoid the commission of an offence in respect of a deficiency in those or other goods.
[Weights and Measures Act 1985, s 36.]

1. See note to "prove" in s 34 above.

8–31857 **37. Provisions as to testing.** (1) If proceedings for an offence under this Part of this Act, or any instrument made under this Part, in respect of any deficiency or excess in the quantity—

(*a*) of any goods made up for sale (whether by way of pre-packing or otherwise) in or on a container marked with an indication of quantity, or

(*b*) of any goods which have been pre-packed or otherwise made up in or on a container for sale or for delivery after sale, or which have been made for sale, and which are required by or under this Part of this Act to be prepacked, or to be otherwise so made up, or to be so made, as the case may be, only in particular quantities,

are brought with respect to any article, and it is proved that, at the time and place[1] at which that article was tested, other articles of the same kind, being articles which, or articles containing goods which, had been sold by the person charged or were in that person's possession for sale or for delivery after sale, were available for testing, the person charged shall not be convicted of such an offence with respect to that article unless a reasonable number[2] of those other articles was also tested.

(2) In any proceedings for such an offence as is mentioned in subsection (1) above, the court—

(*a*) if the proceedings are with respect to one or more of a number of articles tested on the same occasion, shall have regard to the average quantity in the articles tested,

(*b*) if the proceedings are with respect to a single article, shall disregard any inconsiderable[3] deficiency or excess, and

(*c*) shall have regard generally to all the circumstances of the case.

(3) Subsections (1) and (2) above shall apply with the necessary modifications to proceedings for an offence in respect of the size, capacity or contents of a container as they apply to proceedings for an offence in respect of the excess or deficiency in the quantity of certain goods.

(4) Where by virtue of section 32 above a person is charged with an offence with which some other person might have been charged, the reference in subsection (1) above to articles or goods sold by or in the possession of the person charged shall be construed as a reference to articles or goods sold by or in the possession of that other person.
[Weights and Measures Act 1985, s 37.]

1. As to the time and place of the start of the test, see *Sears v Smith's Food Group Ltd* [1968] 2 QB 288, [1968] 2 All ER 721.

2. Where 56 loaves had been weighed, and evidence given of deficiency in weight of 37 of them but no evidence of the weight of the other 19, which were either of correct or excess weight, it was held that a reasonable number had been weighed (*Cave v Dudley Co-operative Society Ltd* (1934) 98 JP 265).

3. A deficiency of $2^1/_2$ oz in a 2 lb loaf is not inconsiderable (*Cave v Dudley Co-operative Society Ltd* (1934) 98 JP 265).

Miscellaneous and supplementary

8–31858 **41. Check-weighing of certain road vehicles.** Where any road vehicle is loaded with goods for sale by weight to a single buyer of the whole of the vehicle's load, or for delivery to the buyer after they have been so sold, the buyer or seller of the goods, or any inspector who shows that he is authorised so to do by the buyer or seller of the goods, may require the person in charge of the vehicle to have it check-weighed, and if that person fails without reasonable cause to comply with any such requirement he shall be guilty of an offence[1].
[Weights and Measures Act 1985, s 41.]

1. For penalty see s 84, post.

8–31859 **42.** *Power to make test purchases.*

8–31860 **43. Beer and cider.** (*Repealed*).

8–31861 **44. Selling by quantity.** Where any goods are required by or under this Part of this Act to be sold only by quantity expressed in a particular manner—

(*a*) it shall be a sufficient compliance with that requirement in the case of any sale of, or agreement to sell, any such goods if the quantity of the goods expressed in the manner in question is made known to the buyer before the purchase price is agreed; and

(*b*) no person shall be guilty of an offence under section 25(1) above by reason of the exposing or offering for sale of such goods at any time if both the quantity of the goods expressed in the

manner in question and the price at which they are exposed or offered for sale are made known at that time to any prospective buyer.
[Weights and Measures Act 1985, s 44.]

8–31862 45. Making quantity known to a person. (1) For the purposes of this Part of this Act, without prejudice to any other method of making known to a person the quantity of any goods expressed in a particular manner, that quantity shall be taken to be made known to that person—

(*a*) if the goods are weighed or otherwise measured or counted, as the case may require, in the presence of that person,
(*b*) if the goods are made up in or on a container marked with a statement in writing of the quantity of the goods expressed in the manner in question and the container is readily available for inspection by that person, or
(*c*) upon such a statement in writing being delivered to that person.

(2) The Secretary of State may by order[1] provide that subsection (3) below shall apply, in the case of such goods in such circumstances as are specified in the order, to any requirement so specified of, or of any instrument made under, this Part of this Act with respect to the making known to the buyer of the quantity by weight of such goods sold by retail.

(3) In any case to which this subsection applies, the requirement specified in the order shall be taken to be satisfied if the goods are bought at premises at which weighing equipment of such description as may be prescribed—

(*a*) is kept available by the occupier of those premises for use without charge by any prospective buyer of such goods for the purpose of weighing for himself any such goods offered or exposed for sale by retail on those premises, and
(*b*) is so kept available in a position on those premises which is suitable and convenient for such use of the equipment, and
(*c*) is reserved for use for that purpose at all times while those premises are open for retail transactions,

and a notice of the availability of the equipment for such use is displayed in a position on the premises where it may be readily seen by any such prospective buyer.
[Weights and Measures Act 1985, s 45.]

1. See the Weights and Measures (Weighing Equipment for Use by Customers) Regulations 1976, SI 1976/2061.

8–31863 46. Weighing in presence of a person. For the purpose of this Part of this Act, a person shall not be taken to weigh or otherwise measure or count any goods in the presence of any other person unless he causes any equipment used for the purpose to be so placed, and so conducts the operation of weighing or otherwise measuring or counting the goods, as to permit that other person a clear and unobstructed view of the equipment, if any, and of the operation, and of any indication of quantity given by any such equipment as the result of that operation.
[Weights and Measures Act 1985, s 46.]

PART V[1]
PACKAGED GOODS

Quantity control

8–31864 47. Duty of packers and importers as to quantity. (1) It shall be the duty of a person who is the packer or importer of regulated packages to ensure that when a group of the packages marked with the same nominal quantity is selected in the prescribed manner and the packages in the group or such a portion of the group as is so selected are tested in the prescribed manner by an inspector—

(*a*) the total quantity of the goods shown by the test to be included in the packages tested divided by the number of those packages is not less than the nominal quantity on those packages, and
(*b*) the number of non-standard packages among those tested is not greater than the number prescribed as acceptable in relation to the number tested.

(2) It is hereby declared that a person discharges the duty imposed on him by subsection (1) above in respect of a group of packages if the quantity of goods in each package is or exceeds the nominal quantity on the package.

(3) Regulations[2] in pursuance of subsection (1) above with respect to the manner of selecting or testing packages may, without prejudice to the generality of the powers to make regulations conferred by that subsection or to the generality of section 66(*b*) below, make provision by reference to a document other than the regulations (which may be or include a code of practical guidance issued by the Secretary of State).

(4) Where, as a result of a test in respect of a group of packages which is carried out when the packages are in the possession of the packer or importer of the packages or another person, it is shown that the packer or importer of the packages has failed to perform the duty imposed on him by

subsection (1) above in respect of the packages, then, without prejudice to the liability of the packer or importer under section 50(1) below in respect of the failure, it shall be the duty of the person in possession of the packages to keep them in his possession—

(*a*) except so far as he is authorised by or under regulations to dispose of them, or

(*b*) if he is the packer or importer of them, until he has performed his duty under subsection (1) above in respect of the group.

[Weights and Measures Act 1985, s 47.]

---

1. Part V comprises ss 47–68.

Part V of the Act and the Weights and Measures (Packaged Goods) Regulations 1986 (SI 1986/2049 amended by 1987/1538, SI 1992/1580, SI 1994/1258 and 1852 and SI 2000/3236), make provision for implementing the system of quantity control (commonly known as "the average system") applicable to the packaging of goods sold by weight or volume. The average system requires the actual contents of packages to be not less, on average, than the nominal quantity marked on the package. Part V of the Act gives effect to the requirements of Council Directives No 75/106/EEC (OJ No L42, 15.2.1975, p 1) and No 76/211/EEC (OJ No L46, 17.2.1976, p 1) as amended. It provides for the duties to be complied with by packers and importers of packaged goods, in particular as to the making up and checking of packages, the quantity of goods which packages must contain, and for the statement of quantity to be marked on them.

Part II of the Regulations lays down the coverage of the average system and in reg 3 specifies that it only applies to goods made up by weight or by volume to a predetermined constant quantity. Regulation 4 divides packages into two classes. Class A packages for which the provisions of Part V of the Act and the Regulations are mandatory and Class B packages for which they are made to apply (by virtue of the modifications to Pt V of the Act provided by reg 5(2)) only if the packages are voluntarily marked with a statement of quantity and with the EEC mark referred to in s 54(7) of the Act.

Regulation 5 of the Weights and Measures (Packaged Goods) Regulations 1986 provides exemptions from, and modifications to, Pt V of the Act. Regulations 6–8 make detailed provision with respect to the limits of quantity (reg 6) the importation into the United Kingdom (reg 7) and the export from the United Kingdom (reg 8), of packages marked with the EEC mark. Regulation 9 prescribes the periods in which packers or importers may object (to the Secretary of State) against instructions given by an inspector of weights and measures with respect to the procedures for making up and checking packages which they are required to apply under s 49(1) or (2) of the Act.

2. See Pt V of the Weights and Measures (Packaged Goods) Regulations 1986, SI 1986/2049 amended by SI 1987/1538, SI 1992/1580, SI 1994/1258 and 1852 and SI 2000/3236.

8–31865 **48. Duty of packers and importers as to marking of containers.** (1) It shall be the duty of a person who is the packer or importer of a regulated package to ensure that the container included in the package is marked before the prescribed time and in the prescribed manner with—

(*a*) a statement of quantity in prescribed units either of weight or of volume, as regulations[1] require, and

(*b*) his name and address or a mark which enables his name and address to be readily ascertained by an inspector, or—

(i) if he is the packer of the package, the name and address of a person who arranged for him to make up the package or a mark which enables that name and address to be readily ascertained by an inspector,

(ii) if he is the importer of the package, the name and address of the packer of the package or of the person who arranged for the packer to make up the package or a mark which enables the name and address of the packer or that person to be readily ascertained by an inspector, and

(*c*) if regulations so provide, a mark allocated to him by a scheme in pursuance of section 58 below for the purpose of enabling the place where the package was made up to be ascertained.

(2) If at the time when a regulated package is made up or imported the container included in the package is not marked with such a statement as is mentioned in paragraph (*a*) of subsection (1) above, it shall be the duty of the packer or, as the case may be, the importer of the package—

(*a*) to decide what statement he proposes to mark on the container in pursuance of that paragraph, and

(*b*) to make at that time, and to maintain for the prescribed period[2], a record of the statement.

(3) Until the time mentioned in subsection (1) above or any earlier time at which the container is actually marked in the prescribed manner in pursuance of paragraph (*a*) of that subsection, it shall be treated for the purposes of this Part of this Act as marked with the statement in the record.

(4) A statement applied to a package in pursuance of subsection (1)(*a*) above shall be deemed not to be a trade description within the meaning of the Trade Descriptions Act 1968.

[Weights and Measures Act 1985, s 48.]

---

1. See Pt II of the Weights and Measures (Quantity Marking and Abbreviation of Units) Regulations 1987, SI 1987/1538 amended by SI 1988/627 and SI 1994/1852.

2. See reg 10(6) of the Weights and Measures (Packaged Goods) Regulations 1986, SI 1986/2049 amended by SI 1987/1538, SI 1992/1580, SI 1994/1258 and 1852 and SI 2000/3236.

8–31866 **49. Duties as to equipment, checks and documentation.** (1) It shall be the duty of a person who makes up packages either—

(*a*) to use suitable equipment of the prescribed kind in an appropriate manner in making up the packages, or (*b*) to carry out at the prescribed time a check which is adequate to show whether he has performed the duty imposed on him by section 47(1) above in respect of the packages and—

(i) to use suitable equipment of the prescribed kind in an appropriate manner in carrying out the check, and

(ii) to make, and to keep for the prescribed period, an adequate record of the check.

(2) It shall be the duty of a person who is the importer of regulated packages—

(*a*) to carry out at the prescribed time such a check as is mentioned in paragraph (*b*) of subsection (1) above and to comply with sub-paragraphs (i) and (ii) of that paragraph in connection with the check, or

(*b*) to obtain before the prescribed time, and to keep for the prescribed period, documents containing such information about the packages as is adequate to show that the person is likely to have complied with his duty under section 47(1) above in relation to the packages.

(3) Without prejudice to the generality of the powers to make regulations conferred by subsection (1) or (2) above or to the generality of section 66 below, regulations[1] may provide—

(*a*) for equipment not to be suitable equipment for the purposes of the subsection in question unless it is made from materials and on principles specified in the regulations and is inspected, tested and certified as provided by the regulations,

(*b*) for questions as to the suitability of equipment, the appropriate manner of using equipment and the adequacy of checks, records and information to be determined for those purposes by reference to documents other than the regulations (which may be or include codes or parts of codes of practical guidance issued or approved by the Secretary of State), and

(*c*) that the use and the possession for use, for the purposes of subsection (1) or (2) above, of a thing which is suitable equipment for the purpose of the subsection in question shall not constitute a contravention of section 8(1)(*b*) above.

(4) Where regulations made by virtue of subsection (3)(*a*) above provide for inspection, testing and certification of equipment, a local weights and measures authority may charge such reasonable fees as they may determine for the inspection, testing and certification of equipment.
[Weights and Measures Act 1985, s 49.]

1. See Pt IV of the Weights and Measures (Packaged Goods) Regulations 1986, SI 1986/2049 amended by SI 1987/1538, SI 1992/1580, SI 1994/1258 and 1852 and SI 2000/3236.

Enforcement of control

8–31867 **50. Offences, etc.** (1) A person who fails to perform a duty imposed on him, by section 47, 48 or 49 above shall be guilty of an offence[1].

(2) If a person purports to comply with his duty under—

(*a*) sub-paragraph (ii) of subsection (1)(*b*) of section 49 above, or

(*b*) that sub-paragraph as applied by subsection (2)(*a*) of that section,

by making a record which he knows is false in a material particular, he shall be guilty of an offence[1].

(3) If a person purports to comply with his duty under section 49(2)(*b*) above by reference to a document containing information which he knows is false in a material particular, he shall be guilty of an offence[1].

(4) If a person, with intent to deceive, alters—

(*a*) any record kept for the purposes of section 48(2) or 49(1)(*b*)(ii) above or section 49(1)(*b*)(ii) above as applied by section 49(2)(*a*) above, or

(*b*) any document kept for the purposes of section 49(2)(*b*) above,

he shall be guilty of an offence[1].

(5) If a person has in his possession for sale, agrees to sell or sells a regulated package which is inadequate and either—

(*a*) he is the packer or importer of the package, or

(*b*) he knows that the package is inadequate,

he shall be guilty of an offence[1].

(6) If the packer of a regulated package which is inadequate and which was made up by him in the course of carrying out arrangements with another person for the packer to make up packages delivers the package to or to the order of a person to whom it falls to be delivered in pursuance of the arrangements, the packer shall be guilty of an offence[1].

(7) No action shall lie in respect of a failure to perform a duty imposed by section 47, 48 or 49 above.
[Weights and Measures Act 1985, s 50.]

1. For penalty see s 84, post.

8–31868 **51. Defences to certain charges under section 50.** (1) Where a person is charged with an offence under section 50(1) above of failing to perform the duty imposed on him by section 47(1) above in respect of any packages, it shall be a defence to prove that the test in question took place when the packages were not in his possession and by reference to a nominal quantity which was not on the packages when they were in his possession.

(2) Where the importer of packages is charged with an offence under section 50(1) above of failing to perform the duty imposed on him by section 47(1) above in respect of the packages, it shall be a defence to prove—

(*a*) that in respect of the packages the accused performed the duty imposed on him by paragraph (*b*) of section 49(2) above, and

(*b*) that within the prescribed period after obtaining the documents mentioned in that paragraph relating to the packages he took all reasonable steps to verify the information contained in the documents and that when the relevant test in pursuance of section 47(1) above began he believed and had no reason to disbelieve that the information was true, and

(*c*) that before the beginning of the period of seven days ending with the date when the hearing of the charge began he served on the prosecutor a copy of the said documents and a notice which stated that the accused intended to rely on them in proving a defence under this subsection, and

(*d*) that he took all reasonable steps to ensure that the quantity of goods in each of the packages did not alter while the packages were in his possession.

(3) Where a person is charged with an offence under section 50(1) above of failing to perform the duty imposed on him by paragraph (*b*) of section 48(1) above in respect of a package, it shall be a defence to prove—

(*a*) that the container included in the package was marked at the time and in the manner mentioned in that subsection with a mark as to which he had, before that time, given notice to an inspector stating that the mark indicated a name and address specified in the notice, and

(*b*) that at that time the name and address were such as are mentioned in relation to him in that paragraph.

(4) Where a person is charged with—

(*a*) an offence under subsection (1) of section 50 above, or

(*b*) an offence alleged to have been committed by him, as the packer or importer of a package, under subsection (5) or (6) of that section,

it shall be a defence to prove[1] that he took all reasonable precautions[1] and exercised all due diligence[1] to avoid the commission of the offence.

[Weights and Measures Act 1985, s 51.]

1. In relation to proof, and as to "reasonable precautions" and "due diligence", see footnotes to s 34(1), ante.

8–31879 **52. Enforcement of Part V by local weights and measures authority.** (1) It shall be the duty of a local weights and measures authority to enforce the provisions of this Part of this Act within the area of the authority[1].

(2) *Scotland.*

[Weights and Measures Act 1985, s 52.]

1. Powers of Inspectors and the local weights and measures authority under Pt V (packaged goods) are set out in Sch 8, post.

Special provision for certain packages

8–31880 **54. Special provision for certain packages.** (1) Subsections (2) to (7) below apply only to packages containing goods of a prescribed[1] quantity, and references to packages in those subsections shall be construed accordingly.

(2) If in the course of carrying on a business—

(*a*) a person marks a package with the EEC mark and is neither the packer nor the importer of the package nor a person acting on behalf of the packer or importer of the package, or

(*b*) a person marks a package with a mark so closely resembling the EEC mark as to be likely to deceive,

he shall be guilty of an offence.

(3) For the purposes of this Part of this Act a person who brings a package marked with the EEC mark into the United Kingdom does not import the package if he shows that the package is from a member State of the Economic Community in which it was liable to be tested under a law corresponding to section 47(1) above and, except in such cases as are determined by or under regulations[2], has not since leaving that State been in a country which is not such a member State.

(4) Subject to subsection (6) below, it shall be the duty of—

(*a*) the packer of packages which are marked with the EEC mark and which he intends to export from the United Kingdom,

(*b*) a person who intends to import packages which are so marked and to export them from the United Kingdom to a place in another member State of the Economic Community, and

(*c*) a person who intends to import packages, to mark them with the EEC mark and to export them as mentioned in paragraph (*b*) above,

to give before the prescribed[3] time and in the prescribed[3] manner, to the local weights and measures authority for the area in which the packages were packed or, as the case may be, in which the place of intended import is situated, a notice containing such information about the packages as is prescribed[3] and, in the case of a person who has given such a notice in pursuance of paragraph (*b*) or (*c*) above, such further information about the packages in question as an inspector may specify in a notice served on the person by the inspector.

(5) A person who fails without reasonable cause to perform a duty imposed on him by subsection (4) above shall be guilty of an offence.

(6) Regulations[4] may enable an inspector to give notice to any person providing that, until an inspector informs the person in writing that the notice is cancelled, any paragraph of subsection (4) above which is specified in the notice shall not apply to the person or shall not apply to him as respects packages of a kind specified in the notice or a place so specified.

(7) In this section "the EEC mark" means such mark as may be prescribed; and, without prejudice to the generality of section 66 below, regulations[5] prescribing a mark in pursuance of this subsection—

(*a*) may contain such provisions as the Secretary of State considers appropriate with respect to the dimensions of the mark and the manner and position in which it is to be applied to the container included in a package, and

(*b*) may provide for a mark which is not in accordance with those provisions to be disregarded for the purposes of prescribed provisions of this section.

[Weights and Measures Act 1985, s 54.]

---

1. See reg 6 of the Weights and Measures (Packaged Goods) Regulations 1986, SI 1986/2049 amended by SI 1987/1538, SI 1992/1580, SI 1994/1258 and 1852 and SI 2000/3236.
2. See reg 7 of the Weights and Measures (Packaged Goods) Regulations 1986, SI 1986/2049 amended by SI 1987/1538, SI 1992/1580, SI 1994/1258 and 1852 and SI 2000/3236.
3. See reg 8(1) of the Weights and Measures (Packaged Goods) Regulations 1986, SI 1986/2049 amended by SI 1987/1538, SI 1992/1580, SI 1994/1258 and 1852 and SI 2000/3236.
4. See reg 8(2) of the Weights and Measures (Packaged Goods) Regulations 1986, SI 1986/2049 amended by SI 1987/1538, SI 1992/1580, SI 1994/1258 and 1852 and SI 2000/3236.
5. See reg 12(1) of the Weights and Measures (Packaged Goods) Regulations 1986, SI 1986/2049 amended by SI 1987/1538, SI 1992/1580, SI 1994/1258 and 1852 and SI 2000/3236.

Instructions by inspectors

8–31882 63. Instructions by inspectors. (1) If an inspector has reasonable cause to believe that a person has failed to perform the duty imposed on him by section 47(1) above in relation to a group of packages, the inspector may give to the person in possession of the packages instructions in writing—

(*a*) specifying the packages, and

(*b*) requiring that person to keep the packages at a place specified in the instructions and at the disposal of the inspector for the period of twenty-four hours beginning with the time when the inspector gives him the instructions or for such shorter period as the inspector may specify.

(2) If an inspector has reasonable cause to believe that a person has failed to perform the duty imposed on him by section 49(1) or (2) above, the inspector may give to that person such instructions in writing as the inspector considers appropriate with a view to ensuring that that person does not subsequently fail to perform that duty.

(3) Instructions given to a person by an inspector under subsection (2) above shall not come into force until the expiration of the prescribed[1] period beginning with the day when the instructions are given to him and, if during that period that person gives notice to the inspector that he objects to the instructions, they shall not come into force except as agreed in writing by that person or as directed by the Secretary of State.

(4) Where under subsection (3) above a person gives to an inspector notice of objection to instructions, it shall be the duty of the inspector to refer the instructions to the Secretary of State.

(5) (*Repealed*).

(6) Where instructions are referred to the Secretary of State in pursuance of subsection (4) above, it shall be his duty—

(*a*) to invite representations in writing about the instructions, from the inspector who gave them and from the person to whom they were given,

(*b*) to consider any representations made in response to the invitations within the periods specified in the invitations,

(*c*) to direct that the instructions shall come into force, without modifications or with modifications specified in the direction, on a day so specified or that they shall not come into force, and (*d*) to give notice of the direction, to the inspector and to the person in question.

(7) Where—

(*a*) instructions have been given to a person under subsection (1) above, or

(*b*) instructions given to a person under subsection (2) above have come into force (or have come into force with modifications) in accordance with subsections (3) to (6) above,

he shall be guilty of an offence[2] if without reasonable cause he fails to comply with those instructions (or, as the case may require, those instructions with modifications).

[Weights and Measures Act 1985, s 63 as modified by SI 1987/2187.]

---

1. This is 21 days: reg 9(*a*) of the Weights and Measures (Packaged Goods) Regulations 1986, SI 1986/2049 amended by SI 1987/1538, SI 1992/1580, SI 1994/1258 and 1852 and SI 2000/3236.

2. For penalty see s 84, post.

Miscellaneous

8–31883 64. Disclosure of information. (1) If a person discloses information which—

(*a*) relates to a trade secret or secret manufacturing process, and

(*b*) was obtained by him by virtue of this Part of this Act when he was—

(i), (ii) (*Repealed*).

(iii) an inspector,

(iv) a person who accompanied an inspector by virtue of paragraph 3(1) of Schedule 8 to this Act, or

(v) a person appointed by the Secretary of State in pursuance of section 59(4)(*b*)(iii) above,

he shall be guilty of an offence[1] unless the disclosure was made in the performance of his duty as a member, inspector or other person mentioned in paragraph (*b*) above, or, in the case of an inspector, was made to the Secretary of State in consequence of a request by him.

(2) For the purposes of subsection (1) above information disclosing the identity of the packer of a package or the identity of the person who arranged with the packer of a package for the package to be made up shall be treated as a trade secret unless the information has previously been disclosed in a manner which made it available to the public.

[Weights and Measures Act 1985, s 64 as modified by the National Metrological Co-ordinating Unit (Transfer of Functions and Abolition) Order 1987, SI 1987/2187.]

---

1. For penalty see s 84, post.

8–31884 65, 66. *Regulations*[1] *modifying or under, Part V.*

---

1. The Weights and Measures (Packaged Goods) Regulations 1986, SI 1986/2049 amended by SI 1987/1538, SI 1992/1580, SI 1994/1258 and 1852 and SI 2000/3236, have been made.

8–31885 67. Service of documents. (1) Any document required or authorised by virtue of this Part of this Act to be served on a person may be so served—

(*a*) by delivering it to him or by leaving it at his proper address or by sending it by post to him at that address, or

(*b*) if the person is a body corporate, by serving it in accordance with paragraph (*a*) above on the secretary or clerk of that body, or

(*c*) if the person is a partnership, by serving it in accordance with paragraph (*a*) above on a partner or on a person having the control or management of the partnership business.

(2) For the purposes of subsection (1) above and of section 7 of the Interpretation Act 1978 (which relates to the service of documents by post) in its application to that subsection, the proper address of any person on whom a document is to be served by virtue of this Part of this Act shall be his last known address except that—

(*a*) in the case of service on a body corporate or its secretary or clerk, it shall be the address of the registered or principal office of the body, and

(*b*) in the case of service on a partnership or a partner or a person having the control or management of a partnership business, it shall be the principal office of the partnership;

and for the purposes of this subsection, the principal office of a company registered outside the United Kingdom or a partnership carrying on business outside the United Kingdom is its principal office within the United Kingdom.

[Weights and Measures Act 1985, s 67.]

8–31886 68. Interpretation of Part V. (1) In this Part of this Act—

"container" includes any wrapping;

"goods", in relation to a package, excludes the container included in the package;

"importer", in relation to a package, means, subject to section 54(3) above, the person by whom or on whose behalf the package is entered for customs purposes on importation;

"modifications" includes additions, omissions and alterations;

"nominal quantity", in relation to a package, means the units of weight or volume prescribed for the package and the number of them in the statement of quantity marked on the container included in the package (any other matter in the statement being disregarded);

"notice" means notice in writing;

"package" means, subject to section 54(1) above, a container containing prescribed[1] goods together with the goods in the container in a case where—

(*a*) the goods are placed for sale in the container otherwise than in the presence of a person purchasing the goods, and

(*b*) none of the goods can be removed from the container without opening it;

"packer" means, in relation to a package, the person who placed in the container included in the package the goods included in it;

"regulated package" means any package which—

(*a*) was made up in the United Kingdom on or after the date on which the goods in package became prescribed[1] goods, or

(*b*) was imported on or after that date;

"regulations" means regulations made by the Secretary of State by virtue of this Part of this Act;

"the Unit" means the National Metrological Co-ordinating Unit.

(2) For the purposes of this Part of this Act a package—

(*a*) is non-standard if the quantity of the goods it contains is less by more than a prescribed amount than the nominal quantity on the package, and

(*b*) is inadequate if the quantity of the goods it contains is less by more than twice that amount than the nominal quantity on the package.

(3) Regulations may make provision, in relation to a package which contains more than one container or goods of more than one kind, as to which of the containers or goods shall be disregarded for the purposes of prescribed provisions of this Part of this Act.

(4) If two or more different nominal quantities are marked on a package, each of those quantities except the one which indicates the larger or largest quantity shall be disregarded for the purposes of this Part of this Act.

[Weights and Measures Act 1985, s 68.]

1. See reg 3 of the Weights and Measures (Packaged Goods) Regulations 1986, SI 1986/2049 amended by SI 1987/1538, SI 1992/1580, SI 1994/1258 and 1852 and SI 2000/3236.

PART VI
ADMINISTRATION

8–31887 This Part, comprising ss 69–78, is chiefly concerned with the functions of weights and measures authorities and the appointment of inspectors.

8–31888 75. Offences in connection with office of inspector. (1) Any inspector who—

(*a*) stamps any weighing or measuring equipment in contravention of any provision of this Act or of any instrument made under this Act or without duly testing it, or

(*b*) derives any profit from, or is employed in, the making, adjusting or selling of weighing or measuring equipment, or

(*c*) knowingly[1] commits any breach of any duty imposed on him by or under this Act or otherwise misconducts himself in the execution of his office,

shall be guilty of an offence[2].

(1A) Any approved verifier who—

(*a*) stamps any weighing or measuring equipment in contravention of any provision of this Act or of any instrument made under this Act or without duly testing it, or

(*b*) commits any breach of any duty imposed on him by or under this Act,

shall be guilty of an offence[2].

(2) If any person who is not an inspector, or is not an approved verifier, acts or purports to act as such, he shall be guilty of an offence.[1]

(3) Section 34 of this Act shall apply in relation to proceedings for an offence under subsection (1A)(*b*) above as it applies in relation to proceedings for an offence under Part IV of this Act.

[Weights and Measures Act 1985, s 75, as amended by SI 1999/503.]

1. A person acts knowingly if, intending what is happening, he deliberately looks the other way (*Ross v Moss* [1965] 2 QB 396, [1965] 3 All ER 145, 129 JP 537.

2. For penalty see s 84, post.

PART VII[1]
GENERAL

Enforcement and legal proceedings

8–31889 79. General powers of inspection and entry. (1) Subject to the production if so requested of his credentials, an inspector may, within the area for which he was appointed inspector, at all reasonable times—

(*a*) inspect and test any weighing or measuring equipment which is, or which he has reasonable cause to believe to be, used for trade or in the possession of any person or upon any premises for such use, or which has been, or which he has reasonable cause to believe to have been, passed by an approved verifier, or by a person purporting to act as such a verifier, as fit for such use

(*b*) inspect any goods to which any of the provisions of Part IV of this Act or any instrument made under that Part for the time being applies or which he has reasonable cause to believe to be such goods, and

(*c*) enter any premises at which he has reasonable cause to believe there to be any such equipment or goods, not being premises used only as a private dwelling-house[2].

(2) Subject to the production if so requested of his credentials, an inspector may at any time within the area for which he was appointed inspector seize and detain—

(*a*) any article which he has reasonable cause to believe is liable to be forfeited under Parts II or IV of this Act, and

(*b*) any document or goods which the inspector has reason to believe may be required as evidence in proceedings for an offence under this Act (except an offence under Part V).

(3) If a justice of the peace, on sworn information in writing—

(*a*) is satisfied that there is reasonable ground to believe that any such equipment, goods, articles or documents as are mentioned in subsection (1) or (2) above are on any premises, or that any offence under this Act or any instrument made under it (except an offence under Part V or any instrument made under that Part) has been, is being or is about to be committed on any premises, and

(*b*) is also satisfied either—

(i) that admission to the premises has been refused, or a refusal is apprehended, and that notice of the intention to apply for a warrant has been given to the occupier, or

(ii) that an application for admission, or the giving of such a notice, would defeat the object of the entry, or that the case is one of urgency, or that the premises are unoccupied or the occupier temporarily absent,

the justice may by warrant under his hand, which shall continue in force for a period of one month, authorise an inspector to enter the premises, if need be by force.

(4) *Scotland.*

(5) An inspector entering any premises by virtue of this section may take with him such other persons and such equipment as may appear to him necessary.

(6) An inspector who leaves premises which he has entered by virtue of a warrant under subsection (3) above and which are unoccupied or from which the occupier is temporarily absent shall leave the premises as effectively secured against trespassers as he found them.

(7) If any inspector or other person who enters any workplace by virtue of this section discloses to any person any information obtained by him in the work-place with regard to any secret manufacturing process or trade secret, he shall, unless the disclosure was made in the performance of his duty, be guilty of an offence[3].

(8) In exercising his functions under this Act at any mine of coal, stratified ironstone, shale or fire-clay, an inspector shall so exercise those functions as not to impede or obstruct the working of the mine.

(9) Nothing in this Act shall authorise any inspector to stop any vehicle on a highway.

[Weights and Measures Act 1985, s 79, as amended by SI 1999/503.]

---

1. Part VII comprises ss 79–99.
2. He may not go on to private property to instruct a coal merchant not to tip a suspect sack he wants to weigh (*Brunner v Williams* [1975] Crim LR 250).
3. For penalty see s 84, post.

8–31890 80. Obstruction of inspectors. Any person who wilfully obstructs[1] an inspector acting in pursuance of this Act shall be guilty of an offence[2].

[Weights and Measures Act 1985, s 80.]

---

1. Mere passive conduct is not obstruction unless there is a duty to act (*Swallow v LCC* [1916] 1 KB 224, 80 JP 164).
2. For penalty see s 84, post.

8–31891 **81. Failure to provide assistance or information.** (1) Any person who—

(*a*) wilfully fails to comply with any requirement properly made of him by an inspector under section 38, 39 or 40 above, or

(*b*) without reasonable cause fails to give to any inspector acting in pursuance of this Act any other assistance or information which the inspector may reasonably require of him for the purposes of the performance by the inspector of his functions under Parts II, III, IV or VI of this Act or under this Part of this Act,

shall be guilty of an offence[1].

(2) If any person, in giving to an inspector any such information as is mentioned in subsection (1) above, gives any information which he knows to be false, he shall be guilty of an offence[1].

(3) Nothing in this section shall be construed as requiring a person to answer any question or give any information if to do so might incriminate him.

(4) Subsection (1) of section 14 of the Civil Evidence Act 1968 (which relates to the privilege against self-incrimination) shall apply to the right conferred by subsection (3) above as it applies to the right described in subsection (1) of that section; but this subsection does not extend to Scotland.
[Weights and Measures Act 1985, s 81.]

---

1. For penalty see s 84, post.

8–31892 **82. Offences by corporations.** (1) Where an offence under, or under any instrument made under, this Act which has been committed by a body corporate is proved to have been committed with the consent or connivance of, or to be attributable to any neglect on the part of, any director, manager, secretary or other similar officer of the body corporate, or any person who was purporting to act in any such capacity, he as well as the body corporate shall be guilty of that offence and shall be liable to be proceeded against and punished accordingly.

(2) In subsection (1) above "director" in relation to any body corporate established by or under any enactment for the purpose of carrying on under national ownership any industry or part of an industry or undertaking, being a body corporate whose affairs are managed by its members, means a member of that body corporate.
[Weights and Measures Act 1985, s 82.]

8–31893 **83. Prosecution of offences.** (1) Subject to subsection (2) below, in England and Wales, proceedings for any offence under this Act or any instrument made under this Act, other than proceedings for an offence under section 64, shall not be instituted except by or on behalf of a local weights and measures authority or the chief officer of police for a police area.

(2) Proceedings for an offence under section 57(2) above shall not be instituted in England or Wales except by or on behalf of the Director of Public Prosecutions or the National Metrological Co-ordinating Unit.

(3) Proceedings for an offence under any provision contained in, or having effect by virtue of, Part IV or V of this Act, other than proceedings for an offence under section 33(6), 57(2) or 64 or proceedings by virtue of section 32, shall not be instituted—

(*a*) unless there has been served on the person charged a notice in writing of the date and nature[1] of the offence alleged and, except in the case of an offence under section 50, 54 or 63 or Schedule 8, where the proceedings are in respect of one or more of a number of articles of the same kind tested on the same occasion, of the results of the tests of all those articles; or

(*b*) except where the person charged is a street trader, unless the said notice was served before the expiration of the period of thirty days beginning with the date when evidence which the person proposing to institute the proceedings considers is sufficient to justify a prosecution for the offence came to his knowledge; or

(*c*) after the expiration of the period—

(i) of twelve months beginning with the date mentioned in paragraph (*a*) above, or

(ii) of three months beginning with the date mentioned in paragraph (*b*) above,

whichever first occurs.

(4) Such a notice as is mentioned in subsection (3)(*a*) above may be served on any person either by serving it on him personally or by sending it to him by post at his usual or last known residence or place of business in the United Kingdom or, in the case of a company, at the company's registered office.

(5) For the purposes of subsection (3) above—

(*a*) a certificate of a person who institutes proceedings for an offence mentioned in that subsection which states that evidence came to his knowledge on a particular date shall be conclusive evidence of that fact; and

(*b*) a document purporting to be a certificate of such a person and to be signed by him or on his behalf shall be presumed to be such a certificate unless the contrary is proved.
[Weights and Measures Act 1985, s 83.]

1. The section requires that "the nature", "not particulars", of the alleged offence shall be served on the defendant; see *Milner v Allen* [1933] 1 KB 698, [1933] All ER Rep 734, 97 JP 111.

8–31894 **84. Penalties.** (1) A person guilty of an offence under any of the provisions of this Act specified in subsection (2) below shall be liable on summary conviction to a fine not exceeding **level 3** on the standard scale.

(2) The provisions of this Act to which subsection (1) above refers are—
section 8(4);
section 9(4);
section 10(2);
section 11(3);
section 11(14);
section 13(1);
section 13(2);
section 13(3);
section 14(3);
section 14(5);
section 15(3);
section 15(5);
section 15A(3);
section 18(3);
section 20(2);
section 20(4);
section 20(7);
section 20(8);
paragraphs 4 and 5 of Schedule 4;
paragraph 28(3) of Schedule 5.

(3) A person guilty of an offence under paragraph 24(4) of Schedule 5 to this Act shall be liable on summary conviction to a fine not exceeding **£2,000**.

(4) A person guilty of an offence—

(*a*) under section 17(3), 20(3)(*b*) or 50(2), (3) or (4) above, or
(*b*) under paragraph 10 of Schedule 5 to this Act,

shall be liable[1] on summary conviction to a fine not exceeding **level 5** on the standard scale or to imprisonment for a term not exceeding **six months** or to **both**.

(5) A person guilty of an offence under section 64 or 79(7) above shall be liable, on summary conviction, to a fine not exceeding the **statutory maximum** and, on conviction on indictment, to imprisonment for a term not exceeding **two years** or to a **fine** or to **both**.

(6) A person guilty of an offence under any provision of this Act other than those mentioned in subsections (1) to (5) above shall be liable on summary conviction to a fine not exceeding **level 5** on the standard scale.

(7) The Secretary of State may by order alter the penalty imposed by subsection (3) above but such an order shall not impose any penalty exceeding that provided by subsection (6) above.
[Weights and Measures Act 1985, s 84, as amended by SI 1999/503.]

1. For procedure in respect of an offence triable either way see Magistrates' Courts Act 1980, ss 17A–21 in PART I: MAGISTRATES' COURTS, PROCEDURE, ante.

8–31895 **85. Determination of certain questions by Secretary of State.** (1) Where in any proceedings for an offence under this Act or any instrument made under it, except proceedings for an offence under Part V or any instrument made under that Part, any question arises as to the accuracy of any weighing or measuring equipment, the court shall at the request of any party to the proceedings, and may if it thinks fit without any such request, refer the question to the Secretary of State, whose decision shall be final.

(2) Except where in any particular proceedings the Secretary of State waives his rights under this subsection, any expenses incurred by the Secretary of State in making any test for the purpose of determining any question referred to him under subsection (1) above shall be paid by such of the parties to the proceedings as the court may by order direct.
[Weights and Measures Act 1985, s 85.]

Miscellaneous and supplementary

8–31896 **88. Application to Crown.** (1) Her Majesty may by Order in Council provide for the application to the Crown of such of the provisions of this Act or of any instrument made under it as may be specified in the Order, with such exceptions, adaptations and modifications as may be so specified.

(2), (3) *Orders in Council.*
[Weights and Measures Act 1985, s 88.]

8–31897 89. Saving for use of certain units in wholesale transactions. (1) Except as the Secretary of State may by order otherwise provide, and subject to subsection (2) below, nothing in this Act shall make unlawful the use in any transaction, by agreement between the parties to that transaction, of any unit of measurement which—

(*a*) was customarily used for trade in the like transactions immediately before 31st July 1963, and
(*b*) is not inconsistent with anything for the time being contained in Schedule 1 to this Act,

notwithstanding that the unit in question is not included in Parts I to V of that Schedule.

(2) Subsection (1) above shall not apply in relation to—

(*a*) any retail transaction, or
(*b*) any transaction with respect to which provision to the contrary effect is made by or under Part IV of this Act.

[Weights and Measures Act 1985, s 89.]

8–31898 92. Spelling of "gram", etc. No provision contained in or made under this or any other Act prevents the use of "gram" or "gramme" as alternative ways of spelling that unit, and the same applies for other units in the metric system which are compounds of "gram".
[Weights and Measures Act 1985, s 92.]

8–31909 94. General interpretation. (1) Except where the context otherwise requires, in this Act—

"approved verifier" has the meaning given by section 11(6A) above;
"capacity measurement" means measurement in terms of a unit of measurement included in Part IV of Schedule 1 to this Act;
"check-weighed", in relation to any vehicle, means weighed with its load by means of the nearest suitable and available weighing equipment, and weighed again after it has been unloaded by means of the same or other suitable weighing equipment;
"chief inspector" means a chief inspector of weights and measures appointed under section 72(1) above;
"container" except in Part V, includes any form of packaging of goods for sale as a single item, whether by way of wholly or partly enclosing the goods[1] or by way of attaching the goods to, or winding the goods round, some other article, and in particular includes a wrapper or confining band;
"contravention", in relation to any requirement, includes a failure to comply with that requirement, and cognate expressions shall be construed accordingly;
"credentials", in relation to an inspector, means authority in writing from the local weights and measures authority who appointed him for the exercise by that inspector of powers conferred on inspectors by this Act;
"Department of Trade and Industry standards" means the secondary, tertiary and coinage standards maintained by the Secretary of State under section 3 above;
"drugs" and "food" have the same meanings respectively as for the purposes of the Food Safety Act 1990, Sch 3;
"gross weight", in relation to any goods, means the aggregate weight of the goods and any container in or on which they are made up;
"indication of quantity", in relation to any container in or on which goods are made up, means a statement in writing to the effect that those goods are of, or of not less than, a specified quantity by net weight, gross weight or other measurement or by number, as the case may require;
"industrial use", in relation to any goods, means the use of those goods in the manufacture of, or for incorporation in, goods of a different description in the course of the carrying on of a business;
"inspector" means an inspector of weights and measures appointed under section 72(1) above;
"intoxicating liquor" means spirits, beer, wine, made-wine or cider as defined in section 1 of the Alcoholic Liquor Duties Act 1979;
"local standard" means a standard maintained under section 4 above;
"mark" includes label;
"occupier", in relation to any stall, vehicle, ship or aircraft or in relation to the use of any place for any purpose, means the person for the time being in charge of the stall, vehicle, ship or aircraft or, as the case may be, the person for the time being using that place for that purpose;
"premises", except in section 45 above, includes any place and any stall, vehicle, ship or aircraft;
"pre-packed" means made up in advance ready for retail sale in or on a container;
"prescribed" means prescribed by the Secretary of State by regulations;
"secondary standard" means a standard maintained under section 3(2) above;
"ship" includes any boat and any other description of vessel used in navigation;
"stamp" means, subject to section 15A(4) above, a mark for use as evidence of the passing of weighing or measuring equipment as fit for use for trade, whether applied by impressing, casting, engraving, etching, branding, or otherwise, and cognate expressions shall be construed accordingly;

"tertiary standard" means a standard maintained under section 3(3) above;
"testing equipment" means testing equipment maintained under section 5 above;
"United Kingdom primary standard" means a standard maintained under section 2 above;
"use for trade" shall be construed in accordance with section 7 above;
"weighing or measuring equipment" means equipment for measuring in terms of length, area, volume, capacity, weight or number, whether or not the equipment is constructed to give an indication of the measurement made or other information determined by reference to that measurement;
"working standard" means a standard maintained under section 5 above.

(2) In any provision of this Act "designated country" means such, if any, of the following, that is to say, Northern Ireland, any of the Channel Islands and the Isle of Man, as the Secretary of State, having regard to the law for the time being in force there, thinks it proper to designate for the purposes of that provision by order.

(3) On any premises where articles of any description are—

(*a*) made up in advance ready for retail sale in or on a container, or
(*b*) kept or stored for sale after being so made up,

any article of that description found made up in or on a container shall be deemed to be pre-packed unless the contrary is proved; and it shall not be sufficient proof of the contrary to show that the container has not been marked in accordance with the requirements of this Act or any instrument made under it with respect to the pre-packing of such articles.

(4) Except where the context otherwise requires, any reference in this Act to any person, other than a reference to an inspector, shall be construed as a reference to that person or some other person acting on his behalf in the matter in question.

[Weights and Measures Act 1985, s 94, as amended by the Food Safety Act 1990, Sch 3, the Statute Law (Repeals) Act 1993, Sch 1 and SI 1999/503.]

1. For a case in which a piece of greaseproof paper adhering to goods was held not to be "packaging", see *Lucas v Rushby* [1966] 2 All ER 302, 130 JP 279.

8–31910 96. Transitional provisions and savings. (1) Schedule 11 to this Act (which contains transitional provisions and savings) shall have effect.

(2) The re-enactment—

(*a*) in section 84(3) of, and Part IV of Schedule 5 to, this Act, of provisions contained in the Weights and Measures (Solid Fuel) (Carriage by Rail) Order 1966, and
(*b*) in paragraphs 12 to 17, 22 and 25 of Schedule 11 to this Act, of provisions contained in the Units of Measurement Regulations 1978 and the Units of Measurement Regulations 1980,

shall be without prejudice to the validity of those provisions; and any question as to the validity of any of those provisions shall be determined as if the re-enacting provision of this Act were contained in a statutory instrument made under the powers under which the original provision was made.

(3) The provisions of Schedule 11 to this Act are without prejudice to the operation of sections 16 and 17 of the Interpretation Act 1978 (which relate to the effect of repeals).

[Weights and Measures Act 1985, s 96.]

8–31911

SCHEDULES

Sections 1(2), 8(1)

SCHEDULE 1
DEFINITIONS OF UNITS OF MEASUREMENT
(*As amended by SI 1994/2867.*)

PART I
MEASUREMENT OF LENGTH

Metric units
Kilometre = 1000 metres.
METRE is the length of the path travelled by light in vacuum during a time interval of 1/299 792 458 of a second.
Decimetre = 1/10 metre.
Centimetre = 1/100 metre.
Millimetre = 1/1000 metre.

PART II
MEASUREMENT OF AREA

Metric units
Hectare = 100 ares.
Decare = 10 ares.
Are = 100 square metres.
SQUARE METRE = a superficial area equal to that of a square each side of which measures one metre.
Square decimetre = 1/100 square metre.
Square centimetre = 1/100 square decimetre.
Square millimetre = 1/100 square centimetre.

PART III
MEASUREMENT OF VOLUME

Metric units

Hectare = 100 ares.
Decare = 10 ares.
Are = 100 square metres.
SQUARE METRE = a superficial area equal to that of a square each side of which measures one metre.
Square decimetre = 1/100 square metre.
Square centimetre = 1/100 square decimetre.
Square millimetre = 1/100 square centimetre.

PART IV
MEASUREMENT OF CAPACITY

Imperial unit

PINT = 0.568 261 25 cubic decimetre.

Metric units

Hectolitre = 100 litres.
LITRE = a cubic decimetre.
Decilitre = 1/10 litre.
Centilitre = 1/100 litre.
Millilitre = 1/1000 litre.

PART V
MEASUREMENT OF MASS OR WEIGHT

Imperial unit

OUNCE TROY = 0.031 103 476 8 kilogram.

Metric units

Tonne, metric tonne = 1000 kilograms.
KILOGRAM is the unit of mass; it is equal to the mass of the international prototype of the kilogram.
Hectogram = 1/10 kilogram.
Gram = 1/1000 kilogram.
Carat (metric) = 1/5 gram.
Milligram = 1/1000 gram.

PART VI
DEFINITIONS OF CERTAIN UNITS WHICH MAY NOT BE USED FOR TRADE EXCEPT AS SUPPLEMENTARY INDICATIONS

MEASUREMENT OF LENGTH

Mile = 1760 yards.
Furlong = 220 yards.
Chain = 22 yards.
YARD = 0.9144 metre.
Foot = 1/3 yard.
Inch = 1/36 yard.

Measurement of area
Square mile = 640 acres.
Acre = 4840 square yards.
Rood = 1210 square yards.
Square yard = a superficial area equal to that of a square each side of which measures one yard.
Square foot = 1/9 square yard.
Square inch = 1/144 square foot.

Measurement of volume
Cubic yard = a volume equal to that of a cube each edge of which measures one yard.
Cubic foot = 1/27 cubic yard.
Cubic inch = 1/1728 cubic foot.

Measurement of capacity
Bushel = 8 gallons.
Peck = 2 gallons.
GALLON = 4.546 09 cubic decimetres.
Quart = 1/4 gallon.
Gill = 1/4 pint.
Fluid ounce = 1/20 pint.
Fluid drachm = 1/8 fluid ounce.
Minim = 1/60 fluid drachm.

Measurement of mass or weight		
Ton	=	2240 pounds.
Hundredweight	=	112 pounds.
Cental	=	100 pounds.
Quarter	=	28 pounds.
Stone	=	14 pounds.
POUND	=	0.453 592 37 kilogram.
Ounce	=	1/16 pound.
Dram	=	1/16 ounce.
Grain	=	1/7000 pound.
Pennyweight	=	24 grains.
Ounce apothecaries	=	480 grains.
Drachm	=	1/8 ounce apothecaries.
Scruple	=	1/3 drachm.
Metric ton	=	1000 kilograms.
Quintal	=	100 kilograms.

PART VII
MEASUREMENT OF ELECTRICITY

1
(*a*) AMPERE is that constant current which, if maintained in two straight parallel conductors of infinite length, of negligible circular cross-section and placed 1 metre apart in vacuum, would produce between these conductors a force equal to 2 x 10 (to the power of minus seven) newton per metre of length.

(*b*) OHM is the electric resistance between two points of a conductor when a constant potential difference of 1 volt, applied between the two points, produces in the conductor a current of 1 ampere, the conductor not being the seat of any electromotive force.

(*c*) VOLT is the difference of electric potential between two points of a conducting wire carrying a constant current of 1 ampere when the power dissipated between these points is equal to 1 watt.

(*d*) WATT is the power which in one second gives rise to energy of 1 joule.

2
Kilowatt = 1000 watts.
Megawatt = one million watts.

8–31912

Section 2(3)

SCHEDULE 2
EXISTING UNITED KINGDOM PRIMARY STANDARDS AND AUTHORISED COPIES

....

8–31913

Section 8(1)

SCHEDULE 3
MEASURES AND WEIGHTS LAWFUL FOR USE FOR TRADE

(*As amended by SI 1994/1883 and 2866.*)

PART I
LINEAR MEASURES

1. *Revoked*

Metric system

2. Measures of—

50 metres	2 metres
30 metres	1.5 metres
20 metres	1 metre
10 metres	0.5 metre
5 metres	1 decimetre
3 metres	1 centimetre

PART II
SQUARE MEASURES

1. *Revoked*

Metric system

2. Measures of, or of any multiple of, 1 square decimetre.

PART III
CUBIC MEASURES

Metric system

1. Measures of, or of any multiple of, 0·1 cubic metre.
2. Measures of—

any multiple of 10 litres
10 litres
5 litres
2.5 litres
2 litres
1 litre
500 millilitres
250 millilitres
200 millilitres
100 millilitres
50 millilitres
25 millilitres
20 millilitres
10 millilitres
5 millilitres
2 millilitres
1 millilitre

PART IV
CAPACITY MEASURES

Imperial system

1. Measures of—

16 pints
8 pints
4 pints
2 pints
1 pint
1/2 pint
1/3 pint
2/5 gill
1/3 gill
1/5 gill

Metric system

2. Measures of—

any multiple of 10 litres
10 litres
5 litres
2.5 litres
2 litres
1 litre
500 millilitres
250 millilitres
200 millilitres
175 millilitres
150 millilitres
125 millilitres
100 millilitres
50 millilitres
35 millilitres
25 millilitres
20 millilitres
10 millilitres
5 millilitres
2 millilitres
1 millilitre

PART V
WEIGHTS

Imperial system

1. *Repealed.*
2. Weights of—
500 ounces troy
400 ounces troy
300 ounces troy
200 ounces troy
100 ounces troy
50 ounces troy
40 ounces troy
30 ounces troy
20 ounces troy
10 ounces troy
5 ounces troy
4 ounces troy
3 ounces troy
2 ounces troy
1 ounce troy
0.5 ounce troy
0.4 ounce troy
0.3 ounce troy
0.2 ounce troy
0.1 ounce troy
0.05 ounce troy
0.04 ounce troy
0.03 ounce troy
0.025 ounce troy
0.02 ounce troy
0.01 ounce troy
0.005 ounce troy
0.004 ounce troy
0.003 ounce troy
0.002 ounce troy
0.001 ounce troy

Metric system

3. Weights of—

25 kilograms	3 grams
20 kilograms	2 grams
10 kilograms	1 gram
5 kilograms	500 milligrams
2 kilograms	400 milligrams
1 kilogram	300 milligrams
500 grams	200 milligrams
200 grams	150 milligrams
100 grams	100 milligrams
50 grams	50 milligrams
20 grams	20 milligrams
15 grams	10 milligrams
10 grams	5 milligrams
5 grams	2 milligrams
4 grams	1 milligram

4. Weights of—

500 carats (metric)	1 carat (metric)
200 carats (metric)	0.5 carat (metric)
100 carats (metric)	0.25 carat (metric)
50 carats (metric)	0.2 carat (metric)
20 carats (metric)	0.1 carat (metric)
10 carats (metric)	0.05 carat (metric)
5 carats (metric)	0.02 carat (metric)
2 carats (metric)	0.01 carat (metric)

8–31914

Section 11A

SCHEDULE 3A
APPROVALS UNDER SECTION 11A

(*As inserted by SI 1999/503.*)

PART I
APPROVALS: GENERAL

8–31914A

Section 21

SCHEDULE 4
SAND AND OTHER BALLAST

(*As amended by SI 1994/2866.*)

PART I
GENERAL PROVISIONS

1. In this Schedule, "ballast" means any of the following materials, that is to say—

(*a*) sand, gravel, shingle, ashes and clinker of any description,

(*b*) broken slag, slag chippings, granite chippings, limestone chippings, slate chippings and other stone chippings (including such materials which have been coated with tar, bitumen or cement),

(*c*) any other material commonly used in the building and civil engineering industries as a hardcore or an aggregate, and

(*d*) any other material commonly known in those industries as ballast.

2. Subject to paragraphs 3 and 11 below, ballast shall be sold only by volume in a multiple of 0·2 cubic metre or by net weight.

3. There shall be exempted from the requirements of paragraph 2 above—

(*a*) ballast in a quantity both less than 1 tonne and less than one cubic metre.

(*b*) any sale with a view to its industrial use of ballast of any description mentioned in paragraph 1 (*b*), (*c*) or (*d*) above,

(*c*) any sale in the case of which the buyer is to take delivery in or from a ship,

(*d*) any sale as a whole of ballast produced in the demolition or partial demolition of a building where the buyer is responsible for the removal of the ballast from the site of the building, and

(*e*) any sale in the state in which it was produced of clinker or ashes produced as a by-product, or of any other ballast produced as a casual product, of the carrying on of an industrial process on any premises or of the mining of coal where the buyer is responsible for the removal of the ballast from those premises or, as the case may be, from the colliery tip.

4. Without prejudice to section 15 of this Act, no article shall be used for trade as a cubic measure of ballast other than a receptacle (which may, if so desired, form part of a vehicle) which conforms with such requirements as to form, capacity, calibration and other matters as may be prescribed[1]; and any person who uses for trade, or has in his possession for use for trade, as a cubic measure of ballast any article other than such a receptacle shall be guilty of an offence[2].

5. In measuring any ballast against a calibration mark on such a receptacle as mentioned in paragraph 4 above, the ballast shall be filled into all parts of the receptacle as far as, and be levelled off against, that calibration mark as nearly as the nature of the ballast will permit; and where any ballast is measured for the purposes of trade in such a receptacle, any person who—

(*a*) being the person carrying out the measuring, fails so to level off the ballast when it is loaded into the receptacle, or

(*b*) causes or permits a heaped load to be sent out in the receptacle,

shall be guilty of an offence[2].

---

1. See the Cubic Measures (Ballast and Agricultural Materials) 1978, SI 1978/1962 amended by SI 1988/765.
2. For penalty see s 84, ante.

PART II
CARRIAGE OF BALLAST BY ROAD

6. This Part of this Schedule shall have effect with respect to the carriage of ballast by a road vehicle on a journey any part of which is along a highway.

7. (1) If any of the ballast is being carried for delivery to a buyer in pursuance of, or of an agreement for, its sale and paragraph 2 above applies to the sale, the following provisions of this paragraph shall have effect with respect to that ballast.

(2) There shall, before the journey begins, be delivered to the person in charge of the vehicle a document signed by or on behalf of the seller (in this paragraph referred to as "the delivery document") stating—

(*a*) the name and address of the seller,

(*b*) the name of the buyer, and the address of the premises to which the ballast is being delivered,

(*c*) the type of the ballast,

(*d*) subject to sub-paragraph (4) below, the quantity of the ballast either by net weight or by volume,

(*e*) sufficient particulars to identify the vehicle, and

(*f*) the place, date and time of the loading of the ballast in the vehicle.

(3) Where the quantity of the ballast is stated in the delivery document by volume, the ballast shall be carried on the vehicle only in such a receptacle as is mentioned in paragraph 4 above.

(4) The statement referred to in sub-paragraph (2)(*d*) above shall not be required at any time while the vehicle is travelling between the place where it was loaded and the nearest suitable and available weighing equipment if the whole of the vehicle's load is being delivered to the same person at the same premises and the delivery document states that the quantity of the ballast is to be expressed by net weight determined by means of that equipment and specifies the place at which the equipment is situated.

(5) In any case to which sub-paragraph (4) above applies, the person in charge of the vehicle at the time when the net weight of the ballast is determined shall forthwith add to the delivery document a statement of that net weight, and if he fails so to do he shall be guilty of an offence[1].

(6) If any of the provisions of sub-paragraph (2) or (3) above is contravened, the seller shall be guilty of an offence[1].

(7) If the vehicle is carrying ballast as mentioned in sub-paragraph (1) above for delivery to each of two or more persons, sub-paragraphs (1) to (3) above shall apply separately in relation to each of those persons; but this sub-paragraph shall not be construed as prohibiting the use of the same receptacle such as is mentioned in sub-paragraph (3) above for the carriage of ballast for delivery to two or more different persons.

8. (1) Subject to sub-paragraph (2) below, if all or any of the ballast on the vehicle is being carried in such circumstances that paragraph 7 above does not apply to it, there shall before the journey begins be delivered to the person in charge of the vehicle a document containing a statement to that effect signed by or on behalf of the person causing that ballast to be carried and giving the name and address of the last-mentioned person, and if this paragraph is contravened the last-mentioned person shall be guilty of an offence[1].

(2) Sub-paragraph (1) above shall not apply where all the ballast in the vehicle is being carried in such circumstances that paragraph 7 does not apply to it and is being so carried in a container which does not form part of the vehicle.

9. Any document required by paragraph 7 or 8 above shall at all times during the journey be carried by the person for the time being in charge of the vehicle and shall be handed over by him to any other person to whom he hands over the charge of the vehicle in the course of the journey; and in the case of any document such as is mentioned in paragraph 7 above, on the unloading of the ballast to which the document relates at the premises to which that ballast is to be delivered—

(*a*) before any of that ballast is so unloaded, the document shall be handed over to the buyer, or

(*b*) if the document cannot be so handed over by reason of the absence of the buyer, it shall be left at some suitable place at those premises;

and if at any time any of the provisions of this paragraph is contravened without reasonable cause, the person in charge of the vehicle at that time shall be guilty of an offence[1].

10. In the case of any document such as is mentioned in paragraph 7 above, if at any time during the journey or on unloading at the place of delivery the quantity of the ballast to which the document relates is found to be less than that stated in the document, the statement shall nevertheless be deemed for the purposes of this Act to be correct if, but only if, it is proved that the deficiency is solely attributable to the draining away of normal moisture from, or the consolidation of, the ballast during the journey.

PART III

Application to Scotland

---

1. For penalty see s 84, ante.

Section 21

SCHEDULE 5

(Printed as amended by SI 1987/216, the Coal Industry Act 1987, Sch 1, the Coal Industry Act 1994, Schs 9 and 11 and SIs 1994/2866 and 2867.)

8–31915

SOLID FUEL

PART I
GENERAL

Introductory

1. This Schedule applies to goods of any of the following descriptions (in this Schedule referred to as "solid fuel"), that is to say—

(*a*) coal,
(*b*) coke, and
(*c*) any solid fuel derived from coal or of which coal or coke is a constituent.

Sales by net weight

2. (1) Subject to sub-paragraphs (2) and (3) below, solid fuel shall be sold only by net weight.

(2) There shall be exempted from the requirements of sub-paragraph (1) above—

(*a*) briquettes in a quantity not exceeding 7.5 kilograms, and
(*b*) any solid fuel pre-packed in a securely closed container marked with an indication of quantity by net weight.

(3) In the case of any area in Scotland which the Secretary of State may by order specify for the purposes of this sub-paragraph, solid fuel for delivery in that area may be sold by volume in a quantity of 0·2 cubic metre or a multiple of 0·2 cubic metre.

Quantities in containers

3. (1) Solid fuel shall be made up in a container for sale, or for delivery after sale, only if it is made up in one of the following quantities by net weight, namely—

(*a*) 25 kilograms;
(*b*) 50 kilograms;
(*c*) any multiple of 50 kilograms.

(2) This paragraph shall not apply to any solid fuel pre-packed in a quantity not exceeding 30 kilograms in a securely closed container.

(3) *Revoked.*

(4) This paragraph and paragraphs 4, 5 and 6 below have effect subject to the exemptions in paragraph 7.

Indication of quantity

4. (1) This paragraph applies to solid fuel made up in a container for sale, or for delivery after sale, except where it is made up in a container which is not securely closed.

(2) The solid fuel shall be made up in a container for sale, or for delivery after sale, only if the container is marked with an indication of quantity by net weight.

Loads on vehicles

5. *Revoked.*

Information about containers

6. (1) This paragraph applies where solid fuel is carried on a road vehicle on a highway for sale, or for delivery after sale, and is made up in containers which are not securely closed or is delivered from the vehicle in such containers.

(2) There shall be displayed on the vehicle—

(*a*) an indication of the quantity, or quantities, by net weight of the fuel comprised in the containers (other than any securely closed containers) on, or delivered from, the vehicle, and
(*b*) a statement of the name and address of the seller.

(3) Regulations[1] under section 23 of this Act may prescribe the manner in which the information required by sub-paragraph (2) above is to be displayed, and a person who contravenes any such regulation shall be guilty of an offence[2].

(4) If this paragraph is contravened, the seller, and any other person who is in charge of the vehicle at the time of the contravention, shall each be guilty of an offence[2].

Exemptions

7. There shall be exempted from all the requirements of paragraphs 3, 4, 5 and 6 above—

(*a*) solid fuel supplied under arrangements made in the coal industry for the supply of solid fuel to persons who are or have been employed in that industry or to the dependants of such persons;
(*b*) solid fuel made up in a container only for ease of handling as part of the load of a vehicle or ship where the whole of that load so far as it consists of solid fuel is being delivered to a single buyer.

Vending machines

8. Solid fuel shall be sold by means of, or offered or exposed for sale in, a vending machine only if there is displayed on or in the machine—

(*a*) an indication of the quantity by net weight of the fuel comprised in each item for sale by means of that machine; and

(*b*) except where the machine is on premises at which the seller carries on business, a statement of the name and address of the seller.

Byelaws

9. A local weights and measures authority may make byelaws, subject to the confirmation of the Secretary of State—

(*a*) for securing that on any premises within their area on or from which solid fuel available for purchase in a quantity of 100 kilograms or less is sold or kept or exposed for sale there is displayed a notice specifying the price of the fuel;

(*b*) prohibiting the sale on or from any such premises of any such fuel at a higher price than that so displayed in relation to that fuel; and

(*c*) prescribing penalties not exceeding level 2[3] on the standard scale for any offence under such byelaws.

Damping of fuel

10. Any person who with intent to defraud or deceive[4] damps any solid fuel shall be guilty of an offence[2].

Sale of fuel from vehicles

11. (1) This paragraph applies to any vehicle which is used on highways for carrying solid fuel for sale, or for delivery after sale; and in this paragraph "container" means any container in which solid fuel is carried on such a vehicle, or is delivered from such a vehicle.

(2) The Secretary of State may by order make provision—

(*a*) for securing the display on any such vehicle of an indication of the quantities in which solid fuel is made up in containers;

(*b*) for requiring all containers carried on or delivered from any one vehicle to be made up in the same quantity, or for regulating in any other way the quantities in which they are made up;

(*c*) for imposing any requirement as to the loading of the vehicle, or the delivery of solid fuel from the vehicle, which appears to the Secretary of State appropriate for securing that purchasers are not misled as to the quantity of fuel they purchase.

(3) Any order under sub-paragraph (2) above may—

(*a*) make provision for any of the purposes mentioned in that sub-paragraph by means of amending, or of applying with or without modifications, or of excluding the application in whole or in part of, any of the preceding paragraphs of this Schedule;

(*b*) contain such consequential, incidental or supplementary provision, whether of such kinds as aforesaid or otherwise, as appear to the Secretary of State to be expedient;

(*c*) may in particular make provision, in respect of contraventions of the order for which no penalty is provided by this Act, for the imposition of penalties not exceeding those provided by section 84(6) of this Act for an offence under this Act.

12. An order under section 22 of this Act may amend or repeal any of the preceding paragraphs of this Schedule.

---

1. The Weights and Measures (Solid Fuel) Regulations 1978, post, have been made.
2. For penalty see s 84, ante.
3. A byelaw in force at 17th July 1978 and then providing for a maximum fine of £20 now has a maximum of £50 (Criminal Law Act 1977, s 31(2) and (3). Where the maximum was an amount less than £20 it remains the same. This provision is continued in force by Sch 11 para 24 of this Act.
4. To deceive is by falsehood to induce a state of mind; to defraud is by deceit to induce a course of action whether in doing something or refraining from something (*Re London and Globe Finance Corpn Ltd* [1903] 1 Ch 728, 82 JP Jo 447; *R v Wines* [1953] 2 All ER 1497, 118 JP 49). This statement of law was discussed at length in *Welham v DPP* [1961] AC 103, [1960] 1 All ER 805, 124 JP 280, HL; affg sub nom *R v Welham* [1960] 2 QB 445, [1960] 1 All ER 260, 124 JP 156, CCA, in which it was held that it was not an ingredient of an intent to defraud that there shall be economic loss; the intention may be by deceit to induce a person to act to his detriment in a manner contrary to his duty.

PART II
WEIGHING OF SOLID FUEL AT BUYER'S REQUEST

13. If in the case of any solid fuel sold otherwise than by means of a vending machine the buyer so requests—

(*a*) with respect to any of that fuel the delivery of which has not at the time of the request been completed, or

(*b*) if the request is made before the departure from the premises at which the fuel is delivered of the person delivering it, with respect to any of that fuel the delivery of which has been completed but which is still capable of identification,

the seller shall cause the fuel to be weighed by means of suitable weighing equipment in the presence of the buyer and, in the case of any fuel such as is mentioned in sub-paragraph (*a*) of this paragraph, before the delivery of that fuel is completed; and if this paragraph is contravened, the seller shall be guilty of an offence.

14. Where a request under paragraph 13 above is made in respect of the whole load of a vehicle, the requirements of that paragraph shall be deemed to be satisfied, notwithstanding that the weighing is not done in the presence of the buyer, if the seller causes the vehicle to be check-weighed and the statements of the weights found by the person or persons attending to the check-weighing to be delivered to the buyer.

15. Where after any weighing in pursuance of a request under paragraph 13 above the weight of the solid fuel is found to be not less than that marked on any container in which the fuel was made up or than that stated by the seller in any document delivered to the buyer at or before the delivery of the fuel to him, the buyer shall be liable to repay to the seller all costs reasonably incurred by the seller in connection with the weighing.

PART III
CARRIAGE OF SOLID FUEL BY ROAD

16. This Part of this Schedule shall have effect with respect to the carriage by a road vehicle on a journey any part of which is along a highway of any solid fuel required by paragraph 2 above to be sold only by net weight (in this Part of this Schedule referred to as "relevant goods").

17. (1) If the vehicle is carrying any relevant goods for delivery to a buyer in pursuance of, or of an agreement for, a sale of a quantity exceeding 110 kilograms, then, subject to sub-paragraph (6) below, there shall before the journey begins be delivered to the person in charge of the vehicle a document signed by or on behalf of the seller (in this paragraph referred to as "the delivery document") stating—

(*a*) the name and address of the seller,
(*b*) the name of the buyer and the address of the premises to which the goods to which the document relates are being delivered,
(*c*) the type of those goods,
(*d*) subject to sub-paragraph (2) below, the aggregate net weight of those goods, and
(*e*) where any of those goods are made up in containers—

(i) the number of those containers, and
(ii) except where the whole of the relevant goods carried on the vehicle are for delivery to a single buyer, and except where the whole of the vehicle's load consists of such solid fuel as is mentioned in paragraph 7(*a*) above, the net weight of the goods in each of those containers;

and if this sub-paragraph is contravened the seller shall be guilty of an offence[1].

(2) Where the whole of the vehicle's load consists of relevant goods not made up in containers and is being delivered to the same person at the same premises, the statement referred to in sub-paragraph (1)(*d*) above shall not be required at any time while the vehicle is travelling between the place where it was loaded and the nearest suitable and available weighing equipment if the delivery document states that the quantity of the relevant goods is to be expressed by net weight determined by means of that equipment and specifies the place at which the equipment is situated.

(3) In any case to which sub-paragraph (2) above applies, the person in charge of the vehicle at the time when the net weight of the relevant goods is determined shall forthwith add to the delivery document a statement of that net weight, and if he fails so to do he shall be guilty of an offence[1].

(4) Subject to sub-paragraph (5) below, if the vehicle is carrying relevant goods to which sub-paragraph (1) above applies for delivery to each of two or more buyers—

(*a*) that sub-paragraph shall apply separately in relation to each of those buyers, and
(*b*) the relevant goods for delivery to each respectively of those buyers shall be carried on the vehicle made up separately in containers or in separate compartments;

and if paragraph (*b*) of this sub-paragraph is contravened the seller shall be guilty of an offence[1].

(5) Sub-paragraph (4)(*b*) above shall not apply where the vehicle is constructed or adapted for the mechanical making up in containers of the fuel carried thereon and incorporates weighing equipment approved by the Secretary of State for that purpose.

(6) Sub-paragraph (1) above shall not apply to any goods which to the knowledge of the seller are to be loaded into a ship before their delivery to the buyer.

18. (1) Subject to sub-paragraph (2) below, if all or any of the relevant goods on the vehicle are being carried in such circumstances that paragraph 17(1) above does not apply, there shall, before the journey begins, be delivered to the person in charge of the vehicle a document signed by or on behalf of the person causing the goods to be carried giving the name and address of the last-mentioned person and containing a statement to the effect that all or part of the relevant goods on the vehicle are goods to which paragraph 17(1) above does not apply, and if this paragraph is contravened the last-mentioned person shall be guilty of an offence[1].

(2) Sub-paragraph (1) above shall not apply where the total quantity of the relevant goods carried on the vehicle does not exceed 110 kilograms.

19. Any document required by paragraph 17 or 18 above shall at all times during the journey be carried by the person for the time being in charge of the vehicle and shall be handed over by him to any other person to whom he hands over the charge of the vehicle in the course of the journey; and in the case of any document such as is mentioned in paragraph 17 above, on the unloading of the goods to which the document relates at the premises to which those goods are to be delivered—

(*a*) before any of those goods are so unloaded, the document shall be handed over to the buyer, or
(*b*) if the document cannot be so handed over by reason of the absence of the buyer, it shall be left at some suitable place at those premises[2];

and if at any time any of the requirements of this paragraph is contravened without reasonable cause, the person in charge of the vehicle at that time shall be guilty of an offence[1].

1. For penalty, see s 84, ante.
2. In connection with this paragraph, reference may be made to the following cases decided under s 21 of the Weights and Measures Act 1889 (repealed and replaced by this Part of this Schedule); *Stangoe v Slatter* (1896) 60 JP 342; *Kyle v Dunsdon* [1908] 2 KB 293, 72 JP 293; *Lucas v Hodson* [1919] 1 KB 6, 83 JP 15.

PART IV
CARRIAGE OF SOLID FUEL BY RAIL

20. Where any seller of solid fuel causes that fuel to be loaded into a rail vehicle by way of, or for the purpose of, the delivery of that fuel to, or to a person nominated in that behalf by, the buyer, and the fuel is not carried on the vehicle made up in containers, then, except where at the time of loading it is known to the seller that before the fuel is delivered to the consignee it is to be loaded into a ship, paragraphs 21 to 25 below shall apply in relation to that vehicle.

21. Subject to paragraphs 22 and 28 below, the vehicle shall not be loaded until its tare weight has been determined or redetermined by means of suitable weighing equipment at the place of loading.

22. (1) Paragraph 21 above shall not apply to any rail vehicle which forms part of or is intended to form part of a train conveying only fuel destined for a particular generating station, gas works or other industrial undertaking if—

(*a*) the vehicle is loaded by equipment which weighs the fuel and discharges it directly into the vehicle, or

(*b*) the buyer has agreed with the seller that the weight of the load shall be ascertained at the vehicle's destination, or

(*c*) the buyer has agreed to accept as the tare weight of the vehicle a tare weight ascertained not more than three months before the time of loading and the vehicle has marked upon it in durable lettering a statement of the weight so ascertained and of the date and place at which it was ascertained, or

(*d*) all the vehicles comprised in the train are coupled together in such a manner that they may be weighed while in motion by equipment designed to determine the total weight of the train, and the buyer has agreed with the seller that the total net weight of fuel carried in the train shall be ascertained by deducting the total weight of the train so determined before loading from the total weight thereof so determined when loaded.

(2) Nothing in sub-paragraph (1)(*c*) above shall afford any exemption from the requirements of paragraph 21 above in the case of a vehicle which has undergone repairs or modification or has suffered substantial damage since its tare weight was last ascertained and marked as mentioned in that sub-paragraph.

23. (1) Subject to subparagraph (2) and paragraph 24 below, as soon as the loading has been completed and the seller has ascertained the weight of the vehicle with its load and the identity of the consignee, the seller shall cause to be attached to the vehicle a document stating—

(*a*) the name of the seller and the place and date of weighing,

(*b*) the name of the consignee and the destination of the vehicle,

(*c*) sufficient particulars to identify the vehicle,

(*d*) the tare weight of the vehicle as determined or redetermined in pursuance of paragraph 21 above or, if by virtue of paragraph 28 below paragraph 21 does not apply to the vehicle, the tare weight of the vehicle expressed to be as estimated by the seller,

(*e*) the weight attributed to the solid fuel in the vehicle by the seller for the purpose of calculating its purchase price, and

(*f*) the type of that fuel.

(2) Subparagraph (1) above shall not apply if, at the time of departure of the vehicle from the place of loading, the seller causes to be transmitted to the buyer, for receipt not later than the time of arrival of the vehicle at the buyer's premises, the information required by subparagraphs (*a*) to (*f*) of subparagraph (1) above:

Provided that where such information is transmitted otherwise than in a legible form—

(*a*) the seller and the buyer have agreed in writing that the information may be so transmitted;

(*b*) the places of loading and destination of the vehicle are suitably equipped for the transmission and receipt of information in such form; and

(*c*) the information is capable of being reproduced in a permanent legible form by the system effecting the transmission, and is so reproduced if required by an inspector, subject to the production, if so requested, of his credentials.

24. (1) Paragraph 23 above shall not apply to any vehicle forming part or intended to form part of any such train as is mentioned in paragraph 22 above, but the seller shall either (*a*) before the departure of the train which includes that vehicle deliver to the authority responsible for railway traffic at the place of loading for carriage on that train a document (in this paragraph and paragraph 25 below referred to as "a train bill") giving the information specified in sub-paragraph (2) below or, in the case of any such train as is mentioned in paragraph 22(1)(*d*) above, sub-paragraph (3) below or (*b*) at the time of departure of the train which includes that vehicle transmit to the buyer, for receipt not later than the time of arrival of the train at the buyer's premises, the information required by subparagraph (2) or, as the case may be, subparagraph (3) below:

Provided that where such information is transmitted otherwise than in a legible form—

(*a*) the seller and the buyer have agreed in writing that the information may be so transmitted;

(*b*) the places of loading and destination of the train are suitably equipped for the transmission and receipt of information in such form; and

(*c*) the information is capable of being reproduced in a permanent legible form by the system effecting the transmission, and is so reproduced if required by an inspector, subject to the production, if so requested, of his credentials.

(2) Except in a case to which sub-paragraph (3) below applies, the train bill shall contain the following information—

(*a*) the names of the seller and of the consignee and the destination of the train,

(*b*) sufficient particulars to identify each vehicle in the train,

(*c*) the date and place of loading of each vehicle,

(*d*) a statement of the type of fuel in each vehicle,

(*e*) except in the case of fuel which a buyer has agreed shall be weighed at the train's destination, the weight attributed by the seller to the fuel in each vehicle for the purpose of calculating its purchase price,

(*f*) where any vehicle is not exempted from paragraph 21 above, the tare weight of that vehicle,

(*g*) where any vehicle has been loaded by equipment which weighs fuel and discharges it directly into vehicles, a statement as to the vehicle which has been so loaded, (*h*) where any vehicle is loaded with fuel the weight of which is to be ascertained at the train's destination, a statement as to the vehicle so loaded,

(*i*) where any vehicle is exempted from paragraph 21 above by reason of paragraph 22(1)(*c*) above, a statement of the tare weight and related particulars marked upon that vehicle, and

(*j*) where any vehicle is so exempt by reason of any certificate or direction under paragraph 28 below, a weight stated to be the seller's estimate of the tare weight of that vehicle.

(3) In the case of any such train as is mentioned in paragraph 22(1)(*d*) above, the train bill shall contain the following information—

(*a*) the names of the seller and the consignee and the destination of the train,
(*b*) the date and place of loading of the train,
(*c*) the number of vehicles in the train,
(*d*) the total net weight of fuel carried in the train,
(*e*) a statement of the type of fuel carried in the train, and
(*f*) a statement that the buyer has agreed that the total net weight of fuel carried in the train shall be ascertained in the manner mentioned in paragraph 22(1)(*d*) above.

(4) If the requirements of sub-paragraph (1) above are contravened, the seller shall be guilty of an offence[1].

25. (1) The following provisions of this paragraph apply—

(*a*) in a case where by virtue of paragraph 24 above a train bill is carried, when the train reaches its destination, and
(*b*) in any other case, when the vehicle in question reaches its destination.

(2) The authority responsible for railway traffic at the destination of the train or vehicle, as the case may be, shall—

(*a*) permit the consignee and, subject to the production if so requested of his credentials, any inspector to inspect the document required by paragraph 23 or, as the case may be, 24 above.
(*b*) permit the consignee either to take possession of that document after the train or vehicle is unloaded or to make a copy of the particulars stated therein, and
(*c*) if so requested by the consignee with respect to any such copy which the authority is satisfied is accurate, certify the accuracy thereof,

and if any of the provisions of this sub-paragraph is contravened the authority shall be guilty of an offence[1].

(3) Subject to sub-paragraphs (5) and (6) below, any of the following persons, that is to say—

(*a*) any inspector, subject to the production if so requested of his credentials, or
(*b*) the consignee, subject to his undertaking to pay any cost reasonably incurred,

may require the vehicle to be weighed either before or after or both before and after it is unloaded, and the vehicle shall be weighed accordingly unless it is certified by or on behalf of the authority mentioned in sub-paragraph (2) above that in the circumstances of the particular case the carrying out of the weighing would cause undue dislocation of railway traffic at the vehicle's destination; and any inspector who is present at any such weighing shall if so requested certify the weight found.

(4) If when the fuel is unloaded from the vehicle it is weighed accurately with accurate weighing equipment in the presence of an inspector, the inspector shall if so requested certify that it was so weighed and state in his certificate the weight found.

(5) Where by virtue of paragraph 24 above a train bill is carried and the buyer has agreed that the weight of the fuel in any vehicle is to be ascertained at the train's destination, sub-paragraph (3) above shall not apply in relation to that vehicle.

(6) In a case falling within paragraph 22(1)(*d*) above, sub-paragraph (3) above shall have effect—

(*a*) with the omission of paragraph (*b*), and
(*b*) as if any reference to a vehicle were a reference to a train.

26. Where, in the case of any rail vehicle used on a journey to carry solid fuel which is not made up in containers, paragraphs 21 to 25 above do not apply, the consignor shall cause to be attached to the vehicle before it starts on the journey a document stating the name of the consignor and the place of loading of the vehicle.

27. (1) If paragraph 21 or 23 above is contravened, the seller shall be guilty of an offence[1].

(2) If paragraph 26 above is contravened, the consignor shall be guilty of an offence[1].

(3) If, in the case of any rail vehicle used on a journey to carry solid fuel—

(*a*) the authority responsible for railway traffic at the place of loading or any person employed by that authority wilfully prevents or impedes the attachment to the vehicle of the document required by paragraph 23 or 26 above, or
(*b*) any person, being a person concerned in the sale, carriage or delivery of that fuel, wilfully removes, defaces or alters any such document attached to the vehicle,

that authority or person shall be guilty of an offence[1].

28. (1) (*Repealed*).

(2) If any seller of solid fuel who uses any place, for causing solid fuel to be loaded as mentioned in paragraph 20 above makes representations to the Secretary of State that the provision at that place of weighing equipment suitable for determining the tare weight of rail vehicles is not reasonably practicable or would be unjustified on economic grounds and the Secretary of State is satisfied that there are grounds for those representations, the Secretary of State may direct, that subject to such conditions and for such period as may be specified in the direction, paragraph 21 above shall not apply to any vehicle loaded at that place.

(3) (*Repealed*).

1. For penalty, see s 84, ante.

8–31916

Section 21

SCHEDULE 6
MISCELLANEOUS GOODS OTHER THAN FOODS

(*As amended by SI 1994/1884 and 2866.*)

PART I
LIQUID FUEL AND LUBRICANTS

1. This Part of this Schedule applies to—

(*a*) liquid fuel, lubricating oil and any mixture of such fuel and oil, and
(*b*) lubricating grease.

2. Subject to paragraph 3 below, goods to which this Part of this Schedule applies—

(*a*) unless pre-packed, shall be sold only by net weight or by capacity measurement,
(*b*) shall be pre-packed only if the container is marked with an indication of quantity either by net weight or by capacity measurement, and
(*c*) in the case of lubricating oil in a quantity of one litre or less, shall be made up in a container for sale otherwise than by way of pre-packing only if the container is marked with an indication of quantity by capacity measurement.

3. Notwithstanding anything in paragraph 2 above, liquid fuel—

(*a*) when not pre-packed may be sold by volume, and
(*b*) may be pre-packed in a container marked with an indication of quantity by volume,

being in either case the volume of the gas which would be produced from the fuel in question at such temperature and such atmospheric pressure as are specified in regulations made by the Secretary of State with respect to fuel of the type in question or, if no such regulations are in force, as may be made known by the seller to the buyer before he pays for or takes possession of the fuel; and there shall be exempted from all requirements of paragraph 2 above goods of any description in a quantity of less than 250 grams or of less than 250 millilitres.

PART II
READY-MIXED CEMENT MORTAR AND READY-MIXED CONCRETE

4. This Part of this Schedule applies to ready-mixed cement mortar and ready-mixed concrete.

5. (1) Subject to the following provisions of this Part of this Schedule, any goods to which this Part of this Schedule applies shall be sold only by volume in a multiple of 0·1 cubic metre.

(2) There shall be exempted from the requirements of this paragraph any goods in a quantity of less than one cubic metre.

6. Part II of Schedule 4 to this Act, except sub-paragraph (3) of paragraph 7, shall apply for the purposes of this Part of this Schedule as if—

(*a*) any reference in the said Part II to ballast included a reference to goods to which this Part of this Schedule applies; and
(*b*) the reference in sub-paragraph (1) of paragraph 7 to paragraph 2 of Schedule 4 were a reference to paragraph 5 of this Schedule.

7. Paragraphs 5 and 6 above shall not have effect in any area in Scotland specified by the Secretary of State by order.

PART III
AGRICULTURAL LIMING MATERIALS, AGRICULTURAL SALT AND INORGANIC FERTILISERS

8. This Part of this Schedule applies—

(*a*) to agricultural liming materials, other than calcareous sand,
(*b*) to agricultural salt,
(*c*) to, and to any mixture consisting mainly of, inorganic fertilisers, other than such fertilisers or such a mixture made up into pellets or other articles for use as individual items, and
(*d*) to any mixture of any of the foregoing.

9. (1) Goods to which this Part of this Schedule applies which are not pre-packed, other than liquid fertilisers, shall be sold only by quantity, being—

(*a*) quantity by net weight; or
(*b*) if the goods are sold in a container which does not exceed the permitted weight and the gross weight of the goods is not less than 25 kilograms, quantity either by net weight or by gross weight; or
(*c*) quantity by volume.

(2) Goods to which this Part of this Schedule applies shall be pre-packed only if the container is marked with an indication of quantity, being—

(*a*) in the case of liquid fertilisers, quantity by capacity measurement;
(*b*) in any other case, quantity by net weight or, if the container does not exceed the permitted weight and the gross weight of the goods is not less than 25 kilograms, quantity either by net weight or by gross weight.

(3) In this paragraph, "the permitted weight" means a weight at the rate of 650 grams per 50 kilograms of the gross weight.

(4) There shall be exempted from all requirements of this paragraph any sale of goods with a view to their industrial use.

10. Paragraphs 4 and 5 of Schedule 4 to this Act shall have effect as if any reference in those paragraphs to ballast included a reference to any goods to which this Part of this Schedule applies.

PART IV
WOOD FUEL

11. Subject to paragraphs 12 and 13 below—

(*a*) wood fuel which is not made up in a container for sale shall be sold by retail only by net weight;
(*b*) in the case of a sale by retail of wood fuel made up in a container for sale, the quantity by net weight of the fuel sold shall be made known to the buyer before he pays for or takes possession of it.

12. (1) Paragraph 11 above shall not have effect in any area unless the local weights and measures authority for that area so direct by byelaw.

(2) Not less than one month before making any byelaw by virtue of this paragraph, the local weights and measures authority shall give public notice of their intention to make it by advertisement in one or more newspapers circulating in the area to which the byelaw is to apply.

(3) The local weights and measures authority by whom any byelaw is made by virtue of this paragraph shall give notice of the making of the byelaw to the Secretary of State.

13. There shall be exempted from the requirements of paragraph 11 above any sale of wood fuel in a quantity which does not exceed 7.5 kilograms or which exceeds 500 kilograms.

14. Paragraphs 9 and 10 of Schedule 5 to this Act shall have effect as if any reference in those paragraphs to solid fuel included a reference to wood fuel.

PART V
COSMETIC PRODUCTS

15. In this Part of this Schedule, "cosmetic product" means any substance or preparation intended to be placed in contact with the various external parts of the human body (that is to say, the epidermis, hair system, nails, lips and external genital organs) or with the teeth and the mucous membranes of the oral cavity with a view exclusively or mainly to cleaning them, perfuming them, changing their appearance, correcting bodily odours, protecting them or keeping them in good condition.

16. (1) Subject to sub-paragraph (2) below, cosmetic products shall be pre-packed only if the container is marked with an indication of quantity either by net weight or by volume.

(2) There shall be exempted from the requirements of sub-paragraph (1) above—

(*a*) cosmetic products in quantities of less than 5 grams or 5 millilitres;
(*b*) cosmetic products in sachets or other containers for single use only; and
(*c*) cosmetic products normally sold as a number of items for which particulars of weight or volume are not significant if—

(i) the number of items is marked on the package, or
(ii) the number of items may readily be seen without opening the package, or
(iii) the items are normally sold only individually.

(3) Cosmetic products which are not pre-packed shall be sold only by quantity expressed as net weight, volume or number.

PART VI
SOAP

16A. In this Part of this Schedule "soap" does not include any soap which is a cosmetic product as defined in paragraph 15 above.

17. Subject to paragraph 18 below—

(*a*) soap in the form of a cake, tablet or bar shall be pre-packed only if the container is marked with an indication of quantity by net weight,
(*b*) liquid soap shall be pre-packed only if the container is marked with an indication of quantity by capacity measurement, and
(*c*) soap in any other form—

(i) unless pre-packed, shall be sold by retail only by net weight, and
(ii) shall be pre-packed only if the container is marked with an indication of quantity by net weight.

18. There shall be exempted from the requirements of this Part of this Schedule—

(*a*) liquid soap in a quantity of less than 125 millilitres, and
(*b*) soap in any other form in a quantity of less than 25 grams.

PART VII
MISCELLANEOUS GOODS TO BE SOLD BY OR MARKED WITH LENGTH

19. This Part of this Schedule applies to goods of any of the following descriptions, that is to say, bias binding, elastic, ribbon, tape and sewing thread.

20. Subject to paragraph 21 below, goods to which this Part of this Schedule applies—

(*a*) unless pre-packed, shall be sold by retail only by length, and
(*b*) shall be pre-packed only if the container is marked with an indication of quantity by length.

21. There shall be exempted from all requirements of paragraph 20 above goods of any description in a quantity of less than one metre.

PART VIII
MISCELLANEOUS GOODS TO BE SOLD BY OR MARKED WITH NET WEIGHT

22. This Part of this Schedule applies to—

(*a*) distemper,
(*b*) articles offered as feed for household pets, being manufactured feed or bird feed, other than animal feed in biscuit or cake form pre-packed in a quantity by number not exceeding sixteen,
(*c*) nails,
(*d*) paste paint,
(*e*) seeds, other than pea or bean seeds, and
(*f*) rolled oats.

23. Subject to paragraphs 24 and 25 below, goods to which this Part of this Schedule applies—

(*a*) unless pre-packed, shall be sold by retail only by net weight, and
(*b*) shall be pre-packed only if the container is marked with an indication of quantity by net weight.

24. The following shall be exempted from the requirements of this Part of this Schedule—

(*a*) distemper or paste paint in a quantity of less than 250 grams,
(*b*) bird seed in a quantity of less than 125 grams, and
(*c*) any other goods in a quantity of less than 25 grams.

25. Notwithstanding anything in paragraph 24 above, nails—

(*a*) when not pre-packed may be sold by retail by number, and
(*b*) may be pre-packed in or on a container marked with an indication of quantity by number.

PART IX
MISCELLANEOUS GOODS TO BE MARKED WHEN PRE-PACKED WITH NET WEIGHT

26. This Part of this Schedule applies to—

(*a*) Portland cement,
(*b*) cleansing powders and scouring powders,
(*c*) detergents, other than liquid detergents, and
(*d*) paint remover, other than liquid paint remover.

27. Subject to paragraph 28 below, goods to which this Part of this Schedule applies shall be pre-packed only if the container is marked with an indication of quantity by net weight.

28. There shall be exempted from the requirements of this Part of this Schedule goods of any description in a quantity of less than 25 grams.

PART X
MISCELLANEOUS GOODS TO BE SOLD BY OR MARKED WITH CAPACITY MEASUREMENT

29. This Part of this Schedule applies to antifreeze fluid for internal combustion engines, linseed oil, paint (other than paste paint), paint thinner, turpentine, turpentine substitute, varnish, and wood preservative fluid (including fungicides and insecticides).

30. Subject to paragraph 31 below, goods to which this Part of this Schedule applies—

(*a*) unless pre-packed, shall be sold by retail only by capacity measurement, and
(*b*) shall be pre-packed only if the container is marked with an indication of quantity by capacity measurement.

31. There shall be exempted from all requirements of this Part of this Schedule goods of any description in a quantity of less than 150 millilitres.

PART XI
MISCELLANEOUS GOODS TO BE MARKED WHEN PRE-PACKED WITH CAPACITY MEASUREMENT

32. This Part of this Schedule applies to enamel, lacquer, liquid detergents, liquid paint remover, petrifying fluid and rust remover.

33. Subject to paragraph 34 below, goods to which this Part of this Schedule applies shall be pre-packed only if the container is marked with an indication of quantity by capacity measurement.

34. The following shall be exempted from the requirements of paragraph 33 above—

(*a*) liquid detergents in a quantity of less than 125 millilitres, and
(*b*) goods of any other description in a quantity of less than 150 millilitres.

PART XII
MISCELLANEOUS GOODS TO BE SOLD BY OR MARKED WITH NET WEIGHT OR CAPACITY MEASUREMENT

35. This Part of this Schedule applies to—

(*a*) polishes,
(*b*) dressings, analogous to polishes, and
(*c*) pea seeds and bean seeds.

36. Subject to paragraph 37 below, goods to which this Part of this Schedule applies—

(*a*) unless pre-packed, shall be sold by retail only by net weight or by capacity measurement, and
(*b*) shall be pre-packed only if the container is marked with an indication of quantity either by net weight or by capacity measurement.

37. The following shall be exempted from all the requirements of this Part of this Schedule, that is to say—

(*a*) pea or bean seeds in a quantity of less than 250 grams or of less than 250 millilitres, and
(*b*) any other goods in a quantity of less than 30 grams or of less than 30 millilitres.

PART XIII

MISCELLANEOUS GOODS TO BE MARKED WHEN PRE-PACKED WITH QUANTITY BY NUMBER

38. This Part of this Schedule applies—

(*a*) to cheroots, cigarettes and cigars,
(*b*) to postal stationery, that is to say, paper or cards for use in correspondence, and envelopes,
(*c*) to, and to any mixture consisting mainly of, inorganic fertilisers, being such fertilisers or such a mixture made up into pellets or other articles for use as individual items, and
(*d*) to manufactured animal feed in biscuit or cake form pre-packed in a quantity by number of sixteen or less.

39. Subject to paragraphs 40 and 41 below, goods to which this Part of this Schedule applies shall be pre-packed only if the container is marked with an indication of quantity by number.

40. In relation to postal stationery, the reference to number in paragraph 39 above shall be construed as a reference to the number of sheets of paper, cards or envelopes, as the case may be, in the pad, confining band or other form of container; and postal stationery shall be exempted from the requirements of that paragraph if pre-packed as part of a collection of articles made up for sale together and including any article other than postal stationery and blotting or other paper.

41. There shall be exempted from the requirements of this Part of this Schedule any goods in a quantity by number of one.

Section 21

SCHEDULE 7

(As amended by SI 1994/2866)

8–31917

COMPOSITE GOODS AND COLLECTIONS OF ARTICLES

1. (1) This paragraph applies to any goods which, not being pre-packed, and not themselves being goods—

(*a*) required by or under Part IV of this Act, except this paragraph, to be sold (whether on any sale or on a sale of any particular description) only by quantity expressed in a particular manner, or
(*b*) on a sale of which (whether any sale or a sale of any particular description) the quantity of the goods sold expressed in a particular manner is required by or under Part IV of this Act, except this paragraph, to be made known to the buyer at or before a particular time, or
(*c*) expressly exempted by or under Part IV of this Act, except this paragraph, from all such requirements as mentioned in paragraph (*a*) or (*b*) above which would otherwise apply to them,

consist of a mixture constituted wholly or mainly of goods of one or more descriptions to which there applies any such requirement made by reference to any of the following (whether exclusively or otherwise), that is to say, weight, capacity measurement or volume.

(2) Subject to paragraph 5 below, goods to which this paragraph applies shall be sold only by net weight or by capacity measurement or by volume.

2. (1) This paragraph applies to any goods which, not being aerosol products and not themselves being goods—

(*a*) required by or under Part IV of this Act, except this paragraph, to be pre-packed only if the container is marked with an indication of quantity, or
(*b*) in the case of which when sold pre-packed (whether on any sale or on a sale of any particular description) the quantity of the goods sold expressed in a particular manner is required by or under Part IV of this Act, except this paragraph, to be made known to the buyer at or before a particular time, or
(*c*) expressly exempted by or under Part IV of this Act, except this paragraph, from all such requirements as mentioned in paragraph (*a*) or (*b*) above which would otherwise apply to them,

consist of a mixture constituted wholly or mainly of goods of one or more descriptions to which there applies any such requirement made by reference to any of the following (whether exclusively or otherwise), that is to say, weight, capacity measurement or volume.

(2) Subject to paragraph 5 below, goods to which this paragraph applies shall be pre-packed only if the container is marked with an indication of quantity either by net weight or by capacity measurement or by volume.

3. (1) This paragraph applies to aerosol products containing any goods required by or under Part IV of this Act, except this paragraph, to be pre-packed only if the container is marked with an indication of quantity expressed in a particular manner.

(2) Subject to paragraph 5 below, any aerosol product to which this paragraph applies shall be pre-packed only if the container is marked with an indication of the quantity by net weight of the entire contents of the container.

4. (1) This paragraph applies to any collection of two or more items which, not itself being—

(*a*) required by or under Part IV of this Act, except this paragraph, to be pre-packed only if the container is marked with particular information, or
(*b*) expressly exempted by or under Part IV of this Act, except this paragraph, from any such requirement which would otherwise apply to it,

contains one or more articles to which any such requirement applies.

(2) Any collection to which this paragraph applies shall be pre-packed only if—

(*a*) the container in which the collection is pre-packed is marked with an indication of the quantity of each of any such articles as mentioned in sub-paragraph (1) above contained in it, or
(*b*) each of any such articles contained in the container is made up in an individual container marked with an indication of quantity,

being in either case the like indication of the quantity of each respectively of those articles as would have been required if that article had itself been pre-packed.

5. There shall be exempted from any requirement of paragraph 1, 2 or 3 above food of any description in a quantity of less than five grams or of less than five millilitres and goods of any other description in a quantity of less than 25 grams or of less than 25 millilitres.

Section 53

SCHEDULE 8

8–31918 POWERS OF INSPECTORS AND LOCAL WEIGHTS AND MEASURES AUTHORITY UNDER PART V

Powers of entry and inspection

1. An inspector may, within the area for which he is appointed an inspector and on production if so requested of his credentials, at all reasonable times—

(*a*) enter any premises (except premises used only as a private dwelling-house) as to which he has reasonable cause to believe that packages are made up on the premises or that imported packages belonging to the importer of them are on the premises or that regulated packages intended for sale are on the premises;

(*b*) inspect and test any equipment which he has reasonable cause to believe is used in making up packages in the United Kingdom or in carrying out a check mentioned in subsections (1) and (2) of section 49 of this Act;

(*c*) inspect, and measure in such manner as he thinks fit, any thing which he has reasonable cause to believe is or contains or is contained in a package and, if he considers it necessary to do so for the purpose of inspecting the thing or anything in it, break it open;

(*d*) inspect and take copies of, or of any thing purporting to be, a record, document or certificate mentioned in section 48(2) and subsections (1) to (3) of section 49 of this Act;

(*e*) require any person on premises which the inspector is authorised to enter by virtue of paragraph (*a*) of this paragraph to provide such assistance as the inspector reasonably considers necessary to enable the inspector to exercise effectively any power conferred on him by paragraphs (*a*) to (*d*) above;

(*f*) require any person to give to the inspector such information as the person possesses about the name and address of the packer and of any importer of a package which the inspector finds on premises he has entered by virtue of this sub-paragraph or paragraph 2 below.

2. If a justice of the peace, on sworn information in writing—

(*a*) is satisfied that there is reasonable ground to believe that—

(i) a package or a thing containing a package, or

(ii) any such equipment, record, document or certificate as is mentioned in paragraph 1 above,

is on any premises or that an offence under section 50 or 63 of this Act is being or is about to be committed on any premises, and

(*b*) is also satisfied either—

(i) that admission to the premises has been refused or that a refusal is apprehended and that notice of the intention to apply for a warrant has been given to the occupier, or

(ii) that an application for admission or the giving of such a notice would defeat the object of the entry or that the premises are unoccupied or that the occupier is temporarily absent and it might defeat the object of the entry to await his return,

the justice may by warrant under his hand, which shall continue in force for a period of one month, authorise an inspector to enter the premises if need be by force.

Application to Scotland.

3. (1) An inspector entering any premises by virtue of paragraph 1 or 2 above may take with him such other persons and such equipment as he considers necessary.

(2) It shall be the duty of an inspector who leaves premises which he has entered by virtue of paragraph 2 above and which are unoccupied or from which the occupier is temporarily absent to leave the premises as effectively secured against trespassers as he found them.

Power of seizure

4. Where an inspector has reasonable cause to believe that an offence under section 50, 54 or 63 of this Act or this Schedule has been committed and that any equipment, record, document, package or thing containing or contained in a package may be required as evidence in proceedings for the offence he may seize it and detain it for as long as it is so required[1].

Power to require information

5. (1) An inspector may serve, on any person carrying on business as the packer or importer of packages in the area for which the inspector is appointed an inspector, a notice requiring that person—

(*a*) to furnish the inspector from time to time with particulars of the kind specified in the notice of any marks which, otherwise than in pursuance of section 48(1)(*c*) of this Act, are applied from time to time to packages made up in that area by that person or (as the case may be) to packages imported by him, for the purpose of enabling the place where the packages were made up to be ascertained, and

(*b*) if the person has furnished particulars of a mark in pursuance of the notice and the mark ceases to be applied to such packages for that purpose, to give notice of the cesser to the inspector.

(2) A notice given by an inspector under this paragraph shall not require a person to furnish information which he does not possess.

Purchase of goods

6. (1) A local weights and measures authority shall have power to purchase goods, and to authorise any of its officers to purchase goods on behalf of the authority, for the purpose of ascertaining whether an offence under section 50, 54(2) or 63 of this Act has been committed.

(2) If an inspector breaks open a package in pursuance of paragraph (1)(*c*) above otherwise than on premises occupied by the packer or importer of the package and the package is not inadequate, it shall be the duty of the inspector, if the owner of the package requests him to do so, to buy the package on behalf of the local weights and measures authority for the area in which he broke it open.

Failure to provide assistance or information

7. Any person who without reasonable cause fails to comply with a requirement made of him in pursuance of paragraph 1(*e*) or (*f*) or 5 above shall be guilty of an offence[2].

---

1. See the Criminal Justice and Police Act 2001, Part 2 (PART I, ante). These provisions (summarised at para 1-180, ante) confer, by ss 50 and 51, additional powers of seizure of property in relation to searches carried out under existing powers. However, s 57 (retention of seized items) does not authorise the retention of any property which could not be retained under the provisions listed in s 57(1), which include para 4 of Sch 8 to the Weights and Measures Act 1985, if the property was seized under the new powers (ie those conferred by ss 50 and 51) in reliance on one of those powers (ie those conferred by the provisions listed in s 57(1)). Section 57(4) further provides that nothing in any of the provisions listed in s 57(1) authorises the retention of anything after an obligation to return it has arisen under Part 2.
2. For penalty see s 84, ante.

Weights and Measures (Solid Fuel) Regulations 1978[1]

(SI 1978/238)

8–32140 **1, 2.** *Citation, operation, interpretation.*

---

1. These Regulations are made under the Weights and Measures Act 1963, s 21(4) and Sch 6, para 3C (3), as amended. Reference should now be made to the 1985 Act.

8–32141 **4.** (1) The information required by paragraph 3C (2) (*a*) shall be in the following terms—
"All open sacks on this vehicle contain either 25kg or 50kg".

(2) The information—

(*a*) shall be marked on the vehicle or on a durable material securely affixed to the vehicle;
(*b*) shall be clearly and permanently inscribed in characters of a height of not less than 6 cm; and
(*c*) shall be easily read from either side of the vehicle.

8–32142 **5.** The statement required by paragraph 3C(2)(*b*) of the said Schedule 6, as so amended, to be displayed on a vehicle shall comply with the provisions of paragraph (2) of Regulation 4 above with the substitution in subparagraph (*b*) of that paragraph of 3 cm for 6 cm.

Weights and Measures Act 1963 (Cheese, Fish, Fresh Fruits and Vegetables, Meat and Poultry) Order 1984[1]

(SI 1984/1315 amended by 1985/988 and 1980 and the Criminal Justice Act 1988, s 52)

8–32160 **1.** *Citation, commencement, revocation.*

---

1. Made under the Weights and Measures Act 1963, ss 21(2), (3) and (5) and 54(1) and (4). Reference should be made to the 1985 Act.

Interpretation

8–32161 **2.** In this Order—

"cheese" means cheese, whether or not containing flavouring or colouring matter, and whether or not coated or mixed with other food for the purpose of giving the cheese a distinctive appearance or flavour, and includes processed cheese and cheese spread;
"countable produce" means fruit or vegetables specified in Part I of Schedule 1 to this Order;
"meat" means any part of an animal of any of the following descriptions, that is to say, cattle, sheep and swine; and
"soft fruits" means fruits of the following descriptions, that is to say, bilberries, blackberries, blackcurrants, boysenberries, brambles, cherries, cranberries, gooseberries, loganberries, mulberries, raspberries, redcurrants, strawberries, tayberries and whitecurrants.

8–32162 **3.** *Revoked.*

Cheese, fish, meat and poultry

8–32163 **4.** (1) This Article applies to food of any of the following descriptions that is to say—

(*a*) cheese;

(*b*) fish, meat or poultry of any description, whether fresh, chilled, frozen, salted, cooked or processed;
(*c*) sausage-meat in any form, whether cooked or uncooked; and
(*d*) any article which, though it also contains other food, consists substantially of cheese, fish, meat, poultry or sausage-meat,

other than dripping, lard, fish paste, meat paste, poultry paste and shredded suet, and any reference in this Article to poultry includes a reference to any part of any poultry.

(2) Subject to paragraphs (7) to (9) below, any food to which this Article applies which is not pre-packed, shall, if sold by retail, be sold only—

(*a*) by net weight; or
(*b*) if it is sold in a container which does not exceed the appropriate permitted weight specified in Table A of Schedule 2 to this Order, either by net weight or by gross weight.

(3) Subject to paragraphs (7) and (8) below, any food (other than cheese and fish) to which this Article applies shall, if sold otherwise than by retail, be sold only—

(*a*) by net weight; or
(*b*) if it sold in a container which does not exceed the appropriate permitted weight specified in Table A of Schedule 2 to this Order, either by net weight or by gross weight.

(4) Subject to paragraph (7) below, any food (other than cheese) to which this Article applies shall be pre-packed only if the container is marked with an indication of quantity by net weight: Provided that there shall be exempted from the requirements of this paragraph any food in a quantity of less than 5 g.

(5) Subject to paragraph (9) below—

(*a*) processed cheese;
(*b*) cheese spread; and
(*c*) natural cheese of any of the following descriptions, that is to say, Caerphilly, Cheddar, Cheshire, Derby, Double Gloucester, Dunlop, Edam, Gouda, Lancashire, Leicestershire and Wensleydale,

shall be pre-packed only if the container is marked with an indication of quantity by net weight.

(6) On or after 1st January 1986, cheese of any description other than that specified in paragraph (5) above shall be pre-packed only if the container is marked with an indication of quantity by net weight:

Provided that there shall be exempted from the requirements of this paragraph—

(*a*) whole Stilton cheese;
(*b*) any cheese in a quantity of less than 25 g and more than 10 kg; and
(*c*) any cheese sold by gross weight in a container which does not exceed the appropriate permitted weight specified in Table A of Schedule 2 to this Order, if the quantity is made known to the buyer before he pays for or takes possession of the goods.

(7) There shall be exempted from the requirements of paragraphs (2) to (4) of this Article—

(*a*) bath chaps, cheese, fish, meat or poultry pies, puddings and flans and sausage rolls, provided that in the case of more than one item of food pre-packed in a container not marked with an indication of quantity by net weight the number of items in the container is marked on the container or is clearly visible and capable of being easily counted through the container;
(*b*) any other goods (other than cheese) in a quantity of less than 5 g.

(8) There shall be exempted from the requirements of paragraphs (2) and (3) of this Article—

(*a*) cooked poultry;
(*b*) shellfish in shell, jellied fish, pickled fish and fried fish;
(*c*) any sale of fish made otherwise than from a market, shop, stall or vehicle;
(*d*) single cooked sausages in natural casings less than 500 g in weight; and
(*e*) sausage-meat products other than in sausage form when offered or exposed for sale as a single item in a quantity of less than 500 g.

(9) There shall be exempted from the requirements of paragraphs (2) and (5) of this Article any cheese in a quantity of less than 25 g.

Fresh fruits and vegetables other than potatoes

8–32164 **5.** (1) This Article applies to food consisting of fruits or vegetables of any description, other than potatoes—

(*a*) in the state in which they were harvested;
(*b*) in the said state apart from cleaning or trimming;
(*c*) in the case of beetroots, in the said state apart from having been cooked; or
(*d*) in the case of peas, in the said state apart from having been shelled.

(2) Where fruits or vegetables of any description to which this Article applies have been divided into pieces or have had part thereof removed or both, then, subject to paragraph 7 below, paragraph 6 shall apply to any food consisting of, or including any part of, any of those fruits or vegetables which have not been subjected to any further process.

(3) Subject to paragraphs (7) to (9) below, fruits and vegetables of any description, other than soft fruits and mushrooms, shall be pre-packed only if the container is marked with an indication of quantity by net weight or, in the case of countable produce, either by net weight or by number.

(4) Subject to paragraphs (7) and (9) below, fruits and vegetables of any description, other than soft fruits and mushrooms, which are not pre-packed, shall, if sold by retail, be sold only—

(*a*) by net weight;
(*b*) in the case of countable produce either by net weight or number; or
(*c*) if the food is sold in a container which does not exceed the appropriate permitted weight specified in Table A of Schedule 2 to this Order, either by net weight or by gross weight.

(5) Subject to paragraph (7) below, any fruits or vegetables consisting of soft fruits or mushrooms shall, if sold by retail, be sold only—

(*a*) by net weight; or
(*b*) if the food is sold in a container which does not exceed the appropriate permitted weight specified in Table B of Schedule 2 to this Order, either by net weight or by gross weight,

and the quantity shall be made known to the buyer before he pays for or takes possession of the food.

(6) Any food to which this paragraph applies by virtue of paragraph (2) above, shall—

(*a*) if not pre-packed and if sold by retail, be sold only by net weight or, in the case of countable produce, either by net weight or by number; or
(*b*) be pre-packed only if the container is marked with an indication of quantity by net weight or, in the case of countable produce, either by net weight or by number.

(7) The following shall be exempted from any requirement of paragraph (3), (4) or (5) above which would otherwise apply thereto, that is to say—

(*a*) food pre-packed in the same container with other goods (except potatoes) to which none of those requirements applies;
(*b*) food pre-packed in the same container with goods of two or more other descriptions to which some requirement of this Article would otherwise apply or which include potatoes;
(*c*) any food in a quantity of more than 5 kg;

and there shall be exempted from all requirements of this Article any goods in a quantity of less than 5 g.

(8) There shall be exempted from the requirements of paragraph (3) above a pre-packed collection of not more than eight articles of countable produce, if the container is such that all the articles can be clearly seen by a prospective buyer.

(9) There shall be exempted from the requirements of paragraphs (3) and (4) above any vegetables specified in Part II of Schedule 1 to this Order, if sold in a bunch.

(10) Where at any premises other than a vehicle or ship any food to which this Article applies has been sold by weight when made up in a container, and the sale is otherwise than by retail, the buyer may require all or any of the following weighings to be carried out at those premises, that is to say—

(*a*) a weighing of that container while the food is therein;
(*b*) a weighing of that container after the removal of the food therefrom;
(*c*) a weighing of a similar container which is empty,

and thereupon the seller shall either carry out or permit the buyer to carry out the weighing or weighings so required; and if the seller without reasonable cause contravenes this requirement he shall be guilty of an offence.

(11) The occupier of any premises at which any food to which this Article applies is made up in a container for sale by weight otherwise than by retail, or of any premises (other than a vehicle or ship) at which such food so made up is so sold, shall provide suitable weighing equipment and make that equipment available for any weighing or weighings required under the foregoing paragraph to be carried out at those premises; and if he without reasonable cause contravenes any of the requirements of this paragraph he shall be guilty of an offence.

(12) Except as provided in paragraph (13) below, any person guilty of an offence under paragraph (10) or (11) above shall be liable on summary conviction to a fine not exceeding **level 5** on the standard scale.

(13) Any person guilty of such an offence committed before 1st May 1984 shall be liable on summary conviction to a fine not exceeding **level 4** on the standard scale.

Multipacks

8–32165 **6.** Nothing in the previous provisions of this Order shall require any container to be marked with any information if all the following provisions are satisfied—

(*a*) the contents of the container in which any foods to which this Order applies are pre-packed consist of two or more packs of goods;
(*b*) where any pack, if sold individually, would be required by the Order to be marked with an indication as to the quantity of the goods, the pack is so marked;
(*c*)

(i) the container is marked with a description of the goods in each pack, the total number of packs containing goods of each description and where paragraph (*b*) above applies with an indication as to the quantity of the goods in each such pack; or

(ii) where each pack to which paragraph (*b*) above applies contains the same quantity of identical goods, an indication as to the quantity of the goods in at least one such pack is clearly visible, and the total number of such packs is clearly visible and capable of being easily counted, through the container; or

(iii) where each pack does not contain goods of the same description or does contain such goods but does not contain them in the same quantity, an indication as to the quantity of any goods in each pack to which paragraph (*b*) above applies, or if there are two or more identical such packs an indication as to the quantity of the goods in at least one of them, is clearly visible, and the total number of such packs of each description is clearly visible and capable of being easily counted, through the container.

8–32166 7. *Spent.*

8–32167

Articles 2 and 5(9)

SCHEDULE 1

PART I

COUNTABLE PRODUCE

COUNTABLE PRODUCE

Apples
Apricots
Artichokes (globe)
Aubergines
Avocados

Bananas
Beetroots (including cooked)

Cabbage
Cauliflower
Capsicum
Celery
Coconuts
Corn on the cob
Cucumber
Fennel
Figs (fresh)

Garlic
Grapefruit
Guavas

Kiwi fruit
Kohlrabi

Lemons
Lettuce
Limes

Mangoes
Marrows
Melons

Nectarines
Onions (other than spring)
Oranges

Passion fruit
Pawpaw
Peaches
Pears
Pineapple
Plums
Pomegranates
Pomelo
Pumpkins

Radishes

Shaddock
Soft citrus fruits

Tomatoes
Ugli

PART II

VEGETABLES WHICH MAY BE SOLD BY THE BUNCH

VEGETABLES WHICH MAY BE SOLD BY THE BUNCH

Asparagus
Beetroots
Carrots
Chives
Endives
Garlic
Mint
Mustard and cress
Onions (including spring)
Parsley
Radishes
Salad cress
Turnips
Watercress

8–32168

Articles 4 and 5

SCHEDULE 2

TABLES OF PERMITTED WEIGHTS FOR CONTAINERS

TABLE A

Gross weight	**Permitted weight of container**
Not exceeding 500 g	5 g
Exceeding 500 g	a weight at the rate of 10 g per kg of the gross weight.

TABLE B

Gross weight	**Permitted weight of container**
Not exceeding 250 g	a weight at the rate of 120 g per kg of the gross weight.
Exceeding 250 g but not exceeding 1 kg	a weight at the rate of 100 g per kg of the gross weight.
Exceeding 1 kg but not exceeding 3 kg	a weight at the rate of 90 g per kg of the gross weight.
Exceeding 3 kg	a weight at the rate of 60 g per kg of the gross weight.

Weights and Measures Act 1963 (Intoxicating Liquor) Order 1988[1]

(SI 1988/2039 amended by SI 1990/1550 and SI 1994/1883 and 2868)

8–32320 **1.** *Citation and commencement.*

(2) In this Order except where the context expressly otherwise requires—

"the Act" means the Weights and Measures Act 1985;

"beer", "cider", "made-wine" and "wine" have the same meanings respectively as in section 1 of the Alcoholic Liquor Duties Act 1979 but, in the case of "cider", as if the definition in section 1(6) did not include the words "(or perry)" in either place where they occur or "or pear"; and

references to a subheading are references to a subheading of the Combined Nomenclature of the European Economic Community.

(3) *Revocations.*

---

1. Made by the Secretary of State under ss 22(1) and (2), 24(1) and 86(1) of the Weights and Measures Act 1985.

8–32321 **2.** (1) Unless pre-packed in a securely closed container and except when sold as a constituent of a mixture of two or more liquids, beer or cider shall be sold by retail—

(*a*) only in a quantity of $^1/_3$ pint, $^1/_2$ pint or a multiple of $^1/_2$ pint; and

(*b*) subject to paragraph (2) below, where sold for consumption on the premises of the seller, only in a capacity measure of the quantity in question.

(2) Paragraph 1(*b*) above shall not apply where—

(*a*) the quantity of the intoxicating liquor the subject of the sale is ascertained by means of measuring equipment stamped in accordance with Regulation 16(2) of the Measuring Equipment (Intoxicating Liquor) Regulations 1983;

(*b*) the liquor in question is delivered directly from the measuring equipment into the container in which it is intended the buyer should receive it;

(*c*) the liquor in question is so delivered after the buyer has ordered it; and

(*d*) the measuring equipment (or that part of it from which the liquor is delivered) is installed in such a position that the delivery of the liquor into the container can readily be seen by customers in that part of the premises where the buyer ordered the liquor.

8–32322 **3.** (1) Subject to paragraphs (2) and (3) below, unless pre-packed in a securely closed container intoxicating liquor of any of the following descriptions, that is to say, gin, rum, vodka and whisky, shall be sold by retail for consumption on the premises at which it is sold only—

(*a*) in, or in a multiple of, one of the following quantities, which shall be the same for those parts of any licensed premises or licensed canteen within the meaning of the Licensing Act 1964 or the Licensing (Scotland) Act 1976 of which any person is the licensee and for all those liquors, that is to say, $^1/_4$ gill, $^1/_5$ gill and $^1/_6$ gill, 25 ml or 35 ml; and

(*b*) if there is displayed on those premises, in such a position and manner as to be readily available without special request for inspection by the buyer before the sale is made, a statement in writing showing in which of those quantities those liquors are offered for sale on those premises.

Provide that the quantities of $^1/_4$ gill, $^1/_5$ gill and $^1/_6$ gill referred to in sub-paragraph (*a*) of this paragraph shall not be permitted after 31st December 1994.

(2) Any such liquor shall be exempted from the requirements of this Article when it forms a constituent of a mixture of three or more liquids.

(3) Nothing in this Article shall make unlawful the sale at the express request of the buyer of any mixture of liquids containing any of those liquors in a quantity not otherwise permitted by this Article.

8–32323 **4.** (1) The intoxicating liquor and other liquids specified in column 1 of Schedule 1 to this Order shall be pre-packed or, in the case of those in Part III of Schedule 1, otherwise made up in a container for sale, only if they are made up in one of the quantities by volume specified in column 2, subject to the exceptions specified in column 3.

(2) This article applies to intoxicating liquor specified in column 1 in Part II of Schedule 1 to this Order made up after 31st December 1990, and to intoxicating liquor specified in column 1 in Part III of that Schedule made up after 31st December 1991.

8–32324 **5.** (1) Subject to paragraph (2) of this Article, wine and made-wine for consumption on the premises at which it is sold shall—

(*a*) be pre-packed only in one of the following quantities, that is to say, 25 cl, 50 cl, 75 cl, or 1 L;

(*b*) when not pre-packed, be sold only in those quantities; and (*c*) whether pre-packed or not, be sold only if a statement in writing showing the quantities in which wine or made-wine is for sale is either displayed on those premises in such a position and manner as to be readily available without special request for inspection by the buyer before the sale is made, or is contained in every winelist and menu which is available to the buyer on those premises before the sale is made and which indicates that wine or made-wine is for sale for consumption on those premises.

(2) Paragraph (1) above shall not apply in the case of wine or made-wine which—

(*a*) is pre-packed in a securely closed container whether or not it is to be decanted at the request of the buyer before being served; or
(*b*) subject to article 5A below is sold in the glass or other vessel from which it is intended to be drunk.

8–32325 **5A.** (1) For the purposes of this article "wine" shall mean only the intoxicating liquor and other liquids specified in column 1 of Part I of Schedule I to this Order.

(2) When sold in the glass or other vessel from which it is intended to be drunk, wine for consumption on the premises at which it is sold shall, on or after 1st January 1995, be sold only—

(*a*) in, or in a multiple of, the following quantities, that is to say, 125 ml and 175 ml; and
(*b*) if a statement in writing of the kind required by sub-paragraph (*c*) of article 5(1) above is displayed or otherwise provided as required by that subparagraph.

(3) Nothing in this article shall make unlawful the sale, at the express request of the buyer, of any mixture of liquids containing wine in a quantity not otherwise permitted by this article.

8–32326 **6.** (1) Intoxicating liquor and other liquids specified in column 1 of Schedule 1 to this Order shall be pre-packed in a closed container (or, in the case of those specified in Part III of that Schedule, otherwise made up in such a container for sale) only if the container is marked with an indication of quantity by volume, subject to the exemptions specified in column 4 of that Schedule.

(2) Intoxicating liquor of any other description shall be pre-packed in a closed container in a quantity of 5 ml or more but not exceeding 5 L only if the container is marked with an indication of quantity by volume.

8–32327 **7.** (1) Without prejudice to the provisions of section 25 of the Act, if Article 2(1)(*b*), 3(1)(*b*), 5(1)(*c*) or 5A(2)(*b*) above is contravened, the occupier of the premises in question shall be guilty of an offence.

(2) Any person guilty of an offence under paragraph (1) above shall be liable on summary conviction to a **fine not exceeding £2,000**.

8–32328 **8.** Nothing in this Order shall require any container to be marked with any information or to enclose intoxicating liquor or other liquids of a particular quantity if all the following provisions are satisfied—

(*a*) the contents of the container in which any intoxicating liquor or other liquids is pre-packed consist of two or more packs of goods;
(*b*) where the goods in any pack, if sold individually, would be required by the Order to be made up in a specified quantity, the goods in any such pack are so made up;
(*c*) where any pack, if sold individually, would be required by the Order to be marked with an indication as to the quantity of the goods, the pack is so marked;
(*d*)

(i) the container is marked with a description of the goods in each pack, the total number of packs containing goods of each description and, where paragraph (*c*) above applies with an indication as to the quantity of the goods in each such pack; or
(ii) where each pack to which paragraph (*c*) above applies contains the same quantity of identical goods, an indication as to the quantity of the goods in at least one such pack is clearly visible, and the total number of such packs is clearly visible and capable of being easily counted, through the container; or
(iii) where each pack does not contain goods of the same description or does contain such goods but does not contain them in the same quantity, an indication as to the quantity of any goods in each pack to which paragraph (*c*) above applies, or if there are two or more identical such packs an indication as to the quantity of the goods in at least one of them is clearly visible, and the total number of such packs of each description is clearly visible and capable of being easily counted, through the container.

8–32329

Articles 4 and 6

SCHEDULE

PART I

(1) Description and subheading	(2) Prescribed quantities	(3) Exceptions from prescribed quantities	(4) Exemptions from quantity marking
Wine of fresh grapes; grape must with fermentation prevented or arrested by the addition of alcohol, including wine made of unfermented grape juice blended with alcohol, grape must in fermentation or with fermentation arrested otherwise than by the addition of alcohol, of subheadings 2204 21 21 to 2204 21 39 inclusive, 2204 29 21 to 2204 29 39 inclusive and 2204 30 10	10 cl	(*a*) less than 5 ml, more than 10 L	less than 5 ml, more than 10 L
	18.7 cl (x)	(*b*) when made up in securely closed containers before 1st January 1989	
	25 cl	(*c*) wine to which article 5(1)(*a*) applies	
	37.5 cl	(*d*) not more than 25 cl, when for consumption on the premises of the seller	
	50 cl 75 cl 1 L 1.5 L 2 L 3 4 L 5 L 6 8 L 9 L 10 L (x) for consumption on board aircraft, ships and trains, or for sale duty-free		
"Yellow" wines entitled to use the following designations of origin: "Côtes du Jura", "Arbois", "L'Etoile" and "Château-Chalon"	62 cl		

PART II

(1) Description and subheading	(2) Prescribed quantities	(3) Exceptions from prescribed quantities	(4) Exemptions from quantity marking
Sparkling wine and wine in bottles with "mushroom" stoppers held in place by ties or fastenings, and wine otherwise made up with an excess pressure of not less than one bar but less than three bar, measured at a temperature of 20°C, of subheadings 2204 10 11, 2204 10 19, 2204 10 90, 2204 21 10 and 2204 29 10	12.5 cl	(*a*) less than 5 ml, more than 10 L	less than 5 ml, more than 10 L
	20 cl	(*b*) for consumption on board aircraft, ships and trains, or for sale duty-free	
	37.5 cl	(*c*) when made up in securely closed containers before 1st January 1991	

(1) Description and subheading	(2) Prescribed quantities	(3) Exceptions from prescribed quantities	(4) Exemptions from quantity marking
	75 cl 1.5 L 3 L 4.5 L 6 L 9 L		

PART III

(1) Description and subheading	(2) Prescribed quantities	(3) Exceptions from prescribed quantities	(4) Exemptions from quantity marking
Spirits, liqueurs and other spirituous beverages and compound alcoholic preparations of a kind used for the manufacture of beverages, of subheadings 2208 1010 to 2208 90 79 inclusive	2 cl 3 cl 4 cl 5 cl 7.1 cl 10 cl 20 cl 35 cl 50 cl 70 cl 1 L 1.125 L (x) 1.5 L 2 L 2.5 L 3 L 4.5 L 5 L (x) 10 L (x) (x) for non-retail sales only	(*a*) less than 5 ml, more than 10 L (*b*) less than 10 cl, where aerated water or soda has been added (*c*) for consumption on board aircraft, ships and trains, or for sale duty-free (*d*) when made up in securely closed containers before 1st January 1992	less than 5 ml, more than 10 L

Weights and Measures (Miscellaneous Foods) Order 1988[1]

(SI 1988/2040 amended by SI 1990/1550, SI 1994/2868 and SI 2005/3057)

8–32340 **1.** *Citation, commencement, revocation.*

1. Made by the Secretary of State under ss 22(1) and (2), 24(1) and 86(1) of the Weights and Measures Act 1985.

Interpretation

8–32341 **2.** In this Order, unless the context otherwise requires—

"the Act" means the Weights and Measures Act 1985;

"biscuits" includes wafers, rusks, crispbreads, extruded flatbread, oatcakes and matzos;

"bread" means bread in any form other than breadcrumbs and includes the following, and any part of the following, that is to say, fancy loaves and milk loaves and "loaf" in relation to bread includes a roll and a bap; and for the purposes of this Order any pre-packed sliced bread shall be deemed to be a whole loaf of bread and the pre-packing of sliced bread in any quantity by net weight shall be deemed to be the making for sale of a whole loaf of bread of that net weight;

"casein" and "caseinate" have the same meanings as they have in the Caseins and Caseinates Regulations 1985;

"chicory", "chicory extract paste", "coffee", "coffee mixture", "coffee extract paste", "instant chicory", "instant coffee", "liquid chicory extract" and "liquid coffee extract" have the same meanings as they have in the Coffee and Coffee Products Regulations 1978;

"chocolate confectionery", "flour confectionery" and "sugar confectionery" have the same meanings as they have in the Food Labelling Regulations 1984, except that "flour confectionery" includes food containing a filling which has an ingredient vegetable protein material or microbial protein material;

"cocoa product", "chocolate product", "fancy chocolate product", "container" in relation to these products and "reserved description" have the same meanings as they have in the Cocoa and Chocolate Products Regulations 1976; except that "cocoa product" and "chocolate product" shall include a product specially prepared for diabetics or to which a slimming claim (as defined in the said Regulations) is lawfully applied and which has been specially prepared in connection with that claim by the addition of any ingredient other than an edible substance as so defined;

"coffee bag" means a permeable sealed bag, which is intended to be immersed in water or to have water percolated through it, containing coffee, or a coffee mixture, or a combination of either coffee or a coffee mixture (or both) with a lesser quantity of instant coffee;

"condensed milk" and "dried milk" have the same meanings as they have in the Condensed Milk and Dried Milk Regulations 1977;

"liquid coffee and chicory products" means liquid coffee extract and liquid chicory extract, and blends thereof;

"Member State" means a member State as defined in Part II of Schedule 1 to the European Communities Act 1972, Norway, Iceland or Liechtenstein;

"milk" means cows' milk in any liquid form other than that of condensed milk (including evaporated milk) or of cream;

"potatoes" means potatoes in the state in which they were harvested or in that state apart from cleaning;

"preserved milk" means condensed milk (including evaporated milk) or dried milk;

"solid and paste coffee and chicory products" means instant coffee, coffee extract paste, instant chicory, chicory extract paste, and blends thereof, and extracts of blends of roasted coffee and roasted chicory.

General requirements for certain foods to be pre-packed in prescribed quantities and their containers to be quantity marked or, when not pre-packed, to be sold by retail by quantity

8-32342 **3.** (1) Subject to the following provisions of this Order, the foods specified in column 1 of Schedule 1 to this Order, other than chunk honey and comb honey shall be pre-packed or, in the case of sugar, otherwise made up in a container for sale, only if they are made up in one of the quantities by net weight, or, in the case of milk, by capacity measurement, specified in column 2 in relation to the foods, subject to the exceptions specified in column 3.

(2) Subject to the following provisions of this Order, the foods specified in column 1 of Schedule 1 to this Order, other than milk, shall be pre-packed or, in the case of honey, cocoa products and chocolate products, solid and paste coffee and chicory products and sugar, otherwise made up in a container for sale, only if the container is marked with an indication of quantity by net weight, subject to the exemptions specified in column 4.

(3) Subject to the following provisions of this Order, the foods specified in column 1 of Schedule 1 to this Order, other than bread and chunk honey and comb honey and milk, shall, when not pre-packed, if sold by retail be sold only by net weight, subject to the exceptions specified in column 5.

(4) Paragraph (1) shall not apply to a pre-packed food which is made up in a quantity other than as specified in column 2 of Schedule 1, provided the package was brought into the United Kingdom from another Member State in which a package made up in such a quantity could lawfully be marketed.

Provision for the containers of certain foods not sold by retail to be accompanied by a document indicating quantity

8-32343 **4.** (1) In the case of solid and paste coffee and chicory products, cocoa products and chocolate products, honey, caseins and caseinates or preserved milk for human consumption pre-packed or otherwise made up in a container for sale, the information required by Article 3(2) above or, as the case may be 7, 9(2) or 12 below to be marked on the container may, if—

(*a*) the foods are not sold by retail; and

(*b*) the net weight of the foods is not less than the particular quantities specified in paragraph (2) below in relation to the foods,

be given at the time when they are sold in a document accompanying the container and containing an indication of quantity by net weight.

(2) The quantities referred to in paragraph (1) above are:

solid and paste coffee and chicory products 5 kg
cocoa products and chocolate products .... 10 kg

honey ....10 kg
caseins and caseinates ....10 kg
preserved milk for human consumption ....10 kg

Special provisions in respect of particular foods

Biscuits and shortbread

8–32344 **5.** (1) Article 3(1) and (2) above shall not apply in relation to biscuits which have been pre-packed on the same premises as those on which they were produced, and either:—

(*a*) the biscuits are in the possession of the producer for sale by him by retail on those premises; or

(*b*) if the producer has agreed to sell or has sold the biscuits, he agreed to sell or sold them by retail on those premises.

(2) Biscuits to which paragraph (1) above applies (other than wafer biscuits which are not cream-filled) shall be pre-packed only if the container is marked with an indication of quantity by net weight:

Provided that there shall be exempted from the requirements of this paragraph biscuits pre-packed in a quantity not exceeding 100 g.

(3) Shortbread shall be pre-packed only if the container is marked with an indication of quantity by net weight:

Provided that there shall be exempted from the requirements of this paragraph shortbread—

(*a*) where made up in a quantity not exceeding 50 g; or

(*b*) consisting of a piece or pieces each weighing 200 g or more if the number of pieces in the container, if more than one, is marked on the container or is clearly visible and capable of being easily counted through the container.

(4) Wafer biscuits which are not cream-filled shall be pre-packed only if the container is marked with an indication of quantity by number or, in the case of a container marked with the EEC mark within the meaning of section 54 of the Act, only if it is marked with an indication of quantity by net weight.

(5) Wafer biscuits which are not cream-filled and which are not pre-packed shall if sold by retail be sold only by number.

(6) Shortbread, except where the quantity does not exceed eight pieces, shall, when not pre-packed, if sold by retail be sold only by net weight.

Bread

8–32345 **6.** (1) Subject to paragraph (2) below, a whole loaf of bread of a net weight exceeding 300 g, when not pre-packed, shall be made for sale only if it is of a net weight of 400 g or a multiple of 400 g.

(2) There shall be exempted from the requirements of paragraph (1) above any sale in pursuance of a contract for the supply of bread for consumption on the premises of the buyer if the contract provides for each delivery of bread thereunder to be of a specified aggregate quantity of not less than 25 kg and for the weighing of the bread on delivery.

Caseins and Caseinates

8–32346 **7.** Caseins and caseinates for human consumption in a quantity of not less than 5 g shall be pre-packed or otherwise made up in a container for sale only if the container is marked with an indication of quantity by net weight.

Cocoa and chocolate products

8–32347 **8.** (1) Subject to paragraph (2) below, cocoa products and chocolate products not specified in Schedule 1 to this Order shall be pre-packed or otherwise made up in a container for sale only if the container is marked with an indication of quantity by net weight:

Provided that there shall be exempted from the requirements of this paragraph products pre-packed in a quantity by net weight of less than 50 g.

(2) Nothing in paragraph (1) above shall require a container to be marked with an indication of quantity by net weight if it is a container in which fancy chocolate products are pre-packed, except that when the products are on sale by retail the exemption provided by this paragraph shall apply only if an indication of quantity by net weight is given on a ticket or notice displayed on or in immediate proximity to the products.

(3) Except in the case of an article the net weight of which is less than 50 g cocoa products and chocolate products which are not pre-packed shall, when sold by retail, be sold only by net weight.

Coffee and chicory products

8–32348 **9.** (1) Liquid coffee and chicory products in a quantity of not less than 5 ml shall be pre-packed or otherwise made up in a container for sale only if the container is marked with an indication of quantity by capacity measurement.

(2) Where the contents of a container in which solid and paste coffee and chicory products or liquid coffee and chicory products are pre-packed or otherwise made up for sale consists of packs of such products not intended for individual sale, the container shall, in addition to any marking required by Article 3(2) and paragraph (1) above, be marked with the total number of such packs.

Liquid edible oil

8–32349 **10.** Liquid edible oil shall be pre-packed only if the container is marked with an indication of quantity by volume:
Provided that there shall be exempted from the requirements of this Article liquid edible oil pre-packed in a quantity of less than 5 ml or more than 20 L.

Milk

8–32350 **11.** (1) Milk which is not pre-packed shall be sold only by capacity measurement or by net weight.

(2) If in the case of any pre-packed milk made up in a quantity of less than 250 ml its container is clearly and conspicuously marked with a statement in writing that it is not for sale otherwise than by means of a vending machine, then, notwithstanding that the milk is made up in a quantity other than one of those specified in column 2 of Schedule 1 to this Order in relation to milk, a person shall not by reason only of that fact be guilty of an offence under section 25(2) of the Act—

(*a*) in respect of a sale of that milk by that or any other person if the sale is by means of a vending machine or is otherwise than by retail; or

(*b*) in respect of the possession of that milk by that or any other person if the milk is shown to be in that possession—

(i) for sale by means of a vending machine which complies with paragraph (3) below; or

(ii) for sale otherwise than by retail; or

(iii) for delivery after sale otherwise than by retail.

(3) Milk shall be sold by means of, or offered or exposed for sale in, a vending machine only if there is displayed on or in the machine—

(*a*) an indication of the quantity by capacity measurement of the milk comprised in each item for sale by means of that machine; and

(*b*) except where the machine is on premises at which the seller carries on business, a statement of the name and address of the seller.

Preserved milk

8–32351 **12.** Preserved milk for human consumption in a quantity of not less than 5 g shall be pre-packed or otherwise made up in a container for sale only if the container is marked with an indication of quantity by net weight.

Potatoes

8–32352 **13.** (1) Where at any premises other than a vehicle or ship any potatoes have been sold by weight when made up in a container, and the sale is otherwise than by retail, the buyer may require all or any of the following weighings to be carried out at those premises, that is to say—

(*a*) a weighing of that container while the potatoes are therein;

(*b*) a weighing of that container after the removal of the potatoes therefrom;

(*c*) a weighing of a similar container which is empty,

and thereupon the seller shall either carry out or permit the buyer to carry out the weighing or weighings so required; and if the seller without reasonable cause contravenes this requirement he shall be guilty of an offence.

(2) The occupier of any premises at which any potatoes are made up in a container for sale by weight otherwise than by retail, or of any premises (other than a vehicle or ship) at which such potatoes so made up are so sold, shall provide suitable weighing equipment and make that equipment available for any weighing or weighings required under the foregoing paragraph to be carried out at those premises; and if he without reasonable cause contravenes any of the requirements of this paragraph he shall be guilty of an offence.

(4) Any person guilty of an offence under this Article shall be liable on summary conviction to a fine not exceeding **£2,000**.

8–32353 **14.** Potatoes, which are not pre-packed shall, if sold by retail, be sold only—

(*a*) by net weight; or

(*b*) if the food is sold in a container which does not exceed the appropriate permitted weight specified in the Table in Schedule 2 to this Order, either by net weight or gross weight.

Miscellaneous foods to be marked when pre-packed with quantity by number

8–32354 **15.** (1) Subject to paragraph (2) below, foods of any of the following descriptions, that is to say—

(*a*) cereal biscuit breakfast foods, other than foods in the case of which none of the biscuits weighs more than 10 g;
(*b*) flour confectionery, except when consisting of uncooked pastry or uncooked pastry cases, not containing any filling, or shortbread;
(*c*) fruit preservative tablets, rennet tablets, saccharin tablets, soft drink tablets and sweetening tablets;
(*d*) shell eggs;
(*e*) vanilla pods;
(*f*) capsule and tablet foods,

shall be pre-packed only if the container is marked with an indication of quantity by number.

(2) There shall be exempted from the requirements of this Article—

(*a*) flour confectionery, if the number of items in the container is clearly visible and capable of being easily counted through the container; and
(*b*) any foods in a quantity by number of one.

Other pre-packed foods

8–32355 **16.** (1) This Article applies to foods of any description which are not goods—

(*a*) required by any other provision of this Order or under or by virtue of any other provision of the Act to be pre-packed only if the container is marked with an indication of quantity; or
(*b*) in the case of which when sold pre-packed (whether on any sale or on a sale of any particular description) the quantity of the goods sold expressed in a particular manner is required by or under any such provision to be made known to the buyer at or before a particular time; or
(*c*) expressly exempted by any such provision from all such requirements which would otherwise apply thereto.

(2) Subject to paragraph (3) below, foods to which this Article applies shall be pre-packed only if the container is marked with an indication of quantity either by net weight or by capacity measurement.

(3) The following shall be exempted from the requirements of this Article, that is to say—

(*a*) bread, including bun loaves, fruit loaves, malt loaves and fruited malt loaves;
(*b*) food to which Articles 4 and 5 of the Weights and Measures Act 1963 (Cheese, Fish, Fresh Fruits and Vegetables, Meat and Poultry) Order 1984 apply, other than dates;
(*c*) freeze drinks in a quantity of less than 50 ml;
(*d*) herbs, whole and sifted except saffron, in a quantity of less than 25 g;
(*e*) iced lollies and water ices;
(*f*) intoxicating liquor to which Article 6 of the Weights and Measures (Intoxicating Liquor) Order 1988 applies;
(*g*) milk;
(*h*) potato crisps and other similar products commonly known as snack foods in a quantity of less than 1 oz up to and including 30th June 1989 and thereafter in a quantity of less than 25 g;
(*i*) single portion vending machine beverage packs in a quantity of less than 25 g or of less than 25 ml whether or not they contain other foods to which this Article does not apply;
(*j*) single toffee apples;
(*k*) soft drinks of any description in a syphon;
(*l*) sugar confectionery consisting of rock or barley sugar in sticks or novelty shapes;
(*m*) sugar confectionery not included in paragraph (*l*) above, and chocolate confectionery, in a quantity of less than 50 g;
(*n*) goods of any other description, except saffron, in a quantity of less than 5 g or of less than 5 ml.

Multipacks

8–32356 **17.** (1) Nothing in the previous provisions of this Order shall require any container to be marked with any information or to enclose foods of a particular quantity if all the following provisions are satisfied—

(*a*) the contents of the container in which any foods to which the Order applies are pre-packed or otherwise made up in the container for sale consist of two or more packs of goods;
(*b*) where the goods in any pack, if sold individually, would be required by the Order to be made up in a specified quantity, the goods in any such pack are so made up;
(*c*) where any pack, if sold individually, would be required by the Order to be marked with an indication as to the quantity of the goods, the pack is so marked;
(*d*)

(i) the container is marked with a description of the goods in each pack, the total number of packs containing goods of each description and where paragraph (*c*) above applies with an indication as to the quantity of the goods in each such pack; or
(ii) where each pack to which paragraph (*c*) above applies contains the same quantity of identical goods, an indication as to the quantity of the goods in at least one such pack

is clearly visible, and the total number of such packs is clearly visible and capable of being easily counted, through the container; or

(iii) where each pack does not contain goods of the same description or does contain such goods but does not contain them in the same quantity, an indication as to the quantity of any goods in each pack to which paragraph (*c*) above applies, or if there are two or more identical such packs an indication as to the quantity of the goods in at least one of them, is clearly visible, and the total number of such packs of each description is clearly visible and capable of being easily counted, through the container.

(2) Where the provisions of both Article 4 and paragraph (1) above apply in a particular case, the information permitted by paragraph (1)(*d*)(i) above to be marked on the container may be given in a document accompanying the container.

Application of Section 25 of the Act as modified in relation to certain foods

8–32357 **18.** (1) Section 25(2) and (3) of the Act shall apply in the case of any solid and paste coffee and chicory products, cocoa products and chocolate products, honey, caseins and caseinates or preserved milk for human consumption pre-packed or otherwise made up in a container for sale where the information required by Article 3(2), 7, 9(2) or 12, or permitted by Article 17(1)(*d*)(i), to be marked on the container is given in a document accompanying the container in accordance with Article 4 or 17(2) with the following modifications—

(*a*) in section 25(2) the words "whether the sale is, or is to be, by retail or otherwise" shall be omitted; and

(*b*) in paragraphs (*d*) and (*e*) of section 25(3)—

(i) after the word "information" there shall be inserted the words "or is accompanied by a document containing particular information"; and

(ii) after the words "so marked" there shall be inserted the words "or accompanied".

(2) Where subsections (2) and (3) of section 25 of the Act applies by virtue of paragraph (1) above, a person shall not be guilty of an offence under the said subsection (2) by reason only of—

(*a*) having in his possession for sale, or

(*b*) having in his possession for delivery after sale, or

(*c*) causing or suffering any other person to have in his possession for sale or for delivery after sale,

solid and paste coffee and chicory products, cocoa products and chocolate products, honey, caseins and caseinates or preserved milk for human consumption pre-packed or otherwise made up in a container for sale otherwise than in a container so accompanied.

Article 3

8–32358

SCHEDULE 1

FOODS

(1) **Foods**	(2) **Prescribed quantities (pre-packed foods)**	(3) **Exceptions from prescribed quantities**	(4) **Exemptions from quantity marking (pre-packed foods)**	(5) **Exceptions from quantity requirement (foods not pre-packed)**
Barley kernels, pearl barley, rice (including ground rice and rice flakes), sago, semolina and tapioca.	(1) 125 g, 250 g, 375 g, 500 g or a multiple of 500 g. (2) 125 g, 250 g, 375g, 500 g or a multiple of 500 g.	75 g or less, more than 10 kg.	less than 5 g.	—
Biscuits, other than wafer biscuits which are not cream-filled.	100 g, 125 g, 150 g, 200 g, 250 g, 300 g, or a multiple of 100 g.	85 g or less, more than 5 kg.	50 g or less	8 or less.
Bread in the form of a whole loaf.	400 g or a multiple of 400 g.	(1) where the net weight of each loaf is 300 g or less. (2) any sale in pursuance of a contract for the supply of bread for consumption on the premises of the buyer, if the contract provides for each delivery of bread thereunder to be a specified aggregate quantity of not less than 25 kg and for the weighing of the bread on delivery.	where the net weight of each loaf is less than 300 g and the number of items if more than one in the container is marked on the container or is clearly visible and capable of being easily counted through the container.	—
Cereal breakfast foods in flake form, other than cereal biscuit breakfast foods.	125 g, 250 g, 375 g, 500 g, 750 g, 1 kg, 1.5 kg or a multiple of 1 kg.	50 g or less, more than 10 kg.	less than 5 g.	—
Coffee, coffee mixtures and coffee bags.	57 g, 75 g, 113 g, 125 g, 227 g, 250 g, 340 g, 454 g, 500 g, 680 g, 750 g or a multiple of 454 g or of 500 g. *Note* In the case of coffee bags the prescribed quantities and quantity marking relate to the contents.	less than 25 g, more than 5 kg.	less than 5 g.	—
Coffee extracts and chicory extracts consisting of solid and paste coffee and chicory products.	50 g, 100 g, 200 g, 250 g, (for mixtures of coffee extracts and chicory extracts only), 300 g (for coffee extracts only), 500 g, 750 g, 1 kg, 1.5 kg, 2 kg, 2.5 kg, 3 kg or a multiple of 1 kg.	25 g or less, more than 10 kg.	less than 5 g.	—

SCHEDULE 1 (*Contd*)

FOODS

(1) **Foods**	(2) **Prescribed quantities (pre-packed foods)**	(3) **Exceptions from prescribed quantities**	(4) **Exemptions from quantity marking (pre-packed foods)**	(5) **Exceptions from quantity requirement (foods not pre-packed)**
Dried fruits of any one or more of the following descriptions, that is to say, apples (including dried apple rings), apricots, currants, dates, figs, muscatels, nectarines, peaches, pears (including dried pear rings), prunes, raisins, sultanas and dried fruit salad.	125 g, 250 g, 375 g, 500 g, 1 kg, 1.5 kg, 7.5 kg, or a multiple of 1 kg.	75 g or less, more than 10 kg.	less than 5 g.	—
Dried vegetables of any of the following descriptions, that is to say, beans, lentils and peas (including split peas).	125 g, 250 g, 375 g, 500 g, 1 kg, 1.5 kg, 7.5 kg, or a multiple of 1 kg.	100 g or less, more than 10 kg.	less than 5 g.	—
Edible fats of any of the following descriptions— (*a*) butter, margarine, any mixture of butter and margarine, and low fat spreads (butter or margarine substitutes); (*b*) dripping and shredded suet; (*c*) lard and compound cooking fat and substitutes therefor; (*d*) solidified edible oil (except in gel form).	50 g, 125 g, 250 g, 500 g, or a multiple of 500 g up to and including 4 kg or thereafter a multiple of 1 kg up to and including 10 kg.	(1) in the case of those of the description in paragraph (*a*) 25 g or less, more than 10 kg. (2) in other cases, less than 5 g, more than 10 kg.	less than 5 g.	—
Flour, namely flour of bean, maize, pea, rice, rye, soya bean or wheat and flour products of any of the following descriptions, that is to say— (*a*) cake flour, other than cake mixtures and sponge mixtures; (*b*) cornflour, other than blancmange powders and custard powders; (*c*) self-raising flour.	125 g, 250 g, 500 g, or a multiple of 500 g and in the case of cornflour, in addition 375 g and 750 g.	50 g or less, more than 10 kg.	less than 5 g.	—

SCHEDULE 1 (*Contd*)

FOODS

(1) **Foods**	(2) **Prescribed quantities (pre-packed foods)**	(3) **Exceptions from prescribed quantities**	(4) **Exemptions from quantity marking (pre-packed foods)**	(5) **Exceptions from quantity requirement (foods not pre-packed)**
Honey.	57 g, 113 g, 227 g, 340 g, 454 g, 680 g or a multiple of 454 g.	less than 50 g.	less than 5 g.	—
Jam and marmalade, other than diabetic jam or marmalade. Jelly preserves.	57 g, 113 g, 227 g, 340 g, 454 g, 680 g or a multiple of 454 g.	less than 50 g.	less than 5 g.	—
Milk other than milk in a returnable container	189 ml, 200 ml, 250 ml, 284 ml, 500 ml, 750 ml or a multiple of 284 ml or of 500 ml.	50 ml or less.	—	—
Milk in a returnable container	(1) 1/3 pt, 1/2 pt or a multiple of 1/2 pt. (2) 200 ml, 250 ml, 500 ml, 750 ml or a multiple of 500 ml.	50 ml or less.	—	—
Molasses, syrup and treacle.	57 g, 113 g, 227 g, 340 g, 454 g, 680 g or a multiple of 454 g.	less than 50 g.	less than 5 g.	—
Oat products namely (*a*) flour of oats; (*b*) oatflakes and oatmeal	50 g or less, more than 10 kg.	50 g or less, more than 10 kg.	less than 5 g.	—
Pasta.	125 g, 250g, 375 g, 500 g, or a multiple of 500 g.	50 g or less.	less than 5 g.	—
Potatoes.	500 g, 750 g, 1 kg, 1.5 kg, 2 kg, 2.5 kg or a multiple of 2.5 kg up to and including 15 kg, 20 kg or 25 kg.	(1) where the net weight of each potato is not less than 175 g. (2) less than 5 g, more than 25 kg.	(1) where the net weight of each potato is not less than 175 g and the container is marked with an indication of quantity by number and with a statement to the effect that each potato in the container is of a net weight not less than a weight specified in grams, whether the weight so specified is 175 g or a greater weight. (2) less than 5 g	—

SCHEDULE 1 (*Contd*)

FOODS

(1) **Foods**	(2) **Prescribed quantities (pre-packed foods)**	(3) **Exceptions from prescribed quantities**	(4) **Exemptions from quantity marking (pre-packed foods)**	(5) **Exceptions from quantity requirement (foods not pre-packed)**
Salt.	125 g, 250 g, 500 g, 750 g, 1 kg, 1.5 kg, or a multiple of 1 kg up to and including 10 kg, 12.5 kg, 25 kg or 50 kg.	100 g or less.	less than 5 g.	—
Sugar.	125 g, 250 g, 500 g, 750 g, 1 kg, 1.5 kg, 2 kg, 2.5 kg, 3 kg, 4 kg, or 5 kg.	100 g or less, more than 5 kg.	less than 50 g.	—
Tea in a tea bag, namely a permeable sealed bag, containing tea, which is intended to be immersed in water in the course of preparation to drink.	50 g, 125 g 250 g, 500 g, 750 g, 1 kg, 1.5 kg, 2 kg, 2.5 kg, 3 kg, 4 kg or 5 kg. *Note* In the case of tea in a tea bag the prescribed quantities and quantity marking relate to the contents.	25 g or less, more than 5 kg.	less than 5 g.	
Tea, other than instant tea or tea in a tea bag.	50 g, 125 g, 250 g, 500 g, 750 g, 1 kg, 1.5 kg, 2 kg, 2.5 kg, 3 kg, 4 kg or 5 kg and in the case of tea [(other than instant tea or tea in a tea bag)] packed in tins or glass or wooden containers, in addition 100 g, and 300 g.	25 g or less, more than 5 kg.	less than 5 g.	

8–32359
Article 14

SCHEDULE 2
TABLE OF PERMITTED WEIGHTS FOR CONTAINERS

Gross weight	Permitted weight of container
Not exceeding 500 g	5 g
Exceeding 500 g	a weight at the rate of 10 g per kg of the gross weight

Units of Measurement Regulations 1995[1]

(SI 1995/1804)

8–32360 **1. Citation and commencement.** These Regulations may be cited as the Units of Measurement Regulations 1995 and shall come into force on 1st October 1995.

1. Made by the Secretary of State, being a Minister designated for the purposes of s 2(2) of the European Communities Act 1972.

8–32361 **2. Interpretation.** In these Regulations—

"Act" includes a local and personal or private Act, an Act of the Parliament of Northern Ireland and a Measure of the Northern Ireland Assembly;

"the commencement date", subject to regulation 4 below, means 1st October 1995;

"corresponding metric unit", in relation to a relevant imperial unit, means the unit of measurement specified in relation to the relevant imperial unit in the second column of the Schedule to these Regulations;

"existing provision" means any of the following, namely—

(*a*) a provision of any Act passed, or of any subordinate legislation made, before the commencement date;

(*b*) a provision of any contract, agreement, licence, authority, undertaking or statement made or given before that date; and

(*c*) a provision of any deed, instrument or document made before that date;

"relevant imperial unit" means a unit of measurement specified in the first column of the Schedule to these Regulations;

"subordinate legislation" means Orders in Council, orders, rules, regulations, schemes, warrants, byelaws and other instruments made under any Act; and

"the Units of Measurement Directive" means the Directive of the Council of the European Communities dated 20th December 1979 (No 80/181/EEC) on the approximation of the laws of member States relating to units of measurement.

8–32362 **3. Conversion of imperial units of measurement.** (1) Subject to the following provisions of these Regulations, where—

(*a*) an existing provision authorises or requires a measurement to be made, or an indication of quantity to be expressed, in a relevant imperial unit,

(*b*) the provision has effect for economic, public health, public safety or administrative purposes, and

(*c*) the provision has legal effect on or after the commencement date,

the provision shall, unless the context otherwise requires, be construed on or after that date as authorising or requiring the measurement to be made, or the indication of quantity to be expressed, in the corresponding metric unit.

(2) Subject to the following provisions of these Regulations, where—

(*a*) an existing provision contains a reference to an indication of quantity expressed in a relevant imperial unit,

(*b*) the provision has effect for economic, public health, public safety or administrative purposes, and

(*c*) the provision has legal effect on or after the commencement date,

the provision shall, unless the context otherwise requires, be construed on or after that date as if the indication of quantity concerned were expressed in the corresponding metric unit.

(3) Subject to paragraph (4) below, any conversion of an indication of quantity expressed in a relevant imperial unit which is required to be made by virtue of paragraph (2) above shall be made by using the metric equivalent specified in relation to the relevant imperial unit in the third column of the Schedule to these Regulations.

(4) Any conversion of an indication of quantity expressed in degrees Fahrenheit which is required to be made by virtue of paragraph (2) above shall be made by subtracting thirty-two and multiplying the result by five-ninths.

8–32363 **4. Later application of regulation 3 in relation to certain uses of imperial units.** In relation to any of the following uses of relevant imperial units which are permitted by Article 1(*d*) of the Units of Measurement Directive, that is to say—

(*a*) the use of the fathom for marine navigation,
(*b*) the use of the pint or fluid ounce for beer, cider, water, lemonade and fruit juice in returnable containers,
(*c*) the use of the pound or ounce (avoirdupois) for goods sold loose from bulk, and
(*d*) the use of the therm for the supply of gas,

regulation 3 above shall be treated as coming into force on 1st January 2000 and that date shall be treated as the commencement date for the purposes of these Regulations.

8–32364 5. Exceptions. (1) Nothing in these Regulations shall apply in relation to any supplementary indication; and in this paragraph "supplementary indication" has the same meaning as it has in section 8(5A) of the Weights and Measures Act 1985.

(2) Nothing in these Regulations shall apply in relation to any of the uses of relevant imperial units which are permitted by Article 1(*b*) of the Units of Measurement Directive, that is to say—

(*a*) the use of the mile, yard, foot or inch for road traffic signs, distance and speed measurement,
(*b*) the use of the pint for dispensing draught beer and cider;
(*c*) the use of the pint for milk in returnable containers;
(*d*) the use of the acre for land registration; and
(*e*) the use of the troy ounce for transactions in precious metals.

(3) Nothing in these Regulations shall apply in relation to any use of a relevant imperial unit which is permitted by Article 2(*b*) of the Units of Measurement Directive (use in the field of air and sea transport and rail traffic of units laid down in international conventions or agreements).

(4) Nothing in these Regulations shall apply in relation to any contract to which regulation 11(1) of the Units of Measurement Regulations 1986 applies.

8–32365 6. Revocation. Regulation 4(3) of the Units of Measurement Regulations 1994, and the paragraphs added by it to regulation 11 of the Units of Measurement Regulations 1986, are hereby revoked.

8–32366

Regulations 2 and 3

SCHEDULE

RELEVANT IMPERIAL UNITS, CORRESPONDING METRIC UNITS AND METRIC EQUIVALENTS

Relevant imperial unit	Corresponding metric unit	Metric equivalent
		Length
inch	centimetre	2.54 centimetres
hand	metre	0.1016 metre
foot	metre	0.3048 metre
yard	metre	0.9144 metre
fathom	metre	1.8288 metres
chain	metre	20.1168 metres
furlong	kilometre	0.201168 kilometre
mile	kilometre	1.609344 kilometres
nautical mile (UK)	metre	1853 metres
		Area
square inch	square centimetre	6.4516 square centimetres
square foot	square metre	0.09290304 square metre
square yard	square metre	0.83612736 square metre
rood	square metre	1011.7141056 square metres
acre	square metre	4046.8564224 square metres
square mile	square kilometre	2.589988110336 square kilometres
		Capacity
fluid ounce	millilitre	28.4130625 millilitres
gill	litre	0.1420635125 litre
pint	litre	0.56826125 litre
quart	litre	1.1365225 litres
gallon	litre	4.54609 litres
		Pressure
inch of water	pascal	249.08891 pascals
		Mass
grain	gram	0.06479891 gram
dram	gram	1.7718451953125 grams
ounce (avoirdupois)	gram	28.349523125 grams
troy ounce	gram	31.1034768 grams
pound	kilogram	0.45359237 kilogram
stone	kilogram	6.35029318 kilograms
quarter	kilogram	12.70058636 kilograms
cental	kilogram	45.359237 kilograms
hundredweight	kilogram	50.80234544 kilograms
ton	tonne	1.0160469088 tonnes
		Force
pound-force	newton	4.4482216152605 newtons
ton-force	kilonewton	9.96401641818352 kilonewtons

Relevant imperial unit	Corresponding metric unit	Metric equivalent
	Volume	
cubic inch	cubic centimetre	16.387064 cubic centimetres
cran	cubic decimetre	170.478375 cubic decimetres
cubic foot	cubic metre	0.028316846592 cubic metre
bushel	cubic metre	0.03636872 cubic metre
cubic yard	cubic metre	0.764554857984 cubic metre
	Power	
horsepower	kilowatt	0.7456998715822702 2 kilowatt
	Temperature	
degree Fahrenheit	degree Celsius	(See regulation 3(4))
	Energy	
foot pound-force	joule	1.3558179483314004 joules
British thermal unit	kilojoule	1.05505585257348 kilojoules
therm	megajoule	105.505585257348 megajoules
	Illuminance	
foot candle	lux	10.763910416709 lux
	Speed	
knot (UK)	metres per second	0.51477 metres per second

WITNESSES (PUBLIC INQUIRIES)

8–32799 This title contains the following statute—

8–32810 Inquiries Act 2005

8–32800 The **Witnesses (Public Inquiries) Protection Act 1892** (55 & 56 Vict c 64) protects witnesses who give evidence before any Royal Commission or any committee of either House of Parliament or other public inquiry. A person who threatens, or in any way punishes, damnifies or injures such a witness is liable to a penalty of **level 3** on the standard scale **or three months' imprisonment** (s 2). A prosecution for an offence under this Act may be heard and determined by a magistrates' court.

[Witnesses (Public Inquiries) Protection Act 1892, s 3, as amended by the Criminal Law Act 1977, Sch 13 and the Criminal Justice Act 1982, ss 38 and 46—summarised.]

Inquiries Act 2005[1]

(2005 c 12)

Constitution of inquiry

8–32810 1. Power to establish inquiry. (1) A Minister may cause an inquiry to be held under this Act in relation to a case where it appears to him that—

(a) particular events have caused, or are capable of causing, public concern, or
(b) there is public concern that particular events may have occurred.

(2) In this Act "Minister" means—

(a) a United Kingdom Minister;
(b) the Scottish Ministers;
(c) a Northern Ireland Minister;

and references to a Minister also include references to the National Assembly for Wales.

(3) References in this Act to an inquiry, except where the context requires otherwise, are to an inquiry under this Act.

[Inquiries Act 2005, s 1.]

Inquiry proceedings

8–32811 17. Evidence and procedure. (1) Subject to any provision of this Act or of rules under section 41, the procedure and conduct of an inquiry are to be such as the chairman of the inquiry may direct.

(2) In particular, the chairman may take evidence on oath, and for that purpose may administer oaths.

(3) In making any decision as to the procedure or conduct of an inquiry, the chairman must act with fairness and with regard also to the need to avoid any unnecessary cost (whether to public funds or to witnesses or others).

[Inquiries Act 2005, s 17.]

8–32812 **18. Public access to inquiry proceedings and information.** (1) Subject to any restrictions imposed by a notice or order under section 19, the chairman must take such steps as he considers reasonable to secure that members of the public (including reporters) are able—

(a) to attend the inquiry or to see and hear a simultaneous transmission of proceedings at the inquiry;
(b) to obtain or to view a record of evidence and documents given, produced or provided to the inquiry or inquiry panel.

(2) No recording or broadcast of proceedings at an inquiry may be made except—

(a) at the request of the chairman, or
(b) with the permission of the chairman and in accordance with any terms on which permission is given.

Any such request or permission must be framed so as not to enable a person to see or hear by means of a recording or broadcast anything that he is prohibited by a notice under section 19 from seeing or hearing.

(3) Section 32(2) of the Freedom of Information Act 2000 (c 36) (certain inquiry records etc exempt from obligations under that Act) does not apply in relation to information contained in documents that, in pursuance of rules under section 41(1)(b) below, have been passed to and are held by a public authority.

(4) Section 37(1)(b) of the Freedom of Information (Scotland) Act 2002 (asp 13) (certain inquiry records etc exempt from obligations under that Act) does not apply in relation to information contained in documents that, in pursuance of rules under section 41(1)(b) below, have been passed to and are held by a Scottish public authority.

[Inquiries Act 2005, s 18.]

8–32813 **19. Restrictions on public access etc.** (1) Restrictions may, in accordance with this section, be imposed on—

(a) attendance at an inquiry, or at any particular part of an inquiry;
(b) disclosure or publication of any evidence or documents given, produced or provided to an inquiry.

(2) Restrictions may be imposed in either or both of the following ways—

(a) by being specified in a notice (a "restriction notice") given by the Minister to the chairman at any time before the end of the inquiry;
(b) by being specified in an order (a "restriction order") made by the chairman during the course of the inquiry.

(3) A restriction notice or restriction order must specify only such restrictions—

(a) as are required by any statutory provision, enforceable Community obligation or rule of law, or
(b) as the Minister or chairman considers to be conducive to the inquiry fulfilling its terms of reference or to be necessary in the public interest, having regard in particular to the matters mentioned in subsection (4).

(4) Those matters are—

(a) the extent to which any restriction on attendance, disclosure or publication might inhibit the allaying of public concern;
(b) any risk of harm or damage that could be avoided or reduced by any such restriction;
(c) any conditions as to confidentiality subject to which a person acquired information that he is to give, or has given, to the inquiry;
(d) the extent to which not imposing any particular restriction would be likely—

(i) to cause delay or to impair the efficiency or effectiveness of the inquiry, or
(ii) otherwise to result in additional cost (whether to public funds or to witnesses or others).

(5) In subsection (4)(b) "harm or damage" includes in particular—

(a) death or injury;
(b) damage to national security or international relations;
(c) damage to the economic interests of the United Kingdom or of any part of the United Kingdom;
(d) damage caused by disclosure of commercially sensitive information.

[Inquiries Act 2005, s 18.]

8–32814 **20. Further provisions about restriction notices and orders.** (1) Restrictions specified in a restriction notice have effect in addition to any already specified, whether in an earlier restriction notice or in a restriction order.

(2) Restrictions specified in a restriction order have effect in addition to any already specified, whether in an earlier restriction order or in a restriction notice.

(3) The Minister may vary or revoke a restriction notice by giving a further notice to the chairman at any time before the end of the inquiry.

(4) The chairman may vary or revoke a restriction order by making a further order during the course of the inquiry.

(5) Restrictions imposed under section 19 on disclosure or publication of evidence or documents ("disclosure restrictions") continue in force indefinitely, unless—

(a) under the terms of the relevant notice or order the restrictions expire at the end of the inquiry, or at some other time, or

(b) the relevant notice or order is varied or revoked under subsection (3), (4) or (7).

This is subject to subsection (6).

(6) After the end of the inquiry, disclosure restrictions do not apply to a public authority, or a Scottish public authority, in relation to information held by the authority otherwise than as a result of the breach of any such restrictions.

(7) After the end of an inquiry the Minister may, by a notice published in a way that he considers suitable—

(a) revoke a restriction order or restriction notice containing disclosure restrictions that are still in force, or

(b) vary it so as to remove or relax any of the restrictions.

(8) In this section "restriction notice" and "restriction order" have the meaning given by section 19(2).

[Inquiries Act 2005, s 20.]

8–32815 21. Powers of chairman to require production of evidence etc. (1) The chairman of an inquiry may by notice require a person to attend at a time and place stated in the notice—

(a) to give evidence;

(b) to produce any documents in his custody or under his control that relate to a matter in question at the inquiry;

(c) to produce any other thing in his custody or under his control for inspection, examination or testing by or on behalf of the inquiry panel.

(2) The chairman may by notice require a person, within such period as appears to the inquiry panel to be reasonable—

(a) to provide evidence to the inquiry panel in the form of a written statement;

(b) to provide any documents in his custody or under his control that relate to a matter in question at the inquiry;

(c) to produce any other thing in his custody or under his control for inspection, examination or testing by or on behalf of the inquiry panel.

(3) A notice under subsection (1) or (2) must—

(a) explain the possible consequences of not complying with the notice;

(b) indicate what the recipient of the notice should do if he wishes to make a claim within subsection (4).

(4) A claim by a person that—

(a) he is unable to comply with a notice under this section, or

(b) it is not reasonable in all the circumstances to require him to comply with such a notice,

is to be determined by the chairman of the inquiry, who may revoke or vary the notice on that ground.

(5) In deciding whether to revoke or vary a notice on the ground mentioned in subsection (4)(b), the chairman must consider the public interest in the information in question being obtained by the inquiry, having regard to the likely importance of the information.

(6) For the purposes of this section a thing is under a person's control if it is in his possession or if he has a right to possession of it.

[Inquiries Act 2005, s 21.]

8–32816 22. Privileged information etc. (1) A person may not under section 21 be required to give, produce or provide any evidence or document if—

(a) he could not be required to do so if the proceedings of the inquiry were civil proceedings in a court in the relevant part of the United Kingdom, or

(b) the requirement would be incompatible with a Community obligation.

(2) The rules of law under which evidence or documents are permitted or required to be withheld on grounds of public interest immunity apply in relation to an inquiry as they apply in relation to civil proceedings in a court in the relevant part of the United Kingdom.

[Inquiries Act 2005, s 22.]

8–32817 23. Risk of damage to the economy. (1) This section applies where it is submitted to an inquiry panel, on behalf of the Crown, the Financial Services Authority or the Bank of England, that there is information held by any person which, in order to avoid a risk of damage to the economy, ought not to be revealed.

(2) The panel must not permit or require the information to be revealed, or cause it to be revealed, unless satisfied that the public interest in the information being revealed outweighs the public interest in avoiding a risk of damage to the economy.

(3) In making a decision under this section the panel must take account of any restriction notice given under section 19 or any restriction order that the chairman has made or proposes to make under that section.

(4) In this section—

"damage to the economy" means damage to the economic interests of the United Kingdom or of any part of the United Kingdom;

"revealed" means revealed to anyone who is not a member of the inquiry panel.

(5) This section does not prevent the inquiry panel from communicating any information in confidence to the Minister.

(6) This section does not affect the rules of law referred to in section 22(2).

[Inquiries Act 2005, s 23.]

Supplementary

8–32818 35. Offences. (1) A person is guilty of an offence if he fails without reasonable excuse to do anything that he is required to do by a notice under section 21.

(2) A person is guilty of an offence if during the course of an inquiry he does anything that is intended to have the effect of—

(a) distorting or otherwise altering any evidence, document or other thing that is given, produced or provided to the inquiry panel, or

(b) preventing any evidence, document or other thing from being given, produced or provided to the inquiry panel,

or anything that he knows or believes is likely to have that effect.

(3) A person is guilty of an offence if during the course of an inquiry—

(a) he intentionally suppresses or conceals a document that is, and that he knows or believes to be, a relevant document, or

(b) he intentionally alters or destroys any such document.

For the purposes of this subsection a document is a "relevant document" if it is likely that the inquiry panel would (if aware of its existence) wish to be provided with it.

(4) A person does not commit an offence under subsection (2) or (3) by doing anything that he is authorised or required to do—

(a) by the inquiry panel, or

(b) by virtue of section 22 or any privilege that applies.

(5) Proceedings in England and Wales or in Northern Ireland for an offence under subsection (1) may be instituted only by the chairman.

(6) Proceedings for an offence under subsection (2) or (3) may be instituted—

(a) in England and Wales, only by or with the consent of the Director of Public Prosecutions;

(b) in Northern Ireland, only by or with the consent of the Director of Public Prosecutions for Northern Ireland.

(7) A person who is guilty of an offence under this section is liable on summary conviction to a fine not exceeding level three on the standard scale or to imprisonment for a term not exceeding the relevant maximum, or to both.

(8) "The relevant maximum" is—

(a) in England and Wales, 51 weeks;

(b) in Scotland and Northern Ireland, six months.

[Inquiries Act 2005, s 35.]

8–32819 37. Immunity from suit. (1) No action lies against—

(a) a member of an inquiry panel,

(b) an assessor, counsel or solicitor to an inquiry, or

(c) a person engaged to provide assistance to an inquiry,

in respect of any act done or omission made in the execution of his duty as such, or any act done or omission made in good faith in the purported execution of his duty as such.

(2) Subsection (1) applies only to acts done or omissions made during the course of the inquiry, otherwise than during any period of suspension (within the meaning of section 13).

(3) For the purposes of the law of defamation, the same privilege attaches to—

(a) any statement made in or for the purposes of proceedings before an inquiry (including the report and any interim report of the inquiry), and

(b) reports of proceedings before an inquiry,

as would be the case if those proceedings were proceedings before a court in the relevant part of the United Kingdom.
[Inquiries Act 2005, s 37.]

General

8–32820 43. Interpretation. (1) In this Act—

"assessor" means an assessor appointed under section 11;
"chairman", in relation to an inquiry, means the chairman of the inquiry;
"the course of the inquiry" and similar expressions are to be read in accordance with subsection (2);
"date of conversion" has the meaning given by section 15(1);
"document" includes information recorded in any form (and see subsection (3));
"event", except in sections 13 and 46, includes any conduct or omission;
"inquiry", except where the context requires otherwise, means an inquiry under this Act;
"inquiry panel" is to be read in accordance with section 3(2);
"interested party", in relation to an inquiry, means a person with a particularly significant interest in the proceedings or outcome of the inquiry;
"interim report" means a report under section 24(3);
"joint inquiry" has the meaning given by section 32(2);
"member", in relation to an inquiry panel, includes the chairman;
"Minister" is to be read in accordance with section 1(2) (and see subsection (4) below);
"Northern Ireland Minister" includes the First Minister and the deputy First Minister acting jointly;
"public authority" has the same meaning as in the Freedom of Information Act 2000 (c 36);
"the relevant Parliament or Assembly" means whichever of the following is or are applicable—

(a) in the case of an inquiry for which the Treasury is responsible, the House of Commons;
(b) in the case of an inquiry for which any other United Kingdom Minister is responsible, or one for which the Secretary of State exercising functions by virtue of section 45(2) is responsible, the House of Parliament of which that minister is a member;
(c) in the case of an inquiry for which the Scottish Ministers are responsible, the Scottish Parliament;
(d) in the case of an inquiry for which the National Assembly for Wales is responsible, that Assembly;
(e) in the case of an inquiry for which a Northern Ireland Minister is responsible, the Northern Ireland Assembly;

"the relevant part of the United Kingdom", in relation to an inquiry, means the part specified under section 31(1);
"report" means a report under section 24(1);
"responsible", in relation to an inquiry, is to be read in accordance with subsection (5);
"Scottish public authority" has the same meaning as in the Freedom of Information (Scotland) Act 2002 (asp 13);
"setting-up date" means the date specified under section 5(1)(a);
"statutory provision" means a provision contained in, or having effect under, any enactment, Act of the Scottish Parliament or Northern Ireland legislation;
"terms of reference", in relation to an inquiry under this Act, has the meaning given by section 5(6);
"United Kingdom Minister"—

(a) means the holder of a Ministerial office specified in Part 1, 2 or 3 of Schedule 1 to the Ministerial and other Salaries Act 1975 (c 27) or a Parliamentary Secretary;
(b) also includes the Treasury.

But a reference to a United Kingdom Minister does not include a reference to the Secretary of State discharging functions by virtue of section 45(2).

(2) References in this Act to the course of an inquiry are to the period beginning with the setting-up date, or (in the case of an inquiry converted under section 15) the date of conversion, and ending with the date on which the inquiry comes to an end (which is given by section 14).

(3) References in this Act to producing or providing a document, in relation to information recorded otherwise than in legible form, are to be read as references to producing or providing a copy of the information in a legible form.

(4) References in this Act to "the Minister", in relation to an inquiry, are to the Minister or Ministers responsible for the inquiry.

(5) For the purposes of this Act a Minister is "responsible" for an inquiry if he is the Minister, or one of the Ministers, by whom it was caused to be held under section 1 or converted under section 15.

This is subject to section 34(2)(a).
[Inquiries Act 2005, s 43.]

PART IX

PRECEDENTS AND FORMS

CONTENTS

(1) PRECEDENTS

(2) FORMS

MAGISTRATES' COURTS

MAGISTRATES' COURTS, CRIMINAL PROCEDURE

FAMILY COURTS

Precedents

MAGISTRATES' COURTS, PROCEDURE

9–1 **1. Notice of appeal to Crown Court against conviction, order or sentence**[1]**.** (Magistrates' Courts Act 1980, s 108; Crown Court Rules 1982, r 7). – TO [name and address of the Clerk to the Justices for the magistrates' court] Clerk of the [name] Magistrates' Court sitting at [place]; AND TO [other party's name and address].

On the [*date*], I [*name and address of appellant*] was convicted by the above magistrates' court as follows [*state offence*] for which the court (on the [*date if different from above*]) ordered [*state order or sentence*].

I give notice that I intend to appeal to the Crown court at [*address*] against conviction (*or* the order *or* sentence).

The general grounds of appeal[2] are [*specify*].

Dated the [*date*]. Signed [*signature of appellant*].

---

1. This form may be adapted for appeals not involving convictions, eg under s 301 of the Public Health Act 1936.
2. Grounds of appeal need to be stated only where the appeal is under one of the statutory provisions listed in Part III of Schedule 3 to the Crown Court Rules 1982.

9–11 **2. Application to justices to state case**[1]**.** (Magistrates' Courts Act 1980, s 111 (1); Magistrates' Courts Rules 1981, r 76). – TO [name and address of the Clerk to the Justices for the magistrates' court] Clerk of the [name] Magistrates' Court sitting at [place].

On the [*date*] an information (*or* complaint) wherein (I the undersigned) [*name and address*] was informant (*or* complainant) and (I the undersigned) [*name and address*] was defending was heard before and determined by the above magistrates' court as follows [*set out the information or complaint and the determination of the court*].

I am aggrieved by the conviction (*or* order *or* determination or [*specify other proceeding*] as being wrong in law (and/*or* in excess of jurisdiction) and I apply to the justices composing the said court to state a case for the opinion of the High Court.

The question(s) of law (and/*or* jurisdiction) on which the opinion of the High Court is sought is/are [*specify*].

Dated the [*date*]. Signed [*signature of applicant*].

---

1. The form of a stated case is set out in the section of Forms as form 155. Procedural matters once the case has been stated are contained in Civil Procedure Rules 1998 Part 52, in **Part I: Magistrates' Courts, Procedure**, ante.

9–12 **3. Certificate of refusal to state case.** (Magistrates' Courts Act 1980, s 111(5)). – [Name of county and of magistrates' court].

On the [date] an information (or complaint) was preferred by [name and address of informant or complainant] against [name and address of defendant] that [set out information or complaint] and was determined by us as follows [set out the determination of the court]

The said [name of informant or complainant or defendant] being aggrieved by the determination as being wrong in law (and/or in excess of jurisdiction) has applied to us to state a case for the opinion of the High Court.

We are of opinion that the application is frivolous and so refuse to state a case.

Dated the [*date*]. [*Signature of Justices of the Peace*]

Justices of the Peace for the County of [*specify*].

BAIL

9–13 **4. Absconding.** – Having been released on bail in criminal proceedings on [*date*] by [*state name of court or of police officer and police station*], did fail without reasonable cause[1] to surrender to custody at [*state place, date and time as on bail record*]; contrary to s 6(1) of the Bail Act 1976.

S: Limitation 6 months: fine **level 5** on the standard scale and/or **3 months**[2].

---

1. This form of precedent may be modified for an offence under s 6(2) where the person bailed had reasonable cause for failure to surrender by thereafter failed to surrender as soon after the appointment time as was reasonably practicable. The same penalty applies.
2. A person convicted summarily of this offence may be committed to the Crown Court for sentence where the maximum powers are an unlimited fine and/or twelve months imprisonment.

9–14 **5. Notifying plea**[1]**.** – Read the following instructions carefully. They tell you what you need to do about this summons, and how to avoid unnecessary inconvenience and expense.

(1) If you plead GUILTY, the case will normally be dealt with on the hearing date shown on the summons. If you do not come to court, you will be notified of the result by post within a few days of the hearing.

(2) If you plead NOT GUILTY, the case will be postponed, but a full hearing will be arranged as soon as possible, which you must attend. You will be notified about this. No witnesses need be brought to court on the hearing date shown on the summons. They need attend court only on the date arranged for the full hearing of the case. This saves costs, which you might eventually have to pay.

(3) You should tell the court without delay whether you intend to plead GUILTY or NOT GUILTY. Use the form below. If you are going to be legally represented, you must see your solicitor now, and show him the form before completing it.

*(4) Because of the nature of the offence, you MUST attend court on the date shown on the summons, whether you plead guilty or not guilty[1].

(5) If there is anything you do not understand, you should enquire without delay at my office at [*give address and telephone number*].

* Delete for a purely summary offence.

PLEASE COMPLETE AND RETURN THIS FORM TO:-

The Clerk to the Justices,
[*Address*]

FROM: Full name ....
Address ....
....
Date of Hearing ....

(*a*) I intend to plead GUILTY (Do you intend to come to court? YES/NO)
(OR)
(*b*) I intend to plead NOT GUILTY and understand that the case will be adjourned to a later date when the case can be heard in full.

(Delete (*a*) OR (*b*) as appropriate)

Signed [*signature*]

---

1. This precedent is recommended for use when a system of listing cases for plea is used. In the case of purely summary offence, item (4) will be deleted.

9–15 **6. Plea of guilty by post[1].** –Memorandum from: THE CLERK TO THE JUSTICES, IMPORTANT

1. In connection with the summons(es), notice and statement of facts, now served upon you, will you please acknowledge receipt by signing and returning this form as soon as possible. (No stamp is necessary).

I hereby acknowledge receipt of . . . summons(es), notice, statement of facts and notice of alleged previous convictions.

Signed ....

(Present address) ....

2. Please complete either section A or B. NOTE: If you intend to consult a solicitor you would be well advised to consult him before completing this form.

A If you desire a plea of guilty to be accepted without your attendance at Court, please complete the following:

I have read the statement of facts relating to the charge(s) against me.

I plead guilty to the charge(s) and I desire the Court to deal with the case in my absence, and to take the following circumstances into account.

Signed ....

Mitigating circumstances[2]

(*a*) about the offence-

(*b*) about my financial circumstances-

B If you propose to attend Court considerable saving of time and expense may be effected if you will complete the following:

Do you intend to plead guilty? ....

NOTE: If having completed and returned the form, you change your mind, you should let the Clerk to the Justices know immediately.

---

1. This precedent is recommended in Home Office Circular No 265/1968.
2. The statement of mitigating circumstances as well as the notification of pleas of guilty and the statement of facts must be read out aloud in court (see the Magistrates' Courts Act 1980, s 12(7) in PART I: MAGISTRATES' COURTS, PROCEDURE, ante). It is not sufficient if these documents are passed to the magistrates to read for themselves (R *v Oldham Justices, ex p Morrisey* [1958] 3 All ER 559, 123 JP 38).

9–16 7. **Endorsement for service.** (*Summary Jurisdiction (Process) Act* 1881, *s* 4). – Proof on oath (*or* solemn declaration) having been produced before me that the name of [*name*] subscribed to the within summons (*or* warrant *or* order etc) is of the handwriting of the sheriff (*or* justice of the peace) within mentioned;

I authorise this summons to be served (or warrant to be executed) within the County of [*specify*].

Dated the [*date*]. [*Signature of Justice of the Peace*]

Justice of the Peace for the County of [*specify*].

EVIDENCE

9–17 8. **Affidavit**[1]. – In the matter of ([*specify*] (and other matters)) (R *v* [*name of (first) defendant*] (and others));

I [*name*] of [*address, occupation or description*][2], make oath (*or* do solemnly and sincerely affirm) and say as follows [*state matter of affidavit in numbered paragraphs*][3].

Sworn (Affirmed) at *full address*
this day of 19 . [*signature of maker of affidavit*]

(I having first truly distinctly and audibly read over the contents of this affidavit to the deponent (he being blind) (and explained the nature and effect of the exhibits therein referred to) who appeared perfectly to understand the same and made his mark thereto in my presence).

Before me
[*Signature of Commissioner*]
A Commissioner for Oaths[4].

1. This precedent may be used where for example the law envisages information being placed before the High Court by justices or by the justices' clerk by way of affidavit. Reference must be made to the detailed requirements of Civil Procedure Rules 1998; for example, the affidavit must be in book form, following continuously from page to page, both sides of the paper being used; dates, sums and other numbers must be expressed in figures and not words, alterations, interlineations, erasures etc must be initialled (and the alteration repeated in the margin and initialled).

Any affidavit that does not comply with the Civil Procedure Rules 1998 and *Practice Note* [1983] 3 All ER 33, [1983] 1 WLR 922, amended by Practice Direction [1995] 2 All ER 511, may be rejected by the court or made the subject for an order for costs. The above Practice Direction makes provision in the following terms-

Affidavits

1. *Marking* At the top right-hand corner or the first page of every affidavit, and also on the backsheet, there must be written in clear permanent dark blue or black marking (I) the party on whose behalf it is filed, (ii) the initials and surname of the deponent, (iii) the number of the affidavit in relation to the deponent, (iv) the identifying initials and number of each exhibit to the affidavit, and (v) the date when sworn. For example: "2nd Dft: E W Jones: 3rd: 24.7.82; EWJ 3, 4 and 5."

2. *Binding* Affidavits must not be bound with thick plastic strips or anything else which would hamper filing.

2. The description must be full; for example the following have been held to be insufficient; "gentleman", "esquire", "clerk", "articled clerk", "director of public company", "justice of the peace".

3. Each paragraph should as far as possible be confined to a distinct portion of the subject. The jurat which follows the subject matter should follow immediately after the text and should never begin a fresh page.

4. By the provisions of the Solicitors Act 1974, s 81(1); every solicitor who holds a current practising certificate has the powers of a Commissioner for Oaths under the Comrs for Oaths Act 1889 and 1891 and s 24 of the Stamp Duties Management Act 1891. We note that some courts prefer the signature to be subscribed "a Solicitor of the Supreme Court" instead of "a Commissioner for Oaths". He must not be a party to the proceedings.

9–18 9. **Endorsement on exhibit**[1]. – In the matter of ([*specify*] (and other matters)) (R *v* [*name of (first) defendant*] (and others));

This is the [*name the exhibit*] marked [*specify distinguishing mark if any referred to in the affidavit*] which is referred to as being exhibited to the affidavit of [*name*] sworn (affirmed) on [*date*].

Certified by me

[*Signature of Commissioner*]
A Commissioner for Oaths[2].

1. As to affidavits, exhibits and bundles of documents to be used in proceedings in the Court of Appeal or any division of the High Court, see *Practice Note* [19833] 3 All ER 33, [1983] 1 WLR 922. Failure to comply with this Practice Direction may result in the documents being rejected by the court or made the subject for an order for costs.

2. By the provisions of the Solicitors Act 1974, s 81(1); every solicitor who holds a current practising certificate has the powers of a Commissioner for Oaths under the Comrs for Oaths Act 1889 and 1891 and s 24 of the Stamp Duties Management Act 1891. We note that some courts prefer the signature to be subscribed "a Solicitor of the Supreme Court" instead of "a Commissioner for Oaths". He must not be a party to the proceedings.

STATUTORY DECLARATION

9–19 **10. Statutory declaration**[1]**.** (Statutory Declarations Act 1835[2]).

I [*name*] of [*address*] do solemnly and sincerely declare that:

[*specify matter to be declared*].

And I make this solemn declaration conscientiously believing the same to be true, and by virtue of the provisions of the Statutory Declarations Act 1835.

Dated the [*date*] [*Signature of person making the declaration*]

Declared before me

[*Signature of Justice of the Peace*]
Justice of the Peace for the County of [*specify*]

---

1. Any justice or other person administering an oath when not authorised by law so to do, contravenes the Statutory Declarations Act 1835, s 13, in **PART II: EVIDENCE**, ante. Justices are however empowered to take and receive the voluntary declaration of any person which may be necessary and proper for the confirmation or written instruments of allegations, or of the execution of deeds or other prescribed matters (ibid, s 18). For punishment for making a false declaration see Perjury Act 1911, s 5 in **PART VIII** title **PERJURY**, ante.
2. See STATUTES ON EVIDENCE AND INTERPRETATION in **PART II: EVIDENCE**, ante.

WITNESS DANGEROUSLY ILL

9–20 **11. Notice to accused or prosecutor.** (*Magistrates' Courts Act* 1980, *s* 105; *Magistrates' Courts Rules* 1981, *r* 33). – TO the accused (*or* prosecutor):

In this notice;

The indictable offence is [*specify*]
The prosecutor is
The accused is
The witness is
} [*names and addresses*]

The medical practitioner is

DEPOSITION TO BE TAKEN AT [*state place, date and time*]

Concerning the indictable offence (with which the accused has been charged), it appears to me that the witness is able and willing to give material information.

On the representation of the duly qualified medical practitioner, I am satisfied that the witness is dangerously ill and unlikely to recover, and it is not practicable to take the evidence otherwise in accordance with the Magistrates' Courts Act 1980 and Rules made thereunder.

I give you notice that I intend to take the deposition of the witness as stated above, when you your counsel or solicitor will be given full opportunity of cross-examining the witness.

Date the [*date*]. [*Signature of Justice of the Peace*]
Justice of the Peace for the County of [*specify*].

SENTENCING

9–21

12. Warrant of Commitment: Multiple Sentences of Imprisonment[1]

SCHEDULE FOR TERMS OF IMPRISONMENT WITHOUT OPTION OF FINE

No	Date of Offence	Nature of Offence	Contrary to	Term of Imprisonment	Concurrent or Consecutive

Warrant lodged/executed on..................................date

...............................signed

Maximum Effective Period of Imprisonment on this warrant..

NB The court should indicate whether the effective period of imprisonment on this warrant is consecutive to or concurrent with the effective term on any other warrant issued by the court in respect of this defendant.

---

1. This Schedule is designed to be used with Form 43 of the Magistrates' Courts (Forms) Rules 1981 and was recommended by Home Office Circular No 265/1968, dated 18 December 1968. Where a defendant is committed to prison for a number of offences in respect of which several sentences of imprisonment have been imposed, or where he is committed to prison in default of paying several fines, it was suggested by Home Office Circular No 265/1968 that, in order to simplify the clerical work at courts and prison establishments, only one warrant of commitment should be drawn up for each type of committal, with a schedule on the reverse of the warrant listing the offences, the terms of imprisonment imposed (or periods in default) and whether the terms are concurrent with, or consecutive to other terms of imprisonment.

13. Warrant of Commitment: Fine Default: Multiple Terms of Imprisonment[1]

SCHEDULE FOR IMPRISONMENT FOR NON-PAYMENT OF FINES ETC

No	Date of Offence	Nature of Offence	Contrary to	Fine Imposed and/or costs	Period of imprisonment in Default	Amount Paid Before Reception	Balance of Imprisonment Outstanding	Amount Paid After Reception	Balance of Imprisonment Outstanding	Concurrent/ Consecutive to other terms of Imprisonment

Warrant lodged/executed on ....date
......................................signed
Maximum Effective Period of Imprisonment on this warrant ....

NB The court should indicate whether the effective period of imprisonment on this warrant is consecutive to or concurrent with the effective term on any other warrant issued by the court in respect of this defendant.

1. This Schedule is designed to be used with Forms 51 and 52 of the Magistrates' Courts (Forms) Rules 1981 and was recommended by Home Office Circular No 265/1968, dated 18 December 1968. See note 1 to Precedent 12, ante.

FAMILY

9–34 **25. Notice of Motion to Divisional Court of the Family Division in domestic matters**[1]**.** (*Domestic Proceedings and Magistrates' Courts Act* 1978, s 29; *Guardianship of Minors Act* 1971, s 16(3); *Children Act 1975*, s 101(2); *Maintenance Orders Act* 1958, s 4(7); *Child Care Act* 1980, s 6; *Family Proceedings Rules* 1991, Part VIII).

IN THE HIGH COURT OF JUSTICE No. of 19 .
FAMILY DIVISION (DIVISIONAL COURT)
In the Matter of an appeal under [*state appropriate Act*]
Between [*name*] Appellant and
[*name*] Respondent

TAKE NOTICE that the High Court of Justice, Family Division, Royal Courts of Justice, Strand, London WC2 A2LL will, on a date to be fixed and notified to the parties, consider an appeal by [*name*] (the husband/wife of the respondent or father/mother of the child) against the order of the [*specify*] magistrates' court dated the (*date*).

1. The said order [*here set out details of the magistrates' order*] and [*if appropriate*] the full names, surnames and dates of birth of the children referred to in the order are [*specify*].
2. The appellant appeals against the whole of the said order or [*here set out the part or the parts of the order appealed against*].
3. The appellant seeks an order that [*here set out the order that is sought from the Divisional Court*].
4. [*If appropriate*] Leave to appeal out of time is required because [*here set out briefly the reason giving any dates that are relevant*][2].
5. The ground of the appeal are [*specify*][3].

Dated the [*date*]
This notice was filed by [*name*]
whose address for service
is [*specify*]

Signed (*Signature*)
(Solicitor for the above named appellant).

1. This form is set out as an appendix to *Practice Direction* [1977] 2 All ER 543, [1977] 1 WLR 609, which makes several other additional requirements to Ord 90, r 16.
2. The precedent attached to the Practice Direction states that where the delay is no more than six weeks, ie this notice is being filed within 12 weeks of the hearing, and has been occasioned by the obtaining of documents or legal aid and the respondent has been notified of the likelihood of an appeal, it will normally suffice to say so without giving details.
3. The Practice Direction emphasises the fact that all the grounds should be set out; it is not sufficient to state merely that the finding was against the weight of evidence.

9–35 **26. Application**[1] **for consent to marry.** (Marriage Act 1949 s 3; Magistrates' Courts (Guardianship of Minors Rules 1974 r 5)).

Between [*name and address*] applicant, and [*name and address*] respondent(s):
The applicant wishes to marry [*name and address*].
The person(s) whose consent is required is/are the respondent(s) who has/have (*or* the said *name* has) refused consent.
Wherefore the applicant applies pursuant to s 3 of the Marriage Act 1949 that the [*name and address*] magistrates' court shall consent to the marriage.

Dated the (*date*)

Signed [*signature of applicant*]
Justice of the Peace for the
county of [*specify*] or
or Clerk to the Justices for
[*specify*].

1. See the Magistrates' Courts (Guardianship of Minors) Rules 1974 in **Part IV: Family Law**, ante.

JUSTICES' REASONS

9–36 **27. Reasons for decisions in family proceedings**[1]**.**

In the High Court of Justice
Family Division

(*name*) Magistrates' Court

Name of applicant:

v

Name of respondent:
Date of hearing:
Justices comprising the court:
Clerk of the court:

JUSTICES' REASONS

(*a*) facts not in dispute;
(*b*) disputed facts;
(*c*) facts found proved;
(*d*) the extent to which the parties and witnesses were believed or disbelieved and the information on which the court relied in reaching its decision;
(*e*) authorities cited by the parties;
(*f*) whether a welfare report has been considered;
(*g*) the judgement or findings of fact in relation to each of the heads under the appropriate "checklist" section (eg s 1(3), s 25(1));
(*h*) (where applicable) reasons for departing from the recommendation of the guardian ad litem or welfare officer.

I certify that these reasons were recorded on the date of hearing in accordance with rule 36 of the Magistrates' Courts Rules 1981.

(*Signature of the Justices' clerk*)
Clerk to the Justices.

1. Reasons drawn up pursuant to the Family Proceedings Courts (Children Act 1989) Rules 1991, r 21 and the Family Proceedings Courts (Matrimonial Proceedings) Rules 1991, r 12.

9–37 **28. Family proceedings**[1]. —The court is shortly to hear the family proceedings, details of which are given in the attached summons. In order to assess fairly the amount of any maintenance that might be ordered in this case it is necessary that the Court should know the financial position of both parties. Please complete the following form and bring it with you or post it so as to reach my office before the hearing date.

You should also attach to the form EITHER a statement or earnings during the last 13 weeks, signed by your employer OR your last eight weekly pay slips or last two monthly wage slips AND bring with you to Court any rent book, hire purchase payment card, bills, etc to prove the amounts stated by you below.

DOCUMENTARY PROOF WILL STRONGLY SUPPORT YOUR EVIDENCE.

Name: Hearing date:

Address:

Date of Birth:

Persons living with you now
(if children, give their ages):

WEEKLY INCOME		WEEKLY EXPENDITURE	
Usual pay: (including overtime and bonus payments)		Rent or mortgage:	£
		Rates:	£
		Gas, electricity, coal:	£
1. Gross (before deductions)	£	Hire purchase, clubs, bank loans:	£
2. Net (after deductions)	£		
Social security payments:	£	Court orders (county court, maintenance etc):	£
Any other income: (state source, including payments to you by other members of household)	£	Travelling expenses to and from work:	£
		Any other weekly payments eg insurance, television rental (give full details)	£
TOTAL WEEKLY INCOME	£	TOTAL WEEKLY EXPENDITURE	£

WEEKLY INCOME WEEKLY EXPENDITURE

CAPITAL
If you have a bank balance, savings, bonds or any other capital, state total value: £

Do you want to say anything else about your financial position (for example any changes in the near future)? Write on the back of this form if there is insufficient room on the front.

I believe the above information to be true.

[*date*] [*Signature*]

NOTES: If the proceedings are withdrawn, this form will be returned to you.

If you are to be represented by a solicitor you would be well advised to show the form to him before returning it to my office.

[*Name and address of Clerk to justices*]

1. This form may be adapted for means inquiry for non-payment of fine or maintenance. It should then be pointed out that the defaulter must attend court failing which his attendance will be enforced by other means, unless he has meanwhile paid the whole of the amount outstanding. Space may also be given for him to give reasons for non-payment and for offers for payment.

WARRANTS OF ENTRY, SEARCH WARRANTS AND OTHER EX PARTE APPLICATIONS

MENTAL HEALTH

9–38 **100. Search warrant**[1]. (*Mental Health Act 1983, s 135*). – TO [*name*] a constable of the [*name*] Police Force.

Information on oath (*or* affirmation) has this day been laid by [*name*] an approved social worker of [*name of local social services authority*], that there is reasonable cause to suspect that [*name if available*] a person believed to be suffering from mental disorder (has been or is being ill-treated, neglected or kept otherwise than under proper control) (being unable to care for himself/herself, is living alone at [*specify premises which must be within the justice's jurisdiction*]).

You are hereby authorised to enter, if need be by force, the premises specified herein, accompanied by an approved social worker and by a registered medical practitioner, and if it is thought fit, to remove the said person to a place of safety with a view to the making of an application in respect of him under Part II of the Mental Act 1983, or of other arrangements for his treatment or care.

Dated the [*date*]. [*Signature of Justice of the Peace*]

Justice of the Peace for the County of [*specify*].

1. Note the power under s 135(5) of the Mental Health Act 1983, in PART VIII, title MENTAL HEALTH, ante, to issue a warrant to take or retake a patient without naming him in the information or warrant: the warrant must be adapted to accord with that sub-section if appropriate.

PUBLIC HEALTH

9–39 **105. Warrant of removal of person in need of care and attention**[1]. (*National Assistance Act 1948, s 47; National Assistance (Amendment) Act 1951, s 1*). – For the purposes of this Order,

the council is the [*name*] District Council,
the applicant is
the patient is
the registered medical practitioner is
the hospital is
the officer of the council is

} [*name and addresses*]

The applicant, acting on behalf of (or being the proper officer[2] so authorised of) the council, has certified that in the opinion of the proper officer and of the registered medical practitioner it is in the interests of the patient to remove him without delay.

I am satisfied on the applicant's evidence that the patient is suffering from grave chronic disease (*or* being aged *or* infirm *or* physically incapacitated is living in insanitary conditions) and is unable to devote to himself and is not receiving from other people, proper care and attention; and that in the patient's interests (*or* to prevent injury to the health of *or* prevent serious nuisance to other persons) it is necessary and expedient to remove the patient from the premises in which he is residing; and that the manager of the hospital agrees to accommodate the patient.

I hereby order that the patient be removed to the hospital by the officer of the council, and that the patient be detained therein for the period of [*specify period not exceeding three weeks*] after his removal there.

Dated the [date] [*Signature of Justice of the Peace*]

Justice of the Peace for the County of [*specify*].

1. This form is for the emergency *ex parte* procedure provided for under the 1951 Act. It may be adapted for the court order made solely under the 1948 Act.

2. The proper officer of a local authority replaces the Medical Officer of Health by reason of the Local Government Act 1972, Sch 29, para 4.

9–40 **106. Warrant of entry.** (*Public Health Act 1936, s 287*). – TO any authorised officer of the [*name local authority*]:

Information on oath (or affirmation) and in writing has been laid this day by [*name and address of information*], an authorised officer of [*name of local authority*] that admission has been refused[1] (*or* it is apprehended that admission will be refused[1] *or* the premises are unoccupied *or* the occupier is temporarily absent *or* admission is a case of urgency *or* an application for admission would defeat the object of the entry) and that there is reasonable ground for entry, namely [*specify*].

You are hereby authorised to enter the premises named herein if need be by force.

Dated the [*date*]. [*Signature of Justice of the Peace*]

Justice of the Peace for the County of [*specify*]

1. The justice should be satisfied that if admission has been refused or is apprehended, the occupier should have been given notice of the intention to apply for a warrant.

SEARCH WARRANTS[1]

9–41

9–42 110. Notes for Guidance – application for, and execution of, search warrants under section 8 Police and Criminal Evidence Act 1984 (as amended)[1]

INTRODUCTION

1. These notes concern the template forms for use by courts and police in connection with the application to a Justice of the Peace/District Judge for a search warrants under section 8 PACE. The forms provide a framework which may be adapted to meet local needs for implementing the amendments to sections 8, 15 and 16 PACE made by the Serious Organised Crime & Police Act 2005. These amendments allow a single warrant issued under s 8 PACE to authorise entry to, and search of, more than one set of premises and the entry and search of the same premises on more than one occasion.

1. Annex B to Home Office Circular 56/2005.

2. The template forms are:

Form 1 Application for warrant to enter and search premises under section 8 PACE.
Form 2 Schedule to search warrant/application under section 8 PACE.
Form 3 Warrant to enter and search premises for evidence of an indictable offence.
Form 4 Warrant to enter and search premises for evidence of an indictable offence – COPY FOR OCCUPIER OF THE PREMISES ENTERED.
Form 5 Record of Authority given by inspector or above to execute search warrant issued under section 8 PACE.

MAKING AN APPLICATION
Form 1

3. Complete the form "**Application for warrant to enter and search premises under section 8 PACE**". After completing the court details and indicating the type of warrant (specific premises or all premises) being applied for:

(*a*) Specify the indictable offence; eg *"robbery, s 8 Theft Act 1968"*.
(*b*) Describe the premises where is believed the material sought will be found and describe the material itself so far as it is practicable.
If authority to enter more than one premises is required, complete Form 2 "**Schedule to search warrant/application under section 8 PACE**".
Describe the material in sufficient detail to satisfy the justice/District Judge hearing the application that the material sought:

- is likely to be "relevant evidence" ie admissible in evidence at a trial for the specified offence (see section 8(4) PACE).
- does not consist of or include items subject to legal privilege, excluded material or special procedure material.

(*c*) Indicate the conditions which make the warrant necessary by deleting those that do not apply.
(*d*) Indicate if it is believed necessary to enter the same premises more than once and how many further entries are needed. The justice/District Judge must be satisfied that they are necessary to achieve the purpose for which the warrant is issued and the warrant must state how many entries are allowed (s 15(5A) PACE); this may be once only, a specified maximum or unlimited (see s 8(1C)/1D) PACE).
(*e*) State whether any person(s) should be authorised to accompany the officer executing the warrant (see s 16(2) PACE/Code B3.6(f).

The officer authorising the application (Code B 3.4) should sign in the box provided on the rear of the form.

4. Complete the **FURTHER INFORMATION** section as appropriate to:-
   - explain why it is believed the material sought will be found on the premises to be searched.
   - describe the person(s) to be authorised to accompany the officer executing the warrant and why their presence is necessary.
   - explain why it is believed necessary to search premises that are not specified in the application and why it is not reasonably practicable to specify in the Schedule ALL the premises which might need to be searched. Entry to these premises requires the prior written authority of an inspector or above not involved in the investigation (see s 16(3A) PACE/Code B6.3B).
   - if authority to enter and search the premises on more than one occasion is needed, explain why, and how many, further entries are needed to achieve the purpose for which the warrant is to be issued. Such further entries require the prior written authority of an inspector or above not involved in the investigation (see s 16(3B) PACE/Code B6.3A).

5. The justice/District Judge hearing the application should, when signing it, indicate whether or not a Schedule was included.

Form 2

6. For an application for a warrant to search more than one set of premises: complete Form 2 **"Schedule to search warrant/application under section 8 PACE".**

   (*a*) To avoid duplication, and to ensure that details of the premises set out in the application are exactly the same as in the warrant, this Schedule with the court details signed by the issuing justice/District Judge is to be attached to the warrant (see 7) and a copy retained with the application.
   (*b*) For a "specific premises" warrant, specify all the sets of premises to be entered.
   (*c*) For an "all premises" warrant, specify the name of the person who occupies or controls the premises to be searched. Enter details of each of those premises that can be specified. Entry to those that cannot be specified will require prior written authority of an inspector or above (see s 16(3A) PACE).
   (*d*) The table below the signature of the justice/District Judge is used when the warrant is executed (see 14). It is to be left blank for the application.

COMPLETION OF SEARCH WARRANT AND NEED FOR COPIES
Form 3

7. Information from the application is used to complete the separate warrant (Form 3) "**Warrant to enter and search premises for evidence of an indictable offence**" to which the Schedule (if applicable), is attached. Both the warrant and Schedule are signed by the issuing Justice/District Judge.
8. The instructions below justice's/District Judge's signature, under "Copies to be made" have operational implications for police when executing warrants that authorise entry to more than one premises. They aim to ensure that an occupier of premises entered is not given any information about any other premises to which the warrant authorises entry. This is achieved by the noting the copy warrant (Form 4) given to, or left for, the occupier, to show the premises entered and searched on that particular occasion.

Form 4

9. The Form 4, "**Warrant to enter and search premises for evidence of an indictable offence – COPY FOR OCCUPIER OF THE PREMISES ENTERED**" would be a 'no carbon required' or electronically produced copy of the warrant. The section below the signature of the issuing justice/District Judge is completed by the officer in charge of the search when executing the warrant (see 8).
10. Further copies will needed for each of the officers in charge of the searches made under that warrant give to, or leave for, the occupier on each occasion that premises are searched (including further searches of the same premises) under the warrant.

Simultaneous searches

11. If the warrant authorises entry to more than one premises and police wish to search two or more sets of these premises at the same time, it will also be necessary to make copies of the original warrant (including the endorsement on the reverse) and its Schedule for the officers in charge of those other searches.

EXECUTION

12. BEFORE any premises not specified in an all premises warrant are entered and/or BEFORE any premises are entered for a second or further time under any kind of warrant, the officer in charge of the search must confirm that the prior written authority of an inspector or above required in these cases by s 16(3A) and (3B) PACE respectively, has been given.

Form 5

13. The separate form "**Record of Authority given by inspector or above to execute search warrant issued under s 8 PACE**" allows the authorising officer to give the relevant authorities in writing under s 16(3A) and/or (3B). Both will apply to second and subsequent searches of premises not specified in an application for an all premises warrant. The officer who first gives any such authority in relation to a particular warrant should complete the top section to identify the warrant to which the authority relate. In urgent cases, if the form is not readily available, authorising officers should use their pocket books. Police forces will need to make arrangements to ensure that completed authorisation forms can be linked to the relevant warrants and are available for use in connection with any proceedings (criminal or civil).
14. Where a Schedule (Form 4) is attached and entry to premises not specified in an all premises warrant, or a second or further entry to the same premises is subject to prior written authorisation under s.16(3A) and/or (3B), the officer in charge of the search must confirm that the relevant authority has been given (see 13). The officer should then complete the table in the Schedule below the signature of the issuing justice/District Judge to specify the premises to be entered and the authority or authorities that apply.

ENDORSEMENT OF WARRANT

15. On each occasion that premises are entered and searched under any warrant, the officer in charge of the search must ensure that one of the endorsement boxes on the reverse of the warrant is completed. Copies of the blank endorsements should be made as necessary.
16. If the warrant authorises entry to one set of specified premises on one occasion only (no Schedule), the second box should be deleted and in the first box, against "Authorised by inspector" delete [*Yes] and leave [*Not applicable].
17. If the warrant authorises entry to one set of specified premises on more than one occasion, the first box should be completed as in 15. For any second or subsequent entry, the need for prior authority under s.16(3B) PACE and the fact that the authority has been given is to be indicated against "Authorised by inspector" by leaving [*Yes] and deleting "[*Not applicable]".

Provision of copy warrant for occupier

18. The copy warrant form (see 8) should be given to, or left for, the occupier of the premises entered. If left on the premises, the place where left must be shown in the endorsement (see 14).
19. If the warrant authorises entry to more than one set of premises, including premises which are not specified when the application was made, the table in the section below the signature of the issuing justice/District Judge is to be completed. This gives effect to the instructions on the warrant (see 7) to ensure that the copy warrant for the occupier specifies the one set of premises entered and searched on that particular occasion and does not disclose any information about the other premises.

RETURN OF WARRANT AND SCHEDULE

20. A search warrant and Schedule (if applicable) issued by a Justice of the Peace/District Judge under s 8 PACE search warrant is to be returned to the "appropriate" person in accordance with s 16(10) PACE. Police forces should check that their existing local arrangements with courts ensure compliance with these provisions.
21. The completed endorsement(s) on the warrant (see 17) and if applicable, the Schedule with its completed table (see 16) enable the extended search warrant powers (entry to premises not specified in the application and multiple entries) to be monitored.

Simultaneous searches

22. If more than one set of premises is searched at the same time, each copied warrant (see 12) with completed endorsement (see 16) and its copied Schedule (see 12) with completed authorisation table (see 15) need to be collated for return to the 'appropriate person' in accordance with s 16(10) PACE.

9–43 Form 1. Application for warrant to enter and search premises under section 8 Police and Criminal Evidence Act 1984 *(Section 15 of the Police and Criminal Evidence Act 1984)*

**delete/complete as applicable*

(Specify name of court ....) Magistrates' Court (Code............)

Application is today made before me the undersigned by (specify name of applicant):

....

for the issue of [*a specific premises warrant] [*an all premises warrant] under section 8 Police and Criminal Evidence Act 1984

The applicant says [★on oath] [★affirms] that there are reasonable grounds for believing:

(*a*) that an *indictable* offence, namely (*specify Act & section*)
.... has been committed;

(*b*) that there is on [★the *one* set of premises situated at (*specify premises*);............................
....;]

[★the *sets of premises* described in the Schedule attached;]

material that is likely to be relevant evidence and be of substantial value to the investigation of the offence and does not consist of or include items subject to legal privilege, excluded material or special procedure material, namely (*identify, so far as is practicable, the material sought*)
....
....
....
....
....;

(*c*) ★*delete whichever of (i) to (iv) is NOT applicable:*

★(i) that it is not practicable to communicate with any person entitled to grant entry to the premises;

★(ii) that it is practicable to communicate with a person entitled to grant entry to the premises but it is not practicable to communicate with any person entitled to grant access to the evidence;

★(iii) that entry to the premises will not be granted unless a warrant is produced;

★(iv) that the purpose of a search may be frustrated or seriously prejudiced unless a constable arriving at the premises can secure immediate entry to them; AND

(*d*) that to achieve the purpose for which the warrant is being applied it is necessary that the warrant authorises entry to and search of *each* set of premises;

[★on ONE occasion only.]

★subject to any second and subsequent entry being authorised in writing by an inspector or above,

[★on NOT MORE THAN (enter words & number) .... occasions.]

[★on an UNLIMITED number of occasions.]

(*e*) [★that persons be authorised to accompany the officer executing the warrant.]

FURTHER INFORMATION:

1. **All** applications; explain why it is believed the material sought will be found on the premises to be searched.
2. If applicable, describe any person(s) to be authorised to accompany the officer executing the warrant.
3. If the application is for an "*all premises*" warrant; explain;
   (*a*) Why it is believed necessary to search premises occupied or controlled by the person in question that are not specified in the Schedule; and
   (*b*) Why it is not reasonably practicable to specify in the Schedule ALL the premises the person occupies or controls and which might need to be searched.
4. If authority to enter and search the premises on more than one occasion is needed, explain why, and how many, further entries are needed to achieve the purpose for which the warrant is to be issued.
....
....
....
....

(*continue over*[1] *if necessary*)

Date: .... Signature of Applicant..

This application [★with Schedule] was taken and sworn/affirmed before me

District Judge (Magistrates' Court)
Justice of the Peace.

Application approved by (name and rank) ....
(Inspector or if urgent, next most senior officer, see Code B 3.4)
Signature: .... Date: ....

1. Ie, on the back of the form.

9–44 Form 2. Schedule to search warrant/application under section 8 Police and Criminal Evidence Act 1984

Premises to which entry and search is authorised

**delete/complete as applicable*

(Specify name of court........................) **Magistrates' Court (Code............)**

Date: ....

The premises authorised to be entered and searched under the warrant to which this schedule is attached are:

[*The following specified premises

(1) ....
(2) ....
(3) ....
(4) ....
(5) ....
(6) ....
(7) ....
(8) ....
(9) ....
(10) ....

and/or

*Premises occupied or controlled by (name) ....]
which it is not reasonably practicable to specify in the application. A District Judge/Justice of the Peace may not issue an "all premises" warrant to enter and search premises occupied or controlled by the above named person unless he/she is satisfied that because of the particulars of the offence referred to in the application, there are reasonable grounds for believing that it is necessary to search premises occupied or controlled by that person which are not specified above in order to find the material sought and that it is not reasonably practicable to specify ALL the premises the person occupies or controls and which might need to be searched. Entry to such premises also requires prior authority in writing from an inspector or above.]

Date: ....

District Judge (Magistrates' Court)
Justice of the Peace

The officer in charge of the search (Code B2.10) is to complete this table;

(a) in the case of an ***all premises warrant****, BEFORE entry to any premises which are not specified that warrant; and/or*

(b) in the case of ***a warrant authorising multiple entries****, BEFORE entry to any premises for the second or any subsequent time.*

An inspector or above has given written authority to enter the premises below under the warrant to which this Schedule is attached:

No	Premises (Specify premises to which the authority relates)	Reason for authority (enter *Yes* or *No*)		Officer in charge of the search (Signature/rank/station/date)
		(1)To enter premises not specified in an all premises warrant.	(2)To enter premises on a 2nd or any subsequent time.	
1				
2				
3				
4				
5				
6				
7				
8				
9				
10				
11				

No	Premises (Specify premises to which the authority relates)	Reason for authority (enter *Yes* or *No*)		Officer in charge of the search (Signature/rank/station/date)
		(1)To enter premises not specified in an all premises warrant.	(2)To enter premises on a 2nd or any subsequent time.	
12				
13				
14				
15				

THIS SCHEDULE TO BE RETURNED WITH THE WARRANT TO THE APPROPRIATE PERSON IN ACCORDANCE WITH SECTION 16(10) PACE.

(1). s 16(3A) PACE
(2). s 16 (3B) PACE

9–45 **Form 3. Warrant to enter and search premises for evidence of an indictable offence**

(Section 15 of the Police and Criminal Evidence Act 1984)

**delete/complete as applicable*

(Specify name of court ....) **Magistrates' Court (Code...........)**

Date: ....

On this day an application supported by an information was made by *(specify name of applicant)*: ....for the issue of warrant under section 8 of the Police and Criminal Evidence Act 1984 to enter:

[*the *one set of premises* situated at (specify premises);...]

[*The sets *of premises* described in the Schedule attached]

and search for *(identify so far as is practicable the material sought)*:
....
....
....
....

*Authority is hereby given for any constable, [*accompanied by such other person or persons as are necessary for the purposes of the search], to enter the said premises on the number of occasions specified below within three months* from the date of issue of this warrant and on *each such occasion* to search for the material in respect of which the application is made.

Number of occasions that each set of premises may be entered and searched under this warrant is:

[*on ONE occasion only.]

*subject to any second and subsequent entry being authorised in writing by an inspector or above,

[*on NOT MORE THAN (enter words & number) .... occasions.]

[*on an UNLIMITED number of occasions.]

District Judge (Magistrates' Court)
Justice of the Peace.

COPIES TO BE MADE:

(*a*) For a warrant which specifies only one set of premises and does NOT authorise multiple entries (no Schedule) – TWO copies.

(*b*) For *any other warrant to which a Schedule of the premises to which entry is authorised* – as many copies as are required. An occupier is not entitled to be given details of, or any information about, other premises to which the warrant authorises entry. Whenever premises are entered under a warrant to which a Schedule is attached, the copy that is given to the occupier or left on the premises should be endorsed by the officer in charge of the search to specify the premises entered on *that* occasion.

SEE OVER FOR ENDORSEMENT TO BE MADE AFTER EACH ENTRY & SEARCH UNDER THIS WARRANT

THIS WARRANT AND ITS SCHEDULE (IF APPLICABLE) TO BE RETURNED TO THE APPROPRIATE PERSON – SEE SECTION 16(10) PACE

[REAR OF FORM]

ONE ENDORSEMENT TO BE COMPLETED FOR **EACH** ENTRY AND SEARCH BY A CONSTABLE EXECUTING THE WARRANT (USE CONTINUATION SHEET(S) IF NECESSARY)

**delete/complete as applicable*

Entry No.	Date/Time of Entry: .... Authorised by inspector [*Yes] [*Not applicable] Premises entered & searched on this occasion (specify): ....
1	*1. The following material sought was found (list) *2. The following articles other than article sought were seized (list): *3. No material was found or seized. 4. *Copy of warrant showing the premises entered on this occasion handed to occupier *Copy of warrant showing the premises entered on this occasion left on premises (specify where left) .... *Delete/complete as appropriate Signature(s) of constable(s) executing warrant on this occasion: ....

Entry No.	Date/Time of Entry: .... Authorised by inspector [*Yes] [*Not applicable] Premises entered & searched on this occasion (specify): ....
2	*1. The following material sought was found (list) *2. The following articles other than article sought were seized (list): *3. No material was found or seized. 4. *Copy of warrant showing the premises entered on this occasion handed to occupier *Copy of warrant showing the premises entered on this occasion left on premises (specify where left) .... *Delete/complete as appropriate Signature(s) of constable(s) executing warrant on this occasion: ....

Continuation endorsement sheet? Yes ☐ No. ☐ ✓ Tick one box
Endorsement sheet 1 of (total) ____

9–46 **Form 4. Warrant to enter and search premises for evidence of an indictable offence** *(Section 15 of the Police and Criminal Evidence Act 1984)*

COPY FOR OCCUPIER OF THE PREMISES ENTERED

**delete/complete as applicable*

(Specify name of court ....) **Magistrates' Court (Code...........)**

Date:.............................

On this day an application supported by an information was made by (specify name of applicant): .... for the issue of warrant under section 8 of the Police and Criminal Evidence Act 1984 to enter:

[*the one set of premises situated at (specify premises);..
....]

[*The sets of premises described in the Schedule attached]

and search for (identify so far as is practicable the material sought):
....
....
....
....

Authority is hereby given for any constable, [*accompanied by such other person or persons as are necessary for the purposes of the search,] to enter the said premises on the number of occasions specified below within three months from the date of issue of this warrant and on each such occasion to search for the material in respect of which the application is made.

Number of occasions that each set of premises may be entered and searched under this warrant is:
[*on ONE occasion only.]
*subject to any second and subsequent entry being authorised in writing by an inspector or above,
[*on NOT MORE THAN (enter words & number) .... occasions.]
[*on an UNLIMITED number of occasions.]

District Judge (Magistrates' Court)
Justice of the Peace.

To be completed by the officer in charge of the search if the premises entered are not specified above:
For the information of the occupier, the premises entered on this occasion are:
(Premises: ....
You are not entitled to be given details of, or any information about, other premises to which the warrant authorises entry.
Signed..Date: .... Time: ....
Officer in charge of the search:

9–47 Form 5. Record of authority given by inspector or above to execute search warrant issued under section 8 Police and Criminal Evidence Act 1984 *(See Section [(1)]16(3A) and [(2)](3B) Police and Criminal Evidence Act 1984 and Code B 6.3A and 6.3B)*

Insert Police force references as required

The written authority of an inspector or above not involved in the investigation is required;
(a) in the case of an ***all premises warrant,*** *[(1)]BEFORE entry to any premises which are* ***not specified*** *that warrant; and/or*
(b) in the case of ***a warrant authorising multiple entries,*** *[(2)]BEFORE entry to any premises for the* ***second or any*** *subsequent time.*

Each signed authorisation below applies to the search warrant issued under section 8 of the Police and Criminal Evidence Act 1984 on (date) .... at [Specify name of court...........] Magistrates' Court (Code) on application made by (specify name of applicant)..

No	Premises (Specify premises to which authority relates)	Authority is given as follows to enter: (complete **A** and/or **B** as applicable)		Authorising officer (Signature/rank/station/date)
		[(1)]**A**: Premises not specified in all premises warrant: State reason it was not reasonably practicable to specify these premises when the application for the warrant and why entry now necessary	[(2)]**B** Premises for a 2nd or subsequent time: State number of previous entries why a further entry is necessary to achieve the purpose for which the warrant is issued.	
1				
2				
3				
4				
5				
6				
7				
8				
9				
10				

Forms

MAGISTRATES' COURTS

(Prescribed by the Magistrates' Courts (Forms) Rules 1981. For forms in criminal proceedings, see Annex D to the Practice Direction (criminal: consolidated) [2002].)

Italicised Forms in the list below are not reproduced here. They can be found in the CD-Rom version of this edition.

CIVIL PROCEDURE

Orders other than Civil Debt

Magistrates' Courts (Forms) Rules 1981[1]

(SI 1981/ 553 amended by 1982/246, 1983/524, 1984/1542, 1985/1945, 1986/1333, SI 1990/ 336, SI 1992/729, SI 1994/1481, SI 1995/585 and 1909, SI 1997/707, 1997/2421, 2001/615, SI 2003/1236 and Courts Act 2003, Sch 8)

9–300 **1.** (1) These Rules may be cited as the Magistrates' Courts (Forms) Rules 1981 and shall come into operation on 6th July 1981.

(2) The Rules mentioned in Schedule 1 to these Rules are hereby revoked, but where proceedings were commenced before 6th July 1981 and the old enactments within the meaning of paragraphs 1 and 2(2) of Schedule 8 to the Magistrates' Courts Act 1980 continue to apply by virtue of paragraph 2(1) of the said Schedule 8, the provisions of the Rules so mentioned continue to apply and nothing in these Rules affects those provisions.

1. Made by the Lord Chancellor in exercise of the power conferred on him by s 144 of the Magistrates' Courts Act 1980, as extended by s 145 of that Act. In Wales bi-lingual forms may be used and in certain cases forms may be requested in Welsh; see Magistrates' Courts (Welsh Forms) Rules 1986, SI 1986/1079.

9–301 **2.** (1) The forms contained in Schedule 2 to these Rules or forms to the like effect may be used, with such variation as the circumstances may require, in connection with proceedings in magistrates' courts[1].

(2) Where a requirement is imposed by or under any Act for the use of a form prescribed by rules made under section 144 of the Magistrates' Courts Act 1980, and an appropriate form is contained in Schedule 2 to these Rules, that form or a form to the like effect shall be used.

1. The forms in Sch 2 to the Magistrates' Courts (Children and Young Persons) Rules 1992, post, may be used in lieu of these forms in the youth court.

9–302

Rule 2

SCHEDULE 2

FORMS

9–590

FORM 98

COMPLAINT

(MC Act 1980, ss 51, 52; MC Rules 1981, r 4)

............Magistrates' Court (*Code*)

Date:

Defendant:

Address:

Matter of complaint: (*short particulars and statute*)

The complaint of:

Address: Telephone No.

who (upon oath) states that the defendant was responsible for the matter of complaint of which particulars are given above.

Taken (and sworn) before me

Justice of the Peace

(Justices' Clerk)

9–871

FORM 155

CASE STATED

(MC Act 1980, s 111; MC Rules 1981, rr 78, 81)

In the High Court of Justice
Queen's Bench Division

Between AB, ... Appellant .... CD, ... and .... Respondent.

Case stated by Justices for the (county of ...., acting in and for the Petty Sessional Division of ....), in respect of their adjudication as a Magistrates' Court sitting at ....

CASE

1 On the ....day of ...., 19...., an information (*or* complaint) was preferred by the appellant (*or* respondent) against the respondent (*or* appellant) that he/she (*state shortly particulars of information or complaint and refer to any relevant statutes*).

2 We heard the said information (*or* complaint) on the .... day of ...., 19...., and found the following facts:—(*set out in separate lettered paragraphs*).

* (The following is a short statement of the evidence:— (*set out so as to show relevant evidence given by each witness*)).

**3 It was contended by the appellant that

**4 It was contended by the respondent that

5 We were referred to the following cases

6 We were of opinion that (*state grounds of decision*) and accordingly (*state decision including any sentence or order*).

QUESTION

7 The question for the opinion of the High Court is ....
Dated the ....day of ...., 19.....

EF,...............
GH,...............
Justices of the Peace for the (county) aforesaid (on behalf of all the Justices adjudicating).

Criminal Procedure

Practice Direction (Crime: consolidated) [2002]

ANNEX E

9–986 Form E1

MAGISTRATES' COURT
CASE PROGRESSION

Case committed for trial to the Crown Court under section 6 of the Magistrates' Courts Act 1980

Committed to Crown Court at		on / /
Prosecution advocate:		
D1	[bail] [custody] represented by:	
D2	[bail] [custody] represented by:	
D3	[bail] [custody] represented by:	
D4	[bail] [custody] represented by:	
D5	[bail] [custody] represented by:	
No. of case in Magistrates' Court:		URN:

	D1	D2	D3	D4	D5
Has the defendant been advised about credit for pleading guilty?					
Has the defendant been warned that if he is on bail and fails to attend, the proceedings may continue in his absence?					

1. PLEA AND CASE MANAGEMENT HEARING

The plea and case management hearing will take place on:

2. DIRECTIONS

a. The indictment to be preferred within 28 days and the draft indictment, if not already served, to be served forthwith.
b. If the defence wish a prosecution witness to be called to give evidence in person at the trial, the defence shall so notify the prosecution and the Crown Court within 14 days.
c. Following receipt of the notification referred to in b., the police to notify the prosecution and the Crown Court of the dates when the witness is unavailable to give evidence and the reasons therefor so that the information is available at the plea and case management hearing.
d. The prosecution to comply with its initial duty of disclosure (if not already done) within 14 days.
e. The defence to serve the defence statement, including alibi details if appropriate, within 14 days of the date on which the prosecution complied, or purported to comply, with its initial duty of disclosure.
f. The prosecution to serve any application for special measures within 28 days.
g. The defence to serve any response to the application for special measures within 14 days of service of the application.
h. The prosecution to serve any notice of intention to introduce hearsay evidence within 14 days.
i. The defence to serve any notice opposing the prosecution notice under h., within 14 days of receipt of that notice.
j. The defence to serve any notice of intention to introduce hearsay evidence within 14 days of the date on which the prosecution complied, or purported to comply, with its initial duty of disclosure.
k. The prosecution to serve any notice opposing the defence notice under j. within 14 days of receipt of that notice.
l. The defence to serve any application to introduce the bad character of a prosecution witness within 14 days of the date on which the prosecution complied, or purported to comply, with its initial duty of disclosure.

m. The prosecution to serve any notice opposing the defence application under l. to introduce the bad character of a prosecution witness within 14 days of receipt of the application.

n. The prosecution to serve any notice to introduce the defendant's bad character within 14 days of the service of the prosecution case papers.

o. The defence to serve any application to exclude evidence of the defendant's bad character within 7 days of receipt of the prosecution notice under n.

p. The parties shall, within 14 days, give to the Crown Court case progression officer responsible for this case all the relevant information to enable the Crown Court Case Details form to be completed.

q. *Further orders*:

GUIDANCE NOTES

General notes

These notes accompany the standard directions form for cases committed to the Crown Court.

The Consolidated Criminal Practice Direction states:

V.56.5 . . . a plea and case management hearing ('PCMH') should be ordered in every case ... or committed to the Crown Court for trial. The PCMH should be held within about 7 weeks after committal for trial . . .

Parties must come to the hearing prepared to provide the information set out on page 1 of the form (to the extent that this has not already been done) and to answer the questions in bold. Local practice will determine whether the parties will be required to complete the form and make it available to the District Judge or Magistrate at or before the start of the hearing.

The directions set out in section 2 are default directions, which will apply unless a contrary order is made. Most of these directions are laid down by the Criminal Procedure Rules 2005. The purpose of the directions is to enable the PCMH to be an effective hearing.

The proposed italicised orders should be filled in, if relevant.

Except where otherwise required, a direction in the form to "serve" material means serve on the other party(ies) and file with the Crown Court.

If there are more than 5 defendants use a second form only to record the details on page 1 and the answers to the questions in bold and record the directions on one form only.

Notes relevant to specific sections

1. PLEA AND CASE MANAGEMENT HEARING

1a. This date should be obtained from the Crown Court.

The plea and case management hearing should be fixed for a date within about 7 weeks after committal.

2. DIRECTIONS

2a. See Rule 14.2(1)(d) of the Criminal Procedure Rules 2005.

2b. Section 68 and Schedule 2 of the Criminal Procedure and Investigations Act 1996 ("CPIA") provide that statements served under section 5B of the Magistrates' Courts Act 1980 (committal proceedings) are to be read at trial unless the defence serve notice on the prosecution within **14** days of committal of any objection: see Part 27 of the Criminal Procedure Rules 2005. The Crown Court may extend the period: see Rule 27.2(3).

2e. See regulation 2 of the Criminal Procedure and Investigations Act 1996 (Defence Disclosure Time Limits) Regulations 1997, S.I. 1997 No. 684. If the prescribed period would expire on a weekend, Christmas Day, Good Friday or a bank holiday, the period is treated as expiring on the next working day. By virtue of regulation 3(1): "The period referred to in regulation 2 shall, if the [Crown] court so orders, be extended by so many days as the court specifies". By virtue of regulation 3(2): "The court may only make such an order if an application which complies with paragraph (3) below is made by the accused before the expiration of the period referred to in regulation 2."

2f. See Rule 29.1(4) of the Criminal Procedure Rules 2005. The Crown Court may extend the time: see Rule 29.2; and there is provision for late applications: see Rule 29.3.

2g. See Rule 29.1(6) of the Criminal Procedure Rules 2005. (The Crown Court has no explicit power to extend the time for opposing under 29.1(6): see 29.2(1)).

2h. See Rule 34.3 of the Criminal Procedure Rules 2005. The Crown Court may vary the period, see Rule 34.7.

2i. See Rule 34.5 of the Criminal Procedure Rules 2005. The Crown Court may vary the period, see Rule 34.7.

2j. See Rule 34.4 of the Criminal Procedure Rules 2005. The Crown Court may vary the period, see Rule 34.7.

2k. See Rule 34.5 of the Criminal Procedure Rules 2005. The Crown Court may vary the period, see Rule 34.7.

2l. See Rule 35.2 of the Criminal Procedure Rules 2005. The Crown Court may vary the period, see Rule 35.8.

2m. See Rule 35.3 of the Criminal Procedure Rules 2005. The Crown Court may vary the period, see Rule 35.8.
2n. See Rule 35.4 of the Criminal Procedure Rules 2005. The Crown Court may vary the period, see Rule 35.8.
2o. See Rule 35.6 of the Criminal Procedure Rules 2005. The Crown Court may vary the period, see Rule 35.8.

9–987

Form E2

MAGISTRATES' COURT
CASE PROGRESSION

Case sent to the Crown Court under section 51 of the Crime and Disorder Act 1968

Committed to Crown Court at		on / /
Prosecution advocate:		
D1	[bail] [custody] represented by:	
D2	[bail] [custody] represented by:	
D3	[bail] [custody] represented by:	
D4	[bail] [custody] represented by:	
D5	[bail] [custody] represented by:	
No. of case in Magistrates' Court:		URN:

	D1	D2	D3	D4	D5
Has the defendant been advised about credit for pleading guilty?					
Has the defendant been warned that if he is on bail and fails to attend, the proceedings may continue in his absence?					

1. PRELIMINARY HEARING & PLEA AND CASE MANAGEMENT HEARING
   a. If this is a case for which a preliminary hearing in the Crown Court is necessary the preliminary hearing will take place on: / /
   b. The plea and case management hearing will take place on: / /
   c. If a defendant is likely to plead guilty, and a pre-sentence report would be appropriate, the court orders:
   d. **If a defendant is likely to plead guilty, are there any other matters which should be dealt with at the same time as these proceedings (other offences/TICs)?**
   e. **If yes, give brief details:**
   f. If there are other matters, the court orders:
   g. Further orders (e.g. orders re medical or psychiatric reports):
2. FURTHER DIRECTIONS
   a. The prosecution to serve copies of the documents containing the evidence on which the charge or charges are based ("the prosecution case papers") together with a draft indictment within 50 days where the defendant is in custody and within 70 days in other cases.
   b. The indictment to be preferred within 28 days of the service of the prosecution case papers.
   c. Any notice of application by the defence to dismiss the charges shall be made within 14 days of the service of the prosecution case papers.
   d. If the defence wish a prosecution witness to be called to give evidence in person at the trial, the defence shall so notify the prosecution and the Crown Court within 7 days of receiving the prosecution case papers.
   e. Following receipt of the notification referred to in d., the police to notify the prosecution and the Crown Court of the dates when the witness is unavailable to give evidence and the reasons therefor so that the information is available for the plea and case management hearing.
   f. The prosecution to comply with its initial duty of disclosure at the same time as service of the prosecution case papers.
   g. The defence to serve the defence statement, including alibi details if appropriate, within 14 days of the date on which the prosecution complied, or purported to comply, with its initial duty of disclosure.
   h. The prosecution to serve any application for special measures within 28 days of the service of the prosecution case papers.
   i. The defence to serve any response to the application for special measures within 14 days of service of the application.

j. The prosecution to serve any notice of intention to introduce hearsay evidence within 14 days of the service of the prosecution case papers.

k. The defence to serve any notice opposing the prosecution notice under j. within 14 days of receipt of that notice.

l. The defence to serve any notice of intention to introduce hearsay evidence within 14 days of the date on which the prosecution complied, or purported to comply, with its initial duty of disclosure.

m. The prosecution to serve any notice opposing the defence notice under l. within 14 days of receipt of that notice.

n. The defence to serve any application to introduce the bad character of a prosecution witness within 14 days of the date on which the prosecution complied, or purported to comply, with its initial duty of disclosure.

o. The prosecution to serve any notice opposing the defence application under n. to introduce the bad character of a prosecution witness within 14 days of receipt of the application.

p. The prosecution to serve any notice to introduce the defendant's bad character within 14 days of the service of the prosecution case papers.

q. The defence to serve any application to exclude evidence of the defendant's bad character within 7 days of receipt of the prosecution notice under p.

r. *Any further orders relating to bad character:*

s. The parties shall, within 14 days, give to the Crown Court case progression officer responsible for this case all the relevant information to enable the Crown Court Case Details form to be completed.

t. *Further orders:*

GUIDANCE NOTES

General notes

These notes accompany the standard directions form for cases sent to the Crown Court.

The Consolidated Criminal Practice Direction states:

V.56.4 A preliminary hearing ('PH') is not required in every case sent for trial under section 51 of the Crime and Disorder Act 1998: see rule 12.2 (which altered the Crown Court rule from which it derived). A PH should be ordered only where such a hearing is considered necessary. The PH should be held about 14 days after sending.

V.56.5 Whether or not a magistrates' court orders a PH, a plea and case management hearing ('PCMH') should be ordered in every case sent or committed to the Crown Court for trial. The PCMH should be held ... within about 14 weeks after sending for trial where a defendant is in custody and within about 17 weeks after sending for trial where a defendant is on bail.

Parties must come to the hearing prepared to provide the information set out on page 1 of the form (to the extent that this has not already been done) and to answer the questions in bold. Local practice will determine whether the parties will be required to complete the form and make it available to the District Judge or Magistrate at or before the start of the hearing.

If the defendant intends to plead guilty the court should make appropriate orders so that the defendant can be sentenced at the preliminary hearing if possible.

The directions set out in section 2 are default directions, which will apply unless a contrary order is made. Most of these directions are laid down by the Criminal Procedure Rules 2005. The purpose of the directions is to enable the PCMH to be an effective hearing.

The proposed italicised orders should be filled in, if relevant.

Except where otherwise required, a direction in the form to "serve" material means serve on the other party(ies) and file with the Crown Court.

If there are more than 5 defendants use a second form only to record the details on page 1 and the answers to the questions in bold and record the direction on one form only.

Notes relevant to specific sections

1. PRELIMINARY HEARING & PLEA AND CASE MANAGEMENT HEARING

Where a preliminary hearing is fixed, the date of the plea and case management hearing should be fixed at the same time. Both dates should be obtained from the Crown Court.

Subject to any direction of the Resident Judge, a preliminary hearing should normally only be ordered where:

i) there are case management issues which call for such a hearing;
ii) the case is likely to last for more than 4 weeks;
iii) it would be desirable to set an early trial date;
iv) the defendant is a child or young person;
v) there is likely to be a guilty plea and the defendant could be sentenced at the preliminary hearing; or
vi) it seems to the court that it is a case suitable for a preparatory hearing in the Crown Court (see sections 7 and 9 of the Criminal Justice Act 1987 and sections 29-32 of the Criminal

Procedure and Investigations Act 1996, as amended by sections 43-45 of the Criminal Justice Act 2003).

A preliminary hearing should be fixed for a date about 14 days after sending. The plea and case management hearing should be fixed for a date within about 14 weeks of sending where the defendant is in custody and within about 17 weeks of sending where the defendant is on bail.

No preliminary hearing should be fixed where a case is sent for trial to the Central Criminal Court. If necessary, one will be fixed by that Court.

If the defendant is facing charges in other courts give brief details of offence, court and court number.

2. DIRECTIONS

2a. For a case sent to the Crown Court under section 51 of the Crime and Disorder Act 1998, the Crime and Disorder Act 1998 (Service of Prosecution Evidence) Regulations 2000 (as amended) provide that the prosecution case papers must be served within 50 days of sending where the defendant is in custody and within 70 days of sending in other cases. The Magistrates' Court has no power to enlarge this period: see paragraph 1 of Schedule 3 to the Crime and Disorder Act 1998 ("the 1998 Act"). Only a Crown Court judge can extend the period.

2b. See Rule 14.2(1)(d) of the Criminal Procedure Rules 2005.

2c. See Rule 13.2(2)(c) and Rule 13.3(4)(c) of the Criminal Procedure Rules 2005.

2d. By virtue of section 9(1) of the Criminal Justice Act 1967 a written statement of a witness is "admissible as evidence to the like extent as oral evidence" if, amongst other things, "none of the other parties or their solicitors, within **seven** days from the service of the copy of the statement, serves a notice ... objecting to the statement being tendered in evidence under this section" (s. 9(2)(d)). The period includes weekends and bank holidays. By virtue of s. 9 (4) and (5), a judge in the Crown Court may require that person to attend before the court and give evidence even though the notice was not given in time.

2g. See regulation 2 of the Criminal Procedure and Investigations Act 1996 (Defence Disclosure Time Limits) Regulations 1997, S.I. 1997 No. 684. If the prescribed period would expire on a weekend, Christmas Day, Good Friday or a bank holiday, the period is treated as expiring on the next working day. By virtue of regulation 3(1): "The period referred to in regulation 2 shall, if the [Crown] court so orders, be extended by so many days as the court specifies". By virtue of Regulation 3(2): "The court may only make such an order if an application which complies with paragraph (3) below is made by the accused before the expiration of the period referred to in regulation 2."

2h. See Rule 29.1(4) of the Criminal Procedure Rules 2005. The Crown Court may extend the time: see Rule 29.2; and there is provision for late applications: see Rule 29.3.

2i. See Rule 29.1(6) of the Criminal Procedure Rules 2005. (The Crown Court has no explicit power to extend the time for opposition under 29.1(6): see 29.2(1).)

2j. See Rule 34 3 of the Criminal Procedure Rules 2005. The Crown Court may vary the period, see Rule 34.7.

2k. See Rule 34.5 of the Criminal Procedure Rules 2005. The Crown Court may vary the period, see Rule 34.7.

2l. See Rule 34.4 of the Criminal Procedure Rules 2005. The Crown Court may vary the period, see Rule 34.7.

2m. See Rule 34 .5 of the Criminal Procedure Rules 2005. The Crown Court may vary the period, see Rule 34.7.

2n. See Rule 35.2 of the Criminal Procedure Rules 2005. The Crown Court may vary the period, see Rule 35.8.

2o. See Rule 35.3 of the Criminal Procedure Rules 2005. The Crown Court may vary the period, see Rule 35.8.

2p. See Rule 35.4 of the Criminal Procedure Rules 2005. The Crown Court may vary the period, see Rule 35.8.

2q. See Rule 35.6 of the Criminal Procedure Rules 2005. The Crown Court may vary the period, see Rule 35.8.

2r. Any orders not covered by the bad character provisions in 2n. to 2q should be noted here.

2t. Where a case is sent for trial to the Central Criminal Court the prosecution should be required to serve, 7 days before the plea and case management hearing, an extended case summary prepared or approved by the advocate who will attend that hearing.

9–988

Form E3

MAGISTRATES' COURT
CASE PROGRESSION

Case to be tried in the magistrates' courts

Date of hearing: / /

The court will fix the trial date at (or shortly after) the hearing at which the defendant pleads not guilty. The directions below apply from that hearing unless they are modified or deleted by the court.

DEFENDANT

Name of defendant .... Age ...... Date of Birth ......

Address ....

....

In custody /on bail Contact telephone number (if defendant agrees) ....

CASE

No. of case in Magistrates' Court: [ ] URN: [ ]

Charges: ....

....

....

....

LEGAL REPRESENTATION

Prosecution Reviewing Lawyer: .... Address: ....

Tel.: .... Fax: ....

Email: .... DX ....

Defence Solicitor: .... Solicitors Firm & Address: ....

Tel.: .... Fax: ....

Email: .... DX ....

CASE PROGRESSION OFFICERS

Magistrates' Court	Prosecution	Defence
Name:	Name:	Name:
Address:	Address:	Address:
Tel:	Tel:	Tel:
Fax:	Fax:	Fax:
Email:	Email:	Email:
DX:	DX:	DX:

Has the defendant been advised about credit for pleading guilty? **YES/NO**

Has the defendant been warned that if he is on bail and fails to attend, the proceedings may continue in his absence? **YES/NO**

TRIAL DATE The trial will take place on: and is expected to last for:

DIRECTIONS

Special measures

a. The prosecution to serve any application for special measures within **14 days**.

b. The defence to serve any response to the application for special measures within **14 days** of service of the prosecution application.

Prosecution case and disclosure

c. To the extent it has not done so, the prosecution must serve copies of the documents containing the evidence on which the charge or charges are based, including witness statements and any documentary exhibits, tapes of interview, video tapes and CCTV tapes within **[28] days**.

d. To the extent it has not done so, the prosecution must comply with its initial duty of disclosure within **[28] days**.

Hearsay evidence

e. The prosecution to serve any notice of intention to introduce hearsay evidence at the same time as it complies, or purports to comply with its initial duty of disclosure.

f. The defence to serve any notice opposing the prosecution's notice under e., within **14 days** of receipt of the notice.

g. The defence to serve any notice of intention to introduce hearsay evidence within **14 days** of the date on which the prosecution complied, or purported to comply, with its initial duty of disclosure.
h. The prosecution to serve any notice opposing the defence's notice under g. within **14 days** of receipt of the application.

Bad character evidence

i. The defence to serve any application to introduce the bad character of a prosecution witness within **14 days** of the date on which the prosecution complied, or purported to comply, with its initial duty of disclosure.
j. The prosecution to serve any notice opposing the defence application to introduce the bad character of a prosecution witness under i. within **14 days** of receipt of the application.
k. The prosecution to serve any notice to introduce the defendant's bad character at the same time as it complies, or purports to comply with its initial duty of disclosure.
l. The defence to serve any application to exclude evidence of the defendant's bad character within 7 **days** of receipt of the prosecution application under k.
m. *Any further orders relating to bad character:*

Defence statement

n. If a defence statement is to be given, the defence must serve it within **14 days** of the prosecution complying or purporting to comply with its initial duty of disclosure.

Witness statements

o. If the defence wish a prosecution witness to give evidence in person at the trial, the defence shall so notify the prosecution within **7** days of receiving the prosecution case under c.
p. The defence must serve any statements of defence witnesses who the defence propose not to give evidence in person at the trial within **[14] days** of receiving the prosecution case under c.
q. If a party requires a witness whose statement has been served under p. to give evidence in person at the trial, the party shall so notify the prosecution within **7** days of service of the statement.

Further disclosure

r. The prosecution to complete any further disclosure at least **[14]** days before the trial.

Written admissions

s. The parties must file any written admissions made under section 10 of the Criminal Justice Act 1967 within **[56] days**.

Expert evidence

t. If either party intends to rely on expert evidence, the directions below apply.

Point of law

u. If any point of law is to be taken by a party and a skeleton argument would be helpful, it must be served together with authorities at least **[21] days** prior to the trial.
v. The other party must serve a skeleton argument in reply together with authorities at least **[7] days** prior to the trial.

Trial readiness

w. The parties must certify readiness for trial, by filing a certificate of readiness if appropriate, at least **[7] days** prior to the trial.
x. *Any other orders:*

Further case management

y. *A further case management hearing will take place on:*

EXPERT EVIDENCE

a. A party seeking to rely on expert evidence must serve the expert's report within **[28] days**.
b. A party served with expert evidence must indicate whether the expert is required to attend at the trial, and either serve their own expert evidence in response or indicate that they are not intending to rely on expert evidence within **[28] days** of receipt of the other party's expert evidence.
c. A meeting of experts to agree non-contentious matters and identify issues, if appropriate and if the parties agree, must take place within **[28] days** of service of both parties' expert evidence.
d. The parties must notify the court within **[14] days** of an experts' meeting whether the length of the trial is affected by the outcome of the meeting.

GUIDANCE NOTES

General notes

These notes accompany the standard directions form for cases to be tried in the Magistrates' Court. The directions in this form will apply when a defendant pleads not guilty to a summary offence, or a defendant pleads not guilty to an offence triable either way and it is determined that the case will be tried in the magistrates' court. The timetable begins on the date of the not guilty plea.

The directions in this form allow parties 8 weeks in which to prepare for trial, or 14 weeks where there is to be expert evidence. Not all those directions will be needed in every case. If the court fixes a trial date less than 8 weeks after the date of the not guilty plea then directions relevant to the case will need to be modified.

If the defendant intends to plead guilty but there is a dispute over the facts of the offence, and a Newton Hearing is to be held, the relevant directions will apply and any reference to the trial should be read as a reference to the Newton Hearing. The timetable begins on the date of the guilty plea.

The directions are default directions, which will apply where the defendant pleads not guilty unless the justices, a District Judge (Magistrates' Court), a justices' clerk or an assistant to a justices' clerk, as the case may be, direct otherwise. Except where they appear in square brackets, the time limits are mandatory except to the extent that there is power to vary them.

Parties must come to the hearing prepared to provide the information set out on page 1 of the form (to the extent that this has not already been done) and to answer the questions in bold. Local practice will determine whether the parties will be required to complete the form and make it available to the District Judge or magistrate at or before the start of the hearing.

If the defendant decides later to plead guilty the defence should inform the prosecution and the court immediately and the court should made an appropriate order so that the defendant can be sentenced as soon as possible.

Except where otherwise required, a direction in the form to "serve" material, means serve on the other party(ies) and file with the Magistrates' Court.

If there is more than one defendant use a second form only to record the details on page 1 and the answers to the questions in bold and record the directions on one form only.

Notes relevant to specific sections

a. See Rule 29.1(4) of the Criminal Procedure Rules 2005.
b. See Rule 29.1(6) of the Criminal Procedure Rules 2005.
c. This is a suggested time limit only: the prosecution must provide copies of written statements and a summary of the prosecution case to the defence "as soon as practicable" after a request for advance information by the defence – see rule 21.3 of the Criminal Procedure Rules 2005.
d. This is a suggested time limit only: the prosecution must comply with their initial duty of disclosure "as soon as reasonably practicable"– see section 13 of the Criminal Procedure and Investigations Act 1996.
e. See Rule 34.3 of the Criminal Procedure Rules 2005.
f. See Rule 34.5 of the Criminal Procedure Rules 2005. The court may vary the period, see Rule 34.7.
g. See Rule 34.4 of the Criminal Procedure Rules 2005. The court may vary the period, see Rule 34.7.
h. See Rule 34.5 of the Criminal Procedure Rules 2005. The court may vary the period, see Rule 34.7.
i. See Rule 35 .2 of the Criminal Procedure Rules 2005. The court may vary the period, see Rule 35.8.
j. See Rule 35.3 of the Criminal Procedure Rules 2005. The court may vary the period, see Rule 35.8.
k. See Rule 35.4 of the Criminal Procedure Rules 2005. The court may vary the period, see Rule 35.8.
l. See Rule 35.6 of the Criminal Procedure Rules 2005. The court may vary the period, see Rule 35.8.
m. Any further orders not covered by the bad character provisions in i-l should be set out here.
n. See sections 6 and 12, Criminal Procedure and Investigations Act 1996 and Regulation 3 of the Criminal Procedure and Investigations Act 1996 (Defence Disclosure Time Limits) Regulations 1997. By virtue of Regulation 4, the period may be extended only if the application is made before its expiry.
o. A written statement of a witness served under section 9 Criminal Justice Act 1967 is "admissible as evidence to the like extent as oral evidence" if, amongst other things, "none of the other parties or their solicitors, within **seven** days from the service of the copy of the statement, serves a notice ... objecting to the statement being tendered in evidence under this section" (see section 9(2)(d)). The court may require the witness to give evidence orally notwithstanding a failure to comply with this requirement, see section 9(4).
p. See section 9 Criminal Justice Act 1967. This is a suggested period only and is subject to the discretion of the court.
q. See note o.

r. This is a suggested time limit only: the prosecution must comply with this duty as soon as reasonably practicable – see section 9, Criminal Procedure and Investigation Act 1996.

s. This is a suggested period only and is subject to the discretion of the court.

w. A formal certificate of readiness may not be necessary. The form and timing of confirmation of trial readiness is subject to the discretion of the court.

y. As part of the court's duty to actively manage cases, any unnecessary hearings should be avoided - see Rule 3.2 (2) (f) of the Criminal Procedure Rules 2005.

EXPERT EVIDENCE

a–d. See Rule 24.1 of the Criminal Procedure Rules 2005. These are suggested periods only and subject to the discretion of the court. Expert evidence not disclosed before trial may not be introduced without the court's permission – see Rule 24.3.

Forms

FAMILY COURTS

(prescribed by the Family Proceedings Courts (Children Act 1989) Rules 1991 as amended)

9–1020

Application for an order

Form C1

Children Act 1989

The court

To be completed by the court

Date issued

Case number

The full name(s) of the child(ren)

Child(ren)'s number(s)

1 About you (the applicant)

State
- *your title, full name, address, telephone number, date of birth and relationship to each child above*
- *your solicitor's name, address, reference, telephone, FAX and DX numbers.*

2 The child(ren) and the order(s) you are applying for

For each child state
- *the full name, date of birth and sex*
- *the type of order(s) you are applying for (for example, residence order, contact order, supervision order).*

3 Other cases which concern the child(ren)

If there have ever been, or there are pending, any court cases which concern
- *a child whose name you have put in paragraph 2*
- *a full, half or step brother or sister of a child whose name you have put in paragraph 2*
- *a person in this case who is or has been, involved in caring for a child whose name you have put in paragraph 2*

attach a copy of the relevant order and give
- *the name of the court*
- *the name and* **panel** *address (if known) of the guardian ad litem, if appointed*
- *the name and contact address (if known) of the court welfare officer, if appointed*
- *the name and contact address (if known) of the solicitor appointed for the child(ren).*

4 The respondent(s)

Appendix 3 Family Proceedings Rules 1991; Schedule 2 Family Proceedings Courts (Children Act 1989) Rules 1991

For each respondent state
- *the title, full name and address*
- *the date of birth (if known) or the age*
- *the relationship to each child.*

5 Others to whom notice is to be given

Appendix 3 Family Proceedings Rules 1991; Schedule 2 Family Proceedings Courts (Children Act 1989) Rules 1991

For each person state
- *the title, full name and address*
- *the date of birth (if known) or age*
- *the relationship to each child*

6 The care of the child(ren)

For each child in paragraph 2 state
- *the child's current address and how long the child has lived there*
- *whether it is the child's usual address and who cares for the child there*
- *the child's relationship to the other children (if any).*

7 Social Services

For each child in paragraph 2 state
- *whether the child is known to the Social Services.*
  If so, give the name of the social worker and the address of the Social Services department.
- *whether the child is, or has been, on the Child Protection Register. If so, give the date of registration.*

254698 C*

8 The education and health of the child(ren)

For each child state

- *the name of the school, college or place of training which the child attends*
- *whether the child is in good health. Give details of any serious disabilities or ill health.*
- *whether the child has any special needs.*

9 The parents of the child(ren)

For each child state

- *the full name of the child's mother and father*
- *whether the parents are, or have been, married to each other*
- *whether the parents live together. If so, where.*
- *whether, to your knowledge, either of the parents have been involved in a court case concerning a child. If so, give the date and the name of the court.*

10 The family of the child(ren) (other children)

For any other child not already mentioned in the family (for example, a brother or a half sister) state

- *the full name and address*
- *the date of birth (if known) or age*
- *the relationship of the child to you.*

11 Other adults

State
- *the full name of any other adults (for example, lodgers) who live at the same address as any child named in paragraph 2*
- *whether they live there all the time*
- *whether, to your knowledge, the adult has been involved in a court case concerning a child. If so, give the date and the name of the court.*

12 Your reason(s) for applying and any plans for the child(ren)

State briefly your reasons for applying and what you want the court to order.
- ***Do not** give a full statement if you are applying for an order under Section 8 of Children Act 1989. You may be asked to provide a full statement later.*
- ***Do not** complete this section if this form is accompanied by a prescribed supplement.*

13 At the court

State
- *whether you will need an interpreter at court (parties are responsible for providing their own). If so, specify the language.*
- *whether disabled facilities will be needed at court.*

Signed **(Applicant)** **Date**

C1

9–1021

Application **Form C2**

- **for leave to commence proceedings**
  Family Proceedings Rules 1991 Rule 4.3
  Family Proceedings Courts (Children Act 1989) Rules 1991 Rule 3
- **for an order or directions in existing family proceedings**
  Children Act 1989
- **to be joined as, or cease to be, a party in existing family proceedings**
  Family Proceedings Rules 1991 Rule 4.7(2)
  Family Proceedings Courts (Children Act 1989) Rules 1991 Rule 7(2)

The court	To be completed by the court Date issued Case number
The full name(s) of the child(ren)	Child(ren)'s number(s)

1 About you (the person making this application)

State
- *your title, full name, address, telephone number, date of birth and relationship to each child above*
- *your solicitor's name, address, reference, telephone, FAX and DX numbers*
- *if you are already a party to the case, give your description (for example, applicant, respondent or other).*

2 The order(s) or direction(s) you are applying for

State for each child
- *the full name, date of birth and sex*
- *the type of order(s) you are applying for (for example, residence order, contact order, supervision order).*

3 Persons to be served with this application

For each respondent to this application state the title, full name and address.

4 Your reason(s) for applying and any plans for the child(ren)

State briefly your reasons for applying.
***Do not** give a full statement if you are applying for an order under Section 8 Children Act 1989.*
You may be asked to provide a full statement later.

Signed (Applicant) **Date**

9–1022

Application for an order authorising search for, taking charge of, and delivery of, a child

Form C3

Section 34 Family Law Act 1986

The court	To be completed by the court Date issued Case number
The full name(s) of the child(ren)	Child(ren)'s number(s)

1 About you (the applicant)

State
- *your title, full name, address, telephone number, date of birth and relationship to each child above*
- *your solicitor's name, address, reference, telephone, FAX and DX numbers*

2 The child(ren)

For each child state
- *the full name, date of birth and sex*
- *the title, full name, address, telephone number of the person believed to have actual control of the child*
- *details which identify the child. You may enclose a recent photograph of the child, which should be dated.*

3 The grounds for the application

State
- *whether the application is ex parte and if so, why*
- *particulars of the order being disobeyed*
- *the best information available as to the whereabouts of the child.*

Signed
(Applicant)

Date

C3

9–1023

Application for an order for disclosure of a child's whereabouts

Form C4

Section 33 Family Law Act 1986

The court

To be completed by the court
Date issued

Case number

The full name(s) of the child(ren)

Child(ren)'s number(s)

1 About you (the applicant)

State
- *your title, full name, address, telephone number, date of birth and relationship to each child above*
- *your solicitor's name, address, reference, telephone, FAX and DX numbers.*

2 The child(ren)

For each child state
- *the full name, date of birth and sex*
- *the title, full name, address, telephone number of the person believed to have actual control of the child*
- *details which identify the child. You may enclose a recent photograph of the child, which should be dated.*

3 The order you are seeking

State
- *the name(s) of the person(s) to be directed by the Court to disclose relevant information as to the whereabouts of the child*
- *specific directions you would like the court to give as to when and how the information shall be disclosed to the court.*

4 The grounds for the application

State why you believe that
- ***the court does not have adequate information as to where the child is.***
- ***the person(s) to whom the order is directed may have relevant information.***

Signed (Applicant) **Date**

C4

9–1024

Supplement for an application for an Emergency Protection Order

Form C11

Section 44 Children Act 1989

The court

To be completed by the court

Date issued

Case number

The full name(s) of the child(ren)

Child(ren)'s number(s)

1 Description of the child(ren)

If a child's identity is not known, state details which will identify the child.
You may enclose a recent photograph of the child, which should be dated.

2 The grounds for the application

The grounds are

ANY APPLICANT

A ☐ that there is reasonable cause to believe that [this] [these] child[ren] [is] [are] likely to suffer significant harm if

☐ the child[ren] [is] [are] not removed to accommodation provided by or on behalf of this applicant

or ☐ the child[ren] [does] [do] not remain in the place where [the child] [they] [is] [are] currently being accommodated.

LOCAL AUTHORITY APPLICANTS

B ☐ that enquiries are being made about the welfare of the child[ren] under Section 47(1)(b) of Children Act 1989 **and** those enquiries are being frustrated by access to the child[ren] being unreasonably refused to someone who is authorised to seek access **and** there is reasonable cause to believe that access to the child[ren] is required as a matter of urgency.

AUTHORISED PERSON APPLICANTS

C ☐ that there is reasonable cause to suspect that the child[ren] [is] [are] suffering, or [is] [are] likely to suffer, significant harm **and** enquiries are being made with respect to the welfare of the child[ren] **and** those enquiries are being frustrated by access to the child[ren] being unreasonably refused to someone who is authorised to seek access **and** there is reasonable cause to believe that access to the child[ren] is required as a matter of urgency.

C11

254698 F*2

3 The additional order(s) applied for

☐ information on the whereabouts of the child[ren] (Section 48(1) Children Act 1989).

☐ authorisation for entry of premises (Section 48(3) Children Act 1989).

☐ authorisation to search for another child on the premises (Section 48(4) Children Act 1989).

4 The direction(s) sought

☐ contact (Section 44(6)(a) Children Act 1989).

☐ a medical or psychiatric examination or other assessment of the child[ren] (Section 44(6)(b) Children Act 1989).

☐ to be accompanied by a registered medical practitioner, registered nurse or registered health visitor (Section 45(12) Children Act 1989).

5 The reason(s) for the application

If you are relying on a report or other documentary evidence, state the date(s) and author(s) and enclose a copy.

Signed **Date**
(Applicant)

C11

9–1025

Supplement for an application for a warrant to assist a person authorised by an Emergency Protection Order

Form C12

Section 48 Children Act 1989

The court	**To be completed by the court**
	Date issued
	Case number
The full name(s) of the child(ren)	**Child(ren)'s number(s)**

1 Description of the child(ren)

If a child's identity is not known, state details which will identify the child.
You may enclose a recent photograph of the child, which should be dated.

2 The grounds for the application

An emergency protection order was made on:

(State the date and time, and attach a copy of the order)

and ☐ a person **has been** prevented from exercising powers under the order by being refused entry to premises or access to the child[ren]

or

☐ that a person **is likely to be** prevented from exercising powers under the order by being refused entry to premises or access to the child[ren]

3 The direction(s) sought

State
- *whether you wish to accompany the constable, if the warrant is granted*
- *whether you wish the constable to be accompanied by a registered medical practitioner, registered nurse or registered health visitor, if he so wishes*
- *where the constable is to take the child, if the warrant is executed.*

4 The reason(s) for the application

If you are relying on a report or other documentary evidence, state the date(s) and author(s) and enclose a copy.

Signed
(Applicant)

Date

C12

9–1026

Supplement for an application for a Recovery Order

Form C18

Section 50 Children Act 1989

The court	To be completed by the court
	Date issued
	Case number
The full name(s) and initials of the child(ren)	Child(ren)'s number(s)

1 Particulars of the child(ren)

State whether the child[ren] [is] [are] ☐ in care
or ☐ the subject of an emergency protection order
or ☐ in police protection.

Enclose a copy of the order

If a child's identity is not known, state details that will identify the child.
You may enclose a recent photograph of the child, which should be dated.

2 The order and direction(s) applied for

State

- *whether the child(ren) (is) (are) to be produced to an authorised person specified by the court (Section 50(7) Children Act 1989)*
- *whether you require the court to authorise a constable to enter specified premises (Section 50(3)(d) Children Act 1989).*

3 The grounds for the application

The grounds are that the child[ren]

☐ [has] [have] been unlawfully taken away or [is] [are] being unlawfully kept away from the responsible person

or ☐ [has] [have] run away or [is] [are] staying away from the responsible person

or ☐ [is] [are] missing.

4 The reason(s) for the application

Include your ground(s) for believing that the child(ren) (is) (are) on the premises named in paragraph 2 above (if applicable) (Section 50(6) Children Act 1989).
If you are relying on a report or other documentary evidence, state the date(s) and author(s) and enclose a copy.

Signed (Applicant)　　　Date

9–1027

Application for a warrant of assistance

Form C19

Section 102 Children Act 1989

Section 33 Adoption Act 1976

The court	To be completed by the court
	Date issued
	Case number
The full name(s) of the child(ren) (if known)	Child(ren)'s number(s)

1 About you (the applicant)

State
- *your title, full name, address, telephone number, and relationship to the child(ren) (if any)*
- *your solicitor's name, address, reference, telephone, FAX and DX numbers*
- *whether you are:*
  - ☐ a person authorised by the local authority
  - ☐ a person authorised by the Secretary of State
  - ☐ a supervisor acting under a supervision order

2 Description of the child(ren) (if applicable)

If a child's identity is not known, state details which will identify the child.
You may enclose a recent photograph of the child, which should be dated.

3 The grounds for the application

☐ I am attempting to exercise powers under an enactment within Section 102(6) Children Act 1989 at the following premises *(give full address)*:

and

☐ **I have been** prevented from exercising those powers by

☐ **I am likely to be** prevented from exercising those powers by

PERSON AUTHORISED BY THE LOCAL AUTHORITY

s62(6) ☐ [being, or likely to be, refused entry to accommodation provided by a voluntary organisation]
[being, or likely to be, refused access to a child in accommodation provided by a voluntary organisation]

s64(4) ☐ [being, or likely to be, refused entry to a children's home]
[being, or likely to be, refused access to a child in a children's home]

s67(3) ☐ [being, or likely to be, refused entry to a private foster home]
[being, or likely to be, refused access to a child in a private foster home]

s76(2)

☐ [being, or likely to be, refused entry to domestic premises where child-minding is carried on]
[being, or likely to be, refused access to a child on domestic premises where child-minding is carried on]

☐ [being, or likely to be, refused entry to premises on which day care for children under the age of 8 is provided]
[being or likely to be, refused access to a child in premises on which day care for children under the age of 8 is provided]

s86(5) ☐ [being, or likely to be, refused entry to a residential care, nursing or mental nursing home]
[being, or likely to be, refused access to a child in a residential care, nursing or mental nursing home]

s87(5) ☐ [being, or likely to be, refused entry to an independent school]
[being, or likely to be, refused access to a child in an independent school]

Section 33 Adoption Act 1976 ☐ [being, or likely to be, refused entry to premises on which a protected child is, or is likely to be, kept]
[being or likely to be prevented from visiting a protected child]

PERSON AUTHORISED BY THE SECRETARY OF STATE

s80(8) ☐ [being, or likely to be, refused entry to any of the premises specified by Section 80(1) Children Act 1989]
[being, or likely to be, refused access to a child in any of the premises specified by Section 80(1) Children Act 1989]

SUPERVISOR UNDER THE SUPERVISION ORDER

Paragraph 8(1)(b) Schedule 3 ☐ [being, or likely to be, refused entry to accommodation where a supervised child is living]

Paragraph 8(2)(b) Schedule 3 ☐ [being, or likely to be, refused contact with a supervised child by a responsible person]

4 The respondent(s)

For each respondent state the title, full name, address, telephone number and relationship (if any) to each child.

5 The reason(s) for the application

If you are relying on a report or other documentary evidence, state the date(s) and author(s) and enclose a copy.

6 The direction(s) sought

State
- ***whether you wish to accompany the constable, if the warrant is granted***
- ***whether you wish the constable to be accompanied by a registered medical practitioner, registered nurse or registered health visitor, if he so wishes.***

Signed (Applicant) **Date**

9–1028

Form C23

In the

Case Number:

Child(ren)'s Number(s):

Order

Emergency Protection Order
Section 44 Children Act 1989

The full name(s) of the child(ren)	Boy or Girl	Date(s) of birth

[described as

Warning **It is an offence intentionally to obstruct any person exercising the power under Section 44(4)(b) Children Act 1989 to remove, or prevent the removal, of a child** (Section 44(15) Children Act 1989).

The Court grants an Emergency Protection Order to the applicant who is

The Order gives the applicant parental responsibility for the child[ren].

The Court authorises [the applicant to remove the child[ren] to accommodation provided by or on behalf of the applicant]
[the applicant to prevent the child[ren] being removed from

[This order directs that any person who can produce the child[ren] to the applicant must do so.]

The Court directs that [[a named person] to be excluded from [a named address] [forthwith] [from [date]] so that the child may continue to live there, consent to the exclusion requirement having been given by [a named person]]

[a power of arrest be attached to the exclusion requirement for a period of]

This order ends on at [am] [pm]

Ordered by [Mr] [Mrs] Justice
[His] [Her] Honour Judge
District Judge [of Family Division]
Justice[s] of the Peace

on at [am] [pm]

C23

Form C23 continued

Notes about the Emergency Protection Order

About this order

This is an Emergency Protection Order.

This order states what has been authorised in respect of the child[ren] and when the order will end.

The court can extend this order for up to 7 days but it can only do this once.

Warning

If you are shown this order, you must comply with it. If you do not, you may commit an offence. Read the order now.

What you may do

You may apply to the court

to **change the directions**

or to **end the order.**

You may apply at any time, but the court will only hear an application to end an order **when 72 hours** have passed since the order was made.

If you would like to ask the court to change the directions, or end the order, you must fill in a form. You can obtain the form from a court office.

If the court has directed that the child[ren] should have a medical, psychiatric or another kind of examination, you may ask the court to allow a doctor of your choice to be at the examination.

What you should do

Go to a solicitor as soon as you can.

Some solicitors specialise in court proceedings which involve children. You can obtain the address of a solicitor or advice agency from the Yellow Pages or the Solicitor's Regional Directory.

You will find these books at

- a Citizens Advice Bureau
- a Law Centre
- a local library

A solicitor or an advice agency will be able to tell you whether you may be eligible for legal aid.

9–1029

In the

Case Number:

Child's Number:

Warrant

To assist a person authorised by an Emergency Protection Order

Section 48(9) Children Act 1989

To all Police Constables

The Court was satisfied that

who is the applicant, has been prevented, or is likely to be prevented from exercising powers under an Emergency Protection Order by being refused entry to the named premises or access to the child concerned.

The Court authorises

you to assist the applicant to exercise powers under an Emergency Protection Order made on

You may use reasonable force if necessary.

You may assist the applicant to gain access **to the child**

Name

Boy or Girl *Date of birth*

described as

You may assist the applicant to gain entry **to the premises**

known as

The Court directs

[that you should not be accompanied by the person who applied for the warrant]

[that you may, if you wish, be accompanied by
a registered medical practitioner
or a registered nurse
or a registered health visitor]

You should execute this warrant in accordance with the orders and directions contained in the Emergency Protection Order.

This warrant has [not] been made ex parte.

This warrant ends on

Ordered by [Mr] [Mrs] Justice
[His] [Her] Honour Judge
District Judge [of the Family Division]
Justice[s] of the Peace

on at [am] [pm]

C25

9–1030

In the

Case Number:

Child's Number:

Order

Authority to search for another child

Section 48(4) Children Act 1989

The full name(s) of the child	**Boy or Girl**	**Date of birth**

[who is described as

The Court was satisfied that **[an order had been granted on**
to the applicant for the emergency protection of a child, *known as*

and that the order had authorised the applicant to enter these premises].
[there was reasonable cause to believe that the child named in this order may be on those premises and that an Emergency Protection Order ought to be made in respect of that child].

The Court authorises

who is the applicant

to enter the premises, *known as*

and search for the child.

Warning **It is an offence intentionally to obstruct the applicant from entering or searching the premises specified above (Sections 48(7) and (8) Children Act 1989).**

This order has **[not] been made ex parte.**

This order ends on

Ordered by **[Mr] [Mrs] Justice**
[His] [Her] Honour Judge
District Judge [of the Family Division]
Justice[s] of the Peace

on **at** **[am] [pm]**

C27

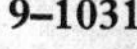

9–1031

In the

Case Number:

Child's Number:

Warrant

To assist a person to gain access to a child or entry to premises

Section 102(1) Children Act 1989

To all Police Constables

The Court authorises you to assist

exercise powers under an enactment as specified on the reverse of this warrant.
You may use reasonable force if necessary.

[You may assist this person to gain access **to the child**

Name

Boy or Girl *Date of birth*

described as

[You may assist this person to gain entry **to the premises**

known as

The Court directs [that you should not be accompanied by the person who applied for the warrant]

[that you may, if you wish, be accompanied by
a registered medical practitioner
or a registered nurse
or a registered health visitor]

This warrant has [not] been made ex parte.

Ordered by [Mr] [Mrs] Justice
[His] [Her] Honour Judge
District Judge [of the Family Division]
Justice[s] of the Peace

on at [am] [pm]

C28

The Court is satisfied that the applicant

☐ has been prevented from exercising those powers by

☐ is likely to be prevented from exercising those powers by

PERSON AUTHORISED BY THE LOCAL AUTHORITY

s62(6) ☐ [being, or likely to be, refused entry to accommodation provided by a voluntary organisation]
[being, or likely to be, refused access to a child in accommodation provided by a voluntary organisation]

s64(4) ☐ [being, or likely to be, refused entry to a children's home]
[being, or likely to be, refused access to a child in a children's home]

s67(3) ☐ [being, or likely to be, refused entry to a private foster home]
[being, or likely to be, refused access to a child in a private foster home]

s76(2) ☐ [being, or likely to be, refused entry to domestic premises where child-minding is carried on]
[being, or likely to be, refused access to a child on domestic premises where child-minding is carried on]

☐ [being, or likely to be, refused entry to premises on which day care for children under the age of 8 is provided]
[being or likely to be, refused access to a child in premises on which day care for children under the age of 8 is provided]

s86(5) ☐ [being, or likely to be, refused entry to a residential care, nursing or mental nursing home]
[being, or likely to be, refused access to a child in a residential care, nursing or mental nursing home]

s87(5) ☐ [being, or likely to be, refused entry to an independent school]
[being, or likely to be, refused access to a child in an independent school]

Section 33 Adoption Act 1976 ☐ [being, or likely to be, refused entry to premises on which a protected child is, or is likely to be, kept]
[being or likely to be prevented from visiting a protected child]

PERSON AUTHORISED BY THE SECRETARY OF STATE

s80(8) ☐ [being, or likely to be, refused entry to any of the premises specified by Section 80(1) Children Act 1989]
[being, or likely to be, refused access to a child in any of the premises specified by Section 80(1) Children Act 1989]

SUPERVISOR UNDER THE SUPERVISION ORDER

Paragraph 8(1)(b) Schedule 3 ☐ [being, or likely to be, refused entry to accommodation where a supervised child is living]

Paragraph 8(2)(b) Schedule 3 ☐ [being, or likely to be, refused contact with a supervised child by a responsible person]

9–1032

In the

Case Number:

Child's Number:

Order

Recovery of a child
Section 50 Children Act 1989

The full name(s) of the child **Boy or Girl** **Date of birth**

The Court is satisfied that [**has parental responsibility for the child by virtue of a [Care Order] [Emergency Protection Order] made on**]

[the child is in police protection and the designated officer is]

[The Court authorises

[a police constable] to remove the child.]

Warning **It is an offence intentionally to obstruct the person from removing the child (Section 50(9) Children Act 1989).**

[The Court authorises **[a police constable to enter the premises,** ***known as***

and search for the child, using reasonable force if necessary.]

[The Court requires **any person who has information about where the child is, or may be, to give that information to a police constable or an officer of the court, if asked to do so.]**

[The Court directs **any person who can produce the child when asked to by**

[a police constable] to do so.]

This order has **[not] been made ex parte.**

Ordered by **[Mr] [Mrs] Justice**
[His] [Her] Honour Judge
District Judge [of the Family Division]
Justice[s] of the Peace

on

C29

9–1033

In the

Case Number:

Child(ren)'s Number(s):

Order

To disclose information about the whereabouts of a missing child

Section 33 Family Law Act 1986

The full name(s) of the child(ren)	Boy or Girl	Date(s) of birth

The adult[s] who [is] [are] believed to have the child[ren] [is] [are]

Warning **Read this Order now. The Court has ordered you to give information and you must give it at once. If you do not, you may be in contempt of court and you may be fined, sent to prison or detained.**

The Court orders and directs **You**

to give all the information you have about where the child[ren] and adult[s]

are now, or where they were when you last knew

and where they are likely to be now.

You must give the information **forthwith, that is as soon as practicable, to an officer of**

Court

[in the following way

]

Ordered by **[Mr] [Mrs] Justice**
[His] [Her] Honour Judge
District Judge [of the Family Division]
Justice[s] of the Peace
[Assistant] Recorder

on

C30

9–1034

In the

Case Number:

Child's Number:

Order

Authorising search for, taking charge of, and delivery of, a child

Section 34 Family Law Act 1986

To [all Police Constables]

[an Officer of the Court]

Notice **You may use reasonable force to execute this order, if necessary.**

The Court authorises you to take charge of the child

Boy or Girl *Date of birth*

whose whereabouts are believed to be

The Court authorises you to enter and search any premises where you believe the child may be found.

The Court authorises you to take charge of the child and deliver the child to

Name

Address

who is entitled to receive the child by virtue of an order made by

Court

on

Ordered by [Mr] [Mrs] Justice

[His] [Her] Honour Judge

District Judge [of the Family Division]

Justice[s] of the Peace

[Assistant] Recorder

on

C31

PART X

STOP PRESS: MISCELLANEOUS LEGISLATION

Material included in Part X was received too late for inclusion under its correct Part and title. The material is listed below in the order in which it would normally appear.

10–1

Criminal Defence Service Act 2006[1]

(2006 c 9)

1. This Act amends the Access to Justice Act 1999, primarily: (*a*) to enable the Legal Services Commission, to the extent regulations define, to take over from courts the grant of rights of representation in criminal cases; and (*b*) to reintroduce a financial eligibility test and contribution orders. These amendments will be brought into force by commencement orders made under s 5. At the time of going to press, no such orders had been made.

10–2

Magistrates' Courts Fees (Amendment) Order 2006[1]

(SI 2006/715)

1. This Order may be cited as the Magistrates' Courts Fees (Amendment) Order 2006 and shall come into force on 6th April 2006.

1. Made by the Lord Chancellor in exercise of the powers conferred by s 92 of the Courts Act 2003.

2. For the Schedule to the Magistrates' Courts Fees Order 2005 substitute the Schedule in the Schedule to this Order.

Article 2

SCHEDULE

Article 2

"SCHEDULE

FEES TO BE TAKEN

Column 1 *Number and description of fee*		*Column 2* *Amount of fee*
1	**Attendance**	
1.1	On a justice of the peace, to view deserted premises in order to affix notice or to give possession thereof, or to view a highway, bridge or nuisance	£44

Column 1 Number and description of fee		Column 2 Amount of fee
2	**Case for the opinion of High Court**	
2.1	On an application to state a case for the opinion of the High Court under section 111 Magistrates' Courts Act 1980: drawing of case, copies, taking recognizance as required by section 114 of that Act and enlargement and renewal of such recognizance	£382
2.2	On a request for a certificate of refusal to state a case	£8
3	**Certificate**	
3.1	On a request for a certificate not otherwise charged	£25
4	**Register of Judgments, Orders and Fines**	
4.1	On a request for a certificate of satisfaction	£15
5	**Council tax and rates**	
5.1	On an application for a liability order (each defendant)	£3
Commitment		
5.2	On a complaint (or application) and the issue of a summons or a warrant of arrest without issuing a summons	£25
5.3	On the issue of a warrant of arrest if the summons is not obeyed	£25
5.4	On the making of a commitment order	£40
6	**Copy Documents**	
6.1	On a request for a copy of any document	
	(a) for the first page (except the first page of a subsequent copy of the same document supplied at the same time)	£1.10
	(b) per page in any other case	55p
	Where a fee has been paid for a summons, order or warrant no fee shall be charged for a copy of that document.	
	(c) each additional copy	10p
7	**Duplicate**	
7.1	For the duplicate of any document	£5
8	**Proceedings under the Domestic Proceedings and Magistrates' Courts Act 1978**	
8.1	On an application for an order for financial provision (excluding an application to vary or revoke such an order or in respect of an application for an order made to the benefit of, or against, a person residing outside the United Kingdom)	£175
9	**Proceedings under the Family Law Act 1986**	
9.1	On an application for a declaration of parentage (each child)	£130
10	**Proceedings under the Children Act 1989**	
10.1	On an application or request for permission under the following provisions of the Children Act 1989—	
	(a) section 4(1)(c) or (3) or 4A(1)(b) or (3) (parental responsibility)	£175
	(b) section 5(1) or 6(7) (guardians)	£175
	(c) section 10(1) or (2) (section 8 orders)	£175
	(d) section 13(1) (change of child's surname or removal from jurisdiction while residence order in force)	£175
	(e) section 14A(3) or (6)(a), 14C(3) or 14D(1) (special guardianship orders)	£140
	(f) section 31 (care or supervision order)	£150
	For the purposes of fee 10.1(f) a care order does not include an interim care order, and a supervision order does not include an interim supervision order.	
	(g) section 33(7) (change of child's surname or removal from jurisdiction while care order in force)	£150
	(h) section 34 (contact with a child in care)	£150
	(i) section 36 (education supervision order)	£150
	(j) section 43 (child assessment order)	£150
	(k) Part XA (affecting the registration of a child minder or day carer including appeals against cancellation or varying the conditions of the registration)	£150
	(l) paragraph 1(1), 2(1), 6(5) or 14(1) of Schedule 1 (financial provision)	£175
	(m) paragraph 8(1) of Schedule 8 (appeals concerning foster parenting)	£150
10.2	On an application to vary, extend or discharge an order relating to provisions to which the following fees apply—	
	(a) fees 10.1(a) to (d) and (l)	£175
	(b) fees 10.1(f) to (j)	£150
	Where an application requires the permission of the court, the relevant fee applies where permission is sought but no further fee may be charged if permission is granted and the application is made.	
	Where an application is made or filed or permission is sought under or relating to provisions of the Children Act 1989 which are listed in two or more different numbered fees, only the highest fee shall be payable.	
	Where an application is made or filed or permission is sought under or relating to two or more provisions of the Children Act 1989 which are listed in the same numbered fee, that fee shall be payable only once.	
	Where the same application is made or filed or permission is sought in respect of two or more children at the same time, only one fee shall be payable in respect of each numbered fee.	
11	**Proceedings under the Human Fertilisation and Embryology Act 1990**	
11.1	On an application under section 30 (parental order)	£175

Column 1 *Number and description of fee*		*Column 2* *Amount of fee*
12	**Proceedings under the Child Support Act 1991**	
12.1	On an application for a liability order	£40
12.2	On commencing an appeal under section 20	£130
12.3	On commencing an appeal against deduction from earnings order	£80
12.4	On a complaint (or application), the issue of a summons and/or a warrant of arrest, and the making of a commitment order (combined fee)	£90
13	**Proceedings under the Adoption and Children Act 2002**	
13.1	On an application or request for permission under Part 1 of the Adoption and Children Act 2002 including applications to vary or revoke an order Where an application requires the permission of the court, the relevant fee applies where permission is sought but no further fee may be charged if permission is granted and the application is made.	£140
14	**Proceedings under Schedule 6 to the Civil Partnership Act 2004**	
14.1	On an application for an order for financial provision (excluding an application to vary or revoke such an order or in respect of an application for an order made to the benefit of, or against, a person residing outside the United Kingdom)	£175
15	**Proceedings to vary, extend or revoke an order made in family proceedings**	
15.1	On an application to vary, extend or revoke an order not otherwise charged	£20
16	**Licences**	
16.1	For every licence, consent or authority not otherwise provided for, to include registration when necessary	£8
16.2	On an application for the revocation of a licence not otherwise provided for	£30
17	**Oaths**	
17.1	On the attestation of constable	£8
17.2	For every oath, affirmation or solemn declaration not otherwise charged (no fee is payable for the swearing in of witnesses in civil proceedings or in any case where an Act directs that no fee shall be taken)	£8
18	**Other civil proceedings**	
18.1	On a complaint (or application)	£25
18.2	On the issue of a summons and copy	£25
18.3	On the issue of a warrant and copy	£25
18.4	On the making of an order and copy	£25
19	**Warrant of Entry**	
19.1	On the application for a warrant of entry	£3

Note: Only one fee is payable where more than one document is issued in relation to a partnership."

10–3

Motor Vehicles (Driving Licences) (Amendment) Regulations 2006[1]

(SI 2006/524)

1. Citation and commencement. (1) These Regulations may be cited as the Motor Vehicles (Driving Licences) (Amendment) Regulations 2006.

(2) Regulation 9(3) shall come into force on 1st July 2007 and all other regulations shall come into force on 1st April 2006.

1. Made by the Secretary of State for Transport in exercise of the powers conferred by ss 89(3) and (4), 97(3), 105(1) and (3) of the Road Traffic Act 1988.

2. Amendment of the Motor Vehicles (Driving Licences) Regulations 1999. The Motor Vehicles (Driving Licences) Regulations 1999 are further amended in accordance with regulations 3 to 9.

3. (1) Regulation 17 (meaning of "qualified driver") is amended as follows.

(2) For paragraph (3)(c) to (f) and the Table substitute—

"(c) "relevant licence" means, subject to sub-paragraph (d), a full licence authorising—

(i) the driving of vehicles of the same class as the vehicle being driven by the provisional licence holder, and

(ii) where sub-paragraph (f) applies—

(aa) where that class of vehicle is included within any sub-category specified in column 1 of the table at the end of this regulation, the driving of vehicles in the sub-category specified in column 2 which is opposite that sub-category, or

(bb) where sub-paragraph (aa) does not apply, the driving of vehicles in the category specified in column 2 of that table which is opposite the category specified in column 1 that includes the class of vehicle being driven by the provisional licence holder;

(d) in the case of a disabled driver who holds a licence authorising the driving of vehicles in category B, a relevant licence must authorise the driving of vehicles other than vehicles in sub-category B1 or B1 (invalid carriages);

(e) a person has relevant driving experience if—

(i) where sub-paragraph (c)(i) only applies, he has held the relevant licence for a period of 3 years, or

(ii) minimum where sub-paragraph (c)(ii) applies, he has held the relevant licence authorising the driving of vehicles—

(aa) of the same class as the vehicle being driven by the provisional licence holder for a minimum period of 1 year, and

(bb) in the category or sub-category specified in column 2 described in sub-paragraph (c)(ii) for a minimum period of 3 years;

(f) this sub-paragraph applies where—

(i) a person holds a full licence authorising the driving of vehicles of the same class as the vehicle being driven by the provisional licence holder;

(ii) that class is included in a category or sub-category specified in column 1 of the table at the end of this regulation, and

(iii) that person has held that licence for less than a minimum period of 3 years;

(g) for the purposes of sub-paragraphs (e) and (f), the minimum period of time for holding a full licence may be met either by holding that licence continuously for that period or for periods amounting in aggregate to not less than that period.

TABLE

Column 1 *Categories and sub-categories which include the vehicle being driven by the provisional licence holder*	*Column 2* *Categories and sub-categories authorised by the relevant licence*
C	D
C1	D1
C + E	D + E
C1 + E	D1 + E
D	C
D1	C1
D + E	C+E
D1 + E	C1 + E"

4. In regulation 22 (interpretation of Part 3) after the definition of "motor bicycle instructor" insert—

""motor car instructor" means a person operating an establishment for providing instruction in the driving of vehicles included in category B, including an establishment which provides tuition to prepare persons for the theory test;".

5. (1) Regulation 26 (applications for theory tests: applicants in person) is amended as follows.

(2) For paragraph (1)(c) omit from "in the case of an application" to "day of the test and".

(3) In paragraph (3), for "regulation 27 or 28" substitute "regulation 27, 28 or 28A".

6. After regulation 28 (applications for theory tests: large vehicle instructors) insert the following new regulation—

"28A. Applications for theory tests: motor car instructors. (1) A motor car instructor who wishes to make an appointment for a theory test prescribed in respect of motor vehicles in category B to be conducted by an appointed person and to be taken by a person who has, or will have, received from that instructor tuition to prepare him for the theory test shall—

(a) apply for such an appointment to the appointed person, specifying the date and time of the appointment which the instructor wishes to reserve and the place where he wishes the test to be conducted,

(b) provide such details relating to himself, the establishment and nature of the test as the appointed person may reasonably require,

(c) pay the fee (recoverable from the person nominated under paragraph (4)) specified in regulation 30.

(2) The appointed person may refuse to accept an application from a motor car instructor (or, where two or more applications have been made on the same occasion, to accept all or any of those applications) where any appointment specified in the application is unavailable, or where, in the opinion of the appointed person, it is reasonably necessary to do so in the general interests of applicants for theory tests.

(3) Subject to paragraphs (2) and (5), upon receipt of such details and such fee the appointed person shall confirm to the motor car instructor the date and time of the appointment.

(4) If, before the expiration of the qualifying period, the appointed person receives from the motor car instructor the name and such further details relating to—

(a) the person receiving tuition from that instructor who will at the appointment submit himself for that test, and
(b) the nature of the test,

as the appointed person may reasonably require, the appointed person shall make the arrangements necessary for the taking of the appropriate test.

(5) A person nominated by a motor car instructor pursuant to paragraph (4) for a theory test prescribed in respect of any category may neither be so nominated nor apply under regulation 26 for a further appointment for such a test unless—

(a) the appointment made pursuant to the first nomination has been cancelled, or
(b) the test due on that appointment does not take place for any reason other than cancellation, or
(c) he has kept that appointment (whether or not the test is completed).

(6) The qualifying period for the purposes of paragraph (4) is the period ending at 16.00 hours on the day which allows one clear working day to elapse between that day and the day for which the appointment is made."

7. (1) Regulation 30(1) (fees for theory tests) is amended as follows.

(2) For "motor car" substitute "motor vehicle".

(3) For "where the test is to be conducted", in both places substitute "where the application is made".

8. In regulation 35(3A) (fees in respect of practical or unitary tests) for "in the case of a test to be conducted" in both places substitute "in the case of an application made".

9. (1) Regulation 37 (test vehicles) is amended as follows.

(2) After paragraph (10B) insert—

"(10C) A person submitting himself for a practical test prescribed in respect of category C or C + E shall provide a motor vehicle in which any seat which is used by the person conducting the test and any seat used by any person authorised by the Secretary of State to attend the test for the purpose of supervising it or otherwise, are each fitted with a properly anchored and functioning two or three-point seat belt.

(10D) A person submitting himself for a practical test prescribed in respect of category B + E, C, C + E, D or D + E shall provide a motor vehicle which is fitted with an exterior nearside mirror and an exterior offside mirror providing adequate rearward vision from the seat occupied by the person conducting the test."

(3) In paragraph (10C), for "C or C + E" substitute "C, + E, D or D + E".

10–4

Equality Act 2006[1]

(2006 c 4)

1. Part 1 of this Act establishes the Commission for Equality and Human Rights, which replaces the Equal Opportunities Commission, the Commission for Racial Equality and the Disability Rights Commission. The new Commission has a general duty, inter alia, to encourage and support the development of equality and to protect individual human rights, dignity and worth. The Commission has investigative powers and may issue 'unlawful act' (ie acts contrary to specified equality enactments) notices which may require the recipients to prepare 'action plans' to avoid repeating or continuing the specified unlawful acts (an appeal procedure is provided). The Commission may also seek injunctions to prevent prospective unlawful acts. The Commission is further empowered to issue 'compliance notices' where it thinks a person has failed to comply with certain, specified duties to eliminate discrimination.

Part 2 of the Act is concerned with discrimination on grounds of religion or belief. It prohibits discrimination (as defined) in the provision of goods, facilities and services. It makes it unlawful for listed educational establishments to discriminate against a person in relation to admission as a pupil and other matters. It further makes it unlawful for any public authority (which is broadly defined) to do any act which constitutes discrimination. It also makes it unlawful to operate discriminatory practices, etc. General exceptions to Part 2 are provided for non-commercial organisations and charities concerned with religious practice or belief, faith schools, etc. A civil enforcement jurisdiction is established, and a criminal offence is created of knowingly or recklessly making a false statement that a proposed act is not unlawful.

Part 3 of the Act is concerned with discrimination on the grounds of sexual orientation. Regulations made under this Part may, inter alia, create criminal offences.

Part 4 contains various amendments to the Sex Discrimination Act 1975.

Part 5 contains general provisions.

The Act will be brought into force in accordance with commencement orders made under s 93. At the date of going to press the Equality Act 2006 (Commencement No 1) Order, SI 2006/1082, had been made, but most of the Act's provisions remain prospective.

10–5

Identity Cards Act 2006[1]

(2006 c 15)

Offences

25. Possession of false identity documents etc. (1) It is an offence for a person with the requisite intention to have in his possession or under his control—

(a) an identity document that is false and that he knows or believes to be false;
(b) an identity document that was improperly obtained and that he knows or believes to have been improperly obtained; or
(c) an identity document that relates to someone else.

(2) The requisite intention for the purposes of subsection (1) is—
(a) the intention of using the document for establishing registrable facts about himself; or
(b) the intention of allowing or inducing another to use it for establishing, ascertaining or verifying registrable facts about himself or about any other person (with the exception, in the case of a document within paragraph (c) of that subsection, of the individual to whom it relates).

(3) It is an offence for a person with the requisite intention to make, or to have in his possession or under his control—
(a) any apparatus which, to his knowledge, is or has been specially designed or adapted for the making of false identity documents; or
(b) any article or material which, to his knowledge, is or has been specially designed or adapted to be used in the making of false identity documents.

(4) The requisite intention for the purposes of subsection (3) is the intention—
(a) that he or another will make a false identity document; and
(b) that the document will be used by somebody for establishing, ascertaining or verifying registrable facts about a person.

(5) It is an offence for a person to have in his possession or under his control, without reasonable excuse—
(a) an identity document that is false;
(b) an identity document that was improperly obtained;
(c) an identity document that relates to someone else; or
(d) any apparatus, article or material which, to his knowledge, is or has been specially designed or adapted for the making of false identity documents or to be used in the making of such documents.

(6) A person guilty of an offence under subsection (1) or (3) shall be liable, on conviction on indictment, to imprisonment for a term not exceeding ten years or to a fine, or to both.

(7) A person guilty of an offence under subsection (5) shall be liable—
(a) on conviction on indictment, to imprisonment for a term not exceeding two years or to a fine, or to both;
(b) on summary conviction in England and Wales, to imprisonment for a term not exceeding twelve months or to a fine not exceeding the statutory maximum, or to both;
(c) on summary conviction in Scotland or Northern Ireland, to imprisonment for a term not exceeding six months or to a fine not exceeding the statutory maximum, or to both;

but, in relation to an offence committed before the commencement of section 154(1) of the Criminal Justice Act 2003 (c 44), the reference in paragraph (b) to twelve months is to be read as a reference to six months.

(8) For the purposes of this section—
(a) an identity document is false only if it is false within the meaning of Part 1 of the Forgery and Counterfeiting Act 1981 (c 45) (see section 9(1) of that Act); and
(b) an identity document was improperly obtained if false information was provided, in or in connection with the application for its issue or an application for its modification, to the person who issued it or (as the case may be) to a person entitled to modify it;

and references to the making of a false identity document include references to the modification of an identity document so that it becomes false.

(9) Subsection (8)(a) does not apply in the application of this section to Scotland.

(10) In this section "identity document" has the meaning given by section 26.

[Identity Cards Act 2006, s 25.]

---

1. This Act makes provision for a national scheme of registration of individuals and for the issue of identify cards. It makes it an offence for a person to be in possession or control of an identity card to which he is not entitled, or of apparatus, etc, to make false identity documents.

Nearly all of the Act's provisions are to be brought into force in accordance with commencement orders made under s 44. At the time of going to press, no such orders had been made.

26. Identity documents for the purposes of s 25. (1) In section 25 "identity document" means any document that is, or purports to be—
(a) an ID card;
(b) a designated document;
(c) an immigration document;
(d) a United Kingdom passport (within the meaning of the Immigration Act 1971 (c 77));
(e) a passport issued by or on behalf of the authorities of a country or territory outside the United Kingdom or by or on behalf of an international organisation;

(f) a document that can be used (in some or all circumstances) instead of a passport;
(g) a UK driving licence; or
(h) a driving licence issued by or on behalf of the authorities of a country or territory outside the United Kingdom.

(2) In subsection (1) "immigration document" means—

(a) a document used for confirming the right of a person under the Community Treaties in respect of entry or residence in the United Kingdom;
(b) a document which is given in exercise of immigration functions and records information about leave granted to a person to enter or to remain in the United Kingdom; or23
(c) a registration card (within the meaning of section 26A of the Immigration Act 1971);

and in paragraph (b) "immigration functions" means functions under the Immigration Acts (within the meaning of the Asylum and Immigration (Treatment of Claimants, etc) Act 2004 (c 19)).

(3) In that subsection "UK driving licence" means—

(a) a licence to drive a motor vehicle granted under Part 3 of the Road Traffic Act 1988 (c 52); or
(b) a licence to drive a motor vehicle granted under Part 2 of the Road Traffic (Northern Ireland) Order 1981 (SI 1981/154 (NI 1)).

(4) The Secretary of State may by order modify the list of documents in subsection (1).

(5) The Secretary of State must not make an order containing (with or without other provision) any provision that he is authorised to make by subsection (4) unless a draft of the order has been laid before Parliament and approved by a resolution of each House.
[Identity Cards Act 2006, s 26.]

27. Unauthorised disclosure of information. (1) A person is guilty of an offence if, without lawful authority—

(a) he provides any person with information that he is required to keep confidential; or
(b) he otherwise makes a disclosure of any such information.

(2) For the purposes of this section a person is required to keep information confidential if it is information that is or has become available to him by reason of his holding an office or employment the duties of which relate, in whole or in part, to—

(a) the establishment or maintenance of the Register;
(b) the issue, manufacture, modification, cancellation or surrender of ID cards; or
(c) the carrying out of the Commissioner's functions.

(3) For the purposes of this section information is provided or otherwise disclosed with lawful authority if, and only if the provision or other disclosure of the information—

(a) is authorised by or under this Act or another enactment;
(b) is in pursuance of an order or direction of a court or of a tribunal established by or under any enactment;
(c) is in pursuance of a Community obligation; or
(d) is for the purposes of the performance of the duties of an office or employment of the sort mentioned in subsection (2).

(4) It is a defence for a person charged with an offence under this section to show that, at the time of the alleged offence, he believed, on reasonable grounds, that he had lawful authority to provide the information or to make the other disclosure in question.

(5) A person guilty of an offence under this section shall be liable, on conviction on indictment, to imprisonment for a term not exceeding two years or to a fine, or to both.
[Identity Cards Act 2006, s 27.]

28. Providing false information. (1) A person is guilty of an offence if, in circumstances falling within subsection (2), he provides false information to any person—

(a) for the purpose of securing the making or modification of an entry in the Register;
(b) in confirming (with or without changes) the contents of an entry in the Register; or
(c) for the purpose of obtaining for himself or another the issue or modification of an ID card.

(2) Those circumstances are that, at the time of the provision of the information he—

(a) knows or believes the information to be false; or
(b) is reckless as to whether or not it is false.

(3) A person guilty of an offence under this section shall be liable—

(a) on conviction on indictment, to imprisonment for a term not exceeding two years or to a fine, or to both;
(b) on summary conviction in England and Wales, to imprisonment for a term not exceeding twelve months or to a fine not exceeding the statutory maximum, or to both;

(c) on summary conviction in Scotland or Northern Ireland, to imprisonment for a term not exceeding six months or to a fine not exceeding the statutory maximum, or to both;

but, in relation to an offence committed before the commencement of section 154(1) of the Criminal Justice Act 2003 (c 44), the reference in paragraph (b) to twelve months is to be read as a reference to six months.
[Identity Cards Act 2006, s 28.]

29. Tampering with the Register etc. (1) A person is guilty of an offence under this section if—

(a) he engages in any conduct that causes an unauthorised modification of information recorded in the Register; and
(b) at the time when he engages in the conduct, he has the requisite intent.

(2) For the purposes of this section a person has the requisite intent if he—

(a) intends to cause a modification of information recorded in the Register; or
(b) is reckless as to whether or not his conduct will cause such a modification.

(3) For the purposes of this section the cases in which conduct causes a modification of information recorded in the Register include—

(a) where it contributes to a modification of such information; and
(b) where it makes it more difficult or impossible for such information to be retrieved in a legible form from a computer on which it is stored by the Secretary of State, or contributes to making that more difficult or impossible.

(4) It is immaterial for the purposes of this section—

(a) whether the conduct constituting the offence, or any of it, took place in the United Kingdom; or
(b) in the case of conduct outside the United Kingdom, whether it is conduct of a British citizen.

(5) For the purposes of this section a modification is unauthorised, in relation to the person whose conduct causes it, if—

(a) he is not himself entitled to determine if the modification may be made; and
(b) he does not have a consent to the modification from a person who is so entitled.

(6) In proceedings against a person for an offence under this section in respect of conduct causing a modification of information recorded in the Register it is to be a defence for that person to show that, at the time of the conduct, he believed, on reasonable grounds—

(a) that he was a person entitled to determine if that modification might be made; or
(b) that consent to the modification had been given by a person so entitled.

(7) A person guilty of an offence under this section shall be liable—

(a) on conviction on indictment, to imprisonment for a term not exceeding ten years or to a fine, or to both;
(b) on summary conviction in England and Wales, to imprisonment for a term not exceeding twelve months or to a fine not exceeding the statutory maximum, or to both;
(c) on summary conviction in Scotland or Northern Ireland, to imprisonment for a term not exceeding six months or to a fine not exceeding the statutory maximum, or to both;

but, in relation to an offence committed before the commencement of section 154(1) of the Criminal Justice Act 2003 (c 44), the reference in paragraph (b) to twelve months is to be read as a reference to six months.

(8) In the case of an offence by virtue of this section in respect of conduct wholly or partly outside the United Kingdom—

(a) proceedings for the offence may be taken at any place in the United Kingdom; and
(b) the offence may for all incidental purposes be treated as having been committed at any such place.

(9) In this section—

"conduct" includes acts and omissions; and
"modification" includes a temporary modification.
[Identity Cards Act 2006, s 29.]

30. Amendments relating to offences. (1) In section 1(2) of the Criminal Justice Act 1993 (c 36) (Group A offences in respect of which jurisdiction is extended for some purposes in relation to conduct outside England and Wales), after paragraph (c) insert—

"(ca)an offence under section 25 of the Identity Cards Act 2006;".

(2) In section 31 of the Immigration and Asylum Act 1999 (defences based on Article 31(1) of the Refugee Convention)—

(a) in subsection (3) (offences in England and Wales and Northern Ireland to which section applies), after paragraph (a) insert—

"(aa) section 25(1) or (5) of the Identity Cards Act 2006;"

(b) in subsection (4) (offences in Scotland to which section applies), after paragraph (b) insert—

"(ba) under section 25(1) or (5) of the Identity Cards Act 2006;".

(3) In section 14(2) of the Asylum and Immigration (Treatment of Claimants, etc) Act 2004 (c 19) (powers of arrest for immigration officers), after paragraph (p) insert—

"(q) an offence under section 25 of the Identity Cards Act 2006."

(4) In Article 26(2) of the Police and Criminal Evidence (Northern Ireland) Order 1989 (SI 1989/1341 (NI 12)) (offences for which an arrest may be made without a warrant), at the end insert—

"(q) an offence under—

(i) section 25(5) of the Identity Cards Act 2006 (possession of false document etc);
(ii) section 27 of that Act (disclosure of information on National Identity Register); or
(iii) section 28 of that Act (providing false information)."

(5) In Article 38(2) of the Criminal Justice (Northern Ireland) Order 1996 (SI 1996/3160 (NI 24)) (which makes provision in relation to conduct outside Northern Ireland corresponding to that made by section 1(2) of the Criminal Justice Act 1993 (c 36)), after sub-paragraph (c) insert—

"(ca) an offence under section 25 of the Identity Cards Act 2006;".

[Identity Cards Act 2006, s 30.]

42. General interpretation. (1) In this Act—

"apparatus" includes any equipment, machinery or device and any wire or cable, together with any software used with it;

"biometric information", in relation to an individual, means data about his external characteristics, including, in particular, the features of an iris or of any other part of the eye;

"card" includes a document or other article, or a combination of a document and an article, in or on which information is or may be recorded;

"the Commissioner" means the National Identity Scheme Commissioner appointed under section 22;

"confirm", in relation to the contents of an individual's entry in the Register, is to be construed in accordance with subsection (4);

"contravention" includes a failure to comply, and cognate expressions are to be construed accordingly;

"crime" means a crime within the meaning of the Regulation of Investigatory Powers Act 2000 (c 23) (see section 81(2) of that Act);

"designated document" means a document of a description designated for the purposes of this Act by an order under section 4;

"designated documents authority" means a person with the power or duty to issue a designated document;

"detection", in relation to crime or serious crime, is to be construed in accordance with subsection (9);

"document" includes a stamp or label;

"enactment" includes—

(a) a provision of Northern Ireland legislation; and34
(b) enactments passed or made after the passing of this Act;

"false", in relation to information, includes containing any inaccuracy or omission that results in a tendency to mislead (and is to be construed subject to section 3(5));

"fingerprint", in relation to an individual, means a record (in any form and produced by any method) of the skin pattern and other physical characteristics or features of any of his fingers;

"ID card" is to be construed in accordance with section 6(1);

"information" includes documents and records;

"issue", in relation to a document or card, and cognate expressions are to be construed in accordance with subsection (5);

"modification" includes omission, addition or alteration, and cognate expressions are to be construed accordingly;

"necessary in the public interest" is to be construed in accordance with section 1(4);

"place of residence" and "resides" and cognate expressions are to be construed subject to any regulations under subsection (10);

"prescribed" means prescribed by regulations made by the Secretary of State;

"public authority" has the same meaning as in section 6 of the Human Rights Act 1998 (c 42);

"public service" is to be construed in accordance with subsection (2);

"the Register" means the National Identity Register established and maintained under section 1;

"registrable fact" has the meaning given by section 1(5) and (6);

"serious crime" means crime that is serious crime within the meaning of the Regulation of Investigatory Powers Act 2000 (c 23) (see section 81(2) and (3) of that Act);

"statutory purposes" means the purposes specified in section 1(3);

"subject to compulsory registration" means required to be entered in the Register in accordance with an obligation imposed by an Act of Parliament passed after the passing of this Act;

"subordinate legislation" has the same meaning as in the Interpretation Act 1978 (c 30).

(2) References in this Act to the provision of a public service are references to—

(a) the provision of any service to an individual by a public authority;

(b) the exercise or performance in relation to an individual of any power or duty of a Minister of the Crown, the Treasury or a Northern Ireland department;

(c) the doing by any other person of anything in relation to an individual which that other person is authorised or required to do for purposes connected with the carrying out of any function conferred by or under an enactment;

(d) the provision of any service to an individual under arrangements made (directly or indirectly) between the person providing the service and a public authority who, for purposes connected with the carrying out of a function so conferred on that authority, bears the whole or a part of the expense of providing the service to that individual; or

(e) the acceptance or acknowledgment of the conduct of an individual as compliance by that individual with a requirement imposed on him by or under an enactment, or the receipt of any notification or information provided by an individual for the purpose of complying with such a requirement.

(3) References in this Act to an application for the provision of a public service include references to any claim, request or requirement for the provision of the service.

(4) References in this Act to an individual confirming the contents of his entry in the Register are references to his confirming that entry to the extent only that it consists of information falling within paragraphs 1 to 5 of Schedule 1 or section 3(3).

(5) References in this Act to the issue of a document or card include references to its renewal, replacement or re-issue (with or without modifications).

(6) References in this Act to a designated document being issued together with an ID card include references to the ID card and the designated document being comprised in the same card.

(7) References in this Act to providing a person with information recorded in an individual's entry in the Register include references to confirming or otherwise disclosing to him—

(a) that the information is recorded in that entry; or

(b) that particular information is not recorded in that entry.

(8) References in this Act to information recorded in an individual's entry in the Register include references to a password or code generated by a method so recorded.

(9) Section 81(5) of the Regulation of Investigatory Powers Act 2000 (c 23) (which defines detection) applies for the purposes of this Act as it applies for the purposes of the provisions of that Act that are not in Chapter 1 of Part 1 of that Act.

(10) The Secretary of State may by regulations make provision for the purposes of this Act as to the circumstances in which a place is to be regarded, in relation to an individual—

(a) as a place where he resides; or

(b) as his principal place of residence in the United Kingdom.

[Identity Cards Act 2006, s 42.]

10–6

Natural Environment and Rural Communities Act 2006[1]

(2006 c 16)

Pesticides harmful to wildlife

43. Possession of pesticides harmful to wildlife. (1) A person is guilty of an offence if he has in his possession a pesticide containing an ingredient that is prescribed for the purposes of this section by an order made by the Secretary of State.

(2) The Secretary of State may not make an order under subsection (1) unless he is satisfied that it is necessary or expedient to do so in the interests of protecting wild birds or wild animals from harm.

(3) It is a defence for a person charged with an offence under this section to prove that his possession of the pesticide was for the purposes of doing anything in accordance with—

(a) provision made by or under the Poisons Act 1972 (c 66);

(b) regulations made under section 16(2) of the Food and Environment Protection Act 1985 (c 48);

(c) the Biocidal Products Regulations 2001 (SI 2001/880) or any regulations replacing those regulations;

(d) the Plant Protection Products Regulations 2005 (SI 2005/1435) or any regulations replacing those regulations.

(4) A person guilty of an offence under this section is liable on summary conviction to imprisonment for a term not exceeding 51 weeks or to a fine not exceeding level 5 on the standard scale (or both).

(5) The court by which a person is convicted of an offence under this section may order the forfeiture of the pesticide in respect of which the offence was committed.

(6) The power to make an order under subsection (1) is exercisable by statutory instrument.

(7) A statutory instrument containing an order under subsection (1) is subject to annulment in pursuance of a resolution of either House of Parliament.

(8) The Secretary of State must take such steps as are reasonably practicable to bring information about the effect of an order under subsection (1) to the attention of persons likely to be affected by the order.

(9) In relation to an offence committed before the commencement of section 281(5) of the Criminal Justice Act 2003 (c 44), the reference in subsection (4) to 51 weeks is to be read as a reference to 6 months.

[Natural Environment and Rural Communities Act 2006, s 43.]

---

1. This Act, except for ss 59 and 99 which came into force on 30 May 2006, is to be brought into force in accordance with orders made under s 107. At the date of going to press no such orders had been made.

44. Enforcement powers in connection with pesticides. (1) An inspector may—

(a) enter any premises if he has reasonable grounds to suspect that he may find there evidence that an offence is being committed under section 43,

(b) require any person whom he reasonably believes has information about the formulation, effects or use of any substance found on the premises to give him that information, and

(c) seize any substance found on the premises, if he has reasonable grounds for believing that it is evidence of an offence under section 43.

(2) "Inspector" means—

(a) a person authorised in writing by the Secretary of State to exercise the powers under this section in relation to England;

(b) a person authorised in writing by the National Assembly for Wales to exercise the powers under this section in relation to Wales.

(3) An authorisation under subsection (2) is subject to any conditions or limitations specified in it.

(4) Schedule 2 to the Food and Environment Protection Act 1985 (officers and their powers), other than paragraph 2A(1)(b) of that Schedule, has effect with respect to inspectors as it has effect with respect to persons authorised to enforce Part 3 of that Act.

(5) Subsections (6) and (7) apply where an inspector seizes a substance under subsection (1)(c).

(6) The inspector must give to a person on the premises, or affix conspicuously to some object on the premises, a notice stating—

(a) what he has seized and the ground for seizing it, and

(b) the address for service for any claim for the return of the substance.

(7) The inspector—

(a) may retain the substance for so long as is reasonably necessary for the purposes of any investigation or proceedings in respect of an offence under section 43;

(b) subject to any order for forfeiture under section 43(5) or any claim made within the relevant period by a person entitled to the return of the substance, may retain the substance or, after the relevant period, destroy or otherwise dispose of it.

(8) "The relevant period" means the period ending 28 days after—

(a) any proceedings in respect of an offence under section 43 are finally determined, or

(b) if no such proceedings are brought, the time for bringing such proceedings expires.

[Natural Environment and Rural Communities Act 2006, s 44.]

45. Codes of practice

46. Interpretation. (1) This section has effect for the interpretation of sections 43 and 44.

(2) "Pesticide" means—

(a) a pesticide as defined by section 16(15) of the Food and Environment Protection Act 1985;

(b) anything to which Part 3 of the 1985 Act applies (by virtue of section 16(16) of the Act) as if it were a pesticide.

(3) "Wild bird" and "wild animal" have the same meaning as in Part 1 of the Wildlife and Countryside Act 1981 (c 69).

(4) "Premises" includes land (including buildings), movable structures, vehicles, vessels, aircraft and other means of transport.

[Natural Environment and Rural Communities Act 2006, s 46.]

Protection of birds

47. Protection for nests of certain birds which re-use their nests. (1) Amend the Wildlife and Countryside Act 1981 (c 69) as follows.

(2) In section 1 (protection of wild birds, their nests and eggs), in subsection (1), after paragraph (a) insert—

"(aa) takes, damages or destroys the nest of a wild bird included in Schedule ZA1;".

(3) At the beginning of the Schedules insert—

"SCHEDULE ZA1

BIRDS WHICH RE-USE THEIR NESTS

Common name	*Scientific name*
Eagle, Golden	Aquila chrysaetos
Eagle, White-tailed	Haliaetus albicilla
Osprey	Pandion haliaetus

NOTE: The common name or names given in the first column of this Schedule are included by way of guidance only; in the event of any dispute or proceedings, the common name or names shall not be taken into account.".

(4) In—

(a) section 4 (exceptions to sections 1 and 3), in subsection (1)(c), and
(b) section 7 (registration etc of certain captive birds), in subsection (3A)(a)(i) and (c)(i),

after "Schedule" insert "ZA1 or".

(5) In section 22 (power to vary Schedules), in subsection (1), for "Schedules 1 to 4" substitute "Schedules ZA1 to 4".

[Natural Environment and Rural Communities Act 2006, s 47.]

48. Birds released into the wild as part of re-population programme. (1) In section 1 of the 1981 Act (protection of wild birds, their nests and eggs), for subsection (6) substitute—

"(6) For the purposes of this section the definition of "wild bird" in section 27(1) is to be read as not including any bird which is shown to have been bred in captivity unless it has been lawfully released into the wild as part of a re-population or re-introduction programme.

(6A) "Re-population" and "re-introduction" have the same meaning as in the Directive of the Council of the European Communities dated 2nd April 1979 (No 1979/409/EEC) on the conservation of wild birds.".

(2) In section 6 of the 1981 Act (sale etc of live or dead wild birds, eggs etc), for subsection (5) substitute—

"(5) Any reference in this section to any bird included in Part 1 of Schedule 3 is a reference to any bird included in that Part which—

(a) was bred in captivity,
(b) has been ringed or marked in accordance with regulations made by the Secretary of State, and
(c) has not been lawfully released into the wild as part of a re-population or re-introduction programme.

(5A) "Re-population" and "re-introduction" have the same meaning as in the Directive of the Council of the European Communities dated 2nd April 1979 (No 1979/409/EEC) on the conservation of wild birds.

(5B) Regulations made for the purposes of subsection (5)(b) may make different provision for different birds or different provisions of this section.".

[Natural Environment and Rural Communities Act 2006, s 48.]

49. Registration etc of certain captive birds. In section 7 of the 1981 Act (registration etc of certain captive birds), in subsection (3A), after paragraph (c) insert—

"(ca) any offence under subsection (1);".

[Natural Environment and Rural Communities Act 2006, s 49.]

Invasive non-native species

50. Sale etc of invasive non-native species. After section 14 of the 1981 Act insert—

"14ZA. Sale etc of invasive non-native species. (1) Subject to the provisions of this Part, a person is guilty of an offence if he sells, offers or exposes for sale, or has in his possession or transports for the purposes of sale—

(a) an animal or plant to which this section applies, or
(b) anything from which such an animal or plant can be reproduced or propagated.

(2) Subject to the provisions of this Part, a person is guilty of an offence if he publishes or causes to be published any advertisement likely to be understood as conveying that he buys or sells, or intends to buy or sell—

(a) an animal or plant to which this section applies, or
(b) anything from which such an animal or plant can be reproduced or propagated.

(3) This section applies to an animal or plant which—

(a) is within section 14(1) or (2) (animals and plants which must not be released etc into the wild),
(b) is of a description prescribed for the purposes of this section by an order made by the Secretary of State, and
(c) is a live animal or live plant.

(4) An order under subsection (3) may be made in relation to a particular area or a particular time of the year.

(5) Subsections (3) and (4) of section 14 (defence of due diligence etc) apply to an offence under this section as they apply to an offence under that section.".

[Natural Environment and Rural Communities Act 2006, s 50.]

51. Codes of practice in connection with invasive non-native species

Enforcement etc of provisions relating to wildlife

52. Enforcement powers in connection with wildlife. Schedule 5 contains amendments relating to enforcement powers in connection with wildlife.

[Natural Environment and Rural Communities Act 2006, s 52.]

53. Wildlife offences: time limits for proceedings. Schedule 6 contains provisions extending the time limit for summary proceedings for certain offences relating to wildlife.

[Natural Environment and Rural Communities Act 2006, s 53.]

PART 4
SITES OF SPECIAL SCIENTIFIC INTEREST

55. Offences in connection with SSSIs. (1) Amend section 28P of the Wildlife and Countryside Act 1981 (c 69) (offences) as follows.

(2) After subsection (5) insert—

"(5A) A section 28G authority which, in the exercise of its functions, permits the carrying out of an operation which damages any of the flora, fauna or geological or physiographical features by reason of which a site of special scientific interest is of special interest—

(a) without first complying with section 28I(2), or
(b) where relevant, without first complying with section 28I(4) or (6),

is, unless there was a reasonable excuse for permitting the carrying out of the operation without complying, guilty of an offence and is liable on summary conviction to a fine not exceeding £20,000 or on conviction on indictment to a fine.

(5B) For the purposes of subsection (5A), it is a reasonable excuse in any event for a section 28G authority to permit the carrying out of an operation without first complying with section 28I(2), (4) or (6) if the operation in question was an emergency operation particulars of which (including details of the emergency) were notified to Natural England as soon as practicable after the permission was given.".

(3) After subsection (6) insert—

"(6A) A person (other than a section 28G authority acting in the exercise of its functions) who without reasonable excuse—

(a) intentionally or recklessly destroys or damages any of the flora, fauna, or geological or physiographical features by reason of which a site of special scientific interest is of special interest, or
(b) intentionally or recklessly disturbs any of those fauna,

is guilty of an offence and is liable on summary conviction to a fine not exceeding level 4 on the standard scale.".

(4) In subsection (7), after "(6)" (in both places) insert "or (6A)".

(5) In section 31 of the 1981 Act (restoration following offence under section 28P), in subsection (1)(b), after "28P(6)" insert "or (6A)".

[Natural Environment and Rural Communities Act 2006, s 55.]

57. Effect of failure to serve certain notices in connection with SSSIs. After section 70A of the 1981 Act insert—

"70B. Effect of failure to serve certain notices. (1) This section applies where the relevant conservation body—

(a) has (whether before or after the commencement of this section) taken all reasonable steps to ensure that, under any provision listed in subsection (2), notice is served on every owner and occupier of any land to which the notice relates, but

(b) has failed to do so.

(2) The provisions are—

(a) section 28(1) (notification of SSSI);

(b) section 28(5) (confirmation or withdrawal of notification of SSSI);

(c) section 28A(3) (notice varying notification under section 28);

(d) section 28A(5) (notice confirming or withdrawing variation of notification);

(e) section 28B(2) (notification of additional land to be included in SSSI);

(f) section 28B(7) (confirmation or withdrawal of notification);

(g) section 28C(2) (notification of enlargement of SSSI);

(h) section 28C(3) (confirmation or withdrawal of notification of enlargement);

(i) section 28D(2) (denotification);

(j) section 28D(5) (withdrawal or confirmation of denotification);

(k) section 28J(3) (notice of proposed management scheme);

(l) section 28J(8) (withdrawal or confirmation of management scheme).

(3) The validity of the notice is not affected by the failure to serve it on every owner and occupier of the land.

(4) For the purposes of sections 28 to 28Q, the time when the notice is to be treated as having been served is the time when the relevant conservation body took the last of the steps referred to in subsection (1)(a).

(5) If the relevant conservation body becomes aware of its failure to serve a notice on an owner or occupier, it must serve a copy of the notice on that owner or occupier.

(6) Nothing in subsection (3) or (4) renders the owner or occupier liable—

(a) in relation to anything done or omitted to be done before the commencement of this section, or

(b) under section 28P(1) or 28Q(4) in relation to anything done or omitted to be done before the copy of the notice is served under subsection (5).

(7) "The relevant conservation body" means—

(a) in relation to land in an area in England—

(i) subject to sub-paragraph (ii), Natural England;

(ii) in relation to any time before the commencement of section 27AA, English Nature;

(b) in relation to land in an area in Wales, the Countryside Council for Wales.".

[Natural Environment and Rural Communities Act 2006, s 57.

58. Notices and signs relating to SSSIs. (1) After section 28R of the 1981 Act insert—

"28S. Notices and signs relating to SSSIs. (1) Natural England may, on any land included in a site of special scientific interest, put up and maintain notices or signs relating to the site.

(2) Natural England may remove any notice or sign put up under subsection (1).

(3) Any other person who intentionally or recklessly and without reasonable excuse takes down, damages, destroys or obscures a notice or sign put up under subsection (1) is guilty of an offence.

(4) A person guilty of an offence under this section is liable on summary conviction to a fine not exceeding level 4 on the standard scale.".

(2) In section 51 of the 1981 Act (powers of entry), in subsection (1), after paragraph (k) insert—

"(ka) for the purposes of putting up, maintaining or removing notices or signs under section 28S;".

(3) In subsection (2) of that section, for "paragraphs (a) to (k)" substitute "paragraphs (a) to (ka)".

[Natural Environment and Rural Communities Act 2006, s 58.]

Section 52

SCHEDULE 5
ENFORCEMENT POWERS IN CONNECTION WITH WILDLIFE

PART 1
AMENDMENTS OF THE WILDLIFE AND COUNTRYSIDE ACT 1981

1. After section 18 insert—

"18A. Wildlife inspectors. (1) In this Part, "wildlife inspector" means a person authorised in writing under this section by—

(a) the Secretary of State (in relation to England), or
(b) the National Assembly for Wales (in relation to Wales).

(2) An authorisation under subsection (1) is subject to any conditions or limitations specified in it.

(3) A wildlife inspector must, if required to do so, produce evidence of his authority before entering any premises under section 18B or 18D.

(4) A wildlife inspector entering premises under either of those sections may take with him a veterinary surgeon if he has reasonable grounds for believing that such a person will be needed for the exercise of powers under section 18C or 18E.

18B. Group 1 offences and licences: power to enter premises. (1) A wildlife inspector may, at any reasonable time, enter and inspect any premises—

(a) for the purpose of ascertaining whether a Group 1 offence is being or has been committed;
(b) for the purpose of—
  (i) verifying any statement or representation made, or document or information supplied, by an occupier in connection with an application for, or the holding of, a Group 1 licence, or
  (ii) ascertaining whether any condition to which a Group 1 licence was subject has been complied with.

(2) In this Part—

"Group 1 offence" means an offence under section 1, 5, 9(1), (2) or (4), 11, 13(1) or 14ZA, and
"Group 1 licence" means a licence authorising anything which would otherwise be a Group 1 offence.

(3) Nothing in this section confers power to enter a dwelling.

18C. Group 1 offences and licences: examining specimens and taking samples. (1) The powers conferred by this section are exercisable where a wildlife inspector has entered any premises for a purpose mentioned in section 18B(1)(a) or (b).

(2) The inspector, or a veterinary surgeon accompanying him, may—

(a) for any such purpose, examine any specimen, and
(b) subject to subsection (5) and section 18F, take a sample from it.

(3) "Specimen" means—

(a) any bird, other animal or plant, or
(b) any part of, or anything derived from, a bird, other animal or plant.

(4) "Sample" means a sample of blood, tissue or other biological material.

(5) No sample may be taken under subsection (2) from a live bird, other animal or plant except for the purpose of establishing its identity or ancestry.

(6) The inspector may require an occupier of the premises to give such assistance as is reasonable in the circumstances for the purpose of—

(a) making an examination under subsection (2)(a), or
(b) taking a sample under subsection (2)(b).

(7) The inspector may take and remove from the premises a specimen which is not a live bird, other animal or plant, if there are reasonable grounds for believing that it is evidence of a Group 1 offence.

18D. Group 2 offences and licences etc: power to enter premises. (1) A wildlife inspector may, at any reasonable time, enter and inspect any premises—

(a) for the purpose of ascertaining whether an offence under section 6, 9(5) or 13(2) is being, or has been, committed on those premises;
(b) where he has reasonable cause to believe that any birds included in Schedule 4 are kept, for the purpose of ascertaining whether an offence under section 7 is being, or has been, committed on those premises;
(c) for the purpose of ascertaining whether an offence under section 14 is being, or has been, committed on those premises;
(d) for the purpose of—
  (i) verifying any statement or representation made, or document or information supplied, by an occupier in connection with an application for, or the holding of, a Group 2 licence or a relevant registration, or
  (ii) ascertaining whether any condition to which a Group 2 licence was subject has been complied with.

(2) In this Part—

"Group 2 offence" means an offence under section 6, 7, 9(5), 13(2) or 14,
"Group 2 licence" means a licence authorising anything which would otherwise be a Group 2 offence, and
"relevant registration" means a registration in accordance with regulations under section 7(1).

(3) In subsection (1)—

(a) paragraphs (a) and (b) do not confer power to enter a dwelling except for purposes connected with—

(i) a Group 2 licence or a relevant registration held by an occupier of the dwelling, or
(ii) an application by an occupier of the dwelling for a Group 2 licence or a relevant registration, and

(b) paragraph (c) does not confer any power to enter a dwelling.

18E. Group 2 offences: examining specimens and taking samples. (1) A wildlife inspector may, for the purpose of ascertaining whether a Group 2 offence is being, or has been, committed in respect of any specimen, require any person who has the specimen in his possession or control to make it available for examination by the inspector or a veterinary surgeon.

(2) A wildlife inspector may, for the purpose of ascertaining whether a Group 2 offence is being or has been committed, require the taking of a sample from a specimen found by him in the exercise of powers conferred by section 18D in order to determine its identity or ancestry.

(3) A wildlife inspector may, for the purpose of ascertaining whether a Group 2 offence is being or has been committed in respect of any specimen ("the relevant specimen"), require any person to make available for the taking of a sample any specimen (other than the relevant specimen) in that person's possession or control which—

(a) is alleged to be, or
(b) which the wildlife inspector suspects with reasonable cause to be,

a specimen a sample from which will tend to establish the identity or ancestry of the relevant specimen.

(4) Where, pursuant to a requirement under this section—

(a) a bird or other animal is to be examined, or
(b) a sample is to be taken from a bird or other animal,

a person who has the bird or animal in his possession or control must give the person making the examination or taking the sample such assistance as he may reasonably require for that purpose.

(5) "Specimen" and "sample" have the same meaning as in section 18C.

(6) This section is subject to section 18F.

18F. Restrictions on taking of samples from live specimens. (1) No sample may be taken by virtue of section 18C, 18E or 19XA from a live bird or other animal except by a veterinary surgeon.

(2) No sample may be taken by virtue of section 18C, 18E or 19XA from a live bird, other animal or plant unless the person taking it is satisfied on reasonable grounds that taking the sample will not cause lasting harm to the specimen.".

2. (1) Amend section 19 (powers of constables to stop, search, enter etc) as follows.

(2) In subsection (2)—

(a) after "is committing" insert "or has committed", and
(b) for "enter any land other than a dwelling-house" substitute "enter any premises other than a dwelling".

(3) After subsection (2) insert—

"(2A) A constable may, for the purpose of assisting him in exercising the powers conferred by subsection (1)(b) and (d) when he has entered any premises under subsection (2), take with him—

(a) any other person, and
(b) any equipment or materials.".

(4) In subsection (3), omit "(with or without other persons)".

3. After section 19 insert—

"19XA Constables' powers in connection with samples. (1) A constable who suspects with reasonable cause that a specimen found by him in the exercise of powers conferred by this section is one in respect of which an offence under this Part is being or has been committed may require the taking from it of a sample.

(2) A constable who suspects with reasonable cause that an offence under this Part is being or has been committed in respect of any specimen ("the relevant specimen") may require any person to make available for the taking of a sample any specimen (other than the relevant specimen) in that person's possession or control which—

(a) is alleged to be, or
(b) the constable suspects with reasonable cause to be,

a specimen a sample from which will tend to establish the identity or ancestry of the relevant specimen.

(3) Where a sample from a live bird or other animal is to be taken pursuant to a requirement under this section, any person who has possession or control of the specimen must give the person taking the sample such assistance as he may reasonably require for that purpose.

(4) "Specimen" and "sample" have the same meaning as in section 18C.

(5) This section is subject to section 18F (restrictions on taking samples).

19XB. Offences in connection with enforcement powers. (1) A person is guilty of an offence if he—

(a) intentionally obstructs a wildlife inspector acting in the exercise of powers conferred by section 18B(1) or 18C(2) or (7), or
(b) fails without reasonable excuse to give any assistance reasonably required under section 18C(6).

(2) A person is guilty of an offence if he—

(a) intentionally obstructs a wildlife inspector acting in the exercise of powers conferred by section 18D(1) or 18E(2), or
(b) fails without reasonable excuse to make available any specimen in accordance with a requirement under section 18E(1) or (3), or

(c) fails without reasonable excuse to give any assistance reasonably required under section 18E(4).

(3) A person is guilty of an offence if he—

(a) fails without reasonable excuse to make available any specimen in accordance with a requirement under section 19XA(2), or
(b) fails without reasonable excuse to give any assistance reasonably required under section 19XA(3).

(4) Any person who, with intent to deceive, falsely pretends to be a wildlife inspector is guilty of an offence.".

4. Omit sections 19ZA (enforcement: wildlife inspectors) and 19ZB (power to take samples).

5. (1) Amend section 21 (penalties etc) as follows.

(2) Omit subsections (4A) and (4D) (penalties in connection with power of entry and powers in connection with examination of specimens and taking samples).

(3) Before subsection (4B) insert—

"(4AA) Except in a case falling within subsection (4B) a person guilty of an offence under section 19XB(1), (2) or (3) shall be liable on summary conviction to a fine not exceeding level 5 on the standard scale.".

(4) In subsection (4B) (penalty for obstructing wildlife inspector to ascertain whether section 14 offence is being or has been committed)—

(a) for "subsection (7) of section 19ZA" substitute "section 19XB(1)(a) or (2)(a)", and
(b) for "acting in the exercise of the power conferred by subsection (3)(c) of that section" substitute "entering premises to ascertain whether an offence under section 14 or 14ZA is being or has been committed".

(5) In subsection (4C) (penalty for pretending to be wildlife inspector), for "19ZA(8)" substitute "19XB(4)".

6. In section 27 (interpretation of Part 1), in subsection (1), in the definition of "wildlife inspector", for "section 19ZA(1)" substitute "section 18A(1)".

PART 2
POWERS OF WILDLIFE INSPECTORS EXTENDED TO CERTAIN OTHER ACTS

Introduction

7. In this Part "the enforcement provisions of the 1981 Act relating to Group 1 offences and Group 1 licences" means the following provisions of the Wildlife and Countryside Act 1981 (c 69)—

(a) section 18A (power to authorise persons to act as wildlife inspectors);
(b) section 18B (power of wildlife inspector to enter premises);
(c) section 18C (power to examine specimens and take samples);
(d) section 18F (restrictions on taking samples from live specimens);
(e) section 21(4AA) to (4C) (penalties for obstructing etc wildlife inspectors).

Destructive Imported Animals Act 1932 (c 12)

8. (1) The enforcement provisions of the 1981 Act relating to Group 1 offences and Group 1 licences apply for the purposes of the 1932 Act as if—

(a) any reference to a Group 1 offence were a reference to any offence under the 1932 Act,
(b) any reference to a Group 1 licence were a reference to a licence under the 1932 Act, and
(c) as if the power to take a sample included power to take a sample from a destructive animal (whether live or dead) for the purpose of testing for disease.

(2) "Destructive animal" means a musk rat or other animal to which the 1932 Act applies.

Conservation of Seals Act 1970 (c 30)

9. The enforcement provisions relating to Group 1 offences and Group 1 licences apply for the purposes of the 1970 Act as if—

(a) the Natural Environment Research Council were required to be consulted about any authorisation of a person to exercise the powers of a wildlife inspector for the purposes of the 1970 Act,
(b) any reference to a Group 1 offence were a reference to any offence under the 1970 Act,
(c) any reference to a Group 1 licence were a reference to a licence under section 10 of the 1970 Act, and
(d) the power to take a sample from a specimen did not include any power to take a sample from a live seal.

Deer Act 1991 (c 54)

10. The enforcement provisions relating to Group 1 offences and Group 1 licences apply for the purposes of the 1991 Act as if—

(a) any reference to a Group 1 offence were a reference to any offence under the 1991 Act,
(b) any reference to a Group 1 licence were a reference to a licence under section 8 of the 1991 Act, and
(c) as if the power to take a sample included power to take a sample from a deer (whether live or dead) for the purpose of testing for disease.

Protection of Badgers Act 1992 (c 51)

11. The enforcement provisions relating to Group 1 offences and Group 1 licences apply for the purposes of the 1992 Act as if—

(a) any reference to a Group 1 offence were a reference to any offence under the 1992 Act,
(b) any reference to a Group 1 licence were a reference to a licence under section 10 of the 1992 Act, and
(c) as if the power to take a sample included power to take a sample from a badger (whether live or dead) for the purpose of testing for disease.

PART 3
CODES OF PRACTICE

12. (1) The Secretary of State may—

(a) issue a code of practice in connection with any of the provisions of sections 18A to 18F of the 1981 Act (including any of those provisions as applied by Part 2 of this Schedule), and
(b) revise or replace such a code.

(2) An inspector must have regard to any relevant provision of a code when discharging any function under any of the provisions mentioned in sub-paragraph (1)(a).

(3) But an inspector's failure to have regard to any provision of a code does not make him liable to criminal or civil proceedings.

(4) A code—

(a) is admissible in evidence in any proceedings, and
(b) must be taken into account by a court in any case in which it appears to the court to be relevant.

PART 4
CONSTABLE'S SEARCH WARRANT POWER EXTENDED TO CERTAIN OTHER ACTS

13. (1) Section 19(3) of the 1981 Act (issue of search warrants for purpose of obtaining evidence of offence) applies in relation to an offence under each of the Acts mentioned in sub-paragraph (2) as it applies in relation to an offence under Part 1 of the 1981 Act.

(2) The Acts are—

(a) the Destructive Imported Animals Act 1932 (c 12);
(b) the Conservation of Seals Act 1970 (c 30);
(c) the Deer Act 1991 (c 54);
(d) the Protection of Badgers Act 1992 (c 51).

Section 53

SCHEDULE 6
WILDLIFE OFFENCES: TIME LIMITS FOR PROCEEDINGS

Destructive Imported Animals Act 1932 (c 12)

1. In section 6 (offences relating to importation etc of musk rats without licence etc), after subsection (2) insert—

"(3) Proceedings in England and Wales for an offence under this section may be brought within the period of 6 months beginning with the date on which evidence sufficient in the opinion of the prosecutor to warrant the proceedings came to his knowledge.

(4) But subsection (3) does not authorise the commencement of proceedings for an offence more than 2 years after the date on which the offence was committed.

(5) For the purposes of subsection (3), a certificate signed by or on behalf of the prosecutor and stating the date on which evidence sufficient in his opinion to warrant the proceedings came to his knowledge shall be conclusive evidence of that fact.

(6) A certificate stating that matter and purporting to be so signed shall be deemed to be so signed unless the contrary is proved.".

Conservation of Seals Act 1970 (c 30)

2. In section 5 (penalties for offences), after subsection (2) insert—

"(3) Proceedings in England and Wales for an offence under this Act may be brought within the period of 6 months beginning with the date on which evidence sufficient in the opinion of the prosecutor to warrant the proceedings came to his knowledge.

(4) But subsection (3) does not authorise the commencement of proceedings for an offence more than 2 years after the date on which the offence was committed.

(5) For the purposes of subsection (3), a certificate signed by or on behalf of the prosecutor and stating the date on which evidence sufficient in his opinion to warrant the proceedings came to his knowledge shall be conclusive evidence of that fact.

(6) A certificate stating that matter and purporting to be so signed shall be deemed to be so signed unless the contrary is proved.".

Wildlife and Countryside Act 1981 (c 69)

3. (1) Amend section 20 (summary prosecutions) as follows.

(2) In subsection (2), for "Summary proceedings for an offence under this Part" substitute "Proceedings for a summary offence under this Part".

(3) In the heading, for "Summary prosecutions" substitute "Proceedings for summary offences".

4. After section 51 insert—

"**51A. Summary prosecutions.** (1) Proceedings in England and Wales for a summary offence under this Part may be brought within the period of 6 months beginning with the date on which evidence sufficient in the opinion of the prosecutor to warrant the proceedings came to his knowledge.

(2) But subsection (1) does not authorise the commencement of proceedings for an offence more than 2 years after the date on which the offence was committed.

(3) For the purposes of this section, a certificate signed by or on behalf of the prosecutor and stating the date on which evidence sufficient in his opinion to warrant the proceedings came to his knowledge shall be conclusive evidence of that fact.

(4) A certificate stating that matter and purporting to be so signed shall be deemed to be so signed unless the contrary is proved.".

Deer Act 1991 (c 54)

5. In section 9 (penalties for offences relating to deer), after subsection (2) insert—

"(3) Proceedings for an offence under this Act may be brought within the period of 6 months beginning with the date on which evidence sufficient in the opinion of the prosecutor to warrant the proceedings came to his knowledge.

(4) But subsection (3) does not authorise the commencement of proceedings for an offence more than 2 years after the date on which the offence was committed.

(5) For the purposes of subsection (3), a certificate signed by or on behalf of the prosecutor and stating the date on which evidence sufficient in his opinion to warrant the proceedings came to his knowledge shall be conclusive evidence of that fact.

(6) A certificate stating that matter and purporting to be so signed shall be deemed to be so signed unless the contrary is proved.".

Protection of Badgers Act 1992 (c 51)

6. After section 12 insert—

"**12ZA Time limit for bringing summary proceedings (England and Wales).** (1) Proceedings in England and Wales for a summary offence under this Act may be brought within the period of 6 months beginning with the date on which evidence sufficient in the opinion of the prosecutor to warrant the proceedings came to his knowledge.

(2) But subsection (1) does not authorise the commencement of proceedings for an offence more than 2 years after the date on which the offence was committed.

(3) For the purposes of this section, a certificate signed by or on behalf of the prosecutor and stating the date on which evidence sufficient in his opinion to warrant the proceedings came to his knowledge shall be conclusive evidence of that fact.

(4) A certificate stating that matter and purporting to be so signed shall be deemed to be so signed unless the contrary is proved.".

10–7

Consumer Credit Act 2006[1]

(2006 c 14)

1. This Act principally amends the Consumer Credit Act 1974 by: providing for the regulation of all consumer credit and hire agreements (with certain exceptions); providing for the licensing of providers of consumer credit, hire and ancillary credit facilities, and making providing in relation to the functions and powers of the Office of Fair Trading in relation to licensing; enabling debtors to challenge unfair relationships with creditors; and providing for an Ombudsman scheme to hear complaints. The Act will be brought into force in accordance with commencement orders made under s 71. At the time of going to press, no such orders had been made.

10–8

Gangmasters Licensing (Exclusions) Regulations 2006[1]

(SI 2006/658)

1. Citation, commencement and interpretation. (1) These Regulations may be cited as the Gangmasters Licensing (Exclusions) Regulations 2006 and come into force on 6th April 2006.

(2) In these Regulations, "the 2004 Act" means the Gangmasters (Licensing) Act 2004.

1. Made by the Secretary of State in exercise of the powers conferred by section 6(2) of the Gangmasters (Licensing) Act 2004.

2. Circumstances in which a licence is not required. A person does not require a licence to act as a gangmaster under section 6(1) of the 2004 Act in the circumstances specified in paragraphs 2 to 15 of the Schedule.

Regulation 2

SCHEDULE

CIRCUMSTANCES IN WHICH A LICENCE IS NOT REQUIRED UNDER THE 2004 ACT

1. In this Schedule—

"catering establishment" means—

(a) a restaurant, canteen, club, public house, school kitchen, prison kitchen, hospital kitchen or similar establishment (including a vehicle or a fixed or mobile stall) where—

(i) food is cooked or made ready for consumption without further preparation; and
(ii) food is prepared for service to the consumer.

(b) other premises used solely for the purpose of cooking or making food ready for consumption, without further preparation, after delivery to the consumer;

"distribution warehouse" means premises where produce is received prior to onward distribution to a wholesale or retail establishment and—

(a) there is no change in the ownership of the produce concerned between receipt and onward distribution; and
(b) the wholesale or retail establishment to which delivery is made is excluded under paragraph 2 of this Schedule; and
(c) the premises are owned by the same company that owns the retail or wholesale establishment to which the produce is delivered;

"farmer" means a person—

(a) who occupies land used for agricultural activities; or
(b) who owns or operates a business that pursues agricultural activities in whole or in part; or
(c) is an employed person with management responsibility for all or part of a business that pursues agricultural activities;

"produce" means produce derived from agricultural work, shellfish, fish or products derived from shellfish or fish;

"Seasonal Agricultural Workers Scheme" means a scheme operated by Work Permits UK, part of the Home Office, which allows farmers and growers in the United Kingdom to recruit overseas workers to undertake work that is both seasonal and agricultural;

"share farming agreement" means an agreement entered into between two or more persons to share the gross receipts of—

(a) their separate business assets; or
(b) services for carrying out specified farming operations,

as divided between them and paid to the businesses in agreed proportions;

"wholesale establishment" means a facility operated solely for the purpose of selling produce for the purposes of resale or to a catering establishment, and includes a cash and carry warehouse.

2. The supply or use of a worker to process or pack produce if the worker is supplied to—

(a) a catering establishment;
(b) a shop or other retail establishment;
(c) a wholesale market;
(d) a wholesale establishment;
(e) a distribution warehouse.

3. The supply of a worker to process or pack a product which includes a derivative of produce but where the product being packed is not a food product, pet food product or a product which is primarily an agricultural, fish or shellfish product.

4. The supply of a worker for agricultural work by a farmer (A) to another farmer (B) where—

(a) the supply is to do work on a farm which is the subject of a share farming agreement between A and B; or
(b) the total hours the worker works for B are not more than twenty per cent of the total hours he worked for A in the three months immediately preceding the commencement of the period of work undertaken for B; or
(c) the worker has been supplied to A by a person (C) who acts as a gangmaster in making that supply, and the supply by A—
  (i) is made with C's agreement to the nature of the work to be undertaken for B; and
  (ii) is a one-off arrangement of less than two weeks.

5. The use of a worker for agricultural work by a farmer (A) in connection with services provided by him to another farmer (B) where—

(a) the services provided involve a one-off arrangement of less than two weeks; and
(b) the total hours the worker works delivering services to B are not more than twenty per cent of the total hours he worked for A in the three months immediately preceding the commencement of the delivery of services to B; or
(c) the worker has been supplied to A by a person (C) who acts as a gangmaster in making that supply, and the use of the worker to deliver services by A is made with C's agreement to the nature of the services to be provided to B.

6. The supply of a worker by a farmer to a contractor to operate machinery supplied by that contractor for the purpose of undertaking agricultural work for that farmer.

7. The supply of a worker by a sole operator in the Seasonal Agricultural Workers Scheme to another Seasonal Agricultural Workers Scheme operator.

8. The use of a worker, for agricultural work by a service provider to provide a service to a farmer—

(a) where the service involves the use of machinery owned or hired by the service provider; and
(b) the worker is employed by the service provider to operate or to support the operation of that machinery.

9. (1) The use of a worker by a service provider, in connection with a food and drink processing and packaging service provided to a service user, where the service provider—

(a) is the worker's employer;
(b) owns, hires or leases any equipment, tools or machinery used by the worker which are necessary to carry out the service; and
(c) owns or leases the premises where the work is carried out.

10. The use of a worker to harvest crops by a person who has transferred title to the land on which the crops are grown, but has retained title to the crops.

11. The supply of a person licensed under the Welfare of Animals (Slaughter or Killing) Regulations 1995 to slaughter animals.

12. The supply of a worker by an educational establishment to undertake agricultural work solely in furtherance of education or training provided to the worker by that establishment leading to an agricultural qualification recognised under sections 96 or 97 of the Learning and Skills Act 2000.

13. The supply by a person (A) to a farmer of a single worker to undertake agricultural work in which that worker is specialised where—

(a) the farmer requires the worker to hold a specific qualification at or above National Vocational Qualification Level 2 or Scottish National Vocational Qualification Level 2 (as recognised under sections 96 and 97 of the Learning and Skills Act 2000), or an equivalent qualification, which is relevant and necessary to ensure the worker can effectively discharge the responsibilities he will be required to undertake; and
(b) the farmer employs the worker following his supply by A; and
(c) on the day the supply is made, no other worker is supplied to the farmer by A.

14. The supply or use of a worker to gather shellfish before 1st October 2006.
15. On and after 1st October 2006 the use of a worker

(a) to dive with the aid of breathing apparatus to gather shellfish from the sea bed; or
(b) to operate a net, dredge or other machinery used to gather shellfish from the sea bed, other than a hand net or hand-held rake, where the worker is using the net, dredge or other machinery on board a fishing vessel which is operating at sea.

10–9

Immigration, Asylum and Nationality Act 2006[1]

(2006 c 13)

21. Offence. (1) A person commits an offence if he employs another ("the employee") knowing that the employee is an adult subject to immigration control and that—

(a) he has not been granted leave to enter or remain in the United Kingdom, or
(b) his leave to enter or remain in the United Kingdom—
  (i) is invalid,
  (ii) has ceased to have effect (whether by reason of curtailment, revocation, cancellation, passage of time or otherwise), or
  (iii) is subject to a condition preventing him from accepting the employment.

(2) A person guilty of an offence under this section shall be liable—

(a) on conviction on indictment—
  (i) to imprisonment for a term not exceeding two years,
  (ii) to a fine, or
  (iii) to both, or
(b) on summary conviction—
  (i) to imprisonment for a term not exceeding 12 months in England and Wales or 6 months in Scotland or Northern Ireland,
  (ii) to a fine not exceeding the statutory maximum, or
  (iii) to both.

(3) An offence under this section shall be treated as—

(a) a relevant offence for the purpose of sections 28B and 28D of the Immigration Act 1971 (c 77) (search, entry and arrest), and
(b) an offence under Part III of that Act (criminal proceedings) for the purposes of sections 28E, 28G and 28H (search after arrest).

(4) In relation to a conviction occurring before the commencement of section 154(1) of the Criminal Justice Act 2003 (c 44) (general limit on magistrates' powers to imprison) the reference to 12 months in subsection (2)(b)(i) shall be taken as a reference to 6 months.
[Immigration, Asylum and Nationality Act 2006, s 21.]

22. Offence: bodies corporate, &c. (1) For the purposes of section 21(1) a body (whether corporate or not) shall be treated as knowing a fact about an employee if a person who has responsibility within the body for an aspect of the employment knows the fact.

(2) If an offence under section 21(1) is committed by a body corporate with the consent or connivance of an officer of the body, the officer, as well as the body, shall be treated as having committed the offence.

(3) In subsection (2) a reference to an officer of a body includes a reference to—

(a) a director, manager or secretary,
(b) a person purporting to act as a director, manager or secretary, and
(c) if the affairs of the body are managed by its members, a member.

(4) Where an offence under section 21(1) is committed by a partnership (whether or not a limited partnership) subsection (2) above shall have effect, but as if a reference to an officer of the body were a reference to—

(a) a partner, and
(b) a person purporting to act as a partner.
[Immigration, Asylum and Nationality Act 2006, s 22.]

32. Passenger and crew information: police powers. (1) This section applies to ships and aircraft which are—

(a) arriving, or expected to arrive, in the United Kingdom, or
(b) leaving, or expected to leave, the United Kingdom.

(2) The owner or agent of a ship or aircraft shall comply with any requirement imposed by a constable of the rank of superintendent or above to provide passenger or service information.

(3) A passenger or member of crew shall provide to the owner or agent of a ship or aircraft any information that he requires for the purpose of complying with a requirement imposed by virtue of subsection (2).

(4) A constable may impose a requirement under subsection (2) only if he thinks it necessary—

(a) in the case of a constable in England, Wales or Northern Ireland, for police purposes, or
(b) in the case of a constable in Scotland, for police purposes which are or relate to reserved matters.

(5) In this section—

(a) "passenger or service information" means information which is of a kind specified by order of the Secretary of State and which relates to—

(i) passengers,
(ii) members of crew, or
(iii) a voyage or flight,

(b) "police purposes" has the meaning given by section 21(3) of the Immigration and Asylum Act 1999 (c 33) (disclosure by Secretary of State), and
(c) "reserved matters" has the same meaning as in the Scotland Act 1998 (c 46).

(6) A requirement imposed under subsection (2)—

(a) must be in writing,
(b) may apply generally or only to one or more specified ships or aircraft,
(c) must specify a period, not exceeding six months and beginning with the date on which it is imposed, during which it has effect,
(d) must state—

(i) the information required, and
(ii) the date or time by which it is to be provided.

(7) The Secretary of State may make an order specifying a kind of information under subsection (5)(a) only if satisfied that the nature of the information is such that there are likely to be circumstances in which it can be required under subsection (2) without breaching Convention rights (within the meaning of the Human Rights Act 1998 (c 42)).

(8) An order under subsection (5)(a)—

(a) may apply generally or only to specified cases or circumstances,
(b) may make different provision for different cases or circumstances,
(c) may specify the form and manner in which information is to be provided,
(d) shall be made by statutory instrument, and
(e) shall be subject to annulment in pursuance of a resolution of either House of Parliament.

[Immigration, Asylum and Nationality Act 2006, s 32.]

33. Freight information: police powers. (1) This section applies to ships, aircraft and vehicles which are—

(a) arriving, or expected to arrive, in the United Kingdom, or
(b) leaving, or expected to leave, the United Kingdom.

(2) If a constable of the rank of superintendent or above requires a person specified in subsection (3) to provide freight information he shall comply with the requirement.

(3) The persons referred to in subsection (2) are—

(a) in the case of a ship or aircraft, the owner or agent,
(b) in the case of a vehicle, the owner or hirer, and
(c) in any case, persons responsible for the import or export of the freight into or from the United Kingdom.

(4) A constable may impose a requirement under subsection (2) only if he thinks it necessary—

(a) in the case of a constable in England, Wales or Northern Ireland, for police purposes, or
(b) in the case of a constable in Scotland, for police purposes which are or relate to reserved matters.

(5) In this section—

(a) "freight information" means information which is of a kind specified by order of the Secretary of State and which relates to freight carried,

(b) "police purposes" has the meaning given by section 21(3) of the Immigration and Asylum Act 1999 (c 33) (disclosure by Secretary of State), and

(c) "reserved matters" has the same meaning as in the Scotland Act 1998 (c 46).

(6) A requirement imposed under subsection (2)—

(a) must be in writing,

(b) may apply generally or only to one or more specified ships, aircraft or vehicles,

(c) must specify a period, not exceeding six months and beginning with the date on which it is imposed, during which it has effect, and

(d) must state—

(i) the information required, and

(ii) the date or time by which it is to be provided.

(7) The Secretary of State may make an order specifying a kind of information under subsection (5)(a) only if satisfied that the nature of the information is such that there are likely to be circumstances in which it can be required under subsection (2) without breaching Convention rights (within the meaning of the Human Rights Act 1998 (c 42)).

(8) An order under subsection (5)(a)—

(a) may apply generally or only to specified cases or circumstances,

(b) may make different provision for different cases or circumstances,

(c) may specify the form and manner in which the information is to be provided,

(d) shall be made by statutory instrument, and

(e) shall be subject to annulment in pursuance of a resolution of either House of Parliament.

[Immigration, Asylum and Nationality Act 2006, s 33.]

34. Offence. (1) A person commits an offence if without reasonable excuse he fails to comply with a requirement imposed under section 32(2) or (3) or 33(2).

(2) But—

(a) a person who fails without reasonable excuse to comply with a requirement imposed under section 32(2) or 33(2) by a constable in England and Wales or Northern Ireland otherwise than in relation to a reserved matter (within the meaning of the Scotland Act 1998 (c 46)) shall not be treated as having committed the offence in Scotland (but has committed the offence in England and Wales or Northern Ireland), and

(b) a person who fails without reasonable excuse to comply with a requirement which is imposed under section 32(3) for the purpose of complying with a requirement to which paragraph (a) applies—

(i) shall not be treated as having committed the offence in Scotland, but

(ii) shall be treated as having committed the offence in England and Wales or Northern Ireland.

(3) A person who is guilty of an offence under subsection (1) shall be liable on summary conviction to—

(a) imprisonment for a term not exceeding 51 weeks in England and Wales or 6 months in Scotland or Northern Ireland,

(b) a fine not exceeding level 4 on the standard scale, or

(c) both.

(4) In relation to a conviction occurring before the commencement of section 281(5) of the Criminal Justice Act 2003 (c 44) (51 week maximum term of sentences) the reference to 51 weeks in subsection (2)(a) shall be taken as a reference to three months.

[Immigration, Asylum and Nationality Act 2006, s 34.]

10–10

London Olympic Games and Paralympic Games Act 2006[1]

(2006 c 12)

Advertising

19–20. *Regulations to be made by the Secretary of State about advertising in the vicinity of London Olympic events.*

1. This Act is to be brought into force in accordance with the provisions of s 40, post.

21. Offence. (1) A person commits an offence if he contravenes regulations under section 19.

(2) It shall be a defence for a person charged with an offence under subsection (1) to prove that the contravention of the regulations occurred—

(a) without his knowledge, or

(b) despite his taking all reasonable steps to prevent it from occurring or (where he became aware of it after its commencement) from continuing.

(3) A person guilty of an offence under subsection (1) shall be liable—

(a) on conviction on indictment, to a fine, or
(b) on summary conviction, to a fine not exceeding £20,000.

(4) A court by or before which a person is convicted of an offence under subsection (1) may require him to pay to a police authority or to the Olympic Delivery Authority sums in respect of expenses reasonably incurred in taking action under section 22(1) in relation to the matters to which the offence relates.
[London Olympic Games and Paralympic Games Act 2006, s 21.]

22. Enforcement: power of entry. (1) A constable or enforcement officer may—

(a) enter land or premises on which they reasonably believe a contravention of regulations under section 19 is occurring (whether by reason of advertising on that land or premises or by the use of that land or premises to cause an advertisement to appear elsewhere);
(b) remove, destroy, conceal or erase any infringing article;
(c) when entering land under paragraph (a), be accompanied by one or more persons for the purpose of taking action under paragraph (b);
(d) use, or authorise the use of, reasonable force for the purpose of taking action under this subsection.

(2) The power to enter land or premises may be exercised only at a time that a constable or enforcement officer thinks reasonable having regard to the nature and circumstances of the contravention of regulations under section 19.

(3) Before entering land or premises a constable or enforcement officer must take reasonable steps to—

(a) establish the identity of an owner, occupier or person responsible for the management of the land or premises or of any infringing article on the land or premises, and
(b) give any owner, occupier or responsible person identified under paragraph (a) such opportunity as seems reasonable to the constable or enforcement officer in the circumstances of the case to end the contravention of the regulations (whether by removing, destroying or concealing any infringing article or otherwise).

(4) The power to enter premises may be exercised in relation to a dwelling only in accordance with a warrant issued by a justice of the peace; and a justice of the peace may issue a warrant only if satisfied on the application of a constable or enforcement officer that—

(a) there are reasonable grounds to believe a contravention of regulations under section 19 is occurring in the dwelling or on land that can reasonably be entered only through the dwelling,
(b) the constable or enforcement officer has complied with subsection (3),
(c) the constable or enforcement officer has taken reasonable steps to give notice to persons likely to be interested of his intention to apply for a warrant, and
(d) that it is reasonable in the circumstances of the case to issue a warrant.

(5) The power to remove an article may be exercised only if the constable or enforcement officer thinks it necessary for the purpose of—

(a) ending the contravention of regulations under section 19,
(b) preventing a future contravention of the regulations,
(c) enabling the article to be used as evidence in proceedings for an offence under section 21, or
(d) enabling the article to be forfeited in accordance with section 143 of the Powers of Criminal Courts (Sentencing) Act 2000 (c 6).

(6) An article removed—

(a) if removed by an enforcement officer, shall as soon as is reasonably practicable be delivered to a constable, and
(b) whether removed by or delivered to a constable, shall be treated as if acquired by the constable in the course of the investigation of an offence.

(7) Having exercised a power under this section a constable or enforcement officer—

(a) shall take reasonable steps to leave the land or premises secure, and
(b) shall comply with any provision of regulations under section 19 about informing specified persons of what the constable or enforcement officer has done.

(8) Regulations under section 19 shall include provision enabling a person whose property is damaged in the course of the exercise or purported exercise of a power under this section (other than a person responsible for a contravention of the regulations or for the management of an infringing article) to obtain compensation from a police authority or the Olympic Delivery Authority; and the regulations may, in particular, include provision—

(a) conferring jurisdiction on a court or tribunal;

(b) about appeals.

(9) A police authority or the Olympic Delivery Authority may recover from a person responsible for the contravention of the regulations, as if it were a debt, the reasonable costs of taking action under this section.

(10) In this section—

"enforcement officer" means a person designated for the purposes of that subsection by the Olympic Delivery Authority (and paragraph 29(1)(a) to (d) of Schedule 1 shall apply to an enforcement officer whether or not he is a member of the Authority's staff), and

"infringing article" means—

(a) an advertisement which contravenes regulations under section 19, and

(b) any other thing that constitutes a contravention of regulations under section 19 or is being used in connection with a contravention of the regulations.

[London Olympic Games and Paralympic Games Act 2006, s 22.]

23. Role of Olympic Delivery Authority. (1) The Olympic Delivery Authority shall make arrangements to have the effect of regulations made or expected to be made under section 19 brought to the attention of persons likely to be affected or interested.

(2) In exercising their function under subsection (1) the Authority shall—

(a) aim to give two years' notice of the general nature of the regulations, and

(b) aim to give six months' notice of the detailed provisions of the regulations.

(3) The Olympic Delivery Authority—

(a) shall make available to persons who are or may be affected by regulations under section 19 advice about the effect or likely effect of the regulations, and

(b) may give assistance (which may include financial assistance) in complying with or avoiding breaches of the regulations.

(4) The Olympic Delivery Authority may institute criminal proceedings in respect of an offence under section 21.

(5) Subsection (4) shall not apply in relation to the institution of proceedings in Scotland or Northern Ireland.

(6) The Olympic Delivery Authority shall—

(a) prepare a strategy for the exercise of their functions under this section and under section 22,

(b) submit the strategy to the Secretary of State,

(c) revise the strategy until it obtains the Secretary of State's approval, and

(d) publish the strategy as approved.

[London Olympic Games and Paralympic Games Act 2006, s 23.]

25–26. *Regulations to be made by the Secretary of State about trading in the vicinity of London Olympic events.*

27. Offence. (1) A person commits an offence if he contravenes regulations under section 25.

(2) A person guilty of an offence under subsection (1) shall be liable—

(a) on conviction on indictment, to a fine, or

(b) on summary conviction, to a fine not exceeding £20,000.

[London Olympic Games and Paralympic Games Act 2006, s 27.]

28. Enforcement: power of entry. (1) A constable or enforcement officer may—

(a) enter land or premises on which they reasonably believe a contravention of regulations under section 25 is occurring;

(b) remove any infringing article;

(c) when entering land under paragraph (a), be accompanied by one or more persons for the purpose of taking action under paragraph (b);

(d) use, or authorise the use of, reasonable force for the purpose of taking action under this subsection.

(2) The power to remove an article may be exercised only if the constable or enforcement officer thinks it necessary for the purpose of—

(a) ending the contravention of regulations under section 25,

(b) preventing a future contravention of the regulations,

(c) enabling the article to be used as evidence in proceedings for an offence under section 27, or

(d) enabling the article to be forfeited in accordance with section 143 of the Powers of Criminal Courts (Sentencing) Act 2000 (c 6).

(3) An article removed shall be returned when retention is no longer justified by a matter specified in subsection (2)(a) to (d); but this subsection does not apply to perishable articles which have ceased to be usable for trade.

(4) An article removed—

(a) if removed by an enforcement officer, shall as soon as is reasonably practicable be delivered to a constable, and

(b) whether removed by or delivered to a constable, shall be treated as if acquired by the constable in the course of the investigation of an offence;

but this subsection is subject to subsection (3).

(5) Having exercised a power under this section a constable or enforcement officer—

(a) shall take reasonable steps to leave the land or premises secure, and

(b) shall comply with any provision of regulations under section 25 about informing specified persons of what the constable or enforcement officer has done.

(6) Regulations under section 25 shall include provision enabling a person whose property is damaged in the course of the exercise or purported exercise of a power under this section (other than a person responsible for a contravention of the regulations) to obtain compensation from a police authority or the Olympic Delivery Authority; and the regulations may, in particular, include provision—

(a) conferring jurisdiction on a court or tribunal;

(b) about appeals.

(7) A police authority or the Olympic Delivery Authority may recover from a person responsible for the contravention of regulations under section 25, as if it were a debt, the reasonable costs of taking action under this section.

(8) In this section—

"enforcement officer" means a person designated for the purposes of that subsection by the Olympic Delivery Authority (and paragraph 29(1)(a) to (d) of Schedule 1 shall apply to an enforcement officer whether or not he is a member of the Authority's staff), and

"infringing article" means—

(a) an article that is being offered for trade in contravention of regulations under section 25 or is otherwise being used in connection with a contravention of the regulations, and

(b) anything (other than a vehicle) containing an article to which paragraph (a) applies.

[London Olympic Games and Paralympic Games Act 2006, s 28.]

29. Role of Olympic Delivery Authority. (1) The Olympic Delivery Authority shall—

(a) make arrangements to have the effect of regulations made or expected to be made under section 25 brought to the attention of persons likely to be affected or interested, and

(b) work with persons likely to be prevented by regulations under section 25 from carrying out their habitual trading activities in attempting to identify acceptable alternatives.

(2) In exercising their function under subsection (1) the Authority shall—

(a) aim to give two years' notice of the general nature of the regulations, and

(b) aim to give six months' notice of the detailed provisions of the regulations.

(3) The Olympic Delivery Authority—

(a) shall make available to persons who are or may be affected by regulations under section 25 advice about the effect or likely effect of the regulations, and

(b) may give assistance (which may include financial assistance) in complying with or avoiding breaches of the regulations.

(4) The Olympic Delivery Authority may institute criminal proceedings in respect of an offence under section 27.

(5) Subsection (4) shall not apply in relation to the institution of proceedings in Scotland or Northern Ireland.

(6) The Olympic Delivery Authority shall—

(a) prepare a strategy for the exercise of their functions under this section and under or by virtue of sections 25 and 28,

(b) submit the strategy to the Secretary of State,

(c) revise the strategy until it obtains the Secretary of State's approval, and

(d) publish the strategy as approved.

[London Olympic Games and Paralympic Games Act 2006, s 29.]

31. Sale of tickets. (1) A person commits an offence if he sells an Olympic ticket—

(a) in a public place or in the course of a business, and

(b) otherwise than in accordance with a written authorisation issued by the London Organising Committee.

(2) For the purposes of subsection (1)—

(a) "Olympic ticket" means anything which is or purports to be a ticket for one or more London Olympic events,

(b) a reference to selling a ticket includes a reference to—

(i) offering to sell a ticket,

(ii) exposing a ticket for sale,

(iii) advertising that a ticket is available for purchase, and

(iv) giving, or offering to give, a ticket to a person who pays or agrees to pay for some other goods or services, and

(c) a person shall (without prejudice to the generality of subsection (1)(a)) be treated as acting in the course of a business if he does anything as a result of which he makes a profit or aims to make a profit.

(3) A person does not commit an offence under subsection (1) by advertising that a ticket is available for purchase if—

(a) the sale of the ticket if purchased would be in the course of a business only by reason of subsection (2)(c), and

(b) the person does not know, and could not reasonably be expected to discover, that subsection (2)(c) would apply to the sale.

(4) A person does not commit an offence under subsection (1) (whether actual or inchoate) only by virtue of making facilities available in connection with electronic communication or the storage of electronic data.

(5) Where a person who provides services for electronic communication or for the storage of electronic data discovers that they are being used in connection with the commission of an offence under subsection (1), the defence in subsection (4) does not apply in respect of continued provision of the services after the shortest time reasonably required to withdraw them.

(6) A person guilty of an offence under subsection (1) shall be liable on summary conviction to a fine not exceeding level 5 on the standard scale.

(7) Section 32(2)(b) of the Police and Criminal Evidence Act 1984 (c 60) (power to search premises) shall, in its application to the offence under subsection (1) above, permit the searching of a vehicle which a constable reasonably thinks was used in connection with the offence.

(8) Subsection (9) applies where a person in Scotland is arrested in connection with the commission of an offence under subsection (1).

(9) For the purposes of recovering evidence relating to the offence, a constable in Scotland may without warrant enter and search—

(a) premises in which the person was when arrested or immediately before he was arrested, and

(b) a vehicle which the constable reasonably believes is being used or was used in connection with the offence.

(10) Subsection (9) is without prejudice to any power of entry or search which is otherwise exercisable by a constable in Scotland.

(11) The London Organising Committee shall make arrangements for the grant of authorisations under subsection (1)(b); and the arrangements may, in particular—

(a) make provision about charges;

(b) enable the Committee to exercise unfettered discretion.

(12) In this section a reference to a London Olympic event includes a reference to an event held by way of a pre-Olympic event in accordance with arrangements made by the London Organising Committee in pursuance of paragraph 7 of the Bye-Law to Rule 49 of the Olympic Charter.
[London Olympic Games and Paralympic Games Act 2006, s 31.]

Miscellaneous

32. Olympic Symbol etc (Protection) Act 1995. Schedule 3 (which amends the Olympic Symbol etc (Protection) Act 1995 (c 32)) shall have effect.
[London Olympic Games and Paralympic Games Act 2006, s 32.]

33. London Olympics association right. Schedule 4 (which creates the London Olympics association right) shall have effect.
[London Olympic Games and Paralympic Games Act 2006, s 33.]

40. Commencement and duration. (1) The following provisions of this Act shall come into force on Royal Assent—

(a) section 1,

(b) sections 3 to 5 and Schedule 1,

(c) section 32 and paragraphs 1 to 11 of Schedule 3,

(d) section 33 and Schedule 4,

(e) sections 34 and 35(1) and (2),

(f) section 36(3)(a) and (d),

(g) section 37, and
(h) section 38.

(2) The other preceding provisions of this Act (including paragraphs 12 to 14 of Schedule 3) shall come into force in accordance with provision made by order of the Secretary of State.

(3) But the following provisions of this Act, so far as they extend to Scotland, shall come into force in accordance with provision made by order of the Scottish Ministers—

(a) sections 19 to 31, and
(b) section 39(2) and (3).

(4) An order under subsection (2) or (3)—

(a) may make provision generally or only for specified purposes,
(b) may make different provision for different purposes,
(c) may include transitional or incidental provision, and
(d) shall be made by statutory instrument.

(5) Despite subsection (1)(c), for the purposes of criminal proceedings under a provision of the Olympic Symbol etc (Protection) Act 1995 (c 32) in respect of anything done before the end of the period of two months beginning with the date on which this Act receives Royal Assent, no account shall be taken of any amendment made of that Act by Schedule 3 to this Act.

(6) Sections 10 to 18 (including any power to make orders or give directions) shall cease to have effect at the end of the London Olympics period.

(7) Paragraph 14 of Schedule 3, which inserts new sections 12A and 12B into the Olympic Symbol etc (Protection) Act 1995, shall have effect in relation to things arriving in the United Kingdom during the period—

(a) beginning with the day specified under subsection (2) above for the commencement of paragraph 14 of Schedule 3, and
(b) ending with 31st December 2012.

(8) Section 33 and Schedule 4 shall cease to have effect at the end of 31st December 2012.

(9) In respect of section 36(3)—

(a) paragraph (a) shall have effect in relation to compulsory purchase orders made on or after 1st October 2005,
(b) an order bringing paragraph (b) into force on a date ("the commencement date")—
    (i) may provide for paragraph (b) to have effect in relation to purchases (whether compulsory or voluntary) completed before, on or after the commencement date, but
    (ii) must include provision modifying section 295 of the Housing Act 1985 in its application by virtue of section 36(3)(b) so that extinguishment of rights and easements takes effect, in the case of a purchase completed before the commencement date, on the commencement date,
(c) an order bringing paragraph (c) into force on a date ("the commencement date")—
    (i) may provide for paragraph (c) to have effect in relation to purchases (whether compulsory or voluntary) completed on or after 1st October 2005, but
    (ii) shall not affect the lawfulness of anything done before the commencement date, and
(d) paragraph (d) shall be treated as having taken effect on 1st October 2005.

[London Olympic Games and Paralympic Games Act 2006, s 40.]

41. Extent and application

42. Short title

10–11

Terrorism Act 2006[1]

(2006 c 11)

PART 1
OFFENCES

Encouragement etc of terrorism

1. Encouragement of terrorism. (1) This section applies to a statement that is likely to be understood by some or all of the members of the public to whom it is published as a direct or indirect encouragement or other inducement to them to the commission, preparation or instigation of acts of terrorism or Convention offences.

(2) A person commits an offence if—

(a) he publishes a statement to which this section applies or causes another to publish such a statement; and

(b) at the time he publishes it or causes it to be published, he—

(i) intends members of the public to be directly or indirectly encouraged or otherwise induced by the statement to commit, prepare or instigate acts of terrorism or Convention offences; or

(ii) is reckless as to whether members of the public will be directly or indirectly encouraged or otherwise induced by the statement to commit, prepare or instigate such acts or offences.

(3) For the purposes of this section, the statements that are likely to be understood by members of the public as indirectly encouraging the commission or preparation of acts of terrorism or Convention offences include every statement which—

(a) glorifies the commission or preparation (whether in the past, in the future or generally) of such acts or offences; and

(b) is a statement from which those members of the public could reasonably be expected to infer that what is being glorified is being glorified as conduct that should be emulated by them in existing circumstances.

(4) For the purposes of this section the questions how a statement is likely to be understood and what members of the public could reasonably be expected to infer from it must be determined having regard both—

(a) to the contents of the statement as a whole; and

(b) to the circumstances and manner of its publication.

(5) It is irrelevant for the purposes of subsections (1) to (3)—

(a) whether anything mentioned in those subsections relates to the commission, preparation or instigation of one or more particular acts of terrorism or Convention offences, of acts of terrorism or Convention offences of a particular description or of acts of terrorism or Convention offences generally; and,

(b) whether any person is in fact encouraged or induced by the statement to commit, prepare or instigate any such act or offence.

(6) In proceedings for an offence under this section against a person in whose case it is not proved that he intended the statement directly or indirectly to encourage or otherwise induce the commission, preparation or instigation of acts of terrorism or Convention offences, it is a defence for him to show—

(a) that the statement neither expressed his views nor had his endorsement (whether by virtue of section 3 or otherwise); and

(b) that it was clear, in all the circumstances of the statement's publication, that it did not express his views and (apart from the possibility of his having been given and failed to comply with a notice under subsection (3) of that section) did not have his endorsement.

(7) A person guilty of an offence under this section shall be liable—

(a) on conviction on indictment, to imprisonment for a term not exceeding 7 years or to a fine, or to both;

(b) on summary conviction in England and Wales, to imprisonment for a term not exceeding 12 months or to a fine not exceeding the statutory maximum, or to both;

(c) on summary conviction in Scotland or Northern Ireland, to imprisonment for a term not exceeding 6 months or to a fine not exceeding the statutory maximum, or to both.

(8) In relation to an offence committed before the commencement of section 154(1) of the Criminal Justice Act 2003 (c 44), the reference in subsection (7)(b) to 12 months is to be read as a reference to 6 months.

[Terrorism Act 2006, s 1.]

---

1. This Act, except s 39, is to be brought into force in accordance with orders made under s 39, post. At the date of press, the following order had been made: (Commencement No 1) SI 2006/1013 which brought into force on 13 April 2006 ss 1 to 22, Sch 1; ss 26 to 36, Sch 2; ss 37(1) to (4) and 38; s 37(5) all of the entries in Sch 3 except those relating to paragraph 36(1) of Schedule 8 to the Terrorism Act 2000 and s 306(2) and (3) of the Criminal Justice Act 2003.

2. Dissemination of terrorist publications. (1) A person commits an offence if he engages in conduct falling within subsection (2) and, at the time he does so—

(a) he intends an effect of his conduct to be a direct or indirect encouragement or other inducement to the commission, preparation or instigation of acts of terrorism;

(b) he intends an effect of his conduct to be the provision of assistance in the commission or preparation of such acts; or

(c) he is reckless as to whether his conduct has an effect mentioned in paragraph (a) or (b).

(2) For the purposes of this section a person engages in conduct falling within this subsection if he—

(a) distributes or circulates a terrorist publication;

(b) gives, sells or lends such a publication;

(c) offers such a publication for sale or loan;
(d) provides a service to others that enables them to obtain, read, listen to or look at such a publication, or to acquire it by means of a gift, sale or loan;
(e) transmits the contents of such a publication electronically; or
(f) has such a publication in his possession with a view to its becoming the subject of conduct falling within any of paragraphs (a) to (e).

(3) For the purposes of this section a publication is a terrorist publication, in relation to conduct falling within subsection (2), if matter contained in it is likely—
(a) to be understood, by some or all of the persons to whom it is or may become available as a consequence of that conduct, as a direct or indirect encouragement or other inducement to them to the commission, preparation or instigation of acts of terrorism; or
(b) to be useful in the commission or preparation of such acts and to be understood, by some or all of those persons, as contained in the publication, or made available to them, wholly or mainly for the purpose of being so useful to them.

(4) For the purposes of this section matter that is likely to be understood by a person as indirectly encouraging the commission or preparation of acts of terrorism includes any matter which—
(a) glorifies the commission or preparation (whether in the past, in the future or generally) of such acts; and
(b) is matter from which that person could reasonably be expected to infer that what is being glorified is being glorified as conduct that should be emulated by him in existing circumstances.

(5) For the purposes of this section the question whether a publication is a terrorist publication in relation to particular conduct must be determined—
(a) as at the time of that conduct; and
(b) having regard both to the contents of the publication as a whole and to the circumstances in which that conduct occurs.

(6) In subsection (1) references to the effect of a person's conduct in relation to a terrorist publication include references to an effect of the publication on one or more persons to whom it is or may become available as a consequence of that conduct.

(7) It is irrelevant for the purposes of this section whether anything mentioned in subsections (1) to (4) is in relation to the commission, preparation or instigation of one or more particular acts of terrorism, of acts of terrorism of a particular description or of acts of terrorism generally.

(8) For the purposes of this section it is also irrelevant, in relation to matter contained in any article whether any person—
(a) is in fact encouraged or induced by that matter to commit, prepare or instigate acts of terrorism; or
(b) in fact makes use of it in the commission or preparation of such acts.

(9) In proceedings for an offence under this section against a person in respect of conduct to which subsection (10) applies, it is a defence for him to show—
(a) that the matter by reference to which the publication in question was a terrorist publication neither expressed his views nor had his endorsement (whether by virtue of section 3 or otherwise); and
(b) that it was clear, in all the circumstances of the conduct, that that matter did not express his views and (apart from the possibility of his having been given and failed to comply with a notice under subsection (3) of that section) did not have his endorsement.

(10) This subsection applies to the conduct of a person to the extent that—
(a) the publication to which his conduct related contained matter by reference to which it was a terrorist publication by virtue of subsection (3)(a); and
(b) that person is not proved to have engaged in that conduct with the intention specified in subsection (1)(a).

(11) A person guilty of an offence under this section shall be liable—
(a) on conviction on indictment, to imprisonment for a term not exceeding 7 years or to a fine, or to both;
(b) on summary conviction in England and Wales, to imprisonment for a term not exceeding 12 months or to a fine not exceeding the statutory maximum, or to both;
(c) on summary conviction in Scotland or Northern Ireland, to imprisonment for a term not exceeding 6 months or to a fine not exceeding the statutory maximum, or to both.

(12) In relation to an offence committed before the commencement of section 154(1) of the Criminal Justice Act 2003 (c 44), the reference in subsection (11)(b) to 12 months is to be read as a reference to 6 months.

(13) In this section—

"lend" includes let on hire, and "loan" is to be construed accordingly;

"publication" means an article or record of any description that contains any of the following, or any combination of them—

(a) matter to be read;
(b) matter to be listened to;
(c) matter to be looked at or watched.

[Terrorism Act 2006, s 2.]

3. Application of ss 1 and 2 to internet activity etc. (1) This section applies for the purposes of sections 1 and 2 in relation to cases where—

(a) a statement is published or caused to be published in the course of, or in connection with, the provision or use of a service provided electronically; or
(b) conduct falling within section 2(2) was in the course of, or in connection with, the provision or use of such a service.

(2) The cases in which the statement, or the article or record to which the conduct relates, is to be regarded as having the endorsement of a person ("the relevant person") at any time include a case in which—

(a) a constable has given him a notice under subsection (3);
(b) that time falls more than 2 working days after the day on which the notice was given; and
(c) the relevant person has failed, without reasonable excuse, to comply with the notice.

(3) A notice under this subsection is a notice which—

(a) declares that, in the opinion of the constable giving it, the statement or the article or record is unlawfully terrorism-related;
(b) requires the relevant person to secure that the statement or the article or record, so far as it is so related, is not available to the public or is modified so as no longer to be so related;
(c) warns the relevant person that a failure to comply with the notice within 2 working days will result in the statement, or the article or record, being regarded as having his endorsement; and
(d) explains how, under subsection (4), he may become liable by virtue of the notice if the statement, or the article or record, becomes available to the public after he has complied with the notice.

(4) Where—

(a) a notice under subsection (3) has been given to the relevant person in respect of a statement, or an article or record, and he has complied with it, but
(b) he subsequently publishes or causes to be published a statement which is, or is for all practical purposes, the same or to the same effect as the statement to which the notice related, or to matter contained in the article or record to which it related, (a "repeat statement");

the requirements of subsection (2)(a) to (c) shall be regarded as satisfied in the case of the repeat statement in relation to the times of its subsequent publication by the relevant person.

(5) In proceedings against a person for an offence under section 1 or 2 the requirements of subsection (2)(a) to (c) are not, in his case, to be regarded as satisfied in relation to any time by virtue of subsection (4) if he shows that he—

(a) has, before that time, taken every step he reasonably could to prevent a repeat statement from becoming available to the public and to ascertain whether it does; and
(b) was, at that time, a person to whom subsection (6) applied.

(6) This subsection applies to a person at any time when he—

(a) is not aware of the publication of the repeat statement; or
(b) having become aware of its publication, has taken every step that he reasonably could to secure that it either ceased to be available to the public or was modified as mentioned in subsection (3)(b).

(7) For the purposes of this section a statement or an article or record is unlawfully terrorism-related if it constitutes, or if matter contained in the article or record constitutes—

(a) something that is likely to be understood, by any one or more of the persons to whom it has or may become available, as a direct or indirect encouragement or other inducement to the commission, preparation or instigation of acts of terrorism or Convention offences; or
(b) information which—
    (i) is likely to be useful to any one or more of those persons in the commission or preparation of such acts; and
    (ii) is in a form or context in which it is likely to be understood by any one or more of those persons as being wholly or mainly for the purpose of being so useful.

(8) The reference in subsection (7) to something that is likely to be understood as an indirect encouragement to the commission or preparation of acts of terrorism or Convention offences includes anything which is likely to be understood as—

(a) the glorification of the commission or preparation (whether in the past, in the future or generally) of such acts or such offences; and

(b) a suggestion that what is being glorified is being glorified as conduct that should be emulated in existing circumstances.

(9) In this section "working day" means any day other than—

(a) a Saturday or a Sunday;
(b) Christmas Day or Good Friday; or
(c) a day which is a bank holiday under the Banking and Financial Dealings Act 1971 (c 80) in any part of the United Kingdom.

[Terrorism Act 2006, s 3.

4. Giving of notices under s 3. (1) Except in a case to which any of subsections (2) to (4) applies, a notice under section 3(3) may be given to a person only—

(a) by delivering it to him in person; or
(b) by sending it to him, by means of a postal service providing for delivery to be recorded, at his last known address.

(2) Such a notice may be given to a body corporate only—

(a) by delivering it to the secretary of that body in person; or
(b) by sending it to the appropriate person, by means of a postal service providing for delivery to be recorded, at the address of the registered or principal office of the body.

(3) Such a notice may be given to a firm only—

(a) by delivering it to a partner of the firm in person;
(b) by so delivering it to a person having the control or management of the partnership business; or
(c) by sending it to the appropriate person, by means of a postal service providing for delivery to be recorded, at the address of the principal office of the partnership.

(4) Such a notice may be given to an unincorporated body or association only—

(a) by delivering it to a member of its governing body in person; or
(b) by sending it to the appropriate person, by means of a postal service providing for delivery to be recorded, at the address of the principal office of the body or association.

(5) In the case of—

(a) a company registered outside the United Kingdom,
(b) a firm carrying on business outside the United Kingdom, or
(c) an unincorporated body or association with offices outside the United Kingdom,

the references in this section to its principal office include references to its principal office within the United Kingdom (if any).

(6) In this section "the appropriate person" means—

(a) in the case of a body corporate, the body itself or its secretary;
(b) in the case of a firm, the firm itself or a partner of the firm or a person having the control or management of the partnership business; and
(c) in the case of an unincorporated body or association, the body or association itself or a member of its governing body.

(7) For the purposes of section 3 the time at which a notice under subsection (3) of that section is to be regarded as given is—

(a) where it is delivered to a person, the time at which it is so delivered; and
(b) where it is sent by a postal service providing for delivery to be recorded, the time recorded as the time of its delivery.

(8) In this section "secretary", in relation to a body corporate, means the secretary or other equivalent officer of the body.

[Terrorism Act 2006, s 4.]

Preparation of terrorist acts and terrorist training

5. Preparation of terrorist acts. (1) A person commits an offence if, with the intention of—

(a) committing acts of terrorism, or
(b) assisting another to commit such acts,

he engages in any conduct in preparation for giving effect to his intention.

(2) It is irrelevant for the purposes of subsection (1) whether the intention and preparations relate to one or more particular acts of terrorism, acts of terrorism of a particular description or acts of terrorism generally.

(3) A person guilty of an offence under this section shall be liable, on conviction on indictment, to imprisonment for life.

[Terrorism Act 2006, s 5.]

6. Training for terrorism. (1) A person commits an offence if—

(a) he provides instruction or training in any of the skills mentioned in subsection (3); and
(b) at the time he provides the instruction or training, he knows that a person receiving it intends to use the skills in which he is being instructed or trained—
(i) for or in connection with the commission or preparation of acts of terrorism or Convention offences; or
(ii) for assisting the commission or preparation by others of such acts or offences.

(2) A person commits an offence if—

(a) he receives instruction or training in any of the skills mentioned in subsection (3); and
(b) at the time of the instruction or training, he intends to use the skills in which he is being instructed or trained—
(i) for or in connection with the commission or preparation of acts of terrorism or Convention offences; or
(ii) for assisting the commission or preparation by others of such acts or offences.

(3) The skills are—

(a) the making, handling or use of a noxious substance, or of substances of a description of such substances;
(b) the use of any method or technique for doing anything else that is capable of being done for the purposes of terrorism, in connection with the commission or preparation of an act of terrorism or Convention offence or in connection with assisting the commission or preparation by another of such an act or offence; and
(c) the design or adaptation for the purposes of terrorism, or in connection with the commission or preparation of an act of terrorism or Convention offence, of any method or technique for doing anything.

(4) It is irrelevant for the purposes of subsections (1) and (2)—

(a) whether any instruction or training that is provided is provided to one or more particular persons or generally;
(b) whether the acts or offences in relation to which a person intends to use skills in which he is instructed or trained consist of one or more particular acts of terrorism or Convention offences, acts of terrorism or Convention offences of a particular description or acts of terrorism or Convention offences generally; and
(c) whether assistance that a person intends to provide to others is intended to be provided to one or more particular persons or to one or more persons whose identities are not yet known.

(5) A person guilty of an offence under this section shall be liable—

(a) on conviction on indictment, to imprisonment for a term not exceeding 10 years or to a fine, or to both;
(b) on summary conviction in England and Wales, to imprisonment for a term not exceeding 12 months or to a fine not exceeding the statutory maximum, or to both;
(c) on summary conviction in Scotland or Northern Ireland, to imprisonment for a term not exceeding 6 months or to a fine not exceeding the statutory maximum, or to both.

(6) In relation to an offence committed before the commencement of section 154(1) of the Criminal Justice Act 2003 (c 44), the reference in subsection (5)(b) to 12 months is to be read as a reference to 6 months.

(7) In this section—

"noxious substance" means—

(a) a dangerous substance within the meaning of Part 7 of the Anti-terrorism, Crime and Security Act 2001 (c 24); or
(b) any other substance which is hazardous or noxious or which may be or become hazardous or noxious only in certain circumstances;

"substance" includes any natural or artificial substance (whatever its origin or method of production and whether in solid or liquid form or in the form of a gas or vapour) and any mixture of substances.

[Terrorism Act 2006, s 6.]

7. Powers of forfeiture in respect of offences under s 6. (1) A court before which a person is convicted of an offence under section 6 may order the forfeiture of anything the court considers to have been in the person's possession for purposes connected with the offence.

(2) Before making an order under subsection (1) in relation to anything the court must give an opportunity of being heard to any person (in addition to the convicted person) who claims to be the owner of that thing or otherwise to have an interest in it.

(3) An order under subsection (1) may not be made so as to come into force at any time before

there is no further possibility (disregarding any power to grant permission for the bringing of an appeal out of time) of the order's being varied or set aside on appeal.

(4) Where a court makes an order under subsection (1), it may also make such other provision as appears to it to be necessary for giving effect to the forfeiture.

(5) That provision may include, in particular, provision relating to the retention, handling, destruction or other disposal of what is forfeited.

(6) Provision made by virtue of this section may be varied at any time by the court that made it.

[Terrorism Act 2006, s 7.]

8. Attendance at a place used for terrorist training. (1) A person commits an offence if—

(a) he attends at any place, whether in the United Kingdom or elsewhere;

(b) while he is at that place, instruction or training of the type mentioned in section 6(1) of this Act or section 54(1) of the Terrorism Act 2000 (c 11) (weapons training) is provided there;

(c) that instruction or training is provided there wholly or partly for purposes connected with the commission or preparation of acts of terrorism or Convention offences; and

(d) the requirements of subsection (2) are satisfied in relation to that person.

(2) The requirements of this subsection are satisfied in relation to a person if—

(a) he knows or believes that instruction or training is being provided there wholly or partly for purposes connected with the commission or preparation of acts of terrorism or Convention offences; or

(b) a person attending at that place throughout the period of that person's attendance could not reasonably have failed to understand that instruction or training was being provided there wholly or partly for such purposes.

(3) It is immaterial for the purposes of this section—

(a) whether the person concerned receives the instruction or training himself; and

(b) whether the instruction or training is provided for purposes connected with one or more particular acts of terrorism or Convention offences, acts of terrorism or Convention offences of a particular description or acts of terrorism or Convention offences generally.

(4) A person guilty of an offence under this section shall be liable—

(a) on conviction on indictment, to imprisonment for a term not exceeding 10 years or to a fine, or to both;

(b) on summary conviction in England and Wales, to imprisonment for a term not exceeding 12 months or to a fine not exceeding the statutory maximum, or to both;

(c) on summary conviction in Scotland or Northern Ireland, to imprisonment for a term not exceeding 6 months or to a fine not exceeding the statutory maximum, or to both.

(5) In relation to an offence committed before the commencement of section 154(1) of the Criminal Justice Act 2003 (c 44), the reference in subsection (4)(b) to 12 months is to be read as a reference to 6 months.

(6) References in this section to instruction or training being provided include references to its being made available.

[Terrorism Act 2006, s 8.]

Offences involving radioactive devices and materials and nuclear facilities and sites

9. Making and possession of devices or materials. (1) A person commits an offence if—

(a) he makes or has in his possession a radioactive device, or

(b) he has in his possession radioactive material,

with the intention of using the device or material in the course of or in connection with the commission or preparation of an act of terrorism or for the purposes of terrorism, or of making it available to be so used.

(2) It is irrelevant for the purposes of subsection (1) whether the act of terrorism to which an intention relates is a particular act of terrorism, an act of terrorism of a particular description or an act of terrorism generally.

(3) A person guilty of an offence under this section shall be liable, on conviction on indictment, to imprisonment for life.

(4) In this section—

"radioactive device" means—

(a) a nuclear weapon or other nuclear explosive device;

(b) a radioactive material dispersal device;

(c) a radiation-emitting device;

"radioactive material" means nuclear material or any other radioactive substance which—

(a) contains nuclides that undergo spontaneous disintegration in a process accompanied by the emission of one or more types of ionising radiation, such as alpha radiation, beta radiation, neutron particles or gamma rays; and

(b) is capable, owing to its radiological or fissile properties, of—

(i) causing serious bodily injury to a person;
(ii) causing serious damage to property;
(iii) endangering a person's life; or
(iv) creating a serious risk to the health or safety of the public.

(5) In subsection (4)—

"device" includes any of the following, whether or not fixed to land, namely, machinery, equipment, appliances, tanks, containers, pipes and conduits;

"nuclear material" has the same meaning as in the Nuclear Material (Offences) Act 1983 (c 18) (see section 6 of that Act).

[Terrorism Act 2006, s 9.]

10. Misuse of devices or material and misuse and damage of facilities. (1) A person commits an offence if he uses—

(a) a radioactive device, or
(b) radioactive material,

in the course of or in connection with the commission of an act of terrorism or for the purposes of terrorism.

(2) A person commits an offence if, in the course of or in connection with the commission of an act of terrorism or for the purposes of terrorism, he uses or damages a nuclear facility in a manner which—

(a) causes a release of radioactive material; or
(b) creates or increases a risk that such material will be released.

(3) A person guilty of an offence under this section shall be liable, on conviction on indictment, to imprisonment for life.

(4) In this section—

"nuclear facility" means—

(a) a nuclear reactor, including a reactor installed in or on any transportation device for use as an energy source in order to propel it or for any other purpose; or
(b) a plant or conveyance being used for the production, storage, processing or transport of radioactive material;

"radioactive device" and "radioactive material" have the same meanings as in section 9.

(5) In subsection (4)—

"nuclear reactor" has the same meaning as in the Nuclear Installations Act 1965 (c 57) (see section 26 of that Act);

"transportation device" means any vehicle or any space object (within the meaning of the Outer Space Act 1986 (c 38)).

[Terrorism Act 2006, s 10.]

11. Terrorist threats relating to devices, materials or facilities. (1) A person commits an offence if, in the course of or in connection with the commission of an act of terrorism or for the purposes of terrorism—

(a) he makes a demand—

(i) for the supply to himself or to another of a radioactive device or of radioactive material;
(ii) for a nuclear facility to be made available to himself or to another; or
(iii) for access to such a facility to be given to himself or to another;

(b) he supports the demand with a threat that he or another will take action if the demand is not met; and
(c) the circumstances and manner of the threat are such that it is reasonable for the person to whom it is made to assume that there is real risk that the threat will be carried out if the demand is not met.

(2) A person also commits an offence if—

(a) he makes a threat falling within subsection (3) in the course of or in connection with the commission of an act of terrorism or for the purposes of terrorism; and
(b) the circumstances and manner of the threat are such that it is reasonable for the person to whom it is made to assume that there is real risk that the threat will be carried out, or would be carried out if demands made in association with the threat are not met.

(3) A threat falls within this subsection if it is—

(a) a threat to use radioactive material;
(b) a threat to use a radioactive device; or

(c) a threat to use or damage a nuclear facility in a manner that releases radioactive material or creates or increases a risk that such material will be released.

(4) A person guilty of an offence under this section shall be liable, on conviction on indictment, to imprisonment for life.

(5) In this section—

"nuclear facility" has the same meaning as in section 10;

"radioactive device" and "radioactive material" have the same meanings as in section 9.

[Terrorism Act 2006, s 11.]

12. Trespassing etc on nuclear sites. (1) The Serious Organised Crime and Police Act 2005 (c 15) is amended as follows.

(2) In sections 128(1), (4) and (7) and 129(1), (4) and (6) (trespassing etc on a designated site in England and Wales or Northern Ireland or in Scotland), for "designated", wherever occurring, substitute "protected".

(3) After section 128(1) (sites in England and Wales and Northern Ireland) insert—

"(1A) In this section 'protected site' means—

(a) a nuclear site; or
(b) a designated site.

(1B) In this section 'nuclear site' means—

(a) so much of any premises in respect of which a nuclear site licence (within the meaning of the Nuclear Installations Act 1965) is for the time being in force as lies within the outer perimeter of the protection provided for those premises; and
(b) so much of any other premises of which premises falling within paragraph (a) form a part as lies within that outer perimeter.

(1C) For this purpose—

(a) the outer perimeter of the protection provided for any premises is the line of the outermost fences, walls or other obstacles provided or relied on for protecting those premises from intruders; and
(b) that line shall be determined on the assumption that every gate, door or other barrier across a way through a fence, wall or other obstacle is closed."

(4) After section 129(1) (sites in Scotland) insert—

"(1A) In this section 'protected Scottish site' means—

(a) a nuclear site in Scotland; or
(b) a designated Scottish site.

(1B) In this section 'nuclear site' means—

(a) so much of any premises in respect of which a nuclear site licence (within the meaning of the Nuclear Installations Act 1965) is for the time being in force as lies within the outer perimeter of the protection provided for those premises; and
(b) so much of any other premises of which premises falling within paragraph (a) form a part as lies within that outer perimeter.

(1C) For this purpose—

(a) the outer perimeter of the protection provided for any premises is the line of the outermost fences, walls or other obstacles provided or relied on for protecting those premises from intruders; and
(b) that line shall be determined on the assumption that every gate, door or other barrier across a way through a fence, wall or other obstacle is closed."

[Terrorism Act 2006, s 12.]

Increases of penalties

13. Maximum penalty for possessing for terrorist purposes. (1) In section 57(4)(a) of the Terrorism Act 2000 (c 11) (10 years maximum imprisonment for possession for terrorist purposes), for "10 years" substitute "15 years".

(2) Subsection (1) does not apply to offences committed before the commencement of this section.

[Terrorism Act 2006, s 13.]

14. Maximum penalty for certain offences relating to nuclear material. (1) In section 2 of the Nuclear Material (Offences) Act 1983 (c 18) (offences involving preparatory acts and threats), for subsection (5) substitute—

"(5) A person guilty of an offence under this section shall be liable, on conviction on indictment, to imprisonment for life."

(2) Subsection (1) does not apply to offences committed before the commencement of this section.
[Terrorism Act 2006, s 14.]

15. Maximum penalty for contravening notice relating to encrypted information. (1) In section 53 of the Regulation of Investigatory Powers Act 2000 (c 23) (offence of contravening disclosure requirement)—

(a) in paragraph (a) of subsection (5), for "two years" substitute "the appropriate maximum term"; and
(b) after that subsection insert the subsections set out in subsection (2).

(2) The inserted subsections are—

"(5A) In subsection (5) 'the appropriate maximum term' means—

(a) in a national security case, five years; and
(b) in any other case, two years.

(5B) In subsection (5A) 'a national security case' means a case in which the grounds specified in the notice to which the offence relates as the grounds for imposing a disclosure requirement were or included a belief that the imposition of the requirement was necessary in the interests of national security."

(3) This section does not apply to offences committed before the commencement of this section.
[Terrorism Act 2006, s 15.]

Incidental provisions about offences

16. Preparatory hearings in terrorism cases. (1) Section 29 of the Criminal Procedure and Investigations Act 1996 (c 25) (power to order preparatory hearing) is amended as follows.

(2) Before subsection (2) insert—

"(1B) An order that a preparatory hearing shall be held must be made by a judge of the Crown Court in every case which (whether or not it falls within subsection (1) or (1A)) is a case in which at least one of the offences charged by the indictment against at least one of the persons charged is a terrorism offence.

(1C) An order that a preparatory hearing shall be held must also be made by a judge of the Crown court in every case which (whether or not it falls within subsection (1) or (1A)) is a case in which—

(a) at least one of the offences charged by the indictment against at least one of the persons charged is an offence carrying a maximum of at least 10 years' imprisonment; and
(b) it appears to the judge that evidence on the indictment reveals that conduct in respect of which that offence is charged had a terrorist connection."

(3) For subsection (3) (no order in serious and complex fraud cases) substitute—

"(3) In a case in which it appears to a judge of the Crown Court that evidence on an indictment reveals a case of fraud of such seriousness or complexity as is mentioned in section 7 of the Criminal Justice Act 1987 (preparatory hearings in cases of serious or complex fraud)—

(a) the judge may make an order for a preparatory hearing under this section only if he is required to do so by subsection (1B) or (1C);
(b) before making an order in pursuance of either of those subsections, he must determine whether to make an order for a preparatory hearing under that section; and
(c) he is not required by either of those subsections to make an order for a preparatory hearing under this section if he determines that an order should be made for a preparatory hearing under that section;

and, in a case in which an order is made for a preparatory hearing under that section, requirements imposed by those subsections apply only if that order ceases to have effect."

(4) In subsection (4) (orders to be capable of being made on application or on the judge's own motion), for the words before paragraph (a) substitute—

"(4) An order that a preparatory hearing shall be held may be made—"

(5) After sub-paragraph (5) insert—

"(6) In this section 'terrorism offence' means—

(a) an offence under section 11 or 12 of the Terrorism Act 2000 (c 11) (offences relating to proscribed organisations);
(b) an offence under any of sections 15 to 18 of that Act (offences relating to terrorist property);
(c) an offence under section 38B of that Act (failure to disclose information about acts of terrorism);
(d) an offence under section 54 of that Act (weapons training);

(e) an offence under any of sections 56 to 59 of that Act (directing terrorism, possessing things and collecting information for the purposes of terrorism and inciting terrorism outside the United Kingdom);
(f) an offence in respect of which there is jurisdiction by virtue of section 62 of that Act (extra-territorial jurisdiction in respect of certain offences committed outside the United Kingdom for the purposes of terrorism etc);
(g) an offence under Part 1 of the Terrorism Act 2006 (miscellaneous terrorist related offences);
(h) conspiring or attempting to commit a terrorism offence;
(i) incitement to commit a terrorism offence.

(7) For the purposes of this section an offence carries a maximum of at least 10 years' imprisonment if—

(a) it is punishable, on conviction on indictment, with imprisonment; and
(b) the maximum term of imprisonment that may be imposed on conviction on indictment of that offence is 10 years or more or is imprisonment for life.

(8) For the purposes of this section conduct has a terrorist connection if it is or takes place in the course of an act of terrorism or is for the purposes of terrorism.

(9) In subsection (8) 'terrorism' has the same meaning as in the Terrorism Act 2000 (see section 1 of that Act)."

[Terrorism Act 2006, s 16.]

17. Commission of offences abroad. (1) If—

(a) a person does anything outside the United Kingdom, and
(b) his action, if done in a part of the United Kingdom, would constitute an offence falling within subsection (2),

he shall be guilty in that part of the United Kingdom of the offence.

(2) The offences falling within this subsection are—

(a) an offence under section 1 or 6 of this Act so far as it is committed in relation to any statement, instruction or training in relation to which that section has effect by reason of its relevance to the commission, preparation or instigation of one or more Convention offences;
(b) an offence under any of sections 8 to 11 of this Act;
(c) an offence under section 11(1) of the Terrorism Act 2000 (c 11) (membership of proscribed organisations);
(d) an offence under section 54 of that Act (weapons training);
(e) conspiracy to commit an offence falling within this subsection;
(f) inciting a person to commit such an offence;
(g) attempting to commit such an offence;
(h) aiding, abetting, counselling or procuring the commission of such an offence.

(3) Subsection (1) applies irrespective of whether the person is a British citizen or, in the case of a company, a company incorporated in a part of the United Kingdom.

(4) In the case of an offence falling within subsection (2) which is committed wholly or partly outside the United Kingdom—

(a) proceedings for the offence may be taken at any place in the United Kingdom; and
(b) the offence may for all incidental purposes be treated as having been committed at any such place.

(5) In section 3(1)(a) and (b) of the Explosive Substances Act 1883 (c 3) (offences committed in preparation for use of explosives with intent to endanger life or property in the United Kingdom or the Republic of Ireland), in each place, for "the Republic of Ireland" substitute "elsewhere".

(6) Subsection (5) does not extend to Scotland except in relation to—

(a) the doing of an act as an act of terrorism or for the purposes of terrorism; or
(b) the possession or control of a substance for the purposes of terrorism.

[Terrorism Act 2006, s 17.]

18. Liability of company directors etc. (1) Where an offence under this Part is committed by a body corporate and is proved to have been committed with the consent or connivance of—

(a) a director, manager, secretary or other similar officer of the body corporate, or
(b) a person who was purporting to act in any such capacity,

he (as well as the body corporate) is guilty of that offence and shall be liable to be proceeded against and punished accordingly.

(2) Where an offence under this Part—

(a) is committed by a Scottish firm, and
(b) is proved to have been committed with the consent or connivance of a partner of the firm,

he (as well as the firm) is guilty of that offence and shall be liable to be proceeded against and punished accordingly.

(3) In this section "director", in relation to a body corporate whose affairs are managed by its members, means a member of the body corporate.

[Terrorism Act 2006, s 18.]

19. Consents to prosecutions. (1) Proceedings for an offence under this Part—

(a) may be instituted in England and Wales only with the consent of the Director of Public Prosecutions; and

(b) may be instituted in Northern Ireland only with the consent of the Director of Public Prosecutions for Northern Ireland.

(2) But if it appears to the Director of Public Prosecutions or the Director of Public Prosecutions for Northern Ireland that an offence under this Part has been committed for a purpose wholly or partly connected with the affairs of a country other than the United Kingdom, his consent for the purposes of this section may be given only with the permission—

(a) in the case of the Director of Public Prosecutions, of the Attorney General; and

(b) in the case of the Director of Public Prosecutions for Northern Ireland, of the Advocate General for Northern Ireland.

(3) In relation to any time before the coming into force of section 27(1) of the Justice (Northern Ireland) Act 2002 (c 26), the reference in subsection (2)(b) to the Advocate General for Northern Ireland is to be read as a reference to the Attorney General for Northern Ireland.

[Terrorism Act 2006, s 19.]

Interpretation of Part 1

20. Interpretation of Part 1. (1) Expressions used in this Part and in the Terrorism Act 2000 (c 11) have the same meanings in this Part as in that Act.

(2) In this Part—

"act of terrorism" includes anything constituting an action taken for the purposes of terrorism, within the meaning of the Terrorism Act 2000 (see section 1(5) of that Act);

"article" includes anything for storing data;

"Convention offence" means an offence listed in Schedule 1 or an equivalent offence under the law of a country or territory outside the United Kingdom;

"glorification" includes any form of praise or celebration, and cognate expressions are to be construed accordingly;

"public" is to be construed in accordance with subsection (3);

"publish" and cognate expressions are to be construed in accordance with subsection (4);

"record" means a record so far as not comprised in an article, including a temporary record created electronically and existing solely in the course of, and for the purposes of, the transmission of the whole or a part of its contents;

"statement" is to be construed in accordance with subsection (6).

(3) In this Part references to the public—

(a) are references to the public of any part of the United Kingdom or of a country or territory outside the United Kingdom, or any section of the public; and

(b) except in section 9(4), also include references to a meeting or other group of persons which is open to the public (whether unconditionally or on the making of a payment or the satisfaction of other conditions).

(4) In this Part references to a person's publishing a statement are references to—

(a) his publishing it in any manner to the public;

(b) his providing electronically any service by means of which the public have access to the statement; or

(c) his using a service provided to him electronically by another so as to enable or to facilitate access by the public to the statement;

but this subsection does not apply to the references to a publication in section 2.

(5) In this Part references to providing a service include references to making a facility available; and references to a service provided to a person are to be construed accordingly.

(6) In this Part references to a statement are references to a communication of any description, including a communication without words consisting of sounds or images or both.

(7) In this Part references to conduct that should be emulated in existing circumstances include references to conduct that is illustrative of a type of conduct that should be so emulated.

(8) In this Part references to what is contained in an article or record include references—

(a) to anything that is embodied or stored in or on it; and

(b) to anything that may be reproduced from it using apparatus designed or adapted for the purpose.

(9) The Secretary of State may by order made by statutory instrument—

(a) modify Schedule 1 so as to add an offence to the offences listed in that Schedule;
(b) modify that Schedule so as to remove an offence from the offences so listed;
(c) make supplemental, incidental, consequential or transitional provision in connection with the addition or removal of an offence.

(10) An order under subsection (9) may add an offence in or as regards Scotland to the offences listed in Schedule 1 to the extent only that a provision creating the offence would be outside the legislative competence of the Scottish Parliament.

(11) The Secretary of State must not make an order containing (with or without other provision) any provision authorised by subsection (9) unless a draft of the order has been laid before Parliament and approved by a resolution of each House.
[Terrorism Act 2006, s 20.]

PART 2
MISCELLANEOUS PROVISIONS
Proscription of terrorist organisations

21. Grounds of proscription. In section 3 of the Terrorism Act 2000 (c 11) (proscription of organisations), after subsection (5) insert—

"(5A) The cases in which an organisation promotes or encourages terrorism for the purposes of subsection (5)(c) include any case in which activities of the organisation—

(a) include the unlawful glorification of the commission or preparation (whether in the past, in the future or generally) of acts of terrorism; or
(b) are carried out in a manner that ensures that the organisation is associated with statements containing any such glorification.

(5B) The glorification of any conduct is unlawful for the purposes of subsection (5A) if there are persons who may become aware of it who could reasonably be expected to infer that what is being glorified, is being glorified as—

(a) conduct that should be emulated in existing circumstances, or
(b) conduct that is illustrative of a type of conduct that should be so emulated.

(5C) In this section—

'glorification' includes any form of praise or celebration, and cognate expressions are to be construed accordingly;

'statement' includes a communication without words consisting of sounds or images or both."
[Terrorism Act 2006, s 21.]

22. Name changes by proscribed organisations. (1) The Terrorism Act 2000 is amended as follows.

(2) In section 3 (proscription of organisations), at the end insert—

"(6) Where the Secretary of State believes—

(a) that an organisation listed in Schedule 2 is operating wholly or partly under a name that is not specified in that Schedule (whether as well as or instead of under the specified name), or
(b) that an organisation that is operating under a name that is not so specified is otherwise for all practical purposes the same as an organisation so listed,

he may, by order, provide that the name that is not specified in that Schedule is to be treated as another name for the listed organisation.

(7) Where an order under subsection (6) provides for a name to be treated as another name for an organisation, this Act shall have effect in relation to acts occurring while—

(a) the order is in force, and
(b) the organisation continues to be listed in Schedule 2,

as if the organisation were listed in that Schedule under the other name, as well as under the name specified in the Schedule.

(8) The Secretary of State may at any time by order revoke an order under subsection (6) or otherwise provide for a name specified in such an order to cease to be treated as a name for a particular organisation.

(9) Nothing in subsections (6) to (8) prevents any liability from being established in any proceedings by proof that an organisation is the same as an organisation listed in Schedule 2, even though it is or was operating under a name specified neither in Schedule 2 nor in an order under subsection (6)."

(3) For subsection (1) of section 4 (applications for deproscription) substitute—

"(1) An application may be made to the Secretary of State for an order under section 3(3) or (8)—

(a) removing an organisation from Schedule 2, or
(b) providing for a name to cease to be treated as a name for an organisation listed in that Schedule."

(4) In subsection (2)(b) of that section (applications may be made by persons affected by the organisation's proscription), after "proscription" insert "or by the treatment of the name as a name for the organisation."

(5) In section 5 (appeals against refusals to deproscribe)—

(a) in subsection (3), after "an organisation" insert "or to provide for a name to cease to be treated as a name for an organisation";
(b) in subsection (4), omit "by or in respect of an organisation";
(c) in subsection (5), after "subsection (4)" insert "in respect of an appeal against a refusal to deproscribe an organisation,".

(6) After subsection (5) of that section insert—

"(5A) Where an order is made under subsection (4) in respect of an appeal against a refusal to provide for a name to cease to be treated as a name for an organisation, the Secretary of State shall, as soon as is reasonably practicable, make an order under section 3(8) providing that the name in question is to cease to be so treated in relation to that organisation."

(7) In section 7 (effect on conviction etc of successful appeal), after subsection (1) insert—

"(1A) This section also applies where—

(a) an appeal under section 5 has been allowed in respect of a name treated as the name for an organisation,
(b) an order has been made under section 3(8) in respect of the name in accordance with an order of the Commission under section 5(4),
(c) a person has been convicted of an offence in respect of the organisation under any of sections 11 to 13, 15 to 19 and 56, and
(d) the activity to which the charge referred took place on or after the date of the refusal, against which the appeal under section 5 was brought, to provide for a name to cease to be treated as a name for the organisation."

(8) In that section—

(a) in subsection (2), after "(1)(c)" insert "or (1A)(c)";
(b) in subsection (4)(a), after "(1)(b)" insert "or (1A)(b)";
(c) in subsection (5), after "(1)(c)" insert "or (1A)(c)";
(d) in subsection (7)(a), after "(1)(b)" insert "or (1A)(b)".

(9) In section 9 (proceedings under the Human Rights Act 1998)—

(a) in subsection (2)(a), for "and (5)" substitute ", (5) and (5A)";
(b) in subsection (4), at the end insert

", and
(c) a reference to a refusal to provide for a name to cease to be treated as a name for an organisation shall be taken as a reference to the action of the Secretary of State which is found to be incompatible with a Convention right".

(10) In section 123(2) (orders and regulations subject to negative resolution procedure), before paragraph (a) insert—

"(za) section 3(6) or (8);".

(11) In paragraph 5(4) of Schedule 3 (the Proscribed Organisations Appeal Commission), after sub-paragraph (a) insert—

"(aa) provide for full particulars of the reasons for—

(i) the making of an order under section 3(6), or
(ii) a refusal to provide for a name to cease to be treated as a name for an organisation,

to be withheld from the organisation or applicant concerned and from any person representing it or him;".

[Terrorism Act 2006, s 22.]

Detention of terrorist suspects

23. Extension of period of detention of terrorist suspects. (1) Schedule 8 to the Terrorism Act 2000 (c 11) (detention of terrorist suspects) is amended as follows.

(2) In sub-paragraph (1) of each of paragraphs 29 and 36 (applications by a superintendent or

above for a warrant extending detention or for the extension of the period of such a warrant), for the words from the beginning to "may" substitute—

"(1) Each of the following—

(a) in England and Wales, a Crown Prosecutor,
(b) in Scotland, the Lord Advocate or a procurator fiscal,
(c) in Northern Ireland, the Director of Public Prosecutions for Northern Ireland,
(d) in any part of the United Kingdom, a police officer of at least the rank of superintendent,

may"

(3) In sub-paragraph (3) of paragraph 29 (period of extension to end no later than 7 days after arrest)—

(a) for "Subject to paragraph 36(3A)" substitute "Subject to sub-paragraph (3A) and paragraph 36"; and
(b) for "end not later than the end of" substitute "be".

(4) After that sub-paragraph insert—

"(3A) A judicial authority may issue a warrant of further detention in relation to a person which specifies a shorter period as the period for which that person's further detention is authorised if—

(a) the application for the warrant is an application for a warrant specifying a shorter period; or
(b) the judicial authority is satisfied that there are circumstances that would make it inappropriate for the specified period to be as long as the period of seven days mentioned in sub-paragraph (3)."

(5) In paragraph 34(1) (persons who can apply for information to be withheld from person to whom application for a warrant relates) for "officer" substitute "person".

(6) In paragraph 36 (applications for extension or further extension), omit the words "to a judicial authority" in sub-paragraph (1), and after that sub-paragraph insert—

"(1A) The person to whom an application under sub-paragraph (1) may be made is—

(a) in the case of an application falling within sub-paragraph (1B), a judicial authority; and
(b) in any other case, a senior judge.

(1B) An application for the extension or further extension of a period falls within this sub-paragraph if—

(a) the grant of the application otherwise than in accordance with sub-paragraph (3AA)(b) would extend that period to a time that is no more than fourteen days after the relevant time; and
(b) no application has previously been made to a senior judge in respect of that period."

(7) For sub-paragraphs (3) and (3A) of that paragraph (period for which warrants may be extended) substitute—

"(3) Subject to sub-paragraph (3AA), the period by which the specified period is extended or further extended shall be the period which—

(a) begins with the time specified in sub-paragraph (3A); and
(b) ends with whichever is the earlier of—
   (i) the end of the period of seven days beginning with that time; and
   (ii) the end of the period of 28 days beginning with the relevant time.

(3A) The time referred to in sub-paragraph (3)(a) is—

(a) in the case of a warrant specifying a period which has not previously been extended under this paragraph, the end of the period specified in the warrant, and
(b) in any other case, the end of the period for which the period specified in the warrant was last extended under this paragraph.

(3AA) A judicial authority or senior judge may extend or further extend the period specified in a warrant by a shorter period than is required by sub-paragraph (3) if—

(a) the application for the extension is an application for an extension by a period that is shorter than is so required; or
(b) the judicial authority or senior judge is satisfied that there are circumstances that would make it inappropriate for the period of the extension to be as long as the period so required."

(8) In sub-paragraph (4) of that paragraph (application of paragraphs 30(3), and 31 to 34), at the end insert

"but, in relation to an application made by virtue of sub-paragraph (1A)(b) to a senior judge, as if—

(a) references to a judicial authority were references to a senior judge; and

(b) references to the judicial authority in question were references to the senior judge in question."

(9) In sub-paragraph (5) of that paragraph, after "authority" insert "or senior judge".

(10) After sub-paragraph (6) of that paragraph insert—

"(7) In this paragraph and paragraph 37 'senior judge' means a judge of the High Court or of the High Court of Justiciary."

(11) For paragraph 37 (release of detained person) substitute—

"**37.** (1) This paragraph applies where—

(a) a person ('the detained person') is detained by virtue of a warrant issued under this Part of this Schedule; and

(b) his detention is not authorised by virtue of section 41(5) or (6) or otherwise apart from the warrant.

(2) If it at any time appears to the police officer or other person in charge of the detained person's case that any of the matters mentioned in paragraph 32(1)(a) and (b) on which the judicial authority or senior judge last authorised his further detention no longer apply, he must—

(a) if he has custody of the detained person, release him immediately; and

(b) if he does not, immediately inform the person who does have custody of the detained person that those matters no longer apply in the detained person's case.

(3) A person with custody of the detained person who is informed in accordance with this paragraph that those matters no longer apply in his case must release that person immediately."

(12) This section does not apply in a case in which—

(a) the arrest of the person detained under section 41 of the Terrorism Act 2000 (c 11) took place before the commencement of this section; or

(b) his examination under Schedule 7 to that Act began before the commencement of this section.

[Terrorism Act 2006, s 23.]

24. Grounds for extending detention. (1) In Schedule 8 to the Terrorism Act 2000, in paragraph 23(1) (grounds on which a review officer may authorise continued detention), after paragraph (b) insert—

"(ba) pending the result of an examination or analysis of any relevant evidence or of anything the examination or analysis of which is to be or is being carried out with a view to obtaining relevant evidence;".

(2) In sub-paragraph (1) of paragraph 32 of that Schedule (grounds on which a judicial authority may authorise further detention), for the words from "to obtain" to "preserve relevant evidence" substitute "as mentioned in sub-paragraph (1A)".

(3) After that sub-paragraph insert—

"(1A) The further detention of a person is necessary as mentioned in this sub-paragraph if it is necessary—

(a) to obtain relevant evidence whether by questioning him or otherwise;

(b) to preserve relevant evidence; or

(c) pending the result of an examination or analysis of any relevant evidence or of anything the examination or analysis of which is to be or is being carried out with a view to obtaining relevant evidence."

(4) In paragraph 23(4) (meaning of "relevant evidence"), for "sub-paragraph (1)(a) and (b)" substitute "this paragraph".

(5) In paragraph 32(2) (meaning of "relevant evidence"), for "sub-paragraph (1)" substitute "this paragraph".

(6) This section does not apply in a case in which—

(a) the arrest of the person detained under section 41 of the Terrorism Act 2000 took place before the commencement of this section; or

(b) his examination under Schedule 7 to that Act began before the commencement of this section.

[Terrorism Act 2006, s 24.]

25. Expiry or renewal of extended maximum detention period. (1) This section applies to any time which—

(a) is more than one year after the commencement of section 23; and

(b) does not fall within a period in relation to which this section is disapplied by an order under subsection (2).

(2) The Secretary of State may by order made by statutory instrument disapply this section in relation to any period of not more than one year beginning with the coming into force of the order.

(3) Schedule 8 to the Terrorism Act 2000 (c 11) has effect in relation to any further extension under paragraph 36 of that Schedule for a period beginning at a time to which this section applies—

(a) as if in sub-paragraph (3)(b) of that paragraph, for "28 days" there were substituted "14 days"; and

(b) as if that paragraph and paragraph 37 of that Schedule had effect with the further consequential modifications set out in subsection (4).

(4) The further consequential modifications are—

(a) the substitution of the words "a judicial authority" for paragraphs (a) and (b) of sub-paragraph (1A) of paragraph 36;

(b) the omission of sub-paragraphs (1B) and (7) of that paragraph;

(c) the omission of the words "or senior judge" wherever occurring in sub-paragraphs (3AA) and (5) of that paragraph and in paragraph 37(2); and

(d) the omission of the words from "but" onwards in paragraph 36(4).

(5) Where at a time to which this section applies—

(a) a person is being detained by virtue of a further extension under paragraph 36 of Schedule 8 to the Terrorism Act 2000,

(b) his further detention was authorised (at a time to which this section did not apply) for a period ending more than 14 days after the relevant time, and

(c) that 14 days has expired,

the person with custody of that individual must release him immediately.

(6) The Secretary of State must not make an order containing (with or without other provision) any provision disapplying this section in relation to any period unless a draft of the order has been laid before Parliament and approved by a resolution of each House.

(7) In this section "the relevant time" has the same meaning as in paragraph 36 of Schedule 8 to the Terrorism Act 2000.

[Terrorism Act 2006, s 25.]

Searches etc

26. All premises warrants: England and Wales and Northern Ireland. (1) Part 1 of Schedule 5 to the Terrorism Act 2000 (searches etc for the purposes of terrorist investigations in England and Wales and Northern Ireland) is amended as follows.

(2) In paragraph 1 (search warrants authorising entry to specified premises), in sub-paragraph (2)(a), for "the premises specified in the warrant" substitute "premises mentioned in sub-paragraph (2A)".

(3) After sub-paragraph (2) of that paragraph insert—

"(2A) The premises referred to in sub-paragraph (2)(a) are—

(a) one or more sets of premises specified in the application (in which case the application is for a 'specific premises warrant'); or

(b) any premises occupied or controlled by a person specified in the application, including such sets of premises as are so specified (in which case the application is for an 'all premises warrant')."

(4) In sub-paragraph (5) of that paragraph—

(a) in paragraph (b), for "premises specified in the application" substitute "premises to which the application relates";

(b) in paragraph (c), at the end insert ", and"; and

(c) after that paragraph insert—

"(d) in the case of an application for an all premises warrant, that it is not reasonably practicable to specify in the application all the premises which the person so specified occupies or controls and which might need to be searched."

(5) In paragraph 2 (warrants as to which special conditions are satisfied), in sub-paragraph (1), after "an application" insert "for a specific premises warrant".

(6) After that paragraph insert—

"**2A.** (1) This paragraph applies where an application for an all premises warrant is made under paragraph 1 and—

(a) the application is made by a police officer of at least the rank of superintendent, and

(b) the justice to whom the application is made is not satisfied of the matter referred to in paragraph 1(5)(c).

(2) The justice may grant the application if satisfied of the matters referred to in paragraph 1(5)(a), (b) and (d).

(3) Where a warrant under paragraph 1 is issued by virtue of this paragraph, the powers under paragraph 1(2)(a) and (b) are exercisable only—

(a) in respect of premises which are not residential premises, and

(b) within the period of 24 hours beginning with the time when the warrant is issued.

(4) For the purpose of sub-paragraph (3) 'residential premises', in relation to a power under paragraph 1(2)(a) or (b), means any premises which the constable exercising the power has reasonable grounds for believing are used wholly or mainly as a dwelling."

(7) In paragraph 11 (applications for search warrants involving excluded or special procedure material), in sub-paragraph (2)(a), for "the premises specified in the warrant" substitute "premises mentioned in sub-paragraph (3A)".

(8) After sub-paragraph (3) of that paragraph insert—

"(3A) The premises referred to in sub-paragraph (2)(a) are—

(a) one or more sets of premises specified in the application (in which case the application is for a 'specific premises warrant'); or

(b) any premises occupied or controlled by a person specified in the application, including such sets of premises as are so specified (in which case the application is for an 'all premises warrant')."

(9) In paragraph 12 (grant of applications where excluded or special procedure material is involved), in each of sub-paragraphs (1) and (2), after "an application" insert "for a specific premises warrant".

(10) After sub-paragraph (2) of that paragraph insert—

"(2A) A Circuit judge or a District Judge (Magistrates' Courts) may grant an application for an all premises warrant under paragraph 11 if satisfied—

(a) that an order made under paragraph 5 has not been complied with, and

(b) that the person specified in the application is also specified in the order.

(2B) A Circuit judge or a District Judge (Magistrates' Courts) may also grant an application for an all premises warrant under paragraph 11 if satisfied that there are reasonable grounds for believing—

(a) that there is material on premises to which the application relates which consists of or includes excluded material or special procedure material but does not include items subject to legal privilege, and

(b) that the conditions in sub-paragraphs (3) and (4) are met."

(11) In sub-paragraph (4)(b) of that paragraph, for "the premises on which the material is situated" substitute "premises to which the application for the warrant relates".

[Terrorism Act 2006, s 26.]

27. All premises warrants: Scotland. *Scotland.*

28. Search, seizure and forfeiture of terrorist publications. (1) If a justice of the peace is satisfied that there are reasonable grounds for suspecting that articles to which this section applies are likely to be found on any premises, he may issue a warrant authorising a constable—

(a) to enter and search the premises; and

(b) to seize anything found there which the constable has reason to believe is such an article.

(2) This section applies to an article if—

(a) it is likely to be the subject of conduct falling within subsection (2)(a) to (e) of section 2; and

(b) it would fall for the purposes of that section to be treated, in the context of the conduct to which it is likely to be subject, as a terrorist publication.

(3) A person exercising a power conferred by a warrant under this section may use such force as is reasonable in the circumstances for exercising that power.

(4) An article seized under the authority of a warrant issued under this section—

(a) may be removed by a constable to such place as he thinks fit; and

(b) must be retained there in the custody of a constable until returned or otherwise disposed of in accordance with this Act.

(5) An article to which this section applies which is seized under the authority of a warrant issued under this section on an information laid by or on behalf of the Director of Public Prosecutions or the Director of Public Prosecutions for Northern Ireland—

(a) shall be liable to forfeiture; and

(b) if forfeited, may be destroyed or otherwise disposed of by a constable in whatever manner he thinks fit.

(6) In Schedule 1 to the Criminal Justice and Police Act 2001 (c 16) (powers which relate to the seizure of property in bulk)—

(a) in Part 1, at the end insert—

"73H. The power of seizure conferred by section 28 of the Terrorism Act 2006."

(b) in Part 3, at the end insert—

"**113.** The power of seizure conferred by section 28 of the Terrorism Act 2006."

(7) Nothing in—

(a) the Police (Property) Act 1897 (c 30) (property seized in the investigation of an offence), or

(b) section 31 of the Police (Northern Ireland) Act 1998 (c 32) (which makes similar provision in Northern Ireland),

applies to an article seized under the authority of a warrant under this section.

(8) Schedule 2 (which makes provision about the forfeiture of articles to which this section applies) has effect.

(9) In this section—

"article" has the same meaning as in Part 1 of this Act;

"forfeited" means treated or condemned as forfeited under Schedule 2, and "forfeiture" is to be construed accordingly;

"premises" has the same meaning as in the Police and Criminal Evidence Act 1984 (c 60) (see section 23 of that Act).

(10) In the application of this section to Scotland—

(a) in subsection (1), for the words from the beginning to "satisfied" substitute "If a sheriff, on the application of a procurator fiscal, is satisfied";

(b) in subsection (5) omit "on an information laid by or on behalf of the Director of Public Prosecutions or the Director of Public Prosecutions for Northern Ireland";

(c) in subsection (9), for the definition of "'premises" substitute—

"'premises' has the same meaning as in the Terrorism Act 2000 (c 11) (see section 121 of that Act)."

[Terrorism Act 2006, s 28.]

29. Power to search vehicles under Schedule 7 to the Terrorism Act 2000. In paragraph 8 of Schedule 7 to the Terrorism Act 2000 (c 11) (search of a person at a port or in the border area to ascertain if he is involved in terrorism), after sub-paragraph (1)(d) insert—

"(e) search a vehicle which is on a ship or aircraft;

(f) search a vehicle which the examining officer reasonably believes has been, or is about to be, on a ship or aircraft."

[Terrorism Act 2006, s 29.]

30. Extension to internal waters of authorisations to stop and search. (1) The Terrorism Act 2000 is amended as follows.

(2) In section 44 (authorisations for stop and search), after subsection (4) insert—

"(4ZA) The power of a person mentioned in subsection (4) to give an authorisation specifying an area or place so mentioned includes power to give such an authorisation specifying such an area or place together with—

(a) the internal waters adjacent to that area or place; or

(b) such area of those internal waters as is specified in the authorisation."

(3) After subsection (5) of that section insert—

"(5A) In this section—

'driver', in relation to an aircraft, hovercraft or vessel, means the captain, pilot or other person with control of the aircraft, hovercraft or vessel or any member of its crew and, in relation to a train, includes any member of its crew;

'internal waters' means waters in the United Kingdom that are not comprised in any police area."

(4) In section 45 (exercise of powers), after subsection (6) insert—

"(7) In this section 'driver' has the same meaning as in section 44."

[Terrorism Act 2006, s 30.]

Other investigatory powers

31. Amendment of the Intelligence Services Act 1994

32. Interception warrants. (1) The Regulation of Investigatory Powers Act 2000 (c 23) is amended as follows.

(2) In section 9(6) (period for which interception warrants can be issued or renewed), after paragraph (a) insert—

"(ab) in relation to an unrenewed warrant which is endorsed under the hand of the Secretary of State with a statement that the issue of the warrant is believed to be necessary on grounds falling within section 5(3)(a) or (c), means the period of six months beginning with the day of the warrant's issue;".

(3) For subsection (6) of section 10 (prohibition on modification of scheduled parts of warrant by the person to whom the warrant is addressed or his subordinates) substitute—

"(6) Subsection (4) authorises the modification of the scheduled parts of an interception warrant under the hand of a senior official who is either—

(a) the person to whom the warrant is addressed, or
(b) a person holding a position subordinate to that person,

only if the applicable condition specified in subsection (6A) is satisfied and a statement that the condition is satisfied is endorsed on the modifying instrument.

(6A) The applicable condition is—

(a) in the case of an unrenewed warrant, that the warrant is endorsed with a statement that the issue of the warrant is believed to be necessary in the interests of national security; and
(b) in the case of a renewed warrant, that the instrument by which it was last renewed is endorsed with a statement that the renewal is believed to be necessary in the interests of national security."

(4) In subsection (9)(b) (modifications made otherwise than by Secretary of State ceasing to have effect after five days), after "(5A)(b)" insert ", (6)".

(5) In section 16 (extra safeguards in the case of certificated warrants)—

(a) in subsection (3)(b) (exception for communications sent during a specified three month period), for "a period of not more than three months specified in the certificate" substitute "a period specified in the certificate that is no longer than the permitted maximum"; and
(b) in subsection (5)(c) (exception for material selected before the end of the first working day after a relevant change of circumstances), for the words from "the first working day" onwards substitute "the permitted period".

(6) After subsection (3) of that section insert—

"(3A) In subsection (3)(b) 'the permitted maximum' means—

(a) in the case of material the examination of which is certified for the purposes of section 8(4) as necessary in the interests of national security, six months; and
(b) in any other case, three months."

(7) After subsection (5) of that section insert—

"(5A) In subsection (5)(c) 'the permitted period' means—

(a) in the case of material the examination of which is certified for the purposes of section 8(4) as necessary in the interests of national security, the period ending with the end of the fifth working day after it first appeared as mentioned in subsection (5)(a) to the person to whom the warrant is addressed; and
(b) in any other case, the period ending with the end of the first working day after it first so appeared to that person."

[Terrorism Act 2006, s 32.]

Definition of terrorism etc

34. Amendment of the definition of "terrorism" etc. In each of—

(a) section 1(1)(b) of the Terrorism Act 2000 (c 11) (under which actions and threats designed to influence a government may be terrorism), and
(b) section 113(1)(c) of the Anti-terrorism, Crime and Security Act 2001 (c 24) (offence of using noxious substances or things to influence a government or to intimidate),

after "government" insert "or an international governmental organisation".

[Terrorism Act 2006, s 34.]

Other amendments

35. Applications for extended detention of seized cash. (1) In paragraph 3 of Schedule 1 to the Anti-terrorism, Crime and Security Act 2001 (application relating to period of detention of seized terrorist cash), after sub-paragraph (3) insert—

"(3A) An application to a justice of the peace or the sheriff for an order under sub-paragraph (2) making the first extension of the period—

(a) may be made and heard without notice of the application or hearing having been given to any of the persons affected by the application or to the legal representative of such a person, and
(b) may be heard and determined in private in the absence of persons so affected and of their legal representatives."

(2) This section applies to applications made after the commencement of this section.
[Terrorism Act 2006, s 35.]

PART 3
SUPPLEMENTAL PROVISIONS

36. Review of terrorism legislation

37. Consequential amendments and repeals

38. Expenses

39. Short title, commencement and extent. (1) This Act may be cited as the Terrorism Act 2006.

(2) This Act (apart from this section) shall come into force on such day as the Secretary of State may by order made by statutory instrument appoint.

(3) An order made under subsection (2) may make different provision for different purposes.

(4) Subject to section 17(6), an amendment or repeal by this Act of another enactment has the same extent as the enactment amended or repealed.

(5) Subject to section 17(6) and to subsection (4) of this section, this Act extends to the whole of the United Kingdom.

(6) Her Majesty may by Order in Council direct that any provisions of this Act shall extend, with such modifications as appear to Her Majesty to be appropriate, to any of the Channel Islands or the Isle of Man.

(7) In subsection (6) "modification" includes omissions, additions and alterations.
[Terrorism Act 2006, s 39.]

Section 20

SCHEDULE 1
CONVENTION OFFENCES

Explosives offences

1. (1) Subject to sub-paragraph (3), an offence under any of sections 28 to 30 of the Offences against the Person Act 1861 (c 100) (causing injury by explosions, causing explosions and handling or placing explosives).

(2) Subject to sub-paragraph (3), an offence under any of the following provisions of the Explosive Substances Act 1883 (c 3)—

(a) section 2 (causing an explosion likely to endanger life);
(b) section 3 (preparation of explosions);
(c) section 5 (ancillary offences).

(3) An offence in or as regards Scotland is a Convention offence by virtue of this paragraph only if it consists in—

(a) the doing of an act as an act of terrorism; or
(b) an action for the purposes of terrorism.

Biological weapons

2. An offence under section 1 of the Biological Weapons Act 1974 (c 6) (development etc of biological weapons).

Offences against internationally protected persons

3. (1) Subject to sub-paragraph (4), an offence mentioned in section 1(1)(a) of the Internationally Protected Persons Act 1978 (c 17) (attacks against protected persons committed outside the United Kingdom) which is committed (whether in the United Kingdom or elsewhere) in relation to a protected person.

(2) Subject to sub-paragraph (4), an offence mentioned in section 1(1)(b) of that Act (attacks on relevant premises etc) which is committed (whether in the United Kingdom or elsewhere) in connection with an attack—

(a) on relevant premises or on a vehicle ordinarily used by a protected person, and
(b) at a time when a protected person is in or on the premises or vehicle.

(3) Subject to sub-paragraph (4), an offence under section 1(3) of that Act (threats etc in relation to protected persons).

(4) An offence in or as regards Scotland is a Convention offence by virtue of this paragraph only if it consists in—

(a) the doing of an act as an act of terrorism; or
(b) an action for the purposes of terrorism.

(5) Expressions used in this paragraph and section 1 of that Act have the same meanings in this paragraph as in that section.

Hostage-taking

4. An offence under section 1 of the Taking of Hostages Act 1982 (c 28) (hostage-taking).

Hijacking and other offences against aircraft

5. Offences under any of the following provisions of the Aviation Security Act 1982 (c 36)—

(a) section 1 (hijacking);
(b) section 2 (destroying, damaging or endangering safety of aircraft);
(c) section 3 (other acts endangering or likely to endanger safety of aircraft);
(d) section 6(2) (ancillary offences).

Offences involving nuclear material

6. (1) An offence mentioned in section 1(1) of the Nuclear Material (Offences) Act 1983 (c 18) (offences in relation to nuclear material committed outside the United Kingdom) which is committed (whether in the United Kingdom or elsewhere) in relation to or by means of nuclear material.

(2) An offence under section 2 of that Act (offence involving preparatory acts and threats in relation to nuclear material).

(3) In this paragraph "nuclear material" has the same meaning as in that Act.

Offences under the Aviation and Maritime Security Act 1990 (c 31)

7. Offences under any of the following provisions of the Aviation and Maritime Security Act 1990—

(a) section 1 (endangering safety at aerodromes);
(b) section 9 (hijacking of ships);
(c) section 10 (seizing or exercising control of fixed platforms);
(d) section 11 (destroying ships or fixed platforms or endangering their safety);
(e) section 12 (other acts endangering or likely to endanger safe navigation);
(f) section 13 (offences involving threats relating to ships or fixed platforms);
(g) section 14 (ancillary offences).

Offences involving chemical weapons

8. An offence under section 2 of the Chemical Weapons Act 1996 (c 6) (use, development etc of chemical weapons).

Terrorist funds

9. An offence under any of the following provisions of the Terrorism Act 2000 (c 11)—

(a) section 15 (terrorist fund-raising);
(b) section 16 (use or possession of terrorist funds);
(c) section 17 (funding arrangements for terrorism);
(d) section 18 (money laundering of terrorist funds).

Directing terrorist organisations

10. An offence under section 56 of the Terrorism Act 2000 (directing a terrorist organisation).

Offences involving nuclear weapons

11. An offence under section 47 of the Anti-terrorism, Crime and Security Act 2001 (c 24) (use, development etc of nuclear weapons).

Conspiracy etc

12. Any of the following offences—

(a) conspiracy to commit a Convention offence;
(b) inciting the commission of a Convention offence;
(c) attempting to commit a Convention offence;
(d) aiding, abetting, counselling or procuring the commission of a Convention offence.

Section 28

SCHEDULE 2

SEIZURE AND FORFEITURE OF TERRORIST PUBLICATIONS

Application of Schedule

1. This Schedule applies where an article—

(a) has been seized under the authority of a warrant under section 28; and
(b) is being retained in the custody of a constable ("the relevant constable").

Notice of seizure

2. (1) The relevant constable must give notice of the article's seizure to—

(a) every person whom he believes to have been the owner of the article, or one of its owners, at the time of the seizure; and
(b) if there is no such person or it is not reasonably practicable to give him notice, every person whom the relevant constable believes to have been an occupier at that time of the premises where the article was seized.

(2) The notice must set out what has been seized and the grounds for the seizure.

(3) The notice may be given to a person only by—

(a) delivering it to him personally;
(b) addressing it to him and leaving it for him at the appropriate address; or
(c) addressing it to him and sending it to him at that address by post.

(4) But where it is not practicable to give a notice in accordance with sub-paragraph (3), a notice given by virtue of sub-paragraph (1)(b) to the occupier of the premises where the article was seized may be given by—

(a) addressing it to "the occupier" of those premises, without naming him; and
(b) leaving it for him at those premises or sending it to him at those premises by post.

(5) An article may be treated or condemned as forfeited under this Schedule only if—

(a) the requirements of this paragraph have been complied with in the case of that article; or
(b) it was not reasonably practicable for them to be complied with.

(6) In this paragraph "the appropriate address", in relation to a person, means—

(a) in the case of a body corporate, its registered or principal office in the United Kingdom;
(b) in the case of a firm, the principal office of the partnership;
(c) in the case of an unincorporated body or association, the principal office of the body or association; and
(d) in any other case, his usual or last known place of residence in the United Kingdom or his last known place of business in the United Kingdom.

(7) In the case of—

(a) a company registered outside the United Kingdom,
(b) a firm carrying on business outside the United Kingdom, or
(c) an unincorporated body or association with offices outside the United Kingdom,

the references in this paragraph to its principal office include references to its principal office within the United Kingdom (if any).

Notice of claim

3. (1) A person claiming that the seized article is not liable to forfeiture may give notice of his claim to a constable at any police station in the police area in which the premises where the seizure took place are located.

(2) Oral notice is not sufficient for these purposes.

4. (1) A notice of claim may not be given more than one month after—

(a) the day of the giving of the notice of seizure; or
(b) if no such notice has been given, the day of the seizure.

(2) A notice of claim must specify—

(a) the name and address of the claimant; and
(b) in the case of a claimant who is outside the United Kingdom, the name and address of a solicitor in the United Kingdom who is authorised to accept service, and to act, on behalf of the claimant.

(3) Service upon a solicitor so specified is to be taken to be service on the claimant for the purposes of any proceedings by virtue of this Schedule.

(4) In a case in which notice of the seizure was given to different persons on different days, the reference in this paragraph to the day on which that notice was given is a reference—

(a) in relation to a person to whom notice of the seizure was given, to the day on which that notice was given to that person; and
(b) in relation to any other person, to the day on which notice of the seizure was given to the last person to be given such a notice.

Automatic forfeiture in a case where no claim is made

5. The article is to be treated as forfeited if, by the end of the period for the giving of a notice of claim in respect of it—

(a) no such notice has been given; or
(b) the requirements of paragraphs 3 and 4 have not been complied with in relation to the only notice or notices of claim that have been given.

Forfeiture by the court in other cases

6. (1) Where a notice of claim in respect of an article is duly given in accordance with paragraphs 3 and 4, the relevant constable must decide whether to take proceedings to ask the court to condemn the article as forfeited.

(2) The decision whether to take such proceedings must be made as soon as reasonably practicable after the giving of the notice of claim.

(3) If the relevant constable takes such proceedings and the court—

(a) finds that the article was liable to forfeiture at the time of its seizure, and
(b) is not satisfied that its forfeiture would be inappropriate,

the court must condemn the article as forfeited.

(4) If that constable takes such proceedings and the court—

(a) finds that the article was not liable to forfeiture at the time of its seizure, or
(b) is satisfied that its forfeiture would be inappropriate,

the court must order the return of the article to the person who appears to the court to be entitled to it.

(5) If the relevant constable decides not to take proceedings for condemnation in a case in which a notice of

claim has been given, he must return the article to the person who appears to him to be the owner of the article, or to one of the persons who appear to him to be owners of it.

(6) An article required to be returned in accordance with sub-paragraph (5) must be returned as soon as reasonably practicable after the decision not to take proceedings for condemnation.

Forfeiture proceedings

7. Proceedings by virtue of this Schedule are civil proceedings and may be instituted—

(a) in England or Wales, either in the High Court or in a magistrates' court;
(b) in Scotland, either in the Court of Session or in the sheriff court; and
(c) in Northern Ireland, either in the High Court or in a court of summary jurisdiction.

8. Proceedings by virtue of this Schedule in—

(a) a magistrates' court in England or Wales,
(b) the sheriff court in Scotland, or
(c) a court of summary jurisdiction in Northern Ireland,

may be instituted in that court only if it has jurisdiction in relation to the place where the article to which they relate was seized.

9. (1) In proceedings by virtue of this Schedule that are instituted in England and Wales or Northern Ireland, the claimant or his solicitor must make his oath that, at the time of the seizure, the seized article was, or was to the best of his knowledge and belief, the property of the claimant.

(2) In any such proceedings instituted in the High Court—

(a) the court may require the claimant to give such security for the costs of the proceedings as may be determined by the court; and
(b) the claimant must comply with any such requirement.

(3) If a requirement of this paragraph is not complied with, the court must find against the claimant.

10. (1) In the case of proceedings by virtue of this Schedule that are instituted in a magistrates' court in England or Wales, either party may appeal against the decision of that court to the Crown Court.

(2) In the case of such proceedings that are instituted in a court of summary jurisdiction in Northern Ireland, either party may appeal against the decision of that court to the county court.

(3) This paragraph does not affect any right to require the statement of a case for the opinion of the High Court.

11. Where an appeal has been made (whether by case stated or otherwise) against the decision of the court in proceedings by virtue of this Schedule in relation to an article, the article is to be left in the custody of a constable pending the final determination of the matter.

Effect of forfeiture

12. Where an article is treated or condemned as forfeited under this Schedule, the forfeiture is to be treated as having taken effect as from the time of the seizure.

Disposal of unclaimed property

13. (1) This paragraph applies where the article seized under the authority of a warrant under section 28 is required to be returned to a person.

(2) If—

(a) the article is (without having been returned) still in the custody of a constable after the end of the period of 12 months beginning with the day after the requirement to return it arose, and
(b) it is not practicable to dispose of the article by returning it immediately to the person to whom it is required to be returned,

the constable may dispose of it in any manner he thinks fit.

Provisions as to proof

14. In proceedings arising out of the seizure of an article, the fact, form and manner of the seizure is to be taken, without further evidence and unless the contrary is shown, to have been as set forth in the process.

15. In proceedings, the condemnation by a court of an article as forfeited under this Schedule may be proved by the production of either—

(a) the order of condemnation; or
(b) a certified copy of the order purporting to be signed by an officer of the court by which the order was made.

Special provisions as to certain claimants

16. (1) This paragraph applies where, at the time of the seizure of the article, it was—

(a) the property of a body corporate;
(b) the property of two or more partners; or
(c) the property of more than five persons.

(2) The oath required by paragraph 9, and any other thing required by this Schedule or by rules of court to be done by an owner of the article, may be sworn or done by—

(a) a person falling within sub-paragraph (3); or
(b) a person authorised to act on behalf of a person so falling.

(3) The persons falling within this sub-paragraph are—

(a) where the owner is a body corporate, the secretary or some duly authorised officer of that body;
(b) where the owners are in partnership, any one or more of the owners;
(c) where there are more than five owners and they are not in partnership, any two or more of the owners acting on behalf of themselves and any of their co-owners who are not acting on their own behalf.

Saving for owner's rights

17. Neither the imposition of a requirement by virtue of this Schedule to return an article to a person nor the return of an article to a person in accordance with such a requirement affects—

(a) the rights in relation to that article of any other person; or
(b) the right of any other person to enforce his rights against the person to whom it is returned.

Interpretation of Schedule

18. In this Schedule—

"article" has the same meaning as in Part 1 of this Act;
"the court" is to be construed in accordance with paragraph 7.

Section 37

SCHEDULE 3

REPEALS

Short title and chapter	*Extent of repeal*
Terrorism Act 2000 (c 11)	In section 5(4), the words "by or in respect of an organisation". In section 9(4), the word "and" at the end of paragraph (b). In section 63A(1)(b), the words "section 54 or". Section 126. In Schedule 5, in each of paragraphs 1(5) and 28(4), the "and" at the end of paragraph (b). In Schedule 8, in paragraph 36(1), the words "to a judicial authority".
Justice (Northern Ireland) Act 2002 (c 26)	In Schedule 7, paragraph 35.
Criminal Justice Act 2003 (c 44)	Section 45(8). Section 306(2) and (3).

10–12

Communications (Television Licensing) (Amendment) Regulations 2006[1]

(SI 2006/619)

1. Commencement, citation, extent and interpretation. (1) These Regulations may be cited as the Communications (Television Licensing) (Amendment) Regulations 2006 and shall come into force on 1st April 2006.

(2) These Regulations, except regulation 3, extend to the Channel Islands and the Isle of Man.

(3) In these Regulations "the 2004 Regulations" means the Communications (Television Licensing) Regulations 2004.

1. Made by the Secretary of State makes the following Regulations in exercise of the powers conferred by s 6(1) of the Wireless Telegraphy Act 1967 and ss 365(1) and (4) and 402(3) of the Communications Act 2003, as extended by the Broadcasting and Communications (Jersey) Order 2004, the Communications (Jersey) Order 2003, the Communications (Bailiwick of Guernsey) Order 2004, the Communications (Bailiwick of Guernsey) Order 2003 and the Communications (Isle of Man) Order 2003.

2. Amendment of the 2004 Regulations. The 2004 Regulations shall be amended in accordance with the following provisions of these Regulations.

3. Amendment of Regulation 11. In regulation 11(1), after "computer apparatus" insert "or a mobile telephone".

4. Amendment of Schedule 1. In Schedule 1 (issue fees for TV licences)—

(a) for "£42.00" in each place where it occurs substitute "£44.00"; and
(b) for "£126.50 in each place where it occurs substitute "£131.50".

5–9. *Amendments to Schs 2–5 and Savings.*

TABLES

AND

INDEX

ABBREVIATIONS

A & E........Adolphus and Ellis's Reports
All ER........All England Law Reports
All ER Rep........All England Law Reports Reprint
AC........Law Reports, Appeal Cases
App Cas........Law Reports (New Series) Appeal Cases
Arch........Archbold's Quarter Sessions Practice
Arch CP........Archbold's Criminal Pleading, Evidence and Practice
Asp MC........Aspinall's Maritime Cases
B & A........Barnewall and Alderson's Reports
B & Ad........Barnewall and Adolphus's Reports
B & C........Barnewall and Cresswell's Reports
B & P........Bosanquet and Puller's Reports
B & S........Best and Smith's Reports
BCC........Bail Court Cases
Bell, CC........Bell's Crown Cases
Bk........Bankruptcy
Bl W........Blackstone's (William) Reports
BTRLR........Brewing Trade Review, Licensing Reports
Burn........Burn's Justice
Burr........Burrow's Reports
CA........Court of Appeal
C & K........Carrington and Kirwan's Reports
C & M........Carrington and Marshman's Reports
C & P........Carrington and Payne's Reports
Cab & E........Cababé and Ellis's Reports
Cald........Caldecott's Settlement Cases
Camp........Campbell's Reports
CB........Common Bench Reports, or Manning, Granger and Scott's Reports
CBNS........Common Bench Reports (New Series)
CCC........Central Criminal Court
CCC (vol)........Reports of the Central Criminal Court
CCR........Crown Cases Reserved
CLR........Common Law Reports
CM & R........Crompton, Meeson and Roscoe's Reports
CPD........Law Reports, Common Pleas Division
Ch........Law Reports, Chancery Division
Ch D........Law Reports (New Series) Chancery Division
CL & Finn........Clark & Finelly's Reports
Com Cas........Commercial Cases
Cowp........Cowper's Reports
Cox, C C........Cox's Criminal Cases
Cr App Rep........Criminal Appeal Reports
Cr & M........Crompton and Meeson's Reports
Crim LR........Criminal Law Review
Cro Eliz........Croke's Reports (*temp* Elizabeth, James and Charles)
D & L........Dowling and Lowndes' Reports
D & M........Davison and Merivale's Reports
D & R........Dowling and Ryland's Reports
Dears........Dearsley's Crown Cases
Dears & B........Dearsley's and Bell's Crown Cases
Den........Denison's Crown Cases
Dow & R........Dowling and Ryland's Magistrates' Cases
DPC........Davies' Patent Cases
ECR........European Court Reports
East........East's Reports
East Pc........East's Pleas of the Crown
El & Bl........Ellis and Blackburn's Reports
El & El........Ellis and Ellis's Reports
El BL & EL........Ellis, Blackburn and Ellis's Reports
Esp........Espinasses's Reports
Ex........Exchequer Reports
Ex D........Law Reports, Exchequer Division
F (Ct of Sess)........Court of Session Cases (Fifth Series)
F & F........Foster and Finlason's Reports
Fam........Family Reports
Fam Law........Family Law
FLR........Family Law Reports

G & D........Gale and Davison's Reports
H & C........Hurlstone and Coltman's Reports
H & N........Hurlstone and Norman's Reports
Hagg........Haggard's Admiralty
Halsbury........Halsbury's Laws of England
Har & Ruth........Harrisin and Rutherfurd's Reports
HL........House of Lords
HL Rep........Clark's House of Lords Cases
Hard........Hardre's Reports
How St Tr........Howell's State Trials
ICR........Industrial Court Reports
IR........Irish Reports
IRLR........Industrial Relations Law Reports
Ir R Ch........Irish Common Law and Chancery Report
JP........Justice of the Peace Reports
JP JO........Justice of the Peace Journal
JPN........Justice of the Peace and Local Government Review (Newspaper)
Jur........Jurist Reports
Jur (NS)........Jurist Reports (New Series)
Just Cas........Justiciary Court Cases
KB........Law Reports, King's Bench
L & C........Leigh and Cave's Crown Cases
LGR........Local Government Reports
Ll L Rep........Lloyd's List Law Reports
LR App........Law Reports, Appeal Cases
LRCCR........Law Reports, Crown Cases Reserved
LR Ch........Law Reports, Chancery Appeals
LRCP........Law Reports, Court of Common Pleas
LR Eq........Law Reports, Equity
LR Ex........Law Reports, Exchequer
LR Ir........Law Reports, (Ireland)
LRKB........Law Reports, King's Bench
LRPC........Law Reports, Privy Council
LRQB........Law Reports, Queen's Bench
LS Gaz........Law Society Gazette
Ld Ken........Kenyon's Reports
Leach........Leach's Crown Cases
Lew CC........Lewin's Crown Cases
LM & P........Lowndes, Maxwell, and Pollock's Cases
LJ........Law Journal
LJ (NS)........Law Journal Reports (New Series), Magistrates' Cases
LJ Bk........Law Journal (Bankruptcy)
LJ CP........Law Journal (Common Pleas)
LJ Ch........Law Journal (Exchequer)
LJ KB........Law Journal (King's Bench)
LJ QB........Law Journal (Queen's Bench)
LT........Law Times Reports (New Series)
LTN........Law Times Journal (Newspaper)
LT (OS)........Law Times (Old Series)
M & M........Moody and Malkin's Reports
M & R........Manning and Ryland's Reports
M & S........Maule and Selwyn's Reports
M & W........Meeson and Welsby's reports
MC........Magistrates' Cases (Law Journal)
Marsh........Marshall's Reports
M'Clel........M'Cleland's Reports
Moo & M........Moody and Malkin's Reports
Moo CC........Moody's Crown Cases
PC........Moore's Privy Council Cases
Moore........Moore's Reports, King's Bench
Mod........Modern Reports
Morrell........Morrell's Bankruptcy Reports
N & M........Neville and Manning's Reports
N & P........Neville and Petty's Reports
NLJ........New Law Journal
New Sess Cas........New Sessions Cases
OJ........Official Journal of the European Communities (reporting legislation of the Council and Commissions of the EEC)
P........Law Reports (Probate Division)
P & CR........Property and Compensation Reports
P & D........Perry and Davison's Reports
PC........Privy Council
PD........Law Reports, Probate Division

Abbreviations

Peakes........Peakes' Reports
Price........Price's Reports
QB........Law Reports, Queen's Bench
QBD........Law Reports, Queen's Bench Division
R........The Reports
RA........Rating Appeals
R & M........Ryan and Moody's
R & R........Russell and Ryan's Crown Cases
(Ct of Justic)........Retties' series of the Scotch Law Judiciary Reports
RPC........Reports of the Patent Cases
RTR........Road Traffic Reports
Russ........Russell on Crime
SC........Court of Session Cases
C (J)........Court of Justiciary Cases
Sc LR........Scottish Law Reporter
Scott NR........Scott's New Reports
SE........Special Edition (digesting legislation of the Council and Commission of the EEC)
Sess Cas........Sessions Cases, or Carrow, Hamerton and Allen's Session Cases
Smith........Smith's Reports
Sol Jo........Solicitors' Journal
Star or Stark........Starkie's Reports
Stra........Strange's reports
Sw & Tr........Swabey and Tristram's Reports
TLR........Times Law Reports
T & M........Temple and Mew's Criminal Appeal cases
TR........Term Reports (Durnford and East)
Taun........Taunton's Reports
Traff Cases........Maxwell and Fay's Traffic Cases
Tyr........Tyrhwhitt's Reports
WLR........Weekly Law Reports
WN........Weekly Notes (Law Reports)
WR........Weekly Reporter
WR Dig........Weekly Reporter Digest
WW & H........Willmore, Wollaston and Hodges' Reports
W Bl........William Blackstone's King's Bench Reports

TABLE OF STATUTES, CONVENTIONS AND TREATIES

Paragraph references in this Table indicate where an Act is set out in part or in full.

C

E

	PARA
Family Law Act 1996—*contd*	
Sch 10	6-3162
Family Law Reform Act 1969	6-502
s 1	6-502
8	6503
9	6-504
12	6-505
20	6-506
21	6-507
23	6-509
24	6-510
25	6-511
26	6-512
Family Law Reform Act 1987	6-1950
s 1	6-1950
2	6-1951
23	6-1957
27	6-1959
30	6-1960
31	6-1961
34	6-1963
Sch 3	
para 1	6-1969
6	6-1974
7	6-1975
8	6-1976
9	6-1977
10	6-1978
Farm and Garden Chemicals Act 1967	8-129
s 2	8-130
3	8-131
4	8-132
Farriers Registration Act 1975	8-1307
Female Genital Mutilation Act 2003	8-23559ZZZJ
s 1	8-23559ZZZJ
2	8-23559ZZZK
3	8-23559ZZZL
4	8-23559ZZZM
5	8-23559ZZZN
6	8-23559ZZZO
7	8-23559ZZZP
8	8-23559ZZZQ
Ferries (Acquisition by Local Authorities) Act 1919	
s 2	7-6191
4	7-6192
Finance Act 1931	
s 28	8-29700
Finance Act 1966	8-6511
s 12	8-6511
15	8-6512
53	8-6513
Sch 3	
Pt I	
para 6	8-6514
Finance Act 1985	
s 10	8-7200
89	8-29700
Finance Act 1988	
s 38	8-29860
40	8-29862
Finance Act 1989	
s 182	8-30070
182A	8-30071
Finance Act 1993	
s 24	8-7210
27	8-7211
28	8-7212
29	8-7213
31	8-7214
32	8-7215
33	8-7216
34	8-7217

	PARA
Finance Act 1993—*contd*	
s 35	8-7218
37	8-7219
40	8-7221
41	8-7222
Finance Act 1994	8-7230
s 8	8-7230
9	8-7230A
10	8-7230B
20	8-7230C
21	8-7231
22	8-7231A
23	8-7231B
24	8-7231C
25	8-7232
26	8-7232A
27	8-7232B
28	8-7232C
29	8-7233
30	8-7233A
31	8-7233B
32	8-7233C
33	8-7234
40	8-7234A
41	8-7234B
42	8-7234C
43	8-7235
48	8-7235B
49	8-7235C
50	8-7236
52	8-7236B
53	8-7236C
70	8-7237
71	8-7237A
72	8-7237B
73	8-7237C
Sch 6	8-7239
Sch 7	8-7239B
Sch 7A	8-7243
Finance Act 1996	8-7245
s 39	8-7245
40	8-7245A
41	8-7245B
47	8-7245E
48	8-7245F
49	8-7245G
50	8-7245GA
64	8-7245H
65	8-7245I
66	8-7245J
67	8-7245K
68	8-7245L
69	8-7245M
70	8-7245N
Sch 5	8-7246
Finance Act 1997	8-7247
s 10	8-7247
11	8-7248
13	8-7250
15	8-7252
Sch 1	8-7253
Finance Act 2000	8-7254
s 20	8-7254
23	8-7255
30	8-7256
144	8-7257
Sch 4	8-7257A
Sch 6	8-7257B
Finance Act 2003	8-7257G
s 24	8-7257G
25	8-7257H
26	8-7257I
27	8-7257J

N

	PARA
Night Poaching Act 1844	
s 1	8-13790
Noise Act 1996	8-26737
s 1	8-26737
2	8-26738
3	8-26739
4	8-26740
7	8-26742
8	8-26743
9	8-26744
10	8-26745
11	8-26746
14	8-26749
Schedule	8-26750
para 1	8-26750
2	8-26751
3	8-26752
4	8-26753
5, 6	8-26754
Noise and Statutory Nuisance Act 1993	8-26650
s 8	8-26650
9	8-26651
Sch 2	8-26652
Sch 3	8-26653
Nuclear Explosions (Prohibition and Inspections) Act 1998	8-22742
Nuclear Installations Act 1965	8-9140
Nuclear Material (Offences) Act 1983	8-9410
s 1	8-9410
2	8-9411
3	8-9412
4	8-9413
6	8-9414
7	8-9415
Schedule	8-9416
Nuclear Safeguards Act 2000	8-9693
s 2	8-9694
3	8-9695
4	8-9696
5	8-9697
6	8-9698
7	8-9698A
8	8-9698B
9	8-9698C
10	8-9698D
Nuclear Safeguards and Electricity (Finance) Act 1978	8-9182
s 2	8-9182
3	8-9183
4	8-9184
Nurses, Midwives and Health Visitors Act 1997	
23	8-22067M
24	8-22067N

O

	PARA
Oaths Act 1978	
s 1	2-1190
3	2-1191
4	2-1192
5	2-1193
6	2-1194
Oaths and Evidence (Overseas Authorities and Countries) Act 1963	
s 5	2-1020
Obscene Publications Act 1959	8-22449
s 1	8-22449
2	8-22450
3	8-22451
4	8-22452
Obscene Publications Act 1964	8-22560
s 2	8-22561
Offences Against the Person Act 1861	8-23079
s 4	8-23080
5	8-23081
16	8-23084
17	8-23085
18	8-23086
20	8-23087
21	8-23088
22	8-23089
23	8-23090
24	8-23091
26	8-23092
27	8-23093
28	8-23094
29	8-23095
30	8-23096
31	8-23097
32	7-7037
33	7-7038
34	7-7039
35	8-23098
36	8-23099
37	8-23112
38	8-23113
44	8-23114
45	8-23115
47	8-23116
57	8-23117
58	8-23118
59	8-23119
60	8-23120
64	8-23121
Offices, Shops and Railway Premises Act 1963	8-14810
s 1	8-14810
2	8-14811
3	8-14812
4	8-14813
5	8-14814
6	8-14815
7	8-14816
8	8-14817
9	8-14818
10	8-14819
11	8-14820
12	8-14821
13	8-14822
14	8-14823
15	8-14824
16	8-14825
17	8-14826
19	8-14828
23	8-14829
27	8-14840
42	8-14841
43	8-14842
44	8-14843
46	8-14844
47	8-14845
49	8-14846
52	8-14847
59	8-14848
59A	8-14848A
63	8-14849
67	8-14850
69	8-14851
72	8-14852
86	8-14857
90	8-14858
Official Secrets Act 1911	8-22751
s 1	8-22751

S

ALPHABETICAL TABLE OF STATUTORY INSTRUMENTS, CODES AND EC REGULATIONS

Paragraph references in this Table indicate where a Statutory Instrument, etc is set out in part or in full

For Chronological List of Statutory Instruments see p [251].

CHRONOLOGICAL LIST OF STATUTORY INSTRUMENTS

Paragraph references in this Table indicate where a Statutory Instrument is set out in part or in full

For Alphabetical Table of Statutory Instruments see p [201]

		PARA
SR&O		
1922/1355	Maintenance Orders (Facilities for Enforcement) Rules 1922	6-4570
1929/952	Petroleum-Spirit (Motor Vehicles, &c..) Regulations 1929	8-16002
SI		
1950/2035	Maintenance Orders Act 1950 (Summary Jurisdiction) Rules 1950	6-4590
1952/2205	Transferred Excise Duties (Application of Enactments) Order 1952	8-7230
1954/1711	Youth Courts (Constitution) Rules 1954	5-1220
1959/3	Magistrates' Courts (Maintenance Orders Act 1958) Rules 1959	6-4640
1960/1701	Betting (Licensing) Regulations 1960	8-13971
1961/248	Evidence by Certificate Rules 1961	1-1002, 7-123, 7-1651
1961/1547	Betting Levy (Particulars of Bookmakers' Permits) Regulations 1961	8-13972
1961/2477	Licensing Rules 1961	6-1624
1962/75	Licensing (Extended Hours Orders) Rules 1962	6-1631
1969/550	Gaming Act (Registration under Part II) Regulations 1969	8-13972B
1969/1109	Gaming Act (Registration under Part III) Regulations 1969	8-13972F
1969/1110	Gaming Clubs (Licensing) Regulations 1969	8-13972H
1970/1958	Functions of Traffic Wardens Order 1970	4-2731
1970/1997	Vehicle and Driving Licences Records (Evidence) Regulations 1970	7-1653
1971/809	Magistrates' Courts (Attachment of Earnings) Rules 1971	1-5794
1971/1538	Gaming Clubs (Permitted Areas) Regulations 1971	8-13972P
1971/1861	Blood Tests (Evidence of Paternity) Regulations 1971	6-3570
1971/1991	Magistrates' Courts (Blood Tests) Rules 1971	6-3590
1972/1217	Motor Vehicles (Third Party Risks) Regulations 1972	4-4061
1973/19	Adoption (Designation of Overseas Adoptions) Order 1973	6-3280
1973/2143	Motor Vehicles (Compulsory Insurance) (No 2) Regulations 1973	4-4071
1974/556	Reciprocal Enforcement of Maintenance Orders (Designation of Reciprocating Countries) Order 1974	6-4690
1974/668	Magistrates' Courts (Reciprocal Enforcement of Maintenance Orders) Rules 1974	6-4694
1974/706	Magistrates' Courts (Guardianship of Minors) Rules 1974	6-4551
1974/1941	Factories Act 1961 etc (Repeals and Modifications) Regulations 1974	8-14610
1974/2211	Rabies (Importation of Dogs, Cats and other Mammals) Order 1974	8-1790
1975/286	Magistrates' Courts (Reciprocal Enforcement of Maintenance Orders) (Republic of Ireland) Rules 1975	6-4720
1975/423	Recovery Abroad of Maintenance (Convention Countries) Order 1975	6-4740
1975/488	Magistrates' Courts (Recovery Abroad of Maintenance) Rules 1975	6-4743
1975/1023	Rehabilitation of Offenders Act 1974 (Exceptions) Order 1975	3-3000
1975/1208	Motor Vehicles (International Circulation) Order 1975	4-4081
1975/2036	Motor Vehicles (Minimum Age for Driving) (Community Rules) Regulations 1975	7-2101
1975/2116	Control of Noise (Appeals) Rules 1975	8-27160
1975/2187	Reciprocal Enforcement of Maintenance Orders (Designation of Reciprocating Countries) Order 1975	6-4760
1976/117	Justices' Allowances Regulations 1976	1-4620
1976/1002	Consumer Credit (Termination of Licences) Regulations 1976	8-5170
1977/276	Carriage of Goods (Prohibition of Discrimination) Regulations 1977	7-7245
1977/1877	Tourism (Sleeping Accommodation Price Display) Order 1977	8-7460
1978/238	Weights and Measures (Solid Fuel) Regulations 1978	8-32140
1978/1644	Licensing (Fees) Order 1978	6-1740
1978/1684	Public Service Vehicles (Lost Property) Regulations 1978	4-2111
1978/1910	European Communities (Services of Lawyers) Order 1978	8-9830
1979/115	Reciprocal Enforcement of Maintenance Orders (Designation of Reciprocating Countries) Order 1979	6-4770
1979/570	Justices' Clerks (Qualifications of Assistants) Rules 1979	1-4630
1979/628	Social Security (Claims and Payments) Regulations 1979	8-29280
1980/108	Magistrates' Courts (Reciprocal Enforcement of Maintenance Orders) (Hague Convention Countries) Rules 1980	6-4789
1981/257	Public Service Vehicles (Conditions of Fitness, Equipment, Use and Certification) Regulations 1981	4-2131
1981/552	Magistrates' Courts Rules 1981	1-5930
1981/553	Magistrates' Courts (Forms) Rules 1981	9-300
1981/917	Health and Safety (First-Aid) Regulations 1981	8-16230
1981/1694	Motor Vehicles (Tests) Regulations 1981	4-3071

SI		PARA
1982/1109	Crown Court Rules 1982	1-6070
1982/1163	Motorways Traffic (England and Wales) Regulations 1982	4-2811
1982/1384	Licensing (Special Hours Certificates) Rules 1982	6-1750
1983/910	Road Vehicles (Marking of Special Weights) Regulations 1983	4-2191
1983/1032	Licensing (Fees) Order 1983	6-1770
1983/1125	Reciprocal Enforcement of Maintenance Orders (Designation of Reciprocating Countries) Order 1983	6-4805
1983/1176	Pedal Cycles (Construction and Use) Regulations 1983	4-3131
1984/145	Pedal Bicycles (Safety) Regulations 1984	8-5250
1984/248	Gaming Clubs (Hours and Charges) Regulations 1984	8-13972T
1984/455	Diseases of Fish Regulations 1984	8-10770, 8-10779
1984/611	Magistrates' Courts (Adoption) Rules 1984	6-3410
1984/748	Road Transport (International Passenger Services) Regulations 1984	4-2241
1984/1315	Weights and Measures Act 1963 (Cheese, fish, fresh fruits and vegetables, meat and poultry) Order 1984	8-32160
1984/1406	Public Service Vehicles (Carrying Capacity) Regulations 1984	4-2271
1985/99	Food Imitations (Safety) Regulations 1985	8-5456
1985/610	Motor Vehicles (International Circulation) Regulations 1985	4-4091
1985/911	Video Recordings (Labelling) Regulations 1985	8-30651
1985/1151	Sports Grounds and Sporting Events (Designation) Order 1985	6-1787
1985/1800	Police and Criminal Evidence Act 1984 (Application to Customs and Excise) Order 1985	1-6140
1986/103	Licensed Betting Offices Regulations 1986	8-13973
1986/178	Local Authorities' Traffic Orders (Exemptions for Disabled Persons) (England and Wales) Regulations 1986	7-1217
1986/834	Gaming Clubs (Multiple Bingo) Regulations 1986	8-13974
1986/1078	Road Vehicles (Construction and Use) Regulations 1986	4-3501
1986/1141	Magistrates' Courts (Child Abduction and Custody) Rules 1986	6-4560
1986/1159	Child Abduction and Custody (Parties to Convention Order 1986	4-1776, 4-1787
1986/1245	Community Bus Regulations 1986	4-2321
1986/1330	Fixed Penalty (Procedure) Regulations 1986	4-4111
1986/1335	Costs in Criminal Cases (General) Regulations 1986	1-6170
1986/1456	Community Drivers' Hours and Recording Equipment (Exemptions and Supplementary Provisions) Regulations 1986	4-2371
1986/1458	Drivers' Hours (Harmonisation with Community Rules) Regulations 1986	4-2391
1986/1459	Drivers' Hours (Goods Vehicles) (Modifications) Order 1986	4-2411
1986/1492	Drivers' Hours (Goods Vehicles) (Exemptions) Regulations 1986	4-2421
1986/1510	Control of Pesticides Regulations 1986	8-12820
1986/1962	Magistrates' Courts (Civil Jurisdiction and Judgments Act 1982) Rules 1986	6-4810
1987/299	Prosecution of Offences (Custody Time Limits) Regulations 1987	1-6220
1987/1421	Drivers' Hours (Goods Vehicles) (Keeping of Records) Regulations 1987	4-2471
1987/2198	Criminal Jurisdiction (Offshore Activities) Order 1987	8-16265
1988/329	Magistrates' Courts (Family Law Act 1986) Rules 1988	6-4840
1988/1324	Furniture and Furnishings (Fire) (Safety) Regulations 1988	8-5330
1988/1478	Goods Vehicles (Plating and Testing) Regulations 1988	4-2491
1988/2019	Criminal Justice Act 1988 (Offensive Weapons) Order 1988	8-22744
1988/2039	Weights and Measures (Intoxicating Liquor) Order 1988	8-32320
1988/2040	Weights and Measures (Miscellaneous Foods) Order 1988	8-32340
1988/2050	Distress for Rent Rules 1988	8-16721
1988/2268	Use of Invalid Carriages on Highways Regulations 1988	4-3711
1989/438	Community charges (Administration and Enforcement) Regulations 19879	1-40
1989/1058	Non-Domestic Rating (Collection and Enforcement) (Local Lists) Regulations 1989	8-20030
1989/1376	Recovery Vehicles (Prescribed Purposes) Regulations 1989	7-1976
1989/1790	Noise at Work Regulations 1989	8-16321
1989/1796	Road Vehicles Lighting Regulations 1989	4-3731
1989/2261	Non-Domestic Rating (Unoccupied Property) Regulations 1989	8-20067
1990/993	Football Spectators (Corresponding Offences in Scotland) Order 1990	8-16337
1990/1020	Public Service Vehicles (Conduct of Drivers, Inspectors, Conductors and Passengers) Regulations 1990	4-2561
1990/1777	Income Support (Liable Relative) Regulations 1990	8-29290
1990/1909	Magistrates' Courts (Social Security Act 1986) Transfer of Orders to Maintain and Enforcement of Maintenance Orders) Rules 1990	6-4848
1990/2260	Magistrates' Courts (Civilian Enforcement Officers) Rules 1990	1-6260
1991/199	Price Indications (Method of Payment) Regulations 1991	8-5460
1991/324	Control of Pollution (Silage, Slurry and Agricultural Fuel Oil) Regulations 1991	8-31741
1991/499	Abortion Regulations 1991	8-23561
1991/1043	Litter (Statutory Undertakers) (Designation and Relevant Land) Order 1991	8-27171
1991/1074	Magistrates' Courts (Criminal Justice (International Co-operation)) Rules 1991	1-6270
1991/1395	Family Proceedings Courts (Children Act 1989) Rules 1991	6-4252
1991/1405	Family Proceedings Courts (Constitution) Rules 1991	6-4450
1991/1414	Emergency Protection Order (Transfer of Responsibilities) Regulations 1991	6-3613
1991/1505	Children (Secure Accommodation) Regulations 1991	6-3618
1991/1677	Children (Allocation of Proceedings) Order 1991	6-4400

SI		PARA
1991/1744	Dangerous Dogs Compensation and Exemption Schemes Order 1991	8-7630
1991/1991	Family Proceedings Courts (Matrimonial Proceedings etc) Rules 1991	6-4521
1991/2034	Children (Secure Accommodation) (No 2) Regulations 1991	6-3637
1991/2096	Magistrates' Courts (Costs Against Legal Representatives in Civil Proceedings) Rules 1991	
1992/613	Council Tax (Administration and Enforcement) Regulations 1992	1-6300
1992/666	Town and Country Planning (Control of Advertisements) Regulations 1992	8-20075
1992/901	Control of Dogs Order 1992	8-31180
1992/1285	Road Vehicles (Prohibition) Regulations 1992	8-7641
1992/1670	Criminal Justice Act 1991 (Notice of Transfer) Regulations 1992	4-2600
1992/1812	Child Support (Information, Evidence and Disclosure) Regulations 1992	1-6340
1992/1989	Child Support (Collection and Enforcement) Regulations 1992	6-4852
1992/2069	Magistrates' Courts (Attendance Centre) Rules 1992	6-4941
1992/2070	Magistrates' Courts (Notice of Transfer) (Children's Evidence) Rules 1992	3-3020
1992/2071	Magistrates' Courts (Children and Young Persons) Rules 1992	1-6380
1992/2182	Fines (Deduction from Income Support) Regulations 1992	5-1310
1992/2643	Child Support (Collection and Enforcement of Other Forms of Maintenance) Regulations 1992	3-3040
1992/2645	Child Support (Maintenance Arrangements and Jurisdiction) Regulations 1992	6-4954
1992/2792	Health and Safety (Display Screen Equipment) Regulations 1992	6-4959
1992/2793	Manual Handling Operations Regulations 1992	8-16342
1992/2823	Firearms Acts (Amendment) Regulations 1992	8-16352
1992/3004	Workplace (Health, Safety and Welfare) Regulations 1992	8-10370
1992/3013	Road Traffic (Courses for Drink-Drive Offenders) Regulations 1992	8-16400
1992/3288	Package Travel, Package Holidays and Package Tours Regulations 1992	4-4401
1993/31	Motor Vehicles (Wearing of Seat Belts by Children in Front Seats) Regulations 1993	8-5494
1993/176	Motor Vehicles (Wearing of Seat Belts) Regulations 1993	4-3791
1993/591	Recovery of Maintenance (United States of America) Order 1993	4-3800
1993/593	Reciprocal Enforcement of Maintenance Orders (Hague Convention Countries) Order 1993	6-4967
1993/594	Reciprocal Enforcement of Maintenance Orders (Republic of Ireland) Order 1993	6-4970
1993/621	Children (Admissibility of Hearsay Evidence) Order 1993	6-4980
1993/627	Family Proceedings Courts (Child Support Act 1991) Rules 1993	6-3653
1993/961	Child Support Appeals (Jurisdiction of Courts) Order 1993	6-4549
1993/1073	Aviation Security (Air Cargo Agents) Regulations 1993	6-4957
1993/1353	Customs and Excise (Transit) Regulations 1993	7-5442
1993/1933	Money Laundering Regulations 1993	8-7261
1993/3223	Lotteries Regulations 1993	8-2435
1994/189	National Lottery Regulations 1994	8-13974C
1994/227	Child Support (Miscellaneous Amendments and Transitional Provisions) Regulations 1994	8-13974Q
1994/576	Railways (Penalty Fares) Regulations 1994	6-5010
1994/1696	Insurance Companies (Third Insurance Directives) Regulations 1994	7-7254
1994/1952	Backing of Warrants (Republic of Ireland) (Rule of Speciality) Order 1994	8-3830, 8-3865
1994/2767	Parental Orders (Human Fertilisation and Embryology) Regulations 1994	8-10340
1994/2811	Magistrates' Courts Committees (Constitution) Regulations 1994	1-3470, 6-3470
1994/3117	Motor Vehicle Tyres (Safety) Regulations 1994	1-3888
1994/3248	Price Indications (Resale of Tickets) Regulations 1994	8-5533
1995/1804	Units of Measurement Regulations 1995	8-5525
1995/2644	Statutory Nuisance (Appeals) Regulations 1995	8-32360
1995/2709	Reciprocal Enforcement of Maintenance Orders (United States of America) Order 1995	8-27180
1995/2802	Magistrates' Courts (Reciprocal Enforcement of Maintenance Orders) (United States of America) Rules 1995	6-5021
1995/2869	Goods Vehicles (Licensing of Operators) Regulations 1995	6-5027
1995/2908	Public Service Vehicles (Operators' Licences) Regulations 1995	4-2609
1995/3163	Reporting of Injuries, Diseases and Dangerous Occurrences Regulations 1995	4-2637
1995/3281	Attendance Centre Rules 1995	8-16491
1996/1455	Disability Discrimination (Meaning of Disability) Regulations 1996	3-3060
1996/1499	Food Labelling Regulations 1996	8-3122
1996/2907	Child Support Departure Directions and Consequential Amendments Regulations 1996	8-13000
1996/2967	Copyright and Related Rights Regulations 1996	4-5030
1996/3267	Children (Reciprocal Enforcement of Prescribed Orders etc (England and Wales and Northern Ireland) (Scotland) Regulations 1996	8-5640
1997/227	Housing (Enforcement Procedures for Houses in Multiple Occupation) Order 1997	4-5030
1997/684	Criminal Procedure and Investigations Act 1996 (Defence Disclosure Time Limits) Regulations 1997	8-17323
1997/1098	New Drivers (Appeals Procedure) Regulations 1997	1-6510
1997/1372	Control of Trade in Endangered Species (Enforcement) Regulations 1997	4-4350
1997/1896	Family Law Act 1996 (Part IV) (Allocation of Proceedings) Order 1997	8-4298
1997/1907	Knives (Forfeited Property) Regulations 1997	6-4550
		8-22746

SI		PARA
1997/1908	Police (Property) Regulations 1997	8-23898
1997/2400	Zebra, Pelican and Puffin Pedestrian Crossings Regulations and General Directions 1997	4-2909
1997/3032	Copyright and Rights in Databases Regulations 1997	8-5925
1998/472	Secure Training Centre Rules 1998	8-24410
1998/473	Secure Training Centres (Escorts) Rules 1998	5-1401
1998/1807	Motor Cycles (Protective Helmets) Regulations 1998	4-3812
1998/1833	Working Time Regulations 1998	8-8584
1998/1941	Firearms Rules 1998	8-10730
1998/2150	Gaming Machines (Maximum Prizes) Regulations 1998	6-920
1998/2682	Magistrates' Courts (Sex Offender and Anti-social Behaviour Orders) Rules 1998	1-6565
1998/3111	Road Vehicles (Authorised Weight) Regulations 1998	4-3813
1998/3132	Civil Procedure Rules 1998	1-5680, 1-6563A
1999/535	Motor Cycles (Eye Protectors) Regulations 1999	4-3824
1999/665	Judicial Committee (Devolution Issues) Rules Order 1999	1-6574
1999/681	Magistrates' Courts (Hearsay Evidence in Civil Proceedings) Rules 1999	2-2334
1999/728	Prison Rules 1999	8-24455
1999/904	Prosecution of Offences Act 1985 (Specified Proceedings Order 1999	1-6635
1999/1265	Secure Remands and Committals (Prescribed Description of Children and Young Persons) Order 1999	5-601
1999/1322	Public Service Vehicles (Community Licences) Regulation 1999	4-4376A
1999/1736	Visiting Forces and International Headquarters (Application of Law) Order 1999	8-2380
1999/2864	Motor Vehicles (Driving Licences) Regulations 1999	4-4377
1999/3413	Road Transport (Passenger Vehicles Cabotage) Regulations 1999	4-2665
2000/441	Community Legal Service (Costs) Regulations 2000	1-5648
2000/442	Legal Services Commission (Disclosure of Information) Regulations 2000	1-619, 1-749
2000/516	Community Legal Service (Financial) Regulations 2000	1-5651
2000/627	Community Legal Service (Funding) Order 2000	1-5654
2000/824	Community Legal Service (Cost Protection) Regulations 2000	1-5655
2000/1119	European Communities (Lawyer's Practice) Regulations 2000	8-29309B
2000/1139	National Police Records (Recordable Offences) Regulations 2000	1-2731
2000/1973	Pollution Prevention and Control (England and Wales) Regulations 2000	8-27184
2000/2126	Football Spectators (Prescription) Order 2000	8-15972A
2000/2329	Football (Offences) (Designation of Football Matches) Order 2000	8-15992
2000/2699	Telecommunications (Lawful Business Practice) (Interception of Communications) Regulations 2000	8-30115
2000/2972	Fixed Penalty Order 2000	4-4381
2000/3371	Young Offender Institution Rules 2000	8-24550
2001/155	Child Support (Maintenance Calculations and Special Cases) Regulations 2000	6-5095A
2001/156	Child Support (Variations) Regulations 2000	6-5096
2001/157	Child Support (Maintenance Calculation Procedure) Regulations 2000	6-5098
2001/561	Road Vehicles (Display of Registration Marks)Regulations 2001	4-4382
2001/786	Local Probation Boards (Miscellaneous Provisions) Regulations 2001	1-4808
2001/855	Criminal Defence Service (Funding) Order 2001	1-5656
2001/856	Criminal Defence Service (Recovery of Defence Costs Orders) Regulations 2001	1-5660
2001/967	Companies (Disqualification Orders) Regulations 2001	8-3940
2001/1035	Local Probation Boards (Appointments and Miscellaneous Provisions) Regulations 2001	1-4810
2001/1077	Community Legal Service (Funding) (Counsel in Family Proceedings) Order 2001	1-5677
2001/1168	Criminal Defence Service (Representation Order Appeals) Regulations 2001	1-5681
2001/1169	Criminal Defence Service (Choice in Very High Cost Cases) Regulations 2001	1-5688
2001/1296	Justices and Justices' Clerks (Costs) Regulations 2001	1-6920
2001/1437	Criminal Defence Service (General) (No 2) Regulations 2001	1-5691
2001/2127	Health and Safety at Work etc Act 1974 (Application outside Great Britain) Order 2001	8-16600
2001/2505	International Criminal Court Act 2001 (Elements of Crimes) Regulations 2001	8-10345
2001/2600	Magistrates' Courts (International Criminal Court) (Forms) Rules 2001	1-6930
2001/3501	Reciprocal Enforcement of Maintenance Orders (Designation of Reciprocating Countries) Order 2001	6-5099F
2001/3928	Civil Jurisdiction and Judgments (Authentic Instruments and Court Settlements) Order 2001	6-5099I
2001/3929	Civil Jurisdiction and Judgments Order 2001	6-5099M
2001/3937	Regulatory Reform (Special Occasions Licensing) Order 2001	6-1840
2001/3948	Protection of the Euro against Counterfeiting Regulations 2001	8-13200
2001/3981	Goods Vehicles (Enforcement Powers) Regulations 2001, SI 2001/3981	4-2680
2001/3998	Misuse of Drugs Regulations 2001	8-22080
2001/4013	Magistrates' Courts (Detention and Forfeiture of Terrorist Cash) (No 2) Rules 2001	1-6940
2001/4051	Driving Licences (Disqualification until Test Passed) (Prescribed Offence) Order 2001	4-4390
2002/233	Police Act 1997 (Criminal Records) Regulations 2002	8-23900T
2002/313	Travel Restriction Order (Prescribed Removal Powers) Order 2002	1-7100

SI		PARA
2005/886	Courts Act 2003 (Consequential Provisions) Order 2005	10-2
2005/898	Materials and Articles in Contact with Food (England) Regulations 2005	8–13065A
2005/910	Courts Act 2003 (Commencement No 10) Order 2005	10-3
2005/911	Courts Act 2003 (Transitional Provisions, Savings and Consequential Provisions) Order 2005	10-4
2005/932	Crime (Sentences) Act 1997 (Commencement No 4) Order 2005	10-13
2005/950	Criminal Justice Act 2003 (Commencement No 8 and Transitional and Saving Provisions) Order 2005	10-5
2005/1012	Courts Act 2003 (Consequential and Transitional Provisions) Order 2005	10-6
2005/1541	Regulatory Reform (Fire Safety) Order 2005	8-16624
2005/1643	Control of Noise at Work Regulations 2005	8-16673
2005/1803	General Product Safety Regulations 2005	8-5535
2005/1970	Air Navigation Order 2005	7-5821
2005/2054	Remand in Custody (Effect of Concurrent and Consecutive Sentences of Imprisonment) Rules 2005	3-3120
2005/2795	Family Procedure (Adoption) Rules 2005	6-3550
2005/3204	Sports Grounds and Sporting Events (Designation) Order 2005	8-27850
2005/3444	Magistrates' Courts Fees Order 2005	1-7510
2005/3595	Register of Judgments, Orders and Fines Regulations 2005	1-7530
2006/14	Food Hygiene (England) Regulations 2006	8-13066
2006/501	Fines Collection Regulations 2006	1-7560
2006/502	Collection of Fines (Pilot Scheme) and Discharge of Fines by Unpaid Work (Pilot Schemes) (Amendment) Order 2006	1-7600

Table of Cases

A

PARA

PARA

B

PARA

B (a child) (sole adoption by unmarried father) [2001] 1 FCR 600, [2001] 1 FLR 589, [2001] Fam Law 174, CA; revsd sub nom B (a minor) (adoption: natural parent), Re [2001] UKHL 70, [2002] 1 All ER 641, [2002] 1 WLR 258, [2002] 1 FCR 150, [2002] 1 FLR 196, [2002] Fam Law 168 6-3434

B (a child) (adoption order), Re [2001] EWCA Civ 347, [2001] 2 FCR 89, [2001] 2 FLR 26, [2001] Fam Law 492 6-1349

B (children) (abduction: new evidence) [2001] EWCA Civ 625, [2001] 2 FCR 531 6-1805D

B (interim care order: renewal), Re [2001] 2 FLR 1217, [2001] Fam Law 802 6-170A

B (a child: interim care order), Re [2002] EWCA Civ 25, [2002] 2 FCR 367, [2002] 1 FLR 545, [2002] Fam Law 252, 146 Sol Jo LB 36, [2002] All ER (D) 29 (Jan) 6-170A

B (children) (residence: interim care order), Re [2002] EWCA Civ 1225, [2002] 3 FCR 562 6-37

B (children: non-accidental injury), Re [2002] EWCA Civ 902, [2002] 2 FCR 654, [2002] 2 FLR 599, [2002] Fam Law 655, [2002] All ER (D) 452 (May)sub nom O and N (children) (non-accidental injury: burden of proof), Re [2002] EWCA Civ 1271, [2002] 3 FCR 418, [2002] Fam Law 1181, [2002] 2 FLR 1167, [2002] All ER (D) 401 (Jul); on appeal sub nom O and N (children) (non accidental injury), Re; Re B (children) (non accidental injury) [2003] UKHL 18, [2004] 1 AC 523, [2003] 2 All ER 305, [2003] 2 WLR 1075, [2003] 1 FCR 673, [2003] 1 FLR 1169, [2003] 23 LS Gaz R 36, (2003) Times, 4 April, [2003] All ER (D) 64 (Apr) 6-165

B (a child) (care proceedings: diplomatic immunity), Re [2002] EWHC 1751 (Fam), [2003] Fam 16, [2003] 2 WLR 168, [2003] 1 FLR 241, [2003] Fam Law 8, [2002] 41 LS Gaz R 27 6-164

B (disclosure to other parties), Re [2002] 2 FCR 32, [2001] 2 FLR 1017, [2001] Fam Law 798 6-29

B (children) (care proceedings: disclosure) [2002] JPN 903, [2002] All ER (D) 167 (Nov), CA 6-29

B (a child) (immunisation), Re [2003] EWCA Civ 1148, [2003] 3 FCR 156, [2003] 2 FLR 1095, 73 BMLR 152, 147 Sol Jo LB 934 4-154

B (children) (removal from jurisdiction), Re [2003] EWCA Civ 1149, [2003] 2 FCR 673, [2003] 2 FLR 1043, [2003] Fam Law 820 6-156

B (children) (care: interference with family life), Re [2003] EWCA Civ 786, [2004] 1 FCR 463, [2003] 2 FLR 813, (2003) Times, 1 July, [2003] All ER (D) 286 (May) 6-170

B (children) (adoption: removal from jurisdiction), Re [2004] EWCA Civ 515, [2004] 2 FCR 129, [2004] All ER (D) 305 (Apr), sub nom A (adoption: placement outside jurisdiction), Re [2005] Fam 105, [2004] 3 WLR 1207, [2004] 2 FLR 337, [2004] Fam Law 560, sub nom B v Birmingham City Council (2004) Times, 10 June 6-2312

B (a child: court's jurisdiction), Re [2004] EWCA Civ 681, [2004] 2 FCR 391, [2004] 2 FLR 741, [2004] All ER (D) 433 (May) 6-1813 6-1835

B (a child) (serious injury: standard of proof). See U (a child) (serious injury: standard of proof), Re

B (care proceedings: notification of father without parental responsibility), Re. See K (care proceedings: joinder of father), Re

B (a child) (immunisation), Re. See C and F (children) (immunisation), Re [2003] EWHC 1376

B v B [1994] 1 FCR 809, [1994] 2 FLR 713, [1994] Fam Law 377 6-19 , 6-24

B v B (minors) [1994] 2 FCR 667, [1994] 2 FLR 489, [1994] 21 LS Gaz R 40, CA 6-142

B v B [1995] 1 WLR 440, [1995] 1 FCR 763, [1995] 1 FLR 459, [1995] Fam Law 233 6-2114, 6-2233, 4-2266

B v B (financial provision for child) [1998] 1 FCR 49, [1998] 1 FLR 373, [1998] Fam Law 131, CA 6-960

B v B (a child) (residence order: condition) [2004] 2 FLR 979, [2004] Fam Law 651, (2004) Times, 7 July, [2004] All ER (D) 387 (May) 6-2110

B (B) v B (M) [1969] P 103, [1969] 1 All ER 891, [1969] 2 WLR 862, 133 JP 245 6-431-2113

B v Birmingham City Council. See B (children) (adoption: removal from jurisdiction), Re

B v C [1995] 2 FCR 678, [1995] 1 FLR 467, [1995] Fam Law 243 1-2158

B v Chief Constable of Avon and Somerset Constabulary [2001] 1 All ER 562, [2001] 1 WLR 340 3-528C, 6-165, 8-17631W

B v Derbyshire County Council [1992] 2 FCR 14, [1992] 1 FLR 538, [1992] Fam Law 287 1-449

B (a minor) v DPP [2000] 2 AC 428, [2000] 1 All ER 833, [2000] 2 WLR 452, [2000] 2 Cr App Rep 65, [2000] Crim LR 403, [2000] 11 LS Gaz R 36, 144 Sol Jo LB 108, HL 8-27981, 8-28180

B v H (children: habitual residence) [2002] 2 FCR 329, [2002] 1 FLR 388, [2002] Fam Law 101 6-1813

B v K [1993] 1 FCR 382, [1993] Fam Law 17 6-1805E

B (a minor) v Knight [1981] RTR 136 4-6

B v United Kingdom (1987) 10 EHRR 87 6-173, 6-2143

B v United Kingdom [2000] 1 FCR 289, [2000] 1 FLR 1, [2000] Fam Law 88, ECtHR 6-11

B v United Kingdom [2000] 2 FCR 97, ECtHR 6-11

B and T (care proceedings: legal representation), Re [2001] 1 FCR 512, [2001] 1 FLR 485, [2001] Fam Law 180, CA 6-164A

BC (a minor) (care order: appropriate local authority), Re [1995] 3 FCR 598 6-2140

B-J (a child) (non-molestation order: power of arrest), Re [2001] Fam 415, [2001] 1 All ER 235, [2001] 2 WLR 1660, [2000] 2 FCR 599, [2000] 2 FLR 443, [2000] Fam Law 807, CA 6-134, 6-3095

B-M (a child) (adoption: parental agreement), Re [2001] 1 FCR 1, CA 6-1355

Babbage v North Norfolk District Council (1988) 153 JP 278, 57 P & CR 237 8-30894

Back v Dick Kerr & Co Ltd [1906] AC 325, 75 LJKB 569, 94 LT 802, 22 TLR 548, 8 WCC 40, HL 8-14683

Back v Holmes (1887) 51 JP 693 1-7427

PARA

PARA

PARA

Belasco v Hannant (1862) 26 JP 823, 3 B & S 13, 31 LJMC 225, 9 Cox CC 203, 8 Jur NS 1226, 10 WR 867, 6 LT 577 6-780
Belgium (Government of) v Postlethwaite [1988] AC 924, [1987] 3 WLR 365, [1987] Crim LR 569; revsd [1988] AC 924, [1987] 2 All ER 985, [1987] 3 WLR 365, 131 Sol Jo 1038, [1987] NLJ Rep 666, [1987] LS Gaz R 2449, HL 8-10195
Belgian Linguistics Case (1967) 1 EHRR 241 . . . . . 8-17631V
Bell, Re (1892) 8 TLR 785 1-761
Bell v Alfred Franks & Barlett Co Ltd [1980] 1 All ER 356, [1980] 1 WLR 340, 123 Sol Jo 804, 39 P & CR 591, 253 Estates Gazette 903 8-28010
Bell v Graham [1907] 2 KB 112, 71 JP 270, 70 LJKB 690, 97 LT 52, 23 TLR 435, 5 LGR 738, 21 for CC 401 8-7824
Bellencontre, Re [1891] 2 QB 122, 60 LJMC 83, 64 LT 461, 55 JP 694, 39 WR 381, 7 TLR 315, 17 Cox CC 253 8-10195
Bellerby v Carle [1983] 2 AC 101, [1983] 1 All ER 1031, [1983] 2 WLR 687, 127 Sol Jo 272, 81 LGR 425, HL 8-31830
Bellerby v Heyworth [1910] AC 377, 74 JP 257, 79 LJ Ch 402, 102 LT 545, 26 TLR 403, 54 Sol Jo 441, HL 8-2027
Benham v United Kingdom (1996) 22 EHRR 293, ECtHR 1-116, 1-600, 1-620, 8-17631W
Benn v Kamm & Co Ltd [1952] 2 QB 127, [1952] 1 All ER 833, [1952] 1 TLR 873, CA 8-14617
Bennett v Bennett [1951] 2 KB 572, [1951] 1 All ER 1088, 115 JP 355, [1951] 1 TLR 873, 95 Sol Jo 286; affd [1952] 1 KB 249, [1952] 1 All ER 413, [1952] 1 TLR 400, CA 6-961A
Bennett v Brown (1980) 71 Cr App Rep 109 8-10446
Bennett v Markham [1982] 3 All ER 641, [1982] 1 WLR 1230, 126 Sol Jo 511, 81 LGR 60, [1982] LS Gaz R 1176 8-31860
Bennett v Richardson [1980] RTR 358 4-6
Bennington v Peter [1984] RTR 383 7-1528
Bensing v Ramsay (1898) 62 JP 613, 14 TLR 345 8-16727
Bensley v Smith [1972] RTR 221, [1972] Crim LR 239 2-34
Benson v Boyce [1997] RTR 226 . . . . . 8-18968, 8-19002
Benson v Northern Ireland Road Transport Board [1942] AC 520, [1942] 1 All ER 465, 111 LJPC 1, 167 LT 408, [1942] NI 61 . . . . . 1-760, 1-821
Bent v Ormerod [1901] 2 KB 290, 65 JP 646, 70 LJKB 747, 84 LT 719, 49 WR 684, 17 TLR 503, 45 Sol Jo 504, 19 Cox CC 725 8-12241
Benthem v Netherlands (1985) 8 EHRR 1, ECtHR 6-200
Bentley v Brudzinski (1982) 75 Cr App Rep 217, [1982] Crim LR 825 8-23824
Bentley v Dickinson (1983) 147 JP 526, [1983] RTR 356, [1983] Crim LR 403, CA 4-1643
Bentley v Mullen [1986] RTR 7 4-1596
Beresford v St Albans Justices (1905) 22 TLR 1 4-1198
Bergin v Bergin [1983] 1 All ER 905, [1983] 1 WLR 279, 147 JP 118, 4 FLR 344, 126 Sol Jo 624 . 6-63
Berkeley v Orchard (1975) 119 Sol Jo 353, [1975] Crim LR 225 3-1690
Berkhamsted RDC v Duerdin-Dutton (1964) 108 Sol Jo 157, [1964] Crim LR 307 . 1-582, 1-753, 2-190
Berkshire County Council v B [1997] 3 FCR 88, [1997] 1 FLR 171, [1997] Fam Law 234 . 6-167, 6-173
Berkshire County Council v Olympic Holidays Ltd (1993) 158 JP 421, [1994] Crim LR 277 . 8-5040
Bernstein v O'Neill [1989] FCR 79, [1989] 2 FLR 1, [1989] Fam Law 275 1-2158
Berridge v Vision Posters Ltd (1994) 159 LG Rev 229, 159 JP 218, sub nom Waverley District Council v Vision Posters Ltd [1994] Crim LR 940 8-31220
Berry v Berry [1987] Fam 1, [1986] 2 All ER 948, [1986] 3 WLR 257, 150 JP 319, [1987] 1 FLR 105, [1986] Fam Law 304, 130 Sol Jo 573, [1986] NLJ Rep 537, [1986] LS Gaz R 3837, CA 1-2158, 6-376, 6-1529
Berryman v Wise (1791) 4 Term Rep 366 . . . . . 2-619, 8-23824
Best Travel Co Ltd v Patterson (1986) 151 JP 619, [1987] BTLC 119 8-4457
Betts v Betts (1917) 33 TLR 200 2-72
Betts v Stevens [1910] 1 KB 1, 73 JP 486, 79 LJKB 17, 101 LT 564, 26 TLR 5, 22 Cox CC 187, 7 LGR 1052 . . . . . 1-768, 1-831, 4-1198, 8-23824
Bevan v Bevan (1923) 87 JP Jo 452 . . . . . 6-72, 6-74
Bevan v Bevan [1955] 3 All ER 332, 119 JP 576, 99 Sol Jo 782 4-74
Bezicheri v Italy (1989) 12 EHRR 210, ECtHR 1-436, 1-465, 1-1560, 1-1579
Bibby v Chief Constable of Essex [2000] RA 384, 164 JP 297, CA 1-183
Bidie, Re, Bidie v General Accident Fire and Life Assurance Corpn Ltd [1948] Ch 697, [1948] 1 All ER 885, 112 JP 257, [1948] LJR 1219, 64 TLR 309, 92 Sol Jo 310, 46 LGR 313; affd [1949] Ch 121, [1948] 2 All ER 995, 113 JP 22, [1949] LJR 386, 65 TLR 25, 92 Sol Jo 705, 47 LGR 465, CA 6-1543
Billington v Billington [1974] Fam 24, [1974] 1 All ER 546, [1974] 2 WLR 53, 138 JP 228, 118 Sol Jo 66 1-1394
Bilon v WH Smith Trading Ltd [2001] EWHC Admin 469, (2001) 165 JP 701, [2001] Crim LR 850 . . . . . 8-30400A
Bindley v Willett [1981] RTR 19 4-3651
Bingham v Bruce [1962] 1 All ER 136, [1962] 1 WLR 70, 126 JP 81, 105 Sol Jo 1086, 60 LGR 79 . . . . . 4-120, 4-916, 4-1212, 4-1598
Binks v Department of the Environment (1975) 119 Sol Jo 304, [1975] RTR 318, [1975] Crim LR 244 4-3
Binks (Maurice) (Turf Accountants) Ltd v Huss [1971] 1 All ER 104, [1971] 1 WLR 52, 135 JP 148, 114 Sol Jo 930 8-13311

PARA

Bond v Chief Constable of Kent [1983] 1 All ER 456, [1983] 1 WLR 40, 147 JP 107, 126 Sol Jo 707, 4 Cr App Rep (S) 324, [1983] Crim LR 166, [1983] LS Gaz R 29 . . . 3-203, 3-1690

Bond v Evans (1888) 21 QBD 249, 52 JP 613, 57 LJMC 105, 16 Cox CC 461, 36 WR 767, [1886-90] All ER Rep 1035, 59 LT 411, 4 TLR 614 . . . 6-777, 6-782

Bone, Re (1994) 159 JP 111 . . . 1-3447

Bonhote v Bonhote [1920] WN 142, 89 LJP 140, 123 LT 174 . . . 6-51

Boniface v Harris (1983) 147 JP 208, 13 Fam Law 117 . . . 1-2102, 1-2110

Boodle v Birmingham Justices (1881) 45 JP 635 . . . 6-566

Booth v DPP [1993] RTR 379 . . . 7-1986, 4-2009ZM

Booth v Howell (1889) 53 JP 678, 5 TLR 449 . . . 8-18835

Boots Cash Chemists (Southern) Ltd v Cowling (1903) 67 JP 195, 88 LT 539, 19 TLR 370, 1 LGR 885, 20 Cox CC 420 . . . 8-12248

Borthwick v Vickers [1973] RTR 390, [1973] Crim LR 317 . . . 2-34

Bosley v Bosley [1958] 2 All ER 167, [1958] 1 WLR 645, 102 Sol Jo 437, CA . . . 6-70

Bosley v Davies (1875) 1 QBD 84, 40 JP 550, 45 LJMC 27, 24 WR 140, [1874-80] All ER Rep 1284, 33 LT 528 . . . 6-777, 6-782

Bosley v Long [1970] 3 All ER 286, [1970] 1 WLR 1410, 114 Sol Jo 571, [1976] RTR 432 . . . 4-1379A

Boss v Kingston [1963] 1 All ER 177, [1963] 1 WLR 99, 106 Sol Jo 1053, 61 LGR 109, [1962] 2 Lloyd's Rep 431 . . . 4-1562

Boss v Measures (1989) 87 LGR 667, [1990] RTR 26, [1989] Crim LR 582 . . . 4-1212

Boston v Boston (1928) 92 JP 44, 138 LT 647, 26 LGR 183 . . . 6-80

Bothamley v Danby (1871) 36 JP 135, 24 LT 656 . . . 7-6028

Botross v Hammersmith and Fulham London Borough Council (1994) 16 Cr App Rep (S) 622, 27 HLR 179 . . . 8-26310

Bottomley, ex p [1909] 2 KB 14, 73 JP 246, 78 LJKB 547, 100 LT 782, 25 TLR 371, 22 Cox CC 106 . . . 1-46

Bottomley v Harrison [1952] 1 All ER 368, 116 JP 113, 96 Sol Jo 90, 50 LGR 172, 159 Estates Gazette 164 . . . 8-17186

Botwood v Phillips [1976] RTR 260, [1976] Crim LR 68 . . . 4-5

Boucher v R [1951] 2 DLR 369 . . . 8-6391

Boucher v Rowsell [1947] 1 All ER 870, 45 LGR 405 . . . 8-13601

Bound v Lawrence [1892] 1 QB 226, 56 JP 118, 61 LJMC 21, 65 LT 844, 40 WR 1, 8 TLR 1, 36 Sol Jo 11, CA . . . 8-14683

Bourke v Davis (1889) 44 Ch D 110, 62 LT 34, 38 WR 167, 6 TLR 87 . . . 8-30733

Bourlet v Porter [1973] 2 All ER 800, [1973] 1 WLR 866, 137 JP 649, 117 Sol Jo 489, 58 Cr App Rep 1, [1973] RTR 293, [1974] Crim LR 53, HL . . . 4-1379A

Bourne v Mendip Concrete Co Ltd (1941) 85 Sol Jo 248 . . . 8-14617

Bourne v Swan and Edgar Ltd, Re Bourne's Trade-Marks [1903] 1 Ch 211, 72 LJ Ch 168, 51 WR 213, 19 TLR 59, 47 Sol Jo 92, 20 RPC 105 . . . 2-205

Bourrasse (criminal proceedings against): C-228, 289/01 [2002] ECR I-10213, [2003] All ER (EC) 465, [2003] RTR 335, ECJ . . . 4-2314

Bowen v Bowen (1908) 73 JP 87 . . . 6-71

Bowen v Jones (1917) 81 JP 178, 86 LJKB 802, 117 LT 125, 15 LGR 517, 25 Cox CC 757 . . . 8-12248

Bowers v Worthington [1982] RTR 400 . . . 7-4040

Bowker v Premier Drug Co [1928] 1 KB 217, 91 JP 118, 96 LJKB 750, 137 LT 347, 43 TLR 516, 25 LGR 306, 28 Cox CC 397 . . . 1-321, 8-12248

Bowker v Woodroffe [1928] 1 KB 217, [1927] All ER Rep 415, 91 JP 118, 96 LJKB 750, 137 LT 347, 43 TLR 516, 25 LGR 306, 28 Cox CC 397 . . . 8-12248

Bowman v DPP [1991] RTR 263 . . . 4-1375

Bowman v Fels [2005] EWCA Civ 226, [2005] 4 All ER 609, [2005] 1 WLR 3083, [2005] 2 Cr App Rep 243, [2005] 2 FLR 247, [2005] Fam Law 546, [2005] NLJR 413, (2005) Times, 14 March, 149 Sol Jo LB 357, [2005] All ER (D) 115 (Mar) . . . 3-1862

Bowman v United Kingdom (1998) 26 EHRR 1, ECtHR . . . 8-7977

Bowron v Bowron [1925] P 187, 89 JP 43, 94 LJP 33, 132 LT 773, 41 TLR 245, 69 Sol Jo 325, 27 Cox CC 769, 23 LGR 223, CA . . . 6-64, 6-74

Boxsius v Goblet Frères [1894] 1 QB 842, 58 JP 670, 63 LJQB 401, 70 LT 368, 42 WR 392, 10 TLR 324, 38 Sol Jo 311, 9 R 224 . . . 8-18632

Boyce v Higgins (1853) 14 CB 1, 17 JP 808, 2 CLR 95, 23 LJCP 5, 22 LTOS 103, 18 Jur 333, 2 WR 73 . . . 8-25225

Boyd v Boyd [1938] WN 336, [1938] 4 All ER 181, 102 JP 525, 108 LJP 25, 159 LT 522, 55 TLR 3, 82 Sol Jo 912, 37 LGR 50 . . . 6-76

Boyd Ltd v Bilham [1909] 1 KB 14, 72 JP 495, 78 LJKB 50, 99 LT 780 . . . 8-16719

Boyle v Wiseman (1855) 10 Exch 647, 24 LJ Ex 160, 24 LTOS 274, 1 Jur NS 115, 3 WR 206, 3 CLR 482 . . . 2-330

Brabham v Wookey (1901) 18 TLR 99 . . . 8-18835, 8-31345A

Bracegirdle v Oxley [1947] KB 349, [1947] 1 All ER 126, 111 JP 131, [1947] LJR 815, 176 LT 187, 63 TLR 98, 91 Sol Jo 27, 45 LGR 69 . . . 1-765, 1-827

Bradford v Wilson (1983) 147 JP 573, 78 Cr App Rep 77, [1984] RTR 116, [1983] Crim LR 482 . . . 4-1375

Bradford Metropolitan District Council v Booth (2000) 164 JP 485 . . . 1-644, 1-805

Bradlaugh v Clarke (1883) 8 App Cas 354, 47 JP 405, 52 LJQB 505, 31 WR 677, 48 LT 681, HL . . . 6-810

Bradley v Baylis (1881) 8 QBD 195, 45 JP 847, 51 LJQB 183, 46 LT 253, 30 WR 823 . . . 8-16727

Bradley v Bradley [1973] 2 All ER 750, [1973] 1 WLR 1291, 117 Sol Jo 632, CA . . . 6-63

PARA

Bradley v Moss [1974] Crim LR 430 8-22630
Bradshaw v Bradshaw [1897] P 24, 61 JP 8, 66 LJP 31, 75 LT 391, 45 WR 143, 13 TLR 82 6-64, 6-65
Bradshaw v Bradshaw [1956] P 274n, [1955] 3 WLR 965n, 99 Sol Jo 890 . . . 6-51
Braham v DPP (1994) 159 JP 527 . . . . 1-768, 1-831
Braintree District Council v Howard [1993] RTR 193 8-18997
Brandas v Barnett (1846) 3 CB 519, [1843-60] All ER Rep 719, 12 Cl & Fin 787, 7 LTOS 525, HL 2-33
Brandon v Barnes [1966] 3 All ER 296, [1966] 1 WLR 1505, 130 JP 389, 110 Sol Jo 669, 64 LGR 456 . . . . 7-6009, 8-31345A
Brasman v Brasman (1975) 5 Fam Law 85 6-1493
Bratty v A-G for Northern Ireland [1963] AC 386, [1961] 3 All ER 523, 105 Sol Jo 865, 46 Cr App Rep 1, HL 1-308
Breed v British Drug Houses Ltd [1947] 2 All ER 613, 112 JP 36, 63 TLR 558, 46 LGR 11 8-12248
Breed v Cluett [1970] 2 QB 459, [1970] 2 All ER 662, [1970] 3 WLR 76, 134 JP 570, 114 Sol Jo 453, 215 Estates Gazette 89 8-4457
Bremme v Duberry [1964] 1 All ER 193, [1964] 1 WLR 119, 128 JP 148, 107 Sol Jo 911 7-7043
Brentwood Borough Council v Gladen [2004] EWHC 2500 (Admin), [2005] RTR 152, (2004) Times, 1 November, [2004] All ER (D) 405 (Oct) 8-18968
Bretherton v United Kingdom Totalisator Co Ltd [1945] KB 555, [1945] 2 All ER 202, 110 JP 45, 114 LJKB 517, 173 LT 126, 61 TLR 468, 89 Sol Jo 414, 43 LGR 169 8-13601M
Brewer v Brewer [1962] P 69, [1961] 3 All ER 957, [1961] 3 WLR 1208, 105 Sol Jo 948, CA 6-74
Brewer v DPP [2004] EWHC 355 (Admin), [2005] RTR 5, (2004) Times, 5 March, [2004] All ER (D) 165 (Feb) 4-5
Brewer v Metropolitan Police Comr [1969] 1 All ER 513, [1969] 1 WLR 267, 133 JP 185, 112 Sol Jo 1022, 53 Cr App Rep 157 4-1680
Brewster v Brewster [1971] 2 All ER 993, [1971] 1 WLR 1102, 135 JP 501, 115 Sol Jo 346 1-2123
Brewster v Sewell (1820) 3 B & Ald 2962-196
Brierley v Brierley and Williams [1918] P 257, 87 LJP 153, 119 LT 343, 34 TLR 458, 62 Sol Jo 704 2-193
Briffet v DPP [2001] EWHC Admin 841, (2001) 166 JP 66, [2002] EMLR 203 . . 5-23, 5-105
Briggs v Swanwick (1883) 10 QBD 510, 47 JP 564, 53 LJMC 63, 31 WR 565 . . . 8-11279
Bright v Ashfold [1932] 2 KB 153, 96 JP 182, 101 LJKB 318, 147 LT 74, 48 TLR 357, 76 Sol Jo 344, 30 LGR 212, 29 Cox CC 455, 43 Ll L Rep 25 4-1565
Brighton and Hove City Council v Woolworth plc [2002] EWHC 2565 (Admin), (2002) 167 JP 21 8-5005
Brighton Stipendiary Magistrate, Re (1893) 9 TLR 522 1-445
Brighty v Pearson [1938] 4 All ER 127, 102 JP 522, 159 LT 619, 82 Sol Jo 910, 36 LGR 664 4-1198
Brigstocke v Rayner (1875) 40 JP 245 . . . . 8-13605, 8-13606
Brinkley v Brinkley [1965] P 75, [1963] 1 All ER 493, [1963] 2 WLR 822, 127 JP 197, 107 Sol Jo 77 2-460
Briscoe v Briscoe [1968] P 501, [1966] 1 All ER 465, [1966] 2 WLR 205, 130 JP 124, 109 Sol Jo 996 . . . . 1-582, 1-753
Briscoe v Shattock [1999] 1 WLR 432, 163 JP 201, [1999] Crim LR 396 . . . 8-7510
Bristol and West Building Society v Hichmott (1980) 144 JP 443 1-766
Bristol Corpn v Sinnott [1917] 2 Ch 340, 81 JP 258; affd [1918] 1 Ch 62, 82 JP 9, 87 LJ Ch 30, 117 LT 644, 62 Sol Jo 53, 15 LGR 871, CA 8-25219
Bristol Corpn v Virgin [1928] 2 KB 622, 92 JP 145, 97 LJKB 522, 139 LT 375, 44 TLR 546, 26 LGR 443 8-25220
Bristow v Cormican (1878) 3 App Cas 641, HL 8-30733
Bristow v Piper [1915] 1 KB 271, 79 JP 177, 84 LJKB 607, 24 Cox CC 553, [1914-15] All ER Rep 1090, 59 Sol Jo 178, 221, 112 LT 426, 31 TLR 80 6-636
Britain v ABC Cabs (Camberley) Ltd [1981] RTR 395 8-18968
British Airways Board v Taylor [1976] 1 All ER 65, [1976] 1 WLR 13, 140 JP 96, 120 Sol Jo 7, [1976] 1 Lloyd's Rep 167, HL 8-4457
British Amusement Catering Trades Association v Westminster City Council [1987] 2 All ER 897, [1987] 1 WLR 977, 131 Sol Jo 941, 86 LGR 1, [1987] 8 TLC 279, [1987] LS Gaz R 1881, CA; affd [1989] AC 147, [1988] 1 All ER 740, [1988] 2 WLR 485, 132 Sol Jo 374, 86 LGR 312, [1988] NLJR 72, [1988] 14 LS Gaz R 49, HL 8-30540
British Car Auctions Ltd v Wright [1972] 3 All ER 462, [1972] 1 WLR 1519, 116 Sol Jo 583, [1972] RTR 540 . . . . 4-1468, 8-11261
British Gas Corpn v Lubbock [1974] 1 All ER 188, [1974] 1 WLR 37, 138 JP 198, 117 Sol Jo 833, 72 LGR 231 8-4448
British Railway Traffic and Electric Lighting Co v CRC Co and LCC [1922] 2 KB 260, 86 JP 70, 91 LJKB 824, 126 LT 602, 38 TLR 190, 20 LGR 102 7-4002
British Railways Board v Liptrot [1969] 1 AC 136, [1967] 2 All ER 1072, [1967] 3 WLR 770, 111 Sol Jo 516, HL 8-14617
British Road Services Ltd v Owen [1971] 2 All ER 999, 135 JP 399, 115 Sol Jo 267, [1971] RTR 372 4-3651
British Telecommunications plc v Nottinghamshire County Council [1999] Crim LR 217 1-387, 7-6162
Broadbent v Broadbent [1927] WN 45, 43 TLR 186 6-80
Broadbent v High (1984) 149 JP 115, [1985] RTR 359 1-460
Bromilley v Bromilley [1987] 2 FLR 207, [1987] Fam Law 165 6-376
Bromilow v Bromilow (1976) 7 Fam Law 16 6-1493

PARA

Budge v Parsons (1863) 3 B & S 382, 27 JP 231, 32 LJMC 95, 1 New Rep 268, 7 LT 784, 9 Jur NS 796, 11 WR 424 — 8-825

Bugge v Taylor [1941] 1 KB 198, 104 JP 467, 110 LJKB 710, 164 LT 312, 85 Sol Jo 82, 39 LGR 100 — 4-5

Bull v Bull [1953] P 224, [1953] 2 All ER 601, [1953] 3 WLR 326, 117 JP 415, 97 Sol Jo 489, CA — 6-79

Bullivant v Bullivant (1902) 18 TLR 317 — 6-81, 6-1492

Bullock v Bullock [1960] 2 All ER 307, [1960] 1 WLR 975, 104 Sol Jo 685 — 6-51

Bulmer (HP) Ltd v J Bollinger SA [1974] 2 All ER 1226, [1974] 3 WLR 202, 118 Sol Jo 404, [1974] 2 CMLR 91, CA — 1-1431

Bunting v British Railways Board (18 November 1971, unreported) — 7-6009

Burden v Harris [1937] 4 All ER 559, 54 TLR 86, 81 Sol Jo 924 — 8-30720

Burden v Rigler [1911] 1 KB 337, 75 JP 36, 80 LJKB 100, 103 LT 758, 27 TLR 140, 9 LGR 71 — 8-27680

Burditt v Joslin [1981] 3 All ER 203, 146 JP 39 — 8-10405, 8-10405A

Burfitt v A & E Killie [1939] 2 KB 743, [1939] 2 All ER 372, 108 LJKB 669, 160 LT 481, 55 TLR 645, 83 Sol Jo 419, 37 LGR 394 — 8-10419

Burge v DPP [1962] 1 All ER 666n, [1962] 1 WLR 265, 106 Sol Jo 198 — 8-28008, 8-28160

Burgess v Bennett (1872) 20 WR 720 — 2-72

Burgess v Home Office [2001] 1 WLR 93, 144 Sol Jo LB 280, CA — 1-1108

Burgess v West [1982] RTR 269, [1982] Crim LR 235 — 4-1680

Burgoyne v Phillips (1982) 147 JP 375, [1983] RTR 49, [1983] Crim LR 265 — 4-8

Burke v Copper [1962] 2 All ER 14, [1962] 1 WLR 700, 126 JP 319, 106 Sol Jo 451 — 1-765, 1-827, 8-22451

Burmingham v Lindsell [1936] 2 All ER 159, 80 Sol Jo 367 — 4-128 4-1619

Burnell v British Transport Commission [1956] 1 QB 187, [1955] 3 All ER 822, [1956] 2 WLR 61, 100 Sol Jo 33, [1955] 2 Lloyd's Rep 549, CA — 2-72

Burns v Bidder [1967] 2 QB 227, [1966] 3 All ER 29, [1966] 3 WLR 99, 130 JP 342, 110 Sol Jo 430 — 4-2933

Burns v Currell [1963] 2 QB 433, [1963] 2 All ER 297, [1963] 2 WLR 1106, 127 JP 397, 107 Sol Jo 272, 61 LGR 356 — 4-3

Burns v Joseph Terry & Sons Ltd [1951] 1 KB 454, [1950] 2 All ER 987, 114 JP 613, [1951] 1 TLR 349, 94 Sol Jo 837, 49 LGR 161, CA — 8-14615

Burns v Scholfield (1922) 87 JP 54, 128 LT 382, 21 LGR 39, 27 Cox CC 378 — 6-632

Burridge v Burridge [1983] Fam 9, [1982] 3 All ER 80, [1982] 3 WLR 552, 12 Fam Law 152, 126 Sol Jo 276 — 6-1492

Burridge v East (1986) 150 JP 347, [1986] RTR 328n, [1986] Crim LR 632 — 7-581

Burrough v Higgins [1936] BTRLR 55 — 6-632

Burrows v Gillingham (1893) 57 JP 423 — 8-13670

Burt v Kirkcaldy [1965] 1 All ER 741, [1965] 1 WLR 474, 129 JP 190, 109 Sol Jo 33 — 2-1216, 4-1642

Burton v Hudson [1909] 2 KB 564, 73 JP 401, 78 LJKB 905, 25 TLR 641 — 1-385

Burton v Plummer (1834) 2 Ad & El 341, 4 Nev & MKB 315, 4 LJKB 53 — 2-72

Bury v Bury (1919) 35 TLR 220, 63 Sol Jo 228 — 6-51

Bushell v Hammond [1904] 2 KB 563, 68 JP 370, 73 LJKB 1005, 52 WR 453, 91 LT 1, 20 TLR 413, CA — 6-121, 6-571, 6-573

Bussey v DPP [1999] 1 Cr App Rep (S) 125, [1998] Crim LR 908 — 1-761, 1-822

Butcher v Catterall (1975) 119 Sol Jo 508, 61 Cr App Rep 221, [1975] RTR 436, [1975] Crim LR 463 — 4-1377A

Butler v Board of Trade [1971] Ch 680, [1970] 3 All ER 593, [1970] 3 WLR 822, 114 Sol Jo 604 — 2-331

Butler v Butler [1917] P 244, 86 LJP 135, 117 LT 542, 33 TLR 494, 61 Sol Jo 631 — 6-78

Butler v DPP [1990] RTR 377 — 4-1655

Butler v DPP [2001] RTR 430, [2001] Crim LR 580 — 4-1378, 4-1379A

Butler v Ford (1833) 1 Cr & M 662, 3 Tyr 677, 2 LJMC 109 — 8-23824

Butler v Glacier Metal Co Ltd (23 October 1924, unreported) — 8-14616

Butler v Gravesend Urban Authority (1894) 58 JP 446 — 8-25215

Butler v Manchester Sheffield and Lincolnshire Rly Co (1888) 21 QBD 207, 52 JP 612, 57 LJQB 564, 60 LT 89, 36 WR 726 — 7-7043, 7-7127

Butterworth v Shorthose [1956] Crim LR 341 — 4-3659

Buxton v Chief Constable of Northumbria (1983) 148 JP 9 — 6-773A

Byrne v Low [1972] 3 All ER 526, [1972] 1 WLR 1282, 116 Sol Jo 762 — 8-6678

Byrne v United Kingdom (1998) EHRLR 626 — 1-643, 1-800, 1-2910

C

C (a minor), Re [1987] 2 FLR 383, [1988] Fam Law 13, CA; revsd [1989] AC 1, [1988] 1 All ER 705, [1988] 2 WLR 474, [1988] FCR 484, [1988] 2 FLR 159, [1988] Fam Law 428, 132 Sol Jo 334, [1988] NLJR 64, [1988] 15 LS Gaz R 35, HL — 6-1349

C, Re (1989) Times, 14 November — 1-2566

C (a minor), Re [1992] 2 FCR 341 — 6-26, 6-141, 6-170, 6-2100, 6-4406

C (a minor), Re [1993] Fam 210, [1993] 3 All ER 259, [1993] 3 WLR 85, [1993] 2 FLR 431, [1993] Fam Law 566 — 6-2109

C (minors), Re [1993] 4 All ER 690, sub nom C v C [1993] 1 FCR 820, [1993] 1 FLR 220, [1993] Fam Law 223, CA — 6-37

C, Re [1994] 2 FCR 1153, [1994] 2 FLR 922 [1995] Fam Law 19 — 6-2134

PARA

PARA

Campbell v Wallsend Slipway and Engineering Co Ltd [1978] ICR 1015, 121 Sol Jo 334, [1977] Crim LR 351 . . . 8-15304
Campbell and Fell v United Kingdom (1984) 7 EHRR 165, ECtHR . . . 1-37
Canada Southern Rly Co v International Bridge Co (1883) 8 App Cas 723, PC . . . 2-742
Cann v Cann [1977] 3 All ER 957, [1977] 1 WLR 938, 7 Fam Law 141, 121 Sol Jo 528 . . . 6-1493
Cannan v Earl of Abingdon [1900] 2 QB 66, 64 JP 504, 69 LJQB 517, 82 LT 382, 48 WR 470, 16 TLR 318, 44 Sol Jo 395 . . . 7-5958
Cannon Street (No 20) Ltd v Singer and Friedlander Ltd [1974] Ch 229, [1974] 2 All ER 577, [1974] 2 WLR 646, 118 Sol Jo 133, 27 P & CR 486, 230 Estates Gazette 1431, 1583 . . . 2-1215
Cant v Harley & Sons Ltd [1938] 2 All ER 768, 36 LGR 465 . . . 8-22450
Caradon District Council v Cheeseman [2000] Crim LR 190 . . . 8-19296
Carasu Ltd v Smith [1968] 2 QB 383, [1968] 2 All ER 529, [1968] 2 WLR 1354, 112 Sol Jo 329 . . . 8-29591
Caravans and Automobiles Ltd v Southall Borough Council [1963] 2 All ER 533, [1963] 1 WLR 690, 127 JP 415, 107 Sol Jo 375, 61 LGR 365, 186 Estates Gazette 717, [1963] RVR 408 . . . 8-31036
Cardiff Revenue Officer v Cardiff Assessment Committee [1931] 1 KB 47, 94 JP 146, 99 LJKB 672, 143 LT 500, 46 TLR 499, 74 Sol Jo 466, 28 LGR 372, [1926-31] 2 BRA 542 . . . 8-14683
Carew-Hunt v Carew-Hunt (1972) Times, 28 June . . . 6-63
Carey v Bexhill Corpn [1904] 1 KB 142, 68 JP 78, 73 LJKB 74, 90 LT 58 . . . 7-6072
Carey v Heath [1952] 1 KB 62, [1951] 2 All ER 774, 115 JP 577, [1951] 2 TLR 797, 50 LGR 227 . . . 7-526, 4-1971
Carey, Smithers v DPP [1989] Crim LR 368, [1989] COD 401 . . . 6-663
Carlin v Carlin (1906) 70 JP 143 . . . 6-51
Carlyle Finance Ltd v Pallas Industrial Finance (Burgess (t/a John Burgess Car Sales), third party) (Wise (t/a HRG Car Sales), fourth party [1999]1 All ER (Comm) 659, [1999] RTR 281, CA . . . 8-4420
Carnill v Rowland [1953] 1 All ER 486, [1953] 1 WLR 380, 117 JP 127, 97 Sol Jo 134, 51 LGR 180, [1953] 1 Lloyd's Rep 99 . . . 4-1560
Carpenter v Campbell [1953] 1 All ER 280, 117 JP 90 . . . 4-1938
Carpenter v Fox [1929] 2 KB 458, 98 LJKB 779, 142 LT 234, 93 JP 239, 45 TLR 571, 27 LGR 601, 29 Cox CC 42 . . . 4-3655
Carpenter v Mason (1840) 12 Ad & El 629, 4 JP 687, 4 P & D 439, 10 LJMC 1 . . . 1-420
Carr v Decca Gramophone Co Ltd [1947] KB 728, [1947] 2 All ER 20, 111 JP 352, [1948] LJR 81, 177 LT 402, 63 TLR 504, 91 Sol Jo 355, 45 LGR 396 . . . 8-14674
Carr v Hackney London Borough Council (1995) 93 LGR 606, 160 JP 402 . . . 8-26310
Carr v Mercantile Produce Co Ltd [1949] 2 KB 601, [1949] 2 All ER 531, 113 JP 488, 65 TLR 503, 93 Sol Jo 588, 47 LGR 642 . . . 8-14617
Carrick District Council v Taunton Vale Meat Traders Ltd (1994) 158 JP 347, 92 LGR 335 . . . 8-12255
Carrington Carr Ltd v Leicestershire County Council (1993) 158 JP 570, [1993] Crim LR 938 . . . 8-4804
Carrol v Bird (1800) 3 Esp 201 . . . 8-8160
Carter v Boehm (1766) 3 Burr 1905 . . . 2-343
Carter v Bradbeer [1975] 3 All ER 158, [1975] 1 WLR 1204, 61 Cr App Rep 275, 139 JP 691, 119 Sol Jo 560, HL . . . 6-165
Carter v Butcher [1966] 1 QB 526, [1965] 1 All ER 994, [1965] 2 WLR 1073, 109 Sol Jo 162, 193 Estates Gazette 639 . . . 8-29320, 8-29321
Carter v Eastbourne Borough Council (2000) 164 JP 273 . . . 2-34, 8-31055
Carter v Richardson [1974] RTR 314, [1974] Crim LR 190 . . . 4-1376
Carter v Secretary of State for the Environment [1994] 1 WLR 1212, [1994] 2 EGLR 194, [1994] 29 EG 124, CA . . . 8-30890
Carter v Walton [1985] RTR 378 . . . 4-280
Carter-Pascoe v Birmingham Justices [2002] EWHC 1202 (Admin), (2002) 166 JPN 498, [2002] All ER (D) 104 (Jun) . . . 6-661
Cartwright v MacCormack [1963] 1 All ER 11, [1963] 1 WLR 18, 106 Sol Jo 957, [1962] 2 Lloyd's Rep 328, CA . . . 2-744
Cartwright v Richardson & Co Ltd [1955] 1 All ER 742, 99 Sol Jo 238 . . . 1-661, 2-69
Case v Storey (1869) LR 4 Ex 319, 33 JP 470, 38 LJMC 113, 20 LT 618, 17 WR 802 . . . 8-13851
Casey v Casey [1952] 1 All ER 453, 116 JP 111 . . . 6-76
Cassady v Morris (Transport) Ltd [1975] RTR 470, [1975] Crim LR 398 . . . 1-321
Cassell v Jones (1913) 77 JP 197, 108 LT 806, 23 Cox CC 327, 11 LGR 488 . . . 8-18835
Cassidy v Cassidy [1959] 3 All ER 187, [1959] 1 WLR 1024, 123 JP 454, 103 Sol Jo 856 . . . 3-1566
Castioni, Re [1891] 1 QB 149, [1886-90] All ER Rep 640, 60 LJMC 22, 64 LT 344, 55 JP 328, 39 WR 202, 7 TLR 50, 17 Cox CC 225 . . . 8-10155
Castle v Cross [1985] 1 All ER 87, [1984] 1 WLR 1372, 128 Sol Jo 855, [1985] RTR 62, [1984] Crim LR 682, [1984] LS Gaz R 3596 . . . 4-1378
Castle v DPP (1998) Times, 3 April . . . 8-10445
Castro v Lushington (1893) 57 JP 168, 68 LT 91, 37 Sol Jo 216, 5 R 180 . . . 8-31450
Caswell v Hundred House Justices (1889) 54 JP 87 . . . 6-802
Caswell v Powell Duffryn Associated Collieries Ltd [1940] AC 152, [1939] 3 All ER 722, 108 LJKB 779, 161 LT 374, 55 TLR 1004, 83 Sol Jo 976, HL . . . 8-14490
Cathcart, Re, ex p Campbell (1870) 5 Ch App 703, 23 LT 289, 18 WR 1056 . . . 2-742
Caton v Community Service Office (1995) 159 JP 444 . . . , 3-1299C
Caurti v DPP [2001] EWHC Admin 867, [2002] Crim LR 131 . . . 8-23469
Cave v Dudley Co-operative Society Ltd [1934] WN 118, [1934] All ER Rep 534, 98 JP 265, 103 LJKB 569, 151 LT 448, 32 LGR 515, 30 Cox CC 151 . . . 8-31857

PARA

Cawley v DPP [2001] EWHC Admin 83 4-1378
Cawley v Frost [1976] 3 All ER 743, [1976] 1 WLR 1207, 141 JP 30, 120 Sol Jo 703, [1976] Crim LR 747 8-27690
Cawthorn v DPP [2000] RTR 45, sub nom Cawthorn v Newcastle upon Tyne Crown Court 164 JP 527 . . . . 4-8, 4-1596
Cawthorn v Newcastle upon Tyne Crown Court. See Cawthorn v DPP 4-8
Caygill v Thwaite (1885) 49 JP 614, 33 WR 581, 1 TLR 386 8-30733
Central Independent Television plc, Re [1991] 1 All ER 347, [1991] 1 WLR 4, 134 Sol Jo 1369, 92 Cr App Rep 154, [1990] NLJR 1641, CA 1-2433
Central Newbury Car Auctions Ltd v Unity Finance Ltd [1957] 1 QB 371, [1956] 3 All ER 905, [1956] 3 WLR 1068, 100 Sol Jo 927, CA 7-4013
Chahal v United Kingdom (1996) 23 EHRR 413, 1 BHRC 405, ECtHR 8-17631Y, 8-17669, 8-17670
Chalkley v United Kingdom [2003] Crim LR 51, ECtHR 2-471
Challis v Newman and Rockman (1937) cited in [1939] 1 All ER 612, 103 JP 126, 160 LT 285 8-13601
Challis v Warrender (1930) 95 JP 39, 144 LT 437, 47 TLR 123, 29 LGR 109, 29 Cox CC 251 8-13601
Chalmers v Johns [1999] 2 FCR 110, [1999] 1 FLR 392, [1999] Fam Law 16, CA . . . 6-127
Chamberlain, ex p (1857) 8 E & B 644, 4 Jur NS 477, sub nom R v Devonshire Justices 21 JP Jo 773, 30 LTOS 150, 6 WR 75 8-2477
Chamberlain v Lindon [1998] 2 All ER 538, [1998] 1 WLR 1252 8-24744
Chambers v Bernasconi (1834) 1 Cr M & R 347, 4 Tyr 531, 3 LJ Ex 373 2-340
Chambers and Edwards v DPP [1995] Crim LR 896 . . . . 8-23067, 8-23466, 8-27724
Champion v Maughan [1984] 1 All ER 680, [1984] 1 WLR 469, 128 Sol Jo 220, [1984] Crim LR 291, [1984] LS Gaz R 586 8-11265
Chan v R [1995] 2 All ER 438, [1995] 1 WLR 251, [1995] 2 Cr App Rep 194, [1995] Crim LR 566, PC 3-31
Chan Man-sin v A-G of Hong Kong (or R) [1988] 1 All ER 1, [1988] 1 WLR 196, 132 Sol Jo 126, 86 Cr App Rep 303, [1988] 2 LS Gaz R 36, [1988] Crim LR 319, PC . . . 8-30693
Chandler v Caisby & Son (30 July 1930, unreported) 8-14615
Chandler v DPP [1964] AC 763, [1962] 3 WLR 694, sub nom R v Chandler [1962] 3 All ER 142, 106 Sol Jo 331, CCA; affd sub nom Chandler v DPP [1964] AC 763, [1962] 3 All ER 142, [1962] 3 WLR 694, 106 Sol Jo 588, 46 Cr App Rep 347, HL 1-763, 8-22751
Chandler v Emerton Justices [1940] 2 KB 261, [1940] 3 All ER 146, 104 JP 342, 109 LJKB 663, 163 LT 80, 56 TLR 790, 38 LGR 329 . . . . 1-765, 1-769, 1-832, 6-257, 6-785
Chandler (Victor) International Ltd v Customs and Excise Comrs [2000] 1 All ER 160, [1999] 1 WLR 2160, [1999] 31 LS Gaz R 42, 143 Sol Jo LB 219; on appeal [2000] 2 All ER 315, [2000] 1 WLR 1296, [2000] 11 LS Gaz R 36, [2000] NLJR 341, 144 Sol Jo LB 127, CA 8-7053
Chandrasekera (otherwise Alisandiri) v R [1937] AC 220, [1936] 3 All ER 865, 106 LJPC 30, 156 LT 204, 53 TLR 137, 80 Sol Jo 1012, 30 Cox CC 546, PC 2-341
Chapman v DPP (1988) 153 JP 27, 89 Cr App Rep 190 1-2728
Chapman v Ingleton (1973) 57 Cr App Rep 476, [1973] Crim LR 296 1-1092
Chapman v Kirke [1948] 2 KB 450, [1948] 2 All ER 556, 112 JP 399, [1949] LJR 255, 64 TLR 519, 92 Sol Jo 558, 46 LGR 507 2-33
Chapman v O'Hagan [1949] 2 All ER 690, 113 JP 518, 65 TLR 657, 93 Sol Jo 694, 47 LGR 717 4-1680
Chappell v DPP (1988) 89 Cr App Rep 82 8-27724
Chappell & Co Ltd v Harrison (1910) 75 JP 20, 103 LT 594, 27 TLR 85 8-16727
Chappell & Co Ltd v Nestlé Co Ltd [1960] AC 87, [1959] 2 All ER 701, [1959] 3 WLR 168, 103 Sol Jo 561, HL 8-31836
Chard v Chard [1956] P 259, [1955] 3 All ER 721, [1955] 3 WLR 954, 99 Sol Jo 890 . . 2-619
Charlton v Crown Prosecution Service: C-116/92 [1994] 2 CMLR 600, sub nom Charlton v DPP 158 JP 766, [1994] RTR 133, ECJ 4-2295
Charlton v Jacob (1925) 89 JP 174, 94 LJKB 855, 134 LT 19, 41 TLR 680, 23 LGR 619, 28 Cox CC 73 8-14475
Charman (FE) Ltd v Clow [1974] 3 All ER 371, [1974] 1 WLR 1384, 138 JP 728, 118 Sol Jo 679 8-31824
Charnock v Merchant [1900] 1 QB 474, 64 JP 183, 69 LJQB 221, 82 LT 89, 48 WR 334, 16 TLR 139, 19 Cox CC 443 2-479
Charter v Charter (1901) 84 LT 272, 65 JP 246, 17 TLR 327 6-67
Chase v Chase (1983) 13 Fam Law 21 6-1493
Chauffeur Bikes v Leeds City Council [2005] EWHC 2369 (Admin), 170 JP 24 . . 8–18970
Chatham Corpn v Wright (1929) 94 JP 43, 142 LT 431, 28 LGR 4 . . . . 1-768, 1-831
Chatters v Burke [1986] 3 All ER 168, [1986] 1 WLR 1321, 150 JP 581, 130 Sol Jo 666, [1986] RTR 396, [1986] NLJ Rep 777, [1986] LS Gaz R 3161 4-1680
Chatterton v Glanford RDC [1915] 3 KB 707, 79 JP 441, 84 LJKB 1865, 113 LT 746, 13 LGR 1352 7-6070
Chatterton v Parker [1914] WN 206, 78 JP 339, 111 LT 380, 12 LGR 1205, 25 Cox CC 312 7-5959
Chechi v Bashier [1999] 2 FCR 241, [1999] 2 FLR 489, [1999] Fam Law 528, 143 Sol Jo LB 113, CA 6-130
Cheeseman v DPP [1992] QB 83, [1991] 3 All ER 54, [1991] 2 WLR 1105, 155 JP 469, 93 Cr App Rep 145, [1991] Crim LR 296 . . . . 8-31345A
Chelsea Vestry v Stoddard (1879) 43 JP 782 . . . . 8-31345A
Cheng v Governor of Pentonville Prison [1973] AC 931, [1973] 2 All ER 204, [1973] 2 WLR 746, 117 Sol Jo 527, sub nom R v Governor of Pentonville Prison, ex p Tzu-Tsai Cheng 137 JP 422, HL 8-10155

PARA

Chepstow Electric Light and Power Co v Chepstow Gas and Coke Consumers' Co [1905] 1 KB 198, 69 JP 72, 74 LJKB 28, 92 LT 27, 21 TLR 35 . . . 1-583, 1-754
Cheshire County Council v B [1992] 2 FCR 572, sub nom Re B (a minor) [1993] 1 FLR 421, [1993] Fam Law 128 . . . 6-173, 6-2143
Cheshire County Council v M [1992] 2 FCR 817, [1993] 1 FLR 463, [1993] Fam Law 207 6-2143
Chesson v Jordan [1981] Crim LR 333 . . . 2-34
Chesterton RDC v Ralph Thompson Ltd [1944] KB 447, [1944] 1 All ER 666, 108 JP 209, 113 LJKB 276, 171 LT 183, 60 TLR 353, 42 LGR 166 . . . 1-2180
Chic Fashions (West Wales) Ltd v Jones [1968] 2 QB 299, [1968] 1 All ER 229, [1968] 2 WLR 201, 132 JP 175, 112 Sol Jo 16, CA . . . 1-180, 8-30725
Chidwick v Beer [1974] RTR 415, [1974] Crim LR 267 . . . 8-4447
Chief Adjudication Officer v Quinn [1996] 4 All ER 72, [1996] 1 WLR 1184, [1996] 37 LS Gaz R 27, 140 Sol Jo LB 207, [1996] NLJR 1150n. HL . . . 8-28561
Chief Constable of Avon and Somerset v Fleming [1987] 1 All ER 318, [1987] RTR 378, 84 Cr App Rep 345, [1987] Crim LR 277 . . . 4-3
Chief Constable of Avon and Somerset Constabulary v Creech [1986] RTR 87, [1986] Crim LR 62 . . . 4-1378
Chief Constable of Avon and Somerset Constabulary v Kelliher [1987] RTR 305, [1986] Crim LR 635 . . . 4-1378
Chief Constable of Avon and Somerset Constabulary v Singh [1988] RTR 107 . . . 4-1378
Chief Constable of Cheshire Constabulary v Hunt (1983) 147 JP 567 . . . 8-21204
Chief Constable of Essex v Germain (1991) 156 JP 109 . . . 8-10409B
Chief Constable of Greater Manchester v Flaherty (1988) 153 JP 242 . . . 6-155, 6-655
Chief Constable of Gwent v Dash [1986] RTR 41, [1985] Crim LR 674 . . . 4-1377
Chief Constable of Hampshire v Mace (1986) 84 Cr App Rep 40, 150 JP 470, [1986] Crim LR 752 . . . 8-27980
Chief Constable of Humberside Police v McQuade [2001] EWCA Civ 1330, [2002] 1 WLR 1347, 165 JP 729, sub nom McQuade v Chief Constable of Humberside Police [2001] 35 LS Gaz R 33 . . . 1-183, 3-541
Chief Constable of Kent v Berry [1986] RTR 321, [1986] Crim LR 748 . . . 4-1378
Chief Constable of Kent v Denyer (1983) 147 JP 403 . . . 6-255, 6-661
Chief Constable of Kent v Mather [1986] RTR 36 . . . 4-1938
Chief Constable of Kent v V [1983] QB 34, [1982] 3 All ER 36, [1982] 3 WLR 462, 126 Sol Jo 536 . . . 1-180, 1-205
Chief Constable of Lancashire v Potter [2003] EWHC 2272 (Admin), [2003] 42 LS Gaz R 31, [2003] All ER (D) 199 (Oct) . . . 1-3804
Chief Constable of Norfolk v Clayton [1983] 2 AC 473, [1983] 2 WLR 555, 127 Sol Jo 222, sub nom Clayton v Chief Constable of Norfolk [1983] 1 All ER 984, sub nom R v Hunstanton Justices, ex p Clayton 147 JP 161, HL . . . 1-4441-445
Chief Constable of Norfolk v Fisher (1991) 156 JP 93, [1991] Crim LR 787 . . . 4-7
Chief Constable of North Wales Police v Evans [1982] 3 All ER 141, [1982] 1 WLR 1115, 147 JP 6, 126 Sol Jo 549, HL . . . 1-770, 1-833
Chief Constable of North Yorkshire Police v Saddington. See DPP v Saddington
Chief Constable of Staffordshire v Lees (1981) 145 JP 208, [1981] RTR 506 . . . 4-1377
Chief Constable of Surrey v Wickens (1984) 149 JP 333, [1985] RTR 277 . . . 4-1656
Chief Constable of West Mercia Constabulary v Boorman [2005] EWHC 2559 (Admin), 169 JP 669, (2005) Times, 17 November, [2005] All ER (D) 28 (Nov) . . . 1-387, 1-3804
Chief Constable of West Mercia Police v Williams [1987] RTR 188 . 4-16947-1043, 8-13142
Chief Constable of West Midlands v White (1992) 157 JP 222, [1992] NLJR 455 . . . 8-23610
Chief Constable of West Midlands Police v Billingham [1979] 2 All ER 182, [1979] 1 WLR 747, 123 Sol Jo 98, [1979] RTR 446, [1979] Crim LR 256 . . . 4-1377
Chief Constable of West Midlands Police v Marsden (1995) 159 JP 405 . . . 6-663, 6-680
Child v Grace (1825) 2 C & P 193 . . . 2-467
Child v Hearn (1874) LR 9 Exch 176, 43 LJ Ex 100, 22 WR 864 . . . 6-320, 8-27672
Childs v Coghlan (1968) 112 Sol Jo 175, [1968] Crim LR 225, 118 NLJ 182 . . . 4-3
Chiltern District Council v Hodgetts. See Hodgetts v Chiltern District Council
Chilvers v Rayner [1984] 1 All ER 843, [1984] 1 WLR 328, 148 JP 50, 128 Sol Jo 130, 78 Cr App Rep 59, [1984] LS Gaz R 741 . . . 8-5609
Chipchase v Chipchase [1939] P 391, [1939] 3 All ER 895, 108 LJP 154, 55 TLR 1067, 83 Sol Jo 798 . . . 2-619, 6-51
Chipchase v Chipchase [1942] P 37, [1941] 2 All ER 560, 110 LJP 65, 165 LT 333, 57 TLR 606, 85 Sol Jo 323 . . . 6-51
Christie v Leachinsky [1947] AC 573, [1947] 1 All ER 567, 111 JP 224, [1947] LJR 757, 176 LT 443, 63 TLR 231, 45 LGR 201, HL . . . 1-2696
Chudley v Chudley (1893) 69 LT 617, 10 TLR 63, 17 Cox CC 697, CA . . . 6-65
Church v Church (1933) 97 JP 91, 148 LT 432, 49 TLR 206, 31 LGR 185, 29 Cox CC 592 . 2-34
Church v Church [1952] P 313, [1952] 2 All ER 441, [1952] 2 TLR 557, 96 Sol Jo 514 . . 6-78
Church v Lee and Co-operative Retail Services (1985) 150 JP 300, [1986] BTLC 91 . . 8-31835
Churcher v Reeves [1942] 1 KB 172, [1942] 1 All ER 69, 106 JP 66, 111 LJKB 136, 166 LT 150, 58 TLR 69, 86 Sol Jo 28, 40 LGR 9 . . . 8-12248
Churchward v Johnson (1889) 54 JP 326 . . . 8-16719, 8-16726
Cichon v DPP [1994] Crim LR 918 . . . 8-7615
City of Oxford Tramway Co v Sankey (1890) 54 JP 564 . . . 1-441, 1-442

PARA

PARA

PARA

D

PARA

PARA

Denard v Abbas (1986) 151 JP 421, [1987] Crim LR 424 . . . 8-4464

Denard v Smith and Dixons Ltd (1990) 155 JP 253, [1991] Crim LR 63 . . . 8-4447

Denerley v Spink [1947] 1 All ER 835, 111 JP 318, 177 LT 503, 91 Sol Jo 572, 45 LGR 473 . . . 8-21033

Denham v Scott (1983) 147 JP 521, 77 Cr App Rep 210, [1983] Crim LR 558 . . . 8-30722

Denneny v Harding [1986] RTR 350, [1986] Crim LR 254 . . . 4-1656

Dennistoun v Charles E Greenhill Ltd [1944] 2 All ER 434 . . . 8-14616, 8-14617

Denny v DPP (1989) 154 JP 460, [1989] 18 LS Gaz R 39 . . . 4-1378

Denny v DPP (2003) 167 JPN 202, [2003] All ER (D) 235 (Mar) . . . 4-1512

Denton v John Lister Ltd [1971] 3 All ER 669, [1971] 1 WLR 1426, 115 Sol Jo 671 . . . 2-910, 8-6644

Department for the Environment, Food and Rural Affairs v Atkinson [2002] EWHC 2028 (Admin), [2002] 3 CMLR 1093, [2002] JPN 802, [2002] 43 LS Gaz R 34 . . . 8-21015

Department of Health and Social Security v Walker Dean Walker Ltd [1970] 2 QB 74, [1970] 1 All ER 757, [1970] 2 WLR 588, 114 Sol Jo 149, 8 KIR 617 . . . 8-29096

Department of Social Security v Butler [1995] 4 All ER 193, [1995] 1 WLR 1528, [1996] 1 FCR 63, [1996] 1 FLR 65, [1996] Fam Law 10, CA . . . 6-2944

Department of Social Services v Taylor (1996) Times, 8 February . . . 6-2944

Department of Transport v Caird Environmental Services Ltd [1999] RTR 137 . . . 4-1971, 4-1984

Department of Transport v Ladd (1995) Times, 29 May . . . 8-6623

Dereham v Strickland (1911) 75 JP 300, 104 LT 820, 9 LGR 528 . . . 8-18835

Derrick v Customs and Excise Comrs [1972] 2 QB 28, [1972] 1 All ER 993, [1972] 2 WLR 359, 136 JP 294, 116 Sol Jo 97, [1972] Crim LR 112, CA . . . 8-6510

Desmond v Thorne [1982] 3 All ER 268, [1983] 1 WLR 163, 126 Sol Jo 783 . . . 8-18650

Despard v Wilcox (1910) 74 JP 115, 102 LT 103, 26 TLR 226, 22 Cox CC 258 . . . 8-23824

Devi v Gaddu (1974) 4 Fam Law 159, 118 Sol Jo 579 . . . 6-67

Devlin v F [1982] 2 All ER 450, [1982] 1 WLR 724, 146 JP 252, 126 Sol Jo 261, 75 Cr App Rep 262 . . . 1-5689

Devlin v Hall (1990) 155 JP 20, [1990] RTR 320, [1990] Crim LR 879 . . . 8-4447

Devon County Council v DB Cars Ltd [2001] EWHC Admin 521, (2001) 166 JP 38, [2002] Crim LR 71 . . . 4-1468

Devon County Council v Gateway Foodmarkets Ltd (1990) 154 JP 557 . . . 7-6009

Devon County Council v George [1989] AC 573, [1988] 3 WLR 1386, 153 JP 375, [1989] 1 FLR 146, [1989] Fam Law 149, 87 LGR 413, [1989] 4 LS Gaz R 41, sub nom George v Devon County Council [1988] 3 All ER 1002, HL . . . 8-7824

Devon County Council v Hawkins [1967] 2 QB 26, [1967] 1 All ER 235, [1967] 2 WLR 285, 131 JP 161, 110 Sol Jo 893, 65 LGR 123 . . . 4-1495

Devon County Council v S [1992] Fam 176, [1992] 3 All ER 793, [1992] 3 WLR 273, [1992] 1 FCR 550, [1992] 2 FLR 244, [1993] Fam Law 190 . . . 6-2100

Devon County Council v S [1993] 2 FCR 36, [1993] 1 FLR 842, [1993] Fam Law 620 . . . 6-4261

Devon County Council v S [1994] Fam 169, [1995] 1 All ER 243, [1994] 3 WLR 183, [1994] 2 FCR 409, [1994] 1 FLR 355, [1994] Fam Law 371 . . . 6-2239

Devonshire (Duke) v Neill (1876) 2 LR Ir 132, 26 WR 91 . . . 8-30733

Devonshire (Duke) v O'Connor (1890) 24 QBD 468, 54 JP 740, 59 LJQB 206, 62 LT 917, 38 WR 420, 6 TLR 155, 34 Sol Jo 190 . . . 2-740

Devonshire (Duke) v Pattinson (1887) 20 QBD 263, 52 JP 276, 57 LJQB 189, 58 LT 392, 4 TLR 164, CA . . . 8-30733

Dew v DPP (1920) 85 JP 81, [1920] All ER Rep 532, 89 LJKB 1166, 124 LT 246, 37 TLR 22, 18 LGR 829, 26 Cox CC 664 . . . 8-13601A

De Wilde, Ooms and Versyp v Belgium (1971) 1 EHRR 373, ECtHR . . . 1-6105

Dibble v Bowater (1853) 2 E & B 564, 17 JP 792, 22 LJQB 396, 17 Jur 1054, 1 WR 435 . . . 8-16724, 8-16726

Dibble v Ingleton [1972] 1 QB 480, [1972] 2 WLR 163, 116 Sol Jo 97, sub nom Ingleton v Dibble [1972] 1 All ER 275, 136 JP 155 . . . 8-23824

Dickenson v Fletcher (1873) LR 9 CP 1, 38 JP 88, 43 LJMC 25, 29 LT 540 . . . 6-777

Dickeson & Co v Mayes [1910] 1 KB 452, 74 JP 139, 79 LJKB 253, 102 LT 287, 26 TLR 236 . . . 6-819

Dickins v Randerson [1901] 1 KB 437, 65 JP 262, 70 LJKB 344, 84 LT 204, 17 TLR 224, 19 Cox CC 643 . . . 8-12248

Dickinson v Dickinson (1889) 62 LT 330 . . . 6-68, 6-76

Dickinson v DPP [1989] Crim LR 741 . . . 4-1378

Dickinson v Ead (1914) 78 JP 326, 111 LT 378, 30 TLR 496, 24 Cox CC 308 . . . 8-13606

Diennet v France (1995) 21 EHRR 554, ECtHR . . . 1-37

Digby v General Accident Fire and Life Assurance Corpn Ltd [1943] AC 121, [1942] 2 All ER 319, 111 LJKB 628, 167 LT 222, 58 TLR 375, 87 Sol Jo 29, 73 Lloyd LR 176, HL . . . 4-1562, 4-1565

Dilieto v Ealing London Borough Council [2000] QB 381, [1998] 2 All ER 885, [1998] 3 WLR 1403, [1998] PLCR 212 . . . 8-31047

Dillon's Case (1886) 31 Sol Jo 136 . . . 3-541

Dimes v Grand Junction Canal (1852) 3 HL Cas 759, 8 State Tr NS 85, 19 LTOS 317, 17 JUR 73 . . . 1-131

Dimond v Lovell [2000] 1 QB 216, [1999] 3 All ER 1, [1999] 3 WLR 561, [1999] RTR 297, [1999] 21 LS Gaz R 40, [1999] NLJR 681, CA; affd [2000] 2 All ER 897, [2000] 2 WLR 1121, [2000] RTR 297, [2000] LJR 740, HL . . . 8-4773

Din v National Assistance Board [1967] 2 QB 213, [1967] 1 All ER 750, [1967] 2 WLR 257, 110 Sol Jo 906 . . . 8-28562

Director-General of Fair Trading v Proprietary Association of Great Britain [2001] EWCA Civ 1217, [2002] 1 All ER 853, [2002] 1 WLR 269, [2001] NLJR 1372 . . . 8-17631F

PARA

DPP v Regional Pool Promotions Ltd [1964] 2 QB 244, [1964] 1 All ER 65, [1964] 2 WLR 209, 128 JP 150, 107 Sol Jo 984, 62 LGR 82 . . . . . 8-13432, 8-13601
DPP v Richards [1988] QB 701, [1988] 3 All ER 406, [1988] 3 WLR 153, 152 JP 333, 132 Sol Jo 623 1-1561
DPP v Robertson [2002] EWHC 542 (Admin), [2002] RTR 383, 166 JP 649, [2002] Crim LR 589, [2002] 15 LS Gaz R 33 4-1375
DPP v Rogers [1953] 2 All ER 644, [1953] 1 WLR 1017, 117 JP 424, 97 Sol Jo 541, 37 Cr App Rep 137 8-27981
DPP v Rogers [1998] Crim LR 202 1-325
DPP v Rose (1988) 156 JP 733 4-1680
DPP v Ryan [1992] RTR 13, 155 JP 456 4-2292
DPP v Saddington [2001] RTR 227, sub nom Chief Constable of North Yorkshire Police v Saddington 165 JP 122, [2001] Crim LR 41 4-3
DPP v Santa-Bermudez [2004] EWHC 2908 (Admin), 168 JP 373, [2004] Crim LR 471 . 8-23061
DPP v Schildkamp [1971] AC 1, [1969] 3 All ER 1640, [1970] 2 WLR 279, 114 Sol Jo 54, HL 2-740
DPP v Scott [1995] RTR 40, 159 JP 261, [1995] Crim LR 91, 16 Cr App Rep (S) 292 3-203, 3-1690
DPP v Seawheel Ltd (1993) 158 JP 444, [1993] Crim LR 707 4-3651
DPP v Selvanayagam (1999) Times, 23 June 8-23466
DPP v Shah [1984] 2 All ER 528, [1984] 1 WLR 886, 149 JP 149, 128 Sol Jo 469, 79 Cr App Rep 162, [1984] Crim LR 626, 4 Tr L 27, [1984] LS Gaz R 2376, HL 1-389
DPP v Short [2001] EWHC Admin 885, (2001) 166 JP 474 . . . . . 1-440, 1-442
DPP v Shuttleworth [2002] EWHC 621 (Admin), (2002) 166 JP 417 . . . 1-463, 1-2038
DPP v Siba [1989] RTR 29 4-1680
DPP v Sikondar (1992) 157 JP 659, [1993] RTR 90, [1993] Crim LR 76 . . . 4-870
DPP v Singh [1988] RTR 209 4-1655
DPP v Skinner (1989) 153 JP 605, [1990] RTR 254 4-1378
DPP v Smith [1961] AC 290, [1960] 3 All ER 161, [1960] 3 WLR 546, 124 JP 473, 104 Sol Jo 683, HL 1-1091, 8-23086
DPP v Smith (Alan) (1993) Times, 1 June 4-1378
DPP v Smith (Robert James) [2000] RTR 341 4-1378
DPP v Smith [2002] EWHC 1151 (Admin), [2002] Crim LR 970 . . . . 4-1661f
DPP v Smith (Michael Ross) [2006] EWHC 94 (Admin), [2006] 2 All ER 16, 150 Sol Jo LB 130, 170 JP 45 8–23116
DPP v Snook [1993] Crim LR 883 4-1655
DPP v Speede [1998] 2 Cr App Rep 108 . . . . 1-2184, 3-541
DPP v Spriggs (1993) 157 JP 1143, [1993] Crim LR 622, [1994] RTR 1 . . . 8-30701
DPP v Spurrier [2000] RTR 60, sub nom R v Crown Prosecution Service, ex p Spurrier 164 JP 369 4-1655
DPP v Stoke on Trent Magistrates' Court [2003] EWHC 1593 (Admin), [2003] 3 All ER 1086, 167 JP 436, [2004] 1 Cr App Rep 55, [2003] Crim LR 804, [2003] 32 LS Gaz R 33, [2003] NLJR 1063 . . . . 1-3822, 8–27824
DPP v Stonehouse [1978] AC 55, [1977] 2 All ER 909, [1977] 3 WLR 143, 141 JP 473, 121 Sol Jo 491, 65 Cr App Rep 192, [1977] Crim LR 544, HL 1-383, 8-30704
DPP v Street (2004) Times, 23 January 8-10389
DPP v Swann (1999) 164 JP 365 4-1512
DPP v T [2006] EWHC 728 (Admin), [2006] All ER (D) 41 (Apr) 1-3804
DPP v Taylor [1992] QB 645, [1992] 1 All ER 299, [1992] 2 WLR 460, 155 JP 713, [1992] Fam Law 377, 95 Cr App Rep 28, [1991] Crim LR 904 . . . . 8-23060, 8-23400
DPP v Teixeira [2001] EWHC Admin 931, (2001) 166 JP 1 4-1655
DPP v Tweddell [2001] EWHC Admin 188, [2002] 1 FCR 438, [2002] 2 FLR 400 . . 1-63
DPP v Upchurch [1994] RTR 336 4-1680
DPP v Varley (1998) 163 JP 443, [1999] Crim LR 753 4-1378
DPP v Vivier [1991] 4 All ER 18, [1991] RTR 205 4-5
DPP v Waite [1997] Crim LR 123 . . . . 8-30105L
DPP v Waller [1989] RTR 112 4-1680
DPP v Ward [1989] RTR 29 4-1680
DPP v Ward (1997) Times, 24 March 7-1379
DPP v Warren [1993] AC 319, [1992] 4 All ER 865, [1992] 3 WLR 884, 157 JP 297, [1993] RTR 58, 96 Cr App Rep 312, [1992] NLJR 1684, [1992] 45 LS Gaz R 26, HL . . 4-1378
DPP v Watkins [1989] QB 521, [1989] 1 All ER 1126, [1989] 2 WLR 966, 154 JP 370, 133 Sol Jo 514, [1989] RTR 324, 89 Cr App Rep 112, [1989] NLJR 365, [1989] 19 LS Gaz R 45 4-1375
DPP v Welsh (1996) 161 JP 57 4-1376
DPP v Whalley [1991] RTR 161, [1991] Crim LR 211 4-1378
DPP v White [1988] RTR 267, 10 Cr App Rep (S) 66 4-1680
DPP v White (1996) 160 JP 726 . . . . 8-30105L
DPP v Whittle [1996] RTR 154 4-1680
DPP v Whyte [1972] AC 849, [1972] 3 All ER 12, [1972] 3 WLR 410, 116 Sol Jo 583, HL . 8-22449
DPP v Williams [1989] Crim LR 382 4-1655
DPP v Wilson [1991] RTR 284, (1991) 156 JP 916, [1991] Crim LR 441 . . . 4-1377
DPP v Wilson [2001] EWHC Admin 198, (2001) 165 JP 715, [2002] RTR 37 . 4-1598, 7-6990
DPP v Winstanley (1993) 158 JP 1062, [1993] RTR 222 4-1379
DPP v Withers [1975] AC 842, [1974] 3 All ER 984, [1974] 3 WLR 751, 118 Sol Jo 862, 60 Cr App Rep 85, [1975] Crim LR 95, HL 8-4011

E

PARA

F

PARA

PARA

G

PARA

PARA

Georgiadis v Greece (1997) 24 EHRR 606, ECtHR . . . 1-27, 1-33, 1-40, 1-47, 1-582, 1-702, 1-753, 1-2031, 1-2093, 1-2124
Geraghty v Morris [1939] WN 153, [1939] 2 All ER 269, 103 JP 175, 160 LT 397, 55 TLR 599, 83 Sol Jo 359, 37 LGR 297, 31 Cox CC 249 4-1493
Germany (Government of) v Kleinschmidt [2005] EWHC 1373 (Admin), [2005] 3 All ER 759, [2006] 1 WLR 1, [2005] All ER (D) 353 (Jun) 8-10299U
Ghafoor v Wakefield Metropolitan District Council (1990) 89 LGR 667, [1990] RTR 389 8-31350
Ghani v Jones [1970] 1 QB 693, [1969] 3 All ER 1700, [1969] 3 WLR 1158, 134 JP 166, 113 Sol Jo 854, CA 1-171, 1-180, 1-205
Gibbins v Skinner [1951] 2 KB 379, [1951] 1 TLR 1159, sub nom Boyd-Gibbins v Skinner [1951] 1 All ER 1049, 115 JP 360, 49 LGR 713 4-1191
Gibbons v Kahl [1956] 1 QB 59, [1955] 3 All ER 345, [1955] 3 WLR 596, 54 LGR 35, 120 JP 1, 99 Sol Jo 782 4-2933
Gibson v Dalton [1980] RTR 410 4-1642
Gibson v Gibson (1859) 23 JP 535, 29 LJP & M 25 6-76
Gibson v Nutter [1984] RTR 8 . . . . 4-1976, 4-2492
Gibson v Wales [1983] 1 All ER 869, [1983] 1 WLR 393, 147 JP 143, 127 Sol Jo 222, 76 Cr App Rep 60, [1983] Crim LR 113, [1983] LS Gaz R 153 8-22630
Giebler v Manning [1906] 1 KB 709, 70 JP 181 1-7427
Gifford v Whittaker [1942] 1 KB 501, [1942] 1 All ER 604, 106 JP 128, 111 LJKB 461, 166 LT 324, 58 TLR 195, 86 Sol Jo 154, 40 LGR 146 4-3651
Gilbert v Gilbert and Boucher [1928] P 1, 96 LJP 137, 137 LT 619, 43 TLR 589, 71 Sol Jo 582, CA 2-741
Gilbey v Great Western Rly Co (1910) 102 LT 202, 3 BWCC 135, CA 2-462
Gilding v DPP (1998) Times, 20 May 3-1587
Gill v Bright (1871) 36 JP 198, 41 LJMC 22, 20 WR 248, 25 LT 591 6-813
Gill v Carson and Nield [1917] 2 KB 674, 81 JP 250, 86 LJKB 1290, 117 LT 285, 15 LGR 567, 25 Cox CC 774 . . . . 4-3655, 8-31345A
Gillard, Re [1986] AC 442, [1985] 3 WLR 936, 150 JP 45, 129 Sol Jo 812, [1986] LS Gaz R 38, sub nom Chief Constable of West Midlands Police v Gillard [1985] 3 All ER 634, HL 1-450, 1-525, 1-2054
Gillick v West Norfolk and Wisbech Area Health Authority [1986] AC 112, [1985] 3 All ER 402, [1985] 3 WLR 830, [1986] 1 FLR 224, 129 Sol Jo 738, [1986] Crim LR 113, [1985] NLJ Rep 1055, [1985] LS Gaz R 3551, HL 6-2107, 8-22279
Gillie v Posho Ltd [1939] 2 All ER 196 . . . . 2-474, 2-617
Gillingham v Walker (1881) 45 JP 470, 44 LT 715, 29 WR 896 7-7043
Gleaves v Deakin [1980] AC 477, [1979] 2 All ER 497, [1979] 2 WLR 665, 123 Sol Jo 320, 69 Cr App Rep 59, HL 8-18620, 8-18631, 8-18632
Gleaves v Insall [1999] 2 Cr App Rep 466, [1999] EMLR 779 . . . . 1-447, 8-18620, 8-18650
Gleeson v Hurley [1916] 2 IR 180 8-13670
Glendyne (Lord) v Rapley [1978] 2 All ER 110, [1978] 1 WLR 601, 122 Sol Jo 247, 246 Estates Gazette 573, CA 8-16880
Glenister v Glenister [1945] P 30, [1945] 1 All ER 513, 109 JP 194, 114 LJP 69, 172 LT 250, 43 LGR 250 . . . . 6-68, 6-78
Glicksman v Lancashire and General Assurance Co Ltd [1927] AC 139, [1926] All ER Rep 161, 62 L Jo 326, 136 LT 263, 43 TLR 46, 70 Sol Jo 1111, 32 Com Cas 62, HL . . . 4-1562
Glimmerveen and Hagenbeek v Netherlands (1979) [171]=22[187], EComHR . . . 8-27737
Gloucester (Bishop) v Cunningham [1943] KB 101, [1943] 1 All ER 61, 112 LJKB 151, 168 LT 68, 59 TLR 83, CA 8-16831
Gloucester Local Board of Health v Chandler (1863) 27 JP 88, 32 LJNC 66, 7 LT 722 . 1-5689
Gloucestershire County Council v P [2000] Fam 1, [1999] 3 WLR 685, [1999] 3 FCR 114, [1999] 2 FLR 61, [1999] Fam Law 444, [1999] 20 LS Gaz R 39, 143 Sol Jo LB 157, CA . 6-2109
Glynn v Simmonds [1952] 2 All ER 47, 116 JP 389, [1952] 1 TLR 1442, 96 Sol Jo 378 . 8-28160
Godfrey v Napier (1901) 18 TLR 31 8-14231
Godlonton v Fulham and Hampstead Property Co [1905] 1 KB 431, 74 LJKB 242, 92 LT 362, 21 TLR 223 8-16727
Godwin v DPP (1992) 157 JP 197, 96 Cr App Rep 244 8-22680
Godwin v Swindon Borough Council [2001] EWCA Civ 1478, [2001] 4 All ER 641, [2002] 1 WLR 997 . . . . 1-6563G
Gojkovic v Gojkovic (No 2) [1992] Fam 40, [1992] 1 All ER 267, [1991] 3 WLR 621, [1991] FCR 913, [1991] 2 FLR 233, [1991] Fam Law 378, CA 6-41
Gold Star Publications v DPP [1981] 2 All ER 257, [1981] 1 WLR 732, 145 JP 289, 125 Sol Jo 376, 73 Cr App Rep 141, [1981] Crim LR 634, HL 8-22449, 8-22451
Golding v Stocking (1869) LR 4 QB 516, 10 B & S 348, 33 JP 566, 38 LJMC 122, 20 LT 479, 17 WR 722 7-6028
Goldsmith v Customs and Excise Comrs [2001] EWHC Admin 285, [2001] 1 WLR 1673, 165 JP 517, 145 Sol Jo LB 124 . . . . 8-6644, 8-17631W
Goldsmith v Deakin [1933] WN 255, [1933] All ER Rep 102, 98 JP 4, 150 LT 157, 50 TLR 73, 31 LGR 420, 30 Cox CC 32 4-7
Goldsmith v Pressdram Ltd [1977] 2 All ER 557, 120 Sol Jo 606 8-18620
Goldsmith's Co v Wyatt [1907] 1 KB 95, [1906] All ER Rep 542, 71 JP 79, 76 LJKB 166, 95 LT 855, 23 TLR 107, 51 Sol Jo 99, CA 2-742

PARA

Gwennap (William) (Agricultural) Ltd v Amphlett [1957] 2 All ER 605, [1957] 1 WLR 910, 55 LGR 557, 121 JP 487, 101 Sol Jo 592 4-3826

H

H (minors), Re (1975) 5 Fam Law 54 6-3425
H (a minor), Re [1985] 3 All ER 1, [1985] 1 WLR 1164, 129 Sol Jo 622, CA 8-22936
H, Re [1986] 1 FLR 476, [1986] Fam Law 193, 130 Sol Jo 128 6-22
H (minors), Re [1992] 1 FCR 70, [1992] 1 FLR 148, [1992] Fam Law 152, CA . . . 6-151
H (a minor), Re [1992] 2 FCR 330, [1993] 1 FLR 440, [1993] Fam Law 200 . . . 6-26, 6-40, 6-4406
H (a minor), Re [1993] 1 FCR 85, [1993] 1 FLR 484, [1993] Fam Law 273, CA . . . 6-146, 6-2103
H (a minor), Re [1993] 1 FCR 671, [1994] 1 FLR 717, [1993] Fam Law 463, CA . . . 6-2110
H (minors), Re [1993] 1 FCR 904, sub nom Birmingham City Council v H (No 2) [1993] 1 FLR 883, [1993] Fam Law 459, CA; revsd sub nom Birmingham City Council v H (a minor) [1994] 2 AC 212, [1994] 1 All ER 12, [1994] 2 WLR 31, 92 LGR 349, [1994] 1 FCR 896, [1994] 1 FLR 224, [1994] 6 LS Gaz R 36, [1994] NLJR 17, 138 Sol Jo LB 13, HL 6-140, 6-173
H, Re [1993] 2 FCR 277 . . . . 6-172, 6-2146
H (a minor), Re [1994] 2 FCR 249, [1994] 2 FLR 979, [1993] Fam Law 673, CA . . . 6-151
H (minors), Re [1994] 2 FCR 1, [1994] 2 FLR 979, [1994] Fam Law 486 6-2321
H (minors), Re [1995] 4 All ER 110, [1995] 1 WLR 667, [1995] 2 FCR 547, [1995] 1 FLR 638, [1995] Fam Law 293, CA 6-152
H (minors) (sexual abuse: standard of proof), Re [1996] AC 563, [1996] 1 All ER 1, [1996] 2 WLR 8, [1996] 1 FCR 509, [1996] 1 FLR 80, [1996] Fam Law 74, 140 Sol Jo LB 24, HL 1-689, 6-165
H (a minor) (blood tests: parental rights), Re [1996] 4 All ER 28, [1996] 3 WLR 506, [1996] 3 FCR 201, [1996] 2 FLR 65, [1996] Fam Law 461, [1996] NLJR 406, CA . . 6-506, 6-509
H (contact: enforcement), Re [1996] 2 FCR 784, [1996] 1 FLR 614, [1996] Fam Law 348 6-151
H (a minor) (parental responsibility order), Re [1996] 3 FCR 49, [1996] 1 FLR 867, [1996] Fam Law 402, CA 6-146
H (shared residence: parental responsibility), Re [1996] 3 FCR 321, [1995] 2 FLR 883, [1996] Fam Law 140, CA 6-153
H (minors) (abduction: acquiescence), Re [1997] 2 All ER 225, [1997] 2 WLR 563, [1997] 2 FCR 257, [1997] 1 FLR 872, [1997] Fam Law 468, HL 6-1805E
H (application to remove from jurisdiction), Re [1999] 2 FCR 34, [1998] 1 FLR 848, [1998] Fam Law 390, CA 6-156, 6-2112
H (child abduction: rights of custody), Re [2000] 2 AC 291, [2000] 2 All ER 1, [2000] 2 WLR 337, [2000] 1 FCR 225, [2000] 1 FLR 374, [2000] Fam Law 310, [2000] 07 LS Gaz R 40, 144 Sol Jo LB 101, HL 6-1805A
H (children) (care proceedings: sexual abuse), Re [2000] 2 FCR 499, CA 6-165
H (abduction: child of sixteen), Re [2000] 3 FCR 404, [2000] 2 FLR 51, [2000] Fam Law 530 6-1805C, 6-1805D
H (child abduction: wrongful retention), Re [2000] 3 FCR 412, [2000] 2 FLR 294, [2000] Fam Law 590 . . . . 6-1805A
H (a child) (adoption: disclosure), Re [2001] 1 FCR 726, [2001] 1 FLR 646, [2001] Fam Law 175, [2000] All ER (D) 2046 6-34234-3434
H (children) (contact order), Re [2001] 1 FCR 49, [2002] 1 FLR 22, [2001] Fam Law 795, CA 6-151
H (children) (contact order) (No 2), Re [2001] 3 FCR 385, [2002] 1 FLR 22, [2001] Fam Law 795 6-151
H (children) (residence order: condition), Re [2001] EWCA Civ 1338, [2001] 3 FCR 182, [2001] 2 FLR 1277, [2001] Fam Law 870 . . . . . 6-156, 6-2110, 6-2112
H (McKenzie friend: pre-trial determination), Re [2001] EWCA Civ 1444, [2002] 1 FLR 39, [2002] Fam Law 17 1-642
H (a child) (adoption: parental consent), Re (2001) 165 JPN 734 . . . . . 6-170A
H (child's name: first name), Re [2002] EWCA Civ 190, [2002] 1 FLR 973, [2002] All ER (D) 247 (Jan) 6-156
H (a child) (care proceedings: children's guardian), Re [2002] 1 WLR 189, sub nom Re MH and SB (supervision orders) [2002] 1 FCR 251, [2001] 2 FLR 1334, [2001] Fam Law 869 1-4003
H (a child: residence), Re [2002] 3 FCR 277, CA 6-37, 6-142, 6-153, 6-155
H (abduction: grave risk), Re [2003] EWCA Civ 355, [2003] 2 FCR 151, [2003] 2 FLR 141 6-1805D
H (a child) (care: local authority), Re [2003] EWCA Civ 1629, [2004] Fam 89, [2004] 2 WLR 419, [2004] 1 FCR 282, [2004] 1 FLR 534, [2004] Fam Law 105, [2004] 02 LS Gaz R 27, (2003) Times, 26 November, [2003] All ER (D) 250 (Nov) 6-2140, 6-2254
H (child abduction: unmarried father: rights of custody), Re [2003] EWHC 492 (Fam), [2003] 2 FLR 153 . . . . 6-1805A
H v Balham Youth Court [2003] EWHC 3267 (Admin), (2003) 168 JP 177, [2003] All ER (D) 173 (Dec) 1-2053, 1-2054
H v DPP [2001] UKHL 10, [2002] 1 AC 285, [2001] 2 All ER 583, [2001] 2 WLR 765, [2001] 2 Cr App Rep 216, 165 JP 437, [2001] Crim LR 491, [2001] 20 LS Gaz R 40, [2001] NLJR 385, 145 Sol Jo LB 101 8-27722
H v DPP [2003] EWHC 878 (Admin), (2003) 167 JP 486, [2003] Crim LR 560 . . . 5-27A
H v H [1928] P 206, 97 LJP 116, 19 LT 412, 44 TLR 711, 72 Sol Jo 598 . . . 6-51

PARA

Hearne v Garton (1859) 2 E & E 66, 23 JP 693, 28 LJMC 216, 33 LTOS 256, 5 Jur NS 648, 7 WR 566 7-7002

Heaton v Costello (1984) 148 JP 688, [1984] Crim LR 485 1-389

Heawood v Bone (1884) 13 QBD 179, 48 JP 710, 51 LT 125, 32 WR 752 . . . 8-16727

Hebden v Hentey (1819) 1 Chit 607 . . . . 8-13653, 8-13822

Hedderwick, Re, Morton v Brinsley [1933] Ch 669, [1933] All ER Rep 73, 102 LJ Ch 193, 149 LT 188, 49 TLR 381 6-1543

Heidak v Winnett [1981] RTR 445 . . . . 4-4379Y

Helle v Finland (1997) 26 EHRR 159, ECtHR 1-27, 1-33, 1-40, 1-47, 1-582, 1-702, 1-753, 1-2031, 1-2093, 1-2124

Hellyer v Hellyer [1997] 1 FCR 340, [1996] 2 FLR 579, [1997] Fam Law 14, CA . . 6-960

Helmers v Sweden (1991) 15 EHRR 285, ECtHR 1-37, 1-777, 1-856, 1-3549

Helson v Barnard 1922 SLT 40 . . . . 4-4399, 7-4038

Henderson v Chief Constable of Cleveland Police [2001] EWCA Civ 225, [2001] 1 WLR 1103 . 1-2208

Henderson v Glasgow Corpn (1900) 2 F 1127, 37 SLR 857, 8 SLT 118 8-14683

Henderson v Jones (1955) 119 JP 304, 53 LGR 319 4-9

Henderson v Preston (1888) 21 QBD 362, 52 JP 820, 57 LJQB 607, 36 WR 834 . 3-244, 3-245

Henderson and Turnbull v Adair (1939) 103 JP 533 8-4448

Henley v Henley [1955] P 202, [1955] 1 All ER 590, [1955] 2 WLR 851, 119 JP 215, 99 Sol Jo 260 2-331

Henn and Darby v DPP [1981] AC 850, [1980] 2 WLR 597, 124 Sol Jo 290, sub nom R v Henn [1980] 2 All ER 166, sub nom DPP v Henn and Darby [1980] 2 CMLR 229, HL 1-1431, 8-6510

Hennen v Southern Counties Dairies Co Ltd [1902] 2 KB 1, 66 JP 774, 71 LJKB 656, 87 LT 51, 18 TLR 538, 20 Cox CC 279 . . . . 1-308, 8-12248

Henry v Taylor [1954] 1 QB 506, [1954] 1 All ER 721, [1954] 2 WLR 601, 118 JP 250, 98 Sol Jo 213, 163 Estates Gazette 242, CA 8-16892

Henshall (John) (Quarries) Ltd v Harvey [1965] 2 QB 233, [1965] 1 All ER 725, [1965] 2 WLR 758, 129 JP 224, 109 Sol Jo 152 . . . . 1-321, 1-329

Henty v Henty (1875) 33 LT 263 6-65

Hepburn v Hepburn [1989] FCR 618, [1989] 1 FLR 373, [1989] Fam Law 271, CA . . 6-1493

Herbage, Re (1985) Times, 25 October 1-770, 1-833

Herbert v Railway Passengers Assurance Co [1938] 1 All ER 650, 158 LT 417, 60 Ll L Rep 143 7-1197

Hereford and Worcester County Council v Newman [1975] 2 All ER 673, [1975] 1 WLR 901, 119 Sol Jo 354, CA 7-5989

Hereford and Worcester County Council v R and G [1994] 2 FCR 981 6-2320

Hereford and Worcester County Council v S [1993] 1 FCR 653, [1993] 2 FLR 360, [1993] Fam Law 573 . . . . 6-2134, 6-3622

Hereford and Worcester County Council v T & S Stores plc (1994) Times, 4 November . 5-84

Heritage v Claxon (1941) 85 Sol Jo 323 8-10442

Herne Bay UDC v Payne and Wood [1907] 2 KB 130, 71 JP 282, 76 LJKB 685, 96 LT 666 . 7-6070

Herniman v Smith [1938] AC 305, [1938] 1 All ER 1, 107 LJKB 225, 82 Sol Jo 192, HL 1-33, 1-221, 1-2020

Herod v Herod [1939] P 11, [1938] 3 All ER 722, 108 LJP 27, 159 LT 530, 54 TLR 1134, 82 Sol Jo 665 . . . . 6-76, 6-78

Heron Service Stations Ltd v Coupe [1973] 2 All ER 110, [1973] 1 WLR 502, 137 JP 415, 117 Sol Jo 305, 226 Estates Gazette 2349, HL 8-31062

Herrington v Slater (1920) 85 JP 83, [1920] Al[171]=22[187]l ER Rep 618, 90 LJKB 265, 124 LT 272, 37 TLR 51, 18 LGR 840, 26 Cox CC 670 8-12248

Hertfordshire County Council v Bolden (1986) 151 JP 252, [1987] BTLC 272 . . . 7-6009

Hertfordshire County Council v W [1992] 2 FCR 885, 136 Sol Jo LB 259, [1992] 39 LS Gaz R 33, sub nom W v Hertfordshire County Council [1993] 1 FLR 118, [1993] Fam Law 75 6-40, 6-2147

Heseltine v Myers (1894) 58 JP 689 8-11293

Hewison v Skegness UDC [1963] 1 QB 584, [1963] 1 All ER 205, [1963] 2 WLR 141, 127 JP 118, 107 Sol Jo 35, 61 LGR 105 2-742

Hewitt v Jervis (1903) 68 JP 54 6-754

Hewlings v McLean Homes East Anglia Ltd [2001] 2 All ER 281, 33 HLR 561, [2000] 39 LS Gaz R 41, [2000] EGCS 100 8-26364

Heywood v Whitehead (1897) 76 LT 781, 13 TLR 503, 18 Cox CC 615 8-12248

Hickman v Maisey [1900] 1 QB 752, 69 LJQB 511, 82 LT 321, 48 WR 385, 16 TLR 274 . . 8-13607

Hicks v Sullam Ltd (1983) 147 JP 373 8-4464

Hicks v Walker (1984) 148 JP 636, [1984] Crim LR 495 8-4800

Hickton v Hodgson (1913) 78 JP 93, 110 LT 380, 30 TLR 221 6-571

Hier v Read [1978] RTR 114, [1977] Crim LR 483 4-1378

Higgins v Higgins and Bannister [1943] P 58, [1943] 2 All ER 86, 112 LJP 55, 169 LT 45, 59 TLR 294, 87 Sol Jo 193 6-64

Higgs v Higgs [1941] P 27, [1941] 1 All ER 214, 105 JP 119, 110 LJP 27, 165 LT 335, 57 TLR 275, 85 Sol Jo 107, 39 LGR 143 6-1492

Higham v Ridgway (1808) 10 East 109 2-340

Highnam v Turier [1951] 2 All ER 850, 115 JP 606, [1951] 2 TLR 951, 95 Sol Jo 729, 50 LGR 69 8-12248

Hill v Anderton. See R v Dartford Justices, ex p Dhesi, R v Edmonton Justices, ex p Hughes and R v Manchester Stipendiary Magistrate, ex p Hill

Hill v Baxter [1958] 1 QB 277, [1958] 1 All ER 193, 122 JP 134, 102 Sol Jo 53, 56 LGR 117, 42 Cr App Rep 51 . . . . 2-34, 4-8

PARA

PARA

I

PARA

J

PARA

K

PARA

Kingdom v Williams [1975] RTR 333, [1975] Crim LR 466 4-3507
Kings v Merris [1920] 3 KB 566, [1920] All ER Rep 628, 85 JP 68, 90 LJKB 161, 124 LT 150, 18 LGR 775, 26 Cox CC 649 8-12248
Kingsley and Kingsley v Hammersmith and Fulham London Borough Council (1991) 156 JP 372, 62 P & CR 589 8-31183
Kingsnorth v DPP (2003) 167 JPN 202, [2003] All ER (D) 235 (Mar) 4-1512
Kingston's (Duchess) Case (1776) 1 Leach 146, 1 East PC 468, 20 State Tr 355, 2 Smith LC 644, 761 . . . . . . 1-60, 1-348
Kingston upon Hull City Council v Wilson (1995) Times, 25 July 8-18968
Kingston-upon-Thames London Borough Council v Marlow (1995) 160 LG Rev 181, [1996] RA 87, 160 JP 502, [1996] 17 EG 187 . . . . . . 8-19671, 8-19690
Kingston-upon-Thames London Borough Council v National Solus Sites Ltd (1993) 158 JP 70, [1994] JPL 251 . . . . . . 8-31062, 8-31216
Kinnaird v Denney (1898) 28 Sol Jo 761 8-13874
Kinnell (Charles P) & Co Ltd v Harding, Wace & Co [1918] 1 KB 405, [1918-19] All ER Rep 594, 87 LJKB 342, 34 TLR 217, 62 Sol Jo 267, CA 1-642
Kinning's Case (1847) 10 QB 730, 16 LJQB 257 1-2159
Kinnis v Graves (1898) 67 LJQB 583, 78 LT 502, 46 WR 480 . . . . . . 1-47, 1-702
Kirkland v Robinson (1986) 151 JP 377, [1987] Crim LR 643 8-4140
Kirklees Metropolitan District Council v S [2006] 1 FLR 333, [2005] Fam Law 768, sub nom A Local Authority v S (a child) (care proceedings: contact) [2005] All ER (D) 24 (Aug) . . . 6-173
Kirkup v DPP [2003] EWHC 2354 (Admin), (2003) 168 JP 255, [2004] Crim LR 230, [2003] All ER (D) 53 (Oct) 7-1378
Kirshenboim v Salmon & Gluckstein Ltd [1898] 2 QB 19, 62 JP 439, 67 LJQB 601, 78 LT 658, 46 WR 573, 14 TLR 395, 42 Sol Jo 538, 19 Cox CC 127 8-4448
Kitcat v Sharp (1882) 52 LJ Ch 134, 48 LT 63, 31 WR 227 2-330
Kite v Brown [1941] 1 KB 26, [1940] 4 All ER 293, 104 JP 458, 109 LJKB 963, 164 LT 221, 57 TLR 82, 84 Sol Jo 705, 38 LGR 504 . . . . . . 1-465, 1-703
Klass v Germany (1978) 2 EHRR 214, ECtHR 8-17631F, 8-17631V
Klucinski v Klucinski [1953] 1 All ER 683, [1953] 1 WLR 522, 117 JP 187, 97 Sol Jo 192 . . 6-83, 6-1493
Knapp v Bedwell (1916) 14 LGR 985, 80 JP 336, 85 LJKB 1507, 115 LT 486, 32 TLR 704 . . 6-632
Knight v Bowers (1885) 14 QBD 845, 54 LJMC 108, 53 LT 234, 49 JP 614, 33 WR 613, 1 TLR 390, 15 Cox CC 728 8-12248
Knight v Halliwell (1874) LR 9 QB 412, 38 JP 470, 43 LJMC 113, 30 LT 359, 23 WR 689 . . 1-831
Knights v London, Chatham and Dover Rly Co (1893) 62 LJQB 378 7-7043
Knole Park Golf Club v Chief Superintendent, Kent County Constabulary [1979] 3 All ER 829, 144 JP 85, [1979] Crim LR 664 . . . . . . 6-255, 6-661
Knott v LCC [1934] 1 KB 126, [1933] All ER Rep 172, 97 JP 385, 103 LJKB 100, 150 LT 91, 50 TLR 55, 31 LGR 395, CA 8-31345A
Knowles v Knowles (1936) 100 JP Jo 736 6-67
Knowles v Knowles [1962] P 161, [1962] 1 All ER 659, [1962] 2 WLR 742, 105 Sol Jo 1011 . . 2-619
Knowles Ltd v Rand [1962] 2 All ER 926, [1962] 1 WLR 893, 126 JP 442, 106 Sol Jo 513, 60 LGR 384 . . . . . . 2-742, 7-1971
Knowles Transport Ltd v Russell [1975] RTR 87, [1974] Crim LR 717 4-7
Knox v Anderton (1983) 147 JP 340, 76 Cr App Rep 156, [1983] Crim LR 114 8-22630
Knupffer v London Express Newspaper Ltd [1944] AC 116, [1944] 1 All ER 495, 113 LJKB 251, 170 LT 362, 60 TLR 310, 88 Sol Jo 143, HL 8-18632
Koch v Koch [1899] P 221, 68 LJP 90, 81 LT 61 6-68
Kokkinakis v Greece (1993) 17 EHRR 397, ECtHR 1-301
Kokosinski v Kokosinski [1980] Fam 72, [1980] 1 All ER 1106, [1980] 3 WLR 55, 124 Sol Jo 16, sub nom K v K (1979) 10 Fam Law 91 6-1493
Kolczynski, Re. See R v Governor of Brixton Prison, ex p Kolczynski
König v Germany (1978) 2 EHRR 170, ECtHR 6-200
Kostovski v Netherlands (1989) 12 EHRR 434, ECtHR 2-466, 2-1470
Kruhlak v Kruhlak (No 2) [1958] 2 All ER 294, [1958] 1 WLR 606, 122 JP 360, 102 Sol Jo 401 . 2-744
Kruse v Johnson [1898] 2 QB 91, 62 JP 469, 67 LJQB 782, 78 LT 647, 46 WR 630, 14 TLR 416, 42 Sol Jo 509, 19 Cox CC 103 8-18835
Krystman v Krystman [1973] 3 All ER 247, [1973] 1 WLR 927, 117 Sol Jo 485, CA . . . 6-1493
Kuhnen v Germany (1988) 56 DR 205, EcomHR 8-27737
Kunnath v The State [1993] 4 All ER 30, [1993] 1 WLR 1315, 137 Sol Jo LB 195, [1993] NLJR 1332, [1993] 37 LS Gaz R 49, PC 1-649, 2-66
Kuruma Son of Kaniu v R [1955] AC 197, [1955] 1 All ER 236, [1955] 2 WLR 223, 119 JP 157, 99 Sol Jo 73, PC 2-206, 2-471
Kutzner v Germany [2003] 1 FCR 249, ECtHR 6-164A
Kyle v Dunsdon [1908] 2 KB 293, 72 JP 292, 77 LJKB 547, 98 LT 752, 24 TLR 505, 6 LGR 578, 21 Cox CC 587 8-31915
Kynaston v Secretary of State for Home Affairs (1981) 73 Cr App Rep 281, [1982] Crim LR 117, CA 8-22297
Kyte v Kyte [1988] Fam 145, [1987] 3 All ER 1041, [1987] 3 WLR 1114, [1988] FCR 325, [1988] 1 FLR 469, [1988] Fam Law 86, 131 Sol Jo 1391, [1987] NLJ Rep 849, [1987] LS Gaz R 3259, CA 6-83, 6-1493

PARA

L

PARA

PARA

M

PARA

M v DPP [2001] UKHL 10, [2002] 1 AC 285, [2001] 2 All ER 583, [2001] 2 WLR 765, [2001] 2 Cr App Rep 216, 165 JP 437, [2001] Crim LR 491, [2001] 20 LS Gaz R 40, [2001] NLJR 385, 145 Sol Jo LB 101 . . . 8-27722
M v London Borough of Islington and L [2002] 1 FLR 95, [2002] Fam Law 103, [2001] NLJR 1665 . . . 1-134
M v M (child of the family) (1980) 2 FLR 39, 10 Fam Law 184 . . . 6-1550
M v W (non-molestation order: duration) [2000] 1 FLR 107, [2000] Fam Law 13 . . . 6-130, 6-134, 6-3095
M v Warwickshire County Council [1994] 2 FCR 121, [1994] 2 FLR 593, [1994] Fam Law 611 . . . 6-168, 4-2324
M and K (child abuse: video evidence), Re [1996] 1 FCR 261, [1995] 2 FLR 571, [1996] Fam Law 13 . . . 6-29
MD and TD, Re [1994] 2 FCR 94, sub nom Re D (minors) [1994] Fam Law 228 . . . 6-24, 6-28
MH (a child), Re [2001] 2 FLR 1334, [2001] Fam Law 869 . . . 1-40036-24
MM (care order: abandoned baby), Re [1996] 2 FCR 521, sub nom Re M (care order: parental responsibility) [1996] 2 FLR 84, [1996] Fam Law 664 . . . 6-165
MFI Furniture Centres Ltd v Hibbert (1995) 160 JP 178 . . . 8-5011
MFI Warehouses Ltd v Nattrass [1973] 1 All ER 762, [1973] 1 WLR 307, 137 JP 307, 117 Sol Jo 143 . . . 8-4457
MGN Ltd v Northamptonshire County Council (1997) 161 JP 735, [1997] Crim LR 882 . . . 8-5012
McAngus, Re [1994] Crim LR 602 . . . 8-30724
M'Attee v Hogg (1903) 5 F 67 (J) . . . 8-11280
McBean v Parker (1983) 147 JP 205, [1983] Crim LR 399 . . . 8-23824
McC (a minor), Re [1985] AC 528, [1984] 3 WLR 1227, 81 Cr App Rep 54, 149 JP 225, [1985] Crim LR 152, 128 Sol Jo 837, [1985] LS Gaz R 117, sub nom McC v Mullan [1984] 3 All ER 908, HL . . . 2-320
McCabe v McCabe [1994] 1 FCR 257, [1994] 1 FLR 410, CA . . . 6-50
McCarthy v The Melita (1923) 130 LT 445, 16 BWCC 222, CA . . . 2-33
McCartney v McCartney [1981] Fam 59, [1981] All ER 597, [1981] 2 WLR 184, 124 Sol Jo 614 . . . 1-669
Macclesfield Corpn v Macclesfield Free Grammar School [1921] 2 Ch 189, 90 LJ Ch 477, 126 LT 15, 65 Sol Jo 663 . . . 8-25219
McCollom v Wrightson [1968] AC 522, [1968] 1 All ER 514, [1968] 2 WLR 578, 132 JP 261, 112 Sol Jo 132, 66 LGR 343, HL . . . 8-13432
McConnell v Chief Constable of the Greater Manchester Police [1990] 1 All ER 423, [1990] 1 WLR 364, 154 JP 325, 134 Sol Jo 457, 91 Cr App Rep 88, CA . . . 8-23824
McCool v Rushcliffe Borough Council [1998] 3 All ER 889, 163 JP 46 . . . 8-18974
McCormack v DPP [2002] EWHC 173 (Admin), [2002] RTR 20, [2002] All ER (D) 88 (Feb) . . . 4-1656
McCormick v National Motor and Accident Insurance Union Ltd (1934) 50 TLR 528, 78 Sol Jo 633, 40 Com Cas 76, 49 Ll L Rep 361, CA . . . 4-1565
McCrone v Riding [1938] WN 60, [1938] 1 All ER 157, 102 JP 109, 158 LT 253, 54 TLR 328, 82 Sol Jo 175, 36 LGR 160, 30 Cox CC 670 . . . 4-9
McCrone v J & L Rigby (Wigan) Ltd [1951] 2 TLR 911, 95 Sol Jo 712 . . . 4-3
McCrory v DPP (1990) 154 JP 520, [1991] RTR 187 . . . 7-2822
McDermott Movements Ltd v Horsfield [1983] RTR 42, [1982] Crim LR 693 . . . 4-3651
Macdonald v Carmichael 1941 JC 27, 1941 SLT 81, 106 JP Jo 53 . . . 4-3
M'Donald v Hughes [1902] 1 KB 94, 66 JP 86, 71 LJKB 43, 20 Cox CC 131, 50 WR 318, 46 Sol Jo 152, 85 LT 727, 18 TLR 79 . . . 6-576
Macdonald v Macdonald (1859) 4 Sw & Tr 242, 164 ER 1508 . . . 6-73
McDonald v Procurator Fiscal, Elgin 2003 SCCR 311, Times, 17 April . . . 1-435, 1-468
McDonald's Hamburger Ltd v Windle (1986) 151 JP 333, [1987] BTLC 362 . . . 8-12248
McDougall v Knight (1889) 14 App Cas 194, 58 JP 691, 58 LJQB 587, 60 LT 762, 38 WR 44 . . . 8-18632
McEachran v Hurst [1978] RTR 462, [1978] Crim LR 499 . . . 4-3
Macey v Macey (1981) 3 FLR 7, 11 Fam Law 248 . . . 6-83, 6-1493
McFarlane v Hulton [1899] 1 Ch 884, 68 LJ Ch 408, 80 LT 486, 47 WR 507 . . . 8-18632
McGrady v McGrady (1977) 1 FLR 67, 8 Fam Law 15, 121 Sol Jo 760 . . . 6-1493
McGrath v Vipas [1984] RTR 58, (1984) 148 JP 405, [1983] Crim LR 628 . . . 4-1377
McGuire v Sittingbourne Co-operative Society Ltd (1976) 140 JP 306, 120 Sol Jo 197, [1976] Crim LR 268 . . . 8-4464
Machent v Quinn [1970] 2 All ER 255, 134 JP 501, 114 Sol Jo 336 . . . 1-5995, 1-686, 1-7426, 8-30693
Machin v Ash [1950] WN 478, 94 Sol Jo 705, 49 LGR 87, 114 JP Jo 604 . . . 1-2174
McInnes v Clarke [1955] 1 All ER 346, [1959] 1 WLR 102, 119 JP 208, 99 Sol Jo 113, 165 Estates Gazette 113 . . . 8-16870
M'Intyre v Henderson 1911 SC (J) 78, 48 SLR 588, 6 Adam 434, 1911 1 SLT 343 . . . 4-1691
McKay v Gillies [1956] 3 All ER 583, [1956] 1 WLR 1402, 120 JP 587, 100 Sol Jo 820 . . . 8-13601A
McKay v Unwin Pyrotechnics Ltd [1991] Crim LR 547 . . . 8-15295
McKay White v DPP [1989] Crim LR 375 . . . 1-2917
McKenzie v DPP [1997] RTR 175 . . . 4-2995
Mackenzie v Mackenzie [1895] AC 384, HL . . . 6-67
McKenzie v McKenzie [1971] P 33, [1970] 3 All ER 1034, [1970] 3 WLR 472, 114 Sol Jo 667, CA . . . 1-139, [171]=22[187]1-639, 1-642
M'Kerrell v Robertson 1956 JC 50, 1956 SLT 290 . . . 4-2933
McKerry v Teesdale and Wear Valley Justices (2000) 164 JP 355, [2000] Crim LR 594, [2000] COD 199, [2001] EMLR 127, sub nom McKerry v DPP [2000] 11 LS Gaz R 36, 144 Sol Jo LB 126, CA . . . 1-47, 1-702, 1-2031, 1-2093, 5-114

PARA

Mantle v Jordan [1897] 1 QB 248, 61 JP 119, 66 LJQB 224, 75 LT 552, 13 TLR 121, 18 Cox CC 467 . . . . 8-18835, 8-31345A
Marco (Croydon) Ltd v Metropolitan Police [1984] RTR 24, [1983] Crim LR 395 . . 1-441, 1-442
Margate Corpn v Roach [1960] 3 All ER 774, [1960] 1 WLR 1380n, 125 JP 34, 104 Sol Jo 1058, 59 LGR 50 7-6071
Marjoram v Marjoram [1955] 2 All ER 1, [1955] 1 WLR 520, 119 JP 291, 99 Sol Jo 320 1-2123, 6-37, 6-67
Markham, ex p (1869) 34 JP 150, 21 LT 748, 18 WR 258 . . . . 1-768, 1-831
Marks v Benjamin (1839) 4 JP 44, 9 LJMC 20, 3 Jur 1195, 5 M & W 565 6-155
Marks v Beyfus (1890) 25 QBD 494, 55 JP 182, 59 LJQB 479, 63 LT 733, 38 WR 705, 6 TLR 406, 34 Sol Jo 619, 17 Cox CC 196 2-330
Marks v West Midlands Police [1981] RTR 471 7-1680
Marlowe Child and Family Services Ltd v DPP [1998] 2 Cr App Rep (S) 438, [1999] 1 FLR 997, [1999] Fam Law 306, [1998] Crim LR 594 3-1697
Marren v Dawson Bentley & Co Ltd [1961] 2 QB 135, [1961] 2 All ER 270, [1961] 2 WLR 679, 105 Sol Jo 383 . . . . 1-387, 2-744
Marsden v Marsden [1968] P 544, [1967] 1 All ER 967, [1967] 3 WLR 230, 111 Sol Jo 436 6-68
Marsh v Hodgson (1973) 137 JP Jo 266 5-87
Marsh v McGee. See Marsh v Police Comr
Marsh v Moores [1949] 2 KB 208, [1949] 2 All ER 27, 113 JP 346, [1949] LJR 1313, 65 TLR 318, 93 Sol Jo 450, 47 LGR 418 4-1560
Marsh v Police Comr [1945] KB 43, [1944] 2 All ER 392, 109 JP 45, 171 LT 331, 61 TLR 15, 88 Sol Jo 391, 42 LGR 305, sub nom Marsh v McGee 114 LJKB 168, CA . . . 8-23610
Marshall, Re (1994) 159 JP 688, [1994] Crim LR 915 1-1566
Marshall v Blackpool Corpn [1935] AC 16, [1934] All ER Rep 437, 98 JP 376, 103 LJKB 566, 151 LT 286, 50 TLR 483, 78 Sol Jo 488, 32 LGR 329, HL 8-25012
Marshall v Ford (1908) 99 LT 796, 72 JP 480, 6 LGR 1126, 21 Cox CC 731 . . 2-205, 2-622
Marshall v Graham [1907] 2 KB 112, 71 JP 270, 76 LJKB 690, 97 LT 52, 23 TLR 435, 5 LGR 738, 21 Cox CC 461 8-7824
Marshall v Matthews [1939] 1 All ER 156, 37 LGR 194 8-31854
Marshall v Smith (1873) LR 8 CP 416, 42 LJMC 108, 28 LT 538 1-387
Marshall v Spicer (1911) 75 JP 138, 103 LT 902 . . . . 6-571, 6-574
Marshall v Tinnelly (1937) 81 Sol Jo 902, (1937) Times, 29 October 8-27680
Marsland v Taggart [1928] 2 KB 447, [1928] All ER Rep 51, 92 JP 118, 97 LJKB 787, 139 LT 192, 44 TLR 543, 26 LGR 377, 28 Cox CC 511 1-5689
Marson v Thompson (1955) 119 JP Jo 172, [1955] Crim LR 319 1-765
Marston Services Ltd v Police Authority (1934) 98 JP Jo 848 4-3503
Martin v Barker (1881) 45 JP 749, 50 LJMC 109, 20 WR 789, 45 LT 214 6-819
Martin v DPP [2000] RTR 188, [2000] 2 Cr App Rep (S) 18, 164 JP 405, [2000] Crim LR 320, 144 Sol Jo LB 5 4-1693
Martin v McIntyre 1910 47 SLR 645, 74 JP Jo 482 . . . . 6-320, 6-343, 8–27672, 8–27677
Martin v Spalding [1979] 2 All ER 1193, [1979] 1 WLR 1164, 143 JP 538, 123 Sol Jo 456 6-255, 6-661
Martin v Watson [1996] AC 74, [1995] 3 All ER 559, [1995] 3 WLR 318, [1995] 31 LS Gaz R 36, [1995] NLJR 1093, 139 Sol Jo LB 190, HL 1-380
Martin v White [1910] 1 KB 665, 74 JP 106, 79 LJKB 553, 102 LT 23, 26 TLR 218, 22 Cox CC 236, 8 LGR 218 . . . . 2-193, 2-205
Martins v Customs and Excise Comrs [2001] EWCA Civ 1040, [2001] 4 All ER 687, [2001] 1 WLR 2253, [2001] STC 1188, [2001] NLJR 1033, 145 Sol Jo LB 174 8-17631W, 8-30086
Mason v Newland and Rosier (1840) 9 C & P 575 8-817
Masper v Brown (1876) 1 CPD 97, 40 JP 265, 45 LJCP 203, 34 LT 254, 24 WR 369 1-448, 8-23115
Massey v S & P Lingwood Ltd (1945) 89 Sol Jo 316 8-14619
Masters v Fraser (1901) 66 JP 100, 85 LT 611, 18 TLR 31 . . . . . 8-16719, 8-16726
Masters v Secretary of State for the Environment [2000] 4 All ER 458, [2000] 3 WLR 1894, [2000] 35 LS Gaz R 39, [2000] NLJR 1422, CA 8-4180
Mathers v Penfold [1915] 1 KB 514, 84 LJKB 627, 112 LT 726, 79 JP 225, 31 TLR 108, 59 Sol Jo 235, 13 LGR 359, 24 Cox CC 642 8-31440
Mathews v Morris (1981) 145 JP 262 . . . . 1-684, 2-75
Matthews v King [1934] 1 KB 505, [1933] All ER Rep 942, 97 JP 345, 103 LJKB 509, 150 LT 133, 50 TLR 62, 31 LGR 379, 30 Cox CC 27 8-27910
Matthews v Matthews [1932] P 103, [1932] All ER Rep 323, 96 JP 290, 101 LJP 41, 147 LT 240, 48 TLR 511, 76 Sol Jo 495, 30 LGR 365, 29 Cox CC 503 6-71
Mattison v Johnson [1916] WN 52, [1916-17] All ER Rep 727, 80 JP 243, 85 LJKB 741, 114 LT 951, 14 LGR 457, 25 Cox CC 373 8-28012
Matto v Crown Court at Wolverhampton [1987] RTR 337, [1987] Crim LR 641 . 4-1378
Maw v Holloway [1914] 3 KB 594, 78 JP 347, 84 LJKB 99, 111 LT 670 8-11279
Mawaz Khan v R [1967] 1 AC 454, [1967] 1 All ER 80, [1966] 3 WLR 1275, 110 Sol Jo 869, PC 2-335
Mawdesley v Chief Constable of Cheshire Constabulary [2003] EWHC 1586 (Admin), [2004] 1 All ER 58, [2004] 1 WLR 1035, [2004] RTR 209, 168 JP 23, [2004] Crim LR 232, [2003] NLJR 1384, (2003) Times, 11 September, [2003] All ER (D) 21 (Aug) . 4-1562, 4-1598, 4-1652
Mawdsley v Walter Cox (Transport) Ltd [1965] 3 All ER 728, [1966] 1 WLR 63, 130 JP 62, 110 Sol Jo 36 4-3535
Mawson v Oxford [1987] RTR 398, [1987] Crim LR 131 . . . . . . 4-1769, 4-2817
Maxwell v DPP [1935] AC 309, 98 JP 387, 103 LJKB 501, 151 LT 477, 50 TLR 499, 32 LGR 335, 30 Cox CC 160, 24 Cr App Rep 152, HL 2-460, 2-477, 2-491

PARA

May v Beeley [1910] 2 KB 722, 74 JP 111, 79 LJKB 852, 102 LT 326, 22 Cox CC 306, 8 LGR 166 . . . 1-642
May v Vincent (1990) 154 JP 997, [1991] 1 EGLR 27, [1991] 04 EG 144 . . . 8-4447
Maydew v Flint (1984) 80 Cr App Rep 49, [1985] Crim LR 502 . . . 1-762, 1-832
Mayer v Harding (1867) LR 2 QB 410, 9 B & S 27n, 31 JP 376, 16 LT 429,15 WR 816 . . . 1-5689
Mayes v Mayes [1971] 2 All ER 397, [1971] 1 WLR 679, 135 JP 487, 115 Sol Jo 111 . . . 1-582, 1-668, 1-753, 1-5943
Mayhew v Wardley (1863) 14 CBNS 550, 2 New Rep 325, 8 LT 504 . . . 8-13607
Mayon v DPP [1988] RTR 281 . . . 4-1655
Meah v Roberts [1978] 1 All ER 97, [1977] 1 WLR 1187, 142 JP 85, 121 Sol Jo 592, [1977] Crim LR 678 . . . 8-12248
Medcalf v Mardell [2002] UKHL 27, [2003] 1 AC 120, [2002] 3 All ER 721, [2002] 3 WLR 172, [2002] 31 LS Gaz R 34, [2002] NLJR 1032 . . . 1-2673
Medicaments and Related Classes of Goods (No 2), Re [2001] 1 WLR 700, [2001] ICR 564, [2001] 07 LS Gaz R 40, 145 Sol Jo LB 29, CA . . . 1-133
Medway Council v BBC [2002] 1 FLR 104, [2001] Fam Law 883 . . . , 6-2100, 5-23
Mee v Cruikshank (1902) 86 LT 708, 66 JP 89, 18 TLR 271, 20 Cox CC 210 . . . 8-23069
Meek v Powell [1952] 1 KB 164, [1952] 1 All ER 347, 116 JP 116, [1952] 1 TLR 358, 96 Sol Jo 91, 50 LGR 247 . . . 1-442
Mehta (otherwise Kohn) v Mehta [1945] 2 All ER 690, 174 LT 63 . . . 6-50
Meigh v Wickenden [1942] 2 KB 160, [1942] 2 All ER 68, 106 JP 207, 112 LJKB 76, 167 LT 135, 58 TLR 260, 86 Sol Jo 218, 40 LGR 191 . . . 8-14683
Melias Ltd v Preston [1957] 2 QB 380, [1957] 2 All ER 449, [1957] 3 WLR 42, 121 JP 444, 101 Sol Jo 481, 55 LGR 366 . . . 8-31854
Mella v Monahan [1961] Crim LR 175 . . . 8-22449, 8-22560
Mellor v Lydiate [1914] 3 KB 1141, 79 JP 68, 84 LJKB 8, 24 Cox CC 443, [1914-15] All ER Rep 762, 111 LT 988, 30 TLR 704 . . . 6-754
Menzies v Wheeler (18 July 1929, unreported) . . . 8-14615
Mepstead v DPP (1995) 160 JP 475, [1996] Crim LR 111 . . . 8-23824
Mercer v Denne [1904] 2 Ch 584, [1904-7] All ER Rep 71, 68 JP 479, 74 LJ Ch 71, 91 LT 513, 58 WR 55, 20 TLR 609, 3 LGR 385; affd [1905] 2 Ch 538, [1904-7] All ER Rep 71, 70 JP 65, 74 LJ Ch 723, 93 LT 412, 54 WR 303, 21 TLR 760, 8 LGR 1293, CA . . . 2-192, 2-208, 2-790
Mercer v DPP [2003] EWHC 225 (Admin), [2004] RTR 103, 167 JP 441, [2003] All ER (D) 13 (Feb) . . . 4-1378
Mercer v Oldham [1984] Crim LR 232 . . . 8-23610
Merchants' and Manufacturers' Insurance Co Ltd v Hunt [1941] 1 KB 295, [1941] 1 All ER 123, 110 LJKB 375, 165 LT 49, 57 TLR 208, 68 Ll L Rep 117, CA . . . 7-1197
Meredith, ex p [1973] 2 All ER 234, [1973] 1 WLR 435, 137 JP 485, 117 Sol Jo 165, 57 Cr App Rep 451 . . . 1-2563
Merriman v Hardy [1987] FCR 44 . . . 6-22
Metford v Edwards [1915] 1 KB 172, 79 JP 84, 84 LJKB 161, 24 Cox CC 490, [1914-15] All ER Rep 653, 112 LT 78, 30 TLR 700 . . . 6-754
Metropolitan Police v Scarlett [1978] Crim LR 234 . . . 4-1643
Metropolitan Police Comr v Caldwell [1982] AC 341, [1981] 1 All ER 961, [1981] 2 WLR 509, 73 Cr App Rep 13, 145 JP 211, 125 Sol Jo 239, HL . . . 1-304 8-24740
Metropolitan Police Comr v Charles [1977] AC 177, [1976] 3 All ER 112, [1977] 3 WLR 431, 140 JP 531, 120 Sol Jo 588, 68 Cr App Rep 334, [1977] Crim LR 615, HL . . . 8-30705
Metropolitan Police Comr v Curran [1976] 1 All ER 162, [1976] 1 WLR 87, 140 JP 77, 120 Sol Jo 49, 62 Cr App Rep 131, HL . . . 7-1389
Metropolitan Police Comr v Hooper [2005] EWHC 340 (Admin), [2005] 4 All ER 1095, [2005] 1 WLR 1995, 169 JP 409, (2005) Times, 3 March, [2005] All ER (D) 245 (Feb) . . . 1-4508, 8-17631W
Metropolitan Properties Co Ltd v Lannon [1969] 1 QB 577, [1968] 3 All ER 304, [1968] 3 WLR 694, 112 Sol Jo 585, 19 P & CR 856, [1968] RVR 490, CA . . . 1-134
Metsoja v H Norman Pitt & Co Ltd (1989) 153 JP 485 . . . 8-4804
Meunier, Re [1894] 2 QB 415, 63 LJMC 198, 71 LT 403, 42 WR 637, 18 Cox CC 15, 10 R 400 . . . 8-10155, 8-10195
Meyer v Meyer [1957] 2 All ER 546, [1957] 1 WLR 927, 121 JP 424, 101 Sol Jo 630 . . . 1-5687
Michael v Gowland [1977] 2 All ER 328, [1977] 1 WLR 296, 141 JP 343, 7 Fam Law 109, 120 Sol Jo 857 . . . 1-766, 6-225
Mickelthwaite v Vincent (1892) 67 LT 225, 8 TLR 685; affd 69 LT 57, CA . . . 8-30733
Middlesbrough Borough Council v Safeer [2001] EWHC Admin 525, [2001] 4 All ER 630, 166 JP 48, [2002] 1 Cr App Rep 266, [2001] Crim LR 922, [2001] 30 LS Gaz R 37 . . . 4-1645, 8-18817
Middleton v Rowlett [1954] 2 All ER 277, [1954] 1 WLR 831, 118 JP 362, 98 Sol Jo 373, 52 LGR 334 . . . 1-684, 2-75
Midelton v Gale (1838) 8 Ad & El 155, sub nom Middleton v Gale 3 Nev & PKB 372, 1 Will Woll & H 352, 7 LJMC 103, 2 JP 328, 2 Jur 819 . . . 8-13677
Midland Bank Ltd v Conway Borough Council [1965] 2 All ER 972, [1965] 1 WLR 1165, 129 JP 466, 109 Sol Jo 494, 63 LGR 346 . . . 8-17185
Midland Greyhound Racing Co Ltd v Foley [1973] 2 All ER 324, [1973] 1 WLR 324, 137 JP 457, 117 Sol Jo 185 . . . 8-13318
Midland Rly Co v Freeman (1884) 12 QBD 629, 48 JP 660, 53 LJMC 79, 32 WR 830 . . . 1-2022
Midlands Electricity Board v Stephenson [1973] Crim LR 441 . . . 7-5959
Mieras v Rees (1975) 139 JP 549 . . . 8-21203

PARA

Moody v Godstone RDC [1966] 2 All ER 696, [1966] 1 WLR 1085, 130 JP 332, 110 Sol Jo 687, 198 Estates Gazette 683 . . . . 2-1216, 8-31036
Moon v Moon (1979) 2 FLR 115, sub nom M v M 10 Fam Law 114 . . . . 6-376, 6-1493
Mooney v Cardiff Magistrates' Court (1999) 164 JP 220, [1999] 42 LS Gaz R 40 . . 1-643, 1-802
Moore v Ball [1984] Fam 41, [1984] 2 All ER 237, [1984] 2 WLR 865, 148 JP 425, [1984] FLR 555, [1984] Fam Law 181, 128 Sol Jo 298, [1984] LS Gaz R 1205 1-2102
Moore v Elphick [1945] 2 All ER 155, 110 JP 66, 48 LGR 142 . . . . 8-13601, 8-13601A
Moore v Gooderham [1960] 3 All ER 575, [1960] 1 WLR 1308, 124 JP 513, 104 Sol Jo 1036 8-10445
Moore v Ray [1951] 1 KB 98, [1950] 2 All ER 561, 114 JP 486, 66 (pt 2) TLR 721, 94 Sol Jo 596, 49 LGR 187 8-12248
Moore v Smith (1859) 1 El & El 597, 23 JP 133, 28 LJMC 126, 7 WR 206, 32 LTOS 314, 5 Jur NS 892 . . . . 1-769, 1-832
Moore, Nettlefold & Co v Singer Manufacturing Co [1904] 1 KB 820, 68 JP 369, 73 LJKB 457, 90 LT 469, 52 WR 385, 20 TLR 366, 48 Sol Jo 328, CA 8-16719
Moores v DPP [1992] 1 QB 125, [1991] 4 All ER 521, [1991] 3 WLR 549, 156 JP 113, 94 Cr App Rep 173, [1992] Crim LR 49 8-7490
Moran v DPP [2002] EWHC 89 (Admin), (2002) 166 JP 467 1-2031
Moorman v Tordoff (1908) 72 JP 142, 98 LT 416, 6 LGR 360 8-18835
Moran v Jones (1911) 75 JP 411, [1911-13] All ER Rep 309, 104 LT 921, 27 TLR 421, 22 Cox CC 474 . . . . 6-320, 8–27672, 8-31441
Morden v Porter (1860) 7 CBNS 641, 25 JP 263, 307, 29 LJMC 213, 1 LT 403, 8 WR 272 8-13606, 8-13677
More O'Ferrall Ltd v Harrow UDC [1947] KB 66, [1946] 2 All ER 489, 110 JP 357, [1947] LJR 520, 175 LT 277, 62 TLR 604, 90 Sol Jo 490, 44 LGR 372 . . . . . 1-767, 1-830
Morgan v Bowker [1964] 1 QB 507, [1963] 1 All ER 691, [1963] 2 WLR 860, 127 JP 264, 107 Sol Jo 155 8-22451
Morgan v Brydges (1818) 2 Stark 314 . . . . 1-664, 2-68
Morgan v DPP [1970] 3 All ER 1053, 135 JP 86, 114 Sol Jo 805 8-2870
Morgan v Edwards (1860) 5 H & N 415, 24 JP 245, 29 LJMC 108, 6 Jur NS 379 1-5689
Morgan v Jackson [1895] 1 QB 885, 59 JP 327, 64 LJQB 462, 72 LT 593, 43 WR 479, 15 R 411 8-13872
Morgan v Lee [1985] RTR 409, 149 JP 583, [1985] Crim LR 515 4-1378
Morgan v London General Omnibus Co (1883) 12 QBD 201, 50 LT 687, 32 WR 416; affd 13 QBD 832, 48 JP 503, 53 LJQB 352, 51 LT 213, 32 WR 759, CA 8-14683
Morgan v Parr [1921] 2 KB 379, [1921] All ER Rep 579, 85 JP 165, 90 LJKB 1199, 125 LT 307, 37 TLR 587, 19 LGR 277, 26 Cox CC 739 . . . . 5-98, 8-7846
Morgan v Quality Tools Engineering (Stourbridge) Ltd [1972] 1 All ER 744, [1972] 1 WLR 196, 116 Sol Jo 98 8-29099
Morgans v DPP [1999] 1 WLR 968, [1999] 2 Cr App Rep 99, 163 JP 543, [1999] Crim LR 490; revsd [2001] 1 AC 315, [2000] 2 All ER 522, [2000] 2 WLR 386, [2000] 2 Cr App Rep 113, [2000] Crim LR 576, [2000] 09 LS Gaz R 39, HL 8-7347, 8-24203
Morphitis v Salmon (1989) 154 JP 365, [1990] Crim LR 48 8-24740
Morris v Blackman (1864) 2 H & C 912, 28 JP 199, 10 Jur NS 520 8-13601
Morris v Corbett (1892) 56 JP 649 8-12248
Morris v Customs and Excise Comrs [2001] EWCA Civ 1040, [2001] 4 All ER 687, [2001] 1 WLR 2253, [2001] STC 1188, [2001] 32 LS Gaz R 37, [2001] NLJR 1033, 145 Sol Jo LB 174 . . . . 8-17631W, 8-30086
Morris v Davies (1837) 5 Cl & Fin 163, 1 Jur 911 6-51
Morris v Jeffries (1866) LR 1 QB 261, 30 JP 198, 35 LJMC 143, 13 LT 629, 14 WR 310 . 7-6028
Morris v Luton Corpn [1946] KB 114, [1946] 1 All ER 1, 110 JP 102, 115 LJKB 202, 174 LT 26, 62 TLR 145, 90 Sol Jo 91, 44 LGR 1, CA 4-9
Morris v Morris (1985) 150 JP 7, [1985] FLR 1176, [1986] Fam Law 24, CA 6-961
Morris v Tolman [1923] 1 KB 166, 86 JP 221, 92 LJKB 215, 128 LT 118, 39 TLR 39, 67 Sol Jo 169, 27 Cox CC 345, 20 LGR 803 1-321
Morrison v Anderson 1913 SC (J) 114, 50 SLR 817, 1913 SLT 124, 7 Adam 201 . . . 8-13670
Morriss v Lawrence (1977) 121 Sol Jo 187, [1977] RTR 205, [1977] Crim LR 170 . . 1-440
Mortimer v M'Callan (1840) 6 M & W 58, 9 LJ Ex 73, 4 Jur 172 2-196
Morton v Chaney [1960] 3 All ER 632, [1960] 1 WLR 1312, 125 JP 37, 104 Sol Jo 1035 . . 8-10380
Morton v Green (1881) 8 R 36, 18 SLR 570 8-12248
Morton v Palmer (1861) 46 JP 150, 51 LJQB 7, 45 LT 426, 30 WR 115, CA 8-16727
Moses v Winder [1981] RTR 37, [1980] Crim LR 232 4-9
Moss v Jenkins [1975] RTR 25, [1974] Crim LR 715 . . . . 1-32, 4-1377
Moss v McLachlan (1984) 149 JP 167, [1985] IRLR 76 . . . . . 1-2698, 8-23824
Mostyn v Fabrigas (1775) 1 Cowp 161 2-344
Motteram v Eastern Counties Rly Co (1859) 7 CBNS 58, 24 JP 40, 29 LJMC 57, 1 LT 101, 6 Jur NS 583, 8 WR 77 . . . . 1-768, 1-831
Motture v Motture [1955] 3 All ER 242n, [1955] 1 WLR 1066, 99 Sol Jo 709 . . . 6-51, 8-23117
Moualem v Carlisle City Council (1994) 158 JP 1110, [1995] ELR 22 8-15293
Mouat v DPP [2001] EWHC Admin 130, [2001] 1 All ER 831, [2001] 1 WLR 1293, [2001] 2 Cr App Rep 427, [2001] Crim LR 741, [2001] NLJR 304 1-63
Moulder v Judd [1974] Crim LR 111 1-442
Mounsey v Campbell [1983] RTR 36 4-3655
Mowe v Perraton [1952] 1 All ER 423, 116 JP 139, 96 Sol Jo 182, 35 Cr App Rep 194 . . 8-30701

PARA

N

PARA

Newspaper Licensing Agency Ltd v Marks & Spencer plc [2001] Ch 257, [2000] 4 All ER 239, [2000] 3 WLR 1256, [2001] RPC 76, [2000] 25 LS Gaz R 38, [2000] NLJR 900, [2000] EMLR 704, CA; affd [2001] UKHL 38, [2003] 1 AC 551, [2001] 3 All ER 977, [2001] 3 WLR 290, [2002] RPC 225, [2001] 31 LS Gaz R 32, [2001] EMLR 991, 145 Sol Jo LB 182 . . . 8-5640

Newton v John Stanning & Son Ltd [1962] 1 All ER 78, [1962] 1 WLR 30, 106 Sol Jo 77, 60 LGR 89, [1962] RVR 58 . . . 8-14683

Newton (G) Ltd v Smith [1962] 2 QB 278, [1962] 2 All ER 19, [1962] 2 WLR 926, 60 LGR 256, 126 JP 324, 106 Sol Jo 287, DC . . . 1-7427

Newton v West Vale Creamery Co Ltd (1956) 120 JP 318 . . . 8-12248

Newton v Woods (1986) 151 JP 436, [1987] RTR 41 . . . 4-1655

Nicholas v Parsonage [1987] RTR 199, [1987] Crim LR 474 . . . 1-2732

Nicholas v Penny [1950] 2 KB 446, 66 TLR 1122, 94 Sol Jo 437, sub nom Penny v Nicholas [1950] 2 All ER 89, 114 JP 335, 48 LGR 535 . . . 2-619, 4-1198

Nicholls v Brentwood Justices. See R v Brentwood Justices, ex p Nicholls

Nicholson v Glasspool (1959) 123 JP 229 . . . 8-18835

Nicholson v Tapp [1972] 3 All ER 245, [1972] 1 WLR 1044, 116 Sol Jo 527 . . . 4-1642

Nicholson v Watts [1973] RTR 208, [1973] Crim LR 246 . . . 4-1655

Nicol and Selvanayagan v DPP (1995) 160 JP 155, [1996] Crim LR 318 . . . 3-541

Nicoll v Catron (1985) 149 JP 424, 81 Cr App Rep 339, [1985] Crim LR 223 . . . 8-24330

Nicoll v Strachan 1913 SC (J) 18 . . . 8-13607

Nielsen, Re [1984] AC 606, [1984] 2 WLR 737, 128 Sol Jo 317, [1984] LS Gaz R 1838, sub nom Government of Denmark v Nielsen [1984] 2 All ER 81, 79 Cr App Rep 1, HL . . . 8-10158, 8-10195

Nimmo v Alexander Cowan & Sons Ltd [1968] AC 107, [1967] 3 All ER 187, [1967] 3 WLR 1169, 111 Sol Jo 668, 3 KIR 277, HL . . . 1-2174

Nobbs, Re [1978] 3 All ER 390, [1978] 1 WLR 1302, 142 JP 624, 122 Sol Jo 714 . . . 8-9921

Noble v Killick (1891) 60 LJMC 61 . . . 7-7043

Noor Mohamed v R [1949] AC 182, [1949] 1 All ER 365, 65 TLR 134, 93 Sol Jo 180, PC . . . 8-27979

Norman (Alec) Garages Ltd v Phillips (1984) 148 JP 741, [1985] RTR 164 . . . 8-4447, 8-4457, 8-4464

Normanshaw v Normanshaw and Measham (1893) 69 LT 468 . . . 2-331

Norris v Ireland (1988) 13 EHRR 186, ECtHR . . . 1-301, 8-17631F

Norris v Manning [1971] Crim LR 419, 115 Sol Jo 407 . . . 6-155

North v Gerrish (1959) 123 JP 313 . . . 1-7427, 4-1596

North West Traffic Area Licensing Authority v Post Office [1982] RTR 304, DC . . . 4–2635

North Yorkshire County Council v G [1994] 1 FCR 737, [1993] 2 FLR 732, [1993] Fam Law 623 . . . 6-2109

North Yorkshire County Council v Holmesterne Farm Co Ltd (1985) 150 JP 124 . . . 8-31838

North Yorkshire County Council v SA [2003] EWCA Civ 839, [2003] 3 FCR 118, [2003] 2 FLR 849, [2003] 35 LS Gaz R 34 . . . 6-165

North Yorkshire County Council v Selby Youth Court Justices [1994] 1 All ER 991, [1995] 1 WLR 1, 93 LGR 226, [1994] 2 FCR 1184, [1994] 2 FLR 169, [1994] Fam Law 490 . . . 5-45, 5-601

North Yorkshire Trading Standards Department v Williams (1994) 159 JP 383 . . . 2-621

North Yorkshire Trading Standards Service v Coleman [2001] EWHC Admin 818, (2001) 166 JP 76, [2001] All ER (D) 190 (Oct) . . . 1-447, 8-4457

Northamptonshire County Council v Islington London Borough Council [2001] Fam 364, [2000] 2 WLR 193, [1999] 3 FCR 385, [1999] 2 FLR 881, [1999] Fam Law 687, CA . . . 6-167, 6-2140

Northamptonshire County Council v Purity Soft Drinks Ltd [2004] EWHC 3119 (Admin), (2004) 169 JP 84 . . . 8–4449

Northern Leisure plc v Schofield [2001] 1 All ER 660, [2001] 1 WLR 1196, 164 JP 613 . . . 6-165, 6-169, 6-663

Northfield v Pinder [1969] 2 QB 7, [1968] 3 All ER 854, [1969] 2 WLR 50, 112 Sol Jo 884 . . . 7-1376

Northumberland County Council v PR Manufacturing Ltd (t/a Paul Rosco) [2004] EWHC 112 (Admin), (2004) 168 JP 209, [2004] All ER (D) 301 (Jan) . . . 8-5003

Nortier v Netherlands (1993) 17 EHRR 273, ECtHR . . . 5-22A

Norton v Knowles [1969] 1 QB 572, [1967] 3 All ER 1061, [1968] 3 WLR 183, 132 JP 100, 111 Sol Jo 890 . . . 8-17030

Norton v Lees (1921) 85 JP Jo 500; on appeal 87 JP Jo 675 . . . 7-5959, 7-6009

Norweb plc v Dixon [1995] 3 All ER 952, [1995] 1 WLR 636 . . . 1-1263, 8-9577

Norwood v DPP [2003] EWHC 1564 (Admin), [2003] Crim LR 888, 167 JPN 522 . . . 8-17631W, 8-27724

Nott v Bound (1866) LR 1 QB 405, 30 JP 564, 14 LT 330 . . . 8-16722

Nott v Nott (1866) LR 1 P & D 251, 36 LJP & M 10, 15 LT 299 . . . 6-73

Nottingham City Council v [171]=22[187] (1998) Times, 28 October . . . 8-18974

Nottingham City Council v Amin [2000] 2 All ER 946, [2000] 1 WLR 1071, [2000] RTR 122, [2000] 1 Cr App Rep 426, [2000] Crim LR 174 . . . 1-768, 1-831, 2-471

Nottingham City Council v Wolverhampton and Dudley Breweries [2003] EWHC 2852 (Admin), [2004] QB 1275, [2004] 1 All ER 1352, [2004] 2 WLR 820, 168 JP 37 . . . 8-12248

Nottingham City Council v Woodings [1994] RTR 72 . . . 8-31354

Nottingham City Council v Zain (a minor) [2001] EWCA Civ 1248, [2002] 1 WLR 607, [2003] HLR 181 . . . 8-18817

Nottingham County Council v P [1994] Fam 18, [1993] 3 All ER 815, [1993] 3 WLR 637, [1994] 1 FCR 624, [1993] 2 FLR 134, 137 Sol Jo LB 147, 92 LGR 72, [1993] 26 LS Gaz R 37, CA . . . 6-150, 6-152, 6-164, 6-2107, 6-2108, 6-2116, 6-2291

Nugent v Ridley [1987] RTR 412, [1987] Crim LR 640 . . . 4-1378

Nurse v Morganite Crucible Ltd [1989] AC 692, [1989] 1 All ER 113, [1989] 2 WLR 82, [1989] ICR 15, [1989] IRLR 88, 153 JP 398, 133 Sol Jo 81, [1989] 5 LS Gaz R 41, HL . . . 8-14683

PARA

PARA

P

PARA

Pearson v Whitfield (1888) 52 JP Jo 708 8-18835

Peckover v Defries (1906) 71 JP 38, 21 Cox CC 323, 95 LT 883, 23 TLR 20 6-754

Peddubriwny v Cambridge City Council [2001] EWHC Admin 200, [2001] RTR 461 8-18974

Pedro v Diss [1981] 2 All ER 59, 145 JP 445, 72 Cr App Rep 193 1-2696

Peek v De Rutzen (1882) 46 JP 313 1-443

Peek v Towle [1945] KB 458, [1945] 2 All ER 611, 109 JP 160, 114 LJKB 540, 173 LT 360, 61 TLR 399, 43 LGR 286 4-1596

Pelladoah v Netherlands (1994) 19 EHRR 81, ECtHR 1-423

Pelling, Re [1997] 2 FCR 585, [1997] 2 FLR 458, [1997] Fam Law 655 8-29561

Pender v Smith [1959] 2 QB 84, [1959] 2 All ER 360, [1959] 2 WLR 794, 123 JP 351, 103 Sol Jo 433 6-632

Penman v Parker [1986] 2 All ER 862, [1986] 1 WLR 882, 130 Sol Jo 357, [1986] RTR 403, [1986] NLJ Rep 538, [1986] LS Gaz R 2492 4-1656

Pennell v Churchwardens of Uxbridge (1862) 26 JP 87, 31 LJMC 92, 5 LT 685, 10 WR 319, 8 Jur NS 99 1-5689

Penrice v Brander 1921 JC 63, 58 SLR 307 8-12248

Penton Park Homes Ltd v Chertsey UDC (1973) 72 LGR 115, 26 PCR 531 8-30893

Penwarden v Palmer (1894) 10 TLR 362 1-385 8-13606

People's Hostels Ltd v Turley [1939] 1 KB 149, [1938] 4 All ER 72, 108 LJKB 66, 102 JP 509, 159 LT 557, 55 TLR 27, 82 Sol Jo 870, 36 LGR 641, 31 Cox CC 152 8-17333

Pepper v Hart [1993] AC 593, [1993] 1 All ER 42, [1992] 3 WLR 1032, [1993] ICR 291, [1993] IRLR 33, [1993] RVR 127, [1992] STC 898, [1993] NLJR 17, HL 1-6970, 2-742

Pepper v Pepper [1960] 1 All ER 529, [1960] 1 WLR 131, 124 JP 184, 104 Sol Jo 190 1-1394

Percival v Ball [1937] WN 106, 107 JP Jo 614 4-1642

Percival v Stanton [1954] 1 All ER 392, [1954] 1 WLR 300, 118 JP 171, 98 Sol Jo 114 8-11296

Percy v DPP [1995] 3 All ER 124, [1995] 1 WLR 1382, 159 JP 337, [1995] Crim LR 714, [1995] 09 LS Gaz R 38 3-540, 3-541

Percy v DPP [2001] EWHC Admin 1125, (2001) 166 JP 93, [2002] Crim LR 835 8-17631W, 8-27724

Percy v DPP [2005] EWHC 684 (Admin), [2005] 3 All ER 330, [2005] 3 WLR 628, [2005] Crim LR 959, [2005] All ER (D) 279 (Apr); affd sub nom R v Jones [2004] EWCA Crim 1981, [2005] QB 259, [2004] 4 All ER 955, [2004] 3 WLR 1362, [2005] 1 Cr App Rep 154, [2005] Crim LR 122, [2004] 34 LS Gaz R 29, (2004) Times, 30 July, 148 Sol Jo LB 1149, [2004] All ER (D) 374 (Jul); affd [2006] UKHL 16, [2006] All ER (D) 419 (Mar) 1-1071, 8-24907

Percy v Hall [1996] 4 All ER 523, [1997] 3 WLR 573, [1996] 23 LS Gaz R 36, 140 Sol Jo LB 130, CA 2-193

Percy v Smith [1986] RTR 252 4-3

Perks v Perks [1946] P 1, [1945] 2 All ER 580, 110 JP 94, 115 LJP 7, 173 LT 340, 62 TLR 26, 89 Sol Jo 577, CA 6-27, 6-84, 6-1527

Perring & Co v Emerson [1906] 1 KB 1, 75 LJKB 12, 93 LT 748, 54 WR 47, 22 TLR 14, 50 Sol Jo 14 8-16719

Perrins v Smith [1946] KB 90, [1945] 2 All ER 706, 110 JP 91, 74 LT 38, 62 TLR 72, 90 Sol Jo 44 8-1279

Perry v Garner [1953] 1 QB 335, [1953] 1 All ER 285, 117 JP 104, 97 Sol Jo 98, 51 LGR 171 8-25354

Perry v McGovern [1986] RTR 240 4-1655

Perry v Perry [1920] P 361, 89 LJP 192, 123 LT 586 6-51, 6-79, 8-23117

Perry v Perry [1952] P 203, [1952] 1 All ER 1076, 116 JP 258, [1952] 1 TLR 1633, 96 Sol Jo 358, CA 6-41

Perth General Station Committee v Ross [1897] AC 479, [1895-9] All ER Rep 1267, 66 LJPC 81, 77 LT 226 7-6979

Peters v General Accident Fire and Life Assurance Corpn Ltd [1938] 2 All ER 267, [1938] WN 158, 158 LT 476, 54 TLR 663, 82 Sol Jo 294, 36 LGR 583, 60 Ll L Rep 311, CA 4-1562

Peters v Yiewsley and West Drayton UDC [1963] 2 QB 133, [1963] 1 All ER 843, [1963] 2 WLR 702, 127 JP 278, 107 Sol Jo 176, 61 LGR 271, [1963] RVR 392, 14 P & CR 140, 186 Estates Gazette 175 8-30895

Peterssen v Royal Society for the Prevention of Cruelty to Animals [1993] Crim LR 852 8-811

Pettigrew v Northumbria Police Authority [1976] RTR 177, [1976] Crim LR 259 4-1378

Pettit v Lilley. See Lilley v Pettit

Pharmaceutical Society v London and Provincial Supply Association (1880) 5 App Cas 857, 45 JP 20, 49 LJQB 736, 43 LT 389, 28 WR 957, HL 1-329, 2-1244

Pharmaceutical Society of Great Britain v Storkwain Ltd [1986] 2 All ER 635, [1986] 1 WLR 903, 150 JP 385, 130 Sol Jo 481, 83 Cr App Rep 359, [1986] Crim LR 813, [1986] LS Gaz R 2238, HL 8-21015

Pheasant v Pheasant [1972] Fam 202, [1972] 1 All ER 587, [1972] 2 WLR 353, 116 Sol Jo 120 6-67, 6-74

Phelan v Black [1972] 1 All ER 901, [1972] 1 WLR 273, 136 JP 298, 116 Sol Jo 76 1-629, 1-684, 2-75

Phillips v Autocars Services Ltd (11 April 1936, unreported) 4-7

Phillips v Berkshire County Council [1967] 2 QB 991, [1967] 2 All ER 675, [1967] 3 WLR 565, 131 JP 382, 111 Sol Jo 498, 65 LGR 377 7-6114

Phillips v Canham (1872) 36 JP 310 8-18835

Phillips v DPP [2002] EWHC 2093 (Admin), [2003] RTR 132, [2003] Crim LR 481, [2002] 46 LS Gaz R 34, [2002] All ER (D) 401 (Oct) 8-17631W

Phillips v Eamer (1795) 1 Esp 355 1-664, 2-68

Phillips v Henson (1877) 3 CPD 26, 42 JP 137, 47 LJPC 273, 37 LT 432, 26 WR 214 8-16727

PARA

PARA

Practice Direction (family division: attached powers of arrest) [2000] 1 All ER 544, sub nom Practice Direction (arresting officer: attendance) [2000] 1 WLR 83, sub nom President's Direction (family law act 1996: attendance of arresting officer) [2000] 1 FCR 86, [2000] 1 FLR 270 . . . . 6-134, 6-3095
Practice Direction (family proceedings: court bundles) [2000] 2 All ER 287, [2000] 1 WLR 737, [2000] 1 FCR 521, [2000] 1 FLR 536 . . . . . 6-24, 6-36A, 6-5101, 6-5102, 6-5103
Practice Direction (appeals against sentence: the provision of notice to the prosecution) [2003] 4 All ER 665 1–6970
Practice Direction (crown Court: business) [2001] 4 All ER 635, [2001] 1 WLR 1996 . . . 1-7000
Practice Direction (Family Division: judicial continuity) [2002] 3 All ER 603, [2002] 1 WLR 2183, [2002] 2 FCR 667, [2002] 2 FLR 367 6-5
Practice Direction (criminal: consolidated) [2002] 3 All ER 90, [2002] 1 WLR 2870; amended sub nom Practice Direction (Forms for use in criminal proceedings [2005] 2 All ER 916, [2005] 2 Cr App Rep 17 . . . . 1–6649,1-6970, 1-7764
Practice Direction (Care Cases: Judicial Continuity and Judicial Case Management) [2003] 1 WLR 2209, [2003] 1 FLR 719 6-5102
Practice Direction (Costs: Criminal Proceedings) [2004] 2 All ER 1070, [2004] 1 WLR 2657, [2004] 2 Cr App Rep 395 1-7388
Practice Direction (Criminal Proceedings:Consolidation) [2004] 1 WLR 589 . . 1-7765, 1-7766, 17767
Practice Direction (bail: failure to surrender and trials in absence) [2004] 1 Cr App Rep 402; 1-6970
Practice Direction (guidance to jurors) [2004] 2 Cr App Rep 3 1-6970
Practice Direction (listing of appeals against conviction and sentence in the Court of Appeal Criminal Division) [2004] 2 Cr App Rep 5 1-6970
Practice Direction (explanations for the imposition of custodial sentences) [2004] 2 Cr App R 391; [2004] TLR 396 1-6970
Practice Direction (crime: mandatory life sentences) [2004] 1 WLR 1874; [2004] 2 Cr App R 24 1-6970
Practice Direction (jury service) [2005] 3 All ER 89, [2005] 1 WLR 1361, [2005] 2 Cr App Rep 16 1-6970
Practice Direction (case management) [2005] 3 All ER 91, [2005] 1 WLR 1491, [2005] 2 Cr App Rep 18 1-6970
Practice Direction (crown court: classification and allocation of business) [2005] 1 WLR 2215, [2005] 2 Cr App Rep 33 1-6970
Practice Note (1943) 107 JP Jo 253 1-5687
Practice Note [1946] WN 103 . . . . 1-771, 1-835
Practice Note [1956] 1 QB 451, [1956] 1 All ER 448, 120 JP Jo 119, 100 Sol Jo 187, 40 Cr App Rep 31 1-6017
Practice Note [1962] 1 All ER 448 1-669
Practice Note [1973] 1 WLR 60. See Practice Direction [1973] 1 All ER 61
Practice Note [1974] 3 All ER 528 1-769
Practice Note [1975] 2 All ER 1072, sub nom Practice Direction [1975] 1 WLR 1065, 119 Sol Jo 459, 61 Cr App Rep 260 . . . . 3-54, 3-943, 3-946
Practice Note (criminal evidence: unused material) [1982] 1 All ER 734, (1982) 74 Cr App Rep 302 1-6970
Practice Note [1983] 3 All ER 33, sub nom Practice Direction [1983] 1 WLR 922, 127 Sol Jo 512, CA 1-768, 1-853, 9-17, 9-18
Practice Note (judicial review: affidavits) [1989] 1 All ER 1024, [1989] 1 WLR 358, 153 JP 363 1-774
Practice Note [1993] 1 All ER 41, CA 1-457, 1-547
Practice Note [1995] 2 All ER 511, sub nom Practice Direction [1995] 1 WLR 507, [1995] 16 LS Gaz R 43 1-774
Practice Note [1995] 2 All ER 900, sub nom Practice Direction [1995] 1 WLR 1083, [1995] 2 Cr App Rep 235, [1995] 25 LS Gaz R 40, CA 1-7000
Practice Note (Crown Office list: consent orders) [1997] 2 All ER 799, [1997] 1 WLR 825, [1997] 2 Cr App Rep 338 . . . . 1-2034, 1-5689
Practice Note (crime: antecedents) [1997] 4 All ER 350, sub nom Practice Direction (crime: antecedents) (No 2) [1997] 1 WLR 1482, [1998] 1 Cr App Rep 213, CA . . . 2-193
Practice Note [1998] 3 All ER 384, sub nom Practice Direction (Crown Court: allocation of business) (No 2) [1998] 1 WLR 1244, [1998] 2 Cr App Rep 446 1-7000
Practice Note (applications for return orders by unmarried fathers) [1998] 1 FCR 253, [1998] 1 FLR 491 . . . . 6-1805C
Practice Note (adminsitrative court: establishment) [2000] 4 All ER 1071 1-850
Practice Note (magistrates' court: contempt in face of court) [2001] 3 All ER 94, 165 JP 462 1-600
Practice Note (protocol for judicial case management in public law Children Act cases) [2003] 2 FLR 719 4-5102
Practice Note (Administrative Court) [2004] 2 All ER 994 . . . . . . 1-6563ZG
Practice Statement (Administrative Court: listing and urgent cases) [2002] 1 All ER 633, [2002] 1 WLR 810, [2002] All ER (D) 12 (Feb) 1-770, 1-770A, 1-839
Prager v Prager and Goodison (1913) 108 LT 734, 29 TLR 556 6-51
Pratt v AA Sites Ltd [1938] 2 KB 459, [1938] 2 All ER 371, 102 JP 278, 107 LJKB 478, 158 LT 522, 54 TLR 719, 82 Sol Jo 547, 36 LGR 344, 31 Cox CC 54 . . . . 1-765, 1-827
Pratt v DPP [2001] EWHC Admin 483, (2001) 165 JP 800 8-23466
Pratt v Martin [1911] 2 KB 90, 75 JP 328, 80 LJKB 711, 105 LT 49, 27 TLR 377, 22 Cox CC 442 . . . . 8-13607, 8-13620
Pratt v Pratt [1927] WN 140, [1927] All ER Rep 234, 96 LJP 123, 137 LT 491, 43 TLR 523, 71 Sol Jo 433, 28 Cox CC 413 1-449

PARA

Q

PARA

PARA

R v Backshall [1998] 1 WLR 1506, [1998] RTR 423, [1999] 1 Cr App Rep 35, [1999] Crim LR 662, [1998] 17 LS Gaz R 30, 142 Sol Jo LB 126, CA . . 1-326
R v Bacon (1915) 11 Cr App R 90, CCA . . 2-209
R v Badash (1917) 87 LJKB 732, 118 LT 179, 26 Cox CC 155, 18 Cr App Rep 17, CCA . . 8-30669
R v Bagnall (1985) 7 Cr App Rep (S) 40 . . 3-234A
R v Bagshaw [1984] 1 All ER 971, [1984] 1 WLR 477, 128 Sol Jo 64, 78 Cr App Rep 163, [1984] Crim LR 233, CA . . 2-617
R v Bailey (1850) 4 Cox CC 390 . . 8-13301
R v Bailey (1872) LR 1 CCR 347, 36 JP 324, 41 LJMC 61, 25 LT 882, 20 WR 301, 12 Cox CC 129 . . 8-6351
R v Bailey [1983] 2 All ER 503, [1983] 1 WLR 760, 147 JP 558, 127 Sol Jo 425, 77 Cr App Rep 76, [1983] Crim LR 533, CA . . 1-308
R v Bailey [1989] Crim LR 723 . . 3-946
R v Bailey [2001] EWCA Crim 733, [2001] All ER (D) 185 (Mar) . . 2-471
R v Bailey and Smith [1993] 3 All ER 513, 97 Cr App Rep 365, [1993] Crim LR 681, CA 1-2211, 1-2741, 2-1359
R v Bainbridge [1960] 1 QB 129, [1959] 3 All ER 200, [1959] 3 WLR 656, 123 JP 499, 43 Cr App Rep 194, CCA . . 1-321
R v Baines [1909] 1 KB 258, [1908-10] All ER Rep 328, 72 JP 524, 78 LJKB 119, 100 LT 78, 25 TLR 79, 53 Sol Jo 101, 21 Cox CC 756 . . 1-2169
R v Baker [1895] 1 QB 797, 64 LJMC 177, 72 LT 631, 43 WR 654, 11 TLR 342, 39 Sol Jo 416, 15 R 346 . . 8-22936
R v Baker (1992) 14 Cr App Rep (S) 242, CA . . 3-522
R v Baker [1999] 2 Cr App Rep 335, CA . . 1-307
R v Baker and Wilkins [1997] Crim LR 497, CA . . 1-324, 8-24745
R v Baldessarre [1930] WN 193, 144 LT 185, 29 Cox CC 193, 22 Cr App Rep 70, CCA . . 8-23081
R v Baldwin (1925) 89 JP 116, 133 LT 191, 69 Sol Jo 429, 28 Cox CC 17, 18 Cr App Rep 175, CCA . . 1-664, 2-68, 2-479
R v Baldwin [1973] QB 774, [1973] 2 All ER 624, [1973] 2 WLR 876, 117 Sol Jo 395, 57 Cr App Rep 511, CA . . 2-617
R v Ball [1911] AC 47, sub nom DPP v Ball and Ball 75 JP 180, 80 LJKB 691, 103 LT 738, 104 LT 48, 27 TLR 162, 55 Sol Jo 139, 6 Cr App Rep 32, 22 Cox CC 366 . . 2-463, 8-27977
R v Ball (1989) 90 Cr App Rep 378, [1989] Crim LR 579, CA . . 8-23066
R v Ball [2002] EWCA Crim 2777, [2003] 2 Cr App Rep (S) 92, [2003] Crim LR 122 3-1558G, 3-1703
R v Balogun [1997] Crim LR 500, CA . . 2-206A
R v Ballysingh (1953) 37 Cr App Rep 28, CCA . . 1-389
R v Banks (1873) 12 Cox CC 393 . . 1-322
R v Banks [1916] 2 KB 621, [1916-17] All ER Rep 356, 85 LJKB 1657, 115 LT 457, 80 JP 432, 25 Cox CC 535, 12 Cr App Rep 74, CCA . . 1-642, 2-36
R v Banks [1972] 1 All ER 1041, [1972] 1 WLR 346, 136 JP 306, 116 Sol Jo 80 . . 4-1656
R v Banks [1978] RTR 535, CA . . 4-1685
R v Bannister [1991] RTR 1, [1991] Crim LR 71, CA . . 4-1685
R v Banu and Ali (1994) 16 Cr App Rep (S) 656, CA . . 3-233
R v Barber (1844) 1 Car & Kir 434, 8 JP 644, sub nom R v Richards, Barber, Fletcher & Dorey 3 LTOS 142, 1 Cox CC 62 . . 1-644, 2-61
R v Barker [1962] 1 All ER 748, [1962] 1 WLR 349, 126 JP 274, 106 Sol Jo 289, 46 Cr App Rep 227, CCA . . 8-22449
R v Barking and Dagenham Justices, ex p DPP (1994) 159 JP 373, [1995] Crim LR 953 1-668, 1-669, 1-2031
R v Barking Justices, ex p Goodspeed [1985] RTR 70n . . 1-2169
R v Barking Youth Court, ex p B CO/2692/99 . . 1-461
R v Barley (1989) 11 Cr App Rep (S) 158, [1989] Crim LR 594, CA . . 3-215
R v Barnes (1942) 86 Sol Jo 341, 28 Cr App Rep 141, CCA . . 8-30669
R v Barnes (1986) 83 Cr App Rep 58, [1986] Crim LR 573 . . 3-248
R v Barnes (1992) 14 Cr App Rep (S) 547, CA . . 3-233
R v Barnes [2004] EWCA Crim 3246, [2005] 2 All ER 113, [2005] 1 WLR 910, [2005] 1 Cr App Rep 507, [2005] Crim LR 381, (2005) Times, 10 January, [2004] All ER (D) 338 (Dec) 8–23063
R v Barnet (1850) 4 Cox CC 269 . . 2-203
R v Barnet Juvenile Court, ex p Barnet London Borough Council (1982) 4 Cr App Rep (S) 221, [1982] Crim LR 592, [1982] LS Gaz R 290 . . 1-2141
R v Barnet Magistrates' Court, ex p Cantor [1998] 2 All ER 333, [1999] 1 WLR 334 . . 3-522
R v Barnsley Licensing Justices, ex p Barnsley and District Licensed Victuallers' Association [1959] 2 QB 276, [1959] 3 All ER 635, [1959] 3 WLR 96, 123 JP 365, 103 Sol Jo 529; affd [1960] 2 QB 167, [1960] 2 All ER 703, [1960] 3 WLR 305, 124 JP 359, 104 Sol Jo 583, 58 LGR 285, CA . . 1-119, 1-45, 6-810
R v Barr [1996] 2 Cr App Rep (S) 294, CA . . 3-230
R v Barrie [2005] EWCA Crim 1318, [2006] 1 Cr App Rep (s) 228 . . 3-161
R v Barratt (1873) LR 2 CCR 81, [1861-73] All ER Rep 792, 43 LJMC 7, 29 LT 409, 22 WR 136, 12 Cox CC 498 . . 8-27969
R v Barrett (1863) Le & Ca 269, 1 New Rep 335, 26 JP 805, 32 LJMC 36, 7 LT 435, 11 WR 124, 9 Cox CC 255 . . 8-7490
R v Barrett [1976] 3 All ER 895, [1976] 1 WLR 946, 141 JP 46, 120 Sol Jo 402 . . 8-2870

PARA

R v Barrick (1985) 149 JP 705, 129 Sol Jo 416, 81 Cr App Rep 78, [1985] Crim LR 602, [1985] NLJ Rep 509, [1985] LS Gaz R 3173, CA 3-234A
R v Barrington [1981] 1 All ER 1132, [1981] 1 WLR 419, 125 Sol Jo 218, 72 Cr App Rep 280, [1981] Crim LR 174, CA 2-464
R v Barron [1914] 2 KB 570, 78 JP 311, 83 LJKB 786, 58 Sol Jo 557, 30 TLR 422, 10 Cr App Rep 81, CCA 1-460
R v Bashir [1969] 3 All ER 692, [1969] 1 WLR 1303, 133 JP 687, 113 Sol Jo 703, 54 Cr App Rep 1 2-477
R v Basid [1996] 1 Cr App Rep (S) 421, 160 JP 1, [1996] Crim LR 67, [1995] 40 LS Gaz R 22, 139 Sol Jo LB 247, CA 5-46
R v Basildon Justices, ex p Holding and Barnes plc [1994] RA 157, 158 JP 980 . . . 8-20044, 8-20106
R v Baskerville [1916] 2 KB 658, [1916-17] All ER Rep 38, 80 JP 446, 86 LJKB 28, 115 LT 453, 60 Sol Jo 696, 25 Cox CC 524, 12 Cr App Rep 81, CCA 2-616
R v Bass [1953] 1 QB 680, [1953] 1 All ER 1064, 117 JP 246, 97 Sol Jo 282, 37 Cr App Rep 51, CCA 2-72
R v Bassett (1985) 7 Cr App Rep (S) 75 . . . . 3-236C
R v Bateman (1925) 89 JP 162, 94 LJKB 791, 133 LT 730, 41 TLR 557, 69 Sol Jo 622, 28 Cox CC 33, 19 Cr App Rep 8, CCA 8-23081
R v Bateman (1946) 110 JP 133, 174 LT 336, 90 Sol Jo 224, 44 LGR 121, 31 Cr App Rep 106, CCA 1-640, 2-31
R v Bates [1911] 1 KB 964, 75 JP 271, 80 LJKB 507, 104 LT 688, 27 TLR 314, 55 Sol Jo 410, 6 Cr App Rep 153, 22 Cox CC 459, CCA 8-14186
R v Bates [1952] 2 All ER 842, 96 Sol Jo 785, 36 Cr App Rep 175; affd sub nom R v Russell [1953] 1 WLR 77, 97 Sol Jo 12, CCA 2-740
R v Bath Licensing Justices, ex p Chittenden [1952] 2 All ER 700, 116 JP 569 . . . 6-257, 6-785
R v Bathurst [1968] 2 QB 99, [1968] 1 All ER 1175, [1968] 2 WLR 1092, 112 Sol Jo 272, 52 Cr App Rep 251, CA 2-333
R v Batt [1996] Crim LR 910, CA 8-29309B
R v Battle Magistrates' Court, ex p Shepherd (1983) 147 JP 372, 5 Cr App Rep (S) 124 . . . 1-771, 1-835
R v Baxter [1972] QB 1, [1971] 2 All ER 359, [1971] 2 WLR 1138, 135 JP 345, 115 Sol Jo 246, 55 Cr App Rep 214, CA 1-383, 8-30720
R v Bayes (1994) 16 Cr App Rep (S) 290 3-230
R v Bayliss (1993) 157 JP 1062, 98 Cr App Rep 235, CA 1-2788
R v Bayliss and Oliver [1978] Crim LR 361 8-21204
R v Beacock (1979) 1 Cr App Rep (S) 198, [1979] Crim LR 797 3-248
R v Beaconsfield Magistrates' Court, ex p Westminster Press Ltd (1994) 158 JP 1055 . . . 1-2433
R v Beale (1865) LR 1 CCR 10, 35 LJMC 60, 13 LT 335, 14 WR 57, 12 Jur NS 12, 10 Cox CC 157 8-27973
R v Beaney [2004] EWCA Crim 449, [2004] 2 Cr App Rep (S) 441, [2004] Crim LR 480, [2004] All ER (D) 449 (Feb) 3-239A
R v Beard (1920). See DPP v Beard
R v Beard [1974] 1 WLR 1549, 118 Sol Jo 848 8-21233
R v Beard [1998] Crim LR 585 1-660
R v Beard [2001] EWCA Crim 1774, (2001) 165 JPN 715 . . . . 3-234A
R v Beattie (1989) 89 Cr App Rep 302, CA 2-474, 2-853
R v Bebbington [2005] EWCA Crim 2395, 169 JP 621, [2006] Crim LR 160, (2005) Times, 24 October, [2005] All ER (D) 153 (Oct) 3-527B
R v Beck [1982] 1 All ER 807, [1982] 1 WLR 461, 146 JP 225, 126 Sol Jo 134, 74 Cr App Rep 221, CA 2-617
R v Beck [1985] 1 All ER 571, [1985] 1 WLR 22, 149 JP 260, 128 Sol Jo 871, 80 Cr App Rep 355, [1985] LS Gaz R 762, CA 8-30709
R v Beckett (1913) 29 TLR 332, 8 Cr App Rep 204, CCA 2-344
R v Beckley (1887) 20 QBD 187, 52 JP 120, 57 LJMC 22, 57 LT 716, 36 WR 160, 4 TLR 151, 16 Cox CC 331 . . . . 1-48, 1-460, 1-563
R v Bedding (1994) 16 Cr App Rep (S) 101, CA 3-234A
R v Beddow (1987) 9 Cr App Rep (S) 235, [1987] Crim LR 833, CA 3-203
R v Bedford Prison (Governor), ex p Ames [1953] 1 All ER 1002, 117 JP 237, 97 Sol Jo 282 . . . 1-2127
R v Bedingfield (1879) 14 Cox CC 341 2-341
R v Bedlington Magistrates' Court, ex p Wilkinson (1999) 164 JP 156 1-2910
R v Bee (1993) 14 Cr App Rep (S) 703, [1993] Crim LR 464 3-248
R v Beebe (1925) 89 JP 175, 133 LT 736, 41 TLR 635, 28 Cox CC 47, 19 Cr App Rep 22, CCA . . . 2-616
R v Beech (1912) 76 JP 287, [1911-13] All ER Rep 530, 107 LT 461, 23 Cox CC 181, 7 Cr App Rep 197, CCA 8-23087
R v Beedie [1998] QB 356, [1997] 3 WLR 758, [1997] 2 Cr App Rep 167, 161 JP 313, [1997] 15 LS Gaz R 26, 141 Sol Jo LB 83, CA 1-461
R v Beer [1998] 2 Cr App Rep (S) 248, CA 3-240
R v Beggs (1989) 90 Cr App Rep 430, CA 2-464
R v Beglin [2002] EWCA Crim 1887, [2003] 1 Cr App Rep (s) 21 3-161
R v Belfon [1976] 3 All ER 46, [1976] 1 WLR 741, 140 JP 523, 120 Sol Jo 329, 63 Cr App Rep 59, CA 8-23086
R v Bell (1874) Ir R 8 CL 542 8-23120
R v Bell (1877) 41 JP 455, 36 LT 670, 13 Cox CC 623 8-30671
R v Bell (1994) 16 Cr App Rep (S) 93, CA 3-236

PARA

R v Birch (1989) 90 Cr App Rep 78, 11 Cr App Rep (S) 202, [1989] Crim LR 757, CA 3-491, 8-22237
R v Bird [1985] 2 All ER 513, [1985] 1 WLR 816, 129 Sol Jo 362, 81 Cr App Rep 110, [1985] Crim LR 388, [1985] LS Gaz R 1709, CA 8-23064
R v Bird (1992) 157 JP 488, [1993] RTR 1, [1993] Crim LR 85, CA 3-237
R v Bird (1996) 161 JP 96, CCA 2-200, 2-1470
R v Bird [1996] RTR 22, CA 1-3160, 1-3161
R v Bird [1996] RTR 49, ECJ 4-2297
R v Birkin (1988) 10 Cr App Rep (S) 303, [1988] Crim LR 854, CA 3-230A
R v Birks [2002] EWCA Crim 3091, [2003] 2 Cr App Rep 122, [2003] Crim LR 401 2-475
R v Birmingham and Gloucester Rly Co (1840) 9 C & P 469 1-642, 1-2260
R v Birmingham City Council, ex p Ferrero Ltd [1993] 1 All ER 530, 155 JP 721, 89 LGR 977, [1991] 26 LS Gaz R 32, CA 8-5006
R v Birmingham City Council, ex p Sheptonhurst Ltd [1990] 1 All ER 1026, 87 LGR 830, CA 8-19267
R v Birmingham Justices, ex p Bennett (1982) Times, 13 November 1-2126
R v Birmingham Justices, ex p F (1999) 164 JP 523, [2000] Crim LR 588 5-9, 5-1231
R v Birmingham Justices, ex p Hodgson [1985] QB 1131, [1985] 2 All ER 193, [1985] 2 WLR 630, 149 JP 193, 129 Sol Jo 219, 81 Cr App Rep 231, [1985] Crim LR 226, [1985] LS Gaz R 1085 1-450, 1-525, 1-2046
R v Birmingham Justices, ex p Lamb [1983] 3 All ER 23, [1983] 1 WLR 339, 147 JP 75, 127 Sol Jo 119, [1983] Crim LR 329 1-463
R v Birmingham Justices, ex p DW Parkin Construction Ltd [1981] QB 470, [1981] 1 All ER 1027, [1981] 2 WLR 419, 145 JP 200, 125 Sol Jo 204, 73 Cr App Rep 87 1-27, 1-33
R v Birmingham Justices, ex p Wyatt [1975] 3 All ER 897, [1976] 1 WLR 260, 140 JP 46, 119 Sol Jo 726, 61 Cr App Rep 306 1-835, 3-219, 3-1643
R v Birmingham Juvenile Court, ex p H (1992) 156 JP 445 1-643, 1-801, 1-802
R v Birmingham Magistrat[171]=22[187]es' Court, ex p Bass Mitchells & Butlers Ltd (1988) 152 JP 563 6-116, 6-220, 6-259, 6-569
R v Birmingham Magistrates' Court, ex p Robinson (1985) 150 JP 1 1-137
R v Birmingham Magistrates' Court, ex p Shields (1994) 158 JP 845 1-46, 1-701, 1-2032, 2-333
R v Birmingham Overseers (1861) 26 JP 198, 1 B & S 763, 31 LJMC 63, 8 Jur NS 37, 10 WR 41, 5 LT 309 2-341
R v Birmingham Stipendiary Magistrate, ex p Webb (1992) 157 JP 89, 95 Cr App Rep 75 1-450, 1-525, 1-2054
R v Biron (1884) 14 QBD 474, 49 JP 68, 54 LJMC 77, 51 LT 429, 1 TLR 1 1-46, 1-701
R v Bishop [1975] QB 274, [1974] 2 All ER 1206, [1974] 3 WLR 308, 138 JP 654, 118 Sol Jo 515, CA 2-493
R v Bispham (1830) 4 C & P 392 1-666, 2-70
R v Bitton (1833) 6 C & P 92 1-460
R v Bjornsen (1865) Le & Ca 545, 6 New Rep 179, 29 JP 373, 34 LJMC 180, 12 LT 473, 13 WR 664, 11 Jur NS 589, 10 Cox CC 74, 2 Mar LC 210 1-2021
R v Black (1910) 74 JP 71 2-203
R v Black (1922) 16 Cr App Rep 118, CCA 2-462
R v Blackburn Justices, ex p Holmes (1999) 164 JP 163, [2000] Crim LR 300 1-405, 1-442
R v Blackham [1997] 2 Cr App Rep (S) 275, CA 3-236C
R v Blackpool Borough Council, ex p Red Cab Taxis Ltd [1994] RTR 402, 158 JP 1069, [1994] COD 513 8-18970
R v Blackpool Justices, ex p Charlson and Gregory [1972] 3 All ER 854, [1972] 1 WLR 1456, 137 JP 25, 116 Sol Jo 729 3-520
R v Blake (1844) 6 QB 126, 8 JP 575, 13 LJMC 131, 8 Jur 666 2-335
R v Blake (1978) 68 Cr App Rep 1, [1979] Crim LR 464, CA 8-21203
R v Blake [1997] 1 All ER 963, [1997] 1 WLR 1167, [1997] 1 Cr App Rep 209, [1997] Crim LR 207, CA 8-30105E
R v Blandford Justices, ex p G (an infant) [1967] 1 QB 82, [1966] 1 All ER 1021, [1966] 2 WLR 1232, 130 JP 260, 110 Sol Jo 465 1-461, 1-581, 1-7458, 5-1315
R v Blanshard (1866) 30 JP 280 8-25225
R v Blastland [1986] AC 41, [1985] 2 All ER 1095, [1985] 3 WLR 345, 129 Sol Jo 557, 81 Cr App Rep 266, [1985] Crim LR 727, [1985] NLJ Rep 780, [1985] LS Gaz R 2331, HL 2-466
R v Blaue [1975] 3 All ER 446, [1975] 1 WLR 1411, 139 JP 841, 119 Sol Jo 589, 61 Cr App Rep 271, CA 8-23250
R v Blight [1999] Crim LR 426, CA 3-1733
R v Bloodworth (1913) 9 Cr App Rep 80 8-27977
R v Bloom [1962] 2 QB 245, [1961] 3 All ER 88, [1961] 3 WLR 611, 125 JP 565, 105 Sol Jo 590, CCA 8-7490
R v Bloomfield [1997] 1 Cr App Rep 135, CA 1-447
R v Bloxham [1983] 1 AC 109, [1982] 1 All ER 582, [1982] 2 WLR 392, 146 JP 201, 126 Sol Jo 154, 74 Cr App Rep 279, [1982] RTR 129, [1982] Crim LR 436, HL 8-30721
R v Blyth [1996] 1 Cr App Rep (S) 388, CA 3-236
R v Blyth Valley Juvenile Court, ex p S (1987) 151 JP 805 1-137
R v Blything (Suffolk) Justices, ex p Knight [1970] RTR 218 1-32, 4-2995
R v Boal [1965] 1 QB 402, [1964] 3 All ER 269, [1964] 3 WLR 593, 128 JP 573, 108 Sol Jo 674, 48 Cr App Rep 342, CCA 2-334
R v Board of Trustees of the Science Museum [1993] 3 All ER 853, [1993] 1 WLR 1171, CA 8-15292
R v Boardman (1987) 9 Cr App Rep (S) 74, [1987] Crim LR 430, CA 3-1690

PARA

R v Clow [1965] 1 QB 598, [1963] 2 All ER 216, [1963] 3 WLR 84, 47 Cr App Rep 136, 127 JP 371, 107 Sol Jo 537, CCA . . . 1-7427
R v Cochrane (1994) 15 Cr App Rep (S) 708, [1994] Crim LR 382, CA . . . 3-1231, 3-1721
R v Cockcroft (1870) 11 Cox CC 410 . . . 2-477
R v Coffey (1976) 74 Cr App Rep 168, CA . . . 3-31
R v Cohen [1938] 3 All ER 380, 159 LT 477, 82 Sol Jo 746, 26 Cr App Rep 190, 31 Cox CC 140, CCA . . . 2-490
R v Cohen [1951] 1 KB 505, [1951] 1 All ER 203, 115 JP 91, [1951] 1 TLR 251, 95 Sol Jo 124, 49 LGR 216, 34 Cr App Rep 239, CCA . . . 6-773A, 8-6664, 8-6676, 8-30087
R v Coid [1998] Crim LR 199, CA . . . 8-21207
R v Cokar [1960] 2 QB 207, [1960] 2 All ER 175, [1960] 2 WLR 836, 124 JP 313, 104 Sol Jo 389, 44 Cr App Rep 165, CCA . . . 2-491
R v Colchester Justices, ex p North Essex Building Co Ltd [1977] 3 All ER 567, [1977] 1 WLR 1109, 141 JP 713, 121 Sol Jo 390, 242 Estates Gazette 696, [1977] Crim LR 562 1-439, 1-520, 1-2045
R v Colchester Magistrates' Court, ex p Abbott [2001] EWHC Admin 136, (2001) 165 JP 386, [2001] Crim LR 564 . . . 1-439A, 1-524, 1-2051
R v Colchester Stipendiary Magistrate, ex p Beck [1979] QB 674, [1979] 1 All ER 1035, [1979] 2 WLR 637, 69 Cr App Rep 128, 143 JP 202, [1979] Crim LR 250, 123 Sol Jo 304 1-139, 1-454, 1-540
R v Cole (1941) 105 JP 279, 165 LT 126, 39 LGR 262, 28 Cr App Rep 43, CCA . . . 8-27980
R v Cole [1990] 2 All ER 108, [1990] 1 WLR 866, 154 JP 692, 134 Sol Jo 908, 90 Cr App Rep 478, [1990] 13 LS Gaz R 42, [1990] Crim LR 333, CA . . . 2-1473
R v Cole [1994] Crim LR 582, CA . . . 1-324
R v Cole [1996] 1 Cr App Rep (S) 193, CA . . . 3-235
R v Coleman (1920) 84 JP 112, CCA . . . 8-23087
R v Coleman (1975) 61 Cr App Rep 206, [1975] Crim LR 349, CA . . . 3-230
R v Coleman (1985) 150 JP 175, [1986] Crim LR 56 . . . 8-30721
R v Coll (1889) 25 LR Ir 522 . . . 2-474
R v Collard [2004] EWCA Crim 1664, [2005] 1 Cr App Rep (S) 155, [2004] Crim LR 757, 148 Sol Jo LB 663, (2004) Times, 7 June, [2004] All ER (D) 305 (May) . . . 3-239A
R v Colley (1985) 7 Cr App Rep (S) 264, [1986] Crim LR 72 . . . 3-234A
R v Colley and Marples (1989) 11 Cr App Rep (S) 462, CA . . . 3-234A
R v Collier [2004] EWCA Crim 1411, [2005] 1 WLR 843, [2005] 1 Cr App Rep 129, [2004] 27 LS Gaz R 29, (2004) Times, 13 July, [2004] All ER (D) 82 (Jun) . . . 8-28270
R v Collins (1839) 9 C & P 456 . . . 8-6391
R v Collins [1947] KB 560, [1947] 1 All ER 147, 111 JP 154, 63 TLR 90, 91 Sol Jo 133, 45 LGR 104, 32 Cr App Rep 27, CCA . . . 3-55, 4-1693
R v Collins (1960) 44 Cr App Rep 170, CCA . . . 2-196
R v Collins [1973] QB 100, [1972] 2 All ER 1105, [1972] 3 WLR 243, 136 JP 605, 116 Sol Jo 432, 56 Cr App Rep 554, CA . . . 8-30698
R v Collins (1994) 16 Cr App Rep (S) 156, CA . . . 5-61
R v Collins [2004] EWCA Crim 83, [2004] 1 WLR 1705 . . . 2-472
R v Collinson (1931) 23 Cr App Rep 49, CCA . . . 4-1375, 8-28160
R v Collister (1955) 39 Cr App Rep 100, CCA . . . 1-642, 2-36
R v Collyer [1996] 2 Cr App Rep (S) 238, CA . . . 3-230
R v Colohan [2001] EWCA Crim 1251, [2001] 3 FCR 409, [2001] 2 FLR 757, [2001] Fam Law 732, 165 JP 594, [2001] Crim LR 845 . . . 8-23466
R v Coltress (1979) 68 Cr App Rep 193, [1979] Crim LR 170 . . . 2-491
R v Colville-Scott [1990] 1 WLR 958, 91 Cr App Rep 174, [1990] 26 LS Gaz R 37, CA . . . 3-1703
R v Colwell (1993) 15 Cr App Rep (S) 323, CA . . . 3-233
R v Colyer [1974] Crim LR 243 . . . 8-21204
R v Conde (1868) 10 Cox CC 547 . . . 2-462
R v Condron and Condron [1997] 1 WLR 827, [1997] 1 Cr App Rep 185, 161 JP 1, [1997] Crim LR 215, CA . . . 2-497
R v Coney (1882) 8 QBD 534, 46 JP 404, 51 LJMC 66, 46 LT 307, 30 WR 678, 15 Cox CC 46 1-321, 8-23063, 8-23065
R v Connatty (1919) 83 JP 292 . . . 8-23117
R v Connolly and Costello [1910] 1 KB 28, 74 JP 15, 79 LJKB 90, 101 LT 784, 26 TLR 31, 54 Sol Jo 130, 22 Cox CC 215, 3 Cr App Rep 27, CCA . . . 8-8160
R v Connor [2004] UKHL 02, [2004] 1 AC 1118, [2004] 1 All ER 925, [2004] 2 WLR 201, [2004] 2 Cr App Rep 112, [2004] 07 LS Gaz R 34, [2004] NLJR 145, 16 BHRC 279, [2004] 5 LRC 171, (2004) Times, 23 January, [2004] All ER (D) 189 (Jan) . . . 1-2437
R v Consett Justices, ex p Postal Bingo Ltd [1967] 2 QB 9, [1967] 1 All ER 605, [1967] 2 WLR 184, 131 JP 196, 110 Sol Jo 850 . . . 1-32
R v Considine (1980) 124 Sol Jo 46, 70 Cr App Rep 239, [1980] Crim LR 179, CA . . . 1-2051
R v Constantinou (1989) 153 JP 619, 91 Cr App Rep 76, [1989] Crim LR 571, CA . . . 2-207
R v Constanza [1997] 2 Cr App Rep 492, [1997] Crim LR 576, CA . . . 8-23061
R v Conti (1973) 58 Cr App Rep 387, CA . . . 2-334
R v Conteh [2003] EWCA Crim 962, [2004] RTR 1 . . . 4-1372
R v Conway [1989] QB 290, [1988] 3 All ER 1025, [1988] 3 WLR 1238, 152 JP 649, 88 Cr App Rep 343, [1989] RTR 35, CA . . . 1-326
R v Cook (1870) 22 LT 216, 11 Cox CC 542 . . . 8-23120
R v Cook [1987] QB 417, [1987] 1 All ER 1049, [1987] 2 WLR 775, 131 Sol Jo 21, 84 Cr App Rep 369, [1987] LS Gaz R 339, CA . . . 2-207

PARA

PARA

PARA

R v Crown Court at Inner London, ex p Sitki (1993) 157 JP 523, [1994] COD 342, CA . . 6-52, 6-60, 6-560, 6-563
R v Crown Court at Ipswich, ex p Baldwin [1981] 1 All ER 596, [1981] RTR 298, sub nom R v Felixstowe Justices, ex p Baldwin 72 Cr App Rep 131, [1981] Crim LR 242 . . 1-770, 1-833
R v Crown Court at Ipswich, ex p Reddington [1981] Crim LR 618 1-1566
R v Crown Court at Isleworth, ex p Buda [2000] 1 Cr App Rep (S) 538, [2000] Crim LR 111 . . . . 1-438, 1-507, 3-560
R v Crown Court at Isleworth, ex p Clarke [1998] 1 Cr App Rep 257 1-3447
R v Crown Court at Isleworth, ex p Marland (1997) 162 JP 251 3-946
R v Crown Court at Kingston upon Thames, ex p Scarll (1989) Times, 28 April . . . 4-1596
R v Crown Court at Knightsbridge, ex p Customs and Excise Comrs [1986] Crim LR 324 . . 1-6082
R v Crown Court at Knightsbridge, ex p Dunne [1993] 4 All ER 491, [1994] 1 WLR 296, 158 JP 213, [1993] Crim LR 853, [1993] NLJR 1479n 8-7615
R v Crown Court at Knightsbridge, ex p Foot [1999] RTR 21 . . . . . . 8-30105L
R v Crown Court at Knightsbridge, ex p Goonatilleke [1986] QB 1, [1985] 2 All ER 498, [1985] 3 WLR 553, 129 Sol Jo 589 1-835
R v Crown Court at Knightsbridge, ex p International Sporting Club (London) Ltd [1982] QB 304, [1981] 3 All ER 417, [1981] 3 WLR 640, 125 Sol Jo 589 . . . . . 1-2563, 8-13457
R v Crown Court at Knightsbridge, ex p Marcrest Ltd [1983] 1 All ER 1148, [1983] 1 WLR 300, CA 8-13395, 8-13440
R v Crown Court at Knutsford, ex p Jones, Gains and Garstang (1985) 7 Cr App Rep (S) 448 1-761, 1-822
R v Crown Court at Leeds, ex p Bradford Chief Constable [1975] QB 314, [1975] 1 All ER 133, [1974] 3 WLR 715, 139 JP 156, 118 Sol Jo 849 . . . . 6-60, 6-563
R v Crown Court at Leeds, ex p Briggs [1998] 2 Cr App Rep 413, 162 JP 623, [1998] Crim LR 744 1-2917
R v Crown Court at Leeds, ex p Briggs (No 2) [1998] 2 Cr App Rep 424, [1998] Crim LR 746, [1998] 14 LS Gaz R 23, 142 Sol Jo LB 109 1-2917
R v Crown Court at Leeds, ex p Wardle [2001] UKHL 12, [2002] 1 AC 754, [2001] 2 All ER 1, [2001] 2 WLR 865, [2001] 2 Cr App Rep 301, 165 JP 465, [2001] 21 LS Gaz R 39, [2001] NLJR 386, 145 Sol Jo LB 117 1-6223
R v Crown Court at Leeds, ex p Whitehead (1999) 164 JP 102 1-2917
R v Crown Court at Leeds, ex p Wood (1989) Times, 17 July 2-741
R v Crown Court at Leicester, ex p DPP [1987] 3 All ER 654, [1987] 1 WLR 1371, 131 Sol Jo 1390, [1987] LS Gaz R 3173 1-2794
R v Crown Court at Leicester, ex p Phipps (1997) 161 JP 505, [1997] COD 299 6-577
R v Crown Court at Lewes, ex p Hill (1990) 93 Cr App Rep 60 1-2794
R v Crown Court at Lewes, ex p Rogers [1974] 1 All ER 589, [1974] 1 WLR 196, 138 JP 249, 118 Sol Jo 100 1-1370
R v Crown Court at Lincoln, ex p Jones [1990] COD 15, (1989) Times, 16 June 1-1250
R v Crown Court at Lincoln, ex p Jude [1997] 3 All ER 737, [1998] 1 WLR 24, [1998] 1 Cr App Rep 130, 161 JP 589, 141 Sol Jo LB 138 . . . . 3-540, 3-541
R v Crown Court at Liverpool, ex p Cooke [1996] 4 All ER 589, [1997] 1 WLR 700, [1997] 1 Cr App Rep (S) 7, 29 HLR 249 . . . . 3-203, 8-26310
R v Crown Court at Liverpool, ex p Roberts [1986] Crim LR 622 1-835
R v Crown Court at Liverpool, ex p Wimpey plc [1991] Crim LR 635 1-2703
R v Crown Court at Luton, ex p Neaves (1992) 157 JP 80, 136 Sol Jo LB 174, [1992] 26 LS Gaz R 30, [1992] Crim LR 721 1-2917
R v Crown Court at Maidstone, ex p Lever [1995] 2 All ER 35, [1995] 1 WLR 928, [1996] 1 Cr App Rep 524, [1994] NLJR 1661n, CA 1-1567
R v Crown Court at Maidstone, ex p Schulz and Steinjkellner (1992) 157 JP 601 . . . 1-2917
R v Crown Court at Manchester, ex p Cambros Enterprises Ltd (1973) 137 JP Jo 266, 117 Sol Jo 222 8-13440
R v Crown Court at Manchester, ex p DPP [1993] 1 All ER 801, [1993] 1 WLR 693, [1992] 3 CMLR 329, 136 Sol Jo LB 235, 96 Cr App Rep 210, [1993] 3 LS Gaz R 42, [1993] Crim LR 377; revsd sub nom DPP v Crown Court at Manchester and Ashton [1993] 2 All ER 663, [1993] NLJR 687, sub nom R v Crown Court at Manchester, ex p DPP [1993] 2 WLR 846, 157 JP 497, 137 Sol Jo LB 144, [1993] 24 LS Gaz R 40, HL 1-462
R v Crown Court at Manchester, ex p H and D [2000] 2 All ER 166, [2000] 1 WLR 760, [2000] 1 Cr App Rep 262 1-2563
R v Crown Court at Manchester, ex p Hill (1984) 149 JP 257 . . . . . . 1-761, 1-822
R v Crown Court at Manchester, ex p McDonald [1999] 1 All ER 805, [1999] 1 WLR 841, [1999] 1 Cr App Rep 409, 163 JP 253, [1999] Crim LR 736, 143 Sol Jo LB 55 1-2917
R v Crown Court at Manchester, ex p Rogers [1999] 4 All ER 35, [1999] 1 WLR 832, [1999] 2 Cr App Rep 267, [1999] Crim LR 743 . . . . 1-2704, 2-331
R v Crown Court at Manchester, ex p Taylor [1988] 2 All ER 769, [1988] 1 WLR 705, 132 Sol Jo 899, [1988] 26 LS Gaz R 42, [1988] Crim LR 386 1-2794
R v Crown Court at Manchester, ex p Welby (1981) 73 Cr App Rep 248 1-6082
R v Crown Court at Merthyr Tydfil , ex p Chief Constable of Dyfed Powys [1998] 46 LS Gaz R 35, 142 Sol Jo LB 284 6-230
R v Crown Court at Middlesex , ex p Khan (1996) 161 JP 240 3-541
R v Crown Court at Middlesex Guildhall, ex p Okoli [2001] 1 Cr App Rep 1, 165 JP 144, [2000] Crim LR 921, 144 Sol Jo LB 228 1-3447

PARA

R v Crown Court at Middlesex Guildhall, ex p Tamosius & Partners (a firm) [2000] 1 WLR 453, [2000] Crim LR 390, sub nom R v IRC, ex p Tamosius & Partners (a firm) [1999] STC 1077, [1999] 45 LS Gaz R 34, 143 Sol Jo LB 279 . . . 8-29714
R v Crown Court at Norwich, ex p Cox (1992) 157 JP 593, 97 Cr App Rep 145; on appeal (1992) Times, 3 November, CA . . . 1-2917
R v Crown Court at Norwich, ex p Parker (1992) 156 JP 818, 96 Cr App Rep 68, [1992] Crim LR 500 . . . 1-2917, 1-2918
R v Crown Court at Norwich, ex p Russell [1993] Crim LR 518 . . . 1-761, 1-822
R v Crown Court at Nottingham, ex p DPP [1996] 1 Cr App Rep (S) 283, 160 JP 78, [1995] Crim LR 902 . . . 3-230, 8-23400
R v Crown Court at Portsmouth, ex p Ballard (1989) 154 JP 109 . . . 1-761, 1-822
R v Crown Court at Preston, ex p Lancashire County Council [1998] 3 All ER 765, [1999] 1 WLR 142 . . . 1-2910
R v Crown Court at Preston, ex p Pamplin [1981] Crim LR 338 . . . 1-1051
R v Crown Court at Reading, ex p Hutchinson [1988] QB 384, [1988] 1 All ER 333, [1987] 3 WLR 1062, 152 JP 47, 131 Sol Jo 1455, 86 LGR 71, 87 Cr App Rep 36, [1987] LS Gaz R 3172, [1987] Crim LR 827 . . . 2-193, 8-18835, 8-18837
R v Crown Court at Reading, ex p Malik [1981] QB 451, [1981] 1 All ER 249, [1981] 1 WLR 473, 145 JP 132, 125 Sol Jo 97, 72 Cr App Rep 146 . . . 1-5738, 1–6564K
R v Crown Court at St Albans, ex p Cinnamond [1981] QB 480, [1981] 1 All ER 802, [1981] 2 WLR 681, 145 JP 277, 125 Sol Jo 289, [1981] RTR 139, [1981] Crim LR 243 1-835, 1-2562, 1-2567
R v Crown Court at St Albans, ex p O'Donovan [2000] 1 Cr App Rep (S) 344 . . . 4-1680
R v Crown Court at Sheffield, ex p Clarkson (1986) 8 Cr App Rep (S) 454 . . . 5-44
R v Crown Court at Sheffield, ex p Mecca Leisure Ltd (1983) 148 JP 225 . . . 6-574
R v Crown Court at Shrewsbury, ex p Venables [1994] Crim LR 61 . . . 8-4447
R v Crown Court at Snaresbrook, ex p DPP [1988] QB 532, [1988] 1 All ER 315, [1987] 3 WLR 1054, 131 Sol Jo 1487, 86 Cr App Rep 227, [1987] LS Gaz R 3335 . . . 1-2704
R v Crown Court at Snaresbrook, ex p Input Management Ltd (1999) 163 JP 533, 143 Sol Jo LB 113 . . . 1-761, 1-822
R v Crown Court at Snaresbrook, ex p Metropolitan Police Comr (1984) 148 JP 449, 79 Cr App Rep 184 . . . 8-22451
R v Crown Court at Southwark, ex p Customs and Excise Comrs [1990] 1 QB 650, [1989] 3 All ER 673, [1989] 3 WLR 1054 . . . 1-2726, 8-22065U
R v Crown Court at Southwark, ex p Godwin [1991] 3 All ER 818, 94 Cr App Rep 34, 156 JP 86, [1991] Crim LR 302, 135 Sol Jo LB 28, CA . . . 5-23
R v Crown Court at Southwark, ex p Tawfick (Crown Prosecution Service intervening) (1994) Times, 1 December . . . 8-29560
R v Crown Court at Southwark, ex p Watts (1989) 153 JP 666, 88 LGR 86 . . . 8-19293
R v Crown Court at Stafford, ex p Chief Constable of Staffordshire Police [1998] 2 All ER 812, [1999] 1 WLR 398, 162 JP 501 . . . 6-165, 6-663
R v Crown Court at Stafford, ex p Shipley [1998] 2 All ER 465, [1998] 1 WLR 1438, 162 JP 429, [1998] 02 LS Gaz R 22, 142 Sol Jo LB 70, (1998) Licensing Review, CA 6-165, 6-169, 6-663, 6-666
R v Crown Court at Stafford, ex p Wilf Gilbert (Staffs) Ltd [1999] 2 All ER 955 . . . 1-6083, 8-13321
R v Crown Court at Swansea, ex p Stacey (1989) 154 JP 185, [1990] RTR 183, [1990] Crim LR 260 . . . 1-761, 1-822
R v Crown Court at Swindon, ex p Murray (1997) 162 JP 36 . . . 1-761, 1-822
R v Crown Court at Swindon, ex p Patwittar Singh [1984] 1 All ER 941, [1984] 1 WLR 449, 148 JP 221, 128 Sol Jo 203 . . . 1-1250
R v Crown Court at Wakefield, ex p Oldfield [1978] Crim LR 164 . . . 8-10376
R v Crown Court at Warrington, ex p RBNB (a company) [2002] UKHL 24, [2002] 4 All ER 131, [2002] 1 WLR 1954, 167 JP 6, [2002] 30 LS Gaz R 39, [2002] NLJR 999 . . . 6-562
R v Crown Court at Warwick, ex p Smalley [1987] 1 WLR 237, 84 Cr App Rep 51, [1987] Crim LR 112, 131 Sol Jo 257, [1987] LS Gaz R 654 . . . 1-7439
R v Crown Court at Winchester, ex p B (a minor) [1999] 4 All ER 53, [1999] 1 WLR 788, [2000] 1 Cr App Rep 11, 143 Sol Jo LB 31 . . . 1-2563, 5-23
R v Crown Court at Winchester, ex p Lewington [1982] 1 WLR 1277, 126 Sol Jo 608, 4 Cr App Rep (S) 224, [1982] Crim LR 664 . . . 1-766, 1-2180
R v Crown Court at Wolverhampton, ex p Crofts [1983] 3 All ER 702, [1983] 1 WLR 204, 76 Cr App Rep 8 . . . 1-835
R v Crown Court at Wood Green, ex p Howe [1992] 3 All ER 366, [1992] 1 WLR 702, 155 JP 652, 93 Cr App Rep 213, [1991] Crim LR 694 . . . 1-1566, 1-7439, 3-1699
R v Crown Court at Woolwich, ex p Gilligan [1998] 2 All ER 1 . . . 8-9921
R v Crown Court at York, ex p Coleman and How (1987) 86 Cr App Rep 151, [1987] Crim LR 761 . . . 1-1567
R v Crown Prosecution Service, ex p Warby (1993) 158 JP 190, [1994] Crim LR 281, DC 2-38A
R v Croydon Crown Court, ex p Lewis (1994) 158 JP 886, [1995] Crim LR 44 . . . 1-2917
R v Croydon Justices, ex p Dean [1993] QB 769, [1993] 3 All ER 129, [1993] 3 WLR 198, 157 JP 975 . . . 1-447
R v Croydon Justices, ex p Holmberg (1992) 157 JP 277, [1992] Crim LR 892 . . . 1-380, 1-2901
R v Croydon Justices, ex p Lefore Holdings Ltd [1981] 1 All ER 520, [1980] 1 WLR 1465, 145 JP 151, 124 Sol Jo 848, [1980] Crim LR 722, CA . . . 1-766
R v Croydon Justices, ex p W H Smith Ltd (2000) Times, 22 November, [2000] 46 LS Gaz R 39 8-15331
R v Croydon Magistrates' Court, ex p Morgan (1996) 161 JP 169 . . . 1-766

PARA

PARA

PARA

PARA

PARA

PARA

R v Harris [1951] 1 KB 107, [1950] 2 All ER 816, 49 LGR 37, 34 Cr App Rep 184, 114 JP 535, 94 Sol Jo 689, 66 (pt 2) TLR 739, CCA . . . 3-1566
R v Harris [1963] 2 QB 442, [1963] 2 All ER 294, [1963] 2 WLR 851, 127 JP 357, 107 Sol Jo 217, 47 Cr App Rep 125, CCA . . . 8-13301
R v Harris [1969] 2 All ER 599, [1969] 1 WLR 745, 133 JP 442, 113 Sol Jo 363, CA . . . 1-465, 1-703
R v Harris (1979) 69 Cr App Rep 122, CA . . . 8-21203
R v Harris (1988) 10 Cr App Rep (S) 164, CA . . . 3-233
R v Harris [1996] 1 Cr App Rep 369, [1996] Crim LR 36, CA . . . 8-21238
R v Harris [2001] Crim LR 227, CA . . . 2-1355
R v Harrison (1992) 14 Cr App Rep (S) 419, CA . . . 3-522
R v Harrison [1997] 2 Cr App Rep (S) 174, CA . . . 3-240
R v Harrow Justices, ex p DPP [1991] 3 All ER 873, [1991] 1 WLR 395, 155 JP 979, 93 Cr App Rep 388, [1991] 23 LS Gaz R 34 . . . 1-2142, 3-209A
R v Hart (1932) 23 Cr App Rep 202, CCA . . . 1-664, 2-68
R v Hart (1957) 42 Cr App Rep 47 . . . 1-2169
R v Hartley [1941] 1 KB 5, 104 JP 470, 110 LJKB 85, 164 LT 344, 57 TLR 98, 85 Sol Jo 32, 38 LGR 487, 28 Cr App Rep 15, CCA . . . 2-463, 8-27977, 8-27979
R v Hartnett [2003] EWCA Crim 345, [2003] Crim LR 719, [2003] All ER (D) 14 (Feb) . . . 1-67
R v Harvey (1869) 1 Cox CC 546 . . . 2-72
R v Harvey, ex p Select Livestock Producers Ltd (1985) 149 JP 389, [1985] Crim LR 510, 4 Tr L 162 . . . 1-32
R v Hasan [2005] UKHL 22, [2005] 4 All ER 685, [2005] 2 Cr App Rep 314, [2006] Crim LR 142, (2005) Times, 21 March, 149 Sol Jo LB 360 . . . 1-324, 1-325, 1-326, 2-1363
R v Hashi (1994) 16 Cr App Rep (S) 121, [1994] Crim LR 618, CA . . . 3-1231, 3-1721
R v Hastings and Rother Justices, ex p Anscombe (1998) 162 JP 340, [1998] Crim LR 812 1-2142, 3-208A, 3-1699
R v Hastings Justices, ex p Mitchell (1925) 89 JP Jo 86 . . . 8-25215
R v Hastings Licensing Justices, ex p John Lovibond & Sons Ltd [1968] 2 All ER 270, [1968] 1 WLR 735, 66 LGR 422, 132 JP 332, 112 Sol Jo 313, 206 Estates Gazette 211 . . . 6-574
R v Hastings Magistrates' Court, ex p McSpirit (1994) 162 JP 44 . . . 3-946, 6-569
R v Hatch (1933) 24 Cr App Rep 100, CCA . . . 8-30724
R v Hatfield Justices, ex p Castle [1980] 3 All ER 509, [1981] 1 WLR 217, 145 JP 265, 125 Sol Jo 165, 71 Cr App Rep 287, [1980] Crim LR 579 . . . 1-2051
R v Hatton [1925] 2 KB 322, [1925] All ER Rep 396, 89 JP 164, 94 LJKB 863, 133 LT 735, 41 TLR 637, 28 Cox CC 43, 19 Cr App Rep 29, CCA . . . 5-80
R v Hatton (1976) 64 Cr App Rep 88, [1977] Crim LR 218 . . . 2-494
R v Havant Justices, ex p Palmer (1985) 149 JP 609, [1985] Crim LR 658 . . . 1-2441
R v Havering Magistrates' Court, ex p DPP [2001] 3 All ER 997, [2001] 1 WLR 805, [2001] 2 Cr App Rep 12, 165 JP 391, [2001] Crim LR 902, [2000] All ER (D) 2307 . . . 1-1566
R v Hawkes (1931) 22 Cr App Rep 172, CCA . . . 7-13735
R v Hawkins (1985) 150 JP 6, 82 Cr App Rep 141, [1986] BTLC 142, [1985] LS Gaz R 3696, [1986] Crim LR 168, CA . . . 8-4459
R v Hawkins (1985) 7 Cr App Rep (S) 351, [1986] Crim LR 194, CA . . . 1-583
R v Hay Halkett, ex p Rush [1929] 2 KB 431, 93 JP 209, 98 LJKB 497, 141 LT 519, 45 TLR 507, 27 LGR 523, 28 Cox CC 648 . . . 1-440
R v Hayden [1975] 2 All ER 558, [1975] 1 WLR 852, 139 JP 564, 119 Sol Jo 390, 60 Cr App Rep 304, CA . . . 1-1231
R v Hayes (1976) 64 Cr App Rep 82, [1977] Crim LR 691, CA . . . 8-30694
R v Hayes [2004] EWCA Crim 2844, [2005] 1 Cr App R 33 . . . 2-1359
R v Hayhurst, ex p Machin (1897) 61 JP Jo 88 . . . 6-102, 6-205
R v Hayles [1969] 1 QB 364, [1969] 1 All ER 34, [1968] 3 WLR 1106, 112 Sol Jo 860, 53 Cr App Rep 36, CA . . . 5-80
R v Haynes [2003] EWCA Crim 3247, [2004] 2 Cr App Rep (S) 36 . . . 8-7618
R v Hayter [2003] EWCA Crim 1048, [2003] 1 WLR 1910, [2003] 2 Cr App Rep 435, [2003] Crim LR 887, [2003] 25 LS Gaz R 45, 147 Sol Jo LB 537 . . . 2-469
R v Hayter [2005] UKHL 6, [2005] 1 WLR 605, [2005] All ER (D) 36 (Feb) . . . 2-335
R v Hayward (1908) 21 Cox CC 692 . . . 8-23081
R v Hayward [1999] Crim LR 71, [1998] 25 LS Gaz R 33, 142 Sol Jo LB 187, CA . . . 8-6676
R v Hayward [2001] EWCA Crim 168, [2001] QB 862, [2001] 3 WLR 125, [2001] 2 Cr App Rep 156, 165 JP 281, [2001] 09 LS Gaz R 38, 145 Sol Jo LB 53 . . . 1-423
R v Hayward and Hayward [2000] 2 Cr App Rep (S) 149, [2001] 04 LS Gaz R 49, [2001] Crim LR 236, 145 Sol Jo LB 22, CA . . . 3-1666
R v Head [1976] 63 Cr App Rep 157, [1976] Crim LR 157, CA . . . 3-56,
R v Headington Union (1883) 47 JP Jo 756, 28 Sol Jo 250 . . . 1-768, 1-831
R v Headley [1996] RTR 173, 160 JP 25, [1995] Crim LR 736, [1995] 13 LS Gaz R 31, CA 8-23567
R v Healey (1944) 109 JP Jo 39 . . . 1-460, 1-563
R v Healy [1998] 1 Cr App Rep (S) 107, CA . . . 3-232A
R v Hearne [1976] Crim LR 753 . . . 1-583
R v Heath [2000] Crim LR 109, CA . . . 1-307
R v Heaton (1896) 60 JP 508 . . . 8-23097
R v Hedley (1989) 90 Cr App Rep 70, 11 Cr App Rep (S) 298, [1989] Crim LR 842 . . . 3-236
R v Hemingway (1912) 77 JP 15, 29 TLR 13, CCA . . . 2-490
R v Hemingway (1993) 15 Cr App Rep (S) 67, CA . . . 3-234A

PARA

PARA

PARA

R v Johnstone [2002] EWCA Crim 194, [2002] JPN 118, [2002] 13 LS Gaz R 25, 146 Sol Jo LB 60, [2002] All ER (D) 34 (Feb); affd [2003] UKHL 28, [2003] 3 All ER 884, [2003] 1 WLR 1736, [2003] 2 Cr App Rep 493, [2003] FSR 42, 167 JP 281, [2004] Crim LR 244, [2003] 26 LS Gaz R 36, 147 Sol Jo LB 625 . . . . . . 1-700, 8-5898, 8-17631W, 8-18415
R v Johnstone [2003] UKHL 28, [2003] 3 All ER 884, [2003] 1 WLR 1736, [2003] 2 Cr App Rep 493, [2003] FSR 42, 167 JP 281, [2004] Crim LR 244, [2003] 26 LS Gaz R 36, (2003) Times, 29 May, 147 Sol Jo LB 625, [2003] All ER (D) 323 (May), [2003] IP & T 901 8-5898
R v Jolie [2003] EWCA Crim 1543, [2004] 1 Cr App Rep 44, 167 JP 313, [2003] Crim LR 730 8-22630, 8-22680
R v Jones (1883) 11 QBD 118, 47 JP 535, 52 LJMC 96, 48 LT 768, 31 WR 800, 15 Cox CC 284 8-23117
R v Jones (1925) 19 Cr App Rep 39, CCA 8-27974
R v Jones (Evan) (1933) 149 LT 143, [1933] All ER Rep 644, 77 Sol Jo 236, 29 Cox CC 637, 24 Cr App Rep 55, CCA 8-27977
R v Jones [1960] 3 All ER 457, [1960] 1 WLR 1169, 124 JP 505, 104 Sol Jo 893, 45 Cr App Rep 5, CCA 2-69
R v Jones [1969] 2 QB 33, [1969] 1 All ER 325, [1968] 2 WLR 105, 53 Cr App Rep 87, 133 JP 144, 112 Sol Jo 984, CA 3-1555
R v Jones [1969] 3 All ER 1559, [1970] 1 WLR 16, [1970] RTR 35, 54 Cr App Rep 63, 134 JP 124, 113 Sol Jo 962, CA 4-1377A
R v Jones [1970] 3 All ER 815, [1970] 1 WLR 1494, 135 JP 36, 114 Sol Jo 867, 55 Cr App Rep 32, CA 3-55, 4-1693
R v Jones (John) [1976] 3 All ER 54, [1976] 1 WLR 672, 140 JP 515, 120 Sol Jo 299, CA . 8-30698
R v Jones [1987] 2 All ER 692, [1987] 1 WLR 692, 131 Sol Jo 504, [1987] LS Gaz R 820, CA 8-6611
R v Jones (1988) 10 Cr App Rep (S) 95, [1988] Crim LR 390, CA 3-522
R v Jones (1990) 12 Cr App Rep (S) 218, CA 3-758
R v Jones (Terence) [1992] Crim LR 365, CA 2-1938
R v Jones (MA) (1993) 158 JP 293, 138 Sol Jo LB 51, [1994] 12 LS Gaz R 38, CA . . 2-1938
R v Jones (1994) 15 Cr App Rep (S) 856, CA 3-236A
R v Jones [1995] QB 235, [1995] 3 All ER 139, [1995] 2 WLR 64, 159 JP 94, [1995] Crim LR 416, [1994] 39 LS Gaz R 38, 138 Sol Jo LB 194, CA 8-10389
R v Jones [1996] 1 Cr App Rep (S) 153, CA 3-173
R v Jones [1997] QB 798, [1997] 2 WLR 792, [1997] 1 Cr App Rep 46, [1997] Crim LR 510, [1996] 37 LS Gaz R 26, 140 Sol Jo LB 206, CA 8-10385
R v Jones (Keith) (1997) 161 JP 597, [1998] Crim LR 56, CA 8-21204
R v Jones (2000) 164 JP 293, CA 8-10387
R v Jones [2001] EWCA Crim 168, [2001] QB 862, [2001] 3 WLR 125, [2001] 2 Cr App Rep 156, 165 JP 281, [2001] 09 LS Gaz R 38, 145 Sol Jo LB 53 1-428
R v Jones [2002] UKHL 5, [2003] 1 AC 1, [2002] 2 All ER 113, [2002] 2 WLR 524, [2002] 2 Cr App Rep 128, 166 JP 333, 146 Sol Jo LB 61, [2002] 13 LS Gaz R 26, (2002) Times, 21 February, [2002] 5 LRC 50, [2002] All ER (D) 275 (Feb), HL . . 1-423, 1-428, 1-6970
R v Jones [2003] EWCA Crim 1609, [2004] 1 Cr App Rep (S) 126, 167 JP 536, [2003] Crim LR 639 . . . . 3-1660, 5-41A
R v Jones [2004] EWCA Crim 1981, [2005] QB 259, [2004] 4 All ER 955, [2004] 3 WLR 1362, [2005] 1 Cr App Rep 154, [2005] Crim LR 122, [2004] 34 LS Gaz R 29, (2004) Times, 30 July, 148 Sol Jo LB 1149, [2004] All ER (D) 374 (Jul) 1-1071, 8-24744
R v Jones, ex p Daunton [1963] 1 All ER 368, [1963] 1 WLR 270, 127 JP 349, 107 Sol Jo 76 8-7510
R v Jones, ex p Davies (1895) 59 JP 87 6-562
R v Jones, ex p Thomas [1921] 1 KB 632, 19 LGR 354, 85 JP 112, 90 LJKB 543, 26 Cox CC 706, 124 LT 668, 37 TLR 299, DC 1-7427
R v Jones and Bowerbank [1896] 1 QB 4, 60 JP 89, 65 LJMC 28, 73 LT 584, 44 WR 110, 40 Sol Jo 85, 18 Cox CC 207 8-27980
R v Jordon [1998] 2 Cr App Rep (S) 83, [1998] Crim LR 353, CA . . . 3-1299C, 3-1732
R v Jory (1985) 150 JP 65, 82 Cr App Rep 141, [1986] BTLC 142, [1985] LS Gaz R 3696, [1986] Crim LR 168, CA 8-4459
R v Josephs and Christie (1977) Times, 26 February 8-21207
R v Joyce [1991] RTR 241, 11 Cr App Rep (S) 253, CA 3-521, 3-1703
R v Joyce [2001] EWCA Crim 2433, [2002] 1 Cr App Rep (S) 582 3-230
R v Judd (1888) 37 WR 143 8-18632
R v Judd [1971] 1 All ER 127, [1971] 1 WLR 89, 55 Cr App Rep 14, CA . . . 3-244, 3-245
R v Judge Clements, ex p Ferridge [1932] 2 KB 535, 101 LJKB 603, 147 LT 353, 76 Sol Jo 414 8-16723
R v Judge Radcliffe, ex p Oxfordshire County Council [1915] 3 KB 418, 79 JP 546, 84 LJKB 2196, 113 LT 991, 31 TLR 610, 13 LGR 1192 . . . . . . 6-320, 8-27672
R v Julien [1969] 2 All ER 856, [1969] 1 WLR 839, 133 JP 489, 113 Sol Jo 342, CA . . . 8-23065
R v Jura [1954] 1 QB 503, [1954] 1 All ER 696, [1954] 2 WLR 516, 118 JP 260, 98 Sol Jo 198, 38 Cr App Rep 53, CCA 8-22630
R v K (1983) 148 JP 410, 78 Cr App Rep 82, [1983] Crim LR 736, CA 1-2169
R v K [2001] 1 Cr App Rep 446, 165 JP 306, [2001] Crim LR 398, CA 1-457, 1-548, 1-3160, 3-1253, 5-14
R v K [2001] UKHL 41, [2002] 1 AC 462, [2001] 3 All ER 897, [2001] 3 WLR 471, [2001] 1 Cr App Rep 35, [2001] 3 FCR 115, [2001] 34 LS Gaz R 39, 145 Sol Jo LB 2028-27973, 8-27981, 8-27986
R v Kabariti (1990) 92 Cr App Rep 362, CA 2-494
R v Kakelo [1923] 2 KB 793, [1923] All ER Rep 191, 87 JP 184, 92 LJKB 997, 129 LT 477, 39 TLR 671, 68 Sol Jo 41, 27 Cox CC 454, 17 Cr App Rep 149, CCA 1-684, 2-75
R v Kalia [1975] Crim LR 181, Cr App Rep 200, CA 1-628, 2-20

PARA

PARA

R v Kneeshaw [1975] QB 57, [1974] 1 All ER 896, [1974] 2 WLR 432, 138 JP 291, 118 Sol Jo 218, CA 3-204, 3-1690
R v Knight (1990) 12 Cr App Rep (S) 319 3-240
R v Knight [1998] 2 Cr App Rep (S) 23, CA 3-236C
R v Knight [2003] EWCA Crim 1977, [2004] 1 WLR 340, [2003] Crim LR 799, [2003] 37 LS Gaz R 31 2-496
R v Knights [2001] EWCA Crim 1694, [2001] All ER (D) 174 (Jul) 2-239A
R v Knockaloe Camp Commandant, ex p Forman [1917] WN 283, 82 JP 41, 87 LJKB 43, 117 LT 627, 34 TLR 4, 62 Sol Jo 35, 16 LGR 295, 26 Cox CC 58 8-17708
R v Knutton (1992) 97 Cr App Rep 115, [1993] Crim LR 208, CA 2-920
R v Koeller [2001] EWCA Crim 1854, [2001] All ER (D) 21 (Aug) 3-239A
R v Kohn (1979) 69 Cr App Rep 395, [1979] Crim LR 675, CA 8-30692, 8-30693
R v Kolawole [2004] EWCA Crim 3047, [2005] 2 Cr App Rep (S) 71, (2004) Times, 16 November, 148 Sol Jo LB 1370, [2004] All ER (D) 439 (Nov) 3-240
R v Kolton [2000] Crim LR 761, CA 1-1093, 2-190
R v Komsta and Murphy (1990) 154 JP 440, [1990] Crim LR 434, CA 1-1264, 3-1699
R v Konzani [2005] EWCA Crim 706, [2005] 2 Cr App Rep 14, (2005) 169 JPN 227, [2005] All ER (D) 292 (Mar) 8-23063
R v Korie [1966] 1 All ER 50 8-28009
R v Kovacs [1974] 1 All ER 1236, [1974] 1 WLR 370, 138 JP 425, 118 Sol Jo 116, CA 8-30705
R v Kowalski [1988] 1 FLR 447, [1988] Fam Law 259, 86 Cr App Rep 339, 9 Cr App Rep (S) 375, [1988] Crim LR 124, CA 8-27981
R v Kraus [1982] Crim LR 468; affd 4 Cr App Rep (S) 113, CA 8-17692
R v Krause (1902) 66 JP 121, 18 TLR 238 . . . . 1-322, 8-23080
R v Krebbs [1977] RTR 406, CA 4-1680
R v Kuechenmeister, ex p Bottrill. See R v Bottrill, ex p Kuechenmeister
R v Kumar [2004] EWCA Crim 3207, [2005] 1 WLR 1352, [2005] 1 Cr App Rep 566, [2005] Crim LR 470, (2005) Times, 10 January, [2004] All ER (D) 249 (Dec) 3-1783
R v Kurasch [1915] 2 KB 749, 79 JP 399, 84 LJKB 1497, 113 LT 431, 25 Cox CC 55, 11 Cr App Rep 166, CCA 2-464
R v Kurasch [1937] 2 All ER 130, 53 TLR 441, 81 Sol Jo 296, 26 Cr App Rep 25, CCA 8-30669
R v L (Steven Donald) [2002] EWCA Crim 628, [2002] 2 Cr App Rep (S) 506 3-160
R v L [2005] EWCA Crim 2487, [2005] All ER (D) 132 (Nov), sub nom R v Lamb [2006] Crim LR 256, (2005) Times, 1 December 3-241
R v LM [2002] EWCA Crim 3047, [2003] 2 Cr App Rep (S) 124, [2003] Crim LR 205 . . . . 5-41A
R v Labouchere (1884) 12 QBD 320, 48 JP 165, 53 LJQB 362, 50 LT 177, 32 WR 861, 15 Cox CC 415 8-18620
R v Lack (1987) 84 Cr App Rep 342, CA 8-13148
R v Lady Scott (1897) Times, 8 January 8-18631
R v Lalani [1999] 1 Cr App Rep 481, [1999] Crim LR 992, CA 8-23567
R v Lamb [1968] 2 QB 829, [1968] 3 All ER 206, [1968] 3 WLR 833, 132 JP 575, 112 Sol Jo 783, 52 Cr App Rep 667, CA 3-248
R v Lambert [2002] QB 1112, [2001] 1 All ER 1014, [2001] 2 WLR 211, [2001] 1 Cr App Rep 205, [2000] 35 LS Gaz R 36, 144 Sol Jo LB 226, CA; affd [2001] UKHL 37, [2002] 2 AC 545, [2001] 3 All ER 577, [2001] 3 WLR 206, [2001] 2 Cr App Rep 511, [2001] 31 LS Gaz R 29, 145 Sol Jo LB 174 8-17631, ... 8-17631B, 8-17631W, 8-21204, 8-21234, 8-23251
R v Lambeth London Borough Council, ex p Caddell [1998] 2 FCR 6, [1998] 1 FLR 253, [1998] Fam Law 20, [1997] 30 LS Gaz R 30, 141 Sol Jo LB 147 4-2133
R v Lambeth Metropolitan Stipendiary Magistrate, ex p McComb [1983] QB 551, [1983] 1 All ER 321, [1983] 2 WLR 259, 76 Cr App Rep 246 . . . . 1-455, 1-541, 1-7430
R v Lambie [1982] AC 449, [1981] 2 All ER 776, [1981] 3 WLR 88, 125 Sol Jo 480, 73 Cr App Rep 294, [1981] Crim LR 712, HL 8-30705
R v Lamont [1989] Crim LR 813, CA 2-1358
R v Lancashire Justices, ex p Customs and Excise Comrs (1934) 32 LGR 265, 98 JP 307, [1934] All ER Rep 542, 151 LT 376 . . . . 6-256, 6-638
R v Lancashire Justices, ex p Tyrer [1925] 1 KB 200, [1924] All ER Rep 304, 89 JP 17, 94 LJKB 331, 132 LT 382, 41 TLR 103, 69 Sol Jo 194, 27 Cox CC 711, 23 LGR 32 . . . . 1-836, 1-2126
R v Lancashire Quarter Sessions Appeal Committee, ex p Huyton-with-Roby UDC [1955] 1 QB 52, [1954] 3 All ER 225, [1954] 3 WLR 597, 118 JP 526, 98 Sol Jo 735, 53 LGR 46 8-25228
R v Land [1999] QB 65, [1998] 1 All ER 403, [1998] 3 WLR 322, [1998] 1 Cr App Rep 301, [1998] 1 FLR 438, [1998] Fam Law 133, [1998] Crim LR 70, [1997] 42 LS Gaz R 32, CA 8-28240, 8-28241
R v Landow (1913) 77 JP 364, 109 LT 48, 29 TLR 375, 23 Cox CC 457, CCA 8-27988
R v Lane and Lane (1985) 82 Cr App Rep 5, [1985] Crim LR 789 5-80
R v Lanfear [1968] 2 QB 77, [1968] 1 All ER 683, [1968] 2 WLR 623, 132 JP 193, 112 Sol Jo 132, 52 Cr App Rep 176, CA 4-1375
R v Lang [2005] EWCA Crim 2864, [2006] Crim LR 174, (2005) Times, 10 November, 149 Sol Jo LB 1450, [2005] All ER (D) 54 (Nov) 1-2053, 3-241B, 5-12
R v Langford [1990] Crim LR 653 2-330
R v Langton (1876) 2 QBD 296, 41 JP 134, 46 LJMC 136, 35 LT 527, 13 Cox CC 345 2-619
R v Lanyon (1872) 27 LT 355 . . . . 1-583, 1-754
R v Larkin [1943] 1 KB 174, [1943] 1 All ER 217, 112 LJKB 163, 168 LT 298, 59 TLR 105, 87 Sol Jo 140, 29 Cr App Rep 18, CCA 2-474

PARA

PARA

R v Lovegrove [1920] 3 KB 643, 85 JP 75, 90 LJKB 285, 124 LT 288, 26 Cox CC 683, 15 Cr App Rep 50, CCA . . . 8-23118
R v Loveridge [2001] EWCA Crim 973, [2001] 2 Cr App Rep 591, 145 Sol Jo LB 120 . . . 1-995, 8-17631W
R v Lovet (1797) 7 Term Rep 152 . . . 8-13653
R v Lovett [1973] 1 All ER 744, [1973] 1 WLR 241, 137 JP 275, 117 Sol Jo 124, 57 Cr App Rep 332, CA . . . 2-494
R v Lowe (1989) Times, 14 November, CA . . . 3-31
R v Lowes (1988) 10 Cr App Rep (S) 175, CA . . . 3-560
R v Lucas [1981] QB 720, [1981] 2 All ER 1008, [1981] 3 WLR 120, 125 Sol Jo 426, 73 Cr App Rep 159, CA . . . 2-617
R v Lucas [1995] Crim LR 400, CA . . . 8-21204
R v Lucien [1995] Crim LR 807, CA . . . 8-6607
R v Luffe (1807) 8 East 193 . . . 2-33
R v Lumley (1869) LR 1 CCR 196, 33 JP 326, 38 LJMC 86, 20 LT 454, 17 WR 685, 11 Cox CC 274 . . . 8-23117
R v Lumsden [1951] 2 KB 513, [1951] 1 All ER 1101, 115 JP 364, [1951] 1 TLR 987, 95 Sol Jo 355, 49 LGR 749, 35 Cr App Rep 57, CCA . . . 8-31441
R v Lund (1921) 16 Cr App Rep 31, CCA . . . 8-23117
R v Lunderbech [1991] Crim LR 784, CA . . . 8-22430
R v Lundt-Smith [1964] 2 QB 167, [1964] 3 All ER 225, [1964] 2 WLR 1063, 128 JP 534, 108 Sol Jo 425, 62 LGR 376 . . . 4-1680
R v Lunt (1986) 85 Cr App Rep 241, [1987] Crim LR 405, CA . . . 2-464, 2-465
R v Luton Magistrates' Court, ex p Sullivan [1992] 1 FCR 475, [1992] 2 FLR 196, [1992] Fam Law 380 . . . 1-2155, 3-209B
R v Luttrell [2004] EWCA Crim 1344, [2004] 2 Cr App Rep 520, [2004] Crim LR 939, 148 Sol Jo LB 698, (2004) Times, 9 June, [2004] All ER (D) 454 (May) . . . 2-344
R v Luxford [1996] 1 Cr App Rep (S) 186, CA . . . 3-240
R v Lyall (1994) 16 Cr App Rep (S) 600, CA . . . 3-236C
R v Lydeard St Lawrence Inhabitants (1841) 1 Ad & El 616, 1 Gal & Dav 191, 10 LJMC 147, 6 Jur 32 . . . 2-467
R v Lydon (Sean) (1987) 87 Cr App Rep 221, [1987] Crim LR 407, CA . . . 2-206, 2-206A, 2-462
R v Lymington and New Forest Justices, ex p Armstrong [1953] Brewing Tr Rev 501 . . . 6-155
R v Lymm Justices, ex p Browne [1973] 1 All ER 716, [1973] 1 WLR 1039, 137 JP 269, 117 Sol Jo 547 . . . 1-835
R v Lynn (1788) 2 Term Rep 733, 1 Leach CC 497 . . . 8-2991
R v Lynn [1964] 1 QB 164, [1963] 3 All ER 659, [1963] 3 WLR 946, 48 Cr App Rep 42, 128 JP 48, 107 Sol Jo 833, CCA . . . 1-171
R v Lynsey [1995] 3 All ER 654, [1995] 2 Cr App Rep 667, 159 JP 437, CA . . . 1-3160, 8-23060
R v Lyon, ex p Skinner (1898) 62 JP 357, 14 TLR 357, CA . . . 6-562
R v Lyons [2001] EWCA Crim 2860, [2002] 2 Cr App Rep 210; affd sub nom [2002] UKHL 44, [2003] 1 AC 976, [2002] 4 All ER 1028, [2002] 3 WLR 1562, [2003] 1 Cr App Rep 24, [2003] Crim LR 623, 146 Sol Jo LB 264 . . . 8-17631
R v Lyth (1994) 16 Cr App Rep (S) 68, CA . . . 3-236A
R v M [2000] 1 WLR 421, sub nom R v TM [2000] 2 Cr App Rep 266, CA . . . 2-460, 2-476
R v M [2001] EWCA Crim 1505, (2001) 165 JPN 455 . . . 5-50A
R v M [2001] EWCA Crim 2024, [2002] 1 WLR 824, [2002] 1 Cr App Rep 283, [2002] Crim LR 57, 145 Sol Jo LB 236; affd [2003] UKHL 1, [2003] 1 All ER 497, [2003] 1 WLR 411, [2003] 2 Cr App Rep 25, 167 JP 125, [2003] Crim LR 817, 71 BMLR 146, [2003] 12 LS Gaz R 30, 147 Sol Jo LB 146 . . . 8-17631W, 8-22232
R v M [2002] JPN 963, [2002] All ER (D) 35 (Dec), CA . . . 3-180, 3-1656, 3-1660
R v M (KJ) [2003] EWCA Crim 357, [2003] 2 Cr App Rep 322 . . . 2-1472
R v M [2004] EWCA Crim 2002, [2005] 1 Cr App Rep (S) 284 . . . 3-233
R v Maben [1997] 2 Cr App Rep (S) 341, CA . . . 3-230
R v McAllister [1974] RTR 408, 59 Cr App Rep 7, [1974] Crim LR 716, CA . . . 4-1378
R v McBride [1962] 2 QB 167, [1961] 3 All ER 6, [1961] 3 WLR 549, 45 Cr App Rep 262, 125 JP 544, 105 Sol Jo 572, CCA . . . 7-9
R v McCalla (1988) 152 JP 481, 87 Cr App Rep 372, CA . . . 8-22630
R v McCallum [2001] EWCA Crim 2352, [2002] 1 Cr App Rep (S) 488 . . . 3-240
R v McCarthy [1964] 1 All ER 95, [1964] 1 WLR 196, 128 JP 191, 108 Sol Jo 17, 48 Cr App Rep 111, CCA . . . 8-14183
R v McCarthy (1993) 158 JP 283, CA . . . 1-608, 2-38A
R v McCarthy [1998] RTR 374, CA . . . 4-1961
R v McCartney and Hansen (1928) 20 Cr App Rep 179, CCA . . . 2-197
R v McCay [1991] 1 All ER 232, [1990] 1 WLR 645, 154 JP 621, 134 Sol Jo 606, 91 Cr App Rep 84, [1990] 19 LS Gaz R 39, [1990] Crim LR 338, CA . . . 2-1938
R v McClelland [1951] 1 All ER 557, 115 JP 179, 49 LGR 227, CCA . . . 3-200, 3-206
R v McCluskie (1992) 13 Cr App Rep (S) 334, CA . . . 4-1680
R v McCormick (1994) 16 Cr App Rep (S) 134, [1994] Crim LR 612, CA . . . 3-234A
R v McCraig (1925) 90 JP 64, 134 LT 160, 42 TLR 215, 28 Cox CC 109, 19 Cr App Rep 68, CCA . . . 2-490
R v McCullum (1973) 117 Sol Jo 525, 57 Cr App Rep 645, [1973] Crim LR 582, CA . . . 8-30721
R v MacDonagh [1974] QB 448, [1974] 2 All ER 257, [1974] 2 WLR 529, 138 JP 488, 118 Sol Jo 222, CA . . . 4-8

PARA

PARA

PARA

PARA

PARA

PARA

R v Newcastle upon Tyne Justices, ex p John Bryce (Contractors) Ltd [1976] 2 All ER 611, [1976] 1 WLR 517, 140 JP 440, 120 Sol Jo 64, [1976] RTR 325, [1976] Crim LR 134 . . . 1-63, 1-442, 1-447
R v Newcastle upon Tyne Justices, ex p Skinner [1987] 1 All ER 349, [1987] 1 WLR 312, 151 JP 92, 131 Sol Jo 194, 84 Cr App Rep 311, [1987] LS Gaz R 412 . . . 1-766
R v Newham Justices, ex p C [1993] Crim LR 130 . . . 1-63, 1-447
R v Newham Justices, ex p Knight [1976] Crim LR 323 . . . 1-2053, 5-14
R v Newham Juvenile Court, ex p F (a minor) [1986] 3 All ER 17, [1986] 1 WLR 939, 130 Sol Jo 526, [1986] Crim LR 557, [1986] LS Gaz R 2160 . . . 1-2053, 5-13
R v Newington (1990) 134 Sol Jo 785, 91 Cr App Rep 247, [1990] Crim LR 593, CA . . . 8-22275
R v Newley [1984] Crim LR 509 . . . 1-2682
R v Newman (1853) 1 E & B 558, 17 JP 84, Dears CC 85, 22 LJQB 156, 22 LTOS 76, 17 Jur 617 . . . 8-18631
R v Newman and Newman [1980] Crim LR 55 . . . 3-20
R v Newport Pagnell Justices, ex p Smith (1988) 152 JP 475 . . . 1-2142, 3-209B
R v Newport (Salop) Justices, ex p Wright [1929] 2 KB 416, 93 JP 179, 98 LJKB 555, 141 LT 563, 45 TLR 477, 73 Sol Jo 384, 27 LGR 518, 28 Cox CC 658 . . . 1-765, 1-827
R v Newton [1974] RTR 451 . . . 4-1680
R v Newton (1983) 77 Cr App Rep 13, 4 Cr App Rep (S) 388, [1983] Crim LR 198 . . . 1-508, 1-583
R v Newton (1982) 77 Cr App Rep 13, 4 Cr App Rep (S) 388, [1983] Crim LR 198, CA . . . 3-50, 1-5659A
R v Ngan [1998] 1 Cr App Rep 331, [1997] 33 LS Gaz R 27, CA . . . 8-30692
R v Nicholls [1960] 2 All ER 449, [1960] 1 WLR 658, 124 JP 343, 104 Sol Jo 547, 44 Cr App Rep 188, CCA . . . 1-420
R v Nicholson (1993) 15 Cr App Rep (S) 226, CA . . . 3-235
R v Nicholson (Andrew) [2000] 1 Cr App Rep 182, 164 JP 29, [1999] 34 LS Gaz R 33, CA . . . 2-1938
R v Nicklin [1977] 2 All ER 444, [1977] 1 WLR 403, 141 JP 391, 121 Sol Jo 286, 64 Cr App Rep 205, CA . . . 8-30721
R v Nickolson [1999] Crim LR 61, CA . . . 2-496
R v Nixon [1969] 2 All ER 688, [1969] 1 WLR 1055, 133 JP 520, 113 Sol Jo 388, 53 Cr App Rep 432, CA . . . 4-1655
R v Noble [2002] EWCA Crim 1713, [2003] RTR 115, [2003] 1 Cr App Rep (S) 312, [2002] Crim LR 676, [2002] 32 LS Gaz R 33 . . . 3-244, 3-245
R v Nokes (1977) 66 Cr App Rep 3, [1978] RTR 101, CA . . . 3-237
R v Nolan (1992) 13 Cr App Rep (S) 144, CA . . . 3-236A
R v Norcott [1917] 1 KB 347, 86 LJKB 78, 116 LT 576, 81 JP 123, 25 Cox CC 698, 12 Cr App Rep 166, CCA . . . 2-475
R v Nordeng (1975) 62 Cr App Rep 123, [1976] Crim LR 194, CA . . . 8-30705
R v Norfolk Justices, ex p Davidson (1925) 69 Sol Jo 558 . . . 1-837
R v Norfolk Justices, ex p DPP [1950] 2 KB 558, 94 Sol Jo 436, 48 LGR 483, 34 Cr App Rep 120, sub nom R v South Greenhoe Justices, ex p DPP [1950] 2 All ER 42, 114 JP 312, 66 (pt 2) TLR 452 . . . 1-836, 1-2235
R v Norfolk Quarter Sessions, ex p Brunson [1953] 1 QB 503, [1953] 1 All ER 346, [1953] 2 WLR 294, 117 JP 100, 97 Sol Jo 98, 37 Cr App Rep 6 . . . 1-454, 1-460, 1-540, 1-563
R v Norfolk Stipendiary Magistrate, ex p Keable [1998] Crim LR 510 . . . 1-3581
R v Norfolk Stipendiary Magistrate, ex p Taylor (1997) 161 JP 773, [1998] Crim LR 276, DC 1-605, 1-608, 2-38, 2-38A
R v Norham and Islandshire Justices, ex p Sunters Bros Ltd [1961] 1 All ER 455, [1961] 1 WLR 364, 125 JP 181, 105 Sol Jo 234 . . . 1-2034
R v Normanton [1998] Crim LR 220, CA . . . 1-3535
R v Norris (1916) 86 LJKB 810, 116 LT 160, 25 Cox CC 601, 12 Cr App Rep 156, CCA . . . 8-30669
R v Norris [2001] 1 Cr App Rep (S) 401, 164 JP 689, [2001] Crim LR 48, CA . . . 3-1661, 5-60A
R v North [2001] Crim LR 746, CA . . . 8-10387
R v North, ex p Oakey [1927] 1 KB 491, 96 LJKB 77, 136 LT 387, 43 TLR 60, 70 Sol Jo 1181, CA . . . 1-405, 1-770, 1-833
R v North East Essex Justices, ex p Lloyd [2001] 2 Cr App Rep (S) 86, 165 JP 117, 144 Sol Jo LB 274 . . . 1-438AA, 1-508, 3-560, 3-1555
R v North Hampshire Youth Court, ex p DPP (2000) 164 JP 377 . . . 1-835, 1-2053, 5-61
R v North London Metropolitan Magistrates, ex p Haywood [1973] 3 All ER 50, [1973] 1 WLR 965, 117 Sol Jo 547 . . . 3-541
R v North Sefton Magistrates' Court, ex p Marsh (1994) 159 JP 9, 16 Cr App Rep (S) 401, [1994] Crim LR 865, CA . . . 3-560
R v Northallerton Magistrates' Court, ex p Dove [2000] 1 Cr App Rep (S) 136, 163 JP 657, [1999] Crim LR 760 . . . 3-522, 3-3080
R v Northampton Juvenile Court, ex p London Borough of Hammersmith and Fulham [1985] FLR 193, [1985] Fam Law 124 . . . 6-2134
R v Northampton Magistrates' Court, ex p Customs and Excise Comrs (1994) 158 JP 1083, [1994] Crim LR 598 . . . 1-835
R v Northampton Magistrates' Court, ex p Newell [1992] RA 283, 157 JP 869, CA . . . 8-20107
R v Northumberland Justices, ex p Thompson (1923) 87 JP 95, 92 LJKB 321, 39 TLR 455, 67 Sol Jo 660, [1923] WC & Ins Rep 191, sub nom R v Spicer, ex p Thompson 129 LT 28, 27 Cox CC 413 . . . 8-29045, 8-29095
R v Norton [1977] Crim LR 478 . . . 8-10385
R v Norwich Magistrates' Court, ex p Elliott [2000] 1 Cr App Rep (S) 152 . . . 1-438AA, 1-508
R v Norwich Magistrates' Courts, ex p Lilly (1987) 151 JP 689 . . . 1-2142, 3-209B

PARA

R v Notice [2000] 1 Cr App Rep (S) 75, CA 3-230
R v Notman [1994] Crim LR 518, CA 8-23061
R v Nottingham County Court [1993] 1 FCR 576, [1993] 2 FLR 6, [1993] Fam Law 625 6-35, 6-4268
R v Nottingham County Justices, ex p Bostock [1970] 2 All ER 641, [1970] 1 WLR 1117, 134 JP 535, 114 Sol Jo 433 2-331
R v Nottingham Justices, ex p Brown [1960] 3 All ER 625, [1960] 1 WLR 1315, 125 JP 49, 104 Sol Jo 1036 8-7510
R v Nottingham Justices, ex p Fraser (1995) 159 JP 612 1-2169
R v Nottingham Justices, ex p Lynn (1984) 79 Cr App Rep 238, [1984] Crim LR 554 . . . 2-199
R v Nottingham Justices, ex p Taylor [1992] 1 QB 557, [1991] 4 All ER 860, [1991] 3 WLR 694, 155 JP 623, 135 Sol Jo 444 . . . . 1-439, 1-523, 1-2053, 5-12
R v Nottingham Magistrates' Court, ex p Davidson [2000] 1 Cr App Rep (S) 167, [2000] Crim LR 118 . . . . 1-438AA, 1-508
R v Nottingham Magistrates' Court, ex p Fohmann (1986) 151 JP 49, 84 Cr App Rep 316 . 3-522
R v Nottingham Magistrates' Court, ex p Furnell (1995) 160 JP 201 1-37
R v Nowaz [1976] 3 All ER 5, [1976] 1 WLR 830, 140 JP 512, 120 Sol Jo 402, 63 Cr App Rep 178, [1974] Crim LR 510, CA 2-196
R v Nowell [1948] 1 All ER 794, 112 JP 255, 64 TLR 277, 92 Sol Jo 351, 46 LGR 386, 32 Cr App Rep 173, CCA 4-1375
R v Nunu (1991) 12 Cr App Rep (S) 752, [1991] Crim LR 653, CA 8-17695
R v Nurdin (1979) 69 Cr App Rep 254, CA 8-2870
R v O. See R v Oulds
R v Oakes [1959] 2 QB 350, [1959] 2 All ER 92, [1959] 2 WLR 694, 123 JP 290, 103 Sol Jo 373, 43 Cr App Rep 114, CCA 2-742, 2-743, 8-22773, 8-24269
R v Oakley [1979] LS Gaz R 731 . . . . 1-583, 2-344
R v Oakley (1990) 12 Cr App Rep (S) 215, CA 3-239
R v Oatridge (1991) 94 Cr App Rep 367, [1992] Crim LR 205 8-23250
R v O'Boyle [1973] RTR 445, (1973) 137 JP 280, CA 4-1377, 4-1378
R v O'Brien (1911) 7 Cr App Rep 29 2-197
R v O'Brien [2000] Crim LR 676, CA 2-344
R v O'Connell (1991) 94 Cr App Rep 39, [1991] Crim LR 771, CA 8-30691
R v O'Connor (1986) 85 Cr App Rep 298, [1987] Crim LR 260, CA 2-1359
R v O'Connor and Brown (1881) 46 JP 214, 45 LT 512, 15 Cox CC 3 8-13301
R v Oddy [1974] 2 All ER 666, [1974] 1 WLR 1212, 138 JP 515, 118 Sol Jo 329, CA . 3-203, 3-204
R v O'Doherty [2003] 1 Cr App Rep 77, NICA 2-344
R v O'Farrell (1988) 10 Cr App Rep (S) 74, CA 3-1703
R v Offen [2001] 2 All ER 154, [2001] 1 WLR 253, [2001] 1 Cr App Rep 372, [2001] 2 Cr App Rep (S) 44, [2001] Crim LR 63, [2001] 01 LS Gaz R 23, 144 Sol Jo LB 288, CA . . . 3-235
R v Ogden, ex p Long Ashton UDC [1963] 1 All ER 574, [1963] 1 WLR 274, 127 JP 206, 107 Sol Jo 77, 61 LGR 253 . . . . 1-385, 7-6009, 7-6107
R v O'Gorman [1999] 2 Cr App Rep (S) 280, CA 3-233
R v O'Grady [1987] QB 995, [1987] 3 All ER 420, [1987] 3 WLR 321, 131 Sol Jo 887, 85 Cr App Rep 315, [1987] NLJ Rep 565, [1987] LS Gaz R 2044, CA 8-23066
R v Okafor [1994] 3 All ER 741, 99 Cr App Rep 97, [1994] Crim LR 221, [1993] 43 LS Gaz R 47, 137 Sol Jo LB 244, CA 2-1359
R v Okike [1978] RTR 489, CA 4-1642
R v Okinikan [1993] 2 All ER 5, [1993] 1 WLR 173, 157 JP 131, [1993] NLJR 90, 14 Cr App Rep (S) 453, [1993] Crim LR 146, CA 3-52,
R v Okuya and Nwaobi (1984) 6 Cr App Rep (S) 253, [1984] Crim LR 766 3-31
R v Oldbury Justices, ex p Smith (1994) 159 JP 316 . . . . 8-20107, 8-20108
R v Oldham Justices, ex p Cawley[1997] QB 1, [1996] 1 All ER 464, [1996] 2 WLR 681, 160 JP 133 . . . . 1-750, 1-821, 3-209B
R v Oldham Justices, ex p Mellor (1909) 73 JP 390, 101 LT 430 1-836
R v Oldham Justices, ex p Morrissey [1958] 3 All ER 559, [1959] 1 WLR 58, 123 JP 38, 103 Sol Jo 55 . . . . 1-2034, 9-15
R v O'Leary (1986) 82 Cr App Rep 341 8-30699
R v O'Leary (1988) 153 JP 69, 87 Cr App Rep 387, CA 2-1359
R v Olifier (1866) 10 Cox CC 402 8-27984
R v Oliver [1944] KB 68, [1943] 2 All ER 800, 108 JP 30, 113 LJKB 119, 170 LT 110, 60 TLR 82, 42 LGR 37, 29 Cr App R 137, CCA 1-2174, 1-7427, 8-21202
R v Oliver [1993] 2 All ER 9, [1993] 1 WLR 177, 157 JP 119, [1993] NLJR 89, [1993] Crim LR 147, CA . . . . , 3-218, 3-1733
R v Oliver [1999] 1 Cr App Rep (S) 394, [1998] 40 LS Gaz R 37, [1998] 43 LS Gaz R 32, 142 Sol Jo LB 262, CA 3-240
R v Oliver, Hartrey and Baldwin [2002] EWCA Crim 2766, [2003] 1 Cr App Rep 463, [2003] 2 Cr App Rep (S) 64, [2003] Crim LR 127 . . . . 3-239A
R v Ollerenshaw [1999] 1 Cr App Rep (S) 65, [1998] Crim LR 515, CA 3-234B, 3-235A,
R v Olliver and Olliver (1989) 153 JP 369, [1989] Crim LR 387, CA . . . 3-204, 3-206, 5-45
R v Ondhia [1998] 2 Cr App Rep 150, [1998] Crim LR 339, CA 8-13140
R v Onufrejczyk [1955] 1 QB 388, [1955] 1 All ER 247, [1955] 2 WLR 273, 99 Sol Jo 97, 39 Cr App Rep 1, CCA 8-23250
R v Oransaye [1993] Crim LR 772, CA 2-1916
R v Ord and Ord (1990) 12 Cr App Rep (S) 12, CA 3-230

PARA

PARA

PARA

PARA

PARA

PARA

PARA

R v Staniforth [1975] Crim LR 291 . . . 8-22449
R v Stannard (1863) Le & Ca 349, 28 JP 20, 33 LJMC 61, 9 LT 428, 12 WR 208, 9 Cox CC 405 8-7490
R v Stannard [1965] 2 QB 1, [1964] 1 All ER 34, [1964] 2 WLR 461, 128 JP 224, 48 Cr App Rep 81, CCA . . . 2-494
R v Stanton [1994] Crim LR 834, CA . . . 2-493
R v Starkie [1922] 2 KB 275, 86 JP 74, 91 LJKB 663, 38 TLR 181, 66 Sol Jo 300, 16 Cr App Rep 61, CCA . . . 8-23118
R v Statutory Committee of the Pharmaceutical Society of Great Britain, ex p Pharmaceutical Society of Great Britain [1981] 2 All ER 805, [1981] 1 WLR 886, 125 Sol Jo 428 . . . 3-1566
R v Steadman (1985) 7 Cr App Rep (S) 431 . . . 5-61
R v Steane [1947] KB 997, [1947] 1 All ER 813, [1947] LJR 969, 111 JP 337, 111 LT 122, 63 TLR 403, 91 Sol Jo 279, 45 LGR 484 . . . 7-7043
R v Steed [1990] Crim LR 816, CA . . . 5-3
R v Steel (1875) 39 JP Jo 357 . . . 8-18632
R v Steel (1992) 158 JP 439, [1993] RTR 415, 96 Cr App Rep 121, 14 Cr App Rep (S) 218, CA 4-1371
R v Steele [1993] Crim LR 298, CA . . . 8-10370
R v Steer [1988] AC 111, [1987] 2 All ER 833, [1987] 3 WLR 205, 151 JP 793, 131 Sol Jo 939, 85 Cr App Rep 352, [1987] NLJ Rep 640, [1987] LS Gaz R 2359, HL . . . 8-24740
R v Stephenson [1912] 3 KB 341, 76 JP 408, 82 LJKB 287, 107 LT 656, 23 Cox CC 214, 56 Sol Jo 764, 8 Cr App Rep 36, CCA . . . 8-27981
R v Stephenson [1947] NI 110 . . . 2-341
R v Stephenson (1998) 162 JP 495, [1998] Crim LR 576, CA . . . 1-2053
R v Stephenson [2001] EWCA Crim 1360, (2000) 165 JPN 435 . . . 3-52
R v Stevens [1981] Crim LR 568, CA . . . 8-21240
R v Stevens [1995] Crim LR 649, CA . . . 2-460, 2-476
R v Stevens [1997] 2 Cr App Rep (S) 180, CA . . . 3-173
R v Stevens (2006) Times, 24 February, 150 Sol Jo LB 167, [2006] All ER (D) 23 (Feb), CA 3-241
R v Steventon (1992) 13 Cr App Rep (S) 127, CA . . . 3-236A
R v Stewart [1896] 1 QB 300, 65 LJMC 83, 74 LT 54, 60 JP 356, 44 WR 368, 40 Sol Jo 259, 18 Cox CC 232 . . . 1-380, 1-420
R v Stewart (1984) 6 Cr App Rep (S) 166, [1984] Crim LR 510, CA . . . , 3-248
R v Stewart [1987] 2 All ER 383, [1987] 1 WLR 559, 131 Sol Jo 538, 85 Cr App Rep 66, [1987] LS Gaz R 1333, CA . . . 2-616, 3-240, 8-28006, 8-29091, 8-30704
R v Stewart (1990) 12 Cr App Rep (S) 15, CA . . . 3-230
R v Stewart [1995] 3 All ER 159, [1995] 1 Cr App Rep 441, [1995] Crim LR 420, CA . . . 1-321
R v Stewart [1995] Crim LR 500, CA . . . 2-1359
R v Stewart [1999] Crim LR 746, CA . . . 2-1355
R v Steyning Magistrates' Court, ex p Hunter (1985) 150 JP 129 . . . 1-2142
R v Stillwell and Jewell (1991) 94 Cr App Rep 65, 156 JP 335, CA . . . 3-1715
R v Stimpson (1863) 4 B & S 301, 27 JP 678, 32 LJMC 208, 8 LT 536, 10 Jur NS 41, 9 Cox CC 356 . . . 8-30733
R v Stobbart [1951] 2 All ER 753, 50 LGR 127, 35 Cr App Rep 125, 115 JP 561, 95 Sol Jo 655, [1951] 2 TLR 823, CCA . . . 3-1566
R v Stockport Justices, ex p Conlon [1997] 2 All ER 204, 161 JP 81 . . . 3-209B
R v Stockport Justices, ex p Hardy's Crown Brewery Ltd [1936] BTRLR 90 . . . 6-574
R v Stocks [1921] 2 KB 119, [1921] All ER Rep 602, 85 JP 203, 90 LJKB 583, 124 LT 830, 37 TLR 417, 65 Sol Jo 554, 26 Cox CC 717, 15 Cr App Rep 134, CCA . . . 8-23117
R v Stockwell (1993) 97 Cr App Rep 260, CA . . . 2-344
R v Stoddart (1909) 73 JP 348, 25 TLR 612, 53 Sol Jo 578, 2 Cr App Rep 217 . . . 1-689
R v Stoddart [1998] 2 Cr App Rep 25, 162 JP 78, [1997] 46 LS Gaz R 29, 141 Sol Jo LB 248, 142 Sol Jo LB 13, CA . . . 8-10388
R v Stoke on Trent Justices, ex p Wilby (1998) 163 JP 369 . . . 1-2567
R v Stokes [1983] RTR 59, [1982] Crim LR 695, CA . . . 8-30701
R v Stokesley (Yorks) Justices, ex p Bartram [1956] 1 All ER 563, [1956] 1 WLR 254, 100 Sol Jo 188 . . . 1-930
R v Stone (1910) 6 Cr App Rep 89, CCA . . . 8-27977
R v Stone [1977] QB 354, [1977] 2 All ER 341, [1977] 2 WLR 169, 141 JP 354, 121 Sol Jo 83, 64 Cr App Rep 186, [1977] Crim LR 166, CA . . . 8-23081
R v Stones [1989] 1 WLR 156, [1989] 1 LS Gaz R 38, 89 Cr App Rep 26, CA . . . 8-30699
R v Storey [1973] 3 All ER 562, [1973] 1 WLR 1045, 137 JP 811, 117 Sol Jo 600, CA . . . 3-1651
R v Storrow and Poole [1983] Crim LR 332 . . . 8-30693
R v Straffen [1952] 2 QB 911, [1952] 2 All ER 657, [1952] 2 TLR 589, 116 JP 536, 96 Sol Jo 749, CCA . . . 2-463
R v Stratford Justices, ex p Imbert [1999] 2 Cr App Rep 276, 163 JP 693 1-461, 1-425, 1-604, 1-3581, 1-7441, 2-38A
R v Stratford Youth Court, ex p Conde [1997] 1 WLR 113, 161 JP 308, [1997] 2 Cr App Rep 1, [1997] Crim LR 212 . . . 3-1560, 5-34
R v Stratford Youth Court, ex p S [1998] 1 WLR 1758, 162 JP 552, [1999] Crim LR 146, [1998] NLJR 870 . . . 1-6223
R v Stretton (1986) 86 Cr App Rep 7, CA . . . 2-320
R v Stride [2003] EWCA Crim 996, [2003] 3 All ER 40, [2003] RTR 483, [2003] 2 Cr App Rep 275, [2004] 1 Cr App Rep (S) 1, [2003] Crim LR 564, [2003] 23 LS Gaz R 36 . . . 3-237
R v Stringer and Banks (1991) 94 Cr App Rep 13, [1991] Crim LR 639, CA . . . 8-30690

PARA

PARA

PARA

PARA

PARA

PARA

PARA

PARA

Robertson v Rosenberg (1951) 49 LGR 210, [1951] WN 97, 115 JP 128, 95 Sol Jo 138, [1951] 1 TLR 417, DC 1-7427
Robey v Vladinier (1935) 99 JP 428, [1935] All ER Rep 695, 154 LT 87, 52 TLR 22, 80 Sol Jo 76, 18 Asp MLC 560, 33 LGR 474, 53 Ll L Rep 121 . . . . . . 7-6313, 7-6368, 7-6486
Robinson v Cowpen Local Board (1893) 63 LJQB 235, 9 R 858, CA 8-31345A
Robinson v DPP [2003] EWHC 2718 (Admin), 168 JP 522, [2004] Crim LR 670, [2003] All ER (D) 05 (Nov) 4-1680
Robinson v Everett and W & F C Bonham & Son Ltd [1988] Crim LR 699 8-4140
Robinson v Gregory [1905] 1 KB 534, 69 JP 161, 74 LJKB 367, 92 LT 171, 20 Cox CC 781, 3 LGR 308 1-769
Robinson v Hill [1910] 1 KB 94, 73 JP 514, 79 LJKB 189, 101 LT 573, 26 TLR 17, 7 LGR 1065 5-91
Robinson v Hughes [1987] Crim LR 644 8-4144
Robinson v Jones (1879) 4 LR Ir 391, 28 Sol Jo 805 8-18632
Robinson v Murray [2005] EWCA Civ 935, [2005] 3 FCR 504, [2006] 1 FLR 365, [2005] Fam Law 859, (2005) Times, 19 August, [2005] All ER (D) 129 (Jul) 1-2113
Robinson v Waddington (1849) 13 QB 753, 18 LJQB 250, 13 LTOS 281, 13 Jur 537 . . . 8-16725
Robinson v Whittle [1980] 3 All ER 459, [1980] 1 WLR 1476, 144 JP 444, 124 Sol Jo 807 . . 1-766
Robinson (Thomas) Sons & Co Ltd v Allardice [1944] WN 41, 108 JP 101, 170 LT 297, 60 TLR 196, 42 LGR 91 8-12248
Robson v Biggar [1907] 1 KB 690, 71 JP 164, 76 LJKB 248, 96 LT 271, 23 TLR 276, 51 Sol Jo 249; on appeal [1908] 1 KB 672, 77 LJKB 203, 97 LT 859, 24 TLR 125, 52 Sol Jo 76, CA 8-16722
Robson v Hallett [1967] 2 QB 939, [1967] 2 All ER 407, [1967] 3 WLR 28, 131 JP 333, 111 Sol Jo 254, 51 Cr App Rep 307 8-23824
Robson v Ribton Turner [1960] 3 All ER 660, [1961] 1 WLR 162, 105 Sol Jo 110 . . . 8-23824
Robson v Sykes [1938] 2 All ER 612, 54 TLR 727, 82 Sol Jo 493 . . . . . . 7-6281, 7-6341
Roche v Willis (1934) 32 LGR 286, 98 JP 227, 30 Cox CC 121, [1934] All ER Rep 613, 151 LT 154 1-7427
Rodbourn v Hudson [1925] 1 KB 225, 89 JP 25, 94 LJKB 129, 132 LT 444, 41 TLR 132, 69 Sol Jo 275, 27 Cox CC 678, 23 LGR 22 8-12248
Rodewald v Rodewald [1977] Fam 192, [1977] 2 All ER 609, [1977] 2 WLR 191, 75 LGR 280, CA 6-1493
Rodgers v Pickersgill (1910) 74 JP 324, 103 LT 33, 26 TLR 493, 54 Sol Jo 564 . . . 8-811
Roe v Hemmings [1951] 1 KB 676, [1951] 1 All ER 389, 115 JP 126, [1951] 1 TLR 365, 95 Sol Jo 77, 49 LGR 206 2-742
Roe v Kingerlee [1986] Crim LR 735 8-24740
Rogers v Islington London Borough Council (1999) 32 HLR 138, [1999] 34 LS Gaz R 33, [1999] 37 EG 178, CA 8-17272
Rogers v Secretary of State for the Home Department [1973] AC 388, [1972] 2 All ER 1057, [1972] 3 WLR 279, 136 JP 574, 116 Sol Jo 696, HL 2-330
Rogers, Eungblut & Co v Martin [1911] 1 KB 19, 75 JP 10, 80 LJKB 208, 103 LT 527, 27 TLR 40, 55 Sol Jo 29, CA 8-16727
Rogerson v Stephens [1950] 2 All ER 144, 115 JP 372, 94 Sol Jo 421, 48 LGR 644 . . . 4-1560
Rolls v Miller (1884) 27 Ch D 71, [1881-5] All ER Rep 915, 53 LJ Ch 682, 50 LT 597, 32 WR 806, CA 8-14683
Romford Ice and Cold Storage Co Ltd v Lister [1956] 2 QB 180, [1955] 3 All ER 460, [1955] 3 WLR 631, 99 Sol Jo 794, [1955] 2 Lloyd's Rep 325, CA; on appeal sub nom Lister v Romford Ice and Cold Storage Co Ltd [1957] AC 555, [1957] 1 All ER 125, 121 JP 98, HL 4-1560
Roper v Sullivan [1978] RTR 181, [1978] Crim LR 233 4-1596
Roper v Taylor's Central Garages (Exeter) Ltd. See Taylor's Central Garages (Exeter) Ltd v Roper
Rose v Matt [1951] 1 KB 810, [1951] 1 All ER 361, 115 JP 122, [1951] 1 TLR 474, 95 Sol Jo 62, 49 LGR 199, 35 Cr App Rep 1 8-30671
Rose v Welbeck Motors Ltd [1962] 2 All ER 801, [1962] 1 WLR 1010, 126 JP 413, 106 Sol Jo 470, 60 LGR 423 8-31351
Ross v Collins [1982] Crim LR 368 8-10389
Ross v Evans [1959] 2 QB 79, [1959] 2 All ER 222, [1959] 2 WLR 699, 123 JP 320, 103 Sol Jo 393, 57 LGR 137 . . . . 8-31345A
Ross v Hodges [1975] RTR 55 . . . . 1-32, 4-1378
Ross v Moss [1965] 2 QB 396, [1965] 3 All ER 145, [1965] 3 WLR 416, 129 JP 537, 109 Sol Jo 475, 63 LGR 321 . . . 1-768, 1-831, 8-13302, 6-755, 6-773A, 8-13386, 8-17293, 8-17305, 8-22276, 8-30087, 8-31888
Ross v Rivenall [1959] 2 All ER 376n, 123 JP 352, 103 Sol Jo 491 8-30701
Ross Hillman Ltd v Bond [1974] QB 435, [1974] 2 All ER 287, [1974] 2 WLR 436, 138 JP 428, 118 Sol Jo 243 4-7
Rossi v Edinburgh Corpn [1905] AC 21, 91 LT 668 8-18835
Rossiter v Conway (1893) 58 JP 350 8-6351
Rotherham Metropolitan Borough Council v Raysun (UK) Ltd (1988) 153 JP 37, [1988] BTLC 293, [1989] CCLR 1 8-4464
Rous de Horsey v Rignell [1963] 1 QB 914, [1963] 1 All ER 38, [1963] 2 WLR 162, 61 LGR 173, 127 JP 108, 106 Sol Jo 1070 . . . . 6-160, 6-657
Routledge v Hislop (1860) 2 E & E 549, 24 JP 148, 29 LJMC 90, 2 LT 53, 8 WR 363, 6 Jur N S 398, HL 1-60, 1-384

S

PARA

PARA

Schtraks v Government of Israel [1964] AC 556, [1962] 3 All ER 529, [1962] 3 WLR 1013, 106 Sol Jo 833, HL . . . 8-10155
Scotcher v Scotcher [1947] P 1, 110 JP 342, [1948] LJR 147, 62 TLR 517, 90 Sol Jo 490, 44 LGR 351 . . . 6-66, 6-78
Scott v Denton [1907] 1 KB 456, 71 JP 66, 76 LJKB 330, 96 LT 760, 23 TLR 73, 51 Sol Jo 82, 5 LGR 251 . . . 8-16721
Scott v Dickson (1939) 83 Sol Jo 317 . . . 4-1623
Scott v DPP [1914] 2 KB 868, 78 JP 267, 83 LJKB 1025, 111 LT 59, 30 TLR 396, 24 Cox CC 194 . . . 8-13601
Scott v Jameson 1914 SC (J) 187, 51 SLR 808 . . . 4-1198
Scott v Jelf [1974] RTR 256, [1974] Crim LR 191 . . . 4-1512
Scott v M'Intosh 1935 SC 199, 1935 SLT 171 . . . 4-9
Scott v Pilliner [1904] 2 KB 855, 68 JP 518, 73 LJKB 998, 91 LT 658, 53 WR 284, 20 TLR 662 8-18835
Scott v Sampson (1882) 8 QBD 491, [1881-5] All ER Rep 628, 46 JP 408, 51 LJQB 380, 46 LT 412, 30 WR 451 . . . 8-18632
Scott (otherwise Morgan) v Scott [1913] AC 417, [1911-13] All ER Rep 1, 82 LJP 74, 109 LT 1, 29 TLR 520, 57 Sol Jo 498, HL . . . 1-36, 1-113
Scott v Warren [1974] RTR 104, [1974] Crim LR 117 . . . 4-9
Scott v Westminster City Council [1995] RTR 327, [1995] 08 LS Gaz R 41, CA . . . 7-6022
Seaboard Offshore Ltd v Secretary of State for Transport, The Safe Carrier [1994] 2 All ER 99, [1994] 1 WLR 541, [1994] 1 Lloyd's Rep 589, [1994] NLJR 461n, [1994] 18 LS Gaz R 43, HL . . . 7-6365
Seager v White (1884) 48 JP 436, 51 LT 261 . . . 6-754
Seal v British Orphan Asylum Trustees (1911) 75 JP 152, 104 LT 424, 22 Cox CC 392, 9 LGR 238 . . . 8-14683
Sealey v Tandy [1902] 1 KB 296, 66 JP 19, 71 LJKB 41, 20 Cox CC 57, 50 WR 347, 85 LT 459, 18 TLR 38 . . . 8-13311, 6-571, 6-779
Seaman v Netherclift (1876) 2 CPD 53, 41 JP 389, 46 LJCP 128, 35 LT 784, 25 WR 159, CA . . . 2-330, 8-18632
Seamark v Prouse [1980] 3 All ER 26, [1980] 1 WLR 698, 144 JP 423, 124 Sol Jo 167, 70 Cr App Rep 236, [1980] Crim LR 240 . . . 6-320, 8-27672
Searle v Reynolds (1866) 31 JP 4, 7 B & S 704, 14 LT 518 . . . 6-777
Sears v Smiths Food Group Ltd [1968] 2 QB 288, [1968] 2 All ER 721, [1968] 2 WLR 1255, 112 Sol Jo 329, 66 LGR 416 . . . 8-31857
Seay v Eastwood [1976] 3 All ER 153, [1976] 1 WLR 1117, 140 JP 589, 120 Sol Jo 734, HL 8-13370-
Secretary of State for Defence v Percy [1999] 1 All ER 732 . . . 2-193, 8-18835
Secretary of State for Social Security v Harmon [1999] 1 WLR 163, [1999] 1 FCR 213, [1998] 2 FLR 598, [1998] Fam Law 519, [1998] 25 LS Gaz R 32, 142 Sol Jo LB 183, CA 6-2903, 6-2905
Secretary of State for Social Security v Shotton [1996] 3 FCR 346, [1996] 2 FLR 241, [1996] Fam Law 530 . . . 6-2944
Secretary of State for the Environment v Hooper [1981] RTR 169 . . . 4-1764
Secretary of State for the Environment, Transport and the Regions v Elsy [2000] RTR 29, 164 JP 61, 164 JPN 127 . . . 4-1524
Secretary of State for the Environment, Transport and the Regions, ex p Holt [2000] RTR 309 4-1938
Secretary of State for Transport v Richards [1998] RTR 456, 162 JP 682 . . . 4-1998
Secretary of State for Transport, Local Government and the Regions v Snowdon [2002] EWHC 2394 (Admin), [2003] RTR 216, [2002] 47 LS Gaz R 29 . . . 4-1526
Secretary of State for War v Wynne [1905] 2 KB 845, [1904-7] All ER Rep 352, 75 LJKB 25, 93 LT 797, 54 WR 235, 22 TLR 8, 50 Sol Jo 13 . . . 8-16719
Secretary of State for Work and Pensions v Jones [2003] EWHC 2163 (Fam), [2004] 1 FLR 282, [2003] Fam Law 881, [2003] 35 LS Gaz R 34 . . . 6-509
Sekanina v Austria (1993) 17 EHRR 221, ECtHR . . . 1-643, 1-800, 1-2910
Selby v Atkins (1926) 90 JP 117, 135 LT 45, 42 TLR 475, 24 LGR 366, 28 Cox CC 202 . . . 1-2127
Selby v DPP (1989) 154 JP 566 . . . 7-5958
Selfe v Isaacson (1858) 1 F & F 194 . . . 1-641, 2-32
Selvey v DPP [1970] AC 304, [1968] 2 All ER 497, [1968] 2 WLR 1494, 132 JP 430, 112 Sol Jo 461, 52 Cr App Rep 443, HL . . . 2-493
Senat v Senat [1965] P 172, [1965] 2 All ER 505, [1965] 2 WLR 981 . . . 2-72
Senator Hanseatische Verwaltungsgessellschaft, Re [1996] 4 All ER 933, [1997] 1 WLR 515, [1996] 2 BCLC 562, CA . . . 8-13601
Seneviratne v Bishop [1978] RTR 92 . . . 4-1377A
Senior v Twelves (1958) 122 JP Jo 379 . . . 8-25216
Sennar, The. See DSV Silo- und Verwaltungsgesellschaft mbH v Sennar (Owners), The Sennar
Serio v Serio (1983) 4 FLR 756, 13 Fam Law 255, CA . . . 6-512
Serves v France (1998) 28 EHRR 265, ECtHR . . . 1-605, 1-648
Sewell v Taylor (1859) 23 JP 792, 7 CBNS 160, 29 LJMC 50, 6 Jur NS 582, 8 WR 26, 1 LT 37 6-800
Shackleton v Chief Constable of Lancashire Constabulary (2001) 165 JPN 875, CA . . . 4-1512
Shallow v Shallow [1979] Fam 1, [1978] 2 All ER 483, [1978] 2 WLR 583, 121 Sol Jo 830, CA 6-1493
Shanks McEwan (Midlands) Ltd v Wrexham Maelor Borough Council (1996) Times, 10 April 8-26271
Shanks & McEwan (Teeside) Ltd v Environment Agency [1997] 2 All ER 332, [1998] 2 WLR 452, [1997] Crim LR 684 . . . 8-26271
Sharp v Fowle (1884) 12 QBD 385, 48 JP 680, 53 LJQB 309, 50 LT 758, 32 WR 539 . 8-16727
Sharp v Sparkes (1926) 70 Sol Jo 1069 . . . 6-831

PARA

PARA

PARA

Spicer v Holt [1976] RTR 1, [1976] Crim LR 139; affd [1977] AC 987, [1976] 3 All ER 71, [1976] 3 WLR 398, 140 JP 545, 120 Sol Jo 572, 63 Cr App Rep 270, [1976] RTR 389, [1976] Crim LR 139, HL 1-181, 1-2204-1377A
Spiers and Pond Ltd v Green [1912] 3 KB 576, 77 JP 11, 82 LJKB 26, 29 TLR 14 . . 8-12056
Spittle v Kent County Constabulary [1986] RTR 142, [1985] Crim LR 744 . . 4-1191, 4-1193
Spittle v Spittle [1965] 3 All ER 451, [1965] 1 WLR 1156, 109 Sol Jo 556 . . . 2-617
Spivack v Spivack (1930) 94 JP 91, [1930] All ER Rep 133, 99 LJP 52, 142 LT 492, 46 TLR 243, 74 Sol Jo 155, 28 LGR 188, 29 Cox CC 91 . . . 6-50, 6-51, 8-23117
Spokes v Grosvenor Hotel Co [1897] 2 QB 124, 66 LJQB 572, 76 LT 679, 45 WR 545, 13 TLR 431 2-196
Springate v Questier [1952] 2 All ER 21, 116 JP 367, 102 L Jo 318, 213 LTN 315 . . 4-1642
Spurgeon v Spurgeon (1930) 46 TLR 396 6-51
Square v Model Farm Dairies (Bournemouth) Ltd [1939] 2 KB 365, [1939] 1 All ER 259, 108 LJKB 198, 160 LT 165, 55 TLR 384, 83 Sol Jo 152, CA 8-12248
Squire v Midland Lace Co [1905] 2 KB 448, 69 JP 257, 74 LJKB 614, 93 LT 29, 53 WR 653, 21 TLR 466, 49 Sol Jo 430 8-14683
Squires v Mitchell [1983] RTR 400 . . . . 7-576, 4-1976
Squirrell Ltd v National Westminster Bank plc (Customs and Excise Comrs intervening) [2005] EWHC 664 (Ch), [2005] 2 All ER 784, [2005] 1 All ER (Comm) 749, [2006] 1 WLR 637, [2005] 2 Lloyd's Rep 374, (2005) Times, 25 May, [2005] All ER (D) 314 (Apr) . . 3-1862
Stacey v Whitehurst (1865) 18 CBNS 344, 29 JP 136, 34 LJMC 94, 11 LT 710, 13 WR 384 1-321, 1-389, 8-13670
Stacey v Wilkins [1946] KB 271, [1946] 1 All ER 293, 110 JP 182, 115 LJKB 222, 174 LT 227, 62 TLR 243, 90 Sol Jo 201, 44 LGR 84 . . . . 8-13601A
Stallard v Marks (1878) 3 QBD 412, 42 JP 359, 47 LJMC 91, 26 WR 694, 38 LT 566 . . 6-754
Stamp v United Dominions Trust (Commercial) Ltd [1967] 1 QB 418, [1967] 1 All ER 251, [1967] 2 WLR 541, 131 JP 177, 110 Sol Jo 904 3-520
Standerwick (W C) Ltd v Smith [1962] 2 QB 278, [1962] 2 All ER 19, [1962] 2 WLR 926, 60 LGR 256, 126 JP 324, 106 Sol Jo 287, DC 1-7427
Stangoe v Slatter (1896) 60 JP 342, 12 TLR 335 8-31915
Stanhope v Thorsby (1866) LR 1 CP 423, 30 JP 342, 1 Har & Ruth 459, 35 LJMC 182, 14 LT 332, 14 WR 651, 12 Jur NS 374 1-766
Stanley v Farndale (1892) 56 JP Jo 709 . . . . 8-31345A
Stansfeld (or Stansfield) & Co Ltd v Andrews (1909) 73 JP 167, 22 Cox CC 84, 100 LT 529, 25 TLR 259 6-754
Stanton v Brown [1900] 1 QB 671, 64 JP 326, 69 LJQB 301, 48 WR 333, 16 TLR 156 . . 8-13874
Stanton & Sons Ltd v Webber (1972) 116 Sol Jo 667, [1973] RTR 86 1-321
Star Cinema (Shepherds Bush) Ltd v Baker (1921) 20 LGR 158, 86 JP 47, 126 LT 506 . . 6-632
Staravia Ltd v Gordon [1973] Crim LR 298 8-10415
Starey v Chilworth Gunpowder Co (1889) 24 QBD 90, 54 JP 436, 59 LJMC 13, 62 LT 73, 38 WR 204, 6 TLR 95, 17 Cox CC 55 8-4448
Starkey v Starkey [1938] WN 316, [1938] 3 All ER 773, 108 LJP 1, 159 LT 490, 54 TLR 1117, 82 Sol Jo 745 . . . . 6-70, 6-71
Starkey v Starkey [1954] P 449, [1954] 1 All ER 1036, [1954] 2 WLR 907, 118 JP 279, 98 Sol Jo 303 . . . . 1-2156, 1-5687
State v Coetzee [1997] 2 LRC 593, SA Const Ct 8-17631W
Staunton v Coates (1924) 88 JP 193, 94 LJKB 95, 132 LT 199, 41 TLR 33, 69 Sol Jo 126, 27 Cox CC 663, 23 LGR 6 4-1642
Stead v Ackroyd [1911] 1 KB 57, 74 JP 482, 80 LJKB 78, 103 LT 727 8-13309
Steadman v DPP [2002] EWHC 810 (QB), [2003] RTR 10, [2002] 21 LS Gaz R 31, 146 Sol Jo LB 118 4-1378
Stear v Scott [1992] RTR 226n 8-24744
Steel v United Kingdom (1998) 28 EHRR 603, [1998] Crim LR 893, ECtHR . 1-2184, 3-540, 3-580
Steele v Rogers (1912) 76 JP 150, 106 LT 79, 28 TLR 198, 22 Cox CC 656 . . . 8-825
Steele Ford & Newton v Crown Prosecution Service (No 2). See Holden & Co (a firm) v Crown Prosecution Service (No 2)
Stefan v General Medical Council [1999] 1 WLR 1293, 49 BMLR 161, [1999] Lloyd's Rep Med 90, 143 Sol Jo LB 112, PC 1-27, 1-33, 1-47, 1-582, 1-701, 1-753, 1-2031, 1-2093, 1-2124
Stein (John G) & Co Ltd v O'Hanlon [1965] AC 890, [1965] 1 All ER 547, [1965] 2 WLR 496, 109 Sol Jo 152, HL 2-743
Stenhouse v Dykes 1908 SC (J) 61 8-13309
Stephens v Snell [1939] WN 296, [1939] 3 All ER 622, 161 LT 266, 55 TLR 962, 83 Sol Jo 656 8-30733
Stephenson v Johnson [1954] 1 All ER 369, [1954] 1 WLR 375, 118 JP 199, 98 Sol Jo 128, DC 7-1427
Stephenson v W J Rogers Ltd (1899) 63 JP 230, 80 LT 193, 15 TLR 148 6-754
Sternberg v Sternberg [1963] 3 All ER 319, [1936] 1 WLR 1036, 127 JP 523, 107 Sol Jo 515 1-449
Stevenage Borough Council v Younas [1990] RTR 405n 8-31350
Stevens v Dickson [1952] 2 All ER 246, 116 JP 439, 96 Sol Jo 449 6-256, 6-320, 6-661, 6-830, 8-27672
Stevens v Stevens (1929) 93 JP 120, 27 LGR 362 6-66
Stevens & Sons v Timber and General Mutual Accident Insurance Association Ltd (1933) 102 LJKB 337, [1933] All ER Rep 806, 148 LT 515, 49 LTR 224, 77 Sol Jo 116, 45 Ll L Rep 43, CA 4-1565
Stevens and Stevens v Christy (1987) 151 JP 366, 85 Cr App Rep 249, [1987] Crim LR 503 8-28009
Stevenson v Stevenson [1911] P 191, 80 LJP 137, 105 LT 183, 27 TLR 547, CA . . . 6-64

PARA

PARA

Suffolk County Council v Hillary's Blinds Ltd [2002] EWHC 87 (Admin), (2002) 166 JP 380 . . . 8-5012
Suffolk County Council v Mason (1977) Times, 16 March . . . 4-5
Suffolk County Council v Rexmore Wholesale Services Ltd (1994) 159 JP 390 . . . 1-643, 1-803, 8-4464
Sullivan v Earl of Caithness [1976] QB 966, [1976] 1 All ER 844, [1976] 2 WLR 361, 140 JP 277, 120 Sol Jo 8, 62 Cr App Rep 105 . . . 8-10370
Sullivan v Sullivan [1956] 1 All ER 611n, [1956] 1 WLR 277, 120 JP 161, 100 Sol Jo 210 . . . 6-80
Sunday Times v United Kingdom (1979) 2 EHRR 245, ECtHR . . . 1-301, 1-310, 8-17631V
Sunderland Borough Council v A [1993] 1 FCR 396 . . . 6-4403
Sunter Bros Ltd v Arlidge [1962] 1 All ER 510, [1962] 1 WLR 199, 60 LGR 142, 126 JP 159, 106 Sol Jo 154 . . . 4-3881
Sunworld Ltd v Hammersmith and Fulham London Borough Council [2000] 2 All ER 837, [2000] 1 WLR 2102, [2000] Crim LR 593 . . . 1-765, 1-826
Surrey County Council v Burton Retail Ltd (1997) 96 LGR 262, 162 JP 545 . . . 8-5011
Surrey County Council v Clark (1991) 156 JP 798, 11 Tr LR 147, [1991] COD 430 . . . 8-4449
Surrey County Council v Ministry of Education [1953] 1 All ER 705, 117 JP 194, 97 Sol Jo 191, 51 LGR 319 . . . 8-7824
Surrey Free Inns plc v Gosport Borough Council [1999] LGR 610, sub nom SFI Group plc (formerly Surrey Free Inns) v Gosport Borough Council [1999] EGCS 51, [1999] Env LR 750, [1999] BLGR 610, CA . . . 8-26308
Sussex Peerage Case (1844) 11 Cl & Fin 85, [1843-60] All ER Rep 55, 6 State Tr NS 79, 3 LTOS 277, 8 Jur 793, HL . . . 2-742
Sutcliffe v Chief Constable of West Yorkshire [1996] RTR 86, 159 JP 770, CA . . . 1-2713
Suter v Suter and Jones [1987] Fam 11, [1987] 2 All ER 336, [1987] 3 WLR 9, 151 JP 593, [1987] FCR 52, [1987] 2 FLR 232, [1987] Fam Law 239, 131 Sol Jo 471, [1987] LS Gaz R 1142, CA . . . 6-960
Sutherland v James Mills Ltd Executors [1938] 1 All ER 283, 36 LGR 167 . . . 8-14617
Sutherland v United Kingdom (1997) 24 EHRR CD 22, ECtHR . . . 1-301
Sutherland v United Kingdom (1998) EHRLR 117 . . . 8-17631F
Sutton London Borough Council v Davis [1994] Fam 241, [1995] 1 All ER 53, [1994] 2 WLR 721, [1994] 1 FLR 737, [1994] Fam Law 493, [1994] 19 LS Gaz R 33 . . . 4-2200, 4-2206
Sutton London Borough Council v Davis (No 2) [1995] 1 All ER 65, [1994] 1 WLR 1317, 92 LGR 746, [1994] 2 FCR 1199, [1994] 2 FLR 569, [1994] Fam Law 616, [1994] 31 LS Gaz R 36, 138 Sol Jo LB 140 . . . 6-41
Sutton London Borough Council v S [2004] EWHC 2876 (Admin), (2004) Times, 1 November, [2004] All ER (D) 358 (Oct) . . . 8-7824
Swain v DPP [1966] AC 591, [1965] 3 All ER 587, [1965] 3 WLR 1131, 130 JP 48, 109 Sol Jo 872, 50 Cr App Rep 36, HL . . . 7-7060
Swain v DPP [2005] EWHC 684 (Admin), [2005] 3 All ER 330, [2005] 3 WLR 628, [2005] Crim LR 959, [2005] All ER (D) 279 (Apr); affd [2004] EWCA Crim 1981, [2005] QB 259, [2004] 4 All ER 955, [2004] 3 WLR 1362, [2005] 1 Cr App Rep 154, [2005] Crim LR 122, [2004] 34 LS Gaz R 29, (2004) Times, 30 July, 148 Sol Jo LB 1149, [2004] All ER (D) 374 (Jul); affd [2006] UKHL 16, [2006] All ER (D) 419 (Mar) . . . 1-1071, 8–24907
Swain v Gillett [1974] RTR 446, [1974] Crim LR 433 . . . 4-1198
Swain v McCaul [1997] RTR 102, 140 Sol Jo LB 142 . . . 4-2292
Swales v Cox [1981] QB 849, [1981] 1 All ER 1115, [1981] 2 WLR 814, 125 Sol Jo 133, 72 Cr App Rep 171, [1981] Crim LR 235 . . . 1-180, 1-205
Swan v Saunders (1881) 45 JP 522, 50 LJMC 67, 44 LT 424, 29 WR 538 . . . 8-825
Swan v Vehicle Inspectorate [1997] RTR 187, 161 JP 293, [1997] 02 LS Gaz R 25, 140 Sol Jo LB 263 . . . 4-1647
Swansea City Council v Jenkins (1994) 158 JP 952 . . . 8-26118
Swanston v DPP (1996) 161 JP 203 . . . 8-27723
Sweet v Williams [1922] WN 313, [1922] All ER Rep 111, 87 JP 51, 128 LT 379, 67 Sol Jo 183, 21 LGR 23, 27 Cox CC 373 . . . 5-98, 8-7846
Swindells v Cheshire County Council (1993) 91 LGR 582, 157 JP 802, 15 BMLR 84 . . . 8-15650, 8-15654
Swinfen v Swinfen (1857) 24 Beav 549, 21 JP 773 . . . 1-151, 1-641
Swithland Motors Ltd v Peck [1991] RTR 322, [1991] Crim LR 386 . . . 8-4447
Sykes v DPP [1988] RTR 129 . . . 4-1378
Sykes v Holmes and Maw (1985) 84 LGR 355, [1985] Crim LR 791 . . . 8-19236
Sykes v White [1983] RTR 419 . . . 4-1378
Symonds v Incorporated Law Society (1884) 49 JP 212 . . . 8-29320
Synge v Synge [1900] P 180, 64 JP 454, 69 LJP 106, 83 LT 224, 16 TLR 388 402; affd [1901]P 317, [1900-3] All ER Rep 452, 70 LJP 97, 85 LT 83, 17 TLR 718 . . . 6-78
Szakal, Re [2000] 1 Cr App Rep 248, sub nom R v Manchester Magistrates' Court, ex p Geza Szakal [2000] Crim LR 47 . . . 1-3447

T

T (a minor), Re [1993] 4 All ER 518, [1993] 3 WLR 602, [1993] 2 FCR 445, [1993] 2 FLR 278, [1993] Fam Law 568, [1993] NLJR 776, CA . . . 6-4263
T (a minor), Re [1993] 1 FCR 973, [1993] 2 FLR 450, [1993] Fam Law 572, CA . . . 6-2230
T (a minor), Re [1994] 2 All ER 526, [1994] 2 WLR 594, [1994] 1 FLR 632 . . . 6-19, 6-2161

PARA

Turner & Son Ltd v Owen [1956] 1 QB 48, [1955] 3 All ER 565, [1955] 3 WLR 700, 120 JP 15, 99 Sol Jo 799, 54 LGR 69 . . . . 1-769, 1-832
Tweney v Tweney [1946] P 180, [1946] 1 All ER 564, 115 LJP 60, 174 LT 335, 62 TLR 266 6-51
Twickenham UDC v Munton [1899] 2 Ch 603, 68 LJ Ch 601, 81 LT 136, 47 WR 660, 15 TLR 457, 43 Sol Jo 673, CA 7-6072
Twyford v Puntschart [1947] 1 All ER 773, 111 JP 315, 97 LJMC 221, 177 LT 30, 63 TLR 329, 91 Sol Jo 264, 45 LGR 279 8-21743
Tyler v Ferris [1906] 1 KB 94, 70 JP 88, 75 LJKB 142, 93 LT 843, 54 WR 469, 22 TLR 181, 4 LGR 201, 21 Cox CC 73 4-915
Tyler v Whatmore [1976] RTR 83, [1976] Crim LR 315 4-8
Tynan v Balmer [1967] 1 QB 91, [1966] 2 All ER 133, [1966] 2 WLR 1181, 110 Sol Jo 129 8-23824
Tynan v Jones [1975] RTR 465, [1975] Crim LR 458 . . . . 1-688, 4-1480
Tyrrell v Tyrrell (1928) 92 JP 45, [1928] All ER Rep 422, 138 LT 624, 26 LGR 188, 28 Cox CC 485 . . . . 1-570, 1-750

U

U, Re [1993] 2 FCR 64, [1993] 2 FLR 992, [1994] Fam Law 71, CA . . . . , 6-1355
U (T) (a minor), Re [1993] 2 FCR 565, [1994] Fam Law 316 6-37
U (a child) (serious injury: standard of proof), Re [2004] EWCA Civ 567, [2005] Fam 134, [2004] 3 WLR 753, [2004] 2 FCR 257, [2004] 2 FLR 263, [2004] Fam Law 565, [2004] NLJR 824, (2004) Times, 27 May, [2004] All ER (D) 197 (May); affd sub nom Re Uddin (a child) (serious injury: standard of proof), [2005] EWCA Civ 52, (2005) 149 Sol Jo LB 266, [2005] NLJR 325, [2005] All ER (D) 385 (Feb) 1-689, 6-165
U v W (A-G intervening) [1998] Fam 29, [1997] 3 WLR 739, [1997] 2 CMLR 431, [1998] 1 FCR 526, [1997] 2 FLR 282, 38 BMLR 54, [1997] 11 LS Gaz R 36, 141 Sol Jo LB 57 6-2807
UK Waste Management Ltd v West Lancashire District Council (1996) 95 LGR 484, [1997] RTR 201, [1996] NPC 54, [1996] 14 LS Gaz R 29, 140 Sol Jo LB 118 . . . 4-1158
Uberoi v Middlesex Justices (2 November 1995, unreported) 3-209B
Uddin (a child) (serious injury: standard of proof), Re. See U (a child) (serious injury: standard of proof), Re
Ullah v Luckhurst [1977] RTR 401, [1977] Crim LR 295 4-1680
Union Cartage Co v Heamon [1937] 1 All ER 538, 25 Ry & Can Tr Cas 137 7-851
United Dairies (London) Ltd v Beckenham Corpn [1963] 1 QB 434, [1961] 1 All ER 579, [1961] 2 WLR 737, 125 JP 218, 105 Sol Jo 130, 59 LGR 252 8-12248
United Dairies (London) Ltd v Fisher & Sons Ltd [1963] 1 QB 434, [1961] 1 All ER 579, [1961] 2 WLR 737, 125 JP 218, 105 Sol Jo 130, 59 LGR 252 8-12248
United States Government v McCaffery [1984] 2 All ER 570, [1984] 1 WLR 867, 128 Sol Jo 448, 80 Cr App Rep 82, [1984] LS Gaz R 2457, HL 8-10195
Unitt v Unitt (1979) 10 Fam Law 119, 124 Sol Jo 80 1-2094
Universal Salvage Ltd and Robinson v Boothby (1983) 148 JP 347, 5 Cr App Rep (S) 428, [1984] RTR 289 . . . . 1-765, 1-827, 4-2292
Urwin v Toole (1976) 75 LGR 98, [1976] Crim LR 583 8-31854
Usill v Hales (1878) 3 CPD 319, 42 JP 113, 47 LJQB 323, 38 LT 65, 26 WR 371, 14 Cox CC 61 8-18632

V

V (a minor), Re [1987] Fam 57, [1986] 1 All ER 752, [1986] 3 WLR 927, 130 Sol Jo 879, CA ,
V (care or supervision order), Re [1996] 2 FCR 555, [1996] 1 FLR 776, [1996] Fam Law 269, CA 6-168
V (a child) (care proceedings: human rights claims), Re [2004] EWCA Civ 54, [2004] 1 All ER 997, [2004] 1 WLR 1433, [2004] 1 FCR 338, [2004] 1 FLR 944, [2004] Fam Law 328, [2004] 11 LS Gaz R 33, (2004) Times, 17 February, [2004] All ER (D) 52 (Feb) 6-11, 6-164, 6-167, 6-2100
V v United Kingdom (1999) 30 EHRR 121, [2000] Crim LR 187, ECtHR 5-16, 5-22A
V v V (children) (intractable contact dispute) [2004] EWHC 1215 (Fam), [2004] 2 FLR 851, (2004) Times, 28 May, [2004] All ER (D) 304 (May) 6-151
V and T v United Kingdom [2000] 2 All ER 1024n, 30 EHRR 121, [2000] Crim LR 187 ECtHR 3-1650, 5-12, 5.16, 5-22A
V-B (abduction: rights of custody), Re [1999] 2 FCR 371, [1999] 2 FLR 192, [1999] Fam Law 372, CA 6-1805C
Vacher & Sons Ltd v London Society of Compositors [1913] AC 107, [1911-13] All ER Rep 241, 82 LJKB 232, 107 LT 722, 29 TLR 73, 57 Sol Jo 75, 50 Sc LR 649, HL . . . 2-740, 2-742
Valentine v Bell 1930 JC 51 6-636
Valentine v Jackson [1972] 1 All ER 90, [1972] 1 WLR 528, 116 Sol Jo 334 6-802
Vallancey v Fletcher [1897] 1 QB 265, 61 JP 183, 66 LJQB 297, 76 LT 201, 45 WR 367, 13 TLR 158, 41 Sol Jo 210, 18 Cox CC 512 8-27910
Van den Boogaard v Laumen: C-220/95 [1997] QB 759, [1997] 3 WLR 284, [1997] All ER (EC) 517, [1997] 3 FCR 493, [1997] 2 FLR 399, [1997] Fam Law 599, ECJ 6-230

W

PARA

PARA

PARA

X

Y

Z

Decisions of the European Court of Justice are listed below numerically. These decisions are also included in the preceding alphabetical Table.

INDEX

K

T